# 1988
# Britannica
# Book of the Year

Encyclopædia Britannica, Inc.
Chicago
Auckland/Geneva/London/Manila/Paris/Rome
Seoul/Sydney/Tokyo/Toronto

# CONTENTS

# CALENDAR 1988

## JANUARY

1 New Year's Day; 125th anniversary of the issuance of the Emancipation Proclamation
7 Coptic Orthodox Christmas
13 Centenary of the founding of the (U.S.) National Geographic Society
18 Martin Luther King Day, a U.S. federal holiday
22 Bicentennial of the birth of Lord Byron, English Romantic poet who died at the age of 36
26 Australia Day
30 40th anniversary of the slaying of Mohandas Gandhi by a fanatic fellow Hindu. Gandhi, an advocate of nonviolence, led India's struggle for independence from Britain

## FEBRUARY

11 Japan's National Foundation Day
12 Abraham Lincoln's birthday (1809)
13 The winter Olympic Games get under way in Calgary, Alta. Canada had never before played host to the world's greatest winter athletes.
14 Valentine's Day in U.S.
16 Mardi Gras, also called Shrove Tuesday and other names; an occasion for gala celebrations on the eve of Ash Wednesday
17 Chinese New Year, ushering in the Year of the Dragon
22 George Washington's birthday (1732)
25 75th anniversary of the 16th Amendment to the U.S. Constitution; it authorized federal income taxes

## MARCH

3 Hina Matsuri, annual Japanese folk festival during which girls display dolls handed down from generation to generation
5 World Day of Prayer, an ecumenical Christian day of prayer
6 Independence Day in Ghana (1957)
13 50th anniversary of the death of Clarence Darrow, U.S. lawyer who gained fame as a defense counsel in many celebrated criminal trials
17 St. Patrick's Day, Ireland's national holiday
23 Pakistan Day, a national holiday
27 Palm Sunday
31 75th anniversary of the death of J. P. Morgan, U.S. financier

## APRIL

1 Good Friday
2 Jewish festival of Passover
3 Easter in Western churches
4 20th anniversary of the death of Martin Luther King, Jr., U.S. civil rights activist
10 Easter in Eastern churches
11 60th presentation of the Academy Awards by the Academy of Motion Picture Arts and Sciences
18 Projected first day of Ramadan, a month of fasting observed by Muslims
21 150th anniversary of the birth of John Muir, U.S. naturalist
24 The (U.S.) National Academy of Sciences begins a four-day celebration of its 125th anniversary

## MAY

1 May Day, celebrated as International Labour Day in many countries
8 Mother's Day in U.S.
11 100th birthday of Irving Berlin, prolific U.S. composer
11 25th anniversary of the historic two-day demonstration in Birmingham, Ala., by civil rights activists
14 40th anniversary of the founding of the state of Israel
16 'Id al-Fitr, end of the monthlong Muslim fast of Ramadan
22 175th anniversary of the birth of Richard Wagner, German composer who deeply influenced Western music
23 Victoria Day in Canada
30 U.S. Memorial Day

## JUNE

6 20th anniversary of the slaying of Robert Kennedy in Los Angeles
11 Official celebration of the birthday of Queen Elizabeth II of Britain
19 Father's Day in U.S.
21 Bicentennial of the founding of the United States, which formally came into being when New Hampshire became the ninth state to ratify the Constitution
26 40th anniversary of the Berlin airlift, the U.S. response to Soviet efforts to force the Western powers out of Berlin by blocking access roads
28 150th anniversary of the coronation of Britain's Queen Victoria, who ruled from 1837 to 1901

## JULY

1 Canada Day, commemoration of the unification of Canada's provinces
4 U.S. Independence Day
6 Republic Day in Malawi (1964)
12 Orangemen's Day, commemoration in Northern Ireland of the victory of William of Orange's Protestant forces over Roman Catholic troops
14 Bastille Day in France
25 Tenth birthday of Louise Joy Brown, the first "test-tube" baby, born in England to parents who had been childless for nine years
30 125th anniversary of the birth of Henry Ford, U.S. industrialist who revolutionized factory production with the assembly line

## AUGUST

6 Annual Peace Festival in Hiroshima, Japan; the dropping of the atomic bomb on the city is remembered with prayers for world peace in Shinto, Buddhist, and Christian services
15 Centenary of the birth of Lawrence of Arabia (T. E. Lawrence), British archaeological scholar, military strategist, and author of legendary military exploits
17 Independence Day in Indonesia
23 40th anniversary of the founding of the World Council of Churches
25 Independence Day in Uruguay (1825)
31 Tercentennial of the death of John Bunyan, British author of *The Pilgrim's Progress*

## SEPTEMBER

5 Labor Day in U.S. and Canada
5 Tenth anniversary of the meeting between Egyptian Pres. Anwar as-Sadat and Israeli Prime Minister Menachem Begin in Maryland. The summit concluded with the historic Camp David accords
11 Coptic Orthodox New Year, observed mainly in Egypt
12 Rosh Hashana, Jewish New Year
17 Opening of the summer Olympic Games in Seoul, South Korea
21 Yom Kippur, Jewish Day of Atonement
26 Centenary of the birth of T. S. Eliot, influential American-English poet, playwright, literary critic, and editor

## OCTOBER

10 Thanksgiving Day in Canada
10 175th anniversary of the birth of Giuseppe Verdi, Italian composer of operas
16 Tenth anniversary of the elevation of Karol Cardinal Wojtyla to the papacy; as Pope John Paul II he became the first non-Italian Roman pontiff in 455 years
16 Centenary of the birth of Eugene O'Neill, U.S. playwright
24 United Nations Day
30 50th anniversary of Orson Welles's radio drama *War of the Worlds,* which many listeners believed was a true report of an invasion by creatures from outer space

## NOVEMBER

10 50th anniversary of the death of Kemal Ataturk, first president of the Republic of Turkey
11 Veterans Day in U.S.
18 Tenth anniversary of the mass suicide in Guyana of about 1,000 followers of Jim Jones, the founder and cult leader of the People's Temple
19 125th anniversary of Abraham Lincoln's Gettysburg Address
22 25th anniversary of the assassination of U.S. Pres. John F. Kennedy while he was riding in an open car in Dallas, Texas. He was 46 years old and had held the office of president less than three years
29 Liberation Day in Albania (1944)

## DECEMBER

4 First day of Hanukka, Jewish festival also called the Festival of Lights
5 55th anniversary of the 21st Amendment to the U.S. Constitution. It repealed Prohibition, which had become law in January 1920, giving birth to bootlegging and speakeasies
24 125th anniversary of the death of William Thackeray, British novelist best known for *Vanity Fair*
25 Christmas Day
25 Constitution Day in the Republic of China; observed in Taiwan
27 Tenth anniversary of the death of Houari Boumedienne, one of the leaders in the fight for Algerian independence from France

# World Revolution in Agriculture

BY NORMAN E. BORLAUG AND CHRISTOPHER R. DOWSWELL

In recent years the international news media have focused on the cruel realities of famine in drought-stricken Africa. To most citizens of the affluent nations—who have never personally known hunger—the tragic scenes of starving people and their dying animals are deplorable and incomprehensible. The situation seems especially paradoxical when parts of the world are awash in surplus food and farmers in many of the developed countries are struggling with the economic consequences of over-production. Though many individuals, organizations, and governments have responded generously with emergency food aid, these are only stopgap measures. The only long-term solution is sustained agricultural development in areas where food is in short supply.

**Agriculture and Population.** In geologic terms, the domestication of plant and animal species is a recent event. Archaeological evidence indicates that all the major cereals, economically important legumes, root crops, and animal species that are still our principal sources of food were domesticated over a period of only 2,000–3,000 years. The process may well have begun when Neolithic women, faced with shortages when their menfolk failed to bring home enough food from hunting forays, decided that something had to be done and began searching for a means to assure a more permanent and reliable supply. It was achieved by sowing seed of the same wild grain species they had been collecting for untold millennia to supplement their meat diet. Thus, agriculture was born. With the development of agriculture some 8,000 to 10,000 years ago, the condition of humankind began to improve markedly, and human numbers, estimated to have been 15 million at that time, began to increase at an accelerated rate. A more stable food supply resulted in better nutrition and the development of a settled way of life, leading to higher survival rates and yet more rapid population growth.

World population presumably doubled four times from the beginning of agriculture to the start of the Christian era (to about 250 million). It had doubled again, to 500 million, by about 1650. The next doubling required only 200 years, producing a population of one billion by 1850. At about that time the discovery of the nature and cause of infectious diseases—the dawn of modern medicine—began to lower death rates. It took only 80 years for the next doubling, to two billion, which occurred

*Norman E. Borlaug, Distinguished Professor of International Agriculture at Texas A & M University, was awarded the Nobel Prize for Peace in 1970 for his achievement in laying the groundwork for the Green Revolution. Christopher R. Dowswell is a consultant in agricultural communications.*

about 1930. Shortly thereafter, the development of sulfa drugs, antibiotics, and improved vaccines led to a further substantial reduction in death rates, especially among infants and children. The next doubling of population took only 45 years—to about 1975, when the global population reached four billion, representing a 256-fold increase since the discovery of agriculture.

While the growth of world population overall has begun to slow, the current rates in the less developed world remain frighteningly high. In 1985, with world population approaching the five billion mark, global food production of all types stood at about 4.3 billion metric tons, representing some 2.2 billion tons of edible dry matter. (*See* TABLE I.) Of this total, 98% was produced on the land; only 1% came from the oceans and the inland waters. (A third source of food, microbial fermentation, is used primarily to produce certain vitamins and amino acids. These products are important nutritionally, but the quantity is small, and they are not included in this survey.)

Plant products constituted 92% of the human diet, with about 30 crop species providing most of the world's calories and protein. These included eight species of cereals, which collectively accounted for 52% of the world food supply. Animal products, constituting 7% of the world's diet, come indirectly from plants.

**Production, Distribution, and the Role of Science.** There are two aspects to the problem of feeding the world's people. The first is the complex task of producing sufficient quantities of the desired foods to satisfy

**Table I. World Food Production, 1984**

In 000 metric tons

| Commodity | Gross | Edible dry matter[1] | Protein[1] | % increase 1979–84 |
|---|---|---|---|---|
| Cereals | 1,802 | 1,500 | 155 | 16 |
| Wheat | 522 | 459 | 54 | 23 |
| Corn (maize) | 449 | 395 | 41 | 14 |
| Rice, rough | 470 | 319 | 27 | 24 |
| Barley | 172 | 151 | 15 | 0 |
| Sorghum/millet | 103 | 92 | 8 | 3 |
| Roots and tubers | 593 | 160 | 10 | 8 |
| Potato | 312 | 68 | 7 | 10 |
| Sweet potato | 117 | 35 | 2 | 3 |
| Cassava | 129 | 47 | 1 | 10 |
| Legumes, oilseeds, nuts | 243 | 162 | 55 | 10 |
| Sugarcane and sugar beets (sugar content only) | 113 | 113 | 0 | 11 |
| Vegetables and melons | 387 | 47 | 5 | 14 |
| Fruits | 300 | 39 | 2 | 5 |
| Animal products | 936 | 180 | 77 | 40 |
| Milk, meat, eggs | 856 | 158 | 59 | 37 |
| Fish | 80 | 21 | 14 | 7 |
| All food | 4,374 | 2,201 | 297 | 17 |

[1]At zero moisture content, excluding inedible hulls and shells.
Source: FAO *Production Yearbook.* Format adapted from L. T. Evans (ed.), *Crop Physiology* (1975).

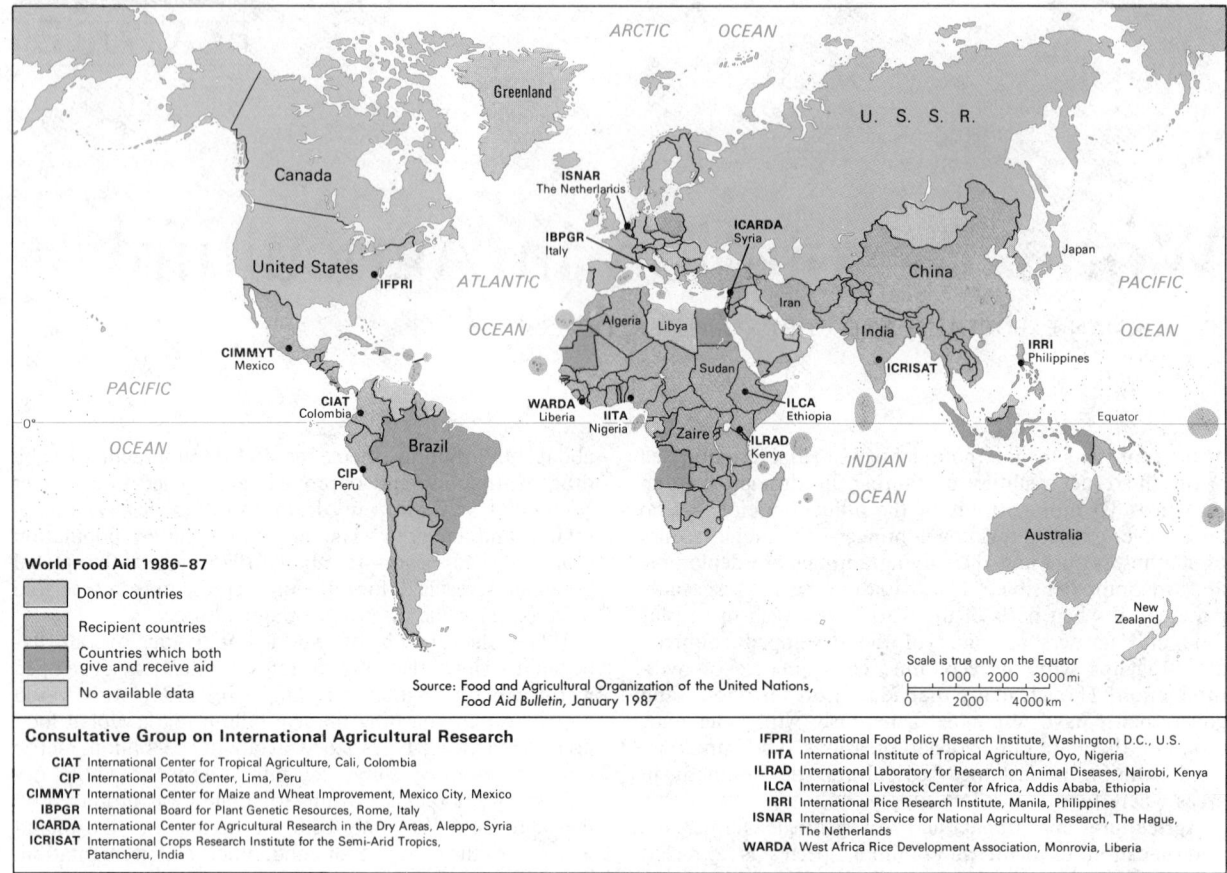

**World Food Aid 1986–87**

- Donor countries
- Recipient countries
- Countries which both give and receive aid
- No available data

Source: Food and Agricultural Organization of the United Nations, *Food Aid Bulletin*, January 1987

Scale is true only on the Equator
0 1000 2000 3000 mi
0 2000 4000 km

**Consultative Group on International Agricultural Research**

CIAT International Center for Tropical Agriculture, Cali, Colombia
CIP International Potato Center, Lima, Peru
CIMMYT International Center for Maize and Wheat Improvement, Mexico City, Mexico
IBPGR International Board for Plant Genetic Resources, Rome, Italy
ICARDA International Center for Agricultural Research in the Dry Areas, Aleppo, Syria
ICRISAT International Crops Research Institute for the Semi-Arid Tropics, Patancheru, India

IFPRI International Food Policy Research Institute, Washington, D.C., U.S.
IITA International Institute of Tropical Agriculture, Oyo, Nigeria
ILRAD International Laboratory for Research on Animal Diseases, Nairobi, Kenya
ILCA International Livestock Center for Africa, Addis Ababa, Ethiopia
IRRI International Rice Research Institute, Manila, Philippines
ISNAR International Service for National Agricultural Research, The Hague, The Netherlands
WARDA West Africa Rice Development Association, Monrovia, Liberia

people's needs. The second task, equally or even more complex, is to distribute the food equitably. The chief impediment to equitable food distribution is poverty—lack of purchasing power—resulting from unemployment or underemployment, which, in turn, is made more severe by rapid population growth. We feel that only by increasing agricultural productivity in food-deficient areas can both aspects of the world food problem be ameliorated. Further, we are convinced that science-based, high-yielding, sustainable agriculture is the key to the required increase.

This type of agriculture is a 20th-century invention. It is important to understand the role it has already played in increasing food production and reducing food prices for consumers. For without a continuing stream of productivity improvements, especially in areas with food shortages, an adequate diet for all humankind cannot be assured.

Until the 19th century, crop improvement was in the hands of farmers who selected seed from the most desirable plant types for sowing the following season. By the early decades of the 19th century, a number of progressive farmers in North America were busy developing and selling seeds from superior varieties based on their individual plant selections. The groundwork for more sophisticated genetic improvement of crop-plant species was laid by Charles Darwin in his writings on the variation of life species (published in 1859) and by Gregor Mendel through his discovery of the laws of genetic inheritance (reported in 1865). While Darwin's book immediately generated a great deal of interest, discussion, and controversy, Mendel's work was largely ignored for 35 years. The rediscovery in 1900 of the laws he had un-

covered, however, provoked tremendous scientific interest and research in plant genetics. Armed with a growing knowledge of genetics, soil chemistry and physics, plant physiology, plant pathology, and entomology, 20th-century agricultural scientists have made enormous contributions to increased food production throughout the world.

As recently as the 1930s, U.S. agriculture followed a traditional pattern for increasing food production. As sons and daughters of farm families married and formed new families, and as immigrants moved to the United States, they opened new land to cultivation. During much of the country's history there was an abundance of available land, and the demand for agricultural products was rising. Improvements in farm machinery expanded the size of a farm that could be cultivated by one family. They also made possible better seedbed preparation, conservation and utilization of moisture, timing of plantings, and weed control, resulting in modest increases in yield per hectare.

The institutional foundations for the development of high-yield agriculture in the United States were laid in the latter half of the 19th century and the early part of the 20th. In 1862 Pres. Abraham Lincoln signed into law three bills that played a vital role in raising U.S. agriculture to its current preeminent position: a law establishing the U.S. Department of Agriculture (USDA), a government agency charged with responsibilities for guiding and coordinating agricultural development; the Morrill Act, which established the publicly supported land-grant colleges of agricultural and mechanical arts in every state; and the Homestead Act, which made land available to landless persons who committed themselves to living on the property and developing it. These laws were supplemented in 1887 by the Hatch Act, which provided for the establishment of agricultural colleges, as well as for closer collaboration between the colleges and the USDA. In 1889 the USDA was raised to Cabinet status. In 1914 a final key organization, the Extension Service, was set up as the educational agency of the USDA and was charged with the responsibility of introducing new technologies to farmers and ranchers.

By the 1930s much of the scientific knowledge needed for high-yield agricultural production was available, but its utilization was delayed by the Great Depression of the 1930s, which paralyzed the agricultural economy. It was not until World War II brought a great demand for food to support the Allied war effort that these research findings began to be applied widely in the United States. Between 1940 and 1980 the combined production of 17 major food crops in the United States rose 142%—from 252 million to 610 million metric tons—with only a 3% increase in cultivated land. Had the 1940 yield levels persisted, an additional 177 million ha (437 million ac) of good quality cropland—an area almost equal in size to all the land east of the Mississippi River minus Illinois, Michigan, and Wisconsin—would have been needed to produce the 1985 harvest. The most impressive gain in the U.S. has been the 251% increase in corn (maize) yields, due in large part to the introduction of high-yielding hybrid varieties. As a result of the new technology, U.S. farmers in 1980 produced 120 million metric tons more corn from 6.6 million ha (16.3 million ac) less land than in 1940. The yields of wheat and other crops have also risen dramatically.

The driving forces behind these production gains have been new practices based on scientific research. They include the use of newly developed high-yielding crop varieties, increased reliance on irrigation and improved techniques for conserving moisture, a 14-fold increase since 1938 in the use of chemical fertilizers to restore soil fertility, more effective weed control through the use of improved cultural practices and herbicides, improved control of diseases and insects, and economic incentives to farmers to adopt these new practices. While the agricultural universities provided much of the basic scientific information underpinning the new technologies, it was the private sector that played the major role in the development, introduction, and distribution of improved seed, fertilizer, weed killers, and pesticides, as well as in the development of better farm machinery. Today U.S. farmers and ranchers, representing less than 2% of the country's economically active population, provide the nation with abundant food supplies that cost consumers only 12% of their disposable income, besides producing a huge exportable surplus.

During the past several decades, improved agricultural technology has also reached the farmers of Western Europe, Oceania, Canada, and Japan, as well as Eastern Europe and the U.S.S.R. Surprisingly, from 1950 to the early 1970s, agricultural production—starting from a low base—grew more rapidly in Eastern Europe and the Soviet Union than in Western Europe and North America, as mechanization and expanded use of fertilizers and pesticides were given high priority in the centrally planned economies. After the mid-1970s, however, this situation changed markedly, with agricultural production increasing sharply in the market-oriented countries and stagnating in the centrally planned, Communist bloc countries, the notable exception being the People's Republic of China. Today, the cereal-yield levels of the developed market economies are the highest in the world. They have been achieved through a combination of private-sector initia-

tives—aggressive agribusiness development and efficient, independent farmers and ranchers—and the research and policy support from public-sector organizations and government needed to stimulate the development and adoption of ever improving technology. In contrast, the lack of individual incentives, inefficient government planning, and government control over agriculture have held back progress in many Communist bloc countries.

**The Third World's Green Revolution.** For a variety of reasons, agricultural development, especially of food crops, was given a low priority in much of the third world until quite recently. In many cases, colonial powers had emphasized the production of cash crops such as cocoa, tea, coffee, and rubber, grown chiefly for export, and little attention had been paid to food crops. Following independence, the governments of the new nations tended to identify economic development with growth of the industrial sector. Despite the fact that 70–90% of the work force in most less developed countries was engaged in agriculture, development funds were channeled into industrial projects, many of them nonviable. Those agricultural development efforts that did occur usually met little success, since they attempted to transfer directly from high-income, temperate zone countries agricultural technologies that were unsuited to the labour-intensive, tropical and semitropical farming systems of the third world.

By the early 1960s declining per capita cereal production—the result of rapid population growth and stagnant agricultural output compounded by several years of drought—had led to acute food shortages in the third world, especially Asia. Most of the affected countries were too poor to purchase imports. It appeared that without perpetual food aid from the developed nations, millions of people in the third world faced continuing, and probably worsening, famine. With their backs to the wall, political leaders became more receptive to focusing on their nations' agricultural problems. In doing so they began to accept some views they had previously rejected. These included the possibility that productive agriculture was essential to economic growth and that supposedly tradition-bound peasant farmers would ultimately accept new technologies, if the technologies were appropriate.

Evidence to support this "radical" thinking about agricultural development was first produced in Mexico, where the Rockefeller Foundation, in conjunction with the government of Mexico, initiated the first cooperative international agricultural research program in 1943. During the 1950s Mexican farmers made great strides in applying new technology—improved varieties and modern cultivation techniques—developed by the foundation to increase yields, and by the late 1950s the country had become self-sufficient in most food commodities.

In 1960, after helping to develop a well-trained corps of agricultural scientists and a national research infrastructure that would provide a continuing flow of new technologies for Mexico's farmers, the Rockefeller Foundation joined forces with the Ford Foundation to create the first full-fledged international agricultural research organization, the International Rice Research Institute (IRRI), located in the Philippines. Shortly thereafter, the international parts of the Rockefeller Foundation corn and wheat programs in Mexico were reorganized, leading to the creation in 1966 of the International Center for Maize and Wheat Improvement (CIMMYT), with headquarters in Mexico.

With their commodity-oriented, interdisciplinary research and training programs focused on solving the most pressing food-production problems in the third world,

Various strains of rice grow at the International Rice Research Institute (IRRI) in Los Bãnos, Philippines. The IRRI has developed high-yield rice plants with high disease resistance and the ability to withstand strong winds.

GENE HETTEL

CIMMYT and IRRI were unique research institutions. They became the models for other international research centres, each concerned with major commodities and food-production problems relevant to third world agricultural development. This network, which has grown to 13 international agricultural research centres, has been a vital force in stimulating appropriate technology development for the major food crops and farming systems in the less developed world.

By the mid-1960s CIMMYT and IRRI scientists had developed disease-resistant, semidwarf wheat and rice varieties with radically improved yields. These new short varieties were much more efficient than their tall predecessor varieties in converting sunlight and nutrients into grain production. Furthermore, their superior plant architecture provided resistance against lodging (falling over) in heavy winds and under improved conditions of soil fertility and moisture. Even when farmers used traditional methods of cultivation, the new wheats and rices yielded more grain than the traditional local varieties. However, when these new varieties were grown with adequate moisture and soil fertility, they yielded up to four times as much. Nevertheless, many agricultural scientists were skeptical about the willingness of farmers to accept the new varieties. Not only did they look different from the traditional types, but they also required substantially different care, especially in the use of fertilizer, in water management, and in weed control.

Despite the misgivings of many local researchers, national leaders in India and Pakistan, facing desperate and deteriorating food situations, decided to embark on major programs to introduce the new varieties and farming techniques as quickly as possible. In the beginning they authorized the purchase of large quantities of the new seeds and massive amounts of fertilizer. Extensive farm demonstration programs were established, and once farmers saw the results of the new technologies, they themselves became the major spokesmen for the new methods. At the same time, national leaders radically changed national investment policies in order to build up domestic seed- and fertilizer-production facilities and assure farmers a price for their grain at harvest similar to that prevailing on the international market, all critical factors for sustaining growth in food production.

The gamble taken by courageous leaders in India and Pakistan—and later in many other countries—has paid

off handsomely. The combined rice and wheat output of the less developed countries increased by 220 million tons, or 74%, between 1965 and 1980, with only a 20% increase in the area planted. (*See* TABLE II.) High-yielding crop varieties, much higher levels of fertilization, markedly higher investments in agriculture, more efficient use of irrigation, and fair prices for grain at harvest were the driving forces behind the improvement. Productivity gains on the farm, in combination with improved systems for delivering fertilizers, pesticides, and other inputs to farmers and for conveying their produce to the markets, greatly expanded the availability of food for consumers while reducing its real price. In addition, rural economic development was stimulated as more bountiful harvests brought expanded job opportunities and higher wage levels.

This breakthrough in wheat and rice production has come to be known as the Green Revolution. Many early reports of the Green Revolution depicted it as a wholesale transfer of high-yield technology from developed countries to peasant farmers in the third world. This was incorrect. In reality, the Green Revolution was the start of a process of using principles of modern agricultural science to develop technologies appropriate to the conditions of third world farmers.

While India, Pakistan, and the Philippines received world attention for their agricultural progress during the 1960s and 1970s, the greatest third world success story of the 1980s has been China, home to one-fifth of the world's people. By changing from a system of centralized planning and control over agricultural production to a regional system based on market incentives, and by making widespread use of appropriate high-yield technology, China has moved ahead of the U.S. and the U.S.S.R. to become the world's biggest food producer. New agricultural policies have brought farmers higher prices, wider markets, and greater individual freedom to decide what to produce. The reform, called the production responsibility system, has resulted in what amounts to a de facto privatization of Chinese farming. While farmland is still collectively owned and the government continues to set production targets for basic crops, the rewards that a farmer receives are now directly linked to output. This encourages initiative, innovation, investment, efficiency, and risk-taking by individuals.

CIMMYT

Wheat researchers in India work with the International Center for Maize and Wheat Improvement. CIMMYT cooperates with scientists in each country where its research is being implemented, exchanging information and training agricultural workers.

**Table II. Estimated Changes in Production, Yield, and Use of Inputs for Wheat and Rice Production in Less Developed Countries, 1965–80**

|  | 1965 | 1975 | 1980 | % change 1965–80 |
|---|---|---|---|---|
| Wheat and rice production (000,000 tons) | 303 | 451 | 527 | 74 |
| Yield (t/ha) | 1.54 | 1.77 | 2.25 | 46 |
| Area (000,000 ha) | 196 | 228 | 234 | 20 |
| Fertilizer (000,000 tons) | 1.8 | 6.7 | 10.3 | 572 |
| Machinery (000,000 units) | 0.319 | 0.763 | 1.12 | 351 |
| Draft animals (000,000) | 301 | 317 | 332 | 10 |
| Labour (000,000 person-yrs) | 230 | 242 | 234 | 9 |

Source: CGIAR Impact Study, 1985.

A second factor in China's agricultural success story is the rapid increase in agricultural research since the end of the Cultural Revolution in 1977. This has led to the development and widespread adoption of high-yielding modern varieties, much higher levels of fertilizer use, improved water management, and more effective practices of weed, disease, and insect control. Since 1978 agricultural production in China has risen by nearly 8% a year—the highest rate in the world—and average incomes in rural areas have grown by about 70%; without much fanfare, 800 million Chinese peasants have become 70% richer.

The Green Revolution, however, has not progressed at the same rate everywhere, nor has it reached all crops or all farming areas. Crop yields in many areas in less developed countries—generally, regions with precarious growing environments and no irrigation facilities—remain abysmally low. While the environmental problems in some of these regions are too great for science to overcome with current technologies, many marginal farming areas could be made substantially more productive through a combination of wise scientific methods and government policies.

**Prospects for World Agriculture.** Future world food demand will be determined by two factors: expanding population and increases in per capita food consumption. Sometime in 1987 world population reached the five billion mark, and by the year 2000 it will have passed six billion. Eighty percent of this growth will occur in less developed nations, in rural areas, and among the poor.

In the more developed market economies, such as the United States, Canada, and the European Communities (EC), population is growing very slowly. The people are already well fed, and little increase in per capita food consumption is expected. In the more developed centrally planned countries of Eastern Europe and the U.S.S.R., population is also growing slowly, although per capita food consumption, especially of meat products, continues to increase. More feed grain will be required if per capita meat consumption there is to rise.

In much of the less developed world—in both market-oriented and centrally planned economies—the population is continuing to grow rapidly, and substantial increases in per capita food consumption are still needed, especially for the poor. It is projected that between 1987 and the year 2000 the population of the third world will grow by more than one billion people, or 20%. Thus, total food supplies in the less developed world will have to increase by at least 33% just to maintain current—and often inadequate—per capita food-consumption levels. If economic development succeeds and incomes rise, demand for food in the third world will be much higher. A considerable portion of this increased demand, if it materializes, will be for poultry and livestock products, commodities that are typically associated with higher living standards. This will require much larger quantities of cereals, grain legumes, and oilseeds for feed.

During the period 1979–81, world grain production stood at some 1,590,000,000 tons. In 1983 the Winrock International Institute for Agricultural Development, an independent research organization with headquarters in Arkansas, published *World Agriculture: Review and Prospects into the 1990s.* The study estimates that between 1979–81 and 1993 world grain production will rise by 30%, or 446 million tons, with half of this growth occurring in the third world. The projections made in this study, while only a few years old, are already out of date for some regions, especially the Far East, where China, India, and Indonesia have achieved much greater than expected growth in cereal production since the late 1970s. (*See* TABLE III.)

Approximately 80% of the projected gains will occur on farmlands currently in production. There are still some vast, largely unpopulated tracts, especially in sub-Saharan Africa and South America, that may eventually come into agricultural production. However, the cost of settling these areas, with their generally fragile ecosystems, makes them unlikely candidates for significant food production during the remainder of the century.

In all the more developed countries—both market-oriented and centrally planned—population growth is very modest. These nations should be able to increase per capita production relatively easily without expanding the area under cultivation, provided suitable technologies continue to be introduced. However, the spectacular increases in crop yields achieved during the 1960s and 1970s probably will not be matched in the 1980s and 1990s. In the United States, Australia, and Argentina—countries that currently export much of their agricultural products—considerable capacity exists to increase grain surpluses provided reasonable prices can be obtained in international markets. In the United States, the prairies and Corn Belt of the Midwest contain some of the best farmland in the world for growing grain. The U.S. government has attempted to avoid overproduction and the collapse of world grain prices through programs designed to keep land out of production. In 1984, 11 million ha (30 million ac) were lying fallow, enrolled in special government programs to set aside land.

The current surpluses of grain, meat, and dairy products in the EC countries are the result of an expensive program of subsidies to European farmers provided through the EC's common agricultural policy (CAP). To encourage self-sufficiency in basic food supplies, the CAP established domestic producer prices for grain, meats, and dairy products that are considerably above world prices. When world prices fall, as they have in recent years, the cost of the farm subsidies to EC taxpayers becomes exorbitant. Currently the subsidized surpluses are sold primarily in the third world, often at prices so low that third world farmers are discouraged from increasing their own output. While the EC remains committed to subsidizing European farmers in order to achieve self-sufficiency, it did not intend the CAP to promote costly overproduction for export, and it seems unlikely that the EC will allow this overproduction to continue. Already a quota system has been imposed on dairy farmers, and the introduction of similar quotas for grain and meat production seems probable. Under such quotas, each EC country would have a predetermined amount of agricultural output authorized at official prices. Any excess would have to be sold on world markets at international prices.

**Table III. Cereal Production, by Regions, Between 1976–78 and 1982–84**

In 000 metric tons

| Region | 1976–78 | 1979–81 | 1982–84 |
|---|---|---|---|
| North America | 309,893 | 343,999 | 333,220 |
| Western Europe | 154,484 | 169,682 | 188,307 |
| Oceania | 19,923 | 21,921 | 25,586 |
| Other developed market economies (Japan, Israel, S. Africa) | 28,326 | 28,476 | 23,280 |
| Eastern Europe and U.S.S.R. | 290,789 | 249,931 | 264,387 |
| Sub-Saharan Africa (excl. S. Africa) | 45,968 | 49,235 | 47,748 |
| Latin America | 85,919 | 92,354 | 104,020 |
| North Africa/Middle East | 53,903 | 56,661 | 56,245 |
| Far East less developed economies | 250,734 | 271,371 | 304,369 |
| Asia centrally planned economies | 276,870 | 308,869 | 369,154 |
| Developed (incl. E. Europe and U.S.S.R.) | 803,416 | 814,010 | 834,772 |
| Less developed (incl. Asia CPE) | 728,717 | 778,533 | 881,576 |
| World | 1,516,846 | 1,592,542 | 1,716,348 |

Source: FAO 1982–1984 Production Yearbooks.

Agricultural production in the U.S.S.R. and most Eastern European countries has stagnated in recent years, and yields have actually declined in many areas. The rapid growth of grain imports by these nations during the past decade is largely a result of the rising demand for livestock feed. Given the prevailing Soviet bloc policy of maintaining artificially low consumer prices, it is reasonable to expect continued growth of grain imports in these countries in the coming years. While the disappointing performance of Soviet agriculture is partly attributable to difficult climatic conditions and overcentralization in agricultural planning, the lack of incentives for individual farmers is the major factor limiting increases in productivity. The new Soviet leader, Mikhail Gorbachev—who is frequently pictured in the Western press as a reformer—until very recently has given no indication that radical reforms in Soviet agriculture would be forthcoming. Instead of moving toward a free market system, like the "reformed" centrally planned economies of China and Hungary, the U.S.S.R. has emphasized fine tuning of the planning process. If Soviet food production does not begin to show improvement, the U.S.S.R. may be forced to consider a more market-oriented solution. Even if this occurs, however, it seems likely that the U.S.S.R. and Eastern Europe will continue to be large food importers for the remainder of the century and beyond.

In contrast, given appropriate investments and policies, the prospects for increased food production in the less developed world are good, although growth rates over the rest of the century probably will not be as strong as those in the 1970s and 1980s. From a strictly technical standpoint, the third world countries have significant agricultural potential on which to capitalize, if appropriate incentives and the required inputs, such as fertilizer, are provided.

In China, where population growth is slowing and the "market-oriented" incentives introduced since 1978 have spurred spectacular expansion in the agricultural sector, per capita production should continue to increase. Production in most other East Asian countries is also expected to rise faster than population. On the other hand, Latin America will have more difficulty raising per capita production. Considerable yield increases are still attainable if suitable economic incentives are offered to farmers, especially in Argentina, Brazil, and Uruguay. But because of the heavy debt burden of these nations, it is unlikely that yield increases can match the area's rapid population growth.

In Asia and Latin America the critical tasks in agricultural development are to continue broadening the use of high-yielding varieties and improved agronomic practices—especially the use of more fertilizer of the correct kind—expand irrigation potential, maintain food-price stability, and develop more employment opportunities off the farm. Assuming that per capita incomes resume their upward trend, there will be strong growth in the demand for food grains and livestock products. The bulk of this demand can be met through increased domestic production, although cereal grain and livestock imports will probably continue the upward trend of the past 20 years. Growth in agricultural production will help to expand rural employment opportunities, increase per capita incomes, lower food costs (the major expenditure item for the poor), and release scarce resources for other development projects.

Agriculture in North Africa and the Middle East suffers from overcentralization and the uncertainties resulting from political unrest. With population growth rates expected to remain quite high, it is unlikely that food production can outstrip population unless important reforms occur. Assuming that the oil glut is a short-range problem, higher oil revenues should permit many countries to increase their food imports. The Winrock Institute study cited above predicts a 50% increase in food imports in this region between 1979–81 and 1993.

In sub-Saharan Africa extreme poverty, poor soils, low and uncertain rainfall, increasing population pressures, changing ownership patterns for land and cattle, and weak national agricultural research and production systems all make agricultural improvements difficult. Too many officials in African nations—as well as at the international level—seem to think that once the drought that precipitated famine in Ethiopia, The Sudan, and more than 20 other countries is over, agricultural production will promptly recover and harvests will again be sufficient for people's needs. This will not happen automatically, and those holding such views fail to comprehend the magnitude and complexities of the interacting forces—of which drought is only one—that have contributed to the current tragic situation.

For more than 15 years, food production in most sub-Saharan countries has not kept pace with demand, as explosive population growth has overwhelmed the traditional agricultural systems. The present crisis is largely the result of neglect by political leaders. Despite the fact that 70–85% of the people in most African countries are engaged in agriculture, development of agricultural and rural sectors was given a low priority. Investment in distribution and marketing systems and in agricultural research and education was woefully inadequate. Furthermore, many governments pursued a policy of providing cheap food for the politically volatile urban dwellers at the expense of production incentives for farmers.

Despite the formidable challenges in Africa, the elements that worked in Asia and Latin America will also work there. Past experience in other parts of the third world provides us with greater knowledge of what to do. In many cases, researchers have developed improved technologies for sub-Saharan farming systems. Sadly, few of these "research products" are being extended to farmers. If effective seed-production and fertilizer-supply industries are developed, the nations of sub-Saharan Africa can make great strides in improving the nutritional and economic well-being of their desperately poor populations.

To capitalize on the unexploited agricultural potential of the third world—and on the significant new technologies in the pipeline—continued investment in agricultural research, water resource development, input production and distribution systems, and grain marketing and storage facilities is essential. This must be complemented by economic policies that stimulate agricultural productivity in ways consistent with the wise use of natural resources. It should be stressed, however, that pursuing policies that encourage high production without, at the same time, introducing technologies that will increase yields and reduce costs will defeat the purpose.

The evidence of the Green Revolution is that improved technology and effective policy must go together; manipulation of prices alone will not ensure success in agricultural development. The development of improved technology, moreover, does not necessarily assure its adoption by most farmers. Linking agricultural research and production activities so as to promote the generation and dissemination of more effective technology remains a major institutional challenge facing policymakers in the third world.

**A Look in the Research Pipeline.** Ten to 15 years usually elapse between the time research and development is funded and the point when the results show up in production figures; thus, gains in the remainder of the 20th century will be largely the result of research investments already made.

In addition to continuing breakthroughs in wheat and rice, improved varieties of corn, field beans, cassava, potatoes, cowpeas, sorghum, and pearl millet are being developed. These varieties have heightened disease and insect resistance, as well as higher yields and greater yield stability under difficult conditions, such as drought and heat. Triticale, a high-yielding, protein-rich hybrid of wheat and rye, has great potential for expanding grain production to such marginal areas as the cool Himalayan foothills and the acid-soil *campos cerrados* of South America. Also in the pipeline are wheat varieties tolerant to high levels of soluble aluminum, characteristic of many tropical soils where wheat traditionally has not flourished. New varieties of rice—the principal food grain in the third world—will make it possible to increase production in upland areas. Research on legume and pasture species, a more recent undertaking, is producing new varieties and production technologies that will permit higher levels of livestock production in the semiarid tropics, particularly the drought-prone zones of Africa and Latin America. The development of faster maturing varieties will allow two or three harvests a year in many areas where only one or two are now possible.

Another promising avenue of research, crossing domesticated crop species with related wild species, may lead to varieties with greater yield potential and dependability in marginal areas. Generally, such "wide crosses" involve breaking down natural barriers between species in order to introduce useful genes from alien plant genera—providing, for example, resistance to certain diseases and insects and tolerance to salinity, high temperatures, and drought—into domesticated species. One probable benefit would be greater year-to-year stability in third world food production.

More efficient methods of tillage and cultivation and more productive crop-rotation patterns are also being developed and made available to farmers; for example, improved production systems to manage heavy impermeable clay soils and soils that are highly oxidized and acidic. These technologies not only stand to increase yield levels markedly, especially in areas dependent on rainfall for their water supply, but can also help to reduce soil erosion. It should be noted, however, that crop-management research in the third world is one of the weakest links in the research chain. Research programs in less developed countries are not easy to organize and direct, since they must contend with a set of difficult and often complex circumstances—environment limitations, poverty, land-ownership patterns, labour, energy/power constraints, shortages of fertilizers and other inputs and of credit. Nevertheless, such research is essential.

International and national research efforts are also under way to increase tropical livestock production, especially in sub-Saharan Africa. The work to develop vaccines or other methods of controlling trypanosomiasis, or sleeping sickness, and East Coast fever, which make large tracts in Africa unusable for livestock raising, is especially important. If successful, it would vastly extend the domain and increase the productivity of livestock in sub-Saharan Africa, as well as reducing the incidence of related human diseases. The male sterile technique of insect control, in which male insects are sterilized by irradiation and then released to mate, was used successfully to eradicate the screwworm from livestock in the United States a decade ago and is now being used to eradicate it from Mexico. It shows promise for control of several fruit flies and possibly the cotton boll weevil and the tsetse fly, the carrier of sleeping sickness.

CIMMYT

Norman Borlaug (right) confers with a CIMMYT wheat pathologist in Ecuador. Research has led to higher crop yields and greater yield stability under difficult conditions, such as drought and heat.

African student examines corn as part of her six-month basic training at CIMMYT. Sub-Saharan Africa needs more agricultural researchers to help offset the effects of its extreme poverty, poor soils, low and uncertain rainfall, and weak national agricultural systems.

CIMMYT

**What to Expect from Biotechnology.** The new genetic-engineering techniques of tissue culture, cell fusion, and gene splicing and DNA transfer, widely publicized in recent years, open new horizons for solving some of the most frustrating problems of animal, human, and plant health. But how soon will they begin to affect food production?

Great progress has been made in employing these techniques with bacteria and yeasts to produce insulin, interferon, and growth hormones. Current research with somatotrophin bovine hormone indicates it may play an important role in increasing milk production within the next 15 years. Similarly, microbiologically produced growth hormones may increase the production of meat within the next two decades. It will be possible to produce improved vaccines for many bacterial and viral diseases of humans and animals more safely and efficiently, and there is hope that effective vaccines against some of the complex vector-borne parasitic diseases, such as trypanosomiasis and malaria, will be developed within 20 or 30 years.

Some enthusiasts predict that these techniques will make it possible to increase the level of disease and insect resistance in higher plants, decreasing the need for chemical fungicides and insecticides. They also predict the development of cereal varieties that, like legumes, can fix atmospheric nitrogen (*i.e.,* convert nitrogen from the air into usable compounds in the soil), thus substantially reducing the need for chemical nitrogen fertilizer. While significant breakthroughs will undoubtedly come from these new lines of research, it is our view that such achievements will not be realized until well into the 21st century, if then. There is a tendency to overpromise the potential of a new technology; overzealous efforts to secure more research funds are partly responsible.

Researchers have shown that bacteria of the *Azospirillum* species inhabit the root zones of tropical grasses and fix a considerable amount of the nitrogen used by these plants. They are sometimes present in the roots of wheat, corn, and sorghum, and if their presence could be increased, more nitrogen could be fixed biologically for these vitally important cereal crops. There is also interest in a number of other biologic systems for fixing atmospheric nitrogen, such as the *Azolla* floating fern–blue-green alga system for paddy rice, as well as beneficial root fungi. The information generated to date merits additional intensive research, and it may well be that scientists will eventually succeed in developing cereal varieties capable of fixing a substantial portion of the nitrogen they require. However, that day is still far in the future, if, indeed, it ever comes.

As for plant breeding, leaving aside asexually propagated species such as potatoes, there is little or no firm evidence as yet that molecular genetic techniques will produce superior, higher-yielding field crop varieties with greater disease and insect resistance within the next 15 years. Many genes and interactions among genes influence the productive potential of cereal crop species, but far fewer basic studies have been undertaken on the genetic makeup of higher plants than on humans and animals, which have been studied intensively in the course of cancer research. This lack of fundamental knowledge limits the effective use of many biotechnological techniques for plant improvement.

Transfers of genes providing disease and insect resistance into crop species through genetic-engineering techniques, while no doubt quicker than conventional plant breeding, will not necessarily result in more durable resistance than has been achieved with conventional methods. Disease-causing organisms and insect pests, when faced with extinction, mutate into new races capable of attacking previously resistant varieties. This biologic reality will continue in force even in the "new age" of genetic engineering. Fortunately, much can be and is being done to exploit conventional plant-breeding methods to improve disease and insect resistance, enhance tolerance to severe environmental conditions, and increase genetic yield potential in the major food and feed grains. Meanwhile, much remains to be done in making better use of the improved varieties and cultural practices currently available.

**Agricultural Trade Prospects.** Despite the large surpluses of grain currently in the marketplace, the Winrock study describes a striking picture emerging in the world grain economy. Although the number of countries with exportable food surpluses has risen temporarily, the general trend is toward fewer exporting countries and increasing food deficits in many nations. The United States, Canada, Australia, Argentina, Thailand, and, more recently, the EC account for about 95% of the grain traded in international markets. When these traditional surplus-producing regions are excluded from world grain-production data, the global cereal-grain deficit in 1969–71 equaled 40 million tons or 4.3% of consumption. By 1979–81 this deficit had grown to 133 million tons or 10.7% of consumption, and it is projected at 224 million tons or 13.6% of consumption by 1993.

Recent projections (1986) by the International Food Policy Research Institute on the demand for cereal feed grains in the third world to the year 2000 predict very strong growth in these commodities. By the end of the century the demand for cereal feeds in less developed countries (excluding China) is expected to increase two and a half times, from 100 million tons in 1980 to 245 million tons. On the basis of this analysis, an 86 million-ton feed-grain deficit is forecast for the third world. These projections point to the vital role that agricultural exports will have to play in future decades.

Despite the large surpluses of grains, milk, and butter in the world marketplace—and the resulting depressed agricultural commodity prices—the long-term global trends point to considerably greater agricultural trade volumes in the years ahead. The greatest potential buyers of food commodities are the Pacific Rim countries of Asia, including China; the U.S.S.R. and the Eastern European countries; and the countries of North Africa and the Middle East. Of the countries with domestic shortages, only those in sub-Saharan Africa will be likely to have difficulty financing food imports. According to the Winrock study, domestic food production in sub-Saharan Africa supplied 92% of total demand in the period 1979–81, with the remainder made up through imports; by 1993 domestic production is expected to account for only 75% of demand. It is unlikely that the poor African nations will be able to pay for large amounts of food, so continuing foreign aid will probably be needed at least for the remainder of this decade.

Even with the Green Revolution, less developed countries have been the most significant growth market for U.S. agricultural products during the past 20 years. In 1977 third world countries accounted for only 30% of U.S. food exports. Today they account for almost 50% of total U.S. export trade, with most of the increase going to the newly industrializing nations and the oil-exporting countries. Interestingly, those less developed countries with the highest agricultural growth rates have also increased their agricultural imports the most; rising incomes have sparked a stronger demand for feed grains and livestock products than domestic producers could supply, and increased amounts of agricultural inputs and machinery, as well as other manufactured goods, have been purchased from industrialized nations. In addition, some of the more agriculturally prosperous less developed countries have tended to concentrate on producing those crops they can grow best while relying on imports for commodities produced more efficiently elsewhere—an example of the economic principle of comparative advantage. Brazil is a case in point: while domestic soybean production and exports have increased rapidly, so have Brazilian imports of wheat as traditional wheatlands have been shifted into soybean production. As improved wheat varieties are developed with adequate disease resistance and tolerance to acid soils, Brazilian wheat could become more profitable and production could rebound.

**The Environmental Issue.** The techniques that made the Green Revolution possible rely heavily on chemicals, mainly fertilizers, and there has been public concern, mostly in the developed countries, about the possible adverse effects of modern, high-yield agricultural technology on the environment, public health, and the survival of wildlife. In our opinion, some members of the environmental movement have played on the public's fears with propaganda campaigns designed to convey the idea that civilization is about to be poisoned out of existence. They often leave the impression that the environment is making us sick, but a look at the record suggests that the opposite is closer to the truth. People today live longer and more pleasant lives than those of any previous generation. In 1900 average life expectancy in the United States at birth was 47.3 years, 46.3 years for males and 48.3 for females. By 1940 average life expectancy at birth had increased to 62.9 years (60.8 for males, 65.2 for females), and by 1982 life expectancy for the entire population had risen to 74.5 years (70.8 for males, 78.2 for females). It continues to increase.

Two factors have added to the confusion: (1) tests used today for detecting the presence of various chemicals in the environment are highly sensitive and thus reveal very small amounts of a contaminant (*e.g.,* a fraction of a part per billion), and (2) testing procedures used to determine safety, based on high dosages of a chemical over a long period of time, tend to magnify the risks of exposure at lower levels. Modern methods of chemical analysis have also shown that many foods included in the human diet since the preagricultural epoch of the hunter-gatherers contain naturally occurring organic compounds that are toxic, mutagenic, carcinogenic, or otherwise harmful at high dosages. On the basis of current knowledge, nevertheless, it appears that at low levels they normally do no harm.

Antitechnology activists seem to imply that the world can, and should, go back to producing its food with pre-World War II technology. However, the agricultural technology of the 1930s, which was adequate to produce food for a world of two billion people, could not produce the food required by five billion. To return to the methods of 50 years ago would be to plunge the world into famine and into social, economic, political, and—yes—environmental chaos. The general public, especially the urban part of it, does not understand the complexities and difficulties of producing and protecting our crops, most of which could not be grown at all or would not

CIMMYT

A Pakistani researcher examines a stalk of wheat. Crossing domestic species with related wild species may lead to domesticated varieties with greater resistance to disease and insects and tolerance for salinity, high temperatures, and drought.

produce reasonable yields without modern husbandry. This ignorance unless corrected poses a serious threat to the food supply of future generations.

An educational program is needed to explain the realities of modern farming to the nonrural public. Such a program should emphasize that the vast tracts of primeval wilderness are gone forever—victims of the encroachment of so-called civilization and humankind's propensity to "be fruitful and multiply." Indeed, we would submit that the "population explosion"—rather than the depredations of materialistic, consumer-oriented, high-income societies—is the greatest environmental threat to planet Earth. If the vestiges of primeval wilderness that remain are to be preserved, all sectors of society must become more supportive of efforts to increase the productivity of land now being used to produce our food and fibre while, at the same time, slowing demographic growth to manageable levels. The protection of our environment against the damage resulting from overpopulation depends in large measure on the ingenuity of scientists in developing new technologies to manage and increase the productivity of our natural resource base.

An attempt to turn back the clock invites disaster. For example, if U.S. farmers used the agricultural technology of the 1930s and 1940s to produce the harvest of 1985, they would have to convert 75% of the permanent pasturelands in the U.S. or 60% of American forests and woodland areas to cropland. Even this may be an underestimation, since the pasture and forestlands are potentially less productive than the land now planted to crops. This would greatly accelerate soil erosion and destroy wildlife habitats and recreational areas. Rather than increasing the amount of land in crop production, the need is to cut back. During the 1970s the cultivated area in the U.S. was expanded by 30%, much of it marginal and highly susceptible to erosion. The environmental damage caused by this land use was recognized in 1985 U.S. farm legislation, which provides a land set-aside program that pays farmers to return these more fragile lands to permanent pasture for at least ten years. This is environmentally sound, but how long it can be sustained politically is another matter.

Without doubt, the single most important factor limiting crop yields worldwide is soil infertility. The use of chemical fertilizers to restore soil fertility is a contentious issue, but unless soil fertility is restored, farmers will gain little benefit from the use of improved varieties and more productive cultural practices. Among the major plant nutrient deficiencies in soils, the lack of sufficient nitrogen is by far the most widespread, although phosphorus and potassium deficiencies are also pervasive. Though they are encountered less frequently, deficiencies of secondary nutrients, sulfur, calcium, magnesium, and minor elements such as zinc, iron, copper, molybdenum, manganese, and boron, depress yields in certain areas, especially where intensive cropping is practiced. Essential nutrients may be removed from the soil as a result of weathering followed by leaching, soil erosion, or "extractive" farming practices, or chemical reactions in the soil may tie up nutrients so that plants cannot utilize them.

Many of the traditional farming systems of the third world are essentially "mining" operations whereby crops are harvested year after year and little or none of the crop residues or animal wastes—which would partially restore soil fertility—are returned to the soil. The Chinese, Japanese, and South Koreans have done an excellent job of maintaining a moderate level of fertility through the use of organic wastes and residues, but even in these countries, large amounts of chemical fertilizers are needed. Without huge quantities of chemical nitrogenous and phosphatic fertilizer, China could not have achieved the spectacular production increases of the last 15 years.

Soil fertility can be restored effectively by applying the right amounts of the right kind of fertilizer—either chemical or organic or, preferably, a combination of the two—according to the requirements of different crops, soil types, and environments. With the per capita base of arable land shrinking in densely populated countries, all the available land must be used for food crops and cannot be allowed to regain fertility by lying fallow. Moreover, in many countries most animal manure is used as a home fuel for cooking and thus is not available as a fertilizer. A recent survey by the U.S. Agency for International Development estimated that 400 million tons of animal manure were being used annually for cooking fires. Hence, if the world's food needs are to be met during the next several decades, it will be necessary to increase the use of chemical fertilizers on the infertile and nutrient-depleted soils of less developed nations. Fortunately, breakthroughs in fertilizer-production technology—especially for nitrogenous fertilizers—during the past 20 years have kept real prices relatively low. Improved methods of application at the farm level can eliminate overuse, reducing costs and also helping to prevent runoff into streams and lakes.

Despite irrefutable scientific evidence that chemical fertilizers, used wisely, do not harm the soil, some organic gardening enthusiasts insist that organic fertilizers could satisfy all our needs. Organic manures are very effective for growing backyard vegetable gardens, but it does not follow that the same procedure can be used to produce food for five billion people in a land-hungry world. It would take about 4.4 billion tons of composted organic animal manure (1.5% nitrogen on a dry-weight basis) to produce the equivalent of the 65 million metric tons of chemical nitrogen used today—quite a dung heap and quite an aroma, were it available. To produce it would require a three- to fourfold increase in world animal production, necessitating, in turn, huge increases in the output of feed grains and pasturage. Furthermore, the transportation costs associated with distributing these fertilizers would be prohibitive.

The point is not that there should be no safeguards to protect the environment and human health from the possible damaging side effects of modern agricultural technology. On the contrary, governments should make every effort to protect the health and welfare of their citizens. But we must also become more knowledgeable and realistic about science and technology and their relationship to food production in our interdependent world. In our view, the antiscience and antitechnology bias so prevalent in affluent countries is both hypocritical and potentially damaging to the third world. In effect, the haves are telling the have-nots that they should stay with their pristine, rural, bucolic, miserable life-styles, since greater material well-being isn't what it's made out to be. Yet people in the developed world are healthier and have the prospect of leading longer, more productive, more comfortable lives than ever before. To trade places with peasants in the less developed world would be to cut their life spans by one half or more, see up to half of their children die before reaching the age of ten, often as a result of minor and easily curable illnesses, live in illiteracy with substandard clothing, shelter, and sanitation, and face poor prospects of improved economic well-being for themselves and their children. Unwittingly, this is the continuing fate that the affluent antitechnology groups are wishing on the third world's people.

## Blainey, Geoffrey

Through three decades of readable and authoritative books, the historian Geoffrey Blainey has interpreted Australian economic and social history and anthropology. The son of a clergyman, Blainey was born March 11, 1930, in Melbourne. After graduating from Queens College of the University of Melbourne, he set out to be a free-lance writer and took a job in Tasmania on the Mt. Lyell mining field. From that experience came his first book, *The Peaks of Lyell* (1954).

WARRNAMBOOL STANDARD

His second book, *A Centenary History of the University of Melbourne* (1957), took him back to academe, and in 1961 he began his teaching career as reader in economic history at the University of Melbourne. He was made professor in 1968, and in 1977 he was given the Ernest Scott chair in history, which he continues to hold. For six years he was also dean of the faculty of arts. His lucid and imaginative writing has won him numerous awards and helped make him a television presence in explaining economic history and international affairs. He has served on many public agencies, as chairman of the Australia Council (the main patron of the arts in Australia) and chairman of the Australia-China Council. In 1982–83 he was visiting professor at Harvard University. His later books include *The Causes of War* (1973), *Triumph of the Nomads* (1975), and *A Land Half Won* (1980).

MIN ZHONGJIE—XINHUA NEWS AGENCY

## Fei Xiaotong

Fighting his way back from the obscurity to which the Cultural Revolution condemned him, Fei Xiaotong (Fei Hsiao-t'ung), China's foremost social anthropologist, has revived the scientific study of village life in China.

Born Nov. 2, 1910, in Wujiang (Wu-chiang) District, Jiangsu (Kiangsu) Province, Fei was graduated in 1933 from Yanjing (Yen-ching) University in Beijing (Peking) and did graduate work at Quinghua (Chi'ing-hua) University in Beijing, the London School of Economics, and the University of London. He became professor of anthropology at Quinghua in 1945 and deputy dean there in 1949. His star appeared to be rising until he made the mistake of taking Mao Zedong's (Mao Tse-tung's) Hundred Flowers movement too literally. He rebounded from these troubles but fell victim to the Cultural Revolution in 1967. Fei reappeared, fully rehabilitated, in 1972 and is now professor and director of the Institute of Sociology of Beijing

University and chairman of the Chinese Democratic League.

In addition to his writings, Fei's effectiveness in communicating knowledge in recent years has resided in his scholarly contacts with Western colleagues. Among his books originally written in English are *Peasant Life in China* (1939), *China's Gentry* (1953), *Chinese Village Close-up* (1983), and *Small Towns in China* (1986).

JIM KALETT

## Galbraith, John Kenneth

Economist, diplomat, author, critic, and consummate communicator, John Kenneth Galbraith, for almost 40 years, has been an articulate and influential force in the moderate-liberal wing of the U.S. political spectrum. He was born Oct. 15, 1908, in Iona Station, Ont., earned a B.S. in economics at the University of Toronto in 1931, and then went to the University of California at Berkeley for an M.S. (1933) and Ph.D. (1934). For five years he was an instructor at Harvard, taking time for postdoctoral studies at Cambridge in 1937–38.

In 1939 he went to Princeton University as an assistant professor of economics and quickly found his way into the bureaucracy gathering in Washington as World War II approached. He held a variety of government posts in the wartime and postwar years. He was named to the board of editors of *Fortune* magazine (1943–48) and in 1948 returned to Harvard as lecturer. Professor of economics (from 1949), Paul M. Warburg professor (1959–75), and professor emeritus thereafter, he still found time to play a prominent role in public life. In 1961–63 he was U.S. ambassador to India. Upon his retirement in 1975 he was made a fellow of Trinity College, Cambridge.

His vast literary output includes titles that have passed into the language (*American Capitalism: The Concept of Countervailing Power*, 1951; *The Affluent Society*, 1958; *The New Industrial State*, 1967). His most recent books are *The Anatomy of Power* (1983) and *Economics in Perspective: A Critical History* (1987).

THOMAS STUDIOS

## Jacobs, Jane

An acute observer of urban life and problems, Jane Jacobs has brought to the study of city planning a distinctive vision that made her widely celebrated even while it infuriated those whose oxen were being gored. Born Jane Butzner on May 4, 1916, in Scranton, Pa., the daughter of a physician, she got a job after high school graduation as a reporter on the *Scranton*

*Tribune.* About a year later she went to New York City, where she built a reputation as a competent and versatile free-lance writer.

In 1944 she married Robert Hyde Jacobs, Jr., an architect. Already keenly interested in city neighbourhoods and their vitality, both as writer and—increasingly—as community activist, she explored urban design and planning at length with her husband. In 1952 she became an associate editor of *Architectural Forum,* where she worked for a decade. Near the end of her tenure there she contributed a chapter, "Downtown Is for People," to a book produced by the editors of *Fortune* magazine, *The Exploding Metropolis* (1958), and three years later published her first full-length book, *The Death and Life of Great American Cities,* a brash and passionate reinterpretation of the actual needs of modern urban places. Translated into Japanese and several European languages, it established her as a force to be reckoned with by planners and economists.

In 1969 she moved to Canada with her husband and later took Canadian citizenship. Her *The Economy of Cities* was published in 1969 and *Cities and the Wealth of Nations* in 1984.

INSTITUTO NACIONAL DE BELLAS ARTES, MEXICO

## Paz, Octavio

Some indication of Octavio Paz's versatility can be gained from his many roles—poet, essayist, polemicist, diplomat, probably Mexico's most respected living intellectual, and a popular television personality. Born March 31, 1914, in Mexico City, Octavio Paz began writing when very young and helped to found "a little magazine," *Barandal.* Like most writers of his generation, he experienced a period of radicalism during the 1930s. However, the controversies of the time, particularly those pertaining to freedom in art, distanced him from his radical friends. The final breakup came with the German-Soviet nonaggression pact and Leon Trotsky's assassination.

In 1946 Paz moved to Paris, where he remained for ten years, befriending the poets and writers of the Surrealist movement. He joined the Mexican diplomatic service, but in 1968 he resigned to protest the bloody repression of student unrest in Mexico. During this time he founded and edited *Plural* magazine, published by the daily newspaper *Excelsior.* In 1975, when Pres. Luis Echeverría engineered the ouster of the paper's editor in chief and other staff members, Paz resigned and, with a group of independent writers, founded *Vuelta.* He has received a number of prizes, including the Premio Cervantes.

Among his books of poetry are (dates are for English translations) *Sun Stone* (1962), whose influence has been compared with that of T. S. Eliot's *The Waste Land; Eagle or Sun?* (1976); and *The Monkey Grammarian* (1981). Prose works include *The Labyrinth of Solitude* (1961), an influential essay about the character, history, and culture of Mexico; *Conjunctions and Disjunctions* (1976); and *One Earth, Four or Five Worlds* (1985).

15

# Chronology of 1987

## JANUARY

**9** **Iran launches new offensive.** Iranian troops mounted a new offensive against Iraq, attacking south of Basra after crossing the Shatt al-Arab waterway. Both sides reported that the enemy had sustained numerous casualties. Although Iranian leaders predicted that it would bring Iraq to its knees by late March, many impartial observers doubted that the war, which had begun in September 1980, would end soon with a victory for either side.

**Nicaragua gets new constitution.** Nicaraguans began to live under a new constitution that guaranteed the right to strike, to receive uncensored news, and to hold meetings and lawful demonstrations. The president, however, was given authority to suspend these and other provisions of the new charter during war or when the national security, economic conditions, or a national catastrophe required it. Among the 96 deputies in the National Assembly, 13 refused to sign the document. The ceremony was attended by Peruvian Pres. Alan García Pérez, the first elected Latin-American head of state to visit Nicaragua since Daniel Ortega Saavedra was elected president in November 1984.

**11** **French strikes lose momentum.** A series of strikes that at times severely disrupted France's transportation system and, later, supplies of electricity and gas appeared to be tapering off. Fears of an impending crisis were first voiced in mid-December when leftist-led railway workers opposed a plan to base future promotions on merit rather than on seniority. Gradually the demands of certain groups for higher wages and better working conditions shifted to calls for new elections. Conservatives thereupon organized countermarches in support of Jacques Chirac, who had been appointed prime minister by Socialist Pres. François Mitterrand after the conservatives won control of the National Assembly in 1986.

**13** **Court rules on pregnant workers.** The U.S. Supreme Court, in a 6–3 vote, upheld a California law that required employers to grant up to four months unpaid leave to women disabled by pregnancy and childbirth, even though similar job protection was not provided for other disabilities. Justice Thurgood Marshall, speaking for the majority, said California's preferential treatment of pregnant employees promoted equal employment opportunity because it "allows women, as well as men, to have families without losing their jobs."

**Mafia leaders go to prison.** Eight men, convicted of being key figures in an organized crime commission, were sentenced to long prison terms by a New York federal district judge. Seven defendants, described as ruthless racketeers who served as "the board of directors" of the Mafia, were given 100-year sentences. The other defendant was given 40 years. Anthony ("Fat Tony") Salerno, Anthony ("Tony Ducks") Corallo, and Carmine ("Junior") Persico were all reputed to be heads of "Mafia families." In a separate hearing on January 16, nine other crime figures were given lesser prison sentences for racketeering.

**14** **Seoul police kill student activist.** A 21-year-old student activist was tortured and killed by South Korean police during the course of an interrogation. Some hours before his death, Park Chong Chol had been arrested on suspicion of harbouring a fugitive radical. He died of suffocation when the police forced his head under water and in the process crushed his neck against the rim of the bathtub. News of Park's death ignited public outrage and led to the resignations on January 20 of the interior minister and the national police chief.

**15** **Geneva arms talks resume.** Representatives of the Soviet Union and the U.S. met in Geneva to resume the 22-month-old negotiations on arms control. The Soviet delegation was headed by Yuly M. Vorontsov, a new appointee, while the U.S. continued to have Max M. Kampelman as its chief negotiator. It appeared that the Soviet Union wanted to initiate a new phase in the stalled negotiations and perhaps even achieve a breakthrough by upgrading the level of its chief representative, who held the title of first deputy foreign minister.

**Truce declared in Afghanistan.** The government of Afghanistan declared the first cease-fire in its seven-year-old war against intransigent guerrillas. Doubts that the rebels would accept the offer of peace were reinforced on January 26 when leaders of the antigovernment forces confirmed that fighting was continuing apace throughout the country. There was, moreover, little likelihood that the most prominent guerrilla leaders would ever agree to share power with the government's Soviet-backed officials, as had been suggested. On January 18 the leader of Afghanistan, known as Najib, declared that a rejection of the cease-fire would be a crime against the people. At the same time, he pledged

to keep Soviet troops in the country until the civil war ended.

**Greek strikers challenge Papandreou.** At least one and a half million workers joined a 24-hour strike in Greece to protest wage curbs imposed by the Socialist government of Prime Minister Andreas Papandreou. It appeared that after a period of relative peace, the Communists and other leftist groups were preparing to challenge the government's program of austerity. The plan included measures to reduce inflation, lower the nation's foreign debt, and restrain deficit spending.

**16** **Hu Yaobang loses post.** During an expanded meeting of the Political Bureau of the Central Committee of the Communist Party of China (CPC), Hu Yaobang (Hu Yao-pang) resigned as general secretary of the CPC after acknowledging that he had made grave errors involving political principles. Although Premier Zhao Ziyang (Chao Tzu-yang) was then named head of the CPC, Hu remained one of five members composing the Standing Committee of the Political Bureau of the CPC. Hu's downfall was generally ascribed to his disregard for China's principle of collective leadership and, more immediately, to his reluctance or inability to control several weeks of nationwide turmoil that began in early December 1986 when university students took to the streets to demand greater freedom and democracy. Hu's forced resignation demonstrated the power of those conservatives in government who were determined to combat openly and forcefully "bourgeois liberalism" and to resist any attempt to undermine the country's socialist system. At the same time, China's leaders made it clear that the current program of reforms would not be delayed or abandoned.

**Ecuador's president kidnapped.** Ecuadoran Pres. León Febres Cordero and some 30 others in his party were taken hostage by air force commandos after a gunfight at the Taura air force base near Guayaquil. Four persons were reported killed. The commandos demanded the release of air force Gen. Frank Vargas Pazos, who had led two rebellions in March 1986 and was still being held in a military prison near Quito even though Congress had granted him amnesty the following October. Twelve hours later, after the president had agreed to free Vargas and to take no action against the commandos, he and the other hostages were set free.

French transportation strikers argue with unimpressed gendarmes about their labour demands. The growing dissent eventually disrupted the French transportation system.
BERNARD BISSON—SYGMA

**22** **Troops kill 18 in Manila.** Government troops opened fire on a group of about 10,000 leftist demonstrators who were trying to force their way to the residence of Pres. Corazon Aquino. Gen. Fidel Ramos, the armed forces chief of staff, later stated that the troops overreacted when they shot and killed 18 of the demonstrators and injured scores of others. Tensions in the country were already running high as voters prepared to cast ballots on February 2 for or against a proposed new constitution. On January 27 rebel soldiers launched an unsuccessful bid to seize control of several key military installations, the power company, and several radio and television stations.

**23** **Japan drops cap on military spending.** The government of Japanese Prime Minister Yasuhiro Nakasone formally abandoned a long-standing policy of limiting annual military expenditures to less than 1% of the gross national product (GNP). In December 1986 the government had already approved a $23 billion military budget for 1987, which was calculated to be 1.004% of the 1987 GNP. Although military spending was not expected to deviate appreciably from the 1% figure during the next few years, the government nonetheless issued a statement saying that Japan, under its Peace Constitution, would maintain an exclusively defensive posture and not become "a military power that presents a threat to other nations."

**25** **West Germans retain Kohl.** West German Chancellor Helmut Kohl's centre-right coalition won 269 seats in elections to the Bundestag (federal parliament), thereby ensuring its control of the government for an additional four years. Although Kohl's Christian Democrats (CDU/CSU) continued to lose favour with the electorate, garnering only 44.3% of the popular vote, the Free Democratic Party (FDP) strengthened the coalition by capturing 9.1% of the total ballots. That left the left-of-centre Social Democrats (SPD) as the main opposition party with 37% of the popular vote. Like the FDP, the Greens, who among other things opposed West German membership in NATO, experienced an upsurge of popularity, winning 8.3% of the vote, compared with only 5.6% in 1983.

**27** **Gorbachev insists on change.** Mikhail Gorbachev, general secretary of the Soviet Communist Party, told a plenary session of the party's Central Committee that changes had to be made to revitalize Soviet society. Countering criticism from some quarters that he was making "too sharp a turn," Gorbachev reassured his listeners that he was firmly committed to the basic principles of Communism. During his long speech, Gorbachev proposed new laws to institutionalize some of the changes he had already set in motion, and he blamed deeply rooted "conservative sentiments, inertia, and a tendency to brush aside everything that did not fit into conventional patterns" as contributing to the nation's stagnation. He also suggested that the party adopt secret balloting and that the name of more than one candidate appear on ballots for elective offices.

**Fate of Terry Waite in doubt.** Robert Runcie, the archbishop of Canterbury, expressed concern in London over the safety of Terry Waite, who had gone to Lebanon as the prelate's personal lay representative in hopes of securing the release of Western hostages kidnapped by terrorist groups. Waite, who had not been heard from since he left his hotel in West Beirut on January 20, had on earlier humanitarian missions managed to contact certain terrorist kidnappers and had eventually persuaded them to free some of the innocent persons they were holding.

# FEBRUARY

**2** **Filipinos approve constitution.** Philippine voters went to the polls in a nationwide plebiscite to approve or reject a proposed new constitution that was supported by Pres. Corazon Aquino and opposed by the far right and the radical left. With early returns indicating overwhelming approval of the charter, Aquino's government was assured of a momentous victory in most regions of the country. The new constitution replaced the 1973 constitution, which Aquino had abolished after defeating Pres. Ferdinand Marcos in the February 1986 election. Among other things, the new charter provided for a two-chamber legislature, whose members would be elected in May. It also stipulated that the president serve a six-year term and that the military play no role in politics.

**China to monitor only party members.** A long front page editorial in China's official newspaper, *Renmin ribao* ("People's Daily"), informed readers that the government's campaign against "bourgeois liberalism" would be limited to members of the Communist Party (CPC) and would focus mainly on politics and ideology. Two days later the CPC's propaganda chief, a proponent of liberalization, was dismissed from his post. Several weeks earlier foreign reporters had begun filing stories about what appeared to them to be a wholesale attack against intellectuals, especially those who had supported the recent student demands for greater freedom and democracy. Among those expelled from the CPC at that time were: Fang Lizhi (Fang Li-chih), an astrophysicist who was vice-president of the University of Science and Technology in Hefei (Ho-fei); Wang Ruowang (Wang Jo-wang), a Shanghai writer whose "major mistakes" extended to calling China's socialist system feudal or semifeudal; and Liu Binyan (Liu Pin-yen), a reporter for the *Renmin ribao* who had gained notoriety for his scathing attacks on corruption, decadence, and selfishness within the CPC. On January 22 both the president and vice-president of the Academy of Sciences were also dismissed from their positions.

**4** **Colombia extradites drug kingpin.** Colombian soldiers captured Carlos Enrique Lehder Rivas, a 37-year-old former state senator and a reputed billionaire drug dealer, after a shoot-out with 15 of Lehder's bodyguards. Lehder was immediately extradited to the U.S. to face multiple charges related to cocaine trafficking. He was the 13th person Colombia had turned over to U.S authorities for prosecution since the two countries signed an extradition treaty in 1979. One casualty of the battle between the government and drug dealers had been Rodrigo Lara Bonilla, the Colombian minister of justice, who was murdered in 1984 after helping work out the details of the treaty. Drug dealers were also blamed for the assassination of a Supreme Court justice who had approved such extraditions. Some 20 other judges who had presided over drug cases in lower courts were also murdered.

**10** **Koop speaks candidly about AIDS.** C. Everett Koop, the U.S. surgeon general, told members of the House Subcommittee on Health and the Environment that television messages were necessary to combat the spread of AIDS (acquired immune deficiency syndrome). Koop urged the use of television advertisements to promote the proper use of condoms. He said they were the best protection against the deadly AIDS virus for those who would not practice abstinence or monogamy. Representatives of the nation's three major networks were among those who argued that a significant number of viewers would find such messages offensive. One committee member, however, accused the networks of hypocrisy, saying they "refuse to describe disease control as they promote disease transmission." He noted that the networks portray "thousands of sexual encounters each year in programming" and market thousands of products by using sex appeal.

**11** **Sikh leaders in open conflict.** The five head priests of Sikhism in India announced the excommunication of Surjit Singh Barnala, who, as chief minister of the strife-torn state of Punjab, was the highest ranking elected Sikh official in the country. Barnala, a moderate, was accused of defying the political orders of the religious hierarchy. Sikhs everywhere were ordered to shun Barnala, thereby strengthening the hand of the militants if the order was widely obeyed. At the heart of the conflict was a demand by militant Sikhs for an independent Punjab, where Sikhs constitute a majority of the population. During the long months of bitter rivalry, hundreds of Sikhs and Hindus had been ruthlessly murdered by their respective political enemies.

**12** **Klan hard hit by court verdict.** An all-white jury hearing a civil case in a federal court in Mobile, Ala., assessed a $7 million fine against the United Klans of America (UKA) after deciding it was responsible for illegal acts committed by its members. Two Klansmen had earlier been convicted in criminal court of murdering Michael Donald, a 19-year-old black, and then hanging him from a tree. The boy's family and the local National Association for the Advancement of Colored People then sued the Klan organization for damages. The lawyers for the plaintiffs argued that the UKA was as responsible for the illegal actions of its members as a commercial corporation is for its employees. The unexpectedly large assessment was sure to have a devastating effect on the UKA and on the six past and present members of the Klan mentioned in the suit. It would also presumably have a profound effect on the behaviour of similar organizations.

**15** **Mexican students end strike.** Students attending the National Autonomous University of Mexico in Mexico City ended a strike that since January 29 had interrupted regular classes for some 340,000 students. The showdown between university officials and students became inevitable when student representatives rejected proposed changes in certain school policies because they had not been consulted in advance. The planned changes included an end to open admissions, a limit on the number of years a student could stay in school, the introduction of standardized examinations, and an increase in student fees, which had been less than one dollar a year for undergraduates. The confrontation ended with school officials withdrawing most of their proposals and the government agreeing to double its funding for the university.

**Superconductive compound found.** The National Science Foundation in Washington, D.C., announced that two teams of scientists, one led by Paul C. W. Chu of the University of Houston, Texas, and the other by Maw-Kuen Wu of the University of Alabama, Huntsville, had cooperated to develop a superconductive compound that could become one of the great scientific breakthroughs of the 20th century. The compound became superconductive at 98 K and thus could be refrigerated with liquid nitrogen rather than liquid helium, which was currently widely used and was about ten times more expensive. Among other benefits, the discovery was expected to reduce dramatically the cost of transmitting electricity.

**17** **Fianna Fail wins in Ireland.** Fine Gael, the party of Irish Prime Minister Garret FitzGerald, was soundly defeated in parliamentary elections, capturing only 51 seats in the 166-seat legislature. Charles J. Haughey led Fianna Fail, the opposition party, to victory by focusing attention on Ireland's numerous economic problems, including high unemployment and budget deficits. Fianna Fail won 81 seats, three short of an absolute majority. The Progressive Democrats won 14, the Labour Party 12, the Workers' Party 4, and independents 4. Haughey assumed the office of prime minister for the third time on March 10.

**Vietnam changes top leaders.** Vietnam announced more than a dozen changes among its top-ranking government officials. According to a radio broadcast from Hanoi, Foreign Minister Nguyen Co Thach assumed the additional responsibility of deputy chairman of the Council of Ministers; Le Duc Anh, who commanded Vietnamese forces in Kampuchea, replaced Gen. Van Tien Dung as defense minister; and Mai Chi Tho replaced Pham Hung as minister of the interior. Other deputy prime ministers were also affected by the changes. In December 1986 the country's Communist Party hierarchy had been similarly revamped.

**19** **U.S. lifts Polish sanctions.** Pres. Ronald Reagan lifted economic sanctions that had been imposed on Poland in 1981 and 1982 after the country was placed under martial law. Tariffs on certain Polish goods exported to the U.S. would be reduced. It was unclear how much permanent damage Poland had suffered; the imposition of sanctions had not only halved Poland's exports to the U.S. to $250 million a year but had opened traditional Polish markets to new competitors. Poland, moreover, had a poor credit rating that would influence decisions when Warsaw officials applied for U.S. credits and government guarantees of private loans. The president's action was welcomed even by ardent opponents of Poland's Communist regime.

**22** **Syrian troops enter Beirut.** An estimated 7,000 Syrian troops supported by about 100 Soviet-built tanks moved into West Beirut in an effort to end a week of vicious fighting between Shi'ah Amal militia and mainly Druze militia of the Progressive Socialist Party, which received armed support from the Lebanese Communist Party. Some

MAHER ATTAR—SYGMA

Syrian troops enter West Beirut, Lebanon, to force an end to the fighting that broke out between the Muslim Shi'ah Amal and Druze militias.

300 persons were reported killed and 1,300 wounded during the furious combat. Heavy artillery and tanks were called into play as both sides maneuvered to seize control of key positions. The Syrians were under the command of Brig. Gen. Ghazi Kanaan, the head of Syrian military intelligence in Lebanon. Although only a few hundred Syrian soldiers had been quartered in Beirut, about 30,000 were in the country, mostly in the Bekaa (al-Biqaʿ) Valley. The first contingent had arrived in 1976 as peacekeepers under an Arab League mandate.

**Ethiopia becomes Marxist state.** Lieut. Col. Mengistu Haile Mariam, the military ruler of Ethiopia, announced that 81% of the ballots cast in a national referendum favoured the adoption of a new constitution providing for civilian rule. In effect, Mengistu's declaration established a one-party Marxist state to be called the People's Democratic Republic of Ethiopia. Later in the year, party-approved candidates would compete for seats in the Shengo (parliament), whose members would then elect a president to a five-year term.

**26** **Tower commission issues report.** A presidential review board made up of former senators John Tower and Edmund Muskie and retired air force general Brent Scowcroft released its report after investigating the role of the National Security Council (NSC) in planning and carrying out the secret sale of U.S. military equipment to Iran that had begun in August 1985. (A broader and more detailed investigation by congressional committees was scheduled for a later date.) Although the Tower panel blamed President Reagan for not keeping informed about the NSC's activities, it concluded that White House Chief of Staff Donald Regan had to bear "primary responsibility for the chaos that descended upon the White House" because "he was personally active in national security affairs and attended almost all of the relevant meetings regarding the Iran initiative." Among other persons criticized for what they did or failed to do were William Casey, former director of the CIA; George Shultz, secretary of state; Vice-Adm. John Poindexter, former head of the NSC; and Marine Lieut. Col. Oliver North, Poindexter's aide at

the NSC. On February 27 Reagan won bipartisan approval when he announced that former senator Howard Baker, Jr., of Tennessee would replace Regan as White House chief of staff.

**28** **France gives terrorist life sentence.** A seven-judge French court sentenced Georges Ibrahim Abdallah, a leading Lebanese Christian terrorist, to life imprisonment for complicity in the 1982 murders of two diplomats, an American and an Israeli. The harshness of the sentence surprised many because the French prosecutor had requested that Abdallah be given no more than ten years. In handing down the maximum sentence allowed by French law, the judges were aware that their decision could jeopardize the lives of French hostages held in Lebanon. There was also the possibility that revenge assassinations could occur as well as bombings similar to those that killed 13 persons in Paris and injured 200 others after Abdallah was apprehended in 1984. Such considerations, however, did not deter the court from taking a strong stand in its fight against terrorism.

# MARCH

**3** **Craxi government falls.** Italian Prime Minister Bettino Craxi, a Socialist, resigned as head of the ruling five-party coalition. He had given the nation an unusually long period of postwar political stability by remaining in office for about three and a half years. It was not certain whether Foreign Minister Giulio Andreotti, a Christian Democrat who had already served the country as prime minister five times, or any other seasoned politician could form a government if asked to do so by Pres. Francesco Cossiga. If none succeeded, parliamentary elections would have to be held within a few months.

**4** **Reagan discusses Iran-*contra* affair.** President Reagan addressed the nation on the U.S. sale of arms

PIERO GUERRINI—GAMMA/LIAISON

Socialist Bettino Craxi announces his resignation as prime minister of Italy, a move likely to end Italy's recent political stability.

to Iran and the subsequent diversion of money from the arms deal to *contra* guerrillas fighting the Sandinista government in Nicaragua. During the speech, which followed by six days the report of the Tower commission, the president called the board's findings "honest, convincing and highly critical" and said he accepted them along with "full responsibility for my own actions and for those of my administration." Reagan went on to say that although certain activities had been undertaken without his knowledge and that secret bank accounts and diverted funds were personally distasteful to him, he could not escape responsibility because those things had happened on his watch. A far clearer and more detailed revelation of the entire affair was expected when committees of both houses of Congress held public hearings.

**10** **Vatican speaks out on procreation.** The Vatican issued a document on human reproduction that was certain to spark animated discussion, even within the Roman Catholic Church. Entitled *Instruction on Respect for Human Life in Its Origin and on the Dignity of Procreation: Replies to Certain Questions of the Day,* it addressed in specific terms some of the most common, most recent, and most controversial medical procedures related to human reproduction. During the course of its wide-ranging discussions, the Vatican condemned "test-tube" fertilization and artificial insemination, and it advocated laws prohibiting such practices as surrogate motherhood and experiments on living embryos.

**15** **Tamils sabotage Indian train.** At least 22 persons were killed and some 150 injured when saboteurs blew up a train bridge in southern India as the Rockfort Express was crossing it.

Officials reported that posters affixed to bridge supports and leaflets left at the scene indicated that the terrorists were supporters of the Tamil minority fighting for autonomy in Sri Lanka. Though the Tamils in that Indian Ocean republic numbered about 2.5 million, there were four times as many Sinhalese. Religion also separated the two groups; whereas most Tamils were Hindu, the majority of Sinhalese were Buddhists. The guerrillas also demanded that the Indian government sanction wider official use of Tamil in the areas where it was the native language, rather than Hindi, which, along with English, had been declared Sri Lanka's national language.

**19** **Evangelist resigns over scandal.** The Rev. Jim Bakker, an Assemblies of God television evangelist, resigned his ministry in the wake of accusations that he was guilty of sexual misconduct and had paid blackmail to keep the matter secret. Bakker, the spiritual and financial head of the PTL Club ("Praise the Lord," or "People That Love"), contended that he had been "wickedly manipulated by treacherous former friends" who had conspired to betray him into a sexual encounter in Florida in 1980. Other television evangelists quickly took sides, some supporting Bakker and his wife, Tammy Faye, who was cohost on his programs, while others made new accusations of impropriety and supported the Rev. Jerry Falwell, a Baptist, who had agreed to take over Bakker's ministry temporarily, even though its future was very much in doubt. Bakker's apparent misuse of funds also seemed to disturb many who contributed to such religious programs; in the weeks that followed, virtually every television evangelist reported a dramatic drop in donations as a result of the public controversy.

**22** **Chad routs Libyan forces.** Chadian officials announced the capture of Libya's most important military installation in northern Chad. The base at Ouadi Doum, which was reportedly protected by some 5,000 troops, fell after what was called "an unforgettable" battle. When the Libyans fled, they abandoned millions of dollars worth of matériel, including tanks, vehicles, various types of aircraft, and radar and communications equipment. The capture of Ouadi Doum was facilitated by the destruction on March 19 and 20 of two Libyan task forces about 50 km (30 mi) southeast of the air base. Libyan troops had been sent to Chad to support forces loyal to former president Goukouni Oueddei, who was attempting to overthrow Pres. Hissen Habré. Chad's military might had been bolstered by France, which sent 2,400 soldiers to its former colony when the presence of Libyan forces posed a serious threat to the government.

**23** **Canada approves seal hunting.** Canadian Fisheries Minister Thomas Siddon announced that large-scale commercial seal hunting could resume on ice floes off Newfoundland, provided the hunters used rifles and restricted their harvest to black-coated harp seals. The government, which set a quota of 57,000 seals, had virtually closed down the Canadian seal industry four years earlier, in part because various animal welfare groups had organized protests, especially against the clubbing to death of white-coated seal pups. In 1983 the antihunting campaigners won a significant victory when they persuaded the European Communities to bar the importation of pup skins.

**24** **Kenya ousts illegal aliens.** The *Kenya Times* reported that the nation's police commissioner had reaffirmed the government's intention to continue deporting illegal aliens until all of them had been expelled. Pres. Daniel arap Moi had personally ordered the deportation of all illegal residents because, he said, they were disrupting Kenya's peace. Most came from the neighbouring countries of Somalia, Ethiopia, Rwanda, Uganda, and Tanzania; still others came from Zaire in central Africa. The hundreds of thousands of aliens living legally in Kenya would not be affected by the expulsion order.

**25** **Zhao Ziyang addresses Congress.** Chinese Premier Zhao Ziyang (Chao Tzu-yang), in an opening address to members of the National People's Congress (NPC), reaffirmed the government's commitment to its new economic policies and to expanding contacts with the West. At the same time, however, Zhao emphasized the importance of rejecting "pernicious" Western ideologies. During his speech he blamed China's continuing economic problems on low productivity, widespread inefficiency, inordinate emphasis on construction projects, and government budget and trade deficits. Some days earlier Peng Zhen (P'eng Chen), a lukewarm supporter of China's new economic policies, had successfully urged fellow members of the Standing

A crowd in southern India views the wreckage of the Rockfort Express, which was crossing a train bridge when it was blown up by supporters of the Tamil minority in Sri Lanka.
KASTURI—GAMMA/LIAISON

Committee of the NPC not to request the NPC to pass a law preventing Communist Party officials from intervening in the day-to-day operation of state factories and enterprises.

**28** **Greece and Turkey avoid showdown.** The spectre of armed conflict between Turkey and Greece began to recede when both countries agreed not to explore for oil in disputed waters of the Aegean Sea. In 1976 both had signed an accord stipulating that their territorial disputes be adjudicated by the International Court of Justice. The present crisis underscored but one of several persistent problems that had soured relations between the two NATO allies. A potential confrontation was set in motion when Greece declared that it planned to extend its territorial waters from 6 to 12 mi and that it would nationalize the North Aegean Petroleum Corp., a foreign consortium that was preparing to drill for oil 11 mi off the east coast of Thasos, one of numerous Greek islands in the Aegean Sea. Turkey, challenging the legality of Greece's action, insisted that the potential oil fields were part of its own continental shelf and said it was prepared to send a petroleum seismic research vessel into the area under military escort.

**29** **Haitians approve new charter.** All but a small fraction of the hundreds of thousands of Haitians who went to the polls approved a new constitution that, it was hoped, would be the first step toward the establishment of a democratic government. The outcome of the election was interpreted as a condemnation of the nearly 30-year rule of the Duvalier family, a rejection of the current regime, and a yearning for a new life in what had long been the Western Hemisphere's poorest nation. Among many other things, the new constitution outlined procedures for a presidential election, which was scheduled for November, and promised personal liberties and a right to free education, decent housing, and a fair living wage.

**31** **Judge decides "Baby M" case.** Harvey R. Sorkow, a superior court judge in Hackensack, N.J., issued a historic ruling in the widely publicized case of "Baby M." He admitted that he was "creating law" when he awarded custody of a one-year-old girl to her biologic father and denied all parental rights to the biologic mother, who had signed a contract to serve as a surrogate mother because the man's wife was a victim of multiple sclerosis and feared the consequences of pregnancy. The judge's decision did not end the heated controversy that raged over the morality and legality of surrogate parentage, nor did it satisfy the biologic mother, who had changed her mind and wished to keep the baby she had delivered. Some of those who opposed surrogate parentage, or who simply sided with the biologic mother, questioned the validity of the contract she had signed. Among other arguments, they contended that an agreement to bear a child for a $10,000 fee violated U.S. laws prohibiting the sale of children. Many others supported the judge's decision, but among their number were some who felt uncomfortable with certain aspects of surrogate parentage, including, for example, the notion that volunteer mothers would be evaluated on the basis of physical features as well as other attributes.

**Pakistan downs Afghan plane.** The Pakistani Defense Ministry announced that two of its F-16 fighters had intercepted and shot down an Afghan military plane that had violated the nation's airspace the day before. The Pakistani government had been vigorously protesting recent Afghan bombing raids along the border and warned that it would retaliate if its borders were violated. Although the air raids had been directed against Afghan guerrillas who had sought safe haven in friendly Pakistan, many Pakistanis were among the hundreds who had been killed. It was no secret that Pakistani Pres. Mohammad Zia-ul-Haq was sympathetic to the Afghan guerrillas, who for years had steadfastly opposed Soviet control of their country.

# APRIL

**3** **Chileans battle during pope's mass.** An estimated one million people attended an outdoor mass celebrated by Pope John Paul II in Santiago, Chile. The event was marred by violent clashes between antigovernment demonstrators, some armed with clubs and stones, and the police, who used tear gas and water cannons in an attempt to crush protests against the regime of Pres. Augusto Pinochet Ugarte. Earlier in the day, during a visit to a Roman Catholic hospice, the Roman pontiff warmly embraced a badly scarred young woman who reportedly had been doused with a flammable liquid and set afire by security police in July 1986 and had since become a symbol of the government's human rights abuses. A male companion had died of his injuries. After the mass, the pope met with 19 opposition leaders who had requested an audience; they ranged from the extreme right to the Marxist left.

**Greece seeks church lands.** The Greek Parliament approved legislation that would permit the Socialist government of Prime Minister Andreas Papandreou to take over some 150,000 ha (370,000 ac) of forest and agricultural lands belonging to Greek Orthodox (Church of Greece) monasteries and convents. The estates would then be turned over to failing agricultural cooperatives, which were largely under the control of the Panhellenic Socialist Movement. In addition, the new law would institute lay control of church organizations that bore responsibility for a wide range of church investments. Clerical reaction to the new legislation was predictably defiant and emotional. Leading members of the hierarchy vowed to boycott committees dominated by nonclericals and said they would rather give their lands away than turn them over to the government. More astonishing still was the church's threat to affiliate itself with the ecumenical patriarchate of Constantinople, which was not subject to Greek law. If such a step were actually taken, it would restore ecclesiastical ties between the Orthodox Church of Greece and the ecumenical patriarchate—ties that had been severed in the 19th century.

**5** **Switzerland to limit refugees.** In a national referendum Swiss voters backed, by a 2–1 margin, government proposals to restrict the influx of refugees into the country and to be more judicious in granting political asylum to those who requested it. The government, which noted that there had been a tenfold increase in the number of applications for asylum during the past decade, was chided by church and human rights groups but found support among those who felt that a substantial number of foreigners seeking entry into Switzerland were motivated by financial reasons alone. Belgium was one of several other countries that had placed restrictions on the admission of refugees.

**13** **Chun suspends debate on constitution.** South Korean Pres. Chun Doo Hwan announced that dis-

cussions with opposition politicians about possible changes in the constitution would be postponed until after the summer Olympic Games in Seoul in 1988. The presidential election scheduled for mid-December, however, would be held as planned in accordance with the present constitution, and a new president would be inaugurated in late February 1988. The announcement came less than a week after the two most prominent opposition politicians, Kim Dae Jung and Kim Young Sam, broke away from the New Korea Democratic Party and took with them more than two-thirds of the party's 90 members of the National Assembly. They then founded the Reunification Democratic Party. Although Chun's political foes had profound policy differences among themselves, they were one in denouncing the unilateral suspension of talks on revising the constitution, especially regarding the question of electing Chun's successor by popular vote rather than by the electoral college (which would guarantee victory for the government's candidate). The prospect of street demonstrations, possibly violent, seemed likely because neither side appeared ready to compromise.

**China to take over Macau.** Portuguese Prime Minister Aníbal Cavaco Silva and Chinese Premier Zhao Ziyang (Chao Tzu-yang) signed a declaration in Beijing (Peking) that would restore the Portuguese overseas territory of Macau to Chinese sovereignty on Dec. 20, 1999. Macau had been part of Guangdong (Kwangtung) Province before China was forced to cede it to Portugal in 1887. About 97% of the territory's 400,000 residents were Chinese.

**17** **U.S. taxes Japanese imports.** President Reagan, seeking "to enforce the principles of free and fair trade," imposed a 100% tariff on certain Japanese computers, television sets,

JOHN CHIASSON—GAMMA/LIAISON

A customer considers purchasing a Japanese power drill, one of the many imports subject to a new U.S. tariff.

and power tools. U.S. consumers could generally avoid paying higher prices for such products, a White House spokesman noted, by purchasing equivalent products not manufactured in Japan. Even though the new tariffs affected only a small fraction of Japan's exports to the U.S., they were an embarrassment to one of the U.S. government's closest allies and did little to mollify congressmen who still felt the need for a tough trade bill to solve the nation's huge trade deficit. Calls for trade sanctions against Japan had grown louder in recent months amid charges that Japan, despite its denials, had failed to comply with the terms of a semiconductor agreement it had signed in July 1986.

**Tamils ambush civilians.** Tamil guerrillas waylaid three buses, two trucks, and a van carrying civilians and servicemen on vacation on a remote jungle road about 185 km (115 mi) northeast of Colombo, the capital of Sri Lanka. They then used machine guns and grenades to kill 127 of the passengers; about 60 others were wounded in the attack. Three days later at least 15 Sinhalese villagers were killed in the same district, which had been the site of many massacres since July 1983. Then, on April 21, more than a hundred persons were killed and twice that number injured, some seriously, when a bomb exploded in Colombo's main bus station. The Sri Lankan Air Force retaliated by bombing suspected Tamil guerrilla bases in the northern part of the country, leaving at least 80 dead.

**23** **Indonesians go to polls.** Indonesians cast ballots for national, provincial, and local legislatures after an abbreviated 25-day period of campaigning followed by a week during which no public gatherings were allowed. As expected, Golkar ("functional groups" representing various segments of the general population) overwhelmed candidates of the two opposition political parties by winning 299 of the 400 elected seats in the House of Representatives. The United Development Party won 61 seats and the Indonesian Democratic Party 40. An additional 100 seats would be filled by military appointees. The election guaranteed that President Suharto would be awarded another five-year term when the People's Consultative Assembly convened to choose the leader of the world's fifth most populous nation.

**24** **South African court voids decrees.** The Natal division of the Supreme Court ruled that South African Pres. P. W. Botha had exceeded his authority on Dec. 11, 1986, when he granted extensive censorship powers to the police commissioner. The court's decision voided key features of the government strategy of curtailing freedom of the press and outlawing campaigns for the release of political detainees, a large number of whom were children. Even though the government immediately appealed the ruling, many lawyers believed that the press could resume photographing and reporting actions by the security forces against those who openly opposed the government's policy of apartheid. In a separate ruling on April 28, a Natal Province Supreme Court justice dealt the government another major blow by nullifying regulations that prohibited protests and appeals on behalf of persons arrested and held without charges.

**25** **Iceland holds election.** In elections to Iceland's unicameral legislature, both partners in the ruling centre-right coalition—the Independence Party and the Progressive Party—lost ground to the opposition Social Democrats and the Women's Alliance. The strength of the coalition was further diluted by the one-month-old Citizens' Party, which did well under the leadership of Albert Gudmundsson (who had deserted the Independents after a tax scandal forced him to resign as minister of industry and energy). Steingrímur Hermannsson, a Progressive, resigned as prime minister on April 28 because his coalition commanded only 31 of 63 seats in the expanded Althing (parliament), compared with 38 of 60 before the election. Negotiations leading to the formation of a new government were expected to consume many weeks.

**26** **Palestinians compromise on differences.** The Palestinian National Council (PNC), which the Palestine Liberation Organization (PLO) considered its parliament-in-exile, ended a meeting in Algiers after heated discussions and dramatic compromises that, generally speaking, brought the rival Palestinian factions closer together. Yasir Arafat was reelected chairman of the PLO, but he had to accede to demands that were more radical than he wished in order to secure the endorsements he needed. Among other things, the delegates agreed to give more seats on the executive council to hardliners who had long opposed Arafat's more moderate policies. Arafat's authority was further diluted by the establishment of a secretariat to handle the PLO's day-to-day operations. In addition, the PNC took a much less conciliatory position toward Egypt because it had refused to abrogate the Camp David accords that led to the

Palestinians gather in Algiers for the opening session of the Palestinian National Council, the parliament of the Palestine Liberation Organization.

ALEXIS DUCLOS—GAMMA/LIAISON

1979 peace treaty with Israel. Egypt closed PLO offices in that country the following day in response.

**27** **U.S. bars Waldheim.** The U.S. Justice Department added the name of Austrian Pres. Kurt Waldheim to the list of those persons not allowed to enter the United States. The two-term (1972–81) secretary-general of the United Nations had been accused of hiding his role as an interpreter and intelligence officer for a German Army unit during World War II. Evidence tied Waldheim to brutal reprisals against Yugoslav partisans and civilians and to the mass deportation of the Jewish population of Thessaloniki, Greece, to Nazi death camps in 1943. Waldheim denied that he had played any role in such wartime atrocities. Nonetheless, he became the first head of state ever to be forbidden entry into the U.S.

**30** **Holkeri assumes office in Finland.** Harri Holkeri, a member of the conservative National Coalition Party, was sworn in as prime minister of Finland heading a new four-party coalition

that commanded a solid majority in the Eduskunta (parliament). Other members of the coalition were the Social Democratic Party, the Swedish People's Party, and the Rural Party. Holkeri replaced Kalevi Sorsa, a Social Democrat, whose party joined the new coalition and, with 56 seats, remained the largest single party in the national legislature. The National Coalition Party held 53 seats, having gained 9 seats in the March 15–16 elections. The Centre Party won 40 seats, a gain of 2, but was no longer a partner in the ruling coalition.

**U.S. Lutherans form new church.** The Evangelical Lutheran Church in America came into existence when three denominations—the American Lutheran Church, the Lutheran Church in America, and the Association of Evangelical Lutheran Churches—formally merged in Columbus, Ohio. Together they had a combined membership of 5.3 million and thus became the fourth largest Protestant denomination in the country, surpassed only by the Southern Baptists, the United Methodists, and the National Baptist Convention. The conservative Lutheran Church-Missouri Synod chose to maintain its own identity.

# MAY

**1** **Quebec recognized as distinct society.** Canadian Prime Minister Brian Mulroney received a standing ovation when he informed Parliament that the French-speaking province of Quebec had finally agreed to sign the Canadian constitution. A long impasse was broken when all of Canada's provincial premiers agreed to include a provision in the constitution acknowledging Quebec as a "distinct society" within the confederation. The compromise agreement also diminished the powers of the central government by expanding the rights of all provinces in such matters as immigration, appointments to the nation's Supreme Court, and modifications of the constitution. Formal approval of the proposals was expected.

**6** **South African whites elect Assembly.** South African whites went to the polls in unexpectedly large numbers to elect their all-white House of Assembly, one of three segregated legislatures that comprise the nation's Parliament. Although Pres. P. W. Botha had become the target of growing opposition both at home and abroad because of his defense of apartheid, he managed to lead his National Party to an impressive victory. The relatively liberal Progressive Federal Party suffered the greatest losses in Parliament and was displaced as the official opposition by the extreme right-wing Conservative Party. With fewer practical options open to them, many white voters apparently felt that the moment of decision had arrived. They then moved

to the right and endorsed, some for the first time, Botha's government. The black majority, which had no representation in Parliament, had called for a "subdued and dignified" two-day work stoppage to protest the government's racial policies. The success of the strike, which began on May 5, suggested that blacks were becoming more impatient with their situation and were working closer together to achieve their goals.

**Bakker dismissed as minister.** The Rev. Jim Bakker, a prominent television evangelist who resigned his ministry in March after revelations of sexual misconduct, was formally dismissed as a minister of the Assemblies of God. The Rev. Richard Dortch, Bakker's close associate, was also dismissed by the church's national board after it consulted district officials in North Carolina. Dortch was punished for concealing information about the immoral conduct of a fellow minister. He had also been involved in negotiating blackmail payments to the church secretary with whom Bakker had been involved.

**8    Gary Hart halts campaign.** Gary Hart, a former two-term U.S. senator from Colorado, abruptly terminated his campaign for the Democratic Party's presidential nomination in 1988. The decision came less than a week after the *Miami* (Fla.) *Herald* reported that he had spent part of a weekend with Donna Rice, a part-time model and actress from Miami. The scandal made headlines because Hart was married and the father of two children. During a press conference in Denver, Hart said his campaign could not continue because the situation had become intolerable. "I refuse," he said, "to submit my family and my friends and innocent people to further rumours and gossip." Hart was clearly leading his Democratic rivals when he dropped out of the race.

**9    Malta gets new leadership.** In a hotly contested election, the Nationalist Party regained power in Malta after 16 years of rule by the Labour Party. The election returns had world significance because the outgoing Socialists had fostered close ties with Libya and in 1979 had reversed the Nationalist Party's pro-Western policies by closing the British-operated NATO naval base. In the 1981 election the Nationalists had won a majority of the popular vote but failed to gain control of the government because constituency boundaries gave the Labour Party a majority in Parliament. An agreement worked out in January 1987 stipulated that henceforth any party winning 50% of the popular vote had the right to govern. The constitution, however, was amended to make neutrality and nonalignment national policies. Since a two-thirds majority would be needed to change this provision, it did not appear likely that Malta would again become part of the NATO defense system.

**11    Philippines holds national elections.** Philippine voters went to the polls to elect the nation's legislators in the first truly democratic election since 1971. Early returns indicated that at least 22 of the 24 Senate seats would be occupied by candidates endorsed by Pres. Corazon Aquino. All candidates had to campaign for votes nationwide. The Senate results, all admitted, were an eloquent testimonial to Aquino's personal popularity and to the confidence Filipinos placed in her ability to restore democracy and find ways gradually to solve the country's most serious and pressing problems. Election returns on races for 200 of the 250 seats in the House of Representatives were not expected to be known soon because voters had to use write-in paper ballots.

**14    Egypt breaks relations with Iran.** Egypt announced that it was severing all diplomatic ties with Iran because that country was financing Islamic fundamentalists who were thought to be responsible for the attempted murder of Hassan Abu Basha. As head of internal security in 1981, Basha had rounded up Muslim extremists after one of their underground army units assassinated Pres. Anwar as-Sadat. Relations between Iran and Egypt had deteriorated substantially when Sadat offered Egyptian hospitality to the shah of Iran after he was overthrown by followers of Ayatollah Ruhollah Khomeini.

**Sihanouk steps aside for one year.** Prince Norodom Sihanouk announced from his residence in Beijing (Peking) that for a period of one year he would "perform no mission, make no journey, engage in no activity" on behalf of those fighting the Vietnamese-sustained government in his native Kampuchea. Sihanouk had given respectability to an unlikely three-party coalition of resistance forces that included, besides his own followers, the Khmer Rouge (remnants of the discredited and detested Pol Pot regime) and the Khmer People's National Liberation Front under Son Sann. With Sihanouk as an active participant, the coalition had received the support of the UN, the Association of Southeast Asian Nations, China, and the U.S., all of whom opposed Vietnam's occupation of Kampuchea. There was speculation that Sihanouk might now attempt to negotiate directly and personally with the Vietnamese, a step that he felt was necessary but that other members of the coalition had not allowed him to take.

**Fiji coup produces chaos.** Determined not to allow ethnic Indians to dominate Fijian politics as they already dominated the island nation's business community, Lieut. Col. Sitiveni Rabuka invaded Parliament with ten armed soldiers and took recently elected Prime Minister Timoci Bavadra and other members of the government into custody. Rabuka then called for a new constitution that would keep control of the government in the hands of ethnic Fijians, even though they were slightly outnumbered by ethnic Indians. The bloodless coup produced total chaos because Rabuka, Bavadra, and Ratu Sir Penaia Ganilau, the governor-general (who represented Queen Elizabeth II, Fiji's chief of state), all claimed to be in charge. On May 21 an agreement was reached to bring Fiji back to a state of normality, but it was impossible to ascertain with certainty to what the various parties in the dispute had agreed.

**17    Iraqi missiles hit U.S. frigate.** The U.S. Navy frigate *Stark* was severely damaged and 37 of its sailors were killed when two Exocet missiles fired from an Iraqi Mirage F-1 fighter-bomber hit it broadside. Although the *Stark*'s officers knew their ship was being tracked as it moved through the Persian Gulf and were aware that a missile had been fired, they took no evasive or retaliatory action. Why they did not use the *Stark*'s highly sophisticated defense capabilities was not immediately known. Iraqi Pres. Saddam Hussein, whose country had been at war with neighbouring Iran for seven years, apologized for the "unintentional accident" and expressed hope that the incident would not adversely affect U.S. relations with his country.

**19    Hawke closes Libyan mission.** Australian Prime Minister Robert Hawke ordered Libya to close its diplomatic mission in Canberra because it had engaged in clandestine activities that could no longer be tolerated. The two persons attached to the mission were given ten days to leave the country. During April an Australian Aborigine had gone to Tripoli to attend a revolutionary conference. He reported receiving assurances from Libyan leader Mu'ammar al-Qaddhafi that money would be provided for a revolution aimed at establishing an independent Aboriginal nation within Australia. Although Hawke made no men-

SYGMA

Smoke billows from the U.S. Navy frigate *Stark* after two Iraqi Exocet missiles hit it broadside. Thirty-seven U.S. sailors were killed in this "unintentional accident."

tion of this particular incident, he hinted at broader and more persistent problems, saying Australia had previously protested "the nature and direction of Libyan activities in the South Pacific region," where it had no legitimate national interest.

**25** **Canada welcomes Mitterrand.** French Pres. François Mitterrand arrived in Canada for a five-day state visit, the first such visit since Pres. Charles de Gaulle outraged many Canadians by calling for a "free Quebec" in 1967. Quebec was the only province in Canada where French was more prevalent than English. It was generally agreed that Mitterrand's visit was a notable success. He noted that times had changed (since Quebecers had been agitating for independence), and he refrained from any remarks that might be construed as inimical to Canadian unity. Nonetheless, he reaffirmed France's policy of maintaining a "direct and privileged" relationship with Quebec. Mitterrand concluded his address to Parliament with the words "Long live Canada!" By contrast, de Gaulle had been ordered out of the country by Prime Minister Lester Pearson after he shouted to French-speaking residents in Montreal, "Vive le Québec libre!"

**26** **Chun Doo Hwan revamps Cabinet.** South Korean Pres. Chun Doo Hwan accepted the forced resignations of 26 high-ranking members of his government, then confirmed all but 8 in their current positions. Lee Han Key, a law professor, replaced Lho Shin Yong as prime minister, and Chong In Yong, finance minister in the old Cabinet, was named deputy prime minister with responsibility for economic planning. Other affected ministries included Justice, Finance, and Home Affairs. In addition, new persons were named to head the National Security Planning Agency, formerly known as the Korean Central Intelligence Agency, the prosecutor general's office,

Curious people view the plane flown into Red Square by Mathias Rust. The West German pilot flew over more than 600 kilometres (400 miles) of Soviet territory without incident.
SYGMA

and the Legislative Administration Agency. Chun's action was apparently motivated by a need to mitigate public resentment that followed, for the most part, from revelations that a 21-year-old student, Park Chong Chul, had been tortured by police before dying in their custody in January. It was also becoming clear that officials had attempted to hide the fact that more persons had been involved in the murder than the two policemen who had been initially arrested.

**30** **Top Soviet military officers replaced.** Aleksandr Koldunov, commander of the Soviet Union's Air Defense Command, was relieved of his post after the Politburo rebuked the military for allowing a young West

German pilot to land a small civilian aircraft in Moscow's Red Square without being challenged. The Politburo castigated the defense forces command for its "intolerable unconcern and indecision" when the nation's airspace was being violated. In another development, Marshal Sergey Sokolov resigned as minister of defense. He had not been a conspicuous supporter of Mikhail Gorbachev's efforts to restructure Soviet society. Sokolov was replaced by Gen. Dmitry Yazov, who had recently been transferred to Moscow by Gorbachev. Since Yazov was considered an outsider by the military hierarchy, his unexpected promotion was seen as a rebuff to the military top brass and an indication that Gorbachev intended to continue making changes that advanced his goals.

# JUNE

**1** **Karami slain in Lebanon.** Lebanese Prime Minister Rashid Karami was killed when a bomb exploded aboard the military helicopter carrying him from Tripoli to Beirut. It was unclear whether the bomb had been planted inside his attaché case or beneath the seat. Karami, who had been prime minister ten times in 32 years, had submitted his resignation to Pres. Amin Gemayel on May 4, but Gemayel had refused to accept it. At the time of his assassination, Karami was siding with other Muslim leaders who refused to deal with the president. They hoped this ploy would win for them a greater share of political power. By law the president had to be a Maronite Christian, the prime minister a Sunni Muslim, and the speaker of the National Assembly a Shi'ah Muslim. Karami's death did little to help solve the numerous political and economic problems that had overwhelmed the country during 12 years of violent civil war.

**2** **Greenspan replaces Volcker.** President Reagan announced that Paul Volcker would be stepping down as chairman of the Federal Reserve Board. During his two four-year terms, Volcker had won worldwide respect for the success of his monetary policies. Alan Greenspan, a 61-year-old economist, was nominated as Volcker's successor. Greenspan was well known on Wall Street and had been chairman of the Council of Economic Advisers during the Richard Nixon and Gerald Ford administrations. Because Volcker and Greenspan held similar views on many basic issues, the policies of the Federal Reserve Board were not expected to change significantly in the foreseeable future.

**3** **Sullivan repudiates his Principles.** The Rev. Leon Sullivan, minister of the Zion Baptist Church in Philadelphia, publicly repudiated the so-called Sullivan Principles he had drawn up in 1977 as norms for companies

doing business in South Africa. The 127 companies that had formally agreed to adhere to Sullivan's code of conduct committed themselves to desegregating the workplace, improving the training of blacks and their prospects for promotion, and upgrading such things as health care, housing, and education. Sullivan, adhering to a timetable he had set for himself, concluded that the condition of blacks was improving so slowly that the time had come for the companies to end all business ties to South Africa. Sullivan also urged the Reagan administration to sever diplomatic relations with South Africa and embargo trade until Pretoria had abandoned its policy of racial segregation and given blacks basic human rights and the right to vote. On June 27 conservative members of the Dutch Reformed Church, meeting in Pretoria, voted by a 4–1 margin to form an all-white church. The leaders of the Dutch Reformed Church had proposed opening membership to persons of all races.

**4** **West Germany accepts "double-zero" plan.** The West German Bundestag (federal parliament) formally endorsed a decision taken on June 1 by Chancellor Helmut Kohl's coalition to back a Soviet-U.S. plan to eliminate from Europe missiles with a range exceeding 500 km (310 mi). Earlier, the NATO countries had supported the removal of missiles with a range over 1,000 km (620 mi). West Germany's decision significantly enhanced the possibility that the U.S. and the Soviet Union would reach an arms control agreement during their negotiations in Geneva.

**5** **Canada to expand military.** The Canadian government announced that it was prepared to begin a long-term program of military spending to upgrade and expand the nation's long-neglected armed forces. With the approval of Parliament, Canada would increase its military budget of $7.8 billion by 2% above inflation during each of the next 15 years. A key element in the plan to "reestablish Canada as a responsible and reliable" partner in the NATO alliance would be the allocation of billions of dollars for nuclear-powered submarines that would not, however, carry nuclear weapons.

**10** **New protests rock South Korea.** News that Roh Tae Woo, a close friend of Pres. Chun Doo Hwan, had been nominated as the Democratic Justice Party's presidential candidate touched off violent demonstrations in South Korea. The protests were directed against the Chun government because it had taken a decisive step toward holding elections in December according to rules set down in the constitution. Chun's opponents had adamantly demanded that the constitution be changed to permit direct election of the president by popular vote rather than by the electoral college. Chun had angered his political rivals in

April when he unilaterally suspended talks on revising the constitution. The president said he felt it necessary to act because the opposition was in disarray and unable to present a unified front. Chun therefore decided to suspend discussions on the constitution until after the 1988 summer Olympic Games in Seoul. By that time his successor would have taken office. During the latest demonstrations some 6,000 persons were arrested, most briefly, as police used tear gas to control the students, some of whom were throwing stones and Molotov cocktails. About 200 students who had claimed sanctuary in the Roman Catholic Myongdong Cathedral in Seoul moved out on June 15 after police agreed not to arrest them. To make sure that promise was kept, thousands of people shielded the students as they boarded buses that carried them to safety on university campuses.

**Spanish Socialists lose support.** In local elections throughout Spain, the Socialist Party of Prime Minister Felipe González lost outright control of Madrid, Valencia, Salamanca, and 18 other major cities. The vote was seen as a reflection of widespread dissatisfaction with the government's economic policies and with its program of austerity in particular. There would now be increased pressure to modify those policies and to enter into coalitions with opposition parties. The Socialists, however, fared better in elections to the European Parliament, winning 28 of the 60 seats. The true measure of the Socialists' hold on the electorate would probably not be known until the 1989 national elections.

**11** **Thatcher wins third term.** Margaret Thatcher was assured of a third consecutive five-year term as Britain's prime minister when her Conservative Party won a comfortable but reduced majority of seats in national elections to the House of Commons. It marked the first time in the 20th century

that a prime minister would hold office for so many years without interruption. The Labour Party, effectively led by Neil Kinnock, captured about one-third of the popular vote, some four percentage points better than it had done in 1983. The Alliance, a centrist coalition of Liberals and Social Democrats, not only failed to achieve its goal of supplanting the Labour Party as the ruling party's main opposition but faced an uncertain future after losing almost 3% of its former support.

**Panama declares state of emergency.** Panama imposed a state of emergency throughout the country to counter growing antigovernment protests. Civil and political rights were suspended, and schools were closed to make it difficult for students and teachers to organize. The protests, which presented the most serious challenge to the military since it seized power in 1968, began on June 7 after recently retired Col. Roberto Díaz Herrera claimed that he had cooperated with Gen. Manuel Antonio Noriega, commander of the National Guard, in perpetrating fraud in the 1984 election. Díaz also confirmed persistent rumours that Noriega had engineered the 1985 murder of Hugo Spadafora, a prominent critic, and had planned the killing of Gen. Omar Torrijos Herrera, the Panamanian strongman who died in a plane crash in the jungle in 1981. Noriega, who was Panama's de facto ruler, also stood accused of dealing in illegal drugs and weapons, of laundering money, and of selling U.S. intelligence secrets to Cuba. Noriega characterized the allegations as "high treason."

**13** **Venice summit ends uneventfully.** The leaders of seven democratic industrialized nations (Canada, France, Great Britain, Italy, Japan, the U.S., and West Germany) concluded their 13th annual conference in Venice after exchanging views on a variety of economic and political topics. The meeting in Italy was relatively uneventful. President Reagan, however, announced that the U.S. was partially lifting the tariffs imposed on Japanese electronic products in April. One of the most delicate issues not fully discussed was the U.S. conviction that the shipping lanes used by oil tankers in the Persian Gulf had to be protected. The mounting crisis was a direct outgrowth of hostilities between Iran and Iraq.

**16** **Goetz wins acquittal.** A New York state Supreme Court jury, consisting of ten whites and two blacks, acquitted 39-year-old Bernhard Goetz of all but one of the 13 charges brought against him for the shooting of four black youths on a subway train in December 1984. Goetz, who was found guilty only of carrying the unlicensed weapon he had purchased after being mugged in 1981, claimed self-defense. Jurors later said they believed Goetz had reasonably concluded that the youths' request for five dollars was a prelude to robbery or a beating. The case, which the judge described as "the most difficult of our times," made international news and sparked heated arguments for and against Goetz's course of action. Commentators noted that the circumstances of the case were so unusual

MAHER ATTAR—SYGMA

Supporters and military personnel surround the flag-draped coffin of Lebanese Prime Minister Rashid Karami. A bomb exploded aboard a military helicopter in which he was traveling.

that the verdict could not be cited as a precedent to justify indiscriminate use of lethal force in defense of one's person or property.

**19** **Pindling wins in The Bahamas.** Lynden Pindling won reelection as prime minister of The Bahamas despite accusations during a bitter campaign that he was involved in government corruption and drug trafficking. Pindling countered by charging that his opponents were lackeys of the U.S., which "ought to stop trying to run our country for us." Pindling derided the Free National Movement party, saying it substituted "bootlicking for foreign relations and Uncle Tomism for foreign policy." Incomplete election returns indicated that Pindling's Progressive Liberal Party would win a large majority in the 49-seat Parliament.

**23** **Argentina upholds amnesty.** The Argentine Supreme Court upheld a new law, passed on June 8, that granted immunity to military officers accused of violating human rights while the military ruled the country from 1976 to 1983. At least 9,000 persons disappeared during that time. The court case directly involved three officers who had appealed their 1985 convictions on the grounds that they had simply carried out the orders of their commanding officers. Opponents of the law angrily denounced the court decision, saying the law granted de facto amnesty to all those guilty of crimes against humanity. A leading human rights lawyer called the court's decision historic "because from now on Argentina is the only nation in the world where the use of torture is legal."

**25** **Pope meets Waldheim.** Pope John Paul II received Austrian Pres. Kurt Waldheim at the Vatican and commended his efforts to promote peace in the world, both as a diplomat and as secretary-general of the United Nations from 1972 to 1981. The pope made no public mention of Waldheim's service in the German Army during World War II, during which time he allegedly participated in Nazi atrocities against Yugoslavs and Greek Jews. Even though Waldheim was head of state of a country that was 85% Roman Catholic, Jews were outraged at the pope's apparent insensitivity to their feelings. The fact that John Paul had previously spoken privately with Mehmet Ali Agca, the Turkish national who attempted to assassinate him in 1981, and had granted an audience to Yasir Arafat, the guerrilla leader of

An enthusiastic Margaret Thatcher greets the press after winning her third consecutive term as prime minister of Great Britain.
DEREK HUDSON—SYGMA

the Palestine Liberation Organization, did little to calm the emotions that were aroused by Waldheim's state visit.

**Gorbachev demands change.** Soviet leader Mikhail Gorbachev used unusually blunt language during an address to the Communist Party Central Committee "On the Party's Tasks in Fundamentally Restructuring Management of the Economy." He said serious and inexcusable miscalculations had already been made during the year by the State Planning Committee under Nikolay Talyzin and by the State Committee for Material and Technical Supply headed by Lev Voronin. He noted that drunkenness was again rife among workers and that "loafers, spongers and pilferers—people who live at the expense of others—again feel at ease." He blamed the situation on negligence, mismanagement, irresponsibility, and lack of discipline. He went on to say that this lackadaisical attitude had adversely affected public transportation, tourism, housing, repairs of home appliances, and the manufacture of footwear, clothing, and a host of other things and had spawned a huge underground economy. Gorbachev then called for a series of reforms, including granting broad rights to factories to ensure their true economic independence based on full-scale financial accountability. Most important of all, he said, was a radical readjustment of the price structure in order to eliminate the often great disparity between the true value of products and their current controlled prices. Gorbachev also warned that henceforth wages and bonuses would have to be earned by the workers.

**Hungary revamps leadership.** The Hungarian government announced that Karoly Grosz, the Communist Party boss in Budapest, would replace Gyorgy Lazar as chairman of the Council of Ministers (prime minister). The promotion marked Grosz as a likely successor to Janos Kadar, who became first secretary (head) of the country's Communist Party in 1956. The outgoing prime minister, Gyorgy Lazar, replaced Karoly Nemeth, who relinquished his duties as Kadar's deputy to become chief of state. The post became vacant with the retirement of Pres. Pal Losonczi. These and other changes in the political hierarchy had been decided by the Communist Party's Central Committee on June 25 and were ratified by Parliament before the public announcement.

**29** **Haitians call general strike.** A general strike, organized by scores of political, religious, and other groups, paralyzed Port-au-Prince, the capital of Haiti, and led to violent confrontations with police in other major cities. The strike was called to protest a decree, issued on June 23, giving the three-man military-civilian council headed by Lieut. Gen. Henri Namphy full control over elections. The constitution stipulated that authority to organize and set rules for elections rested with the nine-member Provincial Electoral Council. Local elections were scheduled for late August and national elections for November. The crisis created by demands for a return to democracy was considered the most important political development in Haiti since the overthrow of Pres. Jean-Claude Duvalier in February 1986.

# JULY

**1** **Top executives resign from Toshiba.** Shoichi Saba, the chairman of Toshiba Corp., and Sugiichiro Watari, the company's president, resigned after a Toshiba subsidiary was found guilty of illegally selling high technology items to the Soviet Union. A few hours earlier the U.S. Senate had voted to ban Toshiba imports for two to five years; the estimated loss to Toshiba

would be between $1 billion and $3 billion annually. On July 14 Prime Minister Yasuhiro Nakasone accused Toshiba of betraying Japan.

**2** **Haiti leaders yield to protesters.** Haiti's military government, headed by Lieut. Gen. Henri Namphy, attempted to end a serious political crisis by restoring control of the

electoral process to an independent nine-member civilian council as stipulated in the nation's constitution. At least 11 persons had been killed during protests the previous few days as political organizations of virtually every political persuasion came together to oppose the government's usurpation of power. The government's effort to restore peace, however, failed to placate those who were determined to oust the country's military leaders. The general chaos also contributed to other violence, most frequently involving soldiers, politicians, innocent bystanders, protest marchers, rich landowners, and land reform activists.

**4** **Klaus Barbie convicted in France.** Klaus Barbie, the head of the Gestapo in Lyon, France, during World War II, was convicted of crimes against humanity and sentenced to life imprisonment. Judge André Cerdini pronounced the 73-year-old former Nazi chief guilty of all the charges set down in the indictment. These included the deportation and torture of Jews and members of the French Resistance between 1942 and 1944 while German forces occupied the area. After the war Barbie worked for the U.S. Army Counterintelligence Corps and reportedly escaped with his family to Bolivia with U.S. assistance. In February 1983 the "butcher of Lyon" was deported to French Guiana, where French authorities arrested him and took him to Lyon to stand trial.

**7** **Oliver North gives public testimony.** Lieut. Col. Oliver North finally appeared before the congressional committees investigating the U.S. sale of arms to Iran and the diversion of funds from those sales to *contra* guerrillas fighting the Sandinista government in Nicaragua. North, who had been granted limited immunity, told the panel and the general public (which had the opportunity to watch the entire proceedings on television) that he had "never carried out a single act, not one" in which he did not have the authority of his superiors. Responding to one critical question, North said that at the time he had believed that President Reagan had been consulted about all major details of the complex operation, though he had no firsthand knowledge that this was so. Reagan had repeatedly insisted that he had never known that money was being diverted to the *contras* and that secret Swiss bank accounts had been opened for that purpose. North, a former National Security Council aide, was so convincing during his days of testimony that thousands of Americans were moved to send telegrams, letters, and flowers as tokens of their support. The public reaction was so unexpected and so overwhelming that the major networks, newspapers, and newsmagazines felt compelled to give the

story top billing. Most admitted that, for the moment at least, North had become something of a folk hero. A minority, according to several polls, believed that North had lied when he answered several crucial questions. It was expected that after all the witnesses were called, the committees would issue a report setting forth their final conclusions.

**11** **Australians reelect Hawke.** In national elections to Australia's 148-seat House of Representatives, the Australian Labor Party (ALP) of Prime Minister Robert Hawke increased its majority from 16 to 18 seats. It was the first time a Labor government had won three consecutive elections. Dissent within the Liberal Party and within the conservative coalition formed by the Liberals and members of the National Party appeared to have benefited the ALP. The main issues during the campaign were economic, including high interest rates, a large trade deficit, and a growing foreign debt. Hawke argued that the country's problems would gradually disappear as Australia changed its emphasis from exporting raw commodities to manufactured goods.

**12** **Soviet diplomats visit Israel.** Eight Soviet diplomats arrived without fanfare in Tel Aviv, Israel, ostensibly to survey property in Jerusalem that belonged to the Russian Orthodox Church and to renew the passports of Soviet citizens. It appeared, however, that the Soviet delegation intended to remain indefinitely. Observers speculated that, despite public denials, the U.S.S.R. might be considering de facto, if not formal, normalization of relations with Israel. The Soviet Union had broken off diplomatic relations in 1967 when the Arab nations and Israel went to war.

**14** **Taiwan rescinds military decree.** The Chinese Nationalist government on Taiwan ended the emergency decree it had promulgated in 1949 following the defeat of its military forces on the mainland and the establishment of the People's Republic of China. The announcement was widely hailed as a significant step toward the establishment of full democracy in the only province of China not controlled by the Communist regime. One of the practical consequences of the government's new policy was that opposition political parties became legal. The Democratic Progressive Party had,

in fact, already openly participated in elections without harassment and had captured more than one-fifth of the popular vote in the December 1986 elections to the legislature. The abolition of the emergency decree also meant that military courts would no longer have jurisdiction over cases normally tried in civilian courts.

**17** **France severs ties to Iran.** France formally severed diplomatic ties with Iran and took steps to prevent diplomats and staff members in Iran's Paris embassy from leaving the country. The previous day Iran had threatened to break off diplomatic relations unless France withdrew the police cordon it had placed around the embassy on June 30. France had acted to prevent the escape of an Iranian national who did not have diplomatic immunity and was believed to be a top agent involved in the terrorist bombings that killed 13 persons in Paris in September 1986. Iran had long been upset with France because it was supplying arms to Iraq, which had been at war with Iran for the past seven years.

**19** **Social Democrats win in Portugal.** The Social Democrats under Portuguese Prime Minister Aníbal Cavaço Silva won an impressive victory in parliamentary elections, increasing their share of the popular vote to 50.2% from 29% in 1985 and raising their representation to 148 seats from the 88 they previously held in the 250-seat legislature. The election gave the country its first majority government since democracy was restored in 1974. The Socialist Party gained 3 seats and remained the second largest party, with 60 seats. Silva's victory devastated the Democratic Renewal Party, which got only 4.7% of the vote, compared with 18% in 1985, and the Christian Democratic Party, which, with only 4.9% of the vote, lost half of its previous supporters. The Communists were also weakened, winning 11.7% of the vote, compared with 15% in 1985.

**20** **Security Council orders cease-fire.** The United Nations Security Council voted unanimously in favour of a resolution demanding that Iran and Iraq observe an immediate cease-fire so that negotiations to end the seven-year-old war could begin. The Security Council deplored the bombing of civilian centres, attacks on neutral shipping and aircraft, the use of chemical weapons, and the heavy loss of lives and property. Should the resolution be ignored, the Security Council appeared ready to go one step further and urge a worldwide arms embargo against either or both parties refusing to enter into peace talks.

**28** **Goria forms government in Italy.** Giovanni Goria, a Christian Democrat, announced the formation of a coalition government in Italy, thereby ending a political crisis that had begun on March 3 with the resignation of Prime Minister Bettino Craxi, a Socialist. Goria, a 43-year-old economist, had served as treasury minister for five years. Once again the Socialists, Social Democrats, Republicans, and Liberals would be part of a ruling coalition, but their differences

TORIN BOYD—GAMMA/LIAISON

Toshiba Corp.'s chairman, Shoichi Saba (left), and president, Sugiichiro Watari, announce their resignations at a Tokyo press conference after a scandal arose because of the sale of high-technology goods to the Soviet Union.

with the Christian Democrats clouded the future of Goria's government. An attempt to end the political stalemate in mid-June had failed when the Christian Democrats held their own in parliamentary elections. Although the Socialists made substantial gains, the Communists, Italy's second largest party after the Christian Democrats, suffered a major defeat.

**29** **India and Sri Lanka sign pact.** Sri Lankan Pres. J. R. Jayawardene and Indian Prime Minister Rajiv Gandhi signed an agreement in Colombo, Sri Lanka, that, it was hoped, would end four years of violent conflict between the majority Sinhalese, who were overwhelmingly Buddhist, and ethnic Tamils, who were for the most part Hindu. The most controversial feature of the accord created a semiautonomous administrative unit in Sri Lanka's Northern and Eastern provinces, where Tamil separatists sought independence. The agreement, which was opposed by Sri Lanka's prime minister, so infuriated many Sinhalese that they went on a rampage burning buildings, vehicles, banks, courthouses, police stations, an army barracks, and shops owned by Tamils. Prospects for peace depended in large part on Tamil guerrillas, some of whom indicated that they had reservations about laying down their arms. India, however, had agreed to send troops to Sri Lanka if they were needed to subdue intransigent Tamil separatists.

Klaus Barbie, head of the Gestapo in Lyon, France, during World War II, was convicted of crimes against humanity and sentenced to life in prison.
SYGMA

**Tanaka conviction upheld.** The three-judge Tokyo High Court upheld the 1983 conviction of Kakuei Tanaka for accepting bribes from the Lockheed Corp. in 1973 and 1974 while he was prime minister. Tanaka had been sentenced to four years in prison and fined 500 million yen by the Tokyo District Court for influencing All Nippon Airways Co. to purchase Lockheed aircraft. The verdict of the High Court definitively ended 69-year-old Tanaka's role as Japan's legendary

political kingmaker, virtually eliminating his influence in choosing Prime Minister Yasuhiro Nakasone's successor. Earlier in the month Tanaka's powerful faction within the ruling Liberal-Democratic Party had split into three groups; 114 of the faction's 141 members of the Diet (parliament) supported the election of Noburu Takeshita, while others chose to back Kiichi Miyazawa or Shintaro Abe.

**31** **Hundreds die in Mecca riot.** Thousands of Iranian demonstrators clashed with Saudi Arabian riot police near the Great Mosque in Mecca, Islam's most sacred shrine. Of the more than 400 persons killed, 275 were identified as Iranians and 85 as Saudis. Many apparently were trampled to death. The confrontation occurred on the eve of the annual hajj (pilgrimage). Iran's spiritual leader, Ayatollah Ruhollah Khomeini, had urged his followers to stage marches to "disavow the pagans," an apparent reference to Saudi Arabia's Sunni Muslims, whose religious tenets and political policies differed from those of the Iranian Shi'ahs. Iran's reaction to news of the violent deaths was to attack the Saudi, Kuwaiti, and French embassies in Tehran and call for the overthrow of the Saudi royal family. Important details of what actually happened would probably never be known with certainty. Nonetheless, most Arab leaders tended to blame Iran for the occurrence.

# AUGUST

**2** **Third world's problems discussed.** The United Nations Conference on Trade and Development ended a monthlong meeting in Geneva after approving a joint strategy for alleviating some of the third world's most urgent economic problems. The plan called for such things as a more generous and flexible treatment of nations burdened by huge foreign debts, for greater participation of private enterprises in economic development, and for more emphasis on free world trade.

**3** **Iran-*contra* hearings end.** The House and Senate select committees concluded their public Iran-*contra* hearings in Washington, D.C., after listening to some 250 hours of testimony from 28 witnesses over a period of 11 weeks. Most committee members agreed that the most crucial and dramatic testimony was provided by Marine Lieut. Col. Oliver North and by his former superior at the National Security Council, Rear Adm. John Poindexter. North said he had assumed that President Reagan was being fully informed of all that was taking place, but he pointedly added that he had no firsthand information that this was so. Poindexter then swore under oath that he had made a deliberate decision not to tell the president everything, especially that funds from the sale of U.S. arms to Iran were being diverted to the *contra* guerrillas in Nicaragua. The committees were not expected to issue a written report for several months.

Troops loyal to Pres. Corazon Aquino wait outside the general headquarters of the Philippines armed forces, which was damaged during a coup attempt led by Col. Gregorio Honasan.
A. TANNENBAUM—SYGMA

**7** **Arias announces peace plan.** Oscar Arias Sánchez, president of Costa Rica, announced that he and four other presidents of Central American nations had reached agreement on a plan to end hostilities in their region of the world. The wide-ranging document was signed in Guatemala by the leaders of Costa Rica, El Salvador, Guatemala, Honduras, and Nicaragua. Though vague on certain details, it specified a timetable for a cease-fire and for the establishment of international commissions to verify that the plan was being systematically implemented. Initial reaction to the plan was generally positive, in part because the peace initiative had been taken by those

most directly involved in the region's conflicts. For this reason, the peace proposal put forward by President Reagan on August 4 was likely to receive less serious consideration.

**15** **New Zealanders reelect Lange.** The Labour Party of New Zealand Prime Minister David Lange won 58 seats in elections to the 97-seat Parliament, thereby assuring Lange of a second three-year term in office. The National Party captured 39 seats. Although New Zealand's role in the Anzus alliance and the maintenance of law and order were significant issues during the campaign, the principal focus was on Lange's economic policies. He had devalued the New Zealand dollar by 20%, removed controls on interest rates and foreign exchange, and revamped the tax structure. This latter program included a 10% sales tax on goods and services and the phasing out of agricultural subsidies.

**17** **Rudolf Hess dies in prison.** Rudolf Hess, Adolf Hitler's former deputy, died in Spandau prison, West Berlin, at the age of 93. He had been in Spandau for 40 years and was its sole inmate for the last 21 years of his life. Because a prison guard reportedly found Hess with an electric cord wrapped around his neck, the death appeared to be a suicide. In 1941 Hess was arrested after he parachuted into Scotland. His purpose, he said, was to make peace between Great Britain and Germany. After the war Hess was tried at Nürnberg and sentenced to life imprisonment.

**18** **Bulgaria reorganizes government.** Bulgaria approved a fundamental reorganization of its central and regional governmental structures that was expected to be incorporated into the nation's constitution. The changes, both political and economic, included the establishment of tariff-free zones to attract foreign capital. Several key ministries were either merged or suppressed; others were given broader responsibilities. Among the new agencies were an Economy and Planning Ministry and a Ministry of Foreign Economic Relations.

**22** **North Korea defaults on loans.** International bankers revealed that North Korea had been formally notified that it was in default on payment of debts amounting to some $770 million and that some of its foreign property would be subject to seizure unless an agreement on repayment was reached within a few weeks. U.S. banks were not involved because they were forbidden by law from making loans to North Korea. The European bankers said they had been reluctant to act, even though North Korea had paid no principal or interest on the loans since March 1984. Their hand had been forced, they said, when North Korea demanded additional loans during a meeting in London and then walked out.

**24** **Marine spy given 30-year term.** Marine Sgt. Clayton Lonetree was sentenced to 30 years in prison

on charges of spying for the Soviet Union. The sentence was subject to approval by the base commander and to an automatic review by a military court. The jury of eight Marine Corps officers in Quantico, Va., found Lonetree guilty on 13 counts of espionage carried out while he served as a guard at the U.S. embassy in Moscow. He had, among other things, provided Soviet agents with the names, photographs, addresses, and phone numbers of U.S. intelligence personnel.

**28** **Coup fails in the Philippines.** In predawn assaults against the presidential palace in Manila and against three major military bases, several thousand rebel soldiers attempted to overthrow the government of Pres. Corazon Aquino. Loyal troops led by Gen. Fidel Ramos, the armed forces chief of staff, quickly responded with ground and air attacks that by midday had virtually ended the fifth, and most serious, violent challenge to the 18-month-old Aquino presidency. More than 50 persons were killed. Simultaneous but smaller rebellions in other parts of the country collapsed when news spread that the coup in Manila had failed. Col. Gregorio Honasan, the acknowledged organizer of the attempt, escaped in a helicopter. For some time, dissatisfaction had been growing over the "ineffectual" steps Aquino was taking to solve the nation's economic and social problems. Just two days before, there had been a nationwide strike of telephone, public transportation, school, factory, and government employees in protest against increases in fuel prices. Various segments within the military had also been demanding higher pay, greater respect, and a more organized and vigorous campaign against the New People's Army—Communist guerrillas whose numbers had been steadily increasing for years. To the embarrassment of the Philippine Army, some guerrilla units were operating with relative impunity, often catching government troops in deadly ambushes.

**29** **Iraq ends Gulf cease-fire.** Iraq ended an informal cease-fire in the Persian Gulf by bombing Iranian offshore oil installations. Iran immediately vowed to take reprisals. The raids, which set an Iranian supertanker ablaze, were the first since July 20, when the UN Security Council called for a cease-fire and negotiations to end the seven-year-old war. An escalation of the conflict, however, appeared inevitable after Iran

began to lay mines in sea-lanes used by oil tankers. Meanwhile, the U.S. was escorting reflagged Kuwaiti tankers through the vital waterways that were being searched by minesweepers. Although Kuwait was not directly involved in the hostilities, it had given assistance to Iraq and thereby angered Iran.

**30** **South African miners end strike.** More than a quarter of a million black South African miners ended their three-week-old strike without winning the 30% pay increases they had demanded. Even with such an increase, blacks would have continued to make substantially less than their white coworkers. The job action, which was the most massive black protest over wages in the country's history, was led by Cyril Ramaphosa, the general secretary of the National Union of Mineworkers. During negotiations mining officials held fast to their original offer to increase wages up to 23% for certain workers, but loss of production during the strike resulted in huge losses for the industry. It was generally agreed that the union's success in shutting down or seriously disrupting production, especially of gold, in a large number of mines had permanently altered relations between management and black workers.

**31** **South Koreans agree on new charter.** Leaders of the ruling Democratic Justice Party and the opposition Reunification Democratic Party, the two major political forces in South Korea, reached agreement on the basic outline of a new constitution. The final written version would be submitted to voters for their approval. Though certain issues were still unresolved, major changes would be incorporated into the new charter. The president would be elected by popular vote, rather than by the electoral college, and would serve one five-year term, two years less than the present constitution provided. The president, moreover, would no longer have power to dissolve the National Assembly, and legislators would have the right to investigate government affairs. In addition, the military would be formally directed to protect the nation's security while observing political neutrality. The announcement of the compromise agreement, important as it was, was not expected to have any direct effect on the hundreds of strikes that were seriously affecting the nation's economic and social stability.

# SEPTEMBER

**2** **French-speaking nations confer.** Leaders of 41 French-speaking nations and territories gathered in Quebec to foster bonds of unity despite profound differences that threatened to destroy the fledgling 18-month-old organization called La Francophonie. Because human rights was an especially divisive issue, it was decided not to make it a subject of debate. Angry demonstrators, however, made sure that all the delegates were made aware that their decision to set

aside a discussion of human rights would not go unnoticed or unchallenged.

**3** **Burundi's president is overthrown.** The president of Burundi, Jean-Baptiste Bagaza, was "relieved of his duties as head of state, party, and Army" by a group of military officers led by Maj. Pierre Buyoya. Bagaza had been accused both at home and abroad of keeping his fellow Tutsis in power by rigging elections, censoring the press,

and suppressing dissent. The Hutus, who comprised about 85% of the population, had revolted on several occasions without success. On the day before the coup, while Bagaza was attending a conference in Quebec, a group of Burundi citizens staged a demonstration to denounce Bagaza's alleged participation in the Army's wholesale killing of Hutus in the early 1970s. Even so, it was not entirely clear how great a role tribal issues played in the president's ouster.

Pope John Paul II waves to followers during his second visit to the U.S. since becoming pope in 1978.

J. L. ATLAN—SYGMA

**5** **U.S. seeks data on MIAs.** Officials of the Reagan administration said the U.S. would be willing to encourage private humanitarian assistance to Vietnam if Hanoi were more cooperative in resolving cases of U.S. soldiers still listed as missing in action (MIA). The U.S. was especially anxious to clear up about 70 "very compelling" cases, but it continued to ignore Vietnam's repeated demands for economic aid or war reparations. The latest U.S. offer was made after an official U.S. delegation gave a favourable report on its visit to Vietnam. The group included the head of an international charitable organization and two doctors who specialized in prosthetic devices that would enhance the lives of Vietnamese soldiers who had lost limbs.

**6** **Argentines go to polls.** Argentines went to the polls to elect members of the national legislature and numerous other provincial and local officers. The opposition Partido Justicialista, popularly known as Peronists, gained five seats in the Chamber of Deputies and four additional governorships, giving them control of 16 of the 22 provinces. Few expected that the Unión Civica Radical (UCR), led by Pres. Raúl Alfonsín, would win only 37.3% of the congressional vote, compared with 41.4% for Peronist candidates. With only half of the 254 seats in the Chamber of Deputies at stake, the UCR's loss of 13 seats still left it the largest single bloc, with 117 seats. The Peronists would control 105, but since 128 seats constituted a majority, the UCR would be forced to seek political allies to enable it to carry out its policies.

**Turks revoke political bans.** By a very narrow margin, Turkish voters approved the removal of the ten-year political bans that had been imposed, by a provision of the constitution, on former prime ministers Suleyman Demirel and Bulent Ecevit and on some 200 other political opponents of Prime Minister Turgut Ozal. In urging a negative vote, Ozal continued to blame Demirel and Ecevit for the violence that disrupted the nation during the late 1970s. Even before the ballots were tabulated, Ozal announced that new elections would be held in November, a year ahead of schedule.

**7** **Honecker visits West Germany.** East German leader Erich Honecker arrived in Bonn to begin an official five-day state visit to West Germany. The historic meeting between Honecker and Chancellor Helmut Kohl was the first of its kind since West Germany became a self-governing republic in 1949 following the amalgamation of the British, French, and U.S. zones of occupation. During Honecker's visit agreements were signed to further scientific and technological cooperation, to protect the environment, and to ensure the safety of nuclear reactors. Both leaders pledged to foster peace and expand contacts between the two Germanys. The latter accord included a reciprocal visit to East Germany by Kohl at an unspecified date.

**8** **Danish coalition crumbles.** The ruling coalition of Danish Prime Minister Poul Schlüter and an allied party won only 81 of 179 seats in the Folketing (parliament), making it impossible to maintain the status quo. After formally resigning, Schlüter immediately set to work to form a new coalition. On September 10 he presented his new government to Queen Margrethe II. The difficulty of winning an absolute majority in the Folketing was aggravated by the fact that any party winning 2% of the vote was assured of a seat. Minor parties thereby gained greater influence in the creation of a coalition government than their sheer numbers warranted.

**9** **Aquino's Cabinet resigns.** Philippine Pres. Corazon Aquino's entire Cabinet resigned along with other top government officials. The action had not been expected, but it facilitated Aquino's removal of Joker Arroyo, her executive secretary, and of Teodoro Locsin, Jr., her chief legal counsel, on September 17. Both had become objects of caustic criticism. The previous day Vice-Pres. Salvador Laurel confirmed that his resignation as foreign minister was irrevocable because he and the president had "basic, fundamental differences of opinion."

SYGMA

**13** **New Caledonia to remain French.** Residents of the Pacific islands of New Caledonia overwhelmingly approved a referendum to remain a territory of France, but the true sentiments of the overall population were not reflected in the vote because a large number of native Kanaks refused to participate. Resentment against the "outsiders" (white French settlers and immigrants from such places as Indonesia and Vietnam) had led to violence in recent years and to demands by Kanaks for total independence for New Caledonia. Although French Prime Minister Jacques Chirac expressed great satisfaction after the ballots were counted, he reiterated his commitment to a new statute that would grant generous autonomy to the territory. French Pres. François Mitterrand had expressed much greater sympathy for the Kanak cause.

**16** **Pact signed to protect ozone.** During an international conference in Montreal, 24 nations signed an agreement to protect the Earth's environment by restricting the use of certain chemicals that, most scientists believed, were gradually destroying the mantle of atmospheric ozone molecules enveloping the Earth. By blocking out certain types of ultraviolet rays, this natural shield of ozone protected life on Earth from harmful solar radiation.

**19** **Pope concludes U.S. visit.** Pope John Paul II ended his second visit to the U.S. since being elected Roman pontiff in 1978. He began his tour in Miami, Fla., on September 10, then traveled to Columbia, S.C.; New Orleans, La.; San Antonio, Texas; and Phoenix, Ariz. In California he visited Los Angeles, Monterey, and San Francisco. His final U.S. stop was in Detroit. The pope then traveled to Edmonton, Alta., before flying to Fort Simpson, N.W.T., where he met with Indians. When weather conditions prevented him from making the trip during his first visit to North America, the pope promised the Indians that he would see them during his next visit. The pope's visit was characterized by his meetings

U.S. Navy men inspect mines on the *Iran Ajr*. The Iranian ship, surprised while allegedly laying mines in the Persian Gulf, was disabled by a U.S. helicopter and then seized.

with a wide variety of religious, ethnic, and social groups. These included Jewish and Protestant leaders; black, Hispanic, and Indian communities; bishops from the Americas; Roman Catholic nuns and lay workers; and members of the gay community, some dying of AIDS (acquired immune deficiency syndrome).

**21** **U.S. seizes Iranian ship.** A U.S. Army helicopter set an Iranian landing craft ablaze in the Persian Gulf, then seized the vessel and 26 Iranian sailors, four of whom were wounded. Three others were reported killed and two missing. The vessel, which reportedly had already planted six mines in international waters sometimes used as an anchorage

by U.S. warships, still had several mines on board. The following day Iranian Pres. Sayyed Ali Khamenei denounced the U.S. before the United Nations General Assembly and pledged that "the United States shall receive a proper response for this abominable act." That same day Britain announced the closing of the Iranian Military Procurement Office in London because Iran had attacked a British tanker in the Gulf. After a six-week lull the "tanker war" had begun to escalate in late August when Iran and Iraq attacked some 20 ships. For that reason UN Secretary-General Javier Pérez de Cuéllar undertook a peace mission to the Gulf on September 11, but he was unable to bring about a cessation of hostilities.

**25** **Fijian colonel stages second coup.** For the second time in five months, Sitiveni Rabuka, an army colonel, took over the Fijian government with a promise that indigenous Fijians would have permanent control of Parliament even though they were slightly outnumbered by ethnic Indians. Since the first coup on May 14, the country had been ruled by a caretaker government headed by the governor-general, Ratu Sir Penaia Ganilau, who represented Queen Elizabeth II, the official chief of state. On September 29 Rabuka announced his intention to declare Fiji a de facto republic outside of the Commonwealth. Then, on October 6, he declared himself the chief of state.

# OCTOBER

**1** **Tibetans demand independence.** Thousands of Tibetans became involved in violence during the latest of several recent protests against Chinese rule. The official Chinese news agency reported that 6 persons were killed and 19 policemen seriously injured during the upheaval. The agency claimed that the demonstrators used guns wrested from police who had obeyed orders not to fire their weapons. Tourists, however, reported that police fired into a crowd of lamas and Buddhist laymen near Jokhang Temple, Tibet's most sacred Buddhist shrine, in Lhasa, the capital. China blamed the turmoil on the Dalai Lama, the spiritual leader of Tibetan Buddhism, who was in the U.S. calling for negotiations to end Chinese control over the land his predecessors had ruled as both spiritual and temporal leaders. After China effectively regained control of Tibet in 1950, an agreement was signed giving Tibetans control over internal affairs and China authority to handle foreign affairs and defense. After an abortive rebellion in 1959, however, the Dalai Lama fled into exile and the Chinese set about destroying Buddhist temples and monasteries. Some of the damage had been repaired in recent years, and efforts were made to build roads and complete other major projects, but Tibetan animosity toward the Chinese had never abated.

**4** **Mexico to have new leader.** The Partido Revolucionario Institucional, which had ruled Mexico without interruption since 1929, unanimously chose 39-year-old economist Carlos Salinas de Gortari to be its presidential candidate in the 1988 general election. There was no doubt that Salinas, who had served as minister of budget and planning, would be elected easily to a single six-year term, succeeding Miguel de la Madrid Hurtado as Mexico's chief of state and head of government.

**6** **Mubarak reelected in Egypt.** Egyptian Interior Minister Zaki Badr announced to a national television audience that 97.1% of those who had cast ballots the day before had approved a referendum granting Pres. Hosni Mubarak six more years in office.

Mubarak had been endorsed by his own National Democratic Party, by three opposition parties, and by the Muslim Brotherhood, an outlawed fundamentalist group that had gained representation in the People's Assembly by allying itself with legal parties.

**16** **Ousted African leader executed.** Capt. Blaise Compaoré declared a national holiday in Burkina Faso following the execution of Capt. Thomas Sankara, who had been ousted as president of the West African nation the previous day. Twelve other officials were also killed. Compaoré, Sankara's chief adviser, said he had been forced to act before the president could carry out a plan to execute those who opposed his military regime. Compaoré also announced that a new president would be selected by representatives of the country's 30 provinces. Burkina Faso, which had been known as Upper Volta before changing its name in 1985, gained independence from France in 1960.

**17** **Commonwealth ends conference.** The 49 members of the Commonwealth of Nations ended their meeting in Vancouver, B.C., with British Prime Minister Margaret Thatcher refusing to endorse new economic sanctions against South Africa. Thatcher, in fact, continued to insist that sanctions already adopted by Britain and other Commonwealth nations were more likely than not to harden

South Africa's resistance to demands that it end apartheid, the government's policy of racial separation. The Commonwealth as a group did affirm the need for "wider, tighter, and more intensified applications" of sanctions worldwide, but it noted in its declaration that Britain, which had the most extensive financial ties to South Africa, did not concur.

**18** **Spaniard to head Unesco.** The executive board of the United Nations Educational, Scientific and Cultural Organization (Unesco) nominated 53-year-old Federico Mayor Zaragoza, a Spanish biochemist, to succeed Amadou Mahtar M'Bow as director general of the international organization. The nomination came on the fifth ballot after bitter wrangling. Mayor received 30 votes, but 20 of M'Bow's supporters voted against him. Nonetheless, members of the general conference were expected to approve the choice. Both Great Britain and the U.S. had withdrawn from Unesco after accusing M'Bow, a native of Senegal, of wasteful spending, inefficient management, and anti-Western bias.

**19** **U.S. stock market collapses.** In a day of frantic trading on Wall Street, the Dow Jones Industrial Average fell a dramatic 508.32 points to 1,738.74, a drop of 22.6%. With 604 million shares changing hands, the volume was nearly double the previous one-day

JAMES COLBURN—PHOTOREPORTERS
The U.S. Senate rejected the controversial nomination of Robert Bork to the Supreme Court by a vote of 58–42.

record. Although the Great Depression followed a 12.82% drop in the stock market on Oct. 28, 1929, and an additional 11.7% drop the following day, analysts were quick to point out that ominous analogies were unjustified because the overall financial situation was significantly better in 1987. Nonetheless, there was serious talk about a possible economic recession, and intense discussions were held about what had to be done to calm the hysteria in order to restore confidence in the U.S. economy. Among the blue chip stocks that suffered dramatic losses were International Business Machines (IBM), which dropped $31 to $104; General Motors, which fell $13.875 to $52.125; and Exxon, which sold for $33.50 a share after dropping $10.25. Overall, stock portfolios lost an estimated $500 billion. Stock markets in other parts of the world also suffered dramatic losses because of the panic on Wall Street.

**U.S. attacks Iranian boat base.** Four U.S. destroyers bombarded two Iranian oil installations in the Persian Gulf after warning the Iranian crews of the impending attack. Some hours later a party of naval commandos boarded a third oil platform and destroyed the radar and communications equipment. A military response was necessary, the U.S. said, because Iran had without provocation attacked ships in the Gulf. Some of the vessels were carrying the U.S. flag, others the flags of neutral nations not involved in Iran's seven-year war with Iraq. The Iranian speedboats that preyed on Gulf shipping reportedly used the platforms as their base. U.S. officials said the targets had been carefully chosen to avoid unnecessary casualties. U.S. Secretary of Defense Caspar Weinberger, however, warned Iran that if it continued its attacks the U.S. would respond with stronger countermeasures. On October 22 Kuwait's Sea Island offshore oil terminal, which serviced supertankers, was severely damaged in a missile attack presumed to have been launched by Iran from the Fao Peninsula. The U.S. said it was not obliged to respond to a situation that involved only Kuwait.

**Goetz sentenced to prison.** Bernhard Goetz, who in June was acquitted on 12 of 13 charges arising from his shooting of four black youths on a New York subway train in December 1984, was fined $5,000 and sentenced to six months in prison and five years' probation for carrying an unlicensed concealed weapon at the time of the shooting. The judge, who also ordered Goetz to undergo psychiatric counseling, remarked that "a nonjail sentence would invite others to violate the gun laws."

**20** **Takeshita to succeed Nakasone.** Japanese Prime Minister Yasuhiro Nakasone chose 63-year-old Noboru Takeshita as his successor. Nakasone had been asked to make the selection after leaders of the ruling Liberal-Democratic Party (LDP) could not reach agreement after several days of negotiations. Takeshita, the secretary-general of the LDP, was picked over Shintaro Abe, chairman of the executive council, and Kiichi Miyazawa, the finance minister. Takeshita was formally elected president of the LDP on November 6. Although

The Communist Party of China held its 13th national congress, the first in five years. During the congress, Deng Xiaoping (Teng Hsiao-p'ing) resigned from two of his three offices.
ANDERSON—GAMMA/LIAISON

the LDP was deeply split by competing factions, its absolute majority in the House of Representatives guaranteed Takeshita the prime ministership.

**22** **Reagan curtails sales to China.** The Reagan administration announced that it was curtailing the sale of certain high-technology items to China because that country continued to sell Silkworm missiles to Iran. These weapons were then allegedly used to attack ships in the Persian Gulf. China strongly denied the U.S. charges. An Iranian official acknowledged that Iran did possess an arsenal of Silkworm missiles, but he insisted that the weapons had been captured from Iraqi troops. He also remarked that Iran had far more U.S.-made surface-to-air Stinger missiles than the 16 that had been reported. Even though the U.S. intended, at least temporarily, to modify its policy of gradually expanding the range of high-technology items made available to China, it apparently desired to downplay any differences with China and to keep relations between the two countries as normal as possible.

**23** **Senate rejects Bork nomination.** By a vote of 58–42 the U.S. Senate rejected Robert Bork's nomination to the Supreme Court. President Reagan had chosen Bork, a judge on the U.S. Court of Appeals for the District of Columbia, to fill a vacancy created by the retirement of Justice Lewis Powell, Jr., in June. Although five other nominees to the Supreme Court had been rejected by the Senate during the 20th century, and 21 others earlier in U.S. history, none was so fiercely attacked by his opponents or so ardently defended by his supporters as was Bork. The judge's legal expertise was never questioned, but his legal views on civil liberties and other issues were vigorously denounced by those who opposed his elevation to the Supreme Court. On October 29 Reagan named Judge Douglas Ginsburg as his second choice, but on November 7 Ginsburg asked that his name be withdrawn after admitting that he had smoked marijuana as a student and as a law professor. An embarrassed president

then sent the name of Judge Anthony Kennedy to Capitol Hill on November 11. The Senate, however, was not expected to consider his qualifications until early in 1988.

**25** **China holds party congress.** In his opening address to members of the Communist Party of China's (CPC's) 13th national congress, the first in five years, Zhao Ziyang (Chao Tzu-yang), China's premier and acting head of the CPC, said that China had to intensify its efforts to restructure its economy and overhaul its governmental bureaucracy if it hoped to achieve its goal of modernization. Reform, Zhao insisted, was the only way to revitalize the country. He pointedly added that the process, already under way, was irresistible because it was demanded by the people and was appropriate to the times. During the congress, a new Central Committee of 175 full members and 110 alternates was elected, as was also a Central Advisory Commission of 200 members and a 69-member Central Committee for Discipline Inspection. In an important development, China's preeminent leader Deng Xiaoping (Teng Hsiao-p'ing) resigned from the CPC Central Committee and from the Standing Committee of the Political Bureau; the only position he retained was that of chairman of the committee's Military Commission. On many occasions Deng had declared that it was time for him and other leaders of advanced age to turn over their responsibilities to younger persons. As previously agreed, Li Xiannian (Li Hsien-nien) and Chen Yun (Ch'en Yün) also resigned from the party Central Committee. Deng's decision to step aside was widely interpreted as proof that Deng now felt that others could be safely entrusted to carry out the social and economic reforms he had introduced. On November 2, the day after the congress ended, Zhao was elected general secretary of the CPC despite often-repeated protestations that he was better suited to oversee economic affairs than to direct the Communist Party. Zhao remained premier, but it was expected that he would be relieved of the duties of that office in the near future.

**26** **U.S. bans Iranian imports.** President Reagan announced a U.S. ban on all Iranian imports because Iran had, among other things, refused to accept a cease-fire mandated by the United Nations and had made unprovoked attacks in the Persian Gulf against ships of neutral nations and against ships flying the U.S. flag. Iran was also accused of sponsoring international terrorism. On October 6 the U.S. Congress had voted to ban the importation of all Iranian products. The Senate vote was 93–0, while that in the House was 407–5. During the first seven months of the year, the U.S. had imported more than $1 billion worth of Iranian oil in addition to a variety of other products of lesser value.

**27** **Koreans approve direct election.** More than 93% of some 20 million South Korean voters approved a new constitution for the country that provided for direct election of the president by popular vote; the old constitution had stipulated that the nation's leader be chosen by members of an electoral college. The change had been one of the chief demands of those who opposed the government of Pres. Chun Doo Hwan. They had even staged violent protests to force the issue. The outcome of the December presidential election was difficult to predict, however, because the two most prominent opponents of Roh Tae Woo, the candidate of the ruling Democratic Justice Party, both seemed determined to run for president. If neither Kim Young Sam nor Kim Dae Jung stepped aside, the presidential race would feature a contest between three major candidates with near-equal followings.

# NOVEMBER

**5** **Pretoria frees black leader.** The South African government granted 77-year-old Govan Mbeki his freedom after 23 years of confinement. The former leader of the African National Congress (ANC) had been convicted in 1964 of plotting the violent overthrow of South Africa's white rulers. After his release Mbeki was allowed a one-hour visit with Nelson Mandela, another ANC leader, who was serving time in a different prison on similar charges. During a news conference—an unusual concession by the government—Mbeki reaffirmed his membership in the ANC and said that he still embraced the ideas that sent him to prison. Mbeki also said that he viewed apartheid as the greatest obstacle to finding a workable solution to South Africa's racial conflict.

**7** **Tunisia's president ousted.** Habib Bourguiba, Tunisia's president for life, was deposed by Prime Minister Zine al-Abidine Ben Ali, who claimed the 84-year-old ruler was too ill and senile to remain in office. Bourguiba had been the nation's only ruler since it gained independence from France in 1956. Ben Ali, a former army general and interior minister, was expected to continue Tunisia's moderate, pro-Western policies. He informed the nation that there was now an urgent need to change the constitution, which had been amended to permit a lifetime president. "Our people are worthy of a developing and institutionalized political life," he said, "founded in reality on a multiparty system and plurality of popular organizations."

**8** **Arabs forge greater unity.** Leaders of the Arab world gathered in Amman, Jordan, to discuss the practical ramifications of the war between Iraq and Iran and to reevaluate the Arab League's relationship with Egypt, whose membership in the organization had been suspended when it signed a peace treaty with Israel in 1979. One of the most dramatic outcomes of the meeting was the apparent reconciliation between Iraqi Pres. Saddam Hussein and Syrian Pres. Hafez al-Assad. The latter added substantially to Arab unity when he agreed to cease supporting Iran militarily and politically. Arab solidarity was further bolstered when individual leaders appeared ready to normalize relations with Egypt. Within a few days the United Arab Emirates, Iraq, Kuwait, and Morocco had taken that step. Jordan, Oman, and The Sudan were already dealing with Egypt on a normal basis.

**9** **Bomb kills 11 in Ulster.** Eleven persons were killed and at least 60 others were wounded when a bomb exploded in Enniskillen, Northern Ireland. The victims were among those gathering for a wreath-laying ceremony on Remembrance Sunday to honour British soldiers who had died during World Wars I and II. The bombing was blamed on the outlawed Irish Republican Army (IRA), whose terrorist attacks had been condemned even by the Irish government. Irish Prime Minister Charles Haughey, fearful of a new onslaught of violence at home as well as across the border, ordered 7,000 soldiers and police to raid suspected IRA havens along the border in search of illegal arms and explosives.

**10** **Death claims Niger's president.** Seyni Kountché, president of the West African nation of Niger, died of a brain tumour in a Paris hospital at the age of 56. He was immediately replaced by Col. Ali Seibou, the army chief of staff and a cousin of the late president. Kountché had been head of Niger's military government since he seized power in 1974. During his rule Niger and Chad, both former French territories, continued to maintain close ties with France. When Libyan troops moved into northern Chad in 1980, Kountché had quietly aided Chadian Pres. Hissen Habré, whose troops also had the support of French paratroopers when the government's survival was threatened.

**Spain to close U.S. bases.** Spain formally notified the U.S. that it would not extend the defense treaty the two countries had been observing for 34 years. If negotiations over the next six months failed to resolve outstanding differences, the treaty would expire in May 1988 and the U.S. would be obliged to vacate two air force bases, a naval station, and various communications facilities. Spain's Socialist government placed special emphasis on the removal of 72 U.S. F-16 jet fighters assigned to the Torrejón air base near Madrid. Although the U.S. argued that the planes were a vital part of NATO's defense system, it offered to move one-third of the planes to a location outside Spain. This compromise, however, was deemed inadequate and consequently unacceptable.

**11** **Gorbachev appointee loses post.** Boris Yeltsin, who had been appointed head of the Moscow

SCOTT ROBINSON—SYGMA

Smoke billows from the federal penitentiary in Atlanta, Georgia. The fire was set by rioting Cuban inmates, angered by the U.S.-Cuban agreement to repatriate "excludable" Cubans.

Communist Party organization by Soviet leader Mikhail Gorbachev, was unexpectedly dismissed from his post. The demotion was linked to a meeting of the party's Central Committee on October 21, when Yeltsin openly criticized Gorbachev and other top officials for introducing change at too slow a pace. On November 15, during an open forum in Moscow, members of the audience expressed anger that Yeltsin should have been punished for urging speedy implementation of Gorbachev's own plan to restructure the economy and political system. On November 18 the Soviet news agency TASS reported that Yeltsin had been named to the prestigious position of first deputy chairman of the State Committee for Construction, a field in which he excelled.

**Bomb kills five in Beirut.** At least five persons were killed and about 70 others injured when a bomb exploded in a crowded passenger terminal in the international airport in Beirut, Lebanon. It was the first such incident of the year. Though no group claimed responsibility for the attack, a Sunni Muslim Lebanese woman who died in the blast was believed to have carried the bomb into the terminal in a suitcase.

**12** **Sri Lankan Tamils win concessions.** The Sri Lankan Parliament approved two bills establishing provincial councils in Tamil-dominated areas in the northern and eastern regions of the country. The concessions had been worked out in July in an effort to end four years of bloody conflict between the ethnic Indian Tamils, who were mainly Hindus, and the majority Sinhalese, who were mostly Buddhists. It was quickly evident that many Sinhalese resented the concessions made to the minority Tamils. Police in one northern city felt it necessary to arrest 95 demonstrators and use tear gas to disperse angry crowds. That same day 25 Tamils were killed when the bus in which they were riding hit a land mine. A few days earlier at least 32 persons had been killed and more than 75 injured when a bomb exploded in a busy section of Colombo, the capital.

**15** **Yugoslavia faces crisis.** In an effort to control Yugoslavia's spiraling inflation—at 140% the highest in Europe—the government froze wages and dramatically increased the prices of such basic commodities as flour, milk, bread, sugar, cooking oil, coal, and gasoline. The cost of transportation and electricity also rose substantially. Some prices increased threefold. The action, which was approved by both the Federal Chamber (121–28) and the Council of Republics and Provinces (58–14), jeopardized the political future of Prime Minister Branko Mikulic. Even if he were forced to resign, few believed the country's economic condition was likely to improve in the foreseeable future under a new leader.

**Romanians ransack city hall.** Several thousand Romanian workers ransacked the city hall in Brasov to protest substantial wage cuts and the likelihood of food and energy shortages for the third consecutive winter. Although the government's drastic economic policies were proclaimed necessary for raising production up to quota levels and wiping out the country's foreign debt, workers vented their anger with the first violent demonstration in ten years. Since 1981 Pres. Nicolae Ceausescu had halved the country's foreign debt to about $5.5 billion, much of which was the result of uneconomical industrial expenditures. However, consumers had suffered in the process and, according to certain experts, poor planning and inferior equipment were critical problems still waiting to be addressed.

**18** **Iran-*contra* report issued.** The U.S. Senate and House committees investigating the Iran-*contra* affair released a 690-page final report that was critical of President Reagan and his administration. Eight Republican committeemen, two from the Senate and six from the House, repudiated the report, calling it biased and hysterical. The main focus of the inquiry was to determine what, if anything, Reagan had known about the sale of U.S. arms to Iran and the subsequent clandestine transfer of funds from those sales to the *contras*, guerrillas fighting the Sandinista government in Nicaragua. Most committeemen preferred to say simply that no evidence directly linked the president to *contra* funding. The dissident Republicans, who issued their own report, insisted that the sworn testimony of key witnesses proved that the president had had no knowledge of the operation. Another point of disagreement involved the interpretation of a law forbidding aid to the *contras*. The majority claimed that the law also applied to the National Security Council (NSC), to which Adm. John Poindexter and his aide Marine Lieut. Col. Oliver North had been assigned. Others argued that the law did not apply to the NSC because it was not mentioned among the groups specifically forbidden to aid the *contras*, directly or indirectly. They pointed out that the NSC was simply a presidential advisory group with no ties to the Department of Defense, the CIA, or any other government agency engaged in intelligence activities. All, however, agreed that the president had a responsibility to know what was being done by the NSC, that private individuals had no right to formulate and carry out policies that by their very nature involved the government, and that the sale of arms to Iran was wrong. With the publication of the report, the work of the congressional committees ended, but special prosecutor Lawrence Walsh still had the option to seek criminal indictments against such witnesses as North, Poindexter, or others who had been interrogated under oath after being granted limited immunity.

**21** **Cubans held in U.S. prisons riot.** About 1,000 Cubans in a federal detention centre in Oakdale, La., set fire to the prison and took about 30 employees hostage. The riot was in response to news that Cuba and the U.S. had reached an agreement that called for the repatriation of some 2,600 "excludable" Cubans (most accused of crimes or mentally ill) who had arrived in the U.S. during the port of Mariel boatlift in 1980. The U.S. would, according to the understanding, accept as many as 27,000 legal Cuban immigrants each year. On November 23, Cubans held in a federal penitentiary in Atlanta, Ga., also rioted; as in Louisiana, they took hostages and set fire to the facility. On November 29, after talking with Agustin Roman, the Cuban-born Roman Catholic auxiliary bishop of Miami, Fla., representatives of the Oakdale inmates agreed to release their 26 remaining hostages. On December 3 an agreement was reached in Atlanta. The basis of the settlement was a signed statement that the U.S. would conduct a "full, fair, and equitable" review of each individual's record. Some detainees were expected to be set free, while others would be returned to Cuba or sent to some other country willing to accept them.

**27** **Ershad decrees emergency.** Lieut. Gen. H. M. Ershad, president of Bangladesh, declared a state of emergency and banned all strikes and protests because, he said, the country was being torn asunder by internal strife that produced insecurity and endangered the economy. Violent demonstrations to force Ershad's resignation had been going on for months. On November 9 the government had arrested at least 1,100 persons, including five members of Parliament; two days later prominent members of the opposition were placed under house arrest. Virtually all dissident groups appeared to have come together to oppose Ershad, who had seized power in 1982 and had won election as president in 1986 amid charges of widespread vote fraud. Despite the vigour of their protests, antigovernment groups did not appear to be winning their battle, especially in the face of a severe crackdown that included curfews, control of the news media, and the suspension of fundamental rights.

**French hostages freed in Beirut.** Two French hostages, one held for 20 months, the other for 11 months, were released in Beirut, Lebanon, after negotiations that apparently involved French, Syrian, Iranian, and perhaps Algerian officials. The little-known Organization of Revolutionary Justice said it decided to free the two men after France promised it would cease supporting Iraq in its war against Iran. Two days later an Iranian suspected of involvement in a series of bombings in Paris was allowed to leave France. He had fled to the Iranian embassy in June, at which time France sealed off the premises and broke diplomatic relations with Iran. Following the release of the two French hostages and the departure of the Iranian suspect, French Prime Minister Jacques Chirac announced that France was moving to settle a $1 billion loan made by Iran in 1974 and was discussing other issues that stood in the way of normalizing relations. Chirac's new policy of reaching accommodation with Iran was severely criticized by Britain, the U.S., and Arab nations.

**29** **Election halted in Haiti.** Haiti's first presidential election in 30 years was halted when weeks of political violence reached a new intensity as voters went to the polls. Fear gripped the nation during indiscriminate attacks on voting stations, on radio broadcasting facilities, and on churches that had been designated as polling places. At least 34 persons were killed and 75 wounded, some by bullets fired from speeding cars. Many of the thugs were believed to be former members of the feared Tontons Macoutes, the private military force of the dictators François Duvalier, who died in 1971, and his son Jean-Claude Duvalier, who was deposed in 1986. The government, which had done little to control the campaign of terror or to assist those entrusted with organizing the election, disbanded the civilian electoral commission for jeopardizing "the unity of the nation." The commission called the order illegal and unconstitutional. In fact, five months earlier the military government had been forced by widespread protests to restore control of the electoral process to the civilian council as stipulated in the constitution. The head of Haiti's provisional government, Lieut. Gen. Henri Namphy, tried to reassure the nation by reiterating his pledge to relinquish power to civilians in February 1988. On December 12 nine civilians were sworn in as members of a new electoral council to oversee elections on Jan. 17, 1988. However, the military government indicated it planned to take an active part in the political process.

**Poles fail to support referendum.** Polish voters failed to support in sufficient numbers a national referendum that proposed a program of severe economic austerity together with moderate political changes. The government did not hide the fact that two or three years of hardship would be needed before permanent improvement in the standard of living could be provided. The defeat of a national referendum on a major government-sponsored program was unprecedented in an Eastern bloc nation. Leaders of the banned Solidarity trade federation had urged Poles not to vote. Abstention was in fact indirect rejection of the government's proposals because Polish law required that referenda win the approval of a majority of eligible voters. On December 5 Prime Minister Zbigniew Messner told parliament that because the referendum had failed, food prices would not rise as sharply as planned in 1988, but the cost of rent, fuel, and heat would increase 140–200% as previously scheduled. Higher wages, however, were expected to soften somewhat the financial burden on Polish workers.

**Korean plane disappears.** A South Korean Boeing 707 airliner carrying 115 persons from Baghdad, Iraq, to Seoul, South Korea, mysteriously disappeared near the Thai–Burmese border. The following day a young woman and an elderly man, who carried false Japanese passports and had left the plane during a stopover in Abu Dhabi, took suicide pills while waiting to be questioned by authorities in Bahrain. The man died almost immediately; the woman went into a deep coma but survived. On December 4 a Thai newspaper reported that the plane's fuselage had been found by a band of Karen guerrillas in Burma. At the beginning of their investigation, South Korean officials believed that the two suspects, most likely acting as agents for North Korea, had probably planted a time bomb in the plane.

# DECEMBER

**2 Kampuchean peace discussed.** Prince Norodom Sihanouk, former leader of Cambodia (now called Kampuchea), met outside Paris with Kampuchean Prime Minister Hun Sen. It was the first meeting between Sihanouk and an official of the regime that was installed by the Vietnamese after they successfully invaded Cambodia in December 1978 and ended a three-year reign of terror by Pol Pot and his Communist Khmer Rouge regime. Sihanouk, having taken a one-year leave of absence as head of a three-party alliance fighting the Vietnamese-backed Kampuchean government, was technically acting in a private capacity when he and Hun Sen began talks on how to end the guerrilla warfare. No settlement would be possible without agreement on such basic issues as free elections and the withdrawal of some 140,000 Vietnamese troops. Further talks were planned at a later date.

**8 U.S.S.R. and U.S. sign INF treaty.** Soviet leader Mikhail Gorbachev and President Reagan signed a historic treaty in Washington, D.C., that would, when ratified by the Supreme Soviet and the U.S. Senate, gradually reduce the size of each nation's nuclear arsenals. The intermediate-range nuclear forces (INF) treaty provided for unprecedented on-site inspection of missile bases and for verification of the systematic destruction of specific missiles. The complex accord, which was years in the making and left each side with awesome nuclear weapons, was warmly received in most capitals of the world. Ratification, which could be delayed by amendments in the U.S. Senate, was expected to be followed by prolonged negotiations on further arms controls, especially on long-range nuclear weapons and on the Soviet Union's conventional forces in Europe, which were of deep concern to many Western politicians.

**9 Honasan captured in Manila.** Col. Gregorio Honasan was captured in a Manila town house without any shots being fired. Four other military officers and two civilians were also taken into custody. Honasan had led a bloody rebellion against the government of Pres. Corazon Aquino in August, but he managed to escape when it became evident that loyal government troops would defeat his followers. Gen. Fidel Ramos, chief of staff of the armed forces, announced that Honasan would face due process of law. On December 10 Sen. Juan Ponce Enrile said his law firm would defend Honasan during the court-martial. The news was not a surprise because the two men were close friends and Honasan had been Enrile's security chief until Enrile was dismissed as Aquino's minister of defense. On December 18 the president signed an order dismissing Honasan from the ranks of the military. There was, however, a possibility that Honasan would be granted clemency because, as some pointed out, he had served the country well during the tumultuous events that led to the removal of Pres. Ferdinand Marcos from power in February 1986.

**13 Palestinians challenge Israel.** The Israeli Cabinet met to discuss growing violence on the part of Palestinians who had grown frustrated by 20 years of occupation in the West Bank and Gaza Strip. By December 17 at least 17 protesters had been killed and scores wounded. When Israel responded to the rioting with increased patrols and curfews, the Palestinians called a general strike. On December 19 the riots spread to the old Arab section of Jerusalem. Two days later hundreds of thousands of Arabs living in Israel staged a general strike in support of the Palestinians. The U.S. was among those who criticized Israel's "harsh security measures and excessive

Gary Hart addresses the press and a group of his supporters in his renewed bid for the Democratic presidential nomination.
RUBEN PEREZ—SYGMA

use of live ammunition." Israeli Prime Minister Yitzhak Shamir, however, was as determined as ever to use whatever means were necessary to restore order. By December 25 nearly 1,000 Palestinians had been arrested for alleged involvement in the riots that continued to flare despite intensified efforts to suppress the unrest. Arab defense lawyers announced on December 30 that they would not participate in the military trials of those who had been arrested because they would thereby appear to legitimize the proceedings.

**Belgium holds election.** In national parliamentary elections, Belgium's centre-right coalition government held onto 110 seats in the 212-seat Chamber of Deputies, but Prime Minister Wilfried Martens was disheartened by Socialist gains. French-speaking Socialists won 40 seats, a gain of 5, while their Flemish-speaking counterparts retained 32. This meant that for the first time in half a century, the Socialist bloc would hold more seats than Roman

Crowds of supporters jam the streets of Seoul, South Korea, to hear presidential candidate Roh Tae Woo of the ruling Democratic Justice Party. Owing to a voter split between opposition candidates, Roh won the election with 35.9% of the popular vote.

H. EDWARD KIM—TIME MAGAZINE

Catholic parties. Martens, who had already headed seven governments since 1979, would once again try to form a new coalition with his Christian Democrats (43 Flemish-speaking, 19 French-speaking) as the base.

**15** **Gary Hart resumes campaign.** Gary Hart, former U.S. senator from Colorado, announced that he was resuming the presidential campaign he had abandoned in May. At the time, Hart was leading his rivals in the race for the Democratic nomination. The situation had become intolerable, Hart complained, because the press continued to focus its attention on revelations that he had been involved with a Florida model rather than on his political views. Hart's decision to reenter the race was supported by his wife and two children, but it caused consternation and resentment in the Democratic camp. Several candidates were incensed when Hart said his decision was motivated by the fact that other Democratic candidates were not addressing the most important issues facing the nation and the world. When asked if the scandal had destroyed his credibility, Hart replied: "Let's let the people decide."

**ASEAN conference ends.** The Association of Southeast Asian Nations (ASEAN) ended a two-day meeting in Manila that was only the third in the 20-year history of the organization and the first in a decade. Simply holding the conference was considered a major triumph. The six members of ASEAN (Brunei, Indonesia, Malaysia, Philippines, Singapore, and Thailand) recognized that much had changed in recent years, including their relationships to the U.S. and their views of the Soviet Union and China. Before adjourning, the Asian leaders signed a Manila Declaration of ASEAN resolve, which included the goal of creating a nuclear-free Zone of Peace, Freedom, and Neutrality in the region. Japanese Prime Minister Noboru Takeshita traveled to Manila to offer ASEAN investments and loans valued at about $2 billion.

**16** **Roh Tae Woo wins election.** Roh Tae Woo, candidate of South Korea's ruling Democratic Justice Party, was elected president with 35.9% of the popular vote. Kim Young Sam, head of the Reunification Democratic

Party, finished second with 27.5%. Kim Dae Jung, the leader of the Party for Peace and Democracy, captured 26.5%. Although antigovernment factions charged that the election had been rigged, few took the accusations seriously because the two main opposition candidates won nearly 54% of the vote. It was highly probable that either would have been elected had they not split the vote. During the campaign both Kims had repeatedly promised that only one of them would oppose Roh, but because their personal rivalry was so strong, neither was willing to yield to the other. Regional loyalties were so powerful that each of the Kims won a massive majority in his native area and neither was able to campaign in the other's territory without meeting violent resistance. Kim Jong Pil, the fourth major candidate and head of the New Democratic Republican Party, also won a plurality in his home province, but he could not muster wide support. After his victory Roh promised to work for national reconciliation and pledged to resign if the people did not give him a vote of confidence in a national plebiscite to be held after the summer Olympic Games in Seoul. By that time, he said, voters would have had sufficient time to judge whether he was truly committed to democracy.

**Italy convicts Mafia chiefs.** The longest and most significant trial of Mafia leaders in Italian history concluded in Palermo, Sicily, with the convictions of 338 of 452 defendants. Nineteen men were given life sentences, the maximum penalty allowed by law, for operating a vast criminal empire that involved illicit drug trafficking and murder. The court also imposed fines amounting to nearly $10 million. Michele Greco, nicknamed "the pope" because he headed the organization, was found guilty of ordering 78 murders. The victims included several prominent government officials. The most damaging evidence against the defendants was supplied by two former members of the Mafia. Although no one believed the trial had destroyed the Mafia, it showed that the government was determined to wage all-out war against Italy's most feared and fearless criminals.

**Deaver found guilty of perjury.** After a seven-week trial, a federal jury in Washington, D.C., convicted Michael Deaver on three counts of perjury, but it acquitted

him on two other charges of lying under oath. Deaver was a personal friend of the Reagans and had served the president as White House deputy chief of staff from 1981 to May 1985. After leaving the administration, he had become a highly paid lobbyist and used his contacts in government to benefit his clients. The trial, however, did not focus on illegal influence peddling but on perjury. Specifically, the jury found Deaver guilty of lying to a House subcommittee about his efforts to arrange a meeting between the president and a South Korean trade representative, of lying to a federal grand jury about contacts made on behalf of Trans World Airlines, and of lying to a federal grand jury about attempts to retain a tax provision that favoured U.S. manufacturers producing goods in Puerto Rico. Sentencing was scheduled for Feb. 25, 1988, but Deaver's chief counsel said the verdict would be appealed.

**17** **Czechoslovak leader resigns.** The official Czechoslovakian news agency reported that 75-year-old Gustav Husak had resigned as secretary-general of the country's Communist Party. He was replaced by 65-year-old Milos Jakes, a member of the party's ruling Presidium. Jakes was expected to adopt Soviet leader Mikhail Gorbachev's policies for revitalizing the economy and restructuring the government bureaucracy to make them more efficient and more responsive to current needs. If he did so, it would mark a profound change in Jakes's political views. After the Soviet invasion of Czechoslovakia in 1968, Jakes headed the Central Control and Auditing Commission that purged tens of thousands from the Communist Party because they espoused a more liberal interpretation of Communism.

**22** **Zimbabwe rivals end feud.** Joshua Nkomo, leader of Zimbabwe's main opposition group, reached a "unity agreement" with Prime Minister Robert Mugabe. The two men had become bitter rivals after the white government of what was then called Rhodesia had been overthrown in 1978. The merger of Mugabe's Zimbabwe African National Union and Nkomo's Zimbabwe African People's Union was expected to diminish violence and perhaps reduce ethnic divisions within the country. On December 31, as agreed, Mugabe was inaugurated as the first executive president of a one-party state. He would be both head of government and head of state. Nkomo became vice-president and second secretary of the united party.

**29** **Cosmonaut sets record.** Soviet cosmonaut Yuri Romanenko returned to Earth in a Soyuz TM-3 capsule after establishing an endurance record of 326 days aboard the Mir space station. Two other cosmonauts still in the space station were expected to eventually surpass Romanenko's record. Scientists were clearly elated that Romanenko had apparently survived his experience without any serious problems. The success of the long experiment increased the possibility of a Soviet manned flight to Mars, which would take about three years.

# Major Revisions from the 1988 *Macropædia*

The purpose of this section is to introduce to continuing *Book of the Year* subscribers selected *Macropædia* articles or portions of them that have been completely revised or written anew. It is intended to update the *Macropædia* in ways that cannot be accomplished fully by reviewing the year's events or by revising statistics annually, because the *Macropædia* texts themselves—written from a longer perspective than any yearly revision—supply authoritative interpretation and analysis as well as narrative and description.

Three articles have been chosen from the 1988 printing: the extensively revised and newly illustrated *Advertising* section of MARKETING AND MERCHANDISING; the wholly new section of MOTION PICTURES dealing with the history of silent film; and BAGHDAD. Each is the work of a distinguished scholar, and represents the continuing dedication of the *Encyclopædia Britannica* to bringing such works to the general reader. A bibliographical updating of the *Macropædia* begins on page 61.

# Marketing and Merchandising

ADVERTISING

Advertising is a form of mass communication intended, in its usual meaning, to promote the sale of a product or service. The term is also used for mass communication intended to influence public opinion, to gain political support, to advance a particular cause, or to elicit some other response desired by the advertiser, although these practices may involve different techniques, measures, and legal requirements. The advertising message, or advertisement, is delivered to its intended audience through the various media, including newspapers, magazines, television, radio, billboards, and direct mail. Advertising is distinguished from other forms of communication in that the advertiser pays the medium to deliver the message. For this payment the advertiser receives the opportunity to control the message. Within legal constraints designed to prevent deception and assure fair competition, and within standards of practice enforced by the media, the advertiser is free to say what he wants to say the way he wants to say it. Within limits set by availability, he can select the particular issue of a newspaper or magazine in which the message will run; in the case of television and radio, he can select the hour and even the minute when the message will be broadcast. The style of presentation usually identifies the message as an advertisement. In some countries if the message is not readily distinguishable from a medium's editorial or program content, the notation "This is an advertisement" and the name of the advertiser or sponsoring organization are included.

Users of advertising    Different kinds of businesses use advertising to motivate different kinds of markets toward different kinds of responses. A retailer such as a department store advertises to build store traffic and patronage and to keep his regular customers informed about available merchandise. The manufacturer of a branded item such as soap advertises to build a brand preference—that is, to add value

to his brand in the consumer's mind. The manufacturer of industrial goods, such as steel, machinery, lubricants, and office equipment, advertises to other business firms to get them to use his product in their operations. The producer of ethical drugs, building materials, or textbooks advertises to doctors, architects, or educators to induce these professional people to prescribe, specify, or recommend his product to patients, clients, or students. An association of firms in a particular industry, such as sugar refiners, orange growers, or dairies, advertise to stimulate consumption of a generic product such as sugar, orange juice, or milk. All business firms, whether they be retailers, manufacturers, or service institutions such as banks, insurance companies, and airlines, advertise to build a respected corporate identity, to make their corporate name well known and highly regarded.

Advertising is also used to awaken, enlighten, and activate the public at large concerning matters that affect society generally. Private, nonprofit organizations in some countries create and distribute various public service advertisements including those for forest fire prevention, rehabilitation of the handicapped, traffic safety, drug abuse information, crime prevention, and continuing education.

Generally speaking, advertising is more prevalent in highly industrialized countries where consumer purchasing power is broadly distributed, where the economic system is competitive, and where mass communications media are more generally available. Although consumer advertising exists in many Communist countries, its volume is relatively insignificant.

**Establishment of modern advertising.** The first advertising was by public criers in ancient times who circulated through the streets calling attention to the sale of such items as slaves, cattle, and imports. A written advertisement, perhaps 3,000 years old, was discovered by an archaeologist delving in the ruins of Thebes. It offered a "whole gold coin" as the reward for the return of a runaway slave named Shem. During the Middle Ages there was little of the activity that is now called advertising. The invention of movable type about 1450 by Johannes Gutenberg made it possible to produce many copies of books and periodicals cheaply and quickly and ushered in the modern era of advertising.

Printed
advertise-
ments

Printing made possible the transition from simple announcement to the system of argument and suggestion that constitutes modern advertising, and the medium of this development was the newspaper. The weekly papers sometimes carried a few advertisements, including the first offerings of coffee (1652), chocolate (1657), and tea (1658) in England. In June 1666 the *London Gazette,* No. 62, announced the first advertisement supplement as follows:

An Advertisement—Being daily prest to the publication of Books, Medicines, and other things not properly the business of a Paper of Intelligence. This is to notifie once for all, that we will not charge the *Gazette* with Advertisements, unless they be matter of state; but that a Paper of Advertisements will be forthwith printed apart, and recommended to the Publick by another hand.

Advertising was prospering by the follqwing century, and in 1758 Samuel Johnson could write in "The Idler":

Advertisements are now so numerous that they are very negligently perused, and it is therefore become necessary to gain attention by magnificence of promise and by eloquence sometimes sublime and sometimes pathetick.

The 19th century was a period of expansion in advertising as well as in business generally. The Industrial Revolution expanded the output of factories, and advertising helped market this output. The growth of the penny press and of magazines, combined with an increase in the educational level in the Western nations, brought forth an increase in audiences. Improvements in transportation made possible vast increases in circulation and reductions in price. Slogans and jingles became favourite advertising techniques. Some of the trademarks famous today were popularized during this period.

During the first two decades of the 20th century, advertising was reexamined. The common use of excessive, false, or deceptive claims caused widespread resentment. Regulation came both from within industries and from governments. After World War I came the era of salesmanship; advertising became "salesmanship in print." Advertising was accepted as an essential tool in selling the booming output of all the nations' factories. "It pays to advertise" became a standard slogan. It was discovered that testimonials by movie stars were effective in selling such items as perfumes, soaps, and cigarettes.

An advertisement for sewing machines in a 19th-century English magazine.
Mary Evans Picture Library, London

"War Gardens Victorious," a World War I poster intended to influence public opinion in favour of victory gardens.

A major new advertising medium, radio, was added during the 1920s. At first, most radio commercials were indirect and there was doubt as to whether advertising would be allowed on the air. In such countries as Great Britain and France, it was banned from public-owned radio; in the United States, however, commercial radio thrived.

Another new medium, television, was added to the advertising scene immediately after World War II. It had a spectacular growth in the United States and became the second largest advertising medium (after newspapers) in terms of total dollars spent and the largest in the top national advertisers' budgets. In the postwar era, too, American advertising agencies began popularizing the concept of the "brand image." According to one agency president, "Every advertisement should be thought of as a contribution to the complex symbol which is the brand image. . . . Every advertisement is . . . a long-term investment in the total personality of the brand." The concept of a brand image was extended to building favourable images for corporations, retail stores, service institutions, and political candidates.

**Development of the advertising agency.** An advertising agency, Reynell and Son, was founded in London as early as 1812. In 1841 Volney Palmer, who had been an editorial writer and later a member of the advertising staff of the *Pottsville* (Pa.) *Miner's Journal,* opened in Philadelphia what is generally considered to have been the first advertising agency in the United States. Unlike modern agents, he was primarily an agent for newspaper publishers, who paid him a commission of 25 percent for selling space, although he did not assume liability for the credit extended to advertisers. Shortly after he had begun operations, he had several competitors.

Adver-
tising
agencies

George P. Rowell, who opened an agency in 1865, added two features—wholesaling and the "list system." He contracted with a large number of weekly newspapers to sell him a column of space for a certain period of time; he then offered this space to advertisers in smaller units at retail rates that were below rates charged by competitors. He was, like Palmer, primarily a seller of space, but he offered exclusive lists of newspapers and magazines, and any advertiser who bought space in these had to buy through the exclusive agent.

In 1875 N.W. Ayer & Son of Philadelphia developed marketing policies that gave advertisers access to the true rates charged by the publishers. Ayer thus put the emphasis on the agency's service to the advertiser rather than on selling space for the media.

The next major step was the development of a full line of services for the advertiser. In the late 19th and early 20th century the emphasis was on the creation of advertising copy. After copy came art services, advertising production, and the selection of media. By 1920 most agencies could plan complete campaigns for their clients, including research and budgeting, and could also execute these campaigns by preparing the advertisements and arranging for their insertion in the various media, which now included outdoor advertising and direct mail.

The typical advertising agency today is staffed to perform the following services for its clients: (1) planning marketing and advertising strategies; (2) writing copy; (3) preparing artwork, layouts, and television storyboards; (4) buying artwork; (5) arranging for mechanical reproduction of printed advertisements; (6) producing television commercials; (7) budgeting expenditures; (8) selecting media; (9) contracting for space and time; (10) checking, billing, and paying media; (11) researching markets, media, copy, and results; (12) merchandising promotional programs to the trade; (13) counseling and engaging in public relations activities. Agencies performing all of these functions are referred to as full-service agencies and are likely to be the larger firms. Many smaller agencies concentrate on planning, preparing, and placing advertising.

**Advertising media.**   Advertising media can be classified as follows: newspapers, magazines (consumer magazines, business publications, farm publications, professional journals), television, radio, direct mail, outdoor media (signs, posters, painted bulletins, electric displays), transit media (car cards, outside displays, station posters), and miscellaneous (dealer displays, theatre-screen advertising, specialties, directories, point of sale).

There is no single best medium for all advertising situations. Each has its own character, and each advertising situation presents a unique set of circumstances. Each medium must therefore be considered in terms of how well it meets the individual advertiser's requirements.

*Newspapers.*   Newspapers, because of their large and general circulations, are the most widely used advertising medium. Through advertising, newspapers keep their readers informed of the myriad goods and services available in the marketplace, including the apartment for rent, the house for sale, and the employment opportunity appearing in the classified section.

The three main kinds of newspapers suit different advertisers. National newspapers are ideal for national brands and, given that different newspapers appeal to different readerships, the advertiser can be broadly selective about the income and social characteristics of his readers. International newspapers like the *International Herald Tribune* and the *Financial Times* reach across national bound-

"*I don't know who you are.*
*I don't know your company.*
*I don't know your company's product.*
*I don't know what your company stands for.*
*I don't know your company's customers.*
*I don't know your company's record.*
*I don't know your company's reputation.*
*Now—what was it you wanted to sell me?*"

**MORAL:** Sales start **before** your salesman calls—with business publication advertising.

**McGRAW-HILL MAGAZINES**
BUSINESS•PROFESSIONAL•TECHNICAL

A magazine advertisement for McGraw-Hill magazines dating from 1958 to the present.
© McGraw-Hill Publications Company; reprinted with permission

aries and reach cosmopolitan consumers of internationally distributed products. Local newspapers, with their limited geographic distribution, are better suited to local distributors and retailers, whose marketing area they may match quite closely. There are a growing number of "free sheets"—newspapers that carry comparatively little news and are paid for entirely by advertising. These can be distributed on a tightly defined geographic or demographic basis and can thus be used by the advertiser to reach very specific target audiences.   *Local newspapers*

*Magazines.*   Magazines offer a wide range of advertising opportunities. General magazines such as *Reader's Digest* (U.S.), *Paris-Match* (France), *Der Spiegel* (West Germany), and *Asahi* (Japan) are edited to serve the interests of many different population segments, thereby offering advertisers the opportunity to reach a broad cross section of people in all parts of a nation. Women's magazines such as *Elle* (France), *Ms.* (U.S.), and *Vogue* (both U.S. and France) appeal to various special interests of women, thereby offering advertisers the opportunity to reach these important consumers in a variety of editorial environments. There are magazines that concentrate on sports, business, science, or virtually any other subject, serving virtually every interest group imaginable. Each type of magazine offers the advertiser an opportunity to reach his best prospects when they are reading subject matter relevant to the advertiser's product. A manufacturer of milking machines, for example, can reach dairymen in a receptive frame of mind when he advertises in a dairymen's journal. The many professional journals read by doctors, dentists, engineers, architects, and educators appeal to advertisers who wish to influence those who are in a position to prescribe, recommend, or specify what others will buy.

The geographic selectivity of consumer magazines has been increased through regional editions that enable advertisers to place an advertisement in a part of the circulation that goes into a particular market area. The advertiser must buy a certain minimum circulation, but this is likely to be sufficiently low to permit him to advertise in only

By courtesy of Levi Strauss & Co.

**LEVI STRAUSS & CO.**
SAN FRANCISCO,CAL
**ORIGINAL RIVETED**
**QUALITY CLOTHING.** XX
TRADE   MARK
**PATENTED   MAY 20 1873**

Label bearing the registered trademark of Levi Strauss & Co., which dates from the 1870s.

one of the major cities. Regional editions let local and regional advertisers benefit from the prestige of a national publication.

The ideal measure of a newspaper's or magazine's value to a given advertiser would be the number of his prospective customers who read it. It would be extremely difficult, however, to isolate and count prospects for each and every advertiser. Therefore, research organizations that measure advertising for advertisers report the composition of magazine audiences in rather standard demographic terms such as age, sex, occupation, income, and family size. Using these breakdowns the advertiser selects newspapers and magazines whose audiences best match the demographic characteristics of his market.

*Television.* In the affluent nations today, more people spend more time with television than any other medium. In the United States, for example, during the peak viewing hours of an average winter evening, more than 50 percent of the households are tuned in. Viewing per household averages six hours daily. Viewing declines about 20 percent during the summer months. Changes in the hour-by-hour activities of various members of the family influence the composition and size of the television audience. Men do most of their viewing at night and on weekends. Preschool-age children watch more daytime television than school-age children. Women usually do more viewing than men in all time categories. The older age groups, 50 and over, do more viewing than younger groups. The audience composition also varies by program types, whether drama, comedy, feature film, documentary, or other.

**Units of advertising time**

Television advertisers buy units of time: a minute, 30 seconds, 20 seconds, 10 seconds, a quarter hour, a half hour, an hour or longer. They may buy time from a single station or from a network of stations. The cost of a unit varies by time of day and from program to program, depending on the size of the audience. In such countries as West Germany all commercials are placed between programs; there are no program interruptions. In the United States they are placed both between programs and within programs. The advertiser may specify the time his commercial is to be broadcast, or for a lower rate he may leave its placement to the station's discretion. Program time units may be bought for exclusive sponsorship or multiple sponsorship.

There are many methods for measuring television audiences. The "Audimeter," for instance, developed in the United States by the A.C. Nielsen Company, is an electronic device that is connected to all television receiving sets in a representative sample of households. The Audimeter makes a minute-by-minute record on photographic film of the time periods when each set is turned on, the specific stations to which the set is tuned, the dialing from one station to another, and the length of time spent with each station. The film cartridges are sent in every two weeks to the Nielsen organization where the data are tabulated and matched against the program schedules of the television stations involved. Although the Audimeter provides a precise record of set tuning, it does not show how many (or if any) people were viewing nor which members of the family were doing so. The "coincidental telephone" method consists of telephoning a sample of households and asking if a television receiver is turned on and, if so, to what station or program. This method is relatively inexpensive and therefore is used extensively in local market areas. The "roster-recall" method involves personal interviews in which a roster of all stations and programs readily available in the area is presented to a sample of people. The respondents are asked to check those programs or stations they recall having watched. The "diary" method requires that individual members of the family use a prepared diary form and keep a record of their viewing as it occurs. This method makes it possible to estimate the composition as well as the size of the audience.

Commonly used measurements of television audiences are the following: "program rating," which reveals the percentage of all households in the sample tuned to the particular program; "share-of-audience," which gives the percentage of households using television tuned to each program; "projected-audience," which gives the estimated number of households reached by a program (a projection of the program rating to total population); and "audience-composition," which offers a breakdown by sex, age, family size, income, and so forth.

*Radio.* Radio is ubiquitous. Battery-operated radios are found in the remotest regions of Africa and Asia, and in the developed countries it is scarcely possible to escape the blare of portable radios. Many governments have considered radio an important medium for education and public information and severely restricted its use for commercial advertising. Some, however, such as Great Britain, have more recently permitted the establishment of commercial stations. Radio advertising time is sold in much the same way as is television time, and the same methods of audience measurement are used.

*Direct mail.* By mail the advertiser can send his message directly to individual prospects. The message can take one of many forms: letter, folder, booklet, brochure, postcard, catalog, or coupons. In letter form the message can be personalized by addressing the recipient by name, by appealing to his personal concerns, and by using the language and style of a personal letter. The advertiser also can single out special groups for special appeals. He can be fairly certain that the message will be at least partly read by most recipients and that it will be read on the date it is received.

**The mailing list**

The mailing list is a critical factor in direct-mail advertising. Frequently used sources of names and addresses are telephone and city directories, trade directories, professional directories, commercial rating books, tax lists, club membership lists, and the records of local governmental bodies. Some firms make a business of compiling lists and selling them to advertisers.

*Other media.* Organized outdoor media include painted signs, electric displays, and printed posters, the latter being the most important. The standard poster or billboard is located mainly on heavily traveled routes in and around urban markets. The fleeting exposure to motorists and passersby demands a brief message, one that can be seen or read in a glance. A single, simple, visual idea with a caption usually is most appropriate. This brevity of message, however, limits the use of posters to reminder advertising.

Transit advertising, including car cards, outside displays, and station posters, reaches the millions of riders of public

Car card advertising Wrigley's chewing gum by Otis Shepard, 1949.

transportation in urban areas. Like outdoor advertising, transit advertising offers frequent exposure to large numbers of people at low cost. Its limitations are brevity of message and an environment low in prestige.

Dealer displays reach consumers at the point of purchase and therefore serve as a reminder or as an invitation to immediate buying action. Display space, however, in crowded, self-service supermarkets is at a minimum.

Theatre-screen advertising offers the opportunity to reach a captive audience with the impact of sound and motion pictures on a big screen.

Advertising "specialties" include calendars and other useful items that are imprinted with the advertiser's name. They include ashtrays, lighters, thermometers, key chains, ballpoint pens, memo pads, paperweights, and rulers. Being items that are used frequently, they serve as frequent reminders and engender some goodwill.

**Advertising strategy.** Advertising strategy is based on a series of key questions: (1) To whom should the advertising be addressed? (2) What communication objectives should be sought? (3) What should the message contain? (4) What media should be employed? (5) How should expenditures be budgeted? Advertising often is characterized as a means of selling to the masses. This leads to the misconception that all advertising should be addressed to everyone. Any population, however, is composed of different individuals with different needs and wants, different life-styles, and different tastes. The most efficient strategy is thus to single out those segments of the population who are the best prospects and to address the advertising to them. Communication objectives include the central idea that is to be learned, the image that is to be perceived, and the action that is to be taken by the target audience. Strategic decisions on message content concern visual, verbal, and aural devices, tone or style, and technique of presentation. Media selection includes the classes of media to be used—for example, daytime television, billboards, or women's magazines. Budgeting involves deciding how much to spend and how expenditures are to be allocated to markets, to media, and to dates. Thus, advertising is essentially a decision-making process. To aid the decision maker, research is used in a variety of ways.

*Research* Researching the consumer gives the advertiser a better understanding of the people whom he wants to influence. Motivations that underlie their buying behaviour, their attitudes toward particular product categories and brands, their perceptions of competitive brands, their satisfactions and dissatisfactions with the products they use, their reactions to new product concepts—these are some of the kinds of information that help the advertiser to identify his best prospects and to select the strongest appeal, thereby increasing the effectiveness of his advertising.

Motivational research utilizes depth interviewing and projective techniques such as word associations, sentence completions, and various other tests drawn from clinical psychiatry. Use of these techniques to educe subconscious motives led to the fear in the 1950s that advertisers were gaining the power to manipulate consumer behaviour. The fear was not well founded, for it overlooked the power of the individual to resist persuasion against his own perceived interest. To the degree that techniques of persuasion have become more sophisticated and effective, people have developed sophisticated awareness of and resistance to manipulation.

Traditionally, market segments have been described in demographic terms such as sex, age, income, and occupation. Recently there have been more attempts to use psychological measurements such as personality traits and motivational variables. Geographically, the market for most products is concentrated in urban areas, where most of industrial populations now live. Regional differences in climate, ethnic groups, and life-style produce different sales potentials for different products. Because markets are dynamic, however, continuing research is necessary to keep up with the changes.

A company's advertisement is best viewed as one of a series building a consistent identity for the product or the company. Creative strategy, therefore, should produce a central idea or unifying theme for a continuing campaign.

The theme may be expressed verbally in the form of a brief proposition, a headline, or slogan. It may also be expressed visually in pictorial content, layout style, graphic treatment, and such details as trademarks and logos.

Creative requirements have important implications in media selection. If superior full-colour reproduction in print is required, magazines have an advantage over newspapers. New product introductions benefit from the "news" format of newspapers, radio, and television. If the copy approach seeks to inspire confidence or dispel doubt, an authoritative medium such as a professional journal is appropriate. The environment in which the message appears has an appreciable influence on the effectiveness of the message itself. *Media strategy*

The basic variables of media strategy are "reach" and "frequency." Reach refers to the number of households or individuals exposed to the advertising message in a given period of time. Frequency is the average number of times that they are exposed. These variables are interdependent. With a given budget it is possible to reach more people less often or fewer people more often. The optimum combination depends on the requirements of the particular advertising situation. When introducing a new product whose market is unknown, for example, one may try to reach as many people as the budget permits. When the market is well defined, however, one may try to "expose" the message as frequently as possible.

The contribution of advertising to sales and profits cannot be readily isolated from all the other variables in the marketing mix. Determining the size of the advertising budget is, therefore, a rather arbitrary procedure. Assuming that a relation exists between advertising and sales (even though it cannot be precisely measured), a common practice is to express the advertising budget as a percentage of sales. The percentage is high for some products—about 20 percent for cosmetics—and low for others—about 1 percent for insurance. The size of the advertising budget tends to be greater when most of the selling burden is placed on advertising instead of personal selling, when a new product is introduced, when there is little or no discernible difference among competing brands, or when competitive practice requires heavy advertising.

(VERNON R. FRYBURGER, JR./PHILIP J.S. LAW)

**Advertising design.** Advertising requires that its ideas be given a visual form by artistic and graphic design. The means used to this end are typography, drawing, photog-

By courtesy of The Procter & Gamble Company

Magazine advertisement in *Ladies' Home Journal,* July 1958, by Norman Rockwell, from a three-year Crest toothpaste campaign with a unifying theme; Benton and Bowles, 1957–59.

*U.S. registered trademarks, 1914 to the 1970s.*
The Morton Salt girl and slogan (centre) first appeared together on the Morton Salt package in 1914. To keep her fashionable, the girl was given new dresses and hairstyles in 1921, 1933, 1941, 1956, and 1968. The other trademarks date from the 1940s, Hallmark greeting cards; the mid-1960s, United Airlines; 1971, American Cotton Producers; and the 1960s, Allstate Insurance Company.

By courtesy of (top left) Hallmark Cards; (centre) Morton Thiokol, Inc. ("The Little Morton Salt Girl" and the slogan "When It Rains It Pours" are registered trademarks of Morton Thiokol, Inc.); (top right) United Airlines; (bottom left) Cotton, Inc., the Fiber Company of American Cotton Producers; (bottom right) Allstate Insurance Company

raphy, and colour. The secret of good and effective design is to conceive the composition as a whole in which form and content, and representation and expression, are interdependent and matched to each other.

*General considerations.* The function of advertising design is primarily a practical one directed toward a particular end. It must communicate quickly and clearly and, in so doing, (1) attract attention; (2) lodge the advertising message in the conscious or unconscious mind; (3) induce an active, positive attitude to the message instead of a passive one; and (4) impress a favourable memory of the message on the mind. Because advertising design is aimed at producing an effect desired by an advertiser, it is obviously not free to choose its theme as the fine arts are. Even so, both advertising design and art use the same resources for the realization of their ideas: form, colour, and composition. Advertising design may use these effects successfully without necessarily producing art; it has served its purpose if image and text create the desired effect. A free work of art, on the other hand, becomes true art only when all the components of the design have genuine qualities of form and colour and together make up a vital composition which is complete in itself. Advertising design, however, can also rise to art if the designer has a strong artistic personality and an original imagination and if the commission allows the artist a certain freedom in the way he presents his theme and selects his artistic means— for example, the famous posters of Toulouse-Lautrec.

Both the nature of advertising design and the tasks that it has to perform have been profoundly influenced by advancing technology. New sophisticated techniques of reproducing and representing acoustic and visual material have given advertising new scope. To relief, intaglio, lithography, and silk-screen printing now have been added computer graphics. Hand composition, monotype, and linotype have been supplemented by computerized phototypesetting techniques. Cinema slides and advertising films have been joined by television commercials and holograms. . . .

The success of advertising design depends on the topicality of what is depicted, on the quality of the design, and, to no less extent, on psychological factors. These largely determine the reactions of the person to whom the advertisement is addressed. Consciously perceived information is capable of inducing moods and feelings that are in harmony with the intention of the advertisement or at variance with it. The static use of the designer's resources in a composition, for instance, may express rest, solidity, conservatism, security, and trust, whereas a dynamic use

**Techniques used in design**

may evoke love of experiment, flexibility, a forward-looking attitude, aggressiveness, and youthfulness. The correct choice of colours is especially important. Colours with a symbolic significance in politics or religion are taboo and must be used with caution, depending on the country and religion involved.

With the increasing sophistication of advertising after World War II, the importance of the free-lance advertising designer naturally diminished. Advertising campaigns, some of which have become very extensive and complex, can be planned and carried out only by specialists working as a team. A full-service advertising agency handles all the problems arising in connection with an advertising assignment, including budgeting, and thus has a far greater capacity than the designer working on his own. The free-lance advertising designer, generally speaking, can only execute commissions for smaller firms or take on jobs assigned to him by the agencies in connection with advertising campaigns. . . .

*Design media.* These include advertisements in periodicals, posters, brochures, leaflets, pamphlets, buttons, and the like. Frequently they contain a "device," "trademark," or "trade name" used to denote the maker or supplier of the product or service. The device or trademark represents the most concise graphic form that a particular subject can be given. It should be simple, unmistakable, applicable,

Photo, courtesy of NIKE, Inc.

Lester Hayes, U.S. football player, endorsing Nike athletic shoes on a billboard; Chiat & Day, 1985.

*Poster design from 1893 to 1935.*
(Left) "Hermann Scherrer Breechesmaker Sporting-Tailor," realistic poster by Ludwig
Hohlwein, 1911; lithograph. (Centre) "Nicolas," experimental poster by A.M. Cassandre for a
French wine merchant, 1935; offset lithograph. (Right) "Divan Japonais," illustrative poster by
Henri de Toulouse-Lautrec, 1893; lithograph.
By courtesy of the Museum of Modern Art, New York City, (left) gift of Peter Muller-Munk, (right) Abby Aldrich Rockefeller Purchase Fund

and timeless. The trade word has the advantage over the device in that it can be read at once, whereas the meaning of the device must first be made known. Its disadvantages, of course, are that it contains more formal elements (depending on the length of the name) and that the designer's freedom to shape it at will is limited by the demands of legibility; it thus usually has a weaker impact.

Each medium has its own demands. Whereas a poster designed to produce an effect at a distance, for instance, must be drawn and coloured on a generous scale, a newspaper advertisement has to be worked out with greater attention to details. In any case, the idea is to achieve the maximum of clarity and impact with the minimum resources of colour and form. The illustrative poster, for example, presents the theme or object with an atmospheric appeal; the realistic poster supplies objective information through its copy and the truthful depiction of the object; the constructivist poster arranges its pictorial elements in accordance with their thematic importance. The experimental poster surprises the viewer by the novel way in which it presents a problem or by the new techniques it employs.

Television commercials and other kinds of films afford the advertising designer a variety of interesting opportunities. If the film or tape consists of live action, then titles, subtitles, possibly functional diagrams, statistics, movie sets, and so on have to be designed. If the film consists of an animated cartoon, then the designer's imagination is given almost unlimited scope; every type of drawing can be used, from fairy-tale illustration to surrealistic montage, and every kind of style can be employed—naturalism, simplified and stylized presentation, abstract symbolism, and so on. But, in any event, it is important that the designer depict his pictorial ideas clearly and simply, that they not change too quickly, and that he not present more than one or two ideas in the picture at the same time. He must consider colours and their sequences with the same care. In all types of films, lettering, image, word, and sound must complement one another.

In parades and demonstrations there are posters, transparencies, banners, and boards, but, unlike most ordinary posters, they are continually in motion and must be visible from various angles. Lettering and images must be recognizable and legible at a distance.

One of the most interesting jobs in advertising design is the creation of a uniform "image" for a business or organization. All advertising aids from visiting cards through commercial forms and newspaper advertisements to outdoor signboards should be given an unmistakable character with regard to graphic form, typography, and colour, so that each element is seen as part of an overall conception. All these different impressions must have a family resemblance, so that their effect is cumulative and produces a clear image in the eye of the beholder. Uniform advertising is a powerful aid in the creation of a firm's image.

Creating the "image" of the firm

In comparing lettered signs on doors, windows, buildings, factories, and so on, the advertising designer is confronted by three specific problems: the lettering must be visible at a certain distance; it must make an impact by reason of its formal originality; and it must be integrated with the architecture in size, form, colour, and material. If the lettering is to be visible at night, the designer can make his choice between neon lettering and spotlighted lettering. If he chooses neon lettering, he must adapt the shape of his letters to technical or engineering requirements.

In composing lettered signs on delivery vans, trucks, and so on, the designer must take the factor of movement into account: the letters must be somewhat spaced out so that they will not run together when read on the moving vehicle. Similar care is also needed in selecting colours; as a rule dark colours are more suitable because they produce more contrast. . . .

There is an enormous variety of items that an advertiser can distribute in order to attract the attention of the public it addresses. These include calendars, matchbooks, glassware, ashtrays, notebooks, writing instruments, playthings, and decorative items of all sorts. Such items may be distributed year-round or be used as holiday gifts.

How long an object will continue to attract attention depends on the quality of the material, its workmanship, and the timelessness of its form or colour arrangement. The designer must be guided by aesthetic considerations in affixing the name of the firm, which may be stamped or printed on the object, attached to it on a label, or cast in its interior if the material is transparent. A decorative version of the name may be a factor in determining the form of the object, but often it is placed discretely on the underside.

(JOSEF MÜLLER-BROCKMANN/
PHILIP JAMES STOPFORD LAW)

# Motion Pictures

A remarkable effective medium in conveying drama and especially in the evocation of emotion, motion pictures consist of the projection of luminous moving images onto a screen. The art of motion pictures is exceedingly complex, requiring contributions from nearly all of the other arts as well as countless technical skills. Nonetheless, probably no other art has proliferated as much in the 20th century nor can any other equal it in popularity or influence.

The motion picture is the newest of the generally recognized "fine arts." It is the product of photographic and technological developments that culminated by 1900 in practical devices for the recording of a moving image and its projection onto a flat surface. During its early development, the motion picture was discounted by many critics for its subservience to commercial interests, for the immediacy of its appeal to the uninstructed, for its mechanical technique, and for its apparent lack of an identifiable artist as its primary creator. After the middle of the 20th century, however, increasing attention was devoted to it as a form of artistic endeavour that is as legitimate as the theatre, literature, music, or the visual arts.

History
   Early years: 1830–1910
      Origins
      Edison and the Lumière brothers
      Méliès and Porter
      Early growth of the film industry
   The silent feature: 1910–27
      Pre-World War I U.S. cinema
      Pre-World War I European cinema
      Griffith
      Post-World War I European cinema
      Post-World War I U.S. cinema

## History

### EARLY YEARS: 1830–1910

*Persistence of vision and the phi phenomenon*

**Origins.** The illusion of motion pictures is based on the optical phenomena known as persistence of vision and the phi phenomenon. The first of these causes the brain to retain images cast upon the retina of the eye for a fraction of a second beyond their disappearance from the field of sight, while the latter creates apparent movement between images when they succeed each other rapidly. Together, these phenomena permit the succession of still frames on a motion-picture film strip to represent continuous movement when projected at the proper speed (usually 16 frames per second for silent films and 24 frames per second for sound films). Before the invention of photography, a variety of optical toys exploited this effect by mounting successive phase drawings of things in motion on the face of a twirling disk (the phenakistoscope,

c. 1832) or inside of a rotating drum (the zoetrope, c. 1834). In 1839, however, Louis-Jacques-Mandé Daguerre perfected the positive photographic process known as daguerreotypy, and as negative photography was innovated and refined over the next few decades, it became possible to replace the phase drawings in the early devices with individually posed phase photographs, which was widely and popularly done.

There would be no true motion pictures, however, until live action could be photographed spontaneously and simultaneously as it occurred. This required a reduction in photographic exposure time from Daguerre's 15 minutes to William Henry Fox Talbot's one-hundredth (and, ultimately, one-thousandth) of a second in 1870, as well as the development of the technology of series photography by the British-American photographer Eadweard Muybridge between 1872 and 1877. During that time, Muybridge was employed by Governor Leland Stanford of California, a zealous racehorse breeder, to prove that at some point in its gallop a running horse lifts all four hooves off the ground at once. Conventions of 19th-century illustration suggested otherwise, and the movement itself occurred too rapidly for perception by the naked eye; so Muybridge experimented with multiple cameras to take successive photographs of horses in motion. Finally, in 1877, he set up a battery of 12 cameras along a Sacramento racecourse with wires stretched across the track to operate their shutters. As a horse strode down the track, its hooves tripped each shutter individually to expose a successive photograph of the gallop, confirming Stanford's belief. When Muybridge later mounted these images on a rotating disk and projected them on a screen through a magic lantern, they produced a "moving picture" of the horse at full gallop as it had actually occurred in life.

*Series photography*

The French physiologist Étienne-Jules Marey took the first series photographs with a single instrument in 1882; once again, the impetus was the analysis of motion too rapid for perception by the human eye. Marey invented the chronophotographic gun, a camera shaped like a rifle that recorded 12 successive photographs per second, in order to study the movement of birds in flight. These images were imprinted on a rotating glass plate (later, paper roll film), and Marey subsequently attempted to project them. Like Muybridge, however, Marey was interested in deconstructing movement rather than synthesizing it, and he did not carry his experiments much beyond the realm of high-speed, or instantaneous, series photography. Muybridge and Marey, in fact, conducted their work in the spirit of scientific inquiry; they extended and elaborated existing technologies in order to probe events that occurred beyond the threshold of human perception. Those who came after would return their discoveries to the realm of normal human vision and exploit them for profit.

In 1887 in Newark, N.J., an Episcopalian minister named Hannibal Goodwin first used celluloid roll film as a base for photographic emulsions, and within the year his idea had been appropriated by the industrialist George East-

An early series of photographs by Eadweard Muybridge (1887).

man, who in 1888 began to mass-produce celluloid roll film for still photography at his plant in Rochester, N.Y. This event was crucial to the development of cinematography: series photography such as Marey's chronophotography could employ glass plates or paper strip film because it recorded events of short duration in a relatively small number of images, but cinematography would inevitably find its subjects in longer, more complicated events, requiring thousands of images and therefore just the kind of flexible but durable recording medium represented by celluloid. It remained for someone to combine the principles embodied in the apparatuses of Muybridge and Marey with celluloid strip film to arrive at a viable motion-picture camera—an innovation achieved by William Kennedy Laurie Dickson in the West Orange, N.J., laboratories of the Edison Company in 1888.

**Edison and the Lumière brothers.** Thomas Alva Edison invented the phonograph in 1877, and it had quickly become the most popular home entertainment device of the century. It was to provide a visual accompaniment to the phonograph that Edison commissioned Dickson, a young laboratory assistant, to invent a motion-picture camera in 1887. Dickson built upon the work of Muybridge and Marey, a fact that he readily acknowledged, but he was the first to combine the two final essentials of motion-picture camera and projection technology. These were a device, adapted from the escapement mechanism of a clock, to ensure the intermittent but regular motion of the film strip through the camera and a regularly perforated celluloid film strip to ensure precise synchronization between the film strip and the shutter. Dickson's camera was patented as the Kinetograph in 1893, and it initially imprinted up to 50 feet of celluloid film at the rate of about 40 frames per second.

*The Kineto-graph*

Because Edison had originally conceived of motion pictures as an adjunct to his phonograph, he did not commission the invention of a projector. Rather, he had Dickson design a type of peep-show viewing device called the Kinetoscope in which a continuous 47-foot film loop ran on spools between an incandescent lamp and a shutter for individual viewing. Starting in 1894, Kinetoscopes were marketed commercially through the firm of Raff and Gammon for $250 to $300 apiece, and the Edison Company established its own Kinetograph studio (a single-room building called the "Black Maria" that rotated on tracks to follow the Sun) in West Orange, N.J., to supply films for the Kinetoscopes that Raff and Gammon were installing in penny arcades, hotel lobbies, amusement parks, and other such semipublic places. In April of that year the first Kinetoscope parlour was opened in a converted storefront in New York City. The parlour charged 25 cents for admission to a bank of five machines.

The syndicate of Maguire and Baucus acquired the foreign rights to the Kinetoscope in 1894 and began to market the machines. Edison had declined to file for international patents on either his camera or viewing device, and as a result, the machines were widely and legally copied throughout Europe, where they were modified and improved far beyond the American originals. In fact, it was a Kinetoscope exhibition in Paris that inspired the Lumière brothers, Auguste and Louis, to invent the first commercially viable projector. Their *cinématographe,* which also functioned as a camera and printer, ran at the economical speed of 16 frames per second. It was given its first commercial demonstration on Dec. 28, 1895.

*The cinéma-tographe*

Unlike the Kinetograph, which was battery-driven and weighed more than 1,000 pounds, the *cinématographe* was hand-cranked, lightweight (less than 20 pounds), and relatively portable. This naturally affected the kinds of films that were made with each machine: Edison films initially featured material such as circus or vaudeville acts that could be brought into a small studio and played out before an inert camera, while early Lumière films were mainly documentary views, or "actualities," shot outdoors on location. In both cases, however, the films themselves were composed of a single, unedited shot emphasizing lifelike movement; they contained little or no narrative content. (After a few years design changes in the machines made it possible for Edison and the Lumières to shoot the same

kinds of subjects.) In general, Lumière technology became the European standard during the early primitive era, and because the Lumières sent their cameramen all over the world in search of exotic subjects, the *cinématographe* became the founding instrument of such far-flung cinemas as the Russian, the Australian, and the Japanese. (It also, of course, is the source for the word cinema.)

In the United States, the Kinetoscope installation business had reached saturation point by the summer of 1895, although it was still quite profitable for Edison as a supplier of films. Raff and Gammon persuaded Edison to buy the rights to a state-of-the-art projector, developed by Thomas Armat of Washington, D.C., which incorporated a superior intermittent movement mechanism and a loop-forming device (known as the Latham loop, after its earliest promoters, Grey and Otway Latham) to reduce film breakage, and in early 1896 Edison began to manufacture and market this machine as his own invention. Given its first public demonstration on April 23, 1896, at Koster and Bial's Music Hall in New York City, the Edison Vitascope brought projection to the United States and established the format for American film exhibition for the next several years. It also encouraged the activities of such successful Edison rivals as the American Mutoscope and Biograph Company, which was formed in 1896 to exploit the Mutoscope peep-show device and the American Biograph camera and projector patented by W.K.L. Dickson in 1896. During this time, which has been characterized as the "novelty period," emphasis fell on the projection device itself, and films achieved their main popularity as self-contained vaudeville attractions. Vaudeville houses, among which there was intense competition at the turn of the century, headlined the name of the machines rather than the films (The Vitascope—Edison's Latest Marvel, The Amazing Cinématographe). The projectors came supplied from the producer, or manufacturer, with an operator and a program of shorts. These films, whether they were Edison-style theatrical variety shorts or Lumière-style actualities, were perceived by their original audiences not as motion pictures in the modern sense of the term but as "animated photographs" or "living pictures," emphasizing their continuity with more familiar media of the time.

*The novelty period*

During the novelty period, the film industry was autonomous and unitary, with production companies leasing a complete film service of projector, operator, and shorts to the vaudeville market as a single, self-contained act. Starting around 1897, however, manufacturers began to sell both projectors and films to itinerant exhibitors who traveled with their programs from one temporary location (vaudeville theatres, fairgrounds, circus tents, lyceums) to another as the novelty of their films wore off at a given site. This new mode of screening by circuit marked the first separation of exhibition from production and gave the exhibitors a large measure of control over early film form, since they were responsible for arranging the one-shot films purchased from the producers into audience-pleasing programs. The putting together of these programs—which often involved narration, sound effects, and music—was in effect a primitive form of editing, so that it is possible to regard the itinerant projectionists working between 1896 and 1904 as the earliest directors of motion pictures. Several of them, notably Edwin S. Porter, were, in fact, hired as directors by production companies after the industry had stabilized in the first decade of the 20th century.

By encouraging the practice of peripatetic exhibition, the U.S. producers' policy of outright sales inhibited the development of permanent film theatres in the United States until nearly a decade after their appearance in Europe, where England and France had taken an early lead in both production and exhibition. Britain's first projector, the theatrograph (later, the animatograph), had been demonstrated in 1896 by the scientific instrument maker Robert W. Paul. In 1899 Paul formed his own production company for the manufacture of actualities and trick films, and until 1905 Paul's Animatograph Works, Ltd., was England's largest producer, turning out an average of 50 films per year. Between 1896 and 1898, two Brighton photographers, George Albert Smith and James Williamson, constructed their own motion-picture cameras and began producing trick films featuring superimpositions (*The Corsican Brothers,* 1897) and interpolated close-ups (*Grandma's Reading Glass,* 1900; *The Big Swallow,* 1901). Smith subsequently developed the first commercially successful photographic colour process (Kinemacolor, *c.* 1906–08, with Charles Urban), while Williamson experimented with parallel editing as early as 1900 (*Attack on a Chinese Mission Station*) and became a pioneer of the chase film (*Stop Thief!,* 1901; *Fire!,* 1901). Both Smith and Williamson had built studios at Brighton by 1902 and, with their associates, came to be known as members of the "Brighton school," although they did not represent a coherent movement. Another important early British filmmaker was Cecil Hepworth, whose *Rescued by Rover* (1905) is regarded by many historians as the most skillfully edited narrative produced before the Biograph shorts of D.W. Griffith.

**Méliès and Porter.** The shift in consciousness away from films as animated photographs to films as stories, or narratives, began to take place around the turn of the century and is most evident in the work of the French filmmaker Georges Méliès. Méliès was a professional magician who had become interested in the illusionist possibilities of the *cinématographe;* when the Lumières refused to sell him one, he bought an animatograph projector from Paul in 1896 and reversed its mechanical principles to design his own camera. The following year he organized the Star Film company and constructed a small glass-enclosed studio on the grounds of his house at Montreuil, where he produced, directed, photographed, and acted in more than 500 films between 1896 and 1913.

Méliès'
"trick"
films

Initially, Méliès used stop-motion photography (the camera and action are stopped while something is added to or removed from the scene, then filming and action are continued) to make one-shot "trick" films in which objects disappeared and reappeared, or transformed themselves into other objects entirely. These films were widely imitated by producers in England and the United States. Soon, however, Méliès began to experiment with brief multi-scene films, such as *L'Affaire Dreyfus (The Dreyfus Affair;* his first, 1899), which followed the logic of linear temporality to establish causal sequences and tell simple stories. By 1902 he had produced the influential 30-scene narrative *Le Voyage dans la lune (A Trip to the Moon).* Adapted from a novel by Jules Verne, it was nearly one reel in length (about 825 feet, or 14 minutes).

The first film to achieve international distribution (mainly through piracy), *Le Voyage dans la lune* was an enormous popular success. It helped to make Star Film one of the world's largest producers (an American branch was opened in 1903) and to establish the fiction film as the cinema's mainstream product. In both respects Méliès dethroned the Lumières' cinema of actuality. Despite his innovations, Méliès' productions remained essentially filmed stage plays. He conceived them quite literally as successions of living pictures or, as he termed them, "artificially arranged scenes." From his earliest trick films through his last successful fantasy, *La Conquête du pole* ("The Conquest of the Pole," 1912), Méliès treated the frame of

the film as the proscenium arch of a theatre stage, never once moving his camera or changing its position within a scene. He ultimately lost his audience in the late 1910s to filmmakers with more sophisticated narrative techniques.

The origination of many such techniques is closely associated with the work of Edwin S. Porter, a free-lance projectionist and engineer who joined the Edison Company in 1900 as production head of its new skylight studio on East 21st Street in New York City. For the next few years, he served as director-cameraman for much of Edison's output, starting with simple one-shot films (*Kansas Saloon Smashers,* 1901) but progressing rapidly to trick films (*The Finish of Bridget McKeen,* 1901) and short multi-scene narratives based on political cartoons and contemporary events (*Sampson-Schley Controversy,* 1901; *Execution of Czolgosz, with Panorama of Auburn Prison,* 1901). Porter also filmed the extraordinary *Pan-American Exposition by Night* (1901), which used time-lapse photography to produce a circular panorama of the exposition's electrical illumination, and the 10-scene *Jack and the Beanstalk* (1902), a narrative that simulates the sequencing of lantern slides to achieve a logical, if elliptical, spatial continuity.

Continuity
editing

It was probably Porter's experience as a projectionist at the Eden Musee theatre in 1898 that ultimately led him in the early 1900s to the practice of continuity editing. The process of selecting one-shot films and arranging them into a 15-minute program for screen presentation was very much like that of constructing a single film out of a series of separate shots. Porter, by his own admission, was also influenced by other filmmakers—especially Méliès, whose *Le Voyage dans la lune* he came to know well in the process of duplicating it for illegal distribution by Edison in October 1902. Years later, Porter claimed that the Méliès film had given him the notion of "telling a story in continuity form," which resulted in *The Life of an American Fireman* (about 400 feet, or six minutes, produced in late 1902 and released in January 1903). This film, which was also influenced by James Williamson's *Fire!,* combined archival footage with staged scenes to create a nine-shot narrative of a dramatic rescue from a burning building. It was for years the subject of controversy because in a later version the last two scenes were intercut, or crosscut, into a 14-shot parallel sequence. It is now generally believed that in the earliest version of the film these scenes, which repeat the same rescue operation from an interior and exterior point of view, were shown in their entirety, one after the other. This repetition, or overlapping continuity, which owes much to magic lantern shows, clearly defines the spatial relationships between scenes but leaves temporal relationships underdeveloped and, to modern sensibilities, confused. Contemporary audiences, however, were conditioned by lantern slide projections and even comic strips; they understood a sequence of motion-picture shots to be a series of individual moving photographs, each of which was self-contained within its frame. Spatial relationships were clear in such earlier narrative forms because their only medium was space.

Motion pictures, however, exist in time as well as space, and the major problem for early filmmakers was the establishment of temporal continuity from one shot to the next. Porter's *The Great Train Robbery* (1903) is widely acknowledged to be the first narrative film to achieve such continuity of action. Comprised of 14 separate shots of noncontinuous, nonoverlapping action, the film contains an early example of parallel editing, two credible back, or rear, projections (the projection from the rear of previously filmed action or scenery onto a translucent screen to provide the background for new action filmed in front of the screen), two camera pans, and several shots composed diagonally and staged in depth—a major departure from the frontally composed, theatrical staging of Méliès.

*The Great
Train
Robbery*

The industry's first spectacular box-office success, *The Great Train Robbery* is credited with establishing the realistic narrative, as opposed to Méliès-style fantasy, as the commercial cinema's dominant form. The film's popularity encouraged investors and led to the establishment of the first permanent film theatres, or nickelodeons, across the country. Running about 12 minutes, it also helped to

By courtesy of the Museum of Modern Art/Film Stills Archive, New York City

*Le Voyage dans la lune* (1902), directed by Georges Méliès.

*The Great Train Robbery* (1903), directed by Edwin S. Porter.
By courtesy of the Museum of Modern Art/Film Stills Archive, New York City

boost standard film length toward one reel, or 1,000 feet (about 16 minutes at the average silent speed). Despite the film's success, Porter continued to practice overlapping action in such conventional narratives as *Uncle Tom's Cabin* (1903) and the social-justice dramas *The Ex-Convict* (1904) and *The Kleptomaniac* (1905). He experimented with model animation in *Dream of a Rarebit Fiend* (1906) and *The Teddy Bears* (1907) but lost interest in the creative aspects of filmmaking as the process became increasingly industrialized. He left Edison in 1909 to pursue a career as a producer and equipment manufacturer. Porter, like Méliès, could not adapt to the linear narrative modes and assembly-line production systems that were developing.

Industrial-<br>ization<br>of<br>European<br>cinema **Early growth of the film industry.** Méliès' decline was assisted by the industrialization of the French and, for a time, the entire European cinema by the Pathé Frères company, founded in 1896 by the former phonograph importer Charles Pathé. Financed by some of France's largest corporations, Pathé acquired the Lumière patents in 1902 and commissioned the design of an improved studio camera that soon dominated the market on both sides of the Atlantic (it has been estimated that, before 1918, 60 percent of all films were shot with a Pathé). Pathé also manufactured his own film stock and in 1902 established a vast production facility at Vincennes where films were turned out on an assembly-line basis under the managing direction of Ferdinand Zecca. The following year, Pathé began to open foreign sales agencies, which would soon become full-blown production companies—Hispano Film (1906), Pathé-Rouss, Moscow (1907), Film d'Arte Italiano (1909), Pathé-Britannia, London (1909), and Pathé-America (1910). He acquired permanent exhibition sites, building the world's first luxury cinema (the Omnia-Pathé) in Paris in 1906. In 1911 Pathé became Méliès' distributor and helped to drive Star Film out of business.

Pathé's only serious rival on the Continent at this time was Gaumont Pictures, founded by the engineer-inventor Léon Gaumont in 1895. Though never more than a quarter the size of Pathé, Gaumont followed the same pattern of expansion, manufacturing its own equipment and mass-producing films under a supervising director (through 1906, Alice Guy, the cinema's first woman director; afterward, Louis Feuillade). Like Pathé, Gaumont opened foreign offices and acquired theatre chains. From 1905 to 1914 its studios at La Villette, Fr., were the largest in the world. Pathé and Gaumont dominated pre-World War I motion-picture production, exhibition, and sales in Europe, and they effectively brought to an end the artisanal mode of filmmaking practiced by Méliès and his British contemporaries.

The<br>formation<br>of film<br>exchanges In the United States a similar pattern was emerging through the formation of film exchanges and the consolidation of an industry-wide monopoly based on the pooling of patent rights. Around 1897 producers had adopted the practice of selling prints outright, which had the effect of promoting itinerant exhibition and discriminating against the owners of permanent sites. In 1903, in response to the needs of theatre owners, Harry J. and Herbert Miles

opened a film exchange in San Francisco. The exchange functioned as a broker between producers and exhibitors, buying prints from the former and leasing them to the latter for 25 percent of the purchase price (in subsequent practice, rental fees were calculated on individual production costs and box-office receipts). The exchange system of distribution quickly caught on because it profited nearly everyone: the new middlemen made fortunes by collecting multiple revenues on the same prints; exhibitors were able to reduce their overheads and vary their programs without financial risk; and, ultimately, producers experienced a tremendous surge in demand for their product as exhibition and distribution boomed nationwide. (Between November 1906 and March 1907, for example, producers increased their weekly output from 10,000 to 28,000 feet and still could not meet demand.)

The most immediate effect of the rapid rise of the distribution sector was the nickelodeon boom, the exponential growth of permanent film theatres in the United States from a mere handful in 1904 to between 8,000 and 10,000 by 1908. Named for the Nickelodeon (ersatz Greek for "nickel theatre"), which opened in Pittsburgh in 1905, these theatres were makeshift facilities lodged in converted storefronts. They showed approximately an hour's worth of films for an admission price of five to 10 cents. Originally identified with working-class audiences, nickelodeons appealed increasingly to the middle class as the decade wore on, and they became associated with the rising popularity of the story film. Their spread also forced the standardization of film length at one reel, or 1,000 feet, to facilitate high-efficiency production and the trading of products within the industry.

By 1908 there were about 20 motion-picture production companies operating in the United States. They were constantly at war with one another over business practices and patent rights, and they had begun to fear that their fragmentation would cause them to lose control of the industry to the two new sectors of distribution and exhibition. The most powerful among them—Edison, Biograph, Vitagraph, Essanay, Kalem, Selig Polyscope, Lubin, the American branches of the French Star Film and Pathé Frères, and Kleine Optical, the largest domestic distributor of foreign films—therefore entered into a collusive trade agreement to ensure their continued dominance. On Sept. 9, 1908, these companies formed the Motion Picture Patents Company (MPPC), pooling the 16 most significant U.S. patents for motion-picture technology and entering into an exclusive contract with the Eastman Kodak Company for the supply of raw film stock. The<br>Motion<br>Picture<br>Patents<br>Company

The MPPC, also known as the "Trust," sought to control every segment of the industry and therefore set up a system to issue licenses and assess royalties therefrom. The use of its patents was granted only to licensed equipment manufacturers; film stock could be sold only to licensed producers; licensed producers and importers were required to fix rental prices at a minimum level and to set quotas for foreign footage to reduce competition; Patents Company films could be sold only to licensed distributors, who could lease them only to licensed exhibitors; and only licensed exhibitors had the right to use Patents Company projectors and rent company films. To further ensure their control, in 1910—the same year in which motion-picture attendance in the United States rose to 26,000,000 persons a week—the MPPC formed the General Film Company, which integrated the licensed distributors into a single corporate entity. Although it was clearly monopolistic in practice and intent, the MPPC helped to stabilize the American film industry during a period of unprecedented growth and change by standardizing exhibition practice, increasing the efficiency of distribution, and regularizing pricing in all three sectors. Its collusive nature, however, provoked a reaction that ultimately destroyed it.

In a sense, the MPPC's iron-clad efforts to eliminate competition merely fostered it. Almost from the outset there was widespread resistance to the Patents Company on the part of independent distributors (numbering 10 or more in early 1909) and exhibitors (estimated at 2,000 to 2,500); and in January 1909 they formed their own trade association, the Independent Film Protective Association—reorganized that fall as the National Independent Moving Picture Alliance—to provide financial and legal support against the Trust. A more effective and powerful anti-Trust organization was the Motion Picture Distributing and Sales Company, which began operation in May 1910 (three weeks after the inception of General Film) and which eventually came to serve 47 exchanges in 27 cities. For nearly two years, independents were able to present a united front through the Sales Company, which finally split into two rival camps in the spring of 1912 (the Mutual Film Corporation and the Universal Film Manufacturing Company).

By imitating Patents Company practices of joining forces and licensing, the early independents were able to compete effectively against the Trust in its first three years of operation, netting about 40 percent of all American film business. In fact, their product, the one-reel short, and their mode of operation were initially fundamentally the same as the MPPC's. The independents later revolutionized the industry, however, by adopting the multiple-reel film as their basic product, a move that caused the MPPC to embrace the one-reeler with a vengeance, hastening its own demise.

### THE SILENT FEATURE: 1910–27

Introduction of the feature film

**Pre-World War I U.S. cinema.** Multiple-reel films had appeared in the United States as early as 1907, when Adolph Zukor distributed Pathé's three-reel *Passion Play;* but when Vitagraph produced the five-reel *The Life of Moses* in 1909, the Patents Company forced it to be released in serial fashion at the rate of one reel a week. The multiple-reel film—which came to be called a "feature," in the vaudevillian sense of a headline attraction—achieved general acceptance with the smashing success of Louis Mercanton's three-and-one-half-reel *Les Amours de la Reine Elizabeth* (*Queen Elizabeth,* 1912), which starred Sarah Bernhardt and was imported by Adolph Zukor (who founded the independent Famous Players production company with its profits). In 1912 Enrico Guazzoni's nine-reel Italian super-spectacle *Quo Vadis?* was road-shown in legitimate theatres across the nation at a top admission price of one dollar, and the feature craze was on.

At first, there were difficulties in distributing features, because the exchanges associated with both the Patents Company and the independents were geared toward cheaply made one-reel shorts. Owing to their more elaborate production values, features had relatively higher negative costs. This was a disadvantage to distributors, who charged a uniform price per foot. By 1914, however, several national feature-distribution alliances that correlated pricing with a film's negative cost and box-office receipts were organized. These new exchanges demonstrated the economic advantage of multiple-reel films over shorts. Exhibitors quickly learned that features could command higher admission prices and longer runs; single title packages were also cheaper and easier to advertise than programs of multiple titles. As for manufacturing, producers found that the higher expenditure for features was readily amortized by high volume sales to distributors, who in turn were eager to share in the higher admission returns from the theatres. The whole industry soon reorganized itself around the economics of the multiple-reel film, and the effects of this restructuring did much to give motion pictures their characteristic modern form.

Feature films, for example, made motion pictures respectable for the middle class by providing a format that was analogous to that of the legitimate theatre and was suitable for the adaptation of middle-class novels and plays. This new audience had more demanding standards than the older lower-class one, and producers readily increased their budgets to provide high technical quality and elaborate productions. The new viewers also had a more refined sense of comfort, which exhibitors quickly accommodated by replacing their storefronts with large, elegantly appointed new theatres in the major urban centres (one of the first was Mitchell L. Marks's 3,300-seat Strand, which opened in the Broadway district of Manhattan in 1914). Known as "dream palaces" because of the fantastic luxuriance of their interiors, these houses had to show features

rather than a program of shorts to attract large audiences at premium prices. By 1916 there were more than 21,000 movie palaces in the United States. Their advent marked the end of the nickelodeon era and foretold the rise of the Hollywood studio system, which dominated urban exhibition from the 1920s to the 1950s. Before the new studio-based monopoly could be established, however, the patents-based monopoly of the MPPC had to expire, and this it did as a result of its own basic assumptions in about 1914.

End of the nickelodeon era

As conceived by Edison, the basic operating principle of the Trust was to control the industry through patents pooling and licensing, an idea logical enough in theory but difficult to practice in the context of a dynamically changing marketplace. Specifically, the Trust's failure to anticipate the independents' widespread and aggressive resistance to its policies cost it a fortune in patent-infringement litigation. Furthermore, the Trust badly underestimated the importance of the feature film, permitting the independents to claim this popular new product as entirely their own. Another issue that the MPPC misjudged was the power of the marketing strategy known as the "star system." Borrowed from the theatre industry, this system involves the creation and management of publicity about key performers, or stars, to stimulate demand for their films. Trust company producers used this kind of publicity after 1910, when Carl Laemmle of Independent Motion Pictures (IMP) promoted Florence Lawrence into national stardom through a series of media stunts in St. Louis, Mo., but they never exploited the technique as forcefully or as imaginatively as the independents. Finally, and most decisively, in August 1912 the U.S. Justice Department brought suit against the MPPC for "restraint of trade" in violation of the Sherman Antitrust Act. Delayed by countersuits and by World War I, the government's case was finally won and the MPPC formally dissolved in 1918, although it had been functionally inoperative since 1914.

The rise and fall of the Patents Company was concurrent with the industry's move to southern California. As a result of the nickelodeon boom, exhibitors had begun to require as many as 20 to 30 new films per week, and it became necessary to put production on a systematic year-round schedule. Because most films were still shot outdoors in available light, such schedules could not be maintained in the vicinity of New York City or Chicago, where the industry had originally located itself in order to take advantage of trained theatrical labour pools. As early as 1907, production companies, such as Selig Polyscope, began to dispatch production units to warmer climates during winter. It was soon clear that what producers required was a new industrial centre—one with warm weather, a temperate climate, a variety of scenery, and other qualities (such as access to acting talent) essential to their highly unconventional form of manufacturing.

Various companies experimented with location shooting in Jacksonville, Fla., in San Antonio, Texas, in Santa Fe, N.M., and even in Cuba, but the ultimate site of the American film industry was a Los Angeles suburb (originally a small industrial town) called Hollywood. It is generally thought that Hollywood's distance from the MPPC's headquarters in New York City made it attractive to the independents, but Patents Company members such as Selig, Kalem, Biograph, and Essanay had also established facilities there by 1911 in response to a number of the region's attractions. These included the temperate climate required for year-round production (the U.S. Weather Bureau estimated that an average of 320 days per year were sunny and/or clear); a wide range of topography within a 50-mile radius of Hollywood, including mountains, valleys, forests, lakes, islands, seacoast, and desert; the status of Los Angeles as a professional theatrical centre; the existence of a low tax base; and the presence of cheap and plentiful labour and land. This latter factor enabled the newly arrived production companies to buy up tens of thousands of acres of prime real estate on which to locate their studios, standing sets, and backlots.

Hollywood

By 1915 approximately 15,000 workers were employed by the motion-picture industry in Hollywood, and more than 60 percent of American production was centred there. In that same year, the trade journal *Variety* reported that capital investment in American motion pictures—the business of artisanal craftsmen and fairground operators only a decade before—had exceeded $500,000,000. The most powerful companies in the new film capital were the independents, who were flush with cash from their conversion to feature production. These included the Famous Players-Lasky Corporation (later Paramount Pictures, *c.* 1927), which was formed by a merger of Adolph Zukor's Famous Players Company, Jesse L. Lasky's Feature Play Company, and the Paramount distribution exchange in 1916; Universal Pictures, founded by Carl Laemmle in 1912 by merging IMP with Powers, Rex, Nestor, Champion, and Bison; Goldwyn Picture Corporation, founded in 1916 by Samuel Goldfish (later Goldwyn) and Edgar Selwyn; Metro Picture Corporation and Louis B. Mayer Pictures, founded by Louis B. Mayer in 1915 and 1917, respectively; and the Fox Film Corporation (later 20th Century-Fox, 1935), founded by William Fox in 1915. After World War I, these companies were joined by Loew's, Inc. (parent corporation of MGM, by merger of Metro, Goldwyn, and Mayer companies cited above, 1924), a national exhibition chain organized by Marcus Loew and Nicholas Schenck in 1919; First National Pictures, Inc., a circuit of independent exhibitors who established their own production facilities at Burbank, Calif., in 1922; Warner Bros. Pictures, Inc., founded by Harry, Albert, Samuel, and Jack Warner in 1923; and Columbia Pictures, Inc., incorporated in 1924 by Harry and Jack Cohn.

These organizations became the backbone of the Hollywood studio system, and the men who controlled them shared several important traits. They were all independent exhibitors and distributors who had outwitted the Trust and earned their success by manipulating finances in the post-nickelodeon feature boom, merging production companies, organizing national distribution networks, and ultimately acquiring vast theatre chains. They saw their business as basically a retailing operation modeled on the practice of chain stores such as Woolworth's and Sears. Not incidentally, these men were all first- or second-generation Jewish immigrants from eastern Europe, most of them with little formal education, while the audience they served was 90 percent Protestant and Catholic. This circumstance would become an issue during the 1920s, when the movies became a mass medium that was part of the life of every American citizen and when Hollywood became the chief purveyor of American culture to the world.

**Pre-World War I European cinema.**  Before World War I European cinema was dominated by France and Italy. At Pathé Frères, director-general Ferdinand Zecca perfected the *course comique,* a uniquely Gallic version of the chase film, which inspired Mack Sennett's Keystone Kops, while the immensely popular Max Linder created a comic persona that would deeply influence the work of Charlie Chaplin. The episodic crime film was pioneered by Victorin Jasset in the "Nick Carter" series, produced for the small Éclair Company, but it remained for Gaumont's Louis Feuillade to bring the genre to aesthetic perfection in the extremely successful serials *Fantômas* (1913–14), *Les Vampires* (1915–16), and *Judex* (1916).

French
film d'art
movement

Another influential phenomenon to appear from prewar France was the *film d'art* movement. It began with *L'Assassinat du duc de Guise* (1908), directed by Charles Le Bargy and André Calmettes of the Comédie Française for the Société Film d'Art, which was formed for the express purpose of transferring prestigious stage plays starring famous performers to the screen. *L'Assassinat*'s success inspired other companies to make similar films, which came to be known as *films d'art*. These films were long on intellectual pedigree and short on narrative sophistication. The directors simply filmed theatrical productions in toto, without adaptation. Their brief popularity nevertheless created a context for the lengthy treatment of serious material in motion pictures and was directly instrumental in the rise of the feature.

Italian
super-
spectacles

No country, however, was more responsible for the popularity of the feature than Italy. The Italian cinema's lavishly produced costume spectacles brought it international prominence in the years before the war. The prototypes of

the genre, by virtue of their epic material and lengths, were the Cines company's six-reel *Gli ultimi giorni di Pompei* (*The Last Days of Pompei*), directed by Luigi Maggi in 1908, and its 10-reel remake, directed by Ernesto Pasquali in 1913; but it was Cines' nine-reel *Quo vadis?* (1912), with its huge three-dimensional sets of ancient Rome and 5,000 extras, that established the standard for the superspectacle and briefly conquered the world market for Italian motion pictures. Its successor, the Italia company's 12-reel *Cabiria* (1914), was even more extravagant in its historical reconstruction of the Second Punic War, from the burning of the Roman fleet at Syracuse to Hannibal crossing the Alps and the sack of Carthage. The Italian superspectacle stimulated public demand for features and influenced such important directors as Cecil B. deMille, Ernst Lubitsch, and especially D.W. Griffith.

**Griffith.**  There has been a tendency in modern film scholarship to view motion-picture narrative form as being governed by the operations of an overall production system. Although narrative film was and continues to be strongly influenced by a combination of economic, technological, and social factors, it also owes a great deal to the individual artists who viewed film as a medium of personal expression. Chief among these innovators was D.W. (David Wark) Griffith. It is true that Griffith's self-cultivated reputation as a Romantic artist—"the father of film technique," "the man who invented Hollywood," "the Shakespeare of the screen," and the like—is somewhat overblown. It is also true that by 1908 film narrative had already been systematically organized to accommodate the material conditions of production. Griffith's work nevertheless transformed that system from its primitive to its classical mode. He was the first filmmaker to realize that the motion-picture medium, properly vested with technical vitality and seriousness of theme, could exercise enormous persuasive power over an audience, or even a nation, without recourse to print or human speech.

Griffith began his film career in late 1907 as an actor. He was cast as the lead in the Edison Company's *Rescued from an Eagle's Nest* (1907) and also appeared in many Biograph films. He had already attempted to make a living as a stage actor and a playwright without much success, and his real goal in approaching the film companies seems to have been to sell them scripts. In June 1908 Biograph gave him an opportunity to replace its ailing director, George "Old Man" McCutcheon, on the chase film *The Adventures of Dollie.* With the advice of the company's two cameramen, G.W. "Billy" Bitzer (who would become Griffith's personal cinematographer for much of his career) and Arthur Marvin (who actually shot the film), Griffith turned in a fresh and exciting film. His work earned him a full-time director's contract at Biograph, where, over the next five years, he directed more than 450 one- and two-reel films.

In the Biograph films, Griffith experimented with all of the narrative techniques he would later use in the epics *The Birth of a Nation* (1915) and *Intolerance* (1916)—techniques that helped to formulate and stabilize Hollywood's classical narrative style. A few of these techniques were already in use when Griffith started; he simply refined them. Others were innovations Griffith devised to solve practical problems in the course of production. Still others resulted from his conscious analogy between film and literary narrative, chiefly Victorian novels and plays. In all cases, however, Griffith brought to the practice of filmmaking a seriousness of purpose and an intensity of vision, which, combined with his intuitive mastery of film technique, made him the first great artist of the cinema.

Griffith's
innova-
tions
in editing

Griffith's first experiments were in the field of editing and involved varying the standard distance between the audience and the screen. In *Greaser's Gauntlet,* made one month after *Dollie,* he first used a "cut-in" from a long shot to a full shot to heighten the emotional intensity of a scene. In an elaboration of this practice, he was soon taking shots from multiple camera set-ups—long shots, full shots, medium shots, close shots, and, ultimately, close-ups—and combining their separate perspectives into single dramatic scenes. By October 1908, Griffith was practicing parallel editing between the dual narratives of *After Many*

*Years,* and the following year he extended the technique to the representation of three simultaneous actions in *Lonely Villa,* cutting rapidly back and forth from a band of robbers breaking into a suburban villa, to a woman and her children barricaded within, to the husband rushing from town to the rescue. This type of crosscutting or intercutting came to be known as the "Griffith last-minute rescue" and was employed as a basic structural principle in both *The Birth of a Nation* and *Intolerance.* It not only employed the rapid alternation of shots but also called for the shots themselves to be held for shorter and shorter durations as the parallel lines of action converged; in its ability to create the illusion of simultaneous actions, the intercut chase sequence prefigured Soviet theories of montage by at least a decade, and it remains a basic component of narrative film form to this day.

**Griffith's use of camera movement and placement**

Another area of experiment for Griffith involved camera movement and placement, most of which had been purely functional before him. When Biograph started sending his production unit to southern California in 1910, Griffith began to practice panoramic panning shots not only to provide visual information but also to engage his audience in the total environment of his films. Later, he would prominently employ the tracking, or traveling, shot, in which the camera—and therefore the audience—participates in the dramatic action by moving with it. In California, Griffith discovered that camera angle could be used to comment upon the content of a shot or to heighten its dramatic emphasis in a way that the conventionally mandated head-on medium shot could not; and, at a time when convention dictated the flat and uniform illumination of every element in a scene, he pioneered the use of expressive lighting to create mood and atmosphere. Like so many of the other devices he brought into general use, these had all been employed by earlier directors, but Griffith was the first to practice them with the care of an artist and to rationalize them within the overall structure of his films.

Griffith's one-reelers grew increasingly complex between 1911 and 1912, and he began to realize that only a longer and more expansive format could contain his vision. At first he made such two-reel films as *Enoch Arden* (1911), *Man's Genesis* (1912), *The Massacre* (1912), and *The Mothering Heart* (1913), but these went virtually unnoticed by a public enthralled with such recent features from Europe as *Queen Elizabeth* and *Quo Vadis?.* Finally, Griffith determined to make an epic himself, based on the story of Judith and Holofernes from the Apocrypha. The result was the four-reel *Judith of Bethulia* (1913), filmed secretly on a 12-square-mile set in Chatsworth Park, Calif. In addition to its structurally complicated narrative, *Judith* contained massive sets and battle scenes unlike anything yet attempted in American film. It cost twice the amount Biograph had allocated for its budget. Company officials, stunned at Griffith's audacity and extravagance, tried to relieve the director of his creative responsibilities by promoting him to studio production chief. Griffith quit

**Griffith's departure from Biograph**

instead, publishing a full-page advertisement in *The New York Dramatic Mirror* (Dec. 3, 1913), in which he took credit for all of the Biograph films he had made from *The Adventures of Dollie* through *Judith,* as well as for the narrative innovations they contained. He then accepted an offer from Harry E. Aitken, the president of the recently formed Mutual Film Corporation, to head the feature production company Reliance-Majestic; he took Bitzer and most of his Biograph stock company with him.

As part of his new contract, Griffith was allowed to make two independent features per year, and for his first project he chose to adapt *The Clansman,* a novel about the Civil War and Reconstruction by the Southern clergyman Thomas Dixon, Jr. (As a Kentuckian whose father had served as a Confederate officer, Griffith was deeply sympathetic to the material, which was highly sensational in its depiction of Reconstruction as a period in which mulatto carpetbaggers and their black henchmen had destroyed the social fabric of the South and given birth to a heroic Ku Klux Klan.) Shooting on the film began in secrecy in late 1914. Although a script existed, Griffith kept most of the continuity in his head—a remarkable feat considering

that the completed film contained 1,544 separate shots at a time when the most elaborate of foreign spectacles boasted fewer than 100. When the film opened in March 1915, retitled *The Birth of a Nation,* it was immediately pronounced "epoch-making" and recognized as a remarkable artistic achievement. The complexity of its narrative and the epic sweep of its subject were unprecedented, but so too were its controversial manipulations of audience response, especially its blatant appeals to racism. Despite its brilliantly conceived battle sequences, its tender domestic scenes, and its dignified historical reconstructions, the film also contained shocking images of miscegenation and racial violence that provoked fear and disgust. As the film's popularity swept the nation, denunciations followed, and many who had originally praised it, such as President Woodrow Wilson, were forced to recant. Ultimately, after screenings of *The Birth of a Nation* had caused riots in several cities, it was banned in eight northern and midwestern states. (First Amendment protection was not extended to motion pictures in the United States until the late 1950s.) Such measures, however, did not prevent *The Birth of a Nation* from becoming the single most popular film in history to date; it achieved national distribution in the year of its release and was seen by nearly 3,000,000 people.

*The Birth of a Nation*

Although it is difficult to believe that the film's racism was unconscious, as some have claimed, it is easy to imagine that Griffith had not anticipated the power of his own images. He seems to have been genuinely stunned by the hostile public reaction to his masterpiece, and he fought back by publishing a pamphlet entitled *The Rise and Fall of Free Speech in America* (1915), which vilified the practice of censorship and especially intolerance. At the height of his notoriety and fame, Griffith decided to produce a spectacular cinematic polemic against this flaw in human character as it had endangered civilization throughout history. The result was the massive epic *Intolerance* (1916), which interweaves stories of martyrdom from four separate historical periods. The film was conceived on a scale so monumental as to dwarf all predecessors. Crosscutting freely between a contemporary tale of courtroom injustice, the fall of ancient Babylon to Cyrus the Great in 539 BC, the St. Bartholomew's Day Massacre in 16th-century France, and the Crucifixion of Christ, Griffith created an editing structure so abstract that contemporary audiences could not understand it. Even the extravagant sets and exciting battle sequences could not save *Intolerance* at the box-office. To reduce his losses, Griffith withdrew the film from distribution after 22 weeks; he subsequently cut into the negative and released the modern and the Babylonian stories as two separate features, *The Mother and the Law* and *The Fall of Babylon,* in 1919. (Although ignored by Americans, *Intolerance* was both popular and vastly influential in the Soviet Union, where filmmakers minutely analyzed Griffith's editing style and techniques.)

*Intolerance*

It would be fair to say that Griffith's career as an innova-

By courtesy of the Museum of Modern Art/Film Stills Archive, New York City

The temple of Babylon sequence from *Intolerance* (1916), directed by D.W. Griffith.

tor of film form ended with *Intolerance,* but his career as a film artist certainly did not. He went on to direct another 26 features between 1916 and 1931, chief among them the World War I anti-German propaganda epic (financed, in part, by the British government) *Hearts of the World* (1918), the subtle and lyrical *Broken Blossoms* (1919), and the rousing melodrama *Way Down East* (1920). The financial success of the latter made it possible for Griffith to establish his own studio at Mamaroneck, N.Y., where he produced the epics *Orphans of the Storm* (1921) and *America* (1924), which focused on the French and American revolutions, respectively; both lost money. Griffith's next feature was the independent semidocumentary *Isn't Life Wonderful?* (1925), which was shot on location in Germany and is thought to have influenced both the "street" films of the German director G.W. Pabst and the post-World War II Italian Neorealist movement.

Griffith's last films, with the exception of *The Struggle* (1931), were all made for other producers. Not one could be called a success, although his first sound film, *Abraham Lincoln* (1930), was recognized as an effective essay in the new medium. The critical and financial failure of *The Struggle,* however, a version of Zola's *L'Assommoir* (*The Drunkard*), forced Griffith to retire.

It might be said of Griffith that, like Méliès and Porter, he outlived his genius, but that is not true. Griffith was fundamentally a 19th-century man who became one of the 20th-century's greatest artists. Transcending personal defects of vision, judgment, and taste, he developed the narrative language of film. He lost touch with his contemporaries because his subjects came to seem old-fashioned, but he remains peculiarly, uniquely in touch with the present because the techniques and structure he contributed to the motion-picture medium are still in use.

**Post-World War I European cinema.** Prior to World War I, the American cinema had lagged behind the film industries of Europe, particularly those of France and Italy, in such matters as feature production and the establishment of permanent theatres. During the war, however, European film production virtually ceased, in part because the same chemicals used in the production of celluloid were necessary for the manufacture of gun powder. The American cinema, meanwhile, experienced a period of unprecedented prosperity and growth. By the end of the war it exercised nearly total control of the international market: when the Treaty of Versailles was signed in 1919, 90 percent of all films screened in Europe, Africa, and Asia were American, and the figure for South America was (and remained through the 1950s) close to 100 percent. The main exception was Germany, which had been cut off from American films from 1914 until the end of the war.

*Germany.* Before World War I, the German motion-picture audience was largely uneducated and unemployed or from the working class. Most of the films exhibited were imported from other countries, particularly Denmark. The few German films produced were usually cheaply and crudely made. This impoverished state of the domestic industry became a matter of concern among military leaders during the war, when a flood of effective anti-German propaganda films began to pour into Germany from the Allied countries. Therefore, on Dec. 18, 1917, the German general Erich Ludendorff ordered the merger of the main German production, distribution, and exhibition companies into the government-subsidized conglomerate Universum Film Aktiengesellschaft. UFA's mission was to upgrade the quality of German films. The organization proved to be highly effective, and when the war ended in Germany's defeat in November 1918, the German film industry was prepared for the first time to compete in the international marketplace. Transferred to private control, UFA became the single largest studio in Europe and produced most of the films associated with the "golden age" of German cinema during the Weimar Republic (1919–33).

UFA's first peacetime productions were elaborate costume dramas (*Kostümfilme*) in the vein of the prewar Italian superspectacles, and the master of this form was Ernst Lubitsch, who directed such lavish and successful historical pageants as *Madame Dubarry* (released in the United

**UFA** (margin)

Werner Krauss in *The Cabinet of Dr. Caligari,* directed by Robert Wiene (1919).
By courtesy of the Museum of Modern Art/Film Stills Archive, New York City

States as *Passion,* 1919), *Anna Boleyn* (*Deception,* 1920), and *Das Weib des Pharao* (*The Loves of Pharaoh,* 1921) before emigrating to the United States in 1922. These films earned the German cinema a foothold in the world market, but it was an Expressionist work, *Das Kabinett des Dr. Caligari* (*The Cabinet of Dr. Caligari,* 1919), that brought the industry its first great artistic acclaim. Based on a scenario by the Czech poet Hans Janowitz and the Austrian writer Carl Mayer, the film recounts a series of brutal murders that are committed in the north German town of Holstenwall by a somnambulist at the bidding of a demented mountebank, who believes himself to be the incarnation of a homicidal 18th-century hypnotist named Dr. Caligari. Erich Pommer, *Caligari*'s producer at Decla-Bioskop (an independent production company that was to merge with UFA in 1921), added a scene to the original scenario so that the story appears to be narrated by a madman confined to an asylum of which the mountebank is director and head psychiatrist. To represent the narrator's tortured mental state, the director, Robert Wiene, hired three prominent Expressionist artists—Hermann Warm, Walter Röhrig, and Walter Reimann—to design sets that depicted exaggerated dimensions and deformed spatial relationships. To heighten this architectural stylization (and also to economize on electric power, which was rationed in postwar Germany), bizarre patterns of light and shadow were painted directly onto the scenery and even onto the characters' makeup.

In its effort to embody disturbed psychological states through decor, *Caligari* influenced enormously the UFA films that followed it and gave rise to the movement known as German Expressionism. The films of this movement were completely studio-made and often used distorted sets and lighting effects to create a highly subjective mood. They were primarily films of fantasy and terror that employed horrific plots to express the theme of the soul in search of itself. Most were photographed by one of the two great cinematographers of the Weimar period, Karl Freund and Fritz Arno Wagner. Representative works include F.W. Murnau's *Der Januskopf* (*Janus-Faced,* 1920), adapted from Robert Louis Stevenson's *Dr. Jekyll and Mr. Hyde;* Paul Wegener and Carl Boese's *Der Golem* (*The Golem,* 1920), adapted from a Jewish legend in which a gigantic clay statue becomes a raging monster; Arthur Robison's *Schatten* (*Warning Shadows,* 1922); Wiene's *Raskolnikow* (1923), based on Dostoyevsky's *Crime and Punishment;* Paul Leni's *Das Wachsfigurenkabinett* (*Waxworks,* 1924); and Henrik Galeen's *Der Student von Prag* (*The Student of Prague,* 1926), which combines the Faust legend with a doppelgänger, or double, motif. In addition to winning international prestige for German films, Expressionism produced two directors who would become major figures in world cinema, Fritz Lang and F.W. (Friedrich Wilhelm) Murnau.

Lang had already directed several successful serials, including *Die Spinnen* (*The Spiders,* 1919–20), when he collaborated with his future wife, the scriptwriter Thea

German Expressionism (margin)

von Harbou, to produce *Der müde Tod* ("The Weary Death"; English title: *Destiny,* 1921) for Decla-Bioscop. This episodic Romantic allegory of doomed lovers, set in several different historical periods, earned Lang acclaim for his dynamic compositions of architectural line and space. Lang's use of striking, stylized images is also demonstrated in the other films of his Expressionist period, notably the crime melodrama *Dr. Mabuse, der Spieler* (*Dr. Mabuse, the Gambler,* 1922), the Wagnerian diptych *Siegfried* (1922–24) and *Kriemhilds Rache* (*Kriemhild's Revenge,* 1922–23), and the stunningly futuristic *Metropolis* (1926), perhaps the greatest science-fiction film ever made. After directing the early sound masterpiece *M* (1931), based on child murders in Dusseldorf, Lang became increasingly estranged from German political life. He emigrated in 1933 to escape the Nazis and began a second career in the Hollywood studios the following year.

Murnau made several minor Expressionist films before directing one of the movement's classics, an (unauthorized) adaptation of Bram Stoker's novel *Dracula* entitled *Nosferatu—eine Symphonie des Grauens* ("Nosferatu, a Symphony of Horror," 1922), but it was *Der letzte Mann* ("The Last Man"; English title: *The Last Laugh,* 1924), a film in the genre of *Kammerspiel* ("intimate theatre"), that made him world famous. Scripted by Carl Mayer and produced by Erich Pommer for UFA, *Der letzte Mann* told the story of a hotel doorman who is humiliated by the loss of his job and—more important, apparently, in postwar German society—of his splendid paramilitary uniform. Murnau and Freund, his cameraman, gave this simple tale a complex narrative structure through their innovative use of camera movement and subjective point-of-view shots. In one famous example, Freund strapped a lightweight camera to his chest and stumbled drunkenly around the set of a bedroom to record the inebriated porter's point of view. In the absence of modern cranes and dollies, at various points in the filming Murnau and Freund placed the camera on moving bicycles, fire engine ladders, and overhead cables in order to achieve smooth, sustained movement. The total effect was a tapestry of subjectively involving movement and intense identification with the narrative.

*Der letzte Mann* was universally hailed as a masterpiece and probably had more influence on Hollywood style than any other single foreign film in history. Its "unchained camera" (Mayer's phrase) technique spawned many imitations in Germany and elsewhere, the most significant being E.A. (Ewald André) Dupont's circus-tent melodrama *Variété* (1925). The film also brought Murnau a long-term Hollywood contract, which he began to fulfill in 1927 after completing two last super-productions, *Tartüff* (1925) and *Faust* (1926), for UFA.

In 1924 the German mark was stabilized by the so-called Dawes Plan, which financed the long-term payment of Germany's war reparations debt and curtailed all exports. This created an artificial prosperity in the economy at large, which lasted only until the stock market crash of 1929, but it was devastating to the film industry, the bulk of whose revenues came from foreign markets. Hollywood then seized the opportunity to cripple its only serious European rival, saturating Germany with American films and buying its independent theatre chains. As a result of these forays and its own internal mismanagement, UFA stood on the brink of bankruptcy by the end of 1925. It was saved by a $4,000,000 loan offered by two major American studios, Famous Players-Lasky (later Paramount) and Metro-Goldwyn-Mayer, in exchange for collaborative rights to UFA studios, theatres, and creative personnel. This arrangement resulted in the founding of the Parufamet (Paramount-UFA-Metro) Distribution Company in early 1926 and the almost immediate emigration of UFA film artists and technicians to Hollywood, where they worked for a variety of studios. This first Germanic migration was temporary. Many of the filmmakers returned to UFA disgusted at the assembly-line character of the American studio system, but many—such as Lubitsch, Freund, Murnau, and Kertész—stayed on to launch full-fledged Hollywood careers, and many more would come back during the 1930s to escape Adolf Hitler.

In the meantime, the new sensibility that had entered German intellectual life turned away from the morbid psychological themes of Expressionism toward an acceptance of "life as it is lived." Called *die neue Sachlichkeit* ("the new objectivity"), this spirit stemmed from the economic dislocations that beset German society in the wake of the war, particularly the impoverishment of the middle classes through raging inflation. In cinema, *die neue Sachlichkeit* translated into the grim social realism of the "street" films of the late 1920s, including G.W. Pabst's *Die freudlose Gasse* (*The Joyless Street,* 1925), Bruno Rhan's *Dirnentragödie* (*Tragedy of the Streets,* 1927), Joe May's *Asphalt* (1929), and Piel Jutzi's *Berlin-Alexanderplatz* (1931). Named for their prototype, Karl Grune's *Die Strasse* (*The Street,* 1923), these films focused on the disillusionment, cynicism, and ultimate resignation of ordinary German people whose lives were crippled during the postwar inflation.

The master of the form was G.W. (Georg Wilhelm) Pabst, whose work established conventions of continuity editing that would become essential to the sound film. In such important realist films as *Die freudlose Gasse, Die Liebe der Jeanne Ney* (*The Love of Jeanne Ney,* 1927), *Die Büchse der Pandora* (*Pandora's Box,* 1929), and *Tagebuch einer Verlorenen* (*Diary of a Lost One,* 1929), Pabst created complex continuity sequences using techniques that became key features of the Hollywood "invisible" editing style, such as cutting on action, cutting from a shot of a character's glance to one of what the character sees (motivated point-of-view shots), and cutting to a reverse angle shot (one in which the camera angle has changed 180 degrees; *e.g.,* in a scene in which a man and a woman face one another in conversation, the man is seen from the woman's point of view, then the woman is shown from the man's point of view). Pabst later became an important figure of the early sound period, contributing in his pacifist films *Westfront 1918* (1930) and *Kameradschaft* ("Comradeship," 1931) two significant works. A few years later, however, Pabst found himself making films for the Nazis, a condition that afflicted the entire German film industry after 1933.

By March 1927, UFA was once again facing financial collapse, and it turned this time to the Prussian financier Alfred Hugenberg, a director of both the powerful Krupp industrial empire and the right-wing German National Party, who was sympathetic to the Nazis. Hugenberg bought out the American interests in UFA, acquiring a majority of the company's stock and directing the remainder into the hands of his political allies. As chairman of the UFA board, he quietly instituted a nationalistic production policy that gave increasing prominence to the Nazis and their cause and that enabled the Nazis to subvert the German film industry when Hitler came to power in 1933. German cinema then fell under the authority of Joseph Goebbels and his Ministry of Public Enlightenment and Propaganda. For the next 12 years every film made in the Third Reich had to be personally approved for release by Goebbels. Jews were officially banned from the industry, causing a vast wave of German film artists to emigrate to Hollywood. Los Angeles became known as "the new Weimar," and the German cinema was emptied of the talent and brilliance that had created its golden age.

*The Soviet Union.* Before the Bolshevik Revolution of October 1917, Russia for all practical purposes had no native film industry. In the industrialized nations of the West, motion pictures had first been accepted as a form of cheap recreation and leisure for the working class. From that base, they had reached out successfully to the middle class and gained wide popularity among all classes by about 1914. In prerevolutionary Russia, however, the working class was composed largely of serfs too poor to support a native industry, and the small movie business that did develop was dominated by foreign interests and foreign films—mainly French, German, and Danish.

The first native Russian company was not founded until 1908, and by the time of the Revolution, there were perhaps 20 more; but even these were small, importing all of their technical equipment and film stock from Germany and France. When Russia entered World War I in August

---

*Sidenotes (left column):*

Use of subjective camera movement in *The Last Laugh*

*Sidenotes (right column):*

Pabst's editing techniques

German cinema under the Third Reich

1914, foreign films could no longer be imported, and the tsarist government established the Skobelev Committee to stimulate domestic production and produce propaganda in support of the regime. The committee had little immediate effect, but when the Tsar fell in March 1917 the provisional Kerensky government reorganized it to produce antitsarist propaganda. When the Bolsheviks inherited the group eight months later, they transformed it into the Cinema Committee of the People's Commissariat of Education.

A minority party with approximately 200,000 members, the Bolsheviks had assumed the leadership of 160,000,000 people who were scattered across the largest continuous landmass in the world, spoke more than 100 separate languages, and were mostly illiterate. Vladimir Ilich Lenin and other Bolshevik leaders looked on the motion-picture medium as a means of unifying the huge, disparate nation. Lenin was the first political leader of the 20th century to recognize both the importance of film as propaganda and its power to communicate quickly and effectively. He understood that audiences did not require literacy to comprehend a film's meaning and that more people could be reached through mass-distributed motion pictures than through any other medium of the time. Lenin declared: "The cinema is for us the most important of the arts," and his government gave top priority to the rapid development of the Soviet film industry, which was nationalized in August 1919 and put under the direct authority of Lenin's wife, Nadezhda Krupskaya.

There was, however, little to build upon. Most of the prerevolutionary producers had fled to Europe, taking their equipment and film stock with them, wrecking their studios as they left. A foreign blockade prevented the importation of new equipment or stock (there were no domestic facilities for manufacturing them), and massive power shortages restricted the use of what limited resources remained. The Cinema Committee was not deterred however; its first act was to found a professional film school in Moscow to train directors, technicians, and actors for the cinema.

The Vsesoyuznyi Gosudarstvenyi Institut Kinematografii (VGIK; "All-Union State Institute of Cinematography") was the first such school in the world and is still among the most respected. Initially, it trained people in the production of *agitki,* existing newsreels reedited for the purpose of agitation and propaganda (agitprop). The *agitki* were transported on specially equipped agit-trains and agit-steamers to the provinces, where they were exhibited to generate support for the Revolution. (The state-controlled Cuban cinema used the same tactic after the revolution of 1959.) In fact, during the abysmal years of the Civil War (1918–20), nearly all Soviet films were *agitki* of some sort. Most of the great directors of the Soviet silent cinema were trained in that form, although, having very little technical equipment and no negative film stock, they were often required to make "films without celluloid."

Students at the VGIK were instructed to write, direct, and act out scenarios as if they were before cameras. Then—on paper—they assembled various "shots" into completed "films." The great teacher Lev Kuleshov obtained a print of Griffith's *Intolerance* and screened it for students in his "Kuleshov workshop" until they had memorized its shot structures and could rearrange its multilayered editing sequences on paper in hundreds of different combinations.

Kuleshov further experimented with editing by intercutting the same shot of a famous actor's expressionless face with several different shots of highly expressive content—a steaming bowl of soup, a dead woman in a coffin, and a little girl playing with a teddy bear. The invariable response of film school audiences when shown these sequences was that the actor's face assumed the emotion appropriate to the intercut object—hunger for the soup, sorrow for the dead woman, paternal affection for the little girl. Kuleshov reasoned from this phenomenon, known today as the "Kuleshov effect," that the shot in film always has two values: that which it carries in itself as a photographic image of reality, and that which it acquires when placed into juxtaposition with another shot. He reasoned further that the second value is more important to cinematic

**Soviet *agitki***

**The Kuleshov effect**

signification than the first and that, therefore, time and space in the cinema must be subordinate to the process of editing, or montage (coined by the Soviets from the French verb *monter,* "to assemble"). Kuleshov ultimately conceived of montage as an expressive process whereby dissimilar images could be linked together to create nonliteral or symbolic meaning.

Although Kuleshov made several important films, including *By the Law* (1926), it was as a teacher and theorist that he most deeply influenced an entire generation of Soviet directors. Two of his most brilliant students were Sergey Eisenstein and Vsevolod Illarionovich Pudovkin.

Eisenstein was, with Griffith, one of the great pioneering geniuses of the modern cinema, and like his predecessor he produced a handful of enduring masterworks. Griffith, however, had elaborated the structure of narrative editing intuitively, whereas Eisenstein was an intellectual who formulated a modernist theory of editing based on the psychology of perception and Marxist dialectic. Trained as a civil engineer, in 1920 he joined the Moscow Proletkult Theatre, where he fell under the influence of the stage director Vsevolod Meyerhold and directed a number of plays in the revolutionary style of Futurism. In the winter of 1922–23 Eisenstein studied under Kuleshov and was inspired to write his first theoretical manifesto, "The Montage of Attractions." Published in the radical journal *Lef,* the article advocated assaulting an audience with calculated emotional shocks for the purpose of agitation.

Eisenstein was invited to direct the Proletkult-sponsored film *Strike* in 1924, but, like Griffith, he knew little of the practical aspects of production. He therefore enlisted the aid of Eduard Tisse, a brilliant cinematographer at the state-owned Goskino studios, beginning a lifelong artistic collaboration. *Strike* is a semidocumentary representation of the brutal suppression of a strike by tsarist factory owners and police. In addition to being Eisenstein's first film, it was also the first revolutionary mass-film of the new Soviet state. Conceived as an extended montage of shock stimuli, the film concludes with the now famous sequence in which the massacre of the strikers and their families is intercut with shots of cattle being slaughtered in an abattoir.

*Strike* was an immediate success, and Eisenstein was next commissioned to direct a film celebrating the 20th anniversary of the failed 1905 revolution against tsarism. Originally intended to provide a panorama of the entire event, the project eventually came to focus on a single representative episode—the mutiny of the battleship *Potemkin* and the massacre of the citizens of the port of Odessa by tsarist troops. *Battleship Potemkin* (1925) emerged as one of the most important and influential films ever made, especially in Eisenstein's use of montage, which had improved far beyond the formulaic, if effective, juxtapositions of *Strike.*

Although agitational to the core, *Potemkin* is a work of extraordinary pictorial beauty and great elegance of form. It is symmetrically broken into five movements or acts, according to the structure of Greek tragedy. In the first of these, "Men and Maggots," the flagrant mistreatment of the sailors at the hands of their officers is demonstrated, while the second, "Drama on the Quarterdeck," presents the actual mutiny and the ship's arrival in Odessa. "Appeal from the Dead" establishes the solidarity of the citizens of Odessa with the mutineers, but it is the fourth sequence, "The Odessa Steps," which depicts the massacre of the citizens, that thrust Eisenstein and his film into the historical eminence that both occupy today. Its power is such that the film's conclusion, "Meeting the Squadron," in which the *Potemkin* in a show of brotherhood is allowed to pass through the squadron unharmed, is anticlimactic.

Unquestionably the most famous sequence of its kind in film history, "The Odessa Steps" incarnates the theory of dialectical montage that Eisenstein later expounded in his collected writings, *The Film Sense* (1942) and *Film Form* (1949). Eisenstein believed that meaning in motion pictures is generated by the collision of opposing shots. Building on Kuleshov's ideas, Eisenstein reasoned that montage operates according to the Marxist view of history as a perpetual conflict in which a force (thesis) and a

**Sergey Eisenstein**

**Eisenstein's theory of montage**

counterforce (antithesis) collide to produce a totally new and greater phenomenon (synthesis). He compared this dialectical process in film editing to "the series of explosions of an internal combustion engine, driving forward its automobile or tractor." The force of the Odessa steps sequence arises when the viewer's mind combines individual, independent shots and forms a new, distinct conceptual impression that far outweighs the shots' narrative significance. Through Eisenstein's accelerated manipulations of filmic time and space, the slaughter on the stone steps—where hundreds of citizens find themselves trapped between descending tsarist militia above and Cossacks below—acquires a powerful symbolic meaning. With the addition of a stirring revolutionary score by the German Marxist composer Edmund Meisel, the agitational appeal of *Potemkin* became nearly irresistible, and, when exported in early 1926, it made Eisenstein world famous.

Eisenstein's next project, *October* (1928), was commissioned by the Central Committee to commemorate the 10th anniversary of the Bolshevik Revolution. Accordingly, vast resources, including the Soviet Army and Navy, were placed at the director's disposal. Eisenstein based the shooting script on voluminous documentary material from the era and on John Reed's book *Ten Days That Shook the World.* When the film was completed in November 1927, it was just under four hours long. While Eisenstein was making *October,* however, Joseph Stalin had taken control of the Politburo from Leon Trotsky, and the director was forced to cut the print by one-third to eliminate references to the exiled Trotsky.

Eisenstein had consciously used *October* as a laboratory for experimenting with "intellectual" or "ideological" montage, an abstract type of editing in which the relationships established between shots are conceptual rather than visual or emotional. When the film was finally released, however, Stalinist critics attacked this alleged "formalist excess" (aestheticism or elitism). The same charge was leveled even more bitterly against Eisenstein's next film, *Old and New* (1929), which Stalinist bureaucrats completely disavowed. Stalin hated Eisenstein because he was an intellectual and a Jew, but the director's international stature was such that he could not be publicly purged. Instead, Stalin used the Soviet state-subsidy apparatus to foil Eisenstein's projects and attack his principles at every turn, a situation that resulted in the director's failure to complete another film until *Alexander Nevsky* was commissioned in 1938.

Eisenstein's nearest rival in the Soviet silent cinema was his fellow student Pudovkin. Like Eisenstein, Pudovkin developed a new theory of montage but one based on cognitive linkage rather than dialectical collision. He maintained that "the film is not shot, but built, built up from the separate strips of celluloid that are its raw material."
**Pudovkin's use of montage** Pudovkin, like Griffith, most often used montage for narrative rather than symbolic purposes. His films are more personal than Eisenstein's; the epic drama that is the focus

of Eisenstein's films exists in Pudovkin's films merely to provide a backdrop for the interplay of human emotions.

Pudovkin's major work is *Mother* (1926), a tale of strike-breaking and terrorism in which a woman loses first her husband and then her son to the opposing sides of the 1905 Revolution. The film was internationally acclaimed for the revolutionary intensity of its montage, as well as for its emotion and lyricism. Pudovkin's later films include *The End of St. Petersburg* (1927), which, like Eisenstein's *October,* was commissioned to celebrate the 10th anniversary of the Bolshevik Revolution, and *The Heir to Genghis Khan* (1928; English title: *Storm over Asia*), which is set in Central Asia during the 1920 Civil War. Both mingle human drama with the epic and the symbolic as they tell a story of a politically naive person who is galvanized into action by tsarist tyranny. Although Pudovkin was never persecuted as severely by the Stalinists as Eisenstein, he too was publicly charged with formalism for his experimental sound film *A Simple Case* (1932) and was forced to release the film without its sound track.

Two other seminal figures of the Soviet silent era were Aleksandr Dovzhenko and Dziga Vertov (original name Denis Kaufman). Dovzhenko, the son of Ukrainian peasants, had been a political cartoonist and painter before becoming a director at the state-controlled Odessa studios in 1926. After several minor works, he made *Zvenigora* (1928), a collection of boldly stylized tales about a hunt for an ancient Scythian treasure set during four different stages of Ukrainian history; *Arsenal* (1929), an epic film poem about the effects of revolution and civil war upon the Ukraine; and *Earth* (1930), which is considered to be his masterpiece. *Earth* tells the story of the conflict between a family of wealthy land-owning peasants (kulaks) and the young peasants of a collective farm in a small Ukrainian village, but the film is less a narrative than a lyric hymn to the cyclic recurrence of birth, life, love, and death in nature and in humankind. Although the film is acclaimed today, when it was released Stalinist critics denounced it as counterrevolutionary. Soon after, Dovzhenko entered a period of political eclipse, during which, however, he continued to make films.

Dziga Vertov (a pseudonym meaning "spinning top") was an artist of quite different talents. He began his career as an *agitki* photographer and newsreel editor and is now acknowledged as the father of *cinéma-vérité* (a self-consciously realistic documentary movement of the 1960s and '70s) for his development and practice of the theory of the *kino-glaz* ("cinema-eye"). Vertov articulated **Dziga Vertov's theory of the *kino-glaz*** this doctrine in the early 1920s in a number of radical manifestos in which he denounced conventional narrative cinema as impotent and demanded that it be replaced with a cinema of actuality based on the "organization of camera-recorded documentary material." Between 1922 and 1925, he put his idea into practice in a series of 23 carefully crafted newsreel-documentaries entitled *Kino-Pravda* ("film truth") and *Goskinokalender.* Vertov's most famous film is *Man with a Movie Camera* (1929), a feature-length portrait of Moscow from dawn to dusk. The film plays upon the "city symphony" genre inaugurated by Walter Ruttman's *Berlin, the Symphony of a Great City* (1927), but Vertov repeatedly draws attention to the filmmaking process to create an autocritique of cinema itself.

Unlike most of his contemporaries, Vertov welcomed the coming of sound, envisioning it as a "radio-ear" to accompany the "cinema-eye." His first sound film, *Symphony of the Donbas* (1931), was an extraordinary contribution to the new medium, as was *Three Songs About Lenin* (1934), yet Vertov could not escape the charge of formalist error any more than his peers. Although he did make the feature film *Lullaby* in 1937, for the most part the Stalinist establishment reduced him to the status of a newsreel photographer after 1934.

Many other Soviet filmmakers played important roles in the great decade of experiment that followed the Revolution, among them Grigory Kozintsev and Leonid Trauberg (*The Overcoat,* 1926; *The New Babylon,* 1929), Boris Barnet (*The House on Trubnaya Square,* 1928), Yakov Protazanov (*Aelita,* 1924), Olga Preobrazhenskaya (*Women of Ryazan,* 1927), Abram Room (*Bed and Sofa,* 1927), and

By courtesy of the Rosa Madell Film Library; photograph from the Museum of Modern Art/Film Stills Archive, New York City

The descent of the baby carriage during the "Odessa Steps" sequence from *Battleship Potemkin*, Sergey Eisenstein (1925).

the documentarian Esther Shub (*The Fall of the Romanov Dynasty,* 1927). The period came to an abrupt end in 1929, when Stalin removed the state film trust (then called Sovkino) from the jurisdiction of the Commissariat of Education and placed it under the direct authority of the Supreme Council of the National Economy. Reorganized as Soyuzkino, the trust was turned over to the reactionary bureaucrat Boris Shumyatsky, a proponent of the narrowly ideological doctrine known as socialist realism. This policy, which came to dominate the Soviet arts, dictated that individual creativity be subordinated to the political aims of the party and the state.

**Soviet socialist realism**

**Post-World War I U.S. cinema.** During the 1920s in the United States, motion-picture production, distribution, and exhibition became a major national industry and movies perhaps the major national obsession. The salaries of stars reached monumental proportions, filmmaking practices and narrative formulas were standardized to accommodate mass production, and Wall Street began to invest heavily in every branch of the business. The growing industry was organized according to the studio system that, in many respects, the producer Thomas Harper Ince had developed at Inceville, his studio in the Santa Ynez Canyon near Hollywood, between 1914 and 1918. Ince functioned as the central authority over multiple production units, each headed by a director who was required to shoot an assigned film according to a detailed continuity script. Every project was carefully budgeted and tightly scheduled, and Ince himself supervised the final cut. This central producer system was the prototype for the studio system of the 1920s, and, with some modification, it prevailed as the dominant mode of Hollywood production for the next 40 years.

Virtually all of the major film genres evolved and were codified during the 1920s, but none was more characteristic of the period than the slapstick comedy. This form was originated by Mack Sennett, who, at his Keystone Studios, produced countless one- and two-reel shorts and features (*Tillie's Punctured Romance,* 1914; *The Surf Girl,* 1916; *Teddy at the Throttle,* 1917) whose narrative logic was subordinated to fantastic, purely visual humour. An anarchic mixture of circus, vaudeville, burlesque, pantomime, and the chase, Sennett's Keystone comedies created a world of inspired madness and mayhem, and they employed the talents of such future stars as Charlie Chaplin, Harry Langdon, Roscoe "Fatty" Arbuckle, Mabel Normand, and Harold Lloyd. When these performers achieved fame, many of them left Keystone, often to form their own production companies, a practice still (if briefly) possible in the early 1920s.

**Charlie Chaplin**

Chaplin, for example, who had developed the persona of the "little tramp" at Keystone, went on to direct and star in a series of shorts produced by Essanay in 1915 (*The Tramp, A Night in the Show*) and Mutual between 1916 and 1917 (*One A.M., The Rink, Easy Street*). In 1917 he was offered an eight-film contract with First National that enabled him to establish his own studio. He directed his first feature there, the semiautobiographical *The Kid* (1921), but most of his First National films were two-reelers. In 1919 Chaplin, Griffith, Mary Pickford, and Douglas Fairbanks, the four most popular and powerful film artists of the time, jointly formed the United Artists Corporation in order to produce and distribute—and thereby retain artistic and financial control over—their own films. Chaplin directed three silent features for United Artists: *A Woman of Paris* (1923), his great comic epic *The Gold Rush* (1925), and *The Circus* (1928), which was released after the introduction of sound into motion pictures. He later made several sound films, but the two most successful—his first two, *City Lights* (1931) and *Modern Times* (1936)—were essentially silent films with musical scores.

**Buster Keaton**

Buster Keaton possessed a very different kind of comic talent than Chaplin; but both men were wonderfully subtle actors with a keen sense of the tragic often contained within the comic, and both were major directors of their period. Keaton, like Chaplin, was born into a theatrical family and began performing in vaudeville skits at a young age. Intrigued by the new film medium, he left the stage and worked for two years as a supporting comedian for

Charlie Chaplin in *Modern Times* (1936).
© Roy Export Company Establishment; photograph, the Museum of Modern Art/Film Stills Archive, New York City

Arbuckle's production company. In 1919 Keaton formed his own production company, where, over the next four years, he made 20 shorts (*One Week,* 1920; *The Boat,* 1921; *Cops,* 1922; *The Balloonatic,* 1923) that represent, with Chaplin's Mutual films, the acme of American slapstick comedy. A Keaton trademark was the "trajectory gag," in which perfect timing of acting, directing, and editing propels his film character through a geometric progression of complicated sight gags that seem impossibly dangerous but are still dramatically logical. Such routines inform all of Keaton's major features—*Our Hospitality* (1923), *Sherlock Jr.* (1924), *The Navigator* (1924), *Seven Chances* (1925), and his masterpieces *The General* (1927) and *Steamboat Bill, Jr.* (1928). Keaton's greatest films, all made before his company was absorbed by MGM, have a reflexive quality that indicates his fascination with film as a medium. Although some of his MGM films were financially successful, the factory-like studio system stifled Keaton's creativity, and he was reduced to playing bit parts after the early 1930s.

Important but lesser silent comics were Lloyd, the team of Stan Laurel and Oliver Hardy, Langdon, and Arbuckle. Working at the Hal Roach Studios, Lloyd cultivated the persona of an earnest, sweet-tempered boy-next-door. He specialized in a variant of Keystone mayhem known as the "comedy of thrills," in which—as in Lloyd's most famous features, *Safety Last* (1923) and *The Freshman* (1925)—an innocent protagonist finds himself placed in physical danger. Laurel and Hardy also worked for Roach. They made 27 silent two-reelers, including *Putting Pants on Philip* (1927) and *Liberty* (1929), and became even more popular in the 1930s in such sound films as *Another Fine Mess* (1930) and *Sons of the Desert* (1933). Their comic characters were basically grown-up children whose relationship was sometimes disturbingly sadomasochistic. Langdon also traded on a childlike, even babylike, image in such popular features as *The Strong Man* (1926) and *Long Pants* (1927), both directed by Frank Capra. Arbuckle, however, in his few years of stardom, unfortunately created the character of a leering, sensual adult. Arbuckle's talent was limited, but his persona affected the course of American film history in a quite unexpected way.

By the early 1920s some 40,000,000 Americans—half of them minors—were attending the movies each week. The rapid spread of the medium and its easy accessibility had already caused mild public concern, especially since films had begun to feature increasingly risqué plots and situations. Concern increased as Hollywood became identified in the popular mind with the materialism, cynicism, and sexual license of the Jazz Age. Then, in September 1921 the popular Arbuckle was charged with the rape and manslaughter of a young starlet, and the concern turned into anger and rage. Arbuckle was eventually exonerated, but other Hollywood scandals surfaced—the murder of director William Desmond Taylor, the death from drug addiction of matinee idol Wallace Reid—and the tabloid press screamed for blood.

The Hays Office

In an attempt to stave off probable mass boycotts and government censorship, in March 1922 the studio heads formed a self-regulatory trade organization, the Motion Picture Producers and Distributors of America (MPPDA), and hired the U.S. postmaster general, Will H. Hays, to head it. In practice, the Hays Office, as the MPPDA was known, functioned as an advisory body and engaged in little actual censorship. It promulgated an unenforceable "Purity Code," which was facetiously called the "Don'ts and Be Carefuls," and it endorsed a policy of "compensating values," whereby all manner of screen vileness could be depicted so long as it was shown to be punished by the film's end. Throughout the 1920s, the Hays Office primarily (and successfully) served to mollify pressure groups and to manage public relations.

The leading practitioner of the compensating values formula was the flamboyant director Cecil B. deMille. He first became famous after World War I for a series of sophisticated comedies of manners that were aimed at Hollywood's new middle-class audience (*Old Wives for New,* 1918; *Forbidden Fruit,* 1921). When the Hays Office was established deMille turned to the sex- and violence-drenched religious spectacles that made him an international figure, notably *The Ten Commandments* (1923; remade 1956). DeMille's chief rival in the production of stylish sex comedies was the German émigré Ernst Lubitsch. An early master of the UFA *Kostümfilm,* Lubitsch excelled at sexual innuendo and understatement in such urbane essays as *The Marriage Circle* (1924). Also popular during the 1920s were the swashbuckling exploits of Douglas Fairbanks, whose lavish adventure spectacles, including *Robin Hood* (1922) and *The Thief of Bagdad* (1924), thrilled a generation, and the narrative documentaries of Robert Flaherty, whose *Nanook of the North* (1922) and *Moana* (1926) were unexpectedly successful with the public and with critics.

The most enigmatic and unconventional figure working in Hollywood at the time, however, was without a doubt the remarkable Viennese émigré Erich von Stroheim. Stroheim, who also acted, learned directing as an assistant to Griffith on *Intolerance* and *Hearts of the World.* His first three films—*Blind Husbands* (1918), *The Devil's Passkey* (1919), and *Foolish Wives* (1922)—constitute an obsessive trilogy of adultery; each features a sexual triangle in which an American wife is seduced by a Prussian army officer. Even though all three films were enormously popular, the great sums Stroheim was spending on the extravagant production design and costuming of his next project brought him into conflict with his Universal producers, and he was replaced.

Stroheim then signed a contract with Goldwyn Pictures and began work on a long-cherished project—an adaptation of Frank Norris' grim, naturalistic novel *McTeague.* Shot entirely on location in the streets and rooming houses of San Francisco, in Death Valley, and in the California hills, the film was conceived as a sentence-by-sentence translation of its source. Stroheim's original version ran approximately 10 hours. Realizing that the film was too long to be exhibited, he cut almost half of the footage. The film was still deemed too long, so Stroheim, with the help of director Rex Ingram, edited it down into a four-hour version that could be shown in two parts. By that time, however, Goldwyn Pictures had merged with Metro Pictures and Louis B. Mayer Pictures to become MGM. MGM took the negative from Stroheim and cut out another two hours, destroying the excised footage in the process. Released as *Greed* (1924), the film had enormous gaps in continuity, but it was still recognized as a work of genius in its rich psychological characterization and in its creation of a naturalistic analogue for the novel.

Stroheim made one more film for MGM, a darkly satiric adaptation of the Franz Lehár operetta *The Merry Widow* (1925). He then went to Celebrity Pictures, where he directed *The Wedding March* (1928), a two-part spectacle of imperial Vienna, but his work was taken from him and recut into a single film when Celebrity was absorbed by Paramount. Stroheim's last directorial duties were on the botched *Queen Kelly* (1929) and *Walking Down Broadway* (1932), although he was removed from both films for various reasons. He made his living thereafter by writing screenplays and acting.

Although many of Stroheim's troubles with Hollywood were personal, he was also a casualty of the American film industry's transformation during the 1920s from a speculative entrepreneurial enterprise into a vertically and horizontally integrated oligopoly that had no tolerance for creative difference. His situation was not unique; many singular artists, including Griffith, Sennett, Chaplin, and Keaton, found it difficult to survive as filmmakers under the rigidly standardized studio system that had been established by the end of the decade. The industry's conversion to sound at that time reinforced its big-business tendencies and further discouraged independent filmmakers. The studios, which had borrowed huge sums of money on the very brink of the Great Depression in order to finance the conversion, were determined to reduce production costs and increase efficiency. They therefore became less and less willing to tolerate artistic innovation or eccentricity.

(DAVID A. COOK)

Decline of independent filmmaking

# Baghdad

**B**aghdad (also spelled Bagdad, Arabic Baghdād) is the capital of Iraq and one of the largest cities in the Middle East. Located near the centre of Iraq, about 330 miles (530 kilometres) from the head of the Persian Gulf, Baghdad is famous as the capital of the 'Abbāsid caliphs and the setting of many of the stories in *The Thousand and One Nights.* Baghdad exhibits marked contrasts in architecture and life-styles, combining Oriental bazaars, shrines, and mosques with riverfront cafés, Western-style luxury hotels, and modern high-rise apartments. With almost a third of the country's population, Baghdad is the centre of Iraq's political, economic, and cultural life.

This article is divided into the following sections:

Physical and human geography
  The landscape
    The city site
    Climate
    The city layout
  The people
  The economy
    Industry
    Commerce and finance
    Transportation

Administration and social conditions
  Government
  Public services
  Education
  Cultural life
History
  Foundation and early growth
  Centuries of decline
  Beginnings of modernization
  The modern city

## Physical and human geography

### THE LANDSCAPE

**The city site.** Baghdad is situated on the Tigris River at the river's closest point to the Euphrates, 25 miles to the west. The Diyālā River joins the Tigris just southeast of the city and borders its eastern suburbs. The terrain surrounding Baghdad is a flat alluvial plain 112 feet (34 metres) above sea level. Historically the city has been inundated by periodic floods from the Tigris' tributaries to the north and east. These ended in 1956 with the completion of a dam on the Tigris at Sāmarrā', north of Baghdad, and the ending of the floods has permitted extensive expansion of the city to the east and west. To the north, urban expansion has absorbed the medieval townships of al-A'ẓamīyah on the east bank and al-Kāẓimīyah on the west bank.

**Climate.** The climate is hot and dry in summer, cool and damp in winter. Spring and fall are brief but pleasant. Between May and September the average daily maximum temperature is 105° F (41° C), and the high may reach 120° F (49° C) at midday in July and August. Intense daytime heat is mitigated by low relative humidity (10 to 50 percent) and a temperature decline of 30° F (17° C) or more at night. In winter the average daytime temperature is about 55° F (13° C), and the temperature occasionally drops below freezing. Rainfall is sparse (six inches, or 150 millimetres, annually) and mainly occurs between December and April. There is no rain in summer. In spring and early summer the prevailing northwesterly winds (shamals) bring sandstorms that frequently bathe the city in a dusty mist.

**The city layout.** *The districts.* The city extends along both banks of the Tigris. The east-bank settlement is known as Ruṣāfah, the west-bank as al-Karkh. A series of modern bridges, including one railroad trestle, links the two banks. From a built-up area of about four square miles (10 square kilometres) at the beginning of the 20th century, Baghdad has expanded into a bustling metropolis with suburbs spreading north and south along the river and east and west onto the surrounding plains.

The city centre The older core of the city consists of a rectangle about two miles long and one mile wide located on the east bank. Its length extends between two former city gates, al-Mu'aẓẓam Gate, now al-Mu'aẓẓam Square, in the north and ash-Sharqī Gate, now Taḥrīr Square, in the south. From the Tigris the rectangle runs eastward to the inner bund, or dike, built by the Ottoman governor Nāẓim Pasha in 1910. Rashīd Street in downtown Baghdad is the heart of this area and contains the city's financial district, many government buildings, and the copper, textile, and gold bazaars. South of Rashīd Street a newer commercial area with shops, cinemas, and business offices has spread along Sa'dūn Street. Parallel to Sa'dūn, Abū Nuwās Street on the riverfront is the city's showpiece and its entertainment centre, featuring cafés, restaurants, luxury hotels, and, along its southern reaches, rows of ultramodern townhouses.

Adjacent to these commercial districts are older, middle-class residential areas, such as as-Sulaykh to the north, al-Wizārīyah to the west, and al-Karrādah to the south, now densely settled. Baghdad University and a fashionable new residential area are located on al-Jādrīyah, a peninsula formed by a bend in the Tigris.

Planned neighbourhoods Since the late 1950s the city has expanded eastward beyond the bund. Planned middle-class neighbourhoods are located between the bund and the Army Canal, which connects the Tigris and Diyālā rivers. Beyond the canal, at the eastern edge of the city, is a sprawling low-income housing development inhabited by more than 1,000,000 urban migrants.

On the west bank are a number of residential quarters, including al-Karkh (an older quarter) and several upper middle-class districts with walled villas and green gardens. Chief among these is al-Manṣūr, surrounding the racetrack, which provides boutiques, fast-food restaurants, and sidewalk cafés that appeal to its affluent professional residents.

*Architecture and monuments.* The architecture of the city ranges from traditional two- or three-story brick houses to modern steel, glass, and concrete structures. The traditional Baghdad house, usually located in a crowded narrow street, has latticed windows and an open inner courtyard; a few fine specimens from the late Ottoman period are tucked away in traditional quarters of al-Karkh, Ruṣāfah, and al-Kāẓimīyah. The typical modern middle-class dwelling is built of brick and mortar and has a garden and wall.

Traditional and modern houses

While no monuments survive from the early 'Abbāsid period, examples of late 'Abbāsid architecture include the 'Abbāsid Palace (late 12th or early 13th century) and the Mustanṣirīyah (an Islāmic law college built by the caliph al-Mustanṣir in 1233), both restored as museums, and the Sahrāwardī Mosque (1234). The Wasṭānī Gate, the only remnant of the medieval wall, has been converted into the Arms Museum.

Another group of buildings dates from the late 13th and 14th centuries (the Il-Khanid and Jalāyirid periods). These include the minaret of the caliph's mosque (1289); the 'Aqūlī Mosque (1328); and two superb buildings constructed by the Jalāyirid governor Marjān ibn 'Abd Allah: the Marjān Mosque (1356), partly demolished in 1946, and the Marjān Khān (1359), a restored caravansary (inn). A number of mosques, bazaars, and public baths survive from the Ottoman period.

A cultural revival in the post-1958 period has produced many modern monuments, the work of contemporary artists and sculptors. Among the best known are Jawād Salīm's Liberation Monument in Taḥrīr ("Liberation") Square, depicting the struggle of the Iraqi people to achieve liberty before the 1958 revolution, and Muḥammad Ghānī's "Murjāna Monument," which depicts Murjāna, Ali Baba's housekeeper in *The Thousand and One Nights*, pouring boiling oil on the 40 thieves. Two monuments are dedicated to the war dead. A large, modernistic shield, built by Khālid ar-Raḥḥāl in 1982, commemorates the Unknown Soldier. The Martyr's Monument, a 150-foot split dome built in 1983, commemorates the casualties of the Iraqi-Iranian war.

Commemorative sculpture

### THE PEOPLE

The population of greater Baghdad has grown tremendously since World War II, exceeding 4,000,000 by 1987. The vast majority of the population is Muslim and Arab. The Muslims are divided, however, between the two main sects of Islām, the Sunnites and the Shī'ites. Other ethnic and linguistic groups include Kurds, Armenians, and people of Indian, Afghan, or Turkish origin. A substantial Persian-speaking population departed for Iran in the 1970s and '80s in the wake of troubles between Iran and Iraq. There are several Eastern-rite Christian communities, notably the Chaldeans and Assyrians, and a small Jewish community with ancient roots in Mesopotamia; most Jews left the country for Israel at the beginning of the 1950s.

Baghdad has a large community of foreign Arabs, including hundreds of thousands of Egyptian workers and a sizable number of Palestinians, many of whom are the second generation to live in the city. The Western community, once substantial, has been reduced since 1958 and is limited mainly to businessmen, members of the diplomatic corps, and executives of foreign companies.

Traditionally, people of the same sect, ethnic group, or craft lived together in separate quarters or neighbourhoods, but oil wealth and massive migration from rural areas to the city have resulted in distribution based on socioeconomic stratification. Some patterns persist, however. As the city expanded physically, the government offered parcels of land for a minimal fee to various professional associations. Thus doctors, lawyers, army officers, and those of other occupational groups have tended to concentrate in new neighbourhoods, each with its own mosques, shops, and schools, creating a pattern of cities within the city. In the 1970s the government attempted to curb "horizontal" expansion, and a new phenomenon, high-rise apartments, appeared.

Changes in neighbourhood patterns

Baghdadis have an affinity for gardens and family recreation. On weekends the city's restaurants, cafés, and public parks are filled with people, particularly along Abū Nuwās Street, where restaurants serve the local delicacy *masgūf*,

Tigris fish roasted over an open fire. Other recreational centres include two islands in the Tigris that have swimming pools and cafés, the Lunar Amusement Park, and az-Zawrā' Public Park and Zoo.

## THE ECONOMY

**Industry.** Most of Iraq's industry, finance, and commerce is concentrated in and around Baghdad. At least half of the country's large-scale industry and much of its smaller industry is located in the Baghdad governorate. The exception is heavy industry (petroleum, iron, steel, and petrochemicals), which is situated near the oil fields in the north (Kirkūk) and the south (in Baṣrah and az-Zubayr). Most economic activities are owned or controlled by the government, which both stimulates and monopolizes the country's economic activities.

*Baghdad's modern industry*

Modern industry began in the interwar period, spurred by the Law for the Encouragement of Industry in 1929. Early factory production centred on textiles (cotton ginning, spinning, and weaving), food processing, brick making, and cigarettes. Beginning in the 1950s, the government used increased oil revenues to develop industries. The city now produces a wide variety of consumer and industrial goods, including processed foods and beverages, tobacco, textiles, clothes, leather goods, wood products, furniture, paper and printed material, bricks and cement, chemicals, plastics, electrical equipment, and metal and nonmetallic products. Despite the growth of modern industry, however, a large percentage of Baghdad's labour force still works in traditional economic activities, such as retail trade, production of handmade consumer goods, auto and mechanical repairs, and personal services.

The most important industry in Baghdad is the government, the city's principal employer. Hundreds of thousands of citizens work for the government, directly or indirectly, in the civil service, in government-run educational institutions, and in government-owned industrial and commercial enterprises.

**Commerce and finance.** The main offices of the Central Bank of Iraq, which has the sole right to issue currency, and the commercial Rafidayn Bank are in Baghdad. No foreign banks are allowed. The main offices of the government companies for commerce, trade, and industry are located in Baghdad, as are the branches of foreign companies operating in Iraq.

**Transportation.** Baghdad is the hub of the country's transportation system. Saddam International Airport, west of Baghdad, serves numerous international airlines, including Iraqi Airways. The major railway lines of the state-owned railway meet at Baghdad. These connect Baghdad with Baṣrah and Umm Qaṣr near the Persian Gulf, with Kirkūk and Irbīl in the northeast, with Mosul in the north, and with al-Qā'im near the Syrian border in the northwest. Baghdad is also the centre of a regional road network, connecting the city by overland routes with Turkey, Syria, Jordan, Iran, Kuwait, and Saudi Arabia. Baghdad is also connected by road with Europe. Within the city, a network of expressways completed in the 1980s relieves traffic congestion and links the city centre with its suburbs. The main means of public transportation are the red double-deck bus (introduced by the British) and the public taxi.

## ADMINISTRATION AND SOCIAL CONDITIONS

**Government.** Baghdad is both a national and a provincial capital. The governor (*muḥāfiẓ*) of the Baghdad province is nominated by presidential decree but is responsible to the minister of interior. The city is governed by a mayor, who is appointed by the president. As the seat of the national government, Baghdad contains the offices of the president, the Council of Ministers, the National Assembly, and the headquarters of the governing party.

**Public services.** Since the 1950s the government has greatly expanded public services in Baghdad, providing low-income housing for poor and middle-income families, as well as electricity, water, sewage, and medical facilities. Baghdad has numerous hospitals and clinics, many of them specialized, and a major medical complex, Madīnat aṭ-Ṭub ("Medical City").

**Education.** Public school facilities have expanded rapidly since the 1950s. Education is compulsory through primary school, and statistics show nearly total compliance in Baghdad. The Baghdad governorate has more than 1,000 primary schools, several hundred intermediate and secondary schools, and a number of vocational schools, as well as numerous technical institutes and teachers' training schools. Baghdad is the centre of higher education in Iraq. The University of Baghdad was established in 1957, although some of its faculties were founded much earlier. There are, in addition, three other institutions of higher learning: al-Mustanṣirīyah University, the University of Technology, and al-Bakr Military Academy. Education is free up to and including the university level.

## CULTURAL LIFE

Baghdad has become an active cultural centre for the Arab world, producing some of the most prominent modern sculptors, painters, poets, and writers. Iraqi poets, for example, pioneered the free-verse movement in Arabic.

Among the most important of Baghdad's museums are the Iraqi Museum, containing important archaeological treasures from ancient Mesopotamian history; the National Museum of Modern Art, containing a permanent collection of painting, sculpture, and ceramics by Iraqi artists; and the Museum of Iraqi Art Pioneers, holding the works of Iraqi artists who laid the foundation of the modern Iraqi art movement.

*The city's Muslim shrines*

Several of the most important mosques and shrines in the Islāmic world are found in Baghdad, including the shrine of the Shī'ite imams Mūsā al-Kāẓim and Muḥammad al-Jawād, in al-Kāẓimīyah; the shrine of the Sunnite jurist Abū Ḥanīfah, in al-A'ẓamīyah; and the shrine of 'Abd al-Qādir al-Jīlānī, founder of the Qādirīyah Ṣūfī order, in Ruṣāfah. All contain libraries and are centres of Muslim pilgrimages.

All mass media are controlled by the government. Two major daily newspapers are published in Arabic, and a variety of political, cultural, and professional journals are published. English is the most widely used foreign language, but publications in European and Asian languages can be found. Radio Baghdad broadcasts to the entire country over several frequencies and in several languages. Baghdad's television station began operation in 1956.

The National Theatre, one of the best equipped in the Arab world, has a regular schedule of plays, concerts, musical productions, and cinema. The National Troupe for Popular Arts presents Iraqi dance and folklore and tours world capitals. Cinema plays an important role as a source of popular entertainment in Baghdad. The Baghdad International Fair, held annually in October, includes industrial displays, theatrical productions, and other cultural activities.

# History

## FOUNDATION AND EARLY GROWTH

Archaeological evidence shows that the site of Baghdad was occupied by various peoples long before the Arab conquest of Mesopotamia in AD 637, and several ancient empires had capitals located in the vicinity. The true founding of the city, however, dates from 762, when the site, then occupied by a Persian village called Baghdad, was selected by al-Manṣūr, the second caliph of the new 'Abbāsid dynasty, for his capital. His city, built within circular walls and called Madīnat as-Salām ("City of Peace")—and known as the Round City—was located between present-day al-Kāẓimīyah and al-Karkh. More a government complex than a residential city, it was about 3,000 yards (2,700 metres) in diameter and had three concentric walls. Its four equal quarters were used mainly to house the caliph's retinue. Four main roads led from the caliph's palace and the grand mosque at the centre to various parts of the empire.

*Baghdad's founding in 762*

The limited size of this city resulted in rapid extramural expansion. Merchants built bazaars and houses around the southern gate and formed a district called al-Karkh. From the northeast gate the Khurāsān road was joined by a bridge of boats to the east bank of the Tigris. There, around the palace of al-Manṣūr's heir apparent, al-Mahdī, grew up the three suburbs of Ruṣāfah, ash-Shammāsīyah, and al-Mukharrim, the forerunners of the modern city. By 946 the seat of the caliphate was fully established on the east bank, and Ruṣāfah grew to rival the Round City.

Baghdad reached the zenith of its economic prosperity and intellectual life in the 8th and early 9th centuries, under al-Mahdī, who reigned from 775 to 785, and his successor, Hārūn ar-Rashīd (786–809). It was then considered the richest city in the world. Its wharves were lined with ships from China, India, and East Africa. The caliph al-Ma'mūn (813–833) encouraged the translation of ancient Greek works into Arabic, founded hospitals and an observatory, and attracted poets and artisans to his capital. The glory of Baghdad in this period is reflected in stories in *The Thousand and One Nights.*

From the mid-9th century onward the 'Abbāsid caliphate was gradually weakened by internal strife, by failure of crops caused by neglect of the irrigation system, and finally, in the 10th century, by the intrusion of nomadic elements. A civil war between Hārūn ar-Rashīd's two sons resulted in destruction of much of the Round City. Between 836 and 892 the caliphs abandoned Baghdad for Sāmarrā' in the north, and the city was taken over by the unruly Turks they had imported as bodyguards. When the caliphs returned to Baghdad they made their capital on the east bank. Invasions and rule by alien elements (the Būyids from 945 to 1055 and the Turkish Seljuqs from 1055 to 1152) left parts of the city in ruins.

### CENTURIES OF DECLINE

The Mongol sack of Baghdad

This long, slow decline was merely a prelude to the devastating attacks from which Baghdad would not recover until the 20th century. In 1258 Hülegü, the Mongol conqueror, overran Mesopotamia, sacked Baghdad, killed the Caliph, and massacred hundreds of thousands of residents. He destroyed the surrounding dikes and headworks, making restoration of the irrigation system impossible and thereby destroying Baghdad's potential for future prosperity.

Thereafter Baghdad became a provincial capital, first of the Mongol emperors of Iran, the Il-Khanids (1258–1339), and then of their vassals, the Jalāyirids (1339–1410). In 1401 the city underwent yet another Mongol sack by Timur (Tamerlane), after which it fell under the sway of two successive Turkmen dynasties (1410–1508), both of which did little to restore its fortunes.

In 1508 Baghdad was temporarily incorporated into the new Persian empire created by the Ṣafavid shah Ismā'īl I. The city was not to remain under the Persians, however. In 1534 the Sunnite Ottoman sultan Süleyman I retook the city. Despite repeated Persian attacks, it remained under Ottoman rule until World War I, except for a brief period (1623–38) when it was taken and held by the Persians.

### BEGINNINGS OF MODERNIZATION

In the 19th century European influence grew in Baghdad with the establishment of French religious orders and increased European trade. In 1798 a permanent British

diplomatic residency was established there, and the British residents soon acquired a power and prestige second only to that of the governor.

Prosperity began to be restored to Baghdad with the opening of steamship travel on the Tigris in the 1860s. Between 1860 and 1914 several energetic, reforming Ottoman governors improved the city, especially Midhat Paşa. During his tenure (1869–72), he destroyed the city walls, reformed the administration, started a newspaper, and set up a modern printing press. The telegraph, military factories, and modern hospitals and schools were also established, along with a municipal council.

### THE MODERN CITY

In 1920 Baghdad became the capital of the newly created state of Iraq. Recognizing British conquest of the state in World War I, the League of Nations granted Great Britain a mandate to govern Iraq, and it did so until 1932. British influence remained dominant until 1958, when the Hashemite monarchy that Britain had helped to establish was overthrown in a military coup d'état. For a decade after 1958 Baghdad underwent a period of political turbulence, with a succession of coups and military regimes. In 1968 the Arab Socialist Ba'th Party came to power. The Ba'thist government achieved relative stability and internal development, particularly after 1973, when rises in oil prices greatly increased revenues to the government and the populace. It was in this period that Baghdad saw its greatest expansion and development. Both were curtailed, however, by the eruption in 1980 of a bitter war with neighbouring Iran.

British influence

BIBLIOGRAPHY. GUY LE STRANGE, *Baghdad During the Abbasid Caliphate* (1900, reprinted 1983), remains the standard work on the city's history to 1258. GASTON WIET, *Baghdad: Metropolis of the Abbasid Caliphate,* trans. from French (1971), is a general, more anecdotal account. A.A. DURI, "Baghdad," in *Encyclopaedia of Islam,* new ed., vol. 1 (1960), pp. 894–908, brings the history to the middle of the 20th century and includes a bibliography of original sources. A collection of scholarly articles on the history and culture of the city (in French) can be found in a special issue of *Arabica,* vol. 9 (1962). JACOB LASSNER, *The Topography of Baghdad in the Early Middle Ages* (1970), offers a detailed analysis of the city's early geography and development. ROBERT M. ADAMS, *Land Behind Baghdad: A History of Settlement on the Diyala Plains* (1965), studies the area around the city. A discussion of the architectural monuments of Baghdad, with beautiful photographs, is presented in IHSAN FATHI, *The Architectural Heritage of Baghdad* (1964); and JOHN WARREN and IHSAN FATHI, *Traditional Houses in Baghdad* (1982), is an account of domestic architecture. Modern Baghdad is sparsely covered. FREYA STARK, *Baghdad Sketches* (1937), is a personal account of life and customs, now somewhat dated. Later impressions and good photographs are found in the chapter "Baghdad" in GAVIN YOUNG, *Iraq, Land of Two Rivers* (1980), pp. 25–67; and WILLIAM ELLIS, "The New Face of Baghdad," *National Geographic,* 167 (1):80–109 (January 1985). Useful information and detailed city maps are offered in the guidebook prepared by the BAGHDAD WRITERS GROUP, *Baghdad and Beyond* (1985).

(PHEBE A. MARR/LOUAY Y. BAHRY)

# Bibliography: Recent Books

The following list encompasses some 180 recent books that have been judged significant contributions to learning and understanding in their respective fields. Each citation includes a few lines of commentary to indicate the general tenor of the work. The citations are organized by subject area, using the ten parts of the *Propædia* as an outline.

## Matter and Energy

Robert K. Adair, *The Great Design: Particles, Fields, and Creation* (1987), a readable introduction, with a minimum of mathematics, to the essential concepts of modern physics.

P.C.W. Davies and J.R. Brown, *The Ghost in the Atom: A Discussion of the Mysteries of Quantum Physics* (1986), an effective treatment of the foundations and philosophy of quantum physics based on interviews with prominent physicists.

A. Babloyantz, *Molecules, Dynamics, and Life: An Introduction to Self-Organization of Matter* (1986), a study of modern developments in the science of biologic dynamics.

Lionel Salem, *Marvels of the Molecule*, trans. from the French (1987), an authoritative brief discussion of the structure, motion, and development of molecules.

Robert S. Boikess, Kenneth Breslauer, and Edward Edelson, *Elements of Chemistry: General, Organic, and Biological* (1986), an exposition of basic aspects of chemical processes.

Donald A. McQuarrie and Peter A. Rock, *General Chemistry*, 2nd ed. (1987), a well-illustrated systematic description of chemical elements and phenomena.

Frank Close, Michael Marten, and Christine Sutton, *The Particle Explosion* (1987), a review of modern discoveries in the physics of constituent parts of atoms.

D.S. Jones, *Acoustic and Electromagnetic Waves* (1986), an exhaustive treatment of the mathematical similarities of acoustics and electromagnetism and their mutual influences.

Valerie Burkig, *Photonics, the New Science of Light* (1986), an introduction to the newest area of theoretical optics based on laser technology using the energy of photons.

Michael Zeilik and Elske v.P. Smith, *Introductory Astronomy and Astrophysics*, 2nd ed. (1987), an important survey of both traditional astronomy and modern developments in astrophysics.

Rudolf Kippenhahn, *Light from the Depth of Time* (1987; originally published in German, 1984), an expert but nonmathematical and widely accessible discussion of astronomy, theory of cosmology, and philosophy of space sciences.

John G. Burke, *Cosmic Debris: Meteorites in History* (1986), an enlightening study of the nature of meteorites and the history of their classification.

Marcia Bartusiak, *Thursday's Universe* (1986), an exploration of the present state of modern astronomy and the possibility that other worlds may exist in the superspace.

## The Earth

Anne H. Ehrlich and Paul R. Ehrlich, *Earth* (1987), an authoritative survey of the properties of our planet.

Piers Blaikie and Harold Brookfield, *Land Degradation and Society* (1987), a historical and geographic study of the phenomenon.

Helen Fraquet, *Amber* (1987), an illustrated survey of both the scientific and the artistic aspects of this natural material.

Elizabeth Kay Berner and Robert A. Berner, *The Global Water Cycle: Geochemistry and Environment* (1987), a readable introductory discussion of multiple factors influencing the chemical composition of water.

Mary J. Burgis and Pat Morris, *The Natural History of Lakes* (1987), an illustrated outline of the properties of these water bodies, their origin, geography, ecology, and conservation.

Henry Stommel, *A View of the Sea: A Discussion Between a Chief Engineer and an Oceanographer About the Machinery of the Ocean Circulation* (1987), a concise exploration of oceanography and its applications, intended for the lay reader.

John E. Oliver and Rhodes W. Fairbridge (eds.), *The Encyclopedia of Climatology* (1987), a reference source on diverse aspects of climate and the effects of civilization on it.

Terence P. Scoffin, *An Introduction to Carbonate Sediments and Rocks* (1987), a comprehensive though brief survey of the specific issues of rock geology.

H.W. Menard, *Islands* (1986), a study of oceanic volcanic islands from the point of view of plate tectonic processes, excluding islands with continental structure.

H.W. Menard, *The Ocean of Truth: A Personal History of Global Tectonics* (1986), an exploration of the development of theories of plate tectonics.

Bruce A. Bolt, *Earthquakes*, rev. ed. (1987), a nonmathematical survey of the subject.

David E. Fisher, *The Birth of the Earth: A Wanderlied Through Space, Time, and the Human Imagination* (1987), a discussion of the origin of our planet and of the relevant modern theories.

Stephen Jay Gould, *Time's Arrow, Time's Cycle: Myth and Metaphor in the Discovery of Geological Time* (1987), an immensely readable interpretive study of the system of earth sciences and especially of seminal works in geology.

## Life on Earth

Lynn Margulis and Dorion Sagan, *Microcosmos: Four Billion Years of Evolution from Our Microbial Ancestors* (1986), an informative exploration of current thinking on the origins of life, beginning with microorganisms.

Lynn Margulis and Karlene V. Schwartz, *Five Kingdoms: An Illustrated Guide to the Phyla of Life on Earth*, 2nd ed. (1987), a nontechnical explanation of the classification of living organisms, with good illustrations and a bibliography.

Robert Augros and George Stanciu, *The New Biology: Discovering the Wisdom in Nature* (1987), an exposition of a novel theory of biologic unity, cooperation, and interdependence.

Niles Eldredge, *Life Pulse: Episodes from the Story of the Fossil Record* (1987), an interpretative study of the history of evolution in light of the non-Darwinian theory of punctuated equilibria.

Sergei V. Meyen, *Fundamentals of Palaeobotany* (1987), a beautifully produced and well-organized work with broad coverage.

Robert Burton, *Eggs: Nature's Perfect Package* (1987), a concise overview of embryology and reproduction for the nonspecialist.

L. Dale Van Vleck, E. John Pollak, and E.A. Branford Oltenacu, *Genetics for the Animal Sciences* (1987), a look at animal breeding and a review of the genetic research in the field.

Michael Begon and Martin Mortimer, *Population Ecology: A Unified Study of Animals and Plants*, 2nd ed. (1986), a study in evolutionary dynamics of plants and animals.

David Attenborough, *The First Eden: The Mediterranean World and Man* (1987), a beautifully illustrated historical survey of plants and animals in the area where civilization began.

Richard S. Boardman, Alan H. Cheetham, and Albert J. Rowell (eds.), *Fossil Invertebrates* (1987), an informative and well-illustrated interpretative review of invertebrate paleontology.

Vicki Pearse *et al.*, *Living Invertebrates* (1987), a splendidly illustrated monograph providing broad coverage.

Jeffrey H. Schwartz, *The Red Ape: Orang-Utans and Human Origins* (1987), a study of the morphology, physiology, and behaviour of the higher primates and their place in human evolution.

Herbert L. Roitblat, *Introduction to Comparative Cognition* (1987), a well-organized, readable review of modern research on cognition in animals.

Vernon Ahmadjian and Surindar Paracer, *Symbiosis: An Introduction to Biological Associations* (1986), a comprehensive, well-illustrated survey of broad aspects of modern biology.

Steven M. Stanley, *Extinction* (1987), a concise and clear historicobiologic account of current thinking on the mass destruction of biologic populations.

Michael Lafavore, *Radon: The Invisible Threat* (1987), an informative discussion of a significant health hazard.

James W. Moore, *The Changing Environment* (1986), an analysis of environmental problems and policies worldwide.

Lee Durrell, *State of the Ark* (1986), a readable treatment of diverse issues of environmental conservation.

Bert Bolin *et al.* (eds.), *The Greenhouse Effect, Climatic Change, and Ecosystems* (1986), an authoritative exploration of an important societal problem.

F.I. Woodward, *Climate and Plant Distribution* (1987), a concise analysis of the interdependence between vegetation and climate on Earth.

## Human Life

David Lambert, *The Field Guide to Early Man* (1987), an informative, concise introduction to human evolution.

Charles Darwin, *The Essential Darwin,* ed. by Mark Ridley (1987), excerpts from the great evolutionist's main writings.

Valerie A. Fildes, *Breasts, Bottles, and Babies: A History of Infant Feeding* (1986), a detailed study of infant feeding practices, concentrating on preindustrial Europe.

Pamela S. Eakins (ed.), *The American Way of Birth* (1986), an authoritative analysis of the sociological issues of childbirth.

Elise F. Jones *et al.* (eds.), *Teenage Pregnancy in Industrialized Countries: A Study Sponsored by the Alan Guttmacher Institute* (1986), an important comparative examination of nonmarital teenage pregnancy in 37 countries.

Lennart Nilsson and Jan Lindberg, *The Body Victorious: The Illustrated Story of Our Immune System and Other Defenses of the Human Body,* trans. from the Swedish (1987), a readable introductory survey of human immune reactions.

Solomon H. Snyder, *Drugs and the Brain* (1986), a masterly systematic exploration of psychotropic drugs and their use in the management of mental illnesses.

Alan Gartner and Tom Joe (eds.), *Images of the Disabled, Disabling Images* (1987), a collection of essays critically surveying media attitudes toward the handicapped and disabled.

*Confronting AIDS: Directions for Public Health, Health Care, and Research* (1986), an informative and well-written report by the Committee on a National Strategy for AIDS of the Institute of Medicine, American National Academy of Science.

David R. Slavitt, *Physicians Observed* (1987), an interesting journalistic work surveying the psychological aspects of physicians' professional and public image.

Vincent Mor, *Hospice Care Systems: Structure, Process, Costs, and Outcome* (1987), a comprehensive evaluation of this rapidly developing field in the delivery of special medical care.

Susan Krauss Whitbourne, *Adult Development.* 2nd ed. (1986), an analysis of adulthood as a time of continuing development, focusing on cognition, intimacy, and socialization.

Mark Snyder, *Public Appearances, Private Realities: The Psychology of Self-Monitoring* (1987), an original study of the concept of self-monitoring in social psychology.

Robert J. Sternberg and Richard K. Wagner (eds.), *Practical Intelligence: Nature and Origins of Competence in the Everyday World* (1986), a collection of essays on nonacademic manifestations of intelligence.

Don E. Hamacheck, *Encounters with the Self,* 3rd ed. (1987), a comprehensive introduction to the self-concept theory.

George L. Maddox (ed.), *The Encyclopedia of Aging* (1987), a first-of-its-kind reference work providing 500 entries on subjects related to the processes and problems of aging.

Thomas Szasz, *Insanity: The Idea and Its Consequences* (1987), a controversial book by an academic psychiatrist, revising traditional attitudes toward mental illness and its treatment.

Karen Grandstrand Gervais, *Redefining Death* (1986), an important research into ontological issues of the end of life as opposed to the biologic understanding of death.

## Human Society

Alan Chenevière, *Vanishing Tribes: The Vanishing World of Primitive Man on Earth* (1987), a magnificently illustrated photographic survey of 20 native populations facing the adversity of the modern world.

Pat Caplan (ed.), *The Cultural Construction of Sexuality* (1987), a collection of historicoanthropological studies on sexual identification in different societies.

Hillel Schwartz, *Never Satisfied: A Cultural History of Diets, Fantasies, and Fat* (1986), a comprehensive work of broad scope, both analytical and entertaining.

Michael Lesy, *The Forbidden Zone* (1987), an interesting exploration of social aspects of death and of the people who deal with it professionally.

David Lee, *Language, Children and Society: An Introduction to Linguistics and Language Development* (1986), a nontechnical introduction to state-of-the-art language science and the theory of language acquisition.

E.D. Hirsch, Jr., *Cultural Literacy: What Every American Needs to Know; With an Appendix, What Literate Americans Know* (1987), an intelligent observation in cultural anthropology.

Roger Sawyer, *Slavery in the Twentieth Century* (1986), a summary of human rights issues, addressing the problems of human exploitation throughout the world.

Joni Seager and Ann Olson, *Women in the World: An International Atlas* (1986), a skillfully researched visual and narrative overview of the status of women worldwide.

Barry D. Adam, *The Rise of a Gay and Lesbian Movement* (1987), an important work on the social history of homosexuality and gay activism.

Harold Cruse, *Plural but Equal: A Critical Study of Blacks and Minorities and America's Plural Society* (1987), an insightful if controversial examination of the civil rights movement.

David Allen (ed.), *The Cocaine Crisis* (1987), a history of the development of cocaine addiction in the West.

E.A. Wrigley, *People, Cities, and Wealth: The Transformation of Traditional Society* (1987), a comparative history of the economic development of Western Europe.

Gerald Leach *et al.*, *Energy and Growth: A Comparison of 13 Industrial and Developing Countries* (1986), a comprehensive study of the need for energy at different stages of economic development.

Thomas V. DiBacco, *Made in the U.S.A.: The History of American Business* (1987), a readable, concise survey of the specifically American type of capitalist business enterprise.

Carl H. McMillan, *Multinationals from the Second World: Growth of Foreign Investment by Soviet and East European Enterprises* (1987), a discussion of the role of multinational enterprises in international macroeconomic systems.

Edwin S. Mills, *The Burden of Government* (1986), an examination of the history of state intervention in industrial economic policies, its reasons and outcomes.

Judith Emily Gruber, *Controlling Bureaucracies: Dilemmas in Democratic Governance* (1987), a well-organized survey of political theory and practice.

Michael J. Ross, *State and Local Politics and Policy: Change and Reform* (1987), a study of different levels of government and their interaction with interest groups.

Bert Edward Park, *The Impact of Illness on World Leaders* (1986), an insightful and cautionary historical study of political leadership impaired by serious health problems.

Jenny Teichman, *Pacifism and the Just War: A Study in Applied Philosophy* (1986), an exploration of the doctrines of pacifism and just war, with a survey of the history of opinions.

Avner Cohen and Steven Lee (eds.), *Nuclear Weapons and the Future of Humanity: The Fundamental Questions* (1986), a collection of essays providing a mature consideration of the problems of disarmament and the antinuclear movement.

Eric Semler, James Benjamin, and Adam Gross, *The Language of Nuclear War: An Intelligent Citizen's Dictionary* (1987), a compendium of 1,200 alphabetically arranged definitions of a broad range of concepts and terms of modern warfare.

William H. Rehnquist, *The Supreme Court: How It Was, How It Is* (1987), an informative discussion of the mechanisms and operations of the Supreme Court, by the chief justice.

Franklin E. Zimring and Gordon Hawkins, *The Citizen's Guide to Gun Control* (1987), a significant analysis of the ongoing debate on gun control, by authoritative criminologists.

Seymour W. Itzkoff, *How We Learn to Read* (1986), a fine, balanced discussion of the reading process, addressing problems of illiteracy.

Carol Lasser (ed.), *Educating Men and Women Together: Co-education in a Changing World* (1987), a symposium on the merits of a coeducational setting in higher education.

## Art

Michael J. Parsons, *How We Understand Art: A Cognitive Developmental Account of Aesthetic Experience* (1987), a critical theory of five chronological stages in the development of understanding of aesthetic stimuli.

Brian McHale, *Postmodernistic Fiction* (1987), a study of postmodernist literature of the Americas and Western Europe.

David Perkins, *A History of Modern Poetry: Modernism and After* (1987), a well-written, comprehensive literary history with qualities of a good reference work.

Mary C. Henderson, *Theater in America: 200 Years of Plays, Players, and Productions* (1986), a comprehensive, well-written, and well-organized history with a good chronology section.

Andrey Tarkovsky, *Sculpting in Time: Reflections on the Cinema,* trans. from the Russian (1987), a successfully translated theory of filmmaking by the late Russian director.

Wilfrid Mellers, *The Masks of Orpheus: Seven Stages in the Story of European Music* (1987), a history and analysis of the societal functions of music.

John Schaefer, *New Sounds: A Listener's Guide to New Music* (1987), a clear and balanced appraisal of difficult-to-define genres or styles of modern music, with a discography.

John Musgrove (ed.), *Sir Banister Fletcher's A History of Architecture,* 19th ed. (1987), a newly rewritten classic history providing broader coverage and suggesting new approaches.

Michael Forsyth, *Auditoria: Designing for the Performing Arts* (1987), an introduction to architecture for music and concert halls and theatres, written by a musician/architect.

Antoinette Le Normand Romain *et al., Sculpture: The Adventure of Modern Sculpture in the Nineteenth and Twentieth Centuries* (1986), a richly illustrated, intelligent survey for the lay reader.

Arthur C. Danto, *The State of the Art* (1987), a wide-ranging collection of pertinent critical articles by a philosophically inclined journalist.

Karl Gerstner, *The Forms of Color: The Interaction of Visual Elements,* trans. from the German (1986), a provocative (though not quite firmly founded) illustrated exposition of a fascinating personal approach to the aesthetics of form and colour.

Kenneth Hudson, *Museums of Influence* (1987), a review of 37 prominent art museums in ten countries.

## Technology

Ahmad Y. al-Hassan and Donald R. Hill, *Islamic Technology: An Illustrated History* (1986), an authoritative study on the history of many branches of technology.

Joseph J. Corn (ed.), *Imagining Tomorrow: History, Technology, and the American Future* (1986), a thought-provoking discussion of technological futurism and its role in modern society.

Carl W. Hall, A.W. Farrall, and A.L. Rippen, *Encyclopedia of Food Engineering,* 2nd ed. (1986), a comprehensive reference work on engineering equipment and industrial facilities for production and transportation of food and food products.

David Goodman, Bernardo Sorj, and John Wilkinson, *From Farming to Biotechnology: A Theory of Agro-Industrial Development* (1987), a thorough review of the industrialization of agriculture and changes in rural societies.

Donald L. Plucknett *et al., Gene Banks and the World's Food* (1987), an authoritative examination of technology and policies concerning the creation of crop germ-plasm resources.

K.S. Fu, R.C. Gonzalez, and C.S.G. Lee, *Robotics: Control, Sensing, Vision, and Intelligence* (1987), an in-depth review of the development and uses of robots.

Andrew C. Staugaard, Jr., *Robotics and AI: An Introduction to Applied Machine Intelligence* (1987), a readable exploration of technology that makes applications of true artificial intelligence. as opposed to automation, possible and practical.

Michael Winn, *Architectronics: Revolutionary Technologies for Masterful Building Through Design* (1987), an assessment of applications of computer technology in architecture.

John Fay, *The Helicopter: History, Piloting, and How It Flies,* 4th ed. (1987), a sound, abundantly illustrated study providing a surprising amount of information in a slim volume.

Fred Howard, *Wilbur and Orville: A Biography of the Wright Brothers* (1987), a documented account of the brothers' place in the development of aeronautics.

Robert A. Edmunds, *The Prentice-Hall Encyclopedia of Information Technology* (1987), a useful reference work for a non-expert, illustrated with examples from the business world.

Ray Bonds (ed.), *The Modern U.S. War Machine: An Encyclopedia of American Military Equipment and Strategy* (1987), a well-presented, informative reference source on present-day military technology.

Martin Clifford, *The Complete Compact Disc Player* (1987), a detailed introduction to the theory and technology of digital compact disc sound recording.

Robert H. Rubman and Howard Rothman, *Future Vision: Space-Age Techniques to Save Your Sight* (1987), a nontechnical outline of developments in medical technology.

Gordon R. Woodcock, *Space Stations and Platforms* (1986), an overview of the computer technology of "buildings" for living and working in outer space.

## Religion

Amos Funkenstein, *Theology and the Scientific Imagination from the Middle Ages to the Seventeenth Century* (1986), an interpretative analysis of the methodology of scientific and religious thinking of prominent early scientists.

Isma'il R. al Fārūkī and Lois Lamyā 'al Fārūkī, *Cultural Atlas of Islam* (1986), a detailed introduction based on a phenomenological approach to the essence of the religion.

Leonardo Boff and Clodovis Boff, *Introducing Liberation Theology* (1987; originally published in Portuguese, 1986), a clear introduction to the new theology and its impact.

Arthur A. Cohen and Paul Mendes-Flohr (eds.), *Contemporary Jewish Religious Thought: Original Essays on Critical Concepts, Movements, and Beliefs* (1987), a collection of 130 short essays thoughtfully defining the concepts and issues of Judaism.

John S. Guest, *The Yezidis: A Study in Survival* (1987), a readable, well-researched account of a small. unusual, and obscure religious community.

R. Joseph Hoffmann and Gerald A. Larue (eds.), *Jesus in History and Myth* (1986), a collection of authoritative essays on the history of the Gospels.

Barbara J. MacHaffie, *Her Story: Women in Christian Tradition* (1986), a broad overview of women's position in the Christian religion from early to modern times.

Robert N. Minor (ed.), *Modern Indian Interpreters of the Bhagavadgita* (1986), a collection of articles by Indian religious scholars on modern interpretations of this Hindu scripture.

Jim Obelkevich, Lyndal Roper, and Raphael Samuel (eds.), *Disciplines of Faith: Studies in Religion, Politics, and Patriarchy* (1987), a collection of 35 substantial articles exploring religious influences in modern society.

Stuart E. Rosenberg, *The Christian Problem: A Jewish View* (1986), a readable work of excellent scholarship, by a rabbi and leader in interfaith activity.

Gershom Scholem, *Origins of the Kabbalah,* ed. by R.J. Zwi Werblowsky (1987; originally published in German, 1962), a posthumous scholarly work by an eminent authority on the mystic tradition that originated in the 12th century.

Keith Ward, *Images of Eternity: Concepts of God in Five Religious Traditions* (1987), a study of doctrines of preeminent authorities in Hinduism, Buddhism, Islam, Judaism, and Christianity.

Robert E. Webber, *The Church in the World: Opposition, Tension, or Transformation* (1986), an interpretative critical study of evangelical social ethics.

## The History of Mankind

Tjeerd H. Van Andel and Curtis Runnels, *Beyond the Acropolis: A Rural Greek Past* (1987), a history of a rural location from the Paleolithic Period to the present.

Malcolm Todd, *The Northern Barbarians, 100 BC–AD 300*, 2nd ed. (1987), a history of Early Germanic peoples supported by substantial archaeological evidence.

W.S. Hanson, *Agricola and the Conquest of the North* (1987), an exploration of the Romans' advance to the north and the Roman period of British history.

Robert B. Coote and Keith Whitelam, *The Emergence of Early Israel in Historical Perspective* (1987), a panorama of biblical times.

T.W. Potter, *Roman Italy* (1987), an examination of Roman antiquity to the time of the decline of Roman Italy.

Derick S. Thomson (ed.), *The Companion to Gaelic Scotland* (1987), an exploration of Celtic cultural and social history from the early 6th century to the present.

Katharine Scherman, *The Birth of France: Warriors, Bishops. and Long-Haired Kings* (1987), an informative detailed survey of early French history and culture.

Jonathan Riley-Smith, *The Crusades: A Short History* (1987), a concise study of seven centuries of the Crusades.

Stephen Haliczer (ed. and trans.), *Inquisition and Society in Early Modern Europe* (1987), an authoritative collection of works on the Spanish, Portuguese, and Roman inquisitions.

John Day, *The Medieval Market Economy* (1987), a symposium of essays on the economic history of medieval Europe.

Robert Crummey, *The Formation of Muscovy, 1304–1613* (1987), an informative history touching upon Russian monarchy, religion, economy, life-styles, foreign relations, and culture.

David Morgan, *The Mongols* (1986), a thorough description of the Mongol Empire and its influence.

Simon Schama, *The Embarrassment of Riches: An Interpretation of Dutch Culture in the Golden Age* (1987), a clear, well-illustrated history of the emergence of The Netherlands as a cultural and political entity.

Jonathan Wylie, *The Faroe Islands: Interpretations of History* (1987), scholarly research on a specific European cultural group from the 17th to the beginning of the 20th century.

T.C. Smout, *A Century of the Scottish People, 1830–1950* (1986), a valuable history of the rural and industrial working class.

A.G. Jamieson (ed.), *A People of the Sea: The Maritime History of the Channel Islands* (1986), a collection of definitive essays based on archival research conducted throughout Europe.

Haim Gerber, *The Social Origins of the Modern Middle East* (1987), a search for sociopolitical origins of the modern Middle Eastern states in the history of the former Ottoman Empire.

Peter Hulme, *Colonial Encounters: Europe and the Native Caribbean, 1492–1797* (1986), a history of the colonization of Amerindian cultures.

Brian W. Ilbery, *Western Europe: A Systematic Human Geography*, 2nd ed. (1986), a concise, up-to-date work with an overview of modern economic developments.

Mark Frankland, *The Sixth Continent: Russia and Mikhail Gorbachev* (1987), an exploration of some newer developments and their older roots.

Cameron Ross, *Local Government in the Soviet Union: Problems of Implementation and Control* (1987), a study of deep structural problems in a society said to be undergoing substantial changes.

Frederic Spotts and Theodor Wieser, *Italy, a Difficult Democracy: A Survey of Italian Politics* (1986), a coherent explanation of the complicated political system of contemporary Italy.

Barbara Jelavich, *Modern Austria: Empire and Republic, 1815–1986* (1987), a balanced analysis of the shrinking of the former empire into a national state.

John Ardagh, *Germany and the Germans* (1987), a multifaceted social and cultural history.

Howard M. Sachar, *A History of Israel: From the Aftermath of the Yom Kippur War* (1987), a comprehensive history of the sovereign state.

James G. Abourezk and Hyman Bookbinder, *Through Different Eyes: An American Debate over Middle Eastern Policy* (1987), an open-ended debate between two authors representing different opinions on the Arab-Israeli situation.

Jack W. Hopkins, *Latin America: Perspectives on a Region* (1987), a readable, informative account of developments in religion, culture, education, defense, and other spheres.

Mónica Peralta-Ramos and Carlos H. Waisman (eds.), *From Military Rule to Liberal Democracy in Argentina* (1987), a study of the democratic developments and their future.

Charles F. Keyes, *Thailand, Buddhist Kingdom as Modern Nation-State* (1987), an introductory analysis of the society with emphasis on its minorities.

Mikiso Hane, *Modern Japan: A Historical Survey* (1986), an excellent history of the last 150 years.

John Sender and Sheila Smith, *The Development of Capitalism in Africa* (1986), an economic history of the continent.

Martin Murray, *South Africa: Time of Agony, Time of Destiny: The Upsurge of Popular Protest* (1987), an examination of political events and economic developments in the area.

C.O.C. Amate, *Inside the OAU: Pan-Africanism in Practice* (1986), an impressive description of the Organization of African Unity and an analysis of its activities.

## The Branches of Knowledge

Philip J. Davis and David Park (eds.), *No Way: The Nature of the Impossible* (1987), a collection of imaginative articles on the nature of creativity within scientific disciplines.

Rudy Rucker, *Mind Tools: The Five Levels of Mathematical Reality* (1987), an outline of recent mathematical research in the theory of information.

Masud Mansuripur, *Introduction to Information Theory* (1987), a discussion of state-of-the-art information theory.

Robert Mortimer Gascoigne, *A Chronology of the History of Science, 1450–1900* (1987), a balanced, readable reference source on 1,000 major scientists.

Margaret Alic, *Hypatia's Heritage: A History of Women in Science from Antiquity to the Late Nineteenth Century* (1986), a study of the role of women as a social group in the development of science.

Dorothy Nelkin, *Selling Science: How the Press Covers Science and Technology* (1987), a well-documented critique of science writing and reporting.

Clifford M. Will, *Was Einstein Right?: Putting General Relativity to the Test* (1986), a nontechnical discussion of experimental testing of the theory of relativity.

Gerrit L. Verschuur, *The Invisible Universe Revealed: The Story of Radio Astronomy* (1987), an informative, well-illustrated history.

Ronald B. Parker, *The Tenth Muse: The Pursuit of Earth Science* (1986), an appreciative account of geology—its achievements and its personalities.

Jon Franklin, *Molecules of the Mind: The Brave New Science of Molecular Psychology* (1987), a clear, nontechnical exploration of the molecular nature of behaviour control.

Rainer Born (ed.), *Artificial Intelligence: The Case Against* (1987), an interdisciplinary study of the philosophy and perspectives of artificial intelligence.

Eugene C. Hargrove (ed.), *Beyond Spaceship Earth: Environmental Ethics and the Solar System* (1986), a consideration of moral issues in space exploration.

Richard Rhodes, *The Making of the Atomic Bomb* (1986), an accomplished history of the scientific achievement and its social and political outcome.

Kenneth Baynes, James Bohman, and Thomas McCarthy (eds.), *After Philosophy: End or Transformation?* (1987), a collection of representative essays by American, German, and French philosophers illustrating contemporary philosophical debate.

D.W. Hamlyn, *A History of Western Philosophy* (1987), a broad exposition of an impressive range of human thought.

# People of 1987

## BIOGRAPHIES

### Arias Sánchez, Oscar

For his "outstanding contribution to the possible return of stability and peace" to war-torn Central America, judges awarded the 1987 Nobel Peace Prize to Oscar Arias Sánchez, president of Costa Rica. His nomination for the prize was late, and he had been considered an outside bet in a group of 93 candidates. In designing a regional peace settlement to which the heads of state of Costa Rica, El Salvador, Guatemala, Honduras, and Nicaragua felt able to commit themselves, Arias achieved what had seemed impossible.

The "Arias Plan" was launched on Feb. 15, 1987, at a meeting arranged by Arias for the presidents of El Salvador, Guatemala, and Honduras. The meeting culminated in a list of proposals that were refreshingly evenhanded. This success was the first of many tributes to the Costa Rican president's powers of persuasion, powers that were to be fully tested both before and after the formal signing of the 11-point plan at Guatemala City on August 7. Although major steps toward compliance were taken, notably by Nicaragua, before the stipulated November 7 deadline, an extension to Jan. 7, 1988, was deemed necessary for full compliance.

Born on Sept. 13, 1941, and educated at the London School of Economics and the University of Essex, Colchester, England, Arias won international admiration for his rigorously intellectual and democratic methods. His tireless efforts for regional reconciliation began when he became president-elect of Costa Rica in February 1986; at that time, to the annoyance of the U.S., he refused to allow Nicaraguan *contra* forces to operate on Costa Rican territory. His first act as president was to convene a summit of the ten Latin-American heads of state attending his inauguration in May 1986 to discuss peace proposals. His exhortations to Nicaragua to restore press freedom and talk to the *contras* played an essential role in maintaining momentum after the accord was signed. On Sept. 22, 1987, his address to the U.S. Congress, "Give

SYGMA

peace a chance," warned that continued support for the *contras* could destroy the peace process and astutely placed the ball in the U.S.'s court before the eyes of the world.

Because the Nobel Peace Prize was announced before the November 7 deadline set for the peace plan to take full effect, the award was criticized by U.S. hard-liners as one designed to affect events. Costa Ricans were jubilant, however, and regarded the prize as international recognition of their nation's peace-loving, democratic tradition. (JANET KRENGEL)

### Atwood, Margaret Eleanor

Margaret Atwood became a writer because that was what she wanted to do. Finding satisfaction in writing both novels and poetry, Atwood compared novels to marathons, poems to short sprints. Appropriately, she won the Canadian Governor General's Award for both: for poetry with *The Circle Game* (1966) and for fiction with *The Handmaid's Tale* (1986). In 1982 Atwood won the Welsh Arts Council's International Writer's Prize as a general recognition of her work, and in 1984 she was the first Canadian chosen by the West German Arts Council to participate in its program for foreign artists.

Born Nov. 18, 1939, in Ottawa, Margaret Eleanor Atwood was attracted as a young reader to fairy tales and children's classics. As a writer, she made children's books one outlet for her talent because in them she found room for play. Atwood first published her poems when she was 19. Her first book of poetry, *Double Persephone*, was published in 1961. Educated at the University of Toronto (B.A., 1961) and at Radcliffe College (M.A., 1962), Atwood also did graduate study at Harvard (1962–63, 1965–67). Between 1964 and 1972, she taught English literature at several Canadian universities, and during 1972–73 she was writer in residence at the University of Toronto. Atwood originally prepared *Survival: A Thematic Guide to Canadian Literature* (1972) as the first introductory text on the subject. To her amazement, the book generated considerable critical controversy, as well as setting exceptional sales records.

Atwood's first novel, *The Edible Woman*, was written in 1965, but it was not published until 1969 because the author thought it too daring to be enjoyed by many readers. Once it was published, it became an international success. *Surfacing* (1972) and *Lady Oracle* (1976) had as a theme "growing up female in the 1950s," and *Life Before Man* (1979) dealt with what it meant to be a female in a time of sexual role upheaval. Such novels caused critics to label Atwood a writer of feminist-oriented fiction. The author was quick to respond that she had begun writing before the women's liberation movement was launched.

Atwood's books of poetry, notably *Power Politics* (1971) and *You Are Happy* (1974), were well received by critics.

From 1971 to 1973 Atwood was an editor and member of the board of directors of the House of Anansi Press. She was vice-chairman of the Writers' Union of Canada (1980–81). Outside the literary world, she was a member of Amnesty International and a member of the board of directors of the Canadian Civil Liberties Association (1973–75). (DIANE LOIS WAY)

### Baker, Howard

In 1987 Howard Baker came within 54 steps of the U.S. presidency. That was the distance that separated the desk of new Chief of Staff Baker from the Oval Office—a room he had long wanted to call his own. Scotching plans for a run at the 1988 Republican presidential nomination, Baker took on the chief of staff's job to help Pres. Ronald Reagan tackle the worst problems of his presidency: the Iran-*contra* affair, a suddenly uncertain economy, and an intransigent Congress. In the first big test, however, Baker's renowned negotiating skills and knowledge of the U.S. Senate could not prevent the defeat of Reagan's Supreme Court nominee Robert Bork (*q.v.*).

In the words of his stepmother, Baker was "like the Tennessee River. He flows right down the middle." Representing Tennessee in the Senate from 1966 to 1985, Baker became effective in Washington with his pragmatism and moderate politics. As Senate majority leader during the early 1980s, he united the warring wings of his party behind Reagan's tax and budget agenda. As minority leader in the late 1970s, Baker fought for some of Pres. Jimmy Carter's policies, most notably the Democrat's Panama Canal treaties. Baker's support for that issue enraged Republican conservatives, some of whom were still angry with him for his sharp and persistent questioning of aides of Pres. Richard Nixon during the Watergate hearings in 1973.

A reputation for statesmanship was not enough to win Baker the White House, however. One of nine candidates for the 1980 Republican presidential nomination, he dropped out after gaining only nine delegates in four months of campaigning. Four years earlier the party had rebuffed his bid to be Pres. Gerald R. Ford's running mate. In each case the Republican right wing helped ensure Baker's defeat.

Baker entered the Republican Party on Nov. 15, 1925—the day he was born in Huntsville, Tenn. His staunchly Republican family included a grandmother who was a sheriff and a father who would serve in the U.S. House of Representatives from 1951 to 1964. Young Baker majored in engineering before serving in the Navy during World War II; after the war he entered law school. After graduation he practiced criminal and corporate law and made a fortune on investments. In 1964, campaigning in Tennessee against foreign aid and the Civil Rights Act, Baker lost his first try for a U.S. Senate seat. Running again in 1966, he moderated his politics and became the first popularly elected Republican U.S. senator in the state's history. (MICHAEL AMEDEO)

### Bakker, Jim and Tammy

"Why shouldn't people who love God be successful?" the Rev. Jim Bakker once asked. He had time to answer that question himself after March 19, 1987, the day he resigned as head of the PTL ("Praise the Lord" or "People That Love") television ministry following revelations of adultery with a church secretary and of bribery with church funds. (*See* RELIGION: *Special Report.*) Standing by her man through the scandal was Jim's wife, Tammy, the tiny, bejeweled gospel singer who marketed her own line of cosmetics and published tips on how wives could look sexy and still remain Christian. The Bakkers' fall from grace ended 26 years of phenomenal success, during which time they built a religious broadcasting and entertainment business worth $175 million.

James Orsen Bakker was born in Muskegon, Mich., on Jan. 2, 1940. Raised in the Assemblies of God church, in 1959 he entered North Central Bible College in Minneapolis, Minn. There he met Tammy Faye LaValley, from International Falls, Minn. The two married in 1961, left college, and worked as itinerant preachers in the South. Jim was ordained a minister of the Assemblies of God in 1964. In 1965 the Bakkers joined Pat Robertson's Christian Broadcasting Network, producing "The Jim and Tammy Show" for children and acting as cohosts for "The 700 Club" talk show. In 1973 they helped found a religious network in California, and in 1974 they moved to Charlotte, N.C., to found the PTL Television Network.

The new "Jim and Tammy Show" featured inspirational music, interviews with born-again celebrities, and phone-in prayer and counseling. Frequently weeping on camera, at times even airing their marital difficulties, the Bakkers endeared themselves to their audience as a down-to-earth Christian couple. Donations poured in, and PTL grew from one local station into a network reaching more than 13 million viewers by cable and satellite. In 1978 PTL began construction on Heritage USA, a religious theme park that drew six million visitors in 1986.

Central to the Bakkers' Pentecostal faith were the gifts of the Holy Spirit, such as prophecy, healing, and speaking in tongues. Another gift, they insisted, was a material prosperity that would come to all true believers—especially those who donated to evangelizing ministries. As viewers responded, the Bakkers' standard of living rose conspicuously. In April 1987 the new board of directors of PTL cut off payments to the couple, claiming that their salaries and bonuses for 1986 had totaled $1.6 million and that they had enjoyed such church-bought amenities as luxury automobiles and four homes (one with gold-plated bathroom fixtures and another with an air-conditioned doghouse). In the wake of the scandal, Jim Bakker was defrocked by the Assemblies of God. Claiming that they were innocent, the Bakkers vowed that they would rise again in a new ministry. (ROBERT CURLEY)

**Barbie, Klaus**
It took a jury only about six hours to find Klaus Barbie, known as the "Butcher of Lyon," guilty on July 4, 1987, of committing "crimes against humanity" during World War II. Barbie was chief of the Gestapo in the French city of Lyon when he committed the crimes: the murder and torture of French Resistance fighters and the persecution of French Jews. This was Barbie's third trial—he had been sentenced to death in absentia in two earlier ones. It was held in Lyon and lasted nearly eight weeks, but Barbie withdrew on the third day on the grounds that he had been "kidnapped" from Bolivia, where he had lived as a businessman from 1951 until 1983 under the name of Klaus Altmann. Just before the jury retired, Barbie returned to the court and made a short speech in which he protested his innocence: "I fought the Resistance which I respected, as hard as I could, but it was war; and the war is over." His plea was to no avail. He was convicted on all charges with no extenuating circumstances and sentenced to life imprisonment. His response was, "It's unbelievable."

Barbie was born on Oct. 25, 1913, in Bad Godesberg near Bonn, Germany. In 1935 he joined the SS (Schutzstaffel, the black-shirted elite guard of the Nazi party). Two years later, as a member of the Nazi party, he was sent to The Hague, Neth., as a full lieutenant and then on to Amsterdam, where he allegedly helped to deport about 300 Dutch Jews to a concentration camp in Austria. Between November 1942 and August 1944 he commanded the SS in Lyon, which was the capital of the French Resistance and a centre for Jews fleeing the Nazis. During

this period he committed the three major crimes of which he was convicted in 1987. In February 1943 he was involved in the deportation of at least 76 Jews to concentration camps; in April 1944 he deported 44 Jewish children and 7 Jewish teachers from the village of Izieu; and in August 1944 he sent 650 Jews and Resistance fighters to concentration camps. In June 1943 he was alleged to have tortured to death the Resistance hero Jean Moulin, and it was possible that he would be subjected to a fourth trial on this charge if it could be reclassified as a crime against humanity rather than a war crime, for which prosecution must take place within 20 years under French law. In the postwar period (1947–51) Barbie worked for U.S counterintelligence, which later assisted his escape to Bolivia. Barbie's third trial followed more than four years of debate within the French judiciary as to the crimes for which he could be tried. The verdict was widely expected and approved—with only Barbie himself expressing surprise that he should be found guilty.

(JANET H. CLARK; K. M. SMOGORZEWSKI)

**Bednorz, Johannes Georg**
When the Royal Swedish Academy of Sciences announced the 1987 Nobel Prize for Physics, it admitted that the award might have been the quickest Nobel ever given. Less than two years after the prizewinning breakthrough was made, Johannes Bednorz of West Germany and Karl Alexander Müller (q.v.) of Switzerland were honoured for their discovery of high-temperature superconductivity in oxide ceramic materials. In addition, because the two laureates both worked at the IBM Zürich Research Laboratory, 1987 became the second consecutive year in which scientists from that facility took the Nobel for physics. (Gerd Binnig and Heinrich Rohrer of IBM shared half the 1986 prize for their invention of the scanning tunneling microscope.)

A material is superconducting if it abruptly loses all electrical resistance when cooled below a characteristic temperature, called the transition temperature, which is generally hundreds of degrees below 0° C (32° F). The conventional theory of superconductivity appears to limit transition temperatures to such cold extremes. Indeed, the highest transition temperature found in the "classic" superconductors—generally metals and alloys—was 23.3 K (kelvins; approximately −250° C [−418° F]), observed in the 1970s. In 1983 Bednorz and Müller began a systematic search in an entirely different class of materials—oxides of nickel and copper—and by early 1986 they had succeeded in raising the transition temperature of a barium-lanthanum-copper oxide to 35 K, about 12° higher than the previous record.

Bednorz was born in West Germany on May 16, 1950. He graduated from the University of

ERMA/CAMERA PRESS/PHOTO TRENDS

Münster in 1976 and received his Ph.D. from the Swiss Federal Institute of Technology in Zürich in 1982. He then joined the IBM Zürich laboratory, where he was recruited into the study of superconductivity by Müller, a specialist in oxides.

Scientists were as yet unable to explain the mechanism of high-temperature superconductivity. Nevertheless, not long after Bednorz and Müller's groundbreaking work appeared in print, other researchers succeeded in finding related ceramic materials whose transition temperatures approached 100 K (about −173° C [−279.4° F])—high enough to be achieved with refrigeration using liquid nitrogen, which is cheaper and easier to handle than the liquid helium needed to cool conventional superconductors. Thus, for the first time, superconductors had a real chance to lend themselves to practical applications, including the manufacture of generators and power lines of unprecedented efficiency, tiny supercomputers, and high-speed trains that ride on a magnetic cushion.

(CAROLYN D. NEWTON)

**Ben Ali, Zine al-Abidine**
In a remarkably peaceful coup, engineered to make it constitutional, on Nov. 7, 1987, Gen. Zine al-Abidine Ben Ali took over the Tunisian presidency from Habib Bourguiba, who was declared medically unfit to rule. Ben Ali had been regarded as Bourguiba's most suitable successor for some time—a view endorsed by Bourguiba himself, as reflected in his appointment of Ben Ali as his prime minister in early October. Since April 1986 Ben Ali had been interior minister, and it was his role in cracking down on the Islamic fundamentalists that won him presidential approval. Ben Ali's military background and experience earned him a reputation as a hard-liner capable of establishing law and order. He demonstrated this ability while serving national security during the January 1978 riots and later after the 1984 bread riots.

Ben Ali was born on Sept. 3, 1936, near Sousse in central Tunisia. He was a professional soldier trained at the French military academy of Saint-Cyr and at the prestigious artillery school at Châlons-sur-Marne. His education was completed in the U.S., where he studied electronic engineering. He was head of military security (1958–74), a post that brought him into the leading government circles in Tunis. In 1974 Ben Ali started a three-year term as military attaché to Morocco. He returned to become head of national security under the Nouira government, and in April 1980 he became Tunisian ambassador in Warsaw.

Returning to Tunis in October 1984, Ben Ali was appointed state secretary for national security and, a year later, a Cabinet minister. His widespread support derived from his active role in rooting out the violent fundamentalist Islamic Tendency Movement, which opposed the government and in August 1987 had planted bombs in tourist resorts. Although Ben Ali and Bourguiba both strongly opposed the religious extremists, Ben Ali believed in a more moderate approach; it was Bourguiba's decision to reopen the recently ended trial of 90 Islamic fundamentalists that prompted the coup. Ben Ali's promise to revise the constitution to eliminate the president's role for life, and to liberate the political system to permit an active role for most opposition parties in state affairs, was an important factor in his popular appeal. No elections were promised, however.

(GEORGE JOFFÉ)

**Billington, James Hadley**
In April 1987 James Hadley Billington was appointed by U.S. Pres. Ronald Reagan to become the nation's 13th librarian of Congress. The long-expected nomination occurred while Billington, a scholar specializing in Russian studies, who had frequently consulted with Reagan regarding the Soviet Union, was traveling in Moscow. At the specific time of the announcement, he was studying some mosaics on the wall of the Moscow subway in the midst of

the city's typically frantic rush hour. Named to succeed Daniel J. Boorstin, the new appointee seemed a particularly appropriate choice at a time when the United States was trying to expand its relations with the Soviet Union.

The librarian of Congress is a position as deeply rooted in America's intellectual tradition as was Billington. Formerly the director of the Woodrow Wilson International Center for Scholars, with an office at the Smithsonian Institution, Washington, D.C., Billington had long devoted himself to scholarly pursuits. The Library of Congress plays an important role in preserving the printed word and has always been a repository for the nation's literature, art, and music.

Billington was born in Bryn Mawr, Pa., on June 1, 1929. Although his parents did not attend college, he grew up in a home filled with books and a deep love of learning. After receiving a B.A. degree from Princeton University, he went to the University of Oxford and gained a doctorate from Balliol College, where he was a Rhodes scholar. After serving in the U.S. Army, he taught history at Harvard University and then at Princeton. He published a study of Russian culture entitled *The Icon and the Axe.*

Billington clearly greeted his appointment to the $85,500 job with enthusiasm. He referred to the "glory of this extraordinary facility" and defined the distinguished library's role: "In a general way, the possibilities of the library involve maintaining, enhancing and celebrating this extraordinary collection of human memory. It's a question of bringing out the music that's already there." Sworn in on September 15 by Chief Justice William Rehnquist, Billington reiterated his feelings about the library's role and destiny, describing it as "not just a mausoleum for culture, but a catalyst for civilization."

(BONNIE OBERMAN)

### Bloom, Allan

In one of the year's most talked-about books, *The Closing of the American Mind,* Allan Bloom, a professor of philosophy at the University of Chicago, argued that universities no longer taught students how to think, that those who sought a truly liberal education were unable to get one, and that history or the examination of ideas in a historical context no longer seemed relevant. Bloom's subtitle, *How Higher Education Has Failed Democracy and Impoverished the Souls of Today's Students,* directly states his thesis.

Bloom was born in Indianapolis, Ind., on Sept. 14, 1930. Self-described as an American Jewish kid who was fortunate to grow up with an awareness of history and the great philosophers, Bloom worried about today's students neither knowing nor caring about the lessons of the past or about the self-discovery that is possible through worthwhile and significant literature. He bemoaned contemporary society's apparent lack of desire or capacity to understand itself—either collectively or as individuals.

In addition to being a professor in the Committee on Social Thought, Bloom served as codirector of the University of Chicago's John M. Olin Center for Inquiry into the Theory and Practice of Democracy. He had also taught at Yale University and at Cornell University, Ithaca, N.Y., as well as the Universities of Toronto, Tel Aviv, and Paris. Given his background in philosophy and education, it was not surprising that this 56-year-old professor, best known for his translations of Jean-Jacques Rousseau's *Émile* and Plato's *Republic,* should feel an obligation to express his concerns. Said Bloom: "These great universities, which can split the atom, find cures for the most terrible disease, conduct surveys of whole populations and produce massive dictionaries of lost languages—cannot generate a modest program of general education for undergraduate students."

Bloom focused much of his book on his students, sadly characterizing them as self-centred nonreaders who seemed to live only for the moment. Although he shared his views of why higher education had reached such a sorry state,

he was not as interested in offering solutions as he was in provoking true soul-searching dialogue—not only between himself and the book's readers but also, more importantly, between educators and their students in order to promote inquiry and introspection. Bloom labeled the whole situation a crisis. If the attention accorded his book indicated that at least some portion of society agreed, perhaps he would be responsible for initiating the reform he so clearly desired.

(BONNIE OBERMAN)

### Bork, Robert Heron

On July 1, 1987, when he accepted Pres. Ronald Reagan's offer of the seat of associate justice of the U.S. Supreme Court, Robert Bork set off the most ferocious confirmation battle in the 200-year history of the Constitution. Passions flared especially hot because Bork, an appellate court judge and former law professor who was the premier proponent of "judicial restraint," would be the conservative tiebreaker on a bench evenly divided between liberals and conservatives. At stake were rulings on such contentious issues as abortion, censorship, and affirmative action.

Born in Pittsburgh, Pa., on March 1, 1927, Robert Heron Bork earned both his bachelor's and jurisprudence degrees (in 1948 and 1953, respectively) at the University of Chicago, punctuating his education with two hitches in the U.S. Marine Corps. After working for a large law firm in Chicago as a specialist in antitrust law, in 1962 he began a career teaching antitrust and constitutional law at Yale University. There he developed his doctrine of original intent, or intentionalism. According to this doctrine, courts can protect only those liberties that are guaranteed as rights under the Constitution; all other liberties are subject to limitation by the legislatures. In deciding which liberties are constitutional rights, courts must often be guided by the "original intent" of the document's framers. For example, the 14th Amendment was intended to grant equal protection under the laws to black citizens; therefore, Bork argued, it cannot be used to approve or mandate affirmative action programs for women. Likewise, judicial decisions allowing abortion and pornography or the advocacy of violence are "unprincipled," as they create new rights of privacy and free speech that are not mentioned in the Constitution and were never intended to be protected.

Bork's conservative views caught the attention of Pres. Richard Nixon, who appointed him solicitor general at the U.S. Department of Justice in 1973. Late that year, under order of the president and at the request of the attorney general (who had resigned in protest against the order), he fired special prosecutor Archibald Cox at a crucial stage of the Watergate investigation. In 1977 Bork returned to Yale, but in 1981 he left for private practice in Washington, D.C. The next year Reagan appointed him to the U.S. Court of Appeals, District of Columbia Circuit.

During Senate confirmation hearings in September 1987, Bork's opponents, stymied by his professional competence, focused on his judicial temperament, contending that he was a dogmatic radical who was insensitive to the concerns of minorities. The Senate agreed, refusing to confirm his nomination on October 23 by a vote of 58 to 42.    (ROBERT CURLEY)

### Brodsky, Joseph

Forty-seven-year-old Joseph Brodsky, involuntarily exiled from the Soviet Union in 1972, seven years after serving a year and a half in a labour camp charged with "social parasitism," won the 1987 Nobel Prize for Literature. Regarded by many throughout the world as the greatest living Russian poet, Brodsky, a U.S. citizen since 1977, called the award (worth $330,000 in prize money) "a big step for me, a small one for mankind. . . . Life has a great deal up its sleeve." He was the second youngest person to receive the literature prize (in 1957 Albert Camus was the winner at the age of 44).

Born Iosip Aleksandrovich Brodsky to Jewish parents on May 24, 1940, the poet grew up

in a modest Leningrad apartment shared with other families. A high-school dropout who then took a variety of jobs as a labourer, he was self-taught in Polish and English. At age 24 he was sent to the Gulag but still found time to write poetry. Although Brodsky was not a political dissident, his trouble with Soviet authorities continued after his release, and in 1972 he was exiled. His trial had been well publicized, and he had become widely recognized in the West.

His first major collection of poems translated into English was published in 1973 (*Selected Poems*), the second in 1980 (*A Part of Speech*). He won the 1986 U.S. National Book Critics Circle Award in criticism for *Less Than One,* a volume of essays. A volume of poems, *History of the Twentieth Century,* also published in 1986, was cited by the Nobel committee for "amazing mastery of the English idiom." Currently living in New York City and teaching part of the year at Mount Holyoke College, South Hadley, Mass., he hoped that the award would lead to the legal publication of more of his poetry in his homeland and, more importantly, that he might get to see his 20-year-old son, Andrey, whom he last saw when the boy was 5.

The Nobel Committee cited Brodsky's essays and poetry, honouring him "for an all-embracing authorship, imbued with clarity of thought and poetic intensity." Others, upon hearing of the award, discussed the poet's preoccupation with the fate of civilization and the fragility of human achievement. Brodsky considered classical Russian, modern Polish, and English metaphysical poetry as major influences on his work, pointing also to Marcel Proust, John Donne, W. H. Auden, and Robert Lowell, as well as William Faulkner and Herman Melville. His work emphasized the role of the poet, through whose language people are able to affirm their common needs and desires and their humanity.

(BONNIE OBERMAN)

### Buyoya, Pierre

On Sept. 3, 1987, an unknown army officer, Maj. Pierre Buyoya, seized power in Burundi in a bloodless coup when the head of state, Col. Jean-Baptiste Bagaza, was attending a conference of heads of state of French-speaking nations in Quebec. The reasons Buyoya advanced for the coup were almost identical to those that had been advanced by Bagaza when he overthrew Burundi's first president, Michel Micombero, in 1976. Buyoya denounced the speculation, corruption, and fraud of the Bagaza regime and promised to respect human rights, religious freedom, and constitutional government. His immediate aim was to bring to an end the struggle that had been taking place for some time between the state and the Roman Catholic Church. He promised that his regime would be more liberal than that of his predecessor and that it would be relaxed in its approach to tribal, religious, and political policies.

In his takeover speech immediately after the coup, Buyoya said that those who had plotted the coup—which appeared to have been instigated solely by the military—had objected to the acquisition of too much power by one person. Bagaza had been head of state, chief of the armed forces, and leader of the ruling party, Uprona. Buyoya also condemned the institutional inertia, the "constant violation of the constitution," and the "incoherent" economic policy of his predecessor's regime. He promised religious freedom for all and immediately reopened Roman Catholic places of worship that had been closed down during the church-state row of the preceding year.

Reported to be about 38 years of age, Buyoya belonged to the same Tutsi group as both his predecessors. The Tutsi, who made up some 15% of the population, had dominated the majority Hutu people since independence. Buyoya trained as an army officer in Belgium and studied in both France and West Germany. He was pro-Western in attitude and was expected to court the International Monetary Fund in an effort to improve the country's financial status. After the coup Buyoya became chairman of the

31-member Military Committee for National Salvation, which on September 9 appointed him president of Burundi. His meeting in Zaire the following day with the presidents of neighbouring Zaire and Rwanda had the effect of conferring a certain legitimacy on the new regime.

(GUY ARNOLD)

## Camdessus, Michel

The appointment on Dec. 18, 1986, of Michel Camdessus as the new managing director of the International Monetary Fund (IMF), to take effect from Jan. 16, 1987, followed what was described as the first open contest for the job in the IMF's 42-year history. He replaced Jacques de Larosière, who had held the post since 1978 and had decided that it was appropriate to resign before his term expired in mid-1988. Although the vote for Camdessus by the 22-member executive board was unanimous, his appointment was by no means predictable. Equally likely to be chosen had been the chairman of the IMF's interim committee, The Netherlands' finance minister Hermann Onno Ruding, who had finished close behind Camdessus in a straw vote held a little earlier—at which point he withdrew.

Camdessus was born on May 1, 1933, at Bayonne, France. He studied law at Notre Dame College in Paris and in 1960 began his career as a civil servant in the Treasury. In 1966 he moved to Brussels, where he spent three years as France's financial attaché to the European Economic Community. He returned to the Treasury in 1969 and in 1974 was made deputy director, a position he held until 1982, when he took over the directorship. Simultaneously (1978–84) he was chairman of the "Paris Club," the medium for multilateral debt negotiations. In 1984 he left the Treasury to go to the Banque de France, where he was made governor; he remained there until 1987.

Larosière resigned because he felt that the upcoming debt negotiations would be difficult and lengthy and that a change in leadership in mid-1988 would be unwise. Camdessus faced a formidable task—to restore creditworthiness to debtor countries and improve the monetary system. New strategies were needed for coping with the changed world situation; the emergence of the U.S. as a potential recipient of emergency loans was a new factor.

In his first year of office, Camdessus made a considerable impact and did much to change the hard image of the IMF. He actively promoted the case for more funds to be made available on easy terms to the poorest countries and put considerable pressure on the seven major industrialized countries to donate funds. His campaigning proved successful, and in late December the IMF announced the establishment of an $8.4 billion fund to help the world's poorest countries. Loans were to be subsidized by the donor countries, and the move marked a distinct change in IMF strategy.

(JANET H. CLARK)

## Carlucci, Frank Charles, III

On Nov. 23, 1987, Frank Carlucci succeeded Caspar Weinberger as U.S. secretary of defense, having been nominated by Pres. Ronald Reagan on November 5 and confirmed by the Senate by a vote of 91–1 on November 20. Long associated with Weinberger, Carlucci supported the Reagan administration's policies on defensive missiles, military buildup, and support of the Nicaraguan Democratic Force. He was considered less of a hard-liner than Weinberger, however, and before taking office had secured the resignation of one of Weinberger's most vocally anti-Soviet aides. Nonpartisan and a former appointee of Pres. Jimmy Carter, Carlucci was respected as a civil servant, an administrator, and a negotiator.

Carlucci was born in Scranton, Pa., on Oct. 18, 1930. He received a B.A. from Princeton University in 1952 and became an officer in the U.S. Navy. He studied at Harvard University in 1954 and 1955 and tried several jobs in business before joining the U.S. Department of State as a foreign service officer in 1956. While serving

in the Congo (now Zaire), he used his athletic ability to rescue U.S. citizens from mobs.

In 1969 he accidentally encountered Donald Rumsfeld, whom he had known at Princeton and who was director of the Office of Economic Opportunity (OEO) in the administration of Pres. Richard Nixon, and accepted Rumsfeld's offer of a job at OEO. He succeeded Rumsfeld as director in 1970. In 1971 Carlucci became associate director of the Office of Management and Budget (OMB), and he was named deputy director in 1972. Weinberger, then director of the OMB, came to appreciate Carlucci's skills. Carlucci eventually became under secretary of health, education, and welfare—by invitation of Weinberger, who had become secretary.

Carlucci returned to the State Department in 1975 as ambassador to Portugal. He established ties with military officers who were leftist but not pro-Soviet and apparently helped them to defeat a plot by pro-Soviet officers to take over the government. In 1978 he became deputy to the director of central intelligence. Weinberger became secretary of defense in the new Reagan administration in 1981 and insisted on having Carlucci as his deputy.

From 1983 to 1986 Carlucci worked for a subsidiary of Sears, Roebuck and Co. that had been founded to negotiate international business deals. In December 1986 President Reagan appointed Carlucci as assistant for national security affairs. Carlucci reorganized and reduced the size of the staff of the National Security Council and tried to mediate rivalries between government agencies.

(CHARLES JOHNSON TAGGART)

## Checkland, Michael

Michael Checkland was appointed director general of the British Broadcasting Corporation (BBC) on Feb. 26, 1987, one month after the surprise resignation of his predecessor, Alasdair Milne. His appointment was unexpected, given his managerial background, although he had been deputy director general since July 1985. He competed with several leading broadcasters for one of the most important positions in world broadcasting. The BBC's board of governors, however, faced by a tightening economy and imminent competition from new forms of home entertainment, saw the need for the corporation to undergo a period of reconstruction and careful financial management. Asked how he foresaw the BBC's position at the end of his five-year contract, Checkland quipped, "Smaller."

Checkland was born in Birmingham on March 13, 1936, and was educated there at King Edward's School, Five Ways, and then at the University of Oxford. Although he graduated in modern history, his career began in industry with Parkinson Cowan and later Thorn Electronics, during which period he qualified as a management accountant. He joined the BBC in

1964 as senior assistant in the cost department. By 1971 he was chief accountant of BBC television, and it was in the second half of the 1970s that his organizational abilities were recognized in a series of promotions; in 1982 he became director of television resources, and in July 1985 he became deputy director general, responsible for resource management throughout the corporation.

In 1987 Checkland set about restructuring the BBC's management system. Not all the changes he made were popular, and several senior executives left; he created a new regional structure. A non-BBC man, John Birt, then director of programs at London Weekend Television, was appointed as his deputy with responsibility for overseeing nearly all the BBC's television and radio journalism. Supported by Checkland, he was committed to making BBC journalism "more rigorous." The appointment of "outsiders" to the BBC contributed to a year of upheaval. Checkland, however, was confident that the changes he was instigating would be beneficial. He achieved a reputation for better husbandry aimed at putting more of the BBC's revenue "onto the screen" than into overhead expenses, and he was sympathetic to program makers' aspirations. He was made a fellow of the Royal Television Society, the first accountant to be awarded that honour.

(PETER FIDDICK)

## Chilstrom, Herbert Walfred

The Rev. Herbert Walfred Chilstrom, former bishop of the Minnesota Synod of the Lutheran Church in America, was chosen in May 1987 to head the newly formed Evangelical Lutheran Church in America. The delegates elected their first bishop in a two-day, nine-ballot process that finally produced a leader with a reputation for openness and reconciliation, crucial personality traits for a church merger creating a new denomination with 5.3 million members. Joining forces were the Lutheran Church in America (where Chilstrom was a minister), the American Lutheran Church (where his wife, the Rev. Corinne Chilstrom, was a minister), and the Association of Evangelical Lutheran Churches. Now the fourth largest Protestant denomination in the U.S., the new church had 16,608 pastors and 11,022 congregations, representing nearly two-thirds of the country's Lutherans.

Not all of the 11,000-plus congregations were satisfied with the merger. One of Bishop Chilstrom's first challenges would be reckoning with the 800 conservative congregations who opposed the action and the 100 who were expected to withdraw. Those in the majority looked toward a greatly expanded denomination that included blacks, Hispanics, and persons of Asian descent. Historically, members of the Lutheran Church had been of German and Scandinavian descent (Chilstrom's Swedish ancestors arrived in America 130 years ago).

Chilstrom was born in Litchfield, Minn., on Oct. 18, 1931. He was a graduate of Augsburg College in Minneapolis, Minn., and Illinois' Augustana Seminary, now the Lutheran School of Theology at Chicago, and held advanced degrees from Princeton (N.J.) Seminary and New York University. Before becoming bishop of the Minnesota Synod, Chilstrom served as pastor at several Minnesota churches and was a dean and professor of biblical studies at Luther College, Teaneck, N.J. The bishop and his wife, who became an ordained minister in 1985, had two children in their 20s. A teenaged son committed suicide in 1984, a trauma the Chilstroms survived by virtue of their deep faith.

A major goal of the new denomination was to reach out to other Christian churches. The bishop was also interested in a redefined position on abortion, which he considered a "tragic option." Critics were concerned that Chilstrom would not be forceful enough to lead a major new American religious movement. The bishop, describing himself as an "evangelical conservative with a radical social conscience," planned to nurture and unify his congregations.

(BONNIE OBERMAN)

## Compaoré, Blaise

The coup that brought Capt. Blaise Compaoré to power in Burkina Faso on Oct. 15, 1987, marked the final falling out of the "four musketeers" who had led the West African state since 1983. Compaoré was a longtime friend and confidant of his predecessor as head of state, Capt. Thomas Sankara (*see* OBITUARIES), who perished during the takeover, and had previously been number two in the self-styled "revolutionary" regime. The coup was apparently precipitated by disagreements over security and other strategic issues, although Compaoré professed not to have planned it in advance and to have been devastated by the death of his friend.

A member of the Mossi, one of the dominant ethnic groups of Burkina Faso, Compaoré was born on Feb. 3, 1951, in Ouagadougou. He attended military college in Yaoundé, Cameroon, and from 1977 to 1981 served as head of section and later company commander in the paracommando regiment based at Dedougou. A brief period in charge of the national commando training centre at Po was interrupted when he was reposted in April 1982 to Bobo-Dioulasso, in the far western part of the country. Within a month, however, he was deeply embroiled in national politics, resigning from the national armed forces council when Sankara, then secretary of state for information, left the government of Saye Zerbo. A year later, when another power struggle saw Sankara put in prison, Compaoré returned to Po and, with Ghanaian and Libyan help, organized the coup that was to install Sankara as head of state in August 1983.

Personally quiet and self-effacing, Compaoré had seemed, until the events of October 1987, content to leave the public business of politics to the more charismatic Sankara and the other two "musketeers," Commandant Jean-Baptiste Lingani and Capt. Henri Zongo, both of whom were to back his seizure of power. Early indications that the new regime would be more willing to reach an accommodation with existing political parties and the traditionally strong trade union movement were quietly welcomed by conservative governments in the region, which had sometimes found Sankara's quirky revolution difficult to live with. However, Compaoré faced a difficult task in overcoming his reputation as the murderer of Sankara, who had attracted a considerable following throughout West Africa.          (NIM CASWELL)

## Conner, Dennis Walter

There were tears in Dennis Conner's eyes when his 12-m yacht *Stars & Stripes* crossed the finish line Feb. 4, 1987, and won the America's Cup back from Australia for the United States. His 3½-year battle for redemption had ended in success, but he was wistful because the battle had ended. "That was fun. I'm sorry it's over," Conner told a fellow crew member. The next America's Cup race was 3½ years away.

Conner not only had driven three boats to America's Cup victories but also had changed the rules of the game. Winning the cup was a five-month project that cost about $1.5 million before 1980, when Conner skippered *Freedom* decisively to victory after practicing for two years with two boats. In 1987, $16 million was spent on *Stars & Stripes*, $10 million of it for design research and development. The result was a four-race sweep of Australian defender *Kookaburra III* in the best-of-seven series. *Stars & Stripes* became the first 12-m racing boat in 20 years to lead its rival past every mark in every race.

Dennis Walter Conner was born Sept. 16, 1942, in San Diego, Calif. His father was a tuna fisherman, lacking a yachtsman's wealth, but young Dennis constantly pestered grownups at the San Diego Yacht Club for information and advice. He was 27 before he could afford to spend $1,700 for half ownership of his first boat. Even as he built his carpet- and drape-manufacturing company, sailing was his first interest.

Conner became recognized as the best 12-m skipper of all time, respected especially for attention to detail and mastery of wind shifts and starts. He was coskipper with Ted Hood in *Courageous*'s 1974 America's Cup victory and also won a bronze medal in the Tempest class at the 1976 Olympics. He won two Star class world championships, setting a record in 1977 when he finished first five straight times against 89 boats in Kiel, West Germany.

After 1983, however, Conner was best known as the only U.S. skipper to lose the America's Cup in 132 years. *Australia II*, featuring the technological innovation of a winged keel, beat Conner's *Liberty* in the last three races for a 4–3 victory at Newport, R.I. Conner, a tireless fund-raiser, answered the challenge with *Stars & Stripes*.

In the final challengers' round for the 1987 cup, Conner defeated the fibreglass-hulled *New Zealand,* which had won 37 of 38 previous races. Then he beat *Kookaburra III* by more than a minute in all four races at Fremantle, Western Australia. Losing skipper Iain Murray said, "I didn't see a foot put wrong in any one of the races by any one of their team."
                                   (KEVIN M. LAMB)

## Cram, Donald James

Working independently, American Donald J. Cram of the University of California at Los Angeles, French chemist Jean-Marie Lehn, and American Charles John Pedersen (*qq.v.*) succeeded in creating molecules in the laboratory that mimic the chemical and biologic behaviour typical of molecules found in living systems. For their achievement they were awarded the Nobel Prize for Chemistry in 1987.

Cram was born on April 22, 1919, in Chester, Vt. He received a bachelor's degree from Rollins College, Winter Park, Fla., in 1941 and a master's degree from the University of Nebraska in 1942. For the next three years he worked as a research chemist at Merck & Co., Inc., in New Jersey, studying the antibiotics penicillin and streptomycin. He entered Harvard University in 1945 and received his Ph.D. in organic chemistry two years later. He became assistant professor in the chemistry department of the University of California at Los Angeles in 1948 and full professor in 1956.

Cram won his share of the prize for helping extend Pedersen's ground-breaking discoveries. In his own prizewinning work Pedersen synthesized a group of organic compounds that he dubbed crown ethers—essentially two-dimensional, ring-shaped molecules that are able to recognize and combine selectively with atoms of certain metal elements, much as natural substances do with specific atoms and molecules. Cram then synthesized molecules that took this chemistry into three dimensions. His achievement represented a crucial step toward the synthesis of functional mimics of natural molecules because natural molecules that interact selectively are known to have complementary three-dimensional structures.

According to the accepted "key-lock" model of molecular selectivity, molecules that do not have complementary shapes will not fit together properly and therefore will not react. Enzymes, for example, which are indispensable to life and which regulate nearly all of the chemical reactions that take place in living things, owe much of their characteristic behaviour to their three-dimensional structure. Each enzyme acts on only one kind of substance or group of substances, called the substrate, and catalyzes only one kind of reaction. Scientists believe that the enzyme's shape, at least in part, permits only molecules of a particular substrate to fit into the enzyme's active site. Cram called his own substrate-binding molecules cavitands after their cavity-like binding sites, and he dubbed the behaviour of his molecular systems host-guest chemistry, the host being the cavitand receptor and the guest being the substrate molecule received.

The work of all three laureates has contributed to understanding how biologic molecules recognize the substances with which they react, and their contributions may have far-reaching applications in medicine and industry. Laboratory-made mimics of natural molecules have already been used in experiments to partially detoxify rats poisoned with lead or radioactive strontium. Scientists foresee such developments as the synthesis of artificial enzymes that possess greater stability and selectivity than their natural counterparts and the design of drug molecules that recognize and bind to cancer cells and other specific targets in the body. Other possibilities include the application of highly sensitive compounds to remove contaminants from the environment and to extract gold and other valuable materials from low-grade ores or even seawater.          (CAROLYN D. NEWTON)

## Depardieu, Gérard

Gérard Depardieu cut an unlikely figure as a box-office idol, but by the 1980s he was established as one of the European cinema's few undoubted megastars. In 15 years he had demonstrated a talent that ranged from French classical theatre to drama, melodrama, and comedy, worked with all the major French directors, and silenced critics who had typecast him as a scruffy and insensitive boor. Even before he appeared as the humpbacked Provençal farmer in Claude Berri's *Jean de Florette* (1986), it seemed there was no part beyond his reach. Yet his chief asset remained an animal presence that was far removed from the polished image traditionally projected by the French movie star.

The son of a sheet-metal worker, Depardieu was born in Châteauroux, Indre, on Dec. 27, 1948. While still a teenager he moved to Paris, studied at the Cours d'Art Dramatique de Charles Dullin, and made his debut in the theatre. His early films, from *Les Valseuses* (1974) to *Loulou* (1980), exploited his working-class background and dominating physique to create an image of the sexually aggressive male, seemingly at odds with an increasingly powerful feminist current in France. But he injected, even into these roles, a measure of charm and a disarming hint of vulnerability.

The turning point came in 1980, with a series of outstanding performances. He confirmed his comic gifts in *Inspecteur la Bavure*, put on a suit for *Mon Oncle d'Amérique*, and worked under François Truffaut on *Le Dernier Métro*, winning a César award for best actor. The male chauvinist had, after all, been just an act. Liberated from it, he threw himself into a dazzling variety of parts: medieval peasant in *Le Retour de Martin Guerre* (1982), revolutionary leader in *Danton* (1982), epic hero in *Fort Saganne* (1984). He shared the Best Actor Award at the 1983 Montreal World Film Festival and the next year, after appearing onstage in Molière's *Tartuffe,* directed a film of the play. He delighted French audiences in a series of comedies in which he was teamed with Pierre Richard and, in 1986, played a homosexual thief in Bertrand Blier's *Ménage* (*Tenue de soirée*). Though he still listed boxing among his recreations, the old Depardieu was gone, replaced by a talented and charismatic actor of apparently limitless scope.
                                     (ROBIN BUSS)

## Douglas, Roger Owen

Reform of the New Zealand tax system, removal of subsidies and controls, conversion of many government departments into corporations in the name of efficiency, removal of import barriers, and introduction of other open market concepts—these were some of the changes introduced in the first term (1984–87) of Prime Minister David Lange's Labour government by Finance Minister Roger Douglas. The policies were so closely identified with him that they spawned a new term in finance jargon: "rogernomics." Because they had strained relations with the party's powerful trade union wing, the government had a great deal riding on the Douglas doctrine that moneymakers must be free to make money before a government can use it to provide for the underprivileged. When the government was voted in for a second term in August 1987, Douglas embarked on phase two of his master plan, to look after the low-paid.

In presenting his preelection budget in 1987—

LIZ BROOK—CAMERA PRESS, LONDON

historic because it claimed to have achieved a surplus—Douglas referred to his pride at being the grandson of a member of Parliament in the first Labour administration, 52 years earlier. Born Dec. 5, 1937, in Auckland, son of a trade union secretary and MP, Douglas was educated at Auckland Grammar School and Auckland University, where he took a degree in accountancy, and became company secretary with a carpet manufacturer. He was elected MP for Manukau (now Manurewa) in 1969. During the Labour government of 1972–75 he was given the portfolios of broadcasting and the post office, and in the 1974 reshuffle he took on housing in place of the post office. In opposition again, he moved from the shadow portfolios of trade and industry, and overseas trade, to his abiding interest, finance, in 1983.

In his last budget statement before the 1987 elections, Douglas reaffirmed his finance priorities by emphasizing first the securing of better living standards, then a fairer, more just society that would provide jobs, education, health care, and housing. His third priority was "the opportunity for people to achieve." His economic priority of the first term never wavered as the government entered the second term. It included the reduction of inflation even at the cost of high interest rates, an overvalued New Zealand dollar—which made the lot of exporters more difficult—and wider unemployment, which he saw as a temporary pain.

(JOHN KELLEHER)

**Dukes, Alan**
Following the sudden resignation of Garret FitzGerald as leader of Ireland's Fine Gael, Alan Dukes was elected to the post on March 21, 1987. He assumed the leadership at a time of enormous difficulty for the party. After a stormy and difficult five years in office, and a crushing defeat in the February general elections, Fine Gael was experiencing a crisis of identity that would be hard to resolve. Dukes came from the party's more liberal wing. He faced difficulties in reconciling the traditional values held by the older members of the party with the liberal and social ethos associated with FitzGerald.

Dukes identified five main themes that he hoped to pursue as leader: to bring about economic reform; to improve the welfare of the people; to work for a pluralist Ireland, including the development of the Anglo-Irish agreement on Northern Ireland; to develop Ireland's role in the European Communities (EC); and to promote the case, along with other parties in the Dail (parliament), for a change in the electoral system. However, he soon ran into criticism on economic policy when he pledged the party's

support for the policies of fiscal rectitude being adopted by the Fianna Fail government. It was felt that he had left himself little room to maneuver or to recover the ground won from Fine Gael by the Progressive Democrats in the elections.

Born in Dublin on April 22, 1945, Dukes was educated in Irish-speaking schools and graduated from University College, Dublin, with a degree in economics, politics, and statistics. He was fluent in both French and Irish. Elected to the Dail for the constituency of Kildare on his first attempt in June 1981, he was appointed to the Cabinet immediately, serving as minister for agriculture in the Fine Gael–Labour Party coalition's short-lived administration. On the formation of another coalition government involving the same parties in December 1982, he was appointed minister for finance, a post he held until February 1986, when he became minister for justice. Dukes was regarded as an extremely able man, with a cool, aloof manner. As a former member of the Irish commissioner's *cabinet* in Brussels (1977–80), he was much respected by his peers in the EC for his calm and rational approach to debates of national importance.

(MAVIS ARNOLD)

**Erving, Julius Winfield, II**
Julius ("Doctor J") Erving's retirement party spanned six months from coast to coast. For the last time, fans around the National Basketball Association (NBA) cheered and thanked the man who had added new colour and excitement to professional basketball.

In Phoenix fans wore surgical caps and masks to watch the Doctor operate. In Boston the Celtics gave him a piece of their famous parquet court. In New Jersey Erving cried as the former New York Nets retired his old American Basketball Association (ABA) jersey. And in Philadelphia, where he played his 11 NBA seasons, fans wore tuxedos for his last regular-season home game on April 17, 1987. His season-high 38 points were two more than he needed to become the third player with 30,000 points in a career.

Erving was all-league in 9 of his first 13 seasons and most valuable player (MVP) in both leagues, but he transcended records and trophies. The 2-m, 91-kg (6-ft 6-in, 200-lb) forward suspended time and gravity on his long-distance flights to dunk the ball, performing balletic air sculpture as he made his way around opponents.

"They aren't choreographed," Erving said of his wondrous moves. "They just appear." He took no credit for them, remembering the example of his mother, Callie Mae Lindsey. "The way I played basketball was never about bringing attention to myself but always about proving myself," he said.

Julius Winfield Erving II was born Feb. 22, 1950, in Roosevelt, N.Y. In high school he was a 1.9-m (6-ft 3-in) guard who attracted no major college teams. In three seasons at the University of Massachusetts, however, he became one of only seven players ever to average more than 20 points and 20 rebounds per game in a college career, but he was still generally unknown when he joined the ABA's Virginia Squires in 1971 and the Nets two years later. He won three scoring titles and averaged 28.7 points per game in five ABA seasons, was the league's MVP in its last three years, and led the Nets to championships in 1974 and 1976.

When the ABA merged with the NBA, the Nets sold Erving to the Philadelphia 76ers. In his first NBA season, his 30.3 points per game in the six-game championship finals against Portland nearly led the 76ers to an upset victory. Philadelphia lost three finals in six years before winning the 1983 championship, but Erving was chosen in 1980 for the NBA's 35th-anniversary all-star team and was honoured in 1981 as the NBA's most valuable player, the first in 17 years who was not a centre. Before playing as guard his last two seasons, he never shot below .491 or averaged fewer than 20 points per game.

(KEVIN M. LAMB)

**Fenech Adami, Eddie**
On May 12, 1987, Eddie Fenech Adami was sworn in as Malta's fourth prime minister since the island obtained its independence from Britain in 1964. As leader of the Nationalist Party (then in opposition), he had directed a vigorous political campaign to prevent a repetition of the 1981 general elections, when his party obtained an absolute majority of votes but a minority of parliamentary seats. The same negative result would have emerged from the 1987 elections had not the House of Representatives (parliament) amended the electoral laws. The amendments had been introduced at the behest of the Nationalist Party and eventually agreed to by the government side.

On assuming the office of prime minister, he applied himself to bringing about national reconciliation in an effort to eliminate the polarization dividing his fellow countrymen. His own residence had been ransacked and members of his family manhandled by Socialist government supporters on what became known as Black Monday (Oct. 15, 1979). He also initiated a policy of open government and planned to implement a program of decentralization, giving power and responsibility to local councils, which were to be revived. He expressed great confidence in the role of private enterprise and set in train negotiations for Malta's entry into the European Communities as a full member, provided conditions were favourable.

A lawyer by profession, Fenech Adami was born in Birkirkara on Feb. 7, 1934, the son of a customs officer, and was educated at the University of Malta. After unsuccessfully contesting the 1962 and 1966 elections, he was co-opted to Parliament in 1969, following the death of a Nationalist member, and was shadow minister of labour and social services (1971–77). He rapidly gained popularity within the party and, in the 1976 elections, his vote total was surpassed only by the leaders of the two major parties, George Borg Olivier and Dom Mintoff, Labour Party prime minister at the time. On becoming leader of the Nationalist Party, Fenech Adami immediately began implementing a vast program of reform within the party that raised it to an unequaled level of organization and efficiency. Beneath his unobtrusive manner lay a strong and determined character that had gained him international esteem over the years, especially within Christian Democratic circles.

(ALBERT GANADO)

**Galvin, John Rogers**
In June 1987 John Galvin, a four-star general in the United States Army, became supreme allied commander Europe, head of all military units in Europe assigned to the North Atlantic Treaty Organization. Although Galvin had previously served in Europe, military officers there were apprehensive about him. The unbroken succession of commanders from the U.S. was not resented, but Galvin's predecessor, Bernard Rogers, was appreciated in Europe for questioning U.S. efforts to remove from the continent nuclear warheads of intermediate range. Galvin, more inclined to support the policies of the U.S. government, said on July 30 that the missiles should eventually be removed and that conventional defenses of Europe should be strengthened.

Born in Wakefield, Mass., on May 13, 1929, Galvin graduated from the U.S. Military Academy in 1954 and was commissioned second lieutenant in the Army. He worked his way up through the ranks to general while serving in various parts of the world. Fluent in Spanish, he served as an adviser to the Colombian Army (1956–58) and with the 101st Airborne Division (1958–60). During the 1960s he studied at Columbia University, New York City—from which he received an M.A. in English in 1962—and at the University of Pennsylvania and the Command and General Staff College, and he also taught at the U.S. Military Academy. His research on the Revolutionary War in Massachusetts led to his award-winning book, *The Minute Men*, published in 1967.

Galvin became a plans officer in Vietnam in 1967 and military assistant to the secretary of the army in 1968. In 1974 he published *Three Men of Boston,* a second book about the Revolutionary War, and became military assistant to the supreme allied commander Europe. He was chief of staff of the 3rd Infantry Division from 1976 to 1978, when he became assistant division commander of the 8th Infantry Division. He was in charge of teaching at Ft. Monroe, Virginia, in 1980–81 and commanded the 24th Infantry Division at Ft. Stewart, Georgia, in 1981–83.

In 1983 Galvin returned to Europe as commanding general of the VII Army Corps with headquarters in Stuttgart, West Germany. In 1985 he became commander in chief of the Southern Command with headquarters at Quarry Heights, Panama, and authority over U.S. armed forces in Latin America and the Caribbean. He enthusiastically advocated support for armed insurrection against the Sandinista regime in Nicaragua, in keeping with the Reagan administration's policies.

(CHARLES JOHNSON TAGGART)

### Gavaskar, Sunil Manohar

Statistically, the career of Indian cricketer Sunil ("Sunny") Gavaskar, who in 1987 announced his retirement from first-class cricket, was easy to describe. He had played in 125 test matches, scoring 10,122 runs and 34 centuries. Each of those was a record. The figures bear eloquent testimony to his legendary powers of concentration and his almost flawless technique, but Gavaskar's batting, particularly in the early years of his test career, was more than just a matter of accumulation. He possessed a perfect eye, an apparently fearless disposition (despite being not much over 1.5 m [5 ft] tall), and neat and unhurried footwork. His batting had the hallmarks of genius.

Gavaskar was born in Bombay on July 10, 1949. He was a prodigious scorer of runs while playing cricket in school and was quickly promoted to the Bombay team, for which he made his debut in 1966 at the age of 17. In his test debut on India's 1970–71 tour to the West Indies, after missing the first match he quickly demonstrated his remarkable talent by scoring 774 runs (including two centuries and a double century) in the remaining four tests. That set the pattern for the next 16 years. Providing a fitting finale to his career, he scored his first-ever century at Lord's in the bicentenary test in August 1987.

If Gavaskar's technique and application made him a great batsman and his remarkable reflexes made him a peerless slip catcher, his instinctive caution made him a mediocre captain. (He captained India from 1978 to 1983.) He was a past master at slowing down the over rate in

a game, tactics that frustrated Indian crowds almost as much as they did his opponents. In Calcutta during England's 1984–85 tour, he continued India's first innings into the fourth day, angering the crowd so much that he had to be escorted onto the field by police. Typically, he reacted to the uproar by vowing never to play in Calcutta again.

At different times charming, witty, and temperamental, Gavaskar was one of the first "superstar" cricketers, turning his runs on the field into rupees off it by endorsing many products that had nothing to do with cricket. He seemed destined for a career in politics, where the courage and endless patience he had shown on the cricket field would doubtless stand him in good stead.            (ANDREW LONGMORE)

### Goria, Giovanni

Giovanni Goria's nomination as Italy's prime minister by Pres. Francesco Cossiga in July 1987 came as a surprise to Goria, his Christian

Democrat Party, and the Italian public. When he took office on July 29, he became Italy's youngest prime minister. He was also the first in that office who had not sought it and the first to have no strong personal power base either within or outside his party. After considering the shortlist given him by Christian Democrat leader Ciriaco De Mita, Cossiga apparently chose Goria on his own, perhaps sensing that the public had wearied of seeing the same faces take turns in office for nearly 40 years. Because of a strong Christian Democrat showing at the June election, it was clearly the time to return the office to that party.

Born July 30, 1943, Goria called himself, half-mockingly, "just a bookkeeper from Asti," even after he had served as treasury minister (1983–87). He probably most impressed the public with his television appearances, during which he did not talk like a politician. While studying for his degree at Turin University, Goria was a volunteer worker for the Christian Democrats in Asti. When an Asti party boss declined to run for Parliament in the 1976 general election, Goria was put on the ballot in his place. He served as an under secretary for the budget (1981–83) before becoming treasury minister in the caretaker Cabinet of Amintore Fanfani and retaining the post in the Craxi government. His easygoing style helped him avoid making political enemies.

Goria's first months as prime minister were singularly lacklustre for the much-hailed "new" man at the top. He performed his routine duties but did not appeal at any time directly to the Italian public, which might have been his most effective approach. His potential for providing a new kind of leadership for Italy's largest party was not developed. His major problem was

the lukewarm support offered by his own party except during times of duress. It seemed as if Italy, with a figurehead president, also had a figurehead prime minister.

(GEORGE ARMSTRONG)

### Gottlieb, Robert Adam

In January, in a memo to the magazine's staff, it was announced that Robert A. Gottlieb would become the new editor of *The New Yorker.* Appointed to succeed 79-year-old William Shawn, editor for the past 35 years, Gottlieb left his post as president and editor in chief of Alfred A. Knopf Inc. to become the third editor in the history of the 62-year-old weekly. Before he took over on March 1, he was presented with a memo urging his resignation from 154 *New Yorker* staffers, all of whom felt Gottlieb's appointment was not only undemocratic and sudden but contrary to previous assurances to the staff that an "insider" would be chosen to carry on the editorial policies and traditions established by Shawn and by Harold Ross, the magazine's founding editor. Both Ross and Shawn had exerted powerful influence—Shawn supposedly read every line of every story he approved. While Gottlieb was without experience in getting out a weekly, his supporters nevertheless believed that he was by far the best person for the job—one of the country's leading book editors, a voracious reader, and a *New Yorker* fan since childhood.

Gottlieb was born April 29, 1931, on Manhattan's Upper West Side. An only child whose parents were compulsive readers, Gottlieb described himself as a child who frequently read three or four books a day. He graduated from Columbia University, New York City, in 1952 and then studied for two years at the University of Cambridge. In 1955 he was hired by Simon & Schuster as an editorial assistant, and within two years, at age 26, he had begun what would be a meteoric rise as an editor. (His first major project was Joseph Heller's best-selling *Catch 22.*) Gottlieb became editor in chief in 1965. He moved to Knopf three years later as executive vice-president and editor in chief. The combination of Knopf, one of the most prestigious U.S. publishers, and Gottlieb, expert editor and talent scout, was enough to lure to the publisher several established authors. In 1973 Gottlieb was named president of Knopf.

In spite of staff resistance to an "outsider," Gottlieb, informal in both demeanour and garb, was optimistic about his new challenge. He pointed to his longtime love for the magazine and his basically conservative temperament. In a midsummer interview, *New Yorker* staffers praised simultaneously the new editor's control and accessibility, his informality and directness. A sample of the latter was offered at the time of his appointment: "There are four things in my life. Work, the ballet, reading, and my family. I don't do anything else. I don't have lunches, dinners, go to plays or movies. I don't meditate, escalate, deviate or have affairs. So I have plenty of time."            (BONNIE OBERMAN)

### Graf, Steffi

When the year ended with Steffi Graf ranked number one in women's tennis, it was the first time since computer ranking began in 1975 that the top spot did not belong to Martina Navratilova or Chris Evert. When Graf moved into the lead Aug. 16, 1987, she was the first player to unseat the reigning duo since Tracy Austin, who ranked first for four months in 1980.

"Nobody hits the ball as hard as Steffi does," Evert said of Graf's forehand. Her speed and footwork gave her the best court range among her contemporaries. Her former weaknesses, at the net and on the backhand, were no longer liabilities. Most of all, her single-minded intensity distinguished her from other young challengers who had burned out in their late teens or early 20s.

Graf had willingly sacrificed youthful hobbies and social life to practice at least three hours a day with Pavel Slozil, a Czechoslovak Davis

Cup player. At the same time, her father and coach, Peter, had kept her fresh with a limited schedule and yearly tournament layoffs of nearly two months.

At the age of 13 in 1982, Graf became the second-youngest player ever to earn a computer ranking. However, when she moved up to sixth in 1985, she still had not won a tournament except for the tennis demonstration at the 1984 Olympics. Her breakthrough year was 1986, when the 1.73-m (5-ft 8-in), 52.7-kg (116-lb) right-hander won eight singles championships in 14 tournaments, including final-round victories over Navratilova and Evert.

During 1987 Graf's only defeats in 79 matches were to Navratilova in finals at Wimbledon and the U.S. Open. She won 11 of 13 tournaments and 45 matches in a row before the Wimbledon final. She won the French, Italian, and German opens and the outdoor and indoor championships of the Women's International Tennis Association. Her $1,019,245 in prize money for singles and $44,540 for doubles raised her career totals to $1,771,582 and $137,730.

Graf was born June 14, 1969, in Bruehl, West Germany, near Heidelberg. She won her first match at six and the next year practiced often with eight-year-old Boris Becker, West Germany's future Wimbledon champion. Her mother, Heidi, played tennis until suffering a back injury in 1976, but it was Peter, a soccer star, who moved the sofa to the middle of the family room so that Steffi, at the age of four, could use it as a net. He promised her a party with ice cream and strawberries if she hit the ball back 25 times. The party was held soon thereafter. (KEVIN M. LAMB)

**Greenspan, Alan**
When Paul Volcker resigned as chairman of the U.S. Federal Reserve Board on June 2, 1987, he was commonly regarded as the most powerful and respected man in the financial world. Market analysts had speculated for months on the identity of Volcker's likely successor and the monumental task he would face. Even Volcker's supporters breathed easier, however, when on June 2 Pres. Ronald Reagan named economist Alan Greenspan as the new chairman. Greenspan, an economic adviser (1968–74) to Pres. Richard Nixon and chairman of the Council of Economic Advisers under Pres. Gerald Ford, was considered a free-market theorist with a practical ability to get things done. Despite reservations on the part of some senators, he was confirmed almost unanimously on August 3.

Wall Street responded with new highs, and after the Dow Jones Industrial Average peaked in late August, the Fed raised the bank discount rate 0.5% to cool fears of inflation and, possibly, to establish Greenspan's independence in his new post. Unfortunately, the bull market was nearing its end, and Greenspan appeared in a badly timed optimistic interview in *Fortune* magazine only a few days before the crash came on October 19. The Fed reacted quickly to loosen credit and pledged additional funds to bolster the economy as needed.

Greenspan was born in New York City on March 6, 1926. He studied clarinet at the Juilliard School of Music and played professionally for a short time before entering New York University to study economics. He received his B.S. in 1948 and his M.A. in 1950. (He finally completed his Ph.D. in 1977.) In 1953 he joined Wall Street broker William Townsend to found Townsend-Greenspan and Co., Inc. After Townsend's death in 1958, Greenspan built the consulting firm into a highly influential one-man show, providing valuable advice to about 100 corporations, despite frequently inaccurate economic forecasts.

Greenspan was best known, perhaps, as an ardent follower and close friend of the writer Ayn Rand, whose espousal of laissez-faire capitalism formed the basis of much of Greenspan's economic philosophy. Greenspan favoured a kind of supercapitalism based on decreased government regulation, a balanced budget with strong

defense spending, liberalized banking laws, and a return to the gold standard, but he admitted that this was impossible in a less-than-perfect world. (MELINDA SHEPHERD)

**Grosz, Karoly**
The appointment of Karoly Grosz as prime minister of Hungary on June 25, 1987, was seen by many as a move designed to eliminate him as a successor to Janos Kadar, general secretary of the Hungarian Socialist Workers' (Communist) Party (HSWP), who had led the country for 31 years. The main task confronting Grosz was to reverse the decline in the nation's economy that had been taking place in recent years; he was expected to implement tough austerity measures in a country where the population was already disenchanted by the lack of economic progress. Contrary to expectations, however, in the months following his appointment he became well respected and seemed a natural successor to Kadar.

Grosz was born in 1930 at Miskolc in northeastern Hungary. He adopted his father's trade (printing) and political views and in 1945 joined the Magyar Communist Party. After studying at a teachers college, Grosz joined the party's central organization under Matyas Rakosi, first secretary of the reconstructed Hungarian Workers' Party (HWP), in 1950.

In 1954 Grosz became head of the agitation and propaganda department of the party committee in his native county, Borsod-Abauj-Zemplen. He stayed there during the sombre period of the November 1956 Hungarian uprising, which—according to the party journal *Nepszabadsag*—was caused by Rakosi's "crimes." Grosz remained at Miskolc while fighting was taking place in and around the capital. From 1958 to 1981 he edited the Miskolc daily *Eszak Magyarotszag.*

From 1962 Grosz was secretary of the party committee of Hungarian Radio and Television. In 1968 he became deputy head and in 1974 head of the agitation and propaganda department of the Central Committee of the HSWP (as the HWP was renamed in 1956). In 1973 Grosz was elected first secretary of Fejer County. His rapid promotions then stopped, following disagreements with Kadar, and he was sent back to Miskolc to run the local party. By December 1984, however, he was back in favour and had returned to Budapest to run the capital's party organization. In 1980 he became a member of the HSWP Central Committee, and he was elected to the Politburo in 1985. (K. M. SMOGORZEWSKI)

**Hackney, Roderick Peter**
English architect Rod Hackney was a pioneer of community architecture and a controversial and outspoken architectural critic. His close association with Prince Charles and his obvious influence on the prince's architectural ideas, together with his election in December 1986, to take office in July 1987, as president of the Royal Institute of British Architects (RIBA), focused attention on his nontraditional and antiestablishment philosophy. Hackney's prime concern had been the rejuvenation of inner cities through community involvement and projects that enabled residents to participate in the design and construction of their homes and surroundings. His architectural philosophy included the conviction that if people are involved in choices and decisions that shape their environment, they are more likely to live happily with those choices.

Inner-city rejuvenation in Britain was a serious political and social issue as well as an architectural one. In a widely publicized speech in 1984, Prince Charles praised community architecture while attacking the "buildings in isolation" approach of establishment modern architects. The prince's concern perhaps originated in the shocking scenes of inner-city riots in rundown sections of London, Liverpool, Manchester, and Bristol in 1981. However, disenchantment with modern architecture's solutions to housing problems went back at least

to the 1968 collapse of the Ronan Point tower block in London's East End. The prince's Inner City Trust, of which Hackney was chairman, was established in 1986.

Hackney was born March 3, 1942, in Liverpool and was raised in Wales. He graduated from the School of Architecture at Manchester University in 1967 and worked in Montreal that year on the design of Expo 67 and subsequently in Libya on a public housing project. He worked with Danish architect Arne Jacobsen in Copenhagen (1968–71); in 1972 he returned to England and established his own practice in Macclesfield, Cheshire. The threatened demolition of his own neighbourhood—Black Road, Macclesfield—provided the impetus for his first community architecture project. By 1977 the area had been successfully renovated and was the subject of a television documentary. Similar projects followed in Leicester; Millom, Cumbria; and Clitheroe, Lancashire. His Weaver's Triangle project in Burnley, Lancashire, developed a derelict area of Victorian mills to provide employment, housing, and workshops. Hackney's projects were designed to restore not only buildings but also a sense of community; he believed that architects should live in a community they designed and be as available as the family doctor. (SANDRA MILLIKIN)

**Hansen, Rick**
One goal of the Man in Motion tour was to raise funds for spinal cord research and rehabilitation. When wheelchair athlete Rick Hansen began his five-continent journey at Vancouver, B.C., on March 21, 1985, his main purpose was to create a greater awareness of the potential of disabled persons. Hansen's slogan was: "Being the best we can with what we have." Setting himself a distance of 80 km (50 mi) per day, he wore out the wheelchair, several sets of tires, and numerous pairs of gloves on his 40,000-km (25,000-mi) trip. Both his goals were achieved. On his 26-month journey he raised nearly $20 million, which was placed in a trust fund. An attraction and an inspiration wherever he went, he was honoured in many of the 34 countries he visited. The Chinese government, for instance, designated him a hero of heroes. Canada awarded him the Order of Canada for his achievement (1987).

Born Aug. 26, 1957, in Port Alberni, B.C., Hansen was a promising athlete at age 15, but a traffic accident in 1973 deprived him of the use of his legs. Embittered at first, he then discovered wheelchair sports. He won championship medals in tennis and racquetball and competed in wheelchair basketball and volleyball. He was captain of the British Columbia wheelchair volleyball team that won three Canadian titles. His basketball team won five national titles in six years.

In track Hansen won four medals at the British Columbia Games for the Physically Disabled in 1979. In 1980, at the Olympiad for the Physically Disabled, he won three medals, setting a world record for the 800-m event and an Olympic record for the 4 × 100-m relay. In 1984 he won three medals in track at the World Wheel Chair Games in England. At the Pan American Games in Halifax, Nova Scotia (1984), he set a world record by winning nine gold medals. He was best known, however, for his competition in wheelchair marathons. Between 1980 and 1984 he won 19 marathons—7 in 1983 alone. Canada named him the National Disabled Athlete of the Year in 1979, 1980, 1982, and 1983. In 1983 he was co-winner, with Wayne Gretzky, of the Lou Marsh Trophy for Canada's outstanding male athlete.

In 1976 Hansen was the first disabled person to enroll in the bachelor of physical education program at the University of British Columbia. After completing his world tour, he intended to return to private life and teach physical education. He would continue to have an interest in the Man in Motion program as an administrator of the trust fund. His memoir of his world journey, *Rick Hansen: Man in Motion,* was published in 1987. (DIANE LOIS WAY)

## Hart, Gary

In 1987 the "character issue" seemingly ended Gary Hart's campaign for the U.S. Democratic presidential nomination. Exasperated with rumours that he was a womanizer, Hart invited *New York Times* reporters to "tail" him and see for themselves that he was not unfaithful to his wife. On the May weekend that the invitation saw print, and with his wife away in Colorado, *Miami* (Fla.) *Herald* reporters staked out Hart's Washington home and spotted him leaving it with model Donna Rice, who, they alleged, had stayed there overnight. The front-page story came at a time when Hart already faced public doubts about his character, thanks to his conflicting statements about his name change and age, the womanizing rumour, and his unpaid 1984 campaign debt of $1.3 million. For a week he continued campaigning despite the Rice story, but when the *Washington Post* threatened to release details about an affair between him and yet another woman, Hart quit the race. By December, however, Hart had once again made headlines by dramatically announcing that he was back in the running for president. Whether the public would trust him and be willing to give him another chance was open to question, but the Democratic establishment was notably hostile toward Hart's reemergence. Democrats feared that he would act as a spoiler and throw into further disarray the party's halting efforts to produce a viable candidate for president.

He was born Gary Warren Hartpence in Ottawa, Kan., on Nov. 28, 1936. Raised by a religiously strict family, he earned degrees at Bethany (Okla.) Nazarene College and Yale Divinity School. John Kennedy's 1960 presidential campaign, however, inspired Hart to change his goals from preaching and teaching to law and politics; four years later he was graduated from Yale Law School. Hart first made a name for himself as the campaign manager for George McGovern's run for the presidency in 1972. His organizational and fund-raising strategies enabled the liberal McGovern to surprise everyone by capturing the Democratic nomination. Two years after his candidate lost the general election to Richard Nixon, Hart was elected by Colorado voters to the U.S. Senate. By the time he won reelection in 1980, he was considerably more conservative than the long-haired Hart of the McGovern days.

In 1984 Hart almost landed the Democratic presidential nomination. In the popular vote he won 26 states to Walter Mondale's 19, but superior organization netted Mondale enough delegates for victory. Hart had gained momentum in the campaign until Mondale ridiculed his "new ideas" with the barb "Where's the beef?," which came from a TV commercial criticizing hamburgers that were more bun than beef.

(MICHAEL AMEDEO)

## Headroom, Max

Like any other year, 1987 had its share of talking heads—from anchorpersons to game show hosts. The head of the class, however, belonged to Max Headroom, a smirking stutterer who was part man, part computer-generated image. Shown only from the shoulders up, Max—with his bleached white teeth, sunshine yellow hair, and deep-set video blue eyes—hosted a half-hour series of rock videos and interviews, starred in an adventure series for American network television, and served as spokeshead for Coke in a $25 million ad campaign. Unlike the television talkers he parodied, Max offered viewers unpredictability: he could be solemnly ingratiating one moment and cheerfully insulting the next.

Max was born in Britain to a creative team needing an angle for a new show of rock videos. The team, headed by record executive Peter Wagg, opted to give the show a computer-generated host and decided to name him after a vehicular sign common in Britain: "max. headroom . . . metres."

To explain his origin, they created the television movie *Max Headroom: Twenty Minutes into the Future.* Its (human) hero was a reporter whose mind and image were copied by a network's computer and put on television. Calling itself Max, the televised copy soon took on a life of its own.

The movie and the rock video series, *The Max Headroom Show,* gave Max's career a head start. Shortly after its debut in Britain in the spring of 1985, the series was drawing more than a million viewers and inspiring the creation of Max shirts, books, and other items. Though it later became a hit in the U.S. and other countries, Max did not achieve superstar status until 1986, when his ubiquitous television ads helped Coke supplant Pepsi as the number one sugar cola. His message: "Don't say the 'P' word; say, 'Catch the wave—Coke.'"

The man behind the Max was Matt Frewer, a Canadian actor. To change into Max, he had to spend hours donning a latex mask and other makeup. A computer then scrambled his image and voice, giving him the electronic look and sound that Max's character required.

In March 1987 Frewer/Max reached network television with "Max Headroom," a visually sophisticated series about a future governed—and choked—by television. In this critically acclaimed ironic satire, Max was prone to such remarks as: "Know how to tell when a network president's lying? His lips move." Its speed-of-light pace and arcane language were too much for most viewers, however; the show was later canceled, ranking only 72 in the Nielsen ratings. Millions loved his likeness in commercials, but when it came to a one-hour show, they had no headroom for Max.

(MICHAEL AMEDEO)

GIORGIO KELLER—CAMERA PRESS, LONDON

## Hess, Erika

The most consistently successful woman alpine ski racer during the 1980s, Erika Hess of Switzerland was a powerful yet petite competitor (1.63 m [5 ft 4 in]) who first gained prominence when she placed second in the 1977 Swiss national championships at the age of 14. Three years later she finished third in her first Olympic Games slalom, at Lake Placid, N.Y. She won her first World Cup race, a slalom in Schruns, Austria, on Jan. 13, 1981. During that season she set a World Cup record with six consecutive slalom victories and, because of her elegant style, was described as "the graceful ballerina of the snow."

Born into a farm family in Engelberg on March 6, 1962, Hess was brought up in a skiing environment. Her aunt was a distinguished slalom skier in the 1950s, and a cousin, Monika, two years her junior, began racing for Switzerland in 1982.

The 1982 season was Hess's most triumphant; she won the slalom, giant slalom, and alpine combination titles at the world championships at Schladming, Austria, and dominated the World Cup circuit to win the first of her two overall titles, the other coming in 1984. She was also twice runner-up in the World Cup (in 1981 and 1986), third in 1983, and fourth in 1985 and 1987. The 1984 winter Olympic Games in Sarajevo, Yugos., were disastrous by her high standards—she finished fifth in the slalom and seventh in the giant slalom—but the following year she won the alpine combination at the world championships in Bormio, Italy.

Despite pressure to continue racing until the 1988 winter Olympic Games in Calgary, Alta., Hess announced her retirement after the 1987 season, when she scored victories in the slalom and the alpine combination in the world championships at Crans-Montana in her own country. This brought her career tally of world championship gold medals to six. Though the downhill event had never been Hess's forte, her versatility enabled her to win many combination awards.

(HOWARD BASS)

## Hogan, Paul

Paul Hogan once assessed the stereotypical Australian as a "beer-guzzling, bar-fighting idiot who thinks culture's something you find in a carton of yogurt." Although the star of the phenomenally successful film *Crocodile Dundee* undoubtedly exaggerated the world's perception of Australians, the same man almost single-handedly evoked worldwide fascination with all things Australian, as well as providing his country with a needed dose of national pride.

Born in Lightning Ridge, New South Wales, Australia, in 1941, Hogan was raised in a working-class suburb of Sydney. After dropping out of school at 15, he worked in a variety of jobs that included chauffeur, boxer, and bridge rigger. While he was working on the Sydney Harbour Bridge, some of Hogan's mates dared him to appear on the television program "New Faces," a "talent" show, the real motive of which was to embarrass its guests. Hogan, billing himself as a blindfolded, tap-dancing knife thrower, managed to turn the tables on the rather malicious judges. His original and unpretentious sense of humour kept him from being skewered and earned him several more guest shots. His popularity on "New Faces" brought more offers, and before long Hogan was making commercials and appearing on other programs. He eventually was given his own program, "The Paul Hogan Show," a popular sketch-comedy show that ran for nine years and was syndicated in some 30 countries. By 1984 the comedian had become something of a national folk hero. The same year, he offered to write and appear, free of charge, in commercials for the Australian Tourist Commission and, not coincidentally, American tourism in Australia more than doubled.

As Hogan gained international exposure, a trip to New York City inspired the idea for *Crocodile Dundee,* a variation on the "innocent abroad" theme—a rugged crocodile hunter from the outback is thrown into the urban jungle of New York City and then must adapt his practical Australian know-how to cope with the eccentric realities of everyday life in Manhattan. Hogan's character more than holds his own in the big city and often is able to "enlighten" the hardened urbanites. *Crocodile Dundee* became the most profitable film in Australian history and set money-making records in the U.S. when it was released there. Named Australian of the Year, voted more "credible" in a public-opinion poll than Australia's prime minister, and with both of Australia's political parties interested in him as a future candidate for Parliament, Hogan projected an image in his own country that was stronger than ever before.

(ELIZABETH LASKEY)

## Holkeri, Harri

The appointment on April 30, 1987, of Harri Holkeri as prime minister of Finland marked a watershed in Finnish politics. Holkeri was the first Conservative prime minister since World War II, and in the March election Finnish voters elected the biggest non-Socialist majority since 1930. Although Holkeri had devoted much of his career to politics, he had not been a member of Parliament since 1978; his political activities in the intervening years were limited to the Helsinki City Council, of which he had been chairman since 1981. In 1979 he became

MARKU LEPOLA—CAMERA PRESS, LONDON

a member of the board of management of the Bank of Finland—a not unusual stepping-stone for would-be prime ministers in Finland. The coalition government Holkeri led included the National Coalition Party (NCP; Conservatives) and the Social Democratic Party, the two largest groups, and two smaller non-Socialist parties, the Rural Party and the Swedish People's Party. The coalition parties secured 131 of the 200 seats in Parliament. Holkeri selected six other Conservatives in his 18-person Cabinet.

Holkeri was born on Jan. 6, 1937, in the village of Oripää. His political career began in earnest when he became secretary of the NCP Youth League in 1959, and he then moved up through the Conservative ranks to become information secretary (1960–62). In 1962 he graduated from the Youth League and became information secretary of the NCP. He continued his career progression by becoming research secretary (1964–65), party secretary (1965–71), and in 1971 party chairman—at 34, he was the youngest Conservative Party leader in Europe—a post that he held until 1979. When he left mainstream politics in 1979, his party was not considered a major force. Holkeri's tenure at the central bank was seen as providing the finishing touches to his political experience.

Holkeri had a reputation as a man of integrity with a strong sense of duty. His liberal thinking would undoubtedly distance him from his other Conservative European counterparts but made him well suited to manage a four-party coalition. He was expected to introduce economic reforms designed to preserve the value of the markka and cut back on excess farm production.                    (JANET H. CLARK)

**Honasan, Gregorio**
Col. Gregorio Honasan's attempt, on Aug. 28, 1987, to overthrow the government of Corazon Aquino, president of the Philippines, demonstrated the rifts that divided mainstream Philippine society. Although there was no clear evidence, it was widely assumed that Honasan had hoped to bring to power Juan Ponce Enrile, a popular former minister of defense and one of the two opposition members of the Senate, which had been elected nationwide. Enrile had a large following among those who feared Aquino's conciliatory attitude toward the Communist New People's Army (NPA) and the Islamic rebels. But the failure of Honasan's attempted coup also demonstrated the willingness of most soldiers to support the Aquino government—even by shooting fellow soldiers.

Honasan was believed to have been in his 41st year at the time of his attempted coup. He graduated from the Philippine Military Academy in 1971 and saw action in the conflict against Islamic rebels in Mindanao. In 1982 he started an organization of military officers opposed to the increased control of the Army by cronies of Pres. Ferdinand Marcos. This group came to

be known as Reform the Armed Forces (RAM) and apparently had 300 members in 1986.

By 1986 Honasan had reached the rank of colonel and was chief of security to Enrile, who was then minister of defense. Amid street demonstrations against Marcos's apparent attempt to steal a presidential election from Corazon Aquino, Enrile in February 1986 sealed Marcos's fate by siding with Aquino, who appointed him minister of defense after Marcos left the country. Honasan, perhaps apprehensive that Marcos would find out about RAM, supported Enrile's defection and became a popular hero. In frequent interviews he criticized Aquino's lack of militancy against the NPA and slowness to reform the military. These opinions won him the respect of many soldiers and civilians who admired Enrile. Suspecting Enrile and Honasan of being at least sympathetic to an attempted coup in late 1986, Aquino dismissed Enrile from the Cabinet and sent Honasan to train recruits in central Luzon.

In 1987 most soldiers apparently voted against a proposed constitution favoured by Aquino, and Enrile was elected to the Senate. Possibly encouraged by these events, Honasan on August 28 led supporters in an attempt to take over important points in metropolitan Manila. Within 24 hours, however, most of Honasan's followers had surrendered. He escaped but was captured in Manila by city police on December 9. On December 18 he was dropped from the Army.          (CHARLES JOHNSON TAGGART)

AP/WIDE WORLD

**Jayawardene, J(unius) R(ichard)**
For Pres. J. R. Jayawardene ten years of leadership culminated in 1987 in the worst violence in Sri Lanka's history. The most pressing problem facing him was how to stop the escalating conflict in the north and east of the country, where the Tamils were fighting for independence. Although the Tamils made up only 18% of Sri Lanka's population, the entire country was being affected by the spreading violence.

Jayawardene could well understand the problem that divided the Hindu Tamils and mainly Buddhist Sinhalese. Although he was baptized a Christian, he converted to Buddhism at an early age. In common with Sri Lanka's Buddhist majority, he believed that it was the religion of the country. Traditionally the Sinhalese feared that India might try to impose Hinduism on Sri Lanka.

Against this background Jayawardene and India's Prime Minister Rajiv Gandhi signed a peace accord on July 29—an important agreement for both leaders. For Jayawardene, India posed a threat in that its Tamil homeland in the south was a source of support for Sri Lanka's warring Tamils. For India, it was vital that such a physically close neighbour be a friend. The agreement, however, was a failure. The fighting continued, and Jayawardene was accused by many Sinhalese of "selling out" to India. His own Cabinet did not like the accord.

Threats to law and order were also posed by a small outlawed party in the south dedicated to the overthrow of Jayawardene. They launched a number of attacks and were believed to be responsible for the murder of several members of the ruling United National Party (UNP). Jayawardene took the unprecedented step of setting up a "Home Militia" to protect UNP members.

Jayawardene was born in Colombo on Sept. 17, 1906. He began his career as a lawyer and in 1938 joined the Ceylon National Congress, which later merged with several smaller parties and became the UNP. He served as finance minister after independence from the U.K. was achieved in 1948. He rose to eminence in 1977 when as leader of the UNP he defeated the Sri Lankan Freedom Party. After six months as prime minister, in February 1978 he became Sri Lanka's president and promulgated a new constitution. Because of the conflict with the Tamils, his plan to free the economy from the constraints imposed by his socialist predecessors did not proceed as fast as he had hoped.
                    (JANET H. CLARK)

**Johnson, Ben**
In 1986 *Track and Field News* declared Ben Johnson of Canada to be the best sprinter in the world. In August 1987 Johnson confirmed this appellation. At the world track and field championships in Rome, he ran the 100-m dash in 9.83 sec. This shattered the previous record (set in 1983 by Calvin Smith of the U.S.) by a full one-tenth of a second.

Born Dec. 30, 1961, in Falmouth, Jamaica, Johnson immigrated to Canada in 1976 with his mother and five siblings. His father remained in Falmouth in order to keep his job with the telephone company. In Toronto Johnson was introduced to Canadian track and field competition by his brother Edward. Ben was soon discovered by Charlie Francis, Canada's national sprint coach.

Johnson's love of speed soon blossomed into a total dedication to running. He began competing internationally for Canada at the age of 16. By 1980 he was the top-ranked junior in Canada. In 1981 Johnson competed in the World Cup trials in Venezuela; in 1982 he won a medal at the Commonwealth Games in Brisbane, Australia. At the 1984 Olympic Games in Los Angeles he won bronze medals in the 100-m dash and the 400 × 100-m relay. In 1985 he won the World Cup in Australia, and at the Yomiuri International Indoor Meet held in Osaka, Japan, also in 1985, he ran 60 m in 6.50 sec—a world indoor record.

The next year was a very successful one for Johnson. At the Commonwealth Games in Edinburgh, he won gold medals in the 100-m dash and the 400 × 100-m relay. He also won a gold medal in the 100 m in the Goodwill Games in Moscow. Also during 1986 he won both the Lou Marsh Trophy and the Lionel Conacher Trophy as Canada's top male athlete of the year.

Called "the ultimate running machine" by his coach, Johnson reacted to the starter's pistol faster than any other runner had. He had a single-minded dedication to the achievement of his goal of becoming the fastest man on Earth. He trained six days a week and took up weight lifting to give him added strength and stamina for the end of a race. All this provided Johnson with the perfect combination for excelling at the 100-m dash, which required an explosive start and 100% effort throughout the race.

In 1986 and 1987 the Canadian Track and Field Association awarded Johnson the Jack W. Davis Trophy as the outstanding Canadian athlete and the Phil Edwards Memorial Trophy as the outstanding Canadian track athlete of the year. He was made a Member of the Order of Canada in 1987.          (DIANE LOIS WAY)

**Joyner-Kersee, Jackie**
The first time Jackie Joyner-Kersee set the world heptathlon record, she shattered the old one by 202 points and stunned the experts, who said she could never do that again. Four weeks

later, in August 1986, she broke her new record by 10 points with a 7,158-point finish. When she scored 7,128 in track and field's quadrennial world championships on Sept. 1, 1987, she beat the runner-up by 564 points and remained the only heptathlete who had topped 7,000.

Joyner-Kersee won the long jump at the world championships three days later, becoming the first person since 1924 to win gold medals in single and multiple events at that tournament. With her share of the women's long-jump record, 7.45 m (24 ft 5½ in) at the Pan American games August 13, she became the only U.S. athlete ever to hold world records in single and multiple events.

Her mother, Mary, had foreseen her daughter's success from the day Jacqueline Joyner was born, March 3, 1962, in East St. Louis, Ill. Mary's mother insisted that she name her daughter after U.S. Pres. John F. Kennedy's wife because, she said, "Someday, this girl will be the first lady of something." Mary died of meningitis at 38 when Jackie was an 18-year-old freshman at UCLA, but her memory kept pushing Jackie. "I knew about setting goals and things," Joyner-Kersee said later, "but with her gone, some of her determination passed to me."

In high school Joyner-Kersee set the Illinois women's long-jump record and starred on the volleyball and basketball teams. When she was graduated in the top 10% of her class, UCLA gave her a basketball scholarship.

An early coach had encouraged Joyner-Kersee to be versatile in track and field. She won four national junior championships in the heptathlon, which comprises the shot put, javelin, high jump, long jump, 100-m hurdles, 200-m dash, and 800-m run. At UCLA, however, she focused only on basketball and the long jump until she met Bob Kersee, an assistant track coach eight years her senior. Kersee, whose mother also had died when he was young, was the first to comfort her after Mary's death. He also worried that the muscular 1.8-m (5-ft 10-in) young woman was wasting her multiple talents, and he insisted on developing them in the heptathlon. Kersee's role shifted comfortably from mentor to partner, and Joyner and he were married on Jan. 11, 1986.

Joyner-Kersee nearly won her first world heptathlon championship at the Olympic Games in 1984, on the same day her older brother, Al, won the gold medal in the triple jump. But she lost the climactic 800 m and the gold by just 6,390 points to 6,385. It took two more years for her to become track's first lady. She won the 1986 Jesse Owens Award for the most outstanding U.S. track athlete and in 1987 became the first two-time winner of the Owens. In 1986 Joyner-Kersee won the Sullivan Award for the most outstanding U.S. amateur athlete.

(KEVIN M. LAMB)

## Keating, Paul John

In 1987 Treasurer Paul Keating moved a step nearer his goal of becoming prime minister of Australia. As a reward for his loyalty and in recognition of his key role in the Australian Labor Party (ALP) election victory, Prime Minister Robert Hawke unequivocally pronounced Keating as the man he would most like to have follow him as leader. From being potentially the ALP's greatest electoral liability, Keating had become a star performer, making his mark with a sometimes bizarre blend of earthy attacks on his opponents and high-level explanations and lectures on the more arcane aspects of economics.

Keating appeared to have the capacity, singlehandedly, to both damage and restore the economy. When he described Australia in 1986 as heading for "banana republic" status, support for the economy evaporated almost overnight. He recovered to be the architect of a shaky turnaround. At first he blamed the deterioration in Australia's terms of trade on a decline in world commodity prices, and later he maintained that it was only a matter of time before the effects of currency devaluation would be reversed and the "J-curve" factor would be-

gin to operate. When commodity prices did not improve and the "J-curve" did not operate, Keating introduced a May minibudget and a postelection strategy that were welcomed by foreign and local investors alike.

When Hawke called the 1987 election, the opposition identified Keating as a vulnerable target. His opposition equivalent, Andrew Peacock, said Australians had always known there were two Keatings—one said let's catch tax evaders, while the other forgot to put in his tax return; one said let's improve the balance of trade, while the other imported antique clocks. Keating maintained a relatively low profile during the election campaign, but he made a dramatic impact on the result when he uncovered a multimillion-dollar error in the opposition's estimate of the cost of its radical new tax policies.

Born Jan. 18, 1944, Keating was educated at a Roman Catholic school in working-class Bankstown, New South Wales. His background as an industrial advocate with the Federated Municipal and Shire Council Employees Union led him into Labor politics. Elected member of the House of Representatives for Blaxland in 1969, he was president of the New South Wales branch of the ALP (1979–83) and was opposition spokesman on a number of different matters before becoming federal treasurer at the start of Hawke's first ministry in 1983.

(A. R. G. GRIFFITHS)

## Kinugasa, Sachio

On June 13, 1987, the name of Sachio Kinugasa, the 40-year-old third baseman of the Hiroshima Toyo Carp, was written into the record book. When he trotted onto the field at the Hiroshima Stadium for his 2,131st consecutive game, he broke the 48-year-old record set by Lou Gehrig of the New York Yankees in 1939. It took "Iron Man" Kinugasa 17 years to accomplish his goal, 2 years longer than Gehrig, because the 130-game Japanese season was 24 games shorter than that played in the U.S. in Gehrig's day. Kinugasa ended a 23-year career on Oct. 22, 1987, after playing 2,215 straight games. During his 2,677-game career he posted an embarrassing Japanese record 1,587 strikeouts, was hit by 161 pitches, slammed 504 home runs, had 2,543 hits, and drove in 1,448 runs. His lifetime batting average was .270. He was voted the league's most valuable player in 1984, the year he also won the batting crown. In 1976 he led the league in stolen bases. Before retiring he won three Golden Glove Awards and was named three times each to the League Best Nine and the Japan All-Stars.

Kinugasa was born in Kyoto on Jan. 18, 1947. After graduating from Heian High School in 1965, he joined the Hiroshima club and never missed a game after Oct. 19, 1970, despite slumps, illness, injuries, and a 1974 hitting average that sank to .100. When he signed his first contract, he was considered a show-off and wild spender. He bought a flashy American car with half of his bonus and gave the rest to his parents. He was so crazy about speed that he thought of becoming an auto racer if he failed in baseball. He loved jazz and classical music. Unlike the average Japanese, the 1.75-m (5-ft 9-in) Kinugasa abhorred fish, but his wife, Masako, whom he credited with much of his success, learned to prepare appetizing dishes, even with foods her husband normally disliked.

Kinugasa attributed his achievements to obeying rules and manners and abiding by *nintai* (fortitude), an expression he scribbled with his autographs. He and Masako had two children. Some senior high schools began using an English textbook in 1987 with a chapter about Kinugasa, who considered it a great honour. An even more impressive encomium came his way when he became the sixth person selected for the prime minister's award for distinguished achievement.

(KAY K. TATEISHI)

## Kitaro

Kitaro (real name: Masanori Takahashi) has been called the quintessential musician of the New Age in part because his lush electronic

SANKEI SHINBUM

instrumentals defined the restrained meditative approach of New Age and also because his personality fit the music. He did not personally identify with New Age, however, preferring to term his work "spiritual." He remarked: "I build on my own creativity, seeking a totality of life and cosmos. As long as people listen to my music, I do not care what they call it."

In 1987 New Age—crossover music that defied definition and appeared on classical, jazz, and pop charts—was big business. Kitaro had sold two million albums in the U.S. and some ten million worldwide when he wound up a 24-city debut tour in North America in October 1987. The American market had opened for the Japanese composer and synthesist only two years earlier, when Geffen Records released several albums from an extensive back catalog. Describing the full house at New York City's Radio City Music Hall as "an absolute peak" in his career, Kitaro made plans to tour Australia and Europe in 1988. In years past he had played for audiences in Asia.

Kitaro was born into a farming family in Toyohashi, Aichi Prefecture, Japan, on Feb. 4, 1953. He started playing guitar in high school, inspired by the explosive rhythm and blues tunes of Otis Redding. In the early 1970s Kitaro switched from guitar to keyboard and formed the Far East Family Band, playing psychedelic and progressive rock. It was after meeting Klaus Schulze, innovative German synthesist, that Kitaro changed direction and set out on his own with electronic keyboards. His first solo album, *TenKai* ("Astral Voyage"), appeared in 1978 and quickly created a cult following in Japan. He reached a wider audience in 1980 when he produced the title of several sound tracks for "Silk Road," a long-running documentary series on Japanese national television.

The North American tour coincided with the release of Kitaro's 12th original album, *The Light of the Spirit*. Coproduced with percussionist Mickey Hart of the Grateful Dead, the new record featured an array of American musicians. Arrangements included such Western instruments as the harmonica and, for the first time in Kitaro's music, a singing human voice in the form of wordless gospelizing. This was not a matter of westernization, though, for Kitaro insisted on music with universal appeal. This was one reason he continued to avoid the limiting effects inherent in sung lyrics.

(GERD LARSSON)

## Koop, C(harles) Everett

In the late 1980s U.S. Surgeon General C. Everett Koop became the leading spokesman in the growing fight against AIDS (acquired immune deficiency syndrome). As the chief public health official in the country, Koop advocated improved sex education in schools, including candid discussions of exactly how AIDS is trans-

BRAD MARKEL—GAMMA LIAISON

mitted and an emphasis on the correct use of a condom as the most effective protection against the disease. Koop refused to condone sexual promiscuity, homosexuality, and intravenous drug use, but he stressed education as the only way to control AIDS and rejected widespread testing for the disease as counterproductive. He was widely criticized for his views by his erstwhile conservative supporters.

To most people Koop, a devout evangelical Christian and staunch conservative, was an unlikely champion for such a traditionally liberal cause, but his frank stand on AIDS was consistent with the mix of idealism and pragmatism that he applied to all the major public health issues he faced as surgeon general. When he tackled the subject of smoking in a 1986 report, he bluntly linked all forms of cigarette smoking (including so-called passive smoking) to cancer and actively campaigned for a "smoke-free society by the year 2000."

Koop was born on Oct. 14, 1916, in Brooklyn, N.Y. After graduating (1937) from Dartmouth College, Hanover, N.H., he attended Cornell Medical College, New York City (M.D., 1941), and the University of Pennsylvania (Sc.D., 1947). From 1948 he served as surgeon in chief at Children's Hospital of Philadelphia, specializing in pediatric surgery. He taught concurrently at the University of Pennsylvania School of Medicine from 1942, becoming professor of pediatric surgery in 1959 and professor of pediatrics in 1971. While at Children's Hospital he gained the national spotlight with his innovative diagnostic and surgical techniques on babies with birth defects, particularly his successful separations of Siamese twins. Koop gained Ronald Reagan's attention in the late 1970s when he participated in a national antiabortion campaign. In February 1981 Reagan named him deputy assistant secretary of health in the Department of Health and Human Services as a step to his nomination as surgeon general, despite the fact that legally he was slightly too old to hold the position. His confirmation was held up for months by liberal opponents in the Senate (who criticized his views on abortion and women's rights) and in public health services (who questioned his public health credentials). After passing a law waiving the maximum age limit, however, the Senate finally confirmed him, and he was sworn in early in 1982.

(MELINDA SHEPHERD)

### Lacroix, Christian
In August 1987 fashion was ready for a change, and Christian Lacroix could not have timed his entrance better. With him came a new freshness and a new approach to clothes. "Couture should be fun," proclaimed the designer, "and provide dreams." The mid-thigh "pouf" skirt,

the challenging colours, the innovative prints, the huge hats with bowl-like brims filled with flowers—they were all made to dazzle and excite women into buying new clothes. The impact was universal.

Lacroix was born on May 16, 1951, in Arles, Provence, France. The city had much to offer in the way of art—important relics from its period of prosperity under Roman rule and from the Middle Ages, when it was a religious centre. Lacroix was no doubt influenced by his artistic environment when, as a young man, he chose to take a degree in art history at Montpellier University with a view to becoming curator of a museum. Once he moved to Paris, however, it soon became obvious that fate had other plans for him. In 1978 he entered the Hermès style bureau. He became assistant to ready-to-wear designer Guy Paulin in 1980, and in 1981 he landed at Jean Patou with the title of artistic director. He remained there until 1987.

In January 1986 Lacroix won the French Dé d'Or. In January 1987 he was awarded the best foreign designer award by the Council of Fashion Designers of America. The following month he received an offer, backed with the necessary money, to open his own couture house. The man behind this golden opportunity was Bernard Arnault, chairman of la Financière Agache, which already owned Dior, Boussac, and a few noncouture concerns. From then on, events moved quickly. During the summer

BEN COSTER—CAMERA PRESS, LONDON

Lacroix presented his first haute couture collection under his own name. The salons, on fashionable rue du Faubourg St. Honoré, reflected the designer's feeling for colour: for the carpets, red and orange from his beloved Provence, the bullfights, the theatre; for the walls and sofas, sand beige with a few streaks of black. Three months later Lacroix presented his first ready-to-wear collection, named "Luxe," with equal success. A less expensive ready-to-wear collection was to follow in March 1988.

(THELMA SWEETINBURGH)

### Lee Huan
In 1987 Lee Huan became one of the most important politicians in Taiwan when he was named secretary-general of the ruling Nationalist Party, or Kuomintang (KMT). Under the leadership of Pres. Chiang Ching-kuo he proved to be a moderate, pragmatic, and reform-minded statesman as the KMT introduced important political reforms designed to speed up Taiwan's democratization drive. Lee's appointment, which came after ten years of political inactivity, was a major political development that presented a new challenge to the Democratic Progressive Party, the KMT's most vocal opposition. With democratization the KMT's top priority, Lee was expected to play a major role in the transformation of the party during

its 13th party congress, to be held in late 1988.

Lee Huan was born in Hankow, Hubei (Hupeh) Province, in 1917 and educated at Chengchi and Columbia (New York City) universities. He began working closely with Chiang in the early 1950s and later took charge of the Youth Corps and the KMT's organization and training work. The effort paid handsome dividends, for it produced well-educated future leaders for the party and the government. In the 1970s Lee oversaw the implementation of a reform program, known as Taiwanization (but not localization). Because it emphasized native talents and resources, it led to the appointment of many natives of Taiwan to important positions. These reforms, however, faced a serious setback from growing conservative opposition, especially after the violent Chungli Incident—the 1977 political riots in Chungli that forced Lee's resignation. In 1978 Lee founded National Sun Yat-sen University, which he helped develop into a major institution. His concern for education led to his appointment as education minister in 1984. He soon won popular acclaim for his educational programs and for the respect he accorded intellectuals and educators. As Chiang's right-hand man in the KMT's democratic reforms, Lee enjoyed grass-roots support for his pragmatic and rational approach to Taiwan's problems, including challenges from the political opposition in Taiwan and the Communist regime on the mainland. Though Lee preferred to keep a low profile, he appeared destined to play a major role in the KMT's reforms and Taiwan's program for democratization.

(WINSTON L. Y. YANG)

### Lehn, Jean-Marie
For his role in the laboratory synthesis of molecules that mimic the vital chemical and biologic functions of molecules in living organisms, French chemist Jean-Marie Lehn shared the 1987 Nobel Prize for Chemistry with U.S. researchers Donald James Cram and Charles John Pedersen (qq.v.). Lehn was cited in particular for creating a molecule that combines with the neurotransmitter acetylcholine, a chemical transmitter of nerve signals in the human brain and nervous system.

Pedersen was credited with laying the groundwork for the prizewinning research with his synthesis of a class of two-dimensional, ring-shaped compounds, called crown ethers, capable of selectively recognizing and combining with other molecules. Working independently, Lehn and Cram extended Pedersen's finds to include three-dimensional molecules that imitate and illuminate the ways in which, for example, natural enzymes recognize the molecules they react with, hormones initiate their effects, neurotransmitters carry signals, and components of the immune system recognize and bind to foreign molecules. As Lehn worked to synthesize

TSCHAEN—SIPA PRESS

mimics of natural molecules, he developed a terminology that thereafter became an accepted part of organic chemistry nomenclature. He named the cavities within his molecules crypts, the compounds themselves cryptands, and their complexes cryptates. Although the work of the three laureates had been primarily scientific, practical applications had been emerging in recent years.

Lehn was born on Sept. 30, 1939, in Rosheim, France. He received a Ph.D. in chemistry from the University of Strasbourg in 1963. In 1970 he became a professor of chemistry at the Louis Pasteur University in Strasbourg, where he remained until 1979, when he took a professorship at the Collège de France in Paris.

(CAROLYN D. NEWTON)

**Maclennan, Robert Adam Ross**
On Aug. 29, 1987, Robert Maclennan became the third leader of Britain's Social Democratic Party (SDP). The little-known Scottish politician succeeded the charismatic former foreign secretary, David Owen.

The suddenness of Maclennan's rise was matched only by the weakness of the party he inherited. In the June 1987 general elections, only 22 Alliance (of the Liberal Party and the SDP) candidates won seats in Parliament, and just 5 of these belonged to the SDP. Liberal leader David Steel called for the two parties to merge. Owen opposed the idea, and when SDP members voted by a margin of 57–43% in favour of the principle of merger, he immediately resigned; he indicated that he would create a new, antimerger party and carried two SDP members of Parliament (MPs) with him. Since the party constitution required that the party leader be an MP, this left only two possible candidates for the succession: Charles Kennedy, an enthusiastic supporter of merger, and Maclennan, who had maintained a relatively neutral stance on the issue. Because Kennedy was only 27, though, Maclennan was the only candidate eligible for the post.

Maclennan was born on June 26, 1936, in Glasgow. He studied law at the University of Oxford and was admitted to the bar in 1962. In 1966 he became Labour Party MP for the constituency of Caithness and Sutherland in the Scottish Highlands. Maclennan consistently took positions to the right of the Labour Party. Following Labour's defeat in 1970, he was appointed opposition spokesman, first on Scotland and then on defense, but he resigned in April 1972 over Labour's opposition to Britain's membership in the European Communities. This did not, however, prevent him from being appointed a junior minister in the Department of Prices and Consumer Protection (1974–79) when Labour returned to office.

Maclennan was one of the original group of Labour MPs to leave the party in 1981 to form the SDP. With his quiet, rational manner he made little impact in the House of Commons or on television, but his legal training proved invaluable in drafting the SDP's constitution. That constitution could not, however, contain the feud that erupted between the pro-merger and antimerger factions after the 1987 general elections. In September, in his first speech as SDP leader, Maclennan attacked "the zealots in our midst" on both sides of the argument and insisted, "The raging must stop." Everyone applauded, but few seemed to alter their behaviour. (PETER KELLNER)

**Madonna**
Unlike her "Virgin Tour" two years earlier, when she performed in relatively small U.S. auditoriums, Madonna launched her "Who's That Girl Tour" at Tokyo's Korakuen Stadium in the summer of 1987, singing, purring, and gyrating before a capacity crowd of 35,000 screaming, mostly teenaged fans. This worldwide extravaganza proved to be another jewel in the young entertainer's crown of success.

In only four years Madonna starred in three feature films—*Desperately Seeking Susan* (1985), *Shanghai Surprise* (1986), and *Who's That Girl?* (1987)—and had more than a dozen

smash-hit records. Each one sold well over a million copies, and several reached the top of *Billboard*'s pop charts, including "Borderline," "Into the Groove," "Like a Virgin," "Crazy for You," "Material Girl," and the controversial "Papa Don't Preach," which was criticized by spokespersons for Planned Parenthood and applauded by antiabortionists.

Madonna herself was no stranger to controversy. She was criticized by feminists, who complained that she was setting the women's movement back several years with her sexually provocative, "boy toy" image. And thanks to her combative husband, actor Sean Penn, whom she married on Aug. 16, 1985, and who had a worldwide reputation for confrontations with photographers, she had been party to a number of public spectacles. (She filed for divorce in November 1987 but later withdrew the petition.) A less determined person might grow weary of the pressure of staying on top and having her private life publicly scrutinized, but Madonna became known for taking the trappings of her career in stride.

Born on Aug. 16, 1958, in Bay City, Mich., Madonna Louise Veronica Ciccone was the third child in a family of three girls and three boys born to a first-generation Italian-American father and a French-Canadian mother, who died when Madonna was five. While attending high school, Madonna performed in several musical productions and won a dance scholarship to the University of Michigan, which she attended for a few semesters.

In the summer of 1978 she moved to New York City, where she danced with the Alvin Ailey Dance Theater on a scholarship. Not satisfied with her rate of advancement there, she went to Paris, where she performed as a dancer and background singer. Upon her return to New York she became the drummer-vocalist for the musical group Breakfast Club. After that combination of the group disbanded in late 1982, she recorded the song "Everybody," which was well-received at local dance clubs. This led to a recording contract with Sire Records and the number four hit, "Lucky Star." Madonna's first album, entitled *Madonna,* got national airplay, and the rest is, as they say, musical history.

(EDWARD PAUL MORAGNE)

**Moore, John Edward Michael**
In 1987 many expected that when Margaret Thatcher (*q.v.*) eventually retired as leader of the U.K.'s Conservative Party, the battle to be her successor would be fought between those who wished to continue the course she had started and those who wished to tilt the party back toward a more consensual approach to politics. In that contest the likely carrier of the Thatcherite torch would be John Moore, who was appointed in June 1987 to run the Department of Health and Social Security.

Moore was born on Nov. 26, 1937, in Kentish Town, then a working-class part of London. His father was a manual labourer, his mother a barmaid. He escaped his modest background via a scholarship to the Licensed Victuallers' boarding school and a degree at the London School of Economics. There he met his future wife, Sheila, a student from the U.S. Moore's belief in free-market economics flowed from their courtship; when she returned to Chicago to complete her education, Moore followed, found work in a local bank, and inhaled the values of American capitalism.

Back in Britain, he built a career as a banker and stockbroker. In February 1974 he was elected Conservative member of Parliament for the south London constituency of Croydon Central. In May 1979, when Thatcher became prime minister, Moore was appointed under secretary for energy. The chance to display his political talents came in June 1983, when he was appointed economic secretary to the Treasury, with responsibility for implementing the government's privatization program. In Parliament and on television, he proclaimed the case for selling state-owned companies such as British Telecom and British Airways. The sales

proved remarkably popular with investors, who invariably saw the value of their shares grow—partly because the privatization stocks were generously priced and partly because, at the time, shares in general were rising in Britain's strong bull market.

In 1986 Moore was rewarded with a seat in the Cabinet, as minister of transport; a year later, after Thatcher's third election victory, he took over the Department of Health and Social Security. Responsible for more than half of all central government spending, the department was traditionally a graveyard for ambitious politicians. Within months Moore showed that he intended to dominate the giant ministry when he announced plans to streamline the complex social security system. His political prospects rested in large measure on his success in accomplishing this task. (PETER KELLNER)

**Müller, Karl Alexander**
In order to avoid the pressure of competition and gain more time for further research, Swiss physicist Karl Müller and fellow scientist Johannes Georg Bednorz (*q.v.*) of West Germany tried to keep their superconductivity research a secret, even from their colleagues at the IBM Zürich Research Laboratory. Ironically, by the end of 1987 the whole world knew of their work after they were awarded the year's Nobel Prize for Physics for discovering superconductivity in oxide ceramic compounds at a record high temperature of 35 K (kelvins; about $-238°$ C [$-396°$ F])—some 12° above the previous record.

Müller was born on April 20, 1927, in Basel, Switz., and received his Ph.D. in physics from the Swiss Federal Institute of Technology in 1958. He spent five years as a project manager with Battelle Institute in Geneva before joining, in 1963, the IBM Zürich laboratory, where he worked in solid-state physics. In 1973 he was named manager of the laboratory's physics department. He was appointed IBM fellow in 1982 and soon after recruited Bednorz to assist him in his superconductivity research.

Müller, a specialist in oxides, was prompted to study superconductivity in these materials (all previous superconductors had been metals or metal alloys) as a result of a 1983 scientific conference in Sicily, at which theorists suggested that the molecular structure of oxides might make them suitable for superconductivity. Although the laureates' discovery was initially greeted with skepticism from other scientists in the field, particularly because most oxides normally do not conduct electricity at room temperature, it soon was confirmed in other laboratories and subsequently inspired a frenetic wave of new research. The result was the discovery of ceramics that become superconductors at still higher temperatures—materials that, for the first time, had a strong poten-

AP/WIDE WORLD

tial for practical applications. Because electrical current in a superconductor loses virtually no energy to resistance, some scientists predicted that the new high-temperature superconductors might bring a new era of ultraefficient power generation and transmission.

(CAROLYN D. NEWTON)

### Nguyen Van Linh

The most significant of the sweeping changes made by the sixth congress of the Communist Party of Vietnam was the installation on Dec. 18, 1986, of Nguyen Van Linh as Communist Party general secretary and effective national leader. Linh immediately took pragmatic measures to reform Vietnam's fossilized economy, thus inviting comparisons with China's Deng Xiaoping (Teng Hsiao-p'ing) and Mikhail Gorbachev of the U.S.S.R.

During his first year in office, Linh engineered broad policy changes, set about dismantling entrenched privileges of the northern bureaucracy, and harnessed dormant entrepreneurial spirit in the south. He already had a reputation as an able administrator of Ho Chi Minh City; by extending programs applied in the south throughout Vietnam, he set in motion a radical overhaul of agriculture, industry, trade, and finance. Newspapers carried a column "Things Which Must Be Done Immediately" signed "N.V.L." Asked if this crusading journalist was himself, Linh said the author was Noi Va Lam (literally, "speak and act").

Little was known of Nguyen Van Linh's life. He was born as Nguyen Van Cuc in 1913 near Hanoi, but he spent most of his life in the south and was totally identified with the political struggles there against the French, the Americans, and the government of South Vietnam. Since 1975 he had been a key figure in southern administration. Linh was known by so many aliases that it was not until the mid-1970s that the U.S. Central Intelligence Agency realized that four important cadres were one and the same.

The French sentenced him to life imprisonment for subversion in 1930 when he was 15 years old. He was freed in an amnesty in 1936 but was incarcerated again in 1941–45, both times being held on Con Son Island. At a party seminar in May 1987, Linh told of how, while he was in jail, he had secretly read the works of Marx and Lenin in French so many times that he could recite long passages. In 1982 he was dropped, inexplicably, from the Politburo. He made a triumphant comeback in 1985 and consolidated his position in the months before and after his predecessor Le Duan's death in July 1986.

(ROBERT WOODROW)

### Noriega, Manuel Antonio

In 1987 the alleged activities of a man known as "pineapple face" left anything but a sweet taste in the mouth of the average Panamanian. Earning that nickname for his plump, pockmarked face, Gen. Manuel Antonio Noriega—head of Panama's National Defense Forces and the real power behind the civilian government—was accused by a former military official and other prominent Panamanians of election rigging, drug trafficking, drug-money laundering, murdering a political dissident, and selling U.S. secrets and advanced technology to Cuba and the Soviet Union. But what most enraged Panamanians was the charge that Noriega had plotted the 1981 airplane crash that killed the then military leader Omar Torrijos Herrera, a national hero. The 49-year-old Noriega tried smothering the protests with a "state of urgency" that suspended political and civil rights. That, however, did not stop the National Civic Crusade, a coalition of civic, business, and student groups, from leading a two-day work stoppage that shut down 90% of the nation's shops and offices.

Some of the charges against Noriega were not new. In 1986 the *New York Times,* quoting U.S. intelligence reports, alleged that Noriega and his military cronies intimidated political dissidents and enriched themselves off drug trafficking.

Though the allegations piled up during 1986 and 1987, the U.S. was reluctant to take forceful action against Noriega, in part because he had been a cooperative host for the Southern Command, the U.S. headquarters for military and intelligence operations in Latin America.

Noriega was born to a poor Panamanian family on Feb. 11, 1938, in Panama City. He won a scholarship to study at a military academy in Peru, returning after graduation to join Panama's National Guard (now National Defense Forces) as a first lieutenant. In 1970 Noriega helped crush a coup attempt against Torrijos, who showed his gratitude by naming him intelligence chief. Giving him the power to gather information against political rivals, the post cleared the way for Noriega to become the new commander of the National Defense Forces in 1982. The flamboyant commander, who was known to attend formal events wearing a purple safari suit, repeatedly denied that he was making millions through the drug trade. Yet he managed to maintain several homes in Panama, a luxury apartment in Paris, and a villa in the French Alps—all on an official annual salary of $50,000.

(MICHAEL AMEDEO)

### North, Oliver Laurence

On July 7, 1987, Lieut. Col. Oliver North broke his long silence and took the stand before the U.S. congressional committees investigating the Iran-*contra* affair. Speculation abounded: would he play the scapegoat and take full responsibility, or would he provide the "smoking gun" to implicate Pres. Ronald Reagan in the scandal? In the end he did neither. In six days of nationally televised testimony, North took control of the hearings. Alternately charming and defiant, he defended the covert activities of the National Security Council (NSC), including the arms deal with Iran. He charged that using the Iranian funds for the Nicaraguan rebels was "a neat idea" necessitated by a weak Congress. He admitted that he had shredded important documents "in earnest" as early as October 1986 and that he had repeatedly lied to investigators. He persistently argued that he was only a good marine, following orders in a just cause. His testimony included serious accusations against former national security adviser (NSA) Robert MacFarlane, NSA Rear Adm. John Poindexter, and, particularly, the late CIA chief William Casey. North acknowledged that he believed Reagan had been fully informed of his actions and said that he had sent five memoranda to his superiors seeking the president's approval, but he insisted that he had never seen an answer. North expressed no regrets for his actions but denied charges that he had made personal use of some of the funds.

North's self-assured appearance on television, coupled with his vehement support for the *contra* cause, caught the public's imagination. "Olliemania" swept the country, and he became a folk hero to admiring Americans, even some who disapproved of his actions. Bumper stickers, T-shirts, and other Ollie collectibles appeared everywhere, while over $100,000 poured into his defense fund. Within a few weeks, however, public sympathy waned. Olliemania was over.

North was born on Oct. 7, 1943, in San Antonio, Texas, but grew up in the small town of Philmont, N.Y. He attended the State University of New York at Brockport for two years before enrolling at the Naval Academy at Annapolis, Md. During his 11 months as a platoon leader in Vietnam (1968–69), where he was admired for his courage and devotion to duty, he received the Silver Star, the Bronze Star, and two Purple Hearts. After teaching at the officer's training school in Quantico, Va., and serving on Okinawa in 1973–74, he was hospitalized briefly for "delayed battle stress." In 1981 he joined the NSC as deputy director of the political-military affairs bureau. In the next five years he was involved in numerous covert operations, such as the 1985 capture of the Palestinians who hijacked the Italian liner *Achille Lauro.*

(MELINDA SHEPHERD)

### Pálsson, Thorsteinn

Thorsteinn Pálsson was sworn into office as prime minister of Iceland on July 8, 1987. At the age of 39 he became the youngest prime minister in the history of the Icelandic republic. The leader of the Independence Party, he was at the head of a coalition government in which the two outgoing coalition partners—the Independence Party and the Progressive Party—were joined by the Social Democratic Party. The new government was formed after protracted negotiations following general elections on April 25, which had resulted in the worst parliamentary stalemate in the country's post-World War II history.

Pálsson's previous political career was a relatively short one. He had served in the Althing (parliament) for a single four-year term, having been first elected in the 1983 general elections. He had barely entered the Althing when the previous leader of the Independence Party, former prime minister Geir Hallgrímsson, resigned from the leadership and threw the succession open to the party convention. Pálsson won the contest by a wide margin, defeating two other contenders, and became party chairman on Nov. 8, 1983. In 1985 he became minister of finance in the government led by his predecessor as prime minister, Steingrímur Hermannsson of the Progressive Party, and he remained in that capacity until he became prime minister. Pálsson also served briefly as minister of industry in 1987.

Pálsson was born Oct. 29, 1947. Prior to entering politics he graduated from the University of Iceland in 1974 with a degree in law and subsequently became a journalist. He was editor of the conservative afternoon newspaper *Visir* from 1975 to 1979, and he served as managing director of the Employers' Federation from 1979 to 1983.

Pálsson owed much of the success of his political career to the fact that he was a good orator and had proved to be a patient negotiator, with a reputation for reaching acceptable agreements in difficult circumstances. The new government's program included plans to introduce new indirect taxes in order to offset an expected budget deficit; renewed inflationary pressures were likely to be among its most pressing economic problems. The government announced that its foreign policy would be largely unchanged from that of the previous coalition, though links with the European Communities, which had replaced the U.S. as the country's major trading partner, were strengthened.

(BJÖRN MATTHÍASSON)

### Parkinson, Cecil Edward

On June 13, 1987, one of U.K. Prime Minister Margaret Thatcher's favourite politicians, Cecil Parkinson, returned to her Cabinet as secretary of state for energy, four years after he had been forced to resign and his career, many people believed, had ended. Parkinson and Thatcher had remained close friends, however; Parkinson and his wife were personal guests of the Thatchers over Christmas 1986. Following her third election victory on June 11, 1987, Thatcher decided it was safe to reward her loyal supporter.

Parkinson was born on Sept. 1, 1931, at Carnforth, Lancashire. Like Thatcher—and unlike most leading Conservatives—he was born into a family of modest means; his father was a railway worker. At 16 he joined the Labour Party, but he left three years later and joined the Conservatives in 1959. He first entered Parliament in 1970, having secured his financial future through a construction company he helped to start.

Parkinson came to prominence in 1981 when Thatcher plucked him from junior ministerial office and appointed him chairman of the Conservative Party; she also gave him a place in the Cabinet (as chancellor of the Duchy of Lancaster, an archaic term used to justify a Cabinet place for a minister who has no department to run). The Conservatives were unpopular, and the party machine was not functioning smoothly. Parkinson proved an ideal appointment. His consistent loyalty to Thatcher led to his appointment to the small inner "War Cabinet" set up when Argentina invaded the Falkland Islands/Islas Malvinas in April 1982. Parkinson also overhauled the party machine and planned the campaign that led to the Conservatives' landslide victory in the June 1983 general elections.

During the final days of the campaign, Parkinson learned that his mistress, Sara Keays, was pregnant. He told Thatcher; the only immediate difference it made to his career was that he was appointed secretary of state for trade and industry, not foreign secretary as she had originally intended. Three months later news of Keays's pregnancy leaked to the media, and Keays also claimed that in the course of their long-standing relationship Parkinson had promised to divorce his wife and marry her. Despite Thatcher's attempt to keep Parkinson in his job, he resigned within ten days of the story becoming public. For four years he stayed on the back benches, until June 1987 and Thatcher's invitation for him to rejoin the Cabinet.   (PETER KELLNER)

### Pedersen, Charles John

In the 1960s, while a research chemist for E. I. du Pont de Nemours & Co., American Charles Pedersen synthesized a group of organic compounds that he named crown ethers for their structure—a loose, flexible ring of carbon atoms punctuated at regular intervals with oxygen atoms. By varying the size of the rings, Pedersen found that his crown ethers would bind the atoms of certain metal elements at the centre of the "crown" while taking on a more rigid, platelike shape. The work demonstrated that it was possible to make molecules in the laboratory that would selectively react with other atoms and compounds much as do molecules found in living organisms. His discoveries were expanded independently by two other scientists, American Donald James Cram and Frenchman Jean-Marie Lehn (qq.v.). The result, the laboratory synthesis of molecules that mimic the behaviour of natural biologic molecules, won the three scientists the Nobel Prize for Chemistry in 1987.

In its announcement, the Royal Swedish Academy of Sciences cited Pedersen for initiating what it termed "one of the most active and expanding fields of chemical research." The work of the three laureates has helped scientists understand how biologic compounds recognize

AP/WIDE WORLD

and bind to each other, and it may have applications in the design of catalysts (reaction-promoting substances) for medical and industrial uses.

Pedersen was born on Oct. 3, 1904, in Pusan, Korea. In the 1920s he moved to the U.S. to study chemical engineering at the University of Dayton in Ohio, where he took his bachelor's degree. He received a master's degree in organic chemistry from the Massachusetts Institute of Technology. Rather than pursue a doctorate, Pedersen chose to launch his career as a research chemist for Du Pont, where he remained until his retirement in 1969.

(CAROLYN D. NEWTON)

### Pollard, Jonathan Jay

On March 4, 1987, U.S. District Judge Aubrey Robinson sentenced Jonathan Pollard to life imprisonment on a plea of guilty to having conveyed classified information to Israel. Pollard received the maximum sentence, even though he had cooperated with investigators since pleading guilty to the accusation on June 4, 1986. Secretary of Defense Caspar Weinberger had written to the judge that Pollard had compromised sources of intelligence and had revealed the locations of ships. In 1986 Prime Minister Shimon Peres of Israel had apologized to the U.S. for Pollard's activities, and an intelligence official in the Israeli Ministry of Defense who may have recruited Pollard had been dismissed. But Israel's highest officials may have known about Pollard. Friendly nations commonly spy on each other—though usually without employing agents.

When arrested for espionage in November 1985, Pollard was a civilian employed by the Department of the Navy to analyze intelligence data. At sentencing he claimed to have been motivated by "sectarianism," but Israeli agents apparently had promised to pay him $30,000 each year for a period of ten years and had already paid him over $45,000. Many who knew him said that he admired Israel and told of (unverifiable) adventures as an agent of Israel and the U.S.

Pollard was born in Galveston, Texas, on Aug. 7, 1954. While he was young, his family moved to South Bend, Ind., and he graduated from Stanford University in 1976. In 1977 he was rejected for a job with the Central Intelligence Agency (CIA) after an investigation uncovered his penchant for storytelling, and he began studies at Tufts University in Medford, Mass. In 1979, when he got a job at the Navy Operational Surveillance and Intelligence Center, the CIA did not make its damaging report available to those investigating his fitness. Caught lying on the job in 1981, he was stripped of security clearance and told to seek psychiatric help, but his clearance was restored after he filed a grievance. In 1984 he was assigned to the Navy's Anti-Terrorist Alert Center. With access to all government documents that could help with his job, he apparently supplied Israel with information from the Departments of State, Defense, and Justice, the CIA, and the National Security Agency. On Oct. 25, 1985, he was seen carrying a large bundle from his office and was placed under surveillance. On November 21 he was arrested outside the Israeli embassy in Washington, where he had gone in hope of asylum.

(CHARLES JOHNSON TAGGART)

### Puckett, Kirby

Teammates rubbed his shaved head for good luck. His megawatt smile gave them good cheer. But most of all, Kirby Puckett's improbably rotund body gave them good baseball—at the plate, on the bases, and in centre field. When the Minnesota Twins won the 1987 World Series four games to three, Puckett batted .357 and tied a Series record by scoring four runs in the pivotal sixth game.

He looked more like a mascot than a hero. He stood 1.7 m (5 ft 8 in), wore size 8½ shoes, and weighed 93 kg (205 lb) without a sharp corner on his body. Puckett's pudgy appearance belied his powerful build, however. When he realized as a youth that he would never grow tall, he worked long hours to grow strong.

Even so, Puckett hit only 17 home runs in his first four professional seasons and none as a Twins rookie in 1984. Then, in 1986, his 31 home runs made him the first major leaguer ever to hit more than 30 homers after a 500-at-bat season without any. Also in 1986 he led the Twins in 11 categories on offense and earned his first of two Gold Gloves for his play in centre field. He led the league by producing 14.8% of his team's runs.

With a second all-star season in 1987, Puckett established his consistency. He followed his .328 batting average of 1986 with .332, which

AP/WIDE WORLD

was fourth best in the league and raised his career average to .311. He followed his 1986 total of 96 runs batted in with 99, his 31 homers with 28, and his 119 runs with 96. He stole at least eight opponents' home runs by leaping above the fence.

Puckett became a fans' favourite as the Twins in 1987 won their first American League West championship in 17 years and first league pennant in 22 years. "He's got this charisma," teammate Al Newman said. "He's always smiling. I've never heard him booed."

Puckett was born March 14, 1961, the youngest of nine children, on Chicago's South Side and grew up in a housing project notorious for breeding criminals and drug addicts. He played baseball whenever he could. When he was alone, he hit rolled-up socks in his bedroom. He was voted to the high-school All-American team, but without the size to interest scouts he went to work at a Ford Motor Co. plant.

His break came at a professional tryout camp, at which the coach of Bradley University, Peoria, Ill., offered him a scholarship. He left Bradley after a year, moving closer to suburban Chicago because his father had died, and at Triton Community College, River Grove, Ill., he could not fight the scouts away after batting .472 with 42 stolen bases. In January 1982 the Twins made him the third selection in the draft.   (KEVIN M. LAMB)

### Rabuka, Sitiveni

On May 14, 1987, Sitiveni (Steve) Rabuka led a coup in Fiji that overthrew the recently elected coalition government of Timoci Bavadra. Although Rabuka justified the coup as being necessary to preserve the peace between Indians and ethnic Fijians and to protect the land rights and political power of the latter, his move paved the way for some of the worst violence in the island's history. On September 25 he staged a second military takeover in his effort to consolidate a power base. This move evoked angry responses, particularly from Australia and New Zealand, which imposed economic sanctions on Fiji. Rabuka called a meeting of diplomats from major countries on September 28, but they were prepared to recognize only Gov.-Gen. Ratu (Chief) Sir Penaia Ganilau as head of state. Despite the opposition, Rabuka declared Fiji a republic at midnight on October 6, ending its 113-year link with the British crown and membership in the Commonwealth. Ganilau was forced to resign as governor-general.

Rabuka was born in September 1949 in Cakaudrone Province, where, according to tradition, Ganilau was his high chief. He was educated at the Queen Victoria School, after which he trained at the Army Staff College at Waiouru, N.Z. He attended the Indian Armed Forces Staff College (1979) and then Australia's Joint Staff Service College (1981). Rabuka commanded the Fiji contingent in Lebanon in 1980 and Fiji's 2nd Battalion with the Sinai Peacekeeping Force in 1984. In between, he served as general staff officer in charge of training; in 1985 he became staff officer (Operations and Training) and was ranked third in the Fijian Army. His rank as lieutenant colonel was confirmed in 1982, and after the coup he was promoted to full colonel and made commander of the Fiji military forces by the governor-general. Following the second coup, he was made brigadier-general. Rabuka's rapid rise in the Fijian Army was remarkable, since leadership was normally by high-ranking chiefs only.

Rabuka spent October and November trying to consolidate his position and to run the country with the 22-member Cabinet he had formed. He was having a new constitution drafted that would favour the ethnic Fijians. Internal and foreign confidence in Fiji continued to decline, however, and as the country neared economic collapse, Rabuka admitted defeat and on December 5 announced that he would relinquish power to a civilian government. In the two days prior to his decision, he held intense talks with Ganilau and former prime minister Ratu Sir Kamisese Mara, who became president and prime minister, respectively.

(BARRIE MACDONALD)

**Rafsanjani, Hojatolislam Hashemi Ali Akbar**
During recent years Hojatolislam Rafsanjani had emerged as a major political force in Iranian domestic politics in an atmosphere of expectation of change brought on by the apparent deteriorating health of Iranian leader Ayatollah Ruhollah Khomeini. He was not the only person within the regime playing out a public role as a servant of Khomeini, however, and at all times his strength vis-à-vis other contenders for power derived only from his abilities to relate to and keep the confidence of the ayatollah.

Rafsanjani's position was created rather by default, many of the more influential revolutionary leaders having been killed in the 1981 bomb assassinations in Tehran, and by the ineptitude of his rivals. He showed political skills in avoiding the pitfalls of office in the revolutionary regime and demonstrated considerable pragmatism in dealing with the outside world. While benefiting from unimpeachable Islamic credentials, Rafsanjani did not yet carry great weight in the Shi'ah religious hierarchy, a liability that might exclude him from inheriting directly the mantle of spiritual leader from Khomeini.

Rafsanjani was born in 1935 in Rafsanjan, Kerman Province. He came from a religious family and studied first in Rafsanjan before moving to the holy city of Qom in 1949. He became a disciple of Khomeini in 1958 and studied under him. Rafsanjani was in Qom immediately preceding and during the religious unrest and riots of 1963 that led to the expulsion of Khomeini from Iran. In 1964 he himself was arrested by the authorities for antistatist activities. He was arrested on a number of other occasions and was in prison for four years (1973–78).

After the overthrow of Shah Mohammad Reza Pahlavi in 1979, Rafsanjani was given a

place on the Revolutionary Council and served as acting interior minister during the early years of the revolution. A prime mover in the establishment of the Islamic Republican Party, which came to dominate the Majlis (parliament), he eventually abandoned leadership of the party to develop his role as speaker (and, in effect, leader) of the Majlis, a post to which he was elected in 1980. He took over responsibility for the military wing of the regime and in June 1987 was appointed to the Council of Guardians, a key position in the management of the country's future.

(KEITH S. MCLACHLAN)

**Ramaphosa, (Matamele) Cyril**
In 1987 Cyril Ramaphosa, a 34-year-old lawyer, emerged as a formidable labour leader during the first major strike by black workers in the South African goldfields. Although the miners failed to win all their demands, their show of unity, resolution, and organization improved their future bargaining strength and alerted the country to the new importance of organized black workers in a key industrial area of the republic. When Ramaphosa became secretary of the all-black National Union of Mineworkers (NUM) in 1982, its strength was only 6,000; five years later it had grown to 300,000. Much of this success was due to the organizational skill and leadership qualities of Ramaphosa, who chose to become a labour organizer in preference to a legal career; he had qualified as a lawyer in 1981 following a turbulent career in student politics.

Ramaphosa was born Nov. 17, 1952, the son of a mine policeman, in the black metropolis of Soweto on the outskirts of Johannesburg. He was educated at the local Sekano-Ntoane school, a breeding ground of student militancy, and studied law. As chairman of the South African Students' Organization in 1974, he was involved in a strike that resulted in his detention for 11 months without trial. Arrested again in 1976 for his role in the Soweto students' revolt of that year, he was sentenced to prison for six months.

After his release Ramaphosa joined the Black Peoples' Convention, the black consciousness movement inspired by Stephen Biko, who became a national martyr after dying at the hands of the police while in prison in 1977. Although he remained dedicated to Biko's ideas,

Ramaphosa learned the need for interracial cooperation in mustering support for the miners in their confrontation with the Chamber of Mines, one of the country's most powerful industrial institutions. Ramaphosa owed his success in part to his calm diplomacy as a negotiator and also to his refusal to allow the NUM to engage in overt political—as opposed to direct industrial—activities. Nevertheless, he saw the strike as having a wide political significance. "The struggle we are involved in on the mines is a training ground for our people, for the ultimate goal is liberation," he declared.

(COLIN LEGUM)

**Ratushinskaya, Irina**
In June 1987, eight months after her release from prison and six months after she left the Soviet Union for medical treatment abroad, Irina Ratushinskaya was stripped of her Soviet citizenship for "slander against the state." This echoed the trial sentence of a little more than five years earlier when she was accused of "dissemination of poetry." A talented poet whose books had been appearing only in the West (*Poems,* 1984; *No, I'm Not Afraid,* 1986; *Beyond the Limit,* 1987), Ratushinskaya had gained recognition for her dedication to the cause of human rights and for the severity of her punishment by the Soviet government.

Irina Borisovna Ratushinskaya was born on March 4, 1954, in Odessa (Ukraine). She was brought up in a politically loyal atmosphere but soon showed signs of an independent spirit. After studying physics and mathematics at the University of Odessa, she began teaching in 1976. Her brushes with the authorities started when she refused to report on her friends' activities and continued when she rejected official policies against Jews. She also began writing poetry seriously, and her work was published in samizdat (underground publications).

In 1979 she married Igor Gerashchenko (in a religious ceremony) and moved to Kiev, where she again incurred the authorities' displeasure by living and working without a residence permit. Together with her husband, also a physicist, she became involved in the human rights movement. In 1980 they applied for permission to travel abroad, but the permit was denied by the authorities.

In December 1981 the couple was arrested for taking part in a human rights demonstration in Moscow and spent ten days in prison. She was arrested again in September 1982, and in March 1983 she was sentenced to seven years of labour camp and five years of internal exile, an unusually severe sentence for a woman. Her poems figured prominently in the trial. The three and a half years she spent in a strict-regime camp were characterized by her struggle for human dignity. The spiritual dimension of her life in prison was expressed in poems that were smuggled to the West, where numerous organizations began working for her release.

Ratushinskaya was freed on Oct. 9, 1986. In December 1986 she and her husband left the Soviet Union for Britain, and in March 1987 they went to Evanston, Ill., where she accepted the post of poet in residence at Northwestern University. Traveling extensively, she devoted enormous effort to making the plight of Soviet political prisoners known to the West and was working on a book about her fellow women prisoners.

(LEAH D. HOTIMLANSKA)

**Reagan, Ronald Wilson**
On Jan. 5, 1987, Ronald Reagan underwent prostate surgery. Twenty-two days later, in his state of the union address to Congress, he had to take responsibility for a decision that "did not work"—to sell arms to Iran. (*See* WORLD AFFAIRS [North America]: *United States:* Special Report.) The Congress that he addressed was the first in his six-year tenure as president of the United States in which the Democratic opposition controlled the Senate as well as the House of Representatives. With his usual outward calm, Reagan faced the difficult first month of a difficult year.

On February 26 Reagan's own Special Review Board, chaired by John G. Tower, submitted a report on the sale of arms to Iran and the diversion of profits to the *contras,* armed opponents of the Sandinista regime in Nicaragua. The report implied that Reagan's statements to the board were contradictory and criticized his detached style of management. Always the communicator, Reagan made a televised speech on March 4. He took full responsibility and, according to the CBS News/*New York Times* poll, improved his standing with the public.

On February 28 Mikhail Gorbachev, general secretary of the Communist Party of the Soviet Union, suggested that the U.S. and the U.S.S.R.

might destroy ground-based nuclear missiles without reference to the Strategic Defense Initiative, which Reagan favoured. Negotiators for the two superpowers went to work on a treaty. They continued despite Soviet criticism of Reagan's decision in March to deploy new defensive weapons.

On August 12, because of congressional hearings, Reagan had to make a second televised speech about the sales of arms to Iran. His prestige was injured in October and November by a decline in the stock market and by problems in filling a seat on the Supreme Court. However, Reagan had the support of the public—except, ironically, the most anti-Soviet Republicans—for work on the treaty on ground-based intermediate-range nuclear missiles. On December 8 he received Gorbachev at the White House, and they signed the treaty, the first to require destruction of existing nuclear missiles—albeit of a relatively unimportant class.

Ronald Reagan was born in Tampico, Ill., on Feb. 6, 1911. He received a B.A. from Eureka College in 1932 and then became a broadcaster in Iowa. In 1937 he became a motion-picture actor under contract to Warner Brothers. He served as president of the Screen Actors Guild from 1947 to 1952 and 1959 to 1960 and was a host of dramatic television shows from 1954 to 1965. He was governor of California from 1967 to 1975 and was first inaugurated as president of the United States in 1981.

(CHARLES JOHNSON TAGGART)

**Reisman, Simon**
When U.S. Pres. Ronald Reagan met with Canadian Prime Minister Brian Mulroney at Quebec City in March 1985, they agreed to seek the "broadest possible agreement aimed at the reduction and elimination of trade barriers" between the two countries. Free-trade talks began in Ottawa on May 22, 1986. Appointed as trade ambassador to lead the talks for Canada was Simon Reisman, a tough and experienced negotiator who had long been an advocate of free trade. Following months of difficult talks, an agreement was finally concluded on Oct. 3, 1987—just 20 minutes before the deadline.

Reisman had been involved in almost every significant Canadian trade negotiation since World War II. As a young public servant, he was secretary to the Canadian delegations at the Geneva Trade and Tariff Conference (1947) and at the World Conference on Trade and Employment in Havana (1947–48). He was a member of the Canadian contingent at all sessions of the General Agreement on Tariffs and Trade between 1948 and 1952. Reisman negotiated for Canada at talks that led to the Canada-U.S. Autopact (1965), which created what amounted to a free-trade agreement for the North American automobile industry. From 1955 to 1957 he was assistant director of research for the Royal Commission on Canada's Economic Prospects. Born June 19, 1919, in Montreal, Sol Simon Reisman earned degrees in economics and political science at McGill University (B.A., 1941; M.A., 1942) before serving with the Royal Canadian Artillery in World War II. After attending the London School of Economics (1945), he joined the Canadian civil service in 1946 and rose quickly through the ranks at the Department of Finance. From 1957 to 1961 he was general director of economics and international affairs for that department, and from 1961 to 1964 he was assistant deputy minister. In 1964 he was made deputy minister of the new Department of Industry. He served as secretary of the Treasury Board from 1968 to 1970 before returning to the Department of Finance as deputy minister (1970–75).

Resigning from public service in 1975, Reisman set up a consulting firm in Ottawa, but he was called back several times. In 1978 he was appointed to the royal commission that investigated the Canadian automobile industry, and in 1983 he was chief government negotiator in the agreement concerning aboriginal land claims in the western Arctic. In 1978 he was awarded the Order of Canada.

(DIANE LOIS WAY)

**Rice, Jerry**
His own team had to change quarterbacks, but Jerry Rice kept catching touchdown passes. His opponents changed defenses to blanket him, but Rice kept catching touchdown passes. He caught short ones, sneaking through congested defenses, and long ones, speeding past dejected defenders. He caught 22 touchdown passes in the 1987 season, breaking the old National Football League (NFL) record of 18 even though he played in only 12 games.

With a 23rd touchdown on a running play, Rice was one short of the league's total touchdown record, set in 16 games, and became the third nonkicker in 20 years to lead NFL scorers. He extended his streak of consecutive games with a touchdown catch to 13, breaking the record of 11 that had not even been tied since 1960.

Rice's coach, Bill Walsh of the San Francisco 49ers, called him "the single most dominating player in the game today." Rice won most of the 1987 awards for most valuable player and top offensive player in the NFL. He was all-pro for the second straight year.

His professional career started slowly in 1985. Rice concentrated on the 49ers' intricate pass-route adjustments instead of the ball, which often dropped. The problem was not his hands; they were large and tough. When he was a youth, his job was catching bricks his brothers threw him at houses his father, a mason, was building. His hands started latching onto the ball in the last three games of 1985, when Rice made 21 of his 49 catches and earned National Conference rookie of the year honours.

After that he averaged 5.5. catches for 99.4 yards per game, with 38 touchdown catches in 31 games. His 86 catches in 1986 led the league, and his 1,570 yd receiving ranked third in the record book, trailing only totals of 1,746 and 1,602 from the now-defunct American Football League. Rice's 65 catches for 1,078 yd in 1987 gave him career totals of 200 catches for 3,575 yd and 42 touchdowns, 15 of them for at least 40 yd, plus 24 rushing carries for 149 yd and 3 touchdowns.

Jerry Lee Rice was born Oct. 13, 1962, near rural Crawford, Miss. Lacking stopwatch-popping speed, he was offered a college football scholarship only at Mississippi Valley State College, where he helped the small school gain national recognition as a passing power. Rice set 18 Division I-AA receiving records, with as many as 24 catches in one game.

(KEVIN M. LAMB)

**Roh Tae Woo**
Although the Dec. 16, 1987, presidential election made Roh Tae Woo the most democratically elected leader in South Korea's history, he won only 35.9% of the vote. His success was partly due to the fact that two strong opponents remained in the race despite repeated promises that only one would challenge Roh. Together they claimed 54% of the vote. Roh, however, finished first or second in all nine provinces, in the two "special cities" of Seoul and Pusan, and in such major cities as Taegu, Inchon, and Kwangju.

Roh was born on Dec. 4, 1932, near Taegu, to a middle-class rural family. His background was remarkably similar to that of Pres. Chun Doo Hwan. Both were educated at Taegu Technical High School and the Korean Military Academy and served in Vietnam in the 1960s. It was Chun who named Roh national security minister, home minister, then head of the Olympic committee. Roh retired from the Army in 1981 and became chairman of the ruling Democratic Justice Party (DJP) in 1985.

The year was heavily disrupted by unrest, sparked by Chun's April 13 announcement that political reform would be postponed until after the 1988 summer Olympic Games in Seoul. Roh became the focus of the unrest when Chun named him as his successor in June. Although Roh had aided the putsch that brought Chun to power in 1979 and thereafter remained his right-hand man, he had shown no political ambition.

He declared that he was quite happy organizing the Olympics. An angry public response followed Chun's statement, however, and martial law seemed the only solution to the breakdown in law and order. On June 29 Roh, who had officially become the DJP's presidential candidate less than three weeks earlier, unexpectedly conceded most of the opposition's demands, including those for a popularly elected president. He also declared himself in favour of full democracy. Roh's stunning victory at the polls meant that he would be bound by many promises, including the pledge that in 1993 the DJP presidential candidate would be nominated at an open convention by the ruling party instead of being chosen by the outgoing president, as had happened in his own case. Roh's main task would be to democratize South Korea and achieve political harmony while maintaining the rapid rate of economic growth to which South Koreans had become accustomed. As proof of his sincerity, he told the nation he would call a plebiscite after the Olympics and would resign if he did not receive a vote of confidence.

(ROBERT WOODROW)

**Sandiford, (Lloyd) Erskine**
The sudden death of Errol Barrow (see OBITUARIES), the prime minister of Barbados, on June 1, 1987, brought Erskine Sandiford into the post after a year as Barrow's deputy. The governing Democratic Labour Party (DLP) had gained a sweeping majority in general elections in May 1986, returning Sandiford and his DLP colleagues to office after ten years in opposition.

Sandiford entered politics in 1966 as personal assistant to Barrow, who headed the government between 1961 and 1976. Appointed to Parliament as a senator in 1967, he became minister of education and community development; in 1975 he moved to the Ministry of Health and Welfare. In the 1976 general elections, he retained his seat in Parliament by only 12 votes, but in 1981 he increased his majority. During the years in opposition, he acted as deputy parliamentary opposition leader. He was selected as deputy prime minister in 1986 in preference to other contenders, including Branford Taitt and Richie Haynes.

Born on March 24, 1937, Lloyd Erskine Sandiford was educated in Barbados at Harrison College and attended the University of the West Indies (UWI) in Jamaica, graduating in 1960 with a degree in English. He was the first prime minister of Barbados or any Caribbean Community (Caricom) country to have graduated from the UWI. He subsequently gained a postgraduate degree in economics and government from Manchester (England) University; he taught in Jamaica and Barbados before entering politics. The importance Sandiford attached to education was expected to be reflected in policy; Barbados already had the highest literacy rate in the Caribbean.

In September 1987 Sandiford's leadership was criticized by Haynes, who resigned from his post as finance minister, accusing the prime minister of failure to consult him on key financial appointments and other matters. Sandiford took over the finance portfolio himself in addition to that of economic affairs, a post created and held by Barrow in 1986. He pledged to continue Barrow's policies, but his approach to government was expected to be more technocratic than that of his flamboyant predecessor. One political difference between them had emerged in 1983 when Sandiford led the DLP in support of the U.S. invasion of Grenada, while Barrow, who opposed it, was out of Barbados.

(ROD PRINCE)

**Sessions, William Steele**
On Nov. 2, 1987, William Sessions was sworn in for a ten-year term as director of the U.S. Federal Bureau of Investigation (FBI), ending a surprisingly long vacancy in the most important law-enforcement job in the U.S. After the FBI's previous director, William Webster, became director of central intelligence on May 26, several distinguished citizens, including former

governor Richard Thornburgh of Pennsylvania, refused Pres. Ronald Reagan's request to take over the agency. Sessions finally accepted the nomination, which Reagan formally announced on July 24.

Despite criticism of the delay, Sessions's nomination was well received in the Senate, which confirmed it by a vote of 90–0 on September 25. He was scheduled to be sworn in on October 1, but he fainted on the airplane taking him to Washington for the ceremony. He was taken to George Washington University Medical Center, where doctors diagnosed an ulcer, and released on October 3. Convalescing in San Antonio, Texas—his home since 1971—he was hospitalized again on October 6 but was released in time to be sworn in on November 2.

The FBI's first well-publicized assignment under his leadership was to investigate the background of Douglas Ginsburg, whom President Reagan wanted to appoint to the Supreme Court. The FBI found no impediment, but Ginsburg had to decline after acquaintances said he had used marijuana. Sessions said he was looking into the oversight, adding that the Bureau had had only 5 days, instead of the usual 25, for the investigation.

Despite the glitches, few doubted Sessions's overall fitness for his new job. A well-read judge and former prosecutor whose passion for mountaineering had led him to camp on Mt. Everest, Sessions impressed those who knew him as intelligent, firm, and fair. He was born in Fort Smith, Ark., on May 27, 1930, and spent most of his childhood and adolescence in Kansas City, Mo. After serving in the U.S. Air Force from 1951 to 1955, he was discharged with the rank of captain and decided to make his home in Waco, Texas. There he attended Baylor University, receiving a B.A. in 1956 and a law degree in 1958. After several years in private law practice, he joined the Nixon administration in 1969 as chief of the government operations section of the Department of Justice's criminal division. He became U.S. attorney for the Western District of Texas in 1971 and was appointed by Pres. Gerald R. Ford to the U.S. District Court for that district in 1974. As chief judge from 1980, he took steps to computerize the court's records.

(CHARLES JOHNSON TAGGART)

### Singh, Vishwanath Pratap

In 1987 it was being predicted that Vishwanath Pratap Singh might become prime minister of India. The general election was not scheduled until the end of 1989, but support for Prime Minister Rajiv Gandhi had steadily declined because of the association of the government with corrupt practices and the deterioration in the economy; there was growing dissent in the ruling party, Congress (I). Until his resignation in April, Singh was one of the strongest and most loyal members of the Gandhi Cabinet. As defense minister he had instigated investigations into bribes paid on defense contracts and campaigned vigorously to expose those involved in such deals. He resigned on April 12 when the government refused to give him the necessary support for his investigations.

Singh had a reputation as an honest man, determined to rid India of corruption. Public and political support for him grew as he toured the country making anticorruption speeches, stressing the need for worker participation in management, and demanding that elections be held within the Congress (I), where many members had held their posts uncontested for as many as 18 years. He was a strong advocate of economic liberalization.

By July it was clear to Gandhi that Singh's popularity was becoming a serious threat. In an effort to undermine Singh's position, on July 15 Gandhi expelled from the party three key politicians who supported Singh. Rumours that Singh would be appointed his deputy were short-lived; Singh quickly tendered his resignation from the party. Gandhi refused it, but on July 19 he expelled him—a move that nevertheless left Singh as a member of Parliament.

Born on June 25, 1931, Singh was adopted by Raja Bahudur Ram Gopal Singh of Manda in the politically important state of Uttar Pradesh. He belonged to the important Thakur Rajput caste and was educated at the Universities of Allahabad and Puna. His rise to political eminence started in 1974, when he became the country's deputy commerce minister. In June 1980 he was made chief minister of the Uttar Pradesh government and resigned in June 1982 when he proved unable to end violent outrages in the state. In 1983 he returned to central government as commerce minister. In 1984 he was made president of the Congress (I) in Uttar Pradesh. From 1985 he remained in central government, first as finance minister and then, from January 1987, as defense minister.

(JANET H. CLARK)

### Solow, Robert Merton

Interested in grappling with everyday economic problems, Robert Merton Solow, recipient of the Nobel Memorial Prize in Economic Science, had concerned himself with the quality, rather than the quantity, of economic growth; he believed that improved technology combined with increased efficiency and human skills brought about economic progress. The Nobel Committee was impressed by the fact that his theories of growth were affected not only by increased capital and an expanding labour force but by technological progress as well. The committee emphasized Solow's influence on contemporary economic analysis in a world being bombarded by ever changing technology.

Solow was born in Brooklyn, N.Y., on Aug. 23, 1924. He attended Harvard University but at age 18 interrupted his studies to join the Army Signal Corps. In 1949 he joined the faculty at the Massachusetts Institute of Technology, and in 1951 he completed his doctorate at Harvard. In 1958 he became professor of economics at MIT, where he spent his academic career except for sojourns as Marshall lecturer at the University of Cambridge in 1963–64 and as Eastman visiting professor at the University of Oxford in 1968–69.

Deeply involved in U.S. economic policy and debate for more than 25 years, Solow moved to Washington, D.C., in 1961 to serve as senior economist on the staff of the Council of Economic Advisers. He helped to adopt the framework of economic policy that would dominate the administrations of John F. Kennedy and Lyndon B. Johnson and that echoed the interventionist policies of renowned British economist John Maynard Keynes. Solow also served as a member of President Johnson's Committee on Technology, Automation and Economic Progress. He was a member of Pres. Richard M. Nixon's Commission on Income Maintenance from 1968 to 1970, and from 1975

AFP PHOTO

to 1980 he was a director of the Boston Federal Reserve Bank. In 1980 he served one term as the president of the American Economic Association.

Described by the Nobel Committee as a pioneer in demonstrating that capital accumulation is not the most important factor in economic growth, Solow had pushed the importance, to nations and their governments, of higher education and technical research. As the U.S. stock market plummeted at the time that Solow received his award, his advocacy of the necessity for quality behind quantity to shore up a country's economic resources appeared to be vindicated. While capital accumulation may increase a nation's gross national product, it apparently does not necessarily cause a sustained increase in the economic growth rate.

(BONNIE OBERMAN)

### Stone, Oliver

In 1987 Oliver Stone gave Americans hell—and was honoured for it. His grim and gory *Platoon*, a film about the experiences of the U.S. foot soldier in Vietnam, won him Academy Awards for best picture and best director. Having the look and feel of a documentary, the film focused on the blood, sweat, and fears of a group

JERRY WATSON—CAMERA PRESS/PHOTO TRENDS

of men at war with the Vietnamese—and themselves. *Platoon* was both a box-office hit and a critical success, with one reviewer calling it "the first real Vietnam film and one of the great war movies of all time." However, like the war itself, *Platoon* had its opponents; Pauline Kael in *The New Yorker* criticized Stone for depicting all the film's dopers as good guys and thereby making "a case for the socializing, humanizing qualities" of drugs.

Stone was born on Sept. 15, 1946, in New York City. Seeking to escape his privileged family background, he left Yale University in 1965 for a six-month stint as an English teacher in Saigon. Two years later he joined the U.S. Army and returned to Vietnam but immediately realized he had "made a terrible mistake." The war was "on-the-job training. You learn if you can, and if not you're dead." Though he was awarded a Bronze Star and a Purple Heart, Stone finished his 15-month tour of duty feeling angry and alienated.

Film helped him sublimate those feelings. He studied under director Martin Scorsese at New York University, where he earned a B.A. degree in 1971. After directing his own script of the horror story *Seizure*, Stone in 1976 wrote *Platoon*, a screenplay based on his own experiences in Vietnam. Regarding the story as too negative for commercial audiences, Hollywood producers refused to film it; however, Columbia Pictures liked Stone's work enough to ask him to write the script for *Midnight Ex-*

*press,* a story about an American youth who is jailed in Turkey for drug smuggling. At about the time that that 1978 film won him the Oscar for best screenplay based on material from another source, he was often Oliver stoned, a man increasingly dependent on cocaine. Later, when his career fortunes nose-dived, Stone said "farewell to drugs" by writing the script for *Scarface* (1983), a profane and sometimes profound story about the viciousness of the Miami drug trade. The film was a box-office success.

After writing and directing *Salvador* (1986) for Britain's Hemdale Films, Stone persuaded the company to finance *Platoon.* Subjecting its cast to a two-week boot camp and almost two months of shooting in the Philippine jungle, Stone completed the $6 million film without the cooperation of the U.S. Army, which considered it antimilitary. His next film, released in late 1987, took aim at a different war—the one waged on *Wall Street.*    (MICHAEL AMEDEO)

### Takeshita, Noboru
Noboru Takeshita, who became prime minister of Japan on November 6, was held to lack the international outlook and strong leadership qualities of his predecessor, Yasuhiro Nakasone. Nonetheless, expectations were high that Takeshita would get things done because he possessed legendary negotiating skills and controlled the 114-member Keiseikai, the largest faction within the ruling Liberal-Democratic Party. All in all, Takeshita appeared to have a good chance of implementing the sweeping reforms sketched out by the previous administration.

The urgency of many of those reforms was underscored when the dollar continued to fall and the stock market collapsed. Takeshita's broad recipe for sustaining growth, while shifting the Japanese economy toward domestic demand, was the *furusato* (hometown) concept. This policy focused on public works spending to increase local amenities. The decentralization program also was meant to take pressure off big cities and their skyrocketing land prices.

One of the tasks left unfinished by the Nakasone Cabinet was tax reform, including the introduction of a controversial general sales tax. Takeshita described this as the single most important issue, acknowledging the need to ensure stable fiscal resources. The new prime minister said he hoped to create a truly prosperous Japan in which freedom of choice and creativity were possible. He called his scheme the "double-happiness" plan, an echo of such slogans as "double-income" and "double-assets" put forth by other Japanese politicians. Takeshita made it quite clear when he assumed office that domestic and international affairs were so intertwined that they could not be separated in seeking solutions to the problems facing the nation.

Takeshita maintained strong links to his rural constituency in Shimane, the poor mountainous area where he was born on Feb. 26, 1924. He served seven years on the Shimane prefectural council before being elected to the lower house of the Diet (parliament) in 1958. His first ministerial post was that of chief Cabinet secretary in 1971; he later became minister of construction and spent five terms as minister of finance, showing skill in depoliticizing some of the crucial issues of financial liberalization. It was, however, Takeshita's ability to divide and exhaust opponents that opened the way to the prime ministership. In the months ahead, he would have countless opportunities to test his political talents.    (GERD LARSSON)

### Tange, Kenzo
The retrospective exhibition held in the classical hall of the Parisian École des Beaux-Arts in 1987 symbolized the universal esteem accorded Kenzo Tange, a pioneer of Japanese modern architecture. His early career was in great part tied to the postwar development of Tokyo. After winning a competition to design the Tokyo Metropolitan Government Office in 1952, he successively elaborated completely new models of architecture embodying new technology. The

Tokyo Project of 1960 provided an integrated development of the city, both by land and by sea. The plan included a huge axis crossing Tokyo Bay, the National Gymnasiums for the 1964 Tokyo Olympic Games, and several half-mirrored buildings in the fashionable districts of Akasaka and Aoyama in the 1970s.

Tange was born in Ehime Prefecture in 1913 and studied architecture at the University of Tokyo between 1935 and 1938. After working with Kunio Maekawa, a Japanese Corbusierian, he deepened his theoretical studies at his alma mater. His talent began to be recognized when he won two competitions for Japanese memorials during World War II, but it was after 1945 that he started his restless career as a pioneer of Japanese modern architecture. After the successful restoration of Hiroshima between 1946 and 1955, he initiated a debate on the value of Japanese tradition, citing the Jomon prehistoric earthenware period as a model. Reinterpreting old Japanese architecture, he combined columns and beams to create a series of public buildings in the 1950s, including Kagawa Prefectural Government Office (1958) and the Imabari City Hall (1958). This notion was gradually replaced by a more expressive core system design, first mentioned in his famous Tokyo Project, in which he showed a completely new model megalopolis equipped with new communication and information devices. The Yamanashi Press and Broadcasting Centre in Kofu (1966) and the Dentsu Office Building in Tokyo (1967) embodied this proposal. His inclination toward a geometric composition through mirrored glass and marble surfaces in the 1970s marked an ultimate aesthetic of modernism. Tange's numerous prizes, including the prestigious 1987 Pritzker Architecture Prize, testified to the worldwide esteem in which he was held and suggested that he would be remembered as one of the great architects of his time.
    (RIICHI MIYAKE)

### Thatcher, Margaret Hilda
On Jan. 3, 1988, U.K. Conservative Prime Minister Margaret Thatcher would become the country's longest-serving prime minister in the 20th century, overtaking Herbert Asquith (8 years and 241 days [1908–16]) and Winston Churchill (8 years and 238 days [1940–45 and 1951–55]). Thatcher established another record during 1987: she became the first prime minister since Lord Liverpool 160 years earlier to win three consecutive general election victories.

Thatcher's victory in the June 11 general election was the more remarkable because of the way she fought the campaign. Having been prime minister since 1979—and therefore during a world recession that saw unemployment in the U.K. more than double to three million—she faced advice from many senior Conservatives to play down her radical instincts and seek to consolidate the policies her government had already implemented: limiting the powers of trade union leaders, reducing government borrowing, and selling state industries to private shareholders. Thatcher spurned this advice. She fought a campaign on a manifesto more radical than 1983 or 1979. She also benefited from her international standing. A visit to Moscow in March for extensive talks with Soviet leader Mikhail Gorbachev secured blanket coverage on British television and acted as an effective curtain raiser to the election campaign, which began just six weeks later.

Nevertheless, Thatcher had her problems. She did not trust her party machine entirely and enlisted a separate set of advisers who occasionally conflicted with those engaged by Conservative Central Office. At 61, Thatcher also displayed greater fatigue and showed signs of faltering under questioning. Toward the end of the campaign she criticized the "drooling and drivelling" of people concerned with poverty; when her startled interviewer challenged her use of this phrase, she displayed uncharacteristic remorse and apologized immediately. Her remarks shocked those people who were not going to vote Conservative; they had no measurable

effect on the increasingly affluent middle-class and skilled working-class people who had benefited from successive tax cuts and voted with their pockets.

During the campaign Thatcher was asked if she would retire before the following election, due by 1992. She replied that she planned "to go on and on," although later she was more cautious about her intentions. For the time being, the woman born in Grantham, Lincolnshire, on Oct. 13, 1925, would continue to dominate British politics.    (PETER KELLNER)

### Tonegawa, Susumu
In 1987, for the first time ever, the Nobel Prize for Physiology or Medicine was awarded to a Japanese scientist—Susumu Tonegawa, a molecular biologist at the Massachusetts Institute of Technology (MIT). In addition, Tonegawa was only the second person since 1961 to be the sole laureate in that category. He was recognized for his discovery of the mechanism by which as few as 1,000 gene segments produce as many as a billion different, specialized antibodies in the human immune system. Said the Nobel Committee, "Tonegawa's discoveries have increased our knowledge about [the] structure of our immune defense. They also open up possibilities to increase the immune response against pathogenic microorganisms through vaccination—and also to improve inhibition of unwanted immune reactions."

Tonegawa was born on Sept. 5, 1939, in Nagoya, Japan. He received a bachelor's degree in chemistry from Kyoto University in 1963 and a Ph.D. in biology from the University of California at San Diego in 1969. He remained in San Diego to do postgraduate work at the University of California and later at the Salk Institute. In 1971 Tonegawa moved to the Basel Institute for Immunology in Switzerland, where he began research on the production of antibodies. In 1981 he returned to the U.S. as a full professor at MIT.

Tonegawa's prizewinning work went far toward solving the long-standing mystery of antibody production. Each antibody is a protein molecule composed of two pairs of amino acid chains that form a flexible shape resembling the letter Y. Antibodies attack antigens—foreign particles or microbes in the body—by binding to them at the tips of the arms of the Y. The sequence of amino acids at these antigen-binding sites varies from one antibody to another so that a given antibody can fit and bind to only one particular antigen. By the 1970s it already had been established that the production of antibodies by the white blood cells known as B lymphocytes, or B cells, is governed by genes within the cells. Scientists did not understand,

however, how the variation in amino-acid sequence was effected—that is, how the immense variety of antibodies able to be made by a B cell can far exceed the total number of a B cell's genes. Tonegawa demonstrated that as a B cell matures, segments of its genetic material are selected, shuffled, and recombined to form new genes, giving rise to the millions of various amino-acid sequences responsible for the exquisite selectivity of the body's immune system. (CAROLYN D. NEWTON)

**Trump, Donald John**
In his 1987 book, *Trump: The Art of the Deal,* real estate tycoon Donald Trump offered advice on deal making and self-promotion: "A little hyperbole never hurts." Indeed, the 41-year-old New York developer had raised deal making almost to an art. For Trump every project had to be the best of its kind, and he usually combined sharp instincts and perfect timing with ruthless negotiations. Perhaps his biggest gamble, the spectacular Trump Tower, next door to Tiffany's on Manhattan's Fifth Avenue, opened in 1983 amid widespread criticism, but by 1987 it was valued at some $700 million. The lobby, decorated with Italian pink marble and a waterfall, even became a local tourist attraction.

Trump's billion-dollar business empire ranged from glamorous high rises like Trump Tower and the nearby Trump Parc and more than 24,-000 rental and co-op apartment units in Queens and Brooklyn to ownership of the New Jersey Generals of the U.S. Football League. He owned at least three casinos in Atlantic City, N.J., notably Trump's Castle, where his wife, Ivana (a former fashion model and Czechoslovak Olympic skier), was chief executive officer. His private fortune included a triplex penthouse in Trump Tower, a 15-bedroom house in Connecticut, an $8 million Palm Beach, Fla., retreat, a private Boeing 727 jet, and a French-built Puma helicopter with "Trump" emblazoned on the side.

The son of a successful apartment building developer and manager in Queens, Trump worked for his father while attending military school and the University of Pennsylvania's Wharton School of Finance (B.A. 1968). His first big solo deal, at the age of 28, involved the crumbling Commodore Hotel near Grand Central Station in Manhattan. He convinced Hyatt Corp. to join in the rebuilding, arranged $70 million in financing, and negotiated a $120 million tax break from the city. The resultant Grand Hyatt Hotel triggered redevelopment of the whole area and by 1987 was worth an estimated $300 million.

In 1986 Trump took over renovation of the Wollman ice-skating rink in Manhattan's Central Park. New York City had spent six years and some $12 million without completing the repairs, but Trump cut through the red tape and finished the project well under budget in less than four months. The subsequent embarrassment to the city and a public clash with New York City Mayor Edward Koch over Trump's next project strained their working relationship. In reaction to NBC's plans to move its corporate headquarters to New Jersey, Trump was prepared to offer the firm Television City, a development that would include the world's tallest building. City officials, however, balked at the requested tax incentives.
(MELINDA SHEPHERD)

**Upshaw, Gene**
On Aug. 8, 1987, Gene Upshaw entered the Pro Football Hall of Fame. Six weeks later, on September 22, he directed the players' union that disrupted pro football by going on strike. In both roles Upshaw was at once a team man and a leader.

He started all but one game as an Oakland Raiders guard from 1967 to 1981, including 207 in a row for a team that won two Super Bowls, three championships of the American Football League (AFL) or American Football Conference (AFC), and nine division titles. The Raiders won their first AFL championship in Upshaw's

AP/WIDE WORLD

rookie year with a record of 13–1. He was all-league or all-conference in eight seasons and team captain from his third season on.

Therefore, it was no surprise that Upshaw moved directly from the locker room to the boardroom. As executive director of the National Football League Players Association (NFLPA) and a member of the AFL-CIO's executive council, he was the most significant black executive in both labour and sports. When the NFL's labour-management agreement expired in 1987, Upshaw supported the players' vote to pursue unrestricted free agency, or freedom to choose teams, despite his belief that improvements in job security were more feasible and more important.

Eugene Upshaw, Jr., was born in rural Robstown, Texas, Aug. 15, 1945. Gene and his brother Marvin, who also played pro football, concentrated on baseball as youths, encouraged in their sports pursuits by their father, a former baseball player. Upshaw did not play football until he was a high-school senior. His father insisted that he go to college, and Upshaw received his degree from Texas A&I University. In college he became a versatile offensive centre, tackle, and tight end, but he was not a top pro prospect until the all-star games after his senior year.

The Raiders decided to make Upshaw a guard. At 2 m (6 ft 5 in) and 115.7 kg (255 lb), he was 7.6 cm taller than the stocky prototype guards of that time, but Upshaw became the first full-time guard to make the Hall of Fame.

As the NFLPA's president during the 1982 strike, Upshaw was criticized for threatening dissidents. After executive director Ed Garvey tapped Upshaw to succeed him in 1983, however, Upshaw reestablished cordial communications between labour and management. It did not help avert another strike, though. The 1987 strike dissolved after 24 days when 14% of the 1,585 players had rejoined management's second-rate nonunion teams. Unable to win at the negotiating table, Upshaw took the players' battle for free agency to court.
(KEVIN M. LAMB)

**Vander Zalm, William Nick**
A controversial and colourful politician, William Nick Vander Zalm was once considered by his party as a maverick, barely to be tolerated. Yet on July 30, 1986, he defeated members of the hierarchy to become leader of the British Columbia Social Credit Party. Seven days later he was sworn in as the 27th premier of the province. Having resigned from provincial politics in 1983 over tensions with then premier Bill Bennett, Vander Zalm did not hold a seat in the provincial legislature. This was remedied, however, in the general election of Oct. 22, 1986. His party was returned to power,

and Vander Zalm was elected to represent the riding of Richmond.

Born May 29, 1934, in Noordwijkerhout, Zuid-Holland, Neth., Vander Zalm immigrated to Canada in 1947 to join his father, who had established a tulip bulb business in the Fraser Valley. When his father suffered a heart attack, William assumed control of the business. At age 22 he took over Art Knapp's Garden Center and built it into British Columbia's largest garden centre franchise. His largest project, however, was his Fantasy Garden World, a theme park in Richmond, B.C.

Although he worked tirelessly to expand the family business, Vander Zalm's major career was in politics. He was first elected alderman in Surrey, B.C., in 1965, and in 1969 he became that city's youngest mayor. As a member of the Liberal Party, Vander Zalm ran unsuccessfully in the 1968 federal election. In 1972 he was an unsuccessful candidate for leader of the provincial Liberals. In 1974 he joined the Social Credit (Socred) Party, and the following year he was elected to the provincial legislature in the Socred sweep. Between 1978 and 1983 he held a number of Cabinet posts.

Throughout his political career, Vander Zalm was noted for his blunt statements. In 1982, for instance, he called his fellow Cabinet ministers "gutless" when the legislature defeated a land-use bill he had worked on for two years. Women asking for job training were told they would make better homemakers than plumbers, and welfare recipients were told to pick up a shovel. When he received complaints about this latter remark, Vander Zalm responded by selling silver shovel pins and auctioning off shovels at Socred fund-raisers.

In 1987 Vander Zalm became the first Canadian premier to act as host on a regularly scheduled open-line radio talk show. An impatient politician with a dislike of bureaucracy, he promised "an open and up-front" style of government. (DIANE LOIS WAY)

**Venkataraman, Ramaswamy**
The election in July 1987 of Ramaswamy Venkataraman, a Tamil, as India's eighth president marked the culmination of a political career that began in the 1930s. He had earned widespread respect for his integrity, amiability, espousal of progressive causes, and administrative experience.

Venkataraman was born on Dec. 4, 1910, in Rajamadam village, Madras state (now Tamil Nadu). He studied law and economics at Madras University and then became a lawyer. His political activities started when he became an advocate of the Madras High Court in 1935, and he was associated with the formation of the Congress Socialist Party. In the "Quit India" movement of 1942, his activities led to his imprisonment for two years. By then he was heavily involved in the labour movement and fought for the rights of dock workers, railwaymen, and landless labourers. In 1946, when independence from the U.K. was imminent, Venkataraman was among the team of lawyers who went to Singapore to defend Indian nationals charged with collaboration with the Japanese during World War II. After independence, Venkataraman was elected to the provisional parliament in 1950 and then was elected to the lower house of Parliament (Lok Sabha) in 1952 and again in 1957. He was secretary of the Congress Party (1952–54).

Venkataraman returned to Madras politics at the request of the state's chief minister, who made him minister of industries, labour, power, and transport, and he actively promoted the state's industrialization. In the early 1970s he retired from politics and edited the English weekly *Swarajaya.* He returned to national politics in 1977 when he was elected to the lower house, to which he was reelected in 1980. In the government of Indira Gandhi he held two ministerial posts—finance (from 1980) and defense (from 1982)—before being elected vice-president in August 1984.

Venkataraman gained international experience as India's representative in the International Labour Organization and in the UN General Assembly. He served as a member of the UN Administrative Tribunal from 1955 to 1979 and for the last 12 years held its presidency. Venkataraman's political acumen was such that he was considered a suitable successor to Prime Minister Rajiv Gandhi. His lack of fluency in the national language, Hindi, was seen as a disadvantage.

(H. Y. SHARADA PRASAD)

**Webster, William Hedgcock**
On May 26, 1987, with 273 days to go on his ten-year term as director of the U.S. Federal Bureau of Investigation (FBI), William Webster became director of central intelligence. As such, he was the principal adviser to Pres. Ronald Reagan on intelligence matters and—more importantly—chief executive of the Central Intelligence Agency (CIA). On taking office, Webster talked of "fidelity to the Constitution and the laws." The CIA was in somewhat the same position as the FBI had been when Webster took it over in 1978—low in public esteem because of accusations that employees had exceeded legal authority for partisan and other purposes.

Although inexperienced in international affairs, Webster was highly regarded for his work at the FBI and for his understanding of terrorism. The CIA's previous head, William Casey, had died before he could answer questions about secret sales of arms to Iran and diversion of the profits to armed opponents of the Sandinista government in Nicaragua. Reagan nominated Webster to succeed Casey on March 3, 1987, and praised Webster's understanding of the rule of law. On May 19 the Senate confirmed the nomination by a vote of 94–1. In his new job Webster did not hold Cabinet rank, as Casey had.

Webster was born on March 6, 1924, in St. Louis, Mo., and was raised in suburban Webster Groves. He served as an officer in the U.S. Naval Reserve from 1943 to 1946 and received a B.A. from Amherst (Mass.) College in 1947. In 1949, back in St. Louis, he received a degree in law from Washington University, was admitted to the Missouri bar, and joined a law firm. He served as a legal officer in the Navy in 1951–52 and then returned to the firm, becoming a partner in 1956. He was U.S. attorney for the Eastern District of Missouri in 1960–61 and then returned to his former firm. A Republican, he was appointed by Pres. Richard M. Nixon to the U.S. District Court for the Eastern District of Missouri in 1971 and to the Court of Appeals for the 8th Circuit in 1973.

In 1978 Pres. Jimmy Carter appointed Webster to a ten-year term as director of the FBI. He accepted that term, resigning a lifetime judicial job, after being promised direct access to the U.S. attorney general and authority over subordinates. Though criticized for use of routine wiretaps and paid informers, he was praised for concentrating the FBI's efforts on terrorism, white-collar crime, and narcotics.

(CHARLES JOHNSON TAGGART)

**Whitehead, Mary Beth**
On March 31, 1987, 29-year-old Mary Beth Whitehead of Brick Town, N.J., was stripped of all parental rights as the mother of Baby M. In his ruling Superior Court Judge Harvey R. Sorkow awarded custody of Baby M to her biologic father, William Stern, and signed papers allowing Stern's wife, Elizabeth, to legally adopt the child, officially named Melissa Elizabeth Stern.

Whitehead and Stern had signed a contract on Feb. 6, 1985, that called for her to be inseminated with his sperm. Upon delivery of a child she was to relinquish all rights and responsibilities and receive $10,000. Several times a month the two drove to New York City for the insemination procedure. After conceiving in July 1985, Whitehead gave birth to a girl she named Sara on March 27, 1986. "Seeing her, holding her . . . she was my child," she said. "It overpowered me; I had no control; I had to keep her." The

SIPA PRESS

Sterns went to court and were granted temporary custody of Baby M. Meanwhile, Whitehead and her husband, Richard, fled with the child to Florida, where they remained for 87 days. A private detective hired by the Sterns regained the child for them, and the Sterns and Whiteheads went to court.

The seven-week trial, which began on January 5, was the first case to be tried between two parties to a surrogacy agreement. It drew extensive national and international media coverage and was expected to have a major impact on the legality of surrogate motherhood. Whitehead herself testified before Congress and became a spokesperson for the National Coalition Against Surrogacy.

One of eight children born to Joseph and Catherine Messer, Whitehead dropped out of high school in her sophomore year at age 15. While working part-time at her brother's delicatessen, she met Richard Whitehead, a 23-year-old truck driver and Vietnam war veteran. They married before her 17th birthday in December 1973 and soon had Ryan, now 13, and Tuesday, now 12. After almost 14 years of marriage they were granted a divorce on Nov. 12, 1987, citing the tribulations of the trial as a major cause. Later that same month Whitehead married Dean Gould, a 26-year-old accountant she met while vacationing in the Virgin Islands. They were expecting a child in late May or early June.

(EDWARD PAUL MORAGNE)

**Williamson, David Francis**
The appointment on Sept. 16, 1987, of a new secretary-general of the Commission of the European Communities (EC) filled what was only the second vacancy in this post in the 30-year history of the EC. A leading British government official, David Williamson, was appointed to succeed the Commission's retiring secretary-general, Emile Noël, a distinguished French civil servant who had held the post since 1957. The position of secretary-general was the most powerful in the entire Commission, apart from the 17 political leaders appointed as commissioners by the 12 member nations of the EC every four years. The secretary-general had to manage the sometimes cumbersome multinational and multilingual bureaucracy that ran the Community on a day-to-day basis.

Born May 8, 1934, and educated at Tonbridge School and Exeter College, Oxford, Williamson was no stranger to Brussels and the Commission. Having served in the British Ministry of Agriculture, Fisheries and Food, he was assigned to the Commission during the period 1977–83 as deputy director-general for agriculture. The common agricultural policy (CAP), one of the most important and most controversial policies adopted by the EC, accounted for some 65%

of the EC annual budget of nearly $40 billion. In 1983 he joined the British government Cabinet Office and served as the senior adviser on Community affairs to Prime Minister Margaret Thatcher.

Williamson was appointed to the post of secretary-general against stiff opposition from senior French and West German officials—a tribute to the importance of the post at a time when the Commission, and the EC, faced serious problems of budgetary and policy reform. The most immediate task facing the Commission in 1987 was that of obtaining agreement on radical measures to reduce the cost of the CAP, eliminate the expensive and unpopular food surpluses it had generated during the previous decade, and increase the ceiling on EC budget revenues. Williamson's appointment occurred as the EC began the task of restructuring its internal market by 1992—a process that would involve the abolition of all remaining internal physical, institutional, and fiscal barriers to free trade and the free movement of capital.

(JOHN PALMER)

**Winfrey, Oprah**
There were times during 1987 when one could not have been blamed for thinking that Oprah Winfrey's middle name must be Ubiquitous. She seemed to be everywhere—on magazine covers, in the movies, and, of course, on television. When she became the anchor of the "A.M. Chicago" morning show in January 1984, it had consistently been last in the ratings for its time slot. Three months later it had overtaken the "Phil Donahue Show," which had been the most popular local talk show for 16 seasons. By September 1985 "A.M. Chicago" had been renamed "The Oprah Winfrey Show" and had been expanded to an hour. It went into syndication on 138 stations in September 1986 and a year later appeared in over 180 cities and won three Emmy awards. Some said that Winfrey's success caused Donahue to leave Chicago and move to New York City.

In 1985 Winfrey made her motion-picture debut in *The Color Purple.* Her performance as Sofia received rave reviews and earned her Academy and Golden Globe award nominations. She then appeared in the film *Native Son* as the mother of the main character.

Winfrey was born Jan. 29, 1954, on a farm in Kosciusko, Miss. Her name was to have been Orpah, after a biblical character, but a misspelling on her birth certificate resulted in the name Oprah. Her young parents were not married, and her grandmother raised her for the first six years of her life. Her public-speaking ability revealed itself early; at the age of two she addressed a church congregation. When she was six, she moved to Milwaukee, Wis., to live

AP/WIDE WORLD

with her mother. She continued speaking in public, usually at social clubs and church teas. As she grew up, however, she became a discipline problem, committing acts of rebellion against her mother. Her mother finally sent her to live with her father and his wife in Nashville, Tenn. Winfrey blossomed under her father's encouragement and strict supervision. She excelled in school and won an oratorical contest that guaranteed her a scholarship to Tennessee State University. After graduation in 1976 she moved to Baltimore, Md., to work for the ABC television affiliate as co-anchor and reporter for the evening news. After realizing that she did not have the necessary detachment for reporting the news, she became cohost of a morning talk show, where she remained until moving to Chicago.

Winfrey's style was more energetic, unrestrained, and spontaneous than that of most talk show hosts. She also was not afraid of controversial topics and shared many of the incidents of her own life.    (BARBARA WHITNEY)

### Wright, Jim

In 1987 the U.S. House of Representatives was Wright's field. New Speaker Jim Wright dominated the game of Capitol Hill politics, exhibiting power, aggressiveness, and speed. After setting the House's legislative agenda, the bright-eyed and bushy-browed Wright quickly led his fellow Democrats to victory in votes for an omnibus trade bill, a health plan for the elderly, and two bills providing aid for the homeless. Opposed to more aid for the Nicaraguan rebels, Wright in August wrote a peace plan that—according to many reports— the cosponsoring Reagan administration privately hoped the Nicaraguan government would reject; he later angered the administration by helping Nicaraguan Pres. Daniel Ortega work out a cease-fire proposal. Wright opened the year with a hit, delivering the Democrats' response to Pres. Ronald Reagan's state of the union address. He almost ended it with a strikeout, however, when his October budget legislation, containing a $12 billion tax increase, was defeated 217–203. A few arm-twistings later, however, he reversed the score to 206–205.

Born in Weatherford, Texas, on Dec. 22, 1922, Wright was a competitive spirit from a young age. During high school he thrived as a Golden Gloves amateur boxer and, after winning the Distinguished Flying Cross in World War II, he was elected at age 23 to the Texas state legislature.

In 1954 Wright reached the political big leagues, winning election as a U.S. representative from Texas. A vigorous supporter of a strong, activist government, Wright in 1956 refused to join 100 Southern colleagues in denouncing the U.S. Supreme Court's 1954 desegregation order. He opposed the Civil Rights Act of 1964 but later reversed himself by voting for various other civil rights bills. Wright was a backer of U.S. involvement in Vietnam and, throughout his career, voted in favour of most social welfare programs.

Wright's team play earned him power in the House. Throughout the 1970s and 1980s he raised money and made personal appearances for countless House Democrats running for reelection. His efforts brought him enough support to defeat Phillip Burton for the position of majority leader in 1976. By late 1986 Wright had done so many favours for so many House Democrats that few opposed his succeeding Thomas ("Tip") O'Neill as speaker of the House.    (MICHAEL AMEDEO)

### Yazov, Dmitry Timofeyevich

The election of Dmitry Timofeyevich Yazov as a candidate member of the Politburo of the Communist Party of the Soviet Union (CPSU) in late June 1987 was less of a surprise than his nomination as defense minister a month earlier. The landing of the young West German pilot Mathias Rust in Red Square in Moscow had been the pretext and not the cause of the dismissal of his predecessor, Sergey Sokolov.

CAMERA PRESS, LONDON

Mikhail Gorbachev had appointed Yazov as head of cadres and a deputy defense minister in early 1987. He was then promoted over the heads of the three first deputy ministers of defense: Marshal Sergey Akhromeyev, chief of staff; Marshal Viktor Kulikov, commander in chief of the Warsaw Pact; and Gen. Pyotr Lushev, army chief. Yasov's primary task as defense minister appeared to be the *perestroika* (restructuring) of military personnel. He was reported to be a ruthless administrator, and the restructuring was expected to take several years.

Yazov was born into a Siberian peasant family in 1923 and joined the Red Army in 1941. During World War II he was a deputy company commander and fought on the Leningrad front. He became a member of the CPSU in 1944. After the war he held various command posts and graduated in 1956 from the Frunze Military Academy and in 1967 from the General Staff Academy. He held various posts in the Leningrad Military District (MD) between 1958 and 1965 and, as a major general (lieutenant general in British Army equivalent), commanded a division in the Transbaikal MD (1967–71). He was then promoted to lieutenant general and commanded an army in the Transcaucasian MD in Azerbaijan.

Yazov was transferred to the Defense Ministry in 1974 and worked in the cadres department. He became a colonel general in 1976 and first deputy commander in chief of the Far Eastern MD. In 1979 he became commander in chief of Soviet forces in Czechoslovakia, and in 1980 he was made commander of the Central Asian MD. As such he was elected to the Central Committee and bureau of the Communist Party of Kazakhstan. He became a candidate member (1981) and a full member (1987) of the Central Committee of the CPSU. Yazov became an army general under Yury Andropov in 1984 and commander of the Far Eastern MD. Gorbachev met him in July 1986, and his subsequent rapid promotions suggested that the general secretary was very impressed by him.    (MARTIN MCCAULEY)

### Yu Kuo-hwa

In 1987 Yu Kuo-hwa, premier of the Republic of China in Taiwan, carried out sweeping reforms and changes. These included an end to martial law and foreign exchange controls as well as establishment of the right to form opposition parties, register new newspapers, and travel to mainland China for family reunions. Under the leadership of Pres. Chiang Ching-kuo, Yu's Cabinet took concrete steps toward democratization and liberalization. On the economic front, Yu guided Taiwan to unprecedented prosperity; the country accumulated a trade surplus of about $20 billion and a for-

eign exchange reserve of close to $75 billion. In addition, its per capita income reached $5,000. The country was rapidly becoming an economic giant by maintaining its status as a major exporter and a leading trading partner of the U.S., despite strong American pressure to reduce the trade imbalance between the two countries.

Yu was born in Fenghua, Chekiang (Zhejiang) Province, in 1914 and was educated at Tsinghua (Qinghua), Harvard, and London universities. During World War II he worked closely with Generalissimo Chiang Kai-shek. During the 1960s and '70s he was governor of the central bank in Taiwan, finance minister, and chairman of the Council for Economic Planning and Development. In these capacities he greatly expanded exports, initiated tax reforms, and increased revenues to finance new programs and balance the budget. After becoming premier in 1984, he carried out—despite political and financial scandals and natural disasters—democratic reforms and a 14-project economic development program. His economic policies, including internationalization and liberalization, became the cornerstone of Taiwan's economic development program.

Yu, who led his country through one of its most difficult periods in history, enjoyed President Chiang's trust and confidence even while certain opposition leaders and legislators made him the object of criticism. An honest and austere administrator convinced of the importance of the rule of law as the foundation of democracy, Yu deserved a large share of the credit for Taiwan's growing prosperity and democracy.    (WINSTON L. Y. YANG)

### Zhao Ziyang

Zhao Ziyang (Chao Tzu-yang) became China's paramount leader in November 1987 when the 13th congress of the Communist Party of China (CPC) officially confirmed his appointment as the party's new general secretary. That event, in addition to the retirement of a number of aging conservative leaders, was a major political victory for Zhao and his 83-year-old mentor, Deng Xiaoping (Teng Hsiao-p'ing), even though it entailed necessary compromises. In a major speech to the congress, Zhao reconfirmed that China would continue to stimulate the economy through market mechanisms and private initiative, as well as its opening to the West. His proposals for reforms in China's political structure and a reduced role for the CPC in the government's day-to-day operations were also approved. He stressed that China, far from being well along on the road to socialist paradise, as Mao Zedong (Mao Tse-tung) had envisioned, was still in the "primary stage of socialism," a condition of pronounced underdevelopment, which justified its adoption of capitalist practices.

Born into a family of landlords and grain merchants in Henan (Honan) Province in 1919, Zhao joined the Young Communist League in 1932 and became a member of the CPC in 1938. During World War II he served in local party organizations in northern China. After the establishment of the Communist regime in 1949, he was moved to Guangdong (Kwangtung) Province, where he became provincial first party secretary in 1965. Purged in 1967 during the Cultural Revolution, he was later rehabilitated and sent in 1975 to Sichuan (Szechwan), China's most populous province, where through bold and flexible programs he increased industrial output and raised agricultural production. These results were achieved through such innovative policies as rewarding workers on the basis of work rather than need and providing incentives based on free enterprise and market forces rather than on rigid quotas established by central authorities. In addition, factory managers were given much greater autonomy, and peasants were allowed to benefit from individual initiative. For such achievements as raising Sichuan's industrial output by 81% in three years, Zhao was made a Political Bureau member in 1979 and premier in 1980.

(WINSTON L. Y. YANG)

# OBITUARIES

**Abel, I(orwith) W(ilbur),** U.S. union leader (b. Aug. 11, 1908, Magnolia, Ohio—d. Aug. 10, 1987, Malvern, Ohio), as the influential and formidable third president (1965–77) of the United Steelworkers of America, increased membership from one million to 1.4 million and without a single strike negotiated better benefits and higher wages for steelworkers. During the Depression, Abel worked in a brickyard, firing kilns 12 hours a day, seven days a week, for 16 cents an hour. As a foundryman at the Timken Roller Bearing Co. in Canton, Ohio, he joined the Steelworkers Organizing Committee and in 1936 helped organize Local 1123. In one year he led 42 wildcat strikes. As the protégé of Philip Murray, founder (1942) and first president of the United Steelworkers of America, Abel was named director of the union's Canton district. After Murray's death in 1952, Abel was elected secretary-treasurer of the international union, and for the next 12 years he served as second in command under the fiery president David J. McDonald. During this time Abel traveled throughout the country visiting union locals and earned a reputation as a deft listener to worker concerns. In 1965, in a bitterly contested battle with McDonald, Abel won the union presidency by 10,000 votes. As president, Abel established a strike fund of more than $85 million and signed a historic no-strike agreement intended to end production and stockpiling swings. Abel retired in 1977, just prior to the industry's sudden decline.

**Ali, Salim,** Indian ornithologist (b. Nov. 12, 1896, Bombay, India—d. June 20, 1987, Bombay), was an internationally acclaimed expert on the birds of India and a leading conservationist. His lifelong interest in birds was pursued with great dedication, and he was able to spend most of his working life in his chosen field. He started out, however, as a clerk before studying accounting in Bombay and taking a course in zoology at the same time. Eventually he went to Germany to study ornithology. On his return he undertook surveys for the Bombay Natural History Society and wrote his first studies on Indian bird life. His greatest work, written with S. Dillon Ripley, was the authoritative ten-volume *Handbook of the Birds of India and Pakistan* (1968–74), which was under revision for a second edition at the time of his death. In 1976 Ali was appointed a member of the upper house of the Indian Parliament. His work for conservation brought him many honours in India and abroad. He was the first non-British scientist to receive the medal of the British Ornithologists' Union, and he was awarded the John C. Phillips Medal of the International Union for Conservation of Nature and Natural Resources, The Netherlands Order of the Golden Ark, and the J. P. Getty International Prize for Wildlife Conservation. From 1954 Ali was a member of the permanent executive committee of the International Ornithological Congress. His autobiography, *The Fall of a Sparrow,* was published in 1985.

**Allégret, Yves Edouard,** French film director (b. Oct. 13, 1907, Asnières, Hauts-de-Seine, France—d. Jan. 31, 1987, Asnières), established his reputation after World War II with sombre stories, notably the trilogy *Dédée d'Anvers* (1948), *Une si jolie petite plage* (1949), and *Manèges* (1950). Most of his stories took place in an underworld setting. Allégret began his career as assistant to his elder brother Marc, an outstanding filmmaker of the 1930s; in the prewar period he was associated with the left-wing *groupe octobre.* After making a number of short films, in 1941 he completed his first feature, *Tobie est un ange,* the negative of which was destroyed in a fire. His next two films had featured roles for his second wife, Simone Signoret, and were followed by the trilogy, his major achievement in *film noir.* The final part of the trilogy was particularly pessimistic in its view of women. However, the public was unsympathetic to an apparent revival of the mood of prewar French cinema, and these fatalistic stories of doomed love among gangsters, sailors, and prostitutes were only moderately successful. Allégret went on to film *Les Orgueilleux* (1953), set in Mexico, and a fine adaptation of Émile Zola's novel *Germinal* (1962). Such later works as *La Fille de Hambourg* (1958) and *L'Ambitieuse* (1959) were largely neglected. During the 1970s Allégret worked in television. His last film, *Mords pas, on t'aime,* appeared in 1976.

**Allen, Clabon Walter,** Australian astronomer (b. Dec. 28, 1904, Perth, Western Australia, Australia—d. Dec. 11, 1987, Canberra, Australia), was assistant (1926–51) at the Commonwealth Observatory, Canberra, and first Perren professor of astronomy (1951–72) at University College, London. His major contributions to astronomy, detailed in his important textbook *Astrophysical Quantities* (1955), were based upon careful collation of data obtained through various methods of work: spectroscopy, eclipse studies, and laboratory atomic physics. His chosen subject was the temperature, magnetic fields, and atmosphere of the Sun. Allen expanded knowledge of the effects of both continuous and spasmodic (sunspot and flare) solar emissions on the Earth's atmosphere and on terrestrial radio communications. During World War II Allen helped the Allies by predicting periods of radio disruption. He took part in eclipse expeditions to Japan (1936), South Africa (1940), Sweden (1954), Ceylon (1955), and the Canary Islands (1959). He was responsible for establishing, at University College, the first undergraduate degree course in astronomy available to students in England and Wales. Allen was also noted for his proposal for a new calendar, in which each date would always fall on the same day of the week; the scheme, presented to the UN in 1954, was rejected after it failed to receive backing from the U.S.

**Andersson, Sven Olof Morgan,** Swedish politician (b. April 5. 1910, Göteborg, Sweden—d. Sept. 21, 1987, Stockholm, Sweden), as a leading Social Democrat, served as minister of defense (1957–73) and of foreign affairs (1973–76). In 1987 he headed the commission that had been appointed by Prime Minister Olof Palme to investigate the violation of territorial waters by unidentified submarines; it concluded that the submarines belonged to the Soviet Union. Educated at the Nordic High School, Geneva, Andersson entered politics early. He was president of the Göteborg district Social Democratic Youth Union (1929–32) and a member of its national committee (1934–40). He later served as general secretary of the Social Democratic Party (1945–48). He was a member of Parliament (1940–44, 1948–76) and served as minister without portfolio (1948–51) and then minister of communications (1951–57). During the latter period he presided over a program of railroad reorganization, the launch of nationwide television, and an expansion of hydroelectric power. A supporter of Sweden's traditional neutral stance, Andersson was strongly critical of the U.S. involvement in Vietnam.

**Andrews, Eamonn,** Irish radio and television personality (b. Dec. 19, 1922, Dublin, Irish Free State—d. Nov. 5, 1987, London, England), was an amateur boxing champion and radio sports commentator before becoming one of the most popular and enduring personalities on British television. He was best remembered as the host of "This Is Your Life," a half-hour portrait of an unsuspecting celebrity lured to the studio and confronted with his or her past through the memories and sentimental anecdotes of family and friends. While still at school, Andrews won the All-Ireland amateur junior middleweight boxing title; he left school for a job in an insurance office, working part-time as actor, journalist, and sports commentator for Radio Eireann. He moved to London in 1950 and was chosen the following year to be host of the television show "What's My Line?" His genial personality and soft Irish brogue helped to put guests at their ease and won the sympathy of audiences. "This Is Your Life" ran on the British Broadcasting Corporation (BBC) network from 1955 until 1964, when Andrews moved to Independent Television. He did more serious interviewing on "The Eamonn Andrews Show" and "Today" before "This Is Your Life" was revived in 1969. Meanwhile, he ran his own entertainment business in Ireland and as chairman of Radio Eireann (1960–66) helped set up Irish television. Four times chosen as "TV Personality of the Year," Andrews received a papal knighthood for charitable work (1960) and was a Commander of the Order of the British Empire (1970). He wrote two volumes of autobiography, the first, not surprisingly, entitled *This Is My Life* (1963).

**Anghelis, Odysseus,** Greek army officer (b. Feb. 3, 1912, Chalcis, Greece—d. March 22, 1987, Athens, Greece), was a member of the military junta headed by Col. Georgios Papadopoulos, which ruled Greece during the period 1967–74. Following the return to civilian rule, Anghelis was sentenced in 1975 to 20 years in prison for high treason and insurrection. Although he became eligible to apply for parole in 1986, he refused to do so, maintaining his innocence of the charge. Educated at military establishments, Anghelis was commissioned in 1934 and served during World War II in Albania (1940–41) and the Middle East (1943–45). In the postwar period he was involved in the anti Communist campaign in Greece. He was chief of army general staff (1967–68) and commander in chief, Hellenic Armed Forces (1969–73), before serving as vice-president of Greece for a short period during 1973. Anghelis was found hanged in his cell at Koryllados Prison, and his death was ruled to be a suicide.

**Anouilh, Jean-Marie-Lucien-Pierre,** French playwright (b. June 23, 1910, Bordeaux, France—d. Oct. 3, 1987, Lausanne, Switz.), during a more than 50-year career, became the most skillful exponent in modern European theatre of the well-crafted play. His plays, which were more successful with audiences than with critics, revealed a painful awareness of the darker side of human existence. Anouilh was the son of a tailor and a musician. He moved to Paris at the age of 12; he worked for an advertising agency before writing his first play at 19 and becoming secretary to the actor Louis Jouvet. However, Jouvet did little to further Anouilh's career, and it was not until *Le Voyageur sans bagage* (1937) that he achieved his first success. That was followed by *Le Bal des voleurs* (1938), which confirmed his comic gifts. His plays *Antigone* (1944), *L'Alouette* (1953), and *Becket ou l'honneur de Dieu* (1959) were considered his greatest achievements. *Antigone,* which was first performed during the German occupation of France, was, however, politically ambiguous and, along with his appeal for clemency in the case of the condemned writer Robert Brasillach, made his postwar opinions suspect to many people. In *Pauvre Bitos, ou le dîner de têtes* (1956), he attacked the political right and left indiscriminately. During this period, when critical attention was focused on the experiments of the avant-garde, he remained a master of stagecraft. In later years Anouilh turned to directing, notably Molière's *Tartuffe* in 1960, an homage to the French classical dramatist whom he most admired. His later work showed a lasting fascination with theatrical reality and illusion and an increased preoccupation with the absurdities of life.

**Anquetil, Jacques,** French cyclist (b. Jan. 8, 1934, Mont-Saint-Aignan, Seine-Maritime, France—d. Nov. 18, 1987, Rouen, France), was the first cyclist to win the Tour de France five times (1957 and 1961–64), a feat later equaled, but not surpassed, by Eddy Merckx of Belgium and Bernard Hinault of France. In the 1960s Anquetil's rivalry with his countryman Raymond Poulidor dominated cycling. In contrast to the flamboyant Poulidor, Anquetil showed a calculating determination, which earned him more victories than popularity with the crowds. He was involved in controversy in 1967 when his refusal to take a drug test invalidated a one-hour record of 47.493 km (29.493 mi). The son of a Normandy farmer, Anquetil took part in local races while still a teenager and in 1952 won the French amateur road championship. In the following year he gained the first of nine victories in the Grand Prix des Nations and in 1956 established a new one-hour record of 46.159 km (28.665 mi). He won the Tour of Italy twice (1960 and 1964) and was the first Frenchman to take the title; in 1963 he became the first rider from any country to capture the three main tours (France, Italy, and Spain). After his 1967 record was disallowed, Anquetil admitted having used stimulants during his career. He retired in 1969 to devote his time to his business interests. He was made Chevalier of the Legion of Honour in 1966.

**Armstrong, John Ward,** Irish ecclesiastic (b. Sept. 30, 1915, Belfast, Ireland—d. July 21, 1987, Skerries, County Dublin, Ireland), was Church of Ireland archbishop of Armagh and as primate of all Ireland (1980–86) was a convinced proponent of ecumenism who worked closely with the Roman Catholic primate, Tomas Cardinal O'Fiaich. Armstrong was educated at Belfast Royal Academy and at Trinity College, Dublin, where he won high academic distinction. Ordained in 1938, he subsequently held a series of positions, including the rectorship (1951–58) of Christ Church, Leeson Park, Dublin. A notable liturgical scholar, he was Wallace lecturer at Trinity College (1954–65). He was bishop of Cashel and Emly, Waterford, and Lismore (1968–80) and also had charge (1977–80) of the dioceses of Ossory, Ferns, and Leighlin. Armstrong was the Church of Ireland representative on the Anglican Consultative Council (1971–81).

**Astaire, Fred** (FREDERICK AUSTERLITZ), U.S. dancer (b. May 10, 1899, Omaha, Neb.—d. June 22, 1987, Los Angeles, Calif.), gracefully displayed his sensational wizardry on the dance floor with an air of sophistication and an ease of movement that made him the greatest dancer in the history of motion pictures. Astaire, who bewitched audiences with his fancy footwork, began his professional career at the age of ten dancing with his sister, Adele; the two appeared in vaudeville and on Broadway in *Over the Top* (1917), *The Passing Show of 1918, Smiles* (1930), and *The Band Wagon* (1931). The partnership disbanded when Adele married, but Astaire took a Hollywood screen test that resulted in the notorious verdict "Can't act. Slightly bald. Can dance a little." He earned a small part (as himself) opposite Joan Crawford in *Dancing Lady* (1933). Then he was paired with Ginger Rogers in *Flying Down to Rio* (1933), and their talents blended to make movie magic. In all, their unique chemistry was featured in ten films, including *The Gay Divorcée* (1934), *Roberta* and *Top Hat* (both 1935), and *Swing Time* (1936). Some of his other partners included Rita Hayworth (*You Were Never Lovelier,* 1942), Lucille Bremer (*Yolanda and the Thief,* 1945), Judy Garland and Ann Miller (*Easter Parade,* 1948), Cyd Charisse (*The Band Wagon,* 1953, and *Silk Stockings,* 1957), and Audrey Hepburn (*Funny Face,* 1957). His charm and polished performances were highlighted by his ingenuity; Astaire danced atop a wedding cake in *You'll Never Get Rich* (1941), on roller skates in *Shall We Dance* (1937), while hitting golf balls off a tee in *Carefree* (1938), and on the

PHOTO TRENDS

walls and the ceiling in *Royal Wedding* (1951). After starring in what many consider his last full-fledged musical, *Silk Stockings,* he turned to straight acting in such films as *On the Beach* (1959) and *The Notorious Landlady* (1962). In 1949 he was awarded a special Academy Award for his "unique artistry," and in 1975 he was nominated for an Academy Award for best supporting actor for his role in *The Towering Inferno* (1974). He published his autobiography, *Steps in Time,* in 1959, and in 1981 he was honoured with the American Film Institute's Life Achievement Award.

**Astor, Mary** (LUCILE VASCONCELLOS LANGHANKE), U.S. actress (b. May 3, 1906, Quincy, Ill.—d. Sept. 25, 1987, Woodland Hills, Calif.), was best remembered for her role as the seductive dark-eyed adventuress who played opposite Humphrey Bogart, as Sam Spade, in the 1941 film classic *The Maltese Falcon.* In her most compelling roles she portrayed a double-crosser and a spiteful shrew, and in 1942 she won a best supporting actress Academy Award for her role as the malicious concert pianist bent on destroying Bette Davis's marriage in *The Great Lie* (1941). Astor, who was propelled into show business by her father, had her first screen role (cut from the release print) in *Sentimental Tommy* (1921). She became a star in *Beau Brummel* (1924) as John Barrymore's leading lady and excelled in *Don Q Son of Zorro* (1925) and *Don Juan* (1926), which introduced Vitaphone background music and sound effects. Her transition to talkies, not smooth at first, was a success. Then in 1936 her second husband, Franklyn Thorpe, in an attempt to gain custody of their daughter, brought to light alleged excerpts from her diary about an affair with playwright George S. Kaufman. The public supported her courageous court fight and flocked to her films, even though movie moguls urged her to drop the suit. She was granted custody nine months of the year and went on to make some of the finest films of her career, including *Dodsworth* (1936), *The Prisoner of Zenda* (1937), *The Hurricane* (1937), *Midnight* (1939), *Across the Pacific* (1942), *The Palm Beach Story* (1942), and *Meet Me in St. Louis* (1944). Her stormy personal life, including four marriages and financial pressures, caused her drinking problem to worsen, and she was admitted into a sanatorium for alcoholics in 1949. Her 1959 autobiography, *My Story,* served as a catharsis, and in 1961 she made a triumphant return to movies as the evil mother in *Return to Peyton Place.* She made her last film, *Hush . . . Hush, Sweet Charlotte,* in 1965 and embarked on a moderately successful writing career with *A Life on Film* (1971) and some novels. In later years a heart ailment kept her confined to the Motion Picture Country Home in Woodland Hills, which she entered in 1974.

**Athanasiadis-Novas, Georgios,** Greek politician (b. Feb. 9, 1893, Nafpaktos, Greece—d. Aug. 10, 1987, Athens, Greece), was very briefly prime minister (July 15–August 5, 1965) following King Constantine II's clash with Georgios Papandreou but failed to secure a vote of confidence in the Chamber. Under the name George Athanas he published seven highly acclaimed volumes of poetry, two books of short stories, and one novel. After studying law at Athens University, he worked as a journalist; he entered the National Assembly in 1926. He lived in Italy during the dictatorship of Ioannis Metaxas (1936–41) and again (1945–49) following the destruction of his home by Greek Communists. Athanasiadis-Novas joined the Liberal Party in 1949 and was minister of education (1950–51), minister of industry (1951–52), and in charge of the prime minister's office (1951–52 and 1963). The Liberals merged with Papandreou's Centre Union Party in 1961, so when Papandreou attained power in 1964, he appointed Athanasiadis-Novas president of the Chamber of Deputies. He was deputy prime minister (July 1965–December 1966) but abandoned politics after the military coup of 1967. In 1955 Athanasiadis-Novas was elected a member of the Academy of Athens.

**Awolowo, Chief Obafemi,** Nigerian statesman (b. March 6, 1909, Ikene, Nigeria—d. May 9, 1987, Ikene), was formally elected leader in 1966 of the Yoruba, one of the major tribal groups of Nigeria. He had served as premier of the Western Region (1954–59), but ancient rivalries prevented him from attaining higher office after independence in 1960. Educated in mission schools and at the University of London, he was called to the bar. After stints in teaching, journalism, and commerce, he was solicitor and advocate in the Supreme Court of Nigeria (1947–51). Awolowo was involved in the Nigerian youth movement in the early 1950s; he founded the Action Group and took part in constitutional conferences in London and Lagos that preceded independence. Subsequently, he was leader of the opposition in the federal Parliament until a tribal quarrel led to his arrest in November 1962. He was sentenced to ten years in prison for plotting to overthrow the government. Released and pardoned (August 1966) after Lieut. Col. Yakubu Gowon had established a military government, Awolowo became vice-chairman of the federal executive council and was placed in charge of the Ministry of Finance (1967–71). He ran unsuccessfully as Unity Party of Nigeria candidate in the presidential elections of 1979 and 1983. Awolowo wrote a number of books on the Nigerian constitution and politics and two autobiographical volumes.

**Baird, Bil** (WILLIAM BRITTON BAIRD), U.S. puppeteer (b. Aug. 15, 1904, Grand Island, Neb.—d. March 18, 1987, New York, N.Y.), together with his wife, Cora, led the 20th-century revival of puppet theatre in the U.S. with such classic wooden creations as Charlemane the Lion; Snarkey Parker, the master of ceremonies; the Spider Lady, famed for casting spells by canting "Elia Kazan!"; and Bubbles La Rue, the marionette striptease dancer. Baird plied his craft while working under puppeteer Tony Sarg for five years; he presented his first independent commercial production at the 1933 Century of Progress Exposition in Chicago. In 1936 Orson Welles commissioned him to fashion puppets representing the seven deadly sins for a WPA Federal Theater Project production of "Dr. Faustus." There he met his future bride, Cora Burlar, the voice of Envy, Gluttony, and Sloth. The couple were married in 1937 and together carved, painted, and dressed some 3,000 characters during their 30-year marriage (Cora died in 1967). They also built scenery, wrote scripts, and composed music. In 1966 Bil and Cora opened the Bil Baird Theater for marionette productions in New York City. His "little wooden ones" were featured in such television series as "Life with Snarky Parker,"

"The Whistling Wizard," and "The Bil Baird Show," and they livened the variety shows of Ed Sullivan, Jack Paar, and Sid Caesar. Baird also created the dancing goats featured in the motion picture *The Sound of Music* (1965) and was the author of *The Art of the Puppet* (1965). A gifted teacher, he trained a legion of puppeteers that included Jim Henson, the creator of the Muppets.

**Baker, Carlos Heard,** U.S. teacher, novelist, and critic (b. May 5, 1909, Biddeford, Maine—d. April 18, 1987, Princeton, N.J.), wrote the definitive biography of Ernest Hemingway. Baker, who earned a Ph.D. from Princeton University in 1940, served on the faculty there from 1938 to 1977. An expert on modern English and American literature, he was Woodrow Wilson professor of literature from 1953 until his retirement in 1977. Baker's book *Shelley's Major Poetry: The Fabric of a Vision* (1948) gained critical acclaim as a powerful synthesis of Shelley's inner self and as a revelation of the multifaceted Shelley, whose personal changes were reflected in his poetry. Baker's scholarly *Hemingway: The Writer as Artist* (1952) was a critical commentary on the writer's novels in moral and aesthetic terms. His authorized 1969 biography, *Ernest Hemingway: A Life Story,* was praised for its unbiased account. Baker also wrote many volumes of criticism and was the editor of *Ernest Hemingway: Selected Letters, 1917–1961* (1981).

**Baldwin, James Arthur,** U.S. writer (b. Aug. 2, 1924, New York, N.Y.—d. Nov. 30, 1987, St. Paul de Vence, France), bore fervent witness to racial oppression and turmoil in the U.S. with his acclaimed essays and his novels and plays. His impassioned and profoundly personal early essays appeared in three important collections—*Notes of a Native Son* (1955), *Nobody Knows My Name* (1961), and *The Fire Next Time* (1963)—and gave eloquent voice to the emerging civil rights movement. Baldwin, who was raised in poverty in the Harlem black ghetto in New York City, was a preacher in a small revivalist church during his teenage years, an experience that, though he later "reviled" it, strongly affected his writing. After graduating from high school, he held a variety of jobs before moving to France in 1948 to escape racial bigotry in the U.S. Later in life he became what he termed a "transatlantic commuter," living alternately in France and in the U.S. In 1953 he published his first and perhaps finest novel, *Go Tell It on the Mountain,* a semiautobiographical account of a poor Harlem boy and his life with a tyrannical father, a preacher who hates his son. Two novels about homosexuality, *Giovanni's Room* (1956) and *Another Country* (1962), were followed by *Blues for Mister Charlie,* a

AP/WIDE WORLD

bitter play about racial oppression, which premiered on Broadway in 1964 to mixed reviews. The following year *The Amen Corner,* first performed in 1955 at Howard University, Washington, D.C., gained new life when it made its New York City debut. Baldwin's other works included *Going to Meet the Man* (1965), a collection of short stories; the novels *Tell Me How Long the Train's Been Gone* (1968), *If Beale Street Could Talk* (1974), and *Just Above My Head* (1979); and *The Evidence of Things Not Seen* (1985), an examination of the racist aspects of the Atlanta child murders of 1979–81. *The Price of a Ticket,* a collection of his nonfiction, also appeared in 1985. In 1956 Baldwin won the National Institute of Arts and Letters award for literature, and in 1986 he was made a Commander of the Legion of Honour by the French government.

**Barrow, Errol Walton,** Barbadian politician (b. Jan. 21, 1920, St. Lucy, Barbados–d. June 1, 1987, Bridgetown, Barbados), premier from 1961, led his country to independence (1966) and was prime minister of Barbados (1966–76 and from 1986). An advocate of regional integration, Barrow fostered economic cooperation when political federation had failed and was a cofounder and supporter of the Caribbean Community and Common Market. He opposed U.S. intervention in Caribbean affairs, notably the invasion of Grenada in 1983. Educated at Harrison College, Barbados, he served in the Royal Air Force (1940–47), studied at the London School of Economics, and was called to the bar at Lincoln's Inn in 1949. Returning to Barbados in 1951, he was elected to the House of Assembly in 1951. In 1955 he helped found the Democratic Labour Party (DLP), becoming its chairman (1958–76). After the DLP won power in 1961, Barrow pursued a policy of agricultural diversification, encouraged tourism, and worked to establish a racially integrated society. When the short-lived (1958–62) Federation of the West Indies broke up and a proposed arrangement with smaller islands in the region also failed, he achieved independence for Barbados on its own. Since his return to power in May 1986, he had strongly opposed upgrading the Regional Security System, especially the signing of any formal treaty.

**Bennett, Michael** (MICHAEL BENNETT DI-FIGLIA), U.S. choreographer (b. April 8, 1943, Buffalo, N.Y.—d. July 2, 1987, Tucson, Ariz.), created a dazzling array of images onstage with the masterful use of lights, sets, and costumes in such Broadway smash hits as *A Chorus Line,* the longest-running Broadway show (in its 12th year in 1987) and *Dreamgirls* (1981), both of which became signature productions. Bennett, who began dancing when he was 3, left high school at the age of 16 to dance in the chorus of a production of *West Side Story* touring Europe; two years later he made his Broadway debut dancing in *Subways Are for Sleeping.* He found his niche as a choreographer, however, when at the age of 23 he won a Tony nomination for *A Joyful Noise* (1966). He then worked his magic on such shows as *Promises, Promises* (1968), *Coco* (1969), *Company* (1970), and *Follies* (1971), which also marked his debut as a director (with Hal Prince). He then directed and coproduced the comedy *Twigs* (1971) and served as a "show doctor" to salvage *Seesaw* (1973). Bennett's creation of *A Chorus Line* (1975), in which he drew on his own experiences as a dance-corps gypsy as well as those of other chorus dancers, made an indelible mark on the contemporary Broadway musical. *A Chorus Line* garnered nine Tony awards in 1975 and the 1976 Pulitzer Prize for drama. Though his *Ballroom* (1978) was a critical flop, he returned to glory with *Dreamgirls,* the electrifying saga of a black female singing trio. (In 1987 *Dreamgirls* made a successful return to Broadway, opening four days before Bennett's death.) Though he began casting in 1985 for the British musical *Chess,* he was unable to complete the commission because of poor health. He died of

AIDS-related cancer. Among the many honours he won for his contributions to theatre was his 1986 election to the Theater Hall of Fame.

**Beswick, Frank Beswick,** BARON, British politician (b. Aug. 21, 1911, Hucknall, Nottinghamshire, England—d. Aug. 17, 1987, London, England), was an aviation expert and former pilot who served as first chairman of the nationalized company British Aerospace (1976–80). Created a life peer in 1964, he was the Labour government's chief whip in the House of Lords (1967–70) and opposition chief whip (1970–74). He served as minister of state for industry and deputy leader of the House of Lords (1974–75). The son of a miner, Beswick studied at the Working Men's College, London, becoming a journalist and London county councillor. During World War II he served in the Royal Air Force in the Middle East. A Labour member of Parliament (1945–59), he was parliamentary private secretary to the under secretary of state for air (1946–49) and parliamentary secretary to the minister of civil aviation (1950–51). He also served as one of the U.K.'s observers of the 1946 Bikini atomic tests. Edward Heath's Conservative government appointed him special adviser (1970–74) to the chairman of the British Aircraft Corporation, later part of British Aerospace. Beswick was chairman (1978–80) of the board that supervised the U.K.'s rejoining of the European Airbus consortium.

**Bissell, Patrick,** U.S. dancer (b. Dec. 1, 1957, Corpus Christi, Texas—d. Dec. 29, 1987, Hoboken, N.J.), was an extraordinarily gifted principal dancer with the American Ballet Theatre (ABT) and one of the dance world's most promising stars. Bissell, who joined the company in 1977 as a corps dancer, quickly gained recognition with his electric stage presence and distinctive style; he was promoted to soloist in 1978 and to principal dancer the following year. Tall, classically handsome, and given to passionate interpretations, he was seen as an American-style ballet prince. Bissell's wide and varied repertory included roles as Don José in Roland Petit's *Carmen,* Franz in *Coppélia,* Basil and Espada in *Don Quixote,* Romeo in *Romeo and Juliet,* Prince Siegfried in *Swan Lake,* and Prince Désiré in Sir Kenneth MacMillan's *Sleeping Beauty.* In 1980 and 1981 Bissell was dismissed from ABT because of chronic lateness and missed rehearsals. He figured prominently in ballerina Gelsey Kirkland's autobiography, *Dancing on My Grave* (1987), in which she revealed both her own and Bissell's drug addiction.

**Bolger, Ray(mond) Wallace,** U.S. actor and dancer (b. Jan. 10, 1904, Dorchester, Mass.—d. Jan. 15, 1987, Los Angeles, Calif.), appeared to be truly made of hay as he cavorted down the Yellow Brick Road as the beloved Scarecrow in search of a brain in the 1939 motion-picture classic *The Wizard of Oz* and delighted Broadway theatregoers in such musical comedies as *On Your Toes* (1936), *By Jupiter* (1942), *Three to Make Ready* (1946), and *Where's Charley?* (1948). The rubber-legged Bolger, who preferred to be known as a comedian, combined the best of his abilities in musical comedy. He appeared in vaudeville as a boy, made his debut on Broadway in *The Merry World* (1926), and starred in *George White's Scandals* (1931) and *Life Begins at 8:40* (1934). After making his film debut in *The Great Ziegfeld* (1936), he appeared on screen in *Sunny* (1941), *Stage Door Canteen* (1943), *Where's Charley?* (1952), *Babes in Toyland* (1961), and *The Runner Stumbles* (1979). Both his "Once in Love with Amy," from *Where's Charley?,* and his "If I Only Had a Brain," from *The Wizard of Oz,* became signature songs.

**Bramwell-Booth, Catherine,** British Salvation Army commissioner (b. July 20, 1883, London, England—d. Oct. 4, 1987, Finchampstead, Berkshire, England), was the granddaughter of the Army's founder, William Booth, and served the Army with devotion and distinction for 45 years. In her old age she became known to a wider audience through television appearances. The eldest child of William Bramwell Booth (who served as second general of the Salvation Army from 1912 to 1929), she entered the Army's training college and became a commissioned officer in 1903. She trained cadets and also traveled widely. Appointed international secretary for Europe in 1917, she became involved with helping to care for and resettle refugees. Bramwell-Booth was in charge of women's social work (1926–37) and supervised the Army's homes for mothers and children. She again helped postwar refugees from 1946 until her retirement in 1948. Bramwell-Booth published two volumes of verse and wrote biographies of her paternal grandmother, Catherine Booth (1970), and her father (1933).

**Brattain, Walter Houser,** U.S. scientist (b. Feb. 10, 1902, Amoy, China—d. Oct. 13, 1987, Seattle, Wash.), shared the 1956 Nobel Prize for Physics with John Bardeen and William B. Shockley for their investigations into the properties of semiconductors; this led to the development of the transistor, which they invented on Dec. 23, 1947, at the American Telephone and Telegraph Co.'s Bell Laboratories in Murray Hill, N.J. Though Brattain was born in China, where his father was teaching, he was raised in Spokane, Wash. After earning a B.A. (1924) from Whitman College in Walla Walla, Wash., he earned an M.A. from the University of Oregon and a Ph.D. from the University of Minnesota. In 1929 he joined Bell Telephone Laboratories, where he conducted research on semiconductors, the materials that are used in transistors. The transistor replaced the bulkier vacuum tube and provided the technology for miniaturizing electronic equipment needed for construction of computers. After leaving Bell Laboratories in 1967, Brattain served as adjunct professor at his alma mater, Whitman College, until 1972. He was also elected to the National Inventors Hall of Fame.

**Brenan, (Edward Fitz-)Gerald,** British author (b. April 7, 1894, Malta—d. Jan. 19, 1987, Ahaurín el Grande, near Málaga, Spain), was best known for writings that reflected his wide knowledge of the Spanish people and their history and literature. The son of an army officer, he spent his early childhood in Africa and Asia before returning to England to be educated. He left school to wander through France and Yugoslavia but returned to take a commission in the Army during World War I. After the war Brenan had an unhappy affair in London with the painter Dora Carrington before settling in Spain with his wife, Gamel Woolsey, a U.S. poet. During World War II he returned to England and wrote *The Spanish Labyrinth* (1943), one of the most penetrating studies of the Spanish Civil War. Despite his sympathy for the losing Republican side in the war, Brenan settled permanently near Málaga in 1953. His works included *The Face of Spain* (1950), *The Literature of the Spanish People* (1953), *South from Granada* (1957), and a study of *St. John of the Cross* (1971). He also wrote a novel and two volumes of autobiography. Though Brenan decided to retire to England in 1984, he was persuaded by the Spanish authorities to return. The Gerald Brenan Foundation was established in Málaga in 1986 to continue the study of his work.

**Broglie, Louis-Victor-Pierre-Raymond,** 7th duc de, French physicist (b. Aug. 15, 1892, Dieppe, France—d. March 19, 1987, Louveciennes, Yvelines, France), was awarded the 1929 Nobel Prize for Physics for his discovery of the wave nature of electrons. His discovery, outlined in his doctoral thesis, *Recherches sur la théorie des quanta* (1924), was that elementary particles of matter possess the properties of waves as well as those of particles and that these properties were not contradictory but linked. Broglie, who advanced the work of Albert Einstein and Max

Planck, thus made a fundamental contribution to the development of quantum theory. In 1927 Clinton Davisson and Lester Germer in the U.S. and George Thomson in Scotland found the first experimental evidence of the electron's wave nature. Broglie turned to physics only after obtaining a university degree in history. He earned (1924) a Ph.D. in physics from the Sorbonne and became professor of theoretical physics at the Henri Poincaré Institute (1928). Broglie taught there until his retirement in 1962. He was permanent secretary of the French Academy of Sciences (1942–75), and he was elected to the Académie Française in 1944. In 1952 he was awarded the United Nations Kalinga Prize in recognition of his science writings, which were geared to the general public and explored the philosophical implications of modern physics. Broglie was the author of more than 20 books; some of his popular writings appeared in English translations, including *The Revolution in Physics* (1953) and *Physics and Microphysics* (1960). He succeeded his brother as duc de Broglie in 1960.

**Brú, Hedin** (HANS JAKOB JACOBSEN), Faeroese writer (b. Aug. 17, 1901, Skálevig, Faeroe Islands—d. May 18, 1987, Tórshavn, Faeroe Islands), as the leading writer in Faeroese, contributed greatly to establishing the language, which before the mid-19th century had barely existed in written form, as a literary language. At 14 Brú worked as a fisherman. He attended the Folk High School in Tórshavn (1919–20) and then spent much of the 1920s studying agriculture in Denmark. He began to contribute stories and other writings to the literary periodical *Vardin,* established in 1921. From 1928 he served as an agricultural consultant, becoming chief agricultural adviser to the Faeroese government in 1942 and gaining valuable experience from his visits to the farming communities of the islands. His travels inspired his first two novels, *Longbrá* (1930, "Mirage") and *Fastatøkur* (1937, "Firm Grip"), which dramatized the changing face of Faeroese life as subsistence agriculture gave way to the fishing industry. A similar contrast between old and new was the main theme of his best work, *Fedgar á ferd* (1940, *The Old Man and His Sons*). He played a central role in cultural life as coeditor of *Vardin* and as a member of the Faeroese Scientific Society. Brú also began to acquire an international reputation. He worked from Scandinavian translations to produce Faeroese versions of *Hamlet* and *The Tempest,* wrote a volume of memoirs, and was a lifelong supporter of the Faeroese Social Democratic Party.

**Burnham, James,** U.S. political philosopher (b. Nov. 22, 1905, Chicago, Ill.—d. July 28, 1987, Kent, Conn.), exerted a powerful influence on the development of conservative thought in the U.S. both as a founding (1955) editorial-board member of William F. Buckley's *National Review* and as the author of such riveting books as *The Struggle for the World* (1947) and *The Coming Defeat of Communism* (1950). Burnham, who undertook graduate studies at Balliol College, Oxford, after graduating from Princeton University, joined the philosophy department of New York University in 1929. A one-time Trotskyite, Burnham tried to form an independent Communist Party during the Depression but abandoned left-wing politics after a falling-out with Trotsky. He later became a vociferous opponent of Communism and gave voice to his views in such books as *The Managerial Revolution* (1941), *The Machiavellians* (1943), and *Suicide of the West* (1964). He remained an editor and columnist at the *National Review* until a stroke in 1977 caused him to reduce his activities. In 1983 Burnham was awarded the Presidential Medal of Freedom in recognition of his lasting contribution to American conservative thought.

**Burns, Arthur Frank,** Austrian-born economist (b. April 27, 1904, Stanislau, Austria—d. June 26, 1987, Baltimore, Md.), as chairman of the

Federal Reserve Board (1970–78) was instrumental in shaping economic policy and was widely respected as an adviser to four U.S. presidents. Burns, who earned his Ph.D. in economics from Columbia University, New York City, taught at Rutgers, the State University of New Jersey, and later served as director of research (1945–53) of the National Bureau of Economic Research, bringing to the post his expertise in the field of business cycles. In 1945 he also became a professor at Columbia. He began his longtime government service in 1953 when he became chairman of Pres. Dwight D. Eisenhower's Council of Economic Advisers. A pragmatist, Burns shifted his policy from advocating tight money to doubling the money supply as inflation either increased or decreased. In 1974, when inflation was at double-digit levels, Burns, who had the responsibility for devising the central banking system's interest-rate policies, escalated the rates, a move that caused him to be blamed for helping plunge the U.S. into a recession that same year. In 1969 he was economic adviser to Pres. Richard M. Nixon and later served under Presidents Gerald Ford and Jimmy Carter. In 1980 he was founding chairman of the Committee to Fight Inflation, and from 1981 to 1985 he served as ambassador to West Germany.

**Caldwell, Erskine,** U.S. writer (b. Dec. 17, 1903, Coweta County, Ga.—d. April 11, 1987, Paradise Valley, Ariz.), with such novels as *Tobacco Road* (1932) and *God's Little Acre* (1933), which chronicled the desperate and degenerate lives of poor Georgia farmers during the Depression, was hailed as one of the foremost Southern writers during the 1930s. His works, which were brutally shocking in their depictions of incest, adultery, lynchings, prostitution, lechery, and murder, were banned or censored in several states. Caldwell, the son of a missionary, attended Erskine College, Due West, S.C., and the University of Virginia, but he did not graduate. In 1926 he settled in Maine. There he wrote several books, including *Tobacco Road,* which became a blockbuster, selling 3.5 million copies. It was also a successful New York stage play, running for more than seven years, and a motion picture (1941). The title became synonymous with rural squalor and degradation.

During the late 1930s Caldwell became involved in social causes, particularly on behalf of impoverished sharecroppers, who were the subject of the stirring documentary *You Have Seen Their Faces* (1937; with photographs provided by Margaret Bourke-White, whom Caldwell married in 1939). The couple were in the Soviet Union during the 1941 German invasion and remained there for several months on journalistic assignments. Caldwell recounted his experience in *All Out on the Road to Smolensk* (1942) and *Moscow Under Fire* (1942; photographs by Bourke-White).

In 1945 Caldwell established and served as general editor of *American Folkways,* a series of 25 regional books on the U.S. Of his 55 books, others that gained critical renown include *Journeyman* (1933), *Trouble in July* (1940), *Georgia Boy* (1943), *Tragic Ground* (1944), and *In Search of Bisco* (1965). Caldwell was admired as a proletarian novelist and was widely read in the Soviet Union, but his naturalistic style fell out of favour in the U.S. During the last 20 years of his life, his efforts attracted little critical attention. In 1984, however, he was elected to the American Academy and Institute of Arts and Letters.

**Campbell, Joseph,** U.S. author (b. March 26, 1904, New York, N.Y.—d. Oct. 31, 1987, Honolulu, Hawaii), was a learned scholar who was considered one of the foremost experts on comparative mythology and folklore. As a child, Campbell devoured library books that chronicled American Indian folklore. This avocation eventually became his lifelong pursuit. While researching for his M.A. in literature at Columbia University, New York City, Campbell discovered that the Arthurian legend reflected some of the basic motifs in American Indian folklore. While serving on the faculty (1934–72) at Sarah Lawrence College, Bronxville, N.Y., he also became a prolific writer and editor. Some of his most important works included *The Hero with a Thousand Faces* (1949), the four-volume *Masks of God* (1959–67), *The Flight of the Wild Gander* (1969), *Myths to Live By* (1972), and *The Mythic Image* (1974). His skills as an editor were best evidenced in such books as *Myths and Symbols in Indian Art and Civilization* (1946), *Myths, Dreams, and Religion* (1970), and *The Mystic Vision* (1969). At the time of his death, he was working on the multivolume opus *The Historical Atlas of World Mythology*. The first part, *The Way of the Animal Powers*, was published in 1983, and the second installment, *The Way of the Seeded Earth*, was scheduled to appear in 1988.

**Carroll, Madeleine** (MARIE-MADELEINE BERNADETTE O'CARROLL), British-born actress (b. Feb. 26, 1906, West Bromwich, England—d. Oct. 2, 1987, Marbella, Spain), was a cool blonde beauty who attained stardom in Britain in the Alfred Hitchcock thrillers *The 39 Steps* (1935) and *Secret Agent* (1936) and then became a major star in the U.S., appearing in *Lloyd's of London* (1936), *The Prisoner of Zenda* (1937), and *My Son, My Son!* (1940). Carroll, who graduated from the University of Birmingham, England, with a B.A. degree and honours in French, worked as a hat model before making her British screen debut in *The Guns of Loos* (1928). She showed a particular flair for cinematic espionage and starred as a spy in *I Was a Spy* (1933), *The General Died at Dawn* (1936), and *My Favorite Blonde* (1942). In 1943 she became a U.S. citizen, but she returned to England to work in the war effort after the death of her sister in the London blitz of World War II. She retired to a farm near Paris, was active in Unesco, and was awarded the U.S. Medal of Freedom for her war-relief efforts, which included converting her home into an orphanage and joining the Red Cross to nurse the wounded from Allied fronts in France and Italy. After the war she made three more films before retiring from the silver screen.

**Casey, William Joseph,** U.S. government official (b. March 13, 1913, Elmhurst, Queens, N.Y.—d. May 6, 1987, Glen Cove, N.Y.), was the powerful yet controversial director of the Central Intelligence Agency (CIA) from 1981 until he resigned on Feb. 2, 1987. He was viewed as a pivotal figure in detailing the role of the CIA in the Iran-*contra* affair, in which weapons were sold by the U.S. to Iran and money from the sale was funneled to the Nicaraguan *contras* (in possible violation of U.S. law). Casey, who suffered two seizures on Dec. 15, 1986—the day

before he was to testify to a Senate panel about the CIA's role in the sale of U.S. arms to Iran—underwent brain surgery three days later for the removal of a malignant tumour. His crucial testimony was never heard, and his death occurred less than 24 hours after the congressional hearings on the affair began.

After Casey earned a law degree from St. John's University, Jamaica, N.Y., in 1937, he worked for the Research Institute of America, Washington, D.C., where he exhibited a flair for analyzing business information. During World War II he worked in Europe (1941–46) with the Office of Strategic Services (forerunner of the CIA) to drop agents behind Nazi lines. After the war he lectured on tax law (1948–62) at New York University; he amassed a personal fortune through successful investments and by compiling legal and economic information for corporate customers. After conducting research for Richard M. Nixon's 1968 presidential campaign, Casey helped the new president by establishing the Citizens Committee for Peace with Security. Casey, who compiled an impressive list of credentials, later served as chairman of the Securities and Exchange Commission (1971–73), under secretary of state for economic affairs (1973–74), president and chairman of the Export-Import Bank (1974–75), and a member of the Foreign Intelligence Advisory Board (1976). He was affiliated with the law firm Rogers & Wells from 1976 until 1981 and served as manager of Ronald Reagan's presidential campaign in 1980. Casey was named director of central intelligence in 1981, and under his leadership the agency built up its ability to act militarily and politically outside the U.S. Covert action increased in places such as Afghanistan, Central America, and Angola, and the agency stepped up its support for various anti-Communist insurgent organizations. During his tenure the agency began providing the *contras* with military assistance and clandestine training before such aid was outlawed by Congress in 1984. His death ensured that the role of the CIA in the Iran-*contra* affair would never be fully revealed.

**Cassola, Carlo,** Italian novelist (b. March 17, 1917, Rome, Italy—d. Jan. 29, 1987, Monte Carlo, Monaco), portrayed the landscapes and the ordinary people of rural Tuscany in simple prose, reacting against the excesses of Fascist rhetoric and the obscurity of the avant-garde. With the lack of action and emphasis on detail in his neorealist work, Cassola was regarded as a forerunner of the French *nouveau roman*. After studying at the University of Rome, he fought with the Resistance during World War II. The period formed the background of some of his best-known works, among them the short-story collection *Il taglio del bosco* (1955; *Timber Cutting*, 1959) and the novel *Fausto e Anna* (1952; *Fausto and Anna*, 1960), both of them strongly autobiographical. In 1960 Cassola won the Strega Prize for *La ragazza di Bube* (*Bebo's Girl*, 1962), which was filmed in 1964 with Claudia Cardinale in the title role. These austere novels depicted with sympathy and restraint the bleak and unfulfilled lives of people—especially women. His later concern with the environment and the threat of nuclear war was reflected in essays and in the novel *Il paradiso degli animali* (1979; "Animals' Paradise").

**Chamoun, Camille,** Lebanese politician (b. April 3, 1900, Dayr al-Qamar, ash Shuf, Lebanon—d. Aug. 7, 1987, Beirut, Lebanon), as president of Lebanon from 1952 to 1958, was an influential right-wing Maronite Christian leader who up to the time of his death played a dominant role in the turbulent politics of Lebanon and was an implacable opponent of the Palestine Liberation Organization. Educated in Beirut at French-run Catholic institutions, he was called to the Lebanese bar in 1924. He entered the Chamber of Deputies in 1934 and served as minister of finance (1938) and minister of the interior (1943–44). While ambassador to Britain (1944–47), Chamoun represented Lebanon on the UN Preparatory Commission (1945) and attended

other UN and Unesco meetings. During his presidency he offended Arab opinion by favouring France and Britain during the 1956 Suez conflict. Following Muslim riots in 1957 and the arrival of the U.S. Marines in 1958, Chamoun was replaced by a less controversial figure when his term ended. In 1958 Chamoun founded the National Liberation Party. He reemerged into prominence at the outbreak of civil war in 1975 as deputy prime minister (1975–76), holding a number of portfolios. Chamoun established a Maronite stronghold at Juniyah in northern Lebanon, and his militia band, the Tigers, was active from 1975 to 1980. He attended national reconciliation conferences in Switzerland (1983, 1984) and was strongly opposed to Syrian intervention in Lebanon. He had survived five assassination attempts.

**Chouinard, Julien,** Canadian Supreme Court justice (b. Feb. 4, 1929, Quebec City, Que.—d. Feb. 6, 1987, Ottawa, Ont.), as one of the nine justices of the Supreme Court of Canada (1979–87), dealt mostly with cases concerned with Quebec and Canadian labour law. Chouinard, who was a Rhodes scholar (1953), taught corporation law at Laval University, Quebec City, before becoming a top civil servant in Quebec. He served as deputy justice minister (1965–68) before becoming (1969) secretary-general of the Cabinet, a post created for him by Premier Daniel Johnson. During the October crisis of 1970—when Le Front de Libération du Québec (FLQ), a terrorist organization dedicated to obtaining Quebec's independence, kidnapped James Cross, a British trade commissioner in Montreal, and Pierre Laporte, Quebec minister of labour—Chouinard, as Quebec Premier Robert Bourassa's top adviser, established the Centre d'Analyse et Documentation, an intelligence unit that collected information on suspected terrorists. After serving under Premier Jean-Jacques Bertrand, he became (1975) a judge of the Quebec Court of Appeals; he held that post until his appointment to the Supreme Court in 1979. He was hailed for his "innate sense of justice and fairness."

**Chowdhury, Abu Sayeed,** Bangladeshi judge and politician (b. Jan. 31, 1921, Tangail, Bengal [now Bangladesh]—d. Aug. 1, 1987, London, England), was one of the founders of Bangladesh and the country's president (January 1972–December 1973). He also gave long and distinguished service to the United Nations, becoming chairman of the UN Commission on Human Rights in 1985. Educated in Calcutta at Presidency College and at the university, he then studied law in London and was called to the bar at Lincoln's Inn in 1947. He returned to East Pakistan and rose rapidly in the legal profession, becoming advocate general in 1960 and a judge the following year. In 1971 Chowdhury was in Geneva, representing Pakistan in the UN Commission on Human Rights, when the events leading to the establishment of Bangladesh occurred; he announced his support of the new country and established himself as its high commissioner in London. Although unanimously elected president of Bangladesh for a five-year term in April 1973, Chowdhury resigned at the end of the year because of disagreements with Prime Minister Sheikh Mujibur Rahman. In 1975 he served briefly as foreign minister under Pres. Khandakar Mushtaque Ahmed. Thereafter he was based in Geneva, where he coordinated foreign aid for Bangladesh and was a member (1978–87) of the UN Sub-Commission on Prevention of Discrimination and Protection of Minorities.

**Cohen, Wilbur Joseph,** U.S. government official (b. June 10, 1913, Milwaukee, Wis.—d. May 18, 1987, Seoul, South Korea), was a devoted public servant and aggressive social reformer who helped draft the Social Security Act of 1935 and the Medicare Act of 1965. Cohen earned a degree in economics from the University of Wisconsin in 1934 and the following year became the first employee of the Social

AP/WIDE WORLD

Security Administration. As assistant secretary of health, education and welfare under Pres. Lyndon B. Johnson, Cohen was instrumental in promoting such important social legislation as the Elementary and Secondary Education Act of 1965, the Heart Disease, Cancer and Stroke Amendments of 1965, and the Child Health Act of 1967. From 1968 to 1969 he served as secretary of health, education and welfare and later as a public affairs professor at the University of Texas at Austin.

**Coldstream, Sir William Menzies,** British painter and art administrator (b. Feb. 28, 1908, Belford, Northumberland, England—d. Feb 18, 1987, London, England), worked in oils, producing mainly landscapes but also still life studies. He was Slade professor of fine art at University College, University of London (1949–75), and as chairman of the National Advisory Council on Art Education (1958–71) had a profound influence on the teaching of art in Britain. Educated privately, Coldstream studied at the Slade School (1926–29). He exhibited with the New English Art Club and with the London Group from 1929. In the mid-1930s he worked on documentary films. With Victor Pasmore and Claude Rogers he founded the Euston Road School of Drawing and Painting in 1937. After the outbreak of World War II, the school closed and Coldstream joined the Army; in 1943 he became an official war artist, based in Cairo and later in southern Italy. Subsequently he taught at the Camberwell School of Art and Crafts (1945–49), becoming head of its painting department in 1946. As Slade professor he introduced postgraduate courses, including one on films. At various times he was a trustee of the National Gallery and of the Tate Gallery, a director of the Royal Opera House, and chairman of the British Film Institute. Coldstream was knighted in 1956.

**Colville, Sir John Rupert,** British civil servant (b. Jan. 28, 1915—d. Nov. 19, 1987, Broughton, Hampshire, England), worked closely with three British prime ministers; he was assistant private secretary to Neville Chamberlain (1939–40), Winston Churchill (1940–41, 1943–45), and Clement Attlee (1945), and he returned as joint principal private secretary in Churchill's postwar administration (1951–55). He was private secretary to Princess Elizabeth (1947–49). His diaries, covering virtually the entire period of his public service and published as *The Fringes of Power* (1985), provide illuminating insider comment on personalities and events. Born into a family closely connected with the court and Parliament, Colville was educated at Harrow School and at Trinity College, Cambridge. He entered the diplomatic service in 1937. During World War II he trained as a fighter pilot and served with the Royal Air Force (1941–43 and after the D-Day landings in 1944). Colville was in the Southern Department of the Foreign Office (1945–47) and was first secretary in the British embassy at Lisbon (1949–51). With Baron Soames (*q.v.*), he was largely responsible for concealing from the public the incapacitating nature of Churchill's illness (a stroke) in June 1953. He left the diplomatic service when Churchill resigned (1955), made a second career in merchant banking, and wrote a number of books. Colville was knighted in 1974.

**Cotton, (Thomas) Henry,** British golfer (b. Jan. 26, 1907, Holmes Chapel, Cheshire, England— d. Dec. 22, 1987, London, England), eclipsed the U.S. domination of golf in England by winning the British Open championship three times (1934, 1937, 1948); in 1937 he defeated a field that included the entire U.S. Ryder Cup team. He was the first British professional golfer of middle-class origins, and his career helped to break down the barriers between amateurs and professionals. After ceasing to play in tournaments, he continued to serve golf as a teacher, course designer, media commentator, journalist, and author of a number of books. Educated at Alleyn's School, Dulwich, London, he was

encouraged to play golf by his father, who had him coached by J. H. Taylor, a former leading professional. Leaving school at 17, Cotton held three assistantships before becoming a full professional (1926) at Langley Park, Kent. He was with Belgium's Waterloo Club (1933–36) before returning to the new club at Ashridge in Buckinghamshire. After serving (1939–43) in the Royal Air Force, he played exhibition matches for the Red Cross. He captured 11 European Open championships and captained the U.K.'s Ryder Cup team (1939, 1947); in 1953 he was nonplaying captain. Cotton designed the Penina golf course in Algarve, Port., where he later lived. Shortly before his death, he received word that he was to be granted a knighthood in the 1988 New Year's Honours List.

**Crawley, Frank Radford ("BUDGE"),** Canadian filmmaker (b. Nov. 14, 1911, Ottawa, Ont.— d. May 13, 1987, Perth, Ont.), together with his wife, Judith, founded (1938) Crawley Films, Ltd., a pioneering enterprise that made more than 2,400 sponsored films for more than 400 clients. The Crawleys' first production, *Île d'Orléans,* was made on their honeymoon and won an award for the best amateur Canadian film of 1939. In the 1940s and '50s they established their reputation with an extensive number of documentary and educational films, many of them contracted by the National Film Board. Crawley, one of the country's foremost filmmakers, produced more than 3,500 films and earned 235 national and international awards. Some of his most notable credits include *The Loon's Necklace* (1948), *Newfoundland Scene* (1950), *The Legend of the Raven* (1958), *The Luck of Ginger Coffey* (1964), *The Rowdyman* (1972), and *The Man Who Skied down Everest* (1975), which won an Academy Award for feature-length documentary. Crawley Films, at one time the country's largest independent film company, served as a training ground for a generation of aspiring technicians.

**Crowther-Hunt, Norman Crowther Crowther-Hunt, BARON,** British academic (b. March 13, 1920, Bradford, Yorkshire, England—d. Feb. 16, 1987, Oxford, England), was a notable university teacher of politics and served as rector of Exeter College, Oxford, from 1982; during the 1960s and '70s he worked for the Labour governments headed by Harold Wilson. He was born Norman Crowther Hunt. He was educated at Sidney Sussex College, Cambridge, served in the Royal Artillery during World War II, and in 1952 became a fellow and lecturer in politics at Exeter College. During his membership on the Fulton Committee (1966–68) on the Civil Service, Hunt drafted the report that advocated wider recruitment and a greater use of specialists. As a member of the Kilbrandon Commission on the Constitution (1969–73), which considered the establishment of legislative assemblies for Scotland and Wales, he was the principal author of the memorandum of dissent, arguing that the English regions should receive similar institutions. He was created a life peer in 1973. Lord Crowther-Hunt served as constitutional adviser (March–October 1974) to Wilson's government and as minister of state for education and science (1974–76). He was a skillful radio and television commentator and for some years presented the BBC World Service's weekly program "People and Politics."

**Dalida** (YOLANDE CHRISTINA GIGLIOTTI), Egyptian-born French singer (b. Jan. 17, 1933, Cairo, Egypt—d. May 3, 1987, Paris, France), a versatile performer for 30 years, was a popular film star, music-hall singer, and recording artist. She was the daughter of a violinist in the Cairo Opera. She was chosen "Miss Egypt" at the age of 21 and acted in films before moving to Paris in 1955. Encouraged by Lucien Morisse, who was artistic director of the radio station Europe 1 and to whom she was briefly married in 1961, she achieved her first successes with "Bambino," "Ciao ciao bambina," and other popular hits. Her sultry voice and her accent combined

to produce an image of exotic, but tame, eroticism. Dalida appeared in the films *Parlez-moi d'amour* (1960) and *Ménage à l'italienne* (1964). Though she took her family to France, she maintained ties with Egypt by recording songs in Arabic. The last of her 11 films was *The Sixth Day* (1986), directed by Youssef Chahine. A hard-working professional, Dalida tried to launch her career in new directions, but her efforts were overshadowed by an unhappy private life, and in the 1980s her popularity declined. She had made at least one previous attempt at suicide before she died from an overdose of barbiturates.

**Darrell, Peter** (PETER SKINNER), British dancer and choreographer (b. Sept. 19, 1929, Richmond, Surrey, England—d. Dec. 2, 1987, Glasgow, Scotland), was cofounder and from 1962 sole artistic director of the Scottish Ballet. The breadth of his imaginative power was demonstrated by the great diversity of his work, ranging from classical ballets skillfully presented in a relevant modern idiom to a variety of totally new creations, such as *Mods and Rockers* (1963), with music by the Beatles. Trained at the Sadler's Wells School, he joined the Sadler's Wells Theatre Ballet on its formation in 1946 and danced with it for two years. He later danced in Paris and Sweden. Darrell was based in London with the Ballet Workshop (1951–55) and in 1952 was invited by Anton Dolin to choreograph *Harlequinade* for the Festival Ballet. In 1957, together with Elizabeth West, he founded the Western Theatre Ballet; it was based at Sadler's Wells from 1965 and in 1969 moved to Glasgow. Some of his notable productions included *The Prisoners* (1957), *Sun into Darkness* (1966)—for which he commissioned the score from Malcolm Williamson and the libretto from David Rudkin—*Mary Queen of Scots* (1976), and *Carmen* (1985). Darrell was made a Commander of the Order of the British Empire in 1984.

**Dassler, Horst,** West German businessman (b. March 12, 1936—d. April 10, 1987, Herzogenaurach, near Nürnburg, West Germany), was chairman from 1985 of Adidas, a leading international sportswear manufacturer that evolved from a gym shoe firm founded in 1920 by his father in partnership with his uncle. Horst Dassler's sales drive at the 1956 Olympic Games in Melbourne, Australia, helped to establish the company's reputation among leading athletes. In 1960 he founded Adidas (France), which became that country's leading manufacturer of sports equipment. He also expanded the company's operations into Eastern Europe and worked tirelessly to develop links with sporting authorities and clubs through various forms of sponsorship. The Adidas symbol became universally known, but at a time of controversy over the definition of amateurism in athletics, the company's aggressive marketing policies were subject to criticism. Its Swiss marketing company, ISL, was accused of undue influence with the International Olympic Committee (IOC), particularly after it secured the marketing contract for the 1988 summer Olympic Games in Seoul, South Korea. Dassler held the IOC's Olympic Order, the U.S. Distinguished Service Award, and the award of the French Académie des Sports.

**Delay, Jean,** French psychiatrist (b. Nov. 14, 1907, Bayonne, France—d. May 29, 1987, Paris, France), a physician of international renown, made important advances in determining the neurological bases of mental disorders and pioneered the successful use of chlorpromazine and similar drugs for affective illnesses and schizophrenia. He was president of the first world congresses of psychiatry (1950) and of psychosomatic medicine (1960). Delay was educated at the Collège Saint-Louis-de-Gonzague, Bayonne, and at the University of Paris. He took up his first hospital appointment in 1928, became a consultant in 1938, and was clinical head of the Salpêtrière (1936–38). A professor at the Faculty of Medicine at the University of Paris from 1939, he was professor of mental diseases and encephalography (1946–70) and director of the Institute of Psychology at the Sorbonne (1951–70). Delay was elected a member of the Académie Française in 1959. Among his important psychiatric books were studies on memory and on mood disorders; he also wrote three novels and published psychological studies of a number of literary figures, including André Gide and Eugène Ionesco. His profound disturbance over the student riots of 1968 led him to withdraw from teaching and private practice in order to plan a composite work of psychological literary criticism.

**Den Uyl, Johannes Marten** ("JOOP"), Dutch politician (b. Aug. 9, 1919, Hilversum, Neth.— d. Dec. 24, 1987, Amsterdam, Neth.), was leader of the Labour Party, served as prime minister (1973–77), heading a coalition of left-wing parties, and was twice leader of the opposition (1967–73, 1982–86). He studied economics at the University of Amsterdam and became a journalist. He was a Resistance worker during World War II. Den Uyl joined the newly formed Labour Party (1946) and became director of its Scientific Bureau (1949). He was elected a Labour representative to the Amsterdam city council (1953) and entered Parliament (1956). As minister of economic affairs (1965–66), he encouraged the Dutch North Sea gas- and oil-extraction industries. As premier he had ambitious plans for social reform, but his administration was plagued with economic difficulties. In 1976 he successfully dissuaded Queen Juliana from abdicating when her consort, Prince Bernhard, was implicated in the Lockheed scandal. Although Labour won most gains in the election in 1977, Den Uyl, whose policies were radical and whose style was compromising, proved unable to form a government. He was minister of social affairs, employment, and Antillean affairs in 1981–82.

**Devlin, William George,** British actor (b. Dec. 5, 1911, Aberdeen, Scotland—d. Jan. 25, 1987, Monksilver, Somerset, England) played leading roles in the 1930s, 1940s, and early 1950s but perhaps lacked the ambition to reach the eminence his talent might have won him. Educated at Stonyhurst College and at Merton College, Oxford, Devlin trained at the Embassy Theatre School of Acting (1933–34) and made an immediate hit on the London stage as King Lear in October 1934. He worked with John Gielgud at London's New Theatre (1934–35) and took parts at the Old Vic (1935–39). Among his outstanding roles in this period was that of Peer Gynt. Following World War II, in which he served with the Royal Wiltshire Yeomanry and with the 8th Army in North Africa and Italy, Devlin was the leading male actor at the Bristol Old Vic (1945–48). There he acted major Shakespearean and classical parts and made regular appearances for the company in London until 1953. Devlin performed for two seasons (1954 and 1955) with the Shakespeare Memorial Theatre Company at Stratford-upon-Avon. Already a skilled television actor, he continued to make brilliant cameo appearances in that medium following his retirement in 1957.

**Diokno, Jose Wright,** Philippine politician (b. Feb. 26, 1922, Taal, Phil.—d. Feb. 27, 1987, Manila, Phil.), was one of the country's foremost human rights activists and was a staunch opponent of the presence of U.S. military bases in the Philippines. Diokno, who graduated summa cum laude from De La Salle University, Manila, practiced as a lawyer before serving (1961–62) as justice secretary. In 1963 he was elected to the first of two terms in the Senate. A prominent opposition senator, he was jailed by Pres. Ferdinand E. Marcos when the latter declared martial law in 1972. Diokno spent two years in solitary confinement, part of the time jailed next to Benigno Aquino. After Diokno's release from prison, he defended political prisoners as well as prominent members of the Communist

Party. He was also a member of a select group of opposition politicians known as the Convenors Group, which chose Corazon Aquino to challenge Marcos in the 1986 presidential election. After Aquino became president, Diokno headed the government panel negotiating peace with Communist rebels but left the post later that year because of ill health. He was also chairman of the presidential commission on human rights, but he resigned the post in protest after the "Mendiola massacre" (Jan. 22, 1987), in which security forces fired into a crowd marching on the presidential palace to demand land reform, killing 18. During his last two years he was unable to participate more fully in governmental affairs because of ill health.

**Doumeng, Jean-Baptiste,** French businessman (b. Dec. 2, 1919, Lacasse, Haute-Garonne, France—d. April 5, 1987, Noé, near Toulouse, Haute-Garonne), joined the Communist Party at the age of 16 and built a huge personal fortune in the years following World War II through a union of agricultural cooperatives and through Interagra, a company specializing in trade with Eastern Europe. The "red billionaire," as Doumeng was known, was the son of a tenant farmer and left school with no qualifications. He fought in the Resistance during the war and from 1945 started to develop a cooperative union among the farmers of his home region. During the next decade it extended to embrace 150 cooperatives involving 40,000 farmers in southwestern France. In 1947 Doumeng founded Interagra, which came to exercise a virtual monopoly in French agricultural dealings with the Soviet bloc and several third world countries. Interagra dealt primarily in meat, cereals, butter, and wine, offering an outlet for European Communities surpluses and opportunities for countries with little foreign exchange to benefit from barter and triangular deals. Doumeng, who remained a loyal Communist, claimed to be the last surviving Frenchman to have dined with Stalin and one of the first to predict the rise of Mikhail Gorbachev. He played a role in political negotiations between East and West under successive French presidents but attracted controversy because of unproved accusations of tax irregularities and claims that he used his wealth to finance the Communist Party. He was mayor of Noé (1959–76) and a regional councillor (1970–76).

**Draper, Charles Stark,** U.S. aeronautical engineer (b. Oct. 2, 1901, Windsor, Mo.—d. July 25, 1987, Cambridge, Mass.), was dubbed the "father of inertial navigation," an electronic guidance system that continuously monitors the position and acceleration of aircraft, ships, submarines, missiles, satellites, and space vehicles independently from a base station or other external sources. In order to develop his system, Draper used gyroscopes, which provide fixed reference direction; accelerometers, which measure changes in the velocity of the system; and a computer, which processes information on changes in direction and acceleration of the vehicle and feeds its results to the vehicle's navigation system. Though he earned a B.A. degree in psychology from Stanford University in 1922, Draper became fascinated with aeronautics and enrolled in the Massachusetts Institute of Technology (MIT), where he earned a B.S. (1926) in electrochemical engineering and an Sc.D. (1938) in physics. The following year he became a full professor at MIT and founded its Instrumentation Laboratory, where he developed the Mark 14 gyroscopic gunsight, which was used on most U.S. naval vessels during World War II and enabled gunners to shoot down more than 30 Japanese kamikazes. As a professor, he was known as Doc Draper and was renowned for piloting terrifying airplane missions to demonstrate a principle on aerodynamics to his colleagues. His laboratory also devised the guidance systems for jet fighter planes and for Polaris, Poseidon, and Trident submarines and missiles; in 1961 he began working on the lunar navigation system for the spacecraft of

the Apollo Project. After the moon landing in 1969, Draper resigned his post as director of the Instrumentation Laboratory when protests erupted over the laboratory's role in defense work. In 1973 the laboratory became independent of MIT and was christened the Charles Stark Draper Laboratory. In 1965 Draper received the National Medal of Science.

**Du Pré, Jacqueline,** British cellist (b. Jan. 26, 1945, Oxford, England—d. Oct. 19, 1987, London, England), was a performer of rare and outstanding brilliance whose career was tragically curtailed when she contracted multiple sclerosis at the age of 26. A virtuoso player of concerti and chamber music, she was perhaps best known for her interpretation of the Elgar Cello Concerto in E Minor, which she first performed at London's Festival Hall in 1962. The warmth and vibrance of her playing made the cello attractive to a hitherto often unappreciative lay audience and greatly enhanced cello playing in Britain. Du Pré inherited her musical talent from her mother, a piano teacher at the Royal Academy of Music, and asked for a cello at the age of four. She studied at the London Cello School and, as the youngest contestant, won the first Suggia International Cello Award (1955). Coached by William Pleeth (1955–62), she attended the Guildhall School of Music and Drama, winning its gold medal in 1960. She also studied under Paul Tortelier in Paris and under Mstislav Rostropovich in Moscow. She first toured North America in 1965 and played in many European cities. In 1967 she married the conductor and pianist Daniel Barenboim. The couple, together with the violinist Pinchas Zukerman, performed chamber music. Du Pré taught and gave master classes for a few years after becoming ill, and with Barenboim she established a Multiple Sclerosis Research Fund. She was made an Officer of the Order of the British Empire in 1976.

**Duncan-Sandys, Duncan Edwin Duncan-Sandys,** BARON, British politician (b. Jan. 24, 1908—d. Nov. 26, 1987, London, England), as minister of defense (1957–59) inaugurated the policy of reliance upon nuclear deterrents rather than conventional forces and as secretary of state for Commonwealth relations (1960–64) assisted British colonies as they prepared for independence. He was born Duncan Edwin Sandys. He was educated at Eton College and at Magdalen College, Oxford, and then joined the foreign service (1930–33). He was Conservative member of Parliament for Norwood (1935–45) and for Streatham (1950–74). In World War II he served with the expedition force sent to Norway (1940) but left the Army after injury in an accident in 1941. He was financial secretary to the War Office (1941–43) and to the Ministry of Supply (1943–44). Sandys distinguished himself as chairman of the war Cabinet's committee for defense against German flying bombs (1943–45), and he entered the Cabinet (December 1944) as minister of works. While his party was out of office (1945–51), he worked enthusiastically to promote European unity. As minister of supply (1951–54) he denationalized the iron and steel industry, and as minister of housing and local government (1954–57) he abolished rent-restriction laws. He was chairman (1972–84) and president (from 1984) of Lonrho Ltd. He was created a life peer in 1974.

**Eaker, Ira Clarence,** general (ret.) U.S. Army (b. April 13, 1896, Field Creek, Texas—d. Aug. 6, 1987, Camp Springs, Md.), during World War II was commander of the famed 8th Air Force in Britain (1942–43) and of allied air forces in the Mediterranean (1944–45); he was also credited with being a guiding force in the establishment of the Air Force as a separate service branch in 1947. Eaker entered the Army in 1917 as an enlisted man but soon completed an officers' training program; by the end of that year he had been commissioned a second lieutenant of infantry. He received his pilot's wings in 1918 and demonstrated pioneering aviation daring by piloting (1929) the Army's *Question Mark*, establishing a world endurance record by staying aloft for nearly a week by refueling in the air. In 1930 he made the first transcontinental flight that implemented the same refueling technique, and some years later he made the first "blind" transcontinental flight by relying totally on instruments. During World War II he was the chief advocate of the precision daylight bombing that led to the destruction of much of Germany's war production, and he also devised the plan that called for around-the-clock bombings on enemy targets. He personally led the bombing of Rouen on Aug. 17, 1942—the first American B-17 bomber strike against German occupation forces in France—and in June 1944 he flew the first bombing raid from Italy into Germany. Though he retired one month prior to the official establishment of the Air Force as a separate military branch in 1947, his influence was legendary. Eaker's many sensational wartime exploits were recognized with rapid promotions, the Silver Star, and the Distinguished Flying Cross. He received a Congressional Gold Medal in 1979, and in 1985 Pres. Ronald Reagan made him a four-star general in recognition of his services to his country.

**Efros, Anatoly,** Soviet theatre director (b. June 3, 1925, Kharkov, U.S.S.R.—d. Jan. 12, 1987, Moscow, U.S.S.R.), was one of the outstanding Soviet theatre directors of the post-World War II period. He gained an international reputation as a director at the Leninist Komsomol Theatre and at various leading Moscow theatres before accepting a controversial appointment to succeed Yury Lyubimov at the Moscow Theatre of Drama and Comedy on the Taganka (popularly known as "the Taganka"). Efros trained at the Moscow State Theatre Institute and worked in Ryazan before returning to Moscow in 1954 to take over the Central Children's Theatre. After moving to the Komsomol Theatre in 1963, he attracted official disapproval with controversial productions, including Mikhail Bulgakov's *Molière* and Edward Radzinsky's *104 Pages of Love*. His production of Alexey Arbusov's *The Promise* was an international success. Efros and Lyubimov were seen as two of the leaders of a movement to modernize Soviet theatre. Dismissed from the Komsomol Theatre in 1967, Efros continued to work in Moscow and abroad. Following the dismissal of Lyubimov, he was invited to take over at the Taganka in 1984. After some hesitation he accepted and was subsequently accused by many, including Lyubimov himself (who had previously helped Efros in battles with authority), of having betrayed his friend. Efros was due to take the Taganka company on tour to Paris when he died of a heart attack.

**Ellmann, Richard David,** U.S. literary critic and scholar (b. March 15, 1918, Highland Park, Mich.—d. May 13, 1987, Oxford, England), wrote *James Joyce* (1959; new and revised ed., 1982), which was hailed as the definitive work on the reclusive and complex Irish novelist. Ellmann, who earned his Ph.D. (1947) at Yale University, was also an expert on the life and works of such literary giants as William Butler Yeats and Oscar Wilde. After traveling to Dublin in 1945, on leave from the U.S. Navy after World War II, Ellmann became intrigued with the works of Irish men of letters. His book *Yeats: The Man and the Masks* (1948; reprinted 1978) was a penetrating study of the poet's personality. After Ellmann published Joyce's biography, he edited Joyce's letters and continued to conduct research for the biography's 1982 revised edition, expanded by 100 pages, in celebration of Joyce's centenary. During his scholarly career he taught at Northwestern University, Evanston, Ill. (1951–68), Yale University (1968–70), and the University of Oxford (1970–84). Despite the onset in 1986 of amyotrophic lateral sclerosis (Lou Gehrig's disease), a debilitating degeneration of the nerve cells, Ellmann completed his long-awaited biography of Oscar Wilde, scheduled to appear in 1988.

**Fairfax, Sir Warwick Oswald,** Australian publishing executive (b. Dec. 19, 1901, Sydney, Australia—d. Jan. 14, 1987, Sydney), as chairman (1956–77) of the newspaper group John Fairfax & Sons Ltd., a family concern that included many prestigious newspapers and magazines, expanded the company's empire into radio, television, and the manufacture of newsprint. He was the son of the former proprietor, Sir James Oswald Fairfax. Educated at Sydney University and at Balliol College, Oxford, he joined the staff of the *Sydney Morning Herald* in 1925, becoming a director two years later and managing director in 1930. Although he avoided the appearance of overt control over editorial policy, his newspapers reflected his political views, notably in their sustained opposition to the Liberal-Country Party administration of Prime Minister Sir Robert Menzies. Fairfax demonstrated his religious affiliation and authoritarian attitude when in 1970 he dismissed the editor of the *Sydney Morning Herald* for issuing a humanist rather than a Christian editorial at Easter. He was ousted from the chairmanship in 1977 as the result of a family quarrel. Fairfax was the author of a number of books, including *Men, Parties and Policies* (1943), and of three plays. He was knighted in 1967.

**Ford, Henry, II,** U.S. corporate executive (b. Sept. 4, 1917, Detroit, Mich.—d. Sept. 29, 1987, Detroit), as the powerful and colourful head (1945–79) of the Ford Motor Co., the world's second-largest automobile maker, revived the ailing firm by recruiting a group of talented systems analysts from the U.S. Air Force who became known as the "Whiz Kids." One of that group was Robert S. McNamara, who became Ford's president and later served as U.S. secretary of defense. Ford was the son of Edsel Ford, the only son of the firm's founder, Henry Ford. He studied at Yale University but never earned a degree. In 1941 he joined the Navy, but two years later he was released from service when his father, then head of Ford Motor Co., died of cancer. Under the tutelage of his grandfather, who assumed a caretaker role in the company, Ford learned the basics of industrial management. After he assumed the presidency in 1945, Ford fired the heavy-handed personnel chief, Harry Bennett, and engineered an illustrious recovery for the company, which had been losing some $9 million a month. He presided over the company when the ill-fated 1957 Edsel was introduced, but he was also at the helm when the highly popular and successful Thunderbird (1954) and Mustang (1964) cars were unveiled. His domination of the company led to the release of company presidents Ernest Breech, Semon Knudsen, and Lee Iacocca, all of whom seemed to be exerting too much power in the eyes of the man who settled

KONRAD BAESCHLIN—CAMERA PRESS/PHOTO TRENDS

disputes by proclaiming, "My name is on the building." Ford, who embraced a jet-setting lifestyle that included lavish spending, was married three times—to Anne McDonnell from 1940 to 1964, Maria Cristina Vettore Austin from 1965 to 1980, and Kathleen DuRoss from 1980. After the 1967 Detroit race riots, Ford used his company's prestige and economic clout to establish the Renaissance Center, a major development on the Detroit River, and he formed the National Alliance of Businessmen to solve problems related to black employment. He had previously helped establish the Ford Foundation and had served as its chairman from 1950 to 1956. In later years the firm experienced a downturn with the energy crisis of the 1970s and the importation of small foreign cars, but in recent years it had recaptured some of the market with its aerodynamic Ford Taurus and Mercury Sable. Ford, who stepped down as chairman in 1980, remained chairman of the board of directors' powerful finance committee until his death.

**Fortner, Wolfgang,** West German composer (b. Oct. 12, 1907, Leipzig, Germany—d. Sept. 11?, 1987, Heidelberg, West Germany), was remembered particularly for his operatic compositions, especially *Die Bluthochzeit* (1957) and *In seinem Garten liebt Don Perlimplin Belisa* (1962), adapted from the works of the Spanish playwright Federico García Lorca. Fortner studied at the Leipzig Conservatory and at the University of Leipzig. He taught at the Heidelberg Institute for Evangelical Church Music (1931–53) and later in Detmold (1954–57) and in Freiburg (1957–72). Fortner experimented with various styles, his work showing the influence of church music as well as that of Stravinsky and Hindemith and, for a brief period after World War II, the atonal music of the Viennese school. A member of the Nazi Party, he founded the Heidelberg Chamber Orchestra and, as a composer acceptable to the regime, was the author of the Hitler Youth song "Haste to the Banner" (1940) and other works. After the war he wrote his only symphony and then concentrated on works for the stage, including the ballet *Die weisse Rose* (1949) and the operas *Elisabeth Tudor* (1972) and *That Time* (1977). Fortner's postwar instrumental compositions were also much admired, but it was in opera that he reached the widest public and seemed to reveal his feelings most directly.

**Fosse, Bob** (ROBERT LOUIS FOSSE), U.S. choreographer, dancer, and director (b. June 23, 1927, Chicago, Ill.—d. Sept. 23, 1987, Washington, D.C.), was an ingenious, hard-driving showman who left an indelible mark on musical theatre. His sensual, jazzy dance movements, punctuated by pelvic thrusts, shoulder rolls, and slithering one-hand gestures down an undulating torso, became the centrepieces for a string of Broadway smash hit musicals. The provocative Fosse, who launched his career as an actor and dancer—first in vaudeville, nightclubs, and stage musicals and then in such movies as *Kiss Me, Kate* and *My Sister Eileen*—imprinted his own brand of energy on his dance numbers. As a choreographer he staged *Pajama Game* (1954), *Damn Yankees* (1955), *Bells Are Ringing* (1956), and *New Girl in Town* (1957), and he later also served as director of *Redhead* (1959), *How to Succeed in Business Without Really Trying* (1961), *Little Me* (1962), *Sweet Charity* (1966), *Pippin* (1972), *Chicago* (1975), and *Dancin'* (1978), his last major hit. He also extended his talent to films and directed *Sweet Charity* (1969); *Cabaret* (1972); *Lenny* (1974), the sombre biography of comedian Lenny Bruce; *All That Jazz* (1979), a semiautobiographical sketch of a driven director/choreographer who dies of a heart attack; and *Star 80* (1983), the re-creation of the death of Playboy bunny centrefold Dorothy Stratten. The banner year of 1973 brought Fosse an unprecedented variety of kudos; he won a Tony, an Emmy, and an Academy Award for direction of Broadway's *Pippin*, the television special "Liza with a Z," and the dazzling motion picture *Cabaret*, respectively. In all, he garnered ten Tony awards. His last Broadway show, *Big Deal* (1986), was not a popular success. At the time of his death from a heart attack, Fosse was on his way to the Washington opening night of a revival of *Sweet Charity*.

**Franju, Georges,** French film director (b. April 12, 1912, Fougères, France—d. Nov. 5, 1987, Paris, France) was cofounder of the Cinémathèque Française, the national film archive of France, and a director whose poetic imagination combined with a taste for the macabre in documentaries and feature films, including the horror fantasy *Les Yeux sans visage* (1959; *The Horror Chamber of Dr. Faustus*). Franju trained as a stage designer before meeting Henri Langlois in the early 1930s and collaborating with him first on a documentary, *Le Métro* (1934). Shortly thereafter, with Jean Mitry and Paul-Auguste Harlé, they established the Cinémathèque Française. Franju was secretary of the International Federation of Film Archives (1938–45) and subsequently made 13 documentary films on social topics. *Le Sang des bêtes* (1949), with its scenes of everyday slaughter in a Paris abattoir, was considered a classic of documentary cinema, and it showed the director's characteristic fascination with the bizarre. In *Hôtel des invalides* (1951) he turned a documentary on the Paris army museum into a polemic against the insanity of war, a theme to which he returned in *Thomas l'imposteur* (1965), adapted from Jean Cocteau's novel. Franju's first feature, *La Tête contre les murs* (1958), set in a lunatic asylum, questioned society's treatment of those who reject its rules. His other films included notable versions of novels by Émile Zola and François Mauriac, and he adapted Joseph Conrad's *The Shadow-Line* for television. Franju was a chevalier of the Legion of Honour (1971).

**Fraser, Sir Hugh,** British businessman (b. Dec. 18, 1936, Glasgow, Scotland—d. May 5, 1987, Milngavie, near Glasgow), inherited the vast retail trading empire built up by his father, Lord Fraser of Allander. As chairman (1966–81) of the House of Fraser group, Sir Hugh initially brought a youthful zest and flair to the consortium's operations but later made some ill-judged and controversial deals. Educated at St. Mary's, Melrose, and at Kelvinside Academy, Glasgow, he started work in one of the family-owned stores at the age of 17, becoming a director at 21. When his father died in 1966, he renounced the barony but retained the baronetcy granted in 1961. He effectively modernized many of the retail outlets, notably the London West End store, Harrods, and in 1973 received the *Guardian*'s young businessman of the year award. Thereafter, his judgment and fortunes waned, and he was censured by the Stock Exchange (1976). His financial connection with Roland ("Tiny") Rowland of the controversial Lonrho Group, which in the early 1980s sought to buy House of Fraser, resulted in his dismissal from the chairmanship. A generous supporter of Scottish charities and interests, he made possible the purchase of the island of Iona for the National Trust for Scotland.

**Freyre, Gilberto de Mello,** Brazilian sociologist (b. March 15, 1900, Recife, Brazil—d. July 18, 1987, Recife), with his seminal work *Casa-Grande e Senzala* (1933; *The Masters and the Slaves*, 1946), explored the relationships between the conquering Portuguese plantation owners, their African slaves, and the aboriginal Amerindians during the 16th and 17th centuries. In his 500-page epic he contended that the Brazilian mestizo, the offspring of the inhabitants of the *casa grande* ("big house") and the *senzala* ("slave quarters"), were ideally suited to the Brazilian environment—in contrast to the prevailing view of them as inferior. Freyre and others from the so-called Northeastern school stressed ethnic and racial pride and local custom. After earning his M.A. from Columbia

University, New York City, he returned to Brazil and in 1925 organized the first Northeastern regionalist congress in Recife and published the "Regionalist Manifesto" with other prominent Northeastern writers. He was awarded the Filipe d'Oliveira Award in 1934 for his masterpiece and in the same year organized the first Congress of Afro-Brazilian Studies. Other important works include *Sobrados e Mucambos* (1936; *The Mansions and the Shanties*, 1963), *Brazil: An Interpretation* (1945), and *Ordem e Progresso* (1959; *Order and Progress*, 1970). He was founding professor of social anthropology at the University of Brazil and a visiting professor and lecturer at many other universities. He also served as a member of the Brazilian parliament (1946–50), was a delegate to the UN General Assembly in 1949 and 1964, and served on the UN committee on race relations in South Africa in 1954.

**Fry, (Edwin) Maxwell,** British architect (b. Aug. 2, 1899, Wallasey, Cheshire, England—d. Sept. 3, 1987, Cotherstone, Durham, England), was a pioneer of modern architecture and practiced (1934–36) with Walter Gropius. Their Impington Village College (now a comprehensive school), near Cambridge, was described by Nikolaus Pevsner as "one of the best buildings of its date in England." Fry's other distinguished works in England included blocks of flats and individual houses. He was responsible for much town planning and for many educational buildings in West Africa, including Nigeria's University of Ibadan; and with Le Corbusier he designed (1951–54) the town of Chandigarh as a new capital for India's postpartition section of the Punjab. Educated at the Liverpool Institute and the Liverpool University School of Architecture, Fry graduated in 1923 and went to work in London. He was a founder member in 1931 of the MARS (Modern Architectural Research) group. He served with the Royal Engineers in World War II, and with his second wife, the architect Jane Drew, he spent several years in West Africa in the mid-1940s; they practiced together in London from 1951. Fry was vice-president of the Royal Institute of British Architects (1961–62) and was awarded its gold medal in 1964. His books include *Fine Building* (1944), *Tropical Architecture* (1964), *Art in a Machine Age* (1969), and *Autobiographical Sketches* (1975).

**Frydenlund, Knut,** Norwegian politician (b. March 31, 1927, Drammen, near Oslo, Norway—d. Feb. 26, 1987, Oslo), was foreign minister in the Labour government from 1973 to 1981 and again from May 1986 until his death. He was a strong supporter of the European Economic Community (EEC) and advocated Norwegian membership in the EEC during the debate leading up to the 1972 referendum that resulted in rejection. A career diplomat, Frydenlund joined the Foreign Service in 1953 and served in Bonn (1953–55) and Brussels (1962–63) and as Norway's permanent representative at the Council of Europe (1963–65). In the late 1960s he acted as consultant to the Labour Party Research Office and joined the party's Oslo Executive in 1968 before being elected a member of Parliament for Oslo the following year. Though disappointed by the result of the EEC referendum, Frydenlund worked to maintain party unity. Sometimes known as "the good person from Drammen," he was highly respected for his qualities of statesmanship and diplomacy, his sense of humour, and his moderation in national and party politics. At the time of his death, Frydenlund was acting prime minister in the absence of Gro Harlem Brundtland.

**Gerhardsen, Einer Henry,** Norwegian politician (b. May 10, 1897, Asker, Norway—d. Sept. 19, 1987, Lilleborg, Norway), was prime minister of Norway from 1945 to 1951 and again from 1955 to 1965. His Labour Party government was responsible for the post-World War II reconstruction of the country, its entry into NATO, and the establishment of a welfare state. Largely

self-educated, Gerhardsen was a construction worker and was active in trade union affairs before he was elected to the Oslo town council in 1932. He became secretary of the Labour Party in 1934 and mayor of Oslo in 1940 but was dismissed later that year by the German occupying forces. Gerhardsen then returned to manual labour, using it as a cover for resistance to the occupation. Arrested by the Gestapo in 1941, he spent three and a half years in prisons and concentration camps. On his liberation in 1945 he returned to his post as mayor of Oslo. He became leader of the Labour Party and was asked to form a coalition government, which launched a campaign to repair the damage and divisions of the war years. Despite the Marxist and antimilitarist leanings of his youth, Gerhardsen brought Norway into NATO and resisted Soviet attempts in 1964 to weaken Norway's commitment. Throughout his career he endeavoured to further East-West détente, and he established Norway's opposition to foreign bases and nuclear weapons. His policies, sometimes controversial abroad, gained support at home. Following the Labour Party defeat at the polls in 1965, he remained a prominent figure in Norwegian politics and served as a member of Parliament until he retired in 1972.

**Gingold, Hermione,** British-born character actress (b. Dec. 9, 1897, London, England—d. May 24, 1987, New York, N.Y.), specialized in humorously portraying ancient dames and harpies and was best remembered as Leslie Caron's unconventional grandmother in *Gigi* (1958). In the film Gingold portrayed a retired courtesan and was especially noted for her throaty duet with Maurice Chevalier, "I Remember It Well." Gingold, who first achieved fame on the English stage, became known to U.S. soldiers during World War II as a comedienne in the long-running London revue *Sweet and Low* (1943). In England she appeared in such films as *Someone at the Door* (1936), *Merry Comes to Town* (1937), *Meet Mr. Penny* (1938), and *The Adventures of Sadie* (1955). In the U.S. she made a splash on Broadway starring in *John Murray Anderson's Almanac* (1953). Her notable U.S. film credits included *Around the World in 80 Days* (1956), *Bell, Book and Candle* (1958), *The Naked Edge* (1961), and *The Music Man* (1962). She delighted talk show audiences with her irrepressible tart humour.

**Gleason, Jackie** (HERBERT JOHN GLEASON), U.S. comedian (b. Feb. 26, 1916, Brooklyn, N.Y.—d. June 24, 1987, Fort Lauderdale, Fla.), was best remembered for his portrayal of the rotund, blustering Brooklyn bus driver Ralph Kramden on the television smash hit series "The Honeymooners" (1955–56), which chronicled the lives of Ralph, his wife, Alice, and their neighbours Trixie and Ed Norton. Gleason, who had a natural comic gift, eschewed pranks and pratfalls and instead relied on innuendo and his instinctive timing to immortalize such characters as the Poor Soul, Reginald Van Gleason III, Joe the Bartender, Fenwick Babbitt, Rudy the Repairman, and Stanley R. Sogg. Gleason was raised in Brooklyn; his father left when he was 8, and his mother died when he was 16. He began working as a vaudeville master of ceremonies and later was a barker at carnivals and an emcee in nightclubs. An outsized performer whose weight fluctuated between 91 and 127 kg (200 and 280 lb), he was also a renowned drinker, heavy smoker, and showgirl aficionado. He began his foray into television in 1949 as the title character in "The Life of Riley." In 1950 he became the star of "The Cavalcade of Stars," which launched his career. "The Great One" reached his pinnacle when he took his most popular character, Ralph Kramden, and developed a vehicle for his madcap schemes; "The Honeymooners" became a classic with such catchphrases as "Bang! Zoom! You're going to the moon, Alice!" and "Baby, you're the greatest!" Besides serving as host of his own variety show, "The Jackie Gleason Show" (1952–70), in which he introduced such

PHOTO TRENDS

slogans as "How sweet it is," and "And away we go," Gleason starred on Broadway in *Hellzapoppin* (1938) and *Take Me Along* (1959), for which he earned a Tony award as the hard-drinking Uncle Sid. In motion pictures he gave such critically acclaimed performances as those of the deaf-mute janitor in *Gigot* (1962) and Minnesota Fats in *The Hustler* (1961), for which he was nominated for an Academy Award for best supporting actor.

**Goh, Choo San,** Singaporean-born choreographer (b. 1948, Singapore—d. Nov. 28, 1987, New York, N.Y.), as resident choreographer (1976–87) and associate artistic director (1984–87) of the Washington Ballet was an important influence on modern ballet. His choreography featured speed punctuated with intricate movements and interpolated academic steps and acrobatic tumbling within a partnering technique. He combined elements of modern dance and classical ballet to produce a strong neoclassic style with a streamlined contemporary look. Goh began his ballet training at the Singapore Ballet Academy at the age of ten. He earned a B.A. in biochemistry at the University of Singapore before joining the Dutch National Ballet in 1970 as a dancer. His ballets, including *Configurations* and *Momentum,* were often plotless, yet they contained a strong dramatic undercurrent. Goh also created ballets for the Paris Opera Ballet, the Royal Danish Ballet, American Ballet Theatre, the Alvin Ailey American Dance Theater, Dance Theatre of Harlem, and the Boston, Joffrey, Houston, and Pennsylvania ballets.

**Goldfinger, Erno,** Hungarian-born British architect (b. Sept. 11, 1902, Budapest, Hung.—d. Nov. 15, 1987, London, England), was a second-generation exponent of modern architecture and was deeply influenced by Adolf Loos and Auguste Perret. Goldfinger, who lived in England from 1934, designed mainly high-rise offices or blocks of flats. His Alexander Fleming House, built (1959–60) in London for the Ministry of Health, won a Civic Trust award (1964). He constructed two tower blocks of flats for the Greater London Council but, when the disadvantages of such housing became apparent, its popularity declined. Educated at the Gymnasium in Budapest, he entered the École des Beaux-Arts in Paris in 1922. Later he studied at the Institut d'Urbanisme at the Sorbonne, Paris, and was a pupil of Perret. An early work was his London salon for Helena Rubinstein (1926). Works especially commended include his row of three-story houses (1937) in London's Hampstead and his offices for the *Daily Worker* newspaper (1949). He was a leading member of the Congrès Internationaux d'Architecture Moderne.

**Gordon, Walter,** Canadian government official (b. Jan. 27, 1906, Toronto, Ont.—d. March 21, 1987, Toronto), as the controversial yet visionary Liberal finance minister (1963–65) in the government of Lester B. Pearson, did more than any other person to shape the country's economic policy during the 1960s. Though he studied engineering at the Royal Military College in Kingston, Ont., he joined the family accounting business, Clarkson, Gordon and Co., before receiving his degree. In 1955 Gordon rose to national prominence when he was named chairman of the Royal Commission on Canada's Economic Prospects. The 1957 "Gordon Commission" report decried the foreign domination of the Canadian economy, discussed the exporting of natural resources, and called for more skilled labour and a more equitable geographic distribution of wealth in Canada. As finance minister, Gordon created a furor when he proposed his first budget. He was criticized for circumventing budget secrecy by using three advisers not in the government service and, under pressure from the business community and the U.S., was forced to amend his provisions for control of foreign ownership in Canada. Gordon resigned in 1965 after the Liberals failed to win a majority in the election that he had recommended. He briefly served in the Cabinet (1967–68) as minister without portfolio and returned to business in 1968. During the 1970s he was a founder of the Committee for an Independent Canada, which was influential for almost a decade before it disbanded. Gordon was the author of many books, including *A Choice for Canada: Independence or Colonial Status* (1966) and *Storm Signals: New Economic Policies for Canada* (1975).

**Green, (James) Maurice Spurgeon,** British newspaper editor (b. Dec. 8, 1906, Padiham, Lancashire, England—d. July 19, 1987, Winchester, Hampshire, England), was editor of the London *Daily Telegraph* from 1964 to 1974, the culmination of a career specializing in financial and economic journalism. He became editor of the *Financial News* at the age of 28, after obtaining his degree at University College, Oxford, and helped to create the "30-share index" in 1935. Ten years later, when the paper was taken over by the *Financial Times,* this became the "FT ordinary share index," still quoted as a guide to movements on the stock exchange. By then, Green had left to join *The Times* as financial and industrial editor. He served with the Royal Artillery during World War II and then returned to *The Times,* from 1953 as the paper's assistant editor. In 1961 he moved to the *Daily Telegraph,* the leading "quality" newspaper committed to the Conservative Party. His expertise and interest in economic matters was not, at that time, shared by many Conservative politicians, and Green set out to remedy this, advocating belief in the market economy and campaigning for membership in the European Communities. He advised Margaret Thatcher to campaign for the Conservative Party leadership, and his influence on her and on what were to become orthodox Conservative economic policies could stand as his most enduring achievement. After retiring from the *Telegraph,* he wrote on financial affairs and was president (1976–77) of the Institute of Journalists.

**Greene, Sir Hugh Carleton,** British publisher and broadcasting executive (b. Nov. 15, 1910, Berkhamsted, England—d. Feb. 19, 1987, London, England), as director general (1960–69) of the British Broadcasting Corporation (BBC), freed the organization from the straitjacket of rectitude and unswerving good taste imposed by the first director general, Sir John (afterward Lord) Reith. Greene was responsible for such earthy series as "Steptoe and Son" and "Till Death Us Do Part" and the popular satirical revue "That Was the Week That Was." During his time the BBC acquired its second television channel, BBC 2, in 1964; colour; and an increased number of hours of radio transmission. He was a brother of the novelist Graham

Greene. Educated at Berkhamsted School and at Merton College, Oxford, Greene became correspondent for the *Daily Telegraph* in Berlin (1934–39). He reported the German invasion of Poland in September 1939 and joined the BBC in October 1940 as German news editor for the European Service. After World War II he reorganized German broadcasting, becoming first director general of Nordwest Deutscher Rundfunk. Greene was head of the BBC's East European Service (1949) and a propaganda broadcaster with the British Army in Malaya (1950–52). He was assistant controller (1953–55) and controller (1955–56) of BBC Overseas Services, then director of administration (1956–58) and of news and current affairs (1958–59). When his policy as director general was threatened by the appointment in 1967 of the more traditionally minded Lord Hill as chairman of the BBC's board of governors, Greene retired (1969). He became chairman of the publishing company Bodley Head (1969–81; later honorary president) and of his family's brewery. He was knighted in 1964.

**Greene, Lorne,** Canadian-born actor (b. Feb. 12, 1915, Ottawa, Ont.—d. Sept. 11, 1987, Santa Monica, Calif.), was best remembered for his portrayal of the stern yet caring patriarch of the Cartwright family on television's long-running series "Bonanza" (1959–73). As Ben Cartwright, the white-maned, barrel-chested land baron of the Ponderosa—in a characterization based on Greene's memory of his own father—he firmly guided his three headstrong sons, Adam, Hoss, and Little Joe. Greene later starred in the television series "Griff" (1973–74) as a detective, "Battlestar Galactica" (1978–80) as a space commander, and "Code Red" (1981–82) as a fire chief. His resonant voice—in his early broadcasting days known as "the Voice of Canada"—was showcased on the hit recording "Ringo" (1964), in which he told the tale of a renegade cowboy by talking rather than singing to music. In later years he remained visible to the public on television commercials as a spokesman for dog food.

**Greenwood, Joan,** British actress (b. March 4, 1921, London, England—d. Feb. 27, 1987, London), was best known for her languid, husky, and provocative voice, which she used to remarkable effect in such outstanding British comedy films as *Whisky Galore* (1949; U.S. title, *Tight Little Island*), *Kind Hearts and Coronets* (1949), *The Importance of Being Earnest* (1952), and *Tom Jones* (1963). Greenwood studied at the Royal Academy of Dramatic Arts in London and made her stage debut in 1938. In 1944 she toured with Donald Wolfit's Company, starring as Ophelia in *Hamlet* and Celia in *Volpone.* She made her New York debut in 1954 in T. S. Eliot's *The Confidential Clerk.* Though she played mainly comic roles in films, onstage she demonstrated her dramatic abilities in such productions as *Lysistrata* (1957), *The Grass Is Greener* (1958), *Hedda Gabler* (1960), and *The Chalk Garden* (1971). In later years Greenwood seemed to be denied the opportunities she deserved. Her husband, the actor André Morell, whom she married after they worked together in *Hedda Gabler,* died in 1978. She played in several successful television productions, including the comedy series "Girls on Top," and made her last stage appearance in a charity gala two weeks before her death.

**Grigorenko, Pyotr Grigorevich,** Soviet army officer and dissident (b. Oct. 16, 1907, Borisovka, Ukraine, Russia—d. Feb. 21, 1987, New York, N.Y.), was founder of Ukrainian and Soviet groups established to monitor the 1975 Helsinki Accords. The son of a peasant, Grigorenko joined the Red Army in 1931. He fought against the Japanese in Mongolia (1939) and against Germany (1941–45); he was promoted to major general in 1959. Subsequently, he lectured at the Frunze Military Academy in Moscow but in 1961 was dismissed for opposing the personality cult revived under Soviet leader Nikita

Khrushchev. Arrested for advocating a return to Leninism, Grigorenko was declared paranoid and confined to an asylum in 1964. On his release the following year, he had to work as a labourer, having been deprived of his pension and Communist Party membership. Grigorenko denounced the Soviet invasion of Czechoslovakia in 1968; a year later he was again arrested and declared insane for supporting the displaced Crimean Tatars. Brutally treated, he was released in 1974 after suffering three heart attacks. In 1977 he was permitted to visit the U.S. for medical treatment; while there he was deprived of Soviet citizenship. His *Memoirs* was published in 1982.

**Guedes, Fernando van Zeller,** Portuguese wine maker (b. Feb. 4, 1903, Oporto, Port.—d. July 15, 1987, Oporto), founded the wine company Sogrape in 1942 and created Mateus Rosé, a gently sparkling wine that captured a huge market, especially outside Portugal, among people who previously had not been wine drinkers. Made from red grapes grown near Vila Real and blended and given its characteristic *pétillant* quality with carbon dioxide, Mateus was a light table wine of an alluring pink colour, attractively labeled and bottled in a flask that invited adaptation as a table lamp or candle holder. Some 90% of production was exported. Guedes, who came from a family with a long tradition in wine making, was modest about his success. He studied at a technical high school and worked for Martinez Grassiot before founding his own firm, which at his death was the second largest in Portugal, with an annual production of 38 million bottles of Mateus Rosé and other wines.

**Guttuso, (Aldo) Renato,** Italian painter (b. Jan. 2, 1912, Bagheria, near Palermo, Sicily, Italy—d. Jan. 17, 1987, Rome, Italy), was regarded as the leading Italian exponent of social realism. His work showed evidence of his political commitment and his love of the Sicilian landscape. A member of the Italian Communist Party, he served as a senator from 1976 to 1984. Although he was a precocious artist, Guttuso nonetheless studied law before devoting himself to painting, training first as a picture restorer. In 1939 he exhibited "The Flight from Etna," a major work influenced by Picasso's "Guernica," and two years later came a "Crucifixion" that was openly critical of the Fascist regime. Guttuso served with the partisans from 1943 to 1945, and in the post-World War II period he was a founder member of the group Fronte Nuovo delle Arti, which promoted art that addressed human and social issues. Never committed to a narrow concept of neorealist painting, he adapted various styles to his own purpose and varied his subject matter to include landscapes and still lifes, as well as the monumental crowd scenes that are his most characteristic contribution to art. Guttuso was a member of the World Peace Council and was awarded the Lenin Peace Prize in 1972. He also won prizes at the 24th and 28th Venice Biennales and had a one-man show at the 26th Biennale. Two major retrospectives of his work were held in West Germany (1967) and Eastern Europe (1979).

**Hakim, Tawfiq al-,** Egyptian writer (b. Oct. 9, 1898, Alexandria, Egypt—d. July 26, 1987, Cairo, Egypt), was the founder of contemporary Egyptian drama and a leading figure in modern Arabic literature. He managed to combine classical Arabic with the strengths of the colloquial Arabic dialect in Egypt. Profoundly influenced by his studies in Paris (1925–28), he represented a current of humane liberalism in political ideas, favourable at first to the revolution of 1952 but increasingly opposed to some later, extremist tendencies in Arab politics. Hakim studied as a lawyer and on his return from Europe worked as a public prosecutor, an experience that inspired his novel *The Maze of Justice* (1937). By that time he had already acquired fame with his first novel, *The Return of the Spirit* (1933), and as a playwright with *People of the Cave* (1933), which was regarded as a turning point

in Arabic drama. He continued to write plays, notably the experimental *Tree-Climber* (1962), influenced by the work of Beckett and Ionesco. Though never attached to any political party, Hakim was a prolific and outspoken journalist throughout his life. In his later years he aroused much hostility through his support for Pres. Anwar as-Sadat's rapprochement with Israel and his attacks on Muslim extremism. Continuing his contributions to the newspaper *al-Ahram* until the end of his life, Hakim refused the status of "grand old man" of Egyptian literature to remain a controversial and vital figure.

**Haley, Sir William John,** British journalist, editor, and broadcasting executive (b. May 24, 1901, St. Helier, Jersey, Channel Islands—d. Sept. 6, 1987, Jersey), was an unwavering exponent of high standards of work and of public morality. He was director-general (1944–52) of the British Broadcasting Corporation (BBC), editor of *The Times* (1952–66), chairman of Times Newspapers Ltd. (1967), and editor in chief of *Encyclopædia Britannica* (1968–69). Educated at Victoria College, St. Helier, Haley served in the merchant marine as a wireless operator during World War I. He joined *The Times* in 1919 as a copy-taker in the foreign department. He was soon sent to Brussels to coordinate European news reports, and from there he contributed a weekly letter to the *Manchester Evening News*. Joining that newspaper in 1922, Haley became managing editor and a director in 1930. He was joint managing director of the Manchester Guardian and Evening News Ltd. (1939–43) and also a director of the Press Association and of Reuters Ltd. He moved to the BBC as editor in chief in 1943 and there was responsible for the postwar development of the Light, Home, and Third Programmes. At *The Times* he sought to widen the paper's appeal and first printed news on its front page (1966). His tenure at *Encyclopædia Britannica* coincided with the publication's bicentenary celebrations in 1968. Haley was knighted in 1946.

**Handl, Irene,** British actress (b. Dec. 27, 1901, London, England—d. Nov. 29, 1987, London), was an outstanding comedienne and character actress of irrepressible charm. The simple-minded innocence of her many memorable Cockney characters belied both her foreign parentage (her mother was French, her father an Austrian banker) and her complex personality. She took up acting at 36 and published the first of two remarkable novels when she was in her mid-60s. After her parents died, Handl trained in drama at the Embassy School of Acting and had an immediate stage success as the maid in *George and Margaret* (1937). By the 1950s she had become established, through her film roles in particular, as one of the most endearing of comic actresses. Her films included *The Belles of St. Trinian's; Brothers in Law; I'm All Right, Jack;* and *Morgan: A Suitable Case for Treatment*. In 1965 her first novel, *The Sioux,* an unusual story about an aristocratic French family, generated both critical and critical acclaim. She also wrote a sequel, *The Gold Tip Pfitzer* (1973). Handl starred in the television series "For the Love of Ada," "Supergran," "In Sickness and in Health," and "Never Say Die."

**Hardy, René,** French Resistance leader (b. Oct. 31, 1911, Mortrée, Orne, France—d. April 12–13, 1987, Melle, near Niort, Deux-Sèvres, France), by 1943 was in charge of all rail sabotage in southern France; he was alleged by many, among them Gestapo leader Klaus Barbie, to have betrayed a number of colleagues, including Jean Moulin, chairman of the National Resistance Council, and Antoine Delestraint, the Paris Resistance chief of staff. Hardy was twice acquitted (1947, 1950) of these charges. The 1987 trial in Lyon of Barbie seemed likely to revive the controversy, but the naming of Resistance traitors did not occur during the trial. An employee of the national railroad (SNCF), Hardy worked from 1940 with train-wrecking groups and masterminded the plan to cut some

500 rail links on D-Day. While traveling to visit Delestraint, he was picked up by the Gestapo on a night train (June 7–8, 1943) but was released three days later; meanwhile, Delestraint was arrested. On June 21 a meeting near Lyon of Resistance leaders, among them Moulin, was surprised by the Gestapo under Barbie. Unlike his colleagues, Hardy was not handcuffed, and he escaped, eventually returning to Resistance work until he was imprisoned by the provisional government in December 1944. Following his second acquittal, Hardy became a prizewinning novelist; in his memoirs, *Derniers Mots* (1984), he denied allegations of treachery.

**Hayes, Woody** (WAYNE WOODROW HAYES), U.S. college football coach (b. Feb. 4, 1913, Clifton, Ohio—d. March 12, 1987, Upper Arlington, Ohio), as the hard-nosed and combative coach at Ohio State University for 28 years, led the school's teams to 13 Big Ten championships and eight Rose Bowl games, four of which they won. Hayes, who graduated (1935) from Denison (Ohio) University, was an all-around athlete there, playing tackle in football, guard in basketball, and outfielder in baseball. During his 33 years as a coach at his alma mater (1946–48), Miami University, Oxford, Ohio (1949–50), and Ohio State University (1951–78), he compiled a career record of 238 games won, 72 lost, and 10 tied. At Ohio State University his teams won 205 games, lost 61, and tied 10. The hot-tempered Hayes was noted for his aggressive and defiant behaviour; he quarreled with officials, destroyed sideline yard markers, and was involved in altercations with cameramen and photographers. In 1978 he was relieved of his duties as a coach after he punched Charlie Bauman of Clemson after the latter intercepted an Ohio State pass during the final minutes of a 17–15 Ohio State loss in the Gator Bowl. Hayes, who ranked fifth in the number of victories by college football coaches, was inducted into the football Hall of Fame in 1983.

**Hayworth, Rita** (MARGARITA CARMEN CANSINO), U.S. actress (b. Oct. 17, 1918, New York, N.Y.—d. May 14, 1987, New York), was a provocative auburn-haired dancer who reigned as a "love goddess" during the 1940s and 1950s after appearing as a glamorous seductress in such films as *Blood and Sand* (1941), *Gilda* (1946), and *Miss Sadie Thompson* (1953). Hayworth, who began dancing professionally at the age of 12, made her motion-picture debut under the name of Rita Cansino and had minor roles in such films as *Charlie Chan in Egypt, Dante's Inferno, A Night at the Opera* (all 1935), and *Trouble in Texas* (1937). During World

War II the *Life* magazine photo of her wearing a negligee and kneeling on a bed was reproduced for servicemen, and it became one of the most famous pinup shots of World War II; the picture adorned the first atomic bomb exploded on Bikini Atoll in 1946. After marrying oilman Ed Judson, who dedicated himself to creating her sensual screen persona, she appeared under the name of Rita Hayworth with Cary Grant in *Only Angels Have Wings* (1939), which propelled her to stardom. She danced with Fred Astaire in *You'll Never Get Rich* (1941) and *You Were Never Lovelier* (1942); though she appeared to sing in many of her films, her singing was usually dubbed. Her many film credits include *The Strawberry Blonde* (1941), *My Gal Sal* (1942), *Cover Girl* (1944), *The Lady from Shanghai* (1948), and *Pal Joey* (1957). In 1943 she married "boy genius" Orson Welles; they had a daughter, Rebecca, but the marriage ended after five years, and she began a whirlwind romance with the married playboy Prince Aly Khan, the son of the spiritual leader of millions of Muslims. After the prince was legally divorced, the two were married; seven months later Hayworth gave birth to another daughter, Yasmin. Her fourth marriage, to singer Dick Haymes, lasted two years, and three years later she wed producer James Hill, who starred her in the dramatic film *Separate Tables* (1958). The couple divorced in 1961, and she appeared in several more films. In the 1970s she was diagnosed as an alcoholic, though it is probable that she was suffering the first stages of Alzheimer's disease. Her daughter Yasmin assumed care for her and actively lobbied for congressional funding of research to combat the devastating disease.

**Heifetz, Jascha,** Russian-born violinist (b. Feb. 2, 1901, Vilna, Lithuania—d. Dec. 10, 1987, Los Angeles, Calif.), was a musical prodigy who began playing the violin at the age of three and could perform Mendelssohn's *Violin Concerto* at the age of six; he became the international standard by which fellow violinists measured their musical virtuosity and interpretive mastery. Heifetz entered the St. Petersburg (Russia) Conservatory at the age of nine and studied under violin master Leopold Auer. When Heifetz was only 11 years old, Arthur Nikisch, the celebrated conductor of the Berlin Philharmonic, invited him to perform Tchaikovsky's *Violin Concerto* with the ensemble. He toured Europe before fleeing the Russian Revolution in 1917 and settling in the U.S. In the same year, he made his U.S. debut at Carnegie Hall, New York City, and he became a U.S. citizen in 1925. Heifetz, who eschewed the more flamboyant stances of other violinists, relied on his technical mastery and silken tone to spellbind audiences. Generally regarded as the greatest violinist of his time, he transcribed works of Bach, Vivaldi, and the 20th-century French composer Poulenc for his instrument, as well as commissioning works by such contemporary composers as Sir William Walton and Louis Gruenberg. In 1961, together with cellist Gregor Piatigorsky and violist William Primrose, Heifetz taught master classes at the University of Southern California School of Music, where he regularly taught thereafter and where the Heifetz chair in music was established in 1975. He ceased giving concerts in 1972 and instead recorded numerous works. In 1975 virtually all of his recordings produced between 1917 and 1965 were reissued by RCA records. After a shoulder operation in 1975, Heifetz confined himself to teaching. A veteran of films, television, and radio, Heifetz made his last public appearance in a French television documentary in 1974.

**Heller, Walter Wolfgang,** U.S. economist (b. Aug. 27, 1915, Buffalo, N.Y.—d. June 15, 1987, Silverdale, Wash.), as chairman of the Council of Economic Advisers (1961–64) under Presidents John F. Kennedy and Lyndon B. Johnson, introduced the seminal tax cut of 1964, which spurred an economic upturn that continued for a record 100 months. A Keynesian economist,

Heller was called to government service in 1942 after earning his Ph.D. in economics from the University of Wisconsin a year earlier. A master at simplifying daunting economic jargon, he proclaimed himself an "educator of Presidents." From 1942 until 1953 he was a consultant to the U.S. Treasury, and in 1946 he became a member of the faculty at the University of Minnesota. After Heller's tax cut was implemented, unemployment diminished and inflation remained low. When the war in Vietnam began to spur inflation, however, he advised President Johnson to raise taxes, but the president declined to do so. Heller left his post in 1964 but remained a much-trusted adviser; he served as consultant to the office of the U.S. president (1965–69 and 1974–77) and to the U.S. Congressional Budget Office (from 1975). He retired from the University of Minnesota in 1986.

**Herman, Babe** (FLOYD CAVES HERMAN), U.S. baseball player (b. June 26, 1903, Buffalo, N.Y.—d. Nov. 27, 1987, Glendale, Calif.), was a powerful hitter with the Brooklyn Dodgers professional baseball team (1926–32 and 1945). During his 13-year career with the Dodgers and such teams as the Cincinnati Reds, the Chicago Cubs, the Pittsburgh Pirates, and the Detroit Tigers, he slammed 1,818 hits and earned a lifetime batting average of .324. Though he was an outstanding hitter, Herman was a lacklustre first baseman and centre fielder; in one of his notable misadventures, he wound up on the same base as two other Brooklyn runners. He was a popular Dodger and for many years held the team records for the most home runs in a season, 35; the highest season batting average, .393; and most total bases, 416. In 1945, after a seven-year absence from the major leagues, he rejoined the Dodgers during a player shortage in World War II. After he retired as a player, Herman spent 22 years as a scout for various baseball teams.

**Herman, Woody** (WOODROW CHARLES HERMAN), U.S. bandleader (b. May 16, 1913, Milwaukee, Wis.—d. Oct. 29, 1987, Los Angeles, Calif.), was an accomplished instrumentalist who played the jazz clarinet and saxophone but was best known as the durable front man of a succession of bands he dubbed Herds. Herman, who performed in vaudeville as a child, was billed as the Boy Wonder of the Clarinet; he cut his first record, "Sentimental Gentleman from Georgia," at the age of 16. After studying music at Marquette University, Milwaukee, for one term, he played and sang on the road with the Tom Gerun band before joining the Isham Jones Juniors in 1934. When that group disbanded in 1936, Herman used its most talented sidemen to form his own ensemble, which he publicized as the Band That Plays the Blues. In 1939 his group was propelled to stardom by the success of "Woodchoppers' Ball," which sold more than a million copies and remained a standout favourite for 50 years. During the 1940s his band took on bass player Chubby Jackson, arrangers Neal Hefti and Ralph Burns, tenor saxophonist Flip Phillips, and trombonist Bill Harris. The band, then known as the Thundering Herd, had its own radio show, appeared in motion pictures, and in 1946 performed, at Carnegie Hall, *Ebony Concerto,* a piece written specifically for it by Igor Stravinsky. With the demise of most of the big bands, Herman disbanded in 1946 but about six months later formed his second Herd, featuring Stan Getz and Zoot Sims. This group produced the celebrated Four Brothers arrangement, which pioneered the combination of three tenor saxophones and one baritone saxophone. Later Herds adopted an amplified sound combined with the traditional big band sound. Herman toured extensively during the 1970s and '80s and in 1986 released the album *Woody Herman and His Big Band 50th Anniversary Tour.* In his last days Herman, plagued by financial problems, was nearly forced to vacate his rented home but was rescued from eviction when fellow entertainers established a fund to aid him.

JOHN COATES—CAMERA PRESS, LONDON

**Hess, (Walter Richard) Rudolf,** German politician (b. April 26, 1894, Alexandria, Egypt—d. Aug. 17, 1987, West Berlin), was a leading Nazi and Hitler's private secretary from the early 1920s. He became deputy party leader in April 1933 and entered Hitler's Cabinet in December of that year. Hess was mainly remembered for his extraordinary wartime solo flight to Scotland (May 10, 1941) on a peace mission undertaken, apparently without Hitler's knowledge, only a few weeks before Germany attacked the Soviet Union. In later years he attracted humanitarian concern as the aged, ailing, and, from 1966, sole surviving prisoner from the Nürnberg trials in West Berlin's Spandau prison, kept there by Soviet intransigence. The son of a German exporter, Hess was educated in Alexandria and at Godesberg High School. During World War I he served in a Bavarian infantry regiment, was wounded, and later joined the Air Force, becoming a fighter pilot. While studying economics at the University of Munich, Hess joined Hitler's National Socialist Party (1920). He took part in Hitler's Munich Putsch (1923) and with him was imprisoned at Landsberg, where Hitler dictated to him a large portion of *Mein Kampf.* In the late 1930s his influence with Hitler declined, and in 1939 he was designated to follow Hermann Göring in the Nazi line of succession. His peace mission was dismissed by the British, and he was imprisoned in the Tower of London. Convicted at Nürnberg in 1946 of preparing and waging aggressive war, he was sentenced to life imprisonment. His suicide by hanging had allegedly been preceded by two or three attempts.

**Ho Ying-ch'in,** Chinese general (b. 1889, Guizhou (Kweichow) Province, China—d. Oct. 21, 1987, Taipei, Taiwan), as commander in chief of the Chinese Army, accepted (Sept. 9, 1945) the unconditional surrender of one million Japanese troops in Nanjing (Nanking) at the end of World War II. The scion of a wealthy family, he received his military training at the Japanese Military Academy in Tokyo. After graduating in 1916, shortly after the Chinese Republic was established, he became principal of the Guizhou Military Institute. He later became commander of the 1st Brigade of the Nationalist Army in Guangdong (Kwangtung) and helped repress antigovernment insurrections in southern China by deposed, yet still-powerful, warlords. In 1929 he became a member of the Central Executive Committee of the Kuomintang (Nationalist Party) and chief of staff of the Nationalist Army. In 1944 Ho was made commander in chief of the Chinese Army, and in 1949 he briefly served as prime minister of China before fleeing to Taiwan with the Nationalists when the Communists took control. In Taiwan Ho was defense minister from 1949 to 1958.

**Howser, Dick** (RICHARD DALTON HOWSER), U.S. baseball player, coach, and manager (b. May 14, 1937, Miami, Fla.—d. June 18, 1987, Kansas City, Mo.), was best remembered as the soft-spoken manager of the Kansas City Royals, who captured the American League pennant and the World Series in 1985 after battling back from a 3–1 deficit in both instances. A former shortstop, coach, and manager for the New York Yankees, Howser was chosen as the American League's rookie of the year in 1961 after batting .280 and striking out only 38 times in 158 games. After playing for the Kansas City Athletics (1961–63) and the Cleveland Indians (1963–66), he joined the New York Yankees in 1967. He ended his playing career the following year and served as a Yankee third-base coach for a decade. Howser coached at Florida State University from 1978 to 1979, but in 1980 he was selected to manage the Yankees. He compiled a respectable record of 103 victories but left the organization after the team lost the league play-offs to Kansas City. In 1981 he joined the Kansas City Royals; he led teams to first- and second-place divisional finishes before leading the team in 1985 to its only World Series championship, over the St. Louis Cardinals. Howser, who resigned in February 1987 after two operations for brain cancer had weakened him, underwent a third operation in March.

**Huston, John,** U.S. director, screenwriter, and actor (b. Aug. 5, 1906, Nevada, Mo.—d. Aug. 28, 1987, Middletown, R.I.), was a maverick filmmaker whose box-office and critical flops were overshadowed by such enduring classics as *The Maltese Falcon* (1941), *The Treasure of the Sierra Madre* (1948), *The Asphalt Jungle* (1950), *The Red Badge of Courage* (1951), *The African Queen* (1951), *Fat City* (1972), and *The Man Who Would Be King* (1975). Huston, who embraced a roguish life-style that included hard drinking, chain-smoking, five marriages, and at one time a vagabond existence in Paris, seemed to revel in his adventurous exploits. As the son of actor Walter Huston, he began his film career as an actor but soon turned to writing for the screen; he wrote, with others, the screenplays for such films as *Murders in the Rue Morgue* (1932), *Jezebel* (1938), *High Sierra* (1941), and *Sergeant York* (1941). As a director he used scripts that were lean and fast-paced and dealt with misfits or nonconformists braving danger in the interest of greed or personal gain. Huston directed the Academy Award-winning

KIP RANO—CAMERA PRESS/PHOTO TRENDS

performances of both his father, in *The Treasure of the Sierra Madre,* for which he himself won Oscars for best direction and best writing, and his daughter, Anjelica, in *Prizzi's Honor* (1985). His early Hollywood directing career was interrupted by service as an officer in the Army Signal Corps during World War II, during which he directed three gripping wartime documentaries: *Report from the Aleutians* (1943), *The Battle of San Pietro* (1945), and *Let There Be Light* (1946; suppressed until 1981, when it had its first public showing). Some postwar credits include *Key Largo* (1948), *Beat the Devil* (1953), *The Misfits* (1961), *Freud* (1962), *The Night of the Iguana* (1964), *The Life and Times of Judge Roy Bean* (1972), and *Annie* (1982). He experimented brilliantly with colour in *Moulin Rouge* (1952) and *Moby Dick* (1956) and disastrously in *Reflections in a Golden Eye* (1967). During his later years he increasingly took roles in films, appearing in *The Cardinal* (1963), *The Bible . . . in the Beginning* (1966), *Casino Royale* (1967), *Myra Breckinridge* (1970), *Chinatown* (1974), and *Winter Kills* (1979). In 1980 he published his autobiography, *An Open Book.* Despite his chronic emphysema he continued to make motion pictures and at the time of his death was producing a film of Thornton Wilder's *Theophilus North;* his adaptation of James Joyce's short story "The Dead" was ready for release.

**Imlach, George** ("PUNCH"), Canadian hockey coach (b. March 15, 1918, Toronto, Ont.—d. Dec. 1, 1987, Toronto), as the colourful coach and general manager of the Toronto Maple Leafs professional hockey team, led them to four Stanley Cup victories (1962, 1963, 1964, and 1967) and, as coach (1970–72) of the expansion Buffalo Sabres, was credited with building the team into a respectable contender. Imlach earned the nickname "Punch" when, as a minor league player, he skated into a stray elbow during a game in Windsor, Ont., was knocked out, and as he regained consciousness began swinging at his own trainer, who had come onto the ice to assist him. After his tenure (1958–69) with the Maple Leafs, Imlach spent two years as coach of the Buffalo Sabres and six years as general manager before returning to the Maple Leafs as general manager in 1979. He left the team in 1981 when he underwent quadruple heart bypass surgery. His lifetime record as both a coach and a general manager included 395 victories, 336 losses, and 148 ties. He was inducted into the Hockey Hall of Fame in 1984.

**Jochum, Eugen,** West German conductor (b. Nov. 1, 1902, Babenhausen, Swabia, Germany—d. March 26, 1987, Munich, West Germany), worked regularly with many of the great orchestras of Europe and the U.S. and was particularly noted as an interpreter of Bruckner. Trained at the Augsburg Conservatory and in Munich, Jochum made his conducting debut in 1926 at the Munich Opera and was appointed deputy and then principal conductor of the Kiel Opera (1926–29). He was musical director of Berlin Radio (1932–34) and of Hamburg Opera (1934–49), where he continued to perform works by composers who were out of favour with the Nazi regime. In the post-World War II period Jochum established an international reputation for himself and for the Bavarian Radio Symphony Orchestra during his tenure as musical director of Bavarian Radio (1949–61). He was chief conductor of the Amsterdam Concertgebouw (1961–63) and of the Bamberg Symphony Orchestra (1969–77). In 1977 he was appointed conductor laureate of the London Symphony Orchestra. He made several outstanding recordings, notably the complete Bruckner symphonies, Bach's *Saint John Passion,* and works by Beethoven, Brahms, and Haydn. His interpretations were the result of long meditation, and while he avoided sensationalism, he did not allow the music to become lifeless. Jochum gained many distinctions, including the Brahms Medal and the medal of the International Bruckner Society.

**Johnson, Eleanor Murdock,** U.S. educator and editor (b. Dec. 10, 1892, Washington County, Md.—d. Oct. 8, 1987, Gaithersburg, Md.), was the founder of *The Weekly Reader* (originally called *My Weekly Reader),* which brought current events into the lives of six generations of grade-school students in straightforward yet tantalizing prose. The newsweekly, which was launched by Johnson on Sept. 21, 1928, had been expanded to seven editions by the early 1970s, one for each grade level from preschool to sixth grade. Some nine million children currently subscribed to the 27 issues published during the school year, which cost about $2. A teacher, Johnson held master's degrees in education from the University of Chicago and Columbia University, New York City. She also was a coauthor of such children's books as the *Child Story Readers* and the *Treasury of Literature Readers.* She served as editor in chief of the newsweekly from 1935 until 1961 and was a consultant until 1978.

**Jonathan, Chief (Joseph) Leabua,** Lesotho politician (b. Oct. 30, 1914, Leribe, Basutoland [now Lesotho]—d. April 5, 1987, Pretoria, South Africa), was prime minister from July 5, 1965, until he was deposed in a military coup on Jan. 20, 1986. He was a great-grandson of the Basuto king Moshoeshoe I. Jonathan was educated at a mission school in Leribe and then worked as a clerk in the Rand mines of South Africa. From 1937 he worked in local government in Basutoland and was a member of delegations to London (1959, 1964) that sought self-government for Basutoland. A convert to Catholicism, he was founder (1959) and leader of the church-supported Basutoland National Party, which won a slim majority in elections held in April 1965; Jonathan himself failed to win a seat, but he entered the National Assembly in a by-election in July 1965. After Lesotho gained independence in 1966, Jonathan established full diplomatic relations with South Africa in 1967. Following the apparent victory in the January 1970 general elections of the opposition Basutoland Congress Party, Jonathan suspended the constitution, thereafter ruling by decree. Gradually his subservience to South Africa diminished, and he began to shelter black dissident refugees, notably members of the African National Congress. In retaliation South Africa raided Lesotho's capital, Maseru (1982), blockaded the kingdom (December 1985), and supported (perhaps engineered) the coup in which he fell.

**Jouvenel des Ursins, Bertrand de,** BARON, French political economist (b. Oct. 31, 1903, Paris, France—d. March 1, 1987, Paris), was the author of *Du pouvoir* (1945; *On Power),* in which he developed his conservative version of liberal political theory, and *L'Arcadie*

JULIEN QUIDEAU—CAMERA PRESS, LONDON

(1968), a collection of articles in which he anticipated later concern with the environment and expressed a highly individual vision of the harmonious life. He was remembered particularly, however, for his association with his stepmother, the writer Colette. In 1920, after his father's marriage to Colette, Jouvenel went to stay with her in Brittany and they became lovers, their relationship forming the basis for Colette's novel *Le Blé en herbe* (1923). He was educated at the Lycée Hoche, Versailles, and at the University of Paris, where he studied law and science. A Radical-Socialist in the 1920s, he later advocated a form of monarchy and, from 1936 to 1938, moved close to fascism as a member of the Parti Populaire Français. During the German occupation in World War II, he was linked with collaborationist circles but repudiated them and lived in Switzerland from 1943. Accused long after by an Israeli historian of being a "theoretician of French fascism," he brought a libel action, which he won convincingly in 1983. During his academic career he taught economics at the universities of Oxford, Cambridge, California at Berkeley, and Yale, among others. His other publications included *La Crise du capitalisme américain* (1933) and *Revoir Hélène* (1986), a novel inspired by the death of his wife.

**Jutra, Claude,** Canadian motion-picture director (b. March 11, 1930, Montreal, Que.—death confirmed April 23, 1987, St. Lawrence River, near Quebec), was a celebrated filmmaker whose 1971 classic, *Mon Oncle Antoine,* the sensitive story of a rural Quebec boy coming of age, was deemed the best-ever Canadian film by an international panel in 1986. Jutra attended the University of Montreal (1946–52), where he studied medicine. He joined the National Film Board in the mid-1950s and directed several short films before producing his first feature, *A tout prendre* (1963), which launched the new Quebec cinema by capturing the essence of Quebec society. Some of his other film credits include *Comment savoir* (1966), *Wow* (1969), *Kamouraska* (1972), and *Pour le meilleur et pour le pire* (1976). Jutra, who had been suffering from depression and Alzheimer's disease, had disappeared on Nov. 5, 1986. His decomposed corpse was retrieved from the St. Lawrence River and was positively identified by means of a distinctive tattoo and a note in his money belt that said, "I am Claude Jutra."

**Kabalevsky, Dmitry Borisovich,** Soviet composer (b. Dec. 30, 1904, St. Petersburg, Russia—d. Feb. 14, 1987, Moscow, U.S.S.R.), was prolific rather than brilliant, having produced a steady flow of orchestral and chamber works and operas. Influenced by the government's decree (1948) against "bourgeois formalism," Kabalevsky continued to adopt patriotic and party themes, and much of his work was based on folk music. In performances of his works he often participated as conductor or pianist. Kabalevsky studied at the Moscow Conservatory, completing courses in composition and piano, and he became a professor there in 1939. A Communist Party member from 1940, he was a member of the collegium of the Ministry of Culture of the U.S.S.R. from 1954. In all, his compositions include five operas, four symphonies, three piano concerti, one violin concerto, two cello concerti, and various chamber pieces, suites, and cantatas. His suite *The Comedians* and the overture to his opera *Colas Breugnon* (1937) have been performed in the West.

**Karami, Rashid Abdul Hamid,** Lebanese politician (b. Dec. 30, 1921, Miriata, near Tripoli, Lebanon—d. June 1, 1987, near Beirut, Lebanon), served as prime minister of his country ten times between 1955 and 1987. Four weeks before he was killed in a helicopter crash that was the result of sabotage, Karami had offered his resignation as prime minister, but Pres. Amin Gemayel refused to accept it. A Sunni Muslim and the son of a leading Sunni politician who was prime minister in 1945, Karami devoted himself to advancing the interests of his community. The Lebanese constitution attempts to balance power between Maronite Christians and Sunni and Shi'ah Muslims, and Karami exploited its provisions to block the initiative of Christian presidents. Trained as a lawyer in Cairo, he entered Parliament in 1951 and became justice minister the same year. He was appointed prime minister for the first time in 1955 by Pres. Camille Chamoun (*q.v.*) but resigned the following year after a dispute with Chamoun. He subsequently played a large role in organizing the Muslim opposition. Reappointed prime minister by Pres. Fuad Chehab in 1958, he remained in that office for much of the 1960s under Chehab and his successor, Pres. Charles Helou. In office he demonstrated the passive strength that was the hallmark of his political career, but he was also recognized for his honesty and devotion to his country and to the Arab cause. He resigned again in 1969 but was recalled by Pres. Suleiman Franjieh on the outbreak of civil war in 1975. Though he was backed by the Palestinians, he lacked the solid power base that might have made his government effective in ending the conflict, and he left office in December 1976. Asked by President Gemayel to form a government of national unity in 1983, Karami became prime minister for the last time in April 1984.

**Kaye, Danny** (DAVID DANIEL KAMINSKI), U.S. actor (b. Jan. 18, 1913, New York, N.Y.—d. March 3, 1987, Los Angeles, Calif.), was a brilliant comedian who mastered the art of verbal acrobatics with double-talk, tongue twisters, and rhymes, using his extraordinary gift on Broadway and television and in films. For 30 years he donated his talents to UNICEF, and he entertained children around the world as its good-

will ambassador. Kaye, a limber-limbed rag doll who delighted audiences with his facial contortions and improvisations, made his Broadway debut in *The Straw Hat Revue* (1939). Two years later, in *Lady in the Dark,* he stopped the show with his machine-gun delivery of the patter song "Tschaikowsky," in which he reeled off the polysyllabic names of 49 Russian composers in 39 seconds. He credited much of his success to his wife, Sylvia Fine, who created a large portion of his material. An established star even before his motion-picture debut in *Up in Arms* (1944), he made a series of lavish Technicolor Samuel Goldwyn films that were tailor-made for his talents. His film credits include *Wonder Man* (1945), *The Kid from Brooklyn* (1946), *The Secret Life of Walter Mitty* (1947), *The Inspector General* (1949), *Hans Christian Andersen* (1952), *White Christmas* (1954), and *The Court Jester* (1956), which was considered by some his best film. From 1963 to 1967 he was host of his own television variety program, "The Danny Kaye Show," for which he won an Emmy and a Peabody award. A talented musician, he raised millions of dollars for musicians' pension funds in the U.S. and Canada by comically conducting symphony concerts. In one performance he conducted "The Flight of the Bumblebee" with a flyswatter. Kaye also was a founding partner of the Seattle Mariners baseball team. He was given an honorary Academy Award in 1954, the Jean Hersholt Humanitarian Award of the Academy of Motion Picture Arts and Sciences in 1982, and Kennedy Center Honors for lifetime achievement in the arts in 1984.

**Kaye, Nora** (NORA KOREFF), U.S. dancer (b. Jan. 17, 1920, New York, N.Y.—d. Feb. 28, 1987, Los Angeles, Calif.), as a prima ballerina with Ballet (now American Ballet) Theatre (1939–51 and 1954–61) and with the New York City Ballet (1951–54), was dubbed the "Duse of the dance" for her extraordinary dramatic interpretations. Kaye studied first with Michel Fokine and then at the Metropolitan Opera Ballet school. She joined Ballet Theatre at its 1939 inception, and in 1942 her performance of the role of Hagar in Antony Tudor's *Pillar of Fire* raised her to the status of prima ballerina. Kaye excelled in dramatic classical roles, and some 24 ballets were created especially for her. Some of her most memorable roles were in Tudor's *Jardin aux Lilas,* Agnes deMille's *Fall River Legend,* and Jerome Robbins's *Cage.* After retiring from dancing in 1961, she assisted her third husband, director-choreographer Herbert Ross, in his film and stage projects; when he directed such dance films as *The Turning Point* (1977) and *Nijinsky* (1980), she served as executive producer and coproducer, respectively. From 1977 to 1983 she was associate artistic director of American Ballet Theatre.

**Kaye, Sammy,** U.S. bandleader (b. March 13, 1910, Lakewood, Ohio—d. June 2, 1987, Ridgewood, N.J.), was maestro of one of the swing era's most popular "sweet bands," which delighted audiences with its soothing reedy ensemble sound typified by such signature songs as "The Old Lamp-Lighter" and "Harbor Lights." Kaye, who wrote the band's theme song, "Until Tomorrow," also developed the slogan "Swing and Sway with Sammy Kaye." After the Sammy Kaye Orchestra recorded its first major hit, "Rosalie," in 1937, a string of more than 100 hit records followed, including "Love Walked In," "Penny Serenade," "Remember Pearl Harbor," "Daddy," "I Left My Heart at the Stage Door Canteen," and "Walkin' to Missouri." Kaye, the host of radio's "Sunday Serenade" and television's "The Sammy Kaye Show," was also known for implementing gimmicks and contests, the most popular of which was "So You Want to Lead a Band," a routine in which amateur bandleaders from the audience competed for Sammy Kaye batons and champagne. Kaye later performed at the inaugurations of Presidents Richard M. Nixon and Ronald Reagan.

**Keyserling, Leon H.,** U.S. economist (b. Jan. 22, 1908, Charleston, S.C.—d. Aug. 9, 1987, Washington, D.C.), as the liberal chairman (1950–53) of the president's Council of Economic Advisers, which he helped create, was instrumental in establishing the economic policies of Pres. Harry S. Truman's administration. Keyserling advocated full employment and production and maintained that government spending to stimulate business could achieve these goals. He was not overly concerned with a balanced budget and believed that spending could cure inflation. After graduating in 1928 from Columbia University, New York City, Keyserling earned a degree at Harvard Law School in 1931. As a legislative assistant to Sen. Robert F. Wagner of New York, Keyserling helped draft such New Deal legislation as the National Industrial Recovery Act of 1933, the Social Security Act of 1935, and the National Labor Relations Act, also known as the Wagner Act. During the later years of the Roosevelt administration, he helped write legislation that led to the formation of the federal Department of Housing and Urban Development. Keyserling also wrote an essay on postwar employment that served as the basis for the Employment Act of 1946, which advocated full employment and the establishment of the Council of Economic Advisers. After leaving government service in 1953, Keyserling practiced law, wrote extensively on economic policy, and founded (1954) the privately supported Conference on Economic Progress.

**King, Cecil Harmsworth,** British newspaper publisher (b. Feb. 20, 1901, Totteridge, Hertfordshire, England—d. April 17, 1987, Dublin, Ireland), as chairman of the International Publishing Corp. (1963–68), headed the world's largest newspaper empire. He controlled nearly two dozen British and overseas newspapers and over 200 periodicals and also had extensive paper and printing interests. He was a nephew of Alfred Harmsworth (afterward Lord Northcliffe), founder of the *Daily Mail* and *Daily Mirror*. King was educated at Winchester College and at Christ Church, Oxford. He was soon taken into the family firm, spending three years with the advertising department of the *Daily Mail*. He then moved to the *Daily Mirror* and was made a director in 1929. He became editorial director (1937) and deputy chairman (1942) of the *Sunday Pictorial* (later the *Sunday Mirror*). In a boardroom coup in 1951 he became chairman of Daily Mirror Newspapers Ltd., supplanting Guy Bartholomew, who had transformed the *Daily Mirror* into a successful tabloid. In 1958 King acquired the Amalgamated Press, which necessitated his purchase of its rival, Odham's Press, in 1960. As his uncle had done, King sought to interfere in government; with a signed editorial (May 10, 1968) in the *Daily Mirror*, he attempted to force Prime Minister Harold Wilson to resign. This was counterproductive and resulted in King's own dismissal (May 30). He published his autobiography, *Strictly Personal*, in 1969.

**Kishi, Nobusuke,** Japanese statesman (b. Nov. 13, 1896, Yamaguchi Prefecture, Japan—d. Aug. 7, 1987, Tokyo, Japan), as prime minister of Japan (1957–60), was instrumental in forcing the ratification of a revised U.S.-Japan Treaty of Mutual Cooperation and Security through the Diet (parliament) despite widespread protests by the opposition, which feared Japan would be drawn into nuclear war. While the opposition boycotted the Diet, the ruling party passed the treaty on its own in May 1960. Under the new treaty the U.S. agreed to defend Japan in the event of an attack, and Japan was given veto power over the use of nuclear weapons in that country, although it was not required to defend the U.S. in the event of war. His action was viewed as high-handed, and he was forced to resign his post two months later. Kishi was adopted at the age of 15 by a paternal uncle bearing the Kishi name. He graduated (1920) from the Tokyo Imperial law department and launched his career as a civil servant in the Commerce Ministry. In 1925 he transferred to the newly created Commerce and Industry Department, and he became director of its Industrial Bureau in 1935. The following year he served as a vice-minister of the Manchukuo government's industrial department and helped develop the industrialization of Japanese-occupied Manchuria and China. As commerce and industry minister (1941–44) in the Cabinet of Hideki Tojo, Kishi was one of the signatories of Japan's declaration of war (December 1941) against the U.S., which resulted in the bombing of Pearl Harbor. After the Japanese surrendered in 1945, Kishi was imprisoned for more than three years as an accused war criminal; he was released after a change in occupation policy in 1948. He returned to politics and in 1953 was elected to the Diet as a member of the Liberal Party. Two years later he engineered the merger of the Liberals and the Democratic Party to form the Liberal-Democratic Party, which controlled the government from that time. In 1956

PANA

he was named foreign minister in the Cabinet of Tanzan Ishibashi, and when the latter resigned two months later, Kishi was elevated to prime minister; he remained in that office until his resignation in 1960. Never far from the political helm, Kishi was the older brother of Eisaku Sato, who served as prime minister from 1964 to 1972, and he was the father-in-law of Shintaro Abe, a one-time foreign minister and a leading candidate to assume the post of prime minister in 1987.

**Kolmogorov, Andrey Nikolayevich,** Soviet mathematician (b. April 25 [April 12, old style], 1903, Tambov, Russia—d. Oct. 20, 1987, Moscow, U.S.S.R.), wrote *Grundbegriffe der Wahrscheinlichkeitsrechnung* (1933; *Foundations of the Theory of Probability* [1950]), a seminal work in modern mathematics. Together with his subsequent contributions to probability theory, the ideas developed in this work had wide applications in mathematics, physics, astronomy, and other fields. Kolmogorov's elegant treatment of probability, built up rigorously from fundamental principles in a way that was compared to the methods of the Greek mathematician Euclid, was crucial to contemporary descriptions of randomness and predictability in physical processes. Kolmogorov later extended his basic theories to such diverse physical systems as the motion of the planets and the turbulent behaviour of air in the jet stream of aircraft. In 1941 he published two papers on turbulence that had extensive implications, and in 1954 he developed his work on dynamic systems in relation to planetary motion, demonstrating the crucial role of probability theory in physics. His broad range of interests led him to pursue such topics as form and structure in the poetry of Pushkin and to devote much attention, particularly in his later years, to the mathematical training of Soviet schoolchildren. Kolmogorov graduated from Moscow State University in 1925 and subsequently taught there as instructor and, from 1931, as professor. In 1939 he was elected to the Soviet Academy of Sciences at the early age of 36, and he subsequently was made a foreign member of learned societies in the U.S. and the U.K., among others. He received the Lenin Prize (1965) and the Order of Lenin on six occasions.

**Koruturk, Fahri S.,** Turkish politician and naval officer (b. 1903, Istanbul, Turkey—d. Oct. 12, 1987, Istanbul), was president of Turkey (April 6, 1973–April 6, 1980) during a period of sustained political unrest and violence, frequent changes of government, and serious dispute with Greece over Cyprus and control of the Aegean seabed. A career naval officer, Koruturk was educated at the Naval Academy and graduated in 1923. He was appointed to the intelligence department of the general staff in

1934 and served as military attaché in Berlin (1935), Rome (1936), and Berlin and Stockholm (1942–43). He subsequently held various executive commands and became commander of the Navy and a full admiral in 1957. Retired after the military coup of May 1960, Koruturk served as Turkey's ambassador to Moscow (1960–64) and to Madrid (1964–65). He was in Parliament as an independent senator from 1968. He attained the presidency as a compromise candidate following 14 inconclusive ballots in which no contestant had gained the necessary majority. Following the expiration of his term of office in 1980, Parliament failed to elect a successor; there were fresh political disturbances and, five months later, another military coup.

**Koun, Karolos,** Greek theatre director (b. Sept. 13, 1908, Bursa, Ottoman Empire [now Turkey]—d. Feb. 14, 1987, Athens, Greece), founded the Art Theatre in Athens in 1942 and achieved an international reputation with his interpretations of classical Greek drama, though his determination to make these works relevant for the modern world sometimes shocked conservative audiences. His influence on Greek culture was enormous; known as "the teacher," he introduced many contemporary foreign and Greek playwrights and trained a whole generation of actors. Educated in Istanbul, Koun later studied in Paris and staged student productions of classical plays while working as an English teacher at Athens College. In 1934 he founded the Popular Theatre and then, during the German occupation, the Art Theatre, which was to become the most controversial and innovative company in Greece. His 1959 production of Aristophanes' *The Birds*, with its bawdy humour and contemporary costumes, was banned in Greece but triumphed in Paris in 1962 and in London two years later. The company appeared in London and toured throughout Europe. The 1967 military coup brought fresh restrictions, however, and it was not until the restoration of democracy in 1974 that Koun enjoyed official as well as popular recognition.

**Kountché, Gen. Seyni,** Niger army officer and politician (b. July 1, 1931, Fandou, Niger—d. Nov. 10, 1987, Paris, France), was Niger's head of state and president of the Supreme Military Council from April 1974. He ruled with paternalistic rigour and managed to make his country self-sufficient in grain while increasing its wealth by developing uranium mining. Educated in the French army schools at Kati, Mali, and at St. Louis, Senegal, he joined the French colonial army in 1949 and served in Indochina and Algeria, becoming a sergeant in 1957. After his country became independent (1960), he transferred to the Niger Army (1961). Kountché studied at the officers' training school in Paris (1965–66) and became deputy chief of staff of the Niger armed forces (1966–73) and then chief of staff (1973). He assumed power when he ousted Pres. Hamani Diori in a military coup. At first Kountché retained a large number of ministerial portfolios, and he frequently reshuffled his governments. He survived a number of attempted coups. He visited China and the U.S. (1984) and maintained good relations with France.

**Krige, Uys,** South African writer (b. Feb. 4, 1910, Swellendam, Cape Province, South Africa—d. Aug. 10, 1987, near Hermanus, Cape Province), writing in both Afrikaans and English, portrayed the world of his fellow Afrikaners with accuracy and understanding, notably in his plays *The Wall of Death* (1960), *The Sniper* (1962), and *The Two Lamps* (1964), which explored the effects of Calvinism on the relationship between a man and his son. He studied law at the University of Stellenbosch before entering journalism as a reporter for the *Rand Daily Mail;* he then worked in France and Spain. He later translated Federico García Lorca's play *Yerma* into Afrikaans and edited an anthology of Latin-American poetry. In the late 1930s he joined the Cape Town Afrikaans newspaper *Die*

*Suiderstem* and subsequently became a war correspondent. Captured at the Battle of Tobruk, Krige chronicled his imprisonment and escape in his novel *The Way Out* (1955). After World War II he founded the newspaper *Vandag.* Krige published several collections of poetry in Afrikaans, but he was best known to English-speaking readers for his short stories, collected in *The Dream and the Desert* (1953) and *Orphan of the Desert* (1967). Determined to stay outside politics, he rarely gave nonwhites a prominent role in his fiction, concentrating instead on the enclosed society of Afrikanerdom.

**Landon, Alf(red Mossman),** U.S. politician (b. Sept. 9, 1887, West Middlesex, Pa.—d. Oct. 12, 1987, Topeka, Kan.), served as governor of Kansas (1933–37) but was best remembered as the 1936 Republican presidential candidate who lost to Democrat Franklin D. Roosevelt in an election landslide. Although Landon won 16,679,543 votes, compared with Roosevelt's 27,747,636, he won the electoral votes of only Maine and Vermont, giving him only 8 electoral votes to Roosevelt's 523. After earning a law degree from the University of Kansas in 1908, he entered the oil business in 1912 and by the 1920s had become a millionaire. His interest in politics was sparked when he attended the 1912 Bull Moose convention of the Progressive Party and met leaders of progressive Republicanism; this experience shaped his later career. When he ran for governor of Kansas in 1932, he narrowly defeated Democratic incumbent Harry H. Woodring by 5,637 votes; he was the only Republican gubernatorial candidate west of the Mississippi to win office that year in the wake of the Democratic landslide. When he won re-election in 1934, he became the only Republican gubernatorial candidate in the country to be elected. Because of this victory, the Republican Party nominated him as its presidential candidate in 1936. Landon good-naturedly assessed his two-state victory by remarking, "As Maine goes, so goes Vermont." He never again sought political office but retained an interest in politics and in later years was referred to fondly as the "grand old man of Republican politics." He spent the rest of his life in the Kansas business community. The month before his death, Landon received President and Mrs. Ronald Reagan, who extended their warmest wishes in anticipation of his 100th birthday.

**Lansdale, Edward G.,** U.S. military officer (b. Feb. 6, 1908, Detroit, Mich.—d. Feb. 23, 1987, McLean, Va.), won wide praise for the civic-action programs he implemented during the 1950s to win the allegiance of Filipino peasants and crush a Communist rebellion but was thwarted when he used the same technique in Southeast Asia during the war in Vietnam. Lansdale, a dashing air force major general, felt that he could halt Communist insurgency by "winning the hearts and minds of the people." He was thought to have been the model for the title characters of two books, Graham Greene's *The Quiet American,* whose main character was naive in his views of Vietnamese peasants, and William J. Lederer and Eugene Burdick's *The Ugly American,* which presented its main character as a pied piper, capturing the hearts of the people with his harmonica. Greene, however, denied that Lansdale had been the subject of his book. After graduating from the University of California at Los Angeles, he worked as an advertising executive before joining the Army as a captain in 1943. He left the Army as a major in 1947 and in the same year joined the Air Force as a captain. After his initiative in the Philippines proved successful, Lansdale served (1954–56) as chief of CIA covert operations in Vietnam, where he helped set up the Saigon government of Pres. Ngo Dinh Diem and organized counterrevolutionary cells against the Communists in Hanoi. After he retired from the Air Force, Lansdale served (1965–68) as special assistant to Ambassador Henry Cabot Lodge and as an adviser to a committee of the South Vietnamese government.

**Lash, Joseph P.,** U.S. reporter and biographer (b. Dec. 2, 1909, New York, N.Y.—d. Aug. 22, 1987, Boston, Mass.), was the Pulitzer Prize-winning author of the critically acclaimed *Eleanor and Franklin* (1971), of its sequel, *Eleanor: The Years Alone* (1972), and of biographies of Dag Hammarskjöld (1961) and Helen Keller (1980). After earning an M.A. in philosophy and literature at Columbia University, New York City, Lash served as an officer of the Student League for International Democracy, a Socialist youth group, and from 1936 to 1939 he was executive secretary of the American Student Union. As a leader of this radical youth group, he was summoned to Washington, D.C., to testify before the House Committee on Un-American Activities about Communist infiltration in student organizations. In 1939, on a train en route to the capital, he met Eleanor Roosevelt, and the two established a lifelong friendship. Roosevelt encouraged Lash to cooperate with the committee, and she lent her moral support by appearing in the hearing room. Lash made a favourable impression on Roosevelt; he was invited to the White House and spent time by himself at the Roosevelt family estate in Hyde Park, N.Y. During those years Lash was privy to Roosevelt's recollections and feelings, and with the notes he kept of their meetings, together with her private papers, to which he was given access in 1966, he was able to construct a heartfelt biography of Franklin and Eleanor Roosevelt. From 1950 to 1966 he was with the *New York Post,* first as a general assignment reporter, then as a UN correspondent, and finally as an assistant editor of the editorial page. He left the *Post* in 1966 to write the Roosevelt biography and later penned such works as *Eleanor Roosevelt: A Friend's Memoir* (1964) and *Roosevelt and Churchill, 1939–1941: The Partnership That Saved the West* (1976). His last book, *Dreamers and Dealers,* was to appear posthumously.

**Laurence, Margaret** (JEAN MARGARET WEMYSS), Canadian novelist (b. July 18, 1926, Neepawa, Man.—d. Jan. 5, 1987, Lakefield, Ont.), was regarded as a titan in Canadian literature. She was best known for a quartet of novels—*The Stone Angel* (1964), *A Jest of God* (1966; adapted for the screen as *Rachel, Rachel,* 1968), *The Fire-Dwellers* (1969), and *The Diviners* (1974)—and a collection of linked short stories, *A Bird in the House* (1970), which brought to life the fictional prairie town of Manawaka and a bounty of strong-willed heroines struggling for self-realization while maintaining their dignity. After graduating (1947) from United College, Winnipeg, Man., she married engineer John Laurence, and in 1950 she accompanied him to Africa. Such books as *A Tree for Poverty* (1954), *This Side Jordan* (1960), *The Prophet's Camel Bell* (U.K., 1963; U.S. title, *New Wind in a Dry Land,* 1964), and *The Tomorrow-Tamer* (1963) reflect her experiences in Somaliland (1950–52) and Ghana (1952–57). Besides garnering Governor General's literary awards in 1967 and 1974, Laurence was made a Companion of the Order of Canada and a fellow of the Royal Society of Canada. She served as writer in residence at the University of Toronto (1969–70), the University of Western Ontario at London (1973), and Trent University, Peterborough, Ont. (1974). Her last work, *Heart of a Stranger* (1976), was a collection of essays.

**Lee Byung Chull,** Korean industrialist (b. Feb. 12, 1910, Kyongsangnam-do, Korea—d. Nov. 19, 1987, Seoul, South Korea), was the founder and chairman of the Samsung Business Group, which became one of the world's 50 largest corporations. Lee, who studied at Waseda University in Tokyo, launched his import-export business in 1938 and after the Korean War expanded his operation to include sugar, textiles, electronics, telecommunications, shipbuilding, machinery, semiconductors, and food processing. An influential tycoon, often called "the richest man in Korea," he helped establish the Korean Businessmen's Association, the fore-runner of the Federation of Korean Industries, which he served as first chairman. Lee battled stomach cancer in 1976 and a brain tumour in 1979 before succumbing to lung cancer.

**Leloir, Luis Federico,** Argentine chemist (b. Sept. 6, 1906, Paris, France—d. Dec. 2?, 1987, Buenos Aires, Arg.), was awarded the 1970 Nobel Prize for Chemistry for the discovery of sugar nucleotides and their role in the biosynthesis of carbohydrates. After earning his M.D. at the University of Buenos Aires in 1932, he worked at the university's Institute of Physiology for two years before studying in England for a year under Gowland Hopkins at the Biochemical Laboratory of the University of Cambridge. In 1937 he returned to the Institute of Physiology, where he undertook investigations of the oxidation of fatty acids. In 1943 political pressures caused Leloir to resign his post and work in the U.S. There he spent time at Washington University, St. Louis, Mo., and at the College of Physicians and Surgeons, Columbia University, New York City. He returned to Argentina in 1946 and the following year secured financial support for his own laboratory, the Instituto de Investigaciones Bioquímicas, Buenos Aires. Leloir assembled a dedicated group of scientists and conducted research on the formation and breakdown of lactose, or milk sugar, in the body. This work led to the discovery of sugar nucleotides and their vital role in carbohydrate metabolism.

**LeRoy, Mervyn,** U.S. motion-picture director and producer (b. Oct. 15, 1900, San Francisco, Calif.—d. Sept. 13, 1987, Beverly Hills, Calif.), amassed an impressive list of credits as the director of such gripping dramas as *Little Caesar* (1930) and *I Am a Fugitive from a Chain Gang* (1932) and such romantic tearjerkers as *Waterloo Bridge* (1940) and *Random Harvest* (1942). LeRoy, an impoverished youth, worked as a newsboy and then appeared in vaudeville for nine years before getting work in films from a relative, film pioneer Jesse L. Lasky, as a wardrobe handler. He worked his way up to directing his first feature, *No Place to Go,* in 1927. After establishing his reputation with *Little Caesar,* he turned out scores of films during his 40-year career, including *Tugboat Annie* and *Gold Diggers of 1933* (both 1933), *Anthony Adverse* (1936), and *They Won't Forget* (1937). He also produced such notable films as *The Wizard of Oz* (1939), *The Bad Seed* (1956), and *No Time for Sergeants* (1958). He often touched the public's social conscience with motion pictures decrying such brutalities as lynch mobs and savage prison conditions, and in 1946 he received a special Academy Award for the documentary *The House I Live In,* an indictment of intolerance. Some of his later triumphs include *Thirty Seconds over Tokyo* (1944), *Quo Vadis* (1951), *Mister Roberts* (1955), and *Gypsy* (1962), his last notable film. In 1957 he successfully persuaded Motion Picture Academy officials to allow the Academy rather than studios to choose whether a performer should be nominated in a leading or a supporting role. A memoir, *Mervyn LeRoy: Take One,* written with Dick Kleener, appeared in 1974. At the Oscar ceremonies in 1976, LeRoy received the Irving G. Thalberg Memorial Award for outstanding work as a producer.

**Lévesque, René,** Canadian politician (b. Aug. 24, 1922, New-Carlisle, Que.—d. Nov. 1, 1987, Montreal, Que.), as the dynamic premier (1976–85) of Quebec, championed the predominantly French-speaking province's campaign to secede from Canada in an effort to preserve its distinctive culture. Lévesque studied law at Laval University in Quebec City but during World War II interrupted his education to serve in Europe as a war correspondent and reporter attached to U.S. forces. After the war he joined the French-language service of the Canadian Broadcasting Corporation in Quebec, and from 1956 to 1959 he was the host of the popular television program "Point de Mire." In 1959 he joined the Quebec Liberal Party and was elected to the

Quebec National Assembly as a Liberal member for Montréal-Laurier. Lévesque became one of the most popular members of Jean Lesage's Liberal government, serving as minister of public works and hydraulic resources (1960–61), minister of natural resources (1961–66), and minister of family and social welfare (1966). His influence was instrumental in the government's decision to nationalize private electric utilities. Lévesque became disenchanted with the Liberal

Party's stand on constitutional issues, and he sat as an independent member in 1967. He quit the party that same year to found the Mouvement Souveraineté-Association, which the following year combined with other separatist groups to form the Parti Québécois (PQ). In 1973 the PQ became the official opposition party in Quebec, and in 1976 Lévesque successfully defeated the unpopular government of Robert Bourassa. During his first term in office, Lévesque introduced several important pieces of legislation, notably Bill 101, which established French as the official language of Quebec. His 1980 referendum on sovereignty was decisively defeated by voters, yet Lévesque won reelection in 1981. In his second term, Lévesque's government attempted to curb public spending in order to solve its financial problems. Faced with growing protest from within the party, he resigned as premier in 1985.

**Levi, Primo,** Italian writer (b. July 31, 1919, Turin, Italy—d. April 11, 1987, Turin), survived deportation to the Auschwitz concentration camp during World War II partly because of his training as a chemist. Levi recounted his experiences in works that made an outstanding contribution to modern Italian literature. He was brought up in the small Jewish community in Turin, studied at the University of Turin, and graduated in chemistry in 1941. Two years later Levi joined the Partisans fighting the German occupation of northern Italy and was captured. Sent to Auschwitz, he was chosen to work in a factory attached to the camp producing artificial rubber; of the 650 Italians captured with him, only 24 survived. Liberated by the Soviets in 1945, he returned to Turin and for 30 years worked as an industrial chemist. His first book, *Se questo è un uomo* (*If This Is a Man*), was published in 1947 and showed extraordinary qualities of humanity and detachment in its analysis of the atrocities he had witnessed. The same qualities were evident in his later works, from *La tregua* (1963; *The Truce*) to *I sommersi e i salvati* (1986; *The Drowned and the Saved*). More than once, he expressed the

importance he attached to science as a realm of verifiable truth and "purity" in an unclean world. Perhaps his greatest work, *Il sistema periodico* (1975; *The Periodic Table*), a collection of stories structured according to the table of elements, bridged the divide between the rival cultures of science and art. It won the Viareggio Prize and attracted universal praise. Levi also published poetry, science fiction, and essays. His death was apparently a suicide.

**Liang Shih-ch'iu,** Chinese scholar (b. Dec. 8, 1902, Peking, China—d. Nov. 3, 1987, Taipei, Taiwan), was an eminent writer, critic, and translator whose most ambitious work was the translation of all of Shakespeare's works into Chinese, a project he launched in 1931 and completed in 1967. Though Liang acquired his early education in China, he went to the U.S. and attended Colorado College. He went on to graduate study at Columbia University, New York City, and Harvard University, where he wrote "The Romantic Tendencies in Modern Chinese Literature." In this important paper he castigated what he viewed as romantic excesses in modern Chinese literature. An anti-Communist, he called for a literary emphasis on aesthetics rather than on propaganda and in 1927, together with Hu Shih and Hsü Chih-mo, founded *Hsin-yueh* ("Crescent Moon"), a literary journal that reflected this view. Liang also taught English literature at Peking University (1934–37) before moving to Taiwan when the Communists took control of the mainland in 1949. In addition, Liang made available to Chinese readers such works as Sir James Barrie's *Peter Pan,* Emily Brontë's *Wuthering Heights,* and the 12th-century love letters of the monk Abelard to Héloïse. He was the author of a complete history of English literature in Chinese and a two-volume definitive Chinese-English dictionary. At the time of his death he was working on an English-language history of Chinese literature. In Taiwan he headed the English department of National Taiwan Normal University until his retirement in 1967.

**Liberace** (Wladziu Valentino Liberace), U.S. entertainer (b. May 16, 1919, West Allis, Wis.—d. Feb. 4, 1987, Palm Springs, Calif.), became a multimillionaire and attracted huge audiences with his extravagant performances at the keyboard, which were matched by his glitzy rhinestone-studded jewelry, sequined costumes,

and elaborate candelabra. Liberace, who was best known as an excerpter of classical piano pieces, was a showman without equal. He began playing the piano at the age of four and later performed in nightclubs. After a 1939 concert he delighted the audience by playing "Three Little Fishies" as an encore and punctuated his performance with sly winks and smiles, which introduced what would be the formula for his success. During the 1950s he was host of his own television show and became a matinee idol. Though his foray into films was unremarkable, his concert circuit was unbelievably successful. For some 25 years he earned an average of $5 million annually. His elaborate wardrobe, including a cape that weighed more than 45 kg (100 lb), a fur worth some $60,000, a jacket trimmed with 24-karat gold braid, and a pink feathered ensemble, never failed to astonish and captivate audiences. Liberace sported rings on every finger, including one in the shape of a piano, and owned five homes, 20 cars, and 18 pianos. The "Casanova of the keyboard" made his last professional appearance in November 1986 at Radio City Music Hall in New York City. His death was attributed to AIDS (acquired immune deficiency syndrome).

**Locke, Bobby** (Arthur D'Arcy Locke), South African golfer (b. Nov. 20, 1917, Germiston, Transvaal, South Africa—d. March 9, 1987, Johannesburg, South Africa), during the course of his career won the British Open championship four times (1949, 1950, 1952, and 1957) and was open champion of South Africa (nine times), Ireland, New Zealand, Canada, France, West Germany, Switzerland, and Egypt. His first victory was at the age of 14 in the South African boys' championship; he went on to win the South African amateur and open championships in 1935 and 1937 and turned professional in 1938. During World War II Locke served as a pilot in the South African Air Force. He opened his postwar career by placing third in the 1947 U.S. Open. For the next decade he was recognized as one of the greatest golfers of his generation and one of the greatest putters of all time, his strength on the greens easily compensating for a relative weakness in his long shots. Following a car accident in 1960 he retired. Something of an eccentric, portly and immaculately—if unfashionably—dressed, Locke was one of the few professionals to be made an honorary member, in 1968, of the Royal and Ancient. He wrote *Bobby Locke on Golf* (1953).

**Lubell, Samuel,** Polish-born U.S. public opinion analyst (b. Nov. 3, 1911, Poland—d. Aug. 16, 1987, Los Angeles, Calif.), measured the political pulse of the nation by conducting door-to-door interviews in order to predict winning candidates in elections. Lubell had been a newspaper reporter with the *Long Island Daily Press* (1935–36) and later with the *Washington Herald* (1937–38). He launched his career as a pollster after World War II when *The Saturday Evening Post* asked him to analyze Pres. Harry S. Truman's surprise victory. In order to interpret public opinion, Lubell combined the statistical analysis of the social scientist with doorbell ringing in areas that had showed consistent trends but then dramatically reversed themselves. His technique proved highly successful during the 1950s and '60s. He was also a syndicated columnist and the author of six books, including *The Future of American Politics* (1952) and *The Hidden Crisis in American Politics* (1970).

**Luce, Clare Boothe,** U.S. playwright and public official (b. April 10, 1903, New York, N.Y.—d. Oct. 9, 1987, Washington, D.C.), possessed an irresistible charm, a quick wit, and a sharp intellect; she became one of the most influential women of her time and was regarded as America's first Renaissance woman, donning the mantle of editor, playwright, war correspondent, congresswoman, ambassador, and activist in the women's movement. She enjoyed immense success as the author of such well-received plays as *The Women* (1936), which featured an all-female cast and ran on Broadway for 657 performances; *Kiss the Boys Goodbye* (1938), a satire on American life; and *Margin for Error* (1939), an anti-Nazi comedy-melodrama. She was also a major force in the U.S. Republican Party as a member of the U.S. House of Representatives from Connecticut (1943–47) and as a campaigner for Dwight D. Eisenhower, who named her ambassador to Italy in 1953. Luce married (1923) and divorced (1929) George T. Brokaw. In 1930 she joined the staff of *Vogue* magazine. From 1933 to 1934 she served as managing editor of *Vanity Fair*, and in 1935 she married Henry R. Luce, founder of *Time, Fortune,* and *Life* magazines. For the latter publication, which she reputedly inspired her husband to found, she was a World War II war correspondent. After the death (1944) of her only daughter, Ann Brokaw, Luce withdrew from politics and embraced Roman Catholicism. In 1952 she made an unsuccessful bid for a seat in the U.S. Senate but gained a powerful appointment when she was named ambassador to Italy, only the second woman to serve as a U.S. ambassador and the first to be posted to a major European capital. She resigned in 1957 after she was poisoned by arsenic dust from her villa ceiling. When her husband died a decade later, she retired to Hawaii but returned to the political limelight in 1981 and was made a member of the president's Foreign Intelligence Advisory Board. Besides being awarded (1979) the Sylvanus Thayer Award, West Point's highest civilian honour, Luce received the Presidential Medal of Freedom from Pres. Ronald Reagan in 1983. Luce also served as a consultant to *Encyclopædia Britannica* from 1968 to 1971.

**Ludlam, Charles,** U.S. actor, director, and playwright (b. April 12, 1943, New York, N.Y.—d. May 28, 1987, New York), was an avant-garde performer who founded (1967) and then served as artistic director of the Ridiculous Theatrical Company, which scored successes with such parodies as *The Mystery of Irma Vep, The Artificial Jungle,* and *Camille*. Ludlam, who directed and starred in his own plays, was on the verge of breaking into the theatrical mainstream when he succumbed to pneumonia complicated by AIDS (acquired immune deficiency syndrome). His plays were characterized by cross-dressing, liberal use of the double entendre, comic exaggeration, puns, and clichés. Among those that won critical acclaim were *Bluebeard, The Ventriloquist's Wife,* and *Eunuchs of the Forbidden City.* In addition to performing in his own theatre, Ludlam starred in the title role in the American Ibsen Theater production of *Hedda Gabler* (1984), and he staged the U.S. premiere of *The English Cat* (1985), an opera by Hans Werner Henze.

**McLaren, Norman,** Scottish-born filmmaker (b. April 11, 1914, Stirling, Scotland—d. Jan. 26, 1987, Montreal, Que.), used his creative genius to direct compelling documentary films and unique animated shorts for Canada's National Film Board (NFB). He was internationally acclaimed for his experiments in animation, which yielded a treasure of innovative techniques. McLaren, who immigrated to Canada in 1941 to join John Grierson at the NFB, invented "pixillation," the animation of live images of actors and objects, which he implemented in *Neighbours* (1952), a political fable that decries the use of violence in resolving conflict. He won an Academy Award for the film. During his more than 40-year career with the NFB, he produced over 50 films, including *Alouette* (1944), *Begone Dull Care* (1949), *Blinkety Blank* (1955), *A Chairy Tale* (1957), *Lines Vertical* (1960), and *Lines Horizontal* (1962), in which he engraved directly onto 35-mm film with a penknife, a sewing needle, and a razor blade. McLaren, interested more in the technique and aesthetic aspects of filming, said, "The purpose of my films is to give the intellect a rest." He also experimented with painting directly

on film, cutout animation, three-dimensional animation, and the conversion of animated drawings into synthetic sound waves. Some of his most visually stunning films, featuring the beauty and harmony of movement, include *Pas de Deux* (1968), *Ballet Adagio* (1972), and *Narcissus* (1983). His techniques were recorded in John Halas and Roger Manvell's books *Design in Motion* (1962) and *Art in Movement* (1970), and his work was the subject of a 1971 BBC television documentary entitled "The Eye Hears, the Ear Sees."

**MacLean, Alistair,** British novelist (b. April 28, 1922, Glasgow, Scotland—d. Feb. 2, 1987, Munich, West Germany), was the author of some 29 works, almost all of them best-selling adventure novels. His first novel, *HMS Ulysses* (1955), was based on his experience in the Royal Navy during World War II; he served for five years on the dangerous North Sea convoys, then took a degree at Glasgow University and went into teaching. After winning a short-story competition, he was persuaded to write the novel by an editor at William Collins publishing house. An immediate best-seller, it was followed by another success, *The Guns of Navarone* (1957). These two works established the MacLean formula of fast-moving adventure in a largely masculine world and, like many of his subsequent novels, they were made into popular films. MacLean despised and was despised by the critics. In the 1950s he went to live in Geneva but returned to Britain for a few years in 1963 to run a chain of hotels. An introvert, he lived frugally despite his wealth and found it hard to settle, traveling around Europe and trying his hand at film production, a biography of *Captain Cook* (1972), and work for the British Cancer Council. MacLean continued to write thrillers, including *Ice Station Zebra* (1963), *Force 10 from Navarone* (1968), and *Breakheart Pass* (1974). He also wrote novels under the pseudonym Ian Stuart.

**McNamara, Kevin,** Roman Catholic primate of Ireland (b. June 10, 1926, Newmarket, Fergus, County Clare, Ireland—d. April 8, 1987, Dublin, Ireland), served as archbishop of Dublin from 1984. Already in failing health, conservative in his views, and totally opposed to divorce or family planning, he was apparently a papal nominee, promoted despite the existence of candidates more acceptable locally. Educated at St. Flannan's College, Ennis, McNamara studied for the priesthood at St. Patrick's College, Maynooth, and later at University College, Cork, and the University of Munich, West Germany. Professor of dogmatic theology at Maynooth (1954–76), he had no pastoral experience when he was appointed bishop of Kerry in 1976. He was a consultor to the Pontifical Council for the Family and to the Vatican Secretariat for Christian Unity. Despite his conservatism, he worked to establish good relations with other churches. He was author of a number of theological and devotional books.

**McNeill, Sir James Charles,** Australian businessman (b. July 29, 1916, Hamilton, New South Wales, Australia—d. March 12, 1987, Melbourne, Victoria, Australia), was managing director (1971–77) and chairman (1977–84) of Broken Hill Proprietary Co. Ltd. (BHP), the steel, minerals, and oil and gas company that was Australia's largest corporation. Educated at Newcastle High School, McNeill joined BHP's Newcastle steelworks as an office boy in 1933, beginning a 51-year association with the company. He became company accountant in 1947 and moved rapidly through the management ranks. BHP's acquisition of Utah International Inc. in 1984, negotiated during McNeill's chairmanship, represented a major stage in the company's development; in that same year he relinquished the chairmanship in accordance with the company's compulsory changeover rules. McNeill was knighted for services to industry in 1978 and was created a Companion of the Order of Australia in 1986.

**Mamoulian, Rouben,** Russian-born theatrical and motion-picture director (b. Oct. 8, 1897, Tbilisi, Georgia, Russia—d. Dec. 4, 1987, Los Angeles, Calif.), was a technical innovator who directed such benchmark Broadway musicals as *Porgy and Bess* (1935), *Oklahoma!* (1943), and *Carousel* (1945) and was equally gifted as a pioneering director of such early sound films as *Applause* (1929), *City Streets* (1931), and *Dr. Jekyll and Mr. Hyde* (1932). After studying law in Moscow, Mamoulian trained for the stage at the Moscow Art Theatre. In 1918 he established his own drama studio in Tbilisi, but two years later he moved to London, where he directed several his plays. In 1923 he immigrated to the U.S. and began a three-year appointment at the George Eastman Theatre in Rochester, N.Y. After only one year as a teacher and director with the Theatre Guild, Mamoulian moved to Broadway and beguiled audiences with *Porgy* (1927), a landmark folk drama with an all-black cast. In Mamoulian's first screen credit, *Applause*, he released the movie camera from the soundproof booth and effectively made use of light and shadow. For *Dr. Jekyll and Mr. Hyde* he employed a subjective, 360° revolving camera and created a stunning transformation of a man into a monster. Mamoulian reached the pinnacle of his inventiveness when he directed *Love Me Tonight* (1932), a musical screen comedy in which he ingeniously integrated musical numbers by Rodgers and Hart with a sophisticated and witty script. He skillfully directed Marlene Dietrich in *Song of Songs* (1933) and Greta Garbo in *Queen Christina* (1933). Mamoulian also directed the first three-colour Technicolor motion picture, *Becky Sharp* (1935). Some of his other film credits include *The Mark of Zorro* (1940), *Blood and Sand* (1941), *Summer Holiday* (1948), and *Silk Stockings* (1957).

**Manley, Edna Swithenbank,** Jamaican sculptor (b. Feb. 29, 1900, Bournemouth, England—d. Feb. 9, 1987, Kingston, Jamaica), was regarded as the national sculptor of Jamaica, where she had lived since 1922 with her husband, Norman Manley (d. 1969), leader of the People's National Party. She was the daughter of a Methodist missionary. Manley was educated at West Cornwall College and studied art at the Regent Street Polytechnic and St. Martin's School of Art, both in London. Her first work to receive notice in London was a life-size figure of Eve (now in Sheffield) carved in Jamaican hardwood; because of it she was elected a member of the London Group. She revisited London in 1937 and also exhibited in Germany, Guyana, Puerto Rico, Cuba, Haiti, Canada, and the U.S. In 1950 Manley founded the Jamaica School of Art. While her most famous works were executed in wood, after 1974 she turned to clay and fibreglass as sculpting media. Her "Negro Aroused" (1935) was bought for the Institute of Fine Arts, Kingston, by public subscription, and a later stone carving, "Woman with Basket," was acquired by the Dublin Municipal Gallery of Modern Art. There were major exhibitions of her work shown in 1980 in London and Jamaica.

**Marechera, Dambudzo,** Zimbabwean novelist (b. 1952, Rusape, Rhodesia [now Zimbabwe]—d. Aug. 18, 1987, Harare, Zimbabwe), won critical acclaim with his first novel, *The House of Hunger* (1978), a powerful account of life in his country under white rule. His second novel, *Black Sunlight* (1980), gave an equally critical account of Zimbabwe after independence and was banned by the authorities, allegedly because of its obscenity. The son of a truck driver, Marechera grew up in poverty. He reacted against his upbringing and adopted an increasingly self-destructive life-style. He studied at the University of Rhodesia but was expelled after a demonstration against the low salaries of black university domestic staff members. Marechera obtained a scholarship to New College, Oxford, but he was expelled in 1977 for trying to set fire to the college building. While living in London, he wrote *The House of Hunger;*

he left his mark on the British literary world by throwing plates at the awards ceremony at which he received the London *Guardian* Fiction Prize. There were other such incidents, leading to arrest in West Berlin and investigations by the Zimbabwean secret service. Marechera produced another novel, *Mindblast* (1984), which was not published outside his native Zimbabwe during his lifetime.

**Marvin, Lee,** U.S. actor (b. Feb. 19, 1924, New York, N.Y.—d. Aug. 29, 1987, Tucson, Ariz.), specialized in portraying motion-picture tough guys, notably in *The Man Who Shot Liberty Valance* (1962) and *The Dirty Dozen* (1967), and won an Academy Award as best actor for his dual role in *Cat Ballou* (1965) as a drunken gunfighter and his menacing twin brother. Marvin, whose granite-hewn features and cold stare lent substance to his roles, made his film debut in *You're in the Navy Now* (1951) but scored his first major success when he played a sergeant in *Eight Iron Men* (1952). His private life made headlines in 1979 when his live-in girlfriend of six years, Michelle Triola Marvin, sued him for $1.5 million in a landmark "palimony" suit that established the right of live-in companions to seek support. She was awarded $104,000 in the suit, but two years later a court of appeals reversed the decision. Marvin, who was ejected from a number of prep schools, joined the Marines as an enlisted man during World War II; he reportedly called upon his experiences in the corps for his characterizations of military officers. He appeared in more than 50 films, including *Donovan's Reef* (1963), *The Killers* (1964), *The Professionals* (1966), *Paint Your Wagon* (1969), and *The Iceman Cometh* (1973), and starred on television in "M Squad" (1957–60) and "Lawbreaker" (1963).

**Masson, André Aimé René,** French artist (b. Jan. 4, 1896, Balagny-sur-Thérain, Oise, France—d. Oct. 28?, 1987, Paris, France), was a member of the Surrealist group in the 1920s and a leading figure in contemporary French art. His work reflected many of the changing currents of his time. A close associate of many literary figures from the 1920s onward, he was also a prolific book illustrator and a designer of theatrical sets. Born in northern France, Masson lived as a child in Belgium, studying from the age of 11 at the Académie Royale des Beaux-Arts, Brussels. From 1912 he continued his studies in Paris and later in Italy until the outbreak of World War I; he fought in the war and in 1917 was seriously wounded. He was profoundly affected by his experiences; Masson's disillusionment with rational human behaviour was evidenced by a brutality that appears throughout his work. He met André Breton in 1923, and the following year Masson joined the Surrealist group, which continued to influence his painting even after he broke with Breton in 1929. Masson's association with the Surrealists led him to pro-

duce a series of automatic paintings, some using glue and sand on canvas and others involving squeezing the paint tubes directly onto the canvas. Largely as a result of his friendship with the writer Georges Bataille, Masson began to display a preoccupation with cruelty and eroticism in his works. Masson lived in Spain (1934–36) and in 1941 immigrated to the U.S., where he remained until 1945. Following his return to France, his work took on a less sombre tone. Living alternately in his homes in Paris and Provence, he painted landscapes and redecorated the ceiling of the Théâtre de l'Odéon in Paris. His work was the subject of several major retrospectives in France, in Basel, Switz. (1950), and in New York City at the Museum of Modern Art (1976). Masson was an Officer of the Legion of Honour.

**Medawar, Sir Peter Brian,** British scientist (b. Feb. 28, 1915, Rio de Janeiro, Brazil—d. Oct. 2, 1987, London, England), was co-winner with the Australian physician Sir Macfarlane Burnet of the 1960 Nobel Prize for Physiology or Medicine for the discovery of acquired immunologic tolerance. He was a dedicated biologist whose work made possible many developments

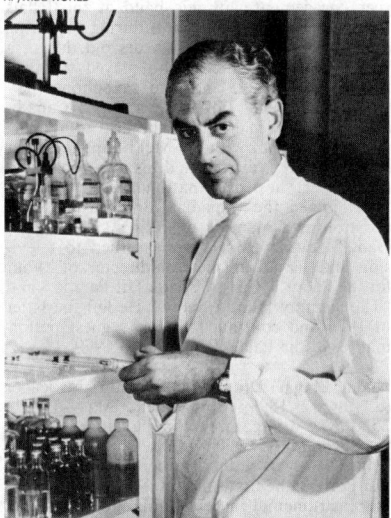

in the grafting of skin and the transplantation of organs. Educated at Marlborough College and at Magdalen College, Oxford, Medawar served as Mason professor of zoology at Birmingham University (1947–51), Jodrell professor of zoology and comparative anatomy at University College, London (1951–62), and director of the National Institute for Medical Research (1962–71). Although he suffered the first of a series of increasingly incapacitating strokes in 1969, he worked with the Medical Research Council's external scientific staff (1971–84) and at the Clinical Research Centre (1984–86). Medawar's work developed from studying the problems of skin-graft rejection in those suffering burns during World War II; he demonstrated that an organism's immune system is not innate but develops during embryonic life and that foreign cells introduced at that stage are not rejected. This discovery laid the foundation for contemporary research into autoimmune disease. A brilliant communicator, Medawar wrote a number of books, including *The Uniqueness of the Individual* (1957) and *Memoir of a Thinking Radish* (1986). He was knighted in 1965 and received the Order of Merit in 1981.

**Mikes, George,** Hungarian-born writer (b. Feb. 15, 1912, Siklos, Hung.—d. Aug. 30, 1987, London, England), satirized the British way of life in *How to Be an Alien* (1946), the first in a series of affectionate and penetrating analyses of national character. His British readers found more humour than he had intended in his portrait of

them and, supported by his illustrator Nicolas Bentley and his publisher André Deutsch, a fellow refugee from Hungary, he went on to explore the peculiarities of the Israelis, French, Italians, Swiss, Germans, Australians, and Japanese. He also wrote an account of the Hungarian revolution (1957) and published *A Study of Infamy* (1959), on the Hungarian secret police. Mikes began to work as a journalist while at Budapest University, where he studied law. In 1938 he was sent to London on a two-week assignment and decided to stay. He worked for the Hungarian Service of the British Broadcasting Corporation (1941–51) and was president of the writers' organization PEN in exile (1972–80). *How to Be Seventy* (1982) chronicled his life with characteristic good humour and detachment.

**Momigliano, Arnaldo Dante,** Italian historian (b. Sept. 5, 1908, Turin, Italy—d. Sept. 1, 1987, London, England), made an outstanding contribution to the study of ancient history and, in particular, to the understanding of how history is written. The son of a Piedmontese Jewish family, Momigliano studied at Turin University, where he wrote a remarkable dissertation on the historian Thucydides before taking a post to teach Greek history at the University of Rome. He went on to write biographies of the Roman emperor Claudius and Philip of Macedon, which established his reputation in England before his arrival there in 1939, a refugee from Fascism. He had been deprived of his professorship in 1938 under racist legislation, and both his parents died in concentration camps. He taught at the University of Bristol (1947–51) and at University College, London (1951–75). He was also professor at the Scuola Normale Superiore in Pisa, Italy, from 1964 until his death and visiting professor at the University of Chicago from 1975. From 1955 onward his name was particularly associated with a series of his collected papers published under the title *Contributi alla storia degli studi classici*, which dealt with Greek, Roman, and Jewish history. This work revealed his fascination with the way in which the cultural and social environment of a historian influences his approach to his work. His longer studies, including *The Conflict Between Paganism and Christianity in the Fourth Century* (1963) and *Alien Wisdom* (1975), made equally important contributions in their field.

**Moss, Howard,** U.S. poet and editor (b. Jan. 22, 1922, New York, N.Y.—d. Sept. 16, 1987, New York), was an influential man of letters who, as poetry editor of *The New Yorker* magazine for almost 40 years, showcased the works and helped establish the careers of such poets as Sylvia Plath, Richard Wilbur, and Elizabeth Bishop. Moss graduated from the University of Wisconsin in 1943 and published the first of his 12 volumes of poetry, *The Wound and the Weather*, in 1946. He joined the staff of *The New Yorker* in 1948 and demonstrated a capacity for choosing works of talented aspiring poets. His own poetry exhibited a technical virtuosity and a lucid, compressed style that sensitively focused on the "mysteries of the commonplace"; he won the National Book Award for poetry for his volume *Selected Poems* (1971). Moss also published such volumes of criticism as *The Magic Lantern of Marcel Proust* (1962) and *Writing Against Time: Critical Essays and Reviews* (1969). He was, in addition, an accomplished playwright; his *The Folding Green* (1958), *The Oedipus Mah-Jongg Scandal* (1968), and *The Palace at 4 A.M.* (1972) were all produced.

**Myrdal, (Karl) Gunnar,** Swedish economist (b. Dec. 6, 1898, Gustafs, Sweden—d. May 17, 1987, Stockholm, Sweden), shared the 1974 Nobel Prize for Economics with Friedrich A. Hayek of Austria. An outstanding figure in modern economic and social studies, Myrdal rejected the idea of economics as an exact science and was committed to the cause of social justice and the eradication of poverty. He was regarded as a major theorist of international economic relations and in particular of third world development policies, which he analyzed in a major work, *Asian Drama* (1968). Myrdal studied law in Stockholm before turning to economics and spending a year (1929–30) in the U.S. as a Rockefeller fellow. He was professor of political economy (1933–50) and of international economy (1960–67) at Stockholm University, where he remained as emeritus professor after 1967. In *The Political Element in the Development of Economic Theory* (1930), as in his later work *Monetary Equilibrium* (1939), he anticipated many of the ideas developed by John Maynard Keynes. Myrdal returned to the U.S. in 1938 to undertake a study for the Carnegie Corporation. The result was *An American Dilemma: The Negro Problem and Modern Democracy* (1944), in which he viewed racial discrimination as incompatible with American democratic ideals. Myrdal was a Social Democratic Party member of Parliament (1935–38 and 1944–47) and served as minister of trade and commerce (1945–47). He left domestic politics to become executive secretary of the UN Economic Commission for Europe (1947–57), and his *Economic Theory and Under-developed Regions* (1957) showed his increasing interest in third world development. His views were not always popular, but he remained convinced that government action was necessary if the evils of poverty and injustice were to be overcome. In 1924 he married Alva Reimer (d. 1986), who was awarded the Nobel Prize for Peace in 1982, and their joint work was recognized with the award of the West German Peace Prize in 1970. Myrdal was chairman of the Stockholm International Peace Research Institute (1967–73).

**Negri, Pola** (BARBARA APOLLONIA CHALUPIEC), Polish-born actress (b. Dec. 31, 1894?, Janowa?, Poland—d. Aug. 1, 1987, San Antonio, Texas), as a tempestuous, green-eyed, raven-haired siren of silent films, titillated audiences with her vampish on-screen roles and her torrid off-screen romances—now generally taken to have been publicity. After dancing with the Russian Imperial Ballet in Poland, she contracted tuberculosis at age 13; when she was cured, she turned to acting. She studied at a school of dramatic arts in Warsaw and became one of Poland's leading actresses by the time she was 17. Her first film, *Slave of Passion, Slave of Vice* (1914), was followed by success on the German stage in Max Reinhardt's *Sumurun* and in a series of Ernst Lubitsch-directed (German) films, the most notable being the German film *Madame DuBarry* (1919), which was released in the U.S. as *Passion* and won her a contract with Paramount studios. She began her Hollywood career with *Bella Donna* (1923) and *The Cheat* (1923). Among her better pictures were *Forbidden Paradise* (1924), *East of Suez* (1925), *Good and Naughty* (1926), *Hotel Imperial* (1927), and *Barbed Wire* (1927). The porcelain-skinned actress was thrice-married, but her most publicized affairs of the heart involved Charlie Chaplin and Rudolph Valentino. Negri, who was adept at interesting movie fans in her doings, often secluded herself from the public eye to ensure that her exoticism became even more intriguing to her admirers. She popularized such fashion fads as turbans, painted toenails, and high boots. After her first American talkie, *A Woman Commands* (1932), met an indifferent reception, she returned (1935) to Germany, where Adolf Hitler is said to have become enamoured of her talents. She reportedly had her German film on mother love, *Mazurka* (1935), run once a week. Near the beginning of World War II, she returned to the U.S. and played a featured comedy role in *Hi Diddle Diddle* (1943), but her popularity had waned and she found no work in films and lived in virtual seclusion until she attempted a last comeback in *The Moon-Spinners* (1964). Negri's autobiography, *Memoirs of a Star*, appeared in 1970.

**Nekrasov, Viktor Platonovich,** Soviet writer (b. June 17, 1911, Kiev, Russia—d. Sept. 3, 1987, Paris, France), won the Stalin Prize for Litera-

ture with his first novel, *V okopakh Stalingrada* (1947; *In the Trenches of Stalingrad,* 1975), but later became a leading dissident before leaving the U.S.S.R. in 1974 to settle in France. He was deprived of his Soviet citizenship in 1979. Nekrasov trained as an architect in Kiev and fought at the siege of Stalingrad, which provided the material for his novel. Despite the award, the novel was criticized for depicting the battle unheroically from the viewpoint of the ordinary soldier. His first serious brush with authority came in 1962 when *Both Sides of the Ocean,* a collection of essays giving his impressions of a visit to Europe and the U.S., aroused the anger of Soviet leader Nikita Khrushchev. In 1972 Nekrasov was expelled from the Writers' Union and from the Communist Party because of his public defense of Aleksandr Solzhenitsyn. From Paris, he edited the journal *Kontinent,* became a leading figure in dissident activities, and continued to write, publishing a volume of memoirs, *Notes of an Idler* (1976). His other works included short stories, journalism, and film scripts.

**Niosi, Bert,** Canadian bandleader (b. 1909, London, Ont.—d. Aug. 3, 1987, Mississauga, Ont.), as Canada's "King of Swing," enjoyed an 18-year engagement with his band at the Palais Royale, Toronto's dance hub during the swing era. When he was only 14 years old, Niosi, a versatile instrumentalist who played trumpet, trombone, clarinet, and alto saxophone, performed with Guy Lombardo's Royal Canadians; while still in his teens he also toured the vaudeville circuit with the McPhillips Buescher Boys. In 1931 Niosi formed his own nine-piece band, which he led on national radio. In 1952 Niosi joined the Canadian Broadcasting Corporation as a member of radio's "The Happy Gang." Seven years later he turned to television and served as musical director of "Four for the Show," "Cross-Canada Hit Parade," and "The Tommy Hunter Show." He left the latter in 1976 and continued to make guest performances at the Palais Royale until 1979.

**Nixon, E(dgar) D(aniel),** U.S. civil rights leader (b. July 12, 1899, Montgomery, Ala.—d. Feb. 25, 1987, Montgomery), was a pioneering activist who in the 1920s with A. Philip Randolph helped to organize the Brotherhood of Sleeping Car Porters, the first successful black union, and was instrumental in persuading the 26-year-old minister Martin Luther King, Jr., to lead the Montgomery bus boycott in 1955. After Rosa Parks, a black woman, was arrested for refusing to yield her bus seat to a white man, Nixon helped post bond for her and formed the Montgomery Improvement Association, which gave rise to the 381-day bus boycott. After Nixon retired as a Pullman porter, he directed a local public housing project. During World War II he established the first USO club for black soldiers, and in 1954 he was the first black since Reconstruction to run for political office in Montgomery County. From 1947 to 1951 he served as president of the Alabama chapter of the National Association for the Advancement of Colored People.

**Northrop, John Howard,** U.S. biochemist (b. July 5, 1891, Yonkers, N.Y.—d. May 27, 1987, Wickenberg, Ariz.), shared with James B. Sumner and Wendell M. Stanley the 1946 Nobel Prize for Chemistry for their work on the purification and crystallization of enzymes, which revealed how proteins aid in digestion, respiration, and general life processes. Their discoveries also later helped in the diagnosis of certain kinds of cancer, heart disease, and some types of leukemia and in the manufacture of antibiotics and detergents. Northrop, who earned a Ph.D. (1915) from Columbia University, New York City, served as a captain in the U.S. Army's Chemical Warfare Service during World War I. In this post he conducted research on fermentation processes that would make possible the industrial production of acetone and ethyl alcohol. In 1930 Northrop crystallized pepsin,

a digestive enzyme present in gastric juice, thus ending the controversy about the chemical nature of enzymes by proving that pepsin is a protein. He later isolated (1938) the first bacterial virus. Northrop, who joined the Rockefeller Institute for Medical Research in New York City as an assistant in 1916, later was a member there until his retirement in 1962, when he became professor emeritus. He also served as a visiting professor at the University of California at Berkeley (1949–58) and as a resident biophysicist at the Donner Lab there (1958–59). He was the author of *Crystalline Enzymes.*

**O'Boyle, Patrick Aloysius Cardinal,** U.S. prelate of the Roman Catholic Church (b. July 18, 1896, Scranton, Pa.—d. Aug. 10, 1987, Washington, D.C.), was the social-minded archbishop of Washington (1948–73) who in 1967 became its first cardinal. After he was ordained a priest in 1921 at St. Patrick's Cathedral in New York City, he undertook charitable and social work assignments. During the 1930s he taught at the Fordham University School of Social Service and became its assistant director. In 1947 he became director of the Catholic Charities of New York and in the following year was named the first archbishop of Washington, D.C., until then part of the diocese of Baltimore. His appointment was unusual in that he had never served as a bishop. O'Boyle, who was a longtime activist, desegregated Washington's churches and parochial schools several years prior to the 1954 Supreme Court ruling that prohibited school segregation. He championed racial integration, protested the living and working conditions of migrant farm workers, and opposed liturgical reform. He was known as a stickler on Catholic doctrine, however. A hard-liner on the use of birth control, he adamantly supported Pope Paul VI's encyclical *Humanae Vitae.* In 1968 he suspended from certain functions some 40 priests who refused to retract a statement that set forth the right of Catholics to follow their own conscience on birth control. O'Boyle retired in 1973.

**Page, Geraldine,** U.S. actress (b. Nov. 22, 1924, Kirksville, Mo.—d. June 13, 1987, New York, N.Y.), performed on both stage and screen but gained her greatest renown for the collection of unforgettable characters she created for Broadway and off-Broadway productions. She played, to critical acclaim, the sexually frustrated spinster Alma Winemiller in the 1952 revival of Tennessee Williams's *Summer and Smoke* and then starred as the idealistic, illiterate Lily in *MidSummer* (1953); as Marcelline, the wife of a homosexual in *The Immoralist* (1954); as Lizzy Curry in *The Rainmaker* (1954); and as Princess Kosmonopolis, the vengeful, decaying motion-picture star in *Sweet Bird of Youth* (1959). Page earned Academy Award nominations for her roles in the films *Hondo* (1953), *Summer and Smoke* (1961), *Sweet Bird of Youth* (1962), *You're a Big Boy Now* (1966), *Pete 'n' Tillie* (1972), *Interiors* (1978), and *The Pope of Greenwich Village* (1984); the honour seemed long overdue when in 1986 she finally won the Academy Award for best actress for her performance in *The Trip to Bountiful.* Some of her other notable stage credits include *Strange Interlude* (1963), *White Lies* and *Black Comedy* (1967), *Absurd Person Singular* (1974), *Clothes for a Summer Hotel* (1980), *Agnes of God* (1982), and *A Lie of the Mind* (1985). Page was also honoured with Emmy awards for her television performances in "A Christmas Memory" and "The Thanksgiving Visitor." At the time of her death, she was appearing on stage as the madcap medium in *Blithe Spirit,* and her last film, *My Little Girl,* had not yet been released.

**Perroux, François,** French economist (b. Dec. 19, 1903, Lyon, France—d. June 2, 1987, Paris, France), was particularly admired for his work on development economics and for a broad vision that encompassed economics, politics, and sociology. Educated at Lyon, he was professor at the University of Lyon (1928–37), at the University of Paris (1935–55), and at the Collège de France (from 1955). He founded the Institut de Science Économique Appliquée, Paris, in 1944. During the post-World War II period, Perroux became known as an advocate of the Marshall Plan and of a wider political role in the world for Europe. In *Economie et société* (1960) he argued that an essential part of an economy was what he described as "solidarity" or "human costs," including the satisfaction of cultural and other needs. Enlarging on this with particular reference to third world countries, he insisted on the distinction between growth and development and on the need for the latter to arise from within a particular society and culture. In later books Perroux analyzed the causes of the economic crises of the 1970s and the relationship between political power and economics. Though little of his work was translated into English, he was an able linguist who taught at many leading economic institutions outside France and received honorary doctorates from some 15 foreign universities. Perroux was a Commander of the Legion of Honour.

**Persichetti, Vincent,** U.S. composer and educator (b. June 6, 1915, Philadelphia, Pa.—d. Aug. 14, 1987, Philadelphia), enjoyed a fruitful dual career as a prolific composer of more than 150 works, including nine symphonies, and an instructor (1947–63), chairman of the composition department (1963–70), and chairman of the literature and materials department (1970–87) at the Juilliard School, New York City. A child prodigy, he entered the Combs Conservatory in Philadelphia at the age of 5 and began composing at the age of 11. Persichetti studied piano under Olga Samaroff and conducting under the tutelage of Fritz Reiner at the Curtis Institute of Music. A musical virtuoso, Persichetti created chamber works for various combinations of instruments, more than a dozen sonatas for piano and harpsichord, choral works, music for chorus and for wind band, and an opera, *The Sibyl,* based on the fable of Chicken Little. His works came to public attention when the Philadelphia Orchestra, under the baton of Eugene Ormandy, began performing them, notably the *Fables* in 1945 and Symphony No. 3 in 1947. Persichetti also wrote the monograph *William Schuman* (1954; with Flora R. Schreiber) and *Twentieth-Century Harmony* (1961).

**Plaza Lasso, Galo,** Ecuadoran politician (b. Feb. 17, 1906, New York, N.Y.—d. Jan 28, 1987, Quito, Ecuador), as president of the country (1948–52) and secretary-general (1968–75) of the Organization of American States (OAS), brought a voice of moderation to these offices. Plaza, the son of Gen. Leonidas Plaza Gutiérrez, who was twice president of Ecuador, was educated at the University of California at Berkeley, the University of Maryland, and later at the Georgetown University School of Foreign Service, Washington, D.C. He served as a senator and as minister of defense before being elected president. Plaza was widely regarded as one of the country's most esteemed diplomats, and he undertook highly successful missions for the UN as an observer and mediator in such charged areas as the Congo (now Zaire), Cyprus, and Lebanon. During his tenure as secretary-general of the OAS, he traveled to member countries (with the exception of Cuba) to reacquaint himself with the needs of each. In later years he was widely respected as an elder statesman and appeared frequently on television and radio.

**Plimsoll, Sir James,** Australian diplomat (b. April 25, 1917, Sydney, New South Wales, Australia—d. May 8, 1987, Hobart, Tasmania, Australia), won international acclaim for his diplomatic skills while serving as the Australian representative on the UN Commission for the Unification and Rehabilitation of Korea (1950–52). He was Australia's permanent representative at the UN (1959–63). Born into the family that had produced the noted Victorian who developed the Plimsoll line, the internationally agreed-upon reference line marking the loading limit for cargo ships, Plimsoll was educated at Sydney High School and at the University of Sydney. He worked in the economics department of the Bank of New South Wales, Sydney, before serving (1942–47) in the Australian Army. Plimsoll returned to Australia in 1953 and was assistant secretary (1953–59) and later secretary (1965–70) at the Department of External Affairs in Canberra. He held such important posts as ambassador to the U.S. (1970–74), the U.S.S.R. and Mongolia (1974–77), and Japan (1981–82) and was Australia's high commissioner in India (1963–65) and the U.K. (1980–81). He became governor of Tasmania in 1982. Plimsoll was knighted in 1962 and was made a Companion of the Order of Australia in 1978.

**Preston, Robert** (ROBERT PRESTON MESERVEY), U.S. actor (b. June 8, 1918, Newton Highlands, Mass.—d. March 21, 1987, Santa Barbara, Calif.), earned a Tony award as the fast-talking Professor Harold Hill, a con man who abandons his scam—selling band instruments in small Midwestern (U.S.) towns—after losing his heart to the River City, Iowa, librarian, in the Broadway smash hit *The Music Man* (1957). Preston, who studied at the theatre school of the Pasadena (Calif.) Community Playhouse, was a durable Hollywood actor who specialized in unsympathetic roles. His early films include *Union Pacific* and *Beau Geste* (both 1939), *North West Mounted Police* (1940), *Reap the Wild Wind* (1942), and *The Macomber Affair* (1947). Between the making of the latter two films, he served in the U.S. Army Air Forces. Then his flair for comedy came to the fore in such Broadway productions as *The Male Animal* (1952), *The Tender Trap* (1954), and *Janus* (1955). He made his musical debut in *The Music Man,* in which a virtuoso performance was highlighted by his renditions of the songs "Trouble," "Seventy-six Trombones," and "Till There Was You." His success in that role assured him of the lead in the 1962 film version of the play. Some of his other Broadway credits include *Ben Franklin in Paris* (1964); *The Lion in Winter* (1966); *I Do! I Do!* (1966), for which he garnered another Tony award; and *Mack and Mabel* (1974). Among his final screen roles were those in *S.O.B.* (1981), *Victor Victoria* (1982), and *The Last Starfighter* (1984).

**Raikin, Arkady Isaakovich,** Soviet comedian (b. Oct. 24, 1911, Riga, Latvia—d. Dec. 19–20, 1987, Moscow, U.S.S.R.), remained a favourite of Soviet leaders from Stalin onward, despite his satires on Soviet political life and bureaucracy. Denounced by some as merely an official "court jester," he enjoyed acceptance even during the grimmest periods of repression, when his humour may have served as a safety valve for the system. He trained as an actor in Leningrad and in 1939 founded his own theatre to perform homilies and satirical skits he called miniatures. His political satire evolved around a cast of typical characters: drunkards, bureaucrats, and others, whom he evoked with an extraordinary gift for minute observation of speech and behaviour. Like some of his characters, he proved able to survive despite his Jewish origin and skepticism about the regime. He performed for the troops during World War II and after the war, as his popularity increased, traveled abroad with his company, notably to the U.K. in 1964 and to the U.S. for the last time in 1987. He was named People's Artist of the U.S.S.R. in 1968, and his other decorations included that of Hero of Socialist Labour.

**Ramachandran, Maruthur Gopalan** ("MGR"), Indian film star and politician (b. Jan. 17, 1917, Kandy, Ceylon—d. Dec. 24, 1987), dominated the cinema in India in his early career and became a key figure in Indian politics. He never lost his star appeal and commanded the kind of adulation normally associated only with much younger stars. MGR, as Ramachandran was known, received little education. He went to India as a child following the death of his father and, with the Madurai Original Boy's Drama Company, toured India for several years. His first major film role was in 1945, when he starred in *Rajakumari*. He became heavily involved in politics in the 1950s and built up support through his fan clubs. Throughout his life he campaigned for the rights of Tamils, and in the 1980s he was closely identified with the Tamil separatist movement in Sri Lanka. In 1972 MGR founded the All-India Anna Dravida Munnetra Kazhagam Party, which promoted the Tamil cause. As chief minister (1977–87) of Tamil Nadu, he introduced some highly controversial populist tactics, including a relaxation of the prohibition laws on alcohol in 1980 and the introduction of free meals for over eight million children and pensioners in 1982.

**Rama Rau, Lady Dhanvanthi,** Indian social worker (b. May 10, 1893, Hubli, India—d. July 19, 1987, Bombay, India), was a pioneer of family planning and of the struggle for women's rights during a time when both were unpopular causes in her native country. She studied at the University of Madras and was assistant professor at Queen Mary's College, Madras (1917–19). In 1917 she joined the Women's Indian Association and dedicated herself to working for health education and services in rural areas, to improving women's education, and to the abolition of child marriage. She later concentrated her efforts on liberating Indian women from the tyranny of unplanned pregnancies, providing advice and contraceptives to rural families. She was founder of the Family Planning Association of India in 1949 and was also president of the All-India Women's Conference. She and Margaret Sanger were named copresidents of the International Planned Parenthood Federation at its founding in 1952, and Lady Rama Rau served as its president (1963–69) and as president emeritus until her death. Married to Sir Benegal Rama Rau, Indian ambassador to the U.S. (1948–49), she was active on many international bodies, including the International Council of Women and the International Alliance of Women for Suffrage and Equal Citizenship. Her memoirs, *An Inheritance,* written with her daughter Santha Rama Rau, were published in 1977.

**Rich, Buddy** (BERNARD RICH), U.S. drummer (b. June 30, 1917, New York, N.Y.—d. April 2, 1987, Los Angeles, Calif.), was a phenomenal jazz technician whose virtuoso drumming, accuracy, and rapid tempo made him a legend in his own time. Rich made his professional debut as a drummer in his parents' vaudeville act, "Wilson and Rich," when he was 18 months old. By the time he was four years old, he had made his Broadway debut as "Baby Traps

the Drum Wonder." A self-taught prodigy, he toured Australia for 18 months when he was 6 years old, and by the time he was 15, he was the second-highest-paid child performer of the 1930s (Jackie Coogan was first). He played with bands fronted by Joe Marsala, Bunny Berigan, Benny Carter, and Artie Shaw in the 1930s, and from 1939 to 1942 he appeared with Tommy Dorsey. After World War II he formed his own band and also toured with the Jazz at the Philharmonic troupe. During the late 1950s and early 1960s, he performed with the band led by trumpeter Harry James. In 1966 he organized another big band, which won national acclaim and became popular on the college concert circuit. Two years later Rich filed for bankruptcy, and in 1970 the Internal Revenue Service sold his house and furnishings to pay his 1961 tax bill. The temperamental Rich dissolved the band in 1974 to open his own Manhattan club, Buddy's Place.

**Robinson, Sir David,** British businessman and philanthropist (b. April 13, 1904, Cambridge, England—d. Jan. 10, 1987, Newmarket, England), made a fortune from television rentals and became a leading racehorse owner who donated much of his enormous wealth to charities and benefactions, including the University of Cambridge college that bears his name. Robinson started in business in 1930 selling bicycles and later sold motorcycles and electrical goods. At the time of the coronation of Queen Elizabeth II in 1953, impressed by the television audience for the event, he anticipated rapid growth in the market by opening a rental business for television sets. When he sold the business in 1968, it was worth more than £8 million. After selling his business, Robinson, a racehorse owner since the 1940s, devoted himself almost entirely to the sport, becoming one of the most successful owners in British racing history. During the period 1960–75 he owned 997 winners. Robinson made substantial donations to the town of Bedford, Papworth Hospital, and Mill Road Maternity Hospital, Cambridge; he also contributed to the fund for the replacement of the lifeboat at Penlee, Cornwall, which had been lost with its entire crew in 1981. His charitable work became widely known only when he donated £17 million to found Robinson College, Cambridge. The decision to name it after him was not his own, and he did not appear in public for its opening by the queen in 1981. His benevolent work was recognized with a knighthood (1985), but he was a shy man who shunned and generally managed to avoid publicity.

**Roca, Blas** (FRANCISCO CALDERÍO), Cuban government official (b. July 24, 1908, Manzanillo, Cuba—d. April 25, 1987, Havana, Cuba), played a leading role as a prominent theoretician of the Cuban revolution and as head of Cuba's clandestine prerevolutionary Communist Party. Roca, a cobbler by trade, became an organizer with the Cuban Shoe Workers' Union (1929–30). When he joined the Communist Party in 1929, he adopted the name Roca, which means "rock." During the 1930s he was imprisoned three times for antigovernment activities, but he later served 12 years in the Cuban legislature. When Gen. Fulgencio Batista was elected president in 1940, Roca and the party supported him. When Batista returned to power, however, in a 1952 military coup, Roca joined with Fidel Castro and others to oust him. Roca later became influential in the evolution of the ruling political party, which emerged as the Communist Party of Cuba in 1965. He served as editor of the official party newspaper and was a member of the ruling directorate. From 1976 to 1981 he served as president of the National Assembly of People's Power. He was the author of *Los Fundamentos del Socialismo en Cuba* (1960; Eng. trans., 1962).

**Rogers, Carl Ransom,** U.S. psychologist (b. Jan. 8, 1902, Oak Park, Ill.—d. Feb. 4, 1987, La Jolla, Calif.), was a pioneer in the development of humanistic psychology, which broke with the

behaviourist and psychoanalytic approaches to psychotherapy and instead focused on the concept of the self and the individual's perception of the world according to his or her own experiences. Rogers stressed that in the development of a personality, an individual strives for "self-actualization (to become oneself), self-maintenance (to keep on being oneself), and self-enhancement (to transcend the status quo)." His influential client-centred approach emphasized the role of the patient, referred to as the client, who actively participates in therapy by determining the course, speed, and duration of treatment. Rogers was also influential in the development of encounter groups in the 1960s. While completing his Ph.D. studies at Teachers College of Columbia University, New York City, he engaged in child study at the Society for the Prevention of Cruelty to Children in Rochester, N.Y. He became director of the agency in 1930 and the following year earned his Ph.D. From 1935 to 1940 he was lecturer at the University of Rochester, and in 1939 he wrote *The Clinical Treatment of the Problem Child.* As professor of psychology at Ohio State University (1940–45), he created a stir with his article "Newer Concepts of Psychotherapy" (1940), which introduced his theory. He expanded on his approach in *Counseling and Psychotherapy* (1942) by suggesting that a trusting relationship between a therapist and client can help resolve difficulties and help the client gain the insight necessary for restructuring his or her life. From 1945 to 1957 he served as a professor at the University of Chicago, where he founded a counseling centre and conducted studies to determine the effectiveness of his therapy. He then joined (1957) the faculty of the University of Wisconsin. In 1961 he wrote his most popular book, *On Becoming a Person,* which became a bible for the humanistic psychology movement. In 1963 he left the university to help found the Center for Studies of the Person in La Jolla, Calif., where he spent the remainder of his professional career. Some of his other books include *Freedom to Learn* (1969), *Personal Power* (1977), and *A Way of Being* (1980).

**Rowan, Dan,** U.S. comedian (b. July 22, 1922, Beggs, Okla.—d. Sept. 22, 1987, Englewood, Fla.), was the straight man in the comedy team of Rowan and (Dick) Martin and served as the cohost of the smash hit television variety show "Rowan & Martin's Laugh-In" (1968–73), an irreverent weekly hour that featured zany antics and routines by regulars Lily Tomlin (as a nasal-voiced telephone operator), Arte Johnson (as a German soldier), Ruth Buzzi (as a frump protecting her virtue), and Goldie Hawn (as a giggling dumb blond). The show, the number one program on the air for its first two full seasons (1968–70), relied on sight gags; a frenetic pace; cameo appearances by such celebrities as Richard M. Nixon, Billy Graham, and Douglas Fairbanks, Jr.; and such catchphrases as "Sock it to me," "You bet your bippy," and "Here come de judge." Rowan toured the nightclub circuit with Martin for a decade before the two became a sensation with their television program, which ended its run when most of its best talent left the show.

**Rustin, Bayard,** U.S. civil rights activist (b. March 17, 1910, West Chester, Pa.—d. Aug. 24, 1987, New York, N.Y.), was a prime mover in the civil rights movement as the adept organizer of the first Freedom Ride (1947; then called a Journey of Reconciliation) and the historic 1963 March on Washington for Jobs and Freedom. A Quaker and a pacifist, Rustin spent 28 months in prison for refusing to serve in the military during World War II. He was imprisoned more than 20 times for his pacifist and civil rights activities. Rustin, who studied at various universities, joined the Young Communist League during the late 1930s but later became disenchanted with the organization's tendencies toward war and discrimination and resigned in 1941. In the same year, he served as a field sec-

retary for the Congress of Racial Equality and criticized A. Philip Randolph, a founder of the modern-day civil rights movement, for canceling a proposed march on Washington. Rustin, who became less militant and adopted a belief in "social dislocation and creative trouble," later became one of Randolph's most fervent supporters. Because Rustin also embraced Jewish, labour, and white liberal causes, he never gained a strong power base among blacks, and in later years he alienated young blacks when he opposed job and college admission quotas. He served (1941–53) as race relations director of the Fellowship of Reconciliation, a group devoted to solving world problems nonviolently, and from 1953 to 1955 he was executive director of the War Resisters League. From 1955 to 1960 he assisted the Rev. Martin Luther King, Jr., and organized several large civil rights demonstrations, among them the 1963 March on Washington. For many years he served as president of the A. Philip Randolph Institute, New York City, and at the time of his death he was cochairman of the institute with Leon Lynch.

**Salas, Rafael Montinola,** Philippine government official and diplomat (b. Aug. 7, 1928, Bago City, Phil.—d. March 4, 1987, Washington, D.C.), as executive director from 1969 of the United Nations Fund for Population Activities, supervised the development of the agency from a small body with a $2.5 million budget to one of the most influential of the UN agencies, spending $150 million a year on collecting and analyzing demographic information, promoting population programs, and providing information on family planning and child health care to less developed countries. Salas, who earned a law degree from the University of the Philippines in 1953, later obtained a master's degree in public administration from Harvard University. In his native country he served (1955–66) as professor of law and economics at the University of the Philippines while concurrently holding the governmental post of executive director of the National Economic Council (1955–61) and functioning as general manager (1963–66) of the *Manila Chronicle.* From 1966 to 1969 he was second in authority to Pres. Ferdinand E. Marcos with the post of executive secretary of the Philippines. He was credited with fostering a "green revolution" in his country while serving (1967–69) as national coordinator of the Philippine National Rice and Corn Sufficiency Program; the country became a rice-sufficient nation under his initiative. In 1969, disenchanted with Marcos's policies, Salas accepted the UN population post and was hailed for transforming family planning into an accepted field of developmental science.

**Sankara, Thomas,** Burkinabe politician and army officer (b. Dec. 21, 1949, Upper Volta—d. Oct. 15?, 1987, Ouagadougou, Burkina Faso), as his country's sixth head of state since independence (1960), held power from Aug. 4, 1983, until his ouster Oct. 15, 1987, in a military coup led by Capt. Blaise Compaoré (*see* BIOGRAPHIES). Sankara and 12 of his aides who had been executed were buried the following day. Sankara was responsible for changing Upper Volta's name to Burkina Faso ("land of the upright people") and made a serious effort to reduce official extravagance and corruption. He had received officer training in Madagascar and first became well known during a border war with Mali in 1974. Sankara served briefly as secretary of state for information under Col. Saye Zerbo in 1981 and was premier (Jan. 10–May 17, 1983) under Maj. Jean-Baptiste Ouedraogo before being dismissed and briefly imprisoned. A captain of paratroopers, Sankara overthrew Ouedraogo and set up a National Revolutionary Council and a predominantly civilian government. He aimed to make his country agriculturally self-sufficient and to improve public health and the position of women. He improved relations with France, which was important for Burkina Faso's economic viability. One of the third world's more charismatic leaders, Sankara was a gifted crowd pleaser and an expert performer on the electric guitar. He based his political style on that of Jerry John Rawlings, chairman of the Provisional National Defense Council government in Ghana, and had hoped to establish a political union with that country.

**Schidlof, Peter,** British musician (b. July 9, 1922, Vienna, Austria—d. Aug. 16, 1987, Sunderland, near Bassenthwaite, Cumbria, England), was the virtuoso viola player in the world-famous Amadeus Quartet. Because he was of Jewish parentage, he was sent to England in 1938 at the time of the Anschluss with Nazi Germany (his parents were subsequently exterminated); he attended Blundell's School at Tiverton, Devon. While interned (1940–41) he met Norbert Brainin (later leader of the Amadeus Quartet) and Siegmund Nissel (who became the second violin player). He became a pupil of Max Rostal, who persuaded him to change from violin to viola. With the cellist Martin Lovett, the group gave concerts as the Brainin Quartet before their first performance as the Amadeus Quartet at the Wigmore Hall, London, in January 1948. Known to students as "eagle ears," Schidlof also performed as a soloist. Noted for producing a warm, rich tone, he was regarded as irreplaceable, and his death caused the Amadeus Quartet to disband.

**Scott, Randolph** (RANDOLPH CRANE), U.S. actor (b. Jan. 23, 1898?, Orange County, Va.— d. March 2, 1987, Los Angeles, Calif.), was a durable and versatile leading man who was best known as the quiet-spoken, quick-drawing cowboy in dozens of B western films. Scott, who served in the military during World War I, studied engineering but embarked on an acting career in films in 1929. In the mid-1930s he became a leading man, appearing in such films as *The Last Round-up* (1934), *She* (1935), *The Last of the Mohicans* (1936), and *High, Wide and Handsome* (1937). He appeared in the musicals *Roberta* (1935) and *Follow the Fleet* (1936), in the comedy *My Favorite Wife* (1940), and in such war films as *Corvette K-225*, *Bombardier*, *Gung Ho!* (all three in 1943), and *China Sky* (1945). Scott's gunslinging persona was on view in such westerns as *Virginia City* (1940), *Belle Starr* (1941), *Abilene Town* (1946), *Colt .45* (1950), and *Sugarfoot* (1951). The latter two became successful television series. It was as an aging cowboy, however, that he made his most important contribution to the western genre; between 1956 and 1960 he brought a new dimension to his character when he starred in seven westerns made by Budd Boetticher, notably *Seven Men from Now* (1956) and *The Tall T* (1957). From 1950 to 1953 Scott was one of Hollywood's top ten box-office draws. In his last film, *Ride the High Country* (1962), Scott portrayed the veteran gunman Gil Westrum, giving what many considered his best performance.

**Segovia, Andrés,** Spanish guitarist (b. Feb. 21, 1893?, Linares, Andalusia, Spain—d. June 2, 1987, Madrid, Spain), was responsible for restoring the acoustic guitar to prominence in classical music from its lowly status as a tavern instrument by using it to play a wide repertoire of music and thus securing it a place on the concert stage. He also accomplished his other ambition: to establish proper teaching of the guitar in musical conservatories and academies. Segovia was self-taught and took up the instrument against opposition from his parents, who felt that his talent would be wasted on it. In 1909 he made his debut, beginning a career that lasted nearly 80 years. He undertook his first international tour in 1919, and five years later he triumphed in Paris. From that time, Segovia came gradually to be recognized as the outstanding modern exponent of the instrument and as a master of guitar technique who had greatly extended its potential. He transcribed classical works for the guitar, persuaded contemporary composers to write for the instrument, played throughout the world, gave lessons and master classes, and made recordings. On the outbreak

RICHARD OPEN—CAMERA PRESS/PHOTO TRENDS

of the Spanish Civil War in 1936, Segovia left Spain to live in Italy and South America and was later based in New York City and Switzerland, returning often and finally permanently to his native Spain. Among the composers influenced by him to write for the guitar were Manuel de Falla, Heitor Villa-Lobos, Francis Poulenc, Benjamin Britten, Manuel Ponce, and Paul Hindemith. He was a major influence on modern guitarists, notably John Williams and Julian Bream. In 1981 Segovia was given the title of marquis of Salobreña by King Juan Carlos of Spain. He was awarded the Grand Cross of Isabel la Católica, the Royal Philharmonic Society Gold Medal, the Japanese Order of the Rising Sun, and the Grand Cross of the Order of Merit of the Italian Republic.

**Silkin, John Ernest,** British politician (b. March 18, 1923, London, England—d. April 26, 1987, London), served as chief whip (1966–69) and as minister of agriculture (1976–79) in Labour Party governments. Silkin studied at the University of Wales, was a lieutenant in the Royal Navy during World War II, and read law at Trinity Hall, Cambridge, before embarking on a career as a solicitor. He was elected to Parliament in 1963 and, though considered a left-winger, was appointed junior whip the following year. He also held office as minister of public buildings and works (1969–70) and minister for planning and local government (1974–76). As minister of agriculture he was noted for his opposition to British membership in the European Communities and fought the hardest battles of his career on this issue. Following the Labour defeat in 1979 and the subsequent resignation of James Callaghan as party leader, Silkin stood unsuccessfully in contests for the party leadership (1980) and deputy leadership (1981). In opposition he held several important posts, including shadow spokesman on defense (1981–84). He was president of Parliamentarians for World Order (1983–84). Under pressure from "hard left" elements in his Deptford constituency, Silkin had decided some time before his death not to stand for Parliament again.

**Singh, (Chaudhuri) Charan,** Indian politician (b. Dec. 23, 1902, Noorpur, Meerut District, United Provinces, India—d. May 29, 1987, New Delhi, India), was champion of the peasant masses and served as prime minister during the final months (July 1979–January 1980) preceding Indira Gandhi's return to power. Singh studied law at Agra University and from 1929 supported Congress Party agitation for independence; he was several times imprisoned by the British. He was elected to the state assembly

of the United Provinces (later Uttar Pradesh) in 1937, held various state ministerial offices (1951–67), and was chief minister (1967–68 and February–October 1970). With other federal opposition leaders, he was imprisoned (1975–76) following Gandhi's declaration of a state of emergency. In 1977 his Bharatiya Kranti Dal merged with others to form the Janata Party, and after Gandhi's electoral defeat in March 1977, he served under Prime Minister Morarji Desai as home minister (1977–78). In this capacity he decided to arrest Gandhi on charges of corruption; he was also finance minister and deputy prime minister (January–July 1979). Following the split in the Janata Party, Singh assumed the premiership with Congress Party backing. This was quickly withdrawn, however, and his administration was rendered powerless. His party (from 1980 renamed Lok Dal) fell into disarray after Singh suffered an incapacitating stroke in 1985.

**Skardon, (William) James,** British counterintelligence officer (b. March 15, 1904, London, England—d. March 9, 1987, Torquay, Devon, England), worked for the British intelligence agency MI-5 during World War II and permanently from 1947 until his retirement in the late 1960s. He played a leading part in all the notable counterespionage cases during that time. It was alleged that the Soviet agent Kim Philby (whose cover he, nevertheless, failed to break before Philby defected to the U.S.S.R.) regarded Skardon, a skilled interrogator, as the official he most feared. Skardon joined the police in 1925 and was seconded from the Criminal Investigation Department of the Metropolitan Police to MI-5 in 1940. Commissioned in the Intelligence Corps in 1944, he was later responsible for the conviction of the British traitor William Joyce ("Lord Haw-Haw"). He again worked briefly for the Metropolitan Police (1946–47). As an official in MI-5 he was concerned mainly with counterespionage in nuclear research establishments. In 1949–50 Skardon successfully interrogated the Harwell nuclear scientist Klaus Fuchs; he was also largely responsible for the destruction in 1960 of the so-called Portland spy ring, bringing to trial and sentence the spy Gordon Lonsdale (Konon Trofimovich Molody) and his associates, the Krogers. The Soviet agents Donald Maclean and Guy Burgess defected to the U.S.S.R. in 1951 before Skardon could interrogate them.

**Snedden, Sir Billy Mackie,** Australian politician (b. Dec. 31, 1926, Perth, Australia—d. June 27, 1987, Sydney, Australia), was an outstandingly successful speaker (1976–83) of the House of Representatives. As leader of the Liberal Party in opposition from December 1972, Snedden had proved insufficiently combative to counter Labor Party Prime Minister Gough Whitlam effectively; Snedden was ousted as party leader by the more abrasive Malcolm Fraser in March 1975. The son of a Scottish immigrant stonemason, Snedden left school in Perth at the age of 15. After serving in the Army during World War II, he studied law at the University of Western Australia under a serviceman's grant. He was admitted a barrister of the Supreme Court of Western Australia (1951) and to the Victorian bar (1955). A member of Parliament for the Melbourne constituency of Bruce (1955–83), Snedden was attorney general (1963–66) under Sir Robert Menzies and served successive Liberal-Country Party prime ministers as minister for immigration (1966–69), minister for labour and national service (1969–71), treasurer (1971–73), and leader of the House (1966–71). Snedden was knighted in 1978.

**Soames, (Arthur) Christopher John Soames,** BARON, British politician and diplomat (b. Oct. 12, 1920, Sheffield Park, East Sussex, England— d. Sept. 16, 1987, North Warnborough, Hampshire, England), was a genial yet astute old-style Tory whose greatest achievements were as ambassador to Paris (1968–72) and as the last governor of Rhodesia (1979–80), where he ended a bitter civil war and presided over the first elections for an independent Zimbabwe. During the period 1973–77 he was a vice-president of the Commission of the European Communities (EC). Educated at Eton College and the Royal Military College, Sandhurst, Soames served with the Coldstream Guards in North Africa. Member of Parliament for Bedford (1950–66), he was parliamentary private secretary (1952–55) to his father-in-law, Sir Winston Churchill (Soames had married Mary Churchill in 1947) and perhaps came closest to real power in Britain during the summer of 1953 when, unknown to the public, the prime minister was incapacitated by a stroke. Soames was minister of agriculture (1960–64) in Harold Macmillan's Cabinet. The Labour government sent him to Paris in 1968 to work toward Britain's entry into the EC. Created a baron in 1978, Soames was leader of the House of Lords (1979–81); soon, however, he became one of the first of a long line of traditional Tories who found themselves in conflict with the Thatcherite style of government.

**Stanford-Tuck, Robert Roland,** British fighter pilot (b. July 1, 1916, London, England—d. May 5, 1987, Sandwich, Kent, England), was one of the highest-scoring fighter pilots in the Battle of Britain, having taken over the leadership of 257 (Hurricane) Squadron at the height of the battle in 1940. After leaving school, Stanford-Tuck served with the merchant navy before joining the Royal Air Force (RAF) in 1935 and getting his wings the following year. When World War II broke out, he was with 92 (Spitfire) Squadron and brought down eight enemy aircraft over Dunkirk. He then moved to 257 Squadron and built up its morale to make it a powerful force in the Battle of Britain. He went on to become wing commander flying at RAF Biggin Hill. Aggressive and apparently fearless, he acquired a reputation equaled only by a select number among "the few," winning the Distinguished Service Order, the Distinguished Flying Cross (DFC) three times, and the American DFC. Stanford-Tuck was forced to bail out several times during operations and was captured in 1942 after crash-landing in occupied territory. He eventually escaped in 1945, on his third attempt. From his return to England in 1945 until his retirement in 1949, he continued to serve with Fighter Command. A biography of Stanford-Tuck, *Fly for Your Life,* was published in 1956.

**Stewart, Michael,** U.S. musical-book writer (b. Aug. 1, 1924, New York, N.Y.—d. Sept. 20, 1987, New York), garnered Tony awards as the author of such smash hit Broadway musicals as *Bye Bye Birdie* (1960) and *Hello, Dolly!* (1964). After attending the Yale School of Drama, Stewart gained renown as the writer of sketches for revues in the 1950s and as a staff writer for Sid Caesar's television program, "Your Show of Shows." His musical credits included *Carnival!* (1961), *George M!* (1968), and *I Love My Wife* (1977). In 1974 Mark Bramble became his musical partner, and in 1980 Stewart wrote the lyrics for Bramble's book *Barnum.* The two also collaborated on the book for *42nd Street* (1980). One of Stewart's last efforts was the book for *Treasure Island* (1986), which premiered in Edmonton, Alta.

**Sullivan, Maxine** (MARIETTA WILLIAMS), U.S. jazz singer (b. May 13, 1911, Homestead, Pa.—d. April 7, 1987, New York, N.Y.), whose inspired and rhythmic rendition of the Scottish folk ballad "Loch Lomond" catapulted her to stardom. Her 1937 recording of the song was arranged by pianist Claude Thornhill, who recognized her singing talent at the Onyx Club in New York City. She followed this triumph with a series of recordings of such swinging folk songs as "Molly Malone," "It Was a Lover and His Lass," and "If I Had a Ribbon Bow." In 1938 she made her motion-picture debut with Louis Armstrong in *Going Places,* and the two introduced the song "Jeepers Creepers." After

appearing in a second film, *St. Louis Blues,* she performed on Broadway with Benny Goodman and Armstrong in *Swingin' the Dream,* a jazz version of Shakespeare's *A Midsummer Night's Dream.* During the 1940s she expanded her repertoire to include such pop songs as "I've Got the World on a String" and "Wrap Your Troubles in Dreams." Though she interrupted her career on two occasions, she made a successful comeback in 1958. She frequently punctuated her performances by playing either a valve-trombone, a miniature trumpet, or a flügelhorn. In 1979 she received a Tony award for her performance in *My Old Friends,* a poignant musical on aging.

**Susskind, David,** U.S. producer and talk show host (b. Dec. 19, 1920, New York, N.Y.—d. Feb. 22, 1987, New York), was the contentious host of "Open End" (1958–66), a freewheeling late-night syndicated conversation show that ran—sometimes for several hours—until members of the panel had exhausted their views. The program was later limited to two hours and in 1966 was renamed "The David Susskind Show." Susskind, who pioneered the talk show forum, often chose subjects that were taboo television topics. He became a household name in 1960 when he interviewed the Soviet leader Nikita S. Khrushchev. Often berated for his fractious and argumentative interviewing style, Susskind nonetheless exerted a powerful influence on the medium that he sometimes harshly criticized. As an independent television producer, he brought quality programs to the screen and earned 27 Emmy awards for such productions as "The Ages of Man" (1966), "Death of a Salesman" (1966), and two for the "Eleanor and Franklin" specials in the 1970s. Some of his other high-quality television credits include "The Crucible" (1967), "The Diary of Anne Frank" (1967), "Mark Twain Tonight" (1967), and "The Glass Menagerie" (1973). As a film producer he presented *A Raisin in the Sun* (1961), *Requiem for a Heavyweight* (1962), and *Alice Doesn't Live Here Anymore* (1974). Susskind ended production of his talk show in 1986.

**Takamatsu, Prince,** member of the Japanese Imperial family (b. Jan. 3, 1905, Tokyo, Japan—d. Feb. 3, 1987, Tokyo), as a younger brother of Emperor Hirohito and as a navy officer during World War II, counseled his brother against war with the United States. After war was declared, however, Takamatsu advocated a buildup in aircraft production, an outgrowth of which was the use of kamikaze pilots on suicide missions in an attempt to sink U.S. warships. The prince, who was named Terunomiya at birth, was given the name Prince Takamatsu at the age of eight. After graduating from the Naval Academy in 1924 and the Naval Staff College in 1936, he was appointed captain in 1942. When the Japanese Navy suffered a crushing defeat in the Battle of Midway in June 1942, Takamatsu reportedly sent a letter to the emperor urging him to "make up your mind to end the war." After World War II the prince was active as a representative of cultural and medical organizations and was for a time president of the Japanese Red Cross Society. He was also prominent as a goodwill ambassador and made trips to Belgium (1958), Hawaii (1960), Canada (1967), Switzerland (1969), and South Korea (1970). The prince was fifth in line to the throne.

**Taylor, Maxwell Davenport,** general (ret.), U.S. Army (b. Aug. 26, 1901, Keytesville, Mo.—d. April 19, 1987, Washington, D.C.), as a daring and heroic military leader, led the 101st Airborne Division in the Normandy invasion on D-Day (June 6, 1944) and was credited with pioneering airborne warfare in Europe during World War II. Taylor, a 1922 graduate of the U.S. Military Academy at West Point, N.Y., had a flair for languages and in 1927 was sent to Paris to perfect his knowledge of French. He taught French and Spanish at West Point and

held various posts before assisting in the formation of the U.S. Army's first airborne division, the 82nd, at the start of World War II. During the war, in a valiant and vital mission, he passed through enemy lines 24 hours before a proposed Allied invasion of Rome (1943) to consult with Italian leaders there; Italian forces had secretly surrendered to the Allies, but Rome was still under enemy control. When he parachuted with the 101st Airborne Division on D-Day, he became the first general to fight in France during World War II. His division also participated in the invasion of The Netherlands on Sept. 17, 1944, and was instrumental in its defense of Bastogne, Belgium, during the Battle of the Bulge in December 1944.

After the war Taylor was installed (1945) as the 37th superintendent of West Point and was credited with reorganizing the curriculum to give cadets a more well-rounded education. In 1953 he saw active duty as commanding general of the 8th Army in Korea during the closing days of the Korean War. He then served as army chief of staff (1955–59) and was appointed chairman of the Joint Chiefs of Staff in 1962. He was a special emissary to South Vietnam for Pres. John F. Kennedy and served as Pres. Lyndon B. Johnson's ambassador to South Vietnam (1964–65) during the U.S. military buildup there; he wielded enormous power in these sensitive posts and more than anyone else was responsible for shaping U.S. military and diplomatic policy in Southeast Asia. After his resignation as ambassador in 1965, he continued to serve as Johnson's special consultant until 1969. An opponent of nuclear conflict, Taylor set forth his views in *The Uncertain Trumpet* (1960), in which he emphasized the infantryman's vital role in fighting small-scale conflicts. Among Taylor's other books are *Responsibility and Response* (1967) and *Precarious Security* (1976).

**Tomás, Américo de Deus Rodrigues,** Portuguese politician and naval officer (b. Nov. 19, 1894, Lisbon, Port.—d. Sept. 18, 1987, Cascais, near Lisbon), was the last notable human relic of the right-wing authoritarian regime of António Salazar and served as president of Portugal from 1958 until toppled by the revolution of April 1974. He also had a distinguished naval career and was largely responsible for the major hydrographic survey of Portugal's coastline, on which he himself worked (1920–36). As minister of the navy (1944–58), he instituted a program of building new merchant ships and lighthouses. Educated at Lisbon Naval Academy, he served during World War I on ships protecting troop convoys for the Western Front. He was appointed special assistant to the minister of the navy in 1936 and president of the National Board for the Merchant Navy in 1940. He became a rear admiral in 1951. Chosen by Salazar to fill the office of president, Tomás defeated Gen. Humberto Delgado in the 1958 elections, which were held under a limited franchise. He was reappointed to the office by an electoral college in 1965 and 1972. Tomás traveled widely in the Portuguese colonies and favoured retention of power by military force. When Salazar became incapacitated by illness in 1968, Tomás replaced him as prime minister with Marcelo Caetano. After being deposed, Tomás spent four years in exile before he was allowed to return to Portugal in 1978.

**Tosh, Peter** (WINSTON HUBERT MCINTOSH), Jamaican reggae singer (b. Oct. 9, 1944, Westmoreland, Jamaica—d. Sept. 11, 1987, Kingston, Jamaica), was an original member, along with Bob Marley and Neville ("Bunny") Livingston, of the Wailers, formed in 1963, the most celebrated of all Jamaican reggae groups. Tosh, rebellious, resolute in his opposition to the political establishment, and aggressive in his defense of Rastafarian principles, found himself at times in conflict with the authorities. On one occasion he was imprisoned for possessing marijuana, and on another he was severely beaten up by the police. His songs, including

"Legalize It" (referring to marijuana), "I'm the Toughest," "Mark of the Beast," and "Get Up, Stand Up," illustrated the close link between music and politics in West Indian culture. Tosh used the 1978 "peace concert" in Kingston, attended by leaders of Jamaica's conflicting political parties, as a platform to defend political freedom and legalization of marijuana and to denounce police brutality. With the Wailers he recorded *Catch a Fire* and *Burnin'*, and his solo albums include *Equal Rights*. Tosh was shot dead during an attempted robbery at his home; his death was followed by accusations that it was politically motivated and by a dispute over his burial place.

**Trapp, Maria von** (AUGUSTA KUTSCHERA), Austrian-born singer (b. Jan. 26, 1905, Vienna, Austria—d. March 28, 1987, Morrisville, Vt.), was the indomitable matriarch of the von Trapp family singers whose life story became the inspiration for the award-winning Broadway musical and motion picture *The Sound of Music*. She was born in a train en route to Vienna. She was graduated (1924) from the State Teachers College for Progressive Education in Vienna before she entered a Salzburg convent. At the age of 20 she was sent by the abbess to teach the seven motherless children of Baron Georg von Trapp, a stern World War I submarine commander 25 years her senior. Maria captured the heart of the baron, and they were married a year later. The family became popular singers in Austria and performed in the Salzburg Festival before fleeing the Nazis and abandoning their home and possessions. In the film version the von Trapps traversed the Alps to freedom, but in reality they left on a train. They settled (1939) in the U.S. and earned a living by giving concerts. In the 1940s they bought property in Stowe, Vt.; they operated a music camp there before opening an Austrian chalet-style resort at the family lodge. A fire destroyed it in 1980, but it was rebuilt. Von Trapp and her husband had three children before his death in 1947. She became a local celebrity after the phenomenally successful motion picture *The Sound of Music* was produced. Some of her writings include *The Story of the Trapp Family Singers* (1949), which was republished as *The Sound of Music: The Story of the Trapp Family Singers* (1976); *A Family on Wheels: Further Adventures of the Trapp Family Singers* (1959); and *Maria* (1972), an autobiography.

**Trend, Burke St. John Trend,** BARON, British civil servant (b. Jan. 2, 1914, London, England—d. July 21, 1987, London), as secretary of the Cabinet (1963–73), was adviser to four successive prime ministers. He carried out (1974–75) the investigation into alleged Soviet penetration of the counterespionage organization MI-5, including the possible treachery of its head, Sir Roger Hollis; he found the evidence inconclusive either way. Educated at Whitgift School, Croydon, and at Merton College, Oxford, Trend entered the home civil service in 1936, working first in the Board of Education. In 1937 he transferred to the Treasury and served as assistant private secretary to the chancellor of the Exchequer (1939–41). He worked on defense equipment during the remainder of World War II. In the postwar Labour governments of Clement Attlee, Trend was principal private secretary to the chancellors of the Exchequer Hugh Dalton and Sir Stafford Cripps before becoming under secretary in charge of the Treasury's Home Finance Division in 1949. He was principal adviser to R. A. Butler (1955–56) when the latter was lord privy seal. Trend was appointed deputy (1956) to Sir Norman Brook, secretary of the Cabinet, but returned to the Treasury in 1959 and became second (*i.e.*, permanent) secretary the following year. Trend was created a life peer in 1974.

**Tsatsos, Konstantinos,** Greek politician, philosopher, and lawyer (b. July 1, 1899, Athens, Greece—d. Oct. 8, 1987, Athens), was president of the Greek Republic from 1975 to 1980 and

the author of more than 20 books on philosophy and law. The son of a lawyer active in public life, he studied law at the Universities of Athens and Heidelberg, where he specialized in the philosophy of law. During the 1930s he taught philosophy at the University of Athens and, following the German occupation of his country, escaped to the Middle East. After serving as adviser to the government-in-exile, Tsatsos served as minister of the interior (1945), minister of the press and air (1945), and minister of education (1949) after World War II. From 1955, as a close associate of Prime Minister Konstantinos Karamanlis, he continued to hold ministerial office and was serving as minister of justice when the 1967 coup precipitated the installation of a military dictatorship. Tsatsos was an active opponent of the regime, and when it was overthrown in 1974, he helped to draft the country's new constitution. A referendum held in December 1974 abolished the monarchy, and the following year Parliament elected Tsatsos as the new republic's chief of state. He was succeeded as president by Karamanlis in 1980 and devoted his retirement to writing and scholarly work.

**Tudor, Antony** (WILLIAM COOK), British-born U.S. dancer and choreographer (b. April 4, 1908, London—d. April 19, 1987, New York, N.Y.), as a ballet dancer was best remembered for his dramatic stage presence but as a choreographer was enormously influential as the creator of the psychological ballet, in which human relationships and emotional conflicts were explored. At the age of 19 Tudor began studying dance with Marie Rambert, and in 1931 he choreographed *Cross-Garter'd* for her company. In 1938 he founded the London Ballet, but the following year he moved to the United States to help establish Ballet Theatre (now American Ballet Theatre). Besides successfully restaging some of his earlier works, including *Jardin aux Lilas* (1936; later retitled *Lilac Garden*), *Dark Elegies* (1937), and *Gala Performance* (1938), he presented such new ballets as *Pillar of Fire* (1942), *Romeo and Juliet* (1943), *Undertow* (1945), and *Nimbus* (1950). His works explored such psychological themes as rejection, frustration, and the lack of communication. In 1950 he became associated with the ballet school of the Metropolitan Opera, and in 1952 he became a faculty member of the dance department of the Juilliard School of Music in New York City. Besides staging ballets for the Royal Swedish Ballet, he also served as its artistic director (1963–64). In 1968 his *Shadowplay*, commissioned for Britain's Royal Ballet, revitalized his career. In 1974 he rejoined American Ballet Theatre as associate artistic director, and the following year he created *The Leaves Are Fading*. In time, however, he concentrated more on restaging his earlier successes. In 1980 he became choreographer emeritus.

**Vaughan-Thomas, (Lewis John) Wynford,** British broadcaster (b. Aug. 15, 1908, Swansea, Wales—d. Feb. 4, 1987, Fishguard, Dyfed, Wales), made his name as a war correspondent during World War II and later became a much-loved commentator on national and often royal occasions. Educated at Swansea Grammar School and at Exeter College, Oxford, Vaughan-Thomas joined the Cardiff regional office of the British Broadcasting Corporation (BBC) as an outside broadcasts assistant in 1937. He moved to London in 1939, where he subsequently covered the Blitz. Later he went overseas, reporting the Allied landings at Anzio in Italy (January 1944) and the crossing of the Rhine by British and Canadian forces (March 1945). One of his postwar assignments was in India at the time of independence (1947). Vaughan-Thomas left the BBC to become a member of Harlech Television, the consortium that in 1968 successfully bid for the independent television franchise in Wales and the West of England; he was Harlech's director of programs (1968–71). Gifted with a sense of occasion and a feel

for places, he later increasingly turned his talents to celebrating the Welsh countryside and culture. He wrote a number of books, including an autobiography, *Trust to Talk* (1980). He was made Commander of the Order of the British Empire in 1986.

**Warhol, Andy** (ANDREW WARHOLA), U.S. pop artist (b. Aug. 6, 1928?, McKeesport?, Pa.—d. Feb. 22, 1987, New York, N.Y.), was an enigmatic, white-wigged artistic genius who was credited with being one of the founders of the Pop Art movement. His silk-screen image of Campbell's soup cans, his wood sculpture painted like a box of Brillo scouring pads, and his vibrant screenprinted paintings of such contemporary icons as Elvis Presley, Marilyn Monroe, and Jacqueline Kennedy made him one of the most famous and influential artists in the world. Warhol studied (1945–49) at the Carnegie Institute of Technology, Pittsburgh, Pa., before briefly working as an illustrator (1949–50) for *Glamour* magazine and then as a commercial artist (1950–57) in New York City. From 1957 he worked as an independent artist, and in 1960 he began producing paintings derived from comic strips and advertising. By 1962 he had become a phenomenon, and he soon abandoned the paint brush in favour of photographic silk screen, a method that allows infinite replication of an image. This depersonalized technique reflected his philosophy of the artist as a detached observer. During the 1960s he also produced a body of works known as "Disaster" pictures, which depicted fatal car wrecks, electric chairs, race riots, and atomic bombs. In 1963 Warhol began experimenting in film and, with Paul Morrissey, produced such underground classics as *Eat* (1963), *My Hustler* (1965), *Chelsea Girls* (1966), and *Blue Movie* (1969), legendary sometimes for their erotic content but other times

for their inordinate length (up to 25 hours) with virtually no action. Although he appeared pale and shy, Warhol's public persona masked a shrewd entrepreneur who was adept at manipulating people and money and at promoting his work as well as securing celebrity status for himself. He once claimed that in the future everyone would be famous for 15 minutes. In 1968 Warhol was shot by Valerie Solanis, a former Factory (the name of his studio) actress. Though some felt that Warhol was never quite as influential after the shooting, in 1969 he founded his monthly journal of fashion and celebrity, *Interview,* which featured large and avant-garde advertisements, many of them by Warhol. He later became a force in music after establishing a touring mixed-media rock revue called The Exploding Plastic Inevitable that featured The Velvet Underground, a forerunner of new wave and punk rock. The artist, whose disquieting and unsettling art revealed a modern culture intent on dehumanization, died of a heart attack in his sleep after undergoing gallbladder surgery. Warhol left an estate of some $15 million, the bulk of which was to be used to establish a foundation for the visual arts.

**Washington, Harold,** U.S. politician (b. April 15, 1922, Chicago, Ill.—d. Nov. 25, 1987, Chicago), became the first black mayor of Chicago on April 12, 1983. Campaigning for reform and an end to city patronage, Washington won nearly 52% of the vote in a record voter turnout tinged with racial overtones. Thousands of Democrats voted for Bernard Epton, a virtually unknown white Republican, many voting for a Republican mayoral candidate for the first time in their lives. In the earlier, hotly contested Democratic primary, Washington had won the nomination by defeating incumbent Mayor Jane Byrne and Cook County State's Attorney Richard M. Daley, whose father, Richard J. Daley, the "last of the big-city bosses," had been Chicago's mayor from 1955 to 1976.

During the primary campaign, voters were reminded that Washington had spent a month in jail for failing to file his federal income tax return for four years and that his law license had been suspended for a time for failure to perform paid legal work. Washington's first term in office was marked by City Council wrangling that was so bitter it became known as the Council Wars. With the opposition controlling a majority of the 50 council seats, Washington was often unable to implement his programs. After a court ruled that several ward boundaries violated the law by disenfranchising minority voters, new elections in those wards finally gave Washington control of the council in 1986. The following year he was easily reelected to a second term even though he had pushed through an unpopular $70 million property tax increase.

Washington graduated from Roosevelt University in Chicago in 1949 and earned a law degree from Northwestern University, Chicago, in 1952. The following year he succeeded his father, a part-time Methodist minister, as Democratic precinct captain. In 1954 he became a city attorney, and from 1960 to 1964 he worked as a state labour arbitrator. He then served in the Illinois House of Representatives (1964–76) and Senate (1976–80) and was elected (1980) to the U.S. House of Representatives. During his second term, he was persuaded by black leaders to enter the mayoral race in Chicago. During his tenure as mayor, he gained national prominence and became a symbol of urban black political power and a folk hero to Chicago's black population.

**Willey, Frederick Thomas,** British politician (b. Nov. 13, 1910, Durham, England—d. Dec. 13, 1987, Bath, Avon, England), held government office under the Labour prime ministers Clement Attlee and Harold Wilson and became chairman (1979–81) of the parliamentary Labour Party. He was educated at Johnston School, Durham, and at St. John's College, Cambridge, and was called to the bar in 1936 and practiced in the northern circuit. During

World War II he was an auxiliary fireman in London's East End, thereby acquiring trade union associations and executive experience. Member of Parliament for Sunderland (1945–50) and for Sunderland North (1950–83), Willey was parliamentary private secretary to the home secretary (1946–50) and parliamentary secretary to the Ministry of Food (1950–51). As opposition spokesman on education (1960–64), he promised that Labour would abolish the 11-plus examination and advance the date for raising the school-leaving age to 16. When Labour regained power in 1964, he was chief of the short-lived Land and National Resources Ministry (1964–67). He chaired parliamentary select committees on estimates, education, members' interests, and race relations. Willey wrote two books on education and *The Honourable Member* (1974), which stressed the potential powers of back-bench (rank and file) members of Parliament.

**Williams, (George) Emlyn,** Welsh actor and playwright (b. Nov. 26, 1905, Pen-y-ffordd, near Mostyn, Wales—d. Sept. 25, 1987, London, England), was the author of such well-made plays as the psychological thriller *Night Must Fall* (1935) and the semiautobiographical *The Corn Is Green* (1938); he was also an actor and appeared in many West End and Broadway productions. In 1951 Williams began giving one-man readings from Dickens—he later added Dylan Thomas and Saki—which he performed in theatres throughout the world during the next three decades. Active on the stage for some 50 years, he was a vital presence in mainstream British theatre.

Williams grew up with Welsh as his first language. Educated at Holywell County School, he won a scholarship to Christ Church, Oxford, and started to act in the university dramatic society. He made his professional debut in 1927 and the following year appeared in his play *Glamour.* Among his other plays were *The Druid's Rest* (1944) and *The Wind of Heaven* (1945). His film appearances included *The Last Days of Dolwyn* (1949), which he also wrote and directed, and *David Copperfield* (1969). Onstage he performed in *The Wild Duck* (1955), *A Man for All Seasons* (1962), and *Forty Years On* (1969). Williams published two volumes of autobiography, *George* (1961) and *Emlyn* (1973), and a novel, *Headlong* (1980). His interest in the macabre was demonstrated in *Beyond Belief* (1967), his study of the couple convicted in the sensational murders of children in the Pennine Moors area during the mid-1960s, and in a fictional diary of a murderer, *Dr. Crippen's Diary* (1987). He was appointed Commander of the Order of the British Empire in 1962.

**Wilson, Earl,** U.S. newspaper columnist (b. May 3, 1907, Rockford, Ohio—d. Jan. 16, 1987, Yonkers, N.Y.), delighted readers for more than 40 years with his gossipy "It Happened Last Night" columns, which revealed spicy tidbits about Broadway and Hollywood starlets. Wilson joined the *New York Post* in 1935, and in 1942 he began his six-times-a-week column, which at the pinnacle of its popularity was carried by 175 newspapers nationwide. Wilson often lured curious readers to his copy by publishing the measurements of female stars. He was also credited with sustaining his readership by capturing the pulse of show business by scrupulously attending scores of motion-picture premieres, Broadway first nights, and cafe openings. Wilson, who wrote several books filled with celebrity anecdotes, including *I Am Gazing into My 8-Ball* (1945), *Let 'Em Eat Cheesecake* (1949), and *The Show Business Nobody Knows* (1971), retired in 1983.

**Wittig, Georg,** West German chemist (b. June 16, 1897, Berlin, Germany—d. Aug. 26, 1987, Heidelberg, West Germany), shared the 1979 Nobel Prize for Chemistry with Herbert C. Brown of Purdue University, West Lafayette, Ind., for the development of a technique that used phosphorus compounds in the synthesis

of natural substances through the regrouping of carbon atoms in the molecules. The "Wittig reaction," which he discovered in 1953, opened the way to the economical production of substances such as Vitamin A on an industrial scale. A gifted pianist, he had at one time considered a musical career. Wittig studied at the University of Tübingen, served in World War I, and eventually graduated from the University of Marburg (1923), where he earned a Ph.D. in 1926. He taught at Marburg (1926–32), at the Braunschweig Technical College (1932–37), and at the Universities of Braunschweig and Freiburg (1937–44) before returning to Tübingen, where he taught for 12 years. In 1956 he became professor and director of the Institute of Organic Chemistry at the University of Heidelberg, where he stayed for the remainder of his academic career. Wittig retired as professor emeritus in 1965 but continued to conduct research. His publications included a *Textbook of Stereochemistry* (1930).

**Yourcenar, Marguerite** (MARGUERITE DE CRAYENCOUR), French writer (b. June 8, 1903, Brussels, Belgium—d. Dec. 17, 1987, Northeast Harbor, Maine), was not only the author of outstanding historical novels (most notably *Mémoires d'Hadrien* [1951]) but also the first woman ever to be elected a member of the French Academy. In her work, from her first novel, *Alexis ou le traité d'un vain combat* (1929; "Alexis, or Treatise on Useless Combat"),

to her last, she developed ideas formulated in her early life; one of her last books, translated into English in 1987 as *Two Lives and a Dream,* was a reworking of stories written some 60 years earlier. Yourcenar was fascinated by real and fictional historical figures like Hadrian and Zeno (the central character in *L'Oeuvre au noir* [1968; *The Abyss*]), who belong to their age and yet manage to transcend its limitations. The daughter of a French aristocrat, she learned Latin and Greek before reaching her teens and spent her childhood exploring Europe with her father. A love of travel remained with her throughout her life, though from 1937 she made her home in the U.S., ultimately settling in Maine with her translator and companion, Grace Frick. During World War II she began teaching at Sarah Lawrence College and did translations, but the success of *Mémoires d'Hadrien* in 1951 allowed her to give up teaching. Her other writings include plays, poetry, essays, memoirs, and a translated anthology of Negro spirituals. In 1980, despite opposition from some academicians based on controversy over her dual U.S.-French nationality, she was elected to the French Academy, the first woman to join the 40 "Immortals" since the Academy was founded in 1635.

# Events of 1987

## Agriculture and Food Supplies

World agricultural and food production showed little gain in 1987, according to preliminary estimates of the United Nations Food and Agriculture Organization (FAO), and per capita output probably fell. Grain production declined for the first time in several years, with the largest reductions occurring in the United States and in South Asia, where the monsoon rainfall was late and inconsistent. China enjoyed another good harvest, but the extraordinary rate of agricultural growth in recent years appeared to be slowing.

Large stocks and depressed world trade prices of farm products encouraged the increased use of policies designed to curb agricultural production in several developed agricultural exporting countries, especially the U.S. Such moves were frequently coupled with aggressive export policies that made heavy use of subsidies to reduce surpluses or to keep them from increasing but that also kept trade tensions high. Government expenditures in support of such policies continued at near-record levels in both the U.S. and the European Communities (EC).

These conditions added urgency to the new round of multilateral trade negotiations aiming at major reform of the world agricultural trading system. The negotiations picked up momentum in the last half of 1987 as the EC and other countries began to respond to a far-reaching U.S. agricultural trade proposal.

**Ethiopian Food Emergency.** Severe crop failures in the north of Ethiopia in late 1987 once again raised fears of famine. The hardest hit regions included Eritrea and Tigrai, areas also devastated by the 1984–85 famine and the scene of continuing civil warfare that again endangered relief efforts. The FAO in December estimated food-aid requirements at 1.3 million tons of cereals, less than half of which was covered by donor pledges. Already pledged aid was deemed sufficient to meet needs until March 1988, but additional fuel, trucks, and spare parts and improved port facilities were urgently needed to ensure its delivery. The FAO warned that urgent action would have to be taken to keep food flowing thereafter.

Grain stocks throughout the world, especially in the exporting countries, were potentially more than ample to meet these and other emergency requirements. Total food-aid shipments of cereals in 1987–88 were expected to equal about 11.2 million tons, a bit under the average for the previous two years, according to a December 1987 FAO estimate. Some of the emergency requirements were likely

### Table I. Selected Indexes of World Agricultural and Food Production
(1976–78 average = 100)

| Region or country | Total agricultural production | | | | | | Total food production | | | | | | Per capita food production | | | | | |
|---|---|---|---|---|---|---|---|---|---|---|---|---|---|---|---|---|---|---|
| | 1981 | 1982 | 1983 | 1984 | 1985 | 1986 | 1981 | 1982 | 1983 | 1984 | 1985 | 1986 | 1981 | 1982 | 1983 | 1984 | 1985 | 1986 |
| Developed countries | 108 | 110 | 102 | 112 | 113 | 111 | 108 | 110 | 103 | 113 | 114 | 112 | 105 | 106 | 99 | 107 | 108 | 105 |
| United States | 113 | 113 | 92 | 109 | 115 | 109 | 113 | 114 | 94 | 110 | 117 | 112 | 108 | 108 | 88 | 102 | 107 | 102 |
| Canada | 113 | 118 | 113 | 110 | 120 | 133 | 113 | 119 | 113 | 110 | 119 | 134 | 108 | 112 | 105 | 101 | 109 | 121 |
| Western Europe | 110 | 113 | 111 | 119 | 117 | 115 | 110 | 113 | 111 | 119 | 117 | 115 | 108 | 111 | 109 | 117 | 114 | 112 |
| EC | 110 | 114 | 111 | 120 | 117 | 116 | 111 | 114 | 111 | 120 | 117 | 116 | 109 | 112 | 109 | 118 | 114 | 113 |
| Japan | 92 | 94 | 94 | 100 | 100 | 100 | 92 | 94 | 94 | 100 | 101 | 101 | 89 | 90 | 90 | 95 | 95 | 94 |
| Oceania | 106 | 98 | 115 | 114 | 116 | 115 | 105 | 95 | 116 | 113 | 113 | 111 | 100 | 89 | 108 | 104 | 103 | 100 |
| South Africa | 119 | 107 | 94 | 102 | 108 | 110 | 121 | 107 | 92 | 102 | 108 | 110 | 109 | 94 | 79 | 86 | 88 | 88 |
| Centrally planned economies | 103 | 110 | 114 | 119 | 118 | 119 | 102 | 109 | 113 | 118 | 116 | 118 | 98 | 103 | 107 | 110 | 108 | 109 |
| U.S.S.R. | 92 | 98 | 102 | 102 | 101 | 107 | 91 | 98 | 102 | 102 | 101 | 108 | 87 | 93 | 96 | 96 | 94 | 99 |
| Eastern Europe | 102 | 105 | 104 | 113 | 109 | 112 | 102 | 105 | 104 | 113 | 109 | 112 | 100 | 102 | 101 | 109 | 104 | 107 |
| China[1] | 126 | 124 | 150 | 164 | 162 | 163 | 124 | 120 | 146 | 156 | 157 | 163 | 118 | 112 | 135 | 142 | 143 | 147 |
| Less developed countries | 112 | 113 | 115 | 120 | 125 | 126 | 112 | 114 | 116 | 121 | 125 | 128 | 102 | 101 | 101 | 102 | 104 | 103 |
| East Asia[2] | 116 | 119 | 123 | 128 | 132 | 133 | 117 | 120 | 122 | 130 | 133 | 135 | 107 | 107 | 107 | 112 | 112 | 111 |
| Indonesia | 131 | 129 | 140 | 149 | 153 | 153 | 133 | 131 | 140 | 152 | 154 | 155 | 120 | 116 | 122 | 129 | 128 | 126 |
| South Korea | 97 | 100 | 102 | 106 | 107 | 111 | 98 | 101 | 103 | 107 | 109 | 112 | 92 | 93 | 94 | 96 | 96 | 98 |
| Malaysia | 121 | 130 | 125 | 131 | 143 | 151 | 132 | 145 | 136 | 147 | 165 | 175 | 120 | 129 | 118 | 125 | 136 | 142 |
| Philippines | 115 | 113 | 114 | 110 | 118 | 124 | 115 | 112 | 111 | 109 | 116 | 123 | 103 | 99 | 95 | 91 | 96 | 99 |
| Thailand | 120 | 121 | 131 | 134 | 139 | 128 | 120 | 120 | 131 | 135 | 138 | 125 | 111 | 108 | 115 | 117 | 117 | 105 |
| Vietnam | 118 | 126 | 132 | 140 | 137 | 140 | 118 | 126 | 132 | 139 | 137 | 140 | 108 | 112 | 115 | 118 | 113 | 113 |
| South Asia | 111 | 108 | 120 | 123 | 126 | 125 | 110 | 108 | 122 | 122 | 124 | 125 | 101 | 97 | 107 | 104 | 104 | 102 |
| Bangladesh | 110 | 114 | 117 | 118 | 124 | 122 | 112 | 116 | 119 | 120 | 124 | 125 | 99 | 100 | 99 | 97 | 98 | 96 |
| India | 111 | 108 | 122 | 124 | 127 | 125 | 110 | 107 | 123 | 124 | 126 | 126 | 101 | 96 | 108 | 106 | 106 | 103 |
| Pakistan | 122 | 124 | 120 | 128 | 132 | 149 | 119 | 118 | 123 | 118 | 118 | 136 | 105 | 101 | 102 | 95 | 92 | 104 |
| West Asia | 103 | 111 | 113 | 115 | 121 | 130 | 105 | 114 | 114 | 117 | 124 | 135 | 94 | 99 | 97 | 96 | 99 | 105 |
| Iran | 89 | 96 | 95 | 94 | 104 | 113 | 89 | 97 | 96 | 95 | 106 | 115 | 79 | 83 | 80 | 76 | 83 | 87 |
| Turkey | 108 | 114 | 114 | 115 | 113 | 121 | 112 | 117 | 116 | 118 | 117 | 127 | 102 | 105 | 101 | 100 | 98 | 103 |
| Sub-Saharan Africa[3] | 111 | 112 | 105 | 111 | 116 | 120 | 111 | 112 | 106 | 110 | 116 | 120 | 99 | 97 | 89 | 90 | 92 | 93 |
| Ethiopia | 108 | 119 | 109 | 98 | 104 | 112 | 108 | 123 | 111 | 102 | 106 | 114 | 102 | 113 | 99 | 89 | 93 | 96 |
| Nigeria | 113 | 115 | 101 | 113 | 114 | 119 | 114 | 115 | 101 | 114 | 115 | 120 | 100 | 98 | 84 | 93 | 91 | 93 |
| Sudan, The | 110 | 98 | 101 | 94 | 118 | 111 | 119 | 98 | 97 | 86 | 117 | 114 | 103 | 82 | 78 | 67 | 87 | 85 |
| North Africa | 105 | 114 | 112 | 115 | 127 | 135 | 104 | 114 | 113 | 117 | 129 | 135 | 92 | 98 | 95 | 95 | 102 | 107 |
| Morocco | 86 | 111 | 106 | 107 | 111 | 130 | 86 | 111 | 106 | 107 | 112 | 131 | 78 | 98 | 91 | 90 | 92 | 105 |
| Egypt | 112 | 115 | 117 | 118 | 124 | 128 | 111 | 116 | 119 | 122 | 126 | 133 | 98 | 99 | 99 | 98 | 99 | 101 |
| Latin America | 116 | 116 | 115 | 122 | 127 | 122 | 115 | 117 | 115 | 122 | 128 | 125 | 105 | 104 | 100 | 103 | 106 | 101 |
| Argentina | 103 | 118 | 114 | 125 | 120 | 122 | 106 | 121 | 117 | 128 | 124 | 127 | 99 | 111 | 106 | 114 | 109 | 109 |
| Brazil | 124 | 120 | 120 | 130 | 145 | 132 | 117 | 121 | 115 | 127 | 139 | 133 | 106 | 106 | 98 | 106 | 113 | 105 |
| Colombia | 123 | 121 | 120 | 122 | 122 | 124 | 122 | 121 | 120 | 123 | 126 | 127 | 113 | 110 | 106 | 106 | 107 | 106 |
| Mexico | 120 | 114 | 119 | 118 | 122 | 122 | 122 | 117 | 122 | 120 | 122 | 126 | 110 | 103 | 104 | 100 | 99 | 100 |
| Venezuela | 110 | 118 | 117 | 120 | 129 | 136 | 110 | 120 | 117 | 123 | 131 | 138 | 96 | 102 | 97 | 99 | 102 | 105 |
| World | 108 | 110 | 110 | 117 | 119 | 119 | 107 | 110 | 110 | 117 | 118 | 120 | 100 | 101 | 100 | 104 | 104 | 103 |

[1]Represents about two-thirds of all field crops (includes all major field crops) but excludes livestock products.  [2]Excludes Japan.  [3]Excludes South Africa.
Source: USDA, Economic Research Service, International Economic Division, December 1987.

to be met from aid already pledged but not allocated, and additional pledges were expected. Total pledges by 72 donors to the regular resources of the World Food Program (WFP) at the end of September equaled $1,026,000,000 of the $1.4 billion target for the 1987–88 biennium; about 75% represented commodities and 25% cash. Pledges by 101 donors in the 1985–86 biennium totaled $1.1 billion, with a target of $1,350,000,000. A little over one-quarter of the total cereal food aid was distributed through multilateral channels, among which the WFP was predominant.

Although conditions elsewhere in Africa were generally far more favourable than during the earlier drought, the FAO estimated that exceptional emergency assistance was needed in Angola, Malawi, Mozambique, and Niger. The Sudan was capable of offsetting a substantial crop shortage from existing stocks but, because of financial difficulties and civil strife in the south, needed external help in moving food supplies to deficit areas. The FAO indicated that several other countries faced similar problems, including Burkina Faso, Chad, Mali, Senegal, Tanzania, and Uganda. The success of the second year of an FAO-coordinated international campaign against far-ranging grasshopper and locust swarms prevented potentially widespread crop losses in much of Africa.

Late and erratic monsoon rainfall in South and Southeast Asia, together with flooding in Bangladesh, damaged crop prospects to varying degrees, producing some increase in emergency food needs. In most cases, however, food stocks were adequate for offsetting the most serious shortages.

**Commodity Developments.** *Grains.* An expected (in December 1987) 5% decline in world grain production in 1987–88 indicated the end of a four-year expansion in output. The low prices for wheat and coarse grains in world trade, resulting from the ample supplies of the previous few years, were acting as a brake to production in many countries. Low prices also appeared to be stimulating both grain use and trade, leading to expectations that use would exceed production for the first time since 1983–84. Exporting countries had to rely on existing stocks to maintain or

expand exports. As a result, total grain stocks were forecast to decline during 1987–88 but to remain large relative to total grain use.

World wheat output declined an estimated 5% in 1987–88, reflecting the third consecutive year of reduced plantings. The area harvested of wheat about equaled that in 1973, although output per unit of land was one-third higher. Wheat production in 1986–87 was expanded or maintained in most wheat-exporting countries; an exception was the U.S. In 1987–88 most major traders of wheat were experiencing reduced production, while the U.S. slightly expanded its output despite lower wheat acreage. The largest reductions were in Australia, Canada, and the Soviet Union. Although world consumption of wheat was projected to level off in 1987–88 after a sharp increase in 1986–87, it was still expected to exceed production for the first time since 1980–81. Expanded trade in low-quality feed wheat, particularly by the EC and Canada, was contributing to the substantial but still partial recovery in world wheat trade.

The U.S. appeared to be benefiting the most from expanding wheat trade. Lower loan rates that provided U.S. farmers less incentive to put their wheat in government stocks, along with subsidized exports under the Export Enhancement Program (EEP), contributed to a 14% rise in U.S. wheat exports in 1986–87. About 25% of U.S. wheat exports moved under the EEP in 1986–87, and about 50% depended on it in the early months of 1987–88. The U.S. was fulfilling a November offer to sell 2.4 million tons of wheat at favourable terms to the Soviet Union under the EEP. Among the other major wheat exporters, only Canada seemed likely to maintain its level of wheat exports in 1987–88. The completion of its new Prince Rupert Port facility on the West Coast added substantial export capacity.

Strong imports of wheat by China and the U.S.S.R. helped stimulate a recovery in world wheat trade. China's imports increased to 8.5 million metric tons in 1986–87 and gave indications of reaching 11.5 million in 1987–88. Its wheat imports had peaked in the early 1980s at about 12 million to 15 million tons but then had contributed to the recent stagnation of world wheat trade by falling to about 6.6 million tons by 1985–86. The decline reflected an accelerated growth of grain production in the early 1980s. The U.S. was the dominant supplier in those earlier years, but Canada and Australia made gains in the Chinese market while the U.S. share declined.

The increased imports in China reflected both the growing consumer demand that was resulting from higher incomes and a general slowdown in the expansion of Chinese agricultural production from about 9% annually between 1978 and 1984 to about 3% thereafter. Between 1978 and 1985 Chinese per capita consumption of all grains increased from 196 to 254 kg (431 to 559 lb). The rapid advances in production in this period in large part represented one-time gains from a broad reform of the Chinese agricultural system. Those reforms included the disbanding of the communes, institution of a contract production system, increased use of private plots, sales to local markets in addition to government procurement, and more favourable producer prices.

World rice production was expected to fall sharply in 1987–88, largely because of adverse weather conditions in South and Southeast Asia. Despite accounting for three-fourths of the reduction, India was more likely to draw from its ample grain stocks and reduce consumption than to import rice or wheat. The greatest impact on rice trade was expected to come from the estimated 2.3 million-

### Table II. World Cereal Supply and Distribution
In 000,000 metric tons

| | 1984–85 | 1985–86 | 1986–87 | 1987–88[1] |
|---|---|---|---|---|
| **Production** | | | | |
| Wheat | 512 | 499 | 529 | 501 |
| Coarse grains | 814 | 842 | 833 | 798 |
| Rice, milled | 319 | 320 | 317 | 302 |
| Total | 1,644 | 1,661 | 1,679 | 1,601 |
| **Utilization** | | | | |
| Wheat | 496 | 487 | 519 | 521 |
| Coarse grains | 783 | 767 | 803 | 818 |
| Rice, milled | 314 | 316 | 319 | 309 |
| Total | 1,593 | 1,570 | 1,641 | 1,648 |
| **Exports** | | | | |
| Wheat | 107 | 85 | 91 | 100 |
| Coarse grains | 101 | 83 | 84 | 86 |
| Rice, milled | 12 | 13 | 13 | 10 |
| Total | 219 | 181 | 188 | 196 |
| **Ending stocks[2]** | | | | |
| Wheat | 125 | 137 | 147 | 127 |
| Coarse grains | 108 | 183 | 213 | 193 |
| Rice, milled | 22 | 26 | 24 | 17 |
| Total | 256 | 347 | 385 | 337 |
| **Stocks as % of utilization** | | | | |
| Wheat | 25.3% | 28.2% | 28.4% | 24.3% |
| Coarse grains | 13.8% | 23.9% | 26.6% | 23.7% |
| Rice, milled | 7.1% | 8.3% | 7.6% | 5.4% |
| Total | 16.1% | 22.1% | 23.5% | 20.4% |
| **Stocks held by U.S. in % of world total** | | | | |
| Wheat | 30.9% | 37.8% | 33.7% | 27.7% |
| Coarse grains | 53.8% | 69.3% | 71.6% | 70.2% |
| Rice | 9.4% | 9.5% | 7.4% | 5.4% |
| Total | 38.7% | 52.3% | 53.0% | 51.0% |

[1] Forecast.
[2] Does not include estimates of total Chinese or Soviet stocks but is adjusted for estimated changes in Soviet stocks.
Source: USDA, Foreign Agricultural Service, December 1987.

metric ton decline in exports from Thailand. China's rice production was expected to rise a little, but not to the peak level reached in 1984. Rice consumption in China was slowing, leading some Chinese officials to suggest that surplus rice could be used for feed manufacturing in southern China. Such surpluses, if exported, could have considerable impact on the low-volume world rice market.

The forecast 35 million-ton drop in world production of coarse grains in 1987–88 was matched by a reduction in U.S. output that resulted in large part from the operation of government programs that took considerable land out of production. Strong increases in Soviet and Chinese coarse-grain production were responsible for expectations that the largest gains in coarse-grain use in 1987–88 would take place there. World trade in coarse grains was expected to continue not much above the low levels of 1985–86 and 1986–87 because of generally large crops outside the U.S. and strong competition by feed wheat.

The U.S. share of world trade in coarse grains, which sank to 44% in 1985–86 before climbing to 57% in 1986–87, could in 1987–88 regain the 60% level of 1983–84. The resulting 17 million-ton drawdown in U.S. coarse-grain stocks would only partially offset the 95 million-ton buildup since 1984–85 and leave the U.S. with more than twice the stocks held in the rest of the world. Tight supplies in Thailand, Argentina, and Australia limited those competitors in world coarse-grain markets.

*Oilseeds.* Countries in the EC and South America were responsible for most of the forecast (in December) rise in oilseed production in 1987–88. The unknown degree of the likely shift from corn (maize) to more favourably priced soybeans in Argentina and Brazil, where plantings were not yet completed, added uncertainty to the forecast. U.S. soybean output rose despite a third consecutive year of acreage reduction. Continuing firm demand for oilseed

meal in 1986–87, reflected in prices for soybean meal (c.i.f., Rotterdam) averaging $191 per ton (4.4% above the average for 1985–86), led to increased crushings of oilseeds in 1986–87, and strengthening prices ($239 per ton in November 1987) offered prospects for a further expansion in 1987–88. As a result, the three-year rise in world oilseed stocks could come to an end in 1987–88.

The resulting expansion in vegetable-oil supplies in 1986–87 led to the third consecutive year of falling prices for vegetable oils, as evidenced by soybean-oil prices (f.o.b., Rotterdam) that at an average of $324 per ton were 14% below the 1985–86 average. However, the low prices appeared to be stimulating consumption of vegetable oils, with the result that prices began to strengthen in 1987–88. Trade in oilseeds expanded 9% in 1986–87 but was slowing in 1987–88, as was trade in oilseed meals, while it seemed likely that trade in vegetable oils would accelerate a little.

The EC Commission's proposal to tax all vegetable and marine oils intended for human consumption as part of its 1987–88 price-setting package (in Portugal and Spain not until 1990) became another irritant in trade relations between the U.S. and the EC and was also displeasing to South American and Asian exporters of oilseed and vegetable-oil products. By year's end the proposal had neither been implemented nor finally shelved. The measure was intended as a means of raising an additional $2.7 billion (ECU equivalent) to finance the EC's subsidization of its oilseed sector. Expenditures on oilseeds represented the fast-growing part of the EC's agricultural budget, rising from about $3 billion in 1980–81 to about $6.3 billion in 1985–86. During that period production of oilseeds also more than doubled, reaching six million tons in 1985–86. Soybean imports fell about 2.4 million tons during the period, with the U.S. taking nearly all the loss. Net imports of oilseed meal into the EC continued to rise during the pe-

## Table III. World Production of Oilseeds and Products

In 000,000 metric tons

| | 1985–86 | 1986–87[1] | 1987–88[2] |
|---|---|---|---|
| Production of oilseeds | 196.0 | 194.1 | 203.0 |
| Soybeans | 96.9 | 98.3 | 102.4 |
| U.S. | 57.1 | 52.8 | 53.3 |
| China | 10.5 | 11.7 | 11.8 |
| Argentina | 7.3 | 7.3 | 8.5 |
| Brazil | 14.1 | 17.3 | 18.3 |
| Cottonseed | 30.4 | 26.9 | 29.5 |
| U.S. | 4.8 | 3.5 | 5.1 |
| U.S.S.R. | 4.9 | 4.7 | 4.4 |
| China | 7.1 | 6.0 | 6.7 |
| Peanuts | 20.6 | 20.3 | 19.3 |
| U.S. | 1.9 | 1.7 | 1.6 |
| China | 6.7 | 5.9 | 6.4 |
| India | 5.6 | 5.9 | 4.4 |
| Sunflower seed | 19.3 | 19.0 | 19.7 |
| U.S. | 1.4 | 1.2 | 1.0 |
| U.S.S.R. | 5.2 | 5.3 | 5.5 |
| Argentina | 4.1 | 2.2 | 2.8 |
| Rapeseed | 18.6 | 19.7 | 22.4 |
| Canada | 3.5 | 3.8 | 3.9 |
| China | 5.6 | 5.9 | 6.1 |
| EC | 3.6 | 3.7 | 5.9 |
| India | 2.6 | 2.8 | 2.9 |
| Flaxseed | 2.4 | 2.7 | 2.4 |
| Copra | 5.3 | 4.7 | 4.6 |
| Palm kernel | 2.6 | 2.5 | 2.7 |
| Crushings of oilseeds | 153.8 | 158.5 | 163.4 |
| Soybeans | 76.2 | 83.2 | 85.5 |
| Ending stocks of oilseeds | 26.8 | 23.7 | 22.8 |
| Soybeans | 23.2 | 20.1 | 18.2 |
| World production[3] | | | |
| Total fats and oils | 61.1 | 61.0 | 62.8 |
| Edible vegetable oils | 47.1 | 47.5 | 49.3 |
| Soybean oil | 13.6 | 14.8 | 15.2 |
| Palm oil | 8.1 | 8.0 | 8.7 |
| Animal fats | 12.0 | 11.6 | 11.4 |
| Industrial and marine oils | 2.1 | 1.9 | 2.1 |
| High-protein meals[4] | 99.8 | 103.9 | 107.5 |

[1] Preliminary.
[2] Forecast.
[3] Processing potential from crops in year indicated.
[4] Converted, based on product's protein content, to weight equivalent to soybeans of 44% protein content.
Source: USDA, Foreign Agricultural Service, June and December 1987.

## Table IV. Livestock Numbers and Meat Production in Major Producing Countries

In 000,000 head and 000,000 metric tons (carcass weight)

| Region and country | 1986 | 1987[1] | 1986 | 1987[1] |
|---|---|---|---|---|
| | Cattle and buffalo | | Beef and veal | |
| World total | 1,042.7 | 1,045.4 | 43.42 | 42.96 |
| Canada | 10.4 | 10.3 | 1.04 | .90 |
| United States | 102.0 | 100.0 | 11.29 | 10.80 |
| Mexico | 33.6 | 35.6 | 1.20 | 1.21 |
| Argentina | 55.7 | 55.0 | 2.85 | 2.65 |
| Brazil | 97.0 | 98.3 | 2.00 | 2.30 |
| Uruguay | 10.3 | 11.0 | .36 | .29 |
| Western Europe | 89.5 | 87.0 | 8.66 | 8.68 |
| EC | 81.8 | 79.5 | 7.98 | 8.03 |
| Eastern Europe | 37.1 | 37.0 | 2.51 | 2.48 |
| U.S.S.R. | 122.1 | 121.5 | 7.70 | 8.10 |
| Australia | 23.6 | 23.7 | 1.48 | 1.42 |
| India | 273.6 | 275.1 | .36 | .37 |
| China | 91.7 | 96.7 | .63 | .69 |
| | Hogs | | Pork | |
| World total | 749.1 | 748.7 | 56.24 | 55.88 |
| Canada | 10.8 | 11.3 | .91 | .94 |
| United States | 51.2 | 55.5 | 6.38 | 6.42 |
| Mexico | 12.4 | 11.4 | .91 | .91 |
| Western Europe | 113.4 | 115.4 | 12.67 | 12.85 |
| EC | 104.0 | 106.0 | 11.52 | 11.72 |
| U.S.S.R. | 79.4 | 78.0 | 5.90 | 5.85 |
| Japan | 11.4 | 11.6 | 1.55 | 1.58 |
| China | 336.9 | 329.3 | 17.97 | 16.91 |
| | Poultry | | Poultry meat | |
| World total | | | 27.30 | 29.00 |
| United States | ... | ... | 8.26 | 9.07 |
| Brazil | | | 1.68 | 1.90 |
| EC | | | 5.41 | 5.55 |
| U.S.S.R. | | | 2.90 | 3.10 |
| Japan | ... | ... | 1.42 | 1.46 |
| | Sheep | | Sheep, goat meat | |
| World total | ... | ... | 5.03 | 5.03 |
| | | | All meat | |
| Total | | | 131.99 | 132.86 |

[1] Preliminary livestock numbers at year's end. Consists of 51 countries for beef and veal, 38 for pork, 50 for poultry meat, 30 for sheep and goat meat; roughly the same coverage for animal numbers. Includes nearly all European producers, the most significant in the Western Hemisphere, and scattered coverage elsewhere.
Source: USDA, Foreign Agricultural Service, September 1987.

riod, but future prospects were less promising because the EC subsidies favoured substitutes for oilseeds and oilseed products.

*Meat and Livestock.* Global production of meat in 1987 was expected (in September) to rise less than 1%, compared with more than 3% in 1986. An acceleration in poultry output more than offset declines in production of red meat.

World beef and veal production probably declined in 1987 after six years of steady growth. Reductions of cattle herds in the U.S., Canada, and Argentina in 1987 suggested a decrease in beef production, as did prospects of the beginning of a small increase in 1988 of U.S. livestock inventories. Herd rebuilding might also have begun in Canada, and the decline in the Argentine cattle herds appeared also to be nearing a halt. The EC's beef production grew modestly because of further slaughter of dairy cows as part of the second year of a program to reduce milk production quotas by 9.5% over two years. The completion of this adjustment and the resulting smaller cattle inventories seemed likely to result in lower beef production in the EC in 1988. Poor pasture conditions in Australia and strong prices for its beef exports kept animals moving to market and provided little incentive for herd rebuilding.

Total beef trade probably declined in 1987, largely because of smaller exports by Brazil, Uruguay, the EC, and Australia. The Australian meat industry faced the problem of adjusting its practices to eliminate the unacceptable levels of DDT found by the U.S. in certain samples of imported Australian beef. The EC appeared ready to implement in January 1988 a ban on imports of red meat from animals treated with hormones for nontherapeutic purposes, but late in December it decided to postpone the ban until January 1989. The U.S. opposed the ban on the grounds that no health hazard had been established. The increased cost to U.S. beef producers of discontinuing the use of growth hormones in meat produced for export to the EC was estimated at 15%.

U.S. beef exports increased in both 1986 and 1987 because of the subsidization of exports designed to prevent the depression of domestic meat prices that would result from the reduction of dairy operations under the U.S. herd buyout. Japan increased its global quota on the importation of beef to a level 20% greater than its commitment under the 1984 Beef-Citrus Understanding with the U.S. Expiration of the understanding in March 1988 was likely to focus attention on U.S. expectations of further liberalization of Japan's meat imports.

After several years of rapid growth, world output of pork declined in 1987 only because of a cutback in Chinese pork production. The decline there came after years of unprecedented growth and resulted from higher feed costs and large supplies of pork that depressed its price. By 1987 China exported more than three million hogs each year as well as about 200,000 tons of pork. The EC's production of pork continued to expand despite three adverse factors: the lowest pork prices since 1980, a 2% excess of output over consumption, and a continued decline in exports to countries outside the EC. Thus the EC announced subsidies for pork storage in January.

The slow expansion in world production of lamb, mutton, and goat meat continued in 1987. The biggest increases in output in 1987 occurred in the U.S. and China. Production and trade were expected to grow modestly in 1988, with New Zealand and Australia continuing as the most important exporters and the EC and Japan as the major import markets.

The U.S. continued to lead the strong growth in world poultry production. World trade in poultry meat also continued to expand in 1987. However, the once booming markets for poultry and eggs in the Middle East had become static because the foreign exchange earnings of those countries had diminished in recent years.

*Dairy Products.* World milk production in major producing countries was estimated (in November) to have declined 1% in 1987, mainly because of the operation of policies aimed at curtailing output in both the EC and the U.S., as well as because of drought in India and New Zealand. Output was expected to continue to fall in the EC because of the 6.5% reduction in milk quotas imposed for 1987–88 and a 3% reduction scheduled for 1988–89. In the U.S. efforts to restrict milk production through a one-time herd buyout that helped reduce the number of dairy cows by 4% in 1986 appeared to be having only short-term success. Genetic improvements in dairy herds and generally low feed prices were expected to boost productivity and output in the U.S. once again in 1988.

The consumption of fluid milk was estimated to have been down 2% in 1987, contrasted with an average annual increase of about 1% over the previous ten years. Most of the decline resulted from fears of radioactive contamination following the accident at the Soviet nuclear power plant at Chernobyl in the spring of 1986.

Production of butter and nonfat dry milk (NFDM) also declined. The manufacture of cheese expanded, partly reflecting strengthened domestic demand in Europe and a diversion of milk from butter to cheese production. The EC's butter surplus remained large in 1987 despite reductions achieved partly by the institution of a new program to feed butter to livestock. International prices for NFDM and casein strengthened in 1987, while those for cheese firmed a little and butter prices remained depressed.

### Table V. World Production and Stocks of Dairy Products[1]

| Region and country | 1985 | 1986 | 1987[2] |
|---|---|---|---|
| Production of cow and buffalo milk | | | |
| In 000,000 metric tons | | | |
| North America | 79.7 | 81.3 | 81.5 |
| United States | 64.9 | 65.5 | 64.5 |
| South America | 19.6 | 19.6 | 20.9 |
| Brazil | 10.4 | 9.8 | 11.0 |
| Western Europe | 131.0 | 132.0 | 126.6 |
| EC | 114.6 | 115.8 | 110.7 |
| France | 26.8 | 27.4 | 26.3 |
| West Germany | 25.7 | 26.4 | 24.8 |
| Italy | 10.2 | 10.3 | 10.3 |
| Netherlands, The | 12.6 | 12.7 | 11.7 |
| United Kingdom | 16.3 | 16.2 | 15.3 |
| Other Western Europe | 16.4 | 16.1 | 15.9 |
| Eastern Europe | 43.5 | 42.7 | 42.8 |
| Poland | 16.6 | 15.7 | 15.4 |
| U.S.S.R. | 98.6 | 102.2 | 103.2 |
| China | 2.5 | 2.9 | 3.5 |
| India | 19.0 | 19.5 | 17.7 |
| Australia/New Zealand[3] | 14.1 | 14.4 | 13.6 |
| Japan/South Africa | 9.7 | 9.7 | 9.5 |
| Total | 417.8 | 424.2 | 419.2 |

| Product/Region | Production | | Year-end stocks | |
|---|---|---|---|---|
| | 1986 | 1987[2] | 1986 | 1987[2] |
| In 000 metric tons | | | | |
| Butter | 6,978 | 6,492 | 2,077 | 1,792 |
| EC | 2,175 | 1,904 | 1,577 | 1,364 |
| U.S. | 545 | 495 | 114 | 70 |
| Cheese | 9,801 | 10,023 | 1,541 | 1,415 |
| EC | 4,057 | 4,152 | 809 | 839 |
| U.S. | 2,363 | 2,385 | 358 | 210 |
| Nonfat dry milk | 4,186 | 3,574 | 1,663 | 1,108 |
| EC | 2,165 | 1,716 | 1,037 | 796 |
| U.S. | 582 | 465 | 312 | 60 |

[1]Based on 38 major producing countries. Those not shown individually include (North America) Canada and Mexico; (South America) Argentina, Chile, Peru, and Venezuela; (EC) Belgium-Luxembourg, Denmark, Greece, Ireland, Portugal, and Spain; (Other Western Europe) Austria, Finland, Norway, Sweden, and Switzerland; and (Eastern Europe) Czechoslovakia, East Germany, and Yugoslavia.
[2]Preliminary.
[3]Year ending June 30 for Australia and May 31 for New Zealand.
Source: USDA, Foreign Agricultural Service, November 1987.

A technician from Advanced Genetic Sciences, Inc., sprays a row of strawberry plants in the first authorized outdoor test of Frostban, genetically altered bacteria that are expected to reduce frost damage.
AP/WIDE WORLD

*Sugar.* World sugar production was expected (in November) to be smaller in 1987–88, largely because of drought in parts of Asia and a cool, wet summer in Europe. Consumption of sugar was expected to exceed production despite slowing to a growth rate of little better than 1% from 2% in 1986–87. The nearly 3% decline in global stocks of sugar in 1986–87 contributed to a rise of two cents per pound in the average annual spot price of freely traded sugar to 6.1 cents in 1986, when it ranged between 4.9 and 8.4 cents. Although sugar stocks could fall an additional 12% in 1987–88 to a level representing 24% of annual consumption, unpromising trade prospects left the price fluctuating in the 5.6-to-7.5-cent range during 1987.

Total world imports of sugar declined about 6% to 26.4 million tons in 1986–87 and were expected to shrink further in 1987–88. Lagging trade reflected slow growth in demand, particularly as influenced by foreign exchange shortages in some less developed countries and by policies in some countries designed to substitute domestically produced sweeteners for imports.

Expanded planting and production of sugar in the U.S. provided a prominent example of the latter. In December the U.S. announced a 1988 import quota for sugar of about 680,000 metric tons, raw value; this was 25% below that of 1987, more than 75% below that of 1984, and the smallest sugar import total since 1875. U.S. legislation forced import quotas to be set at a level that restricted total domestic supplies sufficiently to prevent domestic sugar prices from falling to the point where the U.S. government would have been required to purchase sugar from domestic producers. The U.S. secretary of agriculture warned that "unless the legislation is changed, the trends will continue and cause increasingly adverse consequences for all participants in the domestic sweetener market—exporters, producers, taxpayers, refiners and manufacturers of sugar-containing products." By 1988 lower priced domestic corn

sweeteners, aided by both the support of sugar at a higher level and the low price of corn in recent years, would have captured more than 50% of the U.S. market.

In an apparent move to aid U.S. refiners of cane sugar and also certain countries hurt by the quota reductions, the U.S. Congress late in 1987 authorized the importation of 363,000 metric tons of raw sugar outside the quota. The Philippines would supply about 28% of the sugar and countries in the Caribbean region the remainder. The raw sugar would be imported at the U.S. domestic price (about 21.7 cents per pound in December), refined, and then exported at the world price (about 11.5 cents per pound) under the EEP. To finance the arrangement, "generic certificates" would be issued by the government for the purchase of commodities, such as corn or wheat, from government stocks, presumably sufficient to cover the difference and refining costs (perhaps 4.5 cents per pound).

*Coffee.* World stocks of green coffee fell to a six-year low at the end of 1986–87 because of the 58% drop in Brazil's coffee production, but they were being replenished in 1987–88 as rebounding Brazilian output resulted in a forecast (in December) strong recovery in global coffee production. Exportable production had fallen 23% in 1986–87 but was expected to regain the loss and rise above the previous level in 1987–88. Actual exports declined 5% in 1986–87, but they were also expected to recover. Importing countries built up their coffee stocks in anticipation of the reinstitution of export quotas for coffee under the International Coffee Agreement (ICA) in October 1987.

The increase in world coffee prices following news in 1985 of the prospective large shortfall in Brazil's 1986-87 coffee crop resulted in suspension of export quotas under the ICA in February 1986. The ICA composite indicator price (CIP) had peaked at an average of $2 per pound in January 1986 but then started to fall back. As an anticipatory price-strengthening measure, the ICA Council decided

### Table VI. World Production of Centrifugal (Freed from Liquid) Sugar
In 000,000 metric tons raw value

| Region and country | 1985–86 | 1986–87 | 1987–88[1] |
|---|---|---|---|
| North America | 9.4 | 10.4 | 10.8 |
| United States | 5.6 | 6.2 | 6.5 |
| Mexico | 3.9 | 4.0 | 4.2 |
| Caribbean | 8.7 | 8.6 | 8.7 |
| Cuba | 7.2 | 7.2 | 7.3 |
| Central America | 1.8 | 1.8 | 1.8 |
| South America | 13.1 | 13.8 | 14.2 |
| Argentina | 1.2 | 1.1 | 1.0 |
| Brazil | 8.4 | 8.8 | 9.2 |
| Colombia | 1.2 | 1.3 | 1.3 |
| Europe | 21.3 | 21.6 | 19.8 |
| Western Europe | 15.5 | 15.8 | 14.3 |
| EC | 14.4 | 14.9 | 13.4 |
| France | 4.3 | 3.7 | 4.0 |
| West Germany | 3.4 | 3.5 | 2.9 |
| Eastern Europe | 5.9 | 5.8 | 5.6 |
| Poland | 1.8 | 1.9 | 1.8 |
| U.S.S.R. | 8.3 | 8.7 | 8.3 |
| Africa and Middle East | 10.0 | 10.0 | 10.1 |
| South Africa | 2.2 | 2.1 | 2.2 |
| Turkey | 1.4 | 1.5 | 1.6 |
| Asia | 22.6 | 24.0 | 23.8 |
| China | 5.5 | 5.8 | 5.7 |
| India | 8.0 | 9.1 | 8.9 |
| Indonesia | 1.7 | 1.8 | 1.9 |
| Pakistan | 1.2 | 1.4 | 1.4 |
| Philippines | 1.6 | 1.4 | 1.4 |
| Thailand | 2.6 | 2.6 | 2.5 |
| Oceania | 3.7 | 3.9 | 3.7 |
| Australia | 3.4 | 3.4 | 3.4 |
| Total production[2] | 99.0 | 102.8 | 101.2 |
| Total consumption[2] | 98.4 | 100.4 | 101.7 |
| Total ending stocks[2] | 28.3 | 27.5 | [3] |
| Excluding U.S.[2] | 26.8 | 26.1 | 23.2 |

[1]Preliminary.
[2]Series revised from previous years to be more inclusive. Global totals change relatively little except for stocks that were revised substantially downward.
[3]Not estimated because U.S. import quota had not yet been announced at time of estimates.
Source: USDA, Foreign Agricultural Service, November 1987.

West German farmers, angered by an agreement of the European Communities that they claimed would be very costly to them, dump hundreds of litres of milk in front of the European Patent Office in Munich.
AFP PHOTO

in May 1986 to impose export quotas automatically if the CIP fell to $1.35 per pound. The council reversed itself in September 1986 and could not agree to act when prices fell to $1.18 per pound in January 1987 and then to 96 cents by July, the lowest in "real" terms in more than 25 years.

The deadlock resulted because Brazil would not accept allocations based on "objective criteria," while most consumer members and some producers rejected the traditional "ad hoc" approach to quota distribution. The distribution of coffee export quotas among members had remained nearly stagnant since their reintroduction in October 1980. The distribution then was based roughly on market shares as they existed in the 1960s but also reflected "ad hoc" political considerations. Opponents of the allocations argued that the relative production capacity of the members had changed and that "objective criteria" that assessed national production and stocks available for export over a multiyear period should be used.

Most of the objections to the traditional method came from exporters with quotas that were small relative to their exportable supplies, many of whom had begun to expand output to take advantage of shortages created by the disastrous Brazilian frost in 1975. Because of its poor 1986–87 crop, Brazil's traditional share of about 30% might have been reduced as much as 2% under "objective criteria."

Agreement to reimpose export quotas was finally reached by all but Indonesia in October 1987, the beginning of the 1987–88 coffee year. Prices, in response, had risen to $1.14 per pound by November. The complicated compromise formula did not greatly alter the quota distribution, although some small movement toward "objective criteria" in 1988–89 was accepted. The course to be taken by Indonesia was not certain. The agreement also provided for reductions in the quotas during the early months of the year, intended to boost prices above the $1.20 lower band of the ICA.

*Cocoa.* An expected (in October) record-high cocoa harvest in 1987–88 seemed likely to lead to a buildup in cocoa bean stocks for the fourth consecutive year. Cocoa bean prices (New York futures, nearest three-month average), which averaged 89 cents per pound in 1986, had slipped to a low of 84.8 cents by February 1987. This should have triggered automatic purchases of cocoa for the buffer stock under the new International Cocoa Agreement (ICCA), which became effective provisionally on Jan. 20, 1987.

However, disagreement over new rules for operating the buffer stock prevented purchases of excess cocoa stocks until May and June, when 75,000 tons—two-thirds from

Nigeria—were added. Prices at first strengthened a little but then slipped back to the 87–88-cent range. Questions about graduated prices for different grades of cocoa and whether purchases could be made from nonmembers were at the centre of the controversy. The ICCA inherited from the old agreement a buffer stock of about 100,000 tons of cocoa and $245 million for use in maintaining prices within a range of 1,600 and 2,270 Special Drawing Rights per ton ($0.85 and $1.21 per pound).

The ICCA's governing council in both July and September 1987 considered, but could not reach agreement on, proposals to reduce the ICCA's lower limit, and it suspended purchases by the buffer stock's manager until December. Partly at issue was the question of whether supplies were likely to continue to be so ample as to make the buffer stock's funds insufficient for purchasing enough cocoa to maintain prices within the ICCA range. At a December meeting it could not agree on supplementary measures for stabilizing cocoa prices such as export quotas or increased levies on sales to nonmembers.

*Cotton.* The 1986–87 cotton year opened in August 1986 with large stocks and export prices (Northern European "A" Index) averaging near 37 cents per pound. The previous decline in prices during 1986 had led to a sharp cutback in the cotton harvest in the early part of 1986–87 and to expanded consumption and trade in cotton during the balance of the year. As a result, prices climbed steadily during 1986–87, reaching a peak of 86.6 cents per pound by August 1987. Cotton production throughout the world responded by rising an estimated (in December) 10% in 1987–88. Most of the increase took place in the U.S., where 17% larger plantings resulted in a nearly 47% increase in production, and in China. Both countries had had sharply reduced production the previous year because of large surpluses. Reflecting the prospect of more ample supplies, prices slipped to an average of 75.8 cents per pound in November 1987. World stocks of cotton declined about 18% during 1986–87 to a more normal 25.8 million bales (480-lb bales), and only a modest increase was forecast for 1987–88.

Total exports of cotton climbed 26% in 1986–87 to 25.8 million bales. The U.S. captured most of the gains, its exports jumping from about 2 million bales in 1985–86 to almost 6.7 million in 1986–87. U.S. cotton exports had collapsed because domestic price supports had made it more profitable for farmers to sell their cotton to the federal government than to export it during the period of depressed world prices in 1985–86. The Food Security Act of 1985 authorized the use of government marketing loans that permitted subsidized sales of U.S. cotton at competitive world prices. Export prices had risen above the U.S. support level by the second half of 1987.

**International Trade Policy.** *Canada-U.S. Trade Agreement.* In October 1987 the U.S. and Canada agreed in principle to a broad range of measures that aimed to remove trade barriers and to expand access to each other's markets. The final detailed agreement was to be signed by U.S. Pres. Ronald Reagan and Canadian Prime Minister Brian Mulroney on Jan. 2, 1988, and thereafter submitted to the U.S. Congress. Implementation of the agreement also depended upon ratification by the Canadian Parliament and agreement by Canadian provinces to change certain legislation. The agreement represented an important, but far from complete, movement toward the creation of the North American "free trade area" envisioned by some.

Agricultural trade between Canada and the U.S. accounted for about $4.5 billion of the $124 billion in total two-way trade between the two countries in 1986. The U.S. enjoyed a $500 million net agricultural trade surplus in 1986, but it had been dwindling in the 1980s, in large part because the depreciation of the Canadian dollar made Canada's exports cheaper in the U.S. market.

The provisions of the agreement included the phased elimination of all agricultural tariffs within 10 years, although tariffs on fresh fruits and vegetables could revert to current levels under certain conditions over the next 20 years. Trade in processed, high-value products generally should benefit most because tariffs were highest for such products. Both countries accepted the right to appeal decisions to a bilateral dispute-settlement panel. The two countries decided to leave the negotiation of reductions in programs subsidizing their producers, including most of the nontariff trade barriers associated with them, to the broader multilateral trade talks (*see* below).

Both countries agreed to exempt the other from import restrictions on red meat under their countercyclical domestic import laws, which were designed to limit meat imports when domestic production was large. Both also agreed not to subsidize directly exports of agricultural products to the other and to minimize technical barriers to trade in food and beverages. Canada agreed to end certain transportation subsidies on agricultural commodities moving through western ports to the U.S. markets. U.S. wines and spirits were promised increased access to the Canadian market, while the U.S. guaranteed that it would not apply quantitative restrictions to the importation of Canadian products containing up to 10% of sugar. Canada also agreed to increase its global import quotas for poultry, poultry products, and eggs. A novel feature of the pact involved Canada's agreement to eliminate import licenses for U.S. wheat, barley, and oats as soon as domestic supports for those products in both countries were equalized.

*Multilateral Trade Negotiations.* The agricultural negotiations conducted in 1987 under the auspices of the General Agreement on Tariffs and Trade (GATT) were broader in scope than any previous GATT negotiations. For the first time, the relationship between agricultural trade policies and domestic agricultural policies became a legitimate subject for negotiation. The agreed-upon ground rules called for greater "discipline on the use of all direct and indirect subsidies and other measures affecting directly or indirectly agricultural trade, including the phased reduction of their negative effects and dealing with their causes." Another aim was the reduction of import barriers, including minimization of the adverse trade effects of various sanitary regulations.

The agricultural negotiations were scheduled to continue for four years. The first phase, completed in 1987, considered the nature and causes of problems in agricultural trade along with the basic principles that should govern it and examined proposals by the participants for achieving the negotiating objectives. The second, during 1988, was to begin the negotiation of specific issues dealing with the strengthening of GATT rules and disciplines; with the nature and content of new multilateral commitments, including implementing programs and transitional arrangements; and with the exchange of concessions.

The U.S. in July 1987 was the first to submit a pro-

**Table VII. World Green Coffee Production**

In 000 60-kg bags

| Region and country | 1985–86 | 1986–87[1] | 1987–88[2] |
|---|---|---|---|
| North America | 15,119 | 16,844 | 16,523 |
| Costa Rica | 1,514 | 2,460 | 2,300 |
| El Salvador | 2,300 | 2,375 | 2,350 |
| Guatemala | 2,650 | 2,838 | 2,700 |
| Honduras | 1,062 | 1,500 | 1,480 |
| Mexico | 4,750 | 4,850 | 4,850 |
| South America | 49,608 | 29,913 | 54,162 |
| Brazil | 33,000 | 13,900 | 38,000 |
| Colombia | 12,000 | 11,000 | 11,500 |
| Ecuador | 1,966 | 2,268 | 1,960 |
| Africa | 19,986 | 20,213 | 20,221 |
| Cameroon | 2,067 | 2,417 | 1,700 |
| Côte d'Ivoire | 4,420 | 4,250 | 4,500 |
| Ethiopia | 2,833 | 2,700 | 2,900 |
| Kenya | 2,011 | 1,814 | 1,900 |
| Uganda | 2,700 | 2,700 | 2,800 |
| Zaire | 1,610 | 1,965 | 1,830 |
| Asia and Oceania | 10,757 | 11,565 | 10,301 |
| India | 2,033 | 3,080 | 2,000 |
| Indonesia | 5,800 | 5,800 | 5,500 |
| Total production | 95,470 | 78,535 | 101,207 |
| Exportable[3] | 74,411 | 57,186 | 78,453 |
| Beginning stocks[4] | 37,271 | 42,037 | 32,747 |
| Exports | 69,645 | 66,264 | 69,027 |

[1]Preliminary.
[2]Forecast.
[3]Production minus domestic use.
[4]In exporting countries.
Source: USDA, Foreign Agricultural Service, December 1987.

**Table VIII. World Cocoa Bean Production**

In 000 metric tons

| Region and country | 1985–86 | 1986–87 | 1987–88[1] |
|---|---|---|---|
| North and Central America | 97 | 100 | 96 |
| South America | 555 | 496 | 563 |
| Brazil | 375 | 355 | 400 |
| Ecuador | 112 | 70 | 85 |
| Africa | 1,095 | 1,089 | 1,098 |
| Cameroon | 119 | 125 | 120 |
| Côte d'Ivoire[2] | 580 | 590 | 590 |
| Ghana | 219 | 225 | 225 |
| Nigeria[3] | 130 | 100 | 115 |
| Asia and Oceania | 215 | 250 | 272 |
| Malaysia | 130 | 165 | 185 |
| Total production | 1,963 | 1,935 | 2,029 |
| Beans ground | 1,829 | 1,855 | 1,900 |

[1]Forecast.
[2]Includes some cocoa marketed from Ghana.
[3]Includes cocoa marketed through Benin.
Source: USDA, Foreign Agricultural Service, October 1987.

**Table IX. World Cotton Production**

In 000,000 480-lb bales

| Region and country | 1985–86 | 1986–87 | 1987–88 |
|---|---|---|---|
| Western Hemisphere | 21.0 | 15.6 | 21.7 |
| United States | 13.4 | 9.7 | 14.3 |
| Mexico | 1.0 | 0.6 | 1.0 |
| Brazil | 3.8 | 3.0 | 3.3 |
| Europe | 1.1 | 1.4 | 1.2 |
| U.S.S.R. | 12.3 | 11.7 | 11.0 |
| Africa | 5.7 | 6.0 | 6.0 |
| Egypt | 2.0 | 1.8 | 1.6 |
| Sudan, The | 0.7 | 0.7 | 0.8 |
| Asia and Oceania[1] | 38.9 | 34.9 | 37.0 |
| China | 19.0 | 16.3 | 18.0 |
| India | 8.4 | 7.4 | 7.7 |
| Pakistan | 5.7 | 6.1 | 5.8 |
| Turkey | 2.4 | 2.2 | 2.3 |
| Australia | 1.2 | 1.0 | 1.1 |
| Total | 79.1 | 69.6 | 76.8 |

[1]Includes Middle East.
Source: USDA, Foreign Agricultural Service, December 1987

posal, a broad-ranging plan to reform world agriculture and agricultural trade radically. The EC, the Cairns Group of "nonsubsidizing exporters," Canada, Japan, and the Scandinavian countries responded in October. The following discussion focuses on the major issues that were generated by the positions taken by the U.S. and the EC on agricultural supports and protection. Not covered are such matters as treatment of trade in the less developed countries, health and sanitary border restrictions, GATT rules, and methods for settling disputes.

Central to the U.S. approach was the belief that levels of production and trade should be determined by each country's relative efficiency and comparative advantage as indicated by market forces rather than by the size of government budgets. The U.S. viewed the distortions in world agriculture as being caused by a departure from the principles of free markets; the consequences included large surpluses of commodities, massive government expenditures, inefficient allocation of resources, and spreading trade conflicts. The solution proposed by the U.S. was the comprehensive phased elimination of government intervention in markets for all agricultural commodities, food, beverages, forest products, and fish and fish products. Proposed parallel actions included the complete phasing out over ten years of all agricultural subsidies that directly or indirectly affect trade, the freezing and then phasing out over ten years of the commodities exported with the aid of export subsidies, and the phasing out of all import barriers over ten years.

The key feature of the first of two negotiating phases, the "zero option," was agreement to a schedule for reducing the overall aggregate level of support by countries to agriculture to zero in ten years. This was a major departure from the traditional negotiating method of individually exchanging requests and offers for separate commodities. It required agreement on a yardstick for measuring the aggregate level of benefits, incentives, and financial support that governments afforded their producers. The U.S. advocated the concept of the "producer subsidy equivalent" (PSE), the cash subsidy that would be needed to compensate farmers for the elimination of government support.

The second negotiating phase of the U.S. plan would seek agreement on specific changes in policies for reducing the overall level of support. Individual governments would have flexibility in choosing the means for achieving the reduction, but they would negotiate other commitments "to assure parallel reductions in support" for certain sensitive commodities and programs.

The EC considered the root problem in agricultural trade to be "the imbalance between supply and demand."

The oversupply of commodities that the U.S. regarded as a symptom of the disease of government intervention was what the EC diagnosed as the disease itself. It called for the phased reduction of "the negative effects of support on international markets," as opposed to the U.S. emphasis on the causes. This objective was put on an equal footing with the sociopolitical aims of "providing a sounder framework for continuation of the agricultural activity necessary to economic stability, social cohesion and the environment." It appeared to reflect the EC's traditional resistance to rapid changes in the status of its agricultural sector.

The EC prescribed a two-stage cure that gave highest priority to reducing the effects of supply-demand imbalances in the near term before moving on to more comprehensive reductions of trade barriers and overall domestic support for agriculture. The EC would deal with all raw and processed agricultural products, "giving priority to sectors in structural surplus and those where serious disruptions are foreseeable."

The EC first sought agreements on "emergency measures," to take effect in the next marketing year, which could be renewed; they would deal especially with cereals, rice, sugar, oilseeds, dairy products, and beef and veal. More specifically, they included (1) "price discipline" for cereals, interpretable as actions to stabilize grain prices at higher than current levels, and "corresponding arrangements" for cereal substitutes, an allusion to control of markets for products such as soybeans and corn gluten (major U.S. exports to the EC) whose importation disturbed EC domestic support programs for grains and oilseeds; (2) "disciplines" to reduce sugar supplied to the world market and for maintenance of "present access to traditional import markets," the latter relevant to the tightening of U.S. sugar-import restrictions; and (3) compliance by major exporters of dairy products that do not belong to the GATT's international dairy arrangement (IDA) with IDA "disciplines." The IDA prescribed minimum prices for dairy products in international trade. The U.S. withdrew from the IDA in 1984, protesting that the EC had evaded the limits in a sale of butter to the U.S.S.R.

The EC proposal postponed to some unspecified later stage the "concerted reduction in support" that was "coupled with a readjustment of external protection." This postponement was at the core of disagreement between the EC and the U.S. The EC could accept the PSE yardstick as a measure of support if it dealt only with actions having a significant impact on trade, quantified the effect of production restraints, and dealt with the effect of world price and currency fluctuations.

The proposal by the Cairns Group (comprising Argentina, Australia, Brazil, Canada, Chile, Colombia, Hungary, Indonesia, Malaysia, New Zealand, the Philippines, Thailand, and Uruguay) represented something of a compromise between the EC's concern with alleviating current market conditions and the U.S. desire to begin immediately on fundamental agricultural reform.

The group would end all restrictions on market access not explicitly sanctioned by the GATT. All agricultural tariffs would be bound near zero. Subsidies, both domestic and external, that had a negative impact on trade would be prohibited. The Cairns Group accepted the PSE concept but would expand its use to include a measure of both aggregate support and support for individual commodities.

(RICHARD M. KENNEDY)

*See also* Feature Article: *World Revolution in Agriculture;* Gardening.

This article updates the *Macropædia* article The History of AGRICULTURE.

### Table X. Shipments of Food Aid in Cereals

In 000 metric ton grain equivalent

| Region and country | Average 1982–83, 1984–85 | 1985–86 | 1986–87[1] | 1987–88[1] |
|---|---|---|---|---|
| Australia | 425 | 345 | 368 | 300 |
| Canada | 868 | 1,216 | 1,240 | 1,000 |
| EC | 2,006 | 1,562 | 1,738 | 1,600 |
| By members | 964 | 645 | 791 | ... |
| By organization | 1,042 | 917 | 947 | ... |
| Japan | 414 | 374 | 434 | 350 |
| Sweden | 86 | 69 | 74 | 80 |
| United States | 6,189 | 6,675 | 7,861 | 7,500 |
| Others[2] | 540 | 564 | 382 | 365 |
| Total | 10,527 | 10,805 | 12,097 | 11,195 |
| Percentage to low-income food-deficit countries[3] | ... | 87% | 83% | 86% |

[1]Partly estimated.
[2]Includes Argentina, Austria, China, Finland, India, Norway, OPEC Special Fund, Saudi Arabia, Spain, Switzerland, Turkey, and World Food Program, but not necessarily for all years.
[3]Per capita incomes under U.S. $790 in 1985.
Source: FAO, *Food Outlook*, December 1987.

## FISHERIES

In 1987 the fishing press was preoccupied with the Falkland Islands squid bonanza, fish quotas, and the West's "discovery" of *surimi* (processed minced fish). Demand for *surimi* and for crab sticks and other *surimi* products seemed insatiable. In the U.S. increasingly large vessels were converted to catch and process Alaska pollack, the prime raw material for *surimi;* in Europe ever larger trawlers with refrigerated seawater tanks were being built to catch the still plentiful blue whiting, most of which was destined to become *surimi*.

At 89.2 million metric tons, the world catch in 1986 was 4.7% above that of 1985, reflecting a welcome return to Chile and Peru of the anchovy shoals lost earlier as a result of changes in the El Niño Current. Good catches of this species had been expected for 1987, but by late summer it was apparent that conditions had changed again, and the target of 6.5 million metric tons would not be reached. Peru was forced to buy fish oil to make up the deficit.

In northern waters stocks of the more popular species, such as cod and haddock, were still classed as "pressure stocks," with catches controlled by quota. Even the *Loligo* squid of the South Atlantic, centred on the Falklands, were being fished more cautiously, an attitude supported by the long-awaited report of the UN Food and Agriculture Organization on South Atlantic stocks. More than 200 vessels had been licensed by the Falklands government for the previous season, but the number was now reduced to 90 mostly Spanish vessels—62 for finfish and 28 for squid and finfish. The bonanza of the 1986 fishing season had brought £6 million in revenue to the Falklands, and this was expected to at least quadruple in 1987. Investments were planned for a dry dock, cold store, improved communications, and bunkering facilities.

In the U.S. americanization of the fishery within the 200-mi exclusive economic zone continued, with increased emphasis on the use of U.S. vessels to catch U.S. fish, even if that fish was transferred directly to foreign ships. Alaska pollack was still the main species in demand by Japan for *surimi* production, but there was a trend to market pollack fillets for direct consumption as an alternative to cod. U.S. interests were eager to boost their share of *surimi* production. The prohibitive cost of building new vessels, and the impossibility of building abroad, under the Jones Act, led to a number of conversions at home and in Norway. One was a World War II tanker 100 m (328 ft) in length, only the bow section of which remained after "conversion." The ship was expected to handle 300 metric tons of pollack, producing 60 metric tons of *surimi,* a day. Other operators were converting redundant oil-rig service boats to trawlers and saving hard cash in the process.

On the Pacific coast salmon trollers were finding their position challenged by gill-netters for the first time. In addition, they were having to compete with salmon farm production, which was reaching major proportions in Scandinavia, other parts of Europe, and, more recently, Canada. Farther south the shrimp industry was still unable to satisfy domestic demand, despite bigger catches on the west coast, and U.S. imports rose again, this time by 11% to 67,000 metric tons. The Pacific fishery for herring roe, for export to Japan, was booming, and it was said that the cost of a license sometimes exceeded that of the fishing boat that used it.

The Canadian authorities became more protectionist, and it was made clear that only conservation-minded nations need apply for licenses. It was even suggested that national responsibility for conservation should be extended beyond the internationally agreed 200 mi. The main event for Canada was the restoration of profit and stability to the once-troubled Maritime fisheries. The government-financed Fishery Products International Ltd., an amalgam of troubled companies that were nevertheless vital to the fisheries, was now making a profit and was duly reprivatized by a Can$177 million-share issue. Mexico was making a determined effort to stimulate its tuna fishery with government aid; an 8,000-metric-ton export target to support the 85-strong fleet of tuna boats was planned.

Japan remained the leading fishing nation, with production of about 11 million metric tons, but this was still not enough to satisfy the fish-hungry Japanese, who imported 1.2 trillion yen worth of marine products. The importance of this industry to Japan was reflected in the 305 billion yen budget of its main administrative body, the Fisheries Agency. The wider use of small pelagic species such as sardine, which could be caught in home waters, was encouraged, and efforts continued to boost the natural stocks by the use of hatcheries and of artificial reefs to provide shelter and food for immature fish. The last Japanese commercial whaling expedition returned in 1987 as pressure from foreign environmental lobbies combined with economic factors ended the centuries-old tradition.

The U.S.S.R. had difficulty satisfying home demand. The national catch produced about 5 million metric tons of edible marine products, 2.6 million metric tons of which were frozen and one million metric tons canned. Soviet interest in the waters around New Zealand persisted. Poland remained first in fishing vessel production, mostly for Soviet bloc countries and Europe. Renewal of the ag-

**Table XI. World Fisheries, 1985[1]**
In 000 metric tons

| Country | Catch | | Trade | |
|---|---|---|---|---|
| | Total | Inland | Imports | Exports |
| Japan | 11,443.7 | 205.2 | 1,490.1 | 776.7 |
| U.S.S.R. | 10,552.9 | 905.6 | 421.4 | 640.2 |
| China | 6,778.8 | 2,943.7 | ... | 132.9 |
| Chile | 4,804.4 | 0.6 | 1.0 | 1,312.5 |
| U.S. | 4,766.8 | 74.3 | 1,422.9 | 452.4 |
| Peru | 4,168.4 | 23.1 | 6.2 | 690.8 |
| India | 2,810.0 | 1,080.0 | — | 78.5 |
| South Korea | 2,649.9 | 51.9 | 112.8 | 396.9 |
| Thailand | 2,123.6 | 165.6 | 152.4 | 456.8 |
| Norway | 2,106.8 | 0.4 | 117.8 | 712.7 |
| Indonesia | 2,067.1 | 265.7 | 53.1 | 70.5 |
| Philippines | 1,867.7 | 534.1 | 19.2 | 55.8 |
| North Korea | 1,700.0 | 110.0 | — | 20.6 |
| Denmark | 1,696.3 | 24.0 | 317.6 | 743.7 |
| Iceland | 1,680.2 | 0.5 | 4.4 | 688.8 |
| Canada | 1,425.8 | 44.0 | 118.0 | 533.3 |
| Spain | 1,337.7 | 26.2 | 321.9 | 227.3 |
| Mexico | 1,226.2 | 113.0 | 7.7 | 46.1 |
| Brazil | 959.3 | 211.5 | 37.2 | 58.6 |
| Ecuador | 901.1 | — | | 308.1 |
| France | 844.5 | 29.8 | 569.9 | 199.1 |
| United Kingdom | 832.5 | 13.4 | 891.2 | 304.1 |
| Vietnam | 800.0 | 230.0 | — | 14.8 |
| Bangladesh | 763.7 | 573.3 | — | 20.6 |
| Poland | 683.5 | 28.9 | 177.8 | 119.1 |
| South Africa | 649.9 | 0.8 | 143.0 | 44.7 |
| Burma | 643.7 | 146.8 | | 7.1 |
| Malaysia | 632.2 | 9.3 | 218.0 | 163.5 |
| Turkey | 576.1 | 43.5 | 0.9 | 23.0 |
| The Netherlands | 504.2 | 3.8 | 525.8 | 511.8 |
| Italy | 504.1 | 41.3 | 586.6 | 151.3 |
| Morocco | 473.1 | 1.3 | — | 159.9 |
| Argentina | 410.9 | 7.6 | 13.2 | 146.0 |
| Pakistan | 408.4 | 75.1 | 0.1 | 37.3 |
| Faeroe Islands | 361.6 | — | 2.7 | 135.6 |
| Portugal | 298.5 | ... | 144.6 | 65.2 |
| New Zealand | 283.0 | — | 6.9 | 145.0 |
| Venezuela | 282.8 | 15.3 | 1.2 | 44.7 |
| Panama | 282.5 | — | 3.3 | 41.2 |
| Tanzania | 270.8 | 230.0 | 6.1 | 0.3 |
| Ghana | 254.2 | 40.0 | 21.0 | 28.6 |
| Sweden | 247.6 | 10.8 | 213.4 | 107.9 |
| Senegal | 244.0 | 15.0 | ... | 94.0 |
| Nigeria | 241.6 | 87.4 | 167.6 | 0.7 |
| Other | 6,385.2 | 1,737.3 | 4,170.7 | 1,574.1 |
| World | 84,945.3 | 10,120.1 | 12,467.7 | 12,542.8 |

[1]Excludes whaling.
Source: United Nations Food and Agriculture Organization, *Yearbook of Fishery Statistics*, vol. 60 and 61.

Brian Beal, the environmental resources coordinator at the University of Maine at Machias, displays a young lobster to be used in a hatchery program aimed at helping to augment the diminishing lobster population in New England.

SCOTT PERRY—THE NEW YORK TIMES

ing Baltic fleet was proceeding, with the distant-water fleet next in line. New Zealand waters produced good yields, and exports rose to $NZ 657 million in 1986. Like Australia, New Zealand was exploiting the easily caught shoals of orange roughy, which proved highly marketable in the U.S. Squid was also proving a valuable resource, harvested by 85 licensed squid jiggers with a total allowable catch of 105,000 metric tons.

China was rapidly emerging as a fishing power, with a 13% increase in production for 1986 to some eight million metric tons. Western technology and equipment were acquired, including a high-tech fishing simulator from the Humber College of Technology in England, and many new contacts were made following a fishing exhibition in China. Another was scheduled for 1988 in Shanghai. China was believed to be seeking to expand its distant-water fleet. Taiwan's output in 1986 was constrained by a record loss of 395 fishing vessels and some 1,200 reports of damage, mostly to vessels of under 50 tons. Poor safety standards were blamed. Taiwanese trawlers, squid jiggers, and tuna boats ranged the southern oceans; an application was made for 40 vessels to fish in Argentine waters.

The Indian government continued to press for more deepwater fisheries and was actively seeking joint venture partners; talks with the Soviet Union proved fruitless. India had more vessels built abroad, with several 27-m (88.5-ft) trawlers delivered from The Netherlands. The Australian Shipbuilding Industries led a delegation to India in a quest for sales of expertise and fishing vessels. The value of Indian shrimp exports rose by 15.7% in 1986 as a result of improved quality and price, and during the year the vital U.S. approval for processed shrimp was restored.

World demand for shrimp and prawns continued to be unsatisfied, and countries such as Greenland, the Faeroe Islands, Iceland, and Norway were exploiting the situation by using big stern trawlers able to fish in icy waters and producing frozen packs of both shell-on and peeled shrimp on board. Iceland's shrimp catch rose to over 30,000 metric tons, but Norway experienced a slight reduction. The practice of exporting seafood in refrigerated standard containers, already well established in Spain, was proving popular in Iceland.

Spanish shipyards were enjoying a much-needed boom, stimulated by entry into the European Communities (EC), with its attendant subsidies, and by new fishing opportunities in the Falklands. Construction for joint ventures with other countries and exports to Africa and New Zealand also helped to fill order books. One interesting completion was the 78.5-m (257.5-ft) factory stern trawler *Sil* for the giant Pescanova group of Vigo. This was a new-generation vessel with a fishing and storage capacity far higher than that of its much larger 1960s predecessor. Spain's fisheries agreement with Morocco expired early in 1987, and its renegotiation proved difficult for the EC negotiators, since the matter was clouded by side issues often unconnected with fishing. Rather than suspend fishing operations, it was decided to extend the existing agreement until December 1987 while negotiations continued.

In the U.K. the increased popularity of fish in the diet and improved prices for a well-graded and well-presented catch encouraged fishermen to install weighing, grading, and washing machines on relatively small vessels. The result was a sudden increase in the number of deck shelters, with attendant problems of changed stability.

On the environmental front, a major cleanup was planned for the Mediterranean—none too soon, it appeared, for one Swedish report estimated that the world was putting three times as much garbage into the sea as it was harvesting food from it.          (H. S. NOEL)

This article updates the *Macropædia* article Commercial FISHING AND MARINE PRODUCTS.

## FOOD PROCESSING

The food-processing industry improved its performance during 1987. Although the pace of company amalgamations increased, there were signs of stabilization in employment levels. More significant was the continued rise in profitability. In the U.K., for example, profit margins had increased to 6.8% by the start of the year. Notable, too, was the growing number of orders for new machinery and equipment. During 1987 companies supplying the food industry with capital equipment and manufactured raw materials saw profits and prospects rise to their highest levels in many years.

**Consumer Issues and Trends.** Consumer concern about food additives continued to be a major issue. The number of new products advertised as being—in varying degrees—free from additives reached a record level. The establishment by the U.K. food industry of a food-intolerance data bank was a sign that problems associated with food allergies were being taken more seriously.

Consumer groups increased their opposition to the use of irradiation as a means of preservation. In the U.S. they demanded that Congress impose a ban on this type of processing. In the U.K. the science board of the British Medical Association (BMA) issued warnings about the harmful effects of irradiation. It stated that vitamins C, E, and $B_1$ were broken down by the process and, although harmful bacteria, parasites, and pests would be killed, the toxins they produce would not be eradicated. The BMA board called for a full-scale international investigation into the effects of irradiation before it was made legal in the U.K. In particular, it requested the involvement of doctors from such countries as The Netherlands, where the process was widely used. Production at an irradiation plant at Fucino, southern Italy, which was to have treated 25,000 metric tons of potatoes and 7,000 tons of onions and garlic a year, was stopped as a result of fears arising from the 1986 Chernobyl nuclear power plant disaster in the U.S.S.R.

The emergence of two basic trends in eating habits, the

desire for healthier foods and the desire for convenience, became more marked in all developed countries. Sometimes these trends conflicted. Snacks, a well-established part of the U.S., Japanese, and U.K. diets, spread increasingly to continental Europe. In the U.K. and West Germany, potato-based products continued to dominate the snack market. By the standards of these countries and the U.S., the market in France remained underdeveloped. The fastest growing market for snacks was Australia. The consumption of frozen foods increased worldwide, although unevenly from one country to another. The U.S. had the highest per capita consumption at 39 kg (86 lb). In the U.K., where the market had doubled since 1979, per capita consumption at 21 kg (46 lb) was the highest in Europe. West Germany came next, while the French market, the third largest in Europe, grew by over 20% compared with the previous year.

As health awareness increased among consumers in the U.S. and Western Europe, the consumption of products low in or free from fat and sugar rose significantly at the expense of their more traditional equivalents. Certain dietary fads became evident during the year, notably in the U.S., where calcium fortification of foods and even soft drinks became fashionable. The same trend was becoming evident, to a lesser extent, in other countries.

Health consciousness allied with stricter laws against driving while drunk markedly affected drinking habits, and in all countries a shift in consumer tastes was causing dramatic changes in the beer market, where the light beer segment was developing rapidly. In many countries the trend toward low- and no-alcohol beers was becoming significant; in the U.S. these products accounted for 7% of the total beer market. In the U.K. the low- and no-alcohol sector was still small but grew by 20% over the previous year. The total beer market continued to decline slowly in both countries as well as in West Germany, where per capita consumption was the highest in the world. (See INDUSTRIAL REVIEW: Beverages: Beer.)

**New Products.** In developing new products, manufacturers found many ingenious ways to respond to the growing consumer health awareness. A Swedish company introduced to the rest of Europe a product made from sugar beet that contained 73–84% dietary fibre, with a water-soluble component making it suitable for use in such products as soup and yogurt. A British company launched a high-fibre product made from corn (maize) bran. A Dutch company introduced a product based on potato starch that could be used as a substitute for oil and fat; when mixed with water it formed a fatlike gel that could replace more than half of the oil and fat ingredients in a recipe. A U.S. company launched a milk product, a cross between sour cream and cream cheese, to compete with yogurt. A U.K. dairy company introduced a range of vegetarian cheese ingredients that did not contain animal rennet, and a company in Northern Ireland claimed a technical breakthrough with the introduction of a breaded processed egg product. New products for children appeared in Australia in the form of fruit-flavoured, stick-shaped snacks. They had a high skimmed-milk content, contained rice bran for roughage, used vegetable oil to minimize contact time with the teeth, and avoided decay-inducing sugars.

**Technology.** Products containing a blend of two artificial sweeteners, aspartame and acesulfame-K, came on the market during the year. Aspartame had no lingering aftertaste and had largely replaced saccharin, but it lacked heat and chemical stability, precluding its use in products that were to be heat-treated. Acesulfame-K did not have this disadvantage, and it blended well with aspartame, working synergistically to produce a sweetener blend with sweetening power greater than the sum of the two separate components. It was expected that studies of sweetener synergism would result in the development of a large number of new products with improved flavour and keeping qualities.

A West German company unveiled a technique of sterilizing wine with a laser beam, overcoming the disadvantage of the standard method of preservation with sulfur dioxide, which affected taste. The use of immunoassay techniques in food analysis and quality control was becoming increasingly widespread, and their potential as an alternative to more conventional methods was being recognized. For example, the possibility of detecting 0.5% pork content in beef was good news for importers in Muslim countries.

**Packaging Developments.** Product tampering continued to be a major worry. Japan had been hard hit by this scourge; chocolate boxes had been dosed with cyanide and fruit juice with weed killer, and the Japanese confectionery industry had virtually collapsed. In the U.S. there were 1,700 reported cases of tampering in 1986, 20% of them involving soft drinks and 16% dairy products. In the U.K., where the number of tampering incidents doubled over the previous year, three Edinburgh supermarkets were subjected to a sustained attack over a six-week period during which arsenic and broken glass were found in yogurt, fruit juices, and coleslaw.

Polyethylene terephthalate (PET) bottles for beer were introduced in North America; a Canadian brewery in Ontario was the first to package its products in PET, although U.K. brewers had been using PET for some time. Concern that the world's ozone layer was being depleted by chlorofluorocarbons (CFCs) led the McDonald's fast food chain to announce that it planned to discontinue using rigid foam containers based on CFCs.

**Company Developments.** Notable mergers included the formation of Quest International, the second largest flavour company in the world, through amalgamation of the Dutch flavour company Naarden with the Unilever flavour company PPF; and the merger of U.K. machinery companies APV and Baker Perkins to form the biggest food-machinery manufacturing group in the U.K. In the U.K. soft-drink sector, Coca-Cola and Cadbury Schweppes joined forces to form Coca-Cola & Schweppes Beverages, the largest soft-drink company in the country, while Pepsi-Cola joined with brewers Allied-Lyons, Bass, and Whitbread to form a rival company almost as large called Britvic Corona.

In Italy the wine industry made strenuous efforts to restore its credibility following the scandal of 1986, when at least 20 persons died from drinking wine adulterated with methyl alcohol.

**Legislation.** European food trade associations mounted intense lobbying efforts against proposals by the European Communities (EC) to impose a tax on vegetable oils and fats. Intended to reduce stocks of butter and dairy products, the proposals would have the effect of raising the retail prices of margarine and vegetable cooking oils by up to 60%. The European Court of Justice ruled that West Germany's use of its historic Reinheitsgebot law to block imports of foreign beer was a breach of the EC's principles of free trade. The law, which was promulgated in 1516, laid down that German beer may be made only from hops, barley malt, water, and yeast. A number of brewing companies hitherto excluded from the West German market, including one in Australia, made plans to export beer to West Germany.          (ANTHONY WOOLLEN)

See also Environment; Health and Disease; Industrial Review: Beverages; Textiles; Tobacco.
This article updates the Macropædia article FOOD PROCESSING.

# Anthropology

A recent study released by the American Anthropological Association reported that the statistically typical anthropologist earning a Ph.D. in 1985–86 was 38 years old, married, white, female, and childless. She conducted her fieldwork in North America and, like 51% of her classmates, she held a nonacademic job. Her (statistically modal) name was Judith.

"Judith" and her colleagues throughout the world were participating in 1987 in developments that were altering the face of anthropology. Increased awareness of the impact of historical processes and ecological relationships upon culture was shifting the focus of anthropological inquiry. In 1987 few anthropologists worked with remote, isolated tribal societies, and even fewer continued to regard cultures as static sociocultural laboratories. Most anthropologists were conducting fieldwork in their own society. Wherever they worked they were increasingly emphasizing processes of culture contact and change in their studies.

Anthropologists were also being affected by the worldwide "information revolution." Technological innovations, such as computerized data bases, electronic bulletin boards, and desktop publishing programs, enabled them to share more information with each other faster than ever before. The sheer volume of this information, however, was forcing anthropologists to abandon traditional holistic approaches emphasizing integrated study of all aspects of total human systems in favour of increased specialization.

Advances in knowledge in a rapidly changing world, moreover, were creating new and divergent research interests. Many anthropologists were reaching out beyond traditional disciplinary boundaries to work with scholars in medicine, law, sociology, political science, economics, history, biology, and other fields. These and other forms of interdisciplinary cooperation were helping anthropologists provide new insights into a diverse array of such pressing problems as the spread and containment of AIDS (acquired immune deficiency syndrome), the threat of nuclear war, and the effects of third world debt.

**Theory.** Changing world conditions increasingly were demonstrating that cultural systems behave more as menus offering possible behavioral choices than as prescriptions demanding ideal responses. Recent studies recognizing this aspect of culture were causing anthropologists to reassess many of their traditional theoretical assumptions. In her survey of these developments, "Theory in Anthropology Since the Sixties," ethnologist Sherry B. Ortner shows how growing appreciation of ways people "reinvent" their cultural realities was increasing the importance of the concept of practice as a theoretical tool in anthropology. The subject of a major symposium at the 1987 annual meeting of the American Anthropological Association, Ortner's article had a profound impact upon the discipline.

Ortner begins by tracing the development of influential symbolic, structural, ecological, and materialist theories during the 1960s. Examining the strengths and weaknesses of each approach, she goes on to show how more recent work by linguists, sociologists, historians, and anthropologists has gone beyond analyses of the impact of cultural systems upon people to analyses of ways "society and culture themselves are produced and reproduced through human intention and action." Identifying this viewpoint as practice theory, Ortner suggests that a practice-oriented approach will more effectively reveal relationships between sociocultural ideals and realities by encouraging scholarly debates based upon observable actions in real time and space rather than on idealized abstractions. This process, Ortner maintains, will both foster cooperation among anthropological specialists and enhance interdisciplinary cooperation and understanding.

**Practice.** Ortner's practice-oriented approach was only the most recent expression of the long-standing anthropological impulse to translate theory into action. Helping traditional communities cope with change in Canada, Connecticut, and India, protesting the devastation of tribal lands in Sarawak and Brazil, sponsoring a scholarship fund for Australian Aboriginal women, or reporting on the effects of nuclear fallout among the Saami of Scandinavia, anthropologists throughout the world continued to combine scholarly research with practical concern for the people they studied.

In northern Alberta anthropologist Keltie Paul worked for the Fort Chipewyan band of Cree Indians as their director of social development. Administering federal programs for the Crees, she did many of the jobs formerly performed by government agents. Unlike her predecessors, however,

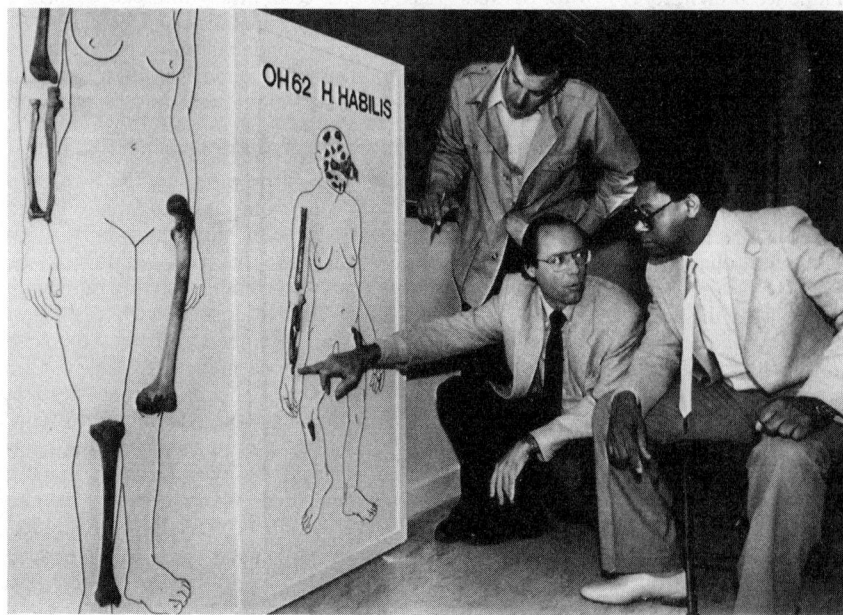

AP/WIDE WORLD

Tim White (pointing) compares the small bones of *Homo habilis* with those of *Homo erectus* in a discussion with a graduate student. Donald Johanson, director of the Institute of Human Origins, listens attentively. The two million-year-old *Homo habilis* bones were discovered in the Olduvai Gorge, Tanzania.

she worked for the Crees as their employee rather than as an administrator employed by the government.

Ethnographer James Wherry served the Mashantucket Pequot tribe of Connecticut in a similar capacity. Working with tribal chairman Richard A. Hayward and an active tribal council, Wherry assisted the Mashantucket Pequots in their successful efforts in 1984 to settle outstanding claims against the government and achieve federal recognition as an Indian tribe. After that, the Mashantucket Pequots increased their reservation land base from 87 to 623 ha (214 to 1,539 ac), established an effective housing authority and several successful business ventures, and were host to a major scholarly convocation devoted to their culture and history.

The Fort Chipewyan Crees and the Mashantucket Pequots employed anthropologists to make development work for them. Half a world away modernization threatened to disrupt the traditional lives of the Tibetan Buddhist Ladakh people living in remote valleys of the north Indian Himalayan plateau. Alarmed by Ladakh abandonment of traditional practices and materials in favour of the more questionable benefits of modernization, the Swedish linguist Helena Norberg-Hodge organized the Ladakh Project. Through this project, Ladakhis were being given assistance in adapting traditional practices and selecting appropriate new technologies in ways that would build upon the strengths of their traditional culture rather than destroy it.

Although government organizations continued to fund most anthropological research, support provided by Survival International and other private foundations was financing and publicizing an increasing amount of applied anthropological research supporting threatened tribal peoples throughout the world. Anthropologists working with Survival International publicized the protests of Penan tribesfolk against logging operations destroying their forests and homes in the Malaysian state of Sarawak. Other anthropologists working with Survival International or Cultural Survival, a similar organization, were focusing international attention upon the Grande Carajas iron mining and development project that was causing turmoil in Brazilian Amazonia, providing scholarship funds for advanced education of Aboriginal and Torres Strait Islands women in Australia, and assessing the environmental impact of radioactive fallout from the Chernobyl nuclear plant accident upon the Saami (also known as Lapps) of Scandinavia.

**Other Developments.** Although practice-oriented studies had become increasingly important in recent years, anthropologists also continued to pursue more traditional areas of interest. Important research continued to be conducted in gender studies. Gilbert Herdt's *The Sambia,* for example, analyzed the role of ritual homosexuality in training young male warriors of a highland New Guinea people. In her study *Oglala Women,* Marla Powers examined contemporary economic, ceremonial, and political roles of Teton Lakota women.

Persistently high unemployment rates and underemployment and part-time employment of anthropologists in academic departments remained major problems. Despite these difficulties, increases in the pace of anthropological research, rising nonacademic employment rates, continued high levels of public interest in anthropological issues, and the growing emphasis upon practical applications of ethnological theory and ethnographic methods suggested that anthropology would continue to experience vigorous growth in the late 1980s.          (ROBERT S. GRUMET)

*See also* Archaeology.

This article updates the *Macropædia* article Human EVOLUTION.

# Archaeology

**Eastern Hemisphere.** During 1987 an increasing number of reports appeared concerning new scientific procedures for recovering evidence of the past. A team of University of California Egyptologists believed they might have located the tomb of several sons of the pharaoh Ramses II by using high-technology equipment designed for oil exploration. Also in Egypt, the still unexposed chamber of the pair containing funerary boats was tapped for samples of its 4,600-year-old air. The boat in the chamber exposed in 1954, near the Great Pyramid of Khufu, was showing signs of deterioration, and it was anticipated that a test of the ancient air might suggest ways to arrest the process. At the 6th–7th-century AD Anglo-Saxon site of Sutton Hoo in England, burials—of which even the bones had disintegrated—were being reconstituted for study by means of a three-dimensional sensor. The sensor's magnetic pulses were recorded by a computer, and a model of the original burial resulted. The first Early Bronze Age tree-ring dating sequence for Anatolia and the Aegean was obtained from oak charcoal at Demircihuyuk in western Turkey.

Considerable restoration activity was being carried on. A huge construction crane and scaffolding were rising within and about the Athenian Parthenon, and the Kampuchean temple complex of Angkor Wat was being restored by a team of Indian archaeologists. The controversy intensified over whether linear cut-mark traces on prehistoric human bones were indications of cannibalism or the cleaning of flesh from bodies as part of a funerary rite. No decision either way was reached. Off the port of Rhodes, divers claimed to have recovered part of a large stone hand that they believed was a fragment of the Colossus of Rhodes. However, Greek archaeologists refuted the claim. In Israel a band of Orthodox Jews disrupted the U.S. archaeological excavations at the Roman port site of Caesarea. The protesters objected to any disturbance of human bones.

The Turkish government filed a lawsuit against the Metropolitan Museum of Art in New York City for the return of illegally excavated and illegally exported 6th-century BC antiquities. The gold and silver objects had been exported in the 1960s. The archaeological community was concerned that the matter might jeopardize the issuance of permits for excavations by U.S. professionals.

*Pleistocene Prehistory.* Although new human paleontological evidence around two million years old appeared during the year at Olduvai Gorge in Tanzania, no associated artifacts had so far been reported. There were, however, claims for hominid occupation at about the same time in northern Pakistan, based on eight "definite" stone artifacts. Should these pieces become generally accepted as positive stone tools, the find would be the earliest evidence of the *Homo habilis* range outside Africa.

Much fine work was done on the restoration and preservation of the famous Magdalenian hunters' campsite adjacent to the Seine in the Paris Basin. The site, Pincevent, gave a remarkably clear picture of what life may have been for the latest Ice Age reindeer hunters of western Europe. Evidence continued to mount concerning the occupation of Australia at a much earlier date than had hitherto been believed. Stone tools recovered in a rock shelter, inland from the MacDonnell Ranges, dated to over 20,000 years ago, and thermoluminescence dating of tools found west of Sydney suggested *c.* 45,000 years ago. There was also evidence suggesting that New Guinea was on the route of this early dispersion, when the whole area was part of the great landmass called Sahul.

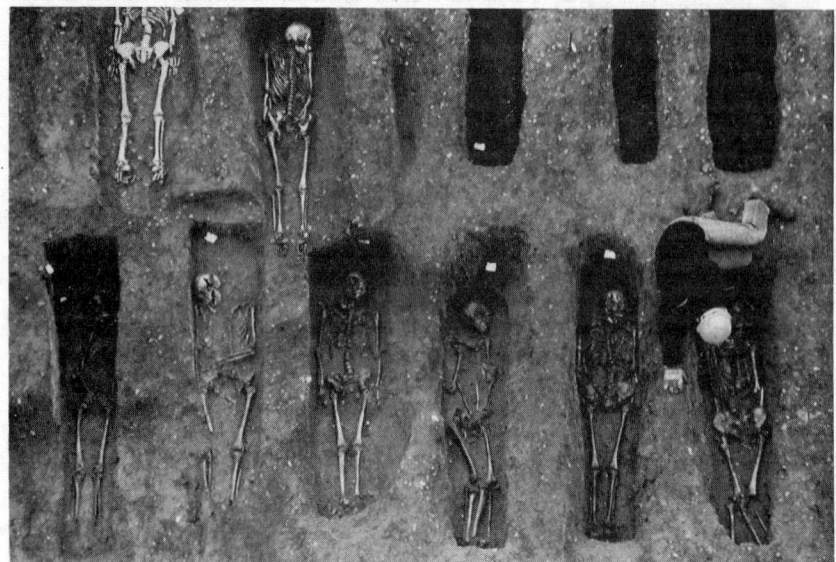

These graves were among the estimated 1,000 graves uncovered near the Tower of London. They contain what was believed to be the remains of persons who died during the Black Death, a plague that swept through Europe during the mid-14th century.
AP/WIDE WORLD

*Middle East.* Understandably, there was little archaeological news from parts of southwestern Asia. Conditions for fieldwork did appear to be improving in Jordan and in the regions of Syria and northern Iraq where salvage efforts were under way on sites soon to be flooded behind new dams. In Egypt teams of investigators from America, Europe (Western and Eastern), and Japan were all at work again, but no news of unusual finds was available. A survey in the Negev highlands of Israel concentrated on 5th–6th millennium BC, Early Bronze Age, and Byzantine sites and also collected evidence of recent Bedouin encampments. An ancient dog cemetery was encountered at the U.S. excavations at ancient Ashqelon.

In southern Jordan the Universities of Berlin and Tübingen (West Germany) were involved in excavations and surveys on sites with important early village-farming community levels. Geneviève Dollfus's French team worked on Tell abu Hamid, an important early 4th-millennium site in the Jordan River valley. More clearances were made by the U.S. excavators on the remarkable 7th-millennium BC early village site of 'Ain Ghazal in the environs of the Jordanian capital, Amman.

In Syria a University of Amsterdam group worked on a site (Hammam at-Turkman) with a full range of Bronze Age materials and also on a site (Sabi Abyad) with an interesting span of early village into Halafian period materials (c. 7th–5th millennium BC). There had long been a tendency to focus only on the brilliant painted pottery style of the Halafian inventory. Now the whole yield from Sabi Abyad, together with the new description of Halafian finds recovered by the Germans at Cavi Tarlasi in Turkey, was providing a fuller idea of the cultural remains of this important developed village-farming range of time.

In Turkey work continued at the early village sites of Cayonu and of Novella Cori in the southeast, with interesting results. A new Dutch excavation was begun at Ilipinar in northwestern Anatolia, also of late prehistoric date. The materials so far exposed promised important new understandings of early Anatolian-southeastern European cultural linkages. A Japanese team was undertaking an important survey in central Anatolia. It was reported that the sources for Near Eastern tin (upon which the copper alloy bronze depended) had at last been located in an ancient mining area in the Taurus Mountains of southern Turkey.

*Late Prehistoric Europe.* There were two interesting reports in the *Scientific American* on a Mesolithic camp in Denmark and on the spread of early farming into northwestern Europe. The Danish site, Vænget Nord, occupied c. 5200–4800 BC, was another indication that preagricultural foraging groups in forested postglacial times were relatively large, affluent, and often quite sedentary. By 4500 BC early agricultural settlements were being occupied in west-central Europe, first on riverside flats with rich soil, later on promontories above river valleys. By 2500 BC fortifications had become common, and a variety of geographic situations were being utilized.

Dutch archaeologists recovered evidence of preagricultural occupation on the island of Sardinia at least 9,000 years ago.

*The Greco-Roman World.* A strong peak of acidity, radiocarbon dated to c. 1645 BC, in the Greenland ice cap was taken to reflect dust-fall from the great volcanic eruption on Thera (Santorini) in the Aegean. This would push back the date of the widespread destruction of Minoan civilization by 150 years. New excavations on a mountain slope on the island of Ithaca were claimed to suggest occupation from Mycenaean to Homeric times and even to suggest that Homer himself had visited the site.

In both Greece and Italy, the normal research activities of the various national archaeological "schools" continued. A joint Italian-Canadian team excavated at the site of Sinuessa on the Via Appia; founded in 296 BC, it came to be an important port town for the export of agricultural products. At Rogozen, in Bulgaria, a splendid hoard of 165 gilded silver vessels, of the 4th century BC, was recovered. The decorations on many pieces were of the "Thracian Animal Style," and some also bore Greek inscriptions. At Sepphoris near Nazareth in Israel, a remarkably fine mosaic portrait of a young woman was recovered. It was being referred to as the "Mona Lisa of Roman Palestine."

*Eastern Asia and Africa.* Little direct news had yet been received of the year's work in India, southeastern Asia, and China, but tourists reported that archaeologists in China were busy. The same dearth of news obtained for Africa. A new survey of sites in the Kalahari (*Science,* Dec. 19, 1986) indicated that pastoralists had long been living in this region of southern Africa. There was evidence of crop cultivation, herding, pottery, metalworking, and long-distance trading going back over more than a thousand years. A sequence of excavations at Shanga on Pate Island, off the coast of Kenya, yielded new information on the role of Swahili traders in bringing gold, ivory, and quartz to Mediterranean ports in the 10th century AD. It was thought that this trade from Africa helped to stimulate the flowering of the Middle Ages in Europe.

(ROBERT J. BRAIDWOOD)

**Western Hemisphere.** Developments in New World archaeology in 1987 were marked by a number of major investigations of both prehistoric and historic-period sites in North America, by the discovery of a major tomb complex in Mexico, and by important new discoveries in the Andean countries of Peru and Bolivia. A common theme in news and scientific reports involved the continuing problem of the illicit antiquities market, especially in Central and South America.

*North America.* Major new insights commonly involve large-scale field programs and/or monumental structures or sites, but sometimes a single small find can significantly alter long-held assumptions concerning the archaeology of a particular period or culture area. Despite years of research and the discovery of thousands of elaborately carved wooden artifacts from sites along the northwestern coast of North America, the discovery of a single small "microblade" of quartz crystal, still bound to its delicate wooden handle by a strand of cherry bark, provided a critical new line of evidence concerning the technology of the northwestern coast cultures. While working to expose and reconstruct a 3,000-year-old village along the Hoko River in Washington State, archaeologists recovered the hafted instrument, which consisted of a worked, razor-sharp quartz crystal still attached to a 15-mm (6-in)-long cedar handle. According to Dale Cross, the Washington State University archaeologist at the site, the mounted tool dates to about 2,800 years before the present and demonstrates for the first time how such tools were used as delicate cutting in-

Although it showed signs of a break-in, a recently discovered Grecian tomb still contained an elaborately carved marble throne. The tomb, discovered by Manolis Andronikos, dated to about 340 BC and was believed to have been the burial place of Queen Eurydice of Macedon.

struments when fine craftsmanship was necessary. Similar quartz blades had been found along the northwest coast, but this was the first instance in the Western Hemisphere of one being found together with a wooden handle.

Two significant discoveries were reported in 1987 for the area of Historic or Colonial Period archaeology of the U.S., both from Florida. In March 1987 excavations directed by Calvin Jones and Charles Ewen of the University of Florida, funded by the Florida Department of State, identified what they believed to be remains of Hernando de Soto's 1539–40 winter encampment at the Martin site near Tallahassee. Artifactual evidence supporting the correlation of the site with de Soto's expedition included the recovery of several hundred chain-mail links, 16th-century Spanish olive jar fragments, 12 historic chevron and blown-glass beads, a crossbow projectile point, and three coins dating to the early 16th century. Associated with these historic artifacts were a number of Native American artifacts identified as belonging to the *c.* 16th-century Walton phase in the early Contact period of Florida's culture history. The site faced impending destruction by private developers, but on July 30, 1987, it was announced that 1.9 ha (4.8 ac) would be purchased with funding from the state Trust for Public Land and set aside for long-term protection and study.

From the same region, a team from the Florida State Museum, University of Florida (under the direction of Kathleen Deagan), reported on the initial results of excavation at the site of Ft. Mose, near modern St. Augustine. Occupied between 1739 and 1763, the fort and town were inhabited and defended by a group of black slaves who had fled the British colonies and had been granted sanctuary by the Spaniards. The excavated artifactual material promised to shed light on some key issues concerning the origins of Afro-American culture, including the question of whether the freed slaves had adopted a Spanish, British, or African style of living more than a century before the Civil War. Evidence recovered to date suggested that the fortifications were formidable and had been put to the test in combat.

*Mexico.* Mexican archaeologists announced what might be the most spectacular find of sculpted clay figures yet discovered in the New World. Initially identified by looters in 1971 and excavated by the Mexican archaeologist Manuel Torres Guzmán in 1975, the collection of 22 figures, ranging in height between 0.8 and 1.8 m (2.5 and 6 ft), was kept out of the public and scientific literature until 1987 for fear of additional destruction by treasure hunters. The majority of the figurines found to date represented half-nude women with long skirts tied at the waist with snakes. Found in a mass grave between two 30.5-m (100-ft)-high mounds known collectively as the El Zapotel site in Veracruz, the ritually smashed figurines were exposed in association with the remains of almost 400 female skeletons. Guzmán speculated in a newspaper interview that they may have been dedicated to the goddess Cihautoetl, who watched over women who died in childbirth. Shown for the first time in public at the opening of the new Jalapa Archaeological Museum, the figurines were distinguished by their delicate features and sculptural detail. They had been compared in quality and potential quantity to the elaborate tomb figurines found in Xian (Sian), China.

The opening of the Jalapa Museum also helped to expose a set of elaborate forgeries of Mexican figurines in the collections of the Dallas (Texas) and St. Louis (Mo.) museums. While working on an article for *Connoisseur Magazine,* two Texas journalists, Mimi Crossley and E. Logan Wagner, interviewed a Mexican sculptor, Brigidio Lara, who admitted to having made thousands of presumably authentic clay figurines, many of which had found their way into the international art market. The Dallas Museum of Art removed from public display three large seated figurines identified by Lara as his work. Of the three forgeries in St. Louis, laboratory testing showed one to be of unfired clay, one to contain post-1935 paint, and the third to be modern.

*South America.* In the first implementation of a bilateral agreement between the U.S. and Ecuador, the U.S. Customs Service confiscated and returned to Ecuador 153 pre-Columbian artifacts worth between $60,000 and $100,000 on the art market. The ancient pieces were confiscated from an Ecuadoran citizen at the Miami (Fla.) airport. According to news-wire accounts, the artifacts had been smuggled with the intent of selling them in exchange for Uzi and Mac-10 submachine guns.

In another development relating to the loss of culturally important evidence of past civilizations, grave robbers in Peru looted what was described as the largest find of ancient gold objects yet discovered in that country. Local grave robbers, near the north coast town of Chiclayo, exposed a Mochica tomb, probably that of a king or noble, dating to *c.* AD 100–700. According to press accounts, the tomb was found some 10.5 m (35 ft) below the modern surface in a 1.8 X 1.8-m (6 X 6-ft) crypt, which contained a skeleton dressed in and surrounded by gold. The artifacts were described in a *Washington Post* news release as having included gold masks of varying sizes, some with silver eyes inlaid with lapis lazuli, gold armbands, necklaces, ear ornaments, gold replicas of plants and other foods, and sheets of gold with raised figures. Most of the collection had already been funneled into the international art market for resale or, possibly, melted down into ingots. However, the son of a local grave robber was shot and killed when police raided his home in search of additional items.

In the southern Andean highlands of the Lake Titicaca Basin of Bolivia, a joint U.S.-Bolivian archaeological team began a major five-year excavation project of the former centre and surrounding agricultural support systems of the pre-Inca capital of the Tiahuanaco empire. While many Bolivian archaeologists considered the site of Tiahuanaco as a major urban centre, until recently most foreign archaeologists had characterized it as a religious centre of a loosely knit confederation of "chiefdoms" struggling to eke out an existence on the harsh high-altitude plateau. However, two lines of evidence from the project, which was being coordinated by the Bolivian archaeologist Osvaldo Rivera and Alan Kolata of the University of Chicago, were causing scholars to make drastic reassessments. First, wherever the team tested on the outskirts of the lake, they encountered dense concentrations of terraced, stone-walled houses and courtyards dotted with tombs, indicating that the area was densely populated. The second line of evidence came from the team's focus on study of the pre-Hispanic agricultural system. Instead of the widely spaced, hand-tilled fields of the modern inhabitants, the archaeologists accumulated evidence that the ancient agriculturists depended on an extensive and sophisticated network of raised fields divided by long irrigation canals. Although estimates varied, conservative projections suggested that this system was capable of producing yields at least 300–400% higher than current farming practices and that these techniques could have supported some 40,000–120,000 inhabitants in the 83-sq km (32-sq mi) valley. Such a population density was more indicative of a major urban centre than of a religious centre characterized only by large ceremonial structures.

(JOEL W. GROSSMAN)

*See also* Anthropology.

# Architecture

In England 1987 was the year of community architecture. The influence of the public interest taken by Prince Charles in architecture continued, and the prince's interest seemed to have brought architecture itself more into the public eye. Concern for the inner cities and concern for the end users of buildings was a theme that had long concerned the prince. In 1987 community architecture finally came of age with the accession of Rod Hackney, whose work the prince had praised, to the presidency of the Royal Institute of British Architecture (RIBA) and the award of the Institute's Royal Gold Medal for Architecture to Ralph Erskine.

The main characteristic of community architecture is the concern of the designer for consultation with and involvement of the end users of an architectural project in all stages of its design and construction. It is about cooperation between various members of the community, from planners and politicians to architects and patrons. Community involvement in the execution and development of a project are paramount factors. Included under the community architecture banner are self-build and cooperative projects as well as those seeking to find new uses for old buildings.

Ralph Erskine, a British architect who had worked in Sweden since 1939, was one of the pioneers of the movement. As early as 1948 he discussed with tenants of a proposed housing scheme how the project would affect them and considered their ideas and suggestions as part of the design process. Erskine's best-known work was the Byker redevelopment, a large housing project in Newcastle upon Tyne, England. The redevelopment of the 80-ha (200-ac) site was approved in 1968, and Erskine's plan was produced in 1970. Close contact was maintained with the residents by the architects. The work was completed in the late 1970s, and its best-known feature was the Byker Wall, an eight-story-high structure around the perimeter of the site. The famous wall was conceived for a dual purpose: to muffle expected noise from a then-proposed highway that would pass near the project and to protect the exposed site from biting northerly winds. Residents remained mostly happy with the design of their open-plan units, and most of their complaints centred on problems with maintenance and security.

Erskine was the first community architect to be honoured with the RIBA Gold Medal. For the first time, a shortlist was announced that was intended to create discussion. Included were I. M. Pei, Richard Meier, and Frei Otto. In accepting the award in March, Erskine described his attitude to architecture as "both functionalist and humanist." His other work included the Stockholm University library, student centre, and sports hall.

**Educational and Cultural Buildings.** The long-running story of the new wing for the National Gallery in London's Trafalgar Square moved ahead with the unveiling in April by the gallery's trustees of the design by Venturi, Rauch & Scott Brown of Philadelphia. The inside and outside of the wing were treated in unrelated ways as separate design problems, and each elevation was also treated in the context of its surroundings but not necessarily with reference to the other elevations. The top galleries, which would house the museum's Early Renaissance collection, would receive natural light through clerestory windows. The outside was adorned with classical columns and pilasters on the facade nearest the famous portico of the main building. The design for the wing, to be known as the Sainsbury

Wing, was roughly a truncated rectangle, and it featured a grand glass-walled staircase.

Museums and galleries were once again among the most noteworthy architectural commissions in 1987. Architect Richard Meier unveiled plans for the J. Paul Getty Center on a 300-ha (742-ac) site in western Los Angeles. All facilities of the J. Paul Getty Trust would eventually be consolidated there. Meier had been chosen as the architect in October 1984, following a worldwide search, and the project was expected to cost at least $100 million. The design featured a campus of low buildings clustered around terraced gardens in Meier's elegant and understated manner. Visitors would leave their cars in an underground garage half a mile away from the complex and would travel from there by shuttle bus.

A controversial design by James Ingo Freed of I. M. Pei & Partners, New York City, for the U.S. Holocaust Memorial Museum was unveiled. The museum was to be built on a prominent site on the Mall in Washington, D.C., one block east of the Washington Monument. The design incorporated a prominent hexagonal Hall of Remembrance that would dominate the west elevation. Critics of the siting claimed that it breached the constitutional separation of church and state. The structure, which would cover 23,-225 sq m (250,000 sq ft), was to include exhibition space, lecture halls, a library, and performance areas.

James Stirling, Michael Wilford & Associates, London, won the competition to design a new gallery for the Thyssen-Bornemisza Collection in Lugano, Switz., from among five invited entrants. The winning design was praised for the harmonious manner in which it integrated the existing 17th-century villa and the 1932 picture gallery and also would blend into the landscape. Barton Myers Associates won a limited competition for the expansion and renovation of the Art Gallery of Ontario in Toronto. The $28 million project would incorporate a high-tech tower and a two-story off-centre entrance court crowned by a skylit pyramid. Striped sandstone would clad the exterior.

In New York City the new Lila Acheson Wallace Wing of the Metropolitan Museum of Art was opened. The wing, by architects Kevin Roche John Dinkeloo & Associates, included a gallery devoted to 20th-century design and was to house the museum's modern art collection. The Los Angeles County Museum of Art also inaugurated a fine new building, the Robert O. Anderson Building by Hardy Holzman Pfeiffer Associates, architects. The design, situated in the courtyard area between the original 1960s structures, was built of buff Minnesota limestone, glass blocks, and green glazed terra-cotta and was reminiscent of the Art Deco and Art Moderne buildings of Wilshire Boulevard in the 1920s and '30s.

Plans were announced in North Adams, Mass., for what would be the largest contemporary art museum in the world. The Massachusetts Museum of Contemporary Art, organized by the Williams College Art Museum, was to be housed in an empty factory complex covering 7 ha (17 ac) and would contain the collection of Count Giuseppe Panza di Biumo, consisting primarily of American art from the 1960s and '70s.

There were several notable projects for educational buildings, including art and architecture schools. The School of Art and Design, Newcastle upon Tyne, designed by the Newcastle City Architects Department, was opened in the spring. The bright, bold building with its high-tech details was intended to appeal to prospective students as much as to community users. Construction was of prefabricated components, allowing the building to be roofed within 11 months. The design reconciled the need for quick construc-

tion with a desire for spatial drama by creating a clean, airy, and light metallic structure.

Aldo Rossi of Italy was chosen as architect for the expansion of the School of Architecture at the University of Miami, Fla. The buildings would be his first in the U.S. The scheme, dubbed by Rossi "The Acropolis in Miami," consisted of a complex of buildings surmounting a plinth with parking underneath. The auditorium was in the form of a rotunda, and a barrel-vaulted pavilion would contain office space. The project was situated by a lake.

In Denmark a new business school and housing complex at Frederiksberg, Copenhagen, by architects Henning Larsen of Copenhagen, would occupy the site of a former factory. The school building would be flanked by two U-shaped housing blocks. It was hoped that the complex would be completed in 1989.

Echoes of H. H. Richardson were noticeable in the new Dolben Library at Northfield Mount Hermon School, Northfield, Mass., by Architectural Resources Cambridge. The building featured round-arched openings, red and brown brick, and a pyramidal-roofed tower, showing a strong interest by the designers in local historical models.

Gwathmey Siegel & Associates, known for their neo-modernist style, seemed to be moving toward a richer and less minimalist approach in a number of their current college and university projects. These included the Dartmouth College gymnasium at Hanover, N.H., completed in the spring, and two buildings for Cornell University at Ithaca, N.Y., the gymnasium fieldhouse and the School of Agriculture administration/academic building, as well as the College of Architecture at the University of North Carolina at Charlotte.

The dramatic visual symmetry of the new Kölner Philharmonie in Cologne, West Germany, reflects a parallel symmetry of sound. In a design by architects Peter Busmann and Godfrid Haberer, sound from the central stage flows evenly over the seating area that encircles it.

The United Airlines terminal at Chicago's O'Hare International Airport owed its clean look to the architectural firm Murphy/Jahn. The dark passageways typical of older terminals were replaced with wide walkways brightened by glass and steel, a look that harked back to 19th-century train stations.
MURPHY/JAHN ARCHITECTS

Formality and symmetry would be significant features of the Indira Gandhi National Center for Arts in New Delhi, India, to be designed by Ralph Lerner of Princeton, N.J. The prominent site was to be organized around a series of courtyards, with the great central court at the heart of the plan surrounded by an arcade.

A new home for the Boston Ballet in the South End area of the city was designed by Graham Gund Architects. It featured a redbrick facade and wide areas of metal-framed windows as well as a curved Baroque parapet, described by the architect as "in the spirit of Queen Anne."

A sports centre in Toronto by Roderick Robbie and Michael Allen was designed with the world's first retractable-roof stadium. The 56,000-seat arena incorporated a 450-room hotel. The telescoping roof of tubular steel covered with corrugated steel decking and an opaque synthetic membrane could be opened or closed in just 20 minutes.

**Public Buildings and Places of Worship.** A competition was held for a new city hall at The Hague, Neth., to replace the existing 30-year-old building, which was to be demolished and replaced by an apartment complex. The new hall would be in the old city. The competition was won by the Dutch architect Rem Koolhaas, but the commission was, surprisingly, awarded to the U.S. firm Richard Meier & Partners.

The Danish firm of Henning Larsen designed a new Ministry of Foreign Affairs for Riyadh, Saudi Arabia. The walled compound containing the chancery, ambassadorial residence, and two residential buildings was organized around a courtyard, with the chancery featuring a two-story skylit octagonal hall. Also in Riyadh the Diplomatic Club was designed by an international consortium comprising Frei Otto, Buro Happold, and Omrania. The club provided social facilities for foreign diplomats and was notable in design terms for the respect given to its desert site. The undulating four-story-high concrete form followed the topography of the desert and enclosed inner terraces and gardens. On the periphery of the structure was a series of fibreglass tents housing lounges and guest rooms. The cost was $32 million.

Monumentality within the classical tradition, a goal increasingly sought by architects of the 1980s, was the keynote of the Cook-Fort Worth Children's Medical Center in Texas, a joint venture by architects David M. Schwarz/ Architectural Services and Karlsberger + Associates. The eight-story hospital was visually conceived as a series of setback pavilions with a two-story base. Oversized windows and bright glazed tiles as well as a large central atrium were incorporated in an effort to minimize the institutional effect of such a large complex.

Historical reference to the Sydney (Australia) Opera House was evident in the Baha'i House of Worship in New Delhi, designed by Iranian architect Fariburz Sahba. The design, with its shell domes intended to be reminiscent of a nine-sided lotus flower—an important cultural symbol— was constructed of cast-in-place concrete with a white marble exterior. The constructional technique, a much simpler one than that employed at Sydney, demonstrated how a high-technology idea could be produced by means of low-technology methods. Concrete was carried in baskets balanced on people's heads.

Historical reference and careful choice of materials were characteristic of the formal symmetrical design for the Kol Israel Synagogue by Robert A. M. Stern Architects, which was under construction in Brooklyn, N.Y. The sanctuary would be underground, maximizing the potential of the small urban site, and the rich yet conservative exterior would be built up of multicoloured brick banks, stone moldings, and mottled roof tiles, all reminiscent of Mediterranean architecture.

**Commercial Buildings.** In London the saga of Peter Palumbo's development of the City's Mansion House site continued. After the rejection in 1984 of a plan by Ludwig Mies van der Rohe for the site, Palumbo commissioned architect James Sirling to produce a new design. The conservation-versus-development debate that had raged around the original proposals appeared likely to be revived. The new plan featured a stone and granite building that would fill the whole triangular site. A circular drum would rise out of an angular glass and stone base, and the corner entrance would feature a high archway. Rustication on the base made reference to the nearby church of St. Mary Woolnoth. It was an exciting design of quality, yet again the project failed to receive planning approval.

Architect John Outram Associates' Harp Group headquarters in Swanley, Kent, demonstrated how simple architectural elements could give distinction to an industrial site. The project comprised a refurbishment of a series of structures to provide unobstructed interior space. The design, incorporating various symbolic features, was executed in brick and concrete and featured a massive portico-like centrepiece supported by whimsical yet massive brick columns, one of which had seemingly "escaped" to form a freestanding gatepost marking the entrance.

Classical precedent reworked was apparent in Quinlan Terry's designs for six villas in Regent's Park, London, to be built in the gardens of Hanover Lodge, itself designed by Regency architect John Nash (1752–1835). The site was originally intended by Nash as a suitable one for villas, and Terry designed each individually in the manner of Nash, including a Doric, an Ionic, a Corinthian, a Veneto, a Gothic, and a Regency villa. The designs were a sure attempt at producing inventive plans that were firmly in the classical tradition without being merely historicist.

A mixed-use project for a 10-ha (25-ac) site was to be developed on a platform projecting over the Hudson River in New York City. To be called Hudson River Center, it was designed by architects Gruzen Samton Steinglass and would eventually comprise three hotels, two apartment houses, a marina, and various retail areas.

In Shanghai plans were announced for a 36-story apartment hotel, to be called Lotus Mansion, which would house visiting Western businessmen. The architect was Vitols Associates of Boston, and the building was said to be the first structure in mainland China that would be constructed entirely with U.S. funds. Financial Square in Hong Kong was to be a quirky complex of two glass-clad office towers, 42 and 46 stories in height, with tripartite elevations intended to reduce the complex into smaller visual units. It was designed by U.S. architect Paul Rudolph with Wong & Ougang. Floors would cantilever from the central core, and faceting would permit the maximum number of corner windows.

**Awards.** Along with the award of the RIBA Gold Medal to Erskine, other prizes presented in 1987 included the Gold Medal of the International Union of Architects to Reima Pietila of Finland and the Pritzker Architecture Prize to Kenzo Tange (see BIOGRAPHIES). Tange, whose designs included St. Mary's Cathedral in Tokyo (1961–64) and the 1964 Olympic Stadia in Tokyo, was praised for his contributions as a teacher, writer, researcher, and historian as well as architect and urban planner.

The American Institute of Architects selected 20 buildings in the U.S. to receive its honour awards. They included the New York Public Library restoration by Davis, Brody & Associates and the O'Hare International Airport Rapid Transit Extension in Chicago, designed by the City of Chicago Department of Public Works, Bureau of Architecture, with Murphy/Jahn as associated architects.

Maxwell Fry (see OBITUARIES), one of the pioneers of modern architecture in the U.K., died in September. He was best known as one of the small group of British architects who in the 1930s promoted the new architecture of the International Style, which had recently emerged in Europe. He was in partnership with Walter Gropius during the latter's stay in England, and in the 1950s he worked closely with Le Corbusier on Chandigarh, the new capital of the Punjab, India. (SANDRA MILLIKIN)

*See also* Engineering Projects; Industrial Review: *Building and Construction.*

This article updates the *Macropædia* article The History of Western ARCHITECTURE.

# Art Exhibitions and Art Sales

Among the most notable art exhibitions in 1987 were a number devoted to Oriental and Far Eastern subjects, some including the loan of objects rarely seen in the West. "Of Ink and Water: Muromachi Period Paintings from Japan 1392–1568" at the Detroit Institute of Arts at the end of 1986 featured masterpieces of ink painting borrowed from 50 museums, temples, and private collections, most of which had never before left Japan. Many of the items lent were classed as "important cultural properties" by the Japanese authorities and were rarely seen even in Japan. During the Muromachi period the influence of Zen Buddhism was strong in Japan, and the artistic influence of China was dominant. Many of the leading Japanese artists of the period were Zen monks. The star of the exhibition was the artist Sesshu, who was represented by 11 paintings. Among the items displayed were some spectacular screens. The exhibition was also seen at the Honolulu Academy of Arts from January to March 1987.

The Philadelphia Museum of Art mounted the greatest display of Chinese ceramic sculpture ever seen outside China. "The Quest for Eternity: Chinese Ceramic Sculpture from the People's Republic of China" was a comprehensive show of 157 objects of great quality found in tombs, ranging in date from the Neolithic Period to the Ming Dynasty. The exhibition was also seen in 1987 at Houston, Texas, and at the Los Angeles County Museum of Art, and it was slated to travel to Cleveland, Ohio, in 1988. The lively figures on show included several fine images of horses.

A total of 155 sculptures in stone, bronze, and clay, representing Buddhist art from Thailand, were exhibited in Tokyo at the Tokyo National Museum in the early autumn. The exhibition was the first on such a scale to be seen outside Thailand, and the pieces on display ranged in date from 2000 BC to the 19th century AD. Another exhibition in Japan was devoted to European influences in 18th-century Japanese art. The show focused on works of Japanese art that had been inspired by Dutch books imported into Japan early in the 18th century, when the ban on importing foreign materials was lifted. The show comprised paintings and sketches depicting European flowers, animals, and people, illustrating how Japanese artists reacted to the opening of their country to European influences at that time. The exhibition was shown at the Suntory Museum of Art, Akasakamitsuke.

The history of the Turkish empire in the first half of the 16th century was the subject of a large-scale exhibition at the National Gallery of Art in Washington, D.C., also seen at the Art Institute of Chicago in the summer and at the Metropolitan Museum of Art in New York City in the autumn and winter. Entitled "The Age of Sultan Suleyman the Magnificent," it drew most of its works from the Topkapi Palace Museum collection in Istanbul. The exhibition was the first major show of Turkish art to be mounted in the U.S. and was made possible by legal changes that, for the first time, allowed such works of art to leave Turkey. The wide range of objects on show included metalwork, jewelry, textiles, maps, calligraphy, and paintings.

The most important exhibition of art from Israel ever allowed to go abroad was seen late in 1986 at the Metropolitan Museum of Art. Jointly organized by the Met and by the Israel Museum, the exhibition of remains from antiquity was entitled "Treasures of the Holy Land: Ancient Art from the Israel Museum." The exhibition was also on view in 1987 at the Los Angeles County Museum of Art and at the Museum of Fine Arts in Houston.

Exhibitions devoted to Russian works of art and to works of art by non-Russian artists in the collections of Soviet museums formed another interesting group of 1987 art exhibitions. At the Grand Palais, Paris, in January and February, "La France et La Russie au Siècle des Lumières" was a collection of works chosen to convey a complete picture of Russian culture in the 18th century as well as to illustrate the close artistic relationship existing at that date between Russia and France. The majority of the works were lent by Soviet museums. Included were portraits of Peter the Great and Catherine I by the French artist Jean-Marc Nattier, as well as a bronze version of Étienne-Maurice Falconet's equestrian statue of Peter. There were also many examples of decorative works of art, including gold, silver, and enameled boxes as well as furniture and textiles. A section devoted to architecture featured a fine bird's-eye view of Moscow's Red Square dating from 1801. The Barbican Art Gallery in London mounted "Russian Style 1700–1920: Court and Country Dress from the Hermitage," the first such exhibition to travel from the Leningrad museum to Western Europe. In this case—as in many others—commercial sponsorship was crucial to the realization of the exhibition. Among the 300 items on display were gowns and uniforms by Russian designers, outfits by French couturiers, and folk costumes.

Without doubt, one of the year's most splendid exhibitions was held at the Villa Favorita, Lugano, Switz., at the private galleries of Baron Thyssen-Bornemisza: a show of 40 Impressionist and Post-Impressionist masterpieces lent by the Pushkin Museum in Moscow and the Hermitage in Leningrad. This was the second time those institutions had lent works for exhibitions in Lugano. In exchange, 40 of the baron's Old Masters would be traveling to Moscow and Leningrad. These splendid exchanges were a tribute to the baron's initiative. The exhibition was so successful that it was necessary to institute an advance booking system. Included in the loan were works by Cézanne, Picasso, and Matisse, and an entire room was devoted to Monet.

Paintings by many of the same artists, but belonging to the Courtauld Institute Galleries in London, traveled to the U.S. Shortly after their return from touring, the works from the Courtauld Institute Galleries were to be transferred to their new home at Somerset House in London. The show was entitled "Impressionist and Post-Impressionist Masterpieces: The Courtauld Collection" and was seen at the Cleveland Museum of Art and four other U.S. museums. Although the pictures, including paintings by virtually all of the major artists of those movements, had been on public display in London for many years, they were not widely known in the U.S., and this traveling exhibition presented a unique and welcome opportunity for Americans to view the splendid works.

"A Magic Mirror: The Portrait of France 1700–1900" at the Museum of Fine Arts, Houston, included 15 portraits never before on view in the U.S. The show featured some excellent portraits lent by U.S. museums, among them works by Jean-Honoré Fragonard and Degas. At the Metropolitan Museum of Art an exhibition devoted to the final 15 months of the life of Vincent van Gogh proved to be one of the most popular shows ever mounted and attracted enormous crowds. The exhibition was entitled "Van Gogh in Saint-Remy and Auvers." A major Paul Klee show organized by the Museum of Modern Art, New York City, included 300 works by the whimsical Swiss artist and was featured in the summer at the Cleveland Museum of Art.

An exhibition at the National Gallery in Washington, entitled "Henri Matisse: The Early Years in Nice, 1916–1930" and comprising 170 pictures by Matisse, was notable for the beauty and vibrant colours of its exhibits. In the summer the National Gallery was host to "American Drawings and Watercolours of the 20th Century: Andrew Wyeth, The Helga Pictures." This exhibition, which attracted considerable attention and many visitors, was devoted entirely to a series of pictures of the artist's neighbour Helga Testorf, painted between 1970 and 1985. The show would later travel throughout the U.S. and to Europe. The long-term study of one model in great depth was characteristic of the artist. The pictures were virtually unknown before they went on show to the public. The announcement of their existence in 1986 had created a major stir in the art world.

Works from Italian museums by such artists as Domenichino and Guido Reni were among 200 or so paintings on view at the Metropolitan Museum of Art in "The Age of Correggio and the Carracci: Emilian Painting of the Sixteenth and Seventeenth Centuries." Some 60% of the pictures were lent from Italian collections, and most had never before been on public view in the U.S. The organization of the exhibition was a joint effort by the Met, the National Gallery in Washington, and the Pinacoteca Nazionale, Bologna, Italy. At the Solomon R. Guggenheim Museum in New York City, "Oskar Kokoschka 1886–1980" was a reduced version of the retrospective devoted to the work of the Austrian artist that had been shown in 1986 at the Tate Gallery, London. It was the first major show devoted to Kokoschka's work to be seen in the U.S. in many years.

There were noteworthy exhibitions in London and in Paris in 1987. In Paris a major exhibition of works by the French Rococo painter Fragonard continued the series of exhibitions at the Grand Palais devoted to major French painters. This show, again helped by major commercial sponsorship, was to travel to New York City in early 1988. One of the most remarkable canvases was an enormous painting entitled "La Fete à Saint-Cloud," dating from the late 1770s and superbly illustrating the delight and beauty of the artist's work. The exhibition was the first retrospective devoted to Fragonard and comprised approximately 100 paintings and the same number of drawings.

The 50th anniversary of the founding of the Musée National des Arts et Traditions Populaires in Paris was commemorated by a large exhibition of traditional French costume through the ages, also shown at the Grand Palais, in the spring of 1987. A number of the items were lent by major provincial folkloric museums. The objects, ranging in date from the 13th century on, included portraits, costumes, and accessories, together with fashion plates and jewelry. Works by the Impressionist Berthe Morisot shown at the Galerie Hopkins-Thomas in Paris in the spring comprised the first important show to be devoted to her intimate pictures since 1961. They formed part of a major Morisot retrospective, which was seen at the National Gallery in Washington in September and was to travel in 1988.

In London the Tate Gallery was the venue for the most comprehensive exhibition devoted to the works of the American Mark Rothko ever held in Britain and the most important Rothko exhibition since 1978–79, when the major retrospective at the Guggenheim Museum took place. Works covered the period from the early 1930s, before Rothko's work became totally abstract, until his death in 1970. Many of the works shown were lent by his estate, though others came from major U.S. collections. The

Marc Chagall's "Over Vitebsk" was one of the many paintings that were displayed in the Chagall exhibit in Moscow. It was the first major exhibit of the artist's work in his own homeland. In addition to paintings, there were numerous lithographs and sketches.
BETTMANN ARCHIVE

earliest painting was "Interior," a preabstract work painted in 1932. Also on view were many canvases featuring his mature style, characterized by large fields of colour, horizontally arranged. The show was seen in the autumn at Madrid. The Tate was also host to an exhibition devoted to the Russian-born Constructivist sculptor Naum Gabo. Sculpture of the same era but very different in style was shown at the Minneapolis (Minn.) Institute of the Arts in a retrospective of 150 works by Jean Arp entitled "The Universe of Jean Arp."

At the Hayward Gallery in London a large exhibition celebrating the centenary of the birth of Le Corbusier focused on that artist and architect's contribution to 20th-century architecture and design. Exhibits illustrated housing schemes, religious buildings, and his work at the Indian city of Chandigarh. An exhibition of 150 drawings by architect Mies van der Rohe, staged to commemorate the centenary of his birth in 1886, was organized by the Art Institute of Chicago and shown in Frankfurt (West Germany), Paris, and Madrid. An exhibition of 50 drawings by Leonardo da Vinci lent by the Royal Library at Windsor, Berkshire, England, was shown at the Centro Cultural de la Caixa in Barcelona, Spain, in October. The drawings had previously traveled to New York, Stockholm, and Tokyo.

"British Art in the 20th Century: the Modern Movement," a survey covering the period from 1910 through the 1970s, was mounted at the Royal Academy in London. Among the art movements represented were the Camden Town Group, the Vorticists, and Pop Art, and the artists whose works were exhibited included Paul Nash, Barbara Hepworth, Francis Bacon, and David Hockney. There were also exhibits by many less well-known names, however. Part of the same period was the focus of "A Paradise Lost—the Neo-Romantic Imagination in Britain 1935–1955" at the Barbican Art Gallery in the summer. The exhibition was devoted to English Neo-Romantic art of the 1940s and 1950s and included 400 paintings, drawings, posters, photographs, designs, and book jackets evocative of a little-remembered phase of British art in the 20th century. Artists represented included Jacob Epstein, Winifred Nicholson, and Ceri Richards.

The British Museum, London, held an exhibition devoted to English drawings entitled "Drawing in England from Hilliard to Hogarth," which was shown later at the

Yale Center for British Art in New Haven, Conn. The show comprised works by 72 artists and included a variety of objects by English and continental artists, primarily dating from the 17th century. Most of the exhibits were drawn from the British Museum's own rich collection, but there were some drawings lent by Queen Elizabeth II and by other private collectors, among them 19 stage designs by Inigo Jones lent from the Chatsworth Collection. An exhibition at the Dulwich College Picture Gallery in London marked the 150th anniversary of the death of Sir John Soane, the

The burial of Sultan Suleyman, from a 16th-century illuminated text, was one of many works in "The Age of Sultan Suleyman the Magnificent," a rare Western tour of Turkish art.
THE CHESTER BEATTY LIBRARY; PHOTOGRAPH, AUTHENTICATED NEWS INTERNATIONAL

architect of the gallery. Plans showing the gallery's design at the time it was built, together with designs for additions and extensions by later architects, were included, as well as exhibits showing the influence of Soane on present-day architects. Back on view at Dulwich were 40 of the finest paintings in the collection, which had traveled to Japan in 1986 and early in 1987.

"Master Drawings from the Woodner Collection" were shown in the summer and early autumn at the Royal Academy of Art. The collection, which was begun in the 1950s, included major drawings by Raphael, Rembrandt, Goya, and Cézanne and was particularly notable for a sheet from Giorgio Vasari's *Libro de'Disegno*, the centrepiece of which was attributed to Botticelli. A splendid exhibition held at the Goldsmith's Hall in the summer was devoted to the jewelry of French designer René Lalique. It was the first major exhibition in the U.K. of the artist's jewelry and the largest of its kind since his own time. Among the more than 230 exhibits was a major group from the Calouste Gulbenkian Museum in Lisbon. The Art Nouveau art jewelry included flamboyant and decorative pieces of gold, gems, and enamels as well as horn and glass. Original drawings by Lalique were also on show.

At the Yorkshire Sculpture Park near Wakefield, Yorkshire, England, an exhibition devoted to the work of Henry Moore, entitled "Henry Moore and the Landscape" and comprising 33 works, was shown. Commercial sponsorship again assisted. The show provided a splendid opportunity to see Moore's work in the landscape of Yorkshire, which inspired so much of his sculpture. Although many pieces were familiar, the landscaped setting enhanced them to a remarkable degree.

In London a loan exhibition was devoted to designs for English frames, the first such show in England. It was mounted by the Morton Morris Gallery and included drawings lent by public and private collectors, among them a group of sketches and documents dating from 1690 to 1712 for carved work at Chatsworth. The Victoria and Albert Museum, London, lent a design for a frame by Thomas Chippendale. An exhibition organized by Sotheby's in association with the Royal Horticultural Society in London was devoted to the glory of the English garden.

(SANDRA MILLIKIN)

## ART SALES

The sale of van Gogh's "Sunflowers" to the Yasuda Fire and Marine Insurance Co. of Japan for £24,750,000 at Christie's in London in March 1987 more than tripled the previous auction price record for a work of art (though that record fell at year's end when the same artist's "Irises" was purchased by an unidentified collector for $53.9 million at Sotheby's in New York). Sotheby's sale of the duchess of Windsor's jewels in Geneva in April caused a similar sensation. The sumptuous love tokens given by the duke to the woman for whom he renounced the British throne fetched $50 million, roughly five times their ordinary retail value as jewels. The two sales combined to make auctions very fashionable.

**Works of Art.** Impressionist and modern pictures comprised the field where most of the serious money was concentrated. The autumn 1986 sales saw an undiscriminating boom. Sotheby's had seven paintings for sale from the collection of James Johnson Sweeney, a former curator at New York City's Museum of Modern Art. A diamond-shaped Mondrian of 1937–38, which Sweeney had first seen in the form of sketches in the artist's studio, made $5,060,000, and one of the series of paintings on the theme of "Femme dans la nuit" by Joan Miró, executed in 1945,

An antique wing chair was sold at auction for $2.7 million, a record price for a piece of furniture. The piece dated to about 1770 and was notable for its intricate carving and hairy paw feet.
AP/WIDE WORLD

made $2,530,000. Among other works sold in the autumn were an 1888 Renoir of a mother dressing her daughter's hair for a party, "La Coiffure," at $3,520,000 and a bronze cast of a reclining figure by Henry Moore at $1,760,000. Christie's sold a 46-cm (18-in) Matisse bronze of 1907, "Nu Couche I," at $1,430,000. The same sense of euphoria was apparent in the London sales at the beginning of December, and the pictures were even more important. A Manet street scene, "La Rue Mosnier aux Paveurs," sold for £7.7 million to a Swiss collector. At Sotheby's a Cubist Braque of 1911 entitled "Femme Lisant" became the most expensive 20th-century painting ever sold at auction at £6.6 million.

The season's Impressionist boom reached a climax with the sale of "Sunflowers" in March. By the time the New York sales began in May, the euphoria was dwindling in the U.S., and only pictures that appealed to the Japanese continued to climb in value. Shigeki Kameyama, a Japanese dealer-collector, bid $3,850,000 to secure a "Portrait of Eugenia Primavesi" by Gustav Klimt. The Fuji Gallery spent $1,045,000 on a Rouault head of a "Clown," and another Japanese bidder spent $2,310,000 on an unfinished Cézanne still life. The end-of-season sales in London saw a third of the paintings offered failing to sell, but exceptional prices were paid for the front-runners. Van Gogh's "Le Pont de Trinquetaille" made £12,650,000 and a Klimt landscape £3.3 million, while "Femme sous les Arbres" by the Japanese Impressionist Seiku Kuroda made £1,760,000—to the surprise of most Westerners, who had never heard of the artist.

Both U.S. and Japanese collectors began to look at Old Master paintings more seriously than in previous years. A little oval portrait of a plump girl by Rembrandt sold in London for £7,260,000 to a U.S. collector in December 1986. In April the Umeda Gallery of Japan spent £638,000 at Christie's on a very standard "Virgin and Child" by Murillo. Two sensational sales of Old Master drawings attracted exceptional interest to this field: the Gaines Collection at Sotheby's in New York in November 1986 and the drawings sent for sale from Chatsworth by the duke of Devonshire at Christie's in London in July 1987. John Gaines had attempted to acquire one drawing by each of the great names of Western art. A page of sketches by Leonardo went to the J. Paul Getty Museum, Malibu, Calif., at $3,630,000; a Rembrandt landscape made $957,000; and three views of a woman's head sketched by Watteau made $852,500. At the Chatsworth sale a preparatory drawing from his "Madonna del Popolo" by Federico Barocci made £1,760,000 and a Rembrandt landscape £1,375,000.

The interest of new millionaires in contemporary art was one of the most remarkable features of the season. Unlike the sales of Impressionists, contemporary art sales were highly successful throughout the year. The trend began with the Scull sale in New York in November. Jasper Johns's "Out the Window," consigned for sale by an ex-wife of U.S. collector Robert C. Scull, secured $3,630,000, while the Pop Art wall paintings—for a large room—by James Rosenquist made $2,090,000. At Sotheby's New York contemporary sale in May, 18 new auction price records for individual artists were set, including $3,630,000 for de Kooning's "Pink Lady." In London new price levels were achieved for postwar European masters. An Anselm Kiefer made £300,000 and a Howard Hodgkin £155,000 at a Sotheby charity sale, roughly doubling current dealers' prices. The following day a large canvas painted blue by Yves Klein made £638,000.

Where exceptional works of art in other fields came up for sale, the general confidence of the market dictated very high prices, especially for anything of U.S. interest. A Chippendale-style wing armchair made in Philadelphia became the most expensive piece of furniture in the world at $2.7 million. A painting by American Symbolist Joseph Stella entitled "Tree of My Life" made $2.2 million. A Houdon plaster bust of Thomas Jefferson became the most expensive "Old Master" sculpture ever sold at auction at $2,860,000, while Giacometti's master bronze "Grande Femme Debout II" topped all other prices on record for sculpture at $3,630,000.

The two sales of T. Y. Chao's collection of Chinese ceramics held by Sotheby's in Hong Kong in December 1986 and May 1987 brought a total of $14.8 million. A late 14th-century underglaze red dish made HK$10,340,-000 in December and a bulbous vase of the same period HK$11,220,000 in May, the highest prices on record for Chinese ceramics. Other record-breaking prices included $308,000 for an Islamic rock-crystal flask, $2,090,000 for a Carlin desk, $792,000 for a Benin bronze head, $198,000 for a Frank Lloyd Wright chair, $440,000 for a Stradivarius violin, $352,000 for a Japanese sculpture, $1,210,000 for a polychrome Boulle marquetry desk, and $242,000 for a Roman marble statue of a maenad with an 18th-century head.

**Book Sales.** In the 1986–87 season the gulf widened between prices in the book trade and prices secured at prestige auctions. A new type of book collector who attended auctions only—and furthermore limited himself to auctions with large, glossy catalogs—tended to distort the market by paying prices far beyond current retail levels. Obviously attractive items, such as natural history books with lavish colour plates, were particularly singled out by this new breed.

Sotheby's fed its appetite with the sale of two sensational collections. The greatest library of books and manuscripts ever devoted to hunting and other country sports, formed by Marcel Jeanson, a French industrialist, between World Wars I and II, made a total of F 44,941,000 in Monte Carlo

in March. The colour-plate books from the celebrated botanical library formed by Robert de Belder of Belgium made £5.9 million at Sotheby's in London in April. The earliest printed book on the subject of hunting, *Livre du roi modus et de la reine ratio*, published in Chambery in 1486, made F 2,664,000 in Monte Carlo. The Getty Museum paid the top price for a manuscript, F 6,882,000, for a richly illuminated copy of the most important medieval treatise on hunting, Gaston Phebus's *Livre de chasse*. The greatest sensation of the de Belder library was the *Hortus Eystettensis* at £605,000. The two large-folio volumes of hand-coloured engravings record the flowers in the early 17th-century garden of the prince bishop of Eichstatt. Other big prices included Christoph J. Trew's sumptuous *Hortus Nitidissimus* of 1750–86 at £308,000 and Robert J.Thornton's relatively common *Temple of Flora* at £187,000.

The high point of Sotheby's year came with the sale of a scruffy paperbound manuscript containing nine of Mozart's symphonies written in his own hand for £2,585,-000. The purchaser was not publicly identified, but the manuscript was subsequently put on loan to the Pierpont Morgan Library, New York City. The British Library spent £165,000 on two and a half vellum pages scribbled with quotations from Shakespeare and dating from the 1590s—the earliest known Shakespeare manuscript. The two-page letter from Albert Einstein to Pres. Franklin D. Roosevelt explaining the theoretical possibility of making an atom bomb sold for $220,000, and the same price was paid for the 1663 edition of the Bible translated into Algonkian.

The complete set of lavishly illustrated bird books published in the 19th century by John Gould and belonging to Gould himself was sold for a total of £397,485 after Sotheby's failed to find a single taker for the set. The 15th-century *Armagnac Breviary* with 47 miniatures and almost 3,000 illuminated initials sold for £704,000.

(GERALDINE NORMAN)

This article updates the *Macropædia* articles The History of Western PAINTING; The History of Western SCULPTURE.

# Astronomy

In the annals of astronomy 1987 would be remembered as the year of the supernova. For the first time in almost four centuries the death of a star was seen with the naked eye from Earth. It was also a year of discoveries that included new findings about the most distant planet in the solar system, Pluto, as well as some of the most distant objects known in the universe.

**Solar System.** Pluto is usually the most distant planet from the Sun. When it was discovered in 1930, it was farther from the Sun than was Neptune. Pluto moves in a highly elliptical orbit, however, so that for roughly 20 years during its 248-year orbital period it is closer to the Sun than is Neptune. In 1979 Pluto moved within the orbit of Neptune; it was expected to reach perihelion—its closest approach to the Sun—in 1989. This circumstance, combined with the most modern telescopes and detectors, gave astronomers their first chance to determine the properties of the mysterious planet. Astronomers were also helped by the transits, or crossings, of the planet by its satellite, Charon (itself discovered only in 1978)—events that were occurring between 1985 and 1989 every 3.19 days. Several groups of astronomers determined the diameter of Pluto to be about 2,200–2,300 km (1,360–1,430 mi), making it significantly smaller than the Earth's Moon. They also found that Pluto and Charon each make one rotation in the time it takes Charon to revolve around Pluto. Thus

The arrow (far left) identifies the supergiant star Sanduleak −69 202 before it transformed into Supernova 1987A (left), the first exploding star visible to the naked eye in almost 400 years.

AP/WIDE WORLD

each body always presents the same face to the other. This contrasts with the Earth-Moon system, wherein the Moon always presents the same face to the Earth while the Earth periodically presents its entire circumference to the Moon.

**Stars.** The first supernova visible to the naked eye since the one seen and described by Johannes Kepler in 1604 was discovered in the early morning of February 24. It was spotted almost simultaneously by astronomers Ian Shelton of the University of Toronto Southern Station, Chile, and Oscar Duhalde of Las Campanas Observatory, Chile, and by amateur sky watcher Albert Jones of Nelson, N.Z. Visible only from the Southern Hemisphere, it lay in the Large Magellanic Cloud, a satellite galaxy of our Galaxy, the Milky Way. Although not the nearest supernova to Earth to have occurred in the past 380 years, it was the brightest. More importantly, it was the first one bright enough for astronomers to really analyze in detail with the use of modern instruments.

Why were scientists so excited about this event? According to extensive observations of supernovas in other galaxies, as well as decades of theoretical analysis, a supernova explosion results from the death of a massive star. As a star evolves, it fuses hydrogen into helium and then to ever heavier elements, eventually converting the material at its core into iron. When this stage has been reached, the core can no longer liberate fusion energy to sustain the star's structure, and the weight of the star causes its centre to collapse inward on itself. As the centre collapses, it liberates gravitational energy, producing a violent outward shock wave that ejects the outside of the star in a gigantic explosion. Whereas the luminosity of a supernova can be greater than 100 billion times that of the Sun, in distant galaxies it is usually visible only for a few months, gradually fading from view. In addition, no one has ever identified a supernova with a particular star that existed before the explosion. Also, supernovas are rare, occurring only about once a century in a galaxy the size of the Milky Way.

The February supernova, which was assigned the name SN 1987A, was initially observed at a magnitude of 4.5, about the limit of unaided human visual perception. It gradually brightened, dimmed somewhat, and then brightened to about magnitude 3 around May 22. It subsequently declined in brightness throughout the rest of the year. It was so bright for many kinds of telescopes, however, that it was studied at virtually every wavelength of the electromagnetic spectrum: radio frequencies, infrared, visible light, ultraviolet, X-rays, and gamma rays. At radio wavelengths several Australian radio telescopes detected a burst of radio waves in the first days of the explosion. In space the International Ultraviolet Explorer satellite detected the supernova within hours of its appearance. The ultraviolet flux declined rapidly, indicating rapid cooling of the expanding shell of material. It subsequently showed the presence of another shell of material far from the supernova itself, presumably the result of mass loss prior to the final death of the star. Ginga, a Japanese satellite capable of detecting X-rays, found the supernova by September. Infrared emission was studied with the Kuiper Airborne Observatory, an astronomically instrumented aircraft. Furthermore, by studying photographic plates taken prior to the explosion, for the first time scientists were able to identify the progenitor of a supernova: a supergiant star whose mass prior to the explosion was perhaps 20 times that of the Sun.

Perhaps most spectacular of all was the detection of a burst of neutrinos from the collapse of the core of the progenitor star. In all, 19 neutrinos—massless, neutral, weakly interacting particles—were counted by two deep underground detectors, one run by a U.S. collaboration in a mine in Ohio and the other by a Japanese-U.S. collaboration in a mine in Japan. Traveling at the speed of light, the neutrinos arrived just before SN 1987A was detected optically, in good agreement with theories of the way in which core collapse leads to the subsequent explosion. They also supported the prediction that the explosion would leave behind a highly collapsed stellar remnant, a neutron star or pulsar, which could show up in the months ahead as a gamma-ray source.

| Earth Perihelion and Aphelion, 1988 | |
|---|---|
| Jan. 4 | Perihelion, 147 million km (91,342,000 mi) from the Sun |
| July 6 | Aphelion, 152,003,000 km (94,450,000 mi) from the Sun |

| Equinoxes and Solstices, 1988 | |
|---|---|
| March 20 | Vernal equinox, 09:39[1] |
| June 21 | Summer solstice, 03:57[1] |
| Sept. 22 | Autumnal equinox, 19:29[1] |
| Dec. 21 | Winter solstice, 15:28[1] |

| Eclipses, 1988 | |
|---|---|
| March 3 | Moon, partial (begins 13:43[1]), visible in Asia, central and eastern Europe, northeastern Africa, parts of Antarctica, Australia, New Zealand, Alaska, and Hawaii. |
| March 17–18 | Sun, total (begins 23:24[1]), visible in eastern Asia, Indonesia, northwestern Australia, New Guinea, Micronesia, and extreme northwestern North America. |
| Aug. 27 | Moon, partial (begins 8:52[1]), visible in eastern Asia, most of Antarctica, Australia, New Zealand, eastern South America, Central America, and western and central North America. |
| Sept. 11 | Sun, total (begins 1:46[1]), visible in extreme eastern Africa, southern Asia, Indonesia, Australia, and New Zealand. |

[1]Universal time.
Source: *The Astronomical Almanac for the Year 1988* (1987).

An image of Pluto and its moon, Charon, was constructed from thermal radiation detected by the Infrared Astronomical Satellite as it scanned across the planet's position. Details in the bright circle, which roughly marks the location of the planet and moon, allowed scientists to infer the existence of polar caps of methane ice.

MARK V. SYKES, STEWARD OBSERVATORY, THE UNIVERSITY OF ARIZONA

Among perplexing aspects of SN 1987A was the observation by a group from Harvard University of a bright companion "mystery" spot near the supernova. Detected with a telescope at the Cerro Tololo Inter-American Observatory in Chile by means of a technique called speckle interferometry, the spot was nearly a tenth as bright as the supernova itself when seen in March and April but became unobservable later in the year. The same group also determined a size for the expanding material for the first time in such a young supernova. If the measurement was correct, it implied that supernova ejecta had already broken up into fragments.

SN 1987A was not the only major find in stellar astronomy during the year. Twenty years earlier, neutron stars called pulsars had first been discovered as pulsating radio beacons in the sky. Typically, these rapidly spinning stellar remnants of supernovas sweep their radio beams past the Earth once every second or so, and several hundred were known. For nearly 15 years the fastest pulsar measured—at 30 pulses per second—was the one in the Crab Nebula, which was associated with a supernova that occurred in 1054. The absence of really fast pulsars had puzzled astronomers because these objects, which are solar-mass stars collapsed to the density of the nucleus of an atom, could in principle rotate as fast as a thousand times per second. In 1982 the first such "millisecond" pulsar was discovered. Subsequently, several more were found, with periods ranging from about 1.5 to 6 milliseconds. In 1987 Andrew Lyne and A. Brinklow of the University of Manchester, England, announced the existence of a three-millisecond pulsar. This object was especially exciting because it was found to lie within a relatively dense globular star cluster, M28. Such star clusters, about 100 of which surround our Galaxy like a halo, are thought to be old and thus somewhat unpromising places to find relatively young objects like pulsars. The discovery of this object (and of a second one in another globular cluster by year's end) suggested that somehow the location of these objects in globular clusters played a significant role in the pulsars' formation, perhaps allowing old "dead" ones to rejuvenate.

**Galaxies and Cosmology.** On the largest scales the universe consists of galaxies, clusters of galaxies, and superclusters of clusters. A typical large spiral galaxy may have a mass equal to that of a few hundred billion stars like the Sun and a diameter of about 100,000 light-years. During the year Roger Lynds of Kitt Peak National Observatory, Arizona, and Vahe Petrosian of Stanford University announced the discovery of three enormous luminous arcs, each some 300,000 light-years long, or about three times the diameter of the Milky Way. These structures, which

were uncovered in a survey of clusters of galaxies, turned up in 3 of 58 clusters that the astronomers examined, suggesting that the phenomenon is not rare. They had not been reported before because the arcs, which appear as essentially perfect segments of a circle in the sky, are quite dim, taking hours of observing time on the largest telescopes for an image to be produced. One theory of their nature suggested that they are not physical structures at all but images of bright galaxies in the clusters produced by gravitational lensing, an effect whereby the gravitational pull of high concentrations of matter bends the paths of light to form images of distant objects. Another theory described them as light "echoes" from giant galactic explosions. Or it could be that the arcs are indeed real objects, consisting of stars torn out of galaxies in the clusters by tidal interaction. At the end of 1987 the arcs remained enigmatic.

The current, generally accepted view of the universe is that, while it consists of galaxies grouped into clusters and superclusters, these largest systems participate as individuals in an overall expansion of the universe. Since the discovery in the 1920s of this expansion, a half century of research has shown that, on the largest scales, groups of galaxies appear to be rushing away from one another at great speeds. Furthermore, the expansion appears to be more or less uniform and unaffected by any unseen mass concentrations, which might tend to make galaxies move in a faster or slower manner than the overall expansion. In 1987, however, Alan Dressler and collaborators of the Mount Wilson and Las Campanas Observatories, Pasadena, Calif., announced that several "local" superclusters, including the Virgo supercluster (which contains the Milky Way), the Perseus supercluster, and the Hydra-Centaurus supercluster, are all moving in the same direction. By "direction" is meant motion with respect to the general expansion of the universe observed in the vicinity. The directed motion suggested that the superclusters were being drawn gravitationally toward a nearby, but unseen, mass concentration, which was dubbed the Great Attractor. If such an object exists, it must be at least ten times more massive than any of the visible superclusters. As to its invisibility, astronomers speculated either that it is not there and there is instead some mistake in the observations or that the Great Attractor consists of "dark" matter of an as yet unknown type.

Finally, the expanding universe model suggests that the universe had a beginning. By measuring the expansion velocity of the galaxies, astronomers have found that the universe could be as old as 18 billion years. A different age-measuring technique, one that involved spectroscopic observations of very long-lived radioactive nuclei in stars, was attempted during the year by Harvey Butcher of the Kapteyn Astronomical Institute, Groningen, Neth. Butcher analyzed the light from the Sun and 20 nearby stars—some older and some younger than the Sun—to determine the relative abundances of the radioactive nuclide thorium-232 (which has a half-life of 14 billion years) and another stellar nuclide, the stable isotope neodymium-142. He found that the ratio of the two isotopes did not vary from star to star, despite their age differences. The result suggested that there had not been time for the thorium to decay, implying an age for the universe of no more than about ten billion years. (KENNETH BRECHER)

*See also* Space Exploration.

This article updates the *Macropædia* articles The COSMOS; GALAXIES; The PHYSICAL SCIENCES: *Astronomy and Astrophysics;* The SOLAR SYSTEM; STARS AND STAR CLUSTERS.

# Botanical Gardens and Zoos

**Botanical Gardens.** The ecosystems of tropical zones were often described as species-rich or highly complex, and for 15 years the international botanical community had expressed its concern over the speed of degradation occurring within these extremely vulnerable habitats. During Aug. 3–7, 1987, 123 delegates from 39 countries attended the tenth general meeting and conference of the International Association of Botanic Gardens (IABG) in Frankfurt am Main, West Germany. The theme for the meeting was "Botanic Gardens and Nature Reserves in the Tropics," and the conference itinerary included the formal opening of the new Tropicarium, a complex of greenhouses exhibiting plants from the various tropical climatic zones.

Conference delegates recognized that knowledge of tropical biology was incomplete and that there was an urgent need to promote the study and understanding of tropical areas for the benefit of humankind. Resolutions were passed urging all governments to support the management of living botanical collections, especially nature reserves and World Heritage areas. Examples were given of cases in which assistance was provided by major institutions of industrialized nations to gardens in less developed countries. Special mention was made of the formation of a Latin-American division of the IABG to foster cooperation in a part of the world that was suffering great degradation of its natural resources.

It was noted that although a high level of botanical knowledge existed in many tropical countries, it was often unavailable to those most in need of it. Such countries also lacked programs for informing people of the value of their fragile natural environment and the need to protect it for future generations. In particular, the deleterious long-term effects of insensitive commercial exploitation on tropical habitats—among them soil infertility, potential erosion problems, and subsequent flooding—were not commonly understood. Many representatives of less developed countries made it known that they required information on existing training programs regarding these and other technical problems. Effective communication within and between botanical gardens was needed, and the conference was informed of recent activities of the newly instituted Botanic Gardens Conservation Secretariat administered by the International Union for Conservation of Nature and Natural Resources (IUCN).

The British Overseas Development Agency agreed to assist in funding redevelopment of the botanical garden at Limbe, southwest Cameroon. Specialist horticultural and botanical staff from the Royal Botanic Gardens, Kew, made a series of visits to assess short- and long-term requirements for revitalizing the botanical garden as a centre for the study of genetic resources in the region. The development of the interrelationship of the botanical garden and the forest nature reserves was regarded as an important step forward that, if successful, would provide guidelines for projects throughout the tropics. Initially, support from overseas would provide the necessary expertise. However, one of the prime objectives would be to provide training opportunities for all levels of Cameroonian staff to enable them to take overall responsibility as soon as possible.

(REGINALD IAN BEYER)

**Zoos.** The two most important international supervisory bodies of zoos—the International Union of Directors of Zoological Gardens (IUDZG) and the Captive Breeding Specialist Group (CBSG), which answered to the Species Survival Specialist Group of the IUCN—met in Bristol, England, in September 1987. Topics discussed at the CBSG meeting included the 80 international studbooks, regional species-management programs, the computerized data programs ISIS and ARKS, and primate-conservation action plans. Also under discussion were a number of species of special concern that had captive-breeding and, in some cases, reintroduction programs; these included all rhinoceros, Asian elephant (*Elephas maximus*), Przewalski's horse (*Equus przewalskii*), Asiatic lion (*Panthera leo persica*), Arabian oryx (*Oryx leucoryx*), kouprey (*Bos sauveli*), tamaraw (*Bubalus mindorensis*), black-footed ferret (*Mustela nigripes*), Spix's macaw (*Cyanopsitta spixii*), and California condor (*Gymnogyps californianus*). The meeting noted the conservation problems of some invertebrates, including the devastating effects in Pacific and Indian Ocean islands of the introduction of alien carnivorous snails on endemic snails.

The IUDZG meeting dealt with wider issues of general zoo policy. Among them was the difficult problem of short-term loans of nonbreeding giant pandas (*Ailuropoda melanoleuca*) from China to Western and Japanese zoos. Opinion was divided as to the worth of such loans; some directors argued that they could have a detrimental effect on captive-breeding programs.

On April 19 scientists from the Condor Research Center in Ventura, Calif., netted the last-known California condor in the wild. The seven-year-old male was taken to the San Diego Wild Animal Park, which, together with the Los Angeles Zoo, held all 27 living condors. Most were still juveniles, but it was hoped that there were now enough adults to begin breeding.

Notable breedings included Louisiana pine snake at Ellen Trout Park Zoo, Lufkin, Texas; bushmaster viper (*Lachesis muta*) at Dallas (Texas) Zoo; lappet-faced vulture (*Torgos tracheliotus*) at Cotswold Wildlife Park, Burford, England; rhinoceros hornbill (*Buceros rhinoceros*) at Audubon Park and Zoological Garden, New Orleans, La.; goliath herons (*Ardea goliath*) from artificially incubated eggs at Dallas Zoo; the 24th Asian elephant to be born at Washington Park Zoo, Portland, Ore.; two giant pandas (both died) at the National Zoological Park, Washington, D.C.; and a Sumatran rhinoceros (*Didermocerus* [or *Dicerorhinus*] *sumatrensis*) at the Melaka Zoo, Malaysia.

The National Zoological Park in Washington succeeded for the first time in producing two litters of European ferrets by artificial insemination. The technique was to be used with the black-footed ferret, the last 18 of which known to exist were housed in Wyoming; two litters were born there naturally in 1987, and seven young survived. The National Zoological Park also reported the production

Yong Yong, a female giant panda, chews idly on a piece of bamboo during her stay at New York City's Bronx Zoo. Yong Yong and her male counterpart, Ling Ling, were visiting from the Beijing (Peking) Zoo in a sister-city program between Beijing and New York City.
RICK MAIMAN—SYGMA

of five domestic cats by in vitro fertilization techniques, the first time "test-tube" fertilization had been successful for any cat or species of carnivore. The first successful nonsurgical transfer of a fresh embryo from an endangered species to a domestic animal resulted in the birth of a male gaur (*Bos gaurus*) at Kings Island Wild Animal Habitat, Ohio. The Zoological Society of London reported the successful hatching of budgerigars (*Melopsittacus undulatus*) and a peregrine falcon (*Falco peregrinus*) through the use of frozen sperm.

New buildings and exhibits included Hippoquarium at Toledo (Ohio) Zoological Gardens; the Himalayan Highlands exhibit at New York Zoological Park (Bronx Zoo); the Lion and Maya Temple Ruins exhibits at Metro Toronto Zoo; the Australian Adventure exhibit at Fort Wayne (Ind.) Children's Zoological Gardens; the Marine Mammal exhibit at Cincinnati (Ohio) Zoological Gardens; Bear Grotto and the Lilah Callan Holden Elephant Museum at Washington Park Zoo, Portland; the Northern Shores exhibit at Denver (Colo.) Zoological Gardens; African Rain Forest at Jackson (Miss.) Zoological Park; the Seven Seas Panorama at Brookfield (Ill.) Zoo; the Monkey complex at Barcelona (Spain) Zoological Park; the Edge of the Reef exhibit at Waikiki Aquarium, Honolulu; and the Discovery Centre at the Whipsnade (England) Park zoo.       (P. J. OLNEY)

*See also* Environment; Gardening.

# Chemistry

**Organic Chemistry.** The discovery and structural elucidation of biologically active molecules remained of great interest during 1987. Not only did chemists find totally new molecules, but they also demonstrated new roles for ones long known.

Salicylic acid, for example, a close relative of aspirin (acetylsalicylic acid), turned out to be involved in a biologic phenomenon first noted more than 200 years earlier. In 1778 the pioneer French biologist Jean-Baptiste Lamarck noticed that some species of *Arum* (lily) generate heat. Subsequently it was found that this thermogenicity is related to the plant's sexual cycle; the heat helps to volatilize molecules whose odour attracts pollinating insects. Dur-

ing the year Axel Ehmann and colleagues of Du Pont, Wilmington, Del., together with Bastiaan Meeuse of the University of Washington, identified salicylic acid as the "calorigen" that triggers this process. Using the voodoo lily, parts of which can become as much as 14° C (25° F) hotter than their surroundings, the researchers were able to prepare a crude extract that, when applied to the lily, produced the heat-generating effect. Mass spectral analysis identified the active ingredient as salicylic acid. When the pure compound was applied to the plant, it had a pronounced thermogenic effect.

Retinoic acid is a molecule with several biologic functions. It had been suspected that it also might be a morphogen; that is, a compound that guides embryonic cells to develop into particular three-dimensional structures—into a finger or a toe, for example. Christina Thaller and Gregor Eichele of Harvard Medical School isolated retinoic acid from forelimb and hindlimb buds of chicks and showed that the amounts of the acid present naturally matched the amounts of exogenous acid used in earlier experiments to induce a particular type of differentiation of limb buds.

A second morphogen was identified later in 1987 by a group from Imperial College, London, the Imperial Cancer Research Fund's Clare Hall Laboratories, Hertfordshire, England, and the MRC Laboratory of Molecular Biology, Cambridge, England. Howard Morris and co-workers identified DIF-1 (differentiation inducing factor 1) as the structure shown in (1). This substance affects the way in which slime mold cells aggregate in response to starvation. (*See* LIFE SCIENCES: *Molecular Biology.*)

An unexpected relationship between the plant and microbial worlds emerged from research on the plant toxin ricin. This highly poisonous protein, found in castor oil seeds, had been used in recent years in conjunction with monoclonal antibodies for selective killing of cells for therapeutic purposes, but its precise mode of action had remained a mystery. During the year Yaeto Endo and his colleagues from Yamanashi (Japan) Medical College showed that part of the molecule selectively removes a particular nucleotide building block (specifically an adenine group) from the RNA of ribosomes, thus disrupting cellular protein synthesis. The investigators found that the same adenine is attacked by several other plant toxins and, perhaps more surprisingly, by the toxin of the dysentery-causing bacterium, *Shigella dysenteriae*. It was suggested that a bacterial ancestor may have borrowed from plants a gene that coded for a ricin-like poison.

Research groups from the pharmaceutical companies Bristol-Myers and Lederle reported structure determinations for a number of potential anticancer agents. The esperamicins and calichemicins are obtained by fermentation from the bacteria *Actinomadura verrucospora* and *Micromonospora echinospora,* respectively. The molecular core of both families of molecules is a bicyclo[7.3.1]tridecane system, and both also carry a methyl trisulfide group. It was suggested that their antitumour activity, which had been demonstrated in mice at very low concentrations, could result from a rearrangement to a free radical compound that removes protons from DNA, leading to breakage of the nucleic acid chain.

A new class of antibacterial compounds was isolated from frog skin by Michael Zasloff of the U.S. National Institute of Child Health and Human Development. Zasloff, who had been carrying out experiments involving surgery on the clawed frog *Xenopus laevis,* observed that the surgical skin wounds healed remarkably well, with no sign of infection. Study of the skin eventually uncovered two peptides (small proteins) that Zasloff dubbed magainins, from the Hebrew word for shield. Each peptide is a chain of 23 amino acids and differs from the other by only two components. The magainins, which proved effective against bacteria, fungi, and protozoans, may work by disrupting fluid transport through cell membranes.

Completely metal-free organic polymers that display ferromagnetism, the ordinary type of magnetism operating in permanent magnets, were reported by A. A. Ovchinnikov and colleagues from Mendeleyev's Institute of Chemical Technology, Moscow, and the Institute of Chemical Physics of the U.S.S.R. Academy of Sciences. Organic ferromagnetism had been considered a possibility for some years; the Soviet group achieved it with a polymer made from a diacetylene substituted with stable radical side groups (2). The yield of ferromagnetic polymer was very small but could be separated magnetically from the other components of the reaction mixture.

**Inorganic Chemistry.** Interest remained high in the behaviour of those elements—silicon (Si), germanium (Ge), tin (Sn), and lead (Pb)—that fall under carbon in the periodic table and that share a little of carbon's versatility. Armin Berndt and his colleagues at Marburg University, West Germany, reported the existence of stable germaethenes and stannaethenes. These are analogues of ethene ($H_2C{=}CH_2$), the simplest double-bonded carbon compound, more commonly known as ethylene. The stable stannaethene, in which a tin atom is double-bonded to a carbon atom, was isolated as red, cubic crystals, while the germaethene, with a germanium-carbon double bond, formed lemon-yellow crystals. The stable parent compound, ethene, possesses two hydrogen atoms attached to each carbon. In order to achieve stability of the C${=}$Sn and C${=}$Ge combinations, it was necessary to surround the core of the molecule with shielding groups much more complex than hydrogen (3). A compound containing a germanium-carbon double bond was also reported by Claude Couret and colleagues from the Université Paul Sabatier, Toulouse, France. Their double-bonded core also had to be stabilized by resonance effects and large protective groups (4). Similarly, in synthesizing the first Si${=}$Si compound to be isolated in a pure, crystalline form, Satoru Masamune, Yuichi Eriyama, and Takeshi Kawasa of the Massachusetts Institute of Technology had to surround the core of the molecule with protective groups (5).

Carbonic acid ($H_2CO_3$) forms when carbon dioxide ($CO_2$) dissolves in water. It is believed that much of the carbon dioxide originally in the Earth's atmosphere dissolved in rain, fell to Earth, and became locked up in carbonate rocks such as dolomite. When carbonate rocks are heated, they release carbon dioxide to give metal oxides. A. Reller, C. Padeste, and P. Hug of the University of Zürich, Switz., showed that if the alkaline earth carbonates are heated in a reducing (hydrogen-containing) atmosphere in the presence of transition metal carbonates, then the major gaseous product is not carbon dioxide but carbon monoxide (CO) or methane ($CH_4$). Unlike carbon dioxide, both of the latter compounds could be of interest to the chemical industry as building blocks for organic chemicals when fossil fuels run out. Such reactions might also prove important at some future date as $CO_2$-trapping systems, should current levels of $CO_2$ release to the atmosphere prove harmful—as in the postulated greenhouse effect.

**Physical Chemistry.** Zeolites are inorganic crystals of aluminum, silicon, and oxygen that can be found as natural minerals or made in the laboratory. Because they are riddled with highly uniform, molecular-sized pores, they have found many important uses as catalysts and molecular sieves. The versatility that zeolites can offer was shown by Heinz Litterer and his colleagues from Hoechst, Frankfurt, West Germany, who used them to convert α-halothiophenes selectively to β-halothiophenes. By using a combination of zeolite conversion and halogenation (addition of halogen atoms, in this case chlorine), they devised ways in which all the possible dichlorothiophenes could be produced in a commercially practicable way. Previous routes, relying on standard chemical reactions, required exhaustive halogenation and then removal of unwanted halogen atoms. The work was significant because the different thiophenes provided useful synthetic intermediates in the production of potential drugs and plant-protection chemicals.

Catalysis, the process by which reactions are speeded up by nonreacting species present in the reaction mix, has been one of the most studied areas of physical chemistry. Not only does all life depend on catalytic processes, mediated primarily by enzymes, but so does most of the chemical industry. By the late 1980s understanding of enzymes had progressed such that it was becoming possible to improve upon natural versions. Alan Russell and Alan Fersht of Imperial College, London, reported that they had produced modified enzymes with higher activity than the "wild" type under certain conditions. As an example, they described modified versions of the enzyme subtilisin that were twice as active as the natural material under the conditions found in a washing machine (most industrially produced subtilisin ended up in laundry detergent). Russell and Fersht's approach was purely physicochemical in that modifications to the enzyme were made in regard to the surface charge of the molecule.

**Analytical Chemistry.** Many common explosives, such as TNT, are based on a benzene ring ($C_6H_6$) whose hydrogen atoms are substituted with nitro ($-NO_2$) and other groups. Using a technique called X-ray-excited Auger electron spectroscopy to probe the electronic structures of such molecules, J. William Rogers, Jr., and his team at Sandia National Laboratories, Albuquerque, N.M., confirmed the long-held hypothesis that adding nitro groups to the benzene ring weakens its carbon-carbon bonds, thus making it sensitive to shock. Other groups, such as amino ($-NH_2$) or methyl ($-CH_3$), have an opposing effect, thus accounting for the differing sensitivities of related explosives.

A natural explosion that took place about 3,500 years ago also caught the attention of analytical chemists during 1987. A team from the University of Copenhagen and Århus (Den.) University analyzed acid fallout in a Greenland ice core in an attempt to date the volcanic eruption that devastated the island of Thera in the Aegean Sea in late Minoan times. They picked a number of acid peaks in the ice core and attributed one dated at 1645 BC to volcanic action because of its sulfuric acid content. Although this date fell within the range of dates for the eruption determined by radiocarbon analysis, it did not agree with the generally accepted archaeological date of about 1500 BC.

(MARTIN A. SHERWOOD)

This article updates the *Macropædia* articles Physical and Chemical ANALYSIS AND MEASUREMENT; BIOCHEMICAL COMPONENTS OF ORGANISMS; CHEMICAL COMPOUNDS; CHEMICAL ELEMENTS; CHEMICAL REACTIONS; Principles, Methods, and Instruments of MEASUREMENT AND OBSERVATION; MOLECULES; The PHYSICAL SCIENCES: *Chemistry*.

# Consumer Affairs

During Sept. 15-20, 1987, nearly 700 consumer leaders and activists represented more than 66 countries at the 12th world congress of the International Organization of Consumers Unions (IOCU) in Madrid. For the first time, both Latin America and the Caribbean and Africa were substantially represented. Also for the first time, economic policy was high on the agenda, with a major seminar on the consumer implications of foreign debt. More than 40 workshops tackled such diverse issues as hazardous technologies, advertising, ozone layer depletion, and inflation. The congress reflected the continuing spread of the consumer movement worldwide. The China Consumers' Association, representing a billion consumers, joined the IOCU. The growth of the Latin-American and Caribbean consumer movement was reflected in the opening of an IOCU regional office in Montevideo, Uruguay. The burgeoning consumer movement in Africa was given added strength through the involvement of pan-African nongovernmental and other grass-roots organizations in consumer protection and education work.

The UN Guidelines for Consumer Protection (1985) continued to provide an important framework for much of the world consumer movement's work; in particular, it supplied a basis for lobbying governments. The most important seminar on consumer protection ever held in Latin America took place under the auspices of the UN. Representatives of 20 governments and at least 20 delegates from various consumer groups from Latin America and the Caribbean met in Montevideo to discuss implementation of the UN guidelines. It was agreed that a network of government officials responsible for consumer protection would be established. Several governments, including Argentina and Ecuador, also decided to establish formal bodies to cover consumer issues.

A report commissioned by the Australian government showed that country's consumer protection legislation to be largely in line with the UN guidelines. The Indian Parliament passed a Consumer Protection Bill aimed at providing consumer councils with the necessary channels for redress and compensation. Seven companion bills covering various aspects of consumer protection were also passed. In the Philippines the new constitution ratified in February included provisions for protecting consumers "from trade malpractices and from substandard or hazardous products" and for regulating mass media and advertising.

Nearly a decade of negotiations brought adoption of the voluntary UN Code of Conduct on Transnational Corporations (TNCs) closer. Agreement had been reached on 80% of the code, which was intended to establish lines of communication between TNCs and their host states in order to minimize the danger of injury to consumers. After much controversy and strenuous efforts by nongovernment representatives, the second issue of the UN Consolidated List of Products Whose Consumption and/or Sales Have Been Banned, Withdrawn, Severely Restricted or Not Approved by Governments was made available. The European Commission proposed tough new regulations that would block exports of banned or hazardous pesticides to third world nations unless authorized by the importing country. However, the UN Conference on Dangerous Chemicals, sponsored by the U.K. government and the UN Environment Program (UNEP), which met in Nairobi, Kenya, in June, adopted the London Guidelines for the Exchange of Information on Chemicals in International Trade without prior informed consent (PIC). The UNEP governing council stated, nevertheless, that "PIC should be incorporated in the London Guidelines as expeditiously as possible."

On March 15 some 135 consumer organizations in 52 countries celebrated the fifth annual World Consumer Rights Day. Food in the consumer interest was the theme chosen by the IOCU. The European Organization of Consumers Unions put forward a complaint against the flagrant violation of consumer rights by the European Communities (EC) in proposals for a levy on margarine, table oils, and fats and many processed foods. The move would seriously affect the poorest consumers and third world countries exporting such products to the EC.

In December 1986, two years after the disaster in Bhopal, India, where toxic fumes escaping from a pesticide plant killed or injured thousands of people, nongovernment organizations from the U.K., the U.S., The Netherlands, Japan, Malaysia, and Hong Kong joined with the IOCU to form the International Coalition for Justice in Bhopal. Its purpose was to protect the interests of the Bhopal victims. The disruption in food production and trade following the Chernobyl nuclear-reactor accident in April 1986 was exacerbated by the lack of uniformity in actions taken by countries to limit exposure to radionuclides in food, water, or air and by the lack of comprehensive information. In response to requests for advice, the UN Food and Agriculture Organization convened an Expert Consultation on Recommended Limits for Radionuclide Contamination in Foods, which recommended adoption of interim International Radionuclide Action Levels for Foods based on accepted international recommendations.

An international seminar on pharmaceutical patents was held in Bangkok, Thailand, on April 4 as part of the Action for Rational Drugs in Asia (ARDA) program. ARDA called for laws on intellectual property that would encourage and stimulate real technical innovation. Health Action International (HAI) launched a worldwide campaign in June for the removal of over 200 antidiarrheal drugs containing antibiotics, which it considered to be ineffective, expensive, and potentially hazardous. A new law on substances harmful to the environment came into force in Switzerland. Batteries and small accumulators containing mercury, cadmium, and nickel could no longer be discarded along with ordinary rubbish, which was usually burned.

Some 30 participants from about 15 countries attended a Dag Hammarskjold Foundation Seminar on "The Sociological Impact of New Biotechnologies on Basic Health and Agriculture in the Third World." The conference acknowledged the potential of biotechnology to improve the quality of life but discussed the need to identify the risks attached. Food irradiation continued to cause concern, and an international meeting in Amsterdam sought to discover how the problem was being approached in various countries. Participants decided to establish a European network for exchanging information and experiences, and the need to establish close contacts with third world organizations was recognized.                        (LÍDIA BARREIROS)

As a result of legislation passed by the U.S. Congress, banks, beginning in 1988, would have to process checks more rapidly so that customers could have access to their funds faster. By 1990 checks drawn on local banks would have to be cleared after one business day, compared with the 5 to 15 working days currently taken by most banks. The Supreme Court ruled that clauses in agreements between investors and their brokers that require customer disputes to be settled by binding arbitration rather than lawsuits can be extended to fraud claims under federal securities laws. The ruling would increase the number of cases decided by independent arbitrators. Congress passed

legislation, to take effect in 1989, cutting from ten to five years the time needed for employees to become vested in pensions. A number of pension portability bills were introduced, including one that would allow employees to set up pension plans with private investment managers who would control workers' pensions during their entire careers, no matter where they were employed.

In July Chrysler Corp., in a nationwide advertising campaign, apologized to consumers for its practice of testing vehicles with the odometer disconnected. Chrysler chairman Lee Iacocca admitted that the automobile manufacturer had made a mistake and announced that Chrysler was extending warranty coverage on such test vehicles, offering free inspections, and replacing vehicles damaged in the test program. Chrysler and two executives faced a federal indictment as a result of the practice. On October 1 Florida became the first state to pass "do not call" legislation allowing residential telephone subscribers to request an additional listing line reading "no sales solicitation calls," at an average cost of $1.20 per month. Telemarketers would be required to obtain all 71 of the state's telephone directories and remove the names and numbers of "do not call" consumers from their calling lists.

A new target for consumer legislation was the marketing of home equity loans through bank advertisements portraying these home-secured loans as the best way to get a tax deduction for financing a major trip or a large purchase. The loans took advantage of a loophole in the new tax law, but it was feared that people would take on too much debt, risking the loss of their homes if they could not make payments. In 1987 Congress approved a provision requiring lenders to set a cap on how much interest rates could increase over the life of the floating-rate home equity loan. Other legislation was introduced that would require full disclosure of closing costs, fees, and rates.

Responding to a sharp rise in consumer complaints about airline service, the U.S. Department of Transportation (DOT) in August threatened to fine airline carriers for flights that were chronically late or canceled or that continually lost luggage. The agency proposed to fine carriers $1,000 for each flight that was late more than half the time (a flight was considered late if it arrived more than 15 minutes after the scheduled time of arrival). Under DOT's plan, airlines were given six months to make their schedules more realistic. DOT also required airlines to disclose on a monthly basis how frequently flights were late or canceled, and the data were made public. A task force of 21 state attorneys general started drawing up national standards concerning deceptive airline practices, including the way airlines advertised discount fares and ran frequent-flier programs. The airlines claimed their activities were not subject to state laws.                (EDWARD MARK MAZZE)

See also Economic Affairs: *World Economy;* Environment; Industrial Review: *Advertising.*

# Crime, Law Enforcement, and Penology

**Violent Crime.** *Terrorism.* The world appeared to experience a limited but welcome respite from terrorist violence in 1987. U.S. State Department figures confirmed that a slight decline had begun a year earlier in the number of terrorist incidents reported worldwide. Experts believed this positive trend was largely the product of greater international cooperation in dealing with the problems of terrorism. However, they also warned that the root causes of terrorism had not been cured and that state-sponsored acts of terror by countries in places like the Middle East posed a continuing threat.

The reality of this threat was apparent in January when an epidemic of terrorist kidnappings occurred in Beirut, the war-torn capital of Lebanon. The abductions began after the January 13 arrest by West German officials of Muhammad Ali Hamadei, an alleged ringleader in the 1985 hijacking of TWA Flight 847. On January 17 two carloads of pistol-wielding terrorists pulled Rudolf Cordes, a West German businessman, out of his cab in a West Beirut suburb. A few days later it was reported that Alfred Schmidt, an engineer employed by Seimens, a West German electronics firm, had been taken at gunpoint from his Beirut hotel bedroom. Then on January 24 a group of well-armed terrorists disguised as Lebanese police officers drove onto the campus of Beirut University College, where they seized three U.S. professors—Robert Polhill, Alann Steen, and Jesse Turner—and Mithileshwar Singh, the Indian-born head of the business department. These kidnap victims became members of a group of more than 20 captives from seven nations held hostage throughout the year by a shadowy network of Lebanese-based terrorists, many with links to the radical Shi'ah regime in Iran. One of the captives was believed to be Terry Waite, the special envoy of the archbishop of Canterbury, who had received widespread acclaim for his skill in negotiating with terrorist groups. Waite was last seen in Beirut on January 20 when he was to hold discussions with Shi'ah Muslim extremists about the release of hostages held in Lebanon.

The fate of these hostages became a major preoccupation of the governments involved. The group holding the two West German businessmen demanded that they be exchanged for Hamadei. Resisting this demand, as well as pressure to extradite Hamadei to the U.S., West Germany announced in June that Hamadei would be tried in Frankfurt. For U.S. Pres. Ronald Reagan, whose political credibility had been seriously compromised by the Iran-*contra* scandal, the situation was rendered still more difficult by the kidnapping of a U.S. journalist, Charles Glass, in June. (*See* WORLD AFFAIRS [North America]: *United States:* Special Report.) However, Glass escaped from his kidnappers after 62 days in captivity. His escape was thought to have been assisted by pressure from Syrian authorities, who were seeking to improve their relations with the West. In June Syria announced that it was shutting down the Damascus office of the Palestinian terrorist leader Abu Nidal.

Representatives of the French government reportedly held many months of secret negotiations with Iran seeking the release of five French citizens being held in Lebanon. However, these discussions broke down in June when evidence came to light that a translator acting as Iran's principal negotiator, Wahid Gordji, may have helped finance and direct the wave of bombing attacks in Paris during September 1986, which killed more than ten people. French officials sought Gordji for questioning, but he fled and took refuge in the Iranian embassy in Paris, which was then surrounded by armed French police. The Iranians reciprocated at the French embassy in Tehran, and the two countries severed diplomatic ties. Gordji was allowed to leave France on November 29, some 48 hours after two French hostages were released in Beirut.

Blame for the 1986 bombings had previously been placed on colleagues of Georges Ibrahim Abdallah, a Lebanese Christian, then in French custody awaiting trial on a number of terrorist-related charges. Abdallah was convicted in February of complicity in the killings of assistant U.S. military attaché Charles Robert Ray and Israeli diplomat Yacov Barsimantov in Paris in 1982 and the attempted murder of U.S. Consul General Robert Homme in Strasbourg in 1984 and was sentenced to life imprisonment.

Other parts of the world continued to experience serious acts of terrorist violence. In July at least 75 people were killed and 300 injured when two massive car bomb explosions ripped through the busiest shopping area in the Pakistani city of Karachi. No group claimed responsibility. In India Sikh extremist groups seeking an independent homeland in the Punjab had been blamed for more than 500 killings by midyear. To the south in the troubled island of Sri Lanka, Tamils engaged in a struggle for an independent homeland in the northern and eastern parts of the country committed a number of terrorist acts against the majority Sinhalese population. (*See* WORLD AFFAIRS [South Asia]: *India; Sri Lanka*).

Terrorist groups were said to finance their activities increasingly from the sale of narcotics in Western Europe and North America. According to a UN report released in January, "narcoterrorism" was spreading rapidly. In February a man described as the "embodiment of a narcoterrorist," Carlos Enrique Lehder Rivas, was captured by Colombian and U.S. law-enforcement officials. Lehder, the alleged leader of the Medellín cartel, a drug network said to be responsible for as much as 80% of the cocaine smuggled into the U.S., was seized after a gun battle with Colombian police and was subsequently taken to Florida to stand trial.

*Murder and Violence.* Trends in serious crime reported to the police in the U.S. moved upward in 1986 for the second consecutive year. The FBI's Crime Index, based on information supplied by more than 16,000 law-enforcement agencies nationwide, showed an overall increase of 6% in serious crime in 1986 over 1985. Violent crime was up 12%, with murder and robbery both rising 9%, forcible rape 3%, and aggravated assault 15%. Law-enforcement officials expressed particular concern about a sharp rise in the number of homicides during 1986 in nine out of ten of the nation's largest cities. Criminologists suggested that the surge in killings was a result of the increasing use of cocaine and, especially, crack, a highly addictive cocaine derivative. In contrast, Canada reported a 20% drop in its homicide rate in 1986. Canadian crime statistics showed that there were 561 killings nationwide, the lowest number in 13 years.

In August, in the worst such incident in recent British history, Michael Ryan went on a shooting rampage in the small Berkshire town of Hungerford, firing bursts from a

(continued on page 145)

Jonathan Jay Pollard, a civilian navy intelligence analyst, was sentenced in March to life imprisonment for selling secret U.S. documents to Israel.

# Crime and High Finance

BY SARAH HOGG

"Velvet-collar crime," as it was soon nicknamed, began to make headlines late in 1986 and continued to haunt the front pages of newspapers in Britain and the U.S. throughout much of 1987. The immediate cause was the sudden remarkable success of the U.S. Securities and Exchange Commission (SEC) in bringing criminal charges against two financiers: Dennis Levine of Drexel Burnham Lambert Inc. in May 1986 and—the big catch—the investor and trader Ivan Boesky in November 1986. From these two men SEC investigators extracted information that led them on a trail of prosecutions throughout Wall Street.

Under pressure from the SEC, Boesky talked freely and even allowed his phone to be tapped. Subsequent investigations involved a number of prominent Wall Street figures, among them Martin Siegel, former head of mergers at Drexel Burnham Lambert. In February 1987 Levine was sentenced to four concurrent two-year prison terms and fined $362,000. In March the SEC announced that it wished to subpoena some of the records of three of the largest financial groups in the U.S.: American Express, its investment banking subsidiary Shearson Lehman Brothers, and Salomon Brothers. Boesky, who had already paid a $100 million civil penalty, was sentenced to three years in prison in December.

The spate of SEC investigations and prosecutions involved a wide range of offenses against the rules covering trading behaviour. These included stock market manipulation during takeovers; "parking" stocks (appearing to buy but in fact merely agreeing to hold stocks for the true buyer for a short time, thus concealing the ownership of the stock); and failure to give sufficiently prompt notification of intended mergers. Perhaps the offense that became most notorious, however, was "insider trading."

Insider trading had been illegal in the U.S. since 1934. Its modern definition depended on case law. SEC officials provided an encapsulation of this to the U.S. Congress in the summer of 1987, in response to a bill seeking to redefine insider trading in law. Their formulation forbade trading "while in possession of material, non-public information" that had been obtained by theft, bribery, misrepresentation, or espionage or obtained or used in breach of a duty to keep the information confidential.

Amid the wealth of information garnered by the SEC was some that enabled it to tip off the British Department of Trade and Industry (DTI) about financial malpractice on the other side of the Atlantic. This led indirectly to the exposure of the biggest financial scandal in Britain for many years.

**The Guinness Affair.** On Dec. 1, 1986, the DTI launched its investigation into the affairs of the Guinness brewing and liquor company. The inquiry was focused on

share movements during Guinness's successful battle with the Argyll Group for control of Distillers Co. in 1986. It led to the downfall of chairman and chief executive Ernest Saunders, who in five years had succeeded in raising Guinness from a sluggish family-run business to Britain's foremost food and drink exporter. It also touched several well-known City institutions, among them the merchant bank Morgan Grenfell, where the chief executive and the head of the corporate finance department resigned and the chairman took early retirement.

The Guinness investigations were focused on three related issues. First, the massive share-support operation that had taken place during the battle for control of Distillers—in particular, the terms on which various individuals and concerns had agreed to buy Guinness shares at the time, or "mop up" shares after the event. Second, the use of Guinness funds not only to indemnify those who bought shares against any possible loss but also to pay fees totaling some $25 million to particular individuals for "services" to the company. And third, the investment of $100 million of Guinness money in a partnership run by Boesky—the move that almost certainly triggered inquiries when Boesky was exposed.

The inquiries were directed toward a variety of possible offenses—ranging from breaches of the Takeover Code to outright fraud—that illustrated both the diversity of what is known as financial crime and the complex structure of authorities intended to keep it in check. The Guinness affair, moreover, came at a particularly critical moment in the history of the City of London: during a spate of inquiries into the incidence of "insider trading," and at a time when the British government's massive privatization program was creating a new breed of private shareholders whom the government was particularly concerned to protect. Most significantly, the scandal broke very shortly after the so-called Big Bang in the London Stock Exchange.

**Effects of the Big Bang.** The wide-ranging changes that came into effect in October 1986 followed similarly radical changes in the U.S. The critical elements in London's Big Bang were the abolition of fixed commissions and of the strict separation between stockbrokers, who acted on behalf of clients, and stockjobbers, with whom brokers dealt. Together with changes in the rules on the ownership of Stock Exchange members, this led to the creation of a few large British-owned financial conglomerates and to the entry into the London market of existing major U.S. and Japanese securities houses.

These changes aroused widespread fears that the "Chinese walls" within these new groups would not be maintained. In particular, it was feared that the barriers might break down between corporate finance departments—advising companies on takeover strategies, for example—and those advising clients to buy or sell shares or doing so on their own account. This might lead to a spread of insider trading on the basis of privileged information, a practice outlawed in Britain since 1980 but very hard to pin down.

**Regulation of Financial Institutions.** The issue of financial misbehaviour was particularly sensitive in that Britain, unlike the U.S., embarked on Big Bang with a system of self-regulation. The new British Securities and Investment Board (SIB), which was very roughly equivalent to the SEC, was designed to operate at arm's length; it would "recognize" a number of self-regulatory organizations—some five in all—which would set rules for their own members. After a certain date (delayed well into 1988) it would be illegal to carry on investment business in Britain without being a member of one of these, unless specifically exempted by the SIB.

*Sarah Hogg is Business and Finance Editor of* The Independent, *London.*

Behaviour during mergers would continue to be monitored by the Takeover Panel, another self-regulatory body. Investigations into insider dealing and breaches of the Companies Act would continue to be the responsibility of the DTI, whose investigatory role might well overlap with that of the newly established Serious Fraud Office. This diverse approach, it was increasingly argued, would prove less effective than the hands-on control of the U.S. securities industry exercised by the SEC.

Changes made to the British system during 1987 reduced the clear-cut distinction between statutory and self-regulation. In particular, the Takeover Panel gained reinforcement from SIB rules. Most notably, the SIB's draft rule book included the "cold shoulder" provision: authorized firms would not be able to act in takeovers for people they had reason to believe would fail to comply with the Takeover Code, and they would be required to cooperate with the panel when requested.

Although the London Stock Exchange claimed that increasing technological sophistication had greatly enhanced its detective powers, New York enjoyed an unrivaled early warning system. The Stopwatch program monitored every transaction and sounded the alarm if trading appeared unusual in size, price, or turnover. In such an event an investigation was automatically launched, parties to the deal were obliged to reveal their clients, and the computer searched for any suspicious links.

Comparisons between the U.S. and the British system did not all work to the disadvantage of the latter, however. It was pointed out that even though insider trading had been illegal for far longer in the U.S., it had taken years—and a lucky break—for the SEC to track down the activities of Boesky. The SEC did not enjoy the same powers to demand answers to its questions as the inspectors appointed by the British DTI—powers rushed into force late in 1986. When he was nominated by U.S. Pres. Ronald Reagan as the new chairman of the SEC in July 1987, David Ruder stressed the need for extra resources. His view of the upsurge in prosecutions was, however, detached: "My experience as a law teacher," remarked Ruder, a former law professor, "informs me that greed and lack of ethical standards will always exist."

Attempts at international cooperation in the prosecution of offenders were hampered by the fact that the main stock markets operated under different regulatory systems, as well as by the existence of small "havens" in which vehicles for investment could be registered. For example, insider trading was not illegal in all stock markets. West Germany had only a "voluntary" code against it. In 1987 the European Commission made it known that it was pressing for a statutory ban in all member countries of the European Communities, but existing rules varied considerably.

Although London and Wall Street appeared to generate—or, rather, to succeed in uncovering—the most notable financial scandals of 1987, the year also saw the exposure of a spectacular fraud in West Germany. Volkswagen announced a total of $259 million in currency losses through alleged foreign exchange fraud. The French government, which was following in Britain's footsteps with an even larger privatization program and simultaneously loosening foreign exchange controls, came alive to the dangers of a simultaneous increase in cross-border financial misbehaviour. Switzerland, too—embarrassed by the use of certain Swiss banks for the channeling of funds in, for example, the Guinness affair—showed a new willingness to join in international talks on financial regulation.

(continued from page 143)

Kalashnikov assault rifle at anything that moved as he walked toward the centre of town. Eventually besieged by police, he took his own life after shooting 30 people, 16 of whom, including his mother, died. Ryan's murderous assault, seemingly patterned after the popular "Rambo" movies, provoked intense debate in England about the influence on human behaviour of violence portrayed on television and movie screens. While experts said evidence of a direct cause-and-effect relationship between the viewing and commission of violent acts was slim, the Hungerford killings were similar to widely publicized mass shootings that had occurred earlier in Australia and the U.S. On August 9, ten days before the British murders, a heavily armed gunman in Clifton Hill, near Melbourne, shot 24 people at random, 6 of whom died, and then surrendered to police, apparently after running out of ammunition. In May a lone gunman went on an eight-hour killing spree in Palm Bay, Fla. The gunman, who fired at shoppers at two supermarkets, was captured alive after six people had been killed and ten others wounded.

In August, Donald Harvey, an orderly at a hospital in Cincinnati, Ohio, pleaded guilty to murdering 24 people, most of them chronically ill patients. Sentenced to three life terms for these crimes, Harvey was believed to have been responsible for the deaths of an additional 30 victims. At year's end investigators were still looking into the December 7 crash of a Pacific Southwest jetliner in California that killed 43 people, but evidence suggested that David Burke, a former employee of Pacific Southwest's parent company, USAir, had smuggled a gun on board, shot the USAir official who had fired him, and then possibly killed or disabled the pilot. In late December, after R. Gene Simmons was arrested in Russellville, Ark., following a shooting spree in which two people died, the bodies of 14 relatives and in-laws were found in his home.

In June a Manhattan jury acquitted Bernhard Goetz, the so-called subway vigilante, of all but one relatively minor charge in the 1984 shooting of four black youths who, Goetz said, had threatened him on a subway train. The case had prompted headlines around the world.

**Nonviolent Crime.** *Political Crime and Espionage.* Two former senior aides of President Reagan were before the criminal courts during the year. In December one-time White House deputy chief of staff Michael Deaver was found guilty of lying under oath about alleged influence peddling. In May, Raymond Donovan, a former secretary of labour, was acquitted along with several associates of charges of defrauding the New York City Transit Authority of $7.4 million in the construction of a subway tunnel in Manhattan. In December three men, including two former associates of Attorney General Edwin Meese, were indicted on racketeering charges in connection with Wedtech, a defense contractor allegedly involved in conspiracies to defraud both the government and the company's stockholders.

Yugoslavia's biggest financial scandal since World War II shook the foundations of the ruling Communist Party. In early September, Vice-Pres. Hamadja Pozderac, who would have been president of Yugoslavia the next year under the rotating leadership system, resigned after being implicated in the scandal, which was said to involve the issuance of up to $850 million in false promissory notes by Agrokomerc, a state-run agro-industry firm. Yugoslav news sources reported that the firm's manager and 8 others had been detained, and 28 more faced criminal charges.

Indian Prime Minister Rajiv Gandhi came under sustained criticism after being accused of seeking to cover up massive bribes totaling $41 million paid by Bofors, the Swedish arms manufacturer, to secure a huge arms contract. Gandhi, who was also defense minister at the time the $1.3 billion contract was signed, denied that he or any of his family had received any of the payoffs, which Bofors admitted making to Indian officials.

In March, Jonathan Pollard (*see* BIOGRAPHIES), a former civilian U.S. Navy intelligence analyst, was sentenced to life imprisonment after pleading guilty to charges of selling Israel hundreds of secret U.S. military documents. Pollard's wife, Anne, who was also involved in the case, received two concurrent five-year prison sentences. The two were sentenced a day after the U.S. filed an indictment against Israeli Air Force Col. Aviem Sella charging that he recruited and paid the Pollards. In Israel a two-member investigative panel appointed by the Cabinet found the entire government responsible for the Pollards' activities. A parliamentary investigation headed by former foreign minister Abba Eban placed the blame on Prime Minister Yitzhak Shamir, Foreign Minister Shimon Peres, and Defense Minister Yitzhak Rabin. Early in the year details began to emerge of what appeared to be a serious security breach. Two Marine guards, Sgt. Clayton Lonetree and Corp. Arnold Bracy, were charged with espionage for allegedly permitting Soviet agents to roam through the U.S. embassy in Moscow in 1986. Both men were said to have been seduced by Soviet women working undercover for the KGB. In March U.S. officials ordered the entire contingent of 28 guards in Moscow to return home and began an extensive investigation, but by July the case seemed to have petered out in a spate of dropped charges and repudiated testimony. An exception was Sergeant Lonetree, who was found guilty of passing secret documents to the Soviets and was sentenced to a 30-year prison term.

*White Collar Crime and Theft.* The massive Wall Street insider trading scandal, which first broke in 1986 with the arrest of Dennis Levine, a senior executive of the investment banking firm Drexel Burnham Lambert Inc., continued to produce fresh revelations. In February Levine, who had cooperated with federal investigators and implicated other high-flying Wall Street players like arbitrageur Ivan Boesky, was sentenced to two years in prison and fined $362,000 after pleading guilty to charges of income tax evasion, securities fraud, and perjury. Boesky, who also cooperated with authorities, pleaded guilty to one count of conspiring to file false documents with the federal gov-

Accused Nazi war criminal Karl Linnas (left) is accompanied by Soviet security personnel after his arrival in the U.S.S.R. Linnas was deported from the U.S. to the U.S.S.R., where he had been sentenced to death in absentia. Linnas died in July in a Leningrad hospital.
AFP PHOTO

ernment and was sentenced in December to three years in prison. An international dimension was added to the scandal in March when the U.S. Securities and Exchange Commission (SEC) charged Nahum Vaskevitch, the head of international mergers in Merrill Lynch's London office, and David Sofer, an Israeli stock speculator, with obtaining more than $4 million in illegal profits from a transatlantic insider trading scheme. The plot provoked new concern about financial crime in both the U.S. and Britain. (*See* Special Report.)

In North America, where protecting the security of automated teller machines had become a problem, researchers were studying more sophisticated means of verifying cardholders' identities. Techniques being considered included scans of certain biologic characteristics of individuals, such as retinal eye scans that could read the unique pattern of blood vessels at the back of a person's eyes. The theft of oil on the high seas was called "a monumental fraud and a cancer on the entire shipping industry" by maritime arbitrators meeting in Madrid in October. One estimate placed the annual loss from oil sold on the black market or used illicitly as tanker fuel at more than $7 billion.

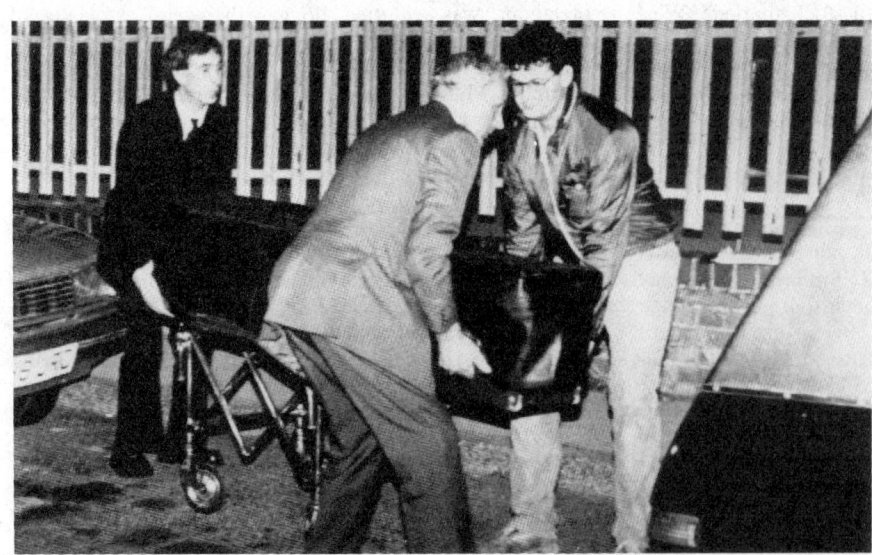

AFP PHOTO

A casket containing one of the victims of Michael Ryan is carried to a waiting hearse. Ryan went on a shooting spree in Hungerford, England, in August, killing 16 people and wounding some 14 others before killing himself.

**Law Enforcement.** Researchers revealed that although overall rates of murder and violence had grown substantially in U.S. cities since the early 1970s, police were less likely to be shot, and less likely to shoot, than they had been 15 years earlier. An extensive study of the situation in Atlanta, Ga., where in 1971 police were fatally shooting more people than their counterparts in any comparable city in the country, showed that by 1986 the number of killings by police had dropped by two-thirds. This change was attributed to new police policies and attitudes. For example, in the early 1970s many police shootings in Atlanta and other big cities took place during stakeouts where police would await armed robbers or burglars, but a new public safety commissioner appointed in 1974 implemented policies prohibiting the shooting of fleeing suspects and permitting the use of deadly force only when the lives of officers or third parties were in jeopardy. By the 1980s most of the nation's big-city police departments had put similar measures in place.

The number of U.S. police departments that dealt with cases of minor domestic assault by arresting one of the parties quadrupled from 1984 to 1986. This change in practice was influenced by an experiment conducted in Minneapolis, Minn., from 1981 to 1982 by the Washington, D.C.-based Police Foundation. The findings showed that arrest was more effective than mediation or inaction in reducing the likelihood of repeated domestic violence over a six-month follow-up period. Since a significant proportion of all homicides arose from domestic disputes, these research results pointed clearly to the need for more assertive police action in dealing with family squabbles.

In Sweden public dissatisfaction with the police investigation into the assassination of Prime Minister Olof Palme, in February 1986, led the government to appoint a parliamentary commission of inquiry to determine what went wrong. Stockholm Police Commissioner Hans Holmer was relieved of his duties as head of the investigation, which seemed no closer to discovering the identity of the individual or group responsible for Palme's death. A confusing array of suspects and motives were still being considered, including a theory that Palme was killed because of his efforts to stop the illegal sale of Swedish weapons to Iran.

The influence of Mikhail Gorbachev's new *glasnost* (openness) policies in the Soviet Union was apparent in the publication in February of graphic accounts of police brutality in the autonomous republic of Karelia. The area's

interior minister was fired, and two policemen received lengthy jail sentences. Soviet authorities published detailed crime statistics for the first time in October. They revealed that in the first six months of the year 4,682 people were convicted of premeditated murder and more than 50,000 of all types of hooliganism. The authorities voiced concern about a rise in drug-related offenses, especially among the young.

A new method of tracing sex killers and rapists by identifying their genetic "fingerprints" began to be used by police forces in a number of countries. The technique involved the analysis of blood, semen, and other bodily fluids left on victims. Even a small amount of fluid contained a DNA signature, the unique genetic code that individuals inherit from their parents. The chance of two individuals' having the same DNA was said to be about one in 560 million.

(DUNCAN CHAPPELL)

**Prisons and Penology.** Punitivism remained dominant in the penological thinking and practice of most countries in 1987, but doubts and controversies persisted. The U.S. Supreme Court pleased conservatives by ruling in April that some accomplices to murder, as well as actual killers, might be sentenced to death and, in May, that federal courts may jail and deny bail before trial to criminal defendants who constituted a danger to the community. In June, however, the court rejected as unconstitutional state laws that made the death penalty mandatory for murder committed by prisoners serving life sentences without the possibility of parole.

A series of cases echoed that of Bernhard H. Goetz, who shot four black youths on a Manhattan subway in 1984, allegedly because he feared they would rob him. Prentice Rashid was also regarded as a hero after his homemade electrical trap killed a burglar in Miami, Fla., and he was freed by a grand jury. Public opinion was outraged when Daniel Canelairo was allowed to begin, from prison, a $2 million suit against the California Savings and Loan Bank for burns suffered when stealing booby-trapped money. The trial and acquittal of Goetz on charges of attempted murder and assault provoked mixed feelings, raising questions about the guilt of the youths he shot and the violence of his response. In the U.K. public reaction was mixed when Eric Butler was given a suspended prison sentence for defending himself with a sword stick against two youths who attacked him in London's underground (subway).

In the U.K. hard-liners, including some prominent

AFP PHOTO

The *Bibby Venture*, a barge once used in the Falkland Islands war, was to be converted into a prison ship to be used by New York City authorities.

judges, policemen, and Cabinet members, favoured restoration of the death penalty, castration of sex offenders, and longer prison sentences for many crimes. Equally hotly debated were proposals for radical changes in criminal law and procedure, such as abolishing the accused's "right to silence" under police questioning, informing trial magistrates and juries of previous convictions, and giving the prosecution a full right of appeal against overlenient sentences so the appellate court could increase the actual sentence, not merely state that it should have been longer. Liberal opinion in the U.K. drew attention to growing doubts about the rightness of the convictions in the 1974 Guildford and Birmingham bombing cases and those of the alleged murderers of Keith Blakelock, a policeman killed in a 1985 London riot. These cases involved what had been capital murders before abolition in 1965, raising anxieties about the problem of wrongful convictions in general and the irrevocability of the death penalty in particular. JUSTICE, the British section of the International Commission of Jurists, long concerned about wrongful convictions, proposed the establishment of a public defender as a reform likely to reduce the number of miscarriages of justice.

*Capital Punishment.* By August 1987, some ten years after the resumption of capital punishment in the U.S., 85 men and one woman had been executed, mainly in Southern states, and some 1,900 people were on death row. Opinion polls continued to show about 75% support for capital punishment. Cases that aroused world attention were those of Warren McCleskey, at whose trial it was demonstrated that blacks who kill whites are disproportionately given the death penalty, and of Paula Cooper, sentenced to die for a murder committed when she was only 15. The U.S. was the only major Western country still using the death penalty.

Parliaments in the U.K. in April and in Canada in June decisively rejected the restoration of capital punishment. Reports from China suggested a diminution in the number of executions there, but some Islamic countries continued rigid enforcement of the severe Shari'ah criminal code; in December 1986 three Iranians were stoned to death in Hamadan for adultery (a fourth escaped). Death sentences reported from the U.S.S.R. mainly involved "white-collar criminals," although a 25-year-old student was executed in Georgia in March for a murder committed while stealing a pair of jeans.

*Prisons.* Most countries continued to experience overcrowding in prisons, often to a point where security was threatened, and in the U.K., France, Italy, and some U.S. jurisdictions, prisoners were discharged early in an effort to alleviate the problem. The weaker control of inmates in overcrowded conditions produced problems that included unchecked drug abuse, the spread of AIDS (acquired immune deficiency syndrome), and increased violence. Rioting in Belgian prisons was the unexpected result of the extradition there from the U.K. of 25 Liverpool football fans charged with involuntary manslaughter in connection with the Heysel stadium soccer riots of 1985; the special treatment they were given for diplomatic reasons drew Belgian prisoners' attention to their own squalor. Cuban inmates in U.S. federal prisons in Atlanta, Ga., and Oakdale, La., rioted in November–December upon hearing of a U.S.-Cuban agreement that might result in their deportation to Cuba. In Yugoslavia and Mexico, prison governors were found to have taken bribes to set prisoners free. In New York and at Harwich, England, surplus prisoners were housed in ships at anchor—recalling the Thames-side "hulks" of Charles Dickens's time.

There were few reports of prison experiments in "reha-bilitation," which had been the staple of recent penological discussion and literature. In the U.S.S.R., *glasnost* (openness) now allowed the official journal *Sovetskaya Rossiya* to condemn the penal system for juveniles as "humiliating" and "tyrannical." Liberal penal reformers urged greater use of noncustodial sentences and of "open" prisons, which were less labour intensive and cheaper to run. There was continued interest in the privatization of prisons.

What was probably the costliest prison term ever served ended in August 1987 with the death at the age of 93 of Rudolf Hess (*see* OBITUARIES), imprisoned for 46 years at Spandau, West Berlin, and the prison's sole occupant after 1966. He was guarded and tended by a staff of more than 600 at a cost to West German taxpayers of more than DM 2.6 million a year. Demolition of the prison began shortly after his death.                    (C. R. M. DAVIES)

*See also* Law.

This article updates the *Macropædia* articles CRIME AND PUNISHMENT; POLICE.

# Dance

**North America.** The prevailing anxieties of 1987 were summed up in the news that Mark Morris—the most inventive and musically disciplined U.S. choreographer to come to international attention in the '80s—had accepted the offer of full-time residency at the Théâtre Royal de la Monnaie in Brussels, Maurice Béjart's former theatre. (See *Europe,* below.) Morris promised annual New York City seasons, but his artistic growth would take place abroad. He had a fertile year: opera ballets, an American Ballet Theatre (ABT) commission, and a richly structured Baroque program for his company at the Brooklyn Academy of Music (BAM).

There were some bright signs. At cofounder Lincoln Kirstein's 80th birthday gala, the New York City Ballet (NYCB) announced plans for a lavish new production of *Sleeping Beauty,* already designed by David Mitchell. Darci Kistler, one likely Aurora, was recovering steadily from a debilitating foot injury. At New York City's Metropolitan Opera House in the spring, ABT pulled in a record $6.2 million in gross ticket sales, with its new production of *Beauty* (staged by Kenneth MacMillan) an important attraction. The dancers of the Dallas (Texas) Ballet, facing economic disaster, performed in the streets to raise a rescuing $535,000. Elsewhere in Texas, Houston's new Wortham Theater Center for opera and ballet was the first such hall to be built since the Kennedy Center, Washington, D.C., in 1971. Legislative appropriations to state arts agencies rose 10.7% in fiscal 1987.

Many companies managed or even thrived. The Minnesota Dance Theatre, threatened with folding, was absorbed by the Pacific Northwest Ballet (now the Northwest Ballet) of Seattle, Wash., and the Milwaukee (Wis.) Ballet became attached to the Pennsylvania Ballet. (There were a score of such two-city arrangements in the U.S.) The newly founded American Indian Dance Theatre, a troupe of 26 Native American dancers and musicians, made its first European tour. Small groups like Ballet Oklahoma found a secure financial footing; large ones like Dance Theatre of Harlem (DTH) were recognized for their management. (DTH's founder-director, Arthur Mitchell, received the prestigious Arnold Gingrich Memorial Award of the Arts and Business Council.)

Still, there were ominous clouds on the dance horizon. The costliness of space was one problem. In New York the Danse Coalition—which publicized the plight of dancers without studios—estimated that during 1985–86 some 55 studio spaces had been eliminated on Manhattan's Upper West Side. A plan for the city to lend performing arts groups money to acquire and renovate rehearsal space was proposed by the comptroller but had yet to be implemented.

However, this loan program—based on a $100,000 contribution from a member of Japan's Shuwa Corp.—led to another grim notion for U.S. dancers: that, with the change in world money patterns, the Zeitgeist of art was lurching to other shores. Much of the sizzle in 1987 was imported. At BAM's Next Wave program, only 4 of the 14 offerings were dance, and only 2 were American dance (Karole Armitage, Nina Wiener). At the Purchase, N.Y., PepsiCo Summerfare, the stir was created by the Frankfurt (West Germany) Ballet dancing work of American expatriate William Forsythe (Forsythe's New Sleep for the San Francisco Ballet was also heralded there). French dancers had been taken to U.S. hearts: the Paris Opéra Ballet (in Rudolf Nureyev's Cinderella) on a large scale and, on the loft level, various ensembles and duets. French dancers also had been hired actively at soloist level in U.S. ballet companies. For many dance-goers untutored by Balanchine, the glamour, thanks to glasnost, came from the U.S.S.R.: the Bolshoi Ballet, members of the Kirov Ballet, the Moscow Ballet (whose Andrey Ustinov defected to the U.S. while on tour), students from the bravura-minded Perm State Ballet School, and, on her own, Maya Plisetskaya, who taught classes at New York's David Howard studio and performed a Ruth St. Denis solo at a Martha Graham gala. Bella Lewitzky's Dance Gallery in Los Angeles announced the formation of an International Presenting Network to facilitate exchanges worldwide. Even so, new, tightened visa regulations by the U.S. immigration service caused many headaches for lesser-known artists and their U.S. producers.

The formula for survival had become collaboration of many kinds; Mikhail Baryshnikov and Nureyev performed together at the Graham gala in Appalachian Spring. At the Armitage and Twyla Tharp companies, ballet, modern, and jazz styles were virtually annealed. Postmodernist David Gordon choreographed Murder for ABT; then Baryshnikov performed with Gordon's Pick-Up Company on a video program. Charles Moulton, whose dancers performed in sneakers, made his first pointe ballet for the North Carolina Dance Theater. Paul Taylor's Sunset was taken into the repertoires of ABT and San Francisco, while his two dances for his own company (Kith and Kin, Syzygy) borrowed elements of classic virtuosity. Among the more outstanding or unusual production matchups: Trisha Brown with artist Donald Judd, Lucinda Childs with artist Tadashi Kawamata and composer Harry de Witt, Jennifer Muller with Keith Haring and Yoko Ono, Wendy Perron with émigré refuseniks Komar and Melamid, Rod Rodgers with protest painter Leon Golub, Yoshiko Chuma with artist Yvonne Jacquette, Ross Winter of Mid America Dance Company with fiction writer Stanley Elkin, and Toni Pimble of the Eugene (Ore.) Ballet with Native American storytellers. Most spectacular was the gala with 13 major New York dance companies, "Dancing for Life," in support of AIDS (acquired immune deficiency syndrome) research.

It was also a year of collaboration with history. The Joffrey Ballet staged a new full-length Nutcracker and presented the Hodson-Archer reconstruction of Nijinsky's Rite of Spring. Tulsa (Okla.) Ballet Theatre reconstructed Balanchine's 1942 Mozart Violin Concerto, never before seen in its entirety in North America. Edward Villella coached Balanchine's Prodigal Son for the Miami (Fla.) City Ballet, and Miami's Dance Umbrella mounted a 20th-century

modernism symposium around it. The Alvin Ailey company produced a retrospective of Katherine Dunham. The Boston Ballet staged the Royal Danish Ballet's traditional Coppélia and mounted a Tales of Hans Christian Andersen by Bruces Wells and Marks. New York Theatre Ballet revived James Waring's Phantom of the Opera. Meredith Monk and Ping Chong revived The Travelogue Series. The Louisville (Ky.) Ballet staged a full-length Sleeping Beauty by Alun Jones. There were old themes, too, at evening length: The Tragedy of Romeo and Juliet at Northwest Ballet (Kent Stowell/Tchaikovsky), The Great Gatsby at Pittsburgh (Pa.) Ballet Theatre (André Prokovsky/Gershwin et al.), the old Russia of Winter Dreams at Pennsylvania Ballet (Robert Weiss/Tchaikovsky). The Herbert Ross feature film Dancers preserved portions of Baryshnikov's and Alessandra Ferri's performances in ABT's Giselle.

Awards went to Fred Astaire, Bob Fosse, Nureyev, Jac Venza (Capezio), Alvin Ailey (Scripps), Merrill Ashley, David White, Trisha Brown, Liz Thompson, Doris Hering (Dance Magazine), John Kelly, Ralph Lemon, Susan Marshall, Patricia Olalde, Stephen Petronio (the first American Choreographer Awards from the National Corporate Fund for Dance). Alwin Nikolais won both the Kennedy Center Honors and the National Medal of Arts. Merce Cunningham received the $50,000 Meadows Award for Excellence in the Arts from Southern Methodist University, Dallas, Texas.

The dance world mourned the deaths of choreographers and dancers Fred Astaire, Michael Bennett, Patrick Bissell, Ray Bolger, Bob Fosse, Nora Kaye, Antony Tudor, Choo San Gho (see OBITUARIES), Raymond Johnson, Maria Swoboda, choreographer and filmmaker Mura Dehn, and critics B. H. Haggin and Barry Laine in 1987 and of choreographers and dancers Dorothy Alexander (founder of Atlanta Ballet), Sanson Candelaria, Peter Fonseca, and Truda Kaschmann in late 1986. New York's 12-year-old

AFP PHOTO

Irek Mukhamedov of the Bolshoi Ballet leaps high during a rehearsal on the stage of the Metropolitan Opera in New York City. The Soviet ballet troupe toured the United States for the first time in eight years.

Christina Johnson and Donald Williams of the Dance Theater of Harlem perform George Balanchine's *Bugaku* at New York's City College. The style of the dance company blended classical foundation and modern adaptation.

MARTHA SWOPE

Riverside Dance Festival, an important showcase for unknowns from the U.S. and abroad, closed its doors.

In Montreal the Festival International de Nouvelle Danse presented, in 12 days, 15 companies from France, Japan, West Germany, the U.S., and Canada. The imagistic French and acrobatic Canadians made powerful impressions on U.S. reporters. Glen Tetley joined the National Ballet of Canada as an artistic associate. Gweneth Lloyd and Arnold Spohr of the Royal Winnipeg Ballet were joint recipients of the $100,000 Royal Bank Award for Canadian Achievement. For the tenth anniversary gala of the National Tap Dance Company of Canada, the stylist Paul Draper choreographed *A Work for Tap Dancers* to a score that included three e. e. cummings poems.

(MINDY ALOFF)

**Europe.** French-born Maurice Béjart, 60, became the first person to transport an entire dance company permanently from one country to another when he moved his Ballet of the Twentieth Century from Brussels—his base for 28 years—to Lausanne, Switz. Forty of the 50 dancers went with their charismatic director and began work in September under the new title of Béjart Ballet Lausanne. Cause of the move was a reduction in public funding from a new administration at the Théâtre Royal de la Monnaie, the Brussels opera house that controlled the dance company's budget. The company's huge popularity meant that for some time most productions had been presented in the larger auditoriums of the Forêt National or the Cirque Royal, and in the Palais des Sports at Paris. Though Lausanne had nothing on this scale, it provided a base at the Théâtre de Beaulieu from which sorties could be made, as well as favourable conditions, funding, and work permits for all the non-Swiss dancers.

Lausanne's bid was through Philippe and Elvire Braunschweig, instigators of the annual Prix de Lausanne, which since 1973 had financed outstanding young dancers for an extra year's training at a leading dance school. From early 1988 this prestigious competition was to be extended by the addition of a competition for choreographers under 35, both classical and modern dance; the Philip Morris Prize was named for the multinational sponsoring company. Finalists would have the Béjart dancers for the creation of their works, and the winner would be taken into the regular company repertory. Béjart's arrival gave a major boost to dance in Switzerland, hitherto centred on the three classical companies at Basel (directed by Heinz Spoerli), Geneva (Oscar Araiz), and Zürich (Uwe Scholz). The last-named reported over 400 applications during the season for any available dancer-vacancy. Modern dance in Switzerland—furnished by numerous small independent groups, as was now customary in most Western European countries—also experienced an upsurge of public interest.

Following Béjart's departure, Belgium was left with two royal-chartered companies of modest reputation, the Ballet Royal de Wallonie at Charleroi and the Ballet of Flanders at Antwerp. The latter remained in some disarray following the enforced departure of its Soviet expatriate director, Valery Panov, but nevertheless undertook a tour of China under his successor, Robert Denvers, an ex-Béjart dancer. Across the border in The Netherlands, the installation of the Dutch National Ballet in the New Music Theatre at Amsterdam (on a sharing basis with Netherlands Opera)

JACK MANNING—THE NEW YORK TIMES

Pierre Advokatoff (left) and Pascale Michelet of the Lyon Opéra Ballet perform William Forsythe's innovative *Steptext* at the City Center in New York.

Mikhail Baryshnikov (left), Maxine Sherman, and Rudolf Nureyev perform Martha Graham's *Appalachian Spring* at New York's City Center.
AP/WIDE WORLD

was followed by the opening of the Spui Dance Theatre at The Hague as a purpose-built dance house. It had facilities for visiting companies, but its primary purpose was to serve as the permanent home of the contemporary-style Netherlands Dance Theatre, whose artistic director, Jiri Kylian, staged his *Perspectives* as the opening production there on September 9.

Patterns of international touring continued unabated, including a month-long Royal Ballet tour of Moscow and Leningrad—the first in the U.S.S.R. by a British ballet company since 1961 (when the company's current director, Anthony Dowell, was a first-year member of the corps de ballet). During the Moscow visit the Bolshoi Theatre was closed "for urgent repair," and performances were given instead at the Operetta Theatre, bringing complaints of inadequate stage conditions and poor musical support by the orchestra provided. This tour came soon after another month-long Royal Ballet tour to South Korea and Japan, while the sister company from London, Sadler's Wells Royal Ballet, was simultaneously making a six-week visit to Czechoslovakia, Poland, East Germany, and Bulgaria. Both companies reported varying degrees of success in what were seen as important steps in the furtherance of East–West cultural relations.

Another British company touring the Far East was the London Contemporary Dance Theatre, directed by Robert Cohan, who took a modern-dance repertory to Malaysia, Singapore, Indonesia, and Hong Kong. On returning to London, the company prepared a home tour with *Phantasmagoria*, Cohan's first full-length production in some years, with music by Barrington Pheloung, aimed successfully at younger audiences. Twenty-one years after changing character and style from classical ballet to modern dance, Britain's Ballet Rambert finally acknowledged the fact with a formal change of title to Rambert Dance Company. In the spirit of founder Dame Marie Rambert, new talents in choreography, music, and design were pioneered in a program titled *Collaboration V,* but the company's major success was a return to Stravinsky's *Pulcinella* in new choreography by artistic director Richard Alston.

Christopher Bruce relinquished his Rambert association after 24 years, first as dancer and later as associate director and choreographer. In The Netherlands a similarly close though shorter association was severed by Hans van Manen's departure from the National Ballet. He took his leave with his new *Symphonies of the Netherlands* (music by Louis Andriessen).

Directorial changes included Robert de Warren's move from Britain's Northern Ballet Theatre to succeed Patricia Neary at La Scala, Milan; his successor at Manchester was Christopher Gable. Scottish Ballet's Peter Darrell (*see* OBITUARIES), who had intended to relinquish his director's post and remain only as choreographer, died before a replacement was found. Yugoslav Zarko Prebil was appointed to the vacancy at the San Carlo Theatre, Naples.

Nureyev's contract as artistic director of the Paris Opéra Ballet, due to expire in 1988, was extended for what was thought to be another three-year period; this would cover the planned changeover of the theatre entirely to dance following the opera company's move to the new Bastille Opera House in late 1989. Another extension was that of Natalia Makarova's performing career beyond previously announced retirement; her widespread guest appearances during 1987 included the ballerina role in London Festival Ballet's revival of Sir Frederick Ashton's *Apparitions* (1936).

Subjects for new dance works continued to range widely, from literary adaptations (Mary Shelley's *Frankenstein*, Lewis Carroll's *Alice in Wonderland*) through calls to social conscience (Rudi van Dantzig's *Sans armes, Citoyens!* at Paris, music by Hector Berlioz) to movement for its own sake (almost every "postmodern" choreographer), often turning into self-indulgence. The boundaries were difficult to define in the many instances when qualities of theatrical communication were explicitly avoided.

Among a plethora of transatlantic visitors to Europe were both the National Ballet of Canada (Toronto) and Les Grands Ballets Canadiens (Montreal). U.S. modern dance was represented by the Martha Graham Company in France, Italy, and Scandinavia and the Merce Cunningham Dancers in London and elsewhere. They became the first dance company to appear as part of the summer series of Henry Wood Promenade Concerts in London, which in 1987 featured dance as the central theme in 53 of 66 programs. Selma Jeanne Cohen moved from New York to Essen, West Germany, to direct an international conference on dance research scholarship under the title "Beyond Performance." It was sponsored by the International Theatre Institute to assist exchange of information and ideas in a field of study that was rapidly acquiring wider significance. (NOËL GOODWIN)

*See* also Music; Theatre.
This article updates the *Macropædia* article The History of Western DANCE.

# Disasters

*The loss of life and property from disasters in 1987 included the following:*

## Aviation

*January 2,* Off the coast of Río Muni, Equatorial Guinea. A Spanish Air Force transport plane crashed into the sea shortly after takeoff; all 18 persons aboard were killed.

*January 3,* Near Abidjan, Côte d'Ivoire. A Brazilian jetliner crashed on its back in a thick tropical jungle moments after the pilot reported that an engine was on fire and that he would dump fuel before attempting an emergency landing; 49 of the 51 persons aboard died on impact when the plane exploded, and one of the two badly burned survivors later succumbed.

*January 13,* Asmera, Eth. An Ethiopian Air Force plane, which developed mechanical problems minutes after takeoff, crashed while attempting to make an emergency landing; all 54 persons aboard died.

*January 15,* Near Salt Lake City, Utah. A midair collision that occurred when a single-engine private plane apparently intruded into the restricted airspace of a twin-engine commuter airliner killed all ten persons aboard the two aircraft.

*April 4,* Medan, Sumatra, Indon. A passenger plane crashed and exploded after striking high-voltage electric wires while attempting to land; 26 of the 45 persons aboard the craft were killed.

*May 5,* Southern Sudan. A small commercial plane carrying 13 persons crashed after apparently being shot down by rebels; all persons aboard perished.

*May 9,* Near Dabrowka, Poland. A Polish jet en route to New York City crashed and exploded in a small forest less than an hour after takeoff despite the pilot's efforts to return to Warsaw after experiencing engine problems; all 183 persons aboard perished in the fire.

*May 28,* Lake Petén Itzá, Guatemala. A Guatemalan Air Force transport plane lost altitude and crashed shortly after takeoff from Santa Elena in Petén department; all 12 persons aboard were killed.

*June 21,* Eastern Burma. A Burma Airways plane crashed into the Menei Mountain some 64 km (40 mi) from Heho in the state of Shan; all 45 persons aboard the craft were found dead.

*June 22,* Fort Hood, Texas. A military helicopter on a routine training flight crashed in rugged terrain; ten persons lost their lives in the crash.

*June 26,* Northern Luzon, Phil. A Philippine Airlines plane slammed into a fog-shrouded mountain and burst into flames just a few miles short of its destination; all 50 persons aboard perished.

*July 4,* Near Flathead Lake, Mont. A twin-engine plane carrying all six members of The Montana Band and four other persons crashed and burned shortly after takeoff; there were no survivors.

*July 30,* Mexico City. A Boeing 377 airplane carrying 18 jumping horses, 7 members of the Mexican junior equestrian team, and 3 crew members skimmed rooftops after failing to gain altitude after takeoff and slammed into a busy eight-lane highway and a crowded restaurant; 54 persons were killed, most of them on the ground, and an additional 30 persons were injured.

*August 16,* Detroit. A Northwest Airlines MD-80 jetliner carrying 154 persons crashed and exploded on takeoff; there was one survivor, a four-year-old girl, and 3 persons were killed on the ground.

*August 31,* Off the coast of Phuket Island, Thailand. A Thai Airways jetliner carrying 83 persons plunged into the Andaman Sea, apparently after trying to avoid hitting a Boeing 737 aircraft that was also descending; all aboard were lost.

*October 11,* Near Pagan, Burma. A Burma Airways twin-engine turboprop plane caught fire in midair and crashed some 32 km (20 mi) south of its destination, Pagan; all 49 persons aboard the aircraft perished.

*October 15,* Near Barni, Italy. An Italian airliner flying from Milan to Cologne, West Germany, slammed into the northern foothills of the Italian Alps during driving rain and heavy fog; all 37 persons aboard the plane were found dead at the crash site on Mount Crezzo.

*October 20,* Indianapolis, Ind. An air force jet plowed into the lobby of a Ramada Inn hotel after the pilot reportedly lost power, tried to make an emergency landing at the airport, and finally ejected from the plane after he lost all engine power; the hotel was engulfed in flames, and nine persons in the lobby died.

*November 15,* Denver, Colo. A Continental DC-9 jetliner, attempting to take off during a severe snowstorm, clipped the runway with its left wing, flipped onto its back, and broke into three pieces; of the 76 passengers and 5 crew members aboard the aircraft, 28 persons lost their lives, including the pilot and copilot, and more than 50 others were injured.

*November 23,* Homer, Alaska. A twin-engine Beechcraft 1900 commuter plane carrying 21 persons was attempting to land when it crashed and plowed through a fence just short of the airport runway; 17 persons lost their lives in the crash.

*November 28,* Indian Ocean. A South African Airways Boeing 747 jetliner carrying 160 persons fell into the ocean some 201 km (125 mi) southeast of Mauritius after the pilot reportedly radioed that smoke was entering the cockpit; all aboard were lost.

*November 29,* Thailand-Burma border. A Korean Air Boeing 707 jetliner carrying 115 persons presumably exploded in midair after a time bomb destroyed the airliner and killed all aboard.

*December 3,* Near Kishwati, Rwanda. A propeller-driven Cessna 404 carrying 12 Americans on a safari to photograph gorillas slammed into the mountains in northwestern Rwanda; all aboard were killed, including the Kenyan pilot.

*December 7,* Near Paso Robles, Calif. A Pacific Southwest Airlines commuter jet carrying 43 persons crashed, apparently after a disgruntled former employee of USAir, the parent company of Pacific Southwest, somehow boarded the plane with a gun, intending to shoot his ex-boss, a passenger on the flight; after firing shots in the passenger compartment, he apparently entered the cockpit and killed the pilot and copilot. The plane then plunged into a hill on a cattle ranch. There were no survivors.

*December 8,* Off the coast of Lima, Peru. An F-27 navy plane carrying Peru's top professional soccer team, including its coach, 16 players, 8 cheerleaders, 12 team employees, and 6 crew members, plunged into the Pacific Ocean after experiencing problems with its landing gear; the pilot was the sole survivor.

*December 21,* Bordeaux, France. A 30-seat French commuter airliner crashed in a wooded area during foggy weather as it approached Mérignac Airport to make a landing; all 16 persons aboard were killed.

*December 21,* Off the coast of Morgan City, La. A helicopter carrying offshore oil workers to an oil rig apparently hit one of the legs on the rig and crashed onto the deck of the oil platform; only one of the 13 workers aboard the chopper survived, and both pilots perished.

## Fires and Explosions

*January 14,* Barranquilla, Colombia. A bus exploded apparently after leftist guerrillas planted a bomb aboard the vehicle; 13 persons were burned to death, and 7 others were injured.

*February 1,* Kaohsiung, Taiwan. A fire gutted a four-story hotel packed with revelers celebrating the Chinese lunar New Year holiday; 17 guests succumbed in the fire, and another person was killed after he jumped from the roof.

*May,* Heilongjiang (Heilungkiang) Province, China. A huge forest fire that raged out of control for nearly two weeks destroyed more than one million hectares (2,470,000 ac) of forest, killed 191 persons, and injured 220 others.

*Late July,* Northern Syria. An explosion on board a train traveling from Aleppo to al-Jazirah ripped through three cars of the train and claimed more than 50 lives.

*September 26,* Surabaya, Indon. An explosion aboard a crowded bus, believed to have been caused by a cooking stove, claimed the lives of 41 passengers and injured 11 others.

*September 30,* Milwaukee, Wis. A fire in a 93-year-old wood-and-cinder-block house claimed the lives of ten children and two adults.

*October 16,* Jakarta, Indon. A fire engulfed a two-story T-shirt factory and trapped workers on the second floor; 21 persons were killed.

*November 18,* London. A fire that started at

SIPA

Two investigators examine the wreckage of a McDonnell Douglas MD-80 jetliner that crashed and exploded while it was taking off from Detroit. Of the 154 passengers and airline personnel aboard the plane, only one person, a four-year-old girl, survived the crash.

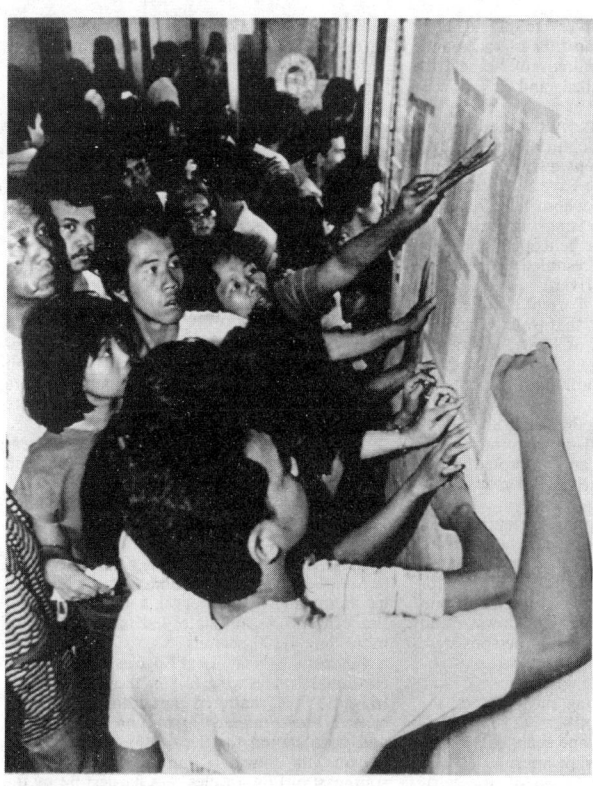

Anxious people search for names of friends and relatives on the passenger manifest of the *Dona Paz*, a Philippine ferry that collided with an oil tanker, the *Victor*, on December 20.

AP/WIDE WORLD

the foot of a 50-year-old wooden escalator in the subway at King's Cross Station resulted in disaster for commuters who boarded the moving stairs and were delivered into the heart of a blazing inferno; 31 persons were killed and 80 persons were injured, 12 of them seriously, as they raced for the smoke-enshrouded exits.

*November 29,* Margarita, Venezuela. A hotel fire claimed the lives of 11 persons attending a wedding reception.

*December 18,* Jiangxi (Kiangsi) Province, China. An explosion at a fireworks factory in Huaizhong (Huai-chung) township claimed the lives of 18 persons.

## Marine

*January 16,* Near Abugan Island, Philippines. A 50-ton boat carrying passengers to a Roman Catholic festival in Cebu, Phil., sank; at least 50 persons were known dead.

*February 5,* Off the coast of Cabo San Quintín, Mexico. A 16-m (53-ft) fishing boat capsized after a 6-m (20-ft) wave swamped the vessel; ten persons were killed.

*February 14,* Off the coast of the Kuril Islands. A South Korean containership with a crew of at least 21 sank in rough seas; there appeared to be no survivors.

*February 19,* Off the coast of the Solomon Islands. An interisland ferry capsized with 49 persons aboard; only 2 persons were rescued.

*February 25,* North Atlantic. A Philippine cargo vessel with 19 crewmen aboard capsized during a storm; one crewman was rescued.

*March 6,* Off the coast of Zeebrugge, Belgium. The car ferry *Herald of Free Enterprise* capsized after an "inrush of water through the open bow doors of the vehicle deck," and many of the 543 passengers aboard were hurled with their vehicles into the icy North Sea water; 188 persons, many of them trapped in the hull, were killed in the worst peacetime ship disaster in the history of English Channel shipping.

*March 15,* Near Guangzhou (Canton), China. A ferry buffeted by heavy rains and strong winds overturned; 22 persons were killed.

*April 11,* Gulf of Thailand. A passenger ferry capsized and sank during a sudden rain and wind squall; 16 persons were known dead, and at least 34 others were missing.

*May 8,* Near Nantong (Nan-t'ung), Jiangsu (Kiangsu) Province, China. A ferryboat carrying 98 passengers and 4 crewmen collided with a tugboat and overturned; 95 persons were feared drowned.

*May 17,* Persian Gulf. The U.S. frigate *Stark* was disabled after an Iraqi missile exploded on the port side of the ship near the bridge; 37 U.S. sailors lost their lives in the attack, which Iraq claimed was an accident.

*May 17,* Off the coast of Burma. A ferry carrying 347 passengers sank in the Andaman Sea; 21 persons were known dead, and 40 others were missing and presumed dead.

*July 5,* Between Zaire and Zambia. A river barge smuggling beer, livestock, and fruit on the Luapula River slammed into a sandbar when the helmsman apparently fell asleep; nearly 390 of the approximately 470 persons aboard were feared drowned although later reports indicated that only 50 had died.

*July 11,* Central Philippines. A 27-ton ferryboat sank in rough seas while traveling from Dumaguete on Negros Island to Larena on Siquijor Island; 8 persons were known dead, and 64 others were missing and feared drowned.

*September 23,* Tongi, Bangladesh. An overloaded ferry sank in the Torag River; seven children and three women drowned.

*October 6,* Near Nagua, Dominican Republic. A wooden fishing boat carrying some 150 people seeking illegal entry to Puerto Rico sank in shark-infested waters after its two outboard motors apparently exploded; as many as 100 passengers were feared drowned or consumed by sharks.

*October 15,* Near Narayanganj, Bangladesh. A double-decker ferry carrying at least twice its normal capacity sank in the Sitalakhya River; of the 200 passengers aboard the vessel, up to 35 were drowned.

*October 26,* Northern Bangladesh. A double-decker ferry jammed with 450 passengers sank in the Ganges River after slamming into a silt island; some 110 persons were feared dead.

*November 28,* Off the coast of Bangladesh. An overcrowded river ferry capsized, and nearly 100 persons were missing and feared drowned.

*December 5,* Off the coast of Cape Finisterre, Spain. A 9,191-ton Panamanian-registered freighter carrying 31 Chinese and Hong Kong seamen from Rotterdam, Neth., to China exploded and emitted poisonous carbon monoxide gas; 23 crew members died.

*December 11,* Hooghly River, India. A ferryboat foundered in strong midstream currents and capsized; 50 persons were feared drowned.

*December 16,* Off the coast of Samar Island, Philippines. A ferryboat capsized and sank after being buffetted by Typhoon Phyllis; 14 of the ship's 50 occupants were missing.

*December 20,* Off the coast of Mindoro, Phil. A ferry believed packed with as many as 3,000 passengers and crewmen collided with an oil tanker with a crew of 13; both vessels exploded and sank, and only 26 badly burned persons survived in one of the century's worst maritime disasters.

*December 27,* Karachi, Pak. A boat carrying 24 picknickers capsized on a lake; 17 persons were known dead, and 4 others were missing.

## Mining

*February 4,* Myslowice, Poland. A methane-gas explosion in a coal mine killed 17 miners and injured 22 others.

*March 26,* Southern Ecuador. A cave-in at the remote Nambija gold mine buried 50 miners; officials believed at least 30 miners perished.

*April 9,* Ermelo, Transvaal, South Africa. An underground explosion in a coal mine claimed the lives of 34 miners; 16 others were hospitalized after the blast.

*August 31,* Welkom, South Africa. An elevator plunged to the bottom of a 1,402-m (4,600-ft) gold mine shaft, apparently after an explosion of unknown origin occurred; 62 miners lost their lives.

## Miscellaneous

*January 15,* Bangladesh. Marauding Bengal tigers became ferocious after being wounded by poachers; the animals killed at least 70 persons.

*Late January,* Madras, India. Toxic illegally distilled liquor killed 30 persons and blinded at least 40 others.

*February 4,* Sri Lanka. Moonshine liquor laced with methyl alcohol killed 20 persons and poisoned more than 170 others.

*March 19,* San Cristóbal, Venezuela. Non-alcoholic punch, presumably poisoned with parathion (an insecticide) by a deranged resident of a home for the elderly, killed 15 persons and hospitalized 119 others in critical condition.

*April 5,* Near Amsterdam, N.Y. At least a 100-m (330-ft) section of a 164-m (540-ft) steel-plate girder bridge covered with steel-reinforced concrete collapsed without warning, killing ten persons when at least two cars and a truck plummeted 18 m (60 ft) into the swiftly moving Schoharie Creek.

*April 8,* Shingak, Pak. An errant shell from a mortar test-firing killed 13 Pakistani tribesmen who were watching the testing near the Afghan border; 26 other tribesmen were injured.

*April 23,* Bridgeport, Conn. A partially finished high-rise apartment building collapsed; 28 construction workers lost their lives.

*May,* Guangxi Zhuang (Kwangsi Chuang) Autonomous Region, China. Wine tainted with methanol poisoned more than 600 persons and killed 33 others.

*July 2,* Sierra Blanca, Texas. The heat in a stifling 49° C (120° F) boxcar carrying 19 illegal Mexican aliens smothered 18 of them.

*July 20–28,* Greece. A brutal eight-day heat wave claimed the lives of more than 700 persons, most of them elderly, who succumbed when temperatures rose above 42° C (107° F).

*December 16,* Marrakech, Morocco. A five-story building under construction collapsed, burying at least 20 persons and injuring 8 others.

*December 16,* Qinghai (Tsinghai) Province, China. Poisonous carbon monoxide exhaust fumes killed ten bus passengers whose symptoms of dizziness and headaches had been mistaken for those of altitude sickness.

*December 30,* Bombay, India. A five-story building collapsed and killed at least 16 residents.

## Natural

*January,* Europe. The continent, subjected to wind-whipped masses of bone-chilling Siberian air and heavy snowfalls, experienced one of its worst winters in nearly a quarter of a century; the record cold disrupted transportation, closed schools, businesses, and government offices, and claimed the lives of more than 265 persons, 81 of them in the Soviet Union, where temperatures plunged below −35° C (−30° F).

*January 22,* East Coast, U.S. A deadly blast of arctic air accompanied by a blizzard struck the East Coast from Maine to Florida and claimed at least 37 lives; North Carolina was hit by 51 cm (20 in) of snow, government offices in Washington, D.C., were closed down, and traffic was crippled in the East and South.

*Late January,* São Paulo, Brazil. A week-long rainfall of 25 cm (10 in) inundated the city and claimed at least 75 lives.

*Early February,* Peru. Torrential rains caused rivers to burst their banks and wash away part of the town of Villa Rica in the foothills of the Andes Mountains; severe flooding and mud slides led to the deaths of more than 100 persons.

*Early February,* Georgian S.S.R. Torrential rains and melting snows precipitated severe flooding that swept away homes and affected some 7,000 persons; 30 persons were known dead and 6 others were missing.

*February 7,* Vanuatu. Deadly Cyclone Uma struck the South Pacific island nation and killed at least 45 islanders.

*February 16,* North Carolina. An ice storm, which caused hundreds of traffic accidents, led to the deaths of at least 17 persons.

*March 5–6,* Ecuador. A series of earthquakes, two of them measuring 7 on the Richter scale, crippled the country by destroying roads and bridges, rupturing a key oil pipeline, and precipitating mud slides that entombed entire villages; some 2,000 persons were believed dead and 75,000 others were injured.

*March 9,* Lima metropolitan area, Peru. Earthen dams weakened by rains collapsed and sent a torrent of water, mud, and boulders on nearby towns; more than 100 persons were killed and 25,000 were left homeless.

*March 16,* Sargazan, Tadzhikistan, U.S.S.R. An avalanche of mud caused a dam to collapse and unleash a reservoir of water on the village; 19 persons were known dead, 9 others were missing, and 6 persons were seriously injured.

*March 19–20,* Mongolia. Severe storms wracked the region and caused human and livestock deaths; because the steppe area of the vast, thinly populated nation was hardest hit by the storm, no casualty figures were available.

*April 3,* Cochancay, Ecuador. A series of mud slides unleashed an avalanche of mud and rocks and buried at least three and as many as five buses on a coastal highway; at least 100 persons were feared dead.

*May 4,* West Sumatra, Indon. Heavy rains and earthquake aftershocks unleashed tons of earth and rocks that engulfed more than 50 homes in two villages; 96 persons were killed and 10 others were missing and feared dead.

*May 22,* Saragosa, Texas. A tornado ravaged the small farming town and leveled a community house where some 100 persons had gathered for a preschool graduation ceremony; about half of the 29 persons killed in the twister perished at the community house.

*July 12–16,* Central Chile. A bridge north of Santiago collapsed when violent floodwaters swept it and 12 persons away; the incident raised to 16 the number of deaths related to the five-day rainstorm.

*July 14,* Le Grand-Bornand, France. A freak flash flood, precipitated by a torrential mountain downpour, descended on a vacation campsite; the raging waters caused the Borne River to break its banks and swept away trailers and cars, heaved huge boulders out of the riverbanks, and claimed the lives of at least 30 persons.

*July 15,* Southern coast of South Korea. Typhoon Thelma rampaged across the southern coast of the country and unleashed sheets of heavy rain that caused rivers to break their banks, boats to capsize, and tons of rocks and mud to cascade onto hundreds of homes; at least 111 persons were killed, and 257 others were also feared dead.

*July 17,* Comfort, Texas. A bus and a van carrying members from a church camp stalled on a bridge and were swept away by swollen waters from the Guadalupe River; six teenagers were known dead, one of whom fell 27 m (90 ft) to her death after releasing her grip on a rope dangling from a rescue helicopter, and four others were missing and presumed drowned in the churning, debris-filled river.

*July 18,* Northern Italy. Torrential rains triggered floods and landslides that isolated several Alpine villages and killed at least 14 persons; hardest hit was the village of Tartano, where a landslide demolished a mountain resort hotel and killed 12 persons.

*July 21–22,* Chungchong Province, South Korea. Two days of torrential rain pummeled the central part of the country and prompted floods and landslides that left nearly 100 persons missing and presumed dead.

*July 24,* Northeastern Iran. Torrential rains caused the Boojhan River to overflow its banks; at least 100 persons were killed.

*July 27,* Seoul, South Korea. The third major storm in three weeks unleashed torrents of rain that inundated streets with waist-high water and touched off landslides; at least 74 persons were known dead.

*July 28,* Zhejiang (Chekiang) Province, China. Typhoon Alex roared along the coast of the province and triggered a 40-km (25-mi) landslide, destroyed 22 bridges, and snapped 32 high-power electricity transmission lines; at least 38 persons were known dead.

*July 31,* Heilongjiang Province, China. A devastating tornado struck 14 towns, killing 16 persons and seriously injuring more than 440 others; 13 others were missing.

*July 31,* Edmonton, Alta. As many as five tornadoes, accompanied by fist-size hail and 100-km/h (60-mph) winds, ravaged a trailer park and a nearby industrial centre; more than 25 persons were killed in the deadly twisters.

*Late July–Early August,* U.S. A blistering heat wave scorched the central part of the nation and led to the deaths of at least 80 persons; in some areas temperatures surpassed 38° C (100° F) for 17 straight days.

*August,* Bangladesh. Monthlong flooding affected 20 million people and was blamed for the deaths of at least 1,000 persons.

*September,* Near Maracay, Venezuela. Heavy flooding caused by torrential rain killed some 500 persons.

*September 25–29,* Natal Province, South Africa. A relentless five-day rainstorm precipitated heavy flooding that caused more than $500 million in damages; 174 persons were known dead, 86 others were missing, and more than 50,000 persons were left homeless.

*September 27,* Medellín, Colombia. Torrential rains touched off an avalanche of red mud and rock that thundered down on the impoverished area of Villa Tina, where an estimated 1,000 people resided in shacks; at least 175 persons were known dead, and as many as 325 others were feared buried under the rubble.

*Late September,* India. Extensive flooding in northern Bihar, West Bengal, and parts of Uttar Pradesh and Assam states led to the deaths of more than 1,200 persons.

*October 1,* Near Los Angeles. A powerful earthquake measuring 6.1 on the Richter scale triggered fires, shattered glass from skyscrapers, caused more than $100 million in damages, and was blamed for the deaths of at least six persons; the town of Whittier, 19 km (12 mi) southeast of Los Angeles, was hardest hit by the quake and by a severe 5.3 aftershock three days later, which caused another death.

*October 3–4,* Spain. Severe storms in the eastern and northern parts of the country led to the deaths of at least ten persons.

AFP PHOTO

People of Bangladesh have to stand in the water as they await government relief in the flood-ridden areas of Dhaka. Shortages of relief supplies caused many to return home empty-handed.

Two children wander through the remains of their home after a series of earthquakes and aftershocks in Ecuador's northeastern mountains caused extensive floods and mud slides that swept through many villages, leaving as many as 110,000 homeless.

EL COMERCIO—SYGMA

*October 15,* England. A fierce storm packing hurricane-force winds knocked out electric power and felled trees across roads and homes; 13 deaths were attributed to the storm, which caused nearly $1 billion in damages and was billed as the worst storm in decades.

*October 19–21,* Tibet. A three-day snowstorm killed 11 persons who froze to death.

*October 24,* Taiwan. Typhoon Lynn swept nine schoolchildren out to sea and was blamed for the death of a man hit by falling rock; 200 homes were destroyed.

*November 3–6,* Andhra Pradesh, India. Cyclone-force winds accompanied by driving rain flattened crops and damaged some 12,000 homes near the coastal town of Nellore; at least 34 persons were known dead.

*November 26,* The Philippines. Typhoon Nina lashed the islands with giant waves that destroyed bridges and knocked down power and communication lines in the port of Matnog; hardest hit was Sorsogon Province in southern Luzon, where as many as 500 persons were feared dead.

*November 26,* Pantar, Indon. An earthquake measuring 5.8 on the Richter scale touched off landslides and a tidal wave on the remote volcanic island of Pantar; 42 persons were known dead, and some 75 others were missing.

*November 29,* Near Los Maitenes, Chile. An avalanche that was started by melting snow high in the mountains thundered down on a camp for workers who were building a hydroelectric plant; some 60 persons were feared dead.

*December 5,* Peru. Mud slides destroyed some 60 homes in four villages in the foothills of the Peruvian Andes Mountains; 15 persons were known dead, and at least 100 others were missing and feared dead.

*December 12–16,* Midwestern U.S. A major snowstorm packing high winds closed airports and schools, knocked down power lines, and spawned tornadoes in Arkansas; 73 deaths were blamed on the storm, which pummeled parts of Wisconsin, Michigan, Missouri, Illinois, Indiana, Minnesota, Ohio, Iowa, and Kansas.

*December 25,* Sulawesi, Indon. Landslides and severe flooding claimed the lives of at least 92 persons.

*Late December,* Minas Gerais, Brazil. Torrential rains caused heavy flooding after a river burst its banks and swept people, animals, and vehicles through the streets; at least 12 persons were known dead.

## Railroad

*January 4,* Chase, Md. A 12-car Amtrak passenger train collided with three Conrail freight engines when the latter train merged onto the same track as the racing passenger train; 15 persons were killed, and more than 175 others were injured in the worst Amtrak rail disaster to date.

*February 17,* Near Itaquera, Brazil. Two commuter trains collided after one of them sped through a warning light near a suburban train station during a driving rainstorm and slammed into the second passenger train; at least 45 persons were killed.

*March 15,* Near Ariyalur, India. An express train derailed after Tamil extremists used remote-controlled bombs to blow up a railway bridge; at least 22 persons were killed, and some 150 others were injured.

*July 2,* Kasumbalesa Shaba, Zaire. A trailer truck plowed headlong into a train at an unguarded crossing; most of the 125 casualties occurred in the first and second cars of the train.

*August 7,* U.S.S.R. A speeding locomotive with defective brakes detached from a freight train and slammed into the rear of a passenger train at more than 130 km/h (80 mph); the impact of the crash destroyed two coaches on the passenger train and killed an unspecified number of passengers.

*October 17,* Near Rajac, Yugos. A speeding freight train ran through a red-light signal and collided head-on with a passenger train carrying 100 passengers; 10 persons were killed and 50 others were seriously harmed.

*October 19,* Near Jakarta, Indon. A passenger train carrying 600 persons crashed head-on into another passenger train carrying 300 persons, apparently after a signaling error diverted both trains to the same track; at least 155 persons were killed and 260 others were injured.

*October 20,* Moro, Pak. A passenger train plowed into a crowded bus at a railroad crossing after the operator of the crossing failed to lower the gate; 50 passengers aboard the bus died.

*November 29,* Georgian S.S.R. A freight train rammed into a stationary passenger train on the Transcaucasian railway near Gardabani; an unknown number of deaths occurred.

*December 16,* Shamboo, India. A stopped passenger train was struck by an engine and then by a 50-car freight train; 10 persons were killed, and 55 others were injured.

*December 22,* Nova Iguacu, Brazil. A speeding commuter train slammed into another train packed with labourers; there were numerous casualties and injuries.

## Traffic

*March 11,* Rajasthan State, India. A bus carrying a wedding party collided with a van; 12 persons were killed and 20 others were injured, 7 seriously.

*March 17,* Eastern Uganda. A bus carrying 150 passengers slammed into a truck and crashed through a bridge railing into a river; 101 persons were killed.

*March 18,* Near Nyamplung, central Java, Indon. A bus struck three pedestrians and plunged 18 m (60 ft) into a ravine after a broken wheel caused the vehicle to go out of control; 12 persons were killed, including one of the pedestrians.

*March 30,* Northwestern China. A bus en route to Gansu (Kansu) Province plunged over a precipice; 19 persons were killed in the crash.

*April 3,* Sinaloa State, Mexico. A bus transporting engineering students to a class project collided with a dump truck near the town of Elota after the driver lost control of the vehicle; 14 persons were killed, and 43 others were injured in the crash.

*May 8,* Port-au-Prince, Haiti. A water truck slammed into a crowd of pedestrians and street vendors; at least 17 persons were known dead, and 5 others were injured.

*June 5,* Uganda. A bus went out of control and overturned after swerving to avoid a large snake on a road; ten persons were killed.

*June 10,* Jammu, India. A bus plunged into a deep gully; 10 persons were killed, and 27 others were injured.

*June 10,* Gujarat State, India. A head-on collision between a bus and a jeep resulted in the deaths of 11 persons.

*June 16,* Near Patiala, India. A crowded bus, loaded with passengers inside and on the roof, slammed through the side of a bridge and plunged into a canal; at least 60 persons were feared drowned.

*June 19,* South Africa. A packed bus collided with a train at a railroad crossing some 50 km (31 mi) west of Pretoria; 18 persons were killed and 84 others injured, 13 of them seriously.

*June 25,* Central India. A tractor pulling guests to a wedding collided with a bus; 21 members of the wedding party were killed.

*July 3,* Near Monterrey, Spain. A bus veered off a mountain road and tumbled 152 m (500 ft) down a mountain cliff; 37 persons aboard were killed and 8 others were injured.

*July 4,* Near Covilhã, Port. A tour bus plunged into a 149-m (490-ft)-deep ravine; 19 persons were killed and 34 others were injured.

*July 18,* Kwamashu, South Africa. A small bus carrying 14 persons slammed into a gasoline truck; 10 persons were killed in the collision.

*August 7,* Uttar Pradesh, India. A bus transporting 110 persons fell into a canal; 90 persons were feared dead in the crash.

*Mid-October,* Central China. A bus carrying 52 passengers careened off a road and plunged down a mountain; the driver and 19 passengers were killed.

*October 28,* Near Preston, England. A gasoline tanker truck slammed into slow-moving traffic and overturned; three other trucks, a minibus, and two cars were involved in the fiery accident, which caused 12 deaths.

*November 13,* Near Mexico City. A crowded bus loaded with schoolchildren and workers skidded off a heavily fog-enshrouded dirt road; 40 persons were killed and 5 others were injured in the crash.

*December 11,* Cairo. A school bus loaded with children returning from a field trip was split in two when a speeding train hit the vehicle at an unmarked railroad crossing; 50 children, 6 teachers, and the bus driver were killed, and at least 58 others were injured.

*December 27,* Near Ain Arnat, Alg. The collision of a truck and a bus resulted in the deaths of 32 persons; 19 others were injured.

# Earth Sciences

## GEOLOGY AND GEOCHEMISTRY

A significant advance in geologic mapping and sedimentary basin analysis was reported in 1987 by a group of scientists from the Jet Propulsion Laboratory (JPL), Pasadena, Calif., who developed and applied a new remote-sensing approach to stratigraphy and structural mapping. They used multispectral-image data acquired from aircraft and satellites, combined with topographic data, to determine the attitude, sequence, thickness, and character of sedimentary strata exposed at the surface in the Wind River and Big Horn basins of Wyoming. The research was made possible by recent advances in remote-sensing instrumentation, including three multispectral systems available only since 1982. An important result of the availability of digital, multispectral data from Earth-resources satellites (beginning in 1972 with the launch of the first Landsat) was the development of systems for computer-image enhancement and display. These systems accentuate spectral contrasts extending outside the range of human vision or photographic film. The JPL group developed such a system, the multimission image processing laboratory (MIPL), and used it in the investigation. The approach had general applicability in regions where the rocks are exposed, not covered by vegetation or alluvial material.

In another JPL study a new multispectral device called a thermal infrared multispectral scanner (TIMS) was flown over Death Valley, California, during the day and at night to collect both spectral-emittance and thermal-inertia data. The images obtained from TIMS permitted researchers to discriminate among some bedrock units and to tell bedrock units from alluvium. Inferences were made about soil moisture and conditions on some of the alluvial fans.

The 19th General Assembly of the International Union of Geodesy and Geophysics, held in Vancouver, B.C., in 1987, served to highlight many developments in geochemistry and the petrologic aspects of geology. Recently recognized tectonic features of the ocean ridges on the scale of kilometres were now associated with significant geochemical and petrologic variations in the basalts forming them. The compositional variations correlate with overlapping ridge axes, propagating ridge tips, deviations from axial symmetry, and transform faults. The emerging picture was one of a series of segmented ridge sections, each with a topographic high point probably representing a volcanic centre; their spacing of 40–70 km (25–43 mi) perhaps reflects separate magma inputs from gravitational instability in a deep, partly molten region. One of the most prominent advances in the study of mantle magmas and their geochemistry was in modeling the segregation of small degrees of partial melt from a deformable solid matrix, with the coupling of phase equilibria and trace-element patterns with fluid dynamical calculations. According to Bruce Marsh of Johns Hopkins University, Baltimore, Md., "We are in the midst of an extremely fertile burst of activity . . . in the steady implementation of newly investigated physical processes into petrological thinking," which includes the theoretical treatment of viscous deformation of partly melted rocks, with upward expulsion of magma, extraction and transport of magmas, the various processes occurring in magma chambers, and the withdrawal of magmas for eruption.

The Continental Deep Drilling Program of West Germany was under way with a pilot hole at a site selected in the Oberpfalz region on the Bohemian Massif. Drilling of the superdeep borehole, expected to reach 12–14 km (7.4–8.7 mi) beneath the surface, was to start in 1989, one major goal being to establish the nature of the crust at a depth of 10–12 km (6.2–7.4 mi), where seismic studies in the German Continental Reflection Program had recorded the presence of highly reflective crust intercalated with low-velocity channels. The borehole was located at an important geologic boundary extending across Europe between two major basement units, and the results were expected to provide information on the fundamental processes of lateral crustal accretion. Another important theme was investigation of rock fluids with respect to thrusting, rock porosity and sealing, mineralization, and recent thermal waters.

Discoveries of two giant impact craters were reported in 1987. Exploration wells drilled into the continental shelf 200 km (125 mi) from Nova Scotia revealed the first known submarine impact crater. Named Montagnais, the structure is 45–65 km (30–40 mi) in diameter, has a central uplift of 1,700 m (5,580 ft), lies buried under 540 m (1,770 ft) of sediment, and is 50 million years old. The second crater, which at 70–80 km (43–50 mi) in diameter proved to be one of the world's largest impact structures, was recognized about 300 km (190 mi) north of Beijing. Known as the Duolun crater, it was believed to have been formed 136 million years ago.

The hypothesis that the mass extinctions of species at the Cretaceous-Tertiary boundary were caused by an energetic collision of an asteroid or comet with the Earth was

G. ROSE—GAMMA/LIAISON

A thin line of dust hangs over the fault line near Whittier, California, after an earthquake on October 1. The quake, which severely shook the Los Angeles area, measured 6.1 on the Richter scale and was the worst temblor to hit southern California since 1971.

strengthened by a 1987 report that shock-disrupted quartz grains indicative of a powerful impact were discovered in the boundary clay at seven widely separated sites. On the other hand, the generality of the impact hypothesis to explain mass extinctions was challenged by an argument that iridium enrichment of boundary clays—the key evidence for collision with an extraterrestrial, iridium-carrying body—had been demonstrated only for the Cretaceous-Tertiary boundary and not for other major mass extinctions that occurred in the past 570 million years. Other reports during the year developed the theme that the Cretaceous-Tertiary extinctions, which included the dinosaurs, coincided with and were caused by intense volcanic activity taking place over hundreds of thousands of years spanning the boundary.

The conditions that led to the sudden release of a deadly cloud of carbon dioxide gas from Lake Nyos, Cameroon, in 1986 was the subject of several reports, wherein the investigators concluded that the origin of the gas was not biogenic but volcanic. The waters of the lake, which occupies a deep volcanic crater, became supercharged with carbon dioxide seeping from the volcanic plumbing system within the crust. Thereafter some minor disturbance sufficed to overturn the water and thus reduce the pressure on the gas-charged water from the bottom levels. Because the hazard of a recurrence persisted, proposals were made to control the gas release, perhaps by inclined drilling into the sediments at the bottom of Lake Nyos and other, similar lakes in the region.

Volcanic carbon dioxide has its source in the Earth's mantle where the volcanic magma is generated. It has been estimated from the compositions of minerals in mantle samples (xenoliths) brought up in lavas that the magma was generated at depths of at least 55 km (34 mi), with the implication that the gas may have come from even greater depths. The mineral compositions in these and similar mantle xenoliths are calibrated in terms of the pressures and depths of formation. In a 1987 report more than a dozen formulations for the mineral barometers and thermometers were evaluated in detail. This refinement of the calibration of minerals in mantle xenoliths provided invaluable information about the variation of temperature as a function of depth in the mantle at the time of eruption of the magmas that carry these samples to the surface; that is, about fossil geotherms. It was now well established that beneath old continents the geotherm is inflected abruptly to higher temperatures at depths approximating the base of the lithosphere, about 130–170 km (80–105 mi).

The mineralogy and composition of mantle xenoliths carried from great depths in lavas like those that made the crater of Lake Nyos and in kimberlites—the magmas that bring diamonds to the surface—also provide direct information about the nature of the upper mantle and the effects of the passage of magmas and more dilute gaseous fluids through the mantle. These fluids cause chemical changes in the host rocks, a process called metasomatism, and xenoliths provide the only firm basis to guide the interpretation of trace element and isotope geochemistry of lavas such as basalts in terms of their source rocks at depth. The intense attention to this topic was manifest in the publication of two volumes during the year, *Mantle Xenoliths,* edited by P. H. Nixon, and *Mantle Metasomatism,* edited by M. A. Menzies and C. J. Hawkesworth, and in the forthcoming proceedings of the Fourth International Kimberlite Symposium held in 1986. Through much of the past decade the isotope data from basaltic rocks had been interpreted in terms of two mantle reservoirs that had remained physically separated from each other for a billion years or

so. By 1987, owing to the availability of more abundant and more detailed isotopic data, the two-reservoir models had been replaced by more complex versions having as many as five distinct reservoirs, or source rocks. One such reservoir is the source of the mid-ocean ridge basalts, depleted in incompatible trace elements. Other basalts were derived from mantle reservoirs that had been enriched in incompatible trace elements, either by metasomatism or by contamination with recycled oceanic crust and sediments.

(PETER JOHN WYLLIE)

## GEOPHYSICS

As it had for the preceding several years, seismic activity remained moderate during 1987. The most devastating earthquake, registering a magnitude 6.9 on the Richter scale, occurred March 6 on the Colombia-Ecuador border. It left several hundred dead, 4,000 missing, and 20,000 homeless while destroying or seriously damaging 28 km (17 mi) of oil pipeline in Ecuador. Other notable quakes included one of magnitude 7 on January 30 near the South Sandwich Islands, one of magnitude 7.4 on February 8 in East Papua New Guinea that left three dead as the result of landslides, one of magnitude 6.1 on October 1 near Los Angeles that killed at least six and caused more than $100 million in damages, and one of magnitude 6.9 on November 17 in the Gulf of Alaska. A shock of magnitude 5.8 struck the Indonesian island of Pantar on November 26, killing at least 42 people, setting off landslides that buried homes, and creating a tsunami (seismic sea wave) that inundated the island's coastal regions. Of two large earthquakes occurring near the coast of northern Chile, the first, on March 8, had a magnitude of 7.3 and caused one death, while the second, on August 8, had a magnitude of 7, killed 6, and injured 62.

Volcanism was exceptionally unspectacular, although the continuously active volcanoes around the world showed some of their usual fire. The most damage was incurred from Kilauea on the island of Hawaii, where yet another episode of the current eruption cycle began in July 1986 and continued into mid-1987. In late 1986, for the first time in 12 years, the accumulated lava flows crossed the coast highway and reached the sea. Within a month they had destroyed 28 houses, caused the evacuation of 400 residents, and inflicted $5 million in damages. After a relatively quiescent period during January 1987, activity increased again on February 1.

The scientific drilling ship *JOIDES Resolution* continued the Ocean Drilling Program (ODP) at an accelerated pace, reporting on ten exploratory legs that had been completed between mid-1986 and mid-1987. It was truly a far-ranging effort, beginning off the northwestern coast of Africa (Leg 108), then to the Mid-Atlantic Ridge (Leg 109), then on to the Tiburon Rise, north of Barbados (Leg 110), through the Panama Canal to the Panama Basin (Leg 111), and finally to the juncture of the South American and Nazca plates off Peru (Leg 112) for the last voyage of 1986. The year 1987 began with Legs 113 and 114 in the Antarctic waters of the Weddell Sea and the South Atlantic immediately to the north near the South Sandwich Islands. Legs 115, 116, and 117 marked the start of a nine-leg schedule of exploration in the Indian Ocean.

Among exceptional physical accomplishments during this odyssey were the occupation of 12 sites on Leg 108, which when combined with previous surveys provided a continuous transept in the eastern Atlantic from the Equator to latitude 54° N, and the recovery of a record 3,850 m (12,630 ft) of drill cores; the penetration on Leg 110 of the detachment surface that marks the boundary between the overriding, eastward-moving Caribbean Plate and the North American Plate in the vicinity of the Tiburon Rise; a fifth visit to Hole 549B, the world's deepest suboceanic hole, in the Panama Basin, where the depth was increased by 212 m (696 ft) to a total of 1,562 m (5,125 ft) below the seafloor; and the successful operations and core recovery, on Leg 114, in extremely high seas and near-hurricane winds.

According to plate tectonic theory, until about 65 million years ago Antarctica and Australia were one landmass, with Antarctica near its present position and connected to South America by a narrow isthmus across what is now the Drake Passage. About 53 million years ago the mass separated, and Australia began to drift north. At that time there was little glaciation in Antarctica, but around 38 million years ago the temperature of the bottom water in the high latitudes dropped abruptly, and an ice cap began to form. Then, some 13 million to 18 million years later, the Drake Passage was formed, creating a path for circumpolar currents that cut off moderating temperate currents and isolated Antarctica both geographically and climatically. Present-day bottom currents from the Weddell Sea have been traced as far north as the latitude of Labrador and are recognized for their role in the development of climate on both sides of the Atlantic. Theories of plate migration and knowledge of past climates were being greatly enhanced by analysis of the cores obtained on Legs 113 and 114, which gave definitive evidence of the sequence of events and more accurately established the times of their occurrences and their far-reaching effects on a large portion of the Southern Hemisphere.

The Indian Ocean contains many plateaus and ridges that drastically affect the circulation of ocean currents and the climatic conditions both at sea and ashore. Some of these features are best explained as remnant island arcs or continental fragments, while others may more logically be attributed to volcanically associated fracture zones or stationary hot spots. Hot spots, which result in holes in the crust through which molten material wells up from the mantle to form primal volcanoes, are regarded as stationary features of the mantle and not affected by plate migration.

Two of the most salient features of the Indian Ocean seafloor are parallel ridges running, almost rectilinearly, due north and south: the Ninetyeast Ridge and the Chagos-Laccadive Plateau, the latter feature extending westward at its south end to link up geologically with the Mascarene Plateau. One theory to explain their formation postulates that the Indian subcontinent was once a part of the Australia-Antarctica landmass. On its journey north to its collision with Asia, it passed over the Kerguelen and Réunion hot spots. The numerous volcanoes thus formed were dragged northward in the subsequent migration. Then, deprived of their primary source of energy, they died and were deposited as parallel chains of islands or subsurface features along the route of the moving plate. Among the many objectives of the drilling program in the Indian Ocean, of which Legs 115–117 were the first of nine, was establishment of the ages of these volcanic features to see whether a north–south sequence could be determined, thus reinforcing the hot-spot theory.    (RUTLAGE J. BRAZEE)

## HYDROLOGY

Below-normal streamflow occurred in much of the western U.S., the Great Lakes region, and the central Southeast during the spring and summer of 1987, whereas only a comparatively small area centred in Kansas experienced above-normal flow during the same period. Such conditions departed sharply from those of the previous fall–winter period, which was dominated by widespread above-normal streamflow comparable with that reported between 1983 and 1986. The combined flow of the Mississippi, St. Lawrence, and Columbia rivers averaged 31,180 cu m (1,101,000 cu ft) per second for 1987, a figure in the normal range. The annual means for the Mississippi and Columbia rivers were in the normal or below-normal range, while the annual mean for the St. Lawrence River at Cornwall, Ont., was the highest for the 108 years of record.

Sharp departures from the generally wet conditions of the previous few years occurred in the Great Lakes-St. Lawrence River basin, the upper Mississippi River basin, the Colorado River basin, and the Great Basin. Mean September elevations for the Great Lakes ranged from 0.23 m (0.74 ft; for Lake Erie) to 0.5 m (1.63 ft; for Lake Ontario) lower than the extremely high levels noted a year earlier. The level of Utah's Great Salt Lake fell to 1,283.1 m (4,209.6 ft) by September 30—a value 0.7 m (2.25 ft) below the record high of 1,283.8 m (4,211.85 ft) of June 3, 1986.

Heavy rains that began March 30, combined with melting snow, caused flooding in much of New England. The hardest hit was Maine, which was declared a federal disaster area on April 8. Record floods also occurred at four sites in Florida between March 30 and April 3, but no damage was reported. On April 5 ten people were killed when floodwaters caused the collapse of a New York State Thruway bridge over Schoharie Creek. Heavy rains near the end of May produced record flooding in parts of Iowa, Oklahoma, and Texas, drowning three people. On August 14 rains totaling 10.2–22.9 cm (4–9 in) in 24 hours caused severe flooding in Du Page and Cook counties in the northeastern part of Illinois. New peaks of record were set, and many roads serving Chicago and surrounding suburbs became impassable.

The ways in which large withdrawals of groundwater profoundly affect flow patterns of some of the major aquifers in the U.S. and contribute to water-quality degradation were emphasized in a report, *National Water Summary 1986—Hydrologic Events and Ground-Water Quality,* published in 1987 by the U.S. Geological Survey. The report focused on groundwater resources and included state summaries giving locations of waste sites and the extent of groundwater contamination in each state. It discussed the many ways in which groundwater can become contaminated from point and nonpoint sources and the water-quality changes that take place as contaminants move through an aquifer. Included in the report's summary of major hydrologic events was a discussion of radon as a health hazard in the home.

Although the U.S. was beginning to clean up contaminated groundwater and to protect it for future generations, more data were needed to describe the extent, character, flow patterns, and quality of water. Scientists still lacked enough information about groundwater to make quantitative assessments of contaminant behaviour and movement in most aquifer systems. Basic, commonly asked questions—for example, the degree of groundwater contamination or whether groundwater quality was becoming better or worse—could not be readily answered. In previous years the U.S. Congress had passed laws authorizing the Environmental Protection Agency (EPA) to regulate substances that were major sources of groundwater contamination. Other federal laws provided money for cleaning up contaminated sites and for setting up programs for protecting groundwater. In 1986 and 1987 Congress amended and reauthorized these environmental laws to strengthen and expand them, in one case overriding a presidential veto of a passed bill to extend and amend the Clean Water Act. In 1987 congressional members introduced new bills to provide additional groundwater protection.

Louisiana's wetlands were being lost at the rate of approximately 130 sq km (50 sq mi) a year, much of it induced by human activity. Levees built to prevent flooding along streams prevented the wetlands from being renewed and replenished by sediment from the streams. State agencies were attempting to stem the loss by regulating land development in coastal zones, creating marshes by breeching levees to allow streamflow into former wetlands, and preserving or building barrier islands along the coast.

About 180 cities in China faced water shortages and deteriorating water quality. The shortages were especially acute in the Beijing-Tianjin (Peking-Tientsin) region, which played an important role in the country's economic future. The Environment and Policy Institute's North China Water Project was examining ways to better manage water supply and demand requirements. The past approach to the problem had been to build more dams and reservoirs, but the institute currently was trying to reduce water use by conservation and better management.

(JOHN E. MOORE)

## METEOROLOGY

Meteorologists from 138 member states and territories gathered in Geneva as the tenth Congress of the World Meteorological Organization (WMO) met in its quadrennial sessions during May 1987. For the first time, the congress approved plans for the next ten years for all of its major programs. The World Weather Watch plan envisaged a major improvement in the global observational system involving more extensive use of both geostationary and polar-orbiting satellites and expansion of the ground-based observing network, especially in the Southern Hemisphere and over the oceans. It also called for the development of cooperative information-processing centres in South America, Africa, and the Far East, so that the advances in sciences that had taken place from the Global Atmospheric Research Program and the advances expected from the World Climate Program could be put into operation to improve services to the people of those regions.

Evidence gathered since the 1970s made it clear that man-made chlorofluorocarbons released into the air play a significant role in depleting the stratospheric ozone layer that shields life on Earth from harmful solar ultraviolet radiation. Scientists who investigated the transient ozone "hole" over Antarctica during the Antarctic spring months of September to November 1987 found that the ozone layer had thinned by 40–50%—the largest decrease ever recorded. Their measurements demonstrated that both chemical and meteorological changes were involved as the hole deepened. While such findings were inconsistent with theories linking the ozone loss to solar activity or solely to meteorological forces, they strengthened the tie between the hole and man-made chlorine compounds in the atmosphere. A greatly expanded multiagency and international research effort would continue to probe the chemistry and dynamics at the stratospheric altitudes where the hole appeared.

The El Niño conditions first detected in the latter part of 1986 continued throughout 1987. El Niño is an anomalous warming of the sea surface in the eastern equatorial Pacific Ocean. Meteorologists and oceanographers believed that an El Niño brings about large-scale climatic aberrations. El Niño events occur at irregular intervals of two to seven years, but no two appear alike in their climatic effects. The previous El Niño of 1982–83 was the most intense of the

century and had a profound influence on the global circulation. The 1986-87 El Niño, which began relatively weak but became moderate to strong as the year progressed, was linked to certain regional responses: consistently above-normal temperatures in southern Alaska, western Canada, and the northern conterminous U.S. from December 1986 to April 1987; the mildest winter and spring in more than half a century for the north-central U.S.; unusually wet weather in parts of South America and very dry conditions in the Philippines and in Australia; and a largely failed or seriously rain-deficient monsoon in India and adjacent Pakistan. Research into the causes of the El Niño, the way it affects climatic conditions worldwide, and the way its influence can be predicted continued as part of the ten-year (1986–95) Tropical Ocean/Global Atmosphere Program (TOGA) under the World Climate Program.

While much of the U.S. enjoyed a mild winter, Europe suffered bitterly cold temperatures during January and February. The extremely low temperatures, the coldest of the century in some locations, dominated all of northern and central Europe reaching to southern France and northern Italy. Record cold weather in April in the central and southern U.S. inhibited the development of tornadoes in that usually high-incident month. The number of tornadoes recorded, 20, was the lowest since 1950 and well below the April average of more than 100. The total number of tornadoes for 1987 was much below normal. The worst tornado of the year was the vicious storm that struck Saragosa, Texas, on May 22, destroying most of the town and killing 29 of its 350 residents.

The 1987 Atlantic hurricane season also was light. The first tropical storm of the season was an unnamed storm that formed in the Gulf of Mexico, came ashore in southeastern Texas on August 10, and brought heavy rains in its slow passage across Louisiana and Mississippi. Arlene barely reached hurricane strength and did not strike land. Bret, Cindy, and Dennis, which never attained hurricane strength, stayed and died over open waters. Hurricane Emily struck the Dominican Republic on September 22, lost much of its strength over the mountains, regenerated over open water, and hit Bermuda on September 25. Floyd, the last storm of the season, formed in the Western

AP/WIDE WORLD

Two men wade along Chicago's Kennedy Expressway after a record rainfall in August. The heavy rains caused flooding throughout Cook and Du Page counties in Illinois and prevented access to O'Hare International Airport.

A woman walks past Istanbul's Blue Mosque during a fierce snowstorm that forced the city to a halt. The winter of 1987 dealt record cold temperatures throughout regions of Asia as well as through northern and central Europe.

FATIH SARIBAS—REUTERS/BETTMANN NEWSPHOTOS

Caribbean on October 9 and reached minimal hurricane strength on October 12 for a 12-hour period as it passed through the Florida Keys. In the Pacific more than 200 people were killed in the Philippines when Typhoon Nina hit that country on November 25.

(RICHARD E. HALLGREN)

This article updates the *Macropædia* article CLIMATE AND WEATHER.

## OCEANOGRAPHY

Understanding the circulation of the ocean near coasts and over continental shelves is of great practical importance because so much of human interaction with the sea occurs there. In past decades oceanographers had conducted a number of intensive experiments aimed at understanding coastal flow. During the year one such study was carried out along several hundred kilometres of the California coast between Cape Mendocino and Point Reyes. A unique feature of the study was careful mapping of the wind over the ocean from aircraft and from anemometers on the buoys that supported instruments in the water. Although the major fieldwork was finished, new results continued to emerge as the data were further analyzed.

Researchers found from the study that the wind field is very different not only from one place to another on the coast but also from the coast out to sea. The coast protrudes out in capes that are separated by abrupt bends. Because the coastal range of mountains is hundreds of metres high, the coast acts as a wall for winds in the stable, near-surface marine layer of the atmosphere. As the wind blows southward along the coast, its strength decreases gradually around capes but increases suddenly at the intervening bends of the coast. The way in which these sudden increases in wind strength extend out to sea was shown to be correctly predicted by a theory very much like one that predicts the shock waves generated in the atmosphere

by supersonic aircraft. Since the atmospheric and coastal conditions important in this theory—a stable marine layer and an unbroken coastal mountain chain—are common along many coasts, most future studies of coastal circulation would have to reckon with the possible occurrence of such extreme variations in the wind as those found in this work. Where they occur, their influence on the coastal ocean may be great.

Since the first atomic explosions in the 1940s, the release of large amounts of radioactive material into the atmosphere has provided oceanographers with the opportunity to follow the fate of material falling onto the ocean. Atmospheric nuclear tests injected large amounts of tritium, a radioactive isotope of hydrogen, into the atmosphere of the Northern Hemisphere, and oceanographers have since been using the isotope to trace the motion of water that sank below the surface in the far-northern Atlantic during the decades of atmospheric nuclear testing. The accident at the Chernobyl nuclear power station in 1986 likewise released radioactive material into the atmosphere. In the North Sea some of this material was found in a sediment trap 222 m (728 ft) below the surface only ten days after the contaminated air had passed overhead. Similarly rapid downward transport of radioactive material was found in the Black Sea and in the Mediterranean. These observations were important because they showed directly that microscopic particles falling onto the ocean can be carried to the bottom much more rapidly than they would be expected to sink by themselves. It was thought that the particles are adsorbed onto microscopic marine plants, which are then eaten by very small marine animals. Incorporated in the animals' fecal pellets, the particles can sink tens or even hundreds of metres in a day.

In 1977 springs of very hot water were discovered at the Galápagos Rift, a volcanically active seafloor spreading centre in the East Pacific. Such hydrothermal vents were found subsequently at a number of Atlantic and Pacific locations. The vented water, which can be hotter than 350° C (660° F), originates as seawater that percolates into the seafloor some distance from the vents to a depth where it is heated by and reacts chemically with the surrounding hot rock. The water then rises back to the surface and emerges from the localized vents. The vented water is thus rich in dissolved minerals, which precipitate out of solution when the vented water mixes with cold seawater. Many vents support local communities of giant tube worms, mussels, and other animals. "Fossil" vent systems—locations surrounded by the shells of such animals but no longer venting hot water—were also discovered. During 1987 a very different kind of vent region was found south of Hawaii. Researchers diving with the research submersible *Alvin* into the underwater depression left by the collapse of an ancient volcano found a hydrothermal vent system around which only bacteria were growing; there were no communities of animals. The carbon dioxide content of the vented water was found comparable to that in carbonated beverages, leading researchers to speculate that this unusually high concentration may be toxic to marine animals.

The discharge from most hydrothermal vents rises several hundred metres above the bottom as a plume before becoming sufficiently diluted by the surrounding seawater that it ceases to rise and instead spreads sideways. By that time its temperature is only a few hundredths of a degree Celsius above that of the surrounding water. Observations taken along the Juan de Fuca Ridge several hundred kilometres seaward of the U.S. Northwest coast and published in 1987 showed the occurrence of a "monster" plume rising 800 m (2,625 ft) above the bottom and having a temperature more than two-tenths of a degree above that of the surrounding water. Several thousand normal vents would have taken a year to inject into the ocean the amount of heat and minerals in this single giant. It was not known what led to its formation; nothing similar had ever been seen before. If such large venting events occur frequently, they may upset present estimates of how much heat and dissolved material is carried from the crust into the ocean by hydrothermal circulation.

Coelacanths are deep-sea fish having a body length of one to two metres (three to six feet). They were abundant from the end of the Permian to the end of the Jurassic periods (225 million to 136 million years ago) and had been thought extinct until 1938, when one was caught in the southwestern Indian Ocean. A second was caught in 1952, and a few more have since been taken, yet such elementary questions as whether the coelacanth crawls along the bottom or swims rapidly through the water remained unanswered. In 1987 the first observations of living coelacanths in their natural environment were published. Made from a research submersible at depths of 100–200 m (330–660 ft) in the Indian Ocean, they showed that the fish usually drift with the current, using their limblike fins to stabilize their bodies in a wide variety of positions and attitudes relative to the direction of drift. When in contact with the bottom, they do not use their fins to crawl. Even so, their paired fins move in alternation, as do the fin pairs of such bottom-crawling fish as lungfish. This pattern of fin motion may be a preadaptation that enabled fish that subsequently evolved air-breathing ability to move on the land when they had emerged from the sea.

(MYRL C. HENDERSHOTT)

*See also* Disasters; Energy; Environment; Life Sciences; Mining; Space Exploration.

This article updates the *Macropædia* articles ATMOSPHERE; The EARTH; EARTHQUAKES; The EARTH SCIENCES; FISHES; GEOCHRONOLOGY; Principles, Methods, and Instruments of MEASUREMENT AND OBSERVATION; OCEANS; PLATE TECTONICS; RIVERS; VOLCANISM.

# Economic Affairs

The world economy experienced a mixed year in 1987. Economic growth slowed down but was maintained at a respectable rate; world trade became relatively sluggish; and the rate of inflation accelerated marginally. At the same time, unemployment declined modestly and output recorded a good increase. However, the international financial system exhibited considerable instability, largely because of the continuing inability to deal with the large current account and budget deficits of the United States and the current account surpluses of West Germany and Japan. This resulted in unstable exchange rates and a rapid depreciation of the dollar against most major currencies.

The problem of the large less developed debtor countries remained as intractable as ever, with the major lenders being forced to make even larger loss provisions. Toward the end of the year the world's major stock markets suffered an unprecedented collapse in equity values. This introduced an additional element of uncertainty into an already uncertain international financial climate and exacerbated existing economic policy disagreements among Organization for Economic Cooperation and Development (OECD) governments. In fact, in the area of international economic cooperation, so vital for continuing growth and prosperity, there was little or no progress; on the contrary, despite a year of talks within the framework of the Uruguay trade liberalization round, protectionist sentiments appeared to

be stronger at the end of 1987 than they had been a year earlier.

World economic growth, as measured by the growth of gross national product (GNP) in OECD countries, was estimated at 2.2% for 1987, as against a rise of 2.5% in 1986. The loss of momentum could be largely attributed to West Germany and France. Despite considerable pressure from other nations and the absence of serious inflationary forces, West Germany did little to stimulate domestic demand and managed only a growth rate of 1–1.5%, compared with 2.5% in the previous year. France also experienced a slowdown, from 2.2 to 1.7%, although—unlike the case of West Germany—an attempt to boost demand further could have had serious inflationary consequences. On the other hand, the economies of Japan, the U.S., and the U.K. performed better than in the previous year. The star performer was the U.K., which managed to secure a GNP gain of 4% (3% in 1986) without significant acceleration in inflation. Japan, responding to overseas pressure to boost domestic demand, went from a GNP gain of 2.5 to 3%, while the U.S.—under attack for financial profligacy—accelerated its growth from 2.5 to over 3%. Most other OECD countries registered a decline in growth; as a bloc they probably gained 2%, as against 2.5% in 1987, with Italy's growth rate remaining broadly stable at 2.7% and that of Canada increasing from 3.3 to 3.6%.

As in 1986 (and 1985), the most buoyant component of demand was private consumption. Although the rise in earnings did not appear to have accelerated markedly, a number of countries—notably the U.K. and Japan—reduced taxation and followed relatively relaxed monetary policies. This had a positive effect on consumers' purchasing power, leading to reasonably buoyant consumer expenditure. As far as other major components of demand were concerned, considerable variations were experienced from country to country. Public consumption was relatively weak (although it still recorded an increase) in both the U.K. and the U.S.—in the case of the U.K. because of the highly successful policy of controlling government expenditure and in the case of the U.S. because of the need to cut the budget deficit. In Japan, however, government spent relatively freely—in fact, extra public expenditure was one of the principal means of supporting growth. Pri-

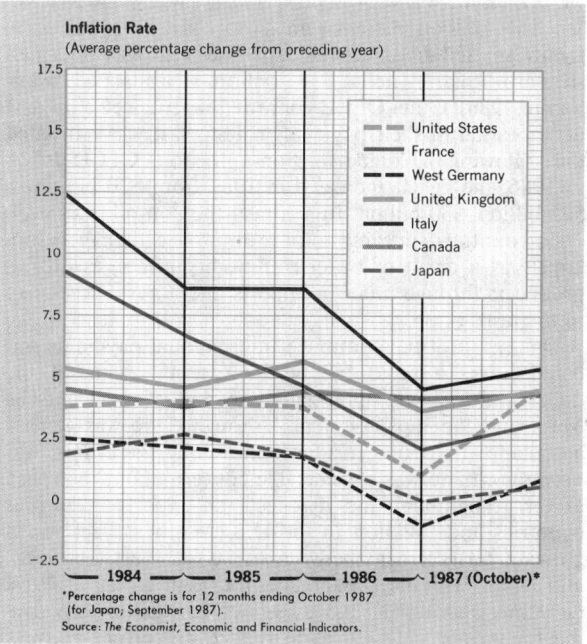

**Inflation Rate**
(Average percentage change from preceding year)

United States
France
West Germany
United Kingdom
Italy
Canada
Japan

1984 — 1985 — 1986 — 1987 (October)*

*Percentage change is for 12 months ending October 1987 (for Japan; September 1987).
Source: *The Economist, Economic and Financial Indicators.*

vate investment also presented a mixed picture. Faced with a strange reluctance to boost demand by the West German government and a steady appreciation in the value of the Deutsche Mark, businesses took a cautious approach and boosted investment by only some 0.5%, compared with 3.3% in 1986. France—also suffering from fragile business confidence—experienced a slowdown from 3.5 to about 2%, while in the U.S. investment was thought to have fallen by about 1%. In sharp contrast, however, the U.K. had a very good growth of 5%, with investment intentions remaining at a high level even after the stock market crash in October.

The trading performances of the principal economic powers also varied greatly. The overall background of considerable exchange rate instability and international financial uncertainty was somewhat unfavourable. Apart from these, the principal influences on world trade were the attempt of the U.S. and the oil-producing countries to slow down the rise in their imports for balance of payments reasons and the somewhat halfhearted policies of the major surplus countries of stepping up their foreign purchases in an attempt to reduce their large positive trade and payments balances. The U.S. was more successful in its import adjusting efforts than were the two principal surplus nations of West Germany and Japan. Thus while U.S. imports grew in volume by only 3.5% in 1987, against 13.5% in 1986, Japan also cut its import growth to 5% (12% in 1986), and in West Germany the growth of imports remained largely unchanged at 5.5–6%. Combined with the rather weak demand from the oil producers, this led to an unexpectedly sluggish advance in world trade. As the year was nearing its close, provisional statistics indicated that the overall gain for 1987 was probably no more than 3–3.5%, compared with a good rise of 4.7% during the preceding year.

Another rather unsatisfactory feature of the world economy was the fact that large payments imbalances—the source of much instability in the world financial system—continued to persist. Despite the relatively slow growth of U.S. imports, combined with an acceleration in the advance of exports, the dollar value of foreign trade was adversely affected by the weakness of the American currency, and the U.S. current account deficit—estimated at $150 billion for 1987—represented a small increase over the $141 billion recorded in 1986. Nor was there any significant reduction in the Japanese and West German surpluses (totaling about $113 billion, as against $126 billion in 1986). Other OECD countries experienced a modest deterioration in their payments balances; it was estimated that following the large reduction in the total OECD deficit in 1986, the deficit increased in 1987 from $20 billion to $25 billion–$30 billion. In contrast, the non-oil less developed countries appeared to have improved their position, largely as a result of better commodity prices, as did oil producers through a cut in imports and a partial recovery in the price of oil.

One result of the continued international payments imbalance was a rapid fall in the external value of the dollar and a strong appreciation in that of the Deutsche Mark and the Japanese yen. Although there was general acceptance that some readjustment along these lines was necessary, there was considerable concern about the speed of the realignment and its effects on exports in surplus countries and inflation in the U.S. Another effect was a growing disagreement between the U.S., West Germany, and Japan, with the U.S. arguing for faster growth in West Germany and Japan, and those two nations in turn calling for greater U.S. efforts to reduce its current account

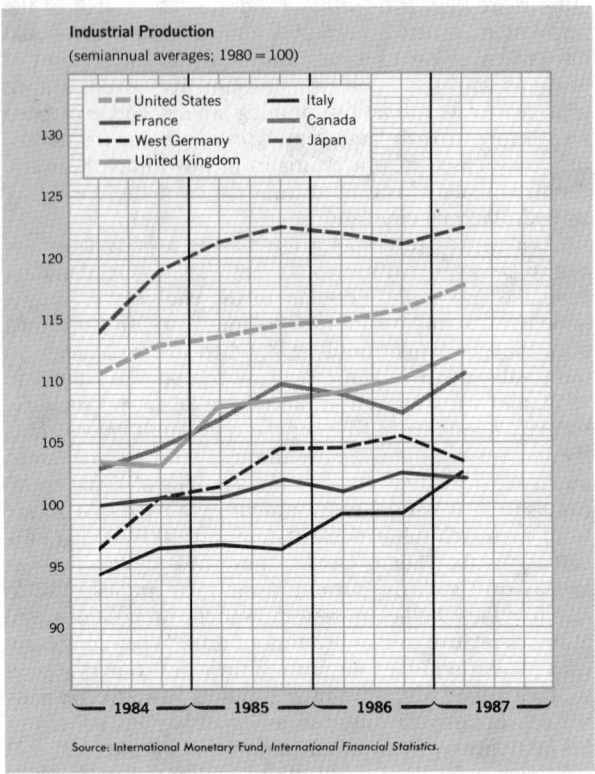

**Industrial Production**
(semiannual averages; 1980 = 100)

Source: International Monetary Fund, *International Financial Statistics.*

and budget deficits. In consequence, protectionist sentiments appeared to have strengthened in the U.S., and the Uruguay round of multilateral trade liberalization negotiations did not make as much headway as was expected after the launch of those negotiations in late 1986. Differences between the principal countries were further accentuated as a result of the stock market crash.

By late November U.S. Pres. Ronald Reagan was able to announce the outlines of a $30 billion budget-reduction package for 1988. International reaction to this was lacklustre owing to the time it took to put the package together and fears that it might not receive congressional approval. For its part, the U.S. made it clear that it expected Europe to boost demand; in response, the European Monetary System (EMS) countries announced a round of modest interest-rate reductions.

Monetary policies during the year were fairly relaxed, with most governments accepting that—contrary to the view previously held—monetary growth in the short term was not a particularly meaningful indicator of the health of the economy. In spite of a fairly fast increase in money stock, many countries experienced a downward trend in interest rates, especially after the stock market crash. In the U.K. base rates dropped from 11 to 8.5%, and in West Germany the Lombard rate was cut from 5.5 to 4.5%. Japanese rates also fell, but the U.S. and France, both suffering from pressure on their currencies, were forced to increase interest rates—the U.S. prime rate, for example, had risen from 7.5 to 8.75% by November. In spite of this, the trade-weighted value of the dollar fell by 14% up to late November, while the values of the currencies of Japan and West Germany rose by 6 and 10%, respectively. Sterling improved by 2.5% against the dollar, but its annual average trade-weighted value declined 0.5%.

Inflation accelerated slightly during the year. This occurred in most countries, with the result that the average for the OECD bloc was estimated to be approximately 3.5%, compared with 2.6% in 1986. The major reason for this was the partial recovery in commodity prices rather than the pressure of demand. Inflation was particularly fast in the U.S. (about 4%), where the weakness of the dollar exacerbated cost pressures; in West Germany and Japan, however, where exchange rates moved in the opposite direction, prices rose by only about 1%. Despite the slowdown in the rate of GNP growth, the level of OECD unemployment was believed to have fallen from 8.3 to 8.1%. Most principal countries saw an improvement, though in France and West Germany the refusal to stimulate the sluggish economy resulted in a rise in the unemployment rate from 8 to about 8.2%.

## NATIONAL ECONOMIC POLICIES

**Developed Market Economies.** *United States.* Although the U.S. economy in 1987 was probably best remembered for the Wall Street crash and its principal cause, the large budget and trade deficits (see *Stock Exchanges,* below), this should not obscure the fact that—in terms of economic growth—the U.S. performed remarkably well. In fact, business activity was unexpectedly buoyant throughout the year. The first quarter got off to a flying start with an annualized GNP gain of 4.4%; this was followed by one of 2.5% in April–June and 4.1% in July–September. Late in the year most indicators pointed to continued progress, and on this basis it was widely expected that 1987 as a whole would register a GNP gain of between 3 and 3.5%. This was a satisfactory performance on several counts. It was in line with the official target of 3.2%; it was (probably) the second fastest rate of growth after that of the U.K. among the major OECD countries, and it represented a satisfactory advance over the previous year's GNP gain of 2.6%.

With the exception of fixed investment, most areas of demand recorded some advance. Average earnings rose a little faster than in the preceding year (about 4%, as against 3.3%), but they were effectively offset by an acceleration in inflation. The effect of this was that—despite further tax cuts—there was only a sluggish growth in disposable incomes. This—on the basis of partial statistics—was thought to have cut back the increase in private consumption to a little over 2%, compared with 4% in 1986 (which was widely regarded as unsustainable and potentially inflationary). Government consumption also rose, but—reflecting the attempts to reduce the budget deficit—the gain was estimated at just over 2%, as against 3.5% in the preceding year.

The investment scenario was mixed. Stock investment was a fairly buoyant feature of the economy, especially in the first half of the year, although the indications for the final six months pointed to some loss of momentum. Fixed investments, on the other hand, were weaker than in 1986. Housing investments, in particular, were fairly sluggish when compared with the 9.4% hike in 1986, largely because of the upward trend of interest rates and the small gain in real disposable incomes. Fixed investment by business was also poor during the first half of 1987, declining to a level that was lower than at any time since 1983. One of the reasons for this (but by no means the whole explanation) appeared to have been the reaction to changes in tax allowances, an explanation that gained some credibility during the third quarter when business investment expenditures rose by a massive 23.7%, the fastest rate of increase for the three years. Nevertheless, the year as a whole was still estimated to have recorded a decrease, though perhaps not quite matching the fall of 1% in 1986.

The most spectacular departure from the previous year's experience, however, was in the area of foreign trade.

### Table I. Real Gross Domestic Products of Selected OECD Countries
% annual change

| Country | 1984 | 1985 | 1986 | 1987* |
|---|---|---|---|---|
| United States† | 6.4 | 2.7 | 2.5 | 2.5 |
| Japan† | 5.1 | 4.7 | 2.5 | 2.0 |
| West Germany† | 3.0 | 2.5 | 2.4 | 1.5 |
| France | 1.5 | 1.4 | 2.0 | 1.2 |
| United Kingdom | 3.0 | 3.5 | 2.7 | 3.2 |
| Canada | 5.5 | 4.0 | 3.1 | 2.2 |
| Italy | 2.8 | 2.3 | 2.7 | 3.0 |
| Total major countries | 5.0 | 3.0 | 2.5 | 2.2 |
| Australia | 7.0 | 5.1 | 1.4 | 2.5 |
| New Zealand | 4.2 | 0.7 | −0.6 | 0.2 |
| Austria | 2.0 | 3.0 | 1.7 | 0.8 |
| Belgium | 1.6 | 1.5 | 2.3 | 1.2 |
| Denmark | 3.5 | 4.2 | 3.4 | −0.8 |
| Finland | 2.8 | 3.0 | 1.8 | 2.8 |
| Greece | 2.8 | 2.1 | 1.3 | −1.0 |
| Iceland | 3.6 | 3.4 | 5.9 | 3.8 |
| Ireland† | 1.8 | 0.2 | −0.5 | 0.8 |
| Luxembourg | −4.8 | 2.9 | 2.0 | 2.5 |
| Netherlands, The | 2.4 | 1.7 | 1.9 | 1.2 |
| Norway | 5.7 | 5.4 | 3.8 | 2.8 |
| Portugal | −1.6 | 3.3 | 4.8 | 3.5 |
| Spain | 1.9 | 2.2 | 3.0 | 3.0 |
| Sweden | 4.0 | 2.2 | 1.3 | 1.8 |
| Switzerland | 1.7 | 4.0 | 2.8 | 1.8 |
| Turkey† | 5.9 | 5.1 | 8.0 | 6.5 |
| Total OECD countries | 4.7 | 3.0 | 2.5 | 2.2 |

*OECD projection.   †GNP.
Source: OECD *Economic Outlook*, June 1987.

Although by the third quarter there were some signs of weakening of exports, on the whole the volume of overseas sales during the year was estimated to have risen by some 12%. This represented a quantum leap over the 1986 gain of 5.7% and was largely the result of a substantial gain in competitiveness that occurred because of the fall in the external value of the dollar. The weaker dollar—together with a slowdown in the rise of private consumption—also helped to restrain the growth of imports, especially of manufactured products. The effect of this—despite an unexpectedly large increase in imports of oil products during the third quarter, attributed to precautionary buying in view of the tension in the Persian Gulf—was to produce a relatively small gain in total imports for the year, estimated at 3.5%, as against 13.5% in 1986.

Larger export deliveries and reduced import demand for non-oil products enabled domestic industry to boost output. Thus in sharp contrast to 1986, when industrial production was largely static, output rose rapidly throughout the year. One highly welcome effect of this was a steady fall in unemployment. At the end of 1986, 6.8% of the labour force was on the unemployment register; by the second quarter of 1987, the figure was down to 6.2%, and the expectation was for a further decrease to just below 6% by the end of the year.

The two main negative aspects of the economy in 1987 were the large budget and current account deficits and an acceleration in inflation. The inflation rate was subject to two powerful influences—a hardening in oil prices and the weakness of the dollar—and started rising quite fast early in the year. Thus consumer prices rose by 1.1% in the first quarter, 1.3% in the second, and 1.2% in the third. The indications were that the final quarter would see a further rise, giving an annual hike of some 4%, as against 2.2% in 1986.

Despite the broadly favourable trend in volume exports and imports, the country's external payments position saw no improvement. This was because, in terms of value, the steady depreciation of the dollar more than offset the benefits derived from the volume changes. Thus in the first quarter of the year, the trade deficit reached $38.3 billion, nearly 10% higher than in the same period of 1986. The second quarter saw a modest improvement, but this was not maintained in the third quarter, and the year-end indicators suggested that the trade deficit was approximately $145 billion for the whole of 1987, as against $147 billion for the preceding year. In terms of the current account of the balance of payments, the position was no better. The surplus of invisible transactions (which included tourism), adversely affected by the large overseas debt-servicing requirements, showed no significant improvement, with the result that the annual current account deficit totaled an estimated $150 billion, compared with $141 billion a year earlier.

Mainly because of the pressure on the dollar but also because of some concern over the trend of inflation, monetary policy was tightened during the year. The trend of interest rates was upward until November, with the prime rate rising gradually from 7.5% in December 1986 to 9% by October 1987. In early November, on the occasion of a small decline in West German interest rates in response to the stock market crash, leading U.S. banks cut their prime rate to 8.75%. This seemed to represent the end of the rising trend, especially as further cuts were announced in Europe in late November, and James Baker, the U.S. secretary of the treasury, made it clear that he was not prepared to raise interest rates and risk a recession in order to defend the dollar.

And yet the dollar certainly needed a little defending. From a trade-weighted index (compiled by the Bank of England) of 110.5 during the closing quarter of 1986, its value fell to 104.2 in January–March 1987. Despite the Louvre Accord (see *International Exchange and Payments,* below), there was a further weakening to 101.1 during the subsequent quarter. Some improvement took place late in the summer, but during the stock market crash the currency lost ground at a spectacular rate despite extensive support operations by the leading central banks. Thus the index stood at 102.4 at the start of October, but by the end of that month it was down to 98.5, and by the end of November there was a further slide to 95.8. The dollar was most vulnerable in terms of the Japanese yen and the Deutsche Mark; between the final quarter of 1986 and end-November 1987, its value against those currencies fell by 17 and 19%, respectively.

The administration's principal response to the collapse of equity prices was to institute, somewhat halfheartedly, a round of talks with Congress aimed at agreement on a substantial reduction in the budget deficit. By late Novem-

ber congressional negotiators and the president had hammered out an agreement to cut the deficit by $76 billion over two years. Although there was considerable opposition in Congress, on December 22 a reconciliation package received congressional approval and was signed by the president. For the 1988 fiscal year the cut was scheduled to be $30 billion (compared with the mandatory expenditure reduction of $23 billion provided for in the Gramm-Rudman legislation). With the passage of the bill, the deficit for fiscal 1988 was expected to reach $156 billion, only marginally in excess of the $148 billion for 1987.

*United Kingdom.* The year 1987 was one of solid achievement for the British economy. For the sixth year in succession gross domestic product (GDP) rose strongly, with the year-end estimates pointing to a growth of 4%, compared with one of 2.7% in 1986 and some 2.2% for the developed world (the OECD). At the same time, living standards rose rapidly, but the rate of inflation recorded only a marginal acceleration. The level of unemployment—although still high by OECD standards—experienced a sharp and welcome fall; government expenditure remained under control, and the public sector borrowing requirement (PSBR) was reduced sharply. The growth of both exports and imports accelerated, and foreign exchange reserves rose rapidly. However, despite the precarious state of the U.S. dollar, the trade-weighted external value of sterling weakened slightly. Another mildly negative aspect of the year was an increase in the current account deficit of the balance of payments, although at an estimated £1.8 billion (as against £1 billion in 1986), this was considerably smaller than had been predicted at the start of the year.

The only major adverse development was the collapse of equity values in October and early November in line with the crash in the world's stock markets. However, because of its strong underlying economic position, the U.K. appeared to be better able to cope with the consequences of the crash in terms of confidence and growth than were most other developed countries.

As encouraging as the strong overall growth rate was the fact that the advance was well spread among the principal sectors of the economy. As in the previous year, consumers' expenditure was a strong performer, fueled by a good increase in personal disposable incomes. This was largely the result of an 8% rise in average wages, compared with a 4% increase in prices, the effect of which was reinforced by the easy availability of credit. In fact, as the year progressed, there were growing fears that the rapid increase in lending could lead to excessive personal consumption, providing a further stimulus to the already strongly expanding imports as well as to inflation. As discussed later, such considerations persuaded the chancellor of the Exchequer to raise base rates by 1% to 10% in July, but it appeared at the year's end that the growth in consumer spending actually fell back from 6% in 1985 to about 5% in 1987.

One of the most cheerful facets of the British economy during 1987 was the upsurge in manufacturing output. Although the year started off relatively poorly, from the second quarter onward output grew rapidly, resulting in a gain of approximately 5% for the whole of 1987, compared with only 1% in the preceding year. The strength of output had a dramatic effect on the level of unemployment. Between December 1986 and September 1987 the seasonally adjusted number of unemployed workers fell from 3.1 million to 2.8 million. The last three months of the year were widely believed to have seen a corresponding improvement, with the result that the unemployment rate for the whole of 1987 was thought to have declined from 11.5 to about 10%. Encouragingly, the fall in unemployment

**Table II. Percentage Changes in Consumer Prices in Selected OECD Countries**

| Country | 1982 | 1983 | 1984 | 1985 | 1986 | 1987* |
|---|---|---|---|---|---|---|
| United States | 6.1 | 3.2 | 4.3 | 3.5 | 2.0 | 4.3 |
| Japan | 2.7 | 1.9 | 2.2 | 2.1 | 0.4 | 0.7 |
| West Germany | 5.3 | 3.3 | 2.4 | 2.2 | -0.2 | 0.8 |
| France | 11.8 | 9.6 | 7.4 | 5.8 | 2.7 | 3.5 |
| United Kingdom | 8.6 | 4.6 | 5.0 | 6.1 | 3.4 | 4.4 |
| Italy | 16.6 | 14.6 | 10.6 | 8.6 | 6.1 | 4.7 |
| Canada | 10.8 | 5.9 | 4.3 | 4.0 | 4.2 | 4.5 |
| Austria | 5.4 | 3.3 | 5.6 | 3.2 | 1.7 | 2.6 |
| Belgium | 8.7 | 7.7 | 6.3 | 4.9 | 1.3 | 2.3 |
| Denmark | 10.1 | 6.9 | 6.3 | 4.7 | 3.6 | 3.9 |
| Finland | 9.6 | 8.3 | 7.1 | 5.9 | 3.6 | 3.4 |
| Greece | 21.0 | 20.2 | 18.5 | 19.3 | 23.0 | 16.4 |
| Iceland | 49.1 | 86.5 | 30.9 | 31.9 | 22.2 | 20.2 |
| Ireland | 17.1 | 10.5 | 8.6 | 5.4 | 3.8 | 3.2 |
| Luxembourg† | 9.4 | 8.7 | 4.6 | 4.1 | 0.3 | 0.3 |
| Netherlands, The | 6.0 | 2.8 | 3.3 | 2.3 | 0.2 | 0.2 |
| Norway | 11.3 | 8.4 | 6.2 | 5.7 | 7.2 | 7.8 |
| Portugal | 22.4 | 25.5 | 29.3 | 19.3 | 11.7 | 9.4 |
| Spain | 14.4 | 12.2 | 11.3 | 8.8 | 8.8 | 4.6 |
| Sweden | 8.6 | 8.9 | 8.0 | 7.4 | 4.3 | 4.9 |
| Switzerland | 5.6 | 3.0 | 3.0 | 3.4 | 0.7 | 1.9 |
| Turkey | 32.7 | 28.8 | 45.6 | 45.0 | 34.5 | 38.9 |
| Australia | 11.1 | 10.1 | 3.9 | 6.8 | 9.1 | 9.3 |
| New Zealand | 7.8 | 7.4 | 6.2 | 15.4 | 13.2 | 18.9 |

*Twelve-month rate of change (not directly comparable with annual changes).
†From 1985, new index.
Sources: OECD, *Economic Outlook,* June 1987; OECD, *Main Economic Indicators,* October 1987.

took place against the background of an acceleration in the growth of labour productivity. Thus output per head in manufacturing rose by over 7% in the first half of the year, as against an improvement of only 3% in 1986. This was only marginally slower than the rise in average wages, with the result that, for the first time since 1982, unit labour costs recorded almost no increase.

This, together with favourable developments in other costs, enabled industry to maintain profit margins and still cut back the rate of growth in wholesale prices, down from 6.5% in 1986 to 4.5% in 1987. This, in turn, made it possible to restrain the rate of retail price inflation, which was estimated at 4% for the year, compared with 3.5% in 1986. However, while this was a considerably better performance than anticipated, it was still well in excess of the 3% average inflation rate for the developed world.

Partly because of industry's improvements in productivity and the relative buoyancy of the world economy, the volume of merchandise exports rose strongly—by 5.5%, as against 3.5% in 1986. Growth would have been even faster had it not been for a decline in oil output and exports. On the import side the consumer boom provided a strong stimulus, resulting in a volume gain of 7.5%, compared with 6.5% in the previous year. As expected, the current account deficit increased in 1987 from £1 billion to about £1.8 billion, but the extent of the increase was well below the pessimistic expectations at the start of 1987. The external value of sterling measured against that of a trade-weighted basket of the major currencies showed little change, with the appropriate index heading for an average of approximately 72.5, as compared with 72.9 in 1986. This, however, disguised a strong downward trend early in the year and a marked recovery from the spring onward, as well as a pronounced weakening against some continental currencies such as the Deutsche Mark and the Swiss franc and a spectacular strengthening against the beleaguered dollar. At the end of 1986, £1 sterling was valued at about $1.44, but the rate was well above this figure for most of the year, and by the end of December—following the crash of world stock markets—it was worth $1.88.

Pres. Ronald Reagan congratulates the new chairman of the Federal Reserve Board, Alan Greenspan. Greenspan, a Wall Street economist and former chairman of the Council of Economic Advisers, was expected to continue the policies established by the retiring Paul Volcker.
HOWARD SACHS—SYGMA

In terms of fiscal and monetary policy, the year was characterized by a gentle relaxation without in any way endangering the government's insistence on "sound money management," as well as its determination to keep inflation at about 4%. In fact, during 1987 the proceeds from the privatization of British Airways, Rolls-Royce Ltd., the British Airports Authority, and British Gas Corp., as well as the unexpectedly rapid growth in tax revenues resulting from the buoyancy of the economy, enabled the chancellor to pursue three normally contradictory objectives. Thus public expenditure constraints were relaxed slightly, taxes were reduced, and the need for deficit financing was cut. In the April budget the basic rate of income tax was reduced by 2% to 27%, and the various tax thresholds and allowances were increased. At the same time, the level of government expenditure benefited from an earlier decision to relax public spending limits, but—in spite of all this—the PSBR, targeted at £4 billion for the 1987–88 financial year, was heading for a figure of only £1 billion.

The underlying trend of interest rates was gently downward. The year opened with a base rate of 11%, but largely because of the strength of sterling and the absence of any major inflationary pressure, the rate was allowed to fall to 9% by June. It was at this point that the chancellor became concerned about the rapid growth of credit and forced the rate up unexpectedly to 10% in July. However, as a result of the world stock market crash, the base rate was cut to 9.5% in October and then 9% in November and 8.5% in early December. The hope was that this would help to stabilize the markets, but share prices continued to languish as investors around the world waited for action to cut the huge U.S. budget deficit. The other main objective of lowering interest rates was to provide a modest stimulus to consumer confidence, which was thought to have been adversely affected by the loss of apparent wealth as a result of the sharp fall in stock market values.

*Japan.* In 1987 the growth of the Japanese economy accelerated modestly in comparison with the preceding year. Although exports were sluggish as a result of the strength of the yen against the dollar, domestic demand—

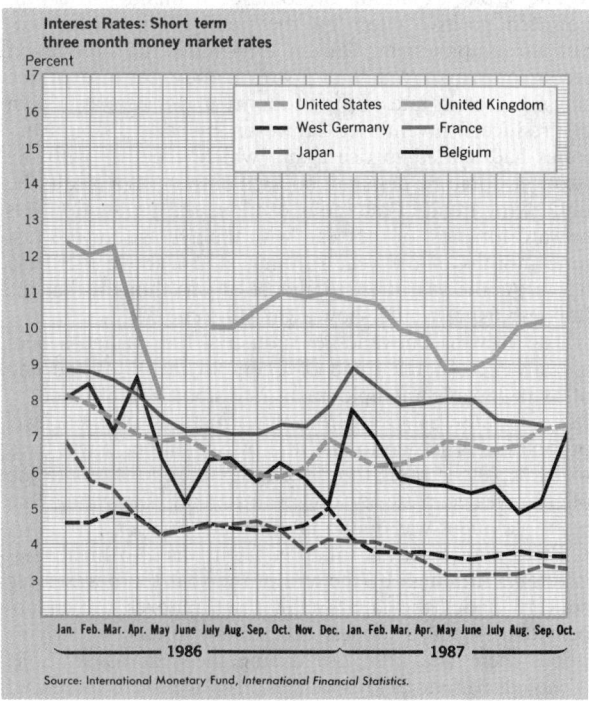

Interest Rates: Short term
three month money market rates
Percent

United States
West Germany
Japan
United Kingdom
France
Belgium

1986    1987

Source: International Monetary Fund, *International Financial Statistics.*

boosted by a series of demand-supporting measures—was strong. Industrial output, which fell in 1986, recorded a small gain, while unemployment—already low by international standards—declined modestly. The underlying rate of inflation appeared to have accelerated marginally but remained one of the lowest among OECD economies. The large trade and current account surplus—which, together with the U.S. deficit, was blamed for the collapse of world equity toward the end of the year—was reduced somewhat but remained at a high level.

Following a fairly indifferent GNP growth of 0.7% in the closing quarter of 1986, the first three months of the year posted a gain of 1.3%. Nevertheless, the government remained under considerable pressure from both business at home and the international community to provide an additional boost to the economy. In contrast to 1986, the authorities acted fairly decisively and announced a 6.5 billion yen business-boosting package in May. This consisted mainly of increased spending on public works programs for the 1987–88 fiscal year, additional public spending, and some tax reductions aimed at strengthening domestic demand at a time when the high international value of the yen was exerting an adverse effect on exports. The need for this package was amply demonstrated a few months later when the GNP figures for the second quarter were announced. These showed that although the volume of domestic demand rose by 4.8%, a fall in exports of goods and services (combined with a rapid rise in imports) offset all the domestic buoyancy. In GNP terms, therefore, the second quarter yielded no increase. The available indicators for the second half of the year, however, suggested a more positive result, mainly because domestic demand was expected to gain further momentum as the cumulative effect of the May business-boosting package came into play. All in all, therefore, it was estimated that for the year as a whole, GNP gained 3%. This was regarded as a fairly satisfactory increase because it represented an acceleration

from the 2.5% growth achieved in 1986 and was broadly in line with the government's original expectations. It was also better than the average growth for all OECD countries, estimated at 2.2%.

As already indicated, the mainstay of the year's growth was domestic demand. Consumer expenditure, although subject to a number of conflicting influences, was estimated to have risen by 3.5%, as against 2.7% in the previous year. On the negative side were the small wage awards secured in the traditional spring wage-bargaining round and the relatively modest summer bonuses. The effects of these factors, however, were more than offset by lower taxation, easy credit, and a strong demand for consumer durables consequent on a fast growth in residential investments. Housing starts were gaining momentum throughout most of the year, and the final figure for private house-building expenditure was expected to show a 12% gain, as against 10% in 1986. The principal reason for this was the easy availability of housing credit and the confidence-boosting effect of the sharp rise in equity prices until October.

Public investment was also buoyant, largely because of the government's enlarged and accelerated spending programs. Private plant and equipment investments, however, proved to be something of a disappointment. The year started off fairly poorly, largely because of industry's caution over such investments in view of the effect of the strong currency on exports. However, thanks to the introduction of the demand-boosting measures referred to above and the steady improvement in corporate profitability, confidence strengthened in the second half, with most of the advance indicators—machinery orders, industrial construction, investment intention surveys—signaling a significantly better performance during the July–December period. As the year drew to an end, there was some concern about the effect of the stock market crash on confidence, but the indications were that this would not necessarily be significant and, in any event, would not affect investment until well into 1988. The estimate, therefore, was for a gain in private plant and equipment investment of about 4% in 1987, smaller than the increase of 6.5% in 1986 but significantly greater than seemed possible at the start of the year.

The strong expansion of domestic demand had a pronounced positive effect on the trend of industrial output and employment. During 1986 industrial production recorded a modest fall of 0.4%, mainly because of the sluggish growth rate of the economy and a running down of producers' inventories. However, by early 1987 inventories had started to rise again, which, together with the stronger domestic demand, boosted output. As a result, the underlying trend of the index of industrial production was upward for most of the year, with the average for the first nine months of the year running at 2% above the 1986 figure. As the year drew to a close, it was thought that the full-year figure would show a gain of some 3%.

The growing buoyancy of industrial output had a beneficial effect on the trend of unemployment. At the end of 1986 Japan's unemployment rate stood at 2.8%, and by May the rate was 3.2%. From that time, however, the level of joblessness started to fall, and by September it was back to 2.8%. At the same time, the index of job seekers to job offers revealed a steady downward trend, suggesting that unemployment was due to fall further.

Performance on the inflation front was also highly satisfactory. Although by the end of the year there was some concern about the latest retail price indexes, which appeared to signal a modest acceleration in the underlying trend, there was little rise during the year as a whole. Although commodity (especially oil) prices were somewhat

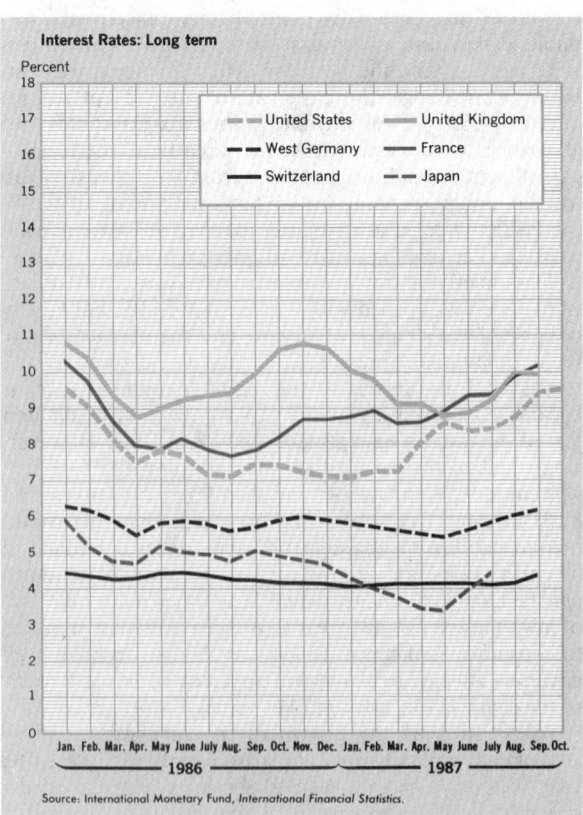

**Interest Rates: Long term**

Percent

Legend:
- United States
- United Kingdom
- West Germany
- France
- Switzerland
- Japan

Jan. Feb. Mar. Apr. May June July Aug. Sep. Oct. Nov. Dec. Jan. Feb. Mar. Apr. May June July Aug. Sep. Oct.
—— 1986 —— —— 1987 ——

Source: International Monetary Fund, International Financial Statistics.

higher than in 1986, the effect of this was offset by the rise in the value of the currency, which made imports cheaper. As a result, the index of retail prices for the first nine months of the year was only 0.2% higher than for the previous year. Given the further rapid rise in the value of the yen in late 1987 in the wake of the stock market upheaval, the year was likely to end with a retail price increase of not more than 0.5%—not an unduly high price to pay for an acceleration of economic growth and a significant boost to domestic demand.

As already indicated, the currency was appreciating for most of the year under review. In the final quarter of 1986 the rate against the dollar was 160 yen, but by the second quarter of 1987 it was up to 148 yen. There followed a period of relative stability, but by the end of September the rate had appreciated further to 146.5 yen. The world stock market crisis further weakened the U.S. currency, and by late December one dollar was worth only 121 yen.

One result of the strong yen was to make exports more expensive in dollar terms and imports cheaper in terms of domestic currency. This resulted in a decline in export volume and a continued increase in the volume of imports. On the basis of partial statistics it was estimated that the volume of merchandise exports fell by about 1%, as against a decline of 2% in 1986. At the same time, imports recorded a major slowdown in growth, from 12% in 1986 to 5% in 1987. In dollar terms the effect of this was to make possible a small reduction in the current account surplus; at the end of 1987 this seemed to be heading for a total of $76 billion, as against $84 billion in the preceding year. Thus, although Japan continued to maintain a large surplus that contributed heavily to international financial instability, the government could at least argue that it was moving in the right direction.

*West Germany.* West Germany's economic performance during 1987 was a major, and largely unexpected, disappointment. There was a marked deceleration in the growth of GDP; the large current account balance became larger; unemployment was thought to have risen; and there was a widespread feeling that the government had no clear strategy to deal with what was an increasingly unfavourable situation. It was against this background that the worldwide collapse of equity prices hit the country's stock market in October–November. This persuaded the authorities to reduce interest rates somewhat after nearly three weeks of relative inaction—a move that was seen as too little and too late and also as symptomatic of the government's longstanding reluctance to provide the required stimulus to the economy. Therefore, as the year neared its end there was not only considerable dissatisfaction with the country's economic performance during 1987 but also increasing uncertainty about the prospects for 1988.

At the end of 1987 the available data, supplemented by some estimates, suggested that GNP for the 12 months to December grew by only 1.5%. Not only was it the weakest performance since 1982 (when GNP recorded an actual fall) but it was significantly below the earlier official expectations, which had suggested that 1987 would match the rather indifferent gain of 2.5% recorded in 1986. It was also, for the sixth year in succession, lower than the average growth of all OECD countries (estimated at approximately 2.2%). In comparison with the preceding year, virtually every area of aggregate demand became weaker, but the real villain of the piece was fixed investment. Earlier expectations had been that growth in this area would exceed the 3.3% gain recorded in 1986, but the 1987 increase was estimated to have been only 0.5%.

Although this was partly the result of the unusually severe winter, which had a highly adverse effect on construction during the first quarter, there were other important factors at work. These included a general lack of confidence in the government's willingness or ability to stimulate economic growth as well as exchange rate uncertainties that had a particularly pronounced effect on the investment plans of export-related industries.

The reluctance of such industries to invest was understandable in view of the fact that overseas sales were sluggish. Principally because of the rapid rise in the external value of the Deutsche Mark, the volume of merchandise exports appeared to have grown by about 1.5%, compared with 1.2% in 1986. At the same time, merchandise imports showed little change; growth was about 5.5%, compared with 6% in the previous year. Overseas transactions, therefore, exerted a powerful negative influence on the rate of domestic growth, and it was only the relatively strong performance of consumer expenditure—together with some acceleration in the rise of public consumption—that made it possible for GNP to record an increase at all.

However, even the growth of private consumption was sluggish compared with 1986. During that year consumption registered a fairly rapid rise of 4.2%. The year 1987, however, opened on a very weak note and, although this was partly explained by vehicle purchases being brought forward into the final quarter of 1986 to take advantage of tax allowances, the latest available evidence pointed to an annual gain of only 2.5%. The indications were that consumers were growing increasingly cautious for a number of reasons. The most important of these was a fairly small increase of about 2.5% in earnings, which—even with near-zero inflation—represented a disappointing rise in purchasing power once the effects of social security contributions and taxes were taken into account.

The consumption climate appeared to have taken a further knock during the last few months of the year as a result of the collapse of stock values. The resulting reduction in nominal wealth was widely expected to lead to the downward revision of expenditure plans. In spite of this, the government refused to yield to pressure to put into effect earlier the tax cuts planned for 1988 as part of the tax reform announced in 1986. Given that the modest increase in wages and the strength of the Deutsche Mark ensured that there were no inflationary pressures to speak of, the reluctance of the authorities to stimulate demand was all the more difficult to understand. One result of this refusal to boost business was an adverse change in the underlying trend of unemployment. Between 1985 and 1986 this underwent an encouraging reduction from 8.3 to 8%, but the latest forecasts suggested that there would be little improvement in 1987.

On the external front the two principal features of the year under review were the failure to do anything about

**Table III. Standardized Unemployment Rates in Selected OECD Countries**

% of total labour force, seasonally adjusted

| Country | 1982 | 1983 | 1984 | 1985 | 1986 | 1987* |
|---------|------|------|------|------|------|-------|
| Canada | 10.9 | 11.8 | 11.3 | 10.5 | 9.6 | 9.2 |
| United States | 9.5 | 9.5 | 7.5 | 7.2 | 7.0 | 6.8 |
| Japan | 2.4 | 2.6 | 2.7 | 2.6 | 2.8 | 3.0 |
| Australia | 7.1 | 9.9 | 8.8 | 8.1 | 8.0 | 8.0 |
| France | 8.1 | 8.3 | 10.0 | 10.2 | 10.5 | 11.2 |
| West Germany | 6.1 | 8.0 | 8.2 | 8.3 | 8.0 | 8.0 |
| Italy | 9.0 | 9.8 | 9.8 | 10.1 | 10.9 | 11.2 |
| Sweden | 3.1 | 3.5 | 2.5 | 2.3 | 2.2 | 2.2 |
| United Kingdom | 11.4 | 12.6 | 11.5 | 11.7 | 11.8 | 11.2 |

*Partially estimated.
Source: OECD, *Economic Outlook*, June 1987.

the country's large balance of payments deficit and the relentless rise in the external value of the currency. Although the volume of exports experienced an actual reduction and the rate of import growth accelerated, the current account surplus was expected to show only a relatively modest reduction from $42 billion in 1986 to around $37 billion. Combined with the huge deficit maintained by the U.S. and the reluctance of the West German government to boost domestic growth and effect a substantial cut in interest rates, this resulted in a rapid rise in the value of the Deutsche Mark. In the final quarter of 1986 the dollar/Deutsche Mark rate was DM 2.008; by the second quarter it was DM 1.805; by early October it stood at about DM 1.850; and by late December—partly because of the effect of the stock market crash on U.S. currency—the rate had fallen to around DM 1.57.

The West German government's reluctance to promote growth and the small reductions in its current account surplus gave rise to considerable criticism of its economic policy and its obsession with inflation when there were no apparent inflationary pressures. However, the West German authorities argued that—despite the U.S.'s failure to take the necessary steps to cut its deficit—they had played their part in reducing international financial pressures by supporting the dollar and by maintaining a relaxed monetary policy. In January 1987 the Bundesbank lowered its discount rate from 3.5 to 3% and the Lombard rate from 5.5 to 5%. However, despite domestic and external pressures, it set its face against further reductions until the October–November stock market crisis—in fact, in early October it allowed some rates to rise, which angered the U.S. secretary of the treasury. But in early November—some three weeks after the start of the stock market crisis—it was persuaded to cut the Lombard rate from 5 to 4.5% and to reduce the repurchase rate (the rate at which the Bundesbank will lend to the domestic money market) from 3.8 to 3.5%. In late November, after the agreement on the U.S. budget reduction package (see *United States,* above), the repurchase rate was cut further to 3.25%.

*France.* Like West Germany, France turned in a fairly disappointing economic performance during 1987. Despite a serious slowdown in the growth of GDP, inflation accelerated and the balance of payments deteriorated markedly. The currency remained vulnerable against most major currencies except the ailing dollar. Industrial production, on the basis of partial data, experienced a relatively small rise, with the result that the level of unemployment continued to rise, probably faster than in 1986. In regard to fiscal policy the position also became less favourable, with increases in social security contributions that were necessary to finance the growing deficit in the social budget offsetting much of the previously announced tax reduction. Given the already precarious state of the economy, the shock of the world stock market crash was thought to have had a particularly serious effect during the closing months of the year.

In general terms 1987 opened on a distinctly unpromising note. GDP was stagnant in the first quarter and, although there was a 0.8% gain during the next three months, the latest available evidence suggested that the advance for the year was unlikely to exceed 1.7%. This compared with a growth of 2.2% in 1986 and an estimated overall improvement of 2.2% for the OECD area as a whole. The slowdown in overall growth was reflected in every principal sector of demand. Consumer expenditure, which was one of the mainstays of growth in 1986, was adversely affected by a combination of smaller wage increases and an acceleration of inflation. Thus average earnings were provisionally calculated to have risen by just over 3.7%,

only marginally faster than the rate of consumer price inflation. Consequently, there was little or no increase in purchasing power. As a result, consumer expenditures, which accounted for over 60% of domestic demand, rose by only about 1.5%, as compared with an increase of 3.1% in 1986.

Even more disappointing was the trend of fixed investment. Although there were some indications that the previous year's rapid decline in residential investment activities was flattening out as 1987 unfolded, business investments were estimated to have fallen by nearly one-third from the growth rate of 4.2% chalked up in the previous year. This was all the more disappointing because the early business intentions surveys—together with an improvement in corporate profitability—had given rise to hopes of a substantially better outcome for 1987. The reasons for the slowdown were something of a mystery—the uncertain international climate and the unexpected failure to cut interest rates largely because of the weakness of the currency in the EMS were two possible reasons—but the net effect was a slowdown in the growth of total investment expenditures to less than 3% in 1987. Government consumption—the third major component of domestic demand—also registered a comparatively sluggish growth; because of the need to cut the deficit while reducing both personal and business taxes, this was estimated to have declined from 3.5% to between 2 and 2.5% in 1987.

The consequence of the above developments was the virtual halving of domestic demand, from 4 to about 2%. Normally, in circumstances such as these the external payments situation tends to improve because weak domestic demand tends to moderate import growth and provides a greater incentive to manufacturers to make up for the weakness of home markets by promoting sales abroad. A weak currency serves to reinforce these forces by making imports more expensive in terms of domestic currency and exports cheaper in the currencies of the purchasing countries. During 1987 the French economy conformed to this pattern, although the relative turnaround in exports

### Table IV. Changes in Output in the Less Developed Countries, 1982–86

In %

| Area | Annual average 1969–78 | Change from preceding year | | | | |
| | | 1982 | 1983 | 1984 | 1985 | 1986 |
| --- | --- | --- | --- | --- | --- | --- |
| All less developed countries | 6.1 | 1.6 | 1.4 | 4.1 | 3.2 | 3.5 |
| Oil-exporting countries | 7.8 | −0.2 | −1.9 | 1.3 | −0.3 | −0.7 |
| Non-oil less developed countries | 5.4 | 2.5 | 3.1 | 5.5 | 4.6 | 5.4 |
| Africa | 5.1 | 0.8 | −1.9 | −1.7 | 2.0 | 1.6 |
| Asia | 5.8 | 5.0 | 7.6 | 7.9 | 5.9 | 5.7 |
| Europe | 6.0 | 2.4 | 1.1 | 3.6 | 2.1 | 3.2 |
| Middle East | 8.2 | −0.2 | 0.2 | 0.9 | −1.0 | — |
| Western Hemisphere | 5.8 | −1.0 | −3.0 | 3.2 | 3.5 | 4.0 |

Source: International Monetary Fund, *World Economic Outlook,* 1987.

### Table V. Changes in Consumer Prices in the Less Developed Countries, 1982–86

In %

| Area | Annual average 1969–78 | Change from preceding year | | | | |
| | | 1982 | 1983 | 1984 | 1985 | 1986 |
| --- | --- | --- | --- | --- | --- | --- |
| All less developed countries | 16.7 | 25.0 | 34.0 | 39.4 | 40.6 | 28.6 |
| Oil-exporting countries | 11.3 | 17.6 | 25.0 | 19.8 | 13.4 | 19.4 |
| Non-oil less developed countries | 19.0 | 28.8 | 38.9 | 50.4 | 55.9 | 33.1 |
| Africa | 11.6 | 11.4 | 19.5 | 20.3 | 12.8 | 14.8 |
| Asia | 8.7 | 6.3 | 6.6 | 7.2 | 7.4 | 5.9 |
| Europe | 11.7 | 23.7 | 23.1 | 28.0 | 28.6 | 27.4 |
| Middle East | 10.8 | 12.7 | 12.3 | 14.9 | 12.2 | 11.1 |
| Western Hemisphere | 31.0 | 68.4 | 106.3 | 129.3 | 150.3 | 86.5 |

Source: International Monetary Fund, *World Economic Outlook,* 1987.

In early October panel members of British Petroleum's (BP's) pathfinder prospectus launch finalize the largest share offering ever, a secondary share sale offering of £7.2 billion. The government's privatization of BP failed to meet expectations because of the depressed state of world markets.

DOD MILLER—CAMERA PRESS/PHOTO TRENDS

...dson ...mited    Rt. Hon. Norman Lamont, M.P.    Peter Cazalet *British Petroleum Company p.l.c.*    David Simon *British Petroleum Company p.l.c.*

and imports appeared to be less pronounced than expected. Imports lost some of their earlier buoyancy, with growth for 1987 estimated at 6%, compared with 7.5% a year earlier. The acceleration in export growth was more modest—from zero to approximately 1%. Therefore, the external sector continued to act as a brake on growth, although the negative impact of all external trade transactions was thought to have been cut from 1.5 to 1%.

In spite of this modestly encouraging performance, the external payments position deteriorated significantly. This was partly because the growth of imports continued to exceed that of exports and because there was modest deterioration in the terms of trade (export prices relative to those of imports). During the first half of 1987 the trade deficit reached F 19.6 billion, as against F 2.5 billion in the same period of the previous year; the final estimates suggested a full-year figure of F 35 billion, nearly ten times larger than that of a year earlier. The growth in net invisible exports was not expected to offset more than a fraction of the deterioration in the trade balance, with the result that the current account was heading for a deficit of $2 billion–$2.5 billion, as against a surplus of $3.8 billion in 1986. As already indicated, during the year the value of the franc against the dollar improved (F 6.01 in the final quarter of 1986 to F 5.32 at the end of December 1987), but against the EMS currencies there was a deterioration. For this reason the expected downward trend in interest rates failed to materialize; on the contrary, rates tended to harden for most of the year and, even after the world stock market crash, when most European countries reacted by a cut in rates, France raised its money market intervention rate from 7.5 to 8.25% in order to lessen pressure on the currency within the EMS. There was, however, a 0.25% reduction in the Bank of France's intervention rate in late November as part of the revision of EMS rates in response to the U.S. deficit-reducing package.

**Less Developed Countries.** In 1986 the economies of the less developed world achieved a GDP gain of 4.2%, as compared with 4.8% in the preceding 12 months. On the basis of incomplete and preliminary statistics, it was estimated that 1987 did not match the growth rate of the previous year; overall GDP gain was put at just above 3.5%, the weakest performance in four years. The most important single reason for the year's disappointing achievement was the slowdown in economic growth in the developed world from 3 to 2.2%. One consequence of this was a weakening in the export demand of the developed countries, which

had an adverse effect on the growth of exports by the less developed economies. On the basis of limited information available at the end of the year, it was estimated that exports of the less developed countries grew by only 5% in 1987, as compared with 6% in 1986. Because exports accounted for about 20% of the total GDP, a slowdown of this magnitude in overseas sales represented a significant weakening of aggregate demand. Also, largely because of fiscal and balance of payments constraints, this decline could not be fully offset by extra domestic stimulus in more than a few countries.

However, some improvement seemed to have taken place in 1987 in the less developed countries' terms of trade. These are governed by world supply and demand conditions and by the movement in currency rates, which had been fairly unfavourable to the less developed countries for several years. Thus, according to the World Bank, prices of exports from the less developed countries fell steadily between 1982 and 1986, yielding an average annual decline of 2.8%. In 1987, however, there was a recovery in the prices of most commodities; those of minerals and metals rose quite rapidly, and agricultural raw material prices also recorded some increase. All in all, it was estimated that industrial raw material prices recorded a rise of 8–10%, although the positive impact of this on the less developed world was blunted by a fall in food prices. Nevertheless, export prices in total probably became stronger in 1987, while those of imports, especially of manufactures, were not believed to have registered a significant increase.

Nevertheless, despite the improvement in the terms of trade, the evidence indicated that, except for the oil producers, the less developed countries faced a further deterioration in their international payments positions. Oil-producing nations appeared to have cut their current account deficit of $30 billion chalked up in 1986 quite substantially because of the partial recovery of oil prices (although the effect of this was greatly reduced by a fall in the volume of oil sales) and by a substantial cutback in their imports. The reduction of imports was, in the main, the delayed effect of the oil-price collapse in 1986 and—according to some estimates—resulted in a decline of 15–17% in the volume of oil producers' imports.

By contrast, non-oil producers faced only a relatively modest slowdown in export growth, from 6% in 1986 to 5% in 1987, largely in response to a weakening of economic growth in the developed countries. Imports also appeared to have grown less rapidly than in 1986—perhaps by 7.5%, as compared with 9%—but, despite the modest improvement in the terms of trade, the combined current account deficit of the non-oil producers was provisionally estimated to have risen from $15 billion to $20 billion. A significant part of the total deficit (and the increase in 1987) was due to the difficulties experienced by Latin-American countries in maintaining export volumes, leading to an estimated increase in their deficit from $8 billion to $12 billion. African economies also faced a (largely unchanged) deficit of $5 billion–$6 billion, but Asia's less developed economies (including some fast-growing industrial exporters such as South Korea, Taiwan, and Singapore) were thought to have achieved a surplus of $5 billion.

During 1986, the last full year for which complete figures were available, economic performance varied widely from country to country, and some of these differences were thought to have been perpetuated in 1987. In 1986 the fastest GDP growth was achieved by exporters of manufactured goods. These, including such relatively prosperous nations as Singapore and South Korea, achieved a growth rate of 7% in the wake of a 7.8% gain in 1985. The second fastest increase, of 6.5%, was recorded by the 37 low-income countries. This group included China and India and most of Africa. Growth rates varied markedly from country to country; India and a number of Asian countries did relatively well, but sub-Saharan Africa increased only 0.5%. The feature common to most countries within the low-income group was the serious deceleration of growth after the rapid increase of 9.1% in 1985. Oil-exporting countries recorded a drop of 1% in GDP as the collapse of oil prices led to an enforced cutback in domestic demand; the evidence in late 1987 was that, while there was an improvement, GNP gain remained below 1%.

In 1986 per capita income growth for the less developed world was 2.5%, which brought income per head to $625, as compared with $12,000 for the developed world. Within the less developed bloc, income levels varied markedly. For low-income countries per capita income was $282, only some 5% higher than in 1980. By contrast, high-income countries such as Brazil, Uruguay, Singapore, and South Korea produced an average of $1,876, representing an increase of 20% since 1980.

As discussed elsewhere, the debt problem of most less developed countries had become more acute in recent years despite a wide variety of (often reluctant) steps by lending countries to ease the debt servicing and repayment burden and to extend new lines of credit. In 1987, for example, the World Bank agreed on a special $4 billion package for 14 African countries, many of which showed very little growth during the year. At the same time, Nigeria, which was thought to have seen a fall in GNP, agreed to a $4,260,000,000 rescheduling plan as well as a new credit facility of $320 million. These and a number of other similar schemes, however, were widely recognized as palliatives rather than as contributions to a structural improvement in less developed countries. The magnitude of the problem was well illustrated by the fact that in 1986 the ratio of debt to GNP in the less developed world was over 35%, a figure that was thought to have increased in 1987. In absolute terms total debt was a staggering $753 billion, which gave rise to a servicing burden that accounted for 5.5% of total GNP, as compared with only 3.7% at the start of the decade.

**Centrally Planned Economies.** The 43rd extraordinary session of the Council for Mutual Economic Assistance (CMEA, or Comecon) was held in Moscow on Oct. 13–14, 1987. The session was attended by the heads of government of Bulgaria, Hungary, East Germany, Mongolia, Poland, Romania, the Soviet Union, and Czechoslovakia, the first deputy prime minister of Vietnam, and the vice-president of the Council of State and the Council of Ministers of Cuba.

Soviet Premier Nikolay Ryzhkov presided over the session. The main subject of the debate was the proposal that the Comecon integration mechanism be "restructured." Although the meeting was the usual annual event, it was announced as being extraordinary to indicate that it was designed to approve measures that would bring about a decisive break with previous practices.

Ryzhkov stated in his opening speech that a restructured Comecon would make cooperation between member nations an economically attractive option. In this way member countries would voluntarily intensify and deepen the process of integration. This would yield, according to Ryzhkov, "a real gain, not only to the Soviet Union, but also to other Comecon countries."

This new Soviet attitude met with varied reactions from the delegates. The Czechoslovak premier, Lubomir Strougal, said at the end of the meeting that the session had resulted in "certain compromises" that were not fully satisfactory. Strougal expressed the hope that member nations would "reach agreement when working out concrete measures in the coming year." Hungarian Prime Minister Karoly Grosz said that although restructuring would result in some new measures, it was not certain whether these would improve conditions of cooperation.

The restructuring of the Comecon institutions was closely connected with the new economic policy of the Soviet Union introduced by the new Soviet leader, Mikhail Gorbachev. It envisioned the strengthening of central planning in regard to strategic and macroeconomic issues. At the same time, it aimed to reduce the scope of direct supervision and intervention by the central planning authority at the level of a business enterprise. It also proposed to substitute administrative supervision by indirect control through greater reliance on markets.

The restructuring of Comecon also aimed at streamlining its institutions and organizations. The Moscow-based secretariat of Comecon was likely to be substantially reduced in size. The central command system was being reshaped but not weakened or abolished. Many national enterprises were to be granted foreign trade rights, which were traditionally the prerogative of the national ministries of foreign trade.

Ryzhkov stated that all delegates agreed that Comecon should concentrate on those key economic problems that required intergovernmental cooperation. It should prepare large-scale agreements and programs. Specific matters should be resolved directly between industrial and commercial enterprises.

During the meeting the reform of the financial system was also discussed. Grosz pointed out the need to introduce currency convertibility. Most Comecon governments

**Table VI. Balances of Payments on Current Account, 1982–86**

In $000,000,000

| Area | 1982 | 1983 | 1984 | 1985 | 1986 |
|---|---|---|---|---|---|
| All less developed countries | −87.3 | −63.8 | −34.2 | −23.8 | −47.6 |
| Oil-exporting countries | −18.2 | −18.7 | −5.4 | 2.6 | −35.7 |
| Non-oil less developed countries | −69.1 | −45.1 | −28.8 | −26.5 | −11.9 |
| Africa | −21.7 | −12.5 | −7.4 | −0.3 | −7.0 |
| Asia | −17.5 | −15.4 | −4.2 | −12.9 | 2.1 |
| Europe | −8.6 | −5.7 | −3.5 | −3.2 | −1.7 |
| Middle East | 2.9 | −19.3 | −16.4 | −2.6 | −24.9 |
| Western Hemisphere | −42.4 | −10.9 | −2.6 | −4.7 | −16.1 |

Source: International Monetary Fund, *World Economic Outlook*, 1987.

supported a long-term program of transition to convertibility, but the implementation of such a program would take at least 10 to 15 years. As of 1987 all foreign transactions within Comecon were conducted in the collective unit called the transferable ruble. This, however, was an accounting device and not a medium for currency convertibility. In order to achieve true convertibility, member nations would probably have to permit greater flexibility in price formation.

The question of convertibility was seen in different ways by the countries of Comecon. Romania publicly rejected the idea of ruble convertibility and stressed that the main problem for Comecon was to widen cooperation in the field of fuels, energy, and raw materials. Czechoslovakia, on the other hand, insisted that it was necessary to have full convertibility in five to seven years. The current transferable ruble did not serve the expansion of foreign trade because it did not reflect real costs of production or the real cost of products.

The council session approved the agreement on economic cooperation between Comecon and Afghanistan. The final communiqué also stressed the need for expanding cooperation with Western countries and for the establishment of official relations between Comecon and the European Communities as well as between member countries of Comecon and the EC.

On October 7 exploratory talks began in Brussels between a group of Soviet officials and members of the European Parliament. The aim of these talks was to establish formal links between Comecon and the EC. This was in accordance with the new Soviet policy that stressed the need for the U.S.S.R. to become more integrated into the international trade system and thus to gain better access to Western markets and Western technology.

The EC was already negotiating trade agreements and economic cooperation with Hungary and Czechoslovakia. Exploratory talks were also held with Poland and Bulgaria. It seemed that Romania and Hungary were ready to conclude separate bilateral agreements with the EC, even if there was no agreement between Comecon and the EC.

There were of course both political and economic obstacles that would have to be resolved before formal links between Comecon and the EC could be established. For example, Comecon differed from the EC because it had no responsibility for the trade policies of its members. Therefore, the EC would have to negotiate trade and economic concessions with individual Comecon countries. Another difficulty, of a political nature, was the EC's insistence that all Comecon countries had to accept the status of West Berlin as an integral part of the EC. The Soviet Union was not ready to accept such a condition.

At the end of the 43rd Comecon session, some political questions were discussed. All the member nations welcomed the Soviet-U.S. accord on the reduction of intermediate-range nuclear forces and declared that the tension in international relations was a major obstacle on the path of the normal development of the world economy. Science and technology, stated the final communiqué, might be used throughout the whole world exclusively for solving urgent economic and social problems.

## INTERNATIONAL TRADE

The evidence available at the end of 1987 suggested that world trade had decelerated significantly during the year. Although the final outcome would not be known before well into 1988, the latest estimates suggested a volume growth of only 3–3.5%, as against 4.7% in 1986. The slowdown was largely the result of the deceleration of economic growth in the developed world; the adverse effect of the fall in oil prices during 1986, which undermined the import capacity of oil producers; and the rapid fall in the value of the dollar, which caused a decline in the volume of U.S. purchases. OECD imports in total were estimated to have grown by only about 4.5%, as against 8% in 1986, while those of the oil producers—despite a modest recovery of oil prices from the low levels of 1986—probably fell by 16%. Non-oil less developed countries, on the other hand, saw an improvement in the prices of their commodities in both 1986 and 1987, but the early figures suggested an import growth of only 5%, as against 10% in 1986.

(continued on page 173)

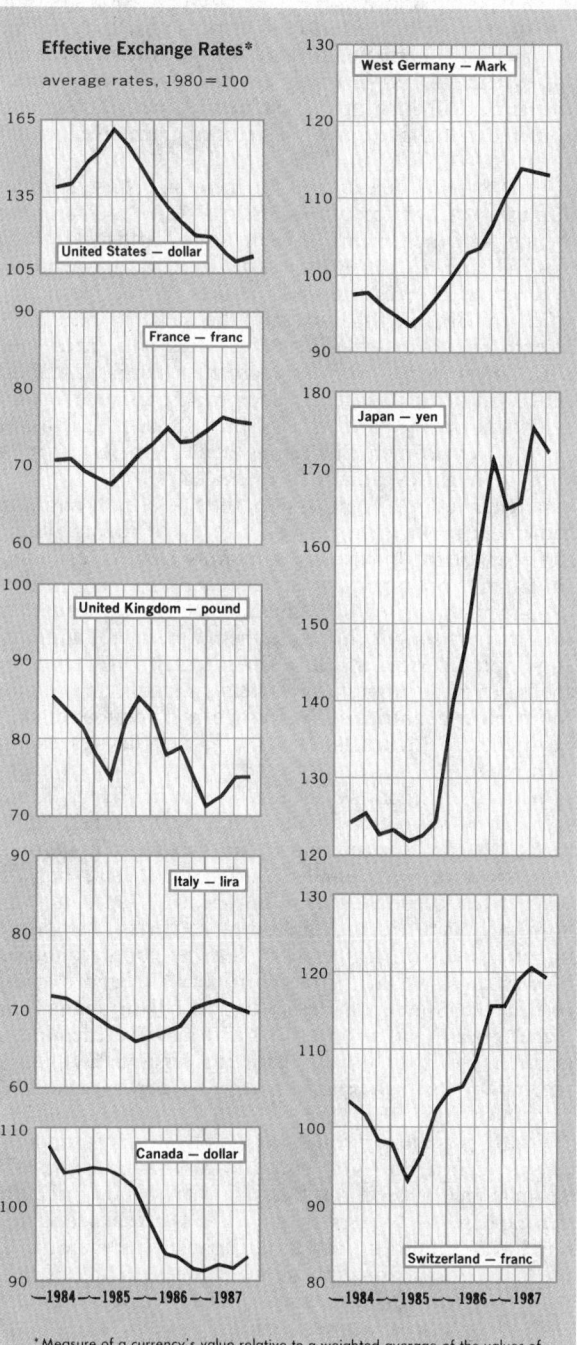

**Effective Exchange Rates***

average rates, 1980 = 100

United States — dollar

France — franc

United Kingdom — pound

Italy — lira

Canada — dollar

West Germany — Mark

Japan — yen

Switzerland — franc

—1984—1985—1986—1987

*Measure of a currency's value relative to a weighted average of the values of the currencies of the country's principal trading partners.

Source: International Monetary Fund, *International Financial Statistics.*

# The Rising Tide of Protectionism

## BY GRAHAM SEARJEANT

In the post-World War II era, the Western world's trading system brought 25 years of improving prosperity, led by growth in international trade. By the 1980s, however, this system had come under attack on two fronts: from threats of deliberate protection to keep out imports and from individual measures that eroded trade freedom bit by bit.

As U.S. trade deficits and Japanese and West German surpluses reached record heights, pledges to maintain the principles of the General Agreement on Tariffs and Trade (GATT) and to resist protection were heard regularly at meetings of Western world leaders. Harder economic times would make the threat and the warnings even more urgent. The threat was identified with bills before the U.S. Congress that would impose high tariffs or import quotas on a wide range of goods or discriminate against individual trading partners. U.S. Pres. Ronald Reagan had pledged to veto such bills before they became law, but he knew he might eventually be overruled.

**Barriers to Free Trade.** As yet, the tide of protectionism had rarely broken through, but the open trading system had been eroded by various "nontariff" barriers, including quota limits on imports, voluntary export restraints agreed to under threat of something worse, and misuse of antidumping actions. Added to these were such traditional anti-import devices as bureaucratic delay, high taxes on goods not made domestically, safety standards, and testing. All member countries of the European Communities (EC) free-trade zone, for instance, still used such devices against each other.

With rare exceptions, such as free-trading Hong Kong, each nation was both perpetrator and victim of these "dirty tricks." Japan was notorious for bureaucratic barriers. Many had been dismantled during the 1980s, but the practice had been taken up in Europe, with Japanese firms now the main victims. Industrial countries maintained import quotas on textiles from less developed countries. Studies suggested that protection in textiles and clothing cost U.S. consumers alone up to $18 billion annually in higher prices. Quotas on textiles and cars also encouraged exporters to switch from basic to high-quality goods, preempting the high-wage importing country's best answer to competition.

GATT signatories could tax goods dumped suddenly outside their normal markets below cost—such as the EC's irregular sale of food surpluses far below world prices, at the expense of farmers in the U.S., Australia, and less developed countries. But this loophole was increasingly used simply to stop competition. Between 1970 and 1974 the U.S. took ten antidumping actions. Between 1980 and 1985 it took or threatened action in almost 100 cases, two-thirds against less developed countries. During that time, Australia initiated even more cases and the EC

*Graham Searjeant is Financial Editor of* The Times, *London.*

almost as many. Many of the European and U.S. cases were against each other. On each side, competitive sectors were penalized and the less efficient protected.

The EC used antidumping actions effectively against imports of Japanese electronic goods, even when these already dominated the market. Japan's distribution and selling system at home was so complex and expensive that goods exported profitably from Japanese factories were sometimes cheaper in Europe than in Japan— a theoretical case of dumping. In recent cases, when Japanese companies set up assembly plants in Europe to avoid this trap, the European Commission deduced that the imported components must be dumped. This strategy aimed to force Japanese companies to manufacture fully in Europe. Plainly, if others followed suit, world trade would shrink drastically.

The World Bank calculated that more than one-sixth of industrial countries' imports were now limited by formal nontariff barriers. If informal barriers were included, the total might be as high as one-third. Open trade had been virtually extinguished in many sectors, from basic goods such as food, textiles, and steel to growth industries like electronic components and computer-related goods. Much of this trade was managed by bilateral "crisis" negotiations rather than through the free market.

The spread of creeping protection made systematic protection more likely. In the U.S., trade threats focused on Japan and on newer Asian manufacturers such as Taiwan and South Korea. But squabbles with Europe, usually over quotas and tariffs to support the EC's common agricultural policy, also influenced U.S. thinking. If Japanese manufacturing success exposed U.S. weakness, European farm protection frustrated its strength. Creeping protection reflected weakness in GATT. Demands for systematic protection arose from the disrupting effects of trade imbalances, caused by volatile and inappropriate exchange rates and ultimately by different countries pursuing incompatible economic and interest-rate policies. Unless protection was fought on both these fronts, the trend to state-managed trade—and ultimately trade wars— could prove irresistible.

**Postwar Moves to Liberalize Trade.** In 19th-century Britain free trade came to be seen as benefiting the country that practiced it, regardless of what others did— a philosophy still echoed in Hong Kong. The postwar trading system had a more limited aim: avoiding a repeat of the trade wars of the 1930s, which prolonged the Great Depression. GATT established mutually agreed-upon rules. Each country (or free-trade zone) would trade with all others on the same basis, without discriminating among them. Trade restraints should be overt tariffs and apply to all. This encouraged people to think protection was an advantage, which they gave up only on a reciprocal basis. Less developed countries, which were allowed exemptions, came to view free trade as a luxury for rich nations. If countries think protection will help their industries, provided others stick to the rules of the game, it is tempting to cheat. Conversely, any successful trading country such as Japan is assumed to cheat.

The 1944 Bretton Woods agreement proposed a regulatory International Trade Organization alongside the World Bank and International Monetary Fund, but leading countries objected. There was therefore only a small GATT secretariat, along with committees to arbitrate disputes. Individual countries decided their own antidumping cases. They could also mutually ignore the rules, as in the Multifibre Arrangement setting individual quotas on textiles from different less developed countries. Lacking power, GATT has held long rounds of negotiations aimed at mutual tariff cuts. The negotiations spawned trade bureaucracies with a vested interest in managing trade through bilateral haggling rather than general agreements and in keeping trade barriers as bargaining counters. They act for local lobbies of producers rather than representing the interests of consumers.

The Japanese government, always close to industrial interests, now had a special responsibility for open trade because, uniquely in modern times, the top trading economy was by no means the most powerful nation. Japan might now have fewer import barriers than Europe or the U.S., but it had not shown leadership in removing them without pressure from abroad. The U.S. Congress had always been prey to local interests. The European Commission favoured protection more than most EC member governments. Hopes of a return to open trade rested on the new GATT multilateral negotiations, dubbed the Uruguay round, which were expected to last until the end of the decade. The agenda aimed to halt spreading protection and break down trade barriers. Success would require such unlikely breakthroughs as reform of farm protection and an end to the textile quota agreement when it expired in 1991.

Conflict seemed more likely unless tensions caused by economic distortions were eased. The trade imbalances that so swiftly turned the U.S. into the world's biggest debtor—and made Japan the biggest creditor—had little to do with fair or unfair trade. Foreigners, however, were easy scapegoats for a trade deficit when politicians could not agree on how to resolve the economic distortions that caused it—in the case of the U.S., the big gap between federal spending and revenue. Japan was blamed, even though the U.S. had smaller trade deficits with almost all other industrial countries. Asian imports were accused of destroying U.S. jobs, even though unemployment in the U.S. had fallen to a historically low level.

This rhetoric revived a fallacy that trade between individual countries should balance, an absurdity in free markets. Fixing bilateral balances is incompatible with open trade, but it suits the trend to state management of trade as practiced by Communist countries. Even in Europe, the EC deficit with Japan is termed "unacceptable," though the EC has a trade surplus with the rest of the world. Xenophobia must ultimately bring protection and probably a breakdown of international trade into American, European, and Far Eastern blocs. Even President Reagan, the champion of open trade, threatened Japan and, while aiming to defuse congressional pressure, helped make public opinion more protectionist. In the worst trade skirmish of 1987, he felt politically obliged to mount discriminatory trade sanctions against Japan, in breach of GATT. Ironically, this followed a fight over a bilateral pact on semiconductors designed to raise prices to the rest of the world.

The rise of the yen, which finally boosted Japanese imports and cut its trade surplus, and the fall in the dollar, which likewise raised U.S. exports, could take some steam out of protectionism, but the effect of the stock market slide in October was more likely to change attitudes. The last great wave of protectionism followed the Wall Street crash of 1929, ensuring depression in America, Europe, and Japan. In 1987 stock markets plummeted round the world simultaneously, showing how national economies depend on each other. Perhaps sudden fears of shared economic difficulties would jolt politicians into thinking of the Western world as an international whole, as they did in 1945.

(continued from page 171)

Reflecting the relative strength of import demand in non-oil less developed countries, OECD exports—especially of manufactured goods—probably recorded a volume advance of 4%, as compared with 3% a year earlier. Oil producers' exports, on the other hand, suffered badly; in reaction to the large rise in oil imports resulting from the low oil prices in 1986 and in response to the hardening of oil prices in 1987, most developed countries reduced their oil purchases. This, it was thought, may have led to a volume drop of 3% in oil producers' exports, as against a gain of just over 13% in 1986. The export performance of non-oil less developed countries also recorded a modest deterioration, with volume growth falling to about 5% from 6% in 1986.

Since trade figures, especially in the less developed countries, are published with a significant time lag and are subject to extensive subsequent revisions, the foregoing figures should be regarded as little more than the best available estimates at the end of 1987. There was, however, little doubt that, in terms of overall trade growth, the developed world did not do as well as in 1986. For oil exporters trade was sluggish in both 1986 and 1987, but non-oil less developed countries did relatively well. Compared with the previous year, the developed world also appeared to have lost out in terms of price movements. Although the dollar prices of their exports rose at about the same rates as in 1986, the increase in import prices—estimated at approximately 12%—was three times faster than it had been a year earlier. This was the result of the partial recovery of oil prices and some improvement in the price of non-oil commodities. These factors went some way toward improving the terms of trade of the less developed countries after the massive adverse swing of 1986.

The relative strength of OECD exports referred to above could be largely attributed to the rapid growth—estimated at 12%, as against 5.7% in 1986—in U.S. shipments abroad. This was principally due to the improvement in U.S. export competitiveness in the wake of the depreciation of the dollar. By the opposite token, both West Germany and Japan experienced an appreciation of their currencies, the effect of which was to cut back their export volumes by between 1 and 2%. The U.K., however, managed an increase of perhaps 5.5% in foreign sales, as compared with a rise of about 3.5% in 1986; so did France and Italy, but the advance in French exports of about 1% was disappointing. Imports, on the other hand, were almost uniformly weaker, reflecting reduced purchases of oil. Once again, the greatest change was seen in the U.S., where the weak dollar made imports relatively expensive and cut their volume growth from 13.5 to approximately 3.5%. The same trend, on a much reduced scale, was also seen in other OECD countries, including West Germany and Japan, where the strength of the currencies might have been expected to give imports a boost. In fact, the only major exception to the general trend was the U.K., where the rapid growth of demand, particularly of consumers' expenditure, was estimated to have yielded an import growth of 7.5%, compared with 6.5% during the previous year.

In terms of trade balances the position of the principal OECD countries vis-à-vis each other did not change much, although the OECD group relative to the rest of the world lost some ground. Thus, as in the previous year, 1987 was characterized by a very large U.S. trade deficit, estimated at $172 billion, as against $170 billion in 1986, largely offset by the Japanese and West German surpluses of about $95 billion and $60 billion, respectively. The U.K. deficit rose modestly from $12 billion to $14.5 billion, and most other

Money dealers work furiously during a hectic session of the Tokyo Foreign Exchange. Trading activity at the foreign exchange was frenzied in early November after the U.S. dollar broke through the 135-yen barrier.

AP/WIDE WORLD

and were expected—in due course—to lead to an easing of trade barriers around the world. However, much of the original optimism, based on the expectation that the world's principal trading countries would display a strong will to push ahead speedily and not allow specific bilateral trade disputes to slow down progress, was a thing of the past by the end of the year. As 1987 drew to a close, it was clear that progress would be hard and slow, with the participants, influenced by short-term domestic constraints, adopting a hard, parochial approach. This was partly explained by the slowdown in world economic growth and trade and the continuing large trade imbalances; clearly, a background of this nature made it difficult to adopt a more conciliatory view of specific disputes or differences.

Thus, against the U.S. administration's better judgment, Congress was busily preparing trade legislation that would intensify the protectionist stance of U.S. policy and reduce the ability of the government to take a liberal view toward trade disputes. The outcome of these moves would not be settled for some time, but the effect on the overall climate was noticeable. Nor was there evidence of an easier approach to bilateral problems. The EC and the U.S. nearly came to blows over trade in pasta during the summer; Japan, whose continued trade surplus attracted much foreign criticism, suffered U.S. sanctions against its sales of semiconductors; Europe and the U.S. continued to be at loggerheads over agricultural trade, aircraft subsidies, and a host of other issues. Japan was threatening action against Europe over a decision to extend its antidumping stance to Japanese typewriters and other products and was facing a critical ruling from the General Agreement on Tariffs and Trade (GATT) over its taxation provisions applying to imported wine and spirits. All in all, there was little evidence of the "new spirit" indicated by the optimistic ministerial declarations at the start of the Uruguay round; in fact, according to the GATT, the number of nontariff barriers in operation in member countries increased rather than declined in the six months following the start of talks initiated in Uruguay.

## INTERNATIONAL EXCHANGE AND PAYMENTS

In the field of international finance 1987 was dominated by the continuing imbalance of international payments, the rapid fall in the external value of the U.S. dollar, and the difficulties of coping with—let alone solving—the debt problems of the less developed economies. It was against this climate of concern and uncertainty that the collapse of world equity prices in October–November introduced another powerful element of tension into the world's financial markets.

The imbalance of international payments did not improve significantly in 1987. Despite a slowdown in the growth of the volume of imports and an acceleration in that of exports, the current account deficit of the U.S. rose to about $150 billion, against $141 billion in 1986. By

OECD countries witnessed either a cut in their surplus or an increase in deficits. The overall result, therefore, was an increase of about $5 billion–$10 billion in the net trade deficit of the OECD area over the $6 million recorded in 1986, with Europe's surplus more than offset by the U.S. deficit.

Because of the difficulty of obtaining up-to-date and accurate trade data for non-OECD countries at the end of the year, it was hard to pinpoint the losers and winners outside the OECD bloc. However, as a group, oil producers were likely to have done significantly better; although they faced a marked fall in the volume of their exports, the effect of this was likely to have been more than counterbalanced by the rise in the price of oil and the significant cutback in their imports. Non-oil less developed countries, however, appeared to have experienced a deterioration. For 1986 UN calculations suggested a total trade surplus of $3 billion, and late in 1987 it was thought that, despite a somewhat slower growth in import volume than in 1986, the relative weakness of their exports was sufficient to cause a small deficit. For the Communist world the net trade position in 1987 was probably stronger, largely because in the previous year its exports had been particularly adversely affected by the Chernobyl nuclear disaster.

The first full year of the Uruguay round of multinational trade liberalization negotiations, initiated, amid considerable optimism, at Punta del Este in September 1986, was completed. The talks progressed on a wide range of issues

### Table VII. Output of Basic Industrial Products in Eastern Europe, 1986
In 000 metric tons unless otherwise stated

| Country | Anthracite (hard coal) | Lignite (brown coal) | Natural gas (000,000 cu m) | Crude petroleum | Electric power (000,000 kw-hr) | Steel | Sulfuric acid | Cement |
|---|---|---|---|---|---|---|---|---|
| Bulgaria | 204 | 35,004 | ... | ... | 41,832 | 2,892 | 806.4 | 5,724 |
| Czechoslovakia | 25,236 | 102,588 | 24,900 | 144 | 85,512 | 15,108 | 1,291.2 | 10,296 |
| East Germany | ... | 311,256 | ... | ... | 115,296 | 7,968 | 883.2 | 11,988 |
| Hungary | 2,328 | 20,808 | 255,336 | 2,004 | 27,984 | 3,720 | 542.4 | 3,864 |
| Poland | 192,084 | 67,260 | 182,724 | 204 | 140,292 | 17,148 | 2,968.8 | 15,828 |
| Romania | ... | ... | ... | ... | ... | ... | ... | ... |
| U.S.S.R. | 511,200 | ... | 23,745,888 | 614,748 | 1,599,000 | 161,004 | ... | 135,108 |

Source: UN, *Monthly Bulletin of Statistics.*

the opposite token, West Germany and Japan did little to reduce their huge surpluses—approximately $113 billion in total, compared with $126 billion in the preceding year. The existence of this imbalance and, even more, the seeming inability/unwillingness of the countries concerned to do anything about it, gave rise to considerable exchange-rate tension that resulted in a rapid depreciation of the dollar during the early months of the year. An attempt was made to stabilize the position at a meeting in Paris of the six principal OECD countries in February, at which the U.S. agreed to work for a reduction in its budget deficit. West Germany and Japan agreed, in principle, to support domestic demand, and the participants expressed their view that the exchange rates then ruling were broadly compatible with economic fundamentals. Given the lack of any clear subsequent evidence that these objectives were being taken seriously, a short period of relief was followed by renewed pressure, and by early May the effective rate of the dollar was nearly 5% lower than at the time of the meeting. The position improved somewhat in the summer, but by the autumn the dollar was on the way down again, a process that was given an additional impetus by the stock market crash in October–November. The effective rate of the dollar fell by 14% between the closing quarter of 1986 and late November 1987, with the rate falling by 17% against the Japanese yen, 19% against the Deutsche Mark, and 25% against sterling. During the same period, the effective rate of the yen rose by 10% and that of the Deutsche Mark by 6%, while the effective rate of sterling recorded a small decline of 0.5%.

The decline in sterling's effective rate was accompanied by a modest increase in the U.K.'s current deficit, from £1 billion to £2.5 billion. Most other OECD countries were in a similar situation; exchange rates, at least against the dollar, tended to harden, but the current balances deteriorated somewhat. Thus in France a surplus of nearly $4 billion in 1986 was turned into a deficit of perhaps $2 billion, while balances in Italy and Canada also deteriorated markedly. It was estimated that the OECD bloc as a whole recorded a current account deficit of $25 billion–$30 billion during 1987, as compared with a shortfall of $20 billion in the preceding year. The mirror image of this deterioration was the improvement in the payments positions of other countries. The balance of payments accounts of the oil producers benefited from a cut in imports and some recovery in oil prices, leading to an estimated improvement in their current account deficit from $30 billion in 1986 to $13 billion in 1987. Non-oil producers, however, appeared to have faced a deterioration, with the deficit widening from $15 billion to about $20 billion.

Interest rates in the developed world moved in response to domestic economic policies, monetary trends, and the pressures of exchange rates. The underlying trend, therefore, did not exhibit a consistent country-to-country pattern. In the U.S. there was some concern about inflation, monetary growth, and the weakness of the dollar. These factors argued for higher interest rates, but the pressure was moderated by the Reagan administration's decision not to slow down the growth of the economy. The result was a moderate upward trend for most of the year, with the prime rate moving from 7.5% in December 1986 to 9% by October. In November and December, however, most countries cut their rates to offset the possible deflationary effects of the stock market crash, and U.S. banks took advantage of this to reduce their prime rate to 8.75%.

The only other major OECD country with rising interest rates was France, where the weakness of the currency within the EMS, even after the October stock market crash, took precedence over the need to boost the nation's rather sluggish economy. In the U.K. the trend was consistently downward except for an unexpected and short-lived increase of 1% in the base rate to 10% in July. The principal influence on U.K. rates was the authorities' desire to prevent an unduly fast appreciation of sterling against the dollar, tempered by some concern about the rapid growth in credit. This latter factor was responsible for the hike in the base rate in July, but it was rescinded after the stock market crash in an attempt to offset the resulting potential loss of consumer confidence. The year, therefore, ended with a rate of 8.5%, as compared with 11% at the start.

West German interest rates also experienced a modest downward trend, but—given the country's sluggish economic growth, lack of serious inflationary pressures, strong currency, and huge external surplus—official policy was widely regarded as far too cautious and came in for much criticism from other countries. In January 1987 the Bundesbank reduced the Lombard rate from 5.5 to 5% but, despite the expansionary noises emanating from the meeting in Paris, it refused to go further until early November, when—in the wake of the stock market crash—it was persuaded to sanction a further reduction of 0.5%. The official repurchase rate was also cut by 0.55% in response to the stock market crash and the U.S. deficit-reducing package.

During 1987 the problem of world debt was managed, but a long-term solution remained elusive. On the contrary, there was a growing recognition by both debtors and creditors that the recent steps taken to enable borrowers to meet their obligations were not working and were unlikely to prevent a further deterioration in the situation. The major shock to world debt management was the decision, early in the year, by Brazil to stop interest payments on its $110 billion debt. Brazil argued that because of a downturn in its international trade, debt-servicing payments could not be kept up and that new, more concessionary arrangements were needed to ensure a structural solution. The Brazilian suggestion was to swap half of its debt for 35-year bonds paying only 5% a year.

In subsequent negotiations Brazil's stance on debt conversion was modified (but the moratorium on interest payments continued), and the latest indications were that a compromise agreement would be reached. Nevertheless, the Brazilian action represented a further intensification in debtor militancy. Increasingly, debtor countries were unwilling (and politically unable) to accept creditor-imposed

**Table VIII. Soviet Trade with Eastern European Countries**

In 000,000 rubles, current prices

| Country | Exports | | | Imports | | |
|---------|---------|---------|---------|---------|---------|---------|
| | 1984 | 1985 | 1986 | 1984 | 1985 | 1986 |
| Bulgaria | 6,124.4 | 6,434.7 | 6,787.8 | 5,608.0 | 6,040.0 | 6,191.3 |
| Czechoslovakia | 6,590.8 | 6,813.3 | 6,947.0 | 6,016.5 | 6,587.3 | 6,556.4 |
| East Germany | 7,481.4 | 7,651.7 | 7,884.2 | 7,367.2 | 7,553.0 | 7,128.1 |
| Hungary | 4,320.8 | 4,560.0 | 4,678.2 | 4,434.4 | 4,850.1 | 4,873.4 |
| Poland | 6,069.2 | 6,516.7 | 6,813.8 | 5,296.8 | 5,525.0 | 6,127.2 |
| Romania | 1,807.2 | 1,948.8 | 2,823.3 | 1,755.2 | 2,276.5 | 2,415.2 |

Source: U.S.S.R. Foreign Trade Statistics/Moscow.

**Table IX. Soviet Crude Petroleum and Products Supplied to Eastern Europe**

In 000 rubles

| Country | 1984 | 1985 | 1986 |
|---------|------|------|------|
| Bulgaria | 2,020,887 | 2,211,090 | 2,256,362 |
| Czechoslovakia | 2,746,953 | 2,924,466 | 2,994,622 |
| East Germany | 3,124,839 | 3,106,406 | 3,126,569 |
| Hungary | 1,396,398 | 1,476,068 | 1,494,733 |
| Poland | 2,520,403 | 2,653,655 | 2,742,241 |
| Romania | 283,596 | 388,533 | 974,947 |

Source: U.S.S.R. Foreign Trade Statistics/Moscow.

austerity packages and argued that their obligation to repay should be related to economic growth and to the current, discounted, value of their debts rather than to the original capital sum. They pointed to the fact that such debts were traded in the secondary market at discounts ranging from 20% for Colombia to 65% for Argentina and that this had to be a factor in future arrangements.

Needless to say, the lenders disagreed, but there was a reluctant acceptance that some movement toward the borrowers' viewpoint would be inevitable. It was partly for this reason that most large lenders increased their bad-debt provisions—Citicorp, for example, increased its loan-loss facility by $3 billion in May—and were beginning to discuss not the concept but the terms attached to the conversion of existing loans into long-term securities.

The 1987 world debt picture was not uniformly dismal. Mexico, the beneficiary of a rescheduling package in 1986 along the lines advocated by U.S. Secretary of the Treasury Baker, improved its situation (although if the price of oil had not risen, the position could have been very different). Colombia, with $15 billion of debt, managed to reduce its debt burden from 43% to approximately 35% of GDP in one year, while Chile succeeded in reducing its debt (currently $20 billion) through a $2 billion package of debt/equity swaps. Argentina, on the other hand, appeared to be immensely vulnerable, and Peru continued to take an extremely hard line on debt servicing. As the year drew to its end, there was little doubt that the world debt problem remained acute and that lenders would be called upon to make further concessions without any conviction that these would lead to a lasting improvement in the situation.

This article updates the *Macropædia* articles BANKS AND BANKING; ECONOMIC GROWTH AND PLANNING; GOVERNMENT FINANCE; INTERNATIONAL TRADE.

## STOCK EXCHANGES

In October 1987 stock exchanges across the world experienced the sharpest falls since the Wall Street crash of 1929. The prices of fixed-income securities were lower as well, but commodity price indexes, in dollar terms, were sharply higher. At the end of 1987 only three of the world's major stock price indexes (TABLE X) ended the year at a higher level than they started it. In commodity markets the main features were volatile oil and soft commodity prices contrasted with higher values for gold and platinum.

During the early part of the year, share prices moved sharply higher in response to the strength of the major economies, in particular the U.S., the U.K., and Japan. Gently falling interest rates and expansionary fiscal and monetary policies coupled with rising corporate earnings and dividends created a favourable backdrop. Investors' interest was also stimulated by the privatization programs in many Western countries. Attractively priced and facilitated by installment payments, the shares of a number of previously government-owned companies in the U.K. and France were largely oversubscribed, giving instant profits to investors.

However, in the early summer the prices of fixed-interest securities weakened when investors' concern over the prospects of higher interest rates increased following the sharp fall in the value of the dollar against the Japanese yen and the Deutsche Mark. Thus the real rate of return (interest rate minus the inflation rate) rose, reducing the attraction of equity investments. Surprisingly, the raging bull markets ignored this development throughout the summer and continued to focus on rising corporate earnings, higher dividends, and prospects of continuing high levels of economic activity.

The trigger for the October crash was provided by the comments of U.S. Secretary of the Treasury Baker following the publication of the U.S. trade figures for August. The monthly deficit of $15.7 billion was far worse than market expectations, and Baker's comments implied that the dollar needed to fall faster and farther in order to correct the widening trade deficit. The nervous markets interpreted this to mean the end of the Louvre accord, under which a group of industrialized countries led by Japan, West Germany, and the United Kingdom had been supporting the dollar with the aim of achieving its orderly and gradual depreciation. The prospects of a free-fall of the dollar led to fears of higher interest rates in order to attract the necessary external funds (mostly Japanese) to finance the monumental trade deficit. Higher interest rates increase borrowing costs for corporations and ordinary consumers alike. A cutback on spending for private consumption coupled with lower corporate investment leads to a recession and in turn to a fall in corporate earnings. Thus the equity risk premium, that is, the difference between bond interest and equity dividend income, looked alarmingly large and unsustainable. Investors in New York panicked and began selling equities heavily, driving the Dow Jones industrial average (DJIA) down by almost 1,000 points from its August high.

The slump in Wall Street share prices spread around the world with frightening speed. Even those countries not closely involved with U.S. financial affairs saw their stock markets nosedive. The first reason for this behaviour was

**New York Stock Exchange Common Stock Index Closing Prices**
Stock prices (Dec. 31, 1965 = 50)

High
Close
Low

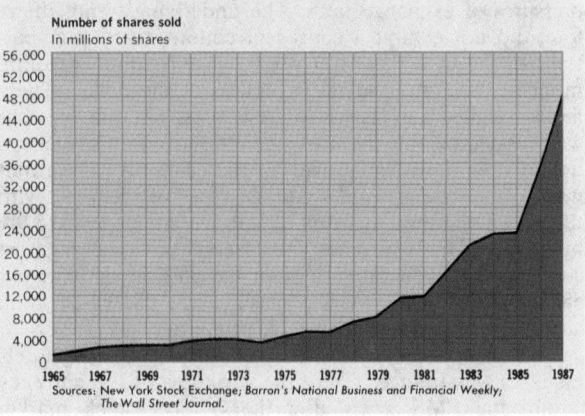

**Number of shares sold**
In millions of shares

Sources: New York Stock Exchange; *Barron's National Business and Financial Weekly*; *The Wall Street Journal*.

The scene on the floor of the New York Stock Exchange is one of utter chaos minutes before the close of trading on October 19, "Black Monday," which saw the Dow Jones industrial average fall a record 508.32 points.

BILL FOLEY—TIME MAGAZINE

the overwhelming importance of the U.S. on the world economic stage. With a recession in the U.S., the rest of the world could not sustain a high level of economic activity. The second reason was the integrated nature of the world's large stock markets. Diversified portfolio investments, with large proportions of foreign participation in each market made possible by technological developments providing instant information throughout the world, "globalized" the securities business. Just as the world's markets marched up together during the long bull phase, so they crashed together.

Although the downward spiral seemed unstoppable, a swift and positive move by the world's monetary authorities to inject liquidity into the system avoided a far worse crash that could have led to a prolonged slump like that of the 1930s. As the year drew to a close, the *Financial Times* Actuaries World Index had declined 30% since "Black Monday" despite lower interest rates and an agreement to cut the budget deficit in the U.S.                                   (IEIS)

**United States.** The stock market crash on "Black Monday," Oct. 19, 1987, when the DJIA fell 508.32 points, was the major event of the year. Although the stock market ended 1987 about where it began, the year was the most volatile and chaotic since 1929. The five-year-old bull market entered 1987 with the DJIA at 1,895.95 and then surged ahead rapidly. The 2,000 mark was passed on January 8 and 2,100 on January 19. The momentum was sustained, and the DJIA peaked at 2,722.42 on August 25. The crash wiped out more than $500 billion (36%) of market values in a single day, however, as the DJIA fell by a startling 22.61%. With heavy trading volume and abnormal volatility, the DJIA then crept back to close at 1,938.83 at the year's end, up 2.26% for 1987 but down 29% from its peak in August.

Bond prices declined irregularly until the October meltdown and then rose sharply for several weeks as investors rushed into bonds and other fixed-income securities. Total return for 1987, as measured by Shearson Lehman Brothers' index of government and corporate bonds, was little more than 2%, compared with 15.6% in 1986 and 21.3% in 1985.

The October crisis in the stock market prompted major investigations by a presidential commission, a U.S. congressional committee, and the New York Stock Exchange (NYSE). All concluded that the capacity of the markets to absorb extraordinary and sudden trading activity needed to be improved.

The euphoria of the bull market gave way after the crash to bearish sentiments as investors contemplated the huge budget and trade deficits, the weakness of the dollar, and the apparent inability of the U.S. to compete effectively in the world markets. While most economic indicators still gave positive signals in the last quarter of 1987, recession talk was in the air, and market uncertainty disheartened many investors.

Merger and acquisition activity, which had been a major concern among regulators for several years, continued unabated in 1987 but virtually halted after October because buyers and sellers could not agree on what constituted a fair price. Two of the biggest completed mergers were British Petroleum's acquisition of the remainder of Stan-

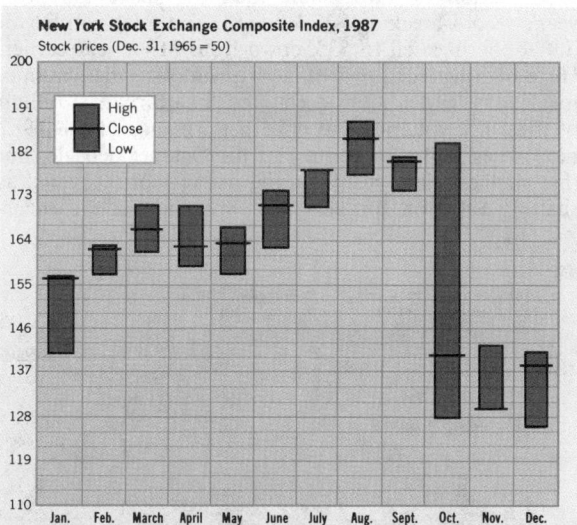

**New York Stock Exchange Composite Index, 1987**
Stock prices (Dec. 31, 1965 = 50)

High
Close
Low

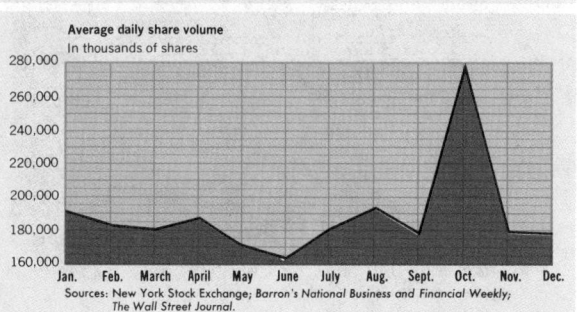

**Average daily share volume**
In thousands of shares

Sources: New York Stock Exchange; *Barron's National Business and Financial Weekly*; *The Wall Street Journal.*

dard Oil Co. for $7,560,000,000 and AV Holdings Corp.'s takeover of Borg-Warner Corp. for $3,760,000,000. There were 243 major leveraged buyouts having a total value of $29.4 billion, compared with 331 deals with a value of $46.4 billion in 1986.

Share repurchases by major corporations proliferated in 1987 as more than 1,400 companies announced plans to buy back shares valued at more than $80 billion. This more than doubled the number of 1986 transactions and almost doubled their dollar value. Early in the year the rationale for buybacks included corporate restructurings, resistance to hostile takeovers, and increasing returns on equity. After October the buybacks were designed to exploit the opportunity to reacquire shares at favourably depressed prices.

Program trading, a strategy employed by major institutions to trade simultaneously in the stock market and in stock index futures contracts in order to profit from discrepancies between the two markets, was a major cause of the October crash. The strategy depended upon the availability of continuous liquidity in the market, and so, when the avalanche of sell orders was placed on the NYSE, those responsible for making orderly markets in a given security were unable to respond adequately. Traders on the Chicago Mercantile Exchange also were unable to handle the volume of activity on a minute-by-minute basis. The result was uncompleted orders and a breakdown of the program-trading strategy. Portfolio insurance, a technique for reducing risk by selling covered options, also failed because of the inability to handle the tremendous volume of computer-generated sell orders flooding into the markets. Intervention by the Federal Reserve Board to ease credit restrictions and promises to provide banks with the liquidity they needed to weather the financial crisis provided reassurance for the markets.

New-issue underwriters set a dollar-volume record of $23.8 billion in 1987, more than 6% above the prior year's record-breaking $22.4 billion. The total number of initial offerings fell to 533, down from 719 a year earlier. Huge offerings for pools of government securities, municipal bonds, and utilities accounted for nearly $10 billion of the 1987 volume. The price performance of the 1987 new issues was poor because of the October debacle, but they neither fell as steeply as the market nor recovered as sharply. Salomon Brothers, Inc., was the leading under-

U.S. Attorney Rudolph Giuliani announces the arrests of three prominent Wall Street executives on charges of conspiracy to commit illegal insider stock trading.
CHIAS—GAMMA/LIAISON

writer for U.S. corporations in 1987, with a total volume of $40.8 billion, down 24% from the previous year's $53.6 billion. Total underwriting volume for 1987 was $281.9 billion, down 11% from the previous year's record $318.4 billion.

Trading volume of stocks on the NYSE rose 30% in 1987 to 47,801,314,120, up from 36,680,016,341 the prior year. An all-time record volume was recorded October 20, when 608.1 million shares changed hands. This contrasted with the 52-week low daily figure of 86,360,000 on November 27. The most active Big Board issues in 1987 were AT&T, 693,221,500; IBM, 520,727,000; General Electric, 410,-637,900; Texaco, 367,425,200; and Navistar, 357,759,400. There were 810 advances, 1,444 declines, and 25 stocks unchanged for the year, with 2,279 issues traded, down from 2,318 in 1986. Bond volume declined to $9,726,244,500 in 1987, a drop of 9.2% from the $10,475,399,000 achieved a year earlier. At the year's end the NYSE was considering a recommendation, by the Katzenbach Commission, that stock indexes be traded on the floor of the exchange. The commission also proposed consolidating regulatory authority over all U.S. financial markets under one government agency and raising margin and capital requirements for trading on the futures exchanges.

On the American Stock Exchange stock sales totaled 3,505,950,000 shares, up 17.9% from the 2,978,540,000 achieved in 1986. The Amex Index ended the year at 260.35, down 1.1% from its 1986 close of 263.27. It reached a record high of 365.01 on August 13; its low, 231.90, was set on December 4. Bond trading was light on the Amex, with 1987 sales of $686,922,000. Trading in the over-the-counter market continued its steep year-by-year gains with 35,597,292,000 shares traded on the National Association of Securities Dealers automated quotation system, commonly known as Nasdaq, up 33.5% from 26,658,897,000 shares in 1986. The 1987 volume was more than double that of 1984 and earlier years. On average, the 5,500 stocks traded on Nasdaq did not do well in 1987. In spite of rallies at the start and end of the year, the broad market as measured by the Nasdaq composite index lost 5.3% of its value, to 330.47, from its 1986 close. Mutual fund sales were off sharply, with sales for the year estimated at $188.3 billion, down from the record $215.8 billion of 1986 but higher than any other year. The bulk of the sales occurred in the first half of the year.

The Standard & Poor's Index of 500 stocks ranged between a high of 336.77 and a low of 223.92 during 1987 and ended the year at 247.08, slightly above the corresponding figure for 1986. The composite index of 500

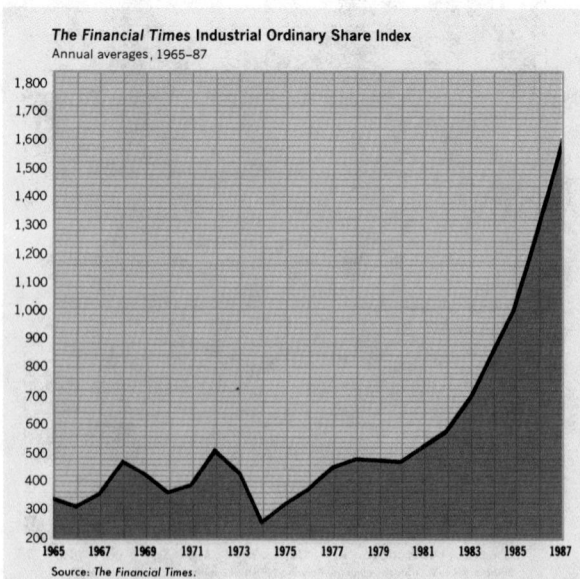

**The Financial Times Industrial Ordinary Share Index**
Annual averages, 1965–87

Source: The Financial Times.

shares (TABLE XI) began the year at 264.51, up 27% from the corresponding month in 1986. The index moved up to 292.47 in March and after a brief slowdown moved upward again to its peak in August. The October crash brought the index down 26.6% in a single day. The industrial index had an uninterrupted climb from October 1986 until August 1987, when it topped out on average at 384.94, well ahead of the 1986 highs. Public utility stocks did not fare as well in 1987. Starting the year at 120.09 in January, the average slid month by month to 108.06 in May, then climbed irregularly to 117.70 in August. The high for the year was 124.04, and the low was 91.80. The year-end figure was only 102.12. Transportation stocks rose from the 1986 levels, but they lost most of their gains in the last quarter.

U.S. government bond yields in 1987 (TABLE XII) rose steadily through September, from a January level of 7.6% to a high of 9.58% in September. By the end of the year these rates had fallen to 8.93%. U.S. corporate bond yields (TABLE XIII) paralleled those of government bonds, climbing from 8.36% in January to a peak of 10.18% in September before falling back after the crash caused an influx of buy orders in this market.

The options markets, which flourished and expanded during the first three quarters of 1987, came under extraordinary pressure in the fourth quarter as a result of the crash. On October 19 prices of stock-index futures and options collapsed along with the stock market. On the following day stock-index trading on the Chicago Mercantile Exchange and the Chicago Board Options Exchange was suspended for nearly an hour. A record volume of trading occurred on the futures exchanges. The Chicago exchanges, offering a variety of contracts on financial futures, benefited from the stock market's volatility in October. Chicago Board of Trade volume jumped 26.1% to a record 127,092,990 contracts from 100,813,833 contracts in 1986, while the Chicago Mercantile Exchange reported that volume rose 22.7% to a record 84,367,214 contracts from 68,775,524 the previous year.

In a year of concentrated attention on the functioning of the stock exchanges, the Securities and Exchange Commission (SEC) negotiated an agreement with Canadian securities regulators to expand cooperation of the two countries in securities fraud cases, similar to agreements with Switzerland, Japan, and others providing for mutual assistance in enforcement cases involving such violations as insider trading.

A by-product of the October crash was a flurry of controversial recommendations for strengthening the market system. Among the proposals were developing a unified clearing system; establishing consistent margin requirements between the stock and options markets; establishing "circuit breakers," like price limits or coordinated trading halts; and creating new information systems to monitor transactions and market conditions.

**Canada.** Financial market developments in Canada paralleled those in the U.S. in 1987, although the market indexes fared slightly better. The Toronto Stock Exchange's broad-based 300 composite index rose 34% from the beginning of 1987 to its all-time high in August of 4,112.9, but the crash in late October reduced it by more than 30%. Some of the losses were recovered in volatile trading during the last two months of the year, so that the composite ended 1987 at 3,160.05 for a net gain in 1987 of 3.1%. The gold mining stocks index increased 42% on rising bullion prices. Other mining stocks were up 36%, and forest products stocks rose 19.4%. Petroleum stocks were flat, and the capital goods and consumer products sectors were lower.

Share volume on the Toronto Stock Exchange established records for both volume and value. Volume was 7,390,-000,000 and aggregate value was $100,220,000,000, up 51 and 57%, respectively, from 1986.

Deregulation of Canada's securities industry in 1986 was expected to attract a flood of foreign investment in local brokerage firms. This did not occur. Instead, Canada's big domestic banks acquired the major stock brokerage firms, such as Wood Gundy Corp., McLeod Young Weir Ltd., and Nesbitt Thomson, Inc. (IRVING PFEFFER)

## Table X. Selected Major World Stock Price Indexes*

| Country | 1987 range† High | 1987 range† Low | Year-end close | Percent change from 12/31/86 |
|---|---|---|---|---|
| Australia | 2,306 | 1,151 | 1,322 | − 4 |
| Austria | 232 | 172 | 181 | −20 |
| Belgium | 5,413 | 3,527 | 3,803 | −12 |
| Denmark | 220 | 180 | 185 | − 1 |
| France | 460 | 285 | 296 | −23 |
| West Germany | 677 | 400 | 444 | −34 |
| Hong Kong | 3,949 | 1,961 | 2,194 | −15 |
| Italy | 767 | 476 | 532 | −26 |
| Japan | 26,646 | 18,544 | 23,286 | +20 |
| Netherlands, The | 334 | 192 | 213 | −18 |
| Norway | 592 | 307 | 351 | − 8 |
| Singapore | 1,505 | 780 | 814 | −11 |
| South Africa | 2,266 | 1,403 | 1,433 | −11 |
| Spain | 325 | 202 | 214 | + 3 |
| Sweden | 3,550 | 2,068 | 2,236 | −12 |
| Switzerland | 730 | 451 | 495 | −30 |
| United Kingdom | 2,443 | 1,565 | 1,652 | − 2.5 |
| United States | 2,722 | 1,739 | 1,939 | + 2.3 |

*Index numbers are rounded.
†Based on daily closing price.
Source: The Financial Times.

## Table XI. U.S. Stock Market Prices

| Month | Railroads (6 stocks) 1987 | Railroads (6 stocks) 1986 | Industrials (400 stocks) 1987 | Industrials (400 stocks) 1986 | Public utilities (40 stocks) 1987 | Public utilities (40 stocks) 1986 | Composite (500 stocks) 1987 | Composite (500 stocks) 1986 |
|---|---|---|---|---|---|---|---|---|
| January | 148.13 | 142.49 | 296.10 | 230.37 | 120.09 | 92.06 | 264.51 | 208.19 |
| February | 158.02 | 150.10 | 318.18 | 241.91 | 119.87 | 97.51 | 280.93 | 219.37 |
| March | 163.02 | 156.43 | 334.65 | 256.25 | 117.65 | 102.01 | 292.47 | 232.33 |
| April | 160.27 | 148.69 | 335.43 | 263.89 | 109.97 | 103.78 | 289.32 | 237.98 |
| May | 169.22 | 142.02 | 336.10 | 266.38 | 108.06 | 102.39 | 289.12 | 238.40 |
| June | 174.05 | 144.23 | 349.58 | 274.55 | 112.63 | 106.65 | 301.38 | 245.30 |
| July | 186.70 | 134.52 | 362.36 | 266.17 | 110.93 | 112.13 | 310.09 | 240.18 |
| August | 195.96 | 131.50 | 384.94 | 270.23 | 117.70 | 118.53 | 329.36 | 245.00 |
| September | 191.61 | 133.04 | 372.49 | 263.62 | 114.98 | 113.11 | 318.66 | 238.27 |
| October | ... | 135.51 | ... | 263.09 | ... | 114.10 | ... | 237.36 |
| November | ... | 141.50 | ... | 272.79 | ... | 114.10 | ... | 245.09 |
| December | ... | 140.70 | ... | 276.69 | ... | 115.52 | ... | 248.61 |

Sources: U.S. Department of Commerce, Survey of Current Business; Board of Governors of the Federal Reserve System, Federal Reserve Bulletin. Prices are Standard & Poor's monthly averages of daily closing prices, with 1941–43 = 10.

## Table XII. U.S. Government Long-Term Bond Yields

| Month | Yield (%) 1987 | Yield (%) 1986 | Month | Yield (%) 1987 | Yield (%) 1986 |
|---|---|---|---|---|---|
| January | 7.60 | 9.50 | July | 8.70 | 7.86 |
| February | 7.69 | 9.07 | August | 8.97 | 7.72 |
| March | 7.62 | 8.13 | September | 9.58 | 8.08 |
| April | 8.31 | 7.59 | October | ... | 8.04 |
| May | 8.79 | 8.02 | November | ... | 7.81 |
| June | 8.63 | 8.23 | December | ... | 7.67 |

Source: U.S. Department of Commerce, Survey of Current Business. Yields are for U.S. Treasury bonds that are taxable and due or callable in ten years or more.

## Table XIII. U.S. Corporate Bond Yields

| Month | Yield (%) 1987 | Yield (%) 1986 | Month | Yield (%) 1987 | Yield (%) 1986 |
|---|---|---|---|---|---|
| January | 8.36 | 10.05 | July | 9.42 | 8.88 |
| February | 8.38 | 9.67 | August | 9.67 | 8.72 |
| March | 8.36 | 9.00 | September | 10.18 | 8.89 |
| April | 8.85 | 8.79 | October | ... | 8.86 |
| May | 9.33 | 9.09 | November | ... | 8.68 |
| June | 9.32 | 9.13 | December | ... | 8.49 |

Source: U.S. Department of Commerce, Survey of Current Business. Yields are based on Moody's Aaa domestic corporate bond index.

**Western Europe.** Stock markets in Europe were generally lower at the end of the year. Until October extremely bullish conditions prevailed in Great Britain, Belgium, and the Scandinavian countries. Conversely, only marginal modest gains were in evidence in West Germany, The Netherlands, Spain, and France. In fact, bearish was an accurate description of the state of many stock markets in Europe after late spring.

Following the October crash, the European markets declined 25–30%. According to the *Financial Times* Actuaries World Indexes, European markets, in local currency terms, declined 15% from the beginning of the year, but the index, in dollar terms, was largely unchanged, reflecting the appreciation of the European currencies against the dollar.

The eight-year-old bull market in the U.K. came to a sudden and unexpected halt on Monday, October 19. Prior to the crash, the *Financial Times* industrial share index reached 2,360, only 5% below the all-time high in mid-July. The year had opened strongly as investors realized that the outlook for economic growth was stronger than had previously been expected. Forecasts for 1987 all pointed to a continuing rapid rate of economic activity, falling unemployment, moderate inflation, and lower interest rates. Firm oil prices and buoyant tax revenues, together with plans for further privatizations, greatly improved the government's ability to borrow. Another favourable development was the easing of the pressure on sterling. Thus the way was clear for the government to reduce interest rates and cut taxes while staying within its long-range economic plans. However, the widely anticipated large-scale foreign buying of British securities in the spring did not materialize. Japanese investors were busy improving their liquidity, while the other international investors were cautious ahead of the summer holidays.

In early August renewed concern over the increased likelihood of the economy's overheating led the U.K. chancellor of the Exchequer, Nigel Lawson, to move swiftly and unexpectedly engineer a rise of 1% in interest rates. The commercial banks raised their base rates to 11%. The London stock market then fell by more than 8% as investors digested a set of poor trade and money supply figures. Eventually, the higher interest rates were seen as a strategic, preemptive move and not a panic measure. This positive interpretation enabled the market to rally as the countdown for the sale of government's remaining stake in British Petroleum got under way. (*See* WORLD AFFAIRS [Western Europe]: *United Kingdom.*) The *Financial Times* index recovered from 2,200 to 2,400.

The mood of investors was cautiously optimistic in mid-October when Wall Street reacted to the slump in the value of the dollar following the worst-ever trade figures for the U.S. The rest is history. Equity securities were no longer attractive, and the London market went into a free-fall as investors dumped them. In the first two days the *Financial Times* index lost 500 points, or 22%. A technical rally on the third day, sparked by lower interest rates in the U.S., proved short-lived, and the headlong decline continued. The trend until the end of the second week was downward, interrupted by occasional technical rallies. The bottom was reached at about 1,515. A hesitant recovery that began early in November enabled the market to recoup about a quarter of the losses.

Worried by the continuing weakness of the dollar, the lame-duck administration in the U.S., and a worldwide slowdown in economic activity, if not an outright recession, the London stock market approached 1988 in an extremely bearish mood. Few observers expected the *Financial Times* index to move much above a 1,650–1,750 trading range.

In West Germany the situation was different until October. The Frankfurt stock market opened the year on a weak note and drifted aimlessly until the summer, when it rallied to reach the December–January levels. Following the October crash and a 30% correction, it retreated to 430 levels. The West German stock markets were influenced for most of the year not by the sound economic fundamentals—that is, the relatively higher pace of economic activity (GDP growth of about 2.5%, low inflation [around 1%], higher investment, and stronger private consumption)—but by the rising value of the Deutsche Mark against the U.S. dollar. A rise of 15% during the first six months, following the 25% appreciation in the previous 18 months, was viewed by investors as a negative development. Loss of competitiveness, it was feared, would hurt West Germany's large export-oriented industries. Furthermore, the Bundesbank's efforts to slow the Deutsche Mark's appreciation against the dollar, by buying dollars and selling Deutsche Marks, was perceived to be inflationary.

During the summer the dollar's apparent stability put new heart in the markets and led to a gradual recovery. The Frankfurt FAZ index increased from the spring level of 550 to about 650, a gain of over 18%. In early October independent economic forecasts pointed to the continuation of the general economic buoyancy, aided by a package of modest tax cuts planned for 1988 and 1989. However, the ultracautious West German economic policymakers, egged on by Chancellor Helmut Kohl's coalition government, tightened their monetary policy on October 6 in response to the renewed strength of the Deutsche Mark against the dollar. It could be argued that the downturn in West German stock markets dated from this event, for it signaled the disagreement between the U.S. and West Germany over the Louvre Accord. As the year drew to a close, the Frankfurt Stock Exchange was shell-shocked. The international investors, who had previously accounted for about 40% of all transactions, had retreated to their domestic markets after the October crash. The dollar continued to weaken, and the West German government was still reluctant to stimulate the economy to help prevent a global recession.

The French stock market charted a contrasting course to that of West Germany in the period from January to October. The Paris Bourse opened the year on an optimistic note buoyed by the upcoming privatizations and cheerful economic news. Inflation was pointing down, and investment and corporate profitability were good. Despite a weak trade position, the franc was stable against the Deutsche Mark. Thus the Paris CAC General Index rose more than 15% in the first quarter, enabling the first three privatization issues, Saint-Gobain, Banque Paribas, and Sogenal, to be floated with immense popularity and instant profits for the investors.

However, the CAC index peaked at 460 in March and after drifting for a month fell sharply, losing most of the gains. There was little gain from then on before October, when the Paris Bourse marched down in step with stock markets throughout the world.

As in West Germany, foreign investors were responsible for more than one-third of the transactions on the Paris exchange. Furthermore, markets were made in London for many of the leading French stocks. The internationalization of the French stocks exaggerated the extent of the price falls when the crash came. The Paris CAC index declined by 35% to about 270 before recovering slightly to the 300 level. In the absence of foreign buying interest and also of the government's intention to press on with its privatization schemes, the market was not expected to stage a recovery in the short to medium term.

In Belgium the bullish pattern was similar to that of Great Britain. Despite political uncertainty, international investors chased the Belgian stocks to dizzy heights. By September the Brussels Bourse index had risen 30% from the January level, but it ended the year down 13%. This swing of 43% was one of the greatest in Europe and in part reflected the dollar exposure of some of the largest companies traded on the exchange.

The Netherlands and Switzerland generally followed the West German stock markets, reflecting the fact that both belonged to Deutsche Mark bloc countries. The Amsterdam stock market, after a hesitant spring, rallied by nearly 20% during the summer, encouraged by the stability of the dollar. However, the realization that many Dutch companies had significant exposure to the dollar and that their earnings growth would be limited owing to sluggish economic activity led to a larger than expected fall in the October crash. In early December the Amsterdam stock market was down 18% from the beginning of the year and 33% below its peak, notwithstanding the fact that even at the peak it was modestly priced. Switzerland ended the year 30% down, having reached an all-time high on September 23. Unlike other exchanges, however, the all-time high was only marginally higher than the January level.

The Scandinavian countries' stock markets were generally stronger in the pre-October period. Norway, having lagged behind in 1986, surged ahead during 1987. Firm oil prices, lower inflation, and improving trade deficits provided a favourable background. Before the crash the Oslo stock exchange index had risen 70% since January, but it ended the year down 8%. In neighbouring Sweden the Stockholm market rose by 42% but lost all the gains in the October crash and ended the year down 12%. Denmark fared better; the upsurge was a modest 20%, and it ended the year 3% below the January level.

The Spanish stock market surged for the fifth consecutive year. The Madrid Stock Exchange index added a 113% gain during the first nine months, having doubled the previous year. Rapid industrialization of the economy, increased foreign investment opportunities, and a decline in the unemployment levels continued to improve the attractions of the shares of the limited number of companies traded on the exchange. After the October crash the Spanish market fared relatively well and ended the year showing a modest 3% gain.

The Italian stock market faltered in 1987 following several years of strong performance. The Milan Stock Exchange index at its best was only 15% above the January level, and even then it was 8% below the all-time high reached in May 1986. After the October crash there was a 25% decline.

**Other Countries.** The stock market in Mexico was easily the most volatile in the world. Between January and October 5, the Bolsa Stock Exchange soared by more than 625% as investors sought to protect their savings from the ravages of inflation, which was running at an annual rate of 120%. The Bolsa then lost 75% of its value in five weeks. Just as swiftly, on November 18, it rallied for a 25% gain; this was followed by another gain of 18% the next day, after which the market became more stable. The extreme volatility in November was largely caused by the collapse of the peso against the dollar following withdrawal of official support that had previously cushioned its fall. Investors liked the cheaper peso, for it would benefit the growing number of industrial exporters, mining companies, and cement mak-

ers. Despite the crash, the Bolsa index at the year's end was 200% higher than on January 1, but measured in sterling terms it was unchanged.

Ironically, the stock market in Japan, which was generally perceived in Europe and the U.S. to be at the greatest risk from a possible correction, performed best. The Nikkei Dow Jones average surged by 40%, comfortably breaching the 25,000 level, during the first six months of the year, but as investors rushed to take profits in July, it fell back more than 10%. However, as the dollar's weakness continued, touching $1 = 145 yen in September, Japanese investors preferred to invest their strong cash flows in the domestic market despite lower earnings yields. In mid-October the Tokyo market was at an all-time high, but in the five weeks after the October crash, it fell by only 20% and approached the year's end registering a 20% gain. The high liquidity of Japanese investment institutions and the support they provided to the market by actually buying equity securities during the crisis explained why the Japanese market performed better.

In Australia the Sydney Stock Exchange raced ahead, reflecting the higher demand for gold mining shares and the nation's improved economic prospects. In early October the index had risen 40% since January, but after that it gave up all the gains and limped to the year's end with a 5% loss. The other major economy that depended on mining and primary products, South Africa, mirrored Australia closely. The Johannesburg Stock Exchange index soared by over 50% before being felled by the October crash. At the year's end the market was almost 10% below the January level.

Hong Kong was another example of a spectacular rise followed by a dramatic fall. The Hang Seng Index at its highest level had risen nearly 55%, yet at the year's end there was a loss of 15%. After the Wall Street and London crash, the Hong Kong authorities attempted to calm the market by suspending all dealings for nearly a week, but to no avail. When trading was resumed, the international investors sold equity securities as if there were no tomorrow. The market fell by 44% in one day.

**Commodity Markets.** The general trend of world commodity indexes was sharply upward during 1987. The *Economist* commodity price index, which measured spot prices in U.S. dollars and sterling for 28 internationally traded foodstuffs, nonfood agricultural products, and metals, rose by nearly 32% in dollar terms during the first 50 weeks of the year. (In sterling terms the increase was a more modest 5%.)

The two major sectors of the *Economist* index once again moved at different rates. The food index increased by 13%, while industrial raw materials surged up by nearly 50%. Within the latter category, nonfood agricultural raw materials prices rose 30%, and metal prices increased 62%.

Gold registered strong gains in the opening quarter of the year and quickly moved from $398 per ounce to $460. By the summer, as the dollar stabilized and oil prices weakened, gold looked less attractive in relation to the booming stock markets. As it fell below the $440 level, investors moved out of gold into equities and fixed-interest securities. After the crash the increased risk of inflation—reflecting liquidity pumped into the system by the central banks, declining interest rates, and a slump in the dollar—made gold attractive once more. Toward the end of the year, gold was trading at $495 per ounce, a net gain for 1987 of 25%.                (IEIS)

*See also* Crime, Law Enforcement, and Penology: *Special Report.*

This article updates the *Macropædia* article MARKETS.

# Education

In most of the leading industrial countries of the world, there was renewed recognition in 1987 that an improved educational system was one of the key ingredients of better economic performance. At the same time, education was being made the scapegoat for unemployment, social disorder, and economic underperformance. This love-hate relationship between governments and their educational systems was analyzed by John Lowe, head of the country education and policy review section at the Organization for Economic Cooperation and Development in Paris. Lowe, who retired in the autumn of 1987 after spending more than ten years studying the world's educational systems, drew attention to the revival of interest in education among politicians—especially in the U.S., the U.K., France, West Germany, and Japan. There was a worldwide tendency to blame the schools and the teachers for social ills, and politicians made headlines with educational reforms and reports that emphasized crises in education.

Lowe maintained that the link between education and economic performance was now taken for granted in most countries. There was also a growing perception of education and training as an interrelated and even unified activity. The persistent problem of youth unemployment in most Western countries had focused attention on "upper secondary" education (ages 14 to 19) and the relationship of the curriculum to the world of work. In most nations the school-leaving age was being steadily increased, to 18 or 19, for all secondary students. In Japan the percentage of this age group in full-time education was more than 90%, and in West Germany it was only a few percent less. In the U.K., by contrast, the percentage was actually going down; in England the latest figures available showed that in 1985–86 only 30% of students stayed in full-time education beyond the age of 16, a 3% decline from three years earlier. In that country, however, as in many others, special work experience and training programs were being developed to meet the needs of school leavers and young adults.

**Primary and Secondary Education.** While many countries looked to Japanese education for the answers to economic success, the Japanese were becoming increasingly concerned that their system had many social defects. The first

and second reports of the Provisional Council on Educational Reform were heavily critical of the school curricula for being too narrow and inflexible, overemphasizing uniformity and competitiveness. The social side effects of the pressure to compete and gain a place in Japan's higher education system manifested themselves in an increase in bullying in primary and middle schools and in suicides among students in secondary schools. Bullying (*Ijime*) became a subject of serious psychological study in Japan and the theme of frequent newspaper headlines. In many cases the phenomenon appeared to be caused by children picking on the slowest or weakest member of a class because they felt that that person was holding the others back.

Other harmful influences were brought to bear on Japanese young people through the widespread use of after-school tutoring in order to pass exams. In 1986 an estimated 86% of middle-school-age and 90% of secondary-age children living in urban areas were involved in time-consuming, expensive extra coaching. In order to reduce these pressures, Japanese reformers were trying to introduce more creative methods of curriculum organization and were turning to computer-assisted learning in order to encourage self-assessment and independent study.

In the U.K., on the other hand, the Conservative Party government won the general election in June 1987 with the clear commitment to bringing greater uniformity and central direction into the educational systems of England and Wales, which had been largely run by local councils for more than 80 years. In November the U.K. secretary of state for education and science, Kenneth Baker, introduced legislation in Parliament to set up the first "national curriculum" for all pupils from 5 to 16. Although such a curriculum had existed in many other nations for some time—in France since the days of the Emperor Napoleon—this was the first time such an idea had been put into practice in an English-speaking country. In addition to the three "core subjects" of English, mathematics, and science, there would be seven or eight foundation subjects that all pupils would have to study up to the age when they could leave school. For the first time, a foreign language would be compulsory for all students, and so would technology. As of 1987, only 38% of 14-to-16-year-olds studied a foreign language, usually French.

Baker had been much impressed by a report from the British school inspectors on education in France and West

DAGMAR FABRICUS—PHOTOREPORTERS

Mexican students protest the lack of student participation in policy-making during a strike in February. Student representatives rejected proposed policy changes, which included an increase in student fees, an end to open admissions, and the introduction of standardized exams. University officials eventually withdrew their proposals, and the government agreed to double its university funding.

Germany. He announced that he wanted to set "national standards" in each subject of the curriculum, with tests for all pupils at the ages of 7, 11, 14, and 16. The model for these tests was to be the six-point *Notenskala,* which had been used in West Germany for many years. At the same time, Baker introduced legislation to "free" the schools and colleges from control by local councils.

Parents, who had already achieved much more influence on school governing bodies under the 1986 Education Act, were to be given increased control over the budgets and staff appointments of their schools. They would also be allowed to decide by vote whether to "opt out" of local council control completely. There would be fewer controls on school admission policies so that popular establishments could accept more pupils, but there were widespread fears that this might lead to racially segregated schools. The legislative reforms were criticized and resisted by a wide spectrum of professional opinion, from the churches to the teacher unions, local councillors, and many parent groups.

In Scotland a proposal to phase in parent-dominated school boards was even more fiercely resisted. but the Scottish minister responsible for education, Michael Forsyth, used the example of parent councils in Denmark to show that a shift of power from professionals to consumers was both feasible and desirable.

The extent to which the proposed reforms of education in the U.K. would actually affect the need to raise standards in the schools remained an open question for many educationalists. The same applied in Spain, where an even more radical set of proposals was under active consideration in 1987. Minister of Education José María Maravall began holding a series of consultations that were intended to culminate in a white paper on "school education up to the year 2000"; it was to contain practical proposals that should be applied by 1990–91. Education in Spain, argued Maravall, had become excessively rigid. He proposed that the core curriculum in secondary schools at first embrace some 80% of a student's total class work and then decrease to 50–60% of the total toward the end of secondary school. Student failure, which sometimes ran as high as 50%, would have to be reduced, and so would class sizes from their average (in 1987) of 30. The practice of repeating years was prevalent in Spain, and the intention was that no student should repeat more than two years in his or her ten-year school career.

The U.S. National Endowment for the Humanities reported that recent educational reform movements had neglected the humanities. The report said that students had become thinkers without knowledge and advocated increased emphasis on subject matter and less on teaching students how to learn. It criticized teacher certification based on completion of college-based training programs, too much reliance on textbooks, and textbook selection by committees.

Three reports were released on poor showings of U.S. students in mathematics. The Mathematical Sciences Education Board said that, in comparison with those in 21 other countries, U.S. students' performance was "lackluster" in all math skills except computation.

To improve performance, teachers should create chatter-filled classrooms that reduce student boredom, according to Albert Shanker, president of the American Federation of Teachers. He wanted teachers to be liberated to provide students with more individual attention. Technological aids such as videocassettes were cited as desirable tools for bringing about needed changes. Shanker said that half of the nation's 2.2 million teachers would leave the profession within six years unless major changes were made.

In New Zealand, education became one of the central issues in the general election held in August 1987. The opposition argued strongly for such right-wing policies as vouchers. The Labour Party was reelected, however, and, surprisingly, Prime Minister David Lange himself assumed the post of minister of education. He was presented by his own Treasury Department with a 300-page briefing paper that made a series of demands concerning education, including, curiously, the advocacy of larger classes on the grounds that U.S. evidence demonstrated them to be more efficient. Lange, however, rejected the paper.

The year was also notable for the way in which several European countries began to take a close look at the examinations they gave to those leaving school. France had made the most progress in this respect with various reforms of the *baccalauréat* examination, making it much more flexible than the old classical *baccalauréat,* which was wholly designed for university entrants. In England and Wales, too, the government took steps to reform the so-called advanced-level examinations by setting up a committee under the chairmanship of the vice-chancellor of the University of Southampton, G. R. Higginson. The A-level examination, taken at the age of 18, was the most specialized in Europe because students were expected to study only three, or at most four, subjects without any compulsory requirements. Thus a student could study physics, pure mathematics, and applied mathematics and nothing else from the age of 16 to 18.

In West Germany the *abitur* required students to take eight subjects (generally at the age of 19) after three years in the sixth form (or high school). The composition of the *abitur* was subject to bitter disputes, settled by the West German government in October. The arguments were based largely on political differences—those states governed by the Social Democratic Party (SPD) ranged against those ruled by the Christian Democratic Union (CDU). The SPD wanted to introduce more vocational elements into the curriculum, whereas the CDU favoured a return to a more traditional, broadly based *abitur* as an academic foundation for later specialization. When it was finally made, the actual change was not great; chiefly it required two compulsory subjects in the *abitur*—chosen from mathematics, a foreign language, and German—plus six others, making eight in all. The reform was intended to begin operation in 1989.

In Denmark the equivalent of the *abitur* was the *studentereksamen.* The Danish reform was aimed at making the curriculum more flexible, thereby providing a better blend of science and arts subjects. English would remain the first compulsory foreign language for all Danish gymnasium (high school) students, but students would in the future be required to have real proficiency in two foreign languages.

The study of languages and their political overtones continued to be an issue in a number of countries, perhaps most tragically in Belgium, where the separation between Flemish and French speakers led to a number of clashes. In former European colonies such as Pakistan, the issue was rather different. Government policy in Pakistan, it was announced, would ensure that by 1989 matriculation examinations would be written in Urdu. The country's constitution called for a complete switch from English to Urdu as the public examination medium, retaining English only as a second language. Urdu was, however, the mother tongue of only about 10% of Pakistanis, although it was the nearest to a national language in the country. Literacy in English remained the passport to a good job, and all public service examinations were in English. In addition, since Pakistani workers were constantly called upon to go abroad and send money home to boost foreign exchange, it was clear that English was widely needed. It seemed unlikely, therefore, that the matriculation exams would be given in Urdu in 1989.

As part of its emphasis on the disadvantaged, the U.S. government in 1987 prepared a document on improving education for disadvantaged students. U.S. Secretary of Education William Bennett said that the document offered strategies for breaking "the cycle of poverty," in which 12.5 million U.S. students were trapped. A survey of U.S. teachers revealed that they believed that poverty was the second most important cause of students' classroom difficulties. The teachers said that the major cause of difficulties was the widespread practice of leaving children unsupervised at home while parents were away for long periods.

Minority students continued to drop out of school at an alarming rate, according to the U.S. National Education Association. The NEA blamed crowded classes, harmful stereotyping, and insufficient numbers of bilingual teachers. Of particular concern were the rates for Hispanics (often 50% or higher) and Native Americans (commonly 70% or higher). Concluding that Boston schools were now in compliance with the landmark 1974 guidelines of Judge W. Arthur Garrity, a U.S. Circuit Court of Appeals released the schools from the lower court order. Garrity had mandated social guidelines in assigning students and assumed considerable direct control of school operations for many years. The appeals judges said that Boston had made an effort to eliminate racial discrimination within the "realities" of urban life.

The U.S. Supreme Court let stand a lower court decision that Norfolk, Va., could drop its 15-year-old court-ordered busing plan. The school board then adopted a neighbourhood school plan, in which 10 of 36 grade schools would have either all or almost all black students. In an Oklahoma City case, the justices upheld a lower court decision that required the school board to seek court approval before ending busing and returning to neighbourhood schools. The Supreme Court left intact the option of courts to require busing as a way to desegregate school systems.

Another curricular issue that remained in the forefront in 1987 was religious education. In many countries this was compulsory, nowhere more so than in Italy, an overwhelmingly Roman Catholic country. During the year the Italian minister of education, Giovanni Galloni, produced a document on religious education that the Vatican considered a threat to the status of the subject in the schools. Galloni's argument was that the timing of the religious education period should be during the first hour (8 to 9 AM) or the last hour (noon to 1 PM) of the school day. This would be convenient for those pupils who wished to be exempted from the "religious hour" (no more than 10%). They would simply arrive at school late or leave early. The Vatican's anxiety was that this would lead to a gradual reduction in the number of students in religion classes as more and more pupils put pressure on parents to seek exemption and get an hour off from school. At the year's end no clear directive had emerged from the minister of education, and school principals were, not surprisingly, angry at having to make the decision themselves.

Claiming that 44 textbooks used in Alabama schools promoted the "religion of secular humanism," a U.S. federal judge banned them. Judge W. Brevard Hand found secular humanism to be a religion and to be in violation of the U.S. Constitution's ban on government-established religion. Hand criticized both what was included in the books and what was left out. He objected to the claim of one book that an individual can make decisions without

divine intervention. He also objected to some content that was left out; for example, the role of the Puritans and of great religious revivals in the early history of the U.S. In its appeal of the decision, Alabama said that removing the textbooks in question would disrupt classes and that funds for replacing them were unavailable. The appeals court overturned Judge Hand's opinion.

In Tennessee a federal judge ruled in favour of some religious fundamentalist parents. He held that their children should not have been expelled from school for refusing to study from textbooks that they found objectionable to their faith. The judge said that compulsory use of the books violated children's free religious choice, which was guaranteed by the First Amendment to the Constitution. A federal appeals court rejected the decision. It said that the children were not forced to believe in what was studied or to act in ways contrary to their religion.

The Supreme Court struck down a Louisiana law that required "creation science" to be taught as an alternative to the scientific theory of evolution. Claiming that the doctrine that the world was created by a supernatural power in six days had as much scientific basis as evolution, religious fundamentalists in several states had sought to have it included in the science curriculum. The justices ruled that the Louisiana law advanced a particular religious belief and was in violation of the First Amendment.

In Western Europe there were fewer reports of major disputes between teachers and governments. Indeed, in Britain and France teachers gained salary increases, and much of the steam was thus taken out of teacher union protests. In France the education budget was expanded by some 4% for the 1987–88 academic year. Most of the extra money was allocated to teachers' salaries. Five thousand new teaching posts were provided for in the budget, 3,000 of them in the lycées (college-preparatory secondary schools), which were expecting an increase of 79,000 pupils in September 1988.

In parts of Latin America, however, it was a different story, notably in Argentina. Extreme inflation in that country led to vigorous demands for higher pay for teachers. The teachers believed themselves to be the worst afflicted within the public services and could point with some justice to the much higher pay increases received by the military. Massive protests were reported from Buenos Aires, and in one province, Tucuman, prolonged strikes took place.

According to a report by the NEA, teachers' salaries in the U.S. increased 5.9% in 1986–87 to an average of $26,704. The NEA president, Mary Futrell, claimed that the increases amounted to catch-up money in relation to inflation. Nationwide, salaries ranged from a low of $18,781 in one state to Alaska's $43,970. The federal share of education budgets was 6%. Schools in five states were affected by strikes. Chicago and Detroit were the largest districts affected. Arkansas had its first-ever teacher strike.

The NEA's annual convention went on record as opposing corporal punishment. About two million students a year were paddled in the 41 states that in 1987 permitted corporal punishment, according to the National Center for the Study of Corporal Punishment in Schools. Other painful punishments included ear twisting and hair pulling. The center found that painful punishment was often used for such offenses as whispering and noncompletion of homework. Nine states prohibited corporal punishment.

In October the Los Angeles board of education voted to put its 618 schools and 592,000 students on a year-round schedule, replacing the long summer vacation by frequent short holidays. The plan was expected to save money by allowing more efficient use of facilities. Two weeks later,

Pres. Ronald Reagan presents Donna H. Oliver with the 1987 National Teacher of the Year Award as her husband and daughter watch. Oliver was a biology teacher at the Hugh M. Cummings High School in Burlington, North Carolina. The award is sponsored by the Encyclopædia Britannica Companies, *Good Housekeeping* magazine, and the Council of Chief State School Officers.

AP/WIDE WORLD

however, the board rescinded its decision and decided to hold four months of public hearings before voting on the issue again in the spring of 1988.

**Higher Education.** Throughout Europe there was a growing movement toward a united series of policies on higher (postsecondary) education. In 1976 an attempt to establish an education policy within the European Communities (EC) failed. Eleven years later, however, with the expansion of the EC from 9 member nations to 12 upon the admission of Greece, Portugal, and Spain, a new mood began to prevail. The most important breakthrough occurred in the summer of 1987 when all the EC members approved a program of student mobility among institutions of higher education in Europe. Known as "Erasmus," the program began on a small scale in July but was ultimately intended to increase to a point where 10% of the students in each country would come from other European nations. Information technology was another area in which member nations began to collaborate, a move spurred by economic competition from the U.S. and the countries of the Pacific Rim.

The strong element of competition between countries continued to dominate national policies on overseas students. The admission of students from less developed countries had become a key weapon in national economic and foreign policies. The future long-term benefits of overseas students were no longer questioned—even in the U.K., which had greatly reduced its intake by increasing student fees in 1981.

In 1987 the U.S. led the field in educating overseas students, with 360 government-funded counseling services in more than 30 countries. In China alone there were 13 educational advisory centres; it was not, therefore, surprising that 18,000 Chinese students were studying in the U.S. higher education system. France, the next largest importer of students, regarded higher education as an important part of cultural diplomacy, especially in French-speaking African countries. Italy, Australia, and Japan were all intent on attracting more overseas students; Japan decided to increase the number of students studying there by 100,000 by the end of the century.

Two books sharply critical of higher education in the U.S. reached the best-seller lists in 1987. *The Closing of the American Mind* by University of Chicago professor Allan Bloom (*see* BIOGRAPHIES) charges that U.S. universi-ties have capitulated to special-interest activist groups and abandoned sound liberal arts teaching for trendy "relevant" courses in which all ideas have equal value. In *Cultural Literacy,* E. D. Hirsch, Jr., a professor at the University of Virginia, advances the thesis that colleges have given up teaching the unifying facts, values, and writings of Western culture, thus creating a generation of cultural illiterates.

College tuition in the U.S. climbed 10% per year in the 1980s, according to the American Council on Education. Though the rate of increase was lower than that for medicine, energy, and new homes, it was 50% higher than the rise in personal income and double the inflation rate. College costs were the most expensive item in the budget of families with children in college.

There were fewer jobs available to the nation's one million 1987 graduates, but the salaries were higher. As the U.S. continued to shift from a manufacturing to a service economy, liberal arts graduates benefited. Job offers for humanities graduates increased 29%. In contrast, engineers, especially petroleum majors, experienced drastic drops in job openings; however, their beginning salaries continued to be the highest among those in the various professional fields.

The American Council on Education created plans for increasing enrollments of minority students, minority graduation rates, and awareness of how to promote racial harmony on campus. Representatives of the council's 1,445 collegiate members responded to concerns about the decline of minority enrollments and some increases in racial tensions. In 1987 minorities comprised 17% of college students, compared with 21% of the total U.S. population.

In the U.K. the Open University doubled its student population to 140,000 by offering short courses for updating skills and expertise in engineering, management, and other professional and scientific areas. The university's new school of management aimed to double the number of managers with master's degrees within five years. In September the British Open College opened to offer learning opportunities to adults below degree level and vocational qualifications in business and technical subjects.

Conflicts continued in some of the major universities in South Africa. Near the end of the year, the universities were told by the South African government that if they did not restrict political activities on the campuses, they would lose some of their government subsidies. Universities were asked to deal firmly with any form of disruption, protest, boycott, or seditious behaviour by staff or students. The new regulations seemed to be aimed chiefly at five universities—Cape Town, Witwatersrand, Rhodes, Natal, and Western Cape. Several academics and academic bodies, including all the university senates, stated that they would refuse to apply the regulations. At the root of the conflict seemed to be the government's policy of imposing racial quotas on universities. The five universities in question had refused to apply these quotas.

The reign of Amadou Mahtar M'Bow, the Senegalese director general of Unesco, came to an end. M'Bow had long been a controversial administrator, having been accused of being anti-Western and inefficient in managing Unesco's affairs. This resulted in the withdrawal of U.S. and British support for the agency in 1984–85. Unesco thus lost about 30% of its income. After a convoluted series of votes, a Spanish biochemist, Federico Mayor, emerged as the new director general.

(JOEL L. BURDIN; TUDOR DAVID; GEORGE LOW)

*See also* Libraries; Motion Pictures.

This article updates the *Macropædia* articles History of EDUCATION; TEACHING.

---

# Energy

The most important event in the field of energy in 1987 was a breakthrough in the technology of superconductivity, the complete absence of resistance to the flow of electricity. The phenomenon had long been known, but its practical application had been severely limited because it was producible only at temperatures close to absolute zero. It could be maintained only if the electrical conductor was continuously bathed in liquid helium. The technology was thus both costly and complicated.

The early months of the year witnessed the demonstration of superconductivity at appreciably higher temperatures, which could be attained and maintained with the use of liquid nitrogen. This new technology opened up the possibility of the economic application of superconductivity in the generation and transmission of electricity and in many of its uses. After the initial flurry of excitement over the new discovery had subsided, researchers settled down to the long and difficult task of translating the new superconductivity from the laboratory to the marketplace. Although no one could say what the ultimate consequences would be, the prospects were considered favourable for eventual widespread changes in the ways electricity would be used. (*See* PHYSICS: *Sidebar.*)

At a more mundane level, prolonged heat waves over much of the U.S. in July caused record-setting consumption of electricity, as air conditioners were used extensively. In Europe a West German utility put into operation a 1,330-MW turbine-generator, the world's largest at a nuclear power plant. The electric grids of the U.K. and France were linked with a submarine cable across the English Channel. With a capacity of 2,000 MW and operating with direct current, the cable was the largest of its type.

Events in the world oil industry were, as usual, dominated by the actions of the Organization of Petroleum Exporting Countries (OPEC). After the disastrous market collapse of 1986, OPEC reestablished market control at the end of that year by setting production quotas for its members that were designed to maintain a market price for crude oil of $18 per barrel. In the early months of 1987, prices stabilized around that level as demand firmed, reflecting in part the coldest winter in Europe in many years.

By midyear, rising military tension in the Persian Gulf, occasioned by increased attacks on oil tankers by both Iran and Iraq, caused prices to move upward. Some OPEC countries took advantage of this opportunity to increase their revenues by raising their production above quota levels. In the absence of increased consumption, this additional supply ended up in inventories, and when it became apparent in late August that inventories were approaching saturation, prices promptly weakened. In September quota discipline was resumed, and this, together with naval activities by the United States and some European countries to minimize the harassment of shipping in the Gulf, restored price stability. At its December meeting OPEC extended its pricing and production policies through the first half of 1988. New oil pipelines under construction by Iraq, Turkey, and Saudi Arabia were expected to reduce the importance of the Gulf in moving Middle Eastern oil to the West and Japan.

In January a new international producer group, the African Petroleum Producers' Association, was inaugurated. The new organization declared that its purpose was not to function as a rival to OPEC but to serve as a forum for exchanging views on matters affecting the oil interests of its members.

Rebounding from the depressed levels of 1986, oil exploration in the North Sea yielded a surprising number of discoveries, including the largest discovery in that area in

A scientist at the Argonne National Laboratory, Batavia, Illinois, prepares to put electrical current through a superconducting wire at 77 Kelvin (−321° Fahrenheit). This was the highest temperature at which any wire had carried electricity without resistance.

A diving boat is moored alongside the supertanker *Bridgeton* while divers examine underwater damage caused by a mine in the Persian Gulf. The ship was one of 11 Kuwaiti oil tankers reflagged by the U.S. in an effort to protect Gulf shipping.
AFP PHOTO

more than a decade. In May the U.S.S.R. set a world record for the daily oil output of an individual country by producing 12.6 million bbl a day. In March the Prudhoe Bay field on the north coast of Alaska, the largest ever discovered in North America, produced its five billionth barrel of crude oil, displacing the East Texas field as the most productive in U.S. history. The Endicott field, just northeast of Prudhoe Bay, began production as the first commercial oil field in the Beaufort Sea. Commercial production also began from the first giant field discovered in the Atlantic Ocean some 300 km (200 mi) northeast of Rio de Janeiro. One of the wells, at 419 m (1,348 ft), established a record water depth for a commercial producing well.

In April the U.S. Department of the Interior announced a five-year plan that would open up millions of hectares of the outer continental shelf for oil and gas exploration. The plan included areas in the Pacific off the coasts of California, Oregon, and Washington; the Georges Bank, a rich fishing area off New England; and waters around the Florida Keys. Critics of the plan complained that it would not adequately protect marine and coastal environments.

A warm winter in the United States, combined with the persistence of an excess supply, resulted in a weak natural gas market. Prices in the spot market dropped to their lowest levels since the development of that market in the early 1980s. In an attempt to increase the productivity of a Siberian gas field, the Soviet Union detonated a 20-kiloton nuclear device in the western part of the Yakut Autonomous Republic. Results were not announced. In Sweden the attempt to test a radical theory on the origin and occurrence of natural gas in the Earth's crust encountered difficulties. Drilling of the well in the Siljan crater, in south-central Sweden, was suspended in September when backers of the project ran out of money. The well had reached 6,600 m (21,780 ft) of the target depth of 7,500 m (24,600 ft) and had yielded tantalizing suggestions of the possible correctness of the theory but no definitive results.

Like that of gas, the coal market continued in a depressed state, although in this instance the circumstance was worldwide. Exporters throughout the world competed with domestic producers in North America and Europe. The first major delivery of Australian coal to the U.S. market took place in January. Alaskan producers hoped

that test burns of coal in Taiwan would result in a new customer for their product. In May the largest single coal shipment in history was loaded on a ship at an export terminal near Vancouver, B.C. The 240,000 metric tons of metallurgical coal were destined for a steel plant in South Korea. The Soviet Union completed its first coal slurry pipeline in the Kuznetsk Basin in Siberia.

Events in the nuclear power industry were of minor note compared with the disastrous reactor explosion at the Chernobyl power station in the Soviet Union during the preceding year. As a follow-up to that event, the Soviets announced that no new units of the Chernobyl design would be built. New nuclear units went into operation in the United States, France, Japan, West Germany, and Canada. The U.S. reactor industry scored a coup when the United Kingdom's Central Electricity Generating Board chose the pressurized water reactor design for its new nuclear unit. This constituted abandonment of the previous reliance on British-developed gas-cooled reactor designs for additions to nuclear generating capacity. Austria decided to begin decommissioning of the Zwentendorf nuclear power station. The station was completed in 1978 but, because of a referendum decision against its use, was never loaded with nuclear fuel and never produced power.

In the United States the decision was made to convert yet another stalled nuclear plant into a fossil fuel plant for generating electricity. Construction of the Midland plant in Michigan had been halted in 1984, when the facility was 85% complete, and completion had been canceled in 1986 in the face of a variety of problems. Plans were made to convert the plant into a combined-cycle, cogeneration facility to be fueled by natural gas. In November Maine voters, for the third time in seven years, decisively rejected a referendum calling for a shutdown of the state's only nuclear reactor because it was a source of nuclear waste.

Several actions took place in the field of energy policy. In March U.S. Pres. Ronald Reagan signed the National Appliance Energy Conservation Act. The new law mandated minimum energy efficiency standards for most of the larger gas and electric appliances and heating-cooling equipment used in the home. It was estimated that the new standards would ultimately save more than $28 billion for consumers on their gas and electric bills. In May the president signed a bill repealing the Fuel Use Act of 1978, thus permitting electric utilities to burn oil or natural gas in new large plants, providing their design permitted future conversion to coal. The act also repealed certain pricing provisions of the 1978 Natural Gas Policy Act. The new law was welcomed by all the fossil fuel industries, which had campaigned vigorously for its passage. In Canada the National Energy Board relaxed the constraints on the export of natural gas. Previously, natural gas reserves could not be committed to export if to do so would reduce total Canadian gas reserves below 15 times annual production. Under the new policy, market forces would be allowed to operate freely unless it was shown that the ability to satisfy Canadian gas needs would be jeopardized.

Texaco Inc., the third largest oil company in the U.S., filed for bankruptcy in April as a consequence of its legal battle with rival Pennzoil Co. In 1984 Texaco acquired Getty Oil Co. soon after Pennzoil had reached what it considered to be a binding agreement to obtain three-sevenths of Getty. Pennzoil sued Texaco for interfering in its agreement with Getty, and a Texas state court jury in 1985 ruled in Pennzoil's favour. Texaco was ordered to pay Pennzoil $10,530,000,000, plus interest, in damages. Texaco appealed the verdict, and its declaration of bankruptcy prevented Pennzoil from seizing any Texaco assets while the case was moving through the courts. In November the Texas Supreme Court refused to hear the case, and Texaco considered appealing to the U.S. Supreme Court. In December, however, it filed a reorganization plan in Federal Bankruptcy Court that included a $3 billion settlement with Pennzoil. Texaco shareholders would vote on the plan early in 1988.                    (BRUCE C. NETSCHERT)

*See also* Engineering Projects; Industrial Review; Mining; Transportation.

This article updates the *Macropædia* articles ENERGY CONVERSION; FOSSIL FUELS.

# Engineering Projects

**Bridges.** San Francisco's most famous landmark, the Golden Gate Bridge, was 50 years old in 1987 and attracted a quarter of a million people to celebrations with fireworks, concerts, and illuminations. With a main span of 1,280 m (1 m = 3.3 ft), it had the longest span in the world until the Verrazano-Narrows Bridge (1,298 m) was opened in 1964, but it still had the tallest towers, at 227 m above sea level. The bridge was built to withstand the worst gales of the Pacific coast and an earthquake at least as severe as the one that devastated San Francisco in 1906. It was still thought to be the safest refuge in the area should a similar earthquake occur.

By the mid-1980s, however, construction of big bridges had become very much a Japanese prerogative. In March 1988 the Kojima-Sakaide road-and-rail route between the country's principal islands of Honshu and Shikoku was to be opened. All the bridges along the route were completed, including the Minami and Bisan Strait bridges. They were twin suspensions, built end-to-end, with main spans of 1,100 m and 990 m and with a common anchorage between them. There, uniquely, the main cables of each bridge were anchored at opposite ends of the chamber, having passed each other and therefore eliminated the threat of both bridges collapsing if one failed. The combined length of the two bridges was 3.4 km (2.1 mi). Also in the crossing were the Hitsuishi Island and Iwakuro Island bridges. They too were built end-to-end with a short land-based connecting span; each had a main span of 420 m. These two bridges were by far the longest cable-stayed bridges in the world for combined road and rail service. A third suspension bridge, the Shimotsui Strait Bridge, with a main span of 940 m and two steel truss viaducts over land, completed the 10-km (6.2-mi)-long crossing of the Seto Inland Sea, serving two smaller islands en route as well as Honshu and Shikoku.

In 1988 a start was to be made on the construction of the Akashi Kaikyo suspension bridge, which would have a main span of 1,990 m, 580 m longer than the 1,410 m of the Humber Bridge in the U.K., currently the world's longest single-span bridge. The Akashi Kaikyo Bridge, scheduled for completion in the late 1990s, would complete the second fixed crossing between Honshu and Shikoku.

Japanese bridge building was not restricted to Japan itself. In Bangkok, Thailand, 1987 saw the completion by a Japanese contractor of a European-designed cable-stayed road bridge that had a main span of 450 m over the Chao Phraya River. It had six traffic lanes and a single-plane

PANA

The Kojima-Sakaide route, which connects Japan's Honshu and Shikoku islands, was said to be the world's longest road-and-rail bridge chain. The 37.3-kilometre (23.3-mile) system was completed in August and was scheduled to open to the public in 1988.

cable system along the centre line of the bridge, which resulted in a particularly elegant structure. The Chao Phraya Bridge was easily the longest-span bridge of its kind anywhere. In Turkey construction on the second suspension bridge over the Bosporus Straits continued, and the main deck was completed. The erection of the bridge, by a Japanese consortium, was remarkably quick since major site work on the land-based tower foundations and the anchorages did not start until midsummer 1986. The construction work was directed by the U.K. A third 1,200-m bridge was being planned.

By contrast with the inspiring work on the big international bridges, the majority of bridge engineers were involved in the more mundane maintenance of existing structures and the assessment of their load-carrying capacities. Many of the concrete bridges built during the previous 30 years exhibited cracks in the concrete, spalling, and exposure of rusting steel reinforcement and prestressing cables. Similarly, many steel bridges built during the same period revealed cracked and corroded welds. The advantage of the steel bridges was that the repairs were easier to make and usually more durable. From the 1950s to the early 1980s, there was a strong preference for building concrete bridges for all spans of short and medium length, with steel being used only for the very longest spans (over 400 m). Since then there had been a return to using steel. Major objectives were to cut the time and cost of construction while at the same time producing stronger and longer-lasting bridges. Improved design and erection techniques did little to help the engineers responsible for the older bridges. In the U.S. the Federal Highway Administration reported that over 40% of the country's bridges were defective or obsolete, and the same was true in most industrialized countries. (DAVID FISHER)

**Buildings.** During 1987 engineering work was at a peak on the cube-shaped "Grande Arche" project at the western end of the Champs-Elysées in Paris. The building, 80,000 sq m (864,000 sq ft) in floor area, took the form of a cube having two opposite faces that are 20-m-wide 35-story towers, a roof, and the two other opposite faces open. The 70-m opening was the same width as the Champs-Elysées. Foundation problems were formidable, as two roads, a railway, and three subway tunnels ran under the site. The solution was to carry 12 piles, of up to 30,000 tons capacity each, down to limestone bedrock. As construction of the structural elements proceeded, the facades were erected. The gables of the sides, roof, and floor were white marble, and the exterior walls were clad in reflective glass to give the effect of two mirrors with an area of one hectare (2.47 ac).

In western Canada the new Olympic Oval, built primarily for staging events in the 1988 winter Olympic Games, was completed. Containing the world's first 400-m covered speed-skating track, it had a shape significantly different from that of other long-span sports facilities. The roof was 200 m by 90 m and had rounded ends, thus taking the form of an arch with a span of 90 m and a rise of 13 m, and the ends of the building were half domelike. The novel main frame of the roof was a grid of 1.8-m-deep concrete arches spaced at 18.5 m with three rows of nodes along the building. By forming the hollow box roof elements in precast concrete, the builders limited the staging works for construction to scaffold towers at the joints. The nodes themselves were cast at the site, incorporating cable ducts for posttensioning the whole network of arches on completion.

The Baha'i House of Worship in New Delhi, India, was completed and dedicated. Described as a shining example

of the combination of computer technology, human craftsmanship, and inspiration, the building was modeled on a lotus flower. The structure was composed of three layers of nine petals each, springing from a podium around an interior dome 34 m in diameter. The concrete shells rose 34 m high and varied in thickness from 60 mm to 200 mm. Advanced stress analysis using computer models was essential to production of such a refined design and was necessary to assure stability. The main contributors to the building represented many nations, which was appropriate given the international appeal of the Baha'i faith.

In the U.K. work proceeded on restoration of the 14th-century Salisbury Cathedral, with essential engineering repairs being carried out on the 123-m spire. The spire appeared solid but was, in fact, hollow and of relatively thin stonework, with the original medieval timber internal scaffold still in place. In places the stonework had been seriously eroded by weather and had to be replaced. This required the installation of permanent steel space frames at several levels so that the load could be bypassed around areas needing extensive stone replacement.

A new method of basement construction in fine water-bearing soils was used at the Victoria Insurance building in Düsseldorf, West Germany. Because the frequently used chemical grouts for forming cutoffs in such soil had been banned for environmental reasons, a grouting technique using traditional cement-based materials was developed. A cylindrical void was formed by a high-pressure water jet emanating from a probe. As the probe was withdrawn, cement grout was pumped in to fill the void while the jetting water and displaced soil were washed to the surface. In this way, a perimeter wall and a one-metre-thick slab at a depth of five metres below finished excavation levels was formed. The latter consisted of interlocking "stub columns" and formed a more or less continuous water cutoff.

Along with the exciting new developments in 1987, there were also tragedies that served as reminders that hazard-free building engineering could not be taken for granted. In April what was to have been the focal point of the L'Ambiance Plaza development in Bridgeport, Conn., collapsed during construction, killing 28 workers. Two adjacent 13-story buildings were being constructed by means of the lift slab system, whereby concrete floors are cast at ground level one on top of another and are progressively jacked up the columns to their final position. At some stage during the slab-lifting process, a too-high length of columns was left unbraced against sway. It was found that overloading had caused the ninth-floor slab to slip and crack, thus leading to a collapse of the whole structure. This type of accident emphasized the need for better coordination of design and construction procedures.

(GEOFFREY M. PINFOLD)

**Dams.** In spite of the unrest in the Middle East, dam construction continued there. Iraq started work on the Baghdadi Dam on the Euphrates River and the Bekne Dam on the Great Zab River, 400 km (250 mi) north of Baghdad. Jordan awarded a contract for a 42-m-high dam in the Mallahah Valley near Karmen. Iran completed a 27-m-high dam near Mianeh to irrigate 800 ha and started another at Khordad to store 200 million cu m (1 cu m = 35.3 cu ft) of water near the city of Qom. Two other Iranian dams, Saveh in Central Province and Jiroft in Kerman Province, were scheduled for completion in 1988. In Syria work was completed on the Abdeen Dam on the Yarmuk River to irrigate 300 ha and the Ba'ath Dam near ar-Raqqah on the Euphrates downstream from Thawra Dam, which would provide 50 MW of electricity and irrigate the valley lands. A new dam was proposed on the Euphrates to store 1.3 billion cu m of water at a cost of $500 million.

Algeria, with its 22 million population, was taking major strides toward providing drinking water to its expanding population and industrial water to its new factories. Irrigation water would provide for food production on 50,000 ha of new lands. The latest five-year government program included 17 new dams to be started at the rate of 4 per year. These dams were by no means small; one would be 160 m high and have a storage capacity of 110 million cu m. The 40-m-high Hammam Ghrouz Dam was to have a reservoir of 45 million cu m of water, and the 55-m-high Ain Zada Dam would store 125 million cu m. Morocco completed the Qued Arib Dam, which would store 700,000 cu m of water for use in Khemisset Province. King Hassan outlined a plan to start 14 new dams. The Ait Youb earth-fill dam was started and would take three years to complete.

Indonesia commissioned the Saguling Dam and hydroelectric plant, which cost $700 million. It was the largest dam in Indonesia, an earth- and rock-fill dam 98 m high with a reservoir of 609 million cu m and a generating capacity of 700 MW of power. This power would save more than four million barrels of oil annually, and more than 200,000 ha of rice fields would be irrigated.

Lesotho reached an agreement with South Africa to construct a water-transfer project involving four dams. This would shift water from the Sengu catchment basin in Lesotho to the Vaal River catchment in South Africa. It would generate power and provide considerable revenue for Lesotho.

Zimbabwe was speeding up completion of its highest dam, which was designed to be 64 m high, have a crest length of 320 m, and store 365 million cu m of water. There were also plans to raise the height of the present 40-m-high Sebakwe Dam by 6 m, thus increasing its ability to capture and store more water. The original dam was completed in 1957.

China continued to expand its hydroelectric potential on the Huang Ho. It has an exploitable potential of 24,000 MW, with only 2,400 MW developed as of the end of 1987. One of the sites studied was that of the present Sanmenxia (San-men-hsia) Dam. This site could have a 106-m-high dam that could produce 1,200 MW. One of the deterrents

## Major World Dams Under Construction in 1987[1]

| Name of dam | River | Country | Type[2] | Height (m) | Length of crest (m) | Volume content (000 cu m) | Gross reservoir capacity (000 cu m) |
|---|---|---|---|---|---|---|---|
| Altinkaya | Kizilirmak | Turkey | E,R | 195 | 634 | 16,000 | 5,763,000 |
| Arachtas/Kalaritikos | Arachtos | Greece | E | 185 | 238 | 1,500 | 1,840,000 |
| Ataturk | Euphrates | Turkey | E,R | 184 | 1,820 | 84,500 | 48,700,000 |
| Bakun | Rajang | Malaysia | R | 210 | 900 | 29,400 | 43,800,000 |
| Boruca | Terraba | Costa Rica | E,R | 267 | 700 | 43,000 | 14,960,000 |
| Bureya | Bureya | U.S.S.R. | G | 139 | 810 | 3,561 | 20,900,000 |
| Casa de Piedra | Rio Colorado | Argentina | E | 56 | 10,000 | 16,500 | 4,000,000 |
| Chapeton | Paraná | Argentina | E,G | 35 | 224,000 | 296,200 | 60,600,000 |
| Chisapani | Karnali | Nepal | E,R | 210 | 850 | 35,000 | 15,100,000 |
| Cipasang | Cimanuk | Indonesia | E,R | 200 | 1,860 | 90,000 | 860,000 |
| Corpus Posadas | Paraná | Argentina/Paraguay | E,G | 65 | 8,474 | 18,200 | 13,000,000 |
| Corumba | Corumba | Brazil | R | 150 | 600 | ... | 675,000 |
| Dabaklamm | Dorferbach | Austria | A | 220 | 332 | 1,000 | 235,000 |
| Dongfeng | Yachi He | China | A | 168 | 251 | 622 | 1,020,000 |
| Dongjiang | Laishui | China | A | 157 | 438 | 940 | 8,120,000 |
| Ertan | Yalang | China | A | 240 | 763 | 4,740 | 5,800 |
| Gallito Ciego | Jequetepeque | Peru | E,R | 112 | 750 | 15,000 | 400,000 |
| Garabi | Uruguay | Argentina/Brazil | E,G | 60 | 3,960 | 19,884 | 5,810,000 |
| Guavio | Guavio | Colombia | E,R | 243 | 390 | 17,755 | 1,020,000 |
| Guayllabamba | Guayllabamba | Ecuador | A | 165 | 413 | 704 | 105,000 |
| Hrusov-Dunakiliti | Dunaj | Czechoslovakia/Hungary | E,G | 29 | 31,500 | 18,340 | 199,000 |
| Ilha Grande | Paraná | Brazil | E,G | 29 | 7,060 | 11,573 | 30,000,000 |
| Ingapata | Paute | Ecuador | G | 166 | 430 | 1,600 | 413,000 |
| Kabalebo | Kabalebo | Suriname | E,R | 45 | 1,650 | 3,790 | 19,000,000 |
| Kayraktepe | Goksu | Turkey | E,R | 199 | 580 | 17,000 | 4,800,000 |
| Kilickaya | Kelkit | Turkey | E,R | 135 | 405 | 6,030 | 15,000,000 |
| Kishau | Tons | India | E,R | 253 | 360 | 18,400 | 2,400,000 |
| Kouilou | Kouilou | Congo | A | 137 | 345 | 390 | 35,000,000 |
| La Vueltosa | Caparo | Venezuela | E | 118 | 1,200 | 15,000 | 5,300,000 |
| Li Jia Xia | Huang He | China | A | 165 | 430 | 1,300 | 1,700,000 |
| Lower Tunguska | Lower Tunguska | U.S.S.R. | E,G | 210 | 6,200 | 23,000 | 45,000,000 |
| Menzelet | Ceyhan | Turkey | E,R | 151 | 425 | 8,530 | 19,500,000 |
| Michihuao | Limay | Argentina | E | 70 | 6,700 | 29,840 | 5,860,000 |
| Nan Choan | Quae Yai | Thailand | R | 187 | 430 | 12,200 | 5,950,000 |
| Pati | Paraná | Argentina | E,G | 36 | 174,900 | 230,180 | 38,000,000 |
| Piedra del Aquila | Limay | Argentina | G | 174 | 795 | 2,764 | 12,800,000 |
| Potrerillos | Mendoza | Argentina | E | 146 | 550 | 17,120 | 860,000 |
| Rocandor | Uruguay | Brazil/Argentina | E,R | 78 | 1,598 | 9,940 | 33,580,000 |
| San Roque | Agno | Philippines | E | 210 | 1,130 | 43,150 | 990,000 |
| Sardar Sarovar | Narmada | India | G | 163 | 1,199 | 7,472 | 9,500,000 |
| Tehri | Bhagirathi | India | E,R | 261 | 570 | 22,750 | 2,600,000 |
| Tian Sheng Qia | Nan Pan | China | R | 180 | 1,250 | 19,300 | 10,800,000 |
| Urra II | Sinu | Colombia | R | 170 | 275 | 23,500 | 34,300,000 |
| Yacyreta-Apipe | Paraná | Paraguay/Argentina | E,G | 42 | 82,000 | 61,200 | 21,000,000 |
| **Major World Dams Completed in 1986 and 1987[1]** | | | | | | | |
| Dorna | Lerez | Spain | G | 151 | 163 | 68 | 27,500 |
| El M'Jara | Ouergha | Morocco | E | 87 | 1,600 | 25,000 | 4,000,000 |
| Kara Kaya | Euphrates | Turkey | A | 173 | 462 | 2,000 | 9,580,000 |
| Khudoni | Inguri | U.S.S.R. | A | 201 | 545 | 1,475 | 365,000 |
| Lhakwar | Yamuna | India | G | 192 | 440 | 2,000 | 580,000 |
| Longyangxia | Huang He | China | A,G | 178 | 396 | 1,570 | 24,700,000 |
| Lower Usuma | Usuma | Nigeria | E | 49 | 1,350 | 93,000 | 100,000 |
| Maqarin | Yarmuk | Jordan | E,R | 164 | 700 | 21,000 | 486,000 |
| Mazar | Paute | Ecuador | G | 180 | 400 | 1,650 | 500,000 |
| Planicie Banderita | Neuquen | Argentina | E | 35 | 350 | 1,194 | 43,000,000 |
| Rogun | Vakhsh | U.S.S.R. | E,R | 335 | 602 | 71,000 | 13,300,000 |
| São Felix | Tocantins | Brazil | E,R | 160 | 1,950 | 34,000 | 55,200,000 |
| Thein | Ravi | India | E,G | 160 | 565 | 16,187 | 3,280,000 |
| Upper Wainganga | Wainganga | India | E | 43 | 181 | 6,290 | 50,700,000 |
| Warna | Warna | India | E,G | 91 | 1,580 | 15,310 | 964,000 |

[1] Having a height exceeding 150 m (492 ft); or having a volume content exceeding 15 million cu m (19.6 cu yd); or forming a reservoir exceeding 14,800 × 10^6 cu m of capacity (12 million ac-ft).
[2] Type of dam: E = earth; R = rockfill; A = arch; G = gravity.

(T. W. MERMEL)

The Olympic Oval in Calgary, Alberta, with the world's first 400-metre covered speed-skating track, was to be used for events in the 1988 Olympics.
RON WATTS—FIRST LIGHT

to getting the dam approved was that it would require the relocation of about 300,000 people from the reservoir area.

In the U.S.S.R. 19 people were killed when a dam was overtopped in the Tadzhuk S.S.R. and waters flooded the village of Sargozan. Torrential rains caused the sudden flood that destroyed the dam.

Canadian Indians filed suit to stop construction of the Three Rivers Dam in Alberta on the grounds that it violated the rights of the Indians to the waters of the Oldman River and would destroy their way of life. Construction of the 76-m-high dam had already started, and the government claimed that the water storage could increase the available water supplies, irrigate 420,000 ha, increase agricultural production, and create 1,700 new jobs. Protests by the Cree Indians brought a settlement of $160 million for damages caused by flooding by the James Bay Dam in Quebec and for failure to honour commitments to provide replacement facilities. (T. W. MERMEL)

**Roads.** Most national governments were finding it difficult to raise sufficient public funds for construction of new highway systems and improvement of existing roads as fast as needed. As a result, many countries were turning to alternative funding sources, such as tolls and private financing of road projects. On a global basis about $45 billion would be needed in the next decade to pay for rehabilitation of roads in the 85 countries that received highway assistance from the World Bank. This did not include the cost of repairing bridges or rural roads.

In the United States federal funding of up to 35% of the cost of toll road construction was permitted in specified projects in Texas, Pennsylvania, Florida, South Carolina, and California. Privately financed toll roads were also on the increase, such as the $323 million North–South Tollway in the Chicago suburbs and the $722 million, 80-km (1 km = 0.62 mi) E-470 highway around Denver, Colo. Over 97%, or 66,446 km, of the 68,382-km Interstate Highway System of the United States was completed. All remaining Interstate segments were scheduled to be finished or under contract by 1990.

In Canada the province of Quebec planned to spend $300 million more than previously anticipated over the next five years to maintain its roads, which had deteriorated to the point where half of them would have to be completely rebuilt. Mexico planned to have as much as 10,000 km of four-lane highway by the year 2000, including the first toll

highways in the country. Mexico also needed 130,000 km of rural roads.

In Argentina a $384 million eight-lane highway was to be built between La Plata and Buenos Aires, a distance of 87 km. Argentina's National Highway Administration was planning the immediate upgrading of 1,200 km of roads at a cost of $300 million. A similar program in Uruguay, covering 883 km, was to cost $152 million.

Costa Rica expected to spend $73 million to complete the highway between the capital city of San José and Puerto Caldera on the Pacific. The first use of asphalt recycling in Central America was successfully carried out in Costa Rica on the La Sabana–San Ramon Highway.

By 1990 China expected to build or reconstruct 14,000 km of highways, bringing the total network to 2,000 km of expressways and first-class highways, 40,000 km of second-class roads, and 200,000 km of other paved roads. A four-lane expressway was being built from Beijing (Peking) to Tanggu (T'ang-ku), 154 km away. Construction was under way on the 108-km Northern Taiwan Second Freeway Project, which would ease congestion in Taipei.

In Malaysia the $3 billion North–South Toll Expressway, under construction, was the single largest road construction project ever undertaken by the government. The 900-km road, stretching from the Thailand border to the Singapore causeway, was privately financed.

India's first expressway, a 93-km highway between Baroda and Ahmadabad, was under construction. It was expected to reduce travel time between the two cities from two hours to 90 minutes. Completion of paving of a 276-km segment of the Great Northern Highway in Western Australia marked the last link in a 16,000-km surfaced road around Australia.

Britain's road spending for 1987–88 was expected to reach $7,761,000,000. Construction of 725 km of motorways (expressways) and trunk roads by 1990 was planned, including widening of sections of the newly opened but congested M25 ring road around London.

A 57-km stretch of the A23 motorway in Italy, connecting Carnio to Tarvisio and the Austrian border, was opened to traffic in July 1987. It was part of the Trans-European North–South Motorway, extending from Poland to Greece and Turkey and crossing ten countries. The Italian government approved a plan to build a road and rail link across the Strait of Messina between Sicily and the Italian mainland. Work started on the first phase of the 15-km ring road around Budapest, Hung., scheduled for completion in 1990. (HUGH M. GILLESPIE)

**Tunnels.** During 1987 the first work began on site for the £4.7 billion Channel Tunnel (Chunnel) linking England and France across the English Channel. At Sangatte near Calais on the French coast, the well-remembered difficulties experienced in 1974 on the inclined access shaft were circumvented by a simple but imaginative means. A shaft 55 m in diameter and 70 m deep was constructed, using diaphragm-wall combined with classic rock-shaft excavating techniques. The huge shaft was to accommodate the successive launch of all six French tunnel-boring machines (TBMs) in stable chalk marl strata. At Lower Shakespeare Cliff near Dover, England, the first British TBM, weighing 500 metric tons and costing some £3.8 million, was assembled piece by piece, underground. It began driving toward France in late 1987. The final hurdle for the project was the raising of £770 million of investment capital from the general stock market by Eurotunnel, the Anglo-French private-sector group granted the Channel Tunnel franchise. Banks and investment houses worldwide had previously pledged £4 billion, conditional upon the success of the stock market flotation.

This major breakthrough for the concept of private-sector financing of major tunneling projects led to a flurry of interest from developed and third world countries alike, where cuts in public spending had become frequent. In France proposals for a road tunnel under the Pyrenees Mountains to Spain, and others beneath the cities of Marseille, Toulon, and Nice, were arousing private-sector interest. In Norway the city of Bergen was raising funds by tolls to finance road tunnels that otherwise would have to wait up to 30 years for government grants.

In both the U.S.S.R. and China, the latest and longest railway tunnels were completed. The 14.3-km Dayao (Tayao) Shan tunnel on the Beijing–Guangzhou (Canton) line took six years to complete. The 8.3-km tunnel on the line between Idzhevan and Razdan passed through mountainous terrain in Armenia, reaching 2,000 m above sea level.

In the U.S. the proposed $4.4 billion superconducting super collider (SSC) nuclear physics experimental facility moved nearer realization when the federal government invited state governments to indicate their interest in providing sites for the 170-km complex of tunnels and underground chambers. In Switzerland the large electron positron (LEP) project at the European Laboratory for Particle Physics was completed and commissioned. This "machine" was housed in 24 km of tunnels 3.7 m in diameter, formed in a circle, at Meyrin, near Geneva.

The world's demand for tunnel engineering continued to be dominated by the expansion and modernization of urban transportation systems. In the U.S. Los Angeles planned to spend $150 million on 30.2 km of subway linking the downtown area with the San Fernando Valley, and sections of work had already been let to contractors. The Japanese authorities started work on an inclined access shaft at Chinzei that would permit exploratory borings for a tunnel that was to be a massive project 200–250 km long. This undersea gallery would stretch from Fukuoka in Japan to Masan in South Korea, some 100 m below the seabed and connecting Iki island, Tsushima, and Kojedo. The Japanese were not deterred by the enormous task, having proved their determination and tenacity in the past. The Seikan tunnel, 23 km long, had taken 19 years to complete. (GEOFFREY J. NOBLETT)

This article updates the *Macropædia* articles BUILDING CONSTRUCTION; PUBLIC WORKS.

# Environment

Perhaps as a legacy of the Chernobyl nuclear-reactor disaster in the U.S.S.R. in April 1986, which compelled governments and international institutions to work together quickly, openly, and on an unprecedented scale, there was a marked increase in international cooperation on environmental issues in 1987. European governments agreed on limits for vehicle-exhaust emissions, and as the Convention on Long-Range Transboundary Air Pollution came into force, it began to appear that the acid rain problem might be brought under control, at least in Europe. The major agreement of the year, however, concerned the ozone layer and restrictions on the production and use of chemicals suspected of damaging it. The protocol to the Convention on the Protection of the Ozone Layer was initialed by 24 countries in September. The importance of the agreement was largely political, demonstrating that tolerance and compromise on such issues were possible. This success raised the possibility that international action might be coordinated to deal with the more difficult—but more firmly established and much more serious—problem of the "greenhouse effect," the projected increase in the Earth's temperature resulting from pollution of the atmosphere.

## INTERNATIONAL COOPERATION

**World Commission on Environment and Development.** On April 27 Norwegian Prime Minister Gro Harlem Brundtland launched the commission's report, *Our Common Future*. Initiated by the UN in 1983 and compiled by commissioners in 21 countries, it listed environmental threats and called for "sustainable development" to feed a growing world population, alleviate poverty, and safeguard the environment.

**United Nations.** Information from the Global Environment Monitoring Service provided the basis for a joint report by the UN Environment Program (UNEP) and the World Health Organization (WHO). *Global Pollution and Health,* published in June, estimated the number of people throughout the world who were exposed to environmental pollutants at levels higher than the recommended maxima. It stated that 600 million people were exposed to unacceptably high levels of sulfur dioxide and one billion to particulate matter from dust and the burning of carbon-based fuels. European rivers contained 45 times the normal background level of plant nutrients, and one-quarter of all the fresh water monitored contained more than the permitted limit of at least one pollutant. In many countries measurable levels of organochlorine pesticides and polychlorinated biphenyls (PCBs) continued to be found in food and in human milk.

**World Bank.** Following the failure of some of the World Bank's development schemes at least partly because of the severe environmental damage they caused, environmentalists welcomed the announcement in May that the bank was to establish an environment department. The new department would devise a series of conservation programs and make sure that the environmental consequences of projects were taken fully into account before funding was approved.

**UN Economic Commission for Europe.** The Convention on Long-Range Transboundary Air Pollution, which came into force on September 2, obliged the signatories to reduce emissions of sulfur to at least 30% below 1980 levels. Of the 21 signatory and 16 ratifying countries, 10 had already met this goal, although the effects were partly offset by increased emissions elsewhere. Within Europe emissions fell from 51.3 million metric tons in 1980 to 44.7 million tons in 1985, and within North America from 27.8 million tons in 1980 to 24.5 million tons in 1983. The commission met in Geneva in May in the hope of agreeing on a protocol, to be ratified in September, to reduce emissions of nitrogen oxides from all sources. The meeting ended in deadlock, however, and the September meeting was postponed until November, when a protocol was agreed on, although it set no targets or timetable.

**European Communities.** In May the European Commission issued a draft directive defining areas in which fresh water was vulnerable to pollution from nitrates and recommending limits to nitrogen fertilizer use and the size of livestock units in those areas. The limits were related to the type of soil and crops grown but in some cases required farmers to halve the amount of fertilizer they applied. In August the Commission complained to the governments of Belgium, West Germany, Greece, Italy, and the U.K. about their failure to enact existing directives designed to safeguard drinking water, bathing water, and surface water and to protect groundwater from pesticide contamination.

In July environment ministers agreed to new limits for vehicle-exhaust emissions, to be measured as the quantity of each pollutant emitted during a standard test. For large, medium, and small cars, respectively, these were to be 45 g, 30 g, and 25 g of carbon monoxide and 15 g, 8 g, and 6.5 g of hydrocarbons and nitrogen oxides. Steps were also taken aimed at eliminating acid rain throughout the EC area within 20 years.

**The Ozone Layer.** Controversy raged over a depletion of the ozone layer that had been observed over the interior of Antarctica during the early austral spring. (*See* EARTH SCIENCES: *Meteorology.*) Several theories were advanced to explain this "hole in the ozone layer"; some held that it was caused naturally, others that it was due to air pollution, primarily by chlorofluorocarbons (CFCs). By September 1987 the scientific consensus held that as the polar air warms in spring it rises, drawing tropospheric air, with little ozone,

into the stratosphere, where more ozone is soon formed as oxygen is exposed to solar radiation. The depletion was natural but possibly exacerbated by the presence of chemicals that would both accelerate the warming and catalyze ozone destruction. This theory was generally accepted by scientists as explaining local anomalies and the speed with which the chemical composition of the Antarctic air could change.

Evidence was accumulating, however, to suggest that chlorine, probably from CFCs, and bromine, probably from "halons" (chlorofluorobromine compounds used in fire extinguishers), played an important part in causing the Antarctic depletion. The results of high-altitude sampling, released in October, showed relatively high concentrations of chlorine monoxide and dioxide—CFC decay products—in the atmospheric region where ozone was depleted. There was no evidence that the depletion had any implications outside Antarctica. Nevertheless, the press publicized the issue widely, and pressure increased for restrictions on the manufacture and use of the offending compounds.

In April the 31 members of the Vienna Convention on the Protection of the Ozone Layer met in Geneva, under UNEP auspices, to discuss ways of reducing CFC production and use, and in September a protocol to this effect was signed by 24 countries in Montreal. It called for CFC production to be frozen at its 1986 level by 1990, to be reduced by 20% from that level by 1995, and to be cut a further 30% by 1999, while halon production would be frozen at 1986 levels by 1993. Exceptions were made to allow exports of CFC refrigerants to less developed countries and to permit the U.S.S.R. to complete the building of two CFC production plants and to increase its own domestic consumption. CFCs are powerful "greenhouse" gases, and the agreement to reduce production of them was related to increasing concern about the climatic consequences of the greenhouse effect. The UNEP governing council asked director Mostafa Tolba to produce policy options within a year for dealing with the issue.

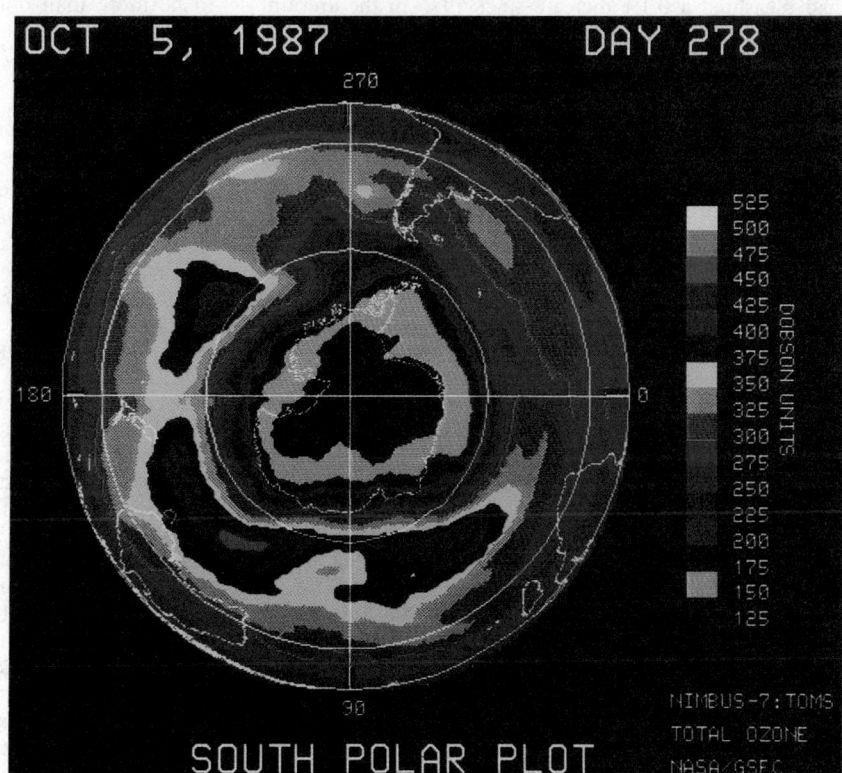

GODDARD SPACE FLIGHT CENTER, NASA

A satellite image shows that the "hole" in the Earth's ozone layer above Antarctica has grown. Ozone helps screen out the Sun's dangerous ultraviolet rays, which cause sunburn and skin cancer and may weaken the immune system. Chlorofluorocarbons (CFCs) and "halons," man-made chemicals found in propellants in aerosol sprays and air-conditioning coolants, were believed to contribute to the ozone depletion.

## NATIONAL DEVELOPMENTS

**The Greenhouse Effect.** Several groups of scientists reported during the year that they had found evidence of changes attributable to a "greenhouse" warming. Bristlecone pines had been growing at an accelerated rate over the previous century; the increases were noted in the growth rate of trees near the tree line over about one million square kilometres (386,000 sq mi) of the U.S., according to Donald Graybill of the University of Arizona Tree Ring Laboratory. He said in January that the increase was probably due to the larger amount of carbon dioxide in the air. In June Frank Woodward of the University of Cambridge reported that his examination of plants stored in a herbarium showed that over the previous 200 years several species had reduced the number of their stomata in response to increasing amounts of carbon dioxide. The results of a study by a team from the Climatic Research Unit, University of East Anglia, the U.S. National Oceanic and Atmospheric Administration (NOAA), and the University of Massachusetts were published in *Science* in July. They showed an increase in precipitation in mid-latitudes in the U.S., Europe, and the U.S.S.R. over the previous 30 to 40 years and a decrease in precipitation in the subtropics. This change was consistent with predictions of the greenhouse effect.

A similar increase in rainfall was reported in Australia. In September Graeme Pearman and Barrie Pittock of the Atmospheric Research Division, Commonwealth Scientific and Industrial Research Organization, launched a program to alert politicians and the public to its implications, especially for Australian farmers. By the year 2030, said Pearman and Pittock, mean average temperatures in Australia could be 2°–3° C (3°–5° F) higher, summer rainfall 50% higher, and sea levels 1.4 m (55 in) higher. Speaking in Vancouver, B.C., in August at a meeting of the International Union of Geodesy and Geophysics, Wayne Evans of the Atmospheric Environment Service of Environment Canada, a Canadian government agency, said he had measured a 0.1% increase since 1975 in the amount of radiation being retained by the Earth. This, he argued, was the first direct evidence of the greenhouse effect, and he maintained that CFCs were a major cause.

**Air Pollution.** Evidence accumulated during the year to show the great distances atmospheric pollutants can travel, and severe pollution problems were reported from several countries. In Britain the increase in road transport was causing a rise in pollution by soot, according to a report issued in March by the Department of the Environment. It showed that about 260,000 tons of soot were released each year, although levels in urban areas were half those recorded ten years earlier. Emissions of sulfur dioxide had fallen 40% in 20 years to 3.6 million tons, close to the 1940 level; lead emissions, at 6,500 tons, had fallen 10% between 1984 and 1985; but emissions of nitrogen oxides, carbon monoxide, and hydrocarbons had increased. In May the government announced a ten-year program to reduce emissions of nitrogen oxides from coal-fired power stations by 30%.

As part of an EC-sponsored survey of European forests, the Forestry Commission announced in July that it was about to begin a new study of pollution damage to British trees. Results from its 1986 survey of Norway spruce showed 1% of trees dead or dying, 31% with moderate or severe damage, and about 36% with slight damage, probably due to pollution. In the same month at a conference in Bergen, Norway, scientists of the Surface Water Acidification Program reported some recovery of acidified Scandinavian lakes since 1975, the year British sulfur emis-

A child is screened for radioactive contamination in Goiânia, Brazil, in October. A junk dealer had opened a discarded cylinder from a cancer-therapy machine that contained a radioactive blue powder and distributed it among friends and neighbours.
SASSAKI—SIPA

sions began to decline. Sponsored by the Royal Society of London, the Royal Swedish Academy of Sciences, and the Norwegian Academy of Science and Letters, the program was funded by the British Central Electricity Generating Board.

Pres. Gustav Husak of Czechoslovakia announced in March that investment in environmental protection was to be more than doubled during the five-year (1986–90) plan period. An official report, leaked in June by members of the Charter 77 dissident group, said sulfur dioxide emissions in Prague were 20 times the permitted limit and were affecting the health of citizens. Severe pollution in Rome led the Italian authorities to close the city centre to private vehicles on Nov. 28, 1986, and again during the morning rush hour in February 1987. A report published in December 1986 said that half of Switzerland's conifers were dead or dying from the effects of acid rain.

The dispute between the U.S. and Canadian governments over acid rain was discussed at meetings in January and April but was not resolved. The preliminary results of a seven-year study by scientists working for the National Acid Precipitation Assessment Program, representing several U.S. government agencies, were published in September. The four-volume report said that 10% of lakes in the Adirondack Mountains were acidified, but in most other parts of the northeastern U.S. sulfur was not accumulating in ecosystems, and further damage to surface waters was unlikely. The report was widely welcomed for its thorough and accurate description of the acid rain situation but was attacked for its allegedly complacent conclusions.

Russell Schnell of NOAA reported in December 1986 that soot and haze from eastern Europe and the U.S.S.R. sometimes covered large areas over the Arctic Ocean and Alaska. He warned that this could warm the atmosphere locally and trigger melting of the ice sheet. The results of the latest forest survey in West Germany, published in October 1986, showed that acid rain damage had increased during the preceding year, especially among oaks, beeches, and other deciduous species. The proportion of trees of all species affected rose around Hamburg from 77 to 80% and around Bremen from 52 to 84%, and in Bavaria 80% of trees were affected. Smog alerts were issued in West Berlin and Hamburg in February when a temperature inversion allowed polluted air to drift from East Germany and then to be augmented by West German emissions.

**Freshwater Pollution.** Deterioration in the quality of water in British rivers was reported by the water authorities in December 1986, much of it due to runoff from farms and from overloaded sewerage works. They estimated that it would cost more than £200 million over 20 years to bring the nitrate content of water down to the EC limit of 50 mg per litre, and in February they said it would cost £1.3 billion over 15 years to bring storm sewage overflows to an acceptable standard. In February 1987 the U.S. Congress overrode Pres. Ronald Reagan's veto of a $20 billion reauthorization of the Clean Water Act. A similar bill passed in late 1986 had lapsed when the president left it unsigned while Congress was not in session (the "pocket veto").

The Canadian and U.S. authorities agreed in February to clean up the Niagara River, described as the most polluted river in either country. It carried municipal and toxic wastes into Lake Ontario, the source of public water supplies on both sides of the border. In February the public was warned against eating fish, especially large fish, caught in the Great Lakes because they contained high levels of organochlorine pesticides and PCBs. On January 29 dieldrin and tri-*n*-butyltin (TBT; an ingredient of antifouling paints) were spilled into Lough Neagh, Northern Ireland. By March 6,000 litres of TBT had been removed from the water, but 3,000–4,000 litres had seeped into drainage systems. Although high levels of contamination were found locally, the public water supply was not seriously affected. Drinking water for thousands of people in Shanxi (Shansi) Province, China, was contaminated on January 2 when toxic chemicals were spilled into the Nanzhang (Nanchang) River near Changzhi (Ch'ang-chih). No one died, but 81 children were seriously poisoned. Radio Prague reported on Nov. 12, 1986, that about 40 tons of heating oil containing sulfur had spilled from the Kunice cement factory in Ostrava, close to Czechoslovakia's border with Poland, into a sewerage system and from there into the Lucina River, a tributary of the Oder. The spillage caused considerable damage in Poland's Katowice Province.

Following the explosions and a fire at the Sandoz AG chemical warehouse at Schweizerhalle, near Basel, Switz., on Nov. 1, 1986, which caused catastrophic pollution of the Rhine, the section of the river between Basel and Karlsruhe was declared dead. Water used to combat the fire had breached a dike, washing 10 to 30 tons of chemicals—including a number of pesticides but mainly disulfoton, an extremely toxic organophosphorus compound— into the river. At a meeting in Zürich on November 12, the Swiss authorities agreed to pay for cleaning the river, and work began a few days later on vacuum-dredging mud from the riverbed. In May 1987 Sandoz agreed to pay £620,000 compensation to French fishermen and £106,000 to finance research and implement projects to clean up the Rhine, as well as more than £3 million in settlement of small claims arising from the incident.

In mid-December 1986 the pressure in a chemical reactor at a Givaudan factory near Geneva overwhelmed the safety system and released pseudoionone, cyclohexane, and phosphoric acid into the Rhône. The chemicals were being used to produce the odour of violets for perfumes, and they perfumed the river itself. Large amounts of phenol and

ammonia contaminated the Sebes Koros River in Hungary in April, and detergents and fungicides were also detected in the water. The source remained a mystery, however.

**Pesticides.** Thallium sulfate, imported by the Guyana Sugar Corporation to kill cane rats on the sugar plantations, was reported in March to have been responsible for about 150 cases of poisoning in humans since 1985 because poor farmers used it as a fertilizer. In Spain some 30,000 birds died of poisoning in October 1986 after feeding in dried-out rice fields contaminated with methyl parathion. The pesticide was banned in Spain but had been used by rice farmers to kill crayfish, which were damaging rice plants and dikes. Dinoseb, a member of the dinitro group of pesticides, was banned by the U.S. Environmental Protection Agency (EPA) after Swiss research showed that it caused birth defects in animals. In February 1987 the National Coalition Against the Misuse of Pesticides joined with Trial Lawyers for Public Justice to recover damages for people claiming to have been injured by heptachlor and chlordane. The EPA was criticized for the inadequacy of its measures to control these insecticides, which are used to kill termites. In Britain antifouling paints used on the hulls of boats and on fishing nets and cages were classified as pesticides rather than paints from July 1. Their toxic ingredient, TBT, was known to harm marine invertebrates.

**Radioactive and Toxic Chemical Wastes.** A radiation leak, described by WHO as the worst ever in the Western Hemisphere and second in severity only to Chernobyl, occurred in Goiânia, capital of the central Brazilian state of Goiás. Details unfolded in early October, when it emerged that during the previous month a cancer-therapy machine had been stolen from an abandoned hospital clinic, and a capsule found in the machine had been smashed open by a scrap metal dealer. Finding a "shiny and pretty" bluish powder inside, he distributed the novelty among neighbours and friends. In some cases the powder was rubbed into the body or ingested. The powder was cesium-137, a highly radioactive material. By late October, 4 people had died, several others were receiving hospital treatment, and a total of almost 250 had been treated for radiation sickness. Some 2,000 sq m (2,400 sq yd) of the town were sealed off for decontamination. A new controversy arose over the government's plans to dispose of the radioactive waste gathered at Goiânia by burying it in a mountain range in the southern Amazon.

Elsewhere the disposal of radioactive wastes and industrial wastes by dumping or incineration at sea dominated the waste-disposal debate. In August the decision by the Belgian government to withdraw permission for the incineration of wastes inside its territorial waters left Britain alone among nations bordering the North Sea in wishing to continue to dispose of wastes at sea. The *Sirius*, a vessel of the environmental action group Greenpeace, sailed from Scotland on September 24 on a six-month campaign to draw attention to pollution in the North and Irish seas and to persuade the British authorities to end dumping within two years and incineration by 1990. On October 7 two demonstrators from the *Sirius* boarded a waste carrier, the *Yarrow*, and chained themselves to its discharge pipe. After 15 hours, when all attempts to dislodge the Greenpeace members had failed, the *Yarrow* gave up its mission and returned to port with the demonstrators still attached.

Disposal of waste at sea was blamed for high levels of pollution along the U.S. Atlantic coast, and there were numerous beach closings, especially in the New York-New Jersey area. Fish kills and algae blooms added to an unpleasant summer, as did the deaths of large numbers of bottlenose dolphins off the Middle Atlantic states. A possi-

Traffic police in Rome direct cars away from the historic centre during the morning rush hour. City officials banned rush-hour traffic from the centre in an attempt to cut down on pollution.
AP/WIDE WORLD

ble clue to these and other mysterious marine deaths came to light in December, when the stomachs of dead humpback whales were found to contain mackerel contaminated by a toxin that originates in the red tide algae bloom. The problem of waste disposal was dramatized by the saga of the garbage scow *Mobro*. Refused permission to dispose of its cargo at an Islip, N.Y., landfill, the *Mobro* traveled some 9,700 km (6,000 mi) and was turned away by six states and three countries before New York officials finally allowed the trash to be burned at a Brooklyn incinerator.

In Britain plans to construct four shallow-burial facilities for the disposal of low-level radioactive wastes were abandoned on May 1, leading to protests from the Radioactive Waste Management Advisory Committee, which had not been consulted about the decision. There was some confusion when on September 14 British Nuclear Fuels Ltd. proposed to build an intermediate-level waste depository beneath the seabed off the Cumbrian coast, close to its Sellafield nuclear reprocessing plant. The Irish government objected, and Nirex, the government agency responsible for radioactive waste disposal, had not completed its own plans. A week later Nirex announced that it was looking for four offshore sites capable of holding 2,000 tons each in either deep mainland mines with galleries extending below the seabed, drift mines sunk diagonally from the shore, or seabed boreholes.

Spanish plans to dispose of radioactive wastes close to the Portuguese border caused considerable disquiet. Following warnings of possible pollution of the Douro River, which provides irrigation water for vineyards and public supplies for Porto, the Portuguese government formally protested to Spain on May 5. Kraftwerk Union, the main West German builder of nuclear plants, announced in July that it planned to dispose of radioactive waste in the Gobi Desert of central Asia.

The sealing of the damaged Chernobyl reactor was completed in November 1986, and in July 1987 six officials held responsible for the accident were tried and imprisoned for terms ranging from two to ten years. The public health implications of the accident were studied intensively once the immediate emergency had passed. At a meeting in Vienna sponsored by the International Atomic Energy Agency (IAEA) in May, it was agreed that the health of 135,000 people evacuated following the accident would be monitored for 50 years. At another IAEA meeting in September, Leonid Ilyin, chairman of the Soviet Com-

mission on Radiation Protection, said that studies in 20 selected regions of the U.S.S.R. showed that over the next 50 years the average Soviet citizen would receive an annual radiation dose of 117 millirems, an increase of 2% above the natural background level of 100 millirems. The consequences for the 550 million Europeans living outside the U.S.S.R. were discussed at a meeting sponsored by WHO in August. Scientists estimated the average exposure as 60 millirems over 50 years, which would cause about 7,000 cancer deaths in addition to the 100 million predicted from other causes, an increase far too small to be detected statistically. In February Robert Gale of the University of California said that no cases of mental retardation had been found in about 300 babies born near Chernobyl since the accident.

Public alarm continued. Consignments of whey powder from West Germany destined for Egypt and Angola were held at Bremen and Cologne in February because they were found to be contaminated. In March Egyptian doctors warned people not to eat imported food, and the consequent alarm was exploited by opposition parties prior to the general elections. During the winter of 1986–87 the levels of cesium-137 in vegetation in the uplands of Cumbria (England), southwestern Scotland, and northern Wales fell to one-tenth of their value immediately following the Chernobyl accident, but in spring and summer levels rose again. The cesium had been washed into wet, peaty soils that contained little clay, which would have trapped and held it, and it was taken up and concentrated by plants. Restrictions on the movement of sheep were reintroduced in July and extended in August.

**Radon.** Concern over high levels of exposure to radon were expressed during the year in the U.S. and Britain. In the U.S. the EPA recommended a maximum exposure limit of 150 becquerels per cubic metre of air (bq/m³). In November 1986 scientists from the Lawrence Berkeley Laboratory in California said that measurements in about 1,400 homes in 38 areas of 21 states indicated that between 100,000 and 200,000 U.S. homes had radon levels above the limit. The *Journal of the American Medical Association* reported in August that another survey of ten states showed that the air in one-fifth of all U.S. homes might exceed the safe limit, in some cases by a wide margin. Peak concentrations of 6,000 bq/m³ had been found in Alabama and of 6,700 bq/m³ in Michigan. The British government announced in January that a limit of 2,000 millirems was the maximum to which people should be exposed in existing homes, and that radiation levels in newly built houses must not exceed 500 millirems. A study by the National Radiological Protection Board and the Committee on the Medical Aspects of Radiation in the Environment had shown that occupants of up to 20,000 homes in Devon and Cornwall might be exposed to unacceptably high radon levels. The government offered to provide a free monitoring service, but householders would have to pay for any necessary modifications to their dwellings.

**Antinuclear Demonstrations.** One protester and 13 police were injured and 40 people arrested during an antinuclear demonstration that turned into a riot outside the Vienna Opera House on February 26. In Britain more than 50,000 people rallied in Hyde Park, London, on April 25 to demonstrate their opposition to nuclear power and mark the anniversary of Chernobyl. In June members of Greenpeace blocked a waste pipe from the Sellafield plant, and on September 30 two members were arrested after they had jumped into the water in the path of a ship they claimed was dumping radioactive waste at sea. Five Greenpeace demonstrators were arrested in Wenceslas Square, Prague, Czech., on April 26 when they attempted to unfurl an antinuclear banner and distribute leaflets. On the same date, some 50,000 demonstrators in Italy joined hands to form a 24-km (15-mi) chain extending from the Caorso nuclear power station, near Milan, to San Bamiano military airfield; and a march and rally by about 16,000 people in Bern, Switz., led to clashes with the police.

There were demonstrations at a nuclear plant at Borssele, Neth., on Dec. 21, 1986, when about 30 protesters chained themselves to the fence, and again on April 26, 1987, when up to 2,000 protesters fought with riot police. About 3,000 people demonstrated at Miedzyrzecz, Poland, on September 6 against plans to construct a nuclear-waste-disposal facility nearby. Antinuclear demonstrations in West Germany were concentrated at the site of the Wackersdorf reprocessing plant in Bavaria. By Oct. 19, 1986, after four days of clashes with police, 494 people had been arrested. There were further clashes on December 26 and a peaceful demonstration on April 26, 1987.

**Green Politics.** In Austria the Green Party won almost 5% of the vote in general elections held in November 1986, giving them eight seats in Parliament. The Green Party

in Finland doubled its number of parliamentary seats to four in the March general elections. In the June 11 general elections in Britain, however, the Green Party fielded 133 candidates but failed to increase the 1% share of the vote it had won in 1983, and none of its candidates was elected.

In April the Polish government established an Ecological Social Movement to coordinate the work of individuals and informal groups concerned with environmental protection. A "Soviet Greenpeace" was formed in June, as part of the Soviet Peace Committee. Its chairman was Sergey Zalygin, a member of the "villagers," a group of writers urging environmental reforms that was credited with a decisive role in persuading the authorities to abandon schemes to divert Siberian rivers.

The dispute between "fundamentalists" and "realists" within the West German Green Party continued, and by June a third group of "neutralists" had emerged. By then the Green Party was represented in the parliaments of eight of the country's ten Länder, but critics complained that in four years they had sponsored only one successful piece of legislation, banning the importation of turtle meat. Electorally, the party made progress, increasing its share of the vote from 5.6 to 8.3% and its representation in the Bundestag to 41 in federal elections in January.

(MICHAEL ALLABY)

## WILDLIFE CONSERVATION

The survival of Spix's macaw (*Cyanopsitta spixii*), a Brazilian bird on the brink of extinction, was further threatened in February 1987 when two young birds were taken from a nest. The fledglings were later confiscated in Paraguay and taken to join three others in the São Paulo (Brazil) Zoo, where it was hoped they would breed. Spix's macaw is the smallest of the all-blue macaws and the only member of its genus. The world's last dusky seaside sparrow (*Ammodramus maritimus nigrescens*) died in Florida on June 16. Five males had been brought into captivity in 1979, but no females were found and, in an effort to save at least some of the dusky sparrow genes, the males were crossed with other seaside sparrow subspecies. The cause of extinction was destruction of the sparrow's habitat in Florida's coastal salt marsh. Aware of the vulnerability of the only population of southern sea otters (*Enhydra lutris nereis*) in Morro Bay, central California, the U.S. Fish and Wildlife

AFP PHOTO

A woman in Basel, Switzerland, pours a glass of clean water into the Rhine River during a demonstration that marked the first anniversary of the fire at a Sandoz AG chemical company that caused catastrophic pollution of the Rhine.

Black rhinoceros calves are fed a milk preparation in a wildlife sanctuary. In Zimbabwe's Zambezi Valley the last viable breeding herd of black rhinos was losing about one animal a day to poachers. The government instructed game rangers to shoot poachers on sight.
WILLIAM CAMPBELL/TIME MAGAZINE

Service decided to capture 70 of the 1,650 individuals to establish a new colony at San Nicolas Island off southern California.

Singapore, one of the world's main centres for wildlife trade, joined the Convention on International Trade in Endangered Species of Wild Fauna and Flora (CITES), effective from February 28. The decision followed imposition of a U.S. embargo on all wildlife products from Singapore, which was lifted when Singapore announced its decision to stop trading in rhinoceros horn and to join CITES. Although the move was welcomed as an important step for rhino conservation, the illegal trade continued in some parts of the world. Armed poachers still devastated rhinos in Africa despite increased vigilance by armed antipoacher patrols. In Zimbabwe poachers were being shot, and Kenya was putting its rhinos behind fences.

The first species to benefit from the World Bank's new approach to the environment was the very rare greater Patagonian conure (*Cyanoliseus patagonus byroni*). It had been collected for the pet trade and killed because it sometimes ate grain crops. Two of its last 12 breeding sites—it nests only in perpendicular soft cliffs—were to be flooded by the Pehuenche hydroelectric project. The World Bank, which was funding the scheme, allocated funds for moving the affected parrots to an abandoned site and for starting a captive-breeding program.

The 39th annual meeting of the International Whaling Commission (IWC), held in Bournemouth, England, in June, confronted the problem of scientific research whaling, which had become the most serious abuse of the commercial whaling moratorium. The meeting adopted a resolution making it possible for the IWC to recommend that governments not issue permits for research whaling unless they were approved by the commission's Scientific Committee. The research whaling programs of South Korea, Iceland, and Japan were rejected, and shortly after the meeting Japan announced its intention to begin its Antarctic whaling in mid-October regardless of the IWC recommendation. Iceland made a deal with the U.S. that allowed it to catch 80 fin whales and 20 sei whales in 1987 without the U.S. inflicting sanctions. In return, Iceland promised to submit its 1988 program to the IWC and abide by its recommendations.

Some reintroductions of native species reported successes. The first fawns were born to the Père David's deer

(*Elaphurus davidianus*) reintroduced to China in 1986, and the scimitar-horned oryx (*Oryx dammah*) reintroduced to Tunisia in 1985 also calved for the first time. Four pairs of captive-bred red wolves (*Canis rufus*) were released into Alligator River National Wildlife Refuge, North Carolina, the first to live in the wild since 1977. They had disappeared from their range in the southeastern U.S. as a result of habitat destruction, persecution, and hybridization with the coyote (*Canis latrans*). The Indian government began a breeding program for five species of freshwater turtles to restock the Ganges River. The turtles' decline had been brought about by pollution, the building of dams, and demand for their meat, and there were too few left to perform the essential task of clearing up the remains of human corpses consigned to the holy river.

A study on the Pacific island of Guam showed that the island's forest birds had been decimated by an introduced brown tree snake (*Boiga irregularis*). Since it first appeared on the island in the 1940s, it had exterminated three species completely and brought the remainder to the brink of extinction. It was questionable whether any of Guam's forest birds would survive. Although two species—the Micronesian kingfisher (*Halcyon c. cinnamomina*) and the endemic Guam rail (*Rallus owstoni*)—were being bred in captivity, the chances of successfully reintroducing them into the wild would depend on whether the snake could be eliminated.

In the Mediterranean the two most important beaches for nesting loggerhead turtles (*Caretta caretta*) were threatened by tourist developments. Although the Greek government banned further development at Lagana Bay on the island of Zakynthos, the local people ignored the decree, and there were violent confrontations when the authorities tried to demolish illegal buildings. Hotels, shops, discos, and restaurants on the beach had halved the number of loggerheads nesting over the previous ten years. At the second most important beach for loggerheads—at Dalyan, Turkey—a proposal for a 600-bed hotel sparked protests. In response to appeals from international conservation organizations, Turkish Prime Minister Turgut Ozal promised to save the turtles.                                                                                                  (JACQUI M. MORRIS)

*See also* Agriculture and Food Supplies; Botanical Gardens and Zoos; Energy; Life Sciences; Transportation.

This article updates the *Macropædia* article CONSERVATION OF NATURAL RESOURCES.

# Fashion and Dress

In fashion history 1987 would go down as the year of the leg. More leg than dress was the theme. Hemlines were up to mid-thigh in spring and summer, with effects that were often ravishing but at times merely startling. It was also the year a new Paris fashion designer rocketed to fame overnight. Christian Lacroix's (*see* BIOGRAPHIES) bubble skirt, christened the "pouf," was front-page news and instantly copied the world over. Haute couture might have lost some of its dignity and purism, but as the designer himself put it: "Couture should be fun. . . . We have to make dreams."

The 1987 mini was light-years away from the mini of the 1960s, introduced by London's Mary Quant and Paris's André Courrèges. Then the line was structured and the mood proper and naive, emphasized by the accompanying white boots and short white gloves. In 1987 the narrow daytime mini, with centre slit low at the back, looked more casual and less urban, though the evening silhouette conveyed a "hat in the ring" attitude on the dance floor, with the skirt rising high in bubbles, rustles, and bustles over a strapless bustier top, sheer black hose, and spiky-heeled pumps. Fabrics for the new mini were also very unlike the whipcords and other stiff materials selected for the loosely fitted mini of the 1960s. Stretch fabrics were extensively used in 1987 to emphasize the body line. Stretch jersey and rubberized fabrics were unrivaled for shaping and snug fitting.

As soon as the harshness of winter eased off, fake fur coats in jungle prints were set aside, together with the extra-wide, extra-long, plain cashmere stoles, usually in natural colours, that had been added for style and warmth in place of a cloak. Colour then took hold of the streets. First to appear was a deep sapphire blue for cropped coats worn over black. For heavy knitwear, sweaters and cardigans with jacquard designs, the same deep blue was combined with a clear emerald green. But it was not long before fireman's red became predominant—in plain woolen fabric for a loose car coat and matching skirt, or in ribbed knitwear for an extra-long or an extra-short cardigan. Red outfits were worn with black shirts, high-necked black sweaters, black miniskirts, or black tights. Frequently seen alternatives to black were charcoal gray and khaki.

Red spread like fire to accessories. First was the hat— a broad-brimmed boater in red felt. Then, in footwear, red kid ballerinas and high-heeled red pumps, always with black hose, replaced the short bootees of winter. Finally, every kind of accessory turned red, from stiff leather belts to soft kid gloves, to bracelets like hoopla rings in red Plexiglass, transparent as ice cubes, to cuff bracelets in red-tinted metal. Earrings appeared in red, flat like flying saucers buttoned to the earlobe or long and dangling. And, of course, handbags followed the red signal, from small pouches to softly gathered nosebags with drawstrings and shoulder straps. Even eyeglasses were rimmed with red. One word summed up accessories: aggressive.

The number one street look for spring was a loosely fitted blazer over a narrow miniskirt, with low back slit, and a bold-striped mannish shirt. Hose were opaque, blended with the outfit or plain black. Later in the season, hose were white, lemon, or vanilla, with a lacy mesh. The rippling peplum from the previous season had lost momentum. The success of the film *Out of Africa* was doubtless responsible for the return of the safari look, with its classic pocketed and belted bush jacket, but in 1987 it was worn with a narrow miniskirt or with shorts in matching gabardine or sand-coloured linen. Long pants were rare. Sweatshirts and T-shirts featured giraffes and elephants. In jewelry, both real and fake, the jungle influence was apparent in wild animal motifs.

For the fashion-minded there were only two options for skirt length—either above the knee or nearing the ankle. In the long version, skirts were gently flared, gathered or pleated. Sandy-toned linen was a favourite; alternatives

(LEFT) JOHN-LUCE HURÉ/THE NEW YORK TIMES; (RIGHT) AFP PHOTO

The miniskirt made a comeback in several forms in 1987, including bold new looks like the satin fichu (right) by overnight sensation Christian Lacroix and the inventive safari evening dress (far right) by Chantal Thomass.

were plain white or black, or printed cotton. Patterns were small; for example, leaves in two different sizes, tiny for the blouse and slightly larger for the skirt, or minute all-over pinhead patterns in black, navy, or beige on contrasting backgrounds. Loose, cardigan-style tops, worn over plain T-shirts, appeared with long, narrow skirts for a 1930s look. Pinhead dots were also featured on very sheer cotton jersey for long T-shirts, with rounded or V-shaped necklines or clearing the shoulders. Hats made an impact—stiff-brimmed boaters in natural straw with ribbon bands or big floppy brims reminiscent of Ascot. From Australia came the akubra, the traditional wide-brimmed farmer's hat in fur felt, seen in the film *Crocodile Dundee* and worn by the U.S. first lady, Nancy Reagan, and her husband.

For town wear in hot weather, the choice occasionally was all black, as in Africa. Brassière tops, baring skin above the waistline, were matched with circular miniskirts cut like skating dresses. Also seen were majorette's outfits with snug, buttoned-up tops and high-rising waistlines or wide belts. With all black, the choice for accessories was wood in various natural shades: for large and bulky bracelets worn in groups and for rings, earrings, and belt buckles. Black was the favourite for tube dresses in stretch-ribbed jersey, high in front and with back cutouts. Black was also used for court shoes tipped with gold, silver, or copper triangles. Heels might be high or mid-height, low with wedge soles, or flat. Sandals and sling shapes went with long skirts.

The beach look was form-fitting. California designer Robin Piccone offered bathing suits made of neoprene, the synthetic rubber used for scuba-diving wet suits, that were guaranteed to streamline the body's imperfections. Colours were fluorescent. Suits were high in front, with surprise cutouts and very high-cut legs. All kinds of strings, lacing, and knots were in evidence; sometimes only a joining band kept a one-piece suit from turning into a two-piece. As cover-ups, transparent voile shirts, in black or a colour matched to the suit, were worn loose and open. Black or charcoal gray replaced blue for denim shorts and blousons. Wigs were the latest craze at Saint-Tropez—long, shaggy mops, curly or frizzy, as if straight from the wilds of Papua New Guinea. In the evening, skirts were all bubbles and ruffles in tiers, while tops were as snug as possible, even corseted as worn by pop star Madonna. Fabrics were glittering, and jewelry was flamboyant.

Despite the success of bubble skirts in shops and at evening parties, Lacroix declared in the summer that the pouf dress was already outdated. Hems did come down in the autumn but still left knees uncovered. Coats were flared and full, often bordered with fox, or belted and with a huge, shoulder-covering, crisscross shawl collar. Colours were strong—bright red, bold yellow, purple. Short was the word for evening wear. The minidress was draped and caught up on one shoulder like a Roman toga or wrapped up high in front and held in place at the waist by a large, soft, pussycat bow or a huge flower. On rare occasions there were back-dipping effects with ruffles cascading to the floor.

Technicolour was the word for makeup. Eyelids were like shimmering butterflies. Eyelashes could be green above and blue below. Black pencil eyeliner was applied with a calligrapher's touch. Lipstick was pale and glossy or bright red to harmonize with earth-tone foundations. The trend in hairdos was shorter at the sides than on top—but not too boyish—or long, straight, and flowing in the breeze.

(THELMA SWEETINBURGH)

**Men's Fashions.** Two significant changes occurred in men's fashions during 1987. The first was that national fashions, especially in Europe, were revived, thereby re-

versing the trend of the early 1980s toward a more international look. Men's fashions in the U.S. were not similarly affected, since they had always been strong enough to stand on their own. The second trend was the increasing polarization between informal casual or leisure wear and the traditional formal styles.

Both these developments were noticed at the men's trade fairs in Europe, which were themselves more national than international in character and content. Most trade fairs enjoyed a measure of success that reflected the buoyant state of the men's clothing and outfitting trades. The numbers of exhibitors and visitors at major fairs in Paris; Cologne, West Germany; Barcelona, Spain; Amsterdam; Florence, Italy; and London showed marked increases over the previous year.

Nostalgia was a keyword. In leisure wear the nautical theme, with plain navy or striped blazers and white trousers, replaced the hunting, shooting, and fishing themes of previous seasons. The embroidered breast-pocket crest or badge emerged as a decoration not only on blazers but also, somewhat surprisingly, on some dinner jackets. Also for leisure wear, white was fashionable for knitted sport shirts and shorts, hose (up to knee length), and leather shoes. Trousers or slacks were baggy at the waist and tapering to the ankle with a narrow turnup.

In formal wear, double-breasted styling continued to make inroads into the suit sector at the expense of single-breasted two-button or three-button models. According to the International Wool Secretariat, the decline in sales of suits generally had been halted. In the U.K. sales of two-piece suits in traditional matching fabrics and of jackets and trousers in contrasting fabrics showed a welcome increase over previous years.

In general, suits were more elegant. What had been dubbed the "worker's look" gave way to a neater, more stylish "management look" for the young and ambitious executive. A broader and wider shoulder for suit jackets was noticed in Italy and Germany. On the other hand, the British look—as interpreted by houses such as Chester Barrie, DAKS, and Aquascutum—kept to the natural shoulder and emphasized elegance. This was also true of the Ivy League styling that was the hallmark of leading suit manufacturers in the U.S.

The trilby proved to be a popular bit of nostalgia, but attempts by hatters in the U.K. to bring back the distinctive panama hat for summer wear were not successful.

(STANLEY H. COSTIN)

*See also* Industrial Review: *Furs.*

This article updates the *Macropædia* article DRESS AND ADORNMENT.

# Gardening

For English gardeners, the most traumatic event of 1987 was the gale that swept over the south of England on the morning of October 16. Winds of more than 160 km/h (100 mph) were recorded, and thousands of mature trees were blown over, particularly in Kent and Sussex, among them many that were exotic and rare. The Royal Botanic Gardens, Kew, was closed for several days while the damage was cleared away.

The National Gardening Survey, taken annually by the Gallup organization, showed that up to 44% of U.S. homeowners engaged in gardening. Gardeners were becoming younger—the median age was in the 30–49-year range—as more members of the "baby boom" generation became householders, and their motivation, by and large, was enjoyment rather than saving money by producing food. As a leisure activity, gardening was preferred over golf, fishing, and tennis. Care of the lawn was given the highest priority, though there was also a trend toward "meadow lawns" planted with wildflowers.

An additional motivation for gardening was evident in real estate estimates showing that improved landscaping significantly increased the value of housing. Statistical analysis indicated that a well-landscaped house rose in value as much as 5–10%, depending on the quality of the plants and how well they were maintained. The value of a property was especially enhanced by large, well-maintained shade trees or specimen flowering trees and shrubs on the lawn.

In food-crop gardens, the trend in the U.S. appeared to be toward "smaller but more selective." Instead of being planted in the traditional regimented rows, vegetables were being tucked into foundation borders, strawberries were sharing the sides of paths, and lettuces, scallions, and other salad greens were filling in spaces around patios. Older vegetable varieties were enjoying a comeback, sparked by the belief that modern varieties had been bred for ease of harvesting, shipping, and marketability at the expense of flavour and vigour. A number of organizations had been formed for the purpose of restoring some of the so-called heritage vegetables to commercial channels.

The number of visitors to gardens in Britain continued to increase, to the point where a few gardens were suffering considerable wear and tear. The task of listing the historically important gardens in all the English counties was completed by the Department of the Environment, and a list of those in Scotland was published at the end of the year. The latest in the series of European garden festivals was held in Düsseldorf, West Germany, from April until October; its legacy was a new park, the Sudpark, for the city. The annual show of the Dutch flower industry, held in early November, marked its 25th anniversary. It continued to be an important occasion for introducing new plants, which were judged under the auspices of the Royal Dutch Horticultural Society.

Among the awards from Fleuroselect, the European seedsmen's organization, a medal was given to the bedding plant Verbena Sandy Scarlet, a bush form showing some resistance to disease. The flowers on test by this organization were grown in countries from Italy to Scandinavia. Nurseries growing bedding plants were increasingly following the practice of buying very young seedlings for growing and later sale to gardeners. Seed companies also offered such young plants directly to amateurs on a limited scale.

More U.S. gardeners were shopping for their supplies through mail-order houses, which offered tools, accessories, and seeds of some of the more unusual and exotic plants. At the same time, the traditional garden centres were beginning to offer more perennials, shrubs, and trees, as well as certain fruit crops. The gardening market in Europe was still expanding, though that for lawn mowers in West Germany was said to be near saturation. The French were the most enthusiastic buyers of tools and equipment, with garden centres at most hypermarkets.

New legislation on the storage and sale of pesticides was introduced in the U.K. in January. Manufacturers of all materials for pest and disease control and related uses were now required to obtain official approval for their products. One of the major changes affecting amateur gardeners was that containers could no longer be split up by unauthorized persons for distribution in smaller quantities. The use of garden chemicals in the U.S. continued to decline in the face of mounting evidence that excessive application of fertilizers and pesticides on lawns and gardens could result in groundwater contamination. Many municipalities were monitoring the use of garden chemicals, and gardeners were turning toward organic gardening and the use of non-toxic pest controls such as hand picking and homemade sprays.

The cut flower and potted plant markets continued to flourish, leading to a continual search for new types of plants. Micropropagation, whereby large numbers of plants were produced under laboratory conditions, had expanded greatly within the flower industry, enabling new plants to be made available to commercial nurseries within a relatively short time. The Gallup survey indicated that tending houseplants was second only to lawn care as the favoured activity of gardening hobbyists, and the U.K. nursery trade reported that the volume of sales of plants in containers had multiplied eight times in the last ten years. Computers were being introduced in some nurseries to help customers choose the right plant for their particular conditions.

(JOAN LEE FAUST; ELSPETH NAPIER)

*See also* Agriculture and Food Supplies; Botanical Gardens and Zoos; Environment; Life Sciences.

This article updates the *Macropædia* article GARDENING AND HORTICULTURE.

ROYAL BOTANIC GARDENS, KEW

A venerable old tree at Kew Gardens was one of the many uprooted in a freak storm that swept through southern England. The storm felled as many as 100,000 trees in the London area and caused nearly $1 billion in property damage.

# Health and Disease

While the worldwide AIDS (acquired immune deficiency syndrome) epidemic continued to dominate the news in 1987, there were nonetheless important advances in the diagnosis and treatment of disease and exciting contributions to basic research. Surgeons in Canada reported the first successful use of a laser to open a blocked coronary artery. In the U.S. the Food and Drug Administration (FDA) authorized limited tests of a potentially promising drug for treating Alzheimer's disease, while another substance, copolymer 1, was shown in preliminary trials to have a beneficial effect on patients in the early stages of multiple sclerosis. In December researchers announced a major breakthrough in the study of muscle contraction, a protein that evidently regulates calcium supply to the muscle cells. This finding was expected to have far-reaching implications for the understanding of a variety of muscle-weakening diseases and, potentially, application in the treatment of such disorders. At years' end an international team of scientists announced that they had isolated a single gene on the Y, or male, chromosome that may be responsible for determining the gender of the developing fetus.

**AIDS.** The pandemic of AIDS continued to challenge both medical science and public health agencies in 1987. The research team of Luc Montagnier at the Institut Pasteur, Paris—codiscoverers of the original AIDS virus (now known as HIV, human immunodeficiency virus)—reported that some cases of the disease in West Africa were caused by a different but related virus. Termed HIV-2, to distinguish it from HIV-1, the new virus seemed to portend the possibility of a second epidemic in Africa, and its spread was being closely monitored.

In the U.S. physicians at Massachusetts General Hospital added another disease to the list of those already known to be seriously aggravated by concurrent AIDS infection. They found neurosyphilis (syphilitic infection of the central nervous system), a disease whose prevalence had otherwise

decreased markedly since the advent of penicillin, in four men with evidence of HIV infection. Another infection first reported in 1987 to be linked to AIDS was disseminated vaccinia—a hitherto rare complication of immunization against smallpox, a disease that is now extinct. Researchers at the Walter Reed Army Institute of Research, Washington, D.C., described a young HIV-positive military recruit in whom both disseminated vaccinia infection and AIDS developed following smallpox vaccination. This finding cast some doubt on the wisdom of current research into "hybrid" vaccines, in which vaccinia virus was used as a carrier of substances that elicit immunity against specific pathogens. If such vaccines were to be used in less developed countries, where HIV infection was becoming increasingly prevalent, they could prove doubly dangerous.

The year 1987 saw some significant improvements in AIDS treatment. Studies in several medical centres in the U.S. and U.K. confirmed that zidovudine (Retrovir; originally called azidothymidine, or AZT) could decrease the death rate of AIDS patients, reduce the frequency of so-called opportunistic infections, and even reverse certain neurological changes (such as chronic dementia) that are among the most horrendous effects of the disease. Approved by the U.S. FDA in March 1987, zidovudine was the first anti-AIDS drug to be marketed in the U.S. Another drug, ampligen, was found to reduce replication of HIV and to partially restore the immune response that is severely impaired in AIDS patients. Laboratory tests indicated that ampligen combined with zidovudine was more potent in inhibiting HIV than either drug used alone. This finding was important because zidovudine, although effective, often had serious immunogenic side effects in the concentrations normally used in AIDS treatment. Zidovudine remained controversial, however, not only because of its potential toxic effects but also because of its expense. The cost per patient of zidovudine treatment was estimated at $8,000–$10,000 a year. In December the Burroughs Wellcome Co., the drug's manufacturer, announced that it would reduce the wholesale price by 20%.

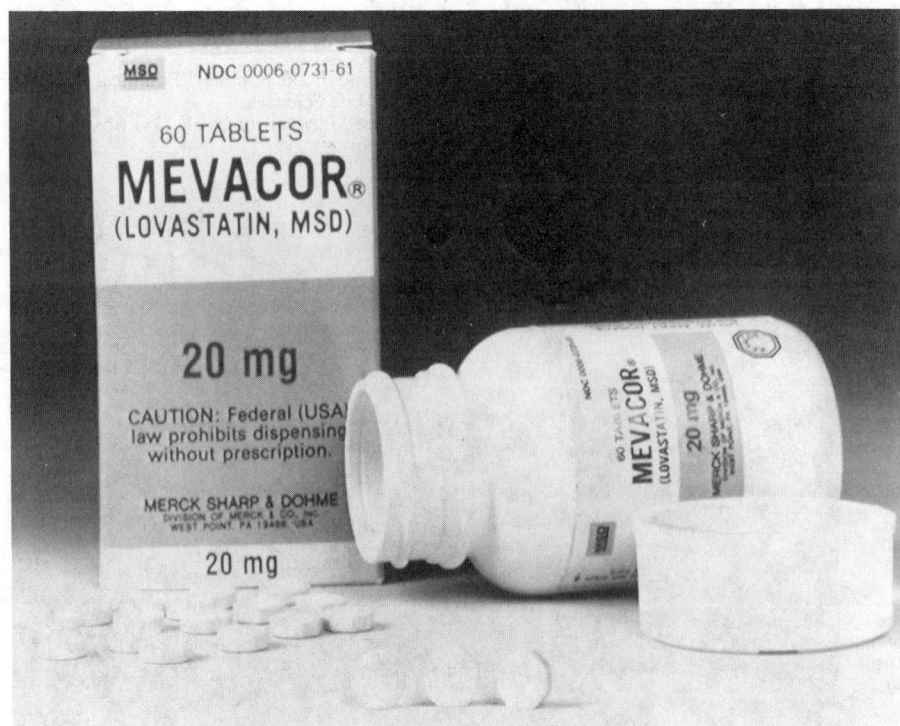

Lovastatin, a new cholesterol-lowering drug, was approved by the Food and Drug Administration (FDA) and was to be marketed under the name Mevacor. The drug blocks cholesterol-producing enzymes in the liver and, according to the FDA, reduces total cholesterol levels by 18 to 34%.

Another substance, known as GM-CSF, granulocyte-macrophage colony-stimulating factor, was found to boost the number and function of circulating white blood cells in AIDS patients. By thus stimulating the body's immune system, it could help to reduce both illness and death caused by the many opportunistic infections that assail the AIDS patient. There were two significant developments in the treatment of pneumocystis pneumonia, a common opportunistic infection in AIDS sufferers. The antibiotic combination trimethoprim-sulphamethoxasole was found to be equally potent—but cheaper and less hazardous when given three days a week than when given daily, which had been routine hitherto. Still another drug, pentamidine, inhaled as an aerosol, proved to be both active against HIV and nontoxic.

Although much had been written of the problems and perils involved in creating a vaccine against AIDS, with predictions that no such agent would be available for many years, the FDA in 1987 approved clinical trials of two experimental vaccines. Both were the products of genetic engineering techniques, and both used protein components of the outer coat of the AIDS virus. A majority of the initial volunteer test subjects were healthy homosexual men with no signs of AIDS infection. The search for an effective vaccine was not confined solely to the U.S. Human trials of experimental vaccines were also under way in France and Zaire.

There were some noteworthy developments in the epidemiological pattern of AIDS during 1987. In October a blood-testing program sponsored by the U.S. government indicated that, in San Francisco at least, the spread of the AIDS virus among the homosexual male population had slowed considerably. The same was apparently true in other cities. At the same time, data on female patients showed that, compared with their male counterparts, women with AIDS tended to be sicker at the time of diagnosis and had dramatically lower survival rates. In one such report, women AIDS patients lived an average of 6 months after diagnosis, while the men studied lived an average of 12–14 months.

Researchers continued to debate the origin of AIDS and to pursue studies to determine how long the virus had been present in humans. The *Journal of the American Medical Association* published a report that attributed the 1969 death of a 15-year-old St. Louis, Mo., youngster to AIDS. The boy's doctors had been baffled by the case but in retrospect realized that his puzzling symptoms were consistent with the picture of AIDS. A study of stored specimens of the boy's blood and tissues confirmed the presence of the AIDS virus. One of the year's most sensational news stories was that of a homosexual Canadian airline steward, known to investigators at the U.S. Centers for Disease Control (CDC) as "Patient Zero," who had had sexual contacts with men in several North American cities; many of these men subsequently died of AIDS. The patient in question died of an AIDS-related infection in 1984.

**Cardiovascular Disease.** On Sept. 1, 1987, the FDA approved the marketing of lovastatin (Mevacor), the first of a new class of cholesterol-lowering drugs, thus ushering in what many believed would be a new era in the prevention of heart disease. As many as 20 million Americans had cholesterol levels high enough to put them at very high risk for heart disease, and before lovastatin the only drug approved in the U.S. for lowering cholesterol levels was cholestyramine, an unpalatable agent not as effective as lovastatin, with undesirable side effects including flatulence and bloating. Cholestyramine comes in the form of a powder that must be mixed with a liquid and swallowed. It

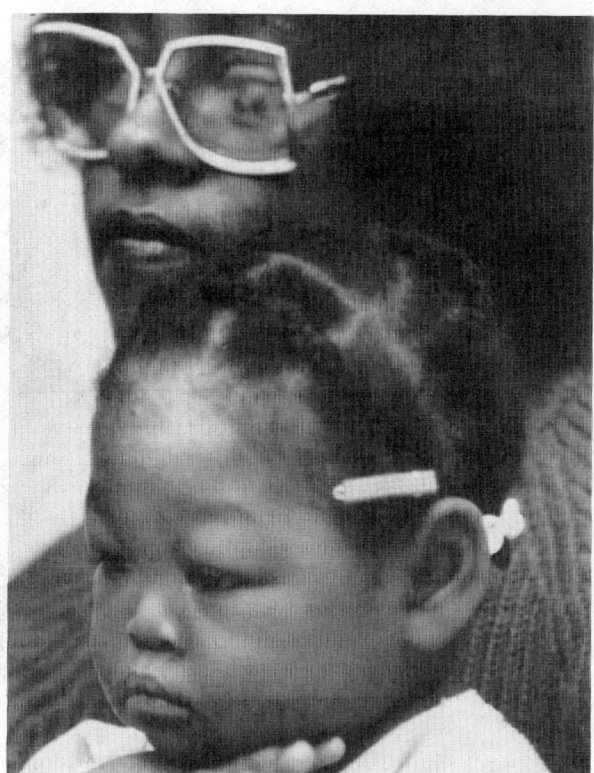

Tabatha Foster, shown with her mother, underwent nearly 15 hours of surgery in the first successful five-organ transplant operation. She received a liver, pancreas, and small intestine and parts of a stomach and colon to correct a digestive-system defect.
AP/WIDE WORLD

forms a concoction so gritty that participants in one study of the drug's effectiveness reportedly joked that drinking it was "like drinking Miami Beach." Because of these many drawbacks, doctors found it difficult to convince patients to take cholestyramine. Lovastatin, in contrast, comes in tablet form and is easy to take.

Lovastatin is one of a class of drugs that block an early step in cholesterol synthesis. They dramatically reduce cholesterol levels and do so by decreasing the amount of low density lipoproteins (LDL), the so-called bad cholesterol, without affecting high density lipoproteins (HDL), which seem to protect against heart disease. Lovastatin is not without side effects, however. About 1% of those who took the drug experienced an increase in liver enzymes, and researchers had not yet determined for certain that the increase did not indicate liver disease. There was also some concern that the drug might cause possible damage to the lens of the eye. Another cholesterol-lowering drug, introduced briefly in the 1960s and then pulled from the market, also blocked cholesterol synthesis, but it caused cataracts. Although lovastatin was shown to cause cataracts in dogs when given in very high doses, there was no evidence that it would have this effect in humans at the dosage currently prescribed. In order to keep a close watch on possible side effects of lovastatin, the FDA ordered that patients taking the drug have blood tests every six weeks to check their liver function and undergo a yearly eye exam for early signs of cataract development.

Not long after the news of lovastatin's approval, doctors at the U.S. National Heart, Lung, and Blood Institute, Bethesda, Md., announced the promising results of a study of still another potential weapon against cholesterol, gemfibrozil (Lopid), which reportedly had fewer adverse effects

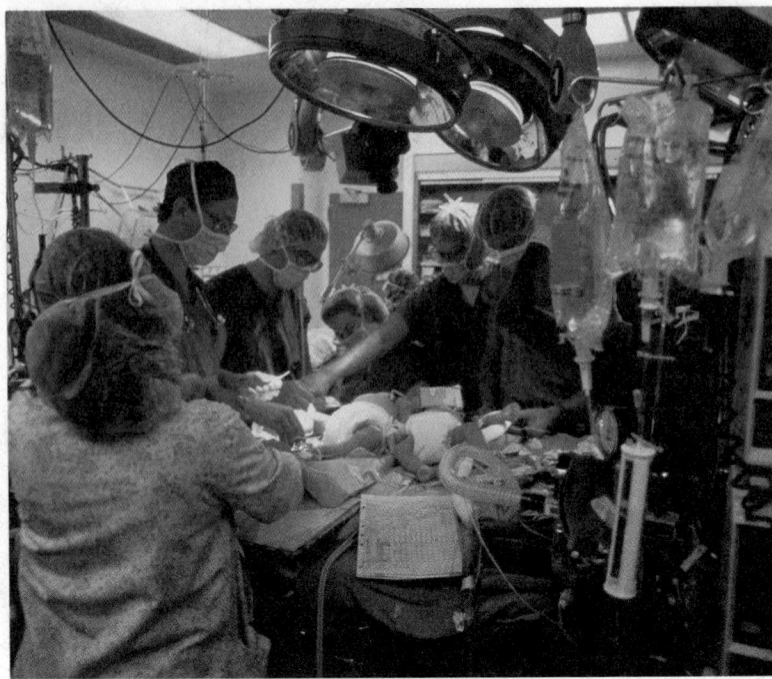

Members of a surgical team at Johns Hopkins Children's Center work to separate Siamese twins joined at the head. Because the infants shared a major vein leading to the heart, the team had to first drain all the twins' blood, stop their hearts, and slow their metabolism by lowering body temperature to 20° C (68° F).
JOHNS HOPKINS CHILDREN'S CENTER; PHOTOGRAPH, J. PAT CARTER

than lovastatin and other existing anticholesterol drugs. Although it had been widely used to treat heart patients with elevated serum cholesterol levels, its safety and effectiveness as a lipid-regulating agent had not been fully documented. Gemfibrozil does not cause dramatic decreases in overall cholesterol level but rather increases the level of "good" HDL while lowering the level of harmful LDL.

In another important development, the FDA approved the use of a new thrombolytic (clot-dissolving) substance, tissue plasminogen activator (TPA, or alteplase; Activase), for the emergency treatment of heart attack victims and, at about the same time, approved the use of an existing thrombolytic agent, streptokinase (Streptase; Kabikinase), for administration during or immediately after a heart attack. Although there are differences in the biochemical actions of the two drugs, both were reported by the FDA to have the potential to reduce the irreversible damage that the heart muscle incurs in the early hours of a heart attack. Despite some controversy over the relative ability of the two substances to improve survival rates among victims of heart attack, U.S. health authorities agreed that their availability represented a major advance in the treatment of heart disease.

Although deaths associated with coronary heart disease had fallen by nearly 40% in the U.S. over the past two decades, there was uncertainty as to how much of this improvement should be attributed to a healthier life-style on the one hand and improved medical therapies on the other. A detailed statistical study from the Minnesota Heart Survey revealed that the four-year survival rate for heart attack victims was 35% better in 1980 than in 1970. This and other findings confirmed that improved long-term survival among patients with severe heart disease had made an important contribution to the decline in deaths due to coronary disease. Evidence from another major study, carried out in Sweden, Norway, and Finland, showed that the antihypertensive drug enalapril (Vasotec) reduced both mortality and symptoms among victims of severe congestive heart failure.

Investigators at Baylor College of Medicine, Houston,

Texas, shed new light on the development of atherosclerosis—the accumulation of fatty plaques that causes the thickening of artery walls and thus narrowing of arteries—which is at the root of much cardiovascular disease. Aside from recognizing the well-documented role of diet and blood cholesterol levels, researchers also suspected that one or another virus may be implicated. The Baylor research highlighted one major contender: cytomegalovirus. The study revealed significantly higher levels of antibodies against this virus in men undergoing surgery for atherosclerosis than in a matched group of individuals who also had high cholesterol levels.

In a study published in August in the *New England Journal of Medicine,* physicians in Göteborg and Uppsala, Sweden, analyzed parental death from stroke in relation to other established risk factors for stroke, such as obesity and high blood pressure, in several hundred men in their 50s. Their findings indicated that a maternal history of stroke is relevant and should probably be added to the existing list of risk factors among middle-aged men. There was also evidence from a joint study by researchers in La Jolla, Calif., and Cambridge, England, that a high intake of dietary potassium may protect individuals against stroke-associated death.

**Infectious Diseases.** In the U.S. there was growing concern over Lyme disease, an infectious form of arthritis first identified in a small town in Connecticut in 1975. It was since found to be the most common tick-borne illness in the country, with cases reported in more than 30 states. A bacterial disease transmitted to humans by certain species of ticks carried by mice and deer, Lyme disease is usually first manifested by a characteristic rash. Subsequently, the victim develops joint pains and such flulike symptoms as chills, fever, headache, muscle aches, and general malaise. Although the symptoms clear up if the patient is promptly treated with antibiotics, Lyme disease can recur and is potentially fatal. More than 5,000 cases had been reported in the U.S. by 1986, and the number seemed to be doubling each year—owing in part to wider recognition of the disease and improved diagnosis. While scientists continued to search for a way to eradicate the species of ticks that spread the disease, people in endemic areas were being urged to take every precaution against tick bites.

The indiscriminate use of antibiotics to promote growth and prevent disease in farm animals had been a subject of debate among epidemiologists and public health officials for several years. In 1987, however, there was major new evidence of the public health dangers arising from this practice. CDC researchers showed that a particular drug-resistant strain of one *Salmonella* species, which was found in hamburgers eaten by people who subsequently developed food poisoning, was the same as that found in slaughterhouses and in sick cattle. This dramatic demonstration of cross infection strengthened the case for restrictions on the use in animal husbandry of drugs that are important in human medicine.

The principles of genetic engineering were applied successfully to the development of several new vaccines. At the Swiss Serum and Vaccine Institute, Bern, Switz., scientists produced an oral vaccine against typhoid fever. It con-

sisted of a greatly weakened strain of the typhoid bacillus, which induced immunity but was not able to invade the body and cause disease. Although the new agent was no more effective than existing vaccines against typhoid fever, it did not induce the adverse reactions associated with the others. From the Centre for Applied Microbiology and Research, Porton Down, England, came a report of successful vaccination of guinea pigs against one of the world's most deadly diseases, Lassa fever. The new vaccine, a hybrid constructed through incorporation of one specific part of the Lassa fever virus into vaccinia virus, was expected to prove invaluable in safeguarding those among the West African population who were likely to be exposed to this rat-borne infection.

**Transplantation.** An infant only hours old became the world's youngest heart transplant patient when doctors at the Loma Linda (Calif.) Medical Center replaced the baby's defective heart with a human donor organ. A three-year-old girl underwent the first successful five-organ transplant;

*(continued on page 208)*

## Antismoking Movement

The battle against smoking in the United States began in 1964 when the surgeon general's report linking smoking to lung cancer and other respiratory diseases was released. At first this resulted only in mandatory health warnings on cigarette packs and restrictions on radio and television tobacco advertisements. Airlines provided "no-smoking" seats, and restaurants in many cities established no-smoking sections, but few real limits were imposed for some 20 years.

In the 1970s and early 1980s, vast advertising campaigns were waged by American antismoking consumer groups and other nonprofit organizations, including the American Lung Association, the American Heart Association, and the American Cancer Society. The first national Great American Smokeout (an annual day set aside for all smokers to quit) was organized in 1977. Tobacco companies mounted aggressive countercampaigns in the print media, ranging from low-key appeals to nonsmokers for tolerance to a slick magazine aimed directly at smokers. Despite this and powerful lobbying by the tobacco industry, the antismoking campaigns did have some effect; smoking peaked at more than 40% of the adult population in the mid-1960s, then declined to only about 30% in the early 1980s.

In the mid-1980s, however, antismoking groups changed their tactics. Instead of trying to persuade more smokers to quit, they focused on restricting where those who continued to smoke could light up. In 1986 the new surgeon general, C. Everett Koop, and the National Research Council published the results of studies linking lung cancer and heart disease risks among nonsmokers to passive smoking (*i.e.*, inhaling second-hand cigarette smoke from the environment), particularly in infants, young children, and nonsmoking spouses of smokers. While the results of these studies remained controversial, with Koop's active support antismoking groups stepped up the fight for a smoke-free society by the year 2000. By late 1987 some 40 states and hundreds of cities and towns had laws restricting or banning smoking in restaurants, schools, and public buildings. More and more

U.S. companies designated limited areas for smoking or banned smoking altogether from corporate offices. Smokers, concerned about the health hazards or faced with new restrictions at work, spent an estimated $100 million in 1987 on prescription nicotine gum, "stop smoking" clinics, and other self-help programs. In some places nonsmokers sued employers for endangering their health, while smokers sued for infringement of their rights. Lawsuits aimed at tobacco companies failed to demonstrate liability for smoking-related deaths—mainly because courts ruled that the warnings on cigarette packs were sufficient notice of health hazards.

Although the antismoking movement in Europe lagged behind that in the United States, Sweden, France, Italy, and the United Kingdom were among those enforcing at least partial smoking bans in 1987, and the UN World Health Organization banned all smoking from its world headquarters in Geneva in April. While Canadian legislators studied the issue, Air Canada banned smoking on many domestic and U.S.-bound flights (the U.S. House of Representatives followed suit for short domestic flights). Even in Japan, where up to 60% of the men smoked (down from a high of 80% in the 1960s), antismoking activists made headway. (MELINDA SHEPHERD)

MICK STEVENS © 1987 HIPPOCRATES MAGAZINE

SMOKING AREA OF THE FUTURE

# AIDS and Society

BY GAIL W. MCBRIDE

Some 75,000 people in the world had succumbed to AIDS by 1987, more than 49,000 in the U.S. alone, according to the World Health Organization and the U.S. Centers for Disease Control (CDC). Estimates of the actual number of cases were far higher, however. And as the writer Susan Sontag noted for other illnesses in the past, the disease had become a metaphor for the problems of society. C. Everett Koop (*see* BIOGRAPHIES), the surgeon general of the United States, couched the same thought in less poetic language: "In some ways the purely scientific issues [of AIDS] pale in comparison to the highly sensitive issues of law, ethics, economics, morality and social cohesion that are beginning to surface." The AIDS epidemic poses "an extremely difficult and complex test of our national character."

The rapid spread of AIDS raised questions that were almost unfathomable: Who will care for the victims and where? Who will love and care for the infected children of infected mothers? How can the spread of a disease be stemmed when the carriers usually do not display any symptoms? How can educational programs be carried out without becoming ensnarled in politics? Who should be tested for AIDS infection, and should testing be mandatory? Is it possible to keep infected people from falling ill? How and on whom should new vaccines and drugs be tested? Where will the money be found to pay for it all?

**The Onslaught and Defense.** AIDS had already afflicted an enormous number of people in Central African countries like Zaire, and in 1987 its incursion into other less developed countries, such as Mexico, and also into certain minority groups within the U.S. and other developed nations, became evident.

A number of countries such as India, Belgium, China, the Soviet Union, and Cuba, and some Eastern European countries forced African—or sometimes all—foreign students to undergo tests for AIDS virus (human immunodeficiency virus, or HIV) antibodies and to leave the country if the test was positive. Foreign workers, noncitizens, and would-be immigrants in countries such as Saudi Arabia, West Germany, and the Soviet Union had to either furnish proof of their HIV-free status or be subject to testing and possible expulsion. In December 1987 the U.S., too, began testing all refugees or aliens seeking to immigrate, denying them permanent legal status if they tested positive. At the same time, U.S. Navy ships began to face possible problems docking in foreign ports because of other countries' fears that the sailors might be carrying the AIDS virus.

As of 1987 the U.S. was testing for HIV antibodies all blood donors, military personnel, Foreign Service officers, and persons entering or getting out of federal prisons. The CDC planned to expand testing of anonymous blood samples from patients at "sentinel" hospitals to other hospitals, drug abuse clinics, and selected other health clinics in 30 U.S. cities during 1988 to assess the extent of infection in the general population. The blood of persons donating organs for transplantation and semen destined for artificial insemination also were tested.

France tested prisoners and the military; Sweden started testing of military recruits and pregnant women; the state of Bavaria in West Germany tested prostitutes, prisoners, drug addicts, and applicants for jobs in the public sector; and the Soviet Union could legally test anyone it chose. However, Latin-American countries, particularly Brazil, which was second to the U.S. in number of reported cases (2,102), had only begun testing and prohibiting the sale of blood. Blood donated at Brazilian public health facilities began to be screened but, unfortunately, that accounted for only 10% of the nation's donated blood.

Certain countries, such as the Soviet Union, were even throwing people, sometimes called "sexual terrorists," into jail if they were HIV-infected and knowingly had sex with healthy partners. In the Soviet Union anyone who did this was jailed for five years; the term lengthened to eight years if the infection was actually transmitted. In the U.S., cases based on such behaviour were in various stages in the courts. Quarantining AIDS victims who were deemed threats to public health began to be discussed, and some states amended or passed new laws allowing this as a "last resort."

**The Sufferers.** The main victims of AIDS in developed countries continued to be homosexual men and intravenous drug abusers, but in the U.S. it was the last group particularly that spawned victims whom Koop felt were desperately in need of society's compassion and largesse and yet unlikely to receive it: prostitutes, blacks and Hispanics already in the underclass, and their children. Some of these victims were also homeless, making them doubly outcast.

In New York City an estimated 60% of drug addicts were infected with HIV, according to Don Des Jarlais of New York State's Division of Substance Abuse Services,

AFP PHOTO

In a bold move to attract attention to the growing AIDS problem in Israel, a giant balloon floats over Tel Aviv, displaying a telephone number that people can call to receive a free handbook on AIDS.

and more addicts than homosexual men died of the disease. In some states, such as New Jersey, about half the prostitutes, many of whom also abused drugs, were infected. Approximately half of infected mothers pass the virus on to their newborns, said the CDC. Doctors in New York who treat such children estimated that about 1,000 were born there in 1987.

CDC figures also showed that blacks and Hispanics now accounted for more than one-third of AIDS cases, though they made up less than one-fifth of the U.S. population. About half of such victims were heterosexual. More than 70% of all women with AIDS were black or Hispanic, as were about 80% of children with AIDS.

Many countries began either distributing free needles to drug abusers or educating them to use bleach—effective in killing the virus—to clean their needles. Another approach, helping such persons to overcome their drug addiction, hit an impasse in the U.S.; underfunded and overworked drug treatment programs were jammed, with the result that applicants had to wait months to get in. Many social support programs were overloaded.

Gay AIDS victims received more sympathy and support, partly because they were often white and articulate and had organized themselves politically, but also partly because the arts and entertainment worlds had been hard-hit by AIDS deaths. This prompted a plethora of artistic works concerning the disease and its victims: plays, books, songs, paintings—as well as many star-studded benefits to raise money for research.

**The New Plague?** Experts tried to assess the spread of AIDS to women and heterosexuals in developed countries. One report in *The Journal of the American Medical Association,* from Nancy Padian at the University of California at Berkeley and co-workers, involved 97 female sexual partners of 93 infected men. It indicated that whether a woman became infected (23% did) was a function of how many times she had sex with the man and whether anal intercourse was practiced. Condom usage was not a factor.

Many experts believed heterosexual spread would occur, but gradually. Others, citing the long latent period before symptoms appear (up to 15 years), believed a pandemic was in the offing, and equated AIDS with the Black Death of the Middle Ages. However, Sandra Panem of the Sloan Foundation, author of a book to be published early in 1988, *The AIDS Bureaucracy,* believed this analogy was "heavily overworked. Unlike the Black Plague, AIDS is a solvable problem. The question is how, when, and with what resolve."

**AIDS Panic.** Whatever the truth, AIDS panic had set in in many areas of the developed world. Monogamy and even abstinence were coming into vogue again. "Safe sex," including use of condoms and spermicides and avoidance of anal intercourse, was on many minds. In the U.S. numerous AIDS-free sex clubs sprang up, based on the premise that a negative test result renders one a safe sexual partner. In fact, such a result means only that a person was not infected some months previously and gives no information about his or her status since then. Still, members believed that if they confined their sexual activities to other members, the danger might be lessened.

AIDS panic had other ramifications as well. Although several studies of families in which members either had AIDS or were infected with HIV showed that no HIV transmission had occurred within the family, many parents refused to let their children go to school with young AIDS victims. In Arcadia, Fla., a family with three school-age hemophiliac boys, infected with HIV from blood products

A sign in a London subway station warns passers-by of the deadly disease AIDS. In hopes of slowing the spread of AIDS, the British government launched a multimillion-pound media campaign to educate the public about its transmission and dangers.
AP/WIDE WORLD

used to control their disease, finally left town after their house was burned down. Neither parent was infected.

Also, out of fear, certain health care professionals, primarily heart surgeons, in the U.S. were refusing to treat AIDS patients. Koop criticized them, and the American Medical Association finally said that physicians could not ethically refuse to treat AIDS or HIV-infected patients. The AMA did, however, uphold the right of physicians to refuse to treat AIDS patients if they felt unqualified to administer treatment.

Getting the correct information about AIDS out to every household had been accomplished by some countries, such as England, but not others. The U.S., embroiled in political controversy, began limited release of an eight-page pamphlet. A longer report, from the surgeon general, was available on request.

**Soaring Costs.** Finally, the costs of dealing with AIDS were staggering. Many insurance companies were asking individual and even group health policy applicants to take the HIV antibody test before the policy was issued. If the applicant tested positive, he or she could not get a regular policy but might, in some states, be allowed to join a subsidized high-risk pool with high premiums and deductibles. In many cases, where insurance companies were not permitted to ask for HIV test results, they were pulling out of the area or raising all policy prices.

Anne Scitovsky, a health economist at the Palo Alto (Calif.) Medical Foundation, said that caring for AIDS victims would cost at least $8.5 billion in 1991, a huge increase from the $1.1 billion that had been spent in 1986. Adding on the costs of research, health education, and blood testing raised the figures to approximately $10 billion–$15 billion. Clearly, new ways to provide and finance care were critically needed.

*Gail W. McBride, a free-lance medical writer and editor, was formerly editor of the Medical News section of* The Journal of the American Medical Association.

*(continued from page 205)*
the youngster, born with a congenital digestive system defect, received a liver, pancreas, and small intestine and part of a stomach and colon. In the first operation of its kind, surgeons at the University of Pennsylvania hospital transplanted an entire human knee, thus enabling them to save the leg of a woman who had a potentially cancerous tumour. Also in 1987, doctors in Mexico and the U.S. reported the results of the first successful experiment in treatment of Parkinson's disease by means of transplantation of tissue from the patient's adrenal gland to the brain.

**Cancer.** There were major developments concerning both the treatment for and the causes of cancer in 1987. The U.S. National Cancer Institute (NCI), Bethesda, Md., and the Biological Therapy Institute and Biotherapeutics Inc. of Memphis and Franklin, Tenn., claimed successes in immunotherapy—the boosting of the body's own system to destroy foreign cells. These advances were based on recent discoveries showing how various specialized cells and substances of the immune system work together to eradicate invading microbes and malignant tissue within the body.

The NCI results came from patients with cancer that was spreading and either was insensitive to standard treatments or had no available routine treatment. Given lymphokine-activated killer cells, together with the so-called immune modulator interleukin-2, 8 of 106 individuals had complete tumour regression, 15 had partial positive responses, and 10 had minor responses. Among those who responded fully, the average duration of regression was 10 months, one patient remaining in remission 22 months after treatment. The Tennessee studies confirmed the activity of interleukin-2 and indicated that constant infusion of the drug into the bloodstream was likely to be safer and more tolerable than the use of larger single doses.

There was new evidence in 1987 linking drinking and breast cancer. A major follow-up study of the U.S. First National Health and Nutrition Examination Survey demonstrated that moderate alcohol consumption by women is associated with a 50–100% increase in the risk of breast cancer. The results of a prospective survey of nearly 90,000 women, reported by Harvard University, suggested that women under age 55 who have no other risk factors for breast cancer face an increased risk of the disease if they consume the equivalent of three drinks a week. The degree of risk rises with the amount of alcohol consumed.

From the University of Edinburgh Medical School came evidence to reinforce the emerging view that one particular cancer, cervical carcinoma, is caused by a virus. Previous investigators had found human papillomavirus in some cases of the disease but had not been able to determine if it had a causal role. Using the technique of nuclear DNA analysis, the Edinburgh team found that the virus does indeed seem to play a major part in the development of cervical cancer. Moreover, because the viral DNA becomes deeply integrated into the cells of the cervix, the Edinburgh researchers suggested that papillomavirus infection should be treated more aggressively than it was at present.

**Medical Genetics.** Improvements continued in disease detection by the identification of genetic marker sequences and allied techniques. One major advance, a joint venture of the Cetus Corp., Emeryville, Calif., and several institutions in that state, was the introduction of a highly sensitive and very rapid prenatal test for sickle cell anemia. In the U.S. alone some 3,000 pregnancies per year were at risk of producing a child with this condition. Although DNA analysis had been applied previously to diagnosis in utero, the technique took several days and was not widely available. The new method was inexpensive and simple and yielded an answer within a few hours.

Researchers at the University of Edinburgh and the Western General Hospital, Edinburgh, announced the development of another DNA hybridization test that could be used in the prenatal diagnosis of genetic disorders carried on the Y (male) chromosome. They proposed that the technique be applied to very early "pre-embryos" obtained during the course of in vitro fertilization programs to separate embryos carrying the disorder from those that were unaffected. The genetically normal embryos would then be transferred back to the uterus. This process would obviate the need to consider abortion at a later stage of development. Toward the end of 1987 scientists at the Howard Hughes Medical Institute, Bethesda, Md., and the University of California at San Francisco claimed a major breakthrough in "amplifying" aberrant DNA sequences as an extremely rapid and accurate technique for the prenatal diagnosis of inherited conditions such as hemophilia A.

Among other noteworthy achievements during the year, researchers studying the possibility of genetic components in various kinds of cancers found a gene defect that might be associated with the development of lung cancer and another gene believed to play a part in colon cancer. Still other groups of investigators identified genetic markers for manic-depressive illness and discovered a genetic defect associated with Alzheimer's disease. (*See* Mental Health, below.) (BERNARD DIXON; GINA KOLATA)

## MENTAL HEALTH

There were important accomplishments during 1987 in the understanding of the genetic and biochemical basis of some forms of mental illness. Studies in the U.S., Great Britain, Iceland, and Belgium identified at least two hereditary determinants believed to be responsible for manic-depressive illness; the possibility of a genetic factor—or factors—had been suggested by previous family and twin studies, but no specific gene had been definitively identified. On the basis of studies of cases among the Old Order Amish of Lancaster County, Pennsylvania (chosen because of the uniquely detailed genealogical records available for this population), researchers at several U.S. centres presented evidence that the condition could be traced to a single gene on the short arm of chromosome 11. However, their finding could not be confirmed by independent researchers studying Icelandic and North American families with a history of the disorder. In another investigation, carried out at the Free University of Brussels, researchers studying DNA samples from Belgian patients and their relatives were able to locate a marker for the disease on the X chromosome. From the four surveys together, however, it seems that at least two different genes may predispose individuals to what may actually be a group of disorders rather than a single illness.

There was also important progress in understanding the molecular basis of Alzheimer's disease, a form of dementia that affects 5% of people over the age of 65. The brains of Alzheimer's patients show characteristic deposits known as plaques, which contain a particular protein. A West German researcher, together with collaborators elsewhere, traced the production of this protein to a specific gene on chromosome 21. This finding was doubly significant because it added to the existing evidence of a link between Alzheimer's disease and Down syndrome, a form of mental retardation caused by an extra copy of chromosome 21; nearly every Down syndrome adult eventually develops brain changes indistinguishable from those seen in victims of Alzheimer's disease. Also in 1987, scientists at the Mt.

Scientists from the Massachusetts General Hospital neurogenetics laboratory scan DNA patterns for genetic markers related to what was thought to be a defective gene on chromosome 21. The gene was suspected of causing familial Alzheimer's disease.

IRA WYMAN—SYGMA

Sinai School of Medicine in New York City confirmed the long-held suspicion that at least some percentage of Alzheimer's cases represent a familial form of the disease.

In Britain, where some three million people are unemployed, there was growing preoccupation with the relationship between joblessness and health, particularly mental health. Researchers at City University, London, augmented an earlier study showing that men seeking work at the time of the 1971 census had a significantly higher death rate during the next decade than those who were employed. The most recent results revealed a similar effect, despite appreciable changes in the size and structure of the labour force, and confirmed that the findings could not be explained simply on the basis of initial poor health among those seeking work. Although death rates for lung cancer and heart disease were higher among the unemployed, particular social and political interest focused on the excess of deaths from suicide, accidents, and violence.

A study of opiate addicts at the Institute of Psychiatry, London, showed that while many of them relapsed soon after treatment, almost half were opiate-free six months later. The first-ever systematic U.K. survey of what happens to addicts after being discharged from dependence centers, it revealed that while many subjects used drugs again within days of leaving the program, this did not necessarily lead to a full relapse into addiction. Nevertheless, the authors argued for greatly increased measures to support drug rehabilitation patients during the period immediately after their return to the community.    (BERNARD DIXON)

This article updates the *Macropædia* article MENTAL DISORDERS and Their Treatment.

## DENTISTRY

A survey released by the National Institute of Dental Research (NIDR) in March 1987 confirmed that the oral health status of U.S. adults was continuing to improve. Among other signs of encouragement, the NIDR report showed that toothlessness had been almost eliminated in middle-aged Americans. Only 4% of the employed adults surveyed were missing all their teeth, while half had lost, at most, one tooth, a significant decrease in tooth loss from that seen in a 1971–74 NIDR study. The new survey was the most comprehensive of its kind ever conducted and the first to look at the prevalence of tooth root caries (decay)

and periodontal (gum) disease in detail. During the course of a one-year period, NIDR-trained dentists performed oral examinations on about 21,000 persons aged 18 to 103. The examinations were conducted at 800 business establishments and 200 senior centres in the continental U.S.

Researchers at the University of Florida College of Dentistry at Gainesville invented an electronic periodontal probe that measures very subtle loss of supportive gum tissues around the teeth. With the device, dentists can instantly and accurately measure the depth between the gum surface and the level of connective gum tissue attachment to the teeth. Measurement of this "pocket depth" is one of the most precise methods for detecting periodontal disease and for assessing the state of the disease. The probe is connected to a microcomputer that instantly displays the measurements on a multicoloured screen, records the data, and provides a printout of results, facilitating long-term monitoring of the condition and accurate assessment of the results of treatment.

Fear of dental treatment often prevents people from seeking regular dental care. In an attempt to evaluate ways to overcome this phobia, an experimental study was conducted in Göteborg, Sweden, on 99 adults who had managed to avoid setting foot in a dentist's office for as long as 15 years. The subjects were divided into two groups; one group received broad-based behavioral therapy along with their dental treatment, while the other group underwent dental treatment with the help of general anesthesia. Reduction in dental anxiety was substantial in both groups but significantly greater among those receiving behavioral therapy. Overall, investigators considered 80 of the 99 patients cured of their dental phobia.    (LOU JOSEPH)

## VETERINARY MEDICINE

Veterinary education was one of the main themes at the 23rd World Veterinary Congress held in Montreal, Que., during August 1987 and attended by more than 5,000 persons. The congress heard proposals that veterinary schools in developed countries participate in exchange programs of veterinary scientists that would concentrate on remedying the shortfall in livestock production while maintaining the quality of the environment. However, the problem remained that many of the most promising veterinary scientists from the third world preferred, after training in

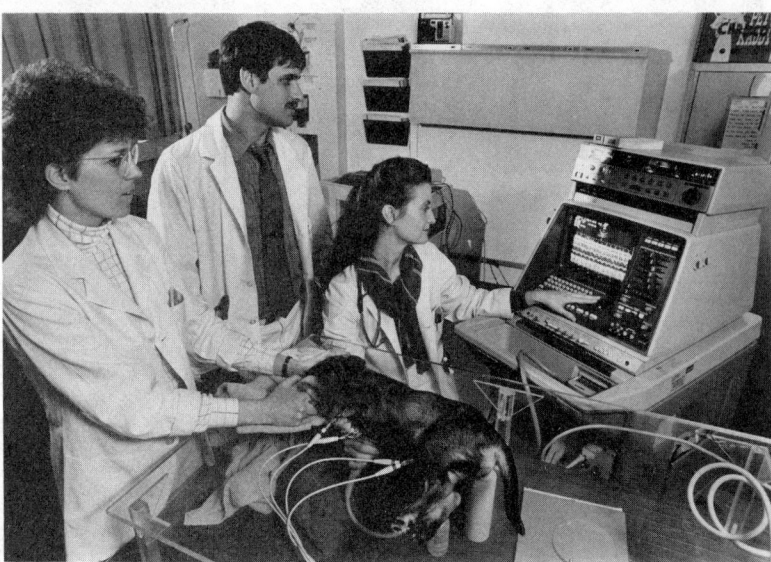

A team of veterinary scientists monitor a dog's heart with the help of an echocardiograph machine. The clinic, outfitted with equipment for EKGs, state-of-the-art anesthesia procedures, a host of complex laboratory diagnostic tests, and more, illustrates a growing trend in veterinary medicine—providing high technology and specialized training in animal care.

NEW YORK STATE COLLEGE OF VETERINARY MEDICINE AT CORNELL; PHOTOGRAPH, DAVID GRUNFELD

the West, to remain there to take advantage of the facilities available for research. There was also a tendency for schools in less developed countries to model training and research programs on those of the West. The most urgent need was for veterinarians who could deal with the basic problems of livestock disease and husbandry necessary for raising standards above those of a survival economy.

The importance of veterinary science in comparative medicine continued to grow. Studies of certain animal viral conditions, notably infectious leukemia of cats, advanced knowledge of the AIDS (acquired immune deficiency syndrome) virus. The behaviour of the virus also showed parallels with other virus-induced diseases in animals. One of those now most familiar—maedi/visna, which was virtually unknown outside Iceland until a few years earlier—causes deterioration of the respiratory and central nervous systems of sheep. Studies of these lentiviruses—that is, slow viruses, so called because their pathological effects can take years to develop—were providing useful parallels with the human immunodeficiency viruses that produce AIDS, the symptoms of which can also be slow to manifest themselves.

For several years the Jockey Club in England funded the compilation of a register of blood types of thoroughbreds, thus enabling cases of doubtful parentage to be settled. The relatively new technique of genetic "fingerprinting"—a method of DNA analysis that allows virtually any sample of body tissue to be used to identify an animal and trace its lineage—although still in its early stages, was expected to revolutionize the solution of equine identity problems.

(EDWARD BODEN)

*See also* Life Sciences; Populations and Population Movements; Social Security and Welfare Services.

This article updates the *Macropædia* articles DISEASE; MEDICINE.

# Industrial Review

Manufacturing activity in the Western world increased in 1986 at about the same rate, just over 3%, as in the previous year. Growth in the developed industrial countries was, at about 2%, more moderate than in 1985, but the manufacturing industries in the less developed countries raised their output by more than 10% in 1986. Manufacturing

production in the centrally planned economies continued to advance at a fairly steady rate of over 4%.

The performance in 1986 was uneven; an increase during the first half of the year was followed in the second by stagnation in the advanced market economies. Preliminary indicators pointed to a renewal of industrial growth in the developed countries in the first half of 1987. The likelihood was that the 1986 trends would continue into 1987, although the record growth rate of manufacturing in the less developed nations was unlikely to be repeated. The pattern of progress in 1986 was different from that in 1985, when the rate of growth was rather similar in the three

**Table I. Annual Average Rates of Growth of Manufacturing Output, 1973–86**

Percent

| Area | 1973–78 | 1978–81 | 1981–84 | 1985 | 1986 |
|---|---|---|---|---|---|
| World[1]: market economies | 2.2 | 1.5 | 2.2 | 3.5 | 3.3 |
| Industrial countries | 1.7 | 1.0 | 1.8 | 2.9 | 1.7 |
| Less industrialized countries | 5.9 | 3.9 | 4.0 | 6.1 | 11.1 |
| Centrally planned economies[1] | 7.6 | 3.3 | 4.0 | 4.6 | 4.8 |

[1] For definition *see* Table IV.
Source: UN, *Monthly Bulletin of Statistics.*

**Table II. Output per Hour Worked in Manufacturing**

1980 = 100

| Country | 1982 | 1983 | 1984 | 1985 | 1986 |
|---|---|---|---|---|---|
| France | 105 | 108 | 115 | 119 | 121 |
| West Germany | 104 | 110 | 113 | 119 | 120 |
| Italy | 104 | 106 | 112 | 115 | 116 |
| Japan | 100 | 103 | 112 | 116 | 116 |
| U.K. | 110 | 119 | 124 | 128 | 131 |
| U.S. | 108 | 114 | 119 | 124 | 127 |

Source: National Institute, *Economic Review.*

**Table III. Manufacturing Production in the U.S.S.R. and Eastern Europe[1]**

1980 = 100

| Country | 1982 | 1983 | 1984 | 1985 | 1986 |
|---|---|---|---|---|---|
| Bulgaria[2] | 110 | 115 | 120 | 124 | 128 |
| Czechoslovakia | 104 | 107 | 111 | 116 | 119 |
| East Germany[2] | 108 | 113 | 117 | 122 | 127 |
| Hungary | 106 | 107 | 110 | 110 | 112 |
| Poland | 84 | 89 | 94 | 98 | 102 |
| U.S.S.R. | 107 | 111 | 116 | 121 | ... |

[1] Romania not available.
[2] All industries.
Source: UN, *Monthly Bulletin of Statistics.*

main Western centres of manufacturing. In 1986 output in Japan stagnated as exports fell because of the strong yen, while production advanced at comparable—albeit moderate—rates in North America and Western Europe.

Within Europe, Switzerland and some of the newer members of the European Communities (EC)—Spain, Portugal, Denmark, and Ireland—achieved relatively fast progress in their manufacturing output. The West German, Italian, and Yugoslav industries also advanced faster than the average, while the growth of the Austrian, Swedish, and British industries was slower; productivity stagnated in Greece and fell in Finland. In the latter, however, an upsurge in mining activity caused overall output to rise.

Many of the less developed countries succeeded in increasing their manufacturing production significantly. They included India by 5%, Argentina, Chile, Indonesia, peninsular Malaysia, and Singapore by 7–8%, Brazil and Barbados by 9–11%, and South Korea, Fiji, and the Philippines by about 20%. Among the centrally planned economies the Soviet, East German, and Bulgarian manufacturing industries progressed the most rapidly in the 1980s.

Most significant was the decline or stagnation in the volume of exports from the U.S., Japan, and West Germany. The annual increase in world exports of manufactures fell from 10% in 1984 to 3.4% in 1985 and only 1.5% in 1986.

Low prices of oil and other primary products reduced the export earnings of oil-producing and other less developed countries; this and mounting indebtedness lowered their import capacities.

The pattern of growth in the developed areas clearly indicated relatively weakened investment activity, particularly in the oil and gas sectors, as well as technological change favouring lighter products and the penetration of new materials into the markets of traditional ones. For example, the rate of growth of the heavy industries was slow, lagging behind the advance of light industries; the production of base metals fell appreciably, and the output of building materials might just about have recovered to the level of 1984.

The light industries of the advanced countries had a better year, with the exception of the clothing and footwear group; the marginal decline there contrasted with the 8% production increase in the less developed countries. Some of the products of the latter continued to penetrate the consumer markets of the industrial nations.

In the centrally planned economies the traditional trends continued; the heavy industries, particularly metal products, grew faster than the light industries, although the gap between them might have narrowed a little in 1986 in comparison with the two previous years.                (G. F. RAY)

## Table IV. Index Numbers of Production, Employment, and Productivity in Manufacturing Industries
1980 = 100

| Area | Relative importance[1] 1980 | 1986 | Production 1985 | 1986 | Employment 1985 | 1986 | Productivity[2] 1985 | 1986 |
|---|---|---|---|---|---|---|---|---|
| World[3] | 1,000 | 1,000 | 111 | 114 | ... | ... | ... | ... |
| Industrial countries | 861 | 836 | 109 | 111 | ... | ... | ... | ... |
| Less industrialized countries | 139 | 164 | 121 | 135 | ... | ... | ... | ... |
| North America[4] | 282 | 285 | 112 | 115 | ... | ... | ... | ... |
| Canada | 22 | 21 | 107 | 109 | 93 | 95 | 115 | 115 |
| United States | 260 | 264 | 117 | 119 | 95 | 94 | 123 | 126 |
| Latin America[5] | 79 | 74 | 102 | 107 | ... | ... | ... | ... |
| Argentina | 12 | 9 | 83 | 90 | ... | ... | ... | ... |
| Brazil | 26 | 24 | 97 | 106 | ... | ... | ... | ... |
| Mexico | 18 | 16 | 107 | 102 | 94 | ... | ... | 114 |
| Asia[6] | 183 | 220 | 129 | 137 | ... | ... | ... | ... |
| India | 11 | 13 | 131 | 137 | 105 | ... | 125 | ... |
| Japan | 131 | 140 | 122 | 122 | 109 | 108 | 112 | 113 |
| South Korea | 6 | 10 | 167 | 199 | ... | ... | ... | ... |
| Europe[7] | 422 | 391 | 103 | 105 | ... | ... | ... | ... |
| Austria | 9 | 9 | 109 | 110 | 90 | 89 | 121 | 123 |
| Belgium | 13 | 12 | 104 | 106 | ... | ... | ... | ... |
| Denmark | 5 | 6 | 122 | 127 | 103 | ... | 119 | ... |
| Finland | 6 | 6 | 118 | 116 | 95 | 94 | 124 | 123 |

| Area | Relative importance[1] 1980 | 1986 | Production 1985 | 1986 | Employment 1985 | 1986 | Productivity[2] 1985 | 1986 |
|---|---|---|---|---|---|---|---|---|
| France | 75 | 64 | 95 | 97 | 88 | 86 | 108 | 113 |
| West Germany | 114 | 107 | 104 | 107 | 90 | 91 | 116 | 118 |
| Greece | 4 | 4 | 101 | 101 | 99 | 99 | 102 | 102 |
| Ireland | 2 | 2 | 130 | 134 | 83 | 82 | 157 | 163 |
| Italy | 54 | 47 | 96 | 99 | ... | ... | ... | ... |
| Netherlands, The | 14 | 14 | 109 | 111 | 86 | ... | 127 | ... |
| Norway | 5 | 5 | 106 | 108 | 89 | ... | 119 | ... |
| Portugal | 3 | 3 | 117 | 122 | ... | ... | ... | ... |
| Spain | 23 | 21 | 101 | 105 | ... | ... | ... | ... |
| Sweden | 13 | 13 | 109 | 110 | 90 | 90 | 121 | 122 |
| Switzerland | 13 | 12 | 103 | 107 | 95 | 94 | 108 | 114 |
| United Kingdom | 58 | 54 | 104 | 105 | 80 | 78 | 130 | 135 |
| Yugoslavia | 10 | 10 | 114 | 117 | ... | ... | ... | ... |
| Rest of the world[8] | 34 | 30 | ... | ... | ... | ... | ... | ... |
| Oceania | 15 | 13 | 97 | 99 | ... | ... | ... | ... |
| Australia | 13 | 12 | 98 | ... | 99 | ... | 99 | ... |
| South Africa | 8 | 7 | 95 | 95 | 94 | 93 | 101 | 102 |
| Centrally planned economies[9] | ... | ... | ... | 120 | 126 | ... | ... | ... |

[1] The 1980 weights are those applied by the UN Statistical Office; those for 1986 were estimated on the basis of the changes in manufacturing output since 1980 in the various countries.
[2] This is 100 times the production index divided by the employment index, giving a rough indication of changes in output per person employed.
[3] Excluding Albania, Bulgaria, China, Czechoslovakia, East Germany, Hungary, Mongolia, North Korea, Poland, Romania, the U.S.S.R., and Vietnam.
[4] Canada and the United States.
[5] South and Central America (including Mexico) and the Caribbean islands.
[6] Asian Middle East and East and Southeast Asia; including Japan, Israel, and Turkey.
[7] Excluding Albania, Bulgaria, Czechoslovakia, East Germany, Hungary, Poland, Romania, and the U.S.S.R.
[8] Africa and Oceania.
[9] These are not included in the above world total and consist of the European countries listed in note 7 above.

## Table V. Pattern of Output, 1983–86
Percent change from previous year

| | World[1] 1983 | 1984 | 1985 | 1986 | Developed countries 1983 | 1984 | 1985 | 1986 | Less developed countries 1983 | 1984 | 1985 | 1986 | Centrally planned economies[2] 1983 | 1984 | 1985 | 1986 |
|---|---|---|---|---|---|---|---|---|---|---|---|---|---|---|---|---|
| All manufacturing | 3 | 7 | 3 | 3 | 3 | 7 | 3 | 2 | 3 | 8 | 6 | 11 | 5 | 5 | 5 | 5 |
| Heavy industries | 3 | 8 | 4 | 2 | 3 | 9 | 4 | 1 | 2 | 9 | 5 | 10 | 5 | 6 | 6 | 6 |
| Base metals | 2 | 9 | 0 | −2 | 3 | 8 | 0 | −4 | 1 | 11 | 3 | 7 | 3 | 4 | 2 | 3 |
| Metal products | 3 | 10 | 5 | 3 | 3 | 10 | 5 | 1 | 2 | 12 | 6 | 14 | 6 | 7 | *7 | 7 |
| Building materials, etc. | 2 | 4 | 1 | 2 | 3 | 3 | −1 | 1 | −2 | 5 | 5 | 6 | 3 | 3 | 3 | 4 |
| Chemicals | 6 | 6 | 3 | 4 | 6 | 6 | 3 | 3 | 5 | 7 | 4 | 8 | 5 | 4 | 3 | 4 |
| Light industries | 3 | 4 | 3 | 5 | 3 | 4 | 1 | 3 | 3 | 7 | 8 | 12 | 4 | 3 | 3 | 4 |
| Food, drink, tobacco | 2 | 3 | 3 | 2 | 1 | 2 | 2 | 2 | 1 | 6 | 5 | 2 | 4 | 3 | 3 | 2 |
| Textiles | 2 | 2 | 2 | 4 | 2 | 1 | 1 | 3 | 3 | 3 | 3 | 6 | 2 | 1 | 3 | 2 |
| Clothing, footwear | 0 | 3 | −1 | 1 | 0 | 1 | 1 | −1 | 2 | 7 | 1 | 8 | 2 | 3 | 3 | 3 |
| Wood products | 7 | 4 | 1 | 5 | 5 | 4 | 0 | 4 | 7 | 3 | 5 | 7 | 5 | 4 | 4 | 4 |
| Paper, printing | 5 | 7 | 3 | 6 | 5 | 7 | 2 | 5 | 2 | 8 | 15 | 12 | 5 | 4 | 4 | 4 |

[1] Excluding centrally planned economies.    [2] Excluding China.
Source: UN, *Monthly Bulletin of Statistics*.

## ADVERTISING

In September 1987 the A. C. Nielsen Co. introduced the "people meter," a new way to measure television viewership patterns. The meter replaced the diary in which people listed the programs they watched. The diaries were considered to be only as reliable as the memories of the people who entered the programs on the appropriate page. With the people meter, each individual who was part of the Nielsen sample pushed a button on a box on the television set each time the set was turned on or the channel was changed. The new system provided a detailed profile of a program's viewers, including their age, sex, income, education, and ethnic background. Nielsen placed 2,000 meters in the homes of its statistically selected national sample.

Since advertising rates for television programs are based on ratings, the switch could have a considerable effect on the television industry. The networks claimed that the people meter had certain built-in biases. In the first people-meter results, the ratings were lower than those provided under the old system. In general, people meters helped programs that appealed to younger, urban viewers, especially men, who had tended to be less faithful in filling out the diaries than older persons and women. At the same time, some viewers considered the constant button-pushing a hardship and neglected the box. This was found to be particularly true of children and teenagers, thus lowering the ratings of programs directed toward those groups.

In June U.S. Pres. Ronald Reagan vetoed a measure that would have written into law the Federal Communications Commission's (FCC's) fairness doctrine, a policy requiring broadcasters to air opposing views on controversial issues. In August the FCC voted to abolish the fairness doctrine on the grounds that it restricted broadcast journalists' First Amendment rights. There was speculation that this might encourage stations to accept advertising that advocated a specific viewpoint.

Congress was concerned that there were few regularly scheduled weekday children's programs on commercial television and that children's programs shown on weekends were mainly cartoon shows designed to sell toys. New to children's television was a show that used a signal in the program's sound track to activate an expensive toy. (See *Games and Toys,* below.) In September a federal appeals court ruled against the FCC position that allowed toy manufacturers to promote their products on cartoon shows without having to say that they paid for the programs. Currently, toy manufacturers produced about 75 different television programs. They did not advertise on cartoon shows based on their products and often received, in payment, free air time for their commercials on other programs. The identification of toy manufacturers as sponsors of programs based on their products would make it difficult for the networks to attract other advertisers for these programs.

The long-standing ban against the advertising of condoms on television was eased somewhat in light of the finding that use of condoms could slow the spread of AIDS (acquired immune deficiency syndrome). Several local stations agreed to accept condom ads, though the networks still refused to air such commercials. Bars to condom advertising in the print media also were eased.

In April 1987 General Motors Corp. and Procter & Gamble Co. joined together in an $8 million advertising campaign using "split 30 second" commercials to promote a car giveaway contest. These commercials were the first to break the barrier against joint television advertising in a 30-second commercial. Joint advertising had been standard for years in newspapers and store displays, where manufacturers teamed up with retailers in what was called cooperative advertising. Among popular television shows, the cost of a 30-second commercial in 1987 was $425,000 for "The Cosby Show," $230,000 for "The Golden Girls," and $265,000 for "Family Ties." A half-hour television show often consisted of 26 minutes of entertainment, 1 minute of network and local promotion time, and 3 minutes of commercials.

*Advertising Age,* the international newspaper of marketing, published its list of the 100 leading national advertisers in the U.S. in September. The newspaper reported that the top 100 increased their U.S. advertising spending 3.4% over the 1985 level to $27,170,000,000 in 1986. Procter & Gamble continued in the number one position even though its spending, at $1.4 billion, declined by 10.3% from 1985. The other four top spenders in order of expenditures were Philip Morris Cos., Sears, Roebuck & Co., RJR/Nabisco, and General Motors (GM). The five top network television advertisers were Procter & Gamble, Philip Morris, GM, Unilever NV, and Kellogg. GM was the largest newspaper advertiser, spending $146 million in this medium in 1986. The top magazine advertiser in 1986 was Philip Morris, spending $230 million.

(EDWARD MARK MAZZE)

## AEROSPACE

A major issue in the air transport industry in 1987 was the problem of insufficient airport capacity, caused by the huge and growing demand for air travel. The problem was most acute in the U.S., where total demand was growing by some 14% annually. This demand was uneven; at Washington (D.C.) Dulles International Airport, for example, it increased by 75%. No fewer than 38 airports recorded traffic growth of more than 10%. In Europe and elsewhere the overall growth was a lower but still rapid 11%, and by October it was clear that world air traffic for the year would break all records.

The financing of airline reequipment was the theme of an international conference in Geneva. The scope of the problem was highlighted by Europe's Airbus Industrie, which calculated a market for some 7,300 airliners over the upcoming 20 years, costing about $4 billion. Increasingly, outside financing was becoming inevitable, with the money market accepting the aircraft as security rather than relying on the creditworthiness of the customers. To secure a loan, United Air Lines gave Boeing Co. a 15% share in its airline in return for part of a 110-aircraft commitment made in November 1985. The deal marked a departure from traditional methods of financing.

Commercial aircraft builders continued to produce new or "derivative" designs. Airbus flew its 150-seat A320 for the first time in February. It was technologically advanced, and Airbus already had orders and options for more than 400 of them. Its success caused concern in the U.S. and provoked accusations that European governments were permitting or helping Airbus to underprice its aircraft, a charge that was vigorously refuted. The grievance was intensified by the impending launch by Airbus of its new A330-A340 family of two- and four-engine airliners; they represented a commercial threat to McDonnell Douglas's MD-11, an updated version of the DC-10 trijet designed in the late 1960s. The MD-11 had been launched in late December 1986; its European rival was given the go-ahead six months later.

However, the revolutionary—as opposed

A 3-D viewfinder, enclosed in a magazine layout, adds a new dimension to advertising. Advertisers were concentrating their efforts more on print, spending funds normally allocated to television on ideas that would make a greater impact on a more select audience.

The new Airbus A320, manufactured by Europe's Airbus Industrie, heightened concern among major U.S. jet producers, which were accustomed to dominance in the market. Its high technology and low cost were typical of Airbus craft that had made the jet firm second in sales only to Boeing.

GRUYAERT—MAGNUM

to evolutionary—shape of things to come was indicated by a new generation of propulsive devices modeled on the previously maligned propeller. During 1987 three aircraft modified to provide improved fuel economy and less noise began or continued experimental flights and demonstration programs: a Boeing 727 with a Pratt & Whitney-Allison unducted fan, a McDonnell Douglas MD-80 with a General Electric unducted fan, and a U.S. National Aeronautics and Space Administration (NASA)-Lockheed Gulfstream 2 with an Allison propfan. The Boeing and McDonnell Douglas experiments were to pave the way for, respectively, the 7J7 and MD-91X commercial follow-ons. Late in the year Boeing announced postponement of certification of the 7J7 from 1992 to 1993, partly to assess the trend in fuel prices; if these continued to be depressed, much of the attraction of the new power plants would vanish, and it would be difficult to recoup heavy investment costs.

In the U.S. continuing airline instability was revealed in a spate of takeovers and mergers. In the U.K. the national carrier, British Airways, was privatized as was Rolls-Royce, which had been under government ownership since its financial collapse in 1971 during development of the RB.211 engine for the Lockheed TriStar. This engine had become the company's most important product.

Corporate and business aviation flourished, with such sophisticated aircraft as the U.S. Gulfstream and Canada's Challenger selling well. At the lower end of the market, however, exemplified by the single- and twin-engined piston types, sales

dipped to their lowest levels since World War II. Part of the reason was the high cost of insurance, required by insurers for combating litigation.

The world's most prestigious transport—the Mach 2.2 Concorde (Mach number 1 corresponds to the speed of sound)—completed 11 years of service on its scheduled routes and excursions. Despite the political and administrative difficulties that destroyed its marketability, U.S. manufacturers predicted a substantial fleet—up to 430 according to McDonnell Douglas—flying at between Mach 2.2 and Mach 5 in the year 2000. That company, along with General Dynamics and Rockwell International Corp., was chosen by NASA and the U.S. Department of Defense in October to begin preliminary design of the proposed National Aero-Space Plane (NASP) as a long-range surface-to-surface transport or orbital-delivery vehicle for commercial and military applications.

On the military scene there was an airship revival, with the U.S. Navy (a traditional operator until the early 1960s) ordering a prototype fleet-surveillance and airborne-early-warning vehicle to be built by a team of Airship Industries of the U.K. and Westinghouse Electric Corp. of the U.S. New interest stemmed from the many technical developments that had taken place since passenger-carrying airships were abandoned 50 years earlier following several disasters. In recent years the U.K. company had successfully operated several airships.

Several years of controversy over escalating costs led the Israeli government to abandon its advanced Lavi fighter in favour

of additional U.S.-supplied F-16s. It also announced the mothballing of some of its Kfir fighters because of lack of funds. Cost problems also caused delays in launching the European Fighter Aircraft (EFA) development venture by the U.K., West Germany, Italy, and Spain and jeopardized its planned 1995 delivery.

U.S. interest focused on the Northrop Advanced Technology Bomber (ATB) and the Lockheed F-19 "stealth" fighter. The former was due to make its first flight at the end of 1987, while several of the latter were believed to be operating nocturnally in the U.S. and Europe. In general the industry was concentrating on upgrading existing combat aircraft; those over a decade old normally underwent structural, engine, or electronics enhancement. Even the F-16—the most recent U.S. Air Force fighter—was equipped with a new engine and flight-control system to improve performance and reliability.

(MICHAEL WILSON)

## AUTOMOBILES

The first nine months of 1987 were a period of strength for most of the world's automobile manufacturers. There were, however, some worrying signals for the powerful Japanese industry, whose exports and total output fell slightly.

In Europe new-car sales seemed certain to reach a record of more than 12 million units in 1987 after a 6.8% rise to 11.5 million in the 11 months through November. This followed a record 11.7 million sales in 1986. Small declines in both car and commercial vehicle output took place in Japan in 1987. This reflected pricing problems in some export markets because of the increasing strength of the yen and trade protectionism, either actual or threatened. Small increases in sales in the Japanese home market were countered by declines in exports of both cars and commercial vehicles, although exports rose sharply at year's end.

Technical innovations in 1987 included four-wheel steering, with Honda and Mazda of Japan joining Nissan in offering production versions, and electronic continuously variable transmissions (ECVTs) from Ford and Fiat in Europe and Subaru in Japan. More cars with four-wheel drive became available in Europe and Japan. There was a notable increase in the availability of high-efficiency multivalve engines in relatively low-cost cars, led by Japan's Toyota.

News of a different kind from Volkswagen was the production of the last of the "Beetles" in Lagos, Nigeria, in mid-1987. The first prototype of the legendary model was produced in 1935. Commercial output started in 1945, and more than 18 million were produced in over 20 countries during the next 42 years.

**Europe and Australia.** Every Western European automobile manufacturing country increased its output in the six months ended June 1987 compared with the same period in 1986. A small decline in commercial vehicle production for the half year took place in West Germany, but France, the U.K., Italy, Sweden, Belgium, The Netherlands, and Spain all increased their output of commercial vehicles as well as cars.

Italy, France, and the U.K. were each

on target to top two million units in sales in 1987 for the first time. Europe's fastest growing market and manufacturing country, Spain, came close to one million sales for the first time. In the European competition for car sales leadership, West Germany's Volkswagen-Audi Group (VAG), which included SEAT of Spain, led Italy's Fiat Group (Fiat-Lancia-Ferrari-Autobianchi-Alfa Romeo). VAG won 14.9% of all Western European car sales, and the Fiat Group gained 14.8%. Ford held a strong third place with 12.1% of total sales, ahead of France's Peugeot Group (Peugeot and Citroën) with 11.6%. The Peugeot Group nevertheless displaced General Motors (Opel and Vauxhall), which totaled 10.8%. Renault of France recorded an above-average increase, moving up to 10.2%. GM, West Germany's Mercedes-Benz and BMW, Sweden's Volvo, and the U.K.'s state-owned Austin Rover all suffered a decreased share of the market. The Japanese share of European car sales declined from 12.1 to 11.5% despite an increase in volume from 1,078,000 to 1,084,000.

Major changes in industry ownership in 1987 included Fiat Group's takeover of state-owned Alfa Romeo. Italy's prestigious Lamborghini was absorbed into Chrysler Corp., which also took over American Motors Corp. (AMC) in the U.S. from France's Renault. Ford bought the British sports and luxury carmaker Aston Martin Lagonda. Toyota and VAG announced that Toyota's light commercial vehicles were to be assembled in West Germany in a joint venture. Thus Japan's top company was to be linked with West Germany's in the same way that it successfully worked with GM in the U.S.

The seven-year-old Nissan-Alfa Romeo joint manufacturing venture, known as ARNA, ended with Fiat's acquisition of Alfa Romeo. The product of the joint venture, an Alfa-engined Nissan Cherry assembled in Italy, failed to achieve the partners' market ambitions.

In Australia sales of both cars and commercial vehicles continued to decline as a result of heavy taxation, a heavily devalued currency, and uncertainty caused by government intervention in the activities of five manufacturers (Ford, GM, Toyota, Nissan, and Mitsubishi). Sales for the first half of 1987 fell to the levels of the late 1960s. Substantial changes in the structure of the Australian industry were expected to take place in late 1987 and 1988 as manufacturers attempted to adjust to low sales and increasing lack of competitiveness in quality and export marketability.

(JOHN R. WEINTHAL)

**U.S.** The year 1987 was one to celebrate for Ford Motor Co. Earnings soared to new records, topping even those of archrival General Motors Corp. (GM), and the best-selling car and truck in the industry both carried the Ford nameplate. The celebration was subdued, however, as Henry Ford II, 70, who was the grandson of the founder of the company and who guided it for 34 years before his retirement in 1980, died of pneumonia on September 29 (*see* OBITUARIES).

During the first nine months of the year alone, Ford earned $3,690,000,000, topping not only the $2.5 billion earned in the same period a year earlier but surpassing

the previous record of $3.3 billion earned in all of 1986. Contributing to the record profits were strong vehicle sales by Ford. In the 1987 model year ended September 30, Ford sold 2.8 million cars and trucks to finish ahead of GM's Chevrolet division, which sold 2.6 million cars and trucks. It was the first time since 1956 that Ford topped Chevrolet in combined sales. Chevrolet sold more cars than Ford, 1.5 million to 1.4 million, but Ford sold more trucks, 1.4 million to 1.1 million.

While Ford did well, the U.S. industry as a whole fared poorly. Domestic automakers sold 7.3 million cars, down from the 8 million sold the previous year. It was the lowest number of cars sold since 6.5 million were sold in 1983.

Import car sales totaled 3.2 million units, topping the record of 3.1 million sold in the 1986 model year. Combined domestic and import car sales totaled 10.5 million units, which represented a sharp decline from the 11.2 million units sold in 1986. By contrast, combined domestic and import truck sales totaled 4.9 million units, topping the record 4.8 million in 1986. Total industry sales—cars and trucks, imports and domestics—were 15.4 million units, down from the record 16.1 million sold in 1986 but still the third highest total in industry history.

Despite a host of incentives throughout the year, from discount financing to cash rebates, sales totals were down from a year earlier except at Ford. GM sold 3.7 million cars in the 1987 model year, an 18% decline from the 4.5 million sold in 1986 and the first time the company had sold fewer than 4 million cars since the 1983 model year. Ford sales totaled 2,070,000 units, a 5% gain from the 1,960,000 sold in 1986. Chrysler Corp. sales, which included those from newly acquired AMC, declined 18% to 1,010,000 units from 1,230,000 in 1986. AMC's contribution to the total was only 49,610 units in the 1987 model year versus 82,292 in 1986.

Honda, which built both the Civic and Accord in Marysville, Ohio, sold 316,812 U.S.-made cars, a 73% gain from 183,629 a year earlier. Nissan, which built the subcompact Sentra in Smyrna, Tenn., sold 123,113 cars, double the 49,325 sold a

year earlier. Volkswagen sold 65,671 cars, a 14% decline from 76,410 a year earlier, and announced that it would close its assembly plant in New Stanton, Pa., in 1988. Toyota, in its first full year of selling U.S.-made Corolla FX-16 cars built at its joint-venture (with GM) plant in Fremont, Calif., sold 37,308 cars.

Among the major imports, Toyota sold the most cars, 597,110, with Honda second at 426,837 and Nissan third at 422,143. Import sales by the Japanese producers all trailed 1986 levels. The producers reduced the number of cars shipped from Japan and increased the number of cars built at their plants in the U.S. in order to offset the effects of the rising value of the yen against the U.S. dollar, which had forced price increases on Japanese imported cars.

The subcompact Ford Escort, with sales of 394,999 units, was the industry's top-selling car for the second year in a row. The Taurus, another Ford nameplate, was the second leading seller, with 376,907 units. Rounding out the top ten were the Honda Accord at 337,076 (built both in the U.S. and abroad), Chevrolet Celebrity (331,647), Chevrolet Cavalier (295,316), Oldsmobile Ciera (264,860), Hyundai Excel (261,392), Nissan Sentra (239,968), Ford Tempo (234,663), and Honda Civic (232,812). The best-selling vehicle overall was the Ford F-Series pickup truck, with sales of 519,704. The Chevrolet truck finished in second place with sales of 405,722.

With the start of the new 1988 model year on Oct. 1, 1987, the automakers brought out a relatively small number of new cars. GM introduced its so-called GM10s, or W-cars—downsized, front-wheel-drive replacements for the Pontiac Grand Prix, Buick Regal, and Oldsmobile Cutlass Supreme. However, GM decided to introduce the Regal first and hold off on the others until 1988.

Pontiac introduced a new top-of-the-line model called the Bonneville SSE and a new four-wheel-drive version of the mid-size 6000STE. Cadillac had no new car but stretched its existing Eldorado by 7.6 cm (3 in) and squared off what had been rounded body lines in an attempt to win back customers who had argued that the 1987 Eldorado looked too much like the

A Chrysler Fifth Avenue assembly line (left) alongside that of the AMC-Renault Alliance symbolizes the Chrysler-American Motors Corp. merger. Chrysler's investment in AMC would help guarantee that there would be enough factories to meet market demand.

A showroom worker in India polishes a new Maruti while prospective customers peruse its price list. The car was produced in India with the cooperation of Japan's Suzuki as part of a plan that India's prime minister hoped would stimulate his nation's economy.

AP/WIDE WORLD

less expensive Buick Riviera or Oldsmobile Toronado.

Oldsmobile brought out a new engine called the Quad 4, which featured the industry's newly popular multiple-valve design. The Quad 4 was a 2.3-litre, four-cylinder engine with four valves per cylinder (two intake and two exhaust) rather than the conventional two valves (one intake and one exhaust).

At Ford there was only one new car, but it was a significant one. Ford brought out a larger, front-wheel-drive replacement for its luxury Continental. In addition to front-wheel drive, the car featured four-wheel antilock brakes. Chrysler introduced a new pair of full-size, front-wheel-drive cars, the Chrysler New Yorker Brougham and the Dodge Dynasty.

Among the imports, Toyota brought out a new sporty Celica featuring four-wheel drive, while both Mazda and Honda introduced cars featuring four-wheel steering, the Mazda MX-6 and the Honda Prelude Si 4WS. With four-wheel steering, front and rear wheels can move in the same or opposite direction depending on vehicle speed and the need to make a sharp or normal turn or corner.

To begin the new model year the automakers raised prices between 1 and 3% but instituted a new pricing strategy in which previously optional equipment was made standard. Thus Chrysler raised the price of its Grand Caravan by $2,800 but said that since $2,500 of that included now-standard air conditioning, automatic transmission, and a larger three-litre V-6 engine, it only considered the increase to be $300.

On March 9 Chrysler announced that it had made an offer to acquire AMC for $4 per share of AMC stock, roughly a $1 billion deal. AMC had become a partner of Renault of France in 1980 when the latter purchased nearly a 46% equity interest in AMC. On August 5 AMC shareholders voted to approve an amended offer of $4.50 a share, bringing the total transaction to about $1.6 billion.

Chrysler said that it was interested in AMC to obtain its car- and Jeep-manufacturing plants as well as its established dealer network. Soon after the merger was completed, Chrysler dropped the subcompact Renault Alliance and compact Eagle four-wheel-drive station wagon. AMC operations were renamed Chrysler's Jeep-Eagle division.

Among other major announcements during the year, Toyota and Nissan said that they planned to bring out full-size luxury cars in 1989 to compete directly with U.S. and European luxury cars. Fuji Heavy Industries (Subaru) announced that it would build a large car at its joint-venture plant with Isuzu of Japan in Lafayette, Ind.

Mazda began building its compact 626 at a plant in Flat Rock, Mich. Ford, which owned an equity interest in Mazda, said that it would obtain a version of the 626 in 1988 from the Flat Rock plant.

The Japanese-built Sprint captured the title of most fuel-efficient vehicle in the industry in 1987 with ratings of 54 mpg for city driving and 58 mpg on the highway. The Sprint was sold under the Chevrolet nameplate. The Honda Civic CRX HF placed second with a 50-mpg city/56-mpg highway rating. The lowest-ranked car was the Lamborghini East Countach with a 6-mpg city/10-mpg highway rating, earning it a $3,850 "gas guzzler" tax.

(JAMES L. MATEJA)

**Japan.** Production of passenger and commercial vehicles in Japan during the first eight months of 1987 declined 1.7% to 8,024,000 units from the corresponding period in 1986. Passenger cars accounted for 5,130,000 units, a 1.4% drop, and commercial vehicles totaled 2,894,000 units, a 2.2% decrease.

Domestic sales of passenger and commercial vehicles reached 2,820,000 units during the same period in 1987. A continuation of this pace would cause domestic sales to reach a new peak of 4.3 million units during 1987, topping the record of 4,297,000 vehicles in 1979.

The domestic sales of "light vehicles" (those of 500-cc displacement), including both passenger and commercial types, rose 3% to 1.1 million units during the same period. A continuation of that pace would result in domestic sales of light vehicles exceeding the previous high of 1,610,000 units in 1986, marking the sixth consecutive record year.

These upturns in domestic sales were attributable to two factors. One was that Japanese automakers gave buyers powerful incentives that induced them into the passenger car market. These included a variety of technological innovations. Another factor was that the package of measures for encouraging domestic demand introduced

by the government helped increase activity in the construction industry, which led in turn to an increased demand for trucks. Sales of trucks, excluding light vehicles, jumped to 64,000 vehicles in the single month of August, a strong 7.6% advance over the same month in 1986.

The industry, however, suffered a downturn in exports, including those to Europe and the U.S. The total fell during the first eight months of 1987 to 4,247,000 vehicles, a 5.8% decline from the corresponding period in 1986. On the other hand, sales of imported cars in the Japanese market rose more rapidly than did those of domestic cars, thanks partly to the government-led "buy imported products" campaign; sales jumped a significant 43% to 62,000 units during the first eight months of 1987. If sales continued at that rate, the total sales of imports would top 90,000 in one year for the first time. This figure seemed particularly significant when compared with totals of 68,457 and 50,172 for 1986 and 1985, respectively. Major reasons for the increased sales of imports included the high value of the Japanese yen in 1987, which devalued the selling prices of imported cars, and increased efforts by overseas automakers to make inroads into the Japanese market; imports gained growing popularity among young consumers.

(NOBUYOSHI YOSHIDA)

## BEVERAGES

**Beer.** In 1987 the trend toward brewing foreign beers under license continued. The small brewer Gibbs Mew became the first British company to license a brew in Germany, to the Bavarian brewer Graf Arco. Budweiser, the main brand of the world's largest brewer, Anheuser-Busch of the U.S., was franchised for brewing in Denmark to United Breweries, while United's main brand, Carlsberg, was to be brewed in Japan by Suntory and in South Korea by the Chosun brewery. U.S. brewer Coors franchised production of its beer in Japan, to the Asahi brewery. A new Amstel brewery inaugurated in Burundi by Heineken of The Netherlands was 40% owned by the Burundian state.

Brazil became the 6th largest brewing nation, moving up from 12th place ten years earlier. In China modernization of the Guangzhou (Canton) brewery was completed, the culmination of a six-year joint project with Danebrew Consult of Denmark and the Carlsberg brewery in Hong Kong.

The major international exhibition was Brew '87, held in London, with some 300 companies participating. U.K. brewers dominated the international awards held in conjunction with the exhibition. Among the more than 900 beers entered, the champion bottled ale award went to Owd Roger, a strong ale from Marston's brewery of Burton upon Trent. The international lager champion was LCL Pils from the Federation brewery in Newcastle. The U.K. government announced its intention to reform the licensing laws in England and Wales. Public houses had to close during the afternoon in accordance with emergency legislation introduced in 1915, during World War I.

The European Court of Justice declared that the West German Reinheitsgebot, which limits the raw materials used in beer, should no longer be used to bar imported beer from West Germany. The case began in 1982 when the French brewer Brasseries du Pecheur lodged a formal complaint alleging discrimination by West Germany against beers from other countries within the EC. (MICHAEL D. RIPLEY)

**Spirits.** With emphasis on healthier living and concern about drinking and driving still in the news, the worldwide trend toward lower-strength spirits persisted in 1987. The U.S. spirits market was particularly hard hit as changing drinking habits combined with the adverse effects of a record 19% increase in liquor tax imposed in 1986. Apart from imported vodkas, single malt whiskies, and the rapidly emerging peach schnapps product sector, spirit sales were depressed. Distilled spirit shipments to the U.S. fell from their 1980 high of 1.7 billion litres to 1.6 billion litres, and 19 of the top 25 U.S. brands recorded sales declines. An exception was De Kuyper liqueurs, led by the phenomenally successful original Peachtree Schnapps.

Imported whisky sales also fell sharply in the important Japanese market because of unfavourable taxation and the increased popularity of the lower-strength traditional *shochu* white spirit. Worldwide cognac shipments declined 1.6% in 1986 to 9.9 million cases, and revenue fell 3.6%. Some 80% of the finest-quality cognac continued to be destined for the Asia-Pacific market.

In the U.K. whisky's share of total spirit sales fell below 50%, and this, together with the threat of tougher legislation, was a source of concern for the Scotch Whisky Association. A ministerial group established to study alcohol misuse was urged not to make drink the scapegoat for violent crime. The U.K. government set up an investigation into the £2.7 billion takeover of Distillers by Guinness in 1986, and criminal charges were brought against a former Guinness chief executive. (*See* CRIME, LAW ENFORCEMENT, AND PENOLOGY: *Special Report.*)

Takeovers in 1987 included Whitbread's purchase of the Beefeater gin firm

"Buffalo Bill" Owens was one of many "microbrewers" taking advantage of new direct-sales laws that allowed people to market their own beer.

JAMES D. WILSON—WOODFIN CAMP & ASSOCIATES

James Burrough, Grandmet's purchase of Heublein, the Guinness Group's $480 million bid for Schenley Industries, and the Moët-Hennessy acquisition of Hine cognac. (ANTONY C. WARNER)

**Wine.** Output of wine in 1987 was provisionally estimated at between 315 million and 320 hectolitres (hl; 1 hl = 26.4 U.S. gal). This compared with actual production of 330,196,000 hl in 1986. The decline in 1987 was largely attributable to lower than expected output in the EC countries. Adverse weather constrained production, which was estimated at 205 million hl. With France particularly badly affected, Italy became the world's biggest producer with 73.5 million hl, followed by France (70.6 million hl), Spain (38.9 million hl),

Portugal (9.7 million hl), and West Germany (8.5 million hl).

Eastern European output totaled 38.3 million hl, believed to be well below 1986 production because of a reduction in Soviet output to half the 1986 level of 34.4 million hl; the Soviet government's anti-alcohol campaign was responsible for the decline. Output of other European producers (Austria, Switzerland, and Yugoslavia) was estimated at 10 million hl. In North America the U.S. accounted for 16.5 million hl of the 17.2 million-hl total, while South America added another 28.4 million hl. There was little change in South Africa (8.7 million hl), Australia (4.1 million hl), or New Zealand (500,000 hl). In Algeria, Morocco, and Tunisia, where output was mainly table wine, the total was 1.9 million hl. In Asia both Japan (500,000 hl) and China were trying to develop their wine industries, and there was a small overall rise.

The area planted to grapes for wine had been declining since 1980, but better yields ensured that wine production continued to rise. World consumption of wine, however, continued to fall. In the EC countries there were problems of oversupply, and the financial support given to wine producers was a continuing source of controversy. Average annual consumption worldwide was 285,746,000 hl in the period 1976–80, but in 1986 it was only 274,923,000 hl. The supply imbalance was likely to become worse given the trend in many countries toward lower alcohol consumption. (MARIE-JOSE DESHAYES)

**Soft drinks.** Soft drinks continued their reign as the favourite choice of beverage in the U.S., with per capita consumption increasing to 44.8 gal in 1986. This upward trend continued into 1987, with soft drink sales rising 4.5% from 1986 totals. Though due largely to strong marketing and advertising, much of this increase could be attributed to the industry's effective distribution system. U.S. soft drink manufacturers had made it easier to buy their products than any other beverage.

The necessity of realizing economies of

| Table VI. Estimated Consumption of Beer in Selected Countries | | | |
|---|---|---|---|
| In litres[1] per capita | | | |
| Country | 1984 | 1985 | 1986 |
| West Germany | 144.7 | 145.5 | 146.6 |
| East Germany | 142.2 | 141.6 | 140.0 |
| Czechoslovakia | 140.1 | 130.8 | 133.4 |
| Denmark | 129.75 | 121.26 | 125.78 |
| New Zealand | 116.9 | 115.2 | 123.5 |
| Belgium | 126.3 | 121.0 | 119.9 |
| Luxembourg | 120.7 | 120.4 | 119.3 |
| Austria | 107.7 | 111.6 | 118.5 |
| Australia[2] | 114.5 | 115.5 | 111.3 |
| United Kingdom | 110.1 | 108.9 | 108.1 |
| Hungary | 87.1 | 92.4 | 99.4 |
| United States | 90.7 | 90.3 | 90.8 |
| Netherlands, The | 83.4 | 84.5 | 86.0 |
| Ireland | 108.4 | 100.0 | 80.0 |
| Canada[3] | 81.8 | 83.0 | ... |
| Switzerland | 68.6 | 69.2 | 69.4 |
| Finland | 59.5 | 61.7 | 65.4 |
| Bulgaria | 63.6 | 63.3 | 64.3 |
| Spain | 59.0 | 61.0 | 62.0 |
| Venezuela | 70.2 | 59.5 | 60.7 |
| Colombia | 50.0 | 55.2 | 52.0 |
| Norway | 46.82 | 47.52 | 50.78 |
| Sweden | 44.5 | 46.8 | 50.0 |
| Romania | 50.0 | 50.0 | 48.0 |
| Yugoslavia | 48.8 | 45.9 | 47.5 |

[1] One litre = 1.0567 U.S. quart = 0.8799 imperial quart.
[2] Years ending June 30.
[3] Years ending March 31.

| Table VII. Estimated Consumption of Spirits in Selected Countries | | | |
|---|---|---|---|
| In litres[1] per capita | | | |
| Country | 1984 | 1985 | 1986 |
| Hungary | 5.1 | 5.4 | 5.3 |
| East Germany | 4.6 | 4.8 | 4.7 |
| Poland | 4.2 | 4.6 | 4.7 |
| Bulgaria | 3.17 | 3.21 | 3.41 |
| Czechoslovakia | 3.28 | 3.52 | 3.4 |
| Finland | 3.1 | 3.01 | 3.17 |
| Spain | 2.8 | 3.0 | 3.0 |
| Canada[2] | 2.66 | 2.61 | ... |
| Luxembourg | 2.5 | 2.5 | 2.5 |
| United States | 2.81 | 2.72 | 2.45 |
| Iceland | 2.21 | 2.26 | 2.44 |
| Japan | 2.47 | 2.4 | 2.38 |
| France[3] | 2.22 | 2.33 | 2.34 |
| West Germany | 2.32 | 2.37 | 2.3 |
| Cyprus | 2.3 | 2.1 | 2.3 |
| Netherlands, The | 2.36 | 2.24 | 2.21 |
| Sweden | 2.1 | 2.06 | 2.12 |
| Switzerland | 2.11 | 2.18 | 2.08 |
| Romania | 2.0 | 2.0 | 2.0 |
| Yugoslavia | 2.1 | 1.9 | 2.0 |
| Belgium | 1.91 | 2.12 | 1.98 |
| U.S.S.R. | 3.7 | 3.1 | 1.9 |
| United Kingdom | 1.61 | 1.72 | 1.71 |
| New Zealand | 1.75 | 1.71 | 1.7 |
| Denmark | 1.49 | 1.61 | 1.58 |

[1] One litre = 1.0567 U.S. quart = 0.8799 imperial quart.
[2] Years ending March 31.
[3] Including aperitifs.

| Table VIII. Estimated Consumption of Wine in Selected Countries | | | |
|---|---|---|---|
| In litres[1] per capita | | | |
| Country | 1984 | 1985 | 1986 |
| France | 82.0 | 79.7 | 78.4 |
| Italy | 90.5 | 84.8 | 73.3 |
| Portugal | 84.2 | 87.0 | 70.8 |
| Argentina | 66.3 | 60.1 | 60.0 |
| Luxembourg | 52.5 | 57.3 | 55.4 |
| Switzerland | 49.9 | 49.6 | 48.6 |
| Spain | 48.0 | 48.0 | 45.0 |
| Chile | 39.7 | 40.0 | 40.0 |
| Greece | 43.9 | 37.3 | 37.0 |
| Austria[2] | 36.4 | 34.3 | 35.0 |
| Romania | 28.0 | 28.0 | 28.0 |
| Uruguay | 28.0 | 28.0 | 28.0 |
| Yugoslavia | 26.5 | 17.4 | 25.0 |
| West Germany | 25.7 | 25.6 | 23.3 |
| Hungary | 30.7 | 24.8 | 23.2 |
| Bulgaria | 23.4 | 20.2 | 22.1 |
| Belgium | 22.9 | 22.7 | 21.7 |
| Australia[2] | 21.3 | 21.6 | 20.6 |
| Denmark | 18.86 | 20.71 | 19.82 |
| New Zealand | 14.1 | 14.3 | 16.2 |
| Netherlands, The | 15.22 | 14.96 | 14.9 |
| Czechoslovakia | 15.5 | 16.0 | 12.3 |
| Sweden | 11.61 | 11.7 | 11.96 |
| Cyprus | 11.8 | 11.9 | 11.7 |
| United Kingdom | 9.55 | 9.96 | 10.4 |

[1] One litre = 1.0567 U.S. quart = 0.8799 imperial quart.
[2] Years ending June 30.

Source: Produktschap voor Gedistilleerde Dranken, *Hoeveel alcoholhoudende dranken worden er in de wereld gedronken?*

scale was both a principal cause and an effect of the recent wave of mergers and acquisitions that had swept the industry. Bottlers remaining independent were becoming involved in cooperative ventures in which bottling and canning of the product were done in one central location.

A deep consumer concern for health and fitness was a hallmark of the 1980s, and the soft drink industry responded to that concern with juice-added, low-calorie, caffeine-free, and natural-flavoured soft drinks. The juice-added category was capturing an increasing share of the U.S. market and was expected soon to exceed 10% of total sales.

Bottled water became the fastest growing sector of the beverage market, reflecting the consumer's attraction to more natural and health-enhancing products. A new and booming beverage segment emerged in 1987 in the form of sweetened seltzers, which created industry controversy in light of the traditional definition by the U.S. Food and Drug Administration (FDA) of seltzer as unsweetened sodium-free carbonated water.

The low-calorie soft drink segment captured 25% of the U.S. soft drink market. Two promising new sweeteners, alitame and sucralose, were under review by the FDA for use in soft drinks. In 1987 only two sweeteners were available for this use, saccharin and aspartame.

(FREDERICK L. WEBBER)

## BUILDING AND CONSTRUCTION

Dollar outlays for new construction in the U.S. in 1987 exceeded the record levels attained in 1986, according to U.S. Department of Commerce reports for the first three quarters of the year. It appeared that total dollar outlays for construction in 1987 would be close to the $388.8 billion expended in 1986. In midyear, however, concerns over the health of the economy indicated a possible decline, especially in the fourth quarter.

While total construction outlays had fallen only slightly at mid-1987, there were large declines in multifamily and nonresidential building construction. In view of the widespread overbuilding of apartment and office buildings and the adverse effects of the new tax law on construction projects, it appeared that these segments of the industry would continue to weaken. Residential construction continued at near-record levels in the first half of 1987, but sales of new houses fell sharply in May and June. Analysts predicted that the number of units sold in 1987 would be below 700,000, compared with 750,000 sold in 1986. The U.S. Department of Commerce attributed the decline to increases in mortgage interest rates and in the average prices of new houses.

In June 1987 the average effective fixed interest rate on 25-year conventional home mortgage loans (75% loan-to-price ratio) was 10.85%. The average fixed rate reached a low of 9.47% in March but moved up significantly in the second quarter of the year. Adjustable mortgage rates stood at 8.74% in June. The median sale price of a new house sold in the U.S. reached an all-time high of $110,000 in June. In that month the monthly principal and interest payment for a median-priced house, based on the average commitment interest rate,

was $755, placing the purchase of a new house beyond the financial reach of many middle- and lower-income families.

In Canada the construction and building industries showed mixed developments in 1986. Business investment was down 2.2%, while investment in housing rose 13.1%. Housing demand had been strong in 1985 and continued strong into 1987. The outlook was for business investment to decline somewhat more in 1987 than in 1986.

In Great Britain fixed investment fell in the manufacturing and the petroleum and natural gas industries in 1986 and showed a negligible increase in the distribution, financial, and business service industries. The one area of fixed investment to show a marked rise was private-sector housing. Although real interest rates were high, the housing market had continued strong. Housing investment totaled £7,329,000,-000 (1980 prices) in 1986, compared with expected investment of £8,048,000,000 in 1987. The expectation was that housing demand would continue to be strong in 1987 and that business investment would improve. However, the sharp stock market decline cast a cloud over these predictions.

In West Germany investment rose 3.3% in 1986, but no increase was foreseen in 1987. The housing market was expected to be depressed throughout the year, although public construction would be stimulated by the government's urban renewal program. In Italy it appeared that private investment would increase more in 1987 than the 1.2% recorded in 1986. Housing investment in France was down 3.4% in 1986 and was expected to decline about 0.6% in 1987.

In Japan private investment in housing rose 10.1% in 1986, and a similar increase was predicted for 1987. Business investment rose 6.5% in 1986, considerably less than the 12.3% reported in 1985, and it was predicted that in 1987 the increase would be less than 1%.

(CARTER C. OSTERBIND)

## CERAMICS

U.S. ceramic industry sales for 1986 totaled just over $28 billion, an annual increase of about 2%, and 1987 sales suggested a similar rise. The glass industry's share fell slightly, to about 61.6%. Advanced ceramics sales increased substantially, accounting for slightly over 15% of the total. Porcelain enamels retained a 13.5% share of the market, and whiteware's segment increased to almost 10%.

Most glass continued to be sold in the form of containers (25%), flat glass (23%), fibreglass (22%), and lighting products (17%). Competition from alternative container materials eased as consumers returned somewhat to glass, particularly for beverages such as wine coolers. Flat glass shipments remained at levels near industry capacity, with about one-third going to construction and about 60% to automotive use. (See *Glass,* below.)

Porcelain enamel sales rose slightly, to about $3.8 billion in 1986. Because more than 90% of the sales were for appliances and about 7.6% were for sanitary ware, they were closely tied to new home starts and consumer interest in remodeling. Although appliance sales had been up for several years, industry projections called for a slowdown in late 1987 and 1988.

Overall, whiteware sales rose about 13% to about $2.7 billion in 1986. Ceramic tile sales were up substantially. Ceramic plumbing fixture sales, almost 46% of all U.S. whitewares sold, rose more than 10% despite extreme pressure from imports, primarily from Canada, Mexico, and Taiwan. Dinnerware, fine china, and artware sales were virtually unchanged.

U.S. advanced ceramic sales increased more than 10% to about $4.3 billion in 1986 and showed continued strong growth in 1987. The electrical, electronic, and optical ceramic segment share declined slightly to about 52%, but the outlook for the future remained bright. Electrical porcelain sales, at 25%, were fairly level, with most continuing to be for automotive spark plugs. The engineering ceramic sector, including ceramics for structural applications, cutting tools, wear and die parts, and bioceramics, expanded substantially to a more than 23% share of all advanced ceramics.

Although about 70% of all integrated circuits were packaged in plastics, ceramic chip carriers remained the materials of choice for high-temperature, high-performance applications, and they accounted for the majority of all electronic ceramic sales. Most of the other electronic ceramics sold were for capacitors. Ceramics were used as the dielectric element of more than 80% of all capacitors.

The electrical and optical ceramic segments of advanced ceramics consisted primarily of sensors, magnetic ceramics, piezoelectric ceramics, and optical fibres. The major growth in this sector occurred in the areas of ceramic sensors for a wide variety of industrial, residential, and automotive applications; piezoelectric ceramics for use as electroacoustic signal devices, precision actuators, and small motors; and optical fibres for telecommunications. Worldwide piezoelectric ceramic and optical fibre sales were forecast to grow at about 10 and 20%, respectively, with U.S. sales accounting for about 50% of the total.

While it was too soon to anticipate sales of the high-temperature ceramic superconductors that burst upon the scene in 1987,

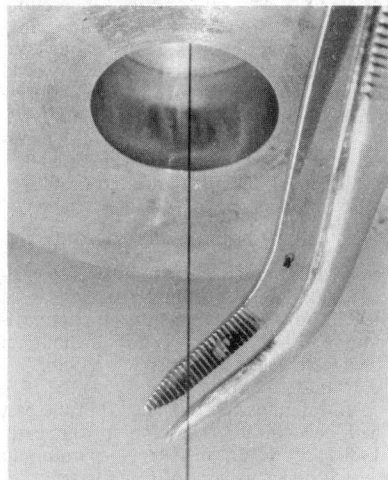

ARGONNE NATIONAL LABORATORY

A ceramic superconductor wire, formed and being chilled at the Argonne National Laboratory, is a first step toward production of such a wire for commercial use.

their ability to operate above liquid nitrogen temperatures provided tremendous economic opportunities. Their potential for use in high-speed computers, magnetic-field sensors, high-power magnets, and a host of other devices led major corporations around the world to invest heavily in their development and early commercialization. (*See* PHYSICS: *Sidebar.*)

U.S. and worldwide sales of advanced ceramics for structural applications were well ahead of the 1985 figures but grew far less than expected. The automotive market was particularly disappointing. A few companies—for example, Nissan and Porsche—continued cautious efforts to introduce ceramic components into their engines. U.S. companies, however, appeared still to be waiting for increased reliability, lower cost, and greater marketing incentives. Fortunately, disappointing ceramic sales in the automotive sector were at least partly compensated by strong sales in the cutting tool and wear and die markets, where advanced ceramics continued to post significant gains.

(NORMAN M. TALLAN)

## CHEMICALS

For 1986 and most of the first three quarters of 1987, the chemical industries in the industrialized countries of the world exhibited generally good health. However, the plunge in major stock markets followed by the gyrations in those markets during the last weeks of October 1987 cast considerable doubt on the short- and medium-term prospects for the industry.

In 1986, according to the European Council of Chemical Manufacturers' Federations (CEFIC), chemical sales for major producing countries—those in Western Europe, the U.S., Japan, Australia, and Canada—were $579,898,000,000, 16.2% higher than they were in 1985. The CEFIC sales figures in dollars were somewhat misleading, however, because of wide fluctuations in the values of the various currencies.

By the middle of October 1987, the chemical industry in the U.S. had nearly completed three quarters of what appeared to be a satisfying year in terms of volume and profits, and many managers in the industry were optimistic that 1988 would prove to be as good or better. Uncertainty about the stock market led to uncertainty about the economy as a whole, however, and because the chemical industry had become so large, its fortunes were closely linked to those of the general economy.

The size and health of the U.S. chemical industry were evident in the figures it posted in shipments, trade, and profits. In 1985 shipments of chemicals, as reported by the U.S. Department of Commerce, amounted to $197,314,000,000. They increased only marginally in 1986 to $198,-348,000,000. In the first six months of 1987, however, shipments of chemicals rose to $107,134,000,000, 5.5% higher than they were in the same period of 1986.

In trade the hefty surplus that the U.S. chemical industry had achieved in the past had been steadily eroding in the early 1980s. However, in 1986, according to the U.S. Department of Commerce, it rebounded significantly, thanks in part to the weakening of the U.S. dollar against the currencies of the nation's major trading partners.

Profits of U.S. chemical companies increased substantially. In 1985 after-tax profits, as compiled by the Census Bureau, were $9,542,000,000. In 1986 they rose to $12.9 million, an increase of 35.2%. During the first quarter of 1987, they reached a record high of $4,251,000,000.

The high earnings reflected a number of factors. Demand for chemical products in a variety of end uses was strong. More important, however, was the sharp reduction in prices that the chemical industry was paying for energy.

The weaker dollar was providing solace to U.S. chemical managers by strengthening the industry's export posture, but in Japan executives in the chemical and other industries were concerned about the other side of the coin, the strong yen. For instance, CEFIC showed that the Japanese chemical industry registered a 34.7% sales increase in 1986 in dollar terms to $115,-660,000,000, but that represented a 4.8% drop in yen. Production volume increased in 1986 by 0.4% from 1985.

The strong yen notwithstanding, there was no shortage of positive signs for Japan's chemical industry. Despite the country's stunning achievement in building the second largest chemical industry in the non-Communist world with almost no indigenous material resources, and despite its tradition of exporting, Japan had run a deficit in chemical trade until 1984, when it managed to balance chemical imports and exports. By 1986, according to figures of the Japan Chemical Exporters' Association and the Japan Chemical Importers' Association, the country had a favourable chemical trade balance of $3.4 billion.

Like their counterparts in other countries, Japan's chemical leaders had undertaken substantial restructuring. As a result, capacity reductions in 11 industries had been completed by the end of 1986, and capacity-utilization rates had improved. For instance, between 1981 and 1985 Japan's ethylene capacity was cut by 42%. The Ministry of International Trade and Industry reported that the operating rate for ethylene, which had been a satisfactory 90.7% in the first quarter of 1986, was a remarkable 98.1% for the first quarter of 1987.

In West Germany, too, the weakened U.S. dollar was causing a set of problems, not the least of which was trying to quantify its effect. For instance, the weaker dollar meant that German companies had to spend fewer marks to buy raw materials that were priced in dollars. However, it also meant that the earnings of the German chemical subsidiaries in the U.S., which were substantial, would be lowered when they were converted into marks. Fluctuations in the value of the mark relative to the dollar made it difficult to compare the performance of German companies with their counterparts in the U.S. and elsewhere. This was particularly difficult with German companies that had always depended heavily on exports.

Overall, CEFIC reported, the West German chemical industry recorded sales of $64,470,000,000 in 1986, 27.6% above the level of 1985. As in Japan, however, sales in the national currency, the Deutsche Mark, dropped from DM 148,751,000,000 in 1985 to DM 139,997,000,000 in 1986. The principal reason for the lower sales

value in West Germany, as in Japan, was lower petrochemical prices brought about by the drop in prices for crude oil. Prices for organic chemicals fell by 23% after the oil price tumbled.

The West German industry maintained a strong export position in chemicals, as reported by the Verband der Chemischen Industrie (VCI), the chemical industry association. VCI's tabulation of trade revealed 1986 chemical exports of $40.5 billion and chemical imports of $23 billion for a favourable balance of trade of $17.5 billion.

The outlook for chemicals in West Germany during 1987 was one of cautious optimism. VCI reported that chemical sales during the first nine months amounted to $58 billion, 2% lower than they were in the same period in 1986. The expectation was that the full year would be similar to 1986, which was not a bad year by most measures.

In the U.K. 1986 turned out to be better than had been expected. Demand for chemicals was flat in the first half of the year but picked up in the second half. By the year's end, supply and demand were approximately in balance, and plants were operating at a satisfying rate. CEFIC's figures showed a 17.2% increase in dollar sales, from $26,090,000,000 in 1985 to $30,572,000,000 in 1986. Production increased by 1.1%. (DONALD P. BURKE)

## ELECTRICAL

World output of electricity was expected to have risen in 1987. In 1986 it declined by 0.7% to 9,605,000,000,000 kw-hr following the all-time record in 1985. Most of the major producer countries recorded increases (the U.S., the U.S.S.R., China, West Germany, and the U.K.), as did such newly industrializing nations as Brazil and South Korea. Japan's output in 1986 fell, however, reflecting the decline in manufacturing—the first in a decade—but recovery was expected in 1987.

At the end of 1987, major moves in the restructuring of the electrical manufacturing industry were awaited. As the year ended, the world's large electrical manufacturing firms were still assessing the implications of the merger of the Swedish ASEA Group and the Swiss Brown Boveri Company (BBC) Group. The surprise announcement of the merger came in August, and in October the respective governments gave their approval.

The new ASEA-BBC (ABB) Group had sales totaling more than $16 billion, 50% greater than Siemens, Hitachi, or General Electric Co. (GE), each of which had sales of about $10 billion of equivalent electrical power and industrial equipment. ASEA had grown quickly in the 1980s; at the beginning of the decade, it had 2,500 employees, and by the end of 1986, 15,000 were employed worldwide. About 7,000 of this increase resulted from ASEA's acquisition of the Finnish electrical equipment manufacturer Stromberg in 1986. About a year before the merger with BBC, it had been rumoured that ASEA wanted to buy the heavy power interests of either Westinghouse or GE.

ASEA and BBC claimed that they complemented each other in product lines and technology. BBC was best known for turbine generators, while ASEA was strong in nuclear power and high-voltage direct-current transmission. They were to benefit from economies of scale and the pooling of $1 billion to spend on research and development (R and D). ABB's headquarters were to be in Zürich, Switz., and the new group was to start trading on Jan. 1, 1988, becoming fully operational a year later.

In 1986 GE's main acquisition was RCA Corp. (solid-state electronics) for $6.4 billion. RCA's business, however, had no significant effect on GE's industrial equipment and power systems sectors ($9,973,-000,000 combined sales in 1986 against $10,586,000,000 in 1985). The decline in the 1986 sales occurred in the industrial sector despite the success following the formation in 1986 of a 50-50 joint venture with Fanuc Ltd. of Japan in factory automation products and systems. However, with greatly increased sales in its aerospace and engines sectors, GE ended 1986 with total sales of $36.7 billion, an increase of 26% over 1985; earnings, at $2,492,000,-000, were up 9%. In 1986 GE spent a total of $1.3 billion from its resources on research and development ($1,069,000,000 in 1985). Less than 50% of the R and D total was believed to be related to the electrical sector.

Westinghouse Electric Corp. devoted $246 million in 1986 to R and D, the same amount as in 1985. Sales, at $10,731,000,-000, were up only 0.3% over 1985, but net income increased by 11% to $670.8 million. The U.K.'s General Electric Co. (GEC) had sales of £5,247,000,000 for the year ended March 31, 1987, down £6 million from the previous year. Net income declined £8 million to £420 million.

The proposed privatization of the U.K. public electricity supply industry was being viewed with concern by British plant manufacturers. Just as it seemed that a decade of low ordering of large electricity generating stations was about to come to an end, worries were mounting that the industry, if privatized, would delay investment or bring in foreign competition. A repetition of the problems that affected the British telecommunications industry when the state-owned British Telecom (BT) was privatized seemed likely. Before privatization BT always bought from British suppliers, but subsequently some contracts went to Ericsson of Sweden, and the prices of the new electronic exchanges were halved in the process.

Technically the main development in 1986 was the discovery that the superconducting phenomenon (the property of some materials to allow electricity to flow through them without any losses because of resistance) was not confined to extremely low temperatures, only a few degrees above absolute zero ($-273.15°$ C [$-459.67°$ F]). (See PHYSICS: *Sidebar*.) By the end of 1986, most of the world's leading materials laboratories had produced superconducting wires working at $-173°$ C ($-279.4°$ F). As a result of the discovery, it was believed that motors and generators with efficiencies of almost 100% and power cables with negligible losses could be a reality within five years. In its annual report for 1986–87, GEC noted: "These new materials could have far-reaching importance in a wide range of GEC activities including microelectronics and power engineering."

(T. C. J. COGLE)

## FURNITURE

The final quarter of 1987 was a time of reassessment for the furniture industry as it attempted to evaluate the possible effects of the October stock market crash. On the whole, however, industry executives tended to be optimistic, according to a survey conducted by industry observers. Most optimistic was the American Furniture Manufacturers Association, which, in November, projected a 6.9% increase in retail sales for the entire year. This meant an expected total of $27.8 billion in receipts. The association described the year as strong and cited employment stability as the major reason for consumer confidence. The Consumer Confidence Index had advanced to 114.8, its highest level in 15 years, and dropped only a few points after the crash.

General retail sales in the U.S. at midyear were 9.3% above a year earlier, but there was a dip in sales in July, according to the Census Bureau. Sales of consumer electronics, a major competitor with furniture for the consumer dollar, were up by 7%, and some analysts believed this was cutting into the furniture industry's profits. Furniture manufacturers were seeing a drop in orders in the latter part of the year, even before the crash. In general, the results of the mergers, buyouts, and consolidations that took place in 1986 were still being evaluated.

One of the most positive changes that took place during 1987 was an increased emphasis on customer service, with particular attention being given to quicker delivery. A Management Horizons survey of over 300 retailing and consumer-goods marketing executives in the U.S. cited service as the most important strategy for the 1990s. The survey noted that service, across the board, was at a historic low, but companies that provided good service had enviable financial records.

Reasons given for the decline in service in past years were rapid store expansion in the 1960s and '70s and an overemphasis on merchandising and quick profits. The introduction into the marketplace of new forms of self-service outlets offering much lower retail prices was also a factor. Some experts believed that the gap between stores of the warehouse (low-price/no- or low-service) variety and the designer-oriented (high-price/full-service) outlets would continue to widen.

With renewed emphasis being placed on service, computers emerged as a business's best friend and the single most important differentiating factor among companies. According to major computer systems experts, the furniture industry in 1987 was eight to ten years behind the technology, and it was predicted that those manufacturers and retailers that did not invest in major computer systems soon would be unable to compete in the marketplace.

At the two major style markets held in April and October in High Point, N.C., the emphasis was, once again, on traditional and transitional designs rather than contemporary. Of note was the growing interest in Victorian designs and Victorian-influenced designs, particularly wicker. Eighteenth-century traditional designs and their variations continued to hold their own, and the new version of Early American, known as Country, kept its share of the market. There was also a renewed interest in Art Moderne and Art Deco styles.

One significant style trend was the increased use of leather as an upholstery fabric. Although this material was once considered a luxury, it was now being prized for its virtues: feel, durability, and long-term beauty. Demand was so great that one leading U.S. tanner had to double production to keep up with orders.

(ABBY CHAPPLE)

## FURS

The year 1987 proved difficult for the fur industry in many Western countries. Sharp increases in the price of mink, which accounted for most of the retail fur business, led to hesitation among customers whose means were not unlimited. Many also were confused by the shorter coat lengths advocated by leading fashion designers and were waiting for the style picture to crystallize.

Nevertheless, retail sales were running ahead of the previous year and, in the U.S., were expected to reach or exceed the $2

JACK MANNING/THE NEW YORK TIMES

The new chair-and-a-half with its ottoman combines the traditional camel-back style with a modern "rumpled" look. This trend in furniture for 1987 placed an emphasis on transitional designs, producing a style midway beween traditional and contemporary.

billion mark for the first time. The rapidly growing Japanese market was looking for at least a 10% increase. Sales were showing a slight improvement in West Germany, Italy, Switzerland, Spain, and Scandinavia.

For the U.S. trade, the effects of higher skin prices were compounded by the further weakening of the dollar in relation to the other major currencies. Since the dollar was the principal medium for international trade in furs, Americans were at a clear disadvantage at virtually all of the skin auctions. In addition, considerably larger capital outlays were required for the same number of pelts as in the previous year.

A sharp increase in imports of fur apparel into the U.S. in 1987 also put a severe strain on finances. At year's end it appeared that imports had soared about 25% to approximately $500 million. Since most of the Far Eastern suppliers required payment before shipment, this contributed significantly to the industry's cash drain. Profits dropped sharply, and there were some insolvencies.

Nevertheless, furs continued to increase in popularity, especially among younger customers. This was especially evident in the rising sales of such "affordable" furs as beaver, raccoon, lamb, coyote, rabbit, and shearling, often sold outside the conventional fur salons and departments. This reflected not only wider use of furs by designers but also a greater ability of women to buy their own. Stepped-up activities by animal rights and other antifur activists seemed to have little effect on this trend.

World production of ranched mink increased 3% in 1987 to a total of 34,165,000 pelts. The four Scandinavian countries accounted for 16,515,000, while the U.S. contributed 4.4 million. The U.S.S.R., which marketed only a fraction of its production, came up with 4.5 million; China contributed 2.2 million; and Canada, 1.5 million. The world crop of ranch-raised foxes declined slightly to 5,149,500, with Scandinavia accounting for more than 80%.

According to a report prepared for the Convention on International Trade in Endangered Species, a five-month study of African leopard populations indicated that the current population of between 700,-000 and 850,000 could easily sustain an annual harvest of 30,000. No move was made, however, to take leopard off the endangered list.          (SANDY PARKER)

## GAMES AND TOYS

World toy markets witnessed a high degree of technological advancement in 1987. The success during the previous year of talking toys was followed up with a wide variety of new toys that interacted with television sets. For example, Captain Power and the Soldiers of the Future by Mattel Inc. came complete with its own syndicated TV series, which gave off high-frequency signals to activate the toys. Action for Children's Television argued that these toys created a mandate for all toys and TV programming to become inextricably commercially linked. (See *Advertising,* above.)

Despite increased investment worldwide in the marketing of figures and plush toys, fewer of these achieved blockbuster status than in previous years. Multinational firms concentrated their efforts on diversifying existing product lines in order to reduce dependence on one or two, which gave the

consumer a far greater breadth of choice. An exception was Pictionary, produced by Western Publishing Co., a drawing and guessing game that was the most successful game since Trivial Pursuit; its sales of $60 million in the U.S. in 1986 accounted for 27% of the board-game market. Worlds of Wonder Inc., maker of Teddy Ruxpin the talking bear and Laser Tag, failed to produce a third hit and filed for bankruptcy.

Talking dolls, operated by cassette players, batteries, or microchips, continued to be popular. Baby Heather from Mattel giggled, sneezed, and had a 400-word vocabulary that could be switched from that of a six-month-old to that of a one- or two-year-old. Coleco's Cabbage Patch Talking Kids could "converse" when they were within 6 m (20 ft) of one another. New lines of action figures included SilverHawks and the highly successful Ghostbusters, both by Kenner Parker, and Hasbro's Visionaries and Tonka's SuperNaturals, each equipped with holographic faces or shields. Mr. GameShow from Lewis Galoob Toys featured a battery-operated game-show host with a 600-word vocabulary.

Apart from the U.S., toy sales on a worldwide basis were expected to fall. The child population in both West Germany and the U.K. was likely to have declined 25% by 1990. Children were also becoming increasingly sophisticated and were spending more on such other goods as phonograph records and fashion items.

In 1986 the total value of sales in the U.S., the U.K., Italy, France, and West Germany was $17.4 billion. The U.S. accounted for over 70% of the market, followed by France with 11%. World markets grew in the first half of 1987, according to the annual meeting of the International Committee of Toy Industries (ICTI) held in Taipei, Taiwan, in June. U.S. shipments during the first three months rose 5.5% compared with the same period in 1986. U.K. exports had risen to £146.8 million in 1986, up 21.1%, led by sales of plastic toys and games. Imports increased to £325.4 million, nearly equal to sales of home-produced toys, at £326 million, with demand for textile and fabric toys up 52%.

Hong Kong, Taiwan, and South Korea remained the largest exporters of toys to Europe and the U.S.

U.S.-owned Tonka became a major force following its acquisition of the Italian company Polistil and the U.S. multinational Kenner Parker. The group's sales of approximately $800 million made it the largest U.S. toy company after Hasbro and Mattel. The U.K. toy-retail sector was active. Hamleys was acquired by Harris Queensway, which planned to open its first U.S. store in New York, and the first Boots children's superstore, Children's World, was launched.

Safety matters were the focus of attention worldwide and were high on the agenda of the annual ICTI meeting. In the U.S., potential problems for the toy industry were the filing of a petition with the Consumer Product Safety Commission that would require an amendment to the small parts regulations and the introduction in the New York state legislature of a hazardous toy labeling bill. There was a movement to ban realistic toy guns after some were used to commit crimes.

Counterfeiting continued to cause the industry problems, and in an effort to stop the practice, Lego issued a warning to imitators. The British International Toy and Hobby Fair followed the U.S. lead and refused space to any company that had been prosecuted for manufacturing counterfeit products.          (KATE STEVENS)

## GEMSTONES

During 1986–87 signs of returning confidence could be observed in the gem trade of a number of Western countries. More diamonds were being sold, and the stockpiles accumulated at De Beers and at manufacturers were showing signs of running down. Gem shows were also useful indicators of reviving interest in unusual stones, though the use of fine and rare stones for investment had not recovered from downturns in the U.S. economy and unfavourable interest taken by tax authorities.

The jewels of the duchess of Windsor, sold at Geneva in April 1987, realized far more than the previously estimated prices.

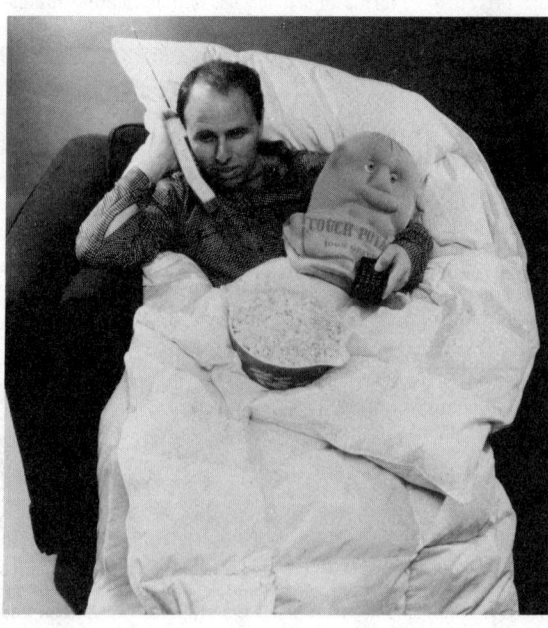

PETER FREED

Two couch potatoes prepare for a quiet evening with popcorn, telephone, and television. The Couch Potato Pal, a spud-shaped doll by Coleco, is named after people who spend their leisure time watching television.

An emerald and diamond necklace with matching pendant brought over £1,350,000 at an auction featuring the duchess of Windsor's jewels. The duchess's jewels may have generated renewed interest in all jewelry.

CAMERA PRESS, LONDON

It appeared that this was not entirely due to the historical interest of the pieces, since prices went well over most estimates at other sales as well. The exceptional media treatment of the Windsor jewels clearly helped to attract public attention to the world of jewelry in general. In the U.K. an exhibition of Lalique jewelry showed how this small and select form of applied art stimulated trade.

A number of important gem-producing countries experienced less than ideal political and economic conditions during the year. The serious internal strife occurring in Sri Lanka had not yet affected exports of gems, but it seemed likely to be only a matter of time before some impact was felt. The gem scene in Thailand was marked chiefly by the continued heat treatment of corundum, and it was no longer easy to tell, without laboratory testing, whether the colour of a particular ruby or sapphire had been artificially improved. This caused problems with trade descriptions, and no final agreement had been reached on how such goods should be described. Major rubies and even some sapphires were beginning to have their place of origin described in salesroom catalogs, and proof of unaltered colour was also likely to be required.

Probably the most important development on the gemstone scene was the introduction of synthetic yellow gem-quality diamonds. The Japanese firm of Sumitomo had produced yellow diamond crystals for industrial use, and some had been cut into faceted stones experimentally. When the faceted stones were tested by several laboratories, they were found to have enough distinguishing features for the stones to be identified. As of late 1987 no other firm was reported to be working on these types of diamond.    (MICHAEL O'DONOGHUE)

## GLASS

The recovery in the glass industry noted in 1986 continued in 1987, with growth taking place in most sectors. The year was characterized by further concentration of the industry in the developed Western economies.

Sales of flat glass set a world record in 1986, and demand remained strong in 1987. European demand was approximately 4 million metric tons, while the U.S. market experienced its fifth successive year of growth, reaching about 390 million sq m (4.2 billion sq ft). Demand was particularly strong for coated glasses for architectural use and double glazing. Low emissivity (low-E) glass was becoming particularly popular in North America for double glazing to reduce heat loss. The market for automotive safety glass also grew in 1987.

The market for glass containers continued to recover from the impact of new competitive packaging products in the early 1980s. Substantial restructuring and modernization left the glass container industry in the major Western nations much more competitive and profitable than it had been in recent years. The year 1987 was marked by two major structural changes in the U.S. industry—the takeover of Brockway, Inc., the second largest supplier in the country, by Owens-Illinois, Inc., the largest, to form a company with 40% of the market; and the merger between Anchor Glass Container Corp. and Diamond-Bathurst Inc. to make another giant supplier. With only modest growth forecast for the U.S. glass container market, the stage was clearly set for a major battle for market share.

In regard to fibreglass, a reasonably strong demand in the home insulation sector and very strong demand for reinforcement fibres took place in the U.S. In Europe there was a gradual drop in capacity, but governments were withdrawing grants for energy conservation measures such as home insulation, and this led to reduced demand.

The U.S. glassware industry was significantly affected by the fall in the value of the dollar and reduced U.S. tourism. The U.S. and Europe were the main markets for the industry, but sales fell there because of strong competition from Far Eastern imports. China continued to develop its domestic glassware industry with new Western technology, and it could become a major competitor in the coming years.

Special high-performance glasses for optical, surgical, information technology, and solar energy uses were a small but rapidly developing sector of the industry. For example, Japanese chemical companies were developing glass susstrate technology in the production of computer disks, which would enable them to offer ten times the storage capacity by virtue of the smoother surface.

Finally, in a more prosaic example of new uses for glass, New York City was planning to pave three blocks in Brooklyn in 1988 with a new asphalt material called glasphalt. It contained 40% glass, made from recycled crushed glass bottles. A street in Liège, Belgium, had been similarly paved ten years earlier and did not yet show signs of wear.

(ALLEN F. BROBYN)

## INSURANCE

Global sales by 13,500 insurers in the private markets expanded to approximately $700 billion in 1987. Although almost one-half of worldwide premiums were written in the U.S. and one-fourth in Europe, Japan retained its position as the growth leader, having quadrupled its share of world premiums to nearly 20% during the last two decades. One setback for private insurance was the nationalization of insurance companies in Peru during October.

Insured catastrophe losses rose in 1987, following the record low of $870 million in 1986. Heading the list were the San Juan, P.R., hotel disaster on New Year's Eve ($400 million in damages sought); the second-worst U.S. airline crash, in Detroit, with 156 dead and a lone four-year-old survivor; a California earthquake ($100 million damage, about one-third insured); a hurricane in Bermuda (estimated $50 million damages); and a freak storm in southern England (nearly $1 billion damages).

In the U.K. a significant development was the implementation of the new Financial Services Act, regulating conduct of the investment business, including life insurance, under the Securities and Investment Board. Life insurance companies would be subject to the Life Assurance and Unit Trust Regulatory Organisation, and insurance agents and brokers to the Financial Intermediaries, Managers and Brokers Regulatory Organisation. Intermediaries had to choose between selling the products of one company or giving "best advice" on the whole market. Although Lloyd's was excluded from this regulation, the Council of Lloyd's agreed to 79 recommendations.

Under Lloyd's three-year accounting system, the latest published results showed premiums of £2,959,000,000 for 1984, with record profits of £300 million despite losses of £170 million on general liability and £25 million on U.K. motor insurance business. Accounts for other U.K. insurance companies showed that general insurance premiums rose in 1986 by 19%, with investment income exceeding underwriting losses by approximately £1 billion, the best result since the early 1980s. During 1987 automobile insurance rates increased sharply. Long-term life insurance premiums rose by almost 25% to about £21 billion, with the most marked increase for single-premium contracts, up 47% to more than £7 billion. The cost of professional liability insurance rose sharply. Appeals were made to the government to limit liabilities and to consider no-fault compensation for medical malpractice, such as had been adopted some years earlier in Sweden.

By midyear U.S. life insurance premiums were up about 15% compared with those of a year earlier, largely owing to substantial market gains for universal and variable life insurance and a 250% surge in the sale of tax-sheltered single-premium life insurance contracts. Although a new Federal Reserve Board decision would allow banks to sell insurance directly, a judicial review was in progress to determine if bank holding companies would be permitted to purchase state-chartered banks that had insurance subsidiaries.

Many employers were feeling the pinch of a 20% or more increase in their group health insurance premiums. Various cost-containment techniques and strong competition with health maintenance organizations (HMOs) and other new health care providers had failed to offset rising costs. One-third of small (under 500 employees) and 85% of the very large (over 40,000)

"Irises," by Vincent Van Gogh, sold for a record $53.9 million, the highest price ever paid for an artwork at auction. The soaring amounts paid for such works made them increasingly more difficult to insure for exhibitions and were literally forcing such works of art "out of sight."

SOTHEBY'S/AUTHENTICATED NEWS INTERNATIONAL

employers had chosen self-funding for part or all of their health benefits.

The spread of AIDS (acquired immune deficiency syndrome) was expected to have serious effects on both life and health insurers. Although individual life claims were still under 1% of all claims, by 1991 they could exceed 8%. Health care costs of $30,-000 annually per victim could cause group rates to soar. Another increased health cost burden was the mandated coverage of up to three years for discontinued employees and dependents under the Consolidated Omnibus Budget Reconciliation Act.

The U.S. property-liability business rebounded in the first half of 1987 to achieve $7.5 billion net income from underwriting and investments, up almost 30% from a year earlier. Premium growth slowed from a 26 to a 12% increase, which was good news for policyholders. The liability insurance crisis eased, but self-insurance in commercial lines continued to expand from an estimated 25 to 30% of the market. A number of states passed legislation aimed at easing the liability insurance situation. State guaranty funds reported 60 insurer insolvencies totaling $946 million in the last 3 years, compared with $454 million paid out for 86 insolvencies in the previous 14 years. Automobile insurance rates were rising in many territories, partly because some states had returned to 65-mph speed limits. Insurance exchanges for hazardous risks had increasing problems in New York, and the Florida exchange was closed in February with 23 lawsuits pending.

The U.S. stock market crash of October and subsequent market volatility could have pronounced effects on insurance company operations in 1988. With 25% or more of assets in stocks, property-liability insurers would have less capacity to accept risks. Although their investment portfolios included only about 10% stocks, life insurance companies also would have to make major adjustments.

(DAVID L. BICKELHAUPT)

## IRON AND STEEL

In 1987 there was a recovery in world production of crude steel, which had declined by 0.7% in 1986 after three years of slow but steady growth. Lower output in the European Coal and Steel Community (ECSC), the U.S., and Japan was largely offset by increases in China, South Korea, Turkey, South America, and some Eastern European countries. The slowing of production in the industrialized countries was more marked at the end of 1986 and continued into early 1987, but the subsequent recovery led to predictions that world output in 1987 would rise 2% over that of 1986. Prices had fallen throughout 1986, but as 1987 progressed demand improved more rapidly than expected and even led to a temporary tightness of supply for some important products. Prices recovered, and financial results toward the end of 1987 were much improved.

Despite this optimistic short-term situation, steel producers continued to operate with the knowledge that a number of forecasts, including one by the Organization for Economic Cooperation and Development (OECD), predicted that in 1990 steelmaking capacity of about 910 million metric tons would exceed demand by 180 million–200 million metric tons. Thus the need to restructure and further reduce capacity continued to preoccupy many producers and governments, especially in industrialized countries, during 1987.

Within the ECSC the difficulties faced by steel producers in 1986 continued into 1987, with only the U.K. showing resilience. The devaluation of the U.S. dollar resulted in an unsustainable difference between prices on the ECSC internal market and those in export markets. The European Commission had imposed increasingly restrictive production quotas on producers in an attempt to sustain prices during this period. As 1987 progressed, internal and export demand recovered somewhat so that by the end of 1987 total production levels were close to those of the previous year. Because of the weakening of sterling, the U.K. was comparatively unaffected by the devaluation of the dollar. The completed renovation of British Steel Corporation's (BSC's) largest blast furnace, together with continued strong growth of the U.K. economy, allowed BSC to increase production of crude steel by 20% in the first eight months of 1987 compared with the previous year.

Production and delivery quotas imposed by the European Commission were due to expire at the end of 1987. Although 30 million metric tons of steelmaking capacity had already been eliminated since 1980, further reductions were necessary. At the end of 1987 ECSC governments were considering the possible extension of production quotas for certain steel products for an additional three years, but this was being made conditional upon satisfactory commitments that further necessary plant closures would take place. Employment in the ECSC steel industry (excluding the three newest member countries) had declined by 200,000 to 400,000 by the end of 1986, and additional job losses of over 100,000 were expected. The ECSC was introducing measures to alleviate the regional effects of the lost employment.

In the U.S. 1986 production of crude steel fell by 8%. This was largely accounted for by a strike at USX (formerly U.S. Steel Corp.), the largest U.S. producer, which began in August 1986 and continued until February 1987. The U.S. did not suffer any serious shortage of steel products during the strike, and there were fears that prices would fall as USX fought to regain its share of the market after the strike. This did not happen. USX staged a gradual return to the market, at the same time announcing a major restructuring plan that meant that some production units would not reopen. This had the effect of cutting production capacity by some 25%, equal to about seven million metric tons of steelmaking. With firmer prices and market demand through the remainder of 1987, all the major U.S. steel producers finished the year in stronger positions than in the previous year.

The strengthening of the Japanese currency had a particularly serious effect on Japanese steel producers during 1986, especially because of their dependence on exports of steel and goods made of steel. Weaker demand and lower prices resulted in large losses for five of the six major producers during their 1986–87 financial year, and plans for restructuring were vigorously pursued. Nippon Steel, the world's largest steel company, disclosed plans to cease production at five blast furnaces and to reduce the number of jobs in its steelworks by 30%.

In the newly industrialized countries, production continued to increase. In South Korea crude steel production rose by 8% in 1986 and by a similar amount in 1987. The inauguration of the first stage of a new steel plant at Kwangyang during 1989 seemed certain to confirm South Korea's position among the top ten steel-producing countries. In Brazil the rate of growth in crude steel production slowed following dramatic increases in previous years—from 13 million metric tons in 1982 to 21 million metric tons in 1986. Turkey

**Table IX. World Production of Crude Steel**
In 000 metric tons

| Country | 1982 | 1983 | 1984 | 1985 | 1986 | 1987 Year to date | No. of months | Percent change 1987/86 |
|---|---|---|---|---|---|---|---|---|
| World | 644,870 | 663,200 | 710,320 | 719,460 | 714,500 | | | |
| U.S.S.R. | 147,150 | 152,510 | 154,200 | 154,650 | 161,000* | 40,120 | 3 | +4.8 |
| Japan | 99,550 | 97,170 | 105,580 | 105,280 | 98,275 | 63,760 | 8 | −3.4 |
| U.S. | 67,640 | 76,760 | 84,500 | 80,070 | 73,750 | 51,400 | 8 | −0.5 |
| China | 37,120 | 40,020 | 43,360 | 46,720 | 51,900 | † | † | † |
| West Germany | 35,880 | 35,730 | 39,390 | 40,500 | 37,140 | 24,350 | 8 | −4.5 |
| Italy | 24,010 | 21,810 | 24,060 | 23,870 | 22,870 | 15,050 | 8 | −1.4 |
| France | 18,400 | 17,580 | 19,000 | 18,820 | 17,900 | 11,610 | 8 | −1.4 |
| Czechoslovakia | 14,990 | 15,020 | 14,830 | 15,040 | 15,110 | 3,840 | 3 | −1.0 |
| Poland | 14,790 | 16,240 | 16,530 | 16,130 | 17,200 | 3,980 | 3 | −7.9 |
| U.K. | 13,700 | 14,990 | 15,120 | 15,720 | 14,810 | 11,160 | 8 | +20.2 |
| Spain | 13,180 | 13,010 | 13,500 | 14,230 | 11,980 | 7,500 | 8 | −5.1 |
| Romania | 13,060 | 12,590 | 14,440 | 13,800 | 14,300 | † | † | † |
| Brazil | 13,000 | 14,670 | 18,390 | 20,450 | 21,230 | 14,190 | 8 | +3.2 |
| Canada | 11,870 | 12,830 | 14,700 | 14,640 | 14,080 | 9,820 | 8 | +4.5 |
| South Korea | 11,760 | 11,920 | 13,030 | 13,540 | 14,560 | 10,680 | 8 | +11.0 |
| India | 11,000 | 10,240 | 10,550 | 11,540 | 11,870 | 8,220 | 8 | +3.1 |
| Belgium | 9,990 | 10,150 | 11,300 | 10,680 | 9,720 | 6,350 | 8 | −2.9 |
| South Africa | 8,280 | 7,180 | 7,730 | 8,510 | 9,060 | 5,970 | 8 | −1.4 |
| East Germany | 7,170 | 7,220 | 7,573 | 7,850 | 7,970 | 2,020* | 3 | +1.0 |
| Mexico | 7,060 | 6,920 | 7,480 | 7,260 | 7,170 | 4,750 | 8 | −5.5 |
| Australia | 6,370 | 5,680 | 6,300 | 6,610 | 6,670 | 3,940 | 8 | −8.1 |
| North Korea | 5,800 | 6,100 | 6,500 | 8,400* | 9,000* | † | † | † |
| Netherlands, The | 4,350 | 4,480 | 5,740 | 5,520 | 5,280 | 3,360 | 8 | −5.3 |
| Austria | 4,260 | 4,410 | 4,870 | 4,660 | 4,290 | 2,806 | 8 | −5.1 |
| Taiwan | 4,150 | 5,030 | 5,010 | 5,090 | 5,550 | 3,700 | 8 | +0.1 |
| Sweden | 3,900 | 4,210 | 4,705 | 4,810 | 4,710 | 2,800 | 8 | −5.9 |
| Yugoslavia | 3,840 | 4,130 | 4,290 | 4,480 | 4,520 | 2,970 | 8 | −2.5 |
| Hungary | 3,700 | 3,620 | 3,750 | 3,650 | 3,730 | 900 | 3 | −4.3 |
| Luxembourg | 3,510 | 3,290 | 3,990 | 3,945 | 3,710 | 2,210 | 8 | −10.9 |
| Turkey | 3,180 | 3,830 | 4,330 | 4,950 | 5,980 | 4,390 | 8 | +12.4 |
| Argentina | 2,910 | 2,940 | 2,650 | 2,940 | 3,240 | 2,370 | 8 | +16.4 |
| Bulgaria | 2,590 | 2,830 | 2,870 | 2,930 | 2,830 | 770 | 3 | +6.9 |
| Finland | 2,410 | 2,420 | 2,640 | 2,520 | 2,590 | 1,710 | 8 | +1.6 |
| Venezuela | 2,278 | 2,320 | 2,770 | 3,060 | 3,460 | 2,490 | 8 | +15.2 |
| Iran | 1,200* | 1,200* | 1,200* | 1,200* | 1,200* | † | † | † |
| Greece | 930 | 870 | 900 | 990 | 1,010 | 580 | 8 | −10.8 |
| Switzerland | 840 | 840 | 980 | 990 | 1,010 | † | † | † |
| Norway | 780 | 900 | 920 | 940 | 850 | 540 | 8 | +2.5 |

*Estimated. †1987 figures not yet available.
Sources: International Iron and Steel Institute; United Nations.

**Table X. World Production of Pig Iron**
In 000 metric tons

| Country | 1982 | 1983 | 1984 | 1985 | 1986 |
|---|---|---|---|---|---|
| World | 452,350 | 457,830 | 489,740 | 498,955 | 488,840 |
| U.S.S.R. | 106,720 | 110,450 | 110,800 | 109,980 | 113,600 |
| Japan | 77,660 | 72,940 | 80,400 | 80,570 | 74,650 |
| U.S. | 39,281 | 44,210 | 47,090 | 45,760 | 39,770 |
| China | 35,510 | 37,380 | 40,000 | 43,540 | 47,000 |
| West Germany | 27,620 | 26,600 | 30,200 | 31,530 | 28,590 |
| France | 14,720 | 13,500 | 14,710 | 13,710 | 13,710 |
| Italy | 11,540 | 10,310 | 11,630 | 11,660 | 11,900 |
| Brazil | 10,830 | 12,950 | 17,220 | 18,960 | 15,840 |
| India | 9,640 | 9,160 | 9,460 | 9,840 | 10,510 |
| Czechoslovakia | 9,530 | 9,470 | 9,560 | 9,560 | 9,600 |
| Romania | 8,640 | 8,180 | 9,560 | 9,210 | 9,500 |
| South Korea | 8,440 | 8,020 | 8,760 | 8,830 | 9,000 |
| U.K. | 8,330 | 9,480 | 9,490 | 10,380 | 9,713 |
| Poland | 8,110 | 9,470 | 9,540 | 9,440 | 10,220 |
| Canada | 8,000 | 8,570 | 9,640 | 9,670 | 9,250 |
| Belgium | 7,830 | 8,070 | 9,010 | 8,750 | 8,090 |
| South Africa | 6,760 | 5,220 | 5,530 | 5,040 | 5,770 |
| Spain | 6,000 | 5,420 | 5,340 | 5,480 | 4,803 |
| Australia | 5,950 | 5,060 | 5,330 | 5,600 | 5,850 |
| North Korea | 5,250 | 5,500 | 5,750 | 7,750* | 8,500* |
| Netherlands, The | 3,620 | 3,750 | 4,930 | 4,820 | 4,630 |
| Mexico | 3,600 | 3,540 | 3,870 | 3,530 | 3,730 |
| Austria | 3,120 | 3,320 | 3,745 | 3,700 | 3,350 |
| Yugoslavia | 2,700 | 2,840 | 2,850 | 3,110 | 3,070 |
| Taiwan | 2,700 | 3,420 | 3,290 | 3,430 | 3,740 |
| Luxembourg | 2,590 | 2,320 | 2,770 | 2,750 | 2,650 |
| Hungary | 2,200 | 2,060 | 2,100 | 2,100 | 2,080 |
| Turkey | 2,170 | 2,720 | 2,900 | 3,190 | 3,670 |
| East Germany | 2,150 | 2,210 | 2,360 | 2,580 | 2,625 |
| Finland | 1,940 | 1,900 | 2,030 | 1,900 | 1,980 |
| Sweden | 1,780 | 2,010 | 2,210 | 2,420 | 2,440 |
| Bulgaria | 1,560 | 1,630 | 1,580 | 1,710 | 1,600 |
| Algeria | 1,100 | 1,100 | 1,100 | 1,100 | 1,100 |
| Egypt | 1,070 | 990 | 940 | 950 | 950 |
| Argentina | 1,020 | 910 | 920 | 1,310 | 1,640 |
| Norway | 480 | 600 | 550 | 610 | 570 |
| Zimbabwe | 480 | 580 | 400 | 670 | 640 |
| Chile | 450 | 540 | 590 | 580 | 590 |
| Venezuela | 200 | 170 | 330 | 440 | 490 |

*Estimated.
Source: International Iron and Steel Institute.

continued the rapid expansion of its steel industry, with production rising 12% during 1987. Increased production in China was offset by greater consumption, and that nation remained a large net importer of steel. (IAN D. MATTHEWS)

## MACHINERY AND MACHINE TOOLS

Machine tool production can be considered one gauge of the rate of industrialization of the world, and it is also useful as a measure of the rate of factory modernization. It is therefore interesting to note that the value of worldwide production of machine tools in 1986 soared to a record $29 billion. Builders in Western Europe accounted for more than one-third of this total, while Japan alone accounted for one-fourth and the United States for one-tenth. Total production rose one-third from the $22 billion of a year earlier.

In 1986 the U.S. produced machine tools valued at $2.7 billion, up about 3% from the previous year. Order backlogs stood at $1.2 billion at the end of 1986. (Because of their many specialized features, machine tools are often built to order, and thus an order backlog is created.)

The U.S. imported machine tools valued at $2.2 billion in 1986. Imports came principally from Japan, with a 52% share of the total; West Germany, with a 16% share; and Italy, Taiwan, and Switzerland, each with about a 5% share.

In 1986 U.S. export sales increased by 30% over the prior year to about $600 million. The increase was due in part to the recent more favourable currency exchange rates. Principal receiving nations were Mexico, Canada, Japan, China, the United Kingdom, and West Germany.

The largest producer of machine tools in 1986 was Japan, with a total output worth over $7 billion. Cutting machines accounted for $5.7 billion of this total. Nearly $3 billion of Japan's total production was destined for export trade. Japan's imports were valued at less than one-tenth of its exports.

The second largest producer in 1986 was West Germany, with an output value totaling $5.2 billion. Of this, 60% was produced for export trade. Imports were valued at one-third of exports.

The third largest producer in 1986 was believed to have been the Soviet Union, with total output having an estimated value of $3.7 billion. Additional imports of approximately $1.7 billion made this country the largest consumer of machine tools. The Soviet Union installed machines valued at about one-sixth of total world production. (JOHN B. DEAM)

## MICROELECTRONICS

Sales of semiconductors climbed more than 18% in 1987, reflecting a rebuilding of inventories and increased activity in the computer, communications, and other sectors of the electronics industry. This represented an increase from $31 billion in 1986 to $36.5 billion in 1987, according to Dataquest, a marketing research firm. This included the value of microchips made both by companies that used their own output and by companies that sold their output to others.

Semiconductor consumption in the U.S. reached an estimated $12 billion in 1987, up from $10.2 billion in 1986. Sales to user companies totaled $10.2 billion and $8.5 billion, respectively, according to the Semiconductor Industry Association. Consumption figures in Japan totaled $13.6 billion in 1987, compared with $12.3 billion in 1986. However, the dollar value of microchips produced by Japan and other nations was artificially inflated by a decrease in the value of the dollar in relation to the yen and other currencies.

Inventories of semiconductors became depleted late in 1986, and users began to restock in early 1987. The buying spree coincided with a pickup in sales of computers and communications equipment.

A new generation of microprocessors helped spark the growth of computer sales. These chips, which process 32 bits of information simultaneously, can handle two million to three million instructions per second, compared with 500,000 to one million for the predecessor 16-bit chips. The 32-bit chips provide desktop computers with the power to perform tasks that once could be done only by much larger, more expensive machines; these include the design and manufacture of products, control of robots, creation of high-quality graphics, and solution of difficult scientific and business problems. Engineers were working on developing microcomputers that would allow two or more 32-bit chips to work on a task simultaneously or in parallel. This would provide an enormous increase in efficiency over present computers, which solve problems linearly, or one step at a time.

Microprocessors manipulate data stored on memory chips, which also increased in capacity in 1987. IBM introduced an experimental chip that holds four mil-

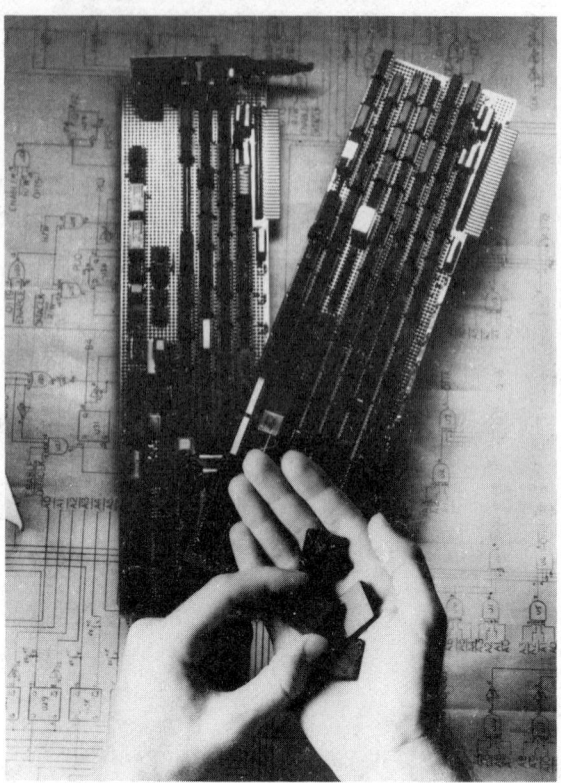

Computer chip makers during the past year showed increased interest in producing application-specific integrated circuitry—customized computer chips (in hand) able to perform the same functions as large circuit boards (background).

THE NEW YORK TIMES

lion bits of information, or four times as much as the newest chips in commercial use. Nippon Telegraph and Telephone of Japan topped this with a new 16-megabit dynamic random-access memory (DRAM) chip.

DRAMs continued to be a focus of U.S.-Japanese competition. As a result of such competition and pressure from the U.S. government, the Japanese agreed in 1986 to permit more sales of U.S.-made microchips in Japan and to stop dumping (selling below the production cost) Japanese-made chips in the U.S. In March the U.S. concluded that Japan was not abiding by the agreement and imposed tariffs that raised the prices of certain imports from Japan, such as TV sets and personal computers. By June Japan had reduced barriers against imports of U.S.-made semiconductors, and the U.S. lifted part of the tariffs.     (WILLIAM J. CROMIE)

## NUCLEAR INDUSTRY

Figures released by the International Atomic Energy Agency revealed that 23 reactors began operation during 1986, adding 25,138 MW to the world's total nuclear generating capacity. At the beginning of 1987 there were 397 nuclear units with a total generating capacity of 273,715 MW operating in 26 countries. In those countries nuclear electricity accounted for 15.4% of all the electricity generated in 1986.

A broad restructuring of the world's major nuclear reactor vendors and associated companies reflected the general slowdown in orders for power plants and the deteriorating public image of nuclear power. West Germany's Kraftwerk Union (KWU), which had become wholly owned by Siemens near the end of 1986, became in 1987 Siemens-Kraftwerk Umwelt (contriv-

ing to maintain the familiar KWU name with a new meaning), a massive reorganization that combined all of Siemens's nuclear, conventional, and renewable energy operations in one new company. KWU earlier had announced a planned reduction in its staffing levels of nearly 25% by 1991. KWU also formed a "strategic alliance" with the U.S. engineering firm Bechtel to provide operating plant services to companies in the U.S. and purchased Exxon Nuclear, a U.S. reactor fuel manufacturer.

A second international restructuring took place in 1987 when the Swedish and Swiss power plant giants, ASEA and Brown Boveri, respectively, announced a merger. Westinghouse Nuclear International in Europe changed its name to Westinghouse Energy Systems to indicate its diversification into fossil, solar, and waste combustion as well as nuclear technologies.

Work in the Soviet Union on the entombment of the Chernobyl Unit 4 reactor, which exploded in April 1986, was reported as completed just before the beginning of 1987. The 60-m (200-ft)-high walls of reinforced concrete that surrounded it were constructed by remotely operated cranes. Sensors were installed throughout the tomb to indicate the conditions inside, and the structure included an exhaust ventilation system with air injected through one shaft and vented from a second through filters and monitors to prevent the escape of radioactivity. Units 1 and 2 at the plant were restarted before the end of 1986, but it was decided later in 1987 to abandon construction of Units 5 and 6 on the site.

Several fundamental design changes to the water-cooled graphite-moderated (RBMK) series of reactors were introduced by Soviet engineers as a result of the Chernobyl accident. The most important of these was the automatic prevention of

withdrawal of the control rods beyond safe limits, additional permanent absorber rods, new reactivity indications in the control room, and increased uranium enrichment to reduce the positive void coefficient at low power that led to the runaway effect at Chernobyl.

One trend in reactor design in the rest of the world that had become more marked since the Soviet accident was the growth of filtered/vented containments. These were being fitted, and backfitted, to plants in Sweden, France, and West Germany and were being actively considered in other countries.

An international conference in Paris in October reached an agreement between virtually all the world's nuclear power utilities to establish an international fault-reporting scheme. Similar in intent to the U.S. Institute of Power Operations (Inpo), an organization that had attracted many members from outside the U.S., the new scheme would link four regional centres in Paris, Tokyo, Atlanta, Ga., and Moscow, with an international coordinating centre in either London or Vienna. These would provide rapid communication of details and data on incidents that resulted in power outages of greater than a specified length at any nuclear station in a member country.

The first report of Inpo on its U.S. power plant performance indicator program showed that there had been a steady improvement in operations since 1980. The forced outage rate declined by more than 26% over the years 1980 to 1985, and collective radiation exposure was reduced from 1,230 man-rem per unit for boiling-water reactors (BWRs) in 1980 to 784 in 1985 and for pressurized-water reactors (PWRs) from 597 to 405 man-rem per unit.

A 450-mm (17.6-in)-diameter feedwater pipe ruptured at the Surry Unit 2 in Virginia, with nonradioactive water and steam scalding eight workers, four of whom later died. This accident drew attention to the need for improved inspection and maintenance in the nonnuclear parts of power stations.

Unloading of the Three Mile Island Unit 2 core reached the halfway mark. A new type of cask was used to transport the fuel and rubble to the Idaho National Engineering Laboratory, where the debris from the 1979 accident would be studied as part of the Department of Energy's accident evaluation and research program.

In Canada the Unit 1 reactor at Pickering, near Toronto, was restarted after a four-year refurbishment. The number 1 and 2 reactors were shut down following a failure of one of the Unit 2 pressure tubes in August 1983 because of a materials problem.

By 1987 more than 70% of France's electricity was supplied by nuclear power stations, but the French government announced that the rate of ordering of new nuclear plants would have to be reduced to at least one per 18 months, instead of one per year as planned by the previous administration. Also in France a leak of liquid sodium from the fuel-storage carousel in the full-scale commercial prototype Superphénix fast-breeder reactor at Creys-Malville prevented the unit from reaching its full output of 1,200 MW. The government later warned that fast breeders would have to prove themselves commercially viable if their development was to be continued.

General Electric of the United States was notified that two 1,356-MW reactors of its advanced BWR design were to be ordered for the Kashiwazaki Kariwa Units 6 and 7 in Japan. GE's last direct reactor order that was completed was placed in 1974.

A new nuclear-waste vitrification plant at Mol, Belgium, began operation, processing liquid high-level radioactive waste resulting from the old Eurochemic reprocessing plant operations on the site. The plant was operated by the West German company DWK, and its success was needed to support the application by DWK to build a similar facility at Wackersdorf, West Germany.

A six-month safety audit of the British Nuclear Fuels' reprocessing plant at Sellafield, by the Nuclear Installations Inspectorate, concluded that the company had to clean up some operations at the plant. One year was allowed for acceptable standards to be reached. Failure to comply with the standards demanded might result in the closing of some parts of the plant.

The long-awaited report of the inspector at the two-year public inquiry into the building of Britain's first PWR power station at Sizewell recommended that the project be approved by the government. Shortly after the publication of the report, Peter Walker, secretary of state for energy, gave Britain's Central Electricity Generating Board the go-ahead for the project.

Little progress was made during the year in negotiations for new projects in many of the emerging nuclear power nations. Egypt again postponed a decision on its al-Dabaa station, and negotiations with the Canadian government for a build-operate-and-transfer (b.o.t.) deal for the two Akkuyu Candu reactors in Turkey failed to reach a conclusion.

A $5.5 million deal was signed by Argentina with Iran for the transfer of nuclear technology. It included the development of a new core for the research reactor at the University of Tehran. The possibility of Argentina's completing the 1,300-MW Bushehr PWR plant abandoned by KWU at the time of the Iranian revolution was also being negotiated.

(RICHARD A. KNOX)

## PAINTS AND VARNISHES

Paint industries steered an uneasy course between near-saturated markets, aging technologies, and a rising tide of regulatory constraints in 1987. Acquisitions and divestments continued, with many targeted to achieve functional lines of specialization. In the U.K. the sector of medium-sized companies shrank as the number of acquisitions rose. The third largest paint maker, Crown Decorative Producers Ltd., was sold by Reed International to the industrial conglomerate Williams Holdings for a record £285 million. With the acquisition of Berger (a subsidiary of Hoest) for £133 million, Williams became the U.K.'s second largest paint manufacturer. Macpherson sold its UV wood-finishing line and its Drynamels powder-coating facility to Crown and to the U.S. Ferro Corp., respectively. The American Porter Paint Co. was bought by International Paint of

the U.K.; Denmark's leading paint maker, Sadolin & Holmblad Ltd., was taken over by Casco of Sweden, part of Nobel Industries Sweden; and Casco went on to purchase the French manufacturer Duco and CdF Chimie.

EC directives continued to wind their way through various stages of revision as previous amendments gained national approval. The year's major event was the appearance of the eight-volume *European Inventory of Existing Commercial Substances,* which had full legal status and listed more than 100,000 chemical substances found on the EC market between January 1971 and September 1981.

The U.K. government's ban on triorganotin-containing antifouling paints for fishing nets and small boats proved controversial. Made in response to the oyster lobby, the move surprised the industry. Paint products featured prominently in two lawsuits. In the U.K. the Beaulieu River Oyster Nurseries sued six paint companies for damages to its oyster beds from antifouling paints. In the U.S. the ill health of a shipyard worker, allegedly resulting from exposure to glycol ether-containing paint, became the centre of legal controversy involving seven paint companies.

With the maturing of markets in the West, growth was increasingly concentrated in the East, where demand for paint and associated know-how was growing in most countries. In the U.S.S.R.—where demand exceeded supplies—technology and capital transfer from the West became possible with the authorization of joint Soviet-Western enterprises on a 60:40 basis.

Appropriately, in the year of the superconductor, the first superconductive coating was developed—a process from IBM utilizing plasma-spraying techniques on high-temperature-resistant wire coatings.

(HELMA JOTISCHKY)

## PHARMACEUTICALS

Pharmaceuticals precipitated a mild parliamentary crisis in Canada in 1987 when a bill to amend the mandatory licensing law for Canadian drug manufacturers, the majority of which were U.S.-based multinationals, was held up in the Liberal-dominated Senate on the grounds that it would raise prices. The new legislation would provide ten years of patent protection for new drugs, after which they could be copied by generic-drug manufacturers, subject to compulsory licensing and payment of a 4% royalty. The matter even became an issue in the U.S.-Canada trade pact negotiations. (*See* WORLD AFFAIRS [North America]: *Canada.*)

Brazil became the target of indirect political pressure from U.S. pharmaceutical manufacturers. As part of its anti-inflation program, Brazil had instituted rigid price controls on prescription drugs, although other consumer goods were not subject to the same regulations. Also, since 1969 drugs had not enjoyed the same patent protection as other inventions. The major U.S. pharmaceutical trade association, the Pharmaceutical Manufacturers Association, filed a complaint petition under the U.S. Trade Act seeking to have Brazil's curbs declared an unreasonable trade barrier. If this was upheld, it could open the way for the imposition of protective tariffs on Brazilian goods entering the U.S.

Major U.S. drug companies showed signs of frustration with their cosmetic subsidiaries, in part because of low profitability resulting from higher new-product costs and flat fragrance and cosmetic sales. This probably accounted for the sale of cosmetic subsidiaries by four drug companies: Elizabeth Arden by Eli Lilly & Co.; Jacqueline Cochran by American Cyanamid Co.; Charles of the Ritz Group by Squibb & Co.; and Diane Von Furstenberg, Lancaster Cosmetics, and Germaine Monteil by Beecham Group.

Cosmetic manufacturers strayed into the territory of drug regulation during the year by escalating claims for their skin-care products, particularly those relating to the suppression of wrinkles and other signs of aging. In April the Center for Drugs and Biologics of the FDA began issuing "regulatory letters" warning that specific products were indeed "drugs" because of claims relating to "cell regeneration," "wrinkle smoothing or elimination," and other allegations of therapeutic benefits. In all, 22 companies received such letters; one discontinued the product line in question and sold off a skin-care subsidiary.

The regulatory establishment was somewhat kinder to pharmaceutical manufacturers. The FDA, pressed for half a dozen years to speed up the new-drug approval process, on June 22 made effective regulations to allow drug manufacturers to recover the costs of research by selling experimental drugs that merely showed promise. So-called investigational new drugs could now be sold after the FDA had been given 30 days' notice, though companies conducting clinical studies still had to get specific FDA permission. The agency had previously instituted a "fast track" approval system for drugs for AIDS (acquired immune deficiency syndrome), Alzheimer's disease, and cancer, but even this required months for approval. Some major drug companies indicated that they had no plans to charge patients for experimental drugs. (DONALD A. DAVIS)

## PLASTICS

The plastics industry in 1987 had its best year since the oil crises of the 1970s. This followed the good performance in 1986 that was stimulated by the fall in oil prices, and as a result there were shortages of many materials, including the important thermoplastics commodity. Thus the lower petrochemical feedstock costs were not reflected in plastics prices, which rose sharply. Because the increase in demand was worldwide, established manufacturers were able to take a fairly relaxed view of imports from new producers in, for example, the Middle East.

Efficiency, which had been the main corporate objective of the thermoplastics materials industry during the previous years of the decade, became a lower priority for the time being with the disappearance of overcapacity. The major news of 1987 in this area was the buyout by Montedison (Italy) of the stake held by its joint-venture partner, Hercules (U.S.), in Himont, the world's largest polypropylene producer with an annual capacity of 1.6 million metric tons. This move surprised observers because polypropylene, with its great versatility for use in moldings, films, and fibres, was the star material of the year. Himont technology, moreover, had already been licensed to more than 40 other companies and accounted for about two-thirds of world output.

A number of major expansion projects for polypropylene were announced during the year. Himont itself formed a link with Statoil, an existing polypropylene producer, to build a substantial plant in Antwerp, Belgium. This choice of partner had much to do with the Norwegian firm's strong position regarding access to North Sea oil and gas and, hence, petrochemical feedstocks. ICI and Shell Chemicals were among others contributing to a sharp upturn in planned world polypropylene capacity, causing some to worry about the prospect of overcapacity in the event of a cyclical downturn. However, the rate of growth for polypropylene in 1987—and prospects that it would continue in the 5–10% range for at least the rest of the decade—bolstered confidence within the industry. There were few plans for expanding capacity for the other main thermoplastics. Manufacturers concentrated on using their expertise to make more expensive materials with superior properties rather than basic commodity grades.

Interest in the more specialized engineering and high performance plastics was as strong as ever, with steadily increasing use in the aerospace, automotive, and electronics industries. The materials contending for this area now seemed to be more or less settled, and a feeling emerged that reorganization with an eye toward greater efficiency was due in this sector also. An exception to this was Hoechst, the major West German chemical group, which took over the Celanese Corp. (U.S.), a leader in engineering thermoplastics.

There was a marked trend in 1987 toward more use of plastics alloys and blends, over 200 of which had now appeared on the market; world consumption was about 700,000 tons per year. The objective was

to maximize the potential and cost effectiveness of existing polymers rather than introducing new (and more expensive) materials. Phenolics, one of the oldest plastics, made a comeback on the basis of its qualities of strength, stability, and nonflammability; this was especially true of phenolic foams used for insulation and other applications in the building industry.

(ROBIN C. PENFOLD)

## PRINTING

Representatives of the world's communications industries meeting at Comprint in Vienna in June 1987 heard that there were more book titles, more new publications, and more uses for printed communications than ever before. The only negative factor was that press-run lengths continued to decline, but even this was forcing technological change. Presses that previously took hours to change over from one job to another were being switched within half an hour.

To cater to packaging markets, sheetfed offset manufacturers introduced special versions of standard multicolour machines for folding-box printing, such as the Heidelberg CD range, which met with instant success. The world's largest and most modern cigarette-pack printing unit was installed at Gudang Garam in Indonesia.

In France *Le Figaro* and its sister newspaper, *France-Soir*, placed orders with M.A.N.-Roland of West Germany for a unique Uniman/Colorman configuration and the first of Rockwell International's Colorliner press lines outside North America. Colour transmission of news pictures by Scitex Satlight and via Crosfield-Muirhead Datrax data compression systems was used increasingly. Dr.Ing. Rudolf Hell of West Germany linked the digital minifloppy image disk storage in the Fujix video still camera directly into a telephone transmitter to transmit pictures into a Chromacom page-composition system. Ba-

sic Densitogragraph of Japan produced a personal computer program allowing full-colour reproduction on paper or transparent plastic at the density standards of an original colour transparency.

At Toppan Printing in Japan, desktop publishing was integrated to introduce a total text and image process, including laser platemaking and black-and-white offset printing. Matsushita/National Panasonic and other Japanese manufacturers utilized laser fax principles to design low-cost colour-separation methods. Mitsubishi of Japan introduced the Silver Digiplate working directly from the digital impulses of the electronic image- and type-generating systems. Black-and-white flatbed scanners became popular, with Autokon leading the field in number of installations. Dai Nippon Printing of Japan became the world's largest printing group, followed by R. R. Donnelley in the U.S. and Robert Maxwell's BPCC in the U.K.

(W. PINCUS JASPERT)

## RUBBER

The rubber industry returned to the problem of tight supplies in 1987 after a period of restructuring, shutting down excess capacity, and fending off arbitrageurs. Shortages of butadiene monomer, a key ingredient in styrene-butadiene rubber (SBR) and polybutadiene rubber, triggered numerous price increases during the year and in the last quarter caused delivery delays of up to nine weeks in North America and Europe. Prices of SBR, the most widely used elastomer, rose more than 40%. Contributing factors were the devaluation of the dollar relative to other currencies and more efficient ethylene processing (butadiene is a by-product of ethylene production). The lower value of the dollar increased exports for U.S. producers; U.S. exports of all synthetic rubber were 35% higher than in the previous year.

Worldwide production and consumption of all rubber rose for the fifth straight year. Estimates were for rubber consumption of nearly 12.9 million metric tons, with synthetic rubber accounting for 8.6 million metric tons and natural rubber, 4.3 million metric tons. North American consumption totaled nearly 3 million metric tons; Western Europe, Africa, and the Middle East consumed almost 2.5 million metric tons; Asia and Oceania, the fastest growing region for rubber consumption, used over 2.7 million metric tons; and Latin-American consumption reached 780,000 metric tons. Estimates of consumption for the centrally planned economies of Eastern Europe and Asia were pegged at just over 4 million metric tons. The ratio of synthetic to natural rubber used remained roughly 2:1.

The International Natural Rubber Agreement (INRA) was ratified during 1987, extending the pact that had been in danger because of dissatisfaction on the part of both producing and consuming nations. Kuala Lumpur, Malaysia, would remain the headquarters of the International Natural Rubber Organization (INRO). The INRO council authorized the buffer stock manager to implement a modest sales program of the buffer stock, which had reached 360,000 metric tons. The manager was to sell about 2,000 tons per month beginning in November. Prices

SIKORSKY AIRCRAFT

Technicians work on a helicopter rotor blade composed of a plastic composite weave. The plastics industry was developing new materials designed to be lighter than steel but strong enough to make not only rotors but also bridges and parts of car engines.

for natural rubber continued to increase in 1987 and were reaching the levels of 1983. Tire grades of natural rubber were 33% higher than in the previous year as a result of some production declines in Indonesia and a strong buying program on the part of manufacturers. Higher grades were in plentiful supply, however, and premium prices stayed flat.

Malaysia was the top producer of natural rubber, followed by Indonesia, Thailand, India, China, and Sri Lanka. During 1987 all were producing more than in the previous year except Sri Lanka, where production was off 5%. The U.S.S.R. was the largest producer of synthetic rubber, followed by the U.S., Japan, France, and West Germany.

The tire industry was affected by a decline in auto sales, especially in the U.S., where shipments of original equipment tires were off more than 2%, but this was offset by a 13% increase in shipments of replacement tires. Shipments of truck and bus tires were up almost 13%. Imports of passenger radial tires into the U.S. increased 14%, other passenger tires rose 55%, and light truck radial imports were up 29% during the year. France's Michelin, which turned a profit in the U.S. for the first time in 1986, announced that it was increasing U.S. production capacity by 30%. Michelin also planned to invest more than $138 million to double production capacity at its Campo Grande and Resende, Brazil, operations. Japan's Bridgestone said that it would begin producing radial passenger and light-truck tires at its heavy-truck tire facility in Tennessee, and Dunlop announced that it would spend $100 million to modernize two of its U.S. plants.

Continental of West Germany acquired the General Tire division of GenCorp, creating the fourth largest tire company by sales. Goodrich closed its Akron, Ohio, operations, signifying the end of commercial tire production in the city known as the rubber capital of the world, and in December announced that it would quit the tire business entirely. Firestone closed two of its tire-manufacturing facilities, and Carlisle stopped making bicycle tires, ending bike-tire production in the U.S. Polysar of Canada built a hydrogenated nitrile plant in Orange, Texas, with a 3.5 million-lb-per-year capacity, and Bayer built a similar plant in Leverkusen, West Germany, with an annual capacity of 2 million lb. Exxon Chemical expanded ethylene propylene capacity by 30% at its plant in Notre-Dame-de-Gravenchon, France, and Copolymer Rubber increased capacity for ethylene propylene diene monomer elastomers at its Addis, La., facility to 130 million lb per year from 92 million lb.

(DONALD SMITH)

## SHIPBUILDING

There was some evidence that the shipbuilding recession was bottoming out in 1987. For the first time in a decade, world order books showed a small upturn in the second quarter of 1987 to 21,345,516 gross tonnage (gt), 752,744 gt more than in the previous quarter but only one-third of the 1976 total. Nevertheless, the world's major shipyards continued either to close or to suffer heavy trading losses. Some went into receivership, while others chose

The MACS 3000, a luxurious cruise liner designed by the Nippon Kokan KK Co., was planned to accommodate 3,000 passengers and featured parks, gardens, four tennis courts, and a heliport.
AP/WIDE WORLD

to undertake major restructuring to meet competition from the Far East.

South Korea became increasingly competitive and would not contemplate artificial curbs on production. It continued to erode Japan's share of the market and accounted for 23.8% of the world tonnage on order, compared with 24.8% for Japan. Because of the fierce competition and the strength of the yen, Japan's major shipbuilding companies incurred pretax losses in the fiscal year ended March 1987, and prospects for an improvement were gloomy.

In Europe shipbuilders considered a range of options for countering competition, most of which involved subsidies. In West Germany the four coastal states urged the federal government to increase shipbuilding subsidies, and plans were announced for a merger of three of West Germany's leading shipbuilders—Blohm & Voss, Thyssen Nordseewerke, and HDW of Kiel. The Greek government offered its shipbuilders subsidies of up to 28% toward the cost of new ships or ship conversions. British Shipbuilders announced a loss of £148 million, incurred because it took over a £45 million crane barge ordered by a firm that subsequently became bankrupt; it later sold the vessel. The U.K. received an order for 25 diesel-electric "superflex" ferries from Denmark; the vessels' power packs were located on deck. Despite low prices from subsidized yards, owners were not tempted to engage in speculative building, and banks continued to be cautious about providing loans.

Japan remained first among the major shipbuilding nations with its order book of 5.3 million gt, or 24.8% of world tonnage. It was closely followed by South Korea with over 5 million gt, which was an amazing achievement considering that in 1977 Japan's order book was 13.7 million gt and Korea's was 900,000 gt. In third place

was Yugoslavia (1.2 million gt), followed by Italy (1.1 million gt), Brazil (920,000 gt), Poland (910,000 gt), and China (790,000 gt). Taiwan (690,000 gt) fell back from fifth to ninth place behind Romania (710,000 gt). These nine countries accounted for 78.3% of all orders. Italy's strong position reflected the restructuring of its shipbuilding industry. By contrast, the United Kingdom fell to 17th place, reflecting the sharp decline that had taken place there in recent years.

The pattern of demand changed with a shift away from bulk carriers, which declined from 43.1% of the total order book in 1986 to 24%. The oil tanker share rose from 22.7% of the order book to 39.9%, while cargo ships maintained their 20% share. The cruise-ship sector of the market remained buoyant, with strong demand in the Caribbean. Finland's Wartsila yard continued to gain orders in this sector, and the Japanese entered into the competition. After delivering the 31,000-gt cruise ferry *Norsea*, British Shipbuilders was also planning to enter this highly competitive market.

Out of total orders of 21.3 million gt, 55.3%, or 11.8 million gt, was for registration in countries outside those in which the ships were being built. This 11.8 million gt included 3.1 million gt for Liberia, 3 million gt for Panama, and 1.1 million gt for the U.S.S.R.    (EDWARD CROWLEY)

## TELECOMMUNICATIONS

Several technical developments during 1987 raised expectations for future improvements in communications. The breakthrough in superconductors, improved optical fibre communications, and digital network developments all pointed to an expanded worldwide communications capability in the years ahead. However, the telecommunications picture was not all rosy. An international trade dispute erupted around an optical fibre communications system, and critics in the U.S. Congress turned back an information embargo advocated by the administration of U.S. Pres. Ronald Reagan. The administration, concerned about national security, proposed a new telecommunications protection policy and limits to the accessing of computer data bases.

Materials scientists provided the most exciting technical development in telecommunications during 1987. They discovered a new class of ceramics that exhibit superconducting properties—almost zero resistance to electrical current—at higher temperatures than had been thought possible. These new superconductors were expected to have widespread applications in telecommunications equipment in the years ahead. (*See* PHYSICS: *Sidebar*.)

Undersea optical fibre cable, telephone office switching gear, and satellite communications all would benefit from the application of superconducting materials to telecommunications. Optical fibre cable was expected to remain the favoured means of long-distance undersea communications because it has superior information-carrying capacity, speed, and security. Some industry observers, however, believed that superconducting wire might play a role in powering the repeaters used to regenerate optical signals as they travel over long distances. The first applications, though, seemed likely to take place in computer and central office digital-circuit technology.

Optical fibre technology continued to improve in 1987, with several successful laboratory demonstrations of transmission of coherent light waves at British, Japanese, and U.S. laboratories. Though still experimental, this technology improved discrimination between the light signals traveling through a fibre. Such improvement promised to increase the number of voice conversations that could be carried on a single fibre and also extend the distance between the costly repeaters. A hundred-fold improvement in performance was anticipated when the new technology was put to work, which probably would not be before 1990.

Optical fibres were also at the centre of an international trade dispute in 1987 as Britain and the U.S. charged Japan with closing its markets to foreign competition. A new undersea optical fibre cable, to link Alaska and Japan, was being planned by Japan's Ministry of Posts and Telecommunications. Two consortia—one all-Japanese, the other Japanese with sizable British and U.S. interests—were bidding for the job. The government said that only one competitor would be able to bid profitably against the state-owned optical fibre monopoly. Therefore, it was asking the two consortia to merge under Japanese management, a move that the Japanese-British-U.S. consortium was resisting.

Though some spots along the road to international cooperation in telecommunications were bumpy in 1987, the worldwide push to develop the Integrated Services Digital Network (ISDN) kept rolling along. ISDN, the movement to convert all of the world's telephones from analog to digital technology, gained considerable momentum in the U.S. Each of the seven regional Bell operating companies was actively engaged in testing the new digital telecommunications technology, while more than 20 semiconductor manufacturers from around the world announced the development of chips that would hasten the introduction of new voice, data, and video services for customers.

The development of new telecommunications services received support on the regulatory front. A rule that had barred the regional Bell operating companies from using the telephone network equipment to store and forward information was lifted in 1987 by the federal judge overseeing the Bell System divestiture. Under the new rule the companies could use their equipment as conduits for information services such as videotex. Videotex used computers, telephone lines, and low-cost terminals to store and distribute text and graphics.

(ROBERT ROSENBERG)

## TEXTILES

In 1987 there was little change in established world trends. The output of yarns continued to shift from the developed to the less developed countries. Total mill consumption was estimated at 33.2 million tons in 1986, with less developed countries accounting for over 47%, compared with an estimated 43% in 1981. In international trade, the less developed countries strengthened their position.

Forecasts based on UN data indicated that these trends would continue to 1990, when mill consumption of 36.4 million tons was expected to be divided evenly between the less developed and developed nations and the trade balance (volume) would have moved even more firmly in favour of the less developed world, particularly China and South Asia. Textiles and clothing consumption would continue to rise most strongly in the less developed countries.

The industrialized countries continued to adopt more technologically advanced machinery. In the less developed countries, investment decisions were complicated by the fact that older machinery met their requirements in terms of job creation and skill availability, but failure to upgrade could erode their competitiveness in qualitative terms. China emerged as a major influence, as both a consumer and a trader. Of most concern to other producers was the prospect of China as a competitor in the market for finished goods of cashmere and silk, and new suppliers of cashmere were sought. (PETER LENNOX-KERR)

**Wool.** As 1987 began there was a growing conviction that the world wool market was exhibiting price strength based on a more favourable demand/supply relationship. The improvement was largely due to increased demand from China, the U.S.S.R., and Japan, with Australian wool exports to these countries up by 37, 32, and 24%, respectively. Softer and uncertain market conditions in the opening months of the 1986–87 wool selling season (starting July 1, 1986) had gradually been replaced by a firming price tendency.

The Australian Wool Corporation (AWC) disposed of most of its stocks, which fell from 894,693 bales greasy basis (1 bale = 348 lb or 158 kg) at the start of the 1986–87 season to 386,369 at the close. The AWC market indicator was 557 cents per kilogram at the end of September 1986 and subsequently rose to 754 at the end of June 1987. After peaking in early April, prices were subdued until soon after the 1987–88 selling season started, when they moved ahead again. A new record was set on August 21, when the AWC indicator reached 945 cents. New Zealand and South Africa, together with other primary markets, showed a similar upward price trend and declines in stocks held by growers. Fine merinos in Australia showed the most spectacular price rises. After a fall in September, wool prices resumed a firmer trend in October.

The world wool clip in 1987–88 was expected to amount to 1,735,000 metric tons (clean basis), reflecting a 1.5% increase over 1986–87, when the final total was estimated at 1,709,000 metric tons.

(H. M. F. MALLETT)

**Cotton.** According to International Cotton Advisory Committee estimates, world output of cotton recovered strongly in 1987, reaching 16.7 million metric tons and reflecting a 10.7% rise from 1986. The revival in Chinese agriculture meant that the significance of cotton for China's agricultural economy continued to increase. China became the world's largest cotton exporter in 1986, with exports rising some 35% over 1985. Recognition of the commercial importance of cotton was reflected in the development of new and finer materials.

High-yield cotton strains were introduced in India. A program was under way to develop short-duration dwarf varieties, which would be less costly to grow and could be grown on land not previously used for cotton. Increased irrigation continued to be an important factor in output. In the U.S. cotton took an increased share of the textile market, representing 28.5% of all fibres used in 1987, compared with 27% in 1986. This included filament yarns as well as staple fibres.

It was predicted that in 1987–88 crops would increase in most of the major cotton-growing countries. Consumption was expected to decrease slightly, suggesting that fibre stocks would rise. This could exert downward pressure on the buoyant raw cotton prices in the longer term, with adverse consequences for some of the poorer less developed countries that were heavily dependent on cotton export revenue.

(PETER LENNOX-KERR)

**Silk.** Demand for silk declined during 1986–87, especially in Italy and France. Commentators blamed the increasingly aggressive selling of silk fabrics and garments at low prices by the Chinese. However, the importation of Chinese silk fabrics was not as buoyant as this explanation would suggest. In dollar terms, prices of raw silk edged upward, and there was little price resistance. Increasing criticism of quality might be explained partly by the greater demands modern weaving and throwing machinery placed on the fibre, which prefers gentle handling.

Reversing the trend of previous years, there was increased demand for spun silk. Insufficient quantities were available from China. Following the spring 1987 Canton fair, stocks of tops and noils became scarce, largely because of Japanese demand. There was evidence of the increasing strength of the protectionist lobby in the U.S., aimed principally at the Far East. Mixed fabrics of Chinese origin were placed in the same quota as ramie and linen, which was already full, causing a de facto embargo on imports. The Japanese government allowed the support price for raw silk to decline to 9,800 yen per kilogram in March 1987 from 12,000 yen a year earlier. This had the beneficial effect of reducing both stockpiles and production.

China remained the world's largest silk producer and dominated international trade in the fabric. World production of raw silk in 1985 totaled 56,727 metric tons, 32,000 tons of which were produced by China. (ANTHONY H. GADDUM)

**Man-Made Fibres.** The measures undertaken to correct overcapacity in the man-made fibre industry were almost completed in 1987, though Japanese makers were still experiencing poor financial results. In many countries, particularly the U.K., there was a tendency for polypropylene fibre capacity to be increased rather dramatically. Polypropylene was a cheaper alternative to nylon, and in the carpet trade a 50:50 blend of polypropylene and wool offered strong competition to the more usual 80:20 wool and nylon blend, although the resilience of polypropylene was inferior to that of nylon and its appearance deteriorated more quickly. For carpets and domestic furnishings such as upholstery, a new type of dirt-resistant nylon was being supplied by fibre producers in Western Europe, the U.S., and Japan.

The rapid growth of industrial or technical textiles, often based on polypropylene, continued, and a new British plant for making spunbonded materials was due to come on stream. The fabric produced by this process had many potential applications; *e.g.,* in carpet backing, roofing felts, and geotextiles (soil and road reinforcement). The manufacture of unknitted nonwovens expanded rapidly. The most recent development, which originated in the U.S. and was in commercial production in Scotland, became known as a powder-bonded nonwoven. The process produced a strong, stable, but soft-handling material. Likely uses were in medical and hygienic textiles, interlining for garments, and possibly soft toys and as a backing or support material for automobile upholstery. Thermoformability was a major feature of such fabrics.

(PETER LENNOX-KERR)

## TOBACCO

During 1987 world cigarette production topped five trillion for the first time and was continuing to rise. The increasing consumption in less developed and centrally planned economy countries, particularly China, more than compensated for stagnant or falling sales in such mature markets as North America, the EC, and Japan. Prices paid to growers for the near-record 6.5 billion kg (14.3 billion lb) of tobacco harvested in 1987 did not increase significantly, but prices for most finished products rose strongly as governments increased their tax take. Nothing suggested that cigars and other forms of tobacco were challenging cigarettes as the most favoured form of smoking, despite the fact that pipes and cigars had been largely ignored in the health debate.

Antitobacco campaigns in advanced countries were as much concerned with the prohibition of smoking in public places as with saving the smokers from themselves. (*See* HEALTH AND DISEASE: *Sidebar.*) The doctrine that "passive smoking" was harmful to health was being widely accepted, as was the need to improve the quality of the environment generally. The tobacco industry in mature markets was concerned that, as smoking populations declined, the smokers who remained included high proportions of younger women and the less affluent, markets it would not want to stimulate on ethical grounds.

Governments of less developed countries were slow to match the antitobacco campaigns of the West because of the high economic and social importance of the industry to them. An international study estimated that nearly 32 million people were employed full- or part-time in growing the crop; another 6.6 million were involved in tobacco manufacture, and a further 21.6 million in distribution and the provision of materials, equipment, and services to the industry. Tobacco also provided massive financial support for governments, with global tobacco-generated tax revenue in 1983 exceeding $75 billion—more than the national budgets of China, Canada, or Australia in that year. The study also showed that in the 60 major tobacco-growing countries, the crop was land-efficient, creating about 1% of the value of agricultural output on only 0.3% of the arable land.

(MICHAEL F. BARFORD)

Soviet tourists bargain with a vendor in a streetside shop in Hanoi. Vietnam was promoting tourism in hopes that the additional revenue would bolster its lagging economy.
AP/WIDE WORLD

## TOURISM

World tourism in 1987 recovered well from the setbacks experienced in 1986. Global international arrivals grew from 336.5 million to 355 million, an increase of 4%. Receipts, boosted by the weakening of the U.S. dollar, advanced by 16.1% from $128 billion to $150 billion. During 1986 global international arrivals had advanced by only 2.4%, although receipts had risen sharply—by 18.2%—in U.S. dollar terms. Anxiety about the consequences of the Chernobyl nuclear accident and fear of terrorism had undermined progress in what was otherwise a year of good economic growth. As a result, worldwide hotel occupancy rates were estimated to have fallen by 2.6 percentage points to 64.5% in 1986. Although average daily room rates jumped by 25% to $56.72, net income before taxes per available room declined 25% to $1,626 in the same year.

A prominent feature of world tourism during 1987 was the recovery in travel from North America to Europe and the Mediterranean basin. Although full-year figures for 1987 were not available, preliminary figures based on the first six to nine months were indicative. The number of arrivals grew in Austria (47%), Portugal (28%), Switzerland (18%), the U.K. (15%), Spain (14%), and West Germany (11%). In France, where U.S. nationals were still subject to a visa requirement, growth was more moderate at 1% (U.S. overnights), and there were 6% fewer U.S. travelers in Italy.

West German expenditure on international travel exceeded $20.6 billion in 1986, surpassing U.S. expenditure, which amounted to $17.8 billion. In 1987 West Germans purchased an all-time record number of 15 million inclusive tours. Top earners of international tourist receipts in 1986 were the U.S. with $12.9 billion and Spain with $12.1 billion, well ahead of Italy in third place at $9.9 billion. Arrivals in Europe from all countries during 1987 marked up the moderate gains character-

istic of a mature market: 13% in the U.K., 6% in Italy, 4% in Austria, West Germany, and Portugal, 2–3% in Spain and Switzerland, and 1% in France.

Destinations in Asia proved much more popular in 1987. This reinforced the trend, visible during most of the 1980s, for travel in Asia to expand faster than in other regions. Arrivals from all countries grew by 24% in India and Thailand (where many special ceremonies marked the Thai king's 60th birthday), 22% in Hong Kong, 16% in China, 15% in Singapore, 10% in the Philippines, and 2–3% in Japan. U.S. ar-

| Table XI. Major Tourism Spenders and Earners in 1986 | |
|---|---|
| Major spenders | Expenditure |
| West Germany | $20,663,000,000 |
| United States | 17,789,000,000 |
| United Kingdom | 8,686,000,000 |
| Japan | 7,229,000,000 |
| France | 6,504,000,000 |
| Netherlands, The | 4,427,000,000 |
| Canada | 4,294,000,000 |
| Switzerland | 3,368,000,000 |
| Austria | 3,257,000,000 |
| Belgium | 2,889,000,000 |
| Sweden | 2,811,000,000 |
| Italy | 2,758,000,000 |
| Mexico | 2,132,000,000 |
| Denmark | 2,119,000,000 |
| Spain | 1,513,000,000 |
| Brazil | 1,464,000,000 |
| Singapore | 652,000,000 |
| Major earners | Receipts |
| United States | $12,927,000,000 |
| Spain | 12,058,000,000 |
| Italy | 9,855,000,000 |
| France | 9,704,000,000 |
| United Kingdom | 7,921,000,000 |
| West Germany | 7,826,000,000 |
| Austria | 6,076,000,000 |
| Switzerland | 4,227,000,000 |
| Canada | 3,860,000,000 |
| Mexico | 2,984,000,000 |
| Belgium | 2,271,000,000 |
| Hong Kong | 2,211,000,000 |
| Netherlands, The | 1,900,000,000 |
| Singapore | 1,842,000,000 |
| Greece | 1,834,000,000 |
| Denmark | 1,759,000,000 |
| Portugal | 1,574,000,000 |
| South Korea | 1,550,000,000 |

Source: World Tourism Organization, 1987.

rivals in most Asian destinations also grew strongly; the exception was Japan, where they declined by 1% as the strength of the yen against the U.S. dollar proved a major deterrent. To reduce its soaring current account surplus, the Japanese government launched its "Ten Million Program," which aimed at doubling overseas travel by the Japanese in five years.

Although worldwide airline passenger traffic had grown by nearly 5% in 1986, with 938 million passengers carried on international and domestic routes of International Civil Aviation Organization (ICAO) member states, passenger traffic on the key North Atlantic route slumped 9% to 21 million, and the load factor declined from 69.1 to 63.6%. Thus there was considerable apprehension about prospects for 1987. In the event, however, tourism from Western Europe revived, helped by the weakening of the U.S. dollar against European currencies. In the U.S. arrivals from Western Europe rose by 27%, while in the Caribbean they soared 36%. A 23% increase in traffic from Asia made an important contribution to the 15% increase in arrivals in the U.S. from all countries. In the Caribbean the corresponding figure was 12%. Visitors to Canada from Europe and Japan increased by 25%, but the overall total was depressed by a drop in arrivals from the U.S.

In North Africa the sharp decline of 1986 was reversed, with increases in both total arrivals and those from the U.S. In Morocco arrivals were up 7% (U.S. arrivals 19%) and in Tunisia, 16% (U.S. 8%). In Africa south of the Sahara, however, only the Côte d'Ivoire reported a rise in U.S. arrivals, by 8%. Arrivals from the U.S. in the Middle East were well above 1986, particularly in Egypt, where they increased by 49%.

World Tourism Day, Sept. 27, 1987, was marked in the 109 member states of the World Tourism Organization (WTO) by events with a tourism and development theme. It underlined the fact that the less developed countries still accounted for only 25% of world tourist receipts while the top ten international earners accounted for 61%. WTO Secretary-General Willibald P. Pahr launched a campaign to eliminate visas "unless they are absolutely necessary for security reasons." A diplomatic conference was planned for 1988–89 to adopt a new, broadly based, international legal instrument on passports, visas, currency, and health formalities. The World Health Organization launched a massive education and information drive to reassure travelers that they need not postpone travel for fear of AIDS (acquired immune deficiency syndrome).          (PETER SHACKLEFORD)

## WOOD PRODUCTS

**Softwood.** Dramatic structural changes in the sawmilling industry in 1987 in both Sweden and Finland raised many questions for the future. In Finland leading banks were forcing reorganization in many forest industry companies in which they held shares. Although cutting capacity was reduced, output was expected to increase by almost 2.8% in 1987, with a consequent rise in exports. In Sweden output was estimated at 12 million cu m (425 million cu ft), with exports topping 8 million cu m (285 million cu ft). Cutbacks in capacity, particularly in the south, were likely to

A power crane lifts a balsam fir designated for shipment to the United States. On Oct. 3, 1987, a trade agreement was reached between the United States and Canada that by 1999 would put an end to tariffs and many other trade restrictions.
KITCHIN—FIRST LIGHT

continue into 1988, but the advantages of shutting down sawmills were being questioned. In both countries, the use of high technology to maximize the utilization of logs was being advocated.

Canadian producers benefited from exchange rate movements that gave them an advantage over Sweden, and their exports of construction-grade softwood rose dramatically. By contrast, mills in southern Sweden geared up to produce carcassing grade softwood and suffered losses in market share, particularly in the U.K. Many stepped up production of more added-value items, such as scaffold boards and graded truss material. Japan and China bought heavily in softwood markets, which allowed prices to move up in the first part of 1987 before stabilizing. Canadian plywood, however, lost considerable market share to the cheaper Southern yellow pine from the U.S., a trend that the mills anticipated would continue. Exporters, therefore, were fully exploiting alternative products such as waferboard and the relative newcomer, oriented strandboard.

There was continued friction between Canada and the U.S. over the softwood market. In January Canada imposed a 15% export duty on sales to the U.S. to placate the U.S., which had threatened to impose a countervailing duty of 15% in October 1986. Twice Canada proved in court that its softwood producers were not subsidized by means of low stumpage charges. Mills in Canada bore the extra duty themselves, but the smaller ones were being squeezed out of business. The forestry industry was fighting further conversion of the export tax into higher provincial stumpage fees, which, it was argued, would be more crippling to the industry.

**Plywood.** In the Far East, Indonesian plywood producers dominated the market in 1987, with exports to Japan, China, and the U.S. exceeding three million cu m (106 million cu ft) and further growth expected in 1988. European buyers were risking future shortfalls in supplies from Indonesia unless they committed themselves to bulk

purchases. Prices were extremely firm, and in September Malaysia followed Indonesia's lead on price and volume controls. New "list" values were set in midyear, but too late to prevent severe overbuying in the U.K., where a glut of plywood and a slump in prices persisted into the summer. Restricted export volumes, however, produced shortages by October.

**Hardwood.** Conservation and the diminishing tropical rain forests became a key international issue in 1987. The International Tropical Timber Organization opened its headquarters in Yokohama, Japan. Its ambitious plans included the introduction of sustained-yield and conservation policies in tropical hardwood-producing countries. The erosion of rain forests and their wildlife and vegetation caught the public imagination. Throughout the year there was extensive radio and television coverage of the debate on who was to blame and how the forests could be saved.

Supply problems in the Far East, Africa, and Brazil led to increased demand for temperate hardwoods, and U.S. producers enjoyed boom conditions. Demand for timber products in the U.S. was lively, allowing producing mills to maintain firm prices at home and for export.

(JEAN CLARK CAMERON KLOOS)

*See also* Agriculture and Food Supplies; Consumer Affairs; Economic Affairs; Energy; Information Processing and Information Systems; Labour-Management Relations; Mining; Photography; Television and Radio; Transportation.

This article updates the *Macropædia* articles BEVERAGE PRODUCTION; ELECTRONICS; ENERGY CONVERSION; FORESTRY AND WOOD PRODUCTION; FURS, LEATHERS, AND HIDES; INDUSTRIAL GLASS AND CERAMICS; Chemical Process INDUSTRIES; Extraction and Processing INDUSTRIES; Manufacturing INDUSTRIES; Textile INDUSTRIES; INSURANCE; MARKETING AND MERCHANDISING; PRINTING, TYPOGRAPHY, AND PHOTOENGRAVING; TELECOMMUNICATIONS SYSTEMS; TOOLS.

# Information Processing and Information Systems

Reflecting its maturity, the U.S. computer industry in 1987 emphasized hardware connectivity, wrangled over intellectual property and foreign trade, and continued the wave of mergers that began during the industry's 1986 doldrums. Those doldrums, however, appeared to be over. The industry posted a 10% increase in revenue in the first half of fiscal 1987 compared with the same period a year earlier. That figure would have reached almost 14% if the subpar earnings of IBM Corp. for the first half of 1987 had been excluded. IBM's first-half earnings of $1,963,000,000 represented a 15.5% decline from the company's first-half performance in 1986.

In 1987 IBM laid the groundwork for its hoped-for recovery by unveiling a new series of mainframes and a new line of personal computers. The new 3090E mainframe family was about 15% faster than the earlier 3090 series and included a model that had six central processors, IBM's most powerful mainframe yet. The new personal computers, the PS/2 series, provided the best colour resolution ever available from an IBM PC and used high-capacity 3½-in (9-cm) diskette drives, although most PC software was still on 5¼-in (13-cm) diskettes. The PS/2s spanned the performance and price range from the $1,350 Model 25, designed for educational and home use, to the Model 80, priced from $6,995 to $10,995 and built around the Intel Corp. 80386 central processing unit (CPU), a chip that would power most personal computers in the 1990s.

All PS/2 models except the 25 and 30 also had the IBM Micro Channel Architecture (MCA), which eliminated the time-consuming setting of switches when the user installed expansion boards. Because the MCA's data path (set of electrical conductors that carry data from one part of the PC to another) was much wider than that of the earlier IBM PC AT, PS/2s with MCA would be able to communicate faster with each other and with mainframe computers. Because IBM had applied for patents on some MCA technology, MCA represented a way that the company could combat the PC and PC AT clones manufactured by other firms, which had been cutting into its sales. In December IBM and the General Electric Co. signed an agreement under which GE would develop and manufacture chips for use in new IBM products.

The leading independent PC software company, Lotus Development Corp. of Cambridge, Mass., also acted in 1987 against competitors it said were selling clones of one of its products, the popular 1-2-3 spreadsheet program. Early in the year Lotus sued Paperback Software International Ltd., the Berkeley, Calif., publisher of the VP-Planner spreadsheet, and Mosaic Software, the Cambridge vendor of a spreadsheet called The Twin. The suits charged the two vendors with pirating the user interface and commands of 1-2-3. In the PC software industry, where program developers often incorporated the commands and appearance of earlier programs into their own software, an uproar resulted. Before the end of the year, a company claiming to represent those who developed the original spreadsheet for personal computers, VisiCalc, had sued Lotus for allegedly stealing VisiCalc's "look and feel." Ironically, when Micropro International Corp. of San Rafael, Calif., introduced in 1987 the long-awaited new version of its popular Wordstar word processor, the program it issued had been a competitor's clone of the Wordstar. Rather than sue the competitor, Micropro had purchased it.

One major software story of 1987 concerned a product that would not be available until early in 1988, the new PC operating system. Called OS/2, it could address up to 16 megabytes of computer memory—almost 25 times the amount addressable with DOS, the current operating system. And it could run nearly all DOS software, though about 10% less quickly.

The new operating system, developed by IBM and Microsoft, of Redmond, Wash., would run on both IBM and competitors' hardware if that hardware used an Intel 80286 or 80386 CPU chip. Eventually, the operating system would gain built-in ability to run on a network, reflecting the connectivity trend in the PC sector.

The new PC operating system, as well as the DOS, would both run on the Apple Computer Inc. Macintosh, thanks to Apple's 1987 introduction of Macintosh models that accepted PC expansion boards. Though potential corporate customers had criticized the Macintosh for its lack of PC compatibility, by 1987 enough Macintosh software was available to make the machine a big success in offices—even without PC compatibility.

For Macintosh users the big news of 1987 was Apple's Multifinder program, which ran as part of the machine's operating system to let the user quickly switch between several applications programs, such as a word processor and a spreadsheet. Apple also introduced a program called Hypercard, which could be used to create Macintosh software that blended images, sound, and text. For example, an entry on U.S. Pres. John F. Kennedy in a computerized encyclopaedia created with Hypercard could display a written biography, a film clip (from an attached laser disc player), and a recording of a speech. Like a stack of index cards, a Hypercard program could also refer users from one entry to several related topics.

In sum, PC hardware and software in 1987 gained more power and usefulness. One Macintosh model introduced by Apple in 1987 used the 32-bit Motorola 68020 CPU, a processor chip more typically found in high-priced Computer Aided Design workstations. IBM's announcement of machines using the 80386 CPU and OS/2 operating system, meanwhile, heralded an era of personal computers that could perform on the level of minicomputers.

The PC developments were not good news to the minicomputer industry, a business already hard hit by declining computer hardware prices. Early in 1987 gloomy financial reports for the close of fiscal year 1986 began to arrive from minicomputer makers. Wang Laboratories Inc., of Lowell, Mass., reported a $78.6 million loss for fiscal 1986 and responded with the elimination of 1,000 jobs worldwide. Unisys, the Detroit company born out of the merger of Sperry Corp. and Burroughs Corp., suffered a net loss in 1986 of $43.4 million. Honeywell Inc. of Minneapolis, Minn., announced a net loss of $492 million, one of the largest losses ever reported in one fiscal year by a U.S. computer vendor.

Before the end of 1987, however, Wang rebounded to profitability, reporting second-quarter revenue of $824 million (its most profitable quarter in 2½ years). Control Data Corp. of Minneapolis also reported its first quarterly net profit, $7.2 million, after eight quarters in the red. Honeywell, however, merged its computer business into a joint venture with Group Bull of France and Japan's NEC Corp., in which it would hold 42% ownership.

As 1987 progressed, other mergers followed. In an effort to unseat Ashton-Tate as the leader in data base software for personal computers, Borland International of Belmont, Calif., purchased Ansa Software, maker of the Paradox data base, in a stock swap valued at $38 million. And, in one of the largest software industry mergers, Computer Associates of Garden City, N.Y., purchased Uccel, a systems software vendor in Dallas, Texas, for a reported $800 million.

While the computer industry was consolidating to improve its competitive stance, it also won from the U.S. government a 100% tariff on personal computers made by its Japanese competitors. Hardest hit by the tariff was Toshiba, which in 1987 had 20% of the U.S. market for laptop portable computers, and Epson, which had an estimated 5% of the market for PC-compatible desktop computers. Toshiba stopped exporting its most popular laptop model to the U.S., and other Japanese vendors raised prices on their personal computers while laying plans to open manufacturing plants in the U.S.

As the year moved to a close, the U.S. computer industry's concern remained focused on how to meet the challenge from foreign competition. The trend toward improved bottom-line performance continued, however, indicating that the industry's worst downturn in years had ended.                                                    (EDWARD S. WARNER)

The American Arbitration Association (AAA), a nongovernmental negotiating organization based in New York City, announced a decision on Sept. 15, 1987, that resolved a bitter copyright dispute between IBM Corp. and Fujitsu Ltd. concerning Fujitsu's use of IBM computer software. Fujitsu, the largest computer firm in Japan, made big mainframe computers capable of running the same programs as IBM's mainframes, and IBM charged that Fujitsu had stolen technology used in IBM's MVS mainframe operating system. The AAA decision called for a transition period of between five and ten years during which Fujitsu would have access to IBM programming information through a tightly controlled procedure designed to protect IBM's rights to "intellectual property." The decision also required adequate compensation to be paid to IBM for such access, the amount to be determined during 1988 by the arbitrators.

According to the announcement released by the arbitrators, the order would provide Fujitsu a reasonable opportunity to obtain the information necessary for the company to develop and maintain IBM-compatible operating systems. In addition, the settlement would allow Fujitsu and its customers to use existing Fujitsu operating system software without interruption.

Although the influence that the AAA settlement would have on the business of both firms had yet to be determined, many industry analysts pointed out that computer software copyrights would be given a great deal of consideration when Japanese computer firms developed new computer programs. It seemed that the ideal solution for computer users would be software products that could be used on many computers. As a step toward that goal, the world computer industry was looking forward to the introduction of an Open System Interconnection standard that would permit the connection of noncompatible computers to one another.                                          (TAKUZO NIWA)

This article updates the *Macropædia* article INFORMATION PROCESSING AND INFORMATION SYSTEMS.

# Labour-Management Relations

The climate of industrial relations in 1987 showed little change from 1986. Economic growth was generally modest, and unemployment remained high in most industrialized countries as traditional industries continued to be run down. Many of the new jobs were part-time or temporary and largely in the service sector.

**United Kingdom.** The Employment Bill published in October envisaged, among other things: removing the right of trade unions to discipline members who cross picket lines; appointment of a commissioner for the rights of trade union members; removal of legal immunity in industrial action where a closed shop is at issue; requirement that trade union members be able to get an injunction to prevent industrial action being called without a vote; requirement that strike votes should apply to each place of work; and provisions concerning postal voting in elections for all members of union governing bodies and in ballots on the use of union funds for political purposes.

A continuing decline in membership and a third successive Conservative victory in the general election combined to make the annual Trades Union Congress a subdued affair. The divisive issue posed by the electricians' union's willingness to enter into single-union, no-strike agreements was sidestepped by its referral to a review body.

A dispute arose over a new disciplinary code introduced by British Coal, especially a clause giving an employer the right to discipline a worker for an offense of which he had been cleared by a court of law. National Union of Mineworkers members voted by a substantial majority for industrial action, and a ban on overtime was imposed. The long-standing dispute in the schools in England and Wales erupted again in connection with the Teachers' Pay and Conditions Act, which received the royal assent in February. The act abolished the old-established "Burnham" collective bargaining machinery and empowered the secretary of state for education to fix the terms of teachers' employment, after consultation with the teachers' unions and local authorities. Substantial pay increases were given, and though these were not enough to satisfy the unions, the centre of the dispute passed to the unions' desire to reestablish collective bargaining for their members.

**United States.** With the Democrats in control of both houses of Congress, it was possible that trade union influence would increase. In the collective bargaining arena, however, gains were frequently won only after concessions by the unions. In the February settlement of a six-month strike at USX, the United Steelworkers of America gained improved health and profit-sharing benefits, retraining funds, and restrictions on contracting work out but accepted wage reductions and large job losses in a new four-year contract.

With both the General Motors (GM) and Ford contracts expiring in September, the United Automobile Workers first tackled Ford, whose financial position was much healthier than that of GM. In a three-year contract that was conditional on reasonable sales, Ford agreed there would be no layoffs of hourly paid workers; at least one of every two workers leaving would be replaced; and workers would not be relocated without union agreement. The cost of surplus workers could not exceed $500 million over the three years. Pay increases were modest, and the union agreed to ease traditional rules and restrictive job classifications. To the surprise of many, a similar three-year contract was signed with GM, though previously announced plant closings were to go ahead.

In October the AFL-CIO executive council voted unanimously to readmit the International Brotherhood of Teamsters, America's biggest union, 30 years after its expulsion.

**Australia and New Zealand.** In Australia the pact between government and the trade unions continued, though toward the end of 1986 a measure of flexibility in national wage adjustment had to be introduced. The 1983 pay and prices accord had yielded wage moderation and social benefits and helped to create 600,000 new jobs. In March 1987 the Australian Conciliation and Arbitration Commission handed down a decision granting a national wage increase of $A 10 a week. Bargaining at enterprise level on an additional productivity-based wage increase up to a general maximum of 4% was allowed. The commission announced new principles based on efficiency and the reduction of restrictive practices.

The Australian Council of Trade Unions continued a searching examination of trade union structure and policies, resulting in a statement entitled "Future Strategies for the Trade Union Movement." On the basis of a visit by senior officials to five European countries, it reviewed a more general report, "Australia Reconstructed." In New Zealand the Labour Relations Act went on the statute book before the general elections. It was heavily criticized by the employers—and to a lesser extent by trade unions. The government's objectives included ensuring that all unions had a minimum membership of 1,000 and encouraging better industrial relations within firms.

**Continental Western Europe.** In early 1987 France was in the grip of major strikes in public services, notably the railways, Paris urban transport, and electricity supply. There was also a seamen's strike. However, the strikes petered out fairly quickly, and only modest concessions were made. Some later "days of action" on various themes received little support, but a series of strikes by air traffic controllers over 15 weeks caused some disruption. The government's displeasure with public-sector strikes resulted in new legislation. Since 1982 public-sector strikers had forfeited pay only for actual strike time. It was proposed that in the future they receive no pay for days on which they stopped work, however short the stoppage. The Constitutional Council, however, considered the measure to be an unjustified infringement of the right to strike, and it was imposed only on the civil service and administrative establishments.

A legislative measure of December 1986 on flexible working hours was declared unconstitutional by the Constitutional Council on January 23, forcing the government to put its proposals forward in a bill; this was duly enacted and became law in June. The new law differed little from the December measure, except that a provision easing restrictions on night work for women was narrowed considerably. A January 1987 agreement in the French metalworking industry required that the (statutory) works committee and health and safety committee be given information and consulted about proposed technological changes before any decision by the employer was put into effect. If a large number of workers were affected, the employer was required to draw up an adjustment plan, which should be discussed with the works committee.

In West Germany there was a renewed attempt by the large metalworkers' union, IG Metall, to achieve its goal of a 35-hour week. There were warning strikes, but a major conflict was avoided. Agreement was reached on April 22 for a reduction of the existing 38.5 hours to 37.5 on April 1, 1988, and to 37 hours on April 1, 1989, accompanied by wage increases of 3.7, 2, and 2.5%, respectively. Similar provisions were agreed to in the printing industry in May.

In Spain at the beginning of the year, elections for plant committees showed the socialist General Union of Workers (UGT) in the lead, but the Communist Workers' Commissions gained considerably improved representation, particularly in large companies. Early negotiations toward a new central agreement broke down, and strikes for wage increases and against layoffs were so substantial, notably around April, that the government considered legal limitations on the right to strike. In October Nicolás Redondo, the influential leader of the UGT, and a colleague resigned their parliamentary seats.

In The Netherlands the most notable strike occurred in Rotterdam and centred on the employers' restructuring plan for general cargo handling, which would necessitate substantial job losses. The subsequent agreement envisaged gradual reduction of the number of dock workers, with incentives for early retirement. There was tension over labour costs in Sweden, and wage drift was a continuing problem. However, the unions decided not to seek reopening of the central collective agreement and, to keep pressures down, on January 30 the finance minister announced a price freeze. The government warned that it would set cash limits on public-sector wage increases and set up a commission to examine the right to strike.

In 1937 the Swiss metal union and the metal employers' federation had agreed to give up the weapons of strike and lockout and to resolve their differences by negotiation and arbitration. The deal spread to other industries. This "Peace at Work" treaty had been reconfirmed at intervals by the parties, and in 1987 the Swiss celebrated its 50th anniversary. In 1986 Switzerland lost 72 working days through strikes.

**Asia.** In Japan labour issues were overshadowed by the problems caused to industry by the appreciation of the yen. On September 20 the Diet approved revisions of the Labour Standards Law calling for phased reductions in working hours. On November 20 a private-sector trade

South African mine workers rally outside the building where negotiations took place between the mine owners' federation and the National Union of Mineworkers. After a three-week strike, the miners were granted upgraded holiday and death benefits, but their pay was not increased.

union was inaugurated that united more than five million workers previously distributed over several trade union federations. South Korea's reputation for industrious workers, low labour costs, and powerless trade unions changed dramatically in 1987. Between July and September, following political disturbances, some 3,200 companies were affected by strikes and claims for higher wages, shorter hours, and stronger trade unions. Many of the strikes were settled quickly—usually with substantial concessions by the employers—but some proved obdurate, notably in the giant industrial groups of Hyundai and Daewoo.

**Africa.** In August the South African gold and coal mines experienced a major strike. Though pay was at the centre of the dispute, the National Union of Mineworkers, led by general secretary Cyril Ramaphosa (*see* BIOGRAPHIES), also sought improvements relating to holidays, safety and health, danger money and death benefits, and replacement of single-sex hostels for workers. More than 40% of the 530,000 black miners took action. After three weeks miners drifted back to work, and the strike was called off. The pay offer was not increased, but the union got improved death and holiday benefits—and proved it had negotiating muscle.                                              (R. O. CLARKE)

The views expressed in this article are the author's and should not be attributed to any organization with which he may be connected.

*See also* Economic Affairs: *World Economy;* Industrial Review.
This article updates the *Macropædia* article WORK AND EMPLOYMENT.

# Law

**Court Decisions.** In 1987 the various judicial tribunals throughout the world decided a number of important cases, most of which involved biologic matters, business, civil rights, criminal law, and women's rights.

*Biology. Matter of Baby M,* handed down by the Supreme Court of New Jersey, attracted international attention among the general population and in legal circles. The case involved the validity of a contract between the biologic father of a child conceived by artificial insemination and his wife on the one side, and the surrogate mother of the child on the other. The alleged contract provided that the surrogate mother should bear the child for a fee and then deliver it to the father and his wife. The surrogate mother, Mary Beth Whitehead (*see* BIOGRAPHIES), bore the child but refused to turn it over, arguing that the contract in question was invalid because it was contrary to public policy. The court recognized the validity of the contract but treated as a separate question the matter of the custody of the child. Using the best interest of the child as its criterion, the court held that custody should be awarded to the biologic father and his wife, with the surrogate mother being allowed visitation rights of two hours per week. Legal scholars in the civil-law countries of the world (*i.e.,* Western Europe, except England, and South and Central America) mainly took the position that, in their respective countries, the contract would be held invalid and the surrogate mother would be entitled to keep the child as a result. Scholars in the common-law countries (roughly the English-speaking world), on the other hand, tended to support the decision.

In the case *In Re B,* the House of Lords, Britain's highest court, upheld a lower court decision authorizing sterilization of a mentally retarded ward of the court. In the decision the court made clear that it was ordering the sterilization not for eugenic or therapeutic reasons but solely for the welfare of the ward. It apparently feared that a pregnancy would injure the ward, and it was satisfied that contraceptive methods were impractical under the circumstances.

In a somewhat related development, the U.S. Supreme Court held in *FEC* v. *Massachusetts Citizens for Life* that a nonprofit, nonstock corporation formed to promote "prolife" (antiabortion) causes could use its treasury funds to support various candidates for public office. The Federal Election Campaign Act prohibits corporations from using treasury funds in connection with any election to public office. Some members of the court found this statute inapplicable to the kind of corporation involved in the case, but a majority said the statute applied but was unconstitutional as a violation of the First Amendment to the Constitution, guaranteeing free speech.

*Business.* In *Asahi Metal Industry Co.* v. *Superior Court,* the U.S. Supreme Court severely limited the jurisdiction that a state court could exercise over a foreign company. Involved was a Japanese company that manufactured valve assemblies in Japan that were sold to a Taiwanese company. The Taiwanese company incorporated these valves into finished tires that were sold throughout the world, including the U.S. The driver of a motorcycle was injured in California, allegedly because of a defective tire manufactured by the Taiwanese seller. The injured party sued the seller in a California court, and the seller filed a cross-complaint seeking indemnification from the Japanese valve manufacturer, contending that it was a defect in the valve that caused the accident. The Japanese company replied that it was not amenable to a lawsuit in California under the circumstances of this case. The Supreme Court of California disagreed and held that its courts had jurisdiction over the Japanese company. On appeal, the U.S. Supreme Court reversed this decision, stating that the decision of the California courts to exercise jurisdiction in the present case violated the due process clause of the U.S. Constitution. It pointed out that the strictures of the due process clause forbid a state court from exercising personal jurisdiction over a nonresident under circumstances that would "offend traditional notions of fair play and substantial justice." Here the contacts between the Japanese company and the state were not sufficiently substantial to allow the latter to assume jurisdiction over controversies involving the former.

In *EC Commission* v. *Germany,* the European Court of Justice held that the Reinheitsgebot of 1516, under which all beer sold in Germany had to comply with certain "purity" standards, was contrary to Article 30 of the Treaty of Rome (establishing the European Economic Community), which prevents barriers to trade. The case arose upon the complaint of a French brewer, which contended that its beer was systematically excluded from Germany because it contained additives prohibited by the Reinheitsgebot. The German government argued that purity of beer is of supreme importance in Germany, since beer forms 26.7% of the average German man's daily nutrition. The court, however, said that the unqualified prohibition of all beers containing any additives was not consistent with the health risks involved and seemed, rather, to be motivated by economic concerns.

*Civil Rights.* Three major cases in this area were decided by the U.S. Supreme Court during the year. In *Edwards* v. *Aguillard* the court invalidated a Louisiana statute that required its public schools to give "balanced treatment" to "creation science" and "evolution science." The court found the statute to advance religious doctrine in violation of the First Amendment.

*School Board of Nassau County* v. *Arline* held that a person suffering from a contagious disease was "handicapped" for purposes of the federal Rehabilitation Act, which prohibits discrimination against an "otherwise qualified handicapped person." The case involved an elementary school teacher who had contracted and recovered from tuberculosis. She was discharged by a local school board because it found that she had a susceptibility to the disease that exposed her students to an unnecessary risk. The court remanded the case for a determination of whether the teacher's condition posed a serious risk to her students. If it did, she could be discharged in spite of her handicap because she would not be "otherwise qualified." In determining this matter, the trial court was directed to make a finding of fact based on medical judgments about (1) the nature of the risk (how the disease is transmitted); (2) the duration of the risk (how long is the carrier infectious); (3) the severity of the risk (what is the potential harm to third persons); and (4) the probabilities that the disease will be transmitted and will cause varying degrees of harm. Although the case involved tuberculosis, the language of the decision seemed to legal scholars to be aimed principally at discrimination against victims of AIDS (acquired immune deficiency syndrome), and it was widely hailed in the gay community.

In *Immigration and Naturalization Service* v. *Cardoza-Fonseca,* the Supreme Court held that an alien is not required to prove "clear probability" of persecution on return to his or her home country in order to be eligible for consideration for asylum. In this case a Nicaraguan citizen sought asylum because she feared persecution if she returned to her home country. She testified that her brother, with whom she fled Nicaragua, had been tortured there and imprisoned because of his opposition to the Sandinista government, and she feared the same fate because of her opposition to that government and her association with her brother. An immigration judge found that she was not entitled to relief because she had not established a "clear probability of persecution." The Supreme Court held that this standard was incorrect; all she needed to prove was a "well-founded fear" of persecution, a standard that is more generous than the "clear probability" test.

William and Elizabeth Stern are clearly pleased after the Supreme Court of New Jersey awarded them custody of "Baby M." Mary Beth Whitehead had agreed to bear Stern's child but, despite that contract, refused to give her up.

*Criminal Law.* In *Booth* v. *Maryland* the Supreme Court invalidated as a violation of the Eighth Amendment to the Constitution a Maryland statute that allowed a jury in deliberating whether to impose a death sentence to consider a "victim impact statement" describing the personal characteristics of the victims and the emotional impact of the crime on the family. The court said this statute required the jury to consider information irrelevant to a capital sentence and created the risk that it might act arbitrarily.

The European Court of Human Rights, in *Monnel and Morris* v. *UK,* sustained the power of the English courts to order that time spent in prison by an offender pending the determination of a frivolous appeal should not count toward the sentence of imprisonment. The court said that this English practice did not violate Article 6 of the European Convention on Human Rights.

In *United States* v. *Salerno,* the Supreme Court validated a provision of the federal Bail Reform Act of 1984 that allows pretrial detention without bail on the ground of dangerousness. The case involved two individuals, alleged by the government to be a "boss" and a "captain," respectively, in an organized crime "family," who were charged with conspiracy to commit murder and numerous racketeering activities. They were denied bail on the ground of "dangerousness," specifically, that "no condition or combination of conditions of release would ensure the safety of the community." This denial was based on standards stated in the Bail Reform Act of 1984. The court sustained these standards against the charge that they violated the Eighth Amendment to the Constitution and the due process clause.

The Eighth Amendment also was interpreted favourably to the government in two other cases handed down by the Supreme Court. In *Tison* v. *Arizona* the court sustained against constitutional attack the felony-murder–death-penalty doctrine. This doctrine provides that a person who has not killed or intended to kill a victim, but who has had a major involvement in the felony that resulted in the victim's death and who has shown reckless indifference to human life, may be sentenced to death by a jury. In *McCleskey* v. *Kemp* the court ruled that statistics showing that a black man charged with killing a white man is 4.3 times more likely to receive the death sentence in Georgia than a black man charged with killing a black man did not prove that the imposition of the death penalty on a black man convicted of killing a white man is arbitrary or unreasonable.

*Women's Rights.* Three significant cases involving women's rights were handed down by the U.S. Supreme Court. *Board of Directors of Rotary International* v. *Rotary Club of Duarte* involved a constitutional review of a California civil rights statute that, in effect, required an all-male nonprofit Rotary club to admit women to membership. The court sustained the statute and denied the power of Rotary International to suspend the charter of the local Rotary club for obeying the statute. The other two cases involved interpretations of the Civil Rights Act of 1964, which generally prohibits unfair discrimination. It has been contended that special considerations based on sex may violate this act, but the court denied this contention in both cases. In *Johnson* v. *Transportation Agency* the court held that a California county did not violate the Civil Rights Act in giving special consideration based on sex to a woman who was promoted over an equally qualified male employee. *California Federal Savings and Loan Ass'n* v. *Guerra* held that a California statute requiring employers to provide leave and then reinstate pregnant employees did not violate the act.           (WILLIAM D. HAWKLAND)

**International Law.** *Territory.* Territorial mergers were prominent during the year. The most far-reaching was the agreement by the governments of seven Caribbean states (Antigua, Dominica, Grenada, Montserrat, Saint Christopher and Nevis, Saint Lucia, and Saint Vincent and the Grenadines) to unite into one country, though it appeared that implementation might be a long-term process. Their neighbours, the heads of government of the 13 member states of the Caribbean Economic Community, agreed to dismantle all internal barriers to trade by September 1988. The Montevideo Act in May included a declaration on economic integration between Argentina and Uruguay, but this was concerned more with cross-border trade than with true integration. More significant was the outline free trade agreement in October between Canada and the U.S., which would remove all tariffs on trade between the two countries over the next ten years. The definitive treaty would be submitted for ratification in 1988 after final details had been worked out.

The European movement toward integration was greatly stimulated by adoption of the Single European Act by the European Communities (EC). This marked a further step toward a quasi-state structure, in particular by extending majority voting in the legislative process, thereby weakening the national powers of veto. (*See* WORLD AFFAIRS [Western Europe]: *Western European Affairs.*) The act, together with the program for completing the internal market by 1992, increased EC morale and caused the surrounding states to give serious consideration to applying for membership. The arrangements to transfer Hong Kong from the U.K. to China were followed by the signature in April of a treaty to transfer the Portuguese colony of Macau to China in December 1999.

Burkina Faso's boundary with Niger was the subject of a joint border demarcation commission, which began sitting in midyear; its boundary with Mali was the subject of a judgment by the International Court of Justice in December 1986 that confirmed the frontier as it was during the French colonial period. The International Court of Justice also began proceedings in the case between El Salvador and Honduras concerning their land, island, and sea frontier. China and Mongolia signed an agreement on the settlement and reduction of border incidents. However, India's decision in December 1986 to grant full statehood to the union territory of Arunachal Pradesh, northeast of Assam, elicited sharp protests by China, which claimed that it was Chinese territory illegally occupied by India.

*The Sea.* After many years' refusal in principle to depart from the old cannon-shot rule (3 mi), the U.K. at last adopted a 12-mi territorial water limit round its coasts (except the Isle of Man and Channel Islands) and redrew its baselines to incorporate low-tide sandbanks. This caused concern within the EC because it was claimed that parts of the Thames Estuary containing rich fishing grounds now became internal waters and were consequently closed to EC fishing vessels. Since France already had a 12-mi limit and Belgium followed the U.K. lead in October, the Straits of Dover now became entirely territorial waters. Passage through that important waterway would therefore depend on the rights of innocent passage and the rules governing international straits rather than high seas rights. The airspace above the Straits of Dover was also closed off, and all flights into the southern North Sea would henceforth require coastal state permission, although in practice that was no great change. Ireland also announced its intention to adopt a 12-mi limit. Since the new British limit applied to both Scotland and Northern Ireland, the whole of the North Channel out of the Irish Sea now became U.K.

territorial waters, and this had security implications for Ireland. The matter was complicated further by Ireland's constitutional claim to regulate the waters around the whole of the island (including Northern Ireland), and the Irish government made a formal protest. Turkey declared a 200-mi economic zone in the Black Sea.

The sea boundary between India and Burma in the Andaman Sea, the Coco Channel, and the Bay of Bengal was settled by treaty in the form of a single continuous equidistant line. Canada and France agreed to refer to international arbitration the boundary between Newfoundland and the islands of Saint Pierre and Miquelon. The dispute between Sweden and the U.S.S.R. over whether the boundary of their respective economic zones in the Baltic should be calculated from the island of Gotland (as Sweden claimed) or from the Swedish mainland (as the U.S.S.R. claimed) continued under discussion, but the U.S.S.R. would not accept reference to arbitration. The equally long-standing dispute between the U.S.S.R. and Norway over their boundary in the Barents Sea also continued under discussion, with some hope that it was nearing conclusion. A fisheries agreement signed by Uruguay and the U.S.S.R. gave the latter fishing rights in the former's 200-mi economic zone.

An agreement on U.S. tuna fishing in the western Pacific was signed, after two years of negotiation, by the U.S. and 12 Pacific states (Australia, New Zealand, Cook Islands, Micronesia, Fiji, Marshall Islands, Nauru, Papua New Guinea, Solomon Islands, Kiribati, Tuvalu, and Western Samoa). A month later nine U.S. tuna boats were seen poaching in Kiribati waters, and one was boarded and arrested. The EC entered into a fishery-management agreement with the International Council for the Exploration of the Sea in respect of its own (European) waters. The 150-mi interim fishery conservation and management zone round the Falkland Islands declared by the U.K. the previous year was supplemented by detailed quota regulations authorizing 215 vessels (mainly Japanese, Polish, South Korean, Spanish, and Taiwanese) to fish for squid, blue whiting, and hake.

Sightings of foreign submarines in Swedish waters and Norwegian fjords continued unabated. There was a further instance of a submerged submarine snagging a trawler's nets in the Irish Sea when the Northern Irish *Summer Morn* was dragged backward for ten miles before it cut itself free, losing its nets. An attachment from the submarine surfaced during the incident bearing a plate showing unequivocal U.S. origin, and this was later confirmed by the Pentagon. In an exchange in the Irish Parliament, the Irish government indicated that it had no means of monitoring or knowing if foreign (in practice U.K. and U.S.) submarines were illegally entering Irish territorial waters.

Incidents of piracy in Far Eastern waters continued. A court in Thailand sentenced to death (the first such sentence) the skipper of a Thai fishing boat for piratical attacks on Vietnamese boat refugees. Polisario Front guerrillas destroyed a British boat off the Western Sahara coast, but the two people on board escaped unhurt. The International Maritime Organization drafted a convention to deal with terrorist actions at sea. Tension rose in the northern Aegean when a Turkish research ship escorted by two warships carried out oil exploration near three Greek islands, disregarding Greek claims to the appurtenant continental shelf. (*See* WORLD AFFAIRS [Western Europe]: *Greece.*) Following the U.S. mining of Nicaraguan waters, a Norwegian vessel that struck such a mine sued the U.S. for damages. A U.S. District Court dismissed the claim on the grounds that the action raised a nonjusticiable political question not appropriate for judicial resolution (*Chaser Shipping Co.* v. *United States*).

*International Violence.* There was a marked deterioration in the position of neutral shipping in the Persian Gulf as the Iran-Iraq war continued. Frequent air attacks were made by Iraq on neutral vessels in neutral and international waters as well as on targets within enemy waters. Incidents included an erroneous missile strike on the U.S. frigate *Stark,* killing 37 crew. Iran also made air attacks on neutrals. The Iranian Navy received orders to fire missiles at neutral ships plying to Kuwait, an Iraq-leaning neutral, and it sometimes did so after having stopped the ship for contraband inspection in the traditional manner. More dangerous were the increasing attacks by patrol boats and speedboats manned by Revolutionary Guards outside naval control. In addition, Iran laid mines in several neutral shipping lanes.

In response, several countries sent warships to the Gulf to escort their ships to the neutral ports. Kuwait went further and persuaded the U.S. to accept a transfer of shipping registration so that many Kuwaiti tankers could fly the U.S. flag and be escorted by U.S. warships. By the autumn some 70 warships belonging to non-Gulf states were active in the Gulf and its entrance. Most were engaged in passive convoy duty, but the U.S. warships went beyond the role of neutral escort and took on an active police role that included one serious act of reprisal (prolonged attack on an Iranian oil platform in retaliation for an Iranian missile attack three days earlier on a U.S.-flagged Kuwaiti tanker); attacks on, sinking, and capturing of Iranian minelayers and patrol boats; and attacks on unidentified boats that were considered to be making hostile maneuvers. The danger to nonbelligerents and to vital international tanker routes led the UN Security Council, acting under Articles 39 and 40 of the UN Charter, to declare the existence of a breach of the peace and to call on the two belligerents to end the war or face an international arms ban. It was not possible, however, for the Security Council to obtain the agreement of all five permanent members for further positive enforcement measures.

In Lebanon, Israel intercepted a Lebanese military aircraft on a rescue mission off the Lebanese coast 48 km (30 mi) from the Israeli border and forced it to land for interrogation in northern Israel. Israeli warships continued to patrol the seas off Lebanon and to halt and search Lebanese fishing boats in an attempt to prevent Palestinian fighters from infiltrating back into Lebanon. In January two Cypriot ferries were stopped and Palestinian fighters removed. A UN Interim Force in Lebanon (UNIFIL) observation post manned by Norwegian troops in southern Lebanon was forcibly entered by Israeli troops in June. A billet in which Irish soldiers of UNIFIL were sleeping was severely damaged by four bombs placed alongside the building, and an Irish soldier was killed in January by Israeli fire. The French contingent withdrew entirely from UNIFIL at the end of 1986 as a result of similar attacks. South African forces penetrated deep into Angola to attack Namibian guerrillas, killing some Angolan troops as well; they also entered Mozambique, killing three Mozambicans. During a December 1986 raid into Swaziland, two Swazi nationals were killed and six people were kidnapped, including a Swiss couple alleged to be involved with the African National Congress; the two Swiss were released after protests from Switzerland. Defending the Swaziland raid, the South African government said that it would have kidnapped the victims even if they had been living in London.

Such invasions of state sovereignty by government agents became more widespread during the year. In late 1986 Israel abducted from Europe an Israeli nuclear technician, Mordechai Vanunu, to stand trial in Israel for breach of official secrets for an article he had written for the London *Sunday Times;* and in September 1987 the U.S. seized a suspected Lebanese terrorist, Fawaz Younis, in the Mediterranean and flew him to the U.S. to be prosecuted under U.S. law.　　　　　(NEVILLE MARCH HUNNINGS)

*See also* Crime, Law Enforcement, and Penology; World Affairs: *United Nations.*

This article updates the *Macropædia* articles CONSTITUTIONAL LAW; INTERNATIONAL LAW.

# Libraries

Libraries in 1987 continued to have financial difficulties, especially those in less developed countries. There were a number of positive developments, however, including the transmission and adaptation of services and ideas from one country to another. Methods of serving ethnic minorities in France, for example, might be adapted for Tunisia or Thailand. Even within one country, a solution found by the profession to a problem in one area could well be adapted elsewhere. The concern with the disadvantaged, for instance, might involve services to prisons, centres for the retired, and hospitals in one area, ethnic minorities, the housebound, and the mentally handicapped in another. Shortages of public money were common, and voluntary bodies became more active in providing services. The Svita Foundation in Thailand gave help in rural areas, both in supporting libraries and in providing a service for publishing. In The Gambia an office for the oral tradition published transcriptions of local material, which was preserved in the National Library.

Such activities highlighted a major problem facing libraries: how to maintain traditional services and at the same time introduce new services, providing information not only in paper form but also in microform and electronically. Demands on the libraries of government departments, educational institutions, and special libraries as well as public libraries were increasing rapidly, in line with the increased scope of education aimed at meeting the need for lifelong development.

In many countries the introduction of microcomputers into schools—a £9 million program had just been completed in the U.K.—impelled libraries to furnish computer facilities for readers. In England many libraries provided the Prestel viewdata service for their users. In France the development of Minitel circumvented the library service, offering a small microcomputer free to each telephone subscriber, though in practice its use was relatively costly. Because automated information was not cheap, many libraries had to charge for services accessing external data bases. In specialized institutions the problem was not so acute, since the need for up-to-date information in such areas as science, technology, economics, administration, and law was recognized. Library administration became increasingly automated, both for internal record keeping, such as acquisitions cataloging and user records, and for access to external bibliographical and full-text data bases. Some libraries, particularly specialized libraries such as those maintained by business establishments, were beginning to give up journal subscriptions and other hard copy and to rely on electronic data bases entirely.

The development of compact disc-read only memory (CD-ROM) had important implications for libraries. *Library and Information Abstracts* was already available in this form. The automation of information also had legal implications, as evidenced in the transborder data-flow program of the International Federation of Library Associations and the more general preoccupation with laws governing rights to intellectual property. It became increasingly difficult to contain information within national boundaries or to restrict unwanted information from entering. At the same time, there was more scope for networking among libraries, and the European parliamentary libraries, under the auspices of the European Parliament and the Council of Europe, were investigating the possibility of establishing a network to facilitate mutual access.

The wide range of library services being offered created conflicts in library and information science, not least because science and technology were fashionable and technology visibly generated income. Culture, therefore, increasingly took second place, and there was a danger that science would dominate subject matter, to the neglect of humanities. Another danger was that education and information would be fragmented among different kinds of institutions. In a number of countries, including Ethiopia, West Germany, Nigeria, and the U.S., separate departments already existed for library science and information services, and the trend was likely to continue. This posed a threat to libraries unless they were prepared to become more active as information centres rather than book collections. International conferences were highlighting this problem, which was of particular concern to librarians in less developed countries who were trying to coordinate services within limited resources.

(PETER HAVARD-WILLIAMS)

In the U.S. James Hadley Billington (*see* BIOGRAPHIES), formerly director of the Woodrow Wilson International Center for Scholars, Smithsonian Institution, was sworn in September 14 as the 13th librarian of Congress, succeeding Daniel J. Boorstin, who chose to step down after nearly 12 years in office. Neither scholar held a library degree, but the American Library Association did not oppose Billington's appointment, as it had Boorstin's.

An all-out "Save the Books" campaign approached its $10 million goal for the Los Angeles Public Library, victim of two 1986 fires and $20 million in damages; new earthquake damage to a processing facility slowed restoration of central services. The library revealed plans for a $144 million, 52,000-sq m (560,000-sq ft) expanded central library to open in 1991. Another major campaign, for about $15 million, was announced by the Harlem-based Schomburg Center for Research in Black Culture of the New York Public Library. In one of the year's worst library disasters, a $10 million arson fire destroyed the Everett (Wash.) Community College library.

Public library circulation growth leveled off at 1,154,-400,000 for 1986, although operating expenditures jumped 10.7% to some $3 billion. The decline in the value of the dollar caused the price of foreign journals to soar. Innovative services included the nation's first library branch inside a supermarket—a 10,000-volume public library branch in Wichita, Kan.; library-based mediation of community disputes as an alternative to court trials, at three branches of the Carnegie Library of Pittsburgh, Pa.; and, at the University of California at Berkeley General Library, a new staff coordinator for AIDS (acquired immune deficiency syndrome) awareness and information. According to a U.S. Department of Education study, California had the largest percentage of school libraries (68%) operating without certified library staff.

(ARTHUR PLOTNIK)

This article updates the *Macropædia* article LIBRARIES AND LIBRARY SCIENCE.

# Life Sciences

During 1987 the growing ability of science to make fundamental changes in the genetic makeup of living organisms was recognized by the U.S. Patent and Trademark Office, which released a memorandum in April announcing its intention to allow the patenting of animals produced by biotechnological techniques. Although humans were to be excluded as candidates for patent review, the Patent Office would consider all other animals—both new forms created in the laboratory and existing species that had been given new genetic traits. Resistance to the policy came from farm groups, which wanted time to study the possible effects of animal patenting on farm economics and on the gene pool of existing farm animals; from religious leaders, who objected to debasing a "gift from God" into a manufactured product; and from animal rightists, who feared increased animal suffering at the hands of biotechnologists determined to create a patentable organism.

In September plant pathologist Gary A. Strobel of Montana State University (MSU) voluntarily destroyed 14 on-campus outdoor elm trees he had inoculated three months earlier with a genetically altered microorganism. Strobel had received reprimands from the U.S. Environmental Protection Agency (EPA) and MSU for not gaining prior federal approval for the experiment. Although Strobel's organism, a modified bacterium that produces a fungicide against Dutch elm disease while living in elm tree sap, was not considered a danger to the environment, its unauthorized environmental release was widely criticized as irresponsible and prompted concern that other scientists might be conducting similar unapproved field tests with engineered microorganisms. In explaining his actions, Strobel voiced impatience with existing regulational red tape that would have forced him to postpone the experiment a year while waiting up to 90 days for an EPA review.

(CHARLES M. CEGIELSKI)

## ZOOLOGY

Understanding the ways in which animal species interact with and are affected by their environments and other species remained a major focus of zoological research in 1987. The behaviour of some species was examined in detail with the aid of improved chemical techniques and laboratory experiments. Major strides also were made in interpreting fossil records and determining the phylogenetic relationships and distribution patterns of animals. Worldwide habitat loss and the threat of extinction of animal species continued to be of concern to zoologists.

Ecologists were beginning to explore the incorporation of predictions of animal behaviour into general theories of the ways in which animal populations and species interact. H. Ronald Pulliam of the University of Georgia reviewed current theories and behavioral findings to consider not only how the abundance and distribution of resources (such as prey or breeding sites) influence the behaviour of individuals but also how behaviour influences resource availability. Using data from research with white-throated sparrows as well as studies of other animals, he demonstrated the way in which prey species may choose poor foraging habitats that are safe from predators in preference to rich food areas having a high risk of predation. To achieve reproductive success, however, the same prey species may be dependent on other habitats where predator risk is high. Pulliam proposed the development of theoretical models that would predict the distribution patterns of animals on the basis of the distribution of various resources in alternative habitats.

An important message from the review was that ecological theories must rely constantly on field observations and laboratory experiments if they are to maintain the essential ingredient of reality.

Research with spiders and insects served to reinforce how intricate the behaviour of animals, even invertebrates, can be and how species are indeed influenced by their mutual interactions. Monica H. Mather and Bernard D. Roitberg of Simon Fraser University, Burnaby, B.C., demonstrated the way in which snowberry flies avoid being eaten by the common zebra spider, a jumping spider that preys on a variety of insects but does not spin a web. In laboratory experiments the investigators found that when exposed to spiders, the flies elevated their striped wings in a manner that resembled the striped legs of the spiders and thereby often managed to avoid being eaten. When the stripes on the flies were obliterated with ink, the behavioral mimicry was less successful, and the fly more likely became a spider's meal. In the study of another predator-prey relationship, bolas spiders were found to lure certain species of male moths by means of chemicals similar to the female moths' own sex attractants. (See *Entomology,* below.)

Claes Andren and Göran Nilson of the University of Göteborg, Sweden, examined the sensitivity of amphibian larvae to different levels of acidity and aluminum in the water in which the animals lived. Mortality increased in eggs and larvae (tadpoles) of three species of frog exposed to high levels of acidity, and many of the survivors were deformed or behaved abnormally. The researchers also reported that changes in the acidity of the water affected the interaction of predator and prey species in ways that could have major effects on the success or failure of certain pond inhabitants. For example, in situations in which fish were eliminated by high acidity, beetle larvae and salamanders became the primary predators on the frog larvae. Furthermore, in waters of increased acidity, the toxic effects of aluminum rose dramatically. Andren and Nilson observed a variation in the frogs' tolerance to high acidity

A thin-spined porcupine, previously thought to be extinct, clings to a tree branch in a tropical forest in Brazil. Its rediscovery emphasized the need to protect such natural habitats, which serve as a last refuge for endangered species.

and suggested that it might indicate a potential for rapid evolutionary change toward increased acid tolerance. Their findings were directly applicable to understanding the effect of acid rain and industrial pollutants on environments in many parts of the world.

In the field of evolutionary ecology, Benoit Heulin of the Station Biologique de Paimpont, France, and Robert Barbault and Thierry Pilorge of the Laboratoire d'Écologie, Paris, investigated the demography of a common European reptile known as the viviparous lizard. Although usually a live-bearing species, females in some localities had been reported to lay eggs. The investigators documented that the species lays eggs in the Pyrenees and Cantabrian mountains. The average number of eggs—five—was found similar to the number of young produced by the live-bearing form, but at the lowest elevations the lizards appeared to have two clutches per year, rather than the one of the live-bearers. To find such different reproductive strategies, live birth and egg laying, within a single animal species is highly unusual and should lead to exciting future research in the ecology, genetics, biogeography, and evolution of this complex system.

Several possibilities had been offered to explain widespread extinctions of major animal groups observed in the fossil record during the past several hundred million years. Further evidence that impacts of large bodies from space may have been responsible in some instances was provided by Bruce F. Bohor, Peter J. Modreski, and Eugene E. Foord of the U.S. Geological Survey, Denver, Colo., who reported the finding of shocked quartz grains at sites in Europe, New Zealand, and the north-central Pacific Ocean. Such grains displayed streaking indicative of a major physical impact. Their worldwide distribution at the end of the Cretaceous Period, 65 million years ago, was considered sufficient evidence that they represent dust particles that settled to Earth following collision with a large meteorite or comet. The shocked quartz pattern coincides with a concentrated layer of the rare element iridium at the end of the Cretaceous, the original evidence suggesting the impact theory. It was speculated that the collision raised a dust cloud of sufficient magnitude to shade the Earth from sunlight for some undetermined period of time, resulting in the extinction of much of the world's flora and fauna, including the dinosaurs.

Several fossil discoveries added to the understanding of world distribution patterns and relationships of animals. The first finding of a fossil anteater from Pleistocene Epoch sediments (between 700,000 and 1,000,000 years old) in northern Mexico, 3,000 km (1,900 mi) north of the present range of any anteater, was reported by Cristopher A. Shaw of the George C. Page Museum, Los Angeles, and H. Gregory McDonald of the Cincinnati (Ohio) Museum of Natural History. The find supported the idea that the region was a more tropical environment during Pleistocene times, when South American species migrated northward across the Panamanian land bridge. The discovery in Colombia of a fossil belonging to the same genus as the present-day owl monkey shed light on the phylogeny of New World monkeys, which some scientists believed originated from those in Africa but whose evolutionary history in the Americas was unknown. The species, described by Takeshi Setoguchi of Kyoto (Japan) University and Alfred L. Rosenberger of the University of Illinois at Chicago, is from Miocene Epoch deposits more than 12 million years old. Significantly, it was the first example of a modern genus of monkey found in rocks from the Tertiary Period and supported a theory that modern New World monkeys have evolved little since that time. Alan J. Charig and Angela C. Milner of the British Museum of Natural History described a new carnivorous dinosaur from Lower Cretaceous rocks about 115 million years old in England. The species, named *Baryonyx walkeri,* represents a new family of large dinosaurs.

The fossil record provided ample evidence that species become extinct through natural causes, but the rapid disappearance of modern species throughout the world due to human activity continued to alarm zoologists. The last dusky seaside sparrow died in Florida, and wildlife officials captured the only California condor that remained in the wild. Several of the latter birds were being maintained in a captive breeding program with the hope of reestablishing the species in its native habitat (see *Ornithology,* below). Following an official decision in 1986 to capture the few remaining individuals of the black-footed ferret, an endangered species of Wyoming, wildlife biologists worked during the year to develop procedures for successfully breeding the animal in captivity. Individuals of the thin-spined porcupine, a Brazilian species believed extinct since the 1960s, were discovered in a tropical forest. The finding prompted reminders from wildlife agencies of the importance of preserving such natural habitats as tropical forests in order to ensure the survival of many species that had become extremely rare.  (J. WHITFIELD GIBBONS)

**Entomology.** In February 1987 the East African Desert Locust Control Organization warned that heavy rains in the dry lowlands of the Ethiopian province of Eritrea were likely to cause an outbreak of the desert locust, *Schistocerca gregaria.* Satellite photographs had shown green patches of vegetation where the locusts were likely to be found, but because the Ethiopian Ministry of Agriculture was short of vehicles and already battling plagues of Quelaquela birds and armyworm attacking cereal crops elsewhere, the warning was not acted upon. By July it was clear that heavy rains had at last broken the drought in East Africa but, meanwhile, the locust had spread virtually unchecked to other parts of Ethiopia, across the Red Sea, and into The Sudan. Simultaneously, an outbreak was under way in West Africa, and various grasshopper pests were attacking crops locally from the Sahel to South Africa. The single most effective remedy for locusts at that stage appeared to be the pesticide dieldrin, a chemical banned from use in countries where it was manufactured. International relief organizations were not prepared to handle it or to risk blame for "dumping" banned pesticides in the third world.

World preoccupation with another plague—AIDS (acquired immune deficiency syndrome)—focused attention on the question of whether blood-sucking insects could transmit the disease. According to studies conducted by Jai Nayar of the Florida Medical Entomology Lab in Vero Beach and co-workers at the U.S. National Cancer Institute, Bethesda, Md., the virus could not survive in the gut of mosquitos and was not transferred to their salivary glands (the route by which malarial parasites and other mosquito-borne diseases were transmitted). Bedbugs were exonerated by Thomas Monath of the Centers for Disease Control, Atlanta, Ga., who pointed out that these insects transfer microbes only by contaminating the skin of their hosts and showed that only diseases 100,000 times more infectious than AIDS could be transmitted this way.

Pheromones, chemicals used by organisms for communication, had already been adapted to a variety of pest-control strategies. Pest controllers used them most often to bait insect traps, but a new approach was adopted by Jeffrey Aldrich of the U.S. Department of Agriculture (USDA), Beltsville, Md., and co-workers. They sprayed crops with a blend of pheromonal compounds that attracted two species

of predacious shield bugs (*Podisus* species) to attack more than 100 species of pests on cotton and soya bean.

One of the more remarkable examples of pheromone exploitation came not from human beings but from bolas spiders. These spiders catch flying moths by whirling a single thread of sticky silk weighted at the end with a ball of gum. Intriguingly, however, only male moths are caught. Mark Stowe of the Museum of Comparative Zoology, Harvard University, and James Tumlinson and Robert Heath of the USDA laboratories in Gainesville, Fla., discovered that one such spider, *Mastophora cornigera,* lured at least 19 species of moth by using components of the sex pheromones of the female moths. Most insect pheromones appeared to be relatively simple derivatives of straight-chain hydrocarbons, and insects had been shown to maintain their species separation by use of "bouquets" containing a number of compounds that differed from one another only in detail. The bolas spiders are apparently able to secrete a variety of such constituents in one combination after another until a susceptible species of moth flying in the vicinity is caught.

Chemicals that imitate or interfere with the hormones that control insect development had been developed as pesticides, but prospects of a very different use motivated Keiko Kadone-Okudo and colleagues at Nagoya (Japan) University to treat silkworms with methoprene, an analogue of the juvenile hormone that keeps immature insects from becoming adults prematurely. Mimics of juvenile hormone were known to induce excessive (supernumerary) larval molts in some insects, including the silkworm, resulting in "superlarvae." Keiko's team wondered whether supersized silk cocoons could be produced in this way, too. Supernumerary molts typically produce physiological monsters, incapable of normal activities. The team found, however, that starving newly molted fourth-stage silkworms for 18 hours and applying a millionth of a gram of methoprene six hours later while the insects were feeding caused all of them to develop in due course into fully functional sixth-stage superlarvae, as much as 46% greater in body weight and producing as much as 40% more silk in their cocoons than normal fifth-stage larvae.

Why should this particular regime have been successful? The team concluded that juvenile hormone, in addition to suppressing adult characters, also stimulates production of molting hormone for the next molt and that, in the silkworm, size determines whether a molt will be to another larva or to a pupa. They proposed that the starvation and methoprene treatment was just right to cause an accelerated molting of somewhat underweight larvae such that they reached what should have been the pupal molt before attaining the required body size, and the resultant extra larval stage then consumed enough food to spin an overweight cocoon when time for the next molt approached.

(PETER W. MILES)

This article updates the *Macropædia* article INSECTS.

**Ornithology.** Birds of a number of different species choose to roost communally at night. One explanation is safety in numbers; numerous watchers are more likely than a solitary one to spot a predator. Another explanation likens the roost gathering to an "information centre." Each morning the less efficient foragers follow those that fed better the previous day and that therefore leave more purposefully in the direction of proven feeding grounds.

During the year support for both theories came from detailed studies at communal nighttime assemblies of the red-winged blackbird in the U.S., the starling in England, and the chough (a kind of crow) in Scotland. It became clear for the first time that within each roost dominant individuals compete for and occupy preferred perching positions. Dominance in birds is known to be related to age (adults dominate adolescents), sex (cocks dominate hens), and weight (heavier birds dominate lighter ones). In the case of the American redwings, which frequently roost in marsh vegetation, it appears that older, more experienced foragers choose to roost communally, rather than individually, and to occupy the central, safer part of the roost. The younger, less experienced foragers accept the more risky periphery and provide a protective buffer in return for guidance to superior feeding areas the next day. For choughs, which roost on vertical cliffs, researchers found that older birds occupy positions not merely in the denser part of the roost but also higher up the cliff face, probably because positions nearer ground level are more vulnerable. The starling study showed that proportionally more birds at the centre of the roost are female and are heavier than those at the periphery. Thus, each nighttime assembly of birds is not merely an amorphous get-together but has a spatially determined social structure based on age, sex, and other factors and is practiced to enhance food gathering and to avoid enemies.

The speeds at which birds can fly, assuming level flight in still air, had long been a subject of popular exaggeration and misinformation. Recently the swift was shown to be among the slower fliers, while the fastest bird known to science became the common eider duck, timed at 24.6 metres/second (55 mph). The speeds at which birds can dive, or stoop, had been overestimated similarly in the popular imagination. With more careful measurements, for example, speeds of 75–100 metres/second (170–225 mph) formerly attributed to the peregrine falcon had to be withdrawn in favour of speeds of 31–39 metres/second (70–87 mph) measured by radar tracking. These observed speeds were well below theoretical estimates of the maximum possible terminal speeds in steep or vertical dives, but by adopting a moderate stooping speed, the peregrine may gain in hunting precision.

The California condor no longer flew wild as of 1987. The last free-living bird was captured in April. Joseph Dowhan, condor recovery coordinator for the U.S. Fish and Wildlife Service, said that the bird had eluded capture for several months. It was placed in the San Diego (Calif.) Wild Animal Park along with 13 others. A further 13, the remainder of the world total of 27, were in the Los Angeles Zoo. It was hoped that the birds might produce sufficient young to enable reintroduction to the wild sometime in the future. No California condor had yet been bred in captivity, but encouraging signs of courtship were observed.

Perhaps the rarest bird with a free-living population was the crested ibis. Its world population stood at 29 following the fledging of seven young from three nests in the Chinese province of Shaanxi (Shensi). In 1981 only seven living birds had been known. Despite the continuing success of the wild population, the future of the bird could depend partly on a new crested ibis breeding centre proposed for the Beijing (Peking) Zoo, which housed two captive ibises.

Each year one or two new species of bird are discovered, adding to the world total of just over 9,000. A new weaver bird was reported from Uganda by John Ash of the Smithsonian Institution, Washington, D.C., and named *Ploceus victoriae*. The longest-lived wild bird known to science was a royal albatross breeding in New Zealand and first individually marked there 56 years earlier. Older captive birds were known. Cared for and protected by humans, aviary birds often live longer than their wild counterparts.

(JEFFERY BOSWALL)

This article updates the *Macropædia* article BIRDS.

## MARINE BIOLOGY

Illustrating how remote-sensing techniques could be used to make assessments of living marine resources, the French Spot satellite mapped New Caledonian reef environments that support *Trochus niloticus*, a mollusk providing a valuable source of mother-of-pearl. A commercially developed, remotely operated vehicle was successfully used to assess densities of pandalid shrimps off the Swedish west coast. A novel in situ method was developed to measure the sizes of particles suspended in estuary waters. It used a submersible laser-diffraction instrument to measure detritus particles, important reaction sites for chemical and microbial activity.

A benthic (ocean-bottom) community in the North Sea that had been studied continuously since 1971 showed, as expected, considerable variability with the passing of time, yet between 1974 and 1980 it exhibited an astonishing steady state. Follow-up studies after the catastrophic oil spill from the tanker *Amoco Cadiz* off the coast of Brittany, France, in 1978 showed that sediment nematodes, marine roundworms regarded as important pollution indicators, took six years to recover, while disturbances of reproductive function in plaice (the flounder *Pleuronectes platessa*) were still apparent after that period. Coelacanths (*Latimeria chalumnae*), primitive fish whose extinct relatives may have been the ancestors of land vertebrates, were photographed for the first time in their benthic habitat in the western Indian Ocean by West German scientists using a small research submarine. Film and videotape records of their sluggish swimming revealed a synchronous motion in the two pairs of limblike fins that resembled movements of four-legged animals.

Swedish workers showed that such aquatic birds as the dunlin (*Calidrus alpina*) and curlew sandpiper (*C. ferruginea*) transfer heavy metals by ingestion from estuarine sediments to terrestrial habitats, often in remote areas, and that cadmium is particularly hazardous to such birds. The search for more specific chemicals to replace wide-spectrum insecticides was advocated. One supposed specific regulator of insect growth, diflubenzuron (DFB), or Dimilin, was shown to disturb growth and reproduction in marine crustaceans and specifically to inhibit burrowing behaviour in fiddler crabs. Common bacterial infections appeared to be the immediate cause of the unprecedented deaths of hundreds of bottle-nosed dolphins along the U.S. East Coast beginning in early summer. Viruses, biologic toxins, man-made pollution, and immunologic disorders were under scrutiny as possible reasons for the dolphins' increased susceptibility to the ordinarily harmless microorganisms. Studies of the continental shelf off central North Carolina fortuitously carried out before, and then after, Hurricane Diana stalled there in 1984 showed unexpectedly that the local coral-reef communities were relatively unaffected.

The reduced light of winter did not, as previously hypothesized, eliminate primary production in the ocean waters around Antarctica. Net primary and bacterial production was demonstrated in and away from sea ice in winter in Antarctica, suggesting that estimates of total annual primary production should be raised 25% to accommodate this unexpected source. More extensive testing of the "outwelling hypothesis" in a South Carolina inlet showed that it was a highly fertile system exporting excess organic material, which supported coastal oceanic productivity.

Investigation of the biology of the spiny lobster (*Palinurus argus*), previously limited by lack of knowledge of the whereabouts of young stages, was advanced by U.S.

findings that such forms settle and live among clumps of highly branched red algae (species of *Laurencia*). Population outbreaks of the coral-feeding starfish *Acanthaster planci,* which had occurred throughout the Indo-West Pacific since the late 1960s, were reported on fringing reefs in Japan, where they produced "rubble reefs" supporting considerably depleted fish communities. Recolonization by new, young corals on such damaged reefs in Australian waters occurred well ahead of the total demise of the previously existing coral populations—that is, before the outbreak of *Acanthaster* had abated.   (ERNEST NAYLOR)

This article updates the *Macropædia* articles CRUSTACEANS; FISHES; MOLLUSKS; etc.

## BOTANY

It had long been recognized that every living organism must have mechanisms by which extracellular signals become converted to events within the cell that ultimately result in a response of the organism to the original environmental cue. Such systems were well documented for animal cells in which the signaling system involves a so-called second messenger; *e.g.,* certain cyclic nucleotides or calcium ions. Until recently the search for a second messenger system in plants had been unsuccessful even though such extracellular signals as light, hormones, and gravity clearly influence plant growth and development in several ways, including cell division, cell elongation, gravitropism (growth toward or away from the direction of gravity), senescence, abscission (leaf fall), enzyme secretion, and spore germination. During the year scientists amassed evidence that calcium acts as a second messenger in converting extracellular signals in plants.

Although it had proved extremely difficult to measure calcium concentrations inside cells, considerable indirect evidence suggested that internal calcium concentrations do change in response to external stimuli. Manipulating calcium concentrations was shown to evoke certain physiological responses in the absence of normal external stimuli, and plants were shown to possess an apparently ubiquitous calcium-binding protein called calmodulin. By 1987 it was apparent that sensitivity to intracellular calcium changes is conferred on physiological-response elements by calmodulin and by other calcium-dependent enzymes. Experimentally blocking the activity of calmodulin inhibited at least some of the responses evoked by such primary signals as light, gravity, and hormones.

Modern biotechnology continued to furnish highly successful methods for inserting new genes into plants, especially dicotyledons. Recent accomplishments included the introduction of genes for herbicide resistance in petunia plants, for resistance to tobacco mosaic virus in tobacco and tomato plants, and for a protein toxic to caterpillar pests in tobacco and tomato. Remarkably, a gene for the light-generating enzyme luciferase was inserted into tobacco plants, allowing the plants light up like fireflies when they were watered with a solution containing the substance on which luciferase acts. Monocotyledonous plants, which include the cereal grains and other food crops, proved more difficult to manipulate in genetic engineering experiments, partly because gene transfers in plants relied on the bacterium *Agrobacterium tumefaciens,* an organism that does not naturally infect cereals or other monocots, as a vector to carry the new genes into plants.

Attempts to circumvent the problem in monocots focused on the use of protoplasts, plant cells that have had their cell walls removed. It had been shown that cell-wall-free protoplasts, including those of rice and maize (corn), can take up new genes directly. It had not been

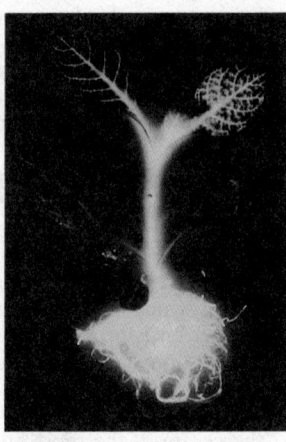

A tobacco plant (left) glows in the dark (right) after a gene for luciferase, a light-generating enzyme found in fireflies, was inserted into the plant. Remarkable in itself, the achievement also heralded the development of a potentially powerful new tool for studying gene expression in both plant and animal cells.
UNIVERSITY OF CALIFORNIA AT SAN DIEGO; PHOTOGRAPHS, KEITH V. WOOD

possible, however, to induce monocot cells manipulated in this way to regenerate into whole plants that carried the newly inserted genes. Success in overcoming this difficulty in rice was recently reported from several laboratories. Regeneration of rice plants from protoplasts would allow not only for the possibility of gene insertion but also for the production of new crosses by fusing protoplasts of plants that cannot be mated sexually. Although regenerating rice plants in this way was still very slow, it was encouraging that for the first time a major cereal crop became subject to modern biotechnological methods.

RuBPCase, shortened form of ribulose-1,5-bisphosphate carboxylase/oxygenase, is the most abundant naturally occurring enzyme. In photosynthetic organisms it is the enzyme that binds atmospheric carbon dioxide and initiates its conversion to useful organic molecules. It is estimated that during the course of a year 100 billion ($10^{11}$) tons of $CO_2$ are fixed into organic compounds by the action of this enzyme. Despite that impressive statistic, RuBPCase is not particularly efficient because it can also catalyze the oxygenation of ribulose-1,5-bisphosphate, which results in photorespiration, a daytime $CO_2$-releasing process that reduces the overall rate of photosynthesis and consequently plant productivity. Although some plants can overcome the dual activity of this enzyme by increasing the concentration of $CO_2$ at the reaction site of the enzyme, most crop plants support significant levels of photorespiration and are therefore relatively inefficient. Were enough known of the structure of RuBPCase, plant scientists might find it possible to specifically eliminate its oxygenase activity. Using X-ray crystallographic and electron microscopic techniques, researchers from three West German institutes reported the detailed structure of RuBPCase from the bacterium *Acaligenes eutrophus.* It was hoped that this discovery would eventually allow scientists to alter the gene for the enzyme in crop plants and thus improve their photosynthetic efficiency.   (PHILIP D. REID)

## MOLECULAR BIOLOGY

**Differentiation and Slime Molds.** Living things can be divided into two major categories, the unicellular and the multicellular. A single cell is a marvelously complex entity capable of many responses and actions, yet by banding together and specializing, cells can give rise to assemblages capable of a much wider range of adaptations. The evolution of both plants and animals must surely have involved a stage during which single cells improved their chances of survival by learning to work together.

The development of an individual animal appears to follow a path that reflects the evolutionary history of the large group to which the individual belongs. For example, the heart within a developing human embryo at first has but one chamber; it later becomes two-chambered and then three- and finally four-chambered. Worms have hearts with one chamber, fish have two chambers, amphibians three, and mammals four. This is but one illustration among many of the way development of the individual (ontogeny) recapitulates evolutionary history (phylogeny). It is not surprising then that every human being begins life as a single cell: the fertilized egg.

Development of the egg into a new adult involves many rounds of cell growth and division with progressive cell differentiation, or specialization, at each cycle of division. In most animals, including humans, each cell division involves duplication of all of its genetic information, so that each cell of the adult contains all of the genes present in the egg. Yet the cells in the adult differ, one from the other, in size, shape, and function. Some provide for movement (muscle), some for signaling (nerve), some for scaffolding (bone), and so on. How is it that cells that differ so dramatically can contain the same complement of genetic information? The answer must lie in mechanisms that specify which genes shall be actively transcribed and which shall remain dormant. Activation of one constellation of genes produces a nerve cell, while activation of a different set produces a muscle cell. When researchers understand this process of differentiation, they will be in a position to appreciate more fully the beautiful complexity of life and to know how cancer cells arise from normal cells and how to prevent and even reverse this process.

Whereas differentiation in humans is dauntingly complex, there still exist relatively simple organisms on the boundary between the unicellular and the multicellular. The cellular slime molds, discovered in the late 1800s, function as independent cells but then become multicellular when conditions demand it. In recent years researchers have worked to unravel the signals and responses that guide the life cycle of these creatures in order to gain clues to the vastly more complex process of differentiation in higher animals.

The cellular slime mold *Dictyostelium discoideum* begins life as a spore that lodges in a favourably damp place. The spore contains a compound that inhibits germination, and not until this compound diffuses away into an appropriately wet environment around the spore does it germinate. The activated spore releases an amoeba, a single-celled organism, which moves about in soil or decaying plant litter seeking bacteria, which it engulfs and digests. It grows and divides into two amoebas, each of which behaves independently of the other. This unicellular life cycle continues as long as there are bacteria to consume.

The search for bacteria is guided by chemotaxis, or movement in response to a chemical gradient; *i.e.,* to changes in the concentration of a chemical with distance. The bacteria secrete chemicals (folic acid and related compounds) that the amoebas can sense and follow up the gradient to their source. While they are seeking bacteria, it would be advantageous for the amoebas to avoid each other and so avoid fruitless competition. Once again chemotaxis comes into play, in this case a negative chemotaxis in response to compounds secreted by the amoebas themselves.

When the supply of bacteria is exhausted, the behaviour of the amoebas changes dramatically. They begin to find each other irresistibly attractive, and they stream together and coalesce into a small sluglike creature, which crawls about in response to gradients in temperature, humidity, and light. The slug then grows upward, like a small mushroom, raising up a cap atop a thin stalk. The cells in the cap divide many times and produce spores that, when ripe, will be released when the cap splits. This process obviously requires differentiation of the amoebas; some form a baseplate, others a stalk, and still others the cap of spores. The advantage of this complex life cycle is not difficult to discern. With the food supply exhausted, the amoebas cannot survive in a vegetative, or growing, state. They must either die or become dormant spores capable of lasting out the unfavourable conditions. Sporulation of each amoeba, however, would leave the already depleted local environment full of spores. Some means of wider dispersal is needed, but to exploit the wind, the spores have to be lifted above the substratum—a task that demands the cooperation of thousands of cells. How this cooperation is achieved has only recently begun to be understood.

During the first few hours of starvation, the amoebas change in many ways. The number of cell-surface receptors for folic acid decreases, with a concomitant loss of responsiveness to folates and hence to bacteria. At the same time, the number of cell-surface receptors for the chemical 3′,5′-cyclic adenylic acid (cAMP) increases 10-fold, and the amount of an enzyme (adenylate cyclase) responsible for the synthesis of cAMP increases 30-fold. There is also a 50-fold increase in another enzyme (phosphodiesterase), which breaks down cAMP, and more than a 100-fold increase in a membrane protein that makes the amoebas mutually adherent once they come into contact. All of these changes set the stage for an ingathering of the amoebas, guided by chemotaxis toward cAMP. Simple chemotaxis will suffice for short-range guidance toward nearby food or away from neighbouring amoebas during feeding, but it is not adequate for the long-range guidance required to bring together thousands of cells over a distance of a centimetre or two (roughly a half to one inch).

Starved amoebas are primed to release a pulse of cAMP, and they can do so either spontaneously or in response to sensing an increase in cAMP in the medium around them. In a large, uniformly dispersed population of amoebas, a few will spontaneously release cAMP before the others, perhaps because they have been starving the longest. The cAMP that diffuses outward from these "focal" cells stimulates neighbouring cells both to move toward the cAMP source and to release a pulse of cAMP in their turn. Since release of cAMP is followed within minutes by its enzymatic breakdown and then by the release of another pulse of cAMP, the result is a series of concentric waves of cAMP traveling outward from the focal cell. These self-propagating waves guide the cells toward the centre, where they coalesce and adhere. Although by 1987 the broad outlines of this process were clear, such details as the way the amoebas follow the cAMP waves remained to be learned.

Once the slug forms, the amoebas become differentiated according to their position. Those at the front end of the slug will become stalk cells, those farther back will constitute the fruiting body, and those at the rear will form the base plate. If the slug is mechanically separated into its constituent cells, the cells will reaggregate and resegregate according to their original positions in the slug. Although by the end of the year the molecular basis of this differentiation and organization was far from clear, researchers believed that it must depend on communications among the amoebas in the slug, which in turn depend on the release and binding of diffusible substances. One of these substances, which are referred to collectively as differentiation inducing factors (DIFs), was isolated and identified during the year. Called DIF-1, it is a relatively simple molecule whose structure nevertheless was very difficult to elucidate, primarily because it was at first available only in minute quantities. Now that it could be synthesized in large quantities, rapid progress in studies aimed at its mechanism of action was anticipated.

Elucidating the minute details of the life cycle of the cellular slime molds should lead to a fuller understanding of cell growth and differentiation, which in turn would likely be applicable to higher animals, including humans. Such knowledge is critical to the control of cancer and many other diseases.            (IRWIN FRIDOVICH)

**Genes That Regulate Form.** Any new parent knows that birth is a miracle, yet even more miraculous is the process that precedes birth—the development of a single fertilized egg into a healthy child. Development can be viewed as the careful orchestration of three processes: growth, the means by which a single cell becomes many cells; differentiation, the assumption of different fates by different cells (so that some become liver cells, some brain cells, and so forth); and morphogenesis, the organization of those cells into the structures that constitute tissues, organs, and ultimately the complete newborn. This section deals with recent advances in understanding morphogenesis.

One of the basic questions in the study of development is the way one-dimensional information stored in the DNA sequence of genes is converted into the three-dimensional form (or four-dimensional form, if one includes time) of an embryo. To date, many genes have been identified that specify structural proteins—the molecular building blocks of cells that control their shape and provide them with mechanical strength. Normal development requires the carefully regulated expression of these genes over both space and time. Cells must make specific structural proteins where and when they are needed. How can the expression of all of these structural genes be regulated so as to be coordinated rather than chaotic? One might predict the existence of certain controlling genes that regulate the activity of groups of structural genes. Such regulatory systems have been found in yeast, where the expression of one gene (MAT) controls the expression of a host of other genes all required for a common purpose: preparing the yeast cell to mate. In the past several years, evidence of similar systems was discovered in higher organisms, including insects and humans. One set of these genes, called homeotic genes, seems to regulate the coordination of gene expression in order to specify the structures of the body plan.

Much of the seminal work in this area has been performed with use of the fruit fly *Drosophila melanogaster.* As early as 1915, mutant flies were recognized that either lack certain body parts or have extra parts where they do not belong. Later, mutants were found that grow extra legs in place of antennas, extra tails in place of heads, extra wings, and so forth. Gradually it became clear that each of these unfortunate flies carries a mutation in one or more genes that regulate the formation of the structures in question. Recently the extensive study of such mutants, permitted by the advent of DNA technology, uncovered an intricate system of regulation that in 1987 was only beginning to be understood.

The most current evidence suggested that homeotic genes may regulate the expression of groups of other genes by coding for proteins that actually bind to DNA sequences of those genes. Although each homeotic gene is different, all share a region of marked similarity that has been designated the homeobox. This region in each gene is about 180 nucleotides long and thus corresponds to 60 amino acids along the length of the encoded protein. The homeobox is striking in a number of respects. First, it represents a small region of DNA sequence that has resisted evolutionary change compared with the surrounding sequence. Second, it codes for an amino acid sequence that is characteristic of proteins taking on a three-dimensional structure called "helix-turn-helix." This structure has been found in a number of proteins known to bind to specific sequences of DNA. Third, all homeobox-containing proteins studied to date have been observed to congregate in the cell nucleus, where the DNA is found.

If homeotic genes serve to coordinate the regulation of groups of other genes, what regulates the expression of the homeotic genes themselves? In other words, the basic question of positional determination—how each cell in the embryo "knows" where it is in relation to the other cells—still needs to be answered. More specifically, how do certain cells know to express the homeotic gene that will direct them to form a leg, while other cells know to express the homeotic gene that will direct them to form a wing? Within the last decade genetic studies of mutant *Drosophila* have identified three classes of genes that are involved in the specification of the body plan. The first are so-called maternal-effect genes, which specify egg polarity (opposite ends) and spatial coordinates of the egg and future embryo. Their name arises from the fact that they are expressed in the ovaries of the mother during oogenesis, or egg production. The second group, called segmentation genes, determines the number and polarity of the body segments. The final group are the homeotic genes, which, as is discussed above, determine the identity and sequence of the body segments.

In 1987 the mechanism by which the first two classes of genes work remained in large part a mystery, but the power of homeotic activity was demonstrated recently in several experiments. Perhaps the most dramatic one was reported by Walter J. Gehring of the University of Basel, Switz., who introduced an additional copy of the homeotic gene *Antp* (for *Antennapedia*) into a fly. Because the gene had been attached to a special inducible "promoter" sequence that functions like an on-off switch, it could be manipulated independently of its normal means of control. When the introduced copy of *Antp* was left silent, the fly developed normally. In contrast, when the gene was induced to expression, it caused the fly to develop an extra pair of legs in place of its antennas. That the aberrant expression of a single gene could cause the substitution of one complex body part for another was remarkable.

Equally remarkable was the amassing of evidence for homeotic genes in organisms ranging in complexity from sea urchins to humans. Comparisons of amino acid sequence specified by the homeobox regions of these genes indicated that the homeobox has been highly conserved through large expanses of evolutionary time. Such conservation of sequence invites speculation that the functions have also been to some degree conserved. But perhaps most remarkable of all is the fact that the many intricate hierarchies of structural and controlling genes do manage to function together to direct the development of something as complex and beautiful as a healthy baby.

(JUDITH L. FRIDOVICH-KEIL)

*See also* Earth Sciences; Environment.

This article updates the *Macropædia* articles Animal BEHAVIOUR; BIOCHEMICAL COMPONENTS OF ORGANISMS; The BIOLOGICAL SCIENCES; CANCER; CONSERVATION OF NATURAL RESOURCES; ECOSYSTEMS; The Principles of GENETICS AND HEREDITY; GEOCHRONOLOGY; Biological GROWTH AND DEVELOPMENT; PHOTOSYNTHESIS; PROTOPHYTES; REPRODUCTION AND REPRODUCTIVE SYSTEMS.

# Literature

The awarding of the 1987 Nobel Prize for Literature to the Soviet-born poet Joseph Brodsky (*see* BIOGRAPHIES) provided an occasion for political comment, for he had been imprisoned in 1964 on a charge of "parasitism," subsequently had been expelled from the U.S.S.R., and then had settled in the U.S. He had then become well known as a poet and critic in the English language, following the example of his friend the late W. H. Auden. A British press report commented: "Official recognition of Brodsky has become a test of the success of *glasnost*." Learning of his award during a visit to London, Brodsky remarked that the quality of his poetry was being ignored in the political "post-Nobel fuss." He said: "You start off trying to talk about art and end up with the Nazis and the Holocaust."

Another Nobel Prize winner, noted for his political commitment, was Knut Hamsun, the Norwegian novelist whose career was exhumed in a new biography by Robert Ferguson. Hamsun died in 1952, a disgraced old man of 93; he had supported Hitler, had spent the years of World War II in German-occupied Norway, and had given his Nobel Prize medal to the Nazi leader Joseph Goebbels. Nevertheless, Ferguson insisted that the old Nazi was a worthy and talented novelist, misled into believing that he was a political thinker.

Hamsun's contemporary, the Viennese novelist Hermann Broch, had often been deemed worthy of the Nobel Prize. He was honoured in 1987 with a new biography by Paul Michael Lützeler and also by a new version of his posthumous novel, *Die Verzauberung*, translated into English as *The Spell* by his son, H. F. Broch; the book had previously been known as *The Tempter* or *The Mountain Story*. It represented Broch's conclusions about the rise of Nazism, which he had observed in Austria before his exile and death in the U.S.

The Prix Goncourt went to the Mo-

Joseph Brodsky

roccan novelist Tahar Ben Jelloun for his novel *La Nuit sacrée*, concerning a North African girl brought up as a boy until her father's death, when she has to contend with her jealous sisters. Jelloun's writing had often dealt with North Africans coming to terms with aspects of modern morals—in this case, feminism. The chairman of the Goncourt judges remarked that it was important that the future of the French language be cherished in Africa; it was noted that the award coincided with political demands that African immigrants be deported from France, and it was generally recognized that the presentation had a political as well as a literary significance. The Prix Renaudot was awarded to René-Jean Clot for his mystical novel *L'Enfant hallucine*.

## ENGLISH

**United Kingdom.** After long deliberation, the Arts Council appointed a new, full-time literature director. The council had announced among its objectives a determination "to treat as a priority Afro-Caribbean and Asian writers and readers." In accordance with this policy, Alastair Niven, a specialist in Commonwealth literature who had been director general of the Africa Centre, was appointed to the post. A reduced sum of money was earmarked for bursaries to individual writers and, for 1987, the only recipients were Africans, Caribbeans, or Asians. The Arts Council continued to subsidize the Poetry Society, but Niven said he would examine the current commitment to literary journals.

The commercial world of publishing was disturbed by a public complaint from the novelist Graham Greene about the defects of his own publisher, Bodley Head, conglomerated with Virago, Jonathan Cape, and Chatto & Windus. Greene was under attack by the right-wing press for attending the Peace Forum in Moscow and for showing a lack of enthusiasm for U.S. policy; it was assumed that he was offering left-wing support for the feminist publisher Virago, squashed by its large partners. Two months later it was announced that the whole conglomerate had been sold to the U.S. giant Random House. Some writers were alarmed by this expansion, nor were they consoled by the very large advances paid out to a few authors in 1987 as gambles on their potential best-seller status.

*Fiction.* The Booker Prize was awarded to Penelope Lively for her novel *Moon Tiger*. This surprised many critics, who had thought other candidates stronger. Derwent May suggested that Lively's book was rather like *Circles of Deceit* by Nina Bawden, another candidate for the prize. Both, he said, told "a story of love and disappointment, but all the characters are like people you hear about in a good conversation"; they were "only people overheard, never really known."

Among other candidates on the shortlist was Brian Moore, with *The Colour of Blood*. His well-known interest in Roman Catholicism had previously been expressed in novels about his native Ireland and his second homeland, Canada. His new story concerned a cardinal in a nameless Communist country (presumably Poland), a man who had come to terms with the government and was now being pursued by terrorists who seemed to be of his own faith.

Hermann Broch

Another striking contender was Peter Ackroyd's *Chatterton;* an accomplished historical time-traveler and pasticheur, Ackroyd was dealing with another pasticheur, the 18th-century poet of that name, talented but fraudulent, famous for his youthful suicide. Ackroyd's century-spanning novel attracted considerable admiration, mixed with a certain irritation at the grotesque and stagey dialogue.

A fifth contender was Dame Iris Murdoch's 23rd novel, *The Book and the Brotherhood*, a swift-moving story of middle-aged Oxford graduates who wish to subsidize an old friend who is writing a great book; elements of farce and melodrama enlivened the plot, which was, though implausible, firmly structured and presented with narrative prose of high distinction. Still more highly favoured was the sixth contender, Chinua Achebe, with *Anthills of the Savannah*, a story of politicians and the populace in modern West Africa. This masterly novel told of three old school friends—men of authority, one of them the president of the nation—and their fall from power.

An older Nigerian writer, Amos Tutuola, presented a fabulous, folklorish tale in his poetic, half-colloquial English; *Pauper, Brawler and Slanderer* concerned three people doomed to failure by the birth oracles that gave them their terrible names. Dan Jacobson, also from Africa, told an equally strange story in a far more complex and modern way with his novel of the past and the future, *Her Story,* presented as a story written in the year 2040 and discovered in 2296. The author's life was described and her story revealed, mysteriously, as a kind of historical romance, set perhaps in the third world of the 20th century or perhaps in the Middle East at the time of Jesus. The mystery was satisfactorily resolved.

William Golding offered *Close Quarters* as a sequel to *Rites of Passage,* published seven years earlier; the 19th-century sailing ship proved to be still in the South Atlantic, and the same gentlemanly passenger was narrating the events—not perhaps so cruelly dramatic as in the first volume but involving one suicide. A third volume was promised. Ian McEwan's *The Child in Time* began poignantly with the loss of a child but developed into a futuristic, dystopian novel about Britain under a harsh Conservative government with no regard for social security and severe ideas about the upbringing of children. *Lenin: The Novel* by Alan Brien, well known as an essayist, was a very ambitious first novel—a long, historical story about the life of the Russian statesman, strengthened by laborious research but generally felt to be lacking in shape and structure.

*Lives, Letters.* With the 50th anniversary of Rudyard Kipling's death, his books came out of copyright, and publishers were enabled to exploit the situation; the National Trust, holders of the Kipling estate, were the only sufferers. His stories were rearranged in many new editions, with new introductions, as *The Complete Supernatural Stories* or *The Best Indian Stories* or *A Choice of Kipling's Prose.* The most valuable contribution to this little Kipling festival was Hugh Brogan's book *Mowgli's Sons: Kipling and Baden-Powell's Scouts,* in which he appreciated Kipling's influence on the Scout movement.

The birth of Rupert Brooke in 1887 was celebrated with two centenary editions of his poetic works and a reprint of his *Letters from America,* with a preface by his admirer Henry James. Brooke's love life was investigated by Paul Delany in *The Neo-Pagans: Friendship and Love in the Rupert Brooke Circle.* An older poet, Alfred Tennyson, was honoured with the second edition of his complete *Poems* and in *The New Oxford Book of Victorian Verse,* both edited by Christopher Ricks. The second volume of Tennyson's letters (1851–70) was edited with brio by Cecil Y. Lang and Edgar F. Shannon.

Robert Louis Stevenson was imaginatively appreciated by Nicholas Rankin in *Dead Man's Chest,* a book in which the young author emulated Stevenson's journeys from Edinburgh through Europe and America to the South Seas in a useful and original exploration of his work. A new study of the depressing life of Oscar Wilde seemed less necessary, but Richard Ellmann (*see* OBITUARIES), the admired biographer of James Joyce, produced one before his death; his *Oscar Wilde* asserted that the playwright had contracted syphilis while at Oxford and remarked that "this conviction is central to my conception of Wilde's character and my interpretation of many things in his later life."

Among the lower ranks, Harry Daley's posthumous memoir, *A Small Cloud,* was released; he had been E. M. Forster's young lover, but his tactful book betrayed nothing about the novelist or any other literary friends. It was simply a well-written account of the life of a homosexual policeman. Almost equally surprising and interesting were the selected *Letters of Conrad Russell: 1897–1947.* Russell had been generally known as a country squire who wrote voluminous letters to unattainable women, but Georgiana Blakiston's selection proved him to have had a strong mind and style, with a deep concern about the wars of the century and the Roman Catholic Church.

Brian Moore
© JERRY BAUER

In the world of the arts, Sir John Vanbrugh, the playwright and architect, was appraised in a biography by Kerry Downes (an art historian, more at ease with the buildings than the plays). Michael Kennedy produced a knowledgeable life of the orchestral conductor Sir Adrian Boult. More attention was paid in the press to a candid biography of Kenneth Tynan by his widow, Kathleen, for Tynan was a talented theatre reviewer, admired by other journalists for his style.

An intriguing book by Anthony Masters was neatly called *Literary Agents: The Novelist as Spy,* an investigation of the many storytellers who have been enlisted in the British secret services, from Graham Greene to Ian Fleming and from Somerset Maugham to John le Carré; the relationship between novel writing and spying was nicely assessed. Writers' autobiographies included George Macbeth's *A Child of the War;* the poet was too young to serve in World War II, but it made a difference to his mind and spirit, narrowing his horizons. A larger, broader memoir was *Little Wilson and Big God: Being the First Part of the Confessions of Anthony Burgess.* Burgess, a prolific novelist, was brought up as a Roman Catholic schoolboy called John Wilson; when he lost his faith, a priest said it was a sad business, "a matter of little Wilson and big God," and this daunting phrase coloured his life.

*Poetry.* With the publication of George Barker's *Collected Poems,* attention was drawn to his "bardic status," a phrase unusually prominent in 1987. John Bayley, Warton professor of English at the University of Oxford, remarked that "as with all bardic poetry, it is the tradition that determines the effect and not the poet's personality." Although Barker had, perhaps, not much grandeur or dignity in himself, he was able to lend these qualities to his subjects, "declaiming in the style that is exactly proper for an important occasion." Bayley's rather equivocal appreciation of Barker was accompanied by an edition of the magazine *Aquarius,* devoted to poetry of the 1940s—remarking "how many outstanding poetic careers had their beginnings in those years" but admitting that the decade was remembered as "a period of unfortunate aberration, a period of sickness from which English poetry fortunately recovered."

One of the stages in the recovery was the period of americanization, powerful in the 1970s but powerfully denounced, remarked Jonathan Raban in the *London Review of Books.* That stage was over, he claimed; reviewing new books by poets between 30 and 45, he found it would be difficult to deduce that Ezra Pound, let alone William Carlos Williams, had ever existed. The model style and tradition had become that of Philip Larkin, the lonely outsider. Raban quoted stanzas from five new elegies for that poet, all the work of men making "a shift, barely imaginable 15 years ago, to the homely, the territory of fiction and reportage, the tight traditional form." Among these poets he seemed to include Blake Morrison and Anthony Thwaite, with their new books, *The Ballad of the Yorkshire Ripper and Other Poems* and *Letter from Tokyo.* Not very domestic titles, these; but Raban held that such poets "seemed to have discovered the delights of family life for the first time," having no intention of echoing Larkin's wistful, involuntary outsiderdom.

Almost echoing Bayley, Ian Hamilton praised the serious Irish poet Seamus Heaney, declaring that he had "redignified the bardic stance" during his career. Heaney's new book, *The Haw Lantern,* showed bardic tendencies "not so much of high vocation as of obedient professionalism." In London a week in May was devoted to whipping up a mass market for poetry with bardic readings. Some took place at Waterloo Station during the rush hour, but policemen urged the more forthright poets to moderate their language. Poets from overseas, including Irina Ratushinskaya (*see* BIOGRAPHIES) and Wole Soyinka, read in the Royal Albert Hall as if they were truly bards, but the audience was too small for that great echo chamber.

(D. A. N. JONES)

**United States.** *Fiction.* An unusual concentration of large, sprawling novels about family life, most of them by Southern writers and set in the South, marked the year. Pat Conroy's *The Prince of Tides,* the story of a South Carolina clan stirred by big emotions and marred by tragedy, spent most of 1987 on the *New York Times* best-seller list. Some critics, such as James Atlas writing in *Vanity Fair,* praised the book to the skies. Others, such as novelist Gail Godwin, tried to shoot the book from the skies. Writing in the *New York Times Book Review,* Godwin faulted Conroy for his melodrama and inflated presentation of Southern family life—and then later in the year published *A Southern Family,* which was greeted with enormous praise but may, in fact, suffer from some of the same flaws as *Prince of Tides.*

Family was the concern of a highly regarded and beautifully told second novel, *Rich in Love,* by Hemingway Prize winner Josephine Humphreys. Humphreys's youthful narrator, wise beyond her 17 years, tells the story of her own initiation into adulthood even as she comes to terms with the vagaries of her delinquent parents.

*You Must Remember This,* Joyce Carol Oates's latest novel, deals with a working-class family in upstate New York in the 1950s. Many critics found it her best book in years. Toni Morrison's *Beloved* received high praise for its exuberant language and historical intelligence; set in southern Ohio just after the slaves were freed, it focuses on the turbulence caused by freedom in the life of a black woman and her children. *First Light,* the first novel by the highly skilled short-story writer Charles Baxter, created a delicate and careful portrait of a brother and sister moving back in time to search out the origins of their disintegrating love for each other. T. C. Boyle, also known for his brilliant short fiction, published *World's End,* set in upstate New York's Hudson Valley. The book showed off Boyle's prowess with language while at the same time producing a rich narrative with scenes out of the late 17th century, the 1940s, and the 1960s, all on the theme of the quest for a missing father. Mona Simpson's brilliant first novel, *Anywhere but Here,* carried the search for family ties and success from the Midwest to California. Another first novel that critics singled out for praise was *The Man Who Owned Vermont* by Bret Lott, the simply narrated but powerful story of a troubled marriage between an energetic wholesale soda pop salesman and his young secretary wife.

Prizewinning poet James Dickey, whose *Deliverance* became a best-seller when it appeared in 1970, brought out *Alnilam,* an avowedly experimental novel, set in the South during World War II, about a Georgia father, gone blind, in search of his missing airman son. At times using double columns on the page, one giving readers the world according to the sighted characters and the other as it seems to the blind protagonist, Dickey created in *Alnilam* an interesting, if never fully satisfying and certainly overlong piece of work. Another enormously long book, experimental to a fault, was Joseph McElroy's *Women and Men,* an attempt at creating a discontinuous narrative about shifting social relations in New York and the Southwest.

Toni Morrison
© BERNARD GOTFRYD—WOODFIN CAMP & ASSOCIATES

Philip Roth published *The Counterlife,* the fourth novel in his Zuckerman series. This proved to be an experiment for him, a book in which the story of Nathan Zuckerman, writer, son, brother, is carried from New Jersey and New York to Israel and England—and in which each successive chapter dismantles the reality of the previous one even as it constructs an alternative. Many critics regarded this often talky, though brilliant, book as Roth's finest in many years. A young experimentalist from Tennessee, Madison Smartt Bell, published two interesting new books in 1987, a collection of impressive stories titled *Zero Db* and a novel, *The Year of Silence,* a technically innovative and compelling story of the effect of the suicide of a young female design artist on the lives of those in her little group of New York friends. *The Year of Silence* put Bell at the head of the class of smart young fiction writers 30 or younger, which also included Bret Easton Ellis, whose novel *The Rules of Attraction* came out during the year to the largest round of undeserved negative reviews seen in a long time; Jill Eisenstadt, who like Ellis was a Bennington (Vt.) College graduate and studied fiction writing with Joe McGinniss, and who was author of *From Rockaway,* a somewhat more humorous and yet more deeply felt novel about college students of the same generation as Ellis's characters; Gary Glickman, whose *Years from Now* focused on family matters among middle-class Jews in New Jersey; and Tama Janowitz, whose *A Cannibal in Manhattan* ran a close second to *The Rules of Attraction* in the scorn and dismissal it received from reviewers.

Winning almost unanimous praise from critics was septuagenarian Wallace Stegner's latest novel, *Crossing to Safety,* the story of the entwined lives of two couples involved in a friendship of nearly half a century. The book's publication marked the 50th year of Stegner's life as a novelist. Unlike the Conroy, Godwin, or Oates novels, Stegner's story of family and friendship is unmarred by violence or near-disaster. In fact, the novelist narrator, Larry Morgan, poses the question that his story itself answers when he asks if it is possible to "make a book that anyone will read out of lives as quiet" as those of his friends.

In *More Die of Heartbreak* Nobel laureate Saul Bellow seemed to slow his

narrative to an almost complete halt in order to have his main character, Kenneth Trachtenberg, a professor in the Midwest, think his way through to a happier view of the world. Another elder statesman of the American novel, Walker Percy of Louisiana, published a new book. *The Thanatos Syndrome,* a seriocomic treatment of a number of problematic themes in American culture—the line between sickness and health, free will versus determinism, and other characteristic Percy motifs—in a story more available to the general reader than most of his other fiction.

Two new and engaging novels by Stephen King—*It* and *Misery*—were popular successes in a single year, as was the absorbing courtroom novel *Presumed Innocent* by Chicago attorney Scott Turow. Chicago writer Larry Heinemann's *Paco's Story* was a powerful story about a Vietnam veteran haunted by the ghosts of his dead comrades who is unable to reintegrate himself into civilian society. Although the late Chicago writer Tomás Rivera's novel *. . . y no se lo tragó la tierra* was published nearly 20 years earlier, it did not appear

© JERRY BAUER
Scott Turow

© JERRY BAUER
Tom Wolfe

in an English version, by southwestern fiction writer Rolando Hinojosa, until 1987, under the title *This Migrant Earth.* This short lyric collage of a book dramatizing the lives of migrant labourers up from the Mexican border was well worth the wait for serious readers who did not know Spanish.

As rich as the year was for novels, short fiction did not suffer, with such highly regarded story writers as Ann Beattie (*Where You'll Find Me*) and Jayne Anne Phillips (*Fast Lanes*) bringing out collections, as did novelists Richard Ford and Richard Bausch, with *Rock Springs* and *Spirits,* respectively, two of the finest volumes of short fiction of this or any recent year. Iowa writer Jane Smiley won praise for *The Age of Grief,* which contains five stories along with the title novella, the story of a dentist and his wife coming to terms with the difficulties of a settled marriage and the onset of early middle age. Ron Carlson, author of two novels, published *The News of the World,* a roundly applauded story collection (six of which were staged off-Broadway under the title "Bigfoot Stole My Wife").

New writers Steve Stern and Pinckney Benedict also published collections of short fiction. Stern's *Lazar Malkin Enters Heaven* was a well-received sheaf of quasi-supernatural tales about Jews in Memphis, Tenn. Benedict, still a student at the Iowa Writers Workshop, set his powerful stories in West Virginia. As the year drew to a close, *The Bonfire of the Vanities,* the first novel by "new journalist" Tom Wolfe, was climbing up the best-seller list. A briskly conducted passage from Park Avenue to the streets of the South Bronx, from expensive dinner parties to foul-smelling jailhouse holding cells, Wolfe's story of a bond broker run afoul of the law gave him the opportunity to write like the Dickens he imagined himself to be. The novel falls short of such greatness, but it is entertaining and would undoubtedly remain on the best-seller lists well into 1988.

*Nonfiction.* Two books, both critiques of U.S. culture in general and the U.S. educational system in particular, captured considerable attention. *Cultural Literacy,* by University of Virginia literary critic E. D. Hirsch, even went so far as to supply a long list of names and catchphrases that, if not recognized, suggested that the reader lacked a sharp understanding of Western culture. *The Closing of the American Mind,* by University of Chicago professor Allan Bloom (*see* BIOGRAPHIES), argued the failure of U.S. schools and the damaged condition of learning in the U.S. Both volumes spent a large part of the year on the best-seller lists, a situation that suggested the paradoxical nature of the national literary culture since neither book is terribly easy to read. San Francisco journalist Randy Shilts offered a controversial and extremely timely account of another crisis, the AIDS (acquired immune deficiency syndrome) epidemic, and its political and social roots and ramifications in *And the Band Played On.*

"Driving though Iowa, mid-May. On both sides of the highway, pale green lines of sprouted soy beans run through the back furrows like basting threads. It doesn't take long to get where we're headed." This was the opening of Patricia Hampl's moving memoir, *Spillville,* about Bohemian composer Antonin Dvorak in the U.S. Pulitzer Prize winner Annie Dillard ventured into memoir with *An American Childhood,* not her best book overall but one that contains some of her best prose. Arthur Miller published his autobiography, *Timebends,* an innovative and fascinating look at his life and times. James D. Houston, a California-based fiction writer and journalist, published *The Men in My Life,* a briskly wrought connected series of sketches about ordinary men, such as his uncle and father, who had a major impact on his education and life. Alan Cheuse—novelist and critic—published *Fall Out of Heaven,* an interlocking memoir of several generations set in the U.S. and the U.S.S.R. Poet Maxine Kumin published *In Deep,* her second collection of essays about country living, which showed her characteristic wit and intelligence. The most provocative literary criticism of the year came from Richard Poirier in *The Renewal of Literature,* subtitled "Emersonian Reflections" on American Writing and Culture.

Aside from Kim Townsend's *Sherwood Anderson,* little important work was done on biographies of major U.S. literary figures, though *A Capote Reader,* the collected nonfiction of Truman Capote, did keep alive the sharp and witty journalism of the late writer.

*Poetry.* Robert Creeley's *Memory Gardens* was published in 1987, as were new volumes of verse by Donald Hall (*The Happy Man*), Charles Simic (*Unending Blues*), and Jane Kenyon (*The Boat of Quiet Hours*). John Ashbery brought out *April Galleons,* and C. K. Williams offered *Flesh and Blood,* the latest of his experiments in poems with uncharacteristically long lines about the workaday life. The latter book also contained a striking elegy to the late poet Paul Zweig. Sharon Olds, in *The Gold Cell,* wrote of the feeling of terror and pleasure that came of family life. One notable volume of translation was the *Brocade River Poems,* selected works of the Tang Dynasty courtesan Xue Tao (Hsüeh T'ao), translated from the Chinese by Virginia poet Jeanne Larsen. Poet and critic David Lehman edited *Ecstatic Occasions, Expedient Forms,* an anthology in which 65 contemporary poets, including Robert Pinsky, Rachel Hadas, Alice Fulton, Edward Hirsch, Frank Bidart, and

Richard Wilbur

Charles Wright, selected one of their own poems and commented upon it.

*Literary Awards.* The Pulitzer Prize for fiction was awarded to Peter Taylor, the dean of American short-story writers, for the second novel of his long career, *A Summons to Memphis* (published in 1986), a beautifully wrought story about the effects on his children in Tennessee and New York of an elderly father's desire to remarry. The Pulitzer for poetry went to Rita Dove for her 1986 narrative sequence *Thomas and Beulah.* The American Book Award for fiction was given to E. L. Doctorow for *World's Fair,* his 1986 novel about a young boy growing up in the Bronx. The National Book Critics Circle gave its fiction prize to Reynolds Price for his novel *Kate Vaiden.* Edward Hirsch won the NBCC award for poetry for his lyric *Wild Gratitude.* Joseph Brodsky took the NBCC criticism prize for *Less Than One,* essays on poetry. Among more recently established awards, the *Los Angeles Times* fiction prize went to Louise Erdrich for her much-lauded novel *The Beet Queen.* Richard Wiley's *Soldiers in Hiding,* an ingenious book about two Japanese-Americans stranded in Japan at the outbreak of World War II, captured the PEN/Faulkner Prize. A half dozen Whiting Awards, each worth $25,000, went to writers and poets, among them novelists Joan Chase and Alice McDermott, story writer Pam Durban, poet Michael Ryan, and essayist Gretel Ehrlich. Richard Wilbur was appointed poet laureate, taking over from the ailing Robert Penn Warren. (ALAN CHEUSE)

**Canada.** More and more poets were turning to and turning out fiction, launching their craft on the wider waters of the short story and novel—and sometimes finding it getting away from them. In Jane Urquhart's collection of short stories, *Storm Glass,* for example, the imagery, rich though it was, sometimes seemed to have been expanded to fit the rectangular demands of the prose page. In Michael Ondaatje's *In the Skin of a Lion,* on the other hand, the complex plot arose from the machinations of nasty characters and the contrivances of nice ones and was carried along on a fine articulation of motive and circumstances.

Four western poets also published prose works during the year. The poet-heroine of George Bowering's *Caprice* tracks her brother's murderer from British Columbia to New Mexico and back again, along a trail strewn with puns and other cunning conceits, while in the shorter fictions of *The Parrot Who Could,* Robin Skelton ranges from the far side of Victoria to "the near side of the Twilight Zone." Susan Musgrave's *The Dancing Chicken,* by contrast, is centred in the black/bleak-humoured hearts of small-town families and institutions. Although Elizabeth Brewster's stories in *Visitations* are also set among ordinary people caught up in the drama of what to others seem ordinary lives, and the insights are as keen, the experience is a gentler one than in Musgrave's book.

Two poets incorporated prose into their work in a slightly different way. Under Gwendolyn MacEwen's deft handling, the long prose poems in *Afterworlds* are passionate mediums for the contemplation and transformation of memory, while Fred Wah's improvisations in *Music at the Heart of Thinking* are apt responses to some exponents of contemporary critical writing.

Prose writers, on the whole, seemed to stick to their last. However, while continuing as a novelist, Jack Hodgins made a major shift in style from magic realism to realistic representation in *The Honorary Patron.* Jane Rule further explored the territory of the desert-hearted who find wellsprings of understanding and compassion in unexpected places in *Memory Board.* In *Unknown Soldier* by George Payerle, the protagonist must learn to reclaim his capacity for love in his present life by finally letting the past die. Two novels set in Alberta—*Getting Married in Buffalo Jump* by Susan Haley, an engaging account of an unusual courtship, and *Swann: A Mystery* by Carol Shields, a grim recounting of an old, unsolved, brutal murder—demonstrated just how different the same landscapes, internal as well as external, can be when presented from different perspectives.

Poetry continued to be a popular cottage industry in Canada, with the year's bounty including Raymond Souster's *The Eyes of Love,* in which poems written about the time of his marriage are accompanied by poems celebrating that marriage through 40 years; the no-doubt-prematurely-titled *Final Reckoning: Poems 1982–1986* by Irving Layton, marking the occasion of his 75th birthday, along with his *In My Father's House,* recollecting the Jews' long and tragic encounters with history; Ralph Gustafson's *Winter Prophecies,* the observations of an intelligence well seasoned but unwearied; the *Word-House of a Grandchild* by Liliane Welch, where the tempestuous exchanges between her Italian grandfather and Belgian grandmother beat about and above the child's head; and Bronwen Wallace's *The Stubborn Particulars of Grace,* in which innocence and experience inform each other. Milton Acorn's posthumous *I Shout Love and Other Poems* contains some of his best forgotten early works. Gary Geddes, continuing to be oriented toward the East, nevertheless threw harsh light on the Canadian conscience in *Hong Kong,* poems honouring those sent to fight and die for a lost cause.

There were several other books dedicated to heroes of heterogeneous manifestation, including Patricia Young's *All I Ever Needed Was a Very Beautiful Room,* a narrative poem about Jean Rhys; Stephen Scobie's *The Ballad of Isobel Gunn,* the biography of the determined woman who joined the Hudson's Bay Company disguised as a man; Paulette Jiles's adroit combination of conjecture and fact in *The Jesse James Poems;* and Marilyn Bowering's *Anyone Can See I Love You, Marilyn Monroe.* (*See also* Biographies: *Atwood, Margaret.*)          (ELIZABETH WOODS)

## FRENCH

**France.** French publishers felt that it had been a bad year, with sales down and some firms involved in takeovers or regrouping, especially in the field of *la bande dessinée,* the cartoon albums that appealed to a wide audience and were in some cases a significant outlet for imaginative expression. This mood did not extend throughout the literary scene, however. The autumn season saw the publication of 54 first novels; there were worthy new books by estab-

Tahar Ben Jelloun
◦DENIS ROCHE—SEUIL

lished writers and signs of a revived interest in poetry.

All was not gloom and despondency, then, though the public apparently read less and some intellectuals, as always, were ready to proclaim a decline in French and European culture: Alain Finkielkraut, for example, in *La Défaite de la pensée,* or Bernard-Henri Lévy with an *Eloge des intellectuels* protesting against the influence of television. Hervé Hamon and Patrick Rotman's *Génération* gave the most penetrating survey of cultural trends since the 1950s. Works on politics and current affairs included books by Emmanuel Breuilhe and Roland Girard on AIDS and the inevitable AIDS novel, Dominique Fernandez's *La Gloire du paria.*

The 350th anniversary of René Descartes's *Discours de la méthode* (1637) provided an opportunity to reexamine the Cartesian tradition, André Glucksmann confidently asserting the philosopher's crucial role in French thought in *Descartes, c'est la France.* One might hesitate to go that far. Biography remained a popular genre and showed the diverse personalities and currents of ideas that had contributed to the making of the country, among them Beaumarchais, the subject of René Pomeau's *Beaumarchais ou la bizarre destinée.* In particular, biographers turned to subjects whose careers had culminated in the grim days of World War II: the Vichy leader Philippe Pétain (Marc Ferro), the politician Pierre Laval (Fred Kupferman), and the writer Robert Brasillach (Anne Brassié). These were complemented, and perhaps contradicted, by Michèle Cointet-Labrousse's *Vichy, un régime fasciste.* Henri Troyat continued his series of powerful biographies of Russian writers with *Gorki,* and there were assessments of Albert Camus (Roger Grenier) and Romain Gary (Dominique Bona).

The publication of Paul Gadenne's collected stories, *Scènes dans le château,* confirmed the reputation of an austere and isolated figure, long neglected after his

death in 1956. Another outsider, Henri Michaux, who died in 1984, was commemorated with a collection titled *Affrontements.* Literary studies included Jacques Roubaud's brilliant essay on the verse art of the troubadours, *La Fleur inverse.*

Several novelists with confirmed reputations pursued favourite themes. Yves Berger recolonized a largely imaginary America in *Les Matins du Nouveau Monde,* only his third novel in 25 years. Françoise Sagan confirmed her "new style" with *Un Sang d'aquarelle,* set against the background of the German occupation. Jacques Roubaud followed *La Belle Hortense* (1985) with *L'Enlèvement d'Hortense,* a further acknowledgment of the influence of Raymond Queneau and the OuLiPo group; and Zoë Oldenbourg, in *La Joie-souffrance,* carried on where she had left off in *Les Amours égarées.* Readers also knew what to expect when André Pieyre de Maniargues contrived an erotic encounter for his hero in the Paris *métro* (*Tout disparaîtra*), while the title of Didier Martin's *Double messieurs* would have prepared them for the writer's familiar ironies and ambiguities.

These were all accomplished works, so the sense of déjà vu was more reassuring than tiresome. It was nevertheless a relief to discover in Simon Leys a first novelist tackling an entirely original theme. *La Mort de Napoléon* started from the premise that the emperor did not die on St. Helena but escaped, eventually ending up in an asylum inhabited entirely by would-be Napoleons. In Guy Hocquenghem's *Eve* a man meets his twin sister, the product of bioengineering. This novel was among those on a shortlist for the Prix Goncourt that also included Marie Cardinal's *Les Grands désordres,* Tahar Ben Jelloun's *La Nuit sacrée* (the eventual winner), and Angelo Rinaldi's *Les Roses de Pline.* (See *Introduction,* above.)

The historical novel, at least in its pure form, seemed to be declining in popularity, though Julien Green's *Les Pays lointains* was set in the American South of the 19th century. The prerevolutionary French court was the background to Claude Grimmer's *Mon tout, mon roi* and Jacques Bressler's *Le Jeu de la reine,* while Paule Langlois-Maire chose a more exotic location for *Le Crépuscule des dieux du Nil.*

The poetry Goncourt went to Yves Bonnefoy, a tribute to the outstanding poet of his generation. Bonnefoy published a collection of poems, *Ce qui fut sans lumière,* and of essays, *Récits en rêve.* The latter, like Philippe Jaccottet's critical writings in *Une Transaction secrète,* seemed to have the underlying concern of defending poetry against the assaults of contemporary criticism. There was less evidence of poets submitting to rigid formal constraints but a good deal of variety in their work, from the brief *retouches* of Daniel Boulanger (*A la marelle*) to the travelogue, myths, poems, and *noèmes* of Xavier Bordes (*La Pierre amour*) and the linguistic sensitivities of Ludovic Janvier (*La Mer à boire*) and Claude Roy (*Le Voyage d'automne*).

(ROBIN BUSS)

**Canada.** The novel scene, in 1987, was dominated by new, young writers, as witnessed by the works of François Gravel (*Benito*), Sylvain Trudel (*Le Souffle de l'Harmattan*), and others. In *Le Souffle de*

Michel Tremblay
CANAPRESS PHOTO SERVICE

*l'Harmattan,* one of the most original novels of the last few years in Quebec, Trudel uses two young children as the main characters, avoiding both narrative and stylistic incongruities as well as facile poetic effects. The plot blends the everyday and the poetic in such a natural manner that the reader is never reluctant to follow the two children in their quest for the promised land, whether it be aboard a custom-made submarine or a train with helium-filled tires. Trudel walks a tightrope between reality and enchantment without ever losing his balance.

It took Fernand Ouellette less than 30 days to write *Les Heures,* a long poem segmented into more than 80 short sections linked by one theme, the death of his father, which occurred seven months prior to the writing of this remarkable text. As always with Ouellette, the subject matter is very serious, dealing with the agony of a man and the reactions to his death of those who love him. One is reminded of the author's recent novel *Lucie, ou un midi en Novembre,* where death was envisaged as an elevation to a mystic existence. The reader is conveyed to what Ouellette himself called in an interview "a sort of exercise of death." *Les Heures* is not a book of revelation but rather the result of an inner quest punctuated by patience and humility, misery and questioning, leading to the final truth of *la vie / qui rompait son pacte.*

The most important theatrical publications of 1987 were the complex works of René-Daniel Dubois (*Le Printemps, Monsieur Deslauriers*) and Michel Tremblay (*Le Vrai monde?*), followed closely by *La Passion de Narcisse Mondou,* a simple and moving play by Gratien Gélinas, the father of modern theatre in Quebec. Another play, however, deserves special notice. In *Un oiseau vivant dans la gueule,* Jeanne-Mance Delisle ruthlessly exposes the sexual inhibitions and taboos of three characters, using a fascinating web of masks, mirrors, and various other deflecting and reflecting devices. (PIERRE HÉBERT)

## GERMAN

The outstanding Austrian novel of the year was Thomas Bernhard's *Die Auslöschung,* a monumental monologue in praise of entropy. With great verve its narrator inveighs against Bernhard's native Austria; seeking to "extinguish" the object of his diatribe, he himself perishes, appropriately enough with his final sentence.

Elsewhere too the National Socialist past continued to be topical. In Jurek Becker's *Bronsteins Kinder,* the father-son theme was given an unusual twist when the son finds that his father, a survivor of the Holocaust, is holding prisoner and torturing a former extermination camp guard. Peter Schneider's controversial *Vati,* portraying a Nazi criminal from the point of view of his son, was based on the visit to the notorious Josef Mengele in Brazil by his son Rolf. The hotel in the title of Eva Demski's *Hotel Hölle* is a symbol of West German society, inherited from a former Nazi, now the scene of jolly congresses but also of encounters with the sinister past. Oliver Storz's *Die Nebelkinder* was an intelligent contribution to the substantial volume of works that describe growing up in the Third Reich.

Post-World War II Germany was sufficiently old to become the subject of novels tracing its history. Through the story of twins who identify with former chancellors Konrad Adenauer and Willy Brandt, respectively, Hans-Josef Ortheil's *Schwerenöter* depicted the Federal Republic from its beginnings to the arrival of the Greens in Parliament. Alfred Cordes's *Caspar Coppenrath* was an entertaining picaresque novel of the postwar years. The division of Germany was the subject of Martin Walser's disappointing *Dorle und Wolf.* Much more ambitious was Libuse Monikova's prizewinning novel *Die Fassade,* which mingled history and fantasy.

Two other stories by women writers proved provocative. Johanna Walser's *Die Unterwerfung* focused on a young woman's determination to be unobtrusive, while Karin Reschke's *Margarete* was a contemporary version of Goethe's *Faust* from the point of view of the innocent girl he seduces. In both cases, the reader's reaction oscillates between irritation at the submissiveness of the victims and anger at the insensitivity of (largely male) society.

Patrick Süskind's novella *Die Taube* was an allegory of the impossibility of finding existential security. It did not, however, have quite the cult success of his *Das Parfum.* Friedrich Dürrenmatt's *Der Auftrag* was an ingenious thriller on a related theme: surveillance, whether by spy satellite, intelligence agencies, or God, as part of the human condition. Both Dieter Wellershoff (*Der Körper und die Träume*) and Adolf Muschg (*Der Turmhahn*) published collections of shorter pieces on the topic of male-oriented love and sexuality. The latter theme was also the subject of Joseph Zoderer's *Dauerhaftes Morgenrot,* a novella that seemed to owe some of its inspiration to the Hermann Hesse of *Steppenwolf.*

This preoccupation with the problems of existence to the exclusion of the problems of society was illustrated in the extraordinarily prolific output of Zoderer's Austrian compatriot Peter Handke. *Die*

*Wiederholung* used the motif of the journey to explore themes of language, nature, and identity, concluding with a vision of a new humanity that would come into being after the nuclear catastrophe. *Die Abwesenheit* was also the story of a journey; its mythical figures are in search of some Holy Grail. Handke also found time to publish the story *Nachmittag eines Schriftstellers* and the long poem and ars poetica *Gedicht an die Dauer.*

Important West German collections of poetry were published by Friederike Mayröcker (*Winterglück*), Jürgen Becker (*Odenthals Küste*), Wolf Biermann (*Affenfels und Barrikade*) and Rolf Haufs (*Felderland*).

Two outstanding novels from East Germany took as their subject the questionable ethics of contemporary science and technology together with the humanizing role that women might play. Helga Königsdorf's *Respektloser Umgang* employed the mode of fantasy; Christa Wolf's *Störfall* was a more obviously autobiographical documentation of the day when news of the Chernobyl nuclear reactor disaster reaches the narrator as she awaits word from the hospital where her brother is undergoing a brain operation—science can be a blessing as well as a curse. In its often harrowing depiction of a death from cancer, Charlotte Worgitzky's story *Heute sterben nur die andern* betrayed similar preoccupations.

Other East German novels were less concerned with the immediate past: Wolfgang Licht's *Die Geschichte der Gussmanns,* a novel of the years 1927–45; Erich-Günther Sasse's *Abgefunden,* on the difficulty of adapting to postwar society; and Jochen Hauser's *Die ruhigen Jahre der Rechlins,* a continuation of his earlier family novel. Major collections of poetry were Wilhelm Bartsch's *Übungen in Joch,* Richard Pietrass's *Spielball,* poems on the threat to the environment, and Volker Braun's *Langsamer knirschender Morgen* on the Sisyphean task of constructing socialism. (J. H. REID)

## SCANDINAVIAN

**Denmark.** A literary event of 1987 was the publication of Kirsten Thorup's *Den yderste grænse,* completing the series of novels that started with *Lille Jonna* in 1977. Defying accepted narrative perspectives, they mirrored Danish society from the 1950s to the present and had been compared to major works such as those of Martin Andersen Nexø.

Two posthumous novels were published in 1986. Albert Dam's long *Mod det ukendte mål,* dating from 1935, needed to have the reputation of its author established before a publisher would undertake it. Uneven, it resembled the Danish *udviklingsroman* but, typically for Dam, had a vision beyond it. The second and more recent posthumous work was Leif Panduro's *Den ufuldendte dommer,* an unfinished novel intended as a sequel to *Høfeber* and once more examining the borderline between sanity and insanity.

Anders Bodelsen's *Guldregn* was developed from his TV thriller of the same name. Bodelsen had earlier shown his skill with TV and radio drama, and three of his radio plays—*Professor Mancinis hemmelighed, Radio,* and *Passageren*—had appeared in book form. While Bodelsen's dramas remained within the realist tradition, those of Inger Christensen were anything but realistic. Of the six plays in *Ufa og andre spil,* five were radio plays that carefully exploit the voice and situation possibilities offered by that medium, while the sixth echoes Chekhov's *Three Sisters.* Bo Green Jensen, once best known for his poetry, published a volume of short stories, *Støjen af virkeligheden,* reflecting a series of attempts to escape an intolerable reality.

Thorkild Bjørnvig's poems *Gennem regnbuen* were less an attempt to escape reality than an attempt to understand it, introducing cosmic perspectives in stark contrast to glimpses of the material world. The young but highly respected Juliane Preisler published *Det tændte hus,* concerned with togetherness, solitariness, and the loneliness of two without contact. Sten Kaaalø's *Spurven. 25 salmer* combined the very earthly with an expression of Christian faith. In his way, Kaalø continued the long Danish tradition of fine hymn writing.

The deservedly celebrated William Heinesen was awarded the Nordic Culture Prize of the Swedish Academy.

(W. GLYN JONES)

**Norway.** Kjell Askildsen's *En plutselig frigjørende tanke,* Sidsel Mørck's *Kikkeren,* and Halldis Moren Vesaas's *Så Nær deg* constituted an exceptionally rich year for the short story. Some of the most unforgettable reading was to be found in Fredrik Skagen's documentary *Purpurhjertene,* based on the horrors of the Vietnam war as experienced by a Norwegian serving in the U.S. Army. A bewitching mixture of Oriental philosophy, myth, cultural history, and poetic sensuality formed the basis of Tor Åge Bringsværd's *Gobi. Djengis Khan.* In a semidocumentary novel, *Sensommer,* Atle Næss recreated the touching but unfulfilled love affair between the teenage Viennese Emilie Bardach and the veteran celebrity Henrik Ibsen.

The final stages of the German occupation in northern Norway and the post–World War II years of reconstruction formed a potent backdrop to Laila and Thor Thorsen's collective novel *Istid.* Herbjørg Wassmo's *Hudløs himmel* provided the heartrending conclusion to the trilogy about Tora, the illegitimate daughter of a German soldier and his Norwegian mistress. In *Katedralen,* Terje Stigen presented a love story lived out against the total devastation of a German town during the last weeks of the war.

The thriller continued to flourish. Fredrik Skagen's *Døden i Capelulo* enters the murky world of secret weapons manufacture, and Norwegians on a package tour to London get into trouble in Ingvar Ambjørnsen's *Heksenes kors.* Lars Saabye Christensen's *Sneglene* focused on terrorism in France. Dag Solstad's semiautobiographical novel *Roman 1987* analyzed the political climate in Norway over the previous two decades. Modern marital mores were the focus of Knut Faldbakken's outspoken play *Livet med Marilyn.*

Tor Obrestad combined Old Norse myth and contemporary polemics in a large collection of poems, *Misteltein.* The loss of his wife was the theme of Sigmund Skard's profound and moving poems in *Atterklang.* Robert Ferguson's *Enigma: The Life of Knut Hamsun,* was a comprehensive,

well-researched, and well-written biography. Valuable scholarship on central aspects of Norwegian literature formed the substance of Daniel Haakonsen's *Tolkning og teori. Festskrift til 70-årsdagen.*

(TORBJØRN STØVERUD)

**Sweden.** The year 1987 saw three fine poetic offerings. In his 78th year Karl Vennberg, uncompromisingly disillusioned and of luminous diction, published *Längtan till Egypten;* Göran Sonnevi's *Oavslutade dikter* thematized states of change and development; while Bengt Emil Johnson's collection *För resten. Improviserade dikter o dyl.* offered clarity, simplicity, and acute perception.

In *Vita bergens barn,* Per Anders Fogelström completed his much-loved historical cycle on the lives of workers in Stockholm, spanning the period 1750 to 1950. Sven Dellbanc's novel *Moria land* presented a frightening scenario for the early 21st century of Sweden under foreign rule, with self-seeking opportunism and betrayal as natural concomitants. A sprightlier satire of the near future was provided by Göran Hägg's portrayal, in *Anders och Dafne,* of bureaucracy in the computer age (supposedly written by a computer). Torgny Lindgren's *Ljuset* presented a mythical northern community with few inhabitants left after a ravaging disease that also attacks justice and morality. In a story of great beauty and inventiveness, righteousness is finally reinstated by this Catholic novelist.

P. C. Jersild's immensely ambitious *Geniernas återkomst* belonged to this same category of chronological projections, in his case both back to Neanderthal times and forward to the rebirth by means of genetic manipulation of Shakespeare, Beethoven, Einstein, and Picasso, as well as certain extinct species. These creatures, isolated on an island (an erstwhile refuge for AIDS sufferers), are unable to reproduce themselves, nor can they function in an entirely foreign environment.

Novels with a contemporary setting included *Smärtprovet,* in which Ingmar Björkstén dealt sensitively with the existential problems of a young homosexual whose self-absorbed father first comes to understand him after he has been killed in Africa. Jonas Gardell's funny, inventive, and moving *Prariehundarna* also featured a homosexual relationship. Inger Edelfeldt wove a persuasive and chilling contemporary tale of a small religious sect and the power exerted by its male leader over its female members.

Fictionalized autobiography formed another category. Loka Enmark's *Inkassererskan* and Birgitta Stenberg's *Spanska trappan* were of the vivid, confessional variety. In *Svarta villan* the poet Ernst Brunner gave a racy account of his childhood haunts of the 1950s and 1960s, with a parent generation of central European refugees from Nazism. Young Mare Kandre's *Bübins unge* was a symbolic-poetic account of a young girl's growing pains.

(KARIN PETHERICK)

## ITALIAN

Piero Chiara's last novel, *Saluti notturni dal passo della Cisa,* appeared soon after his death on Dec. 31, 1986, and became one of the most popular novels of the year. It was a lucid, unpretentious, open-ended thriller—a Pirandellian plot without Piran-

Aldo Busi

dello's metaphysical preoccupations—that once more confirmed Chiara's talents as a narrator. Equally successful was Leonardo Sciascia's *1912 + 1.* It too could be read as a thriller, though it was, like so many of Sciascia's recent works, a piercing reexamination of a real event, a crime passionel that engrossed Italian public opinion in 1913. Sciascia cleverly exploited official records and press reports of the crime and ensuing trial to highlight public hypocrisy and the vagaries, if not the class bias, of the judiciary.

Very few novels were concerned with the past and present history of the country. *I fuochi del Basento,* Raffaele Nigro's first novel, was a remarkable attempt to write the history of southern Italian peasantry through the story of one family from Basilicata between 1784 and 1861. In a style reminiscent of oral narration, mixing legends with historical events, real places with fictional characters, Nigro vividly described the utter misery, violence, and brutality of peasant life. His book won the prestigious Campiello Prize.

Closer to the present was *Gli invisibili* by Nanni Balestrini, a neo-avant-garde writer who had been accused, and later acquitted, of terrorist involvement in the 1970s. His novel described the experiences of a political militant, the reasons and ideals that drove him to embrace terrorist violence, his treatment at the hands of the police, and his imprisonment. Written in short, unpunctuated paragraphs, the book was effective in terms of language and style, but more startling was its refusal to repudiate the violent extremism of the late 1970s at a time when it was being officially obliterated, not least by its former protagonists.

Other novels focused on the present moral and political climate of the country. *La grande Giò* by Alberto Bevilacqua was an ambitious and largely indigestible mixture of real and surreal elements, aiming to be an homage to the eternal feminine and an indictment of the evils of contemporary society. On the same theme, but fresher and more imaginative, was *La delfina bizantina,* Aldo Busi's third novel in three years, a vigorous, overflowing, and overextended pastiche of literary forms and styles, satirizing the male-dominated world of Italian politics. A preoccupation with humanity's violence against nature was at the heart of Carlo Sgorlon's *L'ultima valle*, where the life of a mountain village and its natural environment are first upset by the building of a gigantic dam and then destroyed by its collapse.

However, the trend toward the "private" was more in evidence, often with results of dignified, if not impressive, quality. In this category were *Romanza* by Sergio Zavoli, memories of a youth in Rimini before and after World War II; *Nei mari estremi* by Lalla Romano, retelling the mystery of love and death in the encounter with her husband and his subsequent death; *Il golfo del Paradiso* by Gina Lagorio, about an old painter who lives withdrawn from the world yet in harmony with nature; and *Dogana d'amore* by Nico Orengo, a short novel and fable of crystalline transparency about a man's fascination with a past love. Perhaps the most memorable was *I vetri*, Renato Ghiotto's posthumous novel, where the mind of the narrator merges (or so the narrator believes) with that of a hugely powerful computer—a theme in which Ghiotto, who later died of a brain tumour, achieved moments of haunting intensity.

Among works by younger novelists, there were, besides Busi's book, *Yucatan* by Andrea De Carlo, a rather unconvincing story of the making of a film that is itself turned into a film, and, far more interesting, *Il filo dell'orizzonte* by Antonio Tabucchi, a detective story that intriguingly reveals little about its characters or even about the crime at the plot's centre.

The recent surge in popularity of the essay form was confirmed by the appearance of some works of enduring quality. These included *Jura* by Luigi Meneghello, a collection of essays, mainly about language, that seem to have arisen as a product of the critical self-consciousness that impels and at the same time impedes his writing. The best essay and perhaps the best book of the year was in this genre; *Danubio* by Claudio Magris, at once essay and autobiographical novel, was a sentimental journey from the sources to the delta of the Danube, in which Magris, in compellingly evocative language, brought to life his fascination with the landscapes and the cultures of the peoples who dwell along the course of the river.

Besides Piero Chiara, the writers Carlo Cassola and Primo Levi (*see* OBITUARIES) died during the year.          (LINO PERTILE)

# SPANISH

**Spain.** Late in 1986 the Spanish playwright Antonio Buero Vallejo received the prestigious Miguel de Cervantes Prize, the highest award in international Hispanic letters, for his contribution to the resurgence and steady evolution of postwar theatre, as well as for the enduring social relevance and universality of his work. From his famous *Historia de una escalera* (1949) to his most recent play, *Lázaro en el laberinto* (1986), Buero's central preoccupation had remained constant: man's clouded perception of his moral condition and his resulting doubt about humanity's duty to itself.

In fiction, the historical novel was unusually conspicuous. Néstor Luján won the Plaza & Janés International Novel Prize with a thriller told in a 17th-century voice,

*Decidnos, ¿quién mató al conde?*, based on conflicting accounts of the mysterious assassination in Madrid, in 1622, of the count of Villamediana, a notoriously shady literary figure of the day. The intensely competitive Planeta Prize went to a previously unpublished writer, Juan Eslava, for *En bueca del unicornio*, a first-person narrative in the antique style of a contemporaneous chronicler, about a 15th-century Spanish expedition to Africa in search of a cure for King Enrique IV's impotence. Among established writers, Luis Goytisolo offered another challenging novel, *La paradoja del ave migratoria*, a complex story full of self-canceling experiments with successivity in narration itself. Juan Benet added a third volume to his masterwork, *Herrumbrosas lanzas;* and in *La balada de amor y soledad*, the lyricism of Jesús Fernández Santos's meditations on love, death, war, and nature earned high praise.

Three younger writers attracting serious critical attention were Antonio Muñoz Molina (*El invierno en Lisboa*), Raúl Ruiz (*Hay un lugar feliz lejos, muy lejos* and *El discurso de vivir*), and Jesús Ferrera (*Opium*, 1986).

In poetry, Jaime Siles celebrated the sonorities of speech in the "sonic games" of *Poemas al revés* and *Columnae*, and Francisco Brines won three important awards for the lucidly sensuous and joyful poems of *Otoño de las rosas* (1986). To the collection of his complete works, *Poesías (1970–1985)*, published late in 1986, the psychiatrically troubled poet Leopoldo María Panero added *Poemas del manicomio de Mondragón;* technically rigorous, aesthetically unclassifiable, Panero's deeply introverted poetry stunned readers with the range and power of its ecstasies and horrors.                    (ROGER L. UTT)

**Latin America.** The literary event of most resonance in Latin America was the awarding of the Romulo Gallegos Prize to the Argentine novelist Abel Posse, author of the novels *Los perros del paraiso, Damion,* and other fiction. The major novels to appear were two Mexican works, Sergio Galindo's *Otilia Rauda* and Carlos Fuentes's *Cristóbal nonato,* the Chilean José Donoso's *La desesperanza* (late 1986), and the Colombian Rafael Humberto Moreno-Durán's *Los felinos del canciller.* In Latin America in general, writers were particularly interested in the historical novel.

Galindo and Federico Patán shared the Villaurrutia Novel Prize in Mexico with *Otilia Rauda* (late 1986) and *El último exilio,* respectively. *Otilia Rauda,* set in the rural area of the state of Veracruz, was quite likely the most accomplished work of Galindo's lengthy career. Patán's more experimental *El último exilio* was an introspective treatment of the Spanish presence in Mexico. One of the most discussed and polemical books of the year in Mexico was Fuentes's *Cristóbal nonato,* which featured the playfulness and satire typical of Fuentes's fiction. Joaquin-Armando Chacón won the Diana Novedades Prize with *El recuento de los daños,* a plotless book that examines the city of Cuernavaca. Ricardo Elizondo Elizondo published a family and historical novel, *Setenta veces siete.* Gerardo Laveaga and Silvia Molina also provided well-written historical novels, *Valeria* and *La familia vino del norte,* respectively.

In Colombia Moreno-Durán established his central role in fiction of the 1980s with his fourth novel, *Los felinos del canciller,* a satire of literary and political traditions in early 20th-century Colombia. In *Bulevar de los heroes,* Edgar García Aguilar also satirized the unique relationship between Colombia's literature and political traditions. Tomás González was awarded the Plaza & Janés National Novel Prize for *Para antes del olvido,* a nostalgic evocation of early 20th-century Antioquia. *La ceniza del libertador* by Fernando Cruz Kronfly is an exhaustive treatment of Simón Bolívar's final days in New Granada. Próspero Morales's *Los pecados de Inés de Hinajosa,* which was a rewriting of a scandalous love story set in the Colonial period, was a best-seller in Colombia during much of 1987.

Marvel Moreno offered a feminine perspective of experiences in Barranquilla in *En diciembre llegaban las brisas.* Héctor Rojas Herazo completed his third novel after a hiatus of 20 years, the massive *Celia se pudre.* Juan Gustavo Cobo Borda published a new edition of his poems, *Todos los poetas son santos e irán al cielo,* and Darío Jaramillo Agudelo produced *77 poemas.* The Fundación Guberek published poems by Santiago Mutis Durán (*Soñadores de pájaros*), María Mercedes Carranza (*Vainas*), and Carlos Framb (*Antinoo*) and the essay *Yo vi crecer un país* by Simón Guberek.

In the Southern Cone, Donoso, still writing in Chile, published *La desesperanza* (late 1986) as a response to contemporary social and political conditions in his country. Ariel Dorfman, writing in exile, created a satire of the dictator Pinochet's Chile with *The Last Song of Manuel Sendero* (previously published in Spanish). Isabel Allende, also writing in exile, published her third novel, *Eva Luna,* a work with the magic realism and feminine focus of her previous fiction. Osvaldo Soriano penned his fourth novel in Argentina, *A sus plantas rendido un león* (late 1986), an absurd story dealing with an Argentine in Africa. Manuel Vásquez-Bigi from Argentina wrote an experimental novel with multiple narrators, *Son dos las puertas del destino.*

One of the most significant publications in Central America was *Masas en guerra,* an anthology of poetry, art, and culture from Nicaragua compiled by the Peruvian critic José Miguel Oviedo. The Nicaraguan Sergio Ramírez wrote a Nicaraguan family story of the early 20th century, *Tiempo del fulgor* (late 1986). The venerable Rogelio Sinán, who continued writing in Panama, produced a new edition of his novel from the 1940s, *Plenilunio.* The Panamanian Enrique Jaramillo Levi published a volume of short stories, *La voz despalabrada* (late 1986), and Claribel Alegría of El Salvador created an autobiographical prose/verse novel, *Luisa in Realityland,* originally written in Spanish.

Casa de las Americas published *Jonás y la ballena rosada* by José W. Montes, a story of the decadence of the Bolivian bourgeoisie. Other noteworthy fiction included the Cuban Francisco López Sacha's novel *El cumpleaños del fuego* (late 1986) and the Venezuelan Alejandro Rossi's volume of short fiction, *El cielo Sotero.*

(RAYMOND LESLIE WILLIAMS)

## PORTUGUESE

**Portugal.** The annual output of novels and short stories was increasing, showing a great variety of styles. José Saramago, whose works had been translated into many languages, succeeded admirably in making fantasy the most convincing reality. In his novel *Jangada de Pedra* ("The Stone Raft") he shows the Iberian Peninsula moving adrift, following a cataclysmic fracture that separates it from the rest of Europe. The fortunes of people involved in a floating land and the mysterious encounters that bind some of them together are pursued with great subtlety and humour. But *Jangada de Pedra* is also a complex allegory in which the identity of Iberia, the variety of its cultures, and the vitality of its oral traditions are cleverly fused into a magic and cautionary tale of fascinating originality and a multiplicity of meanings.

The prizewinner of the year for fiction was David Mourão-Ferreira with his novel *Um Amor Feliz* ("A Happy Love Story"). In a fresh and refined return to the direct narrative, Mourão-Ferreira explores with great psychological insight the affair of an artist with a mysterious, beautiful woman. The complexity of this relationship is enhanced in the narrative by the hostility shown to the author by the main character, who tells his own story. This is a subtle device whereby the narrator functions as a mirror of revelations concerning not only other characters but also the society in which they move. The rhythm and sweep of the narrative and the meticulously crafted story make the book refreshing and compelling reading.

The most experimental narrative to appear was *O Apóstolo de Si* ("The Apostle of Oneself") by Júlio Moreira. By questioning the fiction of the character, Moreira explores the solitude of the self and the paths that lead up to the other through love and desire. The poetic quality of the imagery conveys a sense of the uncanny in a way that has rarely been attained in Portuguese literature.  (L. S. REBELO)

**Brazil.** Three of the nation's most internationally respected cultural figures died during the year: Gilberto Freyre (*see* OBITUARIES), Carlos Drummond de Andrade, and Leon Hirszman. Drummond died 12 days after the death of his daughter, Maria Julieta Drummond de Andrade, a *cronista* and university professor of Latin-American literature. Drummond, whose career began in the 1920s along with the modernists of Minas Gerais, defended the Brazilian identity and cultural heritage in his most important poetic works. Eloquent English versions of his poems were rendered by two distinguished American poets, the late Elizabeth Bishop and Mark Strand, both of whose translations appeared in a collection of Drummond's works published late in 1986: *Traveling in the Family.*

Freyre, who was decorated with the French Legion of Honour in 1986, published a volume early in the year, *Os Modos dos Homens, as Modas das Mulheres,* which analyzes the roles and interpersonal relationships between men and women in northeastern Brazilian society. Although many of Freyre's romanticized theories about Brazilian slave society had been disputed over the last decades, he remained a highly respected cultural figure,

perhaps Brazil's last direct link to the age of slavery.

Hirszman's death, at 49 years of age, brought to a close the career of one of Brazil's most innovative film directors. His film version of the dramatist Gianfrancesco Guarnieri's *Eles Ñao Usam Black Tie,* with the author in a leading role, received the Venice Film Festival award in 1981, and his version of the novelist Graciliano Ramos's *São Bernardo* was also highly praised in Brazil and abroad. His final film, *Imagens do Inconsciente,* opened late in 1987. The deaths of the novelist and folklorist Orígenes Lessa and the poet and historian of modernism Joaquim Inojosa were also of note. The centenary of the birth of the composer Heitor Villa-Lobos was celebrated internationally. New studies of his life and works were published by Bruno Kiefer and Luiz Paulo Horta. The poet and novelist Ledo Ivo was elected to the Brazilian Academy of Letters to fill Lessa's seat.

New prose fiction included: Deonísio da Silva's novel *A Cidade dos Padres,* which continues his saga of life in the interior of São Paulo; José Louzeiro's *Devotos do Odio,* dealing with rural violence; a novel about jail life by Frei Betto; and shortstory collections by Luís Vilela and Ivan Ângelo. Women's role in daily life was the continuing theme of new fiction by Lya Luft, *Exílio,* and a collection of poems by Adélia Prado, *O Pelicano.*  (IRWIN STERN)

## RUSSIAN

**Soviet Literature.** Literary developments in 1986–87 were marked by openness and democratic change in Soviet public life. Old works previously published only abroad or not published at all took pride of place in magazines, annual collections, and publishing lists. Noticeable among them were a one-volume selection of Yevgeny Zamyatin, a prosaist who emigrated in 1931; *The Heart of a Dog,* a novella-lampoon by Mikhail Bulgakov; *Foundation Ditch* and *Doubting Makar,* philosophical and satirical fantasies by Andrey Platonov; *The Defense* and *Invitation to a Beheading,* novellas by Vladimir Nabokov; Nikolay Erdman's comedies *Credentials* and *Suicide;* and many of the writings of Nikolay Gumilyov, a poet sentenced to death in 1921.

Major works censored in their time became accessible, among them Aleksandr Bek's novel *A New Appointment,* with its memorable portrait of a Stalinist VIP, and Vladimir Tendryakov's novel *An Attempt on Delusions.* In poetry, Anna Akhmatova's *Requiem,* Aleksandr Tvardovsky's *Authorized by Memory,* and Mikhail Isakovsky's *A Tale of the Truth* were landmarks.

The greatest public acclaim accrued to novels and stories telling the truth about the price paid for socialist transformations. The second part of Boris Mozhayev's novel *Village Men and Women* and the third part of Vasily Belov's novel *The Eyes* were about the advent of collective patterns in Soviet agriculture. Sergey Antonov's novella *Vaska* described the construction of the subway (metro) in Moscow. In his major novel *The Children of Arbat St.,* Anatoly Rybakov presented a broad panorama of Soviet life in the early 1930s. Anatoly Pristavkin's novella *A Golden Cloud Spent the*

Anatoly Rybakov
© JERRY BAUER

*Night* treated a more recent taboo topic, the deportation of North Caucasian ethnic peoples.

Works about contemporary society were also marked by pronounced political content. In particular, Belov's novel *Everything Is to Come* aroused heated debate over its negation of urban culture. Sophisticated irony filled the pages of novels about intellectuals, like Andrey Bitov's *The Pushkin House,* Sergey Yesin's *Procrastinator,* Anatoly Afanasyev's *It Won't Hurt,* and Victor Konetsky's *Nobody'll Encroach on What We Won.* Yury Arakcheyev's *The Pyramid* was the story of a frame-up and its victim. The contemporary man in the street was shown in no ordinary aspect by Anatoly Azolsky in the novels *Stepan Sergeich* and *A Prolonged Shot* and by Sergey Kaledin in his novella *Humble Cemetery.* The Chernobyl nuclear reactor disaster was treated in Vladimir Yavorivsky's novel *Maria and Wormwood Toward the Close of the Century* and Vladimir Gubaryev's play *Sarcophagus.*

Satire was once again becoming one of the most promising trends in Soviet literature. Impressive examples of the genre were Fazil Iskander's *Rabbits and Boa Constrictors* and the Strugatsky brothers' *Lame Fate, A Tale of the Troika,* and *Rainy Time.*  (SERGEY CHUPRININ)

**Expatriate Russian Literature.** The year 1987 was a particularly exciting one where Russian émigré literature was concerned: some interesting titles published; a conference of younger exiled writers; and *glasnost* (openness) in the U.S.S.R. For all its limitations, *glasnost* resulted in freedom for Soviet political prisoners such as the poet Nizameddin Akhmetov and the novelist Leonid Borodin and in the publication of works by long-banned authors who could hitherto appear only in the West. Then in October the Nobel Prize for Literature went to the Leningrad poet Joseph Brodsky (*see* BIOGRAPHIES; *Introduction,* above), now living in the U.S. His latest collection of verse, *Urania,* was brought out earlier in the year by Ardis in Ann Arbor, Mich.

Also in the U.S., Lazar Fleischman published an anthology of the work of Boris Bozhnev, an almost forgotten Russian poet who died in exile 20 years earlier. The book, published by Berkeley Slavic Studies in California, was welcomed by experts as a major literary rediscovery.

*The Memoirs* of Oleg Volkov, recounting his experiences in Stalin's labour camps, was published by Atheneum in Paris. At 88 the oldest member of the Union of Soviet Writers, Volkov spent 27 years in the camps and prisons, which provided the material for his 800-page book. In an exceptionally outspoken article that first circulated in Russian samizdat before being reprinted in the Munich (West Germany)-based magazine *Strana i mir,* he expressed his reservations about *glasnost.* Asking why there were no books about the convicts whose bones were "scattered over the North and Siberia" and why Aleksandr Solzhenitsyn's *Gulag Archipelago* had not been published in the U.S.S.R., Volkov concluded: "Success depends entirely on whether the doors will be thrown wide to *glasnost* in earnest or whether it will all be limited to fine words. It is hard, looking back on the long years that I have lived through, to be optimistic."

The first conference of younger émigré writers (the so-called third wave) took place in Fribourg, Switz., in February, organized by Yury Galperin, who had opened an émigré publishing house in Switzerland. With the sole exception of Andrey Sinyavsky, all the participants were in their 30s or early 40s; they were writers who had done most or all of their writing after leaving the U.S.S.R. and whose work was based on their experiences in the West rather than their earlier life in their native land. Not regarding themselves as dissidents, they had discarded the old ideological preoccupations, taking a more detached view than their older colleagues.

Typical of these younger writers was Zinovy Zinik, a poet and novelist living in London, whose work was about the exile's search for his identity. Another third wave author was Sergey Dovlatov, two of whose books had been published by Slavica in New York: *Predstavlenie i Drugie Rozkazy* ("Performance and Other Stories"), a short story collection, and *Inostranka* ("The Foreign Girl"), a novel about the life of a Russian émigré in New York.

(GEORGE THEINER)

## EASTERN EUROPEAN LITERATURE

As in previous years, Poland and Czechoslovakia continued to bring out by far the greatest number of unofficial and underground titles, both in domestic samizdat and by émigré publishers abroad. The doyen of these publishing houses, the Polish *Kultura* in Paris, celebrated its 40th anniversary. One of its most recent publications, also published in samizdat in Poland, was Igor Newerley's *Zostalo z uczty Bogow* ("Left After God's Feast"), a reminiscence of the revolutionary years after 1917.

One of the best-selling underground titles in Poland was Jan Jozef Szczepanski's *Kadencia* ("Term of Office"), about the period when he was president of the Polish Writers Union. Two other interesting publications were *Obecnoscei* ("The Presence"), an anthology on diverse topics put together as a tribute to the Polish philosopher Leszek Kolakowski on his 60th birth-

day on October 23, and Karl Popper's well-known book *Open Society and Its Enemies,* its full text published for the first time in the Polish underground.

Two books about the first president of Czechoslovakia, T. G. Masaryk, came out: *Masarykuv triumf* ("Masaryk's Triumph") by Jiri Kovtun, who used the extensive Masaryk archive in the Library of Congress in Washington, D.C., to deal with Masaryk's years of exile during World War I; and *Filosof a politik TGM* ("TGM, Philosopher and Politician") by Jaroslav Opat, a Communist historian living in Prague. Kovtun's book was published by 68 Publishers in Toronto, who also brought out Karel Kaplan's *Nekrvava revoluce* ("The Bloodless Revolution"), dealing with the Communist coup in Czechoslovakia in February 1948. Opat's book was published by Index Publishers in Cologne, West Germany. The same émigré publisher also published *Daleko od stromu* ("Far from the Old Block"), a first novel by Zuzana Brabcova.

The energetic Alexander Tomsky published 12 titles in his Rozmluvy series in London. They included Petr Pithart's *Osmasedesaty* ("The Year '68"), about the year of the "Prague Spring" and the Soviet invasion of Czechoslovakia; *Az nakonec Ceska* ("To the End of Bohemia"), the last volume of Rio Preisner's trilogy in which the conservative thinker discussed the Czechoslovak experience with Communist dialectics; and Karel Schulz's *Legendy a invokace* ("Legends and Invocations"). This huge volume contained the entire oeuvre of the author, who died in 1942.

Arkyr publishers in Munich, West Germany, brought out *Generace 35–45,* an anthology of work by 18 "forbidden" Czechoslovak writers, some living in Czechoslovakia and some in exile, all of them aged between 35 and 45. They included Antonin Brousek, Petr Kabes, Eda Kriseova, and Jaroslav Hutka. Ludvik Vaculik's collection of feuilletons, *A Cup of Coffee with My Interrogator,* was published in English translation by Readers International in London. The author, a journalist and writer living in Prague, was awarded the Stockholm-based Charter 77 literary prize for 1987.

In April the Romanian authorities refused two German-Romanian writers, Helmut Frauendorfer and Helmut Seiler, permission to emigrate. Their work had been banned in the country, where increasing harassment was meted out to "politically undesirable" writers. In Yugoslavia a poetry collection called *Flowers on the Balcony* was withdrawn from bookstores when it was discovered that one of the 22 poets represented in it had become an Albanian nationalist. All the poets came from the Kosovo region, where there had been repeated demonstrations and riots by members of the Albanian community.

In Hungary official recognition was withdrawn from the 600-strong Writers Union, which had previously voted most of its Communist Party members off the executive board. The new board, composed of 71 nonparty members, had openly criticized party policies. A new "basic organization of writers, poets, and translators" was later set up to replace the union. New Republic Books in New York published an English translation of Miklos Haraszti's *The Velvet*

*Prison: Artists Under State Socialism,* in which the 42-year-old Hungarian dissident writer warned the West not to be taken in by "apparent liberalization."

(GEORGE THEINER)

## JEWISH

**Hebrew.** The main features of Hebrew literature in 1987 were its impressive productivity and its lively receptivity. Nearly 50,000 copies of A. B. Yehoshua's novel *Molkho* and over 70,000 of Amos Oz's *Kufsa shehora* were sold; four other novels, including *Bahazara miTuicci,* a first work by Yossi Ginsburg, had combined sales of 120,000; and *Tsipor hanefesh,* poetry by Mikhal Senunit, was the best-selling new book of the year with more than 50,000 copies sold.

Other acclaimed novels included David Grossman's *haZman hatsahov,* Hayim Be'er's *Et hazamir,* Sami Michael's *Hatsotsra bavadi,* and Shimon Balas's *haYoresh.* Impressive volumes of stories were Ruth Almog's *Nashim,* Amela Einat's *Ani sone ota doktor,* and Dan Tselka's *Mishak hamal'akhim.* Major poetry collections included the two-volume collected works of the late Amir Gilboa, a posthumous volume of Dan Pagis's last works, *Hamishim shir bamidbar* by Gabriel Preil, and *Ahava amitit* by Dahlia Ravikovitch. Asher Reich and Hazi Leskali published volumes of collected works, and there were new books of poetry by Shulamit Apfel, Shlomo Vinner, Moshe Dor, Aharon Almog, Bat Sheva Sharif-Segal, and the venerable Zerubavel Gilead and Shin Shalom.

Among the eminent works of literary scholarship and criticism published during the year were Boaz Arpali's *haPerahim ve-ha'agartal,* a study of Yehuda Amichai's poetry, and Avraham Balaban's *Bein El lehaya,* an analysis of Amos Oz's fiction. Yair Mazor published a study of Haskalah fiction, Lilly Ratok wrote on Amalia Kahana-Carmon, and Hamutal Bar-Yosef on Zelda. Dan Miron and Dan Laor edited a volume of studies and documents on Uri Nissan Gnessin.

The journals *Proza* and *Iton 77* celebrated, respectively, their 100th issue and tenth anniversary year. Mourned were the children's literature writer Uriel Ofek, the poet Abba Kovner, the scholar-bibliographer Getzel Kressel, and the novelist Rachel Eytan. Several symposia, joint readings, and publications focused on the mutual concerns of Arab and Jewish authors.

(WARREN BARGAD)

**Yiddish.** Poetry accounted for much of the year's literary activity, with Yiddish poets waxing introspective. Shloyme Vorzoger's *Song of Lament* was a finely constructed autobiography, impressive in its imagery. Israeli poet Hirsh Osherovitsh published a meditative selection of his recent work, *Wounded Faith.* Yoysef Papiernikov struck a minor key in his latest volume, *A New Light.* A signal figure in the Bessarabian pleiad, Motl Saktsier, died on Jan. 28, 1987, just days after the appearance of *A Footprint on the Way.* The field of verse was further enriched by Khaym Shvarts's *The Sun over Clouds,* Shmuel Top's *Poems and Ballads,* and Hinde Zaretski's *The Caravan.*

Canadian Yiddish writer Yehuda Elberg's historical fiction, *Between Dawn and Dusk,* led the reader through the experiences of several Polish-Jewish communities against the backdrop of the "final solution." Itskhak Janosowicz penned a riveting description of a major interwar centre of Jewish art, literature—and human pathos—in *The Lodz Years.*

Several Israeli critics made important contributions. *In My Garden* continued Rivke Kahn's role as interpreter of Yiddish letters to Hebrew readers. Shimen Kants's two-volume *The Graciousness of the Word* was a broad-ranging discussion of pets, prose writers, and Hasidism. Major critic Leyzer Podriatshik's *Portraits from Yiddish Literature* was a reevaluation of Early Yiddish writing, while *The Kid and the Goat Motif* by Avrom Beker provided an erudite analysis of this important theme in the Jewish community. Itskhak Ludin wrote a masterful study, *Pearls from Paradise,* on art and artists.

Berl Kagan's *Lexicon of Yiddish Writers* constituted a supplement to the eight-volume *Lexicon of Modern Yiddish Literature* (1956–81), providing much-needed updated information. Three splendid collections of stories rounded out the Yiddish literary scene. Itskhak Guterman wrote the well-crafted *Mama Is Not Mad.* The Jerusalem of Lithuania found its bard in Avrom Karpinovitsh in *On the Paths of Vilna.* Shaye Tenenboym's *Middle of the Night in Warsaw* was an exciting collection of stories, essays, and reminiscences, compelling and difficult to categorize.

(THOMAS E. BIRD)

## CHINESE

**China.** The student movement advocating more freedom and democracy, which erupted in late December 1986 and early January 1987, led to an "anti-capitalist liberalization" campaign marked by the denunciation and purge of a number of prominent liberal writers and intellectuals, among them Liu Binyan (Liu Pin-yen), Fang Lizhi (Fang Li-chih), and Wu Zhuguan (Wu Chu-kuan). Even though attacks on liberal intellectuals subsided under Zhao Ziyang (Chao Tzu-yang), who replaced Hu Yaobang (Hu Yao-pang) as general secretary of the Communist Party of China in January, it had become clear that China would not allow the kind of artistic and intellectual freedom advocated

WANG HUI—SOVFOTO/EASTFOTO

Liu Binyan

by Liu and other liberal writers. As a result of these developments, the fifth congress of writers and artists was postponed indefinitely.

Despite the obvious restraints, Chinese writers continued to expose the dark side of Chinese society, especially the evil deeds of corrupt officials. The fundamental aspects of human nature were emphasized by many writers. Love and passion had also become favourite themes. Among the writers who revealed the sufferings of the Chinese people under Communism were Zhang Xinxin (Chang Hsin-hsin) and Sang Ye (Sang Yeh), whose *Beijing Men* (published in English translation under the title *Chinese Lives*), one of the best examples of China's "documentary literature," became extremely popular. The lives of ordinary Chinese who experienced the extraordinary, and whose stories were tragic, witty, hilarious, small-minded, glorious, and nakedly revealing, were vividly rendered by Zhang and Sang's latest book, which was a complex portrait of a people undergoing peculiar transformations.

**Taiwan.** The lifting in 1987 of martial law, bans on opposition political parties, and travels to mainland China for family reunions created a favourable atmosphere for free artistic expression. Both writers born on the mainland and those native to Taiwan produced a large number of works revealing Taiwan's social, political, and economic realities. Social evils and moral problems became favourite themes of many writers, among them Sung Tze-lai, Huang Fan, and Li An.

Pai Yang (Kuo Yi-tung), a prolific and biting Chinese Voltaire, went to ancient Chinese history to search for the roots of China's contemporary problems. His latest book, *Chinaman, with What Flaws Have You Been Cursed?,* a blend of history and fiction, was nominally about the brutal destruction of a town by a Chinese warlord 1,200 years ago but actually comprised a powerful revelation of and attack on the shortcomings and weaknesses of the Chinese people and their culture. This was in line with his early book, *The Ugly Chinaman,* best known for its scathing criticisms of the Chinese, who were too "ugly," too conformist, too loud, and too cruel to be a great people. The Chinese, in Pai Yang's view, are cursed with serious flaws, and he revived an interest in the reexamination of China's cultural tradition.

Among Taiwan's young poets, Mo Naneng, a member of an eastern mountain tribe who had earned a living as a masseur after he became completely blind several years earlier, revealed, in his simple but original poetry, the history and sufferings of Taiwan's mountain tribes. He stimulated great interest and sympathy.

(WINSTON L. Y. YANG)

## JAPANESE

The most phenomenal success of the year was achieved by a young high school teacher, Machi Tawara, whose *Salad Anniversary* sold more than 1.5 million copies within less than half a year of publication. Amazingly, it was neither a novel nor nonfiction but a collection of short poems, written in the traditional 31-syllable tanka form. Nor was there anything extraordinary or sensational about the content—pleasures and disappointment in young

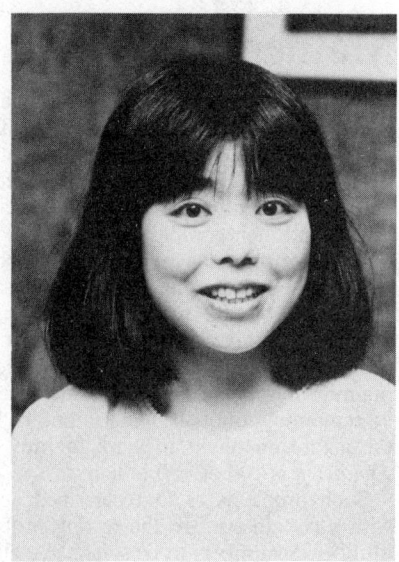

Machi Tawara

love, loneliness, responses to the change of seasons or to a jazz concert. Tawara, however, somehow managed to integrate the spontaneous self-expression of female sensibility with revitalization of the traditional sense of form.

Yuko Tsushima's *Pursued by the Light of the Night* was another remarkable contribution by the female imagination. Tsushima, a divorcée, had lost her young son in an accident a few years earlier, and the novel could be described as a requiem dedicated to him. The main plot was a modern retelling of the classical 11th-century Japanese novel *Awakening at Midnight.* The seemingly curious mixture of highly personal emotion with classical elements turned out to be quite successful.

Atsushi Mori's *As If I Were Going to Die* was a long, sometimes rambling chronological novel dealing with gradual changes in a remote village in northern Japan. While most of the episodes were pathetic, even tragic, the total effect of the novel was curiously affirmative, possibly because of the author's underlying Buddhistic philosophy. Kenzaburo Oe's *Letters to the Good Old Years* could be described as a recapitulation of the author's own career. Some readers might complain of its being too "bookish" and "literary," but the characterization of Brother Guy (obviously, the author's alter ego) was alluring and successful.

In literary criticism, Takeshi Muramatsu's *Cool Flame: The Life of Takayoshi Kido* was remarkable both for the exhaustive investigation of the career of the heroic samurai-statesman and for the reinterpretation of the Meiji Restoration. Koichi Isoda's posthumous biography of the poet *Sakutaro Hagiwara* proved both provocative and readable. Makoto Ooka's *At Midnight, Heaven's Cleaner Coming Down* was a highly enjoyable collection of poems.

(SHOICHI SAEKI)

*See also* Art Exhibitions and Art Sales: *Art Sales;* Libraries; Publishing.

This article updates the *Macropædia* article The History of Western LITERATURE and articles on the literatures of the various languages.

# Mathematics

During the year mathematicians continued to explore computers both as powerful computational tools and as sources of intriguing new problems. Mathematical domains relevant to the efficient use of computers received special emphasis, and one of the more important concerned algorithms and their complexity.

An algorithm is a step-by-step procedure for solving a problem. For example, if a computer is to rearrange, or sort, a list of 100 numbers in increasing order, the algorithm it is given might state, "First, compare the 100 numbers to find the smallest; then compare the 99 remaining numbers to find the smallest; then compare the 98 remaining numbers," and so on. To be useful, however, the algorithm ought to work for any set of $n$ numbers, whether $n$ is 100 or 100 billion.

Such problems as that described above are associated with a certain size. In the sorting problem the size is the number of numbers to be sorted. An algorithm for solving a problem requires a certain number of steps to complete, and the number of steps usually depends on the size of the problem. (Sorting 100 billion numbers takes many more steps than sorting 100.) Since the number of steps is a good measure of the time an algorithm takes to run on a computer, mathematicians interested in the efficiencies of algorithms want to know precisely in what way the number of steps—and thus the running time—depends on the size of the problem. This dependence is called the complexity of the algorithm.

Algorithms are divided into two broad classes depending on complexity. Some have polynomial complexity, which means that the number of steps is never more than some fixed number times a power of $n$, the size of the problem. The sorting algorithm above has polynomial complexity; its running time is a fixed number times $n^2$. Some algorithms have exponential complexity, which means that the number of steps is never more than a fixed number times a number raised to the $n$th power. For algorithms with polynomial complexity, doubling the size of the problem always increases their running time by a fixed multiple, no matter how large $n$ is. By contrast, for algorithms with exponential complexity, doubling the size of the problem increases the running time by ever increasing multiples as $n$ gets larger and larger.

Algorithms for solving a particular class of problems called linear programming problems have attracted mathematical attention in recent years. In such a problem one asks to find the largest (or smallest) value of some quantity, subject to certain real-world constraints. For example, there is a situation in which a large manufacturer makes thousands of products using hundreds of different materials. Each product produces a certain profit; each material is available in limited quantities. The problem is to find how much of each product the manufacturer should produce in order to make his profit as large as possible. The corresponding linear programming problem is so complex that it can be solved only by computer, and even then the solution can take a long time.

In the mid-1940s George Dantzig of Stanford University devised a procedure, called the simplex algorithm, for solving linear programming problems. In some ways the simplex algorithm is similar to the sorting algorithm above—each step is simple to perform, and the algorithm can be implemented easily on a computer. Because linear programming problems are found everywhere, the simplex algorithm is used hundreds of thousands of times each day and has become an essential (albeit hidden) part of modern life.

What is the complexity of the simplex algorithm? The size of a linear programming problem is usually measured by the number of variables and the number of constraints (the number of products and materials in the manufacturing example given above). In the early 1970s the simplex algorithm, surprisingly, was shown to have exponential complexity. This result indicated that, although the algorithm is normally fast and efficient, its running time still can be extraordinarily long for some problems.

Is there a better algorithm for solving linear programming problems? In 1979 Soviet mathematician Leonid G. Khachian described a completely new algorithm for linear programming and showed that it had polynomial complexity. Although the Khachian algorithm is theoretically superior to the simplex algorithm, in practice the simplex algorithm still proved to be much faster. Then a few years later came a startling development. Narendra Karmarkar, working at AT&T Bell Laboratories, Murray Hill, N.J., announced a new algorithm that not only has polynomial complexity but also seemed to work faster in practice than the simplex algorithm—perhaps 50 times faster. The theoretical basis of the algorithm was presented, but some of the practical details remained a mystery. During 1987 mathematicians continued their work on Karmarkar's algorithm and its practical implementation; others pursued the search for new, better algorithms based on different ideas. The stakes were high: an algorithm that could solve linear programming problems 100 times faster than the simplex algorithm would be enormously valuable, saving vast amounts of time and money.          (JOHN EWING)

This article updates the *Macropædia* article The Mathematical Theory of OPTIMIZATION.

# Military Affairs

While public attention focused on the December 1987 superpower summit, the most significant defense development of the year was the expansion of the Iran-Iraq war. It had grown to include, directly or indirectly, all of the Persian (Arabian) Gulf states, the major Middle Eastern powers, the U.S., the U.K., France, Italy, the U.S.S.R., and China. The war was producing complex alliances, symbolized by the accidental Iraqi attack, with French weapons, on a U.S. warship (the *Stark*) that was protecting Iraqi oil tankers against Iranian strikes. However, the basic causes of the war and its expansion could be summarized as control over a major economic resource—oil—and religious ideology in the form of an expansionist, fundamentalist Iranian Shi'ah version of the Muslim faith.

In geopolitical terms, the balance of power in the Persian Gulf had, as its name implied, always been tilted in favour of Iran (Persia). Because of its combination of population (49.9 million), wealth (estimated 1985–86 gross domestic product [GDP] of $147,040,000,000), and armed forces (*see* Table II), Iran had always been the regional superpower. The two other major Gulf powers, Iraq and Saudi Arabia, were both much weaker than Iran, while the smaller Gulf states, including the seven members of the United Arab Emirates (U.A.E.), Kuwait, and Oman, were wealthy but had relatively small populations and armed forces. For these reasons successive U.S. administrations, seeing a developing Iran as the key to regional stability, had supported the shah of Iran until his 1979 overthrow by the Ayatollah Ruhollah Khomeini. The Iranian revolution, however, changed the region's strongest power from

A U.S. Tomahawk cruise missile—captured on film before, during, and after impact with its steel and concrete warehouse target off the coast of California—was fired from a submerged submarine about 645 kilometres (400 miles) away.

a supporter to a challenger of the status quo on religious grounds. This challenge was emphasized by the August 1987 riots in the Muslim holy city of Mecca, in which Iranian pilgrims clashed with Saudi police, despite an absolute religious ban on disrupting the pilgrimage to Mecca or hajj.

The Khomeini regime's ultimate objective was clearly Iranian hegemony over the whole Gulf, including Mecca, replacing existing governments with fundamentalist theocracies and giving Iran control over the Gulf's oil resources. These represented over half of the world's oil reserves.

After seven years of war, Iran's regular armed forces numbered some 654,500, including approximately 300,000 Revolutionary Guards (Pasdaran Inqu), less well trained but still effective, with 1,000 tanks, 750 artillery pieces, and 60 combat aircraft. Iraq's armed forces, all regular, totaled one million, with 4,500 tanks, 3,000 artillery pieces, and 500 combat aircraft. Both sides had suffered heavy casualties, comparable to those of World War I combatants, but Iran could afford these better than could Iraq, with a population of 15.9 million. Similarly, Iran could better afford the economic costs of the war, roughly 12.3% of gross national product (GNP), compared with Iraq's 51.1%. In addition, although the Khomeini regime ruthlessly suppressed any dissent, there was clearly broad-based Iranian support on national and religious grounds for defeating Iraq.

This defeat came much closer in 1987. Successive Iranian offensives made modest but useful gains, notably around Basra and to the north of the main front line from Basra to the Faw Peninsula. These offensives brought the Iraqi Army close to breaking under the strain. Because such an Iraqi collapse would remove the biggest single barrier to Iranian hegemony over the Gulf states, the latter focused on the so-called tanker wars as the only way of stopping Iran's offensive. Since 1984 both Iran and Iraq had been conducting air strikes against tankers carrying their opponents' oil out of the Gulf, oil sold to fund their war effort. Neither side's strikes had been very effective because of the limited forces available and the large numbers of tankers using the Gulf. However, this lack of results masked the potentially decisive effect that the tanker war could have on Iran, which could export oil only by sea and relied on its oil exports to pay for its arms imports. Kuwait's 1987 reflagging of its tankers under the U.S. flag was thus aimed at drawing the U.S. plus the Western European nations (dependent on Gulf oil) into the war to tilt the balance against Iran. Given Iranian hatred of the U.S. and

U.S. hostility toward Iran after the 1979 Iranian seizure of U.S. embassy personnel as hostages, it was likely that their forces would clash in the Gulf. Such clashes could, the Gulf states hoped, lead the U.S. and its allies to use their naval superiority to cut off Iran's seaborne oil exports.

Events from July made such an outcome more likely. Iran mined the Gulf, damaging one tanker in the first U.S.-escorted convoy; increased attacks with fast speedboats armed with rockets, grenades, machine guns, and portable surface-to-air missiles (SAM); and attacked Kuwait's main offshore oil terminal with Chinese Silkworm surface-to-surface missiles (SSM). Meanwhile, the U.S. disabled an Iranian minelayer and three Iranian armed speedboats and destroyed Iranian oil rigs assisting these attacks. These clashes raised fears in the U.S. of another Vietnam-style open-ended U.S. commitment. It was a measure of Iran's basic strength and religious fervour that by the end of 1987, almost totally isolated diplomatically and facing increasing political barriers to buying arms, it was still within sight of defeating Iraq.

## UNITED STATES

U.S. all-volunteer armed forces in 1987 totaled 2,158,000 personnel (203,000 women). Both retention rates and personnel quality remained at record highs. The projected defense budget for fiscal 1987 was $282.9 billion, which represented 6.9% of GDP and approximately 28% of the federal budget.

U.S. strategic and intermediate-range nuclear forces continued their modest modernization programs. Strategic Air Command (SAC) had 54 new Rockwell B-1B strategic bombers that were operational, although they continued to suffer from defects limiting their effectiveness. The elderly B-52 bomber force fell further to 167 B-52Gs and 96 B-52Hs (first deployed in 1959 and 1962, respectively). Of the B-52Gs, 98 carried 12 AGM-86B air-launched cruise missiles (ALCM) each, while 69 were equipped with the Harpoon air-to-surface missile (ASM) and were used in a nonnuclear antishipping role. SAC also had 61 FB-111A medium-range nuclear bombers. Development of the advanced technology (stealth) bomber and the advanced cruise missile continued.

The land-based fixed-silo ICBM (intercontinental ballistic missile) force was almost completely vulnerable to a Soviet attack. The retirement of the last ten obsolete Titan II missiles reduced this force to 1,000 silos, containing M-X Peacekeeper and Minuteman II and III ICBM. The

# The INF Treaty

BY ROBIN RANGER

The intermediate-range nuclear forces (INF) agreement signed by U.S. Pres. Ronald Reagan and Soviet leader Mikhail Gorbachev on Dec. 8, 1987, was a historic document. It was the first major superpower arms control treaty signed since the 1979 SALT II treaty, never ratified and now expired. It was the first to provide for the complete elimination of two classes of weapons systems: longer range (LR)INF (1,000–5,499-km [620–3,415-mi] range) and shorter range (SR)INF (500–999-km [310–620-mi] range)—the double-zero option. Its verification provisions were unprecedented, especially those for on-site inspection of military installations on each other's territory. On paper the INF treaty thus seemed to mark the beginning of a new era in relations between the U.S. and the Soviet Union.

Yet significant doubts remained about whether the treaty would work as advertised in terms of achieving its military and political objectives or whether, even if they were achieved, they were objectives that would contribute to the security of the U.S. and its NATO allies in Western Europe. The U.S. Senate debate on whether to give its advice and consent to the treaty's ratification (by the constitutionally required two-thirds majority) was thus going to be an unusually intense one, recalling the SALT II ratification debate. It seemed likely that the Senate would add reservations to the treaty to remedy its perceived defects, and the document could be amended, thereby requiring its renegotiation with the Soviets. The 1988 presidential election would further complicate the ratification process, particularly for the Republican Party—of their five contenders for the presidential nomination, only one, Vice-Pres. George Bush, supported the treaty. His chief rival, Sen. Robert Dole (Rep., Kan.), favoured attaching such reservations as proved necessary after a careful examination of its text.

The debate on the treaty in the U.S. centred on the question of whether the Soviets would comply with its provisions. Treaty proponents, most notably President Reagan, argued that the Soviets would comply because the treaty's verification provisions guaranteed that the U.S. would quickly detect any Soviet noncompliance. The treaty would eliminate all U.S. LRINF, comprising 108 Pershing II (PII) intermediate-range ballistic missiles (IRBM) and 256 ground-launched cruise missiles (GLCM). As a collateral constraint, 72 Pershing IA short-range ballistic missiles (SRBM) operated by West Germany (with U.S.-controlled nuclear warheads) would be withdrawn after the U.S.-Soviet reductions were completed, a withdrawal already planned because of their age. The Soviet LRINF eliminated would be 441 SS-20 IRBM missiles and their mobile launchers plus an unknown number of SS-20 reload (refire) missiles and 112 obsolete SS-4 IRBM. The Soviet SRINF eliminated would be 110 SS-12 and 20 SS-23 SRBM and their mobile launchers,

plus an unknown number of refire missiles. All of these missiles had single warheads except for the SS-20, which had three; therefore, the U.S. would give up 436 nuclear warheads in exchange for 1,565 known Soviet warheads plus an unknown number of warheads on Soviet refire missiles. This would be a warhead trade in favour of the U.S. and NATO-Europe by at least 4:1.

Treaty supporters also argued that its verification provisions were adequate, enabling the open U.S. society to verify the closed Soviet society's compliance. They included provisions for an annual quota of on-site inspections of sites where the destroyed missiles had been deployed to ensure that they had not been replaced, as well as verification of their destruction. There would be 20 on-site inspections per year in the first three years of the treaty, followed by 15 per year for the next five years and 10 per year for the last five years.

Permanent monitoring teams would also be stationed around the perimeters of plants where the destroyed missiles had been manufactured to ensure that production lines were not restarted. The U.S. would also be allowed to inspect the plant manufacturing the Soviet SS-25 mobile ICBM, similar to the SS-20, to verify that it was not also making SS-20s or the follow-on SS-20 Mod2.

Treaty opponents argued that even these verification provisions might be inadequate for ascertaining Soviet compliance. Since the U.S. did not know how many refire SS-20s the Soviets had, their destruction of 441 SS-20s plus the number of refires they chose to declare would still leave them with an unknown number of refire SS-20s. In addition, the banned SS-20 IRBM was so similar to the permitted SS-25 ICBM that the distinction between the IRBM the Soviets would have to destroy and the ICBM they would continue to deploy was meaningless.

This problem would be compounded by the inherent limitations of on-site inspections. Such a procedure could verify only that the Soviets were not deploying SS-20s at the site of the inspection while it was taking place. Though the treaty provided for inspections on short (48 hours) notice, this notice could still be enough for the Soviets to conceal illegal deployments of mobile missiles carried in closed containers. A leaked U.S. government study reportedly concluded that, even with on-site inspections, U.S. ability to verify Soviet compliance with arms control limits on mobile missiles like the SS-20 and SS-25 would remain limited until the end of the century.

Even more important, in these critics' view, was the fact that the treaty failed to provide any built-in penalties for Soviet violations. Therefore, even if the U.S. detected violations, it would not be committed to taking any compensatory measures to either force the Soviets to reverse their violations or offset their gains from violations. The Senate thus seemed likely to provide for what Senator Dole called "a strong compliance regime."

The treaty's prospects were for ratification by the summer of 1988, probably with the addition of significant reservations by the Senate. These reservations might, or might not, be acceptable to the Soviets. Much would depend, though, on the Senate's intensive analysis of the treaty's long, technically complex text, released only on its signature. This analysis would show the strength of the arguments made by its supporters and critics and clarify the treaty's implications for future arms control negotiations. The most important of these were the Soviet proposals for a 50% reduction in strategic nuclear forces plus an extension of the narrow interpretation of the ABM (antiballistic missile) Treaty for seven to ten years so as to limit President Reagan's Strategic Defense Initiative.

*Robin Ranger is Bradley Resident Scholar at the Heritage Foundation in Washington, D.C. His books include* Arms and Politics 1958–1978.

Peacekeeper was to have been deceptively based, but political pressures had limited deployment to 50 Peacekeepers in vulnerable Minuteman silos. Of these large missiles, 23 were operational, weighing 88,000 kg (195,000 lb) each and carrying ten multiple independently targetable reentry vehicles (MIRV). The 527 Minuteman IIIs were modernized missiles, each carrying three MIRV. The 450 Minuteman II missiles were nearly 20 years old. Development of the small, single-warhead Midgetman ICBM (about 11,350 kg [25,000 lb]) continued.

The ballistic missile nuclear submarine (SSBN) force totaled 36, carrying 640 submarine-launched ballistic missiles (SLBM). The eight new Ohio-class SSBN each carried 24 Trident I/C-4s, to be replaced by the Trident II/D-5 SLBM from 1988 onward. The test of a Trident II with 12 warheads instead of the 10 allowed by the expired, unratified SALT II treaty was controversial but demonstrated the increased capabilities provided by the new missile. Older SSBN included 12 Franklin class (96 Trident I/C-4s, 96 Poseidon C-3s) and 16 Madison and Lafayette class (96 Trident I/C-4s and 160 Poseidon C-3s). Deployment of submarine-launched nuclear cruise missiles continued, with eight nuclear cruise-missile submarines (SSGN) so equipped. Plans called for a total of 700 BGM-109A Tomahawk sea-launched cruise missiles (SLCM). In addition, 2,300 conventionally armed Tomahawk SLCM were being deployed to give each vessel a mix of nuclear and conventionally armed missiles. Dispersing the nuclear SLCM would enhance their survivability.

The U.S. Navy at the end of 1987 totaled 237 principal surface ships, 92 nuclear attack submarines (SSN), and 583,800 personnel. These provided 15 carrier and 3 battleship groups, (to rise to 15 and 4), each carrier having an attack wing of some 86 aircraft plus escorting surface vessels and SSN. Of the 13 modern (post-1955) aircraft carriers, 5 were nuclear powered and 8 were conventionally powered. Modern aircraft included 348 F-14A Tomcat interceptors, 319 A-6 Intruder/Prowler and 222 F/A-18A Hornet strike planes, and 70 E-2C electronic warfare/airborne electronic warning planes. A fourth World War II battleship, the *Wisconsin*, was being recommissioned with Tomahawk SLCM. The 9 nuclear and 27 conventionally powered guided-weapons (GW) cruisers included five new Ticonderoga-class ships equipped with the Aegis fleet air defense missile/radar system. Other major surface combatants included 37 GW and 31 gun/antisubmarine warfare (ASW) Spruance-class destroyers and 56 GW and 59 gun frigates.

The Marine Corps, with 199,600 personnel, was organized in three divisions, each with its air wing. Modern aircraft included 96 F/A-18 Hornet interceptor/strike aircraft, 69 A-6 Intruder strike aircraft, and 73 AV-8A/C Harrier vertical/short takeoff and landing (V/STOL) interceptor/strike aircraft.

The 606,800-strong Air Force had approximately 4,885 combat aircraft. Among modern types were 786 F-15 Eagle interceptors, 1,124 F-16 Falcon fighter-bombers, and 34 E-3A Sentry airborne warning and control systems (AWACS). Older types included 1,404 F-4 Phantom fighter-bombers/reconnaissance, 292 F-111A/D/E/F medium bombers, and 653 A-10A Thunderbolt ground-support aircraft.

The Army, with 774,100 personnel, formed 14 heavy divisions (about 16,000 men each): 4 armoured, 6 mechanized, 1 high-technology motor, 1 regular infantry, 1 air assault, and 1 airborne plus 4 light infantry divisions (about 10,200 men each). The light infantry divisions were easier to transport and were intended as part of the Rapid Deployment Force for use outside NATO-Europe. Armour included 4,500 M-1/1A1 Abrams tanks and 3,600 M-2/-3 Bradley mechanized infantry combat vehicles (MICV), plus 7,352 M-60A3 Patton tanks and 16,800 M-113 armoured personnel carriers (APC).

## U.S.S.R.

The Soviet military machine remained the world's most powerful, with about 5.2 million personnel plus some 25 million in reserves and 570,000 paramilitary personnel. Western, including U.S., estimates of Soviet defense spending put it at 12–20% of GNP, most likely 15–17%, representing some $700 billion. This was a massive burden on the Soviet economy, a burden that had risen steadily.

Soviet leader Mikhail Gorbachev's campaign for *perestroika* (restructuring) was badly handicapped by this high level of defense spending, but it could not be reduced without weakening the U.S.S.R.'s major claim to superpower status, military power. To get the resources needed to make restructuring work and to provide the long-term economic base for Soviet military power, however, the Gorbachev regime might have to reduce military spending temporarily or risk the failure of restructuring. Thus the Soviet government faced a difficult series of choices on defense spending and its reliance on military power.

The difficulties the Soviets faced were dramatized by the daring May 28 landing in Red Square by West German pilot Mathias Rust, flying a Cessna light plane. He had penetrated the entire Soviet air-defense system, the world's most sophisticated, and landed a plane that could theoretically have carried a nuclear weapon just outside the walls of the Kremlin.

The war in Afghanistan, now in its eighth year, underlined the Gorbachev regime's need to make hard defense policy choices and its reluctance to do so. The war was costing the Soviets some $15 million per day to maintain an occupying army of some 115,000, and by the end of 1987 their casualties totaled over 35,000. Gorbachev described the war as "a bleeding wound," but Soviet troops remained in Afghanistan at year's end.

The Strategic Nuclear Forces Command, a separate service with 298,000 troops, further increased its superiority over U.S. and NATO strategic and intermediate-range nuclear forces in missile and warhead numbers and in warhead yields and accuracy. This gave the Soviets a first-strike capability that the U.S. would not have even after the end of the century. The figures shown in Table I underestimate the Soviet advantage because the U.S.S.R. also deployed 1,000–3,000 reload missiles for their ICBM, IRBM, and SLBM launchers. New evidence emerged that this Soviet reload force included SS-II ICBM deployed in railroad trains. New systems being tested and deployed included two ICBM, the SS-24 and SS-25 (both mobile); one SLBM, the SS-N-23; and five long-range cruise missiles, all in the 3,000-km (1,860-mi) range. The four Typhoon-class SSBN, each carrying 20 SS-N-20 MIRVed SLBM, were the world's largest, displacing 25,000 tons each.

The strategic aviation force comprised the new Blackjack A, larger than the U.S. B-1B; 165 older Bears and Bisons; and 160 Tu-26 Backfire B/Cs. Additional medium-range bombers included 135 Tu-22 Blinder A/Bs, 272 obsolete Tu-16 Badgers, and 450 Su-24 strike aircraft. Soviet strategic defensive forces were also large. The Air Defense Troops (VPVO) formed a separate service with some 520,000 personnel, 1,760 interceptors, and more than 9,000 SAM launchers at 1,200 fixed sites. The latest SAM, the SA-12, had a tactical antiballistic missile capability. Soviet upgrading of the ABM system around Moscow, with new

### Table I. U.S./NATO–Soviet Strategic and Intermediate Nuclear Force Balance, July 1987

| Weapons systems | Range (km) | Payload[1] (000 lb) | Warheads, yield[2] | CEP[3] | Speed (Mach) | Number deployed |
|---|---|---|---|---|---|---|
| **UNITED STATES Strategic Forces** | | | | | | |
| Intercontinental ballistic missiles (ICBM) | | | | | | 1,000 |
| Minuteman II | 11,300 | 1.6 | 1 × 1–2 mt | 370 | ... | 450 |
| Minuteman III Mod 1 | 14,800 | 2.2 | 3 × 170 kt | 220 | ... | 227 |
| Mod 2 | 12,900 | 2.4 | 3 × 335 kt | 220 | ... | 300 |
| Peacekeeper (M-X) | 11,000 | 7 | 10 × 300 kt | 100 | ... | 23 |
| Submarine-launched ballistic missiles (SLBM; in 36 nuclear submarines) | | | | | | 640 |
| Poseidon C-3 | 4,000 | 3.3 | 10 × 40 kt or 14 × 40 kt | 450 | ... | 256 |
| Trident I/C-4 | 7,400 | 3.0+ | 8 × 100 kt | 450 | ... | 384 |
| Manned bombers and air-launched cruise missiles (ALCM) | | | | | | |
| B-52G | 12,000 | 45 | 20–24 | ... | 0.95 | 98 |
| B-52H | 12,000 | 45 | 8–12 or 20–24 | ... | 0.95 | 96 |
| FB-111A | 4,700 | 37.5 | 6 | ... | 2.5 | 56 |
| B-1B | 12,000 | 64 | 26–46 | ... | 1.25 | 54 |
| AGM-86B ALCM | 2,400 | 0.60 | 200 kt | ... | 0.7 | 1,380 |
| **U.S./NATO Intermediate Nuclear Forces[4]** (Total: 702 weapons, 342 delivery systems) | | | | | | |
| Intermediate-range ballistic missiles (IRBM) | | | | | | |
| U.S. Pershing II | 1,800 | 3 | 5–50 kt | 40 | ... | 108 |
| Manned bombers and ground-launched cruise missiles (GLCM) | | | | | | |
| U.S. F-111 E/F | 4,700 | 28 | | ... | 2.5 | 160[5] |
| U.S. Tomahawk GLCM | 2,500 | 0.27 | 200 kt | 20 | 0.7 | 256 |
| **BRITAIN (Strategic and INF)[6]** | | | | | | |
| Submarine-launched ballistic missiles (SLBM; in 4 nuclear submarines) | | | | | | |
| Polaris A-3 | 4,600 | 1.5 | 3 × 200 kt | 900 | ... | 64 |
| Strike aircraft | | | | | | |
| Tornado | 2,800 | 16 | 2 | ... | 0.95 | 148 |
| **FRANCE (Strategic and INF)[6]** | | | | | | |
| Submarine-launched ballistic missiles (SLBM; in 5 nuclear submarines) | | | | | | |
| MSBS M-20/TN 60 | 3,000 | ... | 1 × 1 mt | ... | ... | 80 |
| MSBS M-4/TN 70 | 4,400+ | ... | 6 × 150 kt | ... | ... | 16 |
| MSBS M-4/TN 71 | 6,000+ | ... | 6 × 150 kt | ... | ... | — |
| Intermediate-range ballistic missiles (IRBM) | | | | | | |
| SSBS S-3D/TN 61 | 3,500 | ... | 1 × 1 mt | ... | ... | 18 |
| Strike aircraft/Air to surface missiles (ASM) | | | | | | |
| Mirage IVA/P | 3,200 | 16 | 1 × 60/1 × 150 kt ASMP ASM | ... | 2.2 | 22 |
| Mirage IIIE | 2,400 | 19 | 2 × 15 kt | ... | 1.8 | 30 |
| Super Etendard | 1,500 | 2 | 2 × 15/1 × 150 kt ASMP ASM | ... | 1.0 | 36 |
| **SOVIET UNION Strategic Forces** | | | | | | |
| Intercontinental ballistic missiles (ICBM) | | | | | | c. 1,500+ |
| SS-11 Mod 1 | 9,500 | 2 | 1 × 1 mt | 1,400 | ... | } 440 |
| Mod 2/3 | 11–13,000 | 2.5 | 3 × 100–300 kt | 1,100 | ... | |
| SS-16 | 9–10,000 | ... | 3 × 150 kt | ... | ... | c. 100[7] |
| SS-17 Mod 3 | 10,000 | 6.4 | 4 × 500 kt | ... | ... | 150 |
| SS-18 Mod 4 | 11,000 | 16.7 | 10 × 500 kt | 250 | ... | 308 |
| SS-19 Mod 3 | 10,000 | 7.5 | 6 × 550 kt | 300 | ... | 360 |
| SS-24 | 10,000 | 8 | 8–10 × 100 kt | 200 | ... | } c. 100 |
| SS-25 | 10,500 | 1.6 | 1 × 550 kt | 200 | ... | |
| Submarine-launched ballistic missiles (in 62 nuclear plus 14 diesel submarines) | | | | | | c. 1,000 |
| SS-N-5 Sark | 1,400 | ... | 1 × 1 mt | 2,800 | ... | 39 |
| SS-N-6 Mod 1,2 | 2,400 | 1.5 | 1 × 1 mt | 1,300 | ... | } 272 |
| Mod 3 | 3,000 | 1.5 | 2 × 500 kt | 1,300 | ... | |
| SS-N-8 Mod 1 | 7,800 | 1.5 | 1 × 1 mt | 1,500 | ... | } 292 |
| Mod 2 | 9,100 | ... | 1 × 800 kt | 900 | ... | |
| SS-N-17 | 3,900 | 2.5 | 1 × 500 kt | 1,400 | ... | 12 |
| SS-N-18 Mod 1 | 6,500 | 5 | 3 × 500 kt | 1,400 | ... | } 224 |
| Mod 2 | 8,000 | 3.6 | 1 × 500 kt | 900 | ... | |
| Mod 3 | 6,500 | ... | 5 × 500 kt | 900 | ... | |
| SS-N-20 | 8,300 | ... | 6 × 100 kt | 500 | ... | 80 |
| SS-N-23 | 8,300 | ... | 10 × 100 kt | 900 | ... | 48 |
| Manned bombers and air-launched cruise missiles (ALCM) | | | | | | c. 420 |
| Tu-95 Bear B/C/H | 12,800 | 40 | 2–3 + 8 AS-15 ALCM | ... | 0.9 | 150 |
| Mya-4 Bison | 11,200 | 20 | 4 | ... | 0.94 | 20 |
| Tu-26 Backfire B | 11,000 | 17.5 | 4 | ... | 1.9 | 290 |
| AS-15 ALCM | 1,600 | ... | 250 kt | ... | 0.6 | c. 300 |
| **Soviet INF** (Total: c. 4,823 warheads, c. 1,423 delivery systems) | | | | | | |
| Variable/intermediate/medium-range ballistic missiles (V/I/MRBM)[8] | | | | | | |
| SS-4 Sandal | 2,000 | 3 | 1 × 1 mt | 2,300 | ... | 112 |
| SS-20 Mod 1 | 5,000 | 1.2 | 1 × 1.5 mt | ... | ... | } c. 1,423 |
| Mod 2 | 5,000 | ... | 3 × 150 kt | c. 400 | ... | |
| Mod 3 | 7,400 | ... | 1 × 50 kt | ... | ... | |
| Medium/short-range ballistic missiles and ground/sea-launched cruise missiles[9] | | | | | | |
| SS-12/23 MRBM | 900/500 | ... | 1 × 1 mt/ 1 × 100 kt | 300/350 | ... | c. 150 |
| SS-N-12/19 G/SLCM | 550 | ... | 1 × 350/500 kt | ... | ... | c. 280 |
| Manned bombers[10] | | | | | | 745 |
| Tu-16 Badger | 4,800 | 20 | 2 | ... | 0.8 | 502 |
| Tu-22 Blinder | 6,200 | 12 | 2 | ... | 1.5 | 165 |

[1] Payload refers to a missile's throw weight or a bomber's weapons load.

[2] For MIRV and MRV the figure to the left of the multiplication sign gives the number of warheads and the figure to the right is the yield per warhead. For bombers, weapons per bomber are given.

[3] Circular Error Probable: the radius (in metres) of a circle within which at least half of the missile warheads aimed at a specific target will fall.

[4] INF systems are missiles with ranges or aircraft with unrefueled combat radii of 1,000–5,499 km; aircraft combat radii are about one-third or less of the range.

[5] Total deployed worldwide; 100 is the inventory normally based in Europe, or within striking range of Europe.

[6] British nuclear forces are under national control but may be assigned to NATO. French nuclear forces are controlled and targeted independently of NATO.

[7] Mobile SS-16 ICBM reported deployed, based on SS-20 V/IRBM.

[8] Total deployed against both NATO and China theatres; two-thirds are thought to be deployed against NATO. Three missiles per launcher for SS-20. Includes 39 non-SALT counted SS-N-5 theatre missiles in 13 diesel submarines.

[9] Soviet M/SRBM and G/SLCM could hit targets in Western Europe and are therefore shown for illustrative purposes. SS-12/-23 classified as Shorter-Range INF.

[10] Total deployed worldwide. Of these, about half are allocated to Soviet Naval Aviation (some 240 Tu-16, 35 Tu-22, and 120 Tu-26). Two-thirds of the remaining strike bombers and ASM carriers are considered deployed against NATO. Tu-26 Backfire is now counted as strategic.

Sources: International Institute for Strategic Studies, *The Military Balance 1986–1987*; and *Aviation Week and Space Technology*. Figures for Soviet forces, especially INF, can only be estimates.

---

SH-04/08 missiles together with construction of other ABM radars, would enable the U.S.S.R. to field a nationwide ABM system.

The two million-strong Army was organized into 52 tank, 150 motor rifle (mechanized), 18 artillery, and 7 airborne divisions (10,500–12,500 men each). Equipment—at much higher levels than for the U.S., its NATO allies, or China—included 53,000 tanks (modern types comprised 10,800 T-72/-80s and 9,300 T-64s, plus 33,200 older T-54/-55/-62s); 64,700 armoured fighting vehicles (AFV); and 29,000 artillery pieces, including new self-propelled 203-mm, 180-mm, 152-mm, and 130-mm guns.

Soviet Army forces continued to be deployed roughly two-thirds against NATO-Europe and one-third against China. There were three major Strategic Theatre Commands (GTVD), subdivided into five regional theatres of military operations (TVD), and a central strategic reserve military district with 16 divisions.

### WARSAW PACT

Poland maintained the largest military forces of the Eastern European nations, totaling 394,000 personnel and including a 230,000-strong army with 3,670 T-54/-55/-72 main battle tanks (MBT) and an 80,000-strong air force with 665 combat aircraft (400 MiG-21/-21U/-23 interceptors). Czechoslovakia's 201,000-strong forces, the second largest, comprised an army of 145,000 with 3,500 T-54/-55/-72 tanks and an air force of 56,000 with 465 combat aircraft (275 MiG-21/-21U/-23 interceptors).

East Germany's armed forces totaled 176,000, including an army of 120,000 with 1,800 T-54/-55/-62/-72 tanks (plus 1,200 in storage) and an air force of 40,000 with 334 combat aircraft, including 205 MiG-21F/MF/PF/U interceptors. Hungary's armed forces, with 106,000 personnel, included an army of 84,000 with about 1,300 T-54/-55/-72 tanks and an air force of 22,000 with 130 MiG-21/-23 interceptors. All four countries allocated much lower proportions of their GDPs to defense than did the U.S.S.R.

### NATO

The main effect of the superpower intermediate-range nuclear forces (INF) agreement signed on Dec. 8, 1987, was to increase fears of the European NATO nations that the U.S. was becoming less willing to couple its defense against a Soviet attack to that of Western Europe. Because the U.S. agreed to withdraw all the modernized INF deployed as a result of NATO's 1979 INF modernization, an important rung in the coupling ladder of escalation was to be removed, the rung represented by longer range and shorter range (LR/SR)INF and by the 72 Pershing IA short-range ballistic missiles (SRBM) operated by West Germany, with U.S. warheads. Other elements of NATO Theatre Nuclear Forces (TNF) were being withdrawn as a result of the alliance's 1983 Montebello decision. After all of these reductions were completed, by the early 1990s, NATO TNF would consist mainly of aircraft and artillery able to deliver either conventional or nuclear weapons.

The TNF leg of the NATO triad of conventional forces, TNF, and strategic nuclear forces (SNF) would thus be weakened. In addition, the conventional leg could well be weakened by U.S. conventional-force reductions. Pres. Ronald Reagan's Strategic Defense Initiative (SDI) was also seen as a potential shield behind which the U.S. could decouple itself from NATO-Europe. The decoupling issue would thus remain a major one within the alliance, even though many NATO-Europe governments, notably West Germany's, had pressed the U.S. to negotiate any possible reduction in INF. Similarly, many of those raising the

The Rafale, a prototype of a French fighter said to have superior controls and aerodynamics, could develop into the fighter aircraft of the French Air Force and Navy before the turn of the century.
©ALAIN ERNOULT—SERVICE COMMUNICATION-GIFAS/AUTHENTICATED NEWS INTERNATIONAL

decoupling issue had also resisted LR-INF and chemical weapons (CW) modernization. They had also opposed any halt in the reductions in NATO-Europe defense spending as a percentage of GDP. As Table II shows, U.S. defense spending as a percentage of 1985 GDP was, at 6.9%, approximately twice that of France and West Germany (4.1 and 3.2%) and more than three times that of Canada and Denmark. Britain's defense spending, at 5.2% of GDP, was comparable to that of the U.S.

The result of NATO-Europe's refusal to fund a strong conventional-weapon defense was that the new concepts for improving this defense remained paper concepts. The reality, as the recently retired supreme allied commander, Europe (SACEUR), U.S. Gen. Bernard W. Rogers, warned, was that NATO could defend itself with conventional weapons for only a few days before it would have to use nuclear weapons to defeat a Soviet attack.

### UNITED KINGDOM

Prime Minister Margaret Thatcher's 1987 election victory for a third term meant that British defense policy and spending would continue along the lines she had established. Defense expenditure for 1986–87 totaled $27,580,-000,000 (5.2% of 1985 GDP). The Army of 158,700 had 300 new Challenger and 900 Chieftain MBT. The Royal Air Force (RAF), with 93,500 personnel, had about 600 combat aircraft. Some 244 of the new Tornado GR-1 multirole combat aircraft were being deployed in fighter, ground-attack, and reconnaissance models, replacing 150 Phantom fighters. Other modern aircraft included 51 Harrier GR-3/T-4 V/STOL, 132 Jaguar GR-1 ground-attack/reconnaissance planes, and 34 Nimrod MR-2 maritime reconnaissance aircraft.

The Royal Navy was the third largest naval force in the world, with 66,500 personnel, 27 attack submarines (15 nuclear), 59 major surface combatants including 3 carriers with Sea Harriers, 13 GW destroyers, and 35 general-purpose frigates. Royal Marine personnel totaled some 7,700.

### FRANCE

Defense spending in 1987 was estimated at $29,260,000,-000. Modernization of France's national nuclear forces continued, with five SSBN operational, one being refitted, and one under construction. The M-20 SLBM was being replaced with the M-4. Medium-range and tactical nuclear forces were also being increased.

Military personnel totaled 546,900 (279,900 in the Army) as part of the planned reduction of 37,500 from their 1986 strength. Equipment included 1,340 AMX-30 MBT (400 new AMX-30B2), 865 AMX-10P/PC Milan MICV, and about 3,100 APC. These were organized in six armoured, two light armoured, and two motor rifle (APC) divisions, plus a Rapid Action Force for overseas intervention consisting of one parachute, one air portable marine, one light armoured, one alpine, and one air mobile division (averaging 7,500 personnel each). The Air Force of some 96,000 personnel had 520 combat aircraft, newer models including 175 Mirage F-1C and 40 Mirage 200C/N interceptors. The 68,900-strong Navy's 45 major surface combatants included 1 helicopter and 2 light carriers, 16 GW destroyers, and 25 frigates; the Navy also had 16 attack submarines (3 SSN).

### WEST GERMANY

West Germany's defense budget amounted to $27,910,-000,000 in 1987. Standing armed forces totaled 488,400, more than half of them volunteers. The 332,100-strong Army included 12 divisions—6 armoured, 4 armoured infantry, 1 mountain, and 1 airborne, plus 38 5,000-man brigades. Armour included 1,800 new Leopard 2 and 2,440 Leopard 1 MBT, plus about 2,130 MICV and 3,780 APC. Large numbers of artillery, antiaircraft guns and missiles, antitank guns, and guided weapons were also deployed.

The Air Force had 108,700 personnel with 604 combat aircraft. These included 165 new Tornados, 186 older F-4 Phantoms, and 80 obsolete F-104G and 193 Alpha Jet ground-attack fighters. The 36,400-strong Navy, designed for coastal warfare in the Baltic Sea, had 40 fast-attack craft equipped with guided missiles, 7 GW destroyers, 6 GW frigates, and 24 coastal submarines. The naval air arm consisted of 91 combat aircraft, including 72 Tornado attack/reconnaissance planes.

### ARMS CONTROL AND DISARMAMENT

For arms control, 1987 was a year of completely contradictory developments. The positive development was the December 8 INF agreement, which would, if ratified and observed, represent unprecedented progress in arms control. (*See* Special Report.) The negative development was

## Table II. Approximate Strengths of Regular Armed Forces of the World

| Country | Military personnel in 000s | | | Warships[1] | | | Jet aircraft[3] | | Tanks[4] | Defense expenditure as % of 1985 GDP[5] |
|---|---|---|---|---|---|---|---|---|---|---|
| | Army | Navy | Air Force | Aircraft carriers/cruisers | Submarines[2] | Destroyers/frigates | Bombers and fighter-bombers | Fighters/reconnaissance | | |
| **I. NATO** | | | | | | | | | | |
| Belgium | 67.5 | 4.5 | 18.8 | — | — | 4 FFG | 115 FB | 36, 19 R | 320 | 2.9 |
| Canada[6] | 22.5 | 10.0 | 23.0 | — | 3 | 4 DDG, 19 FF | 105 FB, 18 MR | — | 114 | 2.2 |
| Denmark | 17.0 | 5.4 | 6.9 | — | 4 | 5 FFG, 5 FF | 64 FB | 16 R | 210 | 2.2 |
| France[7] | 279.9 | 68.9 | 96.0 | 2 CV, 1 CVH, 1 CG | 14, 3 SSN, 6 SSBN | 16 DDG, 25 FFG | 37 B, 291 FB | 195, 65 R, 53 MR | 1,340 | 4.1 |
| Germany, West | 332.1 | 36.4 | 108.7 | — | 24 | 7 DDG, 6 FFG, 3 FF | 550 FB | 68, 58 R, 19 MR | 4,887 | 3.2 |
| Greece | 165.5 | 19.5 | 24.0 | — | 10 | 14 DD, 2 FFG, 5 FF | 210 FB | 136, 52 R, 12 MR | 1,783 | 7.1 |
| Italy | 265.0 | 50.3 | 73.0 | 2 CVH, 2 CAH | 9 | 4 DDG, 12 FFG, 2 FF | 308 FB | 30 R, 24 MR | 1,720 | 2.7 |
| Luxembourg | 0.7 | — | — | — | — | — | — | — | — | 0.9 |
| Netherlands, The | 68.0 | 17.1 | 18.0 | — | 5 | 16 FFG | 212 FB | 12 R, 15 MR | 913 | 3.1 |
| Norway | 19.0 | 7.0 | 9.1 | — | 14 | 5 FFG | 97 FB | 7 MR | 80 | 3.1 |
| Portugal | 39.0 | 14.2 | 13.4 | — | 3 | 16 FF | 91 FB | — | 80 | 3.2 |
| Spain | 230.0 | 62.5[8] | 32.5 | 2 CVH | 8 | 9 DD, 12 FFG | 67 FB | 122, 13 R, 6 MR | 843 | 2.2 |
| Turkey | 542.0 | 55.0 | 57.4 | — | 17 | 12 DD, 4 FF | 449 FB | 40, 28 R | 3,700 | 4.5 |
| United Kingdom | 158.7 | 66.5[8] | 93.5 | 3 CVH | 13, 15 SSN, 4 SSBN | 14 DDG, 35 FFG | 459 FB | 162, 27 R, 34 MR | 1,200 | 5.2 |
| United States | 774.1 | 783.4[8] | 606.8 | 3 BBG, 5 CVN, 10 CV, 9 CGN, 27 CG, 5 LHA, 7 LPH, 13 LPD, 28 LSD/T | 84 SSN, 36 SSBN, 8 SSGN | 37 DDG, 31 DD, 56 FFG, 59 FF | 317 SB, 353 B, 3,450 FB | 2,410, 270 R, 400 MR/ASW | 13,300 | 6.9 |
| **II. WARSAW PACT** | | | | | | | | | | |
| Bulgaria | 110.0 | 8.8 | 34.0 | — | 4 | 3 FFG | 85 FB | 155, 30 R | 2,100 | ... |
| Czechoslovakia | 145.0 | — | 56.0 | — | — | — | 145 FB | 275, 45 R | 3,500 | 5.0 |
| Germany, East | 120.0 | 16.0 | 40.0 | — | — | 3 FFG | 64 FB | 275, 15 R | 3,000 | 6.9 |
| Hungary | 84.0 | — | 22.0 | — | — | — | 15 FB | 130 | 1,300 | 3.8 |
| Poland | 230.0 | 19.0 | 80.0 | — | 4 | — | 230 FB | 452, 35 R, 15 MR | 3,670 | 4.0 |
| Romania | 140.0 | 7.5 | 32.0 | — | — | 1 DDG, 3 FF | 120 FB | 230, 18 R | 1,430 | 1.6 |
| U.S.S.R. | 3,477.0 | 477.0[8] | 1,272.0[9] | 4 CV, 2 CVH, 3 CGN, 27 CG, 8 CA | 124, 76 SSN, 63 SSBN, 14 SSB, 51 SSGN, 16 SSG | 49 DDG, 14 DD, 32 FFG, 34 FF | 465 SB, 670 B, 4,105 FB | 4,750, 660 R, 180 MR | 53,300 | 12–17 |
| **III. OTHER EUROPEAN** | | | | | | | | | | |
| Albania | 31.5 | 3.3 | 7.2 | — | 2 | — | — | 95 | 190 | ... |
| Austria | 50.0 | — | 4.7 | — | — | — | 32 FB | 5 | 170 | 1.3 |
| Finland | 30.0 | 1.9 | 2.5 | — | — | — | — | 72 | c. 150 | 1.4 |
| Ireland | 11.9 | 0.9 | 0.8 | — | — | — | — | — | — | — |
| Sweden[10] | 47.0/800.0 | 12.0 | 8.0 | — | 13 | — | 82 FB | 194, 51 R | 685 | 3.0 |
| Switzerland[10] | 20.0/1,100.0 | — | 3.0/45.0 | — | — | — | 135 FB | 138, 18 R | 875 | 2.3 |
| Yugoslavia | 165.0 | 12.5 | 36.0 | — | 6 | 4 FFG | 120 FB | 140, 80 R | 1,020 | 3.9 |
| **IV. MIDDLE EAST AND MEDITERRANEAN; SUB-SAHARAN AFRICA; LATIN AMERICA[11]** | | | | | | | | | | |
| Algeria | 150.0 | 7.0 | 12.0 | — | 2 | 3 FFG | 141 FB | 155, 6 R, 10 MR | 910 | 1.9 |
| Egypt | 320.0 | 20.0 | 25.0 | — | 12 | 2 DD, 1 DDG, 4 FFG, 2 FF | 185 FB, 9 B | 161, 20 R | 2,250 | 8.9 |
| Iran[12] | 305.0 | 14.5 | 35.0 | — | — | 3 DDG, 4 FFG | 50 FB | 10 F, 8 R | 1,000 | 10.0 |
| Iraq[12] | 955.0 | 5.0 | 40.0 | — | — | 4 FFG, 1 FF | 15 B, 181 FB | 315, 5 R | 4,500 | 57.1 |
| Israel[10] | 104.0/598.0 | 9.0/10.0 | 28.0/37.0 | — | 3 | — | 521 FB | 19 R | 3,900 | 13.9 |
| Jordan | 70.0 | 0.3 | 10.0 | — | — | — | 66 FB | 32 | 986 | 13.1 |
| Kuwait | 13.0 | 1.1 | 2.0 | — | — | — | 34 FB | 32 | 260 | 9.1 |
| Lebanon[13] | ... | ... | ... | — | — | — | — | — | — | ... |
| Libya[14] | 60.0 | 6.5 | 10.0 | — | 6 | 2 FFG | 6 B, 320 FB | 271, 15 R | 2,280 | ... |
| Morocco | 170.0 | 7.0 | 15.0 | — | — | 1 FFG | 66 FB | — | 110 | 4.2 |
| Oman | 16.5 | 2.0 | 3.0 | — | — | — | 40 FB | — | 39 | 20.1 |
| Qatar | 6.0 | 0.7 | 0.3 | — | — | — | 23 FB | — | 24 | ... |
| Saudi Arabia | 45.0 | 3.5 | 15.0 | — | — | 4 FFG | 70 FB | 45, 10 R | 550 | 18.9 |
| Sudan, The | 54.0 | 1.5 | 3.0 | — | — | — | 32 FB | — | 175 | 8.4 |
| Syria | 300.0 | 2.5 | 45.0 | — | 3 | 2 FF | 207 FB | 275, 6 R | 4,000 | 16.3 |
| Tunisia | 31.0 | 5.0 | 4.1 | — | — | 1 FF | 12 FB | — | 68 | 5.0 |
| United Arab Emirates | 40.0 | 1.5 | 1.5 | — | — | — | 3 FB | 29 | 136 | 8.0 |
| Yemen, North | 35.0 | 0.8 | 1.0 | — | — | — | — | 67 | 683 | 11.7 |
| Yemen, South | 24.0 | 1.0 | 2.5 | — | — | — | 32 FB | 30 | 470 | ... |
| Angola[15] | 49.5 | 1.5 | 2.0 | — | — | — | 99 FB | 38 | 540 | ... |
| Ethiopia[16] | 313.0 | 3.0 | 4.0 | — | — | 2 FF | 138 FB | — | 750 | 9.3 |

that progress in other arms control negotiations seemed even less likely than in previous years, while existing agreements were further weakened by continuing Soviet violations. These violations were also particularly threatening to the future prospects for arms control. Two of the most significant and easily understood were the development and deployment of two new ICBM (SS-24 and SS-25) instead of the one allowed under SALT II and the building of a massive ABM radar facility at Krasnoyarsk.

Under these circumstances it was not surprising that no effective results were achieved in the continuing U.S.-U.S.S.R. negotiations covering strategic offensive forces (START) and weapons in space. It was difficult to see how agreement could be reached on the kinds of major reductions in strategic forces discussed at the 1986 Reykjavík, Iceland, "preliminary" summit meeting between Reagan and Gorbachev. However, a much more limited, poten-

tially useful U.S.-U.S.S.R. agreement was reached on the establishment of crisis management centres in Moscow and Washington.

**MIDDLE EAST**

Syrian armed forces personnel totaled 407,500, with an army of 300,000 comprising five armoured and four mechanized divisions. Equipment included 1,100 new T-72 and 2,900 T-54/-55/-62 MBT and 3,100 BMP/BTR-series MICV/APC. The separate Air Defense Command had 60,000 personnel manning 87 batteries with Soviet SA-2/-3/-5/-6 SAM. The 45,000-strong Air Force had some 480 combat aircraft. Defense spending totaled $3,950,000,000 in 1987.

Israel remained the region's strongest military power, especially in the quality of its weapons. Its defense spending burden, which reached $5,110,000,000 for 1987–88,

| Country | Military personnel in 000s | | | Warships[1] | | | Jet aircraft[3] | | | Defense expenditure as % of 1985 GDP[5] |
|---|---|---|---|---|---|---|---|---|---|---|
| | Army | Navy | Air Force | Aircraft carriers/ cruisers | Submarines[2] | Destroyers/ frigates | Bombers and fighter-bombers | Fighters/ reconnaissance | Tanks[4] | |
| Kenya | 13.0 | 0.35 | 0 | — | — | — | 9 FB | — | 76 | 4.4 |
| Madagascar | 20.0 | 0.55 | 0.5 | — | — | — | 12 FB | — | — | ... |
| Mozambique[17] | 30.0 | 0.7 | 1.0 | — | — | — | 60 FB | — | 250 | ... |
| Nigeria | 80.0 | 5.0 | 9.5 | — | — | 1 FFG | 51 FB | — | 132 | 1.6 |
| Somalia | 61.3 | 1.2 | 2.5 | — | — | — | 96 FB | 38 | 293 | 13.4 |
| South Africa[10] | 75.0 | 9.0 | 13.0 | — | 3 | 1 FF | 12 B, 114 FB | 38 | 250 | 3.6 |
| Tanzania | 38.35 | 0.7 | 1.0 | — | — | — | — | 29 | 30 | ... |
| Zaire | 22.0 | 1.5 | 2.5 | — | — | — | — | 8 | 50 | ... |
| Zimbabwe | 46.0 | — | 1.0 | — | — | — | 7 B, 14 FB | 7 | 43 | 5.0 |
| Argentina | 45.0 | 20.0[8] | 13.0 | 1 CV | 4 | 6 DDG | 7 B, 107 FB | 12 MR | 450 | 3.1 |
| Brazil | 197.0 | 48.0[8] | 50.7 | 1 CVH | 7 | 9 DD, 1 DDG, 6 FFG | 35 FB | 17, 44 MR | — | 0.8 |
| Chile | 57.0 | 25.5 | 15.0 | — | 4 | 5 DDG, 2 DD, 2 FFG | 53 FB | 25, 6 MR | 171 | 7.8 |
| Colombia | 57.0 | 9.0 | 4.2 | — | 2 | 4 FFG | 15 FB | — | 12 | 0.8 |
| Cuba | 145.0 | 12.0 | 18.5 | — | 3 | 2 FFG | 51 FB | 199 | 950 | ... |
| El Salvador | 43.0 | 1.5 | 2.5 | — | — | — | 8 FB | — | — | 4.5 |
| Mexico | 105.0 | 23.0[8] | 6.5 | — | — | 3 DD, 6 FF | — | 11 F, 15 MR | — | 0.7 |
| Nicaragua | 74.0 | 1.0 | 3.4 | — | — | — | — | ... | 150 | 11.1 |
| Peru | 75.0 | 23.0[8] | 15.0 | 2 CA | 12 | 6 DD, 2 DDG, 4 FFG | 17 B, 60 FB | 13 MR | 300 | 4.4 |
| Venezuela | 34.0 | 10.0 | 5.0 | — | 2 | 6 FFG | 19 B, 13 FB | 57 | 81 | 1.7 |
| V. FAR EAST AND OCEANIA[11] | | | | | | | | | | |
| Afghanistan[18] | 45.0 | — | 5.0 | — | — | — | 18 B, 95 FB | — | 450 | ... |
| Australia | 32.0 | 15.7 | 22.8 | — | 6 | 3 DDG, 9 FFG | 22 FB | 72, 20 MR | 103 | 3.0 |
| Bangladesh | 90.0 | 7.5 | 4.0 | — | — | 3 FF | 52 FB | 12 | 50 | 1.2 |
| Burma | 170.0 | 7.0 | 9.0 | — | — | — | — | — | 24 | 3.3 |
| China | 2,300.0 | 340.0[8] | 470.0 | — | 112, 3 SSGN, 2 SSBN | 16 DDG, 28 FFG, 5 FF | 800 B, 500 FB | 4,600, 260 R, 14 MR | 11,450 | 2.9 |
| India | 1,100.0 | 47.0 | 115.0 | 2 CV | 11 | 4 DDG, 10 FFG, 11 FF | 404 FB | 165, 19 R, 6 MR | 2,750 | 3.2 |
| Indonesia | 216.0 | 42.0[8] | 26.0 | — | 2 | 6 FFG, 6 FF | 29 FB | 14, 9 MR | — | 2.7 |
| Japan | 156.0 | 45.0 | 45.0 | — | 15 | 32 DDG, 4 DD, 3 FFG, 15 FF | 77 FB | 220, 10 R, 70 MR | 1,150 | 1.0 |
| Korea, North | 750.0 | 35.0 | 53.0 | — | 27 | 1 FF, 1 FFG | 80 B, 410 FB | 250 | 2,900 | 10.0 |
| Korea, South | 542.0 | 29.0[8] | 33.0 | — | — | 7 DDG, 2 DD, 2 FFG | 280 FB | 65, 10R | 1,300 | 5.2 |
| Laos | 52.5 | 1.0 | 2.0 | — | — | — | 30 FB | — | 30 | ... |
| Malaysia | 90.0 | 11.0 | 12.0 | — | — | 2 FFG, 2 FF | 39 FB | 16, 3 MR, 2 R | — | 5.6 |
| Mongolia | 30.0 | — | 3.5 | — | — | — | — | 17 | 650 | ... |
| New Zealand | 5.8 | 2.6 | 4.2 | — | — | 4 FFG | 22 FB | 6 MR | — | 2.1 |
| Pakistan | 450.0 | 13.0 | 17.6 | — | 6 | 7 DDG | 107 FB | 200, 13 R, 3 MR | 1,600 | 6.9 |
| Philippines | 62.0 | 26.0[8] | 17.0 | — | — | 7 FF | 12 FB | 10, 3 MR | — | 1.4 |
| Singapore | 45.0 | 4.5 | 6.0 | — | — | — | 109 FB | 35 | — | 6.8 |
| Taiwan | 309.0[8] | 38.0 | 77.0 | — | 2 | 18 DDG, 4 DD, 9 FF | 377 FB | 15, 8 R, 29 MR | 309 | 6.6 |
| Thailand | 166.0 | 42.0[8] | 48.0 | — | — | 5 FF, 1 FFG | 18 FB | 36, 13 MR | 89 | 3.9 |
| Vietnam | 1,100.0 | 40.0[8] | 20.0 | — | — | 6 FF, 1 FFG | 83 FB | 200 | 1,600 | ... |

Note: Data exclude paramilitary, security, and irregular forces. Naval data exclude vessels of less than 100 tons standard displacement. Figures are for July 1987. Because of substantive changes in national forces and reassessments of evidence, data may not be comparable with previous editions.

[1] Aircraft carrier (CV); aircraft carrier, nuclear (CVN); helicopter carrier (CVH); general purpose amphibious assault ship (LHA); amphibious transport dock (LPD); amphibious assault ship (helicopter) (LPH); dock/tank landing ship (LSD/T); battleship (BBG); heavy cruiser (CA); guided missile cruiser (CG); guided missile cruiser, nuclear (CGN); helicopter cruiser (CAH); destroyer (DD); guided missile destroyer (DDG); frigate (FF); guided missile frigate (FFG); N denotes nuclear powered.
[2] Nuclear-powered attack submarine (SSN); ballistic missile submarine (SSB); guided (cruise) missile submarine (SSG); coastal (C); N denotes nuclear powered.
[3] Bombers (B), fighter-bombers (FB), strategic bombers (SB), reconnaissance fighters (R); maritime reconnaissance (MR). Data include jet combat aircraft from all services including naval and air defense. MR also includes propeller drive ASW and ECM aircraft; data exclude light strike/counter-insurgency (COIN) aircraft.
[4] Main battle tanks (MBT), medium and heavy, 31 tons and over.
[5] Figures are for Gross Domestic Product (GDP).
[6] Of Canada's other military personnel, approximately 29,000 are not identified by service.
[7] French forces were withdrawn from NATO command structure in 1966, but France remains a member of NATO.
[8] Includes marines.
[9] Figure includes the Strategic Rocket Forces (298,000) and the Air Defense Force (335,000), both separate services.
[10] Second figure is fully mobilized strength.
[11] Sections IV and V list only those states with significant military forces.
[12] Losses in Iran-Iraq war made remaining force estimates uncertain.
[13] Lebanon's civil war and division mean that there are no longer any truly national forces, only militias.
[14] Some advanced Libyan aircraft are maintained and manned by Soviet/Warsaw Pact crews.
[15] Plus 30,000–35,000 Cubans and 500 East Germans serving with Angolan forces.
[16] Ethiopia also has 4,000 Soviet, Cuban plus other Soviet bloc troops, and a 150,000-strong People's Militia.
[17] Plus Cuban, Warsaw Pact, and Chinese advisers and technicians.
[18] Figures approximate, given Soviet occupation of Afghanistan. Excludes about 118,000 Soviet occupation troops, 5,000 Cubans/Czechoslovaks, and 130,000–240,000 mujahidin freedom fighters.

Sources: International Institute for Strategic Studies, 23 Tavistock Street, London, The Military Balance 1987–1988, Strategic Survey 1986–87.

was still difficult to support even with massive U.S. aid, but it had been reduced from earlier levels. Defense had consumed 13.9% of GDP in 1985, compared with 35.5% in 1982. With a population of only about 4,450,000, Israel raised standing armed forces of 141,000 that would increase to 645,000 on mobilization. The Army of 104,000 formed 11 armoured divisions and 9 mechanized infantry, 5 parachute, and 15 artillery brigades. These forces had some 3,900 MBT and 6,300 MICV/APC. The 28,000-strong Air Force had 676 combat aircraft.

Egypt's armed forces totaled 445,000 personnel; defense spending was estimated at $4,570,000,000 in 1987–88. The Army of 320,000 had 750 U.S. M-60A3 and 500 effective Soviet T-54/-55/-62 MBT. Effective aircraft for the 25,000-strong Air Force included 32 F-4E Phantoms, 54 Mirage 5SDE2 and 14 Mirage 2000 EM fighter-bombers, plus 42 F-16A Falcon and 120 MiG-21/J-7 interceptors.

Libya's forces remained numerically large, totaling 76,500 personnel with 2,100 MBT and 544 combat aircraft, but they performed poorly in the war between Libya and Chad during the year.

## SOUTH, EAST, AND SOUTHEAST ASIA

The Soviet occupation of Afghanistan continued in 1987, but the Soviet forces were still unable to gain complete control of the country. Border incidents between Afghanistan and Pakistan and the possibility of Soviet military strikes into the Baluchistan area of Pakistan remained a potential danger. Despite increased U.S. military aid, Pakistan's armed forces totaled only 480,600 personnel, mainly an army of 450,000 with 1,600 MBT (mostly Type-59). The Air Force comprised 17,600 personnel and 381 combat aircraft. The defense budget in 1987–88 totaled $2,540,-000,000.

India's armed forces in 1987 totaled some 1,262,000 personnel. The 1.1 million-strong Army had some 2,800 MBT, including 350 new T-72s. The Air Force of 115,000 had 700 combat aircraft, including 95 MiG-23 Flogger H and 40 Mirage 200H fighter-bombers. Defense spending in 1987–88 amounted to $9,730,000,000.

China's military manpower was being reduced, but more slowly than had been thought, to 3.2 million. Defense expenditure was estimated at about 7% of GNP. The nation's nuclear stockpile was small, with limited numbers of comparatively old, vulnerable delivery systems. These included about 6 ICBM (DF-4/-5), 60 DF-3 IRBM, and 50 DF-2 medium-range ballistic missiles. The Army had 2.3 million personnel but only 11,450 MBT (mostly T-59/-69), while the 470,000-strong Air Force's 5,400 combat aircraft were modifications of old Soviet models, including 3,000 J-6/MiG-19 fighters.

Vietnam remained the largest active military power in Southeast Asia, with armed forces, mostly army, totaling 1,260,000—the fourth largest army in the world. The Army had about 1,600 MBT, and the 20,000-strong Air Force had approximately 270 combat aircraft. Some 140,000 troops were deployed in Kampuchea and 50,000 in Laos.

North Korea's forces were so much larger than those of South Korea that concerns over the danger of a Northern invasion of the South rose to significant levels. The balance was 838,000 personnel, 2,900 MBT, 1,400 APC, and 840 combat aircraft (mostly older types) for the North versus 629,000 personnel, 1,300 MBT, 850 APC, and 476 combat aircraft (mostly modern types) for the South.

The government of outgoing Japanese Prime Minister Yasuhiro Nakasone continued to exceed, marginally, the long-standing spending ceiling of no more than 1% of GNP on defense. Japan's 1987–88 defense expenditure was $24 billion. Armed forces personnel totaled 246,000, including an army of 156,000 with 1,150 MBT. The Air Force and Navy had 45,000 personnel each. Equipment included 77 Japanese-made F-1 fighter-bombers and 90 F-15J/JD and 130 F-EJ Phantom fighter-bombers. Taiwan's armed forces, totaling 424,000 personnel, continued to provide a credible defense against China. The Army, with 270,000 personnel, had 309 MBT, and the 77,000-strong Air Force had 562 combat aircraft. Defense spending in 1986–87 totaled $4,540,000,000.

## AFRICA SOUTH OF THE SAHARA

In September–November the largest-scale fighting in sub-Saharan Africa since the Anglo-Boer War (1899–1902) took place in Angola. Under Soviet Gen. Konstantin Shagnovitch, an 18,000-strong army of Angolans, Cubans, and Soviets launched a long-prepared offensive against the UNITA (National Union for the Total Independence of Angola) rebel capital of Jamba, defended by 14,000 troops led by Jonas Savimbi and supported by South African air and artillery. By November this offensive had failed, UNITA forces holding their line on the Lomba River and inflicting heavy losses on the attackers. South Africa, with artillery fire that proved particularly effective, thus again demonstrated that it was the region's dominant military power, with armed forces totaling 97,000 (rising to 422,000 on mobilization). Equipment included 250 MBT, 1,500 Ratel MICV, and 366 combat aircraft. Defense spending was estimated at $3,290,000,000 for 1987–88.

## LATIN AMERICA

Costa Rica's Pres. Oscar Arias Sánchez (*see* BIOGRAPHIES) received the 1987 Nobel Peace Prize for his Central American peace plan, but the Arias plan failed to deal with the

A weapons transporter carrying nuclear depth bombs for the Royal Navy lies on its side after slipping off an icy road in Wiltshire. Critics later objected to the vehicles' having been sent out in bad weather.
PHOTO TRENDS

two basic causes of instability in Central America. These were depressed economic and social conditions, which encouraged revolutionary movements, plus large-scale Soviet aid to these movements via their Cuban and Nicaraguan proxies.

Central and Latin-American armed forces, primarily internal-security infantry troops with little equipment, were poorly paid and often poorly led. They were also small relative to the size and population of their countries, as is apparent from Table II. Thus the region was vulnerable to outside intervention. Costa Rica had no military forces and only a single Northern Border Security Battalion (9,500 personnel) of paramilitary forces. Honduras had cut its army by 14%, leaving a total armed forces personnel of 16,950, and Guatemala's personnel totaled 40,200. El Salvador's Pres. José Napoleón Duarte had armed forces totaling 47,000, mostly army, supported by U.S. economic and military aid in the government's fight against some 10,000 rebel guerrillas, aided by Cuban and Nicaraguan personnel plus Soviet weapons and supplies.

In sharp contrast, the fifth party to the Arias plan, Nicaragua's Sandinista Pres. Daniel Ortega Saavedra, had increased his army and air force strength by 7 and 70%, respectively. This raised total armed forces to 77,000 personnel, with 150 Soviet T-54/55 tanks and some 50 Mi-8/17/24/25 attack/assault helicopters. Nicaragua's anti-Sandinista guerrillas, the U.S.-backed *contras*, totaled 12,000–15,000 personnel; equipment included the U.S.-supplied Stinger SAM. Cuba was the dominant Latin-American and Caribbean power, with armed forces totaling 175,500 personnel. (ROBIN RANGER)

*See also* Space Exploration.
This article updates the *Macropædia* article The Technology of WAR.

# Mining

According to *Mining Magazine's* 20th Annual Mining Activity Survey, there were in 1986 in the non-Communist world some 1,134 opencut and underground mines, each producing 150,000 tons per year or more of non-energy-related mineral ores and representing in aggregate about

90% of world output for the 29 principal metals and minerals studied. An additional 6,000 to 7,000 mines with lesser capacity were thought to exist, including many significant gold producers. The areas surveyed demonstrated a number of significant aspects of the regional distribution of mining operations. India, for example, operated more than half of Asia's opencut mines for these materials and more than one-third of its underground mines; South Africa had more than half of the major underground mines in Africa but fewer than one-fifth of the opencut; Brazil operated two-fifths of the large opencut mines in Latin America but only one-tenth of the underground mines.

In regard to major development programs, gold continued to attract the most attention, outnumbering projects involving other metals by more than two to one. *Mining Magazine* noted that "attention has turned from many of the more traditional hunting grounds to the new arena of the south-west Pacific." Particularly attractive were prospects for finding gold and copper-gold deposits in areas geologically similar to those of the Bougainville and Ok Tedi operations in Papua New Guinea.

Among nongold minerals, projects calling for capitalization in the $1 billion range included: in Latin America, the Barcarena (aluminum) and Carajas (iron) projects in Brazil and the La Escondida (copper) project in Chile; in Oceania, the Portland, Victoria (aluminum), Yandicoogina, Western Australia (iron), and Olympic Dam, South Australia (uranium), projects; in Africa, the Mount Nimba (iron) operations in Guinea and the Mwanda-Banana (aluminum) prospect in Zaire; and in Asia and North America, a variety of smaller projects.

In 1986, the last year for which reasonably complete data were available, the U.S. Bureau of Mines estimated that of a group of 70 mineral commodities, 25 rose in total world output, 36 fell, and 9 remained unchanged. In the United States, mine output in 1986 was valued at $23 billion as initial production and more than ten times that much as processed mineral commodities, about 5.7% of the gross national product.

**Exploration.** Aside from the extreme emphasis on gold exploration noted above, several other trends were apparent during 1986–87. They included the consequences of failure to explore, apparent in the focus of discussions between Boliden AB and the Swedish government in November on future domestic operations and investment; the increasing

ease and portability of geophysical and geochemical tools; and the increasing availability of computer-related tools.

Boliden AB, a large Swedish mining firm, sought 35% government participation in a strongly exploration-oriented 3 billion kronor ($475 million) domestic development program intended to preserve raw material supplies and jobs in its Swedish operations into the 21st century. Government action on the proposal was expected to turn in large measure upon Boliden's willingness to accede to pressures to improve its environmental record, one of Sweden's worst, particularly at its Ronnskar copper smelter.

A downward trend in exploration budgets for base metals, forced by the expansion of gold and energy exploration budgets, had led to increased use of gravity and electromagnetic geophysical tools and mathematical analytical software for surveying and evaluating large areas with high reliability. Gravity measurements and magnetic anomaly data (both intensities and gradients) had increasingly been subjected to new analytical techniques that provided immediate graphic representations of areas surveyed, resolved shapes and details of subsurface features, and distinguished between anomalous areas of no economic interest or homogeneous areas of differing economic interest. Continuing refinement of techniques for survey or sounding by electrical resistivity or conductivity, radar (useful in either crystalline rock or unconsolidated sediments), and induced polarization (production of a double layer of magnetic or electrical charge at an ore body's interface with the surrounding groundmass) had supplied exploration geologists with tools that were increasingly portable and also increasingly sophisticated in their ability to survey terrain, analyze the data accumulated, and locate sites for boreholes to test their hypotheses.

Software packages of special interest for exploration were developed for the following applications: geologic modeling and interpretation of structure, sedimentology, geochemistry, mineralogy, the geophysical subjects enumerated above, mapping and contouring, statistical analysis and plotting of data, exploration economics, and use of artificial intelligence systems for prospecting. These tools in no way supplanted field geologists but rather extended their capacities for remembering, relating, and interpreting.

**Development and Operations.** Economies of scale had been at the centre of mining economics far longer than in most industries, partly because of the degree of dispersion

## Indexes of Production, Mining and Mineral Commodities
### (1980 = 100)

| | 1982 | 1983 | 1984 | 1985 | 1986 | 1987 1st quarter | 1987 2nd quarter |
|---|---|---|---|---|---|---|---|
| **Mining (total)** | | | | | | | |
| World[1] | 85.6 | 84.9 | 87.9 | 86.5 | 89.1 | 90.6 | . . . |
| Centrally planned economies[2] | 102.7 | 105.1 | 106.9 | 108.6 | 110.3 | 112.9 | 113.5 |
| Developed market economies[3] | 98.9 | 98.3 | 102.4 | 104.1 | 101.5 | 104.5 | 100.3 |
| Less developed market economies[4] | 74.4 | 73.1 | 75.7 | 71.8 | 77.8 | 78.2 | . . . |
| **Coal** | | | | | | | |
| World[1] | 102.2 | 101.7 | 100.3 | 105.6 | 107.1 | 108.0 | . . . |
| Centrally planned economies[2] | 102.9 | 105.2 | 107.0 | 108.9 | 110.4 | 112.1 | 112.9 |
| Developed market economies[3] | 100.8 | 97.7 | 92.7 | 100.4 | 101.6 | 100.2 | 99.5 |
| Less developed market economies[4] | 112.3 | 115.8 | 125.8 | 133.8 | 138.8 | 157.8 | . . . |
| **Petroleum and natural gas** | | | | | | | |
| World[1] | 80.6 | 79.4 | 82.3 | 79.0 | 81.9 | 83.6 | . . . |
| Centrally planned economies[2] | 104.8 | 106.5 | 107.5 | 108.0 | 108.8 | 112.0 | 111.3 |
| Developed market economies[3] | 101.4 | 100.4 | 105.8 | 106.6 | 101.8 | 108.9 | 98.0 |
| Less developed market economies[4] | 71.5 | 70.1 | 72.1 | 67.3 | 73.0 | 72.5 | . . . |
| **Metals** | | | | | | | |
| World[1] | 96.1 | 96.3 | 102.9 | 104.8 | 106.9 | 109.3 | . . . |
| Centrally planned economies[2] | 90.5 | 92.9 | 93.2 | 95.5 | 96.6 | 101.0 | 101.9 |
| Developed market economies[3] | 93.8 | 94.9 | 104.7 | 104.8 | 104.5 | 108.4 | 109.7 |
| Less developed market economies[4] | 101.1 | 99.1 | 101.9 | 106.8 | 112.9 | 112.4 | . . . |
| **Manufacturing (total)** | 98.5 | 101.9 | 108.7 | 112.8 | 117.0 | 118.8 | . . . |

[1] Excluding Albania, China, North Korea, and Vietnam.
[2] Bulgaria, Czechoslovakia, East Germany, Hungary, Poland, Romania, and the U.S.S.R.
[3] North America, Europe (except centrally planned and Yugoslavia), Australia, Israel, Japan, New Zealand, and South Africa.
[4] Caribbean, Central and South America, Africa (except South Africa), Asian Middle East, East and Southeast Asia (except Israel and Japan), and Yugoslavia.
Source: UN, *Monthly Bulletin of Statistics* (November 1987).

In China's Shanxi (Shansi) Province a huge electric shovel loads nearly 50 tons of rock and coal into a mammoth truck during the first day of formal operation of the Antaibao open pit coal mine, a joint venture of U.S. and Chinese interests.
AP/WIDE WORLD

most minerals display in their native form (nine ounces of gold per ton of ore) but also because of the enormous quantities of overburden or spoil that must be handled, the quantities of minerals needed by industries, the distances the ores must be transported, and the unpredictability of cost and price for every element of the equation—labour, equipment, mining rights, transport, environmental protection, market prices, and so on. Much of this was evident during the year, nowhere more clearly than in the $400 million modernization of Kennecott's Bingham Canyon (Utah) copper mine. The mine itself, which had produced some 12 million tons of metal since its opening, more than any other copper mine, was not recognized as an economically viable proposition in view of its low-grade 2% ore until 1903. By 1987 the largest excavation ever undertaken by humans, Bingham Canyon was carrying out improvements necessitated by the closing of the mine in 1985 because of low copper prices. New labour agreements in 1986 and the provision of integrated in-pit crushing, conveyor-belt transport to storage and concentration facilities, concentrate and tailings pipelines, and an on-site refinery (planned to be completed in staged operations by the fall of 1988) were expected to make the facility the most efficient and low-cost in the U.S. and, possibly, the world.

Most elements of mine operations were susceptible to gains in efficiency from economies of scale. One example was excavation machinery; a hydraulic shovel with a capacity of 26 cu m (918 cu ft) was commissioned in January to load trucks regularly exceeding 150 tons in capacity. In other types of mining operations, new large-scale equipment was also being commissioned. Testing began in the late summer on the *Chicago,* the world's largest dredge. Built for Great Lakes Dredge and Dock Co., it incorporated two 4,585-cu m (6,000-cu yd) barges, an 8,800-hp excavator, and a variety of bucket configurations; the dredge could be used for either marine or freshwater applications.

**Safety and Environment.** The Mine Safety and Health Administration (MSHA), responsible for mine safety in the United States, reported that 40 workers had died in metal and nonmetal mining and 87 in coal mining in 1986. While these figures were good by world standards, the MSHA came under criticism for approval of inadequate safety plans offered by mining corporations, lax inspection and enforcement, and a lack of initiative in policy-making that amounted to approval of mine owners' unwillingness to make safety a higher priority. The agency *did* impose a

$111,470 fine in May on the Utah Power and Light Co. for the circumstances of the 1984 fire at its Wilberg mine, in which 27 miners died, but this was viewed by critics mostly as an effort to draw attention away from deficiencies in the day-to-day execution of its mandate.

Once again in 1987, a South African mine disaster was prominent in the world press; the Saint Helena gold mine, near Welkom, Orange Free State, was the site of a fire and explosion on August 31 in which 62 died, mostly as a result of a severed elevator cable. The mine was owned by Gencor, the General Mining Union Corp., at whose Kinross mine only a year earlier 177 miners had died, in consequence of which seven Gencor managers were facing charges of criminal negligence.

**Business and Markets.** The October collapse of the New York Stock Exchange and subsequent market adjustments elsewhere produced consequences of significance to the mining industry. One of the most immediate was the rise in sales of official gold coins; for example, some 218,000 units of the U.S. eagle were sold in the four weeks prior to November 2, while only 63,500 had been sold in the month prior to the stock market collapse. Similar results were reported for the Canadian maple leaf.

The October 1985 collapse of the international tin market had serious consequences throughout 1986 and 1987 for all members of the former International Tin Council (ITC). A new organization comprised largely of ITC members, the Association of Tin Producing Countries (ATPC), provided a cooperative basis for efforts to limit exports by member nations (Australia, Bolivia, Indonesia, Malaysia, Nigeria, Thailand, and Zaire). ATPC members had agreed to limit exports by the group to 96,000 tons during the period from March 1987 through February 1988 in an effort to reduce their stocks, some 70,000 tons at the beginning of the period, over a 2½-year interval and maintain price levels. At the September meeting of the ATPC, the ministers agreed to extend the program beyond February 1988, and it appeared that only some 45,000 tons of the unmarketed stocks would remain at the end of the calendar year. The meeting was attended by representatives of China and Brazil, who, though not members, had voluntarily limited their own exports. Bolivia and its state mining corporation, Comibol, were probably the most seriously affected by the ITC debacle. Tin production by Comibol was off more than 50%, down from 10,060 tons in 1985 to only 4,232 in 1986; its work force had been reduced by more than 70%, from 27,000 to 8,000. The Bolivian government, however, was prepared to continue Comibol's existence, according to a speech at midyear by Jaime Villalobos, Bolivian minister of mining and metallurgy, though without the corruption and mismanagement that had characterized Comibol in the past. The Bolivian industry experienced the lowest levels of productivity among the major tin-producing countries, and a series of reforms imposed on Comibol, such as rental of mines to workers' cooperatives, were already producing dramatic gains in output.

The aluminum industry was largely concentrated in the Western Hemisphere, where in some places it was especially important for the preservation of income to support development (Guyana, Jamaica) or to broaden the export base of the industrializing countries of the region (Brazil and Venezuela). Venezuela was planning a particularly rapid expansion, from its current 405,000 tons per year of primary smelting capacity to one million tons by 1991 and two million tons by the end of the century, according to plans announced in March.

**Technology.** In addition to the technological gains required for bringing to market the large-scale production equipment and high-technology exploration instrumentation referred to above, many other advances became known or passed from the experimental to the commercial during the year. Even the most mundane aspects of the industry were being examined with profit; an example was a vibrating-edge shovel bucket, unveiled in 1986 by Niedermeier of West Germany, that within a year was demonstrating "dramatic" gains in productivity.

One new development had possibilities far beyond the economics of mining alone. The process offered a means of extracting economic value from flue dust and other poisonous wastes (potential value for only six to eight U.S. smelters was estimated at more than $1 billion) while at the same time rendering a toxic-waste site environmentally safe. It would, by the same token, permit ores to be smelted in the future without leaving a toxic site behind. In this process low-cost reagents (limestone [$CaCO_3$], CaO, and $CaCl_2$) were used to process complex arsenical wastes or ores into soluble chlorides of the contained precious and base metals and insoluble (therefore environmentally safe) precipitates of the arsenic compounds. The initial commercial-scale installation was at the old Anaconda, Mont., smelter; the outcome of the program would be closely monitored by both the U.S. Bureau of Mines and the Environmental Protection Agency and by similar agencies worldwide.                   (WILLIAM A. CLEVELAND)

*See also* Earth Sciences; Energy; Industrial Review: Gemstones; Iron and Steel.

This article updates the *Macropædia* article Extraction and Processing INDUSTRIES.

# Motion Pictures

**English-Speaking Cinema.** *United States.* Mainstream Hollywood production continued to respond to a market dominated by a predominantly teenage audience in 1987. The favoured categories were clear-cut: low comedy, the supernatural and science fiction, police melodrama, and high-school films. Sequels and copies proliferated, with such titles as *Police Academy 4: Citizens on Patrol, Beverly Hills Cop II, Penitentiary III,* and *Meatballs III.*

There were some imaginative comic essays, such as Joel Coen's *Raising Arizona,* a surreal and anarchic vision of the American underbelly with the unlikely comic theme of baby theft. Steve Martin updated *Cyrano de Bergerac* in *Roxanne,* with Martin himself playing the proboscis-

plagued romantic hero, now transformed as the chief of a small-town fire brigade. Barry Levinson's *Tin Men* made a rewarding comedy out of the rivalry of aluminum-siding salesmen. *The Witches of Eastwick,* directed by George Miller and adapted from a novel by John Updike, cast Jack Nicholson as the devil, working out the nature of human relationships with three witches.

The social undoing of yuppies inspired Blake Edwards's clumsy slapstick *Blind Date.* In contrast, Herbert Ross's popular *The Secret of My Success* showed the successful yuppie making it to the top of the organization by confidence games and sexual favour. Comedy produced one of the more spectacular commercial disasters of the year: *Ishtar,* directed by Elaine May and with Dustin Hoffman and Warren Beatty as talentless songwriters caught up in North African politics.

Crime maintained its attraction. Ridley Scott's *Someone to Watch over Me* compensated for a conventional story with dazzling technical effects; William Friedkin's *Rampage* used a murder story to argue the case against the insanity defense. A period piece, Brian De Palma's *The Untouchables* was a flamboyant dramatization of the pursuit of Al Capone by an internal revenue agent. Its main merit was the literate script by David Mamet, who made his own debut as writer-director with a stylish story of confidence tricksters, *House of Games.* Paul Verhoeven's *Robocop,* one of the year's box-office successes, combined thriller and science fiction in a cold and violent story about the creation of a robot killer policeman. Achieving both critical and popular success was Adrian Lyne's *Fatal Attraction,* about a woman's increasing obsession with a married man after a brief affair with him.

Following the success of *Platoon,* directed by Oliver Stone (*see* BIOGRAPHIES), there was a rush of films about the Vietnam conflict. Francis Coppola's *Gardens of Stone* viewed the war through the eyes of an instructor in a military academy, dutifully training young men for a war he knows is wrong. John Irvin's *Hamburger Hill* was a conventional "war-is-hell" drama. *Lethal Weapon* was an echo of the aftermath, a tale of cops and villains, all of whom inherited their violence from Vietnam. Barry Levinson's *Good Morning, Vietnam,* with Robin Williams as a disc jockey in Saigon in 1965, offered a view of the developing

GAMMA/LIAISON

Eddie Murphy (left) returned as Axel Foley, as did Judge Reinhold as Billy Rosewood (centre) and John Ashton as John Taggart, in *Beverly Hills Cop II,* one of a bumper crop of sequels and copies.

Glenn Close (left) and Michael Douglas
starred with Anne Archer in *Fatal Attraction*, a
blockbuster thriller about the consequences of
obsessive love resulting from a seemingly casual
illicit affair.
SYGMA

war that gave Williams ample opportunity to express his
comic talents.

A more salutary reflection on the Oriental battleground
was provided by Jonathan Demme's *Swimming to Cambodia*, a straight record of Spalding Gray's stage monologue
about experiences working on *The Killing Fields*. The last
film of John Huston (*see* OBITUARIES) proved an appropriate and moving testament: a sad, comic, reflective
adaptation of James Joyce's "The Dead," with near fault-
less mise-en-scène and acting. Woody Allen's *Radio Days*
evoked the early 1940s, when radio and its stars were a
major focus of interest.

Among the best of the movies released late in the year
were James L. Brooks's *Broadcast News*, a behind-the-
scenes look at television news; Oliver Stone's *Wall Street*,
a morality tale about insider trading on the stock market;
Steven Spielberg's *Empire of the Sun*, about a British boy
in China taken prisoner by the Japanese during World War
II; and Norman Jewison's *Moonstruck*, a comedy about
love and lust in Brooklyn.

At the annual awards ceremony of the Academy of Motion Picture Arts and Sciences in Los Angeles in March,
*Platoon* took four awards, for best picture, best director,
best editing, and best achievement in sound. The Oscars
for best actor and actress went to Paul Newman (*The Color
of Money*) and Marlee Matlin (*Children of a Lesser God*).
Best supporting players were Michael Caine and Dianne
Wiest, both for performances in Woody Allen's *Hannah
and Her Sisters*, which also took the award for the best
original screenplay. James Ivory's *A Room with a View*
received Oscars for best adaptation from another medium,
for costume design, and for art direction.

*Great Britain.* The British film industry could claim one
of its most successful years. At the purely commercial level,
there was the predictable triumph of a new James Bond
picture, *The Living Daylights*, directed by John Glen. A
new Bond, the classical actor Timothy Dalton, made the
world's favourite secret agent a shade more romantic and
a shade less flippant than his predecessors.

Richard Attenborough's *Cry Freedom* was a forthright
attack on the abuses of apartheid in South Africa, through
a dramatization of the killing of the charismatic black
leader Stephen Biko. Stanley Kubrick re-created a stylized
Vietnam, in South London, for *Full Metal Jacket*, which
was made with a technical brilliance that few directors
had equaled. John Boorman made his most personal film

in *Hope and Glory*, recollecting without heroics or high
drama boyhood in wartime Britain. An earlier period piece
was *Maurice*, another E. M. Forster adaptation from James
Ivory, about the confusions and anguish of a young homosexual in post-Edwardian England.

The renaissance of British cinema was mostly due to
modestly budgeted films financed in part by television.
Outstanding in this area was Pat O'Connor's *A Month in
the Country*, a sensitive impression of two soldiers exorcis-
ing the psychological injuries of World War I. Alan Clarke's
*Rita, Sue and Bob Too* was an ambivalent comedy about
the sexual experiments of two schoolgirls from a working-
class housing development with an opportunistic middle-
class man.

Stephen Frears enjoyed a major success with *Prick Up
Your Ears*, a portrait of Joe Orton with script by Alan Bennett, which dealt more with the playwright's provocative
sexual life and violent death than with his art. In *Sammy*

©1987 PARAMOUNT PICTURES CORP.; PHOTOGRAPH, PHOTO TRENDS

Kevin Costner portrays federal agent Eliot Ness in Brian De Palma's
*The Untouchables*. The film's fast pace and strong casting combined
to produce one of the box-office smashes of the summer.

*and Rosie Get Laid,* Frears and screenwriter Hanif Kureishi attempted a broader and fiercer view of racial and political conflicts in contemporary Britain than in their previous collaboration, *My Beautiful Laundrette.* The memoirs of a celebrated suburban madame, Cynthia Payne, inspired two films: *Personal Services,* dealing with her later life and brushes with the law, was written by David Leland and directed by Terry Jones; *Wish You Were Here,* about her adolescence, was a triumphant writer-director debut by Leland. Harry Hook's *The Kitchen Toto*—a well-written picture of the relationships of Britons and Kenyans in late colonial days—took the award for the best first film at the Tokyo Film Festival.

*Australasia.* Australia's most original director, Dutch-born Paul Cox, composed a stylish essay on Van Gogh, *Vincent,* through a montage of the painter's letters, scenes of his life, his paintings, and dramatized incidents—in none of which the figure of the painter himself was personated. Another period piece, Simon Wincer's *The Lighthorsemen,* was an inadequately scripted story of Australian cavalry fighting in the Middle East in 1917, retrieved by the finely handled spectacle of the action sequences. More intimate themes were treated in Carl Schultz's winning, tragicomic study of an elderly man's final romance, *Travelling North,* and in John Duigan's *The Year My Voice Broke,* an unpatronizing picture of the trials of adolescence.

From New Zealand, Barry Barclay's *Ngati,* an assured and well-structured film about a young man who discovers that he is partly Maori, offered an intelligent and humane study of racial relationships.

*Canada.* Giles Walker made a sequel to his brilliant, idiosyncratic comedy *90 Days* in *The Last Straw;* the new film cast the same characters in a bizarre farce about artificial human insemination. Patricia Rozema's assured comedy *I've Heard the Mermaids Singing* related the emotional ups and downs of a naive secretary and her sophisticated boss. Nova Scotian filmmaker Bill MacGillivray made a pleasant, civilized genre comedy, *Life Classes,* about a young woman who leaves Cape Breton for bohemian circles in Halifax. *John and the Missus,* a well-characterized drama of the traumas when a mining community is uprooted, was the debut feature of Gordon Pinsent, a leading Canadian actor.

**Western Europe.** *France.* Broad comedy and slick thrillers, like Jacques Deray's *Le Solitaire* (with Jean-Paul Belmondo), Alexandre Arcady's *L'Été dernier à Tanger,* and Claude Guillemot's *La Brute,* continued to be a staple of French cinema. Very much a cut above the rest was Edouard Niermans's *Poussière d'ange,* a stylish and original thriller about a boozy cop and a beautiful and deadly young femme fatale.

Louis Malle returned to France, after a long stay in Hollywood, to direct one of his best films; *Au revoir, les enfants* was an autobiographical reminiscence, recalling life in a Roman Catholic boys' school in occupied France and the brutal awakening when three Jewish children are taken away by the Gestapo. Claude Chabrol made a minor but satisfying crime comedy, *Masques,* with Philippe Noiret as a popular TV personality who turns out to be a crook.

*Italy.* In Italy 1987 was mostly a year of success and failure for the middle and older generations. After several years of illness, Ermanno Olmi returned with one of his most personal works, *Lunga vita alla signora!,* a comic fantasy about a party of 15-year-old trainee waiters serving at a bizarre dinner in a sinister chateau-hotel. Federico Fellini's *Intervista* was a tribute to Cinecittà studios, a scrapbook of memories of the director's films and collaborators. The Taviani brothers meanwhile paid nostalgic homage to early

Hollywood in *Good Morning, Babylon,* the story of two emigrant Italian stonemasons who created the elephants for the set of D. W. Griffith's *Intolerance.*

Francesco Rosi's *Chronicle of a Death Foretold,* adapted from a Gabriel García Márquez novel, is the story of a man's return to a remote Colombian river township to investigate the circumstances in which his friend was murdered. Bernardo Bertolucci scored a critical success with *The Last Emperor,* about the painful life of the deposed last emperor of China. Among debut films, the most notable was a Franco-Italian coproduction by Giorgio Treves, *Le Mal d'aimer,* a sinister historical drama about sufferers from the newly discovered disease syphilis.

*West Germany.* A generally lacklustre year was relieved by two bright debuts. With a generous and mature sense of the human tragicomedy, Jan Schütte's *Drachenfutter* told a slight story of two immigrants, Chinese and Pakistani, who dreamed of opening a restaurant. Verena Rudolph's feature debut, *Francesca,* was a concocted documentary about a fictitious personality—actress, adventuress, mystic—that brought into question the whole process of mythmaking.

*Spain.* Spanish production flourished, with one of the most noteworthy productions a debut film, Manolo Matji's *La guerra de los locos.* Matji himself scripted the story, set in the Civil War, about a group of escaped lunatics who become involved with Republican guerrillas. The colourful maverick Pedro Almodóvar moved from cult status to box-office success with *The Law of Desire,* a bizarre tale of homosexual passion and transsexualism. On the 50th anniversary of the murder of Federico García Lorca, Mario Camus directed an impressive adaptation of *La casa de Bernarda Alba.*

*Switzerland.* Alain Tanner directed two self-conscious and disappointing films: *Une Flamme dans mon coeur,* the psychodrama of an actress much concerned about her own sexuality, and *La Vallée fantôme,* about a filmmaker looking for an idea and for an actress. The other senior Franco-Swiss director, Claude Goretta, adapted a Charles-Ferdinand Ramuz parabolic novel. The film, *Si le soleil ne revenait pas,* remained remote and unengaging, despite the fine performance of Charles Vanel (95 years old) as the village seer who predicts the death of the Sun.

*Scandinavia.* Biography was a favoured genre. From Sweden, Anders Wahlgren's *Moa* was a tribute to Moa Martinson, a favourite working-class novelist of the 1920s and 1930s. Kjell Grede's *Hip, Hip, Hurra!* was a fantastic interpretation of the life of the late 19th-century painter P. S. Krøyer. From Denmark, Claes Kastholm Hansen's *Peter von Scholten* celebrated an enlightened governor of the Virgin Islands whose support of the emancipation movement resulted in his trial for treason.

Denmark had a major international success with Gabriel Axel's ebullient adaptation of Isak Dinesen's story *Babette's Feast,* about a French female chef in exile who uses all the winnings from a lottery to serve a gargantuan feast to her puritanical Scandinavian employers and neighbours. The Norwegian writer-director Nils Gaup made an effective, polished epic in Lapp language on the 12th-century story of a boy who saves his nomad tribe by leading marauding warriors into an avalanche.

*Turkey.* The outstanding film of the year was Omer Kavur's *Motherland Hotel,* a mesmeric drama of obsession about the mounting madness of a young man who is the entire staff of a shabby hotel, once his family's mansion. A coproduction with West Germany, *Iron Earth, Copper Sky,* directed by the composer Omer Zulfu Livaneli, was a lyrical tale of Anatolian villagers struggling under a repressive landlord.

**Eastern Europe.** *U.S.S.R.* The Soviet cinema underwent a transformation that was as revolutionary as any of the other changes occurring in the country. In May 1985 elections to the Union of Film Makers had replaced the reactionary old guard with new faces, who immediately demanded total reorganization. Their first demand was the release of films that had been banned, sometimes for decades. Not only films but whole careers that had been virtually suppressed were exhumed, including those of Aleksey German and Kira Muratova. *Commissar* (1967), the only film of Aleksandr Askoldov, whose career was ended by official disapproval of it, proved to be a movie of fine technical bravura and humanity. Gennady Poloka's *Intervention* (1968) was a joyous mix of stylization and slapstick, in the vein of the "eccentricism" of the Soviet 1920s.

Soviet audiences were brought face to face with history. Tenghiz Abuladze's *Repentance* (1984) was the first Soviet film to show the workings of the Stalinist terror; it adopted a highly stylized method, mixing absurdist farce with tragedy. For his graduation film Yury Kara directed an adaptation of Boris Vasiliev's *Tomorrow There Was War,* a drama about the paranoia of the 1940s.

Other new films took a fresh, unmoralizing view of young people. From Estonia, Lejda Lajus and Arvo Icho's *Games for Grown-up Children* portrayed life in a children's home. The dropout hero of Karen Shakhnazarov's *Messenger Boy* observes the inequality of society and unashamedly longs for material betterment. Most remarkable of all was a Latvian documentary by Yuris Podnieks, *Is It Easy to Be Young?,* a series of interviews with teenagers who gave their unorthodox views of contemporary Soviet society and their own aspirations.

*Poland.* There was comparable relaxation in other socialist nations. Krzysztof Kieslowski's *Blind Chance* (1982) ingeniously showed three alternative versions of events consequential on a small incident, depending on whether the hero is motivated by party loyalty, subversive involvement, or (most dangerous) easy compromise. Feliks Falk's *Hero of the Year* was an acid satire about a television personality, sacked in 1981 but staging a comeback, who finds himself fatally trapped between truth, compromise, and the shadows of the past. Andrzej Wajda made his first film since the martial law period, *A Chronicle of Love*

*Affairs.* The apparent melancholy nostalgia of this story of young people in 1939 concealed some political barbs; the setting is Lithuanian territory subsequently annexed to the U.S.S.R.

*Hungary.* The outstanding film of the year was *Diary for My Loved One,* the second part of Marta Meszaros's autobiographical diptych, covering the cold war years between 1949 and the Hungarian uprising of 1956. Other films that dealt frankly with history were Peter Gardos's *Whooping Cough,* relating the effects of the 1956 uprising on one ordinary family, and Gyula Maar's *Mills of Hell,* a melodrama about a young student whose romantic and political associations become fatally intertwined. Gyula Gazdag made a finely crafted metaphoric fantasy, *A Hungarian Fairy Tale.* Hungarian law, with the best intentions, assigns fictitious fathers to illegitimate children; Gazdag imagined an orphan unwittingly going in search of his imaginary father. The result is a philosophical essay on identity and bureaucracy.

**Latin America.** Amid Mexico's mass production of melodramas, folk musicals, and comedies, Carlos Enrique Toboada's *Vernerno para las hadas* was a refreshing exception, a disturbing examination of the reverse side of childhood fantasies, with two girls becoming involved in black magic. In Brazil Sergio Toledo made a promising debut with *Vera,* a well-scripted film that sensitively treated the psychological problems of a simple girl tormented by having a male personality in a female body. With Marcos Zurinaga's handsome, accomplished *La gran fiesta,* Puerto Rican cinema made its first successful bid for an international market. The film was a cleverly scripted drama of the country's political schizophrenia in World War II.

Humberto Solas's *Un hombre de éxito* attempted a panorama of Cuban history from 1932 to the revolution through the story of two brothers who always find themselves on politically opposed sides. A Cuban-Soviet coproduction, Manuel Herrera's *Capablanca* related an incident in the life of the 1920s chess champion when he participated in the 1925 Moscow championship.

**Asia.** *India.* The last film of the erratic, talented young Keralan filmmaker John Abraham, who died shortly after completing it, *Report to Mother* was a mesmeric investigation of the malaise of a generation, achieved through a student's quest to discover the reasons for the suicide of a

---

## Hollywood: 100 Years Old

In 1987 Hollywood marked its civic centenary with suitable celebrations and tributes to the memory of its founders, Mr. and Mrs. Horace Henderson Wilcox. The Wilcoxes owned a ranch in the Cahuenga Valley. Wilcox was so impressed by the number of tourists who flocked to admire the prolific local crop of oranges and lemons that he changed the name of his spread to Hollywood and began exploiting the real estate potential of the area. By 1911 Hollywood had grown to become a select and desirable residential settlement, where gasworks, slaughterhouses, drink, and similar indecorous activities were prohibited.

Meanwhile, however, the rest of California was being invaded by the movies. In 1908 a trust was set up to establish a monopoly in motion-picture production and distribution, relying on Edison's patents for the original apparatus. In the fierce patents war that followed, independent producers fled from the East to

avoid the trust's strong-arm men. In California they found good weather, photogenic scenery, cheap labour, lumber, and real estate. Studios began to spring up everywhere.

Hollywood offered charming rural locations and a good hotel. The cowboys and the Keystone Cops moved in, and its days of quiet respectability were over. The first Hollywood studio was Nestor, which took over a roadhouse that had gone out of business because of the local ban on the sale of liquor. The most famous was to be the barn rented in 1913 by Cecil B. deMille, Sam Goldwyn, and Jesse Lasky to make their first big hit, *The Squaw Man.* Within a decade the peaceful old orange groves had been covered over with stages and offices and mansions for the stars, and the once obscure little settlement of Hollywood was established in history and myth as the movie capital of the world. (DAVID ROBINSON)

Yves Montand (left) plays a rich farmer out to swindle away a farm inherited by a tax collector, played by Gérard Depardieu, in the French film *Jean de Florette*. Along with its sequel, *Manon of the Spring*, it was considered by many critics to be one of the best films released in the U.S. in 1987.

GEORGE—SYGMA

young musician. Another outstanding Keralan filmmaker, Aravindan, made *There Was a Village*, which used an anecdote about the introduction of electricity to show the collapse of an entire social fabric.

*Japan.* Several films of 1987 made their mark on international festivals and markets. Kon Ichikawa's *Actress* was a dramatized biography of one of Japan's greatest female stars, Kinuyo Tanaka (1910–77). Ichikawa also completed a decorative historical picture, *Princess from the Moon.* In *A Taxing Woman* Juzo Itami, the comic moralist of Japanese cinema, succeeded in filming a comedy-thriller out of the work of tax-fraud investigators.

Kei Kumai's *The Sea and the Poison* related, with an unsensational sobriety that made it all the more shocking, a wartime atrocity in which the staff of a Japanese hospital performed vivisection on healthy U.S. prisoners of war. Another wartime atrocity was recalled in an exceptional documentary, Kazuo Hara's *Forward God's Army,* recording the peregrinations of a crazy man with a mission to expose the truth about a case of cannibalism.

**Africa.** In *Brightness* Souleymane Cissé of Mali used film techniques and style of high sophistication to convey age-old magic in a story of two sorcerers, father and son, vying for supremacy. (DAVID ROBINSON)

**Nontheatrical Motion Pictures.** In 1987 there were 79 film and video festivals in the United States alone. The Council on International Nontheatrical (film) Events (CINE), on behalf of U.S. producers, submitted 647 films and videos in 82 events in 29 countries abroad.

One such festival of note was the International Industrial Film and Video Congress held in 1987 in Vienna. At this prestigious event France set an unprecedented record, sweeping the Grand Prix, four first-place honours, two seconds, three thirds, and two coveted special prizes.

In the U.S. two documentary subjects captured top honours at the premier nontheatrical American Film Festival. The Emily Award went to a Public Broadcasting System program, *Eyes on the Prize: America's Civil Rights Years 1954–1965: Bridge to Freedom 1965.* Made by Henry Hampton, it involved archival footage coupled to "eloquent interviews with civil rights leaders."

The other film, singled out for the John Grierson Award, was *Contrary Warriors: A Film of the Crow Tribe.* Coproducers Connie Poten and Pamela Roberts built the story, based in southeastern Montana, around the 97-year-old Crow leader Robert Yellowtail. (THOMAS W. HOPE)

*See also* Photography; Television and Radio.
This article updates the *Macropædia* article MOTION PICTURES.

# Museums

There appeared to be no end to the boom in museum building as new museums and additions to existing institutions proliferated, often designed by leading architects. In London in April 1987 both the Theatre Museum and the new Clore Gallery for the Turner Collection at the Tate Gallery opened. Designed by architect James Stirling, the Clore Gallery was opened by Queen Elizabeth II on April 1 and enabled the watercolours, drawings, and sketchbooks of the Turner Bequest—housed "temporarily" at the British Museum since 1928—to be reunited with the oils at the Tate. The new wing was the first step in the expansion of the Tate that would eventually include a modern sculpture museum, a new art museum, and a museum of 20th-century art, as well as a study centre. The cost was approximately £7.8 million, of which the Clore Foundation contributed £6 million.

The Theatre Museum, housed in the old flower market

COURTESY, TATE GALLERY, LONDON

The Clore Gallery, opened by Queen Elizabeth II on April 1, is a new wing of the Tate Gallery in London and the first step in an ambitious program for the Tate's expansion.

An African room in the Menil Collection in Houston, Texas, houses a superb collection of African tribal art, one of three areas, along with surrealism and archaic Mediterranean objects, strongly represented in the museum.

J. CHIAISSON—GAMMA/LIAISON

of Covent Garden, was opened by Princess Margaret on April 23 and housed the largest theatrical collection in the world, including costumes, models, props, memorabilia, puppets, playbills, posters, and books. The basis of the collection was formed by bringing together the Gabrielle Enthoven Collection, given to London's Victoria and Albert (V & A) Museum in 1924; the collection formed by the British Theatre Museum Association and Friends of the Museum of Performing Arts; and the Henry R. Beard Theatre Collection donated to the V & A in 1971.

In Chicago the Terra Museum of American Art unveiled a new 5,580-sq km (60,000-sq ft) space housed in adjacent renovated downtown buildings. The original museum, in suburban Evanston, was to remain open as a branch operation. The museum was intended primarily to display the personal collection of its founder, Daniel J. Terra. Another example of the tendency for important collectors to install their acquisitions in a personal museum was seen in the creation of the Menil Collection in Houston, Texas. This 10,000-item collection, including notable modern works, was opened to the public in a new $25 million building. Three new museums opened in Washington, D.C. The National Museum of Women in the Arts, the first museum to be entirely dedicated to the work of women artists, opened in a $13 million renovated structure. On the Mall, the largest U.S. facility for Asian art was created with the opening of the Arthur M. Sackler Gallery for Asian and Near Eastern Art, a part of the Freer Gallery of Art and thus of the Smithsonian Institution. The entrance to the Sackler museum was on an underground street beneath the Capitol Mall, adjacent to the newly opened National Museum of African Art.

In North Adams, Mass., 28 vacant factory buildings totaling 70,000 sq m (750,000 sq ft) were to be converted into an art museum to house, under long-term loan, one of the world's largest collections of contemporary art, that of Count Giuseppe Panza di Biumo of Milan, Italy. The facility, the Massachusetts Museum of Contemporary Art, would be administered by the nearby Williams College Museum of Art in Williamstown. Count Panza di Biumo was also involved—through the planned loan of 75 large-scale works—in the renovation of the Union Depot in downtown St. Paul, Minn.

Remodelings, extensions, and refurbished displays included, at the V & A, the newly opened Medieval Treasury, a redesigned display of European art and design of the period AD 400–1450, and the new Toshiba gallery devoted to

Japanese art and design. Japanese art was also the subject of major new galleries opened in April at the Metropolitan Museum of Art, New York City, representing the second stage of a campaign begun in 1970 to improve the Met's display of Asian art. The $6.2 million cost was raised entirely from Japanese sources.

Also at the Met, the Lila Acheson Wallace Wing of 20th-century art was opened to the public early in February. The new wing at the southwest corner of the museum had two floors, a mezzanine, and a roof garden and cost approximately $26 million. It was larger than either the Guggenheim Museum or the Whitney Museum of American Art in the same city. Many of the galleries were very large in scale, allowing ideal conditions for the display of late 20th-century paintings.

Following four years of renovation, the Robert Dawson Evans galleries for paintings were reopened at the Museum of Fine Arts in Boston. Structural improvements included the installation of climate-control systems and better lighting. The Art Institute of Chicago opened its European painting galleries, restored to their 1893 Beaux Arts splendour after a three-year renovation. The Memphis (Tenn.) Brooks Museum of Art began a $7.1 million renovation and construction that would more than double its size. On the West Coast, Norton Simon negotiated the transfer of his art collection, valued at $750 million, from the Norton Simon Museum in Pasadena, Calif., to the University of California at Los Angeles. A new museum facility on the campus was planned. At The Hague, Neth., the Mauritshuis reopened in June after being closed five years for extensive renovation. During that time 40 of its paintings had toured the U.S., Canada, and Japan.

In Canada the National Gallery of Art, in Ottawa, closed during the year to prepare for the move to its new facility.

The American Federation of Arts and the Art Museum Association of America merged, under the former's name, to become the largest museum service organization in the U.S., with about 500 museum members. The U.S. museum world worried about a possible decline in donations due to changes in the tax laws. The allowable deduction on the appraised value of artwork given to an institution dropped to 38.5% from 50% and would fall to 28% in 1988. In addition, the difference between the original price and the current value of a work was now subject to a 21% alternate minimum tax. (JOSHUA KIND; SANDRA MILLIKIN)

*See also* Art Exhibitions and Art Sales.
This article updates the *Macropædia* article MUSEUMS.

# Music

**Classical.** Interest in—and spending on—good music increased in 1987, with a sales bonanza led by the compact disc (CD) showing every sign of reawakening a long-dormant interest in live music making. Audio manufacturers, instrument makers, and sheet music publishers all reported solid gains as the year progressed. However, hi-fi and album retailers especially, recalling the steep decline in volume that took place in the late 1970s when consumer spending switched to such nonmusic peripherals as home computers and video games, cautioned that prospects for 1988 appeared less encouraging.

Notable birthdays celebrated during 1987 included those of pianist Wilhelm Kempff (92), cellist-conductor Mstislav Rostropovich (60), and conductor Sir Georg Solti (75). Kempff, doyen among Beethoven specialists, had long since retired to his West German lakeside home but was pleased to give his blessing to what was seen as the beginnings of a major reissue project on CD that would embrace the bulk of his recorded output. By contrast, Rostropovich and Solti still pursued active careers. The former had forged particularly close links with the Paris Orchestra; Solti continued to shoulder a heavy work load, commuting regularly from his London home and the London Philharmonic to Chicago and the Chicago Symphony and to Vienna, where, despite his gradual retirement from the opera house, he continued to appear and record with the city's legendary Philharmonic.

The year also marked the 50th and 10th anniversaries of the deaths of, respectively, French composer Maurice Ravel and soprano Maria Callas. The French monthly *Le Monde de la Musique* published an extended reminiscence by one-time Ravel pupil Manuel Rosenthal, while Angel-EMI announced an ambitious reissue program in which all 40 of Callas's complete opera recordings would be digitally reprocessed and issued on compact disc, along with a quantity of previously unpublished concert materials.

Losses to the world of music included those of violinist Jascha Heifetz; cellist Jacqueline Du Pré; composers Dmitry Kabalevsky, Vincent Persichetti, and Wolfgang Fortner; conductor Eugen Jochum; guitarist Andrés Segovia; and

STEVE J. SHERMAN

Vladimir Feltsman plays at Carnegie Hall five months after being allowed to leave the Soviet Union. His career was blocked for eight years after he applied for an emigration visa.

violist Peter Schidlof (*see* OBITUARIES) and also those of accompanist Gerald Moore; composers Morton Feldman, Federico Mompou, and Phyllis Tate; critics Roger Fiske, John Hammond, Burnett James, and Harold Rosenthal; oboist David Reichenberg; organist and choirmaster George Thalben-Ball; pianists Monique Haas, Louis Kentner, and Erwin Nyiregyházi; recording producer Simon Lawman; recording producer and writer George Marek; sopranos Anni Frind, Maria Ivögun, and Rita Streich; musicologist Hans Gál; and writer Patrick Cairns ("Spike") Hughes.

*Symphonic, Instrumental, and Vocal Music.* Aside from Steven Paulus's novel *Construction Symphony*, premiered at a Los Angeles building site in October and combining live music making with the sounds of such unlikely artifacts as cement mixers, high-power compressors, and the ubiquitous shovel and spade, many of the year's most valuable firsts took place in Europe. Following the success of Olivier Messiaen's *Book of the Blessed Sacrament* for organ, first performed at London's Westminster Cathedral in late 1986, the 79-year-old French master's *Bird Sketches* for piano received its first performance in Paris at the accomplished hands of the composer's wife, Yvonne Loriod. The Henry Wood Promenade Concerts, staged annually at the Royal Albert Hall, London, and a cluster of satellite locations, witnessed numerous premieres, among them that of Robert Saxton's impressive choral work *I Will Awake the Dawn*.

Also of note in London was a summer series of concerts under the generic title "Summerscope," devised by composer Harrison Birtwistle and held at the city's South Bank arts complex. Performance standards, from the likes of Music Projects London and the Hilliard Ensemble, were high. Of particular value was a rare program of live and electronic music that included works by Douglas Fulton (*Red Cup and Rat*), John Lunn (*Echoes*), Richard Taube (*Jub Jub*), and Barry Vercoe (*Synapse*).

Following the death of Sir Peter Pears in 1986, the gradual opening to researchers of the Britten-Pears estate at Aldeburgh, Suffolk, England, continued to bring forth important finds. A prolific composer, Benjamin Britten (who died in 1976) destroyed little, hoarding unused sketches for possible later use. Notable in 1987 was the reappearance of such long-lost snippets as the recitative-song cycle *The Heart of the Matter* and, more crucially, the rediscovery—not at Aldeburgh but in London, among the papers of the late musicologist Erwin Stein—of a setting of the poem "Now Sleeps the Crimson Petal" by Alfred, Lord Tennyson, intended originally for use as part of Britten's *Serenade* for tenor, french horn, and strings of 1942. A premiere at the Queen Elizabeth Hall, London, proved a great success, many observers regarding the "missing" song as being well up to the high standard of the published cycle.

The majority of the world's leading conductors remained with orchestras where they had assumed control of the artistic direction in past seasons. The rapid emergence of Soviet emigré Semyon Bychkov was noted, however, with many Parisians eager to sample the first fruits of his tenure as conductor in chief of the city's Paris Orchestra, which celebrated its 20th anniversary. In London one-time medical doctor Giuseppe Sinopoli continued to forge a strong working relationship with the Philharmonia Orchestra, although public and critics alike continued to divide sharply over certain aspects of his high-tension but, it was felt, often willful music making. With performances of Sir Edward Elgar's intrinsically English symphonic poem *Falstaff* and Second Symphony, Sinopoli was felt to be treading on especially thin ice.

Similar dissension greeted Lorin Maazel's trio of concerts

that opened the 1987–88 season of the London Symphony Orchestra (LSO) at the Barbican Centre. Glitzy readings of Beethoven's *Choral* and Gustav Mahler's *Resurrection* symphonies, coupled with continuing acoustic problems at the LSO's home venue, were not seen as boding well for Maazel's further work with the orchestra. Concern was also expressed about what was viewed as the increasingly moribund nature of much of London's once vibrant musical life. The inclusion of a new or unfamiliar work in a program would, it seemed, lead inevitably to box-office losses.

In the U.S. and on the European continent, matters were considered more healthy. Prior to Paulus's activities, Los Angeles had welcomed Pierre Boulez as guest conductor of the city's symphony orchestra in a quartet of concerts notable for performances of his own *Cummings Is the Poet, Sketch-Message,* and *The Water's Sunlight* and mainstream works by Alban Berg and Igor Stravinsky. A highly successful visit to Japan followed.

Much excitement was generated by the discovery at the Warner Brothers warehouse in downtown Secaucus, N.J., of numerous long-lost manuscript scores by George Gershwin, the 50th anniversary of whose death was marked during 1987. With the help of Gershwin contemporaries and a younger breed of Gershwin scholars and specialists, many vanished gems were rediscovered and programmed in concert halls and recording studios. A number were considered to be of high quality, and titles including the *Damsel in Distress* suite and *Meadow Serenade* seemed destined to enter the canon of Gershwin favourites.

In a year during which pianist Mieczyslaw Horszowski, at 95 years of age, continued to perform concerts extensively and a comparatively youthful Vladimir Horowitz, at 83, roamed as far afield from his New York City apartment as Milan, Italy, to play and record with the La Scala Opera Orchestra, some of the musical world's younger hopefuls also proceeded to carve out positions for themselves. For example, Soviet-born Mariss Jansons toured widely as chief conductor of Norway's fast-improving Oslo Philharmonic Orchestra. Plaudits were widespread, a judgment that was buttressed when Jansons and his orchestra moved from their lively but, in international terms, small recording label and signed a long-term contract with Angel-EMI.

*Opera.* In 1987 the greatest interest for students of voice and stagecraft alike centred on Europe. Controversial producer Harry Kupfer, long established as a lively if unpredictable favourite at The Netherlands Opera, marked the opening of Amsterdam's new "red and white" opera house with characteristically spiky stagings of Handel's unfamiliar *Giustino* and Mussorgsky's epically Dostoyevskyan *Boris Godunov.* These productions had first been seen at the Komische-Oper, Berlin, in 1983 but were revised substantially for Amsterdam. Farther east, at the Wielki Theater in Lodz, Poland, the Lyon Opéra, touring from France, presented what were, remarkably, the first Polish performances of Claude Debussy's landmark *Pélleas and Mélisande,* premiered in Paris as long ago as 1902.

Of particular interest to opera buffs in Western Europe was the creation at Versailles, France, of a Baroque music centre. Although the centre was not intended exclusively for opera, the vast spaces at Versailles, with its castle, fountains, and park and numerous outlying buildings, were ideally suited to productions on the grand scale of operas and ballets by the likes of Jean-Baptiste Lully and Jean-Philippe Rameau, with their elaborate staging and host of complex theatrical effects. In a controversial move Daniel Barenboim was appointed music director at the Bastille Opéra House, Paris, which was to be completed in 1989.

Notable operatic productions during 1987 included stagings in London of Mozart's *The Marriage of Figaro* by the Royal Opera House, Covent Garden, conducted by incoming music director Bernard Haitink, and, imaginatively, of Stephen Sondheim's *Pacific Overtures* by the English National Opera (ENO) at the London Coliseum. Ever in the vanguard of innovative and unexpected productions, ENO also mounted new or updated productions of Georges Bizet's *The Pearl Fishers,* Gilbert and Sullivan's *The Mikado,* and Philip Glass's *Akhnaten.*

Europe's many open-air summer opera festivals provided much enjoyment for vocal aficionados. Particularly memorable were productions at the Aix-en-Provence Festival, France, of Lully's *Psyché* and Christoph Gluck's no less rarely encountered *Iphigénie en Aulide* in performances directed by Lyon Opéra supremo John Eliot Gardiner, while a Ravel double bill *The Child and the Sprites* and *Spanish Time* at Glyndebourne Opera, England, delighted all but the most Francophobic operagoers. Artistic disaster of the year was the staging at Luxor, Egypt, of Verdi's *Aida* on a scale that might have caused even Cecil B. de Mille to balk. Poor acoustics, too much heat, and altogether too much sand did not make for a great operatic event.

*Albums and Recording Technology.* Album collectors with long memories could still recall the industry-destructive "battle of the speeds" that broke out during the early 1950s between the then-standard 78-rpm shellac disc and the new 33⅓-rpm microgroove long-playing (LP) discs. Unhappily, 1987 witnessed first shots in what could prove a new battle, this time between rival digital home music media. Despite numerous attempts at blocking measures, not all of them disinterested, digital audio tape (DAT) was by late 1987 being launched into both the U.S. and European markets. Many industry observers forecast that it was capable within a year of posing a threat—as some saw it—to the continued emergence of the compact disc (CD) as the leading music carrier for the 1990s.

Meanwhile, CD sales soared as both hardware and software prices tumbled. Controversy continued over the proposed introduction of the CBS Copycode system, whereby a spoiler tone would be notched into all future CD, DAT, and LP releases, rendering illegal tape copying impossible. Proponents claimed that Copycode led to no discernible degradation in the original audio signal. Many disagreed, arguing that it produced a small but detectable "pinch" effect on certain tones when heard through high-grade playback systems and was therefore unacceptable.

Outstanding album releases during 1987 included first-ever recordings of Jean-Marie Leclair's opera *Scylla and Glaucus* (RCA-Erato); Albéric Magnard's *Guercoeuer* (Angel-EMI); Messiaen's epic *St. Francis of Assisi* (Cybelia); a 6-CD set of Ferruccio Busoni's piano music (Philips); and a unique 28-CD cycle by Cairo-born Walid Akl of Haydn's complete piano works (Bourg).

(NICHOLAS HARPER)

**Jazz.** In 1987 three of jazz's most venerated elder statesmen celebrated landmark birthdays in a burst of activity. Turning 80, the composer-arranger and multi-instrumentalist Benny Carter toured Europe, Japan, and the U.S. and premiered two extended works, *Central City Sketches* (at an acclaimed New York City concert, leading the American Jazz Orchestra, with which he also recorded) and the *Scottish Suite* (at the Edinburgh Music Festival). Another great composer-arranger, Gil Evans, 75, took his big band to Brazil and Europe and recorded with the rock singer Sting, with whom he also appeared at the Umbria Jazz Festival in Italy and drew a crowd of over 35,000. The 70th birthday of master trumpeter and major influence in bebop Dizzy Gillespie turned into a yearlong celebration highlighted by a European tour with an all-star big band and a tribute concert at Wolf Trap near Washington, D.C., that lasted for six hours and was taped for a PBS television special. Participants included Benny Carter, Stan Getz, Sonny Rollins, Wynton Marsalis, and the trombonist J. J. Johnson, who returned to the performing arena after a 25-year hiatus during which he had pursued a successful career as a composer for films and television. Later in the year, Johnson toured the U.S. with a newly formed quintet, showing that he had lost none of his remarkable instrumental facility.

It was also a banner year for Ornette Coleman, the once controversial pioneer of avant-garde jazz. He was reunited with his 1957 quartet (Don Cherry, trumpet; Charlie Haden, bass; Billy Higgins, drums) for recording and for concert tours of the U.S. and Europe, including an appearance at a symposium in Italy, where musicologists delivered learned papers on his contributions to 20th-century music. In addition, a new Coleman work, *In Honor of NASA and Planetary Soloist,* was premiered in New York City by the Kronos Quartet and oboist Joseph Celli.

Jazz also suffered grievous losses in 1987. The future of big-band jazz was dealt a heavy blow by the deaths of Woody Herman and Buddy Rich (*see* OBITUARIES), among the very few who were still leaders of working bands. Though veteran sidemen (Frank Tiberi for Herman; Steve Marcus for Rich) took over leadership, the uncertain fate of such "ghost bands" was illuminated by the filing for bankruptcy by the Count Basie Band (led by Frank Foster), which nonetheless continued to perform. Guitarist Freddie Green, a mainstay of the Basie band's rhythm section for more than 50 years, also died, as did pioneer arranger and trombonist Eddie Durham, who wrote music for Basie, Jimmie Lunceford, and Glenn Miller; trumpeter Howard McGhee; pianist Dick Wellstood; multi-instrumentalist Victor Feldman; bassist Jaco Pastorius; and Alfred Lion, founder of Blue Note Records, one of the very first labels dedicated to jazz exclusively.

Jazz also lost its greatest talent spotter, record producer John Hammond. His major discoveries during a career that spanned half a century included Billie Holiday, Count Basie, Charlie Christian, Aretha Franklin, Bob Dylan, and Bruce Springsteen, and he was a tireless advocate of recognition and equality for black artists.

A Louis Armstrong Archive was established at Queens College in New York City. Donated by the trumpeter's estate, it contained hundreds of private recordings and tapes, photographs, correspondence, scrapbooks, music scores, and memorabilia. The college was also to operate Armstrong's former home in Corona, Queens, as a memorial to his life and work; it was declared a landmark by New York City.

Jazz continued to benefit from the record industry's success with the compact disc format, chiefly in the area of reissues. Thus Columbia Records released no fewer than 40 discs in its digitally remastered *Jazz Masterpiece* series, for which it claimed impressive sales. These were also issued on conventional analogue LP, but the trend was more and more toward exclusive CD releases, to the chagrin of veteran jazz collectors reluctant to convert to the newer medium.

An unprecedented number of books on jazz were published in 1987, among them autobiographies by guitarist Danny Barker, trumpeters Buck Clayton and Pee Wee Erwin, pianist Sam Price, and saxophonist Arthur Rollini; biographical studies of Sidney Bechet, Duke Ellington, James P. Johnson, Charlie Parker, T-Bone Walker, and singer Alberta Hunter; a collection of essays by pianist Marian McPartland; and a monumental discography of the Verve label.

Jazz festivals continued to thrive in Europe, Japan, and the U.S. Among the biggest of these was the Chicago Jazz Festival, a five-day-long event. Sponsored by the city and free to the public, it was attended by more than 200,000 in its ninth season, presenting performances in every style of jazz, from ragtime to avant-garde. The broad musical spectrum of the festival was exemplified by two notable U.S. debuts: the fine Australian traditional group led by pianist-composer David Dallwitz, founded in 1950, and the West German-based Globe Unity Orchestra, an avant-garde ensemble whose 12 members came from Canada, the U.K., France, East and West Germany, Italy, Japan, and the U.S., underscoring the increasingly international character of jazz. (DAN M. MORGENSTERN)

**Popular.** The popular music scene in 1987 was dominated by one band whose epic brand of guitar rock echoed the power and sheer exhilaration of the best styles of the 1960s. U2, a four-piece band from Dublin, became the most successful rock group in the world, thanks to their fifth studio album, *The Joshua Tree.* Mixing the powerful vocals of singer Bono (Paul Hewson) with the chiming guitar work of The Edge (David Evans), U2 proved that pop music could still be highly emotional, passionate, and even idealistic. The album, a mixture of stirring, religion-tinged anthems with echoes of folk-blues styles, contained

(Left to right) Jo Shabalala, Miriam Makeba, Paul Simon, and Ray Phiri join hands onstage in Harare, Zimbabwe, during a concert tour Simon made with those South African musicians. Simon's *Graceland* album was partly recorded in South Africa.

songs that dealt, often obliquely, with social or political problems, from heroin to Central America.

U2's increase in popularity had been assisted by their appearance in the 1985 Live Aid show, and they had shown their continuing support for the new wave of social concern in pop music by appearing on the 1986 Amnesty International tour of the U.S. By 1987, when U2 simultaneously achieved both the number one album and the number one single (*The Joshua Tree* and "With or Without You") in the U.S., the human-rights organization reported a startling jump in its youth membership.

While U2 dominated white pop, two performers were foremost on the black music scene. Prince produced one of the most unusual, exotic, and inventive collections of songs that the U.S. had heard in years with his double-album *Sign of the Times*, ranging from serious ballads to rap and dance songs, all dressed up with different rhythms and unexpected noises. Rather less exciting, though a massive commercial success, was Michael Jackson's *Bad*, the follow-up to his 1982 best-selling album, *Thriller*. He celebrated its release by embarking on a world tour.

George Michael, previously with the Wham! duo, consolidated his solo success with a new album, *Faith*, and Madonna (*see* BIOGRAPHIES) toured the world with a highly theatrical show, to mixed reviews, but otherwise there was a depressing lack of activity by young artists, allowing a whole series of veterans to make a comeback. In the U.S. those hippie heroes from the 1960s, the Grateful Dead, gained their biggest commercial success to date with *In the Dark*. Their psychedelic-era counterparts in Britain, Pink Floyd, split in two; Roger Waters, former leader of the band, performed yet another concept work, mixed in with a selection of old favourites, to packed stadia in the U.S., while his former colleagues (still calling themselves Pink Floyd) also pulled in the crowds, in tens of thousands, to watch their latest spectacular light show.

Other veterans still proving successful, and releasing good albums during the year, ranged from Van Morrison to the former Beatle George Harrison, whose single "Got My Mind Set on You" was a best-seller. Stevie Wonder, who started his career in the same era, returned to form with his *Characters* album, and even Bruce Springsteen proved that he was part of rock's successful elderly elite. He released a new set of songs, *Tunnel of Love*, that reflected on the pains as well as the pleasures of romance and matrimony. The one veteran to miss out on all the attention was Mick Jagger. His second album recorded away from the Rolling Stones, *Primitive Cool*, met with a decidedly cool response.

Pop music's more serious, political side was reflected during the British general election campaign. A group of musicians including Paul Weller of the Style Council and Billy Bragg had formed a left-wing pressure group, Red Wedge, which set out both to promote the Labour Party and, more ambitiously, to provide a channel through which the ideas of young people could influence party policy. The Wedge team arranged a series of preelection concerts throughout Britain at which bands like the Housemartins, as well as Bragg and the Style Council, appeared under a Red Wedge banner and arranged events at which their audiences could meet prospective Labour candidates.

Bragg was also involved in pop's two main international campaigns of the year, which involved Nicaragua and South Africa. He visited Nicaragua and teamed up with local musical hero Luis Enrique Godoy, a singer who had never experienced the West's confusion as to whether pop should concern itself with political affairs. For the Sandinistas in Nicaragua, popular culture was clearly seen as a

Visitors to Graceland Mansion in Memphis, Tennessee, gaze at Elvis Presley's grave during Elvis International Tribute Week. The special days, filled with dozens of events, marked the tenth anniversary of the death of the "King" on Aug. 16, 1977.

SARA KRULWICH—THE NEW YORK TIMES

revolutionary instrument that should be used to publicize their cause. To this end Godoy appeared alongside Bragg at fund-raising political shows in New York City and in Britain.

Pop's concern with events in Central America coincided with a new musical trend. Mexican-influenced pop and songs in Spanish became popular with English-speaking audiences in the U.S. and Britain. This was largely thanks to the Los Angeles-based band Los Lobos, who appeared in *La Bamba*, a film about the life of Chicano rocker Richie Valens, and scored a massive hit with the title track, a revival of Valens's best-known song.

The musical campaign against the apartheid regime in South Africa was dominated by the continuing controversy surrounding Paul Simon's *Graceland* album, released in 1986. Simon had incurred the wrath of the antiapartheid movement, and such musicians as Bragg and Weller, by recording part of the album in South Africa in contravention of a UN resolution. In 1987 he embarked on a tour, in the company of black South African musicians Miriam Makeba and Hugh Masekela, veteran heroes of the antiapartheid movement. The tour visited Europe, Zimbabwe, and the U.S. and led to furious debates as to whether Simon had damaged the campaign against apartheid or should be forgiven because his album, recorded with the help of South African musicians, helped to increase the worldwide interest in African popular music.

African musicians who benefited from the album included groups from Zimbabwe like the Bhundu Boys, who moved from the small clubs of Harare to join Madonna on her British tour. It was also a good year for South Africans, despite arguments about the cultural boycott. Traditional-style black bands such as Ladysmith Black Mambazo found a new audience outside the country, as did the mixed-race pop band Savuka, led by the political "white zulu" Johnny Clegg. (ROBIN DENSELOW)

*See also* Dance; Motion Pictures; Television and Radio; Theatre.

This article updates the *Macropædia* article THE HISTORY OF WESTERN MUSIC.

# Philately and Numismatics

**Stamps.** The year 1987 was remarkable for the number of important single-country stamp collections offered at auction. Even collections of normally unpopular countries sold well. For instance, the Henry Hibbert collection of Arabia, valued before the sale at £150,000, realized £330,-000, due at least in part to a developing interest in philately in the Middle East. In Europe, other than the U.K., it was trade practice to hold large general auctions at infrequent intervals. Thus Postiljonen of Malmö, Sweden, realized 8.8 million kroner in one sale in March, with Scandinavian stamps and postal history in strong demand. Examples of single-stamp record prices included an 1881 Great Britain 1*d* lilac uniquely used in Bangkok, Siam (Thailand), on cover to England, which sold for £4,900 at Worthing Stamp Auctions, Sussex; an 1865 Italian 20 centesimi inverted surcharge on 15*c* dull blue (one of two known), £23,100 (Harmers of London); and an 1852 Nova Scotia cover to India franked with a pair of the 1*s* cold violet and a 6*d* green, £63,000 (Stanley Gibbons).

The Fédération Internationale de Philatélie (FIP) sponsored the year's major international stamp exhibition, CAPEX 87, held in Toronto in June. The Grand Prix d'Honneur (FIP Championship Class) was awarded to Ryohei Ishikawa (Japan) for a specialized collection of United States 1847–69; the Grand Prix International for the best non-British North America collection to Hassan Shaida (U.K.) for "The Emergence of the World's First Postage Stamps"; and the Grand Prix National for British North America collections to 93-year-old Gerald Wellburn for a specialized collection of British Columbia.

At the British Philatelic Federation (BPF) Congress, held in Eastbourne, Sussex, in September, there were four new signatories to the Roll of Distinguished Philatelists: Ray Chapman (Australia), author of the definitive *History of the Australian Commonwealth Postage;* John O. Griffiths (U.K.), specialist in the stamps of Great Britain and South Australia; Heinz Jaeger (West Germany), president of the Federation of German Philatelists and specialist in the stamps of Baden 1851–71; and Jacques Stibbe (Belgium), president of the Belgian Society of Postal Stationery Collectors for 42 years and president of FIP (1977–80). The BPF Congress Medal was awarded to Roy H. Garland of Beckenham, Kent, for services to British philately.

The activities of the ProPhilForum firm of Bremen, West Germany, were investigated by R. F. Schoolley-West, philatelic curator at the British Library. Peter Winter—later proved to be associated with ProPhilForum—had been provided with top-grade coloured photographs of rarities in the Tapling Collection at the British Library for "private research and study." ProPhilForum admitted using the photographs in the production of "stamps" (quite legally in West Germany, where the reproduction of obsolete, demonetized stamps was permitted) marked "Replika" on the back *in pencil* and subsequently sold. The company and Winter surrendered all unsold stocks of Tapling reproductions, but an unknown quantity remained in circulation.

To protect the standing of past issues of stamps and postal stationery with collectors, the State Congress of San Marino announced the destruction in August of all remaining stocks of 100 past issues of stamps and postal stationery. Following the closing of British *Stamp News,* a new publishing company, Lieuse Publications Ltd., launched *Stamp World* in May. (KENNETH F. CHAPMAN)

**Coins and Paper Money.** Several countries produced gold bullion coins during 1987 in an attempt to capture part of the worldwide market once dominated by South African Krugerrands. The most successful newcomer—the U.S. "American eagle"—outsold all other bullion coins in 1986 and might also rank first in 1987. Eagle sales totaled 1,787,750 troy ounces of gold during the final ten weeks of 1986, the coin's launch period. Precious-metal investors also bought millions of a one-ounce silver eagle that made its debut in November 1986. Although eagle demand moderated during 1987, the U.S. Mint greatly surpassed its initial 12-month sales goals of 2.2 million troy ounces of gold and 4 million troy ounces of silver. Meanwhile, the Royal Canadian Mint attributed a mid-1987 lag in orders for its popular gold maple leaf to competition from a booming stock market and other factors. Two new bullion coins—the Australian nugget and the U.K.'s Britannia—proved popular with some investors.

In mid-1987 the U.S. Mint began selling to collectors gold and silver coins commemorating the U.S. Constitution's 1987 bicentennial. Experts predicted that the special program would generate a multimillion-dollar profit for the U.S. Treasury by the time sales ended in June 1988. South Korea launched a 24-coin program honouring the 1988 Summer Olympics in Seoul, and Canada released the last four in a series of ten silver coins and a gold piece marking the 1988 Winter Olympics in Calgary, Alta. Canada also made plans to phase out $1 bills in 1989, forcing its citizens to use a new dollar coin introduced in late June. The change could greatly reduce the cost of producing money because a dollar coin would last at least 20 years in circulation while a paper dollar wore out in less than 12 months. Canadians dubbed the dollar coin the "loonie" because it depicted a loon, a bird indigenous to Canada.

BRITISH ROYAL MINT

Britain's newly issued gold coin, the Britannia, shows a portrait of Queen Elizabeth II on one side and a personification of ancient Britain on the reverse. The 22-karat gold coins are legal tender in the U.K. and are available in £100, £50, £25, and £10 denominations.

The U.S. Treasury announced in June that technical problems had delayed by as much as two years the printing of Federal Reserve notes featuring two new counterfeiting deterrents. Officials had said that the bills would begin circulating by mid-1987. The additions were expected to make U.S. "greenbacks" more difficult to duplicate on colour copiers. In April the U.S. Commission of Fine Arts—an advisory body appointed by the president—recommended that the government replace designs on the cent through half dollar. Commission members contended that current designs had been in use too long (the Lincoln cent started in 1909 and the Washington quarter in 1932). They also said that fresh images would generate extra revenue for the Treasury and increase interest in coin collecting. Bills pending in Congress in late 1987 called for new designs on the five basic coin types and for introduction of a circulating $1 coin to replace $1 paper notes. Rare-coin prices increased 10.7% in the 12 months ended June 1, according to a Wall Street securities firm, putting coins sixth on a list of 14 investment vehicles. In a midyear California auction, rarities owned by the actor Buddy Ebsen and other collectors fetched about $10 million.          (ROGER BOYE)

This article updates the *Macropædia* article COINS AND COINAGE.

# Photography

Introduction of new autofocus (AF) single-lens-reflex (SLR) 35-mm cameras from Canon, Nikon, Yashica, and Pentax dominated camera design in 1987. Along with existing models from Minolta, Nikon, and Olympus, they established a new generation of automated, highly electronics-dependent cameras that combined sophisticated features with relatively simple operation. Culturally the year was marked by a large number of exhibitions and books, both retrospective and analytical.

**Photo Equipment.** Of particular interest among new autofocus SLRs were Canon's EOS (electro-optical system) 650 and 620 models. Unlike other manufacturers that followed Minolta's lead in locating the AF motor-drive system inside the camera body, Canon placed it inside the lens. Each in a new series of dedicated Canon electrofocus (EF) lenses for the EOS cameras contained two miniature motors (one for autofocusing and one to control lens aperture) of unusual, curved configuration, which permitted the lenses to retain traditional cylindrical shape with little or no added weight or bulk.

Rather than using a CCD (charge-coupled device) for the autofocusing sensor, as did other autofocus SLRs, the EOS cameras employed a Canon-designed hybrid solid-state device called BASIS (base-stored image sensor). The manufacturer claimed that the BASIS system in conjunction with the in-lens motors provided unusually rapid, light-sensitive AF performance with an autofocus illumination threshold of EV 1 at ISO 100 and the ability to focus a 50-mm $f$/1.8 Canon EF lens from infinity to its close-focusing limit of 0.45 m (17.7 in) in $\frac{1}{2}$ second. When the subject was in focus, a green light inside the viewfinder glowed and a beeper sounded. Choices of AF modes included single-shot and continuous, plus manual override. (In single-shot AF mode the camera focused and locked on a centrally located subject but would not allow the shutter to be released until sharp focus was achieved. In continuous mode the AF system continuously tracked a moving subject and allowed an exposure at any time, whether or not the focus was perfect.)

Both EOS models provided a variety of other sophisticated automatic features, while the top-of-the-line 620 also offered an autoexposure program shift, which allowed the user to bias the program in the direction of faster shutter speed or smaller aperture without changing the exposure value. An automatic bracketing exposure mode made three exposures in rapid sequence: one under, one normal, and one over, plus or minus up to five stops, in $\frac{1}{2}$-stop increments. Complementing the EOS models was an assortment of 14 Canon EF lenses, ranging from an EF 15-mm $f$/2.8 fish-eye to an EF 300-mm $f$/2.8L and including the fastest lens available for a 35-mm SLR, an EF 50-mm $f$/1.0L.

Nikon's new autofocus SLR, the N4004 AF, was claimed to provide superior performance in dim light by means of a CCD sensor that included 200 light-gathering elements, about twice the number usually supplied. The elements were arranged diagonally in two rows, the slanting configuration being designed to improve the detection of curves and horizontals. A single-shot AF mode and manual focusing as well as a choice of four autoexposure modes—program, shutter-priority, aperture-priority, and autoflash—plus manual operation were provided. The N4004 AF also included a built-in, pop-up electronic flash unit.

Another new autofocusing SLR camera was the Yashica 230-AF, which provided not only single-shot and continuous AF focusing modes plus manual but also a unique "trap focus" option, which was of particular interest to sports and wildlife photographers. In the trap focus mode the camera tripped its shutter automatically when a sub-

AP/WIDE WORLD

The Kodak Fling is a preloaded, disposable camera developed by Eastman Kodak. When the roll has been completed, both camera and film are sent to the photo finisher. The Fling and a similar camera, the Quick Snap by Fuji, come with a 24-exposure roll of colour print film.

ject—a runner or a flying bird, for example—appeared in a manually prefocused zone.

The Pentax SF1 provided single and continuous autofocusing modes (with a sensitivity threshold of EV 2) plus manual override and included a built-in pop-up thyristor-controlled flash unit. It had a top shutter speed of $^1/_{2000}$ second, programmed automatic exposure modes for "normal," "action," and "depth," shutter and aperture priority modes, manual metering, and autoflash.

Among new compact 35-mm cameras was the dual-lens Ricoh TF-500, which offered an unusually wide spread of focal lengths, from a 35-mm $f/2.8$ to a 70-mm $f/5.6$ lens plus a 1.5× accessory that converted the latter lens to 105 mm. Both Fuji and Kodak introduced novel "disposable" cameras, which the user turned over to a photo finisher after the preloaded film was exposed. Fuji's Quick Snap used Super HR 400 24-exposure 35-mm colour print film and provided a 35-mm $f/11$ lens and a single shutter speed of $^1/_{100}$ second. The Kodak Fling was loaded with a 24-exposure roll of Kodacolor VR-G 200 print film in 110 format and was equipped with a 25-mm $f/8$ lens and a $^1/_{120}$-second shutter.

New all-electronic still cameras using a 47-mm still video floppy disk were shown in prototype and production models. Eastman Kodak announced a major commitment to the new medium with the introduction of an entire system intended primarily for the industrial and professional market, which included a still video camera, recorder-player units, a transceiver, a colour video printer, and a colour monitor. Its camera, shown in prototype form only, used a CCD image sensor that contained 280,000 pixels (picture elements), had a top shutter speed of $^1/_{1000}$ second, and provided four exposure modes—autoexposure program, aperture-priority, shutter-priority, and manual. The Casio VS-101 Electronic Still Camera was designed as a basic model. It used a metal oxide semiconductor (MOS) with 280,000 pixels as an image sensor, had a fixed-focus 11-mm $f/2.8$ lens, and offered programmed automatic exposure covering a range of EV 6 to EV 17. The images it recorded could be played back on a standard TV monitor without the need for a separate playback unit.

Konica introduced SR-V 3200, the fastest colour print film yet available, having twice the speed of the previous two highest, Fuji's Super HR 1600 and Konica's SR 1600. With standard C-41 colour negative processing, it delivered an ISO 3200 speed index with grain and sharpness comparable to that of existing ISO 1600 films. From Agfa came a new ISO 100 colour slide film, Agfachrome CT100, designed for E-6 or equivalent processing, while Fuji made available an ISO 400 black-and-white film, Fuji Neopan 400 Professional. To foster the making of black-and-white prints from colour negatives, Oriental introduced Seagull RP Panchromatic printing paper. Designed for fine-art printers, Gekko Artist paper from Mitsubishi was a fibre-based black-and-white material in grades 1 through 3.

The Japanese photographic industry lost a figure of international importance with the death of Kinji Moriyama, member of the Japanese Diet and founder and president of the Japan Camera and Optical Instruments Inspection and Testing Institute. Moriyama long played an active role in improving the quality of Japanese camera equipment and expanding its export.

**Cultural Trends.** Photographic books and exhibitions included both retrospective-historical efforts and introspective ones that examined photography as a visual medium. *Africa Then: Photographs 1840–1918,* edited by Nicolas Monti, included a variety of images of the dark continent during the colonial era. The photographs, mostly by white Europeans, often revealed as much about the photographers' cultural viewpoint as they did about their African subjects. "Masterpieces of 19th-Century French Photography by Gustave Le Gray and Henri Le Secq," an exhibition at the Metropolitan Museum of Art, New York City, comprised 125 vintage prints by two notable photographers who flourished during the middle years of the century.

The International Center of Photography (ICP) in New York City produced a major retrospective of photographs by master pictorialist Alvin Langdon Coburn, while a less well-known aspect of the work of the late Jacques-Henri Lartigue, his striking experiments with panoramic compositions, was displayed at New York's Museum of Modern Art. *Stopping Time* was a well-reproduced tribute to the photographs of scientist Harold Edgerton (who also received the ICP Life Achievement Award for his pioneering work in electronic flash). Latest in the continuing photographic "a day in the life of" series portrayed the U.S.S.R.

Current trends in photojournalism were explored in "On the Line: The New Color Photojournalism," organized by the Walker Art Center in Minneapolis, Minn. An often amusing look at how photographers sometimes borrow ideas from other photographers was given in "Photographs Beget Photographs" at the Minneapolis Institute of Art. "Photography and Art: Interactions Since 1946" at the Los Angeles County Museum of Art (also a book by Kathleen

From Hollywood Marlene Dietrich speaks to her daughter in Berlin in a 1925 photo by Erich Salomon. Salomon and five other photojournalists were represented in "Photographers of the Weimar Republic," an exhibition of photographs from Germany in the years between the end of World War I and the beginning of the dictatorship of Adolf Hitler. It was held at the Neuberger Museum in Purchase, New York, between February 1 and March 29.
AUTHENTICATED NEWS INTERNATIONAL

Gauss and Andy Grundberg) explored the mutual influences between photography and other visual arts.

The last books of the 12-volume *An Entire Collection of Japanese Photography* were published in Japan during the year. Although flawed in places by confusions in chronology and topical classification, the work nevertheless stood alone in its comprehensive coverage of artistic, documentary, and journalistic photography from the last days of the Tokugawa shogunate to the present. As a result of research conducted for the series, many rare vintage photos were either discovered or rediscovered.

The 1987 Pulitzer Prize for spot news photography was awarded to Kim Komenich of the *San Francisco Examiner* for his coverage of the fall of the Marcos regime in the Philippines, while the Pulitzer for feature photography went to David Peterson of the *Des Moines Register* for his photographic essay "Shattered Dreams," on the crisis facing Iowa farmers. In the 30th annual World Press Photo Contest, the Photo of the Year Award was won by Alon Reininger of Contact Press Images, U.S.A., for his photograph "AIDS in the U.S.A." Free-lancer Jeff Share received the Oskar Barnack Award for his series "Cottonwood Pass—Peace March for Global Nuclear Disarmament."

At the 44th Pictures of the Year competition sponsored by the National Press Photographers Association and the University of Missouri School of Journalism, Bradley Clift of the *Hartford* (Conn.) *Courant* won the Newspaper Photographer of the Year Award, James Nachtwey of *Time* magazine became the second-time recipient of the Magazine Photographer of the Year Award, and Geoffrey Biddle won the Canon Photo Essayist Award for his documentation of New York City's Lower East Side Hispanic community. Mexican photojournalist Graciela Iturbide won the 1987 W. Eugene Smith Grant in Humanistic Photography for her documentation of the unusual matriarchal life-style practiced in Juchitán, Mexico.          (ARTHUR GOLDSMITH)

*See also* Motion Pictures.
This article updates the *Macropædia* article PHOTOGRAPHY.

# Physics

At the end of 1987 there was little disagreement on the most significant development of the year in physics: the discovery of a class of materials that become superconducting at temperatures far higher than previously reported.

Almost overnight a range of new terms entered the scientific vocabulary, including high $T_c$; ceramic superconductors; one-two-three material; and ibco, the shorthand for a compound comprising yttrium (Y), barium (Ba), copper (Cu), and oxygen (O) and having the formula $YBa_2Cu_3O_{7-y}$. "One-two-three" refers to the formula's yttrium, barium, and copper atomic ratios.

Superconductivity, the absence of electrical resistance in a substance, had been strictly a very low-temperature phenomenon since its discovery in 1911. Since 1973 the highest known superconducting critical temperature ($T_c$), the temperature above which superconductivity vanishes and normal resistive conductivity appears, had remained pegged at 23 kelvins (K) for a niobium-germanium alloy. (To convert kelvins to degrees Celsius, subtract 273; thus 23 K = −250° C.) Then, beginning in 1986, the record $T_c$ began to rise—first to 35 K, in itself a major breakthrough, and to more than 90 K by early 1987.

One major surprise was that the new materials are ceramics that can be produced with the most rudimentary technology. The first one found, an oxide of barium, lanthanum (La), and copper, exhibited superconductivity at temperatures below 35 K. It was initially made as a multiphase material—a small fraction of superconducting grains mixed with larger amounts of nonsuperconducting substances. Subsequently the superconducting phase was identified as $Ba_xLa_{2-x}CuO_{4-y}$. For the discovery J. Georg Bednorz and K. Alexander Müller (*see* BIOGRAPHIES) of the IBM Research Laboratory, Zürich, Switz., were awarded the 1987 Nobel Prize for Physics. In March 1987 Paul C. W. Chu of the University of Houston, Texas, and Maw-Kuen Wu of the University of Alabama at Huntsville reported making a ceramic oxide of yttrium, barium, and copper with a $T_c$ of 98 K. Analysis of the superconducting fraction yielded an oxide with the composition $YBa_2Cu_3O_{7-y}$.

Throughout the rest of the year, superconductivity research flourished. At least 800 relevant papers were published in the first six months and a further 30 or so per week thereafter. The reported work included investigations into the physical and microstructural properties of the new materials, the search for yet other ceramic superconductors, growth and study of single crystals of the superconducting phases, fabrication techniques, and fundamental theory. Permeating all was the excitement that fired the imagination with dreams of possible applications. (*See* Sidebar.)

The primary physical properties of a superconducting

material are its critical temperature, critical field ($H_c$), and critical current ($I_c$). $H_c$ and $I_c$ are the maximum magnetic field and maximum electric current that can be supported by the material before superconductivity is lost. These properties are crucial in determining whether the material is of technological importance. A high $T_c$ is of little use if the superconductivity breaks down in the presence of small fields and currents. Measurements indicated that both the $H_c$ and $I_c$ of the new materials were suitable for many applications. In addition to showing no electrical resistance, the ceramics passed an even more stringent test by demonstrating a sharp resistance to magnetization as they were cooled below the critical temperature. This change in magnetic susceptibility is an indication of the Meissner effect, in which a true superconductor expels all magnetic flux from its interior as it cools below its $T_c$.

The quest for materials with even better superconduct-

ing properties concentrated on variations of the Y-Ba-Cu-O compound. For example, it was found that yttrium could be replaced by any of the rare earth elements without destroying the superconductivity or indeed lowering $T_c$. A three-element material comprising only lanthanum, copper, and oxygen also was shown to become superconducting at 40 K. Researchers around the world rushed to publish reports of tantalizing, but inconclusive and unconfirmable evidence for materials having a $T_c$ of 125, 240, or even 300 K (room temperature).

For the physicist searching for fundamental characteristics of the new materials, single crystals were a prime requisite. Small crystals (one to two millimetres across) of $YBa_2Cu_3O_{7-y}$ became readily available. Studies indicated that the material's superconducting properties are anisotropic—strongly dependent on direction in the crystal—a finding not surprising in view of the nature of the

## Why the Fuss over Superconductivity?

A substance that has no electrical resistance is the "stuff of dreams" for engineers and technologists. A wire made of it will transmit electric power without losses. An electromagnet wound from the wire will maintain its magnetic field, once established, with virtually no power draw. A closed ring made of it will store a circulating current without energy loss until needed—the ultimate rechargeable battery. Several hundred of these seemingly magical materials, called superconductors, have been found since 1911, but nearly all of them must be cooled to very low temperatures for the zero-resistance state to be induced. They need expensive and inconvenient liquid-helium refrigeration at 4.2 K, which severely limits their applications. Within the past quarter century these "conventional" superconductors have served primarily as the current-carrying wires in superconducting magnets. Such magnets, which function while immersed in liquid helium, have found use in magnetic separation and extraction pro-

IBM CORP.

A small magnet floats above a ceramic disk that has been chilled in liquid nitrogen. This tabletop demonstration of the Meissner effect came to symbolize the exciting recent breakthroughs in high-temperature superconductivity.

cesses, in prototype high-speed, magnetically levitated trains, in medical imagers, and in the latest generation of high-energy particle accelerators.

The recent discovery of ceramic materials that become superconducting near 100 K is exciting in large part because it offers the freedom to pursue a whole new world of uses that previously had been denied. The relatively high transition temperature means that superconductivity can be maintained with liquid nitrogen, a cheap, plentiful coolant that boils at 77 K, or with closed-cycle refrigeration systems. If the new superconductors can be fully developed, they could make economical a range of applications in electronics, power generation, storage and transmission, and transportation. Furthermore, their discovery suddenly makes the almost mythical goal of room-temperature superconductivity a very real possibility.

Nitrogen-cooled superconductors could find early applications as connections between integrated-circuit chips and boards in computers to increase speed and reduce heat and in smaller, cheaper magnets for medical imaging devices that exploit nuclear magnetic resonance. They could also become integral features of microelectronic devices (*e.g.*, Josephson junctions and ultrasensitive magnetic-field detectors known as SQUIDs) that rely on superconductivity effects. Other possible uses include low-loss underground power cables and data-transmission lines, more compact and efficient generators, and improved "magnetic bottles" for future nuclear fusion reactors.

Although the new superconductors do give much cause to celebrate, physicists and engineers do not expect an easy road from the laboratory to the everyday world. Many basic questions about structure, chemistry, and electrical behaviour need to be answered, and many manufacturing and fabrication problems remain to be solved. In response to these challenges, several nations, notably Japan and the U.S., have called for superconductivity initiatives among business, government, and scientific leaders to promote research and speed commercial development. While work during the year proved that believing in the stuff of dreams was justified, the obligation has now fallen to the future to make the dreams real.

(S. B. PALMER)

structure (a so-called layered perovskite), which has Cu-O-Cu planes lying perpendicular to rows of Ba-Y-Ba.

Fabrication efforts were aimed at producing bulk ceramics, thin films, tape, wires, and single crystals. Virtually every conceivable technique was being employed, from the simple mixing bowls and ovens of high school laboratories to expensive and sophisticated molecular beam epitaxy equipment used in semiconductor research.

Underpinning it all was the need for theoretical understanding. Superconductivity at temperatures as high as 40 K had been satisfactorily explained by the BCS (Bardeen-Cooper-Schrieffer) theory, wherein electrons bind into freely moving pairs by means of an attractive force created by the interaction between the electrons and the vibrations of the material's crystal lattice. To explain superconductivity in the new ceramics, theorists still invoked electron pairs but had yet to clarify the source of the force holding the pairs together. (S. B. PALMER)

This article updates the *Macropædia* articles MATTER: *Low-Temperature Phenomena;* The PHYSICAL SCIENCES: *Physics.*

# Populations and Population Movements

## DEMOGRAPHY

July 11, 1987, was designated the Day of Five Billion by the United Nations Fund for Population Activities to mark the probable passing of this milestone in world population growth—sometime between April and July, according to UN estimates. Annual numbers added about 1987 totaled 87 million, according to Population Reference Bureau estimates, and the world growth rate was 1.73%; both figures were higher than in 1986 because of an increase in the birthrate of China, with 21% of the total world population in 1987. The latest UN medium (most probable) estimates projected that world population would reach six billion in 1999, seven billion in 2010, eight billion in 2022, and stabilize at around ten billion late in the 21st century. Well over 90% of future growth would take place in the less developed countries of Africa, Asia (minus Japan), and Latin America, which accounted for about 73% of world population in 1987. Annual natural increase (births minus deaths) averaged 2.1% in these countries, compared with 0.5% in the more developed countries.

U.S. Census Bureau estimates put the total U.S. population (including armed forces overseas) at 243,773,000 on July 1, 1987, an increase of 2,177,000 over a year earlier. About 1.6 million of this was due to natural increase and the remainder to net immigration (legal plus illegal immigration minus emigration). Census Bureau estimates indicated that black persons made up 12.2% of the U.S. population in 1987 and Hispanics, 7.9%.

**Birth Statistics.** According to provisional data from the National Center for Health Statistics, births in the U.S. in 1986 totaled 3,731,000, 1% fewer than the 3,760,561 births registered in 1985. The birthrate was 15.5 births per 1,000 population, 2% lower than the rate of 15.8 for 1985, and the fertility rate was 64.9 births per 1,000 women aged 15–44, 2% lower than the 1985 figure of 66.2. A slight decline in number of births was still evident in the early part of 1987. For the 12-month period ended in May, there were 10,000 fewer births than during the same period a year earlier. However, for this period the birthrate was still 15.5 and the fertility rate, at 65, was marginally higher than the rate for calendar year 1986. The decline in number of births resulted both from a drop or leveling off in the

number of women aged 15–29, the ages at which more than three-quarters of childbearing typically occurs in the U.S., and continuing fairly steady declines in the birthrates for women of these ages.

Detailed data showed that the total fertility rate, which indicates the average number of lifetime births per woman if current fertility rates were to continue, was 1.8 for U.S. women as a whole in 1985 and 2.2 for black women, unchanged from 1984. The rate for white women had edged up from 1.7 to 1.8. The fact that the total fertility rate had hovered since the mid-1970s at about 1.8, 14% below the "replacement" level of 2.1 births per woman, aroused some concern about a "birth dearth." Although births still outstripped deaths in the U.S. because of the extra-large number of women currently in the childbearing ages (those born during the baby boom of 1946 to 1964), continuation of below-replacement fertility would lead to population decline early in the 21st century, in the absence of immigration. In 1985 there were 828,174 births to unmarried women, 8% more than in 1984. New highs were recorded for the proportion of all births occurring to unmarried women, 22%, and the birthrate per 1,000 unmarried women, 33. The proportion of nonmarital births was still much higher for black women (60%) than for white women (15%). However, this racial difference had narrowed in recent years, and nearly all of the 12% increase in the overall birthrate for unmarried women between 1980 and 1985 was attributable to white women. In these five years, the birthrate for married women fell by 3%.

Estimates reported by the Population Reference Bureau put the world birthrate about 1987 at 28 per 1,000 population, one point higher than a year earlier. The reversal of the previously declining trend resulted from a rise in China's birthrate from 18 in 1985 to 21 in 1986. This was attributed to an easing of China's stringent "one-couple, one-child" policy, together with the arrival in the childbearing ages of the generation born during China's post-Great Leap Forward baby boom of the 1960s. Chinese officials observed that if the current growth rate continued, the official target of 1.2 billion population in 2000 would be exceeded by 100 million. The average birthrate for less developed countries as a whole, including China, also rose one point to 32, while the average for more developed countries was unchanged at 15. Regional rates ranged from 44 in Africa (down one point from the previous annual estimate) to 13 in Europe (unchanged from the last estimate). The latest reported estimates of total fertility rates showed a rise in China's rate from replacement level to 2.4 births per woman and a continuing average of 4.2 for less developed countries. However, apart from China and most of sub-Saharan Africa, this rate continued to fall in many less developed countries. Indonesia, for example, reported that its rate had dropped 23% in just five years, from 4.3 in 1980 to 3.3 in 1985. The average total fertility rate for more developed countries, though still below replacement level, rose slightly from 1.9 to 2.

**Death Statistics.** The provisional count of deaths in the U.S. in 1986 reached a record annual high of 2,099,000. This primarily reflected the continuing rise in the proportion of the total population aged 65 and over. Although the "crude" death rate, at 8.7 deaths per 1,000 population, remained about the same as that of 1985, the provisional age-adjusted death rate of 1986, 540 deaths per 100,000 population, was the lowest on record. Between 1985 and 1986, age-adjusted death rates fell for four leading causes of death—heart disease, cerebrovascular diseases (stroke), diabetes, and atherosclerosis—and rose for the three leading violent causes—accidents and adverse effects, suicide, and homicide and legal intervention. The 15 leading causes of death, accounting for 87.3% of all deaths in 1986, were:

| | Causes of death | Estimated rate per 100,000 population |
|---|---|---|
| 1. | Diseases of the heart | 318.7 |
| 2. | Malignant neoplasms | 193.3 |
| 3. | Cerebrovascular diseases | 61.3 |
| 4. | Accidents and adverse effects | 39.7 |
| 5. | Chronic obstructive pulmonary diseases | 31.3 |
| 6. | Pneumonia and influenza | 29.2 |
| 7. | Diabetes mellitus | 15.1 |
| 8. | Suicide | 13.1 |
| 9. | Chronic liver disease and cirrhosis | 10.9 |
| 10. | Atherosclerosis | 9.2 |
| 11. | Nephritis, nephrotic syndrome, and nephrosis | 9.0 |
| 12. | Homicide and legal intervention | 8.9 |
| 13. | Septicemia | 7.7 |
| 14. | Conditions of the perinatal period | 7.5 |
| 15. | Congenital anomalies | 5.1 |

The average death rate for the world as a whole was 10 per 1,000 population, down one point from the level estimated for the previous several years. Regionally, sub-Saharan Africa's death rates were still highest at 17–18, on average, but since birthrates there were also highest, natural increase still exceeded that of other regions. The latest estimated natural increase rate of Kenya, in eastern Africa, still topped that of all other nations at 3.9%, resulting from a birthrate of 52 and a death rate of 13. At that rate a population doubles in 18 years. At the other extreme, natural increase was negative (fewer births than deaths) in Denmark, Hungary, and West Germany and zero in Austria, Belgium, East Germany, and Luxembourg.

**Infant Mortality.** The provisional infant mortality rate for the U.S. in 1986 was the lowest ever recorded: 10.4 deaths of infants under one year per 1,000 live births. However, the latest international ranking of infant mortality rates, comparing rates reported for 1985, listed the U.S. rate of that year, 10.6, in 18th place. Japan's rate was lowest in 1985 at 5.5, followed by Finland at 6.3. For less developed countries, the latest estimated average was 90, two points below the previous annual estimate.

**Life Expectancy.** Life expectancy at birth for the total U.S. population reached a new high of 74.9 years in 1986. Provisional data showed new records for white females, 78.9 years, and for white males, 72. Both were 0.2 years higher than in 1985, as was the 1986 life expectancy for black males, 65.5. The figure for black females, 73.6, was down by 0.1 years.

### World's 25 Most Populous Urban Areas[1]

| Rank | City and Country | City proper Population | Year | Metropolitan area Population | Year |
|---|---|---|---|---|---|
| 1 | Tokyo, Japan | 8,370,561 | 1987 est. | 27,824,000 | 1985 est. |
| 2 | New York City, U.S. | 7,262,700 | 1986 est. | 17,967,800 | 1986 est. |
| 3 | Mexico City, Mexico | 9,931,413 | 1985 est. | 17,321,800 | 1985 est. |
| 4 | Osaka, Japan | 2,648,166 | 1987 est. | 15,891,000 | 1985 est. |
| 5 | São Paulo, Brazil | 7,032,547 | 1980 cen. | 15,233,492 | 1985 est. |
| 6 | Los Angeles, U.S. | 3,259,300 | 1986 est. | 13,074,800 | 1986 est. |
| 7 | London, England | 6,775,200 | 1986 est. | 12,290,500 | 1986 est. |
| 8 | Shanghai, China | 6,725,700 | 1985 est. | 12,050,000 | 1985 est. |
| 9 | Buenos Aires, Arg. | 2,924,000 | 1986 est. | 10,750,000 | 1985 est. |
| 10 | Calcutta, India | 3,305,006 | 1981 cen. | 10,462,000 | 1985 est. |
| 11 | Rio de Janeiro, Brazil | 5,090,700 | 1980 cen. | 10,190,384 | 1985 est. |
| 12 | Paris, France | 2,140,000 | 1985 est. | 10,173,400 | 1985 est. |
| 13 | Bombay, India | 8,243,405 | 1981 cen. | 10,137,000 | 1985 est. |
| 14 | Seoul, South Korea | [2] | [2] | 9,645,932 | 1985 cen. |
| 15 | Beijing, China | 4,983,000 | 1985 est. | 9,470,000 | 1985 est. |
| 16 | Cairo, Egypt | 6,205,000 | 1985 est. | 9,300,000 | 1985 est. |
| 17 | Rhine-Ruhr, W.Ger. | [3] | [3] | 8,930,000 | 1984 est. |
| 18 | Moscow, U.S.S.R. | 8,527,000 | 1986 est. | 8,714,000 | 1986 est. |
| 19 | Nagoya, Japan | 2,140,648 | 1987 est. | 8,139,000 | 1985 est. |
| 20 | Chicago, U.S. | 3,009,530 | 1986 est. | 8,116,100 | 1986 est. |
| 21 | Tianjin, China | 4,123,800 | 1985 est. | 7,990,000 | 1985 est. |
| 22 | Jakarta, Indonesia | [2] | [2] | 7,829,299 | 1985 est. |
| 23 | Delhi, India | 4,884,234 | 1981 cen. | 6,993,000 | 1985 est. |
| 24 | Manila, Philippines | 1,725,500 | 1983 est. | 6,914,581 | 1985 est. |
| 25 | Tehran, Iran | [2] | [2] | 6,093,900 | 1984 est. |

[1]Ranked by population of metropolitan area.
[2]Administrative unit within which a separate city proper is not distinguished.
[3]An industrial conurbation within which no single central city is defined.

The latest worldwide estimates of life expectancy indicated rises of one year to 63 for the world as a whole and to 59 for less developed countries, on average, with no change in the average of 73 years for more developed countries. The highest national life expectancy for males and females combined was still 77 years, again reported for Japan, Iceland, and Sweden.

**Marriage and Divorce Statistics.** In 1986 the number of marriages in the U.S., 2.4 million, and the marriage rate per 1,000 population, 10, were both down for the second consecutive year. The rate was the lowest since 1977. From the mid-1970s to 1984, the number of marriages had kept pace with population growth. In 1985 and 1986, however, the number of marriages lagged behind population growth, and the marriage rate per 1,000 population consequently fell.

Between 1985 and 1986, the number of divorces in the U.S. dropped 2% to 1,159,000, and the divorce rate declined 4% to 4.8 per 1,000 population, the lowest since 1975. The decline in the divorce rate followed a two-decade rise to a high of 5.3 in 1979 and 1981, a drop to 5 in 1982, and a leveling off at about that rate through 1985.

**Censuses and Surveys.** In 1987 West Germany conducted its first census since 1970, after a four-year delay caused by citizens' concerns about privacy. Similar resistance in The Netherlands continued to make the future of the regular ten-year census uncertain. The last Dutch census was held in 1971. In the U.S. the Census Bureau was being urged to include adjustments to avoid undercounts in the country's 200th-anniversary decennial census of 1990. The undercount of the 1980 census was estimated at only 1% overall but higher among minorities, especially in large cities. New York and other large cities contended that this had cost them their fair share of funds for federal programs keyed to population numbers.

Westinghouse's Institute for Resource Development issued preliminary reports for several of the 35 surveys to be conducted from 1985 to 1990 in 30 less developed countries under the Demographic and Health Surveys program. Total fertility rates in the two to five years before the surveys were 6.6 births per woman in Liberia, 6.5 in Senegal, and 2.8 in Sri Lanka and ranged in six Latin-American countries from 3.1 in Brazil to 4.4 in El Salvador. The proportion of married women of childbearing age using contraception was 6% in Liberia, 12% in Senegal, and 62% in Sri Lanka and ranged in Latin America from 65% in Brazil to 44% in Ecuador.   (JEAN VAN DER TAK)

*See also* World Data.

## INTERNATIONAL MIGRATION

Economic pressure, particularly in third world countries, continued to be an important factor stimulating the movement of people in 1987, but unemployment in the industrialized countries remained at high levels, and governments were more inclined to close doors than to open them. Industrialized countries' labour requirements also continued to change as people were replaced by machinery. The service sectors expanded to provide job opportunities, but not of the kind usually sought by migrant labour. The need to escape threats to life and freedom was emerging as perhaps the greatest stimulus to emigration. Events in 1987 prompted large movements from Sri Lanka and from Fiji, where Indians were trying to return to India. The enormous flow of illegal immigration persisted. In industrialized countries such immigrants fell outside national labour legislation and could easily be exploited.

The drop in demand for labour in the Arab countries following the fall in oil prices continued. The number of immigrant workers in those countries had been estimated at up to seven million in 1985, about half a million of whom were from Europe (mainly Turkey, Italy, and Yugoslavia). The financial effect on Sri Lanka and India, in particular, was severe.

In the Mediterranean region, southern Europe remained the main generator of migrants (particularly Spain, Greece, Portugal, Turkey, and Yugoslavia), but it was also becoming an important host to immigrants. Some 2 million new immigrants were estimated to have entered the area, as well as another 1.3 million illegal workers and refugees. This was partly a response to the restrictive measures being taken in northern Europe and partly because the use of immigrant labour was making the southern European countries more competitive within the European Communities.

The restrictive measures taken in northwestern Europe failed to stop immigration from the South to the North, but they increased the movement of nonactive population elements as the effort to unite families was stepped up. Portugal remained a large potential generator of immigrants with four million of its ten million population living abroad, mainly in Europe. Turkey was also a large potential generator. By contrast, fewer Italians were migrating.

An issue that could have a significant effect on legal immigration was the growing awareness of AIDS (acquired immune deficiency syndrome). Many countries implemented, or proposed to implement, screening of would-be immigrants. (JANET H. CLARK)

In the U.S. immigration issues centred around implementation of the Immigration Reform and Control Act of 1986 and the status of political refugees from Central America. Beginning in May, illegal immigrants who could prove continuous residence in the U.S. since Jan. 1, 1982, could register at offices of the Immigration and Naturalization Service to obtain a temporary resident's permit for a probationary period of 18 months. Then they could apply for permanent residence and after five years for U.S. citizenship. It was estimated that 3.9 million were eligible for amnesty. As of June 1, all employers were required to obtain proof of status from prospective employees.

The U.S. Supreme Court in March ruled that aliens did not have to prove a "clear probability" that they would be killed or tortured for their beliefs if sent home but that asylum should be granted if persecution was "a reasonable possibility." The U.S. government in July announced that 150,000–200,000 Nicaraguan refugees were to be allowed to stay in the U.S. because they had a "well-founded fear of persecution from a Marxist regime." Similar status was not given to the estimated 600,000 Salvadorans not covered by the amnesty, despite their fears about safety as well as the Salvadoran government's claims that it could not survive without the $350 million–$600 million in remittances received from the refugees annually.

The decision by the South African government not to recruit any more Mozambicans and to repatriate some of those already in the country caused concern. Mozambique was heavily dependent on the earnings of the 600,000 employed in South Africa legally and at least a quarter as many illegally. The outward flow of professional labour from South Africa continued; 3,500 left in 1986, mainly bound for Australia. In Australia 120,000 new settlers were to be accepted in 1987–88—an increase of 5,000 over 1986–87. There was a shift from indirect recruitment of skilled migrant workers to a more direct approach and a continued significant increase in the Business Migration Program designed to attract business people from Asia.

Legislation was introduced in the Canadian Parliament to allow immediate deportation of persons considered to be "security risks" and to subject persons convicted of smuggling immigrants to a maximum fine of Can$500,000 and ten years' imprisonment. The government cited an incident on July 12, when 174 people, nearly all Sikhs, arrived in lifeboats from a freighter and claimed refugee status, as proof of the need for legislation.

(LOUIS KUSHNICK)

## REFUGEES

During 1987 some 600,000 people found asylum abroad, while another 200,000 returned to their homelands. The world refugee population by the end of the year reached 12 million. The southern and northeastern parts of Africa witnessed the greatest refugee movements. Conflict and insecurity, exacerbated by sporadic drought, caused a major exodus of refugees from Mozambique, affecting all the neighbouring countries. Toward the end of the year, the number of displaced Mozambicans in Malawi had risen to over 350,000. In addition, an estimated 30,000 settled in Swaziland, 72,000 in Tanzania, 28,000 in Zambia, and up to 150,000 in Zimbabwe. Thousands of Mozambicans also crossed the border into South Africa. In Malawi the

AFP PHOTO

Immigrants form a long, winding line outside an Immigration and Naturalization Service office in response to a new amnesty law that promised U.S. citizenship to certain aliens living in the country illegally.

hospitality of the local population and the response of the authorities in the early stages of the influx had averted an emergency, but by March 1987 the UN High Commissioner for Refugees (UNHCR) had to launch a $2.3 million appeal to provide immediate relief. In Swaziland and Zimbabwe, refugee camps became seriously overcrowded. For reasons of security, both Tanzania and Zambia decided to encourage spontaneously settled refugees to move away from the frontier.

The official voluntary repatriation program from Zaire to Uganda ended after 50,000 had returned home. Over 150,000 Ugandans also returned from The Sudan during 1986–87. In the first half of 1987 more than 15,000 Chadian refugees repatriated from The Sudan, and 17,000 and 9,000 returned from the Central African Republic and Cameroon, respectively. Voluntary repatriation movements continued in the Horn of Africa, with a total of 17,000 returnees benefiting from UNHCR assistance. Nevertheless, refugees in the Horn outnumbered returnees.

In Southeast Asia 130,000 Vietnamese, Kampuchean, and Laotian refugees remained in camps. The arrivals of Vietnamese boat refugees increased, with a large proportion taking the relatively short and safe route to the east coast of Thailand. Laotian asylum seekers still arrived in Thailand at the rate of 300–400 a month, bringing the year-end population to some 75,000. Another 2,100 persons who failed to qualify for refugee status were awaiting permission to return home. About 250 Laotian refugees returned to Laos in 1987 under the voluntary repatriation program. The fate of the 21,000 Kampucheans under UNHCR's care in Thailand was still uncertain; many of them had been repeatedly rejected for resettlement in third countries.

Afghan refugees, estimated at 2.9 million in Pakistan and 2.2 million in Iran, continued to constitute the world's largest single refugee population. In Pakistan successful income-generating projects and self-help activities aimed at refugee self-reliance. Because neither the government nor the refugees wanted permanent settlement in Pakistan, basic relief and maintenance remained the principal component of the assistance program. During 1987 intensified air attacks on the border areas claimed hundreds of lives and forced entire populations to move to safer zones. In Iran UNHCR emergency assistance was provided to 10,000 newly arrived Iraqi refugees. In August a memorandum of understanding was signed between the government of Sri Lanka and UNHCR under which UNHCR would provide emergency assistance to Sri Lankan Tamils who had returned home from India.

Prospects for refugees in Central America improved during the year. With the exception of the Nicaraguan Ladino population, which nearly doubled in Honduras and grew to a lesser degree in Costa Rica, the number of refugees who voluntarily repatriated exceeded new arrivals. Nearly 9,000 Guatemalan, Nicaraguan, and Salvadoran refugees returned home with UNHCR assistance during the first ten months of 1987. Intensified efforts for peace encouraged voluntary repatriation movements, most notably the peace accord signed by the presidents of five Central American nations in August. (*See* WORLD AFFAIRS [Latin America and the Caribbean]: *Latin-American Affairs.*)

In Europe the arrival of large numbers submitting claims for refugee status continued in 1987, albeit at a lower level than in previous years. The concerns of European governments about the nature of these "irregular" flows led to the introduction of unilateral measures designed to prevent or deter the arrival of asylum seekers and to facilitate the removal of those deemed unqualified for refugee

status. At the same time, it became increasingly apparent that unilateral measures did not necessarily prevent the arrival of asylum seekers but simply shifted the burden to countries with a more liberal approach. There was, therefore, a greater willingness to discuss refugee issues within the framework of multilateral consultations.     (UNHCR)

This article updates the *Macropædia* article POPULATION.

# Publishing

In 1987 the world of publishing was marked by feverish activity as the pace of mergers and acquisitions gathered momentum. In the U.K. and the U.S. the Atlantic Ocean proved to be no barrier. In Australia changes in media ownership rules caused a massive upheaval; large sums of money changed hands, and Rupert Murdoch reigned supreme with an estimated two-thirds of the country's newspaper circulation to add to his other interests around the world. The objective of the Australian deregulation was to increase diversity; the result was increased consolidation.

It was also a busy year on the copyright front. In July South Korea passed a domestic copyright law that met international standards, and it acceded to the Universal Copyright Convention (UCC) in September. Indonesia gave notice of an intention to pass laws that would meet international standards in 1988, and Malaysia, Pakistan, the U.S.S.R., and the U.K. were all deeply involved in the redrafting of new copyright laws.

**Newspapers.** In the U.K. in 1987 three newspapers were born and died, another infant flourished, and a fifth, 17 months old, passed to its second set of adoptive parents. Others, meanwhile, were locked in a long legal battle with the U.K. government, which fought on three continents to block the memoirs of a former spy and prevent press coverage.

The rise and fall of titles marked the evolution of the British newspaper industry in 1987. *Today,* launched by the entrepreneur publisher Eddie Shah in 1986 as a challenge to the national publishers and the print unions, was bought within months by the *Observer*'s proprietor, the Lonrho group. A year later, in July 1987, it was sold to Rupert Murdoch's News International Ltd. Hailed a year earlier as the standard-bearer of a new low-cost diversity, *Today* became the fifth national title in the Murdoch stable. The deal provoked protests but proceeded without coming under scrutiny by the Monopolies Commission on the grounds that the paper would otherwise have been closed. Opponents, observing the rival bidders, disputed this. Although *Today*'s sales were little over the 300,000 mark, the purchase gave Murdoch's News International 34% of sales by national newspapers.

The other new 1986 national title, the *Independent,* launched in October, had within a year created a niche among the quality newspapers. Its sales climbed steadily to about 370,000, within 100,000 of both *The Times* and the *Guardian.* The evidence suggested that it had gained a substantial number of new newspaper buyers and taken readership from the middle-market *Daily Mail* and *Daily Express* as well as from its direct upscale rivals. The prospects were for renewed competition in 1988, when price strategies were expected to become more important.

The power of market forces could be seen in the life cycles of three other titles. The *News on Sunday,* launched in April with the idea of creating a popular left-wing weekly, with trade unions among its backers, was torn by internal disagreements from its inception and never achieved its editorial aims or its sales targets. It collapsed in November after suffering losses of £10 million. Robert Maxwell, head of the Mirror Group Newspapers Ltd., in February launched the *London Daily News,* an ambitious attempt at a U.S.-style "24-hour" paper for the region around London. It won professional admiration but was closed after five months, during which it lost an estimated £25 million to £50 million. Maxwell blamed poor distribution and printing problems for the failure. The Associated Newspapers Group Ltd., owners of the established *London Evening Standard,* resuscitated the title of the *Evening News* in a bid to confuse Maxwell's launch and sold it as a low-price downmarket relative of the *Evening Standard.* For a time it seemed as if it would become established, but it only briefly outlived the new rival.

Throughout the year Britain and the world witnessed the efforts of the U.K. government to enforce its code of confidentiality on its secret-service agents and stop publication of Peter Wright's memoirs, *Spycatcher.* (See *Books,* below.) Three British newspapers successfully contested legal injunctions that prevented them from reporting the book's allegations; temporary bans remained in force until the government's appeal, scheduled for early 1988, was heard.

Governments and journalists throughout the world continued to protest against each other's behaviour. In Nigeria *Newswatch* was banned in April for leaking an official report. The West German Supreme Court ruled that journalists must yield notes and film to the police if requested. In the U.S.S.R., alongside more evidence of *glasnost* (openness) in the press, two editors of a magazine called *Glasnost* were arrested. However, while—to choose random examples among many—India's antigovernment *Express* was closed for a period, after official allegations of property irregularities, in Nicaragua *La Prensa* was permitted to reopen on October 1.

The Paris-based *International Herald Tribune,* once the *Paris Herald,* celebrated its centenary and its survival into an era when satellite transmission put it into the new elite of global newspapers. In Australia Rupert Murdoch took over the *Herald* and *Weekly Times* media interests in February, beating off fierce counterbidders. At the year's end, the impact of the worldwide stock market crash, especially on Robert Holmes à Court's Bell Group, foreshadowed further ownership changes.    (PETER FIDDICK)

Though the presidential election was still a year away, U.S. newspapers in 1987 generated considerable controversy by their unprecedented efforts to dig into the backgrounds and personal lives of the leading candidates. Television and magazines were also criticized for those activities, but newspapers led the way. The most prominent example was the *Miami* (Fla.) *Herald* (circulation 433,000), which assigned reporters to an around-the-clock watch of the Washington, D.C., town house of former U.S. senator Gary Hart of Colorado, a leading contender for the Democratic nomination. The newspaper reported that Hart had spent the night in the company of a woman who was not his wife, and the ensuing public furor forced Hart to temporarily drop out of the race. Hart decided to drop out after learning that the *Washington Post* (circulation 748,000) was preparing to run a story about another Hart sexual liaison. When the candidate announced his withdrawal, the *Post's* editors decided not to run a story with details about the affair, describing it merely as a "relationship with a Washington woman."

At about the same time, the *New York Times* (circulation 1,002,000) sent 14 Republican and Democratic presidential contenders an exhaustive questionnaire asking for, among other things, psychiatric records and Federal Bureau

of Investigation files; many candidates quickly complained about the scope of the request. In addition, the *Cleveland Plain Dealer* (circulation 452,000) cited Ohio Gov. Richard Celeste's denials of a "Hart-type personal problem" as justification for running a story about his alleged extramarital affairs; Celeste later said that he would not be a candidate for president. In a disclosure that was less personal but similarly damaging, the *Des Moines* (Iowa) *Register* (circulation 222,000) and the *New York Times* reported that Sen. Joseph Biden (Dem., Del.) had in his speeches used without attribution the words of British Labour Party leader Neil Kinnock; after the story was picked up and elaborated upon by other newspapers, Biden withdrew from the race.

Such disclosures prompted complaints from politicians and public alike that U.S. newspapers were unfairly hounding candidates out of the presidential race over matters that were largely private and had little to do with the contenders' qualifications for office. Editors responded that in an era of slick, media-oriented campaigns that emphasize a candidate's "image" rather than more substantial factors, newspapers had a greater duty to find out what sort of person he or she really was. Nonetheless, a public perception was growing that the press had in some cases abused its power to influence political campaigns and that journalists were not acting responsibly.

That perception may have been at least a minor factor in a decline of total daily circulation, from 62,766,232 to 62,502,036 (0.4%), as reported in the 1987 *Editor & Publisher International Year Book.* The total number of newspapers also dropped, from 1,676 to 1,657. Twelve daily newspapers were merged with others, and 17 discontinued daily publication. Ten new dailies were launched, for a net loss of 19 titles. The long-time trend to morning distribution continued as 20 evening dailies became morning papers, bringing the total number of AM papers to 499. The number of PM newspapers dropped to 1,188. Morning circulation continued to increase, from 36,351,561 to 37,-441,125, a gain of 3%. Evening circulation dropped by 5%, from 26,404,671 to 25,060,911.

Among the newspapers that changed hands during the year, most of the large ones could be traced to a relatively unknown press baron: William Dean Singleton, 36, a Texan whose holdings had previously included mostly small-town dailies. Singleton and his more reclusive partner, Richard Scudder, 73, bought the *Houston* (Texas) *Post* (circulation 316,000) for $150 million. Four days later they acquired the *Denver* (Colo.) *Post* (circulation 227,000) for $95 million. In 1986 the two had made their first major purchase, the *Dallas* (Texas) *Times Herald* (circulation 246,000), for $110 million. All three papers were the second largest in their cities in terms of circulation, and recent experience had shown that it was difficult for a newspaper to be profitable if it faced a larger local competitor. Singleton nonetheless had a reputation for making sick papers financially successful through severe budget cutting. With the Denver acquisition, Singleton and Scudder extended their holdings to 56 newspapers, 29 of them dailies, making their chain the 11th largest in the U.S.

Two newspapers launched with much fanfare in 1982 survived to celebrate their fifth year of publication. The Gannett Co.'s *USA Today* (circulation 1.5 million) marked the occasion with lavish parties in six cities. The paper, a nationally distributed amalgam of short news items, upbeat feature stories, and bits of practical advice, announced that it had begun turning a profit for the first time. The other celebrant was the *Washington* (D.C.) *Times* (circulation 104,000), founded by a group of South Korean investors affiliated with the Rev. Sun Myung Moon's Unification

Church. The paper had lost money consistently, but its owners showed no signs of withdrawing their support.

One source of opinion that disappeared during the year was the newspaper column of James ("Scotty") Reston, who announced his retirement after nearly half a century at the *New York Times*. Reston joined the paper in 1939 as a reporter and since 1953 had written one of the country's most influential political columns.

The big winner in the year's Pulitzer Prize competition was the *Philadelphia Inquirer* (circulation 505,000), which received three awards. Two of them were for feats of investigative reporting: a series by Daniel R. Biddle, H. G. Bissinger, and Fredric N. Tulsky on abuses in the Philadelphia court system; and a reexamination by John Woestendiek of the murder conviction of a local teenager, who as a result of Woestendiek's coverage was given a new trial. The paper was also cited for a feature story by Steve Twomey about life aboard an aircraft carrier. The *New York Times* won two prizes: for its coverage of the aftermath of the *Challenger* space shuttle disaster and for Alex S. Jones's reporting on the breakup of the Bingham family newspaper empire in Louisville, Ky. The *Los Angeles Times* (circulation 1,086,000) also received two awards: for book reviews by Richard Eder and for reporting from South Africa by Michael Parks. *Washington Post* columnist Charles Krauthammer won the prize for commentary, and Berke Breathed, creator of the syndicated comic strip "Bloom County," was cited for editorial cartooning. The Pulitzer gold medal for public service went to the *Pittsburgh (Pa.) Press* (circulation 233,000) for a series by Andrew

One of "The Thousand Faces of Pinochet" is flaunted on the cover of *Apsi*. The magazine was confiscated by the Chilean government before it could appear on newsstands.

Schneider and Matthew Brelis on inadequate screening of airline pilots for drug use and other medical problems.

(DONALD MORRISON)

**Magazines.** The British magazine market remained buoyant, with overall figures boosted by the confirmed success of *Prima,* a women's monthly launched in late 1986 by the West German-based publishing house of Gruner and Jahr. G&J then launched a companion publication, *Best*. Its busy "continental" formula, based on the publishers' French title *Femme Actuelle,* again seemed to find favour with British buyers. Several new glossy magazines were aimed at the financial sector. In October SPL Associates launched *Finance;* Euromoney Publications had earlier launched *Global Investor,* and Robert Maxwell was planning to launch *Global Business* in 1988. The most astonishing indicator of British magazine publishers' own self-confidence was the move into the U.S. market by Reed International, which took over *Variety,* the "showbiz bible" of the U.S.

Two long-established serious weeklies had new editors and one of them, new owners; Stuart Weir was made editor of the left-wing *New Statesman,* while *The Listener,* published since 1929 by the British Broadcasting Corporation as a subsidized extension of its programs, was to be jointly owned with the commercial television network, ITV, and edited by Alan Coren, who gave up editorship of the humorous magazine *Punch*. The editor behind *The Listener's* success for the previous five years, Russell Twisk, left to run the U.K. branch of *Reader's Digest*.

In France the interior minister, Charles Pasqua, created a furor in the press, the public, and among his Cabinet colleagues in March with a move to ban the sale or advertising of several publications that had strong sexual content. In Poland *Res Publica,* a journal that had flowered briefly before the 1981 takeover by the military, became legal again, privately published though still subject to the censorship rules. (PETER FIDDICK)

Changes dominated the U.S. magazine scene in 1987. After 35 years as editor of *The New Yorker,* William Shawn was replaced by Robert Gottlieb (*see* BIOGRAPHIES), editor and president of Alfred A. Knopf, Inc. CBS, which had been criticized as having overspent to purchase 12 magazines from Ziff-Davis for $362.5 million in 1985, agreed to sell CBS Magazines in 1987 for $650 million. The sale, which ended the company's involvement in publishing, was to a group led by the unit's senior executives. Among titles involved were *Woman's Day, Car and Driver,* and *Field & Stream*.

Another change was that public figures would now have to prove actual injury before they could bring a libel suit against a magazine. This ruling of a New Jersey federal judge resulted from a suit filed against Time Inc. concerning a 1982 article that linked a construction company with an FBI investigation.

Despite the widespread belief in the early 1980s that there would be a boom in popular scientific magazines, Time Inc.'s entry, *Discover,* lost money from the start. Its two main competitors, Hearst's *Science Digest* and *Science 86,* both folded in 1986. In 1987 Time sold *Discover* to Family Media (publishers of such titles as *Health*).

For more than two decades the familiar city magazine (from *Dallas* to *New York*) has represented communities, but by 1987 it had rivals. Among these was the local women's magazine. By 1987 some 50 such titles had been introduced. Whether it was *New York Woman* or *San Diego Woman,* they all stressed the community interests of women. With circulations ranging from 10,000 to 50,000,

*(continued on page 290)*

# The Book of the Year: A Retrospective

BY PHILIP W. GOETZ

This volume is the 51st issue of the *Britannica Book of the Year.* The first volume, recounting the events of 1937, was similar in many ways to this one, dissimilar in many others, just as the events of 1937 and those of 1987 are in some ways remarkably convergent and in others unique to their respective times.

In his introduction to that first issue, editor Franklin H. Hooper noted that five generations had come and gone since the first publication of the *Encyclopædia Britannica* in 1768. He went on to write that the interval of time between the succeeding editions "was naturally considerable, and no device was employed to fill the gap. Such a procedure was satisfactory in an age that was more or less static, in which knowledge increased slowly and progress was made at what today would seem a snail's pace. But such a procedure is not suited to the present dynamic era when knowledge increases at an ever faster pace. . . . The *Britannica Book of the Year* bridges the gap between editions . . . it keeps up to date the sets of the *Britannica* in the hands of the public." That remains the intention of this year's edition and of those to come.

For his authors Hooper chose mostly from the ranks of the contributors to the *Britannica,* many of them notable: Bronislaw Malinowski wrote on anthropology; Niels Bohr on the structure of matter; L. Moholy-Nagy on the Bauhaus; Richard E. Byrd on the Antarctic and Vilhjalmur Stefansson on the Arctic; Auguste Piccard on the stratosphere; Charles F. Kettering on motorcars; George Jean Nathan on theatre. Among them were two who would continue to contribute to the *Book of the Year* for more than 30 years: Morris Fishbein on medicine and Hans Kohn on European affairs.

It should be noted here that there was not one book in 1938 but two. A companion volume was published in London for readers in Great Britain. The two books shared a number of articles but included many others that were primarily of interest to local readers. Since space does not permit a review of both, the U.S. version has been the chief source of information for this article.

The division of subject matter in the 1938 book was as fractionalized as it is compact in this one: each of the obituary notices was dropped into alphabetical position, as were the biographies; there were separate articles on the various agricultural and industrial products (RICE; GLASS; GRAPEFRUIT), diseases (SILICOSIS; LEPROSY), and even taxes (GASOLINE TAX; EXCESS PROFITS TAX). The editors also seemed to have a special fascination with the governors of the U.S. states. Each governor had a photograph, some of which suggest that the editors may have been as amused as they were fascinated: one governor is shown cleaning his shotgun, another is playing pool, and one is fearlessly walking under a ladder.

*Philip W. Goetz is Editor in Chief of the* Encyclopædia Britannica.

The hydrogen-filled *Hindenburg* explodes in flame alongside a mooring mast in Lakehurst, New Jersey. The 1938 *Britannica Book of the Year* listed the *Hindenburg* disaster, in which 36 people died, as one of the top ten news stories of 1937.
KEYSTONE

There were also titles that had significance only for the year in question (and perhaps can be seen as the forerunners of the Special Reports like this one): CORONATION (of George VI); HELICOPTER (one had flown for more than an hour in 1937). Many of the titles of articles that catch a reviewer's eye in 1987 reflected the concerns and state of the world—or at least the United States—in 1937: SIT-DOWN STRIKES; REARMAMENT; PROGRESSIVE EDUCATION; BOOTLEGGING; RURAL ELECTRIFICATION; CHILD LABOUR.

But what of the content of these articles? When examined in all of its richness and diversity, every year of the past may be said to be extraordinary, but 1937 does appear to have been a watershed year in a number of respects, though our contributors did not, and probably could not, know that. The ten top stories of the year, as tabulated in the article on newspapers and reflecting the amount of coverage they received in U.S. papers, were: (1) the attempt of U.S. Pres. Franklin Roosevelt to reorganize the Supreme Court; (2) the U.S. steel strikes, the largest in history; (3) the onset of the Sino-Japanese war and the entrance of other nations into the Spanish Civil War; (4) the explosion of the zeppelin *Hindenburg;* (5) a bumper U.S. agricultural crop but a sharp downward break in stock prices; (6) the marriage of the former King Edward VIII of Great Britain to an American divorcée; (7) an explosion that killed 427 children and teachers in a schoolhouse in Texas; (8) the disappearance of Amelia Earhart on a round-the-world flight; (9) the coronation of George VI; and (10) a flood of the Ohio River that resulted in 900 deaths. Some of these events echo in 1987, but two that were not listed at all continue into the present. In Palestine, then under British mandate, the year witnessed a continuation of Arab terrorism directed against Jews. In July a British royal commission proposed a partition of Palestine into two independent states, one Jewish, the other Arab.

But the story that, seen from the vantage point of 1987, overshadowed everything else was the lighting of the fuse that led to World War II. Having repudiated two years earlier the limitations imposed by the Treaty of Versailles at the end of World War I, Germany was rearming. Domestically, the Nazi government seized control of the banks and the railroads and began a persecution of Roman Catholics on the heels of its earlier attacks upon Jews. Chancellor Adolf Hitler entertained the Italian dictator Benito Mussolini, and their partnership was forged. Both signed an anti-Communist pact with Japan, which would become the third major nation on the Axis side in the forthcoming war. Among the Allies, both Great Britain and the U.S. began the year with official speeches about peace and ended it by announcing major rearmament programs. The ARMIES OF THE WORLD article lists the strength of the U.S. Army as fewer than 500,000 men, 20th in the world.

There were those who not only could not see what was happening but also did not believe that it could happen. In the article WARFARE Capt. B. H. Liddell Hart, military correspondent of *The Times,* London, stated that the technological advances in warfare had given the advantage to the defense. He questioned whether the mass armies would ever reach the battlefield because roads and railways could be blocked and supply lines would be too long. He stated that the destructive effect of air power had been overestimated, and he doubted that there would be major battles at sea.

There were other innocent contributors to the 1938 *Book of the Year.* The article PHYSICS began with

Benito Mussolini poses with Adolf Hitler in full military dress. Like most observers at the time, contributors to the first *Book of the Year* missed the significance of their alliance.

this bland sentence: "Nuclear physics was very popular as a subject for research in 1937." Other contributors distinguished themselves by ignoring Britannica's policy of objectivity. The author of the article SALES TAX stated bluntly that the tax "violates practically every principle of justice in taxation." And the author of SOCIALIZED MEDICINE noted that methods of socialization "which disturb the close, direct, personal, confidential relationship between the individual and the physician . . . operate to lessen the quality of the service rendered."

**Here and There in 1937.** The U.S. was producing more than a billion barrels of oil annually, Iran a little more than 50 million. "[T]he only practical use to which television had been put was for a public broadcast in London using a high standard of definition." Two days before the U.S. House of Representatives passed an antilynching bill, two blacks were tied to trees in Mississippi, stripped, and tortured to death. J. R. R. Tolkien's *The Hobbit* was published. The American Medical Association approved of birth control as having a definite place in medical practice. Mickey Mouse was banned in Yugoslavia, but in the U.S.S.R. he was the only product of the U.S. film industry permitted on the state-owned movie screens. If 1937 may be said to be a year of beginnings, it was also a year of endings. Among those who died in that year were George Gershwin, Sir James Barrie, Guglielmo Marconi, Edith Wharton, Ernest Rutherford, Maurice Ravel, and two prominent British statesmen, Austen Chamberlain and Ramsay MacDonald.

In that first issue of the *Book of the Year,* the articles often were encyclopaedic in nature rather than reportorial. Thus, the article SIT-DOWN STRIKES began as follows: "In the twenty-ninth year of King Rameses III (1179 B.C.) workers in the royal cemetery of Thebes sat down behind the temple of Thutmose III and refused to work until given their food allowance. . . ."

**Later Years.** If a review of the year has been a constant for the *Book of the Year,* change in the way the year is reviewed has been the twin constant. The combining of related articles began with the 1939 edition and has continued. The feature articles were introduced in the 1956 *Book of the Year.* Among the many notable authors of these articles since then have been 13 presidents and prime ministers: Betancourt (Venezuela), Deng (China), Gandhi (India), Johnson (U.S.), Kenyatta (Kenya), López Portillo (Mexico), Menzies (Australia), Mugabe (Zimbabwe), Nakasone, Tanaka, and Yoshida (Japan), Park (Korea), and Wilson (U.K.). Most recently, the *Britannica World Data* was added to the volume, making more secure editor Hooper's promise in 1937 that the book would keep sets of the *Encyclopædia Britannica* up-to-date. The regular contributors have changed over the years, but there have been some constants as well: in 1943 Robert Braidwood began writing on archaeology and writes today (his current article will be found on page 125). Editors, too, have come and gone, some 17 of them, but none with a longer tenure than the present editor, Daphne Daume, whose association with the book began with the 1960 issue.

**What of the Future?** Will reviewers of this volume see signs—that we have missed—of another great war, or will the signs point elsewhere? To a planet uninhabitable because of the poisoning of its air, water, and soil? To a world brought closer together by advances in telecommunications and education—or to an Orwellian world of social control made possible by the misuse of technological advance? Or will 1987 be just another year, lacking the excitement and portents of 1937?

*(continued from page 287)*
they offered a mix of topics with a strong emphasis on the women's movement and very little space devoted to recipes and sewing patterns.

*Money* magazine won the coveted public interest category of the annual U.S. National Magazine Awards. The article "Inside the Billion Dollar Business of Blood" was one of 13 winners. Other winners included: *Life,* for reporting; *Consumer Reports,* personal service; *Sports Afield,* special interests; *Elle,* design; *National Geographic,* photography; *Esquire,* fiction; *Outside,* essays and criticism; and *Bulletin of the Atomic Scientists,* single-topic issue (Chernobyl). In addition, *New England Monthly, Common Cause, Elle,* and *People* won general excellence awards.

The average annual price of a magazine published in the U.S. in 1987 was $71.41, up $6.41 from 1986. Prices increased more than five times the rate of inflation, or 11.2%. (WILLIAM A. KATZ)

**Books.** The spate of mergers in world publishing that began in 1986 gathered momentum in 1987. The prestigious British literary group of Chatto & Windus, Virago, Bodley Head, and Jonathan Cape (CVBC) joined with Random House of the U.S. following a public argument over the operation of the CVBC consortium between the novelist Graham Greene and his nephew and the group's chairman, Graham C. Greene. Associated Book Publishers was bought by International Thompson, which promptly put Methuen up for sale; Harper & Row crossed the Atlantic to join the Collins empire, and the U.K.'s Octopus sold out to Reed International.

Even the small publishers were not immune to the activity, with Edward Arnold, one of the last of the independent British publishers, merging with Hodder & Stoughton and medical publishers John Wright being bought out by Butterworths. Publishing in general and U.K. publishing in particular became fashionable businesses, and stock prices of publishing firms were reaching record levels until the dramatic fall in world stock markets in October.

The British government continued its efforts to prevent publication of *Spycatcher,* the memoirs of former secret-service agent Peter Wright, by bringing court cases in Australia, New Zealand, and Hong Kong and applying pressure in Pakistan, India, and Bahrain. Despite these efforts, there were unofficial market infringements that provided the

U.S. Viking edition with world sales that were far higher than expected. In the U.K. the book was not legally available for sale, but imported copies were widely distributed and could be found on library shelves.

The Booker Prize in the U.K. generated growing interest and was increasingly seen as the premier world English-language fiction award. Its impact on sales was felt in Europe, Australia, Japan, and even India and Pakistan. In 1987 an outsider won the prize again. Penelope Lively's *Moon Tiger* unexpectedly finished ahead of Brian Moore's *The Colour of Blood* and Chinua Achebe's *Anthills of the Savannah.*

Despite the new Soviet policy of *glasnost,* censorship continued to be a problem at the sixth Moscow Book Fair, and both British and U.S. publishers' associations made strong protests. Coincidentally, the book that drew the most attention at the Frankfurt (West Germany) Fair was Soviet leader Mikhail Gorbachev's *Perestroika,* in which he discussed *glasnost.* The other major book at Frankfurt was also Soviet; Anatoly Rybakov's *The Children of Arbat St.* was bought by Hutchinson for $300,000, the highest reported bid at Frankfurt in 1987. The Frankfurt Fair was the largest ever, with 7,100 publishers from 88 countries exhibiting 93,000 new titles and 227,000 book list titles. (ANTHONY A. READ)

In the U.S. during 1987 First Amendment (of the U.S. Constitution) issues preoccupied the book publishing industry along with concerns about mergers and acquisitions. The case that overshadowed other First Amendment-related cases involved Random House, which in August 1986 was about to publish *J. D. Salinger: A Writing Life,* a biography by Ian Hamilton. The reclusive Salinger, author of *The Catcher in the Rye,* sought to stop publication on the basis of copyright infringement; Hamilton had quoted or paraphrased from 70 letters, deposited in university libraries by their recipients, to which Salinger held the copyright. A 1986 decision had called the excerpting "fair use" and allowed publication to proceed, but Salinger's appeal to the Second Circuit Court of Appeals barred publication of the Random House biography, on the basis of the court's first application ever of the "fair use" doctrine to unpublished material.

There is no simple formula for what constitutes fair use, but the main criterion usually is damage to the commer-

AP/WIDE WORLD

Paperback copies of *The Tower Commission Report* on the Iran-*contra* affair are added to a display at a bookstore. The first copies were bound and ready to ship only 47 hours 29 minutes after the official report was released in Washington.

cial value of copyrighted material; even if Salinger wanted to keep the letters unpublished, their commercial value might be diminished by Hamilton's use. The court in effect decided that paraphrasing and verbatim quotes are equivalent uses of copyrighted material; publishers feared that this new definition could hinder the use of unpublished material without permission and thus endanger the free exchange of information. Late in the year the U.S. Supreme Court refused to hear Random House's appeal, and the 50,000 copies of Hamilton's biography that had already been bound were shredded.

Throughout the year companies were in the news as they bought, or were bought by, other companies. In late spring British publishing tycoon Robert Maxwell made a $1.7 billion offer for Harcourt Brace Jovanovich (HBJ), a U.S. publishing giant that in 1986 had acquired CBS Publishing for $500 million; William Jovanovich, chairman of the firm, called the hostile takeover bid "preposterous" and later called Maxwell "unfit" to run HBJ. To stave off the Maxwell takeover, HBJ announced a $3 billion recapitalization plan that Maxwell forestalled with a lawsuit; the court found in HBJ's favour in early summer, and in late July Maxwell abandoned his dramatic takeover attempt.

Meanwhile, at HBJ the ramifications of Maxwell's action were felt for the rest of the year; the firm posted a $70 million second-quarter loss, which it claimed was the result of expenses incurred in fighting Maxwell. HBJ later announced that it had sold its business periodicals, trade-show, and school-supply distribution subsidiaries for $334.1 million to a group of investors that included Robert Edgell, a former HBJ director and vice-chairman.

Australian publishing mogul Murdoch was in the news in September and October when he paid $200 million for Martins, a 1,000-store British newsagents chain that also sold books; he later increased to 14% his stake in Pearson, the parent corporation of U.S. publishing subsidiaries Viking Penguin, NAL, and Dutton. A takeover of Pearson was not expected because attempts to own a larger share might provoke regulatory procedures in both Britain and the U.S.

In 1986 and 1987 huge prices were paid for publishers; Time Inc. bought educational publisher Scott Foresman & Co. for $520 million; West German publisher Bertelsmann bought Doubleday & Co. Inc. for $475 million; and, as noted, HBJ bought CBS for $500 million. Analysts said, however, that the high prices reflected the real worth of the companies and were not exorbitant.

VAAP, the copyright agency of the Soviet Union, announced that Boris Pasternak's novel *Doctor Zhivago*, unavailable in the U.S.S.R. since its 1958 publication, would be issued there. Even more surprisingly, the agency noted that the copyright of the novel would stay with Feltrinelli, the Italian publisher that had originally published the book.

Other books in the news were those with big dollar signs attached. The hardcover and paperback rights to a new novel by Judith Rossner, author of *Looking for Mr. Goodbar* and *August,* were sold to Summit Books, a division of Simon & Schuster, for $1,850,000 on the strength of an 80-page outline. *Presumed Innocent,* a first novel by Scott Turow, a Chicago lawyer and author of the nonfiction *One L,* was sold to Farrar, Straus & Giroux for $200,000, a record for that publisher. Before the book was published in July, movie rights had been sold for $1 million; after the book was published and became a number one best-seller (with more than 800,000 copies in print by year's end), paperback rights were sold to Warner Books for $3 million, a record for a first novel and just short of the all-time record of $3,190,000 paid by Bantam for *Princess Daisy* by Judith

Krantz in 1981. In July Warner Books had paid $750,000 for the hardcover and paperback rights to *Promises to Keep,* a first novel by George Bernau that imagines U.S. history after a failed assassination attempt on Pres. John F. Kennedy. During the summer Bantam contracted to pay Arthur C. Clarke $4,050,000 for three books, a record sum all the more surprising because the books were to be written in collaboration with a scientist from the U.S. National Aeronautics and Space Administration.

Best-selling hardcover novels of 1986, as reported in *Publishers Weekly* in March 1987, were Stephen King's *It,* which sold 1,206,266 that year, and Tom Clancy's *Red Storm Rising* (1,025,020 copies). Best-selling hardcover nonfiction books were *Fatherhood* by Bill Cosby (a record 2.4 million copies), Harvey and Marilyn Diamond's diet book, *Fit for Life* (1,350,252 copies), and a biography of Frank Sinatra, *His Way,* by Kitty Kelley, which sold 1,005,000 copies.

According to the Association of American Publishers, 1986 book sales in the U.S. totaled $10.5 billion, a rise of only 5.8% over 1985, less than the 8.3% increase between 1984 and 1985. (WILLIAM W. GOLDSTEIN)

*See also* Literature.

This article updates the *Macropædia* article PUBLISHING.

# Race Relations

In 1987 attempts at achieving racial harmony suffered a number of serious setbacks. Several major trouble spots were in Asia and the Pacific islands.

**Asia and the Pacific Islands.** In Fiji tense relations between the ethnic Melanesian Fijians and the Indian community erupted into open conflict following the election of an Indian-dominated government. Voting was traditionally on ethnic lines, and the Labour Party-National Federation Party coalition's victory over the Alliance Party, which had ruled Fiji since independence in 1970, reflected the rapid growth in the Indian population, which just outnumbered that of the Fijians. Racial harmony in the past had been achieved by the tacit agreement of the two communities: the Fijians ran politics, and the Indians ran business. The change in government raised fears among Fijians that their land and other rights would be threatened. On May 14 a military coup led by Lieut. Col. Sitiveni Rabuka (*see* BIOGRAPHIES) removed the new Indian-dominated government. Within days the capital, Suva, was suffering the worst violence ever known in the country, with Indians and their property under attack by Melanesians. Following a second coup on September 25, in which Rabuka consolidated his power base, he declared a republic and committed himself to the promotion of Fijians in all areas; there were, however, no plans to restructure the Indian-dominated judiciary or trade unions. As the year drew to a close, political dissidents—mainly Indian—were reportedly being tortured and intimidated, and no early solution to the racial conflict appeared likely.

In Sri Lanka racial tensions between the Tamil minority and the Sinhalese reached a climax as the Hindu Tamils stepped up their claim for greater autonomy in the northern and eastern parts of the country, where they were concentrated. The Tamils had relinquished their political power in 1983 when their 18 (out of 168) members of Parliament forfeited their seats rather than renounce separatist activities and pledge allegiance to a unitary state. Intervention by India, which was reportedly fueling the conflict by training guerrillas in its southern Tamil Nadu state, failed despite the signing of a peace accord between the two countries in July. The Sri Lankan government's willingness to give some autonomy to the Tamils was fiercely opposed by the majority of Sinhalese on the grounds that it eroded their sovereignty and also was scorned by the Tamils, who felt betrayed by Indian Prime Minister Rajiv Gandhi. Spasmodic bouts of serious violence continued and were exacerbated by the presence of thousands of Indian "peacekeeping" troops. At least 10,000 Sinhalese had fled the Eastern Province. No solution was in sight, and it could not be proved who the first settlers were, despite claims and counterclaims by each group.

In Malaysia the simmering discontent between the Malay, Chinese, and Indian communities surfaced during the year as the deterioration in the economy heightened grievances. The government's New Economic Policy for several years had favoured the Malays, who made up about half of the population. Religious, industrial, and other policies—such as the appointment of non-Mandarin speakers in Chinese schools—had inflamed racial passions and led to an increase in public protest rallies. On October 27 Prime Minister Mahathir bin Mohamad took unprecedented action when he authorized the arrest of 63 government and opposition politicians and academics, ostensibly to prevent race riots. They were detained without trial under the Internal Security Act. Three newspapers were closed and public rallies were forbidden. By mid-November more than 90 people, mainly Chinese, had been detained, and fears were growing that the move would cause an escalation in racial tension.                                    (JANET H. CLARK)

**Western Europe.** On June 18, 1987, the European Parliament, after citing a pattern of attacks on Greek and Turkish workers in West Germany, condemned the rise of fascist organizations and linked the media with the rise of these organizations. It called on member states to alert the public to the danger of fascist tendencies and to ban reports damaging to the immigrant communities. Nevertheless, racial violence resulting in the deaths of immigrant workers and their families increased in The Netherlands, France, and West Germany.

Nationalist political parties continued to gather support. In France the National Front, led by Jean-Marie Le Pen, entered into an alliance with the right-wing Radical Party in the town of Grasse. Le Pen used his candidacy in the forthcoming presidential elections in May 1988 to blame immigrants for everything from unemployment to moral decadence. During the trial of Klaus Barbie (*see* BIOGRAPHIES), head of the Gestapo in Lyon during World War II, Le Pen stated in an interview that "I do not say that the gas chambers did not exist. I myself have not seen any. I have not specifically studied the question. But I think it is a point of detail in the history of the Second World War." The comment was condemned by all but his own party.

In September the extremist German People's Union (DVU) won a seat in the state assembly in Bremen. It campaigned fiercely, calling for jobs to be given to Germans instead of immigrant workers and for the deportation of foreigners and those who had sought asylum in West Germany.

In the U.K. four nonwhites were elected to Parliament in the 1987 general election, the first to be elected in more than half a century. Diane Abbott became the first black woman MP. In his maiden speech Bernie Grant, one of the four, warned that racial tensions in the inner cities were potentially explosive.

The 1986 annual report of the Commission for Racial Equality (CRE) stated that in the U.K. many symptoms of bad race relations remained to be confronted and that racial attacks continued, as did acts of discrimination.

"Welcome to Forsyth County," are friendly words in contrast to the scene below. National guardsmen form a barrier in front of civil rights demonstrators protesting the all-white status of the Georgia county despite harassment by Ku Klux Klan members and sympathizers.
WEINER—GAMMA/LIAISON

Particularly vulnerable were black polytechnic graduates, entrants to careers in accounting, and applicants for the two-year Youth Training Scheme. Black unemployment remained at twice the level for whites and was much worse in some areas such as Liverpool, where it reached 80%. The housing charity Shelter reported that a disproportionate number of nonwhites were homeless. In an effort to ensure equal employment opportunities, the government was acting to outlaw the use of contract compliance procedures by local councils in England and Wales. At the same time, in Northern Ireland it was introducing legislation to stop religious discrimination.

**South Africa.** In an unexpected move Govan Mbeki, a leader of the African National Congress (ANC), was released in November after nearly a quarter of a century in jail. Top antiapartheid leaders were jubilant and saw the release as possibly preceding that of ANC leader Nelson Mandela. A negotiated settlement to South Africa's black-white problem seemed a possibility, but hopes were dashed when the government imposed a banning order on Mbeki in December.

Earlier events in the year had given little cause for optimism. In June the year-old state of emergency was renewed, and in August the government imposed precensorship on the press for the first time. It was estimated that more than 30,000 people had been detained under the emergency regulations, and 1,424 children aged 12 to 18 were in detention on April 15. There were claims that the figures understated the situation.

The results of the whites-only elections in May, in which the National Party government was reelected, reflected a decline in liberal white opposition and an increase in the extreme right vote from 3% in 1977 to 15% in 1981 and to 27% in 1987. Thus the extreme-right Conservative Party became the official opposition in Parliament. Controversy over sanctions continued and dominated the Commonwealth heads of government meeting in Vancouver, B.C. In the U.S. a special committee appointed by the administration of Pres. Ronald Reagan in February called for international sanctions to isolate South Africa economically, and Congress was considering stronger U.S. sanctions. Sweden planned to impose a total boycott on trade.

**United States.** The split between the Reagan administration and the black community persisted. The Supreme Court's only black justice, Thurgood Marshall, in September said he believed that Reagan was one of the worst presidents for black people in modern times. In October Reagan's nominee for the Supreme Court, Judge Robert Bork (*see* BIOGRAPHIES), was rejected overwhelmingly by the Senate. An important factor was his reticence in supporting the rights of black Americans. Southern senators dependent upon black votes voted against him.

There were confrontations on university campuses and an increasing number of Ku Klux Klan and anti-Klan marches. In January as many as 20,000 civil rights marchers went to Forsyth County, Ga., to demonstrate against racist attacks on an earlier small "freedom march" held to protest the exclusion of blacks from the county. There were also more than 1,000 white counterdemonstrators. In June the Klan marched in Greensboro, N.C., for the first time since Klansmen murdered five anti-Klan activists in 1979. On the day before the Klan march took place, there was a large anti-Klan rally in protest. In September at a rally in Maine, Klan members wearing hoods or military camouflage uniforms burned a large cross. Rallies against the Klan were held in a number of cities in the state.

In June a jury in New York City cleared Bernhard Goetz of attempted murder charges following his 1984 shooting of four black youths on a Manhattan subway. Controversy followed the acquittal, which many saw as a reflection of racial polarization and fear. Also in New York the trial began in September of four white youths accused of participating in a racial attack on three black men in Howard Beach, Queens, in December 1986, causing the death of one of them. On December 21, after 12 days of deliberation, the jury found three of the youths guilty of manslaughter but not guilty of attempted murder. The fourth defendant was acquitted. (LOUIS KUSHNICK)

# Religion

The conflicting passions aroused by different religions helped to ignite "holy wars" around the world in 1987. Some of these wars were raw physical conflicts that resulted in the loss of human life. Others were bloodless battles of words over doctrines or money or places of authority and influence. "Intensity" was the name of all the war games.

Most notably, in the combustible Middle East religious fervour fanned the flames of conflict. In Mecca, Islam's holiest shrine, more than 400 persons died in a July riot that pitted Muslims against Muslims, pilgrims from Iran against Arab riot police. Soon after the fatal clash, Shi'ah Muslims shouted for "revenge, revenge" in a "day of hate" rally in Tehran. Hojatolislam Hashemi Ali Akbar Rafsanjani (*see* BIOGRAPHIES), the speaker of Iran's Majlis (parliament), told the crowd: "We, as soldiers of God and implementers of divine principles, oblige ourselves to avenge [the] martyrs by uprooting Saudi rulers from the region." (See *Islam,* below.)

Meanwhile, four of the five chief priests of the Sikh religion gave their official blessing to the fight being waged

by Sikh militants for a separate Sikh nation in India's Punjab state. As the struggle continued, Indian Prime Minister Rajiv Gandhi seized direct control of Punjab, taking regional power away from moderate Sikh officials. Many small but costly battles were fought in the long war. In two days, Sikh radicals were believed to have been responsible for terrorist attacks that resulted in the deaths of 72 bus passengers in northern India near the Punjab border. (See *Hinduism,* below.)

Violence also erupted in Lhasa, Tibet, where Buddhists led a demonstration calling for Tibetan independence from China. Clashes between Chinese authorities and leaders of the Tibetan independence movement led to the deaths of both Chinese police and Buddhist monks. When monks appealed for world support, the Chinese government issued a sharp attack on the Dalai Lama, Tibet's foremost religious leader and the political leader of Tibetan exiles. Published in the official Communist Party newspaper *People's Daily,* the statement charged that the Dalai Lama and his followers were attempting to "undermine the unification of the motherland."

In the U.S. "holy wars" made the cover of *Newsweek* magazine. In April the newsweekly devoted its cover story, "Holy Wars: Money, Sex and Power," to evangelists Jim and Tammy Bakker (*see* BIOGRAPHIES), who lost their religious television empire after a rival evangelist publicly charged that Jim Bakker had committed adultery with a 21-year-old church secretary. For weeks following Bakker's confession and the subsequent takeover of his PTL ("Praise the Lord") ministry by Jerry Falwell of the Moral Majority, the mass media produced a plethora of stories about the luxurious life-styles of several television evangelists who had "made it big" in the 1970s and 1980s. A special favourite of both serious journalists and TV comedians was Oral Roberts, the veteran preacher-healer, who warned his followers that God might shorten his life and "call Oral Roberts home" if the faithful failed to come up with $8 million for the support of medical missionaries. Included in many of the stories was M. G. ("Pat") Robertson, who worked hard to distance himself from many of the other combatants in the "battle of the airwaves." In preparation for his announcement that he was a candidate for U.S. president, Robertson cut his ties with the flourishing Christian Broadcast Network, which he had headed for 27 years, and resigned as a Baptist minister. (*See* Special Report.)

No one fought the battle for media attention and world influence harder—or more adroitly—than Pope John Paul II. The peripatetic pope made four trips abroad in 1987, bringing to 36 the number of his foreign pilgrimages during his nine-year papacy. His itinerary included his third papal trip to his native Poland and his second to the U.S., as well as journeys to West Germany, Argentina, and Chile.

The potency of his presence was felt the most in his beloved and besieged homeland, where a thriving Catholic Church was building 1,400 new church buildings and had seminaries full of candidates for the priesthood. Because church-state tensions had eased somewhat since his last visit in 1983—at least on the surface—John Paul was able to go to places previously barred to him, including Lublin, near the Soviet border, and Gdansk, birthplace of the now-outlawed Solidarity trade union movement. At the Gdansk shipyard he stirred the masses by saying: "In the name of mankind and of humanity, the word solidarity must be pronounced." At another stop he delivered a coded message of support to the people by invoking the name of Jerzy Popieluszko, an activist priest in the Solidarity movement who was murdered by security police in 1984. While Gen.

*(continued on page 296)*

# Religion, Television, and Money

## BY MARTIN E. MARTY

Two events, one Catholic and one Protestant, one planned and one unplanned, dominated religious news in the U.S. in 1987. The visit of John Paul II was planned and included few surprises. On the Protestant side, controversy over financial practices and scandals in the evangelical television empires was unplanned, and some surprises were revealed.

**"Holy Wars."** Two occasions early in the year led to the controversy. First, Tulsa (Okla.) evangelist and healer Oral Roberts made news by prophesying that God might "call Oral Roberts home" in death if his supporters did not contribute $8 million by the end of March. A large gift from a Florida greyhound racetrack owner helped Roberts produce the money by the deadline. By then, however, his tactics had led to much criticism from fellow evangelists and their followers.

More titillating and engrossing was the second occasion, perhaps because it included surprising disclosures involving sex, a topic that, when mixed with religion, always assures prime-time and front-page interest. South Carolina televangelist Jim Bakker (*see* BIOGRAPHIES), head of the PTL ("Praise the Lord" or "People That Love") enterprise, confessed to a sexual encounter in 1980 with a New York devotee, church secretary Jessica Hahn. She revealed that the PTL leadership had agreed to pay her $265,000 to be silent about Bakker's marital breach.

When rival evangelist Jerry Falwell of the "Old Time Gospel Hour" was invited to step in and rescue PTL—a $172 million television, housing, and "theme park" venture with at least $70 million in debts—there began what the press called a holy war among evangelists. Bakker was soon complaining of betrayal by Falwell through his "hostile takeover." Other TV evangelists, notably Jimmy Swaggart, who had highest audience ratings, were exposed as those who had forced the issue of PTL sex and financial scandals into the public realm.

Soon the Internal Revenue Service was in action, charged with examining whether PTL deserved tax-exempt status as a nonprofit organization. A grand jury was convened to see whether criminal activities were part of the mismanaged South Carolina enterprise. PTL went into bankruptcy, and in October Falwell and his board of directors resigned after a ruling by a federal bankruptcy court seemed to open the way for Bakker's possible return.

After a period in seclusion, Bakker—who had been defrocked by the Assemblies of God—and his wife, Tammy Faye, set up a 900 telephone number for supporters who wished to hear their messages, issued a gospel music video, and planned a national tour (which, however, was subsequently canceled for lack of interest). Hahn, meanwhile, posed seminude for *Playboy* magazine.

---

*Martin E. Marty is Fairfax M. Cone distinguished service professor of history of modern Christianity at the University of Chicago and senior editor of* The Christian Century.

Jim and Tammy Faye Bakker lost their evangelical empire after Jim resigned as head of the PTL enterprise in March. It had been revealed that he had had a brief sexual encounter with a church secretary and that PTL leaders had agreed to pay her for silence.
JOHN BARR—GAMMA/LIAISON

**Where the Money Comes From.** The exposures and controversy led to much public discussion about the support for and financing of the huge "televangelical" empires and about religious fund-raising in general. Whether religious or not, the general public had long been familiar with the needs religious organizations have for funds to support their institutions and carry on their works of education and mercy. Ordinarily, churches and synagogues raise funds through individual or congregational appeals. They encourage members to tithe (giving 10% of their income) or donate other generous and sacrificial amounts. Some institutions prosper through endowments, annuities, and wills, and others might use direct mail, sometimes even bingo and lotteries or leisure-time parish fund-raising events.

Many billions of dollars move through religious channels, which are still the greatest bearers of voluntary financial gifts in the U.S. Because of the moral demands made by and on religious groups, it is ordinarily assumed that they will have the highest standards of accountability. The Roberts and Bakker episodes showed how exceptional the practices of the TV empires are.

That large sums are involved no one questioned. That television demanded other means of fund-raising than local churches and synagogues used was obvious. Razelle Frankl in *Televangelism: The Marketing of Popular Religion* (1987) gave a fair accounting of the televangelists' motives and methods. They deal with a sizable but still confined and not growing market and thus must be highly competitive. A *New York Times/* CBS News Poll in late March found that 65% of the sampled public had a "not favourable" view of most television evangelists. Only 6% of "nonviewers" had a favourable view of them and, surprisingly, 50% of the "viewers" had a "not favourable" opinion.

Such samples suggest why the evangelists, healers, and entertainers must hold the loyalty of their constituents and receive regular and large gifts from them. This the "top ten" televangelists clearly succeeded at doing. Frankl found that they used from 12 to 42.6% of their air time to appeal for funds. They did so not by preaching "hellfire and brimstone" or threatening their loyalists. Instead they offered souvenirs and mementos, personal help or service, healing, success. They announced that funds went for special projects or toward paying for more air time. Some of the appeals were for Christian altruism: to save the world for Jesus Christ, to engage in works of love, to support moral crusades. (This final appeal often but by no means always meant direct engagements in politics, a feature that led many otherwise uninvolved Americans to pay attention to the televangelists and oppose them.)

**Attempting Reform.** In 1979, after exposures of mild scandals, responsible leaders, prompted by Sen. Mark Hatfield, reformed Watergate participant Charles Colson, and a newly chastened evangelist Billy Graham (whose organization was then being criticized but who otherwise had always been above criticism and who stood aside from the current controversy), formed an Evangelical Council for Financial Accountability (ECFA). Critics found it a timid first step, at best, toward producing accountability. Almost none of the top ten organizations belonged to it in any case, and it was very difficult to get anything like accurate accounting from more than one or two of them.

The stakes were high. Researches by Roderick Townley, in the popular *TV Guide,* produced some "best guesses." Jerry Falwell had a small audience but got good support. He was, however, accused of transferring funds given for his political causes (like the Moral Majority) to his religious ventures. Jimmy Swaggart, the only one who regularly criticized many of the others (along with Catholics and others who offended him), reached 3.5 million Americans and raised so much that he could complain of *losing* $50,000 a day after the Bakker scandal.

Oral and his son Richard Roberts—family members are almost always integral to these enterprises—had fewer than a million viewers and had to support not only television programming but a university and medical centre. (Most of these empires start their own universities or other institutions, thus adding to their outreach and cost.) M. G. ("Pat") Robertson, who severed his connection with his television ministry upon becoming a Republican presidential candidate, stressed his businessman status. He well might, for his "The 700 Club" reached 4.4 million people daily. Robertson also acknowledged significant losses of funds after the PTL exposure.

When the ECFA, the consciences of the televangelists, or the demands of their viewers do not force reform or accountability, not much happens. The press is cautious. The *Charlotte* (N.C.) *Observer,* which carried the first and best PTL reports, used especially high standards before it broke the story. Government agencies like the Internal Revenue Service are wary of "violating the separation of church and state" by interfering except when there have been gross and obvious transgressions. The only real hopes for reform come from the hardships created for the broadcasters when the public grows suspicious and withholds money. As a corollary, broadcasters were now likely to hold each other to somewhat higher standards, because the more ethical among them were truly offended by the Roberts and Bakker cases. They also had much to lose if the many existing and few potential viewers regarded them all as being too selfish, too secretive, or possibly as tainted by scandal as PTL was.

The most loyal followers remain loyal through thick and thin. They do respond to the regular "crisis appeals" by their favourites. Their core constituency stayed with Oral and Richard Roberts when competitors or colleagues chided those broadcasters. There were even PTL loyalists ready to forgive Jim Bakker. But it was a hard and perhaps chastening year for organizations that might find new reason to support the ECFA and even to ask that it raise its standards before more public confidence is shaken.

Meanwhile, the scandals did not seem to have hurt local congregations or other religious institutions. Some of them took the opportunity to distance themselves from the TV empires and to demonstrate their own higher standards of accountability and "full disclosure" as televangelism was forced to take long looks at itself.

"A fantastic evangelist was on TV, and I sent him everything."

*(continued from page 293)*

Wojciech Jaruzelski, Poland's chief of state, talked about "constructive coexistence" of the church and the state, the pope stood as a symbol of the church as an alternative to the Marxist system.

In West Germany in May the pope's efforts were concentrated on healing old wounds. In a dramatic ecumenical gesture at Augsburg, where the Diet of Augsburg adopted the basic creed of the Protestant Reformation in 1530, John Paul declared that the confession "provided us with a reminder of how broad and firm the common foundations of our Christian faith still are." To counter the widespread perception that Catholic leaders had failed to speak out strongly against Nazi rule, the pope pointedly paid tribute to Catholics who had suffered at the hands of the Nazis. While in Argentina he praised that country's new democracy, but in Chile he avoided outright criticism of the military dictatorship of Pres. Augusto Pinochet Ugarte. During a meeting with the poor in Santiago, he publicly embraced speakers who had condemned the regime, but he also counseled against the use of violent means to overthrow the government. And he warned against the "politicization" of Catholic "base communities" influenced by Latin-American "liberation theology."

The official theme of the pope's ten-day September trip to the U.S. was "Unity in the Work of Service," but nearly all the extensive media coverage was focused on the differences between official church teaching, as represented by the pope, and the views of American Catholics. Ninety-three percent of the Catholics interviewed in a *Time* magazine poll said they thought it was possible to disagree with the pope and still be a good Catholic, and 78% said it was permissible for Catholics to "make up their own minds" on such moral issues as birth control and abortion. Although he spoke in pastoral tones, the pontiff emphatically reiterated the church's traditional positions opposing birth control, abortion, homosexual acts, married priests, the ordination of women, and the admission to communion of divorced and remarried Catholics. Showing no patience with dissent, he told the American bishops: "Assent [to church teaching] constitutes the basic attitude of the believer, and is an act of will as well as of the mind." The pope's unmoving doctrinal stance was respectfully challenged in San Francisco by Donna Hanson, president of the National Lay Advisory Council, who told John Paul: "Though I know the church is not a democracy ruled by popular vote, I expect to be treated as a mature, educated, and responsible adult."

Prior to his visit, the pope made one conciliatory gesture that reduced the possibilities of public demonstrations by dissenters. He restored the episcopal powers of Archbishop Raymond Hunthausen of Seattle, Wash., who had been stripped of major authority the year before because he had allowed a "permissive" atmosphere to develop in his realm. Left standing, however, was the ban on teaching imposed on theologian Charles Curran of the Catholic University of America in Washington, D.C., because of his views on sexual ethics.

The greatest conflict of the pope's year took place at home. World attention was focused on Rome in June when the pope granted an audience to Pres. Kurt Waldheim of Austria, who had been accused of helping send Jews to Nazi death camps. Outraged Jewish leaders unsuccessfully pressured the pope to cancel the Waldheim visit. After the event the pope felt constrained to make some conciliatory gestures, including an unusually long meeting with Jewish leaders at the Vatican and a meeting with American Jewish leaders in Miami, Fla., at the beginning of his U.S. visit.

Another controversy emanating from Rome resulted when the Vatican issued a detailed document that, in its defense of the "sacredness of life," condemned such modern practices as surrogate motherhood, in vitro ("test-tube") fertilization, and some instances of artificial insemination. A dispute on a related matter arose in December when the administrative board of the U.S. Catholic Conference, representing the nation's bishops, issued a policy paper stating that teaching about the use of condoms could be acceptable in educational programs—even in Catholic schools—aimed at preventing the spread of AIDS (acquired immune deficiency syndrome). Conservative bishops, led by John Cardinal O'Connor of New York, objected, and the question was to be discussed by all the bishops at their meeting in June 1988.

In July there was an easing of the tensions between the Vatican and the government of Italy when Italy's High Court annulled warrants that had been issued for the arrest of Archbishop Paul C. Marcinkus, president of the Institute for Religious Works (the "Vatican bank"), and two other bank officials on the grounds that Italy could not try a citizen of the Vatican City State. In December, however, the magistrates investigating the 1982 collapse of Banco Ambrosiano, in which the Vatican bankers were accused of being involved, filed a constitutional challenge to the treaty provisions granting them immunity. Marcinkus had spent several months within the Vatican to avoid arrest by the Italian police.

In October a monthlong World Synod of Bishops ended inconclusively after extensive debate over the official theme, "The Vocation and Mission of the Laity in the Church and in the World." Without calling for the ordination of women as priests, some of the 200 bishops argued for a greatly expanded role for women in the church, including decision-making positions in the Curia, but the Synod's final recommendations urged few changes. (See *Roman Catholic Church,* below.)

In the U.S. three disputes over religion were settled in federal courtrooms. By a 7–2 vote the Supreme Court held unconstitutional a Louisiana law requiring public schools that taught the theory of evolution also to teach "creation science," based on a literal interpretation of the biblical accounts of creation. Speaking for the court majority, Justice William J. Brennan said the real goal of the Louisiana law "was clearly to advance the religious viewpoint that a supernatural being created humankind." In federal appeals courts fundamentalists also lost two battles for control of public school textbooks. In another courtroom, in Utah, a distressing episode for the Mormon church ended when Mark Hofmann, a dealer in rare documents, pleaded guilty to two counts of murder and two counts of theft by deception. Hofmann, who came from a Mormon family, admitted forging a number of documents that seemed to call into question the accepted version of the church's origins. The murders were committed to prevent the forgeries from being revealed. (See *Church of Jesus Christ of Latter-day Saints,* below.)

In other developments: the Church of England approved the preparation of legislation permitting the ordination of women as priests. Definitive action would not be taken until 1991. (See *Anglican Communion,* below.) And a new denomination with 5.3 million members came into being with the merger of the Lutheran Church in America, the American Lutheran Church, and the Association of Evangelical Lutheran Churches (which had split from the Lutheran Church–Missouri Synod several years earlier) into the Evangelical Lutheran Church in America. (See *Lutheran Communion,* below.) (ROY LARSON)

## PROTESTANT CHURCHES

**Anglican Communion.** The Anglican year ended in sudden high drama and tragedy with the death in December 1987, apparently by suicide, of a distinguished Anglo-Catholic clergyman, Gareth Bennett, of the University of Oxford. His death was the climax to a furious controversy over the preface to the latest edition of *Crockford,* the Church of England's directory of its clergy. The preface bitterly attacked not only the Church of England but also the Communion at large and the leadership of Archbishop of Canterbury Robert Runcie. Bennett repeatedly denied that he had written the preface—which is traditionally anonymous—but after his death church officials admitted that he was the author. It was expected that the General Synod would take up the matter early in 1988.

Until the *Crockford* affair, the principal concern was with the fate of Terry Waite, Runcie's special envoy, who disappeared in Beirut on January 20 during his renewed attempt to secure the release of hostages held in Lebanon. There was no reliable news of him by year's end.

Also in January, the second Anglican-Roman Catholic International Commission (ARCIC II) produced its first agreed statement, "Salvation and the Church," announcing its conviction that, as a result of its work, yet another obstacle on the road to unity had been removed. The statement dealt with issues of salvation and justification that had caused deep divisions between Protestants and Roman Catholics in the 16th century.

The major event of the year was the seventh meeting of the Anglican Consultative Council (ACC-7), held in Singapore in April and May. As part of the preparations for the 1988 Lambeth Conference of bishops, ACC-7's agenda mirrored that set for the conference. It was divided into mission and ministry, dogmatic and pastoral matters, ecumenical relationships, and Christianity and the social order. ACC-7 was remarkable for the degree of consensus reached by the 100 participants from around the Anglican Communion and for the lack of animosity, even on such contentious topics as the ordination of women. From Singapore the archbishop of Canterbury and other dignitaries moved on to Japan for the centenary celebrations of its Anglican church.

The place of women in the church's ministry continued to provoke argument. In February the Church of England's General Synod finally approved legislation allowing women to become deacons, and Runcie ordained the first in Canterbury Cathedral at the end of the month. In August the Australian General Synod rejected by the narrowest of margins legislation that would have opened the priesthood to women. At the same time, a small group of Australian church people announced that it was following other groups in various parts of the world in joining the breakaway church movement espousing strongly traditionalist views.                  (SUSAN YOUNG)

**Baptist Churches.** The American Baptist Churches in the U.S.A. (Northern Baptist), at its biennial meeting in Pittsburgh, Pa., in June 1987, announced that the 1.5 million-member denomination had exceeded its $30 million goal for the Alive in Mission campaign to establish new churches and refurbish mission outreach. Traditionally a white constituency, the denomination had a growing representation of ethnic minorities. After 15 years as general secretary, Robert C. Campbell resigned to become president of Eastern Baptist Theological Seminary in Philadelphia.

The Southern Baptist Convention also met in June, in St. Louis, Mo., with 25,000 messengers (delegates) in attendance. For a decade a battle had been waged between moderates and conservatives for control of the denomination's agencies and institutions, including its six seminaries. By a three-to-two margin, the messengers at St. Louis elected conservative Adrian Rogers president for a second consecutive term. Rogers's victory meant that conservatives had elected their choice for president for nine consecutive years, with the result that conservative trustees now outnumbered their moderate counterparts on all the various boards and institutions except one, Southern Baptist Theological Seminary in Louisville, Ky.

The six million-member National Baptist Convention, U.S.A., Inc., the largest black denomination in the U.S., held its annual meeting in September 1986 in Kansas City, Mo. A feature of the convention was the welcome extended to J. Alfred Smith, Sr., president of the 1.5 million-member Progressive National Baptist Convention Inc., who told the messengers that he hoped the two denominations could work together while maintaining separate identities. Smith's group split from the National Baptist Convention, U.S.A., Inc., in 1961, partly over support of Martin Luther King, Jr., on civil rights issues—support that the then president of the NBC, U.S.A., Inc., J. H. Jackson, had opposed.

In September 1986 the second-largest black denomination, the four million-member National Baptist Convention of America, meeting in Cleveland, Ohio, with 10,000 delegates present, had voted to establish programs for combating teenage pregnancy, halting the deterioration of black family life, and assisting the development of young black males. The denomination's 106th annual meeting also condemned South Africa's apartheid policies.

Edwin T. Dahlberg, past president of the National Council of Churches and of the American Baptist Churches in the U.S.A., died in Phoenix, Ariz., at the age of 93.

(NORMAN R. DE PUY)

**Christian Church (Disciples of Christ).** At its General Assembly held in October 1987 in Louisville, the 1.1 million-member Disciples of Christ adopted a 12-year priority to take the church into the 21st century. Daniel L. Woods of Florida was elected moderator of the church for the next two years.

The church received an $8 million gift from the estate of DeWitt and Othel Fiers Brown, possibly the largest bequest ever made to a Protestant denomination. The church's social service agency, the National Benevolent Association, which celebrated its 100th anniversary during the year, received a grant to fund its second Alzheimer's disease project. Disciples surpassed their goal of establishing 100 new congregations in the 1980s.

The ecumenically minded Disciples continued dialogue with the Roman Catholic Church, and a delegation traveled to the U.S.S.R. for the first in a series of dialogues with the Russian Orthodox Church. The Disciples entered a second year of partnership with the United Church of Christ.

All general units of the church reported complete divestment of stocks in companies doing business in South Africa.

(AUDREY BERTINA LEE)

**Churches of Christ.** Some 13,300 churches of Christ were listed in the 1987 U.S. directory of churches, *Where the Saints Meet.* Although the congregational autonomy of churches of Christ made a complete census difficult, responding churches revealed the greatest increases in membership in Texas and California.

The World Bible School, directed by Reuel Lemmons, sent 300,000 introductory Bible correspondence lessons every 60 days to students in 115 nations during 1987. Five hundred congregations were established through this ministry.

Thirty-two retirement communities supported by members were in operation in the U.S., and 20 were under construction.

AFP PHOTO

Archbishop of Canterbury Robert Runcie stands amid the first 15 women to be ordained as deacons by the Church of England. The momentous occasion took place in Canterbury Cathedral and emphasized the growing importance of women in the church.

Emphasizing that "there is no retirement from Christian service," a group of retirees at the Montgomery Boulevard Church, Albuquerque, N.M., organized to serve widows and senior citizens by repairing homes and providing other assistance.

Colleges and universities supported by members received more than $40 million in gifts, according to the Council for Financial Aid to Education. Lubbock (Texas) Christian College became a university on September 8. Pepperdine University, Malibu, Calif., celebrated its 50th anniversary.

(M. NORVEL YOUNG)

**Church of Christ, Scientist.** Several new publications—including the first major book in over 20 years on Christian Scientists' central practice of spiritual healing—were released in 1987. In July *Spiritual Healing in a Scientific Age* by Robert Peel was welcomed by both students of religion and lay readers. The book confirmed the continuing vitality of Christian Scientists' healing ministry as well as the complexity of the legal and scientific issues involved. Other major publications examining the state of the Church of Christ, Scientist, included items in *Theology Today, Christian Century,* and *The Encyclopedia of Religion.*

At their June annual meeting in Boston, church members were briefed on several new broadcasting efforts, most notably the 1987 launching of worldwide shortwave radio programs. The broadcasts included both religious programming and news reports derived from the *Christian Science Monitor.* A shortwave transmitter was erected in Maine, another was purchased on Saipan in the western Pacific, and plans for the construction of a third were well under way in the southern U.S.

Charles W. Ferris was named to the one-year post of church president.

(NATHAN A. TALBOT)

**Church of Jesus Christ of Latter-day Saints.** During 1987 the 150th anniversary of the introduction of Mormonism into Great Britain was celebrated with a gala banquet in London, with the publication of a history of the Mormon presence in Britain, and by various conferences and other events. The annual meeting of the Mormon History Association was held at the University of Oxford, the first such meeting outside the U.S.

On January 23 the document dealer Mark W. Hofmann pleaded guilty in Salt Lake City to two counts of second-degree murder and two counts of felony theft by deception. The theft by deception related to Hofmann's confessed forgery of the so-called White Salamander letter, supposedly written in 1830 by Martin Harris, an early confidante of Joseph Smith, and the sale of the so-called (nonexistent) McLellin Collection to a Salt Lake City coin dealer. Hofmann later confessed to prosecutors that he had forged hundreds of documents, many of them relating to Mormon history, which had been widely regarded as genuine, including a letter purportedly written by Joseph Smith in 1825.

The Mormon Tabernacle Choir aired its weekly radio broadcast for the 3,000th time on February 15. Brigham Young University's Jerusalem Center for Near Eastern Studies opened on March 8 and was in full operation by September. The First Presidency of the Church announced the

August 31 closing of the church-owned Hotel Utah, a landmark in downtown Salt Lake City for 76 years. The hotel would be converted to an office building for various church departments and affiliated organizations.

The number of church members totaled 6.5 million at the end of 1987, with congregations in 98 countries.

(LEONARD J. ARRINGTON)

**Jehovah's Witnesses.** Jehovah's Witnesses believe that the "Prince of Peace," Jesus Christ, will bring lasting peace. During 1987 the Witnesses worked to bring this message to millions of the Earth's inhabitants. More than three million Witnesses spent in excess of 600 million hours sharing the "good news" with their neighbours in 208 lands.

Faith in the divine promise of world peace was evident in themes selected for Witness conventions. A series of "Divine Peace" district conventions held on all continents during 1986 attracted 6.1 million people. Attendance at the current series of "Trust in Jehovah" conventions was expected to exceed that total. Witnesses believe peace will come from a divine source rather than through political, social, religious, or military efforts. To promote this view, Witness publishing and printing facilities in more than 30 countries turned out over half a billion copies of *The Watchtower* and *Awake!* magazines plus millions of books and Bibles during the year. The society of ministers known as Jehovah's Witnesses was growing at a rate of about 7% annually. (FREDERICK W. FRANZ)

**Lutheran Communion.** The Lutheran World Federation got a new president in July 1987 when the LWF Executive Committee elected a West German bishop, Johannes Hanselmann of Bavaria, to succeed Zoltan Kaldy, presiding bishop of the Lutheran Church in Hungary, who died in May. At its meeting, which marked the 40th anniversary of the formation of the LWF, the committee decided to hold the eighth LWF Assembly in 1990 in Brazil.

In the U.S. the constituting convention of the Evangelical Lutheran Church in America, held April 30–May 3, chose Herbert Chilstrom (*see* BIOGRAPHIES), bishop of Minnesota in one of the ELCA's predecessor bodies, as the first bishop of the new 5.3 million-member denomination, which included about two-thirds of the country's Lutherans. Constituting conventions for the ELCA's 64 regional and one nongeographic (Slovak) synods were held later in the year.

On the global level, Lutheran theological dialogues continued with Reformed, Baptists, Eastern Orthodox, Roman Catholics, and Anglicans. The U.S. Lutheran-Anglican dialogue put the finishing touches on an agreed statement on the gospel and its implications, and the U.S. Lutheran-Methodist dialogue issued a common statement on the role of bishops and others who exercise oversight in the church. The Anglican Consultative Council suggested that the 1988 Lambeth Conference of Anglican bishops commend forms of "interim eucharistic sharing" between Anglicans and Lutherans in other parts of the world like that in effect in the U.S. Lutherans played prominent roles in the *Kirchentage* (church congresses) held in Frankfurt, West Germany, and East Berlin.

Marking the LWF's 40th anniversary, Pope John Paul II spoke of the "real, though imperfect, communion already existing between us." During his visit to West Germany in May, he issued a call to Christian unity at Augsburg, a city closely associated with Lutheran history.

Efforts to end white-minority domination in South Africa and Namibia continued to be high on many Lutheran agendas. In Geneva early in the year, LWF General Secretary Gunnar Stålsett and Namibian church leaders met with Sam Nujoma and other officials of the South West Africa People's Organization, the principal group fighting South African rule in Namibia.

New criteria for counting dropped the total of Lutherans worldwide from 68.4 million to 58.6 million. This resulted from a decision not to continue to estimate the number of people in United Landeskirchen (regional churches) in East and West Germany who still have a Lutheran identity.

(THOMAS HARTLEY DORRIS)

**Methodist Churches.** In 1987 there were 25,141,863 members of churches belonging to the World Methodist Council (WMC), compared with 23,816,204 five years earlier, representing a growth of 5.6%. The greatest percentage of regional gains occurred in South America, Africa, Asia, and the Central America-Caribbean region.

The officers of the WMC met in Vienna in January to review plans for the five-year period following the Nairobi (Kenya) Conference in 1986 and appointed a committee to prepare for the 1991 World Council and Conference. Expressing concern about the widening epidemic of AIDS (acquired immune deficiency syndrome), the officers invited Methodists "to affirm the love of God for all people . . . by exercising a ministry of compassion to those who have contracted AIDS" and "to enunciate clearly the traditional teaching of the church about responsible attitudes to human sexuality." Following concern expressed at the WMC about the situation in South Africa, the officers proposed that a Sunday near June 16, Soweto Day, be adopted annually by each Methodist church as a day of prayer for South Africa.

Ecumenical discussions continued. The final report of conversations between the Lutheran World Federation and the WMC, adopted at the Nairobi Conference, included the recommendation that the churches of both communions "take steps to declare and establish full fellowship of word and sacrament." The fifth series of dialogues between the WMC and the Roman Catholic Church was under way, and in July a consultation with representatives of the World Alliance of Reformed Churches discussed historical doctrinal differences between the two traditions.

The WMC Executive Committee met in Jamaica in September. Other international events included the third International Christian Youth Conference in Brisbane, Australia; the third International Seminar on Evangelism in Atlanta, Ga.; the eighth Oxford Institute of Methodist Theological Studies; and the bicentenary of the movement that became the African Methodist Episcopal Church.

The 1987 World Methodist Peace Prize was awarded jointly to Bert Bissell of the U.K. for his "consistent devotion to the life of reconciliation" and to Judge Woodrow

Seals, a supporter of civil and human rights in the U.S. and a founder of the Society of St. Stephen. The United Methodist Church announced plans to establish a new Methodist university in Zimbabwe.

(JOHN C. A. BARRETT)

**Pentecostal Churches.** The Pentecostal and charismatic world mourned the passing of David du Plessis in 1987. Du Plessis died in February in Pasadena, Calif., where he had established the du Plessis Center for Christian Spirituality at Fuller Theological Seminary.

In March the PTL scandal rocked the U.S. in the wake of the resignation of Assemblies of God minister Jim Bakker (*see* BIOGRAPHIES), who confessed to a sexual indiscretion. Both Bakker and Richard Dortch, a former Assemblies of God leader, were defrocked by the Assemblies of God for their attempts to cover up the affair. (See *Introduction,* above; Special Report.)

In June James Gee was elected general superintendent of the Pentecostal Church of God. Rolf McPherson resigned in March as president of the International Church of the Foursquare Gospel, a position he had held since the death of his mother, Aimee Semple McPherson, the founder of the denomination. He was succeeded by John Holland, the first president not from the McPherson family. Pat Robertson declared his candidacy for the Republican nomination for the U.S. presidency, the first time a charismatic Christian had run for the highest office in the land.

The largest Pentecostal gathering of the year was the North American Congress on the Holy Spirit and World Evangelization, which convened in July in the Louisiana Superdome in New Orleans. At this meeting, David Barrett released statistics that claimed 277 million Pentecostal and charismatic Christians in the world in 1987. The congress adopted the goal of converting over half the world population to Jesus Christ by AD 2000.

(VINSON SYNAN)

**Reformed, Presbyterian, and Congregational Churches.** During 1987 the World Alliance of Reformed Churches (WARC) concluded two significant international consultations: with the Disciples Ecumenical Consultative Council and with the World Methodist Council. Both reports declared that no doctrinal obstacles remained to union between the respective partners. International dialogues with the Roman Catholic Church and with the Lutheran World Federation continued.

The first consultation for WARC member churches of Eastern and Central Europe was held at Kecskemet, Hung., in October. Its report affirmed that "ecumenical openness is an integral part of the Reformed heritage." A consultation for representatives of WARC member churches that witnessed within Islamic majorities was held at Geneva in July. The WARC Executive Committee met at Buckow, East Germany, in October and determined the theme of the 1989 General Council: "Who do you say that I am?" The WARC European Area Council was held at Vienna in August on the theme "Bible—Witness—Europe."

The Caribbean and North American Area Council of WARC met in Puerto Rico. Its Committee on Civil and Religious Liberty drew attention to the militarization of the Caribbean Basin and to the situation in Central America. The Presbyterian Church (U.S.A.) and the United Church of Christ both published statements declaring that Christianity had not superseded God's covenant with the Jewish people. (See *United Church of Christ,* below.)

The president of WARC, Allan A. Boesak, was elected moderator of the Nederduitse Gereformeerde Sendingkerk in South Africa. Charges leveled against him by the South African authorities were dropped. Jean-Françoise Bill, moderator of the Evangelical Presbyterian Church in South Africa, was released from detention in March after being held, uncharged, for nine months. The question of claimed rights vis-à-vis church teaching and discipline was raised by the decision of the Remonstrant Brotherhood in The Netherlands to consecrate in church the relationships not only of husbands and wives but also of the unmarried and of homosexuals.

The Presbyterian churches in Cameroon and Mozambique celebrated their centenaries. Erskine Theological Seminary in Due West, S.C., an affiliate of the Associate Reformed Presbyterian Church, celebrated its 150th anniversary. (ALAN P. F. SELL)

**Religious Society of Friends.** The year 1987 marked the 50th anniversary of the establishment of Friends World Committee for Consultation, the only body to provide liaison between Quakers of differing persuasions. Reminders of these divisions surfaced in two major gatherings. At the International Friends Conference on Evangelism in Guatemala in November, Evangelical Friends sought for the first time to invite more liberal Quakers to join in their mission work. The triennial Friends United Meeting at Greensboro, N.C., marked the centenary of the Richmond Declaration of Faith, itself a cause for dissension among British and American Friends in 1887.

In Britain the 1987 London Yearly Meeting discussed the spiritual hurt of poverty in a materialistic society. Its stated wish to work alongside other British churches on this concern was confirmed by the growing enthusiasm with which the Society of Friends endorsed the interchurch process "Not Strangers but Pilgrims."

One concern common to all branches of the Quaker world was the right to conscientious objection to military service. The efforts of the Quaker UN offices seemed crowned on March 10 when the UN Commission on Human Rights passed a general resolution supporting the right to conscientious objection as a step toward its establishment as a human right in international law.

(DAVID FIRTH)

**Salvation Army.** During 1987 there were several changes in the Salvation Army's senior leadership. Commissioner Caughey Gauntlett retired as chief of the staff (second in command of the world movement) and was succeeded by Commissioner Ron Cox. Commissioner Harry Read took office as the Army's British commissioner (head of evangelical and community work in Britain), and Col. Frank Fullarton became leader of Salvation Army Social Services in Great Britain and Ireland. Gen. Eva Burrows, world leader of the Salvation Army, traveled extensively.

The headquarters of the Army's Social Services moved from Hackney, East London, to refurbished premises in King's Cross. General Burrows appointed a personal consultant on unemployment and community affairs to research the subject and make recommendations for increased Army involvement.

The Salvation Army developed its 1987 program for the homeless in line with the UN International Year of the Homeless. In Britain new hostels were opened and new housing complexes were erected. In Los Angeles the Salvation Army created a tented village in an unused sports stadium to provide shelter for street people.

(ROB GARRAD)

**Seventh-day Adventist Church.** On Sept. 1, 1987, General Conference president Neal C. Wilson and government officials participated in ground-breaking ceremonies for a new $25 million world headquarters office building in Silver Spring, Md. In March Adventist World Radio-Asia began shortwave broadcasts to eastern and southern Asia from its new $5 million facility on Guam. Loma Linda University Medical Center, a Seventh-day Adventist hospital in California, announced, on July 30, plans to build a $39 million cancer therapy centre that would contain the world's first hospital-based proton-beam accelerator.

In *Hobbie* v. *Unemployment Appeals Commission of Florida,* the U.S. Supreme Court ruled that the state could not deny unemployment benefits to a Seventh-day Adventist fired for refusing to work on the Sabbath. In December 1986 the prime minister of Italy and a Seventh-day Adventist official signed an agreement defining church-state relationships and acknowledging the church's rights and liberties. Early in 1987 the Soviet government approved plans for an Adventist seminary and publishing centre south of Moscow.

At the Annual Council in Rio de Janeiro, Brazil, in October 1986, the General Conference president called for development of a global strategy for future church growth. An African planning committee adopted a preliminary 15-year strategy designed to serve African members, who were expected to quintuple to five million by the year 2000.

World membership stood at 5,038,671 on Dec. 31, 1986, an increase of 6.8% over 1985. (ROBERT W. NIXON)

**Unitarian (Universalist) Churches.** Highlights of the year, announced at the 1987 General Assembly of the Unitarian Universalist Association (UUA) in Little Rock, Ark., June 22–27, included the granting of charters to 18 new societies, publication of a new title each week by the Beacon Press (which achieved 97% self-sufficiency), and news that 238 theological students were preparing for UU ministry. The three top resolutions selected in a parish poll for study in 1988 were on censorship in public education, housing for the homeless, and the right to die. The denomination's overall resolution theme for 1987–88 was the protection of fundamental human rights to shelter, personal dignity, and self-determination.

The 59th annual General Assembly of the Unitarian and Free Christian Churches, representing 277 congregations and 8 fellowships and groups in Great Britain, Northern Ireland, and the Republic of Ireland, met at the University of Surrey in Guildford, April 3–6. Resolutions were passed urging support for AIDS sufferers and their families, renewed denominational growth emphases, and wider interfaith contacts.

The Canadian Unitarian Council held its annual meeting in May in Halifax, Nova Scotia. The council was working on a way to replace social action resolutions, which often result in no action or may suggest social policies contradicting the denomination's tradition of free search for truth and tolerance of differing ideas.

The International Association for Religious Freedom (IARF) held its triennial World Congress at Stanford University, July 31–Aug. 7, 1987, with 818 registered delegates from 17 countries representing eight major faiths. O. Eugene Pickett, former president of the UUA, was elected president of the IARF for three years.

(JOHN NICHOLLS BOOTH)

**The United Church of Canada.** Clergy and lay delegates at the 12 annual conferences (regional bodies) meeting across Canada in the summer of 1987 struggled with budget restraints and shrinking congregations but, remembering their global commitment, spoke out strongly against capital punishment, poverty, apartheid in South Africa, U.S. testing of cruise missiles on Canadian territory, and aid to the Nicaraguan *contras*. Many conferences made good use of grants from the national peacemaking fund, which in 1986 provided $55,000 for 45 projects. Over 100 men and women candidates for ministry were ordained or commissioned, but officials said this would still leave some pastorates in isolated areas without a full-time minister.

The church followed up the 1986 General Council endorsement of a full-scale ban on tobacco advertising by ruling that, effective early in 1988, its staff of 300 in Toronto would not be permitted to smoke on church premises. At the same time, the church reaffirmed its commitment to providing pastoral care to tobacco farmers who had suffered economic hardship as a result of the reduction in cigarette sales. Early in 1987 the church joined other denominations and socially concerned organizations in protesting to members of Parliament against the proposed reintroduction of capital punishment (abolished in 1976). Thanks in great measure to the efforts of the 31-member coalition, the government bill was defeated 148–127.

In common with other mainline denominations, the United Church had suffered decreases in membership; 1986 statistics revealed a 1% drop (9,024 members) from the previous year to 872,290. At the same time, contributions for all purposes, local and national, rose by 6.1%, or $247,717,-275, over 1985.

Howard M. Mills, a United Church minister who had been serving as president of the United Theological Seminary, New Brighton, Minn., returned to his home church July 1 to take up his appointment as secretary of the General Council, the church's top legislative body.

(NORMAN K. VALE)

**United Church of Christ.** Celebrations of the 30th anniversary of the birth of the United Church of Christ were held throughout 1987, culminating in the church's 16th General Synod, held June 25–30 in Cleveland, site of the Uniting Synod of the Congregational Christian Churches and the Evangelical and Reformed Church. Approved at the Synod was the proposal that the church add to its permanent bodies a Coordinating Center for Women in Church and Society. Other major actions of the biennial meeting included creation of a Council of Youth and Young Adult Ministries, authorization of a Committee on the Location of National Headquarters, and development of a special partnership relationship with the United Church of Christ in the Philippines.

The 700 delegates at the Cleveland meeting adopted more than 40 resolutions. In a resolution on Jewish-Christian relationships, the Synod declared that "Judaism has not been superseded by Christianity" and that "God has not rejected the Jewish people." The Synod also urged an end to the "Arab-Israeli-Palestinian conflict."

The United Church of Christ added "The Homeless Poor" to three other priorities—Justice and Peace, Spiritual Renewal, and Youth and Young Adult Ministries. Influencing the church throughout 1987 was a new mission statement, framed by a consultation of 350 persons held in Houston, Texas, and adopted by the General Synod. Robert D. Sherard was elected moderator.

Under the leadership of Benjamin F. Chavis, Jr., new leader of the church's Commission for Racial Justice, freedom rides were sponsored in Alabama and Illinois to support the participation of all voters in crucial elections. After several years of preparation, the Office for Church Life and Leadership introduced a new Book of Worship.

(AVERY D. POST)

## ROMAN CATHOLIC CHURCH

Events in 1987 were directed toward the Roman Synod of Bishops in October, which was devoted to the role of lay people "in the church and in the world." There were disagreements about the growth of lay ministries and about the importance of lay movements, such as Opus Dei and liberation theology, which claimed to be the modern form of lay involvement in the secular world. Basil Cardinal Hume of Westminster, England, warned, "The People of God travel through history on bread and butter, not caviar, and because of this it is important to look at the local church as the arena for change, not to Rome."

This was a common attitude in a year in which everything seemed to become more complicated and difficult. The euphoria of the Christian-inspired revolutions in the Philippines and Haiti wore off. The Vatican document on bioethics condemned in vitro fertilization, but instead of settling the issue once and for all, it fueled an intense debate. Relationships between the Vatican and the local churches became more tense.

The case of Archbishop Raymond G. Hunthausen of Seattle was brought to a conclusion in 1987. Hunthausen had been informed by the Congregation of Bishops in 1986 that he no longer had any authority over marriage tribunal operations and liturgical and parish programs, and most of his other responsibilities were removed. Bishop Donald Wuerl, the unwelcome auxiliary with whom Hunthausen had been provided, was removed, and Hunthausen's authority was restored on May 27. However, the decision appeared to have been

In May Pope John Paul II beatified Edith Stein, a step toward sainthood. A Jewish-born Catholic convert, she had become a Carmelite nun and died in Auschwitz during World War II.

AP/WIDE WORLD

taken in preparation for Pope John Paul II's visit to the U.S. in September rather than because of a change of heart.

Pope John Paul's international visits began to be seen as "mixed blessings." In Chile in April the pope distressed many in the church by being the first foreign visitor to appear on the balcony of Moneda Palace alongside the president, Gen. Augusto Pinochet Ugarte. But in the National Stadium, where thousands had been held prisoner after the 1973 coup, young people applauded his reference to "this place of pain and suffering in years past."

The pope's next visit was to Argentina, where his reception was equally mixed. On being invited to confess that the church "had not always identified itself with the poor and persecuted," he responded with a call for "reconciliation." He made no mention of Argentina's "dirty war" against subversives in the 1970s. Although he broadly welcomed the return to democracy under the government of Pres. Raúl Alfonsín, the pope denounced proposed legislation on abortion and divorce.

The papal visit to West Germany early in May raised other questions. John Paul beatified (a step toward canonization) Edith Stein, a Jewish convert to Roman Catholicism who became a Carmelite nun as Sister Teresa Benedicta of the Cross and died at Auschwitz. There were objections within the Jewish community on the grounds that Stein had died because of her race and not as a Christian martyr. The pope emphasized that Stein died as a daughter of the Jewish race, and he tried to turn the event into a symbol of Christian-Jewish reconciliation. To some extent he succeeded, as was proved by the presence in Cologne, West Germany, on May 1 of Stein's U.S. relatives. Earlier, a proposal to open a Carmelite convent in Auschwitz had been the cause of controversy since the former death camp is seen by Jews as the site of the *sho'ah*, or Holocaust, and therefore uniquely theirs. The project was abandoned.

More contentious was the state visit of Austrian Pres. Kurt Waldheim to the Vatican on June 25. That the pope should receive a man suspected of involvement in the "final solution" was a cause of great grief to Jews, and for a time it put in jeopardy the pope's meeting with Jewish leaders planned for Miami on September 11. In fact, the meeting took place without incident, but only after backstage work by Jan Cardinal Willebrands, president of the Vatican's Commission for Christian-Jewish Relations, and an agreement to put the *sho'ah* on its agenda in the future.

Even the pope's visit to his Polish homeland in June was not an unalloyed triumph. It was made possible by a meeting between the pope and Gen. Wojciech Jaruzelski at the Vatican early in January. It was expected that the pope would give his support to Jaruzelski in exchange for being allowed to visit Gdansk, home of the now illegal Solidarity trade union movement. The pope went there and delivered a lament for Solidarity. A bemused Jaruzelski said at the airport: "You take away an image of Poland in your heart, Holy Father, but you leave us with all the problems."

The visit to the U.S., which took place September 10–19, was completely different. For the first time, the pope was obliged to listen and watch videos as well as speak. There was a distinct gap between the experience-based presentations that he heard and his own Rome-prepared replies, which seemed rather abstract and academic. There was much talk in advance of his visit about the "feisty dissidents" in the U.S. church and of "cafeteria Catholicism" (which picks and chooses). But in fact the clash was not with obvious dissidents so much as with bishops, priests, sisters, and lay workers who did much of the work of the church in the U.S. (See *Introduction,* above.)

(*See* WORLD AFFAIRS [Western Europe]: *Vatican City State.*)

(PETER HEBBLETHWAITE)

## THE ORTHODOX CHURCH

Throughout 1987 ecumenical patriarch Dimitrios of Constantinople was paying visits to heads of other autocephalous (independent) Orthodox churches. In December he paid a five-day visit to the Vatican and held talks with Pope John Paul II. In the past, travels by the patriarch had been viewed unfavourably by the Turkish government. These trips, together with the recently reported approval for reconstruction of the Patriarchate's buildings in Istanbul, seemed to indicate a more tolerant attitude toward the international position of Dimitrios I as "first among equal" Orthodox patriarchs. Perhaps most significant was his visit to the Russian and Georgian churches in August. It was anticipated that the personal contacts achieved during the trip would facilitate the solution of problems on the agenda of the committee in charge of preparing a future "Holy and Great Council." This agenda included a discussion of the procedure for establishing new independent Orthodox churches and the question of overlapping national jurisdictions in Europe, Australia, and—particularly—the U.S.

Further contacts were anticipated on the occasion of the celebration in June 1988 of the millennium of Russian Christianity in Moscow. All heads of Orthodox autocephalous churches, including Patriarch

Dimitrios, were expected to attend. The Soviet government made some gestures favouring believers, including the liberation of such prominent religious dissidents as Father Gleb Yakunin (who was also restored to his priestly functions) and the poet Irina Ratushinskaya (*see* BIOGRAPHIES).

In Greece massive demonstrations took place, particularly in Thessaloniki and Patras, in support of the church's protests against measures related to church property and administration presented to Parliament. The government proposed to take over the vast areas of land owned by the church and to place the management of parish affairs in the hands of lay committees. A compromise was reached on the first proposal that allowed the church to retain its lands in urban areas, while the second proposal was dropped.

A new Greek patriarch of Alexandria, Egypt—second in rank among Orthodox patriarchs—was elected on March 8 in the person of Parthenios III. Earlier (Nov. 16, 1986), the metropolitan of Moldavia, Teoktist, was enthroned as patriarch of Romania. The internationally respected archbishop of Finland, Paul, resigned for reasons of health. On June 7 a lay theologian, John Zizioulas, was consecrated bishop in Istanbul. In North America Tikhon Fitzgerald and Serafim Storheim, both of whom came to the Orthodox Church as adults, were consecrated bishops of San Francisco and Edmonton, Alta., respectively, by Metropolitan Theodosius, head of the Orthodox Church in America. The trend that these consecrations represented was also strengthened by the acceptance into the Orthodox Church of a group of several hundred former "Evangelicals" who had established, on their own initiative, an "Evangelical Orthodox Church." The leaders of the group were ordained priests by Archbishop Philip Saliba, who belonged to the jurisdiction of the patriarch of Antioch. The group was to be known as the Antiochian Orthodox Mission.

(JOHN MEYENDORFF)

## EASTERN NON-CHALCEDONIAN CHURCHES

The life of the churches in the Middle East was dominated by concerns for survival in an environment dominated by a resurgence of Islam. In an interview published in the Egyptian newspaper *Al Akhbar,* Patriarch Shenuda III of the Coptic Church expressed no hostility toward an eventual adoption of Islamic law in Egypt, as demanded by conservative Muslims, but noted that, if understood properly, this law would recognize particular rights of the "People of the Book," as Christians are called in the Qur'an. In an interview given to a Greek Orthodox newspaper, Shenuda III expressed the view that "the hour is coming" for formal unity to be reestablished between his church and the (Chalcedonian) Orthodox world.

Equally positive hopes seemed to have resulted from discussions between Syrian (Jacobite) and Orthodox representatives in Damascus. The Orthodox patriarch Ignatius IV offered to "reestablish communion" to the Syrian patriarch Ignatius Zakka. The Armenian "Eastern" Diocese of the Armenian Church officially petitioned the catholicos—head of the church residing in Echmiadzin (Soviet Armenia)—to authorize the ordination of women as deacons. (JOHN MEYENDORFF)

## JUDAISM

The vitality of Orthodox Judaism in the State of Israel came to public view in the statistic (*Jerusalem Post,* March 7, 1987) that approximately 5–7% of the nation's young men of military age chose to spend full time in yeshivas—academies for religious sciences—in study of the Torah rather than enter the Army as part of universal military training. As many as 16,000 draft-age men received military deferment in 1986, and more than twice that number briefly left the yeshiva, undertook military training for a few months, and then returned. Thus, in a population of less than four million Jews, the equivalent of a divi-

AFP PHOTO

Rabbi Isaac Neumann (centre) of the U.S. stands with two cantors. All carry sacred scrolls of the Torah to officially reopen the synagogue in East Berlin. Neumann, the first rabbi appointed in East Berlin in 22 years, was to preside over the synagogue.

sion of troops was exempted from military service, and the counterpart of another two divisions received only minimal training, all in the interest of study of the Torah. By comparison, out of seven million Jews in Eastern Europe before 1939, not more than 10,000 young men were in yeshivas at any one time.

The tension between conflicting Judaisms, Reform and Orthodox, was illustrated by a confrontation that took place in Jerusalem in 1986 when an Orthodox (state-supported) rabbi disrupted the worship services of a Reform synagogue. The occasion was the celebration of the Rejoicing of the Torah (Simhat Torah), at the end of the Festival of Tabernacles (Sukkoth). At that time it is customary to take the Torah-scrolls from the holy ark and conduct a ceremonial dance with and about them. On the eve of the festival, 150 worshipers, men and women, engaged in the ritual dances. The Orthodox rabbi of the neighbourhood, Eliahu Abergil, and some score of followers disrupted the services, maintaining that, because women participated along with men, the synagogue worshipers were "sinful" and the synagogue was "a house of prostitution" (*Moment Magazine,* March 1987). The rabbi and his group tried to remove the scrolls from the synagogue, and a riot ensued.

Subsequently, Rabbi Levi Kelman, the rabbi of the synagogue, filed charges against Rabbi Abergil for attempting to steal the Torahs and incitement to violence. The Sephardi (Oriental) chief rabbi of the State of Israel, Mordechai Eliahu, issued a statement to the effect that it is perfectly legitimate to disrupt a Reform worship service because it is a perversion of Judaism, and the Ashkenazi (European) chief rabbi took the same position. Rabbi Abergil, however, issued a letter of apology, Rabbi Kelman dropped the charges, and the two rabbis embraced.

The incident, highlighting the divisions in Judaic religious life, also demonstrated the vitality of religious feeling and commitment among contemporary Jews. It underlined the importance of the efforts of Rabbi Yitz Greenberg, organizer of CLAL, the National Jewish Center for Learning and Leadership, aimed at establishing the basis for reconciliation and unity among Jews who differ. In an address reported in the *Baltimore* (Md.) *Jewish Times* (Jan. 2, 1987), Greenberg argued for pluralism within Judaism.

The Jewish Theological Seminary of America received a new chancellor, inaugurated in September 1987. Rabbi Ismar Schorsch became the sixth leader of the century-old rabbinical school. Schorsch maintained that Conservative Judaism was vital in holding American Jewry together. "Fragmentation will not occur," he said, "as long as there is a dynamic and self-confident middle position."

A second major personnel development was the resignation of Elie Wiesel as chairman of the U.S. Holocaust Memorial Council. Wiesel resigned "because he felt Holocaust survivors had lost control of the Council's museum project to real estate developers who are contributing large sums to the enterprise," according to Larry Cohler in the *Washington Jewish Week* (Jan. 22, 1987). By year's end, substantial progress in raising funds for the Holocaust

Museum on the Mall in Washington had been made, though a design and plan had yet to achieve final acceptance.

Another important personnel change was the resignation of David Gordis as executive of the American Jewish Committee. No public policy issues were cited to explain Gordis's departure, which was brought about by differences between him and the board of directors and members of the committee's long-term senior staff. Bertram Gold, a retired executive, became interim director.

Relations with the Roman Catholic Church underwent some strain during the year, notably with regard to the state visit to the Vatican by Austrian Pres. Kurt Waldheim, suspected of having helped the Nazis during the Holocaust. (See *Roman Catholic Church,* above.)

(JACOB NEUSNER)

## BUDDHISM

One of the most dramatic developments in the Buddhist world during 1987 was the religion's role in the antigovernment protests that rocked South Korea throughout the year. Among Buddhists, especially Buddhist monks, the protest focused on the controversial government management of Buddhist temples and brought to the surface lingering resentment over the military persecution of Korean Buddhism in October 1980. (*See* WORLD AFFAIRS [East Asia]: *Korea.*) In 1986 the Korean Buddhist organizations of North America had issued a joint declaration denouncing the Korean government's oppression of Buddhism.

In strife-ridden Sri Lanka nationalist sentiment ran high among Sinhalese Buddhists. In July and August riots and demonstrations were widespread among the Sinhalese, protesting the Indian-enforced peace accord with the non-Buddhist Tamils signed July 29. These protests were often led by Buddhist monks, who figured prominently among those arrested and among the casualties. (*See* WORLD AFFAIRS [South Asia]: *Sri Lanka.*)

In April Chinese archaeologists announced that two brown pellets discovered near Beijing (Peking) in 1981 are bodily relics of the Buddha. The relics were placed on public display at the headquarters of the Chinese Buddhist Association there, further encouraging the hopes of long-persecuted Buddhists in China and Tibet that the recent restoration of Buddhism would continue. However, the Dalai Lama remained in exile, and the Chinese government accused him of instigating the violent pro-independence demonstrations that rocked Lhasa in September.

Two major leaders among Tibetan Buddhists in the West died in 1987. Dudjom Rimpoche, supreme leader of the Nyingmapa (Rnying-ma-pa) School of Tibetan Buddhism, died in France in January. In April Chogyam Trungpa Rimpoche, founder of the Naropa Institute, Boulder, Colo., and the Dharmadhatu movement, died in Canada. A two-year-old Spanish boy, Osel Hita, was ordained as the world's youngest lama in March after being recognized as the reincarnation of Thubten Yeshe Rimpoche, who had died in California three years earlier.

Three important conferences on Buddhism were held at Berkeley, Calif., in August: the annual conference of the Inter-

national Association of Buddhist Studies, the annual meeting of the International Association of Shin Studies, and a conference in a continuing series devoted to Buddhist-Christian dialogue. The Conference on World Buddhism in North America, held in Ann Arbor, Mich., in July, issued a "Statement of Consensus" affirming the growing unity among Buddhists throughout the world. The World Fellowship of Buddhists held its 15th General Conference in November and December 1986 in Kathmandu, Nepal.

(FRANK E. REYNOLDS;
JONATHAN S. WALTERS)

## HINDUISM

The often bloody conflict between Hindus and Sikhs in India that had raged for a number of years worsened in 1987. Sikh terrorism, formerly confined largely to attacks on politically prominent individuals, took the form of indiscriminate attacks on the Hindu populace and spread beyond the Punjab, where the majority of India's 16 million Sikhs live. The death toll rose to more than 700 by late summer, compared with 60 in 1985, and prospects for an end to the bloodshed appeared bleak. (*See* WORLD AFFAIRS [South Asia]: *India.*)

Internal divisiveness continued to afflict Hinduism during 1987, as did communal conflict with Muslims. An especially ugly expression of the age-old tension between castes took place in the Aurangabad district of Bihar state. On May 29 Yadavs brutally murdered some 54 Rajput men and women. Although inferior to Rajputs in caste ranking, the Yadavs in recent times had become middle-level farmers, like the Rajputs, and thus were in competition with them. Less violent but also expressive of tension within the caste structure was a riot in Rajasthan on July 1 when leaders of Harijans ("untouchables") defiantly entered the important Shree Nathaji temple at Nathdwara. Although they had a constitutional right to enter the temple, Harijans were still commonly regarded as ritually impure.

The city of Meerut in Uttar Pradesh, which saw bloody Hindu-Muslim riots in 1982, was the scene of communal violence again in May. An attempt by police to arrest a Muslim for the murder of a Hindu in a land dispute exploded into ten days of mayhem that left over 150, mostly Muslims, dead. The Meerut violence sparked riots in Gujarat, Uttar Pradesh, and Delhi throughout the summer. Insinuated into the conflict was the Muslim demand that a mosque at Ayodhya, Rajasthan, given to Hindus by court order in 1986 as a shrine marking the birthplace of the deity Rama, be returned. Half a million Hindus, only one-quarter of the expected turnout, celebrated the Rama Navami festival at Ayodhya on April 7.

In Andhra Pradesh the thousand-year-old practice of dedicating women to the service of a temple deity was terminated by law. The Devadasi ("Handmaiden of God") abolition bill made it illegal for young women to serve the patron god of a temple according to the ritual practices of the Devadasi caste, which traditionally included temple prostitution. It remained to be seen whether mere legal ordinance would eradicate this calling. Suttee had been banned since 1829, but in Rajasthan in September an 18-year-old Rajput widow immolated herself on her husband's funeral pyre. Despite the arrest of several of her husband's relatives for their part in the affair, the site was thronged with pilgrims.

(H. PATRICK SULLIVAN)

## ISLAM

The increasing violence among Muslims exploded at the end of July during the annual Pilgrimage rites in Mecca. More than 400 people, most of whom were pilgrims, were killed in what was described as an attempt by Shi'ah Muslim extremists, loyal to Ayatollah Ruhollah Khomeini of Iran, to discredit the (Sunni) Saudi government and also Western nations, particularly the U.S. Differing accounts of the incident were offered, but announcements made in both Iran and Saudi Arabia clearly pointed to the growing militancy of some Shi'ah groups and the widening split between these Shi'ahs and the majority Sunni groups represented by the governments of the Arab countries. Shi'ah militancy, evident in many periods of Islamic history, had in recent years been fueled both by Iranian government policies and by the rising fundamentalist tide evident in practically all Muslim countries.

Fundamentalism attracted many lower class groups, but it was led and supported by members of the middle class who opposed westernization and modernization. Thus religious tensions continued both in Egypt, where the Muslim population was overwhelmingly Sunni, and in Bahrain, where Shi'ahs were in a majority. A number of Shi'ah groups—for example, in Lebanon—were apparently influenced or led by the Iranian government, although it was difficult to be specific. Shi'ah and fundamentalist groups were putting strong pressures on most Muslim Middle Eastern governments. Even Turkey, long declared to be a secular state, experienced fundamentalist demonstrations in Istanbul when, at the beginning of the year, women college students demanded the right to wear head scarves as symbols of Islamic piety. Terrorist groups, difficult to identify, remained active. Within Iran little opposition to the authorities was noted, but rumours continued to circulate that there were tensions within the ruling group, caused in part by Ayatollah Khomeini's deteriorating health. (See WORLD AFFAIRS [Middle East and North Africa]: Iran.)

Elsewhere, governing authorities had to contend with violence between Muslims and non-Muslims. In March, fighting erupted in southern Egypt between Muslims and Christians. Communal violence flared in India; in Meerut and Delhi, for example, clashes between Hindus and Muslims in May resulted in the deaths of more than 150 persons. (See Hinduism, above.) Violence in Nigeria between Christians and Muslims, especially in the north, was reported to be the worst in decades, and in the Philippines, Muslim groups in the south fought the government and each other. (See WORLD AFFAIRS [Southeast Asia]: Philippines.)

Muslim leaders in Indonesia continued to develop a modernizing program for Muslims in that nation, where a national ideology was being promoted in an attempt to bring the country's diverse peoples together. Fundamentalist activities were increasing, however, despite the Muslim leadership's liberalizing stance. In New York City ground was officially broken for a $25 million mosque and cultural centre supported by a number of Muslim nations belonging to the UN.

(REUBEN W. SMITH)

## WORLD RELIGIOUS STATISTICS

The 1987 table below gives details of the global spread of the world's 16 largest faiths or ideologies. It illustrates the articles on the various religions by showing each religion's continental statistics in the overall global context. It also demonstrates an extraordinary religious development of the 20th century—religious pluralism.

As the right-hand column demonstrates, over 14 major religious systems are each now found in over 80 countries. Christianity, Islam, and the Baha'i World Faith are the most global; agnosticism and atheism are also widespread. Hinduism has recently spread to 88 countries, Buddhism to 86.

This 20th-century spread has brought the religions into contact with each other as never before. Thus we find Filipino Catholics and Korean Protestants in Saudi Arabia, Gujarati Hindus in rural England, Tibetan Tantrists in Wales, Muslim mosques in every capital of Western Europe including Rome. The long-term effects of this mass proximity are sure to be profound. They are certainly resulting in unprecedented interest in other people's religions, expressed in seminars, courses, discussion, dialogue, tolerance, and even acceptance. (DAVID B. BARRETT)

This article updates the Macropædia articles The Buddha and BUDDHISM; CHRISTIANITY; EASTERN ORTHODOXY; HINDUISM; Muhammad and the Religion of ISLAM; JUDAISM; PROTESTANTISM; The Study and Classification of RELIGIONS; ROMAN CATHOLICISM; and Micropædia entries on the various denominations.

### Adherents of All Religions by Eight Continental Areas, 1987

| | Africa | East Asia | Europe | Latin America | Northern America | Oceania | South Asia | U.S.S.R. | World | % | Countries |
|---|---|---|---|---|---|---|---|---|---|---|---|
| Christians | 271,035,700 | 78,100,000 | 413,920,700 | 395,554,500 | 232,048,400 | 21,287,100 | 129,076,700 | 103,373,400 | 1,644,396,500 | 32.9 | 254 |
| Roman Catholics | 102,522,200 | 9,204,000 | 257,155,000 | 371,863,600 | 91,209,800 | 7,434,000 | 81,694,100 | 5,111,900 | 926,194,600 | 18.5 | 242 |
| Protestants | 71,883,000 | 32,100,000 | 76,652,000 | 13,960,000 | 94,965,500 | 7,510,000 | 26,142,100 | 8,803,800 | 332,016,400 | 6.6 | 230 |
| Orthodox | 24,746,700 | 81,000 | 35,606,100 | 570,000 | 5,910,000 | 507,400 | 3,200,000 | 89,442,300 | 160,063,500 | 3.2 | 98 |
| Anglicans | 22,389,900 | 334,000 | 32,886,200 | 1,210,000 | 7,511,000 | 5,350,000 | 290,000 | 400 | 69,971,500 | 1.4 | 148 |
| Other Christians | 49,493,900 | 36,381,000 | 11,621,400 | 7,950,900 | 32,452,100 | 485,700 | 17,750,500 | 15,000 | 156,150,500 | 3.1 | 110 |
| Muslims | 245,110,500 | 23,795,000 | 8,901,500 | 645,000 | 2,682,600 | 96,000 | 547,350,500 | 31,807,200 | 860,388,300 | 17.2 | 172 |
| Nonreligious | 1,495,000 | 641,756,600 | 50,923,940 | 13,237,000 | 21,047,700 | 2,884,400 | 20,651,100 | 84,332,030 | 836,327,770 | 16.7 | 220 |
| Hindus | 1,410,000 | 10,100 | 590,000 | 660,000 | 810,000 | 295,000 | 651,918,900 | 1,200 | 655,695,200 | 13.1 | 88 |
| Buddhists | 12,800 | 154,796,300 | 216,000 | 490,000 | 190,000 | 16,000 | 153,585,000 | 320,000 | 309,626,100 | 6.2 | 86 |
| Atheists | 240,000 | 136,886,000 | 17,803,000 | 2,538,000 | 1,073,000 | 512,000 | 5,300,000 | 60,774,500 | 225,126,500 | 4.5 | 130 |
| Chinese folk religionists | 9,500 | 179,103,100 | 49,000 | 60,000 | 110,000 | 16,000 | 8,169,400 | 100 | 187,517,100 | 3.7 | 56 |
| New-Religionists | 13,000 | 42,217,200 | 34,000 | 370,000 | 1,075,600 | 6,100 | 66,990,000 | 200 | 110,706,100 | 2.2 | 25 |
| Tribal religionists | 68,219,450 | 730,000 | 100 | 1,160,000 | 60,000 | 81,000 | 24,508,200 | 0 | 94,758,750 | 1.9 | 98 |
| Jews | 257,000 | 1,800 | 1,483,600 | 990,000 | 8,084,000 | 86,000 | 4,050,000 | 3,123,000 | 18,075,400 | 0.4 | 125 |
| Sikhs | 26,000 | 1,000 | 215,000 | 6,000 | 9,500 | 6,600 | 16,340,000 | 50 | 16,604,150 | 0.3 | 20 |
| Shamanists | 1,000 | 12,500,000 | 400 | 400 | 200 | 200 | 10,000 | 250,000 | 12,762,200 | 0.2 | 10 |
| Confucians | 500 | 5,900,000 | 1,000 | 500 | 10,000 | 200 | 2,000 | 200 | 5,914,400 | 0.1 | 3 |
| Baha'is | 1,265,000 | 48,400 | 70,500 | 570,000 | 310,000 | 59,000 | 2,300,000 | 5,000 | 4,627,900 | 0.1 | 205 |
| Jains | 47,500 | 500 | 9,900 | 2,000 | 2,000 | 900 | 3,400,000 | 20 | 3,462,820 | 0.1 | 10 |
| Shintoists | 50 | 3,400,000 | 360 | 800 | 1,000 | 500 | 200 | 100 | 3,403,010 | 0.1 | 3 |
| Other religionists | 65,000 | 62,000 | 310,000 | 6,768,800 | 750,000 | 25,000 | 230,000 | 6,000 | 8,216,800 | 0.2 | 170 |
| **Total Population** | **589,208,000** | **1,279,308,000** | **494,529,000** | **423,053,000** | **268,264,000** | **25,372,000** | **1,633,882,000** | **283,993,000** | **4,997,609,000** | **100.0** | **254** |

NOTES:

**Continents.** UN demographic practice divides the world into eight continental areas as shown above (see United Nations, World Population Prospects, New York, 1986, with populations of all countries covering the period 1950–2025).
**Countries.** The last column enumerates sovereign and nonsovereign countries in which each religion has a significant following.
**Rows.** The list of religions is arranged by descending order of magnitude of global adherents in 1987 (last two columns but one).
**Adherents.** As defined and enumerated for each of the world's countries in World Christian Encyclopedia (1982), projected to mid-1987.
**Christians.** Followers of Jesus Christ affiliated to churches (church members, including children), plus persons professing in censuses or polls though not so affiliated.
**Other Christians.** Catholics (non-Roman), marginal Protestants, crypto-Christians, and adherents of African, Asian, Black, and Latin-American indigenous churches.
**Muslims.** 83% Sunnis, 16% Shi'ahs, 1% other schools.
**Nonreligious.** Persons professing no religion, nonbelievers, agnostics, freethinkers, dereligionized secularists indifferent to all religion.
**Hindus.** 70% Vaishnavites, 25% Shaivites, 2% neo-Hindus and reform Hindus.
**Buddhists.** 56% Mahayana, 38% Theravada, 6% Tantrism.
**Atheists.** Persons professing atheism, skepticism, disbelief, or irreligion, including antireligious (opposed to all religion).
**Chinese folk religionists.** Followers of traditional Chinese religion (local deities, ancestor veneration, Confucian ethics, Taoism, universism, divination, some Buddhist elements).
**New-Religionists.** Followers of Asiatic 20th-century New Religions, New Religious movements, radical new crisis religions, and non-Christian syncretistic mass religions, all founded since 1800 and mostly since 1945.
**Jews.** 84% Ashkenazim, 10% Orientals, 4% Sephardim.
**Confucians.** Non-Chinese followers of Confucius and Confucianism, mostly Koreans in Korea.
**Other religionists.** Including 50 minor world religions and a large number of spiritist religions, New Age religions, quasi religions, pseudoreligions, parareligions, religious systems, mystic systems, religious and semireligious brotherhoods of numerous varieties.
**Total Population.** UN medium variant figures for mid-1987, as given in World Population Prospects (1986), pages 72–77.

(DAVID B. BARRETT)

# Social Security and Welfare Services

During 1987 many countries continued to search for ways to improve the effectiveness of social security systems while strengthening their financial base. Despite continuing economic constraints, a number of countries were able to improve and even expand programs.

**National Developments in Social Security.** Major reviews of social security were conducted during the year in France and Australia, and in-depth reviews focusing primarily on pensions were undertaken in several other industrialized countries, including Norway, the U.S.S.R., Hungary, and Yugoslavia. In France the large deficit in social security funding anticipated for 1987 prompted the government to appoint a committee of "wise men" to propose measures for solving the financial crisis. Meanwhile, measures taken in May increased workers' contributions to the old-age and health insurance programs, generated income for the social security system through various taxes, and returned financial responsibility for local outpatient psychiatric care to the state.

In Australia the social security review, originally scheduled for completion in 1987, was extended. It was undertaken because major socioeconomic changes in Australian society—for example, the increase in the number of single parents and the aging of the population—required new responses. The review focused on three parts of the system: income support for families with children, social security and labour force issues (primarily unemployment), and income support for the aged, especially the relationship between public and private occupational pensions. In October the government introduced income-testing of family allowances for high-income families. As part of a "family package" in December, supplementary benefits for families were revised to provide a higher level of assistance to a greater number of families with children.

The effort to make programs more effective while restraining costs was exemplified by a reform in The Netherlands. From January 1 the unemployment scheme was completely reorganized. The new program emphasized unemployment insurance, whereas the previous system had been based on a combination of unemployment insurance and assistance. For the long-term unemployed, the new system could provide benefits for a longer period than both the previous schemes combined. However, the duration of benefits was linked to the length of previous employment, and the requirements were made more stringent. Benefits were payable at the rate of 70% of last wages, up to a ceiling, for a period of six months. They could be extended, however, for up to five years, depending on the length of completed or presumed previous employment. Benefits were also payable in cases of partial unemployment. The flat-rate unemployment assistance benefit became payable only as a supplementary benefit to persons aged 50 and over who had exhausted their unemployment insurance or to those with permanent partial disability.

The age at which pensions were granted continued to be of great interest in many countries, although the motivations for change and the measures taken varied. In Luxembourg legislation effective in April established two new types of preretirement pensions: solidarity preretirement pensions and adjustment preretirement pensions. The scheme covered certain workers who at age 57 became entitled to an old-age pension within three years. The solidarity preretirement pension was in most cases paid by the employer, while the adjustment preretirement pension, granted in cases where workers were laid off, was totally paid by the unemployment fund. In both cases the benefit was initially calculated as 95% of gross monthly salary during the first year. It declined to 80% and then to 70% in the second and third years, respectively.

In Belgium the need to reduce costs influenced the decision to eliminate the possibility of receiving an early retirement pension before age 60. Effective January 1, the measure applied only to women because of the difference in the statutory retirement age for women and men (60 and 65, respectively). Thus, men still had the option of receiving a pension up to five years early. Also effective from the beginning of the year, flexibility in pension age was introduced into the Canada Pension Plan. While the normal pensionable age remained at 65, an insured person could retire at age 60 at the earliest or delay retirement until age 70. Benefits were either increased or decreased by a monthly factor of 0.5%, up to a maximum of 30%. The early retirement pension was not granted, however, if income exceeded the maximum retirement pension for that year.

New legislation introduced in the U.S.S.R. would provide additional retirement income for workers. Working persons under retirement age (60 for men and 55 for women) could voluntarily choose the supplementary amount (up to a limit) they wished to receive over and above the existing old-age pension. Their contributions to the new insurance scheme were based on the amount of the supplement chosen. The new supplementary pension insurance required a minimum of five years of contributions, but the insurance could be taken out at retirement age provided the person continued to work for an additional five years.

In several less developed countries social protection was provided in the form of a provident fund, an obligatory savings plan financed from employer and employee contributions. In Singapore, where the Central Provident Fund (CPF) covered most employed persons, a new provision effective from April allowed children to make contributions to their parents' CPF account. The contribution could be made after the parent reached age 55—either as a lump sum or in installments—up to a maximum. Alternatively, a child could transfer amounts from his or her own CPF account into that of the parents, as long as a specified minimum was maintained in the child's account. The children's contributions could be withdrawn only after the parent reached 60 years of age.

Alongside the provident fund that existed for employed persons, Sri Lanka instituted in March a social security program for certain agricultural workers. The plan, which provided old-age, disability, and survivor benefits, was open to small-scale subsistence farmers on a voluntary basis. It was being financed from insured persons' contributions and, in addition, was to receive a state subsidy for ten years. Eligible farmers aged 18 to 59 were to make twice-yearly contributions. The old-age benefit was payable at age 60, in two installments. If an insured person became disabled before pension age, either a lump-sum benefit or a pension could be chosen. In the event of the death of an insured person, a death benefit was paid to the surviving spouse or other eligible family members. The amount of the benefit was calculated according to the length of the contribution period, amount of contributions paid, and age of the insured person.

Important developments in the area of maternity benefits occurred in Switzerland and the U.K. In March the Swiss Parliament approved an act to establish maternity allowances. This new benefit was to be paid to all women, whether employed or not, provided they were Swiss residents, had lived in Switzerland for at least nine months, and were covered by the old-age insurance scheme. The daily allowance was payable for a total of 16 weeks. The minimum allowance was paid to women not in paid employment or whose income was below a specified level. Women earning above this level received 75% of their earnings up to a maximum. The new allowance was financed by an additional contribution of 0.4% of income, to be split equally between employers and employees.

In the U.K. in April, a new benefit, statutory maternity pay, replaced the scheme previously run by the Department of Employment and the maternity allowance administered by the Department of Health and Social Security; the latter, however, would continue to be paid to those who did not qualify for the new benefit. Statutory maternity pay was paid by employers, who recovered the payments by deducting them from National Insurance contributions. The benefit was payable for up to 18 weeks, beginning 11 to 6 weeks before the expected date of birth. The amount was paid at two levels, depending on length of service with the employer. The object of this change, which was part of the Social Security Act of 1986, was to give women more flexibility in deciding when to stop work prior to childbirth and to direct maternity pay more toward working women.

Most industrialized countries remained concerned with the rising cost of health care benefits, but no obvious solutions were found. Developments in 1987 were somewhat contradictory. For example, in France the approach was to tighten the list of diseases exempt from patient cost-sharing and to increase cost-sharing for some pharmaceutical products, while in Italy cost-sharing on laboratory tests was eliminated and the copayment on drugs was reduced.

(LYNN VILLACORTA)

In the U.S. a year that began with a clear consensus for sweeping change in the welfare system ended with reform stalled in Congress and the outlook clouded by budget constraints and political and philosophical disagreements. In his state of the union address in January, Pres. Ronald Reagan said that "this is the time to reform this outmoded social dinosaur." The National Governors' Association devoted virtually its entire midwinter meeting in February to welfare reform, and Democrats introduced comprehensive reform bills in both houses of Congress.

The heart of the Democratic measures was the creation by states of mandatory education, work, and training programs designed to help welfare recipients find jobs in the private sector. The bills also guaranteed day care and continued health benefits for welfare recipients who took part in work and training programs, and they extended benefits to poor households where both parents were unemployed, thus permitting fathers to remain with their families. Efforts to force absent fathers to pay child support would be strengthened, and states would be given broad authority to experiment with new approaches to welfare. The Senate legislation, sponsored by Sen. Daniel Patrick Moynihan (Dem., N.Y.), was expected to add $2,720,000,000 in welfare spending over the next five years, while the House proposal, which included provisions encouraging states to raise benefits, would add $5.3 billion. Republicans in the House introduced their own less costly and less comprehensive version of reform, which was backed by the White House. Meanwhile, New Jersey became the first state to get a federal waiver so that it could begin one of the most sweeping overhauls of welfare in the nation. The program would require nearly all able-bodied welfare recipients to accept job training and seek full-time employment.

A comprehensive portrait of the U.S. welfare population was furnished in a study published in 1987, conducted by William P. O'Hare, director of policy studies at the Population Reference Bureau, a private educational organization. O'Hare reported that 47% of U.S. households had one or more members who received some type of government assistance in 1984, but only 19% actually got "welfare"; i.e., benefits paid to needy persons enrolled in specific means-tested programs. Most government spending on social programs went for Social Security, Medicare, unemployment insurance, and other assistance distributed without regard to the recipient's income or assets. Welfare typically served low-income families with children, the disabled, and the needy elderly and accounted for 11% of the annual federal budget, according to O'Hare. Although it was not the largest program, the heart of the welfare system was Aid to Families with Dependent Children (AFDC), which benefited about 3.8 million families, including 7.3 million children, at an annual cost of roughly $15 billion, about half of which was paid by the federal government.

Other findings in O'Hare's study were that welfare benefits usually came not in the form of cash but as services like medical care, subsidized housing, or food stamps. The welfare population totaled 48 million in 1986. Those most likely to go on welfare were female heads of households, blacks, Hispanics, and persons under 25. The main reason people turned to welfare was to get through a crisis, such as divorce, an out-of-wedlock birth, or a decline in income. Most recipients remained on welfare only a few months or years, but a "significant minority" were there for long periods. In 1986, 13.6% of the U.S. population, or 32,370,-000 people, lived at or below the poverty level, ($11,203 cash income for a family of four). When poverty was first measured in 1960, 22.2% of Americans were poor. The proportion dropped to an all-time low of 11.1% in 1973 and subsequently ranged from about 11 to slightly over 15%. At least 40% of the people with incomes below the poverty level did not receive welfare benefits.

The House and Senate did pass separate versions of a landmark "catastrophic" health care measure that authorized the biggest expansion of coverage for Medicare's 32 million elderly and disabled beneficiaries since the program was enacted in 1965. It set limits on the maximum amount a Medicare patient would have to pay in health care costs and, for the first time, included broad coverage of outpatient prescription drugs. Final action on the measure had not yet been taken at year's end.

The nation's 38 million Social Security recipients would get a boost in benefits in 1988, the biggest since July 1982. A 4.2% cost-of-living increase would raise the average individual's Social Security check from $492 a month to $513. For couples, the average check would rise $35, to $876 a month. Social Security taxes also would go up in 1988. The payroll tax rate would rise from 7.15 to 7.51%, the first rate hike in two years, and the maximum amount of wages subject to the tax would increase to $45,000 from $43,800. This meant that an employee earning the maximum or more would pay $3,379.50 in 1988, an increase of $247.80 from the 1987 maximum. The employers' matching contributions would rise correspondingly. The Social Security old-age and disability insurance trust funds reached an all-time high combined balance of $49.9 billion in January 1987. The total was expected to grow to $247 billion by the end of 1991 and continue expanding until 2032 as the "baby-boom" generation paid taxes into the system.

(DAVID M. MAZIE)

*See also* Education; Health and Disease; Industrial Review: *Insurance.*

This article updates the *Macropædia* article SOCIAL WELFARE.

# Space Exploration

The Soviet Union continued to forge ahead in space during 1987 with its first launch of the world's most powerful rocket launcher and expanded operations aboard the Mir space station. U.S. preparations for the next launch of the space shuttle continued, and the space station program moved slowly under the threat of budget cuts.

Looking to the future, the U.S. National Aeronautics and Space Administration (NASA) established an office of exploration to analyze and define missions that would expand the human race beyond its home planet, according to agency officials. Formation of the office was recommended during a study on future space goals led by astronaut Sally Ride, who left NASA in August. That study, "Leadership and America's Future in Space," clearly stated that the U.S. lead in space had been lost in manned flight and was about to be lost in planetary flight. It outlined four major categories of missions that could be undertaken to reestablish U.S. leadership and to advance space technology on a number of fronts. They included a "mission to planet Earth" to understand the environment better, unmanned exploration of the solar system, a manned base on the Moon, and manned "sprint" flights to Mars.

**Launchers.** The Soviet Union launched the new Energia superbooster on May 15, giving that nation the world's most powerful space launcher. Energia stood almost 60 m (200 ft) tall and had four large strap-on boosters clustered around an 8-m (26-ft)-wide second stage. A large payload carrier was mounted on one side. Thrust at lift-off was about 3 million kg (6.6 million lb), and the payload into low-Earth orbit could weigh 100,000 to 135,000 kg (220,-000 to 300,000 lb). These figures compared favourably with the discontinued U.S. Saturn V Moon rocket (3.4 million and 114,000 kg, respectively). Because of an autopilot problem, the dummy payload did not go into the planned orbit, delaying the second flight until 1988. It was expected that the Soviet space shuttle would be launched by the Energia booster.

In response, NASA initiated advanced studies of an unmanned cargo version of the space shuttle (Shuttle-C), which could launch 45,500 to 70,000 kg (100,000 to 150,-000 lb) into low-Earth orbit. The U.S. Air Force also awarded seven study contracts for looking into an advanced launch system. It started this without consulting NASA, creating a rift between the two agencies. The Air Force and NASA awarded several contracts for refining the design of the X-30, a small forerunner of the National Aerospace Plane that would be able to take off from an airfield and fly into space or around the Earth.

The U.S.S.R. experienced launch mishaps, on January 30 and April 24, with its Proton heavy-lift vehicle. Soviet officials said that the failures were caused by problems in an experimental fourth stage that is not used in the commercial version of the Proton.

Two accidents marred the effort of the U.S. to recover from the accidents in 1986. An Atlas Centaur booster rocket carrying a U.S. Navy communications satellite was destroyed by lightning when it was launched through a thunderstorm on March 26. A replacement launch had to be canceled on July 13 when a handling accident on the launchpad crumpled the last Centaur upper stage that was then available. An investigation board blamed poor procedures and human error.

Other U.S. launch attempts were more successful. A Titan 34D, believed to be carrying a KH-11 spy satellite, was launched October 26 from Vandenberg Air Force Base in California. This followed an extensive Titan improvement program to prevent repeats of the failures in 1985 and 1986 that had seriously degraded the U.S. capability to monitor Soviet activities from space. The last of the old Atlas H launchers boosted a U.S. Navy "White Cloud" ocean surveillance satellite into orbit on May 15. Other Atlas vehicles and rehabilitated Titan II ballistic missiles were expected to provide comparable launch capabilities.

Two Deltas were successfully launched, one on February 26 carrying a geosynchronous operational environment satellite (GOES-H) delayed from 1986 and another on March 19 carrying a Palapa B-2 communications satellite for Indonesia. McDonnell Douglas Astronautics Corp. was awarded a U.S. Air Force contract for building an advanced Delta II as a new "medium launch vehicle" (MLV).

The European Space Agency also recovered from failure with the launch September 15 of an Ariane following the redesign of its third-stage engine, which had caused an accident in 1986. The Ariane V19 vehicle carried two communications satellites. Ariane V20 was launched successfully on November 20, but the communications satellite it carried encountered initial difficulties.

The only nation with a perfect launch record, Japan, inaugurated its H-1 vehicle, a derivative of the U.S. Delta, on August 20. It carried an electronics test satellite (ETS-5) to provide technologies for later spacecraft.

**Science Satellites.** Few science spacecraft were launched during the year. One of the most ambitious was the U.S.S.R.'s Cosmos 1887, which carried two rhesus monkeys, Yerosha and Dryoma, into orbit on September 29 and returned, 3,200 km (2,000 mi) off target, on October 12. Cosmos 1887 also carried U.S. experiments with human cell specimens. During the flight Yerosha freed its left paw and was reported by Soviet ground controllers to be "probing with great curiosity" anything within reach inside its sealed chamber.

On July 25 the U.S.S.R. launched Cosmos 1870, at 15 to 20 tons the largest Earth-observation satellite and apparently the first such civilian effort by the Soviets. Japan orbited two, the ASTRO-C X-ray astronomy satellite on February 5 and the large Momo-1 (Peach) maritime observations satellite for remote sensing of the ocean. China launched its China 20 satellite on August 5 aboard a Long March II rocket and recovered it on August 10. The spacecraft reportedly held Chinese and French materials science experiments conducted under weightlessness.

Several spacecraft originally intended for launch aboard the U.S. space shuttle underwent major redesigns so that they could be placed atop expendable launch vehicles and not suffer further delays. These included the U.S. Cosmic Background Explorer and Extreme Ultraviolet Explorer and the West German-U.S. Roentgensatellit.

The Hubble Space Telescope, which could be launched only by the space shuttle, underwent extensive testing that revealed some flaws and that would help shorten the orbital test period. After another series of tests in early 1988, the telescope was to be placed in storage until a few months before launch in mid-1989. Launch of the U.S. Mars Observer spacecraft was delayed two years until 1992 over protests by the science community. This craft was to map the chemistry of the Martian surface. The Soviets, meanwhile, continued to develop an ambitious unmanned probe to orbit Mars and to sample the surface of its larger moon, Phobos. Japan announced preliminary plans for a spacecraft that was scheduled to be launched in 1990 and make several swings past the Moon. NASA selected scientists for its Comet Rendezvous/Asteroid Flyby mission that would be launched in the 1990s. The Jet Propulsion

Soviet cosmonaut Aleksandr Laveikin (left) smiles bravely with his comrades Aleksandr Viktorenko (centre) and Muhammad Faris after they landed their Soyuz TM-3. Because of heart problems, Laveikin was forced to shorten his mission on the orbiter Mir.

Laboratory awarded four contracts for preliminary design of vehicles that would land on Mars, rove across its surface, and then return to Earth with samples of Martian soil.

Pioneer 12, orbiting Venus, observed Comet Wilson during March and April, and Voyager 2 fired its thrusters for 70 minutes to bring its trajectory to within 5,000 km (3,100 mi) of the north pole of Neptune in 1989. And Pioneer 9, one of the first interplanetary probes, was declared dead on March 3 after engineers could not raise a signal despite intense transmissions. It was launched in 1968 and had last been heard from in May 1983.

**Space Stations.** The Soviets continued to be the only nation with men in space during the year. On February 6 the Soyuz TM-2 spacecraft was launched carrying cosmonauts Yury Romanenko and Aleksandr Laveikin to the Mir space station. From the outset it appeared that they were trying to set a new record for manned endurance in space. At least five Progress resupply missions were launched to Mir during the year, and on April 5 the Kvant astrophysics module was launched. Although the first docking attempt failed, on April 9 the module was successfully docked to the space station. This gave the crew the capability to perform X-ray and ultraviolet astronomy observations.

The Soyuz TM-3 spacecraft on July 23 carried cosmonauts Aleksandr Aleksandrov, Aleksandr Viktorenko, and Muhammad Faris of Syria to Mir. Because Laveikin was experiencing heart problems, he was replaced by Aleksandrov when the crew returned to Earth. In September Romanenko passed the previous endurance record, set by the Soviets, of 237 days in orbit. On December 21 the U.S.S.R. launched Vladimir Titov, Musa Manarov, and Anatoly Levchenko to replace Romanenko and Aleksandrov.

The U.S. space station program inched toward reality as it moved through the final phases of its design competition. On December 1 NASA announced the awarding of contracts for the four packages comprising the program. General Electric and Rocketdyne Division of Rockwell were the winners for building the unmanned platforms and power system, respectively, other competitors for those two packages having withdrawn. Boeing Aerospace was chosen over Martin Marietta Aerospace for the core module, life-support system, and lab module outfitting, and McDonnell Douglas Astronautics won out over Rockwell International for the crew module outfitting and main structure. The design of the station was reduced during the year as a result of analyses that showed the cost would exceed $30 billion for the complete craft. U.S. Pres. Ronald Reagan ordered that development of the upper and lower payload platforms and the advanced solar power system be deferred until the next administration. Even so, the National Research Council questioned NASA's cost estimates, and Sen. William Proxmire (Dem., Wis.) led a strong fight to cancel the program. Only innovative accounting by space supporters allowed the Senate to find sufficient funding to continue the program.

**Space Shuttle.** Recovery of the U.S. space shuttle program moved ahead well, although the first launch since the *Challenger* accident was delayed again, from February to June 1988. In December NASA announced that the boot ring of the shuttle's booster rocket had failed during an apparently successful test firing. This ring is part of an assembly that is essential for maneuvering the rocket. As a result of the failure the first shuttle launch was postponed again, until late 1988.

The crew for the first mission, STS-26, was named early in the year. Veterans made up the five-man team that would fly space shuttle *Discovery* and deploy a Tracking and Data Relay Satellite identical to the one lost aboard *Challenger* in 1986. They were commander Frederick Hauck, pilot Richard Covey, and mission specialists George Nelson, David Hilmers, and John Lounge. The new crew participated in a 54-hour mission simulation in May, marking the resumption of intense training for space missions. *Discovery* was "powered up" for tests at Kennedy Space Center in Florida, and a countdown demonstration test was also held with space shuttle *Atlantis*. Production started on the replacement for *Challenger*, now known as Orbiter 105. Its name was to be selected from among suggestions to be submitted by U.S. schoolchildren in 1987.

Two full-scale rocket motors were test-fired on May 27 and August 30. A heavily instrumented motor almost identical to the one involved in the *Challenger* accident was used in the first in an effort to provide more data on the old joint design that caused the hot gas leak. The second incorporated redesigned joints and triple O-rings (instead of double). After several aborted countdowns, the motor roared to life in the Utah hills and proved the basic concept of the redesign.

Components of the boosters for STS-26 started arriving at the Kennedy Space Center in the fall and were to be stacked in January, with the vehicle being rolled to the launchpad in March. Acceptance testing began on the three main engines that would power *Discovery* on its flight, but a leak developed inside one engine and threatened to delay delivery of the engines and, thus, the launch.

Work proceeded on other safety measures. The orbiter hatch was modified so that it could be blown off to allow the crew to bail out with extraction rockets before a water landing. However, it would not protect them in case of a *Challenger*-type accident. Space shuttle *Enterprise*, the nonspace forerunner of the orbiters, was towed through safety nets and arresting wires at Dulles International Airport, Chantilly, Va., in a study of emergency landings.

During the year two U.S. firms, General Motors and General Electric, urged the U.S. government to withdraw its ban on the launching of U.S.-made satellites by Soviet rockets. Government officials responded that commercial considerations should not override issues of foreign policy and national security. (DAVID DOOLING)

*See also* Astronomy; Earth Sciences; Industrial Review: *Aerospace; Telecommunications;* Military Affairs; Television and Radio.

This article updates the *Macropædia* article EXPLORATION: *Space Exploration.*

# Sports and Games

## AERIAL SPORTS

Two British industrialists made aerial sports history in 1987 with the world's first hot-air balloon flight across the Atlantic. In July the Fédération Aéronautique Internationale (FAI)—the world's official record-keeping body for aerial achievements—validated the flight as a distance record for such a craft. The balloon traveled 4,512 km (2,803.7 mi). Helium balloons had made crossings of the Atlantic in recent years, but the previous distance record for hot-air balloons was only 1,471.2 km (919 mi). The two, Richard Branson, 36, and Swedish-born Per Lindstrand, 38, took off from Sugarloaf Mountain, Maine, in their 21-story, 60-m (200-ft)-high *Virgin Atlantic Flyer* on July 2. Kept aloft with liquid propane burners and the heat from the Sun, they took advantage of strong winds to reach the Irish coast the following day.

The huge balloon failed to make a controlled landfall, however. Instead, it plunged into the Irish Sea a few kilometres off the Scottish coast. Lindstrand jumped from the gondola into the water just before the crash, allowing the aircraft briefly to take flight again until it finally collapsed in the sea with Branson still aboard. Both men were rescued.

The flight was accepted as a record crossing by the *Guinness Book of Records.* Branson and Lindstrand also claimed that the *Virgin Atlantic Flyer* was the largest and fastest hot-air balloon ever flown.

Accompanied by flight instructors, John Kevin Hill, 11, of Arlington, Texas, and Christopher Lee Marshall, 10, of Oceano, Calif., each made coast-to-coast flights across the United States during the summer and filed rival claims for the record as the youngest pilot ever to make the flight. The Marshall attempt caused some controversy because, though a flight plan was filed with the Federal Aviation Administration, the National Aeronautic Association was not notified. The NAA's Col. Milton Brown said that Marshall would undoubtedly receive a certificate of recognition, however.

On January 22 Glenn Tremml, 26, a Connecticut medical student, overcame serious technical difficulties and surpassed his original goal to set a new world distance record for man-powered aircraft of 59.8 km (37.2 mi) in a 2-hr 13-min flight over a desert course at Edwards Air Force Base in California. The previous record was 35.8 km (22.3 mi) set in 1979. One day earlier Tremml's colleague, Lois McCallin, 29, a Boston investment analyst, set a women's record for distance with a flight of 15.44 km (9.6 mi) in the same aircraft.

Al Nels of the U.S. won the World Hot Air Ballooning Championship, held September 5–12 at Schielleiten, Austria. Second place in the competition was taken by Joseph Starkbaum of Austria and third place by his compatriot Leopold Hauer.

On January 10 William Bussey of the U.S. set a world record for distance for Class AX-6 balloons with a 521.34-km (323.95-mi) flight from Longview, Texas, to Philadelphia, Miss. Claude van Hoorebeeck of Belgium set a world AX-3 balloon duration record of 6 hr 5 min 3 sec in a flight in Belgium from Céroux-Mousty to Lillois-Witterzée in a Colt 21A on January 31.

Competitors from 29 nations flying 108 sailplanes participated in the 20th biennial World Gliding Championships, held January 17–29 at Benalla, Australia. Brian Speckley of England won first place in the 15-m competition, while the open-class contest was won by perennial champion

Ingo Renner of Australia. Markku Kuittinen of Finland took first in the standard-class competition.

At the World Relative Work Parachute Championships, held October 1–10 at Foz do Iguaçu, Brazil, the eight-way contest was won by the U.S. with 119 points. France placed first in the four-way challenge with 134 points.

The first-ever World Para-Ski Championships were held in Sarajevo, Yugos., during March. First in men's skiing was T. Saurer of Switzerland, and Joy Burtis of the U.S. won the women's competition. Men's accuracy was taken by Jandel Frantz of France, and top honours in women's accuracy went to Marjolaine DePury of France. The men's overall winner was Joel Yout of France, and the women's champion was Canada's Beverly Watson. The top three winners in the men's national competition were Switzerland, France, and Yugoslavia. In the women's national it was the U.S., France, and Austria.

A world women's parachute record for four-way rotation was set by a team of Libov Isaeva, Elena Logvinenko, Larisa Zelenina, and Irina Belonogova of the U.S.S.R. They completed five rotations in 180 sec in a jump at Donetsk, U.S.S.R., on Oct. 6, 1987.

A six-man team led by Allen E. Paulsen of the U.S. flew a Gulfstream IV around the world in 45 hr 25 min 10 sec June 12–14 to set a world westbound speed record for jet aircraft of 810.79 km/h (503.91 mph).

(MICHAEL D. KILIAN)

## AUTOMOBILE RACING

**Grand Prix Racing.** In international Formula One automobile racing in 1987, the engines of turbocharged cars had to be run at an officially enforced lower boost pressure. Also, a separate class for cars with normally aspirated engines of up to 3½ litres was recognized alongside the turbocharged 1½-litre class.

The 1987 driver's world championship was won by Brazilian driver Nelson Piquet (who had won it in 1981 and 1983) after a long battle between him and his British teammate Nigel Mansell, both of the Williams-Honda team. The championship was undecided until Mansell crashed in a practice session before the Japanese Grand Prix; bruises and a minor injury kept him out of that race and the remaining Australian Grand Prix.

The season opened at Rio de Janeiro, Brazil, in April, where Alain Prost (France) won in a McLaren-Porsche. Piquet, who had the fastest lap at 192.962 km/h (1 km = 0.62 mi), was second. At the San Marino Grand Prix, Mansell won from Ayrton Senna of Brazil in a Williams-Honda. The fastest lap was by the Italian driver Teo Fabi (Benetton-Ford) at 203.303 km/h. In the Belgian Grand Prix, Prost drove the fastest lap at 213.260 km/h and won from Stefan Johansson (Sweden) in a McLaren-Porsche.

Senna won on the Monaco street circuit after making best lap speed, 136.635 km/h. Piquet finished second. The Canadian Grand Prix having been canceled, Formula One racing moved to Detroit for the U.S. Grand Prix over the downtown circuit. Mansell gained pole position for the fifth time in six races, but Senna won the race, setting a new lap record of 144.171 km/h. Piquet finished second. In the French Grand Prix in July, the Williams-Hondas of Mansell and Piquet finished first and second; Piquet had the fastest lap at 197.372 km/h, a course record.

Before an enormous crowd Mansell won the British Grand Prix at Silverstone, passing Piquet two laps from the finish and establishing a new lap record of 246.324 km/h. At the Hockenheimring for the German Grand Prix, Williams-Honda was supreme again, Piquet winning from Johansson. Mansell made best lap with 231.462

| Formula One Grand Prix Race Results, 1987 | | | |
|---|---|---|---|
| Race | Driver | Car | Average Speed |
| Brazilian | A. Prost | McLaren-Porsche | 184.592 km/h |
| San Marino | N. Mansell | Williams-Honda | 195.201 km/h |
| Belgian | A. Prost | McLaren-Porsche | 205.680 km/h |
| Monaco | A. Senna | Lotus-Honda | 132.102 km/h |
| U.S. | A. Senna | Lotus-Honda | 137.915 km/h |
| French | N. Mansell | Williams-Honda | 188.560 km/h |
| British | N. Mansell | Williams-Honda | 235.299 km/h |
| German | N. Piquet | Williams-Honda | 220.394 km/h |
| Hungarian | N. Piquet | Williams-Honda | 153.239 km/h |
| Austrian | N. Mansell | Williams-Honda | 235.421 km/h |
| Italian | N. Piquet | Williams-Honda | 232.636 km/h |
| Portuguese | A. Prost | McLaren-Porsche | 188.224 km/h |
| Spanish | N. Mansell | Williams-Honda | 166.848 km/h |
| Mexican | N. Mansell | Williams-Honda | 193.411 km/h |
| Japanese | G. Berger | Ferrari F187 | 192.847 km/h |
| Australian | G. Berger | Ferrari F187 | 164.631 km/h |

WORLD DRIVERS' CHAMPIONSHIP: Piquet 73 pt, Mansell 61 pt, Senna 57 pt.
CONSTRUCTORS' WORLD CHAMPIONSHIP: Williams-Honda 137 pt,
  McLaren-TAG 76 pt, Lotus-Honda 64 pt.
NONSUPERCHARGED CARS CHAMPIONSHIP: Tyrrell-Cosworth.

km/h, a record. Mansell battled with Piquet in the Hungarian Grand Prix until a wheel nut came adrift, leaving victory and fastest lap (160.295 km/h, a record) to Piquet. Senna finished second. In the Austrian Grand Prix, Mansell and Piquet produced another Williams-Honda double, and Mansell set a course record at 242.207 km/h. The Italian Grand Prix at Monza was won by Piquet, with Senna second.

The Portuguese Grand Prix was won by Prost. Gerhard Berger of Austria placed second in a Ferrari, demonstrating the improvement in the car since British engineers Harvey Postlethwaite and John Barnard redesigned it. Berger set a lap record of 197.523 km/h. Berger's Ferrari again set a lap record of 174.566 km/h in the Spanish Grand Prix at Jerez before its engine failed. Mansell was ahead of Prost.

The Mexican Grand Prix was won by Mansell, with Piquet second. Piquet set a lap record of 201.127 km/h. In the Japanese Grand Prix at Suzuka, the new-found fortunes of Ferrari continued as Berger won. Senna finished second, and Prost set a lap record for the new circuit at 203.116 km/h. In the Australian Grand Prix at Adelaide, Berger won ahead of his teammate Michele Alboreto of Italy. Berger's 169.175 km/h was fastest lap.

**Rallies and Other Races.** The Spa (Belgium) 24-hour race was won by a BMW M3, a car that also was victorious in the Silverstone Tourist Trophy race in England. The Daytona (Fla.) 24-hour race went to a Porsche 962, as did the historic Le Mans 24-hour race in France. The Silk Cut Jaguar XJR-6 cars won the world sports car championship, scoring successes at Brands Hatch (England) in the 1,000-km race, in the Spa 1,000-km race, and in races at Silverstone and Fuji, Japan. Derek Bell (U.K.) took the world sports car drivers' title for the third successive year.

International rallying was dominated by the Lancia Delta HF 4WD, which won the Monte Carlo, Acropolis, Portuguese, Olympus, New Zealand, Argentina, Thousand Lakes, and Lombard RAC rallies. Peugeot won the Paris–Dakar Rally and Audi Quattro, the Safari Rally in Africa. Lancia won the world rally championship, and for the second year in a row, Juho Kankkunen of Finland took the rally drivers' championship. (WILLIAM C. BODDY)

**U.S. Racing.** Al Unser won the Indianapolis 500 for the fourth time in his long career, driving a March-Cosworth. The 47-year-old senior Unser, previously victorious in 1970, 1971, and 1978, averaged 162.175 mph (1 mi = 1.61 km). He led for the first time 17 laps from the finish and was not passed again. Roberto Guerrero of Colombia finished second, the only other car to complete all 200 laps. Third was Fabrizio Barbazza of Italy, rookie of the year. All drove March-Cosworths. Mario Andretti's Lola T87/01 broke down after leading 170 of the first 177 laps.

In the season-long CART (Championship Auto Racing Teams) competition, Bobby Rahal defended his title successfully against Michael Andretti. Although each won three races, Rahal and his TruSports Lola finished high consistently. He won $1,261,098 for the season.

The National Association for Stock Car Auto Racing (NASCAR) also crowned a repeat champion, Dale Earnhardt, driving a Chevrolet Monte Carlo. He won 11 races, finishing ahead of Ford's Bill Elliott. He won $2,069,243 for the season, surpassed in the record books only by Elliott's $2.3 million in 1985. Elliott won NASCAR's richest race, the Daytona 500.

A new generation of NASCAR drivers continued to make headway. Earnhardt, son of former ace Ralph, found his hands full with other second-generation stars. Kyle Petty, son of Richard, won his first classic, the Charlotte Coca-Cola 600, in a Wood Bros. Ford, and Davey Allison, son of Bobby, won twice, including the first Talladega 500. The winner of NASCAR's Grand National circuit was Larry Pearson, son of David, driving a Pontiac.

In road racing a new champion but a familiar maker won the International Motor Sports Association Camel Grand Touring (GT) Prototype crown. He was Chip Robinson, driving the factory Porsche 962, again the season winner over Chevrolet-powered entries. Robinson won three races, including the Daytona 24-hour Classic, where he teamed with Al Unser, Jr., Al Holbert, and Derek Bell.

In the Camel Light class, roughly equivalent to Group C unsupercharged 3-litre prototypes, Jim Downing of Atlanta successfully defended his driver crown in a Mazda rotary-powered Argo, but Pontiac Fiero took the maker championship.

The most competitive classes in U.S. road racing may

AP/WIDE WORLD

Veteran driver Al Unser, Sr., races down the main straightaway to capture his fourth Indianapolis 500. Almost 48 years old, Unser became the oldest driver ever to win the race.

have been for production cars. In GTOver 3-litre class, Toyota finally prevailed over Camaro and Ford as its lead driver, Chris Cord, won the driver title. The Mazda RX-7 won the GTUnder 2.8-litre championship for the eighth straight year. Tom Kendall, driving a Clayton Cunningham RX-7, defended his driver title rather easily.

Driving a Mercury Merkur, Scott Pruitt won the Sports Car Club of America (SCCA) Trans-Am series over teammate Tom Gloy. The SCCA Group B Rally championship was won by Audi Quattro again, with John Buffum driving. In Group A, a Mazda 323, driven by New Zealand expatriate Rod Millen, won.  (ROBERT J. FENDELL)

## BADMINTON

The 1987 world championships of badminton were held May 18–24 in Beijing (Peking). Athletes from 24 countries competed in five events. As some 16,000 spectators watched, all five of the events were won by players from China.

In the men's singles finals, Yang Yang defeated Morten Frost of Denmark by scores of 15–2, 13–15, 15–12. The victory was well deserved and was achieved in great part by Yang Yang's superb fitness. The women's singles finals was an all-China affair between Li Lingwei and Han Aiping. This match was another three-game contest, with Han Aiping winning 10–12, 11–4, 11–7. Although Li Lingwei showed control around the net, her opponent had more accurate and subtle rear-court control.

In the men's doubles finals, the Chinese pair of Tian Bingyi and Li Yongbo faced the Sidek brothers, Razif and Jalani, of Malaysia. After a match of great speed, marked by bounding smashes interspersed with deceptive jumping drops, the Chinese were victorious by scores of 15–2, 8–15, 15–9. The women's doubles provided the fourth gold medal for China when Lin Ying and Guan Weizhen defeated a somewhat depleted Li Lingwei and Han Aiping by scores of 15–7 and 15–8.

In the mixed doubles finals, the South Korean team of Lee Deuk Choon and Chung Myung Hee played against Wang Pengren and Shi Fangjing of China. This match resulted in more gold for the Chinese by scores of 15–8 and 15–7. Thus China established itself as the world's top badminton power in 1987.  (C. R. ELI)

## BASEBALL

Major league baseball's increasing popularity was evident again during the 1987 season, when the 50 million mark in total attendance was achieved for the first time. With all 26 franchises drawing at least one million paid admissions for a second consecutive season, the 1987 aggregate of 52,008,918 was almost five million better than that of the previous year.

The American League, with two more teams, attracted 27,278,076 customers for a per game average of 24,421. The National League counted 24,730,842 spectators for an average of 25,896. Two teams, the New York Mets and St. Louis Cardinals, drew more than three million spectators each for the first time. Previously, only the Los Angeles Dodgers had reached that plateau.

Following a season that saw a record number of home runs, the sport's rules committee changed the strike zone. The lower limit remained the top of the knees, but the upper limit was lowered from the armpit to "the midpoint between the shoulders and the top of the pants."

**World Series.** The Minnesota Twins surprised the baseball world by capturing the World Series; they defeated the St. Louis Cardinals 4–3. The Twins were 75–1 long shots to win the American League pennant and a 150–1 propo-

sition to win the World Series, according to preseason odds. Those calculations reflected the fact that the Twins had won only 71 games and had lost 91 during the 1986 season, when they finished sixth in the American League West division, a distant 21 games out of first place. However, the Twins parlayed their talents and their unusual success in home games to achieve their first championship since moving to Minneapolis-St. Paul from Washington, D.C., in 1961.

On October 17 in game one at the Hubert H. Humphrey Metrodome in Minneapolis, history was made when the first indoor World Series contest was played. The Twins, who roared to a 56–25 record at "the Dome" during the regular season, responded to the occasion with a 10–1 rout of the Cardinals. Frank Viola, Minnesota's ace left-hander, pitched eight strong innings and received equally robust support. The Twins arose for seven runs in the fourth inning; the telling blow was a grand-slam home run by Dan Gladden, only the 13th in World Series history.

One evening later the Twins thrilled a handkerchief-waving Dome crowd of 55,257 by again striking in the fourth inning for six runs toward an 8–4 conquest. ("Homer Hankies," distributed as a promotion, were a feature of the Dome games.) Bert Blyleven, a veteran right-hander, was the winning pitcher for the Twins, who inflicted most of their lusty hitting on St. Louis loser Danny Cox. The Twins thus assumed a commanding lead in the best-of-seven series, but when the venue was changed to St. Louis's outdoor Busch Stadium, the Twins struggled, much as they had on the road during the regular season. Minnesota's record away from home was 29–52.

In game three of the World Series on October 20, the Cardinals downed the Twins 3–1 behind the tidy pitching of starter John Tudor and reliever Todd Worrell. In the seventh inning, speedster Vince Coleman slashed a two-run opposite field double to left for two runs, and Ozzie Smith then singled home Coleman.

It was 5.5° C (42° F) for game four on October 21, but the Cardinals warmed to the occasion with a 7–2 triumph to even the series at two victories each. On this night, the Cardinals enjoyed a profitable fourth inning, scoring six runs against Viola and reliever Dan Schatzeder. Tom Lawless, a relatively anonymous utility player who had collected only two hits all season, cracked a three-run homer during the outburst. The homer was the second in Lawless's career. Bob Forsch, who relieved starter Greg Mathews, was the winning pitcher.

For game five in St. Louis on October 22, the Cardinals utilized their vaunted speed to register a 4–2 victory, their

### Final Major League Standings, 1987

| AMERICAN LEAGUE East Division | | | | | NATIONAL LEAGUE East Division | | | | |
|---|---|---|---|---|---|---|---|---|---|
| Club | W. | L. | Pct. | G.B. | Club | W. | L. | Pct. | G.B. |
| Detroit | 98 | 64 | .605 | – | St. Louis | 95 | 67 | .586 | – |
| Toronto | 96 | 66 | .593 | 2 | New York | 92 | 70 | .568 | 3 |
| Milwaukee | 91 | 71 | .562 | 7 | Montreal | 91 | 71 | .562 | 4 |
| New York | 89 | 73 | .549 | 9 | Philadelphia | 80 | 82 | .494 | 15 |
| Boston | 78 | 84 | .481 | 20 | Pittsburgh | 80 | 82 | .494 | 15 |
| Baltimore | 67 | 95 | .414 | 31 | Chicago | 76 | 85 | .472 | 18½ |
| Cleveland | 61 | 101 | .377 | 37 | | | | | |

| West Division | | | | | West Division | | | | |
|---|---|---|---|---|---|---|---|---|---|
| Club | W. | L. | Pct. | G.B. | Club | W. | L. | Pct. | G.B. |
| Minnesota | 85 | 77 | .525 | – | San Francisco | 90 | 72 | .556 | – |
| Kansas City | 83 | 79 | .512 | 2 | Cincinnati | 84 | 78 | .519 | 6 |
| Oakland | 81 | 81 | .500 | 4 | Houston | 76 | 86 | .469 | 14 |
| Seattle | 78 | 84 | .481 | 7 | Los Angeles | 73 | 89 | .451 | 17 |
| Chicago | 77 | 85 | .475 | 8 | Atlanta | 69 | 92 | .429 | 20½ |
| California | 75 | 87 | .463 | 10 | San Diego | 65 | 97 | .401 | 25 |
| Texas | 75 | 87 | .463 | 10 | | | | | |

Overjoyed Minnesota Twins pile on top of each other after winning the 1987 World Series. The victory stunned baseball pundits, who had set the preseason odds for a Twins championship at 150 to 1.
AFP PHOTO

third straight. The Cardinals broke open a scoreless pitching duel between Blyleven and Cox with three runs in the sixth inning.

In game six back at Minneapolis on October 24, the Cardinals jumped to a 5–2 lead against Les Straker and Schatzeder. Don Baylor pounded a three-run homer in a four-run fifth inning for the Twins, however, and then Kent Hrbek lashed a grand-slam homer during a four-run sixth to provide Minnesota an 11–5 decision that brought the series to 3–3.

The final contest on October 25 was the most stirring of the World Series. The Cardinals scored twice in their half of the second inning, but the Twins tallied once in their second and again in their fifth for a 2–2 tie off rookie Joe Magrane. Then, with Cox pitching for St. Louis in the sixth, the Twins used three bases on balls and Greg Gagne's infield single to build a 3–2 lead. The Twins added an insurance run in the eighth inning, and star reliever Jeff Reardon retired three straight batters in the ninth to secure the Twins' 4–2 victory. Viola, winner in games one and seven, received most valuable player honours for the series, which was the first ever in which the triumphant team did not win at least one road game.

**Play-offs.** The Twins reached their first World Series since 1965 by surprising the Detroit Tigers in the American League Championship Series. The best-of-seven play-off commenced with two games in the Metrodome, and the Twins won both. They scored four runs in the bottom of the eighth to take the first contest 8–5, then defeated Tiger pitching ace Jack Morris 6–3 in the second game. Morris had entered the game with an 11–0 record against the Twins while pitching in his native state, Minnesota.

In the third game at Detroit's Tiger Stadium, Pat Sheridan delivered a two-run homer in the bottom of the eighth to give the Tigers a 7–6 triumph. However, the Twins won the fourth game 5–3 and clinched their second pennant the next day by walloping the Tigers 9–5 to win the play-off series 4–1.

The ailing Cardinals had a much more difficult time dismissing San Francisco's Giants for their third National

League pennant in six years. The Cardinals won the first game at home 5–3, lost the next 5–0, then surged from a 4–0 deficit to take the third game at San Francisco 6–5. However, the Giants then won two in a row at home—by 4–2 behind the excellent pitching of Mike Krukow, and by 6–3 on Jose Uribe's clutch two-run single and five innings of one-hit relief pitching by Joe Price.

The Giants returned to St. Louis needing one victory for their first pennant in 25 years, but they were unable even to score a run. San Francisco's imposing lineup was quieted 1–0 in the sixth game, which Tudor started and won, and in the deciding affair Cox pitched a 6–0 victory. The Cardinals were buoyed by a 4–0 second inning lead after Jose Oquendo cracked a three-run homer, just the third home run of his career.

**Regular Season.** The lightly regarded Twins under Tom Kelly, a 37-year-old rookie manager, were in first place for most of the season. They led the American League West by two games at the All-Star break and by a half game entering September. They beat out the second-place Kansas City Royals by two games, finishing with a mark of 85–77—the poorest of any of the four division champions. That record also stood as the second weakest of any team to enter the World Series.

The Tigers won 98 games, the most in baseball, and took the American League East by two games over the Toronto Blue Jays. The Blue Jays led the division by 3½ games with only eight days to go but lost their last seven contests, four of them to Detroit.

In the National League the Cardinals mounted a substantial margin of 9½ games by late July, but they were bedeviled by injuries and finished only 3 games ahead of the defending champion New York Mets, who never fully recovered from a disastrous start. Experts predicted that the Cincinnati Reds would win the National League West, but the Giants, fueled by a couple of excellent mid-season trades for pitching help, ran off 37 victories in their final 54 regular season games to capture the division by 6 games over the Reds.

**Individual Leaders.** Tony Gwynn of the San Diego Padres led the major leagues in batting with a .370 average; Wade Boggs of the Boston Red Sox paced the American League with .363. Andre Dawson, acquired from the Montreal Expos, hit 49 home runs for the Chicago Cubs to lead the National League. Rookie Mark McGwire hit 49 for the Oakland Athletics, the most ever for a first-year player. Dawson also was the leader in runs batted in with 137, while Toronto's George Bell led the American League with 134.

Rick Sutcliffe of Chicago posted the most victories in the National League, 18, and Steve Bedrosian of the Philadelphia Phillies had 40 saves in relief. The American League featured two 20-game winners—Boston's Roger Clemens and Oakland's Dave Stewart. Tom Henke of Toronto posted the most saves, 34. Coleman of the Cardinals stole 109 bases, by far the best in either league. Philadelphia's veteran third baseman, Mike Schmidt, hit his 500th home run, thus becoming only the 14th player in major league history to have done so.

Bell and Dawson were voted the most valuable players in the American and National Leagues, respectively. Bedrosian won the Cy Young award as the National League's best pitcher, and Clemens gained that honour for the American League. Rookies of the year were McGwire in the American League and Benito Santiago of San Diego in the National. Buck Rodgers of Montreal and Sparky Anderson of Detroit were named National and American league managers of the year.     (ROBERT WILLIAM VERDI)

**Latin America.** The Cibao Eagles, from the Dominican Republic, went undefeated in four games to win the Caribbean Series, played in Hermosillo, Sonora, Mexico, in February. The Dominicans edged the Caracas Lions 3–2 in 11 innings and humiliated, in front of a partisan home crowd, the Mazatlán (Mexico) Deers by the score of 16–2. The Eagles went on to defeat the Caguas Creoles, from Puerto Rico, in a 14–13 cliff-hanger and completed their series sweep with a decisive 8–0 victory over the Caracas Lions. The Caguas Creoles took second place with an even 2–2 record, while the Mazatlán Deers and the Caracas Lions tied for last place with 1–3 records.

The Pan American Games at Indianapolis, Ind., provided the setting for the year's most important challenge against the powerful Cuban national team. Although during first-round play the Cubans suffered their first Pan American defeat ever, after a ninth-inning home run by a member of the young amateur U.S. team, they still managed to reach the final and took the gold medal by beating the U.S. The Cubans got a chance to play in front of a partisan home crowd in October as they won the world amateur championship in Havana, followed by the U.S. and Japan. (SERGIO SARMIENTO)

**Japan.** Tokorozawa's Seibu Lions of the Pacific League defeated Tokyo's Yomiuri Giants of the Central League 4 games to 2 in the best-of-seven postseason contest to win the Japan Series for the second straight year. In the first game of the series, Yomiuri collected 16 hits, including home runs by outfielder Norihiro Komada and first baseman Kiyoshi Nakahata, against the Lions' ace right-hander Osamu Higashio and three relievers to gain a 7–3 victory. Giants starter Masumi Kuwata was hit by a line drive off the bat of Lions third baseman Hiromichi Ishige in the top of the third inning and had to leave the game.

In the second game the Giants sent Takashi Nishimoto to the mound. Though he had won two games in the 1983 Japan Series against the Lions, Nishimoto gave up three runs, including Koji Akiyama's solo homer, in six innings. Ace left-hander Kimiyasu Kudo of the Lions pitched a three-hit shutout, and Seibu won the game 6–0.

Hurler "Orient Express" Taigen Kaku from Taiwan pitched the full nine innings and helped the Lions win the third game of the series 2–1. Right-hander Hiromi Makihara pitched a three-hit shutout and helped the Giants win

THE SPORTS NIPPON NEWSPAPER

Japanese baseball star Sachio Kinugasa smiles amid bouquets after completing his 2,215th consecutive official game, the last of his 23-year career.

Indiana's Keith Smart shoots over a block by Syracuse's Howard Triche (25) to score the go-ahead basket in the final moments of the NCAA championship game.
AP/WIDE WORLD

the fourth game 4–0. The Giants' cleanup man, Tatsunori Hara, hit his first home run of the series.

In the fifth game the Lions collected three hits and scored three runs in the top of the first inning against Giants starter Kuwata. This, combined with the pitching of Higashio (8⅓ innings) and Kudo, led the Lions to a 3–1 victory. Higashio was the winner, and Kudo got the save.

In the sixth game Kudo again hurled a three-hitter and helped the Lions win the game 3–1 and the series 4 games to 2. Kudo was voted most valuable player of the series. (TOSHIHIKO SUZUKI)

## BASKETBALL

**United States.** *College.* Bobby Knight made a "Smart" move that paid off with his third National Collegiate Athletic Association (NCAA) basketball championship. Keith Smart's 4.9-m (16-ft) jump shot in the last five seconds gave Knight's Indiana University Hoosiers a sensational 74–73 victory over Syracuse in the 1987 NCAA final. It capped a comeback that put the Hoosiers in the winner's circle after an uphill climb that had lasted all season.

For Syracuse, another underdog team that apparently had shaken off its NCAA tournament jinx at last, the stunning finish was pure heartbreak. The Orangemen had electrified a New Orleans (La.) Superdome crowd of 64,959 by leading almost all of the way until coach Jim Boeheim's strategy backfired in the waning moments.

All of that drama in the championship game was one more subplot for Indiana's dream come true. Knight, who once scorned the use of junior college transfers at Indiana, brought in 1.85-m (6-ft 1-in) guard Smart and 2.1-m (6-ft 10-in) centre Dean Garrett for the 1986–87 season. Without those junior college additions, Knight would not have joined Johnny Wooden of UCLA and Adolph Rupp of Kentucky as the only coaches to win the tournament more than twice.

Knight achieved one of the best coaching performances

of his career. He began by dropping centre-forward Daryl Thomas from the squad for missing some classes, then reinstating him. While Smart and Garrett were struggling to adjust to their new roles, Knight said he doubted this Indiana team had enough mental toughness. After a narrow 77–75 escape from lowly Northwestern on February 11, Knight cut loose again: "I've forgotten more basketball than any of you will ever know, and I'm telling you now, this is not a good basketball team." After more narrow escapes—especially the first triple overtime in Indiana basketball history, a thrilling 86–85 comeback at Wisconsin—the Hoosiers proved to him and the rest of the country just how good they were.

In the NCAA Midwest Regional final, Indiana needed a lucky basket by Rick Calloway with six seconds left to nip upset-minded Louisiana State 77–76. The Hoosiers thus qualified for the Final Four again, matched against Nevada-Las Vegas (UNLV), the top-ranked team in the country, with a record of 37–1. Favoured over Indiana, UNLV got a superb 32-point, ten-rebound game from All-American forward Armon Gilliam—and lost 97–93. In the other semifinal, Syracuse easily ousted Providence, the tournament's Cinderella team, 77–63.

The stage was thus set for a fitting NCAA climax. Syracuse, ending a long string of early-round eliminations, was ignited by the brilliance of 2.1-m centre Rony Siekaly, a native of Greece, and playmaker Sherman Douglas, a 1.83-m (6-ft) streak of lightning. With 38 seconds left, the Orangemen led 73–70, but Knight's coaching genius turned the tide. He called time out, pressuring Syracuse freshman Derrick Coleman into missing a crucial one-and-one free throw. Inexplicably, Boeheim kept his rebounders off the lane, enabling Thomas to get the ball for Indiana. Everyone in the Superdome expected Hoosier money player Steve Alford to take the decisive shot with his team down by a point and the last seconds ticking away.

Instead, Thomas got the ball in the lane, faked the same 3-m (10-ft) shot he had missed against Louisiana State, and spotted Smart, cutting to the left baseline. Smart took the pass, went up over the frantic lunge of defender Howard Triche, and scored one of the most dramatic baskets in the Hoosiers' storied history. Indiana thus added another NCAA championship to those won in 1981 and 1976 (also Knight-coached), 1953, and 1940.

Alford, by now almost the symbol of Indiana basketball, got the last line on his coach: "We also accomplished the goal of showing we were mentally tough."

In women's basketball freshman guard Tonya Edwards was the spark plug that put Tennessee into overdrive in 1986–87. The Lady Vols did not stop until they had cruised to the national championship with an impressive

The Boston Celtics' Bill Walton guards Los Angeles Laker Kareem Abdul-Jabbar during the sixth and final game of the NBA play-offs. The Lakers exploded in the third quarter and went on to win the 1987 NBA championship.
AP/WIDE WORLD

67–44 rout of Louisiana Tech. Edwards, a guard from Flint, Mich., was named outstanding player of the NCAA Division I Tournament finals in Austin, Texas. Louisiana Tech had knocked out defending champion Texas in the semifinals, but the Lady Techsters could not cope with Tennessee's smothering defense.

"We stayed up until 3 o'clock in the morning trying to devise a defense that would stop their inside game," said Tennessee coach Pat Head Summitt. The solution was alternating Sheila Frost, Kathy Spinks, and Karla Horton to drape a defensive blanket over Louisiana Tech's 1.92-m (6-ft 4-in) Tori Harrison. That forced the Lady Techsters (30–3) to shoot from outside, and they made only 16 of 48 field-goal attempts.

Edwards, Frost, and Bridgette Gordon shared scoring honours for the winners with 13 points each. Tennessee (28–6) snapped Louisiana Tech's 19-game victory streak in the final, also avenging a 72–60 defeat during the regular season.

*Professional.* The Los Angeles Lakers climaxed their championship 1986–87 campaign with the kind of explosive scoring burst that had become their trademark. A 30–12 spree in the third quarter finished the Boston Celtics, enabling the Lakers to frolic to the National Basketball Association (NBA) title with a 106–93 triumph. The partisan crowd of 17,505 in Los Angeles sat back to enjoy the spectacle of their team salting away the best-of-seven championship series in this sixth-game blowout.

The Celtics had nothing left after a bitter 107–106 Boston Garden defeat in the fourth game. Los Angeles took a 3–1 stranglehold on the final round with that escape act, and the Lakers were content to wait until they got home to wrap it up. Their 123–108 setback in the fifth encounter merely delayed the inevitable.

### NBA Final Standings, 1986–87

EASTERN CONFERENCE
Atlantic Division

| Team | Won | Lost |
| --- | --- | --- |
| Boston | 59 | 23 |
| Philadelphia | 45 | 37 |
| Washington | 42 | 40 |
| New Jersey | 24 | 58 |
| New York | 24 | 58 |

Central Division

| Team | Won | Lost |
| --- | --- | --- |
| Atlanta | 57 | 25 |
| Detroit | 52 | 30 |
| Milwaukee | 50 | 32 |
| Indiana | 41 | 41 |
| Chicago | 40 | 42 |
| Cleveland | 31 | 51 |

WESTERN CONFERENCE
Midwest Division

| Team | Won | Lost |
| --- | --- | --- |
| Dallas | 55 | 27 |
| Utah | 44 | 38 |
| Houston | 42 | 40 |
| Denver | 37 | 45 |
| Sacramento | 29 | 53 |
| San Antonio | 28 | 54 |

Pacific Division

| Team | Won | Lost |
| --- | --- | --- |
| L.A. Lakers | 65 | 17 |
| Portland | 49 | 33 |
| Golden State | 42 | 40 |
| Seattle | 39 | 43 |
| Phoenix | 36 | 46 |
| L.A. Clippers | 12 | 70 |

Sparring like a confident heavyweight boxer in the opening half of the sixth game, the Lakers quickly erased a 56–51 deficit, with Earvin ("Magic") Johnson pulling the trigger on their blistering fast break. An 18–2 outburst combined with smothering defense on Celtic stars Larry Bird and Kevin McHale clinched the victory. Johnson led the way with 16 points, 19 assists, and 8 rebounds in the season-ending romp. The magic man from Michigan State thus earned most valuable player laurels in both the regular season and the play-offs, ending Bird's three-year monopoly on the championship series MVP trophy.

As usual, the Lakers' geriatric marvel, 2.18-m (7-ft 2-in) Kareem Abdul-Jabbar, 40, played a pivotal role. He planned to return in a bid to make Los Angeles the first NBA team to win back-to-back crowns since 1969.

Another veteran star, Julius ("Dr. J") Erving, retired at the end of the season after 16 outstanding years in professional basketball (*see* BIOGRAPHIES). The most notable individual effort of the year was that of Chicago's Michael Jordan, who became only the second player in NBA history to score more than 3,000 points in one season; Jordan averaged 37.1 points per game for a total of 3,041.

(ROBERT G. LOGAN)

**World Basketball.** Greece triumphed in the 1987 European men's basketball championships in June, held in Athens for the first time. The host country performed above all expectations to win the gold medal, defeating the Soviet Union 103–101 in overtime in the final. The Greek hero was Nikos Gallis, one of the smallest players in the tournament, who topped the scoring in the final with 40 points and topped the overall tournament scoring list with 296. Greece had lost earlier to Spain and the Soviet Union but had started its remarkable run of victories at the quarterfinal stage, when it met the previously unbeaten Italian team and recorded a surprising 90–78 victory. In the semifinal Greece defeated Yugoslavia 81–77. The Soviet Union was undefeated going into the final. In the play-off for the bronze medal, Yugoslavia beat Spain 98–87.

The world junior men's championships were held in Bormio, Italy, in July–August 1987. Yugoslavia defeated the U.S. 86–76 in the final, and Italy finished third, beating West Germany 77–56. It was the first time that the U.S. had failed to win the gold medal in a world junior men's championship tournament.

In the Pan American Games, held in Indianapolis, Ind., in August, Brazil upset the U.S. 120–115 to win the men's championship. In women's competition the U.S. defeated Brazil 111–87.

The European Champions' Cup was won by Tracer Milan for the first time when it beat Maccabi Tel Aviv 71–69 in the final at Lausanne, Switz. The European Cup Winners' Cup was won by KK Cibona of Zagreb, Yugos., and the Korac Cup by FC Barcelona.

The women's European championship, held in Spain in September, was won by the Soviet Union. Unbeaten in the competition since 1958, the Soviet team defeated Yugoslavia 83–73 in the final. Hungary took the bronze medal. The women's European Champions' Cup was won for the third successive year by AS Vicenza, Italy, which was appearing in its fifth consecutive final. It beat Dinamo Novosibirsk, U.S.S.R., 86–73 in the final in Thessalonika, Greece.

The Universiade held in Zagreb, Yugos., in July 1987 was a triumph for the host country. The Yugoslavian women's team defeated the Soviet Union 80–73 in the final. In the men's tournament Yugoslavia beat the Soviet Union 66–51 in the semifinal and the U.S. 100–85 in the final.

(MELVIN D. WELCH)

## BILLIARD GAMES

**Billiards.** Disagreement and disorder continued to plague three-cushion billiards. The Union Mondial de Billiard (UMB) for more than four decades had organized and sponsored the established premier event in three-cushion, the UMB world amateur championships. In recent years, however, efforts to relax or modify the amateur status of the event (and the sport itself) had been mounted. A struggle for control ensued, with one result being the late cancellation of the world meet as originally scheduled in Tokyo to avoid conflict with a new professional tour. The amateur billiard federation of Egypt, in conjunction with UMB and the Confederation Européene de Billiard (CEB), then scrambled to present a 42nd UMB world event April 1–5 in Cairo.

Despite such efforts, the event was bypassed by the game's dominant players except for the 1986 runner-up, Torbjorn Blomdahl of Sweden. In the greatly weakened field, the 24-year-old Blomdahl was the clear pretournament favourite, and he seized the opportunity, becoming the youngest UMB world champion ever. He lost only one match in the nine-player round-robin of 50-point games, to Arturo Bone of Mexico (third place). Blomdahl was the lone player to average 1.0 or more (1.099) and was untied for a final record of 7–1–0. The runner-up was Frank Torres of the U.S.

Blomdahl had qualified for the UMB world test by winning his fifth Swedish national three-cushion crown, averaging 1.379 to edge out none other than his father, Lennart Blomdahl. In other "amateur" federation national championship tournaments, Torres won the 20th Billiard Federation of the USA title over a field of 28 in San Jose, Calif.; Yoshio Yoshihara achieved a 1.167 average to win the Japanese championship; Raymond Steijlaerts (with Raymond Ceulemans barred) gained his second win in Belgium after 24 years; Christ van der Smissen captured his second national title in The Netherlands with a 1.206 average; and Kurt Thogersen earned the Danish championship, scoring at a 1.302 pace.

Creating a conflict for the majority of the world's top three-cushion players were the Billiard World Cup Association (BWA) international professional tour events, which were resisted by the CEB and some of the national federations. The BWA's $200,000-plus prize money prevailed over national amateur eligibility, however, and the sport's brightest stars toured Paris, Brussels, West Berlin, and Valkenburg, Neth., in late 1986. Raymond Ceulemans of Belgium edged long-time foe Nobuaki Kobayashi of Japan 42–35 in overall tour points to win the championship; each man earned just over $50,000.

**Pocket Billiards.** The game of nine ball held the sole spotlight in U.S. professional pocket billiards because, for the first time, there were no major championships played in the traditional game of 14.1 Continuous (straight pool). The nine-ball battles drummed up a record $465,000 in prize money, however, so players had little time to lament the possible final gasps of life for 14.1. The winter tour opened in Akron, Ohio, with a full field of 64 at the fifth annual Akron Open. The $4,000 top prize was won by the man who would go on to win eight consecutive tournaments as well as the *Pool & Billiard Magazine* and *Billiards Digest* male player of the year awards, Mike Sigel of Towson, Md. In addition, Sigel took two months off to serve as technical adviser for *The Color of Money,* the hit motion picture credited by many with reigniting public interest in pocket billiards and with providing a much-needed boost in consumer sales throughout the industry.

The 34-year-old Sigel also became the first player ever to exceed $100,000 in official tournament winnings in a 12-month period (July 1, 1986–June 30, 1987), with a total of $102,176. Another record, for the largest single tournament prize, went to Sigel as he garnered the $40,000 booty for the crown of the 356-player Resorts Last Call III in Atlantic City, N.J., in December 1986. During that period he also had victories in the Florida Nineball Open (Melbourne, January 1987), the first RAKMUP Classic (Columbia, S.C., February), the Classic Cup VI (St. Charles, Ill., April), the Sands/Regent Open IV (Reno, Nev., December 1986) and the Vitalie Invitational (Los Angeles, June).

Both major billiard magazines also agreed on the woman player of the year, and there was ample support for their choice. Although the women's professional tour had yet to reach the size and prize money levels of the men's circuit, the performance of Jean Balukas of Brooklyn, N.Y., was absolutely stunning. She opened the winter tour with victories at the third U.S. Nineball Open (Norfolk, Va.), the North Carolina Fall Classic (Charlotte), and the eighth Women's Professional Billiard Association National Championship (Sandusky, Ohio), all in November 1986. She continued unbeaten at the rich ($10,000) Resorts Last Call III in December, the third Bi-Annual Cleveland Open in January 1987, the first RAKMUP Classic in February, the Classic Cup VI in April, the fifth McDermott Masters (Davenport, Iowa) in May, and finally the third Glass City Open (Toledo, Ohio) in May. The 27-year-old Balukas then took a break, but her winning streak stood at an incredible 12 since her return from a softball injury in August 1986.

Back on the men's tour, Earl Strickland of Richmond, Ky., and Buddy Hall of Paducah, Ky., also notched victories. Strickland won the third Bowling Green (Ky.) Open (March), the fifth Sands/Regent Open in Reno (June), and the Charlotte Open (May); Hall won at the North Carolina Fall Classic, the third Glass City Open, and the Colorado Open in Denver in July. Still another Kentuckian, Nick Varner of Owensboro, won the fifth McDermott Masters top prize of $10,000; that amount was also won by Jim Rempe of Scranton, Pa., for his victory in the B.C. Open at Binghamton, N.Y., in September. (BRUCE H. VENZKE)

**Snooker.** Steve Davis (England) won the world professional snooker title for the fourth time when he defeated Joe Johnson (England) by 18 frames to 14 in the final at Sheffield, England, in May. Davis, who had earlier won the Canadian Masters title, the U.K. championship, and the Mercantile Credit Classic, earned a record £322,814 and remained the world's top-ranked player. Dennis Taylor (Northern Ireland) won the Masters title at Wembley, London, but lost 10–7 to Scottish champion Stephen Hendry in the Grand Prix final at Reading in October.

(SYDNEY E. FRISKIN)

# BOWLING

**World Tenpins.** At the tenth Asian Games in Seoul, South Korea, on Sept. 20–Oct. 5, 1986, Japanese bowlers captured 6 of the 12 gold medals. In the men's division Masami Hirai of Japan won the singles crown with 1,280 pins. In doubles the Japanese pair of Kengo Tagata and Hirosi Ishihara won with 2,484. The trios title also went to Japan, with a combined score of 3,534. In the five-man event Thailand won with 5,696, while Ishihara won the all-events with 4,758. In the final play-off for the masters' match game title, South Korea's Byun Yong Hwan defeated Japan's Shino Takashi 449–372.

In the women's division Cathrine Che became the first athlete to gain an Asian Games gold medal for Hong Kong, winning the singles with a score of 1,165. Kumiko Inatsu and Yoshiko Ishiba of Japan, with a combined score of 2,287, won the doubles. In trios the Japanese women finished first with 3,364. In the five-woman event the victorious Philippine team scored 5,573. Bong Coo of the Philippines, with 4,612, once again won the all-events title. The gold medal in the masters' match was won by Lee Ji Yeon of Korea; she defeated Che 388–362 in the final.

The 11th world amateur championships took place in Helsinki, Fin., June 3–13, 1987. More than 400 bowlers representing 43 nations took part. The U.S. team walked off with six gold, one silver, and four bronze medals. Twenty-one new championship records, including a perfect game of 300 by Rick Steelsmith (U.S.), were established. In the men's singles Patrick Rolland won France's first world title with 1,332. Ulf Hämnäs and Ulf Bolleby scored a 2,638 doubles victory for Sweden. In the trios competition the U.S. scored 3,873, 78 ahead of Finland. In the five-man team competition Finland lost by 76 pins to Sweden's remarkable 6,272 score. Steelsmith won the 24-game all-events with 4,860. In the masters' match game play-off final, Roger Pieters of Belgium defeated Steelsmith 684–564.

Among the women Mexico's Edda Piccini won the singles with 1,259, but team events were dominated by the U.S.: doubles (Cora Fiebig and Kathy Wodka) 2,566, trios 3,603, and teams of five 6,011. Sandra Jo Shiery of the U.S. won the all-events with a score of 4,895, 53 more than Piccini. In the two-game masters' grand finals, Annette Hagre won Sweden's third gold medal, defeating Japan's Mayumi Hayashi 419–405. (YRJÖ SARAHETE)

**U.S. Tenpins.** The son of one of the greatest bowlers in history surpassed his father's career earnings total at age 24 in one of the most dramatic moments of the 1987 tenpin campaign. Pete Weber of St. Louis, Mo., captured the Firestone Tournament of Champions in Akron, Ohio, to win a $50,000 prize that brought his seven-season total to $733,331; Dick Weber, a member of the Bowling Hall of Fame, had won $731,003 at that point in his career.

Pete Weber won the Professional Bowlers Association (PBA) Firestone meet by defeating four opponents. He topped Mike Aulby 231–205, Mark Roth 217–187, Art Trask 258–203, and Jim Murtishaw 222–190. The victory was Weber's tenth in PBA events, making him the youngest bowler to reach that plateau. Dick Weber, still in competition at 57, had 28 championships.

The American Bowling Congress (ABC) Masters tournament—and its first prize of $43,500—was won by a college student, Rick Steelsmith, a Wichita (Kan.) State University senior. In the final round of the meet in Niagara Falls, N.Y., Steelsmith defeated John Weltzien 237–184 and Brad Snell 258–219. Also at the ABC Tournament, which is open to virtually all nonprofessional male bowlers, the Regular Division winners were: team, Sound Track, Salamanca, N.Y., 3,197; singles, Terry Taylor, Nashville, Tenn., 749; doubles, Ray Betchkal and Dennis Schlichting, Racine, Wis., 1,380; all-events, Ryan Shafer, Elmira, N.Y., 2,044.

An amateur, Cathy Almeida of Blackwood, N.J., won the Queens tournament conducted by the Women's International Bowling Congress (WIBC) in Bloomfield, Conn., by defeating veteran professional Lorrie Nichols 850–817 in the final four-game match. Leanne Barrette, a 19-year-old newcomer to the WIBC tournament, rolled the meet's best nine-game total to win the Open Division all-events crown. Barrette, from Oklahoma City, Okla., totaled 1,972. Other WIBC winners included: team, Tool Warehouse, Hollywood, Fla., 3,033; singles, Regi Jonak, St. Peters, Mo., 728; doubles, Laura Grant, Norwalk, Conn., and Robin Romeo, Van Nuys, Calif., 1,328. (JOHN J. ARCHIBALD)

## BOXING

International boxing became more complicated in 1987 with the introduction of such new weights as super middleweight, mini flyweight, and straw weight plus a new list of junior world champions created by the World Boxing Council (WBC) but not universally recognized. Nevertheless, boxing achieved the unification of the heavyweight title. A series of elimination contests ended the existence of three recognized champions when Mike Tyson (U.S.) won worldwide recognition as the first undisputed heavyweight champion since Muhammad Ali.

Tyson began 1987 as the youngest heavyweight king ever, having at 20 knocked out Trevor Berbick (Canada) in two rounds to win the WBC title at the end of 1986. He soon added the World Boxing Association (WBA) crown by outpointing James ("Bonecrusher") Smith (U.S.). Tyson then successfully defended both versions of the title by stopping Pinklon Thomas (U.S.) in six rounds. When he next outpointed Tony Tucker (U.S.), he was also recognized as champion by the International Boxing Federation (IBF)—a ruling body based in New Jersey but still not recognized by the European Boxing Union (EBU) or the British Boxing Board of Control (BBBC). (After IBF champion Michael Spinks [U.S.] declined to defend his crown against Tucker, the IBF no longer recognized him and matched Tucker with James ["Buster"] Douglas of the U.S. for its version of the title fight, with Tucker winning in ten rounds.) Tyson ended the year by flattening Tyrell Biggs (U.S.), establishing a record of 32 wins in 32 contests.

Carlos de León (P.R.) carried on as WBC cruiserweight (195 lb) champion. A more active Evander Holyfield (U.S.) retained the WBA's cruiserweight (junior heavyweight) title, beating Henry Tillman (U.S.), Rickey Parkey (U.S.), and Ossie Ocasio (P.R.).

Thomas Hearns (U.S.), a former welterweight and junior middleweight champion, won the WBC light-heavyweight crown from Dennis Andries (England). Hearns gave up this title to bid for the WBC middleweight championship. Donny Lalonde (Canada) won the WBC light-heavyweight title in a fight with Eddie Davis (U.S.). The WBA light-heavyweight title changed hands twice. Leslie Stewart (Trinidad) stopped Marvin Johnson (U.S.) but lost his first defense to Virgil Hill (U.S.). Hill successfully defended the title against Rufino Angelo (France). Chong Pal Park (South Korea) became the first WBA champion at super middleweight—a weight previously recognized only by the IBF and still not accepted by the WBC.

The most controversial contest occurred when Sugar Ray Leonard made a comeback at 30 after three years out of the ring and outpointed the undisputed middleweight champion, Marvin Hagler (U.S.). Leonard had fought only once in five years and had twice undergone cataract surgery. Hagler had defended his title 12 times and had been undefeated for 11 years. The WBA, EBU, and BBBC refused to recognize the contest as a championship, but the WBC gave its blessing. Though Hagler was a strong favourite, Leonard won a controversial decision and his third world crown.

Leonard then announced his retirement, and Hearns, challenging Juan Domingo Roldan (Arg.) for the now-vacant WBC middleweight title, scored a fourth-round knockout and became the first boxer ever to win four world titles. The WBA, which had stripped Hagler of the title when he agreed to fight Leonard, matched Iran Barkley (U.S.) against Sumbu Kalambay (Italy) for its version of the championship; Kalambay, born in Zaire, won.

The WBC junior middleweight championship changed twice. Lupe Aquino (U.S.) took it from Duane Thomas (U.S.) but was subsequently outpointed by Gianfranco Rosi (Italy); Mike McCallum (Jamaica) defended the WBA title, defeating Milton McCrory (U.S.) and Don Curry (U.S.), but then gave up the crown to compete as a middleweight. It was won by Julian Jackson (Virgin Islands, U.S.), who stopped In Chul Baek (South Korea).

Lloyd Honeyghan (England), undisputed welterweight champion, surrendered the WBA version rather than defend his title against a South African challenger, Harold Volbrecht. The WBA then matched Volbrecht with Mark Breland (U.S.), and Breland, a former Olympic champion, was the winner. An upset followed when Breland lost the crown in his first defense, against Marlon Starling (U.S.). Honeyghan remained WBC champion, stopping Johnny Bumphus (U.S.) in 2 rounds, outpointing Maurice Blocker (U.S.) over 12, and knocking out Gene Hatcher (U.S.) in 40 seconds—the quickest knockout recorded in a world championship. However, Honeyghan lost the title and his unbeaten record in 32 contests to Jorge Vaca (Mexico), a rank outsider who was fighting as a substitute. The contest ended in the eighth round when Vaca received a severe cut above the right eye following an accidental clash of heads. Under new WBC rules, when such an accident occurs,

AFP PHOTO

Mike Tyson celebrates his victory over Tyrell Biggs, which cemented his status as the first undisputed heavyweight champion since Muhammad Ali and allowed him to wear three championship belts.

Sugar Ray Leonard (right) throws a punch at Marvin Hagler in their contest for the middleweight title. Leonard, who had returned to the ring after an absence of three years, outpointed Hagler to win the title.

KEN REGAN—CAMERA 5

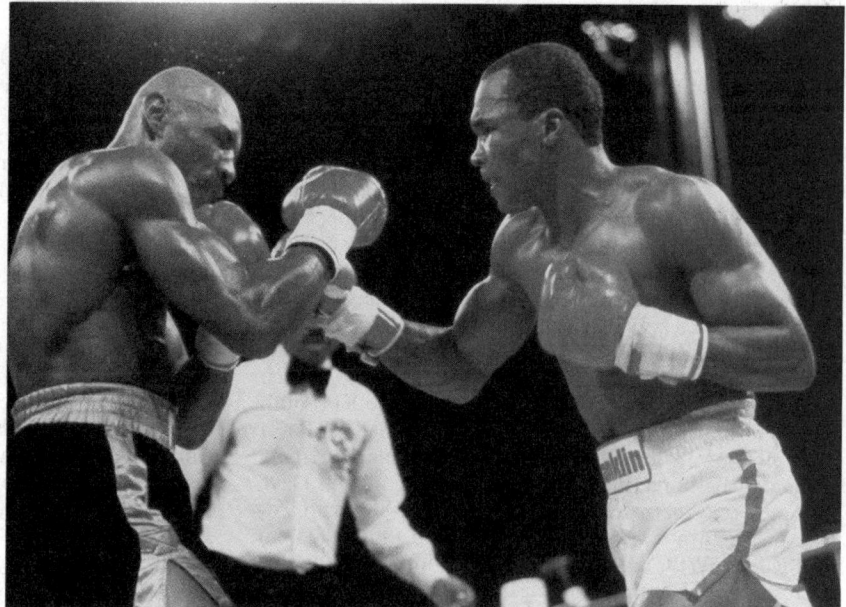

the referee is permitted to halt the contest and call for the scores of the three ringside judges. The boxer leading on points at the end of the previous round is named the winner. The judges voted 2–1 for Vaca.

René Arredondo (Mexico), who had previously lost the WBC junior welterweight crown in one round against Tsuyoshi Hamada (Japan), gained revenge by stopping Hamada in six rounds but lost the title to Roger Mayweather (U.S.) in six. After retaining the WBA championship and an unbeaten record of 48 wins by beating Rodolfo González (Mexico), Patrizio Oliva (Italy) was unexpectedly defeated by Juan Martin Coggi (Arg.) in Sicily.

Hector Camacho (P.R.) gave up the WBC lightweight crown to compete among junior welterweights. The vacant title was won by José Luis Ramírez (Mexico) with a points win against Terrence Alli (Guyana). Ramírez then knocked out Cornelius Boza-Edwards (Uganda) in five rounds. The WBA title remained with Edwin Rosario (P.R.) when he knocked out Juan Nazario (P.R.), but he lost to Julio César Chávez (Mexico) in 11 rounds. Earlier, Chávez defeated Francisco Tomas da Cruz (Brazil) in 3 rounds and Danilo Cabrera (Dominican Republic) over 12, completing nine defenses of the WBC junior lightweight crown. Brian Mitchell (South Africa) defended the WBA version, drawing with Joe Rivera (P.R.), stopping Francisco Fernández

(Panama) in 14, and outpointing Daniel Londas (France).

Azumah Nelson (Ghana) remained one of the WBC's most consistent champions, defeating Mauro Gutierrez (Mexico) in 6 rounds and Marcos Villasana (Mexico) over 12 to retain the featherweight crown he had won in 1984. The WBA title changed hands when Antonio Esparragoza (Venezuela) stopped Steve Cruz (U.S.) in 12 rounds. Esparragoza then retained the championship by knocking out Pascual Aranda (U.S.) in ten. Jeff Fenech (Australia) knocked out Samart Payakarun (Thailand) to take the WBC junior featherweight crown and become the first Australian to win two world titles. Fenech retained the championship with a controversial win over former bantamweight champion Carlos Zarate (Mexico). Fenech received a bad eye cut in the fourth round in an accidental clash of heads. The referee called for the judge's score, and Fenech, leading on points, was declared the winner at the end of the third round. Louie Espinoza (U.S.) took over the vacant WBA version, stopping Tommy Valoy (Dominican Republic) in four rounds. He remained champion by knocking out Aranda in ten rounds but lost the title in a decision to Julio Gervacio (Dominican Republic).

Miguel Lora (Colombia) continued as WBC bantamweight champion, stopping Antonio Avelar (Mexico) in four rounds. After retaining the WBA championship

## World European, Commonwealth, and British Boxing Champions
as of Dec. 31, 1987

| Division | WBC[1] | WBA[2] | Europe | Commonwealth | Britain |
|---|---|---|---|---|---|
| Heavyweight | M. Tyson (U.S.) | M. Tyson (U.S.) | Francesco Damiani, Italy | Horace Notice, England | Horace Notice, England |
| Cruiserweight | C. de León (Puerto Rico) | E. Holyfield (U.S.) | Sammy Reeson, England | Glenn McCrory, England | Tee Jay, England |
| Light heavyweight | D. Lalonde (Canada) | V. Hill (U.S.) | Tom Collins, England | Willie Featherstone, Canada | Tony Wilson, England |
| Super middleweight | — | Chong Pal Park (South Korea) | — | — | — |
| Middleweight | T. Hearns (U.S.) | S. Kalambay (Italy) | Pierre Joly, France | Tony Sibson, England | Tony Sibson, England |
| Junior middleweight | G. Rosi (Italy) | J. Jackson (Virgin I.) | vacant | Troy Waters, Australia | vacant |
| Welterweight | J. Vaca (Mexico) | M. Starling (U.S.) | Mauro Martelli, Switzerland | Wilf Gentzen, Australia | Kirkland Laing, England |
| Junior welterweight | R. Mayweather (U.S.) | J. M. Coggi (Argentina) | Thomas N'Kalankete, France | Tony Laing, England | Lloyd Christie, England |
| Lightweight | J. L. Ramírez (Mexico) | J. C. Chávez (Mexico) | Gert Bo Jacobsen, Denmark | Mo Hussein, England | Alex Dickson, Scotland |
| Junior lightweight | vacant | B. Mitchell (South Africa) | Salvatore Curcetti, Italy | John Sichula, Zambia | Pat Cowdell, England |
| Featherweight | A. Nelson (Ghana) | A. Esparragoza (Venezuela) | vacant | Tyrone Downes, Barbados | Robert Dickie, Wales |
| Junior featherweight | J. Fenech (Australia) | J. Gervacio (Dominican Rep.) | — | — | — |
| Bantamweight | M. Lora (Colombia) | W. Vásquez (Puerto Rico) | vacant | Ray Minus, The Bahamas | Bill Hardy, England |
| Super flyweight | J. Rojas (Colombia) | K. Galaxy (Thailand) | — | — | — |
| Flyweight | S. Chitalada (Thailand) | F. Bassa (Colombia) | Duke McKenzie, England | Nana Yaw Konadu, Ghana | Dave McAuley, Northern Ireland |
| Junior flyweight | Chang Jung Koo (South Korea) | Yuh Myung Woo (South Korea) | — | — | — |
| Straw weight | H. K. Ioka (Japan) | — | — | — | — |

[1]World Boxing Council.  [2]World Boxing Association.

with a points win against Frankie Duarte (U.S.), Bernardo Pinango (Venezuela) retired because of illness. The vacant crown went to Takuya Muguruma (Japan), who knocked out Azael Moran (Panama) but lost in his first defense to Park Chang Young (South Korea). Park also lost the title in his first defense, against Wilfredo Vásquez (P.R.).

The WBC super flyweight championship changed hands twice. After retaining it for the sixth time against Frank Cedeno (Phil.), Gilberto Roman (Mexico) was stopped in 11 rounds by Santos Laciar (Arg.). In his next contest, however, Laciar was outpointed by Jesús Rojas (Colombia), who kept the title by stopping Gustavo Ballas (Arg.) in four. Kaosai Galaxy (Thailand) remained WBA champion with wins against Elly Pical (Indon.) and Chung Byung Kwan (South Korea). Sot Chitalada (Thailand) continued as WBC flyweight king, knocking out Ahn Rae Ki (South Korea) in four rounds. The WBA title went to Fidel Bassa (Colombia) with a points victory against Hilario Zapata (Panama); Bassa retained the crown by knocking out Dave McAuley (Northern Ireland) in 13 and drawing with Zapata in a return contest. Chang Jung Koo (South Korea) retained the WBC junior flyweight title for the 13th time after stopping Efren Pinto (Mexico) and Agustin García (Colombia). Yuh Myung Woo (South Korea) also kept the WBA version, halting Eduardo Tunon (Panama) in one round and Benedicto Murillo (Panama) in 15. Hiro Ki Ioka (Japan) became champion of the WBC's newly instituted straw weight division (maximum of 105 lb) with a unanimous 12-round decision over Mai Thornburifarm (Thailand).                         (FRANK BUTLER)

# CHESS

In an exciting contest that remained in the balance until the last minute of the final game, Garry Kasparov of the U.S.S.R. retained the world chess championship by tying with his Soviet compatriot Anatoly Karpov 12–12 in a match held Oct. 12–Dec. 19, 1987, in Seville, Spain. Under the rules of the Fédération Internationale des Échecs (FIDE), the defending champion needs only a tie to keep the title.

Karpov had appeared to be in the driver's seat before the final match when he took a one-game lead after a series of errors by his opponent. Thus Kasparov had to win the last game in order to remain world champion, and he did so by using his queen to invade Karpov's king position. After eight hours of play, Karpov resigned on his 64th move (*see* box).

In the traditional tournament at Hastings, England, straddling the turn of the year from 1986 to 1987, there was a four-way tie for first place between Jonathan Speelman (England), Murray Chandler (England), Bent Larsen (Denmark), and Smbat Lputian (U.S.S.R.). The first major tournament to begin in 1987 was held at Wijk aan Zee, Neth., where England's Nigel Short started what was to be a phenomenal run of successes by taking first prize ahead of Viktor Korchnoi (Switz.), Tony Miles (England), and Ljubomir Ljubojevic (Yugos.).

Almost immediately afterward, Short and Kasparov took part in an interesting experiment in London. Dressed in dinner jackets (a white one for the player with the white pieces), they contested a six-game match at the London Hippodrome. Each player was allowed 25 minutes for all his moves, and the "intelligent chess board" technology devised in England was used to display the games to the audience. All six games were decisive, and Kasparov was the winner as expected; however, Short's tally of two wins was creditable. All six games were televised live with a running commentary. The experiment was a success.

Soon after this match Short flew to Reykjavík, Iceland, where he decimated a strong field that included Mikhail Tal (U.S.S.R.), Jan Timman (Neth.), Korchnoi, and Lev Polugaevsky (U.S.S.R.), but then at the SWIFT tournament in Brussels he was completely out of form. This tournament was won by Kasparov and Ljubojevic, with Karpov finishing third, and the first Blitz world championship, which took place at the end of the SWIFT event, was won outright by Kasparov.

By the middle of the year the Grand Master Association (GMA) had begun to have conflicts with FIDE. The world body wanted the GMA to affiliate with it, but the grand masters preferred to maintain their independence.

During the summer there were three interzonal tournaments to select most of the qualifiers for the next stage in the world championship cycle. From this cycle the challenger for the 1990 world championship match would eventually emerge. At the Subotica, Yugos., Interzonal, Short, Speelman, and Gyula Sax (Hung.) shared first place. At Szirak, Hung., Valery Salov (U.S.S.R.) and Johann Hjartarson (Iceland) shared first place. Lajos Portisch (Hung.) earned the third qualifying place after a playoff match against John Nunn (England). At Zagreb, Yugos., the veteran Korchnoi qualified, together with Yasser Seirawan (U.S.) and Jaan Ehlvest (U.S.S.R.).

In other major international events played during the summer, the Biel, Switz., tournament was won by Boris Gulko, who now represented the U.S. after emigrating legally from the U.S.S.R. The OHRA tournament in Amsterdam was won by John van der Wiel (Neth.); also in The Netherlands the Tilburg competition was won by Timman. The U.S.S.R. championship ended in a tie for first place; in the play-off match Aleksandr Beljavsky (U.S.S.R.) took the title, with Salov as runner-up. In the U.S. Seirawan again demonstrated that he was that nation's number one player.

Short won the British championship but soon afterward was eliminated in the British Speed championship—another "made for television" event—in which a 50-minute time limit per game was used. The tournament was won by Nunn, who beat Julian Hodgson in the final.

Just as the 1987 world championship match was getting

## 24th (final) game of the world championship match

| White G. Kasparov | Black A. Karpov | White G. Kasparov | Black A. Karpov |
|---|---|---|---|
| 1 c4 | e6 | 34 Qd8+ | Kh7 |
| 2 Nf3 | Nf6 | 35 N×f7 | Ng6 |
| 3 g3 | d5 | 36 Qe8 | Qe7 |
| 4 b3 | Be7 | 37 Q×a4 | Q×f7 |
| 5 Bg2 | 0-0 | 38 Be4 | Kg8 |
| 6 0-0 | b6 | 39 Qb5 | Nf8 |
| 7 Bb2 | Bb7 | 40 Q×b6 | Qf6 |
| 8 e3 | Nbd7 | 41 Qb5 | Qe7 |
| 9 Nc3 | Ne4 | 42 Kg2 | g6 |
| 10 Ne2 | a5 | 43 Qa5 | Qg7 |
| 11 d3 | Bf6 | 44 Qc5 | Qf7 |
| 12 Qc2 | B×b2 | 45 h4 | h5 |
| 13 Q×b2 | Nd6 | 46 Qc6 | Qe7 |
| 14 c×d5 | B×d5 | 47 Bd3 | Qf7 |
| 15 d4 | c5 | 48 Qd6 | Kg7 |
| 16 Rfd1 | Rc8 | 49 e4 | Kg8 |
| 17 Nf4 | B×f3 | 50 Bc4 | Kg7 |
| 18 B×f3 | Qe7 | 51 Qe5+ | Kg8 |
| 19 Rac1 | Rfd8 | 52 Qd6 | Kg7 |
| 20 d×c5 | N×c5 | 53 Bb5 | Kg8 |
| 21 b4 | a×b4 | 54 Bc6 | Qa7 |
| 22 Q×b4 | Qa7 | 55 Qb4 | Qc7 |
| 23 a3 | Nf5 | 56 Qb7 | Qd8 |
| 24 Rb1 | R×d1+ | 57 e5 | Qa5 |
| 25 R×d1 | Qc7 | 58 Be8 | Qc5 |
| 26 Nd3 | h6 | 59 Qf7+ | Kh8 |
| 27 Rc1 | Ne7 | 60 Ba4 | Qd5+ |
| 28 Qb5 | Nf5 | 61 Kh2 | Qc5 |
| 29 a4 | Nd6 | 62 Bb3 | Qc8 |
| 30 Qb1 | Qa7 | 63 Bd1 | Qc5 |
| 31 Ne5 | N×a4 | 64 Kg2 | |
| 32 R×c8+ | N×c8 | | |
| 33 Qd1 | Ne7 | Black resigned | |

under way, the chess world was stirred by a succession of dramatic events. Tony Miles, who had been England's top board for a decade, suddenly announced that in the future he would represent the U.S. Various newspapers speculated that a series of poor results had damaged his chances of regaining top-board status in England and that he had more chance of playing top board for the U.S. Another surprise was the creation of the English Chess Association (ECA), whose chairman was Alexander Kennaway of Imperial College, University of London; ECA wished to make chess as popular as snooker and to bring grass-roots players into closer contact with the country's grand masters and masters.

In addition, there was Kasparov's autobiography, *Child of Change,* which made interesting allegations concerning the way his career as world champion had been stunted by the political influence of his predecessor, Karpov. The publication date was timed to add a touch of spice to the start of the fourth Kasparov versus Karpov world championship match.

Finally, an event took place in 1987 that represented a milestone in chess. Under tournament conditions Joel Lautier (France), world under-14 champion, lost both games in a two-game match to a computer program called Hitech, written at Carnegie-Mellon University, Pittsburgh, Pa., by Hans Berliner, himself a former world champion at correspondence chess. (RAYMOND KEENE)

## CONTRACT BRIDGE

The new laws of duplicate bridge became effective worldwide from October 1987. Perhaps the most revolutionary of the changes related to scoring. The scale of penalties for undertricks in doubled nonvulnerable contracts was altered. Until the new laws the penalties were 100 points for the first undertrick and 200 for each subsequent one. Under the new law the fourth undertrick and each subsequent one would carry a penalty of 300. Redoubled penalties remained twice the doubled amount. For making a redoubled contract the "well-played" bonus, formerly 50, was raised to 100.

The 1987 world bridge championships featured the 28th Bermuda Bowl and the 6th Venice Cup, each played in October at Ocho Rios, Jamaica. In each event ten teams competed: the seven zonal champions, the host country, and the runners-up of the two major zones, Europe and North America. The winners of those two zones were exempted to the semifinal stage. The U.S., defending the Bermuda Bowl it had held since 1976, and European champion Sweden were the exempted teams. After a double round-robin for the other two semifinal spots, these were gained by Great Britain and Taiwan. Great Britain then met Sweden, while the U.S. was opposed by Taiwan. The U.S. had an easy passage, winning by 421–290. In the Sweden versus Great Britain match a bidding misunderstanding by a Swedish pair on the second day resulted in a record penalty of 2,800 on a deal on which the British scored 110 in the replay. The deal (*see* box) indicates the lack of concentration that followed the disaster. With 32 boards to play, the British led by 66 points and emerged with a 358–311 victory.

In the finals Great Britain proved equal to the U.S. almost to the end. With 16 boards to play in the 176-board contest, the U.S. led by only 14 points. The final score was a 354–290 win for the U.S. The gold medal team included Bob Hamman, Bobby Wolff, Chip Martel, Lew Stansby, Hugh Ross, Mike Lawrence, and nonplaying captain Dan Morse. Great Britain's silver medalists were Raymond Brock, Tony Forrester, John Armstrong, Gra-

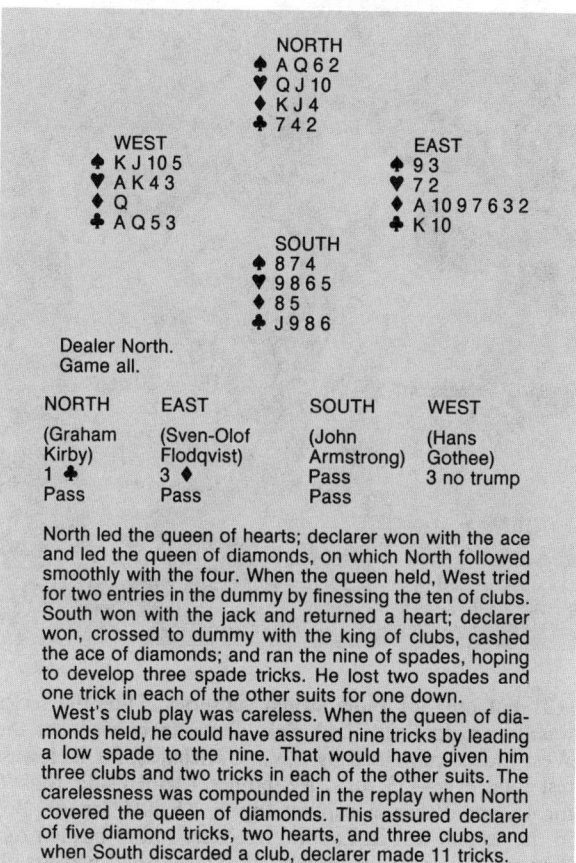

```
                    NORTH
                  ♠ A Q 6 2
                  ♥ Q J 10
                  ♦ K J 4
                  ♣ 7 4 2
  WEST                              EAST
♠ K J 10 5                        ♠ 9 3
♥ A K 4 3                         ♥ 7 2
♦ Q                              ♦ A 10 9 7 6 3 2
♣ A Q 5 3                         ♣ K 10
                    SOUTH
                  ♠ 8 7 4
                  ♥ 9 8 6 5
                  ♦ 8 5
                  ♣ J 9 8 6
```

Dealer North.
Game all.

| NORTH | EAST | SOUTH | WEST |
|---|---|---|---|
| (Graham Kirby) | (Sven-Olof Flodqvist) | (John Armstrong) | (Hans Gothee) |
| 1 ♣ | 3 ♦ | Pass | 3 no trump |
| Pass | Pass | Pass | |

North led the queen of hearts; declarer won with the ace and led the queen of diamonds, on which North followed smoothly with the four. When the queen held, West tried for two entries in the dummy by finessing the ten of clubs. South won with the jack and returned a heart; declarer won, crossed to dummy with the king of clubs, cashed the ace of diamonds; and ran the nine of spades, hoping to develop three spade tricks. He lost two spades and one trick in each of the other suits for one down.

West's club play was careless. When the queen of diamonds held, he could have assured nine tricks by leading a low spade to the nine. That would have given him three clubs and two tricks in each of the other suits. The carelessness was compounded in the replay when North covered the queen of diamonds. This assured declarer of five diamond tricks, two hearts, and three clubs, and when South discarded a club, declarer made 11 tricks.

ham Kirby, Jeremy Flint, Robert Sheehan, and nonplaying captain Tony Priday.

In the Venice Cup the exempted teams were U.S. 1 and France; easy qualifiers from the round-robin were U.S. 2 and Italy. In an all-American semifinal U.S. 2 won 277–251; France beat Italy 276–227 in the other match. In the final U.S. 2 won 251–219. Gold medal winners were Katherine Wei, Judi Radin, Juanita Chambers, Cheri Bjerkan, Beth Palmer, Lynn Deas, and nonplaying captain Carol Sanders. France's silver medalists were Véronique Bessis, Sylvie Willard, Hélène Bordenave, Bénédicte Cronier, Ginette Chevalley, Danielle Gaviard, and nonplaying captain Gérard le Royer. (HAROLD FRANKLIN)

## CRICKET

The balance of power in international cricket in 1986–87 shifted away from the West Indies, which failed to win a series, and toward Pakistan, which beat India and England and drew with the West Indies. England was highly successful in Australia before losing at home to Pakistan.

In the first test match against India, in Madras, Australia's D. M. Jones (210), D. C. Boon (122), and captain A. R. Border (106) built a massive first innings total, and the contest seemed likely to end in a draw. But an enterprising declaration by Border left India 348 to win, a task they appeared to be achieving at 331 for 6. The scores were evened with three balls remaining and, off the second to last ball of the match, G. R. J. Matthews had Maninder Singh out leg before wicket to record test cricket's second tie. The second test in Delhi was ruined by rain. In the third test in Bombay, bat dominated ball; G. R. Marsh (101) for Australia and S. M. Gavaskar (103; *see* BIOGRAPHIES), D. B. Vengsarkar (164 not out), and R. J. Shastri

Members of Pakistan's cricket team congratulate their captain, Imran Khan (facing camera), for fine play during the third match in a five-test series with England.
ADRIAN MURRELL—ALLSPORT

(121 not out) for India scored centuries. Thus the series was drawn. In Faisalabad, Pak., Pakistan bowled out the West Indies, captained by I. V. A. Richards, for its lowest test total ever—53 runs; leg-spinner Abdul Qadir took 6 for 16 and Pakistan captain Imran Khan 4 for 30. But in the second test in Lahore, the West Indies bowled out Pakistan to win by an innings. M. D. Marshall had match figures of 6 for 47, and C. A. Walsh 7 for 77. The final test, in Karachi, ended in controversy when the umpires stopped play because of bad light with 11 overs remaining and Pakistan facing defeat. In an enthralling series no batsman made a century; Khan and Qadir were joint leading wicket-takers with 18.

In the first test in the series for the Ashes urn, held in Brisbane, Australia, England played Australia. England, led by M. W. Gatting and fortified by I. T. Botham (138), G. R. Dilley (5 for 68 in the first innings), and J. E. Emburey (5 for 80 in the second) won comfortably, against all expectations. England's batsmen dominated the next three tests, ensuring draws in Perth and Adelaide and taking the series with a win in the fourth test in Melbourne. England opener B. C. Broad scored centuries in those tests (162, 116, and 112). In Perth, in the second test, D. I. Gower (136) and wicketkeeper C. J. Richards (133) also made centuries for England, while, inevitably, Australia's reply was led by Border (125). In Adelaide, besides Broad, Bor-

**Test Series Results, September 1986–September 1987**

| Test | Host country and its scores | | Visiting country and its scores | | Result |
|---|---|---|---|---|---|
| 1st | India | 397 and 347 | Australia | 574 for 7 wkt dec and 170 for 5 wkt dec | Match tied |
| 2nd | India | 107 for 3 wkt | Australia | 207 for 3 wkt dec | Match drawn |
| 3rd | India | 517 for 5 wkt dec | Australia | 345 and 216 for 2 wkt | Match drawn |
| 1st | Pakistan | 159 and 328 | West Indies | 248 and 53 | Pakistan won by 186 runs |
| 2nd | Pakistan | 131 and 77 | West Indies | 218 | West Indies won by an innings and 10 runs |
| 3rd | Pakistan | 239 and 125 for 7 wkt | West Indies | 240 and 211 | Match drawn |
| 1st | Australia | 248 and 282 | England | 456 and 77 for 3 wkt | England won by 7 wkt |
| 2nd | Australia | 401 and 197 for 4 wkt | England | 592 for 8 wkt dec and 199 for 8 wkt dec | Match drawn |
| 3rd | Australia | 514 for 5 wkt dec and 201 for 3 wkt dec | England | 455 and 39 for 2 wkt | Match drawn |
| 4th | Australia | 141 and 194 | England | 349 | England won by an innings and 14 runs |
| 5th | Australia | 343 and 251 | England | 275 and 264 | Australia won by 55 runs |
| 1st | India | 676 for 7 wkt | Sri Lanka | 420 | Match drawn |
| 2nd | India | 451 for 6 wkt dec | Sri Lanka | 204 and 141 | India won by an innings and 106 runs |
| 3rd | India | 400 | Sri Lanka | 191 and 142 | India won by an innings and 67 runs |
| 1st | India | 527 for 9 wkt dec | Pakistan | 487 for 9 wkt dec and 182 for 3 wkt | Match drawn |
| 2nd | India | 403 and 181 for 3 wkt dec | Pakistan | 229 and 179 for 5 wkt | Match drawn |
| 3rd | India | 465 for 8 wkt dec and 114 for 2 wkt | Pakistan | 341 | Match drawn |
| 4th | India | 323 | Pakistan | 395 and 136 for 2 wkt | Match drawn |
| 5th | India | 145 and 204 | Pakistan | 116 and 249 | Pakistan won by 16 runs |
| 1st | New Zealand | 228 and 386 for 5 wkt dec | West Indies | 345 and 50 for 2 wkt | Match drawn |
| 2nd | New Zealand | 157 and 273 | West Indies | 418 for 9 wkt dec and 16 for 0 wkt | West Indies won by 10 wkt |
| 3rd | New Zealand | 332 and 33 for 5 wkt | West Indies | 100 and 264 | New Zealand won by 5 wkt |
| 1st | Sri Lanka | 397 for 9 wkt dec | New Zealand | 406 for 5 wkt | Match drawn |
| 1st | England | 447 | Pakistan | 140 for 5 wkt | Match drawn |
| 2nd | England | 368 | Pakistan | did not bat | Match drawn |
| 3rd | England | 136 and 199 | Pakistan | 353 | Pakistan won by an innings and 18 runs |
| 4th | England | 521 and 109 for 7 wkt | Pakistan | 439 and 205 | Match drawn |
| 5th | England | 232 and 315 for 4 wkt | Pakistan | 708 | Match drawn |
| Bicentenary test | | | | | |
| | MCC | 455 for 5 wkt dec and 318 for 6 wkt dec | Rest of the World | 421 for 7 wkt dec and 13 for 1 wkt | Match drawn |

der (100 not out), Boon (103), and Gatting (100) scored centuries, but it was the wickets of Botham (5 for 41) and G. C. Small (5 for 48) in Melbourne that brought England victory in the match and the series. Australia won the last test in Sydney, owing mainly to eight wickets by an unknown offspinner, P. L. Taylor, making his test debut, and an unbeaten 184 by Jones. Broad was the outstanding batsman, with 487 runs at an average of 69.57. Australia's B. A. Reid was the leading wicket-taker, with 20. England went on to win the Perth Challenge and the Benson & Hedges World Series cup.

After a draw in the first match India, led by Kapil Dev, thrashed Sri Lanka in the second and third tests. Vengsarkar (2), Gavaskar, M. Azharuddin, Dev, and M. Amarnath scored centuries; the spinners Maninder Singh (18 wickets) and N. S. Yadav (11) completed the rout. But Pakistan proved a better foe for India and, after four draws, won a pulsating final test in Bangalore when 35 of the 40 wickets fell to spin bowlers. Earlier, Vengsarkar, Azharuddin, K. Srikkanth, and Shastri made hundreds for India, while Ijaz Faqih, Khan, Rameez Raja, and Shoaib Mohammad replied for Pakistan. Left-armer Singh, with 20 wickets (10 in the last test), and Pakistan's offspinner Tauseef Ahmed, who shared 18 wickets with Iqbal Qasim in Bangalore, took 16 in the series.

In New Zealand a double century by C. G. Greenidge and six wickets each for Marshall and Walsh in the second test in Auckland gave the West Indies victory. But in the third test at Christchurch, nine wickets by R. J. Hadlee, New Zealand's outstanding bowler, and 83 by its best batsman, M. D. Crowe, to add to his two centuries in the first two tests, leveled the series; Crowe's 328 runs established a record for New Zealand at home against the West Indies. Other centurions were D. L. Haynes for the West Indies (121) and J. G. Wright for New Zealand (138). Hadlee took 17 wickets. Because of local unrest New Zealand's tour of Sri Lanka had to be called off after the drawn first test, in which a double century by D. S. B. P. Kuruppu had been canceled out by the New Zealand captain J. J. Crowe (120 not out) and Hadlee (151 not out).

Rain dominated Pakistan's summer tour of England. Much of the first test at Old Trafford, Manchester, and of the second at Lord's, London, where C. W. J. Athey made his first test century, were washed out. R. T. Robinson scored 166 at Old Trafford. In the third test at Headingley, Leeds, Pakistan's Khan took ten wickets and Wasim Akram five to rout England. In the fourth test at Edgbaston, after Gatting's 124 and seven wickets by Dilley and six by N. A. Foster, England needed to make 124 off the last 18 overs and fell 15 runs short. A massive total in the final test at The Oval, London, inspired by Javed Miandad (260), Salim Malik (102), and Khan (118), ensured Pakistan of the draw it needed to win its first series in England. In Khan (21 wickets) Pakistan had the outstanding individual in the series.

The English season ended with the bicentenary test to celebrate the 200th birthday of the Marylebone Cricket Club (MCC). It was held at Lord's between an MCC team and a Rest of the World XI. Gavaskar recorded his first century at Lord's; G. A. Gooch returned to England's colours with 117; MCC captain Gatting made his third hundred of the summer; and Greenidge scored 122.

(ANDREW LONGMORE)

## CYCLING

Stephen Roche of Ireland was the leading cyclist of 1987, winning the two major national tours, the Tour de France and the Tour of Italy, and the world professional road race

championship in the same season. Only Belgium's Eddy Merckx in 1974 had previously won all three events in one year. The 27-year-old Roche won the 26-day Italian tour after a tense and bitter struggle with teammate Roberto Visentini, the home favourite, who retired with one day remaining in the 3,923-km race (one km = 0.62 mi). The 4,231-km Tour de France, which began in West Berlin 18 days later on July 1, had eight different leaders but narrowed down in the Alps to a struggle between Spain's Pedro Delgado and Roche. At the end of the 21st stage to La Plagne, France, Roche needed oxygen, but he recovered sufficiently to win back the yellow jersey of overall leader on the next to the last stage, a time trial, in Dijon, France, and finished with an advantage of 40 sec in Paris on July 26. The world championship was held at Villach, Austria, over 276 km, and after nearly seven hours of racing Roche finished one second ahead of 1986 champion Moreno Argentin of Italy.

A new event was included in the world championship road program, a 50-km team time trial for women, won by

### 1987 Cycling Champions

| Event | Winner | Country |
|---|---|---|
| **WORLD AMATEUR CHAMPIONS—TRACK** | | |
| Men | | |
| Sprint | L. Hesslich | East Germany |
| Tandem sprint | F. Colas, F. Magne | France |
| Individual pursuit | G. Umaras | U.S.S.R. |
| Team pursuit | V. Ekimov, S. Khmelinine, A. Krasnov, V. Manakov | U.S.S.R. |
| 1,000-m time trial | M. Vinnicombe | Australia |
| 50-km points | M. Ganeev | U.S.S.R. |
| 50-km motor paced | M. Gentili | Italy |
| Women | | |
| Sprint | E. Salumiae | U.S.S.R. |
| Individual pursuit | R. Whitehead | U.S. |
| **WORLD PROFESSIONAL CHAMPIONS—TRACK** | | |
| Sprint | N. Tawara | Japan |
| Individual pursuit | H.-H. Oersted | Denmark |
| 50-km points | U. Freuler | Switzerland |
| One-hour motor paced | M. Hurzeler | Switzerland |
| Keirin | H. Honda | Japan |
| **WORLD AMATEUR CHAMPIONS—ROAD** | | |
| Men | | |
| Individual road race | R. Vivien | France |
| 100-km team time trial | R. Fortunato, E. Poli, M. Scirea, F. Vanzella | Italy |
| Women | | |
| Individual road race | J. Longo | France |
| 50-km team time trial | A. Iakovleva, N. Kibardina, T. Poliakqva, L. Pugovichnikova | U.S.S.R. |
| **WORLD PROFESSIONAL CHAMPION—ROAD** | | |
| Individual road race | S. Roche | Ireland |
| **WORLD CHAMPIONS—CYCLO-CROSS** | | |
| Amateur | M. Kluge | West Germany |
| Professional | K.-P. Thaler | West Germany |
| **MAJOR PROFESSIONAL ROAD-RACE WINNERS** | | |
| Tour de France | S. Roche | Ireland |
| Tour of Italy | S. Roche | Ireland |
| Tour of Spain | L. Herrera | Colombia |
| Paris–Nice | S. Kelly | Ireland |
| Milan–San Remo | E. Maechler | Switzerland |
| Tour of Flanders | C. Criquielion | Belgium |
| Paris–Roubaix | E. Vanderaerden | Belgium |
| Flèche Wallonne | J.-C. Leclercq | France |
| Liège–Bastogne–Liège | M. Argentin | Italy |
| Dauphiné–Libéré | C. Mottet | France |
| Bordeaux–Paris | B. Vallet | France |
| G. P. de Midi Libre | P. Esnault | France |
| Amstel Gold | J. Zoetemelk | The Netherlands |
| Tour of Switzerland | A. Hampsten | U.S. |
| G. P. Frankfurt | D.-O. Lauritzen | Norway |
| Dunkirk 4-day | H. Frison | Belgium |
| Tirenno Adriatico | R. Sorensen | Denmark |
| Ghent–Wevelgem | T. van Vliet | The Netherlands |
| Tour of Romandie | S. Roche | Ireland |
| Paris–Brussels | W. Arras | Belgium |
| Tour of Britain | J. McLoughlin | Great Britain |
| Tour de l'Avenir (EEC Tour)* | M. Madiot | France |
| Tour of Britain Milk Race* | M. Elliott | Great Britain |
| Coors Classic* | R. Alcala | Mexico |
| Warsaw–Berlin–Prague† | U. Ampler | East Germany |
| Tour of Lombardy | M. Argentin | Italy |
| G. P. des Nations | C. Mottet | France |

*Mixed professional and amateur.
†Amateur.

the U.S.S.R. Jeannie Longo of France won the individual women's race for the third successive year; she also won the women's Tour de France for the first time.

Track events for the world championships were held in Vienna at the Ferry-Dusika Stadium. Claudio Golinelli of Italy recorded a time of 10.587 sec to break the world professional indoor 200-m flying-start record, which had stood since 1961. World indoor best pursuit times were set in non-world-record conditions on the 250-m wooden track by Guintautas Umaras of the U.S.S.R. (amateur 4,000 m, 4 min 27.02 sec), Denmark's Hans-Henrik Oersted (professional 5,000 m, 5 min 41.06 sec), and Rebecca Twigg Whitehead of the U.S. (women's 3,000 m, 3 min 41.14 sec). Urs Freuler of Switzerland won his seventh successive professional points race title.          (JOHN R. WILKINSON)

## FIELD HOCKEY

At the ninth Champions Trophy tournament in Amsterdam in June 1987, West Germany won the round-robin series for the second successive year. The Netherlands finished second, Australia third, and Great Britain fourth, ahead of Argentina, Spain, Pakistan, and the Soviet Union. Great Britain won the Lada International Classic at Luton, England, in October. Pakistan was second, Malaysia third, and Poland fourth in the quadrangular tournament.

In August The Netherlands retained the European championship in Moscow after a penalty stroke competition against England in the final. The score was tied at 1–1 after overtime. In the Pan American Games final, Canada defeated Argentina 3–1 in August at Indianapolis, Ind. Kenya won the African Games gold medal in Nairobi. Zimbabwe finished second. In July England won the Home Countries tournament in Dublin. Ireland finished second, Wales third, and Scotland fourth.

The Netherlands won the Indira Gandhi Gold Cup tournament in New Delhi in January. Spain finished second, followed by India, the Soviet Union, South Korea, Poland, and Kenya. England regained the indoor Home Countries championship in Dublin in January. In March West Germany won a six-nation tournament in Buenos Aires. France was second, followed by Australia, Spain, Argentina, and New Zealand.

In women's hockey The Netherlands won the Champions Trophy tournament in Amsterdam in June. Australia was second and South Korea third. In September The Netherlands also won the European championship in London on penalty strokes after the final against England was tied at 2–2. At Wembley, London, in March, England defeated the United States 3–1. Ireland won the Home Countries tournament played at Cardiff, Dublin, and Gateshead. Wales finished second, England third, and Scotland fourth. Indoors, Ireland won the Home Countries tournament in Cardiff.          (SYDNEY E. FRISKIN)

## FOOTBALL

**Association Football (Soccer).** The continuation of the ban on English clubs competing in Europe and the spread of the so-called English disease of hooliganism across the continent posed problems for association football authorities during 1987. Players from England's Football League were attracted to teams on the continent and even to Scotland; Glasgow Rangers benefited notably with six such imports to win the Premier Division championship of the Scottish League. Unruly behaviour among spectators caused disturbances in several countries. The Netherlands, West Germany, Italy, and Greece suffered outbreaks of vandalism and vicious personal assaults. One Dutch game, between Den Haag and Ajax Amsterdam, had to be abandoned at

halftime after 23 spectators and 2 policemen were seriously injured. There were increasing numbers of arrests of fighting spectators at Bundesliga matches in West Germany, and in one regional game rival fans sprayed each other with tear gas. In Italy one Torino youth was stabbed by others because he was wearing shoes in the colours of the rival team Juventus, and in Greece a spectator was killed by a rocket fired from a pistol.

In the first serious instance of trouble in a European cup game involving non-British fans, Dutch followers of the Feyenoord club ran amok on a UEFA Cup visit to Mönchengladbach, West Germany. They rioted before, during, and after the match as well as plundering and looting in the town itself. In England more sophisticated policing and vigilant crowd-control methods reduced the menace without eliminating the problem.

Reorganization of the structure of several European leagues included the reduction from 22 teams to 20 in the English First Division by 1988, the competition's centenary year. Spain split its championship into three groups for end-of-season play-offs, and the Norwegians introduced penalty shoot-outs to eliminate tie games. In East Germany, Dynamo Berlin equaled a European record by winning a ninth successive championship.

At the national level the qualifying tournament for the 1988 European championship neared its completion with the surprise elimination of France, the defending champions. The finals were to be held in West Germany.

*European Champions' Cup.* With a second-half display of flair and imagination rarely seen in the modern game, Portugal's Porto deservedly won the European Champions' Cup for the first time, beating West Germany's Bayern Munich at the Prater Stadium, Vienna, on May 27. The Germans had the Portuguese defense at full stretch for long periods in the opening stages and took the lead after 24 minutes. Hans Pflügler's throw-in was deflected off the head of Porto defender Jaime Magalhaes for Ludwig Kögl to direct a diving header inside the far post. At halftime Porto brought on its Brazilian-born substitute, Juary, and almost immediately forced the Germans on the defensive. Porto was unlucky not to be awarded a penalty in the 58th minute when Paulo Futre was brought down by Helmut Winklhöfer, who was later cautioned for a scything tackle on Futre. However, Porto did tie the game after 77 minutes following neat approach work by Juary and the other substitute, Frasco. The Brazilian crossed for Algerian international Rabah Madjer cheekily to back-heel the ball in. Two minutes later the Portuguese champions were ahead, Madjer returning the favour for Juary to score at the far post from a perfect centre.

*European Cup-Winners' Cup.* Ajax Amsterdam gained a narrow victory over East Germany's Lokomotiv Leipzig in the Cup-Winners' Cup final on a cool evening in Athens on May 13. The Dutch team did most of the attacking but was unable to finish with any accuracy. It scored what proved to be the only goal of the match in the 21st minute. John Silooy overlapped on the right and crossed for Marco van Basten to produce a finely judged near-post header past goalkeeper Rene Muller, the German captain. The East Germans tried to get back into the match but lacked cohesion and often found themselves caught out by swift counterattacks. Muller frequently came to the rescue when it seemed that Ajax might add to its slender lead.

*UEFA Cup.* IFK Göteborg, the first Swedish team to win a European trophy when it took the UEFA Cup in 1982, maintained its excellent record in the competition by overcoming Dundee United, the Scottish League side aiming to achieve a first European honour. In the first leg

### Table I. Association Football National Champions

| Nation | League winners | Cup winners |
|---|---|---|
| Albania | Partizani | Vllaznia |
| Argentina | Rosario Central | |
| Austria | Rapid Vienna | Rapid Vienna |
| Belgium | Anderlecht | Mechelen |
| Bolivia | The Strongest | |
| Brazil | São Paulo | |
| Bulgaria | Sredets | Sredets |
| Chile | Colo Colo | |
| Colombia | América de Cali | |
| Costa Rica | Puntarenas | |
| Cyprus | Omonia | AEL |
| Czechoslovakia | Sparta Prague | Dunajska Streda |
| Denmark | Århus | Århus |
| Ecuador | Nacional Quito | |
| El Salvador | Alianza | |
| England | Everton | Coventry City |
| Finland | Kuusysi | Rovaniemi |
| France | Bordeaux | Bordeaux |
| Germany, East | Dynamo Berlin | Lokomotiv Leipzig |
| Germany, West | Bayern Munich | Hamburg |
| Greece | Olympiakos | Ofi Crete |
| Guatemala | (incomplete) | |
| Honduras | Olimpia | |
| Hungary | MTK/VM | Ujpest Dozsa |
| Iceland | Fram | IA Akranes |
| Ireland | Shamrock Rovers | Shamrock Rovers |
| Italy | Napoli | Napoli |
| Liechtenstein | — | Eischen |
| Luxembourg | Jeuness d'Esch | Avenir Beggen |
| Malta | Hamrun Spartans | Hamrun Spartans |
| Mexico | Guadalajara | |
| Netherlands, The | PSV Eindhoven | Ajax Amsterdam |
| Northern Ireland | Linfield | Glentoran |
| Norway | Lillestrøm | Tromsø |
| Paraguay | Sol de América | |
| Peru | Alianza Lima | |
| Poland | Gornik Zabrze | Slask Wroclaw |
| Portugal | Benfica | Benfica |
| Romania | Steaua Bucharest | Steaua Bucharest |
| Scotland | Glasgow Rangers | St. Mirren |
| Spain | Real Madrid | Real Sociedad |
| Sweden | Malmö | Malmö |
| Switzerland | Neuchatel Xamax | Young Boys |
| Turkey | Galatasaray | Genclerbirligi |
| U.S.S.R. | Dynamo Kiev | Dynamo Kiev |
| U.S. | Dallas | |
| Uruguay | Peñarol | |
| Venezuela | Maritimo | |
| Wales | — | Merthyr Tydfil |
| Yugoslavia | Partizan Belgrade | Hajduk Split |

at the Ullevi Stadium, Göteborg, on May 6, the sun shone but on an uneven, rutted field, scarcely the ideal surface for a European final. The Scottish team defended well and made just one serious mistake, but it proved costly. In the 38th minute Michael Andersson's corner swung to the far post, where Stefan Pettersson headed down for the ball to bounce over goalkeeper Billy Thomson's head and into the net. A one-goal deficit might not have been a problem for United except for the fact that four days before the return leg, the team had played a Scottish Cup final, which went into overtime and ended in defeat. In the return leg at Tannadice Park, Dundee, on May 20, any hopes the Scots had of catching up virtually disappeared in the 22nd minute, when Lennart Nilsson drove hard and accurately inside Thomson's right-hand post to put the Swedish team ahead. John Clark, switched into attack, did spark a revival when he controlled the ball, turned, and scored a goal, but United finished as a tired side, beaten 2–1 on aggregate.

*World Club Championship.* In a match played in Tokyo on December 13, Porto of Portugal defeated Peñarol of Uruguay 2–1 after extra time to take the title.

*North America.* The championship of the nine-year-old Major Indoor Soccer League, which remained the only professional competition of any status, was won by Dallas, which beat Tacoma in the final play-offs. The Canadian Soccer League, a new eight-team competition for 11-a-side, was formed in June. (JACK ROLLIN)

*Latin America.* After years during which Argentina had taken command of Latin-American soccer, the tiny country of Uruguay gained revenge in 1987. Uruguay went to the América Cup—South America's national teams championship—as the reigning titleholder, yet it was clearly an underdog in comparison with the World Cup champion, Argentina, and Brazil, a country with over 40 times the population of Uruguay. As defending champions, the Uruguayans did not have to play in the qualifying round, but they met Argentina in Buenos Aires in the semifinals. They battled the crowd as well as their opponents before achieving a 1–0 victory, and then they went on to defeat Chile by an identical score to regain the South American crown. The Argentines' humiliation was compounded by their 2–1 defeat against low-rated Colombia in the game for third place, also played at Buenos Aires.

If the success of Uruguay's national team was not enough, Peñarol—the traditional powerhouse among the country's professional clubs—also had a remarkable year. After finishing first in the Uruguayan league, this team from Montevideo earned the Libertadores de América Cup, South America's club championship, ending a three-year domination by Argentine teams.

A five-time South American champion, Peñarol had not won the cup since 1982, having been narrowly defeated in the 1983 final. The 1987 title was not won easily, as Peñarol faced a tough rival in América de Cali, the Colombian team that had been the cup's runner-up for two years in a row. América won 2–0 at Cali, and Peñarol prevailed 2–1 at Montevideo. In the deciding game, played at Santiago, Chile, the Colombians needed only a tie to win because of their better goal average, but after battling the Uruguayans to a scoreless tie almost to the end, América allowed a single score by Peñarol in the last minute of the final overtime period.

In Argentina, Rosario Central surprised the powerful Buenos Aires teams by winning the first-division title. The wealthy América de Cali continued its domination of the Colombian league. Colegio San Agustín won the regional and Alianza of Lima the decentralized title in Peru, and the former team went on to earn the national championship.

América of Mexico City won the international club championship organized by the Football Confederation of North America, Central America, and the Caribbean (CON-CACAF) after defeating Defence Force from Trinidad and Tobago. However, it was unable to prevent its traditional Mexican rival, Guadalajara, from winning the Mexican League. (SERGIO SARMIENTO)

**Rugby.** *Rugby Union.* The major event of the 1986–87 period was the staging of rugby's first World Cup in New Zealand and Australia in May and June 1987. The tournament was won by New Zealand, which defeated France 29–9 in the final at Eden Park, Auckland, on June 20. In the game to decide third and fourth places, Wales beat Australia 22–21 at Rotorua, N.Z. There were no preliminary rounds, the participants being decided by invitation from the International Rugby Football Board (IB). South Africa was excluded for political reasons, but the remaining seven IB countries—England, Scotland, Ireland, Wales, New Zealand, Australia, and France—were joined by Argentina, Fiji, Italy, the U.S., Canada, Japan, Tonga, Romania, and Zimbabwe. The 16 countries were divided into four pools of four each. The first- and second-place teams in each group qualified for the quarterfinals, in which Wales beat England 16–3 at Brisbane, Australia defeated Ireland 33–15 at Sydney, France beat Fiji 31–16 at Auckland, and New Zealand triumphed over Scotland 30–3 at Christchurch. In the semifinals New Zealand defeated Wales 49–6 at Brisbane and, in what many people felt was the greatest rugby match they had ever seen, France defeated Australia 30–24 at Sydney.

In the Five Nations' championship, France won its fourth grand slam, beating Wales 16–9 at Paris, England

19–15 at Twickenham, Scotland 28–22 at Paris, and Ireland 19–13 at Dublin. Ireland and Scotland shared second place. Ireland's two victories were against England 17–0 at Dublin and against Wales 15–11 at Cardiff, while Scotland beat Ireland 16–12 and Wales 21–15, both at Murrayfield. Wales and England tied for last place with one win apiece. Wales beat England 19–12 at Cardiff, and England defeated Scotland 21–12 at Twickenham.

Early in the British season, Japan made an eight-match tour of England and Scotland. The Japanese won twice but were defeated 33–18 by a Scotland team at Murrayfield and 39–12 by an England team at Twickenham. In October and November 1986 New Zealand undertook an eight-match tour of France and won the first seven games, including a defeat of France 19–7 at Toulouse in the first of two test matches, but France won the second match, played at Nantes, 16–3. In July 1987 New Zealand traveled to Sydney for the Bledisloe Cup match against Australia. New Zealand won an emphatic victory 30–16.

*Rugby League.* In the 1986–87 Northern Hemisphere season, the Australians made a tour of Britain and France, winning all their matches. Their three test matches against Great Britain brought them victories by 38–16 at Manchester, 34–4 at Leeds, and 24–15 at Wigan. This was Australia's seventh consecutive winning test series. The crowd for the game at Manchester was 50,583, a record for a test match in Britain. Great Britain won both tests against France, 52–4 at Leeds and 20–10 at Carcassonne.

(DAVID FROST)

**U.S. Football.** *College.* Miami of Florida won the national championship of college football by beating Oklahoma 20–14 Jan. 1, 1988, in the Orange Bowl at Miami. Miami, a unanimous choice in both wire-service polls, won all 12 of its games, including a 26–25 victory over second-ranked Florida State (11–1), and was the only major team that had not been defeated or tied. It was the first time in 52 years of Associated Press polls that the top two teams were from the same state.

Big Eight champion Oklahoma (11–1) ranked ahead of number four Syracuse, which had an 11–0–1 record, blemished only by its January 1 tie in the Sugar Bowl, 16–16 against Auburn. The next four spots went, in order, to

Louisiana State (10–1–1), which defeated 8–4 South Carolina in the Gator Bowl 30–13; Nebraska (10–2), the 31–28 Fiesta Bowl loser to Florida State; Southeastern Conference champion Auburn (9–1–2); and Big Ten champion Michigan State (9–2–1), which beat Pacific Ten champion Southern California (8–4) in the Rose Bowl 20–17.

Texas A&M, UCLA, and Clemson also were top ten teams in various polls. Texas A&M, the 10–2 Southwest Conference champion, defeated Notre Dame 35–10 in the Cotton Bowl. UCLA (10–2) won the Aloha Bowl 20–16 against Florida (6–6). Clemson, the Atlantic Coast Conference's 10–2 champion, beat 8–4 Penn State in the Florida Citrus Bowl 35–10.

Oklahoma tied its own one-year-old record by leading the country's biggest (Division I-A) schools in six of eight offensive and defensive categories. The Sooners' offense ranked first with 43.5 points, 499.7 yd, and 428.8 rushing yards per game, and their defense allowed the fewest points (7.5), yards (208.1), and passing yards (102.4) per game. But the defense that had given up only three touchdown passes permitted two against Miami.

Miami's defense tied South Carolina's for second by allowing 10.1 points per game, and its 35.6-point average on offense ranked fifth, behind Oklahoma, Florida State, Nebraska, and UCLA. Michigan State's leading rushing defense gave up 61.5 yd per game. San Jose State's leading pass offense averaged 338.1 yd. Nationally, Division I-A scoring and yardage were at all-time highs of 46.1 points and 715.5 yd per game.

Tim Brown of Notre Dame, a flanker and kick-return specialist, became the third non-back in 53 years to win the Heisman Trophy, awarded annually to college football's best player. Most of his 1,847 total yards came on kick returns and 39 pass catches. Awards for linemen were the Vince Lombardi Trophy to Ohio State linebacker Chris Spielman and the Outland Trophy to Air Force defensive tackle Chad Hennings, who had 24 sacks. Johnny Bailey of Texas A&I won the Harlon Hill Trophy, known as the Heisman for small schools, after leading Division II with 1,598 rushing yards and 20 touchdowns.

Don McPherson, the quarterback for Syracuse and the Heisman runner-up, led Division I-A passers with 10.22

FOCUS ON SPORTS

Quarterback Steve Walsh (centre) of the Miami Hurricanes hands off to Warren Williams (left) during Miami's Orange Bowl victory over Oklahoma. Miami was the only major team to finish the season undefeated and untied.

Quarterback Doug Williams (left) of the Washington Redskins receives the energetic praise of his teammates after a touchdown pass in the second quarter, in which his team took command during the Super Bowl. Williams, whose standout performance got him named most valuable player, led his team to a 42–10 victory against the Denver Broncos.
AP/WIDE WORLD

yd per attempt and a 164.3 efficiency rating. Teammate Tommy Kane led with 14 touchdown catches. San Diego State quarterback Todd Santos's career total of 11,425 passing yards set a record. For the season Santos's 3,932 passing yards, 26 touchdown passes, and 3,688 yd total offense led the division. Santos's teammates included Paul Hewitt, the scoring leader with 24 touchdowns, and Guy Liggins, whose 1,208 yd led receivers. Auburn's Jeff Burger had the highest completion percentage, 66.7, and Long Beach State's Jeff Graham the lowest interception percentage, 2.02.

Elbert Woods of Nevada-Las Vegas won the rushing title with 1,658 yd, only 3 yd more than Pittsburgh's Craig Heyward and fewer than 50 ahead of Oklahoma State's Thurman Thomas. Jason Phillips led receivers with 99 catches for Houston. Tulane's Marc Zeno set a career record with 3,725 yd on 236 catches. Derek Schmidt of Florida State tied South Carolina's Collin Mackie with 23 field goals and led kickers with 116 points for a career scoring record of 393.

Other conference champions were Wyoming (9–3) in the Western Athletic, Eastern Michigan (10–2) in the Mid-American, San Jose State (10–2) in the Pacific Coast Athletic, and Harvard (8–2) in the Ivy League because of its 14–10 victory over Yale. Army's 17–3 defeat of Navy brought the military series to 41–40–7 for Navy.

Holy Cross won the Division I-AA Colonial Conference with an 11–0 record and led the division with 46.5 points and 552.2 yd per game in the senior year of Gordie Lockbaum, who ranked third in Heisman voting for playing both offense and defense. Southland Conference winner Northeast Louisiana (13–2) won the Division I-AA championship 43–42 over Marshall (10–5).

Troy (Ala.) State (12–1–1) defeated Portland (Ore.) State (11–2–1) for the NCAA's Division II championship, and Wagner (13–1) beat Dayton (11–3) in Division III after Dayton had ended Augustana's (Ill.) streaks of four championships and 60 games without defeat. In the National Association for Intercollegiate Athletics, Cameron of Oklahoma (13–1) defeated Carson-Newman of Tennessee (10–4) for the Division I championship, and the Division II title game between Wisconsin-Stevens Point (12–2–1) and Pacific Lutheran (10–1–2) was tied.

Columbia finished the season with 40 straight losses, breaking Northwestern's record of 34. Southern Methodist was not allowed to begin the season. After breaking NCAA rules for amateurism a record seventh time—including twice in five years—Southern Methodist became the first school to be punished by a two-year-old rule that effectively suspended its football program for two years.

*Professional.* The Washington Redskins of the National Football Conference (NFC) won the championship of U.S. professional football by routing the Denver Broncos of the American Football Conference (AFC) 42–10 in the National Football League (NFL) Super Bowl at San Diego, Calif., on Jan. 31, 1988. Redskin quarterback Doug Williams passed for 340 yd, a Super Bowl record, and was voted the game's most valuable player. Other Super Bowl records included 204 yd rushing by Washington's Timmy Smith; 193 yd gained receiving by the Redskins' Ricky Sanders; and, by Washington as a team, 602 total yards, 280 yd rushing, six touchdowns, and 35 points in one quarter.

The 1987 season was the second in six years to be interrupted by a players' strike. The NFL became the first U.S. professional league to use substitute players to continue its schedule. After one week of games was canceled, three were played with nonunion players who had not made final rosters and with strike-breaking union members, who increased from about 85 the first week to about 200 the third week, according to NFL Players Association figures.

The 24-day strike began September 22 after two games and ended without a labour agreement October 15, one day after 89 strikers broke ranks. The NFL Players Association won a court case against the NFL because strikers who returned to work October 15 were not allowed to play in October 18 and 19 games. The union also sued the league under antitrust laws for an end to restrictions on the movement among teams by players whose contracts had expired. Compared with the last games before the strike, attendance for the first week of games during the strike was 28.3%; this grew to 49.7% for the third nonunion games. The NFL agreed to reimburse television networks $60 million, roughly one-eighth of its scheduled income for the season and play-offs.

Games played without most union players counted in

the standings, but those results did not affect the ten teams to make the play-offs. Five play-off teams had not reached the tournament the previous year, the most since the field was expanded to 16 teams after the 1982 strike season. The New Orleans Saints, an NFC wild-card team, had the first winning season and play-off berth of its 21-year history.

The other wild-card teams, the top two teams in each conference that did not win division championships, also had missed the previous play-offs. Seattle had missed the play-offs for two years, Minnesota for four, and Houston for six. AFC East champion Indianapolis's last play-off appearance had been in 1977 as the Baltimore Colts.

The AFC division champions were Indianapolis in the East, Denver in the West, and Cleveland in the Central. NFC Central champion Chicago became the first NFC team since 1981 to win a fourth straight division crown. Washington won the NFC East, and San Francisco won the NFC West with a 13–2 record, the NFL's best. New Orleans tied San Francisco at 10–2 for the best record in union games. The New York Giants had the worst record ever for a defending Super Bowl champion, 6–9, including 0–3 during the strike. In the play-offs Minnesota upset both New Orleans and San Francisco to advance to the NFC finals, where they lost to Washington 17–10. Denver defeated Cleveland for the AFC title 38–33.

In union games only, San Francisco led the league in both points scored and points allowed for the first time since 1972 and in both yards gained and yards allowed for the first time since 1977. However, the NFL included the games without most union players in its official statistics, which ranked San Francisco behind Indianapolis and Cleveland in points allowed. The 49ers averaged 30.6 points per game and gave up 16.9, one point more than the Colts.

In yardage, San Francisco's official rankings were first offensively with 399.1 total and 149.1 rushing yards per game and first defensively with average yields of 273.0 total and 165.6 passing yards. The 49ers ranked second in offensive passing, led by Miami with 258.4 yd per game, and fifth in defensive rushing, led by Chicago's 94.2-yd average. Miami also ranked first with 13 quarterback sacks

allowed, and Chicago ranked first with 70 sacks on defense. New Orleans had the top turnover margin, plus-20.

The nonunion games affected two individual races for yardage leads. They enabled the Los Angeles Rams' Charles White to outrush Eric Dickerson, who was traded from the Rams to Indianapolis, by 1,374 yd to 1,288 and St. Louis's J. T. Smith to outgain San Francisco's Jerry Rice (see BIOGRAPHIES) on pass receptions by 1,117 yd to 1,078. Smith's 91 catches also led the league. White and the New York Jets' Johnny Hector tied with 11 touchdowns rushing, and Rice led all scorers with 23 touchdowns for 138 points. New Orleans' Morten Andersen led kickers with 121 points and 28 field goals. Dean Biasucci's .889 field-goal accuracy on 24 for 27 led the league for the Colts.

Rice, playing in only 12 games, set an NFL record with 22 touchdown catches and at least one in every game, giving him a record streak of 13 games. Seattle's Steve Largent extended his record streak of games with at least one catch to 152 and broke by 2 Charlie Joiner's year-old career record of 750 catches. Philadelphia defensive end Reggie White's 21 sacks in 12 games were one short of the record set in 16 games.

San Francisco quarterback Joe Montana set a record with 22 consecutive pass completions and led the league with a 102.1 passer rating, a .668 completion percentage, and 31 touchdown passes. Other top passing figures were Neil Lomax's 3,387 yd for St. Louis, Phil Simms's 7.91-yd average gain for the Giants, and Ken O'Brien's .020 interception percentage for the New York Jets.

Bo Jackson played half a season for the Los Angeles Raiders after his baseball season for the Kansas City Royals, and his average rushing gain of 6.84 yd was the third highest in NFL history. Other league leaders were Anthony Carter, with 24.3 yd per catch for Minnesota; Barry Wilburn, with nine interceptions for Washington; Herschel Walker, with 1,606 yd from scrimmage for Dallas; Mel Gray, with a 14.7-yd punt return average for New Orleans; and Sylvester Stamps, with a 27.5-yd kickoff return average for Atlanta. Walter Payton of Chicago finished his 13-year career with 16,726 rushing yards, increasing Jim Brown's previous NFL record by 35.9%. He increased other NFL records by more than 30% with final totals of 3,838 rushing attempts, 21,803 combined net yards, 77 100-yd rushing games, and 186 consecutive games at running back, an unofficial record.

Many players used during the strike had played indoor football with new rules on shrunken fields during the spring. The four-team Arena Football League's first season ended with Denver beating Pittsburgh for the championship.

**Canadian Football.** The Edmonton Eskimos won the Canadian Football League's 75th Grey Cup championship game 38–36 over the Toronto Argonauts November 29 in Vancouver, B.C., when Jerry Kauric kicked a 49-yd field goal with 45 seconds remaining. Eskimo quarterback Damon Allen, the brother of Los Angeles Raider running back Marcus Allen, was voted the game's top offensive player. Eskimo Stewart Hill was the top defensive player. Both finalists upset division winners in the play-offs. Toronto finished 11–6–1, behind Winnipeg (12–6) in the Eastern Division, and Edmonton (11–7) trailed British Columbia (12–6) in the Western Division.

Winnipeg dominated the Schenley Awards for outstanding players. Quarterback Tom Clements was most outstanding player, tackle Chris Walby the top offensive lineman, and safety Scott Flagel the top Canadian player. Toronto fullback Gill Fenerty was rookie of the year and British Columbia defensive end Gregg Stumon the top defensive player.

(KEVIN M. LAMB)

---

### Table II. NFL Final Standings and Play-offs, 1987

| AMERICAN CONFERENCE | W | L | T | NATIONAL CONFERENCE | W | L | T |
|---|---|---|---|---|---|---|---|
| **Eastern Division** | | | | **Eastern Division** | | | |
| *Indianapolis | 9 | 6 | 0 | *Washington | 11 | 4 | 0 |
| Miami | 8 | 7 | 0 | Dallas | 7 | 8 | 0 |
| New England | 8 | 7 | 0 | St. Louis | 7 | 8 | 0 |
| Buffalo | 7 | 8 | 0 | Philadelphia | 7 | 8 | 0 |
| New York Jets | 6 | 9 | 0 | New York Giants | 6 | 9 | 0 |
| **Central Division** | | | | **Central Division** | | | |
| *Cleveland | 10 | 5 | 0 | *Chicago | 11 | 4 | 0 |
| *Houston | 9 | 6 | 0 | *Minnesota | 8 | 7 | 0 |
| Pittsburgh | 8 | 7 | 0 | Green Bay | 5 | 9 | 1 |
| Cincinnati | 4 | 11 | 0 | Tampa Bay | 4 | 11 | 0 |
| | | | | Detroit | 4 | 11 | 0 |
| **Western Division** | | | | **Western Division** | | | |
| *Denver | 10 | 4 | 1 | *San Francisco | 13 | 2 | 0 |
| *Seattle | 9 | 6 | 0 | *New Orleans | 12 | 3 | 0 |
| San Diego | 8 | 7 | 0 | Los Angeles Rams | 6 | 9 | 0 |
| Los Angeles Raiders | 5 | 10 | 0 | Atlanta | 3 | 12 | 0 |
| Kansas City | 4 | 11 | 0 | | | | |

*Qualified for play-offs.

**Play-offs**

| Wild-card round | American finals |
|---|---|
| Minnesota 44, New Orleans 10 | Denver 38, Cleveland 33 |
| Houston 23, Seattle 20 (overtime) | |
| **American semifinals** | **National finals** |
| Denver 34, Houston 10 | Washington 17, Minnesota 10 |
| Cleveland 38, Indianapolis 21 | |
| **National semifinals** | **Super Bowl** |
| Washington 21, Chicago 17 | Washington 42, Denver 10 |
| Minnesota 36, San Francisco 24 | |

## GOLF

Europe enjoyed its finest golfing year in 1987. The European team not only successfully defended the Ryder Cup, winning for the first time on American soil as it defeated the United States 15–13, but Nick Faldo of England took the British Open and Laura Davies of England the U.S. Women's Open. These were the principal achievements, but there were supplementary landmarks as well. Sandy Lyle of Scotland became the first British winner of the U.S. Tournament Players' Championship, Ian Woosnam of Wales the first Briton to triumph in the Suntory world match-play championship, England the first British winners of the Dunhill Cup, and Wales only the second British Isles team to win the World Cup (formerly the Canada Cup). It would nevertheless be an exaggeration to suggest that U.S. golf was in disarray. Three of the major championships were won by Americans: Larry Mize won the Masters, Scott Simpson the U.S. Open, and Larry Nelson the Professional Golfers' Association (PGA) championship. The U.S. was also successful in its defense of the Walker Cup between amateurs from the U.S. and Britain.

Europe's Ryder Cup victory was a personal triumph for the captain, Tony Jacklin. Having in 1970 become the first Briton to win the U.S. Open, he could therefore be regarded as the pioneer of a European uprising—one he had successfully maintained even in a nonplaying capacity. Moreover, the victory was achieved against a U.S. team led by Jack Nicklaus on a course—Muirfield Village in Dublin, Ohio—that he had designed himself. It was a historic moment when Severiano Ballesteros of Spain holed the winning putt after what had seemed a disastrous start. On the first morning, the Europeans were at one time down to the U.S. in all four foursomes. One pair, Faldo and Woosnam, were four down after nine holes to Mize and Lanny Wadkins, and as they came back to win by

Laura Davies concentrates on a putt during the U.S. Women's Open golf championship. Davies went on to win the event and became the first British golfer to take the American title.

two holes, it was their recovery that turned the tide. Behind them Ballesteros and his young Spanish partner, José-María Olazabal, were also two down but recovered to beat Nelson and Payne Stewart on the last green. This reprieve at sharing the foursomes 2–2 inspired the Europeans, and in the afternoon they made their first-ever clean sweep, taking the four-ball matches 4–0 for an overall lead of 6–2. (In four-ball competition, teams of two play against each other, and the best score of each player on a team is the one that is counted for each hole.) This was slightly improved in the second series of foursomes the following day and then held in the four-ball competition to leave Europe with a 10½–5½ advantage with 12 singles matches to go. Predictably, the Americans did not go down without a fight, and at one stage it began to look as if they might escape as Andy Bean, Mark Calcavecchia, Stewart, Simpson, and Tom Kite all won. But a valuable early point came from Howard Clark and another crucial one from Eamonn Darcy of Ireland, and then Ballesteros steadied a wallowing ship. Though Faldo was one of the European losers in the singles, the 3½ points he and Woosnam had gained as partners in both the foursomes and four-ball matches played an important part in the overall result.

Already a successful golfer with one victory in the U.S. and many more in Europe, Faldo had in 1985 decided to alter his swing. He was aware that it would be at least two years before he would be fully adjusted and, right on cue, he won the British Open at Muirfield. It was, however, a close contest as Paul Azinger, a young U.S. player making his first appearance in the tournament, led through the second and third rounds. In the fourth round Faldo performed the unusual feat of parring each of the 18 holes. His rounds were 68, 69, 71, 71 for a total of 279, and he won by a stroke from Azinger and Rodger Davis of Australia.

The year had already begun auspiciously for Europe when Lyle, winner of the British Open in 1985, took the U.S. Tournament Players' Championship at Ponte Vedra, Fla. Many considered this event the world's fifth major tournament, and it attracted a top-class field. Lyle came into the tournament with unimpressive recent outings, but rounds of 67, 71, 66, 70, the last demonstrating some resolute golf over the last nine holes, earned him a tie with Jeff Sluman of the U.S. Lyle won on the third hole of the sudden-death play-off.

Two weeks later it looked as if there might be another European success in the Masters at Augusta, Ga., as Ballesteros forced his way into a play-off with Greg Norman of Australia and the less highly rated Mize; the latter was born and raised in Augusta but was not a member of the exclusive National Club. The three of them scored 285 for the 72 holes, and all eyes were on Ballesteros and Norman. Mize beat them both, sinking a long chip shot at the second extra hole against Norman after Ballesteros had eliminated himself by taking three putts on the previous hole.

Ballesteros was also a strong contender for the U.S. Open at the Olympic Club in San Francisco, but again he could not sustain his challenge over the last round, which developed into a two-man contest between Simpson and the more favoured Tom Watson. It was Simpson, with some fine putting over the closing holes, who prevailed, Watson just failing to sink a long putt at the last hole for a birdie and a tie. Simpson's rounds were 71, 68, 70, 68, and Ballesteros was once again third. It was perhaps even more frustrating for Watson, who was in the midst of a three-year slump. Only at the very end of the season did he finally shake himself free when he won the lucrative Nabisco Championships at San Antonio, Texas.

As in the Masters, there was also a tie in the U.S. PGA championship at the PGA National Club in Florida. In a week of extreme heat, Ballesteros was for the third time very much in the thick of things before he met with disaster early in his last round. Instead, Nelson (70, 72, 73, 72) finished in a tie with Wadkins (70, 70, 74, 73) before Nelson won the title for a second time at the first extra hole of a sudden-death play-off.

The outstanding individual performance of the year came from Davies in winning the U.S. Women's Open at Plainfield, N.J. No other British golfer had achieved this distinction. Bad weather and then a tie turned the championship into a marathon, requiring six days to complete. Davies demonstrated a rare talent for the game. This was only her third year as a professional, but she had finished first, first, and second in the European order of merit. Her win in the U.S.—against the best of the world—was on the same level as Jacklin's U.S. Open victory in 1970. She had rounds of 72, 70, 72, 71 for a score of 285 and a tie with Ayako Okamoto of Japan (71, 72, 70, 72) and the U.S. favourite, JoAnne Carner (74, 70, 72, 69). Davies then beat them both in the 18-hole play-off with a 71 to Okamoto's 73 and Carner's 74. Davies had to head for the airport immediately in order to compete in the British Women's Open at St. Mellion in Cornwall. She led for two rounds before being beaten by a stroke by Alison Nicholas, who had rounds of 74, 76, 73, 73 for an aggregate of 296. Davies ranked second in earnings behind Scotland's Dale Reid on the Women's PGA tour in Europe, while Betsy King topped the U.S. tour. Reid's earnings were in excess of £50,000, compared with £28,000 in 1984, the last time that she was leading money winner.

Ian Woosnam set a record on the men's European circuit. The Welshman had six victories during the year with official winnings of £253,717. He had begun the year by becoming the first Briton to win the Hong Kong Open and ended it by becoming the first Briton to win the Suntory world match-play championship. In between he had also taken the Jersey, Madrid, and Scottish opens as well as the Lancôme Trophy. He was the most consistent golfer of the year, jumping from 30th in the Sony world rankings to 6th. Such was the strength of the European tour that four of its members (Woosnam, Lyle, Ballesteros, and Mark McNulty of Zimbabwe) reached the semifinals of the Suntory tournament. For the fourth time in his career, Lyle was a losing finalist, but it was a splendid match, with Woosnam needing a birdie on the last hole to win.

For the second time in three years, Curtis Strange was the leading U.S. money winner, with earnings that were in excess of $900,000. He had three tournament wins, in the Canadian Open at Glen Abbey in Oakville, Ont., the Federal Express at Colonial, Tenn., and the World Series at Akron, Ohio. Generally, however, the U.S. players did not travel well, and the final of the Dunhill Cup, an international team competition, was an all-British affair, England beating Scotland 2–1. Wales defeated Scotland in the final of the World Cup, with Woosnam once again proving outstanding.

The only setback to European golf came in the Walker Cup, which for the first time in Britain was played inland, at Sunningdale. The United States won handsomely by 16½–7½, its biggest margin since the format was modified in 1963 to 18-hole matches, two of foursomes and two of singles, instead of 36 holes. Since the Great Britain and Ireland team had gone into the match with high expectations after the 1985 Ryder Cup and 1986 Curtis Cup successes, this was a disappointment. There was little hope of a recovery after losing the opening series of foursomes 4–0.

Dmitry Belozerchev of the Soviet Union performs on the pommel horse on his way to regaining the world all-around men's gymnastics title.
AFP PHOTO

For once a U.S. player did not win the British Amateur championship, which returned after many years to Prestwick, the first home of the British Open. Instead it was Paul Mayo, one of the British team members, who triumphed, defeating Peter McEvoy, a surprising omission from Britain's Walker Cup team, in the final. However, one of the U.S. players, Billy Mayfair, was later to win the U.S. Amateur championships at the Jupiter Club in Florida.                                    (MICHAEL E. J. WILLIAMS)

## GYMNASTICS

The Soviet Union dominated the men's world gymnastics championships at Rotterdam, Neth., October 19–25. Romania scored a surprising team victory over the U.S.S.R. in the women's competition.

Dmitry Belozerchev of the U.S.S.R. regained the world all-around title that he had won four years earlier at the age of 16. The new women's all-around gold medalist was Aurelia Dobre, 14, of Romania. She was unknown prior to the championships, where she received four perfect scores of ten in eight exercises and also won the gold medal on the balance beam. She was the first non-Soviet winner of the all-around in a world championship in 21 years.

The Romanian women demonstrated their domination of the sport by winning a total of five gold, one silver, and four bronze medals. The U.S.S.R. won two golds, three silvers, and a bronze. East Germany shared the gold medal on the uneven parallel bars and finished third in the team competition. Romania outscored the U.S.S.R. by 395.400 to 394.950.

In 1985 Elena Shushunova of the U.S.S.R. was the cochampion in the all-around. In 1987 she placed second in the all-around and won additional silver medals in the team competition and the balance beam. She won gold medals in the vault and the floor exercise and placed third on the uneven parallel bars. Daniela Silivas of Romania won a gold medal for the team competition and tied for first in the floor exercise.

The U.S.S.R. was a clear-cut victor in the men's team competition, scoring 294.050 to 289.850 for East Germany, 289.800 for China, and 287.800 for Japan and Bulgaria. The Soviets also had the youngest squad in the men's tournament. Belozerchev, who had suffered a broken leg two years earlier, won gold medals in the team competition, the all-around, and the horizontal bar and tied for first place on the pommel horse. Two other Soviet gymnasts were outstanding. Yury Korolev won gold medals for the team competition and the rings and placed second in the all-around. A newcomer, Vladimir Artemov, won gold medals in the team competition and the parallel bars and finished second in the floor exercise and third in the all-around. Lou Yun of China won gold medals in the floor exercise and the vault. The other gold medal went to Silvio Kroll of East Germany, who tied Lou in the vault.

Curtis Hibbert of Canada performed best among North American competitors by placing second in the horizontal bar. The U.S. men and women finished ninth and sixth, respectively, and the men's team probably lost 1984 Olympian Tim Daggett, who broke his leg on the vault dismount. (CHARLES ROBERT PAUL, JR.)

## HORSE RACING

**Thoroughbred Racing and Steeplechasing.** *United States and Canada.* Ferdinand, winner of the 1986 Kentucky Derby, defeated Alysheba, winner of the 1987 Kentucky Derby, by a nose in the Breeders' Cup Classic and subsequently was voted horse of the year, as well as receiving an Eclipse Award as champion older male of the 1987 Thoroughbred racing season. The much-traveled Alysheba lost little prestige by his narrow loss in the climactic contest of the seven-race Breeders' Cup series held at Hollywood Park on November 21. The bay son of Alydar was acclaimed champion three-year-old colt and, together with Ferdinand and Theatrical, was considered a leading contender to succeed Lady's Secret as horse of the year.

Alysheba followed his Kentucky Derby victory with a first in the Preakness, but his attempt to earn Triple Crown honours and a $5 million bonus was thwarted when Bet Twice triumphed in the Belmont Stakes. Alysheba's other victory in ten starts came in the Super Derby, and he completed the year with a world-leading total of $2,511,156 in earnings.

Ferdinand captured three other stakes besides the Breeders' Cup Classic, including the Grade I Gold Cup Handicap at Hollywood Park. He concluded the season with four successive triumphs after failing to win in his first six starts of the campaign. The son of Nijinsky II lost nose decisions in two Grade I events, the Charles H. Strub and Santa Anita handicaps at Santa Anita.

For the fourth successive year, five winners of Breeders' Cup races were voted Eclipse Awards denoting championships by representatives of the Thoroughbred Racing Associations, National Turf Writers Association, and the *Daily Racing Form.* Besides Ferdinand, the others were Epitome, two-year-old filly; Sacahuista, three-year-old filly; Miesque, female turf horse; and Theatrical, male turf horse. Other Eclipse Award equine winners were Forty Niner, two-year-old colt; North Sider, older filly or mare; Groovy, sprinter; and Inlander, steeplechaser. There were no repeat winners from 1986.

Sacahuista and North Sider were trained by D. Wayne Lukas, who won an Eclipse Award as the outstanding trainer for a third consecutive year. Besides Sacahuista, Lukas saddled a second Breeders' Cup victor in Success Express, first in the juvenile colt division. Lukas's chief patrons, Mr. and Mrs. Eugene V. Klein, also were honoured as outstanding owners for a third straight time. Other Eclipse Award winners were Pat Day, jockey, for a third time; Kent J. Desormeaux, apprentice jockey; and Nelson Bunker Hunt, breeder, for a third time. Desormeaux led all jockeys in victories with 450, of which 297 were scored while he held his apprentice allowance.

Lukas-trained horses earned $17,502,206 to break international records that the trainer had set in each of the three previous years. Lukas won 343 races, including 92 stakes to break his own record of 70 set in 1985. Of the 118 Grade I stakes held in North America in 1987, Lukas-trained horses won 22.

The Klein stable won $5,743,134 in purses to break its own single-year earnings record of $5,451,201 set in 1985. Day's mounts earned $12,367,570, that figure being surpassed on the final racing day of the year by José Santos, whose mounts earned $12,375,433 in purses.

Ferdinand, winner of the 1986 Kentucky Derby, noses past Alysheba, winner of the 1987 Kentucky Derby, to win the Breeders' Cup Classic at Hollywood Park. The November event was the first race between Derby winners since Affirmed beat Spectacular Bid in 1979.

Forty Niner, the sole Eclipse Award winner who did not compete in the Breeders' Cup series, won five of six starts, including the Futurity and the Champagne stakes. Epitome won only two other races besides the Breeders' Cup Juvenile fillies, a maiden race at Keeneland and the ungraded Pocahontas Stakes at Churchill Downs. Day rode her to a come-from-behind nose decision over Jeanne Jones in the Breeders' Cup event.

Day also steered Theatrical to a half-length victory over French challenger and Arc de Triomphe victor Trempolino after a long stretch duel in the Breeders' Cup Turf. Theatrical finished first in seven of nine races, won six Grade I stakes, and earned $2,235,500. One of his defeats came in the Budweiser-Arlington Million, in which he finished third to 1986 turf champion Manila. The latter was sidelined by injury late in the summer after winning four of five stakes starts.

Sacahuista captured the Breeders' Cup Distaff and the Spinster, her only triumphs of the season. The five-year-old mare North Sider won 7 of 17 races but was a distant also-ran in the Distaff. In two earlier Grade I stakes, she also finished out of the money, but she won the Santa Margarita, Apple Blossom, and Maskette.

Miesque earned her Eclipse Award with a single appearance in North America. She scored an impressive victory in the Breeders' Cup Mile while establishing a Hollywood Park turf course record of 1 min 32⅘ sec. She won five of seven European races, including four Group I stakes.

Groovy, who lost as the odds-on favourite for the second consecutive year in the Breeders' Cup Sprint, nonetheless was voted the Eclipse Award in that category. Prior to finishing second to Very Subtle in the Breeders' Cup event, Groovy had won all six of his 1987 stakes, setting track records at Belmont Park and Finger Lakes.

Afleet did not win any of Canada's Triple Crown races but won two Sovereign Awards as champion three-year-old colt and as horse of the year. In the Triple Crown competition, Hangin On a Star took the Breeders' Stakes, Market Control the Queen's Plate, and Coryphee the Prince of Wales.

Other Sovereign Award winners were One From Heaven, three-year-old filly; Carotene, turf horse and older mare; Play the King, sprinter and older male; Regal Classic, two-year-old colt; Phoenix Factor, two-year-old filly; Arctic Vixen, broodmare; Kinghaven Farm, owner and breeder; Roger Attfield, trainer; Don Seymour, jockey; James McAleney, apprentice jockey; and Lawrence D. Regan, man of the year. (JOSEPH C. AGRELLA)

*Europe and Australia.* Four horses held claims to be considered the best in Europe at the end of 1987's competitive season: the British-trained Reference Point and Indian Skimmer and the French pair, Miesque and Triptych. Indian Skimmer was the only one of the four not to suffer defeat, but she did not race after June 14, injuring her back in July. That day she extended her winning streak to five with a four-length success over Miesque in the Prix de Diane. The daughter of Storm Bird had gained an equally impressive victory in the Group I Prix Saint-Alary at Longchamp three weeks earlier.

Miesque proved herself a brilliant miler with Group I victories in the One Thousand Guineas, Poule d'Essai des Pouliches, Prix Jacques le Marois, and Prix du Moulin. She took the Moulin from Soviet Star, which had already won the Poule d'Essai des Poulains and Sussex Stakes and later added the Prix de la Forêt to his Group I tally. Miesque handled soft ground at one mile but could never threaten Indian Skimmer over the 1⁵⁄₁₆ mi of the Diane, the sole occasion on which she attempted a longer distance. However, she was unexpectedly beaten by a second British filly, Milligram, in her final race in Europe, the Queen Elizabeth II Stakes at Ascot on September 26. She returned to her brilliant best in the U.S. with her decisive victory in the Breeders' Cup Mile. Milligram had followed her second to Miesque at Newmarket with another second in the Irish One Thousand Guineas, in which a British horse, Forest Flower, beat her by a short head. Forest Flower, the only filly rated above Miesque at two years old, was ill both before and after her Irish triumph and finished last of four in her only other appearance.

Newmarket trainer Henry Cecil and his U.S. jockey Steve Cauthen were associated with both Indian Skimmer and Reference Point, the only colt among the four leading performers. Louis Freedman, who bred and owned the son of Mill Reef, hoped that he would win the Triple Crown (Two Thousand Guineas, Derby, and St. Leger), but Reference Point became sick and had to be operated on for sinus trouble in late March. He made a victorious reappearance in the Dante Stakes and then won the Derby three weeks later, leading all the way. Cecil saddled the winners of 180 races and £1,896,689 first-prize money in Britain, both records, and Cauthen regained the jockeys' championship he had held in 1984 and 1985. Cauthen rode 197 winners, the highest total in Britain since Sir Gordon Richards in 1952, but he had to fight to the very last day to hold off Pat Eddery, who ended the season with 195.

The Irish Derby was won by Sir Harry Lewis. In the Eclipse Reference Point again set off in front, but Mtoto wore him down to win by ¾ length. Reference Point returned to peak form in the King George VI and Queen Elizabeth Diamond Stakes, beating Celestial Storm by three lengths. Then followed comfortable victories in the Great Voltigeur and St. Leger, in the second of which Reference Point gained for his trainer his 147th win, thus surpassing a record that had been set by John Day in 1867. A strong favourite in the Prix de l'Arc de Triomphe, Reference Point faltered more than a furlong from home and finished eighth. It emerged that he had an abscess in a foot, and he was lame afterward. Trempolino galloped on strongly to beat the Italian four-year-old Tony Bin by two lengths and set a new course record. Trempolino's best effort before the Arc de Triomphe was his second by a head in the Prix du Jockey-Club. Trempolino followed his Arc victory with a close second to Theatrical in the Breeders' Cup Turf in the U.S.

Triptych won five Group I races—three in Britain, one in Ireland, and one at home in France. She achieved more good performances in top company than any other horse, but two earlier third-place finishes, in the Eclipse and King George, exposed her limitations. Nevertheless, her toughness and courage, at the age of five, deserved celebration. In mid-November she won a trial race in preparation for the Japan Cup, but disappointment followed in the final race for the cup itself. Triptych was hampered on the final turn and finished fourth, even trailing Le Glorieux, the other French representative.

Other notable milers were Don't Forget Me, which won both the English and Irish Two Thousand Guineas, and Risk Me, a specialist on soft tracks who traveled from England to defeat Soviet Star in the Prix Jean Prat and again to beat Seattle Dancer, the world's most expensive yearling, and Trempolino in the Grand Prix de Paris. Also noteworthy was Half a Year, which beat Soviet Star, Risk Me, and Don't Forget Me in a hard-fought finish to the St. James's Palace Stakes at Royal Ascot.

Among the two-year-olds, the outstanding French filly Ravinella beat her compatriot First Waltz in the Group I

## Major Thoroughbred Race Winners, 1987

| Race | Won by | Jockey |
|------|--------|--------|
| **United States** | | |
| Acorn | Grecian Flight | C. Perret |
| American Derby | Fortunate Moment | E. Fires |
| Arkansas Derby | Demons Begone | P. Day |
| Arlington Classic | Lost Code | G. St. Leon |
| Arlington-Washington Futurity | Tejano | J. Vásquez |
| Arlington-Washington Lassie | Joe's Tammie | C. Perret |
| Belmont | Bet Twice | C. Perret |
| Blue Grass | War | W. McCauley |
| Breeders' Cup Juvenile | Success Express | J. Santos |
| Breeders' Cup Juvenile Fillies | Epitome | P. Day |
| Breeders' Cup Sprint | Very Subtle | P. Valenzuela |
| Breeders' Cup Mile | Miesque | F. Head |
| Breeders' Cup Distaff | Sacahuista | R. Romero |
| Breeders' Cup Turf | Theatrical | P. Day |
| Breeders' Cup Classic | Ferdinand | W. Shoemaker |
| Brooklyn | Waquoit | C. McCarron |
| Budweiser-Arlington Million | Manila | A. Cordero, Jr. |
| Champagne | Forty Niner | E. Maple |
| Coaching Club American Oaks | Fiesta Gal | A. Cordero, Jr. |
| Delaware Handicap | Coup De Fusil | A. Cordero, Jr. |
| Flamingo | Talinum | A. Cordero, Jr. |
| Florida Derby | Cryptoclearance | J. Santos |
| Futurity | Forty Niner | E. Maple |
| Gulfstream Park Handicap | Skip Trial | R. Romero |
| Hialeah Turf Cup | Theatrical | P. Day |
| Hollywood Derby (2 divisions) | Political Ambition | E. Delahoussaye |
| | Stately Don | J. Vásquez |
| Hollywood Futurity | Tejano | L. Pincay, Jr. |
| Hollywood Gold Cup | Ferdinand | W. Shoemaker |
| Jockey Club Gold Cup | Creme Fraiche | L. Pincay, Jr. |
| Kentucky Derby | Alysheba | C. McCarron |
| Kentucky Oaks | Buryyourbelief | J. Santos |
| Man o' War | Theatrical | P. Day |
| Marlboro Cup Invitational | Java Gold | P. Day |
| Meadowlands Cup | Creme Fraiche | L. Pincay, Jr. |
| Metropolitan | Gulch | P. Day |
| Preakness | Alysheba | C. McCarron |
| Santa Anita Derby | Temperate Sil | W. Shoemaker |
| Santa Anita Handicap | Broad Brush | A. Cordero, Jr. |
| Suburban | Broad Brush | A. Cordero, Jr. |
| Travers | Java Gold | P. Day |
| Turf Classic | Theatrical | P. Day |
| Washington (D.C.) International | Le Glorieux | L. Pincay, Jr. |
| Widener | Launch A Pegasus | J. Velásquez |
| Wood Memorial Invitational | Gulch | J. Santos |
| Woodward | Polish Navy | R. Romero |
| | | |
| **England** | | |
| One Thousand Guineas | Miesque | F. Head |
| Two Thousand Guineas | Don't Forget Me | W. Carson |
| Derby | Reference Point | S. Cauthen |
| Oaks | Unite | W. R. Swinburn |
| St. Leger | Reference Point | S. Cauthen |
| Coronation Cup | Triptych | A. Cruz |
| Ascot Gold Cup | Paean | S. Cauthen |
| Eclipse Stakes | Mtoto | M. Roberts |
| King George VI and Queen | | |
| Elizabeth Diamond Stakes | Reference Point | S. Cauthen |
| Sussex Stakes | Soviet Star | G. Starkey |
| Matchmaker International | Triptych | S. Cauthen |
| Dubai Champion Stakes | Triptych | A. Cruz |
| | | |
| **France** | | |
| Poule d'Essai des Poulains | Soviet Star | G. Starkey |
| Poule d'Essai des Pouliches | Miesque | F. Head |
| Prix du Jockey-Club | Natroun | Y. Saint-Martin |
| Prix de Diane | Indian Skimmer | S. Cauthen |
| Prix Royal-Oak | Royal Gait | A. Gibert |
| Prix Ganay | Triptych | A. Cruz |
| Prix Lupin | Groom Dancer | D. Boeuf |
| Grand Prix de Paris | Risk Me | S. Cauthen |
| Grand Prix de Saint-Cloud | Moon Madness | P. Eddery |
| Prix Vermeille | Bint Pasha | P. Eddery |
| Prix de l'Arc de Triomphe | Trempolino | P. Eddery |
| Grand Critérium | Fijar Tango | A. Gibert |
| | | |
| **Ireland** | | |
| Irish Two Thousand Guineas | Don't Forget Me | W. Carson |
| Irish One Thousand Guineas | Forest Flower | T. Ives |
| Irish Derby | Sir Harry Lewis | J. Reid |
| Irish Oaks | Unite | W. R. Swinburn |
| Irish St. Leger | Eurobird | C. Asmussen |
| Phoenix Champion Stakes | Triptych | A. Cruz |
| | | |
| **Italy** | | |
| Derby Italiano | Zaizoom | T. Quinn |
| Gran Premio del Jockey-Club | Tony Bin | C. Asmussen |
| | | |
| **West Germany** | | |
| Deutsches Derby | Lebos | L. Mader |
| Grosser Preis von Baden | Acatenango | G. Bocskai |
| Grosser Preis von Berlin | Le Glorieux | A. Lequeux |
| Puma Europa Preis | Kamiros | P. Alafi |

Cheveley Park Stakes. Britain's Sanquirico was undefeated in his five races, and Ireland's Caerwent won both his outings. Ravinella's success and those of Triptych and Soviet Star helped to balance the work of British horses, who won almost £5 million overseas.

In Australia Rosedale, which had competed in Europe and California, where he was a Group I winner in April, was favoured to win the Melbourne Cup less than two months after his arrival in Australia, but he was beaten by 1 1/2 lengths and a short head by Kensei and Empire Rose. However, he remained in Australia.

The Thinker won the Cheltenham Gold Cup steeplechase after a race that would be remembered more for the fact that it started 81 minutes late because of snowstorms than for the strength of the competition. Maori Venture was a popular winner of the Grand National steeplechase for his 92-year-old owner, Jim Joel.          (ROBERT W. CARTER)

**Harness Racing.** In the million-dollar-plus Hambletonian in 1987, Mack Lobell set a world record of 1 min 54 sec and 1 min 53 3/5 sec for his two heats. He later trotted 1 min 52 1/5 sec, the fastest mile ever, at Springfield, Ill. He was named harness horse of the year and trotter of the year. The Oliver Wendell Holmes for three-year-olds was won by Run The Table. In pacing Jaguar Spur took the Little Brown Jug heat and final. Albert Albert equaled the world-record 1 min 52 4/5 sec winning the two-year-olds' Fox Stake. The Hambletonian Oaks final went to Armbro Fling. Sweden's representative Callit won the $250,000 Roosevelt International Trot, and Napoletano won the World Trotting Derby. Camtastic was chosen pacer of the year.

New Zealand pacer Master Mood won the $275,000 New Zealand Cup and the $300,000 Auckland Cup. The $350,-000 Inter-Dominion Championship was won by Lightning Blue (Australia). Both the $227,500 New Zealand Derby and the Great Northern Derby went to Race Ruler. Landora's Pride won the Rowe Trotting Cup and Tussle the Inter-Dominion Trot final. In Australia Sydney's Miracle Mile was won by Master Mood in a record 1 min 56.1 sec, the Sire Stake colts and geldings event by Tipawin, and the fillies' division by Sweet Papoose. Rocket Jason won the inaugural $100,000 Bathurst Gold Crown for two-year-olds, while in Melbourne the Australian Derby went to Rufus Young Blood, and Bag Limit won the $250,000 Winfield Cup. The $200,000 West Australia Cup was won by Our Ian Mac. Star of Broadway won the Tasmanian Pacing Championship, and Swapzee Bromac took the Australian Pacing Championship at Adelaide.

France's Prix d'Amérique was won by the 1986 winner, Ourasi. The French Critérium for four-year-olds was won by Rangone with a record 2 min 01.3 sec for the 2,100 m, while Quartz succeeded in the Critérium for five-year-olds. In Italy the Gran Permio Lotteria heats at Naples were won by Edyz, Super Play, and Limbo Joe, the latter winning the final. The Italian Premio Repubblica went to Mr. Almo.

The Norwegian Derby was won by Spit Superstar and the Finland Derby by Speedy Butch. In Copenhagen Konsonant took the Danish Derby. Atom Knight easily won the Swedish Derby in a race-record time of 2 min 01.3 sec for the 2,640 m; the German Derby was won by Tappino. West German trotter Diazam Speed won his heat and final of the Matchline Cup in Stockholm and also won against international competition in France and West Germany. Utah Bulwark won the Elitlopp final in Stockholm after Grades Singing and Rex Rodney had each won a heat. Utah Bulwark had previously won the Silver Horse over 2,140 m in a record 2 min 36.9 sec. The Swedish Mare's

Championship was won by Emile Palema. In Helsinki, Fin., Grades Singing lowered the world trotting record on a $^5/_8$-mi track to 1 min 56.2 sec. The Nordic Championship in Helsinki was won by Swedish champion Mac The Knife. In Norway the 1986 Oslo Grand Prix winner Rex Rodney again won the $65,000 event, and Krista Sidney took the V6 Match for Norwegian five-year-olds. The Charlottenlund Open Trot in Copenhagen was won by Garrett Lobell.

In England Dalestar won the National Pacing Derby at York. The Prakas Championship Trot was won by Bucks Frizz; Just a Step scored in the Prakas Trotting Sire Stake; and Silver Glorie won the Roosevelt Cup at Kendal. The fillies' pacing Sire Stake was won by Staly Star and the colts' division by Staly Baron. In August Missing Link became the first British-bred pacer to break the two-minute barrier on British soil when he won the feature Free For All event at York in 1 min 59.99 sec.    (NOEL SIMPSON)

## ICE HOCKEY

**North America.** The Edmonton Oilers regained their National Hockey League (NHL) supremacy during the 1986–87 season. During the regular season the league's 21 teams in the United States and Canada played 80 games each. The Oilers posted the best overall record—50 victories, 24 defeats, and 6 ties. They then swept through the Stanley Cup play-offs, winning 16 games and losing only 5.

This was the Oilers' third Stanley Cup in four years under coach Glen Sather. In the 1985–86 season, when the Montreal Canadiens won the cup, the Oilers were eliminated in the division play-offs.

*Regular Season.* During regular-season play the Oilers were the explosive team of old and won the Smythe Division with 106 points. The Philadelphia Flyers won the Patrick Division with 100 points, the Hartford Whalers the Adams Division with 93, and the St. Louis Blues the Norris Division with 79.

The closest race took place in the Norris Division, where St. Louis finished a point ahead of the Detroit Red Wings. The Red Wings, seeking their first title since the 1964–65 season, had led for the last two months of the season until they lost their final game.

*Play-offs.* The division winners and 12 other teams moved into the play-offs. Edmonton looked unbeatable as it advanced to the final round by routing the Los Angeles Kings (4 games to 1), Winnipeg Jets (4 games to 0), and Detroit (4 games to 1). Philadelphia gained the final round by eliminating the New York Rangers (4 games to 2), the New York Islanders (4 games to 3), and Montreal (4 games to 2).

For the first two games of the finals, Edmonton remained potent on offense. The team then turned to a grinding defense similar to Philadelphia's and took a 3–1 lead in games. Philadelphia won the fifth game 4–3 at Edmonton and the sixth game 3–2 at Philadelphia. Thus the winner of the seventh game, May 31 in Edmonton, would win the Stanley Cup. Edmonton won 3–1 despite excellent goaltending by Ron Hextall of Philadelphia. Hextall won the Conn Smythe Trophy as the play-offs' most valuable player.

There were three especially memorable games in the play-offs. On April 18 in Landover, Md., the seventh and deciding game of the series between the Islanders and the Washington Capitals lasted 6½ hours. The Islanders won 3–2 on Pat LaFontaine's goal in the fourth overtime period. Kelly Hrudey, the Islanders' goalie, stopped 73 of 75 shots, the equivalent of one week's work in one night.

On May 14 in Montreal there was a 15-minute fight before the sixth game between Montreal and Philadelphia.

It involved every player except the two starting goalies, and the league fined the 36 players who took part. Brian O'Neill, the NHL's executive vice-president, said the fight "brought dishonor to the league."

On May 24 in Philadelphia, in the fourth game of the finals, Hextall swung his stick at Kent Nilsson of Edmonton and hit him behind the right knee. The league suspended Hextall for the first eight games of the 1987–88 season.

*Individuals.* At age 26, in his eighth NHL season, Wayne Gretzky again was the league's outstanding player. The Edmonton captain and centre won the Art Ross Trophy as the NHL scoring champion for the seventh consecutive year and the Hart Trophy as the most valuable player for the eighth straight year. Gretzky led in every scoring category—goals (62), assists (121), and total points (183). As usual, he was far ahead of the second leading scorer, this time his line mate Jari Kurri with 108 points.

Gretzky became the NHL's leading career scorer in play-off competition, breaking Jean Beliveau's record of 176 points in 162 games over 17 years with Montreal. Gretzky passed that on April 10 during his 82nd play-off game in eight years.

At age 33, in his 14th NHL season, Denis Potvin of the Islanders became the first defenseman to score 1,000 points and bettered Brad Park's career record for assists. One season earlier he had broken Bobby Orr's career records for goals and total points.

Ray Bourque of the Boston Bruins won the Norris Trophy for defensemen; Hextall of Philadelphia, the Vezina Trophy for goaltending; forward Luc Robitaille of Los Angeles, the Calder Trophy as rookie of the year; forward Joe Mullen of the Calgary Flames, the Lady Byng Trophy for gentlemanly play; Dave Poulin of Philadelphia, the Selke Trophy for defensive forwards; and Jacques Demers of Detroit, the Adams Award as coach of the year. The all-star team consisted of Hextall in goal, Mark Howe of Philadelphia and Bourque on defense, Gretzky at centre, and Michel Goulet of the Quebec Nordiques and Kurri at wing.

An incident involving the Los Angeles Kings, the Vancouver Canucks, and Pat Quinn resulted in punitive action by the league. The league said that during Quinn's last year of a three-year contract as the Los Angeles coach, he accepted a $100,000 signing bonus to become Vancouver's general manager for the 1987–88 season. John Ziegler, the NHL president, fined Vancouver $310,000 and Los Angeles $130,000, the maximum allowed. He also barred Quinn from coaching Vancouver until the 1990–91 season.

(FRANK LITSKY)

**European and International.** Greece became the 37th member nation of the International Ice Hockey Federation (IIHF) in a season during which a record number of 28 countries competed in the 52nd world championships, necessitating the addition of a fourth group. The title, won by Sweden for the first time since 1962, hinged on the final match of the tournament played by the eight Group A nations in Vienna on April 17–May 3, 1987. Czechoslovakia was denied the title when it lost that match 2–1 to the U.S.S.R. The defending champion Soviets, who had been held to a draw by both Sweden and Canada, gained the silver medal. The Czechoslovaks ended with the bronze, followed by Canada.

A stunning 9–0 victory over Canada in the first match of the medals round had put the Swedes firmly in the driver's seat, but they won the gold medal from the Soviets because of the difference in number of goals scored. After the initial round-robin, only subsequent meetings between the four qualifiers for the championship section counted in the competition for medals, but points earned in the opening round were carried forward by teams competing in the relegation section. Awards for the three best players in the group were presented to Dominik Hasek, the Czechoslovak goaltender; Craig Hartsburgh, a Canadian defenseman; and Vladimir Krutov, a Soviet forward.

The eight Group B countries competed at Canazei, Italy, on March 26–April 5. Poland, winning six of its seven games and losing only to East Germany, achieved a one-point margin over Norway to gain promotion to Group A, changing places with the demoted Switzerland for the 1989 competition in Stockholm. (The eight Group A and top four Group B nations qualified for the 1988 Winter Olympics, limited to 12 teams, with no separate world championships.)

### Table I. NHL Final Standings, 1987

| | Won | Lost | Tied | Points |
|---|---|---|---|---|
| **Prince of Wales Conference** | | | | |
| PATRICK DIVISION | | | | |
| *Philadelphia Flyers | 46 | 26 | 8 | 100 |
| *Washington Capitals | 38 | 32 | 10 | 86 |
| *New York Islanders | 35 | 33 | 12 | 82 |
| *New York Rangers | 34 | 38 | 8 | 76 |
| Pittsburgh Penguins | 30 | 38 | 12 | 72 |
| New Jersey Devils | 29 | 45 | 6 | 64 |
| ADAMS DIVISION | | | | |
| *Hartford Whalers | 43 | 30 | 7 | 93 |
| *Montreal Canadiens | 41 | 29 | 10 | 92 |
| *Boston Bruins | 39 | 34 | 7 | 85 |
| *Quebec Nordiques | 31 | 39 | 10 | 72 |
| Buffalo Sabres | 28 | 44 | 8 | 64 |
| **Clarence Campbell Conference** | | | | |
| NORRIS DIVISION | | | | |
| *St. Louis Blues | 32 | 33 | 15 | 79 |
| *Detroit Red Wings | 34 | 36 | 10 | 78 |
| *Chicago Black Hawks | 29 | 37 | 14 | 72 |
| *Toronto Maple Leafs | 32 | 42 | 6 | 70 |
| Minnesota North Stars | 30 | 40 | 10 | 70 |
| SMYTHE DIVISION | | | | |
| *Edmonton Oilers | 50 | 24 | 6 | 106 |
| *Calgary Flames | 46 | 31 | 3 | 95 |
| *Winnipeg Jets | 40 | 32 | 8 | 88 |
| *Los Angeles Kings | 31 | 41 | 8 | 70 |
| Vancouver Canucks | 29 | 43 | 8 | 66 |

*Clinched play-off berth.

### Table II. World Ice Hockey Championships, 1987

| | Won | Lost | Tied | Goals | Goals against | Points |
|---|---|---|---|---|---|---|
| **GROUP A Championship Section** | | | | | | |
| Sweden | 1 | 0 | 2 | 14 | 5 | 4 |
| U.S.S.R. | 1 | 0 | 2 | 4 | 3 | 4 |
| Czechoslovakia | 1 | 1 | 1 | 8 | 7 | 3 |
| Canada | 0 | 2 | 1 | 2 | 13 | 1 |
| **GROUP A Relegation Section** | | | | | | |
| Finland | 5 | 4 | 1 | 32 | 34 | 11 |
| West Germany | 4 | 5 | 1 | 31 | 37 | 9 |
| United States | 4 | 6 | 0 | 36 | 49 | 8 |
| Switzerland | 0 | 10 | 0 | 26 | 71 | 0 |
| **GROUP B** | | | | | | |
| Poland | 6 | 1 | 0 | 39 | 11 | 12 |
| Norway | 5 | 1 | 1 | 33 | 25 | 11 |
| Austria | 5 | 2 | 0 | 41 | 27 | 10 |
| France | 4 | 2 | 1 | 37 | 26 | 9 |
| East Germany | 2 | 3 | 2 | 25 | 31 | 6 |
| Italy | 2 | 4 | 1 | 28 | 30 | 5 |
| Netherlands, The | 1 | 5 | 1 | 30 | 37 | 3 |
| China | 0 | 7 | 0 | 14 | 60 | 0 |
| **GROUP C** | | | | | | |
| Japan | 5 | 1 | 1 | 61 | 13 | 11 |
| Denmark | 5 | 1 | 1 | 47 | 23 | 11 |
| Romania | 5 | 1 | 1 | 48 | 22 | 11 |
| Yugoslavia | 3 | 0 | 4 | 60 | 23 | 10 |
| Hungary | 3 | 4 | 0 | 33 | 28 | 6 |
| North Korea | 2 | 5 | 0 | 13 | 45 | 4 |
| Bulgaria | 1 | 5 | 1 | 21 | 40 | 3 |
| Belgium | 0 | 7 | 0 | 8 | 97 | 0 |
| **GROUP D** | | | | | | |
| Australia | 5 | 0 | 1 | 177 | 6 | 11 |
| South Korea | 4 | 1 | 1 | 130 | 16 | 9 |
| New Zealand | 2 | 4 | 0 | 42 | 143 | 4 |
| Hong Kong | 0 | 6 | 0 | 1 | 185 | 0 |

The Netherlands and China, finishing at the bottom of Group B, were demoted to Group C for 1989. They were to be replaced by Japan and Denmark, which finished first and second, respectively, in the Group C competition at Copenhagen on March 20–29. At Perth, Australia, on March 14–21, the four less experienced nations in the newly formed Group D were unevenly balanced. The result was many one-sided games, most notably Australia's 58–0 defeat of New Zealand, a world championship record. Australia was promoted to Group C, swapping with the demoted Belgium.

An elite tournament for the Canada Cup was contested in Canada on August 27–September 14 between the host nation, the U.S., and the four highest-placed European nations in the world championships. With the North American countries able to call on more NHL players than had been available for the world championships, the tournament was widely regarded as a truer international test.

In a thrill-packed best-of-three final between the host nation and the U.S.S.R., both at full strength, each beat the other 6–5 in overtime before Canada clinched the issue by the same score in the third game. Gretzky topped the tournament point scorers with 21 from 3 goals and 18 assists, but his Canadian teammate Mario Lemieux netted most goals overall (11), including the winners in Canada's two final victories. Sweden and Czechoslovakia were the losing semifinalists after eliminating the U.S. and Finland.

(HOWARD BASS)

## ICE SKATING

Expansion was evident in every aspect of ice skating during 1987. Many more spectators attended major international competitions despite, or perhaps because of, increased television coverage. New rink construction flourished, with increased emphasis on including ice facilities in large, multipurpose arenas. Outdoor speed skating gained impetus from a successful World Cup debut, and short-track racing also gained ground.

**Figure Skating.** Capacity crowds in excess of 14,000 attended every final contest of the 77th world championships in Cincinnati, Ohio, during March 9–14. In the four events 24 nations were represented by 132 skaters. The close-fought singles competition for both men and women riveted interest to the last gasp.

Not for the first time, Katarina Witt of East Germany retrieved a seemingly lost cause—she was in fifth place after the figures—to recapture the women's crown from Debi Thomas, the U.S. runner-up. It was Witt's third title in four years. Another U.S. skater, Caryn Kadavy, took the bronze medal.

Victory was particularly sweet for Brian Orser when the unassuming Canadian mounted the podium as the new men's king after placing second in each of the three previous seasons. Orser set an unprecedented standard of athleticism with six precisely landed triple leaps, including two triple axels. Runner-up was the defending champion, Brian Boitano of the U.S., who tried to be the first person to land a quadruple jump in a desperate effort to win the event. His brave, all-or-nothing attempt ended in an untidy fall, but his five different triples, axel included, proved enough to clinch the silver medal, ahead of Aleksandr Fadeev of the U.S.S.R.

Moscow's diminutive Ekaterina Gordeeva and the giant Sergey Grinkov comfortably retained the pairs title, denying a third win in five years to the Leningrad runners-up, Elena Valova and Oleg Vasiliev. Jill Watson and Peter Oppegard of the U.S. prevented a Soviet clean sweep by finishing third.

Canada's Brian Orser soars over the ice on his way to winning the men's world figure skating championship. Orser surpassed rivals from the U.S. and U.S.S.R. with six precisely landed triple leaps.

AP/WIDE WORLD

The ice dance contest resulted in a third straight victory for Natalia Bestemianova and Andrey Bukin of the U.S.S.R. Their compatriots Marina Klimova and Sergey Ponomarenko finished second. The Soviet dominance was more closely challenged than in 1986 by Tracy Wilson and Robert McCall of Canada, who took the bronze medal for the second successive year.

**Speed Skating.** A highlight of the season was the first men's world championships to be held indoors, on the first covered 400-m circuit, at Heerenveen, Neth., on February 14–15. A capacity crowd of 16,500 watched Nikolay Gulyaev triumph over his Soviet compatriot Oleg Bozhiev. Michael Hadschieff finished third for Austria. In the individual events Gulyaev won the 1,500 m, Leo Visser of the host nation the 5,000 m, Geir Karlstad of Norway the 10,000 m, and Bae Ki Tae of South Korea the 500 m. Protected from the outside elements, the track proved fast enough to produce best-ever times over every distance except the 500 m.

The women's world title was retained by Karin Kania of East Germany at West Allis, Wis., on February 7–8. Her compatriot Andrea Ehrig was runner-up as in the previous season, with Yvonne van Gennip taking the bronze for The Netherlands. Kania won the 500 m and the 1,500 m, and the 3,000 m and the 5,000 m went to Ehrig.

In the separate world sprint championships, at Sainte Foy, Que., on January 31–February 1, Akira Kuroiwa of Japan captured the men's title, with Nick Thometz of the U.S. finishing second and another Japanese, Yukihiro Mitani, third. Kania retained the women's title, defeating Bonnie Blair of the U.S., with Christa Rothenburger third for East Germany.

Following a successful trial run the previous season, the first official World Cup series was contested at 13 sites in ten countries, ending at Inzell, West Germany, on March 12–15, when Thometz emerged the men's winner over both

500 m and 1,000 m. Hans Magnusson took the 1,500 m and Karlstad the long-distance award decided over 5,000 m and 10,000 m. Two women gained double victories, Blair for the 500 m and 1,000 m and van Gennip for the 1,500 m and long distance (3,000 m and 5,000 m).

New world records were established for five men's and three women's distances, all at Heerenveen. Visser reduced the 3,000 m to 3 min 59.27 sec and the 5,000 m to 6 min 47.01 sec. Thometz lowered the 500 m to 36.55 sec. Gulyaev set new figures of 1 min 52.70 sec for the 1,500 m, and Karlstad brought the 10,000 m down to 14 min 3.92 sec. Two of the women's best times were shattered by van Gennip with 4 min 16.85 sec for the 3,000 m and 7 min 20.36 sec for the 5,000 m. The third women's record was clinched by Blair with 39.43 sec for the 500 m.

At the seventh world short-track championships at Montreal on April 4–5, Michel Daignault of Canada and Toshinobu Kawai of Japan shared the men's title. Third for The Netherlands was Charles Veldhoven. Eiko Shishii captured the women's crown for Japan, followed by Nathalie Lambert of Canada in second place and Mariko Kinoshita of Japan in third. Lambert set a new world short-track record of 5 min 31.65 sec for the women's 3,000 m.

(HOWARD BASS)

## LAWN BOWLS

In 1987 lawn bowls continued to be dominated by bowlers from the British Isles, Australia, and New Zealand. The variable British climate assisted the growth of indoor bowls; increased television coverage was stimulating interest and international competition in this form of the game.

David Bryant and Tony Allcock of England, the world's top players, found the television revolution to their taste. Allcock beat Bryant in the Embassy world indoor championship at Coatbridge, Scotland; both men had earlier warded off the challenge of master bowlers from New Zealand, Australia, Canada, Israel, and the British Isles. The pair also retained their Midland Bank world pairs title against similar opposition at Bournemouth, England. Allcock's play in the final was described by his contemporaries as "the best the game has ever seen."

Outdoors at Worthing, England, Bryant won the Gateway Masters for the seventh time, successfully meeting the challenges of Commonwealth Games gold medalist Ian Dickison (New Zealand), Dennis Katunarich (Australia), George Souza (Hong Kong), Peter Fong (Fiji), and Alf Wallace (Canada). England's 1986 champion, Wynne Richards, and Welshman Stephen Rees, the U.K. indoor titleholder, finished second and third, respectively. Earlier, Richards had reached the semifinals of the fifth Hong Kong classic, won by Paul Richards of Australia. The winner was not so fortunate in Australia's Mazda Classic at Adelaide, finishing third in his round-robin section to fellow Australian Ian Schuback, who went on to beat Katunarich.

Norma Shaw, England's former women's world singles gold medalist, defeated Allcock in a televised tournament, and David Holt, aged 20, outbowled him 21–5 in England's outdoor singles final at Worthing. Scotland's Angus Blair won the British Isles title at Llanelli, Wales. Pat and Terry James won the All England mixed pairs at Weston-super-Mare.

(DONALD J. NEWBY)

## MOTORBOATING

Winning his sixth consecutive American Power Boat Association (APBA) Gold Cup trophy, Chip Hanauer and his *Miller American* Unlimited hydroplane turned in only one of the performances that made APBA's 1987 season a true record breaker. At the season's start, Hanauer took a back seat to Jim Kropfeld and *Miss Budweiser.* Not until the second to the last race of the year when the Gold Cup was at stake did the *Miller American* driver really begin to shine. Equipped with a totally redesigned hull, Hanauer clocked the fastest lap in the history of the sport, 155.979 mph (250.970 km/h). In doing so he won his sixth straight Gold Cup, the first driver to have won the championship that many times.

"Never a dull moment" was the key phrase of the year for the 1987 APBA Offshore circuit. Speed records were broken in five of the six national classes. In the first event of the season for Superboats, Tom Gentry broke the old speed record by 18 mph (29 km/h) and went on from there to win the 1987 world championship in that class. However, Gentry had to share the limelight. By again scoring the most points on the U.S. national Superboat circuit, Al Copeland with his *Popeye's/Diet Coke* became the only Offshore driver in any class to have won the U.S. championship four years in a row.

Probably the closest Offshore competition took place in the Modified class, where John Sauselen in *Baja Bandit II* and John D'Elia in *Auto Armor Special Edition* were tied going into their last race. D'Elia finally won when Sauselen could not finish the race.

In the Champ Boat class of the 1987 APBA International Outboard Grand Prix U.S. national circuit, Chris Bush finished second to Billy Seebold in three races out of five but still was the overall winner. Vying for world championship status, the victors of the circuit's SST-140 and Mod VP classes put up a tough battle. In SST-140 a season finale win for Terry Leatherby put him four points above defending champion Harley Wilson. In Mod VP, Rusty Campbell finally overcame his "always a bridesmaid, never a bride" reputation by having his first winning season as a boat racer. With four first-place finishes, one second, and one third, he won the U.S., North American, and world titles.

(RENEE J. MAHN)

## POLO

The young Indios Chapaleufu team (G. Heguy [8], H. Heguy [8], A. Garrahan [8], and M. Heguy [7]) beat La Españada by 13 goals to 12 to win the 1987 Argentine Open championship. U.T.C. defeated La Capilla in the final of the Chilean Open championship. In the U.S., White Birch retained the U.S. Polo Association's Rolex Gold Cup, and in Zimbabwe a Texas team defeated the national team. In the European championship final Great Britain defeated West Germany 5½–5 at the Berlin Olympic Stadium. In a military challenge for the Churchill Trophy in Cyprus, the Royal Jordan Polo Club beat Cyprus 4–2.

In England the Coronation Cup was won by North America (M. Azzaro [6], R. Walton [8], O. Rinehart [9], and D. Smicklas [7]), defeating England (W. Lucas [4], A. Kent [7], J. Hipwood [9], and H. Hipwood [9]) 8–5. In the Silver Jubilee Cup the prince of Wales's team (G. Kent [4], the prince of Wales [4], S. Mackenzie [8], and M. Brown [5]) beat Peru (A. Piaggio [3], J. Pena [6], M. Pena [6], and F. Reusche [6]) 7–5. The Moët and Chandon High Goal Challenge was won by Mexico (C. Gracida [10], M. Gracida [10], A. Herrera [8], and W. Scherer [5]) over the Rest of the World (J. Hipwood [9], A. Kent [7], O. Rinehart [9], and S. Novaes [7]) 8–7, and in the new James Gordon Bennett Challenge Cup, Great Britain (R. Mishcon [0], M. Amoore [4], C. Tomlinson [5], and M. Brown [5]) defeated the U.S. (R. Hissom [2], F. Erb [4], G. Kaywell [5], and J. Ryan [3]) 8–4. In the British Open championship Tramontana beat Windsor Park 9–5.

(COLIN J. CROSS)

## RODEO

Perhaps the most welcome news to professional rodeo cowboys in 1987 came at the end of the year when the Professional Rodeo Cowboys Association (PRCA) governing board announced that the new position of rodeo commissioner had been filled. Lewis Cryer left his job as Pacific Coast Athletic Association commissioner to take the reins at PRCA headquarters in Colorado Springs, Colo., beginning in 1988. The announcement came on the last day of the PRCA's National Finals Rodeo, December 13, in Las Vegas, Nev. PRCA management had been through two years of change and upheaval, and it was hoped that Cryer would bring stability and increased prosperity to the 6,000-member organization.

At the National Finals Rodeo, Lewis Feild of Elk Ridge, Utah, won his third straight world all-around cowboy championship with total year-end earnings of $144,335; his events were saddle bronc and bareback riding. (The all-around title goes to the cowboy who wins the most money throughout the season, including the National Finals, in two or more events.) Other 1987 champions included Clint Johnson of Spearfish, S.D., $86,570 in saddle bronc riding; Bruce Ford of Kersey, Colo., $102,007 in bareback riding (his fifth title in the event); Lane Frost of Quanah, Texas, $105,697 in bull riding; Joe Beaver of Victoria, Texas, $108,586 in calf roping; Steve Duhon of Opelousas, La., $85,450 in steer wrestling; Jake Barnes of Bloomfield, N.M., and Clay O'Brien Cooper of Gilbert, Ariz., $84,148 each in team roping; and Charmayne James of Clayton, N.M., $120,002 in Women's Professional Rodeo Association barrel racing.

Shaun Burchett of Pryor, Okla., was named single steer roping champion two weeks earlier at the National Finals Steer Roping competition in Guthrie, Okla. He won $30,-485 in the event for the year.

In the International Professional Rodeo Association (IPRA), headquartered at Pauls Valley, Okla., Dan Dailey of Peaster, Texas, continued to dominate competition. He reigned as all-around champion for the ninth time in 1987. Duane Daines of Innisfail, Alta., was named Canadian all-around champion in the Canadian Professional Rodeo Association. In the National Intercollegiate Rodeo Association, Roy Cordova of Central Arizona College at Coolidge won the men's all-around, and Sherry Lynn Rosser of Southern Arkansas University at Magnolia took the women's all-around title.

The rodeo world was saddened over the deaths of two prominent competitors in 1987. Warren Granger ("Freckles") Brown of Soper, Okla., died on March 20 at age 66. Brown won only one world title—bull riding, in 1962—but he was 42 years old at the time and competed for a dozen years more after that. The entire country was shocked at the death of Malcolm ("Mac") Baldrige of Woodbury, Conn., on July 25. Baldrige, who had served as U.S. secretary of commerce from the time Ronald Reagan took office as president, was a part-time team roper in the PRCA. He died from injuries sustained when a horse fell on him at a roping session in California.

(RANDALL E. WITTE)

## ROWING

East Germany retained its top position in world rowing in 1987, winning 13 of the 52 championship titles. Italy replaced the Soviet Union in second place with 11 titles, and West Germany finished third with 7 wins, followed by Romania, Bulgaria, Great Britain, the Soviet Union, and the U.S.

(Left) *Stars & Stripes* heads for the first mark in front of Australia's *Kookaburra III* during the fourth race in the America's Cup. (Above) Pres. Ronald Reagan presents skipper Dennis Conner with the cup after the *Stars & Stripes* decisively won, thus returning the cup to the U.S.

(LEFT) AP/WIDE WORLD; (RIGHT) AFP PHOTO

The world championships, held in Copenhagen in August, attracted 283 entries from 34 countries. Six nations shared the men's titles. East Germany scored three wins, its single sculler, Thomas Lange, ending 12 years of supremacy in world sculling by Peter Michael Kolbe of West Germany and Pertti Karppinen of Finland. The East Germans also retained the coxed fours and deposed the U.S. in coxless fours, defeating the Soviet Union for both titles.

The finals were split over two days for the first time, which allowed the rowers to compete for two titles. Andy Holmes and Steve Redgrave of Great Britain made a valiant bid in pairs by taking the coxless title before narrowly surrendering their own coxed title to the Abbagnale brothers of Italy, winners on four previous occasions. Italy lost its double sculls title to Bulgaria, while the Soviet Union retained the quadruple sculls and the U.S. took the eights.

In women's events East Germany lost its three-year hold on the single and double sculls to Bulgaria but retained the quadruple sculls for a third year. Romania comfortably defended the coxed fours and scored its third straight win in coxless pairs; both these crews became the first to win two gold medals at the same championships when they formed part of the triumphant Romanian eight, which ended nine years of unbroken success by the Soviet Union.

In lightweight events Italy lost its men's coxless fours title to West Germany, took the double sculls, and completed its third successive win in eights. Wim van Belleghem of Belgium won the single sculls. In women's events Maria Sava of Romania retained the single sculls, Canada deposed the U.S. in double sculls, and the U.S. took the coxless fours from West Germany.

In the international under-23 championships at Aiguebelette, France, Italy and West Germany won all but 4 of the 17 gold medals—the Italians scoring 7 wins and the Germans 6. Great Britain defeated West Germany in men's eights, and Austria took the coxless pairs. The Netherlands foiled a clean sweep by the Germans and Italians in women's events by winning the quadruple sculls, while

Belgium's double scullers stopped Italy from taking all the lightweight events.

Fifteen nations shared the medals in the world junior championships in Cologne, West Germany, where 162 entries from 30 nations contested 14 titles. East Germany won nine, the Soviet Union took two, and the U.S., Great Britain, and Italy were the other winners.

In England entries for the Henley Royal Regatta reached an all-time record of 371. Soviet crews, in their first appearance since 1974, won four events. Dinamo Moscow took the Double Sculls Cup and the Stewards' Cup (coxless fours), and the Soviet Army won the Grand Challenge Cup (eights) and Prince Philip Cup (coxed fours). Kolbe added the Diamond Sculls to his impressive international singles record. In other events University College, Galway, took the Thames Cup (eights) to Ireland; the Queen Mother Cup (quadruple sculls) went to Ridley College in Canada; and Belmont Hill School in Belmont, Mass., triumphed in the Princess Elizabeth Cup (school eights). In the 133rd University Boat Race, Oxford mastered a fierce head wind to beat Cambridge by four lengths and reduce the latter's lead in the series to 69–63.          (KEITH OSBORNE)

## SAILING

Sailing activity at the start of 1987 was concentrated on the America's Cup selection series for 12-m yachts at Fremantle, Australia. The challengers, with 13 syndicates (six from the U.S., two each from France and Italy, and one each from Great Britain, Canada, and New Zealand), had been dominated by the New Zealand team in *New Zealand* under Chris Dickson. However, in these final elimination races Dennis Conner (*see* BIOGRAPHIES) in *Stars & Stripes* of the San Diego Yacht Club was showing steady improvement and Tom Blackaller in *USA* impressive speed at times, while Britain's *White Crusader* under Harold Cudmore, the New York Yacht Club's *America II* skippered by John Kolius, and France's *French Kiss* under Marc Pajot seemed to be just off the pace. *White Crusader* failed after a series of miscalculations and breakdowns. *America*

*II* seemed to lose speed after its final alterations, and when it too was eliminated, the New York Yacht Club for the first time could not take part in the cup's final races. In the semifinal round New Zealand swept the French aside (4–0), while the U.S.'s Conner beat fellow countryman Blackaller (4–0). In the finals *Stars & Stripes* outsailed *New Zealand* (4–1).

Meanwhile, the defenders' series had established that the two *Kookaburra*s and *Australia IV* were the only consistently fast boats, but the competition was somewhat marred by excessive protesting. Finally and deservedly, *Kookaburra III* under Iain Murray was selected for the attempt to hold off the U.S. challenger. As soon as *Stars & Stripes* and *Kookaburra III* entered the starting zone for the first America's Cup race, Conner took control, and after dominating the pre-start maneuvers he dictated the race to win by 1 min 41 sec. The second race followed the same pattern; Peter Gilmour, the Australian starting helmsman, could not get the better of the Americans, who won by 1 min 10 sec. Race three saw the Australians get away best, but a mainsail zip problem forced them to send a man aloft; Conner soon had *Stars & Stripes* alongside and went ahead to win by 1 min 46 sec. It was clear that the fourth race could be the final one. The U.S. crew started fastest and sailed steadily away from the Australian yacht to win by 1 min 59 sec. The cup was back in U.S. hands.

It was also the year of the Admiral's Cup, the biennial ocean-racing team series sailed off the south coast of England. Fourteen teams, each comprising three yachts, entered. Defending champion West Germany was favoured, but strong challenges were expected from the United Kingdom, the U.S., Australia, and New Zealand. After the first two races it was clear that the West Germans were not going to retain the trophy. On the other hand, the New Zealanders quickly demonstrated that their success in 12-m yacht racing was not just luck. In Bruce Farr and Lawrie Davidson the Kiwis had two exceptionally talented designers and also had the crew to sail against the best. *Propaganda*, a Farr design sailed by Bevan Woolley, moved particularly well. The New Zealanders entered the final race of the cup, the 605-mi (974-km) Fastnet classic, with a substantial lead over the British, who in turn were comfortably ahead of the teams astern; New Zealand took the series, and *Propaganda* won the award for best yacht of the series. It was a particularly notable year for New Zealand, which also won the 12-m world championship and succeeded in many dinghy races. (ADRIAN JARDINE)

## World Class Boat Champions

| Class | Winner | Class | Winner |
|---|---|---|---|
| Catapult | Roger Hodgkinson (United Kingdom) | International 14 | James Hartley (United Kingdom) |
| Contender | Jon Webb (United Kingdom) | J24 | Francesco de Angelis (Italy) |
| Echells 22 | Bruce Burton (United States) | Laser | Stuart Wallace (Australia) |
| 8 Metre | Per Wermelin (Sweden) | OK | Mats Caap (Sweden) |
| Enterprise | Neil Marsden (United Kingdom) | Optimist | Sabrina Landi (Italy) |
| Europe | Thomas Johansson (Sweden) | Soling | Helmar Nauck (East Germany) |
| Flying Dutchman | Luis Doreste (Spain) | Star | Vince Brun (United States) |
| Finn | José-Luis Doreste (Spain) | Tempest | Rolf Bähr (West Germany) |
| 505 | Krister Bergstrom (Sweden) | Tornado | Andreas Hagara (Austria) |
| 470 | Berndt Hoeft (East Germany) | 12 Metre | David Barnes (New Zealand) |
| 420 | Jean-Frere Berthet (France) | 1/2 Ton | Pierre Pasco (France) |
| Hornet | Michael Macnamara (United Kingdom) | 1 Ton | Crown Prince Harald (Norway) |

## SKIING

**Alpine Racing.** Swiss skiers dominated the 29th world championships held on Jan. 27–Feb. 8, 1987, at Crans-Montana, Switz., collecting eight of the ten gold medals. Outstanding were Pirmin Zurbriggen, with two men's golds and two silvers, and Erika Hess (*see* BIOGRAPHIES) and Maria Walliser, each of whom won two women's titles. Zurbriggen's successes were in the giant slalom and supergiant slalom, his runner-up in each being Marc Girardelli of Luxembourg. An Italian, Alberto Tomba, was third in the giant slalom and a West German, Markus Wasmeier, third in the supergiant slalom. Peter Müller was the other Swiss men's victor, taking the downhill ahead of Zurbriggen, with Karl Alpiger completing a national clean sweep. Frank Wörndl became the first West German to win a world championship slalom in 41 years, followed by Günther Mader of Austria and another West German, Armin Bittner. The separate alpine combination was won by Girardelli, ahead of Zurbriggen and Mader.

The Hess triumphs in the slalom and the alpine combination increased her career tally of championships to six. Roswitha Steiner of Austria was the runner-up in the slalom, with Mateja Svet of Yugoslavia third. Another Austrian, Sylvia Eder, narrowly defeated Tamara McKinney of the U.S. for second place in the combination. The versatile Walliser proved supreme in the downhill and the supergiant slalom, her closest rival in each being her fellow Swiss Michela Figini. Third in the downhill was a West German, Regine Mösenlechner, while Svet took the supergiant slalom bronze. Walliser finished third in the giant slalom, won by her compatriot Vreni Schneider with Svet runner-up.

In the 21st Alpine World Cup series, involving 32 men's and 32 women's contests in nine countries, nine of the ten titles went to Swiss racers. Zurbriggen became the second man to win four titles in the same season—downhill, giant slalom, supergiant slalom, and overall—equaling the achievement of Jean-Claude Killy of France in 1967. The one title to elude the man of the season, the slalom, was gained by Bojan Krizaj of Yugoslavia. The Swedish veteran Ingemar Stenmark, second in the slalom, increased his record number of individual race wins to 85, accomplished between 1974 and 1987.

Walliser won the women's overall title, tying for first place in the giant slalom with Schneider. Walliser also took the supergiant slalom. The downhill title went to Figini and the slalom to Corinne Schmidhauser for a Swiss women's grand slam. The concurrently decided Nation's Cup for men and women was retained by Switzerland, ahead of Austria and West Germany, in a repeat of the two previous seasons' results.

**Nordic Events.** Honours in Nordic skiing were widely distributed in the 36th world championships, on February 11–21 at Oberstdorf, West Germany. Thomas Wassberg of Sweden was the most successful men's cross-country racer. He won the 30 km and placed second in both the other individual distances, narrowly losing the 15 km to Marco Albarello of Italy and the grueling 50 km to another Italian, Maurilio DeZolt. Wassberg also was a member of the winning Swedish relay team. Marjo Matikainen of Finland won a gold medal in the women's 5 km and a silver in the 10 km behind Anne Jahren of Norway. Marie-Helene Westin of Sweden took the 20 km. Anfisa Retzova, who was second in both the 20 km and 5 km, anchored the winning Soviet relay team. Andreas Felder of Austria won the 90-m ski jump, Jiri Parma of Czechoslovakia taking the 70-m event. Torbjörn Lökken kept Norway in the picture with a victory in the individual Nordic combination, but his country was beaten by West Germany in the team event.

In the eighth Nordic World Cup series for cross-country racing, comprising 16 men's and 16 women's contests in ten countries, Matikainen retained her title to become the second women's winner for a second time, equaling the feat of her fellow Finn Marja-Liisa Kirvesniemi in 1983 and 1984. The men's title was won by Torgny Mogren of Sweden. The longest recorded ski jump was achieved by Felder when he cleared 630 ft (192 m) at Planica, Yugos., on March 13.

In the world biathlon championships, combining cross-country ski racing with rifle marksmanship, on February 12–15 at Lake Placid, N.Y., Frank-Peter Rötsch of East Germany proved supreme. He won both individual events, 10 km and 20 km, and gained a third gold medal as a member of his national winning relay team.

**Other Events.** Freestyle skiing, with emphasis on specialized acrobatics, continued to prosper, encouraged by acceptance as a demonstration sport in the 1988 winter Olympic Games. Fifteen nations competed in the freestyle World Cup series, contested at nine meetings in six countries. The overall men's and women's winners were Eric Labouriex of France and Conny Kissling of Switzerland.

(HOWARD BASS)

## SQUASH RACKETS

The 1986–87 season would be remembered in squash rackets for the deposition of Jahangir Khan of Pakistan by his 18-year-old compatriot Jansher Khan. Jahangir won the Spanish and British opens, defeating Jansher in both finals, and the Canadian Open but lost the New South Wales Open to Rodney Martin of Australia. Then Jansher took over; he won the Malaysian, Hong Kong, and Pakistan opens, defeating Jahangir in the semifinal and final, respectively, of the last two. In the final of the Australian Open, C. Robertson beat Martin, and in the U.S. Open final, Stuart Davenport of New Zealand beat his compatriot Ross Norman.

The World Open was won by Jansher Khan. He defeated Jahangir Khan in the semifinal and Chris Dittmar of Australia 9–5, 9–4, 4–9, 9–6 in the final to win a world record £10,000 first prize before a record crowd of 3,526 at the National Exhibition Centre, Birmingham, England. In the team event at the Royal Albert Hall in London, Pakistan beat Australia 2–1 and New Zealand beat England 2–1 in the semifinals. Pakistan defeated New Zealand 3–0 in the final, during which Jansher resisted a great challenge from Norman.

In women's squash Susan Devoy of New Zealand again won the French Open and British Open titles, beating England's Lucy Soutter 3–0 and 3–2 in the respective finals. The British national women's championship was won by Lisa Opie, who also repeated as champion in the Australian Open. The Women's World Open and Team events were played in Auckland, N.Z., in October. Devoy retained her individual title, beating Opie 9–3, 10–8, 9–2. In the team event, England overcame Australia 2–1 to repeat as champion.          (ANDREW SHELLEY)

## SWIMMING

In 1987, the year before the Olympic Games in Seoul, South Korea, swimming failed to reach the peaks attained in many previous pre-Olympic years. Swimmers from the United States and Europe combined to set world records on ten occasions.

On August 7, 30-year-old Lynne Cox of Los Alamitos,

Michele Mitchell of the U.S. pushes off the diving platform at the Pan American Games in Indianapolis, Indiana. She won the platform competition and thus earned the 100th gold medal for the U.S.
AP/WIDE WORLD

Calif., made medical, political, and swimming history by swimming the cold 4.35-km (2.7-mi) Bering Strait, between the U.S.'s Little Diomede Island and the U.S.S.R.'s Big Diomede Island, in the time of 2 hours 5 minutes.

The World University Games (FISU) at Zagreb, Yugos., July 9–14, attracted 360 swimmers from 42 nations. Ten tournament records were broken in the new ten-lane Mlodest pool. In spite of the new records, the level of competition was well below that of previous Games, as the early summer date kept many of the world's best swimmers from attending. The U.S. sent swimmers who lacked international experience. Still, the U.S. won the most medals— 9 gold, 10 silver, and 11 bronze out of 32 events. Romania with six gold, two silver, and seven bronze finished second. The top competitor was Noemi Lung, an 18-year-old from Bucharest, with five gold medals. She bettered records in the 400-m and 800-m freestyle and the 200-m and 400-m individual medley. U.S. winners were Tom Williams and

| World Swimming Records Set in 1987 | | | |
|---|---|---|---|
| Event | Name | Country | Time |
| **MEN** | | | |
| 50-m freestyle | Tom Jager | U.S. | 22.32 sec |
| 200-m individual medley | Tamas Darnyi | Hung. | 2 min 00.56 sec |
| 400-m individual medley | David Wharton | U.S. | 4 min 16.12 sec |
| 400-m individual medley | Tamas Darnyi | Hung. | 4 min 15.42 sec |
| 4 × 200-m freestyle relay | West German national team (Peter Sitt, Rainer Henkel, Thomas Fahrner, Michael Gross) | W.Ger. | 7 min 13.10 sec |
| **WOMEN** | | | |
| 800-m freestyle | Janet Evans | U.S. | 8 min 22.44 sec |
| 800-m freestyle | Anke Moehring | E.Ger. | 8 min 19.53 sec |
| 1,500-m freestyle | Janet Evans | U.S. | 16 min 00.73 sec |
| 100-m breaststroke | Silke Hoerner | E.Ger. | 1 min 07.91 sec |
| 4 × 200-m freestyle relay | East German national team (Manuela Stellmach, Astrid Strauss, Anke Moehring, Heike Friedrich) | E.Ger. | 7 min 55.47 sec |

Ann Drolsom in the 50-m freestyle, Mitzi Kremer in the 100-m freestyle, and Alex Mlawsky in the 1,500-m freestyle. The U.S. won five of the six relays.

During the U.S. national championships at Clovis, Calif., held July 27–31, the first world records of 1987 were set by Janet Evans, a 15-year-old from Placentia, Calif. On July 27 she lowered by 2.18 sec the 800-m freestyle, the oldest world record, set Aug. 5, 1978, by Tracey Wickham of Australia, from 8 min 24.62 sec to 8 min 22.44 sec. Four days later she lowered the second-oldest record of 16 min 4.49 sec for the 1,500-m freestyle, set by Kim Linehan of the U.S. on Aug. 19, 1979, to 16 min 0.73 sec.

At the Pan Pacific Championships on August 13–16 at Brisbane, Australia, U.S. swimmers set two world records. On August 13 Tom Jager of Collinsville, Ill., erased the 50-m freestyle mark of 22.33 sec set by Matt Biondi in 1986 at the U.S. championships, clocking 22.32 sec. Two days later David Wharton of Warminster, Pa., lowered by 1.29 sec the 400-m individual medley record of 4 min 17.41 sec set by Alex Baumann of Canada in the 1984 Olympic Games by swimming the distance in 4 min 16.12 sec. The U.S. dominated the championships, winning 24 gold medals out of 32 events. Australia was second with four gold medals, and Canada was third with three.

The European Championships, held in August at Strasbourg, France, produced 6 world records and 13 European records. Wharton's mark lasted only four days as Tamas Darnyi of Hungary on August 19 swam the 400-m individual medley in 4 min 15.42 sec. On August 23 Darnyi set his second world record when he lowered the 200-m individual medley record of 2 min 1.42 sec set by Baumann in the 1984 Olympics to 2 min 0.56 sec. On August 19 the West German quartet of Peter Sitt, Rainer Henkel, Thomas Fahrner, and Michael Gross lowered the 4 × 200-m freestyle relay record by 2.59 sec from 7 min 15.69 sec to 7 min 13.10 sec. The previous record was set by the U.S. in the 1984 Olympics. East Germany continued its mastery in women's swimming, winning 14 of 16 events and setting three world records. On August 21 Silke Hoerner bettered by 0.20 sec the year-old 100-m breaststroke record of 1 min 8.11 sec set by Sylvia Gerasch of East Germany with a time of 1 min 7.91 sec. A day later with a time of 8 min 19.53 sec Anke Moehring slashed 2.91 sec off the 800-m freestyle record set by Janet Evans in July. The East German quartet of Manuela Stellmach, Astrid Strauss, Anke Moehring, and Heike Friedrich on August 18 set a new 4 × 200-m freestyle relay record by cutting 3.86 sec off their year-old record of 7 min 59.33 sec to 7 min 55.47 sec.

East German women strengthened their world domination at the European Championships. In addition to 14 gold medals, they won 9 silver and 3 bronze. Romania with two titles and eight medals was a distant second. In the men's competition East Germany upset West Germany with four titles and 12 medals, compared with West Germany's three titles and 9 medals. The Soviet Union was third with three titles and eight medals. Tamas Darnyi was the outstanding swimmer.

**Diving.** The fifth FINA Cup, held April 23–26 at Amersfoort, Neth., was the first of five major international diving competitions. Greg Louganis of the U.S. won the springboard event, and Tong Hui of China won the platform. Divers from China gained gold medals in women's diving. Gao Min won the springboard title, and teammate Xu Yanmei won the platform. The U.S., with 374 points, was first in team scoring, followed by China with 372 and the Soviet Union with 363.

Louganis swept the 3-m springboard and 10-m platform competitions at the International Meet on May 7–10 at Boca Raton, Fla. The Soviets swept the women's events, with Marina Babkova winning the springboard title and 12-year-old Elena Miroshina the platform.

At the World University Games, divers from China swept all four competitions. Li Kongzheng triumphed on the men's 10-m platform and Tan Liangde off the 3-m springboard. In women's events Li Qiaoxian won the springboard competition, and Lu Wei won the platform.

At the Pan American Games in Indianapolis, Ind., during August, Louganis again demonstrated his superiority by retaining the 3-m springboard and 10-m platform titles. Kelly McCormick successfully defended her springboard title. In platform competition Michele Mitchell of Boca Raton was the gold medalist. In medal counts the U.S. won four gold and three silvers, while Canada gained one silver and two bronze. Argentina and Mexico each won a bronze.

Twelve countries competed at the European Championships. Daphne Jongejans of The Netherlands won the springboard gold medal. Soviet diver Miroshina was the winner in the platform. Albin Killat of West Germany won the men's springboard title, and Georgy Chogovadze of the U.S.S.R. won the gold medal in the platform.

**Synchronized Swimming.** Nine nations competed at the Pan Pacific Championships. Carolyn Waldo of Canada won the solo gold medal; the Canadian pair of Waldo and Michelle Cameron won the duet; and Canada, the U.S., and Japan finished in that order for the team championship.

Eight countries competed in the American Cup III, held at Orlando, Fla., July 27–August 2. The U.S. swept all three events. Tracie Ruiz-Conforto won the solo; the twin sisters Karen and Sarah Josephson won the duet; and the U.S. won the team. Sweden won the "B" competition, and Korea won the "C."

At the Pan American Games Ruiz-Conforto retained her solo title. The Josephson sisters in winning the duet gold medal totaled 192.12 points, the second-highest winning score in the history of the Games. The U.S. completed the sweep, winning the team competition.

Fifteen countries competed in the European Championships. Muriel Hermine of France outscored Alexandre Worisch of Austria for the gold. Hermine paired with Karine Schuler to win the duet. France was the team winner.

Ten countries competed in the third FINA Cup in Cairo, Egypt, on October 1–3. Waldo narrowly outscored Ruiz-Conforto 198.36–197.45 to retain her solo title. Waldo and Cameron retained the duet championship for Canada over the Josephson sisters 195.54–195.06. The U.S. won the team championship. (ALBERT SCHOENFIELD)

## TABLE TENNIS

The biennial world championships got under way in New Delhi, India, in mid-February with 60 men's and 50 women's associations participating in the competition. China retained possession of both the Swaythling and Marcel Corbillon cups, which are awarded to the men's and women's team champions. Sweden's men's team once again finished second, ahead of North Korea, Yugoslavia, Poland, Japan, West Germany, and Taiwan. In the women's team standings South Korea was runner-up, followed by Hungary, The Netherlands, North Korea, the U.S.S.R., Japan, and Yugoslavia.

Chinese athletes also won four of the five individual titles, losing only the women's doubles. In that event the South Korean team of Hyun Jung Hwa and Yang Young Ja defeated Dai Lili and Li Huifen of China in three sets.

In other individual championships Jiang Jialiang retained his men's singles crown by defeating Jan-Ove Waldner (Sweden) in four sets. In the women's singles final He Zhili overcame Yang Young Ja in three sets. Chen Longcan and Wei Qingguang won the men's doubles titles and Hui Jun and Geng Lijuan the mixed doubles.

During the tournament the Congress of the International Table Tennis Federation admitted five new members, bringing the total number of affiliated associations to 131. Options to organize future world championships were granted to West Germany (1989), Japan (1991), and England and Yugoslavia (1993).

In early January the European top 12 players tournament was held in Basel, Switz. After the men's competition Desmond Douglas (England) was ranked number one. Next in order were Waldner, Jorgen Persson (Sweden), Andrzej Grubba (Poland), and Leszek Kucharski (Poland). Csilla Batorfi (Hung.) was ranked first among the women players. Edit Urban (Hung.), who finished second, was followed by Fliora Bulatova (U.S.S.R.), Bettine Vriesekoop (Neth.), and Daniela Guergueltcheva (Bulg.).

The eighth World Cup competition, featuring 16 of the top men players in the world, was held in Macau from July 30 to August 2. In the final rankings Teng Yi (China) was first, Jiang Jialiang second, Grubba third, Kucharski fourth, and Lo Chuen Tsung (Hong Kong) fifth.

(ARTHUR KINGSLEY VINT)

# TENNIS

A legal challenge to the control of the Grand Prix, the worldwide circuit of men's tournaments, was averted in 1987. A suit filed two years earlier by the Volvo North American Corp., former Grand Prix sponsors, and two management companies—the International Merchandising Corp. and ProServe. Inc.—against the Men's International Professional Tennis Council (MIPTC), Philippe Chartier, former chairman of that body, and Marshall Happer, its administrator, was dismissed. The right of MIPTC to regulate tournament tennis for men was confirmed.

A shift from U.S. domination in both the men's and women's games continued. Ivan Lendl, originally from Czechoslovakia, maintained his personal supremacy in men's competition, though he was far from unchallenged. The young West German Steffi Graf (see BIOGRAPHIES) was ranked number one among the women in August and retained the position at year's end. It was the first time since 1980 that a woman other than the naturalized American Martina Navratilova or Chris Evert (the identity reassumed by Chris Evert Lloyd following her divorce from John Lloyd) had been graded first. Australia returned to the fore when Pat Cash won the Wimbledon men's singles, the first Australian success in that event since 1971. Tennis in Europe flourished, in terms of both the achievements of leading players and participation at grass-roots level, though the British did not share in this prosperity.

Disorder marked the Davis Cup match between the U.S.

and Paraguay in Asunción. As a result, Paraguay was excluded from its right to play at home in the next round against Spain. The International Tennis Federation stated that it was "concerned that certain actions by the President of the Paraguayan Association amounted to intimidation of the neutral referee from Denmark." It was the first time that such disciplinary action had been taken. The matches were held in Caracas, Venezuela, and were won by Spain.

**Men's Competition.** The first major tournament of the year was the Australian championships in Melbourne in January. Stefan Edberg of Sweden retained the singles title that he won in December 1985. Cash had notable success in beating Lendl 7–6, 5–7, 7–6, 6–4 in the semifinals and became the first Australian finalist since 1980–81. Edberg beat Cash 6–3, 6–4, 3–6, 5–7, 6–3 in the finals.

Lendl retained his men's singles title in the French championship in Paris, achieving his third success in four years when he beat Mats Wilander (Sweden) 7–5, 6–2, 3–6, 7–6 in the finals. In the semifinals he beat his fellow Czechoslovak Miloslav Mecir 6–3, 6–3, 7–6. Wilander won a quarterfinal 6–4, 6–3, 6–2 against Yannick Noah (France), victor against him in the 1983 finals. Wilander won his semifinal 6–4, 6–1, 6–2 against Boris Becker of West Germany before yielding to Lendl in the finals.

The Wimbledon meeting, with its first week much interrupted by rain, brought defeat to Becker, winner in 1985 and 1986, when Peter Doohan of Australia beat him 7–6, 4–6, 6–2, 6–4 in the second round. Doohan's subsequent loss to Slobodan Zivojinovic of Yugoslavia allowed Jimmy Connors (U.S.) to reach the semifinals and revive old popularity at the age of 34. A win by Connors against Mikael Pernfors (Sweden) was followed by a 7–6, 7–5, 6–3 victory over Zivojinovic in the quarterfinal. In his tenth semifinal appearance since 1972, Connors was, however, no match

Steffi Graf backhands a strong return to Martina Navratilova during the finals of the French Open. Graf won the match and her first Grand Slam title.

for Cash. The Australian, his serve and volley technique thriving on Wimbledon's fast turf, beat Wilander 6–3, 7–5, 6–4 in the quarterfinals and then routed Connors 6–4, 6–4, 6–1. In the finals he met Lendl, who had won a quarterfinal against Henri Leconte (France) 7–6, 6–3, 7–6 and a semifinal against Edberg 3–6, 6–4, 7–6, 6–4. He did not find the same sharp game in the finals, however, and Cash, with unceasing attack, beat him 7–6, 6–2, 7–5. Cash lost only one set in the tournament, in the third round. The last Australian champion was John Newcombe in 1971.

Cash lost in the first round of the U.S. Open at Flushing Meadow, New York City, in September, falling to Peter Lundgren of Sweden. Becker lost in the fourth round to Brad Gilbert of the U.S. Wilander qualified for the finals by defeating Mecir 6–2, 6–7, 7–6, 6–4, 7–6 in the quarterfinals and Edberg 6–4, 3–6, 6–3, 6–4 in the semifinals. Lendl routed John McEnroe (U.S.) 6–3, 6–3, 6–4 in the quarterfinals and Connors 6–4, 6–2, 6–2 in the semifinals. The final was a laboured match in which Lendl beat Wilander 6–7, 6–0, 7–6, 6–4 to gain his third title in three years.

In doubles Edberg and Anders Jarryd (Sweden) won two Grand Slam titles, the Australian and U.S. Edberg also partnered Robert Seguso (U.S.) to win the French. Seguso and Ken Flach (U.S.) won Wimbledon.

The World Team Cup tournament, played in Düsseldorf, West Germany, was won by Czechoslovakia (Mecir, Milan Srejber, Tomas Smid). In the final the Czechoslovaks beat the U.S. (McEnroe, Gilbert, Seguso) 2–1 after McEnroe withdrew in the third set against Mecir.

In the Davis Cup Switzerland, Denmark, Brazil, and New Zealand were zone winners and promoted to the World Group for 1988. In the main group both the U.S. and West Germany lost in the first round, to Paraguay and Spain, respectively. In the Relegation Round at Hartford, Conn., West Germany beat the U.S. 3–2. The U.S. was thereby relegated to the zonal rounds for 1988 along with South Korea, Argentina, and Great Britain.

In the quarterfinals Sweden beat France 4–1, Spain defeated Paraguay 3–2, India beat Israel 4–0, and Australia defeated Mexico 4–1. In the semifinals Sweden (Wilander, Edberg, Jarryd, Jan Gunnarsson) beat Spain (the brothers Emilio and Javier Sánchez) 3–2 to reach the final round for the fifth successive year. India (Ramesh Krishnan, Vijay Amritraj) beat Australia 3–2 in Sydney. Australia was weakened by the restriction of an injured Cash to doubles, John Fitzpatrick and Wally Masur playing singles.

In the finals Sweden dominated India 5–0 to win the Davis Cup for the fourth time. On indoor clay courts in Göteborg, Sweden, in December, Wilander defeated Krishnan 6–4, 6–1, 6–3 and Amritraj 6–2, 6–0. Jarryd triumphed over Amritraj 6–3, 6–3, 6–1 and Krishnan 6–4, 6–3. In the doubles Wilander and Joakim Nystrom beat Amritraj and his brother Anand 6–2, 3–6, 6–1, 6–2.

**Women's Competition.** Graf did not compete in the Australian championship in Melbourne in January, and Navratilova, three times the champion, failed to retain her title. Hana Mandlikova (Czech.), who had gained her first Grand Slam tournament success there at the age of 18 in 1980, won. While Navratilova easily reached the finals, Mandlikova, though winning 6–0, 6–0 in the quarterfinals against Lori McNeil (U.S.), struggled, with three of her five matches going to three sets. She beat Navratilova 7–5, 7–6 in the final match.

Graf won the French championships to take her first Grand Slam title. Her pace and control on the slow courts dominated the event, where Mandlikova lost in the second round to Nathalie Herreman (France). Evert was hoping to win her eighth French singles title, but Navratilova beat her 6–2, 6–2 in the semifinals. It was Navratilova's fourth final in as many years, her last victory having taken place in 1984. Graf had her first difficult match only in the semifinals against Gabriela Sabatini (Arg.), winning 6–4, 4–6, 7–5. Graf beat Navratilova 6–4, 4–6, 8–6 in a hard-fought final.

Navratilova reasserted her dominance at Wimbledon. Until the finals her only danger was against Evert in the semifinals, which she won 6–2, 5–7, 6–4. Graf also reached the finals with only one difficult match, defeating Sabatini in the quarterfinals 4–6, 6–1, 6–1. In the semifinals Graf beat Pam Shriver (U.S.), who had survived 6–7, 7–5, 10–8 against Sylvia Hanika (West Germany) and 4–6, 7–6, 10–8 in her quarterfinal match against Helena Sukova (Czech.). Graf overwhelmed Shriver 6–0, 6–2. In the final Navratilova started slowly but found her best game to beat Graf 7–5, 6–3.

Navratilova's feat made tennis history. She equaled the 1927–38 record of Helen Wills Moody (U.S.) in winning the Wimbledon singles for the eighth time. Uniquely she won it for the sixth successive year.

The U.S. Open was dominated by Navratilova and Graf. Evert was beaten 3–6, 6–2, 6–4 in the quarterfinals by McNeil. It was the first loss before the semifinals by the six-time U.S. champion in 17 years. Graf defeated McNeil 4–6, 6–2, 6–4 in the semifinals, while Navratilova beat Sukova 6–2, 6–2 in the same round. In the finals Navratilova beat Graf 7–6, 6–1 to take the title without the loss of a set. It was her fourth U.S. singles championship in five years.

Navratilova had further success at Flushing Meadow. She won both the women's doubles (with Shriver) and the mixed doubles (with Emilio Sánchez) to become the first triple champion since Margaret Court (Australia) in 1970.

In doubles Navratilova and Shriver were again outstanding. They won the Australian, French, and U.S. titles and failed only at Wimbledon, where Claudia Kohde-Kilsch (West Germany) and Sukova were winners. The U.S. championship was the 17th Grand Slam doubles won by Navratilova and Shriver since 1981, the 26th by Navratilova since 1975.

The Federation Cup, played in Vancouver, B.C., was won by West Germany for the first time. Graf and Kohde-Kilsch led a team that beat Czechoslovakia 2–1 in the semifinals and the U.S. 2–1 in the finals. Graf was unbeaten in five singles matches. Evert and Shriver played for the U.S., and Mandlikova and Sukova for Czechoslovakia. The U.S. beat Great Britain 3–0 in a quarterfinal match.

The 59th Wightman Cup tournament was held in Williamsburg, Va. The U.S. (Shriver, Zina Garrison, McNeil, Gigi Fernandez, Robin White) beat Great Britain (Jo Durie, Anne Hobbs, Sara Gomer, Clare Wood) 5–2 for its ninth win in a row and 49th in all.          (LANCE TINGAY)

## TRACK AND FIELD SPORTS

For the first time ever, the sport of track and field athletics was treated to two world championship meets in a single year. The inaugural indoor championships were held in Indianapolis, Ind., in early March, and six months later the outdoor title meet was held at Rome's Olympic Stadium, site of the 1960 Olympic Games.

**Men's International Competition.** While the indoor championships were a welcome addition to the track and field season, the highlight of the year was the outdoor competition. It had first been held in 1983 and had quickly proved itself to be at least the athletic equal of the quadrennial Olympic Games. It also was able to avoid the politics that had hurt the last four Olympic competitions.

So outstanding were the athletes that 37 of 43 meet records were broken before 518,000 spectators. Of all the records one stood out, and it was the most talked-about event of the tournament. It was set in the 100-m dash, when two of the fastest men in history clashed in a spirited battle to see who would win acclaim as the world's fastest human. The race matched Carl Lewis of the United States and Ben Johnson (*see* Biographies) of Canada. Lewis was rated the number one sprinter in the world for the five-year period ending in 1985. Johnson, third to Lewis in the 1984 Olympics, was ranked first in 1986. Both were considered capable of pressing the world record. The Canadian, recognized as perhaps the fastest starter ever, quickly moved to a lead of almost a metre, and that, give or take a few centimetres, was his margin of victory. Neither Johnson nor Lewis could gain much in the final 30 metres. The official film showed the time to be 9.83 sec, a full tenth of a second under the former record, which had been well aided by the thin air of Colorado Springs, Colo. Lewis ran his best time ever, equaling the former record of 9.93 sec.

While no other event could match the 100 m for thrills and significance, the competition produced many other records. Perhaps the most memorable of these was in the 400-m hurdles. It pitted 32-year-old Edwin Moses, the defending champion and world record holder, against Danny Harris, who had broken Moses's victory string of 107 races, and Harald Schmid, who had been the last man to beat Moses—nine years, nine months, and nine days before Harris's win. The race was a fierce battle all the way, and the outcome was still in doubt minutes after the finish. The phototimer finally revealed that Moses had run the race in 47.46 sec, with both Harris, second, and Schmid clocking 47.48 sec.

Calvin Smith of the U.S. lost his 100-m record but held onto his 200-m title, finishing in 20.16 sec, equal to the time of second-place Gilles Queneherve of France. In one of the major upsets, East Germany's Thomas Schönlebe won the 400 m in a very fast 44.33 sec to defeat Innocent Egbunike of Nigeria and Butch Reynolds of the U.S., who earlier in the season had run a world's best 44.10 sec at low altitude. Another quick finisher was Greg Foster, U.S., who held onto his 110-m hurdle title with a time of 13.21 sec. Quick running by both U.S. relay teams resulted in times of 37.90 sec in the 4 × 100 relay, the third-fastest ever, and 2 min 57.29 sec in the 4 × 400, the second-best ever and the best at low altitude.

Kenya, which had not produced its share of winners for several years, returned to its past form, scoring victories in three events. Billy Konchellah won the 800 m in 1 min 43.06 sec, Paul Kipkoech the 10,000 m in 27 min 38.63 sec, and Douglas Wakiihuru the marathon in 2 hr 11 min 48 sec. Great Britain entered an improving team and had some successes but had to endure the defeat of its two finest athletes. Daley Thompson, king of the decathlon since 1980, was suffering from an injury and finished ninth, while Steve Cram, the leading miler and 1,500-m runner since 1983, also was beset by physical problems and finished eighth in the 1,500. There was considerable irony in Thompson's loss. West Germany's Jurgen Hingsen, a three-time world record breaker but never a winner over Thompson, lost this unusual opportunity when he had to withdraw because of an injury.

Said Aouita of Morocco, holder of the 1,500-m and 5,000-m records, chose to compete in the latter event and talked about lowering his own world record. He was, however, content with a tactical race won in a mediocre 13 min 26.44 sec.

Topping the field events for excitement was the high

Ben Johnson of Canada (right) passes Carl Lewis of the U.S. to set a new 100-metre world record of 9.83 seconds, a full tenth of a second under the former record.

PAUL J. SUTTON—DUOMO

jump, with three men clearing 2.38 m (7 ft 9¾ in) for the first time. The winner was new world-record holder Patrik Sjöberg of Sweden, hard pressed by two Soviets who tied for second—Gennady Avdeyenko, the defending champion, and Igor Paklin. Lewis, who also anchored a winning relay team, won the long jump with a leap of 8.67 m (28 ft 5½ in) in a heated competition.

In the triple jump Khristo Markov of Bulgaria came within 5 cm (2 in) of the world record, jumping 17.92 m (58 ft 9½ in) for an upset win over Mike Conley of the U.S. Another notable upset took place in the discus, in which Jurgen Schult of East Germany, who held the world record but was lightly regarded, won his first major title with a throw of 68.74 (225 ft 6 in). Werner Gunthor of Switzerland came from behind to capture the shot-put title at 22.23 m (72 ft 11¼ in).

Other winners at Rome included Francesco Panetta of Italy, victor in the steeplechase in 8 min 8.57 sec; walkers Maurizio Damilano of Italy, 1 hr 20 min 45 sec for the 20,000 m, and Hartwig Gauder of East Germany, 3 hr 40 min 53 sec for the 50,000 m; Seppo Raty of Finland in the javelin with 83.54 m (274 ft 1 in); and Torsten Voss of East Germany with 8,680 points in the decathlon.

Before the world championships eight additional world records were set in six events. Three of the marks went to Italy's Alessandro Andrei when, in one meet, he put the shot 22.72 m (74 ft 6½ in), 22.84 m (74 ft 11¼ in), and 22.91 m (75 ft 2 in). Aouita was the only man to gain new world records in two events. He lowered the mark for the little-run 2,000 m to 4 min 50.81 sec and broke his own 5,000-m record with 12 min 58.39 sec. The high-jump standard fell to Sjöberg, who cleared 2.42 m (7 ft 11¼ in), while Sergey Bubka of the Soviet Union raised his own pole-vault record to 6.03 m (19 ft 9¼ in) before successfully defending his title at Rome. Least known of the record breakers was Jan Zelezny of Czechoslovakia. He threw the javelin 87.66 m (287 ft 7 in).

Indoors, men broke 11 world records in six events. Johnson and Foster set records at 60 m in the indoor championships, Johnson covering the distance in 6.41 sec and Foster setting the 60-m hurdle record in the semifinals with a time of 7.46 sec. Bubka raised the vault standard to 5.97 m (19 ft 7 in). In the high jump first Carl Thranhardt of West Germany and then Sjöberg set new records, the Swede ending up with 2.41 m (7 ft 10³/₄ in). Conley got the longest of two triple-jump records, reaching 17.76 m (58 ft 3¹/₄ in). Gunthor set a new shot-put mark of 22.26 m (73 ft. ¹/₂ in).

**Women's International Competition.** New world records were established eight times in seven events during the season. The only double winner was the Soviet Union's Natalya Lisovskaya, whose best effort in the shot put was 22.63 m (74 ft 3 in). One mark was set in the world championships at Rome, a high jump of 2.09 m (6 ft 10¹/₄ in) by Stefka Kostadinova of Bulgaria. Earlier she had achieved two indoor bests, the highest being 2.05 m (6 ft 8³/₄ in) in the indoor world meet. New marks were also set in two other field events. Jackie Joyner-Kersee (*see* BIOGRAPHIES) of the U.S. equaled the long-jump mark of 7.45 m (24 ft 5¹/₂ in), and Petra Felke of East Germany regained her javelin record with a throw of 78.90 m (258 ft 10 in). On the track Bulgaria's Ginka Zagorcheva sped over the 100-m hurdles in 12.25 sec. Walking records were achieved by Yan Hong of China with 21 min 20.2 sec for the 5,000 m and by Xu Yongjiu of China, 44 min 26.5 sec for the 10,000 m.

At the outdoor world championships there were three double winners. Joyner-Kersee won the long jump at 7.36 m (24 ft 1³/₄ in) and the heptathlon with 7,128 points, the third-highest total ever. Both sprints were won by Silke Gladisch of East Germany, the 100 m in 10.90 sec and the 200 m in 21.74 sec, just 0.03 sec off the world record. The third double winner was Soviet middle-distance runner Tatyana Samolenko. Her time in the 1,500 m was 3 min 58.56 sec, and in the 3,000 it was 8 min 38.73 sec. Favoured for at least two wins and possibly more, the most disappointed athlete had to be Heike Drechsler of East Germany. An injury held her to second place in the 100 m and third in the long jump.

Other gold medal winners in the world championships were Olga Bryzgina of the Soviet Union, 49.38 sec for the 400 m; Sigrun Wodars of East Germany, 1 min 55.26 sec in the 800 m; Zagorcheva, 12.34 sec in the 100-m hurdles; Sabine Busch of East Germany, 53.62 sec in the 400-m hurdles; Ingrid Kristiansen of Norway, 31 min 5.85 sec in the 10,000 m; Rosa Mota of Portugal, 2 hr 25 min 17 sec in the marathon; Irina Strakhova of the Soviet Union,

Priscilla Welch of the U.K. crosses the finish line of the New York City marathon. Welch, at 42, was the oldest woman to have won the event.
AP/WIDE WORLD

44 min 12 sec in the 10,000-m walk; Martina Hellmann, East Germany, 71.62 m (235 ft) in the discus; Fatima Whitbread of the United Kingdom, 76.64 m (251 ft 5 in) in the javelin; and Lisovskaya, 21.24 m (69 ft 8¹/₄ in) in the shot put.

In the medal count for women at the outdoor world championships, East Germany won 6 gold and 17 other medals to 5 golds and 8 others for the Soviets and 3 golds and 3 others for the U.S. The men's count was six and seven for the U.S., four and four for East Germany, and two and ten for the U.S.S.R.

**U.S. Competition.** National records were set in four outdoor events in the United States, led by Lewis's 9.93 sec in the 100 m, matching what had been the world standard until Johnson broke the record. Had Johnson not run, it would have been the first world mark for Lewis, who dominated the sprints and long jump for seven years but never earned a world record.

Other U.S. records were set by Jim Howard with 2.36 m (7 ft 8³/₄ in) in the high jump, Joe Dial with three new bests in the pole vault, and John Brenner with two records in the shot put. Dial's best vault was 5.96 m (19 ft 6¹/₂ in), and Brenner's longest toss was 22.52 m (73 ft 10³/₄ in). Reynolds's 44.10 sec for the 400 m was the best ever run at low altitude.

U.S. women achieved four national records, with Ramona Pagel twice breaking the shot-put mark; her best distance was 19.22 m (63 ft ³/₄ in). Judi Brown King ran the 400-m hurdles in 54.23 sec, and Louise Ritter matched her own high-jump best, 2.01 m (6 ft 7 in). Also a national record, of course, was Joyner-Kersee's world mark in the long jump.

Indoors, Foster's world record in the hurdles was the only U.S. record achieved by men. Aside from Pagel's shot-putting, the only U.S. indoor record for women was Lesley Welch's 3,000-m run of 8 min 44.05 sec.

In team competition the U.S. National Collegiate Athletic Association's (NCAA's) titles were won by the University of California at Los Angeles for the men and by host team Louisiana State University for the women. At the Athletic Congress championships, which served as the team selection meet for the world tournament, the winners were Athletics West for the men and the Mazda Track Club for the women.

### Table I. World 1987 Outdoor Records—Men

| Event | Competitor and country | Performance |
| --- | --- | --- |
| 100 m | Ben Johnson (Canada) | 9.83 sec |
| 2,000 m | Said Aouita (Morocco) | 4 min 50.81 sec |
| 5,000 m | Said Aouita (Morocco) | 12 min 58.39 sec |
| High jump | Patrik Sjöberg (Sweden) | 2.42 m (7 ft 11¹/₄ in) |
| Pole vault | Sergey Bubka (U.S.S.R.) | 6.03 m (19 ft 9¹/₄ in) |
| Shot put | Alessandro Andrei (Italy) | 22.72 m (74 ft 6¹/₂ in) |
|  | Alessandro Andrei (Italy) | 22.84 m (74 ft 11¹/₄ in) |
|  | Alessandro Andrei (Italy) | 22.91 m (75 ft 2 in) |
| Javelin | Jan Zelezny (Czech.) | 87.66 m (287 ft 7 in) |

### Table II. World 1987 Outdoor Records—Women

| Event | Competitor and country | Performance |
| --- | --- | --- |
| 100-m hurdles | Ginka Zagorcheva (Bulg.) | 12.25 sec |
| 5,000-m walk | Yan Hong (China) | 21 min 20.2 sec |
| 10,000-m walk | Xu Yongjiu (China) | 44 min 26.5 sec |
| High jump | Stefka Kostadinova (Bulg.) | 2.09 m (6 ft 10¹/₄ in) |
| Long jump | Jackie Joyner-Kersee (U.S.) | 7.45 m (24 ft 5¹/₂ in) |
| Shot put | Natalya Lisovskaya (U.S.S.R.) | 22.60 m (74 ft 1³/₄ in) |
|  | Natalya Lisovskaya (U.S.S.R.) | 22.63 m (74 ft 3 in) |
| Javelin | Petra Felke (East Germany) | 78.90 m (258 ft 10 in) |

**Marathon Running and Cross Country.** Ahmed Salah of Djibouti repeated as World Cup marathon champion, winning in 2 hr 10 min 55 sec. Leading the women was Zoya Ivanova of the U.S.S.R. Italy won the men's team competition and the Soviet Union the women's. The Boston marathon was won by Toshihiko Seko of Japan for the men and Mota in the women's competition. Winners of the New York City marathon were Ibrahim Hussein of Kenya for the men and Priscilla Welch of the U.K. for the women.

There was a repeat winner in international cross country competition at Warsaw, the title remaining with John Ngugi of Kenya. Winner of the women's division was Annette Sergent of France. Kenya won the men's team title for the second consecutive year, while the U.S. women were victorious.

In U.S. competition Joe Falcon of Arkansas captured the NCAA men's championship, and Arkansas won the team title. For the women the NCAA winners were Kim Betz of Indiana for the individual gold medal and the University of Oregon as the team leader. In the national championships of the Athletic Congress, the men's winner for the sixth straight time was Pat Porter, with Lynn Jennings leading the women.                                    (BERT NELSON)

## VOLLEYBALL

The major emphasis in volleyball competition in 1987 was on qualifying teams for the 1988 Olympic Games. The United States men and the Chinese women, as the 1984 Olympic champions, and the South Korean men and women, as representatives of the host country, were already qualified. Also already qualified were the Soviet men, second to the U.S. in the 1985 World Cup; the Bulgarian men, third to the U.S. and the U.S.S.R. in the 1986 world championships; and the Cuban women, second to China in the 1986 world championships.

The Argentine men qualified for the 1988 Olympic Games in a tournament organized in Brazil in May 1987. In the European championships in late September, the women of East Germany finished first and qualified for the Olympics, as did the men of France, who were second to the already-qualified Soviets. In the North Central America and Caribbean volleyball championships (Norceca), the Cuban men were victorious and earned a 1988 Olympic position, as did the U.S. women by finishing second to already-qualified Cuba. In Asia both the Japanese men and women gained entry to the Olympics. The Peruvian women and the Brazilian men qualified from South America.

One additional women's team was to be selected at an Olympic qualifying tournament in late May 1988 in Italy to round out the field of eight. For the men's Olympic tournament Africa was to qualify a representative, and then two additional teams would be chosen, one from Olympic qualifying tournament II to be organized in The Netherlands in early 1988 and the other from Olympic qualifying tournament III, to be held in Italy in May 1988.

Other significant world-level competitions included the Pan American Games and the University Games. In the Pan American Games at Indianapolis, Ind., the U.S. men edged Cuba for the title. In the women's competition Cuba finished first, followed by Peru. A U.S. record volleyball crowd of more than 14,500 people attended the finals. The World University Games were held in Zagreb, Yugos. In volleyball competition the host Yugoslav men were first, China second, and Italy third. In the women's tournament China was first, the Soviet Union second, and East Germany third. The U.S. men placed 9th, and the U.S. women were 11th.                          (ALBERT M. MONACO, JR.)

## WEIGHT LIFTING

The world weight-lifting championships in Ostrava, Czech., September 9–16, became essentially a dual meet between Bulgaria and the Soviet Union. Of the 30 medals available, each of the two countries won 9. Bulgaria won five gold medals, the Soviet Union four, and Hungary one. Bulgaria retained its team championship by the narrow margin of 434 to 427 points. Hungary finished third with 302.

Four 1986 world champions retained their laurels, and six new champions were crowned. For Bulgaria the repeat victors were Sevdalin Marinov and Mihail Petrov in the 52.0-kg and 67.5-kg classes, respectively, with total lifts of 262.5 kg (577.5 lb) and 350 kg (770 lb). The Soviet holdover champions were Anatoly Khrapaty, who lifted 417.5 kg (918.5 lb) in the 90-kg class, and Yury Zaharevich with a lift of 445 kg (979 lb) in the 110-kg class.

Bulgaria gained three new champions, the Soviet Union two, and Hungary one. Neno Terziski, 56 kg, Stefan Topurov, 60 kg, and Borislav Gidikov, 75 kg, were the Bulgarians. The new champions from the U.S.S.R. were Pavel Kuznetsov, 100 kg, and superheavyweight Aleksandr Kurlovich. The Hungarian winner was Laszlo Barsi in the 82.5-kg class.

The most significant of the eight world records was the total lift of superheavyweight Kurlovich, 472.5 kg (1,039.5 lb). Vasily Alekseyev of the U.S.S.R., many times world champion, had set an Olympic record of 440 kg (970 lb) in 1976.

In the first women's world championships at Daytona Beach, Fla., China won eight out of nine weight classes. Karyn Marshall of the U.S. in the 82.5-kg class was the other winner.                           (CHARLES ROBERT PAUL, JR.)

## WRESTLING

In one of the most competitive wrestling world championships to be held in recent years, the Soviet Union was again dominant in freestyle competition and placed all ten of its wrestlers as follows: six first places, one second place, two third places, and one fourth place. The United States placed nine wrestlers: two first places, three second places, three third places, and one fifth place. This was the best finish ever for the U.S. team. The team championship went to the Soviet Union with 92 points, followed by the U.S. with 77 points and Bulgaria with 50 points. In Greco-Roman wrestling the Soviets were even more dominant and won with 83 points; Bulgaria was second with 59 points and Poland third with 45 points. The tournament took place at Clermont-Ferrand, France, Aug. 19–29, 1987.

At the U.S. National Collegiate Athletic Association tournament March 19–21 in College Park, Md., Iowa State University ended the winning streak of the University of Iowa, which had won nine straight championships. Iowa State scored 133 points; the University of Iowa was second with 108 points; and Pennsylvania State University was third with 97.75 points.                          (MARVIN G. HESS)

| World Wrestling Champions, 1987 | | |
|---|---|---|
| Weight class | Freestyle | Greco-Roman |
| 48 kg (105.5 lb) | Li Jaesik (N.Kor.) | M. Allakhverdiev (U.S.S.R.) |
| 52 kg (114.5 lb) | V. Jordanov (Bulg.) | P. Roque (Cuba) |
| 57 kg (125.5 lb) | S. Beloglazov (U.S.S.R.) | P. Mourier (France) |
| 62 kg (136.5 lb) | J. Smith (U.S.) | J. Vanguelov (Bulg.) |
| 68 kg (149.5 lb) | A. Fadzaev (U.S.S.R.) | A. Abaev (U.S.S.R.) |
| 74 kg (163 lb) | A. Varaev (U.S.S.R.) | J. Salomaki (Fin.) |
| 82 kg (180.5 lb) | M. Schultz (U.S.) | T. Komaromi (Hung.) |
| 90 kg (198 lb) | M. Khadartsev (U.S.S.R.) | V. Popov (U.S.S.R.) |
| 100 kg (220 lb) | L. Khabelov (U.S.S.R.) | G. Guedekhaorui (U.S.S.R.) |
| 130 kg (286 lb) | A. Khadartsev (U.S.S.R.) | I. Rostorotski (U.S.S.R.) |

# Sporting Record

## ARCHERY

**FITA Outdoor World Target Archery Championships**

| year | men's individual | | men's team | | women's individual | | women's team | |
|------|------------------|--------|-----------|--------|-------------------|--------|-------------|--------|
| | winner | points | winner | points | winner | points | winner | points |
| 1979 | D. Pace (U.S.) | 2,474 | United States | 7,409 | Kim Jin Ho (S.Kor.) | 2,507 | South Korea | 7,341 |
| 1981 | K. Laasonen (Fin.) | 2,541 | United States | 7,547 | N. Butuzova (U.S.S.R.) | 2,514 | U.S.S.R. | 7,455 |
| 1983 | R. McKinney (U.S.) | 2,617 | United States | 7,812 | Kim Jin Ho (S.Kor.) | 2,616 | South Korea | 7,704 |
| 1985 | R. McKinney (U.S.) | 2,601 | South Korea | 7,660 | I. Soldatova (U.S.S.R.) | 2,595 | U.S.S.R. | 7,721 |
| 1987 | V. Esheyev (U.S.S.R.) | 329 | West Germany | 891 | Ma Xiangjun (China) | 330 | U.S.S.R. | 884 |

## ATHLETICS

**World Cup Championship—men**

| | 100 metre | 200 metre | 400 metre | 800 metre | 1,500 metre |
|------|-----------|-----------|-----------|-----------|-------------|
| 1979 | J. Sanford (U.S.) | S. Leonard (Americas) | K. Hassan (Africa) | J. Maina (Africa) | T. Wessinghage (Europe) |
| 1981 | A. Wells (Europe) | M. Lattany (U.S.) | C. Wiley (U.S.) | S. Coe (Europe) | S. Ovett (Europe) |
| 1985 | B. Johnson (Americas) | R. Caetano da Silva (Americas) | M. Franks (U.S.) | S. Koskei (Africa) | O. Khalifa (Africa) |

| | 5,000 metre | 10,000 metre | Steeplechase | 110-m hurdles | 400-m hurdles |
|------|-------------|--------------|--------------|---------------|---------------|
| 1979 | M. Yifter (Africa) | M. Yifter (Africa) | K. Rono (Africa) | R. Nehemiah (U.S.) | E. Moses (U.S.) |
| 1981 | E. Coghlan (Europe) | W. Schildhauer (E.Ger.) | B. Maminski (Europe) | G. Foster (U.S.) | E. Moses (U.S.) |
| 1985 | D. Padilla (U.S.) | W. Bulti (Africa) | J. Kariuki (Africa) | T. Campbell (U.S.) | A. Phillips (U.S.) |

| | 4 × 100 relays | 4 × 400 relays | Triple jump | High jump | Pole vault |
|------|----------------|----------------|-------------|-----------|------------|
| 1979 | Americas | United States | J. de Oliveira (Americas) | F. Jacobs (U.S.) | M. Tully (U.S.) |
| 1981 | Europe | United States | J. de Oliveira (Americas) | T. Peacock (U.S.) | K. Volkov (U.S.S.R.) |
| 1985 | United States | United States | W. Banks (U.S.) | P. Sjoberg (Europe) | S. Bubka (U.S.S.R.) |

| | Long jump | Shot put | Discus throw | Hammer throw | Javelin throw |
|------|-----------|----------|--------------|--------------|---------------|
| 1979 | L. Myricks (U.S.) | U. Beyer (E.Ger.) | W. Schmidt (E.Ger.) | S. Litvinov (U.S.S.R.) | W. Hanisch (W.Ger.) |
| 1981 | C. Lewis (U.S.) | U. Beyer (E.Ger.) | A. Lemme (E.Ger.) | Yu. Sedykh (U.S.S.R.) | D. Kula (U.S.S.R.) |
| 1985 | M. Conley (U.S.) | U. Timmerman (E.Ger.) | G. Kolnootchenko (U.S.S.R.) | Yu. Tamm (U.S.S.R.) | U. Hohn (E.Ger.) |

| | Team |
|------|------|
| 1979 | United States |
| 1981 | Europe |
| 1985 | United States |

**World Cup Championship—women**

| | 100 metre | 200 metre | 400 metre | 800 metre | 1,500 metre |
|------|-----------|-----------|-----------|-----------|-------------|
| 1979 | E. Ashford (U.S.) | E. Ashford (U.S.) | M. Koch (E.Ger.) | N. Shtereva (Europe) | C. Wartenburg (E.Ger.) |
| 1981 | E. Ashford (U.S.) | E. Ashford (U.S.) | J. Kratochvilová (Europe) | L. Veselkova (U.S.S.R.) | T. Sorokina (U.S.S.R.) |
| 1985 | M. Göhr (E.Ger.) | M. Koch (E.Ger.) | M. Koch (E.Ger.) | C. Wachtel (E.Ger.) | H. Korner (E.Ger.) |

| | 3,000 metre | 10,000 metre | 100-m hurdles | 400-m hurdles | 4 × 100 relays |
|------|-------------|--------------|---------------|---------------|----------------|
| 1979 | S. Ulmasova (U.S.S.R.) | — | G. Rabsztyn (Europe) | B. Klepp (E.Ger.) | Europe Select |
| 1981 | A. Zauber (E.Ger.) | — | T. Anisimova (U.S.S.R.) | E. Neumann (E.Ger.) | East Germany |
| 1985 | U. Bruns (E.Ger.) | A. Cunha (Europe) | C. Oschkenat (E.Ger.) | S. Busch (E.Ger.) | East Germany |

| | 4 × 400 relays | High jump | Long jump | Shot put | Discus throw |
|------|----------------|-----------|-----------|----------|--------------|
| 1979 | East Germany | D. Brill (Americas) | A. Stukane (U.S.S.R.) | I. Slupianek (E.Ger.) | E. Jahl (E.Ger.) |
| 1981 | East Germany | U. Meyfarth (Europe) | S. Ulbricht (E.Ger.) | I. Slupianek (E.Ger.) | E. Jahl (E.Ger.) |
| 1985 | East Germany | S. Kostadinova (U.S.S.R.) | H. Daute Drechsler (E.Ger.) | N. Lisovskaya (U.S.S.R.) | M. Optiz (E.Ger.) |

| | Javelin throw | Team |
|------|---------------|------|
| 1979 | R. Fuchs (E.Ger.) | East Germany |
| 1981 | A. Todorova (Europe) | East Germany |
| 1985 | O. Gavrilova (U.S.S.R.) | East Germany |

B. Johnson: 100-m World Cup championship—men (1985)

MARK SHEARMAN

For records of previous years, *see* the entry SPORTING RECORD in the Micropædia.

### World Track-and-Field Championships—men

| event | 1983 | 1987 |
|---|---|---|
| 100 m | C. Lewis (U.S.) | B. Johnson (Can.) |
| 200 m | C. Smith (U.S.) | C. Smith (U.S.) |
| 400 m | B. Cameron (Jam.) | T. Schoenlebe (E.Ger.) |
| 800 m | W. Wülbeck (W.Ger.) | B. Konchellah (Kenya) |
| 1,500 m | S. Cram (U.K.) | A. Bile (Som.) |
| 5,000 m | E. Coghlan (Ire.) | S. Aouita (Mor.) |
| 10,000 m | A. Cova (Italy) | P. Kipkoech (Kenya) |
| steeplechase | P. Ilg (W.Ger.) | F. Panetta (Italy) |
| 110-m hurdles | G. Foster (U.S.) | G. Foster (U.S.) |
| 400-m hurdles | E. Moses (U.S.) | E. Moses (U.S.) |
| marathon | R. de Castella (Australia) | D. Wakihuru (Kenya) |
| 20-km walk | E. Canto (Mex.) | M. Damilano (Italy) |
| 50-km walk | R. Weigel (E.Ger.) | H. Gauder (E.Ger.) |
| 4 × 100 m relay | United States (E. King, W. Gault, C. Smith, C. Lewis) | United States (L. McRae, L. McNeil, H. Glance, C. Lewis) |
| 4 × 400 m relay | U.S.S.R. (S. Lovachev, A. Troschilo, N. Chernetsky, V. Markin) | United States (D. Everett, R. Haley, A. McKay, H. Reynolds) |
| high jump | G. Avdeyenko (U.S.S.R.) | P. Sjoberg (Swed.) |
| pole vault | S. Bubka (U.S.S.R.) | S. Bubka (U.S.S.R.) |
| long jump | C. Lewis (U.S.) | C. Lewis (U.S.) |
| triple jump | Z. Hoffman (Pol.) | C. Markov (Bulg.) |
| shot put | E. Sarul (Pol.) | W. Guenther (Switz.) |
| discus throw | I. Bugár (Czech.) | J. Schult (E.Ger.) |
| hammer throw | S. Litvinov (U.S.S.R.) | S. Litvinov (U.S.S.R.) |
| javelin throw | D. Michel (E.Ger.) | S. Raty (Fin.) |
| decathlon | D. Thompson (U.K.) | T. Voss (E.Ger.) |

### World Track-and-Field Championships—women

| event | 1983 | 1987 |
|---|---|---|
| 100 m | M. Göhr (E.Ger.) | S. Gladisch (E.Ger.) |
| 200 m | M. Koch (E.Ger.) | S. Gladisch (E.Ger.) |
| 400 m | J. Kratochvílová (Czech.) | O. Bryzgina (U.S.S.R.) |
| 800 m | J. Kratochvílová (Czech.) | S. Wodars (E.Ger.) |
| 1,500 m | M. Decker (U.S.) | T. Samolenko (U.S.S.R.) |
| 3,000 m | M. Decker (U.S.) | T. Samolenko (U.S.S.R.) |
| 10,000 m* | | I. Kristiansen (Nor.) |
| 100-m hurdles | B. Jahn (E.Ger.) | G. Zagorcheva (Bulg.) |
| 400-m hurdles | Ye. Fesenko (U.S.S.R.) | S. Busch (E.Ger.) |
| marathon | G. Waitz (Nor.) | R. Mota (Port.) |
| 10-km walk* | | I. Strakhova (U.S.S.R.) |
| 4 × 100 m relay | East Germany (S. Gladisch, M. Koch, M. Göhr, I. Auerswald) | United States (A. Brown, D. Williams, F. Griffith, P. Marshall) |
| 4 × 400 m relay | East Germany (K. Walther, D. Rubsam, M. Koch, S. Busch) | East Germany (D. Neubauer, K. Emmelmann, P. Mueller, S. Busch) |
| high jump | T. Bykova (U.S.S.R.) | S. Kostadinova (Bulg.) |
| long jump | H. Daute (E.Ger.) | J. Joyner-Kersee (U.S.) |
| shot put | H. Fibingerová (Czech.) | N. Lisovskaya (U.S.S.R.) |
| discus throw | M. Opitz (E.Ger.) | M. Hellmann (E.Ger.) |
| javelin throw | T. Lillak (Fin.) | F. Whitbread (U.K.) |
| heptathlon | R. Neubert (E.Ger.) | J. Joyner-Kersee (U.S.) |

*Event added in 1987.

### Boston Marathon

| year | men | h:min:s | women | h:min:s |
|---|---|---|---|---|
| 1983 | G.A. Meyer (U.S.) | 2:09:00 | J. Benoit (U.S.) | 2:22:42 |
| 1984 | G. Smith (Eng.) | 2:10:34 | L. Moller (N.Z.) | 2:29:28 |
| 1985 | G. Smith (Eng.) | 2:14:05 | L. Larsen (Nor.) | 2:34:06 |
| 1986 | R. de Castella (Australia) | 2:07:51 | I. Kristiansen (Nor.) | 2:24:55 |
| 1987 | Seko T. (Japan) | 2:11:50 | R. Mota (Port.) | 2:25:21 |

### New York Marathon

| year | men | h:min:s | women | h:min:s |
|---|---|---|---|---|
| 1983 | R. Dixon (U.S.) | 2:08:59 | G. Waitz (Nor.) | 2:27:00 |
| 1984 | O. Pizzolato (U.S.) | 2:14:53 | G. Waitz (Nor.) | 2:29:30 |
| 1985 | O. Pizzolato (U.S.) | 2:11:34 | G. Waitz (Nor.) | 2:28:34 |
| 1986 | G. Poli (Italy) | 2:11:06 | G. Waitz (Nor.) | 2:28:06 |
| 1987 | I. Hussein (Kenya) | 2:11:01 | P. Welch (U.K.) | 2:30:17 |

### America's Marathon/Chicago

| year | men | h:min:s | women | h:min:s |
|---|---|---|---|---|
| 1983 | J. Nzau (Kenya) | 2:09:45 | R. Mota (Port.) | 2:31:12 |
| 1984 | S. Jones (U.K.) | 2:08:05 | R. Mota (Port.) | 2:26:01 |
| 1985 | S. Jones (U.K.) | 2:07:13 | J. Benoit Samuelson (U.S.) | 2:21:21 |
| 1986 | Seko T. (Japan) | 2:08:27 | I. Kristiansen (Nor.) | 2:27:08 |
| 1987 | not held | | | |

I. Kristiansen: 10,000 m (1987)
MARK SHEARMAN

### World Cross-Country Championship—men (12,000 m)

| year | individual | team |
|---|---|---|
| 1982 | M. Kedir (Eth.) | Ethiopia |
| 1983 | B. Debele (Eth.) | Ethiopia |
| 1984 | C. Lopes (Port.) | Ethiopia |
| 1985 | C. Lopes (Port.) | Ethiopia |
| 1986 | J. Ngugi (Kenya) | Kenya |
| 1987 | J. Ngugi (Kenya) | Kenya |

### World Cross-Country Championship—women (5,000 m)

| year | individual | team |
|---|---|---|
| 1982 | M. Puica (Rom.) | U.S.S.R. |
| 1983 | G. Waitz (Nor.) | United States |
| 1984 | M. Puica (Rom.) | United States |
| 1985 | Z. Budd (U.K.) | United States |
| 1986 | Z. Budd (U.K.) | England |
| 1987 | A. Sergent (Fr.) | United States |

J. Joyner-Kersee: Long jump and heptathlon (1987)
MARK SHEARMAN

# AUTOMOBILE RACING

### United States Auto Club Champions

| year | driver |
| --- | --- |
| 1982/83 | T. Sneva |
| 1983/84 | R. Mears |
| 1984/85 | D. Sullivan |
| 1985/86 | B. Rahal |
| 1986/87 | A. Unser |

### Indianapolis 500

| year | winner | avg. speed in mph |
| --- | --- | --- |
| 1983 | T. Sneva | 162.117 |
| 1984 | R. Mears | 163.612 |
| 1985 | D. Sullivan | 152.982 |
| 1986 | B. Rahal | 170.722 |
| 1987 | A. Unser | 162.175 |

### International Cup for Formula One Manufacturers

| year | car | year | car |
| --- | --- | --- | --- |
| 1982 | Ferrari | 1985 | McLaren/Ferrari |
| 1983 | Ferrari | 1986 | Williams/Honda |
| 1984 | McLaren/Porsche-TAG | 1987 | Williams/Honda |

### World Championship of Drivers

| year | winner | car |
| --- | --- | --- |
| 1983 | N. Piquet (Braz.) | Brabham |
| 1984 | N. Lauda (Austria) | McLaren/Porsche-TAG |
| 1985 | A. Prost (Fr.) | McLaren/Porsche-TAG |
| 1986 | A. Prost (Fr.) | McLaren/Porsche-TAG |
| 1987 | N. Piquet (Braz.) | Williams/Honda |

### Le Mans 24-hour Grand Prix d'Endurance

| year | car | drivers |
| --- | --- | --- |
| 1983 | Porsche | A. Holbert, H. Hayward, V. Schuppan |
| 1984 | Porsche | H. Pescarolo, K. Ludwig |
| 1985 | Porsche | K. Ludwig, J. Winter, P. Barilla |
| 1986 | Porsche | D. Bell, H. Stuck, A. Holbert |
| 1987 | Porsche | H. Stuck, D. Bell, A. Holbert |

### Monte-Carlo Rally

| year | car | driver, codriver |
| --- | --- | --- |
| 1983 | Lancia Rally | Röhrl, Geistdorfer |
| 1984 | Audi Quattro | Röhrl, Geistdorfer |
| 1985 | Peugeot 205 Turbo | Vatanen, Harryman |
| 1986 | Lancia Martini Delta | Toivonen, Cresto |
| 1987 | Lancia Delta HF | Biasion, Siviero |

### National Association for Stock Car Auto Racing (NASCAR) Winston Cup Champions

| year | winner | year | winner |
| --- | --- | --- | --- |
| 1982 | D. Waltrip | 1985 | D. Waltrip |
| 1983 | B. Allison | 1986 | D. Earnhardt |
| 1984 | T. Labonte | 1987 | D. Earnhardt |

H. Toivonen: Monte-Carlo Rally (1986)
ALAIN PATRICE—AGENCE VANDYSTADT/ALLSPORT

D. Earnhardt: National Association for Stock Car Auto Racing (NASCAR) Winston Cup champion (1987)
FOCUS ON SPORTS

# BADMINTON

### World Badminton Championships

| year | men's singles | women's singles | men's doubles | women's doubles |
| --- | --- | --- | --- | --- |
| 1977 | F. Delfs (Den.) | L. Köppen (Den.) | T. Tjun, J. Wahjudi (Indon.) | Toganu E., Ueno E. (Japan) |
| 1980 | R. Hartono (Indon.) | W. Verawaty (Indon.) | A. Chandra, C. Hadinata (Indon.) | N. Perry, J. Webster (U.K.) |
| 1983 | I. Sugiarto (Indon.) | Li Lingwei (China) | S. Fladberg, J. Helledie (Den.) | Lin Ying, Wu Dixi (China) |
| 1985 | Han Jian (China) | Han Aiping (China) | Park Joo Bong, Kim Moon Soo (S.Kor.) | Han Aiping, Li Lingwei (China) |
| 1987 | Yang Yang (China) | Han Aiping (China) | Li Yongbo, Tian Hinghi (China) | Lin Ying, Guan Weizhen (China) |

### All-England Championships—singles

| year | men | women |
| --- | --- | --- |
| 1983 | Luan Jin (China) | Zhang Ailing (China) |
| 1984 | M. Frost (Den.) | Li Lingwei (China) |
| 1985 | Zhao Jianhua (China) | Han Aiping (China) |
| 1986 | M. Frost (Den.) | Kim Yun Ja (S.Kor.) |
| 1987 | M. Frost (Den.) | K. Larsen (Den.) |

### Uber Cup

| year | winner | runner-up |
| --- | --- | --- |
| 1974–75 | Indonesia | Japan |
| 1977–78 | Japan | Indonesia |
| 1980–81 | Japan | Indonesia |
| 1983–84 | China | England |
| 1985–86 | China | Indonesia |

### Thomas Cup

| year | winner | runner-up |
| --- | --- | --- |
| 1975–76 | Indonesia | Thailand |
| 1978–79 | Indonesia | Denmark |
| 1981–82 | China | Indonesia |
| 1983–84 | Indonesia | China |
| 1985–86 | China | Indonesia |

# BASEBALL

New York Mets: World Series (1986)
FOCUS ON SPORTS

### Baseball Hall of Fame

| year elected | members |
|---|---|
| 1983 | Brooks Robinson, Juan Marichal, George Kell, Walter Alston |
| 1984 | R. Ferrell, Pee Wee Reese, H. Killebrew, L. Aparicio, D. Drysdale |
| 1985 | Hoyt Wilhelm, Enos Slaughter, Lou Brock, Joseph Floyd (Arky) Vaughan |
| 1986 | Willie McCovey, Bobby Doerr, Ernie Lombardi |
| 1987 | Willie Stargell |

### World Series*

| year | winning team | losing team | results |
|---|---|---|---|
| 1983 | Baltimore Orioles (AL) | Philadelphia Phillies (NL) | 4–1 |
| 1984 | Detroit Tigers (AL) | San Diego Padres (NL) | 4–1 |
| 1985 | Kansas City Royals (AL) | St. Louis Cardinals (NL) | 4–3 |
| 1986 | New York Mets (NL) | Boston Red Sox (AL) | 4–3 |
| 1987 | Minnesota Twins (AL) | St. Louis Cardinals (NL) | 4–3 |

*AL—American League; NL—National League.

### Japan Series*

| year | winning team | losing team | results |
|---|---|---|---|
| 1983 | Seibu Lions (PL) | Yomiuri Giants (CL) | 4–3 |
| 1984 | Hiroshima Tōyō Carp (CL) | Hankyū Braves (PL) | 4–3 |
| 1985 | Hanshin Tigers (CL) | Seibu Lions (PL) | 4–2 |
| 1986 | Seibu Lions (PL) | Hiroshima Tōyō Carp (CL) | 4–3 |
| 1987 | Seibu Lions (PL) | Yomiuri Giants (CL) | 4–2 |

*CL—Central League; PL—Pacific League.

# BASKETBALL

### National Basketball Association (NBA) Championship

| season | winner | runner-up | results |
|---|---|---|---|
| 1982–83 | Philadelphia 76ers | Los Angeles Lakers | 4–0 |
| 1983–84 | Boston Celtics | Los Angeles Lakers | 4–3 |
| 1984–85 | Los Angeles Lakers | Boston Celtics | 4–2 |
| 1985–86 | Boston Celtics | Houston Rockets | 4–2 |
| 1986–87 | Los Angeles Lakers | Boston Celtics | 4–2 |

### Division I National Collegiate Athletic Association (NCAA) Championship—men

| year | winner | runner-up | score |
|---|---|---|---|
| 1983 | North Carolina State | Houston | 54–52 |
| 1984 | Georgetown | Houston | 84–75 |
| 1985 | Villanova | Georgetown | 66–64 |
| 1986 | Louisville | Duke | 72–69 |
| 1987 | Indiana | Syracuse | 74–73 |

### World Amateur Basketball Championship—men

| year | winner | runner-up |
|---|---|---|
| 1978 | Yugoslavia | U.S.S.R. |
| 1980 | Yugoslavia | Italy |
| 1982 | U.S.S.R. | United States |
| 1984 | United States | Spain |
| 1986 | United States | U.S.S.R. |

### World Amateur Basketball Championship—women

| year | winner | runner-up |
|---|---|---|
| 1979 | United States | South Korea |
| 1980 | U.S.S.R. | Bulgaria |
| 1983 | U.S.S.R. | United States |
| 1984 | United States | South Korea |
| 1986 | United States | U.S.S.R. |

### Division I National Collegiate Athletic Association (NCAA) Championship—women

| year | winner | runner-up | score |
|---|---|---|---|
| 1983 | Southern California | Louisiana Tech | 69–67 |
| 1984 | Southern California | Tennessee | 72–61 |
| 1985 | Old Dominion | Georgia | 70–65 |
| 1986 | Texas | Southern California | 97–81 |
| 1987 | Tennessee | Louisiana Tech | 67–44 |

### National Invitation Tournament (NIT) Championship

| year | winner | runner-up | score |
|---|---|---|---|
| 1983 | Fresno State | DePaul | 69–60 |
| 1984 | Michigan | Notre Dame | 83–63 |
| 1985 | UCLA | Indiana | 65–62 |
| 1986 | Ohio State | Wyoming | 73–63 |
| 1987 | Southern Mississippi | LaSalle | 84–80 |

Los Angeles Lakers: National Basketball Association (NBA) championship (1987)
RICHARD MACKSON/SPORTS ILLUSTRATED

# BILLIARDS

### World Amateur Three-Cushion Championship

| year | winner |
|---|---|
| 1983 | R. Ceulemans (Belg.) |
| 1984 | Kobayashi N. (Japan) |
| 1985 | R. Ceulemans (Belg.) |
| 1986 | A. Rico (Spain) |
| 1987 | T. Blomdahl (Swed.) |

### World Professional (English) Billiards Champions

| year | winner |
|---|---|
| 1983 | R. Williams |
| 1984 | M. Wildman |
| 1985 | R. Edmonds |
| 1986 | R. Foldvari |
| 1987 | N. Dagley |

# BOWLING

### ABC Bowling Championships—Regular Division

| year | singles | score | all-events | score |
|---|---|---|---|---|
| 1984 | R. Antczak | 764 | R. Goike | 2,142 |
| | N. Young | 764 | | |
| 1985 | G. Harbison | 774 | B. Asher | 2,033 |
| 1986 | J. Mackey | 774 | E. Marzka | 2,116 |
| 1987 | T. Taylor | 749 | R. Shafer | 2,044 |

### WIBC Bowling Championship—Open Division

| year | singles | score | all-events | score |
|---|---|---|---|---|
| 1983 | A. Rzepecki-Sill | 726 | V. Norton | 1,922 |
| 1984 | F. Gate | 712 | Saitō S. (Japan) | 1,921 |
| 1985 | P. Schwarzel | 694 | A. Rzepecki Sill | 1,900 |
| 1986 | D. Stewart | 698 | Romeo, Lewis (tie) | 1,877 |
| 1987 | R. Jonak | 728 | L. Barrette | 1,972 |

### FIQ World Bowling Championship—men

| year | singles | pairs | triples | fives | eights |
|---|---|---|---|---|---|
| 1975 | M. Stoudt (U.S.) | United Kingdom | | Finland | West Germany |
| 1979* | G. Bugden (U.K.) | Australia | Malaysia | Australia | |
| 1983 | T. Cariello (U.S.) | Australia | Sweden | Finland | |
| 1987 | P. Rolland (Fr.) | Sweden | United States | Sweden | |

*In 1979 eights were discontinued and triples were introduced.

### Professional Bowlers Association (PBA) Firestone Tournament of Champions

| year | champion | runner-up |
|---|---|---|
| 1983 | J. Berardi | H. Gonzalez |
| 1984 | M. Durbin | M. Aulby |
| 1985 | M. Williams | B. Handley |
| 1986 | M. Holman | M. Baker |
| 1987 | P. Weber | J. Murtishaw |

### FIQ World Bowling Championship—women

| year | singles | pairs | triples | fours | fives |
|---|---|---|---|---|---|
| 1975 | A. Haefker (W.Ger.) | Sweden | | Japan | Japan |
| 1979* | L. de la Rosa (Phil.) | Philippines | United States | | United States |
| 1983 | L. Sulkanen (Swed.) | Denmark | West Germany | | Sweden |
| 1987 | E. Piccini (Mex.) | United States | United States | | United States |

*In 1979 fours were discontinued and triples were introduced.

# BOWLS

### World Lawn Bowls Championships

| year | singles | pairs | triples | fours | team |
|---|---|---|---|---|---|
| 1966 | D. Bryant (Eng.) | Australia | Australia | New Zealand | Australia |
| 1972 | M. Evans (Wales) | Hong Kong | United States | England | Scotland |
| 1976 | D. Watson (S.Af.) | South Africa | South Africa | South Africa | South Africa |
| 1980 | D. Bryant (Eng.) | Australia | England | Hong Kong | — |
| 1984 | P. Bellis (N.Z.) | United States | Ireland | England | Scotland |

# BOXING

### World heavyweight champions—no weight limit

| WBA | WBC |
|---|---|
| Greg Page (U.S.; 12/1/84) | Tim Witherspoon (U.S.; 3/9/84) |
| Tony Tubbs (U.S.; 4/29/85) | Pinklon Thomas (U.S.; 8/31/84) |
| Tim Witherspoon (U.S.; 1/17/86) | Trevor Berbick (Can.; 3/22/86) |
| James Smith (U.S.; 12/12/86) | Mike Tyson (U.S.; 11/22/86) |
| Mike Tyson (U.S.; 3/7/87) | |

D. Andries: WBC light heavyweight champion (1986)
C.COLE—ALLSPORT

### World cruiserweight champions—top weight 195 pounds

| WBA | WBC |
|---|---|
| Ossie Ocasio (P.R.; 2/13/82) | S.T. Gordon (U.S.; 6/27/1982) |
| Piet Crous (S.Af.; 12/1/84) | Carlos de León (P.R.; 7/17/83) |
| Dwight Muhammad Qawi (U.S.; 7/27/85) | Alfonso Ratliff (U.S.; 6/6/85) |
| Evander Holyfield (U.S.; 7/12/86) | Bernard Benton (U.S.; 9/21/85) |
| | Carlos de León (P.R.; 3/22/86) |

### World junior middleweight champions—top weight 154 pounds

| WBA | WBC |
|---|---|
| Roberto Durán (Pan.; 6/16/83) | Thomas Hearns (U.S.; 12/3/82) |
| gave up title in 1984 | gave up title in 1986 |
| Mike McCallum (Jam.; 10/19/84) | Duane Thomas (U.S.; 12/5/86) |
| vacant | Lupe Aquino (Mex.; 7/12/87) |
| Julian Jackson (Virgin Is. U.S.; 11/21/87) | Gianfranco Rosi (Italy; 10/2/87) |

### World light heavyweight champions—top weight 175 pounds

| WBA | WBC |
|---|---|
| Marvin Johnson (U.S.; 2/9/86) | J.B. Williamson (U.S.; 12/10/85) |
| Leslie Stewart (Trinidad and Tobago; 5/23/87) | Dennis Andries (U.K.; 4/30/86) |
| Virgil Hill (U.S.; 9/5/87) | Thomas Hearns (U.S.; 3/7/87) |
| | gave up title in 1987 |
| | Donny Lalonde (Can.; 11/27/87) |

### World welterweight champions—top weight 147 pounds

| WBA | WBC |
|---|---|
| Donald Curry (U.S.; 2/13/83) | Milton McCrory (U.S.; 8/13/83) |
| Lloyd Honeyghan (U.K.; 9/27/86) | Donald Curry (U.S.; 12/6/85) |
| gave up title in 1986 | Lloyd Honeyghan (U.K.; 9/27/86) |
| Mark Breland (U.S.; 2/6/87) | Jorge Vaca (Mex.; 10/28/87) |
| Marlon Starling (U.S.; 8/22/87) | |

### World middleweight champions—top weight 160 pounds

| WBA | WBC |
|---|---|
| Alan Minter (U.K.; 3/16/80) | Alan Minter (U.K.; 3/16/80) |
| Marvin Hagler (U.S.; 9/27/80) | Marvin Hagler (U.S.; 9/27/80) |
| stripped of title in 1987 | Sugar Ray Leonard (U.S.; 4/6/87) |
| vacant | retired |
| S. Kalambay (Italy; 10/23/87) | Thomas Hearns (U.S.; 10/29/87) |

### World junior welterweight champions—top weight 140 pounds

| WBA | WBC |
|---|---|
| Johnny Bumphus (U.S.; 1/22/84) | Lonnie Smith (U.S.; 8/21/85) |
| Gene Hatcher (U.S.; 6/1/84) | René Arredondo (Mex.; 5/6/86) |
| Ubaldo Sacco (Arg.; 7/21/85) | Tsuyoshi Hamada (Japan; 7/24/86) |
| Patrizio Oliva (Italy; 3/15/86) | René Arredondo (Mex.; 7/22/87) |
| Juan Martin Coggi (Arg.; 7/4/87) | Roger Mayweather (U.S.; 11/12/87) |

### World lightweight champions—top weight 135 pounds

| WBA | WBC |
|---|---|
| Arturo Frias (U.S.; 12/5/81) | Edwin Rosario (P.R.; 5/1/83) |
| Ray Mancini (U.S.; 5/8/82) | José Luis Ramírez (Mex.; 11/3/84) |
| Livingstone Bramble (Vir.Is.; 6/1/84) | Hector Camacho (P.R.; 8/10/85) |
| Edwin Rosario (P.R.; 9/26/86) | stripped of title in 1987 |
| Julio César Chávez | José Luis Ramírez (Mex.; 7/19/87) |
| (Mex.; 11/21/87) | |

### World junior lightweight champions—top weight 130 pounds

| WBA | WBC |
|---|---|
| Roger Mayweather (U.S.; 1/19/83) | Bobby Chacon (U.S.; 12/11/82) |
| Rocky Lockridge (U.S.; 2/26/84) | stripped of title in 1983 |
| Wilfredo Gómez (P.R.; 5/19/85) | Hector Camacho (U.S.; 8/7/83) |
| Alfredo Layne (Pan.; 5/24/86) | gave up title in 1984 |
| Brian Mitchell (S.Af.; 9/27/86) | Julio César Chavez (Mex.; 9/13/84) |

### World featherweight champions—top weight 126 pounds

| WBA | WBC |
|---|---|
| Cecilio Lastra (Spain; 12/17/77) | Salvador Sánchez (Mex.; 2/2/80) |
| Eusebio Pedroza (Pan.; 4/15/78) | died in 1982 |
| Barry McGuigan (N.Ire.; 6/8/85) | Juan LaPorte (P.R.; 9/15/82) |
| Steve Cruz (U.S.; 6/23/86) | Wilfredo Gómez (P.R.; 3/31/84) |
| Antonio Esparragoza (Venez.; 3/6/87) | Azumah Nelson (Ghana; 12/8/84) |

### World junior featherweight champions (also called super bantamweight)—top weight 122 pounds

| WBA | WBC |
|---|---|
| Loris Stecca (Italy; 2/22/84) | Jaime Garza (U.S.; 6/15/83) |
| Víctor Callejas (P.R.; 5/26/84) | Juan Meza (Mex.; 11/3/84) |
| stripped of title in 1986 | Guadalupe Pintor (Mex.; 8/18/85) |
| Louie Espinoza (U.S.; 1/16/87) | Samart Payakaroon (Thai.; 1/18/86) |
| Julio Gervacio (Dom.Rep.; 11/28/87) | Jeff Fenech (Australia; 5/8/87) |

### World bantamweight champions—top weight 118 pounds

| WBA | WBC |
|---|---|
| Bernardo Pinango (Venez.; 6/4/86) | Alberto Davila (U.S.; 9/1/83) |
| gave up title in 1987 | stripped of title in 1985 |
| Takuyama Muguruma (Japan; 3/29/87) | Daniel Zaragoza (Mex.; 5/4/85) |
| Park Chang Young (S.Kor.; 5/24/87) | Miguel Lora (Colom.; 8/9/85) |
| Wilfredo Vásquez (P.R.; 10/4/87) | |

### World junior bantamweight champions (also called super flyweight)—top weight 115 pounds

| WBA | WBC |
|---|---|
| Gustavo Ballas (Arg.; 9/12/1981) | Payao Poontarat (Thai.; 11/27/83) |
| Rafael Pedroza (Pan.; 12/5/81) | Watanabe Jiro (Japan; 7/5/84) |
| Watanabe Jiro (Japan; 4/8/82) | Gilberto Román (Mex.; 3/30/86) |
| stripped of title in 1984 | Santos Laciar (Arg.; 5/16/87) |
| Kaosai Galaxy (Thai.; 11/21/84) | Jesús Rojas (Colom.; 8/9/87) |

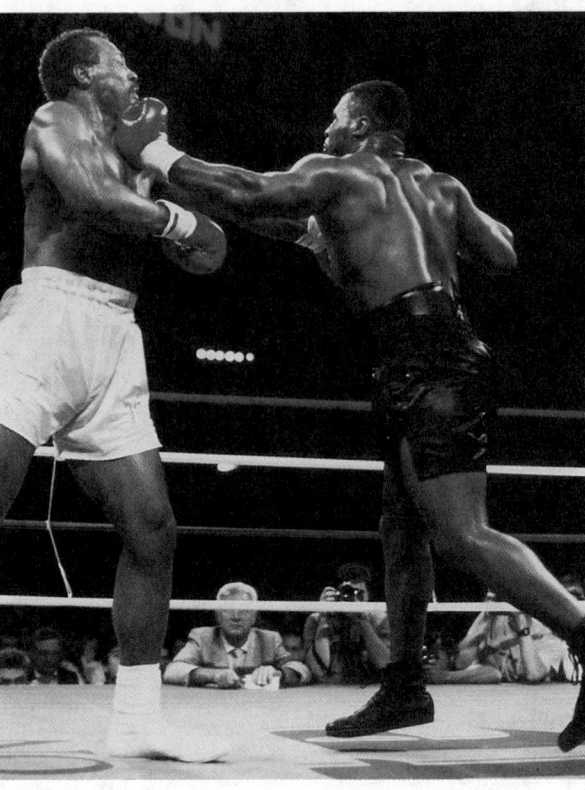

M. Tyson (right): WBA and WBC heavyweight champion (1987)
RICHARD MACKSON/SPORTS ILLUSTRATED

### World flyweight champions—top weight 112 pounds

| WBA | WBC |
|---|---|
| Juan Herrera (Mex.; 9/26/81) | Charlie Magri (U.K.; 3/15/83) |
| Santos Laciar (Arg.; 5/1/82) | Frank Cedeno (Phil.; 9/27/83) |
| gave up title in 1985 | Kobayashi Koji (Japan; 1/18/84) |
| Hilario Zapata (Pan.; 10/5/85) | Gabriel Bernal (Mex.; 4/9/84) |
| Fidel Bassa (Colom.; 2/13/87) | Sot Chitalada (Thai.; 10/8/84) |

### World junior flyweight champions—top weight 108 pounds

| WBA | WBC |
|---|---|
| Tokashiki Katsuo (Japan; 12/16/81) | Hilario Zapata (Pan.; 3/24/80) |
| Lupe Madera (Mex.; 7/10/83) | Amado Ursua (Mex.; 2/6/82) |
| Francisco Quiroz (Dom.Rep.; 5/19/84) | Tomori Tadashi (Japan; 4/13/82) |
| Joey Olivo (U.S.; 3/29/85) | Hilario Zapata (Pan.; 7/20/82) |
| Yuh Myung Woo (S.Kor.; 12/8/85) | Chang Jung Koo (S.Kor.; 3/26/83) |

## CHESS

### World Chess Championships—men

| year | winner | runner-up |
|---|---|---|
| 1975 | A. Karpov (U.S.S.R.)* | * |
| 1978 | A. Karpov (U.S.S.R.) | V. Korchnoy (U.S.S.R.) |
| 1981 | A. Karpov (U.S.S.R.) | V. Korchnoy (U.S.S.R.) |
| 1984–85 | G. Kasparov (U.S.S.R.) | A. Karpov (U.S.S.R.) |
| 1986 | G. Kasparov (U.S.S.R.) | A. Karpov (U.S.S.R.) |
| 1987 | G. Kasparov (U.S.S.R.) | A. Karpov (U.S.S.R.) |

*By default. R. Fischer (U.S.) was stripped of the title for failure to comply with an FIDE ruling, and Karpov was declared the new world champion.

### World Chess Championships—women

| year | winner | runner-up |
|---|---|---|
| 1976 | N. Gaprindashvili (U.S.S.R.) | N. Aleksandriya (U.S.S.R.) |
| 1978 | M. Chiburdanidze (U.S.S.R.) | N. Gaprindashvili (U.S.S.R.) |
| 1981 | M. Chiburdanidze (U.S.S.R.) | N. Aleksandriya (U.S.S.R.) |
| 1984 | M. Chiburdanidze (U.S.S.R.) | I. Levitina (U.S.S.R.) |
| 1986 | M. Chiburdanidze (U.S.S.R.) | E. Akhmilovskaya (U.S.S.R.) |

### International Team Chess Championships—men

| year | winner | runner-up |
|---|---|---|
| 1978 | Hungary | U.S.S.R. |
| 1980 | U.S.S.R. | Hungary |
| 1982 | U.S.S.R. | Czechoslovakia |
| 1984 | U.S.S.R. | United Kingdom |
| 1986 | U.S.S.R. | United Kingdom |

### International Team Chess Championships—women

| year | winner | runner-up |
|---|---|---|
| 1978 | U.S.S.R. | Hungary |
| 1980 | U.S.S.R. | Hungary |
| 1982 | U.S.S.R. | Romania |
| 1984 | U.S.S.R. | Bulgaria |
| 1986 | U.S.S.R. | Hungary |

## CONTRACT BRIDGE

### Bermuda Bowl

| year | winner | runner-up |
|------|--------|-----------|
| 1983 | United States | Italy |
| 1985 | United States | Austria |
| 1987 | United States | United Kingdom |

### World Contract Bridge Pair Championship

| year | open winner | women's winner | mixed winner |
|------|-------------|----------------|--------------|
| 1978 | Brazil | United States | United States |
| 1982 | United States | United States | Canada |
| 1986 | United States | United States | United States |

### World Team Olympiad

| year | open winner | open runner-up | women's winner | women's runner-up |
|------|-------------|----------------|----------------|-------------------|
| 1980 | France | United States | United States | Italy |
| 1984 | Poland | France | United States | United Kingdom |

## CRICKET

### All-time First-class Test Cricket Standings (as of August 31, 1987)

|  | England wins draws losses | | | Australia w d l | | | South Africa w d l | | | West Indies w d l | | | New Zealand w d l | | | India w d l | | | Pakistan w d l | | | Sri Lanka w d l | | |
|---|---|---|---|---|---|---|---|---|---|---|---|---|---|---|---|---|---|---|---|---|---|---|---|---|
| England v. | — | — | — | 88 | 76 | 97 | 46 | 38 | 18 | 21 | 34 | 35 | 30 | 29 | 4 | 29 | 34 | 11 | 13 | 27 | 4 | 1 | 1 | 0 |
| Australia v. | 97 | 76 | 88 | — | — | — | 29 | 13 | 11 | 27 | 16* | 19 | 9 | 7 | 5 | 20 | 17* | 8 | 11 | 9 | 8 | 1 | 0 | 0 |
| South Africa v. | 18 | 38 | 46 | 11 | 13 | 29 | — | — | — | † | | | 19 | 6 | 2 | † | | | † | | | † | | |
| West Indies v. | 35 | 34 | 21 | 19 | 16* | 27 | † | | | — | — | — | 8 | 12 | 4 | 22 | 27 | 5 | 8 | 9 | 5 | † | | |
| New Zealand v. | 4 | 29 | 30 | 5 | 7 | 9 | 2 | 6 | 19 | 4 | 12 | 8 | — | — | — | 4 | 11 | 10 | 3 | 14 | 10 | 4 | 2 | 0 |
| India v. | 11 | 34 | 29 | 8 | 17* | 20 | † | | | 5 | 27 | 22 | 10 | 11 | 4 | — | — | — | 4 | 29 | 7 | 3 | 3 | 1 |
| Pakistan v. | 4 | 27 | 13 | 8 | 9 | 11 | † | | | 5 | 9 | 8 | 10 | 14 | 3 | 7 | 29 | 4 | — | — | — | 5 | 3 | 1 |
| Sri Lanka v. | 0 | 1 | 1 | 0 | 0 | 1 | † | | | † | | | 4 | 2 | 4 | 1 | 3 | 3 | 1 | 3 | 5 | — | — | — |

*Including one tie.  †No matches.

## CURLING

### International Olympic Committee President's Cup

| year | winner | runner-up |
|------|--------|-----------|
| 1983 | Canada | West Germany |
| 1984 | Norway | Switzerland |
| 1985 | Canada | Sweden |
| 1986 | Canada | Scotland |
| 1987 | Canada | West Germany |

### World Curling Championship—women

| year | winner | runner-up |
|------|--------|-----------|
| 1983 | Switzerland | Norway |
| 1984 | Canada | Switzerland |
| 1985 | Canada | Scotland |
| 1986 | Canada | West Germany |
| 1987 | Canada | West Germany |

## CYCLING

### Tour de France

| year | winner | km |
|------|--------|-----|
| 1983 | L. Fignon (Fr.) | 3,568 |
| 1984 | L. Fignon (Fr.) | 3,880 |
| 1985 | B. Hinault (Fr.) | 4,100 |
| 1986 | G. LeMond (U.S.) | 4,091 |
| 1987 | S. Roche (Ire.) | 4,100 |

### Cycling World Track Championships—women (amateur)

| year | sprint | 3-km pursuit |
|------|--------|--------------|
| 1983 | C. Paraskevin (U.S.) | C. Carpenter (U.S.) |
| 1984 | C. Paraskevin (U.S.) | R. Twigg (U.S.) |
| 1985 | I. Nicoloso (Fr.) | R. Twigg (U.S.) |
| 1986 | C. Rothenburger (E.Ger.) | J. Longo (Fr.) |
| 1987 | E. Salumyae (U.S.S.R.) | R. Twigg-Whitehead (U.S.) |

### Cycling World Road-Racing Championships

| year | men (amateur) | men (professional) | women (amateur) |
|------|---------------|--------------------|-----------------|
| 1983 | U. Raab (E.Ger.) | G. LeMond (U.S.) | M. Berglund (Swed.) |
| 1984 | * | C. Criquelion (Belg.) | * |
| 1985 | L. Piasecki (Pol.) | J. Zoetemelk (Neth.) | J. Longo (Fr.) |
| 1986 | U. Ampler (E.Ger.) | M. Argentin (Italy) | J. Longo (Fr.) |
| 1987 | R. Vivien (Fr.) | S. Roche (Ireland) | J. Longo (Fr.) |

*Not held because of Olympic championships.

S. Roche: Tour de France (1987)
BILLY STICK—ALLSPORT

### Cycling World Track Championships—men

| year | sprint (amateur) | sprint (professional) | pursuit (amateur) | pursuit (professional) | motor-paced (amateur) | motor-paced (professional) |
|------|------------------|-----------------------|-------------------|------------------------|-----------------------|----------------------------|
| 1983 | L. Hesslich (E.Ger.) | Nakano K. (Japan) | V. Kupovets (U.S.S.R.) | S. Bishop (Australia) | R. Podlesch (W.Ger.) | B. Vicino (Italy) |
| 1984 | * | Nakano K. (Japan) | * | H.-H. Oersted (Den.) | J. de Nijs (Neth.) | H. Schütz (W.Ger.) |
| 1985 | L. Hesslich (E.Ger.) | Nakano K. (Japan) | V. Ekimov (U.S.S.R.) | H.-H. Oersted (Den.) | R. Dotti (Italy) | B. Vicino (Italy) |
| 1986 | M. Hübner (E.Ger.) | Nakano K. (Japan) | V. Ekimov (U.S.S.R.) | T. Doyle (U.K.) | M. Gentili (Italy) | B. Vicino (Italy) |
| 1987 | L. Hesslich (E.Ger.) | Tawara N. (Japan) | G. Umaras (U.S.S.R.) | H.-H. Oersted (Den.) | M. Gentili (Italy) | M. Huerzeler (Switz.) |

*Not held because of Olympic championships.

# FENCING

### World Fencing Championships—men

| year | individual | | | team | | |
|---|---|---|---|---|---|---|
| | foil | épée | sabre | foil | épée | sabre |
| 1983 | A. Romankov (U.S.S.R.) | E. Bormann (W.Ger.) | V. Etropolski (Bulg.) | West Germany | France | U.S.S.R. |
| 1984 | M. Numa (Italy) | P. Boisse (Fr.) | J.F. Lamour (Fr.) | Italy | West Germany | Italy |
| 1985 | M. Numa (Italy) | P. Boisse (Fr.) | G. Nebald (Hung.) | Italy | West Germany | U.S.S.R. |
| 1986 | A. Borella (Italy) | P. Riboud (Fr.) | S. Mindirgasov (U.S.S.R.) | Italy | West Germany | U.S.S.R. |
| 1987 | M. Gey (W.Ger.) | V. Fischer (W.Ger.) | J.-F. Lamour (Fr.) | West Germany | U.S.S.R. | U.S.S.R. |

### World Fencing Championships—women

| year | individual foil | team foil |
|---|---|---|
| 1983 | D. Vaccaroni (Italy) | Italy |
| 1984 | Luan Jujie (China) | West Germany |
| 1985 | C. Hanisch (W.Ger.) | West Germany |
| 1986 | A. Fichtel (W.Ger.) | U.S.S.R. |
| 1987 | E. Tufan (Rom.) | Hungary |

# FIELD HOCKEY

### World Cup Field Hockey Championships—men

| year | winner | runner-up |
|---|---|---|
| 1982 | Pakistan | West Germany |
| 1986 | Australia | England |

### World Cup Field Hockey Championships—women

| year | winner | runner-up |
|---|---|---|
| 1983 | The Netherlands | Canada |
| 1986 | The Netherlands | West Germany |

# FOOTBALL

### FIFA World Cup

| year | result | | | |
|---|---|---|---|---|
| 1982 | Italy | 3 | West Germany | 1 |
| 1986 | Argentina | 3 | West Germany | 2 |

Argentina (blue): FIFA World Cup (1986)
AGENCE VANDYSTADT/ALLSPORT

### European Cup-Winners' Cup

| season | result | | | |
|---|---|---|---|---|
| 1982–83 | Aberdeen (Scot.) | 2 | Real Madrid | 1 |
| 1983–84 | Juventus (Italy) | 2 | Porto (Port.) | 1 |
| 1984–85 | Everton (Eng.) | 3 | Rapid Vienna | 1 |
| 1985–86 | Dinamo Kiev | 3 | Atlético Madrid | 0 |
| 1986–87 | Ajax Amsterdam | 1 | Lokomotiv Leipzig | 0 |

### The European Cup of Champion Clubs

| season | result | | | |
|---|---|---|---|---|
| 1983–84 | Liverpool* | 1 | Roma | 1 |
| 1984–85 | Juventus (Italy) | 1 | Liverpool | 0 |
| 1985–86 | Steaua Bucharest* | 1 | Barcelona | 0 |
| 1986–87 | Porto (Port.) | 2 | Bayern Munich | 1 |

*Won on penalty kicks.

### Libertadores de América Cup

| year | winner (country) | runner-up (country) | scores |
|---|---|---|---|
| 1984 | Independiente (Arg.) | Grêmio (Braz.) | 1–0, 0–0 |
| 1985 | Argentinos Juniors (Arg.) | América (Colom.) | 1–0, 0–1, 1–1* |
| 1986 | River Plate (Arg.) | América de Cali (Colom.) | 2–1, 1–0 |
| 1987 | Peñarol (Uruguay) | América de Cali (Colom.) | 0–2, 2–1, 1–0 |

*Winner determined in penalty shootout after tiebreaking game.

*U.S. Football—professional*

### Super Bowl

| | season | result | | | |
|---|---|---|---|---|---|
| XVIII | 1983–84 | Los Angeles Raiders (AFC) | 38 | Washington Redskins (NFC) | 9 |
| XIX | 1984–85 | San Francisco 49ers (NFC) | 38 | Miami Dolphins (AFC) | 16 |
| XX | 1985–86 | Chicago Bears (NFC) | 46 | New England Patriots (AFC) | 10 |
| XXI | 1986–87 | New York Giants (NFC) | 39 | Denver Broncos (AFC) | 20 |
| XXII | 1987–88 | Washington Redskins (NFC) | 42 | Denver Broncos (AFC) | 10 |

*U.S. Football—college*

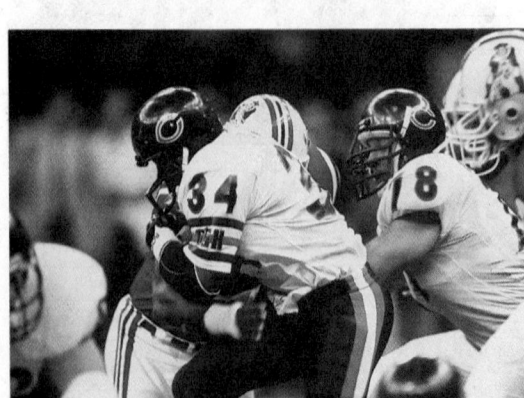

Chicago Bears: Super Bowl (1986)
FOCUS ON SPORTS

### U.S. College Football National Champion

| season | champion |
|---|---|
| 1984 | Brigham Young |
| 1985 | Oklahoma |
| 1986 | Penn State |
| 1987 | Miami |

### Heisman Memorial Trophy winner

| year | player | school |
|---|---|---|
| 1983 | Mike Rozier | Nebraska |
| 1984 | Doug Flutie | Boston College |
| 1985 | Bo Jackson | Auburn |
| 1986 | Vinnie Testaverde | Miami |
| 1987 | Tim Brown | Notre Dame |

### Rose Bowl

| season | result | | | |
|---|---|---|---|---|
| 1983–84 | UCLA | 45 | Illinois | 9 |
| 1984–85 | Southern California | 20 | Ohio State | 17 |
| 1985–86 | UCLA | 45 | Iowa | 28 |
| 1986–87 | Arizona State | 22 | Michigan | 15 |
| 1987–88 | Michigan St. | 20 | Southern California | 17 |

### Orange Bowl

| season | result | | | |
|---|---|---|---|---|
| 1983–84 | Miami (Fla.) | 31 | Nebraska | 30 |
| 1984–85 | Washington | 28 | Oklahoma | 17 |
| 1985–86 | Oklahoma | 25 | Penn State | 10 |
| 1986–87 | Oklahoma | 42 | Arkansas | 8 |
| 1987–88 | Miami | 20 | Oklahoma | 14 |

### Sugar Bowl

| season | result | | | |
|---|---|---|---|---|
| 1983–84 | Auburn | 9 | Michigan | 7 |
| 1984–85 | Nebraska | 28 | Louisiana State | 10 |
| 1985–86 | Tennessee | 35 | Miami (Fla.) | 7 |
| 1986–87 | Nebraska | 30 | Louisiana State | 15 |
| 1987–88 | Auburn | 16 | Syracuse | 16 |

### Cotton Bowl

| season | result | | | |
|---|---|---|---|---|
| 1983–84 | Georgia | 10 | Texas | 9 |
| 1984–85 | Boston College | 45 | Houston | 28 |
| 1985–86 | Texas A&M | 36 | Auburn | 16 |
| 1986–87 | Ohio State | 28 | Texas A&M | 12 |
| 1987–88 | Texas A&M | 35 | Notre Dame | 10 |

## *Canadian football—professional*

### Grey Cup

| year | result | | | |
|---|---|---|---|---|
| 1983 | Toronto Argonauts (EFC) | 18 | British Columbia Lions (WFC) | 17 |
| 1984 | Winnipeg Blue Bombers (WFC) | 47 | Hamilton Tiger-Cats (EFC) | 17 |
| 1985 | British Columbia Lions (WFC) | 37 | Hamilton Tiger-Cats (EFC) | 24 |
| 1986 | Hamilton Tiger-Cats (EFC) | 39 | Edmonton Eskimos (WFC) | 15 |
| 1987 | Edmonton Eskimos (WFC) | 38 | Toronto Argonauts (EFC) | 36 |

## *Rugby Union football*

### Record of International Test matches 1871 to September 30, 1987

| | England wins | draws | losses | Scotland wins | draws | losses | Ireland wins | draws | losses | Wales wins | draws | losses | British Isles wins | draws | losses |
|---|---|---|---|---|---|---|---|---|---|---|---|---|---|---|---|
| England v. | | | | 49 | 16 | 38 | 55 | 8 | 36 | 36 | 12 | 45 | — | | |
| Scotland v. | 38 | 16 | 49 | | | | 49 | 4 | 44 | 38 | 2 | 51 | — | | |
| Ireland v. | 36 | 8 | 55 | 44 | 4 | 49 | | | | 30 | 5 | 55 | — | | |
| Wales v. | 45 | 12 | 36 | 51 | 2 | 38 | 55 | 5 | 30 | | | | — | | |
| British Isles* v. | | | | | | | | | | | | | | | |
| South Africa v. | 6 | 1 | 2 | 5 | 0 | 3 | 8 | 1 | 1 | 6 | 1 | 0 | 20 | 6 | 14 |
| New Zealand v. | 12 | 0 | 3 | 11 | 2 | 0 | 8 | 1 | 0 | 9 | 0 | 3 | 24 | 3 | 5 |
| Australia v. | 8 | 0 | 5 | 4 | 0 | 7 | 6 | 0 | 6 | 5 | 0 | 8 | 2 | 0 | 12 |
| France v. | 23 | 7 | 32 | 28 | 3 | 27 | 30 | 5 | 25 | 21 | 3 | 36 | — | | |

| | South Africa wins | draws | losses | New Zealand wins | draws | losses | Australia wins | draws | losses | France wins | draws | losses |
|---|---|---|---|---|---|---|---|---|---|---|---|---|
| England v. | 2 | 1 | 6 | 3 | 0 | 12 | 5 | 0 | 8 | 32 | 7 | 23 |
| Scotland v. | 3 | 0 | 5 | 0 | 2 | 11 | 7 | 0 | 4 | 27 | 3 | 28 |
| Ireland v. | 1 | 1 | 8 | 0 | 1 | 8 | 6 | 0 | 6 | 25 | 5 | 30 |
| Wales v. | 0 | 1 | 6 | 3 | 0 | 9 | 8 | 0 | 5 | 36 | 3 | 21 |
| British Isles* v. | 14 | 6 | 20 | 5 | 3 | 24 | 12 | 0 | 2 | — | | |
| South Africa v. | | | | 20 | 2 | 15 | 21 | 0 | 7 | 12 | 4 | 3 |
| New Zealand v. | 15 | 2 | 20 | | | | 58 | 4 | 21 | 19 | 0 | 5 |
| Australia v. | 7 | 0 | 21 | 21 | 4 | 58 | | | | 6 | 2 | 10 |
| France v. | 3 | 4 | 12 | 5 | 0 | 19 | 10 | 2 | 6 | | | |

*The British Isles ("British Lions") is a combined team from the four "Home Unions" (England, Ireland, Scotland, and Wales).

### Five Nations Championship

| year | result |
|---|---|
| 1983 | France, Ireland* |
| 1984 | Scotland† |
| 1985 | Ireland† |
| 1986 | France, Scotland* |
| 1987 | France‡ |

*Tied. †Triple Crown (all three matches, excluding France) and Grand Slam (all four matches) winner. ‡Grand Slam winner.

## *Rugby League football*

### Record of Test matches from January 25, 1908, to September 30, 1987

| | Great Britain wins | draws | losses | Australia wins | draws | losses | New Zealand wins | draws | losses | France wins | draws | losses |
|---|---|---|---|---|---|---|---|---|---|---|---|---|
| Great Britain v. | — | | | 49 | 4 | 46 | 45 | 3 | 24 | 28 | 3 | 13 |
| Australia v. | 46 | 4 | 49 | — | | | 38 | 0 | 21 | 24 | 3 | 12 |
| New Zealand v. | 24 | 3 | 45 | 21 | 0 | 38 | — | | | 15 | 3 | 11 |
| France* v. | 13 | 3 | 28 | 12 | 3 | 24 | 11 | 3 | 15 | | | |

*France began playing in this series of matches in 1954.

# GOLF

### British Open Golf Tournament—men

| year | winner |
|---|---|
| 1984 | S. Ballesteros (Spain) |
| 1985 | S. Lyle (Scot.) |
| 1986 | G. Norman (Australia) |
| 1987 | N. Faldo (U.K.) |

### United States Open Golf Championship—men

| year | winner |
|---|---|
| 1984 | F. Zoeller (U.S.) |
| 1985 | A. North (U.S.) |
| 1986 | R. Floyd (U.S.) |
| 1987 | S. Simpson (U.S.) |

### Masters Tournament

| year | winner |
|---|---|
| 1983 | S. Ballesteros (Spain) |
| 1984 | B. Crenshaw (U.S.) |
| 1985 | B. Langer (W.Ger.) |
| 1986 | J. Nicklaus (U.S.) |
| 1987 | L. Mize (U.S.) |

### U.S. Professional Golfers' Association (PGA) championship

| year | winner |
|---|---|
| 1984 | L. Trevino (U.S.) |
| 1985 | H. Green (U.S.) |
| 1986 | B. Tway (U.S.) |
| 1987 | L. Nelson (U.S.) |

L. Mize: Masters tournament (1987)
FOCUS ON SPORTS

N. Faldo: British Open golf tournament (1987)
COLORSPORT

**British Amateur Golf Championship—men**

| year | winner |
|------|--------|
| 1983 | P. Parkin (U.K.) |
| 1984 | J.-M. Olazabal (Spain) |
| 1985 | G. McGimpsey (Ire.) |
| 1986 | D. Curry (U.K.) |
| 1987 | P. Mayo (U.K.) |

**United States Amateur Golf Championship—men**

| year | winner |
|------|--------|
| 1983 | J. Sigel (U.S.) |
| 1984 | S. Verplank (U.S.) |
| 1985 | S. Randolph (U.S.) |
| 1986 | B. Alexander (U.S.) |
| 1987 | B. Mayfair (U.S.) |

**Ladies' British Open Golf Championship**

| year | winner |
|------|--------|
| 1983 | not held |
| 1984 | Okamoto A. (Japan) |
| 1985 | B. King (U.S.) |
| 1986 | L. Davies (U.K.) |
| 1987 | A. Nicholas (U.K.) |

**British Ladies Amateur Golf Championship**

| year | winner |
|------|--------|
| 1983 | J. Thornhill (U.K.) |
| 1984 | J. Rosenthal (U.S.) |
| 1985 | L. Behan (Ire.) |
| 1986 | J. Thornhill (U.K.) |
| 1987 | J. Collingham (U.K.) |

**United States Women's Open champions**

| year | winner |
|------|--------|
| 1983 | J. Stephenson (Australia) |
| 1984 | H. Stacy (U.S.) |
| 1985 | K. Baker (U.S.) |
| 1986 | J. Geddes (U.S.) |
| 1987 | L. Davies (U.K.) |

**United States Women's Amateur Golf Championship**

| year | winner |
|------|--------|
| 1983 | J. Pacillo (U.S.) |
| 1984 | D. Richard (U.S.) |
| 1985 | Hattori M. (Japan) |
| 1986 | K. Cockerill (U.S.) |
| 1987 | K. Cockerill (U.S.) |

**Ladies' Professional Golf Association (LPGA) champions**

| year | winner |
|------|--------|
| 1983 | P. Sheehan (U.S.) |
| 1984 | P. Sheehan (U.S.) |
| 1985 | N. Lopez (U.S.) |
| 1986 | P. Bradley (U.S.) |
| 1987 | J. Geddes (U.S.) |

*Team events*

**Walker Cup**

| year | result | tied | place |
|------|--------|------|-------|
| 1979 | United States 14, Britain and Ireland 7 | 3 | Muirfield, East Lothian, Scot. |
| 1981 | United States 15, Britain and Ireland 9 | 0 | Monterey, Calif., U.S. |
| 1983 | United States 13, Britain and Ireland 10 | 1 | Hoylake, Cheshire, Eng. |
| 1985 | United States 13, Britain and Ireland 11 | 2 | Pine Valley, N.J., U.S. |
| 1987 | United States 16, Britain and Ireland 7 | 1 | Sunningdale, Berkshire, Eng. |

**World Cup**

| year | winner |
|------|--------|
| 1983 | United States (R. Caldwell and J. Cook) |
| 1984 | Spain (J. Cañizares and J. Rivero) |
| 1985 | Canada (D. Halldorson and D. Barr) |
| 1986 | not held |
| 1987 | Wales (I. Woosnam and D. Llewellyn) |

**Ryder Cup**

| year | result | tied | place |
|------|--------|------|-------|
| 1979 | United States 16, Great Britain 10 | 2 | White Sulphur Springs, W.Va., U.S. |
| 1981 | United States 18, Great Britain 9 | 1 | Walton Heath, Surrey, Eng. |
| 1983 | United States 13, Great Britain 12 | 3 | Palm Beach Gardens, Fla., U.S. |
| 1985 | Europe 16, United States 11 | 1 | Belfry, West Midlands, Eng. |
| 1987 | Europe 13, United States 11 | 4 | Dublin, Ohio, U.S. |

**Curtis Cup**

| year | result | tied | place |
|------|--------|------|-------|
| 1978 | United States 12, Britain and Ireland 4 | 2 | Rye, N.Y., U.S. |
| 1980 | United States 11, Britain and Ireland 3 | 4 | Chepstow, Gwent, Wales |
| 1982 | United States 14, Britain and Ireland 3 | 1 | Denver, Colo., U.S. |
| 1984 | United States 9, Britain and Ireland 8 | 1 | Muirfield, East Lothian, Scot. |
| 1986 | Britain and Ireland 11, United States 3 | 4 | Hutchinson, Kan., U.S. |

## GREYHOUND RACING

**British Greyhound Derby**

| year | winning dog | time (s) | year | winning dog | time (s) |
|------|-------------|----------|------|-------------|----------|
| 1980 | Indian Joe | 29.69 | 1984 | Whisper Wishes | 29.43 |
| 1981 | Parkdown Jet | 29.57 | 1985 | Pagan Swallow | 29.04* |
| 1982 | Laurie's Panther | 29.60 | 1986 | Tico | 28.69 |
| 1983 | I'm Slippy | 29.40 | 1987 | Signal Spark | 28.83 |

*In 1985 the distance was lowered from 500 m to 480 m.

# GYMNASTICS

**World Gymnastics Championships—men**

| year | all-around team | all-around individual | horizontal bar | parallel bars |
|------|------|------|------|------|
| 1983 | China | D. Bilozerchev (U.S.S.R.) | D. Bilozerchev (U.S.S.R.)* A. Pogotrlov (U.S.S.R.)* | Lou Yun (China)* V. Artemov (U.S.S.R.)* |
| 1984 | United States | Gushiken K. (Japan) | Morisue S. (Japan) | B. Conner (U.S.) |
| 1985 | U.S.S.R. | Y. Korolyov (U.S.S.R.) | Tong Fei (China) | S. Kroll (E.Ger.)* V. Mogilny (U.S.S.R.)* |
| 1987 | U.S.S.R. | D. Bilozerchev (U.S.S.R.) | D. Bilozerchev (U.S.S.R.) | V. Artemov (U.S.S.R.) |

| year | pommel horse | rings | vault | floor exercise |
|------|------|------|------|------|
| 1983 | D. Bilozerchev (U.S.S.R.) | D. Bilozerchev (U.S.S.R.) | A. Akopyan (U.S.S.R.) | Tong Fei (China) |
| 1984 | Li Ning (China)* P. Vidmar (U.S.)* | Gushiken K. (Japan)* Li Ning (China)* | Lou Yun (China) | Li Ning (China) |
| 1985 | V. Mogilny (U.S.S.R.) | Li Ning (China)* Y. Korolyov (U.S.S.R.)* | Y. Korolyov (U.S.S.R.) | Tong Fei (China) |
| 1987 | D. Bilozerchev (U.S.S.R.) Z. Borkai (Hung.) | Y. Korolyov (U.S.S.R.) | S. Kroll (E.Ger.) Lou Yun (China) | Lou Yun (China) |

*Tied.

O. Omelyanchik: (1985)
EILEEN LANGSLEY—SUPERSPORT

Y. Korolyov: all-around individual world gymnastics championships (1985)
EILEEN LANGSLEY—SUPERSPORT

**World Gymnastics Championships—women**

| year | all-around team | all-around individual | balance beam |
|------|------|------|------|
| 1983 | U.S.S.R. | N. Yurchenko (U.S.S.R.) | O. Mostepanova (U.S.S.R.) |
| 1984 | Romania | M.L. Retton (U.S.) | E. Szabo (Rom.)* S. Pauca (Rom.)* |
| 1985 | U.S.S.R. | E. Shushunova (U.S.S.R.)* O. Omelyanchik (U.S.S.R.)* | D. Silvas (Rom.) |
| 1987 | Romania | A. Dobre (Rom.) | A. Dobre (Rom.) |

| year | uneven parallel bars | vault | floor exercise |
|------|------|------|------|
| 1983 | M. Gnauck (E.Ger.) | B. Stoyanova (Bulg.) | E. Szabo (Rom.) |
| 1984 | J. McNamara (U.S.)* Ma Yanhong (China)* | E. Szabo (Rom.) | E. Szabo (Rom.) |
| 1985 | G. Fahnrich (E.Ger.) | E. Shushunova (U.S.S.R.) | O. Omelyanchik (U.S.S.R.) |
| 1987 | D. Silvas (Rom.) E. Thuemmler (E.Ger.) | E. Shushunova (U.S.S.R.) | E. Shushunova (U.S.S.R.) D. Silvas (Rom.) |

*Tied.

# HORSE RACING

**The Derby**

| year | horse | jockey | owner | trainer |
|------|------|------|------|------|
| 1983 | Teenoso | L. Piggott | E. Moller | G. Wragg |
| 1984* | Secreto | C. Roche | L. Miglitti | D. O'Brian |
| 1985 | Slip Anchor | S. Cauthen | Lord H. de Walden | H. Cecil |
| 1986 | Shahrastani | W.R. Swinburn | Aga Khan IV | M.R. Stoute |
| 1987 | Reference Point | S. Cauthen | L. Freedman | H. Cecil |

*Record time—2 min 12 s.

**The St. Leger**

| year | horse | jockey | owner | trainer |
|------|------|------|------|------|
| 1983 | Sun Princess | W. Carson | Sir M. Sobell | W. Hern |
| 1984 | Comanche Run | L. Piggott | I. Allen | L. Cumani |
| 1985 | Oh So Sharp | S. Cauthen | Sheikh Mohammed | H. Cecil |
| 1986 | Moon Madness | P. Eddery | Duchess of Norfolk | J. Dunlop |
| 1987 | Reference Point | S. Cauthen | L. Freedman | H. Cecil |

**Triple Crown champions—British**

| year | winner |
|------|------|
| 1915 | Pommern |
| 1917 | Gay Crusader |
| 1918 | Gainsborough |
| 1935 | Bahram |
| 1970 | Nijinsky |

**2,000 Guineas**

| year | horse | jockey | owner | trainer |
|------|------|------|------|------|
| 1983 | Lomond | P. Eddery | R. Sangster | V. O'Brien |
| 1984 | El Gran Señor | P. Eddery | R. Sangster | V. O'Brien |
| 1985 | Shadeed | L. Piggott | M. al-Maktoum | M. Stoute |
| 1986 | Dancing Brave | G. Starkey | K. Abdullah | G. Harwood |
| 1987 | Don't Forget Me | W. Carson | J. Horgan | R. Hannon |

*The American Thoroughbred classics*

### The Kentucky Derby

| year | horse | jockey | owner | trainer |
|------|-------|--------|-------|---------|
| 1983 | Sunny's Halo | E. Delahoussaye | D.J. Foster | D. Cross, Jr. |
| 1984 | Swale | L. Pincay | Claiborne Farm | W. Stephens |
| 1985 | Spend a Buck | A. Cordero, Jr. | D. Diaz | C. Gambolati |
| 1986 | Ferdinand | W. Shoemaker | E. Keck | C. Whittingham |
| 1987 | Alysheba | C. McCarron | D. & P. Scharbauer | J. Van Berg |

### The Preakness Stakes

| year | horse | jockey | owner | trainer |
|------|-------|--------|-------|---------|
| 1983 | Deputed Testamony | D. Miller | F.P. Sears | J.W. Boniface |
| 1984 | Gate Dancer | A. Cordero, Jr. | Kenneth Opstein | J. Van Berg |
| 1985 | Tank's Prospect | P. Day | E.V. Klein | D.W. Lukas |
| 1986 | Snow Chief | A. Solis | C. Grinsted, B. Rochelle | M. Stute |
| 1987 | Alysheba | C. McCarron | D. & P. Scharbauer | J. Van Berg |

### The Belmont Stakes

| year | horse | jockey | owner | trainer |
|------|-------|--------|-------|---------|
| 1983 | Caveat | L. Pincay | A. Belmont, others | W. Stephens |
| 1984 | Swale | L. Pincay | Claiborne Farrn | W. Stephens |
| 1985 | Creme Fraiche | E. Maple | E. Moran | W. Stephens |
| 1986 | Danzig Connection | C. McCarren | H. de Kwiatkowski | W. Stephens |
| 1987 | Bet Twice | C. Perret | Cisley Stable | J. Croll |

*Harness racing*

### The Hambletonian Trot

| year | horse | driver |
|------|-------|--------|
| 1983 | Duenna | S. Dancer |
| 1984 | Historic Freight | B. Webster |
| 1985 | Prakas | B. O'Donnell |
| 1986 | Nuclear Kosmos | U. Thoresen |
| 1987 | Mack Lobell | J. Campbell |

*Australian Thoroughbred racing*

### Melbourne Cup

| year | horse | jockey | owner | trainer |
|------|-------|--------|-------|---------|
| 1983 | Kiwi | J. Cassidy | Mr. & Mrs. E.S. Lupton | E.S. Lupton |
| 1984 | Black Knight | P. Cook | R. Holmes A'Court | G.M. Hanlon |
| 1985 | What a Nuisance | P. Hyland | Mr. & Mrs. L.J. Williams | J.F. Meagher |
| 1986 | At Talaq | M. Clarke | Sheikh al-Maktoum | C. Hayes |
| 1987 | Kensei | L. Olsen | Six-man syndicate | L. Bridge |

### Triple Crown champions—U.S.

| year | horse |
|------|-------|
| 1946 | Assault |
| 1948 | Citation |
| 1973 | Secretariat |
| 1977 | Seattle Slew |
| 1978 | Affirmed |

Alysheba (front left): Kentucky Derby (1987)
BILL STRAUS

Edmonton Oilers: Stanley Cup (1987)
CANAPRESS PHOTO SERVICE

## ICE HOCKEY

### The Stanley Cup

| season | winner | runner-up | games |
|--------|--------|-----------|-------|
| 1982–83 | New York Islanders | Edmonton Oilers | 4–0 |
| 1983–84 | Edmonton Oilers | New York Islanders | 4–1 |
| 1984–85 | Edmonton Oilers | Philadelphia Flyers | 4–1 |
| 1985–86 | Montreal Canadiens | Calgary Flames | 4–1 |
| 1986–87 | Edmonton Oilers | Philadelphia Flyers | 4–3 |

### World Amateur Hockey Championships

| year | winner |
|------|--------|
| 1983 | U.S.S.R. |
| 1984 | U.S.S.R. |
| 1985 | Czechoslovakia |
| 1986 | U.S.S.R. |
| 1987 | Sweden |

# ICE SKATING

### World figure skating champions—women

| year | winner |
|------|--------|
| 1983 | R. Sumners (U.S.) |
| 1984 | K. Witt (E.Ger.) |
| 1985 | K. Witt (E.Ger.) |
| 1986 | D. Thomas (U.S.) |
| 1987 | K. Witt (E.Ger.) |

### World figure skating champions—pairs

| year | winners |
|------|---------|
| 1983 | E. Valova, O. Vasilev (U.S.S.R.) |
| 1984 | B. Underhill, P. Martini (Can.) |
| 1985 | E. Valova, O. Vasilev (U.S.S.R.) |
| 1986 | Ye. Gordeyeva, S. Grinkov (U.S.S.R.) |
| 1987 | Ye. Gordeyeva, S. Grinkov (U.S.S.R.) |

### World figure skating champions—men

| year | winner |
|------|--------|
| 1983 | S. Hamilton (U.S.) |
| 1984 | S. Hamilton (U.S.) |
| 1985 | A. Fadeyev (U.S.S.R.) |
| 1986 | B. Boitano (U.S.) |
| 1987 | B. Orser (Can.) |

### World ice dancing champions

| year | winners |
|------|---------|
| 1983 | J. Torvill, C. Dean (U.K.) |
| 1984 | J. Torvill, C. Dean (U.K.) |
| 1985 | N. Bestemyanova, A. Bukin (U.S.S.R.) |
| 1986 | N. Bestemyanova, A. Bukin (U.S.S.R.) |
| 1987 | N. Bestemyanova, A. Bukin (U.S.S.R.) |

K. Kania: World all-around speed skating champion (1987)
DAVID MADISON—DUOMO

Ye. Gordeyeva, S. Grinkov: figure skating (1987)
STEVEN E. SUTTON—DUOMO

N. Bestemyanova, A. Bukin: ice dancing (1986)
AGENCE VANDYSTADT—ALLSPORT

### World all-around speed skating champions—men

| year | winner |
|------|--------|
| 1983 | R. Falk-Larssen (Nor.) |
| 1984 | O. Bozhiev (U.S.S.R.) |
| 1985 | H. Vergeer (Neth.) |
| 1986 | D. Jansen (U.S.) |
| 1987 | N. Gulyaev (U.S.S.R.) |

### World all-around speed skating champions—women

| year | winner |
|------|--------|
| 1983 | A. Schöne (E.Ger.) |
| 1984 | K. Enke (E.Ger.) |
| 1985 | A. Schöne (E.Ger.) |
| 1986 | K. Kania (E.Ger.) |
| 1987 | K. Kania (E.Ger.) |

### World Speed Skating Sprint Championships

| year | men | women |
|------|-----|-------|
| 1983 | Kuroiwa A. (Japan) | K. Enke (E.Ger.) |
| 1984 | G. Boucher (Can.) | K. Enke (E.Ger.) |
| 1985 | I. Zhelezovsky (U.S.S.R.) | C. Rothenburger (E.Ger.) |
| 1986 | I. Zhelezovsky (U.S.S.R.) | K. Kania (E.Ger.) |
| 1987 | Kuroiwa A. (Japan) | K. Kania (E.Ger.) |

# JUDO

### World Judo Championships

| year | open weights | 60 kg | 65 kg | 71 kg |
|------|--------------|-------|-------|-------|
| 1979 | Endo S. (Japan) | T. Rey (Fr.) | N. Solodukhin (U.S.S.R.) | Katsuki K. (Japan) |
| 1981 | Yamashita Y. (Japan) | Moriwaki Y. (Japan) | Kashiwazaki K. (Japan) | Park Chong Hak (S.Kor.) |
| 1983 | Saito H. (Japan) | K. Tletseri (U.S.S.R.) | N. Solodukhin (U.S.S.R.) | Nakanishi H. (Japan) |
| 1985 | Masaki Y. (Japan) | Hosokawa S. (Japan) | Y. Sololov (U.S.S.R.) | Keun Ahn Byung (S. Kor.) |
| 1987 | Ogawa N. (Japan) | Kim Jae Yup (S.Kor.) | Yamamoto Y. (Japan) | M. Swain (U.S.) |

| year | 78 kg | 86 kg | 95 kg | + 95 kg |
|------|-------|-------|-------|---------|
| 1979 | Fujii S. (Japan) | D. Ultsch (E.Ger.) | T. Khubuluri (U.S.S.R.) | Y. Yamashita (Japan) |
| 1981 | N. Adams (U.K.) | B. Tchoullouyan (Fr.) | T. Khubuluri (U.S.S.R.) | Y. Yamashita (Japan) |
| 1983 | Hikage N. (Japan) | D. Ultsch (E.Ger.) | A. Preschel (E.Ger.) | Y. Yamashita (Japan) |
| 1985 | Hikage N. (Japan) | P. Seisenbacher (Austria) | Sugai H. (Japan) | Chul Cho Yong (S.Kor.) |
| 1987 | Okada H. (Japan) | F. Canu (France) | Sugai H. (Japan) | G. Veritchev (U.S.S.R.) |

C. Hanauer: Gold Cup championship (1987)
CARYN LEVY—ALLSPORT

## MOTORBOAT RACING

### Gold Cup Championship

| year | boat | driver |
|---|---|---|
| 1983 | Atlas Van Lines | C. Hanauer |
| 1984 | Atlas Van Lines | C. Hanauer |
| 1985 | Miller American | C. Hanauer |
| 1986 | Miller American | C. Hanauer |
| 1987 | Miller American | C. Hanauer |

## POLO

### Coronation Cup

| year | result | | | | |
|---|---|---|---|---|---|
| 1983 | England | 8 | New Zealand | 6 |
| 1984 | Rest of the World | 8 | England | 7 |
| 1985 | Mexico | 8 | England I | 6 |
| 1986 | Mexico | 8 | England | 4 |
| 1987 | United States | 8 | England | 5 |

### Copa de las Americas

| year | winner |
|---|---|
| 1936 | Argentina |
| 1950 | Argentina |
| 1966 | Argentina |
| 1969 | Argentina |
| 1980 | Argentina |

## RODEO

### Men's World All-Around Rodeo Championship

| year | winner |
|---|---|
| 1983 | R. Cooper |
| 1984 | D. Pickett |
| 1985 | L. Feild |
| 1986 | L. Feild |
| 1987 | L. Feild |

## ROWING

### World Rowing Championship—men

| year | single sculls | min:s | double sculls | min:s | coxed pairs | min:s |
|---|---|---|---|---|---|---|
| 1983 | P.-M. Kolbe (W.Ger.) | 6:49.88 | T. Lange, U. Heppner (E.Ger.) | 6:20.17 | T. Greiner, U. Diessner (E.Ger.) | 6:49.75 |
| 1984 | P. Karppinen (Fin.) | 7:00.24 | B. Lewis, P. Enquist (U.S.) | 6:36.87 | G. Abbagnale, C. Abbagnale (Italy) | 7:05.99 |
| 1985 | P. Karppinen (Fin.) | 6:48.08 | U. Heppner, T. Lange (E.Ger.) | 6:15.49 | G. Abbagnale, C. Abbagnale (Italy) | 6:53.40 |
| 1986 | P.-M. Kolbe (W.Ger.) | 6:54.09 | A. Belgeri, I. Pescialli (Italy) | 6:33.64 | A. Holmes, S. Redgrave (U.K.) | 6:51.66 |
| 1987 | T. Lange (E.Ger.) | 7:36.41 | D. Yorddanov, V. Dadev (Bulg.) | 7:03.33 | G. Abbagnale, C. Abbagnale (Italy) | 7:40.81 |

| year | coxless pairs | min:s | coxed fours | min:s | coxless fours | min:s | eights | min:s |
|---|---|---|---|---|---|---|---|---|
| 1983 | C. Ertel, U. Sauerbrey (E.Ger.) | 6:35.85 | New Zealand | 6:13.89 | West Germany | 5:57.02 | New Zealand | 5:34.39 |
| 1984 | P. Iosub, V. Toma (Rom.) | 6:45.39 | Great Britain | 6:18.64 | New Zealand | 6:03.48 | Canada | 5:41.32 |
| 1985 | N. Pimenov, Yu. Pimenov (U.S.S.R.) | 6:38.39 | U.S.S.R. | 6:07.23 | West Germany | 6:00.19 | U.S.S.R. | 5:33.71 |
| 1986 | Yu. Pimenov, N. Pimenov (U.S.S.R.) | 6:42.37 | East Germany | 6:03.81 | United States | 6:03.53 | Australia | 5:33.54 |
| 1987 | S. Redgrave, A. Holmes (U.K.) | 7:11.20 | East Germany | 6:41.74 | East Germany | 6:39.70 | United States | 5:58.83 |

### World Rowing Championships—women

| year | single sculls | min:s | double sculls | min:s | quadruple sculls | min:s |
|---|---|---|---|---|---|---|
| 1983 | J. Hampe (E.Ger.) | 3:36.51 | J. Schenk, M. Schröter (E.Ger.) | 3:13.44 | U.S.S.R. | 3:02.48 |
| 1984 | V. Racila (Rom.) | 3:40.68 | M. Popescu, E. Oleniuc (Rom.) | 3:26.75 | Romania | 3:14.11 |
| 1985 | C. Linse (E.Ger.) | 7:40.37 | S. Schwabe, M. Schröter (E.Ger.) | 6:58.80 | East Germany | 6:22.47 |
| 1986 | J. Hampe (E.Ger.) | 7:29.60 | S. Schwabe, B. Schramm (E.Ger.) | 6:57.71 | East Germany | 6:13.91 |
| 1987 | M. Georgieva (Bulg.) | 8:59.26 | S. Madina, V. Ninova (Bulg.) | 7:47.89 | East Germany | 6:58.42 |

| year | coxless pairs | min:s | coxed fours | min:s | eights | min:s |
|---|---|---|---|---|---|---|
| 1983 | M. Gasch, S. Fruhlich (E.Ger.) | 3:26.68 | East Germany | 3:11.18 | U.S.S.R. | 2:56.22 |
| 1984 | R. Arba, E. Horvat (Rom.) | 3:32.60 | Romania | 3:19.30 | United States | 2:59.80 |
| 1985 | R. Arba, E. Florea (Rom.) | 7:25.08 | East Germany | 6:50.08 | U.S.S.R. | 6:14.00 |
| 1986 | R. Arba, O. Homeghi (Rom.) | 7:12.20 | Romania | 6:43.86 | U.S.S.R. | 6:08.76 |
| 1987 | R. Arba, O. Homeghi (Rom.) | 8:00.73 | Romania | 7:30.12 | Romania | 6:55.61 |

### The Diamond Challenge Sculls

| year | winner | min:s |
|---|---|---|
| 1983 | S. Redgrave (Marlow R.C.) | 8:23 |
| 1984 | C.L. Baillieu (Leander Club) | 7:57 |
| 1985 | S. Redgrave (Marlow R.C.) | 8:28 |
| 1986 | B. Eltang (Den.) | * |
| 1987 | P.-M. Kolbe (Ruder-Club Hamburg) | 7:52 |

*Not rowed out.

### Grand Challenge Cup

| year | winner | min:s |
|---|---|---|
| 1983 | London R.C. and University of London | 6:26 |
| 1984 | Leander Club and London R.C. | 6:22 |
| 1985 | Harvard University, U.S. | 6:27 |
| 1986 | Nautilus R.C. | 6:18 |
| 1987 | Soviet Army | 6:11 |

## SKIING

### World Nordic Skiing Championships—men

| year | 15-km cross-country | 30-km cross-country | 50-km cross-country | relay |
|---|---|---|---|---|
| 1980 | T. Wassberg (Swed.) | N. Zimyatov (U.S.S.R.) | N. Zimyatov (U.S.S.R.) | U.S.S.R. |
| 1982 | O. Braa (Nor.) | T. Eriksson (Swed.) | T. Wassberg (Swed.) | Norway; U.S.S.R. (tied) |
| 1984 | G. Svan (Swed.) | N. Zimyatov (U.S.S.R.) | T. Wassberg (Swed.) | Sweden |
| 1985 | K. Haerhoenen (Fin.) | G. Svan (Swed.) | G. Svan (Swed.) | Norway |
| 1987 | M. Albarello (Italy) | T. Wassberg (Swed.) | M. De Zoll (Italy) | Sweden |

### World Nordic Skiing Championships—women

| year | 5-km cross-country | 10-km cross-country | 20-km cross-country | relay |
|---|---|---|---|---|
| 1980 | R. Smetanina (U.S.S.R.) | B. Petzold (E.Ger.) | | E.Ger. |
| 1982 | B. Aunli (Nor.) | B. Aunli (Nor.) | R. Smetanina (U.S.S.R.) | Norway |
| 1984 | M.-L. Hämäläinen (Fin.) | M.-L. Hämäläinen (Fin.) | M.-L. Hämäläinen (Fin.) | Norway |
| 1985 | A. Boe (Nor.) | A. Boe (Nor.) | G. Nykelmo (Nor.) | U.S.S.R. |
| 1987 | M. Matikainen (Fin.) | A. Jahren (Nor.) | M.-H. Westin (Swed.) | U.S.S.R. |

### World Nordic Skiing Championships—ski jump

| year | jump | special jump | combined |
|---|---|---|---|
| 1980 | A. Innauer (Austria) | J. Törmänen (Fin.) | U. Wehling (E.Ger.) |
| 1982 | A. Kogler (Austria) | M. Nykänen (Fin.) | T. Sandberg (Nor.) |
| 1984 | J. Weissflog (E.Ger.) | M. Nykänen (Fin.) | T. Sandberg (Nor.) |
| 1985 | J. Weissflog (E.Ger.) | P. Bergerud (Nor.) | H. Weinbach (W.Ger.) |
| 1987 | J. Parma (Czech.) | A. Felder (Austria) | T. Loekken (Nor.) |

### World Alpine Skiing Championships—slalom

| year | men's slalom | men's giant slalom | women's slalom | women's giant slalom |
|---|---|---|---|---|
| 1980 | I. Stenmark (Swed.) | I. Stenmark (Swed.) | H. Wenzel (Liech.) | H. Wenzel (Liech.) |
| 1982 | I. Stenmark (Swed.) | S. Mahre (U.S.) | E. Hess (Switz.) | E. Hess (Switz.) |
| 1984 | P. Mahre (U.S.) | M. Julen (Switz.) | P. Magoni (Italy) | D. Armstrong (U.S.) |
| 1985 | J. Nilsson (Swed.) | M. Wasmaier (W.Ger.) | P. Pelen (Fr.) | D. Roffe (U.S.) |
| 1987 | F. Woerndl (W.Ger.) | P. Zurbriggen (Switz.) | E. Hess (Switz.) | V. Schneider (Switz.) |

P. Zurbriggen: world alpine skiing
championships—giant slalom (1987)
STEVE POWELL—ALLSPORT

### World Alpine Skiing Championships—downhill

| year | men | women |
|---|---|---|
| 1980 | L. Stock (Austria) | A. Moser-Proell (Austria) |
| 1982 | H. Weirather (Austria) | G. Sorensen (Can.) |
| 1984 | B. Johnson (U.S.) | M. Figini (Switz.) |
| 1985 | P. Zurbriggen (Switz.) | M. Figini (Switz.) |
| 1987 | P. Müller (Switz.) | M. Walliser (Switz.) |

### World Alpine Skiing Championships—combined

| year | men | women |
|---|---|---|
| 1974 | F. Klammer (Austria) | F. Serrat (Fr.) |
| 1976 | G. Thoeni (Italy) | R. Mittermaier (W.Ger.) |
| 1978 | A. Wenzel (Liech.) | A. Moser-Proell (Austria) |
| 1982 | M. Vion (Fr.) | E. Hess (Switz.) |
| 1987 | M. Girardelli (Lux.) | E. Hess (Switz.) |

E. Hess: world alpine skiing championships—combined (1987)
DAVID CANNON—ALLSPORT

### Alpine World Cup

| year | men | women |
|---|---|---|
| 1983 | P. Mahre (U.S.) | T. McKinney (U.S.) |
| 1984 | P. Zurbriggen (Switz.) | E. Hess (Switz.) |
| 1985 | M. Girardelli (Lux.) | M. Figini (Switz.) |
| 1986 | M. Girardelli (Lux.) | M. Walliser (Switz.) |
| 1987 | P. Zurbriggen (Switz.) | M. Walliser (Switz.) |

### Nordic World Cup

| year | men | women |
|---|---|---|
| 1983 | A. Zavyalov (U.S.S.R.) | M.-L. Hämäläinen (Fin.) |
| 1984 | G. Svan (Swed.) | M.-L. Hämäläinen (Fin.) |
| 1985 | G. Svan (Swed.) | A. Boe (Nor.) |
| 1986 | G. Svan (Swed.) | M. Matikainen (Fin.) |
| 1987 | T. Mogren (Swed.) | M. Matikainen (Fin.) |

## SQUASH RACKETS

### British Open Championships—men

| year | winner |
|---|---|
| 1982–83 | J. Khan (Pak.) |
| 1983–84 | J. Khan (Pak.) |
| 1984–85 | J. Khan (Pak.) |
| 1985–86 | J. Khan (Pak.) |
| 1986–87 | J. Khan (Pak.) |

### British Open Championships—women

| year | winner |
|---|---|
| 1982–83 | V. Cardwell (Australia) |
| 1983–84 | S. Devoy (N.Z.) |
| 1984–85 | S. Devoy (N.Z.) |
| 1985–86 | S. Devoy (N.Z.) |
| 1986–87 | S. Devoy (N.Z.) |

### World Open Championships—men

| year | winner |
|---|---|
| 1983–84 | Jah. Khan (Pak.) |
| 1984–85 | Jah. Khan (Pak.) |
| 1985–86 | Jah. Khan (Pak.) |
| 1986–87 | R. Norman (N.Z.) |
| 1987–88 | Jan. Khan (Pak.) |

### World Open Championships—women

| year | winner |
|---|---|
| 1979–80 | H. McKay (Australia) |
| 1981–82 | R. Thorne (Australia) |
| 1983–84 | V. Cardwell (Australia) |
| 1985–86 | S. Devoy (N.Z.) |
| 1987–88 | S. Devoy (N.Z.) |

# SWIMMING

## World Swimming Championships—men

|  | freestyle | | | | backstroke | |
|---|---|---|---|---|---|---|
| year | 100 m | 200 m | 400 m | 1,500 m | 100 m | 200 m |
| 1975 | A. Coan (U.S.) | T. Shaw (U.S.) | T. Shaw (U.S.) | T. Shaw (U.S.) | R. Matthes (E.Ger.) | Z. Verraszto (Hung.) |
| 1978 | D. McCagg (U.S.) | B. Forrester (U.S.) | V. Salnikov (U.S.S.R.) | V. Salnikov (U.S.S.R.) | B. Jackson (U.S.) | J. Vassallo (U.S.) |
| 1982 | J. Woithe (E.Ger.) | M. Gross (W.Ger.) | V. Salnikov (U.S.S.R.) | V. Salnikov (U.S.S.R.) | D. Richter (E.Ger.) | R. Carey (U.S.) |
| 1986 | M. Biondi (U.S.) | M. Gross (W.Ger.) | R. Henkel (W.Ger.) | R. Henkel (W.Ger.) | I. Polyansky (U.S.S.R.) | I. Polyansky (U.S.S.R.) |

|  | breaststroke | | butterfly | | individual medley | |
|---|---|---|---|---|---|---|
|  | 100 m | 200 m | 100 m | 200 m | 200 m | 400 m |
| 1975 | D. Wilkie (U.K.) | D. Wilkie (U.K.) | G. Jagenburg (U.S.) | B. Forrester (U.S.) | A. Hargitay (Hung.) | A. Hargitay (Hung.) |
| 1978 | W. Kusch (W.Ger.) | N. Nevid (U.S.) | J. Bottom (U.S.) | M. Bruner (U.S.) | G. Smith (Can.) | J. Vassallo (U.S.) |
| 1982 | S. Lundquist (U.S.) | V. Davis (Can.) | M. Gribble (U.S.) | M. Gross (W.Ger.) | A. Sidorenko (U.S.S.R.) | R. Prado (Braz.) |
| 1986 | V. Davis (Can.) | J. Szabo (Hung.) | P. Morales (U.S.) | M. Gross (W.Ger.) | T. Darnyi (Hung.) | T. Darnyi (Hung.) |

|  | team relays | | | diving | |
|---|---|---|---|---|---|
|  | 4 × 100-m freestyle | 4 × 200-m freestyle | 4 × 100-m medley | springboard | platform |
| 1975 | United States | West Germany | United States | P. Boggs (U.S.) | K. Dibiasi (Italy) |
| 1978 | United States | United States | United States | P. Boggs (U.S.) | G. Louganis (U.S.) |
| 1982 | United States | United States | United States | G. Louganis (U.S.) | G. Louganis (U.S.) |
| 1986 | United States | East Germany | United States | G. Louganis (U.S.) | G. Louganis (U.S.) |

## World Swimming Championships—women

|  | freestyle | | | | backstroke | |
|---|---|---|---|---|---|---|
| year | 100 m | 200 m | 400 m | 800 m | 100 m | 200 m |
| 1975 | K. Ender (E.Ger.) | S. Babashoff (U.S.) | S. Babashoff (U.S.) | J. Turrall (Australia) | U. Richter (E.Ger.) | B. Treiber (E.Ger.) |
| 1978 | B. Krause (E.Ger.) | C. Woodhead (U.S.) | T. Wickham (Australia) | T. Wickham (Australia) | L. Jezek (U.S.) | L. Jezek (U.S.) |
| 1982 | B. Meineke (E.Ger.) | A. Verstappen (Neth.) | C. Schmidt (E.Ger.) | K. Linehan (U.S.) | K. Otto (E.Ger.) | C. Sirch (E.Ger.) |
| 1986 | K. Otto (E.Ger.) | H. Friedrich (E.Ger.) | H. Friedrich (E.Ger.) | A. Strauss (E.Ger.) | B. Mitchell (U.S.) | C. Sirch (E.Ger.) |

|  | breaststroke | | butterfly | | individual medley | |
|---|---|---|---|---|---|---|
|  | 100 m | 200 m | 100 m | 200 m | 200 m | 400 m |
| 1975 | H. Anke (E.Ger.) | H. Anke (E.Ger.) | K. Ender (E.Ger.) | R. Kother (E.Ger.) | K. Heddy (U.S.) | U. Tauber (E.Ger.) |
| 1978 | J. Bogdanova (U.S.S.R.) | L. Kachushite (U.S.S.R.) | J. Pennington (U.S.) | T. Caulkins (U.S.) | T. Caulkins (U.S.) | T. Caulkins (U.S.) |
| 1982 | U. Geweniger (E.Ger.) | S. Varganova (U.S.S.R.) | M.T. Meagher (U.S.) | I. Geissler (E.Ger.) | P. Schneider (E.Ger.) | P. Schneider (E.Ger.) |
| 1986 | S. Gerasch (E.Ger.) | S. Hörner (E.Ger.) | K. Gressler (E.Ger.) | M. Meagher (U.S.) | K. Otto (E.Ger.) | K. Nord (E.Ger.) |

|  | team relays | | | diving | |
|---|---|---|---|---|---|
|  | 4 × 100-m freestyle | 4 × 200-m freestyle | 4 × 100-m medley | springboard | platform |
| 1975 | East Germany |  | East Germany | I. Kalinina (U.S.S.R.) | J. Ely (U.S.) |
| 1978 | United States |  | United States | I. Kalinina (U.S.S.R.) | I. Kalinina (U.S.S.R.) |
| 1982 | East Germany |  | East Germany | M. Neyer (U.S.) | W. Wyland (U.S.) |
| 1986 | East Germany | East Germany | East Germany | Gao Min (China) | Chen Lin (China) |

M. Gross: world swimming championships—200 m (1986)

# TABLE TENNIS

## World Table Tennis Championships—men

| year | St. Bride's Vase (singles) | Iran Cup (doubles) | Swaythling Cup (team) |
|---|---|---|---|
| 1981 | Guo Yuehua (China) | Cai Zhenhua, Li Zhenshi (China) | China |
| 1983 | Guo Yuehua (China) | D. Surbek, Z. Kalinic (Yugos.) | China |
| 1985 | Jiang Jialiang (China) | M. Appelgren, U. Carlsson (Swed.) | China |
| 1987 | Jiang Jialiang (China) | Chen Longcan, Wei Qingguang (China) | China |

## World Table Tennis Championships—women

| year | G. Geist Prize (singles) | W.J. Pope Trophy (doubles) | Corbillon Cup (team) |
|---|---|---|---|
| 1981 | Tong Ling (China) | Cao Yanhua, Zhang Deying (China) | China |
| 1983 | Cao Yanhua (China) | Shen Jianping, Dai Lili (China) | China |
| 1985 | Cao Yanhua (China) | Dai Lili, Geng Lijuan (China) | China |
| 1987 | He Zhili (China) | Hyun Jung Hwa, Yang Young Ja (S.Kor.) | China |

## World Table Tennis Championships—mixed

| year | Heydusek Prize |
|---|---|
| 1979 | Liang Geliang, Ge Xinai (China) |
| 1981 | Xie Saike, Huang Junqun (China) |
| 1983 | Guo Yuehua, Ni Xialian (China) |
| 1985 | Cai Zhenhua, Cao Yanhua (China) |
| 1987 | Hui Jun, Geng Lijuan (China) |

## Table Tennis World Cup

| year | winner |
|---|---|
| 1983 | M. Appelgren (Swed.) |
| 1984 | Jiang Jialiang (China) |
| 1985 | Chen Xinhua (China) |
| 1986 | Chen Longcan (China) |
| 1987 | Teng Yi (China) |

# TENNIS

M. Navratilova: Wimbledon—singles (women) (1987)
ALLSPORT

P. Cash: Wimbledon—singles (men) (1987)
COLORSPORT/SIPA

### All-England (Wimbledon) Tennis Championships—singles

| year | men | women |
|------|-----|-------|
| 1983 | J. McEnroe (U.S.) | M. Navratilova (U.S.) |
| 1984 | J. McEnroe (U.S.) | M. Navratilova (U.S.) |
| 1985 | B. Becker (W.Ger.) | M. Navratilova (U.S.) |
| 1986 | B. Becker (W.Ger.) | M. Navratilova (U.S.) |
| 1987 | P. Cash (Australia) | M. Navratilova (U.S.) |

### French Open Tennis Championships—singles

| year | men | women |
|------|-----|-------|
| 1983 | Y. Noah (Fr.) | C. Evert Lloyd (U.S.) |
| 1984 | I. Lendl (Czech.) | M. Navratilova (U.S.) |
| 1985 | M. Wilander (Swed.) | C. Evert Lloyd (U.S.) |
| 1986 | I. Lendl (Czech.) | C. Evert Lloyd (U.S.) |
| 1987 | I. Lendl (Czech.) | S. Graf (W.Ger.) |

### All-England (Wimbledon) Tennis Championships—doubles

| year | men | women |
|------|-----|-------|
| 1983 | J. McEnroe/P. Fleming | M. Navratilova/P. Shriver |
| 1984 | J. McEnroe/P. Fleming | M. Navratilova/P. Shriver |
| 1985 | H. Gunthardt/B. Taroczy | K. Jordan/E. Smylie |
| 1986 | J. Nystrom/M. Wilander | M. Navratilova/P. Shriver |
| 1987 | R. Seguso/K. Flach | C. Kohde-Kilsche/H. Sukova |

### French Open Tennis Championships—doubles

| year | men | women |
|------|-----|-------|
| 1983 | A. Jarryd/H. Simonsson | R. Fairbank/C. Reynolds |
| 1984 | H. Leconte/Y. Noah | M. Navratilova/P. Shriver |
| 1985 | M. Edmondson/K. Warwick | M. Navratilova/P. Shriver |
| 1986 | J. Fitzgerald/T. Smid | M. Navratilova/A. Temesvari |
| 1987 | R. Seguso/A. Jarryd | M. Navratilova/P. Shriver |

### United States Open Tennis Championships—singles

| year | men | women |
|------|-----|-------|
| 1983 | J. Connors (U.S.) | M. Navratilova (U.S.) |
| 1984 | J. McEnroe (U.S.) | M. Navratilova (U.S.) |
| 1985 | I. Lendl (Czech.) | H. Mandlikova (Czech.) |
| 1986 | I. Lendl (Czech.) | M. Navratilova (U.S.) |
| 1987 | I. Lendl (Czech.) | M. Navratilova (U.S.) |

### Australian Open Tennis Championships—singles

| year | men | women |
|------|-----|-------|
| 1983 | J. Kriek (S.Af.) | C. Evert Lloyd (U.S.) |
| 1984 | M. Wilander (Swed.) | M. Navratilova (U.S.) |
| 1985 | M. Wilander (Swed.) | C. Evert Lloyd (U.S.) |
| 1986 | S. Edberg (Swed.) | M. Navratilova (U.S.) |
| 1987 | S. Edberg (Swed.) | H. Mandlikova (Czech.) |

### United States Open Tennis Championships—doubles

| year | men | women |
|------|-----|-------|
| 1983 | J. McEnroe/P. Fleming | M. Navratilova/P. Shriver |
| 1984 | J. Fitzgerald/T. Smid | M. Navratilova/P. Shriver |
| 1985 | K. Flach/R. Seguso | C. Kohde-Kilsche/H. Sukova |
| 1986 | A. Gómez/S. Zivojinovic | M. Navratilova/P. Shriver |
| 1987 | S. Edberg/A. Jarryd | M. Navratilova/P. Shriver |

### Australian Open Tennis Championships—doubles

| year | men | women |
|------|-----|-------|
| 1983 | J. Alexander/J. Fitzgerald | M. Navratilova/P. Shriver |
| 1984 | M. Edmondson/P. McNamee | M. Navratilova/P. Shriver |
| 1985 | M. Edmondson/S. Stewart | M. Navratilova/P. Shriver |
| 1986 | P. Annacone/C. van Rensburg | M. Navratilova/P. Shriver |
| 1987 | S. Edberg/A. Jarryd | M. Navratilova/P. Shriver |

### Davis Cup

| year | winner |
|------|--------|
| 1983 | Australia |
| 1984 | Sweden |
| 1985 | Sweden |
| 1986 | Australia |
| 1987 | Sweden |

### Wightman Cup

| year | winner |
|------|--------|
| 1983 | United States |
| 1984 | United States |
| 1985 | United States |
| 1986 | United States |
| 1987 | United States |

### Federation Cup

| year | winner | runner-up | results |
|------|--------|-----------|---------|
| 1983 | Czechoslovakia | West Germany | 2–1 |
| 1984 | Czechoslovakia | Australia | 2–1 |
| 1985 | Czechoslovakia | United States | 2–1 |
| 1986 | United States | Czechoslovakia | 3–0 |
| 1987 | West Germany | United States | 2–1 |

# VOLLEYBALL

### World Volleyball Championships

| year | men | women | year | men | women |
|------|-----|-------|------|-----|-------|
| 1976 | Poland | Japan | 1982 | U.S.S.R. | China |
| 1978 | U.S.S.R. | Cuba | 1984 | United States | China |
| 1980 | U.S.S.R. | U.S.S.R. | 1986 | United States | China |

# WRESTLING

## World Wrestling Championships—Freestyle

| year | 48 kg | 52 kg | 57 kg | 62 kg | 68 kg |
|---|---|---|---|---|---|
| 1982 | S. Kornilayev (U.S.S.R.) | H. Reich (E.Ger.) | A. Beloglazov (U.S.S.R.) | S. Beloglazov (U.S.S.R.) | M. Kharachura (U.S.S.R.) |
| 1983 | Kim Hwan Cher (N.Kor.) | V. Iordanov (Bulg.) | S. Beloglasov (U.S.S.R.) | V. Alekseev (U.S.S.R.) | A. Fadzaev (U.S.S.R.) |
| 1984 | R. Weaver (U.S.) | S. Trstena (Yugos.) | Tomiyama H. (Japan) | R. Lewis (U.S.) | You I.T. (S.Kor.) |
| 1985 | Kim Chol Hwan (N.Kor.) | V. Iordanov (Bulg.) | S. Beloglasov (U.S.S.R.) | V. Alekseev (U.S.S.R.) | A. Fadzaev (U.S.S.R.) |
| 1986 | Y. Li (N.Kor.) | K. Sik (N.Kor.) | S. Beloglasov (U.S.S.R.) | K. Isaev (U.S.S.R.) | A. Fadzaev (U.S.S.R.) |
| 1987 | Li Jae Sik (N.Kor.) | V. Iordanov (Bulg.) | S. Beloglasov (U.S.S.R.) | J. Smith (U.S.) | A. Fadzaev (U.S.S.R.) |

| year | 74 kg | 82 kg | 90 kg | 100 kg | 130 kg |
|---|---|---|---|---|---|
| 1982 | L. Kemp (U.S.) | T. Dzgoev (U.S.S.R.) | U. Neupert (E.Ger.) | I. Mate (U.S.S.R.) | S. Khasimikov (U.S.S.R.) |
| 1983 | D. Schultz (U.S.) | T. Dzgoev (U.S.S.R.) | P. Naniev (U.S.S.R.) | A. Khadartzev (U.S.S.R.) | S. Khasimikov (U.S.S.R.) |
| 1984 | D. Schultz (U.S.) | M. Schultz (U.S.) | E. Banach (U.S.) | L. Banach (U.S.) | B. Baumgartner (U.S.) |
| 1985 | R. Cascaret (Cuba) | M. Schultz (U.S.) | B. Scherr (U.S.) | L. Khabelov (U.S.S.R.) | D. Goberdzhishvili (U.S.S.R.) |
| 1986 | R. Cascaret (Cuba) | V. Modozyan (U.S.S.R.) | M. Khadartsev (U.S.S.R.) | A. Khadartsev (U.S.S.R.) | B. Baumgartner (U.S.) |
| 1987 | A. Varaev (U.S.S.R.) | M. Schultz (U.S.) | M. Khadartsev (U.S.S.R.) | L. Khabelov (U.S.S.R.) | A. Khadartsev (U.S.S.R.) |

## World Wrestling Championships—Greco-Roman style

| year | 48 kg | 52 kg | 57 kg | 62 kg | 68 kg |
|---|---|---|---|---|---|
| 1982 | T. Kazarashvili (U.S.S.R.) | B. Pashayan (U.S.S.R.) | P. Mikhalik (Pol.) | R. Swierad (Pol.) | G. Yermilov (U.S.S.R.) |
| 1983 | B. Tsenov (Bulg.) | B. Pashayan (U.S.S.R.) | Ito M. (Japan) | H. Lahtinen (Fin.) | T. Sipila (Fin.) |
| 1984 | V. Maenza (Italy) | Miyahara A. (Japan) | P. Passarelli (W.Ger.) | Kim W.K. (S.Kor.) | V. Lisjak (Yugos.) |
| 1985 | M. Allakhverdiev (U.S.S.R.) | J. Ronningen (Nor.) | S. Balov (Bulg.) | J. Vangelov (Bulg.) | S. Negrisan (Rom.) |
| 1986 | M. Allakhverdiev (U.S.S.R.) | S. Dudyaev (U.S.S.R.) | E. Ivanov (Bulg.) | K. Madzhidov (U.S.S.R.) | L. Dzhulfalakyan (U.S.S.R.) |
| 1987 | M. Allakhverdiev (U.S.S.R.) | P. Roque (Cuba) | P. Mourier (France) | J. Vanguelov (Bulg.) | A. Abaev (U.S.S.R.) |

| year | 74 kg | 82 kg | 90 kg | 100 kg | 130 kg |
|---|---|---|---|---|---|
| 1982 | S. Rusa (Rom.) | T. Abkhasava (U.S.S.R.) | R. Anderson (Swed.) | R. Wroclawski (Pol.) | N. Dinev (Bulg.) |
| 1983 | M. Mamiashvili (U.S.S.R.) | T. Abkhasava (U.S.S.R.) | I. Kanygin (U.S.S.R.) | A. Dimitrov (Bulg.) | E. Arthuine (U.S.S.R.) |
| 1984 | J. Salomaki (Fin.) | I. Draica (Rom.) | S. Fraser (U.S.) | V. Andrei (Rom.) | J. Blatnick (U.S.) |
| 1985 | M. Mamiashvili (U.S.S.R.) | B. Daras (Pol.) | M. Houck (U.S.) | A. Dimitrov (Bulg.) | I. Rostotsky (U.S.S.R.) |
| 1986 | M. Mamiashvili (U.S.S.R.) | not awarded | A. Malina (Poland) | T. Gaspar (Hung.) | T. Johansson (Swed.) |
| 1987 | J. Salomaki (Fin.) | T. Komaromi (Hung.) | V. Popov (U.S.S.R.) | G. Guedekhaorui (U.S.S.R.) | I. Rostorotski (U.S.S.R.) |

# YACHTING

## America's Cup

| year | winning yacht | owner | skipper | losing yacht | owner |
|---|---|---|---|---|---|
| 1970 | Intrepid (U.S.) | Intrepid syndicate | W. Ficker | Gretel II (Australia) | Sir F. Packer and syndicate |
| 1974 | Courageous (U.S.) | Courageous syndicate | T. Hood | Southern Cross (Australia) | A. Bond |
| 1977 | Courageous (U.S.) | Courageous syndicate | T. Turner | Australia (Australia) | A. Bond and syndicate |
| 1980 | Freedom (U.S.) | Maritime College at Fort Schuyler Foundation, Inc. | D. Conner | Australia (Australia) | A. Bond and syndicate |
| 1983 | Australia II (Australia) | A. Bond and syndicate | J. Bertrand | Liberty (U.S.) | Maritime College at Fort Schuyler Foundation, Inc. |
| 1987 | Stars & Stripes (U.S.) | Sail America syndicate | D. Conner | Kookaburra III (Australia) | K. Parry and syndicate |

Stars & Stripes: America's Cup (1987)
LEO MASON—PHOTO TRENDS

## Bermuda Race

| year | winning yacht | owner |
|---|---|---|
| 1978 | Babe | A. Gay |
| 1980 | Holger Danske | R. Wilson |
| 1982 | Brigadoon III | B. Morton |
| 1984 | Pamir | F. Curren, Jr. |
| 1986 | Silver Star and Puritan | D. Clarke D. Robinson |

## Transpacific Race

| year | winning yacht | owner |
|---|---|---|
| 1979 | Arriba | D. Choate |
| 1981 | Sweet Okole | D. Treadway |
| 1983 | Bravura | I. Loube |
| 1985 | Montgomery Street | D. Denning |
| 1987 | Merlin | D. Campion |

## Fastnet Cup

| year | winning yacht | owner |
|---|---|---|
| 1981 | Mordicus | G. Taylor, C. Volters (Belg.) |
| 1983 | Condor | B. Bell (U.K.) |
| 1985 | Panda | P. Whipp (U.K.) |
| 1987 | Irish Independent Pelt | S. Fein (Ire.) |

# Television and Radio

The dominance of radio and television as the source of the world's entertainment and news could be demonstrated by the number of receivers in use. According to the latest statistics provided by Unesco, 1,412,137,000 radio sets and 797,583,400 television sets were providing news and entertainment as of 1983. About one-third of the radio sets—479 million—were in the U.S., and about 180 million were in the Soviet Union. Other countries with large numbers of radios included Japan (85 million), the U.K. (56 million), France (47 million), and West Germany (25 million).

The U.S. and U.S.S.R. also ranked first and second in the number of television sets in use—185.3 million in the U.S. and some 101 million in the U.S.S.R. Japan was third (67.2 million sets), followed by the U.K. (27 million), West Germany (22.1 million), and France (20.5 million).

**Organization of Services.** In August 1987 the U.S. Federal Communications Commission (FCC) took the historic—and controversial—step of repealing the fairness doctrine, a policy that had been in effect since 1949. An outgrowth of the public interest standard set in the Communications Act of 1934, the doctrine required broadcasters to cover controversial issues of public importance and to do so in a balanced manner.

Broadcasters had long complained that the doctrine violated the First Amendment guarantee of freedom of the press. The FCC, following an inquiry in 1985, tended to agree; it concluded that the doctrine inhibited rather than enhanced free speech because it discouraged broadcasters from engaging in controversial programming for fear of generating fairness complaints. Uncertain of its authority in the matter and aware that key members of the U.S. Senate and House of Representatives favoured retention of the doctrine, the commission deferred to Congress on the question of what should be done regarding it. In September 1986, however, a three-judge panel of the U.S. Court of Appeals in Washington, D.C., held that the doctrine was not a binding statutory obligation, as many lawyers had long argued, but a public interest standard. The commission, therefore, was free to repeal it and did so.

The commission's action did not end the matter. During the spring of 1987 both houses of Congress by large margins passed a bill codifying the fairness doctrine into law. U.S. Pres. Ronald Reagan, who had spoken out in support of broadcasters' First Amendment rights, vetoed the legislation in June, and its backers were unable to muster the votes needed to override the veto.

In another controversial action the FCC, responding to complaints about off-colour material on the air, toughened its standards on alleged indecency. In letters to three radio stations and in an accompanying policy statement, a unanimous commission asserted that it would no longer rely on the narrow standard for indecency that had emerged from a U.S. Supreme Court case in 1978 involving a monologue by comedian George Carlin. The monologue, broadcast on a Pacifica Foundation noncommercial station in the afternoon, dealt with the seven words one could never say on television—the so-called seven dirty words. The FCC subsequently interpreted the high court's opinion to mean that broadcasters who aired repeatedly and before 10 PM the words describing sexual or excretory organs or functions contained in the monologue would be in violation of the standard. In the new policy statement, however, the commission said that it would consider indecent any language or material that depicted or described, in terms patently offensive as measured by community standards

for the broadcast medium, sexual or excretory activities or organs if broadcast at a time of day when there was a reasonable risk that children were in the audience. The FCC said that broadcasters could not assume that children would not be in their audience after 10 PM, nor would the repetitive use of the words regarded as offensive be an absolute requirement for a finding of indecency.

The commission's action, in April, received considerable attention in the press and on radio and television programs. Radio executives and on-air personalities throughout the U.S. expressed uncertainty about what kind of programming would violate the new standards and subject their stations to sanctions. They also saw the action as a violation of the First Amendment. The FCC, in response to the protests, agreed to reconsider its action, and in November it ruled that radio and television stations could broadcast indecent programming between the hours of midnight and 6 AM.

The surge of takeovers and mergers that remade much of the structure of the broadcasting business in 1986 slowed in 1987, but changes continued to be made. In January, for instance, the CBS Inc. board made permanent the election of William S. Paley, the company's 85-year-old founder, as chairman and Laurence Tisch, the company's largest stockholder, as president and chief executive officer. The men had held those positions on a temporary basis since former chairman Thomas Wyman was forced out in September 1986.

In July General Electric Co., new parent of NBC, agreed to sell the NBC Radio Network, the oldest broadcast network in the country. Westwood One, a network radio company based in Culver City, Calif., bought the four

RICHARD HOWARD

A family watches television while a people meter records their viewing habits. The new device, which keeps track of which members of a household, as well as how many households, view a particular program, quickly began to influence network programming choices.

Demonstrators at ABC headquarters in New York City protest the airing of "Amerika." The controversial television miniseries, which was set in the U.S. ten years after a Soviet takeover, was attacked months before it was broadcast. While peace activists argued that the miniseries would fuel anti-Soviet hysteria and some right-wing groups claimed it was too soft on Communism, UN representatives criticized its "portrayal of UN peacekeeping forces as brutal oppressors."
SUDHIR—PICTURE GROUP

NBC radio networks, including the 61-year-old NBC Radio Network, for $50 million. In October the FCC conditionally approved the acquisition by George Gillett—group broadcaster and ski-resort owner—of controlling interest in six of Storer Communications Inc.'s television stations for $650 million.

Changes were not confined to the marketplace. An FCC administrative law judge issued an order in August that could, if affirmed, remake a substantial portion of the broadcasting industry. Judge Edward J. Kuhlmann ruled that RKO General Inc., which had been a broadcast licensee for 48 years, lacked the character qualification to be a licensee. The ruling was issued in a 22-year-old case in which RKO had been struggling to hold onto its license for KHJ-TV Los Angeles, but it applied as well to proceedings in which the licenses of 13 other RKO stations were at stake. No case ever before decided by the FCC had involved dishonesty comparable to RKO's, Kuhlmann wrote in his decision. Broadcast station brokers estimated the total worth of the 14 stations at $1 billion. RKO appealed Judge Kuhlmann's decision to the full commission.

Cable television continued to expand. The A. C. Nielsen Co., the leading TV audience measurement service, estimated in July that the number of cable-equipped homes in the U.S. had crept up to 43,260,000, about two million more than 12 months earlier and representing 49.5% of the nation's 87.4 million TV households.

The enthusiasm in the U.S. for videocassette recorders (VCRs), which record and play back television programs as well as playing prerecorded movies and other programming, continued unabated in 1987. The Electronic Industries Association reported that as of June, 45% of all households—about 37,175,000—possessed with the equipment, compared with 35% a year earlier.

One of the major technological developments of the year in television had to do not with the equipment used to record or transmit pictures and sound but, rather, with the means for learning about the viewing audience. People meters were introduced by both A. C. Nielsen Co. and AGB Television Research, a subsidiary of Audits of Great Britain Inc., as the means for informing the television networks and the advertisers not only about how many households were viewing particular programs but which members of those households. Members of the sample

households pushed a button on a key pad that informed a black box on top of the set who was watching what program. The information was relayed daily to the rating service.

In Europe the pace of deregulation of broadcasting services accelerated. The most dramatic change took place in France with the completed privatization of the major state-owned channel, TF1, under the control of the construction magnate Francis Bouygues. However, the two commercial rivals of TF1, La Cinq and M6, both suffered from low audiences and faced a series of financial crises.

Belgium passed legislation to allow advertising on national television, and both the French-speaking and Flemish-speaking regions were given permission to transmit their own private channels. In Finland the third channel, financed by both advertising and subscriptions, opened its service in Helsinki and Tampere as a joint venture between the state broadcasting organization Yleisradio and Nokia, a large Finnish conglomerate. Denmark's second channel began regional transmission, and there were plans for three new private channels in Spain and two in Portugal.

Italian broadcasting was caught up in a fierce competitive battle among the three state-owned networks of RAI, the three private networks of Silvio Berlusconi, and a new private network, Odeon; a number of smaller private channels were also struggling to survive. An extensive reshuffling of senior management at RAI followed an exodus of popular screen performers to the Berlusconi organization.

Satellite broadcasting continued to expand in Europe, though on a shaky financial base. SuperChannel, operated by a consortium of U.K. companies and promising to present the "best of British TV" to continental audiences, was launched in January but within six months faced financial setbacks. The "best of British" promise was abandoned, and the channel began supplying programs in Dutch and German. In July MTV Europe launched a satellite service featuring 24 hours of music video. The channel was owned 50% by British publisher Robert Maxwell's Mirror Group Newspapers, 25% by British Telecom, and 25% by Viscom, the owners of MTV in the U.S.

In the U.K. a management upheaval took place at the British Broadcasting Corporation (BBC) with the departure of the director general, Alasdair Milne, and the arrival of Michael Checkland (see BIOGRAPHIES), an accountant and the first non-program maker to hold the position of director general for 25 years. Checkland introduced a new, young management team, among them John Birt from the Independent Television company London Weekend Television, who announced a controversial merging of the BBC's television and radio news and current affairs departments. Under Checkland the BBC appeared to be taking a more commercial stance, with such innovations as a closed-signal subscription service for medical practitioners during the close-down hours on its second channel.

In Australia, where there had been controversial changes in the management of the state-owned Australian Broadcasting Commission (ABC), there was promise of a new broadcasting bill. It was to be aimed at making the existing legislation easier to administer and pruned of "unnecessary burdens currently suffered by licensees and the Australian Broadcasting Tribunal."

**Programming.** NBC continued to have the most popular television programs in the U.S. in 1987. For the second year in a row, it easily topped its two rivals, winning the ratings competition in 27 of the 30 weeks during the broadcast year that ended in April. NBC was the only network to report an increase in profits. CBS, which once was the undisputed leader in the ratings contest, was second and ABC was third, both with unprecedentedly low figures. CBS's profit dropped by more than $100 million, while ABC actually lost money.

Despite its success during the last two years, NBC began the new season with eight new series. CBS started with nine new ones, and ABC had eight. In spite of network concerns about program costs, 31 of the programs scheduled for the new year were hour-long action shows, the most expensive kind to produce. There was, for instance, CBS's "Tour of Duty," the first regularly scheduled television series about U.S. troops in the Vietnam war. Others were "Private Eye," on NBC, and ABC's "Buck James," which was inspired by a Houston, Texas, surgeon who was also a rancher. All were among the new programs that the three networks had ordered.

The new Fox Broadcasting Co. network was having problems with the competition. Low ratings made it necessary in May to drop comedienne Joan Rivers as host of the late night program that had been introduced on Oct. 9, 1986, as the cornerstone of the network.

The networks were not only competing with one another. They were also competing with cable television—which was offering an increasing amount of original programming—and with videotaped movies for VCRs. Independent stations also were offering competition in the form of original material, rather than reruns of network series. Forty-five new first-run syndicated programs began appearing on the U.S.'s independent stations in September. They covered the spectrum of programming, from situation comedy to drama and adventure to talk show and public affairs.

Public television also remained a source of frequently competitive programming. Public Broadcasting Service said that, according to the Nielsen Television Index, 56.8% of all U.S. television households—that is, 49.6 million households—tuned in to PBS at least once a week during the ten months ended in August. For prime time the comparable figures were 34.3% and 29.9 million households. While some of public broadcasting's major successes in 1987, such as "Eyes on the Prize," "Shoah," and "The Story of English," could be considered educational as well as entertaining, the 1987–88 year included the noncommercial medium's first original comedy anthology, "Trying Times." Aimed at the teenage audience, it was one of 14 new series being broadcast by PBS.

These competitive factors were having an effect on network viewing as the 1987–88 season got under way. The three-network prime time viewing level fell 10% to an average 44.9 rating for the first six weeks of the season compared with the same period a year earlier. The networks' share of those actually watching television in prime time fell four points, to an average 75% over the same period. The loss was attributed in large part to the alternative programming available, but there was also a 2.5% drop—to an average 60.3%—in the level of homes using television. That, in turn, was ascribed to the change in the technology of counting viewers—to the use of people meters—as well as to the comparatively small markets of the two World Series teams—St. Louis and Minneapolis—and to the strike by the National Football League players.

Among the major media events of the year were the hearings held by the special select committees of the U.S. Senate and House of Representatives on the Iran-*contra* affair. The hearings began in May and continued, with some interruptions, into August. Cable News Network, the 24-

A Polish locomotive engineer is one of the many people interviewed in "Shoah," an epic documentary film by Claude Lanzmann shown on Public Broadcasting Service that examines Nazi concentration camps through the accounts of eyewitnesses and participants.

hour all-news service, and public television provided live gavel-to-gavel coverage.

For the first time in several years, the cost of the rights to televise professional and college football did not increase in 1987. According to a survey by *Broadcasting* magazine, the total paid was about $570 million, the same amount as in 1986. The flattening out of costs followed several years of multimillion-dollar losses on the games by ABC, CBS, and NBC. Indeed, the amount that the three networks were paying the National Football League annually under new three-year contracts was $425 million, a 14.1% decrease from 1986. The NFL made up for the loss with a three-year, $153 million contract with cable television sports programmer ESPN, which would cover 13 games during each of the three years. College football cost ABC, CBS, and ESPN $46.5 million under the first year of new four-year contracts. A year earlier the three had paid $40.5 million.

The cost of rights to cover baseball was continuing to rise. According to a *Broadcasting* survey, broadcast and cable rights payments increased about 9%, to $349,850,000. Of that, $153,350,000 was paid by local broadcasters and cable operators, an increase of 9.6%. Most of the remainder came from ABC and NBC.

Basketball also was generating revenue for professional teams and colleges. While precise totals were unavailable, the National Basketball Association had two contracts that would pay its members $56 million in 1987, $43 million from CBS and $13 million from Turner Broadcasting System, whose superstation WTBS Atlanta transmitted the games to cable systems throughout the country. The Atlantic Coast Conference, one of the strongest college leagues in the country, was receiving a reported $35 million over five years under a contract with a joint venture of Raycom Sports and Jefferson Pilot Teleproductions.

One of the major programming stories of 1987 was ABC's production of the miniseries "Amerika," which stretched over 14½ hours in February. A fictional story of the U.S. ten years after a bloodless takeover by the U.S.S.R., the series was attacked, months before broadcast, by representatives of both the left and the right. Even officials of the UN criticized it because of its portrayal of what appeared to be a UN peacekeeping force composed of rapists and arsonists. The controversy was sufficient to persuade Chrysler Corp. to withdraw its $7 million worth of commercials from the film. For his part, the man with primary creative responsibility for the film—writer, executive producer, and director Donald Wrye—defended it as an effort to probe the question of what could happen if the people in the U.S. did not take seriously their role in maintaining the viability of its democracy. The miniseries was not good business for ABC; it lost money on the $40 million production, and ratings were disappointing.

As for radio programming, a *Broadcasting* magazine survey found, as did a similar survey a year earlier, that the broadly based adult contemporary music format was the most widely programmed sound among the top ten stations in the top 50 markets in the country in 1987. The adult-contemporary format was defined as including variations on the soft contemporary and rock music approaches. The second most popular sound was found to be contemporary. However, radio programming was not limited to music. According to an Associated Press study, 70% of the radio listeners paid as much attention to news and information as they did to music. Among radio network personalities, newsman and commentator Paul Harvey of ABC remained the most popular according to Statistical Research Inc.'s annual RADAR spring report.

As in 1986, NBC emerged triumphant not only in the ratings contest but in the number of Emmy awards won— 32, compared with 19 by ABC and 15 by CBS. PBS won eight Emmys and syndicated shows garnered one. A major factor in NBC's success was its new series "L.A. Law." It was named the outstanding drama series and won awards for Alfre Woodard as the outstanding guest performer in a drama series, Gregory Hoblit for outstanding direction in a drama series, and Steven Bochco and Terry Louise Fisher for outstanding writing in a drama series. Another NBC winner was "The Golden Girls," cited in three awards, including outstanding comedy series. ABC's awards included one for Bruce Willis of "Moonlighting" as outstanding lead actor in a drama series and one for Gena Rowlands of "The Betty Ford Story" as outstanding lead actress in a miniseries or special.

The broadcast of the Emmy awards ceremony itself made news in that the new Fox Broadcasting Co. managed to take the event away from the three established networks, which had rotated it among themselves for the previous 31 years. However, the four-hour program was not only the longest in the history of the event; its ratings were the lowest in the event's history.

In Europe peak viewing hours continued to be dominated by imports from the U.S. in the "Dallas" and "Dynasty" genre, together with action-adventure formats and local adaptations of game shows and quiz programs. There were strong indications, however, that viewers were rejecting the more violent U.S. programs, such as "The Equalizer" and "Miami Vice."

This was particularly true in the U.K., where a multiple murder in the Berkshire village of Hungerford appeared to imitate screen violence. This provoked a national debate on the possible link between crime in the streets and fiction on the screen. The debate was aggravated by what was seen as a failure to remove certain offensive and brutalizing scenes from a much-publicized U.S. miniseries, "Sins," which was transmitted during mid-evening family viewing time. In the wake of such concerns, the BBC removed a number of imported programs from the schedules, and the Independent Broadcasting Authority reduced the number of U.S. programs in peak time.

In international competition the U.K. performed exceptionally well in the Prix Italia, winning both drama awards with the BBC's black comedy "After Pilkington" and Yorkshire's "The Scab," based on the previous year's miners' strike. NOS, the network of The Netherlands, won the music prize with "The Flood," and Denmark had the best documentary, "Yesterday." At the Montreux (Switz.) Golden Rose awards, the Swedish network Sverigas Television won with a program aptly entitled "The Prize," a humorous and satirical approach to the history of the Nobel Prize.

In a survey of the year's most popular programs outside the U.S. conducted by *Electronic Media Magazine,* game shows, talk programs, and domestic drama scored highly. In West Germany it was "Die Schwarzwaldklinic" (Black Forest Hospital), a medical drama; in Sweden "Varuhuset" (Department Store), a drama set in a Stockholm store; in Switzerland "Bonsoir," an evening talk program with Thierry Masselet as host; and in France "Le Roue de la fortune," a local version of the U.S. game show "Wheel of Fortune."

One of the remarkable TV events of the year was the screening of "Shoah," a nine-hour epic film by French producer Claude Lansmann of eyewitness accounts of the wartime Nazi persecutions of the Jews in Poland. The film, originally made for theatres, was shown on TV in Poland,

France, the U.K., and the U.S. In Poland it aroused deep passions and was condemned by Polish government leader Gen. Wojciech Jaruzelski as "viciously anti-Polish." In France more than 35 million viewers, the majority under age 36, watched the film when it was screened over four consecutive days in the wake of the Klaus Barbie (*see* BIOGRAPHIES) trial in midyear.

Competition among the privatized channels in France had considerable impact on program policy. La Cinq, the channel owned by publisher Robert Hersant and Silvio Berlusconi of Italy, wooed from the former state-owned TF1 the producer and TV satirist Stephane Collaro, whose weekly program "Collaricocoshow," featuring caricatures of leading politicians, proved to be a popular audience attraction.      (MARTIN JACKSON; LAWRENCE B. TAISHOFF; LEONARD ZEIDENBERG)

**Amateur Radio.** Ham radio operators over the years had put their hobby to use during times of earthquake, flood, and other emergencies. They continued in the tradition in 1987, providing communications services for fire fighters battling forest fires in the western U.S. and in behalf of police and rescue workers at the scene of an airliner crash at Detroit's Metro Airport in August.

The FCC reported 430,201 ham operators in the U.S. as of September 29, up from 421,082 a year earlier. The American Radio Relay League said that there were close to two million ham operators throughout the world, an increase of more than 300,000 over the 1,625,000 reported in 1986.

(LAWRENCE B. TAISHOFF; LEONARD ZEIDENBERG)

*See also* Industrial Review: *Advertising; Telecommunications;* Motion Pictures; Music.

This article updates the *Macropædia* article BROADCASTING.

# Theatre

**Great Britain and Ireland.** Criticism of official arts policies and cuts in grants-in-aid voiced by the Arts Council of Great Britain (ACGB) and by performing arts representatives hardened after the reelection of a Conservative government in the June general elections and the reappointment of Arts Minister Richard Luce for another term. However, Luce silenced much criticism by adopting a three-year funding timetable and boosting the ACGB grant from

April 1988 by 17%, from £138 million to £160 million, and nearly doubling the Business Sponsorship Incentive Scheme to £3 million over a three-year period. Welcome news was the reopening of the rebuilt Playhouse Theatre after 35 years, the go-ahead given to Sam Wanamaker's Globe Theatre project, the Society of West End Theatre (SWET) deal permitting the sale of theatre ticket tokens at post offices, and the launching of the Linbury Prize for Stage Design. The first British Theatre Museum, in Covent Garden, London, was formally opened on April 23, the anniversary of Shakespeare's birth.

Latest ACGB figures for theatre grants revealed a drop in real terms because of inflation; the National Theatre (NT) received £7.8 million and the Royal Shakespeare Company (RSC) £5.2 million. Though attendance at the RSC's three Stratford theatres had risen, the three in London (including the Mermaid, newly leased for the transfer of classical dramas from Stratford) showed a deficit of £1.2 million. This would, however, be offset by the first three-year sponsorship grant of £1.1 million from the Royal Insurance company. A similar attendance increase was realized by the NT, where Sir Peter Hall was to be succeeded as manager by Richard Eyre in 1988. Terry Hands took over from Trevor Nunn as artistic director of the RSC.

The NT won the majority of the annual awards given by the *Evening Standard (ES), Plays and Players (PP), Drama Magazine (DM)*, and *Time Out (TO)*. *Antony and Cleopatra* won Hall the *ES* best director award, Judi Dench three best actress awards as Cleopatra (*ES, PP,* and *DM*), and Michael Bryant the *PP* best supporting actor award as Enobarbus. Alan Ayckbourn's black comedy of corrupt suburban business and sexual morals, *A Small Family Business*, won the *ES* best play award and his production of Arthur Miller's *A View from the Bridge* the *PP* best director award, while Michael Gambon won two awards (*ES* and *PP*) for his towering Eddie in the latter. Two more *DM* awards were captured by the NT; a special prize went to Thelma Holt for organizing the international season with companies from West Berlin, Stockholm, Tokyo, and Moscow, and the best supporting actress award was won by Pernilla Östergren for her moving Ophelia in Ingmar Bergman's *Hamlet* from Stockholm.

The adaptations of Eugène Sue's *The Wandering Jew* and Carlo Goldoni's *Countrymania* staged at the NT by Michael Alfreds compared unfavourably with Michael

JOHN HAYNES

Stock traders vie for shares in *Serious Money,* a play by Caryl Churchill that depicted the London equivalent of Wall Street's insider-trading scandals.

Cast members of *The Music Man* perform at Beijing's (Peking's) Tianchao Theatre. It was the first American musical to be produced in China since the revolution in 1949.

FORREST ANDERSON—GAMMA/ LIAISON

scabrous Hogarthian comedy; José Triana's *Worlds Apart*, a study by an exiled Cuban of crippling tradition back home; Tony Marchant's *Speculators*, a satire on London's financial bullyboys; and Vladimir Gubaryev's *Sarcophagus*, a scathing Soviet view of the Chernobyl disaster. The only awards won by the RSC (all from *DM*) went to Brian Cox for his roles in three Stratford plays, including that of a cynical adman in Doug Lucie's *Fashion*; the latter shared the *DM* best play award with newcomer Stephen Bill's euthanasia comedy, *Curtains*, at the Hampstead. *Curtains* also won the *PP* most promising new play award and earned Ralph Nossek the *DM* best supporting actor award.

In the public sector the Royal Court Theatre picked up three awards (best play and best comedy from *ES*, *PP*, and *TO*) for Caryl Churchill's boisterous verse satire on financial malpractices, *Serious Money*, while the *PP* best supporting actress award was won by Saskia Reeves for her excitable Honey in *Who's Afraid of Virginia Woolf?* at the Young Vic. Other *TO* awards were given to Jacqueline Holborough (author) and Maggie McCarthy (actress) for *The Garden Girls* at the Bush; Caroline Pickles in *Body Cell* at the Soho Poly; and Bruce Myers, for his two-handed *The Dybbuk*, and Patrick Mason, director of the mythic *The Great Hunger*, both at the Almeida.

Other plays at the Almeida included Mario Vargas Llosa's nightmarish *Kathy and the Hippopotamus*, the Robert Wilson/Heiner Müller *Hamletmachine*, and a dramatization of Ted Hughes's poem *Gaudete*. Hugh Ross won a *TO* award for his quaint Malvolio in Declan Donnellan's production of *Twelfth Night* (which also won a *DM* directing award) for the Cheek by Jowl touring company. A similar *DM* award went to Michael Pennington and Michael Bogdanov, founders of the newly formed English Shakespeare Company, for the three King Henry plays. Highlights were, at the Lyric in Hammersmith, Molière's *The Hypochondriac*, with Tom Courtenay; at the Greenwich, Elijah Moshinsky's version of *Three Sisters*; at the Tricycle, *The Amen Corner* by James Baldwin (*see* OBITUARIES); at the Royal Court, the Jonathan Miller/Michael Hastings adaptation of Ryszard Kapuscinski's *The Emperor*; at the Donmar Warehouse, Simon Moore and Jane Prowse's *Up on the Roof*; and at the newly opened Offstage Downstairs, John Logan's *Never the Sinner*.

A record-breaking West End box-office hit was Stephen

Rudman's staging of Turgenev's *Fathers and Sons*, with its authentic Russian atmosphere, and with *Waiting for Godot*, for which Samuel Beckett's recent revisions were used. Maggie Smith returned to the NT for Hall's stimulating production of Stephen Poliakoff's *Coming in to Land*. Two women directors made their debuts at the NT: Di Trevis with Molière's *School for Wives* and Federico García Lorca's *Yerma*, and Sarah Pia Anderson with Ibsen's *Rosmersholm*. Two open-stage productions at the Cottesloe were Nick Darke's Cornish miners' documentary *Ting Tang Mine* and David Edgar's *Entertaining Strangers*.

Most RSC transfers from Stratford, even Michael Bogdanov's modern-dress *Romeo and Juliet*, lacked the usual appeal, but Terry Hands's romantic *The Winter's Tale* and his handling of Genet's *The Balcony* were admirable. Novelties at the Pit were Nick Dear's *The Art of Success*, a

MICHAEL LE POER TRENCH

Sombre staging sets the atmosphere for the lavish "rock opera" version of Victor Hugo's *Les Misérables*. After marked success in London and Washington, it opened on Broadway with $11 million in advanced ticket sales, breaking U.S. theatrical records.

Sondheim's *Follies*, which won four *PP* and *DM* awards for best musical and best design. British novelties included a tour of *King Lear* with Anthony Quayle and Kate O'Mara; the birth of Kenneth Branagh's touring Renaissance Company; Simon Gray's *Melon*, with Alan Bates; Jeffrey Archer's *Beyond Reasonable Doubt;* and Peter Shaffer's *Lettice and Lovage,* starring Maggie Smith.

The news that a bigger and better-funded festival would be staged for the 1988 Dublin millennium offset the year's setbacks in Ireland. The Field Day company's production of Stewart Parker's *Pentecost* won its author the Harvey Irish Theatre best writing award. Acting awards went to Kim McDonnell, performing the Project Theatre's one-man *The Diary of a Madman* from a wheelchair, and to Catherine Byrne for the leads in *Yerma* at the Peacock and in John B. Keane's *The Field*, an Abbey revival. Ben Barnes won the directing award for *The Field* and for *Les Liaisons Dangereuses* at the Gate, while Barbara Bradshaw and Brian Power took the technical award for four Project Theatre plays.

**France, Italy, Spain, Low Countries, Greece.** The City of Paris prizes for playwriting and for acting went to the late Copi (d. 1987) for his dramatic output and to Robin Renucci, playing Camille in the first uncut performance of Paul Claudel's *The Satin Slipper* at the Chaillot. Ariane Mnouchkine's Théâtre du Soleil, presenter of Hélène Sixous's *L'Indiade*, covering 12 years of recent Indian history, received the first European Communities prize ever awarded. The new Molière prizes were shared by dramatist Jasmina Reza; director Jean-Pierre Vincent; actor Philippe Caubère; actress Suzanne Flon; West German guest actress Ute Lampe in *Cabaret*, itself a winner of the best musical prize; and director Jérôme Savary, also for *Cabaret*. The critics' prizes went to Vincent (for *The Marriage of Figaro*); Robert Wilson for best foreign-language play; and Ezio Frigerio for the decor of Giorgio Strehler's revival of *The Threepenny Opera*.

Two new theatres, the city-owned Bastille and the National Theatre on the Hill, were built. However, the flow of new French plays slowed, and a larger number than ever of revivals of works by such veterans as Jean Anouilh (*see* OBITUARIES) and the late André Roussin (d. 1987) held the boards. Mammoth spectacles such as Robert Hossein's *The Lyons Mail Affair* at the Palais des Sports vied in popularity with smaller offerings like Loleh Bellon's *The Alienation*; Françoise Sagan's cynical comedy of old Vienna, *The Contrary Excess*; and Fernando Arrabal's latest theatre of panic drama, *A Weightlifter's Love Manual*. Other highlights were Gildas Bourdet's *Moonspittle* at the Théâtre de Ville; O'Neill's *Welded* at the Rond-Point, where Jean-Louis Barrault appointed Comédie Française actor Francis Huster to succeed him in 1988; and, at the Marigny, Sartre's version of Dumas's *Kean*, which won Sabine Haudepin a Molière award alongside Jean-Paul Belmondo, winner of the prestigious Brigadier prize.

In Italy *The Mechanical Pianola*, a new Italo-Russian version by the Russian Nikita Mikhalkov of Chekhov's untitled play (otherwise often known as *Platonov*), marked the return to the Roman stage after 20 years of Marcello Mastroianni. Among new plays Franco Brusati's *Gallant Conservation*, with Anna Proclemer and Gabriele Ferzetti, was among the most outstanding. Pirandello revivals included *Tonight We Improvise*, staged by Giuseppe Patroni Griffi, and *The Rules of the Game*, with Alberto Lionello. In Barcelona, Spain, the Teatre Josep Maria Flotats, renamed after its new Catalan director, staged *El Dret d'Escollir* (*Whose Life Is It Anyway?*) by Brian Clark. Nuria Espert's revival of *Yerma* was the hit of the East Berlin Festival.

Belgium's Europalia Festival, devoted to Austria, was host to German-speaking companies and local productions of Austrian dramas in French and Flemish. René Hainaux made his comeback at the Rideau in Pietro Pizzuti's *Leonardo*, while Anna Prucnal of France was featured in Joshua Sobol's *Ghetto* at the Belgian national theatre. In Amsterdam the 40th Holland Festival's bumper program ranged from Friedrich Hölderlin's verse-drama about Empedocles to Peter Sellars's updated version of Sophocles' *Ajax*. As an homage to Karolos Koun (*see* OBITUARIES), the Greek Drama Symposium in Delphi revived his famous production of Aristophanes' *The Birds*.

**Switzerland, West and East Germany, Austria.** Hans-Dieter Zeidler as Lear in a staging by France's Bernard Sobel and veteran Maria Becker in Achim Benning's revival of *The Physicists* were featured at the Zürich Schauspielhaus. Seen in Berlin during the city's 750th anniversary celebrations were: in West Berlin, Gaston Salvatore's *Stalin*, Peter Ustinov in the title role in his own *Beethoven's Tenth,* Jutte Lampe as Racine's Phèdre in the Peter Stein production, the Burgtheater's *Richard III* with Gert Voss, and Katharina Talbach's directing debut with *Macbeth* at the Schiller; in East Berlin, Heiner Müller's completion of Brecht's unfinished *The Downfall of Egoist Fatzer* with Ekkehard Schall, the Burgtheater's Heinrich von Kleist drama, *Die Hermannsschlacht,* and Mikhail Bulgakov's *The Master and Margarita*.

The Israeli Habimah's European tour brought it to West Berlin for the first time since 1930. Highlights in Vienna were the world premiere of Edward Albee's *Marriage Play*, directed by himself, in English; Angelika Hurwicz's production of *Puntila* at the People's; and Alfred Kirchner's production of Brecht's *Arturo Ui* at the Akademie Theatres.

**Eastern Europe, Scandinavia, Israel.** In the Soviet Union a prime example of the new policy of *glasnost* (openness) was Mikhail Shatrov's treatment of recent history in the Edward Sturua production at the Vakhtangov Theatre of *The Peace of Brest-Litovsk*, in which Trotsky and Bukharin speak their minds to Lenin. Eugène Ionesco and Beckett were performed for the first time in the U.S.S.R., and the new *Hamlet* at the Moscow Studio in the South West, under Viktor Belyakovich, made a rare impact at the Edinburgh Festival. Nikolay Gubenko became head of the Taganka after the death of Anatoly Efros (*see* OBITUARIES). Kazimierz Dejmek's new production of Mikolaj Rej's *The Life of Joseph* at Warsaw's Polski was presented at the East Berlin Festival, while Maciej Engler staged *The Master and Margarita* at the Contemporary Theatre in Warsaw.

Important productions in Hungary included *Three Sisters* and Jyörjy Szpiro's *Chickenhead* at the Jozsef Katona, Zsigmond Moricz's *Be Good unto Death* at the national theatre, and Barrie Stavis's *Coat of Many Colours* at the Debrecen Csokoni theatre. The Balustrade Theatre of Prague took its version of Mikhail Saltykov-Shchedrin's *The Death of Pazukhin* to the East Berlin Festival. First prize at the Yugoslav "bitef" Festival was shared by Tomás Ascher's Budapest production of *Three Sisters* and Andrzej Wajda's *Crime and Punishment* from Krakow.

At Copenhagen's Royal Theatre, East German director Peter Kupke produced Strindberg's *The Dance of Death* and Sam Besekow produced *Tales from the Vienna Woods*. The first staging of Ibsen's unabridged *Emperor and the Galilean* was seen in Tormod Skagestad's New Norwegian translation in Oslo, where the new manager at the national theatre, Kjetil Bang-Hansen, staged Knut Hamsun's *A Life of Violence*. The Royal Dramatic Theatre in Stockholm launched its bicentenary programs with Peter Oskarsson's fanciful production of C. J. L. Almqvist's *The*

*Queen's Jewels.* Highlights in Finland were the national theatre's *Tales from the Vienna Woods,* staged by Ascher, the Helsinki City Theatre's *Tartuffe,* and Astrid Lindgren's new children's play at the Swedish Theatre in Helsinki.

In Israel the Habimah celebrated its 70th birthday with a European tour of its three top productions—Steven Berkoff's *The Trial,* Yury Lyubimov's *Sunset,* and an Israeli play—while companies from Poland, the U.K., Ireland, and France headed the Jerusalem Festival playbills. The Cameri, seen at Edinburgh in Kleist's *Michael Kohlhaas,* put on *Messianic Agonies,* a critique of Israeli extremists, by Motti Lerner.  (OSSIA TRILLING)

**United States and Canada.** A few days in March were all the British needed to confirm in 1987 what they had begun the previous year—the conquest of America's proud musical theatre. On March 12 *Les Misérables* opened with $11 million worth of tickets already sold, by far the biggest advance sale in U.S. theatrical history. On March 15 Lloyd Webber's *Starlight Express* opened at a cost of $8 million, by far the most expensive production in Broadway history. Its price tag was justified, for within six months it recovered that and more, and if this were not enough to show how thoroughly the English had taken over Broadway's musical stage, by December the box office had opened for yet another Andrew Lloyd Webber show, *The Phantom of the Opera,* due in January 1988. The advance ticket sale for that musical broke the *Les Misérables* record; by year's end nearly $20 million was in the till.

In a real way these astronomical finances characterized the current New York theatre as much as the particular shows. It was as if a $50 ticket demanded lavish production effects for justification. Reviews and intrinsic quality seemed irrelevant. Indeed, *Les Misérables* received mixed notices and *Starlight Express* was roundly panned. No matter. Both were spectacles that satisfied their audiences with settings, costumes, and scenery rather than words, music, and emotional communication. *Starlight Express* was a technological extravaganza performed by a futuristically costumed company on roller skates, whizzing up, around, and across a stageful of erector-set runways. *Les Misérables* was somewhat like the *Nicholas Nickleby* of several years earlier in its out-loud reading of a novel, but here again the show was loaded with stage-filling scenic displays and human tableaux. Although it was written by Frenchmen (book by Alain Boublil, music by Claude-Michel Schönberg), *Les Misérables* mimicked the "rock opera" form pioneered by Lloyd Webber; it had lyrics by the British theatre critic Herbert Kretzmer, was produced by Englishman Cameron Mackintosh, and was codirected by John Caird and Trevor Nunn of the RSC.

Such shows as *Starlight Express,* enormous physically as well as financially, dwarfed traditional Broadway. The only conventional U.S. musical to survive during the season (actually one of the few even produced) was Stephen Sondheim's *Into the Woods.* This tongue-in-cheek amalgam of Grimm's fairy tales may have had uncertainty of purpose and a lesser Sondheim score, but it appealed to audiences as this important composer had not previously managed to do with frequency, perhaps because it was more accessible and less bitter than most of Sondheim's work.

During the year Broadway producers seemed more confused than ever before about whether audiences were even interested in plays. Several London productions were unable to repeat their successes in New York whether they featured the British company (*Les Liaisons Dangereuses*) or the original star (*Breaking the Code* with Derek Jacobi) or were americanized (*Stepping Out*). U.S. plays fared little better. After two consecutive hits Harvey Fierstein had

James Earl Jones and Mary Alice star in August Wilson's *Fences.* The play opened on Broadway to resounding acclaim after an unheard-of four years of productions and revisions. It captured four Tony awards, the New York Drama Critics Circle Award, and the 1987 Pulitzer Prize.
RON SCHERL

his comeuppance when *Safe Sex* failed to amuse audiences on the subject of AIDS (acquired immune deficiency syndrome).

The only drama to survive the Broadway season—indeed it won the Pulitzer Prize—was August Wilson's poetic and powerful *Fences.* Featuring a statuesque performance by James Earl Jones, the play is about a person's sense of frustration—as a man and as a black—and how it affects his relationships with his wife and son. Written with a willingness to be rhapsodic, *Fences* regularly soared into the realm of the majestic.

This play originated at the Yale Repertory Theatre, and a number of Broadway dramas had similar beginnings in regional theatres (because producers like productions proven and paid for). A revival of Noël Coward's *Blithe Spirit* with Richard Chamberlain in the lead moved from the Ahmanson Theatre in Los Angeles to a weak engagement on Broadway. A celebrity production of Shaw's *Pygmalion* was similarly unsuccessful, this one starring the odd couple of Peter O'Toole and Amanda Plummer. Another import from the regions, this one of less than a classic—Arthur Miller's *All My Sons*—also failed to attract Broadway audiences after success at the Long Wharf Theatre in New Haven, Conn. The final failed visitor from the regional theatres was a Great Lakes Theatre Festival production of George Abbott and Philip Dunning's *Broadway.* The lesson learned from these assorted disappointments was that provincial successes simply will not be bought at Broadway prices.

As for New York's home-grown institutional theatres, both the Circle in the Square and the Lincoln Center Theater came up with winners. The former presented Tina Howe's *Coastal Disturbances,* a uniquely disturbing study of romance and love as played out on a beach. The Vivian Beaumont Theater at Lincoln Center, which had recently been revitalized by Gregory Mosher (of Chicago's Goodman Theatre), mounted a revival of Cole Porter's *Anything Goes.* It was good to hear this wonderful music again, but the question to be asked in both cases was whether a not-for-profit institutional theatre should seek long-run hits at the expense of a schedule of other productions.

Less commercial (though its subject is commerce) but perhaps most striking of all was Caryl Churchill's *Serious Money,* imported from England by Joseph Papp's Public Theater. An innovative, tough-minded, and deadly serious playwright, Churchill had developed an ardent audience with such previous works as *Cloud Nine* and *Top Girls.* Her successes demonstrated that while serious drama may not be commercially viable on Broadway, it certainly was in no danger of extinction off-Broadway.

That light on the dramatic landscape generally brightened the year off-Broadway, where a number of producers found it financially possible to present serious plays in smaller theatres. The best and most popular during 1987 was Alfred Uhry's *Driving Miss Daisy,* essentially a two-character tour de force for Dana Ivey and Morgan Freeman covering over 20 years in the relationship between an aging Jewish widow in Atlanta and her black chauffeur. Other striking and successful off-Broadway plays included Terrence McNally's *Frankie and Johnny in the Clair de Lune,* about a couple of ordinary people in love, and Robert Harling's *Steel Magnolias,* a study of life in the microcosm of a Louisiana beauty parlour.

The regional theatres fared better on their own territories than on Broadway for the obvious reason that at home they had developed their own audiences for their own productions in their own styles. Zelda Fichandler, who pioneered the American regional theatre movement with her Arena Stage in Washington, D.C., returned there after an absence to direct Arthur Miller's *The Crucible.* The American Repertory Theatre at Harvard University presented a new play with the fascinating title *Sweet Table at the Richelieu* by the U.S. playwright Ronald Ribman.

As a reminder of time's inevitable passage, Canada's prestigious Stratford Festival celebrated its 35th anniversary. Never certain which artistic direction to take, only sure that it would not upset any applecarts, this entrenched institution went from nearly all Shakespeare in 1986 to only three out of eight productions in 1987. Even those were presented in the secondary Avon Theater, while on the main stage were Molière (*The School for Scandal*), Brecht (*Mother Courage*), and, shame of shames, a Broadway musical (*Cabaret*). In the second year of John Neville's reign as artistic director, this hugely endowed and eminent institution seemed more than ever before in need of a strong hand at the wheel and a sense of invention and of purpose.

Finally—all too finally—the AIDS plague took a devastating toll on the theatre in 1987. First to succumb was Charles Ludlam (*see* OBITUARIES), the playful intellectual who was creator, director, writer, and star of his own Ridiculous Theatrical Company. Next victimized by the disease was Michael Bennett (*see* OBITUARIES), the brilliant choreographer and director of *A Chorus Line* and *Dreamgirls.* Finally struck down was Michael Stewart (*see* OBITUARIES), one of Broadway's finest librettists (*Bye, Bye, Birdie; Hello, Dolly!; I Love My Wife; 42nd Street*). Not victimized by AIDS but brought down nevertheless was Bob Fosse (*see* OBITUARIES), the great director and choreographer of films (*Cabaret, Lenny*) as well as shows (*Sweet Charity, Dancin'*).          (MARTIN GOTTFRIED)

This article updates the *Macropædia* article The History of Western THEATRE.
*See also* Dance; Music.

# Transportation

The privatization of two of the world's largest transportation corporations, Japanese National Railways and Japan Air Lines Ltd., in 1987 established further milestones on the road to wider transport deregulation and privatization in the industrialized nations. The deregulated airlines in the U.S. were generating profits well below 1986 levels. The most exciting development of the year was the start of work on the Channel Tunnel. The 50-km (1 km = 0.62 mi) twin tunnels were expected to be open for service in 1993.

Aircraft crashes in the U.S. (one into a freeway in Detroit), the Indian Ocean, Burma, and Poland were among those contributing to the air transport disaster toll. A larger than usual number of ferries and other craft sank, causing heavy loss of life and necessitating a reassessment of safety procedures. (*See* Sidebar.) The sinking of the *Doña Paz* in the Philippines on December 21 was one of the worst peacetime maritime disasters of the 20th century; as many as 3,000 people may have died.          (DAVID BAYLISS)

## AVIATION

World scheduled airline traffic returned to a more normal development pattern in 1987 after the setbacks of 1986, when extraneous factors caused near stagnation. Those factors included the Chernobyl nuclear accident and an upsurge of terrorism; exchange rate fluctuations and depression in the oil industry also made their mark. On the basis of results for the first half of 1987, the International Air Transport Association (IATA), which represented most of the major international airlines, predicted an increase in its members' traffic (passenger and cargo) of about 9% for the year as a whole.

In the first half of 1987, IATA estimated that the growth in international scheduled traffic (12.5%) exceeded the increase in capacity (6%), which meant the load factor improved by more than one percentage point. If this trend were to last until the end of the year, IATA predicted that, overall, its members' scheduled services would show a positive financial result for the year as a whole. Yield (the rate of revenue per traffic unit) was rising faster than unit cost (per unit of capacity) during 1987. Preliminary results put IATA airlines' revenue for 1986 at $87.9 billion, with an operating surplus of $2.3 billion and a net profit of $100 million. The 1985 net profit was $600 million. IATA members accounted for 64% of world scheduled traffic and 80% of world international scheduled traffic.

Total world scheduled traffic reached 178 billion metric ton-km in 1986, 6% over 1985, according to the International Civil Aviation Organization. Freight traffic accounted for 24% of the total. Capacity increased by 7% to reach 297 billion metric ton-km, resulting in an overall load factor of 60%, little changed from 1985. Charter traffic showed an 8% increase but at 17 billion metric ton-km remained a small proportion of the total. For IATA members, scheduled passenger traffic in 1986 amounted to 865,539,000,000 passenger-km, 5.1% more than in 1985. Capacity offered was 1,371,604,000,000 seat-km, a 7.1% increase. The passenger load factor, at 63.1%, was down 1.2 percentage points. The number of passengers carried on scheduled services rose by 5.8% to 494,429,000. Freight traffic on scheduled services reached 32,090,000,000 metric ton-km, 7.4% above 1985. Total scheduled traffic was 113,497,000,000 metric ton-km, up 5.7%, while the overall load factor was 58%, down 0.5 percentage points.

Growth of passenger traffic was strong in 1986 on routes between Latin America and North America and across the

Airplanes line up for departure at Chicago's O'Hare International Airport. Overloaded timetables and the resulting chronic flight delays led to pressure on many airlines to make drastic schedule changes to improve service.
KEVIN HORAN—PICTURE GROUP

South Atlantic. The Far East and Pacific areas also showed good increases. There was a decline in routes involving the North Atlantic, Africa, and the Middle East and stagnation within Europe. The north- and mid-Pacific routes showed the strongest growth in freight traffic.

In the U.S., which accounted for about 40% of all scheduled traffic, the total number of passengers in 1987 was tentatively estimated at 450 million. The dominant issue in public debate was the deterioration in punctuality and service standards offered by scheduled airlines. Time schedules were disrupted because of the increasingly severe capacity shortage and congestion at the nation's 20 busiest airports. A sharp rise in the volume of consumer complaints may have resulted from the consolidation that had been taking place among major carriers. Since 1985 there had been some 25 mergers among the larger airlines. Following the merger of Piedmont and USAir, approved on October 30, eight of the largest carriers would have an estimated 95% of the nation's traffic.

In June 1987 the member countries of the European Communities (EC) came near to agreeing on a further step toward the liberalization of air transport regulation within the Community, but a dispute between Spain and the U.K. over the status of Gibraltar prevented final agreement until December. Also in December, a six-month battle for control of British Caledonian Airways was won by British Airways, which defeated a rival bid from SAS. Several other European carriers, including Sabena, had been investigating various forms of cooperation that would help strengthen their positions. The battle for control of retail outlets through the marketing of computer reservations systems (CRS) to the travel trade intensified in Europe and was spreading to other parts of the world. Concern over aggressive marketing tactics by U.S. carriers led the major European flag carriers, who had failed to agree on development of a common CRS, to polarize into two groups to develop new systems.                    (DAVID WOOLLEY)

## SHIPPING AND PORTS

During 1987 oil prices were falling as tension in the Gulf rose, a paradoxical situation resulting from overproduction by member countries of the Organization of Petroleum Exporting Countries, whose output rose 13.1%. World trade in coarse grain, which had an important influence in

freight rates, was estimated at 89.9 million metric tons in 1987–88, slightly above the 87 million tons in 1986–87. The demand for grain in July raised hopes of a stronger market, and ultralarge and very large crude carriers' freight rates for cargoes from the Gulf to Europe or the U.S. soared temporarily but fell back later. In the U.K. a new deep-water grain-export facility was opened at Aberdeen port, and the port of Hamburg, West Germany, increased its volume of sacked goods, grain, oilseeds, and fodder by 53% to reach a total of 3.9 million tons.

Although overcapacity in world shipping continued, there was a marked decline in the tonnage of vessels laid up, from 33.6 million deadweight tons (dwt) in mid-1986 to 20.6 million dwt in mid-1987. The cruise market remained strong and was estimated to be growing at 15% a year. In the U.S. cruisers operating out of the ports of Miami, Fla., Los Angeles, Seattle, Wash., and other centres were expected to carry a record three million passengers in 1987—seven times more than in 1970.

The size of the world merchant fleet fell from 405 million gross tonnage (gt) in mid-1986 to 403.5 million gt in mid-1987. The Liberian-registered fleet maintained its lead with 51.4 million gt, followed by Panama (43.3 million gt) and Japan (35.9 million gt). By type of ship, the world fleet was made up of oil tankers (122.7 million gt), bulk-ore carriers (110.6 million gt), oil/bulk-ore carriers (20.5 million gt), general cargo ships (72.2 million gt), containerships (21.1 million gt), liquefied gas carriers (9.8 million gt), oil-chemical tankers (4.9 million gt), and chemical tankers (3.5 million gt).                    (EDWARD CROWLEY)

## FREIGHT AND PIPELINES

Freight activity reflected the gradual shift in world trade to the Asian Pacific Rim countries. Hong Kong was now the world's busiest container port, and the Far East had the most dynamic air freight market. The development of an "air chain" between Detroit and Milan, Italy, as part of General Motors' Cadillac production line was one recent innovation, and a new record was set when 1,080 horses were flown from Bordeaux, France, to Delhi, India, in ten 747 freighters. Computer technology contributed to the increasingly sophisticated air and sea freight networks.

The growth in European rail freight faltered, and better and faster services were planned to regain market shares. In

France the Société Nationale des Chemins de Fer (SNCF) introduced high-speed (up to 160 km/h) freight trains. The main freight rail lines being built were Datong (Ta-t'ung) to Qinhuangdao (Ch'in-huang-tao) in China, Bajor to Bandar 'Abbas in Iran, Abu Tartour to Safagu in Egypt, and Labztrangi to Kharasavey in the U.S.S.R.

Low crude-oil and natural-gas prices curbed construction of new pipelines, and many plans were shelved, especially in Africa and South America. In the Middle East the need to move gas from the U.S.S.R. via Bulgaria to Turkey dominated gas pipeline construction, while crude-oil pipeline construction was dominated by Iraq's need to export oil without going through the Strait of Hormuz. The Iraqi oil pipeline to the port of Yurmurtalik, Turkey, and the Saudi Arabian 1,205-km line between Abqaiq and Yanbu' on the Red Sea were completed. In the U.S.S.R. a 260-km coal-slurry line was opened to supply a steel plant at Novosibirsk. The other unconventional product pipeline to go into operation was a 20-km iron and slurry pipeline in New Zealand.

In the Far East and Pacific area the 1,500-km gas line between Palm Valley and Darwin in Australia was completed, and the 1,750-km Haziri-Bijapur-Jagdispur natural-gas system in India neared completion. Major work in the U.S. included the 1,650-km crude-oil Pacific Texas Line to carry Alaskan North Slope crude from Los Angeles to Midland, Texas.

## ROADS AND TRAFFIC

On the 50th anniversary of the world's most famous bridge—the Golden Gate—annual road traffic in the U.S. reached 1.8 trillion vehicle km, and the Interstate Highway System was 66,450 km in length. Nevertheless, demand still exceeded supply, and shortages of public funds led to the reemergence of a number of private toll road projects, such as the 320-km route between Fort Collins and Pueblo, Colo. Privately funded highway projects were becoming more common in many parts of the world. China's road network reached 927,000 km and handled 73% of all domestic traffic, despite the rapidly expanding railway. Traffic volumes topped 100 billion vehicle km a year, and work started on China's second expressway, from Guangzhou (Canton) to Shenzhen-Zhuhai (Shenchen-Chuhei). India's

first (toll) expressway, between Baroda and Ahmedabad, was under construction.

A World Bank study of 1.8 million km of road in 85 less developed countries concluded that over a quarter needed partial or complete reconstruction, about 40% would soon need reconstruction, and $45 billion would be required over the next decade to deal with future deterioration. New roads in less developed countries sometimes had adverse consequences, however. In western Brazil the new highway through Rondonia stimulated inward migration to poor farming areas, and large areas of forest were destroyed.

Two novel forms of road construction were developed. In Qinghai (Tsinghai) Province in China, 500 km of road was built out of salt, which, because of its abundance in the area, caused other highway surface materials to corrode. In Alaska wood chip embankments were used to prevent road structures from sinking through the permafrost.

## INTERCITY RAIL

The gradual move toward higher rail speeds in Europe was marked by the introduction of a new service between Rome and Milan with speeds up to 250 km/h and the construction of 200-km/h rail sets for the Swedish railways. The concept of a high-speed European network was being stimulated, in part, by the Channel Tunnel project. In Japan there were firm proposals for extending the 1,834-km Shinkansen (national high-speed rail network), and work had started on the 275-km Kyushu Shinkansen with its 125 km of tunnel. By 1987, 13 countries had scheduled intercity routes averaging 120 km/h or more. Japan and France led the field with some services exceeding 200 km/h, while the U.K., West Germany, and the U.S. were in the 150–200 km/h bracket. Other countries with fast rails were Sweden, Italy, Canada, Australia, Finland, Ireland, Belgium, and Austria. In the U.S.S.R. the upgraded 650-km line between Dushanbe and Mubarek ran at 140 km/h, reducing the Moscow–Dushanbe journey by two hours. In Australia a private consortium proposed a Very Fast Train service between Sydney and Melbourne (960 km).

Insufficient capacity affected many less developed countries. There was little intercity rail passenger traffic in Africa. In India 24 coach trains ran between Delhi and Allahabad, and another 26 were being considered. The pri-

A truck boards a full-scale model of the "roll-on, roll-off" train intended for use in the "Chunnel," a railway tunnel connecting France and England beneath the English Channel.

As guards and other workers watch, railway operators test drive a subway train in Egypt. The 4.7-kilometre (2.9-mile) Cairo metro, the first subway system in Africa, was the first stage of a plan to alleviate above-ground traffic by as much as 75%.
AP/WIDE WORLD

vatization of the railways in Japan was accomplished, but buyers were not interested in Malaysian Railways because of its heavy debts. Private high-speed rail projects in the U.S. made little progress. Over 14,000 km of intercity rail routes were under construction, mainly in China and the U.S.S.R.

## URBAN MASS TRANSIT

In Egypt the 4.7-km Cairo metro (subway), the first in Africa, became operational in September. Sendai became the ninth Japanese city to get a metro, making Japan second only to the U.S.S.R. in its metro capacity. In the U.S.S.R. extensions to the Minsk, Moscow, and Tashkent systems were opened. Extensions were also completed in Tokyo; Montreal; Santiago, Chile; Marseille, France; Kyoto, Japan; Buenos Aires, Arg.; Prague, Czech.; Baltimore, Md.; and Pusan, South Korea, and in Beijing (Peking) the Circle Line was completed. A new system was started in Los Angeles. Improvements were made in the New York system, reputedly the worst in the world. In London the world's oldest underground system was undergoing refurbishment; a station fire in November that claimed 31 lives marred its good safety record.

New light-rail systems opened during the year included London's Docklands; Grenoble, France; Valencia, Spain; Tunis, Tunisia; Buenos Aires; and Sacramento and San Jose, Calif. Over 20 systems were at an advanced stage of planning, and the renaissance of light rail was becoming closely linked with urban renewal and docks redevelopment. In the U.K. deregulation of the buses produced neither the chaos nor the major improvements in service that observers had predicted. Many countries watched the effects with interest, since deregulation was seen as a possible means of reducing the heavy transport subsidies that many governments provided. Australia opened its first contraflow bus lane in Perth, and trolley buses were introduced in Hanoi, Vietnam. (DAVID BAYLISS)

*See also* Energy; Engineering Projects; Environment; Industrial Review: *Aerospace; Automobiles.*

This article updates the *Macropædia* article TRANSPORTATION.

---

### Questions Raised by the *Herald of Free Enterprise* Disaster

The 1987 disaster in which a U.K. passenger ferry capsized leaving at least 188 dead raised serious questions about safety precautions throughout the shipping world. The Townsend Thoresen roll on-roll off (ro-ro) ferry *Herald of Free Enterprise* left Zeebrugge Harbour, Belgium, at 8 PM on March 6 bound for Dover, England. Minutes later the ferry capsized so quickly the crew could not signal an SOS. Given that the design and buoyancy of most modern ships is such that, in the event of an imminent capsize or other pending emergency, there should be sufficient time to deploy lifesaving equipment and fully evacuate, the accident had serious implications.

According to the official inquiry promptly ordered by the U.K. government, the fundamental error was that the ship put to sea with its outer and inner bow doors fully open. As speed built up, a flood of seawater entered the vehicle deck and caused the rapid sinking. Blame was attributed to four crew members and the Townsend Thoresen management.

The inquiry recommended the immediate fitting of indicator warning lights on the bridge to show the status of all superstructure doors; the fitting of closed-circuit television; better shore ro-ro berths; improved loading indicators on ferries; more reliable ways of calculating freight weights; and many changes to enhance lifesaving capability. Short-term measures were urged to improve trim and stability. Long-term measures were the investigation and revision of conflicting damage-survivability regulations laid down by the International Maritime Organization and other bodies and a feasibility study of having permanent or portable transverse or longitudinal bulkheads on ro-ro vehicle decks. The possibility of using sponsons or flotation collars to improve buoyancy was raised. (EDWARD CROWLEY)

## World Affairs: Contents

For your convenience this article groups the countries of the world by the geopolitical regions to which they belong. Certain related topics, such as United Nations, Dependent States, and various regional affairs articles (*e.g.,* Latin-American Affairs), are also included. An alphabetical list of these topics appears below, indicating the page where each may be found. Articles on the various countries update the *Macropædia* articles of the same name (except where otherwise noted), as do the more extensive statistical treatments in the *World Data* section.

# World Affairs

After two false starts (the Geneva summit in 1985 and the Reykjavík, Iceland, "presummit" the year after), major advances were made in 1987 in the arms control negotiations between the U.S. and the Soviet Union. Eight rounds of talks in Geneva and a meeting of the foreign ministers in Washington (September 1987) culminated in the signing of the intermediate-range nuclear forces (INF) treaty by U.S. Pres. Ronald Reagan and Soviet leader Mikhail Gorbachev in Washington on December 8. (*See* MILITARY AFFAIRS: *Special Report.*) While in previous U.S.-Soviet agreements ceilings had been set on the future buildup of nuclear weapons, this was the first time that the number of arms was actually to be reduced. Furthermore, agreement in one field seemed to open progress in other directions. Reception in Europe was mixed; while the idea of eliminating some nuclear forces was popular, it raised the question of whether a nonnuclear defense was feasible and whether the zero option agreed on by the two superpowers might not lead to the "decoupling" of Western European defense from the U.S. and thus to the disintegration of NATO.

U.S.-Soviet relations, while far from cordial, improved significantly during the year. The same was true with regard to relations between Moscow and Beijing (Peking). There were no immediate foreign political crises; public attention in the Soviet Union as well as the U.S. and China was centred mainly on the domestic scene. Gorbachev's *glasnost* (openness) and *perestroika* (restructuring) policy, initiated at the 27th congress of the Communist Party of the Soviet Union in 1986, received further impetus at the Central Committee meetings in January and June 1987. However, there was also considerable resistance to reform

and even more indifference. While the revelations on the true state of affairs in the country were astonishingly frank, there were many complaints that not much progress had been made in carrying out substantial changes in the economic, political, and social fields.

U.S. attention during the spring and early summer was focused largely on the Iran-*contra* affair, involving revelations of a scheme to provide arms to Iran in exchange for the release of hostages and secret diversions of profits from the arms deals to fund the Nicaraguan *contras.* (*See* North America: *United States:* Special Report, below.) A related topic that preoccupied the U.S. Congress was financial help for the *contras,* demanded by Reagan but opposed by most congressional Democrats. In the meantime (August), the five Central American governments signed a peace plan (the Arias plan) for the region, which called—among other things—for an end to outside aid to rebel groups in Nicaragua on condition that national reconciliation and political freedom prevail in that country. The plan found enthusiastic support in many quarters in Europe and some in the U.S., but the cooperation of the main principals in the conflict was far from certain. (*See* Latin America and the Caribbean: *Latin-American Affairs,* below.)

China witnessed widespread demonstrations calling for political reform and democratization in December 1986 and January 1987, revealing both major political divisions inside the country and a palpable generation gap. This led to a conservative backlash ("antiliberalization campaign"), but by summer something akin to a compromise had been struck.

As in years past, armed conflict was largely limited to sections of the third world. Neither side in the Iran-Iraq war was strong enough to inflict a decisive blow on the other, but the naval conflict in the Gulf intensified. Iranian forces mined the shipping lanes, and U.S. naval forces began conducting convoys of "reflagged" tankers through Gulf waters. They were joined by minesweepers and other naval craft from various Western European countries. On July 31 a violent demonstration on the part of Iranian pilgrims in Mecca was broken up by Saudi security forces with the loss of more than 400 lives.

The war between Chad and the invading Libyan forces reached a new climax between December 1986 and January 1987 as the Libyans were dislodged from many positions in northern Chad. Even though the Libyan forces succeeded in recapturing some of the lost areas, Col. Mu'ammar al-Qadhdhafi's position seemed to be weakened by these setbacks, and Libyan-sponsored terrorism declined. Other trouble spots that flared up were India (Sikh attacks in the Punjab) and, above all, the Sri Lankan civil war, which led to Indian intervention in July–August 1987 with Sri Lankan agreement. Major student riots took place in South Korea in June, compelling Pres. Chun Doo Hwan to agree to constitutional reforms; direct presidential elections took place in December. In the Philippines attempted military coups threatened the government of Corazon Aquino. Unrest continued in South Africa.

Elections held in western countries during the year produced no major upsets. In the U.K. Margaret Thatcher gained an unprecedented third consecutive victory in June. In April Bettino Craxi, the Socialist leader who had been Italian prime minister longer than any other politician since World War II, resigned; he was succeeded in July by Giovanni Goria of the Christian Democrat Party. One of the main events in German politics was the state visit by Erich Honecker, the East German leader, to West Germany. This led to renewed talk about the prospects of German reunification—more among Germany's neighbours than inside the country itself. Japan's leading party, the Liberal-Democrats, suffered a major defeat in local elections in March, largely as the result of Prime Minister Yasuhiro Nakasone's proposed tax policy. Nakasone was replaced by Noboru Takeshita in the fall.

The international debt crisis continued to worry financial and political experts, and leading banks made large loan-loss provisions. Brazil remained the most indebted country ($111 billion). There were encouraging signs of economic improvement in several African countries, but the continent was adversely affected by falling prices of commodities on world markets during much of the year.

(WALTER LAQUEUR)

This article updates the *Macropædia* article 20th-century INTERNATIONAL RELATIONS.

## UNITED NATIONS

Despite continuing regional strife and persistent worldwide economic and social problems, UN Secretary-General Javier Pérez de Cuéllar reported in September that in 1987 he had seen "occasions in which a greater solidarity among nations was evident in addressing serious problems with global implications." His assessment seemed borne out by events in Central America, by new Soviet initiatives, and even in negotiations over Afghanistan. Financial problems, however, plagued both the UN and the specialized agencies, and the Iran-Iraq conflict did not yield to UN attempts to make peace.

**Central America.** Efforts to end conflict in Central America continued. In January the secretary-general visited five Central American countries, hoping to help the so-called Contadora group of countries devise a peace plan (which ultimately proved stillborn). In October the UN sent a peacekeeping team to Central America to determine how

best to monitor compliance with another peace agreement, largely drafted by Costa Rican Pres. Oscar Arias Sánchez (*see* BIOGRAPHIES) and signed August 7 in Guatemala by five Central American presidents. Under the accord, the 13 Central and Latin-American foreign ministers and the secretaries-general of the UN and the Organization of American States composed an International Verification and Follow-up Commission to monitor progress toward peace. The accord set Jan. 15, 1988, as the deadline for establishing a cease-fire, releasing political prisoners, and putting democratic reforms into effect. (*See* Latin America and the Caribbean: *Latin-American Affairs,* below.)

**Soviet Initiatives.** Mikhail S. Gorbachev, general secretary of the Communist Party of the Soviet Union, outlined a new attitude toward the UN on September 17. He called for states to give the organization expanded authority to regulate, among other matters, military conflicts, economic relations, and the environment; to set standards for reunifying families and regulating visas; and to create a "world space organization." He also suggested that the Security Council assume greater responsibility for preserving military stability, expand its peacekeeping activities, verify compliance with arms control agreements and peace treaties, and help settle economic conflicts; that the International Court of Justice be given "mandatory jurisdiction" in more cases; that the UN create a tribunal to investigate acts of international terrorism; and that the authority of the International Atomic Energy Agency be increased.

**Finances.** In October the Soviet Union followed up these words by paying the UN $197 million owed since 1973 for UN activities of which it disapproved, such as the 1973 Middle East peacekeeping force. It also paid the $28 million needed to bring its current contributions up to date, saying that the payments represented the current Soviet view that "responsible tasks facing the United Nations can only be fulfilled under strict compliance with its Charter and on a solid budgetary and administrative foundation." The U.S.S.R. did not, however, pay for debts (which the UN had already written off) contracted in the 1950s and 1960s for the Congo operations, the UN force in Korea, or the first UN Emergency Force in Palestine.

The secretary-general's budget for fiscal 1988 amounted to $1,680,000,000, slightly less than the 1987 budget of $1,710,000,000. The Committee on Programming and Coordination, enlarged from 21 to 34 members, cut the secretary-general's requests by $53 million, but the decline in the value of the dollar threatened to raise total expenditures to $1,750,000,000. The reduction, reversing past trends that had seen UN budgets grow by 5–7% annually, came in response to U.S. demands in 1986 that the UN severely alter its structure and reduce its staff. In exchange, the Reagan administration had committed itself to using its "best efforts" to restore full financing for the UN in 1987. On October 26 the secretary-general wrote U.S. Pres. Ronald Reagan that the UN faced insolvency if the U.S., the single largest UN debtor and the principal cause of the UN's financial problems, did not quickly pay a substantial portion of the $212 million that it owed the UN for 1987, and he repeated his appeal personally to U.S. Ambassador Vernon A. Walters. On December 3 the Reagan administration, which up to then had paid only $10 million for 1987, contributed $90 million more to allow the UN to continue to pay its 6,500 employees in New York. The U.S. still owed $112 million for 1987, in addition to $147 million owed from 1986 for the general budget and $61 million for Middle East peacekeeping forces. The secretary-general reported on December 2 that if the U.S. did not make these payments, the UN would run out of funds in

August 1988 and would have to borrow money in financial markets for the first time. Despite State Department reminders that the U.S. was legally obligated to pay its full contribution, even the partial payment aroused considerable opposition in the U.S.

In Rome on November 9, Edouard Saouma, reelected that day over U.S., Canadian, and British opposition as director general of the Food and Agriculture Organization (FAO), pointed out that the U.S., nominally the largest contributor to FAO, had paid nothing during 1987. World Health Organization (WHO) officials in Geneva also complained several times during the year that, because the U.S. was still withholding some of its 1986 payment to WHO and had not contributed any of the $62 million due in 1987, the organization's regular work and its special program against AIDS (acquired immune deficiency syndrome) were suffering.

**Afghanistan.** Diplomats speculated that the Soviet Union's new interest in the UN might indicate its need for the organization's help in withdrawing its 115,000 troops from Afghanistan. UN Under Secretary-General Diego Cordovez conducted "difficult, intensive and encouraging" negotiations with all parties during the year and managed to narrow the principal issues to the amount of time the U.S.S.R. needed to withdraw its troops and the nature of an Afghan government of "national reconciliation." In the General Assembly, 123 states (one more than in 1986) called on November 10 for "all foreign troops" to withdraw from Afghanistan, and on November 27, 85 states expressed their "deep distress and alarm" over "continued violations of the right to life, liberty and security" there.

**Iran-Iraq.** The UN Security Council on July 20 unanimously called on Iran and Iraq to cease fire on land, at sea, and in the air and threatened sanctions for noncompliance. Only Iraq accepted the resolution; Iran maintained that the Security Council first had to place the responsibility for starting the conflict on Iraq. The secretary-general, operating under Security Council instructions, went in September to Tehran and Baghdad to talk with Iranian and Iraqi leaders in the hope of ending hostilities before the Council confronted the sanctions question. In accordance with the resolution, he suggested to Iranian leaders the possibility of appointing an impartial commission to determine responsibility for the war at the same time that the cease-fire and troop withdrawals took effect. Conversations continued in New York in December, and on December 24 a Security Council statement indicated that the major powers were closer to agreeing on the need for an arms embargo to force a cease-fire in the Gulf.

At various times during the year, private observers suggested establishing a UN naval presence in the Gulf to replace the U.S. and other Western naval forces ensuring freedom of navigation there. The proposal, opposed by the U.S. State Department, was endorsed on September 23 by Soviet Foreign Minister Eduard A. Shevardnadze.

**South Africa.** On February 20 the U.S. and U.K. vetoed a Security Council resolution that would have imposed mandatory economic sanctions against South Africa. The U.S. explained that it would not risk provoking the collapse of the South African economy and engendering revolution. On April 25 South African army commandos carried out a raid into Zambia in which four Zambians were killed. The secretary-general and the Assembly's Special Committee Against Apartheid condemned that action.

On August 26 Pérez de Cuéllar observed Namibia Day by reiterating the concern the Security Council had expressed five days before over the deteriorating situation in South West Africa/Namibia. He joined the Council in

Members of the UN Security Council vote unanimously in favour of a resolution demanding an end to the Iran-Iraq war. The resolution called for a cease-fire on land, at sea, and in the air, as well as the immediate withdrawal of forces to internationally recognized borders.
AP/WIDE WORLD

condemning all acts of repression and brutality against the Namibian people and in calling for South Africa to end its illegal occupation of the territory. The UN Council for Namibia sponsored the observance, and the council president, Peter D. Zuze (Zambia), accused the U.S. of "complicity" with South Africa because it insisted on making its support for the independence of Namibia conditional on Cuba's withdrawing its 35,000 troops from Angola.

On November 20 the General Assembly adopted (103–29 with 23 abstentions) eight resolutions relating to South Africa and called for an oil embargo against the country. The U.S. voted for only one of the eight, a measure calling for a UN trust fund to provide humanitarian and legal assistance to apartheid victims.

**Cyprus.** On November 22 UN forces in Cyprus interposed themselves between Turkish troops and hundreds of Greek Cypriot women attempting to push into northern Cyprus, which Turkish troops had occupied since 1974.

**Disarmament.** A UN Conference on the Relationship Between Disarmament and Development opened at UN headquarters on August 24. A total of 148 states attended, including all NATO members except the U.S., which opposed linking the two subjects.

**African Economic Problems.** According to a report issued by the World Bank on October 15, cuts in foreign aid, drastically lowered commodity prices, and increasing debts of African states threatened economic gains made since the 1985 famines. The report asserted that, though African states did what the Bank and the developed countries asked of them (devalued currencies, deregulated food production, reduced food subsidies, and cut government spending), the developed countries did not respond adequately. After a brief respite, famine reappeared in Ethiopia. In late October and early November, the rebel Eritrean People's Liberation Front attacked food convoys and destroyed many trucks, including some under UN auspices, carrying emergency food supplies from the U.S. They charged that vehicles accompanying the convoys carried bombs, ammunition, and fuel oil. On November 16 UN World Food Program officials said that, to avert disaster, donors would have to send 15 countries in sub-Saharan Africa 2.7 million tons of food "immediately."

In Paris on December 4, major donors agreed with the Bank and the International Monetary Fund on emergency financial assistance amounting to $1 billion a year for three years in direct aid, debt relief, and new loans for the 20 poorest sub-Saharan countries. On December 18 the Fund established the "Enhanced Structural Adjustment Facility" to receive and disburse an estimated $8 billion as low-interest loans to be repaid over long periods.

**War Crimes.** More than 40,000 files in UN custody that delineated Nazi atrocities in World War II were opened to scholars, writers, and journalists in November. The files had been closed since 1948 by order of the former members of the Allied War Crimes Commission, who argued that they contained unsubstantiated allegations. Israeli officials, maintaining that the archives could contribute "a whole new chapter in Holocaust research," hailed the decision. A declassified copy of the master list to the files found in 1986 in Washington, D.C., listed nearly 25,000 so-called Class A suspects against whom the commission believed it had sufficient evidence to warrant prosecution. The name of Kurt Waldheim, former UN secretary-general and now president of Austria, appeared in that group.

**Human Rights.** On June 26 the UN Convention Against Torture and Other Cruel, Inhuman, or Degrading Treatment or Punishment came into force with 20 signatories. The parties agreed that purported torturers must either be tried or extradited for trial. Parties were also obligated not to return refugees to countries where they risked being tortured, to investigate reliable information about torture, and to establish a ten-member committee to receive individual and interstate complaints about torture. The convention excluded "obedience to superior orders" as a defense against charges of torture.

The General Assembly on November 27 adopted resolutions expressing "deep concern" over human rights violations, not only in Afghanistan (*see* above) but in Iran and Chile as well. The members, voting 58–22 with 42 abstentions, expressed their concern over "numerous and detailed allegations of grave human rights violations by Iran's government." The resolution on Chile, accepted by a vote of 81–5 with 47 abstentions, cited torture, poor legal protection, and violence as tactics the government was using against its political opponents.

On December 22 the Security Council adopted (14–0) a resolution strongly deploring Israeli practices in its occupied territories that "violate the human rights of the Palestinian people, and in particular the opening of fire by the Israeli Army." The resolution called on Israel to treat Palestinians as required in international conventions protecting civilians in time of war. The U.S. abstained because the resolution contained "generalized criticism of Israeli policies and practices" and ignored dangers and provocations that the Israeli security forces faced, but U.S. spokespersons called Israeli measures "unacceptably harsh." Israel denied that it was doing anything improper.

**Micronesia.** In June and August, Trusteeship Council officials observed elections in the archipelago of Palau (Belau), the U.S.-administered Trust Territory of the Pacific Islands (the Marshall Islands and the Federated States of Micronesia had already approved constitutional arrangements). Five times previously the indigenous inhabitants had rejected a compact of free association with the U.S. that would make the area self-governing but leave the U.S. responsible for defense and foreign affairs. In August they approved the compact, albeit under circumstances that led some Palauan legislators to call the vote illegal. The U.S. Congress awaited further observer reports, and ultimately the Security Council would have to agree to terminate the trust. (RICHARD N. SWIFT)

This article updates the *Macropædia* article UNITED NATIONS.

## COMMONWEALTH OF NATIONS

The Commonwealth heads of government meeting held in Vancouver, B.C., on Oct. 13–17, 1987, was the major event on the organization's calendar and one that seriously taxed its unity. As on earlier occasions, South Africa was the issue of contention, and Britain's attitude was the focus of criticism. The level of violence in southern Africa, where four of the six frontline states (Botswana, Tanzania, Zambia, and Zimbabwe) were members of the Commonwealth, had increased markedly since the previous summit, held in Nassau, The Bahamas, in 1985, and even since the Eminent Persons' Group set up there made its report on conditions in South Africa in 1986. Leaders from every continent, with the exception of U.K. Prime Minister Margaret Thatcher, made the need for punitive sanctions against Pretoria the keynote of their addresses.

Paragraph 8 of the Nassau Accord had promised to consider "further effective measures" if Pretoria had not begun to dismantle apartheid. The Commonwealth leaders discerned "increased intransigence" on the part of the South African government and, with the exception of Britain, committed themselves to "continuing efforts to secure a global sanctions program." As Commonwealth Secretary-General Sir Shridath Ramphal put it, the Vancouver meeting adopted a process that would "tighten, widen, intensify, and universalize" the sanctions agreed on at Nassau. These included a ban on new bank loans and on a number of South African imports. But the final communiqué's repeated use of the phrase "with the exception of Britain" was a reflection of the Commonwealth's divided loyalties.

The 47 states that stood against Britain paid a price in British acrimony. So bitter was the atmosphere of confrontation that, in a highly unusual move, four senior Commonwealth leaders—Prime Ministers Bob Hawke of Australia, Rajiv Gandhi of India, and Robert Mugabe of Zimbabwe and Pres. Kenneth Kaunda of Zambia—held a press conference to denounce British press briefings. The four cited a British spokesman's use of Canadian trade figures that purported to show an increase in Canadian trade with Pretoria, whereas, they claimed, the actual current figures showed a sharp decrease.

The other major preoccupation of the Vancouver meeting was the decision by the new leader of the small South Pacific island nation of Fiji, Lieut. Col. Sitiveni Rabuka (*see* BIOGRAPHIES), to declare a republic on October 6. On October 15 Queen Elizabeth II's representative, Gov.-Gen. Ratu Sir Penaia Ganilau, resigned, and on the following day Fiji's membership in the Commonwealth was formally declared to have lapsed. Opinion was divided as to whether the new regime, which had staged a coup against the elected government, would be readmitted should it reapply.

The most positive outcome of the Vancouver meeting was its approval of a decision to set up a Commonwealth Open University, to be run from Canada. A network of satellite or television education was to be made available to all Commonwealth countries, and although it would not give degrees, the university was to provide courses, mainly on technical subjects, that could be part of degree courses within various national universities.

The meeting's economic declaration called for strengthening of the General Agreement on Tariffs and Trade, warned against protectionism, and sought an increase in aid for sub-Saharan Africa as well as additional funds for the International Monetary Fund's structural adjustment facility. This went some way toward compensating for the feelings of acrimony among Commonwealth leaders.

(VICTORIA BRITTAIN)

## POLITICAL PARTIES

The following table is a general world guide to the political parties of the world. All countries that were independent on Dec. 31, 1987, are included; there are a number for which no analysis of political activities can be given; for example, states where only one party is legal. Parties are included in most instances only if represented in parliaments (in the lower house in bicameral legislatures); the figures in the last column indicate the number of seats obtained in the last general election (figures in parentheses are those of the penultimate one). The date of the most recent election follows the name of the country.

The code letters in the affiliation column show the relative political positions of the parties within each country; there is, therefore, no entry in this column for single-party nations. There are obvious difficulties involved in labeling parties within the political spectrum of a given country. The key chosen is as follows: F-fascist; ER-extreme right; R-right; CR-centre right; C-centre; L-non-Marxist left; SD-social democratic; S-socialist; EL-extreme left; and K-Communist.

The percentages in the column "Voting strength" indicate proportions of the valid votes cast for the respective parties, or the number of registered voters who went to the polls in single-party states.

## Political Parties

| Country / Name of party | Affiliation | Voting strength (%) | Parliamentary representation |
|---|---|---|---|
| **Afghanistan** | | | |
| Pro-Soviet government since April 27, 1978 | — | — | — |
| **Albania (February 1987)** | | | |
| Albanian Labour (Communist) | — | 100 | 250 (250) |
| **Algeria (February 1987)** | | | |
| National Liberation Front | — | 87 | 295 (281) |
| **Angola (August 1980)** | | | |
| Movimento Popular de Libertaçao de Angola (MPLA) | — | — | 203 |
| **Antigua and Barbuda (April 1984)** | | | |
| Antigua Labour Party | C | ... | 16 (13) |
| Progressive Labour Movement | L | ... | 0 (3) |
| Independents | — | ... | 1 (1) |
| **Argentina (September 1987)** | | | |
| Movimiento Justicialista Nacional (Peronist) | CR | ... | 105 (103) |
| Unión Cívica Radical | C | ... | 117 (130) |
| Others | — | ... | 32 (21) |
| **Australia (July 1987)** | | | |
| National | R | 11.5 | 19 (21) |
| Liberal | C | 34.3 | 43 (45) |
| Labor | L | 45.8 | 86 (82) |
| **Austria (November 1986)** | | | |
| Freiheitliche Partei Österreichs | R | 9.7 | 18 (12) |
| Österreichische Volkspartei | C | 41.3 | 77 (81) |
| Sozialistische Partei Österreichs | SD | 43.3 | 80 (90) |
| Vereinigte Grüne Österreich (Greens) | — | 4.8 | 8 (0) |
| **Bahamas, The (June 1987)** | | | |
| Progressive Liberal Party | CR | 53 | 31 (32) |
| Free National Movement | L | ... | 16 (8) |
| Others | — | ... | 2 (3) |
| **Bahrain** | | | |
| Emirate, no parties | — | — | — |
| **Bangladesh (May 1986)** | | | |
| Jatiya Party | — | ... | 183 |
| Awami League Party | — | ... | 76 |
| Other parties | — | ... | 39 |
| Independents | — | ... | 32 |
| **Barbados (May 1986)** | | | |
| Democratic Labour Party | C | 59.5 | 24 (7) |
| Barbados Labour Party | L | 40.4 | 3 (17) |
| **Belgium (December 1987)** | | | |
| Vlaams Blok | ER | 1.9 | 2 (1) |
| Volksunie | R | 8.0 | 16 (16) |
| Front Démocratique des Francophones | R | 1.2 | 3 (3) |
| Liberals { Flemish | CR | 11.5 | 25 (22) |
| Liberals { French | CR | 9.4 | 23 (24) |
| Social Christians { Flemish | C | 19.5 | 43 (49) |
| Social Christians { French | C | 8.0 | 19 (20) |
| Socialists { Flemish | SD | 14.9 | 32 (32) |
| Socialists { French | SD | 8.0 | 40 (35) |
| Others | — | 7.1 | 9 (10) |
| **Belize (December 1984)** | | | |
| United Democratic Party | R | ... | 21 (5) |
| People's United Party | C | ... | 7 (13) |
| **Benin (June 1984)** | | | |
| People's Revolutionary Party | — | ... | 196 (336) |
| **Bhutan** | | | |
| A monarchy without parties | — | — | — |
| **Bolivia (July 1985)** | | | |
| Acción Democrática Nacionalista | R | 37.0 | 52 |
| Movimiento Nacionalista Revolucionario | C | 42.0 | 60 |
| Christian Democratic Party | C | 2.0 | 3 |
| Movimiento de la Izquierda Revolucionaria | L | 11.0 | 16 |
| Small left-wing parties | L | 15.0 | 22 |
| **Botswana (September 1984)** | | | |
| Botswana Democratic Party | C | ... | 29 (29) |
| Botswana People's Party | L | ... | 1 (1) |
| Botswana National Front | EL | ... | 4 (2) |

| Country / Name of party | Affiliation | Voting strength (%) | Parliamentary representation |
|---|---|---|---|
| **Brazil (November 1986)** | | | |
| Partido do Movimento Democrático Brasileiro (coalition) | R & L | ... | 479 (200) |
| Partido Democrático Social | SD | ... | 0 — |
| Partido Comunista Brasileiro | K | ... | 0 — |
| 37 other parties | — | ... | 8 (277) |
| **Brunei** | | | |
| Legislative Council (nonelected) | — | — | — |
| **Bulgaria (June 1986)** | | | |
| Fatherland Front | | | |
| Bulgarian Communist Party | | 276 | |
| Bulgarian Agrarian People's Union | } 99.9 { 99 | 400 (400) | |
| Independents | | 25 | |
| **Burkina Faso** | | | |
| National Revolutionary Council since August 1983 | — | — | — |
| **Burma (October 1985)** | | | |
| Burma Socialist Program Party | — | ... | 489 (475) |
| **Burundi** | | | |
| Military Committee for National Salvation took power September 1987 | — | — | — |
| **Cameroon (May 1983)** | | | |
| Cameroonian National Union | — | 99.3 | 120 (120) |
| **Canada (September 1984)** | | | |
| Progressive Conservative | CR | 50.0 | 211 (103) |
| Liberal | C | 28.0 | 40 (147) |
| New Democratic | L | 19.0 | 30 (32) |
| Others | — | ... | 1 (0) |
| **Cape Verde (December 1985)** | | | |
| African Party for the Independence of Cape Verde and independents | — | 94 | 83 (56) |
| **Central African Republic (August 1987)** | | | |
| Rassemblement Démocratique Centrafricain | — | ... | 52 |
| **Chad** | | | |
| Military government since 1975 | — | — | — |
| **Chile** | | | |
| Military junta since Sept. 11, 1973 | — | — | — |
| **China, People's Republic of (March 1985)** | | | |
| Communist (Kungchantang) National People's Congress | — | ... | 2,978 |
| **Colombia (March 1986)** | | | |
| Partido Conservador | R | ... | 82 (84) |
| Partido Liberal | C | 49 | 100 (114) |
| Nuevo Liberalismo | C | ... | 7 — |
| Unión Patriótica | EL | ... | 10 — |
| **Comoros (March 1987)** | | | |
| Federal Assembly | — | 65 | 42 (38) |
| **Congo (August 1984)** | | | |
| Parti Congolais du Travail | — | ... | 153 (115) |
| **Costa Rica (February 1986)** | | | |
| Partido de Liberación Nacional | L | ... | 29 (33) |
| Partido Unidad Social Cristiana | CR | ... | 25 (18) |
| Others | — | ... | 3 (6) |
| **Côte d'Ivoire (November 1985)** | | | |
| Parti Démocratique de la Côte d'Ivoire | — | ... | 175 (100) |
| **Cuba (December 1986)** | | | |
| Partido Comunista Cubano | — | ... | 499 (499) |
| **Cyprus (December 1985)** | | | |
| Greek Zone | | | |
| Democratic Rally | CR | 33.56 | 19 (12) |
| Democratic Party (DIKO) | C | 27.65 | 16 (8) |
| Socialist Party (EDEK) | SD | 11.07 | 6 (3) |
| Communist Party (AKEL) | K | 27.43 | 15 (12) |
| Turkish Zone (June 1985) | | | |
| National Turkish Party | — | ... | 24 |
| Communal Liberation Party | — | ... | 10 |
| Turkish Republican Party | — | ... | 12 |
| New Dawn Party (Renaissance) | — | ... | 4 |

| Country / Name of party | Affiliation | Voting strength (%) | Parliamentary representation |
|---|---|---|---|
| **Czechoslovakia (May 1986)** | | | |
| National Front | — | 99.4 | 200 (200) |
| **Denmark (September 1987)** | | | |
| Conservative | R | 20.8 | 38 (42) |
| Liberal Democratic (Venstre) | CR | 10.5 | 19 (22) |
| Christian People's | CR | 2.4 | 4 (5) |
| Progress | C | 4.8 | 9 (6) |
| Radical Liberal (Radikale Venstre) | C | 6.2 | 11 (10) |
| Centre Democrats | C | 4.8 | 9 (8) |
| Social Democrats | SD | 29.3 | 54 (56) |
| Common Course | L | 2.2 | 4 — |
| Socialist People's | EL | 14.6 | 27 (21) |
| Left Socialists | EL | 1.4 | 0 (5) |
| Faeroe Islands and Greenland | — | — | 4 (4) |
| **Djibouti (April 1987)** | | | |
| Rassemblement Populaire pour le Progrès | — | 87 | 65 (65) |
| **Dominica (July 1985)** | | | |
| Freedom Party | C | 59.0 | 15 (17) |
| Labour Party | L | ... | 5 (2) |
| Independents | — | ... | 1 (2) |
| **Dominican Republic (May 1986)** | | | |
| Partido Reformista Social Cristiano | R | ... | 56 |
| Partido Revolucionario Dominicano | L | ... | 48 |
| Partido de la Liberación Dominicana | EL | ... | 16 |
| **Ecuador (June 1986)** | | | |
| Frente de Reconstrucción Nacional | | | |
| Partido Social Cristiano | | | 15 |
| Partido Conservador | | | 1 |
| Partido Liberal Radical | | | 3 |
| Concentración de Fuerzas Populares | } R & CR 35.3 27 { | | 4 |
| Frente Radical Alfarista | | | 3 |
| Others | | | 1 |
| Frente Progresista Democrática | | | |
| Izquierda Democrática | | | 17 |
| Democracia Popular | | | 8 |
| Partido Socialista Ecuatoriano | | | 6 |
| Movimiento Popular Democrático | } L & EL 55.5 43 { | | 4 |
| Frente Amplio de Izquierda | | | 3 |
| Partido Roldosista Ecuatoriano | | | 5 |
| Others | — | — | 1 |
| **Egypt (April 1987)** | | | |
| New Wafd Party | R | 7.8 | 35 (57) |
| National Democratic Party | CR | 77.2 | 346 (391) |
| Socialist Labour Party and allies parties | L | 13.4 | 60 (0) |
| Independents | — | 1.6 | 7 (0) |
| **El Salvador (March 1985)** | | | |
| Alianza Republicana Nacionalista | R | 29 | 13 (19) |
| Partido Auténtico Institucional Salvadoreño | R | ... | 1 (0) |
| Partido de Conciliación Nacional | CR | 8 | 12 (13) |
| Partido Acción Democrática | CR | ... | 1 (18) |
| Partido Cristiano Democrático | C | 54 | 33 (40) |
| **Equatorial Guinea (August 1983)** | | | |
| National Assembly | — | ... | 41 |
| **Ethiopia (June 1987)** | | | |
| Shengo (National Assembly) | — | 85.4 | 835 |
| **Fiji** | | | |
| Military government suspended constitution May 1987 | — | — | — |
| **Finland (March 1987)** | | | |
| National Coalition Party (Conservative) | R | 23.2 | 53 (44) |
| Swedish People's | R | 5.3 | 13 (11) |
| Centre (including former Liberal) Party | C | 17.6 | 40 (38) |
| Christian Union | C | 2.6 | 5 (3) |
| Rural Party | C | 6.3 | 9 (17) |
| Social Democratic | SD | 24.3 | 56 (57) |
| People's Democratic League (Communist) | K | 9.4 | 16 (17) |
| Green Party | — | 4.0 | 4 (10) |
| Democratic Alternative | — | 4.2 | 4 (10) |
| Others | — | 6.1 | 0 (1) |

# Political Parties

| Country / Name of party | Affiliation | Voting strength (%) | Parliamentary representation |
|---|---|---|---|
| **France (March 1986)** | | | |
| Front National | F | 9.7 | 35 (0) |
| Rassemblement pour la République | R ⎱ 40.98 } 277 | | 147 (83) |
| Union pour la Démocratie Française | R ⎰ | | 130 (64) |
| Diverse right | — | — | 14 (11) |
| Parti Socialiste | SD | 31.0 | 207 (269) |
| Diverse left | — | — | 9 (20) |
| Parti Communiste | K | 9.8 | 35 (44) |
| **Gabon (February–March 1985)** | | | |
| Parti Démocratique Gabonais | — | 95.44 | 111 (84) |
| **Gambia, The (March 1987)** | | | |
| People's Progressive Party | C | 59.2 | 31 (27) |
| National Convention Party | — | ... | 5 (4) |
| **German Democratic Republic (June 1986)** | | | |
| National Front (Sozialistische Einheitspartei and others) | — | 99.7 | 500 (500) |
| **Germany, Federal Republic of (January 1987)** | | | |
| Christlich-Demokratische Union | R | 34.5 | 174 (191) |
| Christlich-Soziale Union | | 9.8 | 49 (53) |
| Freie Demokratische Partei | C | 9.1 | 46 (34) |
| Sozialdemokratische Partei Deutschlands | SD | 37.0 | 186 (193) |
| The Green (Ecology) Party | — | 8.3 | 42 (27) |
| **Ghana** | | | |
| Military dictatorship since Dec. 31, 1981 | — | — | — |
| **Greece (June 1985)** | | | |
| New Democracy Party | CR | 40.8 | 126 (115) |
| Panhellenic Socialist Movement (Pasok) | SD | 45.8 | 161 (172) |
| Greek Communist Party (KKE) | K | 9.4 | 12 (13) |
| Eurocommunists | K | 1.4 | 1 (0) |
| **Grenada (December 1984)** | | | |
| New National Party | C | ... | 14 |
| Grenada United Labour Party | R | ... | 1 |
| **Guatemala (November 1985)** | | | |
| Movimiento de Liberación Nacional | ER | 6.3 | 6 |
| Partido Institucional Democrático | R | 6.3 | 6 |
| Central Auténtica Nacionalista | R | 6.3 | 1 |
| Partido Nacionalista Renovador | CR | 3.2 | 1 |
| Partido Democracia Cristiana | C | 38.7 | 51 |
| Unión del Centro Nacional | C | 20.2 | 22 |
| Partido Revolucionario/Partido de Democrático de Conciliación Nacional | C | 13.8 | 11 |
| Partido Socialista Democrático | SD | 3.2 | 2 |
| **Guinea** | | | |
| Military Committee for National Redress in power since April 1984 | — | — | — |
| **Guinea-Bissau (March–May 1984)** | | | |
| African Party for the Independence of Guinea and Cape Verde | — | ... | 150 |
| **Guyana (December 1985)** | | | |
| People's National Congress | R | 77.0 | 42 (41) |
| People's Progressive Party | L | 11.0 | 8 (10) |
| Others | ... | 0.5 | 3 (0) |
| **Haiti** | | | |
| Civilian-military council in power since February 1986 | — | — | — |
| **Honduras (November 1985)** | | | |
| Partido Nacional | R | ... | 63 (34) |
| Partido Liberal | CR | ... | 67 (44) |
| Others | C | ... | 4 (4) |
| **Hungary (June 1985)** | | | |
| Patriotic People's Front | — | ... | 361 |
| Independents | — | ... | 25 |
| **Iceland (April 1987)** | | | |
| Independence Party | R | 27.2 | 18 (23) |
| Citizen's Party | R | 10.9 | 7 — |
| Progressive (Farmers') Party | C | 18.9 | 13 (14) |
| Social Democratic Party | SD | 15.2 | 10 (6) |
| People's Alliance | K | 13.3 | 8 (10) |
| Women's Alliance | — | 10.1 | 6 (3) |
| Others | — | ... | 1 (4) |
| **India (December 1984; figures incomplete)** | | | |
| Congress (I) | C | ... | 395 (351) |
| Communist Party of India (Marxist) | K | ... | 22 (35) |
| Communist Party (pro-Soviet) | K | ... | 6 (10) |
| Other opposition parties and independents | — | ... | 121 |
| **Indonesia (April 1987)** | | | |
| Golkar (Functional Groups) | — | 73.0 | 299 (246) |
| United Development Party | — | 16.0 | 61 (94) |
| Indonesian Democratic Party (merger of five nationalist and Christian parties) | — | 11.0 | 40 (24) |
| **Iran (May 1984)** | | | |
| Islamic Republican Party | R | ... | 251 |
| Others | — | ... | 19 |
| **Iraq (October 1984)** | | | |
| Ba'th Party | — | ... | 183 |
| Others | — | ... | 67 |
| **Ireland (February 1987)** | | | |
| Fianna Fail (Sons of Destiny) | C | 44.1 | 81 (75) |
| Fine Gael (United Ireland) | C | 27.1 | 51 (70) |
| Progressive Democrats | C | 11.9 | 14 — |
| Irish Labour Party | L | 6.5 | 12 (16) |
| Others | — | 10.4 | 8 (5) |
| **Israel (July 1984)** | | | |
| Tehiya | ER | 4.0 | 5 (3) |
| Kach | ER | 1.2 | 1 — |
| Likud { Herut / Liberal } | R | 31.9 | 41 (48) |
| National Religious | CR | 3.5 | 4 (6) |
| Agudat Israel | C | 1.7 | 2 (4) |
| Yahad | C | 2.2 | 3 — |
| Ometz | C | 1.2 | 1 — |
| Labour Alignment { Labour / Mapam } | SD | 34.9 | 44 (47) |
| Civil Rights | SD | 2.4 | 3 (1) |
| Shinui | SD | 2.6 | 3 (2) |
| Progressive List for Peace | EL | 1.8 | 2 — |
| Hadash | K | 3.4 | 4 (4) |
| Others | — | — | 7 (5) |
| **Italy (June 1987)** | | | |
| Movimento Sociale Italiano | F | 5.9 | 35 (42) |
| Partito Liberale Italiano | CR | 2.1 | 11 (16) |
| Democrazia Cristiana | C | 34.3 | 234 (225) |
| Partito Repubblicano Italiano | C | 3.7 | 21 (29) |
| Partito Social-Democratico Italiano | L | 3.4 | 17 (23) |
| Partito Socialista Italiano | SD | 14.3 | 94 (73) |
| Partito Radicale | EL | 2.6 | 13 (11) |
| Partito Comunista Italiano | K | 26.6 | 177 (198) |
| Democrazia Proletaria | K | 1.7 | 8 (7) |
| Greens | — | 2.5 | 13 — |
| Others | — | ... | 7 (6) |
| **Jamaica (December 1983)** | | | |
| Jamaica Labour Party | L | ... | 60 (51) |
| People's National Party | SD | (Boycotted) | (9) |
| **Japan (July 1986)** | | | |
| Liberal-Democratic Party | R | 49.6 | 300 (250) |
| Komeito (Clean Government) | C | ... | 57 (58) |
| Democratic Socialist Party | SD | ... | 28 (38) |
| Japan Socialist Party | S | ... | 87 (112) |
| Japan Communist Party | K | ... | 27 (26) |
| Others | — | ... | 13 (27) |
| **Jordan** | | | |
| Royal government, no parties | — | — | 142 |
| **Kampuchea (May 1981)** | | | |
| Kampuchean United Front for National Salvation (Vietnamese-backed) | — | 99.0 | 117 |
| **Kenya (September 1983)** | | | |
| Kenya African National Union | — | 48.0 | 158 |
| **Kiribati (March 1987)** | | | |
| House of Assembly, no parties | — | 84.0 | 39 (36) |
| **Korea, North (November 1986)** | | | |
| Korean Workers' (Communist) Party | — | ... | |
| **Korea, South (February 1985)** | | | |
| Korea National Party | CR | 9.2 | 20 (25) |
| Democratic Justice Party | C | 35.3 | 148 (151) |
| New Korea Democratic Party | L | 28.6 | 67 — |
| Democratic Korea Party | L | 17.6 | 35 (81) |
| Independents and others | — | ... | 6 (19) |
| **Kuwait** | | | |
| National Assembly abolished July 1986 | — | — | — |
| **Laos, People's Democratic Republic of** | | | |
| Lao People's Revolutionary Party | — | ... | |
| **Lebanon (April 1972)** | | | |
| Maronites (Roman Catholics) | — | ... | 30 |
| Sunni Muslims | — | ... | 20 |
| Shi'ah Muslims | — | ... | 19 |
| Greek Orthodox | — | ... | 11 |
| Druzes (Muslim sect) | — | ... | 6 |
| Melchites (Greek Catholics) | — | ... | 6 |
| Armenian Orthodox | — | ... | 4 |
| Other Christian | — | ... | 2 |
| Armenian Catholics | — | ... | 1 |
| **Lesotho** | | | |
| Military Council in power from January 1986 | — | — | |
| **Liberia (October 1985)** | | | |
| National Democratic Party of Liberia | R | ... | 45 |
| Opposition | L | ... | 19 |
| **Libya** | | | |
| Military government since Sept. 1, 1969 | — | — | |
| **Liechtenstein (February 1986)** | | | |
| Vaterländische Union | CR | 50.2 | 8 (8) |
| Fortschrittliche Bürgerpartei | C | 42.7 | 7 (7) |
| **Luxembourg (June 1984)** | | | |
| Parti Chrétien Social | CR | ... | 25 (24) |
| Parti Libéral | C | ... | 14 (15) |
| Parti Ouvrier Socialiste | SD | ... | 21 (14) |
| Parti Communiste | K | ... | 2 (2) |
| Ecologists | — | ... | 2 (0) |
| **Madagascar (August 1983)** | | | |
| Advance Guard of the Malagasy Revolution (Arema) | C | 64.8 | 117 (112) |
| Madagascar Independence Congress | L | 8.8 | 9 (16) |
| Movement for Proletarian Power | L | 11.1 | 3 — |
| People's Party for National Unity | L | 10.6 | 6 (7) |
| Madagascar National Independence Movement (Monima) | L | 3.7 | 2 — |
| **Malawi (May 1987)** | | | |
| Malawi Congress Party | — | ... | 112 (101) |
| **Malaysia (August 1986)** | | | |
| National Front (Barisan Nasional) Coalition | | | |
| United Malays National Organization | | 83 } | |
| Malaysian Chinese Association | | 17 } | |
| Malaysian Indian Congress | | 57.4  6 } | 148 (133) |
| Malaysian People's Movement | | 5 } | |
| Sabah and Sarawak parties | | 37 } | |
| Opposition Parties | | | |
| Democratic Action Party | | 15.6  24 } | |
| Pan-Malaysian Islamic Party | | 1 } | 29 (21) |
| Independents | | 4 } | |
| **Maldives (December 1984)** | | | |
| Citizens' Assembly | — | ... | 40 |
| **Mali (June 1985)** | | | |
| Union Démocratique du Peuple Malien | — | ... | 82 |
| **Malta (May 1987)** | | | |
| Nationalist Party | R | 50.9 | 35 (31) |
| Labour Party | SD | 48.9 | 34 (34) |
| **Mauritania** | | | |
| Military government since April 25, 1981 | — | — | |
| **Mauritius (August 1987)** | | | |
| Mouvement Socialiste Mauricien | | 26 } | |
| Mauritius Labour Party | C | 9 } | |
| Parti Mauricien Social Démocrate | | 4 } | (43) |
| Org. du Peuple Rodriguais | | 2 } | |
| Mouvement Militant Mauricien | | } | |
| Mouvement Travailliste Démocrate | L | 21 } | (19) |
| Front des Travailleurs Socialiste | | } | |
| **Mexico (July 1985)** | | | |
| Partido Revolucionario Institucional | CR | 64.8 | 289 (299) |
| Partido Acción Nacional | CR | 16.2 | 41 } |
| Partido Auténtico de la Revolución | CR | 3.1 | 9 } (101) |
| Others | — | ... | 61 } |
| **Monaco (1983)** | | | |
| Union Nationale et Démocratique | — | ... | 18 (18) |
| **Mongolia (June 1986)** | | | |
| Mongolian People's Revolutionary Party | — | 99.9 | 370 (354) |
| **Morocco (September 1984)** | | | |
| Union Constitutionelle | CR | ... | 83 — |
| Rassemblement National des Indépendants | CR | ... | 61 (141) |
| Mouvement Populaire | CR | ... | 47 (44) |
| Istiqlal (Independence) | C | ... | 41 (49) |
| Union Socialiste des Forces Populaires | L | ... | 36 (16) |
| Others | — | ... | 38 (14) |
| **Mozambique (November–December 1986)** | | | |
| Frente da Libertação de Moçambique (Frelimo) | — | ... | 250 (210) |
| **Nauru (January 1987)** | | | |
| Independents | — | — | 18 (18) |
| **Nepal (May 1986)** | | | |
| 140-member Parliament, 122 elected and 28 appointed by the king; no parties | — | — | |
| **Netherlands, The (May 1986)** | | | |
| Christen Democratisch Appèl | CR | 34.6 | 54 (45) |
| Volkspartij voor Vrijheid en Democratie | C | 17.4 | 27 (36) |
| Democraten 1966 | C | 6.1 | 9 (6) |
| Partij van de Arbeid | SD | 33.3 | 52 (47) |
| Others | — | ... | 8 (16) |
| **New Zealand (August 1987)** | | | |
| National (Conservative) Party | CR | 45.0 | 39 (37) |
| Democratic Party | C | 6.0 | 0 (2) |
| Labour Party | L | 47.0 | 58 (56) |
| **Nicaragua (November 1984)** | | | |
| Democratic Conservative Party | CR | 14.0 | 14 |
| Independent Liberal Party | C | 9.6 | 9 |
| Popular Social Christian Party | L | 5.6 | 6 |
| Sandinista National Liberation Front | L | 66.8 | 61 |
| Socialist Party of Nicaragua | EL | 1.4 | 2 |
| Communist Party of Nicaragua | K | 1.5 | 2 |
| Marxist-Leninist Popular Action Movement | K | 1.0 | 2 |

# Political Parties

| Country / Name of party | Affiliation | Voting strength (%) | Parliamentary representation |
|---|---|---|---|
| **Niger** | | | |
| Military government since April 1974 | — | — | — |
| **Nigeria** | | | |
| Military government since December 1983 | — | — | — |
| **Norway (September 1985)** | | | |
| Høyre (Conservative) | R | 30.1 | 50 (53) |
| Kristelig Folkeparti | CR | 8.3 | 16 (15) |
| Senterpartiet (Agrarian) | C | 6.7 | 12 (11) |
| Venstre (Liberal) | C | 3.1 | 0 (2) |
| Progress Party | C | 3.7 | 2 (4) |
| Arbeiderpartiet (Labour) | SD | 41.2 | 71 (66) |
| Sosialistisk Venstreparti (Socialist Left) | S | 5.4 | 6 (4) |
| **Oman** | | | |
| Independent sultanate, no parties | — | — | — |
| **Pakistan (February 1985)** | | | |
| National Assembly (no parties) | — | ... | 237 |
| **Panama** | | | |
| Since July 1982 a civilian president under "indirect" military supervision | — | — | — |
| **Papua New Guinea (June–July 1987)** | | | |
| Pangu Party | — | 14.7 | 26 (51) |
| People's Democratic Movement | — | 10.8 | 18 — |
| National Party | — | 5.1 | 12 (13) |
| Melanesian Alliance | — | 5.6 | 7 (8) |
| People's Action Party | — | 3.2 | 6 (7) |
| People's Progress Party | — | 6.1 | 5 (14) |
| Others | — | ... | 14 (12) |
| Independents | — | 41.2 | 21 (4) |
| **Paraguay (February 1983)** | | | |
| Partido Colorado (A. Stroessner) | R | 90.0 | 40 |
| Opposition parties | — | 10.0 | 20 |
| **Peru (April 1985)** | | | |
| Convergencia Democrática | R | ... | 12 |
| Acción Popular | CR | ... | 10 |
| Alianza Popular Revolucionaria Americana | SD | ... | 107 |
| Izquierda Unida | L | ... | 48 |
| Izquierda Nacionalista | L | ... | 1 |
| Independents | — | ... | 2 |
| **Philippines (May 1987)** | | | |
| House of Representatives | — | ... | 200 |
| **Poland (October 1985)** | | | |
| Front of National Unity | | | |
| Polish United Workers' Party | | | 245 (261) |
| United Peasants' party | | | 106 (113) |
| Democratic Party | — | 78.86 | 35 (37) |
| Non-party | | | 74 (49) |
| **Portugal (July 1987)** | | | |
| Social Democratic Centre Party | R | 4.4 | 4 (22) |
| Democratic Renewal Party | CR | 4.9 | 7 (45) |
| Social Democratic Party | C | 50.2 | 148 (88) |
| Socialist Party | SD | 22.2 | 60 (57) |
| United People's Alliance | K | 12.1 | 31 (38) |
| **Qatar** | | | |
| Independent emirate, no parties | — | — | — |
| **Romania (March 1985)** | | | |
| Social Democracy and Unity Front | — | 99.99 | 369 (369) |
| **Rwanda (December 1983)** | | | |
| National Revolutionary Development Movement | — | ... | 70 |
| **Saint Christopher and Nevis (June 1984)** | | | |
| People's Action Movement | CR | ... | 6 (3) |
| Nevis Reformation Party | CR | ... | 3 (2) |
| Labour Party | L | ... | 2 (4) |
| **Saint Lucia (April 1987)** | | | |
| United Workers' Party | C | 52.7 | 9 (14) |
| St. Lucia Labour Party | S | 38.1 | 8 (2) |
| Progressive Labour Party | EL | 9.2 | 0 (1) |
| **Saint Vincent and the Grenadines (July 1984)** | | | |
| St. Vincent Labour Party | CR | 41.4 | 4 (11) |
| New Democratic Party | C | 51.4 | 9 (2) |
| United People's Movement | L | 3.2 | 0 (0) |
| **San Marino (May 1983)** | | | |
| Communist coalition | | | |
| Partito Comunista | | 15 | (16) |
| Partito Socialista | | ... | (8) |
| Partito Socialista Unitario | | 8 | (8) |
| Christian Democrats | | ... | 26 (26) |
| Social Democratic Party | | ... | 1 (2) |
| Republican Party | | | 1 — |
| **São Tomé and Principe (August–September 1985)** | | | |
| Movimento Libertação | — | — | 40 |
| **Saudi Arabia** | | | |
| Royal government, no parties | — | — | — |
| **Senegal (February 1983)** | | | |
| Parti Socialiste | CR | 79.9 | 111 (83) |
| Parti Démocratique Sénégalais | L | 14.0 | 8 (17) |
| Rassemblement National Démocratique | EL | 2.6 | 1 — |
| Ligue Démocratique | K | 1.1 | 0 — |
| **Seychelles (December 1987)** | | | |
| People's Progressive Front | — | ... | 23 (23) |
| **Sierra Leone (May–June 1986)** | | | |
| All People's Congress and independents | — | ... | 105 (85) |
| **Singapore (December 1984)** | | | |
| People's Action Party | CR | 64.38 | 77 (75) |
| Workers' Party | L | 12.79 | 1 (0) |
| Democratic Party | — | 3.70 | 1 (0) |
| **Solomon Islands (October 1984)** | | | |
| National Democratic Party | L | ... | 1 |
| United Party | — | ... | 13 |
| People's Alliance Party | — | ... | 12 |
| Solomone Ano Sagufenua | — | ... | 4 |
| Independents | — | ... | 7 |
| **Somalia (December 1984)** | | | |
| Somalian Revolutionary Socialist Party | — | 99.86 | 171 (171) |
| **South Africa (May 1987)** | | | |
| Herstigte Nasionale Party | ER | 3.1 | 0 (0) |
| Conservative Party | R | 26.4 | 22 — |
| National Party | R | 52.5 | 123 (131) |
| New Republic Party | C | 1.9 | 1 (8) |
| Progressive Federal Party | L | 14.1 | 19 (26) |
| Independent | | 0.04 | 1 — |
| **Spain (June 1986)** | | | |
| Alianza Popular | R | 26 | 105 (105) |
| Centro Democrático y Social | C | 9 | 19 (11) |
| Convergència (Catalan nationalists) | C | 4 | 18 (12) |
| Partido Socialista Obrero Español | SD | 44.1 | 184 (202) |
| Izquierda Unida (Communists) | K | 4 | 7 — |
| Partido Nacionalista Vasco | — | 1.5 | 6 (8) |
| Herri Batasuna (Basque radicals) | — | 1.1 | 5 (2) |
| Others | — | | 6 (10) |
| **Sri Lanka (July 1977)** | | | |
| United National Party | R | ... | 140 (19) |
| Freedom Party | C | ... | 8 (91) |
| Tamil United Liberation Front | C | ... | 18 (12) |
| Communists and others | — | ... | 2 (44) |
| **Sudan, The (April 1986)** | | | |
| National Islamic Front | R | ... | 51 |
| National Umma Party | C | ... | 99 |
| Democratic Unionist Party | L | ... | 63 |
| South Sudan Political Alliance | — | ... | 9 |
| 39 other parties | — | ... | 42 |
| **Suriname (November 1987)** | | | |
| National Democratic Party | — | ... | 2 |
| Front for Democracy and Development (three-party coalition) | — | ... | 42 |
| Others | — | ... | 7 |
| **Swaziland (November 1987)** | | | |
| House of Assembly, no parties | — | ... | 40 |
| **Sweden (September 1985)** | | | |
| Conservative | R | 21.4 | 76 (86) |
| Centre | CR | 12.5 | 44 (56) |
| Liberal | C | 14.3 | 51 (21) |
| Social Democrats | SD | 44.9 | 159 (166) |
| Communists | K | 5.4 | 19 (20) |
| **Switzerland (October 1987)** | | | |
| Christian Democrats | R | ... | 42 (42) |
| National Campaign | R | ... | 3 (5) |
| Evangelical People's | R | ... | 3 (3) |
| Swiss People's | CR | ... | 25 (23) |
| Radical Democrats | C | ... | 51 (54) |
| League of Independents | C | ... | 8 (8) |
| Liberal Democrats | L | ... | 9 (8) |
| Social Democrats | SD | ... | 41 (47) |
| Progressive Organization (Socialists) | EL | ... | 4 (3) |
| Communist Party | K | ... | 1 (1) |
| Environmentalist Party | — | ... | 9 (3) |
| Others | — | ... | 4 (3) |
| **Syria (February 1986)** | | | |
| Ba'th Party | — | ... | 129 |
| National Progressive Front | — | ... | 57 |
| Communist Party | — | ... | 9 |
| **Taiwan (Republic of China)** | | | |
| Nationalist (Kuomintang) | — | ... | 773 |
| **Tanzania (October 1985)** | | | |
| Chama Cha Mapinduzi | — | ... | 169 (111) |
| **Thailand (July 1986)** | | | |
| Prachakorn Thai | ER | ... | 24 (36) |
| Chart Thai Nation | R | ... | 63 (73) |
| Democratic Party | C | ... | 100 (56) |
| Social Action Party | C | ... | 51 (92) |
| United Democratic Party | C | ... | 38 — |
| United Thai Party | — | ... | 19 (0) |
| Others | — | ... | 52 (67) |
| **Togo (March 1985)** | | | |
| Rassemblement du Peuple Togolais | — | 96.0 | 77 (67) |
| **Tonga (February 1987)** | | | |
| Legislative Assembly (partially elected) | — | ... | 28 |
| **Trinidad and Tobago (December 1986)** | | | |
| People's National Movement | C | 32 | 3 (26) |
| National Alliance for Reconstruction (four parties) | — | 66 | 33 — |
| **Tunisia (November 1986)** | | | |
| National Front (led by the Parti Socialiste Destourien) | — | ... | 138 (136) |
| **Turkey (November 1987)** | | | |
| Right Path | CR | 19.2 | 59 — |
| Motherland | CR | 36.2 | 292 (212) |
| Social Democratic Populist | C | 24.8 | 99 — |
| Democratic Left | L | 8.5 | 0 — |
| Others | — | 10.9 | 0 (188) |
| **Tuvalu (September 1985)** | | | |
| House of Assembly, no political parties | — | ... | 12 |
| **Uganda** | | | |
| Military Council in power since July 1985 | — | — | — |
| **Union of Soviet Socialist Republics (November 1984)** | | | |
| Communist Party of the Soviet Union | — | 99.99 | 1,500 (1,500) |
| **United Arab Emirates** | | | |
| Federal government of seven emirates | — | — | — |
| **United Kingdom (June 1987)** | | | |
| Conservative | R | 42.3 | 375 (397) |
| Alliance | | | |
| Liberal | C | 12.8 | 17 (17) |
| Social Democratic | SD | 9.8 | 5 (6) |
| Labour | L | 30.8 | 229 (209) |
| Communist | K | ... | 0 (0) |
| Scottish National Party | — | 1.3 | 3 (2) |
| Plaid Cymru (Welsh Nationalists) | — | 0.4 | 3 (2) |
| Ulster Unionists (three groups) | — | 1.2 | 13 (15) |
| Social Democratic and Labour Party | — | ... | 3 (1) |
| Sinn Fein (Northern Ireland) | — | ... | 1 1 |
| Other (speaker) | — | ... | 1 — |
| **United States (November 1986)** | | | |
| Republican | CR | ... | 177 (183) |
| Democratic | C | ... | 258 (252) |
| **Uruguay (November 1984)** | | | |
| Colorado Party (Conservative) | R | 38.6 | 40 |
| Unión Cívica | CR | 2.3 | 2 |
| National (Blanco) Party | C | 32.9 | 36 |
| Frento Amplio (Broad Front) | L | 20.4 | 21 |
| **Vanuatu (November 1983)** | | | |
| Vanuaaku Pati | C | ... | 24 (26) |
| Others | — | ... | 15 (13) |
| **Venezuela (December 1983)** | | | |
| COPEI (Social Christians) | CR | 28.31 | ... (88) |
| Acción Democrática | L | 44.25 | 118 (88) |
| Movimiento al Socialismo | SD | ... | ... (11) |
| Partido Comunista Venezolano | K | ... | ... (7) |
| Others | — | ... | ... (7) |
| **Vietnam (April 1987)** | | | |
| Vietnam Fatherland Front | — | ... | 496 |
| **Yemen, People's Democratic Republic of (October 1986)** | | | |
| Yemen Socialist Party and independents | — | ... | 111 |
| **Yemen Arab Republic** | | | |
| Military government since 1974 | — | — | — |
| **Yugoslavia (May 1986)** | | | |
| Communist-controlled Federal Chamber | K | ... | 220 (220) |
| **Zaire (September 1987)** | | | |
| Mouvement Populaire de la Révolution | — | ... | 210 (268) |
| **Zambia (October 1983)** | | | |
| United National Independence Party | — | 67.0 | 125 |
| **Zimbabwe (June–July 1985)** | | | |
| Zimbabwe African National Union | — | 77.0 | 63 (57) |
| Zimbabwe African People's Union | — | 20.0 | 15 (20) |
| United African National Council | — | ... | 0 (3) |
| Zimbabwe African National Union (Sithole) | — | ... | 1 (0) |
| white roll | | | |
| Conservative Alliance of Zimbabwe | — | ... | 15 (20) |
| Independent Zimbabwe | — | ... | 4 — |
| Independent | — | ... | 1 (0) |

(K. M. SMOGORZEWSKI)

# Africa South of the Sahara

## AFRICAN AFFAIRS

Following two seasons of reasonable rainfall during which African countries made some progress toward meeting their food requirements, drought and famine again threatened much of the continent in late 1987. Promise of economic recovery was also impeded by a substantial drop in world prices for the continent's main export crops and minerals. After a slow start in recognizing the extent of AIDS (acquired immune deficiency syndrome), most countries began to take more vigorous measures to face up to this threat. (*See* HEALTH AND DISEASE: *Special Report.*) Despite two successful coups, a degree of internal security prevailed in a majority of sub-Saharan countries; the exceptions were those in southern Africa and the Horn of Africa, as well as Uganda and The Sudan.

**Organization of African Unity.** The annual summit of the Organization of African Unity (OAU), which met in Addis Ababa, Eth., in July–August, was attended by only 20 presidents and 4 prime ministers of the 50 member nations, reflecting the fact that a comparatively low priority was being given to the current deliberations. Although the African Economic Recovery Plan (AERP) was featured prominently on the agenda, the two issues that dominated discussions were the conflicts in southern Africa and Chad. Greater support was pledged to the liberation movements of South Africa and South West Africa/Namibia as well as to South Africa's neighbours in their effort to reduce their dependence on the Pretoria regime. Pres. Kenneth Kaunda of Zambia was elected chairman for 1987–88. The OAU's financial affairs remained in a perilous state because of the failure of members to meet their obligations.

The OAU Defense Commission reported on the difficulties of creating an African peacekeeping force, but it did produce a protocol providing for the establishment of an "African defense organ" as a framework institution for coordinating such activities as uniformity of weapons, local production of armaments, and a common syllabus in African military colleges. The OAU Planning Ministers' Conference, which met in Addis Ababa in April, reviewed progress in implementing the Substantial New Program of Action (SNPA). The SNPA had attracted a grant of $8.6 million annually from the industrial nations to help Africa's officially designated least developed countries (LDCs), whose number rose to 27; they contained 35% of the continent's total population.

**Southern Africa.** There was no lessening of the conflicts inside South Africa or in neighbouring countries—especially Mozambique, Angola, and Namibia. The South African Army continued to make irregular attacks into Angola, Botswana, Zambia, and Zimbabwe. The major security problems, however, were caused by increased rebel activities on the part of the Mozambique National Resistance (MNR, or Renamo) and the unflagging resistance of the National Union for the Total Independence of Angola (UNITA). Both these movements badly crippled the economy and security of the respective countries in which they operated. Although it was not formally renounced, the 1984 Nkomati accord between South Africa and Mozambique was inoperative. South Africa continued to complain about the support given by its neighbours to the guerrilla forces of the African National Congress (ANC) and the South West Africa People's Organization (SWAPO), using this support as the reason for its punitive military and economic actions against its neighbours.

The Commonwealth heads of government meeting in Vancouver, B.C., in October was unanimous in calling for a comprehensive response from the international community to help South Africa's neighbours resist what its final communiqué described as "Pretoria's policy of destabilization and destruction." It stressed the need for international support to address the security needs of the frontline states (Angola, Botswana, Mozambique, Tanzania, Zambia, and Zimbabwe) and to assist in developing safe corridors for their exports to the ports of Mozambique and Tanzania as an alternative to exporting them through South Africa. Mozambique was identified as occupying a key geographic position in the region.

**Horn of Africa.** The People's Democratic Republic of Ethiopia was formally proclaimed as a Marxist-Leninist state in a new constitution adopted in September. Its promise of a measure of autonomy for dissident provinces failed to meet the demands of the major resistance movements in Eritrea and Tigrai, where the scale of fighting remained undiminished. Ethiopia's support for the rebel Sudan People's Liberation Army (SPLA) troubled relations between the two countries. The civil war in The Sudan showed no sign of lessening. Despite the previous year's agreement between Ethiopia and Somalia, rebel forces opposed to the Somalian regime continued to make transborder military attacks from their positions in Ethiopia.

**Coups and Inter-African Affairs.** Pres. Jean-Baptiste Bagaza of Burundi was deposed in a military coup in September, and Capt. Thomas Sankara, president of Burkina Faso, was killed in a successful military coup in

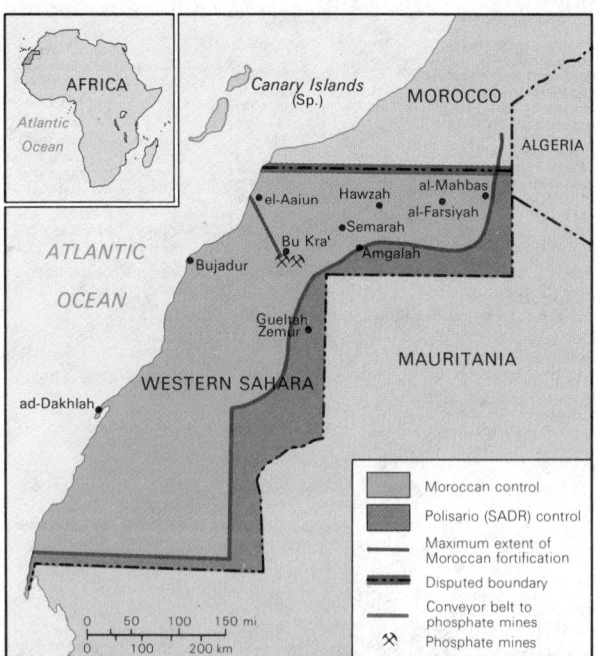

The Polisario Front, formed by native Saharans in 1973, forced Spain's withdrawal from the Spanish Sahara in 1976. The territory became known as Western Sahara and was divided between Morocco and Mauritania. When Mauritania relinquished its claim in 1979, Morocco occupied the entire region. Polisario subsequently declared independence and formed a government, the Saharan Arab Democratic Republic (SADR). By 1987 Morocco controlled most of the original area from behind a barrier of six successively extended walls. The entire territory was considered disputed, but most countries in the Organization of African Unity (OAU) recognized the SADR.

October. Resistance to the military regime of Pres. Yoweri Museveni resulted in the prolongation of violence in Uganda. The repercussions of the struggle seriously troubled Uganda's relations with two of its neighbours, The Sudan and Kenya.

The Chadian Army achieved a notable victory over Libyan forces during the year, thanks in large measure to direct military assistance from France. The Libyans, nevertheless, continued to fight back in support of their claims to sovereignty over the Aozou strip in northern Chad. Although the OAU supported Pres. Hissen Habré's legitimacy, it failed to take a stand on Libya's claim. Chad accused The Sudan of allowing its territory to be used by the Libyans.

Fighting in the Western Sahara between the Moroccan Army and forces of the Popular Front for the Liberation of Saguia el Hamra and Río de Oro (Polisario Front) continued on a much reduced scale as the dispute over the latter's claims to the territory remained unresolved. Attempts by the OAU to mediate led nowhere. Morocco, which had withdrawn from the OAU in 1984 because of its recognition of the Saharan Arab Democratic Republic, Western Sahara's government-in-exile, maintained its claims to sovereignty over the whole territory. Algeria continued to be the principal military supporter of the Polisario Front.

Acting under pressure from the frontline states over its alleged support for the MNR, Malawi reversed its position and committed part of its army to helping defend its rail route to Nacala, Mozambique, against MNR attacks. Accused by the frontline states of allowing U.S. and other military supplies to be shipped across its territory to UNITA, Zaire persisted in denying the accusation. A joint move by Zaire, Zambia, and Angola, with U.S. backing, to open the important Benguela rail route to Lobito—virtually blocked by UNITA since 1976—failed to yield results.

**Political Systems.** In September Ethiopia became the first structured Marxist-Leninist state in the continent with allegiance to the U.S.S.R. as "the leader of the world's progressive forces." Hopes for the consolidation of a multiparty parliamentary democratic system for The Sudan, following the military's withdrawal to the barracks in 1985, remained unfulfilled because of the failure to end the civil war. The main obstacle to agreement was the controversy surrounding Prime Minister Sadiq al-Mahdi's insistence that the proposed new democratic constitution include a system of Shari'ah (laws based on the Qur'an) applicable only to the Muslim population. The rebel SPLA, led by Col. John Garang, as well as all southern political parties and secularist leaders in the north, refused to accept any entrenchment of Islamic law in a new constitution.

Zimbabwe moved close to becoming a one-party state when its Parliament voted to abolish the 20 seats reserved for the white minority. The ruling Zimbabwe African National Union, led by Prime Minister Robert Mugabe, and the Zimbabwe African People's Union, led by Joshua Nkomo, reached a unity agreement in December, and on December 31 Mugabe was sworn in as the country's executive president. Nkomo was made a vice-president.

**External Relations.** The demand for comprehensive international sanctions against South Africa by the OAU and the ANC remained a major divisive factor in relations between a majority of African leaders and the Western community. While welcoming the decision by the U.S. Congress and the European Communities to impose a limited program of sanctions, they accused the Western countries of hanging back because of their economic interests in South Africa.

Soviet bloc countries continued their military aid programs to Angola and to a smaller extent to Mozambique, Zimbabwe, and Zambia, as well as to the ANC and SWAPO. Despite disagreements with the U.S., which was providing military aid to UNITA and supporting South Africa's linkage of Cuban troop withdrawals to Namibian independence, the Angolan regime continued to negotiate with the U.S. over a phased withdrawal of Cuban troops as part of an agreement to secure the withdrawal of South African troops from Angolan territory and to facilitate progress toward Namibian independence. Western countries pledged full support to Mozambique in its struggle against the MNR and South Africa.

**Social and Economic Conditions.** The International Monetary Fund (IMF) predicted that the aggregate real gross domestic product (GDP) of Africa would increase by 2.1% during 1987 and by a further 3.8% in the following year. The IMF warned, however, that 15 of the continent's poorest countries were close to total collapse as a result of rising debt, plummeting living standards, and low world prices for commodities. It noted that the persistence of the debt problem continued to retard the progress of heavily indebted middle-income countries. The total debt of sub-Saharan countries (excluding South Africa and Nigeria) was estimated at $86.2 billion and was expected to reach $92.9 billion in 1988. The ratio of this debt to exports was estimated at 301.5%. The net external financing need for the region was put at $6.9 billion.

A UN report entitled *Africa: One Year Later* showed that 28 African countries had adopted economic policy reforms and structural adjustment measures. Among the measures taken were sharp reductions in social spending and government payrolls, enlargement of the private sector, privatization of state corporations, and reduction of subsidies to state enterprises. According to the report, nearly two-thirds of African governments reached the target of 25% of total investment allocated to agricultural production, which resulted in a 3% increase in food output. The sharpest decline in export earnings since 1950 took place during the year.

The rate of infant deaths continued to drop—from 167 for every 1,000 births in 1965 to 104 in 1985. Over the same period the number of children enrolled in primary schools rose, on average, from 41 to 80%.

President Kaunda highlighted the threat to Africa from AIDS by revealing that his 32-year-old son had died from the disease. Studies showed that among the biggest sufferers were the African middle class—teachers, physicians, engineers, and military officers. In the cities of Central and East Africa, the studies suggested, between 10 and 20% of people aged 15 to 40 years had been exposed to the AIDS virus.                                        (COLIN LEGUM)

See also *Dependent States,* below.

# ANGOLA

A people's republic, Angola is located on the Atlantic coast in southwestern Africa. The small exclave of Cabinda is separated from Angola by a strip of Zaire. Area: 1,246,700 sq km (481,350 sq mi). Pop. (1987 est.): 9,105,000. Cap.: Luanda. Monetary unit: kwanza, with (Oct. 5, 1987) a free rate of 30.53 kwanzas to U.S. $1 (49.58 kwanzas = £1 sterling). President in 1987, José Eduardo dos Santos.

The year 1987 began with the customary announcement of military successes by rebel forces of the National Union for the Total Independence of Angola (UNITA) during the rainy-season offensive that had begun in November 1986. Although such reports were difficult to check and were probably exaggerated, the government's emphasis on South

UNITA rebels fire a mortar at an Angolan government position. The rebels, supported by the U.S. and South Africa, continued to thwart attempts by the Soviet-backed Angolan Army to capture rebel-held territory in southern Angola.
MARK PETERS/THE NEW YORK TIMES

African military incursions over the southern border could not conceal the widespread if limited nature of the UNITA attacks, some of which even took place within the Cabinda enclave, well-guarded by Cuban troops. The effectiveness of UNITA operations was enhanced by arms supplies from the U.S. Accusations that the U.S. was secretly sending arms to UNITA via Zaire were first made in late 1986. By mid-1987 it was openly admitted that U.S. Central Intelligence Agency funds had provided arms to UNITA worth $15 million in the previous year and that further supplies would be made available in 1987. Of particular importance were Stinger antiaircraft missiles, and antitank missiles were also promised to offset the government's acquisition of additional Soviet tanks.

In July Chester Crocker, U.S. assistant secretary of state for African affairs, visited Luanda for discussions with the government after formal contacts between the two countries had been suspended for more than 15 months. It quickly became clear that there had been no change in the U.S. position that Cuban troops would have to leave Angola before the question of Namibian independence could be resolved. The Angolan government rejected equally firmly the right of any foreign power to dictate Angolan policy.

The impact of the civil war on the country's economy continued to be disastrous, though there were hopes that the steadying of oil prices might check the decline in oil revenues. Pres. José Eduardo dos Santos met the presidents of Zaire and Zambia in April to seal an agreement to reopen the Benguela railway, effectively shut down since 1976 because of guerrilla activity. It remained unclear how this was to be achieved, either militarily or financially, but the president discussed the project with French authorities during a visit to Paris in September.

In May talks took place with the Council for Mutual Economic Assistance (Comecon) to consider possible areas of cooperation with the Eastern bloc, and later in the month the U.S.S.R. offered technical assistance to build a hospital in Malange. Gifts of blankets and clothes were received from the Dutch, French, and Spanish national committees of UNICEF, while from India came the offer of a loan of $7.7 million to enable Angola to buy Indian goods to counter possible sanctions by South Africa. This was the result of a visit to Asia by President dos Santos in April. Portugal, in addition to importing 500,000 tons of crude oil from Angola and cooperating in a number

of hydroelectric projects, offered $140 million in credit to assist in the rehabilitation of companies damaged by the flight of European settlers after independence. During his visit to Europe in September, dos Santos became the first president of independent Angola to visit Portugal.

These offers, though helpful, could make little impression on the basic problem of the country's inability to feed its own population. Angola was one of five countries named by the UN Food and Agriculture Organization in February as being in need of emergency food aid; 50% of its food had to be imported. The civil war was the main factor responsible for creating these conditions, and although the government launched its usual dry-weather campaign against the guerrillas in July, there seemed little prospect of a decisive outcome. South Africa's admission in September that it had a military force operating permanently inside Angola's border only exacerbated an already desperate situation. In December South Africa admitted, for the first time, that its troops were fighting alongside those of UNITA.                    (KENNETH INGHAM)

This article updates the *Macropædia* article SOUTHERN AFRICA: *Angola*.

## BENIN

The people's republic of Benin is on the southern coast of West Africa, on the Gulf of Guinea. Area: 112,600 sq km (43,450 sq mi). Pop. (1987 est.): 4,307,000. Cap.: Porto-Novo (official); Cotonou (de facto). Monetary unit: CFA franc, with (Oct. 5, 1987) a par value of CFAF 50 to the French franc and a free rate of CFAF 306.67 to U.S. $1 (CFAF 498 = £1 sterling). President in 1987, Brig. Gen. Mathieu Kérékou.

On Feb. 13, 1987, Pres. Mathieu Kérékou of Benin implemented a major Cabinet reshuffle, replacing 5 members of the 14-strong government and switching the portfolios of 2 more. The changes were generally interpreted as a sign of continued drift away from Marxist ideology. Meanwhile, a call by Amnesty International for the release or trial of nearly 90 detainees—many of whom had been arrested in connection with student demonstrations that started in March 1985—coincided with new demonstrations over living conditions at the university at Abomey-Calavi.

Students were not alone in suffering a drop in living standards. Talks continued with the International Monetary Fund over funding to resolve severe balance of payments difficulties, made worse by a decline in production at the Sèmè oil field following failure of a production deal with the Panocean Company in 1986. Economic matters were high on the agenda when Nigeria's Pres. Ibrahim Babangida visited Cotonou in early July 1987. Relations between the two countries had improved since Nigeria reopened their mutual border in March 1986.　　　(NIM CASWELL)

This article updates the *Macropædia* article WESTERN AFRICA: *Benin.*

## BOTSWANA

A landlocked republic of southern Africa, Botswana is a member of the Commonwealth. Area: 581,730 sq km (224,607 sq mi). Pop. (1987 est.): 1,168,000. Cap.: Gaborone. Monetary unit: pula, with (Oct. 5, 1987) a free rate of 1.71 pula to U.S. $1 (2.77 pula = £1 sterling). President in 1987, Quett Masire.

In 1987 Pres. Quett Masire appealed for international aid to combat the effects of the sixth consecutive year of drought, which had decimated cattle and wiped out crops throughout Botswana. The drought relief program, which was to be extended to the end of 1988, was costing the government $13 million a year.

In July De Beers Consolidated Mines purchased Botswana's diamond stockpile for a mixture of cash and shares. The total value of the deal was not disclosed. Diamonds, which now provided at least 60% of the country's foreign exchange and 50% of government revenue, earned $600 million in 1986–87, more than South Africa earned from the same source. The economy was one of the strongest in Africa; besides diamonds, the main sources of income were the South African Customs Union, which accounted for 14% of revenue, and beef.

Because the economy was deeply penetrated by that of South Africa, Botswana had to perform a more or less constant balancing act; 81% of imports came from South Africa, 90% of trade passed through it, and some 26,000 citizens of Botswana worked there. South Africa exerted constant pressure upon Botswana to deny entry to refugees, whom Pretoria always insisted were terrorists, while the huge open border between the two countries provided another source of friction.　　　(GUY ARNOLD)

This article updates the *Macropædia* article SOUTHERN AFRICA: *Botswana.*

## BURKINA FASO

Burkina Faso is a landlocked country of West Africa. Area: 274,200 sq km (105,869 sq mi). Pop. (1987 est.): 8,308,000. Cap.: Ouagadougou. Monetary unit: CFA franc, with (Oct. 5, 1987) a par value of CFAF 50 to the French franc and a free rate of CFAF 306.67 to U.S. $1 (CFAF 498 = £1 sterling). Chairman of the National Recovery Council (president) to Oct. 15, 1987, Capt. Thomas Sankara; chairman of the Popular Front and head of state from October 15, Capt. Blaise Compaoré.

On Oct. 15, 1987, Capt. Thomas Sankara (*see* OBITUARIES) was killed in a coup that brought Capt. Blaise Compaoré (*see* BIOGRAPHIES), leader of a group of army officers calling itself the Popular Front, to power in Burkina Faso. Some 100 people were reported to have been killed in clashes between rival groups of soldiers in Ouagadougou during the coup. A longtime associate of Sankara, Compaoré had led the rebellion that brought him to power in August 1983 and had been Sankara's second-in-command during his years in power. The 1987 coup was justified by the new regime on the grounds that Sankara had begun to monopolize power and to pursue policies that threatened to lead the country into chaos.

Capt. Blaise Compaoré became the new leader of Burkina Faso after an October coup ended the regime of Capt. Thomas Sankara. Although he was less charismatic than his predecessor, Compaoré was expected to continue similar government policies.
PHILIPPE BOUDIN—GAMMA/LIAISON

The new regime pledged to continue the self-styled revolutionary course of its predecessor but stated that some adjustments would be necessary. The new Cabinet announced on October 31 was predominantly civilian and retained a number of ministers from the Sankara era.

Earlier in 1987 the measures introduced by Sankara in pursuit of economic self-sufficiency had proved increasingly less popular as living standards declined. He remained, however, a charismatic leader whose death was widely mourned at home and throughout much of West Africa.

　　　(NIM CASWELL)

This article updates the *Macropædia* article WESTERN AFRICA: *Burkina Faso.*

## BURUNDI

Burundi is a landlocked republic of central Africa. Area: 27,834 sq km (10,747 sq mi). Pop. (1987 est.): 4,989,000. Cap.: Bujumbura. Monetary unit: Burundi franc, with (Oct. 5, 1987) a free rate of FBu 126.19 to U.S. $1 (FBu 204.92 = £1 sterling). President to Sept. 3, 1987, Col. Jean-Baptiste Bagaza; head of the Military Committee for National Salvation from September 3 to September 9 and president from September 9, Maj. Pierre Buyoya.

On Sept. 3, 1987, while Col. Jean-Baptiste Bagaza was attending a meeting of French-speaking leaders in Canada, he was replaced as Burundi's head of state by Maj. Pierre Buyoya (*see* BIOGRAPHIES) in a bloodless coup. Buyoya justified the coup on the grounds that all power had been vested in the hands of the president, that the constitution was constantly violated, and that massive corruption existed. The same reasons had been advanced in 1976 to justify the overthrow of Michel Micombero by Bagaza. Buyoya promised to increase individual rights and to allow greater religious freedom. A 31-member Military Committee for National Salvation was established, and on September 9 it elected Buyoya president.

Burundi's relations with its neighbours had become increasingly strained during the final months of Bagaza's rule. In April Tanzania expelled some 2,000 illegal Burundi immigrants. At the same time, a long-running dispute between the government and the Roman Catholic Church came to a head; the government banned lay preaching, dissolved the Catholic parish councils, and in June placed a ban on weekday masses. The quarrel led to a deterioration in relations with Belgium, the former colonial power.

(GUY ARNOLD)

This article updates the *Macropædia* article CENTRAL AFRICA: *Burundi.*

## CAMEROON

A republic of western central Africa, Cameroon lies on the Gulf of Guinea. Area: 465,458 sq km (179,714 sq mi). Pop. (1987 est.): 10,759,000. Cap.: Yaoundé. Monetary unit: CFA franc, with (Oct. 5, 1987) a par value of CFAF 50 to the French franc and a free rate of CFAF 306.67 to U.S. $1 (CFAF 498 = £1 sterling). President in 1987, Paul Biya.

The cautious process of political liberalization in Cameroon continued in 1987, with the adoption of legislation permitting multiple candidacies in municipal elections, held in October, and legislative elections scheduled for March 1988. Multiparty politics remained banned, however, and Pres. Paul Biya's Rassemblement Démocratique du Peuple Camerounais remained the sole legal party. In January William Eteki Mboumoua was abruptly dismissed as foreign affairs minister for allegedly acting without presidential authority.

The year was marked by President Biya's first full state visit to France in May. The Canadian and Israeli prime ministers visited Cameroon in February and June, respectively, while Biya visited Morocco in April.

The economy remained in difficulties, despite a recovery in the world oil price. By the time the sixth five-year (1986–91) plan was published early in 1987, its targeted 6.7% average annual growth rate looked overoptimistic. Severe public spending cuts were implemented in midyear.

(NIM CASWELL)

This article updates the *Macropædia* article WESTERN AFRICA: *Cameroon.*

## CAPE VERDE

The republic of Cape Verde occupies an island group in the Atlantic Ocean about 620 km (385 mi) off the west coast of Africa. Area: 4,033 sq km (1,557 sq mi). Pop. (1987 est.): 350,000. Cap.: Praia. Monetary unit: Cape Verde escudo, with (Oct. 5, 1987) a free rate of 89.27 escudos to U.S. $1 (144.97 escudos = £1 sterling). President in 1987, Aristides Pereira; prime minister, Pedro Pires.

As Cape Verde possessed no productive resources, with the exception of fish, it remained heavily dependent upon international aid. Remittances from Cape Verdians abroad provided 40% of government revenue, while 80% of investment was in the form of foreign aid. Revenue was also derived from the provision of services, including landing rights for South African Airways; the U.S. decision to ban flights to and from South Africa cost Cape Verde an estimated $3 million a year. The cost of servicing the national debt was expected to reach $10.9 million by 1990, equivalent to 20% of exports. The high birthrate—an estimated 4.4 children per woman—represented yet another strain on the economy. Despite these adverse conditions, the economy registered some positive growth, and there was a high level of productive investment.

The lifting of visa restrictions on Cape Verdians by Portugal in October 1986 was a sign of the excellent relations between the two countries. During 1987 Cape Verde exchanged ambassadors with Kuwait. Pres. Aristides Pereira visited Brazil and Argentina, and Pres. Joaquim Chissanó of Mozambique paid a five-day visit to Cape Verde. In July a law decriminalizing abortion led to antigovernment demonstrations.

(GUY ARNOLD)

This article updates the *Macropædia* article WESTERN AFRICA: *Cape Verde.*

## CENTRAL AFRICAN REPUBLIC

The Central African Republic is a landlocked state in central Africa. Area: 622,436 sq km (240,324 sq mi). Pop. (1987 est.): 2,774,000. Cap.: Bangui. Monetary unit: CFA franc, with (Oct. 5, 1987) a par value of CFAF 50 to the French franc and a free rate of CFAF 306.67 to U.S. $1 (CFAF 498 = £1 sterling). Head of state in 1987, Gen. André Kolingba.

The first half of 1987 was overshadowed by the trial of Jean-Bedel Bokassa, who had been deposed as leader of the Central African Republic in 1979 and had returned unexpectedly to Bangui in October 1986. Originally scheduled to open in November 1986 and to last just one month, the trial dragged on until June. The one-time dictator and self-styled emperor was charged on 14 counts, and on June 14 he was found guilty of 4, including conspiracy to murder, illegal detentions, and embezzlement. The death sentence passed was, however, widely expected to be commuted by Pres. André Kolingba.

Implementation of the new one-party constitution approved by referendum in November 1986 continued. The founding assembly of the Rassemblement Démocratique Centrafricain (RDC), held in February, was attended by about 840 delegates. An interim council of 44 members was appointed pending an extraordinary congress to elect members to the party's political bureau. Elections to the new 52-seat National Assembly on July 31 passed off peacefully.

(NIM CASWELL)

This article updates the *Macropædia* article CENTRAL AFRICA: *Central African Republic.*

## CHAD

Chad is a landlocked republic of central Africa. Area: 1,284,000 sq km (495,755 sq mi). Pop. (1987 est.): 5,265,000. Cap.: N'Djamena. Monetary unit: CFA franc, with (Oct. 5, 1987) a par value of CFAF 50 to the French franc and a free rate of CFAF 306.67 to U.S. $1 (CFAF 498 = £1 sterling). President in 1987, Hissen Habré.

The year 1987 opened with heavy fighting in northern Chad as forces loyal to Pres. Hissen Habré confronted those of Libya and the rump of the Transitional Government of National Unity (GUNT). Government forces took the town of Fada on January 2 and the heavily fortified air and ground base of Ouadi Doum on March 22. Libyan evacuation of Faya-Largeau soon followed. By mid-April the whole of the northern Borkou-Ennedi-Tibesti region south of the Aozou Strip was in government hands, along with large quantities of captured ammunition and equipment.

This dramatic shift in the military balance between N'Djamena and Tripoli was made possible by a series of political realignments during 1986 and early 1987. By mid-January the last of the southern rebel groups (*codos*) had been integrated into Habré's Chadian National Armed Forces (FANT). In a government reshuffle on August 10, Col. Wadal Abdelkader Kamougue, former vice-president of GUNT, was appointed minister of agriculture, and another *codo* leader, Col. Alphonse Kotiga, became energy minister. The position of Goukouni Oueddei, former president of GUNT, remained ambiguous. Though his faction, the People's Armed Forces, fought alongside the FANT during the early 1987 offensives, he was not brought into the government and remained in Algiers.

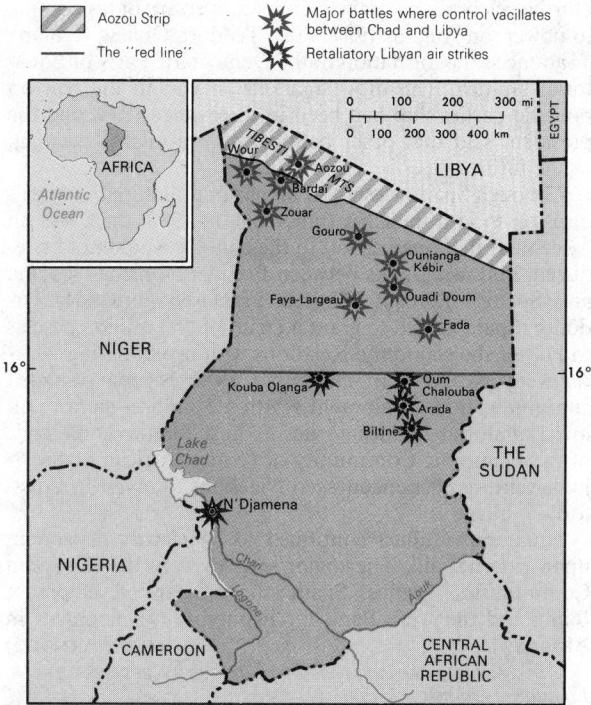

Aozou Strip

The "red line"

Major battles where control vacillates between Chad and Libya

Retaliatory Libyan air strikes

The Aozou Strip in northern Chad, a region rich in uranium and phosphates, has been the subject of a long-standing territorial dispute between Chad and Libya. France has supported the Hissen Habré government of Chad in the area south of the 16th parallel but has not aided in the fight for control of the Aozou Strip because it is considered disputed territory that should be subject to international arbitration. Since its independence in 1960, Chad in general has been the scene of an internal struggle between the northern peoples (largely desert nomads) and the southern peoples (more closely aligned with the rest of sub-Saharan Africa).

A new government offensive on the Aozou Strip began in August. Aozou town was captured briefly on August 8, and on September 5 Chad took the war into undisputed Libyan territory with an attack on the Maaten es Sara air and land base. France shot down a Libyan fighter plane over N'Djamena on September 7 but refused to extend its air cover to the northern offensive and continued to call on Chad and Libya to seek international arbitration on the disputed Aozou Strip. The U.S. took a more hawkish stance, apparently seeing a chance to undermine the Libyan regime. Both countries nevertheless supported a cease-fire sponsored by the Organization of African Unity, which took effect on September 11.      (NIM CASWELL)

This article updates the *Macropædia* article WESTERN AFRICA: *Chad.*

## COMOROS

The republic of Comoros is an island state in the Indian Ocean off the east coast of Africa. Area: 1,862 sq km (719 sq mi), excluding the island of Mayotte, which continued to be a de facto dependency of France. Pop. (1987 est., excluding Mayotte): 422,200. Cap.: Moroni. Monetary unit: Comorian franc, with (Oct. 5, 1987) a par value of CF 50 to the French franc and a free rate of CF 306.67 to U.S. $1 (CF 498 = £1 sterling). President in 1987, Ahmed Abdallah.

Elections to the Comoros' 42-member Federal Assembly took place on March 22, 1987. Early indications by Pres. Ahmed Abdallah that a free vote was planned proved illusory. Members of the president's Union Comorienne pour le Progrès were elected unopposed to all 22 seats on

Anjouan and Mohéli islands. Some limited opposition was permitted in the 20 seats on Grand Comore. However, the only opposition candidate to progress beyond the first ballot stood down before the second round. Two important opposition groupings, the Union pour une République Démocratique aux Comores and Front Démocratique, had been emasculated by arrests and did not participate. The elections appeared to do nothing to defuse political tensions. In early July it was reported that some 20 villagers on Grand Comore had been shot and injured in a clash with the authorities over land rights. An attempted coup was foiled in December, reportedly with some bloodshed.

A visit by the South African defense minister in December 1986 was followed in mid-February by one from the French cooperation minister. Abdallah subsequently met the French president and prime minister in Paris, during a trip that also took him to the Far East.      (NIM CASWELL)

This article updates the *Macropædia* article INDIAN OCEAN ISLANDS: *Comoros.*

## CONGO

A people's republic, Congo is in central Africa on the Atlantic Ocean. Area: 342,000 sq km (132,047 sq mi). Pop. (1987 est.): 2,180,000. Cap.: Brazzaville. Monetary unit: CFA franc, with (Oct. 5, 1987) a par value of CFAF 50 to the French franc and a free rate of CFAF 306.67 to U.S. $1 (CFAF 498 = £1 sterling). President in 1987, Col. Denis Sassou-Nguesso; prime minister, Ange-Édouard Poungui.

The sharp decline in international oil prices in 1986 had both economic and political repercussions for Congo in 1987. On the economic front, gross domestic product was likely to fall again slightly following a massive 10% drop in 1986. The International Monetary Fund, World Bank, and other donors agreed to provide increased support, but only after long negotiations over public spending cuts and civil service staff reductions. Relations with the Western powers generally continued to improve, but at the price of tensions within the nominally Marxist-Leninist ruling party, the Parti Congolais du Travail (PCT).

In early September it was reported that four people had been killed when troops loyal to Pres. Denis Sassou-Nguesso attempted to flush out a rebellious former army captain, Pierre Anga, from his stronghold at Owando, about 400 km (250 mi) north of Brazzaville. The events followed the belated announcement that four army officers had been arrested in July on suspicion of threatening state security. There was, however, no sign of widespread support for Anga within the armed forces.      (NIM CASWELL)

This article updates the *Macropædia* article CENTRAL AFRICA: *Congo.*

## CÔTE D'IVOIRE

A republic of West Africa, Côte d'Ivoire lies on the Gulf of Guinea. Area: 320,763 sq km (123,847 sq mi). Pop. (1987 est.): 11,154,000. Cap., Abidjan; capital designate, Yamoussoukro. Monetary unit: CFA franc, with (Oct. 5, 1987) a par value of CFAF 50 to the French franc and a free rate of CFAF 306.67 to U.S. $1 (CFAF 498 = £1 sterling). President in 1987, Félix Houphouët-Boigny.

During 1987 the official media continued to stress the familiar theme of national unity in preparation for the eventual departure from the scene of the aging Pres. Félix Houphouët-Boigny. There was still no officially designated successor, though if the presidency should fall vacant, the president of the National Assembly, Henri Konan Bédié, would constitutionally become interim president pending new elections. Bédié made a well-publicized visit to France in June, raising new speculation about the succession. All potential candidates, however, continued to maintain a low profile.

Some 32 Ivorians were rounded up in March and interrogated about their role in the semiclandestine Parti Républicain de la Côte d'Ivoire (PRCI). The ruling Parti Démocratique de la Côte d'Ivoire remained the sole legal party, although the PRCI reportedly had been allowed to maintain a discreet presence in Abidjan for some time.

The state of the economy was a continuing preoccupation. By midyear lower-than-forecast export prices for coffee and cocoa—the two key products—forced the government to choose between a further dose of austerity, as recommended by the International Monetary Fund (IMF), and an attempt to renegotiate terms with the country's creditors. On May 25 the government made a declaration of inability to meet even its rescheduled debt service burden. In October, however, it was announced that agreement on rescheduling and resumption of payments had been reached with the World Bank.          (NIM CASWELL)

This article updates the *Macropædia* article WESTERN AFRICA: *Ivory Coast.*

## DJIBOUTI

The republic of Djibouti is in the Horn of northeastern Africa on the Gulf of Aden. Area: 23,200 sq km (8,950 sq mi). Pop. (1987 est.): 470,000. Cap.: Djibouti. Monetary unit: Djibouti franc, with (Oct. 5, 1987) a free rate of DF 176.73 to U.S. $1 (DF 287 = £1 sterling). President in 1987, Hassan Gouled Aptidon; prime minister, Barkat Gourad Hamadou.

Djibouti's second presidential and legislative elections since independence were held on April 24, 1987, amid tight security. Pres. Hassan Gouled Aptidon, the sole candidate, was reelected for another six-year term with 90.3% of the vote, while in elections to the National Assembly the single list of 65 candidates representing the ruling Rassemblement Populaire pour le Progrès (RPP) attracted 87% support. Among the dozen new members elected to the Assembly were two former opponents of the RPP.

There had been fears of a destabilization campaign before the election. At the beginning of March a French priest was found murdered, and on March 18 a bomb exploded in the Historil bar in Djibouti town, killing 11 people (3 French soldiers, 2 French civilians, 3 West Germans, and 3 Djiboutians) and injuring dozens of others. A Tunisian, apparently unconnected with the exiled opposition, unexpectedly appeared in court claiming responsibility for the blast on behalf of a previously unknown group called the Troops of Revolutionaries and Resistance Fighters. The former vice-president of the RPP, Aden Robleh Awaleh, failed to affect the voting from his exile in France, and polling day was reported to have been quiet.

(NIM CASWELL)

This article updates the *Macropædia* article EASTERN AFRICA: *Djibouti.*

## EQUATORIAL GUINEA

The republic of Equatorial Guinea consists of Río Muni, on the Atlantic coast of West Africa, and the offshore islands of Bioko and Annobon. Area: 28,051 sq km (10,831 sq mi). Pop. (1987 est.): 328,000. Cap.: Malabo. Monetary unit: CFA franc, with (Oct. 5, 1987) a par value of CFAF 50 to the French franc and a free rate of CFAF 306.67 to U.S. $1 (CFAF 498 = £1 sterling). President of the Supreme Military Council in 1987, Col. Teodoro Obiang Nguema Mbasogo; prime minister, Capt. Cristino Seriche Bioko.

During celebrations of the eighth anniversary of his coming to power, on Aug. 3, 1987, Pres. Teodoro Obiang Nguema announced the formation of the Democratic Party of Equatorial Guinea. The move marked an end to the ban on political parties that had been in force since 1979, and the president said that other political parties might be set up in the future.

Although Spain was not in favour of Equatorial Guinea's decision to join the CFA franc zone in 1985, there was an agreement that Spanish aid to the country would not be reduced. Following talks between President Obiang Nguema and Spanish Foreign Minister Francisco Fernández Ordóñez, Spain agreed to grant a credit of 750 million pesetas to bolster the economy. Relations with neighbouring Nigeria were excellent. In December 1986 Nigeria provided communications equipment worth 1.5 million naira to allow Equatorial Guinea to act as host for the conference of the Economic Community of Central African States. A joint-venture pact encouraged Nigerians to invest in Equatorial Guinea.

Equatorial Guinea continued to be heavily dependent upon external aid. The major sources were the European Communities, France, Spain, the African Development Bank, and the Arab Bank for Economic Development in Africa.          (GUY ARNOLD)

This article updates the *Macropædia* article WESTERN AFRICA: *Equatorial Guinea.*

## ETHIOPIA

The people's republic of Ethiopia is in the Horn of northeastern Africa, on the Red Sea. Area: 1,223,500 sq km (472,400 sq mi). Pop. (1987 est.): 45,997,000. Cap.: Addis Ababa. Monetary unit: birr, with (Oct. 5, 1987) a par value of 2.07 birr to U.S. $1 (free rate of 3.34 birr = £1 sterling). Head of state and chairman of the Provisional Military Administrative Council to Sept. 10, 1987, Lieut. Col. Mengistu Haile Mariam; president from September 10, Mengistu; prime minister from September 10, Fikre Selassie Wogderess.

The major event of 1987 in Ethiopia was the birth of the People's Democratic Republic and the transfer of power on September 10 from the Provisional Military Administrative Council (PMAC). The process began in January

AFP PHOTO

Mengistu Haile Mariam, newly elected president of the People's Democratic Republic of Ethiopia, holds aloft a flag during the transfer of power from the Provisional Military Administrative Council (PMAC) on September 10.

with registration of participants for a referendum on the constitution drafted during 1986. The referendum took place in February. Of 14.6 million registrations, 14 million voted and 11.4 million voted in favour. The draft constitution was approved by the PMAC three weeks later, after which it appointed an Electoral Commission to organize the choice of deputies for the national Shengo (assembly). A slate of three candidates, evaluated and approved by the Workers Party of Ethiopia (WPE), was presented in each of the 835 constituencies. Registered voters in 25,000 polling stations then selected one. For the benefit of those who were illiterate, candidates were identified by an animal symbol. At this stage 15.2 million were registered and 13.3 million voted. According to these figures, between January and May registrations increased by 4% and the voting rate went up by 17%, supporting the claim of growing participation in national affairs.

At the September 9 inaugural session of the Shengo, the Credentials Commission revealed that 36.5% of deputies were peasants, 12% workers, 23.7% government employees, 12.9% members of the armed forces, 8.5% party activists, and 1.5% artisans; the remainder were not classified; only 6.2% (52) were women. The commission claimed 29.4% as "high-level qualified professionals." It was reported that those elected covered between 70 and 73 of the cultural groups (nationalities) and also provided representation for 46 less developed communities.

The last congress of the PMAC took place on September 3. Its decision to dissolve and hand over power was communicated to the Central Committee (CC) of the WPE two days later. This was very much a case of the same group reporting to itself, and it was repeated at the inaugural session of the Shengo when PMAC Chairman Mengistu Haile Mariam presented a six-hour management report from the PMAC, announcing that power was now in the hands of the people. At the first substantive meeting of the Shengo on September 10, the constitution was unanimously endorsed, and Mengistu, not unexpectedly, became the first president of the People's Democratic Republic of Ethiopia. The Shengo then unanimously approved the appointment of the vice-president (Fisseha Desta), the prime minister (Fikre Selassie Wogderess), 21 members of the Council of State, 21 members of the Council of Ministers, and nearly 100 other senior state officials. The absence of prominent names from the now-dissolved PMAC—such as Legesse Asfaw—among these appointments was explained by their occupancy of top positions in the WPE.

According to the report delivered by Chairman Mengistu, after coming to power in 1974 the PMAC had in early 1975 rejected the option of military dictatorship and adopted the path of creating institutions for popular participation. Thus, Mengistu declared on Sept. 9, 1987, that "the power that was identified as a military regime had more to its content than its form" and that the true nature of the regime "is known not by what it says about itself but as a result of what it stands for, and more so its concrete deeds and its daily actions." In accepting the presidency, Mengistu declared that the purpose of establishing the Shengo was to undertake "the major tasks outlined in the constitution so that the present generation may discharge the historic responsibility entrusted to it and hand over to the succeeding generation a prosperous Ethiopia which is free from destitution, disease, poverty, and other social ills."

The advent of the third major famine since the PMAC's assumption of power and the existence of a level of economic development defined by the World Bank as the lowest among the less developed countries made this statement a formidable challenge for the future. At its clos-

ing meeting on September 18, the Shengo announced a widespread reorganization of Ethiopia's administrative divisions. "Autonomous" status was accorded to five regions (Eritrea, Tigrai, Aseb, Dire Dawa, and Ogaden). The remaining regions were divided into 24 administrative zones, thus changing all regions except Arsi.

Two attempts were made to improve relations with The Sudan and enhance the possibility of peace in the north. At meetings in August and September, chaired by Mengistu, dialogues between various Sudanese political groupings, including the Sudan People's Liberation Army, failed to produce significant results. The absence of high-level Sudanese representation at the September celebrations was noted. The presence of Egyptian Pres. Hosni Mubarak, who delivered a long and friendly address, was applauded.

Poor weather conditions and the worst locust infestation since 1958 created a massive food deficit. As in the famine three years earlier, delivery of food aid to the affected areas was severely hampered by continuing insurgencies, notably in Eritrea and Tigrai.

This article updates the *Macropædia* article EASTERN AFRICA: *Ethiopia.*

## GABON

Gabon is a republic of central Africa, on the Atlantic Ocean. Area: 267,667 sq km (103,347 sq mi). Pop.: in 1987 estimates ranged from 870,000 to 1,450,000 (UN est., 1,195,000). Cap.: Libreville. Monetary unit: CFA franc, with (Oct. 5, 1987) a par value of CFAF 50 to the French franc and a free rate of CFAF 306.67 to U.S. $1 (CFAF 498 = £1 sterling). President in 1987, Omar Bongo; prime minister, Léon Mébiame.

Pres. Omar Bongo reshuffled his Cabinet on Jan. 6, 1987. Three new ministers were appointed and a number of positions were merged or restructured as the Cabinet was reduced from 57 to 45 members. Léon Mébiame was reappointed prime minister, and Simon Essimengane became the new fourth deputy prime minister in line with a decision made at the last congress of the ruling Parti Démocratique Gabonais (PDG). Bongo put an end to rumours early in the year that he was considering converting Gabon to a monarchy, with himself as king. The president paid an official eight-day visit to the U.S. in July–August.

The turnout in local elections held on June 28 was about 88%, compared with 99% officially registered in the presidential election of November 1986. All candidates had to be members of the PDG and resident in the area concerned for at least six months before the poll. The exiled opposition remained largely ineffective, with the main grouping, the Mouvement de Redressement National (Morena), split over whether to seek a reconciliation with the government.

The slump in world oil prices during 1986 continued to have severe repercussions for the economy. The $3 billion Transgabonais railway was nevertheless completed ahead of schedule and was to become fully operational during 1987.                                                    (NIM CASWELL)

This article updates the *Macropædia* article CENTRAL AFRICA: *Gabon.*

## GAMBIA, THE

A republic and member of the Commonwealth, The Gambia extends from the Atlantic Ocean along the lower Gambia River in West Africa; it is surrounded by Senegal, with which it has formed an administrative union called Senegambia. Area: 10,689 sq km (4,127 sq mi). Pop. (1987 est.): 787,000. Cap.: Banjul. Monetary unit: dalasi, with (Oct. 5, 1987) a free rate of 7.51 dalasis to U.S. $1 (12.19 dalasis = £1 sterling). President in 1987, Sir Dawda Jawara.

Elections held on March 11, 1987, resulted in a landslide victory for Sir Dawda Jawara, who was reelected president of The Gambia for another five-year term, and for the People's Progressive Party, which obtained all but 5 seats in the 36-seat Parliament. The opposition National Convention Party took the remainder. During April, while President Jawara was on a six-day visit to China, accusations of election rigging and unconstitutionality were made on the grounds that the president had not at once appointed a new Cabinet. After being sworn in for his new term in May, Jawara appointed a fresh Cabinet in which four new ministers were included. Nineteen petitions to the Supreme Court contesting the results of the election were rejected as improperly filed.

The 1987–88 budget, presented in June, consisted in part of a progress report on the success of the economic recovery program, initiated at the insistence of the International Monetary Fund. According to Minister of Finance Sheriff Sisay, "Overall, the economy is undergoing a dramatic turnaround; confidence has been restored." His view was borne out by the fact that The Gambia attracted increased support from aid donors and additional funds from the IMF.                                    (GUY ARNOLD)

This article updates the *Macropædia* article WESTERN AFRICA: *The Gambia.*

## GHANA

A republic of West Africa and member of the Commonwealth, Ghana lies on the Gulf of Guinea. Area: 238,533 sq km (92,098 sq mi). Pop. (1987 est.): 13,482,000. Cap.: Accra. Monetary unit: cedi, with (Oct. 5, 1987) a free rate of 174.42 cedis to U.S. $1 (283.24 cedis = £1 sterling). Chairman of the Provisional National Defense Council in 1987, Jerry John Rawlings.

The emphasis of the Ghanaian government throughout 1987 was on revamping the economy. In December 1986 Jerry John Rawlings, the chairman of the Provisional National Defense Council, had promised a national debate on the direction of the economy, and this took place in July 1987. Presenting the 1987 budget, Secretary for Finance and Economic Planning Kwesi Botchwey emphasized that the government objective was to deepen the recovery process and deal with underlying structural problems. Gross domestic product grew by 5.3% in 1986 and was expected to grow 5% or more in 1987, while inflation was held

at 15%. At the May 1987 consultations in Paris, donors demonstrated confidence by pledging aid worth $818.6 million.

During the first half of the year, a number of outspoken critics of the regime were imprisoned, and the country's three main universities were closed for three months following student demonstrations. In July the government announced that direct elections to district assemblies would take place in late 1988, although the ban on political parties would remain in force.

The attempted coup in Togo in September 1986 led to a protracted dispute with Togo, which claimed the terrorists had come from Ghana. Both countries closed their common border, which was finally reopened by Togo in February 1987 and by Ghana in May.      (GUY ARNOLD)

This article updates the *Macropædia* article WESTERN AFRICA: *Ghana.*

## GUINEA

The republic of Guinea is located in West Africa, on the Atlantic Ocean. Area: 245,857 sq km (94,926 sq mi). Pop. (1987 est.): 6,380,000. Cap.: Conakry. Monetary unit: Guinean franc, with (Oct. 5, 1987) a free rate of GF 339.71 to U.S. $1 (GF 551.65 = £1 sterling). President in 1987, Brig. Gen. Lansana Conté.

In May 1987 the ruling Military Committee for National Recovery announced that 58 people, former associates of the late president Sékou Touré (d. 1984) or alleged participants in the attempted coup of July 1985, had been sentenced to death, 21 of them in absentia. Another 146 people received sentences ranging from life imprisonment to 28 months in detention. Those named as facing execution included Moussa Diakité, who would probably have become head of state if the coup attempt had succeeded. The alleged leader of the attempt, former premier Diara Traoré, was also apparently among those sentenced to death. It had been widely speculated that about 20 of the best-known accused had been shot within days of the attempted coup. Certainly, there had been no public sighting of Traoré since then. The announcement of the sentences nevertheless closed a painful episode in Guinea's post-Touré era.

The painstaking process of rebuilding the economy continued, with additional measures to reestablish private-

A roadside stand in Accra, Ghana, offers goods such as soft drinks and tomato paste that had been largely unavailable in recent years. The government's emphasis on economic recovery was meeting with marked success.

sector activity and a successful meeting with aid donors in March. A new investment code was adopted, and several foreign companies started gold exploration. Diamond production by the Aredor consortium continued to expand. The government renegotiated the terms under which the Halco group extracted bauxite, Guinea's main export.

(NIM CASWELL)

This article updates the *Macropædia* article WESTERN AFRICA: *Guinea*.

## GUINEA-BISSAU

A republic of West Africa, Guinea-Bissau lies on the Atlantic Ocean. Area: 36,125 sq km (13,948 sq mi). Pop. (1987 est.): 912,000. Cap.: Bissau. Monetary unit: Guinea-Bissau peso, with (Oct. 5, 1987) a free rate of 649 pesos to U.S. $1 (1,055 pesos = £1 sterling). President in 1987, João Bernardo Vieira.

The year 1987 was dominated by the effects of a major change in economic orientation announced at the fourth congress of the ruling African Party for the Independence of Guinea-Bissau and Cape Verde, held in Bissau on Nov. 10–14, 1986. As a result of World Bank and International Monetary Fund (IMF) pressure, the government launched a structural adjustment program to liberalize trade and privatize a large number of state-owned enterprises. The cost was put at $46.4 million.

In May 1987 the government devalued the peso and revealed plans to reduce the civil service by one-third by 1989. The move would require the dismissal of some 5,000 personnel. While energy prices were increased substantially, Pres. João Bernardo Vieira announced that the state would continue to subsidize other basic commodities despite IMF pressure to reduce subsidies. At the end of May the World Bank signaled its support by approving a $15 million structural adjustment loan. Substantial aid contributions were forthcoming from a wide range of donors. The African Development Bank agreed to provide loans to cover essential imports, a credit line for agricultural development, and modernization of the national hospital.

In August, following his return from a visit to Paris for medical treatment, President Vieira denied rumours of an attempted coup. (GUY ARNOLD)

This article updates the *Macropædia* article WESTERN AFRICA: *Guinea-Bissau*.

## KENYA

A republic and member of the Commonwealth, Kenya is in eastern Africa, on the Indian Ocean. Area: 582,646 sq km (224,961 sq mi), including 11,230 sq km of inland water. Pop. (1987 est.): 22,020,000. Cap.: Nairobi. Monetary unit: Kenya shilling, with (Oct. 5, 1987) a free rate of 16.63 shillings to U.S. $1 (27 shillings = £1 sterling). President in 1987, Daniel arap Moi.

Kenya's economic prospects at the beginning of 1987 were better than they had been for some time. The fall in the world price of crude oil in 1986 had benefited the country's oil-refining industry as well as cutting the cost of transport. At the same time, there had been a huge demand for coffee, resulting from the shortfall in Brazil's output, and plentiful rains resulted in a record crop of corn (maize), allowing some to be exported.

These benefits could not be relied on to continue indefinitely, but a successful policy of import control, coupled with a notable increase in productivity, created a favourable balance of payments. This gave the government confidence in its dealings with the International Monetary Fund, to which it had repaid $100 million in 1986, and

with its critics. The latter appeared to Pres. Daniel arap Moi to be increasing in number and in the gravity of the challenge they represented. In practice, the criticisms came primarily from a section of the intelligentsia that favoured more radical policies than those pursued by the regime. The government's reaction was to bring charges of sedition against appreciable numbers of persons alleged to be plotting its overthrow. In particular, membership in or support for a movement said to call itself MwaKenya was regarded as deserving severe punishment.

The most open critics of the government's stringent line were to be found among the members of the National Christian Council of Kenya (NCCK). While condemning all corruption or authoritarianism on the part of government officials, the NCCK particularly opposed a bill that would give the president power to dismiss the attorney general and the controller and auditor general without reference to a tribunal. The government accused the NCCK of meddling in politics and of setting itself up as an opposition party, but reports of harsh methods employed by the police in dealing with its alleged opponents had repercussions outside Kenya. When President Moi visited the U.S. in March, the hitherto friendly U.S. administration was openly critical of events in Kenya, and the president cut short his stay. His reception in Britain afterward was warmer, and the British government agreed to increase its already substantial aid by an additional $80 million.

On his return to Kenya, President Moi promised a cleanup of the police force, but he also accused foreign journalists of misrepresenting the situation in the country. Shortly afterward, however, former vice-president Oginga Odinga broke a long silence to accuse the government of sliding toward tyranny and of using detention without trial to silence opposition. His criticisms were repeated by Amnesty International in a report published in July, which accused the government of serious violations of human rights. Muslims rioted in Mombasa in October when a religious rally was broken up by officials, and the University of Nairobi was closed following student riots in November.

Hopes of reviving the East African Community were fostered by a meeting of ministers of Kenya, Tanzania, and Uganda in February to discuss strategies for renewed economic cooperation. This contrasted with heightened tension that developed along the Kenya–Uganda border in May. Each side accused the other of closing the border, but in fact the difficulty had arisen because of Uganda's demand that all visitors pay an entry fee while Kenya was imposing stricter controls on entry for those who did not possess work permits. At a meeting in June, ministers of the two countries discussed border security and also focused on the welfare of Ugandans in Kenya, many of whom had been required to leave Kenya earlier in the year. Security forces of the two countries fought a gun battle at a border post in December, but the situation was defused when Moi and Ugandan Pres. Yoweri Musaveni agreed to reduce their border forces. (KENNETH INGHAM)

This article updates the *Macropædia* article EASTERN AFRICA: *Kenya*.

## LESOTHO

A constitutional monarchy of southern Africa and member of the Commonwealth, Lesotho forms a landlocked enclave within South Africa. Area: 30,355 sq km (11,720 sq mi). Pop. (1987 est.): 1,628,000. Cap.: Maseru. Monetary unit: loti (plural: maloti), at par with the South African rand, with (Oct. 5, 1987) a free rate of 2.08 maloti to U.S. $1 (3.38 maloti = £1 sterling). King, Moshoeshoe II; chairman of the Military Council in 1987, Maj. Gen. Justin Metsino Lekhanya.

During 1987 Lesotho continued to be politically and economically almost totally dependent upon South Africa. Under Maj. Gen. Justin Lekhanya, brought to power through a military coup in January 1986, relations with South Africa were far smoother than they had been under his predecessor, Chief Leabua Jonathan (*see* OBITUARIES), who died in a Pretoria hospital on April 5, 1987. Among five people abducted and shot dead in Roma town in November 1986 were two of Jonathan's former ministers, Desmond Sixishe (information) and Vincent Makhele (foreign affairs).

Although 80% of the population was dependent upon agriculture, this sector of Lesotho's economy accounted for just 20% of the gross domestic product. Remittances from an estimated 100,000 Basotho working in the South African gold and coal mines remained the country's largest source of income.

In 1986 the $2 billion Lesotho Highlands Water Scheme to divert water to South Africa and also produce enough hydroelectric power to meet most of Lesotho's energy requirements received final approval. A R 15 million loan from the World Bank, announced in March 1987, allowed work to begin on the first phase, which involved the building of access roads. (GUY ARNOLD)

This article updates the *Macropædia* article SOUTHERN AFRICA: *Lesotho*.

## LIBERIA

The republic of Liberia is located in West Africa, on the Atlantic Ocean. Area: 99,067 sq km (38,250 sq mi). Pop. (1987 est.): 2,356,000. Cap.: Monrovia. Monetary unit: Liberian dollar, at par with the U.S. dollar, with a free rate (Oct. 5, 1987) of L$1.62 to £1 sterling. President in 1987, Gen. Samuel K. Doe.

Difficult relations with the U.S. and the deteriorating economic situation combined to make 1987 the most challenging of Gen. Samuel K. Doe's seven-year rule in Liberia. Although U.S. Secretary of State George Shultz praised Doe during his visit to Liberia in January, Shultz later came under fire at home for complimenting what many regarded as a brutal and corrupt regime. In February Doe attacked a U.S. government report that showed that $16.5 million of commodity assistance support provided by the U.S. since 1984 had not been accounted for. Nonetheless, the U.S. provided an additional $38 million in aid for 1987 and late in the year sent a team of financial experts to advise the Liberian government.

In November 1986 the World Bank lifted its suspension on payments to Liberia, and the government proposed an elaborate economic recovery program to last until 1989. Most public utilities were being privatized. West Germany rescheduled Liberia's debts and provided $6 million in aid for ongoing projects. In June 1987 Minister of Finance John Bestman announced an eight-point program of action to improve the economy; the most important objective was to keep expenditures within the budget. Foreign travel for Doe and Cabinet ministers was suspended as an economic measure.

Doe made a number of appeals to the opposition parties for unity. The teachers' union, which was calling for payment of salary arrears, was banned; following a three-day strike by academic staff, also seeking pay arrears, the university was shut down; and a crisis arose over the appointment of Chea Cheapoo as chief justice. The opposition parties and the press protested against harassment and intimidation. (GUY ARNOLD)

This article updates the *Macropædia* article WESTERN AFRICA: *Liberia*.

## MADAGASCAR

The republic of Madagascar occupies the island of the same name and minor adjacent islands in the Indian Ocean off the southeast coast of Africa. Area: 587,041 sq km (226,658 sq mi). Pop. (1987 est.): 10,605,000. Cap.: Antananarivo. Monetary unit: Malagasy franc, with (Oct. 5, 1987) a free rate of FMG 1,152 to U.S. $1 (FMG 1,870 = £1 sterling). President in 1987, Didier Ratsiraka; prime minister, Lieut. Col. Désiré Rakotoarijaona.

The government of Pres. Didier Ratsiraka in Madagascar faced exceptionally serious political and economic problems during 1987. The International Monetary Fund (IMF)-backed economic recovery program, involving such measures as devaluation and market liberalization, coincided with the failure of the 1986 rains in the south to bring about a serious famine by the turn of the year in the Androy, Mahafaly, and Taolanaro regions. An unknown number perished, while tens of thousands fled north to Antananarivo and other regional centres. Food riots in the capital were narrowly avoided by the release of rice from emergency buffer stocks.

Disturbances in Toamasina in November 1986 were followed by renewed rioting, aimed principally at Asian businesses, in February and March 1987. Subsequently, 56 people were convicted for involvement in apparently coordinated explosions in Antsirabe, Farafangana, and Fianarantsoa. Trouble on the university campuses also continued throughout the first half of the year. An already tense political atmosphere was exacerbated by the death, in unclear circumstances, of the chief of general staff of the armed forces at the end of June.

The seven-party coalition that formed the government crumbled in the face of the mounting crisis. In March three of its members staged the founding rally of a "rejectionist front" led by veteran politician Monja Jaona. A fourth party joined them in a May Day rally variously estimated to have been attended by 8,000–25,000 people. President Ratsiraka responded by offering some concessions on the economic program and somewhat widening the sphere of political consultation. The government's economic program nevertheless remained in force, receiving new World Bank and IMF funding in September. (NIM CASWELL)

This article updates the *Macropædia* article INDIAN OCEAN ISLANDS: *Madagascar*.

## MALAWI

A republic and member of the Commonwealth, Malawi is a landlocked state in eastern Africa. Area: 118,484 sq km (45,747 sq mi). Pop. (1987 est.): 7,499,000. Cap.: Lilongwe. Monetary unit: Malawi kwacha, with (Oct. 5, 1987) a free rate of 2.26 kwacha to U.S. $1 (3.67 kwacha = £1 sterling). President in 1987, Hastings Kamuzu Banda.

In elections to Malawi's National Assembly on May 27–28, 1987, all 107 elected seats were filled by candidates of the sole party, the Malawi Congress Party. Pres. Hastings Kamuzu Banda nominated an additional five deputies. Poor prices for Malawi's produce in the world market contributed to an unfavourable balance of payments and a shortage of foreign exchange. To counter this trend the kwacha was further devalued by 20% early in the year, but the only result was increased inflation. Malawi was one of the African countries described by the UN World Food Program in October as facing famine and in need of large quantities of relief supplies.

In February President Banda firmly rejected the idea of

participating in a boycott of South Africa. However, fears that South Africa might cut Malawi's main supply routes while taking reprisals against its more hostile neighbours led the government to reconsider its relations with one of those neighbours, Mozambique. This was made easier because Pres. Joaquim Chissanó of Mozambique seemed more prepared for discussions than his predecessor, Samora Machel, and had signed a security agreement with Malawi in December 1986. President Banda agreed to send troops to help defend the railway line between Malawi and the Mozambican port of Nacala against attacks by the rebel Mozambique National Resistance. Formerly, Banda had been thought to favour the rebels.     (KENNETH INGHAM)

This article updates the *Macropædia* article SOUTHERN AFRICA: *Malawi*.

## MALI

Mali is a landlocked republic of West Africa. Area: 1,240,192 sq km (478,841 sq mi). Pop. (1987 est.): 8,690,000. Cap.: Bamako. Monetary unit: CFA franc, with (Oct. 5, 1987) a par value of CFAF 50 to the French franc and a free rate of CFAF 306.67 to U.S. $1 (CFAF 498 = £1 sterling). President in 1987, Gen. Moussa Traoré; prime minister from June 6, Mamadou Dembelé.

In early 1987 Mali experienced a wave of strikes among health and education workers that threatened to spread throughout the public sector. A political crisis was averted when the government paid the strikers the salaries they had lost during the work stoppage. In January a special congress of the ruling Union Démocratique du Peuple Malien approved a national charter against corruption, and in March a commission of inquiry was established to investigate public corruption.

Though the 1986–87 farming season was a relatively good one, the economy continued to hover on the edge of disaster. A Cabinet reshuffle in mid-February apparently strengthened the hand of those in favour of continued reforms along the lines recommended by the International Monetary Fund and the World Bank. A series of measures approved on September 16, including partial privatization of the state import-export company Somiex, was expected to bring agreement with foreign funders closer.

Both Mali and Burkina Faso welcomed the ruling of the International Court of Justice that the Agacher Strip, over which the two countries fought a brief border war in December 1985, should be split between them. A commission was to map the border.     (NIM CASWELL)

This article updates the *Macropædia* article WESTERN AFRICA: *Mali*.

## MAURITANIA

The republic of Mauritania is on the Atlantic coast of West Africa. Area: 1,030,700 sq km (398,000 sq mi). Pop. (1987 est.): 1,844,000. Cap.: Nouakchott. Monetary unit: ouguiya, with (Oct. 5, 1987) a free rate of 74.73 ouguiya to U.S. $1 (121.36 ouguiya = £1 sterling). President of the Military Committee for National Salvation and prime minister in 1987, Col. Maaouya Ould Sidi Ahmed Taya.

Municipal elections held in Mauritania on Dec. 19 and 26, 1986, went smoothly and with little sign of the racial tensions that had flared earlier in the year between black Mauritanians and the Arab elite. It was the first relatively open poll since former president Moktar Ould Daddah proclaimed a one-party state in 1964. Several changes in the composition of the government were announced during 1987. In May Khadijetou Mint Ahmed became the first woman to head a top economic ministry when she was appointed to the mines and industry portfolio. A more substantial reshuffle on September 21 brought new faces to the key economy and fishing ministries.

The government announced that it had foiled an attempt by a group of black Mauritanian army officers to seize power on October 22. Three officers were executed in December for their part in the coup plot.

Pres. Maaouya Ould Sidi Ahmed Taya's reputation as an international statesman was boosted by his successful handling of a long-running crisis in the West African Economic Community (CEAO), which held its 12th summit under his chairmanship in Nouakchott on April 21–22. A more difficult diplomatic problem also presented itself in April when Morocco completed construction of a new defensive wall, running in places less than one kilometre (0.62 mi) from the Mauritanian border, to keep Polisario Front guerrilla forces out of the Western Sahara. The move threatened to drag Mauritania back into a dispute that raised acutely sensitive political questions in Nouakchott.     (NIM CASWELL)

This article updates the *Macropædia* article WESTERN AFRICA: *Mauritania*.

## MAURITIUS

The constitutional monarchy of Mauritius, a member of the Commonwealth, occupies an island in the Indian Ocean about 800 km (500 mi) east of Madagascar and includes the island dependencies of Rodrigues, Agalega, and Cargados Carajos Shoals. Area: 2,040 sq km (788 sq mi). Pop. (1987 est.): 1,040,000. Cap.: Port Louis. Monetary unit: Mauritian rupee, with (Oct. 5, 1987) a free rate of Mau Rs 13.09 to U.S. $1 (Mau Rs 21.25 = £1 sterling). Queen, Elizabeth II; governor-general in 1987, Sir Veerasamy Ringadoo; prime minister, Aneerood Jugnauth.

The ruling Alliance coalition, comprising Prime Minister Aneerood Jugnauth's Mauritius Socialist Movement and two smaller parties, was returned to power in general elections held in Mauritius on Aug. 30, 1987, a year early. The Alliance took 39 of 62 directly elected seats in the Legislative Assembly, compared with 21 for the opposition Union coalition. (For tabulated results, see *Political Parties*, above.) In a surprise result, Paul Berenger of the Mauritian Militant Movement, joint leader of the Union coalition, lost his Assembly seat.

The government's success was attributed largely to the island's economic recovery. An International Monetary Fund (IMF)-approved strategy that included reductions in subsidies, cuts in government spending, and trade liberalization had produced dramatic results. Economic growth of 7.1% in 1986, following 6.5% in 1985, was the highest recorded in Africa. In line with IMF plans, current expenditure in the 1987 budget was severely restricted. The capital development budget, however, rose by 50% to about $100 million.

As part of its trade-liberalization program, Mauritius lifted import duties on textiles and other goods connected with the textile industry. Mauritius was the world's third largest exporter of woolen knitwear, but its textile exports faced growing protectionist barriers. The vital sugar industry was being reorganized with the aim of reducing annual production to 650,000–700,000 metric tons.

Mauritius was host to a conference attended by 200 potential investors in the islands of the Indian Ocean. Other countries represented were Kenya, Tanzania, Seychelles, Maldives, Comoros, Madagascar, and Sri Lanka.     (GUY ARNOLD)

This article updates the *Macropædia* article INDIAN OCEAN ISLANDS: *Mauritius*.

## MOZAMBIQUE

The people's republic of Mozambique is located in eastern Africa, on the Indian Ocean. Area: 799,380 sq km (308,642 sq mi). Pop. (1987 est.): 14,156,000. Cap.: Maputo. Monetary unit: metical, with (Oct. 5, 1987) a free rate of 403.65 meticais to U.S. $1 (655.49 meticais = £1 sterling). President in 1987, Joaquim Chissanó; prime minister, Mario de Graça Machungo.

The debilitating civil war in Mozambique dragged on throughout 1987, with disastrous implications for the lives of the people and the economy. In mid-January Pres. Joaquim Chissanó visited Zimbabwe for talks with Prime Minister Robert Mugabe, who agreed to step up military aid until the Mozambican rebels were wiped out. In February overseas aid agencies announced that four million Mozambicans faced hunger and destitution unless emergency aid was made available. In Zambézia Province alone, nearly one million people had fled their homes because of the activities of the rebel Mozambique National Resistance (MNR, or Renamo). Many sought refuge in Malawi or Zimbabwe or in the towns, where they added to the almost impossible problem of supplying food.

In February and March the results of the discussions between Chissanó and Mugabe materialized in a strong counteroffensive by government forces, supported by troops from Zimbabwe and Tanzania, which recovered control over the lower Zambezi Valley. Driven from their main area of operation in the centre of the country, MNR guerrillas infiltrated southward, causing disruption in the southern provinces of Maputo, Gaza, and Inhambane. The movement culminated in a major attack in the southern districts of Gaza and Inhambane in August. In July another strong attack on the town of Homoine, 400 km (250 mi) northeast of Maputo, which resulted in the deaths of 386 civilians, was at first attributed by the government to the MNR, but later the president accused South Africa. The South African government denied involvement and demanded an apology but then suggested talks with a view to reviving the 1984 Nkomati accord on border security.

South Africa had been reducing the rates for freight carried by its railways to a point where the lines through Mozambique were seriously threatened by competition. By early 1987 some 85% of all goods to and from the so-called frontline states traveled via South Africa. With the approval of Zimbabwe, proposals to revitalize the port of Beira over a ten-year period at a cost of $590 million were submitted to prospective backers. The Netherlands, Sweden, the European Communities, and the U.S. offered financial assistance for the first stage, which was concerned with the port itself. The restoration of the 290-km (180-mi)-long corridor linking the port with the interior by road, rail, and oil pipeline presented additional problems. In spite of the protection provided by Zimbabwean soldiers, guerrilla attacks on the corridor continued. The Cahora Bassa Dam was operating at only 0.5% of its capacity because of the activities of the MNR, and in June rebel forces launched the first of a series of retaliatory attacks over the Zimbabwean border.

One promising sign was the apparent readiness of outside sources to offer assistance. In January the government, backed by considerable foreign aid, launched a program aimed at checking the economic decline through a series of liberalizing measures, including the lifting of price controls and greater flexibility in the exchange rate. The following month the U.K. promised emergency aid of $2.4 million, and in June it offered an additional $3.2 million, raising its total contribution for 1987 to $22 million. Also in

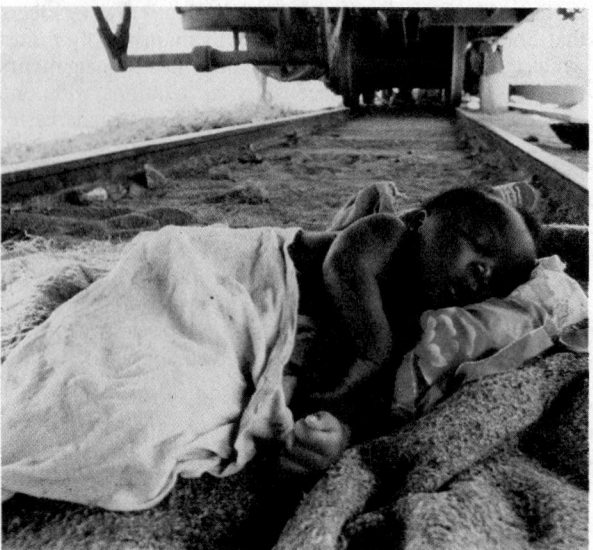

A baby sleeps beneath a train car in a refugee camp in northern Mozambique. Nearly one million people had been forced to leave their homes in the Zambézia Province alone because of the decade-old civil war.
AFP PHOTO

June, the International Monetary Fund made a generous loan, followed in July by a pledge from the Paris Donors' Consultative Group to increase capital inflows in 1987 to $700 million. Mozambique's external debts were rescheduled to reduce the debt-servicing burden. In spite of these measures, the UN Food and Agriculture Organization announced in October that large quantities of relief supplies would be needed to prevent famine.   (KENNETH INGHAM)

This article updates the *Macropædia* article SOUTHERN AFRICA: *Mozambique.*

## NIGER

Niger is a landlocked republic of West Africa. Area: 1,186,408 sq km (458,075 sq mi). Pop. (1987 est.): 6,947,000. Cap.: Niamey. Monetary unit: CFA franc, with (Oct. 5, 1987) a par value of CFAF 50 to the French franc and a free rate of CFAF 306.67 to U.S. $1 (CFAF 498 = £1 sterling). Chiefs of state and presidents of the Supreme Military Council in 1987, Maj. Gen. Seyni Kountché and, from November 10, Col. Ali Seibou; prime minister, Ahmid Algabid.

Niger's political climate was overshadowed during 1987 by the illness of Pres. Seyni Kountché (*see* OBITUARIES), who was hospitalized after falling ill on New Year's Eve. The president made several trips to Paris for treatment, and on November 10 he died in Paris of a brain tumour. Col. Ali Seibou, a cousin of Kountché, was named acting chief of state.

On April 15 former president Hamani Diori, who was deposed in the 1974 coup that brought Kountché to power, was released from detention. He had been in prison or under house arrest since 1974, with the exception of a brief period in 1984–85. The country took another tentative step toward the restoration of democracy on June 14, when the national charter was approved by referendum after more than two years of deliberation. The document had advisory force only, but its adoption opened the way to the drafting of a new constitution to replace the one suspended in 1974.   (NIM CASWELL)

This article updates the *Macropædia* article WESTERN AFRICA: *Niger.*

# NIGERIA

A republic and member of the Commonwealth, Nigeria is located in West Africa, on the Gulf of Guinea. Area: 923,768 sq km (356,669 sq mi). Pop. (1987 est.): 100,596,000. Cap., Lagos; capital designate, Abuja. Monetary unit: naira, with (Oct. 5, 1987) a free rate of 4.16 naira to U.S. $1 (6.75 naira = £1 sterling). President and chairman of the Armed Forces Ruling Council in 1987, Maj. Gen. Ibrahim Babangida.

In July 1987 the Armed Forces Ruling Council (AFRC) announced that return to full civilian rule in Nigeria was to be delayed until 1992, instead of 1990 as previously proposed. The delay was justified in part by the decision to hold a census—an event always fraught with problems in Nigeria—before that date. The government issued a detailed timetable of the various stages that would lead to federal elections in the first half of 1992 and presidential elections and the phasing out of military rule during the second half of that year.

These announcements followed a year of deliberations by the Political Bureau. In September 1987 a Constitutional Review Committee was inaugurated. In a major speech broadcast to the nation at the end of September, Maj. Gen. Ibrahim Babangida, chairman of the AFRC, announced that three broad categories of persons were banned from seeking political office under the new constitution: all those who had held political office during the first (1960–66) and second (1979–83) periods of civilian rule, whether or not they had been dismissed from office for corruption, and all military personnel previously or currently holding political office. The prohibitions therefore included those holding office under the existing AFRC. Babangida said that banning should not be seen as punitive but rather "as a necessary step to give Nigeria a fair chance to develop a new political culture and leadership." In December local elections—the first polling since 1983—candidates stood without party affiliation, and turnout was reported to be high. There were charges of vote rigging in some areas.

By August 1987 Babangida had been head of state for two years, during which time he had demonstrated considerable political capability. In June he visited three neighbouring states—Côte d'Ivoire, Senegal, and Togo—and the tour, concerned with bilateral issues, was considered a success. At the tenth summit of the Economic Community of West African States (ECOWAS), held at Abuja in July, Babangida was given a third consecutive term as chairman.

A major and unresolved scandal during the year concerned the assassination by letter bomb of Dele Giwa, editor in chief of *Newswatch*, on Oct. 21, 1986. In April 1987 *Newswatch* was banned for six months for publishing leaked information from the Political Bureau about the proposals for a return to civilian rule. Later the owners of the magazine apologized to the government, and the banning was lifted two months early.

The government announced the creation of two new states: Katsina, part of Kaduna State in the north, and Akwa Ibom, part of Cross River State in the south. Religious-political riots in Kaduna State were described by Babangida as the equivalent of an attempted civilian coup. The death of Chief Obafemi Awolowo (*see* OBITUARIES) on May 9 signaled the end of a political era.

Government attention throughout the year was concentrated on economic recovery under the structural adjustment program (SAP), which had received the endorsement of the International Monetary Fund in October 1986; this was regarded as an essential first step toward debt rescheduling. The introduction of the second-tier foreign exchange market in the same month led to an effective devaluation of the naira by approximately 60% in a year. The SAP hit lower-paid workers hardest, and there were May Day protests against the decline in the value of wages. Nonetheless, the SAP was judged a success, and the economy was seen as improving. Two rescheduling operations—by the London Club and the Paris Club—between them covered debts worth $10 billion. Recovery had a long way to go, however. During 1986 gross domestic product declined by 3%, gross national income by 16%, and per capita income by 18.5%. One result of the depreciation of the naira was a sharp increase in the naira value of petroleum revenues; this was particularly important in view of the 1986 figures, which showed that oil revenues were halved while imports dropped by 35%.                    (GUY ARNOLD)

This article updates the *Macropædia* article WESTERN AFRICA: *Nigeria*.

# RWANDA

The landlocked republic of Rwanda is situated in central Africa. Area: 26,338 sq km (10,169 sq mi). Pop. (1987 est.): 6,488,000. Cap.: Kigali. Monetary unit: Rwanda franc, with (Oct. 5, 1987) a free rate of RF 79.80 to U.S. $1 (RF 129.59 = £1 sterling). President in 1987, Maj. Gen. Juvénal Habyarimana.

Rwanda's 1987 budget was set at RF 23.7 billion, with an additional RF 4.2 billion allocated to the development budget, which was increased by 11% over that for 1986. However, economic pressures led to reductions in these figures during July. Pres. Juvénal Habyarimana reaffirmed the importance of the peasant farmer in achieving the government's target of food self-sufficiency. A major problem for the economy was the continuing high birthrate, currently running at 3.7% a year. West Germany promised to make available DM 88 million for rural development and water supplies.

At the end of 1986 the trials of 300 members of illegal sects on charges that included incitement to rebellion resulted in sentences of up to 12 years in prison. Members of the Jehovah's Witnesses suffered the heaviest sentences. On July 1, 1987, the 25th anniversary of independence, the president announced an amnesty for certain categories of prisoners. More than one-third of Rwanda's total prison population was freed.

According to the UN High Commissioner for Refugees, there were 110,000 Rwandan refugees in Uganda and probably an equal number who were not registered with the UN body. Rwanda argued that the high number of refugees in Uganda posed a threat to Rwanda's security. In late 1986 Pres. Yoweri Museveni of Uganda made his first visit to Rwanda.                    (GUY ARNOLD)

This article updates the *Macropædia* article CENTRAL AFRICA: *Rwanda*.

# SÃO TOMÉ AND PRÍNCIPE

The republic of São Tomé and Príncipe comprises two main islands and several smaller islets that straddle the Equator in the Gulf of Guinea, off the west coast of Africa. Area: 1,001 sq km (386 sq mi). Pop. (1987 est.): 112,600. Cap.: São Tomé. Monetary unit: dobra, with (Oct. 5, 1987) a free rate of 35.32 dobras to U.S. $1 (57.36 dobras = £1 sterling). President in 1987, Manuel Pinto da Costa.

On a visit to Europe at the end of 1986, Pres. Manuel Pinto da Costa of São Tomé and Príncipe sought support for the government's planned economic liberalization program. Although there was some concern among Western nations over the presence of Soviet radar stations and 1,000

Cuban troops in São Tomé, substantial aid was offered. During his visit to São Tomé in January 1987, Portugal's Pres. Mário Soares said that no limit would be placed on Portuguese credits to boost investment.

The economic recovery program, supported by the World Bank, the International Monetary Fund, and the African Development Bank, was launched in June. It emphasized increased agricultural production and aimed to reduce the trade and budget deficits with a view eventually to rescheduling the foreign debt. As a first measure a devaluation of the dobra was announced.

In January President da Costa made important changes in his Cabinet. Among other changes, a Ministry of Finances was created, the Ministry of Tourism was eliminated, and the president took the portfolio of planning and economy himself.

Aeroflot initiated regular service between Moscow and São Tomé in April.                    (GUY ARNOLD)

This article updates the *Macropædia* article CENTRAL AFRICA: *São Tomé and Príncipe.*

## SENEGAL

The republic of Senegal is located in West Africa, on the Atlantic Ocean; it surrounds the country of The Gambia, with which it has formed an administrative union called Senegambia. Area: 196,722 sq km (75,955 sq mi). Pop. (1987 est.): 6,793,000. Cap.: Dakar. Monetary unit: CFA franc, with (Oct. 5, 1987) a par value of CFAF 50 to the French franc and a free rate of CFAF 306.67 to U.S. $1 (CFAF 498 = £1 sterling). President in 1987, Abdou Diouf.

Signs of political strain increased in 1987 as continued economic difficulties further reduced living standards and Senegal geared up for presidential and legislative elections due in February 1988. At the end of January 1987, students at Cheikh Anta Diop University in Dakar went on strike over campus living conditions and late payment of grants. The protests spread to schools in several areas of the country, and a reported 27 students were injured in clashes with the police. A settlement was reached at the end of February, when the government yielded to the students on most of the immediate points at issue.

In mid-April much of Dakar's police force went on strike to protest prison sentences handed down to two of seven policemen convicted of beating a suspected thief to death. The protests spread outside the capital and threatened at one stage to degenerate into a shooting match between police units and army and paramilitary forces, which remained loyal to the government. Pres. Abdou Diouf responded by suspending the entire police force and dismissing the interior minister, whose functions were temporarily passed to Jean Collin, the secretary-general at the Presidency. The suspensions were subsequently converted into dismissals, although 4,822 out of the 6,265 who lost their jobs were subsequently reemployed.

The 16 opposition parties failed to persuade President Diouf to change the electoral law in time for the 1988 elections and remained divided among themselves. The president faced pressure from within his own Parti Socialiste to relax the government's economic austerity program. A third successive year of good rains resulted in continued recovery in the rural sector, but rock bottom world prices for Senegal's main export commodities, petroleum products and peanut oil, inhibited overall economic recovery. In November the Paris Club agreed to reschedule Senegal's official foreign debt.                    (NIM CASWELL)

This article updates the *Macropædia* article WESTERN AFRICA: *Senegal.*

## SEYCHELLES

A republic and member of the Commonwealth, the Seychelles consists of about 100 islands in the Indian Ocean, 1,450 km (900 mi) from the east coast of Africa. Area: 453 sq km (175 sq mi). Pop. (1987 est.): 66,000. Cap.: Victoria. Monetary unit: Seychelles rupee, with (Oct. 5, 1987) a free rate of SR 5.54 to U.S. $1 (SR 9 = £1 sterling). President in 1987, France-Albert René.

The decline in tourism during 1987 was a setback for the economy of Seychelles. In 1986 tourism accounted for half of gross domestic product and provided 15% of direct employment. The government target was to attract 100,000 visitors in 1989, compared with the 1986 total of 66,626. A new weekly air service was established between Kenya and Seychelles with direct connections to Singapore.

The government was seeking to build up other areas of the economy, and there was increased emphasis on foreign investment in the form of joint ventures. During the year West Germany provided general commodity aid, to be used for importing vital goods and spare parts. Fishing accounted for almost half of all nontourism foreign exchange earnings, and license fees from foreign trawlers in Seychelles waters were a major source of revenue. During 1987 the total debt-servicing bill increased almost 75% over the 1986 total of $44.2 million. The 1987 budget reduced spending by 9%.

In elections to Parliament held on December 6, all candidates were members of the People's Progressive Front, the sole party.                    (GUY ARNOLD)

This article updates the *Macropædia* article INDIAN OCEAN ISLANDS: *Seychelles.*

## SIERRA LEONE

A republic of West Africa and member of the Commonwealth, Sierra Leone lies on the Atlantic Ocean. Area: 71,740 sq km (27,699 sq mi). Pop. (1987 est.): 3,803,000. Cap.: Freetown. Monetary unit: leone, with (Oct. 5, 1987) an official rate of 21.80 leones to U.S. $1 (35.40 leones = £1 sterling). President in 1987, Maj. Gen. Joseph Saidu Momoh.

For much of 1987 political life in Sierra Leone was dominated by the repercussions of an abortive coup attempt on March 23, apparently masterminded by Gabriel Mohammed Tennyson Kai Kai, former head of the antismuggling unit. First Vice-Pres. Francis Minah was dropped from the Cabinet in a reshuffle in April and later was arrested for complicity in the plot. After a trial lasting almost six months, Minah, Kai Kai, and 14 others were sentenced to death on October 17; two others received prison terms. It seemed likely that some of the sentences—though not those against Minah or Kai Kai—would be commuted to life imprisonment.

The economic situation deteriorated markedly. The 1987–88 budget, announced in June, contained measures designed to improve revenue collection and pledged to maintain the floating exchange rate introduced in June 1986. Total spending was to be cut by 3.5% below the actual figure for 1986–87. Primary and secondary school fees were abolished, but there were doubts that the government could find the money to run the educational system. In November Pres. Joseph Momoh declared an economic state of emergency and proposed a 59-point package of measures to deal with the situation. Sierra Leone celebrated its bicentenary in 1987.                    (GUY ARNOLD)

This article updates the *Macropædia* article WESTERN AFRICA: *Sierra Leone.*

# SOMALIA

A republic in the Horn of northeastern Africa, the Somali Democratic Republic, or Somalia, lies on the Gulf of Aden and the Indian Ocean. Area: 637,000 sq km (246,000 sq mi). Pop. (1987 est.): 6,160,000. Cap.: Mogadishu. Monetary unit: Somali shilling, with (Oct. 5, 1987) a free rate of 120.21 Somali shillings to U.S. $1 (195.21 Somali shillings = £1 sterling). President in 1987, Maj. Gen. Muhammad Siyad Barrah; prime minister from February 1, Lieut. Gen. Muhammad Ali Samatar.

Against a background of economic problems and political unrest, the scene in Somalia was dominated in 1987 by rumours of the imminent death or retirement of Pres. Muhammad Siyad Barrah and speculations about his successor. President Barrah, who had held supreme power since the military coup of 1969, was reported to be in his late 70s (though his exact age was not officially disclosed) and had been injured in an automobile accident in 1986.

President Barrah delegated power in a number of key party and government areas during 1987. At an extraordinary session of the Central Committee of the ruling Somali Revolutionary Socialist Party (SRSP) in late January, he appointed Muhammad Ali Samatar, first vice-president, to the newly created post of prime minister. In March Barrah, secretary-general of the SRSP, created a new post of assistant secretary-general.

Discontent was manifest in various parts of the country. Unrest in the north, where local clans and business interests felt themselves disadvantaged under a southern-based regime, was encouraged by the antigovernment Somali National Movement, which launched guerrilla attacks from its base beyond the Ethiopian border. At the beginning of 1987 there were demonstrations in the northern capital, Hargeysa, to which the authorities responded with mass arrests and a curfew. In July rioting in the southern city of Kismaayo was followed by major disturbances in the capital, Mogadishu, which lasted for three days, August 15–17. The disturbances were provoked by fuel shortages and the rising cost of living.

In response, a memorandum released by the Central Committee of the SRSP recommended a number of economic reforms. On September 18 the foreign currency auctions that had been held since the previous September as part of an arrangement with the International Monetary Fund were suspended, and the maintenance of a fixed exchange rate of 100 Somali shillings to the U.S. dollar was announced on October 20.

In April 1987 the government declared a state of emergency owing to a drought in the rangelands of central Somalia. Herdsmen were reported to have lost up to 80% of their livestock, and human deaths were estimated at as many as 600. Emergency supplies were eventually transported to the area by truck.

Somalia's severe debt problem was alleviated in July when the Paris Club of Western creditor nations agreed to reschedule its share of Somalia's debt repayment, amounting to $170 million, on exceptionally favourable terms over 20 years. Despite the agreement, overall repayments due during the upcoming two years remained in excess of estimated export earnings.

During the year there was no perceptible progress in talks with Ethiopia, with which Somalia had a long-standing territorial dispute over the Ogaden region. Somalia claimed that Ethiopia was building up its military presence in the disputed area.                    (VIRGINIA R. LULING)

This article updates the *Macropædia* article EASTERN AFRICA: *Somalia*.

# SOUTH AFRICA

## The Republic

South Africa occupies the southern tip of Africa, with the Atlantic Ocean to the west and the Indian Ocean to the east. It partially surrounds the four republics of Bophuthatswana, Ciskei, Transkei, and Venda (whose independence from South Africa is not recognized by the international community). Area: 1,123,226 sq km (433,680 sq mi). Pop. (1987 est.): 28,881,000. (Area and population figures exclude the four republics.) Executive cap., Pretoria; judicial cap., Bloemfontein; legislative cap., Cape Town. Monetary unit: South African rand, with (Oct. 5, 1987) a commercial rate of R 2.08 to U.S. $1 (R 3.38 = £1 sterling). Executive state president in 1987, Pieter Willem Botha.

**The Republic.** *Domestic Affairs.* The nationwide state of emergency declared in South Africa in June 1986 continued throughout 1987. Repressive action by the police and Army—and also by black vigilantes—brought a halt to the more insurrectionary manifestations of black township resistance that had characterized the previous two years. However, a defiant mood persisted in many black townships, reflected, for example, in a continued rent boycott estimated to have cost local authorities R 720 million in arrears in Transvaal alone by September. Some 650,000 households were involved.

General elections for the white House of Assembly took place on May 6, two years early. While the ruling National Party (NP) was easily reelected, the Conservative Party, to the right of the NP, won 22 seats to 19 for the liberal Progressive Federal Party (PFP) and so replaced the latter as the official opposition. (For tabulated results, see *Political Parties*, above.) Ripples were caused during the election campaign by the defection of some leading NP members, notably Denis Worrall, former ambassador to Great Britain, to campaign as independent candidates attempting to promote a reformist realignment. Worrall lost in a close contest, while Wynand Malan was elected. PFP leader Colin Eglin described the results as "a major setback for the PFP and the concept of a reform alliance developing into an alternative government for South Africa."

The dominant theme of the election campaign was the attitude that the government should take toward the banned African National Congress (ANC): repression or negotiation. The ANC was generally regarded as the most popular political organization among South Africa's black majority. This was emphasized during the year when its program, the Freedom Charter, was adopted by the main groups of the extraparliamentary opposition. These were the 750,000-strong Congress of South African Trade Unions (COSATU), formed in 1985; the United Democratic Front (UDF), formed in 1983; and the South African Youth Congress, launched in March 1987 and claiming more than 600,000 members. According to the government, Umkhonto we Sizwe, the military wing of the ANC, had been responsible for 70 actions up to the end of May, compared with 228 during all of 1986.

An important indication of the changing alignment of forces was the national general strike of some three million black workers and students that took place on May 5–6. The biggest strike in the country's history, it overshadowed the white election in many ways. Touched off by the police shooting of striking railway workers and by raids on trade union offices, including COSATU headquarters, the strike was at the same time a massive expression of protest against the system of white minority rule. On the night of May 6, COSATU headquarters were wrecked by bombs. A second national general strike on a similar scale took place on June 16, the 11th anniversary of the police massacre of schoolchildren in Soweto, a black urban complex near Johannesburg.

A three-month railway strike by up to 25,000 workers was also a major episode in the biggest wave of industrial action in South Africa's history, which was another reflection of deep-rooted social tensions. By the end of August work stoppages had involved about 5.5 million strike-days, compared with 1.3 million in all of 1986. A stimulus to this strike wave was the launching by COSATU of a campaign for a national minimum living wage. The strike wave, together with industrial disputes short of strike action, touched almost every sector of the economy.

The most important single action was the strike of 340,-000 black mine workers—by far the biggest ever on the mines, the nerve centre of the economy. Launched on August 9 by the National Union of Mineworkers under the leadership of general secretary Cyril Ramaphosa (*see* BIOGRAPHIES) and centred on a demand for a 30% wage increase, it was called off on August 30 without achieving further wage concessions. During the strike 46,000 mine workers had been dismissed, mainly by Anglo American Corp., and 50,000 others were threatened with dismissal.

Harassment of trade union and black political organizations by the government and media censorship measures continued, as did detentions of activists, though on a lesser scale than in 1986. While some 25,000–30,000 people were detained during 1986, 30–40% of them under 18, the government stated in April 1987 that 4,244 were then in detention. By mid-October this had been reduced to between one thousand and two thousand. Treason trials were in progress. Among the 40 accused were many UDF leaders, as well as Moses Mayekiso, general secretary of the National Union of Metal and Motor Workers.

Violence by black vigilante groups against opponents of the regime continued in many areas, particularly in Natal, where at least 280 people were estimated to have died during the year in the conflict between supporters of KwaZulu leader Chief Gatsha Buthelezi's Inkatha movement and UDF supporters. A new feature of the situation was vigilante murders of trade unionists by members of the pro-Inkatha United Workers Union of South Africa.

The period up to the white election was characterized by a tough line by Pres. P. W. Botha and the NP government, with no movement toward political reform. Botha sought to identify the white liberal opposition as friends of a "terrorist" and "Moscow-dominated" ANC. After the election the government revived its proposal for a national statutory council, which would include limited elected representation from nonhomeland Africans, to discuss constitutional reform.

In July the government began to introduce Regional Service Councils, "multiracial" bodies responsible for the administration of some services at local government level. It also proposed allowing local choice as to whether residential areas would be racially exclusive, while at the same time making clear its commitment to the perpetuation of "minority group rights"—effective white control.

No significant black leader responded positively to the proposal for a national statutory council. Buthelezi, whose attitude continued to be crucial, reiterated his call for the release of political prisoners such as Nelson Mandela, most popular leader of the ANC, as a precondition for his participation. It was therefore significant that in August President Botha announced in Parliament that the government no longer insisted that such persons would have to renounce violence before they could be released. This was followed on November 5 by the unconditional release from life imprisonment of Govan Mbeki, fellow ANC leader with Mandela and sentenced together with him in 1964. This action was widely seen as a test run for the release of Mandela, to see if it could take place without provoking new explosions of unrest among the black majority. Speculation was dampened, however, when on December 11 Mbeki was served with an order restricting his movements and barring him from talking to the press.

Other political developments included increasing tensions among white liberals. This was caused by the drift to the right among the white electorate on one hand and strengthened and radicalized organization among the black majority on the other, provoking debate on the relative roles of parliamentary and extraparliamentary action in promoting change. In July former PFP leader Frederick van Zyl Slabbert led a delegation of more than 60 prominent "progressives," mainly Afrikaners, to Dakar, Senegal, for talks with ANC representatives. This led to vehement criticism from the far right-wing elements of the white

MARK PETERS—BLACK STAR

Govan Mbeki (left), with wife, Epainette, is released from Robben Island Prison, where he had been serving a life sentence since 1964. Mbeki, Nelson Mandela, and six other leaders of the African National Congress had been convicted of organizing a campaign of sabotage to overthrow the apartheid government of South Africa. His unconditional release on November 5 was widely viewed as a test run for the release of Mandela. Later, however, Mbeki's movements were restricted.

population, particularly the Afrikaanse Weerstandsbeweging. Subsequently, several participants in the talks defected from the PFP. Three of these joined with Malan to launch a new party, the National Democratic Movement. Finding himself excluded from this initiative, Worrall announced plans for another political party in 1988.

Severe floods struck Natal in September–October. They caused at least 250 deaths and massive homelessness.

*Foreign Relations.* The limited sanctions agreed upon against South Africa by major Western powers in 1986 remained in force, though some evasions were documented. Frontline states, in particular Zimbabwe and Zambia, found themselves in too vulnerable a position in relation to South Africa to implement sanctions they had announced.

At the Commonwealth heads of government meeting in October, British Prime Minister Margaret Thatcher vigorously and successfully resisted proposals from the rest of the Commonwealth for the intensification of sanctions. She argued that sanctions were counterproductive in promoting change and labeled the ANC a "terrorist" organization. While the U.S. government continued sanctions, the House of Representatives (but not Congress as a whole) had approved measures restricting ANC activity in the U.S. and opposing UN financial assistance to the ANC.

South Africa's relations with its southern African neighbours continued to be brittle. Shortly before the election, the South African Defense Force mounted a raid in Zambia that they claimed was on ANC centres. The Zambian government replied that the four persons killed were Zambians. While the South African government retreated from its 1986 plan to terminate recruitment of all Mozambican workers to South Africa, the Mozambique government accused South Africa of continuing its support for the Mozambique National Resistance rebellion. In July a South African government commission reported that the plane crash on South African soil that led to the death of Pres. Samora Machel of Mozambique in 1986 had been an accident. The Mozambique government and the U.S.S.R. (of which the pilot was a citizen) did not participate in the commission and maintained that the crash was provoked by air traffic control signals that were deliberately misleading.

South African armed forces were again active in Angola during the year, particularly in the latter months. While the South African government claimed that it was staging a preemptive strike against South West Africa People's Organization guerrillas bound for South West Africa/Namibia, the Angolan government said that the South Africans actually were assisting the National Union for the Total Independence of Angola (UNITA) rebels, a charge that South Africa later acknowledged was true. In early September South Africa and Angola, along with other governments, were involved in a complex exchange of prisoners. Maj. Wynand du Toit of the South African Army was released by Angola in exchange for the release by UNITA of 133 Angolan soldiers. In addition, Klaas de Jonge, a Dutchman who had taken refuge in his embassy in Pretoria after escaping from arrest on arms smuggling charges, was allowed to leave the country, and Pierre Albertini, a Frenchman jailed in Ciskei on political charges, was also released.

*The Economy.* The mild upturn in the economy that had begun in 1986 continued into 1987, but original expectations for a 3% growth in gross domestic product (GDP) were being revised downward by midyear. In 1986 GDP increased by only 0.7%. In his annual address the governor of the Reserve Bank stated that while the economy was poised "technically" for growth, "the inducement to invest and the propensity to consume are not strong enough to

lend real momentum to the economic upswing." Among the favourable factors he mentioned was the large current account surplus and the improvement in the foreign debt repayment situation. The trade surplus for the first eight months of 1987 was R 9.4 billion, leading to an estimated surplus on the current account of the balance of payments of R 5 billion–R 6 billion for the year, compared with R 7.2 billion in 1986. Together with a slowing in capital outflow, this had allowed a strengthening of reserves and the repayment of $4.3 billion of outstanding foreign debt between 1984 and the end of 1986.

There was a continued decline in the amount of gross fixed investment, which had fallen every year since 1981. In the second quarter of 1987 this was 25% lower than that of the corresponding period of 1986. Commentators pointed out that the upturn was not export-led, as it had been in the past, but was based almost wholly on domestic consumer spending. The favourable balance of payments, correspondingly, resulted not from export growth but from the low level of capital-goods imports.

After a mildly stimulatory minibudget in February, the main budget in June was regarded as neutral in its economic effects. Defense spending was increased by 30%, police spending by 43%, and education spending by 20%. The budget deficit was projected at 4.7% of GDP. Unemployment levels continued high, with official estimates of up to 1.5 million and unofficial estimates up to 6 million.

## Bophuthatswana

The republic of Bophuthatswana consists of six discontinuous, landlocked geographic units, entirely surrounded by South Africa except for one unit that borders Botswana on the northwest. Area: 40,000 sq km (15,444 sq mi). Pop. (1987 est.): 1,606,000. Cap.: Mmabatho. Monetary unit: South African rand. President in 1987, Lucas Mangope.

## Ciskei

Bordering the Indian Ocean in the south, Ciskei is surrounded on land by South Africa. Area: 5,386 sq km (2,080 sq mi). Pop. (1987 est.): 1,140,000. Cap.: Bisho. Monetary unit: South African rand. President in 1987, Lennox Sebe.

## Transkei

Bordering the Indian Ocean and surrounded on land by South Africa, Transkei comprises three discontinuous geographic units, two of which are landlocked and one of which borders Lesotho. Area: 43,553 sq km (16,816 sq mi). Pop. (1987 est.): 2,832,000. Cap.: Umtata. Monetary unit: South African rand. President in 1987, Nyangelizwe Vulindlela Ndamase; prime ministers, George Matanzima until September 24 and Stella Sigcau from October 5 to December 30; head of Military Council from December 30, Maj. Gen. Bantu Holomisa.

## Venda

The landlocked republic of Venda is located in extreme northeastern South Africa. Area: 6,198 sq km (2,393 sq mi). Pop. (1987 est.): 516,000. Cap.: Thohoyandou. Monetary unit: South African rand. President in 1987, Patrick Mphephu.

The four former homelands, regarded as politically independent of South Africa only by the South African government, continued to depend overwhelmingly on revenue generated in the central South African economy, on the one hand in the form of wages paid to migrant workers and on the other in the form of direct and indirect payments from the government of the republic. For 1987–88 direct transfers were estimated at R 595 million for Transkei, R

535 million for Bophuthatswana, R 376 million for Ciskei, and R 289 million for Venda. This excluded Development Bank investment, salaries to South African government personnel working in the four republics, special job creation assistance, customs and excise payments, and South African government guaranteed loans. In the 1987–88 fiscal year it was estimated that the proportion of government revenue raised within the areas themselves was only 24% for Transkei, 23% for Bophuthatswana, 10% for Ciskei, and 12% for Venda.

In Transkei two commissions of inquiry found extensive evidence of misuse of state funds—R 120 million—some of it involving Prime Minister George Matanzima directly. These investigations caused political instability, which culminated at the end of September in the flight of Matanzima to South Africa, an unopposed coup by army chief Maj. Gen. Bantu Holomisa, and the enforced resignation of eight Cabinet ministers. Stella Sigcau, who was elected to serve as prime minister, was herself ousted on December 30 by Holomisa, who claimed that she also was implicated in investigations into corruption. These developments had been preceded in April by the deportation from Transkei of a number of white military advisers accused of involvement in a raid on the residence of Pres. Lennox Sebe of Ciskei and by the release of Holomisa from detention to assume control of the Army. In May Kaiser Matanzima, former president of Transkei, announced the formation of a political party in opposition to his brother, who responded by banishing him from the capital.

Following dismissals and detentions of members, the KwaNdebele Assembly reversed its position of 1986 once again and requested independence from the South African government. Because of continued severe divisions on the question, however, President Botha had not responded to this request by the end of 1987.

In elections held in Bophuthatswana in October, the ruling party of Lucas Mangope won 66 seats out of 72. While the government claimed that 47% of eligible voters went to the polls, this was hotly disputed by commentators.

In Ciskei UDF leader Arnold Stofile was sentenced to an effective 11 years in prison on charges of ANC-linked arms offenses. Three others received long sentences in the same trial.                (MARTIN LEGASSICK)

See also *Dependent States,* below.

## SUDAN, THE

A republic of North Africa, The Sudan has a coastline on the Red Sea. Area: 2,503,890 sq km (966,757 sq mi). Pop. (1987 est.): 25,562,000. Cap.: Khartoum. Monetary unit: Sudanese pound, with (Oct. 5, 1987) an official rate of LSd 2.50 to U.S. $1 (LSd 4.06 = £1 sterling). Chairman of the Supreme Council in 1987, Ahmad al-Mirghani; prime minister, Sadiq al-Mahdi.

While civil war continued unabated in the south, The Sudan's economy deteriorated further in 1987. Unable to service the foreign debt and harassed by strikes of public servants in Khartoum and demonstrations in other areas, the government declared a 12-month state of emergency in July. The declared aim of sorting out the economy was received with considerable skepticism by many who believed that the emergency was really intended as a means of controlling rioting and imposing a check on the growing power of the National Islamic Front. This group, widely known as the Muslim Brotherhood, freely admitted that it saw itself as an alternative government and that, in power, it would insist on strict observance of Shari'ah (Islamic law). While the group took every opportunity to criticize the government's mishandling of the civil war, its funda-

mentalist Islamic creed held little attraction for the Sudan People's Liberation Army, the main antigovernment force in the south.

If the state of emergency was intended to reassure the International Monetary Fund, which was about to begin new talks with The Sudan, that hope was destroyed by events in August, when the coalition government collapsed. The immediate cause of the disagreement between the Umma Party, the largest group in Parliament, and its partner, the Democratic Unionist Party (DUP), was the nomination by the DUP of a former supporter of Gen. Gaafar Nimeiry, deposed as president in 1985, as a candidate for membership on the Supreme Council. The nomination reflected the DUP's close alignment with Egypt, where Nimeiry was in exile. More fundamentally responsible for the breakdown was the sense of frustration arising from the government's inability to bring an end to the civil war or to ameliorate the economic crisis. Attempts to engineer a new coalition with the National Islamic Front failed, and in October the Umma Party and the DUP agreed to resume their alliance.

(KENNETH INGHAM)

## SWAZILAND

Swaziland is a landlocked monarchy of southern Africa and a member of the Commonwealth. Area: 17,364 sq km (6,704 sq mi). Pop. (1987 est.): 716,000. Administrative cap., Mbabane; royal and legislative cap., Lobamba. Monetary unit: lilangeni (plural: emalangeni), at par with the South African rand, with (Oct. 5, 1987) a free rate of 2.08 emalangeni to U.S. $1 (3.38 emalangeni = £1 sterling). King, Mswati III; prime minister, Sotsha Dlamini.

A certain stability following the coronation of King Mswati III in 1986, coupled with a clampdown on African National Congress activities, enabled Swaziland to concentrate on economic development in 1987. High world sugar prices and a record crop in 1986–87 boosted the economy. In 1986 gross domestic product increased by an estimated 9%, and international debt stood at $266 million.

The greatest problem facing the country was the generally deteriorating security situation in the whole region and particularly the escalating violence in neighbouring Natal. Swaziland remained highly vulnerable to events in South Africa. The depreciation of the South African rand affected the lilangeni, leading to an increase in the cost of imports and to higher local costs in servicing the country's debts.

Elections to the lower house of the National Assembly took place on November 5. In May, 12 people, including former prime minister Prince Bhekimpi Dlamini and other former ministers and members of the royal family, were arrested and charged with sedition in connection with events in 1983, when a power struggle between different factions of the royal family had taken place following the death of King Sobhuza II a year earlier.    (GUY ARNOLD)

This article updates the *Macropædia* article SOUTHERN AFRICA: *Swaziland.*

## TANZANIA

The republic of Tanzania, a member of the Commonwealth, consists of Tanganyika, on the east coast of Africa, and Zanzibar, just off the coast in the Indian Ocean, which includes Zanzibar Island, Pemba Island, and small islets. Area: 945,037 sq km (364,881 sq mi). Pop. (1987 est.): 23,217,000. Seat of government, Dar es Salaam; capital designate, Dodoma. Monetary unit: Tanzania shilling, with (Oct. 5, 1987) a free rate of 69.74 shillings to U.S. $1 (113.25 shillings = £1 sterling). President in 1987, Ali Hassan Mwinyi; prime minister, Joseph Warioba.

Right up to the annual party conference at the end of October 1987, there was widespread speculation in Tanzania as to whether former president Julius Nyerere would resign the chairmanship of the ruling Chama Cha Mapinduzi (CCM) on completion of the two-year period during which he had agreed to hold office. On more than one occasion he indicated that this was his intention, and some believed that his known opposition to the deal made in 1986 with the International Monetary Fund (IMF) was a serious discouragement to potential foreign investors and a constraint on Pres. Ali Hassan Mwinyi, the leading figure behind the IMF agreement. Nevertheless, Nyerere, who had modified his stance to the extent of stating that he would leave the decision to the party, was nominated unopposed as chairman by Mwinyi at the CCM conference and reelected on October 31. It was a testimony to Nyerere's continuing influence and Mwinyi's reluctance to appear to be challenging it.

The effect of the IMF agreement was not as disastrous as Nyerere had predicted, but this did not mean that Tanzania faced a comfortable future. As an immediate result, the exchange rate of the Tanzania shilling had dropped from 16 to 62 against the U.S. dollar, and prices had soared. Delays in the disbursement of aid and a local shortage of cash for borrowing because of the credit ceiling imposed by the agreement also held up progress. At the same time, the production of many cash crops continued to decline. Coffee output was still falling because of the shortage of insecticides and because farmers were discouraged by the lack of good roads for transporting crops. Sisal production, which had stood at 200,000 metric tons a year in the 1960s, had fallen to 30,431 tons because of the lack of tools and transport and the shortage of sisal cutters. Old cashew nut trees, which should have been replaced, produced only 15,188 tons, compared with 140,000 tons in the 1960s. Cotton output doubled in the 1986–87 season, however, and corn (maize), the staple food crop, was in plentiful supply.

Continuing good weather and the fall in oil prices contributed to an improvement in the economic outlook, as did the government campaign to encourage farmers to rehabilitate farms and smallholders to diversify crops. Promises were made that roads would be improved, that prices for crops would be increased by 25–50%, and that money for the purchase of the crops would be made available in good time for the harvest. There were hopeful signs that export earnings would show an increase of nearly 20% over the previous year, though they still fell far short of the sum spent on imports. In July the Paris Club, having agreed to postpone for five years virtually all of the servicing of the country's debt, promised an additional loan of $1.9 billion, to be spread over two years.

Old habits died hard, however. In July Kingunge Ngomdale-Mwiru, a member of the CCM Central Committee, warned a seminar of representatives of political parties in less developed countries against bilateral and multilateral aid agreements that might conceal the self-interested motives of imperialist powers.　　　　(KENNETH INGHAM)

This article updates the *Macropædia* article EASTERN AFRICA: *Tanzania*.

## TOGO

A republic of West Africa, Togo is situated on the Bight of Benin. Area: 56,785 sq km (21,925 sq mi). Pop. (1987 est.): 3,158,000. Cap.: Lomé. Monetary unit: CFA franc, with (Oct. 5, 1987) a par value of CFAF 50 to the French franc and a free rate of CFAF 306.67 to U.S. $1 (CFAF 498 = £1 sterling). President in 1987, Gen. Gnassingbe Eyadema.

The political atmosphere in Togo relaxed in 1987 following the tensions engendered by a failed coup attempt in September 1986. The 20th anniversary of the coup that brought Pres. Gnassingbe Eyadema to power, Jan. 13, 1987, was marked by the lifting of the five-year-old public-sector wage freeze. In May it was announced that a human rights commission was being established to investigate persistent allegations by Amnesty International, among others, of torture in Togolese prisons. On June 3 an unprecedented meeting was held between Eyadema and former leading members of political parties dissolved after the 1963 and 1967 coups, and several former politicians later participated in an enlarged Council of Ministers. Liberalization moved a step further with the holding on July 5 of direct elections for municipal and prefectural offices.

Togo joined Cameroon, Côte d'Ivoire, Liberia, and Zaire as the fifth sub-Saharan country to reestablish diplomatic relations with Israel. Israeli Prime Minister Yitzhak Shamir visited Lomé in mid-June for talks on subjects that included the resumption of Israeli economic and military cooperation.　　　　(NIM CASWELL)

This article updates the *Macropædia* article WESTERN AFRICA: *Togo*.

## UGANDA

A landlocked republic and member of the Commonwealth, Uganda is located in eastern Africa. Area: 241,040 sq km (93,070 sq mi), including 44,000 sq km of inland water. Pop. (1987 est.): 15,514,000. Cap.: Kampala. Monetary unit: Uganda shilling, with (Oct. 5, 1987) a par value of 60 shillings to U.S. $1 (free rate of 98 shillings = £1 sterling). President in 1987, Yoweri Museveni; prime minister, Samson Kisekka.

After seizing power in 1986 following a five-year civil war waged against two successive governments, Pres. Yoweri Museveni in 1987 experienced armed rebels' disruption of his own attempts to create a stable society in Uganda. Most of the rebel activities took place in the northern half of the country, where loyalty to former presidents Milton Obote and Tito Okello remained strong despite Museveni's claim in March 1986 that the civil war was over. Important towns, including Soroti and Gulu, were attacked, and although government forces were in general victorious, the fighting showed no signs of ending. Nor was Kampala itself free from violence. Many people were murdered, among them Andrew Kayiira, a former leader of the Uganda Freedom Movement guerrilla group who recently had been a member of Museveni's government until treason charges were leveled against him. The charges were withdrawn, but the killing of Kayiira, a Muganda, in March aroused fears of a split within the National Resistance Movement (NRM) along tribal lines. In June the Federal Democratic Movement (Fedemo) broke its links with the NRM and signed an agreement in London with the Uganda People's Democratic Movement that was aimed at overthrowing the government. Fedemo claimed that the NRM was backed by Libya.

By November the threat from a fanatical group based in northern Uganda and led by Alice Lakwena, who claimed God had instructed her to overthrow Museveni, appeared to have receded. The rebels were poorly armed and relied on magic to protect them from bullets. On December 30 the Kenyan authorities announced that Lakwena had been imprisoned after crossing illegally into Kenya.

The many operations in which government troops were involved resulted in accusations that they were using the tactics of torture and murder that they themselves had so vigorously denounced when those tactics were employed by the armies of Obote and Okello. The charges were supported by a report from Amnesty International.

The effect of the continuing insecurity upon the economy was disastrous. Supplies of coffee, overwhelmingly the most important source of foreign exchange, failed to reach the state-run coffee marketing board at the end of 1986, with the result that the board had a cash crisis early in 1987. Faced with an almost total lack of foreign exchange, empty shops, and an inflation rate of 300%, Museveni engaged in lengthy discussions, which in May led to the promise of loans of $78 million from the World Bank and $100 million from the International Monetary Fund, together with a rescheduling of the servicing of the foreign debt. In return, a new currency was introduced, coupled with a devaluation of 76%. Ugandans changing old money for new were required to pay a 30% tax, which, the government hoped, would reduce the money supply. Inevitably, a black market in currency quickly developed.

The 1987–88 budget lowered taxes on many consumer goods, particularly basic necessities, and reduced customs duties on a range of motor vehicles and spare parts. The duty on raw materials for industry was waived, but taxes on beer, cigarettes, and gasoline were increased. Defense still accounted for a high proportion of expenditures. In August Saudi Arabia offered substantial financial aid.

Fears of the recurrence of famine in the Karamoja district were voiced by development workers after torrential rains in May destroyed newly planted crops. This was followed by an unexpectedly dry period in July that led to forecasts of drought later in the year. Settled farming in the area was constantly threatened by armed cattle raiders.

A border dispute with Kenya flared into open conflict in December. Museveni and Pres. Daniel arap Moi of Kenya met at year's end and agreed to resolve the dispute through peaceful means.                    (KENNETH INGHAM)

This article updates the *Macropædia* article EASTERN AFRICA: *Uganda*.

## ZAIRE

The republic of Zaire is located in central Africa with a short coastline on the Atlantic Ocean. Area: 2,344,885 sq km (905,365 sq mi). Pop. (1987 est.): 31,804,000. Cap.: Kinshasa. Monetary unit: zaire, with (Oct. 5, 1987) a free rate of 121.03 zaires to U.S. $1 (196.54 zaires = £1 sterling). President in 1987, Mobutu Sese Seko; first state commissioner (prime minister) from January 22, Mabi Mulumba.

In January and February 1987 Pres. Mobutu Sese Seko of Zaire reshuffled his Cabinet comprehensively. Among numerous changes Mabi Mulumba was appointed to the restored office of prime minister. The post had been abolished in October 1986, when Mulumba's predecessor, Kengo wa Dondo, was treated as a scapegoat for unpopular austerity measures demanded by the International Monetary Fund (IMF). Ekila Liyonda, ambassador to Belgium, became minister for foreign affairs, and Tshunza Mbiye, deputy chairman of the central bank, replaced Nyembo Shabani as minister of finance.

Local and municipal elections were held in midyear, but in August the results were nullified because of irregularities. Particular care was consequently taken with regard to elections to the National Assembly in September, in which all candidates were approved by the Mouvement Populaire de la Révolution, the sole party. Vote counting took place in the presence of representatives of every candidate immediately after polling closed. Kalume Mwana Kahambwe, proposed by President Mobutu, was elected chairman of the new Assembly in place of Kasongo Mukundji. Kahambwe

had been deputy chairman of the previous legislature.

The rebel Congolese National Movement (MNC) claimed in July that its forces had attacked the towns of Watsa and Kisindi in eastern Zaire, inflicting casualties on government troops. At a meeting in Switzerland on September 5–6, 13 opposition movements agreed to form a government-in-exile with the aim of overthrowing Mobutu's regime by any means and of reestablishing democracy in Zaire. Albert-Jerry Mahele was named prime minister. Paul-Roger Mokede, who was nominated president of the constitution, subsequently denied any involvement with the government-in-exile and called for all opponents to return to Zaire.

Economic issues were the main concern of the government throughout the year. In February Mobutu visited Brazil and Argentina to seek information about how those countries were dealing with their debt problems, and he went on to Washington, D.C., for discussions with the IMF and the World Bank. His decision, announced on Oct. 30, 1986, to throw down the gauntlet to the IMF, with which he had formerly cooperated closely, and to limit debt-service payments to 10% of export earnings had not been well received by some Western powers. In Bonn he had friendly discussions with the West German president and with Chancellor Helmut Kohl, but he was left in no doubt of that government's disapproval of his economic measures. Nevertheless, he received a promise of support for any fair agreement he might make with the IMF.

Other countries were less critical. The U.S. had strategic interests in Zaire—including a base from which to dispatch military supplies to the National Union for the Total Independence of Angola (UNITA) guerrillas opposing the Angolan government—and tried to urge the IMF to come to Zaire's assistance. Representatives of the governments of Zaire and Angola, meeting in December 1986, had issued a statement to the effect that they were seeking to prevent any disturbance of the peace along their common border. Despite this, U.S. troops were allowed to carry out training in Zaire's Shaba Province, near the Angolan border, in April in conjunction with Zairian forces. Zaire did not, however, strive to appear submissive to the U.S. Indeed, diplomatic relations were opened with Nicaragua, a technical assistance agreement was signed with Romania, and a parliamentary delegation from the U.S.S.R. discussed the possibility of strengthening bilateral cooperation with Zaire. This did not prevent the expulsion on July 31 of three Soviet diplomats who were accused of spying, an action to which the U.S.S.R. replied by expelling three Zairian diplomats.

An agreement concluded in March with Portugal concerned exchanges of technicians and technical information to promote agricultural development; Portugal also offered to provide a loan for Zairian students. Shortly afterward a tentative agreement was reached with the IMF, which offered $126 million on the understanding that the government would demonstrate a genuine commitment to increasing its financial and budgetary discipline in a way that would attract foreign investment.

In December 1986 two loan agreements were signed with the African Development Fund and the African Development Bank, one loan to be repaid over 40 years and the other over 10 years. The loans were to finance the rehabilitation plan for the Kilo-Moto Gold Mining Corp. and to provide research and technical assistance needed for its management. Zaire also received an International Development Agency credit of $27.6 million to help revive river transportation, and in May the Paris Club agreed to a generous rescheduling of $884 million of debt repayments falling due in 1988.

In his turn, Mobutu created the new post of deputy prime minister, to which he appointed Sambwa Pida Mbagui, who at one time had been governor of the central bank and more recently minister of planning. Mbagui's task was to head a team of four junior ministers to improve economic performance. Without waiting for the team to make any recommendations, however, Mobutu himself dissolved ten state enterprises that he considered nonviable. Further evidence of foreign support followed when private creditors, meeting in Kinshasa in August, agreed to the rescheduling of 95% of Zaire's debt.            (KENNETH INGHAM)

This article updates the *Macropædia* article CENTRAL AFRICA: *Zaire*.

## ZAMBIA

A landlocked republic and member of the Commonwealth, Zambia is in eastern Africa. Area: 752,614 sq km (290,586 sq mi). Pop. (1987 est.): 7,135,000. Cap.: Lusaka. Monetary unit: kwacha, with (Oct. 5, 1987) a free rate of 7.82 kwacha to U.S. $1 (12.70 kwacha = £1 sterling). President in 1987, Kenneth Kaunda; prime minister, Kebby Musokotwane.

In May 1987 Pres. Kenneth Kaunda, deeply disturbed by the high cost of servicing Zambia's foreign debt, broke with the economic austerity policies of the International Monetary Fund (IMF). The government revalued the kwacha, reintroduced price controls, and severely restricted payments to foreign creditors. In response, the World Bank and the IMF refused to make further funds available, while the revaluation of the kwacha had an adverse effect on the export of copper, the main source of foreign exchange earnings. In spite of an appeal from Kaunda for a sympathetic reception for his policy, most countries that had previously given aid to Zambia were openly critical of what he had done.

The economy suffered a further blow in July when Zimbabwe stopped importing electricity from Zambia because of the impossibility of reaching a satisfactory financial agreement. This meant that half the country's generating power would lie idle, with a consequent loss of annual revenue of an estimated $17 million. Kaunda announced an interim national development plan to cover the 18-month period to December 1988. His aim was to set priorities for foreign exchange expenditure; consumption of expensive imported goods and services was severely cut, and luxury goods were heavily taxed.            (KENNETH INGHAM)

This article updates the *Macropædia* article SOUTHERN AFRICA: *Zambia*.

## ZIMBABWE

A republic and member of the Commonwealth, Zimbabwe is a landlocked state in eastern Africa. Area: 390,759 sq km (150,873 sq mi). Pop. (1987 est.): 8,640,000. Cap.: Harare. Monetary unit: Zimbabwe dollar, with (Oct. 5, 1987) a free rate of Z$1.71 to U.S. $1 (Z$2.77 = £1 sterling). President to Dec. 31, 1987, the Rev. Canaan Banana; prime minister to December 31, Robert Mugabe; executive president from December 31, Mugabe.

On Jan. 20, 1987, the national state of emergency was renewed in response to continuing instability in Matabeleland and, increasingly throughout the year, along Zimbabwe's eastern frontier with Mozambique. In March Pres. Joaquim Chissanó of Mozambique paid his first official visit to Zimbabwe in the hope of further strengthening Zimbabwe's commitment to assisting his country with troops. A new antiguerrilla offensive had already been launched in Mozambique, led in part by Zimbabwean forces, and

in response guerrillas from Mozambique attacked bases in Zimbabwe on May 31 in the first of many incursions over the border.

Early in April Ian Smith, former leader of white-ruled Rhodesia, was suspended from the House of Assembly for a year because, while on a visit to South Africa, he had urged South Africans to unite against the sanctions imposed by foreign critics of the government. A month later he resigned as president of the Conservative Alliance of Zimbabwe but said he would continue in politics. It was, however, effectively the end of his 39-year career because in April the constitutional provision that 20 seats in the House of Assembly and 10 in the Senate were to be reserved for representatives elected by white voters was due for revision.

Not until July 15, however, was the bill to deal with the white-voter issue published. It proposed that all other members of Parliament sit as an electoral college to choose replacements for the 30 legislators. All those selected would be under an obligation to support the ruling party, which meant that in the House of Assembly Robert Mugabe's Patriotic Front party, the Zimbabwe African National Union (ZANU [PF]), would control 85 seats, while Joshua Nkomo's Zimbabwe African People's Union (ZAPU) would hold 14. The bill also set out to amalgamate the white voters' roll with the common roll.

In May Edgar Tekere, former chairman of ZANU (PF), was dismissed from his post as provincial party leader on the grounds that he had failed to fulfill his obligations and had tarnished the image of the party. He had been a lively critic of his Cabinet colleagues, and Mugabe was seeking unity among his supporters during the crucial period of constitutional amendment. Early in August, on the eve of the debate on the constitutional bill, it seemed that ZANU (PF) might reach an agreement that would unite the party with Nkomo's ZAPU, but at this stage the two parties once again drew back from merger. The bill was approved by the House of Assembly on August 21 and by the Senate in early September. Pres. Canaan Banana added his signature on September 21.

The following day Enos Nkala, minister for home affairs, made the startling announcement that he had ordered the closing of ZAPU's offices and said that the party's structure would cease to function. He gave as the reason for his action the continuing violence in Matabeleland, which had been widely attributed to bandits who did not represent any political movement. Mugabe intervened personally to support Nkala. While stating that the closure of ZAPU's offices was a temporary measure to enable police to carry out searches, he insisted that enough evidence had been discovered by security forces to link ZAPU firmly with guerrilla activities in Matabeleland.

The government's hostility toward ZAPU was further demonstrated in October when ZANU (PF) refused to support any ZAPU candidates for the vacant seats in Parliament, preferring to nominate whites to both houses. Most of the whites chosen had formerly been among the leading opponents of ZANU (PF) and, indeed, of black rule generally. Those of a more liberal outlook had offended the government by criticizing its hard-line policy against guerrillas in Matabeleland in 1983–84. Nevertheless, two years of on-off discussions between ZANU (PF) and ZAPU culminated in the signing of a merger agreement by Mugabe and Nkomo on December 22. Under the agreement the merged party was to retain the name ZANU (PF), and Mugabe was to be party president and first secretary.

A further constitutional amendment approved in October allowed for the creation of an executive presidency that

Zimbabwe Prime Minister Robert Mugabe (left) and opposition leader Joshua Nkomo embrace after signing a momentous agreement to merge their rival parties.
AFP PHOTO

combined the functions of president and prime minister. Mugabe was the sole candidate for elections that took place on December 30, and he took office the following day.

The final delivery in January of 34,000 metric tons of fuel oil—ordered from South Africa to cover a serious shortfall created largely by acts of sabotage against the pipeline through Mozambique—underlined Zimbabwe's heavy dependence upon its powerful neighbour. This was particularly galling because Mugabe was eager to lead the southern African nations in a sanctions campaign against South Africa and also because Zimbabwe was already suffering from a shortage of foreign exchange. The shortage made it difficult to buy foreign items essential to the effective functioning of a number of industries. The situation was made worse by the deficit budget adopted in 1986. The considerable sums spent on education not only placed a serious burden on the economy but also resulted in the production of thousands of school graduates who were unable to find employment suited to their qualifications.

The International Monetary Fund did not look with favour on the government's policies and consequently suspended payment of a loan. In return for providing export credit funds, the World Bank demanded a wide range of economic reforms, including devaluation of the currency and fewer restrictions on the flow of foreign currency. Finance Minister Bernard Chidzero feared, however, that meeting the World Bank's demands would open the gate to a flood of foreign imports.

In early 1987 there appeared to be some grounds for optimism in spite of these problems. There were reserves of corn sufficient to feed the whole population for two years, with the result that corn farmers had been urged to diversify their crops. Some had turned to the production of oilseeds, a useful foreign exchange earner. The tobacco crop, the country's main earner of foreign exchange, was expected to exceed that of 1986. However, a severe drought, accompanied by high temperatures, resulted in a brittle and flavourless tobacco crop; also, reserve stocks of corn were retained to meet internal demand. At least 1.4 million people were directly affected by drought and the serious unemployment that resulted from it, while inflation was running at 15%.

On June 24 a six-month wage freeze was announced, accompanied by strict price controls. It was hoped that the measures would encourage the World Bank to make a loan. Zimbabwe's businessmen urged Mugabe to try to attract foreign investors by modifying his anticapitalist policy, but the prime minister believed that doing so would only increase the country's debts. Mugabe faced opposition even within his own Cabinet when he appeared in July to be ready to sever all trading links with South Africa in support of his antiapartheid views. Stocks of commodities essential to industry, agriculture, and commerce were wholly inadequate for sustaining such a stand, however, and the proposal was shelved.          (KENNETH INGHAM)

This article updates the *Macropædia* article SOUTHERN AFRICA: *Zimbabwe*.

# Middle East and North Africa

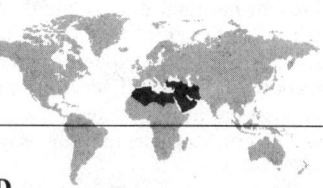

## MIDDLE EASTERN AND NORTH AFRICAN AFFAIRS

The failure of peace efforts in the Gulf war between Iran and Iraq and the frustration of moves toward a settlement between Israel and the Arab states characterized 1987, a year in which Moscow and Washington moved back into the diplomatic arena in the Middle East. The Arab League summit in Amman, Jordan, in November allowed individual Arab countries to decide whether to mend relations with Egypt. Within a week, nine of them gratefully reopened the embassies they had closed when the late president Anwar as-Sadat made peace with Tel Aviv by signing the Camp David accords in 1979.

Egypt's Pres. Hosni Mubarak played skillfully on the growing Arab fear of Iran. On a broad geostrategic level, the 50 million Egyptians were a potential Arab bulwark against Iran, although peace with Israel had affected the growth of the Egyptian Army, which had fewer tanks than Syria and fewer divisions than Iraq. The scale and scope of the escalation of the Gulf war was featured on the agenda of the Gulf Cooperation Council (GCC) summit, held in late December 1987 in Riyadh, Saudi Arabia. The summit took place later in the year than usual because of the Amman Arab summit. The GCC states suffered during the year not only from regional insecurity but also from a slump in the purchasing power of the U.S. dollar, in which oil revenues were expressed.

Saudi Arabia was involved in sharp exchanges with Iran after more than 400 people, mostly Iranian pilgrims, died as a result of clashes with Saudi Arabian security forces in Mecca at the climax of the hajj (annual pilgrimage) in July. (See *Saudi Arabia*, below.)

**The Arab World and Arab-Israeli Relations.** The Amman summit, which began on November 8, was a turning point in Israel's 40-year war against the Arab world. The summit lionized King Hussein of Jordan, the Arab leader who had spent much of the year holding "secret meetings" with Israeli leaders. The meeting implicitly forgave Egypt for the Camp David peace process. Instead of calling for the liberation of Palestine by force, the summit endorsed the Egyptian and Jordanian view that the Arabs should negotiate peace in the forum of an international conference (though an unpublished resolution also called for strategic parity with Israel). This call for an international conference was also supported by Israel's foreign minister, Shimon Peres, who believed that a federal entity should be created uniting Jordan and the occupied West Bank and Gaza Strip. On the negative side the Amman meeting reiterated the Arab view that a comprehensive peace in the Middle East meant regaining "all occupied Arab territory, particularly Jerusalem." Pres. Amin Gemayel of Lebanon received a token acknowledgement of his request to the summit for economic aid.

The summit left the radical Arab states, especially Libya and Syria, exposed as the real obstacles to Arab unity. Pres. Hafez al-Assad of Syria, anxious to shield Iran from too harsh an attack, argued in favour of an evenhanded resolution on the Gulf war. Syria was prepared to allow criticism of Iranian military strikes against Kuwait but would not tolerate a blanket condemnation. The Syrians also recommended the withdrawal of all foreign navies from the Gulf. Libya was represented by the second most important member of the regime, Maj. Abdul Salam Ahmed Jalloud, who said that by restoring relations with Cairo the other Arabs would be turning Egypt into "a bridgehead for the Zionist crossing into the Arab homeland."

The countries that restored relations with Egypt following the summit were Saudi Arabia (whose King Fahd was a notable absentee from the summit because of an angry exchange beforehand with Libya), Kuwait, Morocco, Iraq, the Yemen Arab Republic (North Yemen), the United Arab Emirates, Bahrain, Qatar, and Mauritania. Three Arab countries had never broken relations with Egypt, and two—Jordan and Djibouti—had restored links in 1984 and 1986, respectively. Following the summit Egypt sent a military mission, headed by a major general, to assess Kuwait's security needs. Jordan and Egypt had supplied technical advisers to Kuwait, whose sovereignty was jeopardized in 1987 by Iranian threats and missile attacks on its oil installations.

On October 16–18 U.S. Secretary of State George Shultz visited Israel to discuss efforts to convene an international peace conference, although this appeared to have been rejected in advance by Israeli Prime Minister Yitzhak Shamir. Shultz also appeared to have suggested that key leaders in the Middle East peace process should travel to the United States during the superpower summit in December to relaunch the moribund peace process. Soviet diplomacy in the Middle East had entered a new and more active phase. Moscow played a prominent role in 1987 in the reunification of the Palestine Liberation Organization (PLO) under its chairman, Yasir Arafat. During a visit by President Assad to Moscow in April, Soviet leader Mikhail Gorbachev said, in effect, that the Arab-Israel conflict was not going to be solved by military means; he thus implicitly criticized Syria's foreign policy. In addition, during the year Moscow was assiduously courting Israel; the U.S.S.R. had broken off relations in 1967, at the time of the Six-Day War. There was a marked increase in the number of Jews permitted to leave the U.S.S.R. to make their homes in Israel.

Israel's nuclear potential was discussed by the fifth summit meeting of the Islamic Conference Organization, which opened in Kuwait on January 26. Other motions debated by the 1,500 delegates were critical of the Israeli occupation of Jerusalem and of southern Lebanon. Iran declined to attend because it alleged that the host country was not an impartial state in the Gulf war. Israeli officials had never admitted that the country possessed nuclear weapons. On August 25 Foreign Minister Peres refused to confirm directly that Israel had tested nuclear weapons. He said: "We are facing missiles in the Middle East provided by the Soviet Union to many Arab countries. We have to make a major effort to match this challenge."

A diplomatic success for Israel came on September 14 when Hungary agreed to resume regular diplomatic contacts with Tel Aviv. Yugoslavia was expected to follow Hungary's lead. On August 20 Prime Minister Shamir ended a three-day visit to Romania. As the only Eastern European country that did not break relations with Israel in 1967, Romania had acted as an intermediary with Arab states. A week before the visit, Pres. Nicolae Ceausescu of Romania had held talks with Arafat and agreed to work for PLO participation in the proposed international conference on the Middle East peace process.

In 1987 the Israeli economy was in better shape than it had been for at least 15 years, and it was expected that its need for external support would be reduced further in 1988. The country's foreign exchange reserves reached an unprecedented level of $5.7 billion following the payment in November 1987 of the $1.2 billion civilian portion of aid from the United States, as agreed for the 1987–88 fiscal year; military grants of $1.8 billion were to follow. Nevertheless, in early December Prime Minister Shamir put his argument to U.S. Pres. Ronald Reagan that Israel should be treated as a special case when the administration reviewed its foreign aid program for the 1988–89 fiscal year. Israel was the largest recipient of U.S. aid in absolute terms and had the most to lose from the impending cuts in the U.S. budget deficit.

Israel suffered the backwash of Palestinian attempts to reintroduce the Palestine question as the primary Arab cause, following the Amman summit resolutions. On November 25 a Palestinian guerrilla loyal to the Damascus-based hard-line Popular Front for the Liberation of Palestine (PFLP) mounted an airborne attack in a hang glider on an Israeli army post in northern Galilee, leaving six Israeli soldiers dead. Violence flared in the occupied territories in December when Israeli troops and Palestinians clashed in Gaza and the West Bank; at least 22 Palestinians were killed and over 250 injured. By December 21 unrest had spread to the Arab community inside Israel's pre-1967 borders, and some two million Arabs in Israel and the occupied territories joined in a strike to protest the use of deadly force by the Israelis. Christmas observances in Bethlehem—a prime tourist attraction—were scaled down because of the violence. On June 17 four Israeli leftists who had met PLO officials in Romania in November 1986 went on trial, charged with violating an Israeli law banning contacts with "terrorist groups."

Polarization of attitudes within Israel toward the PLO was exacerbated by the outcome of the late-April meeting of the Palestine National Council (PNC), the Palestinian parliament-in-exile. Libya and Algeria played key roles in mediating between the various PLO factions, thus enabling the meeting to go ahead in Algiers on April 20. In constructing a platform for unity, PLO chairman Arafat accepted demands from opposing factions that he abrogate his 1985 agreement with Jordan's King Hussein. The agreement had been suspended earlier by the Jordanian monarch, who blamed Arafat for the Arab failure to make progress on peace talks with Israel. The PLO had been torn apart after it lost its Beirut base. Three Arab states, however, were dismayed by the outcome of the PNC meeting: Egypt, Morocco, and Jordan. After the PNC meeting Egyptian police closed 14 PLO offices and sealed them with wax. In September it was announced that the PLO office in Washington was to be closed because the PLO was considered to contain elements that supported international terrorism.

**Hostages.** The French government secured the release of two hostages in Lebanon, Jean-Louis Normandin and Roger Auque, who were freed in late November. Final agreement on the package came after two months of delicate negotiations involving French, Syrian, and Iranian officials, but the French government denied reports that a ransom had been paid. (*See* Western Europe: *France,* below.) By early December, 17 Western hostages, excluding 3 who reportedly had been killed, were still in captivity. The most prominent was Terry Waite, the archbishop of Canterbury's special envoy, who disappeared in January after leaving his Beirut hotel. President Assad was eager to play an intermediary role in talks with extremist groups on the fate of some of the hostages in order to increase his leverage with Western governments.

**Gulf War.** Diplomatic efforts to end the Gulf war between Iran and Iraq involved strong support among the conservative Arab states for the July 20 UN Security Council resolution calling for a cease-fire. Iran initially maintained an ambiguous position toward the resolution— neither endorsing nor rejecting it—but later held out for amendments condemning Iraq as the aggressor and calling on all foreign navies to leave the Gulf. The personal mission of UN Secretary-General Javier Pérez de Cuéllar to Iran and Iraq in mid-September hardened Iran's view that peace was impossible without Iraq's identification and punishment as the aggressor. The U.S. increased its profile in the Gulf war following an attack on May 17 by Iraq on the USS *Stark,* although both sides referred to the incident as "accidental." The Reagan administration agreed to reflag 11 Kuwaiti oil tankers as U.S. vessels and also requested more assistance from GCC countries. GCC states backed the UN resolution but had reservations about increasing military cooperation with the superpowers for fear of provoking Iran. In early December Kuwait lent a barge to the U.S. Navy to use as an observation post in the Gulf.

On July 24 the reflagged vessel *Bridgeton* hit a mine while passing through a waterway near the Iranian island of Farsi as it was being escorted by U.S. warships. On September 21 the U.S. Navy intercepted and captured the Iranian landing craft *Iran Ajr,* which was in the process of seeding the Gulf with mines. On October 22 Kuwait's oil terminal at Sea Island was hit by an Iranian missile, the first attack of its kind in the seven-year war. This appeared

to be in retaliation for the shelling of two Iranian oil rigs by U.S. warships on October 19. In addition to the U.S. ships, smaller naval forces belonging to several European nations were present in Gulf waters during the year.

Against this background the ground war was being fought at a low level of intensity in the autumn of 1987, after a determined spring offensive by Iran aimed at isolating Basra. Iran's intentions were spelled out by Hojatolislam Hashemi Ali Akbar Rafsanjani (*see* BIOGRAPHIES), speaker of the Majlis (parliament), on November 13 when he repeated Iran's determination to win a military victory. On the diplomatic front, separate talks with UN officials, involving both Iran and Iraq, took place in New York City in early December.

**North African Affairs.** The ousting on November 7 of the elderly and ailing Pres. Habib Bourguiba of Tunisia and his replacement in a bloodless coup by Prime Minister Zine al-Abidine Ben Ali (*see* BIOGRAPHIES) was likely to ease the path toward wider regional unity in North Africa. Tunisia's closest ally, Algeria, was quick to respond positively to the news, and the new regime in Tunis moved quickly to improve contacts with Libya.

At a summit meeting on May 4, Pres. Chadli Bendjedid of Algeria and King Hassan of Morocco met to discuss the Maghrib's continuing problem: the conflict in the Western Sahara between Moroccan troops and the Algerian-backed guerrillas of the Popular Front for the Liberation of Saguia el Hamra and Río de Oro (Polisario Front), the Saharan people's independence movement. An exchange of prisoners between Morocco and Algeria took place at the border on May 25. Although the two sides agreed to hold further talks, no progress was reported on the central issue. On November 21 a UN technical mission seeking to explore the possibility of holding a referendum in the disputed territory arrived at el-Aaiun in the Western Sahara for talks with Moroccan officials and a tour of the defensive wall built by the Moroccan Army. The visit took place against the background of intensive fighting between Morocco and the Polisario Front. On November 24 Polisario announced a unilateral cease-fire to run from the following day, when the UN delegation was due to visit the portion of the territory controlled by Polisario forces, until December 15. It was only the second occasion that Polisario had declared a cease-fire. The Western Sahara issue was regarded as the greatest stumbling block to closer relations between Algeria and Morocco.

On June 28 Libya's revolutionary leader, Col. Mu'ammar al-Qadhdhafi, arrived in Algiers for a surprise visit aimed at pushing proposals for a merger between the two countries. On July 16 the Algerian Central Committee described the union proposal as "imperative" and answering "the logic of history." This was counter to the previous caution shown by Algerian officials, who had said political union could only follow closer economic cooperation. On September 29 Libya's industry secretary, Ahmad Fathi ibn Shaiwan, began talks with his Algerian counterpart on strengthening various proposed joint ventures.

Algeria was also pivotal to attempts to reconcile Libya and Chad. Fierce fighting during the summer of 1987 in the Aozou Strip, the disputed area on the border between the two countries, was brought to an end by a cease-fire agreement on September 11. The UN General Assembly decided on November 12 not to examine a dossier presented by Chad on Libya's "aggression and occupation of Chad." Pres. Kenneth Kaunda of Zambia, in his capacity as chairman of the Organization of African Unity (OAU), had argued that a UN debate on Chad should not be allowed to disrupt the OAU's mediation efforts.

- ■ Tanker terminals
- ○ Oil refineries
- ⌐ Silkworm missile bases
- ⌣ Silkworm missile ranges
- ✈ Iranian air bases
- ✈ Air bases in Arab countries
- ⚓ Iranian naval bases
- • Iranian patrol boat bases

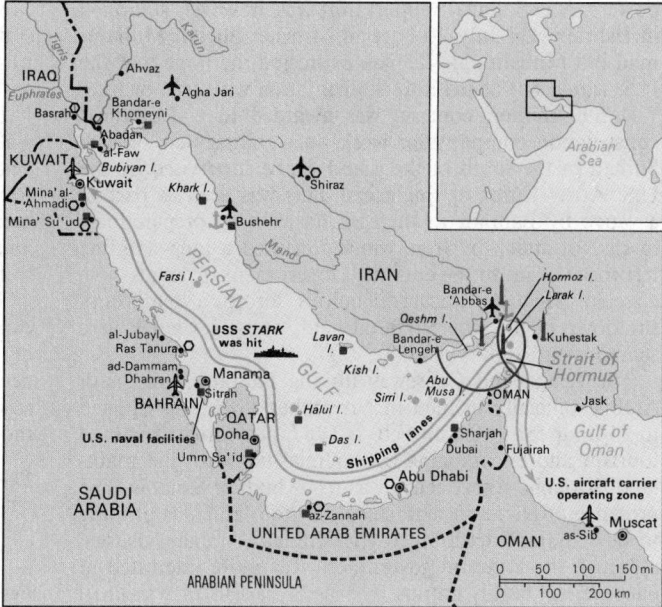

One-seventh of the non-Communist world's crude oil is shipped through the Persian Gulf and the Strait of Hormuz. Since the beginning of the Iran-Iraq war in 1980, both countries have attacked shipping in the Gulf. The escalation of the so-called tanker war throughout 1987 led to an increased U.S. naval presence in the area.

On February 24 Prime Minister Felipe González Márquez of Spain said the Spanish enclave of Melilla, which is surrounded by Moroccan territory, would remain under Spanish rule. Madrid turned down a proposal from King Hassan to establish a committee to discuss the enclave's future. (JOHN WHELAN)

## ALGERIA

Algeria is a socialist republic of North Africa on the Mediterranean Sea. Area: 2,381,741 sq km (919,595 sq mi). Pop. (1987 census): 22,971,000. Cap.: Algiers. Monetary unit: Algerian dinar, with (Oct. 5, 1987) a free rate of 4.67 dinars to U.S. $1 (7.58 dinars = £1 sterling). President in 1987, Col. Chadli Bendjedid; prime minister, Abdelhamid Brahimi.

Despite its ongoing economic problems, Algeria endeavoured to continue to play an active role in regional and international affairs throughout 1987. Within the Maghrib, tensions with Morocco increased at the start of the year as the Moroccan Army extended its defensive wall system in the Western Sahara toward the Mauritanian border. (See *Morocco*, below.) Pres. Chadli Bendjedid visited Nouakchott at the end of April to reassure Mauritanian leaders of support should Morocco threaten Mauritania. The tensions subsided in May in the wake of a meeting between Chadli and King Hassan II of Morocco, brokered by King Fahd of Saudi Arabia.

Relations with Libya continued to improve, and Col. Mu'ammar al-Qadhdhafi paid a state visit to Algiers at the end of June. Although the Libyan leader called for political union between Libya and Algeria, official Algerian sources remained cool. Economic cooperation grew rapidly, however, and 15 joint ventures were planned. Another joint venture—for the export of Algerian gas to Libya—was to involve Tunisia, and extensive lobbying by Algeria was required for suspicious Tunisian diplomats to be persuaded that relations with Libya could safely be improved. Algeria continued to have problems with France because of its failure to establish an acceptable gas price. Nevertheless, France extended a $500 million credit line for the first time. Algeria's decision to accept members of the Basque separatist organization ETA who had been expelled from France cast a shadow over relations with Spain. Gas sales

to Spain's Enagas and Belgium's Distrigas continued to suffer from disputes over price, but new gas deals with West Germany, Yugoslavia, and the U.S. company Panhandle augured well for the future.

Despite an improvement in oil prices from $15 a barrel in 1986 to $18 a barrel, the trade account was likely to be in deficit once again—the deficit of 10.8 billion dinars in 1986 was the first in six years. Reserves had fallen by $1 billion, and foreign debt had grown by 16% in 1986 to $19.8 billion for commercial debt alone. Serious riots in November 1986 and widespread demonstrations in early 1987 forced the government to increase its import budget. Output improved, however, particularly in agriculture, where it rose by 57% in 1986.

As it celebrated the 25th anniversary of Algerian independence, the government continued to reform the economy, with greater decentralization of the state sector and the extension of private ownership in agriculture. Political liberalization began with a new law on associations, although government control was emphasized by the trial of 202 Muslim fundamentalists in Blida in July for threatening state security, and of supporters of former president Ahmed Ben Bella in June for similar offenses. In elections on February 26 to fill the 295-seat National Popular Assembly, all candidates were approved by the Front de Libération Nationale, the sole party. (GEORGE JOFFÉ)

This article updates the *Macropædia* article NORTH AFRICA: *Algeria*.

## BAHRAIN

The monarchy (emirate) of Bahrain consists of a group of islands in the Persian Gulf between the Qatar Peninsula and Saudi Arabia. Area: 691 sq km (267 sq mi). Pop. (1987 est.): 481,000. Cap.: Manama. Monetary unit: Bahrain dinar, with (Oct. 5, 1987) a free rate of 0.38 dinar to U.S. $1 (0.61 dinar = £1 sterling). Emir in 1987, Isa ibn Sulman al-Khalifah; prime minister, Khalifah ibn Sulman al-Khalifah.

During 1987 the government of Bahrain indicated its support for Kuwait's decision to register 11 tankers under the U.S. flag as a means of securing U.S. protection for its shipping in the Gulf. At the same time, it expressed opposition to any use of its own military bases by foreign powers. A U.S. naval support unit was, however, stationed in Bahrain. On July 20 Foreign Minister Sheikh Muhammad ibn Mubarak al-Khalifah expressed the hope that the U.S. would not be led into confrontation with Iran or Iraq.

A $90 million contract was awarded to a Taiwanese construction company for work on a military air base at Suman in the south of the island, to be supervised by the U.S. Army Corps of Engineers. This was seen as part of a move by Bahrain to increase its military preparedness in case of attack by Iran, which nurtured a long-standing territorial claim to the emirate. Government revenues were affected when technical difficulties forced a temporary shutdown of the Abu Safah oil field, whose revenues were shared with Saudi Arabia.

The King Fahd Causeway linking Bahrain with Saudi Arabia, officially opened in November 1986, was opened to 24-hour car traffic on Feb. 1, 1987, providing a boost to tourism and encouraging commercial ties with the mainland. A public resort beach was to be built at Sanabis. The presence of bars and nightclubs on the island was proving to be a major attraction to young Saudi Arabian visitors, although the Bahraini government was more interested in encouraging family groups.            (JOHN WHELAN)

This article updates the *Macropædia* article ARABIA: *Bahrain.*

## CYPRUS

An island republic and member of the Commonwealth, Cyprus is in the eastern Mediterranean Sea. Island area: 9,251 sq km (3,572 sq mi). Island pop. (1987 est.): 719,000. Area of the Turkish Republic of Northern Cyprus (TRNC), which has occupied the northern third of the island since 1974: 3,355 sq km (1,295 sq mi); pop. (1987 est.): 165,000. Cap.: Nicosia. Monetary unit: Cyprus pound, with (Oct. 5, 1987) a free rate of £C 0.48 to U.S. $1 (£C 0.78 = £1 sterling). President in 1987, Spyros Kyprianou. President of TRNC in 1987, Rauf Denktash.

The deadlock in efforts to find a solution to the division of the island between Greek and Turkish Cypriots entered its second year in 1987. UN Secretary-General Javier Pérez de Cuéllar expressed his mounting concern over the situation on the island. In a report to the UN Security Council in June, he said that distrust between the two communities had deepened and that the impasse was not being eased by an increasing military buildup on both sides.

The UN peacekeeping force in Cyprus entered its 24th year on an assignment originally projected to last three months. One of the world's most successful peacekeeping operations, it had become the victim of its own success and appeared headed for a crisis of mounting debt and disillusionment in those countries that supplied troops. Sweden became the first to declare that it had lost patience with the cost of the failure to find a solution in Cyprus and began to pull out its contingent. The Security Council continued to renew the six-monthly mandate for the peacekeeping force, but Pérez de Cuéllar warned that other member states were growing weary of the continuing intransigence of both communities.

Little political movement was to be expected on the island itself, as Greek Cypriots concentrated on forging alliances for presidential elections due in February 1988. The outcome of the election, in which Pres. Spyros Kyprianou was seeking a third five-year term, was thrown open by the rift between Kyprianou and the powerful AKEL (Communist Party), whose 33% of the vote had helped put him in power in 1983. AKEL was backing a new face in politics, independent candidate George Vassiliou, a successful international businessman. Also opposing Kyprianou were the Socialist EDEK candidate, Vassos Lyssarides, and Glafcos Clerides, veteran leader of the right-wing Democratic Rally.

More uncertainty emerged in November when Kyprianou suffered a heart attack. As he recovered, however, he dismissed widespread speculation that he would not run again as "wishful thinking" by his opponents.

In northern Cyprus Turkish Cypriots continued to battle a stagnant economy. There were no significant political developments beyond growing signs that community leader Rauf Denktash was apparently edging toward seeking wider recognition for the Turkish Republic of Northern Cyprus and would presumably thereby abandon any further efforts to federate with Greek Cypriots.

The Greek Cypriot economy recorded a 25% increase in exports to £C 110.4 million during the first seven months of 1987 compared with the previous year, while imports declined marginally to £C 398 million. Tourist arrivals rose for the 12th year; the average increase in the first nine months was 18%.                    (THOMAS O'DWYER)

## EGYPT

A republic of North Africa, Egypt has coastlines on the Mediterranean and Red seas. Area: 997,739 sq km (385,229 sq mi). Pop. (1987 est.): 49,143,000. Cap.: Cairo. Monetary unit: Egyptian pound (LE), with (Oct. 5, 1987) a free rate of LE 2.22 to U.S. $1 (LE 3.61 = £1 sterling). President in 1987, Hosni Mubarak; prime minister, Atef Sedki.

Pres. Hosni Mubarak of Egypt began a second six-year term of office on Oct. 5, 1987, after receiving 97% of the vote in a popular referendum. The economy was given a boost when the International Monetary Fund (IMF) signaled its approval of economic reforms, thus clearing the way for agreement with major creditors. The government was forced to take strong measures against religious dissidents—the most significant trend was the rising Islamic current. On the international front, relations with Israel warmed slightly following the July 20–22 visit to Tel Aviv of Foreign Minister Esmat 'Abd al-Meguid, the most senior Egyptian to go to Israel since 1981. The Arab League summit in Jordan in November passed a resolution that fell short of readmitting Egypt to membership but allowed individual member countries to restore diplomatic relations with Egypt. (See *Middle Eastern and North African Affairs,* above.)

**Domestic Affairs.** National elections to the People's Assembly on April 6 resulted in a clear majority for the ruling National Democratic Party (NDP), which took 346 of the 448 elected seats. The alliance of the Socialist Labour Party, the Liberal Socialist Party, and Muslim Brotherhood candidates took 60 seats and the New Wafd Party, 35. The remaining seven seats went to independents. (For tabulated results, see *Political Parties,* above.) Although the Muslim Brotherhood remained officially banned, individual members were permitted to stand as candidates. The move was designed to broaden the political consensus to include the Islamic mainstream. The election was considered the freest since the 1952 revolution. It was held two years early to head off a constitutional challenge to the legality of the previous Assembly.

A massive crackdown on Muslim fundamentalists was confirmed on June 7 by Interior Minister Zaki Badr, who acknowledged that 500 people had been arrested. This followed three assassination attempts: journalist Makram Muhammad Ahmed was shot at on June 3, two U.S. embassy officials were fired at on May 26, and former interior minister Hassan Abu Basha was hit on May 5. On August 29 police arrested members of a fundamentalist group, El-Nagun min el-Nar ("Saved from Hell"), after a shoot-out north of Cairo. In January Badr announced that in the previous nine months nearly 400 people had been arrested, accused of belonging to outlawed fundamentalist groups. His hard-line view was not necessarily shared by President Mubarak, who in July ordered that emergency laws, which gave sweeping powers to the police, should be used only in exceptional circumstances.

The government also faced continuing sectarian violence. On February 26–27 fighting broke out in Sohag and Beni Suef, Upper Egypt. The incidents erupted when fundamentalists tried to set fire to two Coptic churches following rumours that Copts had started a fire in a mosque.

**The Economy.** On May 22 the Paris Club of Western creditor governments, attended by officials from Kuwait and from member countries of the Organization for Economic Cooperation and Development, agreed on the framework for rescheduling some $12 billion of civilian and military debt-servicing payments over ten years, including a five-year grace period. This paved the way for Egypt to work out details with each creditor country on a bilateral basis. The agreement not only allowed the government to eliminate its financing gap but also permitted export credit agencies to reconsider resuming credit to Egypt.

The historic accord was made possible by the May 15 decision of the IMF board to approve an 18-month standby credit program. Although the amount involved was small by comparison with Egypt's total external debt of some $40 billion, it signaled IMF approval of the government's economic reforms, especially those relating to exchange rates and prices. While central bank governor Salah al-Hamid had made no pledge to abolish the official fixed rate of exchange, on May 11 the Ministry of Economy and Foreign Trade announced reforms to the exchange rate system that were seen as the first step toward complete liberalization. The other central demands of the IMF—raising the prices of energy and agricultural goods and increasing interest rates—were also carried out. The measures were presented as homegrown solutions instead of commitments exacted by the IMF. Egypt was also expected to receive some $800 million in World Bank quick disbursement loans in fiscal 1988.

On September 27 President Mubarak and Prime Minister Jacques Chirac of France opened the Cairo metro (subway), which was expected to reduce traffic congestion in the city centre dramatically when it became fully operational in early 1988. This major achievement symbolized the close ties with France, which managed the project. In August Industry Minister Muhammad Mahmud 'Abd al-Wahab announced that a far-reaching proposal by General Motors Corp. of the U.S. to build an integrated automobile industry had been shelved.

Under the new five-year (1987–92) plan, an ambitious 5.8% annual growth rate was specified. The plan projected that gross domestic product would rise to the equivalent of $40 billion. Yet the two main sources of revenue—remittances from Egyptians working abroad and oil—had come under pressure. Egyptians had been returning home from the Gulf states because of the completion of many projects there. In January Petroleum Minister 'Abd al-Hadi Muhammad Qandil announced that crude oil production would total 870,000 bbl a day, to help the Organization of Petroleum Exporting Countries stabilize world demand, but the actual figure for the first half of 1987 was just above 900,000 bbl a day. Net oil exports in 1987 were expected to reach $1.5 billion. Tourism receipts were said to be recovering from the slump in early 1986, while Suez Canal revenues were holding up at $1 billion a year.

Providing evidence of the close bilateral relationship between Cairo and Washington, in January the U.S. admin-

Staff members of the North Yemen embassy in Cairo raise their country's flag following the restoration of diplomatic relations with Egypt. North Yemen had severed ties eight years earlier when Egypt signed the Camp David accords.
AFP PHOTO

istration offered to refinance some $4.5 billion of military debt to the U.S. at 7.5% interest. U.S. Assistant Secretary of State Richard Murphy visited Cairo early in the same month. The U.S. Congress was formally notified on January 27 of a proposal by the administration to sell Egypt 40 F-16 aircraft in a $1.3 billion contract. In June the Kuwait Fund for Arab Economic Development—the oldest Arab aid fund—approved a $25 million credit facility, the first to be granted to Egypt since credits had been suspended as part of the Arab boycott of Egypt following the 1979 peace treaty with Israel. Other Arab funds were expected to follow the Kuwaiti fund's lead.

**Foreign Affairs.** In dealings with Israel, Egypt continued to press the case for an international conference on the issue of a comprehensive Middle East peace settlement. The foreign minister's visit to Israel in July served to highlight the internal differences between the two wings of Israel's government of national unity. The Egyptian administration rejected Prime Minister Yitzhak Shamir's proposal that Middle East peace talks be confined to Egypt, Israel, Jordan, and the U.S., but its views were considered to be closer to those of Israeli Foreign Minister Shimon Peres.

A charter of fraternity with The Sudan was signed during the February 17–22 visit to Cairo of Sudanese Prime Minister Sadiq al-Mahdi. This replaced the integration charter between the two countries. The new charter outlined possible cooperation in project work and a framework for political relations. The high point of Egypt's attempt to return to the Arab fold was the resolution passed by the Arab League summit in November. Nine member countries immediately restored diplomatic relations with Egypt. Earlier, President Mubarak attended the fifth summit meeting of the Islamic Conference Organization in Kuwait on January 26, where he appeared in public with other Arab leaders.

On the other hand, Egypt's relations with Libya remained strained. A series of defections by Libyan military personnel gave rise to charges and countercharges. When a Libyan helicopter landed in Egypt on July 16, the Libyans said it had crossed the border by mistake, while Egypt claimed the crew was seeking asylum. Palestine Liberation Organization offices in Egypt were closed down by the Egyptian authorities in April after the Palestine National Council attacked the treaty with Israel. President Mubarak's unexpected visit to Amman on June 3 for talks with King Hussein—his second visit in a month—symbolized the growing consensus between Egypt and Jordan on the question of the right course for securing a permanent peace settlement in the Middle East.

Joint Egyptian–U.S. military exercises involving 9,000 U.S. troops were held in mid-August. The purpose of the annual Bright Star maneuvers was to help train local troops to use U.S. equipment. Nevertheless, Egyptian officials were eager to allay fears that policies were becoming too closely allied with Washington. The U.S. was committed to offering Egypt some $2.5 billion a year in aid, its biggest foreign commitment after Israel.          (JOHN WHELAN)

## IRAN

The Islamic republic of Iran is in southwestern Asia on the Caspian and Arabian seas and the Persian Gulf. Area: 1,648,-196 sq km (636,372 sq mi). Pop. (1987 est., including some 2 million Afghan and 450,000 Iraqi refugees): 49,930,000. Cap.: Tehran. Monetary unit: Iranian rial, with (Oct. 5, 1987) an official rate of 72.17 rials to U.S. $1 (117.20 rials = £1 sterling). Supreme *faqih* (spiritual leader) in 1987, Ayatollah Ruhollah Khomeini; president, Sayyed Ali Khamenei; prime minister, Mir Hossein Moussavi.

During 1987 the many political factions and personalities dependent on Ayatollah Ruhollah Khomeini attempted to improve their relative positions within the institutional structure of Iran. The faction supporting Ayatollah Hussein Ali Montazeri, the heir apparent to Khomeini, suffered from its connections with Mehdi Hashemi, who was found guilty of the Islamic crime of "corruption on earth" and was executed on September 28; Hashemi had reportedly been responsible for exposing the clandestine U.S.-Iran arms deals. (*See* North America: *United States:* Special Report, below.) The authority of Hojatolislam Hashemi Ali Akbar Rafsanjani (*see* BIOGRAPHIES), the speaker of the Majlis (parliament), was increased by his appointment to the Council of Guardians of the Revolution in June. Pres. Sayyed Ali Khamenei saw his power base undermined when the Islamic Republican Party was dissolved on June 2. Meanwhile, a balance between radical and conservative Islamic forces in the regime neutralized the political strength of both groups, leaving Khomeini as the sole real power.

The war with Iraq continued. On January 9 Iran launched the Karbala 5 offensive against Iraqi defenses between Khorramshahr and Iraqi territory east of Basra. Iraqi air cover, normally deployed to halt massed infantry attacks, was hindered by the Iranian possession of advanced antiaircraft missiles obtained from the U.S. and other sources. Iranian forces came within a few kilometres of Basra before losing the initiative in February. By the end of the campaign, they held only 150 sq km (58 sq mi) and had lost an estimated 45,000 dead.

Iranian attempts to deter Iraqi air attacks on its tankers moving oil from Kharg Island to terminals in the southern Persian Gulf—and to discourage Arab financial aid to Iraq by harassing Kuwaiti shipping—excited the interest of the superpowers. The U.S. offered to reflag and so provide protection to Kuwaiti tankers, and by midyear Iran found itself in full-scale naval confrontation with the U.S. Despite the presence in the Gulf of minesweepers from several Western countries, Iranian mines continued to cause damage to shipping. On October 19 two Iranian production platforms in the lower Gulf were destroyed by U.S. warships in retaliation for an Iranian missile attack on a U.S.-registered tanker moored in Kuwaiti waters.

International concern over the conflict in the Gulf was manifest in UN Resolution 598, passed unanimously on July 20, which called for an immediate end to all hostilities. UN Secretary-General Javier Pérez de Cuéllar visited Iran and Iraq in mid-September but failed to move Iran toward acceptance of the resolution.

Iran's isolation from the international community increased during 1987. Libya dropped its support for Iran and adopted an evenhanded approach to the parties in the Gulf war. Syria increasingly came under pressure to rejoin the Arab consensus. Following the deaths of some 275 Iranians on July 31 in disturbances during the annual pilgrimage to Mecca, Iran accused Saudi Arabia of killing Iranian pilgrims on behalf of the U.S. The U.S.S.R. made conciliatory gestures in the economic domain, including an offer to open an oil-export pipeline through Baku, but maintained its hard line against the continuance of the war. France broke off diplomatic relations with Iran in July. (*See* Western Europe: *France,* below.) In June the U.K. government closed the Iranian consulate in Manchester and, with the exception of one caretaker, the Iranian embassy in London.

The economy in 1986–87 recorded mixed results, with oil production erratic but mainly averaging over 2.3 million

An Iranian oil rig burns in the Persian Gulf after an attack by the U.S. Navy. U.S. officials claimed that attacks on Gulf shipping had been launched from the rig and that its destruction was thus a "measured and appropriate response."

bbl a day. Income on oil account was estimated at some $9 billion, and non-oil exports approached $1 billion. Civil imports were constrained by shortages of foreign exchange to $5.6 billion, while the cost of imports of war matériel approached $5 billion. Foreign exchange reserves declined slightly to $5 billion, and debt was reported to be $1.5 billion. The inflation rate was officially put at more than 20% but was probably nearer 40%.

(KEITH S. MCLACHLAN)

# IRAQ

A republic of southwestern Asia, Iraq has a short coastline on the Persian Gulf. Area: 438,317 sq km (169,235 sq mi). Pop. (1987 est.): 16,476,000. Cap.: Baghdad. Monetary unit: Iraqi dinar, with (Oct. 5, 1987) a par value of 0.31 dinar to U.S. $1 (free rate of 0.50 dinar = £1 sterling). President in 1987, Saddam Hussein at-Takriti.

During 1987 the Gulf war escalated dangerously at sea, while Baghdad held off a determined Iranian land assault against Basra early in the year. Despite UN mediation and moves by the superpowers, prospects for peace appeared bleak. Internal pressures on Pres. Saddam Hussein at-Takriti were manifest in Cabinet changes, discussions with trade creditors, and evidence of a stiffening of Kurdish resistance to the regime. On May 17 an Iraqi warplane attacked the USS *Stark,* apparently in error, killing 37 sailors. Baghdad apologized for the incident, but subsequently foreign powers began increasing their naval strength in the Gulf. Iraqi attacks on shipping serving Iran resulted in reprisal missile strikes by Iran on Baghdad on October 10 and 13. The latter hit a school and killed 32 people, most of them children.

On land the thrust against Basra started on Dec. 24, 1986, when Iran briefly occupied three Iraqi islands in the Shatt al-Arab, south of Basra. The offensive had run out of steam by early March but at considerable cost to Iraq, which had responded with two-pronged attacks on Iranian oil targets in the Gulf and on military and economic targets in Iran itself. To finance its military requirements, civil spending, and debt servicing in 1987, Iraq required some $15 billion, compared with oil revenue of $8.5 billion. By early October Hikmat Mekhailef al-Hadithi, the newly appointed finance minister, claimed that every outstanding debt was being negotiated or had been settled, although he declined to go into detail. There were a number of Cabinet shake-ups as the president brought in technocrats and party men to oversee his economic reform program, which included commitments to cut public-sector spending and to privatize state assets, among them Iraqi Airways, the state airline. On September 22 Qassem Ahmed Taqi al-Uraibi, the heavy industries minister, and Finance Minister Hassan Tawfiq were dismissed, as was the governor of the central bank. The Agricultural Ministry was reformed to include irrigation under Karim Hassan Redha.

In a speech on June 7 President Hussein presented a new vision of Iraqi socialism radically different from that of the 1968 revolution, particularly in its attempt to reduce the influence of the Ba'th Socialist Party. Industrial efficiency was to be increased and private savings would be tapped to maintain the momentum of development. On March 11 the president told trade unionists that the term "worker" had been replaced by "official." If these moves suggested a softening of the harsher aspects of the regime, a warning against those engaging in corruption was provided by the execution of a former mayor of Baghdad found guilty of accepting bribes from foreign companies.

Although deferment of payments to foreign suppliers

had been a cornerstone of economic policy since 1982, international contractors still appeared willing to engage in projects. On September 20 the contract for the $1 billion second stage of the badly needed crude-oil pipeline across Saudi Arabia was awarded. By then Iraq was exporting 500,000 bbl a day through Saudi Arabia and 1.5 million bbl a day through Turkey. In February Kuwait and Saudi Arabia stopped providing war relief crude oil for Iraq.

More than 400 Iraqi opposition figures, including the two main Kurdish leaders, met in Iran in late December 1986 to unify their struggle against the government. A 17-point resolution was announced on December 28. On May 19 the Iraqi National Assembly passed a bill setting up a new administrative system for the Kurdish autonomous region that would allow the Kurds more freedom to administer their own finances. A government official asserted in August that Iraqi forces were in full control of border areas in the north, but Kurdish reports said a "major war" had been raging in the area for four months.

Relations with Arab governments remained stable. Following an incident on July 28 when a Syrian MiG-21 was shot down near the Syrian border, Iraq complained of continuing Syrian violations of its airspace but reported that it had handed over the captured pilot.   (JOHN WHELAN)

# ISRAEL

A republic of southwestern Asia, Israel is situated on the Mediterranean Sea. Area: 20,700 sq km (7,992 sq mi), not including territory occupied in the June 1967 war. Pop. (1987 est.): 4,449,000. Cap.: Jerusalem (but see Israel table in *World Data* section). Monetary unit: New (Israeli) sheqel, with (Oct. 5, 1987) a free rate of 1.60 sheqalim to U.S. $1 (2.60 sheqalim = £1 sterling). President in 1987, Chaim Herzog; prime minister, Yitzhak Shamir.

The year 1987 proved to be a traumatic one for both the people and the government of Israel. The hopes for progress in the Middle East peace process and consolidation and improvement of economic conditions at home with which 1986 had ended were dissipated during 1987 in the wake of a series of shocks and scandals that seriously undermined the effectiveness and credibility of the government of national unity. An air of inertia appeared to overcome the government, and there were neither domestic nor foreign initiatives. Prime Minister Yitzhak Shamir and Foreign Minister Shimon Peres disagreed publicly about the desirability of holding an international peace conference sponsored either by the superpowers or by the UN Security Council. The idea was advocated and encouraged by Peres and rejected and denounced by Shamir. But this was only the most outwardly visible sign of internal division within the government. There were similar differences over domestic policies, especially, with regard to the handling of the West Bank and Gaza and their Arab populations. The latter were thrown into sharp relief by the disorders that flared in Gaza and the West Bank at year's end.

It was not just that Israel in 1987 had its least effective government since the establishment of the state but that it had, in effect, no real government. It had ministers and ministries, some of which were doing their job and were effective while others were doing little more than bankrolling their supporters and backers. It said much for the basic strength of the Israeli society and economy that, despite failures of leadership and the urgent need for economic adjustment in the spending departments of the government, there was a continuing high rate of economic activity and initiative independent of government. With the country poised for its 40th anniversary celebrations in May 1988, with another general election looming on the horizon, and with a new generation preparing to take over, Israel would be glad to forget 1987 as a year when the causes of national advancement and peace went astray among the self-seeking feuds of politicians and the aggressive intervention of religious partisans.

**Domestic Affairs.** Israeli affairs throughout the year were dominated by a problem that many Israelis had known about but that had never before been discussed in public and officially—Israel's secret government. Israelis had known of the function and success of its secret security services and admired them for ensuring the safety of the state, beset by enemies without and terrorists within. It was assumed and accepted that this could not be done with kid gloves at all times. Given the difficulties and the grave responsibilities involved, a degree of latitude was considered acceptable in the methods used to defend public security and the interests of the state.

The General Security Service (GSS), known as Shin Bet, was Israel's most secret internal security service. Over the years it had acquired the status of a sacred cow; its activities were never mentioned, never discussed, let alone questioned, except in military courts by defense counsel in cases of terrorism. However, these references received little attention and even less credence until the last days of 1986, when the head of the GSS was publicly identified for the first time in a newspaper article published in the U.S. His resignation followed, together with that of other senior officials said to have been involved in the illegal killing in 1984 of two Arab terrorists after they had been taken prisoner; the officials were also said to be guilty of perjury in an elaborate cover-up of the crime. As it developed, this was the beginning, rather than the end, of Israel's newly awakened preoccupation with its secret government.

The revelations of December 1986 proved to be the catalyst for a series of scandals that engaged the Israeli government and public throughout 1987. One accusation in particular surfaced and received wide attention. In 1980 a Circassian lieutenant in the Israel Defense Forces (IDF), Izat Nafsu, had been sentenced to 18 years' imprisonment on charges of treason and espionage for Syria, on the basis of a confession produced by the GSS before a military court. Nafsu maintained that he had been framed by the GSS, that he had confessed under duress, and that GSS witnesses had committed perjury. Because of the immunity of the GSS from scrutiny, he had not been able to obtain a hearing before a higher civilian court for seven years. In 1987 the Supreme Court decided to review his case. On May 24 it confirmed Nafsu's claim that he had been framed and ordered his immediate release and reinstatement in the IDF. The court ruled that GSS interrogations must be bound by the same rules as those of the police.

A new dimension was given to this Supreme Court ruling when a special commission appointed by the government to investigate GSS practices published its findings at the end of October. These shocked the country—and even the government. The commission found that the use of unacceptable violence and subsequent perjury in court had been an approved practice of the GSS for 16 years, and it called for an immediate halt to such practices. It did not spell out in the unclassified section of the report just how far up the scale in government and law these GSS practices had been condoned. The impact of the report was such that a radical change in GSS practice and personnel was inevitable.

In May, as this aspect of the secret government was first being revealed, another was about to be uncovered. On May 26 two committees published their findings in the "Pollard

Palestinian rioters hurl rocks and bottles at Israeli troops in the city of Nabulus in the West Bank. The rioting that took place in Gaza and the West Bank in the last weeks of 1987 focused world attention on the discontent of Palestinians under Israeli rule. Israel's harsh response provoked criticism even among its allies, and no solution was in sight.
AP/WIDE WORLD

affair"—the case of Jonathan Jay Pollard (*see* BIOGRAPHIES), who on March 4 was sentenced by a U.S. court to life imprisonment for espionage on behalf of Israel. Prime Minister Shamir had appointed a two-man committee to advise him as to the facts of the case, which had come to light in the U.S. the previous year, and the Foreign Affairs and Defense Committee of the Knesset (parliament) conducted its own, rather more controversial, inquiry into the question of Israeli responsibility for the Pollard operation. Neither investigation proved really conclusive or highly informative; the one was concerned to limit the damage done to Israeli-U.S. relations, while the other was intent on pinning political responsibility on Peres and Shamir (at the time of the incident, prime minister and foreign minister, respectively). Both reports added to the feeling that there were considerable areas of government being withheld not only from the Knesset but also from the Cabinet.

A daring Palestinian hang glider attack on an Israeli army base in which six Israeli soldiers were killed was credited by some with igniting the riots that erupted in Gaza on December 9 and spread to the West Bank. The Israelis responded with force, and by year's end at least 22 Palestinians had been killed; military trials of the 1,000-odd detainees had begun, and it was suggested that some might be deported. UN and U.S. criticism of Israel's use of lethal force was rejected by Shamir, who maintained that "Israel knows how to defend its . . . security."

The IDF was being streamlined and restructured under a new and highly respected chief of staff, Gen. Dan Shomron. The IDF had taken a firm stand, supported by

Defense Minister Yitzhak Rabin, against production of the Lavi fighter plane on the grounds that the prestige aircraft would drain the country's defense resources.

**Foreign Relations.** Dominating the year were Israel's relations with the U.S., which were strained by a number of issues, not least the Pollard affair. Pollard had been recruited by two very senior Israeli officials and encouraged to pass on relevant information that he had acquired in the course of his work as a naval analyst. He complied with their requests and claimed in court that he had done so as a Jew and a Zionist who felt that vital information relating to Israel's security had been withheld by the U.S. It was this aspect of the affair that created the major strain in relations between the U.S. and Israel. The U.S. claimed that Israel had violated an unwritten agreement between the two countries not to spy on each other. The Israeli government expressed its regret but claimed that a secret Israeli intelligence unit had operated in the U.S. without the knowledge of the Israeli government and with a wide area of discretion. Israel recalled the head of the unit and other senior officials, returned papers that had been obtained from Pollard to the U.S., and hoped that the incident would soon be forgotten.

A more fundamental consequence of the Pollard affair was the shadow it cast over the traditional understanding between U.S. Jews and Israel. It had been understood and accepted since the establishment of the state of Israel in 1948 that U.S. Jews had a special relationship with Israel, based on a form of kinship, but that this in no way affected the U.S. Jews' primary loyalty to the U.S. Following Pollard's arrest, there was evidence of a prevailing suspicion in U.S. security bodies that Pollard was not an exception, and U.S. Jews in sensitive government positions found themselves scrutinized as never before.

Alongside these developments, Israelis were further bemused by a disturbing display in the U.S. of the workings and fallibility of that country's own secret government as it concerned Israeli interests, among others. Those Israelis who had been involved in what became known as the Iran-*contra* affair, in response to a U.S. request to help establish a dialogue with Iran, were dismayed and startled to read the reputedly official U.S. version of this attempt. (*See* North America: *United States:* Special Report, below.) To Israelis it had the makings of a Pollard affair in reverse. The Tower Report, published in February, was supposed to be a full and frank account of the initiative. As Israeli officials who had detailed knowledge of these negotiations read the report that had been produced in Washington, they were beset by two separate and distinct impressions. In the Israeli view, the U.S. participants, for reasons of their own, were apparently transforming the scenario so that Israel would appear as a scapegoat. Instead of the helpful intermediary Peres had sought to be, Israel was depicted as the initiator of the scheme to supply arms to Iran and the party that had inveigled the U.S. into becoming involved. This was primarily a political problem: how far could Israel trust the U.S. regarding such covert approaches in the future?

Another aspect of dealing with the U.S. under conditions of confidentiality gravely concerned Israel. In the longer run, it was the most disturbing element of the Iran-*contra* investigation. Matters of great secrecy that affected the well-being and safety of third parties had been reported in confidence to the president and Congress and then published. This meant that Israel, or any other ally of the U.S., would have to think carefully before passing on sensitive information to the U.S. government or its agencies.

(JON KIMCHE)

# JORDAN

A constitutional monarchy, Jordan is located in southwestern Asia and has a short coastline on the Gulf of Aqaba. Area: 89,206 sq km (34,443 sq mi). Pop. (1987 est.): 2,853,000. Cap.: Amman. Monetary unit: Jordan dinar, with (Oct. 5, 1987) a free rate of 0.35 dinar to U.S. $1 (0.56 dinar = £1 sterling). King, Hussein I; prime minister in 1987, Zaid ar-Rifai.

King Hussein directed his efforts toward ensuring full attendance at the Arab League summit held in Amman on Nov. 8, 1987, and reviving plans for an international peace conference on the Middle East. (See *Middle Eastern and North African Affairs,* above.) The Jordanian monarch entered the 36th year of his reign on August 11. His relations with Pres. Hafez al-Assad of Syria were strengthening after a long period of conflict, and Jordan's profile remained high. On February 18 King Hussein condemned U.S. arms sales to Iran, and in July, expressing his disappointment at Pres. Ronald Reagan's decision to halt weapons sales to Amman, he declared that Jordan had decided "never again to seek weapons from the United States."

Jordan's desire for an international peace conference received backing from Israeli Foreign Minister Shimon Peres, who saw the move as a first step toward bilateral talks with Jordan about the future of the occupied territories. This course was opposed, however, by Israeli Prime Minister Yitzhak Shamir. In April the Israeli press reported that Peres and Defense Minister Yitzhak Rabin had held secret talks with King Hussein. Israel wished, however, to exclude the Palestine Liberation Organization (PLO) from the conference. At the Palestine National Council meeting in Algiers, which began on April 20, PLO chairman Yasir Arafat abrogated his 1985 agreement with King Hussein that had committed him to joint action with Jordan.

In essence, King Hussein had already backed away from his deal with Arafat, but the new mood of unity in the Palestinian movement was thought likely to make his own efforts at diplomacy more difficult. The first meeting in more than two years of the Jordanian-Palestinian committee charged with helping residents of the occupied territories took place in February. The committee was able to resume work because Saudi Arabia provided more than $9 million in grant aid.

King Hussein's links with Gulf nations—particularly Saudi Arabia, the only country to maintain its commitment to assist Jordan under the 1978 Baghdad Arab summit declaration—remained strong. On May 14 the Kuwait Fund for Arab Economic Development signed a $15.8 million loan for Jordan; together with an earlier $10.7 million grant by the Saudi Fund for Development. In December Hussein traveled to Moscow to urge Soviet support for sanctions against Iran.

Gross domestic product grew by 2.3% in 1986, reflecting an improved economic outlook. Agriculture was performing well, and efforts were being made to break into European markets for fruit and vegetables. Unemployment was officially described as being at about 8%, but some estimates put it closer to 12%. Fears that returning expatriates would swell the ranks of the jobless proved unfounded, and expatriate remittances in 1986 remained healthy, at the equivalent of $1.2 billion. Phosphate and fertilizer exports rose in the first half of 1987, compared with those of the same period in 1986. The volume of transit goods through Aqaba, mainly to Iraq, at 2.6 million metric tons for January–June, was also strong. A $150 million Euroloan borrowing by the government in March was well received by Arab and international bankers, demonstrating growing confidence in Jordan's economy and its management. The 1987 budget—the first to exceed 1 billion dinars—was mildly expansionary, with the aims of promoting exports, providing more jobs, and expanding local production.

A major royal event took place on August 10. Prince Faisal, aged 23, second son of King Hussein, married the daughter of a Jordanian businessman.　(JOHN WHELAN)

## KUWAIT

A constitutional monarchy (emirate), Kuwait is in the northeastern Arabian Peninsula, on the Persian Gulf. Area: 17,818 sq km (6,880 sq mi). Pop. (1987 est.): 1,873,000. Cap.: Kuwait City. Monetary unit: Kuwaiti dinar, with (Oct. 5, 1987) a free rate of 0.28 dinar to U.S. $1 (0.46 dinar = £1 sterling). Emir, Sheikh Jabir al-Ahmad al-Jabir as-Sabah; prime minister in 1987, Crown Prince Sheikh Saad al-Abdullah as-Salim as-Sabah.

The escalation of hostilities in the Gulf war between Iran and Iraq, together with growing evidence of urban guerrilla activity at home, provided a troubled background to developments in Kuwait during 1987. There was some evidence of capital flight. Kuwait's decision to reflag 11 tankers belonging to the Kuwait Oil Tanker Company under the U.S. flag was regarded as a provocation by Iran. The reflagging process, which began in June, was balanced by the chartering of three Soviet tankers and by the registration of two tankers under the British flag in Gibraltar. Kuwait also sought protection for its shipping from China.

An unprecedented security exercise staged before the fifth Islamic Conference Organization summit, which opened in Kuwait on January 26, did not prevent disturbances. Saboteurs started fires in the oil fields, and a number of people were arrested for illegal assembly. On June 6 the state security court passed the death sentence on six Kuwaitis—two of them in absentia—for sabotaging oil installations and plotting against the government. The six were all Shi'ah Muslims. Large caches of U.S.-, Soviet-, and Israeli-made weapons were seized in connection with the plot. By July 15, however, eight separate bomb explosions had been reported in Kuwait, indicating the existence of significant underground opposition to the conservative regime.

On April 15 it was announced that conscript camps were being established to train national servicemen. All male Kuwaitis between the ages of 18 and 30 were eligible for conscription. Economic indicators continued to improve. A $106 million loan to the World Bank signed on July 10 represented the first public borrowing in Kuwaiti dinars by a non-Kuwaiti institution since 1982. Oil production was touching 999,000 bbl a day.　(JOHN WHELAN)

This article updates the *Macropædia* article ARABIA: *Kuwait*.

## LEBANON

A republic of southwestern Asia, Lebanon is situated on the Mediterranean Sea. Area: 10,230 sq km (3,950 sq mi). Pop. (1987 est.): 2,762,000 (including Palestinian refugees estimated to number about 270,000). Cap.: Beirut. Monetary unit: Lebanese pound, with (Oct. 5, 1987) a free rate of LL 284.95 to U.S. $1 (LL 462.73 = £1 sterling). President in 1987, Amin Gemayel; prime ministers, Rashid Karami and, from June 1, Selim al-Hoss.

The assassination of Lebanese Prime Minister Rashid Karami (*see* OBITUARIES) on June 1, 1987, by a remote-control device planted in the army helicopter he was using was a further setback for chances of peace. As the civil war entered its 13th year in April 1987, only Syria was making any concerted effort to force the parties to a settlement. On February 22 Pres. Hafez al-Assad of Syria sent troops into West Beirut. The move followed some of the worst street fighting since the Israeli invasion of 1982 as Amal (Shi'ah Muslim) militia laying siege to Palestinian refugee camps were opposed by leftist groups.

On April 7 Syrian troops took an even more significant step by ending the five-month-long siege of the Shatila camp, where the refugees were close to starvation. In early March Amal had partially lifted its blockade of the larger Burj al-Barajinah camp. About 110 Palestinians died during the encirclement of Shatila, but fewer casualties were recorded in the better defended Burj al-Barajinah. In taking this action, Syria moved against groups with which it was apparently in sympathy.

Syria was also motivated by a desire to play the role of broker over foreign hostages seized in Beirut by pro-Iranian fringe groups. On January 20 the special envoy of the archbishop of Canterbury, Terry Waite, who had been involved earlier in negotiations that led to the release of hostages, disappeared in the city and was presumed kidnapped. By the time Syria intervened, some 26 hostages were being held. Some progress in releasing hostages was

AFP PHOTO

Lebanese Red Cross ambulances evacuate wounded from Shatila, a Palestinian refugee camp. On April 7 Syrian troops broke a five-month-long seige of the camp by Amal (Shi'ah Muslim) militia.

made later, although kidnappings continued. On September 7 Alfred Schmidt, a West German, was released, and it was possible that Syria also had a hand in the escape on August 18 of the U.S. journalist Charles Glass, who had spent two months in captivity. Two French hostages were freed in November after what were said to have been extended negotiations. (*See* Western Europe: *France,* below.)

In making fresh efforts to bring about lasting peace in Lebanon, Syria produced little that was new. Proposals introduced in March entailed stripping away some of the powers of the president—by tradition, a Maronite Christian—and ending the bias in favour of Christians in the distribution of seats in the legislature. The assassination of the prime minister was another blow to the peace process, and it was followed by the killing on August 2 of Muhammad Shuqair, Pres. Amin Gemayel's only Muslim adviser. This appeared to be in retaliation for Gemayel's declaration of support for Saudi Arabia over clashes in Mecca on July 31. (See *Saudi Arabia,* below.)

The assassination of Karami provoked the resignation of a key figure in the political process. Hussain al-Hussaini resigned as parliamentary speaker on June 5 because he was dissatisfied with the official investigation into the killing. He was, however, reelected to the office in October. Muslim political leaders had boycotted President Gemayel for the first time after he refused to support Syrian peace plans in January 1986. After Karami's death Selim al-Hoss, who was appointed acting prime minister, declared that he was only the head of a caretaker government and would neither form a new government nor end the boycott of the president. Gemayel was further handicapped in dealing with internal politics by the fact that within the Christian community political maneuvering had already started for the election of his successor in September 1988. Among the early candidates to declare was Dani Chamoun, son of former president and finance minister Camille Chamoun (*see* OBITUARIES), who died in August.

Three Israeli soldiers were killed in a clash with pro-Syrian guerrillas on September 15, the highest casualty toll suffered by Israel in an engagement in Lebanon since 1985. A strong Israeli force raided guerrilla bases in southeast Lebanon on December 15.

The political situation adversely affected the economy. On October 6, after the Finance Ministry announced a doubling of the minimum wage, the Lebanese pound dropped to below LL 300 = U.S. $1 for the first time. The slide continued after that date. The economy was also suffering from a bitter dispute between the banking authorities and the commercial banks about monetary policy. Previous disputes had been settled by political intervention, but the prospect of coordinated action appeared remote. In October Joseph al-Hashem, the acting finance minister, published a draft 1988 budget, but this was considered an academic exercise since neither the 1986 nor the 1987 budget had passed the Chamber of Deputies. The state had virtually lost its ability to tax citizens or collect customs and excise duties, and before April 23 the Cabinet had not met for seven months.                    (JOHN WHELAN)

## LIBYA

A socialist country of North Africa, Libya lies on the Mediterranean Sea. Area: 1,775,500 sq km (685,524 sq mi). Pop. (1987 est.): 4,132,000. Cap.: Tripoli. Monetary unit: Libyan dinar, with (Oct. 5, 1987) a free rate of 0.30 dinar to U.S. $1 (0.49 dinar = £1 sterling). Chief of state in 1987, Col. Mu'ammar al-Qadhdhafi; secretaries-general of the General People's Committee (premiers), Mifta al-Usta Umar and, from March 1, Umar Mustafa al-Muntasir.

Libya was less prominent in international news during 1987 mainly because its economy remained weak as a result of modest oil exports and the comparatively low price of oil. In 1987 the familiar confrontation between the U.S. and Libyan governments was evident in Chad, where the Libyan Army and Air Force faced a Chadian Army supplied with U.S. equipment. The struggle took on new significance in 1987 because, for the first time in more than a decade, Chad reasserted its authority over the Aozou Strip. Despite a 1956 agreement between the Libyan premier at that time and the French authorities running Chad that recognized Chad's claim to the Aozou Strip, Libya preferred to recognize an unratified 1935 deal between the Italian and French colonial governments that placed the border to the south of the 1956 line.

Because the Libyan leadership had the total support of the population in laying claim to the Aozou Strip, its military reverses there in the summer of 1987 were much more significant than its defeats in central Chad earlier in the year. A brief recovery by Libya in late August enabled Libyan leader Col. Mu'ammar al-Qadhdhafi to make optimistic and even conciliatory comments about the Chad relationship in his annual September 1 speech marking the anniversary of the revolution. During the speech he made the surprising remark that Libya had no further territorial claims than those represented by the position held at that time. Since Chad controlled all of the strategic highlands of Tibesti within the Aozou Strip and also at least one-third of its area, the conciliatory tone was not in tune with the general opinion in Libya that the Aozou Strip was Libyan.

With much going against him regionally, Qadhdhafi was eager to cultivate good relations with sympathetic neighbours. In October it was reported that Libya and Algeria had agreed to form a political union, but the announcement was not made as expected on November 1, and indications were that Algeria had decided against such close ties. The new regime in Tunisia restored full diplomatic relations in December. Earlier, Iraq and Jordan also reestablished diplomatic ties with Libya.

The economy remained weak but not as weak as in the previous three years. Recently published data showed that Libya had halved its imports in the four years after 1981 and as a result had managed with much pain to maintain a positive trade balance. An improvement in oil exports and revenues in 1987 eased shortages of some consumer goods such as food, but there were still supply problems with many items. The nation's physical infrastructure was further impaired because of constraints on the supply of parts and maintenance materials.

Although development spending was restricted, some major projects, such as a network of regional hospitals, were being completed, and the "great man-made river," a massive effort to bring water from the south to the coast by the 1990s, was proceeding on schedule. In a speech in February, Qadhdhafi suggested that the project might have to be reconsidered in light of the country's economic difficulties, but there was no evidence that work on it had slowed down. By 1987 as much as one-third of the first phase had been completed.

A major proposal to move a large number of administrative functions and government secretariats (ministries) away from Tripoli, ostensibly to shift population and employment away from the capital, was met with opposition from those potentially affected. The military headquarters was moved to the Jufrah area, more than 300 km (185 mi) to the south, but was apparently returned to Tripoli. The tasks of the Agricultural Secretariat were decentralized to the regional authorities, and other secretariats were directed to move to the Jufrah area or to Surt. Many believed that unstated reasons for this shake-up included the vulnerability of Tripoli to aerial attack, as demonstrated by the 1986 U.S. bombing raid, and fears that the concentration of people and government in Tripoli was not good for the stability of the government.                    (J. A. ALLAN)

This article updates the *Macropædia* article NORTH AFRICA: *Libya.*

## MOROCCO

A constitutional monarchy of North Africa, Morocco has coastlines on the Atlantic Ocean and the Mediterranean Sea. Area: 458,730 sq km (177,117 sq mi). Pop. (1987 est.): 23,119,000. (Area and population figures refer to Morocco as constituted prior to the purported division of Western Sahara between Morocco and Mauritania and the subsequent Moroccan occupation of the Mauritanian zone in 1979.) Cap.: Rabat. Monetary unit: dirham, with (Oct. 5, 1987) a free rate of 8.37 dirhams to U.S. $1 (13.57 dirhams = £1 sterling). King, Hassan II; prime minister in 1987, Azzedine Laraki.

Once again, events connected with the Western Sahara dominated Moroccan concerns in 1987. In April Moroccan Army forces extended the defensive wall system southward to the Mauritanian border in order to deny units of the Popular Front for the Liberation of Saguia el Hamra and Río de Oro (Polisario Front), the Western Saharan national liberation movement, access to the Atlantic Ocean. Polisario forces maintained an active campaign throughout the first eight months of the year, with major attacks in the al-Mahbas region on February 25 and in the south in July and August. Morocco was accused of trying to assassinate Polisario leader Muhammad Abdulaziz in Tindouf, Alg.— a claim that was strongly denied in Rabat. Despite the accusation, Morocco agreed to further "proximity talks" under UN auspices at Geneva in July, though with little apparent result.

Regional tensions created by the extension of the wall were dissipated only after a border meeting between Algerian Pres. Chadli Bendjedid and King Hassan II, arranged by Saudi Arabia's King Fahd. The meeting achieved little, although there was a prisoner exchange between the countries two weeks later. Algeria was also the setting for a dispute between Morocco and the Palestine Liberation Organization (PLO) in April when the Polisario leader shared a platform with PLO leader Yasir Arafat. The PLO later apologized to Morocco over the incident.

Although Rabat accepted as final European Communities (EC) proposals for future relations with its southern Mediterranean members, peripheral improvements were sought. The EC increased aid to Morocco by 62.8% and proposed improved terms for EC access to Moroccan fishing grounds. Spain continued to place a high priority on relations with Morocco, occasioned in part by continued disturbances in the Spanish enclaves of Melilla and Ceuta; Morocco laid claim to the territories but was prepared to wait for an agreed solution. French Pres. François Mitterrand visited the country, and new credit lines were extended. The U.S., which had previously reduced its aid, provided a supplementary grant of about $25 million.

The economy continued to improve, with inflation cut to 4%, compared with 9% in 1986. The trade balance was reduced by 7% in 1986, and similar improvements were expected in 1987. Morocco was also able to reschedule its debt, estimated at $15 billion–$17 billion, in the wake of its December 1986 standby agreement with the International Monetary Fund. The new five-year (1988–92) plan was to involve public-sector privatization and educational reform. Additional tax reforms, this time concerning company tax-

ation, were completed. In political terms the government was able to signal a major triumph with the return to Morocco of the country's most famous dissident, Muhammad Basri.                    (GEORGE JOFFÉ)

This article updates the *Macropædia* article NORTH AFRICA: *Morocco.*

## OMAN

The sultanate of Oman occupies the southeastern part of the Arabian Peninsula, facing the Persian Gulf, the Gulf of Oman, and the Arabian Sea. A small part of the country lies to the north and is separated from the rest of Oman by the United Arab Emirates. Area: 300,000 sq km (120,000 sq mi). Pop.: in 1987 estimates ranged from 1.2 million to an official 2 million; no census has ever been taken (UN est., 1,331,000). Cap.: Muscat. Monetary unit: rial Omani, with (Oct. 5, 1987) a par value of 0.38 rial to U.S. $1 (free rate of 0.62 rial = £1 sterling). Sultan and prime minister in 1987, Qabus ibn Sa'id.

During 1987 Oman maintained a difficult balancing act between East and West while taking a neutral posture in the Gulf war. U.S. use of the Omani Red Crescent to return Iranian sailors detained during incidents in the lower Gulf appeared acceptable to Iran, whose relations with some other Arab Gulf states were poor. Iranian Foreign Affairs Minister Ali Akbar Velayati's visit to Muscat on August 15–16 indicated a stable relationship between the two countries. In October Oman announced the appointment of its first ambassador to the U.S.S.R., and an embassy was opened in Moscow late in the year. Minister of State for Foreign Affairs Yousef al-Alawi visited Yugoslavia in April, and in the same month Soviet Deputy Foreign Minister Vladimir Petrovsky visited Muscat.

Since oil production was at 545,000 bbl a day, the country's finances were being sustained by limited commercial borrowing and aid from friendly Arab countries. In September a $14.3 million loan was extended by the Kuwait Fund for Arab Economic Development to finance a gas project. It was announced in May that a stock exchange was to open in Oman by the end of 1987, but dealings in local securities were expected to be limited. The 1987 budget, announced on January 3, called for spending of $4.2 billion, 14% below 1986.

Eight South Yemenis on border patrol were killed by Omani forces on October 11 when they strayed eight kilometres (five miles) into Omani territory. Sheikh Zaid, president of the United Arab Emirates, mediated between the two countries, which had a long-standing border dispute although diplomatic relations had been reestablished in 1983.                    (JOHN WHELAN)

This article updates the *Macropædia* article ARABIA: *Oman.*

## QATAR

A constitutional monarchy (emirate) on the Arabian Peninsula, Qatar occupies a desert peninsula on the west coast of the Persian Gulf. Area: 11,400 sq km (4,400 sq mi). Pop. (1987 est.): 379,000. Cap.: Doha. Monetary unit: Qatar riyal, with (Oct. 5, 1987) a free rate of 3.63 riyals to U.S. $1 (5.89 riyals = £1 sterling). Emir and prime minister in 1987, Sheikh Khalifah ibn Hamad ath-Thani.

The signing of a contract with two major engineering companies on May 20, 1987, for the design and technical drawings for the North Field gas project provided a fillip for Qatar's depressed economy. Qatar avoided any direct involvement in the Gulf war, maintaining a policy of strict neutrality. Detailed talks on strengthening the country's defense forces took place on June 15–17 when Crown Prince and Minister of Defense Sheikh Hamad ibn Khalifah met

Pres. François Mitterrand of France during a visit to Paris.

With oil production limited, the decision to go ahead with the North Field scheme was expected to boost supplies of gas feedstock to industry when it came on stream in 1991. Many of Qatar's non-oil industries were performing badly, however, owing to high overheads and marketing problems. The initial project work for North Field was being undertaken by Bechtel of the U.S. and Technip of France.

Qatar's reputation for caution in public spending was borne out by the 1987–88 budget, published in March, which set the total at $3.4 billion, 22% below the last-announced budget (1985–86). No budget had been published in 1986–87. Because of the government's uncompetitive pricing policy, oil exports were uneven. The quota of only 299,000 bbl a day set by the Organization of Petroleum Exporting Countries underlined Qatar's continuing need to diversify the economy as well as to provide jobs for young Qataris.                              (JOHN WHELAN)

This article updates the *Macropædia* article ARABIA: *Qatar*.

## SAUDI ARABIA

The kingdom of Saudi Arabia occupies four-fifths of the Arabian Peninsula, with coastlines on the Red Sea and the Persian Gulf. Area: 2,240,000 sq km (865,000 sq mi). Pop. (1987 est.): 12,483,000. Cap.: Riyadh. Monetary unit: Saudi Arabian riyal, with (Oct. 5, 1987) a free rate of 3.75 riyals to U.S. $1 (6.09 riyals = £1 sterling). King and prime minister in 1987, Fahd.

The deaths of 402 people, mainly Iranian pilgrims, at Mecca during the hajj (annual pilgrimage) on July 31, 1987, provoked a sharp exchange with Iran. Political relations with the United States remained close, despite the lack of intervention by Saudi warplanes in the USS *Stark* incident. King Fahd declined to attend the Arab League summit in Amman, Jordan, in November in protest against attacks on the kingdom by the Libyan leadership. Following the summit Saudi Arabia restored diplomatic relations with Egypt, broken in 1979 after the bilateral peace agreement between Egypt and Israel.

**Domestic Affairs.** A total of 275 Iranians and 85 Saudi citizens, including security men, died in clashes started by Iranian marchers when Saudi officials tried to separate Iranian and anti-Iranian pilgrims in Mecca in July. The official Saudi account of the incident was that not a single bullet was fired, the deaths being caused by a panic stampede in the narrow streets around the Great Mosque as the hajj came to a climax. Iran claimed the trouble was started by Saudis who threw stones from the roofs of buildings lining the route of the march.

On the eve of the hajj, Iranian leader Ayatollah Ruhollah Khomeini told Iranian and like-minded pilgrims that they should try to politicize the event. The Iranians had previously used the hajj as a showcase for revolutionary Islam, where converts could be won over to their interpretation of the religion. On August 2 in Tehran, more than one million people heard a speech by the speaker of the Majlis (parliament), Hojatolislam Hashemi Ali Akbar Rafsanjani (*see* BIOGRAPHIES), in which he threatened to uproot the Saudi rulers and called for supervision of the holy shrines by the world Islamic community. The day before angry crowds, said to have included relatives of those killed in Mecca, attacked the Saudi embassy in Tehran.

In the subsequent propaganda war, Saudi Arabia invited representatives of 44 Muslim countries to send envoys to the kingdom to examine the bodies of the dead for any signs of gunshot wounds. Videotape showing weapons discovered on the persons of Iranian pilgrims arriving for the hajj was also released. The Saudi Arabians continued to insist that politics must not be allowed to intrude into the purely religious aspects of the pilgrimage, which involved about two million worshipers each year.

**Foreign Policy.** Saudi Arabia continued its moderate line in Arab and international politics. Recognition of Egypt, following the Amman Arab League summit, was done in concert with other Gulf Cooperation Council countries, although it was presented as a bilateral decision. During the years of political freeze, a number of Saudi leaders had remained on good personal terms with Egypt's Pres. Hosni Mubarak, and private investment flows had remained strong.

No reason was given for King Fahd's absence from the Arab summit, but the kingdom had reacted angrily to accusations on November 3 by the Libyan leader, Col. Mu'ammar al-Qadhdhafi, that the Saudi Arabians had paid for weapons used against Libya by Chadian forces. Crown

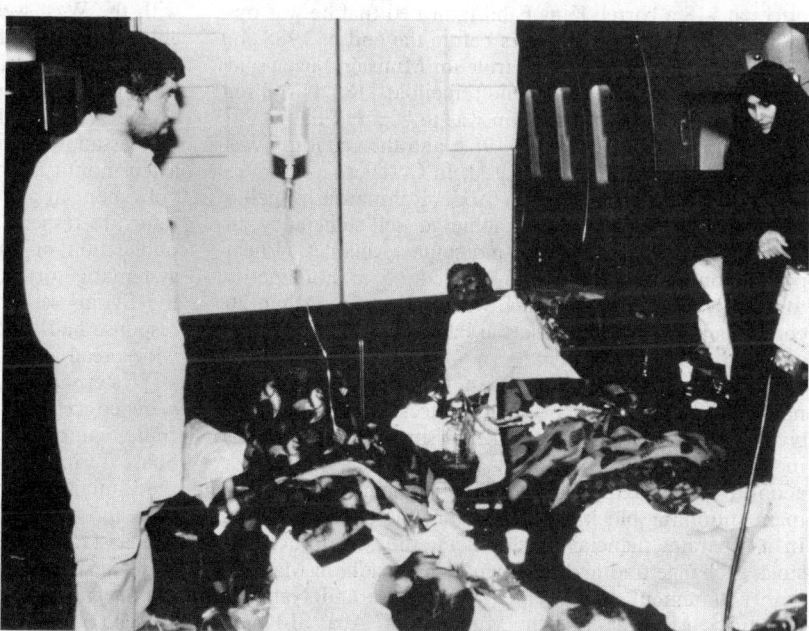

M. SHANDIZ—SYGMA

Wounded Iranian pilgrims are flown back to Iran after a clash with Saudi Arabian security forces in the holy city of Mecca. Over 400 people were killed when a crowd of pilgrims turned the hajj (annual pilgrimage) into a political event that was eventually broken up by the Saudi riot police.

Prince Abdullah, who attended the summit, visited the U.S. on October 18–21—the highest ranking Saudi to visit Washington since King Fahd in 1985. Fahd paid a state visit to the U.K. on March 24–27, followed by a tour of other European countries. Weapons deals with both the U.S. and the U.K. made progress.

Despite the lack of Saudi intervention during the attack by Iraq on the USS *Stark* on May 17, U.S. Pres. Ronald Reagan remained sympathetic to Saudi Arabian requests for advanced weapons systems. There was, nevertheless, a built-in majority in the U.S. Congress opposed to selling arms to Saudi Arabia because they might be used against Israel. In October an arrangement was worked out between the administration and congressional leaders permitting the sale of a $1 billion arms package including 12 new F-15 fighters. However, a proposal to include 1,600 Maverick air-to-ground missiles in the deal was withdrawn.

A similar breakthrough was the signing on October 21 of a memorandum establishing an economic offset program with the U.K. for the supply to Saudi Arabia of Tornado combat aircraft, an agreement originally reached in 1985. This was signed by Defense Aviation Minister Prince Sultan ibn Abdel-Aziz al-Saud and U.K. Secretary of State for Defence George Younger. The talks took time because of the British government's inability to guarantee a specific level of private investment in industrial ventures in the kingdom equal to a percentage of the value of the Tornado deal.

Saudi relations with other European countries remained strong. A West German general was named to oversee security for the 1988 hajj. Links with the Soviet Union were advanced at a meeting on January 20 between Petroleum Minister Hisham Nazer and Soviet Foreign Minister Eduard Shevardnadze. The kingdom said that the removal of Soviet troops from Afghanistan would be the main condition for a resumption of diplomatic relations.

**The Economy.** On February 3 the oil company Aramco announced that it had been authorized by its U.S. stockholders—Exxon Corp., Chevron Corp., Mobil Corp., and Texaco Inc.—to enter into a long-term agreement with the Saudi Arabian government for the purchase of oil. The deal expressed the desire of the four companies to keep on good terms with Saudi Arabia despite the crude oil glut.

For its part Saudi Arabia was anxious to stabilize oil prices at $18 a barrel. King Fahd indicated that he was opposed to any increase in prices before the end of 1988. In Chicago on November 10, Petroleum Minister Nazer said that the price of crude oil should remain at $18 a barrel for some time to come. Production was to begin at the Mahd al-Dhahab gold mine in early 1988, and the economy was already much more broadly based. In October Agriculture and Water Resources Minister Abdel-Rahman ash-Sheikh said that the kingdom had achieved self-sufficiency in wheat, dates, eggs, milk, fish, and some vegetables. Wheat production in the 1987 season totaled 2.5 million metric tons, 1.4 million tons of which were sold to more than 20 countries in the Middle East, the Far East, Africa, Europe, and Latin America.

In October the Saudi Arabian Monetary Agency announced the formation of a committee, comprising three civil servants, to arbitrate issues arising from bad loans in which borrowers were using the Shari'ah law to block action by their creditor banks. This problem had been the main stumbling block to expansion of the banking sector. In a separate financial development, the kingdom's first stock exchange trading floor opened in Riyadh on May 11.

In a statement on November 7, Finance and National Economy Minister Sheikh Muhammad Aba al-Khayl firmly ruled out the possibility of a revaluation of the riyal against the U.S. dollar despite a sharp decline in the value of the U.S. currency on foreign exchange markets during October. Saudi Arabian policy had been to reduce movements in the riyal's value against the dollar in an effort to lessen the uncertainty for importers. In December it was announced that the kingdom would borrow money to finance its budget for the first time since the oil boom began.                                        (JOHN WHELAN)

This article updates the *Macropædia* article ARABIA: *Saudi Arabia.*

## SYRIA

A republic of southwestern Asia, Syria is on the Mediterranean Sea. Area: 185,180 sq km (71,498 sq mi). Pop. (1987 est.): 10,969,000. Cap.: Damascus. Monetary unit: Syrian pound, with (Oct. 5, 1987) an official rate of LS 3.93 to U.S. $1 (LS 6.37 = £1 sterling). President in 1987, Gen. Hafez al-Assad; prime ministers, Abdul Rauf al-Kasm and, from November 1, Mahmoud Zuabi.

Syria's pivotal role with regard to the major Middle East peace questions was reaffirmed at the Arab League summit held in Amman, Jordan, in November 1987. Pres. Hafez al-Assad was forced to agree to a final resolution critical of Iran for occupying Iraqi territory but managed to head off moves to sever relations between Arab nations and Iran. The president also staved off the readmission of Egypt into the Arab League but went along with a resolution allowing individual Arab countries to renew diplomatic relations with that country. The summit's decision to insist on the presence of the Palestine Liberation Organization at any international conference on the Arab–Israel dispute was also opposed by Syria.

Syria reemerged as a central player in the Lebanon crisis in a number of ways. The decision to intervene militarily in Beirut presented Syria as a force for stability in the region and was a major step toward improving Syria's relations with Western countries. Syrian troops ended the siege of the Shatila and Burj al-Barajinah refugee camps in Beirut. Syria's good offices were also believed to have helped gain the release of a number of Western hostages kidnapped in Beirut by pro-Iranian Muslim extremists.

Among the steps taken by Syria to improve relations with the West were the demotion of air force intelligence chief Muhammad al-Khuli, who was responsible for the attempt to plant a bomb on an Israeli airliner in London in April 1986, and the closing of the Damascus office of the Abu Nidal terrorist group. On September 2 U.S. Ambassador William Eagleton returned to his post after a ten-month absence in protest against Syria's alleged involvement in acts of international terrorism. The nation's return to respectability received a jolt in October with the publication of an Amnesty International report alleging systematic torture of political detainees by members of the Syrian security services. The report alleged that no response had been made by the government to charges of widespread abuses of human rights.

Western countries, along with moderate Arab states, were concerned about the close ties between Syria and Iran, reaffirmed by Foreign Affairs Minister Faruq ash-Shara during a visit to Tehran on May 12. At this meeting the Iranians pointed to the friendship that existed between Iraq and the U.S.S.R. On April 23 President Assad began a state visit to Moscow. The joint statement at the end referred to the need to halt hostilities in the Persian Gulf region and to unify Palestinian ranks. The U.S.S.R. pledged continued economic and military assistance.

A Cabinet reshuffle on November 1 suggested growing concern about the economic crisis. Abdul Rauf al-Kasm, who had held the post of prime minister since 1980, was replaced by Mahmoud Zuabi, the speaker of the People's Council since 1981. An agronomist by training, he had been responsible in the 1970s for the Lower Euphrates Irrigation Project, and his appointment reflected a move to improve agricultural output. Earlier, Agriculture and Agrarian Reform Minister Mahmoud al-Kurdi was dismissed for allowing the introduction of the cattle disease rinderpest into Syria, and Supply and Internal Trade Minister Riyad Khalil lost his job for the same reason. Investigations ordered by the People's Council also led to the resignations of Construction Minister Riyad Baghdadi and Industry Minister Ali at-Tarabulsi, blamed respectively for delays on the Euphrates Basin projects and for inflated prices paid for cement factory equipment.

An oil concession awarded to the U.K.'s Tricentrol in May indicated increased international interest in oil prospects after the successful development of Thayyem and other fields in the Dayr az-Zawr area. The Thayyem field was producing some 60,000 bbl a day in 1987.

The first Syrian in space, Muhammad Faris, returned to Earth on July 30 at the end of a nine-day space voyage aboard the Soviet spacecraft Soyuz TM-3. During the journey Faris photographed the Euphrates Valley and the desert to the east as a contribution to research on mineral and groundwater resources. (JOHN WHELAN)

## TUNISIA

A republic of North Africa, Tunisia lies on the Mediterranean Sea. Area: 154,530 sq km (59,664 sq mi). Pop. (1987 est.): 7,662,000. Cap.: Tunis. Monetary unit: Tunisian dinar, with (Oct. 5, 1987) a free rate of 0.85 dinar to U.S. $1 (1.39 dinars = £1 sterling). Presidents in 1987, Habib Bourguiba and, from November 7, Gen. Zine al-Abidine Ben Ali; prime ministers, Rashid Sfar until October 2, General Ben Ali until November 7, and, from November 7, Hedi Baccouche.

The most important development in Tunisia during 1987 was the unexpected resolution of the issue of the succession to Tunisia's 84-year-old president-for-life, Habib Bourguiba, who had led the country to independence in 1956 and retained the reins of power thereafter. On November 7 the president was replaced by Gen. Zine al-Abidine Ben Ali (see BIOGRAPHIES), who had been appointed prime minister one month earlier. The move was justified on the grounds of the president's inability to discharge his duties, because of poor health, as laid down in Article 57 of the Constitution. The new president rapidly consolidated his power by removing known favourites of Bourguiba from public office and by guaranteeing that there would be no radical change in domestic or foreign policy. His actions were welcomed by Algeria, Tunisia's most important regional ally, and the change in regime was accepted by France and the U.S., its most important Western backers.

The move came after several months of rapidly deteriorating domestic political circumstances in which the government had identified the Muslim fundamentalist movement as the major threat to its stability. In March, alleging that Iran was organizing antigovernment fundamentalists, Tunisia broke diplomatic relations with that nation. In August bomb explosions in Monastir and Sousse led to a nationwide search for the perpetrators. This resulted in widespread arrests that culminated in the trial of 90 members of the Tendence Islamique and other fundamentalist groups in September. Seven persons were sentenced to death, five in absentia.

Gen. Zine al-Abidine Ben Ali takes the oath of office as the new president of Tunisia. He replaced Pres. Habib Bourguiba, whose "senility and lingering illness" were cited as reasons for Ben Ali's assumption of office.
AFP PHOTO

The trial mirrored Bourguiba's determination to stamp out what he considered the fundamentalist menace, despite warnings of the political dangers of such a course. It may well have been that replacing the president was designed to prevent further such actions from deepening the social and political divisions in Tunisia. Many government officials, including the new president, were eager to avoid further alienation of the opposition. In November, however, some 76 people identified as fundamentalists were arrested for plotting to assassinate government figures.

The government continued the reformist economic policies initiated by Ben Ali's predecessor as prime minister, Rashid Sfar. The 1987 budget sought cuts in real government expenditure, while subsidies to consumers and to industries associated with the government were cut. Foreign investment was encouraged by cuts in import tariffs and by new investment codes for manufacturing and for the oil sector. The depression in export earnings from oil and phosphates was partly countered by a decline in imports, with a good harvest reducing the need for massive food imports. The seventh five-year plan, announced in July, involved $12.3 billion worth of investment.

Tunisia and Libya restored diplomatic relations in December. (GEORGE JOFFÉ)

## TURKEY

A republic of Asia Minor and southeastern Europe, Turkey has coastlines on the Aegean, Black, and Mediterranean seas. Area: 779,452 sq km (300,948 sq mi), including 23,764 sq km in Europe. Pop. (1987 est.): 52,845,000. Cap.: Ankara. Monetary unit: Turkish lira, with (Oct. 5, 1987) a free rate of 932 liras to U.S. $1 (1,513 liras = £1 sterling). President in 1987, Gen. Kenan Evren; prime minister, Turgut Ozal.

In general elections held in Turkey on Nov. 29, 1987, the ruling Motherland Party of Prime Minister Turgut Ozal won an overwhelming victory, securing 292 seats in the newly enlarged 450-seat National Assembly. (For tabulated results, see Political Parties, above.)

The campaign was dominated by the personal contest between old and new politicians. On the right, Turgut Ozal was pitted against Suleyman Demirel, who had been ousted from office by the military in 1980; on the left, Erdal Inonu, leader of the Social Democratic Populist Party (SDPP), challenged Bulent Ecevit, who had led the left-of-centre Republican People's Party before 1980. The political ban on the old politicians was lifted by a majority

Prime Minister Turgut Ozal of Turkey waves to crowds of supporters during his campaign for reelection. Ozal's Motherland Party won decisively in the November 29 general elections, gaining a secure majority in the National Assembly.
AFP PHOTO

of only 0.3% of the 24.4 million voters who took part in a referendum to decide the issue on September 6. The referendum result allowed formerly banned politicians to become leaders of parties that they had been directing by proxy. Demirel thus became leader of the Right Path Party and Ecevit of the Democratic Left Party. Ozal announced that elections would be held on November 1, a year before the expiration of his five-year mandate, but a decision of the Constitutional Court invalidating a clause in the new electoral law led to a four-week postponement.

The state of the economy was the other main issue in the elections. Rapid economic growth had been bought at the cost of raising the annual inflation rate to some 50%. A rapid devaluation of the Turkish lira encouraged exports; the trade deficit fell to $2.5 billion for the first nine months of the year, and this was largely offset by revenues from tourism and by the remittances of Turkish workers abroad. In December Ozal introduced a plan for further liberalization of the economy.

During the election campaign, several bombs exploded in Motherland Party offices. However, the main terrorist threat continued to come from the Kurdish secessionist PKK gangs operating near the borders with Syria, Iraq, and Iran. Neither the protocol signed during Ozal's visit to Damascus on July 16, when Syria promised to ban anti-Turkish activities on its soil, nor the visit to Turkey in June by the Iranian prime minister had an effect on the number of terrorist attacks. In all, some 500 people had been killed by the PKK since the start of its campaign in August 1984. Nevertheless, martial law was lifted in July from the provinces where it was still in force.

On April 14 Turkey applied formally for full membership in the European Communities (EC), and the EC Council of Ministers referred the application for study to the European Commission. Relations with Europe were strained, however, when the European Parliament approved on June 18 a resolution that listed Armenian and Greek accusations against Turkey as obstacles to Turkey's accession. A crisis in Turkish-Greek relations developed at the end of March when Greece threatened to stop a Turkish ship from prospecting for oil in disputed Aegean waters, where, Turkey believed, Greece was about to start drilling. A clash was avoided when Ozal declared on March 27 that the Turkish ship would stay within Turkish territorial waters if the Greeks would not drill outside theirs. A Greek statement to this effect led to a lengthy exchange of messages on means for resolving the continental shelf dispute. Both parties thereafter abided tacitly by their 1976 Bern agreement to refrain from action likely to disturb negotiations.

A letter extending the defense and economic cooperation agreement between Turkey and the U.S. was signed on March 16, but its implementation was suspended on April 11 after Congress decided to cut aid to Turkey. In May Pres. Kenan Evren postponed his planned visit to the U.S.

(ANDREW MANGO)

This article updates the *Macropædia* article TURKEY AND ANCIENT ANATOLIA.

## UNITED ARAB EMIRATES

Consisting of Abu Dhabi, Ajman, Dubai, Fujairah, Ras al-Khaimah, Sharjah, and Umm al-Qaiwain, the United Arab Emirates is a federation of seven largely autonomous emirates located on the eastern Arabian Peninsula. Area: 77,700 sq km (30,000 sq mi). Pop. (1987 est.): 1,856,000. Provisional cap.: Abu Dhabi. Monetary unit: United Arab Emirates dirham, with (Oct. 5, 1987) a free rate of 3.67 dirhams to U.S. $1 (5.96 dirhams = £1 sterling). President in 1987, Sheikh Zaid ibn Sultan an-Nahayan; prime minister, Sheikh Rashid ibn Said al-Maktum.

Events in the United Arab Emirates (U.A.E.) were dominated by the attempted coup in Sharjah during which the ruler, Sheikh Sultan ibn Muhammad al-Qasimi, was challenged by his elder brother, Sheikh Abdel-Aziz. On June 17 the official news agency WAM said Sheikh Sultan had abdicated after admitting mismanagement of oil revenues and financial policy. The Amiri Guard, loyal to Sheikh Abdel-Aziz, surrounded the palace and denied Sheikh Sultan access, but there was no violence. On June 23 Sheikh Abdel-Aziz was named crown prince and deputy ruler after 56 members of Sharjah's ruling family gave their support to Sheikh Sultan, ruler since 1972.

In the negotiations leading to the settlement, a key role was apparently played by U.A.E. Defense Minister Sheikh Muhammad ibn Rashid. Suggestions of a split between Dubai and Abu Dhabi on the issue were subsequently downplayed, but initially it appeared that Abu Dhabi favoured the replacement of Sheikh Sultan, whose policies involved heavy foreign borrowing and strict adherence to Islamic values. His ban on alcohol sales in hotels had damaged the tourist industry. During the crisis Sharjah announced a rescheduling of its debt to international banks, although negotiations had been under way earlier.

On October 29 the U.A.E.'s fifth international airport, in Fujairah, opened. The long-serving Algerian general manager of the state-owned Abu Dhabi National Oil Company resigned in April and was replaced by an Abu Dhabi national.

(JOHN WHELAN)

This article updates the *Macropædia* article ARABIA: *United Arab Emirates.*

## YEMEN, PEOPLE'S DEMOCRATIC REPUBLIC OF

The People's Democratic Republic of Yemen (Yemen [Aden]; South Yemen) is located in the southern coastal region of the Arabian Peninsula, on the Gulf of Aden and the Arabian Sea. Area: 336,869 sq km (130,066 sq mi). Pop. (1987 est.): 2,285,000. Cap.: Aden. Monetary unit: Yemeni dinar, with (Oct. 5, 1987) a par value of 0.34 dinar to U.S. $1 (free rate of 0.56 dinar = £1 sterling). President in 1987, Haidar Abu Bakr al-Attas; prime minister, Yasin Said Numan.

The Yemen Socialist Party ended its first congress in nearly two years on June 21, 1987, by promising closer ties with the U.S.S.R. The Central Committee was cut from 189 members to 71, and the meeting also expressed the familiar call for speeding up merger talks with North Yemen. This prospect was belied by a series of defections to the North, where supporters of former president Ali Nasir Muhammad Husani, deposed in 1986, were based. In December, after a long trial, Husani was sentenced to death in absentia for treason, together with a number of his followers, many of them also in exile.

In a border clash on October 11, eight South Yemeni soldiers were killed after straying into Oman. Diplomatic efforts helped to contain the consequences of the incident—the worst since the end of the Dhofar rebellion in 1975.

The U.S.S.R. was providing technical assistance to help South Yemen develop its oil fields. The discovery of oil in commercial quantities in the Shabwa field was announced on April 15. By October the field was already producing 10,000 bbl a day.                                        (JOHN WHELAN)

This article updates the Macropædia article ARABIA: *People's Democratic Republic of Yemen.*

## YEMEN ARAB REPUBLIC

The Yemen Arab Republic (Yemen [San'a']; North Yemen) is situated in the southwestern coastal region of the Arabian Peninsula, on the Red Sea. Area: 195,000 sq km (75,300 sq mi). Pop. (1987 est.): 8,386,000. Cap.: San'a'. Monetary unit: Yemen rial, with (Oct. 5, 1987) a free rate of 10.22 rials = U.S. $1 (16.60 rials = £1 sterling). President in 1987, Col. Ali Abdullah Saleh; prime minister, Abdel Aziz Abdel Ghani.

North Yemen celebrated the 25th anniversary of the revolution in September 1987. The country's economic prospects had improved, but hopes for unity with South Yemen again foundered. In talks with South Yemen starting on July 21, Pres. Ali Abdullah Saleh pressed for national reconciliation and urged that former South Yemen president Ali Nasir Muhammad Husani and his supporters, now living in exile in the North, be allowed to return. This was rejected by the ruling party in South Yemen.

On March 28 Saudi Arabia praised President Saleh as a "pillar of stability" in the region. This followed a Saudi denial of clashes on their common border and denials by the Saudi Press Agency that Saudi Arabia had any territorial claims over the Marib al-Jawf area, in which oil had been discovered.

The first deliveries of crude oil from the Marib al-Jawf field to the coastal terminal at Salif took place in mid-November. Initial throughput was 135,000 bbl a day; this was expected to rise rapidly to 200,000 bbl a day. On May 28 President Saleh announced a second substantial discovery in the same basin. These oil finds gave increased hope that the government would fulfill its five-year (1987–91) plan.                                        (JOHN WHELAN)

This article updates the Macropædia article ARABIA: *Yemen Arab Republic.*

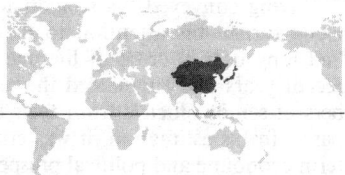

# East Asia

## CHINA

The People's Republic of China is situated in eastern Asia, with coastlines on the Yellow Sea and the East and South China seas. Area: 9,572,900 sq km (3,696,100 sq mi), including Tibet and excluding Taiwan. (See *Taiwan,* below.) Pop. (1987 est., excluding Taiwan): 1,072,330,000. Cap.: Beijing (Peking). Monetary unit: renminbi yuan, with (Oct. 5, 1987) a free rate of 3.73 yuan to U.S. $1 (6.06 yuan = £1 sterling). General secretaries of the Communist Party of China in 1987, Hu Yaobang (Hu Yao-pang) and, from January 16 (acting to November 2), Zhao Ziyang (Chao Tzu-yang); president, Li Xiannian (Li Hsien-nien); premiers, Zhao and, from November 24 (acting), Li Peng (Li P'eng).

Two interrelated processes dominated Chinese politics in 1987: resolving the succession arrangements for the country's aged revolutionary-era leaders, and sustaining efforts at economic and political reform. Political tensions in the aftermath of student demonstrations late in 1986 appeared to threaten momentarily the succession plans advocated by 83-year-old Deng Xiaoping (Teng Hsiao-p'ing), the principal architect of China's extraordinary shifts of the past decade toward market-oriented socialism and away from the dominance of the Communist Party of China (CPC) in all spheres of economic life. However, the CPC's 13th national congress in late October and early November approved Deng's plans for virtually all senior leaders to resign their posts, with the positions filled by leaders in their 50s and 60s. At the same time, China remained strongly committed to its "opening to the outside world," including further expansion of ties with the advanced industrial nations. Relations with the Soviet Union continued to improve, but Chinese displeasure over several congressional actions and U.S. unhappiness over Chinese arms sales to Iran disturbed Sino-U.S. ties. Heightened political and economic tensions also created uncertainties in the Sino-Japanese relationship.

**Domestic Affairs.** Contention over leadership succession dominated the Chinese political agenda for much of the year. Following the student demands for increased freedom of expression, Hu Yaobang (Hu Yao-pang), Deng's handpicked choice as CPC general secretary, resigned in mid-January; the position was filled on an acting basis by Premier Zhao Ziyang (Chao Tzu-yang; *see* BIOGRAPHIES), whom Deng had previously chosen to implement and coordinate the economic reform process. Some party elders, troubled by Hu's departures from ideological orthodoxy, used his resignation as an opportunity to regain political ground. Harsh attacks on "bourgeois liberalization" were followed by renewed limits on intellectual expression and a reemphasis on the "four cardinal principles" that enshrined party dominance over the nation's political life. Although Deng remained a leading advocate of economic change, he also strongly endorsed the curbs on unbridled intellectual expression, which he saw posing a threat to party supremacy. By midwinter, however, key reformists (including Zhao) were seeking to limit the political damage. Zhao insisted that the campaign against "bourgeois liberalization" be strictly confined to internal party matters. In May Deng offered strong support for Zhao, asserting that "ossified leftist thinking" represented a greater threat than any challenge posed by "bourgeois liberalization."

Having conveyed his support for the reformist course, Deng turned his attention to the succession issue. Deng had long been a critic of lifetime tenure in office and in recent years had engineered the resignation of large numbers of senior officials from their entrenched bureaucratic bases. In his estimation, it was crucial for China's longer-term economic and political prospects to bequeath political power to younger, more highly educated officials. He also viewed this step as vital to rejuvenating the party, which now exceeded 46 million members. Having repeatedly emphasized his own desire to retire from various leadership posts, Deng sought to convince other party elders—including conservative critics of rapid economic and political change—to follow suit. Despite resistance in some quarters, Deng ultimately engineered the resignations of virtually all senior CPC officials. In addition to Deng, those stepping down from the Political Bureau included chief of state Li Xiannian (Li Hsien-nien), senior economic planner Chen Yun (Ch'en Yün), legal and security affairs specialist Peng Zhen (P'eng Chen), military leaders Yang Dezhi (Yang Te-chih) and Yu Qiuli (Yü Ch'iu-li), and veteran ideologist Hu Qiaomu (Hu Ch'iao-mu). Deng, however, opted to retain his chairmanship of the party Military Commission.

The new Political Bureau appointed at the party congress was smaller (17 members rather than 20) and younger (an average age of 65 rather than 70). The average age in the Political Bureau Standing Committee dropped from 77 to 64. Zhao, a vigorous 68, was named the new CPC general secretary and head of the Standing Committee. Zhao was joined on the Standing Committee by four newcomers to this ranking leadership body: Li Peng (Li P'eng), a Soviet-trained engineer responsible in recent years for various economic management tasks; party administrator Qiao Shi (Ch'iao Shih); Hu Qili (Hu Ch'i-li), regarded as a leading reform advocate; and veteran economic planner Yao Yilin (Yao Yi-lin). Hu Yaobang, though yielding his seat on the Standing Committee, retained his membership in the Political Bureau.

Following the party congress, Zhao resigned the premiership. He was succeeded on an acting basis by Li Peng, whose appointment would be formally ratified in the spring of 1988. Although most political observers deemed Li more cautious in his approach to economic reform than Zhao, this was not expected to lead to major movement away from the reform objectives. Zhao sought to enshrine many of these objectives in his political report delivered at the party congress. According to Zhao, China remained "in the primary stage of socialism," which would continue at least through the middle of the next century. Thus China would not be able to leapfrog intermediate stages on the road to fully developed socialism. Instead, the country would have to expand its productive capabilities by all possible means, while also undertaking "comprehensive reform" of its political and administrative structure. Zhao placed particular stress on economic restructuring, whereby the direct economic control exercised by the state would steadily diminish. Establishing a "socialist market system" was expected to increase the capability and incentives of enterprises to produce more and to depend less on central planners for resources and policy guidance.

Zhao also gave great emphasis to reform of the political structure. The goal of political reform had proved to be a highly contentious issue in recent years. Zhao stressed the need to separate the functions of party and government, which meant curtailing the party's monopoly of decision-making authority, especially for economic matters and for local-level policy. Other measures would be introduced to reduce the ability of political authorities to exercise their powers arbitrarily and to professionalize numerous bureaucratic appointments through a competitive examination system. Many of these objectives were clearly long-term goals rather than near-term proposals. By setting forth these tasks in a comprehensive manner, the new party leadership hoped to generate political support at all levels.

**The Economy.** Chinese planners continued to grapple with the complexities of the transition to a mixed economy. Although economic reformers sought to limit the powers exercised at a macro level, they had yet to devise an effective means of maintaining indirect control over economic growth, particularly unchecked expenditure by individual enterprises and by local governments in the rural areas. The economy grew rapidly, with industrial output alone increasing more than 11% during the first six months of 1987. However, planners expressed mounting concern about the risks posed by uncontrolled growth, given that demand vastly outstripped available supplies of energy, raw materials, and high-quality producer and consumer goods.

Some of the biggest problems included a major expansion of money supply (a full 50% increase in the first half of the year), rapid price increases in the cities for many foodstuffs and consumer items, excessive consumption, and uncontrolled investment. According to nongovernment estimates, inflation in the cities approached 20%, resulting in soaring living costs for workers. At the same time, it was proving increasingly difficult to regulate the activities of individual enterprises, which, more often than not, sought to return profits to workers through across-the-board wage increases rather than reinvesting them in new production technology.

To curb major excesses, planners sought to reintroduce some of the controls on prices that had been relaxed in recent years, while searching for more effective mechanisms to curb enterprise overinvestment. The central bank reimposed limits on credit and attempted to reclaim some of the surplus funds now in circulation. Efforts were also under way to shift investment to vital but long-neglected infrastructural tasks in transportation, communications, and resource development, as mandated by the seventh five-year (1986–90) plan, but no easy answers to the problem of acquiring sufficient funds for large-scale projects were in sight. Related problems hampered the agricultural sector, the leading success story of the economic reforms of the past decade. The development of small-scale industry and the emergence of a service sector in the Chinese countryside had resulted in major shifts in the labour force, with tens of millions of peasants moving away from agricultural production. Changing patterns of land use and manpower led to higher feed-grain prices and reduced production of pork, necessitating a decision in December to ration pork supplies in most major cities.

China achieved greater success in correcting the nation's trade imbalance. In recent years China's desire for foreign products and advanced technology had vastly outstripped the country's ability to pay for them. At the same time, decentralization of the foreign trade system meant that officials in Beijing (Peking) exercised far less oversight and control over this process. The decline of export earnings from crude oil and petroleum products posed additional problems. As a result, even though exports increased substantially in 1986, China's trade imbalance reached $10 billion, based on two-way trade of $66 billion. China sought to address these problems by three methods: greatly restricting imports of finished products from abroad; launching a major new export push; and increasing the country's for-

China's Premier Zhao Ziyang (Chao Tzu-yang) meets with the press after his confirmation as the new head of the Communist Party of China. Zhao was the only member of the Political Bureau Standing Committee to retain his position of power at the 13th party congress.

ANDERSON—GAMMA/LIAISON

eign borrowing. Purchases of consumer goods (especially automobiles, motorcycles, and household appliances) returned to modest levels. Japan (which alone accounted for more than half of China's trade deficit in 1986) bore the brunt of the cuts.

In the export sector, China attempted to compensate for declining oil revenues by accelerating its sales of textiles, coal, and foodstuffs. Fueled in particular by a major push in textiles, the value of Chinese exports rose more than 30% in the first six months of 1987, though increases were more modest later in the year. Although Japan remained China's largest trading partner, Hong Kong was now China's biggest export market. Trade with the U.S. declined slightly but was still expected to surpass $8 billion for the year. Trade with Western Europe—especially West Germany—registered impressive increases.

China also was looking abroad for loans to help finance major industrial projects. During the first six months of the year, China became the largest borrower among Asian states. In addition, China began more actively to tap new sources of funds, including bond markets in the U.S. Although China's total foreign debt was expected to surpass $32 billion by the end of 1987, most economists believed that (unlike many third world states) the country's debt service was manageable. However, the outlook for direct foreign investment remained somewhat more clouded. Although new regulations for foreign investment introduced in late 1986 seemed attractive, foreign businessmen showed caution, and pledged investments dropped significantly early in the year. To allay fears about the political climate, Chinese leaders repeatedly stressed that recent leadership changes would not alter China's long-term commitment to increasing its involvement in the world economy.

**Foreign Affairs.** Chinese foreign policy priorities continued to emphasize the reduction of military tensions and the enhancement of China's international political and economic contacts to facilitate internal development. Despite progress in both areas, there were uncertainties and complications, especially in relations with Japan but extending in some aspects to Sino-U.S. relations as well.

Chinese-Japanese differences were both economic and political. Although it was China's largest trading partner, Japan remained cautious about investing substantial sums in the Chinese modernization program. As a result, Beijing accused Tokyo of viewing China solely as a market for Japanese goods and of withholding advanced technology from Chinese industry. China combined its efforts to

reduce imports of Japanese goods with calls for Japan to extend additional low-interest loans. China expressed increased concern about the growth of Japan's military power. Japan's decision to exceed 1% of its gross national product in defense expenditure was greeted very warily in Beijing, with China warning against the possibility that Japan might ultimately assume a larger military role. Chinese officials also repeated objections to a Japanese court decision awarding ownership of a student dormitory in Kyoto to the authorities in Taiwan; Beijing decried this step as tantamount to a "two Chinas" policy. Despite such tensions, China reiterated its desire to sustain amicable long-term relations with Japan and invited Noboru Takeshita, the newly elected prime minister, to visit China during 1988.

Closer ties with the U.S. remained a vital policy objective for China, but irritants to the relationship developed. In March Secretary of State George Shultz traveled to Beijing, reassuring Chinese leaders of the U.S. intention to broaden relations in all areas. In May Gen. Yang Shangkun (Yang Shang-k'un), China's most important military leader, made a first-ever visit to the U.S. The importance of the U.S. to China's modernization agenda was underscored by its increased purchases of high technology from U.S. companies, including some in the defense sector. More than 18,000 Chinese students were enrolled in U.S. universities and colleges, especially in science and engineering programs.

Many of the problems in Sino-U.S. ties reflected the growing institutionalization of relations between the two countries. Following a late summer visit by the Dalai Lama, the exiled Tibetan religious leader, to Capitol Hill, violent demonstrations led by Buddhist monks protesting Chinese rule occurred in the Tibetan capital of Lhasa. The Ministry of Foreign Affairs voiced strenuous objections to expressions of congressional support for Tibetan autonomy. Meanwhile, the Reagan administration objected vigorously to Chinese sales of Silkworm missiles to Iran and placed on hold requests for additional modifications in U.S. policy regarding high-technology exports to China. Agreement was reached by the two sides in December limiting future increases in Chinese textile exports to the U.S.

China also sought to enhance its relations with the Soviet Union. Sino-Soviet ties continued their marked improvement of recent years, with the U.S.S.R. now among China's leading trading partners. Sino-Soviet trade in 1987 was expected to approach $3 billion, mostly conducted on a barter basis. Modest steps were begun toward refurbishing industrial facilities constructed with Soviet assistance in the 1950s, but these programs were still dwarfed by the Western contribution to the modernization effort. China expressed a growing interest in Soviet leader Mikhail Gorbachev's efforts at political and economic reform. Many Chinese officials noted that similar challenges confronted the world's two largest socialist societies. However, Beijing insisted that the acid test for future ties remained the "three obstacles": the Soviet military presence in Mongolia and along the Sino-Soviet border; the Soviet occupation of Afghanistan; and Moscow's continued support for the Vietnamese occupation of Kampuchea.

During bilateral talks in August, Moscow and Beijing made some progress toward resolving claims along the eastern sector of the Sino-Soviet border, and the formation of expert groups to further adjudicate various disputes was announced. China described Moscow's limited troop withdrawals from northern Mongolia as an encouraging step but insisted that these measures were much too partial. Beijing also voiced great skepticism about Moscow's supposed readiness to withdraw from Afghanistan. In November Deng Xiaoping reiterated his willingness (notwithstanding his advanced age) to meet with Gorbachev personally should the Soviet leader withdraw Moscow's economic and military support for Vietnamese forces in Kampuchea. Gorbachev, however, insisted that a Sino-Soviet summit should be held without prior conditions.

Vietnam and India were the two major exceptions to Beijing's success in improving relations with its neighbours. Beijing repeatedly insisted that the key to resolving tensions in Southeast Asia was Vietnam's readiness to withdraw its armies from Kampuchea. Chinese spokesmen stated that Vietnam's pledges to withdraw its forces were totally false and warned other Asian states against seeking an accommodation with leaders in Hanoi. Relations with New Delhi took a worrisome turn in the spring when troop reinforcements on both sides of the Sino-Indian border increased appreciably. Although the two sides were subsequently able to defuse tensions, the sudden increase in military deployments reflected underlying Sino-Indian differences that remained unresolved.          (JONATHAN D. POLLACK)

# JAPAN

A constitutional monarchy in the northwestern Pacific Ocean, Japan comprises an archipelago with four main islands (Hokkaido, Honshu, Kyushu, and Shikoku), the Ryukyus (including Okinawa), and minor adjacent islands. Area: 377,801 sq km (145,870 sq mi). Pop. (1987 est.): 122.1 million. Cap.: Tokyo. Monetary unit: yen, with (Oct. 5, 1987) a free rate of 146.87 yen to U.S. $1 (238.50 yen = £1 sterling). Emperor, Hirohito; prime ministers in 1987, Yasuhiro Nakasone and, from November 6, Noboru Takeshita.

**Domestic Affairs.** Despite an impressive victory in the general election of July 1986, the ruling Liberal-Democratic Party (LDP) found itself engaged in a typical leadership struggle in early 1987. After the election the LDP had extended the tenure of Yasuhiro Nakasone as party president (and hence as prime minister) to October 1987 but refused to grant him a third term. Immediately, powerful factions within the LDP began maneuvers toward a "post-Nakasone era." On July 22, 1986, Prime Minister Nakasone had reshuffled his Cabinet to reflect factional strengths within the LDP. Kiichi Miyazawa became finance minister; Tadashi Kuranari, a Nakasone supporter, took the post of foreign minister; Masaharu Gotoda remained as chief Cabinet secretary; and Shin Kanemaru served as deputy prime minister. Noboru Takeshita, LDP secretary-general, and Shintaro Abe, chairman of the party's executive coun-

cil, waited in the wings. Nakasone's successor was expected to be chosen from among Takeshita, Miyazawa, and Abe, known as the "three new leaders."

The 108th regular session of the Diet convened on Jan. 26, 1987. Party strength in the (lower) House of Representatives was LDP (including independent allies) 309; Japan Socialist Party (JSP) 87; Clean Government Party (Komeito) 57; Democratic Socialist Party (DSP) 29; Japan Communist Party (JCP) 27; vacancies 3 (total 512). In the (upper) House of Councillors the LDP held 143 seats; JSP 41; Komeito 25; DSP 12; JCP 16; independents 14; vacancies 1 (total 252).

Troubles for the Nakasone regime began on March 8, when JSP candidate Jinichi Ogawa overwhelmingly won an upper house by-election in conservative Iwate Prefecture. At issue were the economic recession and a controversial sales tax plan sponsored by the prime minister. Although the LDP won most of the prefectural governorships and assembly seats at stake in local elections held April 12, the party lost crucial gubernatorial races in industrial Fukuoka (Kyushu) and in Hokkaido. In fact, the election losses certified a precipitous drop in public support for the LDP and, specifically, for Nakasone and his Cabinet. A Kyodo news service survey released March 28 showed that only 26.9% of those polled supported Nakasone, compared with over 50% in December 1986.

On New Year's Day, Kakuei Tanaka, the ailing former prime minister, made a brief public appearance, his first since February 1985. Found guilty in the so-called Lockheed bribery case but free on appeal, Tanaka was technically not an LDP member but still nominally headed the largest party faction. He welcomed at his residence Susumu Nikaido, former LDP vice-president, but deliberately snubbed Secretary-General Takeshita. On July 29 the Tokyo High Court upheld Tanaka's conviction, subject to further appeal to the Supreme Court. In effect, Tanaka's power within the party fell sharply.

On May 1 Deputy Prime Minister Kanemaru urged Takeshita to establish his own faction in preparation for the presidential race. On May 14 Nikaido announced his candidacy for the LDP leadership, even though he commanded only about 20 members of the old Tanaka faction. On May 21 Takeshita drew 120 faction members to a fund-raising party, and on July 4 he announced formation of the Keiseikai, the first new faction in the LDP in 15 years. Finance Minister Miyazawa in effect announced his candidacy on July 12, when he began a national stumping tour in Aomori. Abe, the third "new leader," bided his time but appeared to be lining up with Takeshita.

On October 20, after negotiations among the "three new leaders" failed to produce a behind-the-screen compromise, Prime Minister Nakasone took the unusual step of naming Noboru Takeshita to be the new LDP president. It was the second time in postwar history that an outgoing party chief had chosen his own successor. Takeshita was formally named president at an extraordinary LDP convention on October 31 and, as head of the majority party, was elected prime minister by the Diet on November 6.

The Socialists, led by the first woman to head a major political party in Japan's history, Takako Doi, adopted an action program for 1987 designed to convert the JSP into a "party of the people." Doi and the new Komeito chairman, Junya Yano, agreed to oppose the LDP government's program for increased defense spending and its plan to participate in the U.S. Strategic Defense Initiative. Later, DSP Chairman Saburo Tsukamoto joined the two opposition leaders in a strategy to "confront" the government on Nakasone's tax proposals.

Noboru Takeshita celebrates after he was formally named as the new prime minister of Japan at an extraordinary convention of the Liberal-Democratic Party. A deadlock among three candidates forced Prime Minister Yasuhiro Nakasone to choose his own successor.
KAKU KURITA

**The Economy.** In February the government approved a draft general account budget with expenditures set at 54,101,000,000,000 yen, an increase of only 0.02% from the previous fiscal year. Defense spending, however, would increase 5.2% to exceed 1% of GNP, a decade-old politically established ceiling. In any case, the budget-making procedure was disrupted by the proposed tax reform.

In December 1986, after two years of preparation, Nakasone had unveiled his tax plan, which provided for a 5% value-added tax. Although individual rates were to be lowered, the *maruyu* exemption on small postal savings accounts would be dropped. Opposition parties immediately staged a boycott of committee proceedings in the Diet. Chairman Takeshi Kurokawa of the General Council of Trade Unions of Japan (Sohyo) mounted a determined fight against the new tax. Major retail business associations, traditionally staunch supporters of the LDP, served notice that they would withdraw support if the government proceeded with the plan. On March 13 opposition parties ended their third boycott of budget proceedings when the LDP agreed to delay public hearings at least until the April 12 local elections. On March 27 the Cabinet was forced to adopt a record 8,830,000,000,000-yen provisional budget to cover the first 50 days of fiscal year 1987 (beginning April 1). Setbacks in the local elections led to concessions by the LDP; on April 23 the government abandoned the sales tax bill in order to secure passage of the budget.

Because of the deflationary impact of the strong yen and a steep plunge in consumer spending, Japan's economy grew a minuscule 0.8% in the last three months of 1986. According to the Economic Planning Agency, inflation-adjusted growth for the year was only 2.5%, the lowest in 12 years. The Bank of Japan carried out a long-awaited 0.5% reduction in the official discount rate to a record low of 2.5% effective February 23. On April 17 the LDP unveiled a package of emergency measures aimed at boosting the domestic economy. Inflation remained relatively low; in March Tokyo's 23-ward consumer index was at 100.6 (1985 = 100). Unemployment, however, reached a record 3% in January, the highest since the Management and Coordination Agency began compiling statistics in 1953.

In April major labour unions in steel, automobile, and electronics industries accepted wage increases averaging slightly over 3%, the lowest rate in the 28-year history of the annual spring labour offensive.

The Nakasone government did enjoy one legislative victory. Late in 1986 the LDP had steered through the Diet a package of bills to reform the Japanese National Railways. JNR deficits had reached over 25 trillion yen by the end of fiscal year 1986. On April 1, seven private-sector railway companies and four auxiliary companies inherited the century-old national system. Some 200,000 employees took over about 200 lines, totaling more than 20,000 km (12,500 mi).

On May 29, just before the Venice summit of the advanced economic powers, Japan announced a $43 billion package of emergency measures. The plan was designed to stimulate domestic demand, reduce the nation's trade surplus, and provide loans to less developed nations.

**Foreign Affairs.** Relations with the U.S. were dominated by trade issues throughout 1987. The Finance Ministry revealed that trade and current account surpluses in fiscal 1986 (ended March 31) reached $101.4 billion and $93.8 billion, respectively. Although exports to the U.S. fell in yen terms, they increased 17.8% in dollars to total a record surplus of $52 billion. On January 21 in Washington, Finance Minister Miyazawa and U.S. Treasury Secretary James Baker had reaffirmed an agreement to coordinate fiscal policies and to stabilize the yen-dollar exchange rate. Nonetheless, during January the Bank of Japan had to spend a record monthly total of $8.5 billion to support the dollar, which closed at 152.30 yen on January 30 (down from 160.10 yen at the end of 1986).

Government and business leaders welcomed a Paris agreement, announced February 21–22 by six of the Group of Seven (G-7) nations. The U.S., Canada, West Germany, Britain, France, and Japan agreed "to cooperate closely" in supporting the dollar. (Italy refused to sign the agreement, complaining that it had been left out of decision making.) Despite the Paris pact, dollar-selling pressure overwhelmed the central banks' intervention, and the dollar plunged to a postwar low of 144.70 yen on March 30. In the wake of another G-7 meeting, April 8 in Washington, the dollar tumbled further to 141.85 yen on April 13. On April 27 the dollar opened in Tokyo at 137.70 yen, a record low since the yen was revalued after World War II. At their summit in Washington April 30–May 1, U.S. Pres. Ronald Reagan and Nakasone agreed that a further decline in the dollar's value would be "unproductive."

Meanwhile, trade frictions stiffened attitudes on both sides of the Pacific. The U.S. began a formal investigation of Japanese barriers to imports of supercomputers and charged that foreigners were shut out of bidding on contracts for the new $8.5 billion Osaka international airport. In February Japan's Ministry of Trade and Industry (MITI) expressed shock over a comprehensive trade bill being prepared by U.S. Sen. Lloyd Bentsen. March 16 saw the collapse of a planned merger between Fujitsu Ltd. and the Fairchild Semiconductor Corp. The primary objection by U.S. Cabinet officers centred on national security, but other officials admitted that the unspoken reason was mounting trade friction with Japan.

On March 27 the U.S. government announced plans for the first retaliation against Japan's trade in postwar history. Japan was charged with failing to live up to a 1986 semiconductor agreement by allowing sale of products in third countries at below cost ("dumping"). On April 15 Tokyo formally warned that sanctions would be in violation of the General Agreement on Tariffs and Trade (GATT).

Nevertheless, on April 17 President Reagan imposed 100% duties on $300 million of Japan-made computers, television sets, and power tools. Although Nakasone failed to have the sanctions lifted, at his meetings with Reagan in Washington April 30–May 1, the president promised to ease the restrictions on the eve of the Venice summit of major industrialized nations. The sanctions were eased in June and again in November, but about $165 million worth of imports were still covered.

Earlier, Japan's response was to threaten to revoke the semiconductor accord, but on March 23 MITI instructed chip makers to cut production of 256K DRAM chips in the second quarter of 1987. Moreover, on January 27 MITI announced the seventh annual renewal of automobile export quotas under the Voluntary Restraint Agreement. Exports of cars were to be limited to 2.3 million units in the year beginning in April.

Several incidents affected relations with both the U.S. and the Soviet Union. In May Tokyo police arrested four Japanese for selling technical manuals on U.S. military aircraft to a Soviet official. Even more serious was the revelation that the Toshiba Machine Co., a major producer of machine tools, had engaged in illegal sales to the U.S.S.R. Apparently Toshiba, between 1982 and 1984, had shipped eight militarily useful machines to the Soviet Union in violation of rules adopted by the Coordinating Committee on Export Controls (including Japan and most NATO members). The company's chairman, Shoichi Saba, and president, Sugiichiro Watari, resigned on July 1 to accept responsibility. This followed the Japanese government's ban of all Toshiba exports to the U.S.S.R. for one year.

Foreign Ministry officials nevertheless continued to feel confident that they could overcome difficulties with the U.S.S.R. in paving the way for Soviet leader Mikhail Gorbachev to visit Tokyo. On March 21 in Moscow, Ambassador Yasue Katori and Soviet Foreign Minister Eduard Shevardnadze resumed negotiations on the visit. The chief obstacle remained Japan's insistence that a dispute over ownership of what Tokyo called "the Northern Territories" be discussed in any Nakasone-Gorbachev talks. The area in question was a group of islands north of Hokkaido, occupied by the Soviet Union since World War II. Soviet diplomatic sources hinted that the Soviet leader would not go to Tokyo unless this request was dropped.

Relations with China were clouded by a decision rendered by the Osaka High Court in February recognizing the right of Taiwan to maintain possession of a Chinese student dormitory in Kyoto. On June 4 in Beijing (Peking), the Chinese leader Deng Xiaoping (Teng Hsiao-p'ing) told Komeito Chairman Yano that the decision violated the 1978 China-Japan treaty of friendship. In meetings with Foreign Minister Kuranari and six other Japanese ministers in Beijing June 26–28, Deng requested the delegation to convey to Tokyo the need to settle the controversial legal dispute. Kuranari in turn relayed Nakasone's pledge that Japan would continue to recognize Beijing as the sole legitimate government of China.

Another incident involving Japan and Taiwan affected relations with the two Koreas. On February 9 the Foreign Ministry expressed the hope that a transfer of 11 North Korean defectors via Japan to South Korea would not aggravate relations between Tokyo, Seoul, and Pyongyang. On February 7 Japan had flown the defectors to Taiwan in the belief that a stay there would reduce the impact of an eventual transfer to Seoul, but to Tokyo's surprise the refugees were flown to Seoul only 20 hours later. The move angered North Korea, which stated that it would therefore be difficult to negotiate the return of two Japanese fishermen being detained in Pyongyang since November 1983. Japan, which recognized South Korea, had no diplomatic relations with North Korea.

On January 10 Nakasone left Tokyo for a week-long journey to Finland, East Germany, Yugoslavia, and Poland. No Japanese leader had previously made an official state visit to Eastern Europe. The Japanese press reported that the trip filled a gap caused by Gorbachev's decision not to go to Tokyo in mid-January. Japan had imposed economic sanctions on Poland after martial law was declared there in 1981. However, Tokyo, which held some $1 billion of the Polish debt, indicated that it was prepared to ease the sanctions by making available to Poland $200 million in loans, to be tied to purchases of Japanese auto-production equipment.

(ARDATH W. BURKS)

## KOREA

A country of northeastern Asia, bordered by the Sea of Japan, the Korea Strait, and the Yellow Sea, Korea is divided into two parts roughly at the 38th parallel.

The Olympic Games, scheduled to open in Seoul, South Korea, in September 1988, overshadowed relations between North and South Korea throughout 1987. It soon became clear that North Korea's threat to organize a boycott by Communist countries was meaningless because it

CHARLIE COLE—PICTURE GROUP

Riot police in Seoul shield themselves from a firebomb. This and other violence marked the struggle between the followers of South Korean Pres. Chun Doo Hwan and his opponents.

did not have sufficient influence with either the U.S.S.R. or China. North Korea then changed its strategy and demanded that the Games be shared between the two Koreas. The International Olympic Committee (IOC)—which selected cities for the games, not countries—initially rejected the suggestion, but to avoid possible reprisals it agreed to a compromise that would allow the North to be host for some of the events. With South Korea's agreement the IOC offered four events, but the North demanded more. One IOC concession, that a long-distance bicycle race begin in the North and cross the demilitarized zone (DMZ), was rejected, as was the next offer, to stage the entire race in the North. Inconclusive haggling continued, and in September the UN warned North Korea against attempting to disrupt the Games.

Both sides agreed to resume bilateral negotiations, suspended since January 1986, but they were called off by the regime of North Korean Pres. Kim Il Sung because of the military exercises that the South conducted with U.S. forces at the beginning of each year. During 1987 relations between China and the South eased further, and trade between the two exceeded that between China and the North, to the evident discomfort of the latter.

Tensions heightened in midyear when the government in the South warned that the Kumgang Dam, being built just ten kilometres (six miles) north of the DMZ, was a threat to its security. Strategists stated that the dam would allow North Korea to flood Seoul at will. Another diplomatic incident raged in January 1987 when a family of 11 fled the North in a small boat and was picked up by a Japanese Coast Guard ship. Eventually the family was flown to Taiwan and from there to Seoul. South Korean officials blamed the North for the November 29 crash of a Korean Air Lines jetliner near the Thai-Burmese border in which 115 persons died. A man and woman carrying false Japanese passports were arrested in Bahrain on suspicion of having planted a bomb aboard the plane. The man died after the pair swallowed poison, but the woman survived and was taken to Seoul. The North denied involvement.

### Republic of Korea (South Korea)

Area: 99,143 sq km (38,279 sq mi). Pop. (1987 est.): 42,082,-000. Cap.: Seoul. Monetary unit: won, with (Oct. 5, 1987) a free rate of 804 won to U.S. $1 (1,305 won = £1 sterling). President in 1987, Chun Doo Hwan; prime ministers, Lho Shin Yong until May 26, Lee Han Key until July 13, and, from July 13, Kim Chung Yul.

For South Korea 1987 proved to be a political watershed, one in which the citizens gained more democratic rights and free elections took place. The events that prompted the moves toward democracy were unhappy ones, marked by violence and widespread demonstrations against the government of Pres. Chun Doo Hwan. The result was a flurry of activity by the government and the political opposition, an amnesty for dissidents, and the abolition of the president's emergency powers.

The unrest was touched off in January by the death in custody of a student activist who had suffered brutal interrogation by the police. Opposition to the government escalated, with religious groups and the normally passive middle classes joining protests and calling for full democracy. Demonstrations gathered momentum in May, June, and July, involving at one time an estimated quarter of a million people in combat with a quarter as many police. Unrest spread to the workplace, with the usually industrious labour force demanding higher wages and better conditions. Employers were surprisingly quick to meet demands

and, when the giant Hyundai Group refused to do so, the government intervened—on behalf of the workers—and the dispute ended. Nevertheless, many companies suffered production losses because of the strikes.

The much-feared return to martial law did not take place, and in this the U.S. exerted its influence. Instead there were rapid moves toward democracy. In June Roh Tae Woo (see BIOGRAPHIES) was endorsed as presidential candidate of the ruling Democratic Justice Party (DJP). He was a former general and close associate of Chun, although he distanced himself from Chun as the election campaign got under way. Chun resigned as president of the DJP in July and was replaced by party chairman Roh.

A new constitution was drawn up and approved by all parties in the National Assembly. The main points included direct presidential elections; new laws on fair balloting; freeing of political prisoners and the restitution of civil and political rights to leading dissidents, including Kim Dae Jung; a guarantee of human rights; freedom of the press; election of provincial and municipal councils; removal of restrictions on political parties; and a campaign against corruption. The new constitution was given overwhelming approval in a national referendum on October 27, and the election campaign gathered momentum.

The three main contenders were Roh, who was widely admired for his role in solving the crisis, and the two major opposition leaders, Kim Young Sam and Kim Dae Jung. The latter were joint leaders of the Reunification Democratic Party, which was formed in April; in early November, however, rivalry led to a split and a decision by Kim Dae Jung to form a breakaway group. At about the same time, Kim Jong Pil, a former prime minister, also announced his candidacy. With the opposition split, Roh won easily in the December 16 election, garnering 35.9% of the 23,070,748 votes cast to 27.5% for Kim Young Sam, 26.5% for Kim Dae Jung, and 7.9% for Kim Jong Pil. Opposition charges of widespread vote fraud were generally discounted by observers, and the result seemed to be accepted by the majority of the population.

The unrest was not able to retard South Korea's economic progress. The elimination of the current account deficit for the first time in 1986, when growth reached 12.5%, had paved the way for yet another surplus and similar growth in 1987. The phenomenal success of South Korean exports, which by mid-1987 were 33% above the levels of a year earlier, producing a trade surplus three times larger, was helped by the strength of the Japanese yen and lower oil prices. Because of the strong yen, Japan's traditional markets were being eroded, and Korean goods became more competitive. International confidence in South Korea persisted as the government gradually reduced its still-high external debt ($42 billion in March), lowered its import barriers, and was successfully diversifying its trade away from dependence on Japan.

### Democratic People's Republic of Korea (North Korea)

Area: 122,370 sq km (47,250 sq mi). Pop. (1987 est.): 21,390,-000. Cap.: Pyongyang. Monetary unit: won, with (Oct. 5, 1987) a nominal exchange rate of 0.94 won to U.S. $1 (1.53 won = £1 sterling). General secretary of the Central Committee of the Workers' (Communist) Party of Korea and president in 1987, Marshal Kim Il Sung; chairman of the Council of Ministers (premier), Li Gun Mo.

The U.S. took the initiative in 1987 in improving its relations with North Korea in an effort to ensure the success of the Olympics in Seoul. During his visit to China in March, U.S. Secretary of State George Shultz asked China to convey to North Korea a detailed proposal of measures conditional on the North's participation in the Olympics. The measures included the approval of visas to North Koreans, a partial lifting of the trade embargo to permit sales of humanitarian goods, an end to U.S. automatic opposition to the North's participation in international organizations, and the lifting of the ban on contact between the two countries' diplomats. Although the initiative produced no tangible result, it was seen as a positive move.

The move was made just before the visit to Beijing (Peking) of Kim Il Sung in May. Kim met Chinese leader Deng Xiaoping (Teng Hsiao-p'ing) and was given a royal welcome. China was anxious to improve relations with North Korea, given the closer links formed between the North and the U.S.S.R.; North Korea had granted the U.S.S.R. overflying rights and local facilities for its warships. The meetings produced nothing of substance, however, and North Korea became increasingly isolated.

Early in 1987 there was much speculation about the well-being of Kim. Mistaken reports from the South that he had been assassinated in late 1986 were followed in 1987 by reports that he had collapsed in June during a meeting with the Bulgarian ambassador, that he required brain surgery, that an official visit to Bangladesh had been canceled, and that he had "disappeared." Speculation abruptly halted following the publication of a photograph of Kim taken during an official visit of Indonesia's Foreign Minister Mochtar Kusumaatmadja on July 6.

Economic progress was slow. Western banks declared North Korea to be in default of debt payments of $770 million following the collapse of talks to reschedule them. The threat of having its assets seized caused the North to agree to sign a rescheduling accord.  (ROBERT WOODROW)

## MONGOLIA

A landlocked people's republic of eastern Asia, Mongolia occupies the geographic area known as Outer Mongolia. Area: 1,565,000 sq km (604,000 sq mi). Pop. (1987 est.): 1,989,000. Cap.: Ulan Bator. Monetary unit: tugrik, with (Oct. 5, 1987) a free rate of 3.36 tugriks to U.S. $1 (5.45 tugriks = £1 sterling). First secretary of the Mongolian People's Revolutionary (Communist) Party and chairman of the Presidium of the Great People's Hural (chief of state) in 1987, Zhambyn Batmunkh; chairman of the Council of Ministers (premier), Dumaagiyn Sodnom.

On Jan. 15, 1987, Marshal Sergey Sokolov, Soviet minister of defense, announced that a complete armoured division and several small units of Soviet troops were to be withdrawn from Mongolia. The Soviet Defense Ministry confirmed on June 7 that the partial evacuation had been completed, though no details of the numbers of troops involved were published.

The move followed an announcement by Soviet leader Mikhail Gorbachev during a speech at Vladivostok in July 1986 that "the question of withdrawing a substantial part of Soviet troops from Mongolia is being examined jointly" by Soviet and Mongolian leaders. Diplomats interpreted the decision as a move by the U.S.S.R. to improve relations with China, which had demanded that all Soviet troops leave Mongolia.

It was announced in June that Mongolian and Chinese officials had signed a treaty agreeing on methods of handling border disputes between the two countries. On January 27 Mongolia and the U.S. established diplomatic relations, and the U.S. was expected to open a diplomatic mission in Ulan Bator by 1988. The Mongolian capital was host to a meeting of senior officials from 21 Asian Communist parties in July.  (K. M. SMOGORZEWSKI)

## TAIWAN

Taiwan, which consists of the island of Taiwan and surrounding islands off the coast of China, is the seat of the Republic of China (Nationalist China). Area: 36,000 sq km (13,900 sq mi), including the island of Taiwan and its 85 outlying islands, 21 in the Taiwan group and 64 in the Pescadores group. Pop. (1987 est.): 19,630,000. (Area and population figures exclude the Quemoy and Matsu groups, which are administered as an occupied part of Fujian [Fukien] Province.) Cap.: Taipei. Monetary unit: new Taiwan dollar, with (Oct. 5, 1987) an official rate of NT$29.88 to U.S. $1 (NT$48.53 = £1 sterling). President in 1987, Chiang Ching-kuo; president of the Executive Yuan (premier), Yu Kuo-hwa.

The year 1987 was one of extraordinary accomplishment for Taiwan. Despite a dwindling diplomatic profile, major breakthroughs in political reform and the island's remarkable economic performance fostered a growing self-confidence and stability. In July martial law was lifted after 38 years, replaced by a National Security Law with much more explicit guarantees of individual rights, increased freedom of movement abroad, relaxation of most foreign exchange controls, and greater opportunities for political participation. Passage of the new law reflected increased flexibility and the pursuit of political reform by the ruling Kuomintang (Nationalist Party) and portended a further opening of the political process.

The Kuomintang's commitment to greater openness reflected increased concerns about the strength of its power base. With most top-level political positions still occupied by aging mainlanders who fled to the island in 1949, new measures were required for rejuvenating support for the party, especially among the increasingly affluent Taiwanese who comprised some 85% of the population. The Kuomintang made clear its resolve to combat calls for Taiwanese independence or self-determination, some of them voiced by the one-year-old Democratic Progressive Party. The opposition forces also pressured the Kuomintang to allow elections for all seats in the legislative body, where at present only a limited number were open to electoral competition.

The role of Chiang Ching-kuo, Taiwan's aging but still powerful president, remained crucial to sustaining the political reform process. Chiang's authority enabled him to overcome resistance among more conservative elements in the party leadership. Numerous observers expressed concern about the succession to Chiang, now 77 and in uncertain health. Most speculation centred on Lee Huan (see BIOGRAPHIES), Chiang's longtime confidant who was named Kuomintang secretary-general. Others noted the prominence given to Vice-Pres. Lee Teng-hui, a Taiwanese native.

Although the Kuomintang insisted that it would continue to reject any official contact with the mainland, these declarations obscured a growing flexibility in unofficial dealings. In late July restrictions on travel to Hong Kong and the Portuguese enclave of Macau were lifted, and in October a new policy was promulgated permitting Taiwanese citizens other than military and government personnel to visit their relatives on the mainland. Approval of this measure produced a flood of requests for such visits, barred for nearly four decades. Indirect trade between China and Taiwan also flourished and was expected to reach $2 billion by year's end.

The key to Taiwan's social and political stability remained its continuing economic success. Led by a further surge in exports, economic growth for the year was projected at 10.6%, with per capita income surpassing $5,000.

Shao Yu-ming, director of Taiwan's government information office, announces the end of 38 years of martial law, which had been imposed by Gen. Chiang Kai-shek.
AFP PHOTO

Trade relations with the U.S. were crucial to this strategy, with nearly 45% of exports shipped to U.S. markets. The U.S. trade deficit with Taiwan was expected to reach $20 billion for the year, second only to that with Japan.

Although many of Taiwan's export gains were registered by local subsidiaries of U.S. companies, the widening trade gap fueled protectionist sentiment in the U.S. Under pressure from the administration of Pres. Ronald Reagan, Taiwan's currency appreciated sharply against the U.S. dollar. Taiwan sought to resist pressures for further shifts by committing itself to larger purchases of U.S. products, lowering tariff barriers to imports, and stimulating domestic demand. Despite such measures, the central bank's hard currency reserves approached $70 billion by year's end, holdings exceeded only by Japan and West Germany.

(JONATHAN D. POLLACK)

# South Asia

## AFGHANISTAN

Afghanistan is a landlocked people's republic in central Asia. Area: 652,225 sq km (251,825 sq mi). Pop. (1987 est.): 14,184,000 (excluding Afghan refugees estimated to number about 2.8 million in Pakistan and 2.2 million in Iran). Cap.: Kabul. Monetary unit: afghani, with (Oct. 5, 1987) a free rate of 61.12 afghanis to U.S. $1 (99.25 afghanis = £1 sterling). Presidents of the Revolutionary Council (head of state), Haji Mohammad Chamkani and, from September 30 to November 30, Mohammad Najibullah; president (head of state) from November 30, Najibullah; general secretary of the People's Democratic (Communist) Party, Najibullah; prime minister, Sultan Ali Keshtmand.

The seven-year-old war in Afghanistan continued in 1987, with no agreement on a timetable for withdrawal of the estimated 115,000 Soviet troops. Two rounds of UN-sponsored talks were held—in March and September—in Geneva, with the UN mediator, Diego Cordovez, acting as liaison between the foreign ministers of Pakistan and Afghanistan. Pakistan continued to refuse to have direct negotiations with Afghanistan since it did not recognize the Soviet-backed Afghan government. Pakistan rejected the Soviet–Afghan offer of a 16-month timetable, maintaining that it should be reduced to 8 months.

The talks followed several months of diplomatic activity. Mohammad Najibullah (also known as Najib), who had led Afghanistan since late 1986—although he was not formally elected president of the Revolutionary Council (head of state) until September 1987—made an unexpected visit to Moscow in July for talks with the Soviet leader Mikhail Gorbachev. His visit came in the wake of failure to reach a cease-fire agreement. Najibullah had announced that a cease-fire would begin on January 15, but all the major anti-Communist forces rejected it. On July 15 the extension of a unilateral government offer of a cease-fire until Jan. 15, 1988, brought no response, and by August even Kabul, the capital, was threatened as resistance was stepped up. The July talks in Moscow were not reported in depth. Najibullah told the press that 60,000 former refugees had been returned, 15,000 guerrillas had given up their arms, and tens of thousands of guerrillas were negotiating with his government. The claims were not believed by the West or supported by the U.S.S.R.

At a meeting of the loyal jirgah (grand national assembly) in late November, Najibullah announced that he would present a revised timetable for the withdrawal of Soviet troops, reduced from 16 months to one year, at UN-sponsored talks scheduled for February 1988. The assembly ratified a new constitution under which the post of president (head of state) was created; Najibullah, the sole candidate, was elected to the post on November 30. The constitution also embodied a call for other parties to partake in government alongside the ruling Communist Party in an effort to promote national reconciliation.

There were conflicting reports on the military successes of both the resistance movements and Soviet-backed Afghan forces. Western diplomats reported fighting in all the major provinces, with heavy casualties on both sides. Widespread violations of human rights continued and attracted the notice of the UN Commission on Human Rights. At year's end some of the fiercest fighting of the war was reported from the garrison town of Khost, eastern Afghanistan, where Soviet-backed government forces were attempting to end a guerrilla siege of the town.

Information on the poor and war-torn economy contin-

A poster shown throughout
Afghanistan shows the two warring
parties laying down their arms and
asks the people to work for peace in
their villages.
CAMERA PRESS/PHOTO TRENDS

ued to be scarce and difficult to verify. The new five-year
(1986–91) plan set growth targets of about 15% for agriculture over the period (compared with 6% achieved in the
previous five-year period) and 38% for industrial output
(26%). Gross national product rose by 3.3% in 1986–87 to
155.3 billion afghanis, with agricultural output increasing
by 1.6%, implying a 2.4% industrial growth. The U.S.S.R.
remained Afghanistan's most important trading partner,
taking nearly 70% of exports in 1986.

The private sector remained extremely important and
generated nearly half of all export goods. Despite the poor
state of the economy, Kabul was reported to be a thriving business centre. Reasonable power supplies were being
maintained in the capital, which had grown from about
350,000 in 1974 to around 2 million in 1987 as rural
dwellers moved in, fleeing from the war or seeking work.

A UNICEF report showed that Afghanis suffered one of
the highest infant and child mortality rates in the world.
For children under one year it was 189 in every 1,000
live births in 1985, compared with 115 in neighbouring
Pakistan.                                    (DILIP GANGULY)

## BANGLADESH

A republic and member of the Commonwealth, Bangladesh
is in the northeastern part of the Indian subcontinent, on the
Bay of Bengal. Area: 143,998 sq km (55,598 sq mi). Pop. (1987
est.): 105,307,000. Cap.: Dhaka. Monetary unit: taka, with (Oct.
5, 1987) a free rate of 30.42 taka to U.S. $1 (49.40 taka = £1
sterling). President in 1987, Lieut. Gen. Hossain Mohammad
Ershad; prime minister, Mizanur Rahman Chowdhury.

In 1987 the position of Bangladesh at the bottom of the
league of the world's poorest countries was consolidated.
In the July–September period the worst flooding in 40
years brought devastation to northern, eastern, and central
regions, destroying and damaging villages and thousands of
miles of roads. The death toll in August was estimated at
at least 1,000, and it continued to rise steadily as epidemics
of waterborne disease swept the affected areas; more than
20 million were made homeless. Government reports estimated flood damage at nearly $1 billion.

Even more severe food shortages than usual were experienced by the population, despite generous food aid
from many countries. Bangladesh's food-grain import requirement in 1987 was put at 3.5 million tons, mostly
of wheat; 2.7 million tons were lost through floods and,

ironically, another 300,000 tons because of drought. A
government rehabilitation program was expected to lead
to the salvaging of around one million tons. Because of
the importance of agriculture to the economy, the International Monetary Fund did not expect growth of gross
domestic product (GDP) to exceed 1.8% in 1987, although
government officials believed 2.5% was possible. Pres. Hossain Mohammad Ershad received the 1987 UN Population
Award in recognition of the fact that the annual population
growth rate had been reduced from 3.2 to 2.4%.

Efforts were under way to upgrade the image of
Bangladesh to that of an industrializing country with an
abundance of labour available to foreign investors at highly
competitive wage rates. The government planned to increase the share of industry from 10% of GDP to 25% and
launched programs to encourage the development of small
and craft industries. Negotiations were under way with
France and West Germany for the construction of a 320-
MW nuclear power plant in the Pabna district.

The poor state of the economy helped to fuel opposition
to the government, and there were several outbursts of
violence. Legislation approved by Parliament on July 12
to allow military officers to sit on the country's 64 district
councils provoked three weeks of antigovernment protests.
The demonstrations and strikes—mainly by students and
unionists—left eight dead and many more injured. The
two major opposition groupings, the Bangladesh Nationalist Party and the Awami League Party, were united in
their attack on the government. They feared the bill was
designed to bring the military back into government, despite the official end, in November 1986, of four and a half
years of martial law. Ershad said the bill would give the
armed forces a greater chance to participate in the country's development programs. On August 2, however, he
succumbed to pressure and asked Parliament to reconsider
the bill. The turnaround was hailed as a "people's victory"
by the two main opposition leaders, Sheikh Hasina Wajad
and Khaleda Zia.

A new wave of antigovernment agitation began in early
December. Ershad declared a state of emergency and
banned all political demonstrations and strikes on November 27. On December 6 he dissolved Parliament and the
following day announced that fresh elections would be held
within 90 days. Wajad and Zia, who were among thousands
of political activists detained in early November, were freed
from house arrest after a month. Both opposition leaders

Police remove an antigovernment demonstrator who took part in protests against legislation to allow the military to sit on Bangladesh's 64 district councils.
AFP PHOTO

declared that they would not take part in the forthcoming elections unless Ershad resigned.

In an unexpected move, a new political party was launched on August 3 by the two main architects of the 1975 military coup. The new Freedom Party was strongly opposed by the Awami League. Its leaders were the former army colonels Faruq Rahman and Abdur Rashid, who had been in exile in Libya since 1975. The former president of Bangladesh, Abu Sayeed Chowdhury (*see* OBITUARIES), died on August 1 at the age of 66.        (DILIP GANGULY)

## BHUTAN

The monarchy of Bhutan is a landlocked state situated in the eastern Himalayas between China and India. Area: 47,000 sq km (18,100 sq mi). Pop. (1987 est.): 1,337,000. Cap.: Thimphu. Monetary unit: ngultrum, at par with the Indian rupee (which is also in use), with (Oct. 5, 1987) a free rate of 12.93 ngultrums to U.S. $1 (21 ngultrums = £1 sterling). Druk gyalpo (king) in 1987, Jigme Singye Wangchuk.

Bhutan gained a little more international recognition in 1987. It established diplomatic relations with Sri Lanka and South Korea, adding those countries to the existing list, which included Japan, India, Bangladesh, and Nepal. Although Bhutan had no relations with China, the two countries had held talks aimed at achieving a formal demarcation of their common border. A fourth meeting in 1987 progressed from discussing principles and procedures to substantive negotiations; the next round of talks was scheduled for 1988, when a formal agreement was likely. The prospect of closer links between China and Bhutan was a cause of concern to India, which guided the tiny kingdom in its external relations.

India provided Bhutan with an annual subsidy worth about £28,000, a not insignificant amount given that the tiny country had the world's lowest per capita income ($100). Tourism continued to be the most important foreign exchange generator. The easing of strict travel laws in 1987 brought a strong rise in the number of visitors, particularly Japanese, estimated at 3,000, compared with 2,400 in 1986, and producing $2.2 million in foreign exchange.

(DILIP GANGULY)

This article updates the *Micropædia* article BHUTAN.

## INDIA

A federal republic of southern Asia and member of the Commonwealth, India is situated on a peninsula extending into the Indian Ocean with the Arabian Sea to the west and the Bay of Bengal to the east. Area: 3,166,414 sq km (1,222,559 sq mi), including the Indian-administered portion of Jammu and Kashmir. Pop. (1987 est.): 783 044,000, including Indian-administered Jammu and Kashmir. Cap.: New Delhi. Monetary unit: Indian rupee, with (Oct. 5, 1987) a free rate of Rs 12.93 to U.S. $1 (Rs 21 = £1 sterling). Presidents in 1987, Zail Singh and, from July 25, Ramaswamy Venkataraman; prime minister, Rajiv Gandhi.

**Domestic Affairs.** In 1987 India grappled with the disaster caused by widespread drought—the worst in a century—and the political uncertainties brought about by challenges to Prime Minister Rajiv Gandhi. In July a new president was elected by an electoral college made up of nearly 5,000 legislators throughout the country. Outgoing president Zail Singh, who had served his five-year term, did not stand for a second term despite requests by several parties. The ruling Congress (I) candidate, Vice-Pres. Ramaswamy Venkataraman (*see* BIOGRAPHIES), was elected by an overwhelming majority, receiving the votes of 2,886 legislators. The principal opposition candidate was V. R. Krishna Iyer, a former Supreme Court judge, who secured 1,439 votes. Venkataraman was sworn in on July 25.

Prior to the election, Singh had been under pressure to use his power to remove Gandhi from office in the wake of corruption scandals. The scandals arose when Swedish radio announced in April that a Swedish weapons manufacturing company, Bofors, had paid 32 million Swedish kronor to middlemen in connection with a contract to supply guns to India. Bofors and the Indian government denied this, and Gandhi declared that neither he nor members of his family had received any payments. Further investigations by the Swedish government revealed that Bofors had made "winding-up" payments of 170 million–250 million kronor. A parliamentary committee was set up by the Indian government to find out, among other things, who had received the payments and whether any Indian laws had been broken. The committee was boycotted by several opposition parties. Just before the Bofors scandal, there had been charges that the West German company Howaldtswerke Deutsche Werft (HDW) had had to pay Rs 300 million in "commissions" on supplies to India of submarines. On August 31 the government announced that it was making inquiries into the allegations.

The scandals had far-reaching effects. The defense minister, Vishwanath Pratap Singh (*see* BIOGRAPHIES), who had been switched from the finance portfolio in January, resigned from the Cabinet in April, after he had announced that he was setting up a Defense Ministry inquiry to look into the HDW affair. He was replaced by K. C. Pant. Following the expulsion from the party on July 15 of three leading dissidents and former ministers who had rallied around Singh, Arun Nehru, Arif Mohammed Khan, and Vidya Charan Shukla, Singh also was expelled. This prompted the resignation of two other Cabinet ministers, A. K. Sen and Mufti Mohammed Syed. Arun Singh resigned for personal reasons, and K. K. Tewari was dismissed. In July N. D. Tiwari was made finance minister and P. Shiv Shankar moved from commerce to planning. Gandhi took over external affairs and water resources.

Speculation about the future of the Congress Party and the prime minister himself dominated the political scene in the ensuing months. The opposition's hopes grew following election victories in Kerala (March), West Bengal (March), and Haryana (May), and efforts to bring down the government and force an election were intensified. By the end of October, however, the threat to Gandhi appeared to have receded.

Three union territories, Arunachal Pradesh, Mizoram, and Goa, were accorded the status of states during the year, bringing the number of constituent states of the union to 25. Other state elections held during the year were in Mizoram (February), won by the Mizo National Front; in Jammu and Kashmir (March), where an alliance of the National Conference and the Congress took power; and in Nagaland (November), won by the Congress.

Violence continued in Punjab. On the basis of a report from the governor that some ministers were involved with extremists, the government was dismissed in May and the state placed under presidential rule. In November Parliament extended presidential rule by another six months. The Ranganath Mishra Commission, which inquired into the riots in Delhi, Kanpur, and elsewhere following Indira Gandhi's assassination in 1984, found the Delhi police culpable of "total passivity, callousness, and indifference." Hindu-Muslim riots erupted in Meerut, Uttar Pradesh, in April–May. Incidents also took place in Ahmedabad. The agitation of the Gurkha National Liberation Front in West Bengal continued.

There was concern over the persistence of the Hindu practice of suttee ("true woman"), whereby a widow burns herself to death on her husband's pyre, a practice made illegal more than 150 years earlier. The problem was highlighted when such an event drew over 5,000 spectators in the town of Deorala in Rajasthan. In December Parliament passed a stringent law imposing a maximum sentence of the death penalty for those found guilty of assisting a widow in committing suttee. (*See* RELIGION: *Hinduism.*) Ceremonial functions were held at the start of celebrations marking the 40th anniversary of independence. Former prime minister Charan Singh (*see* OBITUARIES) died in May at the age of 84.

**The Economy.** The economy grew by 4% in 1986, but the failure of the June–September monsoon meant that the rate would be much lower in 1987. The country experienced the most widespread drought in a century, and in some areas of Gujarat and Rajasthan it was the third successive failure of the monsoon. The summer food-grain crop was estimated to be 14 million metric tons less than in 1976. A comprehensive relief program provided drinking water, cattle fodder, food, and employment. More positively, tea output was expected to set a record. The network of fair-price shops was expanded to prevent rises in the prices of essential commodities.

Inflation, as measured by the wholesale price index at the beginning of October, was rising at an annual rate of 5.8%, compared with 7.1% a year earlier, but consumer prices showed a 9.5% increase. The official estimate of the rise in industrial production was 8.9%. The union government's budget for 1987–88, presented on February 27, offered some tax relief on consumer articles but imposed new levies on luxury items. These changes were calculated to bring in Rs 5.1 billion a year. Total current revenue for 1987–88 was estimated at Rs 366.9 billion against expenditure of Rs 434.3 billion. After allowance for capital inflows, the overall deficit was estimated at Rs 56.9 billion. In June the Aid India Consortium pledged assistance of $5.4 billion instead of the $4.8 billion targeted.

A national water policy was adopted. Major projects approved during the year included the Rs 70 billion Narmada River plan, expected to irrigate 1,915,000 ha (5,688,000 ac) and produce 2,450 MW of power. The plan to cleanse the Ganges made progress. The space program suffered a setback in March when its most advanced satellite launch vehicle plunged into the Bay of Bengal three minutes after lift-off. The defense establishment successfully tested submarine-to-submarine killer equipment and surface-to-air missiles and took delivery of the first batch of MiG-29 jet fighters from the U.S.S.R.

**Foreign Affairs.** India's involvement in Sri Lanka deepened. After prolonged discussions with various Tamil militant groups, including the Liberation Tigers of Tamil Eelam (LTTE), Gandhi visited Colombo on July 29 and signed an agreement with Pres. J. R. Jayawardene (*see* BIOGRAPHIES) calculated to meet the Tamils' demands. The agreement guaranteed the unity and multiethnic character of Sri Lanka, recognized that the Northern and Eastern provinces had been the traditional homes for Sri Lankan Tamils, and provided for the two provinces to form one administrative unit subject to a referendum by the end of 1988. It also accorded Tamil the status of an official language. It envisioned amnesty for militants and their surrender of arms. India promised to provide military assistance to Sri Lanka to implement the agreement. Sri Lanka gave a written undertaking to India that it would not employ foreign military personnel or make the Trincomalee port

BALDEV—SYGMA

Prime Minister Rajiv Gandhi of India (left) and Pres. J. R. Jayawardene of Sri Lanka sign a peace accord on July 29. The accord officially recognized the minority Tamils of Sri Lanka and granted them limited political autonomy.

available to any other country. The next day Gandhi had a narrow escape at the farewell ceremony when a Sri Lankan Navy sailor attacked him with the butt of a rifle. After initially surrendering arms, the LTTE rejected the agreement. Heavy bloodshed followed, and no early solution to the problem was in sight. Jayawardene paid a two-day visit to Delhi in November for talks on implementing the agreement.

Relations with Pakistan continued to be affected by apprehensions about that country's program to produce nuclear weapons. Pres. Mohammad Zia-ul-Haq paid a brief informal visit. Ministerial visits were also exchanged, and there was agreement to increase bilateral contacts. The forces of the two countries clashed on the common border in the Siachen Glacier area of the Karakoram Range. India claimed that 150 Pakistani troops were killed. Both India and China reiterated their desire to find a solution to their border problem.

Relations with the U.S.S.R. remained close. Gandhi's visit to Moscow in July to inaugurate a Festival of India provided the occasion for an exchange of views with Soviet leader Mikhail Gorbachev and the signing of a long-term agreement for cooperation in advanced science and technology. It was also agreed to open an Indian consulate general in Tashkent. Soviet Premier Nikolay Ryzhkov visited Delhi in November to inaugurate a year-long cultural Festival of Russia in India. During Gandhi's visit to the U.S. in October, it was agreed to extend the Indo-U.S. science and technology initiative for a three-year term beyond 1988 and to increase military cooperation. Earlier, the U.S. had issued a license enabling India to import a powerful supercomputer. Gandhi participated in the Commonwealth heads of government meeting at Vancouver, B.C. The Africa Fund, set up under India's chairmanship at the nonaligned movement summit in Zimbabwe in 1986, met in New Delhi in January. India announced a contribution to the fund of Rs 500 million. Gandhi attended the third meeting of the South Asian Association for Regional Cooperation (SAARC) in Nepal, where a convention to combat terrorism was signed. On his way to Canada he conferred with the Japanese prime minister in Tokyo. An extradition treaty was signed with Canada earlier in the year to deal with terrorists.          (H. Y. SHARADA PRASAD)

## MALDIVES

A republic and member of the Commonwealth in the Indian Ocean, the Maldives consists of about 2,000 small islands southwest of the southern tip of India. Area: 298 sq km (115 sq mi). Pop. (1987 est.): 195,000 Cap.: Male. Monetary unit: rufiyaa, with (Oct. 5, 1987) a free rate of 7 rufiyaa to U.S. $1 (11.37 rufiyaa = £1 sterling). President in 1987, Maumoon Abdul Gayoom.

Fishing, tourism, and shipping services remained the chief sources of foreign exchange for Maldives. The economic base was so small, however, that aid remained essential. The 1985–87 development plan concentrated on water improvements—sanitation and the supply of drinking water. The government's attempts to improve conditions in the outlying islands (as opposed to the capital, Male, where 25% of the population lived) produced further economic strains.

The main generator of foreign currency was the fishing industry, which employed two-fifths of the labour force and accounted for 20% of gross national product (GNP). Tourism accounted for 10% of GNP, and the industry expanded further following the introduction in 1984 of direct flights to Europe (the source of 85% of visitors).

Two islands previously reserved for tourists—Villingili and Meerufenfushi—were to be used for housing when the hoteliers' leases expired in 1990. The decision was taken to ease congestion on Male.

Shipping was adversely affected by the Gulf war and trade difficulties. Maldives' main trading partners continued to be Sri Lanka, Singapore, India, Thailand, and Japan.          (GUY ARNOLD)

This article updates the *Macropædia* article INDIAN OCEAN ISLANDS: *Maldives*.

## NEPAL

A constitutional monarchy, Nepal is a landlocked country in the Himalayas between India and the Tibetan Autonomous Region of China. Area: 147,181 sq km (56,827 sq mi). Pop. (1987 est.): 17,567,000. Cap.: Kathmandu. Monetary unit: Nepalese rupee, with (Oct. 5, 1987) a free rate of NRs 20.98 to U.S. $1 (NRs 34.07 = £1 sterling). King, Birendra Bir Bikram Shah Deva; prime minister in 1987, Marich Man Singh Shrestha.

Several events in 1987 served to enhance the international status of Nepal. Kathmandu was inaugurated as the headquarters of the South Asian Association for Regional Cooperation (SAARC), comprising Bangladesh, Bhutan, India, the Maldives, Nepal, Pakistan, and Sri Lanka. Grindlays Bank of the U.K. opened a branch in Nepal, bringing to three the number of foreign banks in the country.

Significant overseas visitors during the year included Japan's Prince Hiro, grandson of Emperor Hirohito, who spent two weeks in Nepal in March, and West German Chancellor Helmut Kohl. King Birendra Bir Bikram Shah Deva toured China in September, making his seventh visit to Beijing (Peking) since he was crowned in 1975.

Little economic progress was made during the year. Agricultural output was constrained by severe flooding and landslides in June that killed at least 98 people and destroyed more than 200 homes. Tourism became increasingly important as a generator of jobs and foreign exchange. More than 223,000 tourists visited Nepal in 1986, 23% more than in 1985 but far short of the one million envisaged for the year 2000. The World Bank and International Monetary Fund provided funding to assist in restructuring the economy.          (DILIP GANGULY)

## PAKISTAN

A federal republic, Pakistan is in the northwestern part of the Indian subcontinent, on the Arabian Sea. Area: 796,095 sq km (307,374 sq mi), excluding the Pakistani-controlled section of Jammu and Kashmir. Pop. (1987 est., including some 3 million Afghan refugees and 1.6 million residents of Pakistani-controlled Jammu and Kashmir): 106,187,000. Cap.: Islamabad. Monetary unit: Pakistan rupee, with (Oct. 5, 1987) a free rate of PRs 17.18 to U.S. $1 (PRs 27.90 = £1 sterling). President in 1987, Gen. Mohammad Zia-ul-Haq; prime minister, Mohammad Khan Junejo.

In 1987 Pakistanis enjoyed the freedom that followed the lifting of martial law in 1985. Although candidates in local elections held on November 30 officially stood without party affiliation, the parties were active in promoting candidates, and the results were seen as the first important test of public opinion since martial law ended. The Pakistan People's Party, led by Benazir Bhutto, ended its boycott and contested the elections but emerged with disappointing results. The Muslim People's Party of Prime Minister Mohammad Khan Junejo was the main victor.

The year was marked by a high level of violence in the form of ethnic riots and terrorist bombings that were particularly serious in Karachi, Lahore, Rawalpindi, Pe-

Ambulances arrive at a crowded shopping bazaar in Karachi, where two bombs had exploded within 20 minutes of each other, killing 75 people and injuring some 300 others.
AFP PHOTO

shawar, and Quetta. More than 200 people were estimated to have been killed. The most serious incident occurred in the port city of Karachi in July when two bombs exploded within 20 minutes in a bazaar and left 75 people dead and some 300 wounded. The government blamed the Afghan secret police KHAD for the attack; it was believed to have been part of a campaign to discredit the Afghan refugees, a theory that was supported by anti-refugee demonstrations in the wake of the Karachi bombing. Criticism that it was not taking measures to stop such terrorism led the government to promulgate an ordinance for quick trials and harsh punishments for terrorists.

Apart from suffering reprisals for the support it gave to the resistance fighters in Afghanistan, Pakistan had problems with India over the disputed Kashmir border. Both countries built up their troops early in the year, and by September there were reports of fighting in the hazardous Karakoram Range. Troops were withdrawn after calls for peace by officials from both countries; the border dispute remained a potential cause for conflict.

Apart from the predictable disputes with its neighbours, Pakistan faced a third, albeit nonviolent, dispute with its traditional ally, the U.S. Shortly after celebrating the 40th anniversary of its independence, Pakistan learned that the U.S. administration had temporarily suspended its six-year aid program; instead of commencing in October, it would not begin until January 1988. There had been considerable pressure in the U.S., particularly from those concerned about nuclear weapons, following the arrest in Philadelphia in July of a Pakistan-born Canadian who allegedly attempted to export to Pakistan a special grade of steel used in nuclear weapons. The U.S. was one of Pakistan's most important trading partners and donated $630 million of aid in 1987. Pakistan was also the route by which the U.S. channeled aid to Muslim guerrillas fighting Soviet troops in Afghanistan, as well as to the three million to four million Afghan refugees who had crossed the border into Pakistan. Pakistan's response to the aid suspension was designed to upset the U.S. It announced a 12-point program that included improved tax collection, import restraint, export expansion, and—most significantly—diversification of foreign trade and extension of commercial links to include more business with socialist countries.

Despite the lifting of martial law, an International Commission of Jurists' report stated that human rights abuses were continuing in Pakistan. The findings were based on a two-week visit to the country in December 1986.

The nation's strong economic performance continued and helped explain the lack of concerted opposition to the government. Industrial growth averaged 9.5% a year in the decade to 1985–86. The share of agriculture in gross domestic product (GDP) had fallen to less than a quarter, while manufacturing had risen to 17.4% and services to nearly half. GDP growth in 1986–87 reached 7% and was expected to be about 6% in 1987–88. Prices were stable, and standards of living continued to rise. Buoyant international demand for all forms of cotton—raw yarn and textiles—boosted exports and, following a record crop in 1987–88 of at least 7.7 million bales (almost 1.4 billion kg [3 billion lb]), Pakistan once again became the world's largest exporter of raw cotton.                    (DILIP GANGULY)

## SRI LANKA

A republic and member of the Commonwealth, Sri Lanka occupies an island in the Indian Ocean off the southeast coast of peninsular India. Area: 65,610 sq km (25,332 sq mi). Pop. (1987 est.): 16,353,000. Legislative and judicial cap., Sri Jayawardenapura; administrative cap., Colombo. Monetary unit: Sri Lanka rupee, with (Oct. 5, 1987) a free rate of SL Rs 29.68 to U.S. $1 (SL Rs 48.20 = £1 sterling). President in 1987, Junius Richard Jayawardene; prime minister, Ranasingne Premadasa.

During 1987 the tension between the Sinhalese and the Tamil community, which wanted greater autonomy for the north and east of Sri Lanka, increased dramatically. War raged in the northeastern regions, and as of midyear some 6,000 lives had been lost since the violence began in 1983. The mainly Hindu Tamils, who made up 18% of Sri Lanka's 16 million population, claimed that the Sinhalese discriminated against them in employment and education. With 50 million Tamils living in its southern state of Tamil Nadu, India continued to play an important role in the search for a peaceful solution to the problem.

A momentous turning point appeared to have been reached when Pres. Junius Richard Jayawardene (see BIOGRAPHIES) and India's Prime Minister Rajiv Gandhi signed a peace accord on July 29. The main points were: an end to hostilities within 48 hours, with arms to be given up by Tamil militants within 72 hours; the Northern and Eastern provinces to form one administrative unit with an elected council within three months; a political amnesty for all Tamil militants; and Tamil and English to share official-language status with Sinhala. India agreed to prevent its territory from being used by Tamil militants—

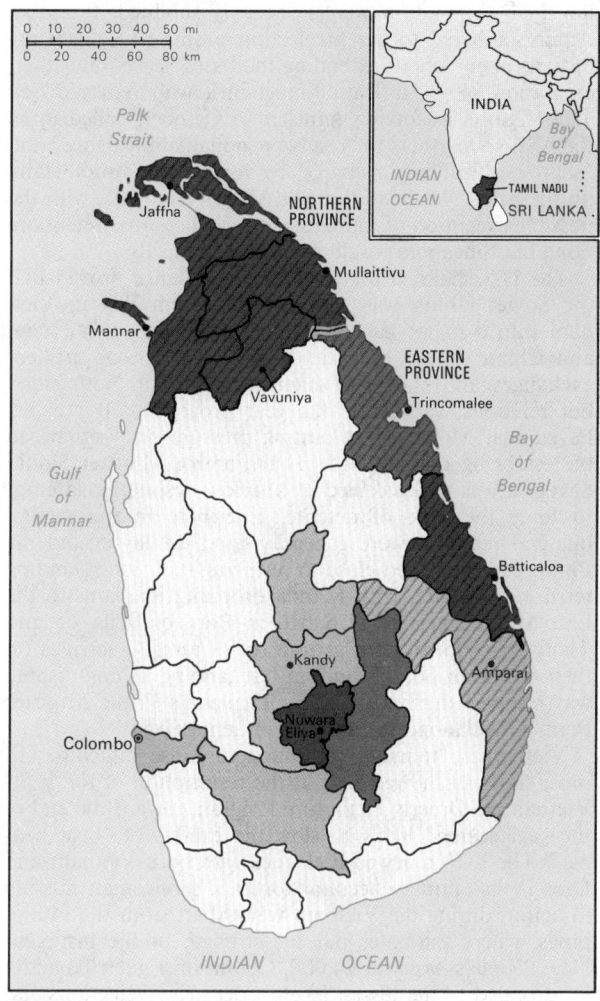

% of Tamil population by district

| | | |
|---|---|---|
| ☐ Less than 10 | ▨ | "Tamil Eelam" Autonomous Region |
| 10–25 | ▬ | Boundary between Northern and Eastern provinces. |
| 25–60 | ▬ | District Boundaries |
| More than 60 | | |

An agreement signed by Sri Lanka and India provided limited autonomy for predominantly Tamil areas of Sri Lanka, where the Hindu Tamil minority was fighting the Buddhist Sinhalese majority. India's interest stemmed from the relationship between Tamils in Sri Lanka and those in the Indian state of Tamil Nadu.

there was substantive evidence to show that they had been given training and shelter there—and to repatriate 130,000 Tamil refugees to Sri Lanka; India was also to provide military assistance to implement the agreement. Sri Lanka in return gave India the right to veto the military use of its ports by foreign powers and agreed to consult India on the employment of foreign military advisers.

The accord was widely opposed both by Tamils and by the Sinhalese, who regarded it as an infringement of Sri Lanka's sovereignty. Many arms were relinquished, but as many were not. The Indian troops sent in to implement the accord numbered more than 10,000 by October, but the result was an increase in bloodshed. An assassination attempt on Jayawardene in the middle of August was made by a previously unknown group claiming it opposed the accord; one member of Parliament was killed and 15 other people were injured, one of whom later died. At the end of September an attempt to salvage the peace accord by recognizing the Tamil group called the Liberation Tigers of

Tamil Eelam as the dominant power in the north and east caused further violence as India ordered its peacekeeping troops to use force to restore order.

On November 12 Parliament approved two bills granting increased autonomy to the Northern and Eastern provinces, as envisaged in the July 29 accord. The move brought intensified violence from Tamil and Sinhalese opponents. A banned Sinhalese group, the People's Liberation Front (JVP), was reported to be responsible for the assassination of the chairman of the ruling United National Party on December 23.

Despite the problems, the economy performed moderately well. An average growth in gross national product (GNP) of 4.7% was achieved in 1981–86. In 1987 GNP growth was expected to fall below 3%. The extended drought badly affected agricultural output, and it was expected that the paddy rice crop might be half the 1986 crop of 2.6 million metric tons. At the same time, cuts in power supplies throughout the country disrupted industrial output. The trade balance deteriorated. In 1986 textile exports rose 21% over the 1985 figure, replacing tea (27.2%) as the country's most important export.

A $10 billion public investment program announced for 1987–91 concentrated on the improvement of irrigation, power, transport, and communications. The country's first totally indigenous bank, the Agro Commercial Bank, started operations late in 1987, unaided by the state. The stock exchange was given increased status with the setting up of a securities commission to ensure professional standards. (DILIP GANGULY)

# Southeast Asia

## SOUTHEAST ASIAN AFFAIRS

The chief focus of diplomatic attention in Southeast Asia during 1987, as in previous years, was the search for an end to the conflict in Kampuchea. The climate for a peaceful settlement seemed more encouraging than at any other time since the Vietnamese Army drove the Khmer Rouge out of Phnom Penh in early 1979. As the year progressed, however, the deteriorating political situation in the Philippines tended to overshadow Indochina as an issue of grave concern, not only in the capitals of neighbouring countries but in Washington and Tokyo. Thus, as fear of Communist aggression spreading from Kampuchea was abating, it was replaced by the threat of destabilization in the Philippines. There were doubts about the government's ability to contain insurgency. For the first time, the possible loss of the two U.S. military bases in the Philippines became a factor in debates about Southeast Asia's security. Fortunately for the governments of the region, neither the Soviet Union nor China was disposed to exploit tensions militarily.

In Vietnam the gradual installation of a more pragmatic, open-minded regime over the first half of the year gave hope of a new flexibility toward reduction or withdrawal of Vietnamese troops in Kampuchea, estimated by the U.S. Defense Department at about 140,000. The Soviet Union, which was footing much of the bill for the occupation forces, appeared responsive to resolving the military impasse, though there were no firm declarations. Soviet leader Mikhail Gorbachev clearly did not wish to be distracted from his restructuring program at home. Moreover, the ascendancy of reformists in China, confirmed at the 13th national Communist Party congress in October, strengthened expectations that the Kampuchea conflict would not be allowed to jeopardize China's own modernization effort. Beijing (Peking) was providing money and matériel for the resistance, especially the Khmer Rouge, the best organized of the three resistance groups fighting the Vietnam-backed Heng Samrin government in Kampuchea.

The U.S. was willing to support a settlement that ensured evacuation of Vietnamese troops but was ill-disposed toward a role for the Khmer Rouge in a coalition government. Japan, too, was eager for a political solution. The Khmer Rouge, led since the eclipse of Pol Pot by Khieu Samphan, was at odds with its two resistance partners— the Sihanoukists, followers of former head of state Prince Norodom Sihanouk, and the Khmer People's National Liberation Front, led by Son Sann. Frustrated by the lack of progress and internal quarreling, Prince Sihanouk, generally considered the only acceptable leader of any compromise coalition, took one year's "leave of absence" in May but was more than once drafted back into the fray.

The Association of Southeast Asian Nations (ASEAN), grouping Indonesia, the Philippines, Thailand, Malaysia, Singapore, and Brunei, kept up sporadic pressure on Vietnam throughout the year. The ASEAN countries, including frontline Thailand, whose army exchanged periodic heavy artillery barrages with Vietnamese troops at the Thai-Laotian-Kampuchean border, were obviously more comfortable with the moderate reformist Nguyen Van Linh (*see* BIOGRAPHIES) as Communist Party general secretary in Vietnam. Nevertheless, they roundly condemned Tokyo for not preventing Japanese companies from taking advantage of Hanoi's trade and investment openings while no concrete settlement for Kampuchea was in sight. They succeeded in having low-level Japanese cooperation with Vietnam put on hold (though there was rapid expansion of ASEAN-Vietnam trade).

Indonesian Foreign Minister Mochtar Kusumaatmadja, the regional bloc's official interlocutor with Vietnam, tirelessly promoted his "cocktail party" plan—a gathering without fixed agenda of all three resistance groups and the Heng Samrin government to explore a peaceful political solution. Mochtar visited Prince Sihanouk in North Korea in July and later had talks in Hanoi with Vietnam's foreign minister, apparently convincing the latter of the usefulness of this approach. Other ASEAN nations, particularly Thailand, expressed reservations, but these and other diplomatic pressures brought about a major breakthrough by the end of the year: a meeting in Paris between Sihanouk and Kampuchean Prime Minister Hun Sen. (See *Kampuchea*, below.)

The six ASEAN heads of government agreed early in the year to meet in Manila in December for their third summit. As the political situation in the Philippines deteriorated, however, fears grew for the safety of the leaders. Heads of government delayed committing themselves to attending but eventually did so after the government of Pres. Corazon Aquino promised the tightest possible security measures. The summit, which took place on December 13–15, was regarded as important primarily for the demonstration of support offered to President Aquino by those attending.

Controversy mounted in the Philippines over the status of the U.S. Air Force base at Clark Field and the U.S. naval base at Subic Bay, both northwest of Manila. No consensus emerged on whether they were providing a bulwark against Communism or exacerbating insurgency. After the August revolt, however, legislators who had been calling

for their elimination were noticeably subdued. President Aquino adhered to her preelection promise to "keep my options open" about extending the bases' leases after their expiration in 1991. Raul Manglapus, who replaced Salvador Laurel as foreign minister in October, called upon the ASEAN partners to "resolve regional ambivalence" and "share political responsibility" by voicing a common stand on the bases. While all the ASEAN governments, with the possible exception of Indonesia, clearly favoured retention, none but Singapore would say so emphatically.

The U.S. claimed that satellite surveillance proved that the Soviet Union was turning Cam Ranh Bay in Vietnam into a major base, but Moscow denied it. Vietnam and China started the year badly, with furious artillery exchanges and claims of high casualties on both sides, but relations warmed as the year progressed. It was believed that Moscow was putting pressure on Vietnam to be less belligerent. In May Thai Foreign Minister Siddhi Savetsila was well received in Moscow despite his attempt to force the pace of détente. Elsewhere in the region, bilateral relations were generally good. Malaysia and the Philippines appeared close to resolving their long-standing territorial dispute, with Manila dropping its claim to the East Malaysian state of Sabah in Borneo. Malaysia and Thailand cooperated in getting rid of jungle guerrillas on their common border, and an outstanding fishing dispute was resolved during a visit by Thailand's Prime Minister Prem Tinsulanond to Malaysia in September.

Vietnamese refugees continued to cause difficulties in most states in the region, but the resumption of the U.S.-Vietnamese Orderly Departure Program toward the end of the year seemed likely to slow the exodus of "boat people." The U.S. renewed dialogues with both Vietnam and Laos in its effort to account for U.S. servicemen missing in action during the Vietnam war. Apart from the Philippines, where estimates put the strength of the insurgent New People's Army at 24,000, Communist guerrilla activity dropped to the lowest level in decades. Defections and defeats reduced the Communist parties of Malaysia and Thailand to a few hundred members each. Some two dozen people were detained in Singapore for alleged connections with the Communist Party of Malaya, but few Singaporeans seriously believed stability was endangered. In Burma both Communist and ethnic-separatist insurgents continued to confront government troops.

An ASEAN ministerial meeting in Singapore in June was also attended by foreign ministers of the "dialogue" countries (the U.S., the European Communities, Japan, Canada, Australia, and New Zealand). U.S. Secretary of State George Shultz warned against declaring Southeast Asia a nuclear-free zone, saying it would undermine U.S. efforts for peace. Only Indonesia and Malaysia still strongly supported the idea rhetorically. In June, as well as at earlier top-level meetings, an attempt was made to put meaningful economic integration on the agenda for the December ASEAN summit. Indonesia continued to oppose the idea on the grounds that it was inappropriate, given existing stages of economic development. The Philippines and Singapore were enthusiastic, while Malaysia and Thailand had reservations. Nevertheless, it was agreed to establish a goal of 50% of intraregional trade to be covered by preferences. It was observed that although some 18,000 items enjoyed preferences, they accounted for a mere 5% of trade. The December summit approved these economic cooperation measures and heard first details of Japan's $2 billion fund for ASEAN aid, announced earlier in the year; the fund was to be used principally for private-sector industrial development. (ROBERT WOODROW)

## BRUNEI

The sultanate of Brunei is located on the northern coast of the island of Borneo, on the South China Sea. Area: 5,765 sq km (2,226 sq mi). Pop. (1987 est.): 241,000. Cap.: Bandar Seri Begawan. Monetary unit: Brunei dollar, with (Oct. 5, 1987) a free rate of Br$2.10 to U.S. $1 (Br$3.41 = £1 sterling). Sultan and prime minister in 1987, Sir Muda Hassanal Bolkiah Mu'izzadin Waddaulah.

Unaccustomed international attention focused on Brunei in May 1987 when it became known that U.S. Assistant Secretary of State Elliot Abrams, who had solicited $10 million from Sultan Hassanal Bolkiah to support the *contra* rebels in Nicaragua, had misplaced the money. An aide in U.S. Pres. Ronald Reagan's National Security Council had inadvertently transposed two digits in a Geneva bank account number, and although the sultan subsequently sued a Swiss businessman for recovery, the amount was dismissed as trivial. The incident generated a spate of press reports about the monarch's wealth. He was believed to be the richest man in the world, with assets of $25 billion.

Brunei was reported to be receptive to joining the Five-Power Defense Arrangement, organized by the U.K. in 1971 after withdrawal of its "east of Suez" forces deployed to confront Indonesia. At the same time, the sultan announced that Brunei would establish a military reserve force. In September Brunei offered a $100 million interest-free loan to Indonesia. The National Bank of Brunei, larger of two local banks and a joint venture between the royal family and Singapore businessman Khoo Teck Puat, was closed down after a dispute involving fraud charges.

(ROBERT WOODROW)

This article updates the *Macropædia* article EAST INDIES: *Brunei.*

## BURMA

Burma is a people's republic of Southeast Asia with coastlines on the Bay of Bengal and the Andaman Sea. Area: 676,577 sq km (261,228 sq mi). Pop. (1987 est.): 39,191,000. Cap.: Rangoon. Monetary unit: kyat, with (Oct. 5, 1987) a free rate of 6.70 kyats to U.S. $1 (10.89 kyats = £1 sterling). Chairman of the State Council in 1987, U San Yu; prime minister, U Maung Maung Kha.

The Burmese political and economic situation reached a new low in 1987, just four decades after independence. Twenty-five years of the "Burmese Road to Socialism" under the charismatic leader Gen. U Ne Win had brought the country—once the richest in Southeast Asia—to unprecedented levels of poverty and isolation from the outside world. Guerrilla insurgency persisted throughout the year, sapping the country's slim financial resources. Government troops killed 640 pro-Communist forces and suffered 175 deaths in four months of particularly bloody offensives on the Chinese border.

Long-overdue recognition of its economic plight was reflected in Burma's request to the UN that it be given least developed country status. In August Ne Win called on leaders to draw up legal and economic reforms. Farmers, unable to survive on the low government prices paid for rice, had begun to leave the land; prospects of severe food shortages prompted the lifting, in September, of 21-year-old controls on internal trade in rice and other foods in an effort to stimulate production.

A financial crisis occurred as foreign exchange reserves dwindled and Burma's foreign debt ran out of control. In an effort to regulate the burgeoning black market,

A woman receives alms near a pagoda in Rangoon. Burma's per capita annual income reached an all-time low of about $190, and the government asked the UN to classify it among the world's least developed countries.
FRED R. CONRAD/THE NEW YORK TIMES

the government, on September 5, declared illegal Burma's largest denominations of currency notes, leaving the highest worth only 15 kyats ($1 = 40 kyats minimum on the black market). The action provoked serious student riots in Rangoon, to which the government responded by closing all schools and universities indefinitely. The unrest was the worst since 1974.

(DILIP GANGULY)

## INDONESIA

A republic of Southeast Asia, Indonesia consists of the major islands of Sumatra, Java, Kalimantan (Indonesian Borneo), Celebes, and Irian Jaya (West New Guinea) and approximately 3,000 smaller islands and islets. Area: 1,919,443 sq km (741,101 sq mi). Pop. (1987 est.): 172,245,000. (Area and population figures include East [former Portuguese] Timor.) Cap.: Jakarta. Monetary unit: rupiah, with (Oct. 5, 1987) a free rate of 1,649 rupiah to U.S. $1 (2,677 rupiah = £1 sterling). President in 1987, Suharto.

The early part of 1987 was dominated by the April 23 parliamentary elections. The result was an overwhelming victory for the government-backed Golkar, which captured 73% of the vote, compared with 64% in the 1982 elections. The fundamentalist Muslim United Development Party (PPP) remained the major opposition party, but its share of the vote declined from 28 to 16%. Major progress was made by the Indonesian Democratic Party, which increased its support from 8 to 11%, with most of the gains in Jakarta, where the electorate was more critical of the government. (For tabulated results, see *Political Parties*, above.) The preelection period was comparatively peaceful, although there were predictable charges of fraud against the government after the election.

Presidential elections were scheduled for 1988, and although there had been a gradual transfer of power to the younger generation, Suharto was expected to stand for another term; by that time he would have completed 20 years as president. Senior government posts were being filled by civilians, and the military image of government was disappearing. Political discontent was largely limited to Jakarta, where the main issue was corruption.

Supporters of the government-backed Golkar gather at Senayan Sports Complex for a final campaign rally for Indonesia's parliamentary elections. The April elections brought a resounding victory for the Golkar, which captured a strong 73% of the vote.
AP/WIDE WORLD

Relations with Portugal over the controversial Indonesian province of East Timor (once a Portuguese colony) eased during the year, and in September the Portuguese government, for the first time, did not include in its program the commitment to self-determination for the people of East Timor. Migration from Java to other islands proceeded. The domestic satellite broadcasting system was threatened with technical failure until the U.S State Department intervened to secure a launch slot for a second satellite on a National Aeronautics and Space Administration Delta rocket ahead of a Pentagon payload.

The economy performed better in 1986 than had been expected, with gross domestic product (GDP) increasing by 2.5%. Economic growth was expected to reach 2% in 1987, helped by improved oil and other commodity prices as well as by increased exports of manufactured goods. Following a substantial devaluation of the rupiah in 1986, financial confidence waned, and fear of a further devaluation led to a flight of capital from the country. The government took measures to stop the outflow; interest rates were pegged among the highest in the world (prime lending rate of 25% on September 21) in order to hold investors' interest and stop the purchase of dollars. Despite the lack of confidence in the local financial markets and a large external debt, which some estimates put at over $30 billion, international confidence in Indonesia remained as strong as ever. This was reflected in the promise of $3.2 billion in foreign aid for 1987.

Restructuring of the economy proceeded, albeit more slowly than in the 1970s and early 1980s, when heavy inflows of revenue from oil exports could fund development. More measures were taken to attract foreign investment, particularly in the manufacturing sector, and to encourage industry in less developed areas where there was a particular need to create jobs. Industrial practices were simplified to allow companies to switch products without ministerial approval. The government appeared to recognize that it could no longer depend on high oil revenues and that it must shift the economy away from its agricultural base, which still generated a quarter of GDP and employed more than half the labour force. Early in the year the 215 state-owned companies were instructed to produce accounts for the previous five years in preparation for privatization and possible liquidation of unprofitable firms. Moves were also made to put life into the traditionally dormant stock market.                              (ROBERT WOODROW)

This article updates the *Macropædia* article EAST INDIES: *Indonesia*.

## KAMPUCHEA

A people's republic of Southeast Asia, Kampuchea occupies the southwestern part of the Indochinese Peninsula, on the Gulf of Thailand. Area: 181,035 sq km (69,898 sq mi). Pop. (1987 est.): 7,688,000. Cap.: Phnom Penh. Monetary unit: riel. Secretary-general of the People's Revolutionary (Communist) Party of Kampuchea and chairman of the Council of State (president) in 1987, Heng Samrin; chairman of the Council of Ministers (prime minister), Hun Sen.

The signs of an end to Kampuchea's long armed struggle were more positive in 1987 than at any other time since the Vietnamese occupation began nine years earlier. In response to new overtures, Vietnam did not automatically rule out peace talks that would include the China-backed Khmer Rouge (KR), largest of the three resistance movements that made up the UN-recognized Coalition Government of Democratic Kampuchea (CGDK). In May CGDK president Prince Norodom Sihanouk, declaring himself exasperated with the lack of progress and disillusioned with his allies, announced his "irrevocable" decision to take "leave of absence" for a year. By August, however, he had made a "special exception" to attend a Beijing (Peking) meeting chaired by Chinese Premier Zhao Ziyang (Chao Tzu-yang). There he had talks with Son Sann, leader of the Khmer People's National Liberation Front (KPNLF), and Khieu Samphan, head of the KR.

Vietnam maintained a tight grip on the country with its 140,000-strong occupying army, despite some publicized withdrawals of battalions and reports of disaffection among its troops. The Hanoi-bolstered Heng Samrin government in Phnom Penh fielded an army of 35,000, but monitored radio broadcasts urging soldiers to grow food and conserve supplies indicated that it was underfed and poorly equipped. It suffered steady attrition through desertion to the Sihanoukist forces, about 10,000 strong and commanded by the former monarch's son, Prince Norodom Ranariddh. Son Sann's KPNLF was also believed to have 10,000 men in the field, though dissidents loyal to Gen. Sak Sutsakhan, who had been commander in chief of the KPNLF until early 1986, effectively split the movement. The factions claimed they had patched up differences in April. The KR, with 40,000 men, remained the largest, best equipped, and best financed guerrilla force. Pol Pot, leader of the KR regime in 1975–78, was reported to be ill, but this might have been a smoke screen. All parties had vowed never to negotiate with him.

Of crucial importance was the U.S.S.R.'s new Asia policy under Mikhail Gorbachev, which included an apparently earnest effort to urge Vietnam to seek a compromise. In January Sihanouk asserted unequivocally that an approach from Hanoi, indicating a willingness to negotiate a cease-fire with all three resistance groups, had been made to him through Pres. Nicolae Ceausescu of Romania. After a short delay, Vietnam denied that it had made the offer. Sihanouk favoured a meeting but said it would be point-less without the Khmer Rouge. In March Soviet Foreign Minister Eduard Shevardnadze, visiting Bangkok and In-donesia before going on to Hanoi, urged conciliation. In December Sihanouk and Hun Sen, prime minister in the Heng Samrin government, held three days of talks near Paris. Although little of substance emerged, the discussions were described as amicable. At year's end the conditions for formal negotiations were under discussion.

Vietnam's Foreign Minister Nguyen Co Thach con-firmed the willingness of Vietnam, Kampuchea, and Laos to hold talks with China and the Association of Southeast Asian Nations (ASEAN). The Thais were opposed to a forum that lacked preconditions, though Indonesia's peri-patetic foreign minister, Mochtar Kusumaatmadja, princi-pal supporter of the "cocktail party" solution (an informal gathering without a preset agenda), seemed receptive.

The economy remained in total disarray, made worse by the drought that affected all of Southeast Asia and presaged food shortages. Following Vietnam's lead, the government put into effect certain free market reforms that proved popular. A satellite ground station installed by the U.S.S.R. facilitated international telephone and telex links—the first since 1975. A trickle of tourists, the first in more than a decade, visited the capital and the temple of Angkor Wat, which was undergoing a $10 million restoration by experts from India.                                    (ROBERT WOODROW)

This article updates the *Macropædia* article Mainland SOUTH-EAST ASIA: *Kampuchea.*

## LAOS

A landlocked people's republic, Laos is in the northern part of the Indochinese Peninsula. Area: 236,800 sq km (91,400 sq mi). Pop. (1987 est.): 3,757,000. Cap.: Vientiane. Monetary unit: new kip, with (Oct. 5, 1987) a par value of 35 kip to U.S. $1 (free rate of 56.84 kip = £1 sterling). President in 1987 (interim), Phoumi Vongvichit; chairman of the Council of Ministers (prime minister), Kaysone Phomvihan.

Though the dominant political influence in the domestic affairs of Laos was the continuing presence of some 40,000 Vietnamese troops, the main focus of foreign policy re-mained Thailand, which had a historically strong cultural influence and continued to be the country's most impor-tant trading partner. In late 1986 relations had seemed to be improving, but the visit to Bangkok in March of Deputy Foreign Minister Soubanh Srithirath produced no encouraging results. Since 1984 the two nations had been involved in a border dispute. In August 1987 a Laotian platoon clashed briefly with Thai soldiers, and a diplo-matic confrontation occurred over the seizure by Laotian authorities of seven villagers.

Thai Foreign Minister Siddhi Savetsila declined to visit Laos but said in September that Thailand would try in "every possible way" to improve relations. Laos accused Thailand of supporting right-wing Lao guerrillas and of complicity in a bomb explosion that marred a visit in March by Soviet Foreign Minister Eduard Shevardnadze. During the year the Thai government reduced from 273 to 61 the items banned in cross-river trade. A road linking

the Laotian capital and the Vietnamese port of Da Nang was scheduled for completion by the end of the year; its purpose was to reduce economic dependence on Thailand.

In global diplomacy Laos remained more neutral than its neighbours, Vietnam and Kampuchea. China's deputy foreign minister visited in January, and in December the two countries agreed to exchange ambassadors. The U.S. reached an agreement with the Laotian government in De-cember to step up the search for the remains of 549 U.S. Air Force personnel missing in action (MIAs) during the war in Vietnam (Laos insisted that no MIAs were alive). In return, the U.S. said it would "respond within the limits of its capabilities" to the Laotians' humanitarian concerns.

The year marked the fading from the scene of "Red Prince" Souphanouvong, replaced as president of the Lao Front for National Reconstruction, his last post of conse-quence, by acting president Phoumi Vongvichit. Political reform that was expected after the fourth party congress of November 1986 was stymied by factional differences.

A commercial dispute over electricity generated by a hydroelectric dam north of Vientiane and sold to Thailand threatened already meagre foreign exchange. In September the Thai authorities disconnected the power after failing to get a favourable price. An agreement was promptly concluded. It was announced that a second dam would be built in the far south with financing from the Asian Development Bank and assistance from Sweden. Thailand was to buy the electricity after 1991. The currency was devalued in September to boost exports and deter black market operations.                           (ROBERT WOODROW)

This article updates the *Macropædia* article Mainland SOUTH-EAST ASIA: *Laos.*

## MALAYSIA

A federal constitutional monarchy of Southeast Asia and member of the Commonwealth, Malaysia consists of the former Federation of Malaya at the southern end of the Malay Peninsula (excluding Singapore) and Sabah and Sarawak on the northern part of the island of Borneo. Area: 330,434 sq km (127,581 sq mi). Pop. (1987 est.): 16,538,000. Cap.: Kuala Lumpur. Monetary unit: ringgit, with (Oct. 5, 1987) a free rate of 2.55 ringgits to U.S. $1 (4.13 ringgits = £1 sterling). Supreme head of state in 1987, with the title of *yang di-pertuan agong,* Tuanku Mahmood Iskandar ibni al-Marhum Sultan Ismail; prime minister, Datuk Seri Mahathir bin Mohamad.

Datuk Seri Mahathir bin Mohamad, prime minister of Malaysia since 1981, came within a whisker of being dropped as leader of the politically dominant United Malays National Organization (UMNO) in fierce and divi-sive polling by some 1,500 delegates at the party's triennial congress in April 1987. A challenge by Trade and Industry Minister Razaleigh Hamzah was supported by the powerful former deputy premier, Musa Hitam. Musa himself was narrowly defeated for the post of deputy president by Gha-far Baba, a Mahathir ally. Mahathir offered no conciliation to his opponent's supporters and, as a result, Razaleigh and former foreign minister Rais Yatim resigned. Three other ministers and four deputy ministers were promptly fired.

A constitutional crisis loomed in August when 84-year-old Tunku Abdul Rahman, Malaysia's first prime minister, supported suggestions by groups of intellectuals that the constitutional immunity from processes of law of the nine hereditary sultans, who elect one of their number to serve as king for a five-year term, be modified. The incumbent, Sultan Mahmood Iskandar of Johore, had been tried for unlawful killing before becoming king, and Malaysians un-derstood that the Tunku, himself the son of a sultan of Kedah, was referring to some of the king's recent actions in advocating the constitutional change. The deputy king, the sultan of Perak, supported the Tunku's move. The prime minister and other leading Malay politicians of his faction rejected it. There may have been a degree of personal animosity involved, as Mahathir had been removed from UMNO by the Tunku in 1969.

There were political crises in both of Malaysia's Borneo states. Sabah's relations with the federal government deteriorated over the contention by some state politicians that the 20-point formula under which the then-British North Borneo had become a part of Malaysia in 1963 was not being observed. (Sabah and Sarawak, where Muslims had no clear majority, were guaranteed more autonomy in their education, religion, and immigration policies than the 11 peninsular states.) Veteran Sabah politician and former chief minister Mustapha Harun returned to politics after winning a by-election, but state politics remained firmly under the control of the mainly Christian Parti Bersatu Sabah. In Sarawak the ongoing political feud between Chief Minister Taib Mahmud and his uncle, former governor Rahman Yakub, led to a dissolution of the state assembly and an inconclusive election that left Taib still in command.

By October a row over a highway-construction contract was threatening the delicate fabric of Malaysia's race-based politics. Lim Kit Siang, head of the Democratic Action Party and leader of the parliamentary opposition, obtained an injunction preventing the award of the multibillion-dollar contract to a company controlled by UMNO after satisfying a judge that he had admissible evidence of corruption. Late in October Lim and more than 100 other critics of the administration were arrested. Three newspapers were closed, and in early November the government introduced a bill tightening curbs on the press. About half the detainees were released, but at year's end it was announced that 33, including Lin, had been placed under two-year detention.

At the end of the year, the economy showed signs of emerging from two years of recession. Gross domestic product increased by some 1% in 1986, and the rate was expected to have doubled in 1987. The manufacturing sector and commodities were doing well, but finance and commerce remained mired in a series of confidence-shaking scandals resulting from disastrous property speculation on a gigantic scale. There was a serious oversupply of office buildings and hotels.                              (ROBERT WOODROW)

This article updates the *Macropædia* article Mainland SOUTHEAST ASIA: *Malaysia*.

## PHILIPPINES

Situated in the western Pacific Ocean off the southeast coast of Asia, the republic of the Philippines consists of an archipelago of about 7,100 islands. Area: 300,000 sq km (115,800 sq mi). Pop (1987 est.): 57,357,000. Cap.: Manila. Monetary unit: Philippine peso, with (Oct. 5, 1987) a free rate of 20.01 pesos to U.S. $1 (32.50 pesos = £1 sterling). President in 1987, Corazon Aquino.

In a plebiscite on Feb. 2, 1987, Filipino voters approved a new constitution by more than three to one. It restored a system that comprised a strong presidency and a two-house Congress, which had existed until Pres. Ferdinand E. Marcos abolished it in 1973. Corazon C. Aquino, who succeeded Marcos in 1986, was confirmed by the constitution as president until June 30, 1992. After that, presidents would be elected for six-year terms and would not be eligible for reelection.

Elections on May 11 chose 200 members of a new 250-member House of Representatives and 24 senators. A coalition of Aquino supporters known as Laban won 162 House seats and 22 Senate seats. With her backing, Ramon Mitra was chosen as speaker of the House. Jovito Salonga, who had won the most votes in nationwide polling for senators, was chosen as Senate president, thus becoming the nation's third-ranking official, after Aquino and Vice-Pres. Salvador H. Laurel.

The power to govern by decree that Aquino had assumed shortly after becoming president lapsed when the new Congress opened on July 27. She had signed 302 decrees—42 of them in the last 24 hours before Congress convened. One of the most important established an Agrarian Reform Council to redistribute not only large rice and corn farms but also—for the first time—sugarcane and coconut lands. Reform was intended to reduce rural poverty, thereby undercutting the appeal of Communist guerrillas, but some big landowners vowed to fight it. Farmers' groups

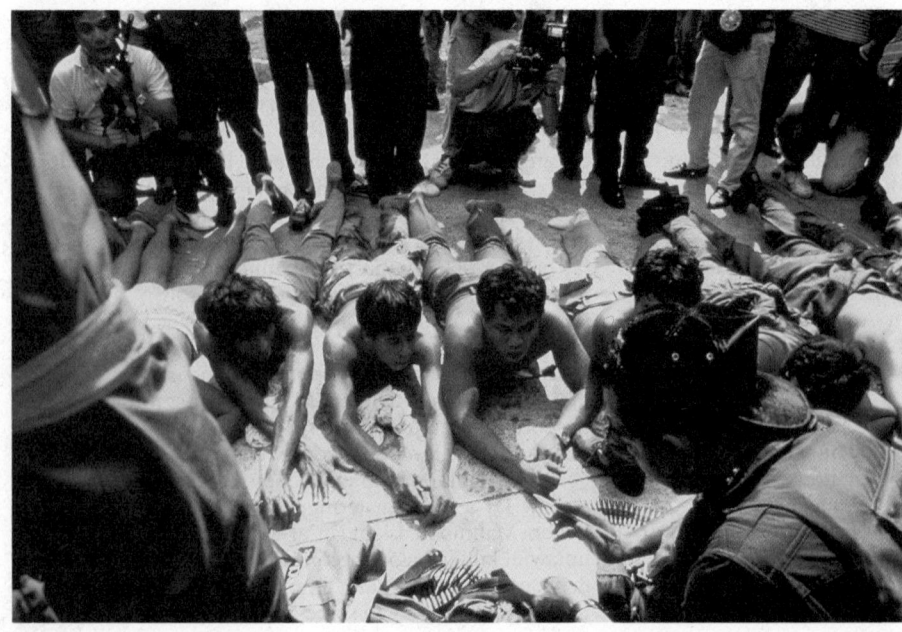

SIPA

A group of Filipino rebels are captured after Col. Gregorio Honasan's unsuccessful coup attempt against Pres. Corazon Aquino.

and others criticized the reform as insufficient. The decree left it to the new Congress to work out politically sensitive details.

Despite the creation of new institutions, the political situation remained unstable. Some observers blamed Aquino, calling her indecisive and too soft on the Communists. On January 27, July 13, and August 28, rebellious troops tried unsuccessfully to seize power. On August 28 more than 50 persons were killed when the rebels attacked the presidential palace and took over other key points. The coup leader, Col. Gregorio Honasan (see BIOGRAPHIES), escaped capture as loyal troops and police rallied to Aquino's support, but he was captured in late October.

Aquino responded to pressure to improve governmental efficiency by making Cabinet changes. On September 16 Laurel resigned the post of foreign secretary but remained vice-president. The next day two key aides whom the military accused of hindering the anti-Communist struggle were fired. The Cabinet secretary for local government, Jaime Ferrer, was murdered on August 2, and on September 19 a prominent leftist leader, Leandro Alejandro, was assassinated. Neither group of killers was identified. In January and again in July, the U.S. acted to prevent Marcos, who was living in Hawaii, from trying to return to the Philippines in an attempt to take power.

Aquino's efforts to negotiate peace with the Communist New People's Army (NPA) failed, and the guerrillas stepped up operations in 1987. Officials estimated that about 25,000 guerrillas controlled a fifth of the country's 42,000 villages. The NPA, with the advantage of surprise, conducted numerous ambushes and sometimes carried fighting into the towns. Anti-Communist vigilantes became strong in Mindanao and some other areas where governmental authority was weak. Communist guerrillas were suspected in the shooting deaths of two U.S. airmen, a retired U.S. serviceman, and a Filipino businessman in separate attacks near Clark Air Base on October 28. Muslim separatists in the southern islands continued to defy the government despite Aquino's peace efforts. One Muslim leader, Nur Misuari, said on September 8 that they would set up a provisional government within a year.

Although poverty remained widespread, economic conditions improved during 1987 as a result of increased investment, a construction boom, and higher prices for sugar and coconut products. However, the foreign debt of some $26 billion from the Marcos era remained a major burden, limiting development programs. Uncertainty over land reform inhibited investment late in the year.

(HENRY S. BRADSHER)

## SINGAPORE

Singapore, a republic of Southeast Asia and member of the Commonwealth, occupies a group of islands, the largest of which is Singapore, at the southern extremity of the Malay Peninsula. Area: 622 sq km (240 sq mi). Pop. (1987 est.): 2,616,000. Monetary unit: Singapore dollar, with (Oct. 5, 1987) a free rate of S$2.10 to U.S. $1 (S$3.41 = £1 sterling). President in 1987, Wee Kim Wee; prime minister, Lee Kuan Yew.

Domestic affairs in 1987 were tinged with drama. On May 26 it was announced that Singapore's Internal Security Department had "uncovered a Marxist conspiracy to subvert the existing social and political system" in order to "establish a Communist state." Official reports stated that five days earlier 16 people had been detained, including several lay workers for Roman Catholic organizations. On June 20 there were six more arrests. None of the accused was brought to trial, and the government said it had no

intention of doing so. Among the detainees were members of a theatre group, the Law Society, and the opposition Workers' Party. By mid-October, 16 of the 22 had been released, but activities of all but one were restricted. The man named by the government as "mastermind" of the conspiracy, Tan Wah Piow, was said to have "fled to the U.K. in 1976." Protests abroad about the detentions were relatively muted.

Workers' Party General Secretary J. B. Jeyaretnam was fined S$5,000 by Parliament for abuse of privilege and contempt while still a member. Jeyaretnam, one of only two opposition members elected to Parliament in the December 1984 elections, had been expelled in 1986 following his conviction for misuse of party funds. It was revealed that the death in December 1986 of former National Development Minister Teh Cheang Wan was by suicide and that at the time he was being investigated for corruption.

Prime Minister Lee Kuan Yew predicted that the declining birthrate would have dire consequences, and there was an ongoing campaign to encourage marriage and larger families. A $9,500 tax rebate for families having a third child marked a reversal of the government's long-standing policy of encouraging families to stop at two; fears of a labour shortage prompted the policy change.

The economy made an impressive recovery from the relatively sluggish 1.9% increase in gross domestic product in 1986 to an expected 5%. Strong export growth was led by sales of electronic components and computer-related products. A government committee recommended a massive program of privatization affecting 41 firms, to take place over ten years. The tourist industry registered a strong revival, although hotel overcapacity continued as the strengthening of the Singapore dollar deterred some tourists and shoppers.                    (ROBERT WOODROW)

This article updates the *Macropædia* article Mainland SOUTHEAST ASIA: *Singapore*.

## THAILAND

Thailand is a constitutional monarchy in Southeast Asia, on the Andaman Sea and the Gulf of Thailand. Area: 513,115 sq km (198,115 sq mi). Pop. (1987 est.): 53,722,000. Cap.: Bangkok. Monetary unit: baht, with (Oct. 5, 1987) a free rate of 25.49 baht to U.S. $1 (41.40 baht = £1 sterling). King, Bhumibol Adulyadej; prime minister in 1987, Gen. Prem Tinsulanond.

For most Thais 1987 was dominated by the year-long series of festivities that preceded the highly auspicious 60th birthday of King Bhumibol Adulyadej on December 5. The hugely successful "Visit Thailand Year," which was promoted in conjunction with the birthday celebrations, was extended until July 2, 1988. It was expected to surpass its target of three million tourists, restoring a measure of prosperity to the hotel industry, long plagued by overcapacity. The position of Crown Prince Maha Vajiralongkorn, 35, in the line of succession to the throne was consolidated during the year. For some time the prince had appeared to be eclipsed by his younger sister, Princess Maha Chakri Sirindhorn. Standing in for his father (who had not left the kingdom since the 1960s), he visited Beijing (Peking) in February and met Chinese leader Deng Xiaoping (Teng Hsiao-p'ing). His visit to Japan in October, however, was marred by breaches of protocol, and he cut short his stay.

In domestic politics the most significant trend was the rise in influence of the commander in chief of the Army, Chaovalit Yongchaiyuth. Contrary to expectations at the time of his appointment in May 1986, Chaovalit became increasingly outspoken in political affairs, giving rise to speculation that he had ambitions to succeed Gen. Prem

Members of the military present Thailand's commander in chief of the Army, Gen. Chaovalit Yongchaiyuth (right), with flowers, a traditional show of support. Chaovalit's public statements increased speculation that he might wish to succeed Gen. Prem Tinsulanond as prime minister.
THE BANGKOK POST/THE NEW YORK TIMES

Tinsulanond as prime minister when Prem's term of office ended in 1990. In February Chaovalit spoke contemptuously of political parties and called for reform, using the emotion-laden term *patiwat*, which could be interpreted as coup d'état as well as social evolution. In April elder statesman and former prime minister Kukrit Pramoj made a disparaging speech about Chaovalit's ambitions and was promptly threatened by paramilitary personnel, who laid siege to his home. Soon afterward, some 400 influential army officers demonstrated their support for Chaovalit. Prem increasingly distanced himself from the political fray. The Democrats, largest party in the four-member coalition government, were badly divided between the mainstream wing led by Deputy Prime Minister Bhichai Rattakul and members of the "January 10" faction. Since Chaovalit had pledged to step down in 1988, the appointment of a new army deputy commander in the annual military reshuffle in October was especially significant. The post went to Gen. Wanchai Ruangtrakul, who had not been regarded as a front-runner.

In March China agreed to sell Thailand, for a "friendship price," T-69 battle tanks and other Chinese weapons for use in confronting Vietnam. At the start of the year, the U.S. and Thailand had announced plans to set up a joint munitions stockpile starting in 1988. Fierce but inconclusive engagements took place between the Thai Army and Vietnamese forces, entrenched in hilly positions at Chong Bok Pass, where the Thai, Laotian, and Kampuchean frontiers converge. Casualties were reportedly heavy, but the number was not disclosed. There was a brief engagement with Laotian soldiers in August at another disputed border location. Thai Communist insurgency continued to decline. In the south some 540 guerrillas surrendered between March and May under an amnesty. In April a special operations group arrested 18 leaders of the Communist Party of Thailand, including Politburo members.

Thailand's economy in 1987 recorded one of the best performances in the less developed world, with gross national product growth expected to reach 6%, compared with 3.8% in 1986. Exports were up 25% in U.S. dollar terms, and though imports rose even more, the trade deficit was small. With strong foreign investment, especially from Japan and Taiwan, the balance of payments was comfortably in surplus, and the declining foreign debt remained manageable. (ROBERT WOODROW)

This article updates the *Macropædia* article Mainland SOUTH-EAST ASIA: *Thailand*.

## VIETNAM

The socialist republic of Vietnam occupies the eastern part of the Indochinese Peninsula in Southeast Asia and is bounded on the south and east by the South China Sea. Area: 331,653 sq km (128,052 sq mi). Pop. (1987 est.): 62,468,000. Cap.: Hanoi. Monetary unit: dong, with (Oct. 5, 1987) a par value of 80 dong to U.S. $1 (free rate of 129.80 dong = £1 sterling). General secretary of the Communist Party in 1987, Nguyen Van Linh; chairmen of the State Council (presidents), Truong Chinh and, from June 18, Vo Chi Cong; chairmen of the Council of Ministers, Pham Van Dong and, from June 18, Pham Hung.

Many of Vietnam's old revolutionaries were removed from office in 1987. The faithful comrades of Ho Chi Minh, who had guided the North to victory and, after 1975, imposed Marxism on the conquered South, had become thoroughly discredited. Critics, not only among the people but within the Communist Party, wanted change, and the U.S.S.R., tired of being paymaster for an ineffectual government, applied discreet pressure. The sixth party congress in December 1986 ousted the old guard, declaring it had failed to raise living standards, curb inflation, check corruption, or modify a rigid, doctrinaire outlook on society. Reformist Nguyen Van Linh (*see* BIOGRAPHIES) replaced 79-year-old Truong Chinh as general secretary of the party and effective head of the nation. He promptly set in motion a massive overhaul of party and government that continued throughout 1987.

The congress secured the resignation from the 13-member Politburo of elderly hard-liners Le Duc Tho (who with Henry Kissinger had been awarded the 1973 Nobel Peace Prize) and Pham Van Dong, chairman since 1955 of the Council of Ministers of first North, then unified Vietnam. Dong remained chairman and Chinh state president until after the general elections in April for a new National Assembly. In February the reformists engineered a total revamp of the Cabinet. Ousted was Defense Minister Gen. Van Tien Dung, conqueror of Saigon, replaced by Le Duc Anh, commander of forces in Kampuchea. Mai Chi Tho, a former mayor of Ho Chi Minh City and brother of Le Duc Tho, was made interior minister. He replaced party veteran Pham Hung, who was, however, chosen as chairman of the Council of Ministers in June by the Assembly. Some saw his appointment—he was closely identified with the old regime—as a brake on the reformist tide. Foreign Minister Nguyen Co Thach was given the concurrent post of deputy chairman, and Vo Chi Cong was made president.

People wait in line outside a Hanoi department store for staples such as tobacco, sugar, and salt. Chronic shortages, symptoms of Vietnam's depressed economy and low level of technology, attest to the country's need for changes, popularly termed "national renovation."

JIM BRYANT—GAMMA LIAISON

Corrupt and incompetent cadres and functionaries were put on trial for bribery, embezzlement, and "decadence." Linh effected liberal economic and social reforms, among them allowing a choice in the April 19 elections from among 829 approved candidates, chosen at open meetings, for the 496 seats. In May Linh visited Moscow and was well received by Soviet leader Mikhail Gorbachev. He reportedly committed himself to more efficient use of an estimated $1 billion a year (in rubles) in economic aid, and a larger amount in military aid, which Vietnam received from the U.S.S.R. Under an amnesty in September, 480 senior civil servants and army officers of the previous government of South Vietnam were released from reeducation camps, along with 6,205 other detainees. Yet there were also condemnations of capitalism, a tightening of party discipline, and a crackdown on extra-party dissent. Certain Catholic groups were harassed; priests were arrested in July and tried in October. In December, 17 people were sentenced to prison for attempting an invasion, allegedly with U.S. and Thai support.

A concerted effort was made to harness the entrepreneurial spirit of the South. A measure of economic freedom was granted to industry, and central planning was lessened. Small businesses were encouraged, even in the North, where private wealth had been nationalized in the 1950s. Western and Japanese investors were wooed with incentives, and trade with non-Communist countries was vigorously promoted. A law passed in December removed long-standing obstacles to foreign investment.

A start was made on creating a tourist industry, and the first trickle of adventurous foreigners sampled the spartan facilities. There was a drive to coax airlines to call at Ho Chi Minh City. Currency-reform measures, already painful, were strengthened to control inflation and suppress the black market. The reforms, especially freer agricultural markets, proved popular with the public, though bureaucrats who lost privileges complained. In September, however, Linh admitted that the reforms had not put an end to "disastrous" inflation. In October Vietnam's first commercial bank was opened.

President Vo Chi Cong made a new call in October for normal relations with China. In May the transport minister had attended an international railway conference in Beijing (Peking), the first visit to China by a high-ranking member of the government since the fierce border war of

1979. However, 1987 had opened with savage fighting at the frontier. Hanoi reported that 74,000 artillery shells were fired by China and claimed that its army had killed 1,500 Chinese troops in repelling an invasion. China dismissed this as boasting, but with no independent observers, there was no way to verify claims.

The commander of the U.S. Pacific Fleet, visiting Sydney, Australia, in February, said U.S. Navy photographs proved that a Soviet military buildup was taking place at Cam Ranh Bay, but Moscow denied it. Though by October there was little to show for its effort, Vietnam seemed more open to a negotiated settlement of the war in Kampuchea. Vietnam had 140,000 troops there, according to the U.S. State Department. In October Hanoi announced a major pullout, thought to involve 20,000 soldiers. However, this was treated with caution by Southeast Asian governments, which considered previous "withdrawals" to have been troop rotations.

There was a thaw in relations with the U.S. The new government in Hanoi exploited to maximum effect its only bargaining tool—the desire of U.S. politicians to account for the 1,776 U.S. servicemen missing after the U.S. withdrawal. Nguyen Van Linh called assertions that some were still alive "absurd." After months of negotiation, a special envoy of U.S. Pres. Ronald Reagan, Gen. John Vessey, Jr., arrived in Hanoi on August 1. Desperate for foreign exchange, Western loans, and aid, and evidently less wedded under Linh to old-style strident rhetoric, Vietnam agreed "to work methodically and seriously to solve humanitarian issues of both sides." The word reparations was carefully avoided, but Hanoi wanted finance for its "war-related humanitarian concerns." Progress was also made in repatriating "Amerasians," the adolescent and young-adult children fathered by U.S. servicemen. Following Vessey's visit, the stalled Orderly Departure Program for emigrants was reinstated.                    (ROBERT WOODROW)

This article updates the *Macropædia* article Mainland SOUTHEAST ASIA: *Vietnam.*

# Western Europe

## WESTERN EUROPEAN AFFAIRS

The year that marked the 30th anniversary of the signing of the Treaty of Rome—the treaty founding the European Economic Community (EEC, which together with the European Coal and Steel Community [ECSC] and Euratom made up the European Communities [EC])—was also one of considerable internal stress over the future reform of the EC's finances and spending policies. However, 1987 also saw the belated adoption of the most significant constitutional amendment to the Treaty of Rome since 1957.

The Single European Act (SEA), which entered into force in July, was intended to increase the effectiveness of the EC's sometimes cumbersome decision-making processes. In the future more decisions were to be taken by the Council of Ministers, representing the 12 member states of the EC, on a majority vote basis, not subject to a single country's veto. Moreover, the directly elected European Parliament was given increased consultative rights as well as some modest additional powers. The SEA was finally adopted after being approved in all 12 member states.

Referenda had to be held in Denmark and Ireland, where considerable opposition developed over fears that the SEA would dilute national sovereignty. It was hoped that the new decision-making procedures would help the EC overcome its long-running but increasingly critical internal financial crisis. The mounting annual deficit in the EC budget, largely caused by the common agricultural policy (CAP), again overshadowed much else during 1987. As the year began, the Community still had not adopted a proper legal budget, and for some months expenditure was on an emergency basis.

The European Commission, which in September acquired a new secretary-general, David Williamson (*see* BIOGRAPHIES), in March unveiled its most radical proposals to date for bringing the EC budget under control. In 1987 the CAP accounted for nearly 70% of the $40 billion annual budget. Under the Commission's proposals, strict limits on the amount of support Europe's farmers could expect would be linked to output targets in order to eliminate massive overproduction and surpluses. Although aspects of the plan won the support of EC heads of state and government when they met in Brussels in June, there was no clear agreement on the precise steps to be taken. The British government in particular held out against agreeing—even in principle—to lift the current ceiling on EC budget revenues without much more detailed evidence of how the agricultural reforms would work in practice.

The failure of the Brussels summit was a bitter disappointment to the Belgian government, which held the six-month presidency of the EC during the first half of 1987. The Danish government took over at the end of June, but there was little optimism that an outline agreement would be reached during its term. In the event, the December EC summit, meeting in Copenhagen, also failed. The 12 EC leaders were unable to agree, and the summit was adjourned until February 1988 in Brussels.

The other major preoccupation of the EC was the commitment to complete the internal market by 1992. This would involve some 300 pieces of legislation removing all remaining physical, political, and fiscal barriers to free trade and the free movement of capital and individuals within the EC. During September the president of the Commission told EC finance ministers meeting in Denmark that the goal of the internal market might be jeopardized if action was not taken to strengthen the European Monetary System (EMS). These warnings were linked to episodic pressures on European currency exchange rates induced by the weakness of the U.S. dollar.

As early as January, the slide in the dollar had forced a realignment of fixed currency rates within the EMS, notably a revaluation of the Deutsche Mark. However, the fall in the value of the dollar, by reducing dollar-denominated world food prices, increased the gap between EC and world prices and thus pushed up the cost of subsidies paid on European farm exports. Concern turned increasingly to the possible economic consequences of the crash on Wall Street and other international stock markets during October. EC economists had warned that European growth rates in 1989 might average only around 2%—barely enough to prevent an increase in unemployment. In early October EC finance ministers took some modest steps to strengthen the EMS currency system, though in the view of many EC governments the moves fell short of what was needed.

The Council of Ministers made only limited progress in adopting liberalizing legislation to complete the internal market. Particular controversy surrounded Commission proposals made in July to narrow the permitted range of value-added tax (VAT) rates charged in different EC countries. The less wealthy, mainly southern, EC governments were concerned over the threat posed by the budget crisis to the EC's nonagricultural policies, notably regional and social development. There were hints that some of these governments might not agree to the timetable of internal liberalization measures unless the richer EC states agreed to the Commission's proposals for a doubling of regional and social spending over the next five years.

Relations between the EC and its principal trading partners were the subject of growing concern. Friction with the U.S. and Japan increased as mutual fears and recriminations about protectionism spread. (*See* ECONOMIC AFFAIRS: *Special Report*.) During January and February there were threats of sanctions and countersanctions between the EC and the U.S. over the effect of Spain and Portugal's accession to the EC on U.S. grain sales. A crisis was narrowly averted by high-level diplomatic exchanges between Brussels and Washington, but trouble developed in midyear over a range of other trade disputes. Among the sources of disagreement were a planned EC tax on vegetable oils, measures to ban hormones in meat, subsidies for the European Airbus project, and discrimination against U.S. suppliers by EC telecommunications authorities. More generally, the U.S. complained that the EC was not giving the priority it should to liberalizing farm trade as part of the so-called Uruguay round of negotiations under the General Agreement on Tariffs and Trade. For its part, the EC charged the U.S. with sliding toward greater de facto protectionism, citing the trade bill pending in Congress. The Europeans also claimed that U.S. farmers were supported by a variety of payments and that the massive U.S. defense research program acted as a de facto subsidy to U.S. aerospace firms.

The Commission imposed a series of penalties on Japanese firms for alleged dumping and also denounced so-called screwdriver plants established in Europe by Japanese firms to assemble goods made in Japan, thus avoiding EC antidumping duties. Alarm was expressed in Brussels during May over the signing of a U.S.-Japanese agreement limiting the export to the U.S. market of computer chips and other high-technology products, since this raised the possibility that Japan would divert its exports to Europe.

As a result of the SEA, EC foreign ministers stepped up their consideration of how increased political cooperation would affect security-related issues. There was an unresolved problem of relating EC policy decisions on the political aspects of arms control to the more defense-oriented discussions taking place in the seven-nation Western European Union (WEU). Comprising Belgium, France, The Netherlands, the U.K., Italy, Luxembourg, and West Germany, the WEU met at foreign and defense minister level twice during the year. Although mainly concerned with drawing up a European security charter, the discussions were all the more significant in view of reservations among some WEU and EC countries about the implications of the Soviet-U.S. agreement eliminating land-based, medium-range nuclear missiles from Europe. (*See* MILITARY AFFAIRS: *Special Report*.) Some WEU governments, notably the U.K. and France, warned against "creeping denuclearization" of Europe's defenses and the potential danger of a decoupling of the U.S. from the defense of Western Europe. Although the U.S. administration denied that it had any intention of reducing its troop commitment in Western Europe, Washington was less than happy with the growing tendency of its European allies to discuss key issues of security strategy in forums outside NATO. Moreover, there were other issues, such as policy toward Central America, where EC and U.S. views diverged.

East German leader Erich Honecker
(right) and West German Chancellor
Helmut Kohl inspect an honour guard
in front of the Bonn Chancellery.
Honecker's five-day visit marked the
first time an East German head of
state had set foot in West Germany
since the division of Germany in 1949.
PATRICK PIEL—GAMMA/LIAISON

EC countries were divided among themselves on other foreign policy issues. In March the 12 reluctantly agreed to impose sanctions on Syria for its alleged involvement in terrorism, but most were subsequently lifted by countries other than the U.K. For its part, the U.K., together with West Germany, opposed calls from other EC countries to strengthen sanctions against South Africa.

Whatever its internal and external difficulties, the EC continued to be a pole of attraction for other European states. This was particularly true for the six remaining members (Austria, Finland, Iceland, Norway, Sweden, and Switzerland) of the European Free Trade Association (EFTA), which met in Interlaken, Switz., in May to discuss future links with the EC. EFTA states feared that they might be adversely affected if the EC moved to complete its internal market. Debates about joining the EC were held in Austria, Norway, Sweden, and Switzerland. It seemed that Norway might be the first to make a move after its general elections, due in 1989. A customs union between the EC and EFTA already existed, and the creation of a single Western European market would represent the emergence of a major economic and trading bloc on the world scene.

At year's end it also seemed probable that the EC and the Council for Mutual Economic Assistance (Comecon), the Eastern bloc trading organization, would sign a mutual recognition treaty. Following the example set by Romania and Yugoslavia, other Comecon countries, such as Hungary, began negotiations aimed at arranging commercial cooperation agreements with the EC. The policy of economic and political liberalization undertaken by the Soviet government awakened interest among EC companies about the prospect of joint economic ventures with state authorities in the U.S.S.R. It was unclear, however, how practical some of these ventures would be in view of the economic difficulties experienced by Eastern bloc countries and the indebtedness of some of them to Western banks.

The European Court of Justice in Luxembourg experienced a greatly increased work load during 1987, partly as a result of challenges by one EC institution about the political authority of others. Important rulings were made on the rights of the European Parliament to amend the budget and the responsibility of the Council of Ministers to fix an annual budget. The European Court ruled against France in a complaint about the West German government's VAT rebates to its farmers and against West Germany in a case affecting national purity standards for beer. The U.K. lost its appeal against an EC decision to ban the use of hormones in stock animals.

Overshadowed to a degree by the EC and the revived WEU, the 21-nation Council of Europe nonetheless had an active year. Based in Strasbourg, France, where it was linked to the European Commission of Human Rights and the European Court of Human Rights, the Council of Europe convened major conferences on education, culture, civil liberties, and international drug traffic.

(JOHN PALMER)

*See also* Economic Affairs; Military Affairs.

## ANDORRA

A landlocked independent coprincipality of Europe, Andorra is in the Pyrenees Mountains between Spain and France. Area: 468 sq km (181 sq mi). Pop. (1987 est.): 48,800. Cap.: Andorra la Vella. Monetary units: French franc and Spanish peseta. Coprinces: the president of the French Republic and the bishop of Urgel, Spain, represented by their *veguers* (provosts) and *batlles* (prosecutors). An elected Council General of 28 members elects the first syndic, in 1987 Francesc Cerqueda Pascuet; chief executive, Josep Pintat-Solans.

During Sept. 7–13, 1987, representatives of six of Europe's smallest nation-states—Andorra, Liechtenstein, Luxembourg, Malta, Monaco, and San Marino—gathered in Andorra la Vella to attend a meeting organized by Andorra's Council of Education and Culture. Though no political resolution was passed at the meeting, the delegates used the occasion to point out the positive aspects of small nationhood, as well as to discuss obvious difficulties, such as lack of resources. In particular, it was stressed that in small countries it was much easier for the individual to influence politics. Luis Mallart, adviser to the Council of Education and Culture, claimed, "It is agreeable to be able to discuss affairs with a minister in the street."

Andorra continued its efforts to resolve the status of its relationship with the European Communities (EC) now that the coprincipality was completely surrounded by EC territory. Much of Andorra's income was derived from trading in duty-free goods—imported in some cases with the aid of EC subsidies—and the economy would be severely affected if EC action brought an end to this trade.

(K. M. SMOGORZEWSKI)

This article updates the *Micropædia* article ANDORRA.

## AUSTRIA

The republic of Austria is a landlocked state of central Europe. Area: 83,855 sq km (32,376 sq mi). Pop. (1987 est.): 7,554,000. Cap.: Vienna. Monetary unit: Austrian Schilling, with (Oct. 5, 1987) a free rate of 12.97 Schillings to U.S. $1 (21.07 Schillings = £1 sterling). President in 1987, Kurt Waldheim; chancellor, Franz Vranitzky.

Following the general elections of Nov. 23, 1986, in which the Socialist Party of Austria (SPÖ) lost support but remained the largest single party in Parliament, a coalition government was formed between the SPÖ and the Austrian People's Party (ÖVP) in January 1987. The elections had been prompted by the SPÖ decision to dissolve the previous coalition government, in which its partner was the Freedom Party (FPÖ), because of the latter's shift from liberal toward nationalist policies. Federal Chancellor Franz Vranitzky (SPÖ) and Vice-Chancellor Alois Mock (ÖVP) headed an administration in which Cabinet posts were divided equally between the two parties and the Justice Ministry was held by an independent.

The most urgent problems facing the government included modernizing the economy, restructuring the industrial and agricultural sectors, and bringing the budget under control—a task that required a solid parliamentary majority. Following years of unprofitability in the nationalized industries, particularly the raw materials sector, the government announced plans to privatize portions of several state-owned companies. In each case, however, Österreichische Industrieholding (ÖIAG), the state holding company, would retain at least a 51% share. Stringent measures, including reductions in staff levels, were to be imposed on the remaining state-owned concerns in an effort to bring them into profit by 1990. Although plans to create new jobs and counteract the social effects of the policies were envisioned, the regions that would be most affected expressed concern. During 1986–87 the issue provoked demonstrations and, on occasion, attacks on politicians.

The government also intended to reduce significantly the existing level of subsidies in the agricultural sector. The challenge of adapting to the needs of the European Communities (EC) market was a longer term aim. Membership in the EC was ruled out by Austria's neutrality, but a customs union was considered a possibility.

The environmental impact of traffic passing through Austria, particularly the western part of the country, was proving increasingly serious. Measures aimed at easing the situation included transferring traffic from road to rail, constructing more tunnels, and making the use of catalytic converters on cars compulsory. In the Alpine regions deforestation caused by acid rain and the clearing of areas for ski runs resulted in extensive bad-weather damage in the summer months. The most spectacular of many demonstrations against the planned nuclear reprocessing plant at Wackersdorf, Bavaria, West Germany, took place during the Vienna Opera Ball in February, when many people were injured. A party of "Greens," including three members of Parliament, was arrested in Budapest, Hung., in May while trying to survey the ecological damage caused by a power station on the Danube.

The attacks on federal Pres. Kurt Waldheim at home and abroad reached new heights. In April the U.S. put him on its watch list of undesirable aliens, and in June the Vienna state branch of the SPÖ passed a resolution calling for his resignation. The watch list decision triggered a fresh wave of anti-Semitic and anti-U.S. feeling in Austria and reinforced the patriotic pronouncements of the

Veteran's Association. Despite the strain on the coalition, its members abided by a policy of supporting Waldheim in order to avoid a national crisis. Pope John Paul II exposed himself to worldwide criticism by receiving Waldheim at the Vatican in June.

The Austrian Centre, one of the most modern and largest conference centres in the world, opened in Vienna in April. Its 14 rooms on four floors provided space for 9,500 people. The ÖVP, which had campaigned against the project, boycotted the inauguration.

(ELFRIEDE DIRNBACHER)

## BELGIUM

A constitutional monarchy, the Benelux country of Belgium is situated on the North Sea coast of northwestern Europe. Area: 30,518 sq km (11,783 sq mi). Pop. (1987 est.): 9,861,000. Cap.: Brussels. Monetary unit: Belgian franc, with (Oct. 5, 1987) a commercial rate of BF 38.24 to U.S. $1 (BF 62.10 = £1 sterling) and a financial rate of BF 38.46 to U.S. $1 (BF 62.45 = £1 sterling). King, Baudouin I; prime minister in 1987, Wilfried Martens.

Throughout 1987 the government of Belgium was confronted with the Voeren (Fourons) controversy. Because of his refusal to speak Dutch, José Happart had been removed from office as mayor of this small township, officially situated in Dutch-speaking Flanders, by a decision of the Council of State. Subsequently, however, Happart was nominated as first alderman and acting mayor by the municipal council. Every time this vote was voided by the governor of Limburg Province, the council repeated its contested vote. An appeal by the minister of the interior to the Supreme Court of Justice against the Council of State ruling was rejected. Following a new ruling by the latter body, Happart abstained from signing official acts until a

AFP PHOTO

Salvage crews dredge up the British car ferry *Herald of Free Enterprise*. At least 188 people died when it capsized off the coast of Belgium in the worst peacetime ship disaster in the history of English Channel shipping.

lower civil court judge ordered him to sign a specific administrative document. Thereafter he again proceeded to function as acting mayor.

The government's attempts to find a satisfactory solution to the problem failed, and on October 19 King Baudouin accepted the resignation of Prime Minister Wilfried Martens, who then formed a caretaker Cabinet to hold office until elections took place. In the elections, which were held on December 13, the ruling coalition parties retained a bare majority of seats. Martens's Flemish Social Christians lost six seats and the French Social Christians one, while the two other coalition members, the Flemish and French Liberals, gained a net two seats. The French Socialists, the biggest winner, added five. (For tabulated results, see *Political Parties,* above.) Negotiations to form a new government were continuing at year's end.

Before leaving office, the government tackled several important issues, including reduction of the budget deficit for 1988, which it managed to limit to 7.4% of gross national product. Cuts were implemented in the employment and social security budgets and in subsidies to industrial enterprises. The government also agreed to introduce a reform of the tax system and took steps to stimulate investments through venture capital. A pension-savings scheme offering tax deductions, to which some 900,000 taxpayers subscribed, was considered a major success.

A dispute over funds allotted to the two ministers of education led to the resignation of the French-speaking minister, André Damseaux. Because of a drop in the number of secondary-school students, the schools' operating expenditures were reduced by 2%, with the prospect that thousands of teachers would be laid off. Trade unions agreed to proposals put forward by the newly appointed general manager of the Limburg coal mines involving the closure of three of the six remaining pits and the merger of two others. Despite protest demonstrations, the government approved the extension of the French (high-speed) Train à Grande Vitesse to Belgium.

In September the government agreed to send Belgian minesweepers to the Gulf region. Revelations about the part played by Belgian arms firms in supplying weapons to the belligerents in the area prompted the House of Representatives to set up a special inquiry commission.

Extradition proceedings launched by Minister of Justice Jean Gol led to the transfer to Brussels of 25 British soccer fans accused of involuntary manslaughter in connection with the deaths of 39 people during riots in the Heysel stadium, Brussels, in May 1985. Their arrival stirred up considerable commotion in Belgian prisons, where inmates objected that the Britons' accommodations were better than those provided for other prisoners.

The British car ferry the *Herald of Free Enterprise* capsized just outside the port of Zeebrugge on March 6. At least 188 people died in the disaster, notwithstanding quick and efficient rescue efforts by the harbour authorities and the navies of several European countries. (*See* Transportation: *Sidebar.*) (JAN R. ENGELS)

This article updates the *Macropædia* article The Low Countries: *Belgium.*

## DENMARK

A constitutional monarchy of north central Europe, Denmark lies between the North and Baltic seas. Area: 43,092 sq km (16,638 sq mi), excluding the Faeroe Islands and Greenland. Pop. (1987 est.): 5,126,000. Cap.: Copenhagen. Monetary unit: krone, with (Oct. 5, 1987) a free rate of 7.09 kroner to U.S. $1 (11.51 kroner = £1 sterling). Queen, Margrethe II; prime minister in 1987, Poul Schlüter.

The major event in Denmark in 1987 was the sudden election called by Prime Minister Poul Schlüter for September 8. Although the government had several more months before its four-year term expired, it chose to strike while the iron was hot. Good trade figures were due to be announced, which gave Denmark a badly needed economic boost. Although it was widely predicted that the government would be returned to office, the result was a disappointment for Schlüter. His ruling four-party coalition lost seven seats, giving it only 70 seats in the Folketing (parliament); the prime minister's own party, the Conservatives, lost four seats for a total of 38. The main opposition party, the Social Democrats, fared little better, losing 2 seats for a total of 54. The opposition Socialist People's Party gained most from the election, winning 27 seats, compared with 21 in 1984.

The result was, therefore, a loss for the government and a failure for the opposition. The stalemate caused a 24-hour panic, but feverish political activity resulted in a typically Danish solution. Schlüter tendered his resignation, but six of the nine parties returned to the Folketing wanted him to form a new government.

The outcome meant that in the future new policies would involve greater debate, and the government would have to enter into negotiations with the Social Democrats. Anker Jørgensen, chairman of the Social Democrats, regarded the two-seat decline for his party as a personal defeat and resigned; he was replaced by Svend Auken, his vice-chairman. The balance of power in the new Folketing was held by the Progress Party, which increased its strength to nine seats.

The new Cabinet of Prime Minister Schlüter included six new ministers and two new ministries. Key ministers were Uffe Ellemann-Jensen (foreign affairs), Palle Simonsen (finance), Erhard Jakobsen (economic coordination), and Knud Enggaard (economy).

Denmark's economic situation deteriorated in 1987 after three years of buoyant growth. Following increases in gross domestic product of 4.2% in 1985 and 3.4% in 1986, output in 1987 was expected to decline by up to 1%. Poor investment was a major cause, with government investment tightly constrained by the need to curb spending. Consumer price inflation remained under control, having fallen to an annual rate of 3%. The rate of unemployment, which declined to 7.9% in 1986, increased in 1987 and was expected to reach an annual average of 8.5%. The government's major achievement was the reduction of the state budget deficit, which in 1982 was one of the largest in Europe—nearly 11% of gross domestic product. In 1986 the budget registered a small surplus (1.2% of GDP), and in 1987 the deficit was only about 0.5%. The major problem continued to be the size of the foreign debt, which reached 262 billion kroner at the end of 1986. In 1987 the interest burden on the debt totaled 30 billion kroner. This represented a major strain on the balance of payments, which suffered a deficit of some 18 billion–20 billion kroner in 1987.

A pact with the Social Democrats brought agreement on the 1988 finance bill and paved the way for lower wage increases in order to improve the competitiveness of export industries. The government agreed to raise old-age pensions and to increase unemployment benefits by 10%. In return, the Social Democrats supported government measures on reducing the employers' liability for social security and sickness benefits. Wage costs for industry were expected to fall by 5% as a result of the measures. The agreement with the opposition strengthened the position of the government and allayed fears of another election. (JENS W. HOLSÖE)

## FINLAND

The republic of Finland is in northern Europe, on the Gulf of Bothnia and the Gulf of Finland. Area: 338,145 sq km (130,559 sq mi). Pop. (1987 est.): 4,942,000. Cap.: Helsinki. Monetary unit: Finnish markka, with (Oct. 5, 1987) a free rate of 4.42 markkaa to U.S. $1 (7.19 markkaa = £1 sterling). President in 1987, Mauno Koivisto; prime ministers, Kalevi Sorsa and, from April 30, Harri Holkeri.

The year 1987 was a watershed in Finnish politics. On April 30 a government was installed in which the Conservatives, who had been out of office for 21 years, joined the Social Democrats, a dominant force in recent coalitions. Discarded was the largely agrarian Centre Party, a key constituent in almost every administration during the previous half century. Within the Cabinet the Social Democrats, claiming most of the strategic ministries, outnumbered the Conservatives 8–7. They had two fewer portfolios than the non-Socialists combined, however, and the prime minister, Harri Holkeri (see BIOGRAPHIES), was a Conservative.

Prior to the general elections of March 15–16, Social Democratic Prime Minister Kalevi Sorsa's fourth coalition had set a record by serving out its entire four-year mandate. A modified system of proportional representation produced some unexpected swings in strength within the 200-seat Eduskunta (parliament). (For tabulated results, see *Political Parties,* above.) The Social Democrats lost 100,000 votes but only one seat, while the Conservatives, gaining just 6,000 votes, expanded their parliamentary base from 44 to 53. The Centre gained some ground, while the split Communists appeared to be a spent force. Most small parties fared poorly. Sorsa, who became foreign minister in the new Cabinet, resigned as leader of the Social Democrats.

The traditional method of selecting the head of state by means of a popularly chosen electoral college was to be dispensed with in the 1988 presidential election, provided a single contender captured most of the votes cast by the nation; otherwise, the college would convene. With his popularity rating fluctuating between 55 and 66% in the opinion polls during 1987, Pres. Mauno Koivisto appeared likely to have a second six-year term within his grasp without college intervention. His closest rival, Holkeri, was hard pressed to gain more than 15% in the polls as his government implemented its policy of "structural change without tears."

There were some chinks in Koivisto's armour. In September, after playing host to Kenyan Pres. Daniel arap Moi, Koivisto attacked neighbouring Norway and, to a lesser extent, Sweden in an outburst that jarred the customary harmony of the Nordic countries. Moi had canceled planned visits to those countries because of their critical attitude toward the human rights situation in Kenya. However, Koivisto's pardoning of an ex-parliamentarian convicted of tax fraud appeared more likely to cost him votes.

Despite a spate of mergers and company closings, the economy was more resilient than expected, with a growth rate of around 3%. Improved sales in Western markets, which accounted for two-thirds of foreign trade, more than offset a contraction in exports to the U.S.S.R. Commercial considerations ranked high during Soviet Premier Nikolay Ryzhkov's visit to Finland in January and President Koivisto's trip to Moscow in October. Apprehension grew that Finland, which had a free trade agreement with the European Communities, might be left out in the cold if the EC succeeded in forming an internal common market by 1992. The government hoped that a barrier-free area could be negotiated between the EC and the European Free Trade Association, of which Finland was a member.

During a prolonged cold spell in January, Helsinki logged the lowest temperature ever recorded there, −34° C (−29° F). Though this was several degrees "milder" than the temperatures registered at many inland stations in most winters, Helsinki's raw climate was a key factor in the dozen deaths attributed to cold. Subsequently, a wretched summer brought one of the worst harvests ever.

(DONALD FIELDS)

## FRANCE

A republic of western Europe, France includes the island of Corsica in the Mediterranean Sea and has coastlines on the English Channel, the Mediterranean, and the Atlantic Ocean. Area: 543,965 sq km (210,026 sq mi). Pop. (1987 est.): 55,623,000. Cap.: Paris. Monetary unit: franc, with (Oct. 5, 1987) a free rate of F 6.13 to U.S. $1 (F 9.96 = £1 sterling). President in 1987, François Mitterrand; prime minister, Jacques Chirac.

**Domestic Affairs.** During 1987 the "cohabitation" between the left-wing Socialist Party (PS) head of state, Pres. François Mitterrand, and the right-wing head of government, Prime Minister Jacques Chirac, continued uneasily. After being criticized by former prime minister Raymond Barre and receiving poor showings in opinion polls, Chirac decided to appeal for grass-roots support in an effort to regain his popularity. He visited several French départements during the year. Taking advantage of the popularity he enjoyed in the opinion polls, President Mitterrand also visited a number of départements, where he was welcomed with warmth and, sometimes, enthusiasm.

In April, a year after Prime Minister Chirac came to power, the right-wing majority in the National Assembly reconfirmed its confidence in him by 294 votes (from his own party, the Rassemblement pour la République [RPR], the Union pour la Démocratie Française [UDF], and other smaller right-wing parties) against 282 (from the PS, the Communist Party [PC], and the far-right National Front). Events that followed clearly had a demoralizing effect on Chirac—particularly France's hostage deal with Iran—and in early December he sought another affirmation of confidence from the Assembly. The result of the December 4 vote was the same as in April.

With the 1988 presidential election only a few months away, a number of arguments broke out between the Élysée Palace and the Hôtel Matignon, the official residences of the president and the prime minister. Barre (UDF) was the leading right-wing rival to Chirac; François Léotard (UDF-Republican Party) confirmed that he would not stand in the 1988 election, thus leaving Chirac and Barre to fight it out on the right. For the time being, it was understood that whichever of them obtained the least satisfactory result in the first round of the election would stand down in favour of the other in the second round.

The Socialist opposition, meanwhile, would have several presidential candidates in the increasingly unlikely event that Mitterrand did not stand for a second seven-year term. His most serious rival was former minister Michel Rocard, but Rocard had said he would withdraw if Mitterrand chose to stand again. The decline of the PC, which obtained only 10% of the vote in the 1986 parliamentary elections, continued. In June Pierre Juquin, leader of the important reformist faction of the party, resigned from the party's Central Committee. The PC had selected a hard-liner, André Lajoinie, as its candidate in the presidential elections, but it was expected that Juquin would present a formidable challenge to him if he decided to run.

The trial of Klaus Barbie (*see* BIOGRAPHIES) was the focus of international attention. After six hours of deliberation, the Rhône Court of Assizes on July 4 sentenced Barbie, the "butcher of Lyon," to life imprisonment after finding him guilty of numerous crimes against humanity. French public opinion felt it essential that, after an interval of more than 40 years, all those who had not yet been born at the time be reminded of the atrocious acts committed by Barbie while he was Gestapo commander in Lyon (1942–44).

Unrest among students and schoolchildren at the end of 1986 was followed by protests against conditions of service by primary-school teachers, 35,000 of whom traveled from all parts of France to march peacefully in Paris. Other industrial disputes included a 15-week action involving strikes and serious disturbances to air traffic. In December a strike at the Banque de France (central bank) was beginning to threaten the French banking system. The summer witnessed violent unrest in prisons, and several detainees were charged.

In September a referendum on whether New Caledonia should remain within the French Republic gave a large majority to the Caldoches, settlers who were opposed to independence. Of the 59% of the electorate who participated in the poll, 98.3% voted to stay with France. About half the 40,000 or so who abstained were indigenous Melanesians (Kanaks), who made up 43% of the population. The election boycott called by Kanak leaders was partially heeded, and the separatist issue remained a problem. Chirac greeted the result as a "victory for France" and went to Nouméa to seek agreement on a new autonomous status for the territory and a new division of its regions, which would give more power to the Kanaks. The French Foreign Office declared its satisfaction that half the member countries of the UN Committee on Decolonization approved the way in which the referendum was conducted. Mitterrand, however, warned during a television interview: "There are risks of conflict if inequalities of a colonial nature are perpetuated. Referendum or no referendum, we must do away with a division of land and wealth which is so inequitable and unjust."

In another French territory, the Pacific island of Tahiti, French Polynesia, riots followed a clash between striking dockers and police, and a state of emergency was declared in the capital. Several hundred French troops and police were sent in to restore order. French officials denied that the involvement of separatists was a major factor.

**The Economy.** The economy performed better than predicted in 1987, and gross domestic product was expected to rise by nearly 2% instead of the 1.5% anticipated in the government's September budget (compared with 2.1% in 1986). The main factors contributing to the country's overall growth were buoyant consumer spending and strong capital investment. Consumer price inflation remained moderate at just over 3% for the year, marking a slight acceleration over 1986. Unemployment stood at 10.5% in September, the same as a year earlier; it had been expected to deteriorate but was eased by job creation and training schemes. The number of job seekers was 2.6 million. The bad news was export performance—sales of manufactured goods were poor because of lack of competitiveness, made worse by the fall in the value of the U.S. dollar. Imports rose strongly, and there was a growing trade deficit—$4.4 billion in the first ten months—compared with a small surplus in 1986.

A major concern for the government was the expected deficit of F 13.8 billion in the social security budget for 1987. The "seven wise men" appointed early in the year

French police guard the Iranian embassy in Paris to prevent the escape of Wahid Gordji, an Iranian interpreter suspected in bombings that killed 13 persons in Paris in 1986. France formally severed diplomatic ties with Iran on July 17.

F. REGLAIN—GAMMA/LIAISON

to review the system gave Chirac a report suggesting more economic management of pensions and health insurance and, above all, proportional contributions from all incomes, to be set annually by Parliament.

The government's privatization program, which began late in 1986, got under way more quickly and smoothly than expected. By June nine state-owned companies had been sold, raising more than F 33 billion. Altogether, 65 companies were scheduled for privatization, but the program came to a halt following the slump in the stock market in October. One of France's major companies, Renault, became the centre of controversy toward the year's end. The company's losses had accumulated, and the government's decision to write off F 12 billion of its debts was the subject of a European Communities (EC) inquiry on whether the move contravened EC rules on state subsidies. Ironically, three years of restructuring had brought Renault to profitability, but its future remained uncertain.

The stock market plunge in October brought a sharp fall of confidence in the Bourse, and there were fears of a de facto devaluation of the French franc. The effect on the economy, however, would not be felt until 1988, when a slowdown in growth was expected.

**Foreign Affairs.** Relations with Iran appeared to turn full circle during the year. On July 17 France broke off diplomatic relations with Tehran. The action followed investigations into a bombing campaign in Paris in 1986, when 13 people were killed and many more seriously injured. During a June police raid Wahid Gordji, who was suspected of organizing a network of terrorists throughout Europe as well as involvement in the Paris bombing, refused to be subjected to questioning and took refuge in the Iranian embassy. On July 13 there was an unprovoked attack on a French containership by two Iranian patrol boats in the Gulf, and French civilians were being prevented from leaving Iran. France's own "Irangate," which broke in early November, was the focus of international attention. It was revealed that there had been large illegal shipments of arms from France to Iran beginning in 1983, with the involvement of the Socialist government and with substantial commissions allegedly diverted to the PS. The sales reportedly continued under the Chirac government at least until mid-1987.

In November, in a surprise move, Gordji was allowed to leave the country, and Chirac said that normal relations with Iran were in prospect. This followed the release of two French hostages by a pro-Iranian group in Lebanon. The deal gave rise to international fears of a softening in the French attitude toward terrorism. Subsequently, the French police arrested scores of opponents of the Iranian government, 17 of whom were deported. Details and implications of the deal were still emerging as the year drew to a close.

Although most of the world greeted the signing of the U.S.-Soviet intermediate-range nuclear forces (INF) disarmament agreement with enthusiasm, France was skeptical. Both Chirac and Mitterrand warned against believing that the U.S.-Soviet agreement represented an important step in the field of security. France took the view that the disparities between the conventional forces of the Warsaw Pact states and those of NATO were such that Europeans should think seriously about common defense policies.

French foreign policy continued to attach great importance to the strengthening of ties between the 12 EC countries, and France welcomed the substantial progress made toward strengthening the Community. The ratification of the Franco-British treaty on the Channel Tunnel was a particular cause of satisfaction. Eighteen months after the treaty was signed in Canterbury Cathedral on Feb. 12, 1986, U.K. Prime Minister Margaret Thatcher and Mitterrand met to exchange the instruments of ratification, thus giving the green light to one of the largest construction projects in the world. The simultaneous flotation of Eurotunnel shares on the U.K. and French markets did not reflect this enthusiasm, however, although the decline of world stock markets may have been a major factor in investor reluctance.

Earlier in the year Mitterrand and Prime Minister Felipe González Márquez had put the seal on the Franco-Spanish rapprochement at a meeting in Madrid. Relations cooled in August following a visit by González to Mitterrand's vacation home, where he appealed in vain for French assistance against the Basque terrorist group ETA. In October, however, France altered its strategy and handed over 40–50 Basque exiles, at the risk of possible repercussions in its own Basque region. Relations with West Germany improved, and cooperation between the two countries was a major factor leading to a solution of the EC budget gap, agreed to at the EC summit in Brussels in June. Together the two countries also helped resolve the deadlock in farm prices for the 1987–88 season. France was successful in starting to dismantle the system of financial compensation, which had protected German farmers against the rise in value of the Deutsche Mark. In early July Chirac and Chancellor Helmut Kohl met in Reims to mark the anniversary of the Franco-German reconciliation. An agreement was later signed for the construction of a Franco-German military helicopter, and Mitterrand and Kohl were considering the eventual establishment of a joint defense council. Mitterrand's visit to West Germany in mid-October dealt largely with cultural links.

Mitterrand attended the 13th summit of the seven leading industrial democracies in Venice along with the heads of state or government of Canada, West Germany, Italy, Japan, the U.K., and the U.S. It was agreed to set up an international ethics committee on AIDS (acquired immune deficiency syndrome) and to strengthen coordination of economic policies. Relations with the U.S.S.R. suffered a setback in April when France expelled six Soviet diplomats for their alleged role in a spy ring that had gathered information on advanced technology. Shortly afterward

Chirac expressed reservations about the U.S.S.R.'s offer to eliminate short-range nuclear missiles from Europe. It was against this background that Chirac went ahead with his planned two-day visit to Moscow in May, and his reception was understandably cool. He had several talks on disarmament with Soviet leader Mikhail Gorbachev and went on Soviet television to express opinions on Soviet shortcomings in the field of human rights.

Following a visit by Mitterrand to Canada to renew cooperation between Paris and Ottawa 20 years after Gen. Charles de Gaulle's call of "Vive le Québec libre!," and a five-day visit to the same country by Chirac, the second summit of French-speaking countries was held in Quebec. The prime minister and president were able to present an apparently united front to the participants as they appeared side by side at the opening of a conference to lay the foundations for what might eventually become a charter for Francophone states.

In Africa the cease-fire in Chad called for by the Organization of African Unity (OAU) was accepted at the beginning of September by the governments of Chad and Libya, greatly to the satisfaction of France, which had long supported the Chad government. However, Paris believed that no lasting solution to the conflict over the Aozou Strip, on the frontier between Chad and Libya, could be found without a legal settlement of the dispute. In December it was revealed that one of the two French security agents detained on the French Polynesian island of Hao, where they were serving sentences for their part in the 1985 sinking of the *Rainbow Warrior* in Auckland Harbour, New Zealand, had been flown to Paris, reportedly for medical treatment. New Zealand accused the French government of breaching the agreement that the prisoners should not be moved from the island without the mutual consent of the French and New Zealand governments.

(JEAN KNECHT)

See also *Dependent States,* below.

## GERMANY, FEDERAL REPUBLIC OF

The Federal Republic of Germany (West Germany) is in central Europe, on the North and Baltic seas. Area: 248,708 sq km (96,027 sq mi). Pop. (1987 est., including West Berlin, which is an enclave within East Germany): 60,924,000. Provisional cap.: Bonn. Monetary unit: Deutsche Mark, with (Oct. 5, 1987) a free rate of DM 1.84 to U.S. $1 (DM 2.99 = £1 sterling). President in 1987, Richard von Weizsäcker; chancellor, Helmut Kohl.

The centre-right coalition government of the Christian Democratic Union (CDU), its Bavarian wing, the Christian Social Union (CSU), and the Free Democratic Party (FDP) was returned to office in the West German federal elections on Jan. 25, 1987. Helmut Kohl, the CDU leader, was subsequently reelected federal chancellor by the Bundestag (federal parliament), receiving 253 of the 486 votes cast.

**Domestic Affairs.** Even though there was no shortage of important issues, it was a dull campaign, mainly because the outcome was never seriously in doubt. The result was nonetheless a disappointment for Kohl. His party and its Bavarian allies polled 44.3%, compared with 48.8% in 1983. The Social Democratic Party (SPD), led by Johannes Rau, the premier of North Rhine-Westphalia who was fighting his first federal election as chancellor candidate, captured 37% of the votes (38.2% in 1983), its lowest share since 1961. The FDP did well, polling 9.1% (7%), and so did the Greens with 8.3% (5.6%). This gave Kohl a parliamentary majority of 45 seats, 15 fewer than in the previous Bundestag. (For tabulated results, see *Political Parties,* above.)

West German Chancellor Helmut Kohl's centre-right coalition won a "Decision for Germany," capturing 269 seats in January elections to the Bundestag and ensuring Kohl's subsequent reelection as chancellor for another four years.

PATRICK PIEL—GAMMA/LIAISON

Several analysts concluded that the government had lost support because many voters saw its leaders as doing little more than administering the status quo. The CDU campaigned under the banner *Deutschland, weiter so* ("keep up the good work"). Still, West Germany's status quo was hardly a matter for concern. The economy was growing for the fourth year in a row, and inflation was negligible.

The election of the state parliament of Hessen in April, the first of five such elections during the year, produced a severe shock for the SPD. The party lost this traditional stronghold of social democracy after 40 years in control. The election followed the breakup of the coalition between the SPD and the Greens over the issue of nuclear energy. The SPD's performance—it polled 40.2%, a fall of 6%—was the worst since World War II. The CDU increased its vote from 39.4 to 42.1%, while the Greens polled 9.4% (5.9%) and the FDP 7.8% (7.6%). The CDU and the FDP formed a coalition with a majority of two seats. Walter Wallmann (CDU), federal environment minister and a former mayor of Frankfurt, became state premier.

It was hard, however, to see a pattern in the year's Länder election results. The CDU lost ground in the state elections in Rhineland-Palatinate and Hamburg in May. In the former the party forfeited its absolute majority, polling 45.1%, compared with 51.9% in the previous election. The SPD remained steady at 38.8% (39.6%), while the Free Democrats, who were not represented in the previous parliament, came back with a 7.3% share of the poll and seven seats. The Greens also gained admittance, polling 5.9% and so comfortably clearing the 5% hurdle. The CDU and the FDP formed a coalition. In Hamburg the Social Democrats, who had been clinging to power with a minority government since 1986, beat off a CDU challenge. The SPD polled 45% (41.7%), the CDU 40.5% (41.9%), the FDP 6.6% (4.8%), and the Greens 7% (10.4%). In this case the Free Democrats formed a coalition with the SPD, demonstrating once again their willingness—if the terms were right—to join forces with either of the main parties.

The events surrounding the Schleswig-Holstein state election caused an uproar that resounded throughout the country. On the eve of polling day, the magazine *Der Spiegel* published an article alleging that the state premier, Uwe Barschel (CDU), had instigated a campaign to denigrate his SPD opponent, Björn Engholm. The disclosures were made by Reiner Pfeiffer, a former member of Barschel's campaign team who said he had been ordered to dig up dirt on Engholm. The media quickly dubbed the scandal the North German Watergate affair. Barschel strongly denied the allegations, but under pressure from his party he resigned the premiership two weeks after the election. Later he gave up his seat in the state parliament. On the day before he was due to appear before a parliamentary commission investigating the allegations, Barschel was found dead in a hotel room in Geneva. He had told relatives he was visiting Geneva to meet a man who could help him clear his name. A postmortem indicated that Barschel had committed suicide. His family did not accept this version, and his brother claimed that he had been murdered.

In the election the CDU's share of the poll was reduced from 49% in 1983 to 42.6%. The SPD emerged as the strongest party, polling 42.5%, an increase of more than 11%. The FDP (5.2%) entered parliament; the Greens again failed to win seats; and the Danish minority party, which was excluded from the minimum 5% clause, won one seat. The CDU and the FDP together had 37 seats and the SPD 36. A fresh election seemed likely. The election in the country's smallest state, Bremen, on the same day confirmed the Social Democrats in power with an absolute majority. They polled 50.5% (51.3%), the CDU 23.4% (33.3%), the FDP 10% (4.6%), and the Greens 10.2% (5.4%).

Former federal chancellor Willy Brandt announced his resignation from the chairmanship of the SPD in March after 23 years. Ostensibly, he stepped down because of opposition to his choice of a Greek woman, who was not a party member, as the party's first press spokeswoman. In fact, the row revealed deep dissatisfaction with his leadership at a time when the battered party badly needed a thorough overhaul. In the circumstances, Brandt's departure was a sad end to a distinguished political career. He was succeeded as chairman by Hans-Jochen Vogel, SPD leader in the Bundestag and chancellor candidate in the 1983 federal elections.

Rudolf Hess (*see* Obituaries), Hitler's former deputy, died in Spandau prison, West Berlin, on August 17 at the age of 93. Convicted by the Nürnberg war crimes tribunal of planning an aggressive war, he had spent 46 years in captivity and was Spandau's sole inmate for his last 21 years. An autopsy showed he had strangled himself, and a note also pointed to suicide. There were minor demonstrations of support by old and new Nazis in West Berlin and at the Hess family home in Bavaria, but the old man, unrepentant to the last, seemed quickly forgotten.

A young West German created a sensation in May by landing a light aircraft in Moscow's Red Square. Mathias Rust, aged 19, had flown solo from Finland, undetected by Soviet defenses. His exploit caused humour in the West, but it came as a shock to those in positions of power in the U.S.S.R. The Soviet defense minister, Marshal Sergey Sokolov, and the chief of air defenses, Aleksandr Koldunov, were dismissed, and Rust, who appeared to have no political motive for what he admitted was a foolhardy escapade, was put on trial for a variety of offenses. He was sentenced to four years' imprisonment in a labour camp. This was considered harsh in West Germany, but it was only half the length of sentence demanded by the prosecution.

The five-day visit of East German leader Erich Honecker to West Germany in September was an event of historic significance. It was the first time an East German head of state had set foot on West German soil. The visit had been in the offing for five years but was repeatedly deferred because, it was said, conditions were unfavourable. Honecker went to Bonn and several other cities and also paid a nostalgic visit to his native town of Wiebelskirchen, in the Saarland, which he had not seen since 1949. Honecker saw his visit primarily as a mission for peace and disarmament. He pressed for a nuclear-free corridor and a central European zone free of chemical weapons; a balance in conventional forces; and a ban on weapons in space. Kohl's main aim was to improve human contacts between the two German states and cooperation on practical problems such as environmental pollution and improving access to West Berlin. From the outset Kohl had said the visit would not change differing views on matters of principle, including the German question. He was right—it did not—but the chancellor said West Germany would never abandon its constitutional mandate to strive for German unity.

Many distinguished guests, among them Queen Elizabeth II, U.S. Pres. Ronald Reagan, and French Pres. François Mitterrand, visited West Berlin for the city's 750th anniversary celebrations. President Reagan, who was there in June, stood in front of the Brandenburg Gate, symbol of a divided Germany, and challenged Soviet leader Mikhail Gorbachev to "open this gate, tear down this wall." As he spoke, West Berlin was littered with smashed glass, burned-out vehicles, and barricades, relics of anti-U.S. riots by young people. The riots, involving about 2,000 *Autonomen* (left-wing dropouts), followed a peaceful demonstration by about 30,000 people.

**Foreign Affairs.** Presenting his new government's statement of policy to the Bundestag on March 18, Kohl said he perceived a persistent military threat from the Warsaw Pact. Strengthening the Western alliance would therefore continue to have high priority. He said the strategic relationship between the superpowers could change as a result of extensive disarmament, but in the foreseeable future there could be no alternative to the alliance strategy of flexible response. Balanced conventional and nuclear forces would continue to be needed if that strategy was to remain effective. Moreover, deterrence and defense in Europe would continue to require the presence of large contingents of U.S. and other allied forces in West Germany.

Kohl described Franco-German friendship as the dynamic force in the process of European reunification. He said there already existed between the two countries an identity of views and interests that should make it possible to embark on the first steps toward a common foreign policy. His government would also continue to develop military cooperation with France. West Germany's desire for closer defense collaboration with France and Britain stemmed from fear that the U.S. would slowly disengage from Europe in the wake of arms agreements with the U.S.S.R. The West Germans were shocked by the outcome of the 1986 Reagan-Gorbachev summit in Reykjavík (Iceland), which had shown that a U.S. president could talk away a substantial part of their security without even consulting them.

The Reykjavík summit involved the proposed removal of medium-range missiles (1,000–5,500 km; 620–3,410 mi) from Europe, but the West Germans became even more alarmed when Gorbachev went on to propose a "double-zero" deal, including weapons between 500 km (310 mi) and 1,000 km as well. That, they felt, would leave frontline West Germany in a far weaker position than the rest of the NATO allies, vulnerable to battlefield weapons, and without the protection of weapons that could threaten Soviet territory. This view irritated West Germany's allies, who pointed out that the proposed reductions would not turn their territories into nuclear-free zones. However, in June the Bundestag approved by a comfortable majority Kohl's reluctant decision to accept talks on the controversial double-zero missile-disarmament plan. West Germany thus became the last of the leading NATO countries to give its consent. Introducing the debate, Kohl said there could be no question of an unconditional acceptance of a shorter-range zero deal; this would be scarcely tolerable for a country in such an exposed position as West Germany. He emphasized that the double-zero proposals would have to be embedded in a comprehensive disarmament process involving all weapons systems.

West Germany's possession of 72 obsolescent Pershing 1A missiles proved to be a sticking point in the superpower negotiations. Gorbachev insisted in July that these missiles be included in the deal; Kohl's position was that they should not. The Pershings were operated by the West German Luftwaffe, but they had U.S. nuclear warheads, controlled by a dual-key arrangement. The stockpiling of U.S. warheads for use by NATO forces had been common since the 1960s. By the end of July the West German government had shifted its position on the Pershings. It said it was willing to renounce them in exchange for an agreement that would eliminate the U.S.S.R.'s capacity to invade its territory. Bonn's offer was evidently designed to draw the U.S.S.R.'s superior conventional forces and its short-range nuclear weapons into the arms control deal. It was also intended to prevent Moscow from using the Pershing problem to drive a wedge between West Germany and the U.S. Kohl later agreed that when the U.S.-Soviet agreement to reduce intermediate-range nuclear forces was implemented, the Pershing 1A missiles would be scrapped. (*See* MILITARY AFFAIRS: *Special Report.*)

The West Germans were assured by a Soviet economic delegation in April that Moscow's policy of *perestroika* (restructuring) would involve closer economic cooperation with West Germany, but Pres. Richard von Weizsäcker, who paid an official visit to the U.S.S.R. in July, found that relations between the two countries were still heavily burdened by the past. Gorbachev himself destroyed the fantasy that he might tolerate movement toward German unity by reaffirming that there were two German states with different political systems. West Germany reached agreement with Albania in September on the establishment of diplomatic relations. The agreement had taken three years to draw up, mainly because of a long-standing Albanian demand for wartime reparations. Albania dropped that demand on condition that the Germans behave generously in developing trade links.

Kohl visited China in July, accompanied by a trade delegation. West Germany earned one-third of its total national income from exports and had long been trying to improve access to the huge Chinese market. There were discussions about West German participation in the modernization and expansion of the Chinese telephone system, the building of a steelworks, and the construction of nuclear power plants, but firm contracts were not signed. Kohl also went to Tibet, a visit that upset the Tibetan government-in-exile. Pres. Chaim Herzog of Israel paid an official visit to West Germany in April, the first Israeli head of state to do so. He said he did not bring forgiveness or forgetfulness: "The only ones who can forgive are the dead. The living have no right to forget." He made this statement at the site of the former concentration camp of Bergen-Belsen, which he had first seen as a British Army officer shortly after its liberation in 1945.                           (NORMAN CROSSLAND)

This article updates the *Macropædia* article GERMANY: *Federal Republic of Germany.*

## GREECE

The republic of Greece occupies the southern part of the Balkan Peninsula and several adjoining island groups in southeastern Europe, in and between the Ionian and Aegean seas. Area: 131,-957 sq km (50,949 sq mi). Pop. (1987 est.): 10,010,000. Cap.: Athens. Monetary unit: drachma, with (Oct. 5, 1987) a free rate of 140.98 drachmas to U.S. $1 (228.93 drachmas = £1 sterling). President in 1987, Christos Sartzetakis; prime minister, Andreas Papandreou.

A dispute over oil rights in the Aegean Sea in late March brought Greece and Turkey, once again, to the verge of war. Conflict was averted, but the confrontation produced significant side effects: it stimulated a spate of message diplomacy between Athens and Ankara that kept tempers cool, and it induced Prime Minister Andreas Papandreou to offer the U.S. the chance to keep its military bases in Greece in exchange for safeguards against what he saw as Turkey's expansionism.

The Aegean crisis erupted when the Greek government decided to take over the offshore oil concession in the northern Aegean from a Canadian-U.S.-West German consortium. Turkey misinterpreted the move. Assuming that Greece intended to drill oil wells outside its territorial waters, Ankara announced that it was dispatching its own research ship into the disputed Aegean continental shelf. Greece threatened to sink the ship and defiantly braced for war. Following Western diplomatic representations, Turkey consented to desist if Greece agreed to drill only within the six-mile national limits. The Greeks obliged and proposed to Turkey that the two countries jointly appeal to the International Court of Justice to seek demarcation of their boundary on the Aegean shelf. In view of the multitude of Greek islands in the Aegean, Turkey preferred a political rather than a legal settlement; it declined but seized the opportunity to propose a bilateral dialogue instead. The resulting exchange of personal messages between the prime ministers of the two countries failed to produce concrete results, although it acted as a hedge against another crisis.

Greece's Western allies were annoyed when, at the height of the Greek-Turkish crisis, Papandreou—instead of turning to the NATO alliance or the European Communities for support—dispatched Foreign Minister Karolos Papou-

lias to Sofia with a personal message for Bulgarian Pres. Todor Zhivkov. Besides generating groundless rumours of Bulgarian promises of military support, the mission was meant to imply mistrust of the U.S. and the West and to remind Turkey that it was also at odds with neighbouring Bulgaria over minorities. It had become clear to Papandreou that Greece's security in the Aegean would be in serious jeopardy without the sustained goodwill of the U.S. and NATO. Nevertheless, the U.S. and Greece continued throughout 1987 to jockey for position. They exchanged snubs and defiance, which merely delayed talks on the future of the U.S. installations after the existing agreement expired at the end of 1988. The most striking, if short-lived, tiff occurred in June when Papandreou postponed the opening of talks until the U.S. officially retracted charges that Greece had granted safe passage to Arab terrorists in return for immunity for Greek-related targets.

Papandreou's real dilemma was that his ruling Panhellenic Socialist Movement (Pasok) stood little chance of surviving in power after the next general elections if it continued to displease its left-wing constituents. This was bound to happen if, despite his pledge to remove all foreign bases after 1988, Papandreou signed a new pact with the U.S. In this context, on May 24 he announced in Parliament that if negotiations produced an agreement that "serves the paramount interests of our nation," it would be put to the people for approval in a national referendum. This maneuver absolved him from blame if the bases remained and also left him facing the Americans with all his options open. Preliminary talks on the future of the bases began on November 9, and the Greek government said at

Anticipating shortages of goods, Greek shoppers jammed supermarkets during a period of tense Greco-Turkish relations. The crisis began when Turkey mistakenly thought that Greece intended to drill offshore oil wells in disputed territorial waters in the Aegean Sea.

the outset that this would be a long-winded negotiation. Many Greeks suspected that Papandreou wanted to keep the issue alive for eventual use in his domestic strategy. For instance, although elections were not due until mid-1989, an abrupt break in talks, combined with a call to the Americans to remove their installations at once, could rally the left behind him in a snap election.

This scenario seemed even more plausible as the Socialist government watched its popularity decline rapidly after a two-year-long economic austerity program. Tight policies reduced government deficits, cut inflation, and boosted business profits, but only at a heavy cost for wage-earners, whose income shrank by 12%. Despite frequent labour strikes, the government decided to persevere with its economic restraint, but it was forced to promise some relaxation by 1988. Budgetary stringency was reflected in worsening conditions in public health and, especially, education, which prompted widespread student unrest. Heavy snowstorms in the spring damaged crops, while a freak heat wave in July caused more than 1,000 deaths.

Hopes of a breakthrough in the struggle against domestic terrorism rose in September following a gun battle between police and alleged terrorists in Athens, in which one man was killed, two were captured, and arms caches were discovered. However, the outcome of investigations remained in doubt. Responsibility for two terrorist attacks against buses carrying U.S. servicemen near Athens, in which 12 people were injured, was claimed by the mysterious "November 17 Revolutionary Organization."

Domestic tensions were heightened by the conflict between the state and the Orthodox Church over legislation that placed monastic property and valuable church-owned urban property under state control. (*See* RELIGION: *The Orthodox Church.*) Popular dissatisfaction was aggravated by a spate of scandals involving corruption in public enterprises. The government resisted pressure for a parliamentary investigation of accusations of embezzlement and fraud. Papandreou tried to react to the general sense of failure, inadequacy, and immorality by reshuffling his Cabinet on two occasions: on February 5 he transferred his principal ministers to the party's executive, and on September 22, quite inexplicably, he moved them back again, some with enhanced powers.     (MARIO MODIANO)

## ICELAND

Iceland is an island republic in the North Atlantic Ocean, near the Arctic Circle. Area: 103,000 sq km (39,769 sq mi). Pop. (1987 est.): 245,000. Cap.: Reykjavík. Monetary unit: Icelandic króna, with (Oct. 5, 1987) a free rate of 39.06 krónur to U.S. $1 (63.44 krónur = £1 sterling). President in 1987, Vigdís Finnbogadóttir; prime ministers, Steingrímur Hermannsson and, from July 8, Thorsteinn Pálsson.

Parliamentary elections were held in Iceland on April 25, 1987, the first in nearly four years. Shortly before the elections the country's largest party, the Independence Party, split after one of its leaders, Industry Minister Albert Gudmundsson, was forced to resign from the Cabinet following allegations of tax evasion. Gudmundsson went on to form his own party, the Citizen's Party, which presented a full slate of candidates.

Gudmundsson and six other candidates of the Citizen's Party were elected, mostly at the expense of the Independence Party. Though the number of seats it held declined from 23 in 1983 to 18, the Independence Party nevertheless remained the single largest party in the new Althing (parliament), enlarged from 60 members to 63. The Social Democratic Party was the only one of the four traditional

parties to emerge with an increased number of seats (ten, compared with six in 1983); its success was explained by the fact that the splinter Social Democratic Alliance had merged back into the party ranks. The Progressive Party and the People's Party lost seats to the smaller parties, the Citizen's Party and the Women's Alliance. The latter, which doubled its representation from three to six seats, ran on a platform advocating sexual and social equality and peace. (For tabulated results, see *Political Parties,* above.)

Despite the split within the Independence Party, a coalition government was formed under its leadership. In the previous Althing the Progressives had led a coalition with the Independents, but since these two parties no longer commanded a parliamentary majority, they were forced to expand the coalition by taking in the Social Democrats, after some ten weeks of discussion. The new government came into office on July 8 under the prime ministership of 39-year-old Thorsteinn Pálsson (*see* BIOGRAPHIES) of the Independence Party. His ten-member Cabinet comprised four Progressives, including former prime minister Steingrímur Hermannsson (foreign affairs), and three ministers each from the Independence and Social Democratic parties.

One of the government's most pressing tasks was to deal with mounting pressures in the economy resulting from rapid growth in 1986 and 1987. In 1986 real gross national product increased by an estimated 6.2%, largely on the basis of substantial growth in exports. The government succeeded in lowering inflation considerably, bringing the rate down to about 12–14% (annualized basis) at the beginning of 1987. However, this rate—low by Icelandic standards—could not be maintained throughout 1987 and rose to some 25% (annualized) by the end of the year. Despite the rapid growth in output, demand in 1986 rose moderately, making possible the achievement of a small surplus on the current account of the balance of payments—unusual for Iceland. In the course of 1987, however, demand pressures began to build up gradually in concert with the production boom. The current account slid into deficit, and the labour market became very tight.

Whaling turned out to be one of the thornier issues of Iceland's foreign policy during 1987. Several years earlier Iceland had decided to bow to international conservationist pressure and cease commercial whaling. Instead, it instituted a scientific whaling program that allowed for a catch of 120 whales per year, compared with an average annual commercial catch of 300–400. Conservationist groups maintained, however, that whaling for scientific purposes was nothing but commercial whaling in disguise and brought considerable pressure upon Iceland to cease its whaling activities entirely. The U.S. government called for urgent consultations with Iceland in midyear—which is also the whaling season—and the implication of the consultations was that if Iceland did not stop catching whales, the U.S. would deny access to its exports. A compromise was finally reached in September when Iceland undertook to abide by the decisions of the Scientific Committee of the International Whaling Commission in the future.

(BJÖRN MATTHÍASSON)

## IRELAND

The republic of Ireland, separated from Great Britain by the North Channel, the Irish Sea, and St. George's Channel, shares its island with Northern Ireland to the northeast. Area: 70,285 sq km (27,137 sq mi). Pop. (1987 est.): 3,560,000. Cap.: Dublin. Monetary unit: Irish pound (punt), with (Oct. 5, 1987) a free rate of Ir£0.69 to U.S. $1 (Ir£1.12 = £1 sterling). President in 1987, Patrick J. Hillery; prime ministers, Garret FitzGerald and, from March 10, Charles Haughey.

Party supporters and fellow candidates applaud Charles Haughey as they await results of the Irish general elections. Haughey's party, Fianna Fail, won 81 seats, and Haughey later became prime minister.
AP/WIDE WORLD

The year 1987 opened with the Irish coalition government of Fine Gael and the Labour Party, led by Prime Minister Garret FitzGerald, in political turmoil. The coalition collapsed on January 20 when the four Labour ministers resigned after refusing to accept proposed cuts in public expenditure contained in the 1987 budget on the grounds that they would hit workers and lower-income groups hardest. FitzGerald went on to form the first minority Fine Gael government in the history of Ireland, but it proved to be short-lived. On January 21 the Dail was dissolved, and general elections were called for February 17.

The general elections resulted in substantially reduced representation for Fine Gael, which secured 51 seats, compared with 70 in 1982. Fianna Fail won 81 seats, 6 more than in 1982, but nevertheless failed to command an overall majority. The Progressive Democrats (PD), formed in December 1985 by former Fianna Fail minister Desmond O'Malley and contesting their first general election, overtook the Labour Party to become the third largest group in the Dail. The PD won 14 seats, compared with the Labour Party's 12. (For tabulated results, see *Political Parties,* above.) Shortly before the election Sinn Fein, which in November 1986 had voted to end its policy of not taking up any seats in the Dail won by its candidates, was officially registered as a political party. However, the ban on political broadcasts by the party—the political wing of the Provisional Irish Republican Army—remained in force. Sinn Fein failed to win any seats.

In the vote to elect the *taoiseach* (prime minister) on March 10, Fianna Fail leader Charles Haughey secured 82 votes (81 Fianna Fail deputies and an independent) to 82 against and finally won when the speaker supported him with his casting vote. Key members of Haughey's 16-member Cabinet included Brian Lenihan (deputy prime minister and foreign affairs), Ray MacSharry (finance and public service), and Gerard Collins (justice). All but five members of the new Cabinet had served in previous administrations under Haughey in 1979–81 and 1982.

The day after the elections, in a decision that took both party members and commentators by surprise, FitzGerald resigned as leader of Fine Gael, a post he had held for ten years. Tributes flowed in from all over the world to

mark the major contribution he had made to the intellectual and political life of the country. The 1985 Anglo-Irish agreement was widely regarded as his main political achievement. On March 21 the parliamentary party elected Alan Dukes (*see* BIOGRAPHIES), former justice minister, to succeed him.

The economy dominated the remainder of the year. Fine Gael pledged its support for the new government's budget, introduced in late March, thus enabling it to be passed and allowing current spending to be cut by Ir£246 million. "Financial rectitude" was the message repeatedly forced on the people by MacSharry, who proved to be tough and uncompromising. Cuts were made across the board—in spending on health, social welfare, education, and the environment—with resultant loss of jobs. In 1987 unemployment stood at 18.6% of the work force. The response to these harsh measures, however, was a fall in interest rates, a forecast of 1% growth in gross national product, an inflation rate of 3.2%, and a measure of optimism that the country's finances were being taken in hand. Further details of cuts amounting to Ir£485 million, at a cost of 8,000 state jobs, were announced in October as part of a three-year plan for economic recovery. Haughey was confident that, as a result of talks with trade unions and employers, these measures could be introduced. There was criticism from some experts, however, that the severity of the cuts would inhibit economic growth.

There were two significant constitutional issues during the year. A Supreme Court case established that the Single European Act, designed to harmonize the laws of the European Communities member states, contravened Ireland's constitution and that a referendum had to be held in order to amend the constitution and allow for ratification. The result of the referendum, held on May 26, was 69.9–30.1% in favour of ratification in a low turnout (44%). Following the tapping of their telephones, three Dublin journalists won an action against the state that established a new constitutional right to privacy.

Controversy over proposed new legislation on extradition erupted in the latter part of the year. In December 1986 the Fine Gael government had secured the passage of a bill providing for Ireland's ratification of the European Convention on the Suppression of Terrorism. As a result, new extradition procedures were to be adopted, but Fianna Fail (then in opposition) had succeeded in inserting an amendment into the bill delaying the adoption of these procedures from June 1987 to December. Fianna Fail had originally delayed implementation because it was seeking reforms from the U.K. on the administration of justice in Northern Ireland. Haughey expressed disappointment over the limited progress that had been made under the Anglo-Irish agreement and, in particular, over the fact that the "Diplock" courts, which had one judge and no jury, continued to try those suspected of terrorist acts. The extradition agreement was approved by the Dail on December 3.

On October 14 John O'Grady was kidnapped by an armed gang, led by Dessie O'Hare, a former member of the Irish National Liberation Army and of the Irish Republican Army. The gang apparently mistook O'Grady for his father-in-law, medical millionaire Austin Darragh. The rescue of O'Grady by police in Dublin on November 5 was marred by the subsequent escape of several of the kidnappers from police custody. O'Hare was captured, following a gun battle with police on November 27.

Irishman of the year was, undoubtedly, Stephen Roche, who was made a freeman of Dublin for his cycling successes in 1987. (*See* SPORTS AND GAMES: *Cycling*.) A market research survey entitled "Perspectives on Irish Society" revealed that the Irish considered themselves to be proud, patriotic, and Christian but less caring than they had been 20 years earlier.                                    (MAVIS ARNOLD)

See also *United Kingdom,* below.

## ITALY

A republic of southern Europe, Italy occupies the Apennine Peninsula, Sicily, Sardinia, and a number of smaller islands in the Mediterranean Sea. Area: 301,277 sq km (116,324 sq mi). Pop. (1987 est.): 57,256,000. Cap.: Rome. Monetary unit: Italian lira, with (Oct. 5, 1987) a free rate of 1,329 lire to U.S. $1 (2,158 lire = £1 sterling). President in 1987, Francesco Cossiga; prime ministers, Bettino Craxi to April 18, Amintore Fanfani, and, from July 29, Giovanni Goria.

General elections took place in Italy on June 14–15, 1987, a year early. It was the fourth consecutive time that Parliament had failed to serve out its five-year term. The government that emerged after the elections comprised the same coalition of five parties—the Christian Democrats, Socialists, Social Democrats, Republicans, and Liberals—that Socialist Bettino Craxi had headed as prime minister for most of the previous four years. The new government was led by a Christian Democrat, Giovanni Goria (*see* BIOGRAPHIES). He took office on July 29, one day before his 44th birthday, making him Italy's youngest prime minister.

The way in which Craxi had become prime minister in 1983, when his Socialist Party won only 11% of the vote, was an essential element in the story of why elections came to be called in 1987. At that time the Christian Democrats, commanding three times the parliamentary strength of the Socialists, had a new leader, Ciriaco De Mita, who had consented to support Craxi as prime minister because he regarded the restructuring of his own party as his main task. De Mita claimed he had a pact with Craxi, made during a Cabinet crisis in July 1986, that the latter would step down in March 1987 to make way for a Christian Democrat prime minister. As the time approached, however, Craxi denied that such a pact existed and said that if it did he was renouncing it. The premiership was not a "relay race" with the baton of command to be passed on to the next man. De Mita replied that Craxi was "not trustworthy in a democracy."

Craxi wanted to preside over the Socialist Party conference, held at the end of March in Rimini, as the sitting prime minister. The Rimini conference saw Craxi bathing in oceans of adoration, bordering on cult worship. It was a personal triumph for the man who had taken over the party little more than ten years earlier. Before the party conference, on March 3, Craxi had delivered a speech to the Chamber of Deputies in praise of Italy's achievements under his guidance. The speech was ambiguous about his status as prime minister, but Pres. Francesco Cossiga interpreted it as a definitive resignation and asked Foreign Minister Giulio Andreotti, a Christian Democrat who had been prime minister five times, to see if he could form a new government. Craxi put obstacles in his way, and the Christian Democrat prime minister designate was surprised to learn that the Socialists had espoused five referenda, which concerned nuclear energy and judicial reform and had been sponsored initially by the Radicals. The Socialists maintained that they would join a new coalition only if the referenda were held before July.

The constitution allowed citizens to abrogate a law by referendum, but no referendum could be held in the same 12 months as general elections. The Christian Democrats were therefore wary of the five referenda. Their wariness also sprang from their belief that the voting in a referendum, whatever the issue, might be taken as a poll of public support for the parties. That was probably Craxi's intention when he became, almost overnight, the white knight defending the people's right to a referendum.

Cossiga summoned Craxi to Rome from the Rimini conference in what looked at first like a presidential appeal to the Socialist to withdraw his implicit resignation. Andreotti having failed in his effort to form an administration, Nilde Iotti, the 67-year-old Communist chairman of the Chamber since 1979, was given an "exploratory mandate" by Cossiga to find out what was going on among the parties. On April 8 the 15 Christian Democrat ministers resigned from the Craxi Cabinet, and at last the president and the public knew that the Craxi government had ended.

Amintore Fanfani, another Christian Democrat who had served five times as prime minister, was able to announce on April 18 that he had formed an "institutional" government—one put together, in effect, to see the country through the now inevitable elections. Fanfani resigned ten days later but remained in office until Goria was sworn in on July 29.

In the elections the Christian Democrats won 34.3% of the national vote (an increase of 1.4% over 1983); the Socialist Party's share increased by 2.9% to 14.3%, while the Communists' vote declined by 3.3%, leaving them with 26.6% and still the second largest party in the Chamber

Italy's president, Francesco Cossiga (left), swears in Giovanni Goria (right) as the new Italian prime minister before Sergio Berlinguer (centre), general secretary of the Quirinale Presidential Palace.

of Deputies, but with a troubled future. Among the other seven parties who won seats in Parliament, the *Verdi* (the Greens), in their maiden ballot, obtained 2.5%, nearly one million votes, and occupied 13 of the 630 seats in the Chamber. The major parties became intensely concerned with ecological matters following the Greens' unforeseen good showing. (For tabulated results, see *Political Parties*, above.)

The results clearly indicated that the next prime minister would be a Christian Democrat. De Mita did not want the job, but he had prepared a shortlist of candidates that did not include Goria, the outgoing treasury minister. Cossiga, whose presidency until then had been placid, took his own Christian Democrats by surprise in asking the relatively young Goria to see if he could form a government. It seemed an acceptable idea to outsiders, even though the Goria Cabinet was not itself a radical change from its predecessors. The Socialists let it be known that they were still pulling the strings of government. That seemed to be the case when Goria decided to send Italian minesweepers and other vessels to the Gulf even though Andreotti, who remained foreign minister in the new government, was firmly opposed.

The referenda had been postponed but, meanwhile, Parliament had changed the law, and they were held five months after the elections, on November 8. Italians voted overwhelmingly in favour of limiting nuclear energy and making judges liable to be penalized for judicial errors. The government had 150 days to alter existing laws to take these views into account.

The government faced its first crisis on November 13 when the Liberals withdrew from the coalition because they disagreed with the proposed budget for 1988. Goria offered his resignation, but in little over a week the quarrel was resolved, and his resignation offer was withdrawn. In December Goria visited Washington and held talks with U.S. Pres. Ronald Reagan.

Goria and seven Cabinet ministers went to Venice in the autumn to sign the necessary documents authorizing the spending of 6.5 billion lire on projects designed to preserve and improve the city, with the provision that the funds be spent by 1995. On three or four holiday weekends each year, the city authorities were forced to close the causeway connecting Venice with the mainland after an estimated 90,000 visitors had crossed. Too many tourists, all parties agreed, made enjoyment of Venice impossible for either visitor or native.

The inquiries in Milan into the suspected fraudulent bankruptcy of the Banco Ambrosiano led in February to the issue of an arrest warrant for Archbishop Paul Marcinkus, the American who headed the Istituto per le Opere di Religione (Institute for Religious Works, otherwise known as the Vatican bank). Warrants were also issued for two of the bank's lay executives. All three had taken up residence within the walls of the extraterritorial Vatican City State. Extradition from the Vatican to Italy was turned down by the Holy See, and its objection was upheld in July by the Italian Supreme Court. The Concordat between the two states did not allow Italian interference in the Vatican's "central administration."

It was thought possible that another extradition sought by the same Milan magistrates, that of Licio Gelli, who turned himself over to the Swiss police in September, might be successful—and with repercussions involving not only the Banco Ambrosiano collapse but wrongdoing in the Italian political world as well. Until 1981 Gelli had been venerable master of the P2 Masonic lodge in Rome. This maverick—subsequently outlawed—lodge, virtually

of Gelli's own invention, had become a clearinghouse for Italian political, military, and financial scandals, all kept on file for Gelli's personal use.

The *maxi-processo*—the trial in Palermo of alleged Mafia members, which opened in February 1986—ended on Dec. 16, 1987. The jury found 338 of the 452 defendants guilty, and 19 people were sentenced to life imprisonment.

In 1987 Italy's Central Institute of Statistics suddenly decided that Italy had become the world's fifth economic power, having overtaken the U.K., which held the position previously. During the final weeks of his administration, Craxi used the claim to press Italy's case for a stronger voice among Western nations. Part of the explanation for the claim lay in the fact that the institute had decided to give legitimacy at last to Italy's long-submerged economy—income from moonlighting and second jobs, which went untaxed and unrecorded in official registers. For example, many bureaucrats in Rome worked from 8 in the morning until 2 in the afternoon, after which they were free to handle a second permanent job. It was estimated that this activity increased total gross domestic product (GDP) by some 15–18%.

Partly as a result of the fall in oil prices and the depreciation of the U.S. dollar, the economy performed well in 1986. Inflation declined to around 6%, and both trade and current accounts were in surplus. Real GDP rose by 2.7%, one of the highest growth rates in the European Communities, and was expected to increase by up to 3% in 1987. The unemployment rate (11.1% in 1986) continued to rise in 1987. (GEORGE ARMSTRONG)

## LIECHTENSTEIN

A landlocked constitutional monarchy of central Europe, Liechtenstein is united with Switzerland by a customs and monetary union. Area: 160 sq km (62 sq mi). Pop. (1987 est.): 27,500. Cap.: Vaduz. Monetary unit: Swiss franc, with (Oct. 5, 1987) a free rate of Sw F 1.53 to U.S. $1 (Sw F 2.49 = £1 sterling). Sovereign prince, Francis Joseph II; deputy head of state in 1987, Prince Hans Adam; head of government, Hans Brunhart.

Liechtenstein was one of six small European nations that met in Andorra la Vella in mid-September 1987 to discuss the virtues and problems of being a tiny state. (See *Andorra*, above.) Like the other states represented at the gathering, the principality depended for many of its services on a larger and more powerful neighbour—in this case, Switzerland. Liechtenstein depended on Switzerland for defense, transportation, and the administration of its postal and telecommunications services. It possessed no army, and the total police force numbered less than 50. Liechtenstein used Swiss currency, and the two countries had been joined by a customs union since 1923.

Much of Liechtenstein's income was derived from its status as a tax haven for foreign companies, from tourism, and from a variety of light industries established since the end of World War II, when a process of rapid industrialization had begun. (K. M. SMOGORZEWSKI)

This article updates the *Micropædia* article LIECHTENSTEIN.

## LUXEMBOURG

The Benelux country of Luxembourg is a landlocked constitutional monarchy in western Europe. Area: 2,586 sq km (999 sq mi). Pop. (1987 est.): 367,000. Cap.: Luxembourg. Monetary unit: Luxembourg franc, at par with the Belgian franc, with (Oct. 5, 1987) a free rate of Lux F 38.24 to U.S. $1 (Lux F 62.10 = £1 sterling). Grand duke, Jean; prime minister in 1987, Jacques Santer.

Eddie Fenech Adami is carried on the shoulders of his supporters at a mass meeting during Malta's tense election campaign. On May 9 Adami's Nationalist Party won the general elections, and he subsequently became prime minister.
M. LOUNES—GAMMA/LIAISON

Although the once all-important steel industry continued to face serious problems, exacerbated by the abolition of the European Communities' compulsory minimum price mechanism, Luxembourg's economy continued to thrive overall. Economic growth rose 2% in 1986 and was estimated at 2.5% in 1987. Several factors contributed to the buoyant economy in 1987: reductions in personal and corporate tax pushed up investment and personal spending, and the latter was also stimulated by high wage settlements.

The financial services sector continued to expand, and the Grand Duchy's first bank was set up by Banque Internationale à Luxembourg and Prominvest. It was to deal only with risk capital, and its objective was to help small companies by providing both finance and expertise. Unemployment remained extremely low (just over 1%) and continued to decline. Consumer price inflation ceased to be a factor—prices stagnated in 1986 and were expected to increase by less than 1% during 1987.

It was announced that a merchant flag would be created in order to develop a registration business. Belgian vessels were expected to switch to a Luxembourg flag by early 1988. On March 25 the defense minister signed a convention under which Luxembourg entered into a defense alliance with Belgium and The Netherlands. Since 1948 the three countries had been joined in a customs union, later widened into a more general economic union.

(K. M. SMOGORZEWSKI)

This article updates the *Macropædia* article The Low Countries: *Luxembourg*.

## MALTA

The republic of Malta, a member of the Commonwealth, comprises the islands of Malta, Gozo, and Comino in the Mediterranean Sea between Sicily and Tunisia. Area: 316 sq km (122 sq mi). Pop. (1987 est.): 345,000. Cap.: Valletta. Monetary unit: Maltese lira (formerly Maltese pound), with (Oct. 5, 1987) a free rate of 0.35 lira to U.S. $1 (0.57 lira = £1 sterling). Presidents in 1987, Agatha Barbara and, from February 15, Paul Xuereb (acting); prime ministers, Carmelo Mifsud Bonnici and, from May 12, Eddie Fenech Adami.

General elections to Malta's House of Representatives held on May 9, 1987, were won by the Nationalist Party, ending 16 years of Labour Party rule. The Nationalists attracted 50.9% of the popular vote but secured only 31 of 65 directly elected seats in Parliament to the Labour Party's 34; however, a constitutional amendment introduced in January stipulated that a party gaining a majority of votes and a minority of seats should be awarded extra seats to allow it to command a majority of one, and four extra seats were awarded to the Nationalists. A harsh and tense electoral campaign, beginning months earlier, was characterized by violent clashes between rival groups of supporters.

The new government of Prime Minister Eddie Fenech Adami (*see* BIOGRAPHIES) embarked on a program of liberalizing the economy, strengthening law and order, and consolidating Malta's foreign policy. In January the principle of neutrality based on a policy of nonalignment was incorporated into the constitution. On October 9 Fenech Adami became the first Maltese prime minister to address the UN General Assembly since his Nationalist predecessor, George Borg Olivier, in 1967. In October he attended the meeting of the Commonwealth heads of government, which was held in Vancouver, B.C.

On the strength of its mandate, the government held talks with a view to obtaining full membership in the European Communities. The financial position was not encouraging; the public deficit stood at 29 million lire in November 1987.

(ALBERT GANADO)

## MONACO

A sovereign principality on the northern Mediterranean coast, Monaco is bounded on land by the French département of Alpes-Maritimes. Area: 1.9 sq km (0.73 sq mi). Pop. (1987 est.): 29,000. Monetary unit: French franc, with (Oct. 5, 1987) a free rate of F 6.13 to U.S. $1 (F 9.96 = £1 sterling). Chief of state, Prince Rainier III; minister of state in 1987, Jean Ausseil.

During 1986 Monaco experienced a drop of 75–80% in the number of summer visitors from the U.S. The decline brought greater urgency to efforts to diversify Monaco's sources of income. In an interview with the London *Financial Times* in March 1987, Prince Rainier III described how Monaco was trying to attract more business from conventions and congresses and to encourage industry. Considering the possibility that Monaco could become an offshore banking centre along the lines of Liechtenstein, Prince Rainier remarked that such a move would have to be made in accordance with the rules of Monaco's treaty with France.

Commenting on the frequent speculation that he would soon make way for his son, Prince Albert, Prince Rainier said, "We have agreed with each other that he will take over when he feels he's ready."

Monaco was one of six small nation-states of Europe that held a week-long meeting in Andorra in September to discuss aspects of being a tiny country.

(K. M. SMOGORZEWSKI)

This article updates the *Micropædia* article MONACO.

## NETHERLANDS, THE

A constitutional monarchy of northwestern Europe, The Netherlands, a Benelux country, is on the North Sea. Area: 41,785 sq km (16,133 sq mi). Pop. (1987 est.): 14,615,000. Cap., Amsterdam; seat of government, The Hague. Monetary unit: Netherlands guilder, with (Oct. 5, 1987) a free rate of 2.07 guilders to U.S. $1 (3.37 guilders = £1 sterling). Queen, Beatrix; prime minister in 1987, Ruud Lubbers.

On March 18, 1987, provincial elections took place in The Netherlands. By means of an indirect election system, the results also determined the composition of the First (upper) Chamber of Parliament. The two government parties—the Christian Democratic Appeal (CDA) and the Liberals (VVD)—both lost nearly 2% of the vote compared with the results of the 1986 general elections. Compared with the provincial elections of 1982, the losses of the VVD were more severe: the party secured 15.5% of the vote, as against 22.2% in 1982. The opposition Labour Party (PvdA) gained 12.2% to reach a total of 33% in 1987, giving it a share of the vote equal to that of the CDA. The regional effect of the election was significant, but in the First Chamber the government coalition partners held a narrow majority of 38 of the 75 seats. The CDA experienced surprising losses in its traditional stronghold, the Catholic province of Limburg, where its support declined from 51.4% in 1982 to 43% in 1987.

Following accusations of large-scale manipulation of building costs in order to secure higher government subsidies for the construction trade, Parliament decided to set up a parliamentary inquiry in October 1986. How much money was involved was not known precisely, but it was estimated that billions of guilders had been spent in this way over the period 1968–75. On Aug. 31, 1987, the parliamentary inquiry—headed by PvdA member Klaas de Vries—began its public hearings. The key question in the investigation turned out to be whether a "gentleman's agreement" had existed with either the government or public officials that had allowed financiers in the construction business to manipulate building costs in order to increase their short-term profits. Clear proof of such an agreement had not been found, but there was evidence of a total lack of government control. The inquiry was expected to be completed by mid-1988.

Having just recovered from a short illness, Queen Beatrix delivered the traditional speech to open the new parliamentary year on September 15. In order to lower the budget deficit, the government planned to reduce spending by 7 billion guilders in 1988. The health service and welfare in particular were hit by the cuts. Prime Minister Ruud Lubbers's Cabinet also proclaimed a slight overall tax decrease. Despite a moderate economic recovery, unemployment was decreasing by less than had been forecast, and the level of unemployed remained at over half a million.

Accompanied by a broad-based delegation of Dutch business people, Prime Minister Lubbers paid an official visit to China on May 10–17. Erich Honecker, the general secretary of the East German Communist Party, paid an official visit to The Netherlands on June 3–5, his third visit to a NATO member since 1985. After Foreign Minister Hans van den Broek failed to persuade members of the Western European Union to join the U.S. Navy in the "tanker war" in the Gulf, the Dutch government decided on September 7 to send two minesweepers to the area.

On September 8 Klaas de Jonge, who had been accused by the South African police of illegally supplying arms to the African National Congress—a charge that he

admitted—returned home from South Africa. After escaping from the custody of the South African police, he had sought refuge in the Dutch embassy in Pretoria, where the Dutch government protected him for nearly two years. Through diplomatic efforts, the Dutch government finally succeeded in getting him out of the country in a complex prisoner exchange that also involved Angola and France.

(KLAAS J. HOEKSEMA)

See also *Dependent States,* below.

This article updates the *Macropædia* article The Low COUNTRIES: *The Netherlands.*

## NORWAY

A constitutional monarchy of northern Europe, Norway occupies the western part of the Scandinavian Peninsula, with coastlines on the Skagerrak, the North Sea, the Norwegian Sea, and the Arctic Ocean. Area: 323,878 sq km (125,050 sq mi), excluding the Svalbard Archipelago and Jan Mayen Island. Pop. (1987 est.): 4,180,000. Cap.: Oslo. Monetary unit: Norwegian krone, with (Oct. 5, 1987) a free rate of 6.73 kroner to U.S. $1 (10.93 kroner = £1 sterling). King, Olav V; prime minister in 1987, Gro Harlem Brundtland.

Norway's minority Labour government led by Prime Minister Gro Harlem Brundtland consolidated its hold on political power during 1987. Growing divisions between the non-Socialist opposition parties in the Storting (parliament) thwarted an attempt to topple the government on June 12 when Labour survived a vote of no confidence. It seemed increasingly likely that Labour would remain in office at least until the next parliamentary elections, due in September 1989.

Labour continued to pursue the austerity policies adopted when it took over in May 1986 from the three-party coalition led by the Conservatives. The draft budget for 1988, introduced on October 6, envisioned higher direct and indirect taxes and lower consumer subsidies. Moreover, it proposed to carry further tax reforms aimed at closing tax-avoidance loopholes, discouraging borrowing, and stimulating saving. The stringent regime was necessary because revenues from the offshore oil and gas industry were hard hit by the 1986 oil price collapse. The government aimed to make the economy less dependent on the petroleum sector by stimulating growth in land-based industry.

Although spring wage settlements were moderate, wage costs were boosted by a reform that shortened the standard workweek for blue-collar employees to 37.5 hours, bringing it into line with that of white-collar workers. The Norwegian Employers' Association estimated that this change created around 2,000 new jobs, led to increased overtime, and raised hourly wages by an average of 5.2%. Unemployment was negligible.

Local government elections held in September saw unexpectedly strong gains by the right-wing, antitax Progress Party. This group, whose two representatives in the Storting held the balance of power between the Socialist and non-Socialist parties, had never previously secured more than 4–5% of the vote. This time the Progress Party scored 10.4%, putting it in third place after Labour (36%) and the Conservatives (23.2%). Both those parties lost ground compared with the 1985 parliamentary elections and the 1983 local government elections. Labour voters were disappointed by the government's tough economic policies and the high level of interest rates maintained to discourage consumer borrowing and to bolster the strength of the Norwegian krone. Conservative voters were disappointed by their party's failure to regain power. The election result led to the resignation of Rolf Presthus as Conservative leader, effective January 1988.

Another factor in the election was the government's liberal policy on third world immigration. This policy, increasingly unpopular with many Norwegians, was to admit virtually anyone claiming political persecution at home and to allow them to remain in Norway until their cases could be investigated. As other nations tightened immigration controls, the number of self-styled "asylum seekers" arriving in Norway rose steadily, putting a heavy burden on public funds. A tougher government line on immigration seemed likely. In October Deputy Justice Minister Tore-Jarl Christensen said Norway would refuse entry to Tamils who had left Sri Lanka after the July peace accord.

In November a government inquiry uncovered attempts by the board of Statoil, the state-owned oil company, to cover up substantial overspending on an oil refinery project. The oil minister refused to dismiss the Statoil board, and a government crisis was averted when several board members resigned on November 20.

In the offshore oil industry, exploration drilling began in the Barents Sea area above the North Cape. Geologists regarded the area as highly promising, but the first two wells proved to be dry. In midyear the platforms on the Ekofisk oil and gas field were raised six metres (20 ft) in a unique engineering operation, made necessary because the seabed had subsided as a result of petroleum extraction. Production in 1987 was forecast to reach 76 million metric tons of oil equivalent, compared with 68 million tons of oil equivalent in 1986.

Thorvald Stoltenberg was appointed foreign affairs minister in March, following the death of Knut Frydenlund (*see* OBITUARIES) on February 26.          (FAY GJESTER)

See also *Dependent States,* below.

## PORTUGAL

A republic of southwestern Europe, metropolitan Portugal is on the Atlantic coast of the Iberian Peninsula, which it shares with Spain. Area: 92,389 sq km (35,672 sq mi), including the Azores and Madeira island groups/archipelagoes in the Atlantic. Pop. (1987 est.): 10,312,000. Cap.: Lisbon. Monetary unit: Portuguese escudo, with (Oct. 5, 1987) a free rate of 145.02 escudos to U.S. $1 (235.50 escudos = £1 sterling). President in 1987, Mário Soares; prime minister, Aníbal Cavaço Silva.

After nearly 18 months in office, Portugal's minority Social Democratic Party (PSD) government was brought down in April 1987. It was defeated by 134–108 on a motion of censure introduced by former president Gen. António Ramalho Eanes's centre-left Democratic Renewal Party (PRD), backed by the Socialist Party (PSP) and the Communists. Following consultations in the Council of State, 12 of the 17 members voted to hold an early election rather than form a new government with the opposition. Pres. Mário Soares voted for dissolution on the grounds that no satisfactory alternative government was offered to him by the parties backing the censure motion. Prime Minister Aníbal Cavaço Silva agreed to head a caretaker administration from April 18 until elections could take place. The Assembly was dissolved, and elections were called for July 19—the fifth snap election to be held in eight years.

The good-tempered but frenetic three-week campaign that ensued ended with Cavaço Silva's PSD receiving 50.15% of the vote, well over the 43% needed for an overall majority in Parliament. The ruling party benefited from Portugal's economic performance in 1986, when economic growth had been the highest in continental Europe, and from a surge of interest from first-time voters, who favoured the government's attempts to modernize the country by attacking problems of heavy overstaffing in the

Portugal's prime minister, Aníbal Cavaço Silva, greets supporters during his campaign for reelection. Cavaço Silva's Social Democratic Party won a controlling majority in the Parliament, producing the country's first stable government since 1974.
FRANCO—PHOTO SPRINT/GAMMA/LIAISON

civil services and public sector, as well as those of the farming sector.

The election gave Cavaço Silva and his PSD a historic majority and provided Portugal with its first stable government since 1974. The PSD increased its seats to 148 from 88 in 1985. The result marked a major defeat for the PRD, which lost 38 seats, and Eanes resigned from the party leadership. The PSP slightly strengthened its position, gaining 3 seats for a total of 60. (For tabulated results, see *Political Parties,* above.)

Elections for the 24 seats in the European Parliament were held simultaneously and showed a similar voting pattern. The PSD led with ten, followed by the PSP with six, the Democratic and Social Centre (CDS) with four, the Communist Party with three, and the PRD with one. Well-known personalities who were elected included former prime minister Maria de Lourdes Pintasilgo and Francisco António Lucas Pires, a former CDS leader.

On August 12 Cavaço Silva named his Cabinet, returning many of the same people but adding two new positions. Former education minister João de Deus Pinheiro became the new foreign minister, replacing Pedro Pires de Miranda, and Miguel Ribeiro Cadilhe retained his post as finance minister. Enrico de Melo was appointed to the new post of deputy prime minister, as well as to the defense ministry, and the newly created minister of youth was António Couto dos Santos. The only non-PSD member of the Cabinet was Roberto Carneiro, a former supporter of the CDS, who took the trouble-ridden education portfolio.

The new government pledged to give priority to building political confidence, reducing regional disparities, and increasing the role of the private sector. Cavaço Silva's pragmatic populist approach to the role of the state in social matters was set to continue, as were his attempts to revise labour legislation, curb state-sector spending, and lessen state control over the industrial and service sectors of the economy. To do so he needed to amend the country's constitution, which provided for absolute job security and widespread public ownership. He had a strong mandate to do this, and the Socialists were quick to express their willingness to negotiate changes.

At the end of a trial that had begun in July 1985, Lieut. Col. Otelo Saraiva de Carvalho, a hero of the 1974 revolution, was sentenced to 15 years in prison in May for his part in organizing the activities of the Popular Forces of April 25 (FP-25) urban guerrilla group. The group had carried out a series of terrorist attacks against NATO and U.S. targets in Portugal in the early 1980s.

The economy continued to expand rapidly following its record 4.8% growth in 1986 and was expected to grow a further 4–4.5% in 1987, boosted by strong investment and consumer spending. The inflation rate continued to decline and was not expected to exceed 10% in 1987, compared with nearly 20% in 1985. Private consumption, which rose by 6.5% in 1986 and by a similar amount in 1987, was stimulated by high wage increases. A less positive effect of buoyant consumer demand was the 30% rise in imports in the first nine months of the year, increasing the trade deficit. Concern that the economy was expanding too fast was a major factor behind the government's 1988 budget, which was designed to cut domestic demand to 4% while at the same time maintaining steady capital investment growth. In November the Cabinet approved a draft privatization law that would give employees and small investors guaranteed shares in certain public corporations.

In foreign policy, the European Communities (EC) continued to receive the highest priority, both from the point of view of maximizing potential aid from the EC to its poorest member and from that of meeting increased competition from EC companies. The EC had designated Portugal as a priority country for its regional development aid. The government was intensifying its efforts to gain better access to EC markets for sensitive products such as textiles, tomato paste, wood pulp, cellulose, and footwear.

Cavaço Silva was attempting to improve the country's benefits from U.S. bases in Portugal; in October he stated that, because he was not happy with U.S. aid, he might renegotiate the lease on the U.S. air base in the Azores, although it did not expire until 1991.

In March Portugal agreed to hand over control of the colony of Macau to China in December 1999. The agreement was expected to be similar to that signed between the U.K. and China on the future of Hong Kong. In a surprise move the government said it would no longer demand self-determination for East Timor, which had been the cause of dispute with Indonesia since 1975.

(MICHAEL WOOLLER)

See also *Dependent States,* below.

## SAN MARINO

The republic of San Marino is a landlocked enclave in northeastern Italy. Area: 61 sq km (24 sq mi). Pop. (1987 est.): 22,100. Cap.: San Marino. Monetary unit: Italian lira, with (Oct. 5, 1987) a free rate of 1,329 lire to U.S. $1 (2,158 lire = £1 sterling). The republic is governed by two *capitani reggenti,* or coregents, appointed every six months by a popularly elected Great and General Council. Executive power rests with the Congress of State, composed of the coregents, three secretaries of state, and seven ministers.

During 1987 San Marino continued to be governed by a coalition of Christian Democrats and Communists, which had come to power in July 1986 following the collapse of the previous coalition of Communists, Socialists, and United Socialists. Elections to the Great and General Council were due to take place in 1988. The 60-member Council elected Renzo Renzi (Communist) and Carlo Franciosi (Christian Democrat) to serve as coregents for the six-month period beginning April 1, 1987. They were succeeded by Rossano Zafferani (Communist) and Gian

Franco Terenzi (Christian Democrat), who would serve until the end of March 1988.

The economy was almost entirely dependent on tourism. Some three million tourists visited the tiny republic each year. The coalition government planned a major development of hotel and recreational facilities, and it was proposed that a gambling casino be opened in order to finance the plans. Within the republic the suggestion provoked deep feelings both for and against, while it was widely assumed that the government of Italy would be strongly opposed to the move. Previous efforts to run a gambling casino in 1949 had been thwarted when the Italian government first withheld its annual grant and subsequently imposed a blockade that effectively discouraged tourists from making the trip. (K. M. SMOGORZEWSKI)

This article updates the *Micropædia* article SAN MARINO.

## SPAIN

A constitutional monarchy of southwestern Europe with coastlines on the Bay of Biscay, the Atlantic Ocean, and the Mediterranean Sea, Spain shares the Iberian Peninsula with Portugal; it includes the Balearic and Canary island groups, in the Mediterranean and the Atlantic, respectively, and enclaves in northern Morocco. Area: 504,783 sq km (194,898 sq mi). Pop. (1987 est.): 38,832,000. Cap.: Madrid. Monetary unit: Spanish peseta, with (Oct. 5, 1987) a free rate of 122.21 pesetas to U.S. $1 (198.45 pesetas = £1 sterling). King, Juan Carlos I; prime minister in 1987, Felipe González Márquez.

Prime Minister Felipe González Márquez and his Partido Socialista Obrero Español (PSOE; Spanish Socialist Workers' Party) had received overwhelming support in the June 1986 general elections, but political support for both fell dramatically in 1987. The June 10, 1987, municipal, regional, and European parliamentary elections reflected the decline. In the local elections the PSOE lost its absolute majority in 21 out of 27 major cities and in 7 out of 13 of the self-governing regions, forcing it to either share power with the Communists or move into opposition. The second major national party, the right-wing Alianza Popular (AP), and the Centro Democrático y Social (CDS) performed less well than expected. By contrast, regional parties, including Herri Batasuna, the political wing of the Basque separatist group Euzkadi ta Azkatasuna (ETA; Basque Homeland and Liberty), increased their votes. Geographically, it was in the area north of Madrid that the PSOE lost ground, with the Castilla-León and La Rioja regions going to the AP and Aragón to the AP and the regional party. The principal town halls to fall were Salamanca and Toledo to the AP, Segovia and Las Palmas to the CDS, and Pamplona to the regional centre-right party.

Elections to the European Parliament, in which Spain had 60 seats, secured 28 seats for the PSOE, which had 39% of the vote, compared with 44% at the 1986 general elections. The AP won 17 seats on a slightly lower vote than in 1986. The CDS, under former prime minister Adolfo Suárez, secured seven seats; it had not been represented at Strasbourg before.

ETA maintained its campaign of violence. Despite its earlier denial, the government held talks with the group, but little progress was made. A bomb attack on a supermarket in Barcelona on June 19 killed 21 civilians and brought an estimated quarter of a million protesters to the streets of the city. It evoked a public apology from ETA, which then reorganized with real power going to José Antonio Urrutikoetxea. It was known that ETA was split between its veterans, who were seeking an honourable way to lay down their arms, and the younger "commandos" in Madrid and Barcelona. Following the murder of one of its policemen, France involved itself in the anti-ETA campaign for the first time. A meeting between Pres. François Mitterrand of France and González at the end of August produced no immediate result but later led to the deportation of members of the ETA resident command under French antiterrorist legislation. Since Herri Batasuna had gained support in the 1987 elections and had won a seat in the European Parliament, the government was unable to ban it. A state pact to which all Basque parties subscribed offered some hope that a solution might be reached.

There was an upsurge in strike activity during the year as the government tried to control inflation. Following the breakdown in wage negotiations with employers' federations in January, the largest union, the PSOE-affiliated Unión Generale de Trabajadores (UGT), and the Communist-led Comisiones Obreras, the second largest, planned a mass strike of all national services. The protests were directed at the government's attempts to impose a 5% ceiling on wage increases and restructuring measures in some industries that caused job losses. Relations between the government and the UGT reached an all-time low in October, when the veteran UGT secretary-general Nicolás Redondo and another UGT member of the Cortes (parliament) resigned from the government. Another MP who had led the Socialist-left faction of the PSOE had also resigned, against his will, following the publication of injurious remarks he had made about the personal wealth and business activities of key party leaders. González appeared indifferent to the members' actions, reportedly because he saw the sharing of power with the unions as potentially disastrous.

Spain's entry into the European Communities (EC) on Jan. 1, 1986, initially had a positive effect on the economy. Gross domestic product rose by 3% in 1986 and by a similar amount in 1987. The growth was led by an unprecedentedly high level of consumer spending, an influx of foreign investment, and strong industrial output and was accompanied by an increase in jobs. The rate of inflation was under greater control and not expected to exceed 6% in 1987. By the middle of the year, however, the negative effects of the buoyant economy were beginning to become apparent. The consumer spending spree was extremely expensive in terms of imports, which rose 16% in 1986 and in the first few months of 1987 were running well over 30% above year-earlier levels. Export volume growth picked up from the 1% recorded in 1986, however, and the balance of payments position was sound because of record earnings from tourism and lower interest charges. Excessive public spending was a major contributor to the consumer boom, and the government responded with a tighter monetary policy and by increasing bank interest rates. It also tried to impose wage restraint but failed drastically; in the three months to August, average manufacturing wages were rising at a 15% annual rate.

Within the EC Spain was active in blocking a new air transport agreement until its dispute with the U.K. over the sharing of Gibraltar airport was resolved at year's end. (See *Dependent States,* below.) It also opposed spending increases in the EC's common agricultural policy, which it saw as more beneficial to northern European countries.

Talks with the U.S. over its bases continued during the year as the May 1988 expiration date of the treaty governing them approached. The two main bases, the naval-submarine depot at Rota and the air base at Torrejón, were seen as crucial to European defense by the U.S. Although Spain gave formal notice in November of its intention to renounce the treaty, there were conflicting reports as to how serious this intent was.          (MICHAEL WOOLLER)

## SWEDEN

A constitutional monarchy of northern Europe, Sweden occupies the eastern side of the Scandinavian Peninsula, with coastlines on the North and Baltic seas and the Gulf of Bothnia. Area: 449,964 sq km (173,732 sq mi). Pop. (1987 est.): 8,387,000. Cap.: Stockholm. Monetary unit: Swedish krona, with (Oct. 5, 1987) a free rate of 6.45 kronor to U.S. $1 (10.48 kronor = £1 sterling). King, Carl XVI Gustaf; prime minister in 1987, Ingvar Carlsson.

The hunt for the assassin of former prime minister Olof Palme, shot down in a Stockholm street late at night on Feb. 28, 1986, degenerated into farce during 1987. Stockholm police chief Hans Holmér ordered a series of raids on Sweden's Kurdish exile community, in which 20 arrests were made. During a press conference in January attended by journalists representing most of the important international media, Holmér clashed bitterly with the public prosecutor, Claes Zeime—who did not share his conviction that a Kurdish hit squad was to blame—before announcing that all suspects would be released. Holmér was forced to resign in March. Prime Minister Ingvar Carlsson had announced the establishment of a parliamentary commission of inquiry into the affair, and Swedes became increasingly resigned to the likelihood that the killer might never be found. In November the government placed advertisements in major newspapers around the world offering a reward for information leading to solution of the crime.

The country's reputation for efficiency and fair dealing took a further battering when it was revealed that Bofors, the leading Swedish arms manufacturer, had sold weapons, via a subsidiary in Singapore, to countries banned from receiving them under Swedish legislation that forbade weapons sales to "areas of conflict." It was further alleged that Bofors had paid bribes to secure a massive arms order from India. The affair led to several resignations of Bofors executives, a suicide, and a government reshuffle. Carlsson relieved Mats Hellström of the overseas trade portfolio and moved him to the Ministry of Agriculture. Hellström held ultimate responsibility for the Bofors deal, but it seemed that he might ride out the storm.

Police battled with thousands of bored, rioting teenagers in Stockholm at the end of the school holidays in August. Shop windows were smashed, stores plundered, cars overturned, and homemade firebombs hurled. The riots highlighted the human deficiencies of an otherwise efficient, extremely comprehensive welfare state and cast doubts on the country's liberal, antidisciplinarian teaching practices.

In a year that had turned into a chapter of errors, however, one event more than any other deeply shocked and worried Swedes, according to an opinion poll carried out by the authoritative Sifo research institute. This was the disappearance in October of Stig Bergling, the country's best-known spy and its only prisoner serving a full life sentence. Bergling vanished while improperly supervised on "conjugal leave" with his wife. Police did not notice his departure until the middle of the following day and failed to sound a national alarm until that evening. A hired car believed to have been used by the couple was later found in Finland, but there the trail went cold. It was revealed later that Bergling had been provided with a new identity, that of "Eugen Sandberg," by the Swedish authorities in the belief that he would one day be shown clemency. In the aftermath of the affair, Justice Minister Sten Wickbom was forced to resign on October 19, along with four senior civil servants. Anna-Greta Leijon was moved rapidly from the Ministry of Labour to sort out the mess. She was replaced as labour minister by local government politician Ingela Thalén.

The Swedish judicial system came under international attack in the case of Simon Hayward, a captain in the British Life Guards, held for more than four months in solitary confinement before being charged and found guilty of smuggling hashish into the country.

There were anti-American demonstrations during a visit by U.S. First Lady Nancy Reagan to see how Sweden handled its drug abuse problems, but an official visit by Carlsson to Washington in September set the seal on the hoped-for era of greatly improved relations between the two countries. Relations had reached an all-time low during the late 1960s and early 1970s because of Swedish opposition to U.S. involvement in the Vietnam war.

(CHRIS MOSEY)

## SWITZERLAND

A landlocked federal state in west central Europe, Switzerland consists of a confederation of 26 cantons (6 of which are demicantons). Area: 41,293 sq km (15,943 sq mi). Pop. (1987 est.): 6,586,000. Cap.: Bern. Monetary unit: Swiss franc, with (Oct. 5, 1987) a free rate of Sw F 1.53 to U.S. $1 (Sw F 2.49 = £1 sterling). President in 1987, Pierre Aubert.

Switzerland's main preoccupations in 1987 were essentially a continuation of those that marked the previous year: environment, drugs, refugees, and would-be economic migrants. In addition, there was a collection of lesser matters, including abnormally severe summer floods, especially in the Ticino and Grisons, and efforts by the U.S. and Philippine governments to obtain from Swiss banks details of accounts relating, respectively, to the Iran-*contra* affair and the assets accumulated by former Philippine president Ferdinand Marcos. The U.S. government's efforts were successful.

In view of public concern over the environment, the October general elections produced a surprise; the Greens did not fare nearly as well as had been expected, even though they increased their representation in the 200-member lower house, the National Council, by six seats to a total of nine. This outcome was attributed to the espousal by the four parties in the coalition government (the Radical Democrats [Conservatives], Social Democrats, and Christian Democrats, with two seats each in the Federal Council [Cabinet], and the People's Party with one) of the main ecological objectives on which the Greens had been instrumental in sensitizing the public. While both the Radicals and the Socialists lost votes to the Christian Democrats, this did not alter the distribution of portfolios in the Federal Council. (For tabulated results, see *Political Parties*, above.) There was a similar trend in voting for vacant seats in the upper house, the Council of States.

The December quarterly national referendum also produced a surprise, this time more directly encouraging for the Greens; a majority voted to preserve, in effect, what remained of the country's marshlands. The proposal was to prevent the largest peat-bog landscape left in the country, at Rothenthurm (Canton Schwyz), from being designated as a new training ground for the Swiss Army. This was only the ninth time in a century that a proposal resulting from a popular initiative had gained acceptance.

The final referendum of 1987 also produced a firm rejection, by more than two-thirds, of a proposal that would compel the country's sickness insurance funds—all recipients of federal subsidies—to extend their coverage to include maternity payments. The public, holding to the concept of maintaining individual responsibility, was clearly not prepared to have childbirth added to the factors responsible for the inexorable rise in health-care costs and premiums. At the same time, a change in attitudes toward personal spending was indicated by an increased use of credit cards and by Switzerland's losing to Japan its long-held place as the world's leading average per capita saver. The economy remained buoyantly robust on the whole, though the year ended with uncertainty because of the world stock-market plunge in October.

A major issue discernible on the horizon during election campaigning was what form of association Switzerland might eventually have with the European Communities (EC). Many of the 2,400 National Council candidates referred at least in passing to the benefits of eventual membership. Some made the point that the country's prosperity was attributable in no small degree to the closeness of economic links with the EC.

Traditional concepts of neutrality once again reasserted themselves, and Parliament's attitude toward some aspects of such considerations was evident in the refusal (by 104

AFP PHOTO

Arms negotiators Maynard Glitman (left) and Max Kampelman (third from left) of the United States meet in Geneva with Yuly Vorontsov (second from left) and Aleksey Obukhov of the Soviet Union to discuss the reduction of intermediate-range nuclear forces.

votes to 82) of the lower house, following the lead provided by the upper chamber, to allow the government to ratify the European Social Charter, which it had signed 11 years earlier.

Pierre Aubert (Socialist), who had been foreign minister since 1978, left the seven-member Federal Council at the end of the year, as did Leon Schlumpf (People's Party), who had been minister of energy and transport since 1980. Elected by Parliament to replace them were René Felber and Adolf Ogi. Finance Minister Otto Stich, a Social Democrat, was chosen to serve as president in 1988.

(ALAN MCGREGOR)

## UNITED KINGDOM

A constitutional monarchy in northwestern Europe and member of the Commonwealth, the United Kingdom comprises the island of Great Britain (England, Scotland, and Wales) and Northern Ireland, together with many small islands. Area: 244,110 sq km (94,251 sq mi), including 3,218 sq km of inland water but excluding the crown dependencies of the Channel Islands and Isle of Man. Pop. (1987 est.): 56,878,000. Cap.: London. Monetary unit: pound sterling, with (Oct. 5, 1987) a free rate of £0.62 to U.S. $1 (U.S. $1.62 = £1 sterling). Queen, Elizabeth II; prime minister in 1987, Margaret Thatcher.

**Domestic Affairs.** The reelection of the Conservative Party government of Prime Minister Margaret Thatcher (*see* BIOGRAPHIES) on June 11, 1987, was more decisive than seemed likely at the beginning of the year. In January the Conservatives were even with the Labour Party in the opinion polls; at no point since early 1985 had the government commanded sufficient public support to be confident of reelection. A by-election on February 26 in the London constituency of Greenwich appeared to underline the fragility of Conservative support. The party's share of the vote fell from 35% in the June 1983 general election to 11%—a sharper decline than in any other by-election since Thatcher came to power in 1979.

The Conservatives, however, quickly recovered from the Greenwich result; Labour did not. It lost the seat to the Social Democratic Party (SDP), partly because Labour's candidate, Deirdre Wood, had a record of supporting extreme left-wing policies when she was a member of the Greater London Council. Neil Kinnock, Labour's leader, had been developing a moderate image for the party; the Greenwich by-election, fought in the glare of intensive national publicity, reawakened voters' fears about Labour "extremism."

Soon after Labour suffered defeat at Greenwich, a leaked letter written by Patricia Hewitt, Kinnock's press secretary, spoke of the national damage that "the London effect" was doing to Labour. Meanwhile, the Liberal-SDP Alliance was beginning to recover from a disastrous autumn in the previous year, when the Liberal assembly had voted against the party leadership's defense policy. In January 1987 the Alliance was relaunched, with a new slogan ("The time has come"). The SDP victory in Greenwich was followed by a big Liberal win on March 12 in a by-election in the Cornwall constituency of Truro, where the party was defending a seat it had held since 1974.

By the spring the decision facing Thatcher was whether to call an early general election or wait until nearer the end of her five-year term. Her popularity was boosted by a widely publicized visit to the U.S.S.R. (March 28–April 1), during which she held lengthy talks with Soviet leader Mikhail Gorbachev. In April a succession of opinion polls showed the Conservatives to be consistently above the 40% support likely to be necessary to retain power. Local council elections held on May 7 confirmed this trend. On May

11 Thatcher announced the dissolution of Parliament and called a general election for June 11. (For tabulated results, see *Political Parties*, above; *see also* Sidebar.)

Following the Conservatives' victory, Thatcher undertook a partial reconstruction of her Cabinet. The main posts continued to be held by Nigel Lawson (chancellor of the Exchequer), Douglas Hurd (home secretary), and Sir Geoffrey Howe (foreign secretary). However, three prominent figures left the Cabinet: Lord Hailsham, who retired at 79 as lord chancellor; Norman Tebbit, who returned to the back benches after holding the nominal title of chancellor of the duchy of Lancaster while working as chairman of the Conservative Party organization; and John Biffen, who was dismissed as leader of the House of Commons after making various implied criticisms of the style and policies of the prime minister. Cecil Parkinson (*see* BIOGRAPHIES) returned to the Cabinet as energy secretary four years after a sex scandal had forced him to resign from Thatcher's previous administration. One of the main promotions in the new Cabinet was that of John Moore (*see* BIOGRAPHIES), an enthusiastic advocate of Thatcher's free-market policies; he became social services secretary.

Queen Elizabeth II opened the new Parliament on June 25 and set out the government's legislative program for the first 16-month session. The queen's speech contained two of the most controversial proposals in the Conservative election program. The first of these concerned education. More than 90% of children of secondary-school age (11 and over) attended government-supported (state) schools administered by local councils, which have considerable autonomy within broad national guidelines set by the government of the day. The government proposed curbing the power of local councils by establishing a national "core curriculum" that all state schools would have to follow and by allowing parents at individual state schools to vote for their school to withdraw from their local education authority. Such schools would then be financed directly by the central government and administered by independent charitable trusts. (*See* EDUCATION.)

The government's second major reform concerned the rates, Britain's local property tax. The government announced that it would abolish rates and levy a "community charge" instead. This would consist of a flat-rate payment, called a "poll tax" by its critics, that would be equal for every adult within each local authority. Some Conservatives joined with all opposition parties in condemning the proposed charge as regressive; the government responded that the new system would make local councils more responsive to the wishes of local voters.

While the government presented its plans, the opposition parties licked their wounds. The Labour Party met for its annual conference in late September in Brighton in a sombre mood. It attempted to improve its image both by widening the party's internal democracy and by rethinking its policies. The conference decided to give all individual party members the right to take part in a ballot to choose the party's parliamentary candidates. This reform responded to criticisms that local constituency committees had frequently selected candidates who were too left-wing to be acceptable to local voters. Labour also decided to embark on a series of comprehensive policy reviews, covering everything from defense to the economy.

Events within the Liberal-SDP Alliance progressed faster and more dramatically. On the Sunday after the election, David Steel, the Liberal Party leader, called for a "democratic fusion" of the Liberal and Social Democratic parties. David Owen, the SDP leader, opposed Steel, but the SDP national committee decided in July to hold a ballot of party members to determine whether merger talks should proceed. The result, announced on August 6, split the party. It voted by 57.4 to 42.6% in favour of the principle of merger. Owen immediately resigned as SDP leader. After three weeks of untidy haggling, Robert Maclennan (*see* BIOGRAPHIES) emerged as its new leader. Throughout the autumn leading members from the two parties held negotiations to determine the name, principles, and constitution of the new party. Owen and his supporters within the SDP planned to start a new party.

Outside the party battles, two issues involving national security and the media recurred during 1987. The government fought a continuing battle to prevent publication of *Spycatcher,* the memoirs of a former secret service officer, Peter Wright. A lengthy court case in Australia culminated on September 23 in the government's defeat, and the government decided against trying to prevent publication in the U.S. or Ireland. (*See* PUBLISHING.)

A separate controversy arose in January when the British Broadcasting Corporation (BBC) was not allowed to broadcast a television program that disclosed the existence of a secret Ministry of Defence project, known as Zircon, to launch a surveillance satellite that would intercept civilian and radio communications. The government obtained an injunction restraining Duncan Campbell, the journalist who had unearthed the story, from disclosing details about Zircon, but this was too late to prevent an article from appearing in the January 23 issue of the *New Statesman.* Special Branch officers subsequently searched Campbell's home, the offices of the *New Statesman,* and the BBC offices in Glasgow, where the program had been made. Copies of the Zircon film were shown in London to members of Parliament and at various public meetings throughout Britain. In November extracts from the film were shown on U.S. television. By then, however, events had overtaken the controversy; according to a report published in *The Times* (August 6), the government had decided to abandon the Zircon project.

**Economic Affairs.** Like all stock markets round the world, London suffered from the crash of share prices in October. The main immediate domestic consequence was that the sale of the government's remaining 31% stake in British Petroleum (BP) flopped as an exercise in extending stock ownership to more of the general public. The crash took place after underwriters had agreed to guarantee the government its proceeds of £4 billion from the sale—the biggest of any of the government's acts of privatization—but before individual investors had to commit their money.

BP's share price quickly fell below the value at which it would have made sense to make the 120-pence-per-share down payment. Lawson resisted demands by the underwriters to abandon the sale, but on October 29 he agreed that the Bank of England should offer to buy back any shares the financial institutions did not want for 70 pence per share. The immediate effect of this announcement was to steady the London stock market in general and the price of BP shares in particular.

Beyond the London financial district, the real economy grew strongly. In November Lawson announced that the U.K.'s gross domestic product (GDP) was likely to increase by 4% during 1987, more than any other major Western economy, and that the public-sector borrowing requirement during the 1987–88 financial year was likely to be only £1 billion, or 0.25% of GDP, the lowest in 17 years. The rapid growth of the economy led to a sharp reduction in unemployment. In October it stood at 2,750,000, a decline of 500,000 since its peak in July 1986.

Public confidence in the government's handling of the economy was one of the major factors in the Conservatives' election victory—a perception aided by Lawson's decision in March to reduce the standard rate of income tax to 27 pence in the pound. In their election manifesto the Conservatives aimed to reduce the annual rate of inflation to zero. At the end of 1987 it stood at 4%.

**Foreign Affairs.** Thatcher's visit to Moscow at the end of March was more important as a curtain raiser for the U.K. general election than as a major foreign policy initiative. Nevertheless, it confirmed Thatcher's role as Western Europe's senior political leader. The agreements that Thatcher and Gorbachev signed included an upgrading of the London–Moscow hot line and exchanges of cultural and educational information. More important were the informal talks on disarmament. At their meetings, as throughout the year, Thatcher insisted on Britain's right to retain and upgrade its own nuclear weapons regardless of any agreements reached between the U.S. and the U.S.S.R.

AP/WIDE WORLD

The coffin of one of the victims of a bomb blast in Northern Ireland is carried past the site of the explosion. The bomb, planted by the Irish Republican Army, was intended for soldiers who were to march in a Remembrance Day parade but went off early, killing 11 people and leaving some 60 others injured.

Thatcher and Gorbachev established a personal rapport that was unusual between such ideologically opposed leaders. Evidence of this came in December when Gorbachev chose the U.K. for a stopover on his way to sign the U.S.-Soviet intermediate-range nuclear forces treaty. It was the first visit by a Soviet leader to the U.K. in 31 years.

Moscow in March proved more congenial to the prime minister than Vancouver, B.C., in October, scene of the Commonwealth heads of government meeting. The U.K. government found itself more isolated than ever before over sanctions against South Africa. Thatcher refused flatly to extend sanctions. In the final communiqué issued on October 19, all the remaining Commonwealth members agreed to a "wider, tighter, and more intensified application" of sanctions. (See *Commonwealth of Nations,* above.)

**Northern Ireland.** The U.K. general election showed that Provisional Sinn Fein (PSF), the political arm of the Irish Republican Army (IRA), had lost some support among Northern Ireland's Catholics but was still strong enough to win one-third of the Roman Catholic vote and reelect Gerry Adams, president of PSF, for Belfast West. (Adams was first elected in 1983 but had never taken his seat in Parliament.)

The more moderate Catholic group, the Social Democratic and Labour Party (SDLP), won three of Northern Ireland's 17 seats, compared with one in 1983. In Down South the SDLP candidate defeated Enoch Powell, one of the most prominent right-wing figures in post-World War II U.K. politics, who had switched from the Conservative Party to the Ulster Unionists in 1974. Overall, the Official Unionists won nine seats in the general election (down two

from 1983), while the other Protestant party, the Democratic Unionists, won three (no change). The final seat was held by the leader of the tiny Ulster Popular Unionist Party.

Fianna Fail's victory in the Irish Republic's general election in February slowed the pace of discussion between the U.K. and Ireland on the implementation of the Anglo-Irish agreement, signed in November 1985. One stumbling block concerned Britain's wish for a new extradition agreement that would make it easier to bring suspected IRA terrorists to Britain to face trial. Also, Charles Haughey, the new Irish prime minister, wanted Britain to reform the "Diplock" courts in Northern Ireland, which allowed judges to hear certain criminal cases without a jury.

It took an unexpected piece of IRA brutality to bring that argument to a head. On November 8 a bomb exploded at the town of Enniskillen in Northern Ireland, killing 11 people who were attending a Remembrance Day service commemorating the dead of the two World Wars. The IRA admitted responsibility and conceded that it had made a serious mistake in planting the bomb. The following Sunday Catholic priests throughout Northern Ireland as well as in the Irish Republic read a statement by the Irish bishops declaring support for the IRA to be "a sin." Within days Tom King, the U.K.'s Northern Ireland secretary, found Haughey more willing to support a new extradition agreement; it finally received the approval of the Irish Parliament on December 3, although in a weaker form than the U.K. had hoped for.      (PETER KELLNER)

See also *Commonwealth of Nations,* above; *Dependent States,* below.

---

## The 1987 Election

On June 11, 1987, Margaret Thatcher led the U.K. Conservative Party to its third successive general election victory. The vote gave her party a 101-seat majority in the new House of Commons. (For tabulated results, see *Political Parties,* above.)

The Conservatives retained almost exactly the share of support they won in 1983. They consolidated their support in southern England, gaining two seats from Labour in London. Conservative gains exactly matched their losses in all of London, the South, and the Midlands. They won 294 of the 360 seats in this, the more prosperous, half of the United Kingdom.

In the rest of the country, however, it was a different story. Areas with high unemployment swung against the government. The Conservatives lost 22 seats in Wales, northern England, and Scotland, reducing their representation from 103 (out of 273) to 81. Labour won 50 of the 72 seats in Scotland—more than it had ever won before.

Overall, the election was a personal triumph for Thatcher, who became the first party leader in the 20th century to win three consecutive general elections. Since becoming leader of the Conservative Party in 1975, she had identified, exploited, and accelerated a number of social changes that helped her party and weakened Labour. Between 1979, when she came to power, and 1987, the middle and upper-middle classes had grown from 33 to 39% of the electorate; homeowners had risen from 52 to 66%; and owners of shares in corporations had doubled to 20%. Trade union membership, in contrast, had declined from 30

to 22%, while those living in rented public-sector housing (council homes)—traditionally a reliable source of Labour voters—had declined from 35 to 27%.

For Labour's leader, Neil Kinnock, the election result was acutely disappointing. Personally, he had a good campaign; an exit poll for Independent Television News among 4,000 voters on election day found that he was named more often than Thatcher as the party leader who campaigned most effectively. Kinnock's personal appeal, however, was insufficient to counter the adverse social trends, nor could it expunge the reputation of his party for extremism and division—a reputation that persuaded many voters that a Labour government would neither run the economy effectively nor defend Britain adequately.

For the two Alliance leaders, David Steel (Liberal) and David Owen (Social Democratic Party [SDP]), the outcome was even worse. The Liberal-SDP Alliance's support fell, and it was left with just 22 members of Parliament (17 Liberal, 5 SDP). Just six years after the birth of the SDP and the formation of the Alliance, the 1987 election finally extinguished the hopes of many SDP members that their party would be able, as they had originally hoped, "to break the mold" of Conservative and Labour domination of British politics.

The one mold that did start to crack was that of Parliament's domination by white male MPs. Four nonwhite candidates, all Labour, were elected—there had been none for half a century—and 41 women were elected, compared with 23 in 1983.

(PETER KELLNER)

## VATICAN CITY STATE

The independent sovereignty of Vatican City State is surrounded by but is not part of Rome. As a state with territorial limits, it is properly distinguished from the Holy See, which constitutes the worldwide administrative and legislative body for the Roman Catholic Church. Area: 44 ha (109 ac). Pop. (1987 est.): 750. As sovereign pontiff, John Paul II is the chief of state. Vatican City is administered by a pontifical commission of five cardinals headed by the secretary of state, in 1987 Agostino Cardinal Casaroli.

The main events of 1987 were the visit of Austrian Pres. Kurt Waldheim and Pope John Paul II's journeys to Uruguay, Argentina, and Chile, followed by those to West Germany, Poland, and the U.S.

Referring to President Waldheim's visit, the pope stressed that he could not refuse an audience to the head of state of a country with a long Catholic tradition unless he was given proof (as he had requested) of the allegations that Waldheim had taken part in the deportation of Jews during World War II. Faced with the prospect of hostile reaction during his visit to the U.S., the pope granted a private audience to a delegation of American Jews. He established that the question of recognition for the state of Israel no longer would be a theological matter but would be a political one to be dealt with by the State Secretariat.

There were further protests when the pope met Gen. Augusto Pinochet Ugarte of Chile during his visit to Chile and Argentina, where the Vatican's successful mediation in the Beagle Channel dispute between those two countries was celebrated. The pope's third journey to his homeland, Poland, in June was preceded in January by a visit to the Vatican from Polish leader Gen. Wojciech Jaruzelski. Hungarian Prime Minister Gyorgy Lazar, Iraqi Deputy Prime Minister Tariq Aziz, and Pres. Joaquim Chissanó of Mozambique were among others received by the pope during the year. (MAX BERGERRE)

*See also* Religion: *Roman Catholic Church.*

This article updates the *Micropædia* article VATICAN CITY STATE.

FELICI—GAMMA/LIAISON

Pope John Paul II met with Austrian Pres. Kurt Waldheim in June despite allegations that Waldheim had taken part in the deportation of Jews during World War II.

# Eastern Europe and the U.S.S.R

## EASTERN EUROPEAN AFFAIRS

Overshadowing virtually everything else in Eastern Europe in 1987 was the transformed relationship between the Soviet Union and the Eastern European elites. For the first time in two or three decades, the impulse to change appeared stronger in Moscow than in the Eastern European capitals. Whereas for many years Eastern European conservatives had become intellectually comfortable and could justify their resistance to change by pointing to Brezhnevian conservatism, they were increasingly faced with either having no pretext at all for their policies or being forced to feign support for *glasnost* and *perestroika* (openness and restructuring).

The benchmark of change, on the other hand, was not as far-reaching as some feared. The problem for the anti-reformers lay in the new atmosphere, in which reformers of various kinds could enter the political game with relatively strong hands, in a way that had not been possible since the late 1960s. The Soviet benchmark was made public in the speech given by Mikhail Gorbachev at the plenum of the Soviet Communist Party's Central Committee on January 27. In this speech, Gorbachev outlined his conception of reform, which might be summarized as the cautious outward extension of individual and group initiative and the corresponding lifting of the stifling hand of the party and state bureaucracy.

A second important speech made by Gorbachev came during his visit to Prague, Czech., in April. In this speech, he defined his view of the relationship between Soviet restructuring and what the Eastern Europeans should do. He suggested that Soviet experience would be useful to Eastern European countries, but that each country had its own peculiarities and national features. In effect, Gorbachev came close to diluting a traditional Soviet demand, that all Communist parties regard the experience of the Soviet Union as an obligatory model. The symbolic aspects of the speech also were significant inasmuch as it was made in Prague, scene of the most far-reaching experiment in reform ever attempted by a ruling Communist party, the "Prague Spring" of 1968.

For several of the Eastern European states, the Gorbachev project contained little that was new. For Hungary and Poland, in particular, it offered nothing at all, beyond the already noted change in atmospherics. In Hungary, for example, the more outspoken reformers were suggesting that the Hungarian experience implied that what Gorbachev was offering would turn out to be too cautious. The most effective road toward making the Communist system effective was to end the monopoly of the party and to move toward one-party pluralism. There was nothing in the Gorbachev proposals to indicate that the Kremlin would accept anything of the kind.

Among the ideas circulating in Hungary, the one that received the strongest emphasis from the reformers was that the role of the party should be legally redefined and that it should be firmly placed within a genuine legal framework. This, it was hoped, would end the arbitrary power of the party, which officials used to distort the rationality of the market and to exclude other actors from the political arena. The crucial requirement, in the view of the reformers, was to widen the scope of the political system by upgrading the power and authority of existing institutions, thereby providing opportunities for all political conflicts to be articulated openly. The problem with the existing system was that it suppressed conflicts of interest and made it possible for abuses of power to flourish. Furthermore, the genuine aspirations of society and the creative abilities of its members had no room to develop. Despite the strength of the reformers' case and the urgency of the economic deterioration, there was little evidence that the authorities in Hungary were prepared for anything as drastic as permitting the revival of the rule of law.

Despite surface appearance, the package of reforms made public by the Polish authorities in the autumn remained within the broad area of tinkering with the system and avoiding anything that smacked of radical change. This was all the more striking in light of the Polish leadership's manifest need for popular backing, given that the country's economy could not be turned around without a much greater degree of popular involvement and readiness to support official initiatives. The one political gesture, the referendum held on November 29, was regarded as more manipulative than anything else.

Yet the idea that the party should rule at least in consultation with society was being quietly put into effect in Slovenia, in Yugoslavia. The significance of the Slovene experiment should not be exaggerated—it was restricted to one republic of the Yugoslav federation. All the same, its value as a role model was far from negligible. Effectively, the Slovene leadership quietly withdrew party control from a wide range of institutions—trade unions, press, youth movement, local government—in order to allow these bodies to express the views of their members. There was no question that one of the direct benefits of this dispensation, still largely informal, was to raise the stock of the Slovene leadership and to promote a high degree of consent.

These examples were from the countries where the greatest efforts were being made to contemplate reform. Elsewhere in Eastern Europe, even these measures were avoided. Indeed, in East Germany and Romania, the leaderships came close to denouncing the Gorbachev initiatives in support of *glasnost* and *perestroika* as unnecessary. In Czechoslovakia and Bulgaria, rather cautious moves were being made, restricted to the running of the economy; on the other hand, it could be argued that the state of affairs in these two countries corresponded most closely to that in the Soviet Union, making political transformation unnecessary—for the moment. The pace of reform in Czechoslovakia was not expected to speed up following the replacement of Gustav Husak as Communist Party general secretary in December.

All the same, it was hard to see how the existing system could be sustained without major sacrifices on the part of the population—as were already being experienced in Romania—and the threat of economic collapse. That, in turn, could promote instability and stronger pressure for political change. This was hardly in the interests of the Soviet Union, for in this respect Gorbachev did not differ from his predecessors. He was looking for both stability and prosperity among his Eastern European allies and, in the changed domestic and international circumstances of the 1980s (a renewal of economic and, crucially, technological dynamism in the West), this would inevitably involve greater political change than anything openly contemplated by either Gorbachev or his Eastern European colleagues. The longer these reforms were delayed, the more painful they would be.                    (GEORGE SCHÖPFLIN)

*See also* Economic Affairs; Military Affairs.

## ALBANIA

A socialist republic in the western Balkan Peninsula of southeastern Europe, Albania is situated on the Adriatic Sea. Area: 28,748 sq km (11,100 sq mi). Pop. (1987 est.): 3,087,000. Cap.: Tirane. Monetary unit: lek, with (Oct. 5, 1987) a free rate of 6.19 leks to U.S. $1 (10.05 leks = £1 sterling). First secretary of the Albanian (Communist) Party of Labour and chairman of the Presidium of the People's Assembly (president) in 1987, Ramiz Alia; chairman of the Council of Ministers (premier), Adil Carcani.

On Feb. 1, 1987, elections were held to fill the 250 seats in Albania's People's Assembly (parliament). Official sources reported a 100% turnout of registered electors, with all but a single vote, which was declared invalid, cast in favour of candidates on the list approved by the Democratic Front of Albania. Ramiz Alia, first secretary of the Albanian (Communist) Party of Labour, was reelected chairman of the Presidium of the People's Assembly on February 19.

There were signs that Albania was emerging from the diplomatic isolation that had marked the era of Alia's predecessor, Enver Hoxha. Following the establishment of diplomatic relations at the ambassadorial level with Spain, Mozambique, and Singapore in late 1986, Albania agreed to similar ties with Canada and West Germany in September 1987. During negotiations with the latter, Albania's long-standing claim for war reparations was apparently settled, but no details were made known. On August 28 Greece declared an end to the state of war with Albania that had existed since the end of World War II. Albania was also reported to be seeking improved relations with the U.K. and the U.S.

During 1987 Alia's speeches on domestic issues were increasingly critical of inefficiency and incompetence in business and government.                    (K. M. SMOGORZEWSKI)

## BULGARIA

The socialist republic of Bulgaria is on the eastern Balkan Peninsula of southeastern Europe, along the Black Sea. Area: 110,912 sq km (42,823 sq mi). Pop. (1987 est.): 8,983,000. Cap.: Sofia. Monetary unit: lev, with (Oct. 5, 1987) a free rate of 0.85 lev to U.S. $1 (1.39 leva = £1 sterling). General secretary of the Bulgarian Communist Party and chairman of the State Council (president) in 1987, Todor Zhivkov; chairman of the Council of Ministers (premier), Georgy Atanasov.

Bulgaria followed the U.S.S.R.'s lead and cautiously entered into the spirit of restructuring (*perestroika*) of its national economic and political systems. The move had been presaged by Todor Zhivkov, general secretary of the Bulgarian Communist Party, during his speech to the party congress in April 1986, when he announced that a new style of management of the national economy was indispensable. On July 28–29, 1987, Zhivkov presented his reform proposals to a plenary session of the Central Committee. He described the existing system as "a breeding ground for bureaucracy."

Under the proposed revisions, the supreme authority in the state was to be the National Assembly (parliament), while the State Council and the Council of Ministers would merge to form the Presidential Office. Four advisory councils—for economic affairs, social affairs, agriculture and fisheries, and research and technology—attached to the Council of Ministers were dissolved in September. At the end of 1987 the Ministries of Planning, Finance, Trade, Education, and Technology were to be disbanded, leaving a total of ten ministries.

Grisha Filipov, who had been succeeded as chairman of

the Council of Ministers (premier) by Georgy Atanasov in March 1986, commented favourably on Zhivkov's reforms in *Pogled*, the weekly journal of the Union of Bulgarian Journalists. In particular, Filipov approved plans to reduce the power of the Communist Party; ostentatious displays of party power, including the posting of portraits of party leaders and the holding of parades, were criticized. Chudomir Aleksandrov, a member of the Politburo and of the Central Committee Secretariat, was widely regarded as a leader of the reforming group.

In August the National Assembly approved a proposal that from January 1988 Bulgaria would be divided into nine large administrative counties (to be called *obvods*). The new system would supersede that of 28 provinces (*okrugs*) adopted in 1964. (K. M. SMOGORZEWSKI)

## CZECHOSLOVAKIA

The federal socialist republic of Czechoslovakia is a landlocked state of central Europe. Area: 127,905 sq km (49,384 sq mi). Pop. (1987 est.): 15,591,000. Cap.: Prague. Monetary unit: koruna, with (Oct. 5, 1987) a commercial rate of 5.48 koruny to U.S. $1 (8.90 koruny = £1 sterling). President in 1987, Gustav Husak; general secretaries of the Communist Party of Czechoslovakia, Husak and, from December 17, Milos Jakes; federal premier, Lubomir Strougal.

During 1987 Czechoslovakia very gradually moved toward public acceptance of the need for change. It was an extremely tentative and not entirely convincing conversion of the Communist Party leadership's staunchly antireformist position, but Gustav Husak, the aging Communist Party general secretary, did use the word reform in public for the first time in many years. On December 17 Husak was replaced by Milos Jakes, the Central Committee secretary in charge of economic affairs, who was expected to continue the limited reforms of his predecessor.

The first signs that the Czechoslovak leadership had shifted from what had been a position of near-total immobility came in December 1986, when a Central Committee meeting indicated a very cautious readiness to consider change. This was confirmed in January, when a number of minimal changes in the management of enterprises came into effect. These were all rather technical measures aimed at giving the enterprises greater autonomy. How-

AP/WIDE WORLD

A member of Greenpeace is seized by Czechoslovak police on the balcony of Prague's National Museum. The activist was arrested with others for posting a banner against nuclear energy.

ever, speeches by federal Premier Lubomir Strougal in January and Husak in March suggested that the Prague leadership was considering more far-reaching moves. Reflecting on the disappointing economic results for 1986, Strougal called for genuine improvements in productivity and quality. The figure for growth in the national income, 3.4% above 1985, was more or less on target, but the volume measure of economic output did not take qualitative factors into account. Hard currency exports continued to decline.

Economic results made public during 1987 confirmed that the long, slow slide in the public sector had not been halted. Results for the first six months showed that only 63% of all state economic units had met their plan targets. There was widespread skepticism about the country's ability to meet the targets for the 1986–90 five-year plan, which envisaged an average annual increase in national income of 3.5%. Husak sanctioned reform, though of a conservative kind, and noted that reform was not counterrevolution. He promised that the changes under consideration would be the most "significant intervention in the economic system" since the 1948 nationalizations.

The visit to Prague by Soviet leader Mikhail Gorbachev in April was undoubtedly an important factor in the Czechoslovak leadership's change in attitude. Gorbachev evidently favoured change in Czechoslovakia but at the same time declared that the U.S.S.R. would no longer insist that Eastern European countries follow its example unreservedly. This implied encouragement for reform, but no insistence on it.

Husak returned to the theme of reform in a speech in August. Again, the emphasis was on economic rather than political change. He noted that, despite successes, there were still shortcomings—indifference, passivity, dilatoriness, inability to introduce new technology—and concluded that the "present mechanism" of running the country was not in accordance with requirements. The new draft Law on State Enterprises (published in June), the major instrument of change, stressed the central role to be played by the party in all spheres.

There were two main reasons for this greater open-mindedness. Reformism in the Soviet Union effectively removed one of the most widely used excuses for not carrying out change in Czechoslovakia—that the Soviet Union would object. The economic dependence of Czechoslovakia on the U.S.S.R. left it with little choice but to follow suit. Further, there was some recognition in Prague that the minimalist tinkering with policy in previous years had brought little improvement to the economy.

At the same time, opposition to change remained deeply rooted. Any reforms immediately raised the question of the suppression of the 1968 "Prague Spring" reform program—the basis of the Husak regime's rule—albeit suggestions had been made that the post-1969 freeze had been excessive. Also, while a new generation of cadres, perhaps less instinctively hostile to change than the leadership, was beginning to emerge, the conservative middle and top levels of the establishment were firmly entrenched. The harsh reality was that the stabilizers of the 1970s were expected to be the reformers of the 1980s—any attempt by them to adopt this role would be deeply unconvincing. A third factor underlying the political constellation was that Slovakia, which had benefited from the conservatism of the post-1969 era, had no particular reason to support any meaningful alteration.

Against this political background, nothing very radical could be expected. Indeed, Czechoslovakia's proposals for change were rather more conservative than those emerging in either Poland or Hungary or even in the Soviet Union. Change would be directed only at the economy, particularly the running of enterprises and industrial strategy, and there would be no experimentation with greater political *glasnost* (openness), as in the U.S.S.R. In light of the Prague leadership's short-term perspectives, this strategy was perhaps not unrealistic. After a long period of political freeze, change could only be slow. Further, given the conservative nature of the system that had evolved in the Husak period, purely technical improvements could, in fact, bring short-term benefits to the economy, unlike the situation in some other Eastern European countries, where the need for more radical change was urgent.

The Charter 77 dissident organization watched these changes with varying degrees of hope, skepticism, and cynicism. On the anniversary of the Soviet invasion of 1968 (August 20), it issued a document calling for national reconciliation on a democratic basis. The group wanted an amnesty for all political prisoners, free access to employment, and an end to political restrictions, with those forced into emigration after 1968 being encouraged to return. A petition sent in October to the Federal Assembly by 50 signatories returned to those themes, adding to their demands freedom of information and access to public life for all citizens.                    (GEORGE SCHÖPFLIN)

## GERMAN DEMOCRATIC REPUBLIC

A socialist republic, the German Democratic Republic (East Germany) is in central Europe on the Baltic Sea. Area: 108,333 sq km (41,827 sq mi). Pop. (1987 est.): 16,598,000. Cap.: Berlin (East). Monetary unit: Mark of Deutsche Demokratische Republik, with (Oct. 5, 1987) a free rate of M 1.84 to U.S. $1 (M 2.99 = £1 sterling). General secretary of the Socialist Unity (Communist) Party and chairman of the Council of State (president) in 1987, Erich Honecker; chairman of the Council of Ministers (premier), Willi Stoph.

The people of East Germany learned little from their own media in 1987 about the liberalization taking place in the U.S.S.R. The country's leader, Erich Honecker, who received Soviet leader Mikhail Gorbachev in East Berlin in May, stated that there could be no alternative to the already successful brand of socialist democracy in the German Democratic Republic. Nevertheless, Honecker's visit to West Germany was a milestone in political thinking. In late November it was announced that Honecker was to visit Paris, the first trip by an Eastern European leader to one of the three Western allies responsible for Berlin.

Honecker saw his momentous five-day visit to West Germany in September, a long-awaited mission that was finally approved by Gorbachev, as the climax of his tireless efforts to win official recognition of his country and of the division of Germany. He dismissed West Germany's thesis that the German nation continued to exist as a single entity. Nevertheless, he ensured that the conditions surrounding his visit were as favourable as possible. In the first half of the year, more than half a million East Germans under pensionable age had been allowed to travel to West Germany for pressing family reasons. (Until a few years previously, only pensioners had been allowed out.) For the first time, visits to the West were being given as rewards to workers who had performed well, provided they were not critical of their own system. It was expected that the total would reach a million by the end of the year.

Shortly before Honecker left for Bonn, the two German states exchanged five prisoners at the border post near Herleshausen, in Hessen. Among the three handed over by West Germany was Manfred Rotsch, who had been sentenced to eight and a half years' imprisonment in 1986

"Pilgrimage: Olof Palme March for a Nuclear Free Zone" reads a banner carried by protesters in East Berlin. It was the first time East German authorities had allowed a spontaneous demonstration.
AFP PHOTO

for spying for the KGB. He was a former research director with the Messerschmitt-Bölkow-Blohm aerospace group and had supplied the U.S.S.R. with vital military information. One of the prisoners released by the East Germans was Christa-Karin Schumann, who had been sentenced to 15 years' imprisonment for espionage in 1980. She was said to have been the companion of Rear Adm. Winfried Baumann-Zakrzowski, who was executed after being exposed as a spy.

There was evidence that the shoot-to-kill policy of East German border guards had been modified in anticipation of the Honecker visit. More refugees than ever before were reported to be crossing into West Germany, even though conditions in the East appeared to be more relaxed. There was a good deal of open criticism of the country's establishment, especially by pacifist groups, and religious leaders were reported to have more freedom than they would have thought possible ten years earlier.

Honecker's visit to West Germany produced an unexciting communiqué. Agreements were signed promising closer cooperation on environmental protection and radiation protection and in the fields of science and technology. Both sides undertook to maintain good, neighbourly relations and to respect each other's independence and autonomy in internal and external affairs.

Although East Germany had by far the most successful economy of the Warsaw Pact countries, it faced increasing complaints that its factories were not meeting the standards of quality demanded by the West. The range of goods available for export to the West was limited; delivery dates were too long; and the East German economy, measured against Western requirements, remained too inflexible. The U.S.S.R. was the country's biggest customer, taking up to 40% of East German foreign trade. National income increased by 4.3% in 1986 but by only 3% in the first few months of 1987, and targets of the five-year (1986–90) plan were not being met.

One of the main events of Berlin's 750th anniversary celebrations in July was an eight-kilometre (five-mile)-long parade with 40,000 participants, 375 bands, and 760 horses. Soviet Army soldiers reenacted the storming of the Reichstag in April 1945. Perhaps more meaningful were the measures taken to mark the country's 38th anniversary on October 7. The death penalty was abolished, and it was reported that more than 25,000 prisoners were released after July under a wide-ranging amnesty. Under the previous amnesty in 1979, 22,000 had been allowed to go free.

The most serious outbreak of street violence in East Berlin in many years occurred in June when rock fans were dispersed by police on three successive nights. It happened when thousands of youngsters gathered near the Berlin Wall to hear rock concerts being performed on the Western side. As police started picking out people and marching them off, loud protests arose, then angry chants: "The Wall must go!" and "We want freedom!" The East German authorities, already nervous about Gorbachev's reform program, were eager to stifle any notion of political unrest. Officially no trouble was reported, even though the incident had been witnessed by many Western correspondents.

Dissidents claimed that a two-class society was being created by people who managed to get hold of considerable quantities of West German Deutsch Marks with which they could buy Western goods in special shops. They also received preferential treatment in restaurants and when dealing with local tradespeople. A survey showed that the purchasing power of East Germans had been declining in recent years even though they worked longer hours. The volume of goods produced per capita had increased, but exports had risen. The survey also found a lack of innovation and inadequate motivation of the work force.

(NORMAN CROSSLAND)

This article updates the *Macropædia* article GERMANY: *German Democratic Republic.*

## HUNGARY

A socialist republic, Hungary is a landlocked state in central Europe. Area: 93,036 sq km (35,921 sq mi). Pop. (1987 est.): 10,608,000. Cap.: Budapest. Monetary unit: forint, with (Oct. 5, 1987) a free rate of 47.99 forints to U.S. $1 (77.92 forints = £1 sterling). General secretary of the Hungarian Socialist Workers' (Communist) Party in 1987, Janos Kadar; chairmen of the Presidential Council (chiefs of state), Pal Losonczi and, from June 25, Karoly Nemeth; chairmen of the Council of Ministers (prime ministers), Gyorgy Lazar and, from June 25, Karoly Grosz.

Political developments in Hungary were heavily influenced by the continuing deterioration of the economy in 1987. Disenchantment with the progress and implementation of the much-flaunted liberal New Economic Mechanism introduced in 1968 led to banking reforms and severe austerity measures. The Central Committee of the Hungarian Socialist Workers' (Communist) Party declared that more economic and political reforms were needed. This gave rise to speculation about the future of General Secretary Janos Kadar, who had led the country for 31 years and, at the age of 75, apparently had no intention of resigning.

On June 25 the Council of Ministers appointed a new prime minister, Karoly Grosz (*see* BIOGRAPHIES), to replace Gyorgy Lazar. The latter replaced Karoly Nemeth in the relatively uninfluential post of deputy party leader, while Nemeth was appointed chairman of the Presidential Council in succession to the ailing Pal Losonczi, who retired. Janos Berecz, chairman of the Central Committee and regarded as a leading contender to succeed Kadar, was one of two new faces in the 13-member Politburo. The belief that Grosz had been appointed to carry out unpopular economic reforms and thereby eliminate himself as a successor to Kadar was confounded. The directness with which Grosz in September announced the introduction of income and value-added taxes rather appealed to Hungarians. A Cabinet reshuffle in December strengthened Grosz's hold on the management of the economy. Several

ministries were merged or eliminated, and the first Environment Ministry in Eastern Europe was established.

A measure of the relative freedom of the Hungarians as compared with their Soviet bloc neighbours was reflected in the high level of religious tolerance, underlined by the selection of Budapest by the World Jewish Congress (WJC) as the venue for its executive meeting on May 6–7. Some 80,000 Jews were living in Hungary in 1987. Israeli press and delegates attended the WJC meeting, and there was no censorship—both preconditions set by the WJC. Topics on the agenda included a progress report on Jewish emigration from the U.S.S.R. The meeting no doubt prompted a September agreement that formal links with Israel be renewed after 20 years.

Although the Roman Catholic Church was remarkably well established in Hungary, the superficially harmonious relationship with the Vatican had an undercurrent of dissatisfaction. This surfaced in March when a papal envoy visited Budapest to discuss with the new primate, Archbishop Laszlo Paskai, concern over the degree to which the Hungarian church supported the government on such issues as conscription when Catholic conscientious objectors had been imprisoned. Many church officials believed, however, that some compromise of their values was justified if it allowed the church to survive.

There was more *glasnost* (openness) about the problem of AIDS (acquired immune deficiency syndrome). There were reported to be more carriers (137) in Hungary than elsewhere in Eastern Europe, and a "help-line" was set up to answer questions.

Economic growth was sluggish. In 1986 gross national product rose 0.5% instead of the planned 2.3–2.7%. Agricultural output was disrupted by a second year of drought, and industry and construction did not perform well. The prospects of achieving the planned 2% increase in 1987 were poor, although there was some improvement. External account problems persisted, and consumer prices accelerated from 1986 levels (5.3%) following the 30% price rise for many consumer items in July. Unemployment was also becoming a problem as industry restructured—the iron and steel industry alone planned to lay off 10,-000 workers by 1989. Problems were compounded by the growing external debt, the highest in Eastern Europe on a per capita basis. In 1987 the equivalent of three-quarters of Hungary's hard currency export revenue was required to service it. (JANET H. CLARK; K. M. SMOGORZEWSKI)

## POLAND

A socialist republic of eastern Europe, Poland is on the Baltic Sea. Area: 312,683 sq km (120,727 sq mi). Pop. (1987 est.): 37,769,000. Cap.: Warsaw. Monetary unit: zloty, with (Oct. 5, 1987) an official rate of 297.70 zlotys to U.S. $1 (483.43 zlotys = £1 sterling). First secretary of the Polish United Workers' (Communist) Party and chairman of the Council of State (chief of state) in 1987, Gen. Wojciech Jaruzelski; chairman of the Council of Ministers (premier), Zbigniew Messner.

Political events in Poland in 1987 were dominated by the need for change. The government was anxious to introduce economic reforms; there was pressure from the U.S.S.R., where Soviet leader Mikhail Gorbachev was actively promoting *perestroika* (restructuring), as well as from international organizations such as the World Bank, which was concerned about Poland's financial problems and its need to modernize. Access to Western technology and capital was essential for modernization. The government made it clear that no progress could be made without price reforms, an issue that gradually became all-important.

On October 23 the Sejm (parliament) passed a momentous resolution to hold its first national referendum since 1946. The vote, seeking approval for change, was held on November 29. The move followed intense debate between the central committees of the three political parties and the Patriotic Movement of National Revival. Two questions were asked of the voters: one asked for support for the government's radical economic recovery program, aiming to improve living conditions but accepting two to three years of inevitable upheavals; the second wanted support for "the Polish model of democratization which aims to strengthen self-government, widen citizen's rights, and increase their participation in ruling the country."

The vote was the focus of international attention, not least because the credibility of Gen. Wojciech Jaruzelski, the Polish United Workers' (Communist) Party (PUWP) first secretary, was heavily dependent on the result. Of the 26.2 million entitled to vote, 17.6 million (67.3%) did so. The authorities needed the support of 51% of all those entitled to vote.

The economic question was approved by 66% of those who voted and the political question by 69%. When all those eligible to vote were counted, however, only about 45% had voted in favour. The result thus did not give the government a majority, but the referendum was not binding and obliged officials only to use it as an indicator of public feeling. On December 1 the PUWP examined the results and, although Jaruzelski was disappointed that he did not get a majority in favour of reform, he was heartened by the fact that Lech Walesa, leader of the banned trade union Solidarnosc (Solidarity), had been largely ignored in his call for a referendum boycott.

Economic anxieties were reflected in a major restructuring of the government and a Cabinet reshuffle, announced on October 24. Jaruzelski commented that the changes were designed to improve economic strategy. The most significant appointment was that of a nonparty member, Zdislaw Sadowski, as chairman of Poland's top planning body, the State Planning Commission, which was reorganized to focus on overall economic policy. The 62-year-old economist was expected to implement the reforms he had helped shape, which involved the removal of many state subsidies and the freeing of market forces to influence wages and prices. The commission drafted and helped implement all national plans.

In the new government Sadowski also sat as deputy premier along with Zbigniew Szalajda and Jozef Koziol, both members of the previous government. Three departmental ministers—Marian Orzechowski (foreign affairs), Czeslaw Kiszczak (home affairs), and Gen. Florian Siwicki (national defense)—retained their posts. The number of ministries was reduced from 26 to 19.

The Polish economy continued to experience difficulties. National output rose by 5% in 1986, compared with the planned 3.1–3.4%, and was planned to rise 3.2–3.5% in 1987, but in real terms national income had still not reached the 1978 level. The external account was expected to have deteriorated further with Polish products proving noncompetitive on Western markets. The total foreign debt was estimated to have reached $36 billion in 1987 and was a major handicap. Some two-thirds of it was owed to Western governments. At the end of October the Paris Club of Western creditor nations reached a preliminary agreement with Poland on repayments due before the end of 1988.

Prices and price reform became the overriding economic and political issue. With the exception of meat and meat products, basic necessities were no longer rationed, but

Polish leader Gen. Wojciech Jaruzelski (right) greets Pope John Paul II upon his arrival in Poland in June. The seven-day tour was John Paul's third visit to his native country since he became pope.
CAMERA PRESS/PHOTO TRENDS

many foodstuffs were in short supply. Subsidies were gradually being lifted, causing an acceleration in the rate of inflation, which was 18% in 1986 rather than the planned 8.5–9%. In March 1987 the government gave an assurance that food prices would not increase by more than 10% during the year, but by November they were rising by 25% annually. Concern about inflation was a major factor in the negative response to the referendum on economic reform, after which the government scaled down its proposed food price increases to 40% from a planned 110%. It was not clear to what extent wage increases would compensate for the higher prices. Inflation had also been exacerbated by the policy introduced in April 1986 that allowed the national bank to have devaluations of up to 3% when it believed that they were necessary. This caused a fall in the value of the zloty by nearly one-third against the U.S. dollar between early February and mid-December, with the free-market rate plunging far more.

In early June Pope John Paul II made his third visit to Poland since becoming pope. His seven-day tour proved a challenge to the government since on this visit the pope made no attempt to disguise his views on the Communist system, which, he often stated, was incapable of satisfying spiritual demands. Jaruzelski was cordial and stated that Christianity was "a permanent feature" of Poland's culture. In return, the pope warned that "every violation of the rights of man is a threat to peace." Wherever he went, the pope was given a rapturous welcome. The gatherings of millions, however, signified unrest to the government, and alcohol sales were banned in Warsaw during the visit; there were a large number of arrests.

Relations with the U.S. improved following the U.S. decision in February to drop all remaining economic sanctions imposed against Poland in 1982; as a result, Polish imports again achieved most-favoured-nation status. The move preceded a four-day visit to Poland in September by U.S. Vice-Pres. George Bush, who met twice with Jaruzelski and publicly reiterated U.S. support for Solidarity's activities.                    (K. M. SMOGORZEWSKI)

## ROMANIA

A socialist republic on the Balkan Peninsula in southeastern Europe, Romania has a coastline on the Black Sea. Area: 237,500 sq km (91,699 sq mi). Pop. (1987 est.): 22,913,000. Cap.: Bucharest. Monetary unit: leu, with (Sept. 30, 1987) a commercial rate of 14.60 lei to U.S. $1 (23.71 lei = £1 sterling). General secretary of the Romanian Communist Party, president of the republic, and president of the State Council in 1987, Nicolae Ceausescu; chairman of the Council of Ministers (prime minister), Constantin Dascalescu.

The year 1987 was characterized by Romania's increasing self-imposed isolation, against a background of deteriorating economic conditions and growing political unrest. There was evidence of a widening rift between Pres. Nicolae Ceausescu and Soviet leader Mikhail Gorbachev, whose reforms were not welcomed by the Romanian leadership.

In an unprecedented display of public dissatisfaction, on November 15 thousands of workers demonstrated in the industrial city of Brasov, Romania's second largest city, to protest poor living standards, food shortages, and energy conservation measures. The city was closed to Western journalists, but unconfirmed reports suggested that between 6,000 and 20,000 people took part. The demonstrators reportedly shouted anti-Ceausescu slogans and stormed the town hall and Communist Party headquarters. There were reports of unrest in several other Romanian towns, including Bucharest, in early December.

Romanian officials described the unrest as the result of workers' anger at the incompetence of local factory managers, many of whom were subsequently sacked. At a higher level, Alexandru Babe was dismissed from his post of finance minister by presidential decree "for having failed to fulfill his job obligations." The move followed wide-ranging changes in the Council of Ministers that had been announced in the period August–October. Affecting some 20 ministries, the moves were concentrated in the economic field. Gheorghe Petrescu and Ioan Avram were dismissed from their posts as deputy prime minister and minister of electric power, respectively, and were also expelled from the Communist Party.

A major factor in the unrest was the economic privation caused by Romania's efforts to repay its hard-currency debt. Standing at $10.5 billion in 1981, external debt had been reduced to $5.4 billion by the end of 1986, and the plan for 1987 included repayment of a further $1 billion. In 1986 the economy grew substantially, though the ambitious targets of the five-year (1986–90) plan were not achieved, and growth was expected to continue in 1987. At the same time, wage increases of only 1.8% were planned, while one-half of any increase in production in the energy sector was to be exported. Immediately before the Brasov disturbances, the authorities introduced new restrictions on energy supplies to domestic consumers. In early December Romania threatened to suspend repayments on debt owed to the World Bank, which it accused of imposing credit conditions that were "inequitable and discriminatory."

In the aftermath of the Brasov unrest, the Communist Party national conference, due to open on December 7, was delayed for a week. The conference had been called to review party work between quinquennial plenary congresses. In his opening speech, Ceausescu strongly defended central planning and underlined that he would not consider introducing Soviet-style reforms. He stressed that Romania would continue to emphasize repayment of its foreign debt and that efforts to reduce consumption and conserve raw materials would therefore continue as well. In what appeared to be a concessionary move, Ceausescu

promised wage increases of 10% in 1988. At year's end, however, he banned foreign borrowing in 1988, presaging more austerity.

During the year, Ceausescu paid working visits to the leaders of Czechoslovakia, Poland, East Germany, and Bulgaria. He and his wife, Elena, made official visits to five Asian countries (India, Pakistan, Bangladesh, Burma, and Nepal) and three African countries (Angola, The Sudan, and Zaire). In October they visited Turkey.

During Gorbachev's visit to Romania on May 25–27, the extent of the gulf between the Soviet and Romanian leadership became apparent. References in Gorbachev's speech to the need for *glasnost* (openness) and *perestroika* (restructuring) met a cool response. In early December Ceausescu declined to attend the meeting of Warsaw Pact leaders at which Gorbachev briefed his allies on the Washington summit.                    (K. M. SMOGORZEWSKI)

## UNION OF SOVIET SOCIALIST REPUBLICS

The Union of Soviet Socialist Republics is a federal state covering parts of eastern Europe and northern Asia. Area: 22,402,200 sq km (8,649,500 sq mi). Pop (1987 est.): 282,811,000. Cap.: Moscow. Monetary unit: ruble, with (Oct. 5, 1987) a free rate of 0.64 ruble to U.S. $1 (1.04 rubles = £1 sterling). General secretary of the Communist Party of the Soviet Union in 1987, Mikhail S. Gorbachev; chairman of the Presidium of the Supreme Soviet (president), Andrey A. Gromyko; chairman of the Council of Ministers (premier), Nikolay I. Ryzhkov.

The year 1987 was one of success and disappointment for Mikhail Gorbachev, general secretary of the Communist Party of the Soviet Union (CPSU). His greatest success was the signing of the intermediate-range nuclear forces (INF) agreement with the U.S. in Washington on December 8. (*See* MILITARY AFFAIRS: *Special Report.*) This represented the first tangible victory for his "new political thinking" in foreign and security policy. Gorbachev's perception of the world was much more sophisticated than that of his predecessors. He realized that success in foreign relations was vital for advancement in internal affairs. If fewer resources were expended on arms, then more would be available

(continued on page 476)

Soviet Foreign Minister Eduard Shevardnadze (right) and U.S. Secretary of State George Shultz sign a bilateral agreement on cooperation in the exploration and peaceful use of outer space.

# Perestroika and Glasnost—A Progress Report

## BY MARTIN McCAULEY

Until July 1987 everything appeared to be going Mikhail Gorbachev's way. At the January Central Committee (CC) plenum—postponed three times owing to opposition, on the general secretary's own admission—he delivered a devastating critique of the past failings of the Soviet system. He proposed new electoral procedures with the possibility of secret ballots for Communist Party posts (a proposal not included in the CC resolution passed at the end of the plenum); a special national conference was to be held in June 1988 to discuss economic reform and the democratization of Soviet society; a new law was to be enacted to permit citizens to sue officials; and non-Communist Party members were to be encouraged to play a more significant role in Soviet life.

Then on May 1 the law on individual enterprises became effective. Symbolically becoming law on International Labour Day to underline that it was socialist legislation, the new enactment permitted individuals to set up in business on their own but not to hire labour. A license had to be obtained from the local soviet and income tax paid on gross earnings. One part-timer in Moscow paid 300 rubles for a license and then proceeded to sell jeans at 300–400 rubles a pair. He was mystified by the fact that his previously illegal behaviour had suddenly become legal. "There's a lot in it for me," he mused, "but what is there in it for the state?"

On June 30 the Supreme Soviet of the U.S.S.R. passed laws to take effect from Jan. 1, 1988, to "promote a nationwide discussion of important questions of state life"—in other words, to encourage *glasnost* (openness); to encourage individual responsibility and competition in state enterprises; and to enable citizens to take erring officials to court.

**The Vanishing General Secretary.** The political atmosphere began to change in August when Gorbachev was in the northern Caucasus on holiday. Two hard-hitting articles about abuses of *glasnost* appeared, one by Egor Ligachev, Gorbachev's second in command, and the other by Gen. Viktor Chebrikov, head of the KGB. *Pravda* began to reverse its policy of publishing readers' letters that predominantly favoured *glasnost* and chose a majority that were critical of the misuse of openness. Gorbachev remained on holiday longer than expected—a meeting with a well-known American magazine was canceled at short notice without explanation—and when he returned to Moscow in late September, he immediately appeared on Soviet television addressing a French delegation.

On September 30 Gorbachev and his wife, Raisa, traveled to Murmansk to confer on the northern city the title of "hero-city" and the Order of Lenin. Significantly, it should have been Pres. Andrey Gromyko, because the Supreme Soviet had made the awards and Gorbachev held no state office. The general secretary's speech was combative and provided a robust defense of *perestroika* (restructuring) and *glasnost*. He conceded that some were trying to put on the brakes but made it clear that the process of economic change and democratization was irreversible. *Glasnost* was limited, however—it did not extend to explaining why the leader was not at his desk. Gorbachev's holiday had given rise to wild rumours: he was suffering from food poisoning; Raisa had had an operation; even that attempts had been made to poison him. It was noticeable, however, that when he did return to Moscow, he and his wife made themselves very visible. Reports that he extended his holiday in order to finish his book on *perestroika* were disregarded.

**The Yeltsin Affair.** Later Gorbachev revealed that while on holiday he had received a letter from Boris Yeltsin offering to resign as Moscow party leader and candidate Politburo member. Gorbachev had asked Yeltsin to postpone any decision until after the November 7 celebrations marking the 70th anniversary of the Revolution. At the CC plenum on October 21, intended mainly for consideration of Gorbachev's report on 70 years of Soviet history, Yeltsin had attempted to draw CC members into a debate about the bureaucratic obstacles to restructuring and openness. A furious row developed, with Yeltsin harshly criticized by Ligachev and Chebrikov. On November 11 the Moscow city Communist Party committee convened and savagely attacked its first secretary. Yeltsin had been led to make "promises largely fed by excessive conceit" and, driven by the "desire to remain in constant view," he had ended by "losing control." Yeltsin abased himself before the party.

N. IGNATIEV—TIME MAGAZINE

A Soviet artisan puts the finishing touches on a piggy bank. A new "individual labour" law passed in the Soviet Union allowed individuals to set up private businesses but not to hire labour.

A mural in the Soviet Union emphasizes the government's new strong position against the abuse of alcohol.
KELER—SYGMA

"I have lost face as a political leader, as a Communist. I am very guilty before the party organization, very guilty before the city party committee, before you certainly, before the Moscow Bureau and certainly I am very guilty before Mikhail Sergeyevich Gorbachev."

This was political *glasnost* with a vengeance. Such vitriolic language and such self-negation were reminiscent of the Stalinist 1930s but revealed the depth of passion aroused by *perestroika* and *glasnost*. After such a mea culpa, Yeltsin was expected to fade into obscurity, but there was a ground swell of support for him among ordinary Muscovites, and eventually he was given the task of coordinating construction throughout the U.S.S.R. at ministerial rank. It would appear that public opinion did have an impact on his fate.

All members of the political elite favoured an economic revolution, but only some favoured political revolution as well. The conservatives wanted only economic change, but the radicals favoured a thorough democratization of society. Yeltsin was a leading radical who had become frustrated with the slow pace of economic and political change. Gorbachev was also a radical, so the dismissal of Yeltsin caused him to lose authority. Yeltsin had been placed in Moscow by Gorbachev in December 1985.

During his speech in Murmansk on October 1, Gorbachev stated that the current overbureaucratic system fitted many officials like a glove. A whole generation of officials had been nurtured in a political culture that shied away from risk taking and favoured the regulation of every minute detail of economic and social life. Dynamic, efficient, fearless leadership was needed, but the political and economic culture did not produce many people capable of providing it. Most factory managers did not want greater decision-making powers. A new generation was needed to take over, but how was it to be trained? A revealing survey of 141 enterprises was published in *Izvestiya* on September 4. It had been carried out in the Urals by the Academy of Sciences during the summer and provided stark evidence of how far *perestroika* was penetrating the system. Its findings suggested that 45–60% of workers and technical personnel were only vaguely aware of the new economic mechanisms; 45% of managers and 35% of section heads but only 16% of workers were convinced that the reforms would benefit them; only 29%

believed that real progress in restructuring the economy would be achieved by 1990.

**What's in It for Ivan?** *Perestroika* or even *glasnost* was not the main concern of the average Soviet citizen. Food and housing were much more important. Hence the success of economic reform in the long term depended on solving the nation's two most crucial social problems. In real terms, per capita production of foodstuffs was only slightly higher than that of a decade earlier and was less evenly distributed, with the food-deficit zones of the north and centre the hardest hit. Expanding food output was a high priority for Gorbachev, given the shortages and the increase in the number of citizens suffering from vitamin deficiency—a problem that was particularly serious in Siberia. Other consumer goods were very unevenly distributed largely because of nepotism and bribery. The retail trade tended to favour the existing deficit economy since shortages could be exploited to increase incomes.

Housing construction had been neglected for two decades, and according to Abel Aganbegyan, an economic adviser close to Gorbachev, 17% of Soviet families in 1987 did not have their own dwelling. In 1987 about a quarter of city dwellings and 72% of rural homes were privately owned, and there was a 10–15-year wait for a couple wanting state housing. The number of citizens seeking redress for their housing grievances increased in 1986 to a quarter of a million, but courts had no power to allocate housing. Rents were still calculated at the 1928 rate of 13.2 kopecks per square metre, so a 50-sq m (540-sq ft) flat cost 6 rubles 60 kopecks per month, but in major cities subletting could fetch 100–150 rubles a month for a single room.

Living conditions for the average Soviet citizen had not improved over the previous decade. Citizens who could not obtain what they wanted in the first or planned economy moved into the black market. Frustration with the political culture—Gorbachev stated that citizens felt insulted and degraded by being excluded from the political process—led to development of informal discussion groups, societies for the protection of the environment and the like. Gorbachev's goal was to make the first economy so attractive that there would be no need for substitutes, but this would not be achieved in the 20th century. Another stumbling block was the need to increase prices. Food subsidies in 1987 were in excess of 50 billion rubles, with transport and housing adding another 20 billion. The state promised full compensation when these subsidies were lifted, but the average citizen did not believe it. Most people were convinced that they would be worse off, even with promised wage and pension increases. Drinkers were aggrieved by the reduced supplies of vodka in the wake of the government's antialcohol campaign. The introduction of *gospriyomka* (tightening up on the quality of goods acceptable by the state) caused workers to lose bonuses, which in turn prompted strikes in many parts of the country.

Gorbachev stated that the Communist Party had been deaf to the social aspirations of the population in the decade to 1985. The evidence suggested that citizens would need to experience an increase in living standards before they would feel any commitment to *perestroika*. Given the lack of resources, improvements could result only from higher labour productivity, putting Gorbachev in a Catch-22 situation.

*Martin McCauley is Senior Lecturer in Soviet and East European Studies in the School of Slavonic and East European Studies, University of London.*

Crowds of people file past the graves of the firemen who were killed at the Chernobyl nuclear power plant. The ceremony marked the first anniversary of the nuclear disaster, which killed 31 persons and forced the evacuation of more than 135,000 others from the Chernobyl area.
V. MATVIEVSKY—TASS/SOVFOTO

*(continued from page 473)*
for the civilian economy. The U.S.S.R. defense burden, estimated at 15% of gross domestic product in 1987, was about two to three times that of the U.K. and the U.S. The Soviet leadership perceived for the first time that the Soviet arms buildup actually fueled defense expenditure in NATO. The Soviet Union needed to be seen as cutting its nuclear arsenal to convince public opinion in the West that it was a diminishing threat.

**Domestic Affairs.** In 1987 Gorbachev's standing abroad was greater than at home. In an action-packed year he toured the country and made many passionate speeches promoting *perestroika* (restructuring) and *glasnost* (openness). (*See* Special Report.) He was highly visible on television and used that medium very effectively to drive home his message that the processes now under way were irreversible. Since becoming leader of the CPSU in March 1985, Gorbachev had been quietly mastering the art of television presentation. After the 27th party congress in 1986, television had been upgraded and more resources poured into it. "Vremya," the main news program, had become much more international in its coverage and slightly less negative in its reporting on the West. Examples of efficient U.S. industry were televised, and the message was that if the Americans could do it so could the Soviets. Hence the new political thinking not only aimed at changing the West's perception of the U.S.S.R. but also the average Soviet citizen's attitude toward everyday life and work.

Personnel changes during the year in the Politburo favoured Gorbachev. At the June Central Committee (CC) plenum, Nikolay Slyunkov and Aleksandr Yakovlev were promoted from candidate membership to full membership in the Politburo. Viktor Nikonov, CC secretary for agriculture, was made a full member of the Politburo without first having to serve as a candidate member. The new defense minister, General of the Army Dmitry Yazov (*see* BIOGRAPHIES), was elected a candidate member of the Politburo, the same rank as his predecessor, Marshal Sergey Sokolov, who was dropped as a candidate member. Dinmukhamed Kunayev, former first secretary of the Communist Party of Kazakhstan, was removed from the CC for "serious deficiencies" during his period in office. At the October CC plenum, Geidar Aliyev, a full member of the Politburo, was removed, but no one was elected in his place.

There were two key dismissals in 1987, those of Sokolov in May and of Boris Yeltsin, first secretary of the Moscow city Communist Party, in November. The first enhanced Gorbachev's authority, the second diminished it. The defense minister's dismissal was precipitated by his failure to prevent Mathias Rust, a 19-year-old West German, from landing in Red Square in his Cessna 172 light aircraft. The air defense commander in chief, Marshal Aleksandr Koldunov, was also dismissed for dereliction of duty. In the official announcement he was referred to merely as Comrade Koldunov, a slight not only to him but to the whole military establishment. General of the Army Ivan Tretyak was appointed as Koldunov's successor, a surprising move given that Tretyak had no flying experience. The Rust incident occurred while Gorbachev and Sokolov were in East Berlin for a Warsaw Pact meeting. In the communiqué issued at the end of the meeting, Warsaw Pact military doctrine was stated to be "defensive," and the term *necessary military sufficiency* was also employed. All this indicated that the general secretary was asserting his authority over the military.

If everything went Gorbachev's way in May, the reverse was true in November. Apparently Yeltsin had offered to resign his posts in a letter to the CPSU leader in August. This, it could be argued, was a breach of party discipline, since all members are entrusted with their tasks until the party has decided they should go. The Yeltsin affair caused one of the golden rules of Soviet politics to be broken, that the leadership must always appear united. On October 31, just two days before Gorbachev's speech commemorating the 70th anniversary of the Revolution, Anatoly Lukyanov, a CC secretary regarded as a Gorbachev appointee, revealed at a press conference that Yeltsin had offered to resign but had been advised not to raise the issue until after November 7. He had ignored this advice, and this had led to a furious row during the CC plenum on October 21.

Yeltsin's replacement as Moscow city leader was Lev Zaikov, CC secretary for defense industries and already a full Politburo member. His appointment could be seen as a demotion since his previous tasks were more important, and he would have to give up his CC secretaryship. The fact that Zaikov, a previous first secretary of the Leningrad Party organization, took the post revealed that the Politburo could not agree on an outsider as Yeltsin's successor. Since the Moscow city leader was always elected to the Politburo, it was a key post.

Another revelation about Yeltsin was that he had criticized Gorbachev's wife, Raisa, for her extravagant taste in clothes and jewelry and accused her of requiring payment as deputy chair of the Soviet Cultural Foundation, a body that promoted young artistic talent. This was not the first time that she had been vilified. Raisa played the role of a first lady but was also a political figure in her own right. She accompanied her husband in the Soviet Union and abroad and answered political questions. Both the Gorbachevs favoured a more active political and economic role for women, but many men did not share this view, and criticism of Raisa was an indirect attack on Gorbachev.

A man was sentenced to death because of his role in the riots in Alma-Ata, Kazakhstan, in December 1986. Nationalist demonstrations were also reported from Armenia and Lithuania. The number of Jews and Germans granted exit visas to the West rose appreciably during the year. Among those dissidents who left the U.S.S.R. was Anatoly Koryagin, a psychiatrist who had publicly protested the policy of diagnosing opponents of the regime as insane. In November *Komsomolskaya Pravda* carried a denunciation of the abuse of psychiatry in the Soviet Union.

**The Economy.** The 1987 economic results were disappointing. During the first ten months industrial output was reported to have risen by 3.6%, but the crucial machine-building sector rose only 1.6%. Output of light industry was 0.5% above 1986—less than the increase in population. Agriculture was hit by poor weather, and the grain harvest fell short of the targeted 230 million metric tons. Despite heavy investment, the machine-building sector grew sluggishly. The official explanation was that restructuring involved so much change that growth rates were bound to be affected. In fact, however, there had been a real economic decline during the 1980s because of hidden inflation, and a deterioration in quality meant that an increasing volume of goods had to be scrapped.

**Foreign Affairs.** Eastern Europe was preoccupied with the Soviet reforms. In Poland Gen. Wojciech Jaruzelski was an enthusiastic supporter of reform, but his government's failure to receive majority support for proposed changes in a national referendum held on November 29 meant that progress in reform would be slow at best. The referendum

VLASTIMIR SHONE—GAMMA/LIAISON

Mathias Rust, the young West German pilot who made an unauthorized landing in Moscow's Red Square, testifies before the Supreme Court in Moscow about his violation of Soviet airspace.

result was expected to have a similar effect on other Eastern European countries. In Romania Pres. Nicolae Ceausescu dismissed the reforms as irrelevant, and in East Germany many reports of the new policies in the U.S.S.R. were censored. In Czechoslovakia Premier Lubomir Strougal advocated economic change, and reform was thought to be more likely when Milos Jakes replaced Gustav Husak as party leader late in the year. Hungary and Bulgaria showed little enthusiasm for Soviet ideas. Overall, Eastern Europe's economic performance remained weak. In 1987 Gorbachev made a successful visit to Czechoslovakia and an unsuccessful one to Romania.

British Prime Minister Margaret Thatcher visited the U.S.S.R. March 28–April 1 and appeared uncensored on Soviet television. (MARTIN MCCAULEY)

## YUGOSLAVIA

A federal socialist republic, Yugoslavia is in southern Europe on the Adriatic Sea. Area: 255,804 sq km (98,766 sq mi). Pop. (1987 est.): 23,433,000. Cap.: Belgrade. Monetary unit: Yugoslav dinar, with (Oct. 5, 1987) a free rate of 970 dinars to U.S. $1 (1,575 dinars = £1 sterling). Presidents of the Presidium of the League of Communists in 1987, Milanko Renovica and, from June 30, Bosko Krunic; presidents of the Collective Presidency, Sinan Hasani and, from May 15, Lazar Mojsov; president of the Federal Executive Council (premier), Branko Mikulic.

Yugoslavia's political and economic crisis deepened in 1987, causing a rise in social tension. Discord among the six republics and two autonomous provinces continued to grow. Kosovo Province suffered the most severe unrest; the 1.6 million ethnic Albanians (Muslims) stepped up their demands for a separate state, while the minority (about 10%) Serbs agitated for tougher measures to curb what they considered to be systematic intimidation intended to force them out. Kosovo was part of the Serbian Republic and the cause of a power struggle in the Serbian Central Committee under the presidency of Slobodan Milosevic, who favoured a tough response on the Albanian issue. The president of the republic and Milosevic's rival, Ivan Stambolic, was under heavy criticism for being weak in the fight against Albanian nationalism and "irredentism." In Belgrade the secretary of the Communist Party committee was sacked over the issue; a number of officials associated with Stambolic resigned, and Stambolic himself was sacked in mid-December. Antiriot police were moved into Kosovo on October 25 following an escalation in tension prompted by a comment of Fadilj Hoxha, an Albanian and a former vice-president under the late president Tito. Hoxha was dismissed from his honorary post—membership in the Council of the Federation—as well as from the Communist Party on the grounds that he was supporting Albanian separatism.

In August Yugoslavia was shaken by its biggest post-1945 scandal, involving fraud that lost 63 Yugoslav banks $500 million–$850 million. Many of the country's leading politicians were involved, and among the members expelled or forced to resign from the Communist Party was Vice-Pres. Hamdija Pozderac, who was to have become the country's president in May 1988. The banks had accepted promissory notes from one of the biggest and previously most successful food-processing firms, Agrokomerc. The firm subsequently went bankrupt, and its general manager, Fikret Abdic, was expelled from the party and his official posts. Many other party members were under investigation. The incident highlighted the poor financial controls in a country where high inflation and low incomes forced most families to become dependent on credit.

Social unrest was reflected in an unprecedented level of strikes—1,262 by the end of October, compared with 851 in all of 1986. Many strikes were ended quickly, but others dragged on, notably a 33-day stoppage at a coal mine in Croatia, which ended with a 70% wage increase. The poor state of the economy was a major factor in the unrest. Gross domestic product grew by only 1% in 1987 instead of the 3% planned. Inflation reached an annual rate of 175% in November and was expected to be 150% for the year. Following the introduction of a new law on bankruptcies on July 1, unemployment rose, reaching 1.2 million by the end of the year. Industrial output increased only marginally, and agricultural output fell by 5% compared with 1986. On November 14 the government introduced economic austerity measures that included large price increases for essential goods and a restrictive wage policy. The measures brought an angry response from workers. Shortly afterward the government announced a 24.6% devaluation of the dinar. The burden of heavy external debt continued to be a major economic constraint. In July the government was unable to meet its repayment obligations, and in September its creditors were asked to reschedule $19 billion. In December the government decided to seek International Monetary Fund assistance.

Tension with Albania continued because of problems in Kosovo, but Albania did agree to attend the first Balkan conference for foreign ministers in Belgrade in early 1988. Relations with Romania improved following a visit to Belgrade by Pres. Nicolae Ceausescu, but relations with Greece remained cool.                    (K. F. CVIIC)

# North America

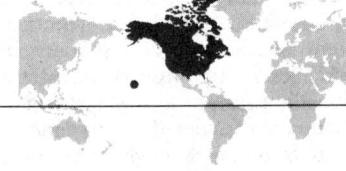

## CANADA

Canada is a federal parliamentary state and member of the Commonwealth covering North America north of conterminous United States and east of Alaska. Area: 9,970,610 sq km (3,849,675 sq mi). Pop (1987 est.): 25,857,000. Cap.: Ottawa. Monetary unit: Canadian dollar, with (Oct. 5, 1987) a free rate of Can$1.31 to U.S. $1 (Can$2.13 = £1 sterling). Queen, Elizabeth II; governor-general in 1987, Jeanne Sauvé; prime minister, Brian Mulroney.

**Domestic Affairs.** The Progressive Conservative government of Prime Minister Brian Mulroney, elected with a landslide majority in 1984, could point to a mixed record of accomplishment in 1987. It presided over a flourishing Canadian economy, devised new arrangements that would make Quebec a full adherent of the 1982 constitution, unveiled a radical reform of Canada's personal tax system, and concluded a free trade agreement with the U.S. Yet the government's popularity in public opinion polls continued to decline. One taken in September showed it possessing the confidence of only 27% of decided voters, compared with 39% for the socialist New Democratic Party (NDP) and 32% for the Liberal Party. Worse, in three by-elections held on July 20, the party lost two seats, one in Newfoundland and one in Yukon, to the NDP. A third seat, in Ontario, was retained by the NDP. These results left party standings in the 282-seat House of Commons: Progressive Conservatives 208; Liberals 40; NDP 33; independent 1.

Most observers attributed the Conservatives' low rating

to the personal image of their leader. Mulroney was seen as less than forthright, untrustworthy, and obsessively concerned with his own popularity. Despite election promises to sweep away patronage, he had rewarded a host of friends and political cronies. A number of ministers had resigned from his Cabinet after being touched by scandal, and there had been administrative bungling. The collapse of Tory support benefited the NDP, which showed unprecedented strength in the polls. Its leader, Edward Broadbent, was judged the most effective political leader in Canada. Whether this could be translated into ballots at the next election was debatable, however; in previous years the party's standing had often been high at by-elections, when it represented a protest vote. The once-dominant Liberal Party of Pierre Trudeau continued to be divided on policy questions, and its leader, John Turner, who had succeeded Trudeau in 1984, seemed unable to pull it together.

Mulroney lost one of the principal pillars of his government when Erik Nielsen, MP for Yukon and a former deputy prime minister, resigned from Parliament in January for health reasons. A Cabinet scandal emerged in the same month when André Bissonnette, secretary of state for transport, was asked to resign by the prime minister because of his part in a multimillion-dollar land speculation in his riding south of Montreal. In February another Quebec minister, Roch LaSalle, resigned from the Cabinet when news reports stated that he had been guest of honour at a party that businessmen had paid to attend in hopes of securing government contracts. LaSalle was the seventh minister, the fourth from Quebec, to resign or be forced from the Mulroney Cabinet. A minor Cabinet shake-up occurred on August 27 when two senior Quebec ministers were moved to new positions. The reconstructed Mulroney Cabinet still contained 40 members, making it the largest in Canadian history.

During the 1986–87 parliamentary session the government introduced 82 bills (with another 11 in the Senate) and saw more than half of them passed. An important and controversial measure was an amendment to the Patent Act giving greater protection to pharmaceutical manufac-

Canadian Prime Minister Brian Mulroney (left) talks with French Pres. François Mitterrand during the first state visit to Canada by a French president since 1967.

turers, most of them U.S.-based multinationals. The period in which these companies could hold a patent on their products would be increased from four to ten years, during which time manufacturers of generic drugs would not be allowed to copy products in return for a royalty payment. The drug companies, in asking for this protection, committed themselves to carrying out increased research in Canada. Passed over strong opposition in the House of Commons, the bill was severely amended by the appointed Senate, whose 104 seats were dominated by 65 Liberal members. The senators claimed, as had the opposition in the Commons, that the bill would result in higher drug prices for Canadian consumers. The Senate's action produced a rare constitutional dispute, since the upper house's right to refuse to pass a bill sent from the Commons is seldom exercised. The government requested that the Commons be recalled on August 11, when the bill was repassed in its original form and returned to the Senate. After long study the Senate eventually gave its assent to the measure on November 19.

The summer session of Parliament also dealt with two controversial bills setting out tougher rules for would-be refugees entering Canada. One established a simpler and speedier refugee determination process. The second gave the government power to impose heavy penalties on smugglers and transportation companies taking illegal immigrants to Canada. The number of persons claiming refugee status was expected to reach as high as 25,000 in 1987, compared with 18,000 the previous year. A flagrant case of what appeared to be abuse of the system occurred on July 12, when 174 Sikhs from northern India were landed on a lonely stretch of Nova Scotia coast.

The Commons held a dramatic debate through the night of June 29–30 on a motion to restore the death penalty, abolished in Canada since 1976. The resolution was defeated in a free vote of MPs, 148–127. It was the fifth time the issue had come before Parliament in 21 years.

A federal-provincial conference, held in Ottawa on March 26 and 27, failed to agree on an amendment to the constitution guaranteeing self-government to the aboriginal peoples of Canada. The conference broke down over demands of leaders representing the 575,000 native peoples of Canada for a constitutional amendment guaranteeing them an "inherent" right to self-government, stemming from their ancestral occupancy of the land. Ottawa and the provinces insisted that only forms of self-rule that had been politically negotiated could be entrenched. The 1987 meeting was the last of three provided for by a 1983 agreement. Its failure meant that the future definition of aboriginal rights would probably be determined by the courts.

The federal and provincial governments reached a historic agreement on April 30 that would make possible Quebec's acceptance of the 1982 constitution and would transfer extensive new powers to all the provinces. In a nine-hour negotiating session in an old stone mansion overlooking Meech Lake, a few miles north of Ottawa, Mulroney and the ten provincial premiers accepted Quebec's key demand that the province be recognized as constituting a "distinct society" within Canada with the right to assert that identity.

A second meeting at Meech Lake on June 3 produced a document, known as the Meech Lake accord, that was signed by Mulroney and the ten premiers. It contained the following provisions: a new amending formula requiring the consent of Ottawa and all the provinces for changes in federal institutions such as the House of Commons, the Senate, and the Supreme Court (the previous formula had involved the federal Parliament and seven provinces

containing 50% of Canada's population), as well as for the creation of new provinces; all provinces to gain new powers over immigration; the provinces to have the right to nominate candidates for the Senate and the Supreme Court, the federal government to have the power to veto the appointments; the provinces to have the right to opt out of new national shared-cost programs, with Ottawa providing compensation if the province undertook a program compatible with national objectives.

The Meech Lake accord represented a compromise between a strong desire to bring Quebec into the constitution, which meant meeting some of its terms, and the conviction that Quebec should not be given special status. This was satisfied by granting to all the provinces the concessions offered to Quebec with the exception of the "distinct society" clause. To become part of the constitution, the Meech Lake accord would have to be ratified by Parliament and the legislatures of all the provinces. The first province to declare its acceptance was Quebec on June 2. A longtime champion of Quebec separatism, former provincial premier René Lévesque (see OBITUARIES), died November 1.

Two provinces held elections in 1987. In Ontario a minority Liberal government headed by David Peterson won a massive vote of confidence on September 10, gaining 95 of the 130 seats in the legislature. In New Brunswick, Richard Hatfield, heading a Progressive Conservative administration that had been in power for 17 years, saw the Liberals under Frank McKenna win a clean sweep of the 58-seat house. There were now four Liberal governments in the ten provinces, four Conservative, one Social Credit, and one NDP.

**The Economy.** During the second quarter of 1987 the Canadian economy grew at a seasonally adjusted annual rate of 6.1%, making it one of the fastest growing in the Western world. Unadjusted for inflation, the gross domestic product stood at $547.2 billion at midyear. Much of the growth came from the consumption of consumer goods, but housing construction was also vigorous. The unemployment rate fell to 8.2% in November, the lowest level since early 1982, and labour shortages in certain occupations began to appear in major centres such as Toronto. Inflation began to edge up, stimulated by sharp increases in energy prices and in consumption taxes. In October the consumer price index stood at 4.3% at an annual rate, representing a leveling off from previous months. The Canadian dollar recovered from its 1986 levels to reach 76 cents U.S. in late September. Interest rates began rising in the third quarter, with the Bank of Canada rate, which determines rates charged by the chartered banks, reaching a plateau around 9.4% in late September.

A short strike of the Canadian Auto Workers union against Chrysler Canada Ltd. was settled on September 17 with a historic agreement providing pensions indexed to the cost of living. There would also be large increases in basic pension payments in the future.

Canada unveiled a new $1 coin on June 30. Gold-coloured and with 11 sides, the new coins would gradually replace $1 bills beginning in 1989.

Presenting the budget on February 18, Finance Minister Michael Wilson revealed that the federal government intended to continue its present economic policies. He predicted that federal spending would climb 5.1% in 1987–88 to $122.6 billion. With revenues estimated at $93.3 billion, this would produce a deficit of $29.3 billion, lower than in 1986–87. The budget postponed major tax changes until a comprehensive tax reform plan could be presented. There were increases in some indirect taxes.

The first phase of the long-awaited tax reform was unveiled on June 18. It dealt with the personal and corporate income tax structure, leaving changes in the sales tax to be announced at a later date. Beginning in 1988 the number of tax brackets for individuals would be reduced from ten to three, and rates in the brackets would run from 17 to 29%. Many tax exemptions and deductions would be eliminated, to be replaced by tax credits. These changes would mean the end of income tax liability for 850,000 low-income individuals and reductions for another 1.2 million taxpayers. Corporate tax rates would be decreased, but a broader base would bring a larger collection from business. Banks, trust companies, and loan, real estate, and insurance companies would have their transactions taxed in a new way. Wilson called on the provinces to meet with him in the fall to discuss a shared sales tax. The federal government indicated that it was considering a value-added tax such as that used in the European Communities.

**Foreign Affairs.** *Canada-U.S. Relations.* After more than 16 months of negotiations, a historic free trade agreement was reached by Canadian and U.S. negotiators on October 3, two hours before U.S. trade law required that the president notify Congress of his intention to enter into such an arrangement. The agreement looked to the elimination of all tariffs between the two countries over a ten-year period beginning in 1989, after it had been approved by the U.S. Congress and the Canadian Parliament. Approval was not expected to come easily. The legal text of the agreement was issued on December 11 and was to be signed by U.S. Pres. Ronald Reagan and Prime Minister Mulroney on Jan. 2, 1988.

Although free trade with Canada was not a major issue in the U.S., it was a burning question in Canada in 1987. Supporting free trade were the business community and most provincial premiers; opposing it were labour unions and groups worried about the effects on Canada's cultural identity. Premier Peterson, before the Ontario provincial election, laid down several conditions for a satisfactory trade agreement, including no weakening of the 1965 Auto Pact and no provisions threatening Canada's cultural identity, agriculture, regional economic assistance policies, and foreign investment guidelines. The Liberal leader interpreted his resounding victory as an endorsement of his cautious approach to free trade.

Addressing the Canadian Parliament during his visit to Ottawa on April 5–6, President Reagan gave a ringing endorsement of the benefits of free enterprise and free trade to the two countries. However, he and Mulroney failed to resolve differences over acid rain and Arctic sovereignty.

*External Affairs.* Canada was host to two important international conferences in 1987: a meeting of La Francophonie in Quebec City, September 2–4, and a Commonwealth heads of government conference in Vancouver, B.C., October 13–17. The meeting of La Francophonie brought together representatives of 37 countries using French as a common language. There was discussion as to whether the organization should assume a more political role comparable to that of the Commonwealth, but France was not receptive to this notion. Prime Minister Mulroney attended, as did the leaders of Canada's two officially bilingual provinces, Quebec and New Brunswick.

The Commonwealth meeting, attended by the leaders of 47 countries, continued the association's focus on measures to end apartheid in South Africa. Additional economic sanctions were ruled out, but the meeting authorized a committee of foreign ministers, chaired by Canada's Joe Clark, to monitor the effectiveness of existing sanctions and to counter South African propaganda. (See *Commonwealth of Nations,* above.)

Canada was the only country in the world that belonged to the Commonwealth, La Francophonie, and the Group of Seven industrialized countries. Mulroney attended the economic summit held in Venice, Italy, June 8–10. The seven leaders present promised to increase coordination in their economic policies, reduce their farm subsidies, and continue the effort to dismantle apartheid in South Africa.

Africa and apartheid continued to play a large part in the Mulroney government's foreign policy. The prime minister journeyed to Zimbabwe on January 27–30 to consult with the leaders of black southern African states hurt by embargoes imposed against South Africa. He was the first Western leader to visit Zimbabwe since it achieved independence in 1980. Canadian aid was given to a hydroelectric project designed to help free the African states from economic dependence on South Africa. Clark also traveled to southern Africa in August, visiting Zambia, Mozambique, and South Africa. In the latter country he and Roelof ("Pik") Botha, South Africa's foreign minister, discussed means of getting negotiations started between the South African government and the black majority in the country, but there was no meeting of minds.

On January 24 an agreement was reached in Paris to settle the dispute over the limits of France's fishing grounds around its island dependency of Saint-Pierre and Miquelon in the Gulf of St. Lawrence. Canada and France would agree on temporary quotas for French fishing; then permanent quotas would be assigned to France within Canada's 200-mi economic zone, and the maritime boundaries of Saint-Pierre and Miquelon would be established. The premier of Newfoundland, Brian Peckford, was enraged by the agreement, which, he said, granted France unwarranted access to fishing grounds Newfoundland considered its own, and he withdrew Newfoundland advisers from the negotiations. When France persisted in overfishing in the disputed waters, Canada closed its ports to French fishing vessels on March 17. France then broke off the negotiations, which remained in abeyance until Mulroney and Prime Minister Jacques Chirac, meeting at the Francophone summit, agreed to resume them.

A long-awaited government statement on defense was introduced in Parliament on June 5. It reiterated Canada's faith in common defense arrangements such as NATO to ensure its security. Earlier, Canada had strengthened its forces committed to NATO in Europe, and it now confirmed its intention to support NATO's Central Front through a brigade group permanently stationed in southern Germany. At the same time, the government announced that it could no longer honour its "unsustainable commitment" to send a brigade group to northern Norway. Defense Minister Perrin Beatty took the occasion to announce a 15-year budget of $183 billion to provide badly needed equipment for the Canadian forces. This included ten nuclear-powered submarines for Arctic and coastal patrols, a fixed under-ice surveillance system for Arctic waters, antisubmarine helicopters, new long-range patrol aircraft, and new battle tanks.          (D. M. L. FARR)

## UNITED STATES

The United States of America is a federal republic composed of 50 states, 49 of which are in North America and one of which consists of the Hawaiian Islands. Area: 9,372,571 sq km (3,618,770 sq mi), including 205,856 sq km of inland water but excluding the 156,492 sq km of the Great Lakes that lie within U.S. boundaries. Pop. (1987 est.): 243,773,000. Cap.: Washington, D.C. Monetary unit: U.S. dollar, with (Oct. 5, 1987) a free rate of U.S. $1.62 to £1 sterling. President in 1987, Ronald Reagan.

Fireworks brighten the sky over Philadelphia's Independence Hall in celebration of the 200th anniversary of the U.S. Constitution.
AP/WIDE WORLD

**Foreign Affairs.** The string of reverses that began to plague the Reagan administration in late 1986 grew still longer in 1987. Both at home and abroad, a number of major White House initiatives either fell short of their announced objectives or were subjected to harsh second-guessing. There was even speculation in Washington as to whether Pres. Ronald Reagan (*see* BIOGRAPHIES) was still fully in command of the federal government's executive machinery. At year's end the summit with Soviet leader Mikhail Gorbachev and the signing of a U.S.-U.S.S.R. treaty on intermediate nuclear forces (INF) restored some lustre to the Reagan presidency, though Senate ratification of the treaty was by no means assured.

Beyond question, the major source of adversity for the White House was the Iran-*contra* affair—the series of secret transactions involving arms shipments to Iran and aid to Nicaraguan rebel groups that first came to public attention in November 1986. (*See* Special Report.) The report of the President's Special Review Board (the Tower Commission), appointed to review the National Security Council's role in the scandal, described U.S. policy as having evolved into "chaos" as "amateurish" staff members failed to subject their complex dealings to comprehensive policy review. One immediate result was the resignation of White House chief of staff Donald Regan. He was replaced by former Senate majority leader Howard Baker (*see* BIOGRAPHIES) of Tennessee, whose appointment was warmly received by members of Congress of both parties. The subsequent congressional hearings into the affair turned up no "smoking gun" evidence that Reagan was personally involved in wrongdoing, though they did little to restore the president's image as a strong and effective leader.

Other events during the year underscored the extent of U.S. involvement in the Middle East, where the Iran-Iraq war seemed no nearer resolution. On May 17 the USS *Stark*, a U.S. Navy frigate on patrol in the Persian Gulf, was struck by missiles fired by an Iraqi warplane. Thirty-seven U.S. sailors were killed in the attack, which officials of both countries described as accidental. The U.S. protested the incident but accepted Iraq's apologies. On June 19 the

Navy announced that the captain and two other officers from the *Stark* were being relieved of duty owing to "lack of confidence in their performance." Notwithstanding the *Stark* incident and the outcry it caused in Congress, the administration proceeded with plans to reflag 11 Kuwaiti oil tankers so that they could be escorted by U.S. Navy ships through Gulf waters. Kuwait, which was considered friendly to Iraq, had been a particular target of Iranian hostility. Washington agreed to the arrangement after Kuwait had made known its plans to lease three Soviet tankers that could be protected by Soviet warships.

The escort operation began July 22. Two U.S.-flagged Kuwaiti tankers were escorted through the Strait of Hormuz by three U.S. Navy ships; a fourth warship joined the convoy when it reached the Gulf. On July 24, two days into the voyage, one of the reflagged tankers, the *Bridgeton,* struck a mine, apparently laid by Iran. The vessel sustained only slight damage, and the convoy was delayed by only a few hours. The *Bridgeton* was repaired and reentered service later in the year. However, the incident pointed up the lack of minesweeping equipment in the Gulf. On July 29 it was announced that Defense Secretary Caspar Weinberger had ordered eight minesweeping helicopters flown to the area. In a later incident, on August 24, U.S. warships accompanying reflagged Kuwaiti tankers out of the Gulf fired warning shots across the bows of two small fishing craft and challenged an Iranian naval vessel. On September 21 a U.S. helicopter attacked an Iranian naval vessel that was allegedly surprised while laying mines. The ship was disabled and seized, together with its crew. Three Iranian sailors were killed, and two others were missing and presumed dead. The survivors, including four wounded, were returned to Iran. The Iranian government denied that the ship was a minelayer.

On October 8 four of the armed patrol boats that constituted Iran's chief naval threat in the Gulf reportedly fired on a U.S. surveillance helicopter. In retaliation, U.S. helicopter gunships sank one of the vessels and disabled two others, which were then seized; one boat escaped. U.S. officials claimed that evidence from the captured ships indicated that Iran possessed the advanced U.S.-made Stinger missile. On October 16 a U.S.-flagged oil tanker sailing in Kuwaiti waters was hit by an Iranian Silkworm missile (a Chinese-made version of the French Exocet), injuring 18 crewmen. Three days later, in what the U.S. described as a retaliatory action, U.S. warships bombarded an offshore oil rig that was being used as a base for Iranian gunboats. Iran responded on October 22 by firing a missile into Kuwait's main offshore oil-loading platform.

These blows and counterblows threatened to bring Washington and Tehran into open military conflict and, in fact, Iran announced that it was actually at war with the U.S. as well as with Iraq. This was vigorously denied by the Reagan administration, which maintained that the U.S. was not actively involved in the Gulf conflict. The administration also resisted invocation of the War Powers Act, although some members of Congress claimed that the situation in the Gulf required such an action. Some commentators suggested that Kuwait and the U.S. had both underestimated the risks involved in the reflagging policy, and that the implications had not been thought through.

Another source of conflict between Congress and the White House during the year was the issue of aid to the Nicaraguan *contras*. The Iran-*contra* affair disclosures that the administration had attempted to evade a congressional ban on *contra* aid stiffened opposition on Capitol Hill to its renewal. The administration, on the other hand, maintained its position that support for the *contras* was vital to

U.S interests. On September 10 Secretary of State George Shultz told the Senate Foreign Relations Committee that the administration intended to ask for $270 million more in *contra* aid when the current funding expired at the end of fiscal 1987 (September 30). Although a Central American peace plan had been signed in Guatemala in August, Shultz said the administration did not believe that the Marxist Nicaraguan government would live up to it. He argued that "it is simply not in our interest to leave the Sandinista regime [in Managua] unconstrained by credible resistance forces on the basis of a hope or a premise."

The administration's strategy on *contra* aid ran into an unexpected and somewhat embarrassing obstacle on October 13 when it was announced that Costa Rican Pres. Oscar Arias Sánchez (*see* BIOGRAPHIES), the principal architect of the Central American peace plan, had been awarded the 1987 Nobel Peace Prize. U.S. House Speaker Jim Wright (Dem., Texas; *see* BIOGRAPHIES) reacted to the news by saying that the award ensured that Congress would not approve the money the White House was seeking for the *contras*. A bitter impasse between the administration and the speaker soon developed, broken only when Wright and Shultz appeared together on November 17 in the Capitol and read a joint statement pledging to "work together" for peace. The statement appeared to quell, at least temporarily, a feud that had threatened to derail whatever bipartisan agreement had developed on U.S. policy in the troubled region. Several days earlier Wright had raised eyebrows by becoming involved in indirect negotiations between Nicaraguan Pres. Daniel Ortega and *contra* leaders over implementation of the Arias plan.

For the short term, the Shultz-Wright accord may have helped the administration's campaign to continue nonlethal aid to the *contras*. On December 22 Congress approved $14 million in nonlethal aid to the *contras* as part of the fiscal 1988 appropriations bill. However, the question of *contra* aid would come before Congress again in February 1988.

U.S.-Soviet relations followed an uneven course in 1987. The low point was a spy scandal at the U.S. embassy in Moscow that initially seemed like the plot of an espionage thriller. It came to public notice on March 30 when Washington announced that the entire contingent of 28 Marine Corps guards at the embassy was to be recalled. Two former Marine guards, Sgt. Clayton J. Lonetree and Cpl. Arnold Bracy, had allegedly allowed Soviets access to the embassy in return for sexual favours from Soviet women, and others were thought to be implicated as well.

Word of the Moscow scandal led Reagan to order a study of security at the new U.S. embassy compound under construction in the Soviet capital. Some $100 million had already been spent on the complex, which was due to be completed in 1989. Under a 1977 agreement, the Soviets could not move into the office sections of their new embassy in the U.S. (on an elevated site in the Mount Alto neighbourhood of Washington, D.C.) until U.S. personnel were able to move into their new quarters in Moscow. The investigation produced evidence that sophisticated Soviet listening devices, implanted in precast concrete pillars and beams that had been molded away from the construction site, were hidden throughout the new U.S. chancery. Former defense secretary James R. Schlesinger, head of a State Department investigative panel, called on June 8 for a thorough overhaul of the Moscow chancery building to rid it of the eavesdropping equipment. In his report, Schlesinger said the U.S. had overestimated its ability to counteract Soviet espionage efforts with "superior U.S. technology and ingenuity." If the building were to be usable, the top three floors would have to be demolished and rebuilt under tight

security. Schlesinger also recommended construction of a six-story secure annex adjacent to the chancery.

Espionage charges against Bracy were dropped June 12. The Marine Corps explained that it lacked sufficient evidence to warrant prosecution. On the same day, U.S. officials were quoted in news dispatches as saying that it was not certain that Soviet agents had actually entered the Moscow embassy or, if the penetration had indeed taken place, whether security had been seriously compromised. Lonetree was not so fortunate. A jury of eight Marine Corps officers sentenced him to 30 years in prison August 24 after his conviction three days earlier on charges of spying for the Soviet Union. The prosecution's case was based largely on a 20-page confession signed by Lonetree. He claimed it was made under duress, but defense efforts to challenge it were unsuccessful.

As the spy case was unfolding, the U.S. and the Soviet Union were engaged in protracted negotiations on a treaty to ban intermediate-range nuclear missiles. After months of preliminary negotiations in Geneva, Reagan announced September 18 in Washington that the two sides had agreed on a pact. The final breakthrough had been achieved by Shultz and Soviet Foreign Minister Eduard A. Shevardnadze September 15–17 in Washington. In addition, Reagan said, the superpowers had agreed to make an "intensive effort" to reach a treaty on a bilateral 50% reduction of strategic (long-range) nuclear weapons. Reagan also announced that Shultz and Shevardnadze would meet in Moscow in October to complete arrangements for a summit meeting in the U.S. between Gorbachev and himself.

Relations took a step backward on October 23, when Shultz was in Moscow to arrange the details of the summit. To his surprise, Gorbachev refused to set a date, justifying the rebuff on the basis of long-standing Soviet objections to the U.S. Strategic Defense Initiative ("Star Wars"). The incident reminded many observers of the rift that destroyed the 1986 "preparatory" summit between the two leaders in Reykjavík, Iceland. A week later, however, the Soviet foreign minister arrived in Washington bearing a letter from Gorbachev saying that he had the authority to agree on the dates and agenda of a summit. Reagan was able to announce that he and his Soviet counterpart would meet in Washington starting December 7. Meeting again in Geneva November 24, Shultz and Shevardnadze announced that both countries had accepted the terms of an accord banning nuclear missiles with ranges between 500 and 5,499 km (310 and 3,415 mi). Under the pact, the Soviet Union would destroy some 441 triple-warhead SS-20 missiles and nearly 250 other missiles, while the U.S. would give up 364 single-warhead Pershing II and cruise missiles. (*See* MILITARY AFFAIRS: *Special Report.*)

The summit took place in Washington December 8–10, and the INF treaty was signed December 8. Although both leaders declared the meeting a success, little else of substance appeared to have been accomplished. Perhaps one of the most notable features of the affair was the Soviets' newfound ability to make use of the media. It was announced that a fourth summit would be held, in Moscow, before the end of Reagan's term, whether or not a treaty covering strategic forces had been completed. Senate leaders expressed qualified optimism over ratification of the INF treaty without "killer" amendments. It appeared, however, that the treaty had cost Reagan support on the right. A number of far-right conservatives, including the fund-raiser Richard Viguerie, announced their belief that Reagan had deserted their cause and their intention to organize to defeat the INF treaty in the Senate.

Reagan visited Ottawa April 5–6 for his third annual summit meeting with Canadian Prime Minister Brian Mulroney. The principal topics of discussion were acid rain and free trade, although other issues—notably defense, Arctic sovereignty, and health research—also figured in the parley. Addressing the Canadian Parliament April 6, Reagan avoided mention of any goals or timetables on reducing U.S. industrial emissions responsible for acid rain, asserting that there were "no quick and easy answers" to the environmental problem. As to free trade, the president said current talks between the countries could serve as a "model of cooperation for the rest of the world."

The talks resulted in an agreement on October 3 covering virtually every sector of trade between the two countries. Of prime importance was a provision calling for the elimination of all bilateral tariffs over a ten-year period, starting Jan. 1, 1989. Under existing arrangements, about 85% of Canadian exports to the U.S. and about 70% of U.S. exports to Canada were duty-free. A major U.S. concession to Canada embodied in the pact was an agreement to establish a binding-arbitration panel to resolve bilateral trade disagreements, using the provisions of the new treaty. Individual U.S. companies could have trade complaints against Canadian industries decided under U.S. trade laws if they chose, but Canada could appeal the decisions to the arbitration panel. The treaty required approval by the legislatures of both countries. At year's end some opposition appeared to be developing on both sides of the border.

The Rev. Leon H. Sullivan, author of an influential antidiscrimination code of conduct for U.S. companies operating in South Africa, called on June 3 for a complete corporate pullout from that country within nine months. He also urged the U.S. government to sever diplomatic relations with Pretoria's white minority government and to impose total economic sanctions until South Africa dismantled the apartheid system of rigid racial separation. Sullivan urged that "stringent penalties" be imposed on such U.S. trading partners as Japan, which had moved into the vacuum created by U.S. companies that already had ceased operating in South Africa. He also criticized President Reagan, saying that if Reagan "had taken the same interest in black South Africans as he does in [the Nicaraguan] *contras,* we wouldn't have the problems we have in South Africa."

**Domestic Affairs.** Filling the U.S. Supreme Court vacancy caused by the retirement of Justice Lewis F. Powell, Jr., proved to be a source of frustration and embarrassment for the White House during the latter half of the year.

Reagan's first choice as Powell's successor was U.S. Court of Appeals Judge Robert H. Bork (*see* BIOGRAPHIES), 60, a prominent conservative jurist and a Nixon administration official during the Watergate scandal period. Though Bork's selection touched off immediate criticism from liberal Democrats, the initial expectation was that he would have little difficulty winning Senate confirmation. Much was at stake, since Powell's surprise retirement for reasons of health presented Reagan with an opportunity to shift the ideological balance of the court decisively to the right. Powell, a moderate, had played a "swing" role on the court, more pronounced in recent years, of casting the deciding vote in many key 5–4 decisions.

An early sign of trouble was the divided vote on the Bork nomination by the American Bar Association's (ABA's) standing committee on the federal judiciary. Although the panel's vote was supposed to be secret, major newspapers reported September 10 that ten of its members gave the nominee its highest rating, "well qualified," while four found him "not qualified" and one chose the noncommittal option, "not opposed." This was the first time in over a decade that the ABA committee had failed to give unanimous approval to a Supreme Court nominee.

In his opening statement before the Senate Judiciary Committee hearings on his nomination, Bork described his legal philosophy as "neither liberal nor conservative." He went on to say that he had changed his mind about a number of previously held positions described by critics as extreme and saw nothing wrong in having done so. Sen. Patrick Leahy (Dem., Vt.) asked Bork if his new-found moderation on certain sensitive issues such as the right of privacy represented "confirmation conversions" to mainstream views, adopted to win Senate approval. Bork replied that he would be "disgraced in history" if he were found to have tailored his views just to get on the court.

Apparently finding Bork's testimony unpersuasive, the committee voted 9–5 on October 6 to reject the nomination. Bork nonetheless declared three days later that he would not withdraw his name from consideration, even though the number of senators on record as planning to vote against him had by then reached a majority of the chamber's membership. "A crucial principle is at stake," Bork said. If he backed down now, "public campaigns of distortion . . . would be seen as a success" and would be "mounted against future nominees." The gesture of defiance was unavailing. The full Senate rejected Bork's nomination on October 23 by a vote of 58–42. Reagan reacted by declaring, in a statement from the White House,

Coffins of the sailors killed aboard the U.S. Navy frigate *Stark* are flown back to the United States for burial. Thirty-seven U.S. sailors were killed after the ship, on patrol in the Persian Gulf, was struck broadside by two Exocet missiles fired from an Iraqi fighter-bomber on May 17.

"My next nominee for the court will share Judge Bork's belief in judicial restraint—that a judge is bound by the Constitution to interpret laws, not make them."

That nominee turned out to be Judge Douglas H. Ginsburg, 41, one of Bork's colleagues on the U.S. Court of Appeals for the District of Columbia. Unlike Bork, who had expressed his views at length in articles and speeches as well as decisions, Ginsburg had been a member of the tribunal for only about a year, and published material embodying his legal views was sparse. He was known primarily as a conservative advocate of a free-market approach to regulatory and antitrust law issues. Also, he was said to be the favoured candidate of Attorney General Edwin Meese III, one of Reagan's closest advisers. The nomination ran into serious trouble almost immediately. An Associated Press report November 1 said that Ginsburg had had an investment of about $140,000 in Rogers Communications Inc. at the time he was in charge of a Justice Department case asking the Supreme Court to extend First Amendment protection to cable television operators. There was no direct relationship between the case and Rogers Communications, but the connection, though tenuous, did raise a question of propriety. Another matter in Ginsburg's background that attracted attention was a disclosure that his wife had performed abortions during her medical training. This revelation was especially mortifying for conservatives, since the 1973 Supreme Court decision (in *Roe* v. *Wade*) legalizing abortions in most circumstances was one they hoped to reverse with the addition of a like-minded jurist to the court.

The last straw came with the disclosure that Ginsburg had smoked marijuana in the past, not only in his youth but when he was on the faculty of Harvard Law School. This final bit of damaging news prompted the nominee to withdraw his name from consideration on November 7. Four days later Reagan announced his third choice to fill the vacant Powell seat—U.S. Court of Appeals Judge Anthony Kennedy, 51, who had been passed over in favour of Ginsburg just two weeks earlier. Closer to the conservative mainstream than Bork and more experienced than Ginsburg, he was treated gently at Judiciary Committee hearings in December. The nomination was expected to go before the Senate in January 1988.

Meanwhile, the revolving personnel door was spinning within the Reagan administration itself—a common enough occurrence during the latter stages of a lame-duck presidency. On February 2 the White House announced the resignation of William J. Casey (*see* OBITUARIES) as director of the CIA and Reagan's nomination of Robert M. Gates, a career intelligence analyst, to succeed him. However, Gates withdrew his name from consideration on March 2, whereupon Reagan named William H. Webster (*see* BIOGRAPHIES), director of the FBI, as the new nominee to head the CIA. Webster was confirmed and sworn into office in May. Succeeding Webster as FBI chief was William S. Sessions (*see* BIOGRAPHIES), a U.S. District Court judge from San Antonio, Texas. Despite Reagan's offer of a third term, Paul A. Volcker stepped down as chairman of the Federal Reserve Board at the end of his second four-year stint. He was replaced by Alan Greenspan (*see* BIOGRAPHIES), who had served as chairman of the Council of Economic Advisers under Pres. Gerald R. Ford.

Tragedy struck the Cabinet when Commerce Secretary Malcolm Baldrige, a rodeo cowboy by avocation, died July 25 after being crushed by a horse that reared and fell over backward on him at a calf-roping competition in Walnut Creek, Calif. Baldrige was succeeded by C. William Verity, Jr., a retired chairman of Armco Inc., the nation's fifth-largest steel producer. Transportation Secretary Elizabeth Hanford Dole resigned effective October 1, saying she wanted to devote herself to the 1988 presidential campaign of her husband, Senate Minority Leader Robert J. Dole (Rep., Kan.). Reagan designated James H. Burnley IV, a deputy secretary of transportation, as Dole's successor. However, the major change in the Cabinet occurred November 5, when Defense Secretary Weinberger, one of Reagan's original appointees, announced that he would step down as soon as a successor was confirmed. The president's choice was Frank C. Carlucci (*see* BIOGRAPHIES), who had succeeded Vice-Adm. John Poindexter as White House adviser on national security after Poindexter resigned during the Iran-*contra* scandal. To fill Carlucci's now-vacant post, Reagan named his deputy, Lieut. Gen. Colin L. Powell. The national security job did not require Senate approval.

Although the next presidential election was more than a year away, 1987 was filled with news of the comings and goings of candidates hoping to become the Democratic or Republican standard-bearer. Those who announced their intention to seek the GOP nomination included Vice-Pres. George Bush, Senator Dole, former secretary of state Alexander M. Haig, Jr., Rep. Jack F. Kemp of New York, former senator Paul Laxalt of Nevada, and the Rev. Marion G. (Pat) Robertson. Former governor Pierre S. (Pete) du Pont IV of Delaware had declared his candidacy in 1986. Laxalt dropped out of the race August 26, citing potential fund-raising problems. The Democratic field was more crowded, including at one time or another former governor Bruce Babbitt of Arizona, Sen. Joseph R. Biden, Jr., of Delaware, Gov. Michael S. Dukakis of Massachusetts, Rep. Richard A. Gephardt of Missouri, Sen. Albert Gore, Jr., of Tennessee, former senator Gary Hart of Colorado, the Rev. Jesse L. Jackson, and Sen. Paul Simon of Illinois.

*(continued on page 486)*

JAMES COLBURN—PHOTOREPORTERS

Lieut. Col. Oliver North is sworn in before a U.S. congressional investigating committee during the Iran-*contra* hearings. North's controversial testimony earned him temporary status as a folk hero.

# The Iran-*Contra* Affair

BY DONALD MORRISON

The first sign that a major scandal was in the making appeared on Nov. 3, 1986, in Lebanon. According to a report in *al-Shiraa,* an obscure Beirut magazine, the U.S. government had negotiated an arms deal with Iran. That was a remarkable disclosure. The U.S., arguing that Iran was a major sponsor of international terrorism, had long maintained a firm policy against aiding Iran in its war with neighbouring Iraq. In addition, Pres. Ronald Reagan had been especially outspoken in urging U.S. allies to avoid selling weapons to Iran. Therefore, when U.S. officials conceded that the *al-Shiraa* report was basically true, foreign allies and American citizens alike were confused and outraged.

**The Scandal Is Disclosed.** Then came an even more amazing disclosure. On November 25, U.S. Attorney General Edwin Meese confirmed that millions of dollars in profits from the Iran arms sale had been sent secretly to the *contras,* the U.S.-backed rebels fighting to overthrow the leftist government of Nicaragua. That news was particularly galling to members of Congress, which in 1984 had passed the Boland Amendment (named after a sponsor, Rep. Edward P. Boland of Massachusetts) banning direct or indirect U.S. military aid to the *contras.* All through the early part of 1987, new details dribbled out about the affair, which was known variously as the Iran-*contra* arms scandal and Irangate, the latter being a reference to the Watergate scandal of the 1970s. Indeed, the parallels with the earlier affair were undeniable. Once again there were allegations of serious misdeeds by White House insiders, of an official cover-up, and of direct presidential involvement. Once again investigations were launched and televised hearings commanded public attention for weeks on end. This time, in fact, there were two official inquiries.

A special panel, headed by former Texas senator John Tower and including former secretary of state Edmund Muskie and Brent Scowcroft, a retired air force general and foreign policy adviser in several administrations, was appointed by Reagan to look into the matter. In February the Tower Commission, as it came to be called, issued a report critical of Reagan and his advisers for failing to control actions by the National Security Council. The NSC, which was created in the late 1940s to advise the president on foreign affairs, was found to be heavily involved in organizing the Iran arms sales and transferring the proceeds to the *contras.* The NSC members most deeply tied to the scandal in one way or another were National Security Adviser Robert C. McFarlane, the council's head; his successor, Vice-Adm. John M. Poindexter; and Lieut. Col. Oliver L. North (*see* BIOGRAPHIES), a member of the NSC staff.

In January special committees of both houses of Congress

---

*Donald Morrison is a Senior Editor on the staff of* Time *magazine.*

undertook their own investigation, which included four weeks of joint televised hearings during the summer. The hearings, plus the committee's 690-page final report, painted a picture of official deception, apparent illegality, and presidential ineptitude. Reagan was widely criticized for allowing the affair to proceed, and in a televised speech he acknowledged mistakes and accepted responsibility. Yet there were few calls for his impeachment or resignation, as there had been for Richard Nixon's over Watergate.

Nonetheless, the Iran-*contra* scandal was destined to be remembered as one of the more bizarre episodes in U.S. history. The affair apparently began more than a year before the *al-Shiraa* article appeared. In early 1985 McFarlane went to Iran to negotiate the eventual sale of 2,004 TOW antitank missiles, 18 Hawk antiaircraft missiles, and more than 200 spare parts for Hawk missile batteries, for which Iran paid $30 million. The weapons were shipped via Israel, which U.S. officials said first suggested the deal. McFarlane later testified that he believed he was dealing with "moderates" in the Islamic fundamentalist government of Ayatollah Ruhollah Khomeini and that the U.S. merely desired to open channels of communication with such factions in the hope of restoring normal relations between the two countries. Eventually, however, the U.S. acknowledged that the arms sale was intended as a straight arms-for-hostages deal to free a number of Americans held captive in Lebanon by Shi'ah terrorist groups loyal to Iran. The effort was a failure. Only three hostages were freed, and three more Americans were soon kidnapped to take their place. In addition, despite the intention of opening a window to "moderates" in Iran, some of the arms went directly to the Revolutionary Guards, Iran's most radical faction. One of the Iranians with whom the U.S. dealt was even implicated in the kidnap-murder of a hostage, William Buckley, a CIA official in Lebanon. McFarlane later resigned and was hospitalized after taking an overdose of sleeping pills.

**The Enterprise.** What the arms sales did accomplish was to generate huge amounts of cash. Of the $30 million Iran paid for the arms, according to congressional testimony, about $12 million went to the U.S. Treasury and $3 million was spent on shipping and other costs, leaving a profit of $15 million to be used on the *contras.* Only $3.8 million of that ever found its way to the rebels, however. Much of the rest went to two U.S. businessmen, retired major general Richard Secord and his Iranian-born partner, Albert Hakim.

Secord and Hakim were engaged by Lieut. Col. North to set up what became known as the "Enterprise," a private network for supporting the *contras* after Congress passed the Boland Amendment. North and others raised $10 million in private contributions for the *contras,* though most of that went for expenses and salaries. The Enterprise at one point had its own airplanes, airfield, ship, and secret Swiss bank accounts. Money from the Iran arms sales began flowing to the Enterprise in 1985 after Israel advanced the U.S. $1 million for a shipment of Hawk missiles. The Enterprise took over responsibility for the Iran arms sales in 1986. In his congressional testimony, North said that former CIA director William Casey saw the Enterprise as a "stand-alone," "off-the-shelf" organization that would carry on covert activities throughout the world while evading congressional review. Many details of the Enterprise's operations were likely to remain secret. Casey died in May 1987 without having been questioned in detail about the affair. North and Poindexter shredded many relevant documents. North testified that he nonetheless thought that what the Enterprise did was justified and that he had assumed that the president was fully aware of his activities.

In response to questions from the congressional panel and in public statements, Reagan denied that he was fully aware of the Enterprise's activities. Though the president clearly did authorize the sale of arms to Iran, no document was found that proved he knew about the diversion of funds to the *contras*. Nonetheless, the congressional group concluded in its majority report that Reagan failed in his constitutional responsibility to see that the laws were faithfully executed. In addition, said the report, he "created or at least tolerated an environment where those who did know of the diversion believed with certainty that they were carrying out the President's policies." The panel also concluded that the raising of money from foreign governments and private individuals for the *contras* was a clear violation of the Boland Amendment, though that law provided no criminal penalties. In addition, Meese was faulted for not having looked into the Enterprise's operations more energetically.

All 15 of the Democrats on the panel signed the report, as did 3 of the 11 Republicans. The other eight Republicans issued a minority report acknowledging that the administration had made "mistakes" but rejecting all charges of illegality.

**Looking for Lessons.** The entire congressional panel endorsed a number of recommendations. Among them: that Congress be notified before the start of a covert U.S. intelligence operation; that the NSC not engage in covert activities; that the CIA have an inspector general confirmed by the Senate to be used for internal investigations; that Congress have the right to ask for the foreign-bank records of U.S. citizens; that contempt statutes be reviewed to allow Congress to compel witnesses to testify and to produce documents; and that the president's national security adviser always be a civilian so that he or she could avoid close ties to the military.

Whether the Iran-*contra* scandal would have any lasting effects on U.S. law or politics was uncertain at year's end. Perhaps the most memorable, and to some Americans disturbing, impression of the televised hearings was the testimony of Lieut. Col. North and others that the cause he pursued—aiding the *contras*—justified almost any illegality. As North's personal secretary, Fawn Hall, who helped with the document shredding, told the congressional panel, "Sometimes you have to go above the written law." Political commentators generally concluded that the affair diminished the effectiveness of President Reagan, already a "lame duck" in the last year of his second and final term. It was uncertain whether any of the congressional committee's recommendations would be enacted into law. Reagan, ignoring the panel's prescription that the national security adviser always be a civilian, appointed Army Lieut. Gen. Colin Powell to the post.

Nonetheless, the Iran-*contra* affair was certain to live on. Early in 1987 Reagan had named a special prosecutor to see if any criminal indictments were warranted. The prosecutor, a veteran Washington lawyer named Lawrence E. Walsh, had not completed his investigation by year's end, but he was expected to bring a number of indictments in 1988. Whatever the result, Walsh's appointment was a reminder that in American politics scandal often breeds reform. Reagan had been compelled to set Walsh's investigation in motion by a relatively recent law requiring that a special prosecutor be named to investigate any serious charges of misdeeds by administration officials. The law had been enacted as a direct result of Watergate.

*(continued from page 484)*

Among those declaring their unavailability were two frequently mentioned possibilities, Gov. Mario M. Cuomo of New York and Sen. Sam Nunn of Georgia.

Both Hart and Biden withdrew from the race under unusual circumstances. Hart formally bowed out May 8, five days after publication of a *Miami* (Fla.) *Herald* story reporting that he had spent much of the weekend alone in his Washington town house with a young woman, later identified as a Miami model, Donna Rice. Hart's wife, Lee, was in Colorado at the time. Up to that point, Hart had been regarded as the front-runner for the 1988 Democratic nomination. The *Herald*'s story sparked controversy not only about Hart's character and judgment but also about the importance of a candidate's private life as a public issue and the proper limits of press investigation into this area. The main focus of media attention, however, remained Hart himself, especially after it transpired that he, Rice, and another couple had spent one night on a yacht in Florida and a second night sailing for Bimini in The Bahamas aboard the luxury craft, appropriately named *Monkey Business.* The Hart story was not over, however. The furor had barely died down when, on December 15, Hart announced that he was reentering the race and filed in the New Hampshire presidential primary.

Biden's downfall began with the disclosure in mid-September that he had borrowed—without attribution—some of his loftiest rhetoric from other politicians, notably British Labour Party leader Neil Kinnock, and had been disciplined while a student at Syracuse (N.Y.) University Law School on plagiarism charges. After *Newsweek* magazine reported a week later that Biden had misstated his academic attainments as a college undergraduate and in law school, he formally withdrew from the race.

Wall Street was the locale of one of the year's wildest dramas as the stock market soared to unprecedented heights and then experienced a crash far greater than the legendary debacle of October 1929 that set off the Great Depression. The market rose sharply as the year opened, carrying the closely watched Dow Jones Industrial Average over the 2000 mark to a record 2002.25 close on January 8. Over subsequent months the Dow continued to climb, even in the face of economic news that ordinarily would have depressed securities prices, but autumn brought reckoning. After reaching a peak above 2700 in August, the Dow lost 261.43 points during October 14–16. The decline of 108.35 points on October 16 set a one-day record, but it was only

Douglas Ginsburg talks with reporters after the announcement of his nomination to the U.S. Supreme Court. Ginsburg later requested that his name be withdrawn when controversy arose over his past use of marijuana.

Frank Carlucci (centre) replaced Caspar Weinberger (left) as secretary of defense in a ceremony with Pres. Ronald Reagan in November. Weinberger resigned from his post to spend time with his seriously ill wife.

DIANA WALKER—TIME MAGAZINE

a preliminary. The main event came on October 19, Black Monday, when the Dow plunged an unprecedented 508.32 points in frenzied selling that was repeated in securities exchanges in other major countries. The Dow recovered 300 points over the next two days, turned downward again on October 22, and remained erratic for the rest of the year. (*See* ECONOMIC AFFAIRS.)

One effect of the stock market crash was to break a long-standing deadlock between the White House and Congress over reducing the federal budget deficit, which some financial analysts had cited as a leading cause of the collapse. In a compromise announced November 20, the two sides agreed on a deal to eradicate $30 billion in red ink from the budget in the current fiscal year and $46 billion the following year. On December 22 legislation was passed in the form of two bills that would realize these targets.

(RICHARD L. WORSNOP)

See also *Dependent States,* below.

## Church Membership in the United States

| Religious body | Total clergy | Inclusive membership | Religious body | Total clergy | Inclusive membership |
|---|---|---|---|---|---|
| Baptist bodies | | | Jehovah's Witnesses | None | 752,404 |
| American Baptist Association | 1,760 | 250,000 | Jews | 6,500 | 5,814,000 |
| American Baptist Churches in the U.S.A. | 7,678 | 1,576,483 | Latter Day Saints (Mormons) | | |
| Baptist Bible Fellowship, International | 4,500 | 1,405,900 | Church of Jesus Christ of Latter-day Saints | 28,598 | 3,860,000 |
| Baptist General Conference | 1,700 | 131,480 | Reorganized Church of Jesus Christ of L.D.S. | 16,585 | 192,077 |
| Baptist Missionary Association of America | 2,450 | 228,125 | Lutherans | | |
| Conservative Baptist Association of America | ... | 225,000 | American Lutheran Church | 7,671 | 2,319,443 |
| Free Will Baptists | 2,895 | 205,546 | Evangelical Lutheran Churches, The Assn. of | 672 | 103,263 |
| General Baptists (General Association of) | 1,444 | 72,263 | Lutheran Church in America | 8,586 | 2,896,138 |
| Liberty Baptist Fellowship | 374 | 130,000 | Lutheran Church—Missouri Synod | 8,044 | 2,630,588 |
| National Baptist Convention of America | 28,574 | 2,668,799 | Wisconsin Evangelical Lutheran Synod | 1,497 | 416,493 |
| National Baptist Convention, U.S.A., Inc. | 27,500 | 5,500,000 | Mennonites | | |
| National Primitive Baptist Convention | 636 | 250,000 | Mennonite Church | 2,399 | 91,167 |
| Primitive Baptists | ... | 72,000 | Old Order Amish Church | ... | 62,640 |
| Progressive National Baptist Convention | 863 | 521,692 | Methodists | | |
| Regular Baptist Churches, General Association of | 2,045 | 300,839 | African Methodist Episcopal Church | 6,550 | 2,210,000 |
| Southern Baptist Convention | 63,200 | 14,613,618 | African Methodist Episcopal Zion Church | 6,396 | 1,195,173 |
| Buddhist Churches of America | 115 | 100,000 | Christian Methodist Episcopal Church | 2,650 | 718,922 |
| Christian and Missionary Alliance | 2,154 | 238,734 | Free Methodist Church of North America | 1,765 | 71,682 |
| Christian Congregation | 1,455 | 105,478 | United Methodist Church | 37,808 | 9,192,172 |
| Church Brethren | 500 | 98,000 | Wesleyan Church | 2,596 | 109,196 |
| Church of God (Anderson, Ind.) | 3,313 | 188,662 | North American Old Roman Catholic Church | 150 | 62,611 |
| Church of the Brethren | 1,963 | 155,967 | Pentecostals | | |
| Church of the Nazarene | 8,667 | 530,912 | Assemblies of God | 26,837 | 2,135,104 |
| Churches of Christ—Christian Churches | | | Church of God | 2,737 | 75,890 |
| Christian Church (Disciples of Christ) | 6,806 | 1,106,692 | Church of God (Cleveland, Tenn.) | 9,638 | 505,775 |
| Christian Churches and Churches of Christ | 6,238 | 1,051,469 | Church of God in Christ | 10,425 | 3,709,661 |
| Churches of Christ | ... | 1,623,754 | Church of God in Christ, International | 1,600 | 200,000 |
| Community Churches, International Council of | 350 | 200,000 | Church of God of Prophecy | 7,573 | 74,122 |
| Congregational Christian Churches, Natl. Assn. of | 826 | 108,115 | Full Gospel Fellowship of Churches and Ministers, Intl. | 850 | 65,000 |
| Eastern Churches | | | International Church of the Foursquare Gospel | 3,482 | 186,213 |
| American Carpatho-Russian Orthodox Greek Catholic Ch. | 68 | 100,000 | Pentecostal Church of God | 1,595 | 90,300 |
| Antiochian Orthodox Christian Archdiocese of N. Am. | 180 | 280,000 | Pentecostal Holiness Church, International | 3,422 | 113,000 |
| Apostolic Catholic Assyrian Ch. of the East, N. Am. Dioc. | 57 | 80,000 | United Pentecostal Church, International | 6,984 | 500,000 |
| Armenian Church of America, Diocese of the | 61 | 450,000 | Polish National Catholic Church of America | 141 | 282,411 |
| Bulgarian Eastern Orthodox Church | 11 | 86,000 | Presbyterians | | |
| Coptic Orthodox Church | 28 | 115,000 | Cumberland Presbyterian Church | 766 | 98,103 |
| Greek Orthodox Archdiocese of N. and S. America | 655 | 1,950,000 | Presbyterian Church in America | 1,702 | 188,083 |
| Orthodox Church in America | 531 | 1,000,000 | Presbyterian Church (U.S.A.) | 19,514 | 3,007,322 |
| Romanian Orthodox Episcopate of America | 67 | 60,000 | Reformed bodies | | |
| Russian Orthodox Church Outside of Russia | 168 | 55,000 | Christian Reformed Church in North America | 1,077 | 219,988 |
| Serbian Eastern Orth. Ch. in the U.S.A. and Canada | 82 | 67,000 | Reformed Church in America | 1,636 | 340,359 |
| Ukrainian Orthodox Church in the U.S.A. | 131 | 87,745 | United Church of Christ | 10,071 | 1,676,105 |
| Episcopal Church | 14,111 | 2,504,507 | Roman Catholic Church | 53,382 | 52,893,217 |
| Evangelical Covenant Church of America | 930 | 86,079 | Salvation Army | 5,195 | 432,893 |
| Evangelical Free Church of America | 1,484 | 95,722 | Seventh-day Adventist Church | 5,481 | 666,199 |
| Friends United Meeting | 595 | 56,475 | Triumph the Church and Kingdom of God in Christ | 1,375 | 54,307 |
| Independent Fundamental Churches of America | 1,366 | 120,446 | Unitarian Universalist Association | 1,069 | 173,167 |

Table includes churches reporting a membership of 50,000 or more and represents the latest information available.
Source: National Council of the Churches of Christ in the U.S.A.

(CONSTANT H. JACQUET)

## Developments in the States in 1987

State governments, buffeted by adverse economic conditions, waded through a tumultuous financial year in 1987. Even while returning to taxpayers 81% of a $5.7 billion windfall from federal tax reform, states were forced to boost taxes by $6.1 billion net, the second largest state tax increase in history. An attempt in Florida to resolve fiscal problems by extending the state sales tax to services ended in failure.

Federal-state relations were particularly uneven, with states filing lawsuits against the federal government over environmental protection, the legal drinking age, highway speed limits, and National Guard assignments. A long-running intergovernmental dispute was eased during the year when Congress approved an increased 65-mph speed limit on rural interstate highways. In a rider attached to a spending bill late in the year, Congress allowed the first 20 states to apply to raise the speed limit to 65 mph on certain rural roads. It was an eventful year for ethics problems, with corruption indictments affecting the legislatures of the two largest states and a serious recall effort mounted against Arizona's governor. The populations of state prisons continued to soar.

Reacting to a perceived slowdown in federal initiatives, states took the lead in tackling such diverse problems as environmental protection, AIDS (acquired immune deficiency syndrome), surrogate parenthood, and problems of the homeless. Forty-nine states (all except Kentucky) staged regular legislative sessions during the year, and 13 (including Kentucky) called special sessions.

**Party Strengths.** Few significant changes in political party lineups were ordered by voters in limited state elections in 1987. After statewide balloting in four states and two special elections, Democrats were left in control of 28 state legislatures, while Republicans enjoyed a two-house majority in only 9. Democrats dominated legislatures in all states except Arizona, Colorado, Idaho, Indiana, Kansas, New Hampshire, South Dakota, Utah, and Wyoming (where Republicans had control in both houses); Alaska, Michigan, Nevada, New York, Ohio, Pennsylvania, and Washington (where Republicans organized the upper house and Democrats the lower chamber); Delaware, New Jersey, and North Dakota (where Democrats controlled the upper body and Republicans the lower house); Montana (Republican house and Senate tied); New Mexico (Democratic house and Senate tied); and Nebraska (a nonpartisan, one-house legislature).

At the year's end Democrats held 4,465 seats and Republicans 2,923 in state legislatures throughout the nation. Women continued to make gains in legislative membership; in 1987 women held 15.6% of state legislative seats, up from 4% in 1969 and 10.3% in 1979.

No statehouses changed party hands in gubernatorial balloting in Kentucky, Louisiana, and Mississippi during the year, leaving the lineup of governorships for 1988 at 26 Democrats and 24 Republicans. Democrats controlled the governorship and both legislative chambers in 14 states, while Republicans enjoyed overall control in 6.

**Government Structures, Powers.** Financial problems, aggravated by reduced federal assistance payments, made 1987 a quiet year for structural change in state governments. Many states authorized studies and set up mechanisms designed to stimulate business investment, competitiveness, and trade for local economies.

The prospect of a rare recall election loomed in Arizona during the year as nearly 300,000 registered voters signed petitions demanding the ouster of Republican Gov. Evan Mecham. Only 217,000 valid signatures were needed to force a recall ballot in May 1988. Mecham, first elected in 1986, initially angered minorities by canceling a state holiday honouring Martin Luther King, Jr.; the resulting protest cost Arizona significant convention business. It was later revealed that Mecham had failed to disclose a $350,000 campaign loan from a Tempe developer, prompting a legislative investigation. Mecham aggravated his opposition by blaming the recall effort on "militant liberals and the homosexual lobby."

Georgia authorities ruled that unless an individual filed notice of his write-in candidacy, his votes would not be counted in future elections. In recent years Mickey Mouse had become a popular protest write-in. An Idaho silver miner, saying he objected to taxpayer-subsidized publicity for a single industry, filed suit to remove "Famous Potatoes" from state license plates. The executive director of the Idaho Potato Commission called the suit "half-baked," and a court dismissed it on April 1.

**Government Relations.** Lawsuits challenging alleged federal encroachment on states' rights fared poorly during the year. South Dakota lodged a legal challenge to the federal government's demand for uniform 21-year-old minimum drinking laws in all states. Similarly, Nevada attempted to void a threatened cutoff of U.S. highway funds after the state announced plans to ignore the mandatory 55-mph speed limit on part of a single interstate highway. Minnesota, reacting to Reagan administration military exercises in Central America, filed suit against a 1986 federal law forbidding governors from interfering in Pentagon assignments of state National Guard units

sent abroad. All three suits were dismissed.

Montana became the 19th state to ratify a long-lost 1789 U.S. constitutional amendment prohibiting self-granted pay increases for the U.S. Congress. Thirty-eight states were needed for ratification, and there was no deadline.

State lobbies unsuccessfully pushed Congress to close a loophole in interstate tax administration by forcing out-of-state mail order firms to collect state sales taxes. State officials estimated that their revenue loss from uncollected sales taxes from interstate mailers amounted to more than $2 billion annually.

**Finances.** Beset by political and economic pressures, states raised taxes by $6.1 billion overall during 1987, the second-largest state tax increase in history. The trend was ironic, because states simultaneously rebated to taxpayers some $4.5 billion of a $5.7 billion windfall provided by federal tax reform.

Most states tied their personal income tax system to U.S. laws. A 1986 federal tax reform law broadened the tax base, eliminating shelters and making additional income subject to taxation. Twenty-two states used the resulting windfall as an opportunity to revamp their tax codes, typically by lowering rates, increasing exemptions and standard deductions, and reducing the number of brackets. Experts called the developments the most significant state tax reform in the 20 years since a majority of states adopted income taxes.

Even so, state treasuries were beset by sluggish and uneven economic conditions, reduced federal assistance, and a continuing business tilt away from their traditional manufacturing tax base and toward a service economy. In a significant response, Florida boldly extended its sales tax to personal and professional services, projecting $750 million in new annual revenue from the step. The tax aroused widespread controversy, however, and some boycotting threats from national advertisers. At the year's end Florida's governor and legislature agreed to eliminate the services tax, substituting a one-cent general sales tax boost in its place, and the experiment was judged a failure.

Overall, 33 states raised taxes by $6.6

Workers from the Safeway Sign Co. remove a speed limit sign from a silkscreen press at their plant in Gardena, California. In April Congress allowed the speed limit, which had been 55 miles per hour, to be increased to 65 miles per hour on designated rural interstate highways.

billion, and 6 states lowered taxes by $500 million during the year. The $6.1 billion net increase was topped only by a $7.4 billion revenue increase levied in the recession year of 1983. Following the federal lead, 13 states reduced their top marginal income tax rates, some of them significantly, and 7 reduced the number of brackets. Attempting to achieve increased progressivity, 12 states raised standard deductions and increased exemptions, often removing low-income individuals from tax rolls.

Two states, New York and Vermont, reduced their personal income tax burden overall. Arkansas, Indiana, and New Mexico raised income tax rates, while Montana and North Dakota imposed income tax surcharges. Corporate income taxes were raised in Colorado, Idaho, Indiana, Montana, and Minnesota but lowered in Oregon and South Carolina.

Sales and excise tax increases were an important source of added revenue. Arkansas, Florida, Minnesota, and South Dakota broadened their sales tax bases, while sales tax rates were raised in Florida, North Dakota, Oklahoma, South Dakota, and Utah. Idaho and Vermont made "temporary" sales tax increases permanent.

Motor fuel taxes were raised in Maryland, Mississippi, Missouri, Montana, Nevada, New Mexico, North Dakota, Oklahoma, South Carolina, and Utah. Cigarette taxes went up in Idaho, Indiana, Minnesota, Nebraska, Nevada, North Dakota, Oklahoma, and Utah; Minnesota's increase from 23 to 38 cents a pack made that state's levy the nation's highest. Alcoholic beverage taxes were increased in Arkansas, Minnesota, and South Dakota, and insurance premium taxes were increased in Arkansas, Minnesota, and North Dakota. In an effort to stimulate oil and gas exploration, severance taxes were reduced in Kansas, Montana, New Mexico, and North Dakota.

Figures compiled in 1987 revealed that state revenue from all sources totaled $481.2 billion in the 1986 fiscal year, an increase of 9.5% over the preceding 12 months. General revenue (excluding state liquor and state insurance trust revenue) was $393.5 billion, up 7.6% from the previous year. Total state expenditures rose 8.6% to $424.2 billion, creating a technical surplus of $57 billion. General expenditures, not including outlays of the state liquor stores and insurance trust systems, amounted to $376.5 billion, up 9.1% for the year. Of general revenue, 58.5% came from state taxes and licenses; 16.7% from charges and miscellaneous revenue, including educational tuition; and 24.8% from intergovernmental revenue, mostly from the federal government.

The largest state outlay was $140.2 billion for education, of which $47.9 billion went to state colleges and universities and $81.9 billion to local public schools. Other major outlays included $72.6 billion for public welfare, $36.7 billion for highways, and $30.2 billion for health and public hospitals.

**Ethics.** New York's legislature was rocked by allegations of payroll irregularities during the year. Senators Ralph Quattrociocchi, Manfred Ohrenstein, and Howard Babush and former senator Joseph Montalto were indicted for alleged payroll abuse, and Assemblywoman Gerdi E. Lipshutz resigned after admitting she had placed two phantom employees on the legislative payroll. A state judge, Francis X. Smith, was convicted of perjury and criminal contempt in connection with a cable television franchise bribery scandal in Queens.

The New York legislature responded by approving a new ethics bill, but Gov. Mario Cuomo vetoed the proposal, calling it loophole-ridden and inexcusably weak. The legislature then approved a new, tougher version that was signed into law late in the year.

Former California assemblyman Bruce E. Young was convicted on five counts of mail fraud for concealing outside income and laundering campaign money to other politicians. Young's was the first conviction of a California legislator in 30 years.

Maryland Sen. Michael Mitchell and his brother, former senator Clarence Mitchell III, were found guilty of wire fraud and attempting to obstruct a congressional investigation of the Wedtech Corp. The 1977 racketeering and mail fraud conviction of former Maryland governor Marvin Mandel was overturned on a technicality late in the year; an earlier decision limited the federal mail fraud statute to protection of property rights.

Ohio Gov. Richard Celeste dropped his proposed U.S. presidential bid after the *Cleveland Plain Dealer* alleged he had been "romantically linked" to three women over the past decade. Oklahoma bank commissioner Robert Y. Empie, accused of using insider information to sell stock in state-regulated banking institutions, was suspended in March by Gov. Henry Bellmon. Empie was reinstated and cleared of wrongdoing in April after he agreed to resign two months later.

Pennsylvania state treasurer R. Budd Dwyer, convicted on charges that he had awarded a state computer contract in return for promise of a $300,000 payoff, shot himself to death in front of a press conference he had called in Harrisburg on January 22. Connecticut liquor commission chairman Charles Kasmer was indicted on charges arising from the bribery of undercover IRS agents. Vermont Gov. Madeleine Kunin asked three of the state's five Supreme Court justices to step aside after they were named in 25 ethics count violations, including sexual advances and interfering with a criminal investigation.

**Education.** Michigan and Wyoming approved the nation's first state-sponsored tuition-guarantee programs, designed to assist parents in saving for college expenses and hedging against the prospect of soaring higher education costs. At the year's end 28 other states were considering or planning similar programs.

**Health, Welfare.** Virtually all states struggled to cope with the onslaught of AIDS during the year. Agencies and legislatures worked to clarify the rights of AIDS victims; to set policy on access to various settings, services, and occupations (especially public schools) for those victims; and to determine how to deal with persons who endanger others. Thirty states appropriated funds for combating AIDS during fiscal year 1987, compared with only five states in fiscal 1983.

Illinois and Louisiana enacted legislation requiring AIDS tests for all those applying for marriage licenses. The Illinois action was part of an AIDS package approved by the state legislature, but Gov. James Thompson vetoed bills that would have required mandatory tests for prisoners and hospital patients and the tracing of all AIDS victims' sexual partners by the state health department. Colorado approved a strict AIDS reporting law, requiring physicians to report incidence of the disease and enforcing confidentiality of the resulting records.

Spurred by the highly publicized Baby M trial in New Jersey, states also wrestled with problems raised by surrogate parenthood during 1987. Twenty-seven states considered 70 bills to regulate, outlaw, or study surrogate parenthood during the year, but only one, a Louisiana measure declaring surrogacy contracts to be unenforceable, became law. Most proposed legislation would discourage or restrict the bearing of children for others on social and moral grounds.

Seven more states, reacting to ever increasing problems of homeless Americans, moved to make easier the commitment of the mentally ill; ten states had approved similar laws in 1985–86.

By a 4–4 tie vote, the U.S. Supreme Court affirmed the voiding of an Illinois law requiring girls under 18 to wait for an abortion for 24 hours while their parents were consulted. Twenty-three states required either parental consent or notification before a minor could obtain an abortion; the high court's vote left unsettled the constitutionality of those laws.

Illinois became the 32nd state to require mumps shots for all schoolchildren. Pennsylvania and Rhode Island approved major new laws assisting the disabled and homebound. Montana became the first state to pass a Uniform Health Care Information Act, protecting patients' right to determine access to their medical records and guaranteeing patients access to their own records.

Oregon and Minnesota approved new laws guaranteeing employment leave for parents of newborns. A landmark California parental leave law was upheld by the U.S. Supreme Court in January. Five other states mandated paid maternity leave through disability insurance, and six more treated failure to provide such leave as a violation of antidiscrimination laws.

**Drugs.** Arkansas, Indiana, Iowa, Maine, and Vermont approved new laws restricting smoking in public places. California banned smoking on commercial planes, trains, and buses. However, a New York court voided a strict, sweeping ban on smoking in public areas promulgated by the state public health council, which had been appointed by the governor. The ban exceeded the council's authority, the court ruled, and invaded legislative prerogatives.

Under pressure of a threatened highway fund cutoff from the federal government, Colorado, the District of Columbia, Louisiana, Montana, Ohio, and South Dakota raised the minimum drinking age to 21 during the year. That left only one state still holding out against the federal decree; Wyoming still allowed persons as young as 19 to purchase beer and hard liquor.

Thirty states considered various drug testing bills. Connecticut, Iowa, Minnesota, Montana, Utah, and Vermont allowed employers to test employees for drug usage, usually on the basis of "reasonable suspicion" of violation.

**Law, Justice.** Reacting to drug-related violence in the state, Florida lawmakers approved a proposed state constitutional amendment guaranteeing rights of crime victims; Rhode Island in 1986 became the first state to enact such an amendment. In a more controversial action, the Florida legislature also approved two laws that effectively removed local control over who can carry concealed weapons. The moves allowed any adult without a criminal record or a history of mental illness or alcoholism to carry a concealed weapon in the state and nullified some 400 local gun-control laws.

A federal court struck down a Utah law prohibiting the broadcasting of pornographic films on cable television. The Oregon Supreme Court banned police roadblocks for the purpose of stopping drivers and testing them for drunkenness, calling the technique a violation of constitutional rights.

Kansas lawmakers voted to allow the sale of liquor by the drink in one-third of the state's counties; that meant that only Utah and West Virginia banned liquor by the drink statewide. Arkansas, Florida, Maryland, and New Jersey joined 23 states enacting amnesty programs for taxpayers who agreed to discharge overdue or unpaid tax obligations.

An outbreak of assaults by pit bull terriers prompted a dozen states to consider legislation during the year, with Illinois, Ohio, Texas, and Washington approving new or tightened vicious-dog laws. The new bills obligated owners of dogs that had threatened the health or safety of individuals and other pets to secure, identify, and leash their animals. The Ohio and Washington laws treated some violations as felony offenses.

**Prisons.** The population of state prisons continued to set new records during 1987. A survey by the Bureau of Justice Statistics found a record 522,866 inmates in state prisons throughout the nation at midyear, a 7.8% increase over a year earlier. California, which had recently begun enforcing new laws mandating minimum sentences for certain crimes, continued its astounding prisoner increase; the state's inmate population swelled by 9,499 to 64,737 during the year, an 18% increase on top of a 17.3% jump in 1986.

The survey found that 5% of prisoners nationwide were women. This was the highest number since record keeping began in 1926.

The National Association for the Advancement of Colored People Legal Defense Fund announced that 1,977 prisoners awaited execution in late 1987, up from 1,788 a year earlier. Twenty-five death row inmates were executed during the year, compared with 17 in 1986; this brought to 93 the number of executions in the U.S. since capital punishment was reinstated by the U.S. Supreme Court in 1976.

**Gambling.** Virginia voters approved a new state-sponsored lottery in a fall election, bringing to 29 the number of jurisdictions nationwide with government-sponsored games of chance. Lottery proposals were also on the ballot for 1988 in Idaho, Indiana, and North Dakota.

Lottery backers noted that ticket sales for state games totaled $11 billion during fiscal 1986, netting governments nearly $5 billion. A New England multistate lottery, designed to increase prizes and buyer interest, more than doubled lottery income for Maine, New Hampshire, and Vermont during the year, and ten other states moved toward a second multistate lottery with enhanced prizes for 1988.

Texas voters approved pari-mutuel betting on horses and greyhounds.

**Environment.** Responding to concerns that the federal government was underfunding environmental protection programs, states moved to leadership positions on numerous pollution questions. Colorado became the first state to require the use of ethanol or oxygenated fuel in the Denver area to combat air pollution. Massachusetts became the first to ban alachlor, the most widely used herbicide in the nation; alachlor was suspected of causing some cancers. New York required lawn-care firms to disclose the chemicals they used, post signs, and warn neighbours about possible hazards.

Colorado, Florida, Illinois, Indiana, Ohio, and Virginia mandated a statewide survey to detect incidence of radon; New Jersey, New York, and Pennsylvania pushed expensive programs of detection and cleanup. Six northeastern states sued the federal Environmental Protection Agency in an attempt to force a reduction of power plant emissions suspected of causing acid rain.

Maine became the first state to outlaw irradiated food preserved with radioactive gamma rays. Vermont required stringent labeling of irradiated food, which was opposed by organic food growers and antinuclear activists.

New Jersey became the third state to require recycling of garbage, mandating the separation of bottles and newspapers from other trash. Rhode Island had similar legislation, and Oregon required recycling in communities with a population of more than 4,000. Iowa approved a tough new groundwater contamination law even though the bill placed added burdens on agriculture at a time when it was already suffering economically. District of Columbia voters turned down a proposal to require a deposit on beverage bottles and cans.

Federal Superfund legislation approved during 1987 required states to plan for evacuation and medical treatment in the event of leaks at toxic chemical plants. The EPA also notified 44 governors that their states violated federal ozone and carbon monoxide standards, and they thus faced possible federal sanctions.

**Energy.** After a decade of increasing state opposition to the federal 55-mph speed limit, Congress relaxed the limit in April. By the end of the year, 37 states had increased the limit on rural interstate highways to 65 mph as permitted in the amended law. Before the vote, Arizona became the first state to be penalized for failure to enforce the 55-mph limit, losing $510,000 in federal highway funds.

By a 3 to 2 margin, Maine voters rejected a referendum aimed at shutting down the state's sole nuclear power reactor.

Twenty-five states moved during the year to compete for the federal Energy De-

partment's superconducting super collider (SSC), billed as the largest single construction project ever envisioned, with costs estimated between $4.4 billion and $6 billion. In late December the field was narrowed to eight states: Arizona, Colorado, Illinois, Michigan, New York, North Carolina, Tennessee, and Texas. Texas voters approved the issuance of $500 million in bonds to help attract the project; the Energy Department was scheduled to announce the SSC site in January 1989.

**Equal Rights.** Massachusetts became the second state to forbid insurance firms to use gender in establishing premiums and policy terms; Montana had been first to enact the controversial restriction two years earlier. Insurers argued that because of actuarial realities women should pay more for health insurance and less for life insurance, and men should pay increased premiums for disability protection.

The U.S. Supreme Court struck down Louisiana's "creation science" law, which required schools teaching evolution to devote equal teaching time to a theory suggesting the abrupt appearance on Earth of most life forms. The 7–2 court majority ruled that the state law employed the "support of government to achieve a religious purpose."

In an extremely close vote Mississippi voters revised their state constitution to permit interracial marriage. As a practical matter, the U.S. Supreme Court had protected interracial marriage in a 1967 decision, so the Mississippi vote was symbolic only.

**Consumer Protection.** Following a permissive Supreme Court ruling upholding an Indiana antitakeover law, Arizona, Florida, Hawaii, Louisiana, Massachusetts, Minnesota, Nevada, North Carolina, Oklahoma, Utah, and Washington approved new bills protecting local businesses from unwelcome suitors. Florida, Louisiana, and North Carolina adopted fair price statutes, assuring that all stockholders would get full value for their shares even after the acquirer obtained control.

Reacting to problems caused by fast-fluctuating interest rates, Connecticut and Maryland approved new laws requiring that mortgage commitments be put in writing.

The National Association of Attorneys General issued in late 1987 guidelines requiring airlines to provide additional disclosure in advertising discount fares and limiting rule changes in frequent-flyer programs under state consumer protection statutes.

Colorado, Montana, Nevada, Oregon, Pennsylvania, Virginia, and Wisconsin approved new laws requiring the use of seat belts in automobiles, bringing to 32 the number of jurisdictions with such legislation. South Dakota mandated seat belts for children under five. Enthusiasm for requiring belts on school buses died after the National Transportation Safety Board issued a report questioning the measure's efficacy. Although 14 states considered joining New York in approving such legislation, none was passed during the year.

Measures to require individual item pricing in grocery stores also met with a chilly reception; although eight states had earlier mandated item pricing, no states were added to that list in 1987.

(DAVID C. BECKWITH)

# Latin America and the Caribbean

## LATIN-AMERICAN AFFAIRS

Little progress was made toward solving Latin America's economic problems during 1987, and the region's external debt continued to cause anxiety. The most important political events were agreement in August on a draft peace plan for Central America, midterm elections in Argentina, tensions over a new constitution and the presidential succession in Brazil, and the naming of a candidate to become the next president of Mexico.

In Argentina the Partido Justicialista (Peronist) won 41% of the vote and the key governorship of Buenos Aires in the September 6 elections for half of Congress and 22 provincial governorships. The ruling Unión Cívica Radical lost its overall congressional majority but remained the largest party, with 118 seats against 107 for the Peronists and 29 for smaller parties. In Brazil the Constituent Assembly deliberated all year on a new constitution, which was expected to be promulgated in April 1988. Pres. José Sarney's position weakened steadily as he tried to construct a political consensus to legitimize his administration.

In Mexico the budget and planning minister, Carlos Salinas de Gortari, was named as candidate of the Partido Revolucionario Institucional (PRI) for the 1988 presidential elections. In Trinidad and Tobago the National Alliance for Reconstruction, headed by A. N. R. Robinson, won general elections in December 1986 and municipal elections in September 1987. Presidential and municipal elections were aborted in Haiti in November, against a background of political violence.

Central America remained bedeviled by social and economic difficulties, and guerrilla activity continued in El Salvador, Guatemala, and Nicaragua. In Guatemala City

Costa Rican Pres. Oscar Arias Sánchez and his wife are greeted enthusiastically after their return from Guatemala, where his Central American peace plan was signed. For his efforts toward achieving peace in the region, Arias was awarded the 1987 Nobel Peace Prize.

on August 7, the presidents of these countries, Costa Rica, and Honduras signed an outline peace accord for the region, initiated by Pres. Oscar Arias Sánchez (*see* BIOGRAPHIES) of Costa Rica. The agreement provided for a number of measures to take place within 90 days, including cease-fires followed by dialogue with and amnesty for guerrilla forces and an end to external military aid and the launching of attacks from other states. Other provisions included the establishment of national reconciliation commissions, free national and municipal elections in accordance with each country's constitution, elections in 1988 to a Central American parliament, "urgent attention" to refugees and displaced persons, negotiations on reduction of troops and weapons, and steps toward increasing political freedom and democracy. A multilateral commission with observers from the Organization of American States and the UN was to verify progress within 120 days. An alternative peace initiative announced by the U.S. on August 5 and focusing on Nicaragua was dropped.

The agreement was not in place by the November 5 deadline. The U.S. administration had refused to forgo aid to the rebel *contras* in Nicaragua, although it agreed to consider delaying the submission of a bill to Congress calling for $270 million in aid to the *contras* during the period 1988–June 1989. The Nicaraguans agreed to negotiate only indirectly with the *contras* on a partial cease-fire. Talks between the El Salvador government and guerrillas made no headway. An informal deadline of January 1988 was agreed for implementation of the proposals in the agreement, to coincide with a summit of the five signatory presidents to monitor progress.

The Central American Common Market (CACM), comprising Costa Rica, El Salvador, Guatemala, Honduras, and Nicaragua, remained in the doldrums. Intraregional trade totaled only $360 million in 1986, the lowest in over ten years. Eight Latin-American countries, including Argentina, Brazil, and Mexico, were expected to announce at year's end the granting of $500 million–$750 million in aid to the CACM countries, mainly Nicaragua. The San José Pact, signed in 1980, whereby Mexico and Venezuela supplied up to 130,000 bbl of oil a day on concessional terms to the CACM, Panama, Barbados, Jamaica, and the Dominican Republic, was renewed for another year from July 30.

Neither the Latin American Integration Association (LAIA; Argentina, Bolivia, Brazil, Chile, Colombia, Ecuador, Mexico, Paraguay, Peru, Uruguay, Venezuela) nor the Andean Group (Bolivia, Colombia, Ecuador, Peru, Venezuela) forged ahead during the year, and bilateral trade became the dominant trend. An example was the launching by Argentina and Brazil in October of a bilateral trading currency, the gaucho, with a value equal to one Special Drawing Right (SDR). A total of SDR 200 million was to be issued, using $260 million of $400 million reciprocal credits under the LAIA central bank clearing system. The only significant event under LAIA aegis was the conclusion of an economic complementation agreement between Mexico and Peru, the sixth under LAIA rules providing for bilateral trade in specific manufactured products. In the Andean Group the main occurrence was the replacement of Decision 24, which governed foreign investment in member countries, by Decision 220, which allowed each country to determine its own national rules for the entry of risk capital.

In October representatives of the member countries of the Inter-American Development Bank (IDB) failed to reach agreement on new resources of $26.7 billion for the IDB for the period 1987–90, seriously threatening its lending operations. The U.S.S.R. launched a diplomatic offensive in Latin America during 1987. Soviet Foreign Minister Eduard Shevardnadze visited Argentina, Brazil, and Uruguay on September 27–October 8, and Soviet leader Mikhail Gorbachev was scheduled to visit the region in 1988.

The agreement in May by the prime ministers of the seven islands of the Organization of Eastern Caribbean States to form a single nation, subject to referendum, proved controversial. The proposed federation, made up of Saint Vincent and the Grenadines, Saint Lucia, Montserrat, Dominica, Grenada, Antigua and Barbuda, and Saint Christopher (St. Kitts) and Nevis, soon faced difficulties. In July the government of Antigua and Barbuda rejected the association as impossible on the grounds that it was a new form of colonialism. Instead, the Antiguan prime minister proposed a smaller grouping of the Leeward Islands (Antigua and Barbuda, St. Kitts and Nevis, and the U.K. colony of Montserrat), which gained the support of Montserrat. Strong opposition to the original union from within some of the islands suggested that any process toward integration would take a long time.

At a meeting in St. Lucia in July, heads of government of the 13 Caribbean Community (Caricom) member countries agreed to dismantle all barriers to trade within the group by September 1988 and to establish a Caribbean Export Credit Facility to begin operations in January 1988 with initial capital from Caricom governments of $16.5 million. In August members of the U.S. Congress called for changes in the U.S. Caribbean Basin Initiative (CBI), an integrated program of trade and tax measures giving duty-free access to the U.S. market for 12 years (from 1984) for a wide range of Caribbean and Central American products, mainly manufactured goods. The proposals included total duty exemption for imports of items manufactured, assembled, or processed from materials and components originating wholly within the U.S. Exports to the U.S. of goods eligible for existing CBI benefits totaled $4.9 billion in 1985, $3.9 billion in 1986, and $900 million in January–March 1987.

During 1986 slower growth in advanced industrial countries and expansionary domestic market policies, especially in Brazil, restricted the region's economic recovery, which had begun in 1984 after the 1981–83 recession. The better performers among the large economies were Colombia and Chile. Regional gross domestic product (GDP) rose by 3.9% in 1986 against 3.4% in 1985. There was very little investment in new capacity, however, and growth resulted from the utilization of idle productive capacity. Income per head was $2,240, 7% lower than in 1980. Consumer prices rose by 69.1%, well below the 275.7% of 1985, mainly because of lower inflation in Argentina, Brazil, Peru, and Bolivia. The external accounts deteriorated sharply. Exports from Latin America reached $78.3 billion, 15% below 1985, largely because of a $14.5 billion drop in the oil-exporting countries' revenue. The trade surplus fell by 45% to $18.4 billion, and the current account deficit rose from $4 billion to $14.2 billion. There was a net capital transfer to creditors of $25.5 billion in 1986, against $31.7 billion in 1985. Total external debt (excluding the International Monetary Fund) rose by 2.4% to $382.1 billion at the end of December 1986. GDP estimates for 1987 envisaged a further slowdown in growth to about 3%.

A total of 12 countries were involved in debt rescheduling negotiations in 1987. Brazil and Mexico remained the world's most indebted less developed countries, with debts of $111 billion and $101 billion, respectively, in November. In February Brazil introduced a moratorium on in-

terest payments on commercial bank medium- and long-term debts of $68 billion. In December an interim finance package with 114 banks was agreed to clear interest arrears under which $1.5 billion would be provided by Brazil and short-term loans of $3 billion by the banks. Initially, October–December interest was to be paid as from Jan. 1, 1987. In August Argentina and commercial bank creditors signed a rescheduling package providing for restructuring of $30.2 billion of principal, new money of $1,950,000,000, and the maintenance of interbank and trade credits of $2.2 billion for two years. In a surprising move, Latin America's main debtors—Brazil, Mexico, Argentina, Venezuela, Peru, Colombia, Uruguay, and Panama—formed themselves into a group at the end of November to renegotiate their combined debt of over $350 billion. The "Acapulco agreement" that they signed was a commitment to have debts revalued to reflect their lower market values and to demand much lower interest rates.　　(ROBIN CHAPMAN)

## ANTIGUA AND BARBUDA

A constitutional monarchy and member of the Commonwealth, Antigua and Barbuda comprises the islands of Antigua, Barbuda, and Redonda in the eastern Caribbean Sea. Area: 442 sq km (171 sq mi). Pop. (1987 est.): 82,400. Cap.: Saint John's. Monetary unit: Eastern Caribbean dollar, with (Oct. 5, 1987) a par value of EC$2.70 to U.S. $1 (free rate of EC$4.38 = £1 sterling). Queen, Elizabeth II; governor-general in 1987, Sir Wilfred E. Jacobs; prime minister, Vere Cornwall Bird.

Divisions within the governing Antigua Labour Party widened throughout 1987, with 8 of the 14 Cabinet members seeking the removal of the public works minister, Vere Bird, Jr., eldest son of Prime Minister Vere Cornwall Bird. An official inquiry into allegations of wrongdoing in connection with a project to resurface the runway at the international airport, conducted by Sir Archibald Nedd, former chief justice of Grenada, reported in August that Vere Bird, Jr., had behaved in a manner unbecoming a minister of government. Prime Minister Bird rejected the calls for his son's dismissal, saying that the Nedd report had not substantiated charges of criminal conduct against him. Lester Bird, a younger son of the prime minister who was deputy prime minister and foreign minister, was among the Cabinet members pressing the resignation demand.

The dissension in the Cabinet drew a statement of concern in August from the country's business sector, which said that day-to-day administration was being adversely affected. Some observers suggested that a general election might have to be called ahead of the April 1989 limit.

Another successful tourist year was expected in 1987. Growth in gross domestic product was forecast at 5.5%.

(ROD PRINCE)

This article updates the *Macropædia* article The WEST INDIES: *Antigua and Barbuda*.

## ARGENTINA

The federal republic of Argentina occupies the eastern section of the Southern Cone of South America, along the Atlantic Ocean. Area: 2,780,092 sq km (1,073,399 sq mi). Pop. (1987 est.): 31,496,000. Cap.: Buenos Aires. Monetary unit: austral, with (Oct. 5, 1987) a free rate of 2.72 australes to U.S. $1 (4.42 australes = £1 sterling). President in 1987, Raúl Alfonsín.

**Domestic Affairs.** The government faced widespread criticism during 1987 for its economic policies and inability to stem inflation. Two 24-hour general strikes were held, in January and November, and many work stoppages took place during the year, particularly in the public sector, which disrupted oil and gas supplies and many services. In a bid to soften labour opposition, Pres. Raúl Alfonsín dismissed Labour Minister Hugo Barrionuevo and replaced him with Carlos Alderete, the Peronist leader of the light and power workers' union. The appointment was not successful, however, and he was replaced after a few months.

Opposition by the military to President Alfonsín's human rights policies erupted in what became known as the Easter rebellion. A revolt of officers in Córdoba and Buenos Aires to force the suspension of trials related to human rights violations during the 1976–83 period of military rule was resolved following the personal intervention of the president. A number of key military personnel were retired, and further military protests followed the appointment of Gen. José Segundo Dante Caridi as the new army chief of staff. However, the security of the nation and the democratic system were not threatened. In November an Amnesty International report was generally favourable but criticized the "due obedience law," passed in June, which granted immunity from prosecution to military officers accused of torture during 1976–83.

The electorate showed its disapproval of the Unión Cívica Radical (UCR) government's policies in September 6 midterm elections for half the seats in Congress and 22 provincial governors. The Partido Justicialista (Peronists) won 41% of the vote and the key governorship of Buenos Aires in a largely unexpected and spectacular rebuttal of the government. The UCR lost its overall majority in Congress but remained the largest party, with 117 seats against 105 for the Peronists and 32 for the smaller parties. The Peronists controlled most of the provinces and were the largest party in the Senate, where seats were not contested.

Immediately after the elections, the Cabinet resigned. Ten days later President Alfonsín named his new Cabinet, retaining the controversial Juan Sourrouille (economy) as well as Dante Caputo (foreign affairs) and Horacio Jaunarena (defense) but accepting the resignations of five others. The electoral result persuaded President Alfonsín to drop his plans for constitutional reform, which would have led to the appointment of a prime minister and given more power to the legislative branch of government.

During the year there were several apparently unrelated terrorist attacks believed to have been carried out mostly by right-wing paramilitary groups. The most bizarre incident was the theft of former president Juan Perón's hands and sword from his grave, for which a ransom demand was made but never paid; the items were retrieved a few weeks later. In November a political scandal exploded with the discovery of the body of twice-kidnapped businessman Osvaldo Sivak, who had been murdered in 1985 after his family paid a ransom to police officers posing as mediators.

**Foreign Relations.** No progress was made in resolving the dispute between Argentina and the U.K. over sovereignty of the Falkland Islands/Islas Malvinas, although the two countries did make some progress in cooperating in fisheries conservation through the mediation of the U.S. government. Argentina and Brazil continued their efforts to increase integration, particularly through reduced tariff barriers and greater trade. In July Pres. José Sarney of Brazil paid an official visit to Argentina and signed agreements to expand the list of capital goods eligible for tariff exemptions and to create a new bilateral trade currency. The currency, the gaucho, was launched on October 30 and had a value equal to one Special Drawing Right (SDR). A total of SDR 200 million was to be issued using reciprocal credits under the Latin American Integration Association central bank clearing system.

**The Economy.** Expectations of 4% economic growth and moderate inflation were not fulfilled. Gross domestic product (GDP) rose 5.3% in 1986 but was likely to reach only 2% in 1987. Floods in the major grain-growing areas of Buenos Aires Province early in 1987 diminished hopes of agricultural growth. Industry continued to suffer from lack of investment and overmanning, particularly in the state sector, although manufactured exports increased as domestic demand declined. The 1987 budget bill aimed to cut the public-sector deficit to 2.5% of GDP by boosting tax revenues, but this was based on GDP growth of 4% and inflation of 42.6%. Following agreement about a 15-month economic program, the International Monetary Fund (IMF) approved a standby loan of $1,420,000,000 and a compensatory financing facility of $670 million for loss of export revenues. Targets were set for government spending, monetary growth, inflation, balance of payments, and the gradual liberalization of prices and wages. The World Bank granted a $2 billion package for structural adjustment in industry, agriculture, and foreign trade.

In January inflation of 7.6% was recorded, and a new

Pres. Raúl Alfonsín declared that Argentina's democracy "cannot be negotiated" during an emergency session of Congress in April. Rebellious soldiers had seized several army bases, demanding amnesty for officers accused of human rights violations.

emergency price and wage freeze was introduced to prevent a similar rise in February. Wages were raised and then frozen for four months, as were public utility rates and the price of gasoline. The exchange rate was raised and frozen for two months, while interest rates were lowered. Congress approved a tax amnesty law under which individuals and companies could pay between 2 and 10% on previously undeclared earnings. The government hoped that this would bring an extra $1 billion in revenues for 1987, but its implementation was delayed, causing revenue shortfalls in the first half of the year.

In April Argentina reached agreement with creditor banks to reschedule $30 billion of debt over 19 years with 7 years of grace, to provide $1,950,000,000 of new money facilities, and to maintain $2.2 billion of money-market and short-term trade lines for 2 years. There were also provisions for debt-to-equity conversion and tradable exit bonds. The agreement was promptly signed in August. Subsequently, the government reached agreement with the Paris Club of Western creditor governments to reschedule 100% of the capital and interest due between Jan. 1, 1986, and June 30, 1988, amounting to about $2.1 billion.

Wages and prices continued to rise as the public-sector deficit grew. By midyear it had become clear that government spending had exceeded targets, and the deficit was about 6.5% of GDP as revenues also fell. Net international reserves declined by about $1.8 billion instead of $800 million. To secure disbursement of IMF funds, a new memorandum of understanding was agreed upon in which new targets were set to cut the deficit by raising fiscal receipts. Wage increases were to be held to 5% a month, and interest rates on deposits were to be maintained at three points above inflation on an annual basis.

The government attempted to reduce the size of the public sector through privatization but without much success. Bids were asked for eight branch railway lines to be operated by the private sector, and more contracts were sought with private companies in the oil industry. State shares in many mixed or state-owned petrochemicals companies were offered for sale, and the government was eager to divest itself of some steel companies. Austral airline was sold to a local company in September, having had its debts assumed by the government and been returned to profit.

The economy failed to recover. The demands of the domestic economy and the poor world market for agricultural exports reduced the trade surplus, and the current account deficit grew. Servicing the foreign debt became difficult even after the favourable rescheduling and new money deals with creditors. President Alfonsín strongly attacked the lending policies of the IMF, the World Bank, and foreign banks and called for a freezing of interest rates at historic levels of 2–3% in real terms.

Another set of IMF targets was missed in the third quarter, which necessitated the granting of a waiver to ensure disbursement of $215 million of IMF funds and $500 million of bank loans and prevent a debt default by the end of the year. New economic measures were introduced in October to cut the budget deficit and boost the external accounts. This included another price and wage increase and subsequent freeze, a steep devaluation of the austral, and the legalization of the parallel exchange rate to be used for most financial transactions except trade. The immediate effect was an inflation rate of 19.5% in October, but the government hoped to reduce this to 5% a month. Success of the program was dependent on approval by Congress of a new package increasing property taxes, renewing a "forced savings" scheme, and raising bank transaction taxes.

(SARAH CAMERON)

## BAHAMAS, THE

A constitutional monarchy and member of the Commonwealth, The Bahamas comprises an archipelago of about 700 islands in the North Atlantic Ocean just southeast of the United States. Area: 13,939 sq km (5,382 sq mi). Pop. (1987 est.): 245,000. Cap.: Nassau. Monetary unit: Bahamian dollar, with (Oct. 5, 1987) a par value of B$1 to U.S. $1 (free rate of B$1.62 = £1 sterling). Queen, Elizabeth II; governor-general in 1987, Sir Gerald Cash; prime minister, Sir Lynden O. Pindling.

Prime Minister Sir Lynden Pindling was returned for a sixth term in a general election on June 19, 1987, when his Progressive Liberal Party won 31 out of 49 seats in an enlarged Assembly. The Free National Movement (FNM) won 16, and 2 seats went to independents. FNM leader Kendal Isaacs resigned after the defeat and was replaced by his deputy, Cecil Wallace-Whitfield. Each party accused the other of involvement in drug trafficking.

Shortly after the election, the government signed a legal assistance treaty with the U.S. providing for cooperation with U.S. drug interdiction efforts. Although U.S. Drug Enforcement Agency officers had been given diplomatic status at the end of 1986, two officers were jailed for two weeks in early 1987 after they made an emergency landing on Andros Island.

Another record tourist year was in prospect for 1987, with total arrivals up by 10% in the first five months; a total of 3,250,000 stopover and cruise visitors was expected for the year, bringing foreign exchange earnings of $1,250,-000,000. The prime minister forecast in July that per capita income would rise from $7,500 to $10,000 by 1992.

(ROD PRINCE)

This article updates the *Macropædia* article The WEST INDIES: *The Bahamas.*

## BARBADOS

The constitutional monarchy of Barbados, a member of the Commonwealth, occupies the most easterly island in the southern Caribbean Sea. Area: 430 sq km (166 sq mi). Pop. (1987 est.): 254,000. Cap.: Bridgetown. Monetary unit: Barbados dollar, with (Oct. 5, 1987) a par value of BDS$2.01 to U.S. $1 (free rate of BDS$3.27 = £1 sterling). Queen, Elizabeth II; governor-general in 1987, Sir Hugh Springer; prime ministers, Errol Barrow to June 1 and Erskine Sandiford.

Prime Minister Errol Barrow (*see* OBITUARIES) died suddenly on June 1, 1987, at the age of 67, the second Barbadian leader to die in office in two years. He was succeeded by his deputy, Erskine Sandiford (*see* BIOGRAPHIES). The governing Democratic Labour Party won the subsequent by-election for Barrow's former parliamentary seat.

In September Finance Minister Richie Haynes resigned, saying that he had not been consulted about new appointments, including that of Kurleigh King, former secretary-general of the Caribbean Community, to replace Courtney Blackman as governor of the central bank.

Hopes of a 4% growth rate in gross domestic product for 1987 were pinned chiefly on tourism, with stopover arrivals expected to surpass the 1979 record of 371,000. Manufacturing remained depressed; at midyear unemployment stood at 18.3%, slightly higher than in June 1986. The trade deficit for the first four months of the year was 21.5% more than for the same period of 1986, raising the prospect of a deficit for the year greater than the 1981 record of BDS$760 million. (ROD PRINCE)

This article updates the *Macropædia* article The WEST INDIES: *Barbados.*

## BELIZE

A constitutional monarchy and member of the Commonwealth, Belize is on the Caribbean coast of Central America. Area: 22,965 sq km (8,867 sq mi). Pop. (1987 est.): 176,000. Cap.: Belmopan. Monetary unit: Belize dollar, with (Oct. 5, 1987) a par value of BZ$2 to U.S. $1 (free rate of BZ$3.28 = £1 sterling). Queen, Elizabeth II; governor-general in 1987, Dame Minita Gordon; prime minister, Manuel Esquivel.

In his 1987–88 budget speech, Prime Minister Manuel Esquivel presented a BZ$266.4 million budget. Salary adjustments to improve conditions of all public officers and primary school teachers became effective in July. The increase was an attempt to dissuade skilled nationals from leaving the country.

In July the government moved to address the troubling problem of refugees and other immigrants. During the previous ten years, there had been a massive wave of immigrants from neighbouring countries. The government tried to curtail this influx by introducing a new Immigration Ordinance that made it more difficult to hire illegal immigrants. Employers would bear the burden of responsibility for carrying out the policy.

The economy showed signs of recovery with renewed confidence as exports surged 24% during the first quarter. Imports rose by 11%. In April swarms of African killer bees threatened honey exports and human life, and from April to June the Mediterranean fruit fly devastated fruit crops. Gold deposits estimated to be worth as much as $200 million were discovered in an isolated area in the Mayan Mountains. Their exploitation awaited the passage of a mining code. (INES T. BAPTIST)

This article updates the *Macropædia* article CENTRAL AMERICA: *Belize.*

## BOLIVIA

Bolivia is a landlocked republic in central South America. Area: 1,098,581 sq km (424,164 sq mi). Pop. (1987 est.): 6,799,000. Judicial cap., Sucre; administrative cap., La Paz. Monetary unit: boliviano, with (Oct. 5, 1987) an official rate of 2.11 bolivianos to U.S. $1 (3.43 bolivianos = £1 sterling). President in 1987, Víctor Paz Estenssoro.

The congressional alliance between Pres. Víctor Paz Estenssoro's Movimiento Nacionalista Revolucionario (MNR) and the Acción Democrática Nacionalista achieved for Bolivia in 1987 what had seemed impossible only two years earlier—political stability without any hint of a military coup, and the lowest rate of inflation on mainland South America. In addition, gross domestic product (GDP) was expected to show positive growth for the first time since 1980. There was little to cheer most Bolivians, however, and the ranks of those living in abject poverty continued to be swollen by mine workers made jobless as a result of the collapse of world tin prices in October 1985. More than 40,000 miners had lost their jobs by the end of 1987, about half from the state-owned mining company Comibol. The once-powerful miners' union, FSTMB, proved unable to reverse the government's drive to end Comibol's drain on public expenditures, and the company's payroll was cut by 75%. Although the remaining 7,000 miners were granted a 15% wage increase at the end of a 37-day strike in May, the government firmly rejected the union's proposals to rehabilitate Comibol. The MNR was heavily defeated in municipal elections held in December.

A detailed plan to reactivate the economy was unveiled in July. It was designed to reduce the country's increasing dependence on the production of coca, the raw material for cocaine, and reorient activity toward agroindustry, forestry, and mining other than tin. Total investments of $1.5 billion over three years were foreseen, to be financed by loans from sympathetic governments, the World Bank, the Inter-American Development Bank, and the International Monetary Fund (IMF). The IMF showed its approval of the government's achievements to date and its plans for the future by agreeing to lend $173 million on an extended three-year basis. The economy looked set to meet the Fund's 1987 targets of 2.2% GDP growth and 12% inflation; inflation had averaged 11,741% in 1985 and 276% in 1986.

On July 10 the government signed with its foreign commercial bank creditors a novel agreement that allowed it to repurchase its $1 billion debt to banks at about 15% of face value, somewhat above the price that then prevailed for Bolivian debt on the so-called secondary market. The funds required for the buy-back scheme were donated by Western governments as part of a $300 million international plan to help Bolivia curb coca production.

The funds were granted on the condition that the government reform Bolivian law to make coca cultivation illegal for all but a few traditional growers. This implied eradication of some 70% of known coca fields and the displacement of 30,000 families. The government had little choice but to agree. However, at a UN conference on drug abuse and trafficking in June, Foreign Minister Guillermo Bedregal expressed concern about the political and social consequences of such a commitment, given the large number of Bolivians who were dependent on the drug trade for their livelihoods. (JANET KRENGEL)

## BRAZIL

Brazil is a federal republic in eastern South America on the Atlantic Ocean. Area: 8,511,965 sq km (3,286,488 sq mi). Pop. (1987 est.): 141,302,000. Cap.: Brasília. Monetary unit: cruzado, with (Oct. 5, 1987) a free rate of 51.63 cruzados to U.S. $1 (83.84 cruzados = £1 sterling). President in 1987, José Sarney.

**Domestic Affairs.** During 1987 the political scene was dominated by tensions over a new constitution and the presidential succession. The Constituent Assembly, formed out of Congress, began its deliberations on the constitution on February 1 under the chairmanship of Ulysses Guimarães, the president of the Brazilian Democratic Movement Party (PMDB), the dominant party in the governing coalition. Several drafts of the document were published during the year, including one in November providing for the introduction of a parliamentary system of government with a prime minister assuming most of the functions of the president. There were also provisions for a reduction in the workweek from 48 hours to 44 hours, the right to strike, and a job-for-life guarantee for those employed for more than three months by companies. The constitution was expected to be passed into law by April 1988.

Pres. José Sarney's position weakened steadily during the year as he unsuccessfully sought a political consensus to legitimize his government. He had assumed office in April 1985 following the death of President-elect Tancredo Neves. In a national television broadcast in May, Sarney asked for his term of office to end in March 1990 instead of March 1991. He initially enjoyed considerable support for this among congressional deputies and state governors. In October he orchestrated the breakup of the coalition between the PMDB and the Liberal Front Party (PFL) in the hope that political power and jobs would be steered to the PFL, of which he was a member. Instead, the

Brazilian men look over a selection of newspapers relating the government decision to suspend interest payments on foreign debts. The middle headline states, "Suspension of payment is for an indefinite period."
AP/WIDE WORLD

PMDB tightened its control of policy, and in its centre-left elements became much more influential. The energy minister, Aureliano Chaves, the PFL presidential candidate, promised only conditional support for the Sarney administration until the Assembly had completed its business. Also in October Sarney tried to form a government of national unity with members supporting the maintenance of existing presidential prerogatives and a term for himself expiring in 1990. A Cabinet reshuffle on October 20 resulted in the dismissal of Minister of Social Welfare Rafael Magalhães and the reshuffling of four others. The army minister, Gen. Leonidas Pires Gonçalves, stated early in November that the armed forces would back the recommendations of the Assembly, even if it voted for a parliamentary system. In the middle of November, however, Sarney decided that he could no longer continue for a full term in office. He stated that he would act as independent arbiter in presidential elections to be held in November 1988.

Labour unrest grew steadily during the year, with many strikes taking place, particularly among public-sector employees. In March the Army was ordered into oil refineries and production centres to break a strike by 55,000 workers, and the Navy took over 11 ports in the face of a national seamen's stoppage. Both strikes ended soon afterward. A general strike on August 20 attracted limited support.

**The Economy.** The economy performed fitfully against this background of political uncertainties. The Cruzado Plan introduced in February 1986, which was designed to produce price stability, finally collapsed on February 6 with the ending of the retail-price freeze. Inflation rapidly gathered pace, averaging 21% a month in March–June. Dilson Funaro resigned as finance minister in April and was replaced by Luíz Carlos Bresser Pereira, a respected banker and economist. Bresser introduced a stabilization package on June 12 including another freeze of up to 105 days on prices and wages and the gradual resumption of full indexation. The package also included measures to ensure that the 1987 operational public-sector deficit reached 3.5% of gross domestic product, including consolidation of the fiscal and monetary budgets and public expenditure cuts. Two further packages were introduced to restrain

public spending in July and August. These involved pay ceilings for senior civil servants and restrictions on lending among state entities. In July the Macroeconomic Control Plan was published defining medium-term economic strategy. It aimed at real growth of 5% in 1987, 6% in 1988, and 7% in 1989–91. Growth in 1987 was expected to be 3.5%, however, with industrial and agricultural output rising by 1 and 11%, respectively. The price and pay freeze was initially successful in curbing inflation, but with relaxation of the price freeze in September and of wage controls in October, prices escalated, and inflation reached a record 366% for the year. Pay raises exceeding 40% for civil servants in October undermined attempts to reach the 1987 operational public-sector deficit target. Bresser resigned on December 18 when he failed to receive backing for proposals to reduce the deficit.

The freezing of prices and fears that jobs for workers would have to be guaranteed did little for business confidence. Dissatisfaction was reflected in a protest by 3,000 business groups on November 10. Industrialists drew some confidence from a decision by the federal court that Autolatina, the largest automobile manufacturer in Latin America, could increase its prices above the government's limits. The company employed nearly 56,000 in Brazil and was threatened with closure because of heavy losses. It had demonstrated its muscle by suspending sales on the domestic market, of which it held a 65% share. The decision was seen as a setback for the government.

The external accounts position remained sound, and in the first nine months of the year, export revenue was up 3.2% from the same period in 1986. The 1987 trade surplus target was $10.3 billion, compared with $8.3 billion in 1986, and the current account deficit was expected to be reduced from $4 billion in 1986 to $2.1 billion in 1987. On February 20 the government announced a moratorium on interest payments on $68 billion of medium- and long-term commercial bank debt. An agreement was reached in December under which the Brazilians were to provide $1.5 billion and 114 commercial banks were to provide short-term loans of $3 billion to finance payment of interest arrears.                                                    (ROBIN CHAPMAN)

# CHILE

The republic of Chile extends along the Pacific coast of the Southern Cone of South America. Area: 756,626 sq km (292,135 sq mi), not including Chile's Antarctic claim. Pop. (1987 est.): 12,536,000. Cap.: Santiago. Monetary unit: Chilean peso, with (Oct. 5, 1987) a free rate of 228.23 pesos to U.S. $1 (370.62 pesos = £1 sterling). President in 1987, Maj. Gen. Augusto Pinochet Ugarte.

In anticipation of Pope John Paul II's visit to Chile in April 1987, Gen. Augusto Pinochet Ugarte eased the repressive measures imposed after the assassination attempt against him in September 1986. The state of siege that ended on Jan. 6, 1987, was not renewed, and some exiles were allowed to return. A new independent newspaper, *La Epoca*, was permitted to start publishing in March. The political parties law was signed on March 11 to coincide with celebrations of the sixth anniversary of the constitution. This followed the opening of electoral registers in late February. The political parties law legalized centrist and right-wing parties, but Marxist parties remained illegal.

The February statements of former army major Armando Fernández Larios lent credence to the opposition. In testimony given in the U.S., top Chilean Army officers were implicated in the killing of former Chilean ambassador to the U.S. Orlando Letelier and a colleague, which occurred in Washington, D.C., in 1976. Many political leaders called for an independent investigation to clarify the officers' involvement. The opposition attempted to regain the initiative with the launching of the Movement for Free Elections on March 11. Coordinated by Sergio Molina, the group of 14 people represented a wide range of political ideologies; its objective was to unite all social and political sectors in the fight for free and fair elections.

On April 1 the pope arrived in Chile for a six-day visit. He avoided supporting any particular faction and stressed the need for reconciliation. On account of his message, the orientation of many political groups shifted perceptibly to the centre. Pinochet took steps to ease the tense relations between the regime and the Roman Catholic Church. Most consequential of all, however, were the declarations of the three civilian members of the government, who indirectly responded to the demands for free elections and to U.S.

pressures for a speedier transition to democracy. They fully supported the 1980 constitution and favoured the nomination of a civilian for the presidential plebiscite planned to take place late in 1988. They did not want the armed forces involved in the electoral process itself—a suggestion that had been made in 1986 but not reiterated after the military closed ranks around Pinochet following the assassination attempt against him and earlier discoveries of arms caches.

The adoption of a populist approach prompted Pinochet to tour the regions extensively, missing no occasion to inaugurate public works and housing developments. The Army and the state bureaucracy mobilized support for the government through job creation, social programs, and attention to local problems. At the same time, its attitude toward dissenters hardened; 12 presumed members of the Manuel Rodríguez Patriotic Front (FPMR), a group linked to the banned Communist Party, were killed by the secret police (CNI) during separate raids in less than 18 hours. Some were allegedly involved in the 1986 assassination attempt on Pinochet. In addition, in a move designed to strengthen his political defenses, Pinochet reshuffled his Cabinet in early July. Seven ministers were replaced. Most notable was the appointment as interior minister of Sergio Fernández, a lawyer who had held the post between 1978 and 1982 and was a key influence on the 1980 constitution. At the same time, he was a "moderate," and his calls for democracy had led to his dismissal in 1982.

The opposition's rallying cry for free elections was superseded by the centrist Christian Democratic Party's call to speed up voter registration following the election of its new president, Patricio Aylwin, in late July. At that time only 1.6 million out of 8 million eligible voters had registered. To overcome the general apathy and create greater political awareness, mock elections were held in the southern cities of Concepción, Talcahuano, and Chillán in early September. Support for the peaceful transition to democracy was given by foreign parliamentarians in the second International Parliamentary Assembly, which took place in Santiago during September 4–6. Labour, grouped under the National Workers Command, confronted the government with demands for higher wages and better bargaining conditions for trade unions; a demonstration of about 20,000 people in Santiago in late August was followed by a poorly supported general strike on October 7.

Demonstrators protest the Chilean government of Pres. Augusto Pinochet in Santiago, where an estimated one million people await a mass celebrated by Pope John Paul II.

Economic recovery continued to gather momentum with a 5.7% growth in 1986 and sustained buoyancy in 1987. The adoption of appropriate foreign-exchange, monetary, and fiscal policies improved the country's competitiveness in foreign markets and caused domestic demand to recover. The current account deficit declined to $1.1 billion, or 6.6% of gross domestic product (GDP), as exports of goods and services, particularly noncopper, rose by 12.7% to $5.3 billion while imports increased only 6.2% to $6.4 billion. Chile remained the world's largest producer and exporter of copper but reduced its dependence on the metal to only 40% in terms of export revenue. Replacing copper were the newer exports of fruit, fish, and machinery. The fiscal deficit was reduced to 2.2% of GDP, helped by efficient tax collections and funds generated by the privatization of state industries. The external debt was $21.6 billion at the end of 1986, its rate of increase held down by the rapid expansion of the debt-conversion program.

During 1986 all the performance criteria under the current International Monetary Fund program, due to expire in mid-1988, were again fully met. In early February 1987 agreement was reached with the IMF concerning the policy objectives for 1987, which included continued economic growth and further reductions in the fiscal deficit, inflation, and the current account deficit. Later that month an agreement with international bank creditors reduced the frequency of interest payments from 6 to 12 months, lowered interest rate spreads, and rescheduled 1988–91 principal payments.    (ALEXANDER JOHNS CAMPBELL)

## COLOMBIA

A republic in northwestern South America, Colombia has coastlines on the Caribbean Sea and the Pacific Ocean. Area: 1,141,748 sq km (440,831 sq mi). Pop. (1987 est.): 28,665,000. Cap.: Bogotá. Monetary unit: Colombian peso, with (Oct. 5, 1987) a free rate of 255.68 pesos to U.S. $1 (415.20 pesos = £1 sterling). President in 1987, Virgilio Barco Vargas.

Adjustment to the new era of one-party government, following Liberal Party victories in both congressional and presidential contests in 1986, continued to dominate politics in Colombia during 1987. Neither the Liberals nor the Conservatives had anticipated the speed with which the Frente Nacional, which had ruled Colombia under coalition governments for almost three decades, would come to an end. Pres. Virgilio Barco Vargas set to work on his plans to eradicate poverty and rehabilitate the violence-stricken regions of the country, but results were slow to materialize. Members of the government party, more interested in the allocation of posts left by the Conservatives than in reform, offered only lukewarm support for government policies, while members of the opposition, unfamiliar with their new role, resorted to obstructive tactics without providing alternatives. It was not until December 1986 that the government's first major tax legislation was passed. By that time, the long-awaited details of the National Plan for the Eradication of Poverty had been announced. Its objectives were the generation of stable and adequately remunerated employment and the meeting of basic needs.

The initial sense of drift of the Barco administration was further exacerbated by a Cabinet working at cross-purposes. Efforts by the Mines and Energy and the Economic Development ministries to attract investment into mining and the free-trade zones were thwarted by the Finance Ministry's attempt to raise government revenues. Also, the interior minister's refusal to answer opposition questions undermined Barco's statement that Congress was the place where constructive public debate should take

Carlos Enrique Lehder Rivas (right) is taken into custody after a shootout with Colombian authorities. Lehder, identified as one of the world's biggest drug traffickers, was extradited to the United States.
EL TIEMPO/SYGMA

place. A workable mix of technocrats, business people, and seasoned politicians was finally achieved in May, following an earlier Cabinet reshuffle in March.

Despite pressures to reach an all-party consensus on how to deal with the key issue of national security, Barco preferred to tackle the outbursts of guerrilla and criminal violence as they occurred. Several rebel groups that had been rivals were closing ranks under the Coordinadora Nacional Guerrillera—about half a dozen guerrilla movements. The three-year-old truce between the government and the Colombian Revolutionary Armed Forces (FARC), the largest guerrilla group, became increasingly fragile, and the number of skirmishes between active factions of the FARC and the Army grew. A turning point was reached in June when hard-line local FARC members in the Caquetá region ambushed a military convoy transporting engineers engaged in a community development program. The government responded by ending the cease-fire in the area. Relations between the government and the FARC deteriorated further following the assassination on October 11 of Jaime Pardo Leal, leader of the Patriotic Union (UP). Formed in 1985, the UP included many amnestied guerrillas, and the FARC vowed to avenge the killing.

The Barco administration launched its campaign against the drug trade in the wake of the assassination of Guillermo Cano Isaza, editor of the national daily *El Espectador,* in December 1986. The newspaper had published several articles on the Medellín drug cartel, said to control a huge share of the world trade in cocaine. In February 1987 Carlos Lehder Rivas, one of the drug barons, was extradited to the U.S. The constitutional validity of the extradition treaty, which had been signed into law by Barco in December 1986, was promptly challenged, however, and in June 1987 the Supreme Court voted against it, rendering it inoperative.

The economic growth rate doubled to 5% in 1986 and, with the momentum of the recovery continuing, a similar expansion was expected in 1987.

(ALEXANDER JOHNS CAMPBELL)

## COSTA RICA

The Central American republic of Costa Rica has coastlines on the Caribbean Sea and the Pacific Ocean. Area: 51,100 sq km (19,730 sq mi). Pop. (1987 est.): 2,613,000. Cap.: San José. Monetary unit: Costa Rican colón, with (Oct. 5, 1987) a free rate of 64.30 colones to U.S. $1 (104.41 colones = £1 sterling). President in 1987, Oscar Arias Sánchez.

As the architect of the Central American peace plan signed unexpectedly by Costa Rica, El Salvador, Guatemala, Honduras, and Nicaragua on Aug. 7, 1987, Pres. Oscar Arias Sánchez (*see* BIOGRAPHIES) gave substance to Costa Rica's proclaimed neutrality in the regional conflict. Shortly after the accord was signed, Nicaragua dropped its suit against Costa Rica in the International Court of Justice; Costa Rica had been accused of sheltering anti-Sandinista (*contra*) forces.

In July a new national park was opened near the border with Nicaragua, on and around the site of an airstrip previously used by *contra* forces. During the Iran-*contra* hearings in the U.S., it was revealed that the airstrip's construction had been authorized by the former U.S. National Security Council aide Lieut. Col. Oliver North and funded by the covert sale of U.S. arms to Iran.

The most pressing domestic problem continued to be that of servicing the country's $4.5 billion foreign debt, one of the highest levels of per capita debt in the world.

GILLES MERMET—GAMMA/LIAISON

Members of the Guardia Civil, responsible for the internal security of Costa Rica, watch over the Rio Frío near the Nicaraguan border. The Guardia is there to prevent the entry of Sandinista or anti-Sandinista (*contra*) forces in order to maintain Costa Rica's neutrality.

Disagreement over the treatment of some $100 million in interest arrears to commercial banks led to delays in finalizing a rescheduling agreement. This in turn delayed final approval from the International Monetary Fund (IMF) for a standby loan. The economy grew 3.2% in 1986, but expansion of only 2% was expected in 1987 because of low prices for coffee exports and the cuts in public expenditure necessary to meet the IMF target. (JANET KRENGEL)

This article updates the *Macropædia* article CENTRAL AMERICA: *Costa Rica*.

## CUBA

The socialist republic of Cuba comprises the island of Cuba and several thousand smaller islands and cays in the Caribbean Sea. Area: 110,861 sq km (42,804 sq mi). Pop. (1987 est.): 10,302,000. Cap.: Havana. Monetary unit: Cuban peso, with (Oct. 5, 1987) a free rate of 0.78 peso to U.S. $1 (1.27 pesos = £1 sterling). President of the Councils of State and Ministers in 1987, Fidel Castro Ruz.

Cuba enjoyed relative political stability during 1987, and Pres. Fidel Castro Ruz remained firmly in charge. The National Assembly of People's Power was inaugurated to a third five-year term on Dec. 27, 1986, and predictably reelected Castro as president of the Council of State; his brother Gen. Raúl Castro Ruz was reelected as first vice-president of the Council. Castro and the Communist Party maintained tight controls, in contrast to the U.S.S.R. and other Eastern European countries where a measure of political and economic liberalization was being encouraged. In September, in response to international pressure and particularly that of the Roman Catholic Church, 348 elderly political prisoners were released, the largest group since 1980, and allowed to go to the U.S.

Cuban-U.S. relations had deteriorated steadily since 1985, when Radio Martí, a Radio Free Europe-style station, began transmission from Miami, Fla. On January 21 the last remaining U.S. diplomat in Havana, the head of the U.S. interests section at the Swiss embassy, was withdrawn and was not expected to be replaced. Relations were further soured when a senior Cuban officer in the defense ministry, Brig. Gen. Rafael del Piño Diáz, defected to the U.S. in May. According to the U.S., del Piño possessed information about the role of the U.S.S.R. and Cuba in the Central American conflict. On November 20, however, it was announced that Cuba and the U.S. had agreed to revive the 1984 immigration pact suspended by Cuba in 1985 in protest against the Radio Martí transmissions. The accord opened the way for some 20,000 Cubans annually, in addition to those seeking political asylum, to immigrate legally to the U.S.; it also allowed for the return home of Cubans who had arrived in the U.S. during the 1980 Mariel exodus and had since been declared "undesirables." Seeking assurances that they would not be deported, Cuban inmates rioted and took control of two U.S. prisons for a number of days. The sieges ended with agreements that cases would be reviewed on an individual basis.

Relations with other Latin-American countries improved during 1986 and 1987; both Brazil and Argentina restored diplomatic links. In August President Castro endorsed the draft Central American peace plan signed by the presidents of Costa Rica, El Salvador, Guatemala, Honduras, and Nicaragua in Guatemala City earlier the same month.

Economic growth was estimated at 1.7% in 1987, compared with 1.4% in 1986—well short of the 5.5% target. The fall in the value of the U.S. dollar against European and Japanese currencies was an important factor in trade since Cuba had to pay for its imports in strengthening

Nicaraguan Pres. Daniel Ortega (left) visited Cuban Pres. Fidel Castro in August to discuss Nicaragua-Cuba relations and the Central American peace plan.
AFP PHOTO

currencies. Oil reexport income failed to recover after falling to $300 million in 1986, as against $574 million in 1985, and sugar accounted for only an estimated 25% of hard currency exports because of poor harvests. In 1987 a prolonged drought, the worst in Camagüey Province in 40 years, caused the loss of 500,000 head of cattle and 100,000 metric tons of the 1987–88 sugar crop. The 1986–87 sugar crop totaled 7.5 million tons, compared with 7.9 million tons in 1985–86. The decline was caused by the drought and the aftereffects of Hurricane Kate, which swept through the country in November 1985.

Cuba continued to be heavily dependent on Soviet economic and financial aid, which amounted to about $4 billion in 1986, excluding military assistance. The level of aid was reduced in 1987, however, in line with a May 1986 agreement; Cuban sugar shipments to Moscow were to remain at four million tons a year in 1986–90, but the price paid was 7% lower than in 1981–85.

Cuba's convertible currency debt rose to over $5.2 billion in March 1987 from $4.7 billion in December 1986. The suspension of interest payments imposed in July 1986 was continued, and by June 1987 arrears were estimated at about $800 million. Commercial banks were reluctant to proceed with rescheduling negotiations unless some interest was paid. Cuba's debt to the U.S.S.R. and other member countries of the Council of Mutual Economic Assistance (Comecon) was not known but was estimated at between $9 billion and $22 billion. Repayment was to begin in 1990. The government attempted to stop the rundown of foreign exchange reserves by introducing stiffer foreign exchange controls, which it hoped would reduce the steadily growing black market for foreign currencies. Anyone found with unregistered currency was liable to be fined.

During the year a program was started to develop the tourism industry, which in the 1950s had been Cuba's second largest foreign exchange earner. The José Martí International Airport in Havana was being expanded to double passenger capacity, and the airports at Varadero

(accessible only from Canada) and Santiago de Cuba were being upgraded to handle international flights. The number of hotel rooms in Havana was to be doubled to 3,700 by 1991. Air Cubana was planning to increase the size of its fleet so that it could expand routes to Western Europe and Latin America. A total of 194,600 tourists visited Cuba in 1986, generating foreign exchange income of $130 million, compared with $110 million in 1985. It was proposed to raise the number of visitors to 250,000 by 1991, still below the 300,000 in 1957. (ROBIN CHAPMAN)

This article updates the *Macropædia* article The WEST INDIES: *Cuba.*

## DOMINICA

An island republic within the Commonwealth, Dominica is in the eastern Caribbean Sea. Area: 750 sq km (290 sq mi). Pop. (1987 est.): 87,700. Cap.: Roseau. Monetary unit: Eastern Caribbean dollar, with (Oct. 5, 1987) a par value of EC$2.70 to U.S. $1 (free rate of EC$4.38 = £1 sterling). President in 1987, Clarence Augustus Seignoret; prime minister, Eugenia Charles.

The governing Dominica Freedom Party (DFP) again strengthened its position in Parliament during 1987, with the decision in July of the sole independent member of Parliament, Eden Durand, to join the party. The move gave the DFP 17 of the 21 elected House of Assembly seats. In September the DFP took control of the municipal council of Portsmouth, Dominica's second largest town and a traditional stronghold of the opposition Dominica Labour Party. The change was effected by legislation allowing the DFP to nominate five council members to sit alongside the eight elected members.

In the 1987–88 budget presented in July, Prime Minister Eugenia Charles raised the income tax threshold to exempt 3,300 people from paying tax. Income tax rates were reduced and consumption taxes increased to compensate. Charles said that agriculture was the leading sector in promoting growth in gross domestic product, which had met the target of 4% in 1986. In June the World Bank approved an interest-free credit of $3 million to support the International Monetary Fund-backed adjustment plan started in 1986.

A new national telephone network and a rural electrification project in the eastern part of the country were completed during the year. (ROD PRINCE)

This article updates the *Macropædia* article The WEST INDIES: *Dominica.*

## DOMINICAN REPUBLIC

The Dominican Republic covers the eastern two-thirds of the Caribbean island of Hispaniola, which it shares with Haiti. Area: 48,443 sq km (18,704 sq mi). Pop. (1987 est.): 6,708,000. Cap.: Santo Domingo. Monetary unit: Dominican peso, with (Oct. 5, 1987) a free rate of 3.19 pesos to U.S. $1 (5.18 pesos to £1 sterling). President in 1987, Joaquín Balaguer.

The Dominican Republic enjoyed political calm but made limited economic progress in 1987. Pres. Joaquín Balaguer proved to be a popular leader, though his ill health caused concern. He had strengthened his control of the Cabinet in November 1986 with the appointment of Gen. Elias Wessín y Wessín as minister of the interior and new commanding officers of the armed forces. The most important political event of the year was the reopening of the border with Haiti in April. In late April Balaguer's predecessor, Salvador Jorge Blanco, sought asylum in the Venezuelan embassy to escape arrest in connection with an investigation of corruption during his administration. Later he was allowed to go to the U.S. for medical treatment.

Gross domestic product was expected to increase by 3% in 1987, compared with 1.4% in 1986. Consumer prices rose by 35% in the year to August 1987. External payments difficulties persisted, and in February it was announced that servicing payments would be limited to what the country could afford. The International Monetary Fund was dissatisfied with economic management, and a policy program had not been agreed on by December 1987.

In October some 100 Dominicans, apparently hoping to be smuggled into Puerto Rico, died when the ship carrying them exploded and sank in shark-infested waters off the Dominican Republic's northeast coast. (ROBIN CHAPMAN)

This article updates the *Macropædia* article The WEST INDIES: *Dominican Republic.*

## ECUADOR

The republic of Ecuador is in western South America, on the Pacific Ocean. Area: 269,178 sq km (103,930 sq mi), including the Galápagos Islands. Pop. (1987 est.): 9,923,000. Cap.: Quito. Monetary unit: sucre, with (Oct. 5, 1987) an official intervention rate of 159.08 sucres to U.S. $1 (258.33 sucres = £1 sterling) and a free rate of 201.02 sucres to U.S. $1 (326.44 sucres = £1 sterling). President in 1987, León Febres Cordero Rivadeneira.

On Jan. 16, 1987, Pres. León Febres Cordero of Ecuador was kidnapped while attending a military review at the Taura air base near Guayaquil. His captors were 75 air force personnel, who demanded an official amnesty for Gen. Frank Vargas Pazos, leader of the brief antigovernment revolt at Quito air base in March 1986. Febres Cordero, apparently under threat of execution, conceded and also guaranteed his kidnappers immunity from arrest; he was released after 12 hours in captivity. The president's fiercely anti-Communist image was tarnished by his swift capitulation.

The incident served to polarize opposition to the president's fragile conservative-liberal coalition government. The deep antipathy between the president and opposition parties led to frequent stormy scenes in Congress. The conflict spilled onto the streets in late October when violent demonstrations accompanied a one-day general strike held under a national state of emergency. The strike was called when Febres Cordero vetoed Congress's impeachment of Interior Minister Luis Robles Plaza.

The political and economic problems were aggravated by a natural disaster. On March 5 and 6 a series of earthquakes in the northeast Amazonian province of Napo released massive mud slides and floods that killed an estimated 2,000 people and left 75,000 injured. Because 27 km (17 mi) of the vital trans-Andean oil pipeline were destroyed, oil exports, which accounted for 45% of total exports in 1986, had to be suspended until August 23. A link to a Colombian pipeline was constructed by May, allowing Ecuador to pump oil for domestic use.

The cost of the disaster was calculated to be $1 billion. As a result, gross domestic product was expected to decline by 2.8% in 1987, following a 1.7% rise in 1986.

(JANET KRENGEL)

Members of Ecuadoran government and opposition blocks shout and gesture in disagreement during a extraordinary session of Congress, which was called by the opposition to censure the conduct of Pres. León Febres Cordero and to demand his resignation.

Thousands of hopeful people assemble in San Salvador near the site of peace negotiations between Pres. José Napoleón Duarte and representatives of the Farabundo Martí National Liberation Front (FMLN) guerrillas.

REUTERS/BETTMANN NEWSPHOTOS

## EL SALVADOR

The republic of El Salvador is situated on the Pacific coast of Central America. Area: 21,041 sq km (8,124 sq mi). Pop. (1987 est.): 4,974,000. Cap.: San Salvador. Monetary unit: Salvadoran colón, with (Oct. 5, 1987) a par value of 5 colones to U.S. $1 (free rate of 8.12 colones = £1 sterling). President in 1987, José Napoleón Duarte.

The Central American peace plan signed in Guatemala City on Aug. 7, 1987, by Pres. José Napoleón Duarte and other Central American leaders did not appear at first to offer much hope of ending El Salvador's eight-year-old civil war. (See *Latin-American Affairs*, above.) The Farabundo Martí National Liberation Front (FMLN) rejected the plan but held talks with the government in October, when it was agreed to form a commission to seek a cease-fire. Major political and ideological differences remained unsolved, however. An amnesty law approved by the National Assembly on October 27 was in compliance with the peace plan but was opposed by the guerrillas. The FMLN also rejected a unilateral cease-fire declared by the government on November 5—the original deadline for implementing the peace plan. The government refused to talk to two leaders of the Democratic Revolutionary Front, political wing of the FMLN, when they returned to El Salvador briefly in late November. Assassinations by right-wing death squads continued; on November 23 Duarte accused Maj. Roberto d'Aubuisson, leader of the right-wing Arena party, of having planned the assassination in 1980 of Oscar Romero, Roman Catholic archbishop of El Salvador.

The war, in which more than 60,000 people had died, continued. The FMLN guerrillas successfully disrupted power supplies, and in March the government announced the rationing of electricity. Military bases were also under attack, and one of the Army's strongest garrisons, at El Paraíso, was devastated. Both sides accepted the need to "humanize" the war; the FMLN was asked to cease laying mines, which maimed both soldiers and civilians, in return for the Army's curtailing its bombing missions, and prisoner exchanges and medical evacuations were sought.

Duarte's popularity reached a low level in January after he introduced a tax bill designed to raise $30 million for the war from the wealthier classes. Strong opposition to the tax by both business and labour unions led to its abandonment in February. Antigovernment protests surfaced again as the economy deteriorated further.          (BEN BOX)

This article updates the *Macropædia* article CENTRAL AMERICA: *El Salvador.*

## GRENADA

A constitutional monarchy within the Commonwealth, Grenada (with its dependency, the Southern Grenadines) is in the eastern Caribbean Sea. Area: 345 sq km (133 sq mi). Pop. (1987 est.): 104,000. Cap.: Saint George's. Monetary unit: Eastern Caribbean dollar, with (Oct. 5, 1987) a par value of EC$2.70 to U.S. $1 (free rate of EC$4.38 = £1 sterling). Queen, Elizabeth II; governor-general in 1987, Sir Paul Scoon; prime minister, Herbert A. Blaize.

The tensions within the governing New National Party (NNP) in Grenada reached a climax in April 1987 with the resignation of three ministers, George Brizan, Francis Alexis, and Tillman Thomas. They left the government and the NNP after criticizing the proposed dismissal of 1,800 of the country's 7,000 civil servants and other public service employees. In July they announced the formation of a new political party, the National Democratic Congress, and in September Brizan became parliamentary opposition leader in place of Phinsley St. Louis. The defections reduced the NNP's parliamentary strength to 9 of the 15 seats.

The annual budget introduced a property tax, land transfer tax, and business levy on sales, but Prime Minister Herbert Blaize said in July that difficulties in collecting the new taxes had led to a fiscal deficit for the first half year of EC$13.9 million. Increased revenue was urgently required for making severance payments to the public servants who were being fired, he said; the number to be sacked was, however, subsequently reduced to about 500. A growth rate of 4.5–5% was expected for 1987.          (ROD PRINCE)

This article updates the *Macropædia* article The WEST INDIES: *Grenada.*

## GUATEMALA

A republic of Central America, Guatemala has coastlines on the Caribbean Sea and the Pacific Ocean. Area: 108,889 sq km (42,042 sq mi). Pop. (1987 est.): 8,434,000. Cap.: Guatemala City. Monetary unit: quetzal, at par with the U.S. dollar, with (Oct. 5, 1987) an official market rate of 1 quetzal to U.S. $1 (1.62 quetzals = £1 sterling), a banking market rate of 2.70 quetzals to U.S. $1 (4.39 quetzals = £1 sterling), and an auction market rate established on an occasional basis by the Bank of Guatemala to govern certain import transactions. President in 1987, Marco Vinicio Cerezo Arévalo.

The tortuous process of bringing political stability to Guatemala, which began with the return to civilian government in January 1986, continued in 1987. The administration of Pres. Marco Vinicio Cerezo Arévalo survived veiled threats of a military coup in January following the appointment of Gen. Héctor Gramajo as defense minister. His predecessor, Gen. Jaime Hernández, had been forcibly retired, partly because he opposed the government's neutral stance on the Central American conflict. Cerezo was influential in ensuring that the regional peace plan initiated by Costa Rica and signed on August 7 was not weighted against the Sandinista regime in Nicaragua.

Deaths and disappearances attributable to right-wing paramilitary squads continued in 1987, while leftist guerrillas staged sporadic attacks on military personnel. Talks between the government and guerrillas held in Madrid in October were inconclusive, but November talks resulted in the declaration of an amnesty for rebels.

Gross domestic product was expected to increase by 1–2%, the first growth in five years. Unemployment fell to 27% from 43% in January 1986, and the inflation rate for 1987 was expected to be under 15%, compared with 26% in 1986. Nonetheless, in May the country was paralyzed by a 15-day strike of about 250,000 state employees demanding pay increases and price controls. The government compromised with an arbitration agreement. Compromise with the powerful business sector subdued protest against a tax-reform program passed by Congress in September. Implementation of the reforms was delayed, but they would eventually raise income from wealthier individuals to pay for increased social spending. (JANET KRENGEL)

This article updates the *Macropædia* article CENTRAL AMERICA: *Guatemala.*

## GUYANA

A republic and member of the Commonwealth, Guyana is situated in northeastern South America, on the Atlantic Ocean. Area: 215,000 sq km (83,000 sq mi). Pop. (1987 est.): 802,000. Cap.: Georgetown. Monetary unit: Guyana dollar, with (Oct. 5, 1987) a free rate of G$8.95 to U.S. $1 (G$14.54 = £1 sterling). President in 1987, Desmond Hoyte; prime minister, Hamilton Green.

The government took a major step in its economic restructuring program in January 1987 with a 56% devaluation of the Guyana dollar. While the official rate moved from G$4.40 to G$10 to the U.S. dollar, the government also announced that commercial banks would be allowed to trade in hard currencies at rates prevailing on the parallel market. By midyear the commercial rate had settled at G$21 to U.S. $1, and the banking system had acquired substantial amounts of foreign exchange previously handled by street traders.

Some tax modifications were announced, together with public-sector wage increases, to offset a portion of the cost-of-living increase resulting from the devaluation. The

trade deficit was expected to increase sharply in 1987, and a growth rate target of no more than 3% was set. The government reiterated its desire for overseas private investment, and agreements were reached for Canadian and Australian mining companies to explore for gold on a large scale. Talks with International Monetary Fund and World Bank officials took place in March, but no agreement was announced. The country experienced a prolonged fuel shortage in August and September. (ROD PRINCE)

This article updates the *Macropædia* article The GUIANAS: *Guyana.*

## HAITI

The republic of Haiti occupies the western one-third of the Caribbean island of Hispaniola, which it shares with the Dominican Republic. Area: 27,400 sq km (10,579 sq mi). Pop. (1987 est.): 5,532,000. Cap.: Port-au-Prince. Monetary unit: gourde, with (Oct. 5, 1987) a par value of 5 gourdes to U.S. $1 (free rate of 8.12 gourdes = £1 sterling). President of the interim governing council in 1987, Lieut. Gen. Henri Namphy.

Haiti's interim governing council, headed by Lieut. Gen. Henri Namphy, canceled presidential elections that were taking place on Nov. 29, 1987, and dissolved the independent electoral council after severe outbreaks of violence disrupted polling. Even before polling day began, voting had been postponed over one-fifth of the country because of attacks on polling stations and candidates. The elections would have been the first in 30 years. On December 9 it was announced that the elections had been rescheduled for Jan. 17, 1988. Shortly thereafter a new electoral council was sworn in, although the leading candidates demanded that the original council be restored.

The interim council was dominated by the Army, which was expanded to about 12,000 men during 1987 with the inclusion of some members of the infamous Tontons Macoutes, the militia created under the Duvalier regime, which had been overthrown in February 1986. Violence occurred all year, with severe outbreaks claiming 34 lives after the electoral council had disqualified 12 candidates closely associated with former president Jean-Claude Duvalier on November 2. Two presidential candidates were assassinated, one in August and the other in October. In June the interim council tried to suspend the electoral council but backed down after a wave of strikes in which

Haitian soldiers guard the Palace of Justice while, inside, a new electoral council selected by the ruling military junta to replace the council that had been dissolved after failed elections is sworn in.

30 people were killed and a U.S. threat to suspend aid. The U.S. cut off virtually all aid on November 29 after the elections were canceled.

A new constitution was approved by the Constitutional Assembly on March 10 and was endorsed in a national referendum on March 29 by 99% of voters in a turnout of 50%. The interim council introduced several economic reforms in 1986 and 1987. However, in 1987 Haiti's economy experienced its fifth year of stagnation.

(ROBIN CHAPMAN)

This article updates the *Macropædia* article The WEST INDIES: *Haiti.*

## HONDURAS

A republic of Central America, Honduras has coastlines on the Caribbean Sea and the Pacific Ocean. Area: 112,088 sq km (43,277 sq mi). Pop (1987 est.): 4,657,000. Cap.: Tegucigalpa. Monetary unit: lempira, with (Oct. 5, 1987) a par value of 2 lempiras to U.S. $1 (free rate of 3.25 lempiras = £1 sterling). President in 1987, José Azcona Hoyo.

On Aug. 7, 1987, Honduras became one of the signatories of the Central American peace plan initiated by Pres. Oscar Arias Sánchez (*see* BIOGRAPHIES) of Costa Rica. At the time of the postponement in June of a meeting of Central American heads of state to consider the plan, Honduras admitted to sharing some of the U.S. administration's misgivings. It was also worried that, if the plan succeeded in bringing to an end the war between the Sandinista government of Nicaragua and the *contra* opposition forces, Honduras would be incapable of coping with the *contras* remaining on its soil.

The presence of the *contras* in Honduras led to tension between the Honduran government, the *contras*, and their U.S. backers. During 1987 it was implied, through the Pentagon's plans for construction projects in Honduras, that the U.S. military presence in the country was not temporary. The 3,700 U.S. troops on tour of duty were bolstered by troops and equipment taking part in such maneuvers as Solid Shield '87. While substantial development aid accompanied the military assistance (an estimated $1 billion in total since 1982), the Honduran government sought assurances from the U.S. that aid would continue should support to the *contras* be cut off. The Iran-*contra* hearings in the U.S. and intensification of an official campaign against corruption in Honduras led the government and the Army to distance themselves from the *contras*. (*See* North America: *United States:* Special Report, above.)

Despite its strong ties with Honduras, the U.S. did not stand in the way of the first bilateral trade pact between Honduras and the U.S.S.R., signed in August. In June Honduras reached provisional agreement with its commercial bank creditors on restructuring its external debt, which had reached $2.9 billion. Besides renegotiating the repayments schedule, the banks agreed to capitalize $30 million in interest arrears or to refinance these arrears by providing new money.

(BEN BOX)

This article updates the *Macropædia* article CENTRAL AMERICA: *Honduras.*

## JAMAICA

A constitutional monarchy within the Commonwealth, Jamaica occupies an island in the Caribbean Sea. Area: 10,991 sq km (4,244 sq mi). Pop. (1987 est.): 2,365,000. Cap.: Kingston. Monetary unit: Jamaica dollar, with (Oct. 5, 1987) a free rate of J$5.37 to U.S. $1 (J$8.72 = £1 sterling). Queen, Elizabeth II; governor-general in 1987, Sir Florizel Glasspole; prime minister, Edward Seaga.

Prolonged negotiations with the International Monetary Fund (IMF) resulted in an agreement in January 1987 giving Jamaica access to $132.8 million by March 1988. The terms of the agreement precluded any currency devaluation as long as inflation was kept to 7% during 1987. At the end of August the central bank indicated that the year-end targets would be met without difficulty. The IMF agreement also featured a 10% limit on pay raises, a reduction in corporate taxation, and progressive reduction of import duties over four years.

Following the IMF agreement, the government negotiated a rescheduling of debts worth $125 million with the Paris Club, and the commercial banks agreed to reschedule $181 million. Plans were announced for conversion of about $400 million of bank debt into equity.

The government's critics concentrated on the rising trade deficit in the first half of the year. Political activity was muted, however, partly because of the illness of the opposition leader, Michael Manley, during the second quarter. In August and September anxiety was expressed over a resurgence in violent crime; well-publicized incidents included armed robberies of foreign tourists and the murder of reggae singer Peter Tosh (*see* OBITUARIES).

(ROD PRINCE)

This article updates the *Macropædia* article The WEST INDIES: *Jamaica.*

## MEXICO

A federal republic of North America, Mexico has coastlines on the Pacific Ocean, the Gulf of Mexico, and the Caribbean Sea. Area: 1,958,201 sq km (756,066 sq mi). Pop. (1987 est.): 81,323,000. Cap.: Mexico City. Monetary unit: Mexican peso, with (Oct. 5, 1987) a free rate of 1,582 pesos to U.S. $1 (2,569 pesos = £1 sterling). President in 1987, Miguel de la Madrid Hurtado.

The Mexican political scene was dominated in 1987 by the nomination of candidates for the 1988 presidential elections. Considerable speculation surrounded the choice of candidates for the ruling Partido Revolucionario Institucional (PRI), which had not lost a major election since it came to power in 1929. In January the PRI overhauled its top organization to strengthen the electoral machinery and avoid favouring any of the aspirants. Humberto Lugo Gil was appointed secretary-general of the PRI's national executive committee, the number-two post in the party hierarchy, and six new members, former or departing state governors, were brought onto the committee for their extensive local campaign experience.

A smooth buildup to the nomination in the latter part of the year was disrupted by the emergence of a dissident wing of the party, known as the Democratic Current, led by Cuauhtémoc Cárdenas, a former state governor and senator, and Porfirio Muñoz Ledo, a former party boss. The Democratic Current campaigned for more internal party democracy and for the presidential candidate to be chosen by the rank and file members rather than by the incumbent president. The attack came at a low point in the popularity of the PRI, beset by accusations of economic failure, corruption, and continuing monopoly of power, and gained support from the populist and nationalist left wing. For all practical purposes, Cárdenas was expelled from the PRI, but he later became a candidate for the small Partido Auténtico de la Revolución.

To improve its image, the PRI leadership adapted its procedures and, in a surprise move, announced six precandidates for the presidential nomination. The six were Ramón Aguirre Velázquez, mayor of Mexico City; Manuel

Carlos Salinas de Gortari, candidate of Mexico's ruling Partido Revolucionario Institucional, was expected to win the July 1988 presidential elections and to follow the course set by Pres. Miguel de la Madrid Hurtado.

PETER JORDAN/TIME MAGAZINE

Nevertheless, the slide in stock market values led to another round of capital flight and a resultant fall in the value of the peso on the open market. After initially trying to support the currency, the government, fearful of depleting its foreign exchange reserves, announced on November 18 that it would let the peso float. The result was a drastic fall in the peso, a spurt in the inflation rate to 144%, and increased restiveness on the part of the labour unions, which threatened a general strike on December 18. On December 14 the central bank lowered the official exchange rate by 22%, to 2,200 pesos to the U.S. dollar, bringing it closer to the open market rate, which then stood at 2,350 pesos. The following day the government granted raises of up to 38% to union workers and announced an "economic solidarity pact" that involved tax increases and cuts in the budget.

(SARAH CAMERON)

## NICARAGUA

A republic of Central America, Nicaragua has coastlines on the Caribbean Sea and the Pacific Ocean. Area: 127,849 sq km (49,363 sq mi). Pop. (1987 est.): 3,502,000. Cap.: Managua. Monetary unit: córdoba, with (Oct. 5, 1987) a market rate of 2,000 córdobas to U.S. $1 (3,248 córdobas = £1 sterling). President in 1987, Daniel Ortega Saavedra.

Bartlett Díaz, minister of the interior; Alfredo del Mazo González, minister of energy and state industries; Sergio García Ramírez, the attorney general; Miguel González Avelar, minister of education; and Carlos Salinas de Gortari, minister of budget and planning. In October Pres. Miguel de la Madrid Hurtado chose Salinas, aged 39, to be the nominee. Salinas had been closely linked to de la Madrid for 15 of his 19 years in politics, and his choice implied continuation of the current economic policies.

Five left-wing parties, the Mexican Unified Socialist Party (PSUM), the Mexican Workers' Party (PMT), and three smaller groups, united in March to create the Mexican Socialist Party (PMS). The Mexican left wing had traditionally been split into several rival factions and had been unable to attract the support of more than a tiny minority of the electorate. The PMS held primary elections for its candidate, which were won by Heberto Castillo, founder and leader of the Mexican Workers' Party. In an unprecedented show of unity, opposition parties from the left and right joined forces in November, launching the Democratic Assembly for Effective Suffrage to challenge the PRI's hold on power. The PRI recognized the importance of the new challenge and, in a departure from its usual policy of ignoring opponents, prepared to set up a team to monitor and debate with the opposition.

The agreement to restructure Mexico's debt to international commercial banks, which had been negotiated in 1986, was signed in April 1987 and legally came into effect in October. In the largest-ever restructuring agreement, Mexico and the banks rescheduled $43.7 billion over 20 years with a 7-year grace period. A flexible financing package from all creditors of $13.2 billion in new loans, up to $7.7 billion of which was to come from banks, included contingency funds if the economy did not grow at the expected rate or if foreign exchange earnings were insufficient. In the event, however, Mexico was able to record a huge trade surplus as oil prices held steady and non-oil exports responded favourably to the devaluation of the peso. Loans from banks were reduced to less than $6 billion, and foreign exchange reserves soared to $14 billion from as low as $2.9 billion in July 1986.

Part of the rise in foreign exchange reserves was accounted for by the repatriation of capital held abroad by Mexicans. As the peso depreciated, interest rates remained high, savings increased, and investors clamoured for profitable instruments. The main beneficiary of this demand was the stock exchange, which became the world's fastest growing market. Even after the world stock market slide in mid-October, the index showed a gain of more than 400% over the previous year.

Fighting between Sandinista government forces and the armed right-wing opposition, or *contra*, forces intensified in 1987. Invigorated by a $100 million package of military aid approved by the U.S. Congress in August 1986, the *contras* infiltrated Nicaragua from their Honduran bases to launch a major offensive in April. They were heavily outnumbered, however, and according to government figures 477 *contras* were killed in June alone, compared with 131 Sandinistas. The government announced in February that 5,066 government soldiers and civilians and 14,914 *contras* had been killed in the five years to 1986. The revelation late in 1986 that money from secret U.S. arms sales to Iran had been illegally diverted to the *contras* placed their future in doubt. They were dealt a further blow on August 7 when the Sandinista government signed a five-nation Central American peace plan stipulating that external powers should cease all military aid to insurgent forces in the region; it was doubted that the *contras* could survive without U.S. funds.

The government took steps to comply with the peace plan. The banned opposition newspaper *La Prensa* was allowed to reopen on October 1; two Catholic clergymen expelled in 1986 were granted reentry; and many political prisoners were freed. Pres. Daniel Ortega Saavedra initially resisted opening a dialogue with the *contras*. However, the prospect that further military aid might be approved by the U.S.—and perhaps also pressure applied by Moscow during Ortega's two-day visit there in October—led him to agree to indirect negotiations, using as mediator an outspoken opponent of the Sandinistas, Miguel Cardinal Obando y Bravo. Two rounds of indirect talks held in the Dominican Republic ended in an impasse on December 22. On December 21 the *contras* launched a major attack in the northeast, which they subsequently described as the most successful of the war. Meanwhile, the U.S. Congress, on December 22, passed legislation that would allow the administration to continue furnishing nonlethal aid to the *contras* until early 1988, when Congress would again review the matter. Apparently encouraged by these developments, the *contras* presented new demands to the government and Cardinal Obando on December 30.

The economy deteriorated further in 1987. Gross domestic product fell by an estimated 2% in the fourth suc-

cessive year of contraction. The rate of inflation accelerated from 747% in 1986 to an estimated 1,500%. Domestic fuel was rationed, and prices rose more sharply following the U.S.S.R.'s decision to reduce oil supplies.

A new constitution went into effect on Jan. 9, 1987, after much debate. While it guaranteed numerous freedoms, it also identified the conditions under which a state of emergency—still in force at year's end—could be imposed.

(JANET KRENGEL)

This article updates the *Macropædia* article CENTRAL AMERICA: *Nicaragua.*

## PANAMA

A republic of Central America, Panama lies between the Caribbean Sea and the Pacific Ocean on the Isthmus of Panama. Area: 77,082 sq km (29,762 sq mi). Pop. (1987 est.): 2,274,000. Cap.: Panama City. Monetary unit: balboa, at par with the U.S. dollar, with a free rate (Oct. 5, 1987) of 1.62 balboas to £1 sterling. President in 1987, Eric Arturo Delvalle.

National Civic Crusade members protest the violent regime of Panama's de facto leader, Gen. Manuel Antonio Noriega, during a two-day general strike that paralyzed the capital and other cities.

Panama's sagging economy was further jeopardized in 1987 by severe political upheaval. On June 6 Col. Roberto Díaz Herrera publicly charged his superior, the commander of the defense forces, Gen. Manuel Antonio Noriega (*see* BIOGRAPHIES), with conspiring to plant a bomb in the small plane that had carried former strongman Brig. Gen. Omar Torrijos Herrera to his death in 1981. Díaz, who was a cousin of Torrijos, also charged Noriega with—among other misdeeds—involvement in the brutal murder of Hugo Spadafora, a severe critic of the military, in 1985.

The accusations brought thousands of protesters into the streets, and demonstrations and strikes continued for months. In response, the government dispatched riot police to restore order, issued a stream of emergency decrees, and clamped down on the news media. Colonel Díaz was tried and sentenced to five years in prison for crimes against state security; in December he was expelled from the country and flown to Venezuela.

The turmoil in Panama prompted the U.S. Senate to call on Noriega to step down and to urge the establishment of civilian rule. Pres. Eric Arturo Delvalle responded that this was unacceptable interference in Panama's affairs and recalled the Panamanian ambassador from Washington. Reports persisted that canal operations had deteriorated, but they did not appear to be directly affected by the unrest.

(ALMON R. WRIGHT)

This article updates the *Macropædia* article CENTRAL AMERICA: *Panama.*

## PARAGUAY

Paraguay is a landlocked republic of central South America. Area: 406,752 sq km (157,048 sq mi). Pop. (1987 est.): 3,897,000. Cap.: Asunción. Monetary unit: guaraní, with (Oct. 5, 1987) an official rate of 320 guaraníes to U.S. $1 (519.71 guaraníes = £1 sterling) and a free market rate of 855 guaraníes to U.S. $1 (1,388 guaraníes = £1 sterling). President in 1987, Gen. Alfredo Stroessner.

Following renewed pressure from the U.S., Pres. Alfredo Stroessner lifted the state of siege in Asunción in April 1987 (it had been nearly continuous for 58 years). More political exiles were allowed to return, most notably Domingo Laíno, leader of the unofficial opposition Authentic Radical Liberal Party, and in December Napoleón Ortigoza Gómez, who had spent 25 years in solitary confinement for plotting against the regime, was released from prison. Nevertheless, a new penal code restored many of the powers just rescinded. Arrests of government opponents continued; the consistently critical Radio Ñandutí was forced off the air; and the only remaining opposition newspaper, the weekly *El Pueblo,* was closed down.

The ruling Colorado Party elected as its new president Interior Minister Sabino Montanaro of the pro-Stroessner *militantes.* This widened the rift between the party's militant faction and the *tradicionalistas,* who favoured greater freedom. A third faction, the *éticos,* sided with opposition parties in subsequent demonstrations. The four-party Acuerdo Nacional (National Agreement) intended to boycott the 1988 elections, while other groups formed a new front and named a candidate. Stroessner was chosen as his party's candidate in November.

Industrialists criticized the government for failing to implement promised economic reforms. The exchange rate system was modified but not unified; the high level of contraband trade was not discouraged; and much of industry, starved of credit, was operating at just 50% of capacity. Economic performance was expected to be better than in 1986 because of agricultural recovery.     (BEN BOX)

## PERU

The republic of Peru is located in western South America, on the Pacific Ocean. Area: 1,285,216 sq km (496,225 sq mi). Pop. (1987 est.): 20,727,000. Cap.: Lima. Monetary unit: inti, with (Oct. 5, 1987) an official rate of 15.89 intis to U.S. $1 (25.81 intis = £1 sterling). President in 1987, Alan García Pérez; prime ministers, Luis Alva Castro until June 22 and, from June 26, Guillermo Larco Cox.

In Peru 1987 started on a familiar note with a series of attacks by the guerrilla group Sendero Luminoso (Shining Path) on economic and political targets in Lima. The problem of how to suppress terrorism without violating human rights proved to be intractable, and Pres. Alan García Pérez's campaign pleased none but his most stalwart supporters. Military discontent was stirred by a bill passed in April that merged the Army, Navy, and Air Force into a single Ministry of Defense under greater civilian control. When Air Force Gen. Luis Abram Cavellerino was dismissed for attempting to organize military and political opposition to the bill, hundreds of military supporters protested by locking themselves into two airfields. The administration's failure to make any headway against the guerrillas was underlined by the increasing number of attacks on officials of the ruling party, the Alianza Popular Revolucionaria Americana (APRA). More than 230 APRA members had been assassinated since President García came to office in July 1985.

Notwithstanding the undiminished viciousness of the guerrilla war, 1987 was dominated by the government's own battle to sustain economic growth. In 1986 large real wage increases had generated growth of 8.5% in gross domestic product (GDP), the highest rate since 1969 and a key factor behind García's popularity. Inflation in 1986 averaged a relatively modest 78%, compared with over 163% in 1985. In January 1987, however, the government relaxed the price freeze and announced that the exchange rate would be devalued by 2.2% a month. Inflation immediately began to accelerate, causing the year's target of 35% to be unattainable; prices rose 88% in the 12 months to August and were expected to exceed 100% in 1987. The export performance was sluggish despite improved world oil and mineral prices, and imports rose for the second consecutive year; trade surpluses of more than $1 billion

Francisco Pardo Mesones, president of Peru's Banco Mercantil, speaks with supporters and members of the media. Pardo's bank was the third to be affected following the enactment of legislation in October nationalizing banks and other financial institutions.
AFP PHOTO

in 1984 and 1985 were transformed into deficits of $50 million in 1986 and an expected $100 million in 1987. Nonetheless, GDP growth of at least 6% was assured for 1987 because of statistical distortions created by the exceptionally rapid growth in the second half of 1986.

These signs of a faltering economy led to dissent within García's inner Cabinet. The resignation on June 22 of Prime Minister Luis Alva Castro, who also held the key post of finance minister, cleared the way for a major reshuffle that brought to the fore politicians prepared to relaunch García's demand-led growth model. Their first economic package, which included large wage increases, a renewed price freeze on basic goods, increased taxation, and a complex system of exchange rates, did little to enhance business confidence or the government's popularity.

García marked the start of his third year in office on July 28 with the announcement that Peru's banks and other financial entities were to be nationalized. The move provoked a fierce national debate that succeeded in revitalizing Peru's dormant right-wing opposition. Despite rumours, lawsuits against the government by banks and private individuals, and mass protests, the legislation was enacted on October 12. Business confidence collapsed, and there was a rapid withdrawal of trade credit lines.

The deteriorating economic outlook, in particular the acute shortage of foreign exchange to pay for vital imports, led to a perceptible shift in the government's attitude toward foreign creditors. An International Monetary Fund (IMF) mission was allowed into Peru in September to make a routine report on the economy. Agreements with two foreign commercial banks to repay debt with commodities were signed in October.     (JANET KRENGEL)

## SAINT CHRISTOPHER AND NEVIS

A constitutional monarchy and member of the Commonwealth, St. Christopher and Nevis comprises the islands of St. Christopher and Nevis in the eastern Caribbean Sea. Area: 267 sq km (103 sq mi). Pop. (1987 est.): 46,500. Cap.: Basseterre. Monetary unit: Eastern Caribbean dollar, with (Oct. 5, 1987) a par value of EC$2.70 to U.S. $1 (free rate of EC$4.38 = £1 sterling). Queen, Elizabeth II; governor-general in 1987, Sir Clement Arrindell; prime minister, Kennedy A. Simmonds.

Moderate economic growth was expected to continue throughout 1987, based principally on the further development of the tourist industry. In the first four months of the year, stopover arrivals increased by 38% over the comparable 1986 period, and there was a slight increase in cruise ship traffic. Several new hotel projects were planned.

Sugar production from the 1987 crop was about 25,000 metric tons, approximately the same as in the previous year; a target of 30,000 tons was set for 1988. Improved revenue collection and expenditure discipline produced a fiscal surplus of EC$900,000 in 1986, and further improvement was expected in 1987. Including capital expenditure, the overall deficit in 1986 declined to EC$1.6 million, financed largely by domestic borrowing; this accounted for 43% of total debt in 1986, as against 33% in 1985.

The ambassador to the U.S., William Herbert, resigned in April in order to fight British newspaper allegations that he was involved in money laundering. He was supported in his efforts to clear his name by Prime Minister Kennedy Simmonds.                                    (ROD PRINCE)

This article updates the *Macropædia* article The WEST INDIES: *Saint Christopher and Nevis.*

## SAINT LUCIA

A constitutional monarchy and member of the Commonwealth, St. Lucia is the second largest of the Windward Islands in the eastern Caribbean Sea. Area: 617 sq km (238 sq mi). Pop. (1987 est.): 143,000. Cap.: Castries. Monetary unit: Eastern Caribbean dollar, with (Oct. 5, 1987) a par value of EC$2.70 to U.S. $1 (free rate of EC$4.38 = £1 sterling). Queen, Elizabeth II; governors-general in 1986, Sir Allen Lewis and, from April 30, Sir Vincent Floissac; prime minister, John Compton.

In two general elections held on April 6 and April 30, 1987, the governing United Workers' Party (UWP) gained a one-seat majority, winning 9 of the 17 parliamentary seats, as against 8 for the St. Lucia Labour Party. In the previous Parliament, the UWP had held 14 seats. Prime Minister John Compton called the April 30 election in an attempt to improve his majority. In June his position was strengthened when an opposition member, Neville Cenac, crossed the floor to join the UWP members. Cenac was immediately appointed foreign minister.

As chairman of the Organization of Eastern Caribbean States (OECS), Compton was active in promoting a proposal for unification of the seven OECS members into a single state. Although opposed by Antigua and Barbuda, the proposal was being discussed in the latter part of 1987 in several countries.

Further economic growth was expected for 1987, following a 6% growth in gross domestic product recorded for 1986. Prospects for the 1987 banana crop were dimmed by bad weather in the first half of the year, but tourism continued to expand, and there were hopes for a revival of manufacturing exports.                          (ROD PRINCE)

This article updates the *Macropædia* article The WEST INDIES: *Saint Lucia.*

## SAINT VINCENT AND THE GRENADINES

A constitutional monarchy within the Commonwealth, St. Vincent and the Grenadines comprises the islands of St. Vincent and the northern Grenadines in the eastern Caribbean Sea. Area: 389 sq km (150 sq mi). Pop. (1987 est.): 112,000. Cap.: Kingstown. Monetary unit: Eastern Caribbean dollar, with (Oct. 5, 1987) a par value of EC$2.70 to U.S. $1 (free rate of EC$4.38 = £1 sterling). Queen, Elizabeth II; governor-general in 1987, Joseph Lambert Eustace; prime minister, James Fitz-Allen Mitchell.

Efforts to develop agriculture, manufacturing, and tourism increased during 1987, with the aid of investment incentives in the 1987–88 budget. A surplus on current account of EC$4 million was projected in the budget, which allowed for a 9% increase in recurrent spending and a slight decline in capital expenditure.

Banana production for the year was expected to increase, following the setback in 1986 when a tropical storm reduced the crop to 37,644 metric tons, as against 41,173 tons in 1985. The government announced a restructuring plan for the arrowroot industry that included rescheduling of its EC$7.2 million debt.

The government was involved in a controversy over press freedom in May, when Information Minister Parnell Campbell issued new editorial directives to the state radio station. Opposition parties condemned the directives; radio station staff took sick leave in an apparent protest action but subsequently returned to work under threat of dismissal.                                (ROD PRINCE)

This article updates the *Macropædia* article The WEST INDIES: *Saint Vincent and the Grenadines.*

## SURINAME

The republic of Suriname is in northeastern South America, on the Atlantic Ocean. Area: 163,820 sq km (63,251 sq mi), not including a 17,635-km area disputed with Guyana. Pop. (1987 est.): 415,000. Cap.: Paramaribo. Monetary unit: Suriname guilder, with (Oct. 5, 1987) a par value of 1.79 Suriname guilders to U.S. $1 (free rate of 2.90 Suriname guilders = £1 sterling). Chairman of the National Military Council in 1987, Dési Bouterse; acting president, L. F. Ramdat Misier; prime ministers, Pretaapnarian Radhakishun to February 12 and Jules Wijdenbosch (temporary).

The major event in 1987 was the general election on November 25, bringing to an end seven years of military rule. Six political parties contested the 51 seats in the National Assembly, and the result was overwhelming defeat for Suriname's military leader Dési Bouterse and a victory for a three-party opposition coalition, the Front for Democracy and Development, made up of the Indonesian, Creole, and Indian minorities. (For tabulated results, see *Political Parties*, above.) A draft constitution approved in a September referendum, however, gave the military a continuing role on an executive council of state, which could override Cabinet decisions, and a security council that had special powers in the event of a threat to national security. A civilian president, who would serve as head of government, was to be chosen early in 1988.

The guerrilla movement led by Ronnie Brunswijk had eroded Bouterse's power and contributed to the deterioration of the economy. Damage to transmission lines caused electricity supply cuts and the closing of an aluminum smelter. Output of bauxite ore, the country's economic mainstay, was curbed. A tightening of links with Libya caused anxiety to France, which had a power station in neighbouring French Guiana.          (KLAUS J. HOEKSEMA)

This article updates the *Macropædia* article The GUIANAS: *Suriname.*

## TRINIDAD AND TOBAGO

A republic and member of the Commonwealth, Trinidad and Tobago consists of two islands in the Caribbean Sea off the coast of Venezuela. Area: 5,124 sq km (1,978 sq mi). Pop. (1987 est.): 1,221,000. Cap.: Port-of-Spain. Monetary unit: Trinidad and Tobago dollar, with (Oct. 5, 1987) a par value of TT$3.60 to U.S. $1 (free rate of TT$5.85 = £1 sterling). Presidents in 1987, Sir Ellis Clarke and, from March 19, Noor Mohammad Hassanali; prime minister, A. N. R. Robinson.

Stringent austerity measures, including tax increases and cuts in public expenditure, were imposed early in 1987 by the newly elected government of Prime Minister Arthur N. R. Robinson, who claimed that his National Alliance for Reconstruction (NAR) had inherited a catastrophic economic situation. Foreign exchange reserves had declined to TT$1.4 billion by May 1987, and the government expected an overall balance of payments deficit of TT$2.8 billion for the year. Policy measures proposed by the government included privatization of a number of unprofitable state companies, improved incentives for overseas investors, and development of a state-owned natural gas platform off the Trinidad coast. The coalition government became increasingly fragile. Robinson asked the 13 members of his Cabinet to resign on November 25 and then reinstated all but one of them—Public Works Minister John Humphrey, who had been critical of the government.

The new government established a constitutional reform commission. The move followed its failure to win support for a bill to amend the constitution that would have forced the resignation of presidential appointees at the end of each president's term of office. Four magistrates and more than 50 police officers were suspended after publication of the report of a commission of inquiry into drug-related corruption.

In local elections in Trinidad in September, the NAR retained control of six out of seven counties and gained the Arima and San Fernando municipal councils from the People's National Movement (PNM). Port-of-Spain and Point Fortin remained in PNM hands.    (ROD PRINCE)

This article updates the Macropædia article The WEST INDIES: Trinidad and Tobago.

## URUGUAY

A republic of eastern South America, Uruguay lies on the Atlantic Ocean. Area: 176,215 sq km (68,037 sq mi). Pop. (1987 est.): 3,058,000. Cap.: Montevideo. Monetary unit: Uruguayan new peso, with (Oct. 5, 1987) a free rate of 247.78 new pesos to U.S. $1 (402.37 new pesos = £1 sterling). President in 1987, Julio María Sanguinetti Cairolo.

Uruguay enjoyed political stability in 1987 and made modest economic progress. The main political issue was a campaign mounted by the centre-left party coalition Frente Amplio, together with trade unions and human rights groups, to overturn a law approved by Congress in December 1986 granting an amnesty to members of the armed forces accused of human rights violations during the period of military rule, 1973 to 1985. The organizers tried to gather sufficient support for a referendum but could not obtain the necessary signatures of 25% of the electorate. A total of 61 officers benefited from the amnesty. The ruling Colorado Party opposed the campaign, and its relations with other political parties deteriorated so that the passage of legislation in Congress was slowed. Pres. Julio María Sanguinetti stated that to try the officers would provoke a constitutional crisis because the military had threatened to defy the courts.

Uruguay successfully completed an 18-month standby arrangement with the International Monetary Fund in December 1986. In November 1987 the government reached an accord with commercial bank creditors that improved the terms of the July 1986 agreement on the rescheduling of $1,760,000,000 of external debt maturing in 1985–89 and also covered almost $100 million of debt maturing in 1990–91. Growth was expected to fall to 3% in 1987 from 6.3% in 1986, mainly because of lower private consumption.    (ROBIN CHAPMAN)

## VENEZUELA

A republic of northern South America, Venezuela lies on the Caribbean Sea. Area: 912,050 sq km (352,144 sq mi). Pop. (1987 est.): 18,272,000. Cap.: Caracas. Monetary unit: bolívar, with (Oct. 5, 1987) a main official rate of 14.50 bolivares to U.S. $1 (23.55 bolivares = £1 sterling). President in 1987, Jaime Lusinchi.

The presidential election due in 1988 dominated Venezuela's politics in 1987 as it had in 1986. Both main parties, the ruling Acción Democrática (AD) and the Social Christian Party (COPEI), had two contenders for party nomination. In October the AD selected former president Carlos Andrés Pérez over Octavio Lepage Barreto, who had the tacit backing of Pres. Jaime Lusinchi. The two COPEI precandidates, former president Rafael Caldera and party general secretary Eduardo Fernández, ran a close race, but Fernández was selected in December after a long and acrimonious contest.

In March the country suffered the most serious unrest in several years. Countrywide riots were sparked by the shooting to death of a university student in Mérida. The looting and violence that followed caused damage estimated at $2 million. Further unrest occurred in June following a buildup of tensions that culminated in student hunger strikes and calls for educational reform. The government blamed subversives, but a slowdown in economic growth and increasing social discontent were believed to be more likely reasons.

Relations between Venezuela and Colombia became strained. In June Colombian gunmen killed at least nine Venezuelan national guards who had destroyed illegal marijuana and coca plantations along the Colombian border. Tension increased in August when a Colombian frigate intruded into Venezuelan waters in the Gulf of Venezuela. Venezuela protested and the ship was withdrawn, but shortly afterward two Colombian jets violated Venezuelan airspace in the same area.

National guardsmen help a woman out of the rushing waters of the Limón River in Venezuela. September rains caused flooding near the city of Maracay that cost some 500 lives.

Although Venezuela's economic problems persisted because of its heavy dependence on oil, gross domestic product in 1986 rose by a spectacular 5.2%. All sectors of the economy recorded strong growth, and the unemployment rate fell to 10.5%. Growth slowed in 1987 and was not expected to exceed 2.5%. The December 1986 devaluation of the main exchange rate from 7.5 bolivares to U.S. $1 to 14.50 bolivares, which affected 75% of imports, was inflationary. The increase in consumer prices accelerated sharply from 12.7% in 1986 to a forecast 35–40% in 1987. To compensate, minimum wages were raised by 25–33% in December 1986; general wage increases amounting to an additional 20–30% and a four-month price freeze were announced at the end of April 1987.

The devaluation had shaken business confidence, and foreign investors were reluctant despite improvements in the investment laws. Although Venezuela had a good record on debt repayment, the foreign debt was still a burdensome $25 billion. The problem of debt servicing was alleviated by restructuring, but there was considerable pressure for new loans from all sectors. Some easing of the debt problem was possible if interest in debt-for-equity swaps increased. The first such deal was announced in September when a U.S. bank agreed to finance a new aluminum plant. Following Japan's announcement that it would lend $30 billion to Latin America, a top-level Venezuelan delegation visited Tokyo in May. In October Japan agreed to provide a $324 million loan for a hydroelectric project on the Caroní River, the largest single loan agreed on in many years.

The budget recorded a deficit in 1986, and another was likely in 1987. For 1988 the budget was set at $12.6 billion, with half the revenue expected to come from oil. A deficit was to be covered by external loans and issuing bonds of around 20 billion bolivares in order to access Venezuela's considerable private-sector savings. Privatization was increasingly seen as a means of generating more funds.

In September Venezuela suffered a natural disaster when torrential rain caused severe flooding near the city of Maracay. Some 500 lives were lost.                    (BEN BOX)

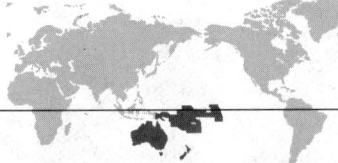

# Oceania

## OCEANIAN AFFAIRS

**The Fijian Crisis.** The two coups that occurred in Fiji in 1987 sent shock waves through the South Pacific region. Following the defeat of the Alliance Party government, which had ruled Fiji since independence in 1970, in the April general elections, the ministers of an Indian-dominated but multiracial coalition led by Timoci Bavadra were arrested and a military regime led by Lieut. Col. Sitiveni Rabuka (*see* BIOGRAPHIES) was installed in the first coup on May 14. Subsequent negotiations seemed close to reaching a compromise when Rabuka led a second coup on September 25.

Within the region, reaction to the first coup was mixed. The region had been unique in the third world in having had no coups, no constitutions overturned, and no military dictatorships. It enjoyed a reputation for stability, and many of the island nations took pride in their democratic institutions modified to operate in accordance with local customs and values. The situation in Fiji challenged this state of affairs and created uneasy precedents for others who might be reluctant to accept the arbitration of the ballot box. Against this, there was widespread sympathy with the rights of an indigenous population to land and political power within its own country. To many Pacific islanders, indigenous rights took precedence over grafted-on democratic institutions; parallels were drawn between the rights of Fijians and those of Kanaks in New Caledonia.

Among South Pacific island governments, however, there was even greater concern over the temptation for metropolitan countries to intervene. A sharp awareness of the U.S. action in Grenada in 1983 (even though under very different circumstances), and the fact that in the days immediately after the coup Australia and New Zealand did not rule out the possibility of military intervention, brought a sharp response from the leaders of Papua New Guinea, the Solomon Islands, and Vanuatu, in particular. The Fijians, they insisted, had the right to solve their own problems without outside interference. The second coup provoked less sympathy because it involved the rejection by radical elements of a compromise that had been worked out between the two leading political parties and seemed to offer a peaceful solution. The Solomon Islands was the first of the region's island nations to join Australia and New Zealand in condemning the coup.

**The South Pacific Forum.** Fiji was absent from the South Pacific Forum meeting held in Western Samoa at the end of May. The Forum offered Fiji the services of a delegation composed of Australian Prime Minister Bob Hawke, Solomon Islands Prime Minister Ezekiel Alebua, and Henry Naisali, director of the South Pacific Bureau of Economic Cooperation (SPEC), the executive arm of the Forum. The offer was rejected by Fiji's governor-general.

The Forum admitted two new members, the Federated States of Micronesia and the Republic of the Marshall Islands, which had embarked on self-government in association with the U.S. Both had attended earlier meetings as observers.

The South Pacific Nuclear Free Zone Treaty became operative in December 1986 when Australia became the eighth Forum member to ratify it. The nuclear powers were asked to sign the protocols to the treaty. These required states possessing nuclear weapons to refrain from using those weapons, or threatening to use them, against any treaty member and to refrain from nuclear testing in the region. The U.S.S.R. immediately signed the treaty, an act with more political than strategic significance; the U.S., the U.K., and France all refused to do so, even though the protocols had been weakened to meet great power objections to any restraint on the rights of passage through international waters.

There was also concern about the delay in implementing an agreement reached between the U.S. and Forum countries over tuna-fishing rights. The island nations all claimed a 200-mi exclusive economic zone, but the U.S. denied the rights of any nation to highly migratory species of fish, especially tuna. The issue had long soured relationships between the U.S. and the South Pacific. In April 1987 a final agreement was reached under which the U.S. agreed to pay an annual fee of $10 million and the U.S. tuna industry $1,750,000 for fishing rights for up to 35 U.S. vessels; the fees were to be divided among the island nations in proportion to the estimated catch from their respective zones. There was delay in ratification by the U.S. Senate, however, and the frustration of the island nations swelled to anger when about a dozen U.S. tuna boats were spotted fishing in Kiribati's waters in May. One vessel was arrested, and its owner and captain were heavily fined.

**External Relations.** In response to a call from the South Pacific Forum for increased dialogue with Japan and other countries on the Pacific Rim, Japanese Foreign Minister Tadeshi Kuranari visited Australia, New Zealand, Vanuatu, and Papua New Guinea early in the year. He pledged $2 million to the UN Development Program specifically to promote telecommunications and transport projects in the region and gave a further $1 million for energy research. Japan also showed interest in annual talks with the chairman of the South Pacific Forum and the director of SPEC.

While Japan's growing interest in the region was welcomed, the island nations closed ranks when faced by Libyan initiatives. Given the potential for violent confrontation in New Caledonia, there was widespread concern over growing contacts between Libya and the Kanak independence movement. Anxious that its regional support not be undermined, the Kanak Socialist National Liberation Front (FLNKS) dismissed its spokesman on foreign affairs because of his reluctance to soft-pedal the issue. Having embarked on a dialogue with Tripoli, Prime Minister Walter Lini of Vanuatu responded to regional pressure by announcing that a decision on the establishment of a Libyan people's bureau (embassy) in Vila had been deferred indefinitely. In May the Libyan bureau in Australia was closed and its diplomats were expelled.

France remained an important focus of regional attention because of its continued nuclear testing at Mururoa, French Polynesia, and its refusal to countenance independence for New Caledonia. At a special meeting in Auckland, N.Z., in March, Forum leaders called on France to defer the referendum on independence planned for September, to allow for decolonization of New Caledonia, and to open a dialogue with the Forum. (See *Dependent States*, below.) The *Rainbow Warrior* affair also resurfaced with an international arbitration decision that France should pay $8 million in compensation to the Greenpeace organization for sinking its ship in 1985 and with news that one of two French military agents serving a sentence in French Polynesia for involvement in the affair had returned to France, reportedly for medical treatment.   (BARRIE MACDONALD)

## AUSTRALIA

A federal parliamentary state (formally a constitutional monarchy) and member of the Commonwealth, Australia occupies the smallest continent and includes the island state of Tasmania. Area: 7,682,300 sq km (2,966,200 sq mi). Pop. (1987 est.): 16,188,300. Cap.: Canberra. Monetary unit: Australian dollar, with (Oct. 5, 1987) a free rate of $A 1.40 to U.S. $1 ($A 2.27 = £1 sterling). Queen, Elizabeth II; governor-general in 1987, Sir Ninian Martin Stephen; prime minister, Robert J. Hawke.

**Domestic Affairs.** In July 1987 the Australian Labor Party (ALP) government of Prime Minister Robert (Bob) Hawke became the first Labor administration to win three successive elections. Until the very eve of the election date announcement, Hawke promised that his government would run for its full term of office, but in a masterly change of tactics in midyear, the prime minister seized the initiative and went to the polls early. (*See* Sidebar.)

Hawke based his decision to call an election on the chaos caused in the National and Liberal parties by the recalcitrant state premier of Queensland, Sir Johannes Bjelke-Petersen. Showing no concern for the effect such an announcement would have on his National Party colleagues, Bjelke-Petersen declared that he would mount a campaign to become federal prime minister himself because of the inadequacy of the Liberal Party, led by John Howard. Before Bjelke-Petersen split the two conservative parties, public opinion surveys showed that the ALP would most likely lose the next election.

Once the election had been called, the two parties tried to submerge their differences for the duration of the campaign, but by then the damage was done. The vigorous and uninhibited criticism of Howard and of Ian Sinclair, leader of the National Party in the House of Representatives, culminated in the decision of Queensland National Party members to walk out of the federal opposition coalition. Sinclair lost considerable public support when he was unable to bridge the gap between the Nationals in Queensland and the Nationals in the rest of Australia. Following

Australian Prime Minister Bob Hawke and his wife, Hazel, smile after Hawke's election in July to a third term. His was the first Labor government in Australia to win three consecutive terms.

a poor showing in a Northern Territory election, Bjelke-Petersen called off his personal campaign to become prime minister, but the attempt to offer an olive branch to the Liberals once Hawke had called the election failed signally. To make matters worse, Howard was under continual open threat from members of his own party, especially from the previous Liberal leader, Andrew Peacock. Howard was forced to banish Peacock from the shadow ministry for disloyalty after a conversation in which he discussed Howard in unflattering terms on a car-telephone system was intercepted, illegally recorded, and subsequently published. After the election Peacock returned to the fold as shadow spokesman on the economy.

Howard was deserted by the press, a traditional friend of Australian conservatives; newspaper proprietors and stockholders had grown richer as a result of Hawke's deregulation of ownership and monopoly rules. Howard made a further error of judgment in an attempt to woo voters by appealing to their greed with promises of tax cuts. The idea of tax cuts had been discredited by Bjelke-Petersen's attempt to convince voters of the merits of a low flat-rate tax coupled with a cut in government enterprises. Bjelke-Petersen finally lost the support of his own National Party in Queensland and resigned as state premier on December 1, a week after he had been replaced as state party leader. He was succeeded in both posts by Mike Ahern.

Hawke was returned with an increased majority and promptly went on the offensive. The ALP's powers within Parliament and the prime minister's supremacy within the ALP meant that in the postelection period no serious obstacle stood in Hawke's way as he attempted to carry out a further installment of what his critics called "Thatcherite Laborism" on account of his penchant for smaller govern-

ment, privatization of government-owned enterprises, and the selling of government assets.

Hawke used his enhanced authority to reform the Cabinet and the public service. He increased the size of the government (Cabinet and non-Cabinet ministers) to 30, included 3 women in it, and insisted both that Tasmania be represented and that the representation of Queensland grow from one to three. Before the new government was sworn in, Hawke announced that he would reduce the number of public service departments from 28 to 17, thus demoting a dozen ministers and departmental heads to junior status and eliminating 3,000 posts. The key to Hawke's new plan was a reorganization of the administration to embrace a system under which senior ministers were backed up by junior ministers. Senior positions within the government were filled by Hawke himself (prime minister), Lionel Bowen (deputy prime minister), John Button (industry, technology, and commerce minister), and Paul Keating (treasurer; *see* BIOGRAPHIES). William (Bill) Hayden became minister for trade as well as foreign minister, and Susan Ryan became special minister of state, minister assisting the prime minister on the status of women and the Bicentenary, and minister assisting the minister for community services and health.

The new system came under pressure almost immediately, leaving the prime minister angry and embarrassed. Two ministers gave contradictory answers, one in the Senate and the other in the House of Representatives, when they were each asked a similar question about the sensitive issue of the coast-watch service: public opinion had become alarmed when the private companies contracted to scan Australia's shores for drug smugglers, illegal immigrants, and other threats fell out with the government.

---

## The General Election Campaign

Following speculation in the press and unhealthy fluctuations in the exchange rate and on the stock exchange, on April 1, 1987, Prime Minister Bob Hawke announced that there would be no early election. He declared that the government would continue in office for its full term and that he would not be drawn into an opportunistic grab for reelection to capitalize on the disunity within the opposition parties. Such a statement, he said, was necessary in the interests of stability and good government.

In the two succeeding months, however, the disunity in the opposition parties reached such a pitch that Hawke could no longer resist the temptation. A well-received minibudget in May, the promise of actual tax cuts at about the date of the election, and the possibility that no more opportune moment would present itself led the prime minister to change his mind, and Hawke announced on May 27 that the election would take place on July 11. Opposition leaders branded Hawke's decision as another broken promise.

Hawke went to the electorate standing on his record and offering little that was new. Under the Australian Labor Party (ALP), existing policies were to be largely maintained. The ALP promised to maintain its strong alliance with the U.S. but to oppose the Reagan administration's Strategic Defense Initiative. It would also support disarmament and a Pacific nuclear-free zone and would resist Soviet expansion into the region. On taxation, Hawke promised to leave the capital gains

tax and fringe benefits tax unchanged. He also pledged support for environmental issues.

The Liberals based their campaign on a reduction in the top rate of income tax from 49 to 38%. They also promised to remove the assets test and to maintain indexation of income-tested pensions. Liberal leader John Howard said that if his party were elected, unemployment benefits would not be paid by the government until severance pay by the former employer was used up, and there would be no unemployment benefits for those who left their jobs voluntarily. The Liberals also said that they would not allow a veto by the Aborigines over resource exploration or development, would abolish export controls on minerals, would oppose reverse discrimination for women, and would sell Australian Airlines and 49% of Qantas.

The ALP government was returned to office with its majority of 16 in the House of Representatives increased to 24. (For tabulated results, see *Political Parties*, above.) There was a national swing of 1% against the party, but it maintained its vote in vital marginal seats, and Hawke was so confident that Labor had achieved an almost dynastic record that he put forward his treasurer, Paul Keating (*see* BIOGRAPHIES), as a likely candidate to succeed him as prime minister. Howard later said that he had spent 75% of his time trying to prevent conflicts between the liberal and National parties, leaving him little time to oppose the government.                              (A. R. G. GRIFFITHS)

Vietnam veterans march past crowds of
supporters during a parade in Sydney.
The October celebration was the first
"Welcome Home" that the Australian vets
had received since their return from the
war.
AFP PHOTO

Hawke called the election after the Senate refused to pass legislation designed to establish an Australia-wide identification system based on an identity number carried on what was to be called the Australia Card. The government argued that the new card would be an effective weapon in the fight against tax evasion and welfare payment fraud. Under the constitution the refusal of the Senate to pass the legislation, already approved by the House of Representatives, gave Hawke the right to call a double dissolution election, in which voters choose members of both houses.

Despite widespread public opinion that the Australia Card was not worth the sacrifice of civil liberties, Hawke maintained after the election that he had a popular mandate to pass the law as soon as possible. While the question had received scant attention during the election campaign, once the new Parliament assembled and Hawke reintroduced the bill, there was talk of little else. The anticard forces mobilized so successfully that by September public opinion polls showed that only 35% of Australians approved the system. In a day of high drama in Parliament, Howard was able to kill off the Australia Card by exposing a technical flaw in the drafting of the bill: it could be implemented only by regulation, and because the government did not have a majority in the Senate, the bill was dead. Within a week Hawke admitted defeat and abandoned the legislation, turning instead to investigate other methods of combating tax fraud.

**Foreign Affairs.** Foreign Minister Hayden successfully steered Australian foreign policy through stormy seas in 1987, remarking wistfully at times that the government's task of handling foreign relations would be made easier if the press would be less uninhibited in its criticism not only of Australia's enemies but also of its friends and neighbours. Referring to Australia's new preoccupation with the Pacific region, Hayden criticized the romantic European illusion that it was "a paradise of bounteous palms, fish positively leaping into nets and naked girls falling all over Fletcher Christian and his mates"; the Pacific was no longer an irrelevant backwater, he maintained, but a scene of conflict between the superpowers.

Australia's relationship with France continued to be among the most difficult of its diplomatic problems. The French refused to lift the ban imposed on ministerial

contact between the two nations imposed after Australia criticized French policies in the Pacific. The two nations continued to snipe at each other and, their mutual disclaimers to the contrary, no headway was made in breaking down the barriers until the end of September, when the French government lifted the ban. The low-water mark of Australian-French relations was reached when, during the buildup to the referendum on the independence issue in New Caledonia, France expelled the Australian consul general from New Caledonia. The French accused the Australian government of meddling in their private affairs by supporting the decolonization of New Caledonia, and the Australian and French prime ministers swapped insults over the issue, with Jacques Chirac going so far as to describe Hawke as "stupid" after Hawke pointed to the inevitability of the independence process in the Pacific. Relations failed to improve after the referendum, when Hawke interpreted the 59% turnout in the voting as a sign that instability would continue in the area for the foreseeable future. The French responded to this observation by attacking Australia's treatment of Aborigines and describing Australians as incorrigible in their support for anticolonialism.

Australia also warned Libya against interference in the South Pacific. Hayden asserted that Libya's commercial interests in the region were almost nil, that Libya was not a member of the region and did not share regional interests and concerns. Hawke subsequently decided to close the Libyan people's bureau (embassy) in Canberra, explaining that his move had become necessary because Libya's activities in Australia and in the Pacific region were destabilizing and divisive. While Australia continued to respect the right of Pacific island nations to establish relations with whatever countries they chose, Hawke concluded that Australia's concern for peace had made the action necessary.

Australian diplomacy was severely tested when the elected government of Fiji was overthrown by a military coup. Australia had always maintained close links with Fiji, a near neighbour and fellow member of the Commonwealth. Hawke quickly ruled out the use of force by Australia to restore the Fijian constitution after the first coup in May and moved to recognize the new regime. In Australia, however, vocal supporters of the Fijian Indian community deplored the discriminatory policies of the new Fijian government. More significant was the effect of the loss of Australian tourist dollars as Australians, until they were lured back by extremely low air fares, avoided holidays in what had been a popular recreational area. Hawke's prestige in the region was recognized by the South Pacific Forum, which immediately elected him head of a possible special mission to Fiji to talk to all parties on the crisis. On the eve of what appeared to be a settlement of the crisis, Lieut. Col. Sitiveni Rabuka (*see* BIOGRAPHIES) staged a second coup. The government immediately condemned the coup and reviewed its policy toward Fiji. Hayden, who was abroad and scheduled to address the UN, was recalled to take charge of the crisis. Because prices had been reduced in order to revitalize tourism following the May coup, many Australian tourists were crowding Fiji's hotel resorts. Hawke called upon Rabuka not to harass Australian citizens, and the Australian Navy was told to prepare its ships to evacuate them from Fiji if necessary.

**The Economy.** During 1987 the economy continued to improve, with the size of the foreign debt the only intractable problem. A crucial element in the government's success was an economic statement in May, at which time the treasurer announced that government assets worth $A 1 billion would be sold. The government also announced in May a major restructuring of unemployment benefits and study allowances, which greatly increased the incentive for young Australians to remain in education and stay within the family system rather than moving onto welfare. The September budget included proposals to provide an extra 5,800 places in higher education for young school-leavers in 1988.

Keating described as essential to the ALP's economic success the reductions in the size of government and in the budget deficit, which had been cut from close to $A 10 billion when the ALP first came to power to a projected $A 27 million in 1987–88. The budget provided $A 250 million to meet the election commitment to a family allowance supplement for low-income families, and it incorporated a 2.4% real reduction in Commonwealth spending, reducing outlays by $A 3.5 billion for both 1987 and 1988. At the same time, there were massive cuts of $A 4.5 billion in personal income tax and the introduction of a new company tax system that eliminated the double taxation of dividends. Keating announced that the government's policy was bearing fruit as Australians responded to the national export effort and successfully sought out new markets. He claimed that the current account deficit had been cut by $A 1 billion from 6% of gross domestic product to 5% and forecast that in the forthcoming year it would decline further to 4%. Although his forecast was doubted by the opposition and by economic experts, the stock exchange responded by reaching record levels before joining in the world stock market slide of October.

While Keating claimed that the needy had been protected and assisted and that welfare cheats had been caught and made to pay their way, Howard described the budget as clever and superficially attractive while in reality being a coat of paint and veneer over a brittle and fragile economy. Equally critical was a professor of economics at Sydney University, who pointed out that improved employment prospects for Australia had been gained at the expense of a reduction in wages; that inflation rates, although falling, were still well above those of Australia's trading partners; that investment in new plant and equipment was not as popular in Australia as in many other countries; and that interest rates might be driven up as the country's external debt level increased.　　　(A. R. G. GRIFFITHS)

# FIJI

A republic from Oct. 6, 1987, Fiji occupies an island group in the South Pacific Ocean. Area: 18,274 sq km (7,056 sq mi). Pop. (1987 est.): 726,000. Cap.: Suva. Monetary unit: Fiji dollar, with (Oct. 5, 1987) a free rate of F$1.28 to U.S. $1 (F$2.08 = £1 sterling). Queen to Oct. 15, 1987, Elizabeth II; governor-general to October 15 and president from December 5, Ratu Sir Penaia Ganilau; prime ministers, Ratu Sir Kamisese Mara to April 13, Timoci Bavadra from April 13 to May 14, and Mara from December 5; military leader from May 14 to December 5, Brig. Gen. Sitiveni Rabuka; normal constitutional government was suspended and a series of interim arrangements succeeded one another from the May 14 coup until December 5.

On May 14, 1987, Lieut. Col. Sitiveni Rabuka (*see* BIOGRAPHIES) used troops to arrest the entire Cabinet and declared himself leader of a military government in Fiji. The coup followed street demonstrations in which indigenous Fijians protested that their rights, though entrenched in the constitution, would be jeopardized under the Indian-dominated government formed after elections in April; Rabuka claimed that his action was necessary to prevent further bloodshed. In the election the Alliance Party government of Ratu Sir Kamisese Mara, which had ruled Fiji since independence, was defeated by a coalition of the Indian-dominated National Federation Party and the new Labour Party, led by Timoci Bavadra. The coalition won 28 seats to the Alliance's 24.

AFP PHOTO

Lieut. Col. Sitiveni Rabuka of Fiji arrives at a news conference in September. He staged two coups—one in May, the second in September—to ensure government control by indigenous Fijians rather than by the ethnic Indian majority.

Following the coup the governor-general, Ratu Sir Penaia Ganilau, declared a state of emergency, established an advisory council, and tried to initiate negotiations among the parties. By September agreement had been reached on the formation of a bipartisan caretaker government, but before these plans could be implemented, Rabuka staged a second coup on September 25. Perhaps the most important factor in this coup was the emergence of the radical Taukei (landowners) movement, which had wide support among rural Fijians of all ranks and among urban commoners.

The second coup was followed by the suspension of the Supreme Court after the judges refused to serve the new regime. Newspapers and radio stations were closed, a curfew was imposed, and nationals were forbidden to leave the country; imprisonment without trial was formalized, and soldiers were promised protection from prosecution should they cause death or injury in carrying out orders. After several attempts to start negotiations had failed, Rabuka declared Fiji a republic at midnight on October 6–7, and the queen, in accepting Ganilau's resignation as governor-general on October 15, stepped down as head of state. There were suggestions that elections might be held early in 1988 under a revised constitution that would ensure Fijian dominance and effectively reduce Indians to the status of second-class citizens. On December 5 Ganilau was appointed president and Mara, prime minister. As minister of home affairs, Rabuka remained in charge of security and the armed forces.

For Fiji 1987 had seemed to offer great economic promise. In 1986 inflation was held to 2%, and there was a balance of payments surplus. As a result of the coup, however, the economy suffered a severe decline.

(BARRIE MACDONALD)

This article updates the *Macropædia* article PACIFIC ISLANDS: *Fiji.*

## KIRIBATI

A republic in the western Pacific Ocean and member of the Commonwealth, Kiribati comprises the former Gilbert Islands, Banaba (Ocean Island), the Line Islands, and the Phoenix Islands. Area: 849 sq km (328 sq mi). Pop. (1987 est.): 66,000. Cap.: Bairiki. Monetary unit: Australian dollar, with (Oct. 5, 1987) a free rate of $A 1.40 to U.S. $1 ($A 2.27 = £1 sterling). President (*berititenti*) in 1987, Ieremia Tabai.

In general elections held in two rounds on March 12 and 19, 1987, Pres. Ieremia Tabai of Kiribati and all but two of his Cabinet ministers were returned to office. Overall, 16 sitting members lost their seats in the House of Assembly, enlarged to 39 members. In subsequent presidential elections, Tabai (51%) defeated his main rival, Teburoro Tito (43%), who represented the opposition Christian Democratic Party. At midyear Tabai reshuffled his Cabinet, bringing in members from the small Liberal Party.

In May the authorities arrested the *Tradition,* a U.S. vessel, for fishing illegally in Kiribati's exclusive economic zone. The captain and charterer were each fined $A 200,-000, the vessel was seized, and the cargo was sold by the government. The ship was later sold back to its owners.

The controversial fishing agreement with the U.S.S.R., which lapsed in October 1986, was not renewed. However, another step toward the development of Kiribati's own tuna-fishing industry was taken with the completion of a new facility at Betio, Tarawa. The $A 10 million Nippon Causeway linking Betio islet to Bairiki, the administrative headquarters, was completed.   (BARRIE MACDONALD)

This article updates the *Macropædia* article PACIFIC ISLANDS: *Kiribati.*

## NAURU

An island republic within the Commonwealth, Nauru lies in the Pacific Ocean about 1,900 km (1,200 mi) east of New Guinea. Area: 21 sq km (8 sq mi). Pop. (1987 est.): 8,100. Cap.: Yaren. Monetary unit: Australian dollar, with (Oct. 5, 1987) a free rate of $A 1.40 to U.S. $1 ($A 2.27 = £1 sterling). President in 1987, Hammer DeRoburt.

Following a close-fought general election in Nauru on Dec. 6, 1986, the members of Parliament elected Kennan Adeang president. Within days, however, the defection of Finance Minister Kinze Clodumar resulted in the downfall of his administration. Hammer DeRoburt was returned as president, but his own majority was continually threatened by defections. Following fresh elections held on Jan. 24, 1987, his position was secured when his group won 11 of the 18 seats in Parliament. DeRoburt's victory ensured the continuity of his economic policies, based on the building of an investment portfolio to see the country through the days ahead when the phosphate deposits were depleted. In a victory on the economic front, the Nauruan Local Government Council successfully concluded its suit for damages against the New Zealand Seaman's Industrial Workers' Union over the union's blacklisting of the *Enna G,* a Nauruan vessel.

President DeRoburt expanded Nauru's foreign policy portfolio by signing the South Pacific Nuclear Free Zone Treaty. Nauru was the ninth of the South Pacific Forum's 15 members to do so.   (A. R. G. GRIFFITHS)

This article updates the *Micropædia* article NAURU.

## NEW ZEALAND

New Zealand, a constitutional monarchy and member of the Commonwealth in the South Pacific Ocean, consists of North and South islands and Stewart, Chatham, and other minor islands. Area: 267,515 sq km (103,288 sq mi). Pop. (1987 est.): 3,341,000. Cap.: Wellington. Monetary unit: New Zealand dollar, with (Oct. 5, 1987) a free rate of $NZ 1.54 to U.S. $1 ($NZ 2.50 = £1 sterling). Queen, Elizabeth II; governor-general in 1987, Sir Paul Reeves; prime minister, David Russell Lange.

New Zealand's fourth Labour government swept back into office with an increased overall majority in the Aug. 15, 1987, general elections. The National Party opposition knocked out the only two minor party representatives, from the Democratic (formerly Social Credit) Party, and the House of Representatives was left divided between the Labour (58 seats) and National (39) parties. Labour's deregulated, more market-oriented, and less protectionist trade policies had tested the loyalty of its trade union base, while its insistence on a nuclear-free policy had angered traditional allies. Unemployment was up, and the administration's prospects for maintaining its majority seemed poor. In the event, Labour ran on its record, National was still recovering from its defeat in the 1984 elections, and the electorate granted Prime Minister David Lange a second term.

In a reconstructed Cabinet, Lange gave up foreign affairs for education, a field he had identified during the campaign as basic to New Zealand's social problems. He left his senior aides Geoffrey Palmer (deputy prime minister) and Mike Moore to their justice and trade portfolios, respectively, and proclaimed confidence in key minister Roger Douglas (*see* BIOGRAPHIES) at finance by appointing finance associates Richard Prebble and David Caygill to other senior work. Prebble took over the newly created Department of State-Owned Enterprises and was also given responsibility for works, island affairs, broadcasting, and railways; Caygill picked up the contentious health portfolio as well as trade and industry. The moves indicated a relaxed approach in the midst of the biggest finance policy changes the country had known.

National opposition leader Jim Bolger, a farmer and former minister of labour, had mounted a sufficiently lusty challenge to consolidate his position as party leader. It was victory enough for him to outpoint the former party boss and prime minister, Sir Robert Muldoon, in opinion polls on leadership quality. National's caucus replaced veteran George Gair with Don McKinnon as deputy leader, and Bolger awarded the key shadow portfolio of finance to Ruth Richardson after she was narrowly defeated by McKinnon in the vote for deputy. When Muldoon declined defense, Bolger sent him to the back benches.

Two months before the elections, Douglas had caused surprise with a budget that provided for a surplus, the first in 35 years. Against an Organization for Economic Cooperation and Development prediction of a $1.2 billion deficit, Douglas provided for more state assets to be sold and for new state corporations to pay back millions more dollars in capital. The privatization policies exacerbated unemployment as new corporations sought profits, but they apparently appealed to investors, shifting Labour's support from traditional working-class to management and investment sectors. Douglas continued to target inflation as the basic danger, but by midyear it had exceeded expectations at 3.3% for the quarter and 18.9% for the year.

Economic policy merged with foreign policy in drawing New Zealand closer to Australia. Apart from differences with the U.S. administration over port access for nuclear-powered or nuclear-armed ships, the main regional issues were the coup in Fiji and developments in New Caledonia. New Zealand welcomed a change of premier in the Cook Islands. One of the most damaging earthquakes in the country's history hit the Bay of Plenty in March. Visitors included Queen Margrethe II of Denmark, the deputy leader of the African National Congress, Oliver Tambo, and British Foreign Secretary Sir Geoffrey Howe. Prime Minister Lange was soon at odds with Howe over New Zealand's antinuclear policy.

An Order of New Zealand with a 20-member limit was instituted. Sir Edmund Hillary, conqueror of Mt. Everest who was now envoy to India, was the best known of the first group to be honoured.　　　(JOHN A. KELLEHER)

See also *Dependent States,* below.

## PAPUA NEW GUINEA

A constitutional monarchy and member of the Commonwealth, Papua New Guinea is situated in the southwestern Pacific Ocean and comprises the eastern part of the island of New Guinea, the islands of the Bismarck, Trobriand, Woodlark, Louisiade, and D'Entrecasteaux groups, and parts of the Solomon Islands, including Bougainville. Area: 462,840 sq km (178,704 sq mi). Pop. (1987 est.): 3.5 million. Cap.: Port Moresby. Monetary unit: kina, with (Oct. 5, 1987) a free rate of 0.89 kina to U.S. $1 (1.45 kinas = £1 sterling). Queen, Elizabeth II; governor-general in 1987, Sir Kingsford Dibela; prime minister, Paias Wingti.

General elections took place in Papua New Guinea in June–July 1987. A total of 2.7 million votes were cast in the elections, which took three weeks to complete. Although a large number of independents were elected, the new Parliament continued to be dominated by two parties, the People's Democratic Movement, led by Prime Minister Paias Wingti, and the Pangu Pati, under former prime minister Michael Somare. (For tabulated results, see *Political Parties,* above.) Wingti remained as prime minister, although his slender majority of 54 to 51 made the implementation of controversial policies difficult. Somare described the Wingti coalition as a ramshackle gaggle of unruly independents.

Law and order continued to be a problem, with some criminologists linking high rates of violent urban crime to a combination of detribalization and unemployment. Wingti proposed to get the economy moving by relending cash from the mining sector to farmers for rural development. In the area of foreign policy, improved relations with Indonesia were offset by deteriorating relations with France, as Wingti supported the campaign against the French presence in New Caledonia. (See *Dependent States,* below.) In a major foreign policy speech in August, Wingti announced that his government wished to strengthen Papua New

AP/WIDE WORLD

New Zealand's Prime Minister David Lange (right) and Finance Minister Roger Douglas celebrate the Labour Party's victory in the August general elections, which signaled a continuation of the economic policies Lange began in 1984.

Papua New Guinea's Prime Minister Paias Wingti campaigns for reelection. Returned to office with a slender majority, Wingti faced difficulty in implementing controversial policies.

AP/WIDE WORLD

Guinea's relations with the U.S., China, and Japan and would consider establishing formal links with the U.S.S.R.

(A. R. G. GRIFFITHS)

This article updates the *Macropædia* article EAST INDIES: *Papua New Guinea.*

## SOLOMON ISLANDS

A parliamentary state and member of the Commonwealth, the Solomon Islands comprises a 1,450-km (900-mi) chain of islands and atolls in the western Pacific Ocean. Area: 27,556 sq km (10,640 sq mi). Pop. (1987 est.): 292,000. Cap.: Honiara. Monetary unit: Solomon Islands dollar, with (Oct. 5, 1987) a free rate of SI$2.01 to U.S. $1 (SI$3.27 = £1 sterling). Queen, Elizabeth II; governor-general in 1987, Sir Baddeley Devesi; prime minister, Ezekiel Alebua.

Prime Minister Ezekiel Alebua, who had assumed power in the Solomon Islands in December 1986 at the head of a Cabinet dominated by the United Party, visited Taiwan at midyear for talks on future aid to the Solomons. The recurrent budget for 1987 was projected at SI$65 million and the development budget at SI$77 million. The main focus was on natural resources development and reconstruction following damage caused by Typhoon Namu in 1986. At the World Bank–International Monetary Fund meeting in Washington in October, Finance Minister George Kejoa criticized the failure of industrialized nations to deliver "real aid" to third world countries. He argued that interest payments on third world debt outweighed the advantages of the aid received.

Having responded to the May coup in Fiji with a declaration that Fiji should be left to solve its problems without outside interference, the Solomon Islands was the first Pacific Island nation to condemn the second coup four months later. Alebua said his government would recognize only a government headed by Fiji's governor-general and

suggested that the coup leaders had taken their proposed protection of ethnic Fijian interests beyond reasonable limits. He called on the South Pacific Forum to reexamine the issues involved.                    (BARRIE MACDONALD)

This article updates the *Macropædia* article PACIFIC ISLANDS: *Solomon Islands.*

## TONGA

A monarchy and member of the Commonwealth, Tonga is an island group in the Pacific Ocean east of Fiji. Area: 747 sq km (288 sq mi). Pop. (1987 est.): 94,800. Cap.: Nuku'alofa. Monetary unit: pa'anga, with (Oct. 5, 1987) a free rate of 1.40 pa'anga to U.S. $1 (2.27 pa'anga = £1 sterling). King, Taufa'ahau Tupou IV; prime minister in 1987, Prince Fatafehi Tu'ipelehake.

In the February 1987 elections a record 55 candidates contested the nine commoners' seats in the Tongan Parliament. There had been considerable discontent with the outgoing government, largely because of tax increases, and only three of eight members seeking reelection were successful. Most of the new members were younger and better educated than those they replaced. Their power would be limited, however, because under Tonga's constitution they were joined in Parliament by nine nobles and ten ministers nominated by the king.

Tonga enjoyed improved economic conditions. Inflation was halved to less than 9% in the second half of 1986, and at the end of that year overseas reserves stood at 29 million pa'anga, an increase of 20% across the year. Tourism earnings totaled 12 million pa'anga, second only to remittances from Tongans working overseas as a source of foreign exchange. In 1987 several new economic initiatives were taken, the most important being a major planning exercise in cooperation with U.S. consultants for future development based on tourism and including the expansion of Tonga's international airport.

During July King Taufa'ahau Tupou IV attended Bastille Day celebrations in Papeete, French Polynesia, and paid a controversial visit to France's nuclear testing site at Mururoa Atoll.                    (BARRIE MACDONALD)

This article updates the *Macropædia* article PACIFIC ISLANDS: *Tonga.*

## TUVALU

A constitutional monarchy within the Commonwealth, Tuvalu comprises nine main islands and their associated islets and reefs in the western Pacific Ocean. Area: 24 sq km (9 sq mi). Pop. (1987): 8,200. Cap.: Fongafale. Monetary unit: Tuvalu dollar, at par with the Australian dollar (also a legal currency), with (Oct. 5, 1987) a free rate of $T 1.40 to U.S. $1 ($T 2.27 = £1 sterling). Queen, Elizabeth II; governor-general in 1987, Tupua Leupena; prime minister, Tomasi Puapua.

In 1987 Tuvalu took a major step toward establishing its economic viability. Budgetary assistance was required to cover approximately one-third of its $A 4 million annual recurrent expenditure. On the initiative of the director of the South Pacific Bureau for Economic Cooperation, Henry Naisali, Tuvalu sought contributions toward a $A 27 million investment fund that would generate income of at least $A 1.5 million. Pledges totaling $A 27 million were received, with major contributions of about $A 8 million each from the U.K., Australia, and New Zealand.

The philatelic bureau, which had provided more than one-quarter of government revenue in the years immediately following independence, suffered a loss for the third year in succession; however, the new tuna-fishing agreement between the island nations and U.S. interests was estimated to produce between $A 300,000 and $A 1 million per year. At its own request Tuvalu was added to the UN list of least developed countries, a status that carried access to concessional World Bank and International Monetary Fund loans.                    (BARRIE MACDONALD)

This article updates the *Macropædia* article PACIFIC ISLANDS: *Tuvalu.*

## VANUATU

The republic of Vanuatu, a member of the Commonwealth, comprises 12 main islands and some 60 smaller ones in the southwestern Pacific Ocean. Area: 12,190 sq km (4,707 sq mi). Pop. (1987 est.): 145,000. Cap.: Vila. Monetary unit: vatu, with (Oct. 5, 1987) a free rate of 106.53 vatu to U.S. $1 (173 vatu = £1 sterling). President in 1987, George Sokomanu; prime minister, the Rev. Walter Lini.

Prime Minister Walter Lini of Vanuatu suffered a cerebral hemorrhage while on an official visit to the U.S. in February 1987. He returned to work in midyear, was reelected president of the Vanuaaku Pati, and led his party into November elections. Lini was returned to office, though with a reduced majority. His party lost ground especially in the capital, Vila, to a coalition of "moderate" pro-French parties.

Vanuatu and the U.S.S.R. announced a fishing agreement permitting eight Soviet vessels to fish Vanuatu's exclusive economic zone (but not within the 12-mile limit) for an annual fee of $1.5 million. There was continuing controversy over Vanuatu's links with Libya. After strong comment from within the region, a decision on Libya's request to establish a diplomatic mission in Vila was postponed indefinitely.

Vanuatu continued to criticize France's nuclear testing at Mururoa Atoll and its policies in New Caledonia. The situation worsened in September when, for the third time since independence in 1980, Vanuatu expelled the French ambassador. In February Cyclone Uma caused damage estimated at $100 million; at least 45 people were killed.
                    (BARRIE MACDONALD)

This article updates the *Macropædia* article PACIFIC ISLANDS: *Vanuatu.*

## WESTERN SAMOA

A constitutional monarchy and member of the Commonwealth, Western Samoa occupies an island group in the South Pacific Ocean. Area: 2,831 sq km (1,093 sq mi). Pop. (1987 est.): 161,000. Cap.: Apia. Monetary unit: Western Samoa tala, with (Oct. 5, 1987) a free rate of 2.03 tala to U.S. $1 (3.30 tala = £1 sterling). Head of state (*O le Ao o le Malo*) in 1987, Malietoa Tanumafili II; prime minister, Va'ai Kolone.

In its budget for 1987, Western Samoa remained dependent on foreign aid for more than one-third of government expenditure, but it was able to encourage new initiatives by lowering both business and personal taxes. Remittances from Western Samoans living in the U.S. and New Zealand exceeded the country's total receipts from overseas aid.

Western Samoa adopted an uncharacteristically high profile on foreign affairs. At the UN in September, Prime Minister Va'ai Kolone criticized French policy in its Pacific dependencies, specifically New Caledonia. Western Samoa's permanent representative also criticized France's nuclear testing policy, arguing that, if the testing was as safe as was claimed, it should take place in metropolitan France. As chairman of the South Pacific Forum, Va'ai called in September for a boycott of the South Pacific

Games planned to take place in New Caledonia in December. Va'ai maintained that the safety of competitors could not be guaranteed, but his statement was also seen as seeking a regional gesture of disapproval of French policies.

Four Western Samoans who joined a rebel South Pacific Barbarians rugby union tour of South Africa were criticized by sporting and political leaders for jeopardizing the international reputation of Western Samoa.

                    (BARRIE MACDONALD)

This article updates the *Macropædia* article PACIFIC ISLANDS: *Samoa.*

# Dependent States

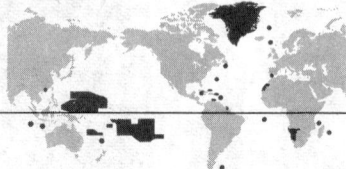

**Europe and the Atlantic.** On Dec. 2, 1987, Britain and Spain settled their long-standing dispute over Gibraltar airport by agreeing on a formula for joint civilian use of the facility. The agreement conceded Spain a consultative role in the development of services. Implementation of the accord depended on approval by Gibraltar's House of Assembly, but it met a cool response from both the Gibraltarian government and opposition politicians. Sir Joshua Hassan resigned as chief minister days after the deal was announced and was succeeded by his deputy, Adolfo Canepa, in a caretaker capacity. The agreement was expected to dominate elections due in 1988. In February the 150-mi "fisheries protection zone" around the Falkland Islands/Islas Malvinas declared by the U.K. came into force. Indirect talks held during the year between U.K. and Argentine representatives had the aim of preventing clashes around the zone, which was policed by British vessels.

Elections took place in Greenland on May 26 following the collapse on March 11 of the ruling left-wing coalition of the Siumut (Forward Party) and the Inuit Ataqatigiit (Eskimo Movement), who disagreed over the new radar equipment being installed at the U.S. air base at Thule. In the new Landsting (parliament), the Siumut lost its status as the largest single party to the centrist Atassut (Unity Party). Following an unsuccessful attempt by the Siumut leader to negotiate a coalition with Atassut, the Siumut and Inuit Ataqatigiit resumed their coalition.

**Caribbean.** At the end of March the British government announced a range of constitutional changes for the Turks and Caicos Islands, which had been recommended by the constitutional commission set up in September 1986. The provisions included electoral reforms, establishment of a public service commission and a committee system to assist ministerial accountability, and the assignment of some power over ministerial appointments to the governor. General elections were to be held in February 1988. Gov. Michael Bradley appointed three new members to the advisory Executive Council in May to replace the original four, who had resigned. One of the four, Clement Howell, was killed in August on a flight from Nassau, The Bahamas.

Anguilla, the British Virgin Islands, and Montserrat all signed information-exchange agreements with the U.S. in the first half of the year, following the earlier examples of the Cayman Islands and Turks and Caicos Islands. The agreements, which could be upgraded to the status of legal assistance treaty, would allow U.S. agents access to bank records to help trace the laundering of drug money. In the

British Virgin Islands a five-year development plan to improve public services and communications, announced in April, was expected to require $50 million in investment. A similar plan was announced in the Cayman Islands. In general elections held in Montserrat on August 25, the People's Liberation Movement headed by John Osborne was returned to power, with four of the seven legislative seats.

French Prime Minister Jacques Chirac indicated that he favoured closer links with France for the overseas départements of Guadeloupe, Martinique, and French Guiana and opposed extending the powers of the elected regional councils. In July the head of the banned Alliance Revolutionnaire Caraibe, Luc Reinette, was arrested with four companions in St. Vincent and flown to prison in France; he had escaped from prison in Guadeloupe in 1985.

The Puerto Rican government convinced the U.S. Congress to preserve benefits contained in Sec. 936 of the Internal Revenue Code in a new tax law approved early in the year. However, U.S. companies operating in Puerto Rico were made liable to a 10% profits tax. Airline traffic was stimulated by the decision of several U.S. airlines to make San Juan the hub of their Caribbean operations.

**Africa.** In April Morocco announced that it had completed the sixth phase of its defensive wall in the Western Sahara, designed to keep out the forces of the Popular Front for the Liberation of Saguia el Hamra and Río de Oro (Polisario Front). A Polisario attack on the northern section of the wall in February was the first major confrontation in the area in two years. On February 27 Muhammad Abdulaziz, the Polisario secretary-general, reportedly escaped an assassination attempt, which, Polisario claimed, involved the Moroccan and French authorities. In November a UN mission arrived in the area to study the feasibility of holding a referendum on its future.

No progress was made toward implementing UN Resolution 435 on independence for South West Africa/Namibia. In July a new constitution was published with the support of four of the parties in the South African-appointed "transitional government" (TG). Though it contained various safeguards for "minorities," it was rejected by one TG party and by the South African government for its inadequate protection of "group rights," particularly the right to segregated education. South Africa proposed new elections to the "ethnic authorities" established under the existing constitution. A notable development was a resurgence of labour organization. Namibia's biggest-ever demonstration, with some 35,000 participants, occurred on May Day. The National Union of Namibian Workers was estimated to have recruited 32,000 members—10% of the industrial work force—in 1986–87. In September, for the first time in Namibia's history, a judge ordered the release of six leaders of the South West Africa People's Organization and the trade union movement detained under the Terrorism Act.

**Pacific.** The U.S. terminated its trusteeship agreements with the Republic of the Marshall Islands and the Federated States of Micronesia on Oct. 21, 1986, and Nov. 3, 1986, respectively, bringing into effect compacts of free association. As a result, the Marshalls and the Federated States had internal self-government, their own citizenship, and control over some aspects of foreign affairs. The U.S. was to provide more than 90% of government revenue and pay compensation for its continuing military presence. The Northern Marianas, another unit of the trusteeship, became on Nov. 3, 1986, a self-governing commonwealth in political union with the U.S., their residents becoming U.S. citizens. The fourth unit, Palau, attempted to reconcile its antinuclear constitution with the compact of free association approved by the U.S. Congress on Oct. 16, 1986. The nuclear clauses of the compact required 75% endorsement by referendum. In a fifth plebiscite, held on Aug. 4, 1987, Palauans voted by a nearly three to one margin to suspend the antinuclear clauses of the constitution, opening the way for simple majority approval of the compact. On August 21, 70% voted in favour of the compact, and the government declared it confirmed. All these developments stirred further controversy, however, leading to court challenges by the compact's opponents. Until the political status of Palau was resolved, the U.S. would continue as administrative authority under the trusteeship agreement.

In American Samoa, Fofo Sunia was reelected as the territory's congressional representative in November 1986. In mid-1987 he protested a review of American Samoa's status by the UN Committee of 24, arguing that Samoans wanted a close relationship with the U.S.

In a referendum held in New Caledonia on September 13, 98% of those who voted rejected independence in favour of remaining a dependency of France. However,

"Don't vote; the referendum is phony. It is death." The indigenous, pro-independence group, FLNKS, urged voters to boycott a referendum on whether New Caledonia should remain a French dependency.

there was only a 59% turnout because of a boycott by the indigenous, pro-independence Kanak population. Leaders of the FLNKS (Kanak Socialist National Liberation Front) said that Kanak opposition to French rule would continue. By the time the referendum took place, more than 8,000 French troops were based in New Caledonia. France's policy there continued to draw criticism from within the region. Throughout the year the economy of French Polynesia was disrupted by a series of dock strikes that culminated in violence, notably in Tahiti. In February Gaston Flosse, who had been criticized for his handling of the strikes, resigned as French Polynesia's president, though he retained his position of minister of state for Pacific affairs in the French government. He was succeeded by Jacques Teuira, his long-time colleague and supporter. Following further violent incidents in late October, the French authorities in Tahiti declared a state of emergency. Teuira resigned in December.

On July 29 Sir Thomas Davis, who had been premier of the Cook Islands for all but a few months since 1978, was forced to resign after a unanimous vote of no confidence in parliament. Davis was succeeded by his former deputy, Pupuke Robati. Criticism of Davis's dictatorial leadership style had been mounting for some months. Another factor was the controversy surrounding the distribution of aid funds received after the island group suffered severe damage from Cyclone Sally in January. In elections in Niue in March, the island's leader for more than 20 years, Sir Robert Rex, and all members of his Cabinet were returned to office. The opposition People's Action Party led by Young Vivian attracted strong support from Niueans living in New Zealand but could win only 4 of the 20 seats in the legislature. In January Tokelau was devastated by Hurricane Tusi, which destroyed nearly one-third of all housing. The UN Committee of 24 reviewed the status of Tokelau and accepted the realism of the island's current relationship with New Zealand, under which self-government was limited to local affairs and exercised through elected island councils.

**East Asia.** Hong Kong's 27th governor, Sir David Wilson, arrived to assume his new office in April. The main task awaiting him was political reform to establish a system that would take the territory beyond 1997, when it was to

became a "special administrative region" of China. Beijing (Peking) was opposed to substantial constitutional changes before a Basic Law was drafted. A committee of experts from Hong Kong and China was not expected to finish this before 1988 or 1989. Strong opposition was voiced in the Legislative Council to the Public Order (Amendment) Law, enacted in March. While dismantling certain old, unenforced restrictions on newspapers, the act kept a provision to punish persons who "maliciously" publish "false news likely to alarm." Opponents labeled it a ready-made instrument for post-1997 suppression of the press. The Council strongly opposed lenient treatment of refugee "boat people" from Vietnam, 6,000 of whom arrived between June and August. The public was generally unsympathetic to the plight of some 8,000 confined to sealed camps. An alarming labour shortage did not modify attitudes appreciably.

In May Joaquim Pinto Machado unexpectedly resigned as governor of Macau after only a year in office. He was succeeded in July by Carlos Melancia, who had held several Cabinet posts in the Portuguese government. In April the prime ministers of China and Portugal signed an agreement in Beijing under which Macau was to return to Chinese sovereignty on Dec. 20, 1999. Like the accord between the U.K. and China over the future of Hong Kong, the agreement guaranteed that Macau could retain its capitalist system for a 50-year period beyond the transfer date.

(MARTIN LEGASSICK; BARRIE MACDONALD; ROD PRINCE; LOUISE WATSON; ROBERT WOODROW)

This article updates the *Macropædia* articles HONG KONG; INDIAN OCEAN ISLANDS; PACIFIC ISLANDS; SOUTHERN AFRICA: *South West Africa/Namibia;* The WEST INDIES.

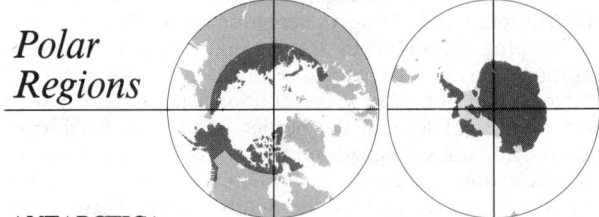

# Polar Regions

## ANTARCTICA

Major research efforts during the 1986–87 summer field season were directed toward the problem of the depletion of the ozone layer above the Antarctic continent in the spring. Four scientific teams were flown to McMurdo Station in August to measure ozone density and other atmospheric characteristics. Initial results indicated that the large hole in the ozone layer was probably due to manmade chlorofluorocarbons in the atmosphere mixing with the intense cold over Antarctica. A similar depletion of nitrous oxide was also determined. Observations in the Arctic revealed a similar ozone depletion centred on Spitsbergen. A joint U.S.-U.S.S.R. research program was formed to pool observations and analysis. U.S.-supplied balloons and measuring equipment would be flown from Molodezhnaya on the Indian Ocean coast so that a broader picture of the ozone-depletion problem could be developed.

The tenth session of the Special Consultative Meeting on Antarctic Mineral Resources was held in Montevideo, Uruguay. At the conclusion of the meeting, it was announced that a final session would be held in Wellington, N.Z., sometime before July 1988 to adopt a draft convention, which would then be circulated to the various governments for ratification.

The international Filchner Ice Shelf Program, involving scientists from West Germany, Austria, Belgium, Norway, and the United States, continued work on the Filchner and

**Dependent States***

| | |
|---|---|
| **Australia** | **South Africa** |
| Christmas Island | South West Africa/Namibia |
| Cocos (Keeling) Islands | **United Kingdom** |
| Norfolk Island | Anguilla |
| **Denmark** | Bermuda |
| Faeroe Islands | British Virgin Islands |
| Greenland | Cayman Islands |
| **France** | Falkland Islands |
| French Guiana | Gibraltar |
| French Polynesia | Guernsey |
| Guadeloupe | Hong Kong |
| Martinique | Isle of Man |
| Mayotte | Jersey |
| New Caledonia | Montserrat |
| Réunion | Pitcairn Island |
| Saint Pierre and Miquelon | Saint Helena |
| Wallis and Futuna | Turks and Caicos Islands |
| **Netherlands, The** | **United States** |
| Aruba | American Samoa |
| Netherlands Antilles | Guam |
| **New Zealand** | Puerto Rico |
| Cook Islands | Trust Territory of the Pacific Islands |
| Niue | Marshall Islands |
| Tokelau | Federated States of Micronesia |
| **Norway** | Northern Marianas |
| Jan Mayen | Palau |
| Svalbard | Virgin Islands (of the U.S.) |
| **Portugal** | |
| Macau | |

*Excludes territories (1) to which Antarctic Treaty is applicable in whole or in part, (2) without permanent civilian population, (3) without internationally recognized civilian government (Western Sahara, Gaza Strip), or (4) representing unadjudicated unilateral or multilateral territorial claims.

Recovery efforts began on a ski-equipped LC-130 Hercules plane that had been buried in Antarctic ice since 1971. Abandoned because of damage and its remote location, the plane was considered salvageable.

ITT ANTARCTIC SERVICES INC.

Ekstrom ice shelves. Two aircraft provided mobility and airborne measurements.

**National Programs.** *Australia.* Research programs away from Australia's three permanent bases were initiated as part of a national policy to learn more about the Australian Antarctic Territory. A multidisciplinary program in the Larsemann Hills began, but heavy pack ice off the Shackleton Ice Shelf forced postponement of the planned work in the Bunger Hills. For the second consecutive year, *Nella Dan* became trapped in the ice and had to be freed by *Mikhail Somov.*

*Chile.* The small-scale research program continued, but major efforts seemed to be devoted to the development of a tourism program based at Teniente Rodolfo Marsh Base on King George Island.

*New Zealand.* Scott Base continued in operation, as did several temporary camps within helicopter range. Botanists working in the dry Garwood Valley discovered two Adélie penguins and fresh seal tracks some 12 km (7.5 mi) from the sea, providing a better understanding of fossil penguins and seals discovered several years earlier.

The CIROS drilling program off Butter Point in McMurdo Sound recovered a sediment core 702 m in length (1 m = 3.3 ft). At 632 m a two-metre-thick asphaltic residue was found in sand, evidence of hydrocarbon formation. The bottom of the core was dated at about 38 million years. The Scott Base husky dog team was removed and shipped to the U.S., where they were to live out their lives.

*South Africa.* The SANAE IV base was maintained, and Sarie Marais, formerly an emergency base in Queen Maud Land, was operated as a summer station. Puma helicopters provided long-range mobility for geologists and surveyors working out of Sarie Marais and Grunehogna, a second summer station.

*Soviet Union.* The seven permanent bases continued to operate. Personnel were delivered to Molodezhnaya by air in early October, much earlier than was possible by ship. One of the aircraft remained to conduct a gravimetric survey in Enderby Land. The missing Druzhnaya I base was located on the new Weddell Sea iceberg. Intense snow drift after the ice had broken off had obscured the station. Teams recovered large quantities of equipment and supplies to be used at a new station, Druzhnaya III, to be built at Norsel Iceport near the Quar Ice Shelf in Queen Maud Land. Workers also built an airstrip for use by the IL-14 airplanes operating from Molodezhnaya. Summer bases were established in the Prince Charles Mountains, in the Larsemann Hills, and on the Amery Ice Shelf.

*United Kingdom.* Three British Antarctic Survey permanent bases were maintained. Three new emperor penguin colonies were discovered on the shores of the Weddell Sea by members of the Weddell Sea winter project. The long-term Offshore Biological Program continued in the waters near South Georgia. Three Twin Otter aircraft were flown in from the United Kingdom and based at Rothera. They operated throughout the Antarctic Peninsula, supporting field parties and transferring personnel and supplies between stations. All the British bases reported heavier snow accumulations and more extensive sea ice than in the previous four years.

*United States.* Three permanent stations were occupied during the 1987 winter by 212 men and women. Shipboard scientists working with Weddell Sea sediment cores discovered that the West Antarctic ice sheet had formed much more recently than the ice sheet covering East Antarctica. Pollen and spores found in the cores revealed that West Antarctica had been covered with temperate vegetation until about 37 million years ago. Paleontologists working nearby on Seymour Island discovered a spectacular cache of fossils, including crocodiles, a two-metre-tall flightless bird, and a nine-metre-long whale about 40 million years old. These discoveries supported the argument for a land bridge between Antarctica and South America. Biologists working on Lake Hoare in the ice-free Taylor Valley near McMurdo Sound reported a two-metre thinning of the lake's ice cover in the past ten years, perhaps an indication of recent climatic warming.

A U.S.-Poland survey of commercial fishing in Antarctic waters warned of severe depletion of some fish species and krill from overfishing, especially by Soviet fleets. The recently begun ten-year program was also studying the impact of atmospheric ozone depletion on plankton productivity.

A ski-equipped LC-130 Hercules airplane, abandoned in 1971 when it was damaged during a jet-assisted take-off accident, was dug out of ten metres of snow and ice some 1,200 km (750 mi) from McMurdo Station. It was hoped that the plane could be returned to the U.S. for reconditioning. During the recovery effort, another LC-130 crashed and burned, killing two navy crewmen.

*West Germany.* Von Neumeyeer station continued in operation as a year-round base. *Polarstern* conducted summer cruises in the Weddell Sea for oceanographic and marine geology and geophysics. During the winter the ship cruised the winter pack-ice zone, providing a rare opportunity for studying the formation and dynamics of sea ice, as well as the open-water areas along the coast. Biologists were able to observe living processes in the winter ice-covered sea. They found that life developed not in the water column, as previously believed, but on the seafloor and on the underside of ice floes, where krill feed on algal mats that develop in the winter darkness.

**Other Expeditions.** East Germany established a research program at Georg Foster Base independent of the Soviet Union's expedition. Research programs in Earth and atmospheric sciences would be emphasized.

The 90 Degree South Expedition, Monica Kristensen's attempt to duplicate Roald Amundsen's trek to the South Pole, ended about 450 km (280 mi) short of the goal and turned back to meet the relief ship at the base at the Bay of Whales.

Italy's first Antarctic expedition set up a summer base in Gerlache Inlet at Terra Nova Bay. Research programs in meteorology, atmospheric physics, physical oceanography, and Earth and biologic sciences were conducted. Automatic weather stations were installed.

Norway fielded a small expedition to Peter I Island to conduct a detailed mapping and aerial photography program. An automatic weather station was established.

Greenpeace, the international environmental organization, successfully established a small base at Cape Evans on Ross Island. During the 1987 winter it was occupied by three men and one woman.

The Footsteps of Scott Expedition evacuated Jack Hayward Base at Cape Evans. The three men who were left behind to pack up the base during the 1986 winter after their ship was lost were finally evacuated by a Twin Otter that flew in from Punta Arenas, Chile.

(PETER J. ANDERSON)

This article updates the *Macropædia* article ANTARCTICA.

## ARCTIC REGIONS

**U.S. and Canada.** Generally weak crude oil prices continued to have a serious effect on oil and gas activities and on the economies of the North American Arctic region. In February Alaska's unemployment rate was reported to be 10.6%, compared with 6% for the U.S. as a whole. It was forecast that about 12,000 jobs in the state would disappear by 1989. Construction, real estate, government, and the petroleum sector in general were especially hard hit. An economist with the Alaska Pacific Bank recommended that the state shift its focus to the private sector, to mining resource industries, and to tourism and commercial fishing,

where there were favourable prospects for growth. Along these lines, Cominco Ltd. and the NANA native development corporation announced plans to proceed with development of the Red Dog mine near Kotzebue, expected to be the largest zinc producer in the Western world.

In April the U.S. secretary of the interior set the stage for a classic environmental confrontation by recommending that the entire 600,000-ha (1.5 million-ac) coastal plain within Alaska's Arctic National Wildlife Refuge be opened to petroleum development. Conservationists in both the U.S. and Canada said such an action would threaten a delicate and irreplaceable ecological system with permanent damage. The Canadian government claimed that the development could disrupt the calving grounds of the 180,-000-strong Porcupine herd of migratory caribou and hurt native communities in northern Canada that depended on the herd for their livelihood. In another area of dispute, the Interior Department invited U.S. oil companies in August to bid for drilling rights in the Beaufort Sea, including a 360-sq km (140-sq mi) area of Canadian territory near the Yukon-Alaska boundary. The dispute could end up being referred to the World Court.

In Canada the gradual increase in crude oil prices and the prospect of future oil shortages led one of the major oil companies—Gulf Canada Resources Ltd.—to renew its oil exploration at the Amauligak project in the Beaufort Sea. In May, as part of the $4.6 billion project, the company announced that it was considering extending production testing into 1988, possibly leading to full production in the early to mid-1990s.

The Canadian minister of external affairs declared in April that Canada had to be prepared to defend the Arctic if it hoped to assert its national sovereignty in the north. The 1985 incursion of the U.S. icebreaker *Polar Sea* into the Northwest Passage had provoked negotiations with Washington over waters claimed by Canada but regarded by the U.S. as an international strait. A U.S.-Canadian agreement negotiated late in the year provided for Canadian consent to the passage of U.S. icebreakers through the disputed waters but apparently did not represent abandonment of either country's claims. Canada announced plans to expand its presence in the Arctic by building additional military bases, improving radar and under-ice surveillance installations, acquiring nuclear-powered submarines capable of operating throughout the Arctic Ocean, increasing environmental research in the north, and creating new na-

A Canadian Army surveyor takes a reading near Ft. Eureka, Northwest Territories. The result of a 40-year project, the soon-to-be-completed, detailed maps were to be used for military and recreational purposes.

A platform marks a site where an oil rig tested for reserves near the Arctic National Wildlife Refuge. The U.S. secretary of the interior urged the opening of the refuge to oil exploration despite contentions by conservationists that such a move would permanently damage the ecological system.

FRAN DURNER/ANCHORAGE DAILY NEWS

tional parks in the region. In August the government gave the go-ahead for the design of the Polar 8—the world's most powerful icebreaker. The $400 million vessel, scheduled for delivery in 1992, would be capable of operating anywhere in the Arctic through ice 2.4 m (8 ft) thick.

**International Affairs.** In a three-year study of the world's environment, the World Commission on Environment and Development, chaired by Gro Harlem Brundtland, now prime minister of Norway, stated that a measure of the success of global survival policies would be how well countries protect their traditional native societies in the circumpolar Arctic, Australia, the Amazon basin, and other isolated regions. The commission report said that protection of the natives' traditional, life-sustaining rights to land and resources was critical to the preservation not only of the environment but also of the vast accumulation of indigenous knowledge and experience. The report was the focus of a major UN debate in October.

Early in the year a study by the World Wildlife Fund showed that in some parts of the Arctic whales had been hunted almost out of existence; in other areas they were still abundant but threatened. The $2 million study estimated that there were up to 30,000 narwhals in the eastern Arctic regions of Canada and 3,000 to 4,000 bowheads and up to 30,000 belugas in the western Arctic. These populations were considered sufficient to meet the hunting requirements of the aboriginal peoples. However, fears were expressed that future developments, such as increased shipping traffic through the Arctic seas and the damming of rivers for hydroelectric projects, could severely affect some whale species.

The U.S. Environmental Protection Agency approved a technique for tracking the origins of Arctic haze, a pollution pocket—many times worse than the pollution commonly found over large cities—that blankets parts of the northern polar regions. By measuring concentrations of seven trace elements commonly produced by industry, it was possible to locate pollution sources within several hundred miles of the polluted area. The method confirmed previous conjectures that Arctic haze is composed mainly of pollutants from smelters and manufacturing plants in the Soviet Union.

In October a Canadian scientist reported that a massive hole in the ozone layer of the atmosphere over the Arctic, first discovered in 1986, did not reappear in 1987. The presence of a similar ozone hole over the Antarctic prompted at least 24 countries to agree to limit the use of industrial chemicals known to destroy ozone. Ozone in

the high atmosphere protects the planet from the harmful effects of the sun's ultraviolet radiation.

Toward the end of the year Soviet leader Mikhail Gorbachev proposed a wide range of measures to turn the Arctic into a "zone of peace." He proposed that the Warsaw Pact and NATO begin consultations on scaling down military activities in the Greenland, Norwegian, and North seas. It was suggested that the Soviet Union might open its Arctic shipping lanes to foreign vessels and provide icebreaking services. It was also proposed that Canada and Norway join with the U.S.S.R. in creating enterprises for extracting oil and gas from the continental shelf of northern Soviet seas.

Pope John Paul II fulfilled his promise to Canadian natives by meeting with them in Fort Simpson, N.W.T., in September after the end of his ten-day visit to the U.S. The promise was made in 1984 when the pope was unable to reach Fort Simpson because of poor weather conditions.

The Reuters news service reported in August that the Soviet Union appeared to have beaten Norway in the race to find oil in the Barents Sea. However, output from the Kolguyey Island oil field was expected to reach only 10,000 bbl a day by 1990 and was not considered to be commercially viable. Norway had exploratory oil rigs in its sector of the Barents but was embroiled in a 15-year dispute with the U.S.S.R. over large areas of the icy, storm-swept sea.

Completion of a 3,000-km (1,860-mi) natural gas pipeline linking the West Siberian Yamburg gas fields with the city of Yelets in the Russian republic was reported by *Oilweek*. This was the second of six large-diameter (about 1,500 mm [60 in]) pipelines planned for 1986–90 that were to supply European U.S.S.R. with Siberian gas. The Yamburg field was expected to become the Soviet Union's most important gas producer.

A five-man expedition retraced the last great Inuit migration from Baffin Island to northwestern Greenland across 2,500 km (1,600 mi) of sea ice, glaciers, and mountain passes 125 years earlier. The three Inuit who participated in the expedition were all related to members of the original migration. The Canadian government approved a joint 11-man, 1,800-km (1,100-mi) Soviet-Canadian ski expedition across the Arctic Ocean between the Severnaya Zemlya Islands and Cape Columbia on Ellesmere Island. The expedition, which would begin in March 1988, aimed to collect scientific data on the Arctic Ocean and to study the effects of the harsh climate on the team members.

(KENNETH DE LA BARRE)

This article updates the *Macropædia* article The ARCTIC.

# CONTRIBUTORS

**Agrella, Joseph C.** Correspondent, *Blood-Horse* magazine and Associated Press; former Turf Editor, *Chicago Sun-Times.*
SPORTS AND GAMES: *Horse Racing (in part)*
**Allaby, Michael.** Free-lance Writer and Lecturer. Author of *Ecology Facts; Who Will Eat?*
ENVIRONMENT *(in part)*
**Allan, J. A.** Reader in Geography, School of Oriental and African Studies, University of London.
WORLD AFFAIRS: *Libya*
**Aloff, Mindy.** Dance Critic, *The Nation;* Senior Critic, *Dance Magazine.* Editor, *Vassar Quarterly.*
DANCE *(in part)*
**Amedeo, Michael.** Writer, Encyclopædia Britannica Educational Corp.
BIOGRAPHIES *(in part)*
**Anderson, Peter J.** Assistant Director, Byrd Polar Research Center, Ohio State University.
WORLD AFFAIRS: *Antarctica*
**Archibald, John J.** Feature Writer, *St. Louis Post-Dispatch;* Adjunct Professor, Washington University, St. Louis, Mo.
SPORTS AND GAMES: *Bowling (in part)*
**Armstrong, George.** Rome Correspondent, *The Guardian.*
BIOGRAPHIES *(in part);* WORLD AFFAIRS: *Italy*
**Arnold, Guy.** Free-lance Writer. Author of *Modern Nigeria; Aid in Africa.*
BIOGRAPHIES *(in part);* WORLD AFFAIRS: *Botswana; Burundi; Cape Verde; Equatorial Guinea; Gambia, The; Ghana; Guinea-Bissau; Lesotho; Liberia; Maldives; Mauritius; Nigeria; Rwanda; São Tomé and Príncipe; Seychelles; Sierra Leone; Swaziland*
**Arnold, Mavis.** Free-lance Journalist, Dublin.
BIOGRAPHIES *(in part);* WORLD AFFAIRS: *Ireland*
**Arrington, Leonard J.** Formerly Church Historian, Church of Jesus Christ of Latter-day Saints.
RELIGION: *Church of Jesus Christ of Latter-day Saints*
**Bahry, Louay Y.** Adjunct Professor of Political Science, University of Tennessee, Knoxville. Author of *Die Bagdad-Bahn: a Study in the Development and Diplomacy of the Baghdad Railway Question.*
*Macropædia:* BAGHDAD *(in part)*
**Baptist, Ines T.** Free-lance Writer.
WORLD AFFAIRS: *Belize*
**Barford, Michael F.** Editor and Director, *Tabacosmos,* London.
INDUSTRIAL REVIEW: *Tobacco*
**Bargad, Warren.** Samuel M. Melton Professor of Jewish Studies and Director, Center for Jewish Studies, University of Florida.
LITERATURE: *Hebrew*
**Barreiros, Lidia.** Head, Central Office, International Organization of Consumer Unions, The Hague, Neth. Coeditor of *Theory and Policy Design for Basic Needs Planning: A Case Study of Ecuador.*
CONSUMER AFFAIRS *(in part)*
**Barrett, David B.** Missions Researcher, Foreign Mission Board, U.S. Southern Baptist Convention.
RELIGION: *World Religious Statistics*
**Barrett, John C. A.** Headmaster, Kent College, Pembury, England; Secretary, British Committee, World Methodist Council. Author of *Family Worship in Theory and Practice.*
RELIGION: *Methodist Churches*
**Bass, Howard.** Journalist and Broadcaster. Editor, *Winter Sports,* 1948–69; author of 15 books on winter sports.
BIOGRAPHIES *(in part);* SPORTS AND GAMES: *Ice Hockey (in part); Ice Skating; Skiing*
**Bayliss, David.** Director of Planning, London

Regional Transport.
TRANSPORTATION *(in part)*
**Beckwith, David C.** White House Correspondent, *Time* magazine, Washington, D.C.
WORLD AFFAIRS: *United States:* Developments in the States in 1987
**Bergerre, Max.** Vatican Affairs Correspondent, *La Vie Catholique,* Paris.
WORLD AFFAIRS: *Vatican City State*
**Beyer, Reginald Ian.** Deputy Curator, Royal Botanic Gardens, Kew, England.
BOTANICAL GARDENS AND ZOOS *(in part)*
**Bickelhaupt, David L.** Professor of Insurance, Faculty of Finance, College of Business, Ohio State University, Columbus.
INDUSTRIAL REVIEW: *Insurance*
**Bird, Thomas E.** Director, Council for the Study of Ethics and Public Policy, Queens College, City University of New York.
LITERATURE: *Yiddish*
**Boddy, William C.** Editor, *Motor Sport.* Full Member, Guild of Motoring Writers.
SPORTS AND GAMES: *Automobile Racing (in part)*
**Boden, Edward.** Editor, *Veterinary Record.*
HEALTH AND DISEASE: *Veterinary Medicine*
**Booth, John Nicholls.** Lecturer and Writer. Author of *The Quest for Preaching Power.*
RELIGION: *Unitarian (Universalist) Churches*
**Borlaug, Norman E.** Distinguished Professor of International Agriculture, Texas A & M University, College Station.
Feature Article: WORLD REVOLUTION IN AGRICULTURE *(in part)*
**Boswall, Jeffery.** Head of Film and Video, Royal Society for the Protection of Birds, Bedfordshire, England.
LIFE SCIENCES: *Ornithology*
**Box, Ben.** Free-lance Writer and Researcher.
WORLD AFFAIRS: *El Salvador; Honduras; Paraguay; Venezuela*
**Boye, Roger.** Coin columnist, *Chicago Tribune.*
PHILATELY AND NUMISMATICS: *Coins and Paper Money*
**Bradsher, Henry S.** Foreign Affairs Writer.
WORLD AFFAIRS: *Philippines*
**Braidwood, Robert J.** Professor Emeritus of Old World Prehistory, Oriental Institute and Department of Anthropology, University of Chicago. Author of *Prehistoric Men.*
ARCHAEOLOGY: *Eastern Hemisphere*
**Brazee, Rutlage J.** Geophysical Consultant.
EARTH SCIENCES: *Geophysics*
**Brecher, Kenneth.** Professor of Astronomy and Physics, Boston University. Coauthor and coeditor of *Astronomy of the Ancients.*
ASTRONOMY
**Brittain, Victoria.** Third World Review Editor, *The Guardian,* London. Coeditor of *Voices from the South.*
WORLD AFFAIRS: *Commonwealth of Nations*
**Brobyn, Allen F.** Assistant Director (Marketing), Glass Manufacturers Federation, London.
INDUSTRIAL REVIEW: *Glass*
**Burdin, Joel L.** Professor of Educational Administration, City College of the City University of New York.
EDUCATION *(in part)*
**Burke, Donald P.** Executive Editor, *Chemical Week,* New York City.
INDUSTRIAL REVIEW: *Chemicals*
**Burks, Ardath W.** Emeritus Professor of Asian Studies, Rutgers University, New Brunswick, N.J.
WORLD AFFAIRS: *Japan*
**Buss, Robin.** Writer and Lecturer. Author of *The French Through Their Films* and critical guides to Vigny's *Chatterton* and Cocteau's

*Les Enfants terribles.*
BIOGRAPHIES *(in part);* LITERATURE: *French (in part)*
**Butler, Frank.** Former Sports Editor, *News of the World,* London. Author of *The Good, the Bad and the Ugly: A Story of Boxing.*
SPORTS AND GAMES: *Boxing*
**Cameron, Sarah.** Economic Advisor, Latin America and the Caribbean, Economics Department, Lloyds Bank PLC, London.
WORLD AFFAIRS: *Argentina; Mexico*
**Campbell, Alexander Johns.** Economist, Economics Department, Lloyds Bank PLC, London.
WORLD AFFAIRS: *Chile; Colombia*
**Carter, Robert W.** Journalist, London.
SPORTS AND GAMES: *Horse Racing (in part)*
**Caswell, Nim.** Deputy Editor (Africa), The Economist Intelligence Unit, London.
BIOGRAPHIES *(in part);* WORLD AFFAIRS: *Benin; Burkina Faso; Cameroon; Central African Republic; Chad; Comoros; Congo; Côte d'Ivoire; Djibouti; Gabon; Guinea; Madagascar; Mali; Mauritania; Niger; Senegal; Togo*
**Cegielski, Charles M.** Senior Editor, Encyclopædia Britannica Yearbooks.
LIFE SCIENCES: *Introduction*
**Chapman, Kenneth F.** Former Editor, *Stamp Collecting* and *Philatelic Magazine.*
PHILATELY AND NUMISMATICS: *Stamps*
**Chapman, Robin.** Senior Economist, Economics Department, Lloyds Bank PLC, London.
WORLD AFFAIRS: *Brazil; Cuba; Dominican Republic; Haiti; Latin-American Affairs; Uruguay*
**Chappell, Duncan.** Director, Australian Institute of Criminology.
CRIME, LAW ENFORCEMENT, AND PENOLOGY: *Crime; Law Enforcement*
**Chapple, Abby.** Writer, Consumer Communications, Annapolis, Md.
INDUSTRIAL REVIEW: *Furniture*
**Cheuse, Alan.** Writing Faculty, English Department, George Mason University, Fairfax, Va. Author of *The Grandmothers' Club; Candide.*
LITERATURE: *English (in part)*
**Chuprinin, Sergey.** Journalist, Novosti Press Agency, Moscow.
LITERATURE: *Russian (in part)*
**Clark, Janet H.** Staff Editor, *Britannica Book of the Year,* London. Former Far East Editor, Economist Publications.
BIOGRAPHIES *(in part);* RACE RELATIONS *(in part);* WORLD AFFAIRS: *Hungary (in part)*
**Clarke, R. O.** Writer, Paris.
LABOUR–MANAGEMENT RELATIONS
**Cleveland, William A.** Editor, Britannica World Data and *Britannica Atlas.*
MINING
**Cogle, T. C. J.** Editor, *Electrical Review,* London.
INDUSTRIAL REVIEW: *Electrical*
**Cook, David A.** Professor and Director of Film Studies Program, Emory University, Atlanta, Ga. Author of *A History of Narrative Film.*
*Macropædia:* MOTION PICTURES: *History (in part)*
**Costin, Stanley H.** British Correspondent, Nykytekstiili, Finland, and others.
FASHION AND DRESS *(in part)*
**Cromie, William J.** Knight Science Journalism Fellow, Massachusetts Institute of Technology; Executive Director, Council for the Advancement of Science Writing.
INDUSTRIAL REVIEW: *Microelectronics*
**Cross, Colin J.** Chairman, European Polo Academy.
SPORTS AND GAMES: *Polo*
**Crossland, Norman.** Former Bonn Correspon-

dent, *The Economist,* London.
WORLD AFFAIRS: *German Democratic Republic; Germany, Federal Republic of*

**Crowley, Edward.** Editor, *100A1* magazine and Annual Report, Lloyd's Register of Shipping.
INDUSTRIAL REVIEW: *Shipbuilding;* TRANSPORTATION *(in part);* TRANSPORTATION: Sidebar

**Curley, Robert.** Assistant Editor, Encyclopædia Britannica, Inc.
BIOGRAPHIES *(in part)*

**Cviic, K. F.** East European Specialist, *The Economist,* London.
WORLD AFFAIRS: *Yugoslavia*

**David, Tudor.** Education Journalist; former Managing Editor, *Education,* London.
EDUCATION *(in part)*

**Davies, C. R. M.** Research Lecturer in Criminology and Penology, University of Liverpool, England.
CRIME, LAW ENFORCEMENT, AND PENOLOGY: *Prisons and Penology*

**Davis, Donald A.** Editor, *Drug & Cosmetic Industry* and *Cosmetic Insider's Report.*
INDUSTRIAL REVIEW: *Pharmaceuticals*

**Deam, John B.** Technical Director, National Machine Tool Builders Association, McLean, Va.
INDUSTRIAL REVIEW: *Machinery and Machine Tools*

**de la Barre, Kenneth.** Director, Katimavik, Montreal.
WORLD AFFAIRS: *Arctic Regions*

**Denselow, Robin.** Rock Music Critic, *The Guardian,* London; Current Affairs Reporter, BBC Television.
MUSIC: *Popular*

**De Puy, Norman R.** Minister, First Baptist Church, Newton Centre, Mass.; Columnist, *American Baptist* magazine.
RELIGION: *Baptist Churches*

**Deshayes, Marie-Jose.** Head of Documentation Service, International Vine and Wine Office, Paris.
INDUSTRIAL REVIEW: *Beverages (in part)*

**Dirnbacher, Elfriede.** Austrian Civil Servant.
WORLD AFFAIRS: *Austria*

**Dixon, Bernard.** Science Writer and Consultant. European Editor, *The Scientist.* Author of *Magnificent Microbes; Health and the Human Body.*
HEALTH AND DISEASE: *Mental Health; Overview (in part)*

**Dooling, Dave.** Manager, Program Development, Alabama Space and Rocket Center, Huntsville.
SPACE EXPLORATION

**Dorris, Thomas Hartley.** Editor, Ecumenical Press Service, Geneva.
RELIGION: *Lutheran Communion*

**Dowswell, Christopher R.** Consultant in Agricultural Communications.
Feature Article: WORLD REVOLUTION IN AGRICULTURE *(in part)*

**Eli, C. R.** Former Executive Director, U.S. Badminton Association.
SPORTS AND GAMES: *Badminton*

**Engels, Jan R.** Director, Centre Paul Hymans; Editor, *Vooruitgang-Progrès* magazine.
WORLD AFFAIRS: *Belgium*

**Ewing, John.** Professor and Chairman, Department of Mathematics, Indiana University. Author of *Puzzle It Out.*
MATHEMATICS

**Farr, D. M. L.** Professor of History, Carleton University, Ottawa.
WORLD AFFAIRS: *Canada*

**Faust, Joan Lee.** Garden Editor, *New York Times.*
GARDENING *(in part)*

**Fendell, Robert J.** Author of *The New Era Car Book and Auto Survival Guide; Encyclopedia of Auto Racing Greats.*
SPORTS AND GAMES: *Automobile Racing (in part)*

**Fiddick, Peter.** Media Editor, *The Guardian,* London.
BIOGRAPHIES *(in part);* PUBLISHING: *Newspapers (in part); Magazines (in part)*

**Fields, Donald.** Helsinki Correspondent, BBC, *Independent,* and *The Sunday Times,* London.
WORLD AFFAIRS: *Finland*

**Firth, David.** Editor, *The Friend,* London; formerly Editor, *Quaker Monthly,* London.
RELIGION: *Religious Society of Friends*

**Fisher, David.** Self-employed Civil Engineer, formerly with Freeman Fox Ltd., Consulting Engineers, London.
ENGINEERING PROJECTS: *Bridges*

**Franklin, Harold.** Bridge Correspondent, *Yorkshire Post.*
SPORTS AND GAMES: *Contract Bridge*

**Franz, Frederick W.** President, Watch Tower Bible and Tract Society of Pennsylvania.
RELIGION: *Jehovah's Witnesses*

**Fridovich, Irwin.** James B. Duke Professor of Biochemistry, Duke University Medical Center, Durham, N.C.
LIFE SCIENCES: *Molecular Biology (in part)*

**Fridovich-Keil, Judith L.** Postdoctoral Fellow, Department of Pharmacology, Harvard Medical School, Dana Farber Cancer Institute.
LIFE SCIENCES: *Molecular Biology (in part)*

**Friskin, Sydney E.** Hockey Correspondent, *The Times,* London.
SPORTS AND GAMES: *Billiard Games (in part); Field Hockey*

**Frost, David.** Rugby Union Correspondent, *The Guardian,* London.
SPORTS AND GAMES: *Football (in part)*

**Fryburger, Jr., Vernon R.** Professor of Advertising and Marketing and Chairman, Department of Advertising, Northwestern University, Evanston, Ill. Coauthor of *Advertising Theory and Practice.*
*Macropædia:* MARKETING AND MERCHANDISING *(in part)*

**Gaddum, Anthony H.** Chairman, H. T. Gaddum and Company Ltd., Silk Merchants, Macclesfield, Cheshire, England.
INDUSTRIAL REVIEW: *Textiles (in part)*

**Ganado, Albert.** Lawyer, Malta.
BIOGRAPHIES *(in part);* WORLD AFFAIRS: *Malta*

**Ganguly, Dilip.** Senior Correspondent, Associated Press (USA), South Asia Bureau, New Delhi, India.
WORLD AFFAIRS: *Afghanistan; Bangladesh; Bhutan; Burma; Nepal; Pakistan; Sri Lanka*

**Garrad, Rob.** Director of Information Services, International Headquarters, Salvation Army.
RELIGION: *Salvation Army*

**Gibbons, J. Whitfield.** Senior Research Ecologist, Savannah River Ecology Laboratory, Aiken, S.C.
LIFE SCIENCES: *Zoology*

**Gillespie, Hugh M.** Director of Communications, International Road Federation, Washington, D.C.
ENGINEERING PROJECTS: *Roads*

**Gjester, Fay.** Free-lance Journalist and Editor; formerly Oslo Correspondent, *Financial Times,* London.
WORLD AFFAIRS: *Norway*

**Goetz, Philip W.** Editor in Chief, Encyclopædia Britannica, Inc.
PUBLISHING: Special Report

**Goldsmith, Arthur.** Editor-at-Large, *Popular Photography,* New York City.
PHOTOGRAPHY

**Goldstein, William W.** Trade News Editor, *Publishers Weekly.*
PUBLISHING: *Books (in part)*

**Goodwin, Noël.** Free-lance Writer and Broadcaster. Associate Editor and Music Editor, *Dance & Dancers.*
DANCE *(in part)*

**Gottfried, Martin.** Drama Critic, New York City. Author of *A Theater Divided; Opening Nights; Broadway Musicals.*

THEATRE *(in part)*

**Griffiths, A. R. G.** Senior Lecturer in History, Flinders University of South Australia. Author of *Contemporary Australia.*
BIOGRAPHIES *(in part);* WORLD AFFAIRS: *Australia; Australia:* Sidebar; *Nauru; Papua New Guinea*

**Grossman, Joel W.** Archaeologist.
ARCHAEOLOGY: *Western Hemisphere*

**Grumet, Robert S.** Senior Historic Preservation Specialist, Office of New Jersey Heritage, Department of Environmental Protection, New Jersey.
ANTHROPOLOGY

**Hallgren, Richard E.** Assistant Administrator for Weather Services, National Oceanic and Atmospheric Administration.
EARTH SCIENCES: *Meteorology*

**Harper, Nicholas.** Music Writer; Foreign Correspondent, *Fanfare,* Tenafly, N.J.
MUSIC: *Classical*

**Havard-Williams, P.** Professor, Department of Library and Information Studies, Loughborough University, Leicestershire, England.
LIBRARIES *(in part)*

**Hawkland, William D.** Chancellor and Professor of Law, Louisiana State University.
LAW: *Court Decisions*

**Hebblethwaite, Peter.** Vatican Affairs Writer, *National Catholic Reporter,* Kansas City, Mo.
RELIGION: *Roman Catholic Church*

**Hébert, Pierre.** Associate Professor, University of Toronto.
LITERATURE: *French (in part)*

**Hendershott, Myrl C.** Professor of Oceanography, Scripps Institution of Oceanography, La Jolla, Calif.
EARTH SCIENCES: *Oceanography*

**Hess, Marvin G.** Executive Vice-President, National Wrestling Coaches Association.
SPORTS AND GAMES: *Wrestling (in part)*

**Hoeksema, Klaas J.** Assistant Professor, Department of Political Science, Free University, Amsterdam.
WORLD AFFAIRS: *Netherlands, The; Suriname*

**Hogg, Sarah.** Business and Finance Editor, *The Independent,* London.
CRIME, LAW ENFORCEMENT, AND PENOLOGY: Special Report

**Holsöe, Jens W.** Diplomatic Correspondent, *Politiken,* Copenhagen.
WORLD AFFAIRS: *Denmark*

**Hope, Thomas W.** President, Hope Reports, Inc., Rochester, N.Y.
MOTION PICTURES *(in part)*

**Hotimlanska, Leah D.** Editorial Bibliographer, Encyclopædia Britannica, Inc.
BIOGRAPHIES *(in part)*

**Hunnings, Neville March.** Editorial Director, European Law Centre, London. Editor, *Common Market Law Reports.*
LAW: *International Law*

**IEIS.** International Economic Information Services, London.
ECONOMIC AFFAIRS: *World Economy; Stock Exchanges (in part)*

**Ingham, Kenneth.** Emeritus Professor of History, University of Bristol, England. Author of *Jan Christian Smuts: The Conscience of a South African.*
WORLD AFFAIRS: *Angola; Kenya; Malawi; Mozambique; Sudan, The; Tanzania; Uganda; Zaire; Zambia; Zimbabwe*

**Jackson, Martin.** Editor in Chief, *Broadcast* magazine, London.
TELEVISION AND RADIO *(in part)*

**Jacquet, Constant H.** Staff Associate, National Council of Churches. Editor of *Yearbook of American and Canadian Churches.*
WORLD AFFAIRS: *United States (table)*

**Jardine, Adrian.** Company Director. Member, Guild of Yachting Writers.
SPORTS AND GAMES: *Sailing*

**Jaspert, W. Pincus.** Technical and Editorial Consultant. International Editor, *American*

*Printer* and *Worldwide Printer*. Author of *Encyclopaedia of Typefaces*.
INDUSTRIAL REVIEW: *Printing*
**Joffé, George.** Journalist and Writer on North African Affairs.
BIOGRAPHIES *(in part)*; WORLD AFFAIRS: *Algeria; Morocco; Tunisia*
**Jones, D. A. N.** Novelist and Critic. Author of *Parade in Pairs; Never Had It So Good.*
LITERATURE: *Introduction; United Kingdom*
**Jones, W. Glyn.** Professor of European Literature, University of East Anglia, Norwich, England.
LITERATURE: *Danish*
**Joseph, Lou.** Senior Science Writer, Hill and Knowlton, Chicago.
HEALTH AND DISEASE: *Dentistry*
**Jotischky, Helma.** Principal Research Officer, Paint Research Association, London.
INDUSTRIAL REVIEW: *Paints and Varnishes*
**Katz, William A.** Professor, School of Library Science, State University of New York, Albany.
PUBLISHING: *Magazines (in part)*
**Keene, Raymond.** Chess Correspondent, *The Times*, London; International Chess Grandmaster.
SPORTS AND GAMES: *Chess*
**Kelleher, John A.** Group Relations Editor, INL (newspapers), Wellington, N.Z.
BIOGRAPHIES *(in part)*; WORLD AFFAIRS: *New Zealand*
**Kellner, Peter.** Political Columnist, *The Independent*, London. Author of *The Civil Servants: An Inquiry into Britain's Ruling Class; Callaghan: The Road to Number Ten.*
BIOGRAPHIES *(in part)*; WORLD AFFAIRS: *United Kingdom; United Kingdom: Sidebar*
**Kennedy, Richard M.** Agricultural Economist, Agriculture and Trade Analysis Division of the Economic Research Service, U.S. Department of Agriculture.
AGRICULTURE AND FOOD SUPPLIES *(in part)*
**Kilian, Michael D.** Washington Columnist, *Chicago Tribune*. Author of *Flying Can Be Fun.*
SPORTS AND GAMES: *Aerial Sports*
**Kimche, Jon.** Formerly Editor, *New Middle East; Afro-Asian Affairs*, London. Author of *Second Arab Awakening; Palestine or Israel.*
WORLD AFFAIRS: *Israel*
**Kind, Joshua B.** Professor of Art History, Northern Illinois University, De Kalb. Author of *Rouault; Geometry as Abstract Art.*
MUSEUMS *(in part)*
**Kloos, Jean Clark Cameron.** Editor, *Timber Trades Journal.*
INDUSTRIAL REVIEW: *Wood Products*
**Knecht, Jean.** Formerly Assistant Foreign Editor, *Le Monde*, Paris.
WORLD AFFAIRS: *France*
**Knox, Richard A.** Technical Author; formerly Editor, *Nuclear Engineering International*, London.
INDUSTRIAL REVIEW: *Nuclear Industry*
**Kolata, Gina.** Writer, *Science* magazine, Washington, D.C. Coauthor of *The High Blood Pressure Book.*
HEALTH AND DISEASE: *Overview (in part)*
**Krengel, Janet.** Economist, Economics Department, Lloyds Bank PLC, London.
BIOGRAPHIES *(in part)*; WORLD AFFAIRS: *Bolivia; Costa Rica; Ecuador; Guatemala; Nicaragua; Peru*
**Kushnick, Louis.** Lecturer, Department of American Studies, University of Manchester, England.
POPULATIONS AND POPULATION MOVEMENTS: *International Migration;* RACE RELATIONS *(in part)*
**Lamb, Kevin M.** Sportswriter, *Chicago Sun-Times.* Author of *Quarterbacks, Nickelbacks & Other Loose Change.*
BIOGRAPHIES *(in part)*; SPORTS AND GAMES: *Football (in part)*

**Laqueur, Walter.** Codirector, Institute of Contemporary History and Wiener Library, London. Author of *Europe Since Hitler.*
WORLD AFFAIRS: *Introduction*
**Larson, Roy.** Editor and Publisher, *The Chicago Reporter.*
RELIGION: *Introduction*
**Larsson, Gerd.** Japan Correspondent, *Dagens Industri.*
BIOGRAPHIES *(in part)*
**Laskey, Elizabeth.** Copy Editor, Encyclopædia Britannica, Inc.
BIOGRAPHIES *(in part)*
**Law, Philip James Stopford.** Senior Lecturer in Marketing, London Business School. Editor of *Product Management Readings.*
*Macropædia:* MARKETING AND MERCHANDISING *(in part)*
**Lee, Audrey Bertina.** Director of Information, Office of Communication, Christian Church (Disciples of Christ).
RELIGION: *Christian Church (Disciples of Christ)*
**Legassick, Martin.** Coordinator (honorary), Southern Africa Labour Education Project; formerly Senior Lecturer in Sociology, University of Warwick, Coventry, England.
WORLD AFFAIRS: *Dependent States (in part); South Africa*
**Legum, Colin.** Associate Editor (1947–81), *The Observer;* Editor, *Africa Contemporary Record* and *Third World Reports*, London.
BIOGRAPHIES *(in part)*; WORLD AFFAIRS: *African Affairs*
**Lennox-Kerr, Peter.** Editor, *High Performance Textiles;* European Editor, *Textile World.* Author of *The World Fibres Book.*
INDUSTRIAL REVIEW: *Textiles (in part)*
**Litsky, Frank.** Sportswriter, *New York Times.*
SPORTS AND GAMES: *Ice Hockey (in part)*
**Logan, Robert G.** Sportswriter, *Chicago Tribune.* Author of *Cubs Win!; So You Think You're a Diehard Cub Fan.*
SPORTS AND GAMES: *Basketball (in part)*
**Longmore, Andrew.** Free-lance Sportswriter, *The Times;* former Assistant Editor, *The Cricketer.*
BIOGRAPHIES *(in part)*; SPORTS AND GAMES: *Cricket*
**Low, George.** Editor, *Education*, London.
EDUCATION *(in part)*
**Luling, Virginia R.** Social Anthropologist.
WORLD AFFAIRS: *Somalia*
**McBride, Gail W.** Free-lance Medical Writer and Editor; formerly Editor, Medical News section, *Journal of the American Medical Association.*
HEALTH AND DISEASE: Special Report
**McCauley, Martin.** Senior Lecturer in Soviet and East European Studies, School of Slavonic and East European Studies, University of London.
BIOGRAPHIES *(in part)*; WORLD AFFAIRS: *Union of Soviet Socialist Republics; Union of Soviet Socialist Republics:* Special Report
**Macdonald, Barrie.** Reader in History, Massey University, Palmerston North, N.Z.
BIOGRAPHIES *(in part)*; WORLD AFFAIRS: *Dependent States (in part); Fiji; Kiribati; Oceanian Affairs; Solomon Islands; Tonga; Tuvalu; Vanuatu; Western Samoa*
**McGregor, Alan.** Geneva Correspondent, *The Times*, London; Swiss Radio International, Bern; ABC, Australia; and RNZ, New Zealand.
WORLD AFFAIRS: *Switzerland*
**McLachlan, Keith S.** Senior Lecturer, School of Oriental and African Studies, University of London.
BIOGRAPHIES *(in part)*; WORLD AFFAIRS: *Iran*
**Mahn, Renee J.** Publications Editor, American Power Boat Association.
SPORTS AND GAMES: *Motorboating*
**Mallett, H. M. F.** Editor, *Wool Record Weekly Market Report*, Bradford, England.
INDUSTRIAL REVIEW: *Textiles (in part)*

**Mango, Andrew.** Orientalist and Broadcaster.
WORLD AFFAIRS: *Turkey*
**Marr, Phebe A.** Senior Fellow, National Defense University, Washington, D.C.; former Associate Professor of History, University of Tennessee, Knoxville. Author of *The Modern History of Iraq.*
*Macropædia:* BAGHDAD *(in part)*
**Marty, Martin E.** Fairfax M. Cone Distinguished Service Professor of the History of Modern Christianity, University of Chicago.
RELIGION: Special Report
**Mateja, James L.** Auto Editor, Columnist, and Financial Reporter, *Chicago Tribune.* Author of *Used Cars: Finding the Best Buy.*
INDUSTRIAL REVIEW: *Automobiles (in part)*
**Matthews, Ian D.** Manager, International Affairs, British Steel Corp.
INDUSTRIAL REVIEW: *Iron and Steel*
**Matthíasson, Björn.** Economist, Central Bank of Iceland.
BIOGRAPHIES *(in part)*; WORLD AFFAIRS: *Iceland*
**Mazie, David M.** Associate of Carl T. Rowan, syndicated columnist. Free-lance Writer.
SOCIAL SECURITY AND WELFARE SERVICES *(in part)*
**Mazze, Edward Mark.** Professor of Marketing, School of Business Administration, Temple University, Philadelphia.
CONSUMER AFFAIRS *(in part)*; INDUSTRIAL REVIEW: *Advertising*
**Mermel, T. W.** Consultant; formerly Chairman, Committee on World Register of Dams.
ENGINEERING PROJECTS: *Dams; Dams table*
**Meyendorff, John.** Professor, Dean of St. Vladimir's Orthodox Theological Seminary; Professor of History, Fordham University, New York City.
RELIGION: *The Orthodox Church; Eastern Non-Chalcedonian Churches*
**Miles, Peter W.** University of Adelaide, Australia.
LIFE SCIENCES: *Entomology*
**Millikin, Sandra.** Architectural Historian.
ARCHITECTURE; ART EXHIBITIONS AND ART SALES: *Art Exhibitions;* BIOGRAPHIES *(in part)*; MUSEUMS *(in part)*
**Miyake, Riichi.** Associate Professor, Department of Architecture and Building Engineering, Shibaura Institute of Technology, Japan.
BIOGRAPHIES *(in part)*
**Modiano, Mario.** Athens Correspondent, *The Times*, London.
WORLD AFFAIRS: *Greece*
**Monaco, Albert M., Jr.** Executive Director, United States Volleyball Association.
SPORTS AND GAMES: *Volleyball*
**Moore, John E.** Hydrologist, Reston, Va.
EARTH SCIENCES: Hydrology
**Moragne, Edward Paul.** Index Editor, Encyclopædia Britannica, Inc.
BIOGRAPHIES *(in part)*
**Morgenstern, Dan M.** Director, Institute of Jazz Studies, Rutgers, The State University of New Jersey. Author of *Jazz People.*
MUSIC: *Jazz*
**Morris, Jacqui M.** Editor, *Oryx* magazine.
ENVIRONMENT *(in part)*
**Morrison, Donald.** Senior Editor, *Time.*
PUBLISHING: *Newspapers (in part)*; WORLD AFFAIRS: *United States:* Special Report
**Mosey, Chris.** Associate Editor, *Sweden Now*, Stockholm; Nordic Correspondent, *The Observer;* Swedish Correspondent, *The Times.*
WORLD AFFAIRS: *Sweden*
**Müller-Brockmann, Josef.** Graphic Designer, Lecturer, and Writer; IBM European Design Consultant. Author of *The Graphic Artist and His Design Problems.*
*Macropædia:* MARKETING AND MERCHANDISING *(in part)*
**Napier, Elspeth.** Editor of publications of the Royal Horticultural Society.
GARDENING *(in part)*

**Naylor, Ernest.** Lloyd Roberts Professor of Zoology, University College of North Wales.
LIFE SCIENCES: *Marine Biology*
**Nelson, Bert.** Editor, *Track and Field News.* Author of *Olympic Track and Field.*
SPORTS AND GAMES: *Track and Field Sports*
**Netschert, Bruce C.** Vice-President, National Economic Research Associates, Inc., Washington, D.C.
ENERGY
**Neusner, Jacob.** University Professor, Brown University, Providence, R.I. Author of *Judaism, The Evidence of the Mishnah.*
RELIGION: *Judaism*
**Newby, Donald J.** Bowls Correspondent, *Daily Telegraph,* London; former Editor, *World Bowls.*
SPORTS AND GAMES: *Lawn Bowls*
**Newton, Carolyn D.** Assistant Science Editor, *Compton's Encyclopedia.*
BIOGRAPHIES *(in part)*
**Niwa, Takuzo.** Deputy Editor, Commentary and Feature Department, *Japan Economic Journal.*
INFORMATION PROCESSING AND INFORMATION SYSTEMS *(in part)*
**Nixon, Robert W.** Director, Communication Department, General Conference of Seventh-day Adventists, Washington, D.C.
RELIGION: *Seventh-day Adventist Church*
**Noblett, Geoffrey J.** Senior Planning Engineer (Tunnels), Channel Tunnel Project Transmanche Link Joint Venture, London.
ENGINEERING PROJECTS: *Tunnels*
**Noel, H. S.** Editor, *World Fishing,* England.
AGRICULTURE AND FOOD SUPPLIES: *Fisheries*
**Norman, Geraldine.** Saleroom Correspondent, *The Times,* London. Author of *The Sale of Works of Art; Nineteenth Century Painters and Painting;* Coauthor of *The Fake's Progress.*
ART EXHIBITIONS AND ART SALES: *Art Sales*
**Oberman, Bonnie.** Writer and Editor.
BIOGRAPHIES *(in part)*
**O'Donoghue, Michael.** Curator, Science Reference Library, London; Lecturer in Gemmology, City of London Polytechnic.
INDUSTRIAL REVIEW: *Gemstones*
**O'Dwyer, Thomas.** Director, Levant Bureau; Writer on East Mediterranean Affairs, Nicosia, Cyprus.
WORLD AFFAIRS: *Cyprus*
**Olney, P. J.** Curator of Birds and Reptiles, Zoological Society of London. Editor, *International Zoo Yearbook.*
BOTANICAL GARDENS AND ZOOS: *Zoos*
**Osborne, Keith.** Editor, *British Rowing Almanack.* Author of *Boat Racing in Britain, 1715–1975.*
SPORTS AND GAMES: *Rowing*
**Osterbind, Carter C.** Associate, Gerontology Center, and Professor Emeritus of Economics, University of Florida.
INDUSTRIAL REVIEW: *Building and Construction*
**Palmer, John.** European Editor, *The Guardian,* London.
BIOGRAPHIES *(in part);* WORLD AFFAIRS: *Western European Affairs*
**Palmer, S. B.** Professor of Experimental Physics, Department of Physics, University of Warwick, England.
PHYSICS; PHYSICS: Sidebar
**Parker, Sandy.** Publisher of weekly international newsletter on fur industry; Copublisher, *Fur World.*
INDUSTRIAL REVIEW: *Furs*
**Paul, Charles Robert, Jr.** Special Assistant to the Secretary-General, U.S. Olympic Committee, Colorado Springs.
SPORTS AND GAMES: *Gymnastics; Weight Lifting*
**Penfold, Robin C.** Free-lance Writer on industrial topics. Editor, *Shell Petrochemicals.* Author of *A Journalist's Guide to Plastics.*
INDUSTRIAL REVIEW: *Plastics*

**Pertile, Lino.** Reader in Italian, University of Sussex, England.
LITERATURE: *Italian*
**Petherick, Karin.** Reader in Swedish, University of London.
LITERATURE: Swedish
**Pfeffer, Irving.** Attorney. Author of *The Financing of Small Business.*
ECONOMIC AFFAIRS: *Stock Exchanges (in part)*
**Pinfold, Geoffrey M.** Director, NCL Stewart Scott Ltd., London. Author of *Reinforced Concrete Chimneys and Towers.*
ENGINEERING PROJECTS: *Buildings*
**Plotnik, Arthur.** Editor, *American Libraries* magazine, American Library Association.
LIBRARIES *(in part)*
**Pollack, Jonathan D.** Senior Staff Member, Political Science Department, Rand Corp., Santa Monica, Calif.
WORLD AFFAIRS: *China; Taiwan*
**Post, Avery D.** President, United Church of Christ, New York City.
RELIGION: *United Church of Christ*
**Prasad, H. Y. Sharada.** Information Adviser to the Prime Minister, New Delhi, India.
BIOGRAPHIES *(in part);* WORLD AFFAIRS: *India*
**Prince, Rod.** Journalist specializing in Caribbean matters. Editor, *Caribbean Insight.*
BIOGRAPHIES *(in part);* WORLD AFFAIRS: *Antigua and Barbuda; Bahamas, The; Barbados; Dependent States (in part); Dominica; Grenada; Guyana; Jamaica; Saint Christopher and Nevis; Saint Lucia; Saint Vincent and the Grenadines; Trinidad and Tobago*
**Ranger, Robin.** Bradley Resident Scholar, The Heritage Foundation, Washington, D.C. Author of *Arms and Politics 1958–1978; Arms Control in a Changing Political Context.*
MILITARY AFFAIRS; MILITARY AFFAIRS: Special Report
**Ray, G. F.** Senior Research Fellow, National Institute of Economic and Social Research, London.
INDUSTRIAL REVIEW: *Introduction*
**Read, Anthony A.** Director, Book Development Council, London.
PUBLISHING: *Books (in part)*
**Rebelo, L. S.** Reader, Department of Portuguese Studies, King's College, University of London.
LITERATURE: *Portuguese (in part)*
**Reid, J. H.** Reader in German, University of Nottingham, England. Author of *Heinrich Böll: Withdrawal and Re-emergence.*
LITERATURE: *German*
**Reid, Philip D.** Professor of Biological Sciences, Smith College, Northampton, Mass.
LIFE SCIENCES: *Botany*
**Reynolds, Frank E.** Professor of the History of Religions and Buddhist Studies, Divinity School, University of Chicago.
RELIGION: *Buddhism (in part)*
**Ripley, Michael D.** Senior Public Relations Officer, Brewers' Society, U.K.
INDUSTRIAL REVIEW: *Beverages (in part)*
**Robinson, David.** Film Critic, *The Times,* London. Author of *A History of World Cinema; Chaplin: His Life and Art.*
MOTION PICTURES *(in part);* MOTION PICTURES: Sidebar
**Rollin, Jack.** Association Football Columnist, *Sunday Telegraph,* London. Coeditor, *Daily Telegraph Football Year Book.* Author of England's *World Cup Triumph; Guinness Book of Soccer Facts and Feats.*
SPORTS AND GAMES: *Football (in part)*
**Rosenberg, Robert.** Computer Editor, *Data Communications* magazine, New York City.
INDUSTRIAL REVIEW: *Telecommunications*
**Saeki, Shoichi.** Professor of Literature, Chuo University, Tokyo. Author of *In Search of Japanese Ego.*
LITERATURE: *Japanese*
**Sarahete, Yrjö.** General Secretary, Fédération Internationale des Quilleurs, Helsinki.

SPORTS AND GAMES: *Bowling (in part)*
**Sarmiento, Sergio.** Editor in Chief, Spanish-language publications, Encyclopædia Britannica Publishers, Inc.
SPORTS AND GAMES: *Baseball (in part); Football (in part)*
**Schoenfield, Albert.** Formerly Publisher, *Swimming World;* Vice-Chairman, U.S. Olympic Swimming Committee; Honoree, International Swimming Hall of Fame.
SPORTS AND GAMES: *Swimming*
**Schöpflin, George.** Lecturer in East European Political Institutions, London School of Economics and School of Slavonic and East European Studies, University of London.
WORLD AFFAIRS: *Czechoslovakia; Eastern European Affairs*
**Searjeant, Graham.** Financial Editor, *The Times,* London.
ECONOMIC AFFAIRS: Special Report
**Sell, Alan P. F.** Theological Secretary, World Alliance of Reformed Churches, Geneva.
RELIGION: *Reformed, Presbyterian, and Congregational Churches*
**Shackleford, Peter.** Chief of Research, World Tourism Organization, Madrid.
INDUSTRIAL REVIEW: *Tourism*
**Shelley, Andrew.** Competitions Manager, Squash Rackets Association, England.
SPORTS AND GAMES: *Squash Rackets*
**Shepherd, Melinda.** Copy Editor, Encyclopædia Britannica, Inc.
BIOGRAPHIES *(in part);* HEALTH AND DISEASE: Sidebar
**Sherwood, Martin A.** Employed in the pharmaceutical industry. Author of *New Worlds in Chemistry.*
CHEMISTRY
**Simpson, Noel.** Managing Director, Sydney Bloodstock Proprietary Ltd., Sydney.
SPORTS AND GAMES: *Horse Racing (in part)*
**Smith, Donald.** Editor, *Rubber World* magazine, Akron, Ohio.
INDUSTRIAL REVIEW: *Rubber*
**Smith, Reuben W.** Dean, Graduate School, and Professor of History, University of the Pacific, Stockton, Calif.
RELIGION: *Islam*
**Smogorzewski, K. M.** Writer on contemporary history. Founder and Editor, *Free Europe,* London.
BIOGRAPHIES *(in part);* WORLD AFFAIRS: *Albania; Andorra; Bulgaria; Hungary (in part); Liechtenstein; Luxembourg; Monaco; Mongolia; Poland; Political Parties; Romania; San Marino*
**Stern, Irwin.** Assistant Professor of Portuguese, Columbia University, New York City.
LITERATURE: *Portuguese (in part)*
**Stevens, Kate.** Director, Gameway Ltd.; former Assistant Editor, *British Toys and Hobbies Briefing.*
INDUSTRIAL REVIEW: *Games and Toys*
**Støverud, Torbjørn.** Honorary Research Fellow, University College, London.
LITERATURE: *Norwegian*
**Sullivan, H. Patrick.** Dean of the College and Professor of Religion, Vassar College, Poughkeepsie, N.Y.
RELIGION: *Hinduism*
**Suzuki, Toshihiko.** Associate Editor, *Newsweek Japan,* TBS-Britannica Co., Ltd., Tokyo.
SPORTS AND GAMES: *Baseball (in part)*
**Sweetinburgh, Thelma.** Fashion Writer, Paris.
BIOGRAPHIES *(in part);* FASHION AND DRESS *(in part)*
**Swift, Richard N.** Professor Emeritus of Politics, New York University, New York City.
WORLD AFFAIRS: *United Nations*
**Synan, Vinson.** Chairman, North American Renewal Services Committee. Author of *The Holiness-Pentecostal Movement.*
RELIGION: *Pentecostal Churches*

**Taggart, Charles Johnson.** Free-lance Writer.
BIOGRAPHIES *(in part)*
**Taishoff, Lawrence B.** President, Broadcasting Publications, Inc., and Publisher, *Broadcasting* magazine and others.
TELEVISION AND RADIO *(in part)*
**Tak, Jean van der.** Formerly Senior Editor, Population Reference Bureau, Inc.
POPULATIONS AND POPULATION MOVEMENTS: *Demography*
**Talbot, Nathan A.** Manager, Committees on Publication, The First Church of Christ, Scientist, Boston.
RELIGION: *Church of Christ, Scientist*
**Tallan, Norman M.** Chief, Metals and Ceramics Division, Materials Laboratory, Wright-Patterson Air Force Base, Dayton, Ohio.
INDUSTRIAL REVIEW: *Ceramics*
**Tateishi, Kay K.** Free-lance Writer and Translator.
BIOGRAPHIES *(in part)*
**Theiner, George.** Editor, *Index on Censorship,* London. Coauthor of *The Kill Dog;* editor of *New Writing in Czechoslovakia.*
LITERATURE: *Eastern European; Russian (in part)*
**Tingay, Lance.** Former Tennis Correspondent, *Daily Telegraph,* London. Author of *100 Years of Wimbledon; Tennis Facts and Feats.*
SPORTS AND GAMES: *Tennis*
**Trilling, Ossia.** Coeditor and Contributor, *International Theatre.* Contributor, BBC, *The Times,* London, and other media.
THEATRE *(in part)*
**UNHCR.** The Office of the United Nations High Commissioner for Refugees.
POPULATIONS AND POPULATION MOVEMENTS: *Refugees*
**Utt, Roger L.** Formerly Assistant Professor of Spanish, Department of Romance Languages and Literatures, University of Chicago.
LITERATURE: *Spanish (in part)*
**Vale, Norman K.** Retired Director of News Services, The United Church of Canada.
RELIGION: *The United Church of Canada*
**Venzke, Bruce E. H.** Associate Editor, *Pool & Billiard Magazine;* Member, Statistics and Records Committee, Billiard Congress of America; President, Billiard Congress of Wisconsin.
SPORTS AND GAMES: *Billiard Games (in part)*
**Verdi, Robert William.** Sports Columnist, *Chicago Tribune.*
SPORTS AND GAMES: *Baseball (in part)*
**Villacorta, Lynn.** Social Security Specialist,

International Labour Office, Geneva.
SOCIAL SECURITY AND WELFARE SERVICES *(in part)*
**Vint, Arthur Kingsley.** Counselor, International Table Tennis Federation.
SPORTS AND GAMES: *Table Tennis*
**Walters, Jonathan S.** Ph.D. Candidate, Divinity School, University of Chicago.
RELIGION: *Buddhism (in part)*
**Warner, Antony C.** Editor, *Drinks Retailing,* London.
INDUSTRIAL REVIEW: *Beverages (in part)*
**Warner, Edward S.** Executive Editor, East Coast, *Infoworld* magazine, Palo Alto, Calif.
INFORMATION PROCESSING AND INFORMATION SYSTEMS *(in part)*
**Watson, Louise.** London Editor, *Britannica Book of the Year.*
WORLD AFFAIRS: *Dependent States (in part)*
**Way, Diane Lois.** Historical Researcher.
BIOGRAPHIES *(in part)*
**Webber, Frederick L.** President, National Soft Drink Association, Washington, D.C.
INDUSTRIAL REVIEW: *Beverages (in part)*
**Weinthal, John R.** Writer on the automotive industry.
INDUSTRIAL REVIEW: *Automobiles (in part)*
**Welch, Melvin D.** Secretary, English Basket Ball Association; Editor (1971–78), *Basketball Magazine.*
SPORTS AND GAMES: *Basketball (in part)*
**Whelan, John.** Publishing Director, *Middle East Economic Digest* and *Africa Economic Digest.*
WORLD AFFAIRS: *Bahrain; Egypt; Iraq; Jordan; Kuwait; Lebanon; Middle Eastern and North African Affairs; Oman; Qatar; Saudi Arabia; Syria; United Arab Emirates; Yemen, People's Democratic Republic of; Yemen Arab Republic*
**Whitney, Barbara.** Senior Copy Editor, Encyclopædia Britannica, Inc.
BIOGRAPHIES *(in part)*
**Wilkinson, John R.** Sportswriter, East Midland Provincial Newspapers Ltd., U.K.
SPORTS AND GAMES: *Cycling*
**Williams, Michael E. J.** Golf Correspondent, *Daily Telegraph,* London.
SPORTS AND GAMES: *Golf*
**Williams, Raymond Leslie.** Professor of Spanish, University of Colorado, Boulder.
LITERATURE: *Spanish (in part)*
**Williamson, Trevor.** Chief Sports Subeditor, *Daily Telegraph,* London.
BIOGRAPHIES *(in part);* SPORTS AND GAMES: *Football (in part)*

**Wilson, Michael.** Free-lance Aviation Writer and Consultant.
INDUSTRIAL REVIEW: *Aerospace*
**Witte, Randall E.** Editor, *The Western Horseman* magazine, Colorado Springs, Colo.
SPORTS AND GAMES: *Rodeo*
**Woodrow, Robert.** Assistant Managing Editor, *Asiaweek,* Hong Kong.
BIOGRAPHIES *(in part);* WORLD AFFAIRS: *Brunei; Dependent States (in part); Indonesia; Kampuchea; Korea; Laos; Malaysia; Singapore; Southeast Asian Affairs; Thailand; Vietnam*
**Woods, Elizabeth.** Writer. Author of *The Yellow Volkswagen; Gone; Men; The Amateur.*
LITERATURE: *English (in part)*
**Woollen, Anthony.** Editor (1959–79), *Food Manufacture,* London. Editor, *Food Industries Manual* (20th ed.).
AGRICULTURE AND FOOD SUPPLIES: *Food Processing*
**Wooller, Michael.** Economist, Economics Dept., Lloyds Bank PLC, London.
WORLD AFFAIRS: *Portugal; Spain*
**Woolley, David.** International Editor, *Airline Executive;* Contributing Editor, *Airport Forum.*
TRANSPORTATION *(in part)*
**Worsnop, Richard L.** Associate Editor, Editorial Research Reports, Washington, D.C.
WORLD AFFAIRS: *United States*
**Wright, Almon R.** Retired Senior Historian, U.S. Department of State.
WORLD AFFAIRS: *Panama*
**Wyllie, Peter John.** Division of Geological and Planetary Sciences, California Institute of Technology.
EARTH SCIENCES: *Geology and Geochemistry*
**Yang, Winston L. Y.** Chairman, Department of Asian Studies, Seton Hall University, South Orange, N.J.
BIOGRAPHIES *(in part);* LITERATURE: *Chinese*
**Yoshida, Nobuyoshi.** Executive Editor, *Industrial Japan,* Tokyo.
INDUSTRIAL REVIEW: *Automobiles (in part)*
**Young, M. Norvel.** Chancellor Emeritus, Pepperdine University, Malibu, Calif. Author of *Preachers of Today.*
RELIGION: *Churches of Christ*
**Young, Susan.** News Editor, *Church Times,* London.
RELIGION: *Anglican Communion*
**Zeidenberg, Leonard.** Chief Correspondent, *Broadcasting* magazine, Washington, D.C.
TELEVISION AND RADIO *(in part)*

# 1988
# Britannica
# World Data

Encyclopædia Britannica, Inc.
Chicago
Auckland/Geneva/London/Manila/Paris/Rome
Seoul/Sydney/Tokyo/Toronto

# CONTENTS

# INTRODUCTION

*Britannica World Data* provides a statistical portrait of some 221 countries and dependencies of the world, at a level appropriate to the size and importance of each. It contains 186 country statements, ranging in length from one to four pages, for the largest and most significant of these, and permits, in the development of more than a score of major thematic subject areas (employment, agriculture, trade), simultaneous comparison among all of these larger countries and 35 additional smaller dependent states.

Updated annually, *Britannica World Data* can be consulted as a separate work of reference developing a particular body of subject matter, but it is particularly intended as direct, structured support for many of Britannica's other reference works—encyclopedias, yearbooks, atlases—at a level of detail that their editorial style or space requirements do not permit.

Like the textual, graphic, or cartographic modes of expression of these other products, statistics possess their own inherent editorial virtues and weaknesses. Two principal goals in the creation of *Britannica World Data* were up-to-dateness and comparability, each possible separately, but not always possible to combine. If, for example, research on some subject (say, registered motor vehicles) is completed during a particular year ($x$), figures may be available for 100 countries for the preceding year ($x-1$), for 140 countries for the year before that ($x-2$), and for 180 countries for the year before that ($x-3$).

Which year should be the basis of a thematic compilation for 221 countries so as to give the best combination of up-to-dateness and comparability? And, should $x-1$ be adopted for the thematic table, ought up-to-dateness in the country table (for which year $x$ is already available) be sacrificed for agreement with the thematic table? In general, the editors have opted for maximum up-to-dateness in the country statistical boxes and maximum comparability in the thematic tables, so as to take the best advantage of late information, published and unpublished.

Comparability, however, also resides in the meaning of the numbers compiled, which may differ greatly from country to country. The headnotes to the thematic tables explain many of these definitional problems; the Glossary serves the same purpose for the country statistical pages. Since the researcher or editor does not always find a neat, unambiguous choice between a datum compiled on two different bases (say, railroad track length, or route length), one of which is wanted and the other not, a choice must be made between the latest official national data (which may be incomplete, published only after a delay of several years, politically suspect, compiled on the wrong basis [for international comparability], or may refer to some time period other than a standard Gregorian calendar year) and some external figure, often only an estimate, compiled by an international organization (such as the UN, FAO, or IMF), on the desired basis, but often at a considerable remove from the country's own most recent data, both in time and distance. Every effort has been made to obtain the best combination of comparability and up-to-dateness from available sources, and, when the completeness of a country's published data permitted, to analyze it further for better agreement in coverage, scope, and datedness, For certain subjects, especially population, the editors have prepared their own estimates.

The published basis of the information compiled is the statistical collections of Encyclopædia Britannica, Inc., some of the principal elements of which are enumerated in the Bibliography. All of these sources are held, and updated continuously for editorial use, in Britannica's editorial offices. The publications themselves are issued in some 75 languages in common use among the countries of the world; the information contained in them is supplemented by unpublished data received in correspondence from the countries concerned. Usual holdings for a country with a well-developed statistical and publishing program may include any of the following kinds of documents: the national statistical abstract; the most recent censuses of population; periodic or occasional reports on vital statistics, social indicators, agriculture, mining, labour, manufacturing, wholesale and retail trade, finance and banking, development planning, foreign trade, transportation, and communication. These primarily statistical sources are supplemented by other kinds of national reference works, such as gazetteers (of place names), national atlases, constitutions, and monographs by domestic or external analysts.

No reference work on the countries of the world can, or should, be used in isolation. To say that the population density of Hungary is about 300 persons per square mile will not be misleading, because the population is rather evenly distributed across the landscape outside the cities. To give a density for Greenland calculated on the same basis (total population ÷ total area) *would* be misleading (and would amount to only 0.06 person per square mile) because much of Greenland is uninhabitable ice cap. Similarly, the great majority of the social, economic, and financial data contained in this work should not be interpreted in isolation. Interpretive text of long perspective, such as that of the *Encyclopædia Britannica* itself; political, geographic, and topical maps; and recent analysis of political events and economic trends, such as that contained in the articles of the *Book of the Year*, will all help to supply balance, physical framework, and analytical focus that numbers alone cannot provide. By the same token, study of those sources will be amplified and made more concrete by use of the *Britannica World Data* to supply up-to-date geographic, demographic, economic, and financial data to illuminate the generalized and more impressionistic methodology of those works.

# GLOSSARY

A number of terms that are used to classify and report data in the "Nations of the World" section require some explanation.

Those italicized terms that are used regularly in the country compilations to introduce specific categories of information (*e.g., birth rate, budget*) appear in this glossary in italic boldface type, followed by a description of the precise kind of information being offered and how it has been edited and presented.

All other terms are printed here in roman boldface type. Many terms have quite specific meanings in statistical reporting, and they are so defined here. Other terms have less specific application as they are used by different countries or organizations. Data in the country compilations based on definitions markedly different from those below will usually be footnoted.

Terms that appear in small capitals in certain definitions are themselves defined at their respective alphabetical locations.

Terms whose definitions are marked by an asterisk (*) refer to data supplied only in the larger two- to four-page country compilations.

***access to services,*** a group of measures indicating the general population's level of access to public services, including electrical power, treated public drinking water, sewage removal, and fire protection.*

**activity rate,** *see* participation rate.

***age breakdown,*** the distribution of a given population by age, usually reported here as percentages of total population in each of six 15-year age brackets. When substantial numbers of persons censused do not know, or state, their exact age, reported distributions may not total 100.0%.

***area and population,*** a tabulation usually including the first-order administrative subdivisions of the country (such as the states of the United States), with capital or administrative seat, area, and population. When these subdivisions are especially numerous, or, occasionally, nonexistent, a regional, political, electoral, census, or other nonadministrative scheme of subdivisions has been substituted.

**associated state,** *see* (free) association; *see* state.

**balance of payments,** a statistical statement for a given period showing the balance among: (1) transactions in goods, services, and income between a country and the rest of the world, (2) changes in ownership or valuation of that country's monetary gold, SPECIAL DRAWING RIGHTS, and claims on and liabilities to the rest of the world, and (3) unrequited transfers and counterpart entries needed (in an accounting sense) to balance transactions and changes among any of the foregoing types of exchange that are not mutually offsetting. The United Nations *System of National Accounts* (SNA) provides a framework for international comparability in classifying such transactions, but detail of local law as to what constitutes a transaction, basis of valuation, reporting periods, and the size of a transaction visible to fiscal authorities all result in differences in the meaning of a particular national statement.*

***balance of trade,*** the net value of all international goods trade of a country, usually excluding reexports (goods received only for transshipment), and the percentage that this net represents of total trade.

Balance of trade refers only to the "visible" international trade of goods as recorded by customs authorities and is thus a segment of a country's BALANCE OF PAYMENTS, which takes all visible and invisible trade with other countries into account. (Invisible trade refers to imports and exports of money, financial instruments, and services such as transport, tourism, and insurance.) A country has a favourable balance of trade when the value of exports exceeds that of imports.

**barrel** (bbl), a unit of liquid measure. The barrel conventionally used for reporting crude petroleum and petroleum products is equal to 42 U.S. gallons or 159 litres. The number of barrels of crude petroleum per metric ton, ranging typically from 6.45 to 8.13, depends upon the specific gravity of the petroleum. The world average is roughly 7.33 barrels per ton.

***birth rate,*** the number of live births annually per 1,000 of midyear population. Birth rates for individual countries may be compared with the world annual average of 29 births per 1,000 population between 1980 and 1985.

***budget,*** the annual receipts and expenditures of the central government for its activities only; does not include state, provincial, or local governments unless otherwise specified. Figures for budgets are limited to ordinary (recurrent) receipts and expenditures and wherever possible exclude capital expenditures, *i.e.,* funds for development and other special projects originating as foreign-aid grants or loans.

When both a recurrent and a capital budget exist for a single country, the former is the budget funded entirely from national resources (taxes, duties, excises, etc.) that would recur (be generated by economic activity) every year. It funds the most basic governmental services, those least able to stand interruption. The capital budget is usually funded, particularly in less developed countries, by external aid and may change its size considerably from year to year. Sometimes a capital budget is funded by transfers from a recurrent budget.

***capital,*** usually the actual seat of administration and government of a state. When more than one capital exists, each is identified by kind; when interim arrangements exist during the creation or movement of a national capital, the de facto situation is described.

Anomalous cases where the de jure designation under the country's laws differs from actual local practice, such as Benin's designation of one capital in constitutional law, but another in actual practice; or where international recognition does not support a country's claim, as with the proclamation by Israel of a capital on territory not fully recognized as part of Israel; or the proclamation of both a state and a capital on territory recognized as part of another state, as with the Turkish Republic of Northern Cyprus, are footnoted.

**capital budget,** see budget.

**causes of death,** as defined by the World Health Organization, "the disease or injury which initiated the train of morbid events leading directly to death, or the circumstances of accident or violence which produced the fatal injury." This principle, the "underlying cause of death," is the basis of the medical judgment as to cause; the statistical classification system according to which these causes are grouped and named is the *International List of Causes of Death,* the latest revision of which is the Ninth, although a number of countries continue to report according to the Eighth, or even earlier, versions. Reporting is usually in terms of events per 100,000 population. When data on actual causes of death are unavailable, information on morbidity, or illness rate, usually given as reported cases per 100,000 of infectious diseases (notifiable to WHO as a matter of international agreement) may be substituted.

**chief of state/head of government,** as prescribed or practiced, although divergences between form and practice may be considerable.

In general usage, the chief of state is the formal head of a national state. The primary responsibilities of the chief of state are usually ceremonial—convening legislatures, greeting foreign officials, hosting state dinners, and bestowing honours. The head of government of a national state is the chief executive officer who effectively exercises the majority of actual executive powers. The head of government of a dependent political unit is the chief executive officer, either appointive or elective, who wields the most local executive powers, regardless of administrative prerogatives reserved elsewhere. In some countries the two functions may be merged.

In communist countries the official given as the chief of state is the chairman of the policy-making organ, and the official given as the head of government is the chairman of the nominal administrative/executive organ.

**c.i.f.** (trade valuation): see imports.

**colony,** an area annexed to, or controlled by, an independent state but not an integral part of it; a non-self-governing territory. A colony has a charter and may have a degree of self-government. A crown colony is a colony originally chartered by the British government.

**commonwealth** (U.S.), a self-governing political entity associated with the United States; examples are the Philippines from 1935 to 1946, Puerto Rico since 1952, or the Northern Marianas since 1979.

**communications,** collectively, the means available for the public transmission of information within a country. Data are provided for daily newspapers, their number and total circulation, and the per capita rate of circulation implied by that total; for radio, television, and telephone receivers, total numbers and rates of availability are supplied.

**constant prices,** an adjustment to the members of a time series (of values) to eliminate the effect of inflation year by year. It consists of referring all data in the series to a single year so that "real" change may be seen.

**constitutional monarchy,** see monarchy.

**consumer price index,** also known as the retail price index or the cost-of-living index, a series of index numbers assigned to the price of a selected "basket," or assortment, of basic consumer goods and services in a country or region to measure changes over time in prices paid by a typical household for those goods and services. Items included in the consumer price index are ordinarily determined by governmental surveys of typical household expenditures, and are assigned weights relative to their proportion of those expenditures. Index values are period averages unless otherwise noted.

**coprincipality,** see monarchy.

**current prices,** the valuation of a financial aggregate as of the year reported, without adjustment for inflation.

**daily per capita caloric intake** (supply), the calories equivalent to the known average daily supply of foodstuffs for human consumption in a given country divided by the population of the country. This estimated measure may differ from actual daily per capita consumption of food as a result of waste, inefficient distribution, and exploitation of sources of food not included in the known supply of foodstuffs. The daily per capita caloric intake of a country may be compared with the corresponding daily per capita caloric requirement. The latter is calculated by the Food and Agriculture Organization (FAO) of the United Nations from the age and sex distributions, average body weights, and environmental temperatures in a given region to determine the calories needed to sustain a person there at normal levels of activity and health. The daily per capita caloric requirement ranges from 2,200 to 2,500.

See also food.

**de facto population,** for a given area, the population composed of those present at a particular time, including temporary visitors and excluding legal residents temporarily absent.

**de jure population,** for a given area, the population composed of those legally resident at a particular time, excluding temporary visitors and including legal residents temporarily absent.

**deadweight tonnage,** the maximum weight of cargo, fuel, fresh water, stores, and persons that may safely be carried by a ship. It is customarily measured in long tons of 2,240 pounds each, equivalent to 1.016 metric tons. Deadweight tonnage is the difference between the tonnage of a fully loaded ship and the fully unloaded tonnage of that ship.

**death rate,** the number of deaths annually per 1,000 of midyear population. Death rates for individual countries may be compared with the world annual average of 11 deaths per 1,000 population between 1980 and 1985.

**density** (of population), usually the total area of the country divided into its DE FACTO POPULATION. Special adjustment is made for inland water or other uninhabitable areas, e.g., excluding the lake area of Finland or the ice area of Greenland.

**department,** a first-order civil administrative subdivision. *Overseas department* (France), an overseas subdivision of the French Republic, almost equivalent to a department of metropolitan France, with elected representation in the French Parliament.

**dependency,** any area outside of and under the jurisdiction of an independent state but not formally annexed to it.

**direct taxes,** taxes levied directly on firms and individuals, such as taxes on income, profits, and capital gains. The immediate incidence, or burden, of direct taxes is on the firms and individuals thus taxed; the incidence of direct taxes on firms may, however, be passed on to consumers and other economic units in the form of higher prices for goods and services, with the result that in practice the distinction between direct and indirect taxes is not always clear.

**distribution of income/wealth,** the portion of personal income or wealth accruing to households or individuals comprising each respective decile (tenth) or quintile (fifth) of a country's households or individuals.*

See also household income and expenditures.

**divorce rate,** the number of legal, civilly recognized divorces annually per 1,000 population.

**doubling time,** the number of complete years required for a country to double its population at its current rate of natural increase; it does

---

## Dependent states[1]

| | |
|---|---|
| **Australia** | **South Africa** |
| Christmas Island | South West Africa/Namibia |
| Cocos (Keeling) Islands | **United Kingdom** |
| Norfolk Island | Anguilla |
| **Denmark** | Bermuda |
| Faeroe Islands | British Virgin Islands |
| Greenland | Cayman Islands |
| **France** | Falkland Islands |
| French Guiana | Gibraltar |
| French Polynesia | Guernsey |
| Guadeloupe | Hong Kong |
| Martinique | Isle of Man |
| Mayotte | Jersey |
| New Caledonia | Montserrat |
| Réunion | Pitcairn Island |
| Saint Pierre and Miquelon | Saint Helena and Dependencies |
| Wallis and Futuna | Turks and Caicos Islands |
| **Netherlands, The** | **United States** |
| Aruba | American Samoa |
| Netherlands Antilles | Guam |
| **New Zealand** | Puerto Rico |
| Cook Islands | Trust Territory of the Pacific Islands |
| Niue | Marshall Islands |
| Tokelau | Federated States of Micronesia |
| **Norway** | Northern Mariana Islands |
| Jan Mayen | Palau |
| Svalbard | Virgin Islands (of the U.S.) |
| **Portugal** | |
| Macau | |

[1]Excludes territories (1) to which Antarctic Treaty is applicable in whole or in part, (2) without permanent civilian population, (3) without internationally recognized civilian government (Western Sahara, Gaza Strip), or (4) representing unadjudicated unilateral or multilateral territorial claims.

not take into account expected demographic change during the period, such as changes in birth rate, death rate, or population migration.

**earnings index,** a series of index numbers comparing average wages in a collective industrial sample for a country or region with the same industries at a previous period to measure changes over time in those wages. It is most commonly reported for wages paid on a daily, weekly, or monthly basis; annual figures represent averages of these shorter periods. The scope of the earnings index varies from country to country; the index is often limited to earnings in manufacturing industries. The index for each country applies to all wage earners in a designated group and ordinarily takes into account basic wages (overtime is normally distinguished), bonuses, cost-of-living allowances, and contributions toward social security. Some countries include payments in kind. Contributions toward social security by employers are usually excluded, as are social security benefits received by wage earners.

*See also* price and earnings indexes.

**economically active population,** *see* population economically active.

*education,* tabulation of the principal elements of the country's educational establishment, classified as far as possible according to the country's own system of primary, secondary, and higher levels (the usual age limits for these levels being identified in parentheses), with total number of schools (physical facilities) and of teachers and students (whether full- or part-time). The student–teacher ratio is calculated whenever available data permit.

*educational attainment,* the distribution of the population age 25 and over with completed educations by the highest level of formal education attained or completed; it is often reported, however, for age groups still in school, or for the economically active only.

**emirate,** *see* monarchy.

**enterprise,** a legal entity formed to conduct a business, which it may do from more than one establishment (place of business or service point).

*ethnic/linguistic composition,* ethnic, racial, or linguistic composition of a national population, reported here according to the most reliable breakdown published in official sources (when available) or external analysis (when the subject is not addressed in national sources [usually because of social or political sensitivities]).

**exchange rate,** the value of one currency compared to another, or to a standardized value such as the SPECIAL DRAWING RIGHT, or as mandated by local statute when one currency is "tied" by a par value to another. Rates given usually refer to market values when the currency itself is traded, or to the value of trade transactions either averaged over the period of a year, or as of a single date during the year.

*exports,* material goods legally leaving a country (or customs area) and subject to customs regulations. The total value and distribution by percentage of the major items (in preference to groups of goods) exported are given, together with the distribution of trade among major trading partners (usually single countries or trading blocs). Figures given for goods exported are free on board (f.o.b.) unless otherwise specified. The value of goods exported and imported free on board (f.o.b.) is calculated from the cost of production and excludes the cost of transport.

**external debt,** public and publicly guaranteed debt with a maturity of more than one year that is owed to nonnationals of a country, and is repayable in foreign currency, goods, or services. The debt may be an obligation of a national or subnational governmental body (or an agency of either), of an autonomous public body, or of a private debtor that is guaranteed

for repayment by a public entity. The debt is usually either outstanding (contracted) or disbursed (drawn).

**external territory** (Australia), *see* territory.

**farm,** economic unit comprising an operator and the land on which agricultural operations are conducted. The legal tenure of the farm may be under the control of a person, partnership, or corporation. In the United States, a farm is such a place with annual gross sales of farm products of $1,000 or more.

**federal,** consisting of first-order political subdivisions that are prior to and independent of the central government in certain functions.

**federal republic,** *see* republic.

**federation,** a union of coequal political entities that retain some degree of autonomy within the union.

**fertility rate,** *see* total fertility rate.

*financial aggregates,* tabulation of seven-year time series, providing principal measures of the financial condition of a country: the exchange rate of the national currency against the U.S. dollar, the pound sterling, and the International Monetary Fund's SPECIAL DRAWING RIGHT (SDR); the amount and kind of international reserves (holdings of SDRs, gold, and foreign currencies) and reserve position of the country in the IMF; principal economic rates and prices (central bank discount rate, government bond yields, and industrial stock [share] prices). For BALANCE OF PAYMENTS, the origin in terms of component balance of trade items and balance of invisibles (net) is given.*

**fish catch,** the live-weight equivalent of the aquatic animals (including fish, crustaceans, mollusks, etc., but excluding whales, seals, and other aquatic mammals) caught in freshwater or marine areas by national fleets and landed in domestic or foreign harbours for commercial, industrial, or subsistence purposes.

**f.o.b.** (trade valuation): *see* exports.

*food, see* daily per capita caloric intake.

*form of government/political status,* the structure of a country's administration provided for in normal constitutional operation, whether or not suspended by extralegal military or civil action, although such de facto administrations are identified; together with the number of members (elected, appointed, and ex officio) for each legislative house, named according to its English rendering. Dependent states (*see* Table) are classified according to the status of their political association with the administering country.

**(free) association,** late stage in the process by which U.K. and U.S. dependencies achieve independence; it usually implies a relation between a largely self-governing dependency and its administering power that is capable of termination in full independence at the instance of the dependent state, though always in consultation with the administering power.

**global social product,** *see* material product.

*gross domestic product* (GDP), the total value of the final goods and services produced by residents and nonresidents within a given country during a given year. The GDP excludes the value of net income earned abroad, which is included in the GROSS NATIONAL PRODUCT (GNP). Unless otherwise noted, the value is given in current prices of the year indicated.

*gross national product* (GNP), the total value of final goods and services produced both from within a given country *and* from external (foreign) transactions in a given year. Unless otherwise noted, the value is given in current prices of the year indicated. GNP is equal to GROSS DOMESTIC PRODUCT adjusted by net factor income from abroad. That income comprises the income residents receive from abroad for factor services (labour, investment, and interest) less similar payments made to nonresidents who contributed to the domestic economy.

**gross output in factor values,** the total market value of goods and services produced by a country, industry, or firm, less all INDIRECT TAXES on production but including all current subsidies received in support of production activity.

**gross output value in producers' prices,** the total market value of goods and services produced by a country, industry, or firm, including all INDIRECT TAXES on production but excluding subsidies.

**gross (register) ton,** unit of measure of the permanently enclosed volume of a ship, less certain exempted spaces such as those devoted to machinery, bunkers, crew accommodations, and so on; the gross register tonnage of a ship is thus a rough estimation of its volumetric cargo capacity. The gross register ton is equivalent to 100 cubic feet or 2.83 cubic metres.

*head of government, see* chief of state/head of government.

**health,** total number of accredited physicians (according to World Health Organization criteria) by specialization and their ratio to the total population; similarly for hospital beds.

*household income and expenditure,* data for average household size (by number of individuals) and average household income. Sources of income and expenditures for major items of consumption are reported as percentages.

In general, household income is the amount of funds, usually measured in monetary units, received by the members (generally those 14 years old and over) of a HOUSEHOLD in a given time period. The income can be derived from (1) wages or salaries, (2) nonfarm or farm SELF-EMPLOYMENT, (3) transfer payments, such as pensions, public assistance, unemployment benefits, etc., and (4) other income, including interest and dividends, rent, royalties, etc. The income of a household is expressed as a gross amount before deductions for taxes. Data on expenditure refer to consumption of personal or household goods and services; they normally exclude savings, taxes, and insurance; practice with regard to inclusion of credit purchases differs markedly.

**households,** groups of related or unrelated individuals living in the same housing unit, distributed by size of household. A family household is one composed principally of individuals related by blood or marriage.*

*immigration,* usually the number and origin of those immigrants admitted to a nation in a legal status that would eventually permit the granting of the right to settle permanently or to acquire citizenship.*

*imports,* material goods legally entering a country (or customs area) and subject to customs regulations; excludes financial movements. The total value and distribution by percentage of the major items (in preference to groups of goods) imported are given, together with the direction of trade among major trading partners (usually single countries), trading blocs (such as the European Economic Community), or customs areas (such as Belgium–Luxembourg). The value of goods imported is given free on board (f.o.b.) unless otherwise specified; f.o.b. is defined above under EXPORTS.

The principal alternate basis for reporting valuation of goods in international trade is that of cost, insurance, and freight (c.i.f.); its use is restricted to imports, as it comprises the principal charges needed to bring the goods to the customs house in the country of destination. Because it inflates the value of imports relative to exports, more countries have, latterly, been providing estimates of imports on an f.o.b. basis as well.

**incorporated territory** (U.S.), *see* territory.

**independent,** of a state, autonomous and controlling both its internal and external affairs.

**indirect taxes,** taxes levied on sales or transfers of selected intermediate goods and services, including excises, value-added taxes, and tariffs, that are ordinarily passed on to the ultimate consumers of the goods and services. Figures given for individual countries are limited to indirect taxes levied by their respective central governments unless otherwise specified.

**infant mortality rate,** the number of children born live who die before their first birthday per 1,000 live births. Total infant mortality includes neonatal mortality, which is deaths of children within one month of birth.

**invisibles (invisible trade),** *see* balance of trade.

**kingdom,** *see* monarchy.

*land use,* distribution by classes of vegetational cover or economic use of the land area only (excluding inland water, for example, but not marshland), reported as percentages.

*leisure,* the principal uses or reported preferences in the use of the individual's free time for recreation, rest, or self-improvement.*

*life expectancy,* the number of years a person born within a particular population group (age cohort) would be expected to live, based on actuarial calculations. Life expectancy at birth is usually lower than after the first year of life because of infant mortality and is often used to compare the general health of populations of different countries.

**literacy,** the ability to read and write a language with some degree of competence; the precise degree constituting the basis of a particular national statement is usually defined by the national census and is often tested by the census enumerator. Elsewhere, particularly where much adult literacy may be the result of literacy campaigns, rather than passage through a formal educational system, definition and testing of literacy may be better standardized, albeit of a lower overall standard.

*major cities,* usually the five largest cities proper whose population is at least one-tenth that of the primate (largest) city; fewer will be listed if the size disparity is very great or there are fewer urban localities in the country. For multipage tables, ten or more* will be listed without regard for the size of the primate city. All populations will refer to the most specific administrative or demographically defined city proper, unless a municipality or METROPOLITAN AREA is specified.

*manufacturing, mining, and construction enterprises/retail sales and service enterprises,* a detailed tabulation of the principal industries in these sectors, showing for each industry the number of enterprises and employees, wages in that industry as a percentage of the general average wage, and the value of that industry's output in terms of value added or turnover.*

*marriage rate,* the number of legal, civilly recognized marriages annually per 1,000 population.

**material (or social) product,** in the national accounting systems of the socialist countries, the aggregate (sometimes "global") value of all "productive" services, generally omitting personal (nonpublic) services, financial activities, and the like that in conventional Western national accounts would contribute to the GROSS DOMESTIC PRODUCT, a more comprehensive measure that not only includes material output but also every identifiable service element of a national economy. Socialist countries that are members of the International Monetary Fund have begun, however, to report gross domestic, and national, product according to the *System of National Accounts* that forms the basis of international reporting of national accounts.

*material well-being,* a group of measures indicating the percentage of households or dwellings possessing certain goods or appliances, including automobiles, telephones, television receivers, refrigerators, air conditioners, and washing machines.*

**merchant marine,** the privately or publicly owned ships of a nation (limited to those in Lloyd's of London statistical reporting of 100 or more GROSS REGISTER TONS) that are employed in commerce.

**metropolitan area,** comprises a city and the region of dense, predominantly urban, settlement around the city; the population of the whole is usually economically dependent upon the central city to some degree, for employment, shopping, transportation services, and the like. Such areas are usually compact and contiguous, containing no physically discontinuous elements.

*military expenditure,* the apparent value of all identifiable military expenditure by the central government on hardware, personnel, pensions, research and development, etc., reported here as a percentage of the GNP, with a comparison to the world average.

**military personnel,** *see* total active duty personnel.

*mobility,* a measure of the rate at which individuals or households change dwellings (or remain in them), usually measured between censuses and including international as well as domestic migration.*

**monarchy,** a government in which the CHIEF OF STATE holds office, usually hereditarily, but sometimes electively, and for life (sometimes electively for a term). The state may be a coprincipality, emirate, empire, kingdom, principality, shaykhdom, or sultanate. The powers of the monarch may range from absolute, *i.e.,* he or she both reigns and rules, through various degrees of limitation of authority, to merely nominal, as in a constitutional monarchy, in which the titular monarch reigns but others, as elected officials, participate in the ruling.

*monetary unit,* currency of issue, or that in official use in a given country; name, spelling, and abbreviation in English according to International Monetary Fund recommendations or local practice; valuation usually according to market or commercial rates.
*See also* exchange rate.

*natural increase,* also called natural growth or the balance of births and deaths, the excess of births over deaths in a population; the rate of natural increase is the difference between the BIRTH RATE and the DEATH RATE of a given population. Natural increase is added to the balance of migration to calculate the total growth of that population.

**net material product,** *see* material product.

*official language(s),* that (or those) prescribed for actual day-to-day conduct and publication of a country's official business. Other languages may have local protection, may be permitted in legal action (such as a trial), or may be "national languages," for the protection of which special provisions have been made, but these are not deemed official.

*official name,* the local official form(s) short or long, of a country's legal name(s) taken from the country's constitution or from other official documents. The English-language form is usually the protocol form in use by the country, the U.S. Department of State, and the United Nations.

*official religion,* generally, any religion prescribed or given special protection by the constitution or legal system of the country.

**organized territory** (U.S.), *see* territory.

**overseas department** (France), *see* department.

**overseas territory** (France), *see* territory.

**parliamentary state,** *see* state.

**part of a realm,** a dependent political entity with some degree of self-government and having a special status above that of a colony (*e.g.,* the prerogative of rejecting for local application any law enacted by the motherland).

**participation/activity rates,** measures defining differential rates of economic activity within a population. Participation rate refers to the percentage of those employed or economically active who possess a particular characteristic (sex, age, etc.); activity rate refers to the fraction of the total population who *are* economically active.

**passenger-miles** or **passenger-kilometres,** carriage by public or commercial means of a single passenger a distance of one mile (or kilometre); in aggregate the total miles or kilometres traveled by all passengers in a given country via specified means of transportation. Figures given for countries are often calculated from ticket sales and ordinarily exclude passengers carried free of charge.

**people's republic,** *see* republic.

*place of birth/national origin,* if the former, numbers of native- and foreign-born population of a country by actual place of birth; if the latter, any of several classifications, including those based on origin of passport at original admission to country, on cultural heritage of family name, on self-designated (often multiple) origin of (some) ancestors, and on other systems for assigning national origin.*

**political status,** *see* form of government/political status.

**population,** the number of persons actually present within the borders of a country, state, or other civil entity at the date of a census of population, survey, cumulation of a civil register, or other estimate. Unless otherwise specified, populations given are DE FACTO, referring to those actually present, rather than DE JURE, those legally resident but not necessarily present on the referent date. If a time series, noncensus year, or per capita ratio referring to a country's total population is cited, it will usually refer to midyear of the calendar year indicated. Populations for cities will usually refer to the city proper, *i.e.,* the legally bounded corporate entity, or the most compact, contiguous, demographically urban portion of the entity defined by the local authorities. Occasionally it has been necessary to provide city figures for METROPOLITAN AREAS when the relevant civil entity at the core of a major agglomeration had an unrepresentatively small population.

*population economically active,* the total number of persons (above a set age for economic labour, usually 10–15 years) in all employment statuses—self-employed, wage- or salary-earning, part-time, seasonal, unemployed, etc. The United Nations' *Yearbook of Labour Statistics* defines the economically active population as "all persons of either sex who furnish the supply of labour for the production of economic goods and services." National practices vary between countries as regards the treatment of such groups as armed forces, inmates of institutions, persons living on reservations, persons seeking their first job, seasonal workers and persons engaged in part-time economic activities. In some countries, all or part of these groups may be included among the economically active while in other countries the same groups may be treated as inactive. However, in general, the data on economically active population do not include students, women occupied solely in domestic duties, retired persons, persons living entirely on their own means, and persons wholly dependent upon others.

*population projection,* the expected population in 1990 and 2000, embodying the country's own projections wherever possible. Estimates of the future size of a population are usually based on assumed future levels of fertility, mortality, and migration. Projections in the tables, whether based on external estimates by the United Nations, World Bank, U.S. Department of Commerce, or on those of the country itself, unless otherwise specified, are medium (*i.e.,* most likely) variants.

**price and earnings indexes,** tabulation comparing the change in the CONSUMER PRICE INDEX over a period of seven years with the change in the general labour force's EARNINGS INDEX for the same period.

**principality,** see monarchy.

**production,** the physical quantity or monetary value of the output of an industry, usually tabulated here as the most important items or groups of items (depending on the available detail) of primary (extractive) and secondary (manufactured) production. When a single consistent measure of value, such as "value added," can be obtained, this is given, ranked by value; otherwise, and usually, quantity of production is given.

**public debt,** the current outstanding debt of all periods of maturity for which the central government and its organs are obligated. Publicly guaranteed private debt is excluded. For many developing countries, only figures for long-term EXTERNAL DEBT are available.

**quality of working life,** a group of measures including weekly hours of work (including overtime); rates per 100,000 for job-connected injury, illness, and mortality; coverage of labour force by insurance for injury, permanent disability, and death; work days lost to labour strikes and stoppages; and commuting patterns (length of journey to work in minutes and usual method of transportation).*

**railroads,** mode of transportation by self-driven or locomotive-drawn cars over fixed rails. Length of track figures given for individual countries ordinarily include the total length of all mainline and spurline running track and exclude switching sidings and yard track. Route length, when given, does not compound multiple running tracks laid on the same trackbed.

**recurrent budget,** see budget.

**religious affiliation,** distribution of practicing or nominal religionists, as a percentage of total population. This usually assigns to children the religion of their parents, since few sources conform to any other practice.

**republic,** a state with elected leaders and a centralized presidential form of government, local subdivisions being subordinate to the national government. *Federal republic* (as distinguished from a unitary republic), a republic in which power is divided between the central government and local subdivisions (e.g., states, provinces, or cantons) in whom it is held to originate, the division of power being defined in a written constitution and jurisdictional disputes usually being settled in a court; sovereignty usually rests with the authority that has the power to amend the constitution. *People's republic,* in the dialectics of Communism, the first stage of development toward a communist state, the second stage being a *socialist republic. Soviet republic,* a republic governed by an elected soviet (council). *Unitary republic* (as distinguished from a federal republic), a republic in which power is held by a central authority and not derived from constituent subdivisions.

**retail price index,** see consumer price index.

**retail sales and service enterprises,** see manufacturing, mining, and construction enterprises/retail sales and service enterprises.

**roundwood,** wood obtained from removals from forests, felled or harvested (with or without bark), in all forms.

**rural,** see urban–rural.

**self-employment,** work in which income derives from direct employment in one's own business, trade, or profession, as opposed to work in which salary or wages are earned from an employer.

**self-governing,** of a state, in control of its internal affairs in degrees ranging from control of most internal affairs (though perhaps not of public order or of internal security) to complete control of all internal affairs (i.e., the state is autonomous) but having no control of external affairs or defense. In this work the term self-governing refers to the final state in the successive stages of increasing self-government, generally followed by independence.

**service/trade enterprises,** see manufacturing, mining, and construction enterprises/retail sales and service enterprises.

**sex distribution,** ratios, calculated as percentages, of male and female population to total population.

**shaykhdom,** see monarchy.

**social deviance,** a group of measures, usually reported as rates per 100,000, for principal categories of socially deviant behaviour, including specified crimes, alcoholism, drug abuse, and suicide.*

**social participation,** a group of measures indicative of the degree of social engagement possessed by a particular population, including rates of participation or membership in public activities such as elections, voluntary work (or non-job-connected organizational memberships), trade unions, and religion.*

**social security,** public programs designed to protect individuals and families from loss of income owing to unemployment, old age, sickness or disability, or death and to provide other assistance, such as medical care or other services. Such programs may include social insurance, health and welfare programs, income maintenance programs, or other modes of public aid.

**socialist republic,** see republic.

**soviet republic,** see republic.

**Special Drawing Right** (SDR), a unit of account utilized by the International Monetary Fund (IMF) to denominate monetary reserves available under a quota system to IMF members to maintain the value of their national currency unit in international transactions.

**state,** an autonomous political entity; also, a first-order civil administrative subdivision, especially of a federated union. *Associated state,* an autonomous state in free association with another that conducts its external affairs and defense. *Parliamentary state,* an independent state in the Commonwealth that is governed by a parliament and that may recognize the British monarch as its titular head.

**structure of gross domestic product and labour force,** tabulation of the principal elements of the national economy, according to standard industrial categories, together with the distribution of the labour force (when possible POPULATION ECONOMICALLY ACTIVE) that generates the GROSS DOMESTIC PRODUCT.

**sultanate,** see monarchy.

**territory,** a noncategorized political dependency; a first-order administrative subdivision; a dependent political entity with some degree of self-government, but with fewer rights and less autonomy than a colony since there is no charter. *External territory* (Australia), a territory situated outside the area of the country. *Incorporated territory* (U.S.), a part of the United States with nonvoting representation in the Congress, but with most constitutional provisions extended to its inhabitants (e.g., Alaska until 1959). *Organized territory* (U.S.), a territory for which a system of laws and a settled government have been provided by an act of the United States Congress. *Overseas territory* (France), an overseas subdivision of the French Republic with elected representation in the French Parliament, having individual statutes, laws, and internal organization adapted to local conditions. *Trust territory,* a non-self-governing former mandate of the League of Nations, administered by an independent state under trust arrangements with the United Nations, with the goal of eventual self-government. *Unincorporated territory* (U.S.), a dependency of the United States with limited self-government, whose inhabitants can claim the fundamental but not all of the procedural rights (e.g., trial by jury) guaranteed by the United States Constitution.

**theocracy,** a state governed by hierarchs, i.e., by religious leaders.

**ton-miles** or **ton-kilometres,** aggregate measure of freight hauled in a specified period of time, equal to tons of freight multiplied by the miles (or kilometres) each ton is transported. Figures given for individual countries indicate the aggregate ton-miles (or ton-kilometres) traveled by freight via the means of transportation indicated. Figures are compiled from way-bills (nationally) and ordinarily exclude mail, specie, passengers' baggage, the fuel and stores of the conveyance in question, and goods carried free of charge.

**total active duty personnel,** full-time active duty military personnel (excluding militias and part-time, informal, or other paramilitary elements), with their distribution by percentages among the major services.
*See also* military expenditure.

**total fertility rate,** the sum of the current age-specific birth rates for each of the child-bearing years (usually 15–49). It is the probable number of births, given present fertility data, that would occur during the lifetime of each woman (should she live to the end of her child-bearing years).

**tourism,** service industry comprising activities connected with domestic and international travel for pleasure or recreation; confined here to international travel and reported as expenditures in U.S.$ by tourists of all nationalities visiting a particular country and, conversely, the estimated expenditures of that country's nationals in all countries of destination.

**transport,** all mechanical methods of moving persons or goods. Data reported for national establishments include: for railroads, length of track and volume of traffic for passengers and cargo (but excluding mail, etc.); for roads, length of network and numbers of passengers cars and of commercial vehicles, i.e., trucks and buses (no data on traffic); for merchant marine, the number of vessels of more than 100 gross tons and their total deadweight tonnage (no data on traffic); for air transport, traffic data for passengers and cargo, and the number of airports with scheduled flights.

**trust territory,** see territory.

**unincorporated territory** (U.S.), see territory.

**unitary republic,** see republic.

**urban–rural,** social characteristic of local or national populations, defined by predominant economic activities, "urban" referring to a group of predominantly nonagricultural pursuits, "rural" to agricultural pursuits. The distinction is usually based on the country's own definition of urban, which may depend only upon the size (population) or a place, or upon factors like employment, administrative status, density of housing, public services, etc.

**value added,** also called value added by manufacture, the GROSS OUTPUT VALUE of a firm or industry minus the cost of inputs—raw materials, supplies, and other inputs for which other firms are paid—required to produce it. Value added is the portion of the sales value or gross output value that is actually created by the firm or industry. Value added generally includes labour costs, administrative costs, and operating profits.

# The Nations of the World

## Afghanistan

*Official name:* Da Afghānestān Dimukratik Jamhawrīyat (Pashto); Jomhūrī-ye Demowkrātīk-e Afghānestān (Dari) (Democratic Republic of Afghanistan).
*Form of government*[1]: unitary single-party people's republic with one transitional legislative body (Revolutionary Council [57]).
*Chief of state*[1]: President of the Revolutionary Council.
*Head of government*[1]: Prime Minister.
*Capital:* Kābul.
*Official languages:* Pashto; Dari Persian.
*Official religion:* Islam.
*Monetary unit:* 1 afghani (AF) = 100 puls (puli); valuation (Oct. 5, 1987) 1 U.S.$ = AF 61.12; 1 £ = AF 99.25.

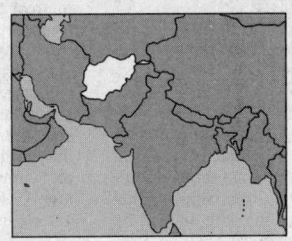

| Area and population | area | | population |
| --- | --- | --- | --- |
| | | | 1984 |
| Regions | sq mi | sq km | estimate |
| Eastern | 28,664 | 74,240 | 1,923,081 |
| North-central | 20,461 | 52,994 | 2,062,677 |
| North-east | 29,911 | 77,468 | 1,442,099 |
| North-west | 50,581 | 131,005 | 2,368,323 |
| South-central | 32,963 | 85,375 | 1,140,390 |
| South-east | 12,546 | 32,494 | 3,875,364 |
| Western | 76,699 | 198,649 | 1,554,500 |
| TOTAL | 251,825 | 652,225 | 14,366,434[2] |

### Demography

*Density*[3] (1987): persons per sq mi 62.5, persons per sq km 24.1.
*Urban–rural*[4] (1985): urban 18.5%; rural 81.5%.
*Sex distribution*[4] (1985): male 51.04%; female 48.96%.
*Age breakdown*[4] (1985): under 15, 45.4%; 15–29, 26.7%; 30–44, 15.6%; 45–59, 8.4%; 60–74, 3.4%; 75 and over, 0.5%.
*Population projection:* (1990) 16,940,000; (2000) 21,664,000.
*Doubling time*[4]: 32 years.
*Ethnic composition* (1983): Pashtun 52.3%; Tadzhik 20.3%; Uzbek 8.7%; Hazāra 8.7%; Chahar Aimak 2.9%; Turkmen 2.0%; Baluchi 1.0%; other 4.1%.
*Religious affiliation* (1986): Sunnī Muslim 74%; Shī'ī Muslim 25%; other 1%.
*Major cities* (1984): Kābul 1,179,341; Qandahār 203,177; Herāt 159,804; Mazār-e Sharīf 117,723.

### Vital statistics

*Birth rate* per 1,000 population (1980–85): 48.9 (world avg. 29.0).
*Death rate* per 1,000 population (1980–85): 27.3 (world avg. 11.0).
*Natural increase rate* per 1,000 population (1980–85): 21.6 (world avg. 18.0).
*Total fertility rate* (avg. births per childbearing woman; 1980–85): 6.9.
*Life expectancy* at birth (1980–85): male 36.6 years; female 37.3 years.
*Major reported illness* (1981–82): tuberculosis 17,499 cases.

### National economy

*Budget* (1981–82). Revenue: AF 40,464,100,000 (internal revenue sources 74.1%, of which natural gas revenues 43.9%; loans and grants-in-aid 25.9%). Expenditures: AF 40,464,100,000 (governmental ministries 50.0%; developmental budget 31.9%; foreign debt service 13.9%; surplus 1.6%).
*Public debt* (external, outstanding; 1985)[5]: U.S.$1,424,000,000.
*Tourism* (1985): receipts from visitors U.S.$1,000,000; expenditures by nationals abroad, n.a.
*Production* (metric tons except as noted). Agriculture, forestry, fishing (1985): wheat 2,850,000, corn (maize) 800,000, grapes 510,000, rice 480,000, barley 340,000; livestock (number of live animals) 20,000,000 sheep, 3,750,000 cattle, 3,000,000 goats, 1,250,000 asses, 410,000 horses, 270,000 camels; roundwood 6,452,000 cu m; fish catch 1,500. Mining and quarrying (1983): salt 8,000; gypsum 5,000; barite 2,000. Manufacturing (by production value in afghanis; 1981–82): food products 3,762,000,000; textiles (all forms) 2,770,000,000; industrial chemicals (including fertilizers) 751,000,000; printing and publishing 539,000,000 cement (metric tons; 1986) 77,000. Construction (1981–82): nonresidential 113,176 cu m, of which educational buildings 29,779, industrial buildings 21,171. Energy production (consumption): electricity (kW-hr; 1985) 1,060,000,000 (1,060,000,000); coal (metric tons; 1985) 151,000 (151,000); petroleum products (metric tons; 1985) 8,000 (450,000); natural gas (cu m; 1985) 2,851,000,000 (596,000,000).
*Household size.* Average household size[4] (1979): 6.2.
*Gross national product* (1985): U.S.$3,520,000,000 (U.S.$230 per capita).

| Structure of net material product and labour force | 1985 | | 1981–82 | |
| --- | --- | --- | --- | --- |
| | in value AF '000,000[6] | % of total value | labour force[4] | % of labour force |
| Agriculture | 65,100 | 64.8 | 2,194,770 | 57.3 |
| Manufacturing, mining, and public utilities | 16,300 | 16.2 | 466,860 | 12.2 |
| Construction | 4,000 | 4.0 | 48,880 | 1.3 |
| Transp. and commun. | 3,100 | 3.1 | 65,650 | 1.7 |
| Trade | 10,200 | 10.2 | 126,100 | 3.3 |
| Public administration | | | 79,260 | 2.1 |
| Public services | 1,700 | 1.7 | 204,940 | 5.3 |
| Other | | | 642,360 | 16.8 |
| TOTAL | 100,400 | 100.0 | 3,828,820 | 100.0 |

*Population economically active*[4] (1981–82): total 3,828,820; activity rate of total population 27.8% (participation rates: ages 10–59, 43.8%; female 12.8%; unemployed 5.5%).

| Price indexes (1980 = 100) | 1979 | 1980 | 1981 | 1982 | 1983 | 1984 | 1985 |
| --- | --- | --- | --- | --- | --- | --- | --- |
| Consumer price index | 99.1 | 100.0 | 104.9 | 111.0 | 107.7 | 116.0 | 126.6 |

*Land use* (1984): forested 2.9%; meadows and pastures 46.3%; agricultural and under permanent cultivation 12.4%; other 38.4%.

### Foreign trade

| Balance of trade (current prices) | 1980 | 1981 | 1982 | 1983 | 1984 | 1985 |
| --- | --- | --- | --- | --- | --- | --- |
| AF '000,000 | 5,432 | 3,555 | 629 | −5,941 | −4,569 | −32,252 |
| % of total | 9.7% | 5.5% | 0.9% | 7.5% | 5.4% | 36.4% |

*Imports* (1985): U.S.$1,194,200,000 (1981–82; vehicles 22.7%, petroleum products 18.0%, sugar 8.1%, woven fabrics of flax or ramie 7.9%, processed animal and vegetable oils 4.2%, tea 4.0%). *Major import sources:* U.S.S.R. 48.8%; Japan 10.7%; West Germany 2.3%; Hong Kong 2.1%; U.K. 1.9%.
*Exports* (1985): U.S.$556,800,000 (natural gas 55.6%, dried fruit and nuts 16.9%, carpets and rugs 4.8%, wool and hides 4.0%). *Major export destinations:* U.S.S.R. 65.0%; U.K. 10.0%; West Germany 3.7%.

### Transport and communications

*Transport.* Railroads (1984): length 6 mi, 10 km. Roads (1981–82): total length 11,789 mi, 18,974 km (paved 42%). Vehicles (1981–82): passenger cars 31,754; trucks and buses 30,997. Merchant marine: none. Air transport (1986): passenger-mi 87,089,000, passenger-km 140,156,000; short ton-mi cargo 5,119,000, metric ton-km cargo 7,473,000; airports (1987) 1.
*Communications.* Daily newspapers (1986): total number 12; total circulation 106,600; circulation per 1,000 population 6.9. Radio (1986): 150,000 receivers (1 per 102 persons). Television (1986): 20,000 receivers (1 per 768 persons). Telephones (1984): 31,200 (1 per 566 persons).

### Education and health

| Education (1984) | schools | teachers | students | student/ teacher ratio |
| --- | --- | --- | --- | --- |
| Primary | 754 | 14,865 | 545,959 | 36.7 |
| Secondary | 332 | 6,943 | 99,729 | 14.4 |
| Voc., teacher tr.[7] | 16 | 666 | 7,360 | 11.1 |
| Higher | 5 | 1,283 | 13,450 | 10.5 |

*Educational attainment* (1980). Percent of population age 25 and over having: no formal schooling 88.5%; some primary education 6.8%; complete primary 0.3%; some secondary 1.2%; postsecondary 3.2%. *Literacy* (1980): total population age 15 and over literate 1,436,000 (20.0%); males 33.2%; females 5.8%.
*Health* (1981–82): physicians 1,215 (1 per 13,092 persons); hospital beds 6,875 (1 per 2,314 persons); infant mortality rate per 1,000 live births (1985) 189.
*Food* (1979–81): daily per capita caloric intake 2,055 (vegetable products 90%, animal products 10%); 84% of FAO recommended minimum.

### Military

*Total active duty personnel* (1986): 50,000 (army 90.0%, air force 10.0%).
*Military expenditure as percent of GNP* (1983): 5.9% (world 6.0%); per capita expenditure U.S.$13.

---

[1]Reflects status before announcement of new constitution on Nov. 30, 1987. [2]Total includes 2,615,000 nomads not distributed by region. Afghan refugees in Pakistan number almost 3,000,000 and in Iran almost 2,000,000. [3]Includes both settled and nomadic population. [4]Based on settled population only. [5]Includes external long-term private debt not guaranteed by the government. [6]At prices of 1978. [7]Includes technical institutes.

# Albania

*Official name:* Republika Popullore Socialiste e Shqipërisë (People's Socialist Republic of Albania).
*Form of government:* unitary single-party socialist republic with one legislative house (People's Assembly [250]).
*Chief of state:* President (Chairman of the Presidium of the People's Assembly).
*Head of government:* Premier (Chairman of the Council of Ministers).
*Capital:* Tiranë.
*Official language:* Albanian.
*Official religion:* none.
*Monetary unit:* 1 lek = 100 qindars; valuation (Oct. 5, 1987) 1 U.S.$ = 6.19 leks; 1 £ = 10.05 leks.

### Area and population

| Provinces | Capitals | area sq mi | sq km | population 1983 estimate |
|---|---|---|---|---|
| Berat | Berat | 396 | 1,026 | 157,300 |
| Dibër | Peshkopi | 605 | 1,568 | 137,800 |
| Durrës | Durrës | 327 | 848 | 220,600 |
| Elbasan | Elbasan | 572 | 1,481 | 213,200 |
| Fier | Fier | 454 | 1,175 | 216,400 |
| Gjirokastër | Gjirokastër | 439 | 1,137 | 61,200 |
| Gramsh | Gramsh | 268 | 695 | 39,300 |
| Kolonjë | Ersekë | 311 | 805 | 22,500 |
| Korçë | Korçë | 842 | 2,181 | 201,300 |
| Krujë | Krujë | 234 | 607 | 94,600 |
| Kukës | Kukës | 514 | 1,331 | 88,400 |
| Lezhë | Lezhë | 185 | 479 | 54,200 |
| Librazhd | Librazhd | 391 | 1,013 | 64,100 |
| Lushnjë | Lushnjë | 275 | 712 | 117,800 |
| Mat | Burrel | 397 | 1,028 | 68,700 |
| Mirditë | Rrëshen | 335 | 867 | 45,800 |
| Përmet | Përmet | 359 | 930 | 37,100 |
| Pogradec | Pogradec | 280 | 725 | 62,700 |
| Pukë | Pukë | 399 | 1,033 | 46,100 |
| Sarandë | Sarandë | 424 | 1,097 | 78,200 |
| Shkodër | Shkodër | 976 | 2,528 | 210,200 |
| Skrapar | Çorovoda | 299 | 775 | 42,500 |
| Tepelenë | Tepelenë | 315 | 817 | 46,100 |
| Tiranë | Tiranë | 478 | 1,238 | 316,100 |
| Tropojë | Bajram | 403 | 1,043 | 40,900 |
| Vlorë | Vlorë | 621 | 1,609 | 158,200 |
| TOTAL | | 11,100[1] | 28,748 | 2,841,300 |

## Demography

*Population* (1987): 3,087,000.
*Density* (1987): persons per sq mi 278.1, persons per sq km 107.4.
*Urban–rural* (1984): urban 33.7%; rural 66.3%.
*Sex distribution* (1984): male 51.60%; female 48.40%.
*Age breakdown* (1985): under 15, 35.8%; 15–29, 29.3%; 30–44, 17.0%; 45–59, 11.1%; 60–74, 5.3%; 75 and over, 1.5%.
*Population projection:* (1990) 3,285,000; (2000) 4,040,000.
*Doubling time:* 28 years.
*Ethnic composition* (1983): Albanian 96.7%; Greek 2.0%; Romanian 0.5%; Macedonian 0.4%; Montenegrin 0.2%; Gypsy 0.2%.
*Religious affiliation* (1980): Muslim 20.5%; Christian 5.4%; atheist 18.7%; nonreligious 55.4%.
*Major cities* (1983): Tiranë 206,100; Durrës 72,400; Shkodër 71,200; Elbasan 69,900; Vlorë 61,100.

## Vital statistics

*Birth rate* per 1,000 population (1985): 26.2 (world avg. 29.0).
*Death rate* per 1,000 population (1985): 5.8 (world avg. 11.0).
*Natural increase rate* per 1,000 population (1985): 20.4 (world avg. 18.0).
*Total fertility rate* (avg. births per childbearing woman; 1980): 3.6.
*Marriage rate* per 1,000 population (1984): 9.0.
*Divorce rate* per 1,000 population (1982): 0.8.
*Life expectancy* at birth (1983): male 67.9 years; female 72.9 years.
*Major causes of death* per 100,000 population: n.a.; however, major health problems include tuberculosis, hypertension, liver and stomach disorders; malaria and syphilis, formerly widespread, are now practically nonexistent.

## National economy

*Budget* (1987). Revenue: 9,350,000,000 leks (surplus from state enterprises 96.3%, other 3.7%). Expenditures: 9,300,000,000 leks (national economy 54.3%, social and cultural services 28.7%, defense 11.3%, administration 1.6%).
*Public debt* (1985): U.S.$5,600,000,000[2].
*Tourism* (1986): number of tourists 8,000; receipts from visitors, n.a.; expenditures by nationals abroad, n.a.
*Production* (metric tons except as noted). Agriculture, forestry, fishing (1985): wheat 530,000, corn (maize) 400,000, vegetables and fruit except grapes 352,000, sugar beets 348,000, potatoes 136,000, grapes 83,000, sunflower seeds 53,000, barley 36,000, oats 31,000, olives 26,000, tobacco 19,000; livestock (number of live animals) 1,204,000 sheep, 703,000 goats, 614,000 cattle, 210,000 pigs, 75,000 mules and asses, 43,000 horses; roundwood

2,330,000 cu m; fish catch 4,000. Mining and quarrying (1985): ferronickel ores 1,130,000; chromite ore 1,100,000; salt 70,000; copper (metal content) 16,200; nickel 9,600. Manufacturing (1984): bitumen (asphalt) 1,800,000; cement 860,000; distillate fuel oils 270,000; nitrogenous and phosphate fertilizers 104,000; raw sugar 37,000; paper and paperboard 21,200; olive oil 5,000; wine 230,000 hectolitres; beer 140,000 hectolitres; cigarettes 6,200,-000,000 units; cotton and woolen fabrics 60,900,000 m3. Construction (1981–83): 1,706,000,000 leks. Energy production (consumption): electricity (kW-hr; 1985) 3,155,000,000 (2,555,000,000); coal (metric tons; 1985) 1,790,000 (2,010,000); crude petroleum (barrels; 1985) 25,032,000 (25,032,-000); petroleum products (metric tons; 1985) 1,375,000 (1,375,000); natural gas (cu m; 1985) 440,000,000 (440,000,000).
*Gross national product* (at current market prices; 1985): U.S.$2,800,000,000 (U.S.$950 per capita).

### Structure of net material product and labour force

| | 1983 value | % of total value | labour force[4] | % of labour force |
|---|---|---|---|---|
| Agriculture | ... | 34.1 | 152,400 | 21.8 |
| Manufacturing, mining, public utilities | ... | 43.3 | 252,700 | 36.2 |
| Construction | ... | 7.8 | 80,700 | 11.6 |
| Transportation and communication | | | 33,400 | 4.8 |
| Trade | ... | 14.8 | 53,900 | 7.7 |
| Pub. admin., defense | | | 87,200 | 12.5 |
| Other | | | 37,500 | 5.4 |
| TOTAL | ... | 100.0 | 697,800 | 100.0 |

*Population economically active* (1983): total 1,090,800; activity rate of total population 38.4% (participation rates: ages 15–64, n.a.; female 46.0%; unemployed, n.a.).
*Price and earnings indexes:* n.a.
*Household income and expenditure.* Average household size (1984) 5.5; income per household: n.a.; sources of income: n.a.; expenditure: n.a.
*Land use* (1984): forested 37.9%; meadows and pastures 14.6%; agricultural and under permanent cultivation 26.0%; other 21.5%.

## Foreign trade

### Balance of trade (current prices)

| | 1978 | 1979 | 1980 | 1981 | 1982 | 1983 |
|---|---|---|---|---|---|---|
| '000,000 leks | ... | 100 | ... | ... | ... | ... |
| % of total | ... | 5.3 | ... | ... | ... | ... |

*Imports* (1982): U.S.$373,500,000 (mineral fuels and lubricants 33.3%, machinery and transport equipment 22.2%, chemicals and related products 16.6%, food and live animals 16.6%, consumer goods 5.9%). *Major import sources:* U.S.S.R. and Eastern European countries 35.6%; European Economic Community countries 28.7%; United States 4.6%; Japan 2.8%.
*Exports* (1982): U.S.$350,700,000 (mineral fuels 27.1%, crude minerals and metalliferous ores 26.2%, electricity 13.2%, food and food preparations 13.2%, consumer products 9.8%). *Major export destinations:* U.S.S.R. and Eastern European countries 35.7%; European Economic Community countries 31.2%; United States 3.8%; Japan 1.1%.

## Transport and communications

*Transport.* Railroads (1984): length 253 mi, 408 km; passenger-mi 181,000,-000[3], passenger-km 291,000,000[3]; short ton-mi cargo 87,000,000[3], metric ton-km cargo 127,000,000[3]. Roads (1981): total length 13,049 mi, 21,000 km (paved 14%). Vehicles (1970): passenger cars 3,500; trucks and buses 11,200. Merchant marine (1986): vessels (100 gross tons and over) 20; total deadweight tonnage 79,940. Air transport: passengers, n.a.; cargo, n.a.; airports (1987) with scheduled flights 1.
*Communications.* Daily newspapers (1985): total number 2; total circulation 145,000[3]; circulation per 1,000 population 52.0[3]. Radio (1986): total number of receivers 210,000 (1 per 14.8 persons). Television (1985): total number of receivers 185,740 (1 per 15 persons). Telephones, n.a.

## Education and health

### Education (1984)

| | schools | teachers | students | student/teacher ratio |
|---|---|---|---|---|
| Primary (age 6–13) | 1,631 | 27,387 | 540,332 | 19.7 |
| Secondary (age 14–17) | 205 | 1,552 | 35,643 | 23.0 |
| Voc., teacher tr. | 313[5] | 5,405 | 123,797 | 22.9 |
| Higher | 8[5] | 1,502 | 21,285 | 14.2 |

*Educational attainment,* n.a. *Literacy* (1970): total population age 15 and over literate 1,234,376 (75.0%).
*Health* (1983): physicians 4,957[6] (1 per 609 persons); hospital beds 17,600 (1 per 161 persons); infant mortality rate per 1,000 live births (1982) 44.0.
*Food* (1980–82): daily per capita caloric intake 3,060 (vegetable products 87%, animal products 13%); 127% of FAO recommended minimum requirement.

## Military

*Total active duty personnel* (1986): 42,000 (army 75.0%, navy 7.9%, air force 17.1%). *Military expenditure as percent of GNP* (1981): 8.1% (world 5.8%); per capita expenditure U.S.$69.

[1]Detail does not add to total given because of rounding. [2]Estimated total since 1949. [3]1981. [4]State sector only. [5]1983. [6]Includes dentists.

# Algeria

*Official name:* al-Jumhūrīyah al-Jazā'irīyah ad-Dīmuqrāṭīyah ash-Sha'bīyah (Arabic) (Democratic and Popular Republic of Algeria).
*Form of government:* socialist republic with one legislative house (The National People's Assembly [295]).
*Head of state and government:* President.
*Capital:* Algiers.
*Official language:* Arabic.
*Official religion:* Islam.
*Monetary unit:* 1 Algerian dinar (DA) = 100 centimes; valuation (Oct. 5, 1987) 1 U.S.$ = DA 4.67; 1 £ = DA 7.58.

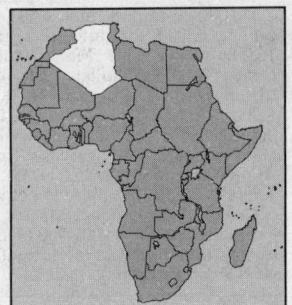

### Population 1987 Census[1]

| Wilāyat | population | Wilāyat | population |
|---|---|---|---|
| Adrar | 216,931 | Médéa | 650,623 |
| Ain Defla | 536,205 | Mila | 511,047 |
| Ain Temouchent | 271,454 | Mostaganem | 504,124 |
| Alger | 1,687,579 | M'Sila | 605,578 |
| Annaba | 453,951 | Naâma | 112,858 |
| Batna | 757,059 | Oran | 916,578 |
| el-Bayadh | 155,494 | Ouargla | 286,696 |
| Béchar | 183,896 | el-Oued | 379,512 |
| Bejaia | 697,669 | Oum el-Bouaghi | 402,683 |
| Biskra | 429,217 | Relizane | 545,061 |
| Blida | 704,462 | Saïda | 235,240 |
| Bordj Bou Arreridj | 429,009 | Sétif | 997,482 |
| Bouira | 525,460 | Sidi bel-Abbès | 444,047 |
| Boumerdes | 646,870 | Skikda | 619,094 |
| ech-Chlef | 679,717 | Souk Ahras | 298,236 |
| Constantine | 662,330 | Tamanrasset | 94,219 |
| Djelfa | 490,240 | el-Tarf | 276,836 |
| Guelma | 353,329 | Tébessa | 409,317 |
| Ghardaïa | 215,955 | Tiaret | 574,786 |
| Illizi | 19,698 | Tindouf | 16,339 |
| Jijel | 471,319 | Tipaza | 615,140 |
| Khenchela | 243,733 | Tissemsilt | 227,542 |
| Laghouat | 215,183 | Tizi Ouzou | 931,501 |
| Mascara | 562,806 | Tlemcen | 707,453 |
| | | TOTAL | 22,971,558 |

## Demography

*Area:* 919,595 sq mi, 2,381,741 sq km.
*Population* (1987): 23,116,000.
*Density* (1987): persons per sq mi 25.1, persons per sq km 9.7.
*Urban–rural* (1987): urban 49%; rural 51%.
*Sex distribution* (1985): male 49.71%; female 50.29%.
*Age breakdown* (1985): under 15, 46.0%; 15–29, 27.2%; 30–44, 12.8%; 45–59, 8.3%; 60–74, 4.4%; 75 and over, 1.4%.
*Population projection:* (1990) 25,280,000; (2000) 34,064,000.
*Doubling time:* 22 years.
*Ethnic composition* (1983): Arab 82.6%; Berber 17.0%; French 0.1%; other 0.3%.
*Religious affiliation* (1980): Sunnī Muslim 99.1%; Roman Catholic 0.5%; other 0.4%.
*Major cities* (1987): Algiers 1,483,000; Oran 590,000; Constantine 438,000; Annaba 310,000; Batna 182,000.

## Vital statistics

*Birth rate* per 1,000 population (1985): 38.9[2] (world avg. 29.0); legitimacy rate, n.a.; marriage, however, is nearly universal.
*Death rate* per 1,000 population (1985): 7.1[2] (world avg. 11.0).
*Natural increase rate* per 1,000 population (1985): 31.8[2] (world avg. 18.0).
*Total fertility rate* (avg. births per childbearing woman; 1984): 6.1.
*Marriage rate* per 1,000 population (1985): 5.7[2].
*Divorce rate* per 1,000 population (1984): 1.1[2].
*Life expectancy* at birth (1983): male 61.6 years; female 63.3 years.
*Major infectious diseases* per 100,000 population (1984): measles 106.8; dysentery 33.5; typhoid fever 23.4.

## National economy

*Budget* (1986–87). Revenue: DA 96,000,000,000 (hydrocarbons 23%). Expenditures: DA 108,000,000,000 (current expenditures 58%, investment 42%).
*Tourism* (1985): receipts from visitors U.S.$143,000,000; expenditures by nationals abroad U.S.$574,000,000.
*Production* (metric tons except as noted). Agriculture, forestry, fishing (1985): wheat 1,650,000, barley 1,295,000, potatoes 800,000, grapes 469,000, tomatoes 305,000, oranges 260,000, dates 220,000; livestock (number of live animals) 13,111,000 sheep, 3,010,000 goats 1,750,000 cattle; roundwood 1,691,000 cu m; fish catch 66,000. Mining and quarrying (1985): iron ore 3,377,000; phosphates 1,221,000; gypsum and plaster 250,000; barite 60,000; silver 120,000 troy oz. Manufacturing (1985): cement 6,096,000; flour 2,293,-000; pig iron and ferroalloys 1,469,900; crude steel 1,245,500; edible oils 269,700. Construction (1981): residential 28,000 units. Energy production (consumption): electricity (kW-hr; 1985) 12,274,000,000 (12,360,000,000); coal (metric tons; 1985) 8,000 (1,608,000); crude petroleum (barrels; 1985) 232,977,000 (173,798,000); petroleum products (metric tons; 1985) 32,840,-000 (5,473,000); natural gas (cu m; 1985) 26,019,000,000 (5,055,000,000).
*Gross national product* (1985): U.S.$55,230,000,000 (U.S.$2,530 per capita).

### Structure of gross domestic product and labour force

| | 1984 | | 1985 | |
|---|---|---|---|---|
| | in value DA '000,000 | % of total value | labour force[3] | % of labour force |
| Agriculture | 19,710 | 8.7 | 990,000 | 25.8 |
| Oil and gas | 63,030 | 27.7 | 510,000 | 13.3 |
| Manufacturing | 29,690 | 13.0 | | |
| Construction | 38,190 | 16.8 | 658,000 | 17.1 |
| Public utilities | | | | |
| Transp. and commun. | 12,240 | 5.4 | 170,000 | 4.4 |
| Trade | 32,070 | 14.1 | 612,000 | 15.9 |
| Finance | | | | |
| Services | | | | |
| Pub. admin., defense | 9,530 | 4.2 | 900,000 | 23.5 |
| Other | 23,360 | 10.3 | ... | ... |
| TOTAL | 227,820 | 100.0[4] | 3,840,000 | 100.0 |

*Public debt* (external, outstanding; 1985): U.S.$13,664,000,000.
*Population economically active* (1987): total 4,204,460[3]; activity rate of population 18.3%[3] (participation rates [1983]: over age 10, 38.9%; female 6.7%; unemployed, n.a.).

### Price and earnings indexes (1980 = 100)

| | 1980 | 1981 | 1982 | 1983 | 1984 | 1985 | 1986 |
|---|---|---|---|---|---|---|---|
| Consumer price index | 100.0 | 114.6 | 122.3 | 127.9 | 136.3 | 156.4 | 173.9 |
| Earnings index | ... | ... | ... | ... | ... | ... | ... |

*Household income and expenditure.* Average household size (1987) 6.9; income per household: n.a.; sources of income: n.a.; expenditure (1979–80): food and beverages 55.7%, housing 11.7%, clothing and footwear 9.2%, transport and communication 6.7%, recreation 3.4%, medical care and health 3.1%.
*Land use* (1984): forested 1.8%; meadows and pastures 13.5%; agricultural and under permanent cultivation 3.1%; built-up, wasteland, and other (mostly desert) 81.6%.

## Foreign trade

### Balance of trade (current prices)

| | 1979 | 1980 | 1981 | 1982 | 1983 | 1984 |
|---|---|---|---|---|---|---|
| DA '000,000 | +6,939 | +19,493 | +19,836 | +11,151 | +14,686 | +18,672 |
| % of total | 10.4% | 19.4% | 19.0% | 10.1% | 13.9% | 17.2% |

*Imports* (1985): DA 49,491,000,000 (raw materials for industry 37.4%; machinery and transport equipment 35.8%, of which transport equipment 10.6%; food and beverages 19.7%; consumer products 5.5%). *Major import sources:* France 26.0%; West Germany 11.2%; Italy 10.9%; United States 6.5%; Japan 5.8%.
*Exports* (1985): DA 64,564,000,000 (mineral fuels and lubricants 98.0%, crude materials 1.3%). *Major export destinations:* European Economic Community 67.4%; United States 10.0%; Spain 5.9%.

## Transport and communications

*Transport.* Railroads (1986): route length 2,337 mi, 3,761 km; passenger-mi 1,265,000,000, passenger-km 2,035,000,000; short ton-mi cargo 2,010,-000,000, metric ton-km cargo 2,934,000,000. Roads (1981): total length 44,795 mi, 72,091 km (paved 54%). Vehicles (1985): passenger cars 712,-700; trucks and buses 471,500. Merchant marine (1986): vessels (100 gross tons and over) 145; total deadweight tonnage 1,018,510. Air transport[5] (1986): passenger-mi 1,518,000,000, passenger-km 2,443,000,000; short ton-mi cargo 3,532,000, metric ton-km cargo 5,157,000; airports (1987) with scheduled flights 22.
*Communications.* Daily newspapers (1986): total number 4; total circulation 480,000; circulation per 1,000 population 23.0. Radio (1986): 3,250,000 receivers (1 per 7 persons). Television (1986): 1,540,000 receivers (1 per 15 persons). Telephones (1985): 769,000 (1 per 28.3 persons).

## Education and health

### Education (1986–87)

| | schools | teachers | students | student/teacher ratio |
|---|---|---|---|---|
| Primary (age 6–11) | 11,692 | 133,250 | 3,635,000 | 27.3 |
| Secondary (age 12–18) | 1,959[6] | 95,113 | 1,877,000 | 19.7 |
| Voc., teacher tr. | 717 | 2,528 | 98,000 | 38.8 |
| Higher | 15[8] | 12,509[9] | 143,300 | 8.3[9] |

*Educational attainment* (1971). Percent of population age 25 and over having: no formal schooling 84.4%; primary education 13.0%; secondary education 2.2%; higher 0.3%; unknown 0.4%. *Literacy* (1980): total population age 15 and over literate 4,342,300 (41.8%); males literate 2,771,400 (55.6%); females literate 1,570,900 (29.1%).
*Health:* physicians (1986) 15,361 (1 per 1,468 persons); hospital beds (1985) 49,280 (1 per 436 persons); infant mortality rate (1984) 81.2.
*Food* (1981–83): daily per capita caloric intake 2,663 (vegetable products 88%, animal products 12%); (1983) 115% of FAO recommended minimum requirement.

## Military

*Total active duty personnel* (1986): 169,000 (army 88.8%, navy 4.1%, air force 7.1%). *Military expenditure as percent of GNP* (1984): 2.7% (world 5.9%); per capita expenditure U.S.$66.

[1]March 20. [2]Algerian population only. [3]Employed persons only. [4]Detail does not add to total given because of rounding. [5]Air Algérie international traffic only. [6]Excludes lycées for general education. [7]1980–81. [8]1981–82. [9]1983–84.

# Andorra

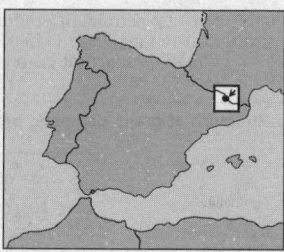

*Official name:* Principat (Co-Principat) or Senyoriu (Co-Senyoriu) d'Andorra; les Valls d'Andorra (Principality [or Co-Principality] of Andorra; the Valleys of Andorra).
*Form of government:* co-principality with one nonpartisan legislative house (General Council of the Valleys [28]).
*Chiefs of state:* President of France; Bishop of Urgel, Spain.
*Head of government:* Chief executive.
*Capital:* Andorra la Vella.
*Official language:* Catalan.
*Official religion:* Roman Catholicism.
*Monetary unit:* There is no local currency of issue; the French franc and Spanish peseta are both in circulation. 1 franc (F) = 100 centimes; 1 peseta (Pta) = 100 céntimos. Valuation (Oct. 5, 1987) 1 U.S.$ = F 6.13, 1 £ = F 9.96; 1 U.S.$ = Ptas 122.21, 1 £ = Ptas 198.45.

| Area and population | | area | | population |
|---|---|---|---|---|
| Parishes | Capitals | sq mi | sq km | 1986 census |
| Andorra la Vella | Andorra la Vella | 49[1] | 127[1] | 18,463 |
| Canillo | Canillo | 74 | 191 | 1,153 |
| Encamp | Encamp | | | 5,766 |
| La Massana | La Massana | 25 | 65 | 3,229 |
| Les Escaldes–Engordany | — | 1 | 1 | 11,734 |
| Ordino | Ordino | 33 | 85 | 1,096 |
| Sant Julià de Lòria | Sant Julià de Lòria | 1 | 1 | 5,535 |
| TOTAL | | 181 | 468 | 46,976 |

## Demography

*Population* (1987): 48,800.
*Density* (1987): persons per sq mi 269.6, persons per sq km 104.3.
*Urban–rural* (1986): urban 64.7%; rural 35.3%.
*Sex distribution* (1986): male 53.12%; female 46.88%.
*Age breakdown* (1986): under 15, 19.0%; 15–29, 27.3%; 30–44, 26.4%; 45–59, 14.8%; 60–74, 9.4%; 75 and over, 3.1%.
*Population projection*[2]: (1990) 57,000; (2000) 96,000.
*Doubling time:* 89 years.
*Ethnic composition* (1986): Spanish 55.1%; Andorran 27.5%; French 7.4%; Portuguese 4.1%; British 1.5%; other 4.4%.
*Religious affiliation* (1980): Roman Catholic 94.2%; Jewish 0.4%; Jehovah's Witnesses 0.3%; Protestant 0.2%; other 4.9%.
*Major cities* (1986): Andorra la Vella 15,639; Les Escaldes 11,955; Encamp 3,535.

## Vital statistics

*Birth rate* per 1,000 population (1986): 11.6 (world avg. 26.0).
*Death rate* per 1,000 population (1986): 3.8 (world avg. 9.9).
*Natural increase rate* per 1,000 population (1986): 7.8 (world avg. 16.1).
*Total fertility rate* (avg. births per childbearing woman): n.a.
*Marriage rate* per 1,000 population (1986): 2.8.
*Divorce rate* per 1,000 population: n.a.
*Life expectancy* at birth: (1980; both sexes) 70 years.
*Major causes of death* per 100,000 population: n.a.; however, health problems are those of a developed country—cardiovascular disease, hypertension, malignant neoplasms (cancers).

## National economy

*Budget* (1986). Revenue: Ptas 6,655,098,711 (1983; excise taxes on imported consumer goods and gasoline 93.9%; additional revenue is derived from a 3% tax on alcoholic beverages). Expenditures: Ptas 6,655,098,711 (primarily administrative services and education; Andorra has virtually no military expenditures).
*Production.* Agriculture, forestry, fishing (1981): potatoes 472 metric tons, tobacco 264 metric tons, and unknown amounts of hay, rye, buckwheat, olives, and grapes; livestock (number of live animals; 1982) 9,000 sheep, 1,115 cattle, 217 horses. Mining and quarrying: building stone, alum, iron, and lead. Manufacturing: ceramics, cigars and cigarettes, alcoholic beverages (including anisette and brandy), clothing, jewelry, textiles (including woolen blankets and scarves), and wooden furniture. Construction (1984): 90 buildings totaling 83,834 sq m were authorized for construction. Energy production (consumption): electricity (kW-hr; 1986) 132,470,000 (166,675,-000[3,4]); coal, none (n.a.); crude petroleum, none (n.a.); petroleum products (metric tons; 1986) none (95,349); natural gas, none (n.a.).
*Population economically active* (1986): total 21,484; activity rate of total population 46.8% (participation rates: ages 15–64, n.a.; female, n.a.; unemployed, n.a.).

| Price and earnings indexes (1980 = 100)[5] | | | | | | | |
|---|---|---|---|---|---|---|---|
| | 1981 | 1982 | 1983 | 1984 | 1985 | 1986 | 1987[6] |
| Consumer price index | 114.6 | 131.0 | 147.0 | 163.6 | 178.0 | 193.6 | 202.2 |
| Earnings index | ... | ... | ... | ... | ... | ... | ... |

*Public debt:* n.a.
*Gross national product* (at current market prices; 1982): U.S.$340,000,000 (U.S.$9,000 per capita)[7].

| Structure of labour force | | |
|---|---|---|
| | 1986 | |
| | labour force | % of labour force |
| Agriculture and forestry | 132 | 0.6 |
| Mining | 571 | 2.7 |
| Manufacturing | 957 | 4.5 |
| Construction | 1,754 | 8.2 |
| Public utilities | 1,266 | 5.9 |
| Transportation and communication | 1,832 | 8.5 |
| Trade | 5,777 | 26.9 |
| Finance | 1,281 | 6.0 |
| Pub. admin., defense | 650 | 3.0 |
| Services and hotel | 5,209 | 24.3 |
| Other | 2,025 | 9.4 |
| TOTAL | 21,454 | 100.0 |

*Household income and expenditure.* Average household size: n.a.; income per household: n.a.; sources of income: n.a.; expenditure: n.a.
*Land use* (1985): forested 23.7%; meadows and pastures 44.2%; agricultural and under permanent cultivation 4.0%; other 28.1%.
*Tourism* (1983): receipts from tourist arrivals, n.a.; expenditures by nationals abroad, n.a.; number of tourist arrivals, approximately 10,000,000 annually, most of whom do not stay overnight; number of hotels 235; number of hotel rooms (1987) 35,000.

## Foreign trade

| Balance of trade (current prices) | | | | | |
|---|---|---|---|---|---|
| | 1980 | 1981 | 1982 | 1983 | 1984 |
| Ptas '000,000 | −25,879 | −28,090 | −30,197 | −32,011 | −35,795 |
| % of total | 91.9% | 94.8% | 91.5% | 91.6% | 92.1% |

*Imports* (1986): Ptas 74,312,755,085, of which from France Ptas 31,525,-222,000, from Spain Ptas 20,036,199,000 (includes fuels, food, perfumes, clothing, and radio and television sets)[8].
*Exports* (1986): Ptas 2,325,252,000, of which to France Ptas 1,261,917,000, to Spain Ptas 762,196,000 (includes wooden furniture, handicrafts, cigarettes, cigars, leather goods, and electricity).

## Transport and communications

*Transport.* Railroads: none; however, both French and Spanish railways stop near the border. Roads (1981): total length 138 mi, 220 km (paved 55%). Vehicles (1986): passenger cars 25,000; trucks and buses 2,583[9]. Merchant marine: vessels (100 gross tons and over) none. Airports with scheduled flights: none; the airport at nearby Seo de Urgel, Spain, has scheduled daily flights to Barcelona and Palma (on Majorca).
*Communications.* Weekly newspapers (1986): total number 1; circulation 4,000; circulation per 1,000 population 86.4. Radio (1986): total number of receivers 8,000 (1 per 5.8 persons). Television (1986): total number of receivers 4,000 (1 per 12 persons). Telephones (1982): 17,719 (1 per 2.1 persons).

## Education and health

| Education (1986–87) | | | | |
|---|---|---|---|---|
| | schools | teachers[10] | students | student/ teacher ratio |
| Primary (age 6–12) | 13 | 214 | 5,344 | ... |
| Secondary (age 12–18) | 10 | 53 | 2,253 | ... |
| Voc., teacher tr. | 5 | 37 | 1,248 | ... |
| Higher | ... | ... | ... | ... |

*Educational attainment,* n.a.; education is compulsory to age 16, however.
*Literacy* (1987): total population literate (virtually 100%).
*Health:* physicians (1984) 53 (1 per 784 persons); hospital beds (1981) 110 (1 per 325 persons); infant mortality rate per 1,000 live births (1986) 3.7.
*Food* (1981–83)[11]: daily per capita caloric intake 3,430 (vegetable products 66%, animal products 34%); (1983) 135% of FAO recommended minimum requirement.

## Military

*Total active duty personnel* (1982): none. France and Spain are responsible for Andorra's external security; a 100-man police force maintains domestic security. *Military expenditure as a percent of central government expenditure* (1981): 0.0001% (world 19.0%).

[1]Andorra la Vella includes Les Escaldes-Engordany and Sant Julià de Lòria. [2]Includes substantial in-migration. [3]1984. [4]Most of the consumption is produced within Andorra; the remainder is imported from Spain. [5]In Spanish pesetas. [6]June. [7]Trade, tourism (including winter-season sports, fairs, and festivals), and the banking system (of some importance as a tax haven for foreign financial investment and transactions) are the primary sources of GNP. [8]Imported manufactured items are less expensive in Andorra than in neighbouring countries because they are duty free. As a result, smuggling remains a profitable sideline for some. [9]1982. [10]1985–86. [11]Composite values derived from Spanish and French food data.

# Angola

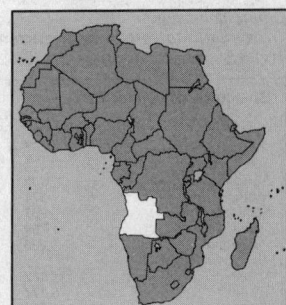

*Official name:* República Popular de Angola (People's Republic of Angola).
*Form of government:* people's republic with one legislative house (People's Assembly [203]).
*Head of state and government:* President.
*Capital:* Luanda.
*Official language:* Portuguese.
*Official religion:* none.
*Monetary unit:* 1 kwanza (Kw) = 100 lwei; valuation (Oct. 5, 1987)
1 U.S.$ = Kw 30.53; 1 £ = Kw 49.58.

### Area and population

| Provinces | Capitals | area[1] sq mi | area[1] sq km | population 1987 estimate[2] |
|---|---|---|---|---|
| Bengo | Caxito | 14,173 | 36,708 | 147,000 |
| Benguela | Benguela | 15,116 | 39,151 | 699,000 |
| Bié | Kuito | 27,149 | 70,317 | 938,000 |
| Cabinda | Cabinda | 2,744 | 7,107 | 112,000 |
| Huambo | Huambo | 12,796 | 33,141 | 1,267,000 |
| Huíla | Lubango | 30,499 | 78,992 | 815,000 |
| Kuando Kubango | Menongue | 76,671 | 198,577 | 169,000 |
| Kuanza Norte | N'Dalatando | 7,717 | 19,988 | 463,000 |
| Kuanza Sul | Sumbe | 21,281 | 55,117 | 692,000 |
| Kunene | N'Giva | 29,327 | 75,956 | 245,000 |
| Luanda | Luanda | 570 | 1,477 | 1,134,000 |
| Lunda Norte | Lucapa | 39,685 | 102,784 | 303,000 |
| Lunda Sul | Saurimo | 29,860 | 77,336 | 146,000 |
| Malanje | Malanje | 33,686 | 87,247 | 829,000 |
| Moxico | Lwena | 77,870 | 201,683 | 277,000 |
| Namibe | Namibe | 22,043 | 57,090 | 77,000 |
| Uíge | Uíge | 23,728 | 61,455 | 589,000 |
| Zaire | M'Banza Kongo | 14,281 | 36,989 | 203,000 |
| TOTAL | | 481,350[3,4] | 1,246,700[3,4] | 9,105,000 |

## Demography

*Population* (1987): 9,105,000.
*Density* (1987): persons per sq mi 18.9, persons per sq km 7.3.
*Urban–rural* (1986): urban 30%; rural 70%.
*Sex distribution* (1987): male 50.90%; female 49.10%.
*Age breakdown* (1987): under 15, 42.2%; 15–29, 27.5%; 30–44, 16.4%; 45–59, 9.5%; 60 and over, 4.4%.
*Population projection:* (1990) 9,978,000; (2000) 13,280,000.
*Doubling time:* 32 years.
*Ethnic composition* (1983): Ovimbundu 37.2%; Mbundu 22.8%; Kongo 13.2%; Luimbe 5.4%; Humbe and Nyaneka 5.4%; Chokwe 4.2%; Luena 3.4%; Luchasi 2.4%; Ambo 2.4%; Lunda 1.2%; MBundu 1.2%; Portuguese 0.5%; mulatto 0.5%; other 0.2%.
*Religious affiliation* (1980): affiliated Christian 65.7%, of which Roman Catholic 55.1%, Protestant 9.2%; nominal Christian 24.3%; traditional beliefs 9.5%; other 0.5%.
*Major cities* (1987)[6]: Luanda 1,134,000; Lubango 105,000[5]; Namibe 77,000.

## Vital statistics

*Birth rate* per 1,000 population (1984): 47.0 (world avg. 29.0).
*Death rate* per 1,000 population (1984): 25.0 (world avg. 11.0).
*Natural increase rate* per 1,000 population (1984): 22.0 (world avg. 18.0).
*Total fertility rate* (avg. births per childbearing woman; 1984): 6.4.
*Marriage rate* per 1,000 population (1972): 4.5.
*Divorce rate* per 1,000 population: n.a.
*Life expectancy* at birth (1985): male 40.4 years; female 43.6 years.
*Major causes of death* per 100,000 population (1973): accidents, poisoning, and violence 89.0; infectious and parasitic diseases 73.2; diseases of the respiratory system 24.6; diseases of the circulatory system 19.2; neoplasms 6.5.

## National economy

*Budget* (1986). Revenue: Kw 103,200,000,000 (1984; taxes 72.9%; state returns from mixed enterprises 14.0%; other 13.1%). Expenditures: Kw 103,200,000,000 (1984; economic and social development 26.7%; education, health, and other social services 21.0%; administration 11.5%; defense 11.5%[7]; other 5.0%).
*Public debt* (external, outstanding; 1985): U.S.$1,106,000,000.
*Tourism:* receipts from visitors, n.a.; expenditures by nationals abroad, n.a.
*Price and earnings indexes:* n.a.
*Production* (metric tons except as noted). Agriculture, forestry, fishing (1985): cassava 1,950,000, sugarcane 350,000, bananas 280,000, corn (maize) 250,000, sweet potatoes 180,000, pulses 40,000, palm oil 40,000, coffee 25,000, peanuts (groundnuts) 20,000; livestock (number of live animals) 3,360,000 cattle, 960,000 goats, 465,000 pigs, 250,000 sheep, 6,000,000 poultry; roundwood (1984) 9,078,000 cu m; fish catch (1984) 70,700. Mining and quarrying (1985): diamonds, of which gem quality 375,000 carats, industrial quality 250,000 carats; cement 350,000; salt 10,000. Manufacturing (1982): raw sugar 35,000; crude steel 10,000; soaps 6,000[8]; paints 5,000[8]; beer 1,250,000 hectolitres[9]; matches 55,000 boxes; cigarettes 2,400,000,000 units; shirts 2,300,000 units; skirts 967,000 units[8]; leather shoes 306,000 pairs[8]. Construction (1980): 164,500 sq m. Energy production (consumption): electricity (kW-hr; 1985) 1,790,000,000 (1,790,000,000); coal (metric tons; 1985) none (negligible); crude petroleum (barrels; 1986) 84,640,400

(10,572,000[10]); petroleum products (metric tons; 1985) 1,035,000 (515,000); natural gas (cu m; 1985) 115,400,000 (115,400,000).
*Gross national product* (at current market prices; 1984): U.S.$6,930,000,000 (U.S. $830 per capita).

### Structure of gross domestic product and labour force

| | 1982 in value Kw '000,000 | 1982 % of total value | 1980 labour force | 1980 % of labour force |
|---|---|---|---|---|
| Agriculture | 77,200 | 38.2 | 2,518,000 | 73.8 |
| Mining | 31,160 | 15.4 | | |
| Manufacturing | 4,690 | 2.3 | | |
| Construction | 3,310 | 1.6 | | |
| Trade, finance | 9,110 | 4.5 | 326,000 | 9.5 |
| Public utilities | 810 | 0.4 | | |
| Transportation and communication | 7,990 | 4.0 | | |
| Pub. admin., defense | 23,580 | 11.7 | | |
| Services | ... | ... | 569,000 | 16.7 |
| Other | 44,120 | 21.8 | | |
| TOTAL | 201,970 | 100.0[4] | 3,413,000 | 100.0 |

*Population economically active* (1980): total 3,413,000; activity rate of total population 44.2% (participation rates: ages 15–64, 73.4%; female 40.6%; unemployed, n.a.).
*Household income and expenditure.* Average household size (1980) 4.8; annual income per household: n.a.; sources of income: n.a.; expenditure: n.a.
*Land use* (1984): forested 42.8%; meadows and pastures 23.3%; agricultural and under permanent cultivation 2.8%; other 31.1%.

## Foreign trade

### Balance of trade (current prices)

| | 1979 | 1980 | 1981 | 1982 | 1983 | 1984 |
|---|---|---|---|---|---|---|
| Kw '000,000 | +11,400 | +4,100 | +3,200 | +22,024 | +32,959 | +41,261 |
| % of total | 16.9% | 3.8% | 3.1% | 26.6% | 41.5% | 52.3% |

*Imports* (1985): U.S.$1,318,900,000 (mostly purchases of military hardware, machinery and transport equipment, bulk iron and ironwork, steel and metals, textile and clothing, medicines, and food). *Major import sources:* Portugal 13.0%; France 11.5%; United States 10.9%; Brazil 10.8%; The Netherlands 6.9%.
*Exports* (1985): U.S.$2,190,300,000 (mainly crude petroleum and petroleum products, diamonds, sisal, fish and fish products, coffee, and cotton). *Major export destinations:* United States 45.3%; Spain 13.7%; The Bahamas 11.4%; France 3.5%.

## Transport and communications

*Transport.* Railroads (1986): route length 1,834 mi, 2,952 km; passenger journeys 7,622,000[8]; cargo transported 725,000 metric tons[8]. Roads (1986): total length 45,877 mi, 73,830 km (paved 51%). Vehicles (1984): passenger cars 56,625; trucks and buses 29,000. Merchant marine (1986): vessels (100 gross tons and over) 100; total deadweight tonnage 127,431. Air transport (1985)[11]: passenger-mi 606,000,000, passenger-km 975,000,000; short ton-mi cargo 23,200,000, metric ton-km cargo 33,900,000; airports (1987) with scheduled flights 19.
*Communications.* Daily newspapers (1984): total number 4; total circulation 111,500; circulation per 1,000 population 13.5. Radio (1986): total number of receivers 400,000 (1 per 22 persons). Television (1986): total number of receivers 32,000 (1 per 276 persons). Telephones (1982): 40,000 (1 per 202 persons).

## Education and health

### Education (1982–83)

| | schools | teachers | students | student/ teacher ratio |
|---|---|---|---|---|
| Primary (age 7–10) | 6,308 | 32,004 | 1,178,430 | 36.8 |
| Secondary (age 11–16) | ... | 3,870[12] | 124,858 | 34.2 |
| Voc., teacher tr. | ... | 410[12] | 7,060 | 12.7 |
| Higher | 1 | 316 | 2,764 | 8.7 |

*Educational attainment,* n.a. *Literacy* (1980): total population over age 15 literate 1,196,000 (about 28%); males literate 771,000 (36.2%); females literate 425,000 (19.3%).
*Health* (1980): physicians 436 (1 per 17,000 persons); hospital beds 20,700 (1 per 359 persons); infant mortality rate per 1,000 live births (1986) 200.0.
*Food* (1979–81): daily per capita caloric intake 2,353 (vegetable products 92%, animal products 8%); 100% of FAO recommended minimum requirement.

## Military

*Total active duty personnel* (1986): 50,000[13] (army 92.9%, navy 3.0%, air force 4.1%). *Military expenditure as percent of GNP* (1984): 14.3% (world 5.9%); per capita expenditure U.S.$119.

---

[1]Provincial detail and totals independently reported and converted. [2]Unified national estimates and projections based on sample surveys, partial censuses, and analysis of provincial vital statistics. [3]Total contains adjustments of unspecified nature amounting to 2,156 sq mi (5,585 sq km). [4]Detail does not add to total given because of rounding. [5]1984. [6]Populations (1970 census) of other important towns were: Huambo 61,885; Lobito 59,258; and Benguela 40,996. [7]According to unofficial estimates, defense consumed more than 60% of the budget in 1983. [8]1981. [9]1979. [10]1985. [11]TAAG airline only. [12]1981–82. [13]In 1986, about 27,000 Cuban troops and several hundred other Soviet-bloc advisers and technicians were assisting government forces.

# Antigua and Barbuda

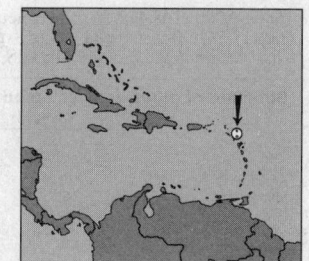

*Official name:* Antigua and Barbuda.
*Form of government:* constitutional
monarchy with two legislative houses
(Senate [17]; House of Representatives
[17]).
*Chief of state:* British Monarch
represented by governor-general.
*Head of government:* Prime Minister.
*Capital:* Saint John's.
*Official language:* English.
*Official religion:* none.
*Monetary unit:* 1 East Caribbean dollar
(EC$) = 100 cents; valuation (Oct. 5,
1987) 1 U.S.$ = EC$2.70;
1 £ = EC$4.38.

| Area and population | area | | population |
|---|---|---|---|
| | | | 1986 |
| Parishes[1] | sq mi | sq km | estimate |
| Saint George | 10.2 | 26.4 | |
| Saint John's | 26.2 | 67.9 | |
| Saint Mary | 25.1 | 65.0 | 80,000 |
| Saint Paul | 17.7 | 45.8 | |
| Saint Peter | 12.8 | 33.2 | |
| Saint Phillip | 16.0 | 41.4 | |
| Islands[1] | | | |
| Barbuda | 62.0 | 160.6 | 1,500 |
| Redonda | 0.5 | 1.3 | 2 |
| TOTAL | 170.5 | 441.6 | 81,500 |

## Demography

*Population* (1987): 82,400.
*Density* (1987): persons per sq mi 483.3, persons per sq km 186.6.
*Urban–rural* (1985): urban 30.8%; rural 69.2%.
*Sex distribution* (1983): male 48.00%; female 52.00%.
*Age breakdown* (1985): under 15, 37.2%; 15–29, 30.8%; 30–44, 12.8%; 45–59
11.5%; 60–74, 6.4%; 75 and over, 1.3%.
*Population projection:* (1990) 86,000; (2000) 98,000.
*Doubling time:* 72 years.
*Ethnic composition* (1980): black 94.4%; mulatto 3.5%; white 1.3%; other
0.8%.
*Religious affiliation* (1980): Anglican 44.5%; other Protestant (largely Mora-
vian, Methodist, and Seventh-day Adventist) 42.2%; Roman Catholic
10.2%; Rastafarian 0.7%; other 2.4%.
*Major cities* (1982): Saint John's 30,000; Codrington 1,200.

## Vital statistics

*Birth rate* per 1,000 population (1985): 14.8 (world avg. 29.0); (1983) legiti-
mate 18.7%; illegitimate 81.3%.
*Death rate* per 1,000 population (1985): 5.0 (world avg. 11.0).
*Natural increase rate* per 1,000 population (1985): 9.8 (world avg. 18.0).
*Total fertility rate* (avg. births per childbearing woman; 1984): 2.1.
*Marriage rate* per 1,000 population (1984): 2.6.
*Divorce rate* per 1,000 population (1983): 0.4.
*Life expectancy* at birth (1980–85): male 70.4 years; female 74.2 years.
*Major causes of death* per 100,000 population (1983): malignant neo-
plasms (cancers) 62.6; hypertensive heart disease 42.2; blood poisoning
30.7; cerebrovascular disease 28.1; pneumonia 25.6; diseases of pulmonary
circulation 25.6.

## National economy

*Budget* (1986). Revenue: EC$158,900,000 (tax revenue 82.9%, of which con-
sumer taxes 24.5%, import duties 19.7%, income and property taxes 12.8%,
taxes on goods and services 12.3%; transfer payments from abroad 4.3%;
nontax revenue 17.1%). Expenditure: EC$248,700,000 (1983; general public
services 18.3%; education 13.8%; transportation and communication 10.3%;
public order 9.3%; health 7.4%; interest on public debt 6.9%; defense 1.7%).
*Public debt* (external, outstanding; 1985): U.S.$64,900,000.
*Production* (metric tons except as noted). Agriculture, forestry, fishing
(1983): sugarcane 4,600[3], sweet potatoes 353, tomatoes 285, yams 273,
carrots 184, pineapples 181, cabbage 166, limes 143[3], cucumbers 140, mangoes 113; livestock (number of live animals; 1985): 17,000 cattle, 13,000
sheep, 12,000 goats; roundwood, n.a.; fish catch 2,246. Mining and quarrying (1983): gravel 49,212. Manufacturing (value of production in EC$;
1983): clothing 24,000,000; mattresses 4,500,000; stoves 3,300,000; refrigerators 1,700,000; rum 1,200,000; electronic components are assembled for
reexport. Construction (1983): total building applications 557; gross value
EC$60,400,000. Energy production (consumption): electricity (kW-hr; 1985)
77,000,000 (77,000,000); coal, none (none); crude petroleum (barrels; 1985)
none (negligible); petroleum products (metric tons; 1985) negligible (48,-
000); natural gas, none (none).
*Population economically active* (1983): total 30,843; activity rate of total
population 39.4% (participation rates: age 16 and over 56.2%; female 39.6%;
unemployed [1984] 21.0%).

| Price and earnings indexes (1980 = 100) | | | | | | | |
|---|---|---|---|---|---|---|---|
| | 1979 | 1980 | 1981 | 1982 | 1983 | 1984 | 1985 |
| Consumer price index | 84.0 | 100.0 | 111.5 | 116.1 | 118.5 | 123.5 | 124.6 |
| Weekly earnings index | 85.8 | 100.0 | ... | ... | ... | ... | ... |

*Household income and expenditure.* Average household size (1970) 4.2;
income per household: n.a.; sources of income: n.a.; expenditure (1969)[4]:
food and nonalcoholic beverages 42.9%, housing 23.3%, transportation
10.0%, clothing and footwear 7.5%, energy 5.5%, alcoholic beverages and
tobacco 3.6%, other 7.2%.
*Tourism:* receipts from visitors (1985) U.S.$84,000,000; expenditures by na-
tionals abroad (1983) U.S.$6,000,000.
*Gross national product* (at current market prices; 1985): U.S.$160,000,000
(U.S.$1,990 per capita).

| Structure of gross domestic product and labour force | | | | |
|---|---|---|---|---|
| | 1986[5] | | 1982 | |
| | in value EC$'000,000 | % of total value | labour force[6] | % of labour force |
| Agriculture, fishing | 10.1 | 3.8 | 2,090 | 9.0 |
| Quarrying | 5.6 | 2.1 | 60 | 0.3 |
| Manufacturing | 15.8 | 5.9 | 1,718 | 7.4 |
| Construction | 22.7 | 8.5 | 2,577 | 11.1 |
| Public utilities | 9.9 | 3.7 | 340 | 1.5 |
| Transp. and commun. | 58.0 | 21.6 | 2,575 | 11.1 |
| Trade, restaurants, and hotels | 71.7 | 26.7 | 5,201 | 22.4 |
| Finance, real estate | 61.2[7] | 22.8[7] | 778 | 3.3 |
| Pub. admin., defense | 23.6 | 8.8 | 7,883 | 33.9 |
| Services | 7 | 7 | | |
| Other | −10.4[8] | −3.9[8] | — | — |
| TOTAL | 268.2 | 100.0 | 23,222 | 100.0 |

*Land use* (1984): forested 16.0%; meadows and pastures 7.0%; agricultural
and under permanent cultivation 18.0%; other 59.0%.

## Foreign trade[9]

| Balance of trade (current prices) | | | | | | |
|---|---|---|---|---|---|---|
| | 1981 | 1982 | 1983 | 1984 | 1985 | 1986 |
| EC$'000,000 | −207 | −189 | −178 | −315 | −379 | −472 |
| % of total | 52.9% | 63.6% | 4.2% | 63.2% | 72.3% | 78.0% |

*Imports* (1983): EC$227,859,000 (food and live animals 24.1%, of which
meat 5.9%, cereals 4.0%, fruits and vegetables 3.8%; machinery and transport equipment 23.9%, of which motor vehicle parts 6.0%; chemicals 8.7%;
clothing 6.4%; beverages 4.1%). *Major import sources:* United States 49.6%;
United Kingdom 13.2%; Caricom states (The Bahamas, Barbados, Belize,
Guyana, Jamaica, and Trinidad and Tobago) other than OECS (Dominica,
Grenada, Montserrat, St. Christopher and Nevis, St. Lucia, St. Vincent
and the Grenadines) 7.9%; Canada 5.5%.
*Exports* (1983): EC$49,688,000 (reexports 39.6%, of which miscellaneous
manufactured articles 17.7%; machinery 15.6%; domestic exports 60.4%,
of which miscellaneous manufactured articles 32.9%, machinery 7.9%,
chemicals 4.7%, beverages and tobacco 4.5%). *Major export destinations:*
Caricom states other than OECS 44.3%; United States 12.9%; OECS 12.9%;
United Kingdom 6.8%.

## Transport and communications

*Transport.* Railroads[10] (1985): 48 mi (78 km). Roads (1984): total length 341
mi, 548 km (paved 44%). Vehicles (1983): passenger cars 7,120; trucks and
buses 1,271. Merchant marine (1986): vessels (100 gross tons and over) 5;
total deadweight tonnage 1,048. Air transport (1983)[11]: passenger arrivals
202,536, passenger departures 200,898; short ton-mi cargo, n.a., metric ton-
km cargo, n.a.; airports (1987) with scheduled flights 2.
*Communications.* Daily newspapers: none. Radio (1986): total number of
receivers 35,000 (1 per 2.3 persons). Television (1986): total number of
receivers 27,000 (1 per 3.0 persons). Telephones (1983): 10,470 (1 per 7.5
persons).

## Education and health

| Education (1983) | schools | teachers | students | student/ teacher ratio |
|---|---|---|---|---|
| Primary (age 5–10) | 48 | 426 | 9,933 | 23.3 |
| Secondary (age 11–16) | 16 | 331 | 4,197 | 12.7 |
| Voc., teacher tr. | 1 | ... | ... | ... |
| Higher | ... | ... | ... | ... |

*Educational attainment* (1970). Percent of total population having: no
schooling 15.0%; primary education 79.2%; secondary 4.5%; higher 1.3%.
*Literacy* (1985): total population age 15 and over literate 45,000 (90.0%).
*Health* (1984): physicians 33 (1 per 2,394 persons); hospital beds 415 (1 per
190 persons); infant mortality rate per 1,000 live births (1982–83 avg.) 19.8.
*Food* (1981–83): daily per capita caloric intake 2,019 (vegetable products
73%, animal products 27%); (1983) 81% of FAO recommended minimum
requirement.

## Military

*Total active duty personnel* (1985): 700-member defense and police force.
*Military expenditure as percent of central government expenditure:* 1.7%.

[1]Community councils are the actual organs of local governments. [2]Uninhabited.
[3]1984. [4]Weights of consumer price index components. [5]At prices of 1977. [6]Wage
earners and self-employed only. [7]Finance, real estate includes services. [8]Less imputed
bank service charges. [9]Excludes crude petroleum and petroleum products for years
1978–83. [10]Private railroad only. [11]Vere Bird Airport.

# Argentina

*Official name:* República Argentina
(Argentine Republic).
*Form of government:* federal republic
with two legislative houses (Senate
[46]; Chamber of Deputies [254]).
*Head of state and government:*
President.
*Capital:* Buenos Aires[1].
*Official language:* Spanish.
*Official religion:* Roman Catholicism.
*Monetary unit:* 1 austral (pl. australes)[2]
(₳) = 1,000 pesos ($a 1,000); valuation
(Oct. 5, 1987) 1 U.S.$ = ₳ 2.72;
1 £ = ₳ 4.42.

## Area and population

| Provinces | Capitals | area sq mi | area sq km | population 1986 estimate |
|---|---|---|---|---|
| Buenos Aires | La Plata | 118,754 | 307,571 | 12,226,000 |
| Catamarca | San Fernando del Valle de Catamarca | 38,984 | 100,967 | 230,000 |
| Chaco | Resistencia | 38,469 | 99,633 | 791,000 |
| Chubut | Rawson | 86,752 | 224,686 | 316,000 |
| Córdoba· | Córdoba | 65,161 | 168,766 | 2,629,000 |
| Corrientes | Corrientes | 34,054 | 88,199 | 724,000 |
| Entre Ríos | Paraná | 30,418 | 78,781 | 968,000 |
| Formosa | Formosa | 27,825 | 72,066 | 338,000 |
| Jujuy | San Salvador de Jujuy | 20,548 | 53,219 | 487,000 |
| La Pampa | Santa Rosa | 55,382 | 143,440 | 231,000 |
| La Rioja | La Rioja | 34,626 | 89,680 | 183,000 |
| Mendoza | Mendoza | 57,462 | 148,827 | 1,344,000 |
| Misiones | Posadas | 11,506 | 29,801 | 690,000 |
| Neuquén | Neuquén | 36,324 | 94,078 | 315,000 |
| Río Negro | Viedma | 78,384 | 203,013 | 477,000 |
| Salta | Salta | 59,759 | 154,775 | 768,000 |
| San Juan | San Juan | 34,614 | 89,651 | 520,000 |
| San Luis | San Luis | 29,633 | 76,748 | 234,000 |
| Santa Cruz | Río Gallegos | 94,187 | 243,943 | 138,000 |
| Santa Fe | Santa Fe | 51,354 | 133,007 | 2,675,000 |
| Santiago del Estero | Santiago del Estero | 52,222 | 135,254 | 660,000 |
| Tucumán | San Miguel de Tucumán | 8,697 | 22,524 | 1,112,000 |
| **Other federal entities** | | | | |
| Distrito Federal | Buenos Aires | 77 | 200 | 2,924,000 |
| Tierra del Fuego | Ushuaia | 8,210 | 21,263 | 50,000 |
| TOTAL | | 1,073,399[3] | 2,780,092 | 31,030,000 |

## Demography

*Population* (1987): 31,496,000.
*Density* (1987): persons per sq mi 29.3, persons per sq km 11.3.
*Urban–rural* (1985): urban 84.6%; rural 15.4%.
*Sex distribution* (1985): male 49.61%; female 50.39%.
*Age breakdown* (1985): under 15, 31.1%; 15–29, 23.0%; 30–44, 19.1%; 45–59, 14.5%; 60–74, 9.5%; 75 and over, 2.8%.
*Population projection:* (1990) 32,880,000; (2000) 37,197,000.
*Doubling time:* 54 years.
*Ethnic composition* (1986): European 85%; mestizo, Amerindian, and other 15%.
*Religious affiliation* (1984): Roman Catholic 92.8%; other 7.2%.
*Major cities* (1980): Buenos Aires 2,922,829 (Greater Buenos Aires 9,766,000[4]); Córdoba 968,829; Rosario 875,664; La Plata 454,884.

## Vital statistics

*Birth rate* per 1,000 population (1985): 25.0 (world avg. 29.0); (1979) legitimate 70.2%; illegitimate 27.4%; unknown 2.4%.
*Death rate* per 1,000 population (1985): 9.0 (world avg. 11.0).
*Natural increase rate* per 1,000 population (1985): 16.0 (world avg. 18.0).
*Total fertility rate* (avg. births per childbearing woman; 1985): 3.4.
*Marriage rate* per 1,000 population (1983): 6.0.
*Life expectancy* at birth (1981): male 68.6 years; female 73.3 years.
*Major causes of death* per 100,000 population (1981): circulatory diseases 371.9; cancers 148.8; respiratory diseases 51.8; accidents 42.8.

## National economy

*Budget* (1984). Revenue: $a 782,348,000,000[5] (excise taxes 29.2%, social security taxes 24.1%, general sales tax 12.0%, export duties 7.7%, import duties 4.4%, income taxes 3.1%, property tax 2.7%). Expenditures: $a 885,773,000,000[6] (social security and welfare 37.8%, economic services 20.3%, general public services 9.9%, education 9.5%, defense 8.8%, health 1.8%).
*Public debt* (external, outstanding; 1985): U.S.$38,391,500,000.
*Tourism* (1984): receipts from visitors U.S.$602,000,000; expenditures by nationals abroad U.S.$681,000,000.
*Production* (metric tons except as noted). Agriculture, forestry, fishing (1986): sugarcane 14,105,000, corn (maize) 12,400,000, wheat 8,700,000, sorghum 4,200,000, sunflower seeds 4,100,000, grapes 2,279,000[4], potatoes 2,000,000[4], soybeans 1,720,000, alfalfa 1,500,000, tomatoes 824,400; livestock (number of live animals; 1985) 54,800,000 cattle, 29,000,000 sheep; roundwood 13,375,000 cu m[6]; fish catch 406,148[6]. Mining and quarrying (1985): uranium 180; silver 2,500,000 troy oz[6]; gold 24,000 troy oz[6]. Manufacturing (by value in $a '000[5]; 1985): motor vehicles 629,978; iron and steel, 475,695; processed sugar 314,056; iron and steel pipes and tubes 291,232; paper and paper products 52,000; cigars and cigarettes 48,443. Construction (authorized; 1985) 1,255,700 sq m[7]. Energy production (consumption): electricity (kW-hr; 1985) 45,265,000,000 (45,259,000,000); coal (metric tons; 1985) 400,000 (1,203,000); crude petroleum (barrels; 1985)

168,960,000 (168,473,000); petroleum products (metric tons; 1985) 20,738,000 (17,761,000); natural gas (cu m; 1985) 16,405,000,000 (18,616,000,000).
*Gross national product* (1985): U.S.$65,080,000,000 (U.S.$2,130 per capita).

## Structure of gross domestic product and labour force

| | 1985[8] in value ₳ '000,000 | 1985[8] % of total value | 1980 labour force | 1980 % of labour force |
|---|---|---|---|---|
| Agriculture | 1,407 | 15.9 | 1,200,992 | 12.0 |
| Mining | 245 | 2.8 | 47,171 | 0.5 |
| Manufacturing | 2,035 | 23.0 | 1,985,995 | 19.9 |
| Construction | 308 | 3.5 | 1,003,175 | 10.1 |
| Public utilities | 418 | 4.7 | 103,256 | 1.0 |
| Transp. and commun. | 1,037 | 11.7 | 460,476 | 4.6 |
| Trade | 1,128 | 12.7 | 1,702,080 | 17.0 |
| Finance | 693 | 7.8 | 395,704 | 4.0 |
| Pub. admin., defense Services } | 1,579 | 17.8 | 2,399,039 | 24.0 |
| Other | ... | ... | 691,302 | 6.9 |
| TOTAL | 8,847[3] | 100.0 | 9,989,190 | 100.0 |

*Population economically active* (1985): total 11,452,444; activity rate of total population 37.5% (participation rates: ages 15–64, 59.2%; female 26.8%; unemployed 5.7%).

## Price and earnings indexes (1980 = 100)

| | 1980 | 1981 | 1982 | 1983 | 1984 | 1985 | 1986 |
|---|---|---|---|---|---|---|---|
| Consumer price index | 100.0 | 204.0 | 541.0 | 2,403 | 17,462 | 134,833 | 256,312 |
| Monthly earnings index[9] | 100.0 | 183.3 | 434.3 | 2,496 | 22,056 | 138,698 | ... |

*Land use* (1984): forested 21.8%; meadows and pastures 52.2%; agricultural and under permanent cultivation 13.0%; other 13.0%.

## Foreign trade[10]

### Balance of trade (current prices)

| | 1980 | 1981 | 1982 | 1983 | 1984 | 1985[5] | 1986[5] |
|---|---|---|---|---|---|---|---|
| $a '000,000 | −270 | +312 | +4,834 | +37,495 | +184,460 | +2,937 | +2,225 |
| % of total | 8.4% | 4.2% | 19.7% | 30.0% | 23.2% | 41.3% | 21.0% |

*Imports* (1985)[11]: U.S.$3,814,229,000 (industrial chemicals 21.9%; nonelectrical machinery 14.4%; petroleum and products 10.0%; electrical machinery 8.4%; iron and steel products 8.1%; road vehicles and transport equipment 7.7%; plastics 6.1%). *Major import sources:* U.S. 17.9%; Brazil 15.9%; W.Ger. 10.5%.
*Exports* (1985)[11]: U.S.$8,396,114,000 (cereals 21.3%; vegetables, fruits, and nuts 15.4%; vegetable oils 12.7%; animal feed 10.0%; meat 6.1%; hides and skins 4.3%; petroleum and petroleum products 4.0%; iron and steel products 2.9%). *Major export destinations:* U.S. 12.5%; U.S.S.R. 11.8%; The Netherlands 10.9%; Brazil 6.0%; Japan 4.3%; Iran 4.0%; Italy 3.7%.

## Transport and communications

*Transport.* Railroads (1986): route length 21,233 mi, 34,172 km; passenger-km 10,740,000,000[4]; metric ton-km cargo 9,504,000,000[4]. Roads (1985): total length 131,321 mi, 211,341 km (paved 26%). Vehicles (1985): passenger cars 3,773,600; commercial vehicles and buses 1,396,000. Merchant marine (1986): vessels (100 gross tons and over) 454; total deadweight tonnage 3,171,154. Air transport (1986)[12]: passenger-km 6,648,000,000; metric ton-km cargo 185,000,000; airports (1987) 65.
*Communications.* Daily newspapers (1984): total number 227; total circulation 2,748,400[13]; circulation per 1,000 population 91. Radio (1985): 19,866,000 receivers (1 per 1.5 persons). Television (1985): 5,925,000 receivers (1 per 5.2 persons). Telephones (1984): 3,593,962 (1 per 8.4 persons).

## Education and health

### Education (1984)

| | schools | teachers | students | student/ teacher ratio |
|---|---|---|---|---|
| Primary (age 6–12) | 20,619 | 218,520 | 4,430,513 | 20.3 |
| Secondary (age 13–17)[14] | 1,987 | 86,874 | 656,521 | 7.6 |
| Vocational | 3,117 | 119,309 | 905,755 | 7.6 |
| Higher | 1,251 | 64,230 | 677,535 | 10.5 |

*Educational attainment* (1980). Percent of population age 25 and over having: no formal schooling 6.0%; less than primary education 32.0%; primary 34.6%; secondary 20.5%; higher 6.9%. *Literacy* (1980): total population age 15 and over literate 94.9%; males literate 95.5%; females literate 94.4%.
*Health* (1980): physicians 72,762 (1 per 388 persons); hospital beds 151,568 (1 per 186 persons); infant mortality rate per 1,000 live births (1984) 36.0.
*Food* (1981–83): daily per capita caloric intake 3,195 (vegetable products 69%; animal products 31%); (1983) 119% of FAO recommended minimum requirement.

## Military

*Total active duty personnel* (1986): 73,000 (army 54.8%, navy 24.7%, air force 20.5%). *Military expenditure as percent of GNP* (1984): 3.7% (world 5.9%); per capita expenditure: U.S.$74.

[1]Legislation has been enacted to move the capital from Buenos Aires to Viedma in northern Patagonia by 1989. [2]Introduced June 14, 1985, at the rate of 1 austral (₳) = 1,000 pesos ($a). [3]Detail does not add to total given because of rounding. [4]1985. [5]In new pesos, which prior to June 14, 1985, had a rate of 1 new peso = 10,000 old pesos. [6]1984. [7]Distrito Federal only. [8]At 1970 prices. [9]Skilled workers in manufacturing only. [10]Import figures are f.o.b. (free on board) in balance of trade and c.i.f. (cost, insurance, and freight) for commodities and trading partners. [11]Commodities breakdown is for 1984. [12]Aerolineas Argentinos only. [13]For 109 newspapers only. [14]Teacher training included with secondary.

# Aruba

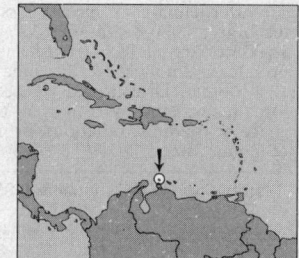

*Official name:* Aruba.
*Political status:* nonmetropolitan
part of The Netherlands realm with
one legislative house (States of
Aruba [21])[1].
*Chief of state:* Dutch Monarch
represented by governor.
*Head of government:* Prime Minister.
*Capital:* Oranjestad.
*Official language:* Dutch.
*Official religion:* none.
*Monetary unit:* 1 Aruban guilder (A f.)
at par with the Netherlands Antillean
guilder (NA f.) = 100 cents; valuation
(Oct. 5, 1987) 1U.S.$ = A f. 1.80;
1 £ = A f. 2.92.

## Area and population

| Island | Capital | area sq mi | area sq km | population 1981 census |
|---|---|---|---|---|
| Aruba | Oranjestad | 75 | 193 | 60,312 |
| TOTAL | | 75 | 193 | 60,312 |

## Demography

*Population* (1987): 62,000.
*Density* (1987): persons per sq mi 826.7, persons per sq km 321.2.
*Urban–rural:* n.a..
*Sex distribution* (1981): male 48.64%; female 51.36%.
*Age breakdown* (1981): under 15, 25.9%; 15–29, 30.6%; 30–44, 21.3%; 45–59,
12.7%; 60–74, 7.4%; 75 and over, 2.1%.
*Population projection:* (1990) 63,000; (2000) 66,000.
*Doubling time:* 59 years.
*Ethnic composition* (1980): mostly Netherlands Antillean (Dutch/Spanish/
black/Amerindian) creole[2].
*Religious affiliation* (1981): Roman Catholic 88.5%; Protestant 7.4%, of
which Lutheran/Reformed tradition 2.5%, Methodist 2.4%; other Christian
(Jehovah's Witness) 1.1%; Jewish 0.2%; nonreligious 1.6%; other 1.2%.
*Major cities* (1986): Oranjestad 19,800; San Nicolas 17,000.

## Vital statistics

*Birth rate* per 1,000 population (1983): 16.9 (world avg. 29.0); (1982) legiti-
mate 41.3%; illegitimate 58.7%.
*Death rate* per 1,000 population (1983): 5.1 (world avg. 11.0).
*Natural increase rate* per 1,000 population (1983): 11.8 (world avg. 18.0).
*Total fertility rate* (avg. births per childbearing woman; 1984): 3.4[3].
*Marriage rate* per 1,000 population (1982): 7.1.
*Divorce rate* per 1,000 population (1982): 2.0.
*Life expectancy* at birth (1981): male 71.6 years; female 76.8 years.
*Major causes of death* per 100,000 population: n.a.

## National economy

*Budget* (1984)[4]. Revenue: NA f. 207,000,000 (taxes on wages 43.5%, taxes
on profits 42.0%, taxes on goods and services 4.6%). Expenditures: NA f.
278,200,000 (current expenditures 82.0%, development expenditures 9.0%,
transfers to central government 9.0%).
*Public debt* (funded debt to The Netherlands; 1984)[4]: U.S.$58,000,000.
*Tourism* (1985): receipts from visitors U.S.$111,000,000; expenditures by
nationals abroad U.S.$17,000,000.
*Production* (metric tons except as noted). Agriculture, forestry, fishing (1986):
aloes are cultivated for export; small amounts of tomatoes, beans, cucumbers, gherkins, watermelons, and lettuce are grown on hydroponic farms;
divi-divi pods, sour orange fruit, sorghum, and peanuts (groundnuts) are
nonhydroponic crops of limited value; livestock (number of live animals;
1984[3]) 23,000 goats, 9,000 cattle, 9,000 sheep, 8,000 pigs; roundwood,
n.a.; fish catch 770. Mining and quarrying: excavation of sand for local
use. Manufacturing: rum, cigarettes, and soft drinks[5]. Construction: n.a.
Energy production (consumption): electricity (kW-hr; 1985[3]) 2,400,000,000
(2,400,000,000); coal, none (none); crude petroleum (barrels; 1985[3,6]) none
(74,400,000); petroleum products (metric tons; 1985[3,6]) 9,670,000 (1,991,-
000); natural gas, none (none).
*Gross national product* (at current market prices; 1985[3]): U.S.$1,610,000,000
(U.S.$6,810 per capita).

## Structure of gross domestic product and labour force

| | 1985 in value U.S.$'000,000 | 1985 % of total value | 1981[7] labour force | 1981[7] % of labour force |
|---|---|---|---|---|
| Agriculture | ... | ... | 40 | 0.2 |
| Mining | ... | ... | 4 | — |
| Manufacturing | ... | ... | 2,020 | 8.6 |
| Construction | ... | ... | 1,882 | 8.0 |
| Public utilities | ... | ... | 484 | 2.1 |
| Transportation and communication | ... | ... | 1,277 | 5.4 |
| Trade, restaurants, hotels | ... | ... | 7,720 | 32.7 |
| Finance | ... | ... | 1,045 | 4.4 |
| Pub. admin., defense | ... | ... } | 9,082 | 38.5 |
| Services | . | ... } | | |
| Other | ... | ... | 22 | 0.1 |
| TOTAL | 454 | 100.0 | 23,576 | 100.0 |

*Population economically active* (1981): total 26,031; activity rate of total
population 43.2% (participation rates: ages 15–64, 62.0%; female 36.7%;
unemployed [end of 1985] 40.0%[6]).

## Price and earnings indexes (1980 = 100)[3]

| | 1979 | 1980 | 1981 | 1982 | 1983 | 1984 | 1985[8] |
|---|---|---|---|---|---|---|---|
| Consumer price index | 87.2 | 100.0 | 112.2 | 119.0 | 122.4 | 125.0 | 125.4 |
| Monthly earnings index[9] | 88.9 | 100.0 | 114.7 | 127.8 | 129.4 | 129.9 | ... |

*Household income and expenditure:* average household size (1981) 3.6; income per household: n.a.; sources of income: n.a.; expenditure (1984)[10]:
food 24.5%, housing 18.4%, transportation and communication 17.4%,
household furnishings 9.1%, clothing and footwear 8.4%, recreation and
education 5.0%, health 2.9%, beverages and tobacco 2.9%, other 11.4%.
*Land use* (1985): forested, negligible; meadows and pastures, negligible; agricultural and under permanent cultivation 5.0%; other (dry savanna and
built-up) 95.0%.

## Foreign trade[11]

### Balance of trade (current prices)

| | 1979 | 1980 | 1981 | 1982 | 1983 | 1984 |
|---|---|---|---|---|---|---|
| NA f. '000,000 | −317 | −23 | ... | +91 | −33 | −68 |
| % of total | 3.9% | 0.2% | ... | 0.9% | 0.4% | 0.9% |

*Imports* (1984): NA f. 3,827,000,000 (crude petroleum and petroleum products 88.1%, machinery and transport equipment 2.8%, food 2.6%, chemicals
2.3%, basic and miscellaneous manufactures 1.8%). *Major import sources*
(1983): Venezuela 83.0%; United States 9.4%; Saudi Arabia 2.2%; The
Netherlands 1.5%.
*Exports* (1984): NA f. 3,759,000,000 (crude petroleum and petroleum products 98.9%, crude materials including sulfur pyrite 0.7%). *Major export
destinations* (1983): United States 55.5%; Puerto Rico 9.7%; United Kingdom 4.5%; Chile 2.7%; Colombia 2.6%.

## Transport and communications

*Transport.* Railroads: none. Roads (1984): total length 236 mi, 380 km
(paved, n.a.). Vehicles (1984): passenger cars 23,409; trucks and buses 582.
Merchant marine: vessels (100 gross tons and over) n.a. Air transport
(1985): passenger arrivals 329,061, passenger departures 333,261; cargo unloaded 2,056 metric tons, cargo loaded 893 metric tons; airports (1987)
with scheduled flights 1.
*Communications.* Daily newspapers (1986): total number 2; total circulation
10,819; circulation per 1,000 population 175. Radio: (1986): total number
of receivers 12,000 (1 per 5.1 persons). Television (1986): total number of
receivers 6,000 (1 per 10 persons). Telephones (1983): 17,000 (1 per 3.6
persons).

## Education and health

### Education (1983)

| | schools | teachers | students | student/ teacher ratio |
|---|---|---|---|---|
| Primary (age 6–12) | 33 | 373 | 6,763 | 18.1 |
| Secondary (age 12–17) | 10 | 189 | 3,082 | 16.3 |
| Voc., teacher tr. | 3 | 65 | 701 | 10.8 |
| Higher | 1 | 20 | 180 | 9.0 |

*Educational attainment* (1981). Percent of population age 25 and over having: no formal schooling or incomplete primary education 34.9%; completed
primary 28.6%; completed secondary/vocational 36.1%; completed higher
0.4%. *Literacy* (1985): total population age 15 and over literate 95.0%.
*Health* (1985): physicians 59 (1 per 1,043 persons); hospital beds 279 (1 per
221 persons); infant mortality rate per 1,000 live births (1982) 8.0.
*Food* (1981–83)[3]: daily per capita caloric intake 2,807 (vegetable products
65%; animal products 35%); (1983) 116% of FAO recommended minimum requirement.

## Military

*Total active duty personnel* (1986): A small Dutch naval contingent is stationed permanently in the Netherlands Antilles and Aruba.

[1]Aruba withdrew from the Netherlands Antilles on Jan. 1, 1986, becoming an autonomous member of the Kingdom of The Netherlands, the same status as that of the
whole of the Netherlands Antilles. [2]Nationality (1981): Dutch 93.8%, of which born
in Aruba or the Netherlands Antilles 88.3%, born in The Netherlands 2.3%, born
elswhere 3.2%; citizen of the United Kingdom 1.3%; Colombian 0.8%; Venezuelan
0.7%; citizen of the Dominican Republic 0.7%; citizen of the United States 0.6%;
other 2.1%. [3]Includes the Netherlands Antilles. [4]Island government of Aruba prior to
withdrawal from the Netherlands Antilles. [5]Servicing facilities, including a petroleum
transshipment terminal and two ship repair and bunkering facilities, are underutilized. [6]Aruba's oil refinery was closed in March 1985. [7]Employed persons only. [8]First
quarter average. [9]Minimum wages in manufacturing as of January 1 of each year.
[10]Weights of consumer price index components. [11]Imports c.i.f. (cost, insurance, and
freight); exports f.o.b. (free on board).

# Australia

*Official name:* Commonwealth of Australia.
*Form of government:* federal parliamentary state (formally a constitutional monarchy) with two legislative houses (Senate [76]; House of Representatives [148]).
*Chief of state:* British Monarch represented by governor-general.
*Head of government:* Prime Minister.
*Capital:* Canberra.
*Official language:* English.
*Official religion:* none.
*Monetary unit:* 1 Australian dollar ($A) = 100 cents; valuation (Oct. 5, 1987) 1 U.S.$ = $A 1.40; 1 £ = $A 2.27.

### Area and population

|  |  | area | | population |
|---|---|---|---|---|
|  |  | | | 1987 |
| **States** | **Capitals** | sq mi | sq km | estimate[1] |
| New South Wales | Sydney | 309,500 | 801,600 | 5,581,300 |
| Queensland | Brisbane | 666,900 | 1,727,200 | 2,616,300 |
| South Australia | Adelaide | 379,900 | 984,000 | 1,378,900 |
| Tasmania | Hobart | 26,200 | 67,800 | 448,600 |
| Victoria | Melbourne | 87,900 | 227,600 | 4,188,300 |
| Western Australia | Perth | 975,100 | 2,525,500 | 1,458,700 |
| **Territories** | | | | |
| Australian Capital | | | | |
| Territory | Canberra | 900 | 2,400 | 267,600 |
| Northern Territory | Darwin | 519,800 | 1,346,200 | 150,300 |
| TOTAL | | 2,966,200 | 7,682,300 | 16,090,000 |

## Demography

*Population* (1987): 16,188,300.
*Density* (1987): persons per sq mi 5.5, persons per sq km 2.1.
*Urban–rural* (1981): urban 85.7%; rural 14.3%.
*Sex distribution* (1987): male 49.89%; female 50.11%.
*Age breakdown* (1987): under 15, 22.7%; 15–29, 25.2%; 30–44, 22.5%; 45–59, 14.6%; 60–74, 11.0%; 75 and over, 4.0%.
*Population projection:* (1990) 16,913,000; (2000) 19,078,000.
*Doubling time:* 84 years.
*Ethnic composition* (1983): white 94.4%; Asian 2.1%; aboriginal 1.1%; other 2.4%.
*Religious affiliation* (1981): Christian 76.4%, of which Anglican Church of Australia 26.1%, Roman Catholic 26.0%, other Protestant 20.8% (Uniting Church 4.9%, Presbyterian 4.4%, Methodist 3.4%), Orthodox 2.9%; Muslim 0.5%; Jewish 0.4%; Buddhist 0.2%; no religion 10.8%; other 11.7%.
*Major cities* (1986): Sydney 3,430,600; Melbourne 2,942,000; Brisbane 1,171,-300; Perth 1,025,300; Adelaide 993,100; Newcastle 429,300; Canberra 285,-800; Wollongong 237,600; Gold Coast 219,300[2]; Hobart 180,300.
*Place of birth* (1985): 78.9% native-born; 21.1% foreign-born, of which United Kingdom 7.5%[3], Italy 1.8%, New Zealand 1.2%, Greece 1.0%, Yugoslavia 1.0%, East and West Germany 0.8%, The Netherlands 0.7%, Poland 0.4%, Malta 0.4%, Lebanon 0.3%, other 6.0%.
*Mobility* (1984). Population living in the same residence as in 1983: 83.2%; different residence, same state 15.5%; different state or territory 1.3%.
*Households* (1985). Total number of households 5,644,900. Average household size 2.8; (1981) 1 person 18.0%, 2 persons 29.2%, 3 persons 16.9%, 4 persons 19.1%, 5 persons 10.5%, 6 persons 4.1%, 7 or more persons 2.2%. Family households (1985): 4,033,100 (71.4%), nonfamily 1,611,800 (28.6%).
*Immigration* (1986): permanent immigrants admitted 80,520, from United Kingdom and Ireland 17.4%, New Zealand 14.3%, Vietnam 7.7%, Philippines 4.5%, Hong Kong 3.4%, South Africa 3.4%, China 3.4%, Lebanon 3.0%, Malaysia and Singapore 2.5%, India 2.3%, Yugoslavia 2.1%, United States 1.8%, East and West Germany 1.1%. Refugee arrivals (1986) 11,810.

## Vital statistics

*Birth rate* per 1,000 population (1987): 15.2 (world avg. 26.0); (1984) legitimate 85.2%; illegitimate 14.8%.
*Death rate* per 1,000 population (1987): 7.5 (world avg. 9.9).
*Natural increase rate* per 1,000 population (1987): 7.7 (world avg. 16.1).
*Total fertility rate* (avg. births per childbearing woman; 1986): 1.9.
*Marriage rate* per 1,000 population (1986): 7.3.
*Divorce rate* per 1,000 population (1986): 2.5.
*Life expectancy* at birth (1986): male 72.3 years; female 78.8 years.
*Major causes of death* per 100,000 population (1984): diseases of the circulatory system 349; malignant neoplasms (cancers) 168; diseases of the respiratory system 50; accidents, poisonings, and violence 47; diseases of the digestive system 24; endocrine, nutritional, and metabolic diseases and immunity disorders 15; diseases of the nervous system and sense organs 10.

## Social indicators

*Educational attainment* (1985). Percent of population age 15 and over having: no formal schooling 0.4%; primary and secondary education 62.0%, of which completed secondary 11.4%; postsecondary, technical, or other certificate/diploma 30.6%; university 7.0%.
*Quality of working life* (1985). Average workweek: 35.8 hours (3.6% overtime). Annual rate per 100,000 workers for: injury or accident, n.a.; industrial illness, n.a.; death, n.a. Proportion of employed persons in-

sured for damages or income loss resulting from: injury 100%; permanent disability 100%; death 100%. Average days lost to labour stoppages per 1,000 workdays (1985): 0.6. Means of transportation to work (1981): 62.2% private automobile; 13.9% public transportation; 1.3% bicycle; 5.4% foot; 17.2% other. Discouraged job seekers among persons not in the labour force (considered by employers to be too young or too old, having language or training limitations, or no vacancies in line of work; 1984): 1.3% of labour force.

### Distribution of family income (1982)

| income group | $A 0–5,000 | $A 6,000–13,000 | $A 14,000–18,700 | more than $A 18,700 |
|---|---|---|---|---|
| % of population | 11.2% | 28.4% | 32.4% | 28.0% |

*Access to services* (1976). Proportion of dwellings having access to: electricity 99.5%; bathroom 96.0%; flush toilet 92.2%; kitchen 97.9%; public sewer 73.4%.
*Social participation.* Eligible voters participating in last national election: 88.0%. Population age 16 and over participating in voluntary work (1982): 4.2%. Trade union membership in total work force (1984): 55%. Practicing religious population in total affiliated population: n.a.
*Social deviance* (1984). Offense rate per 100,000 population for: murder 3.4; rape 13.8; serious assault 58.6; auto theft 584.7; burglary and housebreaking 1,754.3; fraud and forgery 473.8. Incidence per 100,000 in general population of (1984): alcoholism, n.a.; drug and substance abuse (charges) 360.8; suicide 12.3.
*Leisure,* n.a.
*Material well-being* (1983). Households possessing: automobile 86%; telephone 85%; refrigerator 99.6%; air conditioner 32.3%; washing machine 91.7%; hot water 98.7%; central heating 3.9%; swimming pool 10.1%.

## National economy

*Gross national product* (at current market prices; 1985): U.S.$171,170,000,-000 (U.S.$10,860 per capita).

### Structure of gross domestic product and labour force

|  | 1985–86 | | 1985 | |
|---|---|---|---|---|
|  | in value $A '000,000 | % of total value | labour force[4] | % of labour force |
| Agriculture | 9,024 | 4.3 | 393,700 | 5.9 |
| Mining | 10,491 | 5.0 | 93,700 | 1.4 |
| Manufacturing | 36,163 | 17.2 | 1,137,000 | 17.1 |
| Construction | 15,949 | 7.6 | 485,100 | 7.3 |
| Public utilities | 8,031 | 3.8 | 132,900 | 2.0 |
| Transportation and communication | 18,096 | 8.6 | 512,700 | 7.7 |
| Trade | 27,784 | 13.2 | 1,318,500 | 19.9 |
| Finance | 43,881 | 20.9 | 652,200 | 9.8 |
| Pub. admin., defense | 9,788 | 4.7 | 323,900 | 4.9 |
| Services | 35,587 | 17.0 | 1,582,700 | 23.9 |
| Other | −5,021[5] | −2.4[5] | ... | ... |
| TOTAL | 209,773[6] | 100.0[7] | 6,632,400 | 100.0[7] |

*Budget* (1985–86). Revenue: $A 64,100,000,000 (income tax 61.9%, of which individual 51.0%, corporate 10.0%; excise duties 14.0%; sales tax 9.4%). Expenditures: $A 69,100,000,000 (social security and welfare 27.6%; transfers to state governments 19.6%; health 9.7%; interest on public debt 9.7%; defense 9.5%; education 7.2%; general public services 6.9%; economic services 6.3%; housing 2.0%; culture and recreation 1.2%).
*External debt* (1986): $A 55,622,000,000[8].
*Tourism* (1985): receipts from visitors U.S.$1,051,000,000; expenditures by nationals abroad U.S.$1,873,000,000.

### Manufacturing, mining, and construction enterprises (1984–85)

|  | no. of establishments | no. of employees | weekly wages as a % of avg. of all wages | annual value added ($A '000,000) |
|---|---|---|---|---|
| Manufacturing | | | | |
| Food, beverages, and tobacco | 3,387 | 161,260 | 88.2 | 6,794.1 |
| Paper, printing, and publishing | 2,972 | 101,643 | 106.3 | 4,029.0 |
| Basic metal products | 529 | 72,891 | 124.0 | 3,991.0 |
| Transport equipment | 1,308 | 118,486 | 95.1 | 3,805.4 |
| Chemical, petroleum, and coal products | 887 | 52,316 | 112.7 | 3,526.7 |
| Fabricated metal products | 4,137 | 93,000 | 84.3 | 2,905.2 |
| Wood, wood products, and furniture | 4,023 | 72,252 | 76.5 | 2,178.7 |
| Nonmetallic mineral products | 1,711 | 37,483 | 101.5 | 1,966.7 |
| Clothing and footwear | 2,011 | 74,610 | 66.2 | 1,651.6 |
| Textiles | 656 | 31,749 | 86.3 | 1,024.9 |
| Mining | | | | |
| Coal, oil, and gas | 158 | 38,646 ⎫ | 150.5 | 6,924 |
| Metallic minerals | 328 | 31,041 ⎭ | | 2,970 |
| Construction[9] | 51,351 | 246,510 | 104.0 | 3,925 |

*Production* (gross value in $A '000 except as noted). Agriculture, forestry, fishing (1985–86): livestock slaughtered—cattle 2,373,700, sheep and lambs 509,600, pigs 439,900; wool 2,678,100, wheat 2,274,100, sugarcane 491,100, barley 453,600, cotton 330,800, grapes 261,700, potatoes 179,200, sorghum 147,100, oats 117,100, apples 116,300, oranges 93,000, bananas 85,200, rice 79,600, sunflower seeds 47,000, pears 45,600, pineapples 29,500, peanuts (groundnuts) 23,600, peaches 23,000; livestock (number of live animals; 1986) 156,332,000 sheep, 23,217,000 cattle, 2,500,000 pigs, 51,400,000 poultry; roundwood (1985) 18,286,000 cu m; fish catch (1985) 168,900 metric tons. Mining and quarrying (metric tons; 1985–86): iron ore 97,789,000; bauxite 31,245,000; refined metals—aluminum 869,560, zinc 301,836, lead 206,400, copper 161,600, tin 2,208, gold 56,928 kg. Manufacturing (metric tons; 1985–86): raw steel 6,826,000; cement 6,039,000; pig iron 5,925,000;

iron and steel slabs 4,446,000; super phosphate 2,479,000; sulfuric acid 1,788,000; beef and veal 1,384,900; wheat flour 1,173,000; refined sugar 703,200; newsprint 362,954; lamb 300,300; pork 268,500; mutton 257,900; plaster sheets 76,249,000 sq m; textile floor coverings 42,090,000 sq m; woven cotton cloth 39,480,000 sq m; concrete roofing tiles 18,082,000 cu m; woven woolen cloth 11,136,000 sq m; automotive gasoline 156,520,000 hectolitres; furnace fuel 22,640,000 hectolitres; beer 18,630,000 hectolitres; finished and partly finished motor vehicles 365,613 units. Construction (buildings completed by value in $A '000; 1985–86): new dwellings 7,307,000; alterations and additions to dwellings 955,000; nonresidential 7,129,100.

### Retail sales and service enterprises (1979–80)

| | no. of establishments | no. of employees | total wages and salaries ($A '000,000) | annual turnover ($A '000,000) |
|---|---|---|---|---|
| Motor vehicle dealers, gasoline and tire dealers | 26,516 | 175,995 | 1,319 | 18,203 |
| Food stores | 39,416 | 260,266 | 1,131 | 12,747 |
| Department and general stores | 857 | 99,569 | 717 | 4,254 |
| Clothing, fabrics, and furniture stores | 17,908 | 81,797 | 519 | 4,143 |
| Household appliances and hardware stores | 8,196 | 43,542 | 320 | 2,966 |
| Restaurants, hotels and accommodations | 17,702 | 183,310 | 1,022 | 4,670 |
| Licensed clubs | 3,243 | 52,297 | 697 | 1,515 |
| Laundries and dry cleaners | 1,365 | 12,106 | 91 | 224 |
| Motion picture theatres | 577 | 6,777 | 45 | 178 |
| Hairdressers and beauty salons | 2,265 | 12,282 | 78 | 173 |

Energy production (consumption): electricity (kW-hr; 1985–86) 124,369,000,000 (124,369,000,000); coal (metric tons; 1985–86) 192,139,000 (82,443,000[9]); crude petroleum (barrels; 1986) 173,545,000 (212,942,000[9]); petroleum products (metric tons; 1985) 27,866,000 (25,587,000); natural gas (cu m; 1985–86) 14,275,000 (14,275,000).
*Population economically active* (November 1986): total 7,590,200; activity rate of total population 48.1% (participation rates: ages 15–64 [1985] 69.3%; female [1985] 54.2%; unemployed 7.7%).

### Price and earnings indexes (1980 = 100)

| | 1980 | 1981 | 1982 | 1983 | 1984 | 1985 | 1986 |
|---|---|---|---|---|---|---|---|
| Consumer price index | 100.0 | 109.7 | 121.9 | 134.2 | 139.6 | 149.0 | 162.5 |
| Monthly earnings index | 100.0 | 111.4 | 124.5 | 133.3 | 146.0 | 153.4 | 165.3 |

*Household income and expenditure.* Average household size (1985): 2.8; average annual income per household (1985–86) $A 25,300 (U.S.$36,100); sources of income (1985–86): wages and salaries 61.1%, government pensions and benefits 11.7%, self-employment 6.3%, transfer payments 3.2%; expenditure (1985–86): housing 21.9%, food and nonalcoholic beverages 15.9%, transportation and communication 13.4%, household durable goods 6.7%, health 6.4%, clothing and footwear 6.2%, education and recreation 5.2%, energy 2.3%.
*Land use* (1985): meadows and pastures 59.0%; agricultural and under permanent cultivation 4.3%; other 36.7%[10].

### Financial aggregates

| | 1981 | 1982 | 1983 | 1984 | 1985 | 1986 | 1987 (8 mos.) |
|---|---|---|---|---|---|---|---|
| Exchange Rate, $A 1.00 per: | | | | | | | |
| U.S. Dollar | 1.15 | 1.02 | 0.90 | 0.88 | 0.70 | 0.67 | 0.71 |
| £ | 0.57 | 0.50 | 0.59 | 0.64 | 0.54 | 0.46 | 0.44 |
| SDR | 0.97 | 0.89 | 0.86 | 0.84 | 0.62 | 0.54 | 0.55 |
| International reserves (U.S.$) | | | | | | | |
| Total (excl. gold; '000,000) | 1,671 | 6,371 | 8,962 | 7,441 | 5,768 | 7,246 | 9,346 |
| SDRs ('000,000) | 52 | 86 | 81 | 209 | 310 | 332 | 337 |
| Reserve pos. in IMF ('000,000) | 294 | --- | 114 | 183 | 207 | 231 | 239 |
| Foreign exchange ('000,000) | 1,325 | 6,285 | 8,768 | 7,049 | 5,250 | 6,684 | 8,770 |
| Gold ('000,000 fine troy oz) | 7.93 | 7.93 | 7.93 | 7.93 | 7.93 | 7.93 | 7.93 |
| % world reserves | 0.8 | 0.8 | 0.8 | 0.8 | 0.8 | 0.8 | 0.8 |
| Interest and prices | | | | | | | |
| Central bank discount (%) | ... | ... | ... | ... | ... | ... | ... |
| Gov't. Bond yield (%) | 13.8 | 15.2 | 12.8 | 12.2 | 14.0 | 14.0 | 13.25[11] |
| Industrial share prices (1980 = 100) | 104.2 | 79.5 | 100.4 | 117.0 | 143.5 | 193.4 | ... |
| Balance of payments (U.S.$'000,000) | | | | | | | |
| Balance of visible trade | −2,333 | −2,611 | 30 | −862 | −1,277 | −2,171 | ... |
| Imports, f.o.b. | 23,549 | 23,407 | 19,470 | 23,653 | 23,558 | 24,344 | ... |
| Exports, f.o.b. | 21,216 | 20,796 | 19,510 | 22,791 | 22,281 | 22,173 | ... |
| Balance of invisibles | −6,013 | −5,690 | −6,028 | −7,775 | −7,983 | −7,350 | ... |
| Balance of payments, current account | −8,503 | −8,495 | −5,926 | −8,500 | −8,730 | −9,232 | ... |

## Foreign trade

### Balance of trade (current prices)

| | 1980–81 | 1981–82 | 1982–83 | 1983–84 | 1984–85 | 1985–86 |
|---|---|---|---|---|---|---|
| $A '000,000 | −1,755 | −2,099 | +1,331 | +720 | +614 | −1,872 |
| % of total | 4.4% | 4.6% | 3.0% | 1.5% | 1.0% | 2.8% |

*Imports* (1984–85): $A 30,026,400,000 (machinery 25.4%, of which office machines and automatic data-processing equipment 5.3%; transport equipment 14.9%, of which road motor vehicles 7.9%; mineral fuels and lubricants 9.4%; chemicals and related products 8.7%; food and live animals 4.1%; crude materials [inedible] excluding fuels 3.4%; paper and paperboard 2.6%; beverages and tobacco 0.8%). *Major import sources:* Japan 22.1%; United States 21.9%; United Kingdom 7.0%; West Germany 6.0%; New Zealand 3.7%; Italy 2.8%; Saudi Arabia 2.4%; Hong Kong 2.3%; Singapore 2.3%; France 2.2%.
*Exports* (1984–85): $A 30,639,500,000 (metalliferous ores and metal scrap 16.2%; coal, coke, and briquettes 15.6%; cereals 9.6%; textile fibres and

their waste 8.1%; petroleum, petroleum gases, and petroleum products 8.0%; nonferrous metals 7.8%; iron and steel 6.3%; meat 4.6%; sugar and honey 1.9%; dairy products 1.4%). *Major export destinations:* Japan 26.3%; United States 11.1%; New Zealand 5.9%; United Kingdom 3.7%; South Korea 3.6%; Singapore 3.4%; China 3.1%; West Germany 3.0%; Hong Kong 2.9%; Malaysia 2.0%; U.S.S.R. 2.5%; Papua New Guinea 1.9%.

### Trade by commodity group (1984–85)

| SITC Group | imports $A '000,000 | imports % | exports $A '000,000 | exports % |
|---|---|---|---|---|
| 00 Food and live animals | 1,284.1 | 4.3 | 7,284.0 | 23.8 |
| 01 Beverages and tobacco | 225.4 | 0.7 | 72.3 | 0.3 |
| 02 Crude materials, excluding fuels | 932.5 | 3.1 | 7,949.7 | 25.9 |
| 03 Mineral fuels, lubricants, and related materials | 2,300.3 | 7.7 | 7,823.7 | 25.5 |
| 04 Animal and vegetable oils, fat and waxes | 112.0 | 0.4 | 124.0 | 0.4 |
| 05 Chemicals and related products, n.e.s. | 2,215.9 | 7.4 | 548.3 | 1.8 |
| 06 Basic manufactures | 5,786.5 | 19.3 | 2,979.5 | 9.7 |
| 07 Machinery and transport equipment | 11,333.3 | 37.7 | 1,482.9 | 4.8 |
| 08 Miscellaneous manufactured articles | 3,865.8 | 12.9 | 592.8 | 1.9 |
| 09 Goods not classified by kind | 1,000.1 | 3.3 | 952.1 | 3.1 |
| Nonmerchandise trade | 970.5 | 3.2 | 830.2 | 2.7 |
| TOTAL | 30,026.4 | 100.0 | 30,639.5 | 100.0[7] |

### Direction of trade (1984–85)

| | imports $A '000,000 | imports % | exports $A '000,000 | exports % |
|---|---|---|---|---|
| Africa | 146.0 | 0.5 | 655.8 | 2.1 |
| Asia | 12,689.4 | 42.3 | 17,345.4 | 56.6 |
| Japan | 6,644.5 | 22.1 | 8,066.1 | 26.3 |
| South America | 273.5 | 0.9 | 172.6 | 0.6 |
| North and Central America | 7,484.0 | 24.9 | 3,977.4 | 13.0 |
| United States | 6,819.3 | 22.7 | 3,584.1 | 11.7 |
| Europe | 7,743.1 | 25.8 | 5,482.9 | 17.9 |
| EEC | 6,286.4 | 20.9 | 3,873.7 | 12.6 |
| U.S.S.R. | 28.9 | 0.1 | 873.4 | 2.9 |
| Other Europe | 1,427.8 | 4.8 | 735.8 | 2.4 |
| Oceania | 1,157.9 | 3.9 | 1,787.8 | 5.8 |
| New Zealand | 1,116.3 | 3.7 | 1,591.0 | 5.2 |
| Other countries, including destinations unknown | 532.5 | 1.8 | 1,217.6 | 4.0 |
| TOTAL | 30,026.4 | 100.0[7] | 30,639.5 | 100.0 |

## Transport and communications

*Transport.* Railroads[12] (1984): route length 24,389 mi, 39,251 km; passenger-mi 1,359,051,000[13], passenger-km 2,187,120,000[13]; short ton-mi cargo 27,018,000,000, metric ton-km cargo 39,447,800,000. Roads (1984): total length 500,049 mi, 804,753 km (paved 47%). Vehicles (1986): passenger cars 8,770,899; trucks and buses 1,231,359. Merchant marine (1986): vessels (100 gross tons and over) 673; total deadweight tonnage 3,653,670. Air transport (1985): passenger-mi 15,144,000,000, passenger-km 24,372,000,000; short ton-mi cargo 1,821,700,000, metric ton-km cargo 2,659,800,000; airports (1986) with scheduled flights 441.
*Communications.* Daily newspapers (1983): total number 61; total circulation 4,739,500; circulation per 1,000 population 308. Radio (1985): total number of receivers 20,000,000 (1 per 0.8 person). Television (1985): total number of receivers 6,500,000 (1 per 2.3 persons). Telephones (1985): 8,727,000 (1 per 1.8 persons).

## Education and health

### Education (1985)

| | schools | teachers | students | student/ teacher ratio |
|---|---|---|---|---|
| Primary (age 6–12) | 8,460 | 96,087 | 1,727,897 | 18.0 |
| Secondary (age 13–17) | 1,603 | 101,043 | 1,278,272 | 12.7 |
| Voc., teacher tr. | 234 | 52,587 | 859,195 | 16.3 |
| Higher | 95 | 22,234 | 370,707 | 16.7 |

*Literacy* (1980): total population age 15 and over literate 99.5%.
*Health* (1985): physicians (1982) 27,500 (1 per 552 persons); hospital beds 91,541 (1 per 172 persons); infant mortality rate per 1,000 live births (1986) 9.4.
*Food* (1981–83): daily per capita caloric intake 3,382 (vegetable products 61%, animal products 39%); 115% of FAO recommended minimum requirement.

## Military

*Total active duty personnel* (1986): 69,555 (army 45.6%, navy 22.0%, air force 32.4%). *Military expenditure as percent of GNP* (1984): 2.9% (world 5.9%); per capita expenditure U.S.$300.

[1]Beginning of year. [2]Includes Tweed Heads. [3]Includes both Northern Ireland and Republic of Ireland. [4]Employed persons only. [5]Less imputed bank service charges. [6]At factor cost. [7]Detail does not add to total given because of rounding. [8]Fourth quarter. [9]1985. [10]Urban areas, state forests and mining leases, unoccupied land (mainly desert). [11]Five months. [12]Government railways only. [13]1978–79.

# Austria

*Official name:* Republik Österreich
(Republic of Austria).
*Form of government:* federal multi-
party republic with two legislative
houses (Federal Council [63]; National
Council [183]).
*Chief of state:* President.
*Head of government:* Chancellor.
*Capital:* Vienna.
*Official language:* German.
*Official religion:* none.
*Monetary unit:* 1 Schilling (S) = 100
Groschen; valuation (Oct. 5, 1987)
1 U.S.$ = S 12.97; 1 £ = S 21.07.

### Area and population

| States | Capitals | area sq mi | area sq km | population 1985 estimate |
|---|---|---|---|---|
| Burgenland | Eisenstadt | 1,531 | 3,965 | 267,686 |
| Kärnten | Klagenfurt | 3,681 | 9,534 | 540,342 |
| Niederösterreich | Sankt Pölten | 7,402 | 19,172 | 1,423,741 |
| Oberösterreich | Linz | 4,626 | 11,980 | 1,285,955 |
| Salzburg[11] | Salzburg | 2,762 | 7,154 | 456,502 |
| Steiermark | Graz | 6,327 | 16,387 | 1,183,383 |
| Tirol | Innsbruck | 4,883 | 12,647 | 601,618 |
| Vorarlberg | Bregenz | 1,004 | 2,601 | 309,287 |
| Wien | — | 160 | 415 | 1,489,153 |
| TOTAL | | 32,376 | 83,855 | 7,557,667 |

## Demography

*Population* (1987): 7,554,000.
*Density* (1987): persons per sq mi 233.3, persons per sq km 90.1.
*Urban–rural* (1986): urban 55.0%; rural 45.0%.
*Sex distribution* (1985): male 47.41%; female 52.59%.
*Age breakdown* (1985): under 15, 18.2%; 15–29, 24.7%; 30–44, 20.2%; 45–59,
16.9%; 60–74, 13.3%; 75 and over, 6.7%.
*Population projection:* (1990) 7,549,000; (2000) 7,530,000.
*Doubling time:* not applicable; population is declining.
*Ethnic composition* (national origin; 1981): Austrian 96.1%; Yugoslavian
1.7%; Turkish 0.8%; German 0.5%; other 0.9%.
*Religious affiliation* (1981): Roman Catholic 84.3%; Protestant 5.6%; non-
religious and atheist 6.0%; other 4.1%.
*Major cities* (1981): Vienna 1,489,153[1]; Graz 243,166; Linz 199,910; Salzburg
139,426; Innsbruck 117,287.

## Vital statistics

*Birth rate* per 1,000 population (1985): 11.6 (world avg. 29.0); (1985) legiti-
mate 77.6%; illegitimate 22.4%.
*Death rate* per 1,000 population (1985): 11.9 (world avg. 11.0).
*Natural increase rate* per 1,000 population (1985): −0.3 (world avg. 18.0).
*Total fertility rate* (avg. births per childbearing woman; 1985): 1.5.
*Marriage rate* per 1,000 population (1985): 5.9.
*Divorce rate* per 1,000 population (1985): 2.0.
*Life expectancy* at birth (1980–82): male 69.2 years; female 76.4 years.
*Major causes of death* per 100,000 population (1985): heart and circulatory
disease 634.0, of which ischemic heart disease 209.8; malignant neoplasms
(cancers) 253.9; diseases of the respiratory system 65.0; accidents 54.6.

## National economy

*Budget* (1985). Revenue: S 325,700,000,000 (taxes 86.2%, of which indirect
income 48.7%, direct income 31.5%, corporate 6.0%, property income and
entrepreneurship 4.9%). Expenditures: S 341,400,000,000 (transfer payments
41.2%, of which to public authorities 23.0%, to private households 17.8%;
goods and services 27.6%; interest on public debt 10.8%; subsidies 10.2%).
*Tourism* (1985): receipts from visitors U.S.$6,041,000,000; expenditures by
nationals abroad U.S.$3,333,000,000.
*Production* (metric tons except as noted). Agriculture, forestry, fishing (1985):
sugar beets 2,315,000, corn (maize) 1,727,000, wheat 1,563,000, barley
1,521,000, potatoes 1,042,000, rye 339,000, apples 293,000, milk 3,797,000;
livestock (number of live animals) 3,925,935 pigs, 2,650,574 cattle, 14,439,-
835 chickens; roundwood (1984) 14,204,000. Mining and quarrying (1985):
iron ore 3,270,000; magnesite 1,183,409[2]; zinc 24,260[3]; lead 7,510[3]. Manufacturing (value in S '000,000; 1983) machinery 58,160, of which electrical
25,150, transport 12,730; metal products (including steel) 23,140; beverages
and tobacco 20,860; food products 19,590; textiles and apparel 18,290;
chemical products 16,680. Construction (dwellings completed; 1985): residential 3,993,000 sq m; nonresidential, n.a. Energy production (consumption): electricity (kW-hr; 1985) 43,923,000,000 (42,204,000,000); coal (metric
tons; 1985) 3,081,000 (7,019,000); crude petroleum (barrels; 1985) 8,123,000
(53,854,000); petroleum products (metric tons; 1985) 7,708,000 (8,790,000);
natural gas (cu m; 1985) 1,295,600,000 (5,482,400,000).
*Population economically active* (1985): total 3,355,200; activity rate of total
population 44.4% (participation rates: ages 15–64, 65.5%; female 39.5%;
unemployed 3.6%).

### Price and earnings indexes (1980 = 100)

| | 1980 | 1981 | 1982 | 1983 | 1984 | 1985 | 1986 |
|---|---|---|---|---|---|---|---|
| Consumer price index | 100.0 | 106.8 | 112.6 | 116.3 | 122.9 | 126.9 | 129.0 |
| Monthly earnings index | 100.0 | 106.1 | 123.7 | 117.8 | 123.7 | 126.9 | ... |

*Gross national product* (at current market prices; 1985): U.S.$69,060,000,000
(U.S.$9,140 per capita).

### Structure of gross domestic product and labour force

| | 1985 in value S '000,000 | 1985 % of total value | 1985 labour force | 1985 % of labour force |
|---|---|---|---|---|
| Agriculture | 45,450 | 3.3 | 293,800 | 8.8 |
| Mining | 385,040 | 28.2 | 14,500 | 0.4 |
| Manufacturing | | | 947,200 | 28.2 |
| Construction | 90,340 | 6.6 | 290,100 | 8.6 |
| Public utilities | 42,530 | 3.1 | 42,100 | 1.3 |
| Transportation and communication | 79,020 | 5.8 | 212,400 | 6.3 |
| Trade | 216,820 | 15.9 | 451,700 | 13.5 |
| Finance | 200,960 | 14.7 | 182,500 | 5.4 |
| Pub. admin., defense | 195,190 | 14.3 | 750,700 | 22.4 |
| Services | 45,010 | 3.3 | 154,100 | 4.6 |
| Other | 66,280 | 4.8 | 16,100 | 0.5 |
| TOTAL | 1,366,640 | 100.0 | 3,355,200 | 100.0 |

*Household income and expenditure.* Average household size (1985) 2.6;
income per household[4] (1985) S 179,000 (U.S.$8,665); sources of income
(1984): wages and salaries 56.1%, social security benefits and social assistance grants 24.3%, self-employment 19.6%; expenditure (1984): food
22.7%, housing and utilities 21.1%, clothing and footwear 11.8%.
*Land use* (1984): forested 38.9%; meadows and pastures 24.0%; agricultural
and under permanent cultivation 18.4%; other 18.7%.

## Foreign trade

### Balance of trade (current prices)

| | 1981 | 1982 | 1983 | 1984 | 1985 | 1986 |
|---|---|---|---|---|---|---|
| S '000,000 | −69,520 | −53,460 | −55,940 | −55,950 | −57,570 | −47,480 |
| % of total | 12.1% | 9.1% | 9.2% | 8.7% | 7.5% | 6.5% |

*Imports* (1985): S 430,969,325,000 (machinery and transport equipment
29.8%, of which road vehicles 8.7%; manufactured goods 18.2%, of which
textile yarn 4.4%, iron and steel 2.8%; chemicals and related products
10.0%; petroleum and related materials 9.7%). *Major import sources:* West
Germany 40.9%; Italy 8.2%; U.S.S.R. 4.4%; Switzerland 4.0%; France 3.6%;
The Netherlands 2.7%..
*Exports* (1985): S 353,962,448,000 (manufactured goods 33.8%, of which
iron and steel 8.9%, textile yarn 5.4%; machinery and transport equipment 31.3%, of which road vehicles 4.2%; chemicals 9.1%). *Major export
destinations:* West Germany 30.1%; Italy 9.0%; Switzerland 6.8%; United
Kingdom 4.6%; France 4.0%; U.S.S.R. 3.8%.

## Transport and communications

*Transport.* Railroads (1985): length 4,148 mi, 6,676 km; passenger-mi 4,356,-
000,000[1], passenger-km 7,010,000,000[1]; short ton-mi cargo 8,154,000,000,
metric ton-km cargo 11,904,000,000. Roads (1985): total length 66,739 mi,
107,406 km (paved 100%). Vehicles (1985): passenger cars 2,530,800; trucks
and buses 234,925. Merchant marine (1986): vessels (100 gross tons and
over) 26; total deadweight tonnage 210,632. Air transport (1986): passenger-
mi 857,300,000, passenger-km 1,380,000,000; short ton-mi cargo 16,100,000,
metric ton-km cargo 23,500,000; airports (1987) with scheduled flights 6.
*Communications.* Daily newspapers (1985): total number 33; total circulation, n.a.; circulation per 1,000 population, n.a. Radio (1985): total number
of receivers 2,619,318 (1 per 2.9 persons). Television (1984): total number
of receivers 2,418,584 (1 per 3.1 persons). Telephones (1983): 3,330,171 (1
per 2.3 persons).

## Education and health

### Education (1985–86)

| | schools | teachers | students | student/ teacher ratio |
|---|---|---|---|---|
| Primary (age 6–9) | 3,411 | 28,305 | 341,867 | 12.1 |
| Secondary (age 10–18) | 2,066 | 55,932 | 504,326 | 9.0 |
| Voc., teacher tr. | 1,241 | 22,910 | 374,424 | 16.3 |
| Higher | 44 | 10,252 | 168,060 | 16.4 |

*Educational attainment* (1985). Percent of population age 25 and over having: primary education 44.4%; lower secondary 31.7%; higher secondary
15.3%; postsecondary 4.4%; university 4.2%. *Literacy* (1983): virtually 100%.
*Health* (1985): physicians 19,398 (1 per 390 persons); hospital beds 84,125
(1 per 90 persons); infant mortality rate per 1,000 live births 11.2.
*Food* (1981–83): daily per capita caloric intake 3,486 (vegetable products
61%, animal products 39%); (1983) 126% of FAO recommended minimum requirement.

## Military

*Total active duty personnel* (1985): 54,700 (army 91.4%; navy, none; air force
8.6%). *Military expenditure as percent of GNP* (1984): 1.2% (world 5.9%);
per capita expenditure U.S.$105.

[1]1985. [2]1984. [3]Metal content only. [4]Median net household or disposable income.

# Bahamas, The

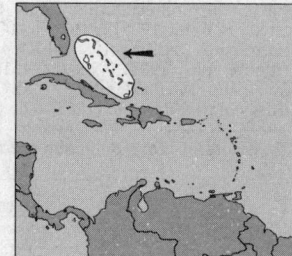

*Official name:* The Commonwealth of The Bahamas.
*Form of government:* constitutional monarchy with two legislative houses (Senate [16]; House of Assembly [49]).
*Chief of state:* British Monarch represented by governor-general.
*Head of government:* Prime Minister.
*Capital:* Nassau.
*Official language:* English.
*Official religion:* none.
*Monetary unit:* 1 Bahamian dollar (B$) = 100 cents; valuation (Oct. 5, 1987) 1 Bahamian dollar = U.S.$1.00 = £0.62.

## Area and population

| Islands and Island Groups[2] | Residence of Commissioner[2] | area[1] sq mi | area[1] sq km | population 1980 census[3] |
|---|---|---|---|---|
| Abaco, Great and Little, and Mores Island and cays | Marsh Harbour | 649 | 1,681 | 7,324 |
| Acklins Island | Pompey Bay | 192 | 497 | 616 |
| Andros Island | Kemps Bay | 2,300 | 5,957 | 8,397 |
| Berry Islands | Nicolls Town | 12 | 31 | 509 |
| Biminis, North and South, Cay Lobos, and Cay Sal | Alice Town | 11 | 28 | 1,432 |
| Cat Island | Arthur's Town | 150 | 388 | 2,143 |
| Crooked Island | Colonel Hill | 84 | 218 | 517 |
| Eleuthera, Harbour Island, and Spanish Wells | Rock Sound | 200 | 518 | 10,600 |
| Exuma, Great and Little, and cays | George Town | 112 | 290 | 3,672 |
| Grand Bahama | Freeport | 530 | 1,373 | 33,102 |
| Inagua, Great and Little | Matthew Town | 599 | 1,551 | 939 |
| Long Cay | ... | 9 | 23 | 33 |
| Long Island | Clarence Town | 230 | 596 | 3,358 |
| Mayaguana | Abraham's Bay | 110 | 285 | 476 |
| New Providence | Nassau | 80 | 207 | 135,437 |
| Ragged Island and cays | Duncan Town | 14 | 36 | 146 |
| San Salvador and Rum Cay | Cockburn Town | 90 | 233 | 804 |
| TOTAL | | 5,382[4] | 13,939[4] | 209,505 |

## Demography

*Population* (1987)[3]: 245,000.
*Density* (1987): persons per sq mi 44.6, persons per sq km 17.2.
*Urban–rural* (1986): urban 54.1%; rural 45.9%.
*Sex distribution* (1980): male 48.77%; female 51.23%.
*Age breakdown* (1985): under 15, 38.0%; 15–29, 27.9%; 30–44, 17.9%; 45–59, 10.5%; 60–74, 4.8%; 75 and over, 0.9%.
*Population projection:* (1990) 262,000; (2000) 327,000.
*Doubling time:* 41 years.
*Ethnic composition* (1980): black 72.3%; mixed 14.2%; white 12.9%; other 0.6%.
*Religious affiliation* (1980): non-Anglican Protestant (mostly Baptist and Church of God [Anderson Ind.]) 48.4%; Roman Catholic 25.5%; Anglican 20.7%; other 5.4%.
*Major cities* (1980): Nassau 110,000; Freeport 25,423.

## Vital statistics

*Birth rate* per 1,000 population (1984): 22.2 (world avg. 29.0); legitimate 37.8%, illegitimate 62.2%.
*Death rate* per 1,000 population (1984): 5.0 (world avg. 11.0).
*Natural increase rate* per 1,000 population (1984): 17.2 (world avg. 18.0).
*Total fertility rate* (avg. births per childbearing woman; 1984): 3.1.
*Marriage rate* per 1,000 population (1984): 7.4.
*Divorce rate* per 1,000 population (1984): 1.6.
*Life expectancy* at birth (1980–85): male 66.9 years; female 70.9 years.
*Major causes of death* per 100,000 population (1984): diseases of the circulatory system 128.8; malignant neoplasms (cancers) 102.2; accidents, poisoning, and violence 65.5.

## National economy

*Budget* (1986). Revenue: B$384,935,000 (customs receipts 57.6%, stamp taxes 8.0%, fines and forfeits 7.7%, service taxes 6.3%, business and professional licenses 3.5%). Expenditures: B$399,677,000 (education 22.2%, health 16.8%, interest on the public debt 11.8%, general administration 10.3%, public order 9.2%, public works 8.5%, defense 3.7%).
*Public debt* (external, outstanding; 1985): U.S.$190,200,000.
*Tourism:* receipts from visitors (1986) U.S.$1,105,000,000; expenditures by nationals abroad U.S.$106,000,000.
*Production* (metric tons except as noted). Agriculture, forestry, fishing, (1985): sugarcane 230,000, tomatoes 9,000, bananas 8,000, onions 2,000, corn (maize) 1,000, pulses 1,000; livestock (number of live animals) 39,000 sheep, 19,000 pigs, 18,000 goats, 4,000 cattle, 1,000,000 chickens; roundwood 115,000 cu m; fish catch 8,188, of which crayfish 6,016, groupers 644, conchs 587. Mining and quarrying (value of production in B$'000; 1986): salt 11,600; aragonite 2,400. Manufacturing (value of production in B$'000; 1986[5]): pharmaceuticals 131,200; rum 13,300. Construction (value of new buildings in B$'000,000; 1986)[6]: residential 88; nonresidential 24. Energy production (consumption): electricity (kW-hr; 1985) 854,000,000 (854,000,-

000); coal (metric tons; 1985) none (negligible); crude petroleum (barrels; 1985) none (26,755,000); petroleum products (metric tons; 1985) 2,930,000 (719,000); natural gas, none (none).
*Gross national product* (at current market prices; 1985): U.S.$1,670,000,000 (U.S.$7,140 per capita).

## Structure of gross domestic product and labour force

| | 1986 in value B$'000,000 | 1986 % of total value | 1980 labour force | 1980 % of labour force |
|---|---|---|---|---|
| Agriculture | 90 | 4.5 | 4,554 | 5.2 |
| Mining | | | 346 | 0.4 |
| Manufacturing | 206 | 10.3 | 4,957 | 5.7 |
| Public utilities | | | 1,271 | 1.5 |
| Construction | 61 | 3.1 | 6,675 | 7.7 |
| Transp. and commun. | 219 | 10.9 | 6,176 | 7.1 |
| Trade | 524 | 26.2 | 24,474 | 28.1 |
| Finance | 245 | 12.2 | 6,441 | 7.4 |
| Pub. admin., defense | 342 | 17.1 | 24,094 | 27.6 |
| Other | 315 | 15.7 | 8,064[7] | 9.3[7] |
| TOTAL | 2,003[8] | 100.0 | 87,052 | 100.0 |

*Population economically active* (1980): total 87,052; activity rate of total population 41.6% (participation rates: ages 15–64, 70.9%; female 44.3%; unemployed [1987] 18.0%).

## Price and earnings indexes (1980 = 100)

| | 1980 | 1981 | 1982 | 1983 | 1984 | 1985 | 1986 |
|---|---|---|---|---|---|---|---|
| Consumer price index | 100.0 | 111.1 | 117.8 | 122.6 | 127.4 | 133.2 | 140.5 |
| Annual earnings index | ... | ... | ... | ... | ... | ... | ... |

*Household income and expenditure.* Average household size (1980) 4.3; income per household (1979) B$13,537 (U.S.$13,537)[6]; sources of income: n.a.; expenditure (1982): food and beverages 20.5%, expenditures in restaurants and hotels 16.1%, transport and communication 15.1%, housing 14.1%, recreation 6.5%, household furnishings 6.0%.
*Land use* (1984): forested 32.2%; meadows and pastures 0.2%; agricultural and under permanent cultivation 0.9%; other 66.7%.

## Foreign trade

### Balance of trade (current prices)

| | 1979 | 1980 | 1981 | 1982 | 1983 | 1984 | 1985 |
|---|---|---|---|---|---|---|---|
| B$'000,000 | +272 | −2,536 | −1,095 | −1,814 | −646 | −705 | −48 |
| % of total | 3.7% | 20.2% | 8.1% | 16.7% | 7.5% | 9.4% | 0.8% |

*Imports* (1985): B$3,081,000,000 (petroleum [all forms] 73.7%, machinery and transport equipment 6.5%, food 5.0%). *Major import sources:* Nigeria 35.4%; United States 27.3%; Angola 5.6%; Gabon 4.9%.
*Exports* (1985): B$3,033,000,000 (petroleum [all forms] 89.3%, nonpetroleum reexports 1.3%, hormones 1.0%, crayfish 0.6%, rum 0.5%). *Major export destinations:* United States 84.9%; Canada 6.2%; Puerto Rico 4.0%; United Kingdom 2.7%.

## Transport and communications

*Transport.* Railroads: none. Roads (1984): total length 2,548 mi, 4,100 km (paved 40%). Vehicles (1984): passenger cars 88,000; trucks and buses 5,600. Merchant marine (1986): vessels (100 gross tons and over) 302; total deadweight tonnage 10,600,356. Air transport (1986)[9]: passenger-mi 245,000,000, passenger-km 394,000,000; short ton-mi cargo, n.a.; airports (1987) with scheduled flights 21.
*Communications.* Daily newspapers (1985): total number 3; total circulation 31,500; circulation per 1,000 population 136. Radio (1986): total receivers 120,000 (1 per 2.0 persons). Television (1986): total receivers 40,000 (1 per 5.9 persons). Telephones (1985): 97,468 (1 per 2.4 persons).

## Education and health

### Education (1983)

| | schools | teachers | students | student/ teacher ratio |
|---|---|---|---|---|
| Primary (age 5–11) | 187 | 1,972 | 37,097 | 18.8 |
| Secondary (age 11–16) | 38 | 1,334 | 23,202 | 17.4 |
| Higher[10] | 1 | 135 | 2,000 | 14.8 |

*Educational attainment* (1970). Percent of population age 25 and over having: no formal schooling 6.7%; primary education only 15.4%; secondary 63.0%; postsecondary or higher 14.9%. *Literacy* (1984): total population age 15 and over literate 125,000 (89.0%).
*Health:* physicians (1983) 218 (1 per 1,018 persons); hospital beds (1985) 999[11] (1 per 235 persons); infant mortality rate per 1,000 live births (1982–84 avg.) 23.1.
*Food* (1981–83): daily per capita caloric intake 2,614 (vegetable products 67%, animal products 33%); (1983) 94% of FAO recommended minimum requirement.

## Military

*Total active duty personnel* (1986): 496[12]. *Military expenditure as percent of GNP* (1984): 0.5% (world 5.9%); per capita expenditure U.S.$40.

[1]Land area only of individual islands or island groups. [2]Out Islands (all islands and island groups other than New Providence) are governed by commissioners assigned by the central government. [3]De jure. [4]Total includes 10 sq mi (27 sq km) unaccounted for in breakdown. [5]Petroleum-refining operations ceased in August 1985. [6]New Providence and Grand Bahama islands only. [7]Includes 1,705 not adequately defined and 6,359 unemployed persons not previously employed. [8]Detail does not add to total given because of rounding. [9]Bahamasair only. [10]1985. [11]Excludes two private hospitals. [12]All paramilitary (coast guard) personnel.

# Bahrain

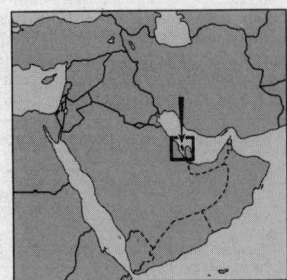

*Official name:* Dawlat al-Baḥrayn (State of Bahrain).
*Form of government:* monarchy (emirate) with a cabinet appointed by the Emir.
*Chief of state:* Emir.
*Head of government:* Prime Minister.
*Capital:* Manama.
*Official language:* Arabic.
*Official religion:* Islam.
*Monetary unit:* 1 Bahrain dinar (BD) = 1,000 fils; valuation (Oct. 5, 1987) 1 BD = U.S.$2.66 = £1.64.

### Area and population

| Regions | area[1] sq mi | area[1] sq km | population 1987 estimate |
|---|---|---|---|
| Central | 13.6 | 35.2 | 29,034 |
| al-Ḥadd | 2.0 | 5.2 | 8,509 |
| Judd Ḥafṣ | 8.4 | 21.6 | 46,741 |
| al-Manāmah | 9.8 | 25.5 | 146,994 |
| al-Muḥarraq | 5.9 | 15.2 | 75,579 |
| Northern | 14.2 | 36.8 | 34,364 |
| Rifā' | 112.6 | 291.6 | 45,530 |
| Sitrah | 11.0 | 28.6 | 35,188 |
| Western | 60.2 | 156.0 | 19,711 |
| **Towns with special status** | | | |
| Ḥammād | 5.1 | 13.1 | ... |
| Madīnat 'Īsā | 4.8 | 12.4 | 39,783 |
| **Islands** | | | |
| Ḥawār and other | 19.3 | 50.0 | ... |
| TOTAL | 266.9 | 691.2 | 481,433 |

## Demography

*Population* (1987): 481,000.
*Density* (1987): persons per sq mi 1,802.2, persons per sq km 695.9.
*Urban–rural* (1984): urban 78.9%; rural 21.1%.
*Sex distribution* (1986): male 59.75%; female 40.25%.
*Age breakdown* (1986): under 15, 32.0%; 15–29, 34.4%; 30–44, 21.3%; 45–59, 8.7%; 60–74, 2.9%; 75 and over, 0.7%.
*Population projection:* (1990) 527,455; (2000) 715,074.
*Doubling time:* 23 years.
*Ethnic composition* (1981): Bahraini Arab 67.9%; Persian, Indian, and Pakistani 24.7%; other Arab 4.1%; European 2.5%; other 0.8%.
*Religious affiliation* (1981): Muslim 85.0%; (1987; Shī'ī 70.0% and Sunnī 30.0%); Christian 7.3%; other 7.7%.
*Major cities* (1987): Manama 146,994; al-Muḥarraq 75,579; Judd Ḥafṣ 46,-741; ar-Rifā' 45,530; Madīnat 'Īsā 39.783.

## Vital statistics

*Birth rate* per 1,000 population (1984): 36.8 (world avg. 29.0); legitimate, n.a.; illegitimate, n.a.
*Death rate* per 1,000 population (1984): 5.9 (world avg. 11.0).
*Natural increase rate* per 1,000 population (1984): 30.9 (world avg. 18.0).
*Total fertility rate* (avg. births per childbearing woman; 1984): 5.3.
*Marriage rate* per 1,000 population (1983): 6.2.
*Divorce rate* per 1,000 population (1983): 1.1.
*Life expectancy* at birth (1980–85): male 65.7 years; female 69.9 years.
*Major causes of death* per 100,000 population (1983): diseases of the circulatory system 97.3; accidents and acts of violence 30.2; malignant neoplasms (cancers) 23.9; respiratory diseases 17.2; diseases of the genito-urinary system 6.5; endocrine, nutritional, and metabolic diseases 6.2; certain causes of perinatal morbidity and mortality 5.2; infectious and parasitic diseases 4.7; ill-defined diseases 29.7%.

## National economy

*Budget* (1984). Revenue: BD 495,000,000 (petroleum company dividends and oil field receipts 64.4%; tax revenue 20.8%, of which taxes on international trade 9.9%; social security contributions 3.9%). Expenditures: BD 543,700,000 (public utilities 12.9%; defense 10.2%; education 10.2%; health 6.4%; roads 6.3%; social security and welfare 2.3%).
*Population economically active* (1984): total 176,853; activity rate of total population 44.2% (participation rates: over age 15, 64.6%; female 13.7%; unemployed [1987] 10.0%).

### Price and earnings indexes (1980 = 100)

| | 1979 | 1980 | 1981 | 1982 | 1983 | 1984 | 1985 |
|---|---|---|---|---|---|---|---|
| Consumer price index | 96.3 | 100 | 111.3 | 121.2 | 124.8 | 125.2 | 122.0 |
| Monthly earnings index | ... | ... | ... | ... | ... | ... | ... |

*Production* (metric tons except as noted). Agriculture, forestry, fishing (1985): fruit excluding melons 44,000, dates 40,000[2], pulses 38,000, melons 29,000, tomatoes 12,000, cow's milk 6,000, cucumbers 3,000, eggplants 3,000, onions 3,000, hen eggs 2,400; livestock (number of live animals) 15,000 goats, 7,000 sheep, 6,000 cattle, 1,000,000 chickens; fish catch (1984) 6,073. Manufacturing (1985): heavy fuel oils 4,579,000; jet fuels 1,479,000; motor gasoline 911,000; kerosene 348,000; aluminum metal 178,000[3]; manufactured gases 3,000,000 barrels[3]; other manufactures include methanol, plastics, and paper products. Construction (permits issued; 1983): residen-

tial 5,896; nonresidential 2,445. Energy production (consumption): electricity (kW-hr; 1985) 2,130,000,000 (2,130,000,000); coal, none (n.a.); crude petroleum (barrels; 1986) 15,484,000 (67,651,000[4]); petroleum products (metric tons; 1985) 7,586,000 (518,000); natural gas (cu m; 1985) 3,568,-000,000 (3,568,000,000).
*Gross national product* (1985): U.S.$4,040,000,000 (U.S.$9,290 per capita).

### Structure of gross domestic product and labour force

| | 1984 value in BD '000,000 | 1984 % of total value | 1984 labour force | 1984 % of labour force |
|---|---|---|---|---|
| Agriculture | 19.4 | 1.0 | 3,600 | 2.0 |
| Mining | 356.1 | 19.0 | 5,022 | 2.8 |
| Manufacturing | 206.3 | 11.0 | 14,654 | 8.3 |
| Construction | 185.4 | 9.9 | 37,565 | 21.2 |
| Public utilities | ... | ... | 3,391 | 2.0 |
| Transp. and commun. | 197.5 | 10.5 | 16,005 | 9.1 |
| Trade | 187.0 | 10.0 | 23,504 | 13.3 |
| Finance | 277.3 | 14.8 | 6,576 | 3.7 |
| Pub. admin., defense | | | ... | ... |
| Services | 446.5 | 23.8 | 64,093 | 36.2 |
| Other | | | 2,443[5] | 1.4[5] |
| TOTAL | 1,875.5 | 100.0 | 176,853 | 100.0 |

*Households.* Average household size (1984) 6.7; income per household: n.a.; sources of income: n.a.; expenditure: n.a.
*Land use* (1984): meadows and pastures 6.5%; agricultural and under permanent cultivation 3.2%; built-on and wasteland (mostly sand plains and salt marshes) 90.3%.
*Public debt* (external, outstanding; 1983): BD 91,200,000.
*Tourism*[6]: receipts from visitors (1985) U.S.$101,000,000; expenditures by nationals abroad (1983) U.S.$99,000,000.

## Foreign trade[7]

### Balance of trade (current prices)

| | 1981 | 1982 | 1983 | 1984 | 1985 | 1986 |
|---|---|---|---|---|---|---|
| BD '000,000 | +238 | +201 | +71 | −16 | −129 | −31 |
| % of total | 7.9% | 7.6% | 3.0% | 0.7% | 5.8% | 1.7% |

*Imports* (1986): BD 916,800,000 (nonpetroleum products 59.3%, petroleum products 40.7%). *Major import sources* (1985): Saudi Arabia 50.3%; United Kingdom 7.8%; Japan 7.1%; United States 4.0%; West Germany 3.7%.
*Exports* (1986): BD 885,600,000 (petroleum products 83.6%, nonpetroleum products [mostly aluminum products] 16.4%). *Major export destinations* (1985): United Arab Emirates 18.9%; India 12.6%; Japan 10.5%; United States 3.2%; country not specified 17.6%.

## Transport and communications

*Transport.* Railroads: none. Roads (1984): total length 155 km (paved 100.0%). Vehicles (1984): passenger cars 72,253; trucks and buses 23,182. Merchant marine (1986): vessels (100 gross tons and over) 98; total deadweight tonnage 64,419. Air transport (1986)[8]: passenger-mi 721,000,000, passenger-km 1,160,000,000; short ton-mi cargo 21,500,000, metric ton-km cargo 31,400,000; airports (1987) with scheduled flights 1.
*Communications.* Daily newspapers (1986): total number 5; total circulation 27,500[9]; circulation per 1,000 population 60.1[9]. Radio (1986): total number of receivers 200,000 (1 per 2.3 persons). Television (1986): total number of receivers 135,000 (1 per 3.4 persons). Telephones (1985): 114,857 (1 per 3.8 persons).

## Education and health

### Education (1984–85)

| | schools | teachers | students | student/ teacher ratio |
|---|---|---|---|---|
| Primary (age 6–11) | 114 | 2,963 | 49,644 | 16.8 |
| Secondary (age 12–17) | 21 | 951 | 32,927 | 34.6 |
| Voc., teacher tr. | 5 | 233 | 2,846 | 12.2 |
| Higher | 2 | 159 | 3,650 | 22.9 |

*Educational attainment* (1981): Percent of population age 10 and over having: no formal education 27.2%; knowledge of reading and writing 26.3%; primary education 24.9%; secondary 13.3%; higher 8.3%.
*Literacy* (1984): total population age 15 and over literate 202,429 (74.0%); males literate 139,715 (81.1%); females literate 62,714 (61.8%).
*Health* (1985): physicians 518 (1 per 839 persons); hospital beds 1,481 (1 per 294 persons); infant mortality rate per 1,000 live births 30.

## Military

*Total active duty personnel* (1986): 2,800 (army 82.1%, navy 10.7%, air force 7.2%). *Military expenditure as percent of GNP* (1984): 3.6% (world 5.9%); per capita expenditure U.S.$358.

[1]Total area includes numerous small uninhabited islands and dependencies of Bahrain. [2]1984. [3]1986. [4]1985. [5]Seeking work for the first time. [6]*Tourism* (1986–87): number of tourist arrivals (1986) 260,000; number of tourist arrivals in first 6 months of 1987 after completion of causeway with Saudi Arabia 1,400,000. [7]Import figures are f.o.b. (free on board) in balance of trade and c.i.f. (cost, insurance, and freight) for commodities and trading partners. [8]One-fourth apportionment of international flights of Gulf Air (jointly administered by the governments of Bahrain, Oman, Qatar, and the United Arab Emirates). [9]Circulation based on three dailies only.

# Bangladesh

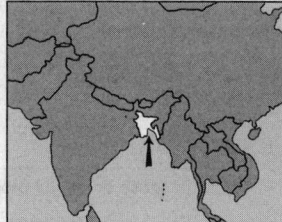

*Official name:* Gana Prajātantrī Bangladesh (People's Republic of Bangladesh).
*Form of government:* unitary multiparty republic with one legislative house (Parliament [330[1]]).
*Head of state and government:* President.
*Capital:* Dhākā (formerly Dacca).
*Official language:* Bengali.
*Official religion:* Islam.
*Monetary unit:* 1 Bangladesh taka (Tk) = 100 paisa; valuation (Oct. 5, 1987) 1 U.S.$ = Tk 30.42; 1 £ = Tk 49.40.

### Area and population

| Divisions[2] | Administrative centres | area sq mi | area sq km | population 1985 estimate |
|---|---|---|---|---|
| Chittagong | Chittagong | 17,535 | 45,415 | 26,062,000 |
| Dhākā | Dhākā | 11,881 | 30,772 | 29,043,000 |
| Khulna | Khulna | 12,963 | 33,574 | 19,792,000 |
| Rājshāhi | Rājshāhi | 13,219 | 34,237 | 24,383,000 |
| TOTAL | | 55,598 | 143,998 | 100,468,000[3] |

## Demography

*Population* (1987): 105,307,000.
*Density* (1987): persons per sq mi 1,894.1, persons per sq km 731.3.
*Urban–rural* (1985): urban 20.3%; rural 79.7%.
*Sex distribution* (1985): male 51.51%; female 48.49%.
*Age breakdown* (1985): under 15, 44.3%; 15–29, 26.6%; 30–44, 15.2%; 45–59, 8.6%; 60 and over, 5.3%.
*Population projection:* (1990) 113,005,000; (2000) 139,693,000.
*Doubling time:* 27 years.
*Ethnic composition* (1983): Bengali 97.7%; Bihārī 1.3%; tribal (Chakmā, Gāro, Khāsi, Santāl, etc.) 1.0%.
*Religious affiliation* (1981): Muslim 86.6%; Hindu 12.1%; Buddhist 0.6%; Christian 0.3%; other 0.4%.
*Major cities* (1986): Dhākā 4,470,000; Chittagong 1,750,000; Khulna 820,000; Rājshāhi 380,000.

## Vital statistics

*Birth rate* per 1,000 population (1986): 42.7 (world avg. 26.0).
*Death rate* per 1,000 population (1986): 16.3 (world avg. 9.9).
*Natural increase rate* per 1,000 population (1986): 26.4 (world avg. 16.1).
*Total fertility rate* (avg. births per childbearing woman; 1986): 5.7.
*Marriage rate* per 1,000 population (1986): 15.9.
*Divorce rate* per 1,000 population: n.a.
*Life expectancy* at birth (1986): male 50.2 years; female 49.2 years.
*Major causes of death* per 100 deaths (1976): diseases of the respiratory system 25.7, of which tuberculosis 4.8; malignant neoplasms (cancers) 19.8; infectious intestinal diseases 15.5; diseases of the liver and kidney 11.4; diseases of the circulatory system 5.9; virus fevers 4.5; childbirth related causes 4.4.; diabetes 3.6.

## National economy

*Budget* (1985–86). Revenue: Tk 37,540,000,000 (tax receipts 79.8%, of which customs duties 30.9%, excise duties 22.0%, sales tax 12.3%, income taxes 11.5%, stamps [nonjudicial] 3.1%; dividends and profits from financial institutions 5.4%; interest receipts 4.5%). Expenditures: Tk 33,130,000,000 (defense 15.1%; education 14.7%; debt service 11.8%; subsidy and grants-in-aid 11.6%; social and community services 5.1%; justice and police 4.1%; health and population control 3.9%; unexpected expenditures 11.8%).
*Production* (metric tons except as noted). Agriculture, forestry, fishing (1985–86): paddy rice 22,204,500, sugarcane 6,535,000, jute 1,366,000, wheat 1,026,000, bananas 680,000, sweet potatoes 602,000, mangoes 156,000, pineapples 126,000, tobacco leaf 46,000, tea 43,000, peanuts (groundnuts) 22,000, sesame seed 20,000; livestock (number of live animals) 23,137,000 cattle, 10,420,000 goats, 605,000 buffalo, 526,000 sheep, 60,845,000 chickens, 28,775,000 ducks; roundwood 27,144,000 cu m; fish catch 763,731. Mining and quarrying (1985): marine salt 489,000; industrial limestone 35,000. Manufacturing (1985–86): chemical fertilizers 945,720; jute manufactures 450,835; cotton yarn 430,520; iron and steel 207,107; sugar 131,850; cotton cloth 116,000; paper and newsprint 48,414; chemicals 19,774; glass sheet 736,000 sq m; matches 13,579,000 gross. Construction: n.a. Energy production (consumption) (kW-hr; 1985) 4,870,000,000 (4,870,-000,000); coal (metric tons; 1985) none (98,000); crude petroleum (barrels; 1985) 161,000 (7,535,000); petroleum products (metric tons; 1985) 813,000 (1,412,000); natural gas (cu m; 1985) 2,948,779,000 (2,948,779,000).
*Land use* (1984): forested 15.7%; meadows and pastures 4.5%; agricultural and under permanent cultivation 68.0%; other 11.8%.
*Household income.* Average household size (1981) 5.7; average annual income per household (1981–82) Tk 13,254 (U.S.$668); sources of income (1977–78): agriculture 44.7%, wages 26.9%, finance and trade 11.8%, real estate 6.0%, gifts and assistance 0.3%, pension 0.2%, other 10.1%; expenditure (1981–82): food and drink 66.1%, housing and rent 8.9%, clothing and footwear 7.9%, fuel and light 5.9%, education 1.2%.
*Gross national product* (at current market prices; 1985): U.S.$14,770,000,000 (U.S.$150 per capita).

### Structure of gross domestic product and labour force

| | 1985–86 in value Tk '000,000 | 1985–86 % of total value | 1984–85 labour force | 1984–85 % of labour force |
|---|---|---|---|---|
| Agriculture | 248,556 | 51.6 | 16,700,000 | 58.3 |
| Mining Manufacturing } | 37,345 | 7.8 | 2,500,000 | 8.7 |
| Construction | 26,456 | 5.5 | 600,000 | 2.1 |
| Public utilities | 2,574 | 0.5 | 28,000 | 0.1 |
| Transp. and commun. | 28,674 | 6.0 | 1,100,000 | 3.8 |
| Trade | 38,092 | 7.9 | 3,300,000 | 11.5 |
| Finance | 8,057 | 1.7 | 400,000 | 1.4 |
| Public admin., defense | 20,864 | 4.3 | 1,400,000 | 5.0 |
| Services and other | 71,004 | 14.7 | 2,600,000 | 9.1 |
| TOTAL | 481,622 | 100.0 | 28,628,000 | 100.0 |

*Population economically active* (1983–84): total 28,493,000; activity rate of total population 29.9% (participation rates: ages 15–64, 49.4%; female 3.9%; unemployed and underemployed 26.5%).

### Price and earnings indexes (1980 = 100)

| | 1981 | 1982 | 1983 | 1984 | 1985 | 1986 | 1987[4] |
|---|---|---|---|---|---|---|---|
| Consumer price index | 116.2 | 130.7 | 143.0 | 158.1 | 175.0 | 194.3 | 205.1 |
| Hourly earnings index[5] | 105.4 | 106.3 | 106.4 | 106.8 | ... | ... | ... |

*Public debt* (external, outstanding; 1985): U.S.$5,967,800,000.
*Tourism:* receipts from visitors (1984) U.S.$27,000,000; expenditures by nationals abroad (1983) U.S.$23,000,000.

## Foreign trade

### Balance of trade (current prices)

| | 1981 | 1982 | 1983 | 1984 | 1985 | 1986 |
|---|---|---|---|---|---|---|
| Tk '000,000 | −29,692 | −28,508 | −30,138 | −40,882 | −41,543 | −47,222 |
| % of total | 51.2% | 45.5% | 45.8% | 46.4% | 42.6% | 46.9% |

*Imports* (1985–86): Tk 62,929,622,000 (machinery and transport equipment 18.2%; chemicals 12.3%; food grains 6.6%, of which wheat 6.1%, rice 0.5%; fertilizers 5.1%; textile yarn 3.2%; cement 2.8%; cotton 2.6%). *Major import sources:* Singapore 16.9%; Japan 14.9%; United States 6.7%; China 4.4%; United Kingdom 4.4%; Hong Kong 1.5%.
*Exports* (1985–86): Tk 27,396,204,000 (jute manufactures 31.3%; ready-made garments 19.7%; fish, shrimp, and frog legs 13.1%; raw jute and mesta 12.5%; leather 8.6%; tea 3.6%). *Major export destinations:* United States 24.4%; Japan 7.4%; United Kingdom 6.0%; Italy 5.7%; Singapore 4.9%; Belgium 3.9%.

## Transport and communications

*Transport.* Railroads (1984–85): route length 1,793 mi, 2,886 km; passenger-mi 3,747,700,000, passenger-km 6,031,300,000; short ton-mi cargo 556,800,-000, metric ton-km cargo 812,900,000. Roads (1982): total length 98,522 mi, 158,551 km (paved 12%). Vehicles (1984): passenger cars 38,665; trucks and buses 23,263. Merchant marine (1986): vessels (100 gross tons and over) 274; total deadweight tonnage 517,772. Air transport (1985)[6]: passenger-mi 1,021,845,000, passenger-km 1,643,924,000; short ton-mi cargo 151,174,000, metric ton-km cargo 220,711,000; airports (1987) 8.
*Communications.* Daily newspapers (1985): total number 54; total circulation 554,000; circulation per 1,000 population 5.5. Radio (1985): 775,000 receivers (1 per 130 persons). Television (1985): 300,000 receivers (1 per 335 persons). Telephones (1985): 151,000 (1 per 665 persons).

## Education and health

### Education (1984–85)

| | schools | teachers | students | student/ teacher ratio |
|---|---|---|---|---|
| Primary (age 5–9) | 43,712 | 184,668 | 10,776,000 | 58.4 |
| Secondary (age 10–14) | 8,793 | 99,016 | 2,745,000 | 27.7 |
| Voc., teacher tr. | 157 | 2,151 | 34,840 | 16.2 |
| Higher | 43 | 3,774 | 44,464 | 11.8 |

*Educational attainment* (1981). Percent of population age 25 and over having: no formal schooling 70.4%; primary education 24.1%; secondary 4.2%; postsecondary 1.3%. *Literacy* (1985): total population age 15 and over literate 18,166,000 (33.1%); males literate 12,272,000 (43.3%); females literate 5,894,000 (22.2%).
*Health:* physicians (1983–84) 14,307 (1 per 6,761 persons); hospital beds (1984) 29,000 (1 per 3,378 persons); infant mortality rate (1986) 133.0.
*Food* (1981–83): daily per capita caloric intake 1,878 (vegetable products 97%, animal products 3%); (1983) 84% of FAO recommended minimum.

## Military

*Total active duty personnel* (1986): 91,300 (army 89.6%, navy 7.1%, air force 3.3%). *Military expenditure as percent of GNP* (1984): 1.9% (world 5.9%); per capita expenditure U.S.$2.

[1]Includes 30 seats reserved for women. [2]Geographic reorganization at the district level took place in 1984; each division is now divided into the following number of new districts: Chittagong 15, Dhākā 17, Khulna 16, and Rājshāhi 16. [3]Detail does not add to total given because of rounding. [4]May. [5]Skilled wage earnings in manufacturing. [6]Bangladesh Biman only.

# Barbados

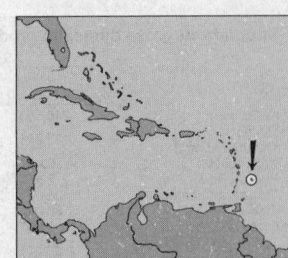

*Official name:* Barbados.
*Form of government:* constitutional monarchy with two legislative houses (Senate [21]; House of Assembly [27]).
*Chief of state:* British Monarch represented by governor-general.
*Head of government:* Prime Minister.
*Capital:* Bridgetown.
*Official language:* English.
*Official religion:* none.
*Monetary unit:* 1 Barbados dollar (BDS$) = 100 cents; valuation (Oct. 5, 1987) 1 U.S.$ = BDS$2.01; 1 £ = BDS$3.27.

### Area and population

| | area | | population |
|---|---|---|---|
| | | | 1980 |
| Parishes[1] | sq mi | sq km | census |
| Christ Church | 22 | 57 | 40,790 |
| St. Andrew | 14 | 36 | 6,731 |
| St. George | 17 | 44 | 17,361 |
| St. James | 12 | 31 | 17,255 |
| St. John | 13 | 34 | 10,330 |
| St. Joseph | 10 | 26 | 7,211 |
| St. Lucy | 14 | 36 | 9,264 |
| St. Michael[2] | 15 | 39 | 99,953 |
| St. Peter | 13 | 34 | 10,717 |
| St. Philip | 23 | 60 | 18,662 |
| St. Thomas | 13 | 34 | 10,709 |
| TOTAL | 166 | 430[3] | 248,983 |

## Demography

*Population* (1987): 254,000.
*Density* (1987): persons per sq mi 1,530, persons per sq km 591.
*Urban–rural* (1985): urban 42.3%; rural 57.7%.
*Sex distribution* (1986): male 47.83%; female 52.17%.
*Age breakdown* (1985): under 15, 27.3%; 15–29, 30.5%; 30–44, 17.2%; 45–59, 12.1%; 60–74, 9.4%; 75 and over, 3.5%.
*Population projection:* (1990) 256,000; (2000) 263,000.
*Doubling time:* 88 years.
*Ethnic composition* (1980): black 91.9%; white 3.3%; mulatto 2.6%; East Indian 0.5%; other 1.7%.
*Religious affiliation* (1980): Anglican 39.7%; other Protestant 25.6% (mainly Methodist, Pentecostal, and Seventh-day Adventist); nonreligious 17.5%; Roman Catholic 4.4%; other 12.8%.
*Major cities* (1980): Bridgetown 7,552 (metropolitan area [1986] 102,000); other cities cannot be identified because no other bounded localities exist.

## Vital statistics

*Birth rate* per 1,000 population (1986): 16.1 (world avg. 26.0); (1978) legitimate 27.9%; illegitimate 72.1%.
*Death rate* per 1,000 population (1986): 8.2 (world avg. 9.9).
*Natural increase rate* per 1,000 population (1986): 7.9 (world avg. 16.1).
*Total fertility rate* (avg. births per childbearing woman; 1984): 1.9.
*Marriage rate* per 1,000 population (1983): 5.0.
*Divorce rate* per 1,000 population (1983): 1.3.
*Life expectancy* at birth (1980–85): male 70.0 years; female 75.4 years.
*Major causes of death* per 100,000 population (1984): diseases of the circulatory system 364.7, of which cerebrovascular disease 129.0, diseases of pulmonary circulation 101.2, acute myocardial infarction 54.8; malignant neoplasms (cancers) 142.1; diabetes mellitus 51.2.

## National economy

*Budget* (1986). Revenue: BDS$657,911,000 (tax revenue 88.2%, of which consumption tax 17.4%, import duties 16.5%, individual income tax 14.8%, corporate tax 9.6%; nontax revenue 11.8%). Expenditures: BDS$818,804,-000 (current expenditure 78.4%, of which education 18.0%, general public services 12.2%, health 11.1%, debt charges 9.0%, roads and other transportation 8.2%, defense 2.3%; development expenditure 21.6%).
*Production* (metric tons except as noted). Agriculture, forestry, fishing (1986): sugarcane 788,000, sweet potatoes 2,192, yams 1,989, carrots 985, cabbages 944, beans 409, cotton lint 161[4]; livestock (number of live animals) 54,000 sheep, 49,000 pigs, 32,000 goats, 18,000 cattle; roundwood, n.a.; fish catch (1986) 2,956, of which flying fishes 1,907. Manufacturing (1985): electronic assembly (including microprocessors and computer chips), n.a.; clothing, n.a.; metal and wooden furniture, n.a.; cement 200,000; raw sugar 111,000[5]; cigarettes 241; beer 74,000 hectolitres; rum 49,000 hectolitres. Construction, n.a. Energy production (consumption): electricity (kW-hr; 1986) 414,000,-000 (356,000,000); coal, none (none); crude petroleum (barrels; 1986) 559,-000 (1,598,000[6]); petroleum products (metric tons; 1985) 205,000 (218,000); natural gas (cu m; 1986) 34,500,000 (25,400,000[6]).
*Population economically active* (1986): total 116,900; activity rate of total population 46.1% (participation rates: ages 15–64, 73.7%[7]; female 47.3%; unemployed 17.8%).

### Price and earnings indexes (1980 = 100)

| | 1981 | 1982 | 1983 | 1984 | 1985 | 1986 | 1987[8] |
|---|---|---|---|---|---|---|---|
| Consumer price index | 114.6 | 126.4 | 133.0 | 139.2 | 144.7 | 146.6 | 146.4 |
| Annual earnings index | 110.5 | 123.0 | 130.1 | 142.0 | 148.9 | ... | ... |

*Household income and expenditure.* Average household size (1980) 3.7; income per household: n.a.; sources of income: n.a.; expenditure (1980)[9]: food 43.2%, housing 13.1%, household operations 9.6%, alcohol and tobacco 8.4%, fuel and light 6.2%, medical and personal care 6.0%, clothing and footwear 5.1%, transportation 4.6%, education, recreation, and other expenses 3.8%.
*Gross national product* (at current market prices; 1985): U.S.$1,180,000,000 (U.S.$4,660 per capita).

### Structure of gross domestic product and labour force

| | 1986 | | 1985 | |
|---|---|---|---|---|
| | in value BDS$'000 | % of total value | labour force | % of labour force |
| Agriculture, fishing | 149,450 | 5.6 | 9,100 | 8.0 |
| Mining | 31,170 | 1.2 } | 16,600 | 14.7 |
| Manufacturing | 229,262 | 8.6 } | | |
| Construction | 131,354 | 4.9 | 8,700 | 7.7 |
| Public utilities | 71,736 | 2.7 | 2,400 | 2.1 |
| Transportation and communication | 211,475 | 7.9 | 5,500 | 4.8 |
| Trade | 719,579 | 26.9 | 24,400 | 21.5 |
| Finance | 311,045 | 11.6 | 3,300 | 2.9 |
| Pub. admin., defense | 379,043 | 14.1 } | 38,600 | 34.1 |
| Services | 94,365 | 3.5 } | | |
| Other | 348,735[10] | 13.0[10] | 4,800 | 4.2 |
| TOTAL | 2,676,914 | 100.0 | 113,400 | 100.0 |

*Public debt* (external, outstanding; 1985): U.S.$351,900,000.
*Tourism:* receipts from visitors (1986) U.S.$326,000,000; expenditures by nationals abroad (1984) U.S.$23,000,000.
*Land use* (1984): forested, negligible; meadows and pastures 9.0%; agricultural and under permanent cultivation 77.0%; other 14.0%.

## Foreign trade[11]

### Balance of trade (current prices)

| | 1980 | 1981 | 1982 | 1983 | 1984 | 1985 | 1986 |
|---|---|---|---|---|---|---|---|
| BDS$'000,000 | −507.1 | −665.1 | −498.6 | −499.0 | −431.3 | −402.7 | −521.0 |
| % of total | 35.8% | 46.0% | 32.5% | 27.9% | 21.5% | 22.1% | 32.0% |

*Imports* (1986): BDS$1,181,000,000 ([12]; electrical components 17.5%, machinery 16.6%, food and beverages 15.2%, construction materials 4.9%, chemicals 4.8%, motor cars 3.2%). *Major import sources:* United States 39.8%; United Kingdom 10.8%; CARICOM 10.7%; Canada 6.6%; Japan 5.6%.
*Exports* (1986): BDS$552,600,000 ([13]; electrical components 57.3%, sugar 12.5%, clothing 8.5%, chemicals 4.5%, rum 2.1%). *Major export destinations:* United States 23.7%; CARICOM 17.4%; United Kingdom 7.6%; West Germany 5.4%; Canada 4.2%.

## Transport and communications

*Transport.* Railroads: none. Roads (1985): total length 996 mi, 1,603 km (paved 90%). Vehicles (1985): passenger cars 32,263; trucks and buses 5,363. Merchant marine (1986): vessels (100 gross tons and over) 34; total deadweight tonnage 8,066. Air transport (1985): passenger arrivals 511,354, passenger departures 514,742; cargo unloaded 7,469 metric tons, cargo loaded 4,881 metric tons; airports (1987) with scheduled flights 1.
*Communications.* Daily newspapers (1986): total number 2; total circulation 39,500; circulation per 1,000 population 156. Radio (1986): total number of receivers 335,000 (1 per 0.8 persons). Television (1986): total number of receivers 60,000 (1 per 4.2 persons). Telephones (1986): 90,708 (1 per 2.8 persons).

## Education and health

### Education (1984–85)

| | schools | teachers | students | student/ teacher ratio |
|---|---|---|---|---|
| Primary (age 5–11) | 130 | 1,464 | 30,792 | 21.0 |
| Secondary (age 12–16) | 36 | 1,449 | 28,815 | 19.9 |
| Vocational | 3 | 154 | 3,592 | 23.3 |
| Higher | 1 | 108 | 1,617 | 15.0 |

*Educational attainment* (1980). Percent of population age 25 and over having: no formal schooling 0.8%; primary education 63.5%; secondary 32.3%; higher 3.3%. *Literacy* (1980): total population age 15 and over literate[14] 169,894 (98.0%); males literate 78,022 (98.3%); females literate 91,872 (97.7%).
*Health* (1983): physicians 213 (1 per 1,179 persons); hospital beds 2,110 (1 per 119 persons); infant mortality rate per 1,000 live births (1984–86) 9.2.
*Food* (1981–83): daily per capita caloric intake 3,215 (vegetable products 74%, animal products 26%); (1983) 132% of FAO recommended minimum requirement.

## Military

*Total active duty personnel* (1986): 154 (paramilitary marine and coast guard components only). *Military expenditure as percent of GNP* (1984): 1.0% (world 5.9%); per capita expenditure U.S.$44.

---

[1]Parishes have no local administrative function. [2]Includes Bridgetown. [3]Detail does not add to total given because of rounding. [4]1986–87. [5]1986. [6]1985. [7]1983. [8]Average of first quarter. [9]Weights of consumer price index components. [10]Net indirect taxes. [11]Import figures are f.o.b. in balance of trade and c.i.f. in commodities and trading partners. [12]Breakdown based on retained imports only valued at BDS$1,049,000,000. [13]Breakdown based on domestic exports only valued at BDS$421,100,000. [14]National literacy standard based solely on school attendance. Functional literacy may be appreciably lower.

# Belgium

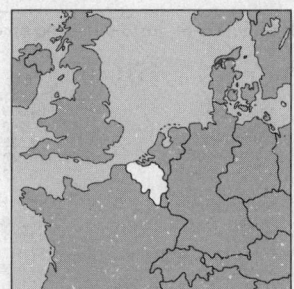

*Official name:* Koninkrijk België (Dutch); Royaume de Belgique (French) (Kingdom of Belgium).
*Form of government:* constitutional monarchy with two legislative houses (Senate [183]; House of Representatives [212]).
*Chief of state:* Monarch.
*Head of government:* Prime Minister.
*Capital:* Brussels.
*Official languages:* Dutch; French; German.
*Official religion:* none.
*Monetary unit:* 1 Belgian franc (BF) = 100 centimes; valuation (Oct. 5, 1987) 1 U.S.$ = BF 38.24; 1 £ = BF 62.10.

| Area and population | | area | | population |
|---|---|---|---|---|
| Provinces | Capitals | sq mi | sq km | 1986 estimate[1] |
| Antwerp | Antwerp | 1,107 | 2,867 | 1,582,786 |
| Brabant | Brussels | 1,297 | 3,358 | 2,218,349 |
| East Flanders | Ghent | 1,151 | 2,982 | 1,328,805 |
| Hainaut | Mons | 1,462 | 3,787 | 1,277,939 |
| Liège | Liège | 1,491 | 3,862 | 991,535 |
| Limburg | Hasselt | 935 | 2,422 | 731,875 |
| Luxembourg | Arlon | 1,715 | 4,441 | 224,988 |
| Namur | Namur | 1,415 | 3,665 | 412,231 |
| West Flanders | Brugge | 1,210 | 3,134 | 1,090,387 |
| TOTAL | | 11,783 | 30,518 | 9,858,895 |

## Demography

*Population* (1987): 9,861,000.
*Density* (1987): persons per sq mi 836.9, persons per sq km 323.1.
*Urban–rural* (1980): urban 72.4%; rural 27.6%.
*Sex distribution* (1986): male 48.81%; female 51.19%.
*Age breakdown* (1984): under 15, 19.3%; 15–29, 23.5%; 30–44, 19.8%; 45–59, 18.2%; 60–74, 13.1%; 75 and over, 6.1%.
*Population projection:* (1990) 9,864,000; (2000) 9,875,000.
*Doubling time:* n.a.; doubling time exceeds 100 years.
*Nationality* (1981): Belgian 91.1%; Italian 2.8%; Moroccan 1.1%; French 1.1%; Dutch 0.7%; Turkish 0.6%; other 2.6%.
*Religious affiliation* (1980): Roman Catholic 91.8%; Protestant 3.5%; Muslim 1.1%.
*Major cities* (1986[1]): Brussels 136,453 (976,536[2]); Antwerp 483,199; Ghent 234,251; Charleroi 210,324; Liège 201,749.

## Vital statistics

*Birth rate* per 1,000 population (1985): 11.7 (world avg. 29.0); (1983) legitimate 93.9%; illegitimate 6.1%.
*Death rate* per 1,000 population (1985): 11.2 (world avg. 11.0).
*Natural increase rate* per 1,000 population (1985): 0.5 (world avg. 18.0).
*Total fertility rate* (avg. births per childbearing woman; 1985): 1.6.
*Marriage rate* per 1,000 population (1985): 5.8.
*Divorce rate* per 1,000 population (1985): 1.9.
*Life expectancy* at birth (1979–82): male 70.0 years; female 76.8 years.
*Major causes of death* per 100,000 population (1984): heart and circulatory diseases 480.0, of which cerebrovascular disease 124.8; malignant neoplasms (cancers) 273.5.

## National economy

*Budget* (1986). Revenue: BF 1,433,100,000,000 (direct taxes 62.2%; value-added, stamp, and similar duties 26.1%; customs and excise duties 7.1%). Expenditures: BF 1,972,934,000,000 (government departments 41.7%; public debt 21.7%; education and culture 14.6%; pension 9.2%; defense 5.5%).
*Public debt* (1986): U.S.$121,291,000,000.
*Tourism* (1985): receipts from visitors U.S.$1,661,000,000; expenditures by nationals abroad U.S.$2,048,000,000.
*Production* (metric tons except as noted). Agriculture, forestry, fishing (1985)[3]: sugar beets 6,000,000, potatoes 1,700,000, wheat 1,204,000, barley 723,000, apples 213,000, tomatoes 138,000, oats 123,000, corn (maize) 90,000, milk 4,075,000; livestock (number of live animals) 3,210,000 cattle, 5,339,000 pigs, 105,000 sheep, 35,000 horses; roundwood 3,086,000 cu m; fish catch 44,621, of which European plaice (flounder) 12,003, Atlantic cod 6,240, Atlantic herring 3,482. Mining and quarrying (1985[3]): quartz 300,000; barite 40,000. Manufacturing (value added in BF '000,000; 1983): metal products and machinery 301,000; food 170,100; chemicals and chemical products 123,200, of which drugs and medicines 16,200; textiles 54,700; furniture and fixtures 38,100; glass and glass products 33,800; iron and steel 32,900; printing and publishing 29,000; paper and paper products 22,200; wearing apparel 21,500. Construction (1984): residential 14,972,000 cu m; nonresidential 18,161,000 cu m. Energy production (consumption): electricity (kW-hr; 1985) 56,356,000,000 (56,310,000,000); coal (metric tons; 1985) 7,666,000 (16,032,000); petroleum (barrels; 1985) none (147,538,000); natural gas (cu m; 1985) 50,000,000 (8,736,550,000).
*Household income and expenditure.* Average household size (1981) 2.7; sources of income (1984): wages and salaries 52.0%, transfer payments 22.5%, self-employment 10.1%, other 15.4%; expenditure (1984): food 23.1%, housing 18.5%, transportation 12.8%, personal care and health 9.3%, clothing and footwear 6.0%, other 30.3%.

*Gross national product* (at current market prices; 1985): U.S.$83,230,000,000 (U.S.$8,440 per capita).

| Structure of gross domestic product and labour force | | | | |
|---|---|---|---|---|
| | 1985 | | 1984 | |
| | in value BF '000,000 | % of total value | labour force | % of labour force |
| Agriculture | 115,500 | 2.4 | 106,085 | 2.5 |
| Mining | 25,900 | 0.6 | 25,548 | 0.6 |
| Manufacturing | 1,103,100 | 22.9 | 821,566 | 19.5 |
| Construction | 248,100 | 5.2 | 203,167 | 4.8 |
| Public utilities | 188,700 | 3.9 | 32,813 | 0.8 |
| Transportation and communication | 384,300 | 8.0 | 263,378 | 6.3 |
| Trade | 969,400 | 20.1 | 696,670 | 16.5 |
| Finance | 278,900 | 5.8 | 271,117 | 6.4 |
| Pub. admin., defense Services | 1,349,600 | 28.0 | 1,214,367 | 28.8 |
| Other | 148,600[4] | 3.1 | 579,619[5] | 13.8 |
| TOTAL | 4,812,100 | 100.0 | 4,214,330 | 100.0 |

*Population economically active* (1984): total 4,214,330; activity rate of total population 42.8% (participation rates: ages 15–64, n.a.; female 39.2%; unemployed 13.0%).

| Price and earnings indexes (1980 = 100) | | | | | | | |
|---|---|---|---|---|---|---|---|
| | 1981 | 1982 | 1983 | 1984 | 1985 | 1986 | 1987[6] |
| Consumer price index | 107.6 | 117.0 | 126.0 | 134.0 | 141.8 | 142.3 | 145.1 |
| Hourly earnings index | 110.1 | 116.9 | 122.0 | 128.0 | 136.4 | 136.3 | ... |

*Land use*[3] (1984): forested 21.4%; meadows and pastures 20.3%; agricultural and under permanent cultivation 25.1%; other 33.2%.

## Foreign trade[3]

| Balance of trade (current prices) | | | | | |
|---|---|---|---|---|---|
| | 1981 | 1982 | 1983 | 1984 | 1985 | 1986 |
| BF '000,000 | −178,000 | −180,400 | −84,800 | −107,600 | −50,300 | +96,800 |
| % of total | 4.1% | 3.6% | 1.6% | 1.8% | 0.8% | 1.6% |

*Imports* (1985): BF 3,315,468,000,000 (machinery and transport equipment 23.1%, of which road vehicles and parts 10.1%; mineral fuels and lubricants 16.6%, of which petroleum and petroleum products 11.9%, natural gas 2.9%; chemicals and chemical products 10.2%; food and live animals 8.9%; nonindustrial (gem) diamonds 5.0%). *Major import sources:* West Germany 21.0%; The Netherlands 18.5%; France 15.0%; U.K. 8.9%; U.S. 5.7%.
*Exports* (1985): BF 3,163,725,000,000 (machinery and transport equipment 23.2%, of which passenger cars 9.0%; chemicals and chemical products 12.8%, of which plastics 4.5%; food and live animals 8.6%; iron and steel 8.4%; petroleum and petroleum products 6.0%; nonindustrial (gem) diamonds 5.9%; textile yarns and fabrics 5.6%). *Major export destinations:* France 19.6%; West Germany 19.2%; The Netherlands 14.7%; U.K. 10.1%; U.S. 6.5%.

## Transport and communications

*Transport.* Railroads (1985): route length 2,325 mi, 3,741 km; passenger-mi 4,071,000,000, passenger-km 6,552,000,000; short ton-mi cargo 5,080,000,000[7], metric ton-km cargo 7,416,000,000[7]. Roads (1985): total length 79,468 mi, 127,893 km (paved 96%). Vehicles (1985): passenger cars 3,342,704; trucks and buses 318,899. Merchant marine (1986): vessels (100 gross tons and over) 355; total deadweight tonnage 3,916,538. Air transport (1986): passenger-mi 3,452,000,000, passenger-km 5,556,000,000; short ton-mi cargo 406,872,000; metric ton-km cargo 594,024,000; airports (1987) with scheduled flights 3.
*Communications.* Daily newspapers (1985): total number 39; total circulation 2,196,011; circulation per 1,000 population 223. Radio (1985): total number of receivers 4,526,291 (1 per 2.2 persons). Television (1985): total number of receivers 3,040,935 (1 per 3.2 persons). Telephones (1986): 4,346,369 (1 per 2.3 persons).

## Education and health

| Education (1984–85) | | | | |
|---|---|---|---|---|
| | schools | teachers | students | student/ teacher ratio |
| Primary (age 6–12) | 4,790 | 45,261[8] | 768,207 | ... |
| Secondary (age 12–18) | 2,272 | 56,719[9] | 858,625 | ... |
| Voc., teacher tr.[9] | 209 | 6,864 | 218,717 | 31.9 |
| Higher[10] | 6 | ... | 102,354 | ... |

*Educational attainment* (1977). Percent of population age 25 and over having: less than secondary education 64.4%; lower secondary 16.0%; upper secondary 10.0%; vocational 3.7%; teacher's college 2.1%; university 3.8%.
*Literacy* (1986): virtually 100% literate.
*Health* (1985): physicians 28,828 (1 per 342 persons); hospital beds (1984) 91,638 (1 per 105 persons); infant mortality rate per 1,000 live births 9.4.
*Food*[3] (1981–83): daily per capita caloric intake 3,679 (vegetable products 60%, animal products 40%); (1983) 139% of FAO recommended minimum.

## Military

*Total active duty personnel* (1986): 91,428 (army 73.7%, navy 4.9%, air force 21.4%). *Military expenditure as percent of GNP* (1984): 3.2% (world 6.1%); per capita expenditure U.S.$248.

[1]January 1. [2]Région Bruxelloise. [3]Includes Luxembourg. [4]Includes imputed bank service charges. [5]Includes 545,720 unemployed. [6]July. [7]1986. [8]1983–84. [9]1982–83. [10]University only.

# Belize

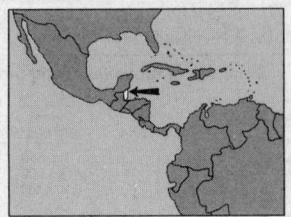

*Official name:* Belize.
*Form of government:* constitutional monarchy with two legislative houses (Senate [9]; House of Representatives [28]).
*Chief of state:* British Monarch represented by governor-general.
*Head of government:* Prime Minister.
*Capital:* Belmopan.
*Official language:* English.
*Official religion:* none.
*Monetary unit:* 1 Belize dollar (BZ$) = 100 cents; valuation (Oct. 5, 1987) 1 U.S.$ = BZ$2.00[1]; 1 £ = BZ$3.28.

### Area and population

| Districts | Capitals | area sq mi | area sq km | population 1985 estimate |
|---|---|---|---|---|
| Belize | Belize City | 1,624 | 4,206 | 54,500 |
| Cayo | San Ignacio | 2,061 | 5,338 | 27,400 |
| Corozal | Corozal | 718 | 1,860 | 28,000 |
| Orange Walk | Orange Walk | 1,829 | 4,737 | 26,600 |
| Stann Creek | Dangriga | 840 | 2,176 | 16,500 |
| Toledo | Punta Gorda | 1,795 | 4,649 | 13,400 |
| TOTAL | | 8,867 | 22,965[2] | 166,400 |

## Demography

*Population* (1987): 176,000.
*Density* (1987): persons per sq mi 19.8, persons per sq km 7.7.
*Urban–rural* (1980): urban 51.7%; rural 48.3%.
*Sex distribution* (1985): male 50.62%; female 49.38%.
*Age breakdown* (1985): under 15, 44.9%; 15–29, 28.0%; 30–44, 12.0%; 45–59, 7.8%; 60–74, 5.0%; 75 and over, 2.3%.
*Population projection:* (1990) 190,000; (2000) 249,000.
*Doubling time:* 20 years.
*Ethnic composition* (1980): Creole (predominantly black) 39.7%; mestizo (Spanish-Indian) 33.1%; Mayan Indian 9.5%, of which Kekchi 2.7%; Garifuna (black-Carib Indian) 7.6%; white 4.2%; East Indian 2.1%; other 3.8%.
*Religious affiliation* (1980): Roman Catholic 61.7%; Protestant 28.9%, of which Anglican 11.8%, Methodist 6.0%, Mennonite 3.9%, Seventh-day Adventist 3.0%; Bahá'í 2.5%; Jewish 1.2%; other Christian 1.0%; other 4.7%.
*Major cities* (1985): Belize City 47,000; Corozal 10,000; Orange Walk 9,600; Dangriga 7,700; Belmopan 4,500.

## Vital statistics

*Birth rate* per 1,000 population (1985): 40.1 (world avg. 29.0); (1984) legitimate 46.1%; illegitimate 53.9%.
*Death rate* per 1,000 population (1985): 4.0 (world avg. 11.0).
*Natural increase rate* per 1,000 population (1985): 36.1 (world avg. 18.0).
*Total fertility rate* (avg. births per childbearing woman; 1985): 4.9.
*Marriage rate* per 1,000 population (1985): 5.9.
*Divorce rate* per 1,000 population (1985): 0.4.
*Life expectancy* at birth (1980–85): male 63.3 years; female 67.1 years.
*Major causes of death* per 100,000 population (1985): malignant neoplasms (cancers) 40.9; pneumonia 39.1; perinatal mortality 37.3; heart diseases 33.1; accidents 33.1; cerebrovascular disease 29.4; diabetes mellitus 23.4.

## National economy

*Budget* (1986–87). Revenue: BZ$213,800,000 (local revenue sources 65.8%, foreign sources 34.2%). Expenditures: BZ$213,800,000 (capital projects 45.8%, administration 11.9%, public debt payment 11.5%, education 9.0%, security 5.0%, health 4.9%).
*Public debt* (external, outstanding; June 1986): U.S.$94,200,000.
*Tourism* (1985): receipts from visitors U.S.$11,000,000; expenditures by nationals abroad, n.a.
*Production* (metric tons except as noted). Agriculture, forestry, fishing (1985): sugarcane 977,000, oranges 43,000, grapefruits 17,000, corn (maize) 16,000, bananas 12,000, rice 6,000, coconuts 3,000, red kidney beans 1,040, honey 315; livestock (number of live animals) 52,000 cattle, 23,000 pigs, 350,000 chickens[3]; roundwood 164,000 cu m; fish catch 1,389, of which spiny lobster 730, marine fishes 388, conchs 215. Mining and quarrying (1985): limestone 600,000; sand and gravel 500,000. Manufacturing (1985): sugar 102,000; molasses 28,100; fertilizer 3,670; citrus concentrate 39,015 hectolitres; beer 22,700 hectolitres; cigarettes 74,000,000 units; garments 2,734,000 units. Construction (1984): residential 6,185 sq m, nonresidential, n.a. Energy production (consumption): electricity (kW-hr; 1985) 60,000,000 (60,000,000); coal, none (none); crude petroleum, none (none); petroleum products (metric tons; 1985) none (59,000); natural gas, none (none).
*Population economically active* (1983–84): total 47,325; activity rate of total population 29.6% (participation rates: ages 15–64, n.a.; female 32.5%; unemployed [1984] 13.6%).

### Price and earnings indexes (1980 = 100)

| | 1981 | 1982 | 1983 | 1984 | 1985 | 1986 |
|---|---|---|---|---|---|---|
| Consumer price index | 111.2 | 118.8 | 124.8 | 129.4 | 134.1 | 135.4 |
| Earnings index | ... | ... | ... | ... | ... | ... |

*Gross national product* (at current market prices; 1985): U.S.$180,000,000 (U.S.$1,080 per capita).

### Structure of gross domestic product and labour force

| | 1984 in value BZ$'000 | 1984 % of total value | 1983–84 labour force[4] | 1983–84 % of labour force |
|---|---|---|---|---|
| Agriculture | 64,999 | 19.9 | 13,070 | 32.1 |
| Mining | 760 | 0.2 | 80 | 0.2 |
| Manufacturing | 34,685 | 10.6 | 4,190 | 10.3 |
| Construction | 18,040 | 5.5 | 1,990 | 4.9 |
| Public utilities | 10,339 | 3.2 | 610 | 1.5 |
| Transportation and communication | 32,037 | 9.8 | 2,040 | 5.0 |
| Trade | 57,358 | 17.5 | 4,560 | 11.2 |
| Finance | 42,991 | 13.1 | 570 | 1.4 |
| Pub. admin., defense | 37,517 | 11.5 | 6,270 | 15.4 |
| Services | 34,948 | 10.7 | 6,510 | 16.0 |
| Other | −6,645 | −2.0 | 810 | 2.0 |
| TOTAL | 327,029 | 100.0 | 40,700 | 100.0 |

*Household income and expenditure.* Average household size (1984) 5.2; income per household: n.a.; sources of income: n.a.; expenditure (1980): food and beverages 51.5%, clothing and footwear 11.1%, household furnishings 10.1%, transportation and communication 6.5%, energy and water 6.0%, health care 3.4%, housing 2.3%, other 9.1%.
*Land use* (1984): forested 44.4%; meadows and pastures 1.9%; agricultural and under permanent cultivation 2.3%; other 51.4%.

## Foreign trade

### Balance of trade (current prices)

| | 1980 | 1981 | 1982 | 1983 | 1984 | 1985 | 1986 |
|---|---|---|---|---|---|---|---|
| BZ$'000,000 | −51.0 | −56.5 | −50.6 | −47.8 | −50.2 | −52.9 | −40.9 |
| % of total | 10.3% | 10.6% | 12.2% | 13.3% | 11.9% | 12.8% | 10.1% |

*Imports* (1985): BZ$256,300,000 (1984; manufactured goods 26.2%; food 18.8%; machinery and transport 17.7%; fuels 15.5%; chemicals 8.0%). *Major import sources:* United States 48.2%; United Kingdom 9.3%; The Netherlands 5.2%; Mexico 4.1%.
*Exports* (1985): BZ$180,200,000 (domestic exports 71.5%, of which sugar 38.0%, garments 24.3%, citrus fruits 18.8%, fish, crustaceans, and mollusks 11.4%, bananas 5.1%; reexports 28.5%). *Major export destinations:* United States 57.9%; United Kingdom 22.7%; Trinidad and Tobago 5.9%; Canada 5.0%.

## Transport and communications

*Transport.* Railroads: none. Roads (1984): total length 1,639 mi, 2,637 km (paved 16%). Vehicles (1984): passenger cars 3,707; trucks and buses 1,855. Merchant marine (1986): vessels (100 gross tons and over) 3; total deadweight tonnage 805. Air transport (1985)[5]: passenger arrivals 55,348, passenger departures 53,702; cargo loaded 523 metric tons, cargo unloaded 934 metric tons. Airports (1987) with scheduled flights 8.
*Communications.* Daily newspapers: none. Radio (1986): total number of receivers 88,000 (1 per 1.9 persons). Television: total number of receivers, n.a. Telephones (1984): 9,350 (1 per 17 persons).

## Education and health

### Education (1985)

| | schools | teachers | students | student/teacher ratio |
|---|---|---|---|---|
| Primary (age 5–14) | 225 | 1,582 | 38,512 | 24.3 |
| Secondary (age, n.a.) | 24 | 504 | 6,676 | 13.2 |
| Voc., teacher tr. } | 5 | 62 | 765 | 12.3 |
| Higher | | | | |

*Educational attainment* (1980). Percent of population age 25 and over having: no formal schooling 10.7%; primary education 75.3%; secondary 11.7%; higher 2.3%. *Literacy* (1985): total population age 15 and over literate 85,000 (93%).
*Health* (1985): physicians 78 (1 per 2,133 persons); hospital beds 583 (1 per 285 persons); infant mortality rate per 1,000 live births (1983–85 avg.) 21.8.
*Food* (1981–83): daily per capita caloric intake 2,645 (vegetable products 72%, animal products 28%); (1983) 117% of FAO recommended minimum requirement.

## Military

*Total active duty personnel* (1986): 600 (army 90.8%, maritime wing 6.7%, air wing 2.5%); British troops 1,500. *Military expenditure as percent of GNP* (1984): 2.1% (world 5.9%); per capita expenditure U.S.$22.

[1]The Belize dollar is officially pegged to the U.S. dollar. [2]Detail does not add to total given because of rounding. [3]1984. [4]Employed labour force only. [5]Belize International Airport only.

# Benin

*Official name:* République Populaire du Bénin (People's Republic of Benin).
*Form of government:* unitary single-party people's republic with one legislative house (National Revolutionary Assembly [196]).
*Head of state and government:* President.
*Capitals*[1]: Porto-Novo (official); Cotonou (de facto).
*Official language:* French.
*Official religion:* none.
*Monetary unit:* 1 CFA franc (CFAF) = 100 centimes; valuation (Oct. 5, 1987) 1 U.S.$ = CFAF 306.67; 1 £ = CFAF 498.00.

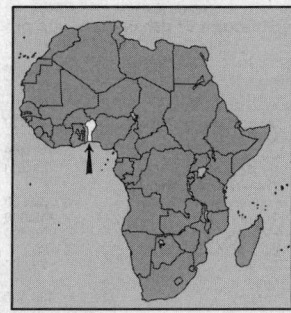

### Area and population

| Provinces | Capitals | area sq mi | area sq km | population 1985 estimate |
|---|---|---|---|---|
| Atacora | Natitingou | 12,050 | 31,200 | 568,000 |
| Atlantique | Cotonou | 1,250 | 3,200 | 824,000 |
| Borgou | Parakou | 19,700 | 51,000 | 577,000 |
| Mono | Lokossa | 1,450 | 3,800 | 560,000 |
| Ouémé | Porto-Novo | 1,800 | 4,700 | 738,000 |
| Zou | Abomey | 7,200 | 18,700 | 670,000 |
| TOTAL | | 43,450 | 112,600 | 3,937,000 |

## Demography

*Population* (1987): 4,307,000.
*Density* (1987): persons per sq mi 99.1, persons per sq km 38.3.
*Urban–rural* (1985): urban 19.0%; rural 81.0%.
*Sex distribution* (1985): male 49.11%; female 50.89%.
*Age breakdown* (1985): under 15, 46.5%; 15–29, 25.7%; 30–44, 14.8%; 45–59, 8.5%; 60 and over, 4.5%.
*Population projection:* (1990) 4,733,000; (2000) 6,532,000.
*Doubling time:* 22 years.
*Ethnic composition* (1983): Fon 65.6%; Bariba 9.7%; Yoruba 8.9%; Somba 5.4%; Fulani 4.0%; other 6.4%.
*Religious affiliation* (1980): traditional beliefs 61.4%; Christian 23.1%, of which Roman Catholic 18.5%, Protestant 2.8%; Muslim 15.2%; other 0.3%.
*Major cities* (1982): Cotonou 487,000; Porto-Novo 208,000; Parakou 66,000; Abomey 54,000; Kandi 53,000.

## Vital statistics

*Birth rate* per 1,000 population (1984): 49.0 (world avg. 29.0).
*Death rate* per 1,000 population (1984): 17.0 (world avg. 11.0).
*Natural increase rate* per 1,000 population (1984): 32.0 (world avg. 18.0).
*Total fertility rate* (avg. births per childbearing woman; 1984): 6.5.
*Marriage rate* per 1,000 population (1980–85): 12.8.
*Divorce rate* per 1,000 population (1980–85): 0.8.
*Life expectancy* at birth (1984): male 47.0 years; female 51.0 years.
*Major causes of death* per 100,000 population (1977): malaria 227.7; diseases of the respiratory system 206.5; diseases of the digestive system 200.7.

## National economy

*Budget* (1986). Revenue: CFAF 57,000,000,000 (indirect taxes 59.8%, direct taxes 31.8%, other 8.4%). Expenditures: CFAF 57,000,000,000 (administration and services 74.2%, economic development 9.2%).
*Production* (metric tons except as noted). Agriculture, forestry, fishing (1985–86): yams 812,057, cassava 793,961, corn (maize) 449,828, seed cotton 107,143, millet and sorghum 90,000, palm kernels 75,000, peanuts (groundnuts) 58,000, sweet potatoes 55,968, tomatoes 53,158, dry beans 52,000, coconuts 20,000, taro 13,000, oranges 13,000, bananas 13,000, paddy rice 10,256, pineapples 3,000, coffee beans 3,000, cacao beans 1,300, tobacco 263[2]; livestock (number of live animals; 1985) 1,131,000 sheep, 1,079,000 goats, 925,000 cattle, 576,000 pigs, 21,000,000 chickens; roundwood (1985) 4,401,000 cu m; fish catch (1985) 20,306. Mining and quarrying (1984–85): marine salt 100. Manufacturing (1985): cement 318,000; meat 56,000; sugar 51,000; palm oil and palm kernel oil 37,000; cotton fibre 16,000. Construction: n.a. Energy production (consumption): electricity (kW-hr; 1985) 172,276,000 (142,242,000); coal, none (n.a.); crude petroleum (barrels; 1985) 3,298,000 (n.a.); petroleum products (metric tons; 1985) none (168,200).
*Gross national product* (at current market prices; 1985): U.S.$1,080,000,000 (U.S.$270 per capita).

### Structure of gross domestic product and labour force

| | 1983 in value CFAF '000,000 | 1983 % of total value | 1982 labour force | 1982 % of labour force |
|---|---|---|---|---|
| Agriculture | 159,895.0 | 36.4 | 1,092,800 | 64.0 |
| Mining and manufacturing | 32,627.0 | 7.4 | | |
| Public utilities | 1,674.0 | 0.4 | 172,300 | 10.1 |
| Construction | 20,832.0 | 4.8 | | |
| Trade | 80,143.0 | 18.2 | | |
| Transportation and communication | 51,137.0 | 11.6 | 441,900 | 25.9 |
| Pub. admin., defense Other | 93,077.0 | 21.2 | | |
| TOTAL | 439,385.0 | 100.0 | 1,707,000 | 100.0 |

*Tourism* (1985): receipts from visitors U.S.$10,000,000; expenditures by nationals abroad U.S.$4,000,000.
*Population economically active* (1985): total 1,964,000; activity rate of total population 48.5% (participation rates: ages 15–64, 86.6%; female 48.3%; unemployed, n.a.).

### Price and earnings indexes (1977 = 100)

| | 1979 | 1980 | 1981 | 1982 | 1983 | 1984 | 1985 |
|---|---|---|---|---|---|---|---|
| Consumer price index | 117.8 | 130.7 | 147.8 | ... | ... | ... | ... |
| Hourly earnings index | 100.0 | 115.0 | 115.0 | 115.0 | 180.4 | 180.4 | 180.4[3] |

*Land use* (1984): forested 34.5%; meadows and pastures 4.0%; agricultural and under permanent cultivation 16.3%; other 45.2%.
*Public debt* (external, outstanding; 1986): U.S.$676,700,000.
*Household income and expenditure.* Average household size (1979) 5.4; income per household (1983): U.S.$240; sources of income: n.a.; expenditure: n.a.

## Foreign trade[4]

### Balance of trade (current prices)

| | 1981 | 1982 | 1983 | 1984 | 1985 | 1986 |
|---|---|---|---|---|---|---|
| CFAF '000,000 | −119,120 | −124,800 | −109,470 | −81,830 | −100.47 | −98.23 |
| % of total | 86.7% | 94.1% | 64.0% | 46.2% | 42.9% | 55.5% |

*Imports* (1982): CFAF 152,552,500,000 (manufactured goods 45.6%, of which cotton yarn and fabric 15.8%, chemical products 6.1%; machinery and transport equipment 22.8%, of which nonelectrical equipment 8.7%, electrical equipment 7.8%, transport equipment 6.3%; tobacco 13.7%; food products 11.8%, of which cereals 4.4%). *Major import sources* (1985): France 19.0%; United States 15.1%; The Netherlands 6.9%; Japan 5.8%; Austria 5.5%; Italy 4.7%; India 4.6%; Brazil 4.1%; West Germany 2.5%; United Kingdom 2.5%; Spain 2.3%; China 2.0%.
*Exports* (1982): CFAF 7,837,000,000 (food products 32.1%, of which coffee 11.6%, cocoa beans 3.6%; palm kernel oil and palm oil 19.7%; cotton 18.7%; energy 7.0%; machinery and transport equipment 7.0%; cement 1.0%, chemical products 0.9%). *Major export destinations* (1985): Spain 27.1%; West Germany 21.9%; France 10.4%; Portugal 10.1%; Italy 7.3%; The Netherlands 5.9%; United Kingdom 5.0%.

## Transport and communications

*Transport.* Railroads (1985): length 360 mi, 580 km; passenger-mi 85,500,-000[2], passenger-km 137,600,000[2]; short ton-mi cargo 121,100,000[2], metric ton-km cargo 176,800,000[2]. Roads (1985): total length 4,626 mi, 7,445 km (paved 11%). Vehicles (1985): passenger cars 2,740; trucks and buses 567. Merchant marine (1986): vessels (100 gross tons and over) 15; total deadweight tonnage 4,880. Air transport[5] (1985): passenger-mi 144,226,000, passenger-km 232,109,000; short ton-mi cargo 27,420,000, metric ton-km cargo 40,035,000; airports (1987) with scheduled flights 5.
*Communications.* Daily newspapers (1984): total number 3; total circulation 12,000[6]; circulation per 1,000 population 3.5[6]. Radio (1984): total number of receivers 290,000 (1 per 14 persons). Television (1984): total number of receivers 17,250 (1 per 203 persons). Telephones (1985): 17,082 (1 per 237 persons).

## Education and health

### Education (1984)

| | schools | teachers | students | student/ teacher ratio |
|---|---|---|---|---|
| Primary | 2,667 | 13,269 | 444,232 | 33.5 |
| Secondary | 133[7] | 2,409 | 112,267 | 46.6 |
| Voc., teacher tr. | 30[7] | 609 | 8,315 | 13.7 |
| Higher[8] | 1 | 803 | 6,818 | 8.4 |

*Educational attainment* (1979): Percent of population age 25 and over having: no formal schooling 89.2%; primary education 8.3%; some secondary 1.4%; secondary 0.8%; postsecondary 0.3%. *Literacy* (1980): total population age 15 and over literate 530,000 (27.9%); males literate 368,000 (39.8%); females literate 162,000 (16.6%).
*Health* (1982): physicians 270 (1 per 13,570 persons); hospital beds 4,902 (1 per 749 persons); infant mortality rate per 1,000 live births (1984) 116.0.
*Food* (1981–83): daily per capita caloric intake 2,073 (vegetable products 95%, animal products 5%); (1983) 83% of FAO recommended minimum requirement.

## Military

*Total active duty personnel* (1986): 3,510 (army 91.2%, navy 4.3%, air force 4.5%). *Military expenditure as percent of GNP* (1984): 3.9% (world 5.9%); per capita expenditure U.S.$7.

---

[1]Porto-Novo is the official capital established under the constitution, but Cotonou, where the president and most government ministers reside, is de facto capital. [2]1984–85. [3]January. [4]Figures do not include unaccountable reexports of black market goods, which originate mainly in Nigeria and amounted to an estimated 90% of Benin's actual exports in 1981. Cross-border trade has been adversely affected by the recession in Nigeria and by the closure of the border in 1984; the border was reopened in March 1986. [5]Cotonou airport only. [6]Circulation for government daily only. [7]1982. [8]1983.

# Bermuda

*Official name:* Bermuda.
*Political status:* colony (United
Kingdom) with two legislative houses
(Senate [11]; House of Assembly [40]).
*Chief of state:* British Monarch,
represented by Governor.
*Head of government:* Premier.
*Capital:* Hamilton.
*Official language:* English.
*Official religion:* none.
*Monetary unit:* 1 Bermuda dollar
(Ber$) = 100 cents; valuation (Oct. 5,
1987) 1 U.S.$ = Ber$1.00[1];
1 £ = Ber$1.62.

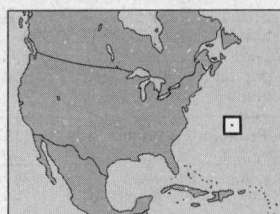

| Area and population | area | | population |
|---|---|---|---|
| | | | 1980 |
| Municipalities | sq mi | sq km | census |
| Hamilton | 0.3 | 0.8 | 1,617 |
| St. George | 0.5 | 1.3 | 1,647 |
| Parishes | | | |
| Devonshire | 1.9 | 4.9 | 6,843 |
| Hamilton | 2.0 | 5.2 | 3,784 |
| Paget | 2.0 | 5.2 | 4,497 |
| Pembroke[2] | 1.8 | 4.7 | 10,443 |
| St. George's[3] | 1.7 | 4.4 | 2,940 |
| Sandys | 1.9 | 4.9 | 6,255 |
| Smith's | 1.9 | 4.9 | 4,463 |
| Southampton | 2.2 | 5.7 | 4,613 |
| Warwick | 2.2 | 5.7 | 6,948 |
| TOTAL | 21.0[4,5] | 54.0[4,5] | 54,050[6] |

## Demography

*Population* (1987): 57,800.
*Density* (1987): persons per sq mi 2,752, persons per sq km 1,070.
*Urban–rural* (1987): urban 100.0%; rural, none.
*Sex distribution* (1985): male 48.81%; female 51.19%.
*Age breakdown* (1985): under 15, 21.3%; 15–29, 24.6%; 30–44, 25.0%; 45–59,
16.1%; 60–74, 9.7%; 75 and over, 3.3%.
*Population projection:* (1990) 59,000; (2000) 64,000.
*Doubling time:* 80 years.
*Ethnic composition* (1980): black 61.3%; white 37.3%; other 1.4%.
*Religious affiliation* (1980): Protestant 72.5%, of which Anglican 37.3%,
Methodist 16.3%; Roman Catholic 13.8%; nonreligious 7.8%; other 5.9%.
*Major cities* (1985): St. George 1,707; Hamilton 1,676.

## Vital statistics

*Birth rate* per 1,000 population (1985): 16.1 (world avg. 29.0); legitimate
68.7%; illegitimate 31.3%.
*Death rate* per 1,000 population (1985): 7.4 (world avg. 11.0).
*Natural increase rate* per 1,000 population (1985): 8.7 (world avg. 18.0).
*Total fertility rate* (avg. births per childbearing woman; 1980): 1.7.
*Marriage rate* per 1,000 population (1985): 12.2.
*Divorce rate* per 1,000 population (1984): 3.8.
*Life expectancy* at birth (1980): male 68.8 years; female 76.3 years.
*Major causes of death* per 100,000 population (1984): diseases of the circu-
latory system 354.0; malignant neoplasms (cancers) 163.0; accidents and
violence 39.0; diseases of the respiratory system 37.0.

## National economy

*Budget* (1986). Revenue: Ber$214,200,000 (customs duty 39.4%, hospital levy
11.7%, employment tax 9.1%, land tax 4.8%, hotel occupancy tax 4.6%,
international companies tax 4.2%). Expenditures: Ber$216,500,000 (health
and social services 20.6%, education 17.0%, public works and agriculture
15.6%, police 8.9%, tourism 7.4%).
*Tourism* (1986): receipts from visitors U.S.$407,000,000; expenditures by
nationals abroad, n.a.
*Production* (value in Ber$ except as noted). Agriculture, forestry, fishing
(1985): vegetables 3,770,000, milk 1,053,000, fruits 900,000, eggs 800,000,
meat 400,000, honey 175,000, flowers 55,000[7]; livestock (number of live
animals) 3,000 pigs, 1,000 cattle, 1,000 horses; roundwood, n.a.; fish
catch (1984) 481 metric tons. Mining and quarrying: limestone quarried
for construction material. Manufacturing: major industries include pharmaceuticals, electronics wares, fish processing, handicrafts, woodworking,
small boat building, and textiles. Construction (value in Ber$; 1986)[8]:
residential 6,400,000; nonresidential 42,500,000. Energy production (consumption): electricity (kW-hr; 1985) 395,000,000 (355,000,000); coal, none
(none); crude petroleum, none (none); petroleum products (metric tons;
1985) none (144,000); natural gas, none (none).
*Population economically active* (1985): total 32,190; activity rate of total
population 56.6% (participation rates: ages 16–64 [1980] 82.1%; female
45.8%; registered unemployed [1986] 0.1%).

| Price and earnings indexes (1985 = 100) | | | | | | | |
|---|---|---|---|---|---|---|---|
| | 1980 | 1981 | 1982 | 1983 | 1984 | 1985 | 1986 |
| Consumer price index | 71.8 | 80.4 | 86.6 | 91.8 | 96.6 | 100.0 | 104.1 |
| Weekly earnings index[9] | ... | 67.8 | 78.3 | 86.4 | 93.0 | 100.0 | ... |

*Gross national product* (at current market prices; 1985): U.S.$1,030,000,000
(U.S.$18,100 per capita).

| Structure of gross domestic product and labour force | | | | |
|---|---|---|---|---|
| | 1978–79 | | 1985 | |
| | in value Ber$'000 | % of total value | labour force | % of labour force |
| Agriculture, fishing | 2,900 | 0.7 | 222 | 0.7 |
| Quarrying | 1,300 | 0.3 | 117 | 0.4 |
| Manufacturing | 19,500 | 4.4 | 1,172 | 3.6 |
| Construction | 21,400 | 4.9 | 2,378 | 7.4 |
| Public utilities | 7,400 | 1.7 | 425 | 1.3 |
| Transportation and communication | 30,500 | 6.9 | 2,176 | 6.8 |
| Trade | 143,900 | 32.8 | 10,997 | 34.2 |
| Finance | 96,600 | 22.0 | 4,386 | 13.6 |
| Pub. admin., defense | 35,800 | 8.2 } | 9,998 | 31.0 |
| Services | 79,200 | 18.1 } | | |
| Other | ... | ... | 319[10] | 1.0[10] |
| TOTAL | 438,500 | 100.0 | 32,190 | 100.0 |

*Public debt* (external, outstanding; 1985): none.
*Household income and expenditure.* Average household size (1982) 2.7; income per household Ber$34,944 (U.S.$34,944); sources of income (1982):
wages and salaries 72.2%, imputed income from owner occupancy 9.7%, investments including rents 8.0%, self-employment 6.7%; expenditure (1982):
housing 20.8%, food and nonalcoholic beverages 17.3%, household furnishings 11.9%, transportation 10.6%, gifts, contributions, and life insurance
8.2%, foreign travel 6.4%, recreation 5.4%, clothing and footwear 5.3%.
*Land use* (1985): forested 14.7%; meadows and pastures, 1.4%; agricultural
and under permanent cultivation, 3.9%; built-on, wasteland, and other
80.0%.

## Foreign trade

| Balance of trade (current prices) | | | | | | |
|---|---|---|---|---|---|---|
| | 1980 | 1981 | 1982 | 1983 | 1984 | 1985 |
| Ber$'000,000 | −274.7 | −293.4 | −334.1 | −355.0 | −373.5 | −379.4 |
| % of total | 78.9% | 83.3% | 90.8% | 88.6% | 80.4% | 89.2% |

*Imports* (1985): Ber$402,491,000 (food 16.0%, of which meat and meat
preparations 4.9%; petroleum and petroleum products 14.1%; electrical machinery, including apparatus and appliances 8.4%; clothing 7.4%; transport
equipment 6.0%; nonelectrical machinery 4.7%; pharmaceutical products
4.4%). *Major import sources:* United States 60.1%; United Kingdom 10.1%;
Canada 6.3%; Netherlands Antilles 5.8%.
*Exports* (1985): Ber$23,054,000 (reexports 98.4%, of which drugs and
medicine 57.1%, personal effects 8.0%, electrical supplies 5.2%, books and
papers 4.6%, electronic supplies 4.0%; Bermuda-originated exports 1.6%).
*Major export destinations:* United States 22.7%; Italy 22.0%; Canada 9.5%;
United Kingdom 6.9%; Hong Kong 6.4%.

## Transport and communications

*Transport.* Railroads: none. Roads (1985): total length 139 mi, 224 km
(paved 100%). Vehicles (1985): passenger cars 17,240; trucks and buses
4,224. Merchant marine (1986): vessels (100 gross tons and over) 97; total
deadweight tonnage 1,759,709. Air transport (passengers, 1985): arrivals
508,679, departures 509,190; metric tons cargo unloaded 7,161, metric tons
cargo loaded 567; airports (1987) with scheduled flights 1.
*Communications.* Daily newspapers (1985): total number 1; total circulation
16,882; circulation per 1,000 population 297. Radio (1986): total number
of receivers 100,000 (1 per 0.6 person). Television (1986): total number of
receivers 67,000 (1 per 0.9 person). Telephones (1984): 52,067 (1 per 1.1
persons).

## Education and health

| Education (1985–86) | | | | |
|---|---|---|---|---|
| | schools | teachers | students | student/ teacher ratio |
| Primary (age 5–11) | 22 | 307 | 5,329 | 17.4 |
| Secondary (age 11–16) | 13 | 367 | 4,106 | 11.2 |
| Vocational } Higher | 1 | 68 | 550 | 8.1 |

*Educational attainment* (1980). Percent of total population age 25 and over
having: no formal schooling, primary education, or incomplete secondary
57.4%; completed secondary 19.5%; completed higher 18.5%; other 4.6%.
*Literacy* (1980): total population age 15 and over literate 39,577 (96.9%);
males literate 19,026 (96.7%); females literate 20,551 (97.0%).
*Health* (1985): physicians 70 (1 per 813 persons); hospital beds 325 (1 per
175 persons); infant mortality rate per 1,000 live births (1983–85 avg.) 9.0.
*Food* (1981–83): daily per capita caloric intake 2,540 (vegetable products
59%, animal products 41%); (1983) 107% of FAO recommended minimum requirement.

## Military

*Total active duty personnel:* British (1985) 700; U.S. (1986) 1,600.

[1]The Bermuda dollar is at par with the U.S. dollar. [2]Excludes the area and population of the city of Hamilton. [3]Excludes the area and population of the town of St.
George. [4]Grand total includes 2.3 sq mi (5.4 sq km) leased to the United States for
military bases. [5]Detail does not add to total given (less area for the military bases)
because of rounding. [6]Excludes 10,918 short-term visitors, 2,173 on-base military
personnel, 620 institutionalized persons, and Bermudians residing abroad. [7]1982.
[8]Excludes residential developments valued below Ber$500,000. [9]Unofficial estimate.
[10]Employment inadequately defined.

# Bhutan

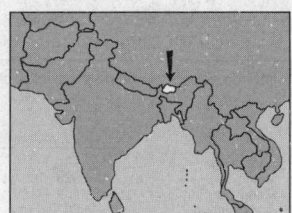

*Official name:* Druk-Yul (Kingdom of Bhutan).
*Form of government:* constitutional monarchy with one legislative house (National Assembly [150]).
*Head of state and government:* Monarch (*druk gyalpo*).
*Capital:* Thimphu.
*Official language:* Dzongkha (a Tibetan dialect).
*Official religion:* Mahāyāna Buddhism.
*Monetary unit:* 1 Ngultrum[1] (Nu) = 100 chetrum; valuation (Oct. 5, 1987) 1 U.S.$ = Nu 12.93; 1 £ = Nu 21.00.

### Area and population

| Districts | Capitals | area[2] sq mi | area[2] sq km | population[3] 1985 estimate |
|---|---|---|---|---|
| Bumthang | Jakar | 1,150 | 2,990 | 23,900 |
| Chirang | Damphu | 310 | 800 | 108,800 |
| Dagana | Dagana | 540 | 1,400 | 28,400 |
| Gasa | Gasa | 2,000 | 5,180 | 16,900 |
| Gaylegphug | Gaylegphug | 1,020 | 2,640 | 111,300 |
| Haa | Paro | 830 | 2,140 | 16,700 |
| Lhuntsi | Lhuntshi | 1,120 | 2,910 | 39,600 |
| Mongar | Mongar | 710 | 1,830 | 73,200 |
| Paro | Paro | 580 | 1,500 | 45,600 |
| Pema Gatsel | Pema Gatsel | 150 | 380 | 37,100 |
| Punakha | Punakha | 330 | 860 | 16,700 |
| Samchi | Samchi | 830 | 2,140 | 172,100 |
| Samdrup Jongkhar | Samdrup Jongkhar | 900 | 2,340 | 73,100 |
| Shemgang | Shemgang | 980 | 2,540 | 44,500 |
| Tashigang | Tashigang | 1,640 | 4,260 | 177,700 |
| Thimphu | Thimphu | 630 | 1,620 | 58,700 |
| Tongsa | Tongsa | 570 | 1,470 | 26,000 |
| Wangdi Phodrang | Wangdi Phodrang | 1,160 | 3,000 | 47,200 |
| TOTAL | | 18,150 | 47,000 | 1,285,300[4] |

## Demography

*Population* (1987): 1,337,000.
*Density* (1987): persons per sq mi 73.7, persons per sq km 28.4.
*Urban–rural* (1985): urban 13.1%; rural 86.9%.
*Sex distribution* (1985): male 51.59%; female 48.41%.
*Age breakdown* (1985): under 15, 40.0%; 15–29, 26.9%; 30–44, 17.4%; 45–59, 10.4%; 60–69, 3.6%; 70 and over, 1.7%.
*Population projection:* (1990) 1,420,000; (2000) 1,731,000.
*Doubling time:* 35 years.
*Ethnic composition* (1983): Bhutia 62.5%; Gurung 15.5%; Assamese 13.2%; other 8.8%.
*Religious affiliation* (1980): Buddhist 69.6%; Hindu 24.6%; Muslim 5.0%; other 0.8%.
*Major cities* (1985): Thimphu 20,000; Phuntsholing 10,000[5].

## Vital statistics

*Birth rate* per 1,000 population (1986): 37.8 (world avg. 26.0); legitimate, n.a.; illegitimate, n.a.
*Death rate* per 1,000 population (1986): 17.3 (world avg. 9.9).
*Natural increase rate* per 1,000 population (1986): 20.5 (world avg. 16.1).
*Total fertility rate* (avg. births per childbearing woman; 1986): 5.5.
*Marital status* of population 15 years and over (1985): married 71.2%; single 19.7%; widowed 7.5%; divorced 1.6%.
*Divorce rate* per 1,000 population: n.a.
*Life expectancy* at birth (1986): male 47.7 years; female 46.3 years.
*Major causes of death* per 100,000 population: n.a.; however, major health problems include malaria, tuberculosis, gastrointestinal infectious diseases, goitre, and pneumonia.

## National economy

*Budget* (1985–86). Revenue: Nu 863,000,000 (grants from government of India 45.3%, internal sources 30.6%, loans 12.9%, grants from UN and other international agencies 11.2%). Expenditures: Nu 863,390,000 (public works 19.3%, agriculture 18.8%, education 10.7%, health 6.2%, district administration 3.7%, foreign affairs 2.3%).
*Public debt* (external, outstanding): n.a.
*Tourism* (1985): receipts from visitors U.S.$1,692,000; expenditures by nationals abroad, n.a.
*Production* (metric tons except as noted). Agriculture, forestry, fishing (1985): corn (maize) 86,000, rice 62,000, fruit 50,000, potatoes 27,000, wheat 11,000, vegetables and melons 11,000, millet 7,000, barley 5,000, jute 4,000, tobacco 1,000; livestock (number of live animals) 347,000 cattle, 60,000 pigs, 46,000 goats, 44,000 sheep, 31,000 yaks, 29,000 buffalo, 16,000 horses; roundwood (1984) 3,224,000 cu m; fish catch (1983) 1,000. Mining and quarrying: details n.a.; however, some slate is quarried, and gypsum and graphite are mined. Manufacturing (value in Nu; 1980–81): distillery products 47,000,000; cement 36,000,000; chemical products 19,000,000; processed food 14,000,000; forest products 3,000,000. Construction (number of buildings completed; 1977–78): residential 10; nonresidential (guest house) 1. Energy production (consumption): electricity (kW-hr; 1985) 30,000,000 (35,000,000); coal (metric tons; 1985), none (1,000); crude petroleum, none (n.a.); petroleum products (metric tons; 1985) none (10,000); natural gas, none (n.a.).

*Household income and expenditure.* Average household size (1980): 5.4; income per household: n.a.; sources of income: n.a.; expenditure (1979): food 72.3%, clothing 21.2%, energy 3.7%, household durable goods 0.7%, personal effects and other 2.1%.
*Gross national product* (at current market prices; 1985): U.S.$190,000,000 (U.S.$150 per capita).

### Structure of gross domestic product and labour force

| | 1984 in value Nu '000,000 | 1984 % of total value | 1981–82 labour force | 1981–82 % of labour force |
|---|---|---|---|---|
| Agriculture | 1,016.2 | 50.5 | 613,000 | 94.3 |
| Mining | 6.7 | 0.3 | | |
| Manufacturing | 79.1 | 3.9 | 6,000 | 0.9 |
| Construction | 268.5 | 13.3 | | |
| Trade | 230.7 | 11.5 | 9,000 | 1.4 |
| Public utilities | 3.2 | 0.2 | | |
| Transportation and communication | 50.3 | 2.5 | | |
| Finance | 175.5 | 8.7 | 22,000 | 3.4 |
| Pub. admin., defense | 221.1 | 11.0 | | |
| Other | −38.57 | −1.9 | | |
| TOTAL | 2,012.8 | 100.0 | 650,000 | 100.0 |

*Population economically active* (1984): total 664,000; activity rate of total population 52.7% (participation rates: ages 15–64, 94.8; female 55.0; unemployed, n.a.).

### Price and earnings indexes (1980 = 100)

| | 1981 | 1982 | 1983 | 1984 | 1985 |
|---|---|---|---|---|---|
| Consumer price index | 112.2 | 127.1 | 137.2 | 150.9 | 157.8 |
| Earnings index | ... | ... | ... | ... | ... |

*Land use* (1984): forested 69.9%; meadows and pastures 4.6%; agricultural and under permanent cultivation 2.1%; other 23.4%.

## Foreign trade

### Balance of trade (current prices)

| | 1980–81 | 1981–82 | 1982–83 | 1983–84 | 1984–85 |
|---|---|---|---|---|---|
| Nu '000,000 | −263.0 | −414.2 | −487.1 | −662.6 | −644.8 |
| % of total | 50.0% | 54.7% | 60.4% | 67.3% | 64.1% |

*Imports* (1981–82): Nu 404,521,000 (machinery and equipment 22.1%, petroleum products 14.2%, iron and steel products 8.1%, motor vehicles 7.3%, rice 3.9%, fabrics 3.0%, stationery and books 2.2%, wheat and wheat flour 1.6%). *Major import source* (1984–85): India 87.9%.
*Exports* (1981–82): Nu 177,981,000[8] (cement 26.6%, oranges 9.6%, sawn timber 9.0%, potatoes 8.7%, talcum powder 6.1%, cardamom 6.1%, rosin 4.0%, menthol products 2.7%). *Major export destination* (1984–85): India 95.9%.

## Transport and communications

*Transport.* Railroads: none. Roads (1985): total length 1,091 mi, 1,755 km (paved about 61%). Vehicles (1985): passenger cars 1,587; trucks and buses 889. Merchant marine: none. Air transport: n.a.; airports (1987) with scheduled flights, none[9].
*Communications.* Daily newspapers: none[10]. Radio (1987): total number of receivers 12,800 (1 per 104 persons). Television (1983): total number of receivers 200 (1 per 6,180 persons). Telephones (1985): 1,880 (1 per 684 persons).

## Education and health

### Education (1985)

| | schools | teachers | students | student/ teacher ratio |
|---|---|---|---|---|
| Primary (age 7–11) | 143 | 1,082 | 33,934 | 31.4 |
| Secondary (age 12–16) | 30 | 589 | 16,377 | 27.8 |
| Voc., teacher tr. | 8 | 103 | 688 | 6.7 |
| Higher | 2 | 18[11] | 55[11] | 3.1[11] |

*Educational attainment,* n.a. *Literacy* (1977): total population age 15 and over literate 124,000 (18.0%); males literate 98,000 (31.0%); females literate 26,000 (9.0%).
*Health* (1985): physicians 70 (1 per 18,360 persons); hospital beds 857 (1 per 1,500 persons); infant mortality rate per 1,000 live births (1986) 137.0.
*Food* (1975–77): daily per capita caloric intake 2,058 (vegetable products 98%, animal products 2%); 89% of FAO recommended minimum requirement.

## Military

*Total active duty personnel* (1985): about 4,000 (army 100%).

[1]Indian currency is also accepted legal tender; the Ngultrum is at par with the Indian rupee. [2]2,700 sq mi (7,000 sq km) are not included in the district area totals. [3]Rural only. [4]Includes urban population. [5]1982. [6]Includes irrigation, animal husbandry, and forestry. [7]Imputed bank service charges. [8]An additional Nu 6,432,000 in commodities was exported to countries other than India. [9]An airport at Paro receives unscheduled air service from Calcutta. [10]A government weekly is published from Thimphu in Dzongkha, Nepalese, and English, circulation (1984) 5,000. [11]1983.

# Bolivia

*Official name:* República de Bolivia (Republic of Bolivia).
*Form of government:* unitary, multiparty republic with two legislative houses (Chamber of Senators [27]; Chamber of Deputies [130]).
*Head of state and government:* President.
*Capital:* La Paz (administrative); Sucre (judicial).
*Official languages:* Spanish, Aymara, Quechua.
*Official religion:* Roman Catholicism.
*Monetary unit:* 1 boliviano[1] ($b) = 100 centavos; valuation (Oct. 5, 1987) 1 U.S.$ = $b 2.11; 1 £ = $b 3.43.

### Area and population

| Departments | Capitals | area sq mi | area sq km | population 1985 estimate |
|---|---|---|---|---|
| Beni | Trinidad | 82,458 | 213,564 | 240,000 |
| Chuquisaca | Sucre | 19,893 | 51,524 | 463,000 |
| Cochabamba | Cochabamba | 21,479 | 55,631 | 979,000 |
| La Paz | La Paz | 51,732 | 133,985 | 2,091,000 |
| Oruro | Oruro | 20,690 | 53,588 | 413,000 |
| Pando | Cobija | 24,644 | 63,827 | 47,000 |
| Potosí | Potosí | 45,644 | 118,218 | 878,000 |
| Santa Cruz | Santa Cruz | 143,098 | 370,621 | 1,048,000 |
| Tarija | Tarija | 14,526 | 37,623 | 270,000 |
| TOTAL | | 424,164 | 1,098,581 | 6,429,000 |

## Demography

*Population* (1987): 6,799,000.
*Density* (1987): persons per sq mi 16.0, persons per sq km 6.2.
*Urban–rural* (1987): urban 49.0%; rural 51.0%.
*Sex distribution* (1985): male 49.25%; female 50.75%.
*Age breakdown* (1985): under 15, 43.4%; 15–29, 26.4%; 30–44, 15.7%; 45–59, 9.3%; 60–74, 4.4%; 75 and over, 0.8%.
*Population projection:* (1990) 7,400,000; (2000) 9,837,000.
*Doubling time:* 25 years.
*Ethnic composition* (1982): mestizo 31.2%; Quechua 25.4%; Aymara 16.9%; white 14.5%; other 12.0%.
*Religious affiliation* (1981): Roman Catholic 94.0%; Bahá'í 2.6%; other 3.4%.
*Major cities* (1985): La Paz 992,592; Santa Cruz 441,717; Cochabamba 317,251; Oruro 178,393; Sucre 86,609.

## Vital statistics

*Birth rate* per 1,000 population (1980–85): 44.0 (world avg. 29.0).
*Death rate* per 1,000 population (1980–85): 15.9 (world avg. 11.0).
*Natural increase rate* per 1,000 population (1980–85): 28.1 (world avg. 18.0).
*Total fertility rate* (avg. births per childbearing woman; 1980–85): 6.3.
*Marriage rate* per 1,000 population (1980): 4.8.
*Divorce rate* per 1,000 population: n.a.
*Life expectancy* at birth (1980–85): male 48.6 years; female 53.0 years.
*Major causes of death* per 100,000 population: n.a.; however, major diseases are diseases of the respiratory system, gastrointestinal infections, measles, diphtheria, malaria, and tetanus.

## National economy

*Budget* (1985). Revenue: $b 193,034,591,500,000 (royalties on petroleum 66.2%, internal taxes 12.1%, customs duties 11.8%, mining royalties 3.0%). Expenditures: $b 909,185,433,200,000 (currency adjustment 76.6%, public services 15.3%, transfers and contributions 4.0%, public debt service 1.6%, materials and equipment 1.6%).
*Production* (metric tons except as noted). Agriculture, forestry, fishing (1985): sugarcane 2,000,000, potatoes 721,000, corn (maize) 554,000, bananas 260,000, rice 184,000, wheat 68,000, oranges 38,000; livestock (number of live animals): 9,413,000 sheep, 5,851,000 cattle, 3,200,000 goats, 1,112,000 pigs, 600,000 asses, 311,000 horses; roundwood 1,317,000 cu m; fish catch (1984) 5,617. Mining and quarrying (metric tons of pure metal; 1985): zinc 37,110; tin 16,136; antimony 8,925; lead 6,242; copper 1,665; tungsten 1,643; gold 993 kilograms. Manufacturing (gross value in $b; 1981): food and beverages 16,080,982,808, of which food 12,254,780,842; nonferrous metals 7,606,061,069; nonmetallic mineral products 1,328,121,249; metal products 1,194,120,108; wood and wood products 999,542,335; machinery and equipment 516,844,375. Construction[2] (1983): residential dwellings 323. Energy production (consumption): electricity (kW-hr; 1985) 1,725,000,000 (1,727,000,000); coal (metric tons; 1985) none (1,000); crude petroleum (barrels; 1985) 7,227,000 (7,660,000); petroleum products (metric tons; 1985) 1,008,000 (1,005,000); natural gas (cu m; 1985) 2,238,700,000 (175,053,000).
*Population economically active* (1985): total 1,923,726; activity rate of total population 29.9% (participation rates: over age 15, 52.5%; female 12.0%; unemployed 18.0%).

### Price and earnings indexes (1980 = 100)

| | 1979 | 1980 | 1981 | 1982 | 1983 | 1984 | 1985 |
|---|---|---|---|---|---|---|---|
| Consumer price index | 50.0 | 100.0 | 204.0 | 541.0 | 2,403 | 17,462 | 134,833 |
| Monthly earnings index | ... | ... | ... | ... | ... | ... | ... |

*Gross national product* (at current market prices; 1985): U.S.$3,010,000,000 (U.S.$470 per capita).

### Structure of gross domestic product and labour force

| | 1985 in value $b '000,000 | 1985 % of total value | 1982 labour force[3] | 1982 % of labour force |
|---|---|---|---|---|
| Agriculture | 657,284 | 27.4 | 792,600 | 46.4 |
| Mining | 167,920 | 7.0 | 76,200 | 4.5 |
| Manufacturing | 461,809 | 19.2 | 155,500 | 9.1 |
| Construction | 85,803 | 3.6 | 56,500 | 3.3 |
| Public utilities | 13,754 | 0.6 | 7,200 | 0.4 |
| Transportation and communication | 137,575 | 5.7 | 94,700 | 5.5 |
| Trade | 356,266 | 14.8 | 128,800 | 7.5 |
| Finance | 241,827 | 10.1 | 13,300 | 0.8 |
| Pub. admin., defense | 179,026 | 7.4 | | |
| Services | 78,382 | 3.3 | 382,600 | 22.4 |
| Other | 22,921[4] | 0.9[4] | | |
| TOTAL | 2,402,567 | 100.0 | 1,707,400 | 100.0[5] |

*Public debt* (external, outstanding; 1985): U.S.$3,259,300,000.
*Tourism* (1985): receipts from visitors U.S.$36,000,000; expenditures by nationals abroad U.S.$38,000,000.
*Land use* (1984): forested 51.6%; meadows and pastures 24.8%; agricultural and under permanent cultivation 3.1%; other 20.5%.

## Foreign trade[6]

### Balance of trade (current prices)

| | 1980 | 1981 | 1982 | 1983 | 1984 | 1985 |
|---|---|---|---|---|---|---|
| U.S.$'000,000 | +261.8 | +229.0 | +399.0 | +282.0 | +311.9 | +160.6 |
| % of total | 16.1% | 14.4% | 31.8% | 23.0% | 27.4% | 14.8% |

*Imports* (1985): U.S.$551,900,000 (capital goods 42.0%, of which capital goods for industry 20.0%, transport equipment 13.5%; raw materials 33.0%, of which raw materials for industry 30.0%; consumer goods 24.0%, of which durable consumer goods 14.5%, nondurable consumer goods 9.5%). *Major import sources:* United States 22.0%; Brazil 21.0%; Argentina 15.0%; West Germany 7.2%; Japan 7.0%; Chile 5.0%; Peru 5.0%; United Kingdom 2.0%; France 1.8%; The Netherlands 1.7%.
*Exports* (1985): U.S.$672,536,000 (natural gas 55.4%; tin 27.7%; zinc 4.4%; coffee 2.1%; silver 1.5%; tungsten 1.5%). *Major export destinations:* Argentina 55.9%; United States 13.5%; United Kingdom 8.9%; West Germany 5.0%; The Netherlands 3.2%; Belgium 2.1%; Peru 1.9%; Chile 1.6%; Switzerland 1.6%; France 1.2%.

## Transport and communications

*Transport.* Railroads: route length (1986) 2,198 mi, 3,538 km; (1985) passenger-mi 457,000,000, passenger-km 736,000,000; (1985) short ton-mi cargo 357,000,000, metric ton-km cargo 521,000,000. Roads (1984): total length 25,468 mi, 40,987 km (paved 4%). Vehicles (1983): passenger cars 40,638; trucks and buses 36,951. Merchant marine (1986): vessels (100 gross tons and over) 2; total deadweight tonnage 18,934. Air transport (1986): passenger-mi 549,394,000, passenger-km 884,166,000; short ton-mi cargo 19,031,000, metric ton-km cargo 27,785,000; airports (1987) with scheduled flights 19.
*Communications.* Daily newspapers (1984): total number 14; total circulation 253,000; circulation per 1,000 population 40. Radio (1983): total number of receivers 3,500,000 (1 per 1.7 persons). Television (1984): total number of receivers 387,000 (1 per 16 persons). Telephones (1984): 213,716 (1 per 29 persons).

## Education and health

### Education (1983)

| | schools | teachers | students | student/ teacher ratio |
|---|---|---|---|---|
| Primary (age 6–13) | 8,514 | 50,703 | 1,154,819 | 22.8 |
| Secondary (age 14–17) | 845 | 8,091 | 174,982 | 21.6 |
| Higher | 25 | 1,487 | 13,388 | 9.0 |

*Educational attainment* (1976). Percent of adult population age 25 and over having: no formal schooling 48.6%; primary education 28.5%; secondary 17.9%; higher 5.0%. *Literacy* (1976): total population age 15 and over literate 1,706,718 (63.2%); males literate 990,408 (75.8%); females literate 716,310 (51.4%).
*Health* (1978): physicians 3,410 (1 per 1,555 persons); hospital beds 9,353 (1 per 523 persons); infant mortality rate per 1,000 live births (1985) 110.0.
*Food* (1981–83): daily per capita caloric intake 2,061 (vegetable products 83%, animal products 17%); (1983) 82% of FAO recommended minimum requirement.

## Military

*Total active duty personnel* (1986): 27,600 (army 72.5%, navy 13.0%, air force 14.5%). *Military expenditure as percent of GNP* (1984): 2.2% (world 5.9%); per capita expenditure U.S.$19.

[1]Effective Jan. 1, 1987, a new currency, the boliviano, was introduced at a rate of one boliviano = 1,000,000 old Bolivian pesos. [2]National government sponsored only. [3]Employed persons only. [4]Includes imputed bank service charges. [5]Detail does not add to total given because of rounding. [6]Import figures are f.o.b. (free on board) in balance of trade and c.i.f. (cost, insurance, and freight) for commodities and trading partners.

# Botswana

*Official name:* Botswana (Tswana), Republic of Botswana. (English).
*Form of government:* multiparty republic with one legislative body (National Assembly [39]).
*Head of state and government:* President.
*Capital:* Gaborone.
*Official languages:* Tswana; English.
*Official religion:* none.
*Monetary unit:* 1 pula (P) = 100 thebe; valuation (Oct. 5, 1987)
1 U.S.$ = P 1.71; 1 £ = P 2.77.

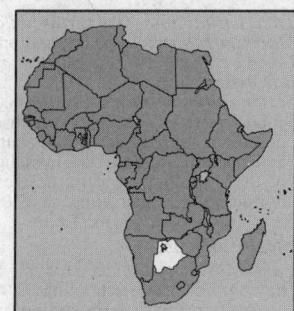

## Area and population

| Districts | Capitals | area sq mi | area sq km | population 1984 estimate |
|---|---|---|---|---|
| Central | Serowe | 57,039 | 147,730 | 355,000 |
| Ghanzi | Ghanzi | 45,525 | 117,910 | 21,000 |
| Kgalagadi | Tsabong | 41,290 | 106,940 | 26,000 |
| Kgatleng | Mochudi | 3,073 | 7,960 | 49,000 |
| Kweneng | Molepolole | 13,857 | 35,890 | 128,000 |
| North East | Masunga | 1,977 | 5,120 | 40,000 |
| North West | | | | |
| Chobe | Kasane | 8,031 | 20,800 | 9,000 |
| Ngamiland | Maun | 42,135 | 109,130 | 75,000 |
| Southern | Kanye | 10,992 | 28,470 | 138,000 |
| South East | Ramotswa | 687 | 1,780 | 34,000 |
| Towns[1] | | | | |
| Francistown | — | 31 | 79 | 36,000 |
| Gaborone | — | 37 | 97 | 79,000 |
| Lobatse | — | 12 | 30 | 22,000 |
| Orapa | — | 4 | 10 | 5,800 |
| Selebi-Pikwe | — | 19 | 50 | 33,000 |
| TOTAL | | 224,607[2] | 581,730 | 1,051,000[2] |

## Demography

*Population* (1987): 1,167,800.
*Density* (1987): persons per sq mi 5.2, persons per sq km 2.0.
*Urban–rural* (1986): urban 20.6%; rural 79.4%.
*Sex distribution* (1986): male 48.51% female 51.49%.
*Age breakdown* (1985): under 15, 48.1%; 15–29, 25.9%; 30–44, 12.7%; 45–59, 7.5%; 60–74, 3.1%; 75 and over, 2.7%.
*Population projection:* (1990) 1,302,600; (2000) 1,817,400.
*Doubling time:* 20 years.
*Ethnic composition* (1983): Tswana 75.5%; Shona 12.4%; San (Bushman) 3.4%; Khoikhoin (Hottentot) 2.5%; Ndebele 1.3%; other 4.9%.
*Religious affiliation* (1980): folk religionist 48.7%; Protestant 26.6%; indigenous Christian 11.8%; Roman Catholic 9.4%; other Christian 2.6%; other 0.9%.
*Major cities* (1986): Gaborone 96,100; Francistown 39,600; Selebi-Pikwe 34,700; Lobatse 24,300; Palapye 13,500.

## Vital statistics

*Birth rate* per 1,000 population (1986): 45.6 (world avg. 26.0); legitimate, n.a.; illegitimate, n.a.
*Death rate* per 1,000 population (1986): 11.1 (world avg. 9.9).
*Natural increase rate* per 1,000 population (1986): 34.5 (world avg. 16.1).
*Total fertility rate* (avg. births per childbearing woman; 1986): 6.8.
*Life expectancy* at birth (1986): male 54.7 years; female 61.2 years.
*Major causes of death* (as percent of total deaths; 1977): measles 16.3%; heart disease 8.4%; influenza and pneumonia 7.6%; diarrheal diseases 7.5%; malignant neoplasms (cancers) 6.0%.

## National economy

*Budget* (1986–87)[3]. Revenue: P 1,195,000,000 (mineral royalties and dividends 57.4%; customs and excise taxes 16.2%; nontax revenue 13.2%; other income taxes 9.1%; foreign aid grants 3.4%). Expenditures: P 902,000,000 (recurrent expenditure 58.4%; development expenditure 38.7%, of which public works and communications 11.1%, mineral resources and water affairs 5.1%, drought relief 1.8%, education 12.0%, police and defense 1.6%).
*Population economically active* (1984–85): total 334,428; activity rate of total population 33.6% (participation rates: ages 15–64, 72.7%; female 54.6%; unemployed [1981] 10.2%).

## Price and earnings indexes (1982 = 100)

| | 1981 | 1982 | 1983 | 1984 | 1985 | 1986 | 1987[4] |
|---|---|---|---|---|---|---|---|
| Consumer price index | 90.0 | 100.0 | 110.5 | 119.9 | 129.7 | 142.7 | 156.4 |
| Earnings index[5] | ... | 100.0 | 109.1 | 120.4 | 127.3 | 145.5 | ... |

*Production* (metric tons except as noted). Agriculture, forestry, fishing (1985–86): cereals 20,800 (of which sorghum 16,000, corn [maize] 3,200, millet 1,600), vegetables and melons 17,000, pulses 17,000, fruit 11,000, roots and tubers 9,000, seed cotton 3,000, cotton seed 2,000, peanuts (groundnuts) 1,000; livestock (number of live animals) 2,685,000 cattle, 890,000 goats, 171,000 sheep, 146,000 mules and asses, 25,000 horses; roundwood (1984) 798,000 cu m; fish catch (1984) 1,500. Mining and quarrying (1986): diamonds 13,100,000 carats; nickel–copper matte 41,263, of which copper 21,703, nickel 19,560; cobalt 259[6]. Manufacturing (1984): beer 155,000 hectolitres. Construction (1984): residential 70,200 sq m; nonresidential 80,700 sq m. Energy production (consumption): electricity (kW-hr; 1985) 438,000,-

000 (621,000,000); coal (metric tons; 1985) 437,000 (n.a.); crude petroleum, none (n.a.); petroleum products, n.a. (n.a.); natural gas, none (n.a.).
*Public debt* (external, outstanding; 1985): U.S.$334,200,000.
*Tourism* (1985): receipts from visitors U.S.$51,000,000; expenditures by nationals abroad U.S.$18,000,000.
*Gross national product* (at current market prices; 1985): U.S.$900,000,000 (U.S.$830 per capita).

## Structure of gross domestic product and labour force

| | 1985–86 in value P '000,000 | % of total value | labour force[7] | % of labour force |
|---|---|---|---|---|
| Agriculture | 84.0 | 3.9 | 4,000 | 3.4 |
| Mining | 1,005.3 | 46.9 | 7,300[8] | 6.2 |
| Manufacturing | 129.4 | 6.0 | 10,100 | 8.6 |
| Construction | 61.3 | 2.9 | 11,600 | 9.9 |
| Public utilities | 40.0 | 1.9 | 1,900 | 1.6 |
| Transportation and communication | 42.5 | 2.0 | 5,700 | 4.9 |
| Trade | 377.0 | 17.6 | 18,300 | 15.6 |
| Finance | 109.5 | 5.1 | 6,800 | 5.8 |
| Pub. admin., defense | 284.8 | 13.3 } | 5,400 | 4.6 |
| Services | 49.1 | 2.3 } | | |
| Other | −38.0 | −1.8 | 46,000[9] | 39.3[9] |
| TOTAL | 2,144.9 | 100.0[2] | 117,100 | 100.0[2] |

*Household income and expenditure.* Average household size (1981) 5.7; average annual income per household, n.a.; sources of income (1981): wages and salaries 65.6%, transfers 19.6%, self-employment 14.8%; expenditure (1985): food, beverages, and tobacco 40.1%, rent and services 13.1%, clothing 10.8%, transportation 10.5%, health 1.3%.
*Land use* (1984): forested 1.6%; meadows and pastures 75.2%; agricultural and under permanent cultivation 2.3%; other 20.9%.

## Foreign trade[10]

### Balance of trade (current prices)

| | 1981 | 1982 | 1983 | 1984 | 1985 | 1986 |
|---|---|---|---|---|---|---|
| P '000,000 | −239.0 | −122.7 | 27.5 | 122.4 | 444.9 | 510.9 |
| % of total | 26.2% | 11.5% | 2.0% | 7.5% | 19.1% | 19.3% |

*Imports* (1986): P 1,276,000,000 (machinery and electrical goods 17.9%; food, beverages, and tobacco 16.9%; vehicles and transport equipment 14.0%; mineral fuels 10.3%; metal and metal products 10.0%; chemical and rubber products 9.2%; textiles and footwear 7.1%; wood and paper 3.4%). *Major import sources* (1985): CUSA (Customs Union of Southern Africa, which includes Botswana, Lesotho, South West Africa/Namibia, South Africa, and Swaziland) 75.8%; United Kingdom 4.6%; United States 2.8%.
*Exports* (1986): P 1,575,900,000 (diamonds 77.8%; meat and meat products 8.0%; copper–nickel matte 6.3%). *Major export destinations* (1985): European countries 82.9%, of which United Kingdom 5.1%; United States 7.1%; CUSA 5.8%.

## Transport and communications

*Transport.* Railroads (1984–85): length 442 mi, 712 km; number of passengers 542,692; short ton-mi cargo 888,133, metric ton-km cargo 1,296,735. Roads (1985): total length 4,987 mi, 8,026 km (paved 25%). Vehicles (1985): passenger cars 14,283; trucks and buses 23,987. Merchant marine: none. Air transport (1986)[11]: passenger-mi 13,953,000, passenger-km 22,456,000; short ton-mi cargo 100,000, metric ton-km cargo 146,000; airports (1987) with scheduled flights 4.
*Communications.* Daily newspapers (1985): total number 1; total circulation 24,000; circulation per 1,000 population 22. Radio (1985): total number of receivers 77,000 (1 per 14 persons). Television (1985): none. Telephones (1985): 19,109 (1 per 90 persons).

## Education and health

### Education (1985–86)

| | schools | teachers | students | student/ teacher ratio |
|---|---|---|---|---|
| Primary (age 7–13) | 528 | 6,980 | 223,608 | 32.0 |
| Secondary (age 14–19) | 65 | 1,283 | 32,172 | 25.1 |
| Voc., teacher tr. | 24 | 283 | 3,099 | 11.0 |
| Higher | 1 | 142 | 1,434 | 10.1 |

*Educational attainment* (1981). Percent of population age 25 and over having: no formal schooling 54.7%; some primary education 31.0%; complete primary 9.4%; some secondary 3.1%; complete secondary 1.3%; postsecondary 0.5%. *Literacy* (1985): total population over age 15 literate 385,000 (70.8%); males literate 179,000 (72.6%); females literate 206,000 (69.5%).
*Health* (1984): physicians 155 (1 per 6,748 persons); hospital beds 2,367 (1 per 442 persons); infant mortality rate per 1,000 live births (1981) 68.4.
*Food* (1981–83): daily per capita caloric intake 2,152 (vegetable products 83%, animal products 17%); 93% of FAO recommended minimum requirement.

## Military

*Total active duty personnel* (1986): 3,000 (army 95.0%; navy, none; air force 5.0%). *Military expenditure as percent of GNP* (1984): 2.2% (world 5.9%); per capita expenditure U.S.$20.

[1]Areas included with respective district area totals. [2]Detail does not add to total given because of rounding. [3]Projected. [4]May. [5]Excludes government sector. [6]1984. [7]Paid employees only. [8]16,397 Botswana were employed in South African mines in 1985. [9]Central and local government employees not distributed by industry. [10]Import figures are f.o.b. in balance of trade and c.i.f. in commodities and trading partners. [11]Air Botswana only.

# Brazil

*Official name:* República Federativa do Brasil (Federative Republic of Brazil).
*Form of government:* multiparty federal republic with 2 legislative houses (Federal Senate [72]; Chamber of Deputies*[487]).
*Chief of state and government:* President.
*Capital:* Brasília.
*Official language:* Portuguese.
*Official religion:* none.
*Monetary unit:* 1 cruzado (Cz$) = 100 centavos; valuation (Oct. 5, 1987) 1 U.S.$ = 51.63 cruzados; 1 £ = 83.84 cruzados.

### Area and population

| States | Capitals | area[1] sq mi | area[1] sq km | population 1987 estimate |
|---|---|---|---|---|
| Acre | Rio Branco | 58,915 | 152,589 | 374,000 |
| Alagoas | Maceió | 10,707 | 27,731 | 2,335,000 |
| Amazonas | Manaus | 604,035 | 1,564,445 | 1,833,000 |
| Bahia | Salvador | 216,613 | 561,026 | 11,170,000 |
| Ceará | Fortaleza | 58,159 | 150,630 | 6,100,000 |
| Espírito Santo[2] | Vitória | 17,605 | 45,597 | 2,381,000 |
| Goiás | Goiânia | 247,913 | 642,092 | 4,659,000 |
| Maranhão | São Luís | 126,897 | 328,663 | 4,863,000 |
| Mato Grosso | Cuiabá | 340,156 | 881,001 | 1,599,000 |
| Mato Grosso do Sul | Campo Grande | 135,347 | 350,548 | 1,687,000 |
| Minas Gerais | Belo Horizonte | 226,708 | 587,172 | 15,021,000 |
| Pará | Belém | 482,906 | 1,250,722 | 4,476,000 |
| Paraíba | João Pessoa | 21,765 | 56,372 | 3,102,000 |
| Paraná | Curitiba | 77,048 | 199,554 | 8,228,000 |
| Pernambuco | Recife | 37,946 | 98,281 | 6,992,000 |
| Piauí | Teresina | 96,886 | 250,934 | 2,532,000 |
| Rio Grande do Norte | Natal | 20,469 | 53,015 | 2,204,000 |
| Rio Grande do Sul | Pôrto Alegre | 108,952 | 282,184 | 8,732,000 |
| Rio de Janeiro | Rio de Janeiro | 17,092 | 44,268 | 13,278,000 |
| Rondônia | Pôrto Velho | 93,840 | 243,044 | 818,000 |
| Santa Catarina | Florianópolis | 37,060 | 95,985 | 4,256,000 |
| São Paulo | São Paulo | 95,714 | 247,898 | 31,263,000 |
| Sergipe | Aracaju | 8,492 | 21,994 | 1,339,000 |
| **Other federal entities** | | | | |
| Distrito Federal | Brasília | 2,245 | 5,814 | 1,720,000 |
| Amapá | Macapá | 54,161 | 140,276 | 227,000 |
| Fernando de Noronha[3] | Fernando de Noronha | 10 | 26 | 1,000 |
| Roraima | Boa Vista | 88,844 | 230,104 | 112,000 |
| TOTAL | | 3,286,487[4] | 8,511,965 | 141,302,000 |

## Demography

*Population* (1987): 141,302,000.
*Density* (1987): persons per sq mi 43.0, persons per sq km 16.6.
*Urban–rural* (1987): urban 74.2%; rural 25.8%.
*Sex distribution* (1985): male 49.92%; female 50.08%.
*Age breakdown* (1985): under 15, 36.4%; 15–29, 28.9%; 30–44, 17.8%; 45–59, 10.3%; 60–74, 5.2%; 75 and over, 1.4%.
*Population projection:* (1990) 150,368,000; (2000) 179,487,000.
*Doubling time:* 28 years.
*Ethnic composition* (1980): Brazilian white 53.0%, of which Portuguese 15.0%, Italian 11.0%, Spanish 10.0%, German 3.0%; mulatto 22.0%; mestizo 12.0%; black 11.0%; Japanese 0.8%; indigenous Indian 0.1%; other 1.1%.
*Religious affiliation* (1980): Roman Catholic 87.8%, of which Spiritist Catholic 15.7%[5], Evangelical Catholic 9.0%[6]; Protestant (mostly Assemblies of God, other Pentecostal, and Baptist) 6.1%; Afro-American Spiritist 2.0%[7]; Spiritist 1.7%[8]; nonreligious 1.0%; atheist 0.4%; Buddhist 0.3%; Jewish 0.2%; other 0.5%.
*Major cities (municipio;* 1985)[9]: São Paulo 10,099,086 (15,280,375); Rio de Janeiro 5,615,149 (10,217,269); Belo Horizonte 2,122,073 (3,059,727); Salvador 1,811,367 (2,125,792); Fortaleza 1,588,709; Brasília 1,576,657; Nova Iguaçu[10] 1,324,639; Recife 1,289,627; Curitiba 1,285,027; Porto Alegre 1,275,483.

### Other principal *municipios* (1985)

| | population | | population | | population |
|---|---|---|---|---|---|
| Belém | 1,120,777 | Santo André[11] | 637,010 | Teresina | 476,102 |
| Goiânia | 928,046 | Osasco[11] | 594,249 | Santos | 461,096 |
| Campinas | 845,057 | São Bernardo | | São João de | |
| Manaus | 834,541 | do Campo | 565,620 | Meriti[10] | 459,103 |
| São Gonçalo | 731,061 | São Luís | 564,434 | Niterói[10] | 442,706 |
| Guarulhos[11] | 717,723 | Natal | 512,241 | Jaboatão | 411,341 |
| Duque de Caxias[10] | 666,128 | Maceió | 484,094 | João Pessoa | 397,715 |

*Place of birth/national origin* (1980): 99.07% native-born; 0.93% foreign-born, of which Portugal 0.33%, Japan 0.12%, Italy 0.09%, Spain 0.08%.
*Mobility* (1980). Population living in same residence as in 1970: 25.0%.
*Families* (1983). Average family size 4.3; 1–2 persons 23.7%, 3 persons 19.7%, 4 persons 19.6%, 5–6 persons 23.1%, 7 or more persons 13.9%.
*Immigration* (1982–84): permanent immigrants admitted 7,673, from Portugal 28.4%, Uruguay 8.7%, Argentina 8.2%.

## Vital statistics

*Birth rate* per 1,000 population (1985): 32.0 (world avg. 29.0).
*Death rate* per 1,000 population (1985): 7.0 (world avg. 11.0).
*Natural increase rate* per 1,000 population (1985): 25.0 (world avg. 18.0).

*Total fertility rate* (avg. births per childbearing woman; 1984): 3.6.
*Marriage rate* per 1,000 population (1984): 7.1.
*Divorce rate* per 1,000 population (1984): 0.2.
*Life expectancy* at birth (1980–85): male 60.9 years; female 66.0 years.
*Major causes of death* per 100,000 population (1980): diseases of the circulatory system 156.2, of which cerebrovascular disease 51.5, diseases of pulmonary circulation 40.5, acute myocardial infarction 30.7; infectious and parasitic diseases 57.4; malignant neoplasms (cancers) 49.3; diseases of the respiratory system 36.9, of which pneumonia 29.3; accidents 32.0; homicide and other violence 22.6; ill-defined conditions 133.0.

## Social indicators

*Educational attainment* (1980)[4]. Percent of population age 25 and over having: no formal schooling 32.9%; incomplete primary education 50.4%; complete primary 4.9%; secondary 6.9%; higher 5.0%.

### Distribution of income (1984)[12]

| | percent of national income by decile | | | | | | | | |
|---|---|---|---|---|---|---|---|---|---|
| 1 | 2 | 3 | 4 | 5 | 6 | 7 | 8 | 9 | 10 (highest) |
| 1.0 | 2.0 | 2.6 | 3.6 | 4.4 | 5.2 | 7.6 | 10.5 | 16.5 | 46.6 |

*Quality of working life.* Average workweek (1980): 80.6% of the labour force works 40 or more hours per week. Annual estimated rate per 100,000 insured urban workers (1982) for: injury or accident 5,500; industrial illness, n.a.; death 21. Proportion of labour force participating in national social insurance system: 51.8%. Average days lost to labour stoppages per 1,000 workdays: n.a: Average duration of journey and method of transport to work: n.a. Rate per 1,000 workers of discouraged (unemployed no longer seeking work): n.a.
*Access to services* (1984). Proportion of households having access to: electricity 79.4%, of which urban households having access 94.2%, rural households having access 34.4%; safe public (piped) water supply 66.2%, of which urban households having access 85.6%, rural households having access 7.4%; public sewage collection 30.8%, of which urban households having access 40.5%, rural households having access 1.3%; public fire protection, n.a.
*Social participation.* Eligible voters participating in last (November 1986) national election: 85.0%. Population participating in voluntary work: n.a. Trade union membership in total work force n.a. Practicing religious population in total affiliated population: most men, and in particular Portuguese-Brazilian men, attend Mass only on special occasions. They believe religion is the domain and duty of women.
*Social deviance:* The incidence of crime is not accurately reported. Crimes resulting in imprisonment (1983): 243,958, of which murder 4.3%, rape 1.0%, other assault 19.5%, burglary and housebreaking 21.6%, armed robbery 0.3%, narcotics trafficking 3.8%, narcotics usage 4.5%. Suicides (1984): 4,432.
*Leisure.* Favourite leisure activities: n.a.
*Material well-being* (1980). Households possessing: automobile 22.4% (urban 28.3%, rural 9.5%); telephone 12.4% (urban 17.5%, rural 0.9%); television receiver 56.1% (urban 73.0%, rural 15.7%); refrigerator 50.4% (urban 65.7%, rural 13.6%); air conditioner, n.a.; washing machine, n.a.

## National economy

*Gross national product* (at current market prices; 1985): U.S.$222,010,000,000 (U.S.$1,640 per capita).

### Structure of gross domestic product and labour force

| | 1985[13] in value U.S.$'000,000 | 1985[13] % of total value | 1984 labour force[14] | 1984 % of labour force |
|---|---|---|---|---|
| Agriculture | 25,147 | 10.1 | 14,974,441 | 29.8 |
| Mining | 2,680 | 1.1 | 7,997,553 | 15.9 |
| Manufacturing | 68,893 | 27.6 | | |
| Construction | 13,645 | 5.5 | 2,926,441 | 5.8 |
| Public utilities | 9,667 | 3.9 | | |
| Transportation and communication | 19,124 | 7.7 | 1,818,407 | 3.6 |
| Trade | 40,757 | 16.4 | 5,354,165 | 10.7 |
| Pub. admin., defense | 17,323 | 6.9 | 2,133,540 | 4.3 |
| Finance | 24,797 | 9.9 | 13,445,733 | 26.8 |
| Services | 27,103 | 10.9 | | |
| Other | — | — | 1,558,485 | 3.1 |
| TOTAL | 249,136 | 100.0 | 50,208,765 | 100.0 |

*Budget* (1986). Revenue: Cz$656,126,000,000 (current revenue 63.6%, of which property taxes 25.8%, taxes on goods and services 13.6%, social security contributions 5.9%, customs duties 3.7%; capital revenue 32.2%). Expenditures: Cz$656,126,000,000 (administration and planning 31.4%; transportation 14.3%; regional development 11.5%; education and culture 9.9%; social welfare 6.5%; agriculture and water supply 6.4%; national defense and public security 5.0%; health and sanitation 2.5%).
*Public debt* (external, outstanding; 1985): U.S.$73,893,600,000.
*Population economically active* (1984): total 52,443,100; activity rate of total population 40.9% (participation rates: ages 15–60, 65.6%; female 33.1%; unemployed [1986] 3.5%).

### Price and earnings indexes (1980 = 100)

| | 1981 | 1982 | 1983 | 1984 | 1985 | 1986 | 1987[15] |
|---|---|---|---|---|---|---|---|
| Consumer price index | 206 | 407 | 984 | 2,924 | 9,556 | 23,436 | 47,987 |
| Earnings index[16] | 203 | 403 | 865 | 2,374 | 8,018 | ... | ... |

*Land use* (1984): forested 66.9%; meadows and pastures 19.5%; agricultural and under permanent cultivation 8.9%; other 4.7%.
*Tourism* (1985): receipts from visitors U.S.$1,739,000,000; expenditures by nationals abroad U.S.$1,145,000,000.

## Manufacturing enterprises (1981)

| | no. of enterprises | number of labourers | wages of labourers as a % of avg. of all wages | value added in producer's prices (in '000s of cruzados) |
|---|---|---|---|---|
| Chemicals | 2,813 | 122,739 | 157.5 | 1,161,916 |
| Metallurgy | 9,032 | 391,670 | 113.9 | 799,797 |
| Mechanical products | 7,835 | 405,690 | 162.7 | 784,716 |
| Food products | 22,942 | 419,215 | 61.3 | 768,480 |
| Textiles | 5,295 | 380,828 | 73.8 | 458,510 |
| Transportation equipment | 2,634 | 196,632 | 153.6 | 531,123 |
| Electric and communications equipment | 2,752 | 186,490 | 120.2 | 500,213 |
| Combustible fuels (not metals) | 15,043 | 257,892 | 75.2 | 402,914 |
| Clothing and footwear | 8,966 | 354,625 | 55.3 | 314,594 |
| Paper and paper products | 1,377 | 80,498 | 102.4 | 183,214 |
| Publishing and printing | 5,004 | 103,074 | 117.5 | 207,294 |
| Lumber | 9,085 | 165,420 | 58.8 | 158,575 |
| Plastics | 2,145 | 104,301 | 89.6 | 158,452 |
| Pharmaceutical products | 443 | 22,688 | 113.7 | 145,835 |
| Furniture | 5,812 | 122,015 | 64.9 | 116,353 |

*Production* (value of production in '000,000s of cruzados except as noted). Agriculture, forestry, fishing (1984): soybeans 5,404, sugarcane 4,443, corn (maize) 3,515, coffee 3,217, rice 2,474, beans 1,894, cassava 1,873, cotton (all forms) 1,687, oranges 1,602, cocoa beans 1,020, wheat 916, bananas 645, potatoes 497, tomatoes 425, cashews 205, grapes 184, onions 166, pineapples 157, papayas 152, coconuts 144, black pepper 141, babassu oil 141, castor beans and oil 141, peanuts (groundnuts) 135; livestock (number of live animals; 1985) 134,500,000 cattle, 30,000,000 pigs, 17,500,000 sheep, 8,500,000 goats, 5,200,000 horses; roundwood (1985) 225,905,000 cu m; fish catch (metric tons; 1985) 959,302, of which sardines 249,362. Mining and quarrying (1984): iron ore 1,437; gold 1,073; tin 465; phosphate fertilizers 425; limestone 411; bauxite 371; granite 302; manganese 185; clay 147; magnesium 121. Manufacturing (1980): chemicals 1,850; food products 1,333; iron and steel and other worked metals 1,318; transport equipment 753; electric and nonelectric machinery 729; textiles 616; electrical goods (including computers, televisions, and radios) 498; cement and other worked nonmetals 403; clothing and footwear 370; paper and paper products 258; lumber 195; plastic products 194; tires and other rubber products 144. Construction (new buildings completed; 1984) residential 14,304,000 sq m; nonresidential 3,698,000 sq m.

## Retail trade enterprises (1980)

| | no. of enterprises | total no. of employees | annual wage as a % of all wages | annual value of sales (in '000 of cruzados) |
|---|---|---|---|---|
| General merchandise stores (including food products) | 16,186 | 274,379 | 145.5 | 658,096 |
| Gasoline stations | 21,588 | 140,865 | 127.6 | 594,063 |
| Food, beverages, and tobacco stores | 538,638 | 963,106 | 16.5 | 586,249 |
| Automobile dealers and auto parts stores | 25,284 | 157,285 | 205.4 | 581,354 |
| Stores selling clothing, fabrics, and textiles | 117,595 | 452,641 | 102.3 | 434,793 |
| Hardware stores | 37,396 | 208,783 | 134.5 | 407,266 |
| Stores selling radios, televisions, and related electronic goods | 26,114 | 168,431 | 180.1 | 353,169 |
| Drugstores | 33,631 | 142,030 | 118.0 | 217,781 |
| Agricultural machinery and heavy equipment dealers | 6,565 | 59,244 | 329.5 | 204,332 |
| General merchandise stores (excluding food products) | 3,367 | 58,729 | 239.9 | 124,359 |
| Book, magazine, and office supply stores | 20,192 | 63,529 | 123.1 | 60,327 |

Energy production (consumption): electricity (kW-hr; 1985) 192,945,000,000 (195,724,000,000); coal (metric tons; 1985) 7,712,000 (16,814,000); crude petroleum (barrels; 1986) 216,610,000 ([1985] 402,520,000); petroleum products (metric tons; 1985) 46,758,000 (37,881,000); natural gas (cu m; 1986) 3,700,000,000 ([1985] 2,482,000,000); alcohol[17] (hectolitres; 1986) 102,000,000 (n.a.).

*Household income and expenditure.* Average household size (1984) 4.4; income per household of families having income (1983)[12,18,19] 5,794 cruzados (U.S.$2,599); sources of income: n.a.; expenditure (1974)[20,21]: food 29.7%, housing and public utilities 22.5%, transportation 8.3%, clothing and footwear 7.8%, health and hygiene 7.7%, education 3.3%, tobacco 2.4%, recreation 2.3%, other 16.0%.

## Financial aggregates[22]

| | 1982 | 1983 | 1984 | 1985 | 1986 | April 1987 |
|---|---|---|---|---|---|---|
| Exchange rate, cruzados per: | | | | | | |
| U.S. dollar | 0.253 | 0.984 | 3.184 | 10.490 | 14.939 | 25.434 |
| £ | 0.408 | 1.427 | 3.682 | 15.153 | 22.028 | 42.355 |
| SDR | 0.279 | 1.030 | 3.121 | 11.522 | 18.273 | 33.223 |
| International reserves (U.S.$) | | | | | | |
| Total (excl. gold; '000,000) | 3,928 | 4,355 | 11,508 | 10,605 | 5,803 | 4,178 |
| SDRs ('000,000) | — | — | 1 | 1 | — | 7 |
| Reserve pos. in IMF ('000,000) | 287 | … | … | … | … | … |
| Foreign exchange ('000,000) | 3,641 | 4,355 | 11,507 | 10,604 | 5,803 | 4,171 |
| Gold ('000,000 fine troy oz) | 0.15 | 0.54 | 1.47 | 3.10 | 2.43 | 2.34 |
| % world reserves | 0.02 | 0.06 | 0.16 | 0.33 | 0.26 | 0.25 |
| Interest and prices | | | | | | |
| Central bank discount (%) | 49.0 | 156.6 | 215.3 | 219.4 | 50.7 | 95.5 |
| Gov't. bond yield (%) | … | … | … | … | … | … |
| Industrial share prices | … | … | … | … | … | … |
| Balance of payments (U.S.$'000,000) | | | | | | |
| Balance of visible trade | 778 | 6,469 | 13,086 | 12,466 | … | … |
| Imports, f.o.b. | 19,395 | 15,429 | 13,916 | 13,168 | … | … |
| Exports, f.o.b. | 20,173 | 21,898 | 27,002 | 25,634 | … | … |
| Balance of invisibles | −17,082 | −13,414 | −13,215 | −12,894 | … | … |
| Balance of payments, current account | −16,312 | −6,837 | +42 | −273 | … | … |

## Foreign trade[23]

### Balance of trade (current prices)

| | 1981 | 1982 | 1983 | 1984 | 1985 | 1986 |
|---|---|---|---|---|---|---|
| U.S.$'000,000 | +1,202 | +780 | +6,470 | +13,089 | +12,486 | +7,950 |
| % of total | 2.6% | 2.0% | 17.3% | 32.0% | 32.2% | 21.6% |

*Imports* (1984): U.S.$15,210,000,000 (mineral fuels 54.5%, of which crude petroleum 49.1%; chemicals 10.6%, of which organic chemicals 4.6%, fertilizers 2.0%; food products 8.5%, of which cereals 6.1%; electrical and nonelectrical machinery 6.6%; electrical and electronic goods 4.9%; transport equipment 3.5%, of which road vehicles 1.3%, boats [all kinds] 1.2%; metals [all forms] 2.9%, of which iron and steel 1.2%, copper 1.1%; photographic, surgical, and scientific instruments and apparatus 1.3%; plastics 1.2%; natural and synthetic rubber materials 1.1%). *Major import sources* (1985): United States 21.2%; Iraq 12.7%; Nigeria 9.5%; Saudi Arabia 7.2%; West Germany 5.9%; Japan 4.4%; Canada 3.6%; China 3.6%; Argentina 3.4%; Mexico 2.9%.

*Exports* (1984): U.S.$27,005,000,000[24] (metals [all forms] 10.9%, of which iron and steel 8.5%, bauxite 1.2%; coffee 9.5%; animal feedstuffs 5.9%; nonspecific vegetable and food products 5.5%; electrical and nonelectrical machinery 5.2%; textiles 4.5%, of which cotton products 1.8%; road vehicles 4.3%; footwear 4.0%; animal and vegetable fats and oils 3.2%; paper and paper products 2.8%; cocoa beans and cocoa 2.6%; sugar and confectionery 2.4%; organic chemicals 2.4%; electrical and electronic goods 2.2%; fresh and frozen meat 2.0%; tobacco products 1.7%; seeds of diverse fruits and products of industrial plants 1.7%; plastics 1.6%; lumber and wooden furniture 1.2%). *Major export destinations* (1985): United States 26.6%; The Netherlands 6.1%; Japan 5.4%; West Germany 5.0%; Italy 4.4%; Nigeria 3.3%; China 3.2%; France 3.0%; United Kingdom 2.6%; Iraq 2.5%.

## Transport and communications

*Transport.* Railroads (1984): route length 17,984 mi, 28,942 km; passenger-mi 9,578,000,000, passenger-km 15,415,000,000; short ton-mi cargo 63,303,000,000, metric ton-km cargo 92,421,000,000. Roads (1985): total length 984,736 mi, 1,583,172 km (paved 7%). Vehicles (1984): passenger cars 10,008,000; trucks and buses 1,082,000. Merchant marine (1986): vessels (100 gross tons and over) 697; total deadweight tonnage 10,277,850. Air transport (1986)[25]: passenger-mi 14,719,000,000, passenger-km 23,688,000,000; short ton-mi cargo 787,686,000, metric ton-km cargo 1,150,000,000; airports (1987) with scheduled flights 110.

*Communications.* Daily newspapers (1986): total number 279; total circulation 8,528,000; circulation per 1,000 population 62. Radio (1986): total number of receivers 50,540,000 (1 per 2.7 persons). Television (1986): total number of receivers 36,000,000 (1 per 3.8 persons). Telephones (1985): 11,427,863 (1 per 12 persons).

## Education and health

### Education (1985)

| | schools | teachers | students | student/ teacher ratio |
|---|---|---|---|---|
| Primary (age 7–14) | 187,274 | 1,040,566 | 24,769,736 | 23.8 |
| Secondary (age 15–17) | 9,260 | 206,111 | 3,016,138 | 14.6 |
| Higher | 859 | 122,486 | 1,367,609 | 11.2 |

*Literacy* (1985)[26]: total population age 15 and over literate 66,255,000 (79.3%); males literate 32,757,000 (80.4%); females literate 33,498,000 (78.3%).

*Health:* physicians (1981) 103,000 (1 per 1,200 persons); hospital beds (1986) 492,519 (1 per 287 persons); infant mortality rate per 1,000 live births (1985) 64.0.

*Food* (1981–83): daily per capita caloric intake 2,564 (vegetable products 85%, animal products 15%); (1983) 106% of FAO recommended minimum requirement.

## Military

*Total active duty personnel* (1986): 283,400 (army 64.5%, navy 17.6%, air force 17.9%). *Military expenditure as percent of GNP* (1984): 0.8% (world 5.9%); per capita expenditure U.S.$13.

[1]Total area, including 1,035 sq mi (2,680 sq km) in dispute between the states of Amazonas and Pará and 1,009 sq mi (2,614 sq km) in dispute between Ceará and Piauí. Land area excluding inland water is 3,265,075 sq mi (8,456,508 sq km). [2]Includes the islands of Trinidade and Martin Vaz. [3]Includes Rocas atoll and the rocks of São Pedro and São Paulo. [4]Detail does not add to total given because of rounding. [5]Spiritist Catholics are actively and regularly involved in the practice of medium religions; about 60,000,000 Roman Catholics defer to spiritist dogma and participate in organized spiritism occasionally. [6]Evangelical Catholics are persons who are officially regarded as Roman Catholic but who are affiliated to Protestant churches. [7]Non-Christian followers of Afro-Brazilian syncretistic religions ("low spiritism"). [8]Non-Christian followers of Kardecism ("high spiritism"). [9]First population cited refers to the *municipio*, an officially delimited area including a central city and adjacent urban and rural districts; second (parenthetical) figure refers to the metropolitan area, defined as the adjoining predominantly urban *municipios* that are economically dependent on the central city. [10]*Municipio* within Rio de Janeiro metropolitan area. [11]*Municipio* within São Paulo metropolitan area. [12]Excludes rural population of Acre, Amazonas, Pará, Rondônia, Amapá, and Roraima. [13]1984 prices. [14]Employed persons aged 10 years and over. [15]April. [16]Minimum wages paid in the *municipio* of São Paulo. [17]Fuel produced from sugarcane used in the operation of locally produced automobiles as either hydrous alcohol or gasohol. [18]Prices of September 1984. [19]Excludes pensioners, domestic servants, and relatives of domestic servants. [20]State of Rio de Janeiro only. [21]Excludes nonmonetary expenditures comprising 16% of total expenditure. [22]Based on end-of-period figures. [23]Import figures are f.o.b. in balance of trade and c.i.f. in commodities and trading partners. [24]Soybeans and products are 9.5% of total exports. [25]Cruzeiro do Sul, TransBrasil, Varig, and Vasp airlines only. [26]Per official estimate, 1986 functional literacy may be as low as 42.0% of total population over age 15.

# Brunei

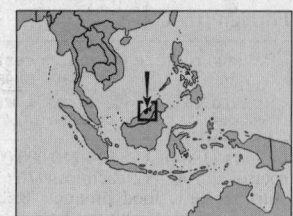

*Official name:* Negara Brunei Darussalam (State of Brunei, Abode of Peace).
*Form of government:* monarchy (sultanate).
*Head of state and government:* Sultan.
*Capital:* Bandar Seri Begawan.
*Official language:* Malay.
*Official religion:* Islam.
*Monetary unit:* 1 Brunei dollar (Br$) = 100 cents; valuation (Oct. 5, 1987) 1 U.S.$ = Br$2.10; 1 £ = Br$3.41.

### Area and population

| Districts | Capitals | area sq mi | area sq km | population 1984 estimate |
|---|---|---|---|---|
| Belait | Kuala Belait | 1,053 | 2,727 | 57,000 |
| Brunei and Muara | Bandar Seri Begawan | 220 | 570 | 129,400 |
| Temburong | Bangar | 503 | 1,303 | 6,800 |
| Tutong | Tutong | 450 | 1,165 | 22,700 |
| TOTAL | | 2,226 | 5,765 | 215,900 |

## Demography

*Population* (1987): 241,000.
*Density* (1987): persons per sq mi 108.3, persons per sq km 41.8.
*Urban–rural* (1981): urban 59.4%; rural 40.6%.
*Sex distribution* (1985): male 53.40%; female 46.60%.
*Age breakdown* (1985): under 15, 37.0%; 15–29, 30.3%; 30–44, 19.6%; 45–59, 8.5%; 60–69, 2.7%; 70 and over, 1.9%.
*Population projection:* (1990) 269,000; (2000) 388,000.
*Doubling time:* 26 years.
*Ethnic composition* (1985): Malay 64.6%; Chinese 20.0%; other indigenous 8.3%; other 7.1%.
*Religious affiliation* (1982): Muslim 63.4%; Buddhist 14.0%; Christian 9.7%; other 12.9%.
*Major cities* (1981): Bandar Seri Begawan 55,000[1]; Seria 23,511; Kuala Belait 19,281; Tutong 6,161.

## Vital statistics

*Birth rate* per 1,000 population (1985): 30.1 (world avg. 29.0); (1978) legitimate 99.3%; illegitimate 0.7%.
*Death rate* per 1,000 population (1985): 3.6 (world avg. 11.0).
*Natural increase rate* per 1,000 population (1985): 26.5 (world avg. 18.0).
*Total fertility rate* (avg. births per childbearing woman): n.a.
*Marriage rate* per 1,000 population (1985): 8.5.
*Divorce rate* per 1,000 population (1985): 0.7[2].
*Life expectancy* at birth (1986): male 70.1 years; female 72.7 years.
*Major causes of death* per 100,000 population (1985): cardiovascular disease 69.0; malignant neoplasms (cancers) 64.0; cerebrovascular disease 40.0; pneumonia 29.0; bronchitis, emphysema, and asthma 25.0; hypertension 23.0; motor vehicle accidents 21.0; tuberculosis 19.0; signs, symptoms, and other ill-defined conditions 268.0.

## National economy

*Budget* (1985). Revenue: Br$7,533,000,000 (government property 64.2%[3]). Expenditures: Br$4,317,900,000 (defense 12.8%[4], public works 8.7%[4], education 8.2%[4], development expenditure 7.7%).
*Public debt* (external, outstanding; 1987): none.
*Tourism* (1985): number of visitors 6,418.
*Production* (metric tons except as noted). Agriculture, forestry, fishing (1985): vegetables and melons 9,000, eggs 1,900, rice 1,065, cassava 1,000, roots and tubers 1,000, sago 210, pepper 3, 108,810,000 fruits, 1,045,000 coconuts; livestock (number of live animals) 13,000 pigs, 12,000 buffalo, 4,000 cattle, 2,000 goats, 2,000,000 chickens; roundwood 294,000 cu m; fish catch 2,986. Mining and quarrying (1985): other than petroleum and natural gas (see below), none except sand and gravel for construction. Manufacturing (1985): gasoline 104,600; distillate fuel oils 83,300; liquefied natural gas 29,400[4]; naphtha 6,800. Construction (number of buildings completed; 1984): residential 195; nonresidential 5. Energy production (consumption): electricity (kW-hr; 1985) 949,000,000 (949,000,000); coal, none (none); crude petroleum (barrels; 1985) 57,993,000 (n.a.); petroleum products (metric tons; 1985) 794,000 (737,000); natural gas (cu m; 1985) 8,950,600 (1,307,100).
*Population economically active* (1981): total 70,690; activity rate of total population 36.4% (participation rates: ages 15–64, 61.1%; female 23.8%; unemployed [1984] 3.4%).

### Price and earnings indexes (1980 = 100)

| | 1979 | 1980 | 1981 | 1982 | 1983 | 1984 | 1985 |
|---|---|---|---|---|---|---|---|
| Consumer price index | ... | 100.0 | 129.0 | 137.2 | 138.8 | 143.1 | 146.4 |
| Monthly earnings index[5] | 86.4 | 100.0 | 107.5 | 111.7 | 139.3 | ... | ... |

*Household income and expenditure.* Average household size (1981) 5.8.; income per household: n.a.; sources of income: n.a.; expenditure (1977): food 45.1%; transportation and communication 17.2%; recreation, education, and cultural services 8.9%; household furnishings 8.3%; clothing and footwear 6.1%; rent and utilities 5.0%.

*Gross national product* (at current market prices; 1985): U.S.$3,940,000,000 (U.S.$17,570 per capita).

### Structure of gross domestic product and labour force

| | 1984 in value Br$'000,000 | 1984 % of total value | 1981 labour force | 1981 % of labour force |
|---|---|---|---|---|
| Agriculture | 89.7 | 1.1 | 3,440 | 4.9 |
| Mining | } 5,583.1 | 69.3 | 3,860 | 5.5 |
| Manufacturing | | | 2,780 | 3.9 |
| Construction | 375.4 | 4.7 | 12,650 | 17.9 |
| Public utilities | 18.2 | 0.2 | 1,960 | 2.8 |
| Transportation and communication | 69.5 | 0.9 | 4,530 | 6.4 |
| Trade | 835.3 | 10.4 | 7,360 | 10.4 |
| Finance | 249.1 | 3.1 | 2,010 | 2.8 |
| Services | 944.5 | 11.7 | 29,280 | 41.4 |
| Other | −113.3[6] | −1.4[6] | 2,820[7] | 4.0[7] |
| TOTAL | 8,051.5 | 100.0 | 70,690 | 100.0 |

*Land use* (1984): forested 54.1%; meadows and pastures 1.1%; agricultural and under permanent cultivation 1.3%; other 43.5%.

## Foreign trade

### Balance of trade (current prices)

| | 1980 | 1981 | 1982 | 1983 | 1984 | 1985 |
|---|---|---|---|---|---|---|
| Br$'000,000 | +8,622 | +7,327 | +6,582 | +5,629 | +5,482 | +5,184 |
| % of total | 77.8% | 74.3% | 67.7% | 64.6% | 67.3% | 65.8% |

*Imports* (1985): Br$1,348,400,000 (machinery and transport equipment 33.8%, manufactured goods 21.5%, food and live animals 14.5%, miscellaneous manufactured articles 10.8%, chemicals 7.1%, beverages and tobacco 5.2%, mineral fuels 1.8%, animal and vegetable oils and fats 0.6%). *Major import sources:* Singapore 24.4%; Japan 19.8%; United States 15.6%; United Kingdom 9.2%; Malaysia 4.5%[8]; West Germany 3.8%; Thailand 3.1%; Australia 2.7%; Taiwan 2.7%.
*Exports* (1985): Br$6,532,900,000 (crude oil 54.4%, liquefied natural gas 42.6%, petroleum products 1.5%, other 1.5%). *Major export destinations:* Japan 61.2%; Thailand 10.6%; Singapore 8.7%; United States 7.3%; South Korea 7.0%; Taiwan 3.5%.

## Transport and communications

*Transport.* Railroads[9] (1984): length 12 mi, 19 km. Roads (1985): total length 958 mi, 1,542 km (paved 35%). Vehicles (1985): passenger cars 79,428; trucks and buses 10,663. Merchant marine (1986): vessels (100 gross tons and over) 5; total deadweight tonnage 1,728. Marine transport (1985): cargo loaded 49,455,000 metric tons, cargo unloaded 680,400 metric tons. Air transport (1985): passenger-mi 153,500,000, passenger-km 247,000,000; short ton-mi cargo 3,014,000, metric ton-km cargo 4,400,000; airports (1987) with scheduled flights 1.
*Communications.* Daily newspapers (1986): none. Radio (1986): total number of receivers 74,000 (1 per 3.1 persons). Television (1986): total number of receivers 48,000 (1 per 4.8 persons). Telephones (1985): 32,865 (1 per 6.8 persons).

## Education and health

### Education (1984)

| | schools | teachers | students | student/ teacher ratio |
|---|---|---|---|---|
| Primary (age 5–11) | 149 | 2,131 | 34,372 | 16.1 |
| Secondary (age 12–20) | 27 | 1,526 | 18,565 | 12.2 |
| Voc., teacher tr. | 6 | 275[10] | 1,339 | 4.9 |
| Higher | 1 | [10] | 187 | ... |

*Educational attainment* (1981). Percent of population age 25 and over having: no formal schooling 32.1%; primary education 28.3%; secondary 30.1%; postsecondary and higher 9.4%. *Literacy* (1984): total population age 15 and over literate 108,900 (80.3%); males literate 64,300 (86.5%); females literate 44,600 (72.8%).
*Health* (1985): physicians 149 (1 per 1,505 persons); hospital beds 876 (1 per 256 persons); infant mortality rate per 1,000 live births 12.1.
*Food* (1981–83): daily per capita caloric intake 3,061 (vegetable products 81%, animal products 19%); 139% of FAO recommended minimum requirement.

## Military

*Total active duty personnel* (1986): 4,050[11] (army 83.5%, navy 11.6%, air force 4.9%). *Military expenditure as percent of GNP* (1983): 5.8% (world 6.1%); per capita expenditure U.S.$1,200.

---

[1]1985 estimate. [2]For Muslim population only. [3]In 1983 more than 98% of state revenue was derived from exports of oil and gas. [4]1984. [5]Nonagricultural sectors only. [6]Imputed bank service charge. [7]Includes unemployed. [8]Peninsular Malaysia only. [9]Privately owned. [10]Vocational and teacher training includes higher. [11]All services form part of the army.

# Bulgaria

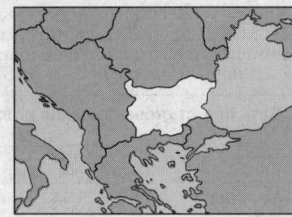

*Official name:* Narodna Republika
Bŭlgaria (People's Republic of
Bulgaria).
*Form of government:* unitary
single-party socialist republic with
one legislative house (National
Assembly [400]).
*Chief of state:* Chairman of the State
Council (president).
*Head of government:* Chairman of the
Council of Ministers (premier).
*Capital:* Sofia.
*Official language:* Bulgarian.
*Official religion:* none.
*Monetary unit:* 1 lev (leva) = 100
stotinki; valuation (Oct. 5, 1987)
1 lev = U.S.$0.85; 1 £ = 1.39 leva.

| Area and population | | area | | population |
|---|---|---|---|---|
| | | | | 1986 |
| Provinces | Capitals | sq mi | sq km | estimate[1] |
| Blagoevgrad | Blagoevgrad | 2,506 | 6,490 | 346,266 |
| Burgas | Burgas | 2,972 | 7,697 | 449,314 |
| Gabrovo | Gabrovo | 786 | 2,035 | 175,120 |
| Khaskovo | Khaskovo | 1,547 | 4,007 | 301,249 |
| Kŭrdzhali | Kŭrdzhali | 1,558 | 4,036 | 302,578 |
| Kyustendil | Kyustendil | 1,174 | 3,041 | 190,410 |
| Lovech | Lovech | 1,597 | 4,136 | 202,708 |
| Mikhaylovgrad | Mikhaylovgrad | 1,393 | 3,609 | 223,292 |
| Pazardzhik | Pazardzhik | 1,720 | 4,455 | 326,315 |
| Pernik | Pernik | 923 | 2,391 | 174,419 |
| Pleven | Pleven | 1,673 | 4,332 | 362,130 |
| Plovdiv | Plovdiv | 2,177 | 5,639 | 754,393 |
| Razgrad | Razgrad | 1,030 | 2,668 | 198,007 |
| Ruse | Ruse | 992 | 2,570 | 304,443 |
| Shumen | Shumen | 1,309 | 3,390 | 254,789 |
| Silistra | Silistra | 1,097 | 2,842 | 174,052 |
| Sliven | Sliven | 1,395 | 3,614 | 239,479 |
| Smolyan | Smolyan | 1,360 | 3,523 | 164,223 |
| Sofiya | Sofia (Sofiya) | 2,766 | 7,165 | 305,251 |
| Stara Zagora | Stara Zagora | 1,956 | 5,066 | 411,506 |
| Tolbukhin | Tolbukhin | 1,816 | 4,704 | 257,298 |
| Tŭrgovishte | Tŭrgovishte | 1,055 | 2,732 | 171,167 |
| Varna | Varna | 1,477 | 3,825 | 464,701 |
| Veliko Tŭrnovo | Veliko Tŭrnovo | 1,807 | 4,680 | 339,120 |
| Vidin | Vidin | 1,161 | 3,006 | 166,388 |
| Vratsa | Vratsa | 1,527 | 3,955 | 287,841 |
| Yambol | Yambol | 1,587 | 4,110 | 203,754 |
| **City Commune** | | | | |
| Sofiya | Sofia (Sofiya) | 461 | 1,194 | 1,199,405 |
| TOTAL | | 42,823[2] | 110,912 | 8,949,618 |

## Demography

*Population* (1987): 8,983,000.
*Density* (1987): persons per sq mi 209.7, persons per sq km 81.0.
*Urban–rural* (1986): urban 64.8%; rural 35.2%.
*Sex distribution* (1986): male 49.51%; female 50.49%.
*Age breakdown* (1985): under 15, 22.2%; 15–29, 20.4%; 30–44, 20.4%; 45–59,
19.4%; 60–74, 13.1%; 75 and over, 4.5%.
*Population projection:* (1990) 9,050,000; (2000) 9,276,000.
*Doubling time:* not applicable; population stable.
*Ethnic composition* (1985): Bulgarian 88.2%; Turkish 8.5%; other 3.3%.
*Religious affiliation* (1982): Eastern Orthodox 26.7%; Muslim 7.5%; Protestant 0.7%; Roman Catholic 0.5%; other 0.1%; atheist 64.5%.
*Major cities* (1986): Sofia 1,114,962; Plovdiv 342,131; Varna 302,211; Ruse
183,746; Burgas 182,570.

## Vital statistics

*Birth rate* per 1,000 population (1985): 13.2 (world avg. 29.0); (1980) legitimate 89.1%; illegitimate 10.9%.
*Death rate* per 1,000 population (1985): 12.0 (world avg. 11.0).
*Natural increase rate* per 1,000 population (1985): 1.2 (world avg. 18.0).
*Total fertility rate* (avg. births per childbearing woman; 1984): 2.0.
*Marriage rate* per 1,000 population (1985): 7.4.
*Divorce rate* per 1,000 population (1985): 1.6.
*Life expectancy* at birth (1978–80): male 68.3 years; female 73.5 years.
*Major causes of death* per 100,000 population (1984): diseases of the circulatory system 673.0; malignant neoplasms (cancers) 160.6.

## National economy

*Budget[3]* (1984). Revenue: 17,500,000,000 leva (turnover tax, taxes from
state enterprises, and income tax 64.8%). Expenditures: 17,400,000,000 leva
(economy 51.2%, education and health 18.1%, social security 17.4%).
*Public debt* (external, outstanding; 1985): U.S.$1,670,000,000.
*Tourism* (1985): number of tourist arrivals 7,295,244; receipts from visitors
(1984) U.S.$288,000,000; expenditures by nationals abroad, n.a.
*Production* (metric tons except as noted). Agriculture, forestry, fishing (1985):
wheat 3,068,000, vegetables 1,506,000, corn (maize) 1,350,000, sugar beets
824,000, barley 800,000; livestock (number of live animals; 1986) 9,724,-
000 sheep, 3,912,000 pigs, 1,735,000 cattle; roundwood (1984) 4,841,000 cu
m; fish catch 135,000. Mining and quarrying (1985): iron ore 2,063,000;
lead 95,000; copper 75,000; zinc 68,000; manganese 45,000. Manufacturing
(1985): cement 5,296,000; crude steel 2,945,000; pig iron 1,712,000; fertilizers 640,000; wood pulp and paper 544,700; cigarettes 94,000; cotton fabrics

349,300,000 m; motor vehicles 15,000 units; wine 3,451,000 hectolitres.
Construction (1985): residential 4,219,000 sq m. Energy production (consumption): electricity (kW-hr; 1985) 41,633,000,000 (45,937,000,000); coal
(metric tons; 1985) 31,015,000 (38,934,000); crude petroleum (barrels; 1985)
2,220,000 (94,720,000); petroleum products (metric tons; 1985) 11,405,000
(13,320,000); natural gas (cu m; 1985) 127,872,000 (5,533,000,000).
*Gross national product* (1985): U.S.$25,530,000,000 (U.S.$2,860 per capita).

| Structure of net material product and labour force | | | | |
|---|---|---|---|---|
| | 1985 | | | |
| | in value '000,000 leva | % of total value | labour force | % of labour force |
| Agriculture | 3,512.0 | 13.8 | 816,200 | 17.0 |
| Mining | } | | 1,724,100[4] | 35.9[4] |
| Manufacturing | 15,170.0 | 59.6 } | | |
| Public utilities | | | 53,600 | 1.1 |
| Construction | 2,490.0 | 9.8 | 376,600 | 7.8 |
| Transp. and commun. | 1,807.0 | 7.1 | 326,400 | 6.8 |
| Trade | 1,801.0 | 7.1 | 397,100 | 8.3 |
| Finance | — | — } | 332,500 | 6.9 |
| Pub. admin., defense | — | — } | | |
| Services | — | — | 702,800 | 14.6 |
| Other | 671.0[5] | 2.6[5] | 72,700 | 1.5 |
| TOTAL | 25,451.0 | 100.0 | 4,802,000 | 100.0[2] |

*Population economically active* (1985): total 4,802,000; activity rate of total
population 53.7% (participation rates: working age [male 16–60; female 16–
55] 82.4%; female 47.6%; unemployed, n.a.).

| Price and earnings indexes (1980 = 100) | | | | | | | |
|---|---|---|---|---|---|---|---|
| | 1979 | 1980 | 1981 | 1982 | 1983 | 1984 | 1985 |
| Consumer price index | 87.7 | 100.0 | 100.5 | 100.7 | 102.0 | 105.0 | ... |
| Monthly earnings index | 85.5 | 100.0 | 105.0 | 107.0 | 107.0 | 110.0 | 111.0 |

*Household income and expenditure.* Average household size (1982) 3.3;
income per household (1985) 7,197 leva (U.S.$7,268); sources of income
(1985): wages and salaries 60.8%, transfer payments 19.5%, self-employment 14.3%; expenditure (1981): food 45.0%, clothing 9.7%, housing 7.2%.
*Land use* (1984): forested 34.9%; meadows and pastures 18.4%; agricultural
and under permanent cultivation 37.5%; other 9.2%.

## Foreign trade

| Balance of trade (current prices) | | | | | | |
|---|---|---|---|---|---|---|
| | 1980 | 1981 | 1982 | 1983 | 1984 | 1985 |
| '000,000 leva | +618.6 | −97.6 | +95.9 | −148.5 | +145.0 | −266.3 |
| % of total | 3.5% | 0.5% | 0.4% | 0.6% | 0.6% | 1.0% |

*Imports* (1985): 14,002,300,000 leva (fuels, mineral raw materials, and metals 46.9%; machinery and equipment 33.2%; food and consumer goods
9.5%; chemical fertilizers and rubber 5.8%). *Major import sources:* U.S.S.R.
56.1%; East Germany 5.3%; Poland 4.5%; Czechoslovakia 4.1%; West Germany 3.9%; Libya 2.9%; Cuba 1.7%; United States 1.1%.
*Exports* (1985): 13,736,000,000 leva (machinery and equipment 53.5%; fuels,
mineral raw materials, and metals 10.0%; consumer goods 9.7%; chemicals
5.8%). *Major export destinations:* U.S.S.R. 56.5%; East Germany 5.2%;
Libya 4.5%; Czechoslovakia 4.5%; Poland 3.5%; Iraq 3.1%; Romania 2.1%.

## Transport and communications

*Transport.* Railroads (1986): length 2,670 mi, 4,297 km; passenger-km
8,909,000,000[6]; metric ton-km cargo 18,172,000,000[6]. Roads (1985): total
length 23,384 mi, 37,633 km (paved 91%). Vehicles (1985): passenger cars
1,030,090; trucks and buses 587,400. Merchant marine (1986): vessels (100
gross tons and over) 205; total deadweight tonnage 1,989,051. Air transport (1985): passenger-km 3,231,000,000; metric ton-km cargo 43,900,000;
airports (1987) 13.
*Communications.* Daily newspapers (1985): total number 17; total circulation 2,274,000; circulation per 1,000 population 254. Radio (1986): 2,018,-
000 receivers (1 per 4.4 persons). Television (1986): 1,697,200 receivers (1
per 5.3 persons). Telephones (1986): 1,946,000 (1 per 4.6 persons).

## Education and health

| Education (1985–86) | | | | |
|---|---|---|---|---|
| | schools | teachers | students | student/ teacher ratio |
| Primary (age 6–14) | 3,040 } | 71,400 | 1,248,000 | 17.4 |
| Secondary (age 15–17) | 481 } | | | |
| Voc., teacher tr. | 506 | 17,884[7] | 216,000 | ... |
| Higher | 33 | 11,800 | 80,400 | 6.8 |

*Educational attainment* (1983): Percent of employed population having:
postsecondary vocational certificate 15.6%; 4-year college 7.5%. *Literacy*
(1980): total population age 15 and over literate 95.5%.
*Health* (1986): physicians 25,700 (1 per 348 persons); hospital beds 84,300
(1 per 106 persons); infant mortality rate per 1,000 live births 15.4.
*Food* (1981–83): daily per capita caloric intake 3,663 (vegetable products
78%, animal products 22%); (1983) 146% of FAO minimum requirement.

## Military

*Total active duty personnel* (1986): 148,500 (army 70.7%, navy 5.7%, air force
23.6%). *Military expenditure as percent of GNP* (1984): 3.9% (world 5.9%);
per capita expenditure U.S.$166.

[1]Beginning of year. [2]Detail does not add to total given because of rounding. [3]Budget
detail is for 1983. [4]Includes fishing and forestry. [5]Includes other material activities.
[6]1985. [7]1983–84.

# Burkina Faso[1]

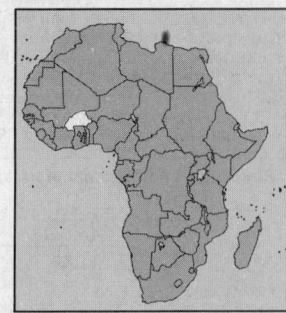

*Official name:* Burkina Faso
(Burkina Faso).
*Form of government:* military
regime[2].
*Head of state and government:*
President.
*Capital:* Ouagadougou.
*Official language:* French.
*Official religion:* none.
*Monetary unit:* 1 CFA franc
(CFAF) = 100 centimes; valuation
(Oct. 5, 1987) 1 U.S.$ = CFAF 306.67;
1 £ = CFAF 498.00.

### Area and population

| Provinces | Capitals | area sq mi | area sq km | population 1985 census |
|---|---|---|---|---|
| Bam | Kongoussi | 1,551 | 4,017 | 164,263 |
| Bazèga | Kombissiri | 2,051 | 5,313 | 306,976 |
| Bougouriba | Diébougou | 2,736 | 7,087 | 221,522 |
| Boulgou | Tenkodogo | 3,488 | 9,033 | 403,358 |
| Boulkiemde | Koudougou | 1,598 | 4,138 | 363,594 |
| Comoé | Banfora | 7,102 | 18,393 | 250,510 |
| Ganzourgou | Zorgho | 1,578 | 4,087 | 196,006 |
| Gnagna | Bogandé | 3,320 | 8,600 | 229,249 |
| Gourma | Fada N'Gourma | 10,275 | 26,613 | 294,123 |
| Houet | Bobo-Dioulasso | 6,360 | 16,472 | 585,031 |
| Kadiogo | Ouagadougou | 451 | 1,169 | 459,138 |
| Kénédougou | Orodara | 3,207 | 8,307 | 139,722 |
| Kossi | Nouna | 5,088 | 13,177 | 330,413 |
| Kouritenga | Koupéla | 628 | 1,627 | 197,027 |
| Mouhoun | Dédougou | 4,032 | 10,442 | 289,213 |
| Nahouri | Pô | 1,484 | 3,843 | 105,273 |
| Namentenga | Boulsa | 2,994 | 7,755 | 198,798 |
| Oubritenga | Ziniaré | 1,812 | 4,693 | 303,229 |
| Oudalan | Gorom Gorom | 3,879 | 10,046 | 105,715 |
| Passoré | Yako | 1,575 | 4,078 | 225,115 |
| Poni | Gaoua | 4,000 | 10,361 | 234,501 |
| Sanguie | Réo | 1,994 | 5,165 | 218,289 |
| Sanmatenga | Kaya | 3,557 | 9,213 | 368,365 |
| Sèno | Dori | 5,202 | 13,473 | 230,043 |
| Sissili | Léo | 5,303 | 13,736 | 246,844 |
| Soum | Djibo | 5,154 | 13,350 | 190,464 |
| Sourou | Tougan | 3,663 | 9,487 | 267,770 |
| Tapoa | Diapaga | 5,707 | 14,780 | 159,121 |
| Yatenga | Ouahigouya | 4,746 | 12,292 | 537,205 |
| Zoundwéogo | Manga | 1,333 | 3,453 | 155,142 |
| TOTAL | | 105,869[3] | 274,200 | 7,967,019 |

## Demography

*Population* (1987): 8,308,000.
*Density* (1987): persons per sq mi 78.5, persons per sq km 30.3.
*Urban–rural* (1985): urban 7.0%; rural 93.0%.
*Sex distribution* (1985): male 48.23%; female 51.77%.
*Age breakdown* (1985): under 15, 44.5%; 15–29, 26.2%; 30–44, 14.4%; 45–59, 9.4%; 60–74, 4.5%; 75 and over, 1.0%.
*Population projection:* (1990) 8,994,000; (2000) 11,719,000.
*Doubling time:* 24 years.
*Ethnic composition* (1983): Mossi 47.9%; Mande 8.8%; Fulani 8.3%; Lobi 6.9%; Bobo 6.8%; Senufo 5.3%; Grosi 5.1%; Gurma 4.8%; Tuareg 3.3%; other 2.8%.
*Religious affiliation* (1980): traditional beliefs 44.8%; Muslim 43.0%; Christian 12.2%, of which Roman Catholic 9.8%, Protestant 2.4%.
*Major cities* (1985): Ouagadougou 442,223; Bobo-Dioulasso 231,162; Koudougou 59,644; Ouahigouya 41,595; Banfora 16,843.

## Vital statistics

*Birth rate* per 1,000 population (1980–85): 47.8 (world avg. 29.0).
*Death rate* per 1,000 population (1980–85): 20.1 (world avg. 11.0).
*Natural increase rate* per 1,000 population (1980–85): 27.7 (world avg. 18.0).
*Total fertility rate* (avg. births per childbearing woman; 1980–85): 6.5.
*Marriage rate* per 1,000 population (1975): 9.4.
*Divorce rate* per 1,000 population (1975): 1.3.
*Life expectancy* at birth (1980–85): male 43.7 years; female 46.8 years.
*Morbidity* (percent of reported cases of illness; 1984): measles 39.6%; malaria 12.4%; tetanus 5.7%; diarrheal diseases 5.3%.

## National economy

*Budget* (1987). Revenue: CFAF 86,000,000,000 (taxes 88.6%, of which indirect 63.1%; direct 22.6%; other 1.1%). *Expenditures:* CFAF 98,600,000,000 (administration 45.0%; debt payment 18.8%; capital equipment 12.6%; material purchases 8.2%).
*Public debt* (external, outstanding; 1985): U.S.$496,300,000.
*Tourism:* receipts from visitors (1984) U.S.$3,000,000; expenditures by nationals abroad (1983) U.S.$32,000,000.
*Production* (metric tons except as noted). Agriculture, forestry, fishing (1985): sorghum 900,000, millet 500,000, sugarcane 340,000, pulses 177,000, corn (maize) 130,000, seed cotton 80,000, peanuts (groundnuts) 77,000, rice 45,000, cassava 44,000, sweet potatoes 43,000, sesame 6,000; livestock (number of live animals) 2,800,000 cattle, 2,600,000 goats, 2,000,000 sheep, 16,000,000 chickens; roundwood 6,691,000 cu m; fish catch 7,000. Mining and quarrying (1985): phosphates 3,000. Manufacturing (1985): flour 25,682; soap 13,456; cotton yarn 392; motorcycles and scooters 12,372 units; footwear 1,317,800 pairs; beer 623,160 hectolitres[4]; soft drinks 122,611 hectolitres[4]. Construction (value added in CFAF; 1983): 7,749,300,000.

*Energy production (consumption):* electricity (kW-hr; 1985) 115,000,000 (115,000,000); coal, none (n.a.); crude petroleum, none (n.a.); petroleum products (metric tons; 1986) none (153,000); natural gas, none (n.a.).
*Gross national product* (1985): U.S.$1,080,000,000 (U.S.$140 per capita).

### Structure of gross domestic product and labour force

| | 1984 in value CFAF '000,000 | 1984 % of total value | 1985 labour force | 1985 % of labour force |
|---|---|---|---|---|
| Agriculture | 157,843.8 | 43.4 | 3,397,518 | 91.8 |
| Mining | 303.8 | 0.1 | | |
| Manufacturing | 50,860.6 | 13.9 | 148,040 | 4.0 |
| Construction | 4,933.7 | 1.4 | | |
| Public utilities | 4,246.2 | 1.2 | | |
| Transp. and commun. | 23,554.0 | 6.5 | | |
| Trade | 42,186.8 | 11.6 | 155,442 | 4.2 |
| Pub. admin., defense Services | } 63,652.4 | 17.5 | | |
| Other | 16,219.3[5] | 4.4[5] | ... | ... |
| TOTAL | 363,800.6 | 100.0 | 3,701,000 | 100.0 |

*Population economically active:* total (1985) 3,701,000; activity rate of total population 47.1% (participation rates: over age 15 85.4%; female 40.9%; unemployed, n.a.).

### Price and earnings indexes (1980 = 100)

| | 1981 | 1982 | 1983 | 1984 | 1985 | 1986 | 1987[6] |
|---|---|---|---|---|---|---|---|
| Consumer price index | 107.6 | 120.5 | 130.6 | 133.4 | 146.3 | 142.5 | 137.5 |
| Hourly earnings index | 100.0 | 126.7 | 126.7 | 126.7 | 126.7 | 126.7 | 126.7 |

*Household income and expenditure.* Average household size (1984) 4.9; average annual income per household CFAF 303,000 (U.S.$640); sources of income: n.a.; expenditure (1985)[7]: food 38.7%; transportation 18.6%; electricity and fuel 13.7%; beverages 9.0%; health 5.2%; housing 5.1%.
*Land use* (1984): forested 25.4%; meadows and pastures 36.5%; agricultural and under permanent cultivation 9.6%; other 28.5%.

## Foreign trade

### Balance of trade (current prices)

| | 1980 | 1981 | 1982 | 1983 | 1984 | 1985 |
|---|---|---|---|---|---|---|
| CFAF '000,000 | −42,910 | −55,030 | −75,340 | −68,100 | −48,050 | −115,086 |
| % of total | 52.9% | 58.0% | 67.5% | 61.1% | 46.7% | 64.9% |

*Imports* (1985): CFAF 146,243,000,000 (machinery and transport equipment 19.6%, of which road transport equipment 9.1%, nonelectrical machinery 6.2%; manufactured goods 17.6%; cereals 15.8%; petroleum products 12.7%; chemicals 10.1%; greases and lubricants 4.6%; dairy products 3.5%; raw materials 2.9%). *Major import sources* (1984): France 26.0%; Côte d'Ivoire 22.4%; U.S. 10.0%; The Netherlands 4.6%; Japan 3.8%; China 3.2%.
*Exports* (1985): CFAF 31,157,000,000 (raw cotton 37.4%; manufactured goods 24.5%; live animals 11.2%; karite nuts 7.0%; vegetable food products 3.1%). *Major export destinations* (1984): Taiwan 25.2%; Côte d'Ivoire 14.8%; France 10.5%; United Kingdom 8.8%; West Germany 8.0%; Japan 7.2%; China 4.7%; Italy 3.6%.

## Transport and communications

*Transport.* Railroads (1984)[8]: length 321 mi, 517 km; passenger-mi 422,-401,000, passenger-km 679,790,000; short ton-mi cargo 321,701,000, metric ton-km cargo 469,675,000. Roads (1985): total length 8,249 mi, 13,276 km (paved 11.1%). Vehicles (1983): passenger cars 21,182; trucks and buses 5,729. Merchant marine: none. Air transport (1985): passenger-mi 153,000,-000, passenger-km 246,000,000; short ton-mi cargo 28,000,000, metric ton-mi cargo 41,000,000; airports (1987) with scheduled flights 2.
*Communications.* Daily newspapers (1982): total number 1; total circulation 1,500; circulation per 1,000 population 0.2. Radio (1986): 311,000 receivers (1 per 26 persons). Television (1986): 41,500 receivers (1 per 196 persons). Telephones (1984): 14,191 (1 per 534 persons).

## Education and health

### Education (1984–85)

| | schools | teachers | students | student/ teacher ratio |
|---|---|---|---|---|
| Primary | 1,037 | 5,354 | 313,520 | 58.6 |
| Secondary | 68 | 1,213 | 41,559 | 26.8 |
| Vocational | 27 | 504 | 4,186 | 8.3 |
| Higher | 1 | 255 | 3,669 | 14.4 |

*Educational attainment,* n.a. *Literacy* (1985): total population age 15 and over literate 509,700 (13.2%); males 392,100 (20.7%); females 119,900 (6.1%).
*Health* (1984): physicians 180 (1 per 42,128 persons); hospital beds 5,580 (1 per 1,359 persons); infant mortality rate per 1,000 live births (1985) 137.0.
*Food* (1981–83): daily per capita caloric intake 2,137 (vegetable products 95%, animal products 5%); (1983) 85% of FAO recommended minimum.

## Military

*Total active duty personnel* (1986): 4,000 (army 97.5%; navy, none; air force 2.5%). *Military expenditure as percent of GNP* (1984): 2.7% (world 5.9%); per capita expenditure U.S.$4.

[1]Known as Upper Volta before Aug. 4, 1984. [2]The functions of the legislative house (National Assembly [57]) and all political parties have been suspended since 1980. [3]Detail does not add to total given because of rounding. [4]1984. [5]Import duties. [6]First semester. [7]Weights of consumer price index components; Ouagadougou only. [8]Passenger-mi and short ton-mi cargo figures are based on traffic between Abidjan, Côte d'Ivoire, and Ouagadougou.

# Burma

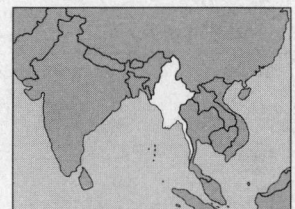

*Official name:* Pyeidaungzu Socialist Thammada Myanma Naingngandaw (Socialist Republic of the Union of Burma).
*Form of government:* single-party people's republic with one legislative house (People's Assembly [489[1]]).
*Chief of state:* President (Chairman).
*Head of government:* Prime Minister.
*Capital:* Rangoon.
*Official language:* Burmese.
*Official religion:* none.
*Monetary unit:* 1 Burmese kyat (K) = 100 pyas; valuation (Oct. 5, 1987) 1 U.S.$ = K 6.70; 1 £ = K 10.89.

### Area and population

| Divisions | Capitals | area sq mi | area sq km | population 1983 census |
|---|---|---|---|---|
| Irrawaddy | Bassein | 13,567 | 35,138 | 4,994,061 |
| Magwe | Magwe | 17,305 | 44,820 | 3,243,166 |
| Mandalay | Mandalay | 14,295 | 37,024 | 4,577,762 |
| Pegu | Pegu | 15,214 | 39,404 | 3,799,791 |
| Rangoon | Rangoon | 3,927 | 10,171 | 3,965,916 |
| Sagaing | Sagaing | 36,535 | 94,625 | 3,862,172 |
| Tenasserim | Tavoy | 16,735 | 43,343 | 917,247 |
| **States** | | | | |
| Chin | Falam | 13,907 | 36,019 | 368,949 |
| Kachin | Myitkyinä | 34,379 | 89,041 | 904,794 |
| Karen | Pa-an | 11,731 | 30,383 | 1,055,359 |
| Kayah | Loi-kaw | 4,530 | 11,733 | 168,429 |
| Mon | Moulmein | 4,748 | 12,297 | 1,680,157 |
| Rakhine (Arakan) | Sittwe (Akyab) | 14,200 | 36,778 | 2,045,559 |
| Shan | Taunggyi | 60,155 | 155,801 | 3,716,841 |
| TOTAL | | 261,228 | 676,577 | 35,307,913[2] |

## Demography

*Population* (1987): 39,218,000.
*Density* (1987): persons per sq mi 150.1, persons per sq km 58.0.
*Urban–rural* (1985): urban 23.9%; rural 76.1%.
*Sex distribution* (1985): male 50.10%; female 49.90%.
*Age breakdown* (1985): under 15, 41.2%; 15–29, 27.2%; 30–44, 15.3%; 45–59, 10.3%; 60–74, 5.0%; 75 and over, 1.0%.
*Population projection:* (1990) 41,114,000; (2000) 48,553,000.
*Doubling time:* 36 years.
*Ethnic composition* (1983): Burman 69.0%; Shan 8.5%; Karen 6.2%; Rakhine 4.5%; Mon 2.4%; Chin 2.2%; Kachin 1.4%; other 5.8%.
*Religious affiliation* (1983): Buddhist 89.4%; Christian 4.9%; Muslim 3.8%; tribal religions 1.1%; Hindu 0.5%; other 0.3%.
*Major cities* (1983): Rangoon 2,458,712; Mandalay 532,895; Moulmein 219,991; Pegu 150,447; Bassein 144,092.

## Vital statistics

*Birth rate* per 1,000 population (1986): 32.9 (world avg. 26.0).
*Death rate* per 1,000 population (1986): 13.4 (world avg. 9.9).
*Natural increase rate* per 1,000 population (1986): 19.5 (world avg. 16.1).
*Total fertility rate* (avg. births per childbearing woman; 1986): 4.4.
*Marriage rate* per 1,000 population, n.a.
*Divorce rate* per 1,000 population, n.a.
*Life expectancy* at birth (1986): male 51.6 years; female 54.6 years.
*Major causes of death* per 100,000 population (1978): pneumonia 16.1; heart diseases 10.5; enteritis and other diarrheal diseases 10.0; tuberculosis 9.4; malignant neoplasms (cancers) 6.5; cerebrovascular disease 4.1; malaria 3.5.

## National economy

*Budget* (1984–85). Revenue: K 8,145,000,000 (taxes on goods and services 38.5%; property income 25.4%; import duties 14.2%; fees and charges 13.1%; grants 5.0%; corporate and individual income taxes 3.8%). Expenditures: K 8,509,000,000 (agriculture, forestry, and fishing 25.4%; defense 18.5%; general public services 13.3%; education 11.7%; health 7.3%; social security and welfare 6.1%).
*Public debt* (external, outstanding; 1984): U.S.$2,219,300,000.
*Tourism* (1985): receipts from visitors U.S.$12,000,000; expenditures by nationals abroad U.S.$5,000,000.
*Production* (metric tons except as noted). Agriculture, forestry, fishing (1985): rice 15,400,000, sugarcane 3,767,000, vegetables and melons 2,060,000, fruits 1,088,000, peanuts (groundnuts) 667,000, pulses 626,000 (of which dry beans 330,000, chick peas 215,000), plantains 438,000, corn (maize) 403,000, roots and tubers 262,000 (of which potatoes 173,000), sesame seed 232,000, wheat 206,000, seed cotton 125,000, millet 88,000, tobacco leaves 70,000, sunflower seed 65,000, jute 52,000, natural rubber 16,000; livestock (number of live animals) 9,550,000 cattle, 2,750,000 pigs, 2,100,000 water buffalo, 1,100,000 goats, 34,000,000 chickens; roundwood 18,876,000 cu m; fish catch 643,750, of which marine fishing areas 496,950. Mining and quarrying (by metal content except as noted; 1985): lead 21,935; copper 16,700; zinc 4,353; tin 622; tungsten 171; jadeite 12,079 kg; silver 568,000 troy oz. Manufacturing (1984–85): cement 328,000; fertilizer 150,000[3]; sugar 62,000; soap 48,200; cotton yarn 14,100; cigarettes 2,760,000,000 units. Construction[4] (units; 1976): residential 73; nonresidential 50. Energy production (consumption): electricity (kW-hr; 1985) 1,756,000,000 (1,756,000,000); coal (metric tons; 1985) 78,000 (258,000); crude petroleum (bar-

rels; 1985) 11,618,000 (10,343,000); petroleum products (metric tons; 1985) 1,115,000 (1,116,000); natural gas (cu m; 1985) 979,960,000 (979,960,000).
*Gross national product* (1985): U.S.$7,080,000,000 (U.S.$190 per capita).

### Structure of gross domestic product and labour force

| | 1985–86 in value K'000,000 | 1985–86 % of total value | 1984–85 labour force | 1984–85 % of labour force |
|---|---|---|---|---|
| Agriculture | 27,594 | 47.8 | 9,772,000 | 66.1 |
| Mining | 661 | 1.2 | 85,000 | 0.6 |
| Manufacturing | 5,735 | 9.9 | 1,234,000 | 8.3 |
| Construction | 968 | 1.7 | 240,000 | 1.6 |
| Public utilities | 317[5] | 0.5[5] | 16,000 | 0.1 |
| Transp. and commun. | 2,191 | 3.8 | 488,000 | 3.3 |
| Trade | 14,009 | 24.3 | 1,444,000 | 9.8 |
| Finance, public admin., services | 6,258[5] | 10.8[5] | 885,000 | 6.0 |
| Other | | | 628,000 | 4.2 |
| TOTAL | 57,733 | 100.0 | 14,792,000 | 100.0 |

*Population economically active* (1983–84): total 15,900,000; activity rate of total population 43.4% (participation rates: over age 15 [1983] 56.0%; female [1983] 36.0%; unemployed 4.6%).

### Price and earnings indexes (1980 = 100)

| | 1981 | 1982 | 1983 | 1984 | 1985 | 1986 | 1987[6] |
|---|---|---|---|---|---|---|---|
| Consumer price index | 100.3 | 105.6 | 111.6 | 117.0 | 125.0 | 136.5 | 166.7 |
| Monthly earnings index[7] | 101.9 | 105.1 | 111.7 | ... | ... | ... | ... |

*Household income and expenditure.* Average household size (1983) 5.2; average annual income per household: n.a.; sources of income: n.a.; expenditure (1976)[8]: food and beverages 75.5%, fuel and power 7.5%, clothing 3.7%, household rent and utilities 3.4%, charities and ceremonials 1.9%, medical care 1.0%, education 1.0%, travel 0.8%.
*Land use* (1984): forested 48.9%; meadows and pastures 0.5%; agricultural and under permanent cultivation 15.3%; other 35.3%.

## Foreign trade[9]

### Balance of trade (current prices)

| | 1981 | 1982 | 1983 | 1984 | 1985 | 1986 |
|---|---|---|---|---|---|---|
| K '000,000 | −1,984.3 | +172.9 | +1,084.1 | +1,338.1 | +393.2 | +160.0 |
| % of total | 22.3% | 2.9% | 21.7% | 26.7% | 8.3% | 3.8% |

*Imports* (1983–84): K 5,197,300,000 (nonelectrical machinery and transport equipment 21.1%; base metals and manufactures 8.8%; chemicals, fertilizers, and pharmaceuticals 5.4%; electrical machinery 3.9%). *Major import sources* (1984): Japan 37.3%; West Germany 13.3%; Singapore 9.9%; United Kingdom 4.5%; United States 3.3%.
*Exports* (1983–84): K 3,419,500,000 (rice and rice products 40.8%; teak 24.6%; base metals and ores 8.8%; rubber 1.8%). *Major export destinations* (1984): Singapore 17.9%; Indonesia 5.5%; United States 4.0%; The Netherlands 2.9%.

## Transport and communications

*Transport.* Railroads (1986): route length 1,949 mi, 3,137 km; passenger-mi 2,356,000,000, passenger-km 3,792,000,000; short ton-mi cargo 395,000,000, metric ton-km cargo 576,000,000. Roads (1984–85): total length 14,333 mi, 23,067 km (paved 17%). Vehicles (1980): passenger cars 43,300; trucks and buses 44,700. Merchant marine (1986): vessels (100 gross tons and over) 106; total deadweight tonnage 150,880. Air transport (1985): passenger-mi 142,000,000, passenger-km 229,000,000; short ton-mi cargo 16,000,000, metric ton-km cargo 23,000,000; airports (1987) with scheduled flights 21.
*Communications.* Daily newspapers (1986): total number 6; total circulation 509,000; circulation per 1,000 population 14. Radio (1986): total receivers 800,000 (1 per 49 persons). Television (1986): total receivers 64,000 (1 per 612 persons). Telephones (1984–85): 52,604 (1 per 710 persons).

## Education and health

### Education (1984–85)

| | schools | teachers | students | student/teacher ratio |
|---|---|---|---|---|
| Primary (age 5–9) | 27,499 | 104,754 | 4,855,963 | 46.4 |
| Secondary (age 10–15) | 2,238 | 41,668 | 1,251,482 | 30.0 |
| Voc., teacher tr. | 74 | 1,036 | 14,570 | 14.1 |
| Higher | 35 | 5,524 | 174,279 | 31.5 |

*Educational attainment* (1983). Percent of population age 25 and over having: no formal schooling 55.8%; primary education 39.4%; secondary 4.6%; religious 0.1%; postsecondary 0.1%. *Literacy* (1983): total population age 15 and over literate 16,472,494 (78.5%); males literate 8,816,031 (85.8%); females literate 7,656,463 (71.6%).
*Health* (1984–85): physicians 9,481 (1 per 3,937 persons); hospital beds 25,599 (1 per 1,458 persons); infant mortality rate per 1,000 live births (1986) 104.
*Food* (1981–83): daily per capita caloric intake 2,464 (vegetable products 95%, animal products 5%); (1983) 114% of FAO recommended minimum.

## Military

*Total active duty personnel* (1987): 186,000 (army 91.4%, navy 3.8%, air force 4.8%). *Military expenditure as percent of GNP* (1984): 2.9% (world 5.9%); per capita expenditure U.S.$5.

[1]Includes 14 nonelected members. [2]Includes 7,710 persons not distributed by area. [3]1983–84. [4]Government building activity only. [5]Gas and water are included with finance, public admin., services, and other. [6]April. [7]Males in manufacturing only. [8]Based on five rural townships. [9]Import figures are f.o.b. in balance of trade and c.i.f. in commodities and trading partners.

# Burundi

*Official name:* Republika y'u Burundi (Rundi); République du Burundi (French) (Republic of Burundi).
*Form of government:* unitary single-party republic with one legislative house (National Assembly [100])[1].
*Head of state and government:* President.
*Capital:* Bujumbura.
*Official languages:* Rundi; French.
*Official religion:* none.
*Monetary unit:* 1 Burundi franc (FBu) = 100 centimes; valuation (Oct. 5, 1987) 1 U.S.$ = FBu 126.19; 1 £ = FBu 204.92.

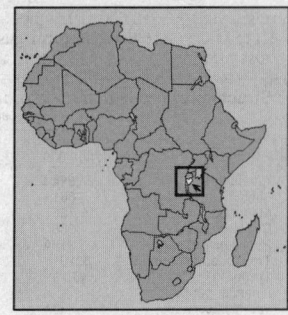

### Area and population

| Provinces | Capitals | area sq mi | area sq km | population 1987 estimate[2] |
|---|---|---|---|---|
| Bubanza | Bubanza | 422 | 1,093 | 200,420 |
| Bujumbura | Bujumbura | 515 | 1,334 | 584,812 |
| Bururi | Bururi | 971 | 2,515 | 374,660 |
| Cankuzo | Cankuzo | 749 | 1,940 | 129,275 |
| Cibitoke | Cibitoke | 633 | 1,639 | 235,279 |
| Gitega | Gitega | 768 | 1,989 | 561,950 |
| Karuzi | Karuzi | 563 | 1,459 | 258,811 |
| Kayanza | Kayanza | 475 | 1,229 | 446,219 |
| Kirundo | Kirundo | 661 | 1,711 | 359,485 |
| Makamba | Makamba | 761 | 1,972 | 155,676 |
| Muramvya | Muramvya | 591 | 1,530 | 437,846 |
| Muyinga | Muyinga | 705 | 1,825 | 315,008 |
| Ngozi | Ngozi | 567 | 1,468 | 476,408 |
| Rutana | Rutana | 733 | 1,898 | 179,302 |
| Ruyigi | Ruyigi | 913 | 2,365 | 206,933 |
| TOTAL LAND AREA | | 10,026[3] | 25,967 | 4,922,084 |
| INLAND WATER | | 721 | 1,867 | |
| TOTAL AREA | | 10,747 | 27,834 | |

## Demography

*Population* (1987): 4,989,000.
*Density*[4] (1987): persons per sq mi 497.6, persons per sq km 192.1.
*Urban-rural* (1985): urban 8.2%; rural 91.8%.
*Sex distribution* (1985): male 48.83%; female 51.17%.
*Age breakdown* (1985): under 15, 44.8%; 15–29, 24.9%; 30–44, 15.5%; 45–59, 9.5%; 60–74, 4.5%; 75 and over, 0.8%.
*Population projection:* (1990) 5,425,000; (2000) 7,170,000.
*Doubling time:* 25 years.
*Ethnic composition* (1983): Rundi 97.3%, of which Hutu 82.7%, Tutsi 13.6%; Twa Pygmy 1.0%; other 2.7%.
*Religious affiliation* (1980): Christian 85.5%, of which Roman Catholic 78.3%, Protestant 7.1%; traditional beliefs 13.5%; Muslim 0.9%; other 0.1%.
*Major cities* (1986): Bujumbura 272,600; Gitega 95,300; Ngozi 20,000[5].

## Vital statistics

*Birth rate* per 1,000 population (1980–85): 47.2 (world avg. 29.0).
*Death rate* per 1,000 population (1980–85): 19.0 (world avg. 11.0).
*Natural increase rate* per 1,000 population (1980–85): 28.2 (world avg. 18.0).
*Total fertility rate* (avg. births per childbearing woman; 1980–85): 6.4.
*Marriage rate* per 1,000 population: n.a.
*Divorce rate* per 1,000 population: n.a.
*Life expectancy* at birth (1980–85): male 44.9 years; female 48.1 years.
*Major causes of death* per 100,000 population (1983)[6]: measles 45.1; bacillary dysentery 26.2; other diarrheal diseases 7.9; malaria 7.4; pulmonary tuberculosis 2.6.

## National economy

*Budget* (1986). Revenue: FBu 20,000,000,000 (1984; customs duties 31.7%, income tax 25.9%, other indirect taxes 22.6%, excise duties 14.9%, administrative receipts 4.3%, property tax 0.6%). Expenditures: FBu 20,000,000,000 (1984; goods and services 57.4%, subsidies and transfers 17.6%, loans 0.5%, other 24.5%).
*Public debt* (external, outstanding; 1985): U.S.$415,300,000.
*Tourism:* receipts from visitors (1985) U.S.$31,000,000; expenditures by nationals abroad (1983) U.S.$18,000,000.
*Production* (metric tons except as noted). Agriculture, forestry, fishing (1985): bananas 1,250,000, sweet potatoes 520,000, cassava 520,000, pulses 322,000, sorghum 240,000, corn (maize) 150,000, yams and taros 112,000, peanuts (groundnuts) 80,000, coffee 36,000, millet 35,000, rice 20,000, wheat 6,000, sugarcane 6,000, palm kernels 2,300, cotton lint 2,000; livestock (number of live animals) 798,000 goats, 415,000 cattle, 369,000 sheep, 3,000,000 chickens; roundwood 3,635,000 cu m; fish catch 14,900. Mining and quarrying (1984): peat 14,000; kaolin clay 1,990; lime 42; gold 1,115 troy oz. Manufacturing (1983): beer 89,486,600 bottles; carbonated beverages 1,952,400 cases; cigarettes 293,950,000 units; blankets 358,800 units; footwear 300,-900 pairs. Construction: n.a. Energy production (consumption): electricity (kW-hr; 1985) 2,000,000 (152,000,000); coal, none (n.a.); crude petroleum, none (n.a.); petroleum products (metric tons; 1985) none (47,000); natural gas, none (n.a.); peat (metric tons; 1985) 10,000 (10,000).
*Land use* (1984): forested 2.5%; meadows and pastures 35.5%; agricultural and under permanent cultivation 51.0%; other 11.0%.

*Gross national product* (at current market prices; 1985): U.S.$1,110,000,000 (U.S.$240 per capita).

### Structure of gross domestic product and labour force

| | 1986 in value FBu '000,000[7] | 1986 % of total value | 1979 labour force | 1979 % of labour force |
|---|---|---|---|---|
| Agriculture | 19,761.2 | 63.1 | 2,246,200 | 93.1 |
| Mining | 142.6 | 0.5 | 1,400 | 0.1 |
| Manufacturing | 3,200.4 | 10.2 | 36,700 | 1.5 |
| Construction | 1,675.0 | 5.3 | 14,700 | 0.6 |
| Public utilities | ... | ... | 1,700 | 0.1 |
| Transportation and communication | 774.4 | 2.5 | 6,400 | 0.2 |
| Trade | 2,217.0 | 7.1 | 20,900 | 0.9 |
| Finance | ... | ... | 1,300 | 0.1 |
| Pub. admin., defense | 3,129.0 | 10.0 | 80,700 | 3.3 |
| Services | 418.1 | 1.3 | | |
| Other | ... | ... | 3,100 | 0.1 |
| TOTAL | 31,317.7 | 100.0 | 2,413,100 | 100.0 |

*Population economically active* (1984): total 2,752,070; activity rate of total population 60.9% (participation rates: ages 15–64 [1979] 94.4%; female 52.6%; unemployed, n.a.).

### Price and earnings indexes (1980 = 100)

| | 1981 | 1982 | 1983 | 1984 | 1985 | 1986 | Sept. 1987 |
|---|---|---|---|---|---|---|---|
| Consumer price index | 112.0 | 118.4 | 128.3 | 146.7 | 152.1 | 154.9 | 168.3 |
| Monthly earnings index[8] | 110.0 | 103.0 | 143.4 | 170.0 | ... | ... | ... |

*Household income and expenditure.* Average household size (1980) 4.9; income per household: n.a.; sources of income: n.a.; expenditure[9]: food 59.6%, clothing and footwear 11.1%, furniture and household goods 6.0%, energy and water 5.8%, housing 4.4%, other 13.1%.

## Foreign trade[10]

### Balance of trade (current prices)

| | 1981 | 1982 | 1983 | 1984 | 1985 | 1986 |
|---|---|---|---|---|---|---|
| FBu '000,000 | −5,873 | −8,864 | −7,354 | −7,145 | −6,324 | −6,893 |
| % of total | 30.3% | 35.9% | 32.9% | 22.5% | 19.0% | 20.6% |

*Imports* (1984): FBu 22,383,000,000 (intermediate goods 42.8%, consumer goods 31.8%, capital goods 25.4%). *Major import sources:* Belgium–Luxembourg 14.7%; France 14.0%; West Germany 8.8%; United States 5.5%; Japan 5.3%; Italy 4.0%.
*Exports* (1984): FBu 11,828,100,000 (coffee 83.6%; tea 7.3%; raw cotton 0.7%; animal hides and skins 0.7%). *Major export destinations:* West Germany 33.5%; Italy 2.9%; Belgium–Luxembourg 2.8%; United Kingdom 2.3%; United States 1.6%; The Netherlands 0.4%; France 0.3%.

## Transport and communications

*Transport.* Railroads: none. Roads (1981): total length 3,196 mi, 5,144 km (paved 7%). Vehicles (1984): passenger cars 7,533; trucks and other vehicles 6,188. Merchant marine (1979): vessels (100 gross tons and over) 1; total gross tonnage 385. Air transport (1984): passenger arrivals 19,050, departures 19,091; cargo loaded 3,528 short tons (3,201 metric tons), unloaded 5,766 short tons (5,231 metric tons); airports (1987) with scheduled flights 1.
*Communications.* Daily newspapers (1986): total number 1; total circulation 20,000; circulation per 1,000 population 4.1. Radio (1986): total number of receivers 230,000 (1 per 21 persons). Television (1986): total number of receivers 4,000 (1 per 1,207 persons). Telephones (1983): 6,033 (1 per 750 persons).

## Education and health

### Education (1985–86)

| | schools | teachers | students | student/teacher ratio |
|---|---|---|---|---|
| Primary (age 6–11) | 1,023 | 7,245 | 387,710 | 53.5 |
| Secondary (age 12–18) | 62 | 795 | 13,037 | 16.4 |
| Voc., teacher tr. | 47 | 1,064 | 12,902 | 12.1 |
| Higher | 8 | 468 | 2,783 | 5.9 |

*Educational attainment,* n.a. *Literacy* (1982): total population age 10 and over literate 991,600 (33.8%); males literate 601,500 (42.8%); females literate 390,100 (25.7%).
*Health* (1983): physicians 216 (1 per 20,942 persons); hospital beds 5,709 (1 per 792 persons); infant mortality rate per 1,000 live births (1980–85) 124.
*Food* (1981–83): daily per capita caloric intake 2,394 (vegetable products 98%, animal products 2%); (1983) 102% of FAO recommended minimum requirement.

## Military

*Total active duty personnel* (1986): 5,700 (army 96.5%, navy 0.9%, air force 2.6%). *Military expenditure as percent of GNP* (1984): 3.5% (world 5.9%); per capita expenditure U.S.$8.

[1]Constitution suspended on Sept. 3, 1987. [2]January 1. [3]Detail does not add to total given because of rounding. [4]Based on land area. [5]1982. [6]Data shown is for four provinces only. [7]At prices of 1970. [8]Nonagricultural activities in Bujumbura only; includes family allowances. [9]Weights of consumer price index components. [10]Import figures are f.o.b. in balance of trade and c.i.f. in commodities and trading partners.

# Cameroon

*Official name:* République du Cameroun (French); Republic of Cameroon (English).
*Form of government:* republic with one legislative house (National Assembly [120]).
*Head of state and government:* President.
*Capital:* Yaoundé.
*Official languages:* French; English.
*Official religion:* none.
*Monetary unit:* 1 CFA franc (CFAF) = 100 centimes; valuation (Oct. 5, 1987) 1 U.S.$ = CFAF 306.67; 1 £ = CFAF 498.00.

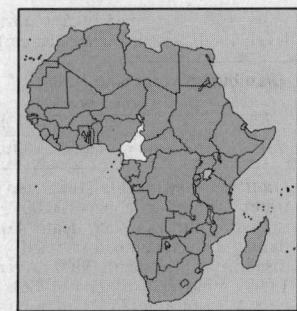

### Area and population

| Provinces | Capitals | area sq mi | area sq km | population 1984 estimate |
|---|---|---|---|---|
| Adamaoua | Ngaoundéré | 23,979 | 62,105 | 355,800 |
| Centre | Yaoundé | 26,655 | 69,035 | 1,764,400 |
| Est | Bertoua | 42,086 | 109,002 | 420,000 |
| Extrême-Nord | Maroua | 12,477 | 32,316 | 1,400,000 |
| Littoral | Douala | 7,810 | 20,229 | 1,829,900 |
| Nord | Garoua | 26,134 | 67,686 | 508,200 |
| Nord-Ouest | Bamenda | 6,722 | 17,409 | 1,009,100 |
| Ouest | Bafoussam | 5,360 | 13,883 | 1,197,700 |
| Sud | Ebolowa | 18,200 | 47,137 | 356,400 |
| Sud-Ouest | Buea | 9,540 | 24,709 | 700,900 |
| LAND AREA | | 178,963 | 463,511 | 9,542,400 |
| INLAND WATER | | 751 | 1,947 | |
| TOTAL AREA | | 179,714 | 465,458 | |

## Demography

*Population* (1987): 10,759,000.
*Density* (1986)[1]: persons per sq mi 60.1, persons per sq km 23.2.
*Urban–rural* (1985): urban 42.4%; rural 57.6%.
*Sex distribution* (1985): male 49.26%; female 50.74%.
*Age breakdown* (1984): under 15, 44.6%; 15–29, 25.2%; 30–44, 15.6%; 45–59, 9.0%; 60 and over, 5.6%.
*Population projection:* (1990) 11,757,000; (2000) 15,801,000.
*Doubling time:* 26 years.
*Ethnic composition* (1983): Fang 19.6%; Bamileke and Bamum 18.5%; Duala, Luanda, and Basa 14.7%; Fulani 9.6%; Tikar 7.4%; Mandara 5.7%; Maka 4.9%; Chamba 2.4%; Mbum 1.3%; Hausa 1.2%; French 0.2%; other 14.5%.
*Religious affiliation* (1980): Roman Catholic 35%; Protestant 18%; animist 25%; Muslim 22%.
*Major cities* (1985): Douala 852,700; Yaoundé 583,500; Nkongsamba 105,200; Maroua 100,200; Garoua 96,200.

## Vital statistics

*Birth rate* per 1,000 population (1980–85): 42.9 (world avg. 29.0).
*Death rate* per 1,000 population (1980–85): 15.8 (world avg. 11.0).
*Natural increase rate* per 1,000 population (1980–85): 27.1 (world avg. 18.0).
*Total fertility rate* (avg. births per childbearing woman; 1980–85): 5.8.
*Life expectancy* at birth (1980–85): male 49.2 years; female 52.6 years.
*Major causes of death* per 100,000 population: n.a.; however, major health problems include measles, malaria, tuberculosis of respiratory system, anemias, meningitis, intestinal obstruction and hernia, avitaminoses and other nutritional deficiency diseases.

## National economy

*Budget* (1987–88). Revenue: CFAF 650,000,000,000[2] (direct and assimilated taxes 49.5%; customs duties and taxes 26.9%; receipts for services 8.6%; indirect taxes 8.1%). Expenditures: CFAF 650,000,000,000 (current expenditure 61.5%, of which education 10.3%, defense 6.9%, health 3.9%, agriculture 2.6%).
*Public debt* (external, outstanding; 1986): U.S.$2,268,900,000.
*Gross national product* (1985): U.S.$8,300,000,000 (U.S.$810 per capita).

### Structure of gross domestic product and labour force

| | 1983–84 in value CFAF '000,000,000 | 1983–84 % of total value | 1982 labour force | 1982 % of labour force |
|---|---|---|---|---|
| Agriculture | 702.0 | 22.0 | 2,594,800 | 73.2 |
| Mining | 520.5 | 16.3 | 1,580 | 0.1 |
| Manufacturing | 358.5 | 11.2 | 159,560 | 4.5 |
| Construction | 192.6 | 6.0 | 62,860 | 1.8 |
| Public utilities | 35.2 | 1.1 | 3,230 | 0.1 |
| Transp. and commun. | 147.3 | 4.6 | 47,400 | 1.3 |
| Trade | 414.9 | 13.0 | } 149,200 | 4.2 |
| Finance | 396.8 | 12.4 | | |
| Public admin., defense | 212.8 | 6.7 | | |
| Services | 79.4 | 2.5 | } 524,370 | 14.8 |
| Other | 135.0[3] | 4.2[3] | | |
| TOTAL | 3,195.0 | 100.0 | 3,543,000 | 100.0 |

*Household income and expenditure.* Average household size (1980) 5.2; average annual income per household[4] (1983): U.S.$420; sources of income: n.a.; expenditure[4] (1983): food 33.6%, clothing and footwear 16.3%, housing 14.6%, transportation and communication 10.5%, recreation 5.1%, health 5.0%.

*Population economically active* (1985): total 3,958,000; activity rate of total population 40.1% (participation rates: ages 15–64, 59.5%; female 20.5%; unemployed, n.a.).

### Price index (1980 = 100)

| | 1979 | 1980 | 1981 | 1982 | 1983 | 1984 | 1985 |
|---|---|---|---|---|---|---|---|
| Consumer price index | 91.3 | 100.0 | 110.7 | 125.4 | 146.3 | 162.9 | 165.0 |
| Earnings index | ... | ... | ... | ... | ... | ... | ... |

*Production* (metric tons except as noted). Agriculture, forestry, fishing (1985): sugarcane 1,200,000, plantains 980,000, cassava 670,000, corn (maize) 530,000, millet 440,000, vegetables and melons 420,000, yams 380,000, coffee 370,000, potatoes 180,000, peanuts (groundnuts) 140,000, sweet potatoes 140,000, cocoa 115,000, dry beans 110,000, palm oil 90,000, rice 90,000, bananas 67,000, palm kernels 50,000; livestock (number of live animals) 3,642,000 cattle, 1,930,000 goats, 1,900,000 sheep, 800,000 pigs; roundwood 10,752,000 cu m; fish catch 50,000. Mining and quarrying (1985): marble 504,000; aluminum 86,296; pozzolana 95,700; limestone 78,800; tin ore and concentrate 13.0. Manufacturing (1983–84): cement 645,850; palm oil 64,500; sugar 58,655; rubber 16,233; fish products 8,331; cigarettes 2,795; sawnwood 463,497 cu m; beer 3,577,900 hectolitres. Construction (1983): residential 230,400 sq m; nonresidential 51,100 sq m. Energy production (consumption): electricity (kW-hr; 1985) 2,237,000,000 (2,237,000,000); coal (metric tons; 1985) 1,000 (2,000); petroleum (barrels; 1985) 48,310,000 (24,677,000); petroleum products (metric tons; 1985) 3,022,000 (2,856,000); natural gas, none (n.a.).
*Land use* (1984): forested 53.7%; meadows and pastures 17.7%; agricultural and under permanent cultivation 14.8%; other 13.8%.
*Tourism:* receipts from visitors (1985) U.S.$69,000,000; expenditures by nationals abroad (1983) U.S.$70,000,000.

### Foreign trade

### Balance of trade (current prices)

| | 1980 | 1981 | 1982 | 1983 | 1984 | 1985 |
|---|---|---|---|---|---|---|
| CFAF '000,000,000 | −47.0 | −89.3 | −65.7 | −94.8 | −44.2 | −140.8 |
| % of total | 7.5% | 13.0% | 9.2% | 11.3% | 4.8% | 17.9% |

*Imports* (1984): CFAF 484,646,000,000 (machinery and transport equipment 34.3%, of which road transport equipment and parts 10.0%, drilling equipment 6.1%; chemical and pharmaceutical products 6.7%; textile yarn 6.6%; iron and steel 5.0%; cement 1.4%). *Major import sources:* France 42.8%; United States 10.2%; Japan 7.1%; West Germany 6.7%; Italy 4.6%; United Kingdom 3.5%; Belgium–Luxembourg 3.0%; The Netherlands 1.7%.
*Exports* (1984): CFAF 440,470,000,000 (cacao 22.8%; crude petroleum 21.6%; coffee 21.2%; aluminum and aluminum products 8.0%; sawnwood and logs 4.2%; cotton yarn and fabrics 3.2%; cocoa pulp and butter 3.2%; rubber 1.6%; bananas 1.5%). *Major export destinations:* France 33.3%; The Netherlands 24.9%; United States 12.4%; Belgium–Luxembourg 6.7%; Italy 6.3%; West Germany 6.1%; Japan 0.9%; United Kingdom 0.8%.

### Transport and communications

*Transport.* Railroads (1986): route length 729 mi, 1,173 km; passenger-mi 268,000,000, passenger-km 432,000,000; short ton-mi cargo 518,000,000, metric ton-km cargo 756,000,000. Roads (1985): total length 40,330 mi, 64,905 km (paved 5%). Vehicles (1985): passenger cars 72,449; trucks and buses 41,301. Merchant marine (1986): vessels (100 gross tons and over) 49; total deadweight tonnage 88,679. Air transport (1985): passenger-mi 360,000,000, passenger-km 580,000,000; short ton-mi cargo 76,000,000, metric ton-km cargo 111,000,000; airports (1987) with scheduled flights 10.
*Communications.* Daily newspapers (1986): 1; total circulation 66,000; circulation per 1,000 population 6.3. Radio (1986): total number of receivers 800,000 (1 per 12.0 persons). Television (1986): total number of receivers 2,000 (1 per 5,223 persons). Telephones (1984): 49,180 (1 per 201 persons).

### Education and health

### Education (1984–85)

| | schools[5] | teachers | students | student/ teacher ratio |
|---|---|---|---|---|
| Primary (age 6–14) | 5,582 | 32,082 | 1,638,569 | 51.1 |
| Secondary (age 15–24) | 365 | 8,381 | 238,075 | 28.4 |
| Voc., teacher tr. | 199 | 3,239 | 77,555 | 23.9 |
| Higher[6] | 1 | 572 | 13,753 | 24.0 |

*Educational attainment* (1976). Percent of population age 15 and over having: no schooling 51.1%; primary education 41.7%; some postprimary 0.2%; secondary 5.7%; some postsecondary 0.3%; higher 0.2%; other 0.8%.
*Literacy* (1980): total population age 15 and over literate 2,344,100 (55.2%); males literate 1,453,200 (70.2%); females literate 890,900 (41.0%).
*Health:* physicians (1982) 604 (1 per 14,800 persons); hospital beds (1984–85) 26,832 (1 per 377 persons); infant mortality rate per 1,000 births (1980–85) 103.0.
*Food* (1981–83): daily per capita caloric intake 2,106 (vegetable products 95%, animal products 5%); (1983) 88% of FAO recommended minimum.

### Military

*Total active duty personnel* (1986): 7,300 (army 90.4%, navy 4.8%, air force 4.8%). *Military expenditure as percent of GNP* (1984): 1.9% (world 5.9%); per capita expenditure U.S.$10.

[1]Based on land area. [2]Revenue breakdown is for 1982–83. [3]Includes import duties less imputed bank service charges. [4]Capital city only. [5]1983–84. [6]University of Yaoundé only.

# Canada

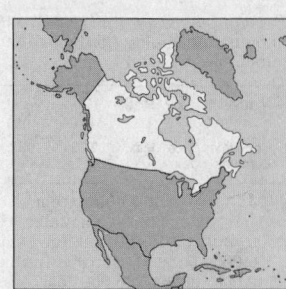

*Official name:* Canada.
*Form of government:* federal multiparty parliamentary state with two legislative houses (Senate [104]; House of Commons [282]).
*Chief of state:* British Monarch represented by governor-general.
*Head of government:* Prime Minister.
*Capital:* Ottawa.
*Official languages:* English; French.
*Official religion:* none.
*Monetary unit:* 1 Canadian dollar (Can$) = 100 cents; valuation (Oct. 5, 1987) 1 U.S.$ = Can$1.31; 1 £ = Can$2.13.

### Area and population

| Provinces | Capitals | area sq mi | area sq km | population 1986 census |
|---|---|---|---|---|
| Alberta | Edmonton | 248,800 | 644,390 | 2,375,278 |
| British Columbia | Victoria | 358,971 | 929,730 | 2,889,207 |
| Manitoba | Winnipeg | 211,723 | 548,360 | 1,071,232 |
| New Brunswick | Fredericton | 27,834 | 72,090 | 710,422 |
| Newfoundland | Saint John's | 143,510 | 371,690 | 568,349 |
| Nova Scotia | Halifax | 20,402 | 52,840 | 873,119 |
| Ontario | Toronto | 344,090 | 891,190 | 9,113,515 |
| Prince Edward Island | Charlottetown | 2,185 | 5,660 | 126,646 |
| Quebec | Quebec | 523,859 | 1,356,790 | 6,540,276 |
| Saskatchewan | Regina | 220,348 | 570,700 | 1,010,198 |
| **Territories** | | | | |
| Northwest Territories | Yellowknife | 1,271,442 | 3,293,020 | 52,238 |
| Yukon Territory | Whitehorse | 184,931 | 478,970 | 23,504 |
| TOTAL LAND AREA | | 3,558,096 | 9,215,430 | 25,354,064 |
| INLAND WATER | | 291,579 | 755,180 | |
| TOTAL AREA | | 3,849,675 | 9,970,610 | |

## Demography

*Population* (1987): 25,857,000.
*Density*[1] (1987): persons per sq mi 7.3, persons per sq km 2.8.
*Urban-rural* (1985): urban 75.9%; rural 24.1%.
*Sex distribution* (1985): male 49.45%; female 50.55%.
*Age breakdown* (1985): under 15, 21.5%; 15–29, 26.5%; 30–44, 22.5%; 45–59, 14.7%; 60–74, 10.7%; 75 and over, 4.1%.
*Population projection:* (1990) 26,826,000; (2000) 29,028,000.
*Doubling time:* 88 years.
*Ethnic origin* (1981): British 40.2%; French 26.7%; German 4.1%; Italian 3.1%; Ukrainian 2.2%; Dutch 1.7%; other European 8.5%; Asiatic 2.1%; Amerindian and Inuktitut (Eskimo) 1.7%; multiple origin and other 9.7%.
*Religious affiliation* (1981): Roman Catholic 46.5%; Protestant 41.2%; Eastern Orthodox 1.5%; Jewish 1.2%; Muslim 0.4%; Hindu 0.3%; Sikh 0.3%; nonreligious 7.4%; other 1.2%.
*Major metropolitan areas* (1986): Toronto 3,427,168; Montreal 2,921,357; Vancouver 1,380,729; Ottawa–Hull 819,263; Edmonton 785,465; Calgary 671,326; Winnipeg 625,304; Quebec 603,267; Hamilton 557,029; Saint Catharines–Niagara 343,258.

### Other metropolitan areas (1986)

| | population | | population | | population |
|---|---|---|---|---|---|
| Chicoutimi-Jonquière | 158,458 | Oshawa | 203,543 | Sudbury | 148,877 |
| Halifax | 295,990 | Regina | 186,521 | Thunder Bay | 122,217 |
| Kitchener | 311,195 | Saint John's | 161,901 | Trois Rivières | 128,888 |
| London | 342,302 | Saskatoon | 200,665 | Victoria | 255,547 |
| | | Sherbrooke | 129,960 | Windsor | 253,988 |

*Place of birth* (1981): 83.9% native-born; 16.1% foreign-born, of which United Kingdom 3.7%, other European 8.6%, Asian countries 1.7%, other 2.1%.
*Mobility* (1981). Population living in the same residence as in 1976: 52.4%; different residence, same province 24.9%; different province 22.7%.
*Households* (1985). Total number of households 9,079,000. Average household size 2.8; 1 person 20.5%, 2 persons 30.8%, 3 persons 18.0%, 4 persons 18.8%, 5 persons 8.1%, 6 or more persons 3.8%. Family households: 6,827,400 (75.2%), nonfamily 2,251,600 (24.8%, of which 1 person 20.5%).
*Immigration* (1986): permanent immigrants admitted 98,620, from Asia 41.5%, Europe 22.8%, West Indies 8.9%, United States 7.3%, other 19.5%; refugee arrivals (1986) 18,282.

## Vital statistics

*Birth rate* per 1,000 population (1986): 14.8 (world avg. 26.0); (1983) legitimate 91.0%; illegitimate 9.0%.
*Death rate* per 1,000 population (1986): 7.3 (world avg. 9.9).
*Natural increase rate* per 1,000 population (1986): 7.5 (world avg. 16.1).
*Total fertility rate* (avg. births per childbearing woman; 1984): 1.7.
*Marriage rate* per 1,000 population (1986): 7.4.
*Divorce rate* per 1,000 population (1986): 2.8.
*Life expectancy* at birth (1983): male 73.0 years; female 79.0 years.
*Major causes of death* per 100,000 population (1985): diseases of the circulatory system 309.6; malignant neoplasms (cancers) 170.6; diseases of the respiratory system 55.4; accidents and violence 52.9.

## Social indicators

*Educational attainment* (1981). Percent of population age 25 and over having: no formal schooling 2.0%; less than full primary education 14.2%; primary 9.5%; secondary 39.6%; postsecondary 34.7%, of which (graduates by level; 1986): 4-year higher degree 102,300, master's 15,480, doctorate 2,070.

### Distribution of income (1984)

percent of national income by quintile

| 1 | 2 | 3 | 4 | 5 (highest) |
|---|---|---|---|---|
| 2.5% | 8.5% | 15.1% | 25.5% | 48.4% |

*Quality of working life* (1986). Average workweek: 38.8 hours (3.1% overtime). Annual rate per 100,000 workers for (1981): injury, accident, or industrial illness 4,956; death 4.0. Proportion of labour force insured for damages or income loss resulting from (1984): injury 99%; permanent disability 99%; death 99%. Average days lost to labour stoppages per 1,000 employee-workdays (1986): 1.2. Average duration of journey to work (1983): 23 minutes[2] (17.3% public transportation, 72.8% automobile, 9.9% other). Rate per 1,000 workers of discouraged (unemployed no longer seeking work; 1983): 10.5.
*Access to services* (1985). Proportion of households having access to: electricity 100.0%; public water supply 99.7%; public sewage collection 99.3%; public fire protection (1978) 90.4%.
*Social participation.* Eligible voters participating in last national election (1984): 69.7%. Population over 18 years of age participating in voluntary work (1980): 15.0%. Trade union membership in total work force (1985): 29.0%. Practicing religious population in total affiliated population: 92.7%.
*Social deviance* (1982). Offense rate per 100,000 population for: murder 6.5; rape 10.2; auto theft 352.8; burglary and housebreaking 1,500.2. Incidence per 100,000 in general population of: alcoholism (1981) 2,405; drug and substance abuse 322.4; suicide (1984) 13.7.
*Leisure* (1981). Favourite leisure activities (hours weekly): television 13.3; social time 10.7; reading 3.5; recreation and culture 2.7.
*Material well-being* (1985). Households possessing: automobile 81.9%; telephone 98.2%; television receiver 98.4%; refrigerator 99.2%; central air conditioner 17.8%; automatic washing machine 77.4%; cable television 62.4%; videocassette recorders (1986) 35.1%.

## National economy

*Gross national product* (at current market prices; 1985): U.S.$347,360,000,000 (U.S.$13,700 per capita).

### Structure of gross domestic product and labour force

| | 1986 in value Can$'000,000 | 1986 % of total value | 1985 labour force | 1985 % of labour force |
|---|---|---|---|---|
| Agriculture | 15,585.0 | 4.3 | 590,000 | 4.7 |
| Mining | 21,114.2 | 5.8 | 191,000 | 1.5 |
| Manufacturing | 71,179.7 | 19.5 | 1,980,000 | 15.7 |
| Construction | 25,368.8 | 7.0 | 587,000 | 4.6 |
| Public utilities | 11,287.0 | 3.1 | 124,000 | 1.0 |
| Transportation and communication | 27,983.7 | 7.7 | 760,000 | 6.0 |
| Trade | 42,585.5 | 11.7 | 2,634,000[3] | 20.8[3] |
| Finance | 51,862.8 | 14.2 | 1,126,000 | 8.9 |
| Pub. admin., defense | 23,400.9 | 6.4 | 3,319,000 | 26.3 |
| Services | 74,154.8 | 20.3 | | |
| Other | — | — | 1,328,000[4] | 10.5[4] |
| TOTAL | 364,522.4[5] | 100.0 | 12,639,000 | 100.0 |

*Budget* (1986–87). Revenue: Can$87,275,000,000 (personal income tax 43.2%; corporation income tax 13.4%; sales tax 13.4%; excise taxes and import duties 11.2%). Expenditures: Can$116,740,000,000 (education, health, and welfare 47.0%; public debt interest 23.4%; economic development 9.5%; defense 8.4%).
*National debt* (1986): Can$217,903,000,000.
*Tourism* (1985): receipts from visitors U.S.$3,056,000,000; expenditures by nationals abroad U.S.$4,125,000,000.

### Manufacturing, mining, and construction enterprises (1986)

| | no. of enterprises[6] | no. of employees | hourly wages as a % of avg. of all wages | annual shipments (Can$'000,000) |
|---|---|---|---|---|
| Manufacturing | | | | |
| Transport equipment | 1,202 | 187,088 | 119.4 | 43,150.4 |
| Food and beverages | 4,372 | 220,168 | 90.3 | 38,118.3 |
| Paper and related products | 773 | 121,426 | 125.3 | 19,145.9 |
| Primary metals | 446 | 99,667 | 127.1 | 16,596.0 |
| Chemicals and related products | 1,221 | 92,048 | 114.8 | 18,166.8 |
| Metal fabricating | 5,150 | 149,490 | 96.5 | 14,428.4 |
| Electrical products | 1,116 | 112,564 | 105.0 | 12,765.4 |
| Wood | 3,353 | 95,822 | 93.8 | 11,853.4 |
| Printing, publishing, and related products | 4,620 | 179,480 | 105.4 | 9,483.1 |
| Machinery | 1,679 | 81,749 | 101.3 | 7,598.8 |
| Rubber and plastic | 1,036 | 66,761 | 91.8 | 7,348.1 |
| Clothing | 2,107 | 88,840 | 56.5 | 6,153.4 |
| Furniture and fixtures | 2,489 | 57,960 | 73.5 | 3,472.6 |
| Knitting mills | 255 | 18,318[6] | 82.3 | 2,700.6[7] |
| Textile | 989 | 62,330 | 82.3 | 2,983.4 |
| Tobacco products industries[6] | 24 | 8,711 | 90.5 | 1,645.1 |
| Leather industries | 419 | 20,632 | 58.4 | 1,374.0 |
| Mining | 125 | 145,994 | 149.3 | 20,545.0 |
| Construction | ... | 395,676 | 112.3 | 21,428.0 |

*Production* (farm cash receipts in Can$'000 except as noted). Agriculture, forestry, fishing (1986): wheat 2,504,970, rapeseed 905,780, corn (maize) 575,350, vegetables 549,350, barley 532,660, floriculture 384,270, fruit 288,560, potatoes 272,650, soybeans 229,850, tobacco 158,000; livestock (number of live animals) 11,465,000 cattle, 10,708,000 pigs, 722,000 sheep, 96,300,000 poultry; roundwood (1984) 144,300,000 cu m; pelts (1985) 4,102,533 metric tons; fish catch 1,186,545 metric tons. Mining and quarrying (metric tons; 1986): iron ore 37,313,000; zinc 1,096,200; copper 743,100;

lead 303,700; nickel 174,200; molybdenum 12,500; uranium 11,110; silver 1,086; gold 104. Manufacturing (metric tons; 1986): wood pulp 21,504,000; crude steel 14,081,000; cement 10,272,000; pig iron 9,276,000; newsprint 9,264,000; sulfuric acid 3,898,000; caustic soda 1,769,000; synthetic rubber 111,200[7]; road motor vehicles 1,845,776 units, of which passenger cars 1,060,884 units, truck and buses 784,892 units; washing machines and dryers 830,520 units; refrigerators 568,960 units; footwear 43,087,000 pairs; beer 235,470,000 hectolitres. Construction (building permits; 1986): residential Can$14,218,900,000; nonresidential Can$10,471,000,000.

### Service enterprises (1986)

| | no. of enterprises | no. of employees[8] | weekly wages as a % of all wages | annual sales (Can$'000,000) |
|---|---|---|---|---|
| Retail trade | | | | |
| Food stores | ... | 213,400 | ... | 34,622.7 |
| Motor vehicle dealers | ... | 79,800 | ... | 28,675.2 |
| Department stores | ... | [9] | ... | 12,667.7 |
| Service stations | ... | 63,700 | ... | 12,230.4 |
| Clothing stores | ... | 50,200 | ... | 6,540.5 |
| Pharmacies | ... | 52,400 | ... | 6,031.8 |
| Furniture and appliance stores | ... | 62,100 | ... | 3,622.9 |
| Automotive stores | ... | 31,500 | ... | 3,094.6 |
| General merchandise | ... | 231,700[9] | ... | 2,910.1 |
| General stores | ... | [9] | ... | 2,089.4 |
| Sporting goods | ... | ... | ... | 2,067.1 |
| Variety stores | ... | 45,100 | ... | 1,249.8 |
| Shoe stores | ... | 18,400 | ... | 1,411.5 |
| Hardware stores | ... | 17,300 | ... | 1,325.4 |
| Jewelry stores | ... | 14,000 | ... | 1,038.3 |

Energy production (consumption): electricity (kW-hr; 1986) 455,820,000,000 (418,436,000,000); coal (metric tons; 1986) 56,508,000,000 (44,683,000,000); crude petroleum (barrels; 1986) 573,076,000 (492,204,500); petroleum products (metric tons; 1985) 86,634,000 (77,997,000); natural gas (cu m; 1986) 71,690,000,000 (48,052,900,000).

*Population economically active* (1986): total 12,870,000; activity rate of total population 50.3% (participation rates: over age 15, 65.7%; female [1985] 42.6%; unemployed 9.6%).

### Price and earnings indexes (1981 = 100)

| | 1981 | 1982 | 1983 | 1984 | 1985 | 1986 | 1987[10] |
|---|---|---|---|---|---|---|---|
| Consumer price index | 100.0 | 110.8 | 117.2 | 122.3 | 127.2 | 132.4 | 137.8 |
| Monthly earnings index | 100.0 | 111.8 | 118.1 | 123.3 | 127.6 | 131.4 | ... |

*Household income and expenditure.* Average household size (1986) 2.7; average annual income per household (1984) Can$35,800 (U.S.$27,500); sources of income: wages and salaries 64.1%, social welfare 14.9%, interest, dividends, and other investment income 13.1%, other 7.9%; expenditure (1983): housing and energy 22.1%, food 17.8%, transportation and communication 15.4%, recreation 7.9%, household durable goods 7.4%, clothing 6.8%, health 3.5%, education 2.8%.

*Land use* (1984): forested 35.4%; meadows and pastures 2.6%; agricultural and under permanent cultivation 5.0%; built-on, wasteland, and other 57.0%.

### Financial aggregates

| | 1981 | 1982 | 1983 | 1984 | 1985 | 1986 | 1987 (8 mos.) |
|---|---|---|---|---|---|---|---|
| Exchange rate, Can$ per: | | | | | | | |
| U.S. dollar | 1.20 | 1.23 | 1.23 | 1.29 | 1.37 | 1.39 | 1.33 |
| £ | 2.42 | 2.15 | 1.88 | 1.50 | 1.78 | 2.04 | 2.12 |
| SDR | 1.38 | 1.36 | 1.30 | 1.30 | 1.54 | 1.69 | 1.71 |
| International reserves (U.S.$) | | | | | | | |
| Total (excl. gold; '000,000) | 3,492 | 3,000 | 3,465 | 2,491 | 2,503 | 3,251 | 6,387 |
| SDRs ('000,000) | 174 | 71 | 21 | 72 | 218 | 247 | 547 |
| Reserve pos. in IMF ('000,000) | 402 | 365 | 703 | 678 | 711 | 686 | 646 |
| Foreign exchange ('000,000) | 2,916 | 2,564 | 2,741 | 1,741 | 1,574 | 2,318 | 5,194 |
| Gold ('000,000 fine troy oz) | 20.46 | 20.26 | 20.17 | 20.14 | 20.11 | 19.72 | 18.75 |
| % world reserves | 2.00 | 2.14 | 2.13 | 2.13 | 2.13 | 2.12 | 2.12 |
| Interest and prices | | | | | | | |
| Central bank discount (%) | 14.66 | 10.26 | 10.04 | 10.16 | 9.49 | 8.49 | 9.24 |
| Gov't. bond yield (%) | 15.22 | 14.26 | 11.79 | 12.75 | 11.04 | 9.52 | 10.44 |
| Industrial share prices (1980 = 100) | 97.4 | 76.8 | 111.4 | 110.2 | 130.5 | 143.9 | 178.0[10] |
| Balance of payments (U.S.$'000,000) | | | | | | | |
| Balance of visible trade, of which: | 6,578 | 14,955 | 14,959 | 16,558 | 13,287 | 7,718 | 2,150[11] |
| Imports, f.o.b. | 65,940 | 55,491 | 60,672 | 72,328 | 79,917 | 81,228 | 20,957[11] |
| Exports, f.o.b. | 72,518 | 70,446 | 75,631 | 88,986 | 90,204 | 881,946 | 23,107[11] |
| Balance of invisibles | −12,795 | −13,813 | −13,429 | −14,768 | −14,033 | −15,041 | −3,143[11] |
| Balance of payments, current account | −5,110 | 2,303 | 2,388 | 2,514 | −432 | −5,990 | −2,852[11] |

### Foreign trade

#### Balance of trade (current prices)

| | 1980 | 1981 | 1982 | 1983 | 1984 | 1985 | 1986 |
|---|---|---|---|---|---|---|---|
| Can$'000,000,000 | 6.9 | 4.5 | 15.8 | 19.4 | 16.6 | 14.3 | 7.8 |
| % of total | 4.7% | 2.8% | 9.9% | 11.8% | 8.0% | 6.4% | 3.3% |

*Imports* (1986): Can$112,678,000,000 (machinery and transport equipment 49.3%, of which road motor vehicles and parts 29.6%, electrical equipment 10.4%, nonelectrical machinery 9.3%; food, feed, beverages, and tobacco 5.7%; chemicals 5.2%; mineral fuels 4.5%, of which crude petroleum 2.8%; nonferrous metals 2.3%; iron and steel 1.7%). *Major import sources:* United States 68.6%; Japan 6.8%; United Kingdom 3.3%; West Germany 3.1%; South Korea 1.6%; Taiwan 1.5%; France 1.4%; Hong Kong 0.9%.
*Exports* (1986): Can$120,494,900,000 (transportation and communication equipment 33.7%, of which road motor vehicles and parts 28.4%; crude

materials 12.7%, of which crude petroleum 3.1%, natural gas 2.1%; food 7.9%, of which wheat 2.4%; newsprint 4.7%; lumber 4.1%; wood pulp 3.4%; machinery 3.2%; chemicals 2.2%; iron and steel 2.1%; aluminum 1.9%). *Major export destinations:* United States 77.3%; Japan 4.9%; United Kingdom 2.3%; West Germany 1.1%; U.S.S.R. 1.0%; China 0.9%; The Netherlands 0.8%; South Korea 0.8%; Belgium–Luxembourg 0.7%; France 0.7%; Brazil 0.7%.

### Trade by commodities (1986)

| SITC Group | | imports Can$'000,000 | % | exports Can$'000,000 | % |
|---|---|---|---|---|---|
| 00 | Food and live animals | 5,841.8 | 5.2 | 9,188.6 | 7.9 |
| 01 | Beverages and tobacco | 517.7 | 0.5 | 322.0 | 0.3 |
| 02 | Crude materials, excluding fuels | 2,011.6 | 1.8 | 8,353.2 | 7.2 |
| 03 | Mineral fuels, lubricants, and related materials | 5,125.4 | 4.5 | 6,256.9 | 5.4 |
| 04 | Animal and vegetable oils, fat, and waxes | 708.0 | 0.6 | 718.1 | 0.6 |
| 05 | Chemicals and related products, n.e.s. | 5,840.0 | 5.2 | 5,078.4 | 4.3 |
| 06 | Basic manufactures | 41,015.0 | 36.4 | 33,287.9 | 28.5 |
| 07 | Machinery and transport equipment | 42,977.6 | 38.1 | 44,459.0 | 38.1 |
| 08 | Miscellaneous manufactured articles | 7,436.7 | 6.6 | 4,271.3 | 3.7 |
| 09 | Goods not classified by kind | 1,204.2 | 1.1 | 4,626.3 | 4.0 |
| TOTAL | | 112,678.0 | 100.0 | 116,561.7[12] | 100.0 |

### Direction of trade (1986)

| | imports Can$'000,000 | % | exports Can$'000,000 | % |
|---|---|---|---|---|
| Africa | 1,009.9 | 0.9 | 886.7 | 0.7 |
| Asia | 14,463.8 | 12.8 | 10,162.8 | 8.4 |
| Americas | 81,316.4 | 72.2 | 96,555.8 | 80.1 |
| United States | 77,337.0 | 68.6 | 93,182.3 | 77.3 |
| South America | 1,894.7 | 1.7 | 1,782.0 | 1.5 |
| Central America | 2,084.7 | 1.9 | 1,558.9 | 1.3 |
| Europe | 15,201.8 | 13.5 | 12,056.3 | 10.0 |
| EEC | 12,811.7 | 11.4 | 8,161.0 | 6.8 |
| U.S.S.R. and Eastern Europe | 360.7 | 0.3 | 2,823.2 | 2.3 |
| Other Europe | 2,029.4 | 1.8 | 1,072.1 | 0.9 |
| Oceania | 686.1 | 0.6 | 833.3 | 0.7 |
| TOTAL | 112,678.0 | 100.0 | 120,494.9 | 100.0[13] |

### Transport and communications

*Transport.* Railroads (1985): length 74,564 mi, 120,000 km; passenger-mi 1,447,000,000, passenger-km 2,328,000,000; short ton-mi cargo 158,921,000,000, metric ton-km cargo 232,036,000,000. Roads (1984): total length 549,445 mi, 884,249 km (paved 81%). Vehicles (1985): passenger cars 11,118,071; trucks and buses 3,095,243. Merchant marine (1986): vessels (100 gross tons and over) 1,249; total deadweight tonnage 3,829,724. Air transport (1985): passenger-mi 45,528,555,000, passenger-km 73,271,248,000; short ton-mi cargo 3,233,289,000, metric ton-km cargo 4,720,522,000; airports (1987) with scheduled flights 61.
*Communications.* Daily newspapers (1986): total number 108; total circulation 5,411,743; circulation per 1,000 population 211. Radio (1985): total number of receivers 28,800,000 (1 per 0.9 person). Television (1986): total number of receivers 15,300,000 (1 per 1.7 persons). Telephones (1984): 16,480,000 (1 per 1.5 persons).

### Education and health

#### Education (1987–88)

| | schools | teachers | students | student/teacher ratio |
|---|---|---|---|---|
| Primary and secondary (age 6–18) | 15,512 | 273,190 | 4,959,000 | 18.1 |
| Postsecondary and higher | 266 | 59,300 | 795,730 | 13.4 |

*Literacy* (1975): total population age 14 and over literate 16,185,000 (95.6%); males literate 8,003,000 (95.6%); females literate 8,182,000 (95.7%).
*Health* (1982): physicians 45,542 (1 per 538 persons); hospital beds 180,935 (1 per 135 persons); infant mortality rate per 1,000 live births (1984) 9.3.
*Food* (1981–83): daily per capita caloric intake 3,421 (vegetable products 63%, animal products 37%); (1983) 130% of FAO recommended minimum requirement.

### Military

*Total active duty personnel* (1986): 83,000 (army 25.3%, navy 6.6%, air force 18.4%, not identified by service 49.7%). *Military expenditure as percent of GNP* (1984): 2.2% (world 5.9%); per capita expenditure U.S.$300.

[1]Based on land areas. [2]Urban areas. [3]Includes restaurants and hotels. [4]Unemployed. [5]At factor cost in 1981 prices. [6]1982. [7]1985. [8]1984. [9]Department and general stores included with general merchandise. [10]June. [11]First quarter. [12]Domestic exports only. Reexports of Can$3,933,200,000 are excluded. [13]Detail does not add to total given because of rounding.

# Cape Verde

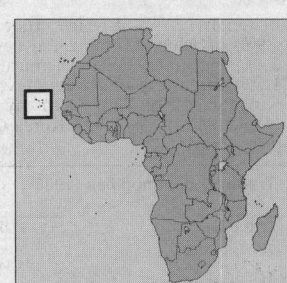

*Official name:* República de Cabo Verde (Republic of Cape Verde).
*Form of government:* unitary single-party republic with one legislative house (People's National Assembly [83]).
*Chief of state:* President.
*Head of government:* Prime Minister.
*Capital:* Praia.
*Official language:* Portuguese.
*Official religion:* none.
*Monetary unit:* 1 escudo (C.V. Esc) = 100 centavos; valuation (Oct. 5, 1987) 1 U.S.$ = C.V. Esc 89.27; 1 £ = C.V. Esc 144.97.

### Area and population

| Islands Counties | Capitals | area sq mi | area sq km | population 1980 census |
|---|---|---|---|---|
| Boa Vista | | 239 | 620 | 3,372 |
| Boa Vista | Sal Rei | | | 6,985 |
| Brava | | 26 | 67 | |
| Brava | Nova Sintra | | | 30,978 |
| Fogo | | 184 | 476 | |
| Fogo | São Filipe | | | 4,098 |
| Maio | | 104 | 269 | |
| Maio | Porto Inglês | | | 5,826 |
| Sal | | 83 | 216 | |
| Sal | Santa Maria | | | 145,957 |
| Santiago | | 383 | 991 | |
| Praia | Praia | | | 57,748 |
| Santa Catarina | Assomada | | | 41,012 |
| Santa Cruz | Pedra Badejo | | | 22,995 |
| Tarrafal | Tarrafal | | | 24,202 |
| Santo Antão | | 301 | 779 | 43,321 |
| Paúl | Pombas | | | 7,983 |
| Porto Novo | Porto Novo | | | 13,236 |
| Ribeira Grande | Ponta Sol | | | 22,102 |
| São Nicolau | | 150 | 388 | |
| São Nicolau | Ribeira Brava | | | 13,572 |
| São Vicente | | 88 | 227 | |
| São Vicente | Mindelo | | | 41,594 |
| TOTAL | | 1,557[1] | 4,033 | 295,703 |

## Demography

*Population* (1987): 350,000.
*Density* (1987): persons per sq mi 224.8, persons per sq km 86.8.
*Urban–rural* (1980): urban 35.1%; rural 64.9%.
*Sex distribution* (1985): male 46.32%; female 53.68%.
*Age breakdown* (1985): under 15, 45.6%; 15–29, 31.8%; 30–44, 7.9%; 45–59, 8.0%; 60–74, 4.6%; 75 and over, 2.1%.
*Population projection:* (1990) 376,600; (2000) 478,800.
*Doubling time:* 30 years.
*Ethnic composition* (1986): mixed 71%; black 28%; white 1%.
*Religious affiliation* (1985): Roman Catholic 97.8%; Protestant and other 2.2%.
*Major cities* (1980): Praia 49,500[2]; Mindelo 36,746; São Filipe 4,370.

## Vital statistics

*Birth rate* per 1,000 population (1986): 32.0 (world avg. 26.0); (1975) legitimate 55.2%; illegitimate 44.8%.
*Death rate* per 1,000 population (1986): 8.7 (world avg. 9.9).
*Natural increase rate* per 1,000 population (1986): 23.3 (world avg. 16.1).
*Total fertility rate* (avg. births per childbearing woman; 1980–85): 2.6.
*Marriage rate* per 1,000 population (1975): 5.4.
*Divorce rate* per 1,000 population: n.a.
*Life expectancy* at birth (1980–85): male 60.3 years; female 64.0 years.
*Major causes of death* per 100,000 population (1980): enteritis and other diarrheal diseases 85.5; heart disease 51.9; cerebrovascular disease 45.7; malignant neoplasms (cancers) 43.8; measles and other infectious and parasitic diseases 34.6; pneumonia 27.2; bronchitis, emphysema, and asthma 20.4; avitaminoses and other nutritional deficiencies 14.5.

## National economy

*Budget.* Revenue (1986): C.V. Esc 3,277,295,000 (indirect taxes 38.4%, of which import duties 16.0%; direct taxes 21.4%, of which taxes from industry 6.8%; receipts from petroleum 2.9%). Expenditures (1984): C.V. Esc 2,134,500,000 (no breakdown available).
*Public debt* (external, outstanding; 1985): U.S.$90,600,000.
*Tourism:* n.a.
*Production* (metric tons except as noted). Agriculture, forestry, fishing (1985): coconuts 10,000, sugarcane 9,000, fruit except bananas 9,000, pulses 5,000, vegetables 5,000, bananas 3,000, potatoes 3,000, sweet potatoes 2,000, cassava 2,000, dates 2,000, corn (maize) 1,000; livestock (number of live animals) 78,000 goats, 24,000 pigs, 13,000 cattle, 8,000 asses and mules, 2,000 horses, 1,000 sheep; roundwood, n.a.; fish catch (1984) 9,131, of which tuna 4,109 (45.0%), other marine fishes 5,032 (55.0%). Mining and quarrying (1986): salt C.V. Esc 9,710,000. Manufacturing (C.V. Esc; 1986): flour 199,918,000; cigars 189,757,000; cacao powder 94,439,000; canned fish 62,710,000; bread 35,530,000; alcoholic beverages 31,152,000; soft drinks 6,091,000 litres. Construction (1982): residential C.V. Esc 365,800,-000; nonresidential C.V. Esc 1,700,000. Energy production (consumption):

electricity (kW-hr; 1986) 28,402,379 (27,562,777); coal, none (none); crude petroleum, n.a. (n.a.); petroleum products (metric tons; 1985) n.a. (31,000); natural gas, n.a. (n.a.).
*Gross national product* (at current market prices; 1985): U.S.$140,000,000 (U.S.$420 per capita).

### Structure of gross domestic product and labour force

| | 1981 in value C.V. Esc '000,000 | % of total value | labour force | % of labour force |
|---|---|---|---|---|
| Agriculture, forestry, and fishing | 560.0 | 17.6 | 58,000 | 55.8 |
| Manufacturing and public utilities | 125.0 | 3.9 | 1,700 | 1.6 |
| Mining | 9.0 | 0.3 | | |
| Construction | 645.0 | 20.3 | | |
| Pub. admin., defense | 550.0 | 17.3 | 44,300 | 42.6 |
| Trade, finance, and other | 1,290 | 40.6 | | |
| TOTAL | 3,179 | 100.0 | 104,000 | 100.0 |

*Population economically active* (1985): total 121,000; activity rate of total population 37.1% (participation rates: ages 15–64, 60.6%; female 28.9%; unemployed 25.2%).

### Price and earnings indexes (1975 = 100)

| | 1976 | 1977 | 1978 | 1979 | 1980 | 1981 |
|---|---|---|---|---|---|---|
| Consumer price index | 101.2 | 108.3 | 122.7 | 131.2 | 150.4 | 167.7 |
| Monthly earnings index | ... | ... | ... | ... | ... | ... |

*Household income and expenditure.* Average household size (1980) 4.3; income per household: n.a.; sources of income: n.a.; expenditure (1985)[3]: food 63.4%, clothing and footwear 9.2%, beverages and tobacco 6.7%, other 20.7%.
*Land use* (1984): forested 0.2%; meadows and pastures 6.2%; agricultural and under permanent cultivation 9.9%; other 83.7%.

## Foreign trade

### Balance of trade (current prices)

| | 1980 | 1981 | 1982 | 1983 | 1984 | 1985 |
|---|---|---|---|---|---|---|
| C.V. Esc '000,000 | −2,743 | −3,300 | −3,978 | −5,482 | −5,766 | −6,983 |
| % of total | 99.9% | 91.5% | 89.8% | 92.0% | 92.8% | 94.2% |

*Imports* (1985): C.V. Esc 7,444,961,000 (foodstuffs and beverages 28.5%; machinery and transport equipment 18.1%, of which transport equipment 10.5%; mineral products 15.5%; chemical products 6.1%; metals 5.9%; textiles and textile products 3.7%; plastics and resins 3.4%). *Major import sources:* Portugal 26.7%; The Netherlands 21.9%; Italy 8.7%; France 6.9%; Spain 6.5%; Brazil 6.4%; West Germany 4.3%; Argentina 2.0%; Belgium–Luxembourg 1.8%.
*Exports* (1985): C.V. Esc 462,345,000 (foodstuffs [principally processed fish] 71.6%; textiles and textile products 26.7%). *Major export destinations:* Algeria 30.9%; Portugal 30.2%; Italy 13.9%; Nigeria 7.0%; United Kingdom 7.0%; Niger 4.7%.

## Transport and communications

*Transport.* Railroads: none. Roads (1984): total length 1,398 mi, 2,250 km (paved 29%). Vehicles (1981): passenger cars 4,000; trucks and buses 1,343. Merchant marine (1986): vessels (100 gross tons and over) 25; total deadweight tonnage 22,092. Air transport (1985): passenger-mi 16,148,000, passenger-km 25,987,000; short ton-mi cargo 1,606,000, metric ton-km cargo 2,345,000; airports (1987) with scheduled flights 9.
*Communications.* Daily newspapers: none. Radio (1985): total number of receivers 47,000 (1 per 6.9 persons). Television: (1985): total number of receivers 500 (1 per 650 persons). Telephones (1984): 2,384 (1 per 137 persons).

## Education and health

### Education (1982–83)

| | schools | teachers | students | student/ teacher ratio |
|---|---|---|---|---|
| Primary (age 7–10) | 436 | 1,459 | 50,000 | 34.3 |
| Secondary (age 10–17) | 16 | 603 | 10,454 | 17.3 |
| Voc., teacher tr. | 4 | 76 | 923 | 12.1 |
| Higher | ... | ... | ... | ... |

*Educational attainment,* n.a. *Literacy* (1981): total population age 15 and over literate 78,839 (49.3%); males literate 43,814 (55.3%); females literate 35,025 (43.4%).
*Health* (1980): physicians 51 (1 per 5,820 persons); hospital beds 632 (1 per 470 persons); infant mortality rate per 1,000 live births (1985) 76.5.
*Food* (1981–83): daily per capita caloric intake 2,535 (vegetable products 88%, animal products 12%); (1983) 100% of FAO recommended minimum requirement.

## Military

*Total active duty personnel* (1986): 1,185 (army 84.4%, navy 13.5%, air force 2.1%). *Military expenditure as percent of GNP* (1982): 2.2% (world 6.0%); per capita expenditure U.S.$7.

[1]Detail does not add to total given because of rounding. [2]1985. [3]Praia only.

# Central African Republic

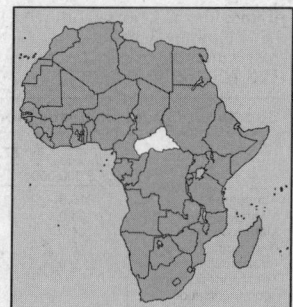

*Official name:* République Centrafricaine (Central African Republic).
*Form of government:* unitary single-party republic with one legislative house (National Assembly [52]).
*Head of state and government:* Chairman.
*Capital:* Bangui.
*Official language:* French.
*Official religion:* none.
*Monetary unit:* 1 CFA franc (CFAF) = 100 centimes; valuation (Oct. 5, 1987) 1 U.S.$ = CFAF 306.67; 1 £ = CFAF 498.00.

## Area and population

| Prefectures | Capitals | area sq mi | area sq km | population 1985[1] estimate |
|---|---|---|---|---|
| Bamingui-Bangoran | Ndélé | 22,471 | 58,200 | 29,400 |
| Bangui | Bangui | 26 | 67 | 473,800 |
| Basse-Kotto | Mobaye | 6,797 | 17,604 | 187,200 |
| Gribingui-Économique | Kaga-Bandoro | 7,720 | 19,996 | 85,700 |
| Haut-Mbomou | Obo | 21,440 | 55,530 | 52,200 |
| Haute-Kotto | Bria | 33,456 | 86,650 | 233,100 |
| Haute-Sangha | Berbérati | 11,661 | 30,203 | 37,400 |
| Kemo-Gribingui | Sibut | 6,642 | 17,204 | 78,300 |
| Lobaye | Mbaïki | 7,427 | 19,235 | 160,700 |
| Mbomou | Bangassou | 23,610 | 61,150 | 132,900 |
| Nana-Mambere | Bouar | 10,270 | 26,600 | 197,600 |
| Ombella-Mpoko | Bimbo | 12,292 | 31,835 | 127,900 |
| Ouaka | Bambari | 19,266 | 49,900 | 216,200 |
| Ouham | Bossangoa | 19,402 | 50,250 | 269,300 |
| Ouham-Pendé | Bozoum | 12,394 | 32,100 | 242,100 |
| Sangha-Économique | Nola | 7,495 | 19,412 | 59,600 |
| Vakaga | Birao | 17,954 | 46,500 | 24,200 |
| TOTAL | | 240,324[2] | 622,436 | 2,607,600 |

## Demography

*Population* (1987): 2,774,000.
*Density* (1987): persons per sq mi 11.5, persons per sq km 4.5.
*Urban–rural* (1984): urban 34.1%; rural 65.9%.
*Sex distribution* (1985): male 48.42%; female 51.58%.
*Age breakdown* (1985): under 15, 42.5%; 15–59, 25.5%; 30–44, 15.9%; 45–59, 10.1%; 60 and over, 6.0%.
*Population projection:* (1990) 2,965,000; (2000) 3,736,000.
*Doubling time:* 28 years.
*Ethnic composition* (1983): Banda 28.6%; Baya (Gbaya) 24.5%; Ngbandi 10.6%; Azande 9.8%; Sara 6.9%; Mbaka 4.3%; Mbum 4.1%; Kare 2.4%; French 0.1%; other 8.7%.
*Religious affiliation* (1980): Protestant 50.0%; Roman Catholic 33.1%; traditional 12.0%; Muslim 3.2%; Baha'i 0.3%; other 1.4%.
*Major cities* (1985): Bangui 473,800; Bambari 44,500; Bouar 42,000; Berberati 38,000; Bossangoa 35,800.

## Vital statistics

*Birth rate* per 1,000 population (1983): 41.0 (world avg. 29.0); legitimate, n.a.; illegitimate, n.a.
*Death rate* per 1,000 population (1983): 17.0 (world avg. 11.0).
*Natural increase rate* per 1,000 population (1983): 24.0 (world avg. 18.0).
*Total fertility rate* (avg. births per childbearing woman; 1983): 5.5.
*Marriage rate* per 1,000 population: n.a.
*Divorce rate* per 1,000 population: n.a.
*Life expectancy* at birth (1983): male 46.0 years; female 49.0 years.
*Morbidity* (as percent of reported cases of illness; 1984): malaria 13.3%; dysentery, enteritis, and other intestinal diseases 12.5%; respiratory diseases 9.9%, of which pneumonia 2.7%.

## National economy

*Budget* (1987). Revenue: CFAF 46,230,000,000 (1982; indirect taxes 52.4%, nonfiscal receipts 21.1%, direct taxes 20.3%). Expenditures: CFAF 56,610,-000,000 (1982; education and culture 13.9%, defense 8.3%, repayment of public debt 8.1%).
*Public debt* (external, outstanding; 1985): U.S.$296,000,000.
*Tourism:* receipts from visitors (1985) U.S.$2,000,000; expenditures by nationals abroad (1982) U.S.$26,000,000.
*Production* (metric tons except as noted). Agriculture, forestry, fishing (1985): cassava 920,000, yams 198,000, peanuts (groundnuts) in shell 140,-000, cocoa beans 115,000, bananas 82,000, plantains 62,000, seed cotton 62,000, millet 60,000, taro 58,000, corn (maize) 50,000, cotton seed 40,000, cotton lint 22,000, coffee 18,000, rice 14,000, pulses 6,000; livestock (number of live animals) 1,800,000 cattle, 970,000 goats, 150,000 pigs, 83,000 sheep, 2,000,000 chickens; roundwood 3,418,000 cu m; fish catch 13,000. Mining and quarrying (1986): diamonds 357,379 carats, of which 258,701 gem quality and 98,678 industrial; gold (1985) 239.7 kg. Manufacturing (1984): household aluminum articles 876; paints 556; hides and skins 368; footwear 381,136 pairs; motorcycles 4,030 units; bicycles 2,977 units; beer 234,241 hectolitres; soft drinks 50,472 hectolitres; cigarettes 20,654,-000 units. Construction: n.a. Energy production (consumption): electricity

(kW-hr; 1985) 75,000,000 (75,000,000); coal, none (n.a.); crude petroleum, none (n.a.); petroleum products (metric tons; 1985) none (60,000); natural gas, none (n.a.).
*Land use* (1984): forested 57.6%; meadows and pastures 4.8%; agricultural and under permanent cultivation 3.2%; other 34.4%.
*Gross national product* (at current market prices; 1985): U.S.$700,000,000 (U.S.$270 per capita).

## Structure of gross domestic product and labour force

| | 1983 in value U.S.$'000,000 | 1983 % of total value | 1983 labour force | 1983 % of labour force |
|---|---|---|---|---|
| Agriculture | 177 | 35.5 | 1,114,000 | 85.8 |
| Mining | 16 | 3.2 | | |
| Manufacturing | 39 | 7.8 | 55,000 | 4.2 |
| Construction | 22 | 4.4 | | |
| Public utilities | 8 | 1.6 | | |
| Transportation and communication | | | | |
| Trade | | | | |
| Finance | 236 | 47.4 | 130,000 | 10.0 |
| Pub. admin., defense | | | | |
| Services | | | | |
| TOTAL | 498[3] | 100.0[2] | 1,299,000 | 100.0 |

*Population economically active* (1985): total 1,282,000; activity rate of total population 49.8% (participation rates: over age 15 [1975] 50.2%; female 45.3%; unemployed, n.a.).

## Price and earnings indexes (1980 = 100)

| | 1981 | 1982 | 1983 | 1984 | 1985 | 1986 | Jan. 1987 |
|---|---|---|---|---|---|---|---|
| Consumer price index | 112.6 | 127.5 | 144.5 | 151.1 | 171.3 | 184.3 | 193.0 |
| Earnings index | ... | ... | ... | ... | ... | ... | ... |

*Household income and expenditure.* Average household size (1980) 4.3; average annual income per household CFAF 91,985 (U.S.$435); sources of income: n.a.; expenditure[4] (1983): food 70.5%, clothing 9.5%, energy 6.5%, transportation and communication 4.1%, recreation 1.3%, health 1.0%, housing 0.6%.

## Foreign trade

### Balance of trade (current prices)

| | 1981 | 1982 | 1983 | 1984 | 1985 | 1986 |
|---|---|---|---|---|---|---|
| U.S.$'000,000 | −2.2 | −16.1 | −11.9 | −9.4 | −41.7 | −40.4 |
| % of total | 1.1% | 7.0% | 6.2% | 4.9% | 31.4% | 25.6% |

*Imports* (1984): CFAF 77,700,000,000 (1980; machinery and equipment 33.9%, food 20.9%, chemicals and plastics 12.2%, textiles 8.4%, fuels and lubricants 1.8%). *Major import sources:* France 45.9%; Zaire 12.4%; Japan 6.3%; West Germany 3.8%; Italy 1.7%.
*Exports* (1984): CFAF 50,000,000,000 (1983; coffee 29.0%, diamonds 24.0%, wood 18.5%, cotton 12.8%). *Major export destinations:* France 30.3%; Belgium–Luxembourg 29.3%; Japan 11.4%; Italy 6.4%; West Germany 6.4%; Spain 4.0%; United States 3.2%.

## Transport and communications

*Transport.* Railroads: none. Roads (1985): total length 12,600 mi, 20,278 km (paved 2%). Vehicles (1984): passenger cars 43,321; trucks and buses 3,861. Merchant marine: vessels (100 gross tons and over) none. Air transport (1982): passenger-mi 105,804,000, passenger-km 170,276,000; short ton-mi cargo 20,677,000, metric ton-km cargo 30,188,000; airports (1987) with scheduled flights 1.
*Communications.* Daily newspapers: total number 1; total circulation 200. Radio (1986): total number of receivers 125,000 (1 per 22 persons). Television (1982): total number of receivers 1,200 (1 per 2,000 persons). Telephones (1985): 6,952 (1 per 380 persons).

## Education and health

### Education (1984–85)

| | schools | teachers | students | student/ teacher ratio |
|---|---|---|---|---|
| Primary (age 6–11) | 960 | 4,263[5] | 308,022 | ... |
| Secondary (age 12–18) | 39 | 675 | 55,787 | 82.6 |
| Voc., teacher tr. | 4 | 122 | 2,514 | 20.6 |
| Higher[6] | 7 | 297 | 4,571 | 15.4 |

*Educational attainment* (1975). Percent of population age 15 and over having: no formal schooling 73.5%; primary education 22.8%; lower secondary 3.0%; upper secondary 0.6%; higher 0.1%. *Literacy* (1980): total population age 15 and over literate 447,800 (38.5%); males literate 322,800 (58.8%); females literate 125,000 (20.4%).
*Health* (1984): physicians 112 (1 per 22,997 persons); hospital beds 3,774 (1 per 682 persons); infant mortality rate per 1,000 live births (1983) 142.0.
*Food* (1981–83): daily per capita caloric intake 2,106 (vegetable products 93%, animal products 7%); (1983) 91% of FAO recommended minimum requirement.

## Military

*Total active duty personnel* (1986): 2,300 (army 87.0%; navy, none; air force 13.0%). *Military expenditure as percent of GNP* (1983): 2.0% (world 6.1%); per capita expenditure U.S.$5.

[1]Beginning of year. [2]Detail does not add to total given because of rounding. [3]At current factor cost. [4]Capital city only. [5]1983–84. [6]1981–82.

# Chad

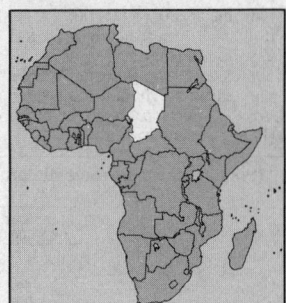

*Official name:* République du Tchad (Republic of Chad).
*Form of government:* pending adoption of a constitution, republican in form with one political party and a single advisory organ (National Consultative Assembly [30]).
*Head of state and government:* President.
*Capital:* N'Djamena.
*Official language:* French.
*Official religion:* none.
*Monetary unit:* 1 CFA franc (CFAF) = 100 centimes; valuation (Oct. 5, 1987) 1 U.S.$ = CFAF 306.67; 1 £ = CFAF 498.00.

| Area and population | | area | | population |
|---|---|---|---|---|
| | | sq mi | sq km | 1984 estimate |
| **Préfectures** | **Capitals** | | | |
| Batha | Ati | 34,285 | 88,800 | 410,000 |
| Biltine | Biltine | 18,090 | 46,850 | 200,000 |
| Borkou-Ennedi-Tibesti | Faya | 231,795 | 600,350 | 103,000 |
| Chari-Baguirmi | N'Djamena | 32,010 | 82,910 | 719,000 |
| Guéra | Mongo | 22,760 | 58,950 | 234,000 |
| Kanem | Mao | 44,215 | 114,520 | 234,000 |
| Lac | Bol | 8,620 | 22,320 | 158,000 |
| Logone Occidental | Moundou | 3,355 | 8,695 | 324,000 |
| Logone Oriental | Doba | 10,825 | 28,035 | 350,000 |
| Mayo-Kebbi | Bongor | 11,625 | 30,105 | 757,000 |
| Moyen-Chari | Sarh | 17,445 | 45,180 | 582,000 |
| Ouaddaï | Abéché | 29,435 | 76,240 | 411,000 |
| Salamat | Am Timan | 24,325 | 63,000 | 121,000 |
| Tandjilé | Laï | 6,965 | 18,045 | 341,000 |
| TOTAL | | 495,755[1] | 1,284,000 | 4,944,000 |

## Demography

*Population* (1987): 5,265,000.
*Density* (1987): persons per sq mi 10.6, persons per sq km 4.1.
*Urban–rural* (1986): urban 23.9%; rural 76.1%.
*Sex distribution* (1985): male 49.24%; female 50.76%.
*Age breakdown* (1985): under 15, 42.5%; 15–29, 26.0%; 30–44, 15.8%; 45–59, 9.9%; 60–74, 4.9%; 75 and over, 0.9%.
*Population projection:* (1990) 5,668,000; (2000) 7,308,000.
*Doubling time:* 33 years.
*Ethnic composition* (1983): Bagirmi, Sara, and Kreish 30.5%; Sudanic Arab 26.1%; Tubu 7.3%; Mbum 6.5%; Masalit, Maba, and Mimi 6.3%; Mubi 4.2%; Tama 6.3%; Kanuri 2.3%; Hausa 2.3%; Masa 2.3%; Kotoko 2.1%; other 3.8%.
*Religious affiliation* (1980): Muslim 44.0%; Christian 33.0%, of which Roman Catholic 21.0%, Protestant 11.6%; traditional beliefs 22.8%; other 0.2%.
*Major cities* (1986): N'Djamena 511,700; Sarh 100,000; Moundou 90,000; Abéché 71,000; Kélo 27,000[2].

## Vital statistics

*Birth rate* per 1,000 population (1984): 43.0 (world avg. 29.0); legitimate, n.a.; illegitimate, n.a.
*Death rate* per 1,000 population (1984): 21.0 (world avg. 11.0).
*Natural increase rate* per 1,000 population (1984): 22.0 (world avg. 18.0).
*Total fertility rate* (avg. births per childbearing woman; 1984): 5.6.
*Marriage rate* per 1,000 population: n.a.
*Divorce rate* per 1,000 population: n.a.
*Life expectancy* at birth (1984): male 43.0 years; female 45.0 years.
*Major causes of death* per 100,000 population: n.a.; however, major diseases include malaria, sleeping sickness, leprosy, venereal diseases, and tuberculosis.

## National economy

*Budget* (1987). Revenue: CFAF 17,800,000,000 (1984; indirect taxes 73.2%, of which customs receipts 60.1%; direct taxes 21.7%). Expenditures: CFAF 25,400,000,000 (1984; defense 46.5%; education 10.9%; community projects 9.1%; health 3.8%).
*Public debt* (external, outstanding; 1986): U.S.$171,800,000.
*Tourism* (1981): receipts from visitors U.S.$2,000,000; expenditures by nationals abroad, n.a.
*Production* (metric tons except as noted). Agriculture, forestry, fishing (1985): millet 600,000, cassava 260,000, yams 195,000, sugarcane 180,000, seed cotton 112,000, peanuts (groundnuts) 80,000, pulses 56,000, corn (maize) 48,000, lint cotton 40,000, sweet potatoes 35,000, mangoes 32,000, dates 32,000, rice 21,000, onions 14,000, potatoes 13,000, sesame seed 11,000; livestock (number of live animals) 3,400,000 cattle, 2,250,000 sheep, 2,000,000 goats, 3,000,000 chickens; roundwood 3,567,000 cu m; fish catch 115,000. Mining and quarrying: clay, natron, tungsten, bauxite, and gold. Manufacturing (1984): beef and veal 24,000; refined sugar 23,000; salted, dried, or smoked fish 20,000[3]; mutton and lamb 8,000; goat meat 7,000; wheat flour 1,000[3]; woven cotton fabrics 13,075,000 metres[3]; beer 130,000 hectolitres[3]; cigarettes 259,000,000 units[3]. Construction: n.a. Energy production (consumption): electricity (kW-hr; 1985) 65,000,000 (65,000,000); coal, none (n.a.); crude petroleum, none (n.a.); petroleum products (metric tons; 1985) none (69,000); natural gas, none (n.a.).
*Household income and expenditure.* Average household size (1980) 3.9; average annual income per household CFAF 96,806 (U.S.$458); sources of income: n.a.; expenditure[4] (1983): food 45.3%, health 11.9%, energy 5.8%, clothing 3.3%.
*Gross national product* (at current market prices; 1984): U.S.$560,000,000 (U.S.$110 per capita).

| Structure of gross domestic product and labour force | | | | |
|---|---|---|---|---|
| | 1983 | | | |
| | in value U.S.$'000,000 | % of total value | labour force | % of labour force |
| Agriculture | 316.0 | 51.6 | 1,476,000 | 81.0 |
| Mining | 3.0 | 0.5 | | |
| Manufacturing | 44.0 | 7.2 | 151,000 | 8.3 |
| Construction | 8.0 | 1.3 | | |
| Public utilities | 3.0 | 0.5 | | |
| Transportation and communication | | | | |
| Trade | 238.0 | 38.9 | 196,000 | 10.7 |
| Finance | | | | |
| Pub. admin., defense | | | | |
| Services | | | | |
| TOTAL | 612.0[5] | 100.0 | 1,823,000 | 100.0 |

*Population economically active* (1984): total 1,862,000; activity rate of total population 38.0% (participation rates: ages 15–64 [1980] 56.5%; female [1981] 23.6%; unemployed, n.a.).

| Price and earnings indexes (1975 = 100) | | | | | | | |
|---|---|---|---|---|---|---|---|
| | 1972 | 1973 | 1974 | 1975 | 1976 | 1977 | 1978 |
| Consumer price index | 73.7 | 77.7 | 86.5 | 100.0 | 103.3 | 112.0 | 128.6 |
| Earnings index | ... | ... | ... | ... | ... | ... | ... |

*Land use* (1984): forested 10.5%; meadows and pastures 35.7%; agricultural and under permanent cultivation 2.5%; built-on, wasteland, and other 51.3%.

## Foreign trade[6]

| Balance of trade (current prices) | | | | | | |
|---|---|---|---|---|---|---|
| | 1979 | 1980 | 1981 | 1982 | 1983 | 1984 |
| CFAF '000,000 | +644 | −534 | −6,684 | −19,255 | −31,793 | −26,239 |
| % of total | 1.7% | 1.7% | 12.9% | 36.1% | 36.1% | 21.3% |

*Imports* (1983): CFAF 74,802,000,000 (petroleum products 16.8%; cereal products 16.8%; pharmaceutical products and chemicals 11.5%; machinery and transport equipment 8.5%, of which transport equipment 7.3%; electrical equipment 5.7%; textiles 2.9%; raw and refined sugar 2.3%). *Major import sources:* France 16.6%; Cameroon 9.2%; United States 8.9%; Italy 4.5%; West Germany 3.2%; United Kingdom 2.4%; The Netherlands 1.9%.
*Exports* (1983): CFAF 48,563,000,000 (raw cotton 91.1%; live cattle and frozen bovine meat 1.8%). *Major export destinations:* United States 36.6%; West Germany 8.0%; Portugal 8.0%; Cameroon 4.0%; France 3.1%; Italy 1.6%; Spain 1.3%; Japan 1.2%.

## Transport and communications

*Transport.* Railroads: none. Roads (1983): total length 24,855 mi, 40,000 km (paved 1%). Vehicles (1982): passenger cars 7,000; trucks and buses 5,000. Merchant marine vessels (100 gross tons and over) none. Air transport[7] (1985): passenger-mi 144,226,000, passenger-km 232,109,000; short ton-mi cargo 27,420,000, metric ton-km cargo 40,035,000; airports (1987) with scheduled flights 2.
*Communications.* Daily newspapers (1986): total number 1; total circulation 1,500; circulation per 1,000 population 0.3. Radio (1986): total number of receivers 100,000 (1 per 51 persons). Television: none. Telephones (1981): 900 (1 per 5,085 persons).

## Education and health

| Education (1984) | schools | teachers | students | student/ teacher ratio |
|---|---|---|---|---|
| Primary (age 6–12) | 1,231 | 4,494 | 288,479 | 64.2 |
| Secondary (age 13–19) | ... | 590[8] | 43,053 | ... |
| Voc., teacher tr. | ... | ... | 2,559 | ... |
| Higher | 1 | 141 | 1,643 | 11.6 |

*Educational attainment,* n.a. *Literacy* (1980): total population age 15 and over literate 466,500 (17.8%); males literate 459,700 (35.6%); females literate 6,800 (0.5%).
*Health:* physicians (1980) 94 (1 per 47,640 persons); hospital beds (1978) 3,553 (1 per 1,190 persons); infant mortality rate per 1,000 live births (1984) 139.
*Food* (1980–82): daily per capita caloric intake 1,821 (vegetable products 92%, animal products 8%); 77% of FAO recommended minimum requirement.

## Military

*Total active duty personnel* (1987): 17,200 (army 98.8%; navy, none; air force 1.2%). *Military expenditure as percent of GNP* (1984): 1.6% (world 5.9%); per capita expenditure U.S.$1.8.

[1]Detail does not add to total given because of rounding. [2]1979. [3]1983. [4]Capital city only. [5]At current factor cost. [6]Imports c.i.f. (cost, insurance, and freight); exports f.o.b. (free on board). [7]The airport at N'Djamena is underutilized because of the political and military unrest in Chad. [8]1976–77.

# Chile

*Official name:* República de Chile (Republic of Chile).
*Form of government:* military regime.
*Head of state and government:* President (general) assisted by a four-member junta.
*Capital:* Santiago.
*Official language:* Spanish.
*Official religion:* none.
*Monetary unit:* 1 peso (Ch$) = 100 centavos; valuation (Oct. 5, 1987) 1 U.S.$ = Ch$228.23; 1 £ = Ch$370.62.

## Area and population

| Regions | Capitals | area[1] sq mi | sq km | population 1986 estimate |
|---|---|---|---|---|
| Tarapacá | Iquique | 22,697 | 58,786 | 314,800 |
| Antofagasta | Antofagasta | 48,360 | 125,253 | 366,300 |
| Atacama | Copiapó | 28,844 | 74,705 | 194,500 |
| Coquimbo | La Serena | 15,697 | 40,656 | 452,500 |
| Valparaíso | Valparaíso | 6,331 | 16,396 | 1,314,300 |
| Libertador General Bernardo O'Higgins | Rancagua | 6,354 | 16,456 | 621,700 |
| Maule | Talca | 11,839 | 30,662 | 792,900 |
| Bío-Bío | Concepción | 14,262 | 36,939 | 1,609,700 |
| Araucanía | Temuco | 12,334 | 31,946 | 745,200 |
| Los Lagos | Puerto Montt | 26,350 | 68,247 | 896,200 |
| Aisén del General Carlos Ibáñez del Campo | Coihaique | 42,084 | 108,997 | 73,000 |
| Magallanes y de la Antártica Chilena | Punta Arenas | 50,979[2] | 132,034[2] | 141,700 |
| Región Metropolitana de Santiago | Santiago | 6,003 | 15,549 | 4,804,200 |
| TOTAL | | 292,135[2,3] | 756,626[2] | 12,327,000 |

## Demography

*Population* (1987): 12,475,000.
*Density* (1987): persons per sq mi 42.7, persons per sq km 16.5.
*Urban–rural* (1985): urban 83.6%; rural 16.4%.
*Sex distribution* (1986): male 49.36%; female 50.64%.
*Age breakdown* (1986): under 15, 31.1%; 15–29, 28.6%; 30–44, 19.9%; 45–59, 12.1%; 60–74, 6.4%; 75 and over, 2.0%[3].
*Population projection:* (1990) 13,109,000; (2000) 15,462,000.
*Doubling time:* 45 years.
*Ethnic composition* (1983): mestizo 91.6%; Indian (mostly Araukan) 6.8%; others (mainly European) 1.6%.
*Religious affiliation* (1982): Roman Catholic 79.2%; Protestant 6.0%; atheist and nonreligious 2.0%; other 12.8%.
*Major cities* (1986): Greater Santiago 4,804,200; Viña del Mar 294,100; Concepción 292,700; Valparaíso 277,900; Talcahuano 229,500; Temuco 215,400; Antofagasta 203,100; Rancagua 170,800; Arica 167,300.

## Vital statistics

*Birth rate* per 1,000 population (1985): 21.7 (world avg. 29.0); (1980) legitimate 72.4%; illegitimate 27.6%.
*Death rate* per 1,000 population (1985): 6.1 (world avg. 11.0).
*Natural increase rate* per 1,000 population (1985): 15.6 (world avg. 18.0).
*Total fertility rate* (avg. births per childbearing woman; 1981): 3.0.
*Marriage rate* per 1,000 population (1985): 7.5.
*Divorce rate* per 1,000 population (1985): 0.4.
*Life expectancy* at birth (1985–90): male 68.1 years; female 75.1 years.
*Major causes of death* per 100,000 population (1984): diseases of the circulatory system 177.6; malignant neoplasms (cancers) 100.9; accidents and poisonings 76.6; diseases of the respiratory system 65.8.

## National economy

*Budget* (1985). Revenue: Ch$752,080,000,000 (excise taxes 39.6%, nontax revenue 23.3%, income taxes 11.3%, import and export duties 10.8%, social security contributions 7.3%, stamp taxes 4.5%). Expenditures: Ch$806,080,-000,000 (social security and welfare 39.0%, education 13.2%, defense 11.5%, public services 11.3%, economic services 7.1%, health 6.1%).
*Tourism* (1985): receipts from visitors U.S.$115,000,000; expenditures by nationals abroad U.S.$269,000,000.
*Production* (metric tons except as noted). Agriculture, forestry, fishing (1985): sugar beets 2,124,000, wheat 1,165,000, grapes 1,100,000, potatoes 909,000, corn (maize) 772,000, apples 401,000, oats 170,000, tomatoes 162,000; livestock (number of live animals) 5,800,000 sheep, 3,400,000 cattle, 1,100,000 pigs; roundwood 15,493,000 cu m; fish catch 4,986,000. Mining (1986): iron ore 6,377,900; copper 1,395,800; manganese 30,800; molybdenum 16,300; zinc 10,300; silver 492,400 kilograms; gold 17,800 kilograms. Manufacturing (1986): cement 1,440,500; cellulose 668,200; sugar 383,700; newsprint 180,900; detergents 47,300; margarine 27,500; carbonated drinks 3,697,900 hectolitres; tires 862,000 units. Construction[4] (value in '000,000 of Ch$; 1984) residential 19,703; nonresidential 5,462. Energy production (consumption): electricity (kW-hr; 1986) 14,887,200,000 (14,887,200,000); coal (metric tons; 1985) 1,218,000 (1,764,000); crude petroleum (barrels; 1985) 11,942,000 (27,945,000); petroleum products (metric tons; 1985) 3,938,000 (4,441,000); natural gas (cu m; 1985) 961,175,000 (961,175,000).
*Gross national product* (at current market prices; 1985): U.S.$17,230,000,000 (U.S.$1,430 per capita).

## Structure of gross domestic product and labour force

| | 1986 in value Ch$'000,000[5] | % of total value | labour force[6] | % of labour force |
|---|---|---|---|---|
| Agriculture | 37,107 | 9.9 | 801,400 | 20.6 |
| Mining | 31,523 | 8.4 | 84,100 | 2.2 |
| Manufacturing | 78,507 | 20.8 | 530,900 | 13.6 |
| Construction | 20,852 | 5.5 | 184,100 | 4.7 |
| Public utilities | 9,744 | 2.6 | 24,300 | 0.6 |
| Transportation and communication | 21,571 | 5.7 | 230,200 | 5.9 |
| Trade | 62,919 | 16.7 | 650,100 | 16.7 |
| Finance | | | 155,900 | 4.0 |
| Pub. admin., defense Services | 114,404 | 30.4 | 1,233,900 | 31.7 |
| Other | | | 800 | ... |
| TOTAL | 376,627 | 100.0 | 3,895,700 | 100.0 |

*Public debt* (external, outstanding; 1985): U.S.$12,734,500,000.
*Population economically active* (1985): total 4,018,700; activity rate of total population 33.6% (participation rates: ages 15–64 [1984] 52.9%; female [1984] 16.4%; unemployed 12.0%).

## Price and earnings indexes (1980 = 100)

| | 1981 | 1982 | 1983 | 1984 | 1985 | 1986 | 1987[7] |
|---|---|---|---|---|---|---|---|
| Consumer price index | 119.7 | 131.6 | 167.5 | 200.7 | 262.3 | 313.4 | 368.1 |
| Monthly earnings index | 130.3 | 142.9 | 162.5 | 195.0 | ... | ... | ... |

*Household income and expenditure.* Average household size (1982) 4.5; income per household, n.a.; expenditure (1978): food 41.9%, housing 13.3%, transportation and communication 11.8%, recreation and education 8.2%, household goods 7.8%, clothing and footwear 7.6%.
*Land use* (1984): forested 20.7%; meadows and pastures 15.9%; agricultural and under permanent cultivation 7.4%; other 56.0%.

## Foreign trade[8]

### Balance of trade (current prices)

| | 1980 | 1981 | 1982 | 1983 | 1984 | 1985 | 1986 |
|---|---|---|---|---|---|---|---|
| U.S.$'000,000 | +329 | −1,487 | +720 | +1,320 | +953 | +1,473 | +1,620 |
| % of total | 3.6% | 16.0% | 10.7% | 20.8% | 15.0% | 24.1% | 27.7% |

*Imports* (1986): U.S.$2,914,400,000 (intermediate goods 62.5%; capital goods 23.0%; consumer goods 14.5%). *Major import sources* (1985): United States 23.9%; Venezuela 9.8%; Brazil 9.1%; West Germany 7.6%; Japan 6.9%; Argentina 3.9%; Spain 3.8%; United Kingdom 3.1%.
*Exports* (1986): U.S.$4,222,300,000 (mining 54.5%, of which copper 41.9%; fruits and vegetables 13.0%; fish meal 7.5%; paper and paper products 6.5%; chemical and petroleum products 2.8%). *Major export destinations* (1985): United States 22.9%; Japan 10.3%; West Germany 9.8%; United Kingdom 6.8%; Brazil 5.5%; Italy 5.2%; France 3.8%; The Netherlands 3.8%.

## Transport and communications

*Transport.* Railroads (1986): route length 5,037 mi, 8,107 km; passenger-mi 790,000,000, passenger-km 1,272,000,000; short ton-mi cargo 1,701,000,000, metric ton-km cargo 2,484,000,000. Roads (1985): total length 49,227 mi, 79,224 km (paved 12%). Vehicles (1985) passenger cars 624,738; trucks and buses 257,298. Merchant marine (1986): vessels (100 gross tons and over) 255; total deadweight tonnage 907,538. Air transport (1986): passenger-mi 1,218,000,000, passenger-km 1,960,000,000; short ton-mi cargo 93,982,000, metric ton-km cargo 137,212,000; airports (1987) with scheduled flights 13.
*Communications.* Daily newspapers (1983): total number 66; total circulation 1,407,300; circulation per 1,000 population 120. Radio (1986): 14,000,-000 receivers (1 per 1.1 persons). Television (1984): 2,645,000 receivers (1 per 4.5 persons). Telephones (1985): 761,087 (1 per 16 persons).

## Education and health

### Education (1984)

| | schools | teachers[9] | students | student/ teacher ratio |
|---|---|---|---|---|
| Primary (age 6–13) | 8,862 | 62,746 | 2,092,069 | ... |
| Secondary (age 14–17) | 1,401 | ... | 581,243 | ... |
| Vocational | 369 | ... | 129,817 | ... |
| Higher | 24 | 10,372 | 126,197 | ... |

*Educational attainment* (1970). Percent of population age 25 and over having: no formal schooling 12.4%; primary education 57.2%; secondary 26.6%; higher 3.8%. *Literacy* (1983): total population age 12 and over literate 8,301,000 (95.6%); males 4,100,000 (95.0%)[10]; females 4,201,000 (93.8%)[10].
*Health* (1985): physicians 12,334 (1 per 983 persons); hospital beds (1986) 33,136 (1 per 372 persons); infant mortality rate per 1,000 live births 19.5.
*Food* (1981–83): daily per capita caloric intake 2,662 (vegetable products 83%, animal products 17%); (1983) 105% of FAO recommended minimum requirement.

## Military

*Total active duty personnel* (1986): 101,000 (army 56.4%, navy 28.7%, air force 14.9%). *Military expenditure as percent of GNP* (1984): 4.2% (world 5.9%); per capita expenditure: U.S.$69.

---

[1]Preliminary. [2]Excludes the territory of Antártica Chilena and inland water areas. [3]Detail does not add to total given because of rounding. [4]Private new construction only. [5]In constant 1977 pesos. [6]Employed persons only. [7]May. [8]Import figures are f.o.b. (free on board) in balance of trade and c.i.f. (cost, insurance, and freight) for commodities and trading partners. [9]1982. [10]Calculated from the 1981 literacy rate of 94.4%.

# China

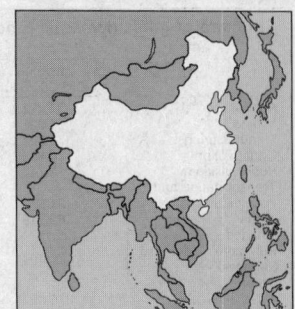

*Official name:* Chung-hua Jen-min Kung-ho-kuo (People's Republic of China).
*Form of government:* single-party people's republic with one legislative house (National People's Congress [2,978]).
*Chief of state:* President.
*Head of government:* Premier.
*Capital:* Peking (Beijing).
*Official language:* Mandarin Chinese.
*Official religion:* none.
*Monetary unit:* 1 Renminbi (yuan) (Y) = 10 jiao = 100 fen; valuation (Oct. 5, 1987) 1 U.S.$ = Y 3.73; 1 £ = Y 6.06.

## Area and population[1,2]

| Provinces | Capitals | area sq mi | area sq km | population 1986[3] estimate |
|---|---|---|---|---|
| Anhwei (Anhui) | Ho-fei (Hefei) | 54,000 | 139,900 | 51,560,000 |
| Chekiang (Zhejiang) | Hangchow (Hangzhou) | 39,300 | 101,800 | 40,300,000 |
| Fukien (Fujian) | Foochow (Fuzhou) | 47,500 | 123,100 | 27,130,000 |
| Heilungkiang (Heilongjiang) | Harbin (Harbin) | 179,000 | 463,600 | 33,110,000 |
| Honan (Henan) | Cheng-chou (Zhengzhou) | 64,500 | 167,000 | 77,130,000 |
| Hopeh (Hebei) | Shih-chia-chuang (Shijiazhuang) | 78,200 | 202,700 | 55,480,000 |
| Hunan (Hunan) | Ch'ang-sha (Changsha) | 81,300 | 210,500 | 56,220,000 |
| Hupeh (Hubei) | Wu-han (Wuhan) | 72,400 | 187,500 | 49,310,000 |
| Kansu (Gansu) | Lan-chou (Lanzhou) | 141,500 | 366,500 | 20,410,000 |
| Kiangsi (Jiangxi) | Nan-ch'ang (Nanchang) | 63,600 | 164,800 | 34,600,000 |
| Kiangsu (Jiangsu) | Nanking (Nanjing) | 39,600 | 102,600 | 62,130,000 |
| Kirin (Jilin) | Ch'ang-ch'un (Changchun) | 72,200 | 187,000 | 22,980,000 |
| Kwangtung (Guangdong) | Canton (Guangzhou) | 89,300 | 231,400 | 62,530,000 |
| Kweichow (Guizhou) | Kuei-yang (Guiyang) | 67,200 | 174,000 | 29,680,000 |
| Liaoning (Liaoning) | Shen-yang (Shenyang) | 58,300 | 151,000 | 36,860,000 |
| Shansi (Shanxi) | T'ai-yüan (Taiyuan) | 60,700 | 157,100 | 26,270,000 |
| Shantung (Shandong) | Tsinan (Jinan) | 59,200 | 153,300 | 76,950,000 |
| Shensi (Shaanxi) | Sian (Xi'an) | 75,600 | 195,800 | 30,020,000 |
| Szechwan (Sichuan) | Ch'eng-tu (Chengdu) | 219,700 | 569,000 | 101,880,000 |
| Tsinghai (Qinghai) | Hsi-ning (Xining) | 278,400 | 721,000 | 4,070,000 |
| Yunnan (Yunnan) | K'un-ming (Kunming) | 168,400 | 436,200 | 34,060,000 |
| **Autonomous regions** | | | | |
| Inner Mongolia (Nei Monggol) | Hu-ho-hao-t'e (Hohhot) | 454,600 | 1,177,500 | 20,070,000 |
| Kwangsi Chuang (Guangxi Zhuang) | Nan-ning (Nanning) | 85,100 | 220,400 | 38,730,000 |
| Ningsia Hui (Ningxia Hui) | Yin-ch'uan (Yinchuan) | 25,600 | 66,400 | 4,150,000 |
| Sinkiang Uighur (Xinjiang Uygur) | Urumchi (Urumqi) | 635,900 | 1,646,900 | 13,610,000 |
| Tibet (Xizang) | Lhasa (Lhasa) | 471,700 | 1,221,600 | 1,990,000 |
| **Municipalities** | | | | |
| Peking (Beijing) | — | 6,500 | 16,800 | 9,600,000 |
| Shanghai (Shanghai) | — | 2,400 | 6,200 | 12,170,000 |
| Tientsin (Tianjin) | — | 4,400 | 11,300 | 8,080,000 |
| **TOTAL** | | 3,696,100[4] | 9,572,900[4] | 1,045,320,000[5] |

## Demography

*Population* (1987): 1,064,135,000.
*Density* (1987): persons per sq mi 287.9, persons per sq km 111.2.
*Urban–rural* (1985): urban 36.6%; rural 63.4%.
*Sex distribution* (1985): male 51.67%; female 48.33%.
*Age breakdown* (1982): under 15, 33.6%; 15–29, 29.1%; 30–44, 17.5%; 45–59, 12.2%; 60–74, 6.3%; 75 and over, 1.3%.
*Population projection:* (1990) 1,099,190,000; (2000) 1,253,000,000.
*Doubling time:* 62 years.
*Ethnic composition* (1982): Han (Chinese) 93.30%; Chuang 1.33%; Hui 0.72%; Uighur 0.59%; Yi 0.54%; Miao 0.50%; Manchu 0.43%; Tibetan 0.39%; Mongolian 0.34%; Tuchia 0.28%; Puyi 0.21%; Korean 0.18%; Tung 0.14%; Yao 0.14%; Pai 0.11%; Hani 0.11%; Kazakh 0.09%; Tai 0.08%; Li 0.08%; other 0.44%.
*Religious affiliation* (1980): nonreligious 59.2%; Chinese folk-religionist 20.1%; atheist 12.0%; Buddhist 6.0%; Muslim 2.4%; Christian 0.2%; other 0.1%.
*Major cities* (1986)[3]: Shanghai 6,980,000; Peking 5,860,000; Tientsin 5,380,000; Shen-yang 4,200,000; Wu-han 3,400,000; Canton 3,290,000; Chungking (Chongqing) 2,780,000; Harbin 2,630,000; Ch'eng-tu 2,580,000; Sian 2,330,000; Nanking 2,250,000; T'ai-yüan 1,880,000; Ch'ang-ch'un 1,860,000; Ta-lien (Dalian) 1,630,000; Cheng-chou 1,590,000; K'un-ming 1,490,000; Tsinan 1,430,000; Lan-chou 1,350,000; An-shan (Anshan) 1,280,000; Ch'ing-tao (Qingdao) 1,250,000; Hangchow 1,250,000.
*Households* (1985). Average rural household size 5.1; urban household size 3.8. Family households (1982): 220,100,755 (99.5%); collective 1,073,010 (0.5%).

## Vital statistics

*Birth rate* per 1,000 population (1985): 17.8 (world avg. 29.0).
*Death rate* per 1,000 population (1985): 6.6 (world avg. 11.0).
*Natural increase rate* per 1,000 population (1985): 11.2 (world avg. 18.0).
*Total fertility rate* (avg. births per childbearing woman; 1986): 2.4.
*Marriage rate* per 1,000 population (1985): 8.0.
*Divorce rate* per 1,000 population (1985): 0.4.
*Life expectancy* at birth (1981): male 66.4 years; female 69.3 years.

*Major causes of death* per 100,000 population (percent distribution; 1985)[6]: diseases of the heart 25.5%; diseases of the circulatory system 15.6%; malignant neoplasms (cancers) 15.2%; diseases of the respiratory system 12.3%; digestive diseases 5.5%; poisoning 3.8%; tuberculosis 3.7%; trauma 3.4%.

## Social indicators

*Educational attainment* (1982). Percent of population age 25 and over having: no schooling 44.5%; completed primary 32.7%; completed junior secondary 16.1%; completed senior secondary 5.6%; postsecondary 1.1%.

### Distribution of rural household income (1985)

by per capita income group (avg. Y 398)

| Y 150 and under | Y 151–Y 300 | Y 301–Y 500 | over Y 500 |
|---|---|---|---|
| 4.4% | 33.5% | 39.8% | 22.3% |

*Quality of working life* (1984). Average workweek: 48 hours. Annual rate per 100,000 workers for: injury or accident, n.a.; industrial illness, n.a.; death, n.a. Expenditure on pensions and social welfare relief (1983): Y 2,404,000,000. Average days lost to labour stoppages per 1,000 workdays: n.a. Average duration of journey to work: n.a. Method of transport: n.a. Rate per 1,000 workers of discouraged (unemployed no longer seeking work): n.a.
*Access to services* (1979). Proportion of communes having access to: electricity 87.1%; safe public water supply (1985) 81.1%; public sewage collection, n.a.; public fire protection, n.a.
*Social participation.* Eligible voters participating in last national election: n.a. Population participating in voluntary work: n.a. Trade union membership in total labour force (1985): 17.0%. Practicing religious population in total affiliated population: n.a..
*Social deviance.* Annual reported offense rate per 100,000 population (1979–81) for: theft 60.0; violent crime (including murder, rape, and robbery) 4.5; other 10.5[7].
*Leisure.* Favourite leisure activities: n.a.
*Material well-being* (1985). Urban families possessing (number per family): wristwatches 2.9; bicycles 1.6; sewing machines 0.7; radios 0.8; televisions 0.9. Rural families possessing (number per family): wristwatches 1.3; bicycles 0.8; sewing machines 0.4; radios 0.5; televisions 0.01.

## National economy

*Gross national product* (at current market prices; 1985): U.S.$318,920,000,000 (U.S.$310 per capita).

### Structure of national income[8] and labour force

| | 1985 in value Y '000,000,000 | 1985 % of total value | 1986[3] labour force ('000)[9] | 1986[3] % of labour force |
|---|---|---|---|---|
| Agriculture | 282.8 | 41.5 | 311,870 | 62.5 |
| Mining | ... | ... | 1,060 | 0.2 |
| Manufacturing | 283.1 | 41.5 | 83,490 | 16.7 |
| Construction | 37.6 | 5.5 | 20,690 | 4.1 |
| Public utilities | ... | ... | 4,370 | 0.9 |
| Transp. and commun. | 23.6 | 3.5 | 12,220 | 2.5 |
| Trade | 55.1 | 8.1 | 23,630 | 4.7 |
| Finance | — | — | 1,380 | 0.3 |
| Pub. admin., defense | — | — | 7,990 | 1.6 |
| Services | — | — | 18,840 | 3.8 |
| Other | ... | ... | 13,190 | 2.6 |
| **TOTAL** | 682.2 | 100.0[10] | 498,730 | 100.0[10] |

*Budget* (1987). Revenue: Y 237,930,000,000 (taxes 92.2%; funds collected for energy and transport projects 7.4%). Expenditures: Y 245,950,000,000 (capital construction 26.7%; culture, education, public health 15.8%; defense 8.3%).
*Tourism* (1986): receipts from visitors U.S.$1,530,000,000; expenditures by nationals abroad, n.a.

### Retail and service enterprises (1985)

| | no. of enterprises | no. of employees | annual wage as a % of all wages | annual gross output value (Y '000,000) |
|---|---|---|---|---|
| Retail trade | 7,783,000 | 17,960,000 | ... | ... |
| Grocery stores | 159,000 | 1,158,000 | ... | ... |
| Department stores | 148,000 | 1,454,000 | ... | ... |
| Other food shops | 110,000 | 774,000 | ... | ... |
| Agricultural supplies stores | 67,000 | 314,000 | ... | ... |
| Household supplies stores | 62,000 | 336,000 | ... | ... |
| Grain and oil shops | 47,000 | 460,000 | ... | ... |
| Electrical appliances stores | 43,000 | 437,000 | ... | ... |
| Textile stores | 36,000 | 220,000 | ... | ... |
| Book stores | 24,000 | 107,000 | ... | ... |
| Drug stores | 23,000 | 179,000 | ... | ... |
| Coal stores | 13,000 | 145,000 | ... | ... |
| Service trade | 1,534,000 | 3,539,000 | ... | ... |
| Repair shops | 693,000 | 1,085,000 | ... | ... |
| Barber shops | 202,000 | 414,000 | ... | ... |
| Hotels | 121,000 | 807,000 | ... | ... |
| Photo studios | 76,000 | 186,000 | ... | ... |

*Production* (metric tons except as noted). Agriculture, forestry, fishing (1985): grains—rice 171,479,000, wheat 85,286,000, corn (maize) 62,250,000, sorghum 6,835,000, millet 6,302,000, barley 2,701,000; oilseeds—peanuts (groundnuts) 6,757,000, rapeseed 5,587,000, sunflower seed 1,901,000, sesame seed 692,000; fruits and nuts—apples 3,215,000, pears 2,331,000, oranges 1,700,000, bananas 560,000; others—roots and tubers 141,136,000, sugarcane 58,665,000, seed cotton 12,453,000, soybeans 10,519,000, sugar beets 8,091,000, pulses 5,840,000, jute fibre 3,200,000, tobacco leaves 2,036,000, tea 465,000; livestock (number of live animals) 313,010,000 pigs, 95,191,000 sheep, 63,427,000 goats, 51,375,000 cattle, 19,547,000 water buffalo, 10,978,000 horses, 9,962,000 asses, 531,000 camels; roundwood (1984)

231,650,000 cu m; fish catch (1984) 5,927,000, of which 2,250,000 freshwater fish, 1,509,000 marine fish, 413,000 clams, 321,000 marine crabs. Mining and quarrying (1985): metals (metal content of ores)—zinc 190,000, copper 185,000, lead 160,000, tin 15,000, tungsten 15,000, molybdenum 2,000; other metals—iron ore 66,000,000, bauxite 1,650,000, nickel 22,000, gold 1,900,000 troy oz; nonmetals—salt 14,450,000, gypsum 5,000,000, barite 1,000,000, talc 950,000, fluorspar 650,000, graphite 185,000, asbestos 160,-000. Manufacturing (1985): cement 145,950,000; steel 46,790,000; chemical fertilizer 13,222,000; sugar 4,510,000; cloth 14,670,000,000 metres; wristwatches 54,311,000 units; bicycles 32,277,000 units; sewing machines 9,912,000 units; television sets 16,676,600 units. Construction (1985): residential 791,075,000 sq m; nonresidential 170,265,000 sq m. Distribution of industrial production (percent of total value of output by sector; 1978 [1985]): state-operated enterprises 80.6% (70.4%); collectives 19.2% (27.7%); privately operated enterprises 0.2% (1.9%). Retail sales (percent of total sales by sector; 1978 [1985]): state-operated enterprises 90.5% (40.4%); collectives 7.4% (37.2%); privately operated enterprises 2.1% (22.4%).

### Manufacturing and mining enterprises (1985)

| | no. of enterprises | no. of employees[11] | annual wages as a % of avg. of all wages[12] | annual gross output value (Y '000,000)[13] |
|---|---|---|---|---|
| Manufacturing | | | | |
| Machinery, transport equipment, and basic manufactures, | 111,000 | 10,091,000 | 96.7 | 217,389 |
| of which, | | | | |
| Industrial equipment | 14,900 | ... | ... | 40,233 |
| Transport equipment | 5,000 | ... | ... | 22,298[14] |
| Electronic goods | 4,100 | 1,043,000[14] | ... | 28,905 |
| Metalware for daily use | 12,500 | ... | ... | 19,448 |
| Textiles, | 22,000 | 4,229,000 | 95.5 | 123,058 |
| of which, | | | | |
| Cotton | 6,600 | ... | ... | 65,524 |
| Foodstuffs, | 79,800 | 3,133,000 | 87.5 | 85,722 |
| of which, | | | | |
| Grains and edible oils | 29,600 | ... | ... | 23,981 |
| Processed meat | 4,000 | ... | ... | 13,247 |
| Tobacco manufactures | 300 | 232,000 | ... | 14,471 |
| Chemicals, | 33,800 | 2,591,000 | 92.1 | 91,142 |
| of which, | | | | |
| Organic chemicals | 4,800 | ... | ... | 21,444 |
| Fertilizers | 3,000 | 1,110,000[14] | ... | 11,522 |
| Building materials, | 63,200 | 2,498,000 | 93.0 | 32,322 |
| of which, | | | | |
| Brick, tile, other | 37,400 | ... | ... | 12,086 |
| Cement (all forms) | 17,600 | 856,000[14] | ... | 11,673 |
| Secondary forest products (including paper and stationery) | 28,900 | 1,081,000 | 96.1 | 30,446 |
| Primary forest products | 24,700 | 1,295,000 | 114.3 | 11,881 |
| Mining | | | | |
| Nonferrous and ferrous metals | 7,200 | 3,559,000 | 107.6 | 65,914 |
| Petroleum, | 500 | 819,000 | 114.0 | 37,184 |
| of which, | | | | |
| Crude petroleum | 24[14] | 522,000 | ... | 14,250[14] |
| Coal | 10,800 | 4,479,000 | 119.8 | 20,474 |

Energy production (consumption): electricity (kW-hr; 1985) 410,700,000,000 (411,750,000,000); coal (metric tons; 1985) 845,000,000 (839,170,000); crude petroleum (barrels; 1985) 914,231,000 (696,242,000); petroleum products (metric tons; 1985) 67,924,000 (62,214,000); natural gas (cu m; 1985) 12,-865,000,000 (12,864,000,000).
*Population economically active* (1982): total 513,625,000; activity rate of total population 51.2% (participation rates: ages 15–64, 51.2%; female 36.7%; unemployed [1985] 1.8%[15]). Urban work force by sector of employment, 1978 (1985): state-run enterprises 74,500,000 (89,895,000); collectives 20,-000,000 (33,243,000); self-employment or privately run enterprises 150,000 (4,501,000).

### Price and earnings indexes (1980 = 100)

| | 1979 | 1980 | 1981 | 1982 | 1983 | 1984 | 1985 |
|---|---|---|---|---|---|---|---|
| Consumer price index | 96.2 | 100.0 | 96.6 | 96.1 | 95.8 | 97.0 | 102.6 |
| Earnings index[16] | 87.7 | 100.0 | 101.3 | 104.7 | 108.4 | 127.8 | 143.0 |

*Land use* (1984): forested 14.5%; meadows and pastures 30.6%; agricultural and under permanent cultivation 10.8%; other 44.1%.

### Financial aggregates[17]

| | 1981 | 1982 | 1983 | 1984 | 1985 | 1986 | April 1987 |
|---|---|---|---|---|---|---|---|
| Exchange rate, Y per: | | | | | | | |
| U.S. dollar | 1.75 | 1.92 | 1.98 | 2.80 | 3.20 | 3.72 | 3.72 |
| £ | 3.33 | 3.10 | 2.87 | 3.23 | 4.62 | 5.49 | 6.18 |
| SDR | 2.03 | 2.12 | 2.07 | 2.74 | 3.52 | 4.55 | 4.86 |
| International reserves (U.S.$) | | | | | | | |
| Total (excl. gold; '000,000) | 5,048 | 11,339 | 14,853 | 15,081 | 12,728 | 11,453 | 12,487 |
| SDRs ('000,000) | 275 | 214 | 335 | 406 | 483 | 569 | 604 |
| Reserve pos. in IMF ('000,000) | — | — | 176 | 223 | 332 | 370 | 395 |
| Foreign exchange | 4,773 | 11,125 | 14,342 | 14,420 | 11,913 | 10,514 | 11,488 |
| Gold ('000,000 fine troy oz) | 12.7 | 12.7 | 12.7 | 12.7 | 12.7 | 12.7 | 12.7 |
| % world reserves | 1.3 | 1.3 | 1.3 | 1.3 | 1.3 | 1.3 | 1.3 |
| Interest and prices | | | | | | | |
| Central bank discount (%) | ... | ... | ... | ... | ... | ... | ... |
| Gov't bond yield (%) | ... | ... | ... | ... | ... | ... | ... |
| Industrial share prices | ... | ... | ... | ... | ... | ... | ... |
| Balance of payments (Y '000,000) | | | | | | | |
| Balance of visible trade, | 3,030 | 8,610 | 5,130 | 1,590 | −54,310 | −28,930 | −2,620 |
| of which: | | | | | | | |
| Imports, f.o.b. | 33,730 | 32,820 | 38,700 | 56,370 | 176,820 | 137,510 | 40,460 |
| Exports, f.o.b. | 36,760 | 41,430 | 43,830 | 57,960 | 122,510 | 108,580 | 37,840 |
| Balance of invisibles | ... | ... | ... | ... | ... | ... | ... |
| Balance of payments, current account | ... | ... | ... | ... | ... | ... | ... |

*Household income and expenditure.* Average household size (1985) 4.3; rural household 5.1, urban household 3.8. Average annual income per household, n.a.; rural household Y 2,036, urban household Y 3,138. Sources of income (1985): rural household—income from the collective and nonproductive sources 8.4%, sideline production 81.1%, of which farming 48.2%, livestock raising 11.2%, labour service 6.7%; urban household[11]—time wages 59.5%, subsidies 15.2%, bonuses 12.9%, piece-rate wages 9.9%. Expenditure (1985): rural household—food 57.7%, housing 12.4%, personal effects 11.4%, clothing 9.9%, fuel 5.7%, cultural activities 2.9%; urban household—food 53.3%, clothing 15.3%, personal effects 11.1%, cultural activities 8.8%, fuel 2.4%, transportation and communication 1.3%, housing 1.1%, other 6.7%.

## Foreign trade[18]

### Balance of trade (current prices)

| | 1980 | 1981 | 1982 | 1983 | 1984 | 1985 |
|---|---|---|---|---|---|---|
| Y '000,000 | −2,760 | −10 | +5,660 | +1,650 | −3,480 | −70,220 |
| % of total | 4.8% | 0.0% | 7.3% | 1.9% | 2.9% | 22.3% |

*Imports* (1985): Y 125,780,000,000 (rolled steel 14.8%; motor vehicles and chassis 6.3%; manufactured fertilizer 3.6%; synthetic fibres 3.4%; aluminum, copper, and zinc [all forms] 3.1%; television sets 2.4%; synthetic polymers 2.2%; wheat 2.1%; logs 1.9%; ships 1.3%). *Major import sources:* Japan 35.6%; United States 12.0%; Hong Kong 11.4%; West Germany 5.7%; Canada 2.7%; Australia 2.7%; Brazil 2.3%; U.S.S.R. 2.3%; Italy 2.2%; United Kingdom 1.8%; France 1.7%.
*Exports* (1985): Y 80,930,000,000 (crude oil 19.2%; petroleum products 5.3%; cereals 5.0%; garments 4.4%; cotton cloth 3.6%; knitted fabrics 1.8%; canned foods 1.4%; polyester and cotton blend cloth 1.3%; cotton yarn 1.1%; silk and satins 1.1%; tea 1.1%). *Major export destinations:* Hong Kong 26.3%; Japan 22.3%; United States 8.6%; Singapore 7.6%; Jordan 3.6%; U.S.S.R. 3.6%; West Germany 3.1%; Brazil 1.6%; United Kingdom 1.3%; The Netherlands 1.2%; Philippines 1.2%.

## Transport and communications

*Transport.* Railroads (1986): length 35,200 mi, 56,600 km; passenger-mi 160,440,000,000, passenger-km 258,204,000,000; short ton-mi cargo 598,-945,000,000, metric ton-km cargo 874,500,000,000. Roads (1986)[3]: total length 584,000 mi, 940,000 km (paved 20%). Vehicles (1985): passenger cars 794,452; trucks 2,231,981. Merchant marine (1986): vessels (100 gross tons and over) 1,562; total deadweight tonnage 24,007,044[19]. Air transport (1985): passenger-mi 7,270,000,000, passenger-km 11,700,000,000; short ton-mi cargo 288,000,000, metric ton-km cargo 420,000,000; airports (1987) with scheduled flights 77.
*Communications.* Daily newspapers (1986)[3]: total number 222; total circulation, n.a.; circulation per 1,000 population, n.a. Radio (1985): total number of receivers 223,730,000 (1 per 4.6 persons). Television (1986): total number of receivers 69,650,000 (1 per 15 persons). Telephones (1985): 6,259,829 (1 per 166 persons).

## Education and health

### Education 1985

| | schools | teachers | students | student/teacher ratio |
|---|---|---|---|---|
| Primary (age 7–13) | 832,309 | 5,377,000 | 133,702,000 | 24.9 |
| Secondary (age 13–17) | 93,221 | 2,652,000 | 47,060,000 | 17.7 |
| Secondary specialized | 12,655 | 361,000 | 4,424,000 | 12.3 |
| Higher | 1,016 | 344,000 | 1,703,000 | 5.0 |

*Literacy* (1982): total population age 15 and over literate 609,283,011 (72.6%); males literate 358,744,834 (83.5%); females literate 250,538,177 (61.2%).
*Health* (1985): physicians 1,413,000 (1 per 737 persons); hospital beds 2,487,000 (1 per 419 persons); infant mortality rate per 1,000 live births (1985–90) 39.0.
*Food* (1983): daily per capita caloric intake 2,877 (vegetable products 92%, animal products 8%); 133% of FAO recommended minimum requirement.

## Military

*Total active duty personnel* (1986): 2,950,000 (army 71.5%, navy 11.9%, air force 16.6%). *Military expenditure as percent of GNP* (1983): 8.6% (world 6.1%); per capita expenditure U.S.$34.

[1]Names of the provinces, autonomous regions, and municipalities are stated in conventional form, followed by Pinyin transliteration; names of capitals are stated in conventional form or Wade–Giles transliteration, followed by Pinyin transliteration. [2]Data for Taiwan, Quemoy, and Matsu are excluded. [3]Beginning of the year. [4]Includes 4,600 sq mi (11,900 sq km) not shown separately. [5]Total includes servicemen not assigned to any political division. [6]Based on rural sample population. [7]Excludes arrests for anti-Communist activities. [8]Application of term differs from functional definition in a market economy. [9]Employed only. [10]Detail does not add to total given because of rounding. [11]In state-owned industries only. [12]1979. [13]In constant 1980 prices. [14]1984. [15]In urban areas only. [16]Average annual wage of staff and workers in state-owned enterprises. [17]Exchange rates and international reserves are based on end-of-year figures. [18]Imports, c.i.f. (cost, insurance, and freight); exports, f.o.b. (free on board). [19]Deadweight tonnage includes 587 vessels of Taiwan (100 gross tons and over).

# Colombia

*Official name:* República de Colombia (Republic of Colombia).
*Form of government:* unitary, multiparty republic with two legislative houses (Senate [114]; House of Representatives [199]).
*Head of state and government:* President.
*Capital:* Bogotá.
*Official language:* Spanish.
*Official religion:* none.
*Monetary unit:* 1 peso (Col$) = 100 centavos; valuation (Oct. 5, 1987) 1 U.S.$ = Col$255.68; 1 £ = Col$415.20.

| Area and population | | area | | population |
|---|---|---|---|---|
| | | sq mi | sq km | 1985 census |
| **Commissariats** | **Capitals** | | | |
| Amazonas | Leticia | 42,342 | 109,665 | 30,327 |
| Guainía | San Felipe (Obando) | 27,891 | 72,238 | 9,214 |
| Guaviare | Guaviare | 16,342 | 42,327 | 35,305 |
| Vaupés | Mitú | 25,200 | 65,268 | 18,935 |
| Vichada | Puerto Carreño | 38,703 | 100,242 | 13,770 |
| **Departments** | | | | |
| Antioquia | Medellín | 24,561 | 63,612 | 3,888,067 |
| Atlántico | Barranquilla | 1,308 | 3,388 | 1,428,601 |
| Bolívar | Cartagena | 10,030 | 25,978 | 1,197,623 |
| Boyacá | Tunja | 8,953 | 23,189 | 1,097,618 |
| Caldas | Manizales | 3,046 | 7,888 | 838,094 |
| Caquetá | Florencia | 34,349 | 88,965 | 214,473 |
| Cauca | Popayán | 11,316 | 29,308 | 795,838 |
| Cesar | Valledupar | 8,844 | 22,905 | 584,631 |
| Chocó | Quibdó | 17,965 | 46,530 | 242,768 |
| Córdoba | Montería | 9,660 | 25,020 | 913,636 |
| Cundinamarca | Bogotá | 8,735 | 22,623 | 1,382,360 |
| Huila | Neiva | 7,680 | 19,890 | 647,756 |
| La Guajira | Riohacha | 8,049 | 20,848 | 255,310 |
| Magdalena | Santa Marta | 8,953 | 23,188 | 769,141 |
| Meta | Villavicencio | 33,064 | 85,635 | 412,312 |
| Nariño | Pasto | 12,845 | 33,268 | 1,019,098 |
| Norte de Santander | Cúcuta | 8,362 | 21,658 | 883,884 |
| Quindío | Armenia | 712 | 1,845 | 377,860 |
| Risaralda | Pereira | 1,598 | 4,140 | 625,451 |
| Santander | Bucaramanga | 11,790 | 30,537 | 1,438,226 |
| Sucre | Sincelejo | 4,215 | 10,917 | 529,059 |
| Tolima | Ibagué | 9,097 | 23,562 | 1,051,852 |
| Valle | Cali | 8,548 | 22,140 | 2,847,087 |
| **Intendancies** | | | | |
| Arauca | Arauca | 9,196 | 23,818 | 70,085 |
| Casanare | Yopal | 17,236 | 44,640 | 110,253 |
| Putumayo | Mocoa | 9,608 | 24,885 | 119,815 |
| San Andrés y Providencia | San Andrés | 17 | 44 | 35,936 |
| **Special District** | | | | |
| Bogotá | | 613 | 1,587 | 3,982,941 |
| TOTAL | | 440,831[1] | 1,141,748 | 27,867,326 |

## Demography

*Population* (1987): 28,655,000.
*Density* (1987): persons per sq mi 65.0, persons per sq km 25.1.
*Urban-rural* (1985): urban 67.2%; rural 32.8%.
*Sex distribution* (1985): male 49.49%; female 50.51%.
*Age breakdown* (1985): under 15, 36.1%; 15–29, 31.2%; 30–44, 17.2%; 45–59, 9.5%; 60–74, 4.6%; 75 and over, 1.4%.
*Population projection:* (1990) 30,095,000; (2000) 35,436,000.
*Doubling time:* 34 years.
*Ethnic composition* (1985): mestizo 58.0%; white 20.0%; mulatto 14.0%; black 4.0%; mixed black-Indian 3.0%; Amerindian 1.0%.
*Religious affiliation* (1984): Roman Catholic 94.8%; other 5.2%.
*Major cities* (1985): Bogotá 3,974,813; Medellín 1,418,554; Cali 1,323,944; Barranquilla 896,649; Cartagena 491,368.

## Vital statistics

*Birth rate* per 1,000 population (1983–88): 27.9 (world avg. 26.0); (1982) legitimate 75.2%; illegitimate 24.8%.
*Death rate* per 1,000 population (1983–88): 7.4 (world avg. 9.9).
*Natural increase rate* per 1,000 population (1983–88): 20.5 (world avg. 16.1).
*Total fertility rate* (avg. births per childbearing woman; 1981–86): 3.4.
*Marriage rate* per 1,000 population (1977): 3.5.
*Life expectancy* at birth (1980–85): male 61.4 years; female 66.0 years.
*Major causes of death* per 100,000 population (1977): diseases of the circulatory system 129.2; infectious and parasitic diseases 86.6.

## National economy

*Budget* (1986). Revenue: Col$974,699,000,000 (indirect taxes 43.2%, credit resources 23.8%, direct taxes 19.0%). Expenditures: Col$954,176,000,000 (transfer payments 35.3%, capital investments 27.0%, debt service 20.9%).
*Public debt* (external, outstanding; 1985): U.S.$9,377,000,000.
*Tourism* (1985): receipts from visitors U.S.$286,000,000; expenditures by nationals abroad U.S.$168,000,000.
*Production* (metric tons except as noted). Agriculture (1986): sugarcane 13,529,000[2], potatoes 2,295,100, plantains 2,290,500, rice 1,743,200, cassava 1,513,400[2], bananas 1,026,000, corn (maize) 728,800, coffee (green) 642,700, sorghum 582,400; roundwood (1985) 17,224,000 cu m; fish catch (1985) 69,736; livestock (number of live animals; 1985) 21,935,000 cattle, 2,714,-

000 sheep, 2,378,000 pigs. Mining and quarrying (1986): iron ore 508,082; gold 1,279,242 troy oz; silver 187,187 troy oz. Manufacturing (value added in Col$'000,000; 1984): processed food 418,207; chemicals 221,655; beverages 156,947; textiles 142,521; transport equipment 89,308; paper and paper products 75,784. Construction (1986)[3]: residential 6,340,675 sq m; nonresidential 1,124,039 sq m. Energy production (consumption): electricity (kW-hr; 1985) 26,800,000,000 (26,798,000,000); coal (metric tons; 1985) 6,500,000 (5,900,000); crude petroleum (barrels; 1985) 64,514,000 (70,890,-000); petroleum products (metric tons; 1985) 8,822,000 (6,833,000); natural gas (cu m; 1985) 4,459,137,000 (4,459,137,000).
*Gross national product* (1985): U.S.$37,610,000,000 (U.S.$1,360 per capita).

| Structure of gross domestic product and labour force | 1986 | | 1980 | |
|---|---|---|---|---|
| | in value U.S.$'000,000 | % of total value | labour force | % of labour force |
| Agriculture | 8,136 | 21.1 | 2,412,413 | 28.5 |
| Mining | 1,008 | 2.6 | 49,740 | 0.6 |
| Manufacturing | 8,398 | 21.7 | 1,136,735 | 13.4 |
| Construction | 1,448 | 3.7 | 242,191 | 2.9 |
| Public utilities | 400 | 1.0 | 44,233 | 0.5 |
| Transp. and commun. | 3,734 | 9.7 | 352,623 | 4.2 |
| Trade | 4,805 | 12.4 } | 1,539,843 | 18.1 |
| Finance | 2,739 | 7.1 } | | |
| Pub. admin., defense | 3,079 | 8.0 | 1,998,460 | 23.6 |
| Services } | 4,887 | 12.7 | 690,762 | 8.2 |
| Other } | | | | |
| TOTAL | 38,634 | 100.0 | 8,467,000 | 100.0 |

*Population economically active* (1985): total 9,552,067; activity rate 34.3% (participation rates: over age 12, 49.4%; female 16.2%; unemployed 4.3%).

| Price and earnings indexes (1980 = 100) | 1981 | 1982 | 1983 | 1984 | 1985 | 1986 | 1987[4] |
|---|---|---|---|---|---|---|---|
| Consumer price index | 127.5 | 158.8 | 190.2 | 220.8 | 273.9 | 325.7 | 396.8 |
| Monthly earnings index[5] | 102.4 | 106.2 | 112.2 | 119.3 | 116.7 | 121.4 | ... |

*Average household size* (1985) 4.7.
*Land use* (1984): forested 48.0%; meadows and pastures 28.9%; agricultural and under permanent cultivation 5.5%; other 17.6%.

## Foreign trade

| Balance of trade (current prices) | 1981 | 1982 | 1983 | 1984 | 1985 | 1986 |
|---|---|---|---|---|---|---|
| U.S.$'000,000 | −1,729.0 | −1,841.8 | −1,390.7 | −590.4 | −179.9 | +1,537.6 |
| % of total | 22.6% | 22.9% | 18.4% | 7.9% | 2.5% | 17.7% |

*Imports* (1986): U.S.$3,852,085,000 (machinery 24.9%, chemicals 10.4%, transport equipment 9.2%, iron and steel products 7.5%, plastic products 4.0%, crude petroleum 3.9%). *Major import sources:* U.S. 36.1%; West Germany 6.6%; Venezuela, 4.9%; Spain 4.3%; France 4.0%; Brazil 3.6%.
*Exports* (1986): U.S.$5,107,936,000 (coffee 58.5%, crude petroleum and petroleum products 13.0%, fruits, mainly bananas 3.9%, fresh-cut flowers 2.9%, cotton 1.7%, textile apparel 1.3%). *Major export destinations:* U.S. 30.0%; West Germany 20.6%; The Netherlands 5.2%; Venezuela 2.9%; United Kingdom 2.6%; France 2.6%.

## Transport and communications

*Transport.* Railroads (1985): route length 2,023 mi, 3,255 km; passenger-mi 39,512,000, passenger-km 63,589,000; short ton-mi cargo 132,688,000, metric ton-km cargo 193,721,000. Roads (1983): total length 65,369 mi, 105,201 km (paved 28%). Vehicles (1983): cars 509,478; trucks and buses 520,085. Merchant marine (1986): vessels (100 gross tons and over) 90; total deadweight tonnage 486,423. Air transport (1986): passenger-km 1,974,658,000; metric ton-km cargo 252,042,000; airports (1987) 78.
*Communications.* Daily newspapers (1984): 31; circulation 1,323,800; circulation per 1,000 population 47. Radio (1986): 7,980,000 receivers (1 per 3.5 persons). Television (1986): 3,800,000 receivers (1 per 7.4 persons). Telephones (1985): 2,096,996 (1 per 13 persons).

## Education and health

| Education (1986) | schools | teachers | students | student/ teacher ratio |
|---|---|---|---|---|
| Primary | 36,979 | 135,924 | 4,002,543 | 29.4 |
| Secondary[6] | 6,336 | 107,084 | 2,136,239 | 19.9 |
| Higher | 231 | 43,447 | 402,438 | 9.3 |

*Educational attainment* (1985). Percent of population age 25 and over having: no schooling 15.3%; primary education 50.1%; secondary 25.4%; higher 6.8%; not stated 2.4%. *Literacy* (1985): population age 18 and over literate 10,714,936 (69.1%).
*Health* (1983): physicians 21,778 (1 per 1,969 persons); hospital beds (1982) 28,880 (1 per 586 persons); infant mortality rate 40.0.
*Food* (1981–83): daily per capita caloric intake 2,543 (vegetable products 86%, animal products 14%); (1983) 111% of FAO minimum requirement.

## Military

*Total active duty personnel* (1986): 66,200 (army 80.1%, navy 13.6%, air force 6.3%). *Military expenditure as percent of GNP* (1984): 1.1% (world 5.9%); per capita expenditure U.S.$15.

[1]Detail does not add to total given because of rounding. [2]Preliminary. [3]Includes 11 urban centres. [4]May. [5]Real wages in the industrial sector. [6]Secondary includes vocational and teacher training.

# Comoros[1]

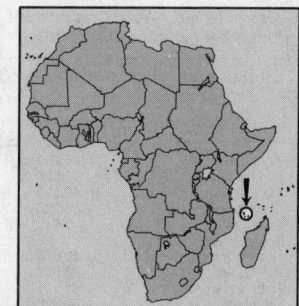

*Official name:* Jumhurīyat al-Qumur al-Ittihādīyah al-Islāmīyah (Arabic); République Fédéral Islamique des Comores (French) (Federal Islamic Republic of the Comoros).
*Form of government:* federal Islamic republic with one legislative house (Federal Assembly [42]).
*Head of state and government:* President.
*Capital:* Moroni.
*Official languages:* Arabic; French.
*Official religion:* Islam.
*Monetary unit:* 1 Comorian franc (CF) = 100 centimes; valuation (Oct. 5, 1987) 1 U.S.\$ = CF 306.67; 1 £ = CF 498.00.

### Area and population

| Governorates/Islands[2] | Capitals | area sq mi | area sq km | population 1987 estimate |
|---|---|---|---|---|
| Moili (Mohéli) | Fomboni | 112 | 290 | 21,803 |
| Ngazidja (Grande Comore) | Moroni | 443 | 1,148 | 226,874 |
| Ndzouani (Anjouan) | Mutsamudu | 164 | 424 | 173,494 |
| TOTAL | | 719 | 1,862 | 422,171 |

## Demography

*Population* (1987): 422,000.
*Density* (1987): persons per sq mi 587.2, persons per sq km 226.7.
*Urban–rural* (1985): urban 27.1%; rural 72.9%.
*Sex distribution* (1985): male 49.72%; female 50.28%.
*Age breakdown* (1985): under 15, 48.3%; 15–29, 24.8%; 30–44, 13.6%; 45–59, 8.1%; 60–74, 4.1%; 75 and over, 1.1%.
*Population projection:* (1990) 466,000; (2000) 650,000.
*Doubling time:* 24 years.
*Ethnic composition* (1980): Comorian (a mixture of Bantu, Arab, and Malagasy peoples) 96.9%; Makua (a Bantu people from East Africa) 1.6%; French 0.4%; other 1.1%.
*Religious affiliation* (1980): Sunnī Muslim 99.7%; Christian 0.2%; Bahā'ī 0.1%.
*Major cities* (1980): Moroni 17,267; Mutsamudu 16,883; Domoni 7,147; Ouani 6,936; Tsembehou 6,578.

## Vital statistics

*Birth rate* per 1,000 population (1985): 44.0 (world avg. 29.0).
*Death rate* per 1,000 population (1985): 15.0 (world avg. 11.0).
*Natural increase rate* per 1,000 population (1985): 29.0 (world avg. 18.0).
*Total fertility rate* (avg. births per childbearing woman; 1984): 7.0.
*Marriage rate* per 1,000 population: n.a.
*Divorce rate* per 1,000 population: n.a.
*Life expectancy* at birth (1980): male 54.2 years; female 53.9 years.
*Major causes of death* per 100,000 population: n.a.; however, major diseases (1980) include malaria (afflicts 80% of the adult population), tuberculosis, leprosy, and kwashiorkor (a nutritional deficiency disease).

## National economy

*Budget* (1984). Revenue: CF 14,305,600,000 (grants from abroad 57.6%; tax revenue 36.7%, of which consumption tax on imported items 19.6%, export duties 4.0%, customs duties 2.8%; nontax revenue 5.7%, of which property income 4.8%). Expenditures: CF 25,730,300,000[3] (economic services 54.5%, of which roads 16.8%, inland and coastal waterways 15.9%, agriculture, forestry, and fishing 8.9%; education 18.6%; general public services 10.2%; health 5.3%; defense 3.0%).
*Public debt* (external, outstanding; 1985): U.S.\$129,100,000.
*Tourism* (1985): tourist arrivals 2,310.
*Production* (metric tons except as noted). Agriculture, forestry, fishing (1985)[4]: cassava 92,000, coconuts 47,000, bananas 35,000, sweet potatoes 18,000, rice 16,000, corn (maize) 6,000, copra 3,000, pulses 3,000, cloves 1,124[5, 6], vanilla 181[5, 6], ylang-ylang 60[5, 6], coffee 8[5, 6], basil 2[5, 6]; livestock (number of live animals) 94,000 goats, 85,000 cattle, 9,000 sheep, 4,000 asses; roundwood, n.a.; fish catch (1984) 4,000. Mining and quarrying: sand and gravel for local construction. Manufacturing (1985): products include cement, handicrafts, soaps, soft drinks, aluminum kitchen utensils, and clothing. Construction: n.a. Energy production (consumption): electricity (kW-hr; 1985) 12,300,000 (10,000,000); coal, none (none); crude petroleum, none (none); petroleum products (metric tons; 1985) none (12,000); natural gas, none (none).
*Population economically active* (1985): total 117,216; activity rate of total population 29.6% (participation rates: ages 15–64, 53.1%; female 26.2%; unemployed [1985] 13.3%).

### Price and earnings indexes (1979 = 100)

| | 1977 | 1978 | 1979 | 1980 | 1981 | 1982 | 1983 |
|---|---|---|---|---|---|---|---|
| Consumer price index | 75.5 | 87.9 | 100.0 | 111.2 | 131.9 | 177.2 | 188.5 |
| Daily earnings index[7] | ... | ... | 100.0 | ... | ... | ... | 133.3 |

*Household income and expenditure.* Average household size (1985) 5.6; income per household: n.a.; sources of income: n.a.; expenditure (1983)[8]: food and beverages 56.0%, energy 14.4%, clothing and footwear 10.0%,

transportation and communication 6.6%, health care 5.0%, recreation 3.0%, tobacco 3.0%, other 2.0%.
*Gross national product* (at current market prices; 1985): U.S.\$110,000,000 (U.S.\$280 per capita).

### Structure of gross domestic product and labour force

| | 1985 in value CF '000,000 | 1985 % of total value | 1980 labour force | 1980 % of labour force |
|---|---|---|---|---|
| Agriculture | 18,037 | 37.0 | 53,063 | 53.3 |
| Mining | ... | ... | 62 | 0.1 |
| Manufacturing | 1,950 | 4.0 | 3,946 | 4.0 |
| Construction | 4,875 | 10.0 | 3,267 | 3.3 |
| Public utilities | | | 129 | 0.1 |
| Transportation and communication | 1,950 | 4.0 | 2,118 | 2.1 |
| Trade, restaurants, hotels | 12,188 | 25.0 | 1,873 | 1.9 |
| Finance, insurance | ... | ... | 237 | 0.2 |
| Public admin., defense, services | 7,800 | 16.0 | 7,081 | 7.2 |
| Other | 1,950 | 4.0 | 27,687[9] | 27.8 |
| TOTAL | 48,750 | 100.0 | 99,463 | 100.0 |

*Land use* (1984)[4]: forested 16.0%; meadows and pastures 7.0%; agricultural and under permanent cultivation 43.0%; other 34.0%.

## Foreign trade[10]

### Balance of trade (current prices)

| | 1980 | 1981 | 1982 | 1983 | 1984 | 1985 |
|---|---|---|---|---|---|---|
| CF '000,000 | −4,185 | −4,330 | −4,291 | −5,680 | −15,700 | −9,433 |
| % of total | 51.6% | 32.5% | 25.0% | 27.7% | 71.7% | 40.1% |

*Imports* (1985): CF 16,481,000,000 (rice 34.3%, petroleum products 8.8%, cement 3.9%, meat 3.7%, iron and steel products 3.0%, unspecified commodities 46.3%). *Major import sources:* France 41.4%; Madagascar 19.9%; Pakistan 9.4%; Kenya and Tanzania 8.4%; China 4.0%.
*Exports* (1985): CF 7,048,000,000 (vanilla 66.5%, cloves 19.5%, ylang-ylang 9.3%, copra 0.9%). *Major export destinations:* France 65.5%; United States 21.4%; Madagascar 5.0%; West Germany 3.4%.

## Transport and communications

*Transport.* Railroads: none. Roads (1985): total length 466 mi, 750 km (paved 53%). Vehicles (1983): passenger cars, 3,600; trucks and buses, 2,000. Merchant marine (1986): vessels (100 gross tons and over) 3; total deadweight tonnage 2,194. Air transport (1983)[11]: passenger arrivals and departures 30,537; cargo loaded and unloaded 172 metric tons; airports (1987) with scheduled flights 3.
*Communications.* Daily newspapers: none. Radio (1986): total number of receivers 41,000 (1 per 10 persons). Television: total number of receivers, none. Telephones (1981): 1,650 (1 per 208 persons).

## Education and health

### Education (1980–81)

| | schools | teachers | students | student/ teacher ratio |
|---|---|---|---|---|
| Primary (age 7–13) | 236 | 1,292 | 59,709 | 46.2 |
| Secondary | 32 | 434 | 13,528 | 31.2 |
| Voc., teacher tr. | 4 | 27 | 327 | 12.1 |

*Educational attainment* (1980). Percent of total population age 25 and over having: no formal schooling 56.7%; Qur'anic school education 8.3%; primary 3.6%; secondary 2.0%; higher 0.2%; not specified 29.2%. *Literacy* (1980): total population age 15 and over literate 82,053 (46.3%); males literate 46,586 (54.2%); females literate 35,467 (39.0%).
*Health* (1982): physicians 20 (1 per 17,300 persons); hospital beds 813 (1 per 439 persons); infant mortality rate per 1,000 live births (1985) 111.0.
*Food* (1981–83)[4]: daily per capita caloric intake 2,214 (vegetable products 95%, animal products 5%); (1983) 91% of FAO recommended minimum requirement.

## Military[12]

*Total active duty personnel* (1986): 700–800 (army 100%). *Military expenditure as percent of GNP* (1983): 1.9% (world 6.1%); per capita expenditure U.S.\$6.

[1]Excludes Mayotte, a *collectivité territoriale* ("territorial collectivity") of France, unless otherwise indicated. [2]Island names in Comorian Swahili and French, respectively. [3]Development expenditures comprise 75.2% of total expenditures. [4]Includes Mayotte. [5]Excludes Mayotte. [6]Export only. [7]Construction sector only. [8]Weights of consumer price index components. [9]Not adequately defined. [10]Import figures c.i.f. (cost, insurance, freight); export figures f.o.b. (free on board). [11]Air Comores only. [12]In 1983 France assumed sole responsibility for the defense of the Comoros.

# Congo

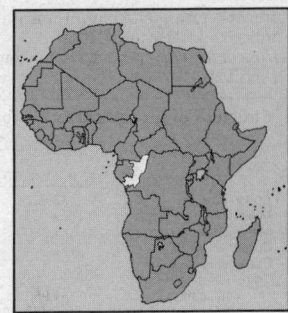

*Official name:* République Populaire du Congo (People's Republic of the Congo).
*Form of government:* people's republic with one legislative body (People's National Assembly [153]).
*Head of state and government:* President (Chairman of the Central Committee).
*Capital:* Brazzaville.
*Official language:* French.
*Official religion:* none.
*Monetary unit:* 1 CFA franc (CFAF) = 100 centimes; valuation (Oct. 5, 1987) 1 U.S.$ = CFAF 306.67; 1 £ = CFAF 498.00.

### Area and population

| | | area | | population |
| --- | --- | --- | --- | --- |
| | | | | 1984 |
| Regions | Capitals | sq mi | sq km | census |
| Bouenza | Madingou | 4,734 | 12,260 | 150,603 |
| Cuvette | Owando | 28,900 | 74,850 | 135,744 |
| Kouilou | Pointe-Noire | 5,274 | 13,660 | 74,870 |
| Lékoumou | Sibiti | 8,089 | 20,950 | 68,287 |
| Likouala | Impfondo | 25,500 | 66,044 | 49,505 |
| Niari | Loubomo | 10,011[1] | 25,930[1] | 110,003 |
| Plateaux | Djambala | 14,826 | 38,400 | 109,663 |
| Pool | Kinkala | 13,124 | 33,990 | 184,263 |
| Sangha | Ouesso | 21,544[2] | 55,800[2] | 34,213 |
| **Communes** | | | | |
| Brazzaville | — | 25 | 65 | 585,812 |
| Loubomo | — | 5 | 12 | 49,134 |
| Mossendjo | — | 1 | 1 | 14,469 |
| Nkayi | — | 2 | 5 | 36,540 |
| Ouesso | — | 2 | 2 | 11,939 |
| Pointe-Noire | — | 13 | 34 | 294,203 |
| TOTAL | | 132,047 | 342,000 | 1,909,248 |

## Demography

*Population* (1987): 2,180,000.
*Density* (1987): persons per sq mi 16.5, persons per sq km 6.4.
*Urban–rural* (1984): urban 51.1%; rural 48.9%.
*Sex distribution* (1985): male 49.31%; female 50.69%.
*Age breakdown* (1985): under 15, 43.6%; 15–29, 25.8%; 30–44, 15.6%; 45–59, 9.5%; 60–74, 4.6%; 75 and over, 0.9%.
*Population projection:* (1990) 2,447,400; (2000) 3,600,000.
*Doubling time:* 18 years.
*Ethnic composition* (1983): Kongo 51.5%; Teke 17.3%; Mboshi 11.5%; Mbete 4.8%; Punu 3.0%; Sanga 2.7%; Maka 1.8%; Pygmy 1.5%; other 5.9%.
*Religious affiliation* (1980): Roman Catholic 53.9%; Protestant 24.9%; African Christian 14.2%; traditional beliefs 4.8%; other 2.2%.
*Major cities* (1984): Brazzaville 585,812; Pointe-Noire 294,203; Loubomo 49,134; Nkayi 36,540; Owando 16,021.

## Vital statistics

*Birth rate* per 1,000 population (1980–85): 44.5 (world avg. 29.0); legitimate, n.a.; illegitimate, n.a.
*Death rate* per 1,000 population (1980–85): 18.6 (world avg. 11.0).
*Natural increase rate* per 1,000 population (1980–85): 25.9 (world avg. 18.0).
*Total fertility rate* (avg. births per childbearing woman; 1980–85): 6.0.
*Marriage rate* per 1,000 population: n.a.
*Divorce rate* per 1,000 population: n.a.
*Life expectancy* at birth (1980–85): male 44.9 years; female 48.1 years.
*Morbidity* (reported cases per 100,000 population; 1985): malaria 2,306.0; diarrhea 845.6; measles 491.2; gonorrhea 300.9; tuberculosis 36.3.

## National economy

*Budget* (1985). Revenue: CFAF 311,000,000,000 (petroleum revenue 58.0%, domestic taxes 19.3%, customs duties 15.0%). Expenditures: CFAF 311,000,000,000 (public works, construction, and housing 29.6%, hydraulic energy 18.1%, civil aviation and transport 9.5%, industries and crafts 6.5%, agriculture and livestock 6.1%, health 6.0%, defense 3.8%).
*Public debt* (external, outstanding; 1985): U.S.$1,760,400,000.
*Tourism* (1985): receipts from visitors U.S.$13,000,000; expenditures by nationals abroad U.S.$55,000,000.
*Production* (metric tons except as noted). Agriculture, forestry, fishing (1985): cassava 610,000, sugarcane 510,000, pineapples 107,000, bananas 33,000, palm oil 15,000, peanuts (groundnuts) 15,000, yams 14,000, sweet potatoes 13,000, corn (maize) 7,000, coffee 3,000, cacao beans 2,000, rice 2,000; livestock (number of live animals) 183,000 goats, 70,000 cattle, 62,000 sheep; roundwood 2,381,000 cu m; fish catch 33,539. Mining and quarrying (1985): lead 6,100; copper 35[3]; gold 13 kilograms. Manufacturing (1985): cement 62,000; raw sugar 46,000; wheat flour 8,000[3]; soap 1,900; cigarettes 1,027; peanut oil 1,000; beer 882,000 hectolitres; soft drinks 279,000 hectolitres; veneer sheets (1984) 65,000 cu m; footwear 1,128,000 pairs. Construction: n.a. Energy production (consumption): electricity (kW-hr; 1985) 237,000,000 (264,000,000); coal, none (n.a.); crude petroleum (barrels; 1985) 43,376,000 (375,000); petroleum products (metric tons; 1985) 49,000 (91,000); natural gas (cu m; 1985) 34,000,000 (n.a.).
*Land use* (1984): forested 62.4%; meadows and pastures 29.3%; agricultural and under permanent cultivation 2.0%; other 6.3%.

*Gross national product* (at current market prices; 1985): U.S.$1,910,000,000 (U.S.$950 per capita).

### Structure of gross domestic product and labour force

| | 1984 | | 1981 | |
| --- | --- | --- | --- | --- |
| | in value CFAF '000,000 | % of total value | labour force | % of labour force |
| Agriculture | 70,299 | 7.7 | 180,200 | 34.0 |
| Mining | 395,854 | 43.0 | | |
| Manufacturing | 42,509 | 4.6 | | |
| Construction | 65,096 | 7.1 | | |
| Public utilities | 9,510 | 1.0 | 137,800 | 26.0 |
| Transportation and communication | 68,576 | 7.5 | | |
| Trade, finance | 98,659 | 10.7 | | |
| Pub. admin., defense | | | | |
| Services | 169,625 | 18.4 | 212,000 | 40.0 |
| Other | | | | |
| TOTAL | 920,128 | 100.0 | 530,000 | 100.0 |

*Population economically active* (1985): total 710,000; activity rate of total population 40.8% (participation rates: ages 15–64, 69.4%; female [1985] 39.3%; unemployed, n.a.).

### Price and earnings indexes (1980 = 100)

| | 1980 | 1981 | 1982 | 1983 | 1984 | 1985 | 1986 |
| --- | --- | --- | --- | --- | --- | --- | --- |
| Consumer price index | 100.0 | 117.0 | 132.0 | 142.3 | 160.3 | 170.1 | 174.3 |
| Earnings index | | | | | | | |

*Household income and expenditure.* Average household size (1980) 4.7; income per household, n.a.; sources of income: n.a.; expenditure: n.a.

## Foreign trade[4]

### Balance of trade (current prices)

| | 1980 | 1981 | 1982 | 1983 | 1984 | 1985 |
| --- | --- | --- | --- | --- | --- | --- |
| CFAF '000,000,000 | 92.1 | 121.5 | 120.4 | 194.9 | 297.2 | 182.2 |
| % of total | 31.5% | 38.0% | 22.6% | 31.8% | 40.4% | 22.9% |

*Imports* (1985): CFAF 306,198,400,000 (machinery and transport equipment 29.6%, of which transport equipment 9.2%; food and beverages 15.4%; iron and steel 11.8%; chemicals and related products 6.7%; textiles 2.8%; petroleum products 2.7%; plastic and rubber goods 2.3%; precision instruments 2.1%). *Major import sources:* France 38.8%; Italy 7.0%; United States 5.6%; West Germany 4.0%; Japan 2.9%; The Netherlands 2.3%; Belgium–Luxembourg 2.0%.
*Exports* (1985): CFAF 488,365,700,000 (crude petroleum 93.3%; wood and wood products 2.5%; pearls and precious stones 1.0%; coffee, cocoa, and tobacco 0.2%). *Major export destinations:* United States 60.0%; Spain 13.9%; France 10.9%; The Netherlands 6.0%; Italy 1.8%; Belgium–Luxembourg 1.0%.

## Transport and communications

*Transport.* Railroads (1985): length 498 mi, 802 km; passenger-mi 268,000,000, passenger-km 432,000,000; short ton-mi cargo 353,000,000, metric ton-km cargo 516,000,000. Roads (1985): total length 6,835 mi, 11,000 km (paved 5.1%). Vehicles (1982): passenger cars 30,500; trucks and buses 78,600. Merchant marine (1986): vessels (100 gross tons and over) 21; total deadweight tonnage 10,840. Air transport[5] (1985): passenger-mi 144,226,000, passenger-km 232,109,000; short ton-mi cargo 27,422,000, metric ton-km cargo 40,035,000; airports (1987) with scheduled flights 17.
*Communications.* Daily newspapers (1986): total number 3; total circulation 24,000; circulation per 1,000 population 11. Radio (1985): total number of receivers 200,000 (1 per 10 persons). Television (1986): total number of receivers 5,500 (1 per 381 persons). Telephones (1983): 18,093 (1 per 103 persons).

## Education and health

### Education (1984–85)

| | schools | teachers | students | student/ teacher ratio |
| --- | --- | --- | --- | --- |
| Primary (age 6–13) | 1,522 | 7,612 | 458,338 | 60.2 |
| Secondary (age 14–18) | 247 | 5,188 | 199,073 | 38.4 |
| Voc., teacher tr. | 19 | 1,073 | 5,477 | 22.2 |
| Higher | 1 | ... | 9,385 | ... |

*Educational attainment*[6] (1974). Percent of population age 15 and over having: secondary education 30%, of which males 37%, females 23%. *Literacy* (1985): total population age 15 and over literate 620,000 (62.9%); males literate 332,000 (71.4%); females literate 288,000 (55.4%).
*Health:* physicians (1980) 278 (1 per 5,986 persons); hospital beds (1978) 6,876 (1 per 224 persons); infant mortality rate per 1,000 live births (1980–85) 81.0.
*Food* (1981–83): daily per capita caloric intake 2,470 (vegetable products 93%, animal products 7%); (1983) 109% of FAO recommended minimum requirement.

## Military

*Total active duty personnel* (1987): 8,750 (army 91.4%, navy 2.9%, air force 5.7%). *Military expenditure as percent of GNP* (1985): 2.5% (world 5.9%); per capita expenditure U.S.$28.

---

[1]Mossendjo is included with Niari. [2]Ouesso is included with Sangha. [3]1983. [4]Import figures are c.i.f. (cost, insurance, and freight). [5]Air Afrique only. [6]For the Commune of Brazzaville only.

# Costa Rica

*Official name:* República de Costa Rica (Republic of Costa Rica).
*Form of government:* unitary multiparty republic with one legislative house (Legislative Assembly [57]).
*Head of state and government:* President.
*Capital:* San José.
*Official language:* Spanish.
*Official religion:* Roman Catholicism.
*Monetary unit:* 1 Costa Rican colón (₡) = 100 céntimos; valuation (Oct. 5, 1987) 1 U.S.$ = ₡64.30; 1 £ = ₡104.41.

### Area and population

| Provinces | Capitals | area sq mi | area sq km | population 1984 census |
|---|---|---|---|---|
| Alajuela | Alajuela | 3,766 | 9,753 | 427,962 |
| Cartago | Cartago | 1,206 | 3,125 | 271,671 |
| Guanacaste | Liberia | 3,915 | 10,141 | 195,208 |
| Heredia | Heredia | 1,026 | 2,656 | 197,575 |
| Limón | Limón | 3,548 | 9,188 | 168,076 |
| Puntarenas | Puntarenas | 4,354 | 11,277 | 265,883 |
| San José | San José | 1,915 | 4,960 | 890,434 |
| TOTAL | | 19,730 | 51,100 | 2,416,809 |

## Demography

*Population* (1987): 2,613,000.
*Density* (1987): persons per sq mi 133.2, persons per sq km 51.4.
*Urban–rural* (1986): urban 50.3%; rural 49.7%.
*Sex distribution* (1984): male 49.99%; female 50.01%.
*Age breakdown* (1984): under 15, 36.6%; 15–29, 31.1%; 30–44, 16.7%; 45–59, 9.1%; 60–74, 4.9%; 75 and over, 1.6%.
*Population projection:* (1990) 2,811,000; (2000) 3,587,000.
*Doubling time:* 26 years.
*Ethnic composition* (1980): European 86.8%; mestizo 7.0%; black/mulatto 2.0%; Chinese 1.9%; Amerindian 0.5%; other 1.8%.
*Religious affiliation* (1984): Roman Catholic 92.4%; other (mostly Protestant) 7.6%.
*Major cities* (1984): San José 241,464; Limón 33,925; Alajuela 29,273; Puntarenas 28,390; Cartago 23,928.

## Vital statistics

*Birth rate* per 1,000 population (1984): 31.4 (world avg. 29.0).
*Death rate* per 1,000 population (1984): 4.1 (world avg. 11.0).
*Natural increase rate* per 1,000 population (1984): 27.3 (world avg. 18.0).
*Total fertility rate* (avg. births per childbearing woman; 1984): 3.3.
*Marriage rate* per 1,000 population (1984): 8.5.
*Divorce rate* per 1,000 population (1983): 1.0.
*Life expectancy* at birth (1980–85): male 70.5 years; female 75.7 years.
*Major causes of death* per 100,000 population (1983): diseases of the circulatory system 111.5; malignant neoplasms (cancers) 78.4; respiratory diseases 39.5; accidents 37.2; birth trauma and other conditions originating from perinatal period 26.7; infectious and parasitic diseases 17.5.

## National economy

*Budget* (1985). Revenue: ₡41,010,600,000 (taxes on goods and services 30.2%, social security contributions 26.5%, taxes on foreign trade 20.3%, income taxes 12.3%). Expenditures: ₡43,135,500,000 (health, social security, and welfare 37.5%, education 18.7%, roads 12.5%, general public services 9.6%, defense 2.7%).
*Public debt* (external, outstanding; 1985): U.S.$3,665,200,000.
*Gross national product* (at current market prices; 1985): U.S.$3,340,000,000 (U.S.$1,340 per capita).

### Structure of gross domestic product and labour force

| | 1985 in value U.S.$'000,000[1] | 1985 % of total value | labour force | % of labour force |
|---|---|---|---|---|
| Agriculture | 843 | 19.6 | 238,207 | 26.8 |
| Mining Manufacturing } | 948 | 22.0 | 142,187 | 16.1 |
| Construction | 199 | 4.6 | 47,465 | 5.3 |
| Public utilities | 141 | 3.3 | 53,421 | 6.0 |
| Transp. and commun. | 308 | 7.1 | | |
| Trade | 708 | 16.4 | 164,863 | 18.6 |
| Finance | 562 | 13.0 | | |
| Public admin. and defense | 419 | 9.7 | 222,845 | 25.1 |
| Services | 182 | 4.2 | | |
| Other | — | | 18,468 | 2.1 |
| TOTAL | 4,310 | 100.0[2] | 887,456 | 100.0 |

*Production* (metric tons except as noted). Agriculture, forestry, fishing (1985): sugarcane 2,951,000, bananas 977,000, rice 235,000, coffee 124,000, corn (maize) 109,000, sorghum 49,000, palm oil 24,000, dry beans 23,000, palm kernels 7,100, cocoa beans 5,000, other products include cut flowers and ornamental plants grown for export; livestock (number of live animals): 2,553,000 cattle, 220,000 pigs, 6,000,000 chickens; roundwood (1984) 3,395,000 cu m; fish catch (1984) 11,976. Mining and quarrying (1985): gold 35,000 troy oz. Manufacturing (value added in ₡'000,000; 1983):

food products 7,649; alcoholic and nonalcoholic beverages 2,592; industrial chemicals 1,904; drugs and medicines 1,660; paper and paper products 1,341; wearing apparel 1,303; textiles 985. Construction (1983): residential 664,000 sq m; nonresidential 128,000 sq m. Energy production (consumption): electricity (kW-hr; 1985) 2,826,000,000 (2,776,000,000); coal, none (none); crude petroleum (barrels; 1985) none (3,049,000); petroleum products (metric tons; 1985) 392,000 (637,000); natural gas, none (none).
*Population economically active* (1985): total 887,456; activity rate of total population 35.7% (participation rates: ages 15–69, 55.8%; female 26.1%; unemployed [1986] 6.0%).

### Price index (1980 = 100)

| | 1981 | 1982 | 1983 | 1984 | 1985 | 1986 | 1987[3] |
|---|---|---|---|---|---|---|---|
| Consumer price index | 137.1 | 260.6 | 345.6 | 386.9 | 445.1 | 497.8 | 550.3 |
| Earnings index[4] | 120.7 | 183.1 | 269.0 | 323.1 | 406.5 | ... | ... |

*Tourism:* receipts from visitors (1985) U.S.$118,000,000; expenditures by nationals abroad (1983) U.S.$36,000,000.
*Family income and expenditure:* average family size (1977) 5.0[5]; income per family ₡29,318 (U.S.$3,421); sources of income: n.a.; expenditure (1975)[6]: food 40.8%, housing 12.3%, clothing and footwear 10.0%, education and recreation 9.2%, household operations 8.2%, energy 6.6%, transportation 6.5%, other 6.4%.
*Land use* (1984): forested 30.8%; meadows and pastures 42.8%; agricultural and under permanent cultivation 12.6%; other 13.8%.

## Foreign trade[7]

### Balance of trade (current prices)

| | 1980 | 1981 | 1982 | 1983 | 1984 | 1985 | 1986 |
|---|---|---|---|---|---|---|---|
| ₡'000,000 | −3,297 | −1,728 | +2,628 | −411 | +814 | −810 | +4,607 |
| % of total | 16.1% | 3.8% | 4.2% | 0.6% | 0.9% | 0.8% | 3.8% |

*Imports* (1984): ₡48,705,000,000 (primary materials for industry 42.5%, consumer nondurables 15.7%, oil and fuel 7.6%, consumer durables 6.6%, capital goods for industry 6.3%, transport equipment 4.7%). *Major import sources:* United States 36.3%; Venezuela 8.6%; Japan 7.6%; Mexico 7.0%; Guatemala 5.4%.
*Exports* (1984): ₡44,818,000,000 (industrial products 31.1%, coffee beans 26.6%, bananas 24.9%, cattle and meat 4.3%, raw sugar 3.5%, other agricultural products 9.0%). *Major export destinations:* United States 37.8%; West Germany 13.3%; Guatemala 7.7%; Honduras 4.5%; El Salvador 4.5%.

## Transport and communications

*Transport.* Railroads (1986): route length 590 mi, 950 km; passenger-mi 56,000,000, passenger-km 90,000,000; short ton-mi cargo 108,600,000, metric ton-km cargo 158,500,000. Roads (1985): total length 21,914 mi, 35,267 km (paved 13%). Vehicles (1985): passenger cars 113,230; trucks and buses 72,816. Merchant marine (1986): vessels (100 gross tons and over) 25; total deadweight tonnage 9,539. Air transport (1986)[8]: passenger-mi 347,000,000, passenger-km 558,000,000; short-ton mi cargo 20,163,000, metric ton-km cargo 29,437,000; airports (1987) with scheduled flights 8.
*Communications.* Daily newspapers (1986): total number 5; total circulation 200,500; circulation per 1,000 population 78. Radio (1986): total number of receivers 200,000 (1 per 13 persons). Television (1986): total number of receivers 470,000 (1 per 5.4 persons). Telephones (1985): 314,895 (1 per 7.9 persons).

## Education and health

### Education (1984)

| | schools | teachers | students | student/ teacher ratio |
|---|---|---|---|---|
| Primary (age 5–11) | 3,068 | 12,223 | 353,958 | 29.0 |
| Secondary (age 12–17) Vocational } | 241 | 9,152 | 148,032 | 16.2 |
| Higher | 14[9] | ... | 54,466 | ... |

*Educational attainment* (1984). Percent of economically active population age 25 and over having: no formal schooling 8.3%; incomplete primary education 28.6%; complete primary 26.3%; secondary 22.6%; postsecondary and higher 14.2%. *Literacy* (1984): total population age 15 and over literate 1,419,365 (92.6%); males literate 702,045 (92.6%); females literate 717,320 (92.6%).
*Health* (1982): physicians 1,929 (1 per 1,198 persons); hospital beds 7,706 (1 per 300 persons); infant mortality per 1,000 live births (1984) 18.9.
*Food* (1981–83): daily per capita caloric intake 2,548 (vegetable products 83%, animal products 17%); (1983) 114% of FAO recommended minimum requirement.

## Military

*Military expenditure as percent of GNP* (1984): 1.0% (world 5.9%); per capita expenditure U.S.$14. The army was officially abolished in 1948. About 9,500 long-term volunteers made up of 6,000 civil guards and 3,500 rural guards conduct both police and paramilitary activities.

---

[1]At prices of 1984. [2]Detail does not add to total because of rounding. [3]February average. [4]Wages of insured persons in nonagricultural activities. [5]Average household size (1984) 4.7. [6]Based on the components of the consumer price index in San José only. [7]Import figures are f.o.b. (free on board) in balance of trade and c.i.f. (cost, insurance, and freight) for commodities and trading partners. [8]LACSA (Costa Rican Airlines) only. [9]1983.

# Côte d'Ivoire

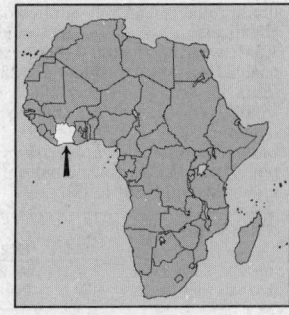

*Official name:* République de Côte
d'Ivoire (Republic of Côte d'Ivoire
[Ivory Coast][1]).
*Form of government:* republic with
one legislative house (National
Assembly [175]).
*Head of state and government:*
President.
*Capital:* Abidjan
(Capital designate: Yamoussoukro).
*Official language:* French.
*Official religion:* none.
*Monetary unit:* 1 CFA franc
(CFAF) = 100 centimes; valuation
(Oct. 5, 1987) 1 U.S.$ = CFAF 306.67;
1 £ = CFAF 498.00.

| Area and population | | area | | population |
|---|---|---|---|---|
| Departments | Capitals | sq mi | sq km | 1975 census[2] |
| Abengourou | Abengourou | 2,664 | 6,900 | 177,692 |
| Abidjan | Abidjan | 5,483 | 14,200 | 1,389,141 |
| Aboisso | Aboisso | 2,413 | 6,250 | 148,823 |
| Adzopé | Adzopé | 2,019 | 5,230 | 162,837 |
| Agboville | Agboville | 1,486 | 3,850 | 141,970 |
| Biankouma | Biankouma | 1,911 | 4,950 | 75,711 |
| Bondoukou | Bondoukou | 6,382 | 16,530 | 296,551 |
| Bongouanou | Bongouanou | 2,151 | 5,570 | 216,907 |
| Bouaflé | Bouaflé | 2,189 | 5,670 | 164,817 |
| Bouaké | Bouaké | 9,189 | 23,800 | 808,048 |
| Bouna | Bouna | 8,290 | 21,470 | 84,290 |
| Boundiali | Boundiali | 3,048 | 7,895 | 96,449 |
| Dabakala | Dabakala | 3,734 | 9,670 | 56,230 |
| Daloa | Daloa | 4,483 | 11,610 | 265,529 |
| Danané | Danané | 1,776 | 4,600 | 170,249 |
| Dimbokro | Dimbokro | 3,293 | 8,530 | 258,116 |
| Divo | Divo | 3,058 | 7,920 | 202,511 |
| Ferkessedougou | Ferkessedougou | 6,845 | 17,728 | 90,423 |
| Gagnoa | Gagnoa | 1,737 | 4,500 | 174,018 |
| Guiglo | Guiglo | 5,463 | 14,150 | 137,672 |
| Issia | Issia | 1,386 | 3,590 | 104,081 |
| Katiola | Katiola | 3,637 | 9,420 | 77,875 |
| Korhogo | Korhogo | 4,826 | 12,500 | 276,816 |
| Lakota | Lakota | 1,054 | 2,730 | 76,105 |
| Man | Man | 2,722 | 7,050 | 278,659 |
| Mankono | Mankono | 4,116 | 10,660 | 82,358 |
| Odienné | Odienné | 7,954 | 20,600 | 124,010 |
| Oumé | Oumé | 927 | 2,400 | 85,486 |
| Sassandra | Sassandra | 6,768 | 17,530 | 116,644 |
| Séguéla | Séguéla | 4,340 | 11,240 | 75,181 |
| Soubré | Soubré | 3,193 | 8,270 | 75,350 |
| Tingréla | Tingréla | 849 | 2,200 | 35,829 |
| Touba | Touba | 3,367 | 8,720 | 77,786 |
| Zuénoula | Zuénoula | 1,093 | 2,830 | 98,792 |
| TOTAL | | 123,847[3] | 320,763 | 6,702,866 |

## Demography

*Population* (1987): 11,154,000.
*Density* (1987): persons per sq mi 90.1, persons per sq km 34.8.
*Urban–rural* (1986): urban 47.0%; rural 53.0%.
*Sex distribution* (1985): male 51.09%; female 48.91%.
*Age breakdown* (1985): under 15, 45.1%; 15–29, 25.4%; 30–44, 15.6%; 45–59,
9.2%; 60–74, 4.0%; 75 and over 0.7%.
*Population projection:* (1990) 12,657,000; (2000) 19,290,000.
*Doubling time:* 23 years.
*Ethnic composition* (1975): Akan 41.4%; Kru 16.7%; Voltaic 15.7%; Malinke
14.9%; Southern Mande 10.2%; other 1.1%.
*Religious affiliation* (1980): folk religionist 43.8%; Christian 32.0%; Muslim
24.0%; other 0.2%.
*Major cities* (1984): Abidjan 1,850,000; Bouaké 220,000; Yamoussoukro
120,000; Gagnoa 93,500[4]; Daloa 59,500.

## Vital statistics

*Birth rate* per 1,000 population (1984): 45.0 (world avg. 29.0).
*Death rate* per 1,000 population (1984): 14.0 (world avg. 11.0).
*Natural increase rate* per 1,000 population (1984): 31.0 (world avg. 18.0).
*Total fertility rate* (avg. births per childbearing woman; 1984): 6.5.
*Life expectancy* at birth (1984): male 51.0 years; female 54.0 years.
*Major causes of death* per 100,000 population: n.a.; however, the major
infectious diseases include malaria, dysentery, yaws, pneumonia, leprosy.

## National economy

*Budget* (1987). Revenue: CFAF 626,859,000,000. Expenditures: CFAF 626,-
859,000,000.
*Public debt* (external, outstanding; 1985): U.S.$5,699,600,000.
*Tourism:* receipts from visitors (1984) U.S.$72,000,000; expenditures by na-
tionals abroad (1983) U.S.$180,000,000.
*Production* (metric tons except as noted). Agriculture (1985): cassava 1,500,-
000, sugarcane 1,300,000, plantains 1,000,000, cacao beans 563,300, rice
522,000, corn (maize) 520,000, coconuts 300,000, coffee 265,700, pineapples 210,000, cotton 189,300, palm oil 151,000; livestock (number of live
animals) 1,450,000 goats, 1,450,000 sheep, 843,000 cattle; roundwood 12,-
486,000 cu m; fish catch 93,098. Mining and quarrying (1985): diamonds
700,000 carats. Manufacturing (1983–84): cement 1,000,000; wheat flour
148,000; raw sugar 126,500; cocoa powder 74,000; cotton fibre 58,400. Construction (in CFAF; 1982): 229,000,000,000. Energy production (consump-

tion): electricity (kW-hr; 1985) 1,785,000,000 (1,785,000,000); coal, none
(n.a.); crude petroleum (barrels; 1985) 10,335,000 (12,314,000); petroleum
products (metric tons; 1985) 1,671,000 (1,285,000).
*Gross national product* (1985): U.S.$6,250,000,000 (U.S.$610 per capita).

| Structure of gross domestic product and labour force | | | | |
|---|---|---|---|---|
| | 1983 | | 1985[5] | |
| | in value CFAF '000,000,000 | % of total value | labour force | % of labour force |
| Agriculture | 709.0 | 26.8 | 2,792,000 | 70.9 |
| Mining | 83.0 | 3.1 | | |
| Manufacturing and public utilities | 385.0 | 14.5 } | 346,830 | 8.8 |
| Construction | 136.0 | 5.1 } | | |
| Transp. and commun. | 182.0 | 6.9 | | |
| Trade, finance Pub. admin., defense, and services | 984.0 | 37.1 } | 799,180 | 20.3 |
| Other | 170.0 | 6.4 | | |
| TOTAL | 2,649.0 | 100.0[3] | 3,938,010 | 100.0 |

*Population economically active* (1985): total 4,053,000[6]; activity rate of total
population 41.3% (participation rates: ages 15–64 71.4%; female 34.7%;
unemployed, n.a.).

| Price and earnings indexes (1980 = 100) | | | | | | | |
|---|---|---|---|---|---|---|---|
| | 1981 | 1982 | 1983 | 1984 | 1985 | 1986 | 1987 |
| Consumer price index | 108.8 | 116.8 | 123.7 | 129.0 | 131.4 | 140.1 | 145.6[7] |
| Annual wage index | 107.0 | 117.4 | 117.4 | 117.4 | 117.4 | 117.4 | 117.4 |

*Household income and expenditure.* Average household size (1980) 4.5;
average annual income per household CFAF 500,000; sources of income:
self-employment 49.9%, wages 44.9%, transfers and other resources 5.2%;
expenditure (1979): food 51.1%, housing 11.6%, clothing 8.4%.
*Land use* (1984): forested 26.3%; meadows and pastures 9.4%; agricultural
and under permanent cultivation 12.5%; other 51.8%.

## Foreign trade

| Balance of trade (current prices) | | | | | | |
|---|---|---|---|---|---|---|
| | 1980 | 1981 | 1982 | 1983 | 1984 | 1985 |
| CFAF '000,000,000 | +49.5 | +7.8 | +36.8 | +92.5 | +525.8 | +545.0 |
| % of total | 3.9% | 0.6% | 2.0% | 6.2% | 28.5 | 26.1% |

*Imports* (1985): CFAF 772,987,000,000 (machinery and transport equipment
22.1%, of which transport equipment 11.8%, nonelectrical machinery 7.0%,
electrical machinery 3.3%; crude petroleum 20.3%; food products 15.1%;
chemicals 13.2%). *Major import sources:* France 32.1%; Nigeria 11.1%;
United States 6.9%; Japan 5.0%; West Germany 4.8%.
*Exports* (1985): CFAF 1,318,060,000,000 (cacao beans 30.2%; coffee 21.1%;
energy products 9.0%; wood 6.9%; cacao butter 6.7%; cotton 2.5%; chemicals 2.3%; canned fish 1.4%). *Major export destinations:* The Netherlands
17.1%; France 16.6%; U.S. 11.7%; Italy 9.2%; West Germany 5.6%; United
Kingdom 4.3%.

## Transport and communications

*Transport.* Railroads (1986): length 1,314 km; passenger-km 857,800,000[8];
metric ton-km cargo 530,200,000[8]. Roads (1986): total length 55,000 km
(paved 9%). Vehicles (1984): passenger cars 182,956; trucks and buses 52,-
491. Merchant marine (1986): vessels (100 gross tons and over) 58; total
deadweight tonnage 151,496. Air transport[9] (1985): passenger-km 338,-
590,000; metric ton-km cargo 57,396,000; airports (1987) with scheduled
flights 14.
*Communications.* Daily newspapers (1984): total number 1; total circulation 80,000; circulation per 1,000 population 8.2. Radio (1986): 1,210,000
receivers (1 per 8.8 persons). Television (1986): 550,000 receivers (1 per 19
persons). Telephones (1980): 88,000 (1 per 94 persons).

## Education and health

| Education (1984–85) | schools[10] | teachers | students | student/ teacher ratio |
|---|---|---|---|---|
| Primary (age 7–12) | 4,419 | 31,297[11] | 1,179,456 | ... |
| Secondary (age 13–19) | 218 | 4,569[10] | 245,342 | ... |
| Voc., teacher tr. | 38 | 1,947[12] | 44,481[10] | ... |
| Higher | 1 | 1,204[11] | 12,755 | ... |

*Educational attainment* (1975). Percent of population age 6 and over having: no formal schooling 75.3%; primary education 17.3%; secondary 5.1%;
higher 0.5%. *Literacy* (1985): total population age 15 and over literate
57.3%.
*Health* (1982): physicians 502 (1 per 17,847 persons); hospital beds 10,062
(1 per 891 persons); infant mortality rate per 1,000 live births (1984) 106.
*Food* (1980–81): daily per capita caloric intake 2,590 (vegetable products
93%, animal products 7%); 1983 112% of FAO recommended minimum.

## Military

*Total active duty personnel* (1986): 7,720 (army 79.0%, navy 8.9%, air force
12.1%). *Military expenditure as percent of GNP* (1984): 1.3% (world 5.9%);
per capita expenditure U.S.$8.

[1]From 1986, Côte d'Ivoire has requested that the French version of the country's
name be utilized as the official protocol version in all languages. [2]Preliminary.
[3]Detail does not add to total given because of rounding. [4]1986. [5]Employed only.
[6]ILO estimate; other sources estimate as many as 5,500,000. [7]February. [8]1984. [9]Air
Afrique only. [10]1979–80. [11]1982. [12]1981.

# Cuba

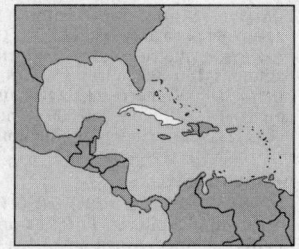

*Official name:* República de Cuba (Republic of Cuba).
*Form of government:* unitary socialist republic with one legislative house (National Assembly of the People's Power [510]).
*Head of state and government:* President.
*Capital:* Havana.
*Official language:* Spanish.
*Official religion:* none.
*Monetary unit:* 1 peso = 100 centavos; valuation (Oct. 5, 1987) 1 peso = U.S.$1.28 = £0.78.

### Area and population

| Provinces | Capitals | area sq mi | area sq km | population 1986 estimate[1] |
|---|---|---|---|---|
| Camagüey | Camagüey | 6,174 | 15,990 | 706,675 |
| Ciego de Avila | Ciego de Avila | 2,668 | 6,910 | 343,290 |
| Cienfuegos | Cienfuegos | 1,613 | 4,178 | 344,642 |
| Ciudad de la Habana[2] | — | 281 | 727 | 2,013,746 |
| Granma | Bayamo | 3,232 | 8,372 | 763,975 |
| Guantánamo | Guantánamo | 2,388 | 6,186 | 476,858 |
| Holguin | Holguin | 3,591 | 9,301 | 953,457 |
| La Habana[3] | Havana | 2,213 | 5,731 | 614,533 |
| Las Tunas | Las Tunas | 2,544 | 6,589 | 464,327 |
| Matanzas | Matanzas | 4,625 | 11,978 | 584,256 |
| Pinar del Río | Pinar del Río | 4,218 | 10,925 | 666,815 |
| Sancti Spíritus | Sancti Spíritus | 2,604 | 6,744 | 414,244 |
| Santiago de Cuba | Santiago de Cuba | 2,382 | 6,170 | 951,084 |
| Villa Clara | Santa Clara | 3,345 | 8,662 | 787,461 |
| **Special municipality** | | | | |
| Isla de la Juventud | Nueva Gerona | 926 | 2,398 | 67,522 |
| TOTAL | | 42,804 | 110,861 | 10,152,885 |

## Demography

*Population* (1987): 10,290,000.
*Density* (1987): persons per sq mi 240.4, persons per sq km 92.8.
*Urban–rural* (1986): urban 70.8%; rural 29.2%.
*Sex distribution* (1986): male 50.38%; female 49.62%.
*Age breakdown* (1986): under 15, 25.9%; 15–29, 29.9%; 30–44, 19.8%; 45–59, 13.1%; 60 and over, 11.3%.
*Population projection:* (1990) 10,683,000; (2000) 11,801,000.
*Doubling time:* 68 years.
*Ethnic composition* (1981): white 66.0%; mulatto 21.9%; black 12.0%; other 0.1%.
*Religious affiliation* (1980): nonreligious 48.7%; Roman Catholic 39.6%; atheist 6.4%; Protestant 3.3%; Afro-American Spiritist 1.6%; other 0.4%.
*Major cities* (1986): Havana 2,013,746; Santiago de Cuba 358,764; Camagüey 260,782; Holguín 194,728; Santa Clara 178,278.

## Vital statistics

*Birth rate* per 1,000 population (1986): 16.3 (world avg. 26.0).
*Death rate* per 1,000 population (1986): 6.1 (world avg. 9.9).
*Natural increase rate* per 1,000 population (1986): 10.2 (world avg. 16.1).
*Total fertility rate* (avg. births per childbearing woman; 1984): 2.0.
*Marriage rate* per 1,000 population (1986): 8.1.
*Divorce rate* per 1,000 population (1986): 3.1.
*Life expectancy* at birth (1983–84): male 72.6 years; female 76.1 years.
*Major causes of death* per 100,000 population (1985): heart disease[4] 189.1; malignant neoplasms (cancers) 116.6; cerebrovascular disease 62.1; pneumonia and influenza 45.2; accidents 42.2; suicide 21.6.

## National economy

*Budget* (1986). Revenue: 12,018,200,000 pesos. Expenditures: 11,996,900,000 pesos (production capital 33.0%; education and public health 21.9%; social, cultural, and scientific activities 16.4%; defense, internal security 10.9%; housing, community services 6.6%).
*Public debt* (external, outstanding; 1984[5]): U.S.$5,403,000,000.
*Production* (metric tons except as noted). Agriculture, forestry, fishing (1986): sugarcane 67,000,000, roots and tubers 675,000, rice 571,000, oranges 390,000, tomatoes 254,000, grapefruit 240,000, bananas 205,000, tobacco 46,000, jute 27,000, coffee 21,000; livestock (number of live animals; 1985): 6,400,000 cattle, 2,400,000 pigs, 749,000 horses; roundwood (1984) 3,132,000 cu m; fish catch 244,600, of which spiny lobster 11,800. Mining and quarrying (1985): chromite 40,000; nickel 32,400; cobalt 1,420. Manufacturing (1986): cement 3,305,200; fertilizers 1,045,200; crude steel 411,500; corrugated steel bars 312,000; cigarettes 16,840,800,000 units; cigars 340,600,000 units; tires 436,000 units; televisions 102,400 units; buses 2,351 units; sugarcane harvesters 613 units; beer 3,091,500 hectolitres; rum (1985) 463,900 hectolitres. Construction (1984): residential 989,000 sq m; nonresidential 1,145,000 sq m. Energy production (consumption): electricity (kW-hr; 1985) 12,199,000,000 (12,199,000,000); coal (metric tons; 1985) none (84,000); crude petroleum (barrels; 1985) 5,598,000 (50,342,000); petroleum products (metric tons; 1985) 6,057,000 (9,846,000); natural gas (cu m; 1985) 6,535,000 (6,535,000).
*Household income and expenditure.* Average household size (1981) 4.2; average annual income per household (1982) 3,680 pesos (U.S.$4,330); sources of income (1982): wages and salaries 57.3%, bonuses and other payments 42.7%; expenditure: n.a.

---

*Population economically active* (1981): total 3,617,620; activity rate of total population 37.2% (participation rates: ages 15–64, 58.5%; female 31.5%; unemployed [1982] 3.4%).

### Price and earnings indexes (1980 = 100)

| | 1979 | 1980 | 1981 | 1982 | 1983 | 1984 | 1985 |
|---|---|---|---|---|---|---|---|
| Consumer price index | ... | ... | ... | ... | ... | ... | ... |
| Annual earnings index | 97.0 | 100.0 | 114.7 | 119.1 | 121.7 | 125.7 | 126.9 |

*Tourism* (1984): receipts from visitors U.S.$108,000,000; expenditures by nationals abroad, n.a.
*Gross national product* (at current market prices; 1984): U.S.$26,920,000,000 (U.S.$2,690 per capita).

### Structure of net material product and labour force

| | 1985 in value '000,000 pesos | % of total value | labour force[6] | % of labour force |
|---|---|---|---|---|
| Agriculture | 1,366 | 9.8 | 581,200 | 18.3 |
| Mining | } | | | |
| Manufacturing | 5,018 | 36.0 | 709,300 | 22.3 |
| Public utilities | } | | | |
| Construction | 1,352 | 9.7 | 314,700 | 9.9 |
| Transp. and commun. | 1,032 | 7.4 | 216,200 | 6.8 |
| Finance | — | — | 18,700 | 0.7 |
| Trade | 5,088 | 36.5 | 367,200 | 11.6 |
| Public administration | — | — | 161,300 | 5.1 |
| Services | — | — | 757,600 | 23.9 |
| Other | 847[7] | 0.6 | 43,700 | 1.4 |
| TOTAL | 13,940 | 100.0 | 3,169,900 | 100.0 |

*Land use* (1984): forested 17.5%; meadows and pastures 22.4%; agricultural and under permanent cultivation 29.2%; other 30.9%.

## Foreign trade

### Balance of trade (current prices)

| | 1979 | 1980 | 1981 | 1982 | 1983 | 1984 | 1985 |
|---|---|---|---|---|---|---|---|
| '000,000 pesos | −187 | −578 | −1,290 | −597 | −693 | −1,745 | −2,000 |
| % of total | 2.6% | 6.8% | 13.2% | 5.7% | 5.9% | 13.8% | 14.3% |

*Imports* (1985): 7,983,200,000 pesos (mineral fuels and lubricants 33.2%, machinery and transport equipment 30.2%, basic manufactures 12.6%, foodstuffs and beverages 11.0%). *Major import sources:* U.S.S.R. 67.2%; East Germany 3.5%; China 2.9%; Japan 2.8%; Czechoslovakia 2.5%.
*Exports* (1985): 5,983,000,000 pesos (sugar 74.1%, petroleum products 10.4%, nickel ore 4.9%, citrus 2.4%, fish products 2.0%). *Major export destinations:* U.S.S.R. 74.7%; East Germany 3.9%; Bulgaria 3.0%; China 2.7%.

## Transport and communications

*Transport.* Railroads (1986): route length[8] 3,038 mi[9], 4,889 km[9]; passenger-mi 1,374,000,000, passenger-km 2,212,000,000; short ton-mi cargo 1,693,000,000, metric ton-km cargo 2,472,000,000. Roads (1984): total length 21,000 mi, 34,000 km (paved 30%). Vehicles (1984): passenger cars 200,100; trucks and buses 164,500. Merchant marine (1986): vessels (100 gross tons and over) 422, total deadweight tonnage 1,274,167. Air transport (1986): passenger-mi 1,639,000,000, passenger-km 2,637,000,000; short ton-mi cargo 23,000,000[9], metric ton-km cargo 33,600,000[9]; airports with scheduled flights (1987) 12.
*Communications.* Daily newspapers (1985): total number 17; total circulation 1,409,000; circulation per 1,000 population 140. Radio (1986): 3,232,000 receivers (1 per 3.2 persons). Television (1986): 1,525,000 receivers (1 per 6.7 persons). Telephones (1985): 515,100 (1 per 20 persons).

## Education and health

### Education (1985–86)

| | schools | teachers | students | student/ teacher ratio |
|---|---|---|---|---|
| Primary (age 6–11) | 10,187 | 77,100 | 1,077,200 | 14.0 |
| Secondary (age 12–17) | 1,287 | 65,900 | 807,600 | 12.3 |
| Voc., teacher tr. | 639 | 27,500 | 307,100 | 11.2 |
| Higher | 35 | 19,600 | 235,200 | 12.0 |

*Educational attainment* (1981). Percent of population age 25 and over having: no formal schooling and some primary education 39.6%; completed primary 26.6%; secondary 29.6%; higher 4.2%. *Literacy* (1980): total population age 15 and over literate 6,087,000 (91.1%); males literate 3,101,000 (91.1%); females literate 2,986,000 (91.1%).
*Health* (1986): physicians 25,418 (1 per 401 persons); hospital beds 56,055 (1 per 182 persons); infant mortality rate per 1,000 live births 13.6.
*Food* (1981–83): daily per capita caloric intake 2,874 (vegetable products 78%, animal products 22%); (1983) 126% of FAO recommended minimum requirement.

## Military

*Total active duty personnel* (1986): 162,000 (army 80.3%, navy 8.3%, air force 11.4%)[10]. *Military expenditure as percent of GNP* (1984): 5.9% (world 5.9%); per capita expenditure: U.S.$160.

---

[1]January 1. [2]Province contiguous with the city of Havana. [3]Province bordering the city of Havana on the east, south, and west. [4]Includes acute myocardial infarction, ischemic heart diseases, and diseases of pulmonary circulation. [5]Includes external long-term private debt not guaranteed by the government. [6]State sector only. [7]Includes other activities of the material sphere. [8]Figures exclude (1984) 4,895 mi (7,878 km) of nonpublic railways serving mostly sugar plantations or sugar factories. [9]1985. [10]Soviet forces total 8,000.

# Cyprus

## Island of Cyprus

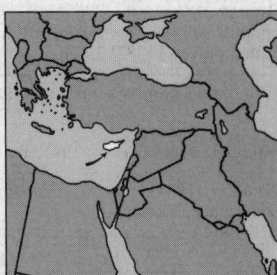

*Area:* 3,572 sq mi, 9,251 sq km.
*Population* (1987): 719,000.

Two states currently exist de facto on the island of Cyprus: the predominantly Greek Republic of Cyprus, in the southern two-thirds of the island, which is the original and still the internationally recognized government of the whole island; and the Turkish Republic of Northern Cyprus (TRNC), proclaimed unilaterally Nov. 15, 1983, on territory originally secured for the Turkish Cypriot population by the July 20, 1974, intervention of Turkey, one of the guarantor powers entitled by Cyprus' 1960 independence treaties to act unilaterally "with the sole aim of reestablishing the state of affairs created by the . . . treaty." The TRNC has received no international recognition and the two ethnic communities have been unable to negotiate the reestablishment of a single state. Provision of separate data below is necessitated by the decade-long lack of unified data.

## Republic of Cyprus

*Official name:* Kipriakí Demokratía (Greek); Kıbrıs Cumhuriyeti (Turkish) (Republic of Cyprus).
*Form of government:* unitary multiparty republic with a unicameral legislature (House of Representatives [80]).
*Head of state and government:* President.
*Capital:* Nicosia.
*Official languages:* Greek; Turkish.
*Monetary unit:* 1 Cyprus pound (£C) = 1,000 mils; valuation (Oct. 5, 1987) 1£C = U.S.$2.08 = £1.28.

### Area and population
(under government control; includes UN Buffer Zone and U.K. Sovereign Base Areas)

| Districts | Capitals | area sq mi | area sq km | population 1982 census |
|---|---|---|---|---|
| Famagusta | Famagusta | ... | ... | 24,187 |
| Larnaca | Larnaca | 433 | 1,121 | 83,151 |
| Limassol | Limassol | 538 | 1,393 | 143,847 |
| Nicosia | Nicosia | ... | ... | 207,290 |
| Paphos | Paphos | 539 | 1,396 | 45,023 |
| TOTAL | | 2,276 | 5,896 | 503,498 |

## Demography

*Population* (1987): 554,000.
*Urban–rural* (1982): urban 63.6%; rural 36.4%.
*Age breakdown* (1982): under 15, 24.7%; 15–29, 26.6%; 30–44, 20.1%; 45–59, 13.8%; 60–74, 10.4%; 75 and over, 4.0%.
*Population projection:* (1990) 591,000; (2000) 732,000.
*Ethnic composition* (1982): Greek 99.2%; other 0.8%.
*Religious affiliation* (1987): predominantly Greek Orthodox.
*Major cities* (1982): Nicosia 123,298; Limassol 100,254; Larnaca 35,823.

## Vital statistics

*Birth rate* per 1,000 population (1986): 19.5[1] (world avg. 26.0).
*Death rate* per 1,000 population (1986): 7.9[1] (world avg. 9.9).
*Natural increase rate* per 1,000 population (1986): 11.6[1] (world avg. 16.1).
*Life expectancy* at birth (1979–81): male 72.3 years; female 76.0 years.

## National economy

*Budget* (1987). £C 404,100,000 (1986; indirect taxes 34.6%, direct taxes 23.1%). Expenditures: £C 540,300,000 (ordinary 81.3%, development 12.6%).
*Household expenditure* (1981): food and beverages 28.1%, transportation and communication 23.2%, household goods 11.8%, clothing and footwear 10.8%, housing 8.4%, restaurants and hotels 8.4%.

### Structure of gross domestic product and labour force

| | 1986 in value £C '000,000 | % of total value | labour force | % of labour force |
|---|---|---|---|---|
| Agriculture | 117.4 | 7.4 | 35,700 | 14.7 |
| Mining | 6.0 | 0.4 | 1,000 | 0.4 |
| Manufacturing | 245.1 | 15.5 | 44,000 | 18.1 |
| Construction | 159.5 | 10.1 | 21,600 | 8.9 |
| Public utilities | 33.2 | 2.1 | 1,500 | 0.6 |
| Transp. and commun. | 155.5 | 9.8 | 13,000 | 5.4 |
| Trade | 296.6 | 18.7 | 49,500 | 20.4 |
| Finance | 226.5 | 14.3 | 11,700 | 4.8 |
| Pub. admin., defense | 117.4 | 7.4 } | 42,500 | 17.5 |
| Services | 158.0 | 9.9 } | | |
| Other | 69.6 | 4.4 | 22,300 | 9.2 |
| TOTAL | 1,584.8 | 100.0 | 242,800 | 100.0 |

*Tourism:* receipts from visitors (1985) U.S.$298,000,000; expenditures by nationals abroad (1984) U.S.$53,000,000.
*Production* (metric tons except as noted). Agriculture (1986): grapes 161,000, potatoes 160,000, citrus fruit (mainly oranges) 126,000; livestock (head; 1984) 334,000 sheep, 235,000 goats, 234,700 pigs. Manufacturing (1986): cement 864,000; wine 280,000 hectolitres; footwear 7,314,000 pairs; clothing £C 41,039,000. Energy production: electricity (kW-hr; 1986) 1,423,000,000.

## Foreign trade

*Imports* (1986): £C 659,070,000 (consumer goods 23.3%, petroleum and petroleum products 12.6%, transport equipment 9.7%). *Major import sources:* United Kingdom 13.4%; Italy 11.8%; West Germany 10.0%.
*Exports* (1986): £C 260,200,000 (clothing 15.8%, potatoes 7.8%, footwear 5.5%, citrus fruit 5.4%). *Major export destinations:* United Kingdom 22.6%; Lebanon 9.8%; Saudi Arabia 6.2%.

## Transport and communications

*Transport.* Roads (1985): total length 11,740 km (paved 48%). Vehicles (1986): passenger cars 127,300; trucks and buses 54,600. Merchant marine (1986): vessels (100 gross tons and over) 940; total deadweight tonnage 18,762,952. Air transport (1986): passenger-km 1,404,000,000; metric ton-km cargo 28,128,000; airports (1987) 3.
*Communications.* Daily newspapers (1986): 12; total circulation 78,224; circulation per 1,000 population 144. Radio (1985): 300,000 receivers (1 per 1.8 persons). Television (1985): 158,300 receivers (1 per 3.4 persons). Telephones (1986): 153,300 (1 per 3.5 persons).

## Education and health

### Education (1985–86)

| | schools | teachers | students | student/ teacher ratio |
|---|---|---|---|---|
| Primary (age 5–12) | 380 | 2,225 | 50,990 | 22.9 |
| Secondary (age 12–18) | 92 | 2,622 | 41,399 | 15.8 |
| Vocational | 15 | 463 | 4,907 | 10.6 |
| Higher | 16 | 289 | 3,134 | 10.8 |

*Literacy* (1980): population age 15 and over literate 93.1%.
*Health* (1984): physicians 797 (1 per 671 persons); hospital beds 3,588 (1 per 149 persons); infant mortality rate per 1,000 live births (1985) 16.

## Turkish Republic of Northern Cyprus

*Official name:* Kuzey Kıbrıs Türk Cumhuriyeti (Turkish) (Turkish Republic of Northern Cyprus).
*Capital:* Lefkoşe (Nicosia).
*Official language:* Turkish.
*Monetary unit:* 1 Turkish lira (LT) = 100 kurush; valuation (Oct. 5, 1987) 1 U.S.$ = LT 932.00; 1£ = LT 1,513.00.

### Area and population

| Provinces | Administrative centres | area sq mi | area sq km | population 1978 estimate |
|---|---|---|---|---|
| Lefkoşe (Nicosia) | Lefkoşe | ... | ... | 68,286 |
| Gazimagosa (Famagusta) | Gazimagosa | ... | ... | 55,647 |
| Girne (Kyrenia) | Girne | 247 | 640 | 22,807 |
| TOTAL | | 1,295 | 3,355 | 146,740 |

*Population* (1987): 165,000.
*Ethnic composition* (1985): Turkish 98.7%, other 1.3%.

### Structure of gross domestic product and labour force

| | 1985 in value LT '000,000 | % of total value | labour force | % of labour force |
|---|---|---|---|---|
| Agriculture | 26,143 | 20.9 | 20,595 | 33.6 |
| Manufacturing | 11,641 | 9.3 | 6,213 | 10.1 |
| Construction | 5,308 | 4.3 | 4,454 | 7.3 |
| Transp. and commun. | 9,578 | 7.7 | 4,004 | 6.5 |
| Trade | 30,642 | 24.5 | 5,386 | 8.8 |
| Finance | 5,113 | 4.1 | 1,531 | 2.5 |
| Real estate | 3,569 | 2.9 | ... | ... |
| Pub. admin. | 18,404 | 14.8 | 14,475 | 23.6 |
| Services | 5,630 | 4.5 | 4,641 | 7.6 |
| Other (customs duties) | 8,796 | 7.0 | — | — |
| TOTAL | 124,824 | 100.0 | 61,299[2] | 100.0 |

*Budget* (1987). Revenue: LT 103,079,616,000 (1985; indirect taxes 19.6%, direct taxes 18.8%, grants 53.1%). Expenditures: LT 45,788,700,000 (current expenditures 78.1%, defense 7.8%).
*Imports* (1986): U.S.$153,169,500 (machinery and transport eqpmt. 24.6%). *Major import sources:* Turkey 45.8%; United Kingdom 14.8%; Italy 7.2%.
*Exports* (1986): U.S.$52,007,823 (food and live animals 74%). *Major export destinations:* United Kingdom 63.1%; Turkey 14.8%.

### Education (1986–87)

| | schools | teachers | students | student/ teacher ratio |
|---|---|---|---|---|
| Primary (age 7–12) | 161 | 751 | 20,781 | 27.7 |
| Secondary (age 13–18) | 35 | 706 | 11,103 | 15.7 |
| Vocational | 10 | 192 | 1,748 | 9.1 |
| Higher | 4 | 84 | 1,649 | 19.6 |

*Health* (1986): physicians 118 (1 per 1,379 persons); hospital beds 755 (1 per 215 persons); infant mortality rate per 1,000 live births 19.0.

[1]Includes imputed adjustment for de jure population of Turkish sector. [2]Total of available detail.

# Czechoslovakia

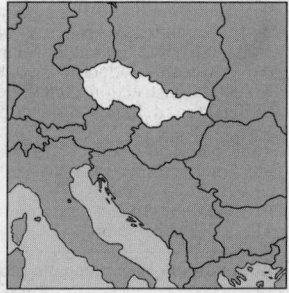

*Official name:* Československá Socialistická Republika (Czechoslovak Socialist Republic).
*Form of government:* federal socialist republic with two legislative houses (House of the People [200]; House of Nations [150]).
*Chief of state:* President.
*Head of government:* Premier.
*Capital:* Prague.
*Official languages:* Czech; Slovak.
*Official religion:* none.
*Monetary unit:* 1 koruna (Kčs) = 100 halura; valuation (Oct. 5, 1987) 1 U.S.$ = Kčs 5.48; 1 £ = Kčs 8.90.

### Area and population

| Republics Regions | Capitals | area sq mi | area sq km | population 1986 estimate |
|---|---|---|---|---|
| Czech Socialist Republic | Prague | | | |
| Jihočeský | České Budějovice | 4,380 | 11,345 | 695,066 |
| Jihomoravský | Brno | 5,802 | 15,028 | 2,058,020 |
| Severočeský | Ústí nad Labem | 3,019 | 7,819 | 1,183,145 |
| Severomoravský | Ostrava | 4,273 | 11,067 | 1,958,877 |
| Středočeský | Prague | 4,245 | 10,994 | 1,137,086 |
| Východočeský | Hradec Králové | 4,340 | 11,240 | 1,244,452 |
| Západočeský | Plzeň | 4,199 | 10,875 | 873,239 |
| Slovak Socialist Republic | Bratislava | | | |
| Středoslovenský | Banská Bystrica | 6,944 | 17,986 | 1,581,144 |
| Východoslovenský | Košice | 6,253 | 16,196 | 1,463,333 |
| Západoslovenský | Bratislava | 5,595 | 14,492 | 1,715,861 |
| **Capital Cities** | | | | |
| Prague | — | 192 | 496 | 1,193,513 |
| Bratislava | — | 142 | 367 | 417,103 |
| TOTAL | | 49,384 | 127,905 | 15,520,839 |

## Demography

*Population* (1987): 15,591,000.
*Density* (1987): persons per sq mi 315.7, persons per sq km 121.9.
*Urban–rural* (1985): urban 74.1%; rural 25.9%.
*Sex distribution* (1986): male 48.70%; female 51.30%.
*Age breakdown* (1986): under 15, 24.4%; 15–29, 21.1%; 30–44, 22.3%; 45–59, 15.8%; 60–74, 11.7%; 75 and over, 4.7%.
*Population projection:* (1990) 15,728,000; (2000) 16,194,000.
*Doubling time:* n.a.; population growth is negligible.
*Ethnic composition* (1986): Czech 63.2%; Slovak 31.5%; Hungarian 3.8%; Polish 0.5%; German 0.4%; Ukrainian 0.3%; other 0.3%.
*Religious affiliation* (1980): Roman Catholic 65.6%; atheist 20.1%; Czechoslovak Church 4.4%; Evangelist Church of Czech Brethren 1.4%; other 8.5%.
*Major cities* (1986): Prague 1,193,500; Bratislava 417,100; Brno 385,700; Ostrava 327,800; Košice 222,200.

## Vital statistics

*Birth rate* per 1,000 population (1985): 14.5 (world avg. 29.0); (1984) legitimate 93.1%; illegitimate 6.9%.
*Death rate* per 1,000 population (1985): 11.8 (world avg. 11.0).
*Natural increase rate* per 1,000 population (1985): 2.7 (world avg. 18.0).
*Total fertility rate* (avg. births per childbearing woman; 1982): 2.3.
*Marriage rate* per 1,000 population (1985): 7.7.
*Divorce rate* per 1,000 population (1985): 2.5.
*Life expectancy* at birth (1985): male 67.2 years; female 74.4 years.
*Major causes of death* per 100,000 population (1985): cerebrovascular disease 340.4; ischemic heart disease 325.1; malignant neoplasms (cancers) 234.0; bronchitis, emphysema, and asthma 86.4; accidents, poisoning, and violence 79.6, of which suicides 18.9; diseases of the digestive system 47.1.

## National economy

*Budget* (1985). Revenue: Kčs 359,692,000,000 (receipts from enterprises 71.8%; taxes 13.1%). Expenditures: Kčs 358,028,000,000 (education, health, social welfare, and culture 28.0%; national economy 27.8%; defense 7.7%).
*Tourism:* receipts from visitors (1985) U.S.$307,000,000; expenditures by nationals abroad (1983) U.S.$229,000,000.
*Production* (metric tons except as noted). Agriculture, forestry, fishing (1985): sugar beets 7,667,000, wheat 2,665,000, potatoes 1,614,000, barley 1,047,000, corn (maize) 235,000; livestock (number of live animals) 6,743,-000 pigs, 5,150,000 cattle, 48,519,000 chickens; roundwood 19,652,000 cu m; fish catch 20,003. Mining and quarrying (1985): iron ore 1,900,000; copper 26,500; lead 21,500; zinc 9,250. Manufacturing (1986): crude steel 15,112,000; rolled steel 11,180,000; cement 10,298,000; sulfuric acid 1,292,-000; plastic and resins 1,140,000; chemical fertilizers 921,361; cotton fabrics 606,457,000 m; beer 22,789,000 hectolitres; other alcoholic beverages 1,224,-000 hectolitres; road motor vehicles 245,229 units. Construction (1985): 5,498,000 sq m. Energy production (consumption): electricity (kW-hr; 1985) 80,628,000,000 (82,960,000,000); coal (metric tons; 1985) 128,532,000 (133,-108,000); crude petroleum (barrels; 1985) 834,000 (116,800,000); petroleum products (metric tons; 1985) 13,315,000 (13,428,000); natural gas (cu m; 1985) 731,000,000 (10,386,000,000).
*Land use* (1985): agricultural 40.4%; forested 35.8%; meadows and pastures 13.0%; other 10.8%.
*Gross national product* (at current market prices; 1985): U.S.$85,960,000,000 (U.S.$5,550 per capita).

### Structure of net material product and labour force

| | 1985 in value Kčs '000,000 | % of total value | labour force | % of labour force |
|---|---|---|---|---|
| Agriculture | 42,130 | 7.5 | 1,040,000 | 13.7 |
| Mining and manufacturing | 334,145 | 59.7 | 2,845,300 | 37.4 |
| Construction | 62,903 | 11.2 | 726,300 | 9.5 |
| Public utilities | — | — | 141,000 | 1.9 |
| Transportation and communication | 28,540 | 5.1 | 501,100 | 6.6 |
| Trade | 88,679 | 15.8 | 832,300 | 10.9 |
| Finance | — | — | 33,000 | 0.4 |
| Pub. admin., defense | — | — | 173,700 | 2.3 |
| Services | — | — | 1,313,300 | 17.3 |
| Other | 3,577[1] | 0.6[1] | ... | ... |
| TOTAL | 559,974 | 100.0[2] | 7,606,000 | 100.0 |

*Public debt* (external, outstanding, to the West; 1985): U.S.$2,800,000,000.
*Population economically active*[3] (1986): total 7,648,900; activity rate of total population 49.3% (participation rates: working age 87.5%; female 46.1%; unemployed, n.a.).

### Price and earnings indexes (1977 = 100)

| | 1979 | 1980 | 1981 | 1982 | 1983 | 1984 | 1985 |
|---|---|---|---|---|---|---|---|
| Consumer price index | 106.4 | 109.5 | 110.4 | 116.0 | 117.1 | 118.2 | 120.9 |
| Monthly earnings index | 105.5 | 107.9 | 109.5 | 112.0 | 114.1 | 116.1 | 118.1 |

*Household income and expenditure.* Average household size (1985) 3.1; income per household Kčs 77,970 (U.S.$12,100); sources of income: wages and salaries 62.1%, welfare 20.2%, other 17.7%; expenditure (1985): food 25.9%, clothing and footwear 11.7%, services 12.1%.

## Foreign trade

### Balance of trade (current prices)

| | 1980 | 1981 | 1982 | 1983 | 1984 | 1985 | 1986 |
|---|---|---|---|---|---|---|---|
| Kčs '000,000 | −1,377 | +1,413 | +1,345 | +826 | +493 | −505 | +3,672 |
| % of total | 0.9% | 0.8% | 0.7% | 0.4% | 0.2% | 0.2% | 1.5% |

*Imports* (1985): Kčs 120,323,000,000 (machinery and transport equipment 31.3%, of which industrial machinery 9.5%, agricultural and construction machinery 8.3%, transport equipment 7.2%; fuels and other energy 30.7%; consumer goods 8.9%; mineral ores 8.3%; food 7.0%; chemicals 6.8%). *Major import sources:* U.S.S.R. 46.0%; East Germany 9.7%; Poland 8.0%; Hungary 5.8%; West Germany 4.2%.
*Exports* (1985): Kčs 119,818,000,000 (machinery and transport equipment 53.6%, of which industrial machinery 13.4%, road vehicles and parts 9.2%; consumer goods 16.8%; chemicals 6.0%; mineral fuels and lubricants 4.3%). *Major export destinations:* U.S.S.R. 43.7%; East Germany 9.2%; Poland 7.7%; Hungary 4.7%; West Germany 4.5%; Yugoslavia 3.5%; Bulgaria 3.0%; Austria 2.6%; Romania 2.0%.

## Transport and communications

*Transport.* Railroads (1985): length 8,149 mi, 13,114 km; passenger-mi 12,327,000,000, passenger-km 19,839,000,000; short ton-mi cargo 45,345,-000,000, metric ton-km cargo 66,203,000,000. Roads (1985): total length 46,535 mi, 74,891 km (paved 100%). Vehicles (1985): passenger cars 2,694,-994; trucks and buses 425,174. Merchant marine (1986): vessels (100 gross tons and over) 20; total deadweight tonnage 299,270. Air transport (1985): passenger-mi 723,500,000, passenger-km 1,164,364,000; short ton-mi cargo 41,746,000, metric ton-km cargo 60,948,000; airports (1987) 14.
*Communications.* Daily newspapers (1985): total number 30; total circulation 4,263,000[4]; circulation per 1,000 population 2754. Radio (1985): 4,208,538 receivers (1 per 3.7 persons). Television (1985): 4,346,022 receivers (1 per 3.6 persons). Telephones (1986): 3,591,000 (1 per 4.3 persons).

## Education and health

### Education (1985–86)

| | schools | teachers | students | student/ teacher ratio |
|---|---|---|---|---|
| Primary (age 6–14) | 6,332 | 96,414 | 2,074,403 | 21.5 |
| Secondary (age 15–18) | 343 | 9,465 | 134,392 | 14.2 |
| Voc., teacher tr. | 562 | 16,740 | 261,422 | 15.6 |
| Higher | 36 | 19,131 | 168,699 | 8.8 |

*Educational attainment* (1980). Percent of adult population having: less than full primary education 1.2%; primary and less than full secondary 52.6%; full secondary 41.2%; higher 5.0%. *Literacy* (1980): total population age 15 and over literate 11,524,716 (99.6%); males literate 5,525,860 (99.6%); females literate 5,998,856 (99.5%).
*Health* (1986): physicians 47,569 (1 per 326 persons); hospital beds 123,194 (1 per 126 persons); infant mortality rate per 1,000 live births (1985) 14.0.
*Food* (1981–83): daily per capita caloric intake 3,534 (vegetable products 67%, animal products 33%); (1983) 145% of FAO recommended minimum requirement.

## Military

*Total active duty personnel* (1986): 201,000 (army 72.1%; navy, none; air force 27.9%). *Military expenditure as percent of GNP* (1984): 5.8% (world 5.9%); per capita expenditure U.S.$478.

[1]Includes other activities of the material sphere. [2]Detail does not add to total given because of rounding. [3]Excludes women on maternity leave and includes workers of working age, which is 15–59 for men and 15–54 for women. [4]27 newspapers only.

# Denmark

*Official name:* Kongeriget Danmark (Kingdom of Denmark).
*Form of government:* parliamentary state and constitutional monarchy with one legislative house (Folketing [179]).
*Chief of state:* Danish Monarch.
*Head of government:* Prime Minister.
*Capital:* Copenhagen.
*Official language:* Danish.
*Official religion:* Evangelical Lutheran.
*Monetary unit:* 1 krone (Dkr; plural kroner) = 100 øre; valuation (Oct. 5, 1987) 1 U.S.$ = Dkr 7.09; 1 £ = Dkr 11.51.

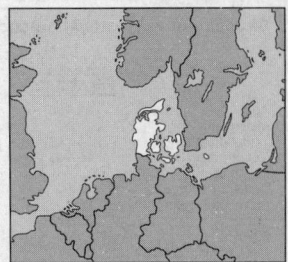

### Area and population[1]

| Counties | Capitals | area sq mi | area sq km | population 1987 estimate[2] |
|---|---|---|---|---|
| Århus | Århus | 1,761 | 4,561 | 589,108 |
| Bornholm | Rønne | 227 | 588 | 46,839 |
| Frederiksborg | Hillerød | 520 | 1,347 | 339,627 |
| Fyn | Odense | 1,346 | 3,486 | 456,483 |
| København | — | 203 | 526 | 606,870 |
| Nordjylland | Ålborg | 2,383 | 6,173 | 483,381 |
| Ribe | Ribe | 1,209 | 3,131 | 216,967 |
| Ringkøbing | Ringkøbing | 1,874 | 4,853 | 266,088 |
| Roskilde | Roskilde | 344 | 891 | 213,476 |
| Sønderjylland | Åbenrå | 1,520 | 3,938 | 249,805 |
| Storstrøm | Nykøbing | 1,312 | 3,398 | 257,880 |
| Vejle | Vejle | 1,157 | 2,997 | 328,849 |
| Vestsjælland | Sorø | 1,152 | 2,984 | 282,397 |
| Viborg | Viborg | 1,592 | 4,122 | 230,760 |
| **Cities** | | | | |
| Copenhagen (København) | — | 34 | 88 | 469,706 |
| Frederiksberg | — | 3 | 9 | 86,558 |
| TOTAL | | 16,638[3] | 43,092 | 5,124,794 |

## Demography

*Population* (1987): 5,126,000.
*Density* (1987): persons per sq mi 308.1, persons per sq km 119.0.
*Urban-rural* (1985): urban 84.3%; rural 15.7%.
*Sex distribution* (1987): male 49.29%; female 50.71%.
*Age breakdown* (1987): under 15, 17.9%; 15–29, 22.8%; 30–44, 22.7%; 45–59, 16.2%; 60–74, 13.8%; 75 and over, 6.6%.
*Population projection:* (1990) 5,136,600; (2000) 5,164,900.
*Doubling time:* n.a.; doubling time exceeds 100 years.
*Ethnic composition* (1987): Danish 97.5%; other Scandinavian 0.5%; Turkish 0.4%; Yugoslavian 0.2%; other 1.4%.
*Religious affiliation* (1986): Evangelical Lutheran 91.1%; Roman Catholic 0.5%; Baptist 0.1%; Jewish 0.1%; other 8.2%.
*Major cities* (1985): Greater Copenhagen 1,358,540; Århus 194,348; Odense 136,803; Ålborg 113,865.

## Vital statistics

*Birth rate* per 1,000 population (1986): 10.8 (world avg. 26.0); (1985) legitimate 57.0%; illegitimate 43.0%.
*Death rate* per 1,000 population (1986): 11.4 (world avg. 9.9).
*Natural increase rate* per 1,000 population (1986): −0.6 (world avg. 16.1).
*Total fertility rate* (avg. births per childbearing woman; 1985): 1.4.
*Marriage rate* per 1,000 population (1985): 5.7.
*Divorce rate* per 1,000 population (1985): 2.8.
*Life expectancy* at birth (1984–85): male 71.6 years; female 77.5 years.
*Major causes of death* per 100,000 population (1985): ischemic heart disease 325.7; malignant neoplasms (cancers) 283.9; cerebrovascular disease 101.6.

## National economy

*Budget* (1987). Revenue: Dkr 245,442,000,000 (customs and excise taxes 48.8%, income and property taxes 41.3%, other 9.9%). Expenditures: Dkr 246,307,000,000 (social services 25.6%, interest payments 19.8%, education 6.8%, defense 5.1%, other 42.7%).
*Public debt* (1985): Dkr 131,346,000,000.
*Tourism* (1985): receipts from visitors U.S.$1,326,000,000; expenditures by nationals abroad U.S.$1,410,000,000.
*Population economically active* (1985): total 2,752,961; activity rate of total population 53.8% (participation rates: ages 15–64, 79.6%; female 45.6%; unemployed 9.0%).

### Price and earnings indexes (1980 = 100)

| | 1981 | 1982 | 1983 | 1984 | 1985 | 1986 | 1987[4] |
|---|---|---|---|---|---|---|---|
| Consumer price index | 111.7 | 123.0 | 131.5 | 139.8 | 146.4 | 151.7 | 157.9 |
| Hourly earnings index | 109.0 | 120.6 | 128.5 | 134.6 | 141.1 | 149.2 | ... |

*Household income and expenditure.* Average household size (1987) 2.3; income per household (1984) Dkr 117,400 (U.S.$11,335); principal sources of income (1982): wages and salaries 65.5%, transfers 12.4%, self-employment 8.8%, other 13.3%; expenditure (1984): food and beverages 21.3%, housing 19.3%, transportation and communication 16.5%, education, recreation, and culture 9.4%, clothing and footwear 5.8%.
*Production* (metric tons except as noted). Agriculture, forestry, fishing (1986): barley 5,134,000, sugar beets 3,195,000, wheat 2,177,000, potatoes 1,129,000; livestock (number of live animals) 2,495,433 cattle, 9,320,533 pigs; roundwood (1985) 2,247,800 cu m; fish catch 1,735,609. Manufacturing (value added in kroner; 1984): fabricated metal products and machinery 33,380,000,000; food, beverages, and tobacco 23,360,000,000; chemicals and petroleum products 10,690,000,000; paper and printed products 9,150,000,000. Construction (1984): residential 2,903,800 sq m; nonresidential 3,370,000 sq m. Energy production (consumption): electricity (kW-hr; 1985) 29,064,000,000 (29,524,000,000); coal (metric tons; 1985) none (12,146,000); crude petroleum (barrels; 1985) 21,198,000 (47,997,000); petroleum products (metric tons; 1985) 6,698,000 (9,961,000); natural gas (cu m; 1985) 1,149,115,000 (670,479,000).
*Gross national product* (at current market prices; 1985): U.S.$57,330,000,000 (U.S.$11,210 per capita).

### Structure of gross domestic product and labour force

| | 1986 in value Dkr '000,000 | 1986 % of total value | 1985 labour force | 1985 % of labour force |
|---|---|---|---|---|
| Agriculture | 30,417 | 5.5 | 176,399 | 6.4 |
| Mining | 4,745 | 0.8 | 4,794 | 0.2 |
| Manufacturing | 113,766 | 20.4 | 550,158 | 20.0 |
| Construction | 35,759 | 6.4 | 188,677 | 6.8 |
| Public utilities | 8,195 | 1.5 | 19,030 | 0.7 |
| Transp. and commun. | 45,107 | 8.1 | 188,021 | 6.8 |
| Trade | 79,010 | 14.2 | 418,676 | 15.2 |
| Finance | 22,041 | 4.0 | 198,816 | 7.2 |
| Pub. admin., defense | 118,719 | 21.3 ⎫ | 968,068 | 35.2 |
| Services | 116,677 | 21.0 ⎭ | | |
| Other | −17,647[5] | −3.2[5] | 40,322 | 1.5 |
| TOTAL | 556,789 | 100.0 | 2,752,961 | 100.0 |

*Land use* (1984): forested 11.6%; meadows and pastures 5.4%; agricultural and under permanent cultivation 62.0%; other 21.0%.

## Foreign trade

### Balance of trade (current prices)

| | 1981 | 1982 | 1983 | 1984 | 1985 | 1986 |
|---|---|---|---|---|---|---|
| Dkr '000,000 | −4,930 | −4,696 | −4,371 | +1,076 | −3,560 | −5,138 |
| % of total | 2.1% | 1.8% | 1.5% | 0.3% | 1.0% | 1.5% |

*Imports* (1986): Dkr 184,640,000,000 (machinery and transportation equipment 31.6%, of which road vehicles 8.9% [of which passenger cars 4.4%, trucks and buses 2.4%]; manufactured goods 9.4%, of which iron and steel 4.4%; chemicals and related products 9.4%; food and live animals 9.4%; mineral fuels 8.7%, of which crude petroleum and petroleum products 6.1%). *Major import sources:* West Germany 23.6%; Sweden 12.3%; U.K. 7.6%; Japan 5.7%; U.S. 5.3%; The Netherlands 5.2%.
*Exports* (1986): Dkr 171,614,900,000 (food and live animals 27.5%, of which meat and meat preparations 11.3%, fish and shellfish 6.0%; dairy products 4.0%, machinery and transport equipment 21.4%; chemicals and related products 8.0%; furniture 3.7%). *Major export destinations:* West Germany 16.8%; U.K. 11.7%; Sweden 11.3%; U.S. 8.5%; Norway 7.6%.

## Transport and communications

*Transport.* Railroads (1985): length 1,535 mi, 2,471 km; passenger-mi 2,921,590,000, passenger-km 4,701,850,000; short ton-mi cargo 1,206,191,000, metric ton-km cargo 1,761,009,000. Roads (1985): total length 43,587 mi, 70,147 km (paved 100%). Vehicles (1985): passenger cars 1,564,450; trucks and buses 346,431. Merchant marine (1986): vessels (100 gross tons and over) 1,063; total deadweight tonnage 6,805,176. Air transport (1986): passenger-mi 1,991,000,000, passenger-km 3,204,000,000; short ton-mi cargo 88,596,000, metric ton-km cargo 129,348,000; airports (1987) with scheduled flights 13.
*Communications.* Daily newspapers (1985): total number 47; total circulation 1,855,000; circulation per 1,000 population 363. Radio (1986): total number of receivers 2,052,467 (1 per 2.5 persons). Television (1986): total number of receivers 1,952,659 (1 per 2.6 persons). Telephones (1986): 4,005,495 (1 per 1.3 persons).

## Education and health

### Education (1984–85)

| | schools | teachers | students | student/teacher ratio |
|---|---|---|---|---|
| Primary (age 7–12) | 2,557 | 34,541 | 415,148 | 12.0 |
| Secondary (age 13–18) | 3,247 | 36,105 | 339,835 | 9.4 |
| Vocational | 282 | ... | 144,024 | ... |
| Higher | 96[6] | 10,411[6] | 124,144 | ... |

*Educational attainment* (1983). Percent of population age 25–62 having: primary education 3.0%; lower secondary 38.3%; upper secondary 41.2%; some postsecondary 13.5%; graduated from university 4.0%. *Literacy* (1986): virtually 100%.
*Health* (1985): physicians 12,975 (1 per 394 persons); hospital beds 35,976 (1 per 142 persons); infant mortality rate per 1,000 live births 7.9.
*Food* (1981–83): daily per capita caloric intake 3,564 (vegetable products 56%, animal products 44%); (1983) 128% of FAO recommended minimum requirement.

## Military

*Total active duty personnel* (1986): 29,525 (army 52.8%, navy 23.5%, air force 23.7%). *Military expenditure as percent of GNP* (1984): 2.5% (world 5.9%); per capita expenditure U.S.$245.

[1]Excluding Greenland (*q.v.*) and the Faeroe Islands. [2]January 1. [3]Detail does not add to total given because of rounding. [4]June. [5]Includes imputed bank service charges. [6]1982–83.

# Djibouti

*Official name:* Jumhūrīyah Jībūtī (Arabic); République de Djibouti (French) (Republic of Djibouti).
*Form of government:* unitary single-party republic with one legislative house (National Assembly [65]).
*Chief of state:* President.
*Head of government:* Prime Minister.
*Capital:* Djibouti.
*Official languages:* Arabic; French.
*Official religion:* none.
*Monetary unit:* 1 Djibouti franc (DF) = 100 centimes; valuation (Oct. 5, 1987) 1 U.S.$ = DF 176.73; 1 £ = DF 287.00.

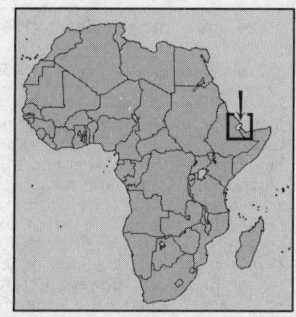

### Area and population

| Districts | Capitals | area[1] sq mi | sq km | population 1982 estimate |
|---|---|---|---|---|
| 'Alī Sabīḥ (Ali-Sabieh) | 'Alī Sabīḥ | 925 | 2,400 | 15,000 |
| Dikhil | Dikhil | 2,775 | 7,200 | 30,000 |
| Djibouti | Djibouti | 225 | 600 | 200,000 |
| Obock | Obock | 2,200 | 5,700 | 15,000 |
| Tadjoura (Tadjourah) | Tadjoura | 2,825 | 7,300 | 30,000 |
| TOTAL | | 8,950 | 23,200 | 335,000[2] |

## Demography

*Population* (1987): 470,000.
*Density* (1987): persons per sq mi 52.5, persons per sq km 20.3.
*Urban-rural* (1985): urban 75.0%; rural 25.0%.
*Sex distribution* (1985): male 50.28%; female 49.72%.
*Age breakdown* (1983): under 15, 38.0%; 15–29, 34.0%; 30–44, 17.0%; 45–50, 3.0%; 51 and over, 8.0%.
*Population projection:* (1990) 513,000; (2000) 690,000.
*Doubling time:* 22 years.
*Ethnic composition* (1984): Issa 47%; Afar 37%; European (mostly French) 8%; Arab (mostly Yemeni) 6%; other 2%.
*Religious affiliation* (1983): Sunnī Muslim 94%; Christian 6%, of which Roman Catholic 4%, Protestant 1%, Orthodox 1%.
*Major city and towns* (1982): Djibouti 200,000[3]; 'Alī Sabīḥ 4,000; Tadjoura 3,500; Dikhil 3,000.

## Vital statistics

*Birth rate* per 1,000 population (1980–85): 49.2 (world avg. 29.0).
*Death rate* per 1,000 population (1980–85): 18.3 (world avg. 11.0).
*Natural increase rate* per 1,000 population (1980–85): 30.9 (world avg. 18.0).
*Total fertility rate* (avg. births per childbearing woman; 1980–85): 6.8.
*Marriage rate* per 1,000 population (1982): 6.7.
*Divorce rate* per 1,000 population (1982): 1.9.
*Life expectancy at birth* (1985): 45 years.
*Major causes of death*[4] (percentage of total deaths; 1984): diarrhea and acute dehydration 16.0%; malnutrition 16.0%; poisoning 11.0%; tuberculosis 6.0%; acute respiratory disease 6.0%; malaria 6.0%; anemia 6.0%; heart disease 2.0%; kidney disease 1.0%; other ailments 19.0%; no diagnosis 11.0%.

## National economy

*Budget* (1985). Revenue: DF 22,585,800,000 (customs duties 47.4%; direct taxes 29.2%, of which licenses and patent fees 7.1%, income tax 6.6%; foreign aid grants 6.6%; excises and stamps 4.1%). Expenditures: DF 22,585,800,000 (general administration 41.7%; defense 21.0%; health 7.5%; education 6.8%; economic development 6.1%; debt payment 3.4%).
*Public debt* (external, outstanding; 1986): U.S.$119,100,000.
*Tourism* (1985): number of tourists staying in hotels 17,037.
*Production* (metric tons except as noted). Agriculture[5], forestry, fishing (1985): vegetables and melons 13,000; livestock (number of live animals) 545,000 goats, 420,000 sheep, 54,000 camels, 45,000 cattle, 1,000 asses, 1,000 horses; fish catch (1984) 426. Mining and quarrying (1985): mineral production limited to locally used construction material and evaporated salt. Manufacturing (1984): detail n.a.; main items produced are furniture, nonalcoholic beverages, light electromechanical goods, and mineral water. Construction (1985): residential 32,214 sq m; nonresidential 21,722 sq m. Energy production (consumption): electricity (kW-hr; 1985) 150,000,000 (150,000,000); coal, none (n.a.); crude petroleum, none (n.a.); petroleum products (metric tons; 1985) none (66,000); natural gas, none (n.a.).
*Population economically active:* n.a.; unemployed (1985) *c.* 60%.

### Price and earnings indexes (1975 = 100)

| | 1977 | 1978 | 1979 | 1980 | 1981 | 1982 | 1983 |
|---|---|---|---|---|---|---|---|
| Consumer price index | 136.6 | 163.4 | 187.6 | 210.5 | 222.2 | 217.0 | ... |
| Monthly earnings index | ... | ... | ... | ... | ... | ... | ... |

*Household income and expenditure.* Average household size[6] (1982) 5.6; income per household: n.a.; sources of income: n.a.; expenditure (expatriate households; 1984): food 50.3%, energy 13.1%, recreation 10.4%, housing 6.4%, clothing 1.7%, personal effects 1.4%, health care 1.0%, household goods 0.3%, other 15.4%.
*Gross national product* (at current market prices; 1984): U.S.$301,540,000 (U.S.$740 per capita).

### Structure of gross domestic product and labour force

| | 1984 in value DF '000,000 | % of total value | 1982 labour force[7] | % of labour force[7] |
|---|---|---|---|---|
| Agriculture | 2,690 | 4.5 | 63 | 0.4 |
| Mining | | | | |
| Manufacturing | 4,920 | 8.2 | 726 | 4.5 |
| Construction | 4,490 | 7.5 | 2,309 | 14.3 |
| Public utilities | 1,942 | 3.2 | 456 | 2.8 |
| Transportation and communication | 6,010 | 10.0 | 2,711 | 17.0 |
| Trade | 9,400 | 15.6 | 3,148 | 19.5 |
| Finance | 6,530 | 10.8 | 1,296 | 8.0 |
| Pub. admin., defense | 16,170 | 26.8 | 3,347 | 20.7 |
| Services | 950 | 1.6 | 915 | 5.6 |
| Other | 7,132[8] | 11.8[8] | 1,168 | 7.2 |
| TOTAL | 60,234 | 100.0 | 16,139 | 100.0 |

*Land use* (1984): forested 0.3%; meadows and pastures 9.1%; agricultural and under permanent cultivation[5]; built-on, wasteland, and other 90.6%.

## Foreign trade[9]

### Balance of trade (current prices)

| | 1977 | 1978 | 1979 | 1980 | 1981 | 1982 | 1983 |
|---|---|---|---|---|---|---|---|
| DF '000,000 | −15,585 | −25,963 | −31,431 | −35,699 | −28,311 | −37,965 | −12,599 |
| % of total | 69.8% | 80.4% | 88.7% | 88.9% | 90.1% | 89.5% | 24.7% |

*Imports* (1983): DF 39,307,000,000 (machinery and transport equipment 23.0%, of which electrical machinery and appliances 10.9%; food and live animals 19.1%; textiles and clothing 12.0%; petroleum products 9.4%; kat [a narcotic leaf] 9.0%; special transactions, including importation of gold coins, personal effects, and military goods, 4.8%; tobacco and tobacco products 4.3%). *Major import sources:* France 35.4%; Ethiopia 9.7%; Japan 7.6%; The Netherlands 5.3%; Italy 4.3%; United Kingdom 3.8%.
*Exports* (1983): DF 1,919,000,000 (unspecified special transactions 89.6%, of which live animals [including camels] 30.8%, food and food products 18.6%). *Major export destinations* (1981): France 31.0%; Yemen (Ṣan'ā') 29.8%; Somalia 9.1%; Ethiopia 7.7%; The Netherlands 6.6%; United States 5.9%.

## Transport and communications

*Transport.* Railroads (1984): length 66 mi, 106 km; short ton-mile cargo 90,140,000, metric ton-km cargo 131,600,000[10]. Roads (1986): total length 1,799 mi, 2,895 km (paved 7%). Vehicles (1985): passenger cars 12,049; trucks and buses 951. Merchant marine (1986): vessels (100 gross tons and over) 7; total deadweight tonnage 2,650. Air transport[11] (1985): passenger arrivals 55,023, passenger departures 48,256; cargo loaded 1,655 metric tons, cargo unloaded 6,627 metric tons; airports (1987) with scheduled flights 3.
*Communications.* Weekly newspapers (1986): total number 1; total circulation 4,000; circulation per 1,000 population 8.8. Radio (1986): total number of receivers 32,000 (1 per 14 persons). Television (1986): total number of receivers 14,000 (1 per 33 persons). Telephone subscribers (1985): 3,986 (1 per 108 persons).

## Education and health

### Education (1985–86)

| | schools | teachers | students | student/ teacher ratio |
|---|---|---|---|---|
| Primary (age 6–14) | 58 | 514 | 25,212 | 49.1 |
| Secondary (age 12–20) | 8 | 306 | 6,234 | 20.4 |
| Voc., teacher tr. | 12 | 110 | 1,984 | 12.5 |
| Higher[12] | — | — | 161 | |

*Educational attainment,* n.a. *Literacy* (*c.* 1980): population age 14 and over literate 11.9% (8.8% if expatriate population is discounted).
*Health* (1985): physicians 68 (1 per 6,323 persons); hospital beds 1,283 (1 per 335 persons); infant mortality rate per 1,000 live births 200.
*Food:* n.a.

## Military

*Total active duty personnel* (1986): 3,000 (army 95.7%, navy 1.3%, air force 3.0%). *Military expenditure as percent of GNP* (1984): 9.0% (world, 5.9%); per capita expenditure U.S.$67.

[1]Approximate figures given in sq km; sq mi equivalent rounded to appropriate level of generality. [2]Including 45,000 unaccounted, not shown separately. [3]District population. [4]Infants and children to age 10, district of Djibouti only. [5]In 1985 only 900 ac (400 ha) of land were cultivated. [6]City of Djibouti only. [7]Salaried employees only. [8]Import duties, less imputed bank service charge. [9]The value of imports includes merchandise destined for Ethiopia and northern Somalia; that of exports excludes reexports coming from those areas. In 1980 the value of reexports from Ethiopia and northern Somalia was approximately five times greater than the value of domestic exports. [10]Based on total weight of Ethiopian exports and imports transported to and from the port of Djibouti. [11]Djibouti International Airport only. [12]1983–84.

# Dominica

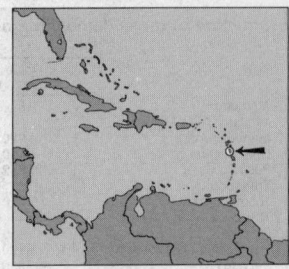

*Official name:* Commonwealth of Dominica.
*Form of government:* multiparty republic with one legislative house (House of Assembly [31][1]).
*Chief of state:* President.
*Head of government:* Prime Minister.
*Capital:* Roseau.
*Official language:* English.
*Official religion:* none.
*Monetary unit:* 1 East Caribbean dollar (EC$) = 100 cents; valuation (Oct. 5, 1987) 1 U.S.$ = EC$2.70;
1 £ = EC$4.38.

### Area and population

| Parishes[2] | area sq mi | area sq km | population 1981 census |
|---|---|---|---|
| St. Andrew | 69 | 179 | 12,748 |
| St. David | 49 | 127 | 7,337 |
| St. George | 21 | 54 | 20,501 |
| St. John | 23 | 60 | 5,412 |
| St. Joseph | 46 | 119 | 6,606 |
| St. Luke | 4 | 10 | 1,503 |
| St. Mark | 4 | 10 | 1,921 |
| St. Patrick | 32 | 83 | 9,780 |
| St. Paul | 26 | 67 | 6,386 |
| St. Peter | 11 | 29 | 1,601 |
| TOTAL | 290[3, 4] | 750[4] | 73,795[5, 6] |

## Demography

*Population* (1987): 87,700.
*Density* (1987): persons per sq mi 302.4, persons per sq km 116.9.
*Urban–rural:* n.a.
*Sex distribution* (1981)[5]: male 49.81%; female 50.19%.
*Age breakdown* (1981)[5]: under 15, 39.8%; 15–29, 28.6%; 30–44, 11.9%; 45–59, 9.2%; 60–74, 7.4%; 75 and over, 3.1%.
*Population projection:* (1990) 93,000; (2000) 114,000.
*Doubling time:* 45 years.
*Ethnic composition* (1981): black 91.2%; mixed race 6.0%; Amerindian 1.5%; white 0.5%; not stated 0.6%; other 0.2%.
*Religious affiliation* (1981): Roman Catholic 76.9%; Protestant 15.5%, of which Methodist 5.0%, Seventh-day Adventist 3.2%, Pentecostal 2.9%; other 7.6%.
*Major towns* (1981): Roseau 8,346; Marigot 3,554; St. Joseph 2,665; Portsmouth 2,220.

## Vital statistics

*Birth rate* per 1,000 population (1984): 20.8 (world avg. 29.0); (1980) legitimate 35.0%; illegitimate 65.0%.
*Death rate* per 1,000 population (1984): 5.2 (world avg. 11.0).
*Natural increase rate* per 1,000 population (1984): 15.6 (world avg. 18.0).
*Total fertility rate* (avg. births per childbearing woman; 1984): 3.4.
*Marriage rate* per 1,000 population: n.a.
*Divorce rate* per 1,000 population: n.a.
*Life expectancy* at birth (1980–85): male 72.8 years; female 76.5 years.
*Major causes of death* per 100,000 population (1984): diseases of the circulatory system 197.8; malignant neoplasms (cancers) 88.6; diseases of the respiratory system 27.9; endocrine and metabolic disorders 26.7; ill-defined conditions 44.9.

## National economy

*Budget* (1985–86). Revenue: EC$124,100,000 (tax revenues 61.5%, of which taxes on international trade 35.0%, income tax 20.8%, consumption tax 5.7%; foreign grants 32.0%; nontax revenue 6.5%). Expenditures: EC$125,-500,000 (wages and salaries 37.5%; capital expenditure 35.4%; goods and services 11.4%; interest on public debt 6.1%; transfer payments 5.7%).
*Gross national product* (1985): U.S.$90,000,000 (U.S.$1,070 per capita).

### Structure of gross domestic product and labour force

| | 1986 in value EC$'000,000[7] | 1986 % of total value | 1981 labour force | 1981 % of labour force |
|---|---|---|---|---|
| Agriculture | 34.0 | 29.5 | 7,843 | 31.0 |
| Mining | 0.9 | 0.8 | 8 | — |
| Manufacturing | 10.2 | 8.8 | 1,417 | 5.6 |
| Construction | 8.6 | 7.4 | 2,306 | 9.1 |
| Public utilities | 2.3 | 2.0 | 245 | 1.0 |
| Transportation and communication | 10.0 | 8.7 | 914 | 3.6 |
| Trade, hotels, restaurants | 15.6 | 13.5 | 1,613 | 6.3 |
| Finance, real estate, insurance | 13.7[8] | 11.9[8] | 257 | 1.0 |
| Pub. admin., defense | 24.2 | 21.0 | 4,980 | 19.7 |
| Services | [8] | [8] | 5,750[10] | 22.7 |
| Other | –4.1[9] | –3.6[9] | | |
| TOTAL | 115.4 | 100.0 | 25,333 | 100.0 |

*Population economically active* (1981): total 25,333; activity rate of total population 34.3% (participation rates: ages 15–64, 61.7%; female 34.1%; unemployed [1984] 13.0%).

### Price and earnings indexes (1980 = 100)

| | 1980 | 1981 | 1982 | 1983 | 1984 | 1985 | 1986 |
|---|---|---|---|---|---|---|---|
| Consumer price index | 100.0 | 113.3 | 118.4 | 123.2 | 125.9 | 128.5 | 132.3 |
| Earnings index | ... | ... | ... | ... | ... | ... | ... |

*Household income and expenditure.* Average household size (1981) 4.3; income per household: n.a.; expenditure (1984)[11]: food and nonalcoholic beverages 43.1%, housing and utilities 16.1%, clothing and footwear 6.5%, alcoholic beverages and tobacco 2.0%, other 32.3%.
*Production* (metric tons except as noted). Agriculture, forestry, fishing (1985): bananas 55,400[12], root crops (mostly dasheens and tanias) 25,000, coconuts 15,000, grapefruits 9,700[12], limes 6,000, oranges 3,000, cucumbers and gherkins 3,000, cocoa 429[13], coffee 366[13], other products include patchouli and cut flowers; livestock (number of live animals) 9,000 pigs, 6,000 goats, 4,000 cattle; roundwood, n.a.; fish catch 446. Mining and quarrying (1985): pumice and volcanic ash 110,000. Manufacturing (1984): galvanized sheets 2,739; laundry soap 2,424; toilet soap, 1,644; coconut meal 789; edible coconut oil 6,600 hectolitres. Construction: n.a. Energy production (consumption): electricity (kW-hr; 1985) 18,000,000 (18,000,-000); coal, none (none); crude petroleum, none (none); petroleum products (metric tons; 1985) none (12,000); natural gas, none (none).
*Public debt* (external, outstanding; 1985): U.S.$45,000,000.
*Tourism:* receipts from visitors (1986) U.S.$7,100,000; expenditures by nationals abroad (1983) U.S.$700,000.
*Land use* (1984): forested 41.0%; meadows and pastures 3.0%; agricultural and under permanent cultivation 23.0%; other 33.0%.

## Foreign trade

### Balance of trade (current prices)[14]

| | 1981 | 1982 | 1983 | 1984[15] | 1985 | 1986 |
|---|---|---|---|---|---|---|
| EC$'000,000 | –82.3 | –62.2 | –53.5 | –77.4 | –66.5 | –36.1 |
| % of total | 44.3% | 32.0% | 28.2% | 33.0% | 29.8% | 13.6% |

*Imports* (1986): EC$150,300,000[16] (1984: food 16.1%, of which meat 5.0%, flour 3.3%, dairy products 2.8%; electric and nonelectric machinery 13.9%; transport equipment 11.1%; metals and their manufactures 9.4%; petroleum products 6.1%; cardboard boxes 4.2%). *Major import sources* (1984): United States 26.7%; United Kingdom 12.8%; Trinidad and Tobago 7.7%; Canada 7.7%; St. Lucia 5.5%; The Netherlands 3.2%.
*Exports* (1986): EC$114,200,000[16] (1984[17]: bananas 44.6%; toilet soap 13.5%; galvanized sheets 9.8%; household soap 8.6%; refined coconut oil 4.3%; crude coconut oil 2.4%; grapefruit 2.3%). *Major export destinations* (1984): United Kingdom 45.7%; Jamaica 15.6%; Trinidad and Tobago 14.1%; Antigua and Barbuda 4.3%; Barbados 3.0%; Grenada 2.7%.

## Transport and communications

*Transport.* Railroads: none. Roads (1984): total length 489 mi, 787 km (paved 60%). Vehicles (1983): passenger cars 2,713; trucks and buses 1,250. Merchant marine (1986): vessels (100 gross tons and over) 7; total deadweight tonnage 2,953. Air transport (1984): passenger arrivals 33,954, passenger departures 34,381; cargo unloaded 196 metric tons, cargo loaded 271 metric tons; airports (1987) with scheduled flights 2.
*Communications.* Daily newspapers: none. Radio (1986): total number of receivers 35,000 (1 per 2.5 persons). Television: total number of receivers, n.a. Telephones (1985): 6,882 (1 per 12.0 persons).

## Education and health

### Education (1982–83)

| | schools | teachers | students | student/ teacher ratio |
|---|---|---|---|---|
| Primary[18] | 66 | 584 | 17,456 | 29.9 |
| Secondary | 8 | 145 | 3,234 | 22.3 |
| Voc., teacher tr. | 1 | 13 | 121 | 9.3 |
| Higher[19] | ... | 17 | 60 | 3.5 |

*Educational attainment* (1981). Percent of population age 25 and over having: no formal schooling 6.6%; primary education 80.6%; secondary 11.1%; higher 1.7%. *Literacy* (1981): total population age 15 and over literate 42,100 (94.9%).
*Health* (1985): physicians 25 (1 per 3,371 persons); hospital beds 292 (1 per 289 persons); infant mortality rate per 1,000 live births (1982–84 avg.) 16.3.
*Food* (1981–83): daily per capita caloric intake 2,391 (vegetable products 83%, animal products 17%); (1983) 100% of FAO recommended minimum requirement.

## Military

*Total active duty personnel* (1986): none[20].

[1]Includes 10 nonelective seats. [2]Dominica is divided into 10 parishes for administrative purposes only. Local government is based on village or town councils. [3]Includes inland water area. [4]Detail does not add to total given because of rounding. [5]Excludes institutionalized population. [6]Total population including institutionalized residents equals 74,785. [7]At constant prices of 1977. [8]Finance, real estate, insurance includes Services. [9]Less imputed service charges. [10]Includes 4,746 unemployed. [11]Weights of consumer price index components. [12]1986. [13]1984. [14]Imports c.i.f. (cost, insurance, and freight); exports f.o.b. (free on board). Exports include reexports. [15]Based on adjusted export figure of EC$78,700,000. [16]Preliminary figure. [17]Breakdown based on domestic exports only, totaling EC$67,307,000. [18]1983–84. [19]1984–85. [20]300-member police force has residual responsibilities for defense.

# Dominican Republic

*Official name:* República Dominicana (Dominican Republic).
*Form of government:* multiparty republic with two legislative houses (Senate [27]; Chamber of Deputies [120]).
*Head of state and government:* President.
*Capital:* Santo Domingo.
*Official language:* Spanish.
*Official religion:* none.
*Monetary unit:* 1 Dominican peso (RD$) = 100 centavos; valuation (Oct. 5, 1987) 1 U.S.$ = RD$3.19; 1 £ = RD$5.18.

### Area and population

| Provinces | Capitals | area sq mi | sq km | population 1987 estimate |
|---|---|---|---|---|
| Azua | Azua | 938 | 2,430 | 178,877 |
| Bahoruco (Baoruco) | Neiba | 531 | 1,376 | 85,356 |
| Barahona | Barahona | 976 | 2,528 | 148,881 |
| Dajabón | Dajabón | 344 | 890 | 62,640 |
| Duarte | San Francisco de Macorís | 499 | 1,292 | 255,672 |
| El Seibo | El Seibo | 641 | 1,659 | 95,333 |
| Espaillat | Moca | 386 | 1,000 | 178,033 |
| Hato Mayor | Hato Mayor | 514 | 1,330 | 76,023 |
| Independencia | Jimaní | 719 | 1,861 | 42,081 |
| La Altagracia | Higüey | 1,191 | 3,084 | 108,667 |
| La Estrelleta | Elías Piña | 690 | 1,788 | 70,971 |
| La Romana | La Romana | 209 | 541 | 149,652 |
| La Vega | La Vega | 916 | 2,373 | 296,039 |
| María Trinidad Sánchez | Nagua | 506 | 1,310 | 122,253 |
| Monseñor Nouel | Bonao | 388 | 1,004 | 121,906 |
| Monte Cristi | Monte Cristi | 768 | 1,989 | 90,534 |
| Monte Plata | Monte Plata | 841 | 2,179 | 170,758 |
| Pedernales | Pedernales | 373 | 967 | 18,459 |
| Peravia | Baní | 626 | 1,622 | 182,489 |
| Puerto Plata | Puerto Plata | 726 | 1,881 | 224,425 |
| Salcedo | Salcedo | 206 | 533 | 107,667 |
| Samaná | Samaná | 382 | 989 | 71,313 |
| Sánchez Ramírez | Cotuí | 453 | 1,174 | 137,382 |
| San Cristóbal | San Cristóbal | 604 | 1,564 | 313,497 |
| San Juan | San Juan | 1,375 | 3,561 | 260,462 |
| San Pedro de Macorís | San Pedro de Macorís | 450 | 1,166 | 184,078 |
| Santiago | Santiago de los Caballeros | 1,205 | 3,122 | 657,729 |
| Santiago Rodríguez | Sabaneta | 394 | 1,020 | 60,146 |
| Santo Domingo[1] | — | 570 | 1,477 | 2,127,496 |
| Valverde | Mao | 220 | 570 | 108,891 |
| TOTAL | | 18,704[2] | 48,443[2] | 6,707,710 |

## Demography

*Population* (1987): 6,708,000.
*Density* (1987): persons per sq mi 358.6, persons per sq km 138.5.
*Urban–rural* (1985): urban 55.7%; rural 44.3%.
*Sex distribution* (1985): male 50.31%; female 49.69%.
*Age breakdown* (1985): under 15, 40.7%; 15–29, 30.7%; 30–44, 15.4%; 45–59, 8.5%; 60–74, 3.7%; 75 and over, 1.0%.
*Population projection:* (1990) 7,223,000; (2000) 9,247,000.
*Doubling time:* 28 years.
*Ethnic composition* (1983): mulatto 73%; white 16%; black 11%.
*Religious affiliation* (1984): Roman Catholic 93.7%; other 6.3%.
*Major cities* (1983): Santo Domingo 1,410,000; Santiago de los Caballeros 285,000; La Romana 101,000; San Pedro de Macorís 81,000.

## Vital statistics

*Birth rate* per 1,000 population (1985–90): 30.9 (world avg. 26.0); (1976) legitimate 32.8%; illegitimate 67.2%.
*Death rate* per 1,000 population (1985–90): 7.1 (world avg. 9.9).
*Natural increase rate* per 1,000 population (1985–90): 23.8 (world avg. 16.1).
*Total fertility rate* (avg. births per childbearing woman; 1984): 4.0.
*Marriage rate* per 1,000 population (1985): 3.4.
*Divorce rate* per 1,000 population (1985): 1.2.
*Life expectancy* at birth (1980–85): male 60.7 years; female 64.6 years.
*Major causes of death* per 100,000 population (1982): infectious and parasitic diseases 47.0; diseases of pulmonary circulation 31.6%; diseases of the respiratory system 29.4; ill-defined conditions 96.3.

## National economy

*Budget* (1986). Revenue: RD$2,133,300,000 (tax revenue 95.3%, of which excise taxes 35.5%, import duties 27.5%, taxes on income and profits 19.7%; nontax revenue 4.7%). Expenditures: RD$2,250,600,000 (administration 31.9%; education 9.9%; agriculture 9.0%; defense 9.0%; health 6.8%).
*Public debt* (external, outstanding; 1985): U.S.$2,500,000,000.
*Tourism:* receipts from visitors (1985) U.S.$297,000,000; expenditures by nationals abroad (1983) U.S.$87,000,000.
*Production* (metric tons except as noted). Agriculture (1985): sugarcane 8,217,000, plantains 610,000, rice 494,000, bananas 320,000, mangoes 185,-000, tomatoes 165,000, cassava 135,000, coffee 68,000, cacao 35,000, tobacco 31,000; livestock (number of live animals) 2,420,000 cattle, 1,850,000 pigs; roundwood (1984) 969,000 cu m; fish catch 18,338. Mining (value of production in RD$'000,000; 1985): ferronickel 123; gold 104. Manufacturing (value of production in RD$'000,000; 1983): food products 1,559; refined petroleum 425; all beverages 362; cement and fertilizers 139; cigarettes 131. Construction (1984): residential 692,000 sq m; nonresidential 312,000 sq m.

*Energy production* (consumption): electricity (kW-hr; 1985) 4,227,000,000 (3,549,000,000); coal, none (none); crude petroleum (barrels; 1985) none (9,667,000); petroleum products (metric tons; 1985) 1,380,000 (2,007,000).
*Gross national product* (at current market prices; 1985): U.S.$5,050,000,000 (U.S.$790 per capita).

### Structure of gross domestic product and labour force

| | 1985 | | 1981 | |
|---|---|---|---|---|
| | in value U.S.$'000,000[3] | % of total value | labour force | % of labour force |
| Agriculture | 1,298 | 16.9 | 420,463 | 22.0 |
| Mining | 333 | 4.3 | 4,743 | 0.2 |
| Manufacturing | 1,298 | 16.9 | 224,437 | 11.7 |
| Construction | 465 | 6.1 | 80,850 | 4.3 |
| Public utilities | 145 | 1.9 | 13,891 | 0.7 |
| Transp. and commun. | 613 | 8.0 | 40,470 | 2.1 |
| Trade | 1,211 | 15.8 | 192,181 | 10.0 |
| Finance, real estate | 735 | 9.6 | 22,369 | 1.2 |
| Pub. admin., defense, services | 1,567 | 20.5 | 363,125 | 18.9 |
| Other | — | — | 552,859[4] | 28.9[4] |
| TOTAL | 7,665 | 100.0 | 1,915,388 | 100.0 |

*Population economically active* (1981): total 1,915,388; activity rate of total population 33.9% (participation rates: ages 15–64, 53.6%; female 28.9%; unemployed [1986] 28.0%).

### Price and earnings indexes (1980 = 100)

| | 1980 | 1981 | 1982 | 1983 | 1984 | 1985 | 1986[5] |
|---|---|---|---|---|---|---|---|
| Consumer price index | 100.0 | 107.5 | 115.8 | 121.3 | 154.0 | 211.8 | 228.3 |
| Monthly earnings index[6] | 100.0 | 107.2 | 118.5 | ... | ... | ... | ... |

*Household income and expenditure.* Average household size (1981) 5.1; average annual income per family (1975) urban family RD$2,299, rural family RD$654; sources of income: n.a.; expenditure (1976–77)[7]: food, beverages, and tobacco 51.7%, housing 23.9%, clothing and footwear 6.0%.
*Land use* (1984): forested 13.0%; meadows and pastures 43.2%; agricultural and under permanent cultivation 30.4%; other 13.4%.

## Foreign trade[8]

### Balance of trade (current prices)

| | 1981 | 1982 | 1983 | 1984 | 1985 | 1986[9] |
|---|---|---|---|---|---|---|
| RD$'000,000 | −262.8 | −491.3 | −493.8 | −389.0 | −557.8 | −389.6 |
| % of total | 9.9% | 24.1% | 23.9% | 18.3% | 27.5% | 27.0% |

*Imports* (1984): RD$1,257,100,000 (crude petroleum 29.3%; petroleum products 8.2%; cereals 3.9%; other [mostly manufactured goods] 58.6%). *Major import sources:* United States 32.4%; Venezuela 26.5%; Mexico 11.7%.
*Exports* (1984): RD$868,100,000 (raw sugar 30.9%; gold alloy 15.1%; ferronickel 12.2%; coffee 10.9%; cacao 7.8%; raw tobacco 2.6%). *Major export destinations:* U.S. 72.1%; The Netherlands 7.0%; Puerto Rico 5.0%.

## Transport and communications

*Transport.* Railroads (1985)[10]: length 994 mi, 1,600 km. Roads (1982): total length 10,788 mi, 17,362 km (paved 29%). Vehicles (1983): passenger cars 94,601; trucks and buses 55,346. Merchant marine (1986): vessels (100 gross tons and over) 35; total deadweight tonnage 67,477. Air transport (1985)[11]: passenger-mi 325,000,000, passenger-km 523,000,000; short ton-mi cargo 36,610,000, metric ton-km cargo 53,450,000; airports (1987) 4.
*Communications.* Daily newspapers (1985): total number 9; total circulation 208,000; circulation per 1,000 population 33. Radio (1986): 800,000 receivers (1 per 8.2 persons). Television (1986): 500,000 receivers (1 per 13 persons). Telephones (1983): 175,054 (1 per 35 persons).

## Education and health

### Education (1983–84)

| | schools | teachers | students | student/ teacher ratio |
|---|---|---|---|---|
| Primary (age 7–12) | 4,846 | 20,607 | 1,121,851 | 54.4 |
| Secondary (age 13–18) | | | 352,328 | ... |
| Voc., teacher tr. | ... | 635 | 27,670 | 43.6 |
| Higher[12] | 6 | 3,107 | 88,024 | 28.3 |

*Educational attainment* (1970). Percent of population age 25 and over having: no formal schooling 40.1%; primary education 45.9%; secondary 12.1%; higher 1.9%. *Literacy* (1985): total population age 15 and over literate 2,860,000 (77.3%); males literate 1,447,000 (77.7%); females literate 1,413,000 (76.8%).
*Health* (1980)[13]: physicians 2,142 (1 per 2,600 persons); hospital beds 8,953 (1 per 620 persons); infant mortality rate per 1,000 live births (1985) 67.0.
*Food* (1981–83): daily per capita caloric intake 2,330 (vegetable products 87%, animal products 13%); 105% of FAO recommended minimum.

## Military

*Total active duty personnel* (1986): 21,300 (army 61.0%, navy 18.8%, air force 20.2%). *Military expenditure as percent of GNP* (1984): 1.2% (world 5.9%); per capita expenditure U.S.$15.

---

[1]National district. [2]Total includes 63 sq mi (163 sq km) of offshore islands not shown separately. [3]At 1984 prices. [4]Includes activities not adequately defined and unemployed. [5]Average of second and third quarters only. [6]Manufacturing only. [7]Weights of consumer price index components. [8]Imports and exports f.o.b. (free on board). [9]Through September only. [10]All track serves the sugar industry only except for 65 mi (104 km) for public transport. [11]CDA (Dominicana) airlines only. [12]1985–86 (universities only). [13]Institute of Social Security only.

# Ecuador

*Official name:* República del Ecuador (Republic of Ecuador).
*Form of government:* unitary multiparty republic with one legislative house (National Congress [71]).
*Head of state and government:* President.
*Capital:* Quito.
*Official language:* Spanish.
*Official religion:* none.
*Monetary unit:* 1 Sucre (S/.) = 100 centavos; valuation (Oct. 5, 1987) 1 U.S.$ = S/. 159.08; 1 £ = S/. 258.33.

### Area and population

| Regions<br>Provinces | Capitals | area | | population |
|---|---|---|---|---|
| | | sq mi | sq km | 1986<br>estimate |
| **Coastal** | | | | |
| El Oro | Machala | 2,281 | 5,908 | 406,800 |
| Esmeraldas | Esmeraldas | 5,854 | 15,162 | 297,400 |
| Guayas | Guayaquil | 8,256 | 21,382 | 2,485,800 |
| Los Ríos | Babahoyo | 2,459 | 6,370 | 533,700 |
| Manabí | Portoviejo | 6,990 | 18,105 | 1,039,400 |
| **Eastern** | | | | |
| Morona-Santiago | Macas | 10,200 | 26,418 | 85,600 |
| Napo | Tena | 20,200 | 52,318 | 151,800 |
| Pastaza | Puyo | 11,687 | 30,269 | 38,500 |
| Zamora-Chinchipe | Zamora | 7,102 | 18,394 | 59,100 |
| **Sierra** | | | | |
| Azuay | Cuenca | 3,124 | 8,092 | 513,300 |
| Bolívar | Guaranda | 1,599 | 4,142 | 164,700 |
| Cañar | Azogues | 1,344 | 3,481 | 198,300 |
| Carchi | Tulcán | 1,446 | 3,744 | 143,300 |
| Chimborazo | Riobamba | 2,338 | 6,056 | 369,200 |
| Cotopaxi | Latacunga | 2,007 | 5,198 | 312,700 |
| Imbabura | Ibarra | 1,921 | 4,976 | 281,000 |
| Loja | Loja | 4,429 | 11,472 | 404,000 |
| Pichincha | Quito | 6,404 | 16,587 | 1,710,300 |
| Tungurahua | Ambato | 1,201 | 3,110 | 374,300 |
| **Island territory** | | | | |
| Galápagos Islands | Puerto Baquerizo<br>Moreno | 3,086 | 7,994 | 8,000 |
| TOTAL | | 103,930[1] | 269,178 | 9,647,100[2] |

## Demography

*Population* (1987): 9,923,000.
*Density* (1987): persons per sq mi 95.5, persons per sq km 36.9.
*Urban–rural* (1986): urban 52.8%; rural 47.2%.
*Sex distribution* (1986): male 50.30%; female 49.70%.
*Age breakdown* (1986): under 15, 41.5%; 15–29, 28.2%; 30–44, 16.1%; 45–64, 10.5%; 65 and over, 3.7%.
*Population projection:* (1990) 10,782,000; (2000) 13,939,000.
*Doubling time:* 24 years.
*Ethnic composition* (1980): Quechua 49.9%; mestizo 40.0%; white 8.5%; Amerindian 1.6%.
*Religious affiliation* (1984): Roman Catholic 92.1%; other 7.9%.
*Major cities* (1987): Guayaquil 1,572,615; Quito 1,137,705; Cuenca 201,490; Machala 144,396; Portoviejo 141,568.

## Vital statistics

*Birth rate* per 1,000 population: (1984) 36.8 (world avg. 29.0); (1982) legitimate 67.9%; illegitimate 32.1%.
*Death rate* per 1,000 population (1984): 8.1 (world avg. 11.0).
*Natural increase rate* per 1,000 population (1984): 28.7 (world avg. 18.0).
*Total fertility rate* (avg. births per childbearing woman; 1985): 4.8.
*Marriage rate* per 1,000 population (1984): 5.9.
*Divorce rate* per 1,000 population (1984): 0.4.
*Life expectancy* at birth (1981): male 59.8 years; female 63.6 years.
*Major causes of death* per 100,000 population (1980): infectious and parasitic diseases 122.1; respiratory diseases 103.2; circulatory diseases 87.4; accidents 60.0; senility without mention of psychosis 48.7.

## National economy

*Budget* (1986). Revenue: S/. 186,824,500,000 (income from petroleum 39.4%, production and sales tax 25.6%, import duties 19.4%, income taxes 10.9%). Expenditures: S/. 235,797,100,000[3] (education 24.3%, debt service 24.0%, public services 23.6%, transport and communication 12.7%, health 6.9%).
*Public debt* (external, outstanding; 1985): U.S.$7,121,100,000.
*Tourism:* receipts from visitors (1985) U.S.$130,000,000; expenditures by nationals abroad (1984) U.S.$155,000,000.
*Production* (metric tons except as noted). Agriculture, forestry, fishing (1985): bananas 1,970,000, corn (maize) 544,000, potatoes 423,000, rice 397,000, oranges 350,000, raw sugar 310,000, cassava 234,000, cacao 131,000, coffee (green) 121,000, pineapples 92,000, palm oil 80,000; livestock (number of live animals) 4,230,000 pigs, 3,378,000 cattle, 2,086,000 sheep, 43,000,000 chickens; roundwood (1984) 8,228,000 cu m; fish catch (1984) 867,496. Mining and quarrying (1985): limestone 3,000,000; silver 2,000 troy oz, gold 1,000 troy oz. Manufacturing (value in S/. '000,000; 1983): food products 19,432; petroleum products 16,446; textiles and clothing 6,495; beverages (including liquors) 2,706. Construction (in S/.4; 1983): residential 12,235,300,000; nonresidential 1,920,000,000. Energy production (consumption): electricity (kW-hr; 1985) 4,806,000,000 (3,817,000,000); crude petroleum (barrels; 1985) 101,809,000 (42,673,000); petroleum prod-

ucts (metric tons; 1985) 4,063,000 (3,661,000); natural gas (cu m; 1985) 140,171,000 (140,171,000).
*Gross national product* (1985): U.S.$10,880,000,000 (U.S.$1,160 per capita).

### Structure of gross domestic product and labour force

| | 1985 | | 1982 | |
|---|---|---|---|---|
| | in value<br>S/. '000,000 | % of total<br>value | labour<br>force | % of labour<br>force |
| Agriculture | 155,887 | 13.6 | 786,530 | 33.0 |
| Mining | 194,634 | 17.0 | 7,050 | 0.3 |
| Manufacturing | 216,805 | 18.9 | 284,780 | 11.9 |
| Construction | 62,258 | 5.4 | 158,530 | 6.6 |
| Public utilities | 2,874 | 0.3 | 14,560 | 0.6 |
| Transp. and commun. | 98,461 | 8.6 | 103,850 | 4.4 |
| Trade | 179,005 | 15.6 | 266,640 | 11.2 |
| Finance | 50,422 | 4.4 | 38,420 | 1.6 |
| Pub. admin., defense | 81,818 | 7.1 | 614,240 | 25.7 |
| Services | 87,061 | 7.6 | | |
| Other | 18,682 | 1.6 | 112,650 | 4.7 |
| TOTAL | 1,147,907 | 100.0[1] | 2,387,250 | 100.0 |

*Population economically active* (1985): total 2,713,000; activity rate of total population 28.9% (participation rates: ages 15–64, 43.3%; female 8.5%; unemployed [1981] 1.9%).

### Price and earnings indexes (1980 = 100)

| | 1981 | 1982 | 1983 | 1984 | 1985 | 1986 | 1987[5] |
|---|---|---|---|---|---|---|---|
| Consumer price index | 116.4 | 135.3 | 200.8 | 263.6 | 337.3 | 415.0 | 535.3 |
| Annual earnings index[6] | 116.3 | 126.9 | ... | ... | ... | ... | ... |

*Household income and expenditure.* Average household size (1982) 5.1; average annual income per household (1982) S/. 28,747 (U.S.$956); sources of income (1982): self-employment 53.6%, wages and salaries 38.0%, interest, dividends, and rent 2.9%, social security 2.9%; expenditure (1985): food, beverages, and tobacco 38.6%, transportation and communication 12.3%, clothing 11.4%, housing and utilities 6.8%.
*Land use* (1984): forested 51.1%; meadows and pastures 17.0%; agricultural and under permanent cultivation 9.1%; other 22.8%.

## Foreign trade[7]

### Balance of trade (current prices)

| | 1981 | 1982 | 1983 | 1984 | 1985 | 1986 |
|---|---|---|---|---|---|---|
| U.S.$'000,000 | +646.4 | +425.8 | +971.6 | +1,124.3 | +1,285.9 | +603.4 |
| % of total | 14.6% | 11.0% | 28.0% | 27.8% | 30.4% | 16.0% |

*Imports* (1986): U.S.$1,533,468,100 (chemical products 16.5%, mineral products 14.6%, industrial machinery 9.2%, transport equipment parts 7.3%, road transport equipment 5.9%). *Major import sources:* United States 29.2%; Japan 11.2%; West Germany 9.5%; Brazil 6.7%; Italy 6.0%.
*Exports* (1986): U.S.$2,185,847,000 (crude petroleum 41.7%, coffee 13.7%, bananas 12.1%, cacao 3.3%, petroleum products 3.2%). *Major export destinations:* United States 60.5%; West Germany 3.6%; Panama 2.7%; Japan 2.6%; Chile 2.2%; Taiwan 1.7%; Colombia 1.4%.

## Transport and communications

*Transport.* Railroads: (1986) route length 600 mi, 965 km; (1982) passenger-mi 26,900,000, passenger-km 43,300,000; (1982) short ton-mi cargo 8,200,000, metric ton-km cargo 11,900,000. Roads (1985): total length 22,486 mi, 36,187 km (paved 28%). Vehicles (1984): passenger cars 248,575; trucks and buses 32,624. Merchant marine (1986): vessels (100 gross tons and over) 155; total deadweight tonnage 611,570. Air transport (1983): passenger-mi 557,000,000, passenger-km 896,000,000; short ton-mi cargo 26,000,000, metric ton-km cargo 37,900,000; airports (1987) 14.
*Communications.* Daily newspapers (1985): total number 7; total circulation 538,000; circulation per 1,000 population 57. Radio (1985): 1,900,000 receivers (1 per 4.9 persons). Television (1985): 600,000 receivers (1 per 16 persons). Telephones (1985): 339,040 (1 per 28 persons).

## Education and health

### Education (1983–84)

| | schools | teachers | students | student/<br>teacher ratio |
|---|---|---|---|---|
| Primary (age 4–12) | 13,011 | 50,347 | 1,677,364 | 33.3 |
| Secondary (age 12–18)[8] | 1,315 | 29,319 | 459,647 | 15.7 |
| Vocational | 466 | 10,590 | 190,631 | 18.0 |
| Higher | 17 | 11,186 | 267,900 | 23.9 |

*Educational attainment* (1982). Percent of population age 25 and over having: no formal schooling 25.4%; primary education 34.1%; secondary 7.9%; higher 7.6%. *Literacy* (1982): total population age 15 and over literate 3,914,694 (69.1%); males 2,005,455 (86.8%); females 1,909,239 (56.9%).
*Health* (1984): physicians 11,000 (1 per 829 persons); hospital beds 15,455 (1 per 590 persons); infant mortality rate per 1,000 live births 68.4.
*Food* (1981–83): daily per capita caloric intake 2,052 (vegetable products 82%, animal products 18%); (1983) 89% of FAO minimum requirement.

## Military

*Total active duty personnel* (1986): 42,000 (army 83.3%, navy 9.5%, air force 7.2%). *Military expenditure as percent of GNP* (1984): 1.6% (world 5.9%); per capita expenditure U.S.$22.

---

[1]Detail does not add to total given because of rounding. [2]Total includes 69,900 persons not shown separately. [3]Breakdown is for 1985. [4]Authorized construction. [5]June. [6]For salaried industrial workers. [7]Import figures are f.o.b. in balance of trade and c.i.f. for commodities and trading partners. [8]Includes teacher training.

# Egypt

*Official name:* Jumhūrīyah Miṣr al-ʿArabīyah (Arab Republic of Egypt).
*Form of government:* republic with one legislative house (People's Assembly [458])[1].
*Chief of state:* President.
*Head of government:* Prime Minister.
*Capital:* Cairo.
*Official language:* Arabic.
*Official religion:* Islam.
*Monetary unit:* 1 Egyptian pound (LE) = 100 piastres = 1,000 millièmes; valuation (Oct. 5, 1987)
1 U.S.$ = LE 2.22;
1 £ = LE 3.61.

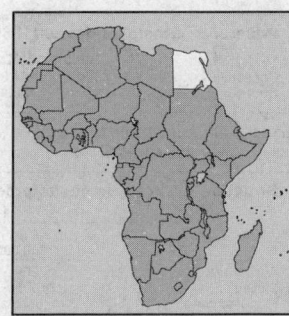

### Area and population

| Regions Governorates | Capitals | area sq mi | area sq km | population 1986 estimate |
|---|---|---|---|---|
| **Desert** | | | | |
| al-Baḥr al-Aḥmar | al-Ghurdaqah | 78,643 | 203,685 | 74,000 |
| Maṭrūḥ | Marsā Maṭrūḥ | 81,897 | 212,112 | 180,000 |
| Sīnāʾ al-Janūbīyah | aṭ-Ṭūr | 12,796 | 33,140 | 24,000 |
| Sīnāʾ ash-Shamālīyah | al-ʿArīsh | 10,646 | 27,574 | 156,000 |
| al-Wādī al-Jadīd | al-Kharijah | 145,369 | 376,505 | 118,000 |
| **Lower Egypt** | | | | |
| al-Buḥayrah | Damanhūr | 3,911 | 10,130 | 3,271,000 |
| ad-Daqahlīyah | al-Manṣūrah | 1,340 | 3,471 | 3,540,000 |
| Dumyāṭ | Dumyāṭ | 227 | 589 | 747,000 |
| al-Gharbīyah | Ṭanṭā | 750 | 1,942 | 2,904,000 |
| Kafr ash-Shaykh | Kafr ash-Shaykh | 1,327 | 3,437 | 1,839,000 |
| al-Minūfīyah | Shibīn al-Kawm | 592 | 1,532 | 2,194,000 |
| al-Qalyūbīyah | Banhā | 387 | 1,001 | 2,262,000 |
| ash-Sharqīyah | az-Zaqāzīq | 1,614 | 4,180 | 3,394,000 |
| **Upper Egypt** | | | | |
| Aswān | Aswān | 262 | 679 | 796,000 |
| Asyūṭ | Asyūṭ | 600 | 1,553 | 2,222,000 |
| Banī Suwayf | Banī Suwayf | 510 | 1,322 | 1,452,000 |
| al-Fayyūm | al-Fayyūm | 705 | 1,827 | 1,527,000 |
| al-Jīzah | al-Jīzah | 32,878 | 85,153 | 3,279,000 |
| al-Minyā | al-Minyā | 873 | 2,262 | 2,746,000 |
| Qinā | Qinā | 715 | 1,851 | 2,194,000 |
| Sawhāj | Sawhāj | 597 | 1,547 | 2,490,000 |
| **Urban** | | | | |
| Būr Saʿīd (Port Said) | — | 28 | 72 | 382,000 |
| al-Iskandarīyah (Alexandria) | — | 1,034 | 2,679 | 2,893,000 |
| al-Ismāʿīlīyah (Ismailia) | — | 557 | 1,442 | 484,000 |
| al-Qāhirah (Cairo) | — | 83 | 214 | 6,325,000 |
| as-Suways (Suez) | — | 6,888 | 17,840 | 265,000 |
| TOTAL | | 385,229 | 997,739 | 47,758,000 |

## Demography

*Population* (1987): 49,143,000.
*Density* (1987): persons per sq mi 127.6, persons per sq km 49.3.
*Urban–rural* (1985): urban 48.8%; rural 51.2%.
*Sex distribution* (1985): male 50.90%; female 49.10%.
*Age breakdown* (1984): under 15, 39.0%; 15–29, 27.8%; 30–44, 16.1%; 45–59, 10.8%; 60–74, 5.3%; 75 and over, 1.0%.
*Population projection:* (1990) 52,536,000; (2000) 63,941,000.
*Doubling time:* 26 years.
*Ethnic composition* (1983): Egyptian 98.8%; other 1.2%.
*Religious affiliation* (1980): Sunnī Muslim 81.8%; Christian 17.8%; other 0.4%.
*Major cities* (1986): Cairo 6,325,000; Alexandria 2,893,000; al-Jīzah 1,670,800; Shubrā al-Khaymah 533,300; al-Maḥallah al-Kubrā 385,300.

## Vital statistics

*Birth rate* per 1,000 population (1984): 37.4 (world avg. 29.0).
*Death rate* per 1,000 population (1984): 10.9 (world avg. 11.0).
*Natural increase rate* per 1,000 population (1984): 26.5 (world avg. 18.0).
*Total fertility rate* (avg. births per childbearing woman; 1984): 5.4.
*Marriage rate* per 1,000 population (1981): 8.9.
*Divorce rate* per 1,000 population (1981): 1.6.
*Life expectancy* at birth (1984): male 58.0 years; female 61.1 years.
*Major causes of death* per 100,000 population (1980): diseases of the digestive system 254.5; diseases of the circulatory system 200.1; senility without mention of psychosis 175.1; diseases of the respiratory system 165.6.

## National economy

*Budget* (1986–87). Revenue: LE 14,451,000,000 (sovereign tax 66.3%, oil revenue 5.3%, Suez Canal revenue 1.6%). Expenditures: LE 20,000,000,000 (debt servicing 13.5%, subsidies 8.7%, increase in the wages in the civil service and the state sector 5.9%).
*Public debt* (external, outstanding; 1985): U.S.$17,751,200,000.
*Tourism:* receipts from visitors (1985) U.S.$990,000,000; expenditures by nationals abroad (1984) U.S.$146,000,000.
*Production* (metric tons except as noted). Agriculture, forestry, fishing (1985): corn (maize) 3,982,000, tomatoes 2,800,000, rice 2,312,000, wheat 1,874,000, watermelons 1,300,000, potatoes 1,300,000, dry onions 850,000, millet 650,000, cotton (lint) 460,000, dates 450,000; livestock (number of live animals) 2,800,000 cattle, 2,650,000 goats, 2,500,000 sheep, 2,415,000 buffalo, 1,850,000 asses, 160,000 camels, 30,000,000 chickens; roundwood 2,011,000 cu m; fish catch 138,782. Mining and quarrying (1985): iron ore 2,000,000; phosphate rock 1,000,000; sodium carbonate 80,000. Manufacturing (1983): cement 3,794,000; cotton yarn 229,200; jute textiles 29,640;

cotton textiles 7,716. Construction (1982–83): residential units 168,577. Energy production (consumption): electricity (kW-hr; 1985) 23,220,000,000 (23,220,000,000); coal (metric tons; 1985) n.a. (1,200,000); crude petroleum (barrels; 1985) 321,528,000 (146,702,000); petroleum products (metric tons; 1985) 18,790,000 (16,525,000); natural gas (cu m; 1985) 3,583,987,000 (3,583,987,000).
*Gross national product* (1985): U.S.$32,220,000,000 (U.S.$690 per capita).

### Structure of gross domestic product and labour force

| | 1986–87 in value LE '000,000 | 1986–87 % of total value | 1984 labour force | 1984 % of labour force |
|---|---|---|---|---|
| Agriculture | 4,660.0 | 16.1 | 4,347,879 | 39.1 |
| Mining | | | 39,730 | 0.3 |
| Manufacturing | 9,598.3 | 33.2 | 1,703,955 | 15.3 |
| Construction | 1,384.0 | 4.8 | 588,267 | 5.3 |
| Public utilities | 266.9 | 0.9 | 76,750 | 0.7 |
| Transp. and commun. | 2,262.3 | 7.8 | 616,013 | 5.5 |
| Trade | 3,811.3 | 13.2 | 954,128 | 8.6 |
| Finance | 1,524.0 | 5.3 | 123,289 | 1.1 |
| Pub. admin., defense | 4,286.4 | 14.8 | 2,098,601 | 18.8 |
| Services | 1,126.8 | 3.9 | | |
| Other | ... | ... | 584,589[2] | 5.3[2] |
| TOTAL | 28,920.0 | 100.0 | 11,133,201 | 100.0 |

*Population economically active* (1984): total 11,133,201; activity rate of total population 24.5% (participation rates: over age 15, 40.2%; female 5.7%; unemployed, n.a.).

### Price and earnings indexes (1980 = 100)

| | 1981 | 1982 | 1983 | 1984 | 1985 | 1986 | 1987[3] |
|---|---|---|---|---|---|---|---|
| Consumer price index | 110.4 | 126.8 | 147.2 | 172.3 | 195.2 | 239.3 | 281.6 |
| Earnings index | 122.1 | ... | ... | ... | ... | ... | ... |

*Household income and expenditure.* Average household size (1984) 5.4; income per household: n.a.; sources of income: n.a.; expenditure[4] (1974–75): food 49.7%, clothing and footwear 14.2%, housing 12.4%, transportation 5.2%, tobacco 4.9%, recreation 1.3%.
*Land use* (1984): meadows and pastures 0.6%; agricultural and under permanent cultivation 2.5%; built-on, wasteland, and other 96.9%.

## Foreign trade

### Balance of trade (current prices)

| | 1981 | 1982 | 1983 | 1984 | 1985 | 1986 |
|---|---|---|---|---|---|---|
| LE '000,000 | −3,924.5 | −4,170.4 | −4,982.0 | −5,338.1 | −4,373.1 | −4,261.8 |
| % of total | 46.4% | 48.8% | 52.3% | 54.8% | 45.7% | 45.2% |

*Imports* (1985–86): LE 6,845,100,000 (foodstuffs 25.6%, machinery and transport equipment 24.2%; chemical products 10.7%; lubricants, fuel, and minerals 9.3%). *Major import sources* (1983): U.S. 16.1%; W.Ger. 10.6%.
*Exports* (1985–86): LE 2,583,300,000 (petroleum and petroleum products 64.5%; raw cotton 9.6%; cotton yarn, textiles, and fabrics 8.8%). *Major export destinations* (1983): Italy 18.1%; France 9.5%; U.S.S.R. 7.3%; U.S. 6.6%; The Netherlands 3.9%.

## Transport and communications

*Transport.* Railroads (1983–84): route length 2,700 mi, 4,346 km; passenger-mi 14,977,200,000, passenger-km 24,103,500,000; short ton-mi cargo 1,779,000,000, metric ton-km cargo 2,597,000,000. Roads (1985): total length 18,999 mi, 30,576 km (paved 50%). Vehicles (1985): passenger cars 719,199; trucks and buses 292,846. Merchant marine (1986): vessels (100 gross tons and over) 422; total deadweight tonnage 1,484,890. Inland water (1985): Suez Canal, number of transits 19,791; metric ton-km cargo 59,233,272,000. Air transport (1986): passenger-km 4,023,130,000; metric ton-km cargo 111,516,000; airports (1987) 11.
*Communications.* Daily newspapers (1986): total number 17; total circulation 4,216,268[5]; circulation per 1,000 population 88[5]. Radio (1986): 15,000,000 receivers (1 per 3.2 persons). Television (1986): 2,010,000 receivers (1 per 24 persons). Telephones (1985): 1,155,269 (1 per 41 persons).

## Education and health

### Education (1982–83)

| | schools | teachers[6] | students | student/ teacher ratio |
|---|---|---|---|---|
| Primary (age 6–11) | 12,613 | 141,562[7] | 5,181,611 | ... |
| Secondary (age 12–17) | 20,106 | 78,086 | 3,108,867 | ... |
| Voc., teacher tr.[6] | 519 | 38,635 | 672,362 | 17.4 |
| Higher | 12 | 11,910 | 666,600 | ... |

*Educational attainment* (1976). Percent of population age 10 and over having: no formal education 82.9%; primary 9.9%; secondary 5.0%; higher 2.1%; postgraduate 0.1%. *Literacy* (1984): total population age 15 and over literate 11,914,209 (43.0%); males 8,230,021 (58.9%); females 3,684,188 (26.8%).
*Health* (1984): physicians 73,300 (1 per 635 persons); hospital beds 85,350 (1 per 545 persons); infant mortality rate per 1,000 live births (1985) 93.0.
*Food* (1981–83): daily per capita caloric intake 3,186 (vegetable products 93%, animal products 7%); (1983) 126% of FAO recommended minimum.

## Military

*Total active duty personnel* (1987): 445,000 (army 71.9%, navy 4.5%, air force 23.6%). *Military expenditure as percent of GNP* (1987): 8.2% (world [1984] 5.9%); per capita expenditure U.S.$106.

[1]Includes 10 nonelective seats. [2]Unemployed seeking work for the first time. [3]May. [4]Urban only. [5]Based on 12 dailies only. [6]1980–81. [7]1981–82.

# El Salvador

*Official name:* República de El Salvador (Republic of El Salvador).
*Form of government:* republic with one legislative house (Legislative Assembly [60]).
*Chief of state and government:* President.
*Capital:* San Salvador.
*Official language:* Spanish.
*Official religion:* none[1].
*Monetary unit:* 1 colón (₡) = 100 centavos; valuation (Oct. 5, 1987) 1 U.S.$ = ₡5.00[2]; 1 £ = ₡8.12.

### Area and population

| Departments | Capitals | area sq mi | area sq km | population 1985 estimate |
|---|---|---|---|---|
| Ahuachapán | Ahuachapán | 479 | 1,240 | 271,990 |
| Cabañas | Sensuntepeque | 426 | 1,104 | 199,229 |
| Chalatenango | Chalatenango | 779 | 2,017 | 256,688 |
| Cuscatlán | Cojutepeque | 292 | 756 | 222,389 |
| La Libertad | Nueva San Salvador | 638 | 1,653 | 440,030 |
| La Paz | Zacatecoluca | 473 | 1,224 | 278,719 |
| La Unión | La Unión | 801 | 2,074 | 346,087 |
| Morazán | San Francisco (Gotera) | 559 | 1,447 | 235,632 |
| San Miguel | San Miguel | 802 | 2,077 | 480,486 |
| San Salvador | San Salvador | 342 | 886 | 1,094,249 |
| Santa Ana | Santa Ana | 781 | 2,023 | 490,367 |
| San Vicente | San Vicente | 457 | 1,184 | 220,630 |
| Sonsonate | Sonsonate | 473 | 1,226 | 364,075 |
| Usulután | Usulután | 822 | 2,130 | 437,325 |
| TOTAL | | 8,124 | 21,041 | 5,337,896[3] |

## Demography

*Population* (1987): 4,974,000.
*Density* (1987): persons per sq mi 612.3, persons per sq km 236.4.
*Urban–rural* (1986): urban 42.8%; rural 57.2%.
*Sex distribution* (1985): male 50.01%; female 49.99%.
*Age breakdown* (1985): under 15, 45.3%; 15–29, 27.8%; 30–44, 14.4%; 45–59, 7.8%; 60–74, 3.7%; 75 and over, 1.0%.
*Population projection:* (1990) 5,171,000; (2000) 6,717,000.
*Doubling time:* 29 years.
*Ethnic composition* (1980): mestizo (white and Indian) 93.7%; Indian 5.3%; white 1.0%.
*Religious affiliation* (1984): Roman Catholic 91.7%; other 8.3%.
*Major cities* (1985): San Salvador 459,902; Santa Ana 137,879; Mejicanos 91,465; San Miguel 88,520; Delgado 67,684.

## Vital statistics

*Birth rate* per 1,000 population (1984): 29.8[4] (world avg. 29.0); (1983) legitimate 32.5%; illegitimate 67.5%.
*Death rate* per 1,000 population (1984): 6.0[5] (world avg. 11.0).
*Natural increase rate* per 1,000 population (1984): 23.8 (world avg. 18.0).
*Total fertility rate* (avg. births per childbearing woman; 1984): 5.3.
*Marriage rate* per 1,000 population (1983): 4.1.
*Divorce rate* per 1,000 population (1983): 0.4.
*Life expectancy* at birth (1981): male 61.7 years; female 65.3 years.
*Major causes of death* per 100,000 population (1984): homicide and other violence 67.3; diseases of the circulatory system 63.9; infectious and parasitic diseases 60.0; accidents 45.0; ill-defined conditions 115.9.

## National economy

*Budget* (1986)[6]. Revenue: ₡3,508,000,000 (indirect taxes 58.6%, of which taxes on coffee exports 27.2%; direct taxes 18.4%; development income 14.3%). Expenditures: ₡3,480,000,000 (current expenditure 73.0%; debt amortization 13.7%; development expenditure 13.3%).
*Public debt* (external, outstanding; 1985): U.S.$1,400,400,000.
*Tourism:* receipts from visitors (1985) U.S.$10,000,000; expenditures by nationals abroad (1983) U.S.$74,000,000.
*Production* (value added in ₡'000,000 except as noted). Agriculture, forestry, fishing (1985): coffee 1,231; corn (maize) 187, sugarcane 151, aviculture 136, cotton 116, *maicillo* (variety of millet) 48, rice 38, beans 29, bananas 55,000 metric tons; livestock (number of live animals) 929,000 cattle, 375,000 pigs, 4,000,000 chickens; forestry 43; fishing 70. Mining and quarrying (1985): very limited amounts of gold, silver, and limestone. Manufacturing (1985): food products 850; beverages 342; petroleum products 200; chemical products 126; nonmetallic products 117; clothing and footwear 116; textiles 114; tobacco products 97. Construction: private residential 206; public and private nonresidential 231. Energy production (consumption): electricity (kW-hr; 1986) 1,750,000,000 (1,675,000,000); coal, none (none); petroleum (barrels; 1985), none (4,545,000); petroleum products (metric tons; 1985) 574,000 (526,000); natural gas, none (none).
*Household income and expenditure.* Average household size (1978) 5.1; income per household ₡8,650 (U.S.$3,460); sources of income: n.a.; expenditure (1978)[7]: food 42.8%, housing 11.7%, household furnishings 8.5%, clothing and footwear 8.4%, transportation 7.7%.
*Population economically active* (1980): total 1,593,353; activity rate of total population 35.4% (participation rates: ages 15–64, 62.4%; female 34.8%; unemployed [1986] 30%).

### Price and earnings indexes (1980 = 100)

| | 1980 | 1981 | 1982 | 1983 | 1984 | 1985 | 1986[8] |
|---|---|---|---|---|---|---|---|
| Consumer price index | 100.0 | 114.8 | 128.3 | 145.3 | 162.1 | 198.2 | 262.4 |
| Hourly earnings index[9] | 100.0 | 106.8 | 107.7 | 125.3 | 126.8 | 136.4 | ... |

*Gross national product* (at current market prices; 1985): U.S.$3,940,000,000 (U.S.$820 per capita).

### Structure of gross domestic product and labour force

| | 1985[10] in value U.S.$'000,000 | 1985[10] % of total value | 1980 labour force | 1980 % of labour force |
|---|---|---|---|---|
| Agriculture | 909 | 24.3 | 636,617 | 40.0 |
| Mining | 5 | 0.1 | 4,394 | 0.3 |
| Manufacturing | 657 | 17.5 | 247,621 | 15.5 |
| Construction | 123 | 3.3 | 80,089 | 5.0 |
| Public utilities | 142 | 3.8 | 9,681 | 0.6 |
| Transportation and communication | 228 | 6.1 | 65,593 | 4.1 |
| Trade | 633 | 16.9 | 256,086 | 16.1 |
| Finance | 313 | 8.4 | 15,863 | 1.0 |
| Public admin., defense | 472 | 12.6 } | 250,158 | 15.7 |
| Services | 264 | 7.0 } | | |
| Other | — | — | 27,251 | 1.7 |
| TOTAL | 3,746 | 100.0 | 1,593,353 | 100.0 |

*Land use* (1984): forested 5.6%; meadows and pastures 29.4%; agricultural and under permanent cultivation 35.0%; other 30.0%.

## Foreign trade[11]

### Balance of trade (current prices)

| | 1980 | 1981 | 1982 | 1983 | 1984 | 1985 |
|---|---|---|---|---|---|---|
| ₡'000,000 | +457.8 | −287.3 | −234.6 | −225.3 | −449.1 | −474.9 |
| % of total | 9.3% | 6.7% | 6.3% | 5.8% | 11.0% | 12.3% |

*Imports* (1985): ₡2,403,444,000 (basic and miscellaneous manufactures 26.9%; chemical products 24.3%, of which medicinal and pharmaceutical products 6.6%; machinery and transport equipment 15.4%; crude petroleum 13.8%; food products 10.0%). *Major import sources:* United States 33.8%; Guatemala 15.6%; Mexico 9.3%; Venezuela 7.6%; Costa Rica 5.6%.
*Exports* (1985): ₡1,697,420,000 (food products 74.6%, of which coffee 66.7%, unrefined sugar 3.4%; chemical products 5.1%; raw cotton 4.5%; petroleum products 2.0%). *Major export destinations:* United States 47.8%; West Germany 21.0%; Guatemala 9.0%; Japan 5.1%.

## Transport and communications

*Transport.* Railroads (1984): route length 374 mi, 602 km; passenger-mi 2,903,000, passenger-km 4,672,000; short ton-mi cargo 17,417,000, metric ton-km cargo 25,429,000. Roads (1985): total length 7,558 mi, 12,164 km (paved 14%). Vehicles (1985): passenger cars 136,163; trucks and buses 19,461. Merchant marine (1986): vessels (100 gross tons and over) 14; total deadweight tonnage 3,318. Air transport (1985)[12]: passenger-mi 274,393,000, passenger-km 441,594,000; short ton-mi cargo 25,434,000, metric ton-km cargo 37,133,000; airports (1987) with scheduled flights 1.
*Communications.* Daily newspapers (1985): total number 6; total circulation 300,000; circulation per 1,000 population 62. Radio (1986): total number of receivers 1,200,000 (1 per 4.1 persons). Television (1986): total number of receivers 400,000 (1 per 12 persons). Telephones (1984): 123,956 (1 per 39 persons).

## Education and health

### Education (1985)

| | schools | teachers | students | student/ teacher ratio |
|---|---|---|---|---|
| Primary (7–15) | 2,883 | 24,295 | 940,963 | 38.7 |
| Secondary (16–18) | 285 | 3,880 | 90,288 | 23.3 |
| Vocational | 17[13] | 667[13] | 9,505 | ... |
| Higher | 34 | 3,404 | 60,994 | 17.9 |

*Educational attainment* (1980). Percent of population over age 10 having: no formal schooling 30.2%; primary education 60.7%; secondary 6.9%; higher 2.3%. *Literacy* (1980): total population over age 15 literate 1,771,431 (69.0%); males literate 880,908 (73.2%); females literate 890,523 (65.3%).
*Health* (1984): physicians 1,592[14] (1 per 3,002 persons); hospital beds 6,525[14] (1 per 732 persons); infant mortality rate per 1,000 live births 35.1[15].
*Food* (1979–81): daily per capita caloric intake 2,155 (vegetable products 88%, animal products 12%); (1983) 91% of FAO recommended minimum requirement.

## Military

*Total active duty personnel* (1986): 42,640 (army 90.6%, navy 3.0%, air force 6.4%). *Military expenditure as percent of GNP* (1984): 6.1% (world 5.9%); per capita expenditure U.S.$53.

[1]Roman Catholicism, although not official, enjoys special recognition per constitution. [2]Official buying rate. [3]De jure population. [4]Registered data; UN est. (1980–85) 40.2. [5]Registered data; UN est. (1980–85) 8.1. [6]Excludes U.S. foreign aid. [7]Weights of consumer price index components for urban households. [8]Average of second and third quarters. [9]Wages in manufacturing for males in San Salvador department. [10]At prices of 1984. [11]Import figures are f.o.b. (free on board) in balance of trade and c.i.f. (cost, insurance, and freight) for commodities and trading partners. [12]TACA airlines. [13]1983. [14]Public sector only. [15]Registered data; UN est. (1980–85) 70.0.

# Equatorial Guinea

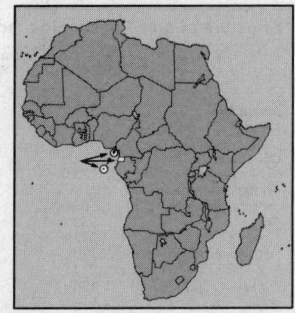

*Official name:* República de Guinea Ecuatorial (Republic of Equatorial Guinea).
*Form of government:* unitary single-party republic with one legislative house (National Assembly [60]).
*Head of state and government:* President.
*Capital:* Malabo.
*Official language:* Spanish.
*Official religion:* none.
*Monetary unit*[1]: 1 CFA franc (CFAF) = 100 centimes; valuation (Oct. 5, 1987) 1 U.S.$ = CFAF 306.67; 1 £ = CFAF 498.00.

## Area and population

| Regions | area | | population |
|---|---|---|---|
| Provinces | sq mi | sq km | 1983 census |
| Insular | 785 | 2,034 | 59,196 |
| Annobón | 7 | 17 | 2,006 |
| Bioko Norte | 299 | 776 | 46,221 |
| Bioko Sur | 479 | 1,241 | 10,969 |
| Continental | 10,045 | 26,017 | 240,804 |
| Centro-Sur | 3,834 | 9,931 | 52,393 |
| Kie-Ntem | 1,523 | 3,943 | 70,202 |
| Litoral | 2,573 | 6,665 | 66,370 |
| Wele-Nzas | 2,115 | 5,478 | 51,839 |
| TOTAL | 10,830 | 28,051 | 300,000 |

## Demography

*Population* (1987): 328,000.
*Density* (1987): persons per sq mi 30.3, persons per sq km 11.7.
*Urban–rural* (1983): urban 27.6%; rural 72.4%.
*Sex distribution* (1983): male 48.09%; female 51.91%.
*Age breakdown* (1985): under 15, 38.1%; 15–29, 26.0%; 30–44, 17.7%; 45–59, 11.5%; 60–74, 5.6%; 75 and over, 1.1%.
*Population projection:* (1990) 351,000; (2000) 445,000.
*Doubling time:* 29 years.
*Ethnic composition* (1983): Fang 72.0%; Bubi 14.7%; Duala 2.7%; Ibibio 1.3%; Maka 1.3%; other 8.0%.
*Religious affiliation* (1980): Christian (mostly Roman Catholic) 88.8%; traditional beliefs 4.6%; atheist 1.4%; Muslim 0.5%; other 0.2%; none 4.5%.
*Major cities* (1983): Malabo 37,500; Ela-Nguema 6,179; Bata 5,633; Campo Yaunde 5,199; Los Angeles 4,079.

## Vital statistics

*Birth rate* per 1,000 population (1980–85): 36.7 (world avg. 29.0); legitimate, n.a.; illegitimate, n.a.
*Death rate* per 1,000 population (1980–85): 12.9 (world avg. 11.0).
*Natural increase rate* per 1,000 population (1980–85): 23.8 (world avg. 18.0).
*Total fertility rate* (avg. births per childbearing woman; 1980–85): 4.8.
*Marriage rate* per 1,000 population: n.a.
*Divorce rate* per 1,000 population: n.a.
*Life expectancy* at birth (1980–85): male 42.4 years; female 45.6 years.
*Major causes of death* per 100,000 population: n.a.; however, major diseases include malaria (affecting about 60% of the population), cholera, leprosy, trypanosomiasis (sleeping sickness), and waterborne (especially gastrointestinal) diseases.

## National economy

*Budget* (1984). Revenue: EK 6,576,000,000 (import and export duties 72.2%). Expenditures: EK 6,838,000,000 (current 69.6%, capital 30.4%).
*Public debt* (external, outstanding; 1985): U.S.$119,300,000.
*Tourism* (1987): Tourism remains undeveloped.
*Gross domestic product* (at current market prices; 1984): U.S.$65,200,000 (U.S.$213 per capita).

## Structure of gross domestic product and labour force

| | 1983 | | | |
|---|---|---|---|---|
| | in value EK '000,000 | % of total value | labour force | % of labour force |
| Agriculture | 2,490 | 41.3 | 86,500 | 85.7 |
| Manufacturing | | | 900 | 0.9 |
| Construction | | | 1,000 | 1.0 |
| Public utilities | 710 | 11.8 | ... | ... |
| Transportation and communication | | | ... | ... |
| Trade | | | 2,600 | 2.6 |
| Finance | | | ... | ... |
| Pub. admin., defense | 2,830 | 46.9 | 7,400 | 7.3 |
| Services | | | 2,500 | 2.5 |
| Other | | | ... | ... |
| TOTAL | 6,030 | 100.0 | 100,900 | 100.0 |

*Production* (metric tons except as noted). Agriculture, forestry, fishing (1985): roots and tubers 90,000 (of which cassava 55,000, sweet potatoes 35,000), bananas 18,000, fruit excluding melons 18,000, coconuts 8,000, coffee 7,000, cacao beans 7,000, palm oil 5,000, palm kernels 2,800; livestock (number of live animals) 35,000 sheep, 7,000 goats, 5,000 pigs, 4,000 cattle, 160,000 chickens; roundwood 607,000 cu m; fish catch 3,600. Mining and quarrying: details n.a.; however, in addition to quarrying for construction materials, unexploited deposits of iron ore, lead, zinc, manganese, and molybdenum are present; traces of gold, diamonds, and radioactive ores have also been located. Manufacturing (1985): palm oil 5,000. Construction: n.a. Energy production (consumption): electricity (kW-hr; 1985) 15,000,000 (15,000,-000); coal, none (n.a.); crude petroleum[2], none (n.a.); petroleum products (metric tons; 1985) none (25,000); natural gas, none (n.a.).
*Population economically active* (1983): total 100,900; activity rate of total population 33.6% (participation rates: over age 15, n.a.; female, n.a.; unemployed, n.a.).
*Price and earnings indexes:* n.a.
*Household income and expenditure.* Average household size (1980) 4.5; income per household: n.a.; sources of income: n.a.; expenditure: n.a.
*Land use* (1984): forested 46.2%; meadows and pastures 3.7%; agricultural and under permanent cultivation 8.2%; built-on, wasteland, and other 41.9%.

## Foreign trade

### Balance of trade (current prices)

| | 1978 | 1979 | 1980 | 1981 | 1982 | 1983 |
|---|---|---|---|---|---|---|
| EK '000,000 | +547.6 | +351.9 | –4,704.0 | –5,400.0 | –6,657.0 | –9,326.0 |
| % of total | 18.6% | 9.8% | 54.8% | 51.1% | 27.5% | 29.3% |

*Imports* (1981): EK 7,982,000,000 (food, beverages, and tobacco 24.9%; petroleum and petroleum products 22.4%; motor vehicles and machinery 17.4%; iron and steel products 12.4%; clothing 6.0%). *Major import sources* (1985): Spain 30.2%; France 23.6%; Italy 14.6%; The Netherlands 4.8%; West Germany 4.1%; Belgium–Luxembourg 3.0%; China 2.4%; United States 1.9%; Japan 1.7%; Norway 1.5%; United Kingdom 1.1%; Switzerland 0.9%.
*Exports* (1981): EK 2,582,000,000 (cacao 71.5%; timber 24.4%; coffee 2.8%). *Major export destinations* (1985): The Netherlands 37.6%; Spain 31.5%; West Germany 16.4%; Italy 5.0%; France 2.2%; Switzerland 1.4%; Portugal 1.3%; Belgium–Luxembourg 0.7%; Greece 0.3%.

## Transport and communications

*Transport.* Railroads: none. Roads (1982): total length 1,715 mi, 2,760 km (paved 12%). Vehicles (1979): passenger cars 4,000; trucks and buses 3,000. Merchant marine (1986): vessels (100 gross tons and over) 2; total deadweight tonnage 6,700. Air transport (1985): passenger-mi 4,000,000, passenger-km 7,000,000; short ton-mi cargo 700,000, metric ton-km cargo 1,000,000; airports (1987) with scheduled flights 2.
*Communications.* Daily newspapers (1986): total number 2; total circulation 1,000; circulation per 1,000 population 3.1. Radio (1984): total number of receivers 90,000 (1 per 3.5 persons). Television (1984): total number of receivers 2,100 (1 per 148 persons). Telephones (1982): 1,366 (1 per 220 persons).

## Education and health

### Education (1980–81)[3]

| | schools | teachers | students | student/ teacher ratio |
|---|---|---|---|---|
| Primary (age 6–11) | 511 | 647 | 40,110 | 62.0 |
| Secondary (age 12–17) | 14 | 288 | 3,013 | 10.5 |
| Voc., teacher tr.[4] | ... | ... | ... | ... |

*Educational attainment,* n.a. *Literacy* (c. 1985): total population literate, about 31%; males literate 46%; females literate 17%.
*Health:* physicians (mid-1980s) 5 (1 per 61,000 persons); hospital beds (1982) 3,200 (1 per 95 persons); infant mortality rate per 1,000 live births (1983) 137.
*Food* (latest): daily per capita caloric intake 2,230; 68% of FAO recommended minimum requirement.

## Military

*Total active duty personnel* (1986): 2,300 (army 87.0%, navy 6.5%, air force 6.5%). *Military expenditure as percent of GNP* (1981): 1.8% (world 5.8%); per capita expenditure U.S.$9.

[1]As of Jan. 1, 1985, Equatorial Guinea became a member of the franc zone, substituting the CFA franc for the previous monetary unit, the ekwele (EK, plural bipkwele), effectively devaluing the latter by 82%. [2]Equatorial Guinea's offshore potential oil areas totaled about 13,450 sq km. [3]In 1982–83 there were 52,021 students in primary; and in 1980–81 there were 175 students in higher education studying abroad. [4]Efforts are being undertaken to provide the training necessary to qualify nondegree teachers for service. Also, teacher training schools are to be expanded in order to increase the number of primary school teachers.

# Ethiopia

*Official name*[1]: YeĒtiyop'iya Hezbawi
Dimokrasīyawī Republēk (People's
Democratic Republic of Ethiopia).
*Form of government:* unitary
single-party people's republic with one
legislative house (Shengo [835]).
*Chief of state:* President.
*Head of government:* Prime Minister.
*Capital:* Addis Ababa.
*Official language:* Amharic.
*Official religion:* none.
*Monetary unit:* 1 Ethiopian Birr
(Br) = 100 cents; valuation (Oct. 5,
1987) 1 U.S.$ = Br 2.07;
1 £ = Br 3.34.

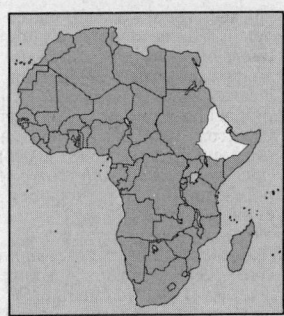

## Area and population

| Regions | Capitals | area sq mi | area sq km | population 1987 estimate |
|---|---|---|---|---|
| Arsi | Asela | 9,500 | 24,600 | 1,808,512 |
| Bale | Goba | 49,500 | 128,300 | 1,095,129 |
| Eritrea[2] | Asmera | 45,300 | 117,400 | 2,951,080 |
| Gemu Gofa | Arba Minch | 15,400 | 40,100 | 1,356,687 |
| Gojam | Debre Markos | 24,900 | 64,400 | 3,530,540 |
| Gonder | Gonder | 28,300 | 73,400 | 3,178,692 |
| Hararge | Harer | 98,400 | 254,800 | 4,527,423 |
| Ilubabor | Metu | 19,600 | 50,800 | 1,048,293 |
| Kefa | Jima | 20,500 | 53,000 | 2,664,557 |
| Shewa[2] | Addis Ababa | 33,000 | 85,500 | 10,394,448 |
| Sidamo | Awasa | 45,100 | 116,700 | 4,123,352 |
| Tigray | Mekele | 25,400 | 65,700 | 2,624,362 |
| Welega | Nekemte | 27,000 | 69,800 | 2,693,623 |
| Welo | Dese | 30,500 | 79,000 | 3,962,018 |
| TOTAL | | 472,400 | 1,223,500 | 45,958,716 |

## Demography

*Population* (1987): 45,959,000.
*Density* (1987): persons per sq mi 97.3, persons per sq km 37.6.
*Urban–rural* (1987): urban 10.6%; rural 89.4%.
*Sex distribution* (1987): male 49.96%; female 50.04%.
*Age breakdown* (1987): under 15, 46.5%; 15–29, 22.8%; 30–44, 15.6%; 45–59, 8.9%; 60–74, 4.5%; 75 and over, 1.7%.
*Population projection:* (1990) 50,133,000; (2000) 66,205,000.
*Doubling time:* 26 years.
*Ethnolinguistic composition* (1983): Amhara 30.0%; Galla 26.0%; Tigrinya 9.0%; Tigre 5.0%; Kafa 4.0%; Somali 3.0%; Gurage 3.0%; Nilotes 3.0%, of which Nuer 1.3%; Arabic 1.3%; Afar 1.0%; other 14.7%.
*Religious affiliation* (1980): Ethiopian Orthodox 52.5%; Muslim 31.4%; traditional beliefs 11.4%; other Christian 4.5%; other 0.2%.
*Major cities* (1984): Addis Ababa 1,423,111; Asmera 275,385; Dire Dawa 98,104; Gonder 68,958; Dese 68,848.

## Vital statistics

*Birth rate* per 1,000 population (1985): 49.7 (world avg. 29.0).
*Death rate* per 1,000 population (1985): 23.1 (world avg. 11.0).
*Natural increase rate* per 1,000 population (1985): 26.6 (world avg. 18.0).
*Total fertility rate* (avg. births per childbearing woman; 1985): 6.7.
*Life expectancy* at birth (1985): male 39.5 years; female 42.6 years.
*Major causes of death* (1977–79)[3]: infectious and parasitic diseases 24.0%; digestive system diseases 17.6%; allergy, endocrine, metabolic, nutritional, and circulatory diseases 14.9%; respiratory diseases 9.9%.

## National economy

*Budget*[4]. (1984–85). Revenue: Br 2,318,500,000 (taxes 71.3%, of which income and profit tax 27.3%, excise tax 14.6%, import duties 12.2%, export duties 7.4%; nontax revenue 28.7%). Expenditures: Br 3,428,000,000 (general services 35.9%; economic development 31.3%, of which agriculture and settlement 11.8%; social services 15.6%, of which education 8.5%, public health 3.1%; debt service 5.6%).
*Tourism:* receipts from visitors (1985) U.S.$9,000,000; expenditures by nationals abroad (1984) U.S.$4,000,000.
*Production* (metric tons except as noted). Agriculture, forestry, fishing (1985): sugarcane 1,700,000, corn (maize) 1,400,000, barley 1,000,000, pulses 944,000, coffee 770,000, wheat 700,000, yams 215,000, potatoes 210,000, millet 200,000, seed cotton 80,000; livestock (number of live animals) 26,000,000 cattle, 22,500,000 sheep, 17,260,000 goats, 6,965,000 horses, mules, and asses, 1,030,000 camels; roundwood 31,154,000 cu m[5]; fish catch 3,900[5]. Mining and quarrying (1985): cement 250,000; salt 135,000; limestone 5,000; kaolin 4,360; gold 829 troy oz; platinum 150 troy oz. Manufacturing (gross value in Br '000[6]; 1984–85): food and beverages 756,400; textiles 352,900; leather and shoes 166,600; metal products 127,300; chemicals 109,400; paper and printing 91,400; cigarettes 89,400; nonmetallic mineral products 56,700. Construction (authorized; 1981): residential 162,000 sq m; nonresidential 32,300 sq m, of which commercial 24,800 sq m. Energy production (consumption): electricity (kW-hr; 1985) 831,000,000 (831,000,000); coal, none (n.a.); crude petroleum (barrels; 1985) n.a. (4,912,000); petroleum products (metric tons; 1984) 653,000 (476,000); natural gas, n.a. (n.a.).
*Land use* (1984): forested 22.7%; meadows and pastures 37.0%; agricultural and under permanent cultivation 11.4%; other 28.9%.
*Gross national product* (at current market prices; 1985): U.S.$4,630,000,000 (U.S.$110 per capita).

## Structure of gross domestic product and labour force

| | 1984–85 in value Br '000,000 | 1984–85 % of total value | 1985 labour force | 1985 % of labour force |
|---|---|---|---|---|
| Agriculture | 3,928.3 | 44.1 | 14,727,000 | 76.8 |
| Mining | 15.8 | 0.2 | | |
| Manufacturing | 1,017.3 | 11.4 | | |
| Construction | 374.5 | 4.2 | | |
| Public utilities | 73.6 | 0.8 | | |
| Transportation and communication | 583.8 | 6.6 | 4,455,000 | 23.2 |
| Trade | 962.1 | 10.8 | | |
| Finance | 347.1 | 3.9 | | |
| Pub. admin., defense | 770.0 | 8.6 | | |
| Services | 644.8 | 7.2 | | |
| Other | 196.7 | 2.2 | | |
| TOTAL | 8,914.0 | 100.0 | 19,182,000 | 100.0 |

*Public debt* (external, outstanding; 1985): U.S.$1,742,200,000.
*Population economically active* (1984): total 18,492,300; activity rate of total population 43.9% (participation .rates: ages 15–64, 74.3%; female 39.2%; unemployed, n.a.).

## Price and earnings indexes (1980 = 100)

| | 1981 | 1982 | 1983 | 1984 | 1985 | 1986 | 1987[7] |
|---|---|---|---|---|---|---|---|
| Consumer price index | 106.1 | 112.4 | 111.6 | 121.0 | 144.1 | 130.0 | 129.9 |
| Monthly earnings index | ... | ... | ... | ... | ... | ... | ... |

*Household income and expenditure.* Average household size (1984) 4.5; income per household c. U.S.$600; sources of income: n.a.; expenditure[8]: food 49.0%, housing 14.6%, household utilities 14.6%, clothing and footwear 6.7%, miscellaneous goods and services 5.4%, transportation 4.5%, recreation and reading 2.6%, medical care 1.8%, personal care 0.8%.

## Foreign trade

### Balance of trade (current prices)

| | 1980 | 1981 | 1982 | 1983 | 1984 | 1985 |
|---|---|---|---|---|---|---|
| Br '000,000 | −614.2 | −723.8 | −775.6 | −980.4 | −1,086.7 | −1,367.0 |
| % of total | 25.9% | 31.0% | 31.7% | 37.0% | 38.6% | 49.8% |

*Imports* (1984–85): Br 1,770,433,000 (food and live animals 19.5%, petroleum and petroleum products 18.0%, machinery 12.7%, motor vehicles 10.1%, metal and metalware 8.1%, chemicals 4.3%, textiles 3.9%). *Major import sources* (1985): U.S.S.R. 17.4%; United States 16.1%; West Germany 10.0%; United Kingdom 8.7%; Italy 8.0%; Japan 6.0%.
*Exports* (1984–85): Br 744,572,000 (coffee 72.6%, hides 12.8%, petroleum products 8.9%, pulses 2.3%, oilseeds 2.1%). *Major export destinations* (1985): West Germany 18.5%; The Netherlands 13.2%; United States 10.5%; Japan 10.3%; South Yemen 8.1%; Italy 7.7%; U.S.S.R. 5.2%.

## Transport and communications

*Transport.* Railroads[9] (1986): length 485 mi, 781 km; passenger-mi 217,000,000, passenger-km 350,000,000; short ton-mi cargo 86,000,000, metric ton-km cargo 125,000,000. Roads (1985): total length 23,532 mi, 37,871 km (paved 34%). Vehicles (1985): passenger cars 41,250; trucks and buses 19,159. Merchant marine (1986): vessels (100 gross tons and over) 23; total deadweight tonnage 84,752. Air transport (1983): passenger-mi 473,697,000, passenger-km 762,343,000; short ton-mi cargo 18,587,000, metric ton-km cargo 27,136,000; airports (1987) with scheduled flights 30.
*Communications.* Daily newspapers (1986): total number 3; total circulation 47,000; circulation per 1,000 population 1.0. Radio (1986): 2,000,000 receivers (1 per 22 persons). Television (1986): 40,000 receivers (1 per 1,119 persons). Telephones (1985): 122,012 (1 per 357 persons).

## Education and health

### Education (1983–84)

| | schools | teachers | students | student/ teacher ratio |
|---|---|---|---|---|
| Primary (age 7–12) | 7,096 | 46,674 | 2,497,114 | 53.5 |
| Secondary (age 13–18) | 1,066 | 13,192 | 579,834 | 44.0 |
| Voc., teacher tr. | ... | ... | ... | ... |
| Higher | 11 | 1,446 | 15,776 | 10.9 |

*Educational attainment,* n.a. *Literacy* (1980)[10]: total population age 15 and over literate 1,000,000 (4.8%); males (9.3%); females (0.5%).
*Health* (1983–84): physicians 539 (1 per 78,740 persons); hospital beds 11,307 (1 per 3,754 persons); infant mortality rate (1980–85) 155.0.
*Food* (1979–81): daily per capita caloric intake 2,149 (vegetable products 93%, animal products 7%); (1983) 84% of FAO recommended minimum requirement.

## Military

*Total active duty personnel* (1986): 220,000[11] (army 96.8%, navy 1.4%, air force 1.8%). *Military expenditure as percent of GNP* (1984): 8.9% (world 5.9%); per capita expenditure U.S.$10.1.

[1]On Feb. 1, 1987, a referendum approved a constitution providing for civilian rule. A National Assembly (Shengo) was elected on June 14, 1987. [2]Eritrea includes Aseb Administration, and Shewa includes Addis Ababa region. [3]Percentage of deaths in a sample population of hospital inpatients. [4]Revenue has increased 8.8% from 1985–86. [5]1984. [6]At constant prices of 1978–79. [7]April. [8]Weights of consumer price index components, Addis Ababa only. [9]Includes 62 mi (100 km) of the Chemin de Fer Djibouti–Ethiopien (CDE) in Djibouti; excludes 190 mi (306 km) of Northern Ethiopia Railway, not in use since 1978. [10]Adult illiteracy is reported to have been reduced to about 37% in 1987. [11]In 1986 about 2,200 Cuban and other Soviet-bloc advisers were assisting government forces.

# Fiji

*Official name:* Fiji.
*Form of government:* republic[1].
*Chief of state:* President[2].
*Head of government:* Prime Minister[2].
*Capital:* Suva.
*Official language:* English.
*Official religion:* none.
*Monetary unit:* 1 Fiji dollar
(F$) = 100 cents; valuation (Oct. 5,
1987) 1 U.S.$ = F$1.28; 1£ = F$2.08.

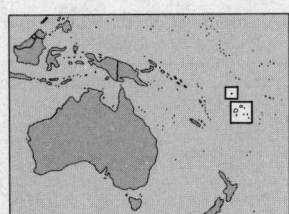

### Area and population

| Divisions Provinces[3] | Capitals | area | | population |
|---|---|---|---|---|
| | | sq mi | sq km | 1986 census |
| Central | Suva | | | |
| Naitasiri | | 643 | 1,666 | 100,227 |
| Namosi | | 220 | 570 | 4,836 |
| Rewa | | 105 | 272 | 97,442 |
| Serua | | 320 | 830 | 13,356 |
| Tailevu | | 369 | 955 | 44,249 |
| Eastern | Levuka | | | |
| Kandavu | | 185 | 478 | 9,805 |
| Lau | | 188 | 487 | 14,203 |
| Lomaiviti | | 159 | 411 | 16,066 |
| Rotuma | | 18 | 46 | 2,688 |
| Northern | Labasa | | | |
| Mathuata | | 774 | 2,004 | 74,735 |
| Mbua | | 532 | 1,379 | 13,986 |
| Thakaundrove | | 1,087 | 2,816 | 40,433 |
| Western | Lautoka | | | |
| Mba | | 1,017 | 2,634 | 197,633 |
| Nandronga-Navosa | | 921 | 2,385 | 54,431 |
| Ra | | 518 | 1,341 | 31,285 |
| TOTAL | | 7,056 | 18,274 | 715,375 |

## Demography

*Population* (1987): 726,000.
*Density* (1987): persons per sq mi 102.9, persons per sq km 39.7.
*Urban–rural* (1986): urban 38.7%; rural 61.3%.
*Sex distribution* (1986): male 50.68%; female 49.32%.
*Age breakdown* (1986): under 15, 38.2%; 15–29, 29.5%; 30–44, 17.8%; 45–59, 9.6%; 60–74, 3.8%; 75 and over, 1.1%.
*Population projection:* (1990) 770,000; (2000) 936,000.
*Doubling time:* 31 years.
*Ethnic composition* (1986): Indian 48.6%; Fijian 46.3%; other 5.1%.
*Religious affiliation* (1980): Christian 51.0%; Hindu 39.2%; Muslim 7.7%; other 2.1%.
*Major cities* (1986): Suva 69,665; Lautoka 28,728; Lami 8,601; Nadi 7,679; Ba 6,518.

## Vital statistics

*Birth rate* per 1,000 population (1985): 27.9 (world avg. 29.0); (1978) legitimate 82.7%; illegitimate 17.3%.
*Death rate* per 1,000 population (1985): 5.3 (world avg. 11.0).
*Natural increase rate* per 1,000 population (1985): 22.6 (world avg. 18.0).
*Total fertility rate* (avg. births per childbearing woman; 1986): 3.3.
*Marriage rate* per 1,000 population (1985): 9.4.
*Divorce rate* per 1,000 population (1979): 0.7.
*Life expectancy* at birth (1986): male 67.8 years; female 72.1 years.
*Major causes of death* per 100,000 population (1985): heart diseases 104.4; hypertensive and cerebrovascular diseases 67.5; malignant neoplasms (cancers) 51.4; diabetes mellitus 29.1; pneumonia 26.5; bronchitis, emphysema, and asthma 16.6.

## National economy

*Budget* (1986). Revenue: F$360,811,000 (income taxes, estate taxes, and gift duties 39.8%; customs duties and port dues 35.0%). Expenditures: F$370,983,000 (departmental expenditure 65.2%, of which education 19.4%; public debt charges 20.1%; pensions and gratuities 4.0%).
*Public debt* (external, outstanding; 1985): U.S.$302,200,000.
*Tourism:* receipts from visitors (1985) U.S.$163,400,000; expenditures by nationals abroad (1981) U.S.$19,000,000.
*Production* (metric tons except as noted). Agriculture, forestry, fishing (1986): sugarcane 4,109,000, paddy rice 24,600, copra 22,510, ginger 5,518; livestock (number of live animals; 1985) 158,000 cattle, 56,000 goats, 29,000 pigs; roundwood (1985) 205,855 cu m; fish catch 9,834. Mining and quarrying (1986): gold 2,856 kilograms; silver 774 kilograms. Manufacturing (1986): refined sugar 502,000; cement 92,200; coconut oil 14,100; soap 6,900; beer 160,200 hectolitres; paint 19,500 hectolitres. Construction (1986): residential 60,000 sq m; nonresidential 48,000 sq m. Energy production (consumption): electricity (kW-hr; 1986) 402,000,000 (311,469,000); coal (metric tons; 1985) none (16,000); crude petroleum, none (n.a.); petroleum products (metric tons; 1985) none (159,000); natural gas, none (n.a.).
*Population economically active* (1986): total 241,160; activity rate of total population 33.8% (participation rates: ages 15–64, 56.9%; female 24.0%; unemployed 8.2%).

### Price and earnings indexes (1980 = 100)

| | 1980 | 1981 | 1982 | 1983 | 1984 | 1985 | 1986 |
|---|---|---|---|---|---|---|---|
| Consumer price index | 100.0 | 111.2 | 119.0 | 127.0 | 133.7 | 139.6 | 142.1 |
| Hourly earnings index | 100.0 | 109.5 | 118.1 | 125.9 | 127.6 | 129.3 | ... |

*Household income and expenditure.* Average household size (1986) 5.7; income per household (1980) F$2,837 (U.S.$3,546); sources of income (1973): wages and salaries 81.5%, self-employment 9.1%, other 9.4%; expenditure (1985): food 33.9%, housing 18.6%, transportation 11.3%, household furnishings 7.6%, clothing and footwear 6.3%, energy 4.9%.
*Gross national product* (at current market prices; 1985): U.S.$1,190,000,000 (U.S.$1,700 per capita).

### Structure of gross domestic product and labour force

| | 1985 | | 1986 | |
|---|---|---|---|---|
| | in value F$'000 | % of total value | labour force | % of labour force |
| Agriculture | 209,875 | 17.3 | 106,305 | 44.1 |
| Mining | 8,306 | 0.7 | 1,345 | 0.5 |
| Manufacturing | 117,837 | 9.7 | 18,106 | 7.5 |
| Construction | 76,508 | 6.3 | 11,786 | 4.9 |
| Public utilities | 42,338 | 3.5 | 2,154 | 0.9 |
| Transportation and communication | 123,192 | 10.2 | 13,151 | 5.4 |
| Trade | 208,172 | 17.2 | 26,010 | 10.8 |
| Finance | 170,900 | 14.1 | 6,016 | 2.5 |
| Pub. admin., defense, services | 287,211 | 23.7 | 36,619 | 15.2 |
| Other | −32,732[4] | −2.7[4] | 19,668[5] | 8.2[5] |
| TOTAL | 1,211,607 | 100.0 | 241,160 | 100.0 |

*Land use* (1984): forested 64.9%; agricultural and under permanent cultivation 13.0%; meadows and pastures 3.3%; other 18.8%.

## Foreign trade

### Balance of trade (current prices)

| | 1981 | 1982 | 1983 | 1984 | 1985 | 1986 |
|---|---|---|---|---|---|---|
| F$'000,000 | −206.2 | −151.0 | −189.0 | −148.4 | −183.2 | −124.7 |
| % of total | 27.7% | 22.0% | 27.8% | 20.9% | 25.8% | 16.6% |

*Imports* (1986): F$496,729,000 (machinery and transport equipment 23.4%; manufactured goods 21.4%; mineral fuels and related materials 16.5%; food, beverages, and tobacco 16.3%; chemicals 8.3%). *Major import sources:* Australia 33.5%; New Zealand 16.7%; Japan 14.4%; United States 4.8%; France 4.4%; United Kingdom 4.4%; Singapore 3.2%; Taiwan 2.8%; West Germany 2.2%; China 2.1%.
*Exports* (1985)[6]: F$242,049,000 (sugar 55.2%; gold 16.0%; fish 6.9%; molasses 3.3%; coconut oil 1.6%; wood and by-products 1.6%). *Major export destinations*[7]: United Kingdom 44.7%; Australia 20.9%; Malaysia 8.4%; New Zealand 6.1%; United States 5.4%; China 2.5%; Japan 2.0%; Canada 2.0%.

## Transport and communications

*Transport.* Railroads[8] (1986): length 660 mi, 1,062 km. Roads (1986): total length 2,564 mi, 4,127 km (paved 13%). Vehicles (1986): passenger cars 32,453; trucks and buses 22,799. Merchant marine (1986): vessels (100 gross tons and over) 56; total deadweight tonnage 26,340. Air transport (1986)[9]: passenger-mi 316,538,000, passenger-km 509,420,000; short ton-mi cargo 4,393,000, metric ton-km cargo 6,414,000; airports (1987) with scheduled flights 20.
*Communications.* Daily newspapers (1985): total number 2; total circulation 53,000; circulation per 1,000 population 76. Radio (1985): total number of receivers 400,000 (1 per 1.8 persons). Television: n.a. Telephones (1986): 56,360 (1 per 12.7 persons).

## Education and health

### Education (1986)

| | schools | teachers | students | student/ teacher ratio |
|---|---|---|---|---|
| Primary (age 5–15) | 672 | 4,315 | 131,221 | 30.4 |
| Secondary (age 16–19) | 140 | 2,551 | 42,200 | 16.5 |
| Voc., teacher tr. | 44 | 257 | 3,793 | 14.8 |
| Higher[10] | 5 | ... | 3,947 | ... |

*Educational attainment* (1986). Percent of population age 25 and over having: no schooling 28.3%; primary only 19.1%; some secondary 44.1%; secondary 4.1%; postsecondary 3.3%. *Literacy* (1985): total population age 15 and over literate 374,300 (85.5%); males literate 197,300 (90.2%); females literate 177,000 (80.9%).
*Health* (1986): physicians 385 (1 per 1,859 persons); hospital beds 1,743 (1 per 410 persons); infant mortality rate per 1,000 live births 18.5.
*Food* (1981–83): daily per capita caloric intake 2,903 (vegetable products 88%, animal products 12%); (1983) 105% of FAO recommended minimum requirement.

## Military

*Total active duty personnel* (1986): 2,670 (army 93.6%; navy 6.4%; air force, none). *Military expenditure as percent of GNP* (1984): 1.3% (world 5.9%); per capita expenditure: U.S.$25.

[1]A military coup overthrew the elected government on May 14, 1987; a second coup, on September 24, deposed the caretaker government. The 1970 constitution was revoked on October 1 and a republic declared on October 7. The Queen's representative in Fiji, the governor-general, resigned on October 15. No constitutional document containing executive, legislative, or judicial machinery had been put forward by December 8. [2]Fiji's first president was appointed Dec. 5, 1987, as was the prime minister, formally returning the nation to civilian rule. [3]The provinces are autonomous only with respect to local affairs. [4]Other activities less imputed bank service charges. [5]Unemployed. [6]Excludes reexports, valued at F$70,403,000. [7]Based on exports of local products only. [8]Owned by the Fiji Sugar Corporation. [9]Domestic airlines only, including South Pacific service. [10]1983.

# Finland

*Official name:* Suomen Tasavalta (Finnish); Republiken Finland (Swedish) (Republic of Finland).
*Form of government:* multiparty parliamentary republic with one legislative house (Eduskunta [200]).
*Chief of state:* President.
*Head of government:* Prime Minister.
*Capital:* Helsinki.
*Official languages:* Finnish; Swedish.
*Official religion:* none.
*Monetary unit:* 1 markka (Fmk) = 100 penni; valuation (Oct. 5, 1987) 1 U.S.$ = Fmk 4.42; 1 £ = Fmk 7.19.

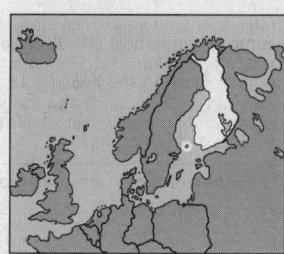

### Area and population

| Provinces | Capitals | land area sq mi | land area sq km | population 1987 estimate[1] |
|---|---|---|---|---|
| Åland (Ahvenanmaa) | Mariehamn (Maarianhamina) | 590 | 1,527 | 23,627 |
| Häme | Hämeenlinna | 6,568 | 17,010 | 680,445 |
| Keski-Suomi | Jyväskylä | 6,266 | 16,230 | 247,905 |
| Kuopio | Kuopio | 6,375 | 16,511 | 256,157 |
| Kymi | Kouvola | 4,163 | 10,783 | 338,537 |
| Lappi | Rovaniemi | 35,930 | 93,057 | 200,275 |
| Mikkeli | Mikkeli | 6,310 | 16,342 | 208,416 |
| Oulu | Oulu | 21,956 | 56,866 | 433,116 |
| Pohjois-Karjala | Joensuu | 6,866 | 17,782 | 177,199 |
| Turku ja Pori | Turku | 8,559 | 22,170 | 714,134 |
| Uusimaa | Helsinki | 3,822 | 9,898 | 1,204,510 |
| Vaasa | Vaasa | 10,211 | 26,447 | 444,466 |
| TOTAL LAND AREA | | 117,616 | 304,623 | 4,928,787 |
| INLAND WATER | | 12,943 | 33,522 | |
| TOTAL AREA | | 130,559 | 338,145 | |

## Demography

*Population* (1987): 4,942,000.
*Density*[2] (1987): persons per sq mi 42.0, persons per sq km 16.2.
*Urban–rural* (1986): urban 61.8%; rural 38.2%.
*Sex distribution* (1986): male 48.43%; female 51.57%.
*Age breakdown* (1985): under 15, 19.5%; 15–29, 22.9%; 30–44, 23.6%; 45–59, 16.7%; 60–74, 12.4%; 75 and over, 4.9%.
*Population projection:* (1990) 5,013,000; (2000) 5,255,000.
*Doubling time:* n.a.; doubling time exceeds 100 years.
*Ethnolinguistic composition* (1985): Finnish 93.6%; Swedish 6.2%; other 0.2%[3].
*Religious affiliation* (1985): Lutheran 89.4%; Greek Orthodox 1.1%; nonaffiliated 8.6%; other 0.9%.
*Major cities* (1987)[1]: Helsinki 487,749; Tampere 170,097; Espoo 162,106; Turku 160,974; Vantaa 147,225.

## Vital statistics

*Birth rate* per 1,000 population (1986): 12.4 (world avg. 26.0); (1985) legitimate 83.6%; illegitimate 16.4%.
*Death rate* per 1,000 population (1986): 9.6 (world avg. 9.9).
*Natural increase rate* per 1,000 population (1986): 2.8 (world avg. 16.1).
*Total fertility rate* (avg. births per childbearing woman; 1985): 1.6.
*Marriage rate* per 1,000 population (1986): 5.3.
*Divorce rate* per 1,000 population (1984): 2.0.
*Life expectancy* at birth (1985): male 70.3 years; female 78.6 years.
*Major causes of death* per 100,000 population (1985): ischemic heart disease 296.5; malignant neoplasms (cancers) 194.6; cerebrovascular diseases 117.9; accidents 47.4; pneumonia 47.0; suicide and self-inflicted injuries 24.6.

## National economy

*Budget* (1986). Revenue: Fmk 100,781,000,000 (tax revenue 76.8%, of which income and property taxes 27.1%, sales tax 26.2%, excise duties 13.1%, vehicle taxes 3.1%, stamp duties 2.9%). Expenditures: Fmk 100,781,000,000 (social security 17.2%; education 15.9%; health 8.4%; agriculture and forestry 8.5%; transportation 8.3%; administration 5.8%; defense 5.2%).
*Public debt* (1987)[4]: U.S.$12,138,000,000.
*Tourism* (1985): receipts from visitors U.S.$501,000,000; expenditures by nationals abroad U.S.$776,000,000.
*Production* (metric tons except as noted). Agriculture, forestry, fishing (1986): barley 1,714,000, oats 1,175,000, sugar beets 792,000, potatoes 773,000, wheat 529,000; livestock (number of live animals) 1,567,300 cattle, 1,322,700 pigs, 201,600 reindeer[5]; roundwood 38,800,000 cu m; fish catch (1985) 160,577. Mining and quarrying (1985)[6]: iron ore 806,000; zinc 60,606; copper 27,897. Manufacturing (value added in Fmk; 1985): machinery 19,987,000,000, of which transport equipment 5,035,000,000; electrical equipment 4,947,000,000; paper and paper products 10,996,000,000; processed food 10,670,000,000; chemical products 3,683,000,000. Construction (1985): residential 17,450,000,000 cu m; nonresidential 27,410,000,000 cu m. Energy production (consumption): electricity (kW-hr; 1985) 47,098,000,000 (51,785,000,000); coal (metric tons; 1985) none (5,207,000); crude petroleum (barrels; 1985) none (73,212,000); petroleum products (metric tons; 1985) 9,107 000 (9,016,000); natural gas (cu m; 1985) none (851,847,000).
*Household income and expenditure.* Average household size (1983) 2.5; income per household Fmk 87,668 (U.S.$15,740); sources of income (1986): wages and salaries 66.4%, self-employment 16.8%, transfer payments 14.2%, income from property 2.6%; expenditure (1985): food 25.4%, housing 18.7%, transportation and communications 18.0%, recreation and education 9.1%, clothing 5.6%.

*Gross national product* (at current market prices; 1985): U.S.$53,450,000,000 (U.S.$10,870 per capita).

### Structure of gross domestic product and labour force

| | 1985 in value Fmk '000,000 | 1985 % of total value | 1986 labour force | 1986 % of labour force |
|---|---|---|---|---|
| Agriculture | 28,800 | 8.6 | 266,000 | 10.2 |
| Mining | 1,700 | 0.5 | 589,000 | 22.5 |
| Manufacturing | 94,800 | 28.3 | | |
| Public utilities | 10,100 | 3.0 | ... | ... |
| Construction | 24,800 | 7.4 | 185,000 | 7.1 |
| Transportation and communication | 26,100 | 7.8 | 183,000 | 7.0 |
| Trade | 38,200 | 11.4 | 355,000 | 13.6 |
| Finance | 52,200 | 15.6 | 160,000 | 6.1 |
| Pub. admin., defense | 50,600 | 15.1 | 690,000 | 26.4 |
| Services | 12,400 | 3.7 | | |
| Other | −4,700[7] | −1.4[7] | 184,000[8] | 7.0[8] |
| TOTAL | 335,000 | 100.0 | 2,612,000 | 100.0[9] |

*Population economically active* (1986): total 2,612,000; activity rate of total population 53.1% (participation rates [1985]: ages 15–64, 78.0%; female 47.5%; unemployed 6.9%).

### Price and earnings indexes (1980 = 100)

| | 1981 | 1982 | 1983 | 1984 | 1985 | 1986 | 1987 |
|---|---|---|---|---|---|---|---|
| Consumer price index | 112.0 | 122.7 | 133.0 | 142.4 | 150.7 | 156.1 | 162.0[4] |
| Hourly earnings index | 113.0 | 124.8 | 137.8 | 150.8 | 163.5 | 174.9 | 182.0[10] |

*Land use* (1984): forested 76.3%; meadows and pastures 0.4%; agricultural and under permanent cultivation 7.7%; other 15.6%.

## Foreign trade

### Balance of trade (current prices)

| | 1981 | 1982 | 1983 | 1984 | 1985 | 1986 |
|---|---|---|---|---|---|---|
| Fmk '000,000 | +1,910 | +1,351 | +1,667 | +9,498 | +6,160 | +10,735 |
| % of total | 1.6% | 1.1% | 1.2% | 6.2% | 3.8% | 6.9% |

*Imports* (1986): Fmk 77,553,000,000 (raw materials and producer goods 58.5%, of which crude petroleum 7.9%; machinery and transport equipment 23.6%, of which transport vehicles 7.2%; fuels and lubricants 5.1%). *Major import sources:* West Germany 17.0%; U.S.S.R. 15.3%; Sweden 13.6%; United Kingdom 6.5%; Japan 6.5%.
*Exports* (1986): Fmk 82,602,000,000 (forestry products 38.2%, of which paper and paper products 29.8%, wood products 8.4%; metal and engineering products 38.6%, of which metal products and machines 31.6%, basic metals 7.0%; chemical products 9.5%; textiles and clothing 6.5%; food and beverages 2.2%). *Major export destinations:* U.S.S.R. 20.3%; Sweden 14.8%; United Kingdom 10.5%; West Germany 9.7%; United States 5.4%; Norway 4.5%.

## Transport and communications

*Transport.* Railroads (1986): length (1985) 5,644 mi, 9,116 km; passenger-mi 1,663,000,000, passenger-km 2,676,000,000; short ton-mi cargo 4,759,000,000, metric ton-km cargo 6,948,000,000. Roads (1985): total length 47,262 mi, 76,061 km (paved 55%). Vehicles (1985): passenger cars 1,546,094; trucks and buses 188,654. Merchant marine (1986): vessels (100 gross tons and over) 276; total deadweight tonnage 1,907,837. Air transport (1986): passenger-mi 1,812,000,000, passenger-km 2,916,000,000; short ton-mi cargo 63,609,000, metric ton-km cargo 92,868,000; airports (1987) 21.
*Communications.* Daily newspapers (1985): total number 65; total circulation 2,661,000; circulation per 1,000 population 543. Radio (1986): total number of receivers 2,515,000 (1 per 2.0 persons). Television (1986): total number of receivers 1,792,382 (1 per 2.7 persons). Telephones (1986): 3,028,000 (1 per 1.7 persons).

## Education and health

### Education (1983–84)

| | schools | teachers | students | student/ teacher ratio |
|---|---|---|---|---|
| Primary (age 7–12) | 4,238 | 25,139 | 369,047 | 14.7 |
| Secondary (age 13–19) | 1,082 | 22,356 | 316,740 | 14.2 |
| Voc., teacher tr. | 550 | 15,000 | 116,906 | 7.8 |
| Higher[11] | 21 | 5,191 | 119,902 | 23.1 |

*Educational attainment* (1983). Percent of population age 15 and over having: lower secondary education 51.5%; higher secondary 28.4%; some postsecondary 8.8%; undergraduate 4.3%; graduate 6.1%; postgraduate 0.6%; other 0.3%. *Literacy* (1987): virtually 100% literate.
*Health* (1985): physicians 10,193 (1 per 481 persons); hospital beds 61,082 (1 per 80 persons); infant mortality rate per 1,000 live births 6.5.
*Food* (1981–83): daily per capita caloric intake 3,077 (vegetable products 57%, animal products 43%); (1983) 111% of FAO recommended minimum requirement.

## Military

*Total active duty personnel* (1986): 34,900 (army 86.0%, navy 5.7%, air force 8.3%). *Military expenditure as percent of GNP* (1984): 1.6% (world 5.9%); per capita expenditure U.S.$168.

---

[1]April 1. [2]Based on land area only. [3]Includes English 0.04%; German 0.04%; Russian 0.04%; Lappish 0.03%; and other 0.1%. [4]June. [5]1985. [6]Metal content of ores. [7]Includes imputed bank service charges. [8]Includes 181,000 unemployed. [9]Detail does not add to total given because of rounding. [10]March. [11]Universities only.

# France

*Official name:* République Française (French Republic).
*Form of government:* republic with two legislative houses (Parliament; National Assembly [577], Senate [319]).
*Chief of state:* President.
*Head of government:* Prime Minister.
*Capital:* Paris.
*Official language:* French.
*Official religion:* none.
*Monetary unit:* 1 Franc (F) = 100 centimes; valuation (Oct. 5, 1987) 1 U.S.$ = F 6.13; 1 £ = F 9.96.

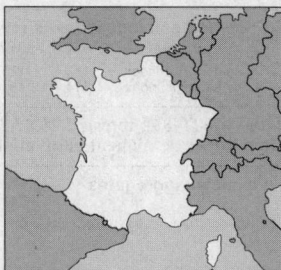

## Area and population

| | | area | | population |
|---|---|---|---|---|
| Regions<br>Departments | Capitals | sq mi | sq km | 1986<br>estimate |
| **Alsace** | | | | |
| Bas-Rhin | Strasbourg | 1,836 | 4,755 | 938,000 |
| Haut-Rhin | Colmar | 1,361 | 3,525 | 661,700 |
| **Aquitaine** | | | | |
| Dordogne | Périgueux | 3,498 | 9,060 | 380,100 |
| Gironde | Bordeaux | 3,861 | 10,000 | 1,166,400 |
| Landes | Mont-de-Marsan | 3,569 | 9,243 | 302,900 |
| Lot-et-Garonne | Agen | 2,070 | 5,361 | 302,300 |
| Pyrénées-Atlantiques | Pau | 2,952 | 7,645 | 566,500 |
| **Auvergne** | | | | |
| Allier | Moulins | 2,834 | 7,340 | 365,000 |
| Cantal | Aurillac | 2,211 | 5,726 | 160,400 |
| Haute-Loire | Le Puy | 1,922 | 4,977 | 207,100 |
| Puy-de-Dôme | Clermont-Ferrand | 3,077 | 7,970 | 601,900 |
| **Basse Normandie** | | | | |
| Calvados | Caen | 2,142 | 5,548 | 604,500 |
| Manche | Saint-Lô | 2,293 | 5,938 | 473,500 |
| Orne | Alen | 2,356 | 6,103 | 295,400 |
| **Bretagne** | | | | |
| Côtes-du-Nord | Saint-Brieuc | 2,656 | 6,878 | 544,600 |
| Finistère | Quimper | 2,600 | 6,733 | 840,600 |
| Ille-et-Vilaine | Rennes | 2,616 | 6,775 | 774,300 |
| Morbihan | Vannes | 2,634 | 6,823 | 604,700 |
| **Bourgogne** | | | | |
| Côte-d'Or | Dijon | 3,383 | 8,763 | 482,700 |
| Nièvre | Nevers | 2,632 | 6,817 | 236,200 |
| Saône-et-Loire | Mâcon | 3,311 | 8,575 | 571,100 |
| Yonne | Auxerre | 2,868 | 7,427 | 317,300 |
| **Centre** | | | | |
| Cher | Bourges | 2,793 | 7,235 | 322,500 |
| Eure-et-Loire | Chartres | 2,270 | 5,880 | 378,800 |
| Indre | Châteauroux | 2,622 | 6,791 | 238,800 |
| Indre-et-Loire | Tours | 2,366 | 6,127 | 520,900 |
| Loiret | Orléans | 2,616 | 6,775 | 561,600 |
| Loir-et-Cher | Blois | 2,449 | 6,343 | 301,800 |
| **Champagne-Ardenne** | | | | |
| Ardennes | Charleville-Mézières | 2,019 | 5,229 | 299,200 |
| Aube | Troyes | 2,318 | 6,004 | 292,100 |
| Haute-Marne | Chaumont | 2,398 | 6,211 | 210,400 |
| Marne | Châlons-sur-Marne | 3,151 | 8,162 | 550,700 |
| **Corse** | | | | |
| Corse-du-Sud | Ajaccio | 1,550 | 4,014 | 113,300 |
| Haute-Corse | Bastia | 1,802 | 4,666 | 135,400 |
| **Franche-Comté** | | | | |
| Doubs | Besançon | 2,021 | 5,234 | 468,900 |
| Haute-Saône | Vesoul | 2,070 | 5,360 | 237,700 |
| Jura | Lons-le-Saunier | 1,930 | 4,999 | 245,500 |
| Territoire de Belfort | Belfort | 235 | 609 | 133,800 |
| **Haute-Normandie** | | | | |
| Eure | Évreux | 2,332 | 6,040 | 486,700 |
| Seine-Maritime | Rouen | 2,424 | 6,278 | 1,206,000 |
| **Île-de-France** | | | | |
| Essonne | Évry | 696 | 1,804 | 1,027,300 |
| Hauts-de-Seine | Nanterre | 68 | 176 | 1,362,700 |
| Paris | Paris | 40 | 105 | 2,127,900 |
| Seine-et-Marne | Melun | 2,284 | 5,915 | 976,300 |
| Seine-Saint-Denis | Bobigny | 91 | 236 | 1,332,400 |
| Val-de-Marne | Créteil | 95 | 245 | 1,182,600 |
| Val-d'Oise | Pontoise | 481 | 1,246 | 973,800 |
| Yvelines | Versailles | 882 | 2,284 | 1,267,800 |
| **Languedoc-Roussillon** | | | | |
| Aude | Carcassonne | 2,370 | 6,139 | 286,000 |
| Gard | Nîmes | 2,260 | 5,853 | 558,100 |
| Hérault | Montpellier | 2,356 | 6,101 | 745,200 |
| Lozère | Mende | 1,995 | 5,167 | 73,500 |
| Pyrénées-Orientales | Perpignan | 1,589 | 4,116 | 349,100 |
| **Limousin** | | | | |
| Corrèze | Tulle | 2,261 | 5,857 | 242,000 |
| Creuse | Guéret | 2,149 | 5,565 | 136,800 |
| Haute-Vienne | Limoges | 2,131 | 5,520 | 357,000 |
| **Lorraine** | | | | |
| Meurthe-et-Moselle | Nancy | 2,024 | 5,241 | 711,700 |
| Meuse | Bar-le-Duc | 2,400 | 6,216 | 198,300 |
| Moselle | Metz | 2,400 | 6,216 | 1,009,400 |
| Vosges | Épinal | 2,268 | 5,874 | 393,800 |
| **Midi-Pyrénées** | | | | |
| Ariège | Foix | 1,888 | 4,890 | 134,700 |
| Aveyron | Rodez | 3,373 | 8,736 | 277,900 |
| Gers | Auch | 2,416 | 6,257 | 173,000 |
| Haute-Garonne | Toulouse | 2,436 | 6,309 | 851,500 |
| Hautes-Pyrénées | Tarbes | 1,724 | 4,464 | 227,100 |
| Lot | Cahors | 2,014 | 5,217 | 156,700 |
| Tarn | Albi | 2,223 | 5,758 | 339,700 |
| Tarn-et-Garonne | Montauban | 1,435 | 3,718 | 194,500 |
| **Nord-Pas-de-Calais** | | | | |
| Nord | Lille | 2,217 | 5,742 | 2,501,300 |
| Pas-de-Calais | Arras | 2,576 | 6,671 | 1,421,900 |

## Area and population (continued)

| | | area | | population |
|---|---|---|---|---|
| | | sq mi | sq km | 1986 estimate |
| **Pays de la Loire** | | | | |
| Loire-Atlantique | Nantes | 2,631 | 6,815 | 1,029,700 |
| Maine-et-Loire | Angers | 2,767 | 7,166 | 700,100 |
| Mayenne | Laval | 1,998 | 5,175 | 276,700 |
| Sarthe | Le Mans | 2,396 | 6,206 | 511,500 |
| Vendée | La Roche-sur-Yon | 2,595 | 6,720 | 499,700 |
| **Picardie** | | | | |
| Aisne | Laon | 2,845 | 7,369 | 535,500 |
| Oise | Beauvais | 2,263 | 5,860 | 689,000 |
| Somme | Amiens | 2,382 | 6,170 | 549,500 |
| **Poitou-Charentes** | | | | |
| Charente | Angoulême | 2,300 | 5,956 | 341,600 |
| Charente-Maritime | La Rochelle | 2,650 | 6,864 | 519,500 |
| Deux-Sèvres | Niort | 2,316 | 5,999 | 344,600 |
| Vienne | Poitiers | 2,699 | 6,990 | 377,900 |
| **Provence-Côte d'Azur** | | | | |
| Alpes-Maritimes | Nice | 1,660 | 4,299 | 894,800 |
| Alpes-de-Haute-Provence | Digne | 2,674 | 6,925 | 122,400 |
| Bouches-du-Rhône | Marseille | 1,964 | 5,087 | 1,740,900 |
| Hautes-Alpes | Gap | 2,142 | 5,549 | 107,000 |
| Var | Toulon | 2,306 | 5,973 | 754,000 |
| Vaucluse | Avignon | 1,377 | 3,567 | 439,700 |
| **Rhône-Alpes** | | | | |
| Ain | Bourg-en-Bresse | 2,225 | 5,762 | 443,100 |
| Ardèche | Privas | 2,135 | 5,529 | 271,600 |
| Drôme | Valence | 2,521 | 6,530 | 404,000 |
| Haute-Savoie | Annecy | 1,694 | 4,388 | 522,000 |
| Isère | Grenoble | 2,869 | 7,431 | 980,600 |
| Loire | Saint-Étienne | 1,846 | 4,781 | 738,200 |
| Rhône | Lyon | 1,254 | 3,249 | 1,460,900 |
| Savoie | Chambéry | 2,327 | 6,028 | 333,200 |
| **TOTAL** | | 210,026 | 543,965 | 55,279,100[1] |

## Demography

*Population* (1987): 55,623,000.
*Density* (1987): persons per sq mi 264.8, persons per sq km 102.2.
*Urban–rural* (1985): urban 73.4%; rural 26.6%.
*Sex distribution* (1986): male 48.76%; female 51.24%.
*Age breakdown* (1986): under 15, 21.1%; 15–29, 23.1%; 30–44, 21.0%; 45–59, 16.5%; 60–74, 11.9%; 75 and over, 6.4%.
*Population projection:* (1990) 56,320,000; (2000) 58,706,000.
*Doubling time:* n.a.; doubling time exceeds 100 years.
*Ethnolinguistic composition* (1980): French (mother tongue) 93.4%, of which fully or substantially bilingual in Occitan 2.7%, German (mostly Alsatian) 2.3%, Breton 1.0%, Catalan 0.4%; Arabic 2.6%; other 4.0%.
*Religious affiliation* (1980): Roman Catholic 76.4%; other Christian 3.7%; atheist 3.4%; Muslim 3.0%; other 13.5%.
*Major cities* (1982): Paris 2,165,892 (metropolitan area 10,210,059); Marseille 868,435 (1,227,901); Lyon 410,455 (1,533,305); Toulouse 344,917 (648,267); Nice 331,165 (865,492); Strasbourg 247,068 (613,380); Nantes 237,789 (558,-814); Bordeaux 201,965 (843,411); Saint-Étienne 193,938 (547,729).
*National origin* (1982): French 90.6%; Algerian 1.5%; Portuguese 1.4%; Moroccan 0.8%; Spanish 0.6%; Italian 0.6%; other 4.5%[2].
*Mobility* (1982). Population living in same residence as in 1975: n.a.; same region 91.7%; different region 5.8%; different country 2.5%.
*Households* (1982). Average household size 2.7; 1 person 24.6%, 2 persons 28.5%, 3 persons 18.8%, 4 persons 16.1%, 5 persons 7.4%, 6 persons or more 4.6%. Family households: 14,118,940 (72.1%); nonfamily 5,471,460 (27.9%, of which 1-person 24.6%).
*Immigration* (1985): permanent immigrants admitted 43,504, from Morocco 19.5%, Turkey 9.4%, Portugal 8.6%, Tunisia 5.4%, Italy 2.9%.

## Vital statistics

*Birth rate* per 1,000 population (1986): 14.1 (world avg. 26.0); (1984) legitimate 82.2%; illegitimate 17.8%.
*Death rate* per 1,000 population (1986): 9.9 (world avg. 9.9).
*Natural increase rate* per 1,000 population (1986): 4.2 (world avg. 16.1).
*Total fertility rate* (avg. births per childbearing woman; 1984): 1.8.
*Marriage rate* per 1,000 population (1986): 4.8.
*Divorce rate* per 1,000 population (1984): 1.9.
*Life expectancy* at birth (1982–84): male 70.9 years; female 79.0 years.
*Major causes of death* per 100,000 population (1985): malignant neoplasms (cancers) 239.1; heart disease 210.4; cerebrovascular disease 156.6.

## Social indicators

*Educational attainment* (1974). Percent of adult employed population having: less than full primary education 36.2%; primary 30.4%; secondary 21.0%; some postsecondary 7.0%; 4-year degree 2.4%; postgraduate 2.8%.

### Distribution of income (1975)

percent of household income by quintile

| 1 | 2 | 3 | 4 | 5 (highest) |
|---|---|---|---|---|
| 5.5% | 11.5% | 17.1% | 23.7% | 42.2%. |

*Quality of working life.* Average workweek (1985): 39.0 hours. Annual rate per 100,000 workers (1984) for: injury or accident 24.2; industrial illness 0.5[3]; death 0.003[3]. Proportion of labour force insured for damages or income loss resulting from: injury, permanent disability, or death, n.a. Average days lost to labour stoppages per 1,000 workers (1985): 30.4. Average duration of journey to work (1974): 53 minutes.
*Access to services* (1982). Proportion of dwellings having: central heating 67.5%; piped water 99.2%; indoor plumbing 85.0%; natural gas 48.9%.
*Social participation.* Eligible voters participating in last national election: 78.0%. Population over 15 years of age participating in voluntary associations: 28.0%.

*Social deviance.* Offense rate per 100,000 population (1985) for: murder 4.2; rape 5.1; other assault 70.7; theft, including burglary and housebreaking, 4,721.7. Incidence per 100,000 in general population of: alcoholism[4] (late 1970s) 3,500–4,000; drug and substance abuse, n.a.; suicide (1985) 22.4.
*Leisure* (1974–75). Favourite leisure activities: television 34%; reading 14%; knitting 10%; conversation 10%; games 8%; walking 4%; radio 4%.
*Material well-being* (1985). Households possessing: automobile 73.3%; television receiver 92.6%, of which colour 69.5%; refrigerator 96.9%; washing machine 83.6%.

## National economy

*Gross national product* (at current market prices; 1985): U.S.$526,630,000,-000 (U.S.$9,545 per capita).

### Structure of gross domestic product and labour force

|  | 1985 | | 1984 | |
|  | in value F '000,000 | % of total value | labour force | % of labour force |
|---|---|---|---|---|
| Agriculture | 169,378 | 3.9 | 1,659,300 | 7.0 |
| Mining | 72,354 | 1.7 | 121,800 | 0.5 |
| Manufacturing | 1,137,975 | 26.0 | 4,991,900 | 21.2 |
| Construction | 249,418 | 5.7 | 1,578,900 | 6.7 |
| Public utilities | 120,481 | 2.8 | 217,200 | 0.9 |
| Transp. and commun. | 237,089 | 5.4 | 1,369,900 | 5.8 |
| Trade | 411,626 | 9.4 | 3,454,400 | 14.7 |
| Finance | 534,776 | 12.2 | 1,655,700 | 7.0 |
| Pub. admin., defense | 616,029 | 14.1 } | | |
| Services | 822,155 | 18.8 } | 8,524,200[5] | 36.2 |
| TOTAL | 4,371,281 | 100.0 | 23,573,300 | 100.0 |

*Budget* (1986). Revenue: F 997,000,000,000 (value-added taxes 47.2%, income tax 23.2%, customs taxes 10.3%). Expenditure: F 1,030,819,000,000 (education 23.4%, health and social services 18.9%, defense 15.9%, administration 12.2%).
*Public debt* (internal; 1986): F 1,195,900,000,000.

### Manufacturing and mining enterprises (1984)

|  | no. of enterprises | no. of employees | hourly wages as a % of avg. of all wages[3] | annual value added (F '000,000) |
|---|---|---|---|---|
| Food products | ... | 546,000 | 100 | 153,200 |
| Transport equipment | 688 | 605,000 | 115 | 132,500 |
| Electrical machinery | 703 | 486,000 | 101 | 82,000 |
| Petroleum refineries | 51 | 27,000 | ... | 66,900 |
| Industrial chemicals | 309 | 124,000 | 117 | 61,300 |
| Metal products | 3,285 | 242,000 | 109 | 52,000 |
| Iron and steel | 140 | 219,000 | ... | 51,800 |
| Textiles | 1,841 | 247,000 | 83 | 35,900 |
| Beverages | ... | 53,000 | 100 | 28,900 |
| Printing, publishing | 1,684 | 218,000 | 117 | 28,700 |
| Paper and products | 602 | 108,000 | 109 | 26,800 |
| Wearing apparel | 2,492 | 228,000 | 79 | 23,500 |
| Rubber products | 166 | 93,000 | 97 | 16,200 |
| Tobacco | ... | 8,000 | 100 | 13,500 |
| Glass products | 150 | 63,000 | 112 | 12,900 |

*Production* (metric tons except as noted). Agriculture, forestry, fishing (1985): wheat 29,030,000, sugar beets 28,476,000, corn (maize) 11,839,000, barley 11,424,000, grapes 10,000,000, potatoes 7,814,000, apples 2,315,000, oats 1,743,000, sunflower seeds 1,510,000, rapeseed 1,400,000, tomatoes 887,000, carrots 580,000, peaches 489,000, pears 450,000, green peas 400,000, rye 298,000, sorghum 192,000; livestock (number of live animals) 23,099,000 cattle, 10,975,000 pigs, 10,824,000 sheep, 962,000 goats; roundwood 38,-999,000 cu m; fish catch 738,813[6]. Mining and quarrying (1986): iron ore 3,700,000[7], potash salts 1,620,000, bauxite 1,380,000, zinc 39,600[7], lead 1,800[7], gold 90,021 troy oz[8]. Manufacturing (1986): cement 22,584,000; crude steel 17,856,000; pig iron 14,052,000; sulfuric acid 3,954,000; rubber products 544,080[8], of which tires 46,224,000 units[8]; aluminum 496,800; automobiles 2,784,000 units[8]. Construction (dwelling units; 1984) 270,793.

### Retail trade enterprises (1983)

|  | no. of enterprises | no. of employees | weekly wages as a % of all wages | annual purchases (F '000,000) |
|---|---|---|---|---|
| Large food stores | 2,381 | 299,404 | ... | 237,568 |
| Small food stores | 129,263 | 347,956 | ... | 122,241 |
|   butcher shops | 48,992 | 140,869 | ... | 40,935 |
| Clothing stores | 72,175 | 194,071 | ... | 44,317 |
| Pharmacies | 20,695 | 100,300 | ... | 32,253 |
| Gas, coal, and other |  |  |  |  |
|   energy products | 4,974 | 20,960 | ... | 28,605 |
| Department stores | 1,919 | 73,032 | ... | 27,885 |
| Furniture stores | 7,762 | 54,063 | ... | 21,270 |
| Electrical and elec- |  |  |  |  |
|   tronics stores | 11,765 | 52,643 | ... | 18,618 |
| Publishing and paper | 20,727 | 59,485 | ... | 12,487 |

*Energy production* (consumption)[9]: electricity (kW-hr; 1985) 326,400,000,-000 (303,000,000,000); coal (metric tons; 1985) 18,964,000 (38,820,000); crude petroleum (barrels; 1985) 19,371,000 (564,109,000); petroleum products (metric tons; 1985) 68,612,000 (76,422,000); natural gas (cu m; 1985) 5,628,800,000 (28,936,000,000).
*Household income and expenditure.* Average household size (1986) 2.7; average annual income per household (1985) F 165,200 (U.S.$18,385). Sources of income (1985): wages and salaries 52.2%, social security 26.3%, self-employment 21.5%; expenditure (1985): housing 28.6%, food 19.7%, health 10.9%, transportation 10.4%, clothing 7.4%, recreation 6.8%.
*Population economically active* (1985): total 23,886,000; activity rate of total population 43.3% (participation rates: ages 15–64 [1984], 65.6%; female [1984] 40.9%; unemployed 10.1%).

### Price and earnings indexes (1980 = 100)

|  | 1981 | 1982 | 1983 | 1984 | 1985 | 1986 | 1987[10] |
|---|---|---|---|---|---|---|---|
| Consumer price index | 113.4 | 126.8 | 139.0 | 149.3 | 157.9 | 161.9 | 165.7 |
| Hourly earnings index | 114.4 | 137.5 | 155.1 | 168.2 | 178.4 | 186.4 | 190.6 |

*Land use* (1985): forested 26.8%; meadows and pastures 22.7%; agricultural and under permanent cultivation 34.4%; other 16.1%.

### Financial aggregates

|  | 1982 | 1983 | 1984 | 1985 | 1986 | 1987[11] |
|---|---|---|---|---|---|---|
| Exchange rate, F per: |  |  |  |  |  |  |
| U.S. dollar | 6.73 | 8.35 | 9.59 | 8.98 | 6.93 | 6.08 |
| £ | 10.87 | 12.11 | 11.09 | 11.65 | 10.17 | 9.91 |
| SDR | 7.42 | 8.74 | 9.40 | 8.30 | 7.90 | 7.80 |
| International reserves (U.S.$) |  |  |  |  |  |  |
| Total (excl. gold; '000,000) | 16,531 | 19,851 | 20,940 | 26,589 | 31,454 | 31,529[12] |
| SDRs ('000,000) | 979 | 442 | 572 | 900 | 1,290 | 1,234 |
| Reserve pos. in IMF ('000,000) | 958 | 1,352 | 1,265 | 1,370 | 1,736 | 1,820 |
| Foreign exchange | 14,594 | 18,057 | 19,102 | 24,319 | 28,428 | 28,436[12] |
| Gold ('000,000 fine troy oz) | 81.85 | 81.85 | 81.85 | 81.85 | 81.85 | 81.85[12] |
| % world reserves | 8.6 | 8.7 | 8.6 | 8.6 | 8.6 | 8.6 |
| Interest and prices |  |  |  |  |  |  |
| Central bank discount (%) | 9.50 | 9.50 | 9.50 | 9.50 | 9.50 | 9.50 |
| Gov't. bond yield (%) | 15.56 | 13.61 | 12.41 | 10.94 | 8.44 | 8.88[12] |
| Industrial share prices |  |  |  |  |  |  |
| (1980 = 100) | 85.5 | 115.8 | 155.8 | 182.0 | 280.6 | 346.4[12] |
| Balance of payments |  |  |  |  |  |  |
| (U.S.$'000,000) |  |  |  |  |  |  |
| Balance of visible trade | −15,785 | −8,754 | −4,089 | −4,532 | −2,120 | ... |
| Imports, f.o.b. | 107,289 | 98,460 | 96,392 | 100,565 | 120,200 | ... |
| Exports, f.o.b. | 91,504 | 89,706 | 92,303 | 96,033 | 118,080 | ... |
| Balance of invisibles | 8,326 | 7,664 | 6,965 | 8,039 | 2,090[13] | ... |
| Balance of payments, |  |  |  |  |  |  |
| current account | −12,082 | −4,904 | −14 | 907 | 837[13] | ... |

*Tourism* (1985): receipts from visitors U.S.$7,942,000,000; expenditures by nationals abroad U.S.$4,557,000,000.

## Foreign trade

### Balance of trade (current prices)

|  | 1981 | 1982 | 1983 | 1984 | 1985 | 1986 |
|---|---|---|---|---|---|---|
| F '000,000,000 | −54.6 | −100.5 | −48.3 | −53.2 | −24.2 | −3.0 |
| % of total | 3.8% | 6.1% | 2.7% | 3.0% | 1.3% | 0.2% |

*Imports* (1986): F 887,459,000,000 (machinery 23.6%; chemicals and chemical products 15.3%; agricultural products 13.1%; fuels 12.5%, of which crude petroleum 6.2%; transport equipment 8.7%, of which automobiles 4.6%). *Major import sources:* West Germany 18.6%; Italy 11.1%; Belgium–Luxembourg 9.0%; U.S. 7.2%; U.K. 6.3%; The Netherlands 5.5%.
*Exports* (1986): F 863,652,000,000 (machinery 27.8%; agricultural products 16.6%; chemicals 15.2%; transport equipment 12.2%, of which automobiles 6.0%). *Major export destinations:* West Germany 16.0%; Italy 11.7%; Belgium–Luxembourg 9.0%; U.K. 8.8%; U.S. 7.3%; The Netherlands 4.9%.

## Transport and communications

*Transport.* Railroads: (1985) route length 21,547 mi, 34,676 km; (1986) passenger-mi 37,073,000,000, passenger-km 59,664,000,000; short ton-mi cargo 40,061,000,000[8], metric ton-km cargo 58,488,000,000[8]. Roads (1985): total length 499,945 mi, 804,650 km (paved 92%). Vehicles (1985): passenger cars 20,940,000; trucks and buses 3,426,000. Merchant marine (1986): vessels (100 gross tons and over) 984; total deadweight tonnage 9,305,297. Air transport[14] (1986): passenger-mi 24,383,000,000, passenger-km 39,240,000,-000; short ton-mi cargo 2,188,746,000, metric ton-km cargo 3,195,516,000; airports (1987) with scheduled flights 69.
*Communications.* Daily newspapers (1986): total number 95; total circulation 11,369,000; circulation per 1,000 population 205. Radio (1985): total number of receivers 20,000,000 (1 per 2.8 persons). Television (1986): total number of receivers 17,950,000 (1 per 3.1 persons). Telephones (1985): 34,347,388 (1 per 1.6 persons).

## Education and health

### Education (1984–85)

|  | schools | teachers | students | student/ teacher ratio |
|---|---|---|---|---|
| Primary (age 2–10) | 66,107 | 300,575 | 6,652,059 | 22.1 |
| Secondary (age 11–18) } Voc., teacher tr. } | 11,184 | 321,128 | 5,310,295 | 16.5 |
| Higher | 1,094[15] | 46,648 | 1,163,903 | 25.0 |

*Literacy* (1980): total population literate 41,112,000 (98.8%); males literate 19,933,000 (98.9%); females literate 21,179,000 (98.7%).
*Health:* physicians (1984) 114,951 (1 per 475.0 persons); hospital beds (1983) 496,896 (1 per 109.9 persons); infant mortality rate per 1,000 live births (1986) 8.0.
*Food* (1981–83): daily per capita caloric intake 3,528 (vegetable products 61%, animal products 39%); 138% of FAO recommended minimum requirement.

## Military

*Total active duty personnel* (1986): 471,785 (army 62.8%, navy 14.1%, air force 20.3%, other 2.8%). *Military expenditure as percent of GNP* (1984): 3.3% (world 5.9%); per capita expenditure U.S.$370.

[1]Detail does not add to total given because of rounding. [2]Includes 2.6% naturalized citizens not designated by national origin. [3]1982. [4]Estimated as per a narrow definition of alcoholism. [5]Includes 2,318,700 unemployed persons. [6]1984. [7]Metal content only. [8]1985. [9]All energy statistics include Monaco. [10]March. [11]June. [12]May. [13]Third quarter. [14]Air France, UTA, and Air Inter only. [15]1980–81.

# French Guiana

*Official name:* Département de la Guyane française (Department of French Guiana).
*Political status:* overseas department of France with two legislative houses (General Council [19]; Regional Council [31]).
*Chief of state:* President of France.
*Heads of government:* Commissioner of the Republic (for France); President of the General Council (for French Guiana); President of the Regional Council (for French Guiana).
*Capital:* Cayenne.
*Official language:* French.
*Official religion:* none.
*Monetary unit:* 1 franc (F) = 100 centimes; valuation (Oct. 5, 1987) 1 U.S.$ = F 6.13; 1 £ = F 9.96.

### Area and population

| Arrondissements | Capitals | area sq mi | area sq km | population 1982 census |
|---|---|---|---|---|
| Cayenne | Cayenne | 17,590 | 45,559 | 61,587 |
| Saint-Laurent-du-Maroni | Saint-Laurent-du-Maroni | 15,809 | 40,945 | 11,435 |
| TOTAL | | 33,399 | 86,504 | 73,022 |

## Demography

*Population* (1987): 88,800.
*Density* (1987): persons per sq mi 2.5, persons per sq km 1.0.
*Urban–rural* (1982): urban 73.4%; rural 26.6%.
*Sex distribution* (1982): male 52.66%; female 47.34%.
*Age breakdown* (1982): under 15, 34.2%; 15–29, 29.2%; 30–44, 19.9%; 45–59, 9.8%; 60–74, 5.1%; 75 and over, 1.8%.
*Population projection:* (1990) 99,000; (2000) 142,000.
*Doubling time:* 32 years.
*Ethnic composition* (1982): Guianese (mixed) Creole 42.6%; Guiana Chinese 14.0%; French (metropolitan) 10.7%; Haitian 7.5%; French West Indian 6.6%; Bush Negro 4.7%; Brazilian 4.6%; Amerindian 4.1%; other (other West Indian, Surinamese, Hmong, and other Southeast Asian) 5.2%.
*Religious affiliation* (1980): Roman Catholic 87.0%; Protestant 3.9%; nonreligious 2.5%; Afro-American spiritist 2.0%; traditional beliefs 1.5%; Chinese folk-religionist 1.3%; Muslim 1.0%; Bahā'ī 0.7%; other 0.1%.
*Major cities* (1982): Cayenne 37,097; Kourou 6,465; Rémire-Montjoly 5,921; Saint-Laurent-du-Maroni 5,042.

## Vital statistics

*Birth rate* per 1,000 population (1986): 27.9 (world avg. 26.0); (1985) legitimate 23.9%; illegitimate 76.1%.
*Death rate* per 1,000 population (1986): 5.7 (world avg. 9.9).
*Natural increase rate* per 1,000 population (1986): 22.2 (world avg. 16.1).
*Total fertility rate* (avg. births per childbearing woman; 1975–79): 3.1.
*Marriage rate* per 1,000 population (1986): 3.9.
*Divorce rate* per 1,000 population (1986): 0.4.
*Life expectancy* at birth (1975–79): male 63.4 years; female 69.7 years.
*Major causes of death* per 100,000 population (1984): diseases of the circulatory system 152.9, of which hypertensive disease 51.4, cerebrovascular disease 40.1%; accidents 76.5%; malignant neoplasms (cancers) 62.7; infectious and parasitic diseases 55.2.

## National economy

*Budget* (1987). Revenue: F 847,000,000 (internal loans and ordered advancements 47.9%, receipts from French central government 18.5%). Expenditures: F 847,000,000 (health and social services 27.2%, public works 12.5%, debt payments 1.7%, unspecified services 47.9%).
*Public debt* (external, outstanding; 1984)[1]: U.S.$18,000,000.
*Tourism:* (1986): number of tourist arrivals 10,237.
*Production* (metric tons except as noted). Agriculture, forestry, fishing (1986): sugarcane 9,000[2], rice 8,874, cassava 8,000[2], plantains 1,000[2], hearts of palm 606, limes 528, bananas 500[3]; livestock (number of live animals) 16,500 cattle, 9,500 pigs, 117,000 chickens; roundwood (1985) 254,000 cu m; fish catch—shrimps and prawns caught by foreign vessels 2,661, local catch of shrimps and prawns 1,073, local fish catch 1,917. Mining and quarrying (1986): gold 326 kg; stone, sand, and gravel 312,000. Manufacturing (1986): yogurt 1,820,000 cups; flans 295,000 units; sawnwood and veneer sheets 35,314 cu m; finished wood products 3,818 cu m; rum 873 hectolitres; other products include leather goods, clothing, passion fruit juice, and beer. Construction (1985): residential 76,799 sq m; nonresidential authorized 28,448 sq m. Energy production (consumption): electricity (kW-hr; 1986) 223,300,000 (189,400,000); coal, none (none); crude petroleum, none (none); petroleum products (metric tons; 1985) none (107,000); natural gas, none (none).
*Household income and expenditure.* Average household size (1982) 3.3; income per household (1980) F 75,762 (U.S.$16,776); sources of income (1980): wages and salaries 76.4%, industrial and commercial profits 12.3%, pensions and rents 3.8%, noncommercial profits 2.5%, income from stocks and bonds 1.6%, other 3.4%; expenditure (1980)[4]: food and beverages 50.0%, clothing and footwear 8.4%, transportation and communication

7.5%, housing 7.3%, household furnishings 6.7%, recreation 4.9%, energy 4.1%, health 2.2%, other 8.9%.
*Land use* (1984): forested 81.9%; meadows and pastures 0.05%; agricultural and under permanent cultivation 0.05%; other 18.0%.
*Gross national product* (at current market prices; 1983): U.S.$180,000,000 (U.S.$2,340 per capita).

### Structure of gross domestic product and labour force

| | 1979 in value F'000,000 | 1979 % of total value | 1982 labour force | 1982 % of labour force |
|---|---|---|---|---|
| Agriculture, forestry fishing | 53.4 | 5.3 | 3,706 | 11.9 |
| Mining | ... | ... | ... | ... |
| Manufacturing | 36.6 | 3.7 | 1,522 | 4.9 |
| Construction | 82.5 | 8.2 | 2,837 | 9.1 |
| Public utilities | −6.4 | −0.6 | 380 | 1.2 |
| Transp. and commun. | 65.1 | 6.5 | 1,347 | 4.3 |
| Trade | 123.2 | 12.3 | 2,025 | 6.5 |
| Finance, real estate | 89.5 | 8.9 | 444 | 1.4 |
| Pub. admin., defense, services | 557.1 | 55.7 | 12,145 | 39.0 |
| Other | — | — | 6,777[5] | 21.7[5] |
| TOTAL | 1,001.0 | 100.0 | 31,183 | 100.0 |

*Population economically active* (1982): total 31,183; activity rate of total population 42.7% (participation rates: ages 15–64, 67.2%; female 37.2%; unemployed [1986] 14.9%).

### Price and earnings indexes (December 1980 = 100)[6]

| | 1980 | 1981 | 1982 | 1983 | 1984 | 1985 | 1986[7] |
|---|---|---|---|---|---|---|---|
| Consumer price index | 100.0 | 116.5 | 130.3 | 151.5 | 163.0 | 172.8 | 174.7 |
| Hourly earnings index[8] | 100.0 | 113.5 | 137.0 | 147.9 | 153.9 | 163.9 | 165.4 |

## Foreign trade

### Balance of trade (current prices)

| | 1981 | 1982 | 1983 | 1984 | 1985 | 1986 |
|---|---|---|---|---|---|---|
| F '000,000 | −1,163 | −1,431 | −1,843 | −1,831 | −1,956 | −1,801 |
| % of total | 75.2% | 77.1% | 75.8% | 73.7% | 74.7% | 77.9% |

*Imports* (1986): F 2,057,000,000 (food products 24.3%; electrical and non-electrical machinery 20.7%; transport vehicles 11.6%; mineral fuels 10.1%; metals and metal products 6.9%; chemicals and chemical products 6.4%). *Major import sources:* France 65.0%; other EEC 11.0%; Trinidad and Tobago 8.0%; United States 5.0%; Japan 4.0%.
*Exports* (1986): F 255,500,000 (shrimps and prawns 59.4%; wood and wood products 6.9%; rice 3.1%; other products [including professional and scientific goods and base-metal products] 30.6%). *Major export destinations:* United States 36.0%; France 23.0%; Martinique and Guadeloupe 22.0%; Japan 16.0%.

## Transport and communications

*Transport.* Railroads (1986): none. Roads (1984): total length 691 mi, 1,112 km (paved 65%). Vehicles (1984): passenger cars 14,440; trucks and buses 625. Merchant marine: n.a. Air transport (1986): passenger arrivals 77,700, passenger departures 78,778; cargo unloaded 2,524 metric tons, cargo loaded 1,487 metric tons; airports (1987): with scheduled flights 1.
*Communications.* Daily newspapers (1985): total number 1; total circulation 16,000; circulation per 1,000 population 194. Radio (1986): 44,000 receivers (1 per 1.9 persons). Television (1986): 6,500 receivers (1 per 13 persons). Telephones (1985): 26,520 (1 per 3.2 persons).

## Education and health

### Education (1984–85)

| | schools | teachers | students | student/ teacher ratio |
|---|---|---|---|---|
| Primary (age 6–11) | 76 | 748 | 15,620[9] | ... |
| Secondary (age 12–18) | 8 | 470 | 5,529[9] | ... |
| Voc., teacher tr. | ... | 177 | ... | ... |
| Higher | 1 | ... | 239 | ... |

*Educational attainment* (1982). Percent of population age 25 and over having: no formal schooling 20.8%; primary education 40.4%; secondary 32.4%; higher 6.4%. *Literacy* (1982): total population age 16 and over literate 38,964 (82.0%); males literate 21,021 (82.5%); females literate 17,943 (81.3%).
*Health* (1984): physicians 122 (1 per 654 persons); hospital beds 1,001 (1 per 80 persons); infant mortality rate per 1,000 live births (1983–85 avg.) 20.6.
*Food* (1981–83): daily per capita caloric intake 2,609 (vegetable products 70%, animal products 30%); (1983) 111% of FAO recommended minimum requirement.

## Military

*Total active duty personnel* (1984): 2,700[10].

---

[1]Includes external long-term private debt not guaranteed by the government. [2]1985. [3]1984. [4]Weights of consumer price index components. [5]Includes 2,017 in categories not clearly defined and 4,760 unemployed. [6]Indexes based on end-of-year figures. [7]End of August. [8]Based on minimum-level wage in public administration. [9]1985–86. [10]Includes French Foreign Legion troops assigned to guard the Kourou Space Centre.

# French Polynesia

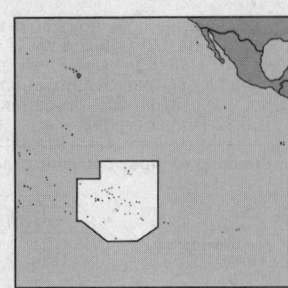

*Official name:* Territoire de la
Polynésie française (French);
Polynesia Farani (Tahitian) (Territory
of French Polynesia).
*Political status:* overseas territory
(France) with one legislative house
(Territorial Assembly [41]).
*Chief of state:* President of France.
*Head of government:* High
Commissioner (for France); President
of the Territorial Assembly (for
French Polynesia).
*Capital:* Papeete.
*Official languages:* French; Tahitian.
*Official religion:* none.
*Monetary unit:* 1 Franc de la Comptoirs
française du pacifique (CFPF) = 100
centimes; valuation (Oct. 5, 1987) 1
U.S.$ = CFPF 108.38; 1 £ = CFPF
176.00.

### Area and population

| Circumscriptions | Capitals | area sq mi | area sq km | population 1983 census |
|---|---|---|---|---|
| Îles Australes | Mataura | 57 | 148 | 6,283 |
| Îles Marquises | Taiohae | 405 | 1,049 | 6,548 |
| Îles sous le Vent | Uturoa | 156 | 404 | 19,060 |
| Îles Tuamotu et Gambier | Papeete | 280 | 726 | 11,793 |
| Îles du Vent | Papeete | 461 | 1,194 | 123,069 |
| TOTAL | | 1,550[1] | 4,000[1] | 166,753 |

## Demography

*Population* (1987): 183,000.
*Density* (1987)[2]: persons per sq mi 134.7, persons per sq km 52.0.
*Urban–rural* (1985): urban 73.4%[3]; rural 26.6%.
*Sex distribution* (1983): male 52.12%; female 47.88%.
*Age breakdown* (1985): under 15, 37.9%; 15–29, 30.0%; 30–44, 16.5%; 45–59, 10.5%; 60–74, 4.3%; 75 and over, 0.8%.
*Population projection:* (1990) 197,000; (2000) 256,000.
*Doubling time:* 29 years.
*Ethnic composition* (1983): Polynesian 68.5%; mixed 14.5%, of which Polynesian-European 9.5%, Polynesian-Chinese 3.8%, European-Chinese 0.3%; European (mostly French) 11.6%; Chinese 4.5%; other 0.9%.
*Religious affiliation* (1980): Protestant 46.6%, of which Evangelical Church of French Polynesia 32.8%; Roman Catholic 39.4%; other Christian 8.2%, of which Mormon 3.5%; nonreligious 5.0%; other 0.8%.
*Major cities* (1983): Papeete 23,496; Faaa 21,927; Punaauia 12,414.

## Vital statistics

*Birth rate* per 1,000 population (1986): 28.9 (world avg. 26.0); (1983) legitimate 41.1%; illegitimate 58.9%.
*Death rate* per 1,000 population (1986): 5.1 (world avg. 9.9).
*Natural increase rate* per 1,000 population (1986): 23.8 (world avg. 16.1).
*Total fertility rate* (avg. births per childbearing woman; 1985): 3.5.
*Marriage rate* per 1,000 population (1986): 6.2.
*Divorce rate* per 1,000 population (1983): 0.8.
*Life expectancy* at birth (1983): male 64.5 years; female 70.4 years.
*Major causes of death* per 100,000 population (1984): diseases of the circulatory system 120.1; malignant neoplasms (cancers) 67.7; accidents, suicide, and violence 58.9; ill-defined conditions 94.2.

## National economy

*Budget* (1987). Revenue: CFPF 52,135,000,000 (indirect taxes 80.7%, of which entry fee 38.9%, social protection tax 15.1%, tax on hydrocarbons 8.3%; direct taxes 14.6%). Expenditures: CFPF 52,135,000,000 (investments 24.2%; public debt service 8.5%; unspecified 67.3%).
*Public debt* (external, outstanding; 1984)[4]: U.S.$149,000,000.
*Tourism* (1985): receipts from visitors U.S.$98,000,000; expenditures by nationals abroad, n.a.
*Production* (metric tons except as noted). Agriculture, forestry, fishing[5] (1986): coconuts 110,000[6], cassava 5,000[6], pineapples 3,000, watermelon 1,666[7], potatoes 1,200, tomatoes 1,053, lettuce 725, cucumbers 549, taros 464, bananas 291, turnips 265, lemons 130, vanilla 25, flowers (value of production) CFPF 655,000,000[8]; livestock (number of live animals) 22,900 pigs, 9,900 cattle, 3,000 goats[6]; roundwood, n.a.; fish catch 1,915 of which skipjack tuna 456, black cultured pearls *c.* 350 kg. Mining and quarrying: none. Manufacturing (1986): copra 13,705; crude coconut oil 8,898; *monoï* oil (a base used in cosmetics and suntan lotions) CFPF 21,000,000[9]; other manufactures include beer, printed cloth, and sandals. Construction (value added in CFPF '000,000; 1986): residential 4,936; nonresidential 3,992. Energy production (consumption): electricity (kW-hr; 1986) 221,700,000 (187,900,000); coal, none (none); crude petroleum, none (none); petroleum products (metric tons; 1985) none (188,000); natural gas, none (none).
*Household income and expenditure.* Average household size (1983) 5.0; average annual income per household (1977) CFPF 2,118,161 (U.S.$23,624); sources of income (1982): salaries 48.0%, self-employment 40.9%, transfer payments 9.4%, other 1.7%; expenditure (1980)[10]: food and beverages 36.5%, transportation 13.1%, household furnishings 9.2%, clothing 9.0%, energy 8.6%.

*Gross national product* (at current market prices; 1985)[11]: U.S.$1,370,000,000 (U.S.$7,830 per capita).

### Structure of gross domestic product and labour force

| | 1982 in value CFPF '000,000 | 1982 % of total value | 1983 labour force | 1983 % of labour force |
|---|---|---|---|---|
| Agriculture | 6,514 | 4.8 | 8,032 | 13.1 |
| Manufacturing | 11,091 | 8.1 | 4,155 | 6.8 |
| Construction | 12,843 | 9.4 | 6,231 | 10.2 |
| Public utilities | 1,330 | 1.0 | 392 | 0.7 |
| Transportation and communication | 8,790 | 6.4 | 3,439 | 5.6 |
| Trade | 33,029 } | 24.1 | 13,698 | 22.4 |
| Finance | | | 1,253 | 2.1 |
| Pub. admin., defense | 32,520 | 23.7 } | 20,663 | 33.8 |
| Services | 30,836 | 22.5 } | | |
| Other[12] | — | — | 3,258 | 5.3 |
| TOTAL | 136,953 | 100.0 | 61,121 | 100.0 |

*Population economically active* (1983): total 61,121; activity rate of total population 36.7% (participation rates: ages 15–60, 66.0%[13]; female 31.6%[13]; unemployed 5.3%).

### Price and earnings indexes (1981 = 100)[14]

| | 1980 | 1981 | 1982 | 1983 | 1984 | 1985 | 1986 |
|---|---|---|---|---|---|---|---|
| Consumer price index | 85.7 | 100.0 | 114.5 | 130.2 | 144.0 | 155.2 | 154.2 |
| Monthly earnings index[15] | ... | 100.0 | 129.9 | 155.2 | 176.1 | 197.6 | 199.8[16] |

*Land use* (1984): forested 31.4%; meadows and pastures 5.5%; agricultural and under permanent cultivation 20.5%; other 42.6%.

## Foreign trade

### Balance of trade (current prices)

| | 1981 | 1982 | 1983 | 1984 | 1985 | 1986 |
|---|---|---|---|---|---|---|
| CFPF '000,000 | −51,962 | −58,957 | −69,399 | −80,392 | −82,300 | −87,555 |
| % of total | 90.0% | 90.0% | 87.0% | 88.1% | 85.7% | 89.0% |

*Imports* (1986): CFPF 92,667,000,000 (electrical machinery and appliances 18.8%; food products 18.3%; transport equipment 15.6%; petroleum products 8.3%; metal manufactures 8.3%; industrial chemicals 5.1%). *Major import sources* (1983): France 46.7%; United States 15.9%; New Zealand 6.1%; Singapore 4.6%; Japan 4.3%.
*Exports* (1986): CFPF 5,112,000,000 (reexports 72.0%, of which petroleum products 68.8%, fish 2.8%; black cultured pearls 19.5%; coconut oil 4.0%; mother-of-pearl 1.0%; vanilla 0.8%). *Major export destinations* (1983): France 58.6%; United States 12.6%; Italy 8.4%; New Caledonia 7.0%.

## Transport and communications

*Transport.* Railroads: none. Roads (1984): total length 495 mi, 797 km (paved 33%[17]). Vehicles (1982): 40,000–45,000. Merchant marine: vessels (100 gross tons and over), n.a. Air transport (1986): passenger arrivals 404,300, passenger departures 387,500; cargo unloaded 7,852 metric tons[18], cargo loaded 840 metric tons[18]; airports (1987) with scheduled flights 32.
*Communications.* Daily newspapers (1984): total number 2; total circulation 21,700; circulation per 1,000 population 128. Radio (1986): total number of receivers 84,000 (1 per 2.1 persons). Television (1986): total number of receivers 26,400 (1 per 6.8 persons). Telephones (1985): 37,730 (1 per 4.6 persons).

## Education and health

### Education (1984–85)

| | schools | teachers | students | student/ teacher ratio |
|---|---|---|---|---|
| Primary (age 6–10) | 198 | 1,337 | 27,401 | 20.5 |
| Secondary (age 11–17) | 24 | 804 | 13,611 | 16.9 |
| Vocational | 17 | 362 | 3,441 | 9.5 |
| Higher[19] | ... | ... | 180 | ... |

*Educational attainment* (1983): Percent of population age 25 and over having: no formal schooling 9.3%; primary education 58.7%; secondary 25.7%; higher 6.3%. *Literacy* (1983): total population age 15 and over literate 98,314 (95.0%); males literate 51,910 (94.9%); females literate 46,404 (95.0%).
*Health:* physicians (1983) 174 (1 per 950 persons); hospital beds (1980) 982 (1 per 154 persons); infant mortality rate per 1,000 live births (1984–86 avg.) 20.2.
*Food* (1981–83): daily per capita caloric intake 2,872 (vegetable products 78%, animal products 22%); (1983) 105% of FAO recommended minimum requirement.

## Military

*Total active duty personnel* (1986): 5,400 French military personnel. *Military expenditure as percent of GNP:* n.a.

---

[1]Approximate total area including inland water; total land area is 1,359 sq mi (3,521 sq km). [2]Based on land area. [3]Urban agglomeration of Papeete. [4]Includes external long-term private debt not guaranteed by the government. [5]Includes marine-produced commodities, *e.g.*, pearls. [6]1985. [7]Commercial production only. [8]Excludes flowers processed for perfume. [9]Export value. [10]Weights of consumer price index components. [11]Gross domestic product. [12]Unemployed. [13]Excludes unemployed. [14]All end-of-year unless footnoted. [15]Manufacturing sector. [16]June. [17]1982. [18]Excludes local interisland traffic. [19]1983–84.

# Gabon

*Official name:* République Gabonaise (Gabonese Republic).
*Form of government:* unitary single-party republic with one legislative house (National Assembly [120]).
*Chief of state:* President.
*Head of government:* Prime Minister.
*Capital:* Libreville.
*Official language:* French.
*Official religion:* none.
*Monetary unit:* 1 CFA franc (CFAF) = 100 centimes; valuation (Oct. 5, 1987) 1 U.S.$ = CFAF 306.67; 1 £ = CFAF 498.00.

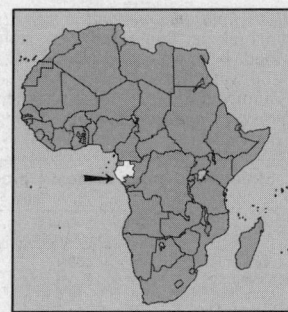

### Area and population

| Provinces | Capitals | area sq mi | area sq km | population 1978 estimate[1] |
|---|---|---|---|---|
| Estuaire | Libreville | 8,008 | 20,740 | 359,000 |
| Haut-Ogooué | Franceville | 14,111 | 36,547 | 213,000 |
| Moyen-Ogooué | Lambaréné | 7,156 | 18,535 | 49,000 |
| Ngounié | Mouila | 14,575 | 37,750 | 118,000 |
| Nyanga | Tchibanga | 8,218 | 21,285 | 98,000 |
| Ogooué-Ivindo | Makokou | 17,790 | 46,075 | 53,000 |
| Ogooué-Lolo | Koulamoutou | 9,799 | 25,380 | 49,000 |
| Ogooué-Maritime | Port-Gentil | 8,838 | 22,890 | 194,000 |
| Woleu-Ntem | Oyem | 14,851 | 38,465 | 166,000 |
| TOTAL | | 103,347[2] | 267,667 | 1,300,000[2] |

## Demography

*Population* (1987)[1]: 1,195,000.
*Density* (1987): persons per sq mi 11.6, persons per sq km 4.5.
*Urban–rural* (1985): urban 40.9%; rural 59.1%.
*Sex distribution* (1985): male 49.14%; female 50.86%.
*Age breakdown* (1985): under 15, 35.4%; 15–29, 24.1%; 30–44, 18.1%; 45–59, 13.1%; 60–74, 7.5%; 75 and over, 1.8%.
*Population projection:* (1990) 1,273,000; (2000) 1,603,000.
*Doubling time:* 35 years.
*Ethnic composition* (1983): Fang 35.5%; Mpongwe 15.1%; Mbete 14.2%; Punu 11.5%; other 23.7%.
*Religious affiliation* (1980): Christian 96.2%, of which Roman Catholic 65.2%, Protestant 18.8%, African indigenous 12.1%; traditional religion 2.9%; Muslim 0.8%; other 0.1%.
*Major cities* (1985): Libreville 235,700; Port-Gentil 124,400; Franceville 58,800.

## Vital statistics

*Birth rate* per 1,000 population (1980–85): 33.8 (world avg. 29.0).
*Death rate* per 1,000 population (1980–85): 18.1 (world avg. 11.0).
*Natural increase rate* per 1,000 population (1980–85): 15.7 (world avg. 18.0).
*Total fertility rate* (avg. births per childbearing woman; 1980–85): 4.5.
*Marriage rate* per 1,000 population: n.a.
*Divorce rate* per 1,000 population: n.a.
*Life expectancy* at birth (1980–85): male 48.0 years; female 51.4 years.
*Major causes of death* per 100,000 population: n.a.; however, major diseases include malaria, measles, shigellosis (infection with dysentery), trypanosomiasis, and tuberculosis.

## National economy

*Budget* (1986). Revenue: CFAF 720,000,000,000 (taxes on petroleum organizations and petroleum fees 50.3%; loans 16.7%; customs duties 14.9%). Expenditures: CFAF 720,000,000,000 (current expenditure 44.4%; development expenditure 33.1%, of which infrastructure 17.8%; public debt 22.5%).
*Public debt* (external, outstanding; 1985): U.S.$871,700,000.
*Tourism:* receipts from visitors (1985) U.S.$5,000,000; expenditures by nationals abroad (1983) U.S.$92,000,000.
*Production* (metric tons except as noted). Agriculture, forestry, fishing (1985): roots and tubers 382,000, cassava 250,000, plantains 165,000, sugarcane 155,000, corn (maize) 10,000, peanuts (groundnuts) 10,000, bananas 8,000, palm oil 3,200, cacao beans 3,000, coffee 1,400; livestock (number of live animals) 150,000 pigs, 80,000 sheep, 60,000 goats, 9,000 cattle, 2,000,000 chickens; roundwood 1,382,000 cu m; fish catch 47,754. Mining and quarrying (1986): manganese 3,000,000; uranium 850. Manufacturing (1984): cement 207,900; flour 21,600; raw sugar 15,000; beer 500,000 hectolitres; soft drinks 198,172 hectolitres; cigarettes 17,800,000 packs; textiles CFAF 2,420,000,000. Construction: n.a. Energy production (consumption): electricity (kW-hr; 1985) 540,000,000 (540,000,000); crude petroleum (barrels; 1985) 63,038,000 (9,000,000); petroleum products (metric tons; 1985) 1,092,000 (717,000); natural gas (cu m; 1985) 201,172,000 (201,172,000); fuelwood and bagasse (cu m; 1984) 1,315,000 (1,315,000).
*Population economically active* (1985): total 518,000; activity rate of total population 45.0% (participation rates: ages 15–64, 68.2%; female 42.8%; unemployed, n.a.).

### Price and earnings indexes (1980 = 100)

| | 1980 | 1981 | 1982 | 1983 | 1984 | 1985 | 1986[3] |
|---|---|---|---|---|---|---|---|
| Consumer price index | 100.0 | 108.7 | 126.8 | 137.0 | 148.2 | 159.1 | 168.5 |
| Earnings index | 100.0 | 101.1 | 126.6 | 156.3 | ... | ... | ... |

*Gross national product* (at current market prices; 1985): U.S.$3,330,000,000 (U.S.$2,890 per capita).

### Structure of gross domestic product and labour force

| | 1983 in value CFAF '000,000 | 1983 % of total value | 1983 labour force | 1983 % of labour force |
|---|---|---|---|---|
| Agriculture | 75,800 | 5.9 | 14,118[4] | 10.2[4] |
| Mining | 605,700 | 47.2 | 3,919 | 2.9 |
| Manufacturing | 57,200 | 4.5 | 4,123 | 3.0 |
| Construction | 93,000 | 7.3 | 13,154 | 9.5 |
| Public utilities | 19,500 | 1.5 | [5] | [5] |
| Transportation and communication | 50,600 | 4.0 | [5] | [5] |
| Trade | 105,000 | 8.2 | 3,732 | 2.7 |
| Finance | 10,000 | 0.8 | [5] | [5] |
| Pub. admin., defense | 102,600 | 8.0 | 42,678 | 31.0 |
| Services | 85,100 | 6.6 | [5] | [5] |
| Other, including taxes on imports | 77,500 | 6.0 | 56,143[5] | 40.7[5] |
| TOTAL | 1,282,000 | 100.0 | 137,867[4] | 100.0 |

*Household income and expenditure.* Average household size (1980) 4.0; income per household: n.a.; sources of income[4] (1983): private sector 73.4%, public sector 26.6%; expenditure[6] (1983): food and tobacco 54.7%, clothing and footwear 17.5%, housing 13.0%, transportation and communication 6.3%.
*Land use* (1984): forested 77.6%; meadows and pastures 18.2%; agricultural and under permanent cultivation 1.8%; other 2.4%.

## Foreign trade

### Balance of trade (current prices)

| | 1981 | 1982 | 1983 | 1984 | 1985 | 1986 |
|---|---|---|---|---|---|---|
| CFAF '000,000 | +371,100 | +252,100 | +421,700 | +492,600 | +492,000 | +140,000 |
| % of total | 45.0% | 32.4% | 39.4% | 40.8% | 39.0% | 18.9% |

*Imports* (1985): CFAF 384,000,000,000 (1983; machinery and mechanical equipment 23.8%; transport equipment and parts 15.1%; food, beverages, and tobacco products 12.3%; metal and metal products 10.7%; household and consumer products 5.3%; clothing and textiles 4.6%). *Major import sources* (1985): France 49.0%; United States 11.0%; West Germany 5.8%; Japan 5.4%; United Kingdom 4.8%; Italy 4.0%; Belgium–Luxembourg 2.9%; The Netherlands 2.5%; Spain 1.9%.
*Exports* (1985): CFAF 876,000,000,000 (crude petroleum and petroleum products 83.0%; wood 6.0%, of which okoumé and ozigo 4.5%; manganese ore and concentrate 6.0%; uranium ore and concentrate 3.0%). *Major export destinations* (1985): France 31.8%; United States 26.3%; Spain 13.2%; United Kingdom 3.0%; South Korea 2.8%; Italy 1.8%; Canada 1.4%; Brazil 1.1%; The Netherlands 1.1%.

## Transport and communications

*Transport.* Railroads (1986): length 403 mi, 648 km; passenger-mi 12,000,000, passenger-km 19,000,000; short ton-mi cargo 71,000,000, metric ton-km cargo 103,000,000. Roads (1986): total length 4,400 mi, 7,082 km (paved 8%). Vehicles (1983): passenger cars 16,043; trucks and buses 10,695. Merchant marine (1986): vessels (100 gross tons and over) 23; total deadweight tonnage 170,176. Air transport (1983): passengers carried 850,000; cargo carried 36,376 short tons (33,000 metric tons); airports (1987) with scheduled flights 25[7].
*Communications.* Daily newspapers (1984): total number 2; total circulation 33,000; circulation per 1,000 population 35. Radio (1985): total number of receivers 100,000 (1 per 12 persons). Television (1985): total number of receivers 21,000 (1 per 55 persons). Telephones (1984): 13,800 (1 per 82 persons).

## Education and health

### Education (1984–85)

| | schools | teachers | students | student/teacher ratio |
|---|---|---|---|---|
| Primary | 940 | 3,837 | 178,811 | 46.6 |
| Secondary | 51 | 1,894 | 25,815 | 13.6 |
| Voc., teacher tr. | 29 | 720 | 13,529 | 18.8 |
| Higher[8] | 1 | 616 | 3,228 | 5.2 |

*Educational attainment,* n.a. *Literacy* (1978): total population age 15 and over literate 800,000 (77%); males literate, n.a.; females literate, n.a.
*Health* (1984): physicians 565 (1 per 2,000 persons); hospital beds 10,980 (1 per 103 persons); infant mortality rate per 1,000 live births (1980–85) 121.6.
*Food* (1981–83): daily per capita caloric intake 2,808 (vegetable products 88%, animal products 12%); (1983) 102% of FAO recommended minimum requirement.

## Military

*Total active duty personnel* (1986): 2,700 (army 70.4%, navy 7.4%, air force 22.2%), not including 600 French troops. *Military expenditure as percent of GNP* (1984): 2.1% (world 5.9%); per capita expenditure U.S.$72.

[1]Population distribution is based on country estimate, which is substantially higher than estimates from external sources (such as the United Nations and the World Bank), which form the basis of the 1987 estimate. [2]Detail does not add to total given because of rounding. [3]Second quarter. [4]Official government figures for salaried workers only, not including traditional agricultural workers; agricultural workers (FAO estimate, 1985) totaled 379,000 (73.1% of the labour force). [5]Public utilities, transportation and communication, finance, and service employees included with other. [6]Libreville only. [7]Includes airfields. [8]1983–84.

# Gambia, The

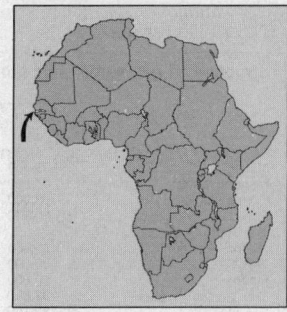

*Official name:* Republic of The Gambia.
*Form of government:* multiparty republic with one legislative house (House of Representatives [36])[1].
*Head of state and government:* President.
*Capital:* Banjul.
*Official language:* English.
*Official religion:* none.
*Monetary unit:* 1 dalasi (D) = 100 butut; valuation (Oct. 5, 1987) 1 U.S.$ = D 7.51; 1 £ = D 12.19.

## Area and population

| Divisions | Capitals | area sq mi | area sq km | population 1983 census[2] |
|---|---|---|---|---|
| Kombo Saint Mary | Kanifing | 29 | 76 | 101,504 |
| Lower River | Mansakonko | 625 | 1,618 | 55,263 |
| MacCarthy Island | Kuntaur/Georgetown | 1,117 | 2,894 | 126,004 |
| North Bank | Kerewan | 871 | 2,256 | 112,225 |
| Upper River | Basse | 799 | 2,069 | 111,388 |
| Western | Brikama | 681 | 1,764 | 137,245 |
| City | | | | |
| Banjul | — | 5 | 12 | 44,188 |
| TOTAL | | 4,127 | 10,689 | 687,817 |

## Demography

*Population* (1987): 787,400.
*Density[3]* (1987): persons per sq mi 236.7, persons per sq km 91.4.
*Urban–rural* (1984): urban 21.2%; rural 78.8%.
*Sex distribution* (1983): male 49.74%; female 50.26%.
*Age breakdown* (1983): under 15, 43.8%; 15–29, 26.5%; 30–44, 15.7%; 45–59, 9.4%; 60–74, 4.0%; 75 and over, 0.6%.
*Population projection:* (1990) 860,000; (2000) 1,156,000.
*Doubling time:* 33 years.
*Ethnic composition* (1983): Malinke 40.4%; Fulani 18.7%; Wolof 14.6%; Dyola 10.3%; Soninke 8.2%; other 7.8%.
*Religious affiliation* (1983): Muslim 95.4%; Christian 3.7%; traditional beliefs and other 0.9%.
*Major cities* (1986): Serekunda 102,600; Banjul 44,188[4]; Brikama 24,300; Bakau 23,600; Basse 5,612.

## Vital statistics

*Birth rate* per 1,000 population (1980–85): 48.4 (world avg. 29.0); legitimate, n.a.; illegitimate, n.a.
*Death rate* per 1,000 population (1980–85): 29.0 (world avg. 11.0).
*Natural increase rate* per 1,000 population (1980–85): 19.4 (world avg. 18.0).
*Total fertility rate* (avg. births per childbearing woman; 1980–85): 6.4.
*Marriage rate* per 1,000 population: n.a.
*Divorce rate* per 1,000 population: n.a.
*Life expectancy* at birth (1980–85): male 40.9 years; female 44.1 years.
*Major causes of death* per 100,000 population: n.a.; however, major infectious diseases include malaria, gonococcal infections and syphilis, leprosy (Hansen's disease), chicken pox, schistosomiasis, tetanus, tuberculosis, and trypanosomiasis (sleeping sickness).

## National economy

*Budget* (1986–87). Revenue: D 498,017,000 (recurrent revenue 296,780,000, of which import and excise duties 67.5%; income tax 11.9%; export duties 2.7%). Expenditures: D 463,864,000 (current expenditure D 262,627,000, of which education, sports, and culture 9.4%; health, labour, and social welfare 6.6%; public works, transport, and communications 4.8%; agriculture, forestry, fisheries, and mineral resources 4.6%).
*Production* (metric tons except as noted). Agriculture, forestry, fishing (1985): peanuts (groundnuts) in shell 120,000, millet and sorghum 54,000, paddy rice 44,000, corn (maize) 29,000, cassava 6,000, palm oil 2,500, palm kernels 2,000; livestock (number of live animals) 290,000 cattle, 194,000 goats, 185,000 sheep, 12,000 pigs, 4,000 asses, 310,000 chickens; roundwood 783,000 cu m, of which fuel wood 528,000 cu m, sawn logs, veneer logs and logs for sleepers 21,000 cu m, industrial wood 7,000 cu m; fish catch 11,512, of which inland water 3,500, Atlantic Ocean 9,200. Mining and quarrying: n.a.; however, deposits of kaolin, tin, ilmenite, zircon, and rutile are significant locally. Manufacturing (value of production in D '000; 1982): processed food, including peanut and palm kernel oil 62,878; beverages 10,546; textiles 3,253; chemicals and related products 1,031; nonmetals 922; printing and publishing 358; leather 150. Construction: n.a. Energy production (consumption): electricity (kW-hr; 1985) 42,000,000 (42,000,000); coal, none (n.a.); crude petroleum, none (n.a.); petroleum products (metric tons; 1985) none (55,000); natural gas, none (n.a.).
*Population economically active* (1983): total 325,600; activity rate of total population 47.3% (participation rates: ages 15–64 78.2%; female 43.6%; unemployed, n.a.).

## Price and earnings indexes (1980 = 100)

| | 1981 | 1982 | 1983 | 1984 | 1985 | 1986 | 1987[5] |
|---|---|---|---|---|---|---|---|
| Consumer price index | 106.1 | 117.6 | 130.1 | 158.9 | 188.0 | 294.3 | 360.1 |
| Earnings index | ... | ... | ... | ... | ... | ... | ... |

*Household income and expenditure.* Average household size (1980) 4.9; income per household: n.a., sources of income: n.a., expenditure[6] (1985): food, beverages, and tobacco 58.0%, clothing and footwear 17.5%, energy and water 5.4%, housing 5.1%, education, health, transportation and communication, recreation and other 14.0%.
*Gross national product* (at current prices; 1985): U.S.$170,000,000 (U.S.$230 per capita).

## Structure of gross domestic product and labour force

| | 1985–86 in value D'000,000 | 1985–86 % of total value | 1983 labour force | 1983 % of labour force |
|---|---|---|---|---|
| Agriculture | 108.4 | 26.2 | 239,940 | 73.7 |
| Mining | — | — | 66 | 0.0 |
| Manufacturing | 18.5 | 4.5 | 8,144 | 2.5 |
| Construction | 13.8 | 3.3 | 4,373 | 1.3 |
| Public utilities | 3.3 | 0.8 | 1,233 | 0.4 |
| Transportation and communication | 36.2 | 8.7 | 8,014 | 2.5 |
| Trade | 111.9 | 27.0 | 16,551 | 5.1 |
| Finance | 26.3 | 6.4 | 4,577 | 1.4 |
| Public administration | 53.6 | 12.9 | 8,295 | 2.5 |
| Services | 7.1 | 1.7 | 9,381 | 2.9 |
| Other | 35.0[7] | 8.5[7] | 25,049 | 7.7 |
| TOTAL | 414.1[8] | 100.0 | 325,623 | 100.0 |

*Tourism:* receipts from visitors (1985) U.S.$21,800,000; expenditures by nationals abroad (1983) U.S.$2,000,000.
*Public debt* (external, outstanding; 1985): U.S.$179,400,000.
*Land use* (1984): forested 19.2%; meadows and pastures 9.0%; agricultural and under permanent cultivation 16.5%; built-on area, wasteland, and other 55.3%.

## Foreign trade[9]

## Balance of trade (current prices)

| | 1981 | 1982 | 1983 | 1984 | 1985 | 1986 |
|---|---|---|---|---|---|---|
| D '000,000 | −156.8 | −90.6 | −133.4 | −140.1 | −189.2 | −221.8 |
| % of total | 60.4% | 31.5% | 34.5% | 30.1% | 35.3% | 29.0% |

*Imports* (1986): D 492,277,000 (food, beverages, and tobacco 33.8%; basic manufactured goods 22.1%; machinery and transport equipment 18.8%; mineral fuels and lubricants 8.2%; chemicals and related products 6.5%; animal and vegetable oils and fats 0.7%). *Major import sources* (1984): United States 15.9%; United Kingdom 14.9%; France 10.0%; China 8.8%; U.S.S.R. and Eastern European countries 7.9%; Thailand 7.2%; West Germany 6.7%; Italy 5.3%; Senegal 4.9%; Japan 4.7%; Algeria 4.2%; The Netherlands 3.7%.
*Exports* (1986): D 270,468,000[10] (peanut oil 28.1%; shelled peanuts 24.5%; peanut meal and cake 2.4%; fish and fish preparations 2.3%). *Major export destinations* (1984): Ghana 26.5%; France 20.3%; Switzerland 19.2%; Belgium–Luxembourg 12.8%; United Kingdom 8.6%; Guinea 6.5%; Italy 5.9%.

## Transport and communications

*Transport.* Railroads: none. Roads (1986): total length 1,484 mi, 2,388 km (paved 21%). Vehicles (1986): passenger cars 5,200; trucks and buses 720. Merchant marine (1986): vessels (100 gross tons and over) 6; total deadweight tonnage 4,046. Air transport: passengers, n.a.; cargo, n.a.; airports (1987) with scheduled flights 1.
*Communications.* Daily newspapers: none. Radio (1986): total number of receivers 110,000 (1 per 7.0 persons). Television: none. Telephones (1980): 3,476 (1 per 182 persons).

## Education and health

## Education (1984–85)

| | schools | teachers | students | student/teacher ratio |
|---|---|---|---|---|
| Primary (age 8–14) | 189 | 2,640 | 66,257 | 25.1 |
| Secondary (age 15–21) | 8 | 235 | 4,348 | 18.5 |
| Secondary vocational | 16 | 502 | 10,102 | 20.1 |
| Postsecondary | 9 | 177 | 1,489 | 8.4 |

*Educational attainment* (1973). Percent of population age 20 and over having: no formal schooling 90.8%; primary education 6.2%; secondary 2.6%; higher 0.4%. *Literacy* (1985): total population age 15 and over literate 74.9%; males literate 35.6%; females literate 15.1%.
*Health* (1981): physicians 66 (1 per 9,900 persons); hospital beds 756 (1 per 865 persons); infant mortality rate per 1,000 live births (1980–85) 174.0.
*Food* (1981–83): daily per capita caloric intake 2,257 (vegetable products 93%, animal products 7%); (1983) 95% of FAO recommended minimum requirement.

## Military

*Total active duty personnel* (1986): 600 (army 87.5%, navy 8.3%, air force 4.2%). *Military expenditure as percent of GNP* (1984): 0.0% (world 5.9%).

[1]Includes 5 nonelective seats. [2]Preliminary. [3]Based on land area, which is 8,613 sq km (3,325 sq mi). [4]1983. [5]May. [6]Low-income population in Banjul and Kombo St. Mary only. [7]Direct taxes less imputed bank charges. [8]At constant market prices. [9]Import figures are f.o.b. (free on board) in balance of trade and c.i.f. (cost, insurance, and freight) for commodities and trading partners. [10]Includes reexports.

# German Democratic Republic

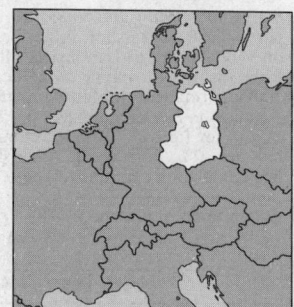

*Official name:* Deutsche Demokratische Republik (German Democratic Republic).
*Form of government:* unitary single-party republic with one legislative house (People's Chamber [500]).
*Chief of state:* Chairman, Council of State.
*Head of government:* Premier.
*Capital:* Berlin.
*Official language:* German.
*Official religion:* none.
*Monetary unit:* 1 Mark of Deutsche Demokratische Republik (M) = 100 Pfennige; valuation (Oct. 5, 1987) 1 U.S.$ = M 1.84; 1 £ = M 2.99.

### Area and population

| Districts | Capitals | area sq mi | area sq km | population 1986 estimate[1] |
|---|---|---|---|---|
| Berlin, capital city | — | 156 | 403 | 1,215,586 |
| Cottbus | Cottbus | 3,190 | 8,262 | 883,308 |
| Dresden | Dresden | 2,602 | 6,738 | 1,775,574 |
| Erfurt | Erfurt | 2,837 | 7,349 | 1,235,546 |
| Frankfurt | Frankfurt | 2,774 | 7,186 | 707,100 |
| Gera | Gera | 1,546 | 4,004 | 741,320 |
| Halle | Halle | 3,386 | 8,771 | 1,790,835 |
| Karl-Marx-Stadt | Karl-Marx-Stadt | 2,320 | 6,009 | 1,875,918 |
| Leipzig | Leipzig | 1,917 | 4,966 | 1,378,456 |
| Magdeburg | Magdeburg | 4,450 | 11,526 | 1,252,143 |
| Neubrandenburg | Neubrandenburg | 4,227 | 10,948 | 619,623 |
| Potsdam | Potsdam | 4,853 | 12,568 | 1,121,099 |
| Rostock | Rostock | 2,732 | 7,075 | 901,722 |
| Schwerin | Schwerin | 3,348 | 8,672 | 592,231 |
| Suhl | Suhl | 1,489 | 3,856 | 549,598 |
| TOTAL | | 41,827 | 108,333 | 16,640,059 |

## Demography

*Population* (1987): 16,598,000.
*Density* (1987): persons per sq mi 396.8; persons per sq km 153.2.
*Urban–rural* (1986): urban 76.6%; rural 23.4%.
*Sex distribution* (1986): male 47.34%; female 52.66%.
*Age breakdown* (1986): under 15, 19.2%; 15–29, 22.0%; 30–44, 19.6%; 45–59, 19.9%; 60–74, 11.0%; 75 and over, 8.3%.
*Population projection:* (1990) 16,530,000; (2000) 16,303,000.
*Doubling time:* not applicable; population is declining.
*Ethnic composition* (1986): German 99.7%; other 0.3%.
*Religious affiliation* (1986): Protestant 47.0%; Roman Catholic 7.0%; unaffiliated and other 46.0%.
*Major cities* (1986): Berlin (East) 1,215,586; Leipzig 553,660; Dresden 519,769; Karl-Marx-Stadt 315,452; Magdeburg 288,965; Rostock 236,011.

## Vital statistics

*Birth rate* per 1,000 population (1985): 13.7 (world avg. 29.0); (1984) legitimate 66.4%; illegitimate 33.6%.
*Death rate* per 1,000 population (1985): 13.5 (world avg. 11.0).
*Natural increase rate* per 1,000 population (1985): −0.2 (world avg. 18.0).
*Total fertility rate* (avg. births per childbearing woman; 1985): 1.6.
*Marriage rate* per 1,000 population (1985): 7.8.
*Divorce rate* per 1,000 population: (1985): 2.9.
*Life expectancy* at birth (1984): male 69.6 years; female 75.4 years.
*Major causes of death* per 100,000 population (1984): circulatory diseases 775.0; malignant neoplasms (cancers) 217.0; accidents 40.0; pneumonia 24.0; stomach and intestinal diseases 8.0; tuberculosis 3.0.

## National economy

*Budget* (1987). Revenue: M 276,779,100,000 (revenue from state-owned enterprises 69.0%, taxes and dues 7.1%, social insurance contributions 6.5%, health care contributions 3.2%). Expenditures: M 276,614,100,000 (economic development 33.4%, social welfare and health 18.0%, economic subsidies and price supports 17.6%, housing construction 5.7%, defense 5.5%, education 3.4%).
*Public debt* (external, outstanding; 1985): U.S.$12,000,000,000.
*Production* (metric tons except as noted). Agriculture, forestry, fishing (1985): potatoes 12,350,300, sugar beets 7,396,900, barley 4,365,700, wheat 3,935,600, rye 2,505,400, oats 746,000; livestock (number of live animals; 1986) 12,946,000 pigs, 5,827,000 cattle, 2,587,000 sheep, 50,700,000 chickens; commercial timber 10,142,200 cu m; fish catch 265,000. Mining and quarrying (metal content except as noted; 1984): bauxite (gross amount) 58,000; iron ore 20,000; copper ore 12,000; nickel 2,000; tin 1,800; silver 1,360,000 troy oz. Manufacturing (1985): cement 11,608,000; steel 7,852,800; fertilizer 4,842,400; pig iron 2,578,200; plastics and synthetic resins 1,047,700; sulfuric acid 882,500; paper 859,900; sugar 843,000; caustic soda 666,600; 1,267,000 vacuum cleaners; 1,132,400 radios; 829,900 refrigerators; 668,100 television receivers; 503,000 washing machines. Construction (sq m; 1985): residential 7,207,000; nonresidential, n.a. Energy production (consumption): electricity (kW-hr; 1985) 113,834,000,000 (117,670,000,000); coal (metric tons; 1985) 312,156,000 (317,254,000); crude petroleum (barrels; 1984) 3,333,000 (3,501,000); petroleum products (metric tons; 1985) 10,652,000 (10,940,000); natural gas (cu m; 1985) 7,780,000,000 (13,981,000,000).

*Gross national product* (at current market prices; 1984): U.S.$93,631,000,000 (U.S.$5,600 per capita).

### Structure of net material product and labour force

| | 1985 in value M '000,000 | 1985 % of total value | 1985 labour force[2] | 1985 % of labour force |
|---|---|---|---|---|
| Agriculture | 19,995 | 8.1 | 922,000 | 10.8 |
| Mining, manufacturing | 174,500[3] | 70.3[3] | 3,499,500 | 41.0 |
| Construction | 14,670 | 5.9 | 577,900 | 6.8 |
| Transportation and communication | 9,760 | 3.9 | 629,800 | 7.4 |
| Trade | 21,970 | 8.9 | 869,100 | 10.2 |
| Services | — | — | 2,040,700[4] | 23.9[4] |
| Other | 7,170[5] | 2.9[5] | | |
| TOTAL | 248,065[6] | 100.0 | 8,539,000 | 100.0[7] |

*Population economically active* (1984): total 8,539,000[2]; activity rate of total population 51.2% (participation rates: ages 15–64, n.a.; female 49.3%; unemployed, n.a.).

### Price and earnings indexes (1980 = 100)

| | 1979 | 1980 | 1981 | 1982 | 1983 | 1984 | 1985 |
|---|---|---|---|---|---|---|---|
| Consumer price index | 99.8 | 100.0 | 100.3 | 100.3 | 100.3 | 100.3 | 100.3 |
| Monthly earnings index | 98.2 | 100.0 | 102.4 | 105.2 | 106.6 | 107.4 | ... |

*Household income and expenditure.* Average household size (1985) 3.1; average annual income per household M 21,000 (U.S.$10,340); sources of income: wages and salaries 68.3%, social welfare 31.7%; expenditure (1985): food 24.1%, household durable goods 22.6%, education and recreation 17.8%, clothing 16.2%, housing 11.6%, energy 1.6%.
*Tourism* (1985): total tourist arrivals 1,060,219.
*Land use* (1984): forested 27.3%; meadows and pastures 11.8%; agricultural and under permanent cultivation 47.3%; other 13.6%.

## Foreign trade

### Balance of trade (current prices)

| | 1980 | 1981 | 1982 | 1983 | 1984 | 1985 |
|---|---|---|---|---|---|---|
| M '000,000 | −5,840 | +1,073 | +5,353 | +8,031 | +6,901 | +6,789 |
| % of total | 4.9% | 0.8% | 3.7% | 5.0% | 4.0% | 3.8% |

*Imports* (1985): M 86,701,000,000 (combustibles, minerals, and unfabricated metals 42.5%; machinery, equipment, and transportation equipment 26.8%; fabricated and partially fabricated industrial materials 16.1%; chemicals and related products 8.4%; consumer goods 6.2%).
*Exports* (1985): M 93,490,300,000 (machinery, equipment, and transportation equipment 46.6%; combustibles, minerals, and unfabricated metals 20.0%; consumer goods 14.1%; chemical products 11.6%; fabricated industrial materials 7.7%). *Direction of total trade*[8]: U.S.S.R. 38.8%; Czechoslovakia 7.2%; West Germany 6.3%; Poland 5.4%; Hungary 4.9%; Bulgaria 2.9%.

## Transport and communications

*Transport.* Railroads (1985): length 8,732 mi, 14,054 km; passenger-mi 13,950,000,000, passenger-km 22,451,000,000; short ton-mi cargo 40,182,000,000, metric ton-km cargo 58,668,000,000. Roads (1985): total length 29,440 mi, 47,380 km (paved 100%). Vehicles (1985): passenger cars 3,306,230; trucks and buses 360,821. Merchant marine (1986): vessels (100 gross tons and over) 403; total deadweight tonnage 1,923,583. Air transport (1985): passenger-mi 1,579,000,000, passenger-km 2,541,000,000; short ton-mi cargo 49,068,000, metric ton-km cargo 71,643,000; airports (1987) with scheduled flights 4.
*Communications.* Daily newspapers (1986): total number 39; total circulation 9,300,000; circulation per 1,000 population 559. Radio (1986): 6,646,500 receivers (1 per 2.5 persons). Television (1986): 6,078,500 receivers (1 per 2.7 persons). Telephones (1986): 3,629,525 (1 per 4.6 persons).

## Education and health

### Education (1983–84)

| | schools | teachers | students | student/teacher ratio |
|---|---|---|---|---|
| Primary (age 6–10) | 5,666 | 54,971 | 766,745 | 13.9 |
| Secondary (age 10–18) | 5,711 | 112,172 | 1,265,349 | 11.3 |
| Vocational | 4,500 | 56,577 | 414,044 | 7.3 |
| Higher | 54 | 29,700 | 434,326 | 14.6 |

*Educational attainment* (1985). Percent of employed population age 20 and over having: primary education, virtually 100%; academic secondary 15.7%; vocational 75.5%; higher 8.8%. *Literacy* (1986): total population age 15 and over literate, virtually 100%.
*Health* (1986): physicians 37,943 (1 per 439 persons); hospital beds 169,112 (1 per 98 persons); infant mortality rate per 1,000 live births (1984) 10.0.
*Food* (1981–83): daily per capita caloric intake 3,697 (vegetable products 64%, animal products 36%); (1983) 142% of FAO recommended minimum requirement.

## Military

*Total active duty personnel* (1986): 179,000 (army 68.7%, navy 9.0%, air force 22.3%). *Military expenditure as percent of GNP* (1984): 7.7% (world 5.9%); per capita expenditure U.S.$457.

[1]Beginning of year. [2]Employed only. [3]Includes public utilities. [4]Includes finance, public administration, and defense. [5]Other material activities. [6]At 1980 prices. [7]Detail does not add to total given because of rounding. [8]Separate figures are not available for import sources and export destinations.

# Germany, Federal Republic of

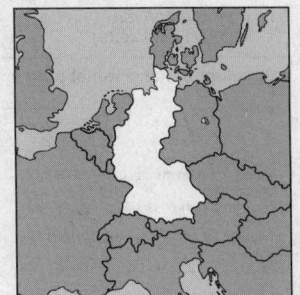

*Official name:* Bundesrepublik
Deutschland (Federal Republic of
Germany).
*Form of government:* federal multiparty
republic with two legislative houses
(Federal Council [45]; Federal
Diet [520]).
*Chief of state:* President.
*Head of government:* Chancellor.
*Capital:* Bonn (provisional).
*Official language:* German.
*Official religion:* none.
*Monetary unit:* 1 Deutsche Mark
(DM) = 100 Pfennige; valuation (Oct.
5, 1987) 1 U.S.$ = DM 1.84;
1 £ = DM 2.99.

| Area and population | | area | | population |
|---|---|---|---|---|
| States | Capitals | sq mi | sq km | 1987 estimate[1] |
| Baden–Württemberg | Stuttgart | 13,804 | 35,751 | 9,321,200 |
| Bayern | Munich | 27,241 | 70,553 | 11,023,000 |
| Bremen | Bremen | 156 | 404 | 654,600 |
| Hamburg | Hamburg | 292 | 755 | 1,571,900 |
| Hessen | Wiesbaden | 8,152 | 21,114 | 5,542,900 |
| Niedersachsen | Hannover | 18,320 | 47,450 | 7,197,200 |
| Nordrhein–Westfalen | Düsseldorf | 13,153 | 34,068 | 16,678,300 |
| Rheinland–Pfalz | Mainz | 7,663 | 19,847 | 3,612,500 |
| Saarland | Saarbrücken | 992 | 2,568 | 1,042,700 |
| Schleswig–Holstein | Kiel | 6,072 | 15,727 | 2,613,500 |
| Berlin (West)[2] | Berlin (West) | 185 | 480 | 1,878,700 |
| TOTAL | | 96,030 | 248,717 | 61,136,500 |

## Demography

*Population* (1987): 60,924,000.
*Density* (1987): persons per sq mi 634.4, persons per sq km 245.0.
*Urban–rural* (1985): urban 85.5%; rural 14.5%.
*Sex distribution* (1987): male 47.90%; female 52.10%.
*Age breakdown* (1986): under 15, 15.0%; 15–29, 24.4%; 30–44, 20.1%; 45–59, 20.1%; 60–74, 13.5%; 75 and over, 6.9%.
*Population projection:* (1990) 60,500,000; (2000) 59,107,000.
*Doubling time:* not applicable; population has been declining since about 1980.
*Ethnic composition* (1987): German 92.6%; Turk 2.3%; Yugoslav 1.0%; Italian 0.9%; Greek 0.5%; Austrian 0.3%; Spanish 0.3%; Dutch 0.2%; other 1.9%.
*Religious affiliation* (1980): Christian 92.8%, of which Protestant 47.3% (including Lutheran-Reformed tradition 23.5%, Lutheran tradition 21.7%, Reformed tradition 0.7%, other 1.4%), Roman Catholic 43.8%, New Apostolic (non-Roman) Catholic 0.6%, Orthodox 1.0%, other Christian 0.1%; nonreligious 3.7%; Muslim 2.4%; atheist 0.9%; Jewish 0.1%; other 0.1%.
*Major cities* (1986): Berlin (West) 1,868,700; Hamburg 1,575,700; Munich 1,269,400; Cologne 914,000; Essen 617,700; Frankfurt am Main 593,400; Dortmund 569,800; Düsseldorf 561,200; Stuttgart 564,500; Bonn 290,800.
*Place of birth:* n.a.
*Mobility:* n.a.
*Households* (1985). Number of households 26,367,000; average household size 2.3; 1 person 33.6%, 2 persons 29.8%, 3 persons 17.1%, 4 persons 13.2%, 5 or more persons 6.3%. Family households: 17,504,000 (66.4%); nonfamily 8,863,000.
*Immigration* (1985): immigrants admitted 512,108, from Poland 17.5%, Turkey 8.2%, Italy 8.2%, German Democratic Republic 5.6%, United States 5.1%, Yugoslavia 4.5%, Romania 3.6%, Iran 3.5%, Austria 3.1%, France 2.8%, United Kingdom 2.7%.

## Vital statistics

*Birth rate* per 1,000 population (1986): 10.2 (world avg. 26.0); legitimate 90.4%; illegitimate 9.6%.
*Death rate* per 1,000 population (1986): 11.5 (world avg. 9.9).
*Natural increase rate* per 1,000 population (1986): −1.3 (world avg. 16.1).
*Total fertility rate* (avg. births per childbearing woman; 1985): 1.3.
*Marriage rate* per 1,000 population (1986): 6.1.
*Divorce rate* per 1,000 population (1985): 2.1.
*Life expectancy* at birth (1983–85): male 71.2 years; female 77.8 years.
*Major causes of death* per 100,000 population (1985): diseases of the circulatory system 588.3, of which cerebrovascular disease 115.0, acute myocardial infarction 134.4; malignant neoplasms (cancers) 266.3, of which stomach, colon, and rectum 64.1, bronchial, lung, and tracheal 43.0, breast 22.4; pulmonary diseases 72.9, of which chronic bronchitis 37.6, pneumonia 26.2; chronic liver disease and cirrhosis 23.8; suicide 20.7.

## Social indicators

*Educational attainment* (1985). Percent of population age 25 and over having: less than full primary education, virtually nil; primary and secondary 26.5%, of which primary with general secondary 15.7%; some postsecondary in preparation for higher education 11.5%; advanced postsecondary vocational education 62.0%, of which trade school graduates with apprenticeship 48.2%, skilled technicians or craftsmen 6.1%, engineers 2.8%, university graduates (all levels) 4.9%.

*Quality of working life* (1985). Average workweek: 40.7 hours. Annual rate per 100,000 workers for: injury or accident at work 5,295; injury or accident on way to work 617; industrial illness 128; death 9.8. Proportion of labour force insured for damages or income loss resulting from: injury, virtually 100%; permanent disability, virtually 100%; death, virtually 100%. Average days lost to labour stoppages per 1,000 workers (1985): 1.3. Principal means of journey to work: private automobile 32.4%; public transportation 19.2%; bicycle 6.2%; foot 37.5%; other 4.7%. Percentage of unemployed workers not eligible for unemployment benefits (1986): 31.9%.

| Distribution of income (1978) | | | | |
|---|---|---|---|---|
| percent of household income by quintile | | | | |
| 1 | 2 | 3 | 4 | 5 (highest) |
| 6.9 | 11.0 | 15.9 | 21.9 | 44.8 |

*Access to services.* Proportion of dwellings having: electricity 99.7%; piped water supply 99.2%; flush sewage disposal 94.2%; public fire protection, virtually 100%.
*Social participation.* Eligible voters participating in last national election 84.4%. Population participating in voluntary work: n.a. Trade union membership in total work force (1985): 26.6%. Practicing religious population in total affiliated population: n.a.
*Social deviance* (1985). Offense rate per 100,000 population for: murder 4.6; sexual abuse 63.1, of which child molestation 17.1, rape 16.0; assault and battery 105.4; larceny 4,308.6, of which burglary 224.5, auto theft 114.2. Incidence per 100,000 in general population (late 1970s) of: alcoholism 2,500 to 3,000; drug and substance abuse 650; suicide 21[3].
*Leisure* (1981). Favourite leisure activities: hiking and walking 27%; reading 27%; yard work 16%; swimming 14%; watching television 14%.
*Material well-being* (1984). Households possessing: automobile 64%; telephone 81%; colour television receiver 82%; refrigerator 82%; washing machine 87%; home freezer 40%.

## National economy

*Gross national product* (at current market prices; 1985): U.S.$667,970,000,-000 (U.S.$10,940 per capita).

| Structure of gross domestic product and labour force | 1986 | | 1985 | |
|---|---|---|---|---|
| | in value DM '000,000 | % of total value | labour force | % of labour force |
| Agriculture | 33,030 | 1.7 | 1,262,000 | 4.4 |
| Mining | 68,380[4] | 3.5[4] | 512,000[4] | 1.8[4] |
| Manufacturing | 649,490 | 33.3 | 8,650,000 | 29.8 |
| Construction | 95,600 | 4.9 | 1,933,000 | 6.7 |
| Public utilities | [4] | [4] | [4] | [4] |
| Transportation and communication | } 280,820 | 14.4 | 1,512,000 | 5.2 |
| Trade | | | 3,268,000 | 11.3 |
| Finance | } 513,010 | 26.4 | 951,000 | 3.3 |
| Services | | | 8,073,000 | 27.8 |
| Pub. admin., defense | 217,850 | 11.2 } | | |
| Other | 85,770 | 4.4 | 2,850,000[5] | 9.8 |
| TOTAL | 1,943,950 | 100.0[6] | 29,012,000[6] | 100.0[6] |

*Budget* (1984). Revenue: DM 515,820,000,000 (tax revenue 93.7%, of which social security contributions from employers 25.6%, from employees 21.5%, taxes on individual wages 13.4%, value added tax on goods and services 12.2%, taxes paid by self-employed or nonemployed 8.1%, mineral oil tax 4.7%, tobacco tax 2.8%; nontax revenue 5.6%, of which income from property 4.4%). Expenditures: DM 538,030,000,000 (social security and welfare 50.2%; health 18.7%; defense 9.2%; economic services 7.1%, of which transportation and communication 3.0%; education 0.7%).
*Total national debt* (1987[7]) DM 425,780,000,000.
*Tourism* (1985)[8]: receipts from visitors U.S.$5,899,000,000; expenditures by nationals abroad U.S.$14,607,000,000.

| Manufacturing, mining, and construction enterprises (1985) | no. of enterprises | no. of tradesmen and professionals | wages as a % of avg. of all wages | annual gross production value (DM '000,000) |
|---|---|---|---|---|
| Road motor vehicle | 1,765 | 808,000 | 111.7 | 186,301 |
| Chemical | 1,155 | 574,000 | 124.6 | 181,614 |
| Machinery (nonelectric) | 4,538 | 952,000 | 105.3 | 159,363 |
| Food and beverage | 3,750 | 448,000 | 86.2 | 154,680 |
| Machinery and appliances (electric) | 2,346 | 977,000 | 102.4 | 154,547 |
| Petroleum and natural gas | 48 | 34,000 | 162.4 | 118,904 |
| Iron and steel | 107 | 228,000 | 107.3 | 56,278 |
| Calculator, computer | 1,990 | 276,000 | 90.8 | 41,737 |
| Textile | 1,381 | 232,000 | 77.2 | 36,520 |
| Mining | 78 | 217,000 | 111.4 | 36,126 |
| Plastics | 1,671 | 197,000 | 89.0 | 34,605 |
| Cement, sand, and gravel | 2,085 | 153,000 | 100.3 | 28,751 |
| Wood and wood products | 2,107 | 190,000 | 86.7 | 26,170 |
| Metalware | 1,243 | 145,000 | 105.1 | 22,395 |
| Construction | 15,020 | 954,000 | 82.2 | ... |

*Production* (metric tons except as noted). Agriculture, forestry, fishing (1985): sugar beets 20,813,000, wheat 9,866,000, barley 9,691,000, potatoes 8,704,000, oats 2,807,000, rye 1,821,000; livestock (number of live animals) 24,282,000 pigs, 15,627,000 cattle, 1,296,000 sheep; roundwood 30,650,000 cu m; fish catch (1984) 326,764, of which Atlantic cod 78,424, blue mussel 59,311, Atlantic redfish 27,947. Mining and quarrying (metal content; 1986): iron ore 230,400; zinc 84,800; lead 16,700; copper 800. Manufacturing (value added at factor cost in DM; 1985): machinery and transport equipment 194,512,000,000, of which transport equipment 60,977,000,000, electrical equipment 60,139,000,000; chemicals (including medicinal products) 48,134,000,000; food and beverages 24,270,000,000; calculators and computers 14,970,000,000; semiprocessed iron and steel 13,545,000,000; plastics and other synthetic products 10,713,000,000; textiles 10,573,000,000; furniture and other wood products 8,993,000,000; printed matter 8,507,000,000; metalware 8,446,000,000; office machines 7,907,000,000; clocks and other precision products 7,336,000,000; clothing 6,666,000,000; cast metals 5,334,-000,000. Construction (1984): residential 193,817,000 cu m; nonresidential 150,794,000 cu m; restoration and conversion 2,797,000 cu m.

| Service enterprises (1985) | no. of enter- prises | no. of employees | weekly wage as a % of all wages | annual turnover (DM '000,000) |
|---|---|---|---|---|
| Gas | 115 | 24,000 | ... | 39,165 |
| Water | 163 | 18,000 | ... | 3,985 |
| Electrical power | 461 | 232,000 | ... | 118,388 |
| Transport | | | | |
| air | 180 | 38,000 | ... | 12,165 |
| buses, trains | 5,736 | 142,000 | ... | 11,164 |
| shipping | 1,851 | 11,000 | ... | ... |
| Communication | | | | |
| press | 2,200 | 211,000 | ... | 27,175 |
| film[9] | 615 | 3,000 | ... | 836 |
| Mail | 17,831 | 506,000 | ... | 47,875 |
| Hotels and restaurants | 186,784 | 839,000 | ... | 50,373 |
| Wholesale trade[10] | 132,000 | 1,239,000 | ... | ... |
| Retail trade[10] | 507,000 | 2,282,000 | ... | ... |
| Health services[10] | 88,000 | 318,000 | ... | ... |
| Financial services[10] | 36,000 | 427,000 | ... | ... |

Energy production (consumption): electricity (kW-hr; 1985) 406,714,000,000 (409,213,000,000); hard coal (metric tons; 1985) 88,489,000 (87,476,000); lignite-brown coal (metric tons; 1985) 120,718,000 (123,176,000); crude petroleum (barrels; 1985) 29,734,000 (505,506,000); petroleum products (metric tons; 1985) 73,921,000 (103,853,000); natural gas (cu m; 1985) 23,-315,000,000 (49,159,000,000).
*Population economically active* (1985): total 29,012,000; activity rate of total population 47.5% (participation rates: ages 15–64, 67.1%; female 39.4%; unemployed 8.2%).

| Price and earnings indexes (1980 = 100) | | | | | | | |
|---|---|---|---|---|---|---|---|
| | 1981 | 1982 | 1983 | 1984 | 1985 | 1986 | 1987[7] |
| Consumer price index | 106.3 | 111.9 | 115.6 | 118.4 | 121.0 | 120.7 | 121.3 |
| Monthly earnings index | 104.9 | 109.2 | 112.7 | 116.1 | 119.4 | 125.5 | ... |

*Household income and expenditure.* Average household size (1985) 2.3; average annual income per household (1985) DM 43,192 (U.S.$14,670); sources of take home income (1985): wages 83.9%, self-employment 7.7%, investments 8.5%; expenditure (1985): food 25.7%, rent 19.6%, transportation 14.8%, entertainment and education 9.0%, clothing and footwear 8.2%, household expenses 8.0%, electricity and gas 7.3%, other 7.4%.
*Land use* (1984): forested 30.0%; meadows and pastures 18.9%; agricultural and under permanent cultivation 30.4%; other 20.7%.

| Financial aggregates | 1981 | 1982 | 1983 | 1984 | 1985 | 1986 | 1987[11] |
|---|---|---|---|---|---|---|---|
| Exchange rate, DM per: | | | | | | | |
| U.S. dollar | 2.2548 | 2.3765 | 2.7238 | 3.1480 | 2.9440 | 2.1715 | 1.8470 |
| £ | 4.3022 | 3.8369 | 3.9511 | 3.6407 | 3.8163 | 3.1856 | 2.973 |
| SDR | 2.6245 | 2.6215 | 2.8517 | 3.0857 | 2.7035 | 2.3740 | 2.3512 |
| International reserves (U.S.$) | | | | | | | |
| Total (excl. gold; '000,000) | 43,719 | 44,762 | 42,674 | 40,141 | 44,380 | 51,734 | 60,891 |
| SDRs ('000,000) | 1,609 | 2,054 | 1,613 | 1,362 | 1,547 | 2,020 | 1,978 |
| Reserve pos. in IMF ('000,000) | 2,465 | 3,088 | 3,748 | 3,750 | 3,808 | 3,848 | 3,891 |
| Foreign exchange | 39,645 | 39,620 | 37,313 | 35,028 | 39,025 | 45,866 | 55,022 |
| Gold ('000,000 fine troy oz) | 95.18 | 95.18 | 95.18 | 95.18 | 95.18 | 95.18 | 95.18 |
| % world reserves | 10.00 | 10.05 | 10.06 | 10.06 | 10.03 | 10.03 | 10.05[7] |
| Interest and prices | | | | | | | |
| Central bank discount (%) | 7.5 | 5.0 | 4.0 | 4.5 | 4.0 | 3.5 | 3.0[7] |
| Gov't. bond yield (%) | 10.6 | 9.1 | 8.0 | 7.8 | 6.9 | 5.9 | 5.6[7] |
| Industrial share prices (1980 = 100) | 100.4 | 99.0 | 133.5 | 150.4 | 199.9 | 270.4 | 241.8[12] |
| Balance of payments (U.S.$ '000,000) | | | | | | | |
| Balance of visible trade | 14.85 | 23.50 | 19.84 | 20.34 | 26.95 | 53.63 | ... |
| Imports, f.o.b. | 150.66 | 141.08 | 138.69 | 139.59 | 145.38 | 175.30 | ... |
| Exports, f.o.b. | 165.51 | 164.58 | 158.53 | 159.93 | 172.73 | 228.93 | ... |
| Balance of invisibles | 10.73 | 10.58 | 7.55 | 4.92 | 4.42 | 5.09 | ... |
| Balance of payments, current account | −5.03 | 3.93 | 4.22 | 6.77 | 13.77 | 35.77 | ... |

## Foreign trade

| Balance of trade (current prices) | | | | | | |
|---|---|---|---|---|---|---|
| | 1981 | 1982 | 1983 | 1984 | 1985 | 1986 |
| DM '000,000 | +14,850 | +23,500 | +19,840 | +20,340 | +26,950 | +53,630 |
| % of total | 4.7% | 7.7% | 6.7% | 6.8% | 8.5% | 13.3% |

*Imports* (1986): DM 413,744,000,000 (machinery and transport equipment 26.3%, of which transport equipment 6.4%, electrical machinery 4.6%, office equipment 3.8%; mineral fuels 11.7%, of which crude petroleum and petroleum products 8.3%, natural gas 2.7%; food and beverages 10.3%, of which fruits and vegetables 3.2%, coffee, tea, and spices 2.0%, meat and meat products 1.3%; chemicals and chemical products 9.3%, of which plastics and synthetics 2.5%, medicinal products 1.0%; clothing and wearing apparel 5.4%; iron and steel 3.7%; textiles and yarn 3.6%; metallic ores and scrap metal 2.6%; paper and paper products 2.2%). *Major import sources:* The Netherlands 11.6%; France 11.4%; Italy 9.2%; United States 7.8%; United Kingdom 7.2%; Belgium–Luxembourg 7.1%; Japan 5.8%.
*Exports* (1986): DM 526,363,000,000 (machinery and transport equipment 47.7%, of which transport equipment 16.9%, specialized equipment for specific industries 6.6%, electrical machinery 6.0%; chemicals and chemical

products 12.9%, of which plastics and synthetics 3.3%, medicinal products 1.4%, dyes and dye products 1.3%; iron and steel 4.4%; food and beverages 4.1%, of which dairy products 1.0%, meat and meat products 0.7%; textiles and yarn 3.4%; paper and paper products 1.9%). *Major export destinations:* France 11.8%; United States 10.5%; The Netherlands 8.6%; United Kingdom 8.5%; Italy 8.2%; Belgium–Luxembourg 7.1%; Austria 5.9%; Switzerland 5.3%.

| Trade by commodity group (1986) | | imports | | exports | |
|---|---|---|---|---|---|
| SITC Group | | DM '000,000 | % | DM '000,000 | % |
| 00 | Food and live animals | 42,743 | 10.1 | 21,704 | 4.1 |
| 01 | Beverages and tobacco | 4,496 | 1.1 | 3,363 | 0.6 |
| 02 | Crude materials, excluding fuels | 26,505 | 6.4 | 9,226 | 1.8 |
| 03 | Mineral fuels, lubricants, and related materials | 48,500 | 11.7 | 8,617 | 1.6 |
| 04 | Animal and vegetable oils, fat, and waxes | 1,519 | 0.4 | 1,690 | 0.3 |
| 05 | Chemicals and related products, n.e.s. | 38,356 | 9.3 | 67,701 | 12.9 |
| 06 | Basic manufactures | 73,411 | 17.7 | 95,143 | 18.1 |
| 07 | Machinery and transport equipment | 108,956 | 26.3 | 251,319 | 47.8 |
| 08 | Miscellaneous manufactured articles | 56,084 | 13.5 | 55,917 | 10.6 |
| 09 | Goods not classified by kind | 13,635 | 3.3 | 11,684 | 2.2 |
| TOTAL | | 414,205 | 100.0[6] | 526,363 | 100.0 |

| Direction of trade (1985) | imports | | exports | |
|---|---|---|---|---|
| | U.S.$'000,000 | % | U.S.$'000,000 | % |
| Africa | 7,094 | 4.5 | 5,261 | 2.9 |
| Asia | 18,761 | 11.9 | 19,283 | 10.5 |
| Middle East | 5,291 | 3.4 | 8,720 | 4.7 |
| Japan | 7,120 | 4.5 | 2,707 | 1.5 |
| other Asia | 6,350 | 4.0 | 7,856 | 4.3 |
| South America | 5,333 | 3.4 | 2,532 | 1.4 |
| North and Central America | 13,262 | 8.4 | 23,246 | 12.6[6] |
| United States | 10,982 | 7.0 | 19,047 | 10.4 |
| other North and Central Am. | 2,280 | 1.4 | 4,199 | 2.3 |
| Europe | 111,678 | 71.0[6] | 131,754 | 71.6[6] |
| EEC | 76,560 | 48.6 | 86,575 | 47.1 |
| U.S.S.R. | 4,690 | 3.0 | 3,603 | 2.0 |
| other Europe | 30,428 | 19.3 | 41,576 | 22.6 |
| Oceania | 1,253 | 0.8 | 1,868 | 1.0 |
| TOTAL | 157,381 | 100.0 | 183,944 | 100.0 |

## Transport and communications

*Transport.* Railroads (1986): length 42,304 mi[3], 68,082 km[3]; passenger-mi 25,928,000,000, passenger-km 41,727,000,000; short ton-mi cargo 41,415,-000,000, metric ton-km cargo 60,465,000,000. Roads (1984): total length 304,499 mi, 490,045 km (paved 99%). Vehicles (1986): passenger cars 26,917,400; trucks and buses 1,364,100. Merchant marine (1986): vessels (100 gross tons and over) 1,752; total deadweight tonnage 7,744,600. Air transport (1986): passenger-mi 16,553,000,000, passenger-km 26,642,000,-000; short ton-mi cargo 2,026,662,000, metric ton-km cargo 2,958,887,000; airports (1987) with scheduled flights 28.
*Communications.* Daily newspapers (1986): total number 660; total circulation 25,439,000; circulation per 1,000 population 417. Radio (1986): total number of receivers 25,916,000 (1 per 2.4 persons). Television (1986): total number of receivers 23,011,000 (1 per 2.6 persons). Telephones (1986): 39,128,000 (1 per 1.6 persons).

## Education and health

| Education (1985–86) | schools | teachers | students | student/ teacher ratio |
|---|---|---|---|---|
| Primary (age 6–10) | 22,420 | 304,702 | 4,316,760 | 14.2 |
| Secondary (age 10–19) | 5,359 | 189,561 | 2,840,938 | 15.0 |
| Voc., teacher tr. | 8,224 | 91,215 | 2,776,435 | 30.4 |
| Higher | 110 | 327,055 | 1,336,395 | 4.1 |

*Literacy* (1986): virtually 100%.
*Health* (1985): physicians 153,895 (1 per 396 persons); hospital beds 674,742 (1 per 90 persons); infant mortality rate per 1,000 live births 8.9.
*Food* (1981–83): daily per capita caloric intake 3,431 (vegetable products 62%, animal products 38%); (1983) 129% of FAO recommended minimum requirement.

## Military

*Total active duty personnel* (1986): 485,800 (army 70.1%, navy 7.5%, air force 22.4%). *Military expenditure as percent of GNP* (1984): 3.3% (world 5.9%); per capita expenditure U.S.$328.

[1]January 1. [2]Berlin (West) is under tripartite (France, United Kingdom, United States) jurisdiction and is only administratively a part of West Germany. [3]1985. [4]Mining includes public utilities. [5]Includes 2,385,000 unemployed. [6]Detail does not add to total given because of rounding. [7]June. [8]Includes West Berlin. [9]1984. [10]1970. [11]July. [12]March.

# Ghana

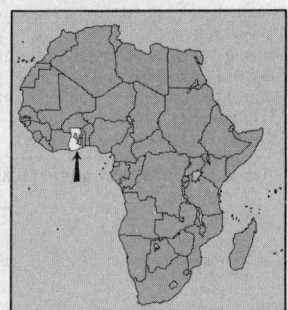

*Official name:* Republic of Ghana.
*Form of government:* republic with one ruling body (Provisional National Defense Council [9]).
*Head of state and government:* Chairman of the Provisional National Defense Council.
*Capital:* Accra.
*Official language:* English.
*Official religion:* none.
*Monetary unit:* 1 cedi (₵) = 100 pesewas; valuation (Oct. 5, 1987) 1 U.S.$ = ₵174.42; 1 £ = ₵283.24.

### Area and population

| Regions | Capitals | area sq mi | area sq km | population 1984 census |
|---|---|---|---|---|
| Ashanti | Kumasi | 9,417 | 24,389 | 2,089,683 |
| Brong-Ahafo | Sunyani | 15,273 | 39,557 | 1,179,407 |
| Central | Cape Coast | 3,794 | 9,826 | 1,145,520 |
| Eastern | Koforidua | 7,461 | 19,323 | 1,679,483 |
| Greater Accra | Accra | 1,253 | 3,245 | 1,420,066 |
| Northern | Tamale | 27,175 | 70,384 | 1,162,645 |
| Upper East | Bolgatanga | 3,414 | 8,842 | 771,584 |
| Upper West | Wa | 7,134 | 18,476 | 439,161 |
| Volta | Ho | 7,942 | 20,570 | 1,201,095 |
| Western | Sekondi-Takoradi | 9,236 | 23,921 | 1,116,930 |
| TOTAL | | 92,098[1] | 238,533 | 12,205,574 |

## Demography

*Population* (1987): 13,482,000.
*Density* (1987): persons per sq mi 146.4, persons per sq km 56.5.
*Urban–rural* (1984): urban 31.3%; rural 68.7%.
*Sex distribution* (1984): male 49.11%; female 50.89%.
*Age breakdown* (1985): under 15, 46.6%; 15–29, 26.1%; 30–44, 14.5%; 45–59, 8.3%; 60–74, 3.8%; 75 and over, 0.7%.
*Population projection:* (1990) 14,500,000; (2000) 18,700,000.
*Doubling time:* 22 years.
*Ethno-linguistic composition* (1983): Akan 52.4%; Mossi 15.8%; Ewe 11.9%; Ga-Adangme 7.8%; Gurma 3.3%; Yoruba 1.3%; other 7.5%.
*Religious affiliation* (1980): Christian 62.6%, of which Protestant 27.9%, Roman Catholic 18.7%, African indigenous 16.0%; traditional beliefs 21.4%; Muslim 15.7%, of which Aḥmadīyah 7.9%; other 0.3%.
*Major cities* (1984): Accra 859,600; Kumasi 348,900; Tamale 136,800; Tema 99,600; Sekondi-Takoradi 93,900.

## Vital statistics

*Birth rate* per 1,000 population (1980–85): 46.9 (world avg. 29.0); legitimate, n.a.; illegitimate, n.a.
*Death rate* per 1,000 population (1980–85): 14.6 (world avg. 11.0).
*Natural increase rate* per 1,000 population (1980–85): 32.3 (world avg. 18.0).
*Total fertility rate* (avg. births per childbearing woman; 1980–85): 6.5.
*Life expectancy* at birth (1980–85): male 50.3 years; female 53.8 years.
*Major causes of death* per 100,000 population: n.a.; however, major infectious diseases include malaria, tuberculosis, leprosy, trypanosomiasis (sleeping sickness), and onchocerciasis (river blindness).

## National economy

*Budget* (1986). Revenue: ₵85,200,000,000 (taxes on international trade 40%; domestic taxes 60%). Expenditures: ₵90,000,000,000 (recurrent expenditures 70.0%; development 29.0%, of which roads and highways 3.2%; health 0.7%; education 0.6%).
*Public debt* (external, outstanding; 1986): U.S.$1,391,300,000.
*Tourism:* receipts from visitors (1984) U.S.$2,000,000; expenditures by nationals abroad (1983) U.S.$25,000,000.
*Production* (metric tons except as noted). Agriculture, forestry, fishing (1985): roots and tubers 3,823,000 (of which cassava 2,373,000, yams 850,000, taro 600,000), bananas and plantains 699,000, cereals 640,000 (of which corn [maize] 460,000, rice 64,000, sorghum 62,000, millet 54,000), cocoa 200,-000, peanuts (groundnuts) 128,000, sugarcane 110,000, coconuts 108,000, oranges 35,000, lemons 30,000, palm kernels 30,000, pulses 11,000; livestock (number of live animals) 2,000,000 goats, 2,000,000 sheep, 820,000 cattle, 375,000 pigs, 14,000,000 chickens; roundwood 8,459,000 cu m; fish catch 254,171 (of which anchovies 43,073). Mining and quarrying (1985): manganese ore 350,270; bauxite 180,286; gold 9,306 kg; diamonds 631,-801 carats. Manufacturing (1985): kerosine, gasoline, and diesel 614,000; cement 336,000; wheat flour 43,306; cocoa cake, cocoa butter, and cocoa liquor 19,852; soap 12,406; iron rods 3,360; margarine 941; toothpaste 122; cloth 12,600,000 metres; beer 429,000 hectolitres; evaporated milk 146,-000 hectolitres; ice cream 1,152 hectolitres; cigarettes 1,942,000,000 units. Construction (value added in ₵'000; 1983): 2,796,100. Energy production (consumption): electricity (kW-hr; 1985) 3,036,000,000 (2,766,000,000); coal (metric tons; 1985) none (2,000); crude petroleum (barrels; 1985) 685,000 (8,188,000); petroleum products (metric tons; 1985) 817,000 (600,000); natural gas, none (n.a.).
*Household income and expenditure.* Average household size (1980) 5.1; average annual income per household (1978) ₵9,600 (U.S.$[2]); sources of income: n.a.; expenditure (1978): food and beverages 35.4%, housing 14.8%, clothing and footwear 14.7%, transport and communication 6.1%, health care 2.3%.

*Gross national product* (at current market prices; 1985): U.S.$4,960,000,000 (U.S.$390 per capita).

### Structure of gross domestic product and labour force

| | 1983 in value ₵'000,000 | 1983 % of total value | 1984 labour force | 1984 % of labour force |
|---|---|---|---|---|
| Agriculture | 109,927 | 59.7 | 2,143,000 | 45.0 |
| Mining | 1,944 | 1.0 | | |
| Manufacturing | 7,101 | 3.9 | 380,000 | 8.0 |
| Construction | 2,798 | 1.5 | | |
| Public utilities | 358 | 0.2 | | |
| Transportation and communication | 7,663 | 4.2 | | |
| Trade | 43,120 | 23.4 | 2,240,000 | 47.0 |
| Finance | 3,311 | 1.8 | | |
| Pub. admin., defense | 7,822 | 4.2 | | |
| Services | 636 | 0.5 | | |
| Other | −640[3] | −0.4[3] | | |
| TOTAL | 184,038[1] | 100.0 | 4,763,000 | 100.0 |

*Population economically active* (1985): total 4,963,000; activity rate of total population 36.5% (participation rates: ages 15–64, 68.1%; female 40.6%; unemployed [1984] 10.8%).

### Price and earnings indexes (1980 = 100)

| | 1981 | 1982 | 1983 | 1984 | 1985 | 1986 | 1987[4] |
|---|---|---|---|---|---|---|---|
| Consumer price index | 216.5 | 264.8 | 590.1 | 824.1 | 909.1 | 1,132.4 | 1,544.3 |
| Earnings index | ... | 139.9 | 240.8 | ... | ... | ... | ... |

*Land use* (1984): forested 36.9%; meadows and pastures 14.9%; agricultural and under permanent cultivation 12.3%; other 35.9%.

## Foreign trade

### Balance of trade (current prices)

| | 1981 | 1982 | 1983 | 1984 | 1985 | 1986 |
|---|---|---|---|---|---|---|
| ₵'000,000 | +79.0 | +588.0 | −85.0 | +637.1 | −4,070.0 | +11,578.0 |
| % of total | 1.4% | 13.9% | 0.4% | 1.6% | 5.8% | 8.1% |

*Imports* (1982): ₵2,781,632,000 (petroleum products 35.6%; machinery and transport equipment 20.8%; chemicals 11.0%; basic manufactures 10.8%; food and live animals 9.9%, of which wheat and flour 1.3%, rice 0.8%). *Major import sources:* Nigeria 21.3%; United States 16.2%; United Kingdom 15.0%; Libya 11.2%; West Germany 7.0%; Togo 4.0%.
*Exports* (1982): ₵2,211,732,000 (cocoa beans 47.6%[5]; gold 14.5%; cocoa products 2.9%; logs and timber 2.0%; industrial diamonds 0.6%). *Major export destinations:* United States 20.3%; Switzerland 16.8%; The Netherlands 16.4%; United Kingdom 14.4%; West Germany 9.9%; Japan 7.8%; U.S.S.R. 6.3%.

## Transport and communications

*Transport.* Railroads (1985): length 592 mi, 953 km; passenger-mi 125,958,-000, passenger-km 201,101,000; short ton-mi cargo 50,500,000, metric ton-km cargo 73,800,000. Roads (1985): total length 17,600 mi, 28,300 km (paved 20%). Vehicles (1983): passenger cars 52,864; trucks and buses 24,-312. Merchant marine (1986): vessels (100 gross tons and over) 137; total deadweight tonnage 178,268. Air transport (1986): passenger-mi 185,497,-000, passenger-km 298,529,000; short ton-mi cargo 6,907,000, metric ton-km cargo 10,084,000; airports (1987) with scheduled flights 4.
*Communications.* Daily newspapers (1986): total number 4; total circulation 460,000; circulation per 1,000 population 35. Radio (1986): 3,000,000 receivers (1 per 4.4 persons). Television (1986): 140,000 receivers (1 per 92 persons). Telephones (1985): 72,022 (1 per 173 persons).

## Education and health

### Education (1984–85)

| | schools | teachers[6] | students | student/ teacher ratio |
|---|---|---|---|---|
| Primary (6–11) | 8,965 | 51,631[7] | 1,464,624 | ... |
| Secondary (12–18) | 5,589 | 32,795[7] | 723,385 | ... |
| Voc., teacher tr. | 61 | 1,727 | 24,827 | ... |
| Higher | 3 | 1,041[8] | 7,878 | ... |

*Educational attainment* (1970). Percent of population age 25 and over having: no formal schooling 77.7%; primary education 5.8%; some secondary 12.8%; complete secondary 3.3%; higher 0.4%. *Literacy* (1985): total population age 15 and over literate 3,835,000 (53.2%); males literate 2,261,000 (64.1%); females literate 1,574,000 (42.8%).
*Health:* physicians (1982) 1,435 (1 per 8,278 persons); hospital beds (1981) 20,582 (1 per 563 persons); infant mortality rate per 1,000 live births (1980–85) 98.
*Food* (1981–83): daily per capita caloric intake 1,621 (vegetable products 94%, animal products 6%); (1983) 66% of FAO minimum recommended requirement.

## Military

*Total active duty personnel* (1986): 11,200 (army 80.4%, navy 10.7%, air force 8.9%). *Military expenditure as percent of GNP* (1984): 0.6% (world 5.9%); per capita expenditure U.S.$29.

---

[1]Detail does not add to total given because of rounding. [2]Unofficial exchange rate (7.5 to 9.9 times the official rate) does not permit meaningful conversion into other currencies. [3]Import duties, less imputed bank service charge. [4]April. [5]In 1984, 1985, and 1986, cocoa beans averaged more than 60% of export earnings. [6]1983–84. [7]Includes untrained teachers. [8]1980–81.

# Greece

*Official name:* Ellinikí Dimokratía
(Hellenic Republic).
*Form of government:* unitary multiparty
republic with one legislative house
(Greek Chamber of Deputies [300]).
*Chief of state:* President.
*Head of government:* Prime Minister.
*Capital:* Athens.
*Official language:* Greek.
*Official religion:* Eastern Orthodox.
*Monetary unit:* 1 drachma (Dr) = 100
leptae; valuation (Oct. 5, 1987)
1 U.S.$ = Dr 140.98; 1 £ = Dr 228.93.

| Area and population[1] | area | | population |
|---|---|---|---|
| | | | 1981 |
| Regions | sq mi | sq km | census |
| Aegean Islands | 3,522 | 9,122 | 428,533 |
| Central Greece and Évvoia | 9,417 | 24,391 | 1,099,841 |
| Crete | 3,219 | 8,336 | 502,165 |
| Greater Athens | 165 | 427 | 3,027,331 |
| Ionian Islands | 891 | 2,307 | 182,651 |
| Ipiros | 3,553 | 9,203 | 324,541 |
| Macedonia | 13,066 | 33,841 | 2,120,481 |
| Pelopónnisos | 8,254 | 21,379 | 1,012,528 |
| Thessalía | 5,420 | 14,037 | 695,654 |
| Thráki | 3,312 | 8,578 | 345,220 |
| **Autonomous administration** | | | |
| Ayion Oros (Mt. Athos) | 130 | 336 | 1,472 |
| TOTAL | 50,949 | 131,957 | 9,740,417 |

## Demography

*Population* (1987): 10,010,000.
*Density* (1987): persons per sq mi 196.5, persons per sq km 75.9.
*Urban–rural* (1985): urban 57.7%; rural 42.3%.
*Sex distribution* (1985): male 49.19%; female 50.81%.
*Age breakdown* (1985): under 15, 20.9%; 15–29, 22.1%; 30–44, 19.1%; 45–59, 19.8%; 60–74, 12.5%; 75 and over, 5.6%.
*Population projection:* (1990) 10,100,000; (2000) 10,600,000.
*Doubling time:* n.a.; doubling time exceeds 100 years.
*Ethnic composition* (1983): Greek 95.5%; Macedonian 1.5%; Turkish 0.9%; Albanian 0.6%; other 1.5%.
*Religious affiliation* (1980): Christian 98.1%, of which Greek Orthodox 97.6%, Roman Catholic 0.4%, Protestant 0.1%; Muslim 1.5%; other 0.4%.
*Major cities* (1981): Athens 885,737; Thessaloníki 406,413; Piraiévs 196,389; Pátrai 142,163; Peristérion 140,858.

## Vital statistics

*Birth rate* per 1,000 population (1986): 11.3 (world avg. 26.0); legitimate 98.1%; illegitimate 1.9%.
*Death rate* per 1,000 population (1986): 9.2 (world avg. 9.9).
*Natural increase rate* per 1,000 population (1986): 2.1 (world avg. 16.1).
*Total fertility rate* (avg. births per childbearing woman; 1986): 2.2.
*Marriage rate* per 1,000 population (1986): 5.9.
*Divorce rate* per 1,000 population (1982): 0.7.
*Life expectancy* at birth (1980): male 72.2 years; female 76.4 years.
*Major causes of death* per 100,000 population (1986): malignant neoplasms (cancers) 184.0; cerebrovascular disease 177.0; diseases of pulmonary circulation and other forms of heart disease 168.8; ischemic heart disease 97.9.

## National economy

*Budget* (1985). Revenue: Dr 1,110,819,000,000 (indirect taxes 65.0%; direct taxes 27.3%; government entrepreneurship 4.7%). Expenditures: Dr 1,500,-940,000,000 (personnel outlays 37.0%, of which salaries 29.2%, pensions 7.8%; servicing of public debt 18.7%; subsidies 11.4%; grants 11.0%).
*Public debt* (1984): U.S.$4,461,745,000.
*Tourism* (1985): receipts from visitors U.S.$1,428,000,000; expenditures by nationals abroad U.S.$368,000,000.
*Production* (metric tons except as noted). Agriculture, forestry, fishing (1985): sugarbeets 2,700,000, tomatoes 2,512,000, corn (maize) 1,800,000, wheat 1,792,000, grapes 1,687,000, olives 1,420,000, potatoes 1,100,000, barley 653,000, oranges 650,000, cotton 181,000, onions 145,000, tobacco 133,000, rice 106,000; livestock (number of live animals) 7,900,000 sheep, 4,660,000 goats, 1,115,000 pigs, 757,000 cattle, 230,000 asses, 38,000,000 chickens; roundwood 2,683,000 cu m; fish catch 102,000. Mining and quarrying (1985): bauxite 2,461,200; iron ore 800,000; zinc ore 22,000; lead ore 20,000. Manufacturing (value added in Dr; 1983): food, beverages, and tobacco 95,100,000,000; textiles 74,270,000,000; chemicals 62,660,000,000; clothing 44,380,000,000; transport equipment 33,919,000,000. Construction (cu m; 1984): residential 28,004,000; nonresidential 12,364,000. Energy production (consumption) (kW-hr; 1985) 27,740,000,000 (28,479,000,000); coal (metric tons; 1985) 35,888,000 (36,279,000); crude petroleum (barrels; 1985) 8,972,000 (88,554,000); petroleum products (metric tons; 1985) 11,-364,000 (9,567,000); natural gas (cu m; 1985) 85,184,000 (85,184,000).
*Household income and expenditure.* Average household size (1982) 3.3; income per household (1982) Dr 252,300 (U.S.$3,777); sources of income (1984): wages and salaries 43.0%, property and entrepreneurship 40.8%, transfer payments 13.3%, other 2.9%; expenditure (1984): food, beverages, and tobacco 42.5%, housing 14.9%, clothing and footwear 8.2%, other 34.4%.
*Gross national product* (at current market prices; 1985): U.S.$35,250,000,000 (U.S.$3,550 per capita).

## Structure of gross domestic product and labour force

| | 1984 | | | |
|---|---|---|---|---|
| | in value Dr '000,000 | % of total value | labour force | % of labour force |
| Agriculture | 615,150 | 18.5 | 1,047,275 | 27.1 |
| Mining | 69,700 | 2.1 | 26,932 | 0.7 |
| Manufacturing | 602,200 | 18.1 | 723,427 | 18.7 |
| Construction | 211,700 | 6.4 | 283,930 | 7.3 |
| Public utilities | 66,950 | 2.0 | 30,585 | 0.8 |
| Transportation and communication | 261,800 | 7.9 | 279,194 | 7.2 |
| Trade | 432,930 | 13.0 | 569,348 | 14.7 |
| Finance | 84,820 | 2.5 | 131,338 | 3.4 |
| Pub. admin., defense | 557,800 | 16.7 | 592,897 | 15.4 |
| Services | 246,850 | 7.4 | | |
| Other | 180,750 | 5.4 | 182,885[2] | 4.7[2] |
| TOTAL | 3,330,650 | 100.0 | 3,867,811 | 100.0 |

*Population economically active* (1984): total 3,867,811; activity rate of total population 39.1% (participation rates: ages 16–64, 57.4%; female 34.6%; unemployed 4.2%).

## Price and earnings indexes (1980 = 100)

| | 1981 | 1982 | 1983 | 1984 | 1985 | 1986 | 1987[3] |
|---|---|---|---|---|---|---|---|
| Consumer price index | 124.5 | 150.6 | 181.1 | 214.5 | 255.9 | 314.8 | 371.0 |
| Hourly earnings index | 127.2 | 169.8 | 202.7 | 256.0 | 306.8 | ... | ... |

*Land use* (1984): forested 20.0%; meadows and pastures 40.2%; agricultural and under permanent cultivation 30.4%; other 9.4%.

## Foreign trade

### Balance of trade (current prices)

| | 1981 | 1982 | 1983 | 1984 | 1985 | 1986 |
|---|---|---|---|---|---|---|
| Dr '000,000 | −199.1 | −303.0 | −356.6 | −416.6 | −621.2 | −614.8 |
| % of total | 29.5% | 34.6% | 31.2% | 27.7% | 33.0% | 28.0% |

*Imports* (1986): Dr 1,587,214,000,000 (machinery and transport equipment 25.8%, of which passenger cars 3.4%; food, beverages, and tobacco 15.7%, of which meat products 4.8%, milk and cream 2.0%, coffee 0.9%; crude petroleum 14.4%; chemical products 10.5%, of which plastics and resins 2.6%, medicinal and pharmaceutical products 1.4%). *Major import sources:* West Germany 21.1%; Italy 11.5%; France 8.1%; The Netherlands 6.8%; Saudi Arabia 6.4%; Japan 6.1%; United Kingdom 4.1%.
*Exports* (1986): Dr 789,994,600,000 (food, beverages, and tobacco 27.2%, of which tobacco 3.8%, olive oil 3.3%, concentrated tomato puree 1.5%; clothing 19.2%; textile yarn 5.8%; petroleum products 4.6%). *Major export destinations:* West Germany 23.7%; Italy 13.5%; France 9.5%; United States 7.1%; United Kingdom 6.8%.

## Transport and communications

*Transport.* Railroads (1986): route length 1,534 mi, 2,469 km; passenger-mi 1,036,000,000, passenger-km 1,668,000,000; short ton-mi cargo 485,000,-000, metric ton-km cargo 708,000,000. Roads (1985): total length 64,191 mi, 103,306 km (paved 83%). Vehicles (1985): passenger cars 1,264,375; trucks and buses 620,724. Merchant marine (1986): vessels (100 gross tons and over) 2,255; total deadweight tonnage 28,390,800. Air transport (1986): passenger-mi 3,967,000,000, passenger-km 6,384,000,000; short ton-mi cargo 69,400,000, metric ton-km cargo 101,352,000; airports (1987) with scheduled flights 29.
*Communications.* Daily newspapers (1983): total number 124; total circulation 981,200[4]; circulation per 1,000 population, n.a. Radio (1985): total number of receivers 4,000,000 (1 per 2.5 persons). Television (1985): total number of receivers 1,725,000 (1 per 5.8 persons). Telephones (1985): 3,529,149 (1 per 2.8 persons).

## Education and health

### Education (1984–85)

| | schools | teachers | students | student/ teacher ratio |
|---|---|---|---|---|
| Primary (age 6–12) | 9,229 | 36,093 | 904,426 | 25.1 |
| Secondary (age 12–18) | 2,613 | 36,851 | 701,711 | 19.0 |
| Voc., teacher tr. | 601 | 8,427 | 101,558 | 12.0 |
| Higher | 102 | 11,735 | 167,967 | 14.3 |

*Educational attainment* (1981). Percent of population age 25 and over having: no formal schooling (illiterate) 11.4%; some primary education 16.8%; completed primary 44.1%; lower secondary 6.0%; higher secondary 13.5%; some postsecondary 2.5%; a degree from institution of higher education 4.9%. *Literacy* (1985): total population age 14 and over literate 7,209,500 (93.8%); males literate 3,555,000 (97.3%); females literate 3,654,500 (90.6%).
*Health* (1984): physicians 28,212 (1 per 351 persons); hospital beds 57,081 (1 per 173 persons); infant mortality rate per 1,000 live births (1986) 12.2.
*Food* (1981–83): daily per capita caloric intake 3,672 (vegetable products 77%, animal products 23%); 143% of FAO recommended minimum requirement.

## Military

*Total active duty personnel* (1986): 209,000 (army 79.2%, navy 9.3%, air force 11.5%). *Military expenditure as percent of GNP* (1984): 7.2% (world 5.9%); per capita expenditure U.S.$237.

[1]For reasons of space, the principal political subdivisions, or departments (*nomoi*), are not included in the table. Regions given are purely geographic entities except for Ayion Oros (Mt. Athos), which is a self-governing monastic community. The creation of 13 new administrative regions was approved by the Greek Cabinet on Jan. 19, 1987. [2]Mostly unemployed. [3]June. [4]For 22 dailies only.

# Greenland

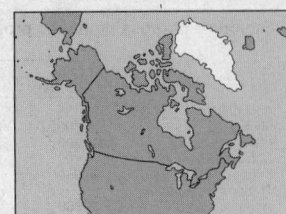

*Official name:* Kalaallit Nunaat (Greenlandic); Grønland (Danish) (Greenland).
*Political status:* integral part of the Danish realm with a local legislative house (Landsting [27]).
*Chief of state:* Danish Monarch.
*Heads of government:* High Commissioner (for Denmark); Prime Minister (for Greenland).
*Capital:* Nuuk (Godthåb).
*Official languages:* Greenlandic; Danish.
*Official religion:* Lutheran Church of Greenland (Evangelical Lutheran).
*Monetary unit:* 1 Danish krone (DKr) = 100 øre; valuation (Oct. 5, 1987) 1 U.S.$ = DKr 7.09; 1 £ = DKr 11.51.

### Area and population

| Counties Communes | area sq mi | area sq km | population 1987 estimate[1] |
|---|---|---|---|
| Avanersuaq (Nordgrønland) | 41,200 | 106,700 | |
| Qaanaaq (Thule) | ... | ... | 794 |
| Kitaa (Vestgrønland) | 46,000 | 119,100 | |
| Aasiaat (Egedesminde) | ... | ... | 3,524 |
| Ilulissat (Jakobshavn) | ... | ... | 4,522 |
| Ivittuut (Ivigtut) | ... | ... | 29 |
| Kangaatsiaq (Kangåtsiaq) | ... | ... | 1,263 |
| Maniitsoq (Sukkertoppen) | ... | ... | 3,992 |
| Nanortalik | ... | ... | 2,653 |
| Narsaq (Narssaq) | ... | ... | 2,131 |
| Nuuk (Godthåb) | ... | ... | 11,649 |
| Paamiut (Frederikshåb) | ... | ... | 2,611 |
| Qaqortoq (Julianehåb) | ... | ... | 3,436 |
| Qasigiannguit (Christianshåb) | ... | ... | 1,778 |
| Qeqertarsuaq (Godhavn) | ... | ... | 1,076 |
| Sisimiut (Holsteinsborg) | ... | ... | 4,948 |
| Upernavik | ... | ... | 2,229 |
| Uummannaq (Umanaq) | ... | ... | 2,583 |
| Tunu (Østgrønland) | 44,800 | 115,900 | |
| Illoqqortoormiut (Scoresbysund) | ... | ... | 549 |
| Tasiilaq (Angmagssalik) | ... | ... | 2,817 |
| TOTAL (ICE-FREE) | 131,900 | 341,700 | 53,733[2] |
| Permanent ice[3] | 708,100 | 1,833,300 | |
| TOTAL | 840,000 | 2,175,000 | |

## Demography

*Population* (1987): 54,000.
*Density*[3] (1987): persons per sq mi 0.41, persons per sq km 0.16.
*Urban–rural* (1987): urban (town) 79.4%; rural (settlement) 20.6%.
*Sex distribution* (1987): male 54.41%; female 45.59%.
*Age breakdown* (1987): under 15, 24.6%; 15–29, 33.0%; 30–44, 23.6%; 45–59, 12.9%; 60–74, 4.8%; 75 and over, 1.1%.
*Population projection:* (1990) 56,000; (2000) 61,000.
*Doubling time:* 60 years.
*Ethnic composition* (by place of birth; 1987): born in Greenland 82.7%; born elsewhere 17.3%.
*Religious affiliation* (1980): Protestant 97.8%; other 2.2%.
*Major towns* (1986): Nuuk (Godthåb) 10,972; Sisimiut (Holsteinsborg) 4,583; Ilulissat (Jakobshavn) 4,043; Aasiaat (Egedesminde) 3,200; Maniitsoq (Sukkertoppen) 3,055.

## Vital statistics

*Birth rate* per 1,000 population (1986): 19.7 (world avg. 26.0); (1985) legitimate 28.8%; illegitimate 71.2%.
*Death rate* per 1,000 population (1986): 8.4 (world avg. 9.9).
*Natural increase rate* per 1,000 population (1986): 11.3 (world avg. 16.1).
*Total fertility rate* (avg. births per childbearing woman; 1985): 2.2.
*Marriage rate* per 1,000 population (1985): 6.5.
*Divorce rate* per 1,000 population (1985): 2.7.
*Life expectancy* at birth (1981–85): male 60.4 years; female 66.3 years.
*Major causes of death* per 100,000 population (1985): heart disease 165.6; malignant neoplasms (cancers) 120.4; suicide 101.5; accidents 90.3%.

## National economy

*Budget* (1985). Revenue: DKr 1,627,500,000 (contributions from Danish government 54.9%, fishing licenses 12.9%, customs duties 12.8%, income tax 11.8%). Expenditures: DKr 1,279,900,000 (education 40.0%, social welfare 30.2%, home-rule subsidies 13.0%, administration 10.7%).
*Public debt* (external, outstanding): n.a.
*Tourism:* receipts from visitors, n.a.; expenditures by nationals abroad, n.a.
*Production* (metric tons except as noted). Agriculture, forestry, hunting, fishing (1985): fish catch 149,424; livestock (number of live animals) 21,443 sheep, 5,980 reindeer; hunting (number of animals killed; 1983) 92,794 seals, 2,308 whales, of which 601 white whales, 492 narwhals; hunting products (number) 50,526 seal skins, 1,182 fox skins, 24 polar bear skins. Mining and quarrying (1985): cryolite 111,500; zinc concentrates 70,711; lead concentrates 50,526; silver 500,000 troy oz. Manufacturing (1985): principally handicrafts and food processing. Construction (1984): residential 39,900 sq m; nonresidential 28,400 sq m. Energy production (consumption): electric-

ity (kW-hr; 1984) 181,700,000 (181,700,000); coal (1983) none (1,000); crude petroleum, none (n.a.); petroleum products (cu m; 1986) none (182,500); natural gas, none (n.a.).
*Gross national product* (at current market prices; 1984): U.S.$390,000,000 (U.S.$7,270 per capita).

### Structure of gross domestic product and labour force

| | 1979 in value DKr '000,000 | 1979 % of total value | 1976 labour force | 1976 % of labour force |
|---|---|---|---|---|
| Agriculture, fishing, hunting, and sheep breeding | 335.3 | 16.0 | 3,222 | 15.1 |
| Mining, manufacturing | 661.2 | 31.6 | 3,205 | 15.0 |
| Construction | 574.9 | 27.4 | 3,112 | 14.5 |
| Transportation and communication | 100.4 | 4.8 | 1,842 | 8.6 |
| Trade | 167.8 | 8.0 | 2,153 | 10.1 |
| Public utilities | | | 293 | 1.4 |
| Public administration, education | 255.0 | 12.2 | 3,233 | 15.1 |
| Social and health services | | | 2,141 | 10.0 |
| Other | | | 2,177 | 10.2 |
| TOTAL | 2,094.6 | 100.0 | 21,378 | 100.0 |

*Population economically active* (1976): total 21,378; activity rate of total population 43.0% (participation rates: ages 15–64, n.a.; female 33.1%; unemployed, n.a.).

### Price and earnings indexes (January 1980 = 100)

| | 1981 | 1982 | 1983 | 1984 | 1985 | 1986 | 1987 |
|---|---|---|---|---|---|---|---|
| Consumer price index[4] | 113.3 | 129.9 | 145.7 | 157.4 | 172.2 | 181.5 | 186.4 |
| Monthly earnings index[4] | 110.9 | 128.4 | 141.2 | 155.8 | 169.7 | 177.6 | ... |

*Household income and expenditure.* Average household size (1976) 3.9; taxable income per taxpayer (1980) DKr 84,160 (U.S.$9,200); sources of income: n.a.; expenditure (1985): food 33.6%, housing 13.8%, clothing 9.2%, fuel and light 7.8%, transportation and communications 7.8%.
*Land use* (1984): forested 0.1%; meadows and pastures 0.7%; agricultural and under permanent cultivation, none; other (principally ice cap) 99.3%.

## Foreign trade

### Balance of trade (current prices)

| | 1981 | 1982 | 1983 | 1984 | 1985 | 1986 |
|---|---|---|---|---|---|---|
| DKr '000,000 | −772 | −875 | −779 | −1,085 | −1,303 | −834 |
| % of total | 22.4% | 23.4% | 19.2% | 23.6% | 26.3% | 16.7% |

*Imports* (1986): DKr 2,912,000,000 (machinery and transport equipment 29.4%, of which ships and aircraft 6.2%, automobiles 1.7%; food 20.1%; metal products and semimanufactures 18.9%; mineral fuels 9.0%). *Major import sources:* Denmark 65.5%; Norway 5.5%; Sweden 5.5%; West Germany 4.8%; Japan 4.6%.
*Exports* (1986): DKr 2,078,000,000 (shrimp, prawns, and mollusks 70.2%; fish and fish products 20.5%; zinc 11.3%; lead 2.2%). *Major export destinations:* Denmark 82.2%; France 6.2%; West Germany 3.1%; Finland 2.5%; United Kingdom 1.4%.

## Transport and communications

*Transport.* Railroads: none. Roads: n.a. Vehicles (1986): passenger cars 1,781; trucks and buses 809. Merchant marine (1986): vessels (100 gross tons and over) 50; total deadweight tonnage, n.a. Air transport (1983): passenger-mi 8,664,000, passenger-km 13,944,000; short ton-mi cargo 162,000, metric ton-km cargo 236,000. Passenger conveyance within Greenland (1985): by ship 31,522[5]; by aircraft 88,688. Airports (1987) with scheduled flights 20.
*Communications.* Daily newspapers: none. Radio (1985): total number of receivers 13,600 (1 per 3.9 persons). Television (1985): total number of receivers 12,000 (1 per 4.4 persons). Telephone subscribers (1984): 11,554 (1 per 4.6 persons).

## Education and health

### Education (1986–87)

| | schools | teachers | students | student/ teacher ratio |
|---|---|---|---|---|
| Primary (age 6–15) | 94 | | 7,065 | ... |
| Secondary (age 15–19) | 37[6] | 1,136 | 2,072[7] | ... |
| Voc., teacher tr. | 5[6] | | 1,469[8] | ... |

*Educational attainment* (1970). Percent of adult population ages 14 through 39 having: primary education 61.7%; secondary 25.9%. *Literacy* (1979): virtually 100%.
*Health* (1985): physicians 61 (1 per 871 persons); hospital beds 570 (1 per 93 persons); infant mortality rate per 1,000 live births 24.6.
*Food:* daily per capita caloric intake, n.a.

## Military

*Total active duty personnel*[9] (1980): 320.

---

[1]January 1. [2]Includes 1,149 people not distributed by county. [3]Area of permanent ice not distributable by county; population density calculated with reference to ice-free area only. [4]Based on January only. [5]For Western Greenland only. [6]1979–80. [7]Does not include 11 students studying in Denmark. [8]1985–86. [9]Foreign troops only. Mostly air force personnel from the United States.

# Grenada

*Official name:* Grenada.
*Form of government:* constitutional
monarchy with two legislative houses
(Senate [13]; House of Representatives
[15]).
*Chief of state:* British Monarch
represented by governor-general.
*Head of government:* Prime Minister.
*Capital:* St. George's.
*Official language:* English.
*Official religion:* none.
*Monetary unit:* 1 East Caribbean dollar
(EC$) = 100 cents; valuation (Oct. 5,
1987) 1 U.S.$ = EC$2.70;
1 £ = EC$4.38.

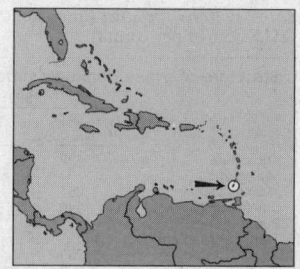

| Area and population[1] | | area | | population |
|---|---|---|---|---|
| | | sq mi | sq km | 1981 census |
| **Parishes** | **Capitals** | | | |
| Carriacou | — | 13 | 34 | 4,671 |
| St. Andrew | — | 35 | 91 | 22,425 |
| St. David | — | 18 | 47 | 10,195 |
| St. George's | — | 26 | 67 | 29,369 |
| St. John | — | 15 | 39 | 8,328 |
| St. Mark | — | 9 | 23 | 3,968 |
| St. Patrick | — | 17 | 44 | 10,132 |
| TOTAL | | 133 | 345 | 89,088 |

## Demography

*Population* (1987): 104,000.
*Density* (1987): persons per sq mi 782.0, persons per sq km 301.4.
*Urban–rural:* n.a.
*Sex distribution* (1981): male 48.58%; female 51.42%.
*Age breakdown* (1985): under 15, 35.1%; 15–29, 35.1%; 30–44, 12.4%; 45–59,
9.3%; 60–74, 6.2%; 75 and over, 2.1%.
*Population projection:* (1990) 111,000; (2000) 134,000.
*Doubling time:* 29 years.
*Ethnic composition* (1983): black 84%; mixed 12%; East Indian 3%; white 1%.
*Religious affiliation* (1980): Roman Catholic 64.4%; Protestant 34.5%, of
which Anglican 20.7%, Seventh-day Adventist 3.1%, Methodist 2.1%; other
1.1%.
*Major locality* (1981): St. George's 4,788.

## Vital statistics

*Birth rate* per 1,000 population (1983): 31.4 (world avg. 29.0); (1979) legiti-
mate 22.5%; illegitimate 77.5%.
*Death rate* per 1,000 population (1983): 6.9 (world avg. 11.0).
*Natural increase rate* per 1,000 population (1983): 24.5 (world avg. 18.0).
*Total fertility rate* (avg. births per childbearing woman; 1984): 3.5.
*Marriage rate* per 1,000 population (1979): 3.9.
*Divorce rate* per 1,000 population (1979): 0.2.
*Life expectancy* at birth (1980–85): male 65.4 years; female 69.4 years.
*Major causes of death* per 100,000 population (1981): diseases of the cir-
culatory system 186.3; malignant neoplasms (cancers) 90.9; endocrine,
nutritional, and metabolic diseases 48.3; diseases of the respiratory system
41.5; diseases of the digestive system 31.4; ill-defined conditions 158.3.

## National economy

*Budget* (1987). Revenue: EC$226,300,000 (internal sources 56.2%; external
loans and grants 43.8%). Expenditures: EC$226,300,000 (current expen-
diture 64.6%, of which debt service 15.1%, education 9.5%, health and
housing 7.4%; development expenditure 35.4%, of which road and bridge
improvement 10.5%).
*Public debt* (external, outstanding; 1985): U.S.$41,400,000.
*Tourism:* receipts from visitors (1986) U.S.$26,200,000; expenditures by na-
tionals abroad (1985) U.S.$3,000,000.
*Gross national product* (1985): U.S.$90,000,000 (U.S.$900 per capita).

| Structure of gross domestic product and labour force | | | | |
|---|---|---|---|---|
| | 1986[2] | | 1981 | |
| | in value EC$'000,000 | % of total value | labour force[3] | % of labour force |
| Agriculture | 41.8 | 16.9 | 7,987 | 28.7 |
| Quarrying | 0.9 | 0.4 | 75 | 0.3 |
| Manufacturing | 11.8 | 4.8 | 1,566 | 5.6 |
| Construction | 22.2 | 9.0 | 2,863 | 10.3 |
| Public utilities | 5.3 | 2.1 | 371 | 1.3 |
| Transportation and communication | 33.4 | 13.5 | 1,689 | 6.1 |
| Trade | 49.2 | 19.9 | 3,902 | 14.0 |
| Finance, real estate | 40.7 | 16.5 | 367 | 1.3 |
| Pub. admin., defense | 54.0 | 21.8 | 1,682 | 6.0 |
| Services | ... | ... | 2,566 | 9.2 |
| Other | −12.0[4] | −4.9[4] | 4,779 | 17.2 |
| TOTAL | 247.3 | 100.0 | 27,847 | 100.0 |

*Production* (metric tons except as noted). Agriculture, forestry, fishing (1985):
coconuts 8,000, bananas 7,800[5], sugarcane 4,000, citrus fruits 4,000, roots
and tubers 4,000, nutmeg 3,400[5], mangoes 2,000, avocados 2,000, cacao
1,700[5], breadfruit 935[6], peas and beans 645[6], soursop 555[6], mace 210[5, 7];
livestock (number of live animals) 17,000 sheep, 14,000 goats, 11,000 pigs,
4,000 cattle, 260,000 chickens[8]; roundwood, n.a.; fish catch 1,243. Mining

and quarrying: excavation of gravel for local use. Manufacturing (1983):
clothing EC$6,500,000 in export sales[8]; beer 11,200 hectolitres; malt 4,700
hectolitres; edible coconut oil 2,600 hectolitres; rum 2,100 hectolitres; coconut meal 105; laundry soap 26. Construction: n.a. Energy production
(consumption): electricity (kW-hr; 1985) 25,000,000 (25,000,000); coal, none
(none); crude petroleum, none (none); petroleum products (metric tons;
1985) none (20,000); natural gas, none (none).
*Household income and expenditure.* Average household size (1970) 4.7;
income per household: n.a.; sources of income: n.a.; expenditure (1979)[9]:
food 59.0%, clothing and footwear 8.0%, housing 6.5%, household furnishings 6.5%, fuel and light 6.0%, transportation 4.0%, alcohol and tobacco
2.5%, other 7.5%.
*Population economically active* (1984): total 46,000; activity rate of total
population *c.* 48.0% (participation rates: ages 15–64, n.a.; female, n.a.;
unemployed [1986] 25–30%).

| Price and earnings indexes (1980 = 100) | | | | | | |
|---|---|---|---|---|---|---|
| | 1982 | 1983 | 1984 | 1985 | 1986 | 1987[10] |
| Consumer price index | 128.0 | 135.9 | 143.5 | 147.2 | 148.0 | 146.9 |
| Earnings index[11] | ... | ... | ... | ... | ... | ... |

*Land use* (1984): forested 9.0%; meadows and pastures 3.0%; agricultural
and under permanent cultivation 41.0%; other 47.0%.

## Foreign trade[12]

| Balance of trade (current prices) | | | | | | |
|---|---|---|---|---|---|---|
| | 1981 | 1982 | 1983 | 1984 | 1985 | 1986 |
| U.S.$'000,000 | −29.8 | −32.2 | −30.9 | −32.0 | −39.5 | −46.5 |
| % of total | 43.9% | 46.4% | 44.9% | 47.0% | 47.1% | 45.6% |

*Imports* (1983): U.S.$55,600,000 (basic manufactures 25.4%; food 22.9%;
machinery and transportation equipment 11.1%; mineral fuels 11.1%;
chemicals 7.8%). *Major import sources* (1984): United States 24.1%; United
Kingdom 17.9%; Trinidad and Tobago 14.6%; Japan 6.7%; Hong Kong
3.8%.
*Exports* (1983): U.S.$18,920,000[13] (domestic exports 97.4%, of which fresh
fruit 21.9%, cocoa beans 21.4%, nutmeg 17.2%, bananas 17.1%, clothing 9.4%, mace 4.0%; reexports 2.6%). *Major export destinations* (1984):
Trinidad and Tobago 36.3%; United Kingdom 33.9%; West Germany 9.8%;
The Netherlands 7.6%; United States 5.2%.

## Transport and communications

*Transport.* Railroads: none. Roads (1984): total length 609 mi, 980 km
(paved 66%). Vehicles (1981): passenger cars 4,784; trucks and buses 981.
Merchant marine (1986): vessels (100 gross tons and over) 3; total deadweight tonnage 577. Air transport (1982): passenger arrivals and departures,
n.a.; cargo loaded 59 metric tons, cargo unloaded 116 metric tons; airports
(1987) with scheduled flights 3.
*Communications.* Daily newspapers: none. Radio (1986): total number of
receivers 50,000 (1 per 2.0 persons). Television: total number of receivers,
n.a. Telephones (1985): 6,367 (1 per 16 persons).

## Education and health

| Education (1983–84) | | | | |
|---|---|---|---|---|
| | schools | teachers | students | student/teacher ratio |
| Primary (age 5–11) | 64 | 775 | 20,460 | 26.4 |
| Secondary (age 12–18) | ... | 321 | 6,799 | 21.2 |
| Vocational | ... | ... | ... | |
| Higher[14] | 2 | 92 | 1,350 | 14.7 |

*Educational attainment* (1981). Percent of population age 25 and over having: no formal schooling 2.2%; primary education 87.8%; secondary 8.5%;
higher 1.5%. *Literacy* (1981): total population age 15 and over literate
46,000 (85.0%).
*Health* (1985): physicians 38 (1 per 2,639 persons); hospital beds 304 (1 per
330 persons); infant mortality rate per 1,000 live births (1981–83 avg.) 16.5.
*Food* (1981–83): daily per capita caloric intake 2,292 (vegetable products
80%, animal products 20%); (1983) 93% of FAO recommended minimum
requirement.

## Military

*Total active duty personnel* (1986):[15]. *Military expenditure as percent of
GNP:* n.a.; per capita expenditure, n.a.

---

[1]Grenada is divided into seven parishes for statistical purposes only. [2]At prices of
1984. [3]Employed labour force only, including 5,932 self-employed. [4]Less imputed
bank charges. [5]1986. [6]1983. [7]First nine months only. [8]1982. [9]Weights of consumer
price index components. [10]March. [11]Grenada does not have a systematically com-
puted index of wage rates. [12]Import figures are f.o.b. in balance of trade and c.i.f. in
commodities and trading partners. [13]Exports (1986): U.S.$27,800,000 (nutmeg 34.8%,
cacoa beans 15.1%, bananas 13.4%, mace 7.1%). [14]1985–86. [15]The 600-member police
force includes a paramilitary unit.

# Guadeloupe

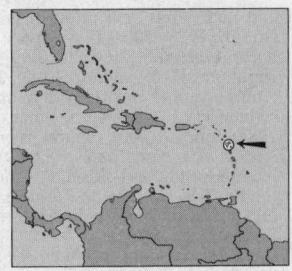

*Official name:* Département de la Guadeloupe (Department of Guadeloupe).
*Political status:* overseas department (France) with two legislative houses (General Council [43]; Regional Council [41]).
*Chief of state:* President of France.
*Heads of government:* Commissioner of the Republic (for France); President of the General Council (for Guadeloupe); President of the Regional Council (for Guadeloupe).
*Capital:* Basse-Terre.
*Official language:* French.
*Official religion:* none.
*Monetary unit:* 1 Franc (F) = 100 centimes; valuation (Oct. 5, 1987) 1 U.S.$ = F 6.13; 1 £ = F 9.96.

| Area and population | | area | | population |
|---|---|---|---|---|
| | | sq mi | sq km | 1982 census |
| **Arrondissements** | **Capitals** | | | |
| Basse-Terre[1] | Basse-Terre | 332 | 861 | 138,242 |
| Pointe-à-Pitre[2] | Pointe-à-Pitre | 297 | 769 | 179,027 |
| Saint-Martin–Saint-Barthélemy[3] | Marigot | 29 | 75 | 11,131 |
| TOTAL | | 687[4] | 1,780[4] | 328,400 |

## Demography

*Population* (1987): 335,000.
*Density* (1987): persons per sq mi 487.6, persons per sq km 188.2.
*Urban–rural* (1985): urban 45.6%; rural 54.4%.
*Sex distribution* (1982): male 49.10%; female 50.90%.
*Age breakdown* (1982): under 15, 31.1%; 15–29, 29.2%; 30–44, 16.6%; 45–59, 12.0%; 60–74, 7.8%; 75 and over, 2.8%; not specified 0.5%.
*Population projection:* (1990) 339,000; (2000) 352,000.
*Doubling time:* 53 years[5].
*Ethnic composition* (1980): Creole (mulatto) 77.0%; black 10.0%; Guadeloupe mestizo (French–Amerindian) 10.0%; white 2.0%; other 1.0%.
*Religious affiliation* (1980): Roman Catholic 90.2%; Protestant (mostly Seventh-day Adventist and Reformed Church of France) 3.9%; Jehovah's Witness 1.9%; Hindu–Catholic spiritist 0.9%; Muslim 0.9%; other 2.2%.
*Major cities* (1982): Les Abymes 51,837; Pointe-à-Pitre 25,151; Le Gosier 13,741; Basse-Terre 13,397.

## Vital statistics

*Birth rate* per 1,000 population (1985): 20.3 (world avg. 29.0); legitimate 43.4%; illegitimate 56.6%.
*Death rate* per 1,000 population (1985): 7.0 (world avg. 11.0).
*Natural increase rate* per 1,000 population (1985): 13.3 (world avg. 18.0).
*Total fertility rate* (avg. births per childbearing woman; 1984): 2.1.
*Marriage rate* per 1,000 population (1985): 4.8.
*Divorce rate* per 1,000 population (1985): 1.1.
*Life expectancy* at birth (1980–85): male 67.8 years; female 73.2 years.
*Major causes of death* per 100,000 population (1983): diseases of the circulatory system 243.0, of which cerebrovascular diseases 97.0; malignant neoplasms (cancers) 105.8; accidents 59.7; diseases of the digestive system 33.9.

## National economy

*Budget* (1985). Revenue: F 1,964,000,000 (receipts from French central government 30.4%, local receipts [including taxes on motor fuels and rum] 21.9%, supplementary receipts 33.3%). Expenditures: F 1,964,000,000 (health and social services 27.4%, capital investments and works 20.1%, supplementary expenses 33.3%).
*Public debt* (external, outstanding; 1984[6]): U.S.$47,000,000.
*Tourism* (1985): receipts from visitors U.S.$95,000,000; expenditures by nationals abroad, n.a.
*Production* (metric tons except as noted). Agriculture, forestry, fishing (1985): sugarcane 712,600[7], bananas 153,000, plants and seedlings 26,800[8], roots and tubers 25,000, fresh-cut flowers 19,200[8], eggplant 6,000, coconuts 3,000, cucumbers 3,000, pineapples 2,000; livestock (number of live animals) 91,000 cattle, 52,000 goats, 46,000 pigs; roundwood (1984) 17,000 cu m; fish catch (1984) 8,940. Mining and quarrying (1985): pozzolan, sand, and gravel for local use. Manufacturing (1985): cement 193,800; raw sugar 65,600[7]; rum 74,900 hectolitres; other products include clothing, wooden furniture and posts, and metalware. Construction (buildings authorized; 1984): residential 250,000 sq m; nonresidential 139,000 sq m. Energy production (consumption): electricity (kW-hr; 1985) 474,000,000 (428,200,000); coal, none (none); crude petroleum, none (none); petroleum products (metric tons; 1985) none (213,000); natural gas, none (none).
*Household income and expenditure.* Average household size (1982) 3.7; income per household (1980) F 72,898 (U.S.$16,142); sources of income: wages and salaries 76.8%, industrial and commercial benefits 9.3%, pensions and rents 4.0%, noncommercial benefits 3.9%, income from stocks and bonds 2.6%, other 3.4%; expenditure (1979)[9]: food 34.4%, transportation 16.3%, housing 12.2%, clothing and footwear 9.2%, education and recreation 6.6%, household furnishings 6.0%, energy 5.7%, other 9.6%.

*Gross national product* (at current market prices; 1984): U.S.$1,205,000,000 (U.S.$3,640 per capita).

| Structure of gross domestic product and labour force | | | | |
|---|---|---|---|---|
| | 1980 | | 1982 | |
| | in value F '000,000 | % of total value | labour force | % of labour force |
| Agriculture | 429 | 7.3 | 12,997 | 10.5 |
| Mining and Manufacturing | 357 | 6.1 | 6,643 | 5.3 |
| Construction | 246 | 4.2 | 9,997 | 8.1 |
| Public utilities | 11 | 0.2 | 703 | 0.6 |
| Transportation and communication | 255 | 4.3 | 4,819 | 3.9 |
| Trade | 1,023 | 17.5 | 10,062 | 8.1 |
| Finance and insurance | 646 | 11.0 | 15,109 | 12.2 |
| Pub. admin., defense | 1,695 | 28.9 } | 28,168 | 22.7 |
| Services | 896 | 15.3 } | | |
| Other | 302 | 5.2 | 35,390[10] | 28.6 |
| TOTAL | 5,860 | 100.0 | 123,888 | 100.0 |

*Population economically active* (1982): total 123,888; activity rate of total population 37.9% (participation rates: ages 15–64, 63.7%; female 42.5%; unemployed [1985] 25.0%).

| Price and earnings indexes (1981 = 100)[11] | | | | | | |
|---|---|---|---|---|---|---|
| | 1981 | 1982 | 1983 | 1984 | 1985 | 1986[12] |
| Consumer price index | 100.0 | 110.2 | 121.2 | 130.6 | 137.4 | 138.8 |
| Earnings index[13] | 100.0 | 120.6 | 130.3 | 135.6 | 144.4 | 145.7 |

*Land use* (1984): forested 40.0%; meadows and pastures 13.0%; agricultural and under permanent cultivation 23.0%; other 24.0%.

## Foreign trade

| Balance of trade (current prices) | | | | | | |
|---|---|---|---|---|---|---|
| | 1980 | 1981 | 1982 | 1983 | 1984 | 1985 | 1986 |
| F '000,000 | −2,628 | −3,025 | −3,569 | −4,412 | −4,480 | −5,076 | −4,684 |
| % of total | 85.9% | 74.8% | 76.5% | 77.9% | 74.9% | 79.1% | 75.2% |

*Imports* (1985): F 5,745,000,000 (food 21.1%, petroleum products 13.6%, electrical machinery 9.9%, transport vehicles 9.7%, chemical products 7.4%, metal manufactures 6.0%). *Major import sources:* France 59.8%; other EEC 11.1%; Martinique 7.5%; Trinidad and Tobago 3.8%.
*Exports* (1985): F 669,000,000 (bananas 43.2%, sugar 10.4%, sport boats 9.2%, wheat flour 8.1%, rum 6.8%). *Major export destinations:* France 63.0%; Martinique 17.6%; St. Lucia 5.0%; United States 2.5%.

## Transport and communications

*Transport.* Railroads: none. Roads (1985): total length 1,284 mi, 2,067 km (paved 80%). Vehicles (1985): passenger cars 95,962; trucks and buses 28,134. Merchant marine: n.a. Air transport (1985)[14]: passenger arrivals 496,239, passenger departures 499,468; cargo loaded 4,226 metric tons, cargo unloaded 7,419 metric tons; airports (1987) with scheduled flights 8.
*Communications.* Daily newspapers (1986): total number 1; total circulation 25,000; circulation per 1,000 population 75. Radio (1986): total number of receivers 96,000 (1 per 3.5 persons). Television (1986): total number of receivers 46,500 (1 per 7.2 persons). Telephones (1985): 95,690 (1 per 3.5 persons).

## Education and health

| Education (1983–84) | schools | teachers | students | student/ teacher ratio |
|---|---|---|---|---|
| Primary (age 6–10) | 230 | 2,173 | 47,733 | 22.0 |
| Secondary (age 11–17) } Vocational | ... | 2,987 | 49,897 | 16.7 |
| Higher[15] | 1 | 92 | 5,212 | 56.7 |

*Educational attainment* (1982). Percent of population age 25 and over having: no formal schooling 10.7%; primary education 54.6%; secondary 29.5%; higher 5.2%. *Literacy* (1982): total population age 15 and over literate 225,400 (90.1%); males literate 108,700 (89.7%); females literate 116,700 (90.5%).
*Health* (1984): physicians 309 (1 per 1,072 persons); hospital beds 4,020 (1 per 82 persons); infant mortality rate per 1,000 live births (1985) 17.5.
*Food* (1981–83): daily per capita caloric intake 2,400 (vegetable products 75%, animal products 25%); (1983) 107% of FAO recommended minimum requirement.

## Military

*Total active duty personnel* (1984): 1,800[16].

[1]Comprises Basse-Terre 327 sq mi (848 sq km) and Îles des Saintes 5 sq mi (13 sq km), pop. 2,901. [2]Comprises Grand-Terre 228 sq mi (590 sq km); Marie-Galante 61 sq mi (158 sq km), pop. 13,757; La Désirade 8 sq mi (20 sq km), pop. 1,602; and the small, uninhabited Îles de la Petite-Terre. [3]Comprises the French part of Saint-Martin 20 sq mi (52 sq km), pop. 8,072; Saint-Barthélemy 8 sq mi (21 sq km), pop. 3,059; and the small, uninhabited island of Tintamarre. [4]Total area includes 29 sq mi (75 sq km) not allocated by arrondissement. [5]Net migration to metropolitan France nearly outweighs natural increase rate. [6]Includes external long-term private debt not guaranteed by the government. [7]1986. [8]Export only. [9]Weights of consumer price index components. [10]Includes 29,427 unemployed. [11]Base and indexes are end of year unless otherwise indicated. [12]End of September. [13]Based on minimum-level wage in public administration. [14]Raizet international airport only. [15]1985–86. [16]Includes police.

# Guam

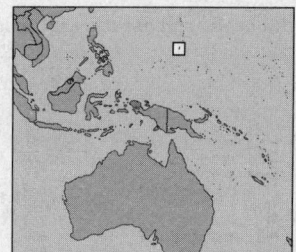

*Official name:* Guam.
*Political Status:* self-governing organized unincorporated territory of the United States with one legislative house (21).
*Chief of state:* President of the United States.
*Head of government:* Governor.
*Capital:* Agana.
*Official language:* English.
*Official religion:* none.
*Monetary unit:* 1 United States dollar (U.S.$) = 100 cents; valuation (Oct. 5, 1987) 1 U.S.$ = £0.62.

### Area and population

| Election Districts | area sq mi | area sq km | population[1] 1987 estimate |
|---|---|---|---|
| Agana | 1 | 3 | 1,000 |
| Agana Heights | 1 | 3 | 3,800 |
| Agat | 10 | 26 | 4,700 |
| Asan | 6 | 16 | 2,400 |
| Barrigada | 9 | 23 | 9,100 |
| Chalan Pago-Ordot | 6 | 16 | 3,600 |
| Dededo | 30 | 78 | 27,600 |
| Inarajan | 19 | 49 | 2,400 |
| Mangilao | 10 | 26 | 8,000 |
| Merizo | 6 | 16 | 1,900 |
| Mongmong-Toto-Maite | 2 | 5 | 6,100 |
| Piti | 7 | 18 | 3,300 |
| Santa Rita | 17 | 44 | 10,700 |
| Sinajana | 1 | 3 | 2,900 |
| Talofofo | 17 | 44 | 2,300 |
| Tamuning | 6 | 16 | 15,800 |
| Umatac | 6 | 16 | 900 |
| Yigo | 35 | 91 | 12,100 |
| Yona | 20 | 52 | 5,000 |
| TOTAL | 209 | 541[2] | 124,000[2] |

## Demography

*Population* (1987): 124,000.
*Density* (1987): persons per sq mi 593.3, persons per sq km 229.2.
*Urban–rural* (1980): urban[3] 39.5%; rural 60.5%.
*Sex distribution* (1985): male 54.31%; female 45.69%.
*Age breakdown* (1980): under 15, 34.9%; 15–29, 30.6%; 30–44, 19.4%; 45–59, 10.5%; 60–74, 3.9%; 75 and over, 0.7%.
*Population projection:* (1990) 132,000; (2000) 165,000.
*Doubling time:* 49 years.
*Ethnic composition* (1980): Chamorro 41.8%; Filipino 21.2%; German 2.1%; Korean 1.8%; Japanese 1.8%; other[4] 31.3%.
*Religious affiliation* (1980): Roman Catholic 79.5%; Protestant 17.3%; other 3.2%.
*Major populated places* (1980): Tamuning 8,862; Apra Harbor 5,633; Andersen Air Force Base 4,892; Mangilao 4,029.

## Vital statistics

*Birth rate* per 1,000 population (1985): 17.8 (world avg. 29.0); legitimate 64.5%; illegitimate 35.5%.
*Death rate* per 1,000 population (1985): 3.4 (world avg. 11.0).
*Natural increase rate* per 1,000 population (1985): 14.4 (world avg. 18.0).
*Total fertility rate* (avg. births per childbearing woman; 1980): 3.2.
*Marriage rate* per 1,000 population (1985): 11.3.
*Divorce rate* per 1,000 population (1985): 5.3.
*Life expectancy* at birth (1980–82): male 69.6 years; female 74.5 years.
*Major causes of death* per 100,000 population (1983): heart disease 117.7; malignant neoplasms (cancers) 51.5; motor vehicle accidents 24.9; cerebrovascular diseases 18.9; pneumonia 14.6; homicide 13.7; other diseases of the central nervous system 12.9; diabetes mellitus 12.9.

## National economy

*Budget* (1984). Revenue: U.S.$212,920,869 (local income taxes 37.9%, gross business receipts taxes 19.6%, revenues from United States agencies[5] 10.4%, federal grants-in-aid 2.3%). Expenditures: U.S.$179,102,238 (general government operations 39.8%, public education 32.1%, law and public safety 12.6%, public health and community services 11.2%, economic development 2.1%).
*Public debt* (external, outstanding): n.a.
*Tourism* (1984): receipts from visitors U.S.$200,000,000; expenditures by nationals abroad, n.a.
*Production.* Agriculture, forestry, fishing (value of production in U.S.$ except as noted; 1984): watermelons 1,197,378, head cabbages 264,567, cucumbers 236,160, bananas 169,715, tomatoes 161,611, long beans 155,100, pepino melons 152,685, sweet potatoes 124,576, pineapples 115,920, eggs 902,462; livestock (number of live animals) 4,120 pigs, 1,300 goats, 650 cattle, 90 carabaos; fish catch (metric tons; 1985) 616. Mining and quarrying (1983): sand and gravel. Manufacturing (value of gross business receipts in U.S.$; 1980): petroleum refining and related products 322,083,000; food processing 11,742,000; printing and publishing 6,039,000; industrial and medical goods and materials 412,000. Construction (gross value of building and construction permits in U.S.$; 1985): residential 33,099,000; nonresidential 30,675,000. Energy production (consumption): electricity (kW-hr; 1985) 1,100,000,000 (1,100,000,000); coal, none (n.a.); crude petroleum (barrels; 1985) none (10,995,000); petroleum products (metric tons; 1985) 1,400,000 (820,000); natural gas, none (n.a.).
*Gross national product* (at current market prices; 1985): U.S.$670,000,000 (U.S.$5,660 per capita).

### Structure of gross business income and labour force

| | 1982 in value U.S.$'000,000 | 1982 % of total value | 1986 labour force[6] | 1986 % of labour force |
|---|---|---|---|---|
| Agriculture | 1.4 | 0.2 | 110 | 0.3 |
| Manufacturing | 107.3 | 13.1 | 1,320 | 3.2 |
| Construction | 64.6 | 7.9 | 3,960 | 9.7 |
| Trade | 422.3 | 51.5 | 7,690 | 18.8 |
| Transp. and commun. | 45.3 | 5.5 | 1,850[7] | 4.5 |
| Finance | 80.8 | 9.9 | 1,690 | 4.1 |
| Pub. admin., defense | ... | ... | 17,640 | 43.1 |
| Services | 99.6 | 12.2 | 6,630 | 16.2 |
| TOTAL | 819.2[2] | 100.0[2] | 40,890 | 100.0[2] |

*Population economically active* (1986): total 35,590[8]; activity rate of total population 29.0% (participation rates: over age 16, 60.4%; female 40.3%; unemployed 6.0%).

### Price and earnings indexes (1980 = 100)

| | 1980 | 1981 | 1982 | 1983 | 1984 | 1985 | 1986 |
|---|---|---|---|---|---|---|---|
| Consumer price index | 100.0 | 114.0 | 128.1 | 132.6 | 144.2 | 149.8 | 153.9[9] |
| Hourly earnings index | 100.0 | ... | ... | 112.8 | 109.3 | 115.2 | 120.8[10] |

*Household income and expenditure.* Average household size (1980) 3.7; median annual income per household (1979) U.S.$16,203; sources of income: n.a.; expenditure (1978): housing 28.6%, food 24.1%, transportation 18.0%, clothing 10.6%, entertainment 5.1%, medical care 4.7%.
*Land use* (1984): forested 18.2%; meadows and pastures 14.5%; agricultural and under permanent cultivation 21.8%; other 45.5%.

## Foreign trade

### Balance of trade (current prices)

| | 1978 | 1979 | 1980 | 1981 | 1982 | 1983 |
|---|---|---|---|---|---|---|
| U.S.$'000 | −236,227 | −403,144 | −483,141 | ... | ... | −571,519 |
| % of total | 76.7% | 82.5% | 79.8% | ... | ... | 87.9% |

*Imports* (1983): U.S.$610,743,985 (mineral fuels 46.9%, of which crude petroleum 28.8%; machinery and transport equipment 19.1%, of which passenger cars 12.4%; food and live animals 12.0%, of which beef and veal 1.5%; beverages and tobacco 4.5%, of which cigarettes 1.3%; manufactured goods 4.4%; chemicals 2.3%). *Major import sources:* United States 23.4%; Japan 19.2%; Taiwan 4.6%; Hong Kong 3.1%; Philippines 1.3%.
*Exports* (1983): U.S.$39,224,728 (clothing 16.9%; beverages and tobacco 12.0%, of which alcoholic beverages 4.4%, cigarettes 3.5%, nonalcoholic beverages 1.9%; machinery and transport equipment 11.4%; travel goods 3.0%; lubricating oils and greases 2.7%; fish and fish products 2.6%; cosmetics 2.6%; watches and watch cases 1.5%; cement 1.5%). *Major export destinations:* United States 24.9%; Japan 4.8%; Hong Kong 2.0%.

## Transport and communications

*Transport.* Railroads: none. Roads (1986): total length 419 mi, 674 km (paved 100%). Vehicles[11] (1984): passenger cars 57,856; trucks and buses 16,521. Merchant marine (1986): vessels (100 gross tons and over), n.a.; surface cargo loaded, unloaded, or transshipped (1984) 977,000 metric tons. Air transport (1984): passenger arrivals 361,423; passenger departures, n.a.; cargo loaded 3,565 metric tons; cargo unloaded 5,797 metric tons; airports (1987) with scheduled flights 1.
*Communications.* Daily newspapers (1986): total number 1; total circulation 18,076; circulation per 1,000 population 149. Radio (1986): total receivers 102,000 (1 per 1.2 persons). Television (1986): total receivers 82,000 (1 per 1.5 persons). Telephones (1984): 23,354 (1 per 5.0 persons).

## Education and health

### Education (1985–86)

| | schools | teachers | students | student/teacher ratio |
|---|---|---|---|---|
| Primary (age 5–10) | 33 | 781 | 14,552 | 18.6 |
| Secondary (age 11–18) | 22 | 814 | 16,223 | 19.9 |
| Vocational | 4 | 146 | 4,377 | 30.0 |
| Higher | 1 | 175 | 2,647 | 15.1 |

*Educational attainment* (1980). Percent of population age 25 and over having: primary education 21.3%; some secondary 13.1%; secondary 31.2%; college 34.4%. *Literacy* (1980): total population age 15 and over literate 66,-537 (96.4%); males literate 35,091 (96.4%); females literate 31,446 (96.5%).
*Health:* physicians (1982) 83 (1 per 1,334 persons); hospital beds (1979) 223 (1 per 470 persons); infant mortality rate per 1,000 live births (1985) 10.6.
*Food:* daily per capita caloric intake, n.a.

## Military

*Total active duty U.S. personnel* (1985): 11,590 (navy 60.6%, air force 34.7%, other 4.7%).

[1]Includes active-duty military personnel, Department of Defense employees, and dependents. [2]Detail does not add to total given because of rounding. [3]Places of 2,500 or more. [4]Includes various Pacific Island groups (mostly Micronesian) and persons of multiple ethnic origin. [5]Consists largely of federal income tax. [6]Employed persons only. [7]Includes public utilities. [8]Excludes nonimmigrant aliens and civilians living on military reservations. [9]First three quarters average. [10]First two quarters average. [11]Excludes military vehicles.

# Guatemala

*Official name:* República de Guatemala (Republic of Guatemala).
*Form of government:* republic with one legislative house (Congress of the Republic [100]).
*Head of state and government:* President.
*Capital:* Guatemala City.
*Official language:* Spanish.
*Official religion:* none.
*Monetary unit:* 1 Guatemalan quetzal (Q) = 100 centavos; valuation (Oct. 5, 1987) 1 U.S.$ = Q 1.00[1]; 1 £ = Q 1.62.

### Area and population

| Departments | Capitals | area sq mi | area sq km | population 1986 estimate |
|---|---|---|---|---|
| Alta Verapaz | Cobán | 3,354 | 8,686 | 506,800 |
| Baja Verapaz | Salamá | 1,206 | 3,124 | 161,500 |
| Chimaltenango | Chimaltenango | 764 | 1,979 | 298,100 |
| Chiquimula | Chiquimula | 917 | 2,376 | 227,800 |
| El Progreso | Progreso | 742 | 1,922 | 98,200 |
| Escuintla | Escuintla | 1,693 | 4,384 | 467,300 |
| Guatemala | Guatemala City | 821 | 2,126 | 1,747,500 |
| Huehuetenango | Huehuetenango | 2,857 | 7,400 | 609,600 |
| Izabal | Puerto Barrios | 3,490 | 9,038 | 278,600 |
| Jalapa | Jalapa | 797 | 2,063 | 168,600 |
| Jutiapa | Jutiapa | 1,243 | 3,219 | 318,800 |
| Petén | Ciudad Flores | 13,843 | 35,854 | 192,800 |
| Quezaltenango | Quezaltenango | 753 | 1,951 | 485,700 |
| Quiché | Santa Cruz | 3,235 | 8,378 | 491,700 |
| Retalhuleu | Retalhuleu | 717 | 1,856 | 206,100 |
| Sacatepéquez | Antigua Guatemala | 180 | 465 | 155,400 |
| San Marcos | San Marcos | 1,464 | 3,791 | 609,600 |
| Santa Rosa | Cuilapa | 1,141 | 2,955 | 242,000 |
| Sololá | Sololá | 410 | 1,061 | 207,400 |
| Suchitepéquez | Mazatenango | 969 | 2,510 | 316,100 |
| Totonicapán | Totonicapán | 410 | 1,061 | 258,100 |
| Zacapa | Zacapa | 1,039 | 2,690 | 147,400 |
| TOTAL | | 42,042[2] | 108,889 | 8,195,100 |

## Demography

*Population* (1987): 8,434,000.
*Density* (1987): persons per sq mi 200.6, persons per sq km 77.5.
*Urban–rural* (1986): urban 32.8%; rural 67.2%.
*Sex distribution* (1985): male 50.56%; female 49.44%.
*Age breakdown* (1985): under 15, 45.9%; 15–29, 26.5%; 30–44, 14.3%; 45–59, 8.6%; 60–74, 3.8%; 75 and over, 0.9%.
*Population projection:* (1990) 9,197,000; (2000) 12,222,000.
*Doubling time:* 21 years.
*Ethnic composition* (1983): Amerindian 55%; Ladino (Hispanic/Amerindian) 42%; white or black 3%.
*Religious affiliation* (1985): Roman Catholic *c.* 75%; Protestant (mostly evangelical churches) *c.* 25%.
*Major cities* (1981): Guatemala City 754,243; Quezaltenango 62,719; Escuintla 36,931; Puerto Barrios 24,235; Retalhuleu 22,001.

## Vital statistics

*Birth rate* per 1,000 population (1985): 41.7 (world avg. 29.0).
*Death rate* per 1,000 population (1985): 7.5 (world avg. 11.0).
*Natural increase rate* per 1,000 population (1985): 34.2 (world avg. 18.0).
*Total fertility rate* (avg. births per childbearing woman; 1984): 5.8.
*Marriage rate* per 1,000 population (1985): 4.8.
*Divorce rate* per 1,000 population (1983): 0.2.
*Life expectancy* at birth (1980–85): male 56.8 years; female 61.3 years.
*Major causes of death* per 100,000 population (1981): infectious and parasitic diseases 256.8; homicide and other violence 170.4; pneumonia 84.1; diseases of the circulatory system 57.2; malnutrition 35.1; ill-defined conditions 143.6.

## National economy

*Budget* (1985). Revenue: Q 1,307,700,000 (tax revenue 51.9%, treasury bills and foreign loans 33.7%). Expenditures: Q 1,187,400,000 (defense 16.6%, education 11.6%, health 6.6%, public works and communication 6.5%, transportation 6.1%, nonspecified categories 49.7%).
*Public debt* (external, outstanding; 1985): U.S.$2,148,100,000.
*Tourism* (1985): receipts from visitors U.S.$67,000,000; expenditures by nationals abroad U.S.$77,000,000.
*Production* (metric tons except as noted). Agriculture, forestry, fishing (1985): sugarcane 5,492,000, corn (maize) 1,096,000, bananas 704,000, coffee 164,000, dry beans 114,000, tomatoes 96,000, sorghum 89,000, cotton lint 67,000; livestock (number of live animals) 2,587,000 cattle, 832,000 pigs, 670,000 sheep, 15,000,000 chickens; roundwood (1984) 7,000,000 cu m; fish catch (1984) 4,284. Mining and quarrying (1985): limestone 990,000; gypsum 16,800[3]; antimony (metal content) 1,057[3]. Manufacturing (1985): raw sugar 542,000; cement 526,000; cheese 14,600[4]; beer 645,000 hectolitres[5]; cigarettes 1,936,000,000 units. Construction (1984)[6]: residential 128,700 sq m; nonresidential 98,800 sq m. Energy production (consumption): electricity (kW-hr; 1985) 1,755,000,000 (1,755,000,000); coal, none (none); crude petroleum (barrels; 1985) 1,327,000 (5,527,000); petroleum products (metric tons; 1985) 665,000 (953,000); natural gas, none (none).
*Gross national product* (1985): U.S.$9,890,000,000 (U.S.$1,240 per capita).

### Structure of gross domestic product and labour force

| | 1985 in value[7] U.S.$'000,000 | % of total value | labour force | % of labour force |
|---|---|---|---|---|
| Agriculture | 2,496 | 25.8 | 1,422,580 | 58.1 |
| Mining | 22 | 0.2 | 2,449 | 0.1 |
| Manufacturing | 1,531 | 15.8 | 332,996 | 13.6 |
| Construction | 175 | 1.8 | 100,388 | 4.1 |
| Public utilities | 187 | 1.9 | 7,345 | 0.3 |
| Transp. and commun. | 680 | 7.0 | 61,213 | 2.5 |
| Trade | 2,448 | 25.3 | 178,741 | 7.3 |
| Finance | 888 | 9.2 | | |
| Pub. admin., defense | 636 | 6.6 | 293,820 | 12.0 |
| Services | 623 | 6.4 | | |
| Other | — | — | 48,970 | 2.0 |
| TOTAL | 9,686 | 100.0 | 2,448,502 | 100.0 |

*Population economically active* (1981)[8]: total 1,683,828; activity rate of total population 27.8% (participation rates: age 15–64, 48.8%; female 14.6%; unemployed [1986] 12.0%).

### Price and earnings indexes (1980 = 100)

| | 1980 | 1981 | 1982 | 1983 | 1984 | 1985 | 1986 |
|---|---|---|---|---|---|---|---|
| Consumer price index | 100.0 | 111.4 | 111.8 | 116.8 | 120.8 | 143.4 | 196.4 |
| Hourly earnings index[9] | 100.0 | 112.1 | 117.6 | 128.6 | ... | ... | ... |

*Household income and expenditure.* Average household size (1981) 5.5; income per household: n.a.; sources of income: n.a.; expenditure (1983)[10]: food 57.3%, housing and energy 12.7%, clothing and footwear 10.4%, household furnishings 6.0%, transportation 5.8%, other 7.8%.
*Land use* (1984): forested 39.0%; meadows and pastures 12.3%; agricultural and under permanent cultivation 16.7%; other 32.0%.

## Foreign trade[11]

### Balance of trade (current prices)

| | 1980 | 1981 | 1982 | 1983 | 1984 | 1985 | 1986 |
|---|---|---|---|---|---|---|---|
| Q '000,000 | +84.5 | −286.3 | −116.7 | +125.0 | −53.3 | −16.6 | +183.0 |
| % of total | 2.8% | 10.2% | 4.8% | 5.6% | 2.3% | 0.8% | 8.9% |

*Imports* (1984): Q 1,277,400,000 (mineral fuels and lubricants 23.7%, chemical products 23.3%, basic manufactures 18.5%, machinery and transport equipment 16.4%). *Major import sources* (1985): United States 30.6%; Mexico 15.1%; Venezuela 14.0%; West Germany 6.3%; Japan 4.3%.
*Exports* (1984): Q 1,127,000,000 (coffee 32.1%, sugar 6.6%, cotton 6.3%, cardamom 5.3%, bananas 5.1%, petroleum 3.0%). *Major export destinations* (1985): United States 35.7%; El Salvador 12.2%; West Germany 6.5%; Italy 4.5%; Costa Rica 4.4%.

## Transport and communications

*Transport.* Railroads (1986): route length 375 mi, 603 km. Roads (1985): total length 11,200 mi, 18,000 km (paved 16%). Vehicles (1983): passenger cars 188,100; trucks and buses 58,500. Merchant marine (1986): vessels (100 gross tons and over) 8; total deadweight tonnage 13,603. Air transport (1986): passenger-mi 84,500,000, passenger-km 136,000,000; short ton-mi cargo 4,910,000, metric ton-km cargo 7,169,000; airports (1987) with scheduled flights 2.
*Communications.* Daily newspapers (1986): total number 9; total circulation 225,500[12]; circulation per 1,000 population 28. Radio (1986): 500,000 receivers (1 per 16 persons). Television (1986): 300,000 receivers (1 per 27 persons). Telephones (1985): 128,179 (1 per 62 persons).

## Education and health

### Education (1984)

| | schools | teachers | students | student/ teacher ratio |
|---|---|---|---|---|
| Primary (age 7–12) | 7,820 | 26,963 | 979,888 | 36.3 |
| Secondary (age 13–18) | ... | 12,023 | 174,653 | 14.5 |
| Voc., teacher tr. | | | | |
| Higher[5] | 5 | 4,490 | 51,556 | 11.5 |

*Educational attainment* (1981). Percent of population age 25 and over having: no formal schooling 52.9%; primary education 34.5%; incomplete secondary 7.1%; complete secondary and higher 2.1%; unknown 3.4%. *Literacy* (1981): total population age 15 and over literate 1,835,379 (55.0%); males literate 1,029,174 (62.8%); females literate 806,205 (47.4%).
*Health:* physicians (1981) 1,250 (1 per 5,691 persons); hospital beds (1982) 9,881 (1 per 740 persons); infant mortality rate per 1,000 live births (1985) 56.0.
*Food* (1981–83): daily per capita caloric intake 2,189 (vegetable products 91%, animal products 9%); (1983) 95% of FAO recommended minimum requirement.

## Military

*Total active duty personnel* (1986): 32,000 (army 94.7%, navy 3.1%, air force 2.2%). *Military expenditure as percent of GNP* (1984): 1.9% (world 5.9%); per capita expenditure U.S.$23.

[1]The official market value of the quetzal is fixed at par with that of the U.S.$; the free market rate is Q 2.70 per U.S.$. [2]Detail does not add to total given because of rounding. [3]Includes data available through July 1986. [4]1984. [5]1983. [6]Authorized construction in Guatemala City metropolitan area. [7]At 1984 prices. [8]Excludes population seeking work for the first time. [9]Wages in manufacturing. [10]Weights of consumer price index components; urban areas only. [11]Import figures are f.o.b. (free on board) in balance of trade and c.i.f. (cost, insurance, and freight) for commodities and trading partners. [12]Five newspapers only.

# Guinea

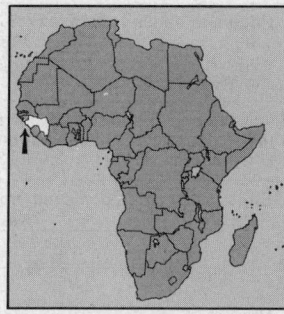

*Official name:* République de Guinée (Republic of Guinea).
*Form of government:* interim military regime ruling through the Military Committee for National Recovery (CMRN [20]).
*Head of state and government:* President.
*Capital:* Conakry.
*Official language:* French.
*Official religion:* none.
*Monetary unit:* 1 Guinean franc[1] (GF) = 100 cauris; valuation (Oct. 5, 1987) 1 U.S.$ = GF 339.71; 1 £ = GF 551.65.

### Area and population

| Regions | Capitals | area sq mi | area sq km | population 1983 census |
|---|---|---|---|---|
| Beyla | Beyla | 6,738 | 17,452 | 161,347 |
| Boffa | Boffa | 1,932 | 5,003 | 141,719 |
| Boké | Boké | 3,881 | 10,053 | 225,207 |
| Conakry | Conakry | 119 | 308 | 705,280 |
| Coyah (Dubréka) | Coyah | 2,153 | 5,576 | 134,190 |
| Dabola | Dabola | 2,317 | 6,000 | 97,986 |
| Dalaba | Dalaba | 1,313 | 3,400 | 132,802 |
| Dinguiraye | Dinguiraye | 4,247 | 11,000 | 133,502 |
| Faranah | Faranah | 4,788 | 12,400 | 142,923 |
| Forécariah | Forécariah | 1,647 | 4,265 | 116,464 |
| Fria | Fria | 840 | 2,175 | 70,413 |
| Gaoual | Gaoual | 4,440 | 11,500 | 135,657 |
| Guéckédou | Guéckédou | 1,605 | 4,157 | 204,757 |
| Kankan | Kankan | 7,104 | 18,400 | 229,861 |
| Kérouané | Kérouané | 3,070 | 7,950 | 106,872 |
| Kindia | Kindia | 3,409 | 8,828 | 216,052 |
| Kissidougou | Kissidougou | 3,425 | 8,872 | 183,236 |
| Koubia | Koubia | 571 | 1,480 | 98,053 |
| Koundara | Koundara | 2,124 | 5,500 | 94,216 |
| Kouroussa | Kouroussa | 4,647 | 12,035 | 136,926 |
| Labé | Labé | 973 | 2,520 | 253,214 |
| Lélouma | Lélouma | 830 | 2,150 | 138,467 |
| Lola | Lola | 1,629 | 4,219 | 106,654 |
| Macenta | Macenta | 3,363 | 8,710 | 193,109 |
| Mali | Mali | 3,398 | 8,800 | 210,889 |
| Mamou | Mamou | 2,378 | 6,160 | 190,525 |
| Mandiana | Mandiana | 5,000 | 12,950 | 136,317 |
| Nzérékoré | Nzérékoré | 1,460 | 3,781 | 216,355 |
| Pita | Pita | 1,544 | 4,000 | 227,912 |
| Siguiri | Siguiri | 7,626 | 19,750 | 209,164 |
| Télimélé | Télimélé | 3,119 | 8,080 | 243,256 |
| Tougué | Tougué | 2,394 | 6,200 | 113,272 |
| Yomou | Yomou | 843 | 2,183 | 74,417 |
| TOTAL | | 94,926[2] | 245,857 | 5,781,014 |

## Demography

*Population* (1987): 6,380,000.
*Density* (1987): persons per sq mi 67.2, persons per sq km 25.9.
*Urban–rural* (1985): urban 26.0%; rural 74.0%.
*Sex distribution* (1985): male 48.63%; female 51.37%.
*Age breakdown* (1985): under 15, 43.1%; 15–29, 26.2%; 30–44, 16.2%; 45–59, 9.6%; 60–74, 4.2%; 75 and over, 0.7%.
*Population projection:* (1990) 6,145,000; (2000) 7,935,000.
*Doubling time:* 30 years.
*Ethnic composition* (1983): Fulani 38.6%; Malinke 23.2%; Susu 11.0%; Kissi 6.0%; Kpelle 4.6%; other 16.6%.
*Religious affiliation* (1980): Muslim 69.0%; traditional beliefs 29.5%; Christian 1.4%, of which Roman Catholic 1.2%; other 0.1%.
*Major cities* (1983): Conakry 705,280; Kankan 88,760; Labé 65,439; Kindia 55,904.

## Vital statistics

*Birth rate* per 1,000 population (1980–85): 46.8 (world avg. 29.0).
*Death rate* per 1,000 population (1980–85): 23.5 (world avg. 11.0).
*Natural increase rate* per 1,000 population (1980–85): 23.3 (world avg. 18.0).
*Total fertility rate* (avg. births per childbearing woman; 1980–85): 6.2.
*Life expectancy* at birth (1980–85): male 38.7 years; female 41.8 years.
*Major causes of death* per 100,000 population: n.a.; however, major diseases include malaria, venereal disease, tuberculosis, intestinal infections, measles, and schistosomiasis.

## National economy

*Budget* (1986). Revenue: GF 109,602,000,000 (customs duties 42.2%, income tax 14.1%, excise tax 3.1%). Expenditures: GF 136,999,000,000 (material expenses 24.1%, wages 22.1%, debt service 17.1%, infrastructure 14.3%, rural development 7.6%, industry and mining development 7.5%).
*Public debt* (external, outstanding; 1985): U.S.$1,292,200,000.
*Tourism:* n.a.
*Production* (metric tons except as noted). Agriculture, forestry, fishing (1985): roots and tubers 663,000 (of which cassava 500,000, yams 61,000), rice 470,-000, vegetables and melons 420,000, plantains 350,000, sugarcane 225,000, citrus fruit 160,000, bananas 104,000, peanuts (groundnuts) 75,000, pulses 45,000, corn (maize) 43,000, palm kernels 35,000, taro 32,000, pineapples 20,000, coconuts 15,000, coffee 15,000, eggs 10,710; livestock (number of live animals) 1,800,000 cattle, 460,000 sheep, 460,000 goats, 460,000 pigs, 11,000,000 chickens; roundwood 3,689,000 cu m; fish catch 30,000. Mining

and quarrying (1985): bauxite 13,100,000; alumina 580,000; gem diamonds 105,000 carats; industrial diamonds 7,000 carats. Manufacturing (value of production in GS '000; 1985): corrugated and sheet iron 571,081; plastics 462,242; tobacco products 375,154; cement 326,138; printed matter 216,511; fruit juice 75,763; beer 69,934; matches 22,449. Construction: n.a. Energy production (consumption): electricity (kW-hr; 1985) 500,000,000 (500,000,-000); coal, none (n.a.); crude petroleum, none (n.a.); petroleum products (metric tons; 1985) none (291,000); natural gas, none (n.a.).
*Gross national product* (at current market prices; 1985): U.S.$1,950,000,000 (U.S.$320 per capita).

### Structure of gross domestic product and labour force

| | 1985 in value GS '000,000[3] | 1985 % of total value | 1983 labour force | 1983 % of labour force |
|---|---|---|---|---|
| Agriculture | 16,195 | 40.0 | 1,968,000 | 82.0 |
| Mining | 5,420 | 13.4 | | |
| Manufacturing | 724 | 1.8 | | |
| Construction | 2,593 | 6.4 | | |
| Public utilities | 133 | 0.3 | 264,000 | 11.0 |
| Transp. and commun. | 531 | 1.3 | | |
| Trade | 8,697 | 21.5 | | |
| Finance | 1,295 | 3.2 | | |
| Pub. admin., defense | 4,765 | 11.8 | 38,400 | 1.6 |
| Services | | | 129,600 | 5.4 |
| Other | 127 | 0.3 | ... | ... |
| TOTAL | 40,480 | 100.0 | 2,400,000 | 100.0 |

*Population economically active* (1984): total 2,306,000; activity rate of total population 43.5% (participation rates: ages 15–64, n.a.; female [1981] 40.7%; unemployed, n.a.).
*Household income and expenditure.* Average household size (1980) 4.7; average annual income per capita (1984) GS 7,660 (U.S.$305); sources of income: n.a.; expenditure (1985): food 61.5%, health care 11.2%, clothing and footwear 7.9%, housing and energy 7.3%, transportation 5.1%, recreation 4.2%, durable goods 2.9%.
*Land use* (1984): forested 41.7%; meadows and pastures 12.2%; agricultural and under permanent cultivation 6.4%; other 39.7%.

## Foreign trade[4]

### Balance of trade (current prices)

| GS '000,000 | 1979 | 1980 | 1981 | 1982 | 1983 | 1984 |
|---|---|---|---|---|---|---|
| | −400 | +1,000 | +1,611 | +2,511 | +2,617 | +3,467 |
| % of total | 2.7% | 4.8% | 9.9% | 16.3% | 16.6% | 18.7% |

*Imports* (1984): GS 7,542,000,000 (food, machinery and transport equipment, petroleum products, building materials, textiles). *Major import sources:* France 31.9%; Brazil 12.3%; U.S. 11.6%; W.Ger. 6.9%; Belgium 6.4%; Spain 5.3%.
*Exports* (1984): GS 11,009,000,000 (bauxite and alumina 90–95%; coffee, pineapples, bananas, palm kernels). *Major export destinations:* U.S. 27.5%; W.Ger. 18.9%; Spain 16.3%; Ireland 10.1%; Italy 5.8%.

## Transport and communications

*Transport.* Railroads (1986): route length 584 mi, 940 km. Roads (1984): total length 17,600 mi, 28,400 km (paved 4%). Vehicles (1982): passenger cars 9,948; trucks and buses 9,992. Merchant marine (1986): vessels (100 gross tons and over) 19; total deadweight tonnage 2,927. Air transport (1985): passenger-mi 99,400,000, passenger-km 160,000,000; short ton-mi cargo 400,000, metric ton-km cargo 600,000; airports (1987) with scheduled flights 1.
*Communications.* Daily newspapers (1986): none. Radio (1986): 200,000 receivers (1 per 31 persons). Television (1986): 11,000 receivers (1 per 566 persons). Telephones (1981): 15,800 (1 per 310 persons).

## Education and health

### Education (1986–87)

| | schools | teachers | students | student/teacher ratio |
|---|---|---|---|---|
| Primary (age 7–12) | 2,204 | 7,493 | 270,140 | 36.0 |
| Secondary (age 13–18) | 225 | 3,577 | 76,493 | 21.4 |
| Voc., teacher tr. | 31 | 758 | 4,929 | 6.5 |
| Higher | 23 | 946 | 7,470 | 7.9 |

*Educational attainment,* n.a. *Literacy* (1985): total population age 15 and over literate 874,000 (28.3%); males literate 603,000 (39.7%); females literate 271,000 (17.2%).
*Health:* physicians (1980) 301 (1 per 17,000 persons); hospital beds[5] (1976) 7,650 (1 per 579 persons); infant mortality rate per 1,000 live births (1980–85) 159.
*Food* (1981–83): daily per capita caloric intake 1,827 (vegetable products 96%, animal products 4%); (1983) 84% of FAO recommended minimum.

## Military

*Total active duty personnel* (1987): 9,900 (army 85.8%, navy 6.1%, air force 8.1%). *Military expenditure as percent of GNP* (1983): 3.3% (world 6.0%); per capita expenditure U.S.$10.

---

[1]In January 1986 the Guinean syli (GS) was replaced at par by the Guinean franc (GF), and its value was depreciated by 92.5% in terms of foreign currency. The exchange rate given for the Guinean franc is the official rate only; the public transaction rate is 11.8% lower. [2]Detail does not add to total given because of rounding. [3]In constant prices of 1981. [4]Trade with the Socialist bloc is not included in major import sources and major export destinations; the U.S.S.R., however, is a major trading partner. [5]Government hospitals only.

# Guinea-Bissau

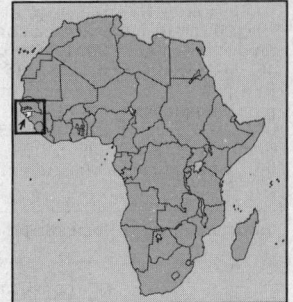

*Official name:* Répública da
  Guiné-Bissau (Republic of
  Guinea-Bissau).
*Form of government:* single-party
  republic with one legislative house
  (National People's Assembly [150]).
*Head of state and government:*
  President.
*Capital:* Bissau.
*Official language:* Portuguese.
*Official religion:* none.
*Monetary unit:* 1 peso (PG) = 100
  centavos; valuation (Oct. 5, 1987)
  1 U.S.$ = PG 649; 1 £ = PG 1,055.

### Area and population

| | | area | | population |
|---|---|---|---|---|
| | | | | 1979 |
| Regions | Capitals | sq mi | sq km | census[1] |
| Bafatá | Bafatá | 2,309 | 5,981 | 115,656 |
| Bissau[2] | Bissau | 324 | 840 | 51,796 |
| Bolama | Bolama | 1,013 | 2,624 | 25,449 |
| Cacheu | Cacheu | 1,998 | 5,175 | 127,514 |
| Gabú | Gabú | 3,533 | 9,150 | 103,683 |
| Oio | Farim | 2,086 | 5,403 | 131,271 |
| Quinara | Fulacunda | 1,212 | 3,138 | 35,567 |
| Tombali | Catió | 1,443 | 3,736 | 55,088 |
| **Autonomous Sector** | | | | |
| Bissau | — | 30 | 78 | 107,281 |
| TOTAL | | 13,948 | 36,125 | 753,305 |

## Demography

*Population* (1987): 912,000.
*Density* (1987): persons per sq mi 65.4, persons per sq km 25.2.
*Urban–rural* (1985): urban 27.0%; rural 73.0%.
*Sex distribution* (1985): male 48.42%; female 51.58%.
*Age breakdown* (1985): under 15, 42.9%; 15–29, 25.6%; 30–44, 15.7%; 45–59,
  10.2%; 60–74, 4.7%; 75 and over, 0.9%.
*Population projection:* (1990) 972,000; (2000) 1,200,000.
*Doubling time:* 37 years.
*Ethnic composition* (1979): Balante 27.2%; Fulani 22.9%; Malinke 12.2%;
  Mandyako 10.6%; Pepel 10.0%; other 17.1%.
*Religious affiliation* (1985): traditional beliefs 65%; Muslim 30%; Chris-
  tian 5%.
*Major cities* (1979): Bissau 109,214; Bafatá 13,429; Gabú 7,803; Mansôa
  5,390; Catió 5,179.

## Vital statistics

*Birth rate* per 1,000 population (1980–85): 40.7 (world avg. 29.0); legitimate,
  n.a.; illegitimate, n.a.
*Death rate* per 1,000 population (1980–85): 21.7 (world avg. 11.0).
*Natural increase rate* per 1,000 population (1980–85): 19.0 (world avg. 18.0).
*Total fertility rate* (avg. births per childbearing woman; 1980–85): 5.4.
*Marriage rate* per 1,000 population: n.a.
*Divorce rate* per 1,000 population: n.a.
*Life expectancy* at birth (1980–85): male 41.4 years; female 44.6 years.
*Major causes of death* per 100,000 population: n.a.; however, major dis-
  eases include tuberculosis of the respiratory system, whooping cough,
  typhoid fever, bacillary dysentery and amebiasis, malaria, pneumonia, and
  meningococcal infections.

## National economy

*Budget* (1985). Revenue: PG 1,000,000,000 (1981; indirect taxes 49.6%; direct taxes 25.8%; duties, fines, and other penalties 3.0%). Expenditures:
  PG 1,000,000,000 (1979; finance 16.3%; defense 15.6%; education 13.3%;
  economic affairs 11.6%; health and social welfare 9.5%; rural development
  5.0%; public works 3.0%).
*Public debt* (external, outstanding; 1985): U.S.$217,400,000.
*Tourism:* n.a.; however, the island of Bubaque is being developed as a
  tourist resort, with 110 rooms in 1979; work began in 1985 on a 180-room
  hotel in Bissau.
*Production* (metric tons except as noted). Agriculture, forestry, fishing
  (1985): rice 110,000, roots and tubers (sweet potatoes and cassava) 40,-
  000, fruit 40,000, peanuts (groundnuts) 30,000, coconuts 25,000, plantains
  25,000, millet 25,000, vegetables 20,000, sorghum 15,000, corn (maize)
  15,000, palm kernels 11,000, cashews 10,000, copra 5,000, sugarcane 5,000,
  papayas 2,000, pulses 2,000; livestock (number of live animals) 225,000
  cattle, 150,000 goats, 133,000 pigs, 65,000 sheep, 420,000 chickens[3]; roundwood 559,000 cu m; fish catch 3,600. Mining and quarrying: n.a.; however,
  prospecting for bauxite, petroleum, and phosphates was being carried out
  in the mid-1980s. Manufacturing (in PG '000,000; 1982): beverages 143.7,
  of which beer 122.3, orangeade and lemonade 16.5; clothing 14.0[4]; peanut
  oil 7.0; palm oil 2.4. Construction (in PG '000,000; 1982): total buildings
  2.5. Energy production (consumption): electricity (kW-hr; 1985) 14,000,-
  000 (14,000,000); coal, none (n.a.); crude petroleum (barrels; 1981) none
  (210,000); petroleum products (metric tons; 1985) none (27,000); natural
  gas, none (n.a.).
*Population economically active* (1979): total 213,010; activity rate of total
  population 38.7% (participation rates: ages 15–64, 41.0%; female 3.6%; unemployed 0.5%).

### Price and earnings indexes (1975 = 100)

| | 1975 | 1976 | 1977 | 1978 | 1979 | 1980 | 1981 |
|---|---|---|---|---|---|---|---|
| Consumer price index | 100.0 | 101.5 | 104.5 | 114.1 | 136.6 | 147.4 | 147.4 |
| Monthly earnings index | ... | ... | ... | ... | ... | ... | ... |

*Land use* (1984): forested 38.2%; meadows and pastures 45.7%; agricultural
  and under permanent cultivation 10.3%; other 5.8%.
*Gross national product* (1985): U.S.$150,000,000 (U.S.$170 per capita).

### Structure of gross domestic product and labour force

| | 1983 | | 1979 | |
|---|---|---|---|---|
| | in value U.S.$'000,000 | % of total value | labour force | % of labour force |
| Agriculture | 37 | 48.7 | 157,320 | 79.2 |
| Mining | 1 | 1.3 | ... | ... |
| Manufacturing | 1 | 1.3 | 3,006 | 1.5 |
| Construction | 2 | 2.6 | 1,727 | 0.9 |
| Public utilities | | | 270 | 0.1 |
| Transportation and communication | | | 2,438 | 1.2 |
| Trade | 35 | 46.1 | 5,250 | 2.6 |
| Finance | | | 207 | 0.1 |
| Pub. admin., defense | | | 27,417 | 13.8 |
| Services | | | | |
| Other | ... | ... | 940 | 0.5 |
| TOTAL | 76[5] | 100.0 | 198,575 | 100.0[6] |

*Household income and expenditure.* Average household size (1981) 4.1; income per household: n.a.; sources of income: n.a.; expenditure: n.a.

## Foreign trade

### Balance of trade (current prices)

| | 1978 | 1979 | 1980 | 1981 | 1982 | 1983 |
|---|---|---|---|---|---|---|
| PG '000,000 | −1,308.8 | −1,588.0 | −1,477.6 | −1,334.1 | −1,500.8 | −1,227.5 |
| % of total | 60.0% | 62.3% | 65.9% | 56.0% | 61.1% | 63.2% |

*Imports* (1983): PG 1,585,600,000 (food and beverages 33.7%, of which
  cereals 22.7%; textiles and clothing 15.8%; transport equipment 12.8%;
  machinery and apparatus, including electrical 8.2%). *Major import sources*
  (1985): Portugal 20.1%; Italy 14.7%; Belgium–Luxembourg 10.9%; France
  6.0%; West Germany 5.8%; The Netherlands 5.5%; Burma 3.3%; Senegal
  2.8%; U.S.S.R. 2.3%; China 2.3%; Eastern European countries 1.5%.
*Exports* (1983): PG 358,100,000 (vegetables and fruits, including peanuts and
  cashew nuts 66.1%; fish, including shrimp 23.7%; cork and wood 4.5%).
  *Major export destinations* (1985): Romania 44.6%; France 16.1%; Portugal
  12.5%; China 12.5%; Spain 4.5%; Senegal 3.7%; Belgium–Luxembourg 3.5%.

## Transport and communications

*Transport.* Railroads: none. Roads (1983): total length 3,143 mi, 5,058 km
  (paved, 8.0%). Vehicles (1982): private motor vehicles 4,100. Merchant marine (1986): vessels (100 gross tons and over) 17; total deadweight tonnage
  2,843. Air transport (1985): passenger-mi 6,000,000, passenger-km 9,000,-
  000; short ton-mi cargo 700,000, metric ton-km cargo 1,000,000; airports
  (1987) with scheduled flights 1.
*Communications.* Daily newspapers (1984): total number 1; total circulation
  6,000; circulation per 1,000 population 7.0. Radio (1986): total number of
  receivers 26,000 (1 per 34 persons). Television: none. Telephones (1986):
  3,000 (1 per 297 persons).

## Education and health

### Education (1984–85)

| | schools | teachers | students | student/ teacher ratio |
|---|---|---|---|---|
| Primary (age 7–13) | 658 | 3,153 | 81,444 | 25.8 |
| Secondary (age 13–18) | 12 | 718 | 11,710 | 16.3 |
| Voc., teacher tr. | 4 | 107 | 1,027 | 9.6 |

*Educational attainment* (1979). Percent of population age 7 and over having:
  no formal schooling or knowledge of reading and writing 90.4%; primary
  education 7.9%; secondary 1.0%; technical 0.5%; higher 0.2%. *Literacy*
  (1985): total population age 15 and over literate 31.4%; males literate
  46.2%; females literate 17.3%.
*Health:* physicians (1980) 108 (1 per 7,287 persons); hospital beds (1983)
  1,593 (1 per 526 persons); infant mortality rate per 1,000 live births
  (1980–85) 143.0.
*Food* (1981–83): daily per capita caloric intake 2,230 (vegetable products
  93%, animal products 7%); (1983) 82% of FAO recommended minimum
  requirement.

## Military

*Total active duty personnel* (1987): 8,550[7] (army 95.9%, navy 3.2%, air force
  0.9%). *Military expenditure as percent of GNP* (1983): 8.4% (world 6.1%);
  per capita expenditure U.S.$11.

[1]Preliminary. [2]Bissau region excludes Bissau city. [3]1982. [4]Production figure for first
three quarters only. [5]At current factor cost. [6]Detail does not add to total given
because of rounding. [7]Includes Gendarmerie.

# Guyana

*Official name:* Co-operative Republic of Guyana.
*Form of government:* unitary multiparty republic with one legislative house (National Assembly [65[1]]).
*Chief of state:* President.
*Head of government:* Prime Minister.
*Capital:* Georgetown.
*Official language:* English.
*Official religion:* none.
*Monetary unit:* 1 Guyana dollar (G$) = 100 cents; valuation (Oct. 5, 1987) 1 U.S.$ = G$8.95; 1 £ = G$14.54.

### Area and population

| Administrative Regions | area | | population |
|---|---|---|---|
| | sq mi | sq km | 1980 census |
| Region 1 (Barima/Waini) | ... | ... | 18,297 |
| Region 2 (Pomeroon/Supenaam) | ... | ... | 42,268 |
| Region 3 (Essequibo Islands/West Demerara) | ... | ... | 104,747 |
| Region 4 (Demerara/Mahaica) | ... | ... | 318,952 |
| Region 5 (Mahaica/Berbice) | ... | ... | 53,862 |
| Region 6 (East Berbice/Corentyne) | ... | ... | 152,517 |
| Region 7 (Cuyuni/Mazaruni) | ... | ... | 14,142 |
| Region 8 (Potaro/Siparuni) | ... | ... | 4,265 |
| Region 9 (Upper Takutu/Upper Essequibo) | ... | ... | 13,051 |
| Region 10 (Upper Demerara/Berbice) | ... | ... | 36,518 |
| TOTAL | 83,000[2] | 215,000[2] | 758,619 |

## Demography

*Population* (1987): 802,000.
*Density* (1987): persons per sq mi 9.7, persons per sq km 3.7.
*Urban–rural* (1986): urban 32.1%; rural 67.9%.
*Sex distribution* (1985): male 50.16%; female 49.84%.
*Age breakdown* (1985): under 15, 37.5%; 15–29, 31.9%; 30–44, 15.8%; 45–59, 8.8%; 60–74, 4.8%; 75 and over, 1.2%.
*Population projection:* (1990) 821,000; (2000) 888,000.
*Doubling time:* 39 years.
*Ethnic composition* (1983): East Indian 51.2%; black (African Negro and Bush Negro) 29.4%; mulatto 13.1%; Amerindian 4.0%, of which Carib 2.8%, Arawak 1.1%; Portuguese 0.8%; Chinese 0.5%; other 1.0%.
*Religious affiliation* (1980): Christian 52.0%, of which Protestant 34.0% [including Anglican 16.0%], Roman Catholic 18.0%; Hindu 34.4%; Muslim 9.0%; traditional beliefs 2.2%; other 2.4%.
*Major cities* (1980): Georgetown 167,839 (200,000[3]); Linden 30,043; New Amsterdam 19,287; Corriverton 13,718; Rose Hall 5,311.

## Vital statistics

*Birth rate* per 1,000 population (1985): 25.5 (world avg. 29.0); legitimate, n.a.; illegitimate, n.a.
*Death rate* per 1,000 population (1985): 7.6 (world avg. 11.0).
*Natural increase rate* per 1,000 population (1985): 17.9 (world avg. 18.0).
*Total fertility rate* (avg. births per childbearing woman; 1984): 3.3.
*Marriage rate* per 1,000 population: n.a.
*Divorce rate* per 1,000 population: n.a.
*Life expectancy* at birth (1980–85): male 66.9 years; female 70.9 years.
*Major causes of death* per 100,000 population (1977): diseases of the circulatory system 236.2; infectious and parasitic diseases 88.1; diseases of the respiratory system 69.3; accidents, poisonings, and violence 67.3; ill-defined conditions 95.9.

## National economy

*Budget* (1985). Revenue: G$962,600,000 (tax revenue 83.9%, of which consumption taxes 21.2%, corporation taxes 20.1%, social security contributions 11.7%; nontax revenue 12.3%). Expenditures: G$1,158,000,000 (economic services 31.5%, of which agriculture, forestry, fishing 10.1%; interest payments 30.1%; defense 12.4%; education 11.1%; health 6.4%).
*Public debt* (external, outstanding; 1986): U.S.$772,200,000.
*Production* (metric tons except as noted). Agriculture, forestry, fishing (1985): sugarcane 3,520,000, rice 300,000, coconuts 40,000, bananas and plantains 20,000, roots and tubers 18,000, oranges 11,000; livestock (number of live animals) 148,000 pigs, 140,000 cattle, 118,000 sheep, 15,000,000 chickens; roundwood 192,000 cu m; fish catch 42,095. Mining and quarrying (1985): bauxite 1,675,000, gold (1986) 14,000 troy oz, diamonds 11,000 carats. Manufacturing (1983): refined sugar 245,000[3]; stock feeds 25,000; soap 1,200; rum 139,000 hectolitres; beer 79,000 hectolitres; cigarettes 408,000,000 units. Construction: n.a. Energy production (consumption): electricity (kW-hr; 1985) 390,000,000 (390,000,000); coal, none (none); crude petroleum, none (none); petroleum products (metric tons; 1985) none (458,000); natural gas, none (none).
*Population economically active* (1980)[4]: total 239,331; activity rate of total population 31.5% (participation rates: ages 15–64, 57.3%; female 24.8%; unemployed [1985] c. 30.0%).

### Price and earnings indexes (1980 = 100)

| | 1978 | 1979 | 1980 | 1981 | 1982 | 1983 | 1984 |
|---|---|---|---|---|---|---|---|
| Consumer price index | 74.4 | 87.7 | 100.0 | 124.7 | 147.8 | 169.9 | 212.7 |
| Weekly earnings index[5] | 85.7 | 95.2 | 100.0 | 110.0 | 168.9 | 160.7 | ... |

*Household income and expenditure.* Average household size (1980) 5.0; income per household: n.a.; sources of income (1974): wages and salaries 73.0%, transfer payments 6.3%, other 20.7%; expenditure (1970)[6]: food, beverages, and tobacco 42.5%, rent and water 21.5%, clothing and footwear 8.6%, education and recreation 6.4%, fuel and light 5.2%, transportation and communication 4.8%, other 11.1%.
*Gross national product* (at current market prices; 1985): U.S.$460,000,000 (U.S.$580 per capita).

### Structure of gross domestic product and labour force

| | 1985 | | 1980 | |
|---|---|---|---|---|
| | in value U.S.$'000,000[7] | % of total value | labour force[4] | % of labour force |
| Agriculture | 154 | 25.9 | 48,603 | 20.3 |
| Mining | 52 | 8.7 | 9,389 | 3.9 |
| Manufacturing | 67 | 11.3 | 27,939 | 11.7 |
| Construction | 44 | 7.4 | 6,574 | 2.8 |
| Public utilities | 8 | 8 | 2,772 | 1.2 |
| Transportation and communication | 44 | 7.4 | 9,160 | 3.8 |
| Trade | 42 | 7.1 | 14,690 | 6.1 |
| Finance | 42 | 7.1 | 2,878 | 1.2 |
| Pub. admin., defense | 134[8] | 22.6[8] | 57,416 | 24.0 |
| Services | 15 | 2.5 | | |
| Other | — | — | 59,910[9] | 25.0 |
| TOTAL | 594 | 100.0 | 239,331 | 100.0 |

*Tourism:* receipts from visitors (1985) U.S.$4,000,000; expenditures by nationals abroad (1983) U.S.$11,000,000.
*Land use* (1984): forested 83.2%; meadows and pastures 6.2%; agricultural and under permanent cultivation 2.5%; other 8.1%.

## Foreign trade[10]

### Balance of trade (current prices)

| | 1981 | 1982 | 1983 | 1984 | 1985 | 1986 |
|---|---|---|---|---|---|---|
| U.S.$'000,000 | −53.2 | −11.9 | −32.4 | +15.3 | +4.9 | −29.9 |
| % of total | 7.1% | 2.5% | 7.7% | 3.7% | 1.2% | 6.7% |

*Imports* (1984): U.S.$222,700,000 (fuels and lubricants 45.9%; capital goods 16.5%, of which industrial and agricultural machinery 5.9%; consumer goods 6.5%, of which food 1.5%). *Major import sources* (1985): Trinidad and Tobago 26.8%; United States 17.6%; Barbados 14.4%; Venezuela 13.3%; United Kingdom 9.8%.
*Exports* (1984): U.S.$207,500,000 (calcined bauxite 33.8%; sugar 28.4%; dried bauxite 10.2%; rice 9.6%; timber 3.4%). *Major export destinations* (1985): United Kingdom 26.7%; United States 21.1%; West Germany 7.6%; Canada 7.4%; Trinidad and Tobago 6.8%.

## Transport and communications

*Transport.* Railroads: length (1985) 65 mi, 109 km; passenger-mi, none; short ton-mi cargo, n.a. Roads (1985): total length 5,524 mi, 8,890 km (paved 9%). Vehicles (1985): passenger cars 25,541; trucks and buses 7,648. Merchant marine (1986): vessels (100 gross tons and over) 103; total deadweight tonnage 22,167. Air transport (1985): passenger-mi 104,000,000, passenger-km 168,000,000; short ton-mi cargo 12,000,000, metric ton-km cargo 18,000,000; airports (1987) with scheduled flights 18.
*Communications.* Daily newspapers (1985): total number 1; total circulation 60,000; circulation per 1,000 population 76. Radio (1986): total number of receivers 350,000 (1 per 2.3 persons). Television (1985): n.a. Telephones (1985): 33,300 (1 per 24 persons).

## Education and health

### Education (1979–80)

| | schools | teachers | students | student/teacher ratio |
|---|---|---|---|---|
| Primary (age 6–11) | 424 | 6,021 | 164,830 | 27.4 |
| Secondary (age 12–17) | 87 | 2,513 | 46,595 | 18.5 |
| Voc., teacher tr. | 15 | 348 | 4,647 | 13.4 |
| Higher | 1 | ... | 1,889 | |

*Educational attainment* (1980). Percent of population age 25 and over having: no formal schooling 8.1%; primary education 72.8%; secondary 17.3%; higher 1.8%. *Literacy* (1980): total population age 15 and over literate 505,300 (95.5%); males literate 255,200 (97.1%); females literate 250,100 (94.0%).
*Health:* physicians (1982) 270 (1 per 2,860 persons); hospital beds (1979) 4,002 (1 per 188 persons); infant mortality rate per 1,000 live births (1985) 41.0.
*Food* (1981–83): daily per capita caloric intake 2,334 (vegetable products 88%, animal products 12%); (1983) 104% of FAO recommended minimum requirement.

## Military

*Total active duty personnel* (1986): 5,450[11] (army 91.7%, navy 5.0%, air force 3.3%). *Military expenditure as percent of GNP* (1984): 4.8% (world 5.9%); per capita expenditure U.S.$31.

[1]Includes 12 seats not popularly elected. [2]Estimated; no dated survey available. [3]1985 estimate. [4]Ages 15–64 only. [5]Wages in nonagricultural activities excluding public utilities, finance and real estate, and services. [6]Weights of consumer price index components. [7]Prices of 1984. [8]Public administration, defense includes Public utilities. [9]Includes 15,260 persons in activities not adequately defined and 44,650 unemployed. [10]Import figures are f.o.b. in balance of trade and c.i.f. in commodities and trading partners. [11]All services are part of the army.

# Haiti

*Official name:* Repiblik Dayti (Haitian Creole): République d'Haïti (French) (Republic of Haiti).
*Form of government:* interim military-civilian regime[1].
*Head of state and government:* President assisted by National Council of Government.
*Capital:* Port-au-Prince.
*Official languages:* Haitian Creole; French.
*Official religion:* none.
*Monetary unit:* 1 gourde (G) = 100 centimes; valuation (Oct. 5, 1987) 1 U.S.$ = G 5.00; 1 £ = G 8.12.

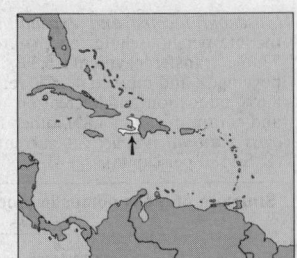

| Area and population | | area | | population |
|---|---|---|---|---|
| | | | | 1987 |
| Departements | Capitals | sq mi | sq km | estimate |
| Artibonite | Gonaïves | 1,750 | 4,532 | 789,019 |
| Centre | Hinche | 1,429 | 3,700 | 393,217 |
| Grande Anse | Jérémie | 1,268 | 3,284 | 514,962 |
| Nord | Cap-Haïtien | 790 | 2,045 | 602,336 |
| Nord-Est | Fort-Liberté | 676 | 1,752 | 197,669 |
| Nord-Ouest | Port-de-Paix | 899 | 2,330 | 320,632 |
| Ouest | Port-au-Prince | 1,795 | 4,649 | 1,808,274 |
| Sud | Les Cayes | 1,117 | 2,894 | 526,420 |
| Sud-Est | Jacmel | 855 | 2,215 | 379,273 |
| TOTAL | | 10,579 | 27,400[2] | 5,531,802 |

## Demography

*Population* (1987): 5,532,000.
*Density* (1987): persons per sq mi 522.9, persons per sq km 201.9.
*Urban–rural* (1986): urban 28.9%; rural 71.1%.
*Sex distribution* (1982): male 48.48%; female 51.52%.
*Age breakdown* (1982): under 15, 39.2%; 15–29, 26.9%; 30–44, 15.6%; 45–59, 10.0%; 60–74, 5.4%; 75 and over, 2.9%.
*Population projection:* (1990) 5,863,000; (2000) 7,118,000.
*Doubling time:* 30 years.
*Ethnic composition* (1983): black 90.0%; mulatto 10.0%.
*Religious affiliation* (1982): Roman Catholic 80.3%[3]; Protestant 15.8%, of which Baptist 9.7%, Pentecostal 3.6%; other 3.9%.
*Major cities* (1987): Port-au-Prince 472,895; Cap-Haïtien 72,161; Gonaïves 37,034; Les Cayes 35,829; Pétionville 35,333[4].

## Vital statistics

*Birth rate* per 1,000 population (1985): 36.0 (world avg. 29.0).
*Death rate* per 1,000 population (1985): 13.0 (world avg. 11.0).
*Natural increase rate* per 1,000 population (1985): 23.0 (world avg. 18.0).
*Total fertility rate* (avg. births per childbearing woman; 1984): 4.5.
*Marriage rate* per 1,000 population (1980): 0.7[5].
*Divorce rate* per 1,000 population (1980): 0.1[5].
*Life expectancy* at birth (1980–85): male 51.2 years; female 54.4 years.
*Major causes of death* per 100,000 population (1982)[6]: infectious and parasitic diseases 46.0, of which tuberculosis 13.1; diseases of the circulatory system 11.9; diseases associated with malnutrition 8.5; diseases of the respiratory system 8.3; endocrine and metabolic disorders 8.0; ill-defined conditions 115.2.

## National economy

*Budget* (1985). Revenue (excluding foreign grants and loans) and nontax revenue[7]: G 1,074,000,000 (excises 24.2%, import duties 23.2%, general sales taxes 17.3%). Expenditures: G 1,808,800,000 (general public services 19.3%, defense 8.4%, education 6.0%, health 5.7%, not published 45.1%).
*Production* (metric tons except as noted). Agriculture, forestry, fishing (1985–86): sugarcane 5,772,000, sweet potatoes 350,000[8], mangoes 340,000[8], plantains 315,000[8], bananas 235,000[8], corn (maize) 196,000, rice 129,000, sorghum 119,000, dry beans 48,000, coffee 38,000, oranges 32,000[8], cacao 5,600; livestock (number of live animals; 1985) 1,350,000 cattle, 1,100,000 goats, 500,000 pigs; roundwood (1985) 5,902,000 cu m; fish catch (1985) 4,400. Mining and quarrying (1986)[9]: limestone 217,000. Manufacturing (value of production in G '000,000; 1985–86): articles assembled for reexport 723 (including garments 261, transformers and switches 202, sports equipment and toys 123); refined flour (1982) 218; cement (1983) 115; leather manufactures (mostly baseballs and softballs) 102[10]; cigarettes (1984) 886,000,000 units; essential oils (1984) 8,500 metric tons. Construction: n.a. Energy production (consumption): electricity (kW-hr; 1985–86) 411,000,000[8] (320,000,000); coal, none (none); crude petroleum, none (none); petroleum products (metric tons; 1985) none (211,000); natural gas, none (none).
*Tourism:* receipts from visitors (1985) U.S.$69,000,000; expenditures by nationals abroad (1983) U.S.$39,000,000.
*Population economically active* (1983): total 2,263,832; activity rate of total population 44.2% (participation rates: ages 15–64, 69.1%; female 42.9% (unemployed [1987] unofficially 60.0%).

| Price and earnings indexes (1980 = 100) | | | | | | | |
|---|---|---|---|---|---|---|---|
| | 1981 | 1982 | 1983 | 1984 | 1985 | 1986 | March 1987 |
| Consumer price index | 110.9 | 119.0 | 131.2 | 139.6 | 159.6 | 159.6 | 143.1 |
| Daily earnings index[11] | 115.0 | 120.0 | 120.0 | 120.0 | 136.4 | ... | ... |

*Household income and expenditure.* Average household size (1982) 4.4; sources of income: n.a.; expenditure (1976): food and beverages 77.9%[12], housing 8.3%, household furnishings 4.0%, clothing and footwear 3.2%, other 6.6%.
*Public debt* (external, outstanding; 1985): U.S.$534,200,000.
*Gross national product* (1985): U.S.$1,900,000,000 (U.S.$360 per capita).

| Structure of gross domestic product and labour force | | | | |
|---|---|---|---|---|
| | 1985[13] | | 1983 | |
| | in value U.S.$'000,000 | % of total value | labour force | % of labour force |
| Agriculture | 560 | 31.9 | 1,299,440 | 57.4 |
| Mining | 2 | 0.1 | 20,374 | 0.9 |
| Manufacturing | 303 | 17.2 | 129,038 | 5.7 |
| Construction | 98 | 5.6 | 22,638 | 1.0 |
| Public utilities | 15 | 0.9 | 2,264 | 0.1 |
| Transp. and commun. | 38 | 2.2 | 18,111 | 0.8 |
| Trade | 314 | 17.9 | 303,353 | 13.4 |
| Finance | 98 | 5.6 | 4,528 | 0.2 |
| Pub. admin., defense | 129 | 7.3 | ... | ... |
| Services | 201 | 11.4 | 133,566 | 5.9 |
| Other | — | — | 330,520[14] | 14.6[14] |
| TOTAL | 1,758 | 100.0[2] | 2,263,832 | 100.0 |

*Land use* (1984): forested 2.0%; meadows and pastures 18.1%; agricultural and under permanent cultivation 32.8%; other 47.1%.

## Foreign trade[15]

| Balance of trade (current prices) | | | | | |
|---|---|---|---|---|---|
| | 1981–82 | 1982–83 | 1983–84 | 1984–85 | 1985–86 |
| G '000,000 | −1,029.8 | −1,115.7 | −1,080.4 | −1,113.2 | −1,016.4 |
| % of total | 36.2% | 37.2% | 33.0% | 33.0% | 34.4% |

*Imports* (1985–86): G 1,985,700,000 (machinery and transport equipment 20.3%; basic manufactures 17.2%; food and live animals 16.3%; petroleum products 11.9%; chemical products 10.4%). *Major import sources:* United States 47.4%; Caribbean area 15.6%; Japan 7.0%; Canada 5.8%; France 3.9%.
*Exports* (1985–86): G 969,300,000 (manufactured goods 33.5%, of which leather products 10.5%; coffee 26.9%; assembled articles for reexport 24.4%; essential oils 2.5%; cocoa 2.1%). *Major export destinations:* United States 53.2%; Italy 12.1%; France 10.7%; Belgium 8.2%; Caribbean area 5.0%.

## Transport and communications

*Transport.* Railroads (1986)[16]. Roads (1985): total length 2,299 mi, 3,700 km (paved 17%). Vehicles (1985): passenger cars 34,669; trucks and buses 11,658. Merchant marine (1986): vessels (100 gross tons and over) 8; total deadweight tonnage 1,705. Air transport (1983)[17]: passenger arrivals 226,000, passenger departures 242,000; cargo unloaded 12,100 metric tons, cargo loaded 14,700 metric tons; airports (1987) with scheduled flights 2.
*Communications.* Daily newspapers (1985): total number 6; total circulation 21,500; circulation per 1,000 population 4.0. Radio (1986): total number of receivers 200,000 (1 per 27 persons). Television (1986): total number of receivers 25,000 (1 per 217 persons). Telephones (1983): 38,400 (1 per 133 persons).

## Education and health

| Education (1983–84) | | | | student/ |
|---|---|---|---|---|
| | schools | teachers | students | teacher ratio |
| Primary (age 6–12) | 3,403 | 18,483 | 783,070 | 42.4 |
| Secondary (age 13–18) | 314 | 5,781 | 134,278 | 23.2 |
| Voc., teacher tr. | 10 | ... | 859 | ... |
| Higher | ... | 818 | 5,492 | 6.7 |

*Educational attainment* (1982). Percent of population age 25 and over having: no formal schooling 76.9%; primary education 15.2%; secondary 7.2%; higher 0.7%. *Literacy* (1982): total population age 15 and over literate 1,066,966 (34.7%); males literate 547,318 (37.1%); females literate 519,648 (32.5%).
*Health* (1985): physicians 803 (1 per 6,539 persons); hospital beds (1982) 3,608 (1 per 1,397 persons); infant mortality rate per 1,000 live births 107.0.
*Food* (1981–83): daily per capita caloric intake 1,901 (vegetable products 95%, animal products 5%); (1983) 83% of FAO recommended minimum requirement.

## Military

*Total active duty personnel* (1986): 6,900 (army 92.8%, navy 4.3%, air force 2.9%). *Military expenditure as percent of GNP* (1984): 1.6% (world 5.9%); per capita expenditure U.S.$5.

[1]Implementation of constitution approved by referendum on March 29, 1987, was pending at year end. [2]Detail does not add to total given because of rounding. [3]About 90% of all Roman Catholics also practice Voodoo. [4]1982 preliminary census figure. [5]Registered only. [6]Public health facilities only. [7]Up to 75% of revenue indirectly or directly financed by foreign donors. [8]1985. [9]First nine months only. [10]Export value only. [11]Excludes alcoholic beverages. [12]Minimum wage. [13]In 1984 prices. [14]Includes 54,332 not adequately defined and 276,188 unemployed persons not previously employed. [15]Import figures are f.o.b. in balance of trade and c.i.f. in commodities and trading partners. [16]The only railway is privately owned and used to transport sugarcane. [17]Port-au-Prince airport only.

# Honduras

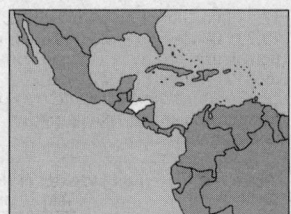

*Official name:* República de Honduras (Republic of Honduras).
*Form of government:* multiparty republic with one legislative house (National Congress [134]).
*Head of state and government:* President.
*Capital:* Tegucigalpa.
*Official language:* Spanish.
*Official religion:* none.
*Monetary unit:* 1 Honduran lempira (L) = 100 centavos; valuation[1] (Oct. 5, 1987) 1 U.S.$ = L 2.00; 1 £ = L 3.25.

## Area and population

| Departments | Administrative centres | area sq mi | area sq km | population 1983 estimate |
|---|---|---|---|---|
| Atlántida | La Ceiba | 1,641 | 4,251 | 242,200 |
| Choluteca | Choluteca | 1,626 | 4,211 | 289,600 |
| Colón | Trujillo | 3,427 | 8,875 | 128,400 |
| Comayagua | Comayagua | 2,006 | 5,196 | 211,500 |
| Copán | Santa Rosa de Copán | 1,237 | 3,203 | 217,300 |
| Cortés | San Pedro Sula | 1,527 | 3,954 | 624,100 |
| El Paraíso | Yuscarán | 2,787 | 7,218 | 206,600 |
| Francisco Morazán | Tegucigalpa | 3,068 | 7,946 | 736,300 |
| Gracias a Dios | Puerto Lempira | 6,421 | 16,630 | 35,500 |
| Intibucá | La Esperanza | 1,186 | 3,072 | 111,400 |
| Islas de la Bahía | Roatán | 100 | 261 | 18,700 |
| La Paz | La Paz | 900 | 2,331 | 86,600 |
| Lempira | Gracias | 1,656 | 4,290 | 174,900 |
| Ocotepeque | Nueva Ocotepeque | 649 | 1,680 | 64,100 |
| Olancho | Juticalpa | 9,402 | 24,351 | 228,100 |
| Santa Bárbara | Santa Bárbara | 1,975 | 5,115 | 286,800 |
| Valle | Nacaome | 604 | 1,565 | 125,600 |
| Yoro | Yoro | 3,065 | 7,939 | 304,300 |
| TOTAL | | 43,277 | 112,088 | 4,092,200[2] |

## Demography

*Population* (1987): 4,657,000.
*Density* (1987): persons per sq mi 107.6, persons per sq km 41.5.
*Urban–rural* (1986): urban 40.7%; rural 59.3%.
*Sex distribution* (1985): male 50.14%; female 49.86%.
*Age breakdown* (1985): under 15, 46.9%; 15–29, 26.9%; 30–44, 13.8%; 45–59, 7.9%; 60–74, 3.7%; 75 and over 0.8%.
*Population projection:* (1990) 5,105,000; (2000) 6,978,000.
*Doubling time:* 21 years.
*Ethnic composition* (1982): mestizo 90.0%; black (including Black Carib) 5.0%; Indian 4.0%; white 1.0%.
*Religious affiliation* (1984): Roman Catholic 96.1%; other 3.9%.
*Major cities* (1985): Tegucigalpa 571,400; San Pedro Sula 372,800; La Ceiba 61,900; Choluteca 57,200; El Progreso 55,500.

## Vital statistics

*Birth rate* per 1,000 population (1985): 41.0 (world avg. 29.0); legitimate, n.a.; illegitimate, n.a.
*Death rate* per 1,000 population (1985): 8.0 (world avg. 11.0).
*Natural increase rate* per 1,000 population (1985): 33.0 (world avg. 18.0).
*Total fertility rate* (avg. births per childbearing woman; 1984): 6.2.
*Marriage rate* per 1,000 population (1983): 4.9.
*Divorce rate* per 1,000 population (1983): 0.4.
*Life expectancy* at birth (1980–85): male 58.2 years; female 61.7 years.
*Major causes of death* per 100,000 population (1981): infectious and parasitic diseases 80.9; accidents and violence 53.9; diseases of the circulatory system 53.1; diseases of the respiratory system 31.9; ill-defined conditions 160.2.

## National economy

*Budget* (1985). Revenue: L 3,004,000,000 (current revenue 61.2%, of which nontax revenue 20.4%, tax on production and internal trade 11.6%, import duties 10.5%, individual income tax 8.0%; development revenue 38.8%). Expenditures: L 3,078,000,000 (current expenditure 57.7%, of which wages and salaries 27.7%; development expenditure 21.7%; debt servicing 17.9%).
*Tourism* (1984): receipts from visitors U.S.$24,000,000; expenditures by nationals abroad U.S.$23,000,000.
*Production* (metric tons except as noted). Agriculture, forestry, fishing (1986): sugarcane 3,226,000[3], bananas 1,300,000, corn (maize) 484,000, mangoes 350,000, plantains 170,000[3], coffee 78,000, dry beans 52,000[3], oranges 47,000, millet 39,000[3], rice 35,000[3], palm kernels 6,000; livestock (number of live animals; 1985) 2,371,000 cattle, 717,000 pigs; roundwood (1985) 5,082 cu m; fish catch (1985) 9,592, of which spiny lobster 4,065, shrimp 2,650. Mining and quarrying (1985)[4]: limestone 500,000; zinc (metal content) 44,026; gypsum 22,000; lead 21,250; silver 2,678,000 troy oz; gold 2,500 troy oz. Manufacturing (1986): cement 360,000; raw sugar 215,600[3]; beef and veal 66,000; palm oil 20,000; steel rods 11,800; beer 514,000 hectolitres; hard liquor 17,000 hectolitres; cigarettes 2,134,000,000 units. Construction (1986)[5]: residential 214,000 sq m; nonresidential 98,000 sq m. Energy production (consumption): electricity (kW-hr; 1985) 1,382,500,000 (1,199,700,000); coal, none (none); crude petroleum (barrels; 1985) none (1,979,000); petroleum products (metric tons; 1985) 264,000 (569,000); natural gas, none (none).
*Gross national product* (at current market prices; 1985): U.S.$3,190,000,000 (U.S.$730 per capita).

## Structure of gross domestic product and labour force

| | 1985 in value L '000,000 | 1985 % of total value | 1984 labour force | 1984 % of labour force |
|---|---|---|---|---|
| Agriculture | 1,607 | 23.9 | 718,505 | 57.2 |
| Mining | 132 | 2.0 | 3,895 | 0.3 |
| Manufacturing | 838 | 12.5 | 167,597 | 13.3 |
| Construction | 356 | 5.3 | 43,470 | 3.5 |
| Public utilities | 148 | 2.2 | 5,151 | 0.4 |
| Transportation and communication | 450 | 6.7 | 37,565 | 3.0 |
| Trade | 786 | 11.7 | 107,292 | 8.5 |
| Finance, real estate | 731 | 10.9 | 12,438 | 1.0 |
| Public admin., defense | 323 | 4.8 | | |
| Services | 548 | 8.2 | 160,436 | 12.8 |
| Other | 800[6] | 11.9[6] | | |
| TOTAL | 6,719 | 100.0[2] | 1,256,349 | 100.0 |

*Public debt* (external, outstanding; 1985): U.S.$2,178,400,000.
*Population economically active* (1984): total 1,256,349; activity rate of total population 29.7% (participation rates: ages 15–64, 53.6%; female 16.7%; unemployed [1986] 25.0%).

## Price and earnings indexes (1980 = 100)

| | 1980 | 1981 | 1982 | 1983 | 1984 | 1985 | 1986 |
|---|---|---|---|---|---|---|---|
| Consumer price index | 100.0 | 109.4 | 119.2 | 129.1 | 135.2 | 139.7 | 145.8 |
| Weekly earnings index[7] | 100.0 | 139.3 | 211.5 | 149.5 | 179.0 | 243.6 | ... |

*Household income and expenditure:* Average household size (1979) 5.7; income per household: n.a.; sources of income (1983): wages and salaries 52.7%, transfer payments 1.7%, other 45.6%; expenditure (1983): food 44.4%, utilities and housing 22.3%, clothing and footwear 9.1%, household furnishings 8.3%, health care 6.9%, other 9.0%.
*Land use* (1984): forested 33.4%; meadows and pastures 30.4%; agricultural and under permanent cultivation 15.9%; other 20.3%.

## Foreign trade[8]

### Balance of trade (current prices)

| L '000,000 | 1980 | 1981 | 1982 | 1983 | 1984 | 1985 |
|---|---|---|---|---|---|---|
| L '000,000 | −179.8 | −201.2 | +10.3 | −84.1 | −239.5 | −47.3 |
| % of total | 5.0% | 6.0% | 0.4% | 2.9% | 7.4% | 1.5% |

*Imports* (1985): L 1,776,200,000 (machinery and transport equipment 22.9%, basic manufactures 21.7%, chemical products 19.9%, mineral fuels 18.4%, food products 9.0%). *Major import sources:* U.S. 35.8%; Venezuela 13.0%; Japan 5.8%; Guatemala 4.9%; Mexico 4.6%.
*Exports* (1985): L 1,560,100,000 (bananas 35.1%, coffee 23.7%, lead and zinc 6.0%, shrimp and lobsters 5.2%, wood 4.4%). *Major export destinations:* U.S. 47.3%; Italy 7.8%; West Germany 7.5%; Japan 6.6%; Belgium 6.6%.

## Transport and communications

*Transport.* Railroads (1986): route length 571 mi, 919 km; passengers, n.a.; cargo, n.a. Roads (1985): total length 10,577 mi, 17,022 km (paved 12%). Vehicles (1985): passenger cars 66,666; trucks and buses 18,759. Merchant marine (1986): vessels (100 gross tons and over) 424; total deadweight tonnage 827,066. Air transport (1984)[9]: passenger-mi 254,500,000, passenger-km 409,500,000; short ton-mi cargo 11,680,000, metric ton-km cargo 17,053,000; airports (1987) with scheduled flights 5.
*Communications.* Daily newspapers (1986): total number 7; total circulation 293,000; circulation per 1,000 population 65. Radio (1986): total number of receivers 300,000 (1 per 15 persons). Television (1986): total number of receivers 90,000 (1 per 50 persons). Telephones (1985): 45,616 (1 per 96 persons).

## Education and health

### Education (1985)

| | schools | teachers | students | student/ teacher ratio |
|---|---|---|---|---|
| Primary (age 7–13) | 6,492 | 20,724 | 858,061 | 41.4 |
| Secondary (age 14–19) Voc., teacher tr. | 452 | 6,799 | 130,277 | 19.2 |
| Higher | 7 | 2,692 | 34,478 | 14.0 |

*Educational attainment* (1983). Percentage of population age 25 and over having: no formal schooling 33.5%; incomplete primary education 51.3%; incomplete secondary 4.3%; complete secondary 7.6%; higher 3.3%. *Literacy* (1980): total population age 15 and over literate 1,309,500 (68.6%); males literate 676,700 (71.1%); females literate 632,800 (66.2%).
*Health* (1985): physicians 1,900 (1 per 2,301 persons); hospital beds 5,220 (1 per 838 persons); infant mortality rate per 1,000 live births 73.0.
*Food* (1981–83): daily per capita caloric intake 2,143 (vegetable products 88%, animal products 12%); (1983) 94% of FAO recommended minimum requirement.

## Military

*Total active duty personnel* (1986): 19,200 (army 88.5%, navy 3.7%, air force 7.8%). *Military expenditure as percent of GNP* (1984): 4.2% (world 5.9%); per capita expenditure U.S.$29.

[1]The Honduran lempira is officially pegged to the U.S. dollar at L 2.00 per U.S.$1. [2]Detail does not add to total given because of rounding. [3]1985. [4]Lead/zinc/silver mine closed in April 1987. [5]Tegucigalpa, San Pedro Sula, and La Ceiba only. [6]Includes net indirect taxes. [7]Wages in nonagricultural activities. [8]Import figures are f.o.b. (free on board) in balance of trade and c.i.f. (cost, insurance, and freight) for commodities and trading partners. [9]TAN and SAHSA airlines only.

# Hong Kong

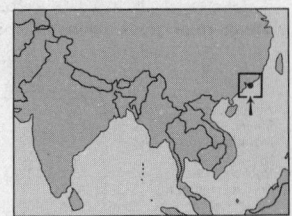

*Official name:* Hsiang Kang (Chinese); Hong Kong (English).
*Political status:* colony (United Kingdom) with three nominated advisory councils (Executive Council [16]; Legislative Council [57]; Urban Council [30]).
*Chief of state:* British Monarch.
*Head of government:* Governor.
*Capital:* Victoria.
*Official languages:* Chinese; English.
*Official religion:* none.
*Monetary unit:* 1 HK dollar (HK$) = 100 cents; valuation (Oct. 5, 1987) 1 U.S.$ = HK$7.81; 1 £ = HK$12.69.

### Area and population

| Districts | area[1] | | population[2] |
|---|---|---|---|
| | sq mi | sq km | 1986 census |
| Hong Kong Island | 30.4 | 78.7 | 1,175,800 |
| Kowloon | 16.3 | 42.2 | 2,301,700 |
| New Territories | 356.6 | 923.7 | 1,918,500 |
| TOTAL | 403.3 | 1,044.6 | 5,396,000 |

## Demography

*Population* (1987): 5,602,000.
*Density[3]* (1987): persons per sq mi 13,890.4, persons per sq km 5,362.8.
*Urban–rural* (1986): urban 92.5%; rural 7.5%.
*Sex distribution* (1986): male 51.49%; female 48.51%.
*Age breakdown[2]* (1986): under 15, 23.1%; 15–29, 29.9%; 30–44, 21.2%; 45–59, 14.3%; 60–74, 9.1%; 75 and over, 2.4%.
*Population projection:* (1990) 5,814,000; (2000) 6,665,000.
*Doubling time:* 84 years.
*Ethnic composition* (1987): Chinese 97.0%; Filipino 0.7%; British 0.3%; other 2.0%.
*Religious affiliation* (1987): predominantly Buddhist and Taoist; some Confucianist; Christian 8.6%.
*Major cities:* no bounded localities exist within Hong Kong.

## Vital statistics

*Birth rate* per 1,000 population (1986): 13.0 (world avg. 26.0).
*Death rate* per 1,000 population (1986): 4.7 (world avg. 9.9).
*Natural increase rate* per 1,000 population (1986): 8.3 (world avg. 16.1).
*Total fertility rate* (avg. births per childbearing woman; 1984): 1.8.
*Marriage rate* per 1,000 population (1986): 8.0.
*Divorce rate* per 1,000 population (1986): 1.0.
*Life expectancy* at birth (1985): male 72.5 years; female 78.4 years.
*Major causes of death* per 100,000 population (1986): malignant neoplasms (cancers) 146.0; diseases of circulatory system 136.2; diseases of respiratory system 76.8; accidents 29.3; diseases of the genitourinary system 21.8; diseases of digestive system 19.7.

## National economy

*Budget* (1986–87 est.). Revenue: HK$43,409,000,000 (earnings and profit taxes 39.1%; indirect taxes 25.9%, of which entertainment and stamp duties 12.9%, excise duties 7.8%; capital revenue 12.0%). Expenditures: HK$48,462,000,000 (education 18.0%; housing 12.0%; medical 8.9%; law and order 8.5%; social welfare 5.8%; defense 4.2%).
*Public debt* (external, outstanding; 1985): U.S.$251,100,000.
*Gross domestic product* (at current market prices; 1985): U.S.$33,770,000,000 (U.S.$6,190 per capita).

### Structure of gross domestic product and labour force

| | 1985 | | | |
|---|---|---|---|---|
| | in value HK$'000,000 | % of total value | labour force | % of labour force |
| Agriculture | 1,238 | 0.5 | 45,100 | 1.7 |
| Mining | 357 | 0.1 | 300 | — |
| Manufacturing | 52,501 | 21.6 | 933,000 | 35.4 |
| Construction | 12,210 | 5.0 | 198,300 | 7.5 |
| Public utilities | 6,665 | 2.7 | 19,200 | 0.7 |
| Transportation and communication | 19,389 | 8.0 | 215,100 | 8.2 |
| Trade | 55,132 | 22.7 | 601,200 | 22.8 |
| Finance | 66,659 | 27.4 | 150,800 | 5.7 |
| Pub. admin., defense, and services | 40,599 | 16.7 | 453,900 | 17.2 |
| Other | −11,468[4] | −4.7[4] | 20,200[5] | 0.8[5] |
| TOTAL | 243,282 | 100.0 | 2,637,100 | 100.0 |

*Production* (metric tons except as noted). Agriculture, forestry, fishing (1986): vegetables 157,000, fruits and nuts 2,040, field crops 1,500, rice 10, milk 2,500; livestock (number of live animals) 560,000 pigs[6], 970 cattle; roundwood (1985) 180,000 cu m; fish catch 161,310, of which marine 155,600. Mining and quarrying (1985): feldspar sand 82,446; feldspar 26,777; kaolin 9,602; quartz 116. Manufacturing (value added in HK$; 1984): wearing apparel 13,171,000,000; textile 7,294,000,000; electrical machinery 6,058,911,000; plastic products 4,809,000,000; publishing and printed material 2,458,000,000; food, beverages, and tobacco 2,181,000,000. Construction (value in HK$; 1985): residential 6,622,000,000; nonresidential

12,536,000,000. Energy production (consumption): electricity (kW-hr; 1985) 19,235,000,000 (18,185,000,000); coal (metric tons; 1985) none (5,223,000); petroleum products (metric tons; 1985) none (3,799,000); natural gas (cu m; 1986) none (231,770,000).
*Population economically active* (1986): total 2,701,500; activity rate of total population 48.9% (participation rates: over age 15, 65.1%; female 48.9%; unemployed 2.8%).

### Price and earnings indexes (1980 = 100)

| | 1981 | 1982 | 1983 | 1984 | 1985 | 1986 | 1987[7] |
|---|---|---|---|---|---|---|---|
| Consumer price index | 117.9 | 130.3 | 143.2 | 154.9 | 159.8 | 164.3 | 169.1 |
| Daily earnings index | 125.0 | 140.4 | 150.7 | 163.8 | 173.9 | ... | ... |

*Household income and expenditure.* Average household size (1986) 3.7; income per household (1983) HK$92,000 (U.S.$11,800); sources of income: n.a.; expenditure (1984–85): food 38.0%, housing 21.0%, clothing and footwear 7.0%, transportation and vehicles 7.0%, durable goods 4.0%, fuel and light 3.0%.
*Tourism* (1986): receipts from visitors U.S.$2,210,800,000; expenditures by nationals abroad, n.a.
*Land use* (1986): forested 20.6%; agricultural and under permanent cultivation 6.8%; fish ponds 2.0%; built-on, scrub lands, and other 70.6%.

## Foreign trade

### Balance of trade (current prices)

| | 1981 | 1982 | 1983 | 1984 | 1985 | 1986 |
|---|---|---|---|---|---|---|
| HK$'000,000 | −16,212 | −15,508 | −14,743 | −1,929 | +3,733 | +575 |
| % of total | 6.2% | 5.7% | 4.4% | 0.4% | 0.8% | 0.1% |

*Imports* (1986): HK$275,954,550,000 (machinery and transport equipment 24.0%, of which electrical machinery 8.6%; textile yarn and fabrics 15.4%; food and live animals 8.1%, of which vegetables and fruits 2.1%; chemicals and related products 7.7%; photographic apparatus, watches, and clocks 6.0%; petroleum and petroleum products 3.2%). *Major import sources:* China 29.6%; Japan 20.4%; Taiwan 8.7%; United States 8.4%; South Korea 4.0%; Singapore 3.9%; United Kingdom 3.4%.
*Exports* (1986): HK$153,983,440,000[8] (clothing accessories and apparel 33.9%; machinery and transport equipment 21.6%, of which electrical machinery 7.3%; photographic apparatus, watches, and clocks 8.5%; textile yarn and fabrics 7.1%; travel goods 1.0%). *Major export destinations:* United States 41.7%; China 11.7%; West Germany 7.1%; United Kingdom 6.4%; Japan 4.0%; Australia 3.2%.

## Transport and communications

*Transport.* Railroads (1984): length 24 mi[9], 39 km[9]; passenger-mi 919,640,000, passenger-km 1,480,020,000; short ton-mi cargo 63,668,000, metric ton-km cargo 92,954,000. Roads (1986): total length 839 mi, 1,350 km (paved 100%). Vehicles (1986): passenger cars 177,961; trucks and buses 93,092. Merchant marine (1986): vessels (100 gross tons and over) 416; total deadweight tonnage 13,664,489. Air transport (1985): passenger arrivals 4,613,145, passenger departures 4,747,804; airports (1987) with scheduled flights 1.
*Communications.* Daily newspapers (1984): total number 67[9]; total circulation 3,189,000[10]; circulation per 1,000 population 602[10]. Radio (1986): total number of receivers 2,740,000 (1 per 2.0 persons). Television (1986): total number of receivers 1,312,000 (1 per 4.1 persons). Telephones (1986): 2,461,000 (1 per 2.2 persons).

## Education and health

### Education (1985–86)

| | schools | teachers | students | student/ teacher ratio |
|---|---|---|---|---|
| Primary (age 6–11) | 736 | 19,404 | 534,903 | 27.6 |
| Secondary (age 12–18) | 407 | 17,724 | 431,781 | 24.4 |
| Vocational | 24 | 1,025 | 18,586 | 18.1 |
| Higher | 11 | 3,262 | 29,977 | 9.2 |

*Educational attainment* (1981). Percent of population age 25 and over having: no schooling 22.5%; primary education 39.9%; secondary 30.5%; postsecondary 7.1%. *Literacy* (1985): total population age 15 and over literate 3,668,000 (88.1%); males literate 2,040,000 (94.7%); females literate 1,628,000 (80.9%).
*Health* (1986): physicians 5,147 (1 per 1,075 persons); hospital beds 24,550 (1 per 225 persons); infant mortality rate per 1,000 live births 7.6.
*Food* (1981–83): daily per capita caloric intake 2,766 (vegetable products 71%, animal products 29%); (1983) 117% of FAO recommended minimum requirement.

## Military

*Total active duty personnel* (1986): 8,945[11] (army 87.7%; navy 9.3%; air force, n.a.). *Military expenditure as percent of GNP* (1984): 0.6% (world 5.9%); per capita expenditure U.S.$39.

[1]Excludes the surface areas of reservoirs. [2]Excludes 26,100 transients and 9,100 Vietnamese refugees. [3]Density based on land area. [4]Less imputed bank service charges. [5]Not employed; previously unemployed. [6]Excludes local pigs not slaughtered in abattoirs. [7]February. [8]Excludes reexports valued at HK$122,546,370,000 in 1986. [9]1986. [10]Thirty-five newspapers only. [11]British forces with a few locally enlisted personnel in the navy.

# Hungary

*Official name:* Magyar Népköztársaság (Hungarian People's Republic).
*Form of government:* unitary single-party republic with one legislative house (National Assembly [386]).
*Chief of State:* President.
*Head of government:* Prime Minister.
*Capital:* Budapest.
*Official language:* Hungarian.
*Official religion:* none.
*Monetary unit:* 1 forint (Ft) = 100 fillér; valuation (Oct. 5, 1987) 1 U.S.$ = Ft 47.99; 1 £ = Ft 77.92.

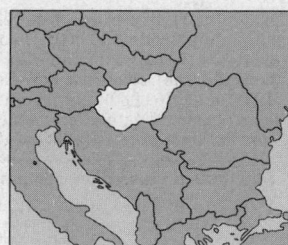

### Area and population

| Counties | Capitals | area | | population |
|---|---|---|---|---|
| | | sq mi | sq km | 1986 estimate[1] |
| Baranya | Pécs | 1,732 | 4,487 | 432,000 |
| Bács-Kiskun | Kecskemét | 3,229 | 8,362 | 558,000 |
| Békés | Békéscsaba | 2,175 | 5,632 | 422,000 |
| Borsod-Abaúj-Zemplén | Miskolc | 2,798 | 7,248 | 791,000 |
| Csongrád | Szeged | 1,646 | 4,263 | 457,000 |
| Fejér | Székesfehérvár | 1,689 | 4,374 | 426,000 |
| Győr-Sopron | Győr | 1,549 | 4,012 | 428,000 |
| Hajdú-Bihar | Debrecen | 2,398 | 6,212 | 551,000 |
| Heves | Eger | 1,404 | 3,637 | 342,000 |
| Komárom | Tatabánya | 869 | 2,250 | 321,000 |
| Nógrád | Salgótarján | 982 | 2,544 | 233,000 |
| Pest | Budapest[2] | 2,469 | 6,394 | 985,000 |
| Somogy | Kaposvár | 2,331 | 6,036 | 353,000 |
| Szabolcs-Szatmár | Nyíregyháza | 2,293 | 5,938 | 578,000 |
| Szolnok | Szolnok | 2,165 | 5,608 | 436,000 |
| Tolna | Szekszárd | 1,430 | 3,704 | 266,000 |
| Vas | Szombathely | 1,288 | 3,337 | 280,000 |
| Veszprém | Veszprém | 1,810 | 4,689 | 388,000 |
| Zala | Zalaegerszeg | 1,461 | 3,784 | 313,000 |
| **Capital City** | | | | |
| Budapest[2] | | 203 | 525 | 2,080,000 |
| TOTAL | | 35,921 | 93,036 | 10,640,000 |

## Demography

*Population* (1987): 10,608,000.
*Density* (1987): persons per sq mi 295.3, persons per sq km 114.0.
*Urban–rural* (1986): urban 56.8%; rural 43.2%.
*Sex distribution* (1986): male 48.28%; female 51.72%.
*Age breakdown* (1986): under 15, 21.4%; 15–29, 19.8%; 30–49, 28.5%; 50–59, 12.1%; 60 and over, 18.2%.
*Population projection:* (1990) 10,553,000; (2000) 10,369,000.
During the intercensal period 1970–80, the average annual growth rate was 0.2%; since 1980, however, the population has been decreasing.
*Ethnic composition* (1983): Magyar 99.4%; other 0.6%.
*Religious affiliation* (1980): Christian 83.2%, of which Roman Catholic 53.9%, Protestant 21.6%; Jewish 0.9%; nonreligious 8.7%; atheist 7.2%.
*Major cities* (1986): Budapest 2,076,000; Debrecen 211,800; Miskolc 211,700; Szeged 182,100; Pécs 177,100.

## Vital statistics

*Birth rate* per 1,000 population (1986): 12.1 (world avg. 26.0); (1984) legitimate 91.2%; illegitimate 8.8%.
*Death rate* per 1,000 population (1986): 13.8 (world avg. 9.9).
*Natural increase rate* per 1,000 population (1986): −1.7 (world avg. 16.1).
*Total fertility rate* (avg. births per childbearing woman; 1984): 1.7.
*Marriage rate* per 1,000 population (1985): 6.9.
*Divorce rate* per 1,000 population (1985): 2.7.
*Life expectancy* at birth (1985): male 65.6 years; female 73.6 years.
*Major causes of death* per 100,000 population (1985): diseases of the circulatory system 747.3; malignant neoplasms (cancers) 267.4.

## National economy

*Budget* (1985). Revenue: Ft 593,500,000,000 (payments by enterprises 48.3%, contributions for social security 22.7%, turnover tax 15.5%, personal income tax 3.7%). Expenditures: Ft 609,300,000,000 (social welfare and health 27.3%, economic tasks 27.0%, education 10.2%, defense 3.9%).
*Tourism* (1985): receipts from visitors U.S.$512,000,000; expenditures by nationals abroad U.S.$208,000,000.
*Production* (metric tons except as noted). Agriculture, forestry, fishing (1985): corn (maize) 6,613,000, wheat 6,548,000, sugar beets 4,024,000, barley 1,040,000, potatoes 971,000, sunflower seeds 669,000, rye 163,000; livestock (number of live animals) 8,280,000 pigs, 2,465,000 sheep, 1,766,000 cattle, 62,000,000 poultry; roundwood 6,600,000 cu m; fish catch 38,976,000. Mining and quarrying (1986): bauxite 3,022,000; dolomite 1,586,000; iron ore 397,000. Manufacturing (1986): cement 3,846,000; crude steel 3,715,000; pig iron 3,414,000; rolled steel 2,903,000; chemical fertilizers 1,040,400; aluminum 72,129; cotton fabrics 314,104,000 sq m; leather footwear 41,-985,000 pairs; buses and trucks 13,028 units. Construction (1985): residential 5,723,500 sq m. Energy production (consumption): electricity (kW-hr; 1986) 27,986,000,000 (38,498,000,000); coal (metric tons; 1986) 23,128,000 (25,617,000[3]); crude petroleum (barrels; 1986) 15,238,000 (64,577,000[3]); petroleum products (metric tons; 1986) 9,002,000 (9,181,000[3]); natural gas (cu m; 1986) 7,098,000,000 (10,462,000,000[3]).
*Gross national product* (1985): U.S.$20,720,000,000 (U.S.$1,940 per capita).

### Structure of net material product and labour force

| | 1985 | | | |
|---|---|---|---|---|
| | in value Ft '000,000,000 | % of total value | labour force | % of labour force |
| Agriculture | 100.3 | 11.9 | 1,035,100 | 21.1 |
| Mining and manufacturing | 329.7 | 39.1 | 1,539,500 | 31.3 |
| Construction | 86.2 | 10.2 | 356,400 | 7.2 |
| Public utilities | 6.4 | 0.8 | 78,200 | 1.6 |
| Transp. and commun. | 60.6 | 7.2 | 396,100 | 8.1 |
| Trade | 101.1 | 12.0 | 508,800 | 10.4 |
| Services | — | — | 998,800 | 20.3 |
| Other | 158.0[4] | 18.8[4] | ... | ... |
| TOTAL | 842.3 | 100.0 | 4,912,900 | 100.0 |

*Population economically active* (1986): total 4,892,500; activity rate of total population 46.0% (participation rates: working age 78.4%; female 45.3%; unemployed, n.a.).

### Price and earnings indexes (1980 = 100)

| | 1980 | 1981 | 1982 | 1983 | 1984 | 1985 | 1986 |
|---|---|---|---|---|---|---|---|
| Consumer price index | 100.0 | 104.6 | 111.8 | 120.0 | 129.9 | 138.9 | 146.4 |
| Monthly earnings index | 100.0 | 107.2 | 114.0 | 119.7 | 127.5 | 141.0 | 151.4 |

*Household income and expenditure.* Average household size (1985) 2.7; income per household Ft 179,300 (U.S.$3,600); sources of income: wages 65.6%, social income 34.0%, other 0.4%; expenditure (1985): food 30.5%, services 29.0%, beverages and tobacco 16.0%, clothing and footwear 9.1%, energy 4.7%.
*Public debt* (external, outstanding; 1985): U.S.$10,137,800,000.
*Land use* (1985): forested 17.7%; meadows and pastures 13.4%; agricultural and under permanent cultivation 56.9%; other 12.0%.

## Foreign trade

### Balance of trade (current prices)

| | 1980 | 1981 | 1982 | 1983 | 1984 | 1985 | 1986 |
|---|---|---|---|---|---|---|---|
| Ft '000,000,000 | +13.6 | −8.4 | +5.5 | +15.0 | +30.0 | +14.5 | −11.8 |
| % of total | 2.4% | 1.2% | 0.8% | 2.0% | 3.8% | 1.7% | 1.4% |

*Imports* (1985): Ft 410,100,000,000 (machinery and transport equipment 27.4%; chemicals and related products 13.4%; crude petroleum and petroleum products 12.6%; food 5.9%; natural gas 3.5%; iron and steel 3.4%; nonferrous metals 2.7%; paper and paperboard 1.6%). *Major import sources:* U.S.S.R. 30.0%; West Germany 11.4%; East Germany 6.5%; Austria 6.4%; Czechoslovakia 5.0%; Poland 4.7%; Yugoslavia 3.5%.
*Exports* (1985): Ft 424,610,000,000 (machinery and transport equipment 33.5%, of which road vehicles and parts 10.0%; food 16.8%, of which meat 5.6%; chemicals 11.5%; petroleum products 4.6%; iron and steel 3.4%). *Major export destinations:* U.S.S.R. 33.6%; West Germany 7.8%; East Germany 6.1%; Czechoslovakia 5.7%; Austria 5.4%; Poland 3.8%; Yugoslavia 3.6%; Italy 2.9%.

## Transport and communications

*Transport.* Railroads (1985): length 8,140 mi, 13,100 km; passenger-mi 6,965,-000,000, passenger-km 11,209,000,000; short ton-mi cargo 15,278,000,000, metric ton-km cargo 22,307,000,000. Roads (1985): total length 18,413 mi, 29,633 km (paved 98.3%). Vehicles (1986): passenger cars 1,435,900; trucks and buses 157,797. Merchant marine (1986): vessels (100 gross tons and over) 22; total deadweight tonnage 122,277. Air transport (1986): passenger-mi 710,226,000, passenger-km 1,143,000,000; short ton-mi cargo 16,225,000, metric ton-km cargo 23,689,000; airports (1987) 4.
*Communications.* Daily newspapers (1985): total number 29; total circulation 2,512,300; circulation per 1,000 population 236. Radio (1985): 5,500,-000 (1 per 2.0 persons). Television (1985): 2,911,000 (1 per 2.7 persons). Telephones (1986): 1,484,500 (1 per 7.2 persons).

## Education and health

### Education (1985–86)

| | schools | teachers | students | student/ teacher ratio |
|---|---|---|---|---|
| Primary (age 6–13) | 3,546 | 88,066 | 1,297,818 | 14.7 |
| Secondary (age 14–18) | 178 | 7,923 | 105,794 | 13.4 |
| Vocational | 737 | 22,120 | 316,529 | 14.3 |
| Higher | 58 | 14,850 | 99,344 | 6.7 |

*Educational attainment* (1984). Percent of population age 7 and over having: no formal schooling 1.3%; primary education 65.5%; secondary 27.1%; higher 6.1%. *Literacy* (1984): total population age 15 and over literate 8,269,850 (98.9%); males literate 3,934,250 (99.2%); females literate 4,335,600 (98.6%).
*Health* (1986): physicians 30,258 (1 per 352 persons); hospital beds 102,348 (1 per 104 persons); infant mortality rate per 1,000 live births 20.4.
*Food* (1981–83): daily per capita caloric intake 3,536 (vegetable products 65%; animal products 35%); (1983) 135% of FAO recommended minimum.

## Military

*Total active duty personnel* (1986): 105,000 (army 79.2%, air force 20.8%). *Military expenditure as percent of GNP* (1984): 4.1% (world 5.9%); per capita expenditure U.S.$298.

[1]Beginning of the year. [2]Budapest has separate county status. The area and population of the city are excluded from the larger county (Pest), which it administers. [3]1985. [4]Includes other material activities, balance of taxes on products and value differences, and cost of nonmaterial services.

# Iceland

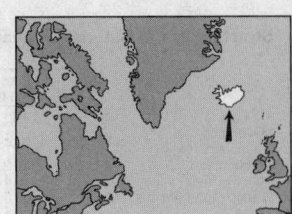

*Official name:* Lýdhveldidh Ísland (Republic of Iceland).
*Form of government:* unitary multiparty republic with two legislative houses (Upper House [21]; Lower House [42]).
*Head of state and government:* President.
*Capital:* Reykjavík.
*Official language:* Icelandic.
*Official religion:* Evangelical Lutheran.
*Monetary unit:* 1 króna (ISK) = 100 aurar; valuation (Oct. 5, 1987) 1 U.S.$ = ISK 39.06; 1 £ = ISK 63.44.

| Area and population | | area | | population |
|---|---|---|---|---|
| **Regions Counties**[1] | **Administrative centres** | **sq mi** | **sq km** | **1986 estimate**[2] |
| Austurland | | 8,683 | 22,490 | 13,131 |
| Austur-Skaftafellssýsla | Höfn | 2,347 | 6,080 | 2,216 |
| Nordhur-Múlasýsla | Seydhisfjördhur | 4,799 | 12,430 | 3,253 |
| Sudhur-Múlasýsla | Eskifjördhur | 1,537 | 3,980 | 7,662 |
| Nordhurland eystra | | 8,370 | 21,680 | 25,764 |
| Eyjafjardharsýsla | Akureyri | 1,602 | 4,150 | 18,853 |
| Nordhur-Thingeyjarsýsla | Húsavik | 2,077 | 5,380 | 1,648 |
| Sudhur-Thingeyjarsýsla | Húsavik | 4,691 | 12,150 | 5,263 |
| Nordhurland vestra | | 4,973 | 12,880 | 10,676 |
| Austur-Húnavatnssýsla | Blönduós | 1,900 | 4,920 | 2,604 |
| Skagafjardharsýsla | Saudhárkrókur | 2,077 | 5,380 | 6,504 |
| Vestur-Húnavatnssýsla | Blönduós | 996 | 2,580 | 1,568 |
| Rekjavíkursvaedhi og Reykjanessvaedhi | | 741 | 1,920 | 148,883 |
| Gullbringusýsla | Keflavík | 405 | 1,050 | 33,977 |
| Kjósarsýsla | Hafnarfjördhur | 336 | 870 | 114,906 |
| Sudhurland | | 9,649 | 24,990 | 20,065 |
| Árnessýsla | Selfoss | 3,401 | 8,810 | 10,491 |
| Rangárvallasýsla | Hvolsvöllur | 3,197 | 8,280 | 8,250 |
| Vestur-Skaftafellssýsla | Vík | 3,050 | 7,900 | 1,324 |
| Vestfirdhir | | 3,676 | 9,520 | 10,193 |
| Austur-Bardhastrandarsýsla | Patreksfjördhur | 444 | 1,150 | 387 |
| Nordhur-Ísafjardharsýsla | Ísafjördhur | 1,181 | 3,060 | 5,113 |
| Strandasýsla | Hólmavík | 1,015 | 2,630 | 1,146 |
| Vestur-Bardhastrandarsýsla | Patreksfjördhur | 598 | 1,550 | 1,979 |
| Vestur-Ísafjardharsýsla | Ísafjördhur | 436 | 1,130 | 1,568 |
| Vesturland | | 3,676 | 9,520 | 14,940 |
| Borgarfjardharsýsla | Borgarnes | 753 | 1,950 | 6,768 |
| Dalasýsla | Budhardalur | 815 | 2,110 | 1,044 |
| Mýrasýsla | Borgarnes | 1,262 | 3,270 | 2,569 |
| Snaefellsnessýsla | Stykkishólmur | 846 | 2,190 | 4,559 |
| TOTAL | | 39,768 | 103,000 | 243,698[3] |

## Demography

*Population* (1987): 245,000.
*Density* (1987): persons per sq mi 6.2, persons per sq km 2.4.
*Urban–rural* (1986): urban 89.7%; rural 10.3%.
*Sex distribution* (1986): male 50.24%; female 49.76%.
*Age breakdown* (1986): under 15, 25.5%; 15–29, 26.1%; 30–44, 20.8%; 45–59, 13.2%; 60–74, 9.9%; 75 and over, 4.5%.
*Population projection:* (1990) 252,000; (2000) 277,000.
*Doubling time:* 76 years.
*Ethnic composition* (1986): native Icelander 96.9%; other European 2.4%; other 0.7%.
*Religious affiliation* (1986): Lutheran 96.7%; Roman Catholic 0.7%; other 2.6%.
*Major cities* (1986): Reykjavík 91,394; Kópavogur 14,609; Akureyri 13,750; Hafnarfjördhur 13,431; Keflavík 6,993.

## Vital statistics

*Birth rate* per 1,000 population (1985): 16.0 (world avg. 29.0); legitimate 52.0%; illegitimate 48.0%.
*Death rate* per 1,000 population (1985): 6.9 (world avg. 11.0).
*Natural increase rate* per 1,000 population (1985): 9.1 (world avg. 18.0).
*Total fertility rate* (avg. births per childbearing woman; 1985): 1.9.
*Marriage rate* per 1,000 population (1985): 5.2.
*Divorce rate* per 1,000 population (1985): 2.2.
*Life expectancy* at birth (1984–85): male 74.7 years; female 80.2 years.
*Major causes of death* per 100,000 population (1984): heart and circulatory diseases 296.0; malignant neoplasms (cancers) 162.8; respiratory diseases 83.5; accidents, suicide, etc. 53.4.

## National economy

*Budget* (1986). Revenue: ISK 38,235,000,000 (indirect taxes 77.1%, of which sales tax 49.4%, import duties 13.3%; income taxes 11.4%). Expenditures: ISK 40,111,000,000 (social services 57.5%, of which social security and welfare 26.0, education 16.1%, health 10.5%; industrial services 21.7%; housing and community amenities 5.0%).
*Public debt* (1986): U.S.$852,470,000.
*Tourism* (1985): receipts from visitors U.S.$75,440,000; expenditures by nationals abroad U.S.$77,660,000.
*Production* (metric tons except as noted). Agriculture, forestry, fishing (1985): fodder crops 3,588,000, potatoes 13,000, milk 128,000; livestock (number of live animals) 709,000 sheep, 72,700 cattle, 52,200 horses; fish catch (1986) capelin 899,300, cod 347,700, herring 64,300, lobster, shrimp, and shellfish 32,900. Mining and quarrying (1984): diatomite 26,486. Man-

ufacturing (1985): frozen fish 122,000; salted fish 75,000; cement 117,000; aluminum, refined 73,400; ferrosilicon 57,700. Construction (1984): residential 812,800 cu m, nonresidential 926,500 cu m. Energy production (consumption): electricity (kW-hr; 1985) 3,837,000,000 (3,837,000,000); coal (1985) none (69,000); petroleum, none (none); petroleum products (1985) none (443,000); natural gas, none (none).
*Gross national product* (1985): U.S.$2,580,000,000 (U.S.$10,700 per capita).

| Structure of gross domestic product and labour force | | | | |
|---|---|---|---|---|
| | 1986 | | 1984 | |
| | in value ISK '000,000 | % of total value | labour force | % of labour force |
| Agriculture | ... | 5.7 } | 23,726 | 20.3 |
| Fishing and processing | ... | 16.1 } | | |
| Manufacturing | ... | 13.4 | 27,813 | 23.9 |
| Construction | ... | 7.6 | 11,614 | 10.0 |
| Transp. and commun. | ... | 9.9 | ... | ... |
| Trade | ... | 20.6[4] | 16,866[4] | 14.5[4] |
| Pub. admin., defense, services, and other | ... | 26.8 | 36,540[5] | 31.3 |
| TOTAL | 111,023 | 100.0[6] | 116,559 | 100.0 |

*Population economically active* (1984): total 116,559; activity rate of total population 48.7% (participation rates: 15–64, n.a.; female [1983] 31.5%; unemployed 1.3%).

| Price and earnings indexes (1980 = 100) | | | | | | | |
|---|---|---|---|---|---|---|---|
| | 1981 | 1982 | 1983 | 1984 | 1985 | 1986 | 1987[7] |
| Consumer price index | 150.6 | 224.7 | 418.2 | 547.0 | 721.8 | 881.9 | 1,006.1 |
| Hourly wages index | 152.7 | 228.5 | 339.0 | 403.2 | 531.6 | 667.7 | ... |

*Household income and expenditure.* Average household size: n.a.; disposable income per person (1982) ISK 82,240 (U.S.$6,660); sources of income (1983): wages and salaries 52.7%, self-employment 45.6%, transfer payments 1.7%; expenditure (1984): food 25.3%, housing 25.3%, transportation and communication 18.8%, education and recreation 10.1%, clothing and footwear 8.8%, health 1.7%, other 9.4%.
*Land use* (1984): forested 1.2%; meadows and pastures 22.7%; agricultural and under permanent cultivation 0.1%; other 76.0%[8].

## Foreign trade

| Balance of trade (current prices) | | | | | | |
|---|---|---|---|---|---|---|
| | 1981 | 1982 | 1983 | 1984 | 1985 | 1986 |
| ISK '000,000 | −274 | −2,109 | −90 | −789 | −356 | +3,910 |
| % of total | 2.1% | 11.1% | 0.2% | 1.6% | 0.5% | 4.5% |

*Imports* (1986): ISK 45,910,000,000 (machinery and transport equipment 19.0%, of which ships and aircraft 4.6%; fuels and lubricants 8.5%, of which gasoline 1.9%; construction materials 5.0%). *Major import sources:* West Germany 15.2%; Denmark 10.4%; Sweden 8.9%; The Netherlands 8.6%; U.K. 8.2%; Norway 7.2%.
*Exports* (1986): ISK 44,968,000,000 (fish and fish products 77.0%, of which frozen fish fillets 29.8%, dried, salted, and smoked fish 14.5%; aluminum, refined 9.2%; agricultural products 1.3%). *Major export destinations:* U.S. 21.7%; U.K. 20.4%; West Germany 9.1%; Portugal 6.5%; France 4.8%.

## Transport and communications

*Transport.* Railroads: none. Roads (1985): total length 7,189 mi, 11,569 km (paved 12%). Vehicles (1985): passenger cars 103,100; trucks and buses 13,160. Merchant marine (1986): vessels (100 gross tons and over) 389; total deadweight tonnage 161,593. Air transport (1985): passenger-mi 1,489,000, passenger-km 2,397,000; short ton-mi cargo 15,398,000, metric ton-km cargo 22,480,000; airports (1987) with scheduled flights 24.
*Communications.* Daily newspapers (1985): total number 6; total circulation c. 100,000; circulation per 1,000 population c. 415. Radio (1985): 72,965 receivers (1 per 3.3 persons). Television (1985): 68,848 receivers (1 per 3.5 persons). Telephones (1986): 102,657 (1 per 2.4 persons).

## Education and health

| Education (1982–83) | schools | teachers | students | student/ teacher ratio |
|---|---|---|---|---|
| Primary (age 7–12) | 187 | 2,600 | 25,000 | 9.6 |
| Secondary (age 12–19) | 157 | ... | 21,800 | ... |
| Voc., teacher tr. | 44 | ... | 4,280 | ... |
| Higher | 4 | 280 | 4,780 | 17.1 |

*Educational attainment,* n.a. *Literacy* (1984): total population age 15 and over literate 175,029 (100.0%).
*Health* (1985): physicians 574 (1 per 420 persons); hospital beds 2,677 (1 per 90 persons); infant mortality rate per 1,000 live births 5.7.
*Food* (1981–83): daily per capita caloric intake 3,142 (vegetable products 54%, animal products 46%); (1983) 113% of FAO recommended minimum.

## Military

Iceland maintains no domestic military forces; external security is guaranteed by the NATO-sponsored U.S.-manned Iceland Defense Force, numbering no more than 2,900 (mostly air force). A domestic coast guard of about 120 is maintained.

[1]Counties include county cities and towns, which are within, but administratively independent of, the counties. [2]Dec. 1, 1986. [3]Includes 46 persons not distributed by county. [4]Trade includes finance and public utilities. [5]Includes 1,480 unemployed. [6]Detail does not add to total given because of rounding. [7]May. [8]Glaciated, covered with peat bogs, or lava desert.

# India

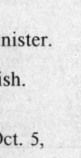

*Official name:* Bhārat (Hindī); Republic of India (English).
*Form of government:* multiparty federal republic with two legislative houses (Council of States [244][1], House of the People [544][2]).
*Chief of state:* President.
*Head of government:* Prime Minister.
*Capital:* New Delhi.
*Official languages:* Hindī; English.
*Official religion:* none.
*Monetary unit:* 1 Indian rupee (Rs) = 100 paisa; valuation (Oct. 5, 1987) 1 U.S.$ = Rs 12.93; 1 £ = Rs 21.00.

## Area and population

| States | Capitals | area sq mi | area sq km | population 1981 census |
|---|---|---|---|---|
| Andhra Pradesh | Hyderābād | 106,204 | 275,068 | 53,549,673 |
| Arunāchal Pradesh | Itanagar | 32,333 | 83,743 | 631,839 |
| Assam | Prāgjyotişapura | 30,285 | 78,438 | 19,896,843[3] |
| Bihār | Patna | 67,134 | 173,877 | 69,914,734 |
| Goa | Panaji | 1,430 | 3,702 | 1,007,749 |
| Gujarāt | Gāndhīnagar | 75,685 | 196,024 | 34,085,799 |
| Haryāna | Chandīgarh | 17,070 | 44,212 | 12,922,618 |
| Himāchal Pradesh | Simla | 21,495 | 55,673 | 4,280,818 |
| Jammu and Kashmir | Srinagar | 39,145[4] | 101,387[4] | 5,987,389 |
| Karnātaka | Bangalore | 74,051 | 191,791 | 37,135,714 |
| Kerala | Trivandrum | 15,005 | 38,863 | 25,453,680 |
| Madhya Pradesh | Bhopāl | 171,215 | 443,446 | 52,178,844 |
| Mahārāshtra | Bombay | 118,800 | 307,690 | 62,784,171 |
| Manipur | Imphāl | 8,621 | 22,327 | 1,420,953 |
| Meghālaya | Shillong | 8,660 | 22,429 | 1,335,819 |
| Mizorām | Aizawl | 8,140 | 21,081 | 493,757 |
| Nāgāland | Kohīma | 6,401 | 16,579 | 774,930 |
| Orissa | Bhubaneswar | 60,119 | 155,707 | 26,370,271 |
| Punjab | Chandīgarh | 19,445 | 50,362 | 16,788,915 |
| Rājasthān | Jaipur | 132,140 | 342,239 | 34,261,862 |
| Sikkim | Gangtok | 2,740 | 7,096 | 316,385 |
| Tamil Nādu | Madras | 50,216 | 130,058 | 48,408,077 |
| Tripura | Agartala | 4,049 | 10,486 | 2,053,058 |
| Uttar Pradesh | Lucknow | 113,673 | 294,411 | 110,862,013 |
| West Bengal | Calcutta | 34,267 | 88,752 | 54,580,647 |
| **Union Territories** | | | | |
| Andaman and Nicobar Islands | Port Blair | 3,185 | 8,249 | 188,741 |
| Chandīgarh | Chandīgarh | 44 | 114 | 451,610 |
| Dādra and Nagar Haveli | Silvassa | 190 | 491 | 103,676 |
| Daman and Diu | ... | 43 | 112 | 78,981 |
| Delhi | Delhi | 572 | 1,483 | 6,220,406 |
| Lakshadweep | Kavaratti | 12 | 32 | 40,249 |
| Pondicherry | Pondicherry | 190 | 492 | 604,471 |
| TOTAL | | 1,222,559[4] | 3,166,414[4] | 685,184,692 |

## Demography

*Population* (1987): 783,044,000.
*Density* (1987)[4]: persons per sq mi 640.5, persons per sq km 247.3.
*Urban–rural* (1985): urban 25.5%; rural 74.5%.
*Sex distribution* (1985): male 51.74%; female 48.26%.
*Age breakdown* (1985): under 15, 36.8%; 15–29, 27.8%; 30–44, 17.2%; 45–59, 11.4%; 60–74, 5.7%; 75 and over, 1.1%.
*Population projection:* (1990) 815,000,000; (2000) 941,000,000.
*Doubling time:* 39 years.
*Linguistic composition* (1971): Hindī 28.1%; Telugu 8.2%; Bengali 8.1%; Marāṭhī 7.6%; Tamil 6.9%; Urdū 5.2%; Gujarāti 4.7%; Malayalam 4.0%; Kannaḍa 3.9%; Oriyā 3.6%; Bhojpurī 2.6%; Punjābī 2.5%; Assamese 1.6%; Chhattisgarhī 1.2%; Magadhī 1.2%; Maithilī 1.1%; other 9.5%.
*Religious affiliation* (1981)[5]: Hindu 82.64%; Muslim 11.35%; Christian 2.43%; Sikh 1.97%; Buddhist 0.71%; Jain 0.48%; Zoroastrian 0.01%; other 0.41%.
*Major cities* (1981): Greater Bombay 8,243,405; Delhi 4,884,234; Calcutta 3,305,006; Madras 3,276,622; Bangalore 2,476,355; Hyderābād 2,150,580; Ahmadābād 2,059,725; Kānpur 1,481,789; Nāgpur 1,219,461; Pune 1,203,351; Jaipur 977,165; Lucknow 895,721; Indore 829,327; New Delhi 273,036.

## Other principal cities (1981)

| | population | | population | | population |
|---|---|---|---|---|---|
| Āgra | 694,191 | Jalapur | 614,162 | Rānchi | 489,626 |
| Ajmer | 375,593 | Jamshedpur | 438,385 | Salem | 361,394 |
| Aligarh | 320,861 | Jodhpur | 506,345 | Sholāpur | |
| Allahābād | 616,051 | Jullundur | 408,196 | (Solapur) | 511,103 |
| Amritsar | 594,844 | Kolhāpur | 340,625 | South Suburban | 378,765 |
| Bareilly | 386,734 | Kota | 358,241 | Srinagar | 586,038 |
| Bhavnagar | 307,121 | Kozhikode | | Surat | 776,583 |
| Bhopāl | 671,018 | (Calicut) | 394,447 | Thāna (Thane) | 309,897 |
| Chandīgarh | 373,789 | Lucknow | 895,721 | Tiruchchirāppalli | 362,045 |
| Cochin | 513,249 | Ludhiāna | 607,052 | Trivandrum | 483,086 |
| Coimbatore | 704,514 | Madurai | 820,891 | Vadodara | |
| Dhārwār-Hubli | 527,108 | Meerut | 417,395 | (Baroda) | 734,473 |
| Durgāpur | 311,798 | Morādābād | 330,051 | Vārānasi | |
| Faridābād | 330,864 | Mysore | 441,754 | (Benares) | 708,647 |
| Guntūr | 367,699 | Patna | 776,371 | Vijayawāda | 454,577 |
| Gwalior | 539,015 | Raipur | 338,245 | Vishākhapatnam | 565,321 |
| Howrah (Haora) | 744,429 | Rājkot | 445,076 | Warangal | 335,150 |

*Place of birth* (foreign born; 1981): other Asia 7,875,399, of which Bangladesh 4,170,524, Pakistan 2,736,038, Nepal 501,292, Sri Lanka 211,514, Burma 134,783; Africa 42,726; Europe 13,046; United States and Canada 5,923.

*Mobility* (1981). Population living in same district but at different residence as in 1971: 47,604,000; different district, same state 22,557,000; different state 10,860,000; moved outside the country 1,179,000.
*Households.* Average household size (1981) 5.7; number of rooms per household (1971): 1 room 47.8%, 2 rooms 28.2%, 3 rooms 12.0%, 4 rooms 6.0%, 5 or more rooms 5.9%, unspecified number of rooms 0.1%. Average number of persons per room (1971) 2.8. Population in households (1981) 665,287,849 (97.1%), houseless population 2,330,000 (0.34%), institutional population (1971) 2,693,000 (0.5%).
*Emigration* (1984): persons living abroad 11,644,000 (accepting foreign citizenship, 7,394,000), of which in Nepal 3,800,000 (2,388,000); Malaysia 1,170,000 (1,030,000); Sri Lanka 1,028,000 (426,000); Middle Eastern countries 949,000 (112,000); United Kingdom 719,000 (359,000); Mauritius 697,000 (696,000); Guyana 500,000 (500,000); United States 440,000 (320,000); Trinidad and Tobago 421,000 (420,000); Burma 350,000 (50,000).

## Vital statistics

*Birth rate* per 1,000 population (1986): 29.6 (world avg. 26.0); legitimate, n.a.; illegitimate, n.a.
*Death rate* per 1,000 population (1986): 11.5 (world avg. 9.9).
*Natural increase rate* per 1,000 population (1986): 18.1 (world avg. 16.1).
*Total fertility rate* (avg. births per childbearing woman; 1986): 3.9.
*Marriage rate* per 1,000 population: n.a.
*Divorce rate* per 1,000 population: n.a.
*Life expectancy* at birth (1986): male 56.2 years; female 57.0 years.
*Major causes of death* (rural areas only; 1985)[6]: senility 21.6%; diseases of the respiratory system 14.8%, of which bronchitis and asthma 8.7%; infectious and parasitic diseases 12.7%, of which tuberculosis 5.8%; all causes peculiar to infancy 10.3%; diseases of the circulatory system 9.9%; diseases of the digestive system 7.6%; diseases of the nervous system 4.2%; malignant neoplasms (cancers) 3.0%.

## Social indicators

*Educational attainment* (1981). Percent of population age 25 and over having: no formal schooling (illiterate) 64.8%; literate population with no formal schooling 0.9%; some primary education only 11.2%; some secondary only 6.2%; completed secondary 7.1%; higher 2.5%; other 7.3%.

### Distribution of income (1975–76)

percent of household income by quintile

| 1 | 2 | 3 | 4 | 5 (highest) |
|---|---|---|---|---|
| 7.0% | 9.2% | 13.9% | 20.5% | 49.4% |

*Quality of working life* (1981). Average workweek: 45 hours. Rate of fatal (nonfatal) injuries per 100,000 workers (1981–82): industrial workers 16 (7,657); miners 34 (371); railway workers 20 (1,531). Employees covered under Employee's State Insurance Scheme (1983) 7,187,000, number of beneficiaries 27,886,000. Average days lost to labour stoppages per 1,000 workdays (1982): 1.4. Average duration of journey to work: n.a. Rate per 1,000 workers of discouraged (unemployed no longer seeking work): n.a.
*Access to services.* Proportion of villages having access to electricity (1984–85) 64.0%; proportion of population having access to safe water supply (1982) 52.0%.
*Social participation.* Eligible voters participating in last (December 1984) national election: 61.5%. Verified trade union membership in total workforce (1981): 2.5%. Practicing religious population in total affiliated population: n.a.
*Social deviance* (1984). Offense rate per 100,000 population for: murder 3.4; dacoity (gang robbery) 1.4; theft and housebreaking 43.7; rape 0.8. Incidence in general population of: alcoholism, n.a.; drug and substance abuse, n.a. Rate per 100,000 population of suicide (1980): 6.1.
*Leisure* (1987). Favourite leisure activities in urban areas: listening to the radio, watching television, reading periodicals, and attending the cinema.
*Material well-being* (1983). Households possessing: automobile 0.8%; telephone 2.3%; television receiver 1.6%; radio receiver 17.2%; air conditioner, n.a.; washing machine, n.a.

## National economy

*Gross national product* (at current market prices; 1985): U.S.$194,820,000,000 (U.S.$260 per capita).

### Structure of gross domestic product and labour force

| | 1985–86 in value Rs '000,000,000 | 1985–86 % of total value | 1981[5] labour force | 1981[5] % of labour force |
|---|---|---|---|---|
| Agriculture | 675.6 | 31.4 | 153,015,000 | 62.5 |
| Mining | 64.8 | 3.0 | 1,264,000 | 0.5 |
| Manufacturing | 358.0 | 16.7 | 25,143,000 | 10.3 |
| Construction | 116.3 | 5.4 | 3,565,000 | 1.5 |
| Public utilities | 47.2 | 2.2 | 974,000 | 0.4 |
| Transportation and communication | 149.2 | 6.9 | 6,069,000 | 2.5 |
| Trade | 318.5 | 14.8 | 12,165,000 | 5.0 |
| Finance, real estate | 172.4 | 8.0 | 1,764,000 | 0.7 |
| Pub. admin., defense | 117.9 | 5.5 | ... | ... |
| Services | 130.3 | 6.1 | 18,557,000 | 7.6 |
| Other | | | 22,089,000[7] | 9.0 |
| TOTAL | 2,150.2 | 100.0 | 244,605,000 | 100.0 |

*Budget* (1985–86). Revenue: Rs 432,741,800,000 (tax revenue 61.5%, of which excise taxes 29.9%, customs duties 21.5%, taxes on corporations 7.2%; nontax revenue 38.5%, of which interest receipts 11.1%). Expenditures: Rs 492,141,400,000 (economic services 31.4%, of which railways 13.2%; transfers to local levels of government 26.4%; interest payments 15.0%; defense 14.6%).

*Public debt* (external, outstanding; 1985): U.S.$26,649,500,000.

*Production* (metric tons except as noted). Agriculture, forestry, fishing (1986): sugarcane 171,681,000, rice 90,000,000, wheat 46,885,000, potatoes 10,696,000, sorghum 10,500,000, mangoes 9,416,000, millet 8,500,-000, corn (maize) 8,000,000, peanuts (groundnuts) 6,400,000, chick-peas 5,683,000, cassava 5,569,000[8], bananas 4,748,000, coconuts 4,550,000[8], rapeseed 3,100,000, dry beans 3,000,000, onions 2,934,000, cottonseed 2,720,000, pigeon peas 2,426,000[8], jute 1,400,000, soybeans 1,300,000, tea 628,000, tobacco 439,000, spices[9]—chilies 525,000, turmeric 173,000, black pepper 26,000, cardamom 5,400; livestock (number of live animals; 1985) 182,410,000 cattle, 81,500,000 goats, 64,500,000 water buffalo, 41,300,000 sheep, 1,100,000 camels; roundwood (1985) 245,029,000 cu m; fish catch (1985) 2,810,000, of which freshwater fishes 1,080,000. Mining and quarrying (1985): iron ore 53,000,000[10]; limestone 48,492,-000; bauxite 2,400,000[10]; dolomite 2,208,000; manganese ore 1,200,000[10]; phosphorite 900,000; kaolin 720,000; chromite 610,000; zinc 74,400[10]; copper (metal content) 55,000; crude mica 6,200; gold 1,930 kg[11]; diamonds 14,000 carats. Manufacturing (1985): cement 33,100,000[12]; steel ingots 11,-332,000[12]; finished steel 7,755,000[12]; refined sugar 7,026,000[12]; nitrogenous fertilizers 4,234,000; paper and paperboard 1,462,000; jute manufactures 1,383,000[12]; vanaspati (hydrogenated vegetable fat) 920,000[12]; soda ash 826,000; soap 372,000; aluminum 260,000; copper cathodes 28,000; bicycles 5,646,000 units; radios 1,212,000 units; motorcycles and scooters 670,000 units; power-driven pumps 512,000 units. sewing machines 334,000 units; typewriters 122,000 units; passenger cars and jeeps 117,000 units; tractors 80,700 units; cotton cloth 92,900,000,000 metres. Construction (value in Rs; 1984) residential 87,010,000,000; nonresidential 40,730,000,000.

### Manufacturing enterprises (1981)

| | no. of factories | no. of employees | annual wages as a % of avg. of all wages | annual value added (Rs '000,000) |
|---|---|---|---|---|
| Chemicals and chemical products | 237 | 730,754 | 109.8 | 14,299 |
| Cotton textiles[13] | 7,189 | 1,070,941 | 124.4 | 13,271 |
| Base metals and alloys | 5,779 | 578,007 | 145.6 | 12,343 |
| Nonelectrical machinery | 7,011 | 401,028 | 115.6 | 8,885 |
| Transport equipment[14] | 2,815 | 484,484 | 144.2 | 8,556 |
| Electrical machinery | 3,406 | 317,349 | 124.4 | 8,339 |
| Food products | 17,067 | 1,289,509 | 36.5 | 7,072 |
| Rubber, plastic, petroleum and coal products | 3,498 | 172,877 | 109.0 | 5,360 |
| Paper, paper products, printing, publishing, etc. | 4,798 | 272,965 | 110.7 | 4,343 |
| Nonmetallic mineral products | 6,440 | 339,713 | 80.7 | 4,033 |
| Wool, silk, and synthetic textiles[13] | 3,743 | 216,282 | 118.2 | 3,787 |
| Metal products | 6,457 | 191,498 | 106.1 | 3,312 |
| Jute, hemp, mesta textiles[13] | 265 | 272,439 | 136.0 | 3,003 |
| Beverages and tobacco products | 8,901 | 403,104 | 41.3 | 2,314 |
| Finished textiles | 2,889 | 98,678 | 77.7 | 1,193 |
| Leather products | 886 | 58,227 | 97.3 | 685 |

Energy production (consumption): electricity (kW-hr; 1985) 188,479,000,000 (188,408,000,000); coal (metric tons; 1985) 157,485,000 (160,476,000); crude petroleum (barrels; 1985) 226,936,000 (313,317,000); petroleum products (metric tons; 1985) 31,740,000 (34,934,000); natural gas (cu m; 1985) 3,863,-000,000 (3,863,000,000).

### Financial aggregates[15]

| | 1981 | 1982 | 1983 | 1984 | 1985 | 1986 | 1987 |
|---|---|---|---|---|---|---|---|
| Exchange rate, Rs per: | | | | | | | |
| U.S. dollar | 9.10 | 9.63 | 10.49 | 12.45 | 12.17 | 13.12 | 12.93[16] |
| £ | 17.36 | 15.55 | 15.22 | 14.40 | 17.59 | 19.35 | 20.82[16] |
| SDR | 10.59 | 10.63 | 10.99 | 12.20 | 13.36 | 16.05 | 16.53[16] |
| International reserves (U.S.$) | | | | | | | |
| Total (excl. gold; '000,000) | 4,693 | 4,315 | 4,937 | 5,842 | 6,420 | 6,396 | 6,730[17] |
| SDRs ('000,000) | 545 | 374 | 110 | 331 | 336 | 356 | 137[16] |
| Reserve pos. in IMF ('000,000) | 384 | 402 | 510 | 477 | 535 | 596 | 623[16] |
| Foreign exchange ('000,000) | 3,764 | 3,539 | 4,318 | 5,034 | 5,549 | 5,444 | 5,924[17] |
| Gold ('000,000 fine troy oz) | 8.594 | 8.594 | 8.594 | 8.737 | 9.397 | 10.449 | 10.449[17] |
| % world reserves | 0.9 | 0.9 | 0.9 | 0.9 | 0.9 | 1.1 | 1.1[17] |
| Interest and prices | | | | | | | |
| Central bank discount (%) | 10.0 | 10.0 | 10.0 | 10.0 | 10.0 | 10.0 | 10.0[18] |
| Gov't. bond yield (%) | 7.2 | 7.6 | 8.0 | 8.7 | 9.0 | ... | ... |
| Industrial share prices (1980 = 100) | 122.7 | 120.1 | 126.2 | 134.8 | 200.0 | 244.3 | 227.8[18] |
| Balance of payments (U.S.$'000,000) | | | | | | | |
| Balance of visible trade | −5,712 | −4,820 | −4,098 | −4,024 | −5,616 | ... | ... |
| Imports, f.o.b. | 14,149 | 14,046 | 13,868 | 14,216 | 15,081 | ... | ... |
| Exports, f.o.b. | 8,437 | 9,226 | 9,770 | 10,192 | 9,465 | ... | ... |
| Balance of invisibles | +7 | −621 | −979 | −1,089 | −1,337 | ... | ... |
| Balance of payments, current account | −2,698 | −2,524 | −1,916 | −2,343 | −4,177 | ... | ... |

*Population economically active* (1981)[5]: total 244,605,000; activity rate of total population 36.8% (participation rates: over age 15, 57.4%; female 26.0%; unemployed [1985] 4.6%).

### Price and earnings indexes (1980 = 100)

| | 1981 | 1982 | 1983 | 1984 | 1985 | 1986 | 1987[17] |
|---|---|---|---|---|---|---|---|
| Consumer price index | 113.0 | 121.9 | 136.3 | 147.7 | 155.9 | 169.5 | 175.9 |
| Daily earnings index[19] | 102.4 | 113.5 | 127.8 | ... | ... | ... | ... |

*Household income and expenditure.* Average household size[5] (1981) 5.6; income per household: n.a.; sources of income (1983–84): self-employment 41.6%, salaries and wages 40.7%, interest 8.1%, profits and dividends 6.0%, rent 3.6%; expenditure (1984): food and beverages 56.8%, transportation and communication 11.0%, clothing and footwear 10.8%, energy 4.8%,

household furnishings 4.5%, housing 2.7%, education 2.2%, health care 1.9%, other 5.3%.

### Service enterprises (1980)

| | no. of enterprises | no. of employees | annual wage as a % of all wages | annual value added (Rs '000,000)[20, 21] |
|---|---|---|---|---|
| Wholesale and retail trade | 6,046,200 | 10,228,700 | ... | 262,270 |
| Transportation | 307,400 | 1,194,300 | ... | 110,280[22] |
| Community and personal services | 3,177,700 | 13,128,800 | ... | 108,670 |
| Construction | 152,000 | 451,200 | ... | 96,290 |
| Finance and insurance | 273,500 | 1,570,800 | ... | 73,970 |
| Electricity, gas, and steam | 33,700 | 363,500 | ... | 35,580 |
| Restaurants and hotels | 807,000 | 2,080,500 | ... | 19,120 |
| Communications | 98,900 | 530,900 | ... | 14,580 |
| Storage and warehousing | 122,400 | 356,900 | ... | ...[22] |

*Tourism:* receipts from visitors (1985) U.S.$1,098,000,000; expenditures by nationals abroad (1983) U.S.$201,000,000.

*Land use* (1985): forested 22.7%; meadows and pastures 4.0%; agricultural and under permanent cultivation 56.6%; other 16.7%.

### Foreign trade[23]

#### Balance of trade (current prices)

| | 1980 | 1981 | 1982 | 1983 | 1984 | 1985 | 1986 |
|---|---|---|---|---|---|---|---|
| Rs '000,000 | −36,983 | −47,682 | −36,841 | −34,733 | −45,147 | −65,352 | −55,120 |
| % of total | 21.5% | 24.9% | 17.2% | 15.8% | 17.4% | 24.8% | 18.8% |

*Imports* (1984–85): Rs 170,921,000,000 (crude petroleum and petroleum products 31.5%; nonelectrical machinery 11.0%; pearls, precious and semi-precious stones [mostly diamonds] 6.0%; edible vegetable oil 4.9%; iron and steel 4.5%; manufactured fertilizers 4.4%; electrical machinery 2.7%). *Major import sources:* U.S.S.R. 10.6%; United States 9.8%; West Germany 7.6%; Japan 7.3%; Saudi Arabia 7.3%; United Kingdom 6.0%; Belgium 4.6%; Iraq 3.9%.

*Exports* (1984–85): Rs 116,569,000,000 (crude petroleum 13.5%; pearls, precious and semiprecious stones [mostly diamonds] 9.5%; ready-made garments 7.4%; tea and maté 6.1%; machinery and transport equipment 4.8%; iron ore 3.8%; leather and leather manufactures 3.6%; cotton fabrics 3.5%; chemicals and chemical products 3.2%). *Major export destinations:* United States 15.2%; U.S.S.R. 14.2%; Japan 9.1%; United Kingdom 5.7%; West Germany 4.0%; United Arab Emirates 2.3%; Saudi Arabia 2.1%; France 1.8%.

### Transport and communications

*Transport.* Railroads (1986): route length (1985) 38,200 mi, 61,478 km; passenger-mi 155,500,000,000, passenger-km 250,300,000,000; short ton-mi cargo 146,200,000,000, metric ton-km cargo 213,400,000,000. Roads (1984–85): total length 1,101,000 mi, 1,772,000 km (paved 47%). Vehicles (1984–85): passenger cars 1,517,000; trucks and buses 952,000. Merchant marine (1986): vessels (100 gross tons and over) 736; total deadweight tonnage 10,691,035. Air transport (1986): passenger-mi 9,580,000,000, passenger-km 15,420,000,000; short ton-mi cargo 387,689,000, metric ton-km cargo 566,016,000; airports (1987) with scheduled flights 94.

*Communications.* Daily newspapers: total number (1984) 1,423; total circulation (1986) 12,895,680[24]; circulation per 1,000 population 26[24]. Radio (1986): total number of receivers 50,000,000 (1 per 15 persons). Television (1986): total number of receivers 5,000,000 (1 per 154 persons). Telephones (1985): 3,761,000 (1 per 201 persons).

### Education and health

#### Education (1984–85)

| | schools | teachers | students | student/teacher ratio |
|---|---|---|---|---|
| Primary (age 5–10) | 519,701 | 1,458,140 | 61,168,620 | 41.9 |
| Secondary (age 10–17) | 188,713 | 1,980,694 | 64,533,244 | 32.6 |
| Voc., Teacher tr. } Higher | 5,215 | ... | 3,033,592 | ... |

*Literacy* (1981): total population age 15 and over literate 168,900,000 (40.8%); males literate 117,600,000 (54.8%); females literate 51,300,000 (25.7%).

*Health:* physicians (1984–85) 297,000 (1 per 2,520 persons); hospital beds (1983) 599,000 (1 per 1,215 persons); infant mortality rate per 1,000 live births (1986) 111.0.

*Food* (1981–83): daily per capita caloric intake 2,088 (vegetable products 95%, animal products 5%); (1983) 96% of FAO recommended minimum requirement.

### Military

*Total active duty personnel* (1986): 1,260,000 (army 87.3%, navy 3.7%, air force 9.0%). *Military expenditure as percent of GNP* (1984): 3.6% (world 5.9%); per capita expenditure U.S.$10.

[1]Includes 13 nonelective seats. [2]Includes 2 nonelective seats. [3]Estimate; state not censused. [4]Excludes 46,660 sq mi (120,849 sq km) of territory claimed by India as part of Jammu and Kashmir but occupied by Pakistan or China. Final status of these claims is not determined. [5]Excludes Assam. [6]Percentage breakdown based on 17,283 deaths recorded at 1,080 nationally dispersed, primary health centre villages. [7]Not adequately defined. [8]1985. [9]1981–82. [10]1986–87. [11]1985–86. [12]1986. [13]Excludes finished products. [14]Includes parts. [15]Exchange rates and international reserves are based on end-of-period figures. [16]June. [17]March. [18]April. [19]Male agricultural workers. [20]1984. [21]Other important service enterprises include real estate and business services 71,180 and water works and supply 1,840. [22]Transportation includes storage and warehousing. [23]Import figures are f.o.b. in balance of trade and c.i.f. in commodities and trading partners. [24]Circulation of 238 main dailies only.

# Indonesia

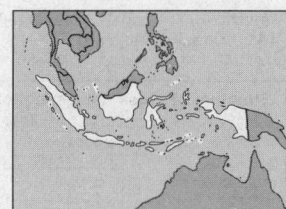

*Official name:* Republik Indonesia (Republic of Indonesia).
*Form of government:* unitary multiparty republic with two legislative houses (People's Consultative Assembly [920]; House of People's Representatives [460[1]]).
*Head of state and government:* President.
*Capital:* Jakarta.
*Official language:* Bahasa Indonesia.
*Official religion:* monotheism.
*Monetary unit:* 1 Indonesian rupiah (Rp) = 100 sen; valuation (Oct. 5, 1987) 1 U.S.$ = Rp 1,649.00; 1 £ = Rp 2,677.00.

| Area and population | | area | | population |
|---|---|---|---|---|
| | | sq mi | sq km | 1986 estimate |
| **Metropolitan district** | **Capitals** | | | |
| Jakarta Raya | Jakarta | 228 | 590 | 8,164,400 |
| **Provinces** | | | | |
| Bali | Denpasar | 2,147 | 5,561 | 2,709,200 |
| Bengkulu | Bengkulu | 8,173 | 21,168 | 985,600 |
| Irian Jaya | Jayapura | 2,928 | 421,981 | 1,363,500 |
| Jambi | Jambi | 7,345 | 44,924 | 1,822,200 |
| Jawa Barat | Bandung | 7,877 | 46,300 | 31,876,400 |
| Jawa Tengah | Semarang | 3,207 | 34,206 | 27,755,900 |
| Jawa Timur | Surabaya | 8,503 | 47,922 | 31,639,300 |
| Kalimantan Barat | Pontianak | 6,664 | 146,760 | 2,827,000 |
| Kalimantan Selatan | Banjarmasin | 4,541 | 37,660 | 2,328,000 |
| Kalimantan Tengah | Palangkaraya | 8,919 | 152,600 | 1,159,000 |
| Kalimantan Timur | Samarinda | 8,162 | 202,440 | 1,690,500 |
| Lampung | Tanjung Karang | 12,860 | 33,307 | 6,422,100 |
| Maluku | Ambon | 28,767 | 74,505 | 1,659,100 |
| Nusa Tenggara Barat | Mataram | 7,790 | 20,177 | 3,107,700 |
| Nusa Tenggara Timur | Kupang | 18,485 | 47,876 | 3,048,900 |
| Riau | Pakanbaru | 36,511 | 94,562 | 2,583,900 |
| Sulawesi Selatan | Ujung Pandang | 28,101 | 72,781 | 6,669,500 |
| Sulawesi Tengah | Palu | 26,921 | 69,726 | 1,604,800 |
| Sulawesi Tenggara | Kendari | 10,690 | 27,686 | 1,122,400 |
| Sulawesi Utara | Menado | 7,345 | 19,023 | 2,406,400 |
| Sumatera Barat | Padang | 19,219 | 49,778 | 3,851,500 |
| Sumatera Selatan | Palembang | 40,034 | 103,688 | 5,586,900 |
| Sumatera Utara | Medan | 27,331 | 70,787 | 9,667,500 |
| Timor Timur[2] | Dili | 5,743 | 14,874 | 618,500 |
| **Special autonomous districts** | | | | |
| Aceh | Banda Aceh | 21,387 | 55,392 | 3,078,400 |
| Yogyakarta | Yogyakarta | 1,224 | 3,169 | 2,913,400 |
| TOTAL | | 741,101[3] | 1,919,443 | 168,662,000 |

## Demography

*Population* (1987): 172,245,000.
*Density* (1987): persons per sq mi 232.4, persons per sq km 89.7.
*Urban–rural* (1985): urban 25.3%; rural 74.7%.
*Sex distribution* (1985): male 49.75%; female 50.25%.
*Age breakdown* (1985): under 15, 39.2%; 15–29, 28.0%; 30–44, 16.8%; 45–59, 10.7%; 60–74, 4.4%; 75 and over, 0.9%.
*Population projection:* (1990) 183,457,000; (2000) 222,753,000.
*Doubling time:* 39 years.
*Ethnolinguistic composition* (1980): Javanese 40.1%; Sundanese 15.3%; Bahasa Indonesian 12.0%; Madurese 4.8%; other 27.8%.
*Religious affiliation* (1980): Muslim 87.1%; Christian 8.8%, of which Roman Catholic 3.0%; Hindu 1.9%; Buddhist 0.9%; other 1.2%.
*Major cities* (1985): Jakarta 7,829,000; Surabaya 2,345,000; Medan 2,110,000; Bandung 1,633,000; Semarang (1984) 1,077,000.

## Vital statistics

*Birth rate* per 1,000 population (1986): 29.8 (world avg. 26.0).
*Death rate* per 1,000 population (1986): 11.7 (world avg. 9.9).
*Natural increase rate* per 1,000 population (1986): 18.1 (world avg. 16.1).
*Total fertility rate* (avg. births per childbearing woman; 1986): 3.7.
*Marriage rate* per 1,000 population (1984): 7.2.
*Divorce rate* per 1,000 population (1984): 1.1.
*Life expectancy* at birth (1986): male 53.9 years; female 56.7 years.
*Major causes of death:* n.a.; however, major diseases include tuberculosis, malaria, dysentery, cholera, and plague.

## National economy

*Budget* (1987–88 est.). Revenue: Rp 22,783,100,000,000 (royalties from energy production 30.5%, foreign aid for development 24.3%, value added tax 15.6%, income tax 14.6%, excise tax 4.7%, nontax revenues 4.6%). Expenditures: Rp 22,783,100,000,000 (development 34.0%, debt service 29.9%, civil service 18.9%, subsidies for autonomous regions 11.6%).
*Public debt* (external, outstanding; 1986): U.S.$32,119,100,000.
*Tourism* (1984): receipts from visitors: U.S.$456,000,000; expenditures by nationals abroad U.S.$511,000,000.
*Production* (metric tons except as noted). Agriculture, forestry, fishing (1985): paddy rice 38,660,000, sugarcane 24,901,000, cassava 14,500,000, corn (maize) 5,300,000, sweet potatoes 2,300,000, copra 1,160,000, palm oil 1,148,000, rubber 1,125,000; livestock (number of live animals) 11,-173,000 goats, 6,859,000 cattle, 4,958,000 sheep, 2,424,000 water buffalo; roundwood 149,008,000 cu m; fish catch 2,067,090. Mining and quarrying (1985): nickel ore 995,604; bauxite 830,471; copper ore[4] 233,446; iron ore[4]

130,930; tin ore[4] 22,414; silver 2,151,821 kg. Manufacturing (1985): cement 9,939,721; fertilizer 5,263,978; paper 96,698; cotton yarn 110,369 bales; beer 608,310 hectolitres; cigarettes 19,013,147,000 units. Energy production (consumption): electricity (kW-hr; 1985) 27,797,000,000 (27,797,000,000); coal (metric tons; 1985) 1,492,000 (918,000); crude petroleum (barrels; 1985) 511,752,000 (196,961,000); petroleum products (metric tons; 1985) 20,950,-000 (21,763,000); natural gas (cu m; 1985) 24,587,000,000 (7,169,000,000).
*Gross national product* (1985): U.S.$86,590,000,000 (U.S.$520 per capita).

| Structure of gross domestic product and labour force | | | | |
|---|---|---|---|---|
| | 1985 | | 1982 | |
| | in value Rp'000,000 | % of total value | labour force | % of labour force |
| Agriculture | 22,650 | 23.6 | 31,593,314 | 54.7 |
| Mining | 15,609 | 16.2 | 390,661 | 0.7 |
| Manufacturing | 12,983 | 13.5 | 6,021,929 | 10.4 |
| Construction | 5,107 | 5.3 | 2,146,210 | 3.7 |
| Public utilities | 781 | 0.8 | 61,666 | 0.1 |
| Transp. and commun. | 6,279 | 6.5 | 1,796,112 | 3.1 |
| Trade | 14,815 | 15.4 | 8,553,919 | 14.8 |
| Finance, real estate | | | 112,859 | 0.2 |
| Pub. admin., defense | 17,843 | 18.6 | 7,126,131 | 12.3 |
| Services and other | | | | |
| TOTAL | 96,066[3] | 100.0[3] | 57,802,801 | 100.0 |

*Population economically active:* total (1982) 59,598,626; activity rate of total population 38.5% (participation rates [1980]: ages 15–64, 59.2%; female 32.8%; unemployed 1.8%).

| Price and earnings indexes (1980 = 100) | | | | | | | |
|---|---|---|---|---|---|---|---|
| | 1981 | 1982 | 1983 | 1984 | 1985 | 1986 | 1987[5] |
| Consumer price index | 112.2 | 122.9 | 137.4 | 151.7 | 158.9 | 168.2 | 182.3 |
| Monthly earnings index[6] | 108.5 | 122.6 | 155.5 | 175.0 | ... | ... | ... |

*Household income and expenditure.* Average household size (1983) 4.7; income per household: n.a.; sources of income: n.a.; expenditure (1984): food 63.3%, housing and utilities 17.4%, clothing 4.6%, durable goods 3.1%.
*Land use* (1983): forested 67.2%; meadows and pastures 6.5%; agricultural and under permanent cultivation 11.5%; other 14.8%.

## Foreign trade

| Balance of trade (current prices) | | | | | | |
|---|---|---|---|---|---|---|
| | 1981 | 1982 | 1983 | 1984 | 1985 | 1986 |
| U.S.$'000,000 | +10,410 | +7,240 | +6,545 | +9,508 | +9,430 | +5,249 |
| % of total | 30.5% | 19.4% | 18.3% | 27.7% | 34.0% | 21.5% |

*Imports* (1985): U.S.$10,259,090,000 (machinery 35.0%, chemicals 14.8%, mineral fuels 14.1%, base metals 13.0%, food and live animals 6.7%). *Major import sources:* Japan 25.8%; U.S. 16.8%; Singapore 8.2%.
*Exports* (1985): U.S.$18,586,712,000 (petroleum and petroleum products 48.9%, natural gas 19.6%, rubber 15.2%, wood products 6.1%, coffee 3.0%). *Major export destinations:* Japan 46.2%; U.S. 21.7%; Singapore 8.7%.

## Transport and communications

*Transport.* Railroads: (1986) length 4,018 mi, 6,466 km; (1985) passenger-km 6,343,000,000; (1984) metric ton-km cargo 1,175,000,000. Roads (1985): total length 127,399 mi, 205,030 km (paved 61%). Vehicles (1985): passenger cars 980,907; trucks and buses 1,055,790. Merchant marine (1986): vessels (100 gross tons and over) 1,707; total deadweight tonnage 2,927,103. Air transport (1985): passenger-km 8,808,000,000; metric ton-km cargo 157,-248,000; airports (1987) 130.
*Communications.* Daily newspapers (1984): total number 55; total circulation 2,878,000; circulation per 1,000 population 18. Radio (1985): 32,800,-000 receivers (1 per 5.1 persons). Television (1985): 4,900,000 receivers (1 per 34 persons). Telephones (1984): 795,647 (1 per 209 persons).

## Education and health

| Education (1984–85) | | | | |
|---|---|---|---|---|
| | schools | teachers | students | student/ teacher ratio |
| Primary (age 7–12) | 136,706 | 986,638 | 26,567,688 | 26.9 |
| Secondary (age 13–18) | 20,229 | 433,750 | 7,042,001 | 16.2 |
| Voc., teacher tr. | 2,708 | 70,026 | 1,002,465 | 14.3 |
| Higher[7] | 475 | 74,044 | 806,470 | 10.9 |

*Educational attainment* (1980). Percent of population age 25 and over having: no formal education 41.1%; less than primary 31.6%; primary 16.8%; some secondary 9.6%; postsecondary 0.8%. *Literacy* (1985): total population over age 15 and over literate 79,197,000 (74.1%); males literate 41,450,000 (83.0%); females literate 33,708,000 (65.4%).
*Health* (1985): physicians 18,447 (1 per 8,953 persons); hospital beds 106,035 (1 per 1,558 persons); infant mortality rate per 1,000 live births (1986) 77.0.
*Food* (1981–83): daily per capita caloric intake 2,401 (vegetable products 98%, animal products 2%); (1983) 110% of FAO recommended minimum requirement.

## Military

*Total active duty personnel* (1986): 281,000 (army 76.9%, navy 13.5%, air force 9.6%). *Military expenditure as percent of GNP* (1984): 2.6%; (world 5.9%); per capita expenditure U.S.$14.

[1]Includes 100 nonelective seats. [2]Indonesian sovereignty over former Portuguese East Timor is not recognized by the United Nations. [3]Detail does not add to total given because of rounding. [4]Concentrates. [5]May. [6]Based on prices received by farmers for sale of produce. [7]1983–84.

# Iran

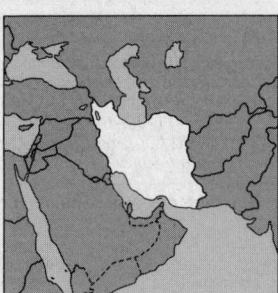

*Official name:* Jomhūrī-ye Eslāmī-ye
Īrān (Islamic Republic of Iran).
*Form of government:* unitary Islamic
republic with a single legislative house
(Islamic Consultative Assembly [270]).
*Chief of state:* Velayat Faghih
(religious leader).
*Head of state:* President.
*Head of government:* Prime Minister.
*Capital:* Tehrān.
*Official language:* Farsī (Persian).
*Official religion:* Islam.
*Monetary unit:* 1 rial (Rls) = 100 dinars;
valuation (Oct. 5, 1987)
1 U.S.$ = Rls 72.17; 1£ = Rls 117.20.

### Area and population

| Provinces | Capitals | area[1] sq mi | area[1] sq km | population 1984 estimate |
|---|---|---|---|---|
| Azārbāijān-e Gharbī | Orūmīyeh | 15,000 | 38,850 | 1,915,000 |
| Azārbāijān-e Sharqī | Tabrīz | 25,909 | 67,103 | 4,097,000 |
| Bakhtarān | Bakhtarān | 9,138 | 23,667 | 1,177,000 |
| Boyer Ahmad-e Kohkilūyeh | Yāsūj | 5,506 | 14,261 | 390,000 |
| Būshehr | Būshehr | 10,677 | 27,653 | 519,000 |
| Chahār Mahāl-e Bakhtiāri | Shahr Kord | 5,741 | 14,870 | 601,000 |
| Esfahān | Esfahān | 40,405 | 104,650 | 3,012,000 |
| Fārs | Shīrāz | 51,467 | 133,298 | 2,806,000 |
| Gīlān | Rasht | 5,679 | 14,709 | 2,069,000 |
| Hamadān | Hamadān | 7,639 | 19,784 | 1,407,000 |
| Hormozgān | Bandar 'Abbās | 25,819 | 66,871 | 694,000 |
| Īlām | Īlām | 7,353 | 19,044 | 308,000 |
| Kermān | Kermān | 69,466 | 179,916 | 1,535,000 |
| Khorāsān | Mashhad | 120,980 | 313,337 | 4,441,000 |
| Khūzestān | Ahvāz | 25,978 | 67,282 | 2,284,000 |
| Kordestān | Sanandaj | 9,652 | 24,998 | 906,000 |
| Lorestān | Khorramābād | 11,121 | 28,803 | 1,306,000 |
| Markazī | Arāk | 15,403 | 39,895 | 1,430,000 |
| Māzandarān | Sārī | 18,292 | 47,375 | 2,880,000 |
| Semnān | Semnān | 34,764 | 90,039 | 370,000 |
| Sīstān-e Balūchestān | Zāhedān | 70,108 | 181,578 | 997,000 |
| Tehrān | Tehrān | 7,381 | 19,118 | 7,243,000 |
| Yazd | Yazd | 27,031 | 70,011 | 569,000 |
| Zanjān | Zanjān | 14,053 | 36,398 | 1,488,000 |
| TOTAL | | 634,562 | 1,643,510 | 44,444,000 |

## Demography

*Population* (1987): 49,930,000.
*Density* (1987): persons per sq mi 78.7, persons per sq km 30.4.
*Urban–rural* (1984–85): urban 51.4%; rural 48.6%.
*Sex distribution* (1984–85): male 51.65%; female 48.6%.
*Age breakdown* (1984–85): under 15, 43.4%; 15–29, 25.9%; 30–44, 15.9%; 45–59, 9.3%; 60–74, 4.4%; 75 and over, 1.1%.
*Population projection:* (1990) 51,315,000; (2000) 65,161,000.
*Doubling time:* 25 years.
*Ethnic composition* (1983): Persian 45.6%; Azerbaijani 16.8%; Kurdish 9.1%; Gīlakī 5.3%; Luri 4.3%; Māzandarānī 3.6%; Baluchi 2.3%; Arab 2.2%; Bakhtiari 1.7%; Turkmen 1.5%; Armenian 0.5%; other 7.1%.
*Religious affiliation* (1985): Muslim 98% (Shī'ī 93%, Sunnī 5%); other 2%.
*Major cities* (1985): Tehrān 5,751,500; Esfahān 1,121,200; Mashhad 1,103,300; Shīrāz 834,800; Ahvaz 508,500.

## Vital statistics

*Birth rate* per 1,000 population (1985–90): 38.5 (world avg. 26.0).
*Death rate* per 1,000 population (1985–90): 10.8 (world avg. 9.9).
*Natural increase rate* per 1,000 population (1985–90): 27.7 (world avg. 16.1).
*Total fertility rate* (avg. births per childbearing woman; 1985): 5.4.
*Marriage rate* per 1,000 population (1984–85): 8.9.
*Divorce rate* per 1,000 population (1984–85): 0.8.
*Life expectancy* at birth (1985): male 58.0 years; female 58.3 years.
*Major causes of death* per 100,000 population (1984–85)[2]: diseases of the circulatory system 52.7; accidents, poisonings, and suicides 29.7; diseases of early infancy 15.2; malignant neoplasms (cancers) 14.0; diseases of the respiratory system 13.1; diseases of the nervous system 5.9.

## National economy

*Budget* (1986–87). Revenue: Rls 3,574,700,000,000 (oil and gas 44.8%, taxes 32.7%). Expenditures: Rls 3,780,000,000,000 (current expenditure 61.9%, economic affairs 25.1%, national defense 11.4%).
*Tourism* (1985): receipts from visitors U.S.$27,000,000; expenditures by nationals abroad, n.a.
*Production* (metric tons except as noted). Agriculture, forestry, fishing (1985): wheat 6,000,000, sugarcane 2,150,000, barley 1,650,000, potatoes 1,550,000, grapes 1,350,000, rice (paddy) 1,100,000, watermelons 960,000; livestock (number of live animals) 34,500,000 sheep, 13,600,000 goats, 8,350,000 cattle, 1,800,000 asses, 316,000 horses, 95,000,000 chickens; roundwood 6,745,000 cu m; fish catch 60,351. Mining and quarrying (1984): iron ore 850,000; copper ore 150,000; kaolin 100,000; barite 90,000; chromium ore (oxide content) 50,000; zinc ore 50,000; lead 28,000. Manufacturing (value in Rls; 1983–84): machinery 513,148,000,000; textiles 388,755,000,000; chemicals 226,085,000,000; iron and steel 135,688,000,000. Construction (1983–84): residential 21,065,000 sq m; nonresidential 1,448,000 sq m. Energy production (consumption): electricity (kW-hr; 1985) 37,300,000,000 (37,300,000,000); coal (metric tons; 1985) 900,000 (1,000,000); crude petroleum (barrels; 1985) 795,865,000 (270,285,000); petroleum products

(metric tons; 1985) 32,579,000 (29,834,000); natural gas (cu m; 1985) 8,303,148,000 (8,303,148,000).
*Gross national product* (1985–86): U.S.$188,200,000,000 ($4,168 per capita).

### Structure of gross domestic product and labour force

| | 1984 in value Rls '000,000 | 1984 % of total value | 1980 labour force | 1980 % of labour force |
|---|---|---|---|---|
| Agriculture | 2,493.9 | 16.6 | 4,026,000 | 36.4 |
| Mining | 1,696.4 | 11.3 | | |
| Manufacturing | 1,167.3 | 7.8 | 3,635,000 | 32.8 |
| Construction | 1,115.2 | 7.4 | | |
| Public utilities | 107.0 | 0.7 | | |
| Transp. and commun. | 1,138.4 | 7.6 | | |
| Trade | 3,205.4 | 21.3 | | |
| Finance | | | 3,411,000 | 30.8 |
| Services | 4,106.0 | 27.3 | | |
| Pub. admin., defense | | | | |
| Other | | | ... | ... |
| TOTAL | 15,029.6 | 100.0 | 11,072,000 | 100.0 |

*Population economically active* (1985): total 13,023,000; activity rate of total population 29.2% (participation rates: ages 15–64, 42.7%; female 7.2%; unemployed [1983–84] 13.9%).

### Price and earnings indexes (1980 = 100)

| | 1980 | 1981 | 1982 | 1983 | 1984 | 1985 | 1986[3] |
|---|---|---|---|---|---|---|---|
| Consumer price index[2] | 100.0 | 124.2 | 147.4 | 176.5 | 198.6 | 207.4 | 227.2 |
| Monthly earnings index[4] | 100.0 | 108.9 | 19.7 | 138.1 | 158.8 | 180.3 | ... |

*Household income and expenditure.* Average household size (1984–85) 4.2; income per household (1975) Rls 298,761 (U.S.$4,235); sources of income: wages 40.8%, self-employment 28.2%, assistance 4.5%; expenditure (1983): food and tobacco 42.1%, housing and energy 22.8%, clothing and footwear 10.4%, furniture and household equipment 7.1%, transportation 6.2%, health care 4.3%, recreation 1.4%.
*Land use* (1984): forested 11.0%; meadows and pastures 26.9%; agricultural and under permanent cultivation 9.1%; other 53.0%.

## Foreign trade

### Balance of trade (current prices)[5]

| | 1980 | 1981 | 1982 | 1983 | 1984 | 1985 |
|---|---|---|---|---|---|---|
| Rls '000,000 | +228,200 | +119,200 | +587,500 | +275,800 | −65.1 | +303.5 |
| % of total | 12.9% | 6.5% | 27.0% | 8.9% | 2.8% | 14.2% |

*Imports* (1983–84): Rls 1,582,719,000,000 (machinery and transport equipment 35.1%, food and live animals 12.5%, chemicals 11.8%). *Major import sources* (1985): West Germany 16.3%; Japan 13.4%; United Kingdom 6.7%; Italy 6.0%; Singapore 3.9%; Australia 2.1%.
*Exports* (1985): Rls 1,218,600,000,000 (petroleum and petroleum products 98.0%). *Major export destinations:* Japan 16.5%; Italy 9.8%; Spain 5.8%; France 5.2%; United States 5.0%; West Germany 4.2%.

## Transport and communications

*Transport.* Railroads (1984–85): route length 2,837 mi, 4,567 km; passenger-mi 1,570,000,000, passenger-km 2,526,000,000; short ton-mi cargo 2,645,000,000, metric ton-km cargo 3,861,000,000. Roads (1983): total length 67,710 mi, 108,970 km (paved 31%). Vehicles (1983): passenger cars 2,113,465; trucks and buses 389,247. Merchant marine (1986): vessels (100 gross tons and over) 359; total deadweight tonnage 5,064,259. Air transport (1986): passenger-mi 2,963,000,000, passenger-km 4,768,000,000; short ton-mi cargo 90,385,000, metric ton-km cargo 131,960,000; airports (1987) 13.
*Communications.* Daily newspapers (1986): 13; circulation 640,000[6]; circulation per 1,000 population 13.2[6]. Radio (1985): 10,000,000 receivers (1 per 4.5 persons). Television (1985): 2,085,000 receivers (1 per 19.4 persons). Telephones (1986): 1,883,570 (1 per 26 persons).

## Education and health

### Education (1985–86)

| | schools | teachers | students | student/teacher ratio |
|---|---|---|---|---|
| Primary (age 7–11) | 48,982 | 268,606 | 6,343,300 | 23.6 |
| Secondary (age 12–18) | 13,818 | 167,769 | 2,922,576 | 17.4 |
| Voc., teacher tr. | 1,325 | 20,683 | 277,609 | 13.4 |
| Higher | 114[7] | 13,698 | 145,809 | 10.6 |

*Educational attainment* (1976). Percent of population age 10 and over having: no formal schooling 16.1%; Qur'anic education 10.7%; primary education 43.0%; secondary 23.7%; higher 6.4%; certificate not reported 0.1%. *Literacy* (1980): total population age 15 and over literate 10,980,000 (42.8%); males literate 7,163,000 (55.4%); females literate 3,817,000 (30.1%).
*Health:* physicians (1982–83) 15,945 (1 per 2,582 persons); hospital beds (1984–85) 70,152 (1 per 616 persons); infant mortality rate (1985) 111.
*Food* (1978–80): daily per capita caloric intake 2,912 (vegetable products 90%, animal products 10%); 121% of FAO recommended minimum requirement.

## Military

*Total active duty personnel* (1987): 654,500 (revolutionary guard corps 45.8%, army 46.6%, navy 2.2%, air force 5.4%). *Military expenditure as percent of GNP* (1984): 7.2% (world 5.9%); per capita expenditure U.S.$252.

[1]Total area excludes the area of Lake Orumiyeh (4,686 sq km [1,809 sq mi]). [2]For urban areas only. [3]April. [4]Compensation paid to employees in large manufacturing establishments. [5]Imports derived from the Direction of Trade Statistics (DOTS). [6]Circulation based on three dailies only. [7]1982–83.

# Iraq

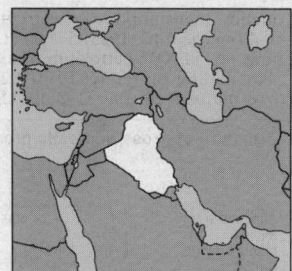

*Official name:* al-Jumhūrīyah al-'Irāqīyah (Republic of Iraq).
*Form of government:* unitary single-party republic with one legislative house (National Assembly [250]).
*Head of state and government:* President.
*Capital:* Baghdād.
*Official language:* Arabic.
*Official religion:* Islam.
*Monetary unit:* 1 Iraqi dinar (ID) = 20 dirhams = 1,000 fils; valuation (Oct. 5, 1987) 1 ID = U.S.$3.23; 1 ID = £1.99.

### Area and population

| Governorates | Capitals | area[1] | | population 1985 estimate |
| | | sq mi | sq km | |
| --- | --- | --- | --- | --- |
| al-Anbār | ar-Ramādī | 53,175 | 137,723 | 582,058 |
| Bābil | al-Hillah | 2,030 | 5,258 | 739,031 |
| Baghdād | Baghdād | 1,992 | 5,159 | 4,648,609 |
| al-Başrah | Basra | 7,363 | 19,070 | 1,304,153 |
| Dhī Qār | an-Nāşiriyah | 5,261 | 13,626 | 725,913 |
| Diyālā | Ba'qūbah | 7,449 | 19,292 | 691,350 |
| Karbalā' | Karbalā' | 1,944 | 5,034 | 329,234 |
| Maysān | al-'Amārah | 5,445 | 14,103 | 411,843 |
| al-Muthannā | as-Samāwah | 19,702 | 51,029 | 253,816 |
| an-Najaf | an-Najaf | 10,751 | 27,844 | 472,103 |
| Nīnawā | Mosul | 14,555 | 37,698 | 1,358,082 |
| al-Qādisiyah | ad-Dīwānīyah | 3,285 | 8,507 | 511,799 |
| Şalāh ad-Dīn | Sāmarrā' | 11,198 | 29,004 | 442,782 |
| at-Ta'mīm | Kirkūk | 4,012 | 10,391 | 650,965 |
| Wasiţ | al-Kūt | 6,683 | 17,308 | 483,716 |
| **Kurdish Autonomous Region** | | | | |
| Dahūk | Dahūk | 2,363 | 6,120 | 330,356 |
| Irbīl | Irbīl | 5,587 | 14,471 | 742,682 |
| as-Sulaymānīyah | as-Sulaymānīyah | 6,083 | 15,756 | 906,495 |
| LAND AREA | | 168,878 | 437,393 | 15,584,987 |
| INLAND WATER | | 357 | 924 | |
| TOTAL AREA | | 169,235 | 438,317 | |

## Demography

*Population* (1987): 16,476,000.
*Density*[2] (1987): persons per sq mi 97.6, persons per sq km 37.7.
*Urban–rural* (1985): urban 70.6%; rural 29.4%.
*Sex distribution* (1985): male 50.92%; female 49.08%.
*Age breakdown* (1985): under 15, 46.9%; 15–29, 26.1%; 30–44, 14.7%; 45–59, 8.0%; 60–74, 3.6%; 75 and over, 0.7%.
*Population projection:* (1990) 18,165,000; (2000) 25,151,000.
*Doubling time:* 20 years.
*Ethnic composition* (1983): Arab 77.1%; Kurd 19.0%; Turkmen 1.4%; Persian 0.8%; Assyrian 0.8%; other 0.9%.
*Religious affiliation* (1980): Muslim 95.8% (of which Shī'ī 53.5%, Sunnī 42.3%); Christian 3.5%; other 0.7%.
*Major cities* (1985): Baghdād 4,648,609; Basra 616,700; Mosul 570,926; Irbīl 333,903; as-Sulaymānīyah 279,424.

## Vital statistics

*Birth rate* per 1,000 population (1980–85): 44.4 (world avg. 29.0).
*Death rate* per 1,000 population (1980–85): 8.7 (world avg. 11.0).
*Natural increase rate* per 1,000 population (1980–85): 35.7 (world avg. 18.0).
*Total fertility rate* (avg. births per childbearing woman; 1980–85): 6.7.
*Marriage rate* per 1,000 population (1982): 4.0.
*Divorce rate* per 1,000 population (1981): 0.1.
*Life expectancy* at birth (1980–85): male 61.5 years; female 63.3 years.
*Major causes of death* per 100,000 population (1975): heart disease (except ischemic) 69.9; accidents (all types) 27.6; pneumonia 27.2; malignant neoplasms (cancers) 19.6; during the early 1980s, however, there were high war casualties and high incidence of trachoma, influenza, measles, whooping cough, and tuberculosis.

## National economy

*Budget* (1981). Revenue: ID 5,025,000,000 (revenue from oil and public enterprises 88.5%, sales tax 7.7%, income tax 1.3%). Expenditures: ID 5,025,000,000 (economic services 44.9%, defense 24.0%, local government 8.3%, internal security 5.2%, health 4.6%, education 2.9%).
*Public debt* (external, outstanding; 1980): U.S.$481,000,000.
*Production* (metric tons except as noted). Agriculture, forestry, fishing (1985): barley 700,000, wheat 650,000, watermelons 630,000, tomatoes 540,000, grapes 440,000, cucumbers and gherkins 300,000, melons 250,000, oranges 157,000, eggplants 150,000, potatoes 115,000; livestock (number of live animals) 8,500,000 sheep, 2,350,000 goats, 1,500,000 cattle, 145,000 buffalo, 55,000 camels, 65,000,000 chickens; roundwood 137,000 cu m; fish catch 21,500. Mining and quarrying (1985): elemental sulfur 500,000; gypsum 300,000. Manufacturing (1985): cement 8,000,000. Construction (1983): authorized residential 9,338,000 sq m; authorized nonresidential 823,000 sq m. Energy production (consumption): electricity (kW-hr; 1985) 18,760,000,000 (18,760,000,000); coal, none (n.a.); crude petroleum (barrels; 1985) 519,011,000 (111,390,000); petroleum products (metric tons; 1985) 12,260,000 (6,480,000); natural gas (cu m; 1985) 589,421,000 (589,421,000).

*Tourism* (1985): receipts from visitors U.S.$181,000,000; expenditures by nationals abroad, n.a.
*Gross national product* (1984): U.S.$34,470,000,000 (U.S.$2,310 per capita).

### Structure of gross domestic product and labour force

| | 1985 | | 1984 | |
| | in value ID '000,000 | % of total value | labour force | % of labour force |
| --- | --- | --- | --- | --- |
| Agriculture | 2,265.8 | 15.6 | 1,121,523 | 29.7 |
| Mining | 3,596.4 | 24.7 | 47,356 | 1.2 |
| Manufacturing | 1,416.2 | 9.7 | 351,391 | 9.3 |
| Construction | 1,094.6 | 7.5 | 387,876 | 10.2 |
| Public utilities | 172.4 | 1.2 | 30,327 | 0.8 |
| Transportation and communication | 783.0 | 5.4 | 229,289 | 6.1 |
| Trade | 1,597.6 | 11.0 | 285,953 | 7.6 |
| Finance | | | 40,272 | 1.1 |
| Pub. admin., defense Services | 3,620.8 | 24.9 | 1,252,184 | 33.1 |
| Other | | | 33,800[3] | 0.9[3] |
| TOTAL | 14,546.8 | 100.0 | 3,779,971 | 100.0 |

*Population economically active* (1985): total 4,259,000; activity rate of total population 26.8% (participation rates: over age 15, 50.2%; female 19.9%; unemployed [1984] 0.9%).

### Price and earnings indexes (1973 = 100)

| | 1981 | 1982 | 1983 |
| --- | --- | --- | --- |
| Consumer price index | 129.4 | 157.9 | 177.1 |
| Earnings index | ... | ... | ... |

*Household income and expenditure.* Average household size (1984) 6.9; income per household: n.a.; sources of income: n.a.; expenditure (1971–72): food and beverages 55.4%, clothing and footwear 10.3%, housing 7.9%, household durable goods 6.2%, transport and communications 5.3%, energy 4.1%, medical care and health 2.4%, recreation 1.2%.
*Land use* (1984): forested 4.4%; meadows and pastures 9.2%; agricultural and under permanent cultivation 12.5%; built-on, wasteland, and other 73.9%.

## Foreign trade[4]

### Balance of trade (current prices)

| | 1978 | 1979 | 1980 | 1981 | 1982 | 1983 |
| --- | --- | --- | --- | --- | --- | --- |
| ID '000,000 | +2,155 | +4,776 | +5,789 | +1,026 | −2,735.6 | −365.2 |
| % of total | 49.2% | 60.6% | 59.5% | 19.8% | 30.9% | 5.7% |

*Imports* (1983): ID 3,407,000,000 (1981; machines electrical and nonelectrical, airplanes, and other 63.2%; consumer goods 20.7%; chemical and pharmaceutical products 3.4%). *Major import sources* (1985): Japan 14.4%; West Germany 9.2%; Italy 7.6%; France 7.5%; United Kingdom 6.3%; United States 4.7%.
*Exports* (1983): ID 3,041,800,000 (1981; foodstuffs 55.9%; rubber, paper, and fertilizers 23.0%). *Major export destinations* (1985): France 13.0%; Italy 11.0%; Spain 10.7%; Yugoslavia 7.9%; United States 4.7%.

## Transport and communications

*Transport.* Railroads (1984): route length 1,268 mi, 2,041 km; passenger-mi 762,000,000, passenger-km 1,227,000,000; short ton-mi cargo 860,000,000, metric ton-km cargo 1,255,000,000. Roads (1984): total length 18,030 mi, 29,017 km (paved 71%). Vehicles (1984): passenger cars 393,473; trucks and buses 225,994. Merchant marine (1986): vessels (100 gross tons and over) 149; total deadweight tonnage 1,699,613. Air transport (1982): passenger-mi 917,000,000, passenger-km 1,476,000,000; short ton-mi cargo 37,463,000, metric ton-km cargo 54,696,000; airports (1987) with scheduled flights 3.
*Communications.* Daily newspapers (1986): total number 6; total circulation 324,000; circulation per 1,000 population 20. Radio (1986): 2,800,000 receivers (1 per 5.7 persons). Television (1986): 605,000 receivers (1 per 26 persons). Telephones (1985): 886,133 (1 per 17 persons).

## Education and health

### Education (1985–86)

| | schools | teachers | students | student/ teacher ratio |
| --- | --- | --- | --- | --- |
| Primary (age 6–11) | 8,142 | 118,442 | 2,816,326 | 23.8 |
| Secondary (age 12–17) | 2,109[5] | 35,143 | 1,038,627 | 29.6 |
| Voc., teacher tr. | 228[5] | 7,855 | 152,206 | 19.4 |
| Higher | 25[6] | 7,176[7] | 126,715[7] | 17.7[7] |

*Educational attainment,* n.a. *Literacy* (1984): total population age 15 and over literate 2,815,895 (45.9%); males literate 2,034,011 (65.9%); females literate 781,884 (26.0%).
*Health* (1984): physicians 4,428 (1 per 3,374 persons); hospital beds 26,657 (1 per 560 persons); infant mortality rate per 1,000 live births (1985) 73.0.
*Food* (1979–81): daily per capita caloric intake 2,789 (vegetable products 88%, animal products 12%); (1983) 121% of FAO recommended minimum requirement.

## Military

*Total active duty personnel* (1986): 845,000 (army 94.7%, navy 0.6%, air force 4.7%). *Military expenditure as percent of GNP* (1984): 42.5% (world 5.9%); per capita expenditure U.S.$980.

[1]Excluding Iraq–Saudi Arabia Neutral Zone. [2]Based on land area only. [3]Unemployed. [4]Balance of trade is based on f.o.b. (free on board) valuation of imports and exports; however, commodities traded and trade partners information are based on c.i.f. (cost, insurance, and freight). [5]1984–85. [6]1982–83. [7]1983–84.

# Ireland

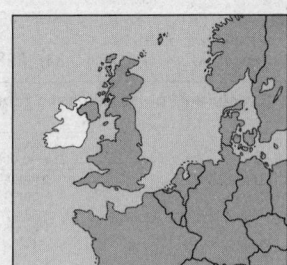

*Official name:* Éire (Irish); Ireland[1] (English).
*Form of government:* unitary multiparty republic with two legislative houses (Senate [60]; House of Representatives [166]).
*Chief of state:* President.
*Head of government:* Prime Minister.
*Capital:* Dublin.
*Official languages:* Irish; English.
*Official religion:* Roman Catholic.
*Monetary unit:* 1 Irish pound (I£) = 100 new pence; valuation (Oct. 5, 1987) 1 I£ = U.S.$1.46 = £0.90.

| Area and population | area | | population |
|---|---|---|---|
| Provinces Counties | sq mi | sq km | 1986 census |
| Connacht | 6,611 | 17,122 | 430,726 |
| Galway[2] | 2,293 | 5,940 | 178,180 |
| Leitrim | 581 | 1,525 | 27,000 |
| Mayo | 2,084 | 5,398 | 115,016 |
| Roscommon | 951 | 2,463 | 54,551 |
| Sligo | 693 | 1,796 | 55,979 |
| Leinster | 7,580 | 19,633 | 1,851,134 |
| Carlow | 346 | 896 | 40,958 |
| Dublin[2] | 356 | 922 | 1,020,796 |
| Kildare | 654 | 1,694 | 116,015 |
| Kilkenny | 796 | 2,062 | 73,094 |
| Laoighis | 664 | 1,719 | 53,270 |
| Longford | 403 | 1,044 | 31,491 |
| Louth | 318 | 823 | 91,698 |
| Meath | 902 | 2,336 | 103,762 |
| Offaly | 771 | 1,998 | 59,806 |
| Westmeath | 681 | 1,763 | 63,306 |
| Wexford | 908 | 2,351 | 102,456 |
| Wicklow | 782 | 2,025 | 94,482 |
| Munster | 9,315 | 24,127 | 1,019,694 |
| Clare | 1,231 | 3,188 | 91,343 |
| Cork[2] | 2,880 | 7,460 | 412,623 |
| Kerry | 1,815 | 4,701 | 123,922 |
| Limerick[2] | 1,037 | 2,686 | 164,204 |
| Tipperary North Riding | 771 | 1,996 | 59,453 |
| Tipperary South Riding | 872 | 2,258 | 77,051 |
| Waterford[2] | 710 | 1,838 | 91,098 |
| Ulster | 3,093 | 8,012 | 235,641 |
| Cavan | 730 | 1,891 | 53,881 |
| Donegal | 1,865 | 4,830 | 129,428 |
| Monaghan | 498 | 1,291 | 52,332 |
| TOTAL LAND AREA | 26,600 | 68,895[3] | 3,537,195 |
| INLAND WATER | 537 | 1,390 | |
| TOTAL AREA | 27,137 | 70,285 | |

## Demography

*Population* (1987): 3,560,000.
*Density* (1987): persons per sq mi 133.8, persons per sq km 51.7.
*Urban–rural* (1985): urban 57.0%; rural 43.0%.
*Sex distribution* (1986): male 49.97%; female 50.03%.
*Age breakdown* (1985): under 15, 30.5%; 15–29, 24.4%; 30–44, 17.4%; 45–59, 12.7%; 60–74, 10.8%; 75 and over, 4.2%.
*Population projection:* (1990) 3,618,000; (2000) 3,817,000.
*Doubling time:* 87 years.
*Ethnic composition* (1981): more than 94% Irish nationality.
*Religious affiliation* (1981): Roman Catholic 93.1%; Church of Ireland (Anglican) 2.8%; Presbyterian 0.4%; other 3.7%.
*Major cities*[4] (1986): Dublin 502,337; Cork 133,196; Limerick 56,241; Galway 47,008; Waterford 39,516.

## Vital statistics

*Birth rate* per 1,000 population (1985): 17.6 (world avg. 29.0); (1984) legitimate 92.2%; illegitimate 7.8%.
*Death rate* per 1,000 population (1985): 9.4 (world avg. 11.0).
*Natural increase rate* per 1,000 population (1985): 8.2 (world avg. 18.0).
*Total fertility rate* (avg. births per childbearing woman; 1980–85): 3.2.
*Marriage rate* per 1,000 population (1985): 5.2.
*Life expectancy* at birth (1980–82): male 70.1 years; female 75.6 years.
*Major causes of death* per 100,000 population (1984): heart and circulatory diseases 454.3; malignant neoplasms (cancers) 189.2; pneumonia 57.8.

## National economy

*Budget* (1986). Revenue: I£6,792,100,000 (income taxes 35.7%, value-added tax 23.0%, excise taxes 20.3%). Expenditures: I£8,042,000,000 (debt service 25.1%, social welfare 19.8%, health 12.8%, education 11.5%, defense 3.5%).
*Public debt* (1986): U.S.$22,957,000,000.
*Tourism* (1985): receipts from visitors U.S.$549,000,000; expenditures by nationals abroad U.S.$422,000,000.
*Production* (metric tons except as noted). Agriculture, forestry, fishing (1985): sugar beets 1,500,000, barley 1,265,000, potatoes 700,000, wheat 500,000, oats 125,000, milk 5,920,000; livestock (number of live animals) 5,835,000 cattle, 2,832,000 sheep, 1,020,000 pigs; roundwood (1984) 1,256,000 cu m; fish catch (1984) 207,615. Mining and quarrying (1985): gypsum 304,100; barite 213,800; zinc ore 191,700[5]; lead ore 34,600[5]. Manufacturing (value added in I£; 1981): food and beverages 899,800,000; machinery and transport equipment 619,800,000; chemical products 511,300,000; nonmetallic mineral products 181,700,000; textiles 159,000,000; printing and publishing 144,100,000. Construction (1984): residential 2,461,000 sq m. Energy pro-

duction (consumption): electricity (kW-hr; 1985) 11,738,000 (11,738,000); coal (metric tons; 1985) 57,000 (1,608,000); crude petroleum (barrels; 1985) none (9,350,000); petroleum products (metric tons; 1985) 1,282,000 (3,783,-000); natural gas (cu m; 1984) 2,272,600,000 (2,276,100,000).
*Gross national product* (1985): U.S.$17,250,000,000 (U.S.$4,900 per capita).

| Structure of gross domestic product and labour force | | | | |
|---|---|---|---|---|
| | 1985 | | | |
| | in value I£'000,000 | % of total value | labour force | % of labour force |
| Agriculture | 1,660 | 10.7 | 169,000 | 13.1 |
| Mining | | | 10,000 | 0.8 |
| Manufacturing | 5,519 | 35.7 | 204,000 | 15.8 |
| Construction | | | 76,000 | 5.9 |
| Public utilities | | | 15,000 | 1.2 |
| Transp. and commun. | 2,943 | 19.0 | 68,000 | 5.3 |
| Trade | | | 209,000[6] | 16.2 |
| Pub. admin., defense | 1,063 | 6.9 | 73,000 | 5.7 |
| Services | | | ...[7] | ... |
| Finance | 4,273 | 27.6 | ...[6] | ... |
| Other | | | 466,000[7,8] | 36.1 |
| TOTAL | 15,458 | 100.0[3] | 1,290,000 | 100.0[3] |

*Population economically active* (1985): total 1,290,000; activity rate of total population 36.6% (participation rates [1984]: ages 15–64, 60.3%; female 29.4%; unemployed 16.8%).

| Price and earnings indexes (1980 = 100) | | | | | | | |
|---|---|---|---|---|---|---|---|
| | 1981 | 1982 | 1983 | 1984 | 1985 | 1986 | 1987[9] |
| Consumer price index | 120.4 | 141.0 | 155.8 | 169.2 | 178.4 | 185.2 | 189.6 |
| Weekly earnings index | 116.7 | 131.7 | 147.1 | 165.1 | 177.5 | 191.6[10] | ... |

*Household income and expenditure.* Average household size (1983) 3.9; income per household: n.a.; sources of income (1984): wages and salaries 59.1%, self-employment 15.1%, interest and dividends 2.9%; expenditure (1984): food 39.8%, rent and household goods 19.0%, transportation 13.2%.
*Land use* (1984): forest 4.9%; pasture 70.6%; agricultural 14.1%; other 10.4%.

## Foreign trade

| Balance of trade (current prices) | | | | | |
|---|---|---|---|---|---|
| | 1981 | 1982 | 1983 | 1984 | 1985 | 1986 |
| I£'000,000 | −1,698 | −1,120 | −420 | −15.3 | +312 | +758 |
| % of total | 15.1% | 9.1% | 2.9% | 0.1% | 1.6% | 4.2% |

*Imports* (1985): I£9,430,492,000 (machinery and transport equipment 31.2%; chemicals 11.7%; petroleum and petroleum products 10.0%; food products 3.7%; textiles 3.6%; paper products 2.8%; iron and steel 1.8%). *Major import sources:* U.K. 42.7%; U.S. 17.0%; W.Ger. 7.7%; France 4.8%; The Netherlands 3.8%; Japan 3.5%.
*Exports* (1985): I£9,743,029,000 (machinery and transport equipment 29.6%, of which office machinery 18.7%, electrical machinery 5.8%; food 13.8%, of which meat 6.2%, dairy products 5.5%). *Major export destinations:* U.K. 33.0%; W.Ger. 10.1%; U.S. 9.8%; France 8.4%.

## Transport and communications

*Transport.* Railroads (1985): length 1,848 mi, 2,975 km; passenger-km 948,-000,000; metric ton-km cargo 552,000,000. Roads (1985): total length 57,354 mi, 92,303 km (paved 94%). Vehicles (1985): passenger cars 709,456; trucks and buses 98,829. Merchant marine (1986): vessels (100 gross tons and over) 154; total deadweight tonnage 148,938. Air transport (1985): passenger-km 2,460,000,000; metric ton-km cargo 86,668,000; airports (1987) 5.
*Communications.* Daily newspapers (1986): 7; circulation 708,682; circulation per 1,000 population 200. Radio (1985): total number of receivers 2,050,000 (1 per 1.7 persons). Television (1986): total number of receivers 918,000 (1 per 3.8 persons). Telephones (1985): 942,000 (1 per 3.7 persons).

## Education and health

| Education (1984–85) | schools | teachers | students | student/ teacher ratio |
|---|---|---|---|---|
| Primary (age 6–14) | 3,387 | 20,933 | 566,289 | 27.0 |
| Secondary (age 12–18) | 565 | 14,078 | 249,253 | 17.7 |
| Voc., teacher tr. | 257 | 5,126 | 81,900 | 16.0 |
| Higher | 25 | 3,690[11] | 46,618 | ... |

*Educational attainment* (1981). Percent of population age 15 and over having: primary education 45.6%; secondary 27.3%; some postsecondary 19.4%; university or like institution 7.6%. *Literacy* (1985): virtually 100% literate.
*Health* (1984): physicians 4,250 (1 per 830 persons); hospital beds (1982) 32,468[12] (1 per 181 persons); infant mortality rate per 1,000 live births 10.1.
*Food* (1981–83): daily per capita caloric intake 3,638 (vegetable products 59%, animal products 41%); (1983) 143% of FAO recommended minimum.

## Military

*Total active duty personnel* (1986): 14,115 (army 87.0%, navy 6.7%, air force 6.3%). *Military expenditure as percent of GNP* (1984): 1.8% (world 5.9%); per capita expenditure U.S.$87.

[1]As provided by the constitution; the 1948 Republic of Ireland Act provides precedent for this longer formulation of the official name but, per official sources, "has not changed the usage *Ireland* as the name of the state in the English language." [2]Includes county borough(s). [3]Detail does not add to total given because of rounding. [4]County boroughs. [5]Metal content only. [6]Trade includes Finance. [7]Other includes Services. [8]Includes unemployed. [9]First quarter. [10]Third quarter. [11]1983–84. [12]Includes an attribution of 13,321 beds based on the average number of long-term resident psychiatric patients.

# Israel

*Official name:* Medinat Yisra'el (Hebrew); Isrā'īl (Arabic) (State of Israel).
*Form of government:* multiparty republic with one legislative house (Knesset [120]).
*Chief of state:* President.
*Head of government:* Prime Minister.
*Capital:* Jerusalem is the proclaimed capital of Israel (from Jan. 23, 1950) and the actual seat of government, but recognition of its status as capital by the international community has largely been withheld pending final settlement of territorial and other issues through peace talks between Israel and the Arab parties concerned.
*Official languages:* Hebrew; Arabic.
*Official religion:* none.
*Monetary unit:* 1 Israeli sheqel (IS) = 100 agorot; valuation (Oct. 5, 1987) 1 U.S.$ = IS 1.60; 1 £ = IS 2.60.

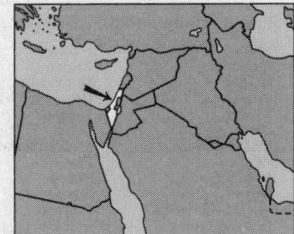

### Area and population

| Districts | Capitals | area[1] sq mi | sq km | population 1985 estimate |
|---|---|---|---|---|
| Central (Ha Merkaz) | Ramla | 479 | 1,242 | 889,100 |
| Haifa (Ḥefa) | Haifa | 330 | 854 | 592,700 |
| Jerusalem (Yerushalayim) | Jerusalem | 215 | 557 | 506,200 |
| Northern (Ha Ẕafon) | Tiberias | 1,347 | 3,490 | 706,700 |
| Southern (Ha Darom) | Beersheba | 5,555 | 14,387 | 510,100 |
| Tel Aviv | Tel Aviv–Yafo | 66 | 170 | 1,015,300 |
| TOTAL | | 7,992 | 20,700 | 4,220,100 |

## Demography[2]

*Population* (1987): 4,449,000.
*Density*[1] (1987): persons per sq mi 556.7, persons per sq km 214.9.
*Urban–rural* (1985): urban 89.4%; rural 10.6%.
*Sex distribution* (1985): male 49.90%; female 50.10%.
*Age breakdown* (1985): under 15, 32.6%; 15–29, 24.6%; 30–44, 18.7%; 45–59, 11.7%; 60–74, 9.1%; 75 and over, 3.3%.
*Population projection*[3]: (1990) 4,739,000; (2000) 5,475,000.
*Doubling time:* 43 years.
*Ethnic composition* (1983): Jewish 83.0%; Arab 16.8%; other 0.2%.
*Religious affiliation* (1985): Jewish 82.5%; Muslim (mostly Sunnī) 13.5%; Christian 2.4%; Druze and other 1.6%.
*Major cities* (1984): Jerusalem 446,500; Tel Aviv–Yafo 323,400; Haifa 224,700; Ḥolon 137,800; Bat Yam 131,200.

## Vital statistics[2]

*Birth rate* per 1,000 population (1986): 23.1 (world avg. 26.0); (1980) legitimate 97.5%; illegitimate 2.5%.
*Death rate* per 1,000 population (1986): 6.7 (world avg. 9.9).
*Natural increase rate* per 1,000 population (1986): 16.4 (world avg. 16.1).
*Total fertility rate* (avg. births per childbearing woman; 1985): 2.9.
*Marriage rate* per 1,000 population (1986): 6.8.
*Divorce rate* per 1,000 population (1986): 1.2.
*Life expectancy* at birth (1984): male 73.5 years; female 77.1 years.
*Major causes of death* per 100,000 population (1983): heart disease 195.6; malignant neoplasms (cancers) 124.6; cerebrovascular disease 74.8.

## National economy

*Budget* (1985–86). Revenue: IS 11,156,500,000,000 (direct taxes 42.4%; indirect taxes 22.7%). Expenditures: IS 12,806,500,000,000 (consumption expenditure 45.6%; interest on loans 35.2%; subsidies 10.8%, of which on credit 3.7%, on exports 3.6%, on price stabilization 3.5%).
*Tourism* (1985): receipts from visitors U.S.$1,109,000,000; expenditures by nationals abroad U.S.$531,000,000.
*Production* (metric tons except as noted). Agriculture, forestry, fishing (1985): oranges 900,000, tomatoes 336,000, potatoes 200,000, wheat 110,000, apples 108,000, grapes 92,000, watermelons 90,000, lemons and limes 65,000, onions 58,000, cucumbers 54,000; livestock (number of live animals) 310,000 cattle, 230,000 sheep, 128,000 goats, 29,000,000 chickens; roundwood 118,000 cu m; fish catch (1984) 22,953. Mining and quarrying (1986–87): phosphate rock 2,550,000; potash 2,100,000; phosphoric acid 190,000; bromine and bromine compounds 162,000; periclase 38,000. Manufacturing (1986): wheat flour 514,000; polyethylene 76,881; writing and printing paper 64,906; cardboard 54,468; ammonium sulfate 46,251; tires 25,111; cotton yarn 14,914. Construction (1986): residential 2,770,000 sq m; nonresidential 1,130,000 sq m. Energy production (consumption): electricity (kW-hr; 1986) 16,277,000,000 (15,908,100,000); coal (metric tons; 1985) none (2,873,000); crude petroleum (barrels; 1986) 89,862 (53,336,000); petroleum products (metric tons; 1985) 5,692,000 (5,152,000); natural gas (cu m; 1985) 48,691,000 (48,691,000).
*Land use* (1984): forested 5.7%; meadows and pastures 40.2%; agricultural and under permanent cultivation 21.5%, other 32.6%.
*Population economically active* (1986)[4]: total 1,472,000; activity rate of total population 33.8% (participation rates: over age 15, 50.6%; female 19.6%; unemployed 7.1%).

### Price and earnings indexes (1980 = 100)

| | 1981 | 1982 | 1983 | 1984 | 1985 | 1986 | 1987[5] |
|---|---|---|---|---|---|---|---|
| Consumer price index | 216.8 | 477.8 | 1,173.5 | 5,560.4 | 22,498 | 33,330 | 38,341 |
| Monthly earnings index | 245.4 | 553.8 | 1,414.8 | 7,028.0 | 24,789 | 39,977 | 48,906 |

*Public debt* (external, outstanding; 1985): U.S.$15,850,400,000.
*Gross national product* (1985): U.S.$21,140,000,000 (U.S.$4,910 per capita).

### Structure of gross domestic product and labour force

| | 1985 in value IS '000,000[6] | 1985 % of total value | 1986 labour force | 1986 % of labour force |
|---|---|---|---|---|
| Agriculture | 1,034,397 | 5.1 | 70,000 | 5.2 |
| Manufacturing, mining | 4,740,568 | 23.4 | 322,400 | 23.7 |
| Construction | 781,234 | 3.9 | 61,800 | 4.5 |
| Public utilities | 424,309 | 2.1 | 12,400 | 0.9 |
| Transp. and commun. | 1,594,038 | 8.0 | 86,700 | 6.4 |
| Trade | 2,926,330 | 14.4 | 178,100 | 13.1 |
| Finance | | | 133,800 | 9.8 |
| Public and community services | 8,725,268 | 43.1 | 405,800 | 29.9 |
| Services, other | | | 87,900 | 6.5 |
| TOTAL | 20,266,144 | 100.0 | 1,358,900 | 100.0 |

*Household income and expenditure* (1984). Average urban household size 3.7; monthly income per household IS 470,900 (U.S.$938); sources of income: salaries and wages 90.8%, property, interest and dividends, pensions, allowances and assistance 8.4%, self-employment 0.8%; expenditure (1986): food, beverages, and tobacco 30.3%, housing and furnishings 25.3%, clothing, footwear, and personal effects 5.6%, fuel and light 3.6%, transportation 3.5%, other goods and services 31.7%.

## Foreign trade

### Balance of trade (current prices)

| | 1983 | 1984 | 1985 | 1986 |
|---|---|---|---|---|
| U.S.$'000,000 | –3,210 | –2,600 | –2,426 | –1,927 |
| % of total | 22.5% | 17.4% | 15.5% | 11.2% |

*Imports* (1986): US$9,635,200,000 (diamonds 18.2%; investment goods 16.6%; fuel and lubricants 9.6%; foodstuffs 3.2%). *Major import sources:* United States 18.6%; Belgium and Luxembourg 13.1%; West Germany 12.6%; United Kingdom 10.2%; Switzerland 8.0%; France 4.0%.
*Exports* (1986): US$7,135,600,000 (metals, machinery, and electronics 30.7%; diamonds 26.3%; agricultural products 7.9%; textiles, clothing, and leather 6.5%; food, beverages, and tobacco 4.7%). *Major export destinations:* United States 32.9%; United Kingdom 7.2%; West Germany 5.2%; France 4.4%; The Netherlands 4.3%; Belgium and Luxembourg 3.7%.

## Transport and communications

*Transport.* Railroads (1986): route length 323 mi, 520 km; passenger-mi 127,000,000, passenger-km 205,000,000; short ton-mi cargo 645,400,000, metric ton-km cargo 942,200,000. Roads (1985): total length 7,930 mi, 12,760 km (paved 100%). Vehicles (1985): passenger cars 613,680; trucks and buses 126,724. Merchant marine (1986): vessels (100 gross tons and over) 64; total deadweight tonnage 679,228. Air transport (1986): passenger-mi 4,183,000,000, passenger-km 6,732,000,000; short ton-mi cargo 394,322,000, metric ton-km cargo 575,700,000; airports (1987) with scheduled flights 4.
*Communications.* Daily newspapers (1986): total number 25; total circulation 1,148,000; circulation per 1,000 population 263. Radio (1986): 700,000 receivers (1 per 6.2 persons). Television (1986): 620,000 receivers (1 per 7.0 persons). Telephones (1986): 1,780,000 (1 per 2.4 persons).

## Education and health

### Education (1985–86)[7]

| | schools | teachers | students | student/ teacher ratio |
|---|---|---|---|---|
| Primary (age 6–13) | 1,843 | 45,016 | 622,056 | 13.8 |
| Secondary (age 14–17)[8] | 936 | 37,717 | 348,262 | 9.2 |
| Voc., teacher tr. | 369 | 3,654[9] | 111,674 | ... |
| Higher | 7[10] | 8,112 | 87,293 | 10.8 |

*Educational attainment* (1982). Percent of population age 25 and over having: no formal schooling 9.7%; primary education 30.6%; secondary 36.6%; postsecondary, vocational, and higher 23.1%. *Literacy* (1983): total population age 15 and over literate 2,542,403 (91.8%); males literate 1,312,258 (95.0%); females literate 1,230,145 (88.7%).
*Health:* physicians (1983) 11,895 (1 per 345 persons); hospital beds (1985) 27,500 (1 per 156 persons); infant mortality rate per 1,000 live births (1986) 11.2.
*Food* (1983–84): daily per capita caloric intake 3,036 (vegetable products 77%, animal products 23%); (1983) 121% of FAO recommended minimum.

## Military

*Total active duty personnel* (1986): 149,000 (army 75.2%, navy 6.0%, air force 18.8%). *Military expenditure as percent of GNP* (1984): 24.4% (world 5.9%); per capita expenditure U.S.$1,380.

[1]Excluding West Bank, Gaza Strip, Golan Heights, and East Jerusalem. [2]De jure; includes population of East Jerusalem and about 25,000 Israeli residents living in occupied territories. [3]Based on migration balance of +5,000 per year in the 1980s and nil in the 1990s. [4]Excludes armed forces; includes Israelis in occupied territories. [5]March. [6]Net domestic product at factor cost. [7]Includes schools run by UNRWA in East Jerusalem. [8]Includes intermediate education age 12–14. [9]Teachers for teacher training only. [10]Universities only.

# Italy

*Official name:* Repubblica Italiana (Italian Republic).
*Form of government:* republic with two legislative houses (Senate [323]; Chamber of Deputies [630]).
*Chief of state:* President.
*Head of government:* Prime Minister.
*Capital:* Rome.
*Official language:* Italian.
*Official religion:* none; Roman Catholicism disestablished 1985.
*Monetary unit:* 1 lira (Lit, plural lire) = 100 centesimi; valuation (Oct. 5, 1987) 1 U.S.$ = Lit 1,329; 1 £ = Lit 2,158.

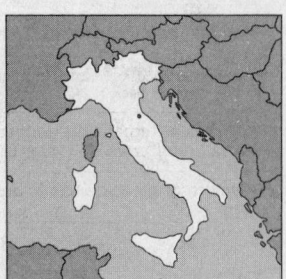

### Area and population

| Regions<br>Provinces | Capitals | area sq mi | area sq km | population<br>1986 estimate |
|---|---|---|---|---|
| Abruzzi | L'Aquila | 4,168 | 10,794 | 1,250,057 |
| Chieti | Chieti | 999 | 2,587 | 381,521 |
| L'Aquila | L'Aquila | 1,944 | 5,034 | 297,791 |
| Pescara | Pescara | 473 | 1,225 | 292,709 |
| Teramo | Teramo | 752 | 1,948 | 278,036 |
| Basilicata | Potenza | 3,858 | 9,992 | 618,647 |
| Matera | Matera | 1,331 | 3,447 | 207,188 |
| Potenza | Potenza | 2,527 | 6,545 | 411,459 |
| Calabria | Catanzaro | 5,823 | 15,080 | 2,131,412 |
| Catanzaro | Catanzaro | 2,026 | 5,247 | 769,461 |
| Cosenza | Cosenza | 2,568 | 6,650 | 772,620 |
| Reggio di Calabria | Reggio di Calabria | 1,229 | 3,183 | 589,331 |
| Campania | Naples | 5,249 | 13,595 | 5,651,200 |
| Avellino | Avellino | 1,078 | 2,792 | 445,670 |
| Benevento | Benevento | 800 | 2,071 | 297,277 |
| Caserta | Caserta | 1,019 | 2,639 | 796,381 |
| Napoli | Naples | 452 | 1,171 | 3,064,607 |
| Salerno | Salerno | 1,900 | 4,922 | 1,047,265 |
| Emilia-Romagna | Bologna | 8,542 | 22,123 | 3,939,289 |
| Bologna | Bologna | 1,429 | 3,702 | 919,591 |
| Ferrara | Ferrara | 1,016 | 2,632 | 374,341 |
| Forlì | Forlì | 1,123 | 2,910 | 607,297 |
| Modena | Modena | 1,039 | 2,690 | 596,437 |
| Parma | Parma | 1,332 | 3,449 | 397,827 |
| Piacenza | Piacenza | 1,000 | 2,589 | 274,726 |
| Ravenna | Ravenna | 718 | 1,859 | 354,600 |
| Reggio nell'Emilia | Reggio nell'Emilia | 885 | 2,292 | 414,470 |
| Friuli-Venezia Giulia | Trieste | 3,030 | 7,847 | 1,219,556 |
| Gorizia | Gorizia | 180 | 467 | 142,232 |
| Pordenone | Pordenone | 878 | 2,273 | 276,354 |
| Trieste | Trieste | 82 | 212 | 272,327 |
| Udine | Udine | 1,890 | 4,895 | 528,643 |
| Lazio | Rome | 6,642 | 17,203 | 5,101,641 |
| Frosinone | Frosinone | 1,251 | 3,239 | 476,611 |
| Latina | Latina | 869 | 2,251 | 457,978 |
| Rieti | Rieti | 1,061 | 2,749 | 145,088 |
| Roma | Rome | 2,066 | 5,352 | 3,747,335 |
| Viterbo | Viterbo | 1,395 | 3,612 | 274,629 |
| Liguria | Genoa | 708 | 5,416 | 1,771,319 |
| Genova | Genoa | 2,091 | 1,834 | 1,015,540 |
| Imperia | Imperia | 446 | 1,155 | 222,925 |
| La Spezia | La Spezia | 341 | 882 | 237,868 |
| Savona | Savona | 596 | 1,545 | 294,986 |
| Lombardia | Milan | 9,211 | 23,857 | 8,881,683 |
| Bergamo | Bergamo | 1,066 | 2,760 | 910,009 |
| Brescia | Brescia | 1,846 | 4,782 | 1,028,999 |
| Como | Como | 798 | 2,067 | 783,007 |
| Cremona | Cremona | 684 | 1,771 | 329,616 |
| Mantova | Mantova | 903 | 2,339 | 373,815 |
| Milano | Milan | 1,066 | 2,762 | 3,984,538 |
| Pavia | Pavia | 1,145 | 2,965 | 504,171 |
| Sondrio | Sondrio | 1,240 | 3,212 | 175,898 |
| Varese | Varese | 463 | 1,199 | 791,630 |
| Marche | Ancona | 3,743 | 9,694 | 1,425,734 |
| Ancona | Ancona | 749 | 1,940 | 437,881 |
| Ascoli Piceno | Ascoli Piceno | 806 | 2,087 | 357,971 |
| Macerata | Macerata | 1,071 | 2,774 | 294,476 |
| Pesaro e Urbino | Pesaro | 1,117 | 2,893 | 335,406 |
| Molise | Campobasso | 1,713 | 4,438 | 333,502 |
| Campobasso | Campobasso | 1,123 | 2,909 | 240,345 |
| Isernia | Isernia | 590 | 1,529 | 93,157 |
| Piemonte | Turin | 9,807 | 25,399 | 4,394,312 |
| Alessandria | Alessandria | 1,375 | 3,560 | 455,263 |
| Asti | Asti | 583 | 1,511 | 211,825 |
| Cuneo | Cuneo | 2,665 | 6,903 | 547,694 |
| Novara | Novara | 1,388 | 3,594 | 503,079 |
| Torino | Turin | 2,637 | 6,830 | 2,289,054 |
| Vercelli | Vercelli | 1,159 | 3,001 | 387,397 |
| Puglia | Bari | 7,470 | 19,348 | 4,005,226 |
| Bari | Bari | 1,980 | 5,129 | 1,507,476 |
| Brindisi | Brindisi | 710 | 1,838 | 404,688 |
| Foggia | Foggia | 2,774 | 7,185 | 697,531 |
| Lecce | Lecce | 1,065 | 2,759 | 803,342 |
| Taranto | Taranto | 941 | 2,437 | 592,189 |
| Sardegna | Cagliari | 9,301 | 24,090 | 1,638,172 |
| Cagliari | Cagliari | 2,662 | 6,895 | 755,771 |
| Nuoro | Nuoro | 2,720 | 7,044 | 276,982 |
| Oristano | Oristano | 1,016 | 2,631 | 159,250 |
| Sassari | Sassari | 2,903 | 7,520 | 446,169 |
| Sicilia (Sicily) | Palermo | 9,926 | 25,708 | 5,084,311 |
| Agrigento | Agrigento | 1,175 | 3,042 | 487,311 |
| Caltanissetta | Caltanissetta | 822 | 2,128 | 294,098 |
| Catania | Catania | 1,371 | 3,552 | 1,051,380 |
| Enna | Enna | 989 | 2,562 | 197,301 |
| Messina | Messina | 1,254 | 3,247 | 684,703 |
| Palermo | Palermo | 1,927 | 4,992 | 1,241,357 |
| Ragusa | Ragusa | 623 | 1,614 | 286,224 |
| Siracusa | Siracusa | 814 | 2,109 | 406,574 |
| Trapani | Trapani | 951 | 2,462 | 435,363 |

### Area and population (continued)

| | | area sq mi | area sq km | population<br>1986 estimate |
|---|---|---|---|---|
| Toscana | Florence | 8,877 | 22,992 | 3,576,508 |
| Arezzo | Arezzo | 1,248 | 3,232 | 313,631 |
| Firenze | Florence | 1,498 | 3,879 | 1,198,400 |
| Grosseto | Grosseto | 1,739 | 4,504 | 220,255 |
| Livorno | Livorno | 468 | 1,213 | 346,257 |
| Lucca | Lucca | 684 | 1,773 | 383,588 |
| Massa-Carrara | Massa-Carrara | 447 | 1,157 | 205,716 |
| Pisa | Pisa | 945 | 2,448 | 389,048 |
| Pistoia | Pistoia | 373 | 965 | 265,637 |
| Siena | Siena | 1,475 | 3,821 | 253,976 |
| Trentino-Alto Adige | Bolzano | 5,259 | 13,620 | 878,590 |
| Bolzano-Bozen | Bolzano | 2,857 | 7,400 | 434,361 |
| Trento | Trento | 2,402 | 6,220 | 444,229 |
| Umbria | Perugia | 3,265 | 8,456 | 816,939 |
| Perugia | Perugia | 2,446 | 6,334 | 589,954 |
| Terni | Terni | 819 | 2,122 | 226,985 |
| Valle d'Aosta | Aosta | 1,259 | 3,262 | 113,714 |
| Veneto | Venice | 7,090 | 18,363 | 4,370,533 |
| Belluno | Belluno | 1,420 | 3,678 | 217,418 |
| Padova | Padova | 827 | 2,142 | 815,586 |
| Rovigo | Rovigo | 691 | 1,789 | 251,544 |
| Treviso | Treviso | 956 | 2,477 | 730,708 |
| Venezia | Venice | 950 | 2,460 | 838,000 |
| Verona | Verona | 1,195 | 3,096 | 781,850 |
| Vicenza | Vicenza | 1,051 | 2,721 | 735,427 |
| TOTAL | | 116,324 | 301,277 | 57,202,345 |

## Demography

*Population* (1987): 57,256,000.
*Density* (1987): persons per sq mi 492.2, persons per sq km 190.0.
*Urban–rural* (1985): urban 67.4%; rural 32.6%.
*Sex distribution* (1985): male 48.96%; female 51.04%.
*Age breakdown* (1985): under 15, 19.9%; 15–29, 22.8%; 30–44, 19.8%; 45–59, 18.7%; 60–74, 13.2%; 75 and over 5.6%.
*Population projection:* (1990) 57,361,000; (2000) 57,388,000.
*Ethnolinguistic composition* (1983): Italian 94.1%; Sardinian 2.6%; Rhaetian 1.3%; other 2.0%.
*Religious affiliation* (1980): Roman Catholic 83.2%; nonreligious 13.6%; atheist 2.6%; other 0.6%.
*Major cities* (1986): Rome 2,823,927; Milan 1,507,877; Naples 1,204,021; Turin 1,030,011; Genoa 731,484; Palermo 722,095; Bologna 435,248.
*National origin* (1980): Italian 98.8%; foreign 1.2%, of which Austrian 0.4%, French 0.2%, Slovene 0.2%, Albanian 0.1%, other 0.3%.
*Mobility* (1977). Population living in the same residence as in 1967: 52.0%.
*Households.* Average household size (1984) 3.0; composition of households (1981) 1 person 17.9%, 2 persons 23.6%, 3 persons 22.1%, 4 persons 21.5%, 5 persons 9.5%, 6 or more persons 5.4%. Family households (1981): 13,088,040 (74.3%); nonfamily 4,527,088 (25.7%), of which 1-person 13.9%.
*Immigration* (1984): immigrants admitted 77,318, from Europe 78.3%, of which West Germany 35.7%, Switzerland 24.4%, France 6.1%; Africa 6.1%; United States 5.1%; Latin America 4.0%; Asia 3.0%.

## Vital statistics

*Birth rate* per 1,000 population (1985): 10.1 (world avg. 29.0); legitimate 94.7%; illegitimate 5.3%.
*Death rate* per 1,000 population (1985): 9.5 (world avg. 11.0).
*Natural increase rate* per 1,000 population (1985): 0.6 (world avg. 18.0).
*Total fertility rate* (avg. births per childbearing woman; 1983): 1.5.
*Marriage rate* per 1,000 population (1985): 5.2.
*Divorce rate* per 1,000 population: (1984): 0.3.
*Life expectancy* at birth (1981): male 71.0 years; female 77.8 years.
*Major causes of death* per 100,000 population (1984): diseases of the circulatory system 429.7; malignant neoplasms (cancers) 226.0; diseases of the respiratory system 60.5; diseases of the digestive system 54.7.

## Social indicators

*Educational attainment,* n.a.

### Distribution of income (1980)

percent of household income by quintile

| 1 | 2 | 3 | 4 | 5 (highest) |
|---|---|---|---|---|
| 7.0 | 11.0 | 16.0 | 22.0 | 45.0 |

*Quality of working life.* Average workweek (1985): 36.6 hours. Annual rate per 100,000 workers (1978) for: injury or accident (1984) 3,737; industrial illness 405; death 66. Proportion of labour force insured for damages or income loss (1982) resulting from: injury 100%; permanent disability 100%; death 100%. Number of working days lost to labour stoppages (1985): 3,830,800. Average duration of journey to work: n.a. Rate per 1,000 workers of discouraged (unemployed no longer seeking work; 1982): 0.9.
*Access to services* (1981). Proportion of dwellings having access to: electricity 99.5%; safe water supply 98.7%; toilet facilities 98.5%; bath facilities 86.4%.
*Social participation.* Eligible voters participating in last national election (1985): 89.7%. Population participating in voluntary work: n.a. Trade union membership in total workforce (1984): *c.* 70%. Practicing religious population in total affiliated population (1980): 65.7%, of which weekly 28.0%.
*Social deviance* (1985). Offense rate per 100,000 population for: murder 11.3; rape 64.7; other assault 47.2; theft, including burglary and housebreaking 2,082. Incidence per 100,000 in general population of: alcoholism (1978) 2.0; drug and substance abuse (1978) 25.1; suicide (1984) 5.6.
*Leisure* (1982). Favourite leisure activities (as percent of public spending on culture): cinema 35.6%; sporting events 16.3%; theatre 10.6%.
*Material well-being.* Rate per 1,000 of population possessing (1985): automobile 391; telephone 447. Households possessing (1979): television 72%; refrigerator 91%; air conditioner 9%; washing machine 88%.

## National economy

*Gross national product* (at current market prices; 1985): U.S.$371,050,000,-000 (U.S.$6,520 per capita).

### Structure of gross domestic product and labour force

| | 1985 | | | |
|---|---|---|---|---|
| | in value 000,000,000 lire | % of total value | labour force | % of labour force |
| Agriculture | 34,243 | 5.0 | 2,296,000 | 9.8 |
| Mining | 21,817 | 3.2 | 209,000 | 0.9 |
| Manufacturing | 157,619 | 23.0 | 4,766,000 | 20.4 |
| Construction | 50,871 | 7.4 | 1,921,000 | 8.2 |
| Public utilities | 36,278 | 5.3 | ... | ... |
| Transportation and communication | 46,624 | 6.8 | 1,091,000 | 4.7 |
| Trade | 107,379 | 15.7 | 4,365,000 | 18.7 |
| Finance | 83,633 | 12.2 | 716,000 | 3.1 |
| Pub. admin., defense | 96,307 | 14.1 } | 5,530,000 | 23.6 |
| Services | 61,175 | 8.9 } | | |
| Other | −11,103[1] | −1.6[1] | 2,472,000[2] | 10.6[2] |
| TOTAL | 684,843 | 100.0 | 23,366,000 | 100.0 |

*Budget* (1985). Revenue: Lit 226,451,000,000,000 (property and income taxes 45.6%, business taxes 23.3%, transfer payments 15.6%, sales taxes 9.2%). Expenditures: Lit 358,924,000,000,000 (social services 17.8%, regional and local subsidies 13.4%, education and culture 9.4%, transportation and communication 8.3%, national defense 4.1%).
*Public debt* (1985): U.S.$390,000,000,000.
*Tourism* (1985): receipts from visitors U.S.$8,758,000,000; expenditures by nationals abroad U.S.$2,283,000,000.

### Manufacturing, mining, and construction enterprises (1982)

| | no. of enterprises | no. of employees | hourly wages as a % of avg. of all wages[3] | annual value added (Lit '000,000,000) |
|---|---|---|---|---|
| Transport equipment | 810 | 386,000 | 117.7 | 11,637 |
| Industrial chemicals | 1,016 | 211,000 | 119.7 | 10,982 |
| Machinery, nonelectrical | 2,420 | 280,000 | 98.0 | 10,558 |
| Electrical machinery | 1,127 | 294,000 | 112.1 | 9,398 |
| Pottery, ceramics, and glass | 2,363 | 197,000 | 83.4 | 7,515 |
| Iron and steel | 848 | 222,000 | 122.6 | 7,321 |
| Textiles | 2,783 | 245,000 | 84.4 | 6,797 |
| Metal products | 2,202 | 174,000 | 86.7 | 6,132 |
| Wearing apparel | 1,657 | 153,000 | 75.0 | 3,679 |
| Printing, publishing | 726 | 79,000 | 103.2 | 3,400 |
| Food products | 1,646 | 166,000 | 92.2 | 3,308 |
| Petroleum and gas | 9 | 8,000 | 138.6 | 2,856 |
| Plastic products | 911 | 68,000 | 84.4 | 2,447 |
| Paper and paper products | 678 | 65,000 | 102.1 | 2,443 |
| Nonmetal mining and quarrying | 275 | 13,000 | 82.9 | 520 |
| Construction | 326,000 | 1,199,000 | ... | 31,920 |

*Production* (metric tons except as noted). Agriculture, forestry, fishing (1985): grapes 10,360,000, sugar beets 9,706,000, wheat 8,602,000, corn (maize) 6,336,300, tomatoes 6,311,000, olives 2,600,000, potatoes 2,494,900, apples 2,092,600, pears 1,874,000, oranges 1,850,000, barley 1,642,700, peaches 1,450,000, rice 1,130,000; livestock (number of live animals) 9,106,000 cattle, 9,500,000 sheep, 9,040,000 pigs, 112,000,000 chickens; roundwood 80,444,000 cu m; fish catch 428,674. Mining and quarrying (1985): rock salt 3,175,700; potash 1,701,500; feldspar 1,116,400; asbestos 136,000; barite 127,200; magnesium 89,400; zinc 82,200; lead 25,000. Manufacturing (1985): cement 37,152,000; crude steel 23,784,000; pig iron 12,036,000; olive oil 3,900,000[4]; plastics and resins 2,640,000; sulfuric acid 2,520,000; pasta 2,485,000[4]; chemical fertilizers 1,830,000[5]; soaps and detergents 1,058,-600[4]; caustic soda 1,031,000; textiles and cloth 253,400[5]; wine 71,200,000 hectolitres[6]; beer 9,333,000 hectolitres[6]; 2,437,300 motorized road vehicles, of which 1,395,500 automobiles, 853,900 motorcycles, scooters, and mopeds[4], 187,800 trucks and buses; 331,500,000 pairs of shoes[4]; 50,000,000 women's dresses[4]. Construction (buildings completed 1985): residential 174,181; commercial, industrial, and other 6,525.

### Service enterprises (1981)

| | no. of enterprises | no. of employees | hourly wage as a % of all wages | annual value added (Lit '000,000,000) |
|---|---|---|---|---|
| Public utilities | 61 | 11,000 | ... | 5,082 |
| Electrical power | 49 | 125,000 | ... | 4,017 |
| Transportation | 195,828 | 1,135,950 | ... | 24,760 |
| Communication } | | | ... | 5,842 |
| Finance | 234,334 | 938,904 | ... | 46,343 |
| Wholesale and retail trade | 1,589,785 | 3,694,238 | ... | 61,884 |
| Pub. admin., services | 494,153 | 3,553,304 | ... | 57,333 |

*Energy production (consumption)*: electricity (kW-hr; 1985) 182,237,000,000 (205,906,000,000); coal (metric tons; 1985) 1,755,000 (24,219,000); crude petroleum (barrels; 1985) 16,118,000 (480,000,000); petroleum products (metric tons; 1985) 66,906,000 (79,054,000); natural gas (cu m; 1985) 13,-755,800,000 (32,423,024,130).
*Population economically active* (1985): total 23,366,000; activity rate of total population 41.1% (participation rates: ages 15–64, 58.2%; female 35.3%; unemployed 10.6%).

### Price and earnings indexes (1980 = 100)

| | 1980 | 1981 | 1982 | 1983 | 1984 | 1985 | 1986 |
|---|---|---|---|---|---|---|---|
| Consumer price index | 100.0 | 117.8 | 137.2 | 157.3 | 174.3 | 190.3 | 201.5 |
| Monthly earnings index | 100.0 | 123.9 | 145.7 | 167.9 | 186.7 | 207.5 | 217.5 |

*Land use* (1984): forested 21.8%; meadows and pastures 16.8%; agricultural and under permanent cultivation 41.6%; other 19.8%.

### Financial aggregates

| | 1982 | 1983 | 1984 | 1985 | 1986 | 1987[7] |
|---|---|---|---|---|---|---|
| Exchange rate, Lit per: | | | | | | |
| U.S. dollar | 1,352.5 | 1,518.8 | 1,757.0 | 1,909.4 | 1,490.8 | 1,304.6 |
| £ | 2,367.6 | 2,304.0 | 2,347.9 | 2,759.1 | 2,187.0 | 2,077.3 |
| SDR | 1,511.3 | 1,737.4 | 1,897.6 | 1,843.7 | 1,661.5 | 1,654.5 |
| International reserves (U.S.$) | | | | | | |
| Total (excl. gold; '000,000) | 14,090 | 19,840 | 20,796 | 15,515 | 19,971 | 25,096 |
| SDRs ('000,000) | 785 | 591 | 633 | 326 | 587 | 645 |
| Reserve pos. in IMF ('000,000) | 696 | 990 | 1,074 | 1,160 | 1,268 | 1,319 |
| Foreign exchange ('000,000) | 12,610 | 18,259 | 19,089 | 14,029 | 18,116 | 23,132 |
| Gold ('000,000 fine troy oz) | 66.67 | 66.67 | 66.67 | 66.67 | 66.67 | 66.67 |
| % world reserves | 7.0 | 7.1 | 7.1 | 7.0 | 7.0 | 7.0[8] |
| Interest and prices | | | | | | |
| Central bank discount (%) | 18.00 | 17.00 | 16.50 | 15.00 | 12.00 | 12.00 |
| Gov't. bond yield (%) | 20.90 | 18.02 | 14.95 | 13.00 | 10.52 | 8.66[8] |
| Industrial share prices (1980 = 100) | 123.1 | 153.1 | 171.9 | 286.7 | 667.4 | 694.4 |
| Balance of payments (U.S.$'000,000) | | | | | | |
| Balance of visible trade | −8,130 | −4,390 | −5,994 | −6,853 | ... | ... |
| Imports, f.o.b. | −80,678 | −75,215 | −78,976 | −85,145 | ... | ... |
| Exports, f.o.b. | 72,548 | 70,827 | 72,982 | 78,292 | ... | ... |
| Balance of invisibles | 1,701 | 2,555 | 2,026 | 1,781 | ... | ... |
| Balance of payments, current account | −5,684 | 555 | −2,871 | −3,980 | ... | ... |

*Household income and expenditure.* Average household size (1984) 3.0; average annual income per household Lit 19,692,000 (U.S.$11,208); sources of income: salaries and wages 49.2%, self-employment 31.1%, social security 11.8%; expenditure (1985): food and beverages 28.1%, housing 26.1%, transport and communications 15.1%, recreation and education 6.1%.

## Foreign trade

### Balance of trade (current prices)

| | 1981 | 1982 | 1983 | 1984 | 1985 | 1986 |
|---|---|---|---|---|---|---|
| Lit '000,000,000 | −14,056 | −16,966 | −11,465 | −19,163 | −23,262 | −3,724 |
| % of total | 6.7% | 7.9% | 4.9% | 16.9% | 7.8% | 1.3% |

*Imports* (1985): Lit 172,816,417,000,000 (machinery and transport equipment 21.5%, of which transport equipment 8.3%, precision machinery 4.7%; crude petroleum 14.7%; chemicals and chemical products 10.1%; food and live animals 8.7%; metal and semiprocessed metal 7.6%; refined petroleum products 7.1%). *Major import sources:* West Germany 16.6%; France 12.5%; United States 6.0%; The Netherlands 5.1%; United Kingdom 4.9%; Switzerland 3.9%.
*Exports* (1985): Lit 149,700,978,000,000 (nontransport machinery 22.6%; textiles 9.1%; metal and processed metal 8.6%; clothing and wearing apparel 8.6%, of which shoes 4.2%; transport equipment 8.3%, of which automobiles 2.8%, tractors and construction equipment 0.8%; chemicals and chemical products 7.9%; refined petroleum products 4.9%). *Major export destinations:* West Germany 16.2%; France 14.0%; United States 12.3%; United Kingdom 7.0%; Switzerland 4.1%; Syria 3.2%.

## Transport and communications

*Transport.* Railroads (1986): route length 12,257 mi, 19,726 km; passenger-mi 25,165,000,000, passenger-km 40,500,000,000; short ton-mi cargo 11,-999,000,000, metric ton-km cargo 17,520,000,000. Roads (1984): total length 187,223 mi, 301,307 km (paved 100%). Vehicles (1985): passenger cars 22,398,000; trucks and buses 1,915,830. Merchant marine (1986): vessels (100 gross tons and over) 1,569; total deadweight tonnage 12,407,125. Air transport (1986)[9]: passenger-mi 8,694,000,000, passenger-km 13,992,000,-000; short ton-mi cargo 589,282,000, metric ton-km cargo 859,000,000; airports (1987) 36.
*Communications.* Daily newspapers (1985): total number 66; total circulation 6,238,000[10]; circulation per 1,000 population 109[10]. Radio (1986): 14,521,-250 receivers (1 per 4.1 persons). Television (1986): 15,000,000 receivers (1 per 3.9 persons). Telephones (1985): 25,614,597 (1 per 2.2 persons).

## Education and health

### Education (1985–86)

| | schools | teachers | students | student/teacher ratio |
|---|---|---|---|---|
| Primary (age 6–10) | 27,748 | 230,698 | 3,715,597 | 16.1 |
| Secondary | 10,033 | 129,980 | 2,764,635 | 21.3 |
| Voc., teacher tr. | 7,564 | 112,876 | 2,607,749 | 23.1 |
| Higher | ... | ... | 1,184,142 | ... |

*Literacy* (1985): total population age 15 and over literate 38,421,342 (97.0%); males literate 18,767,897 (97.9%); females literate 19,653,445 (96.3%).
*Health* (1984): physicians 100,964 (1 per 564.4 persons); hospital beds 481,413 (1 per 118.4 persons); infant mortality rate per 1,000 live births (1985) 10.9.
*Food* (1981–83): daily per capita caloric intake 3,542 (vegetable products 74%, animal products 26%); (1983) 140% of FAO recommended minimum requirement.

## Military

*Total active duty personnel* (1986): 387,800 (army 69.6%, navy 12.2%, air force 18.2%). *Military expenditure as percent of GNP* (1984): 2.7% (world 5.9%); per capita expenditure U.S.$161.

[1]Imputed bank charges less indirect duties on import. [2]Unemployed. [3]1981. [4]1984. [5]1983. [6]1982. [7]March. [8]February. [9]Alitalia only. [10]For 51 newspapers only.

# Jamaica

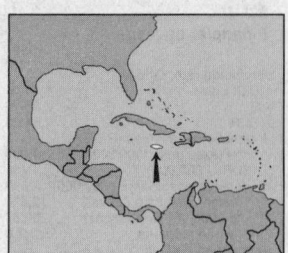

*Official name:* Jamaica.
*Form of government:* constitutional monarchy with two legislative houses (Senate [21]; House of Representatives [60]).
*Chief of state:* British Monarch represented by governor-general.
*Head of government:* Prime Minister.
*Capital:* Kingston.
*Official language:* English.
*Official religion:* none.
*Monetary unit:* 1 Jamaica dollar (J$) = 100 cents; valuation (Oct. 5, 1987) 1 U.S.$ = J$5.37; 1 £ = J$8.72.

### Area and population

| Parishes | Capitals | area sq mi | area sq km | population 1985 estimate |
|---|---|---|---|---|
| Clarendon | May Pen | 462 | 1,196 | 212,100 |
| Hanover | Lucea | 174 | 450 | 64,000 |
| Kingston | 1 | 8 | 22 | 2 |
| Manchester | Mandeville | 321 | 830 | 153,800 |
| Portland | Port Antonio | 314 | 814 | 76,200 |
| Saint Andrew | 1 | 166 | 431 | 625,800[2] |
| Saint Ann | Saint Ann's Bay | 468 | 1,213 | 144,600 |
| Saint Catherine | Spanish Town | 460 | 1,192 | 388,000 |
| Saint Elizabeth | Black River | 468 | 1,212 | 142,400 |
| Saint James | Montego Bay | 230 | 595 | 145,300 |
| Saint Mary | Port Maria | 236 | 611 | 109,900 |
| Saint Thomas | Morant Bay | 287 | 743 | 83,800 |
| Trelawny | Falmouth | 338 | 875 | 72,200 |
| Westmorland | Savanna-la-Mar | 312 | 807 | 125,600 |
| TOTAL | | 4,244 | 10,991 | 2,343,700[3] |

## Demography

*Population* (1987): 2,365,000.
*Density* (1987): persons per sq mi 557.3, persons per sq km 215.2.
*Urban–rural* (1986): urban 49.1%; rural 50.9%.
*Sex distribution* (1982): male 49.06%; female 50.94%.
*Age breakdown* (1982): under 15, 38.4%; 15–29, 28.8%; 30–44, 13.9%; 45–59, 9.4%; 60–74, 6.9%; 75 and over, 2.6%.
*Population projection:* (1990) 2,449,000; (2000) 2,750,000.
*Doubling time:* 38 years.
*Ethnic composition* (1983): black 76.3%; Afro-European 15.1%; East Indian and Afro-East Indian 3.4%; white 3.2%; other 2.0%.
*Religious affiliation* (1980): Protestant (mostly Anglican, Baptist, Seventh-day Adventist) 70.7%; Roman Catholic 9.6%; indigenous Christian 8.6%; spiritist (mostly Rastafarian) 7.1%; other 4.0%.
*Major cities* (1982): Kingston 104,041[4] (metropolitan area 524,638); Spanish Town 89,097; Portmore 73,400; Montego Bay 70,265.

## Vital statistics

*Birth rate* per 1,000 population (1985): 24.3 (world avg. 29.0).
*Death rate* per 1,000 population (1985): 6.0 (world avg. 11.0).
*Natural increase rate* per 1,000 population (1985): 18.3 (world avg. 18.0).
*Total fertility rate* (avg. births per childbearing woman; 1984): 3.3.
*Marriage rate* per 1,000 population (1985): 5.1.
*Divorce rate* per 1,000 population (1985): 0.4.
*Life expectancy* at birth (1980–85): male 67.9 years; female 71.9 years.
*Major causes of death* per 100,000 population (1981): cerebrovascular disease 89.2; ischemic heart disease 87.6; malignant neoplasms (cancers) 74.7; hypertensive disease 34.5; diabetes mellitus 21.9.

## National economy

*Budget* (1986). Revenue: J$3,592,600,000 (tax revenue 97.1%, of which income taxes 42.2%, consumption taxes 23.9%, stamp duties 14.5%; nontax revenue 2.3%). Expenditures: J$4,869,300,000 (public debt service 45.0%; general administration 15.5%; education 11.6%; public order and safety 8.7%; health 6.8%).
*Public debt* (external, outstanding; 1985): U.S.$2,822,700,000.
*Tourism:* receipts from visitors (1986) U.S.$482,400,000; expenditures by nationals abroad (1984) U.S.$20,000,000.
*Production* (metric tons except as noted). Agriculture, forestry, fishing (1985): sugarcane 2,350,000, yams 149,000, coconuts 120,000, bananas 43,-000, oranges 33,000, plantains 29,000, tomatoes 14,000, cabbages 13,000, cocoa 6,000, pimento 3,300, coffee 1,300, tobacco 1,000; livestock (number of live animals) 430,000 goats, 321,000 cattle, 238,000 pigs; roundwood 93,000 cu m; fish catch (1984) 9,431. Mining and quarrying (1986): bauxite 6,854,000; gypsum 200,000[5]. Manufacturing (1986): alumina 1,575,000; cement 240,000; sugar 177,000; stout and beer 473,000 hectolitres[5]; rum 137,000 hectolitres; cigarettes 1,314,000,000 units[5]; tires 210,000 units[5]. Construction (private sector only): residential completions (1983) 54,500 sq m; nonresidential starts (1985) 12,700 sq m. Energy production (consumption): electricity (kW-hr; 1985) 2,400,000,000 (2,400,000,000); coal, none (none); crude petroleum (barrels; 1985) none (7,697,000); petroleum products (metric tons; 1985) 926,000 (1,903,000); natural gas, none (none).
*Land use* (1984): forested 17.6%; meadows and pastures 18.5%; agricultural and under permanent cultivation 24.8%; other 39.1%.
*Gross national product* (at current market prices; 1985): U.S.$2,090,000,000 (U.S.$900 per capita).

### Structure of gross domestic product and labour force

| | 1985 in value J$'000,000 | 1985 % of total value | 1984 labour force | 1984 % of labour force |
|---|---|---|---|---|
| Agriculture | 655.7 | 5.9 | 245,000 | 25.2 |
| Mining | 548.9 | 5.0 | 7,500 | 0.8 |
| Manufacturing | 2,157.5 | 19.6 | 116,200 | 12.0 |
| Construction | 942.7 | 8.6 | 44,700 | 4.6 |
| Public utilities | 365.4 | 3.3 | } | |
| Transportation and communication | 742.0 | 6.7 | 39,600 | 4.1 |
| Trade | 2,563.0 | 23.2 | 119,700 | 12.3 |
| Pub. admin., defense | 1,196.0 | 10.9 | 111,600 | 11.5 |
| Finance, real estate | 1,645.7 | 14.9 | } | |
| Other | 207.9 | 1.9 | 287,100[6] | 29.5 |
| TOTAL | 11,024.8 | 100.0 | 971,400 | 100.0 |

*Population economically active* (1984): total 971,400; activity rate of total population 42.6% (participation rates: ages 14–64, 72.2%; female 46.6%; unemployed [1986] 23.6%).

### Price and earnings indexes (1980 = 100)

| | 1981 | 1982 | 1983 | 1984 | 1985 | 1986 | 1987[7] |
|---|---|---|---|---|---|---|---|
| Consumer price index | 112.7 | 120.1 | 134.0 | 171.3 | 215.3 | 247.8 | 257.4 |
| Monthly earnings index | ... | ... | ... | ... | ... | ... | ... |

*Household income and expenditure.* Average household size (1982) 4.3; income per household, n.a.; sources of income (1982): wages and salaries 70.9%, self-employment 27.3%, transfers 1.8%; expenditure (1982): food and beverages 36.8%, transportation 13.2%, housing 8.5%, cafe and hotel expenditures 7.4%, household furnishings 5.3%, tobacco 4.9%, energy 4.6%, recreation 3.3%, health care 2.5%, clothing 2.3%, other 11.2%.

## Foreign trade[8]

### Balance of trade (current prices)

| | 1981 | 1982 | 1983 | 1984 | 1985 | 1986 |
|---|---|---|---|---|---|---|
| J$'000,000 | −556.1 | −841.2 | −1,071.2 | −1,103.8 | −2,417.5 | −1,370.6 |
| % of total | 13.8% | 24.5% | 27.8% | 16.5% | 28.4% | 17.3% |

*Imports* (1985): J$6,218,800,000 (crude petroleum and petroleum products 31.9%, cereals and cereal preparations 7.9%, transport equipment 7.1%, industrial machinery 3.9%, textile yarn and fabrics 3.1%). *Major import sources:* United States 42.3%; Venezuela 12.2%; Netherlands Antilles 8.4%; Japan 7.1%; United Kingdom 5.2%.
*Exports* (1985): J$3,042,500,000 (alumina 37.3%, bauxite 13.6%, raw sugar 8.7%, food 5.2%, petroleum products 4.9%, rum 1.6%, coffee 1.3%, citrus 1.3%). *Major export destinations:* United States 33.7%; United Kingdom 16.7%; Canada 16.4%; U.S.S.R. 5.0%; Ireland 4.5%.

## Transport and communications

*Transport.* Railroads (1985): length 215 mi, 346 km; passenger-mi 24,887,-000, passenger-km 40,052,000; short ton-mi cargo 88,514,000[9], metric ton-km cargo 129,228,000[9]. Roads (1985): total length 7,680 mi, 12,360 km (paved 39%). Vehicles (1985): passenger cars 42,037; trucks and buses 23,-154. Merchant marine (1986): vessels (100 gross tons and over) 13; total deadweight tonnage 12,878. Air transport (1986): passenger-mi 1,074,000,-000, passenger-km 1,728,000,000; short ton-mi cargo 13,061,000, metric ton-km cargo 19,068,000; airports (1987) with scheduled flights 6.
*Communications.* Daily newspapers (1986): total number 2; total circulation 84,300; circulation per 1,000 population 36. Radio (1986): 910,000 receivers (1 per 2.6 persons). Television (1986): 350,000 receivers (1 per 6.7 persons). Telephones (1985): 143,459 (1 per 16 persons).

## Education and health

### Education (1984–85)[10]

| | schools | teachers | students | student/ teacher ratio |
|---|---|---|---|---|
| Primary (age 6–11) | 785 | ... | 337,231 | ... |
| Secondary (age 12–16) | 132 | 7,435 | 228,241 | 30.7 |
| Voc., teacher tr. | 11 | 501 | 7,856 | 15.7 |
| Higher | 17 | ... | 14,581 | ... |

*Educational attainment* (1981). Percent of population age 14 and over having: no formal schooling 2.0%; primary education 69.7%; secondary and higher 28.3%. *Literacy* (1980): total population age 14 and over literate 1,100,600 (88.6%); males literate 542,600 (88.2%); females literate 558,000 (89.1%).
*Health* (1984): physicians (1985) 317[11] (1 per 7,290 persons); hospital beds 6,298 (1 per 365 persons); infant mortality rate per 1,000 live births 13.2.
*Food* (1981–83): daily per capita caloric intake 2,536 (vegetable products 84%, animal products 16%); (1983) 111% of FAO recommended minimum requirement.

## Military

*Total active duty personnel* (1986): 2,100 (army 84.8%; navy 7.1%; air force 8.1%). *Military expenditure as percent of GNP* (1984): 0.8% (world 5.9%); per capita expenditure U.S.$12.

[1]The parishes of Kingston and Saint Andrew are jointly administered from the Half Way Tree section of Saint Andrew. [2]Kingston included with Saint Andrew. [3]Preliminary estimate; total revised downward to 2,311,000. [4]City of Kingston is contiguous with Kingston parish. [5]1985. [6]Includes 104,000 unemployed not previously employed. [7]February. [8]Import figures are f.o.b. in balance of trade and c.i.f. in commodities and trading partners. [9]1981. [10]Public schools only. [11]Government-employed only.

# Japan

*Official name:* Nihon (Japan).
*Form of government:* constitutional monarchy with a National Diet consisting of two legislative houses (House of Councillors [252]; House of Representatives [512]).
*Chief of state:* Emperor.
*Head of government:* Prime Minister.
*Capital:* Tōkyō.
*Official language:* Japanese.
*Official religion:* none.
*Monetary unit:* 1 yen (¥) = 100 sen; valuation (Oct. 5, 1987)
1 U.S.$ = ¥146.87;
1 £ = ¥238.50.

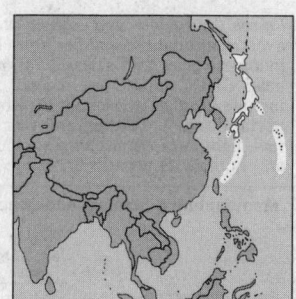

## Area and population

| Regions Prefectures | Capitals | area sq mi | area sq km | population 1986 estimate[1] |
|---|---|---|---|---|
| **Chūbu** | | | | |
| Aichi | Nagoya | 1,984 | 5,138 | 6,507,000 |
| Fukui | Fukui | 1,618 | 4,191 | 820,000 |
| Gifu | Gifu | 4,091 | 10,596 | 2,036,000 |
| Ishikawa | Kanazawa | 1,620 | 4,197 | 1,155,000 |
| Nagano | Nagano | 5,245 | 13,585 | 2,144,000 |
| Niigata | Niigata | 4,857 | 12,579 | 2,479,000 |
| Shizuoka | Shizuoka | 3,001 | 7,773 | 3,596,000 |
| Toyama | Toyama | 1,642 | 4,252 | 1,119,000 |
| Yamanashi | Kōfu | 1,723 | 4,463 | 838,000 |
| **Chūgoku** | | | | |
| Hiroshima | Hiroshima | 3,269 | 8,466 | 2,831,000 |
| Okayama | Okayama | 2,737 | 7,090 | 1,923,000 |
| Shimane | Matsue | 2,559[2] | 6,628[2] | 794,000 |
| Tottori | Tottori | 1,349[2] | 3,493[2] | 617,000 |
| Yamaguchi | Yamaguchi | 2,358 | 6,106 | 1,599,000 |
| **Hokkaidō** | | | | |
| Hokkaidō (Territory) | Sapporo | 32,247 | 83,519 | 5,678,000 |
| **Kantō** | | | | |
| Chiba | Chiba | 1,988 | 5,150 | 5,216,000 |
| Gumma | Maebashi | 2,454 | 6,356 | 1,930,000 |
| Ibaraki | Mito | 2,353 | 6,094 | 2,746,000 |
| Kanagawa | Yokohama | 927 | 2,402 | 7,542,000 |
| Saitama | Urawa | 1,467 | 3,799 | 5,950,000 |
| Tochigi | Utsunomiya | 2,476 | 6,414 | 1,879,000 |
| **Kinki** | | | | |
| Hyōgo | Kōbe | 3,235 | 8,378 | 5,302,000 |
| Mie | Tsu | 2,231 | 5,778 | 1,757,000 |
| Nara | Nara | 1,425 | 3,692 | 1,319,000 |
| Shiga | Ōtsu | 1,551 | 4,016 | 1,167,000 |
| Wakayama | Wakayama | 1,824 | 4,725 | 1,085,000 |
| **Kyūshū** | | | | |
| Fukuoka | Fukuoka | 1,915 | 4,960 | 4,740,000 |
| Kagoshima | Kagoshima | 3,539 | 9,165 | 1,817,000 |
| Kumamoto | Kumamoto | 2,860 | 7,408 | 1,842,000 |
| Miyazaki | Miyazaki | 2,986 | 7,735 | 1,175,000 |
| Nagasaki | Nagasaki | 1,588 | 4,112 | 1,591,000 |
| Ōita | Ōita | 2,447 | 6,337 | 1,250,000 |
| Saga | Saga | 939 | 2,433 | 880,000 |
| **Ryukyu** | | | | |
| Okinawa | Naha | 870 | 2,254 | 1,190,000 |
| **Shikoku** | | | | |
| Ehime | Matsuyama | 2,190 | 5,672 | 1,529,000 |
| Kagawa | Takamatsu | 727 | 1,882 | 1,024,000 |
| Kōchi | Kōchi | 2,744 | 7,107 | 838,000 |
| Tokushima | Tokushima | 1,600 | 4,145 | 835,000 |
| **Tohoku** | | | | |
| Akita | Akita | 4,483[3] | 11,612[3] | 1,249,000 |
| Aomori | Aomori | 3,713[3] | 9,617[3] | 1,520,000 |
| Fukushima | Fukushima | 5,322 | 13,784 | 2,085,000 |
| Iwate | Morioka | 5,899 | 15,279 | 1,431,000 |
| Miyagi | Sendai | 2,815 | 7,292 | 2,190,000 |
| Yamagata | Yamagata | 3,601 | 9,327 | 1,262,000 |
| **Metropolis** | | | | |
| Tōkyō[4] | Tōkyō | 835 | 2,162 | 11,893,000 |
| **Urban prefectures** | | | | |
| Kyōto[5] | Kyōto | 1,781 | 4,613 | 2,596,000 |
| Ōsaka[5] | Ōsaka | 721 | 1,868 | 8,706,000 |
| TOTAL | | 145,870[6,7] | 377,801[6,7] | 121,672,000 |

## Demography

*Population* (1987): 122,100,000.
*Density* (1987): persons per sq mi 837.0, persons per sq km 323.2.
*Urban–rural* (1980): urban 76.2%; rural 23.8%.
*Sex distribution* (1987): male 49.15%; female 50.85%.
*Age breakdown* (1987): under 15, 20.4%; 15–29, 21.0%; 30–44, 23.2%; 45–59, 19.7%; 60–69, 8.5%; 70 and over, 7.2%.
*Population projection:* (1990) 124,275,000; (2000) 132,589,000.
*Doubling time:* n.a.; doubling time exceeds 100 years.
*Composition by nationality* (1986): Japanese 99.4%; other (mainly Korean) 0.6%.
*Place of birth* (1987): 99.4% native-born; 0.6% foreign-born (mainly Korean).
*Religious affiliation* (1985): most Japanese consider themselves to be adherents of both Shintō (93.1%), a body of indigenous beliefs and practices, and Buddhism (73.9%). A small proportion of the population is Christian (1.4%). Most of the others are members of the "new religions," which incorporate to varying degrees Shintō, Buddhist, Taoist, and Christian beliefs.
*Major cities* (1987): Tōkyō 8,366,000; Yokohama 3,089,000; Ōsaka 2,647,000; Nagoya 2,138,000; Sapporo 1,583,000; Kyōto 1,480,000; Kōbe 1,428,000; Fukuoka 1,182,000; Kawasaki 1,121,000; Hiroshima 1,061,000; Kita-Kyūshū 1,047,000.

## Other principal cities (1986)

| | population | | population | | population |
|---|---|---|---|---|---|
| Akashi | 263,031 | Kasugai | 259,689 | Sagamihara | 491,224 |
| Akita | 298,139 | Kawagoe | 289,218 | Sakai | 818,537 |
| Amagasaki | 507,882 | Kawaguchi | 407,520 | Sasebo | 249,973 |
| Aomori | 293,969 | Kōchi | 313,204 | Sendai | 692,404 |
| Asahikawa | 365,843 | Koriyama | 304,435 | Shimonoseki | 268,667 |
| Chiba | 796,668 | Koshigaya | 261,150 | Shizuoka | 470,025 |
| Fujisawa | 333,622 | Kumamoto | 560,263 | Suita | 351,681 |
| Fukushima | 272,305 | Kurashiki | 414,637 | Takamatsu | 328,210 |
| Fukuyama | 361,828 | Machida | 328,567 | Takasaki | 233,090 |
| Funabashi | 512,973 | Maebashi | 279,877 | Takatsuki | 351,988 |
| Gifu | 411,299 | Matsudo | 432,677 | Tokorozawa | 282,869 |
| Hachiōji | 432,431 | Matsuyama | 430,396 | Tokushima | 259,293 |
| Hakodate | 318,734 | Miyazaki | 281,526 | Toyama | 315,338 |
| Hamamatsu | 518,787 | Nagano | 339,086 | Toyohashi | 325,461 |
| Higashi–Ōsaka | 522,144 | Nagasaki | 448,554 | Toyonaka | 416,829 |
| Himeji | 453,636 | Naha | 305,727 | Toyota | 314,222 |
| Hirakata | 385,525 | Nara | 333,222 | Urawa | 382,440 |
| Ibaraki | 253,493 | Neyagawa | 259,280 | Utsunomiya | 411,056 |
| Ichikawa | 407,548 | Niigata | 477,782 | Wakayama | 401,117 |
| Ichinomiya | 259,123 | Nishinomiya | 423,131 | Yao | 276,797 |
| Iwaki | 351,508 | Ōita | 395,346 | Yokkaichi | 265,974 |
| Kagoshima | 531,188 | Okayama | 577,910 | Yokosuka | 427,690 |
| Kanazawa | 433,012 | Okazaki | 289,028 | | |
| Kashiwa | 279,892 | Ōmiya | 378,108 | | |

*Mobility* (1980). Population living in same residence as in October 1975: 77.6%; different residence, same prefecture 17.3%; different prefecture 5.1%.
*Households* (1986). Total households 38,987,773; average household size 3.1; composition of households (1985) 1 person 20.8%, 2 persons 18.4%, 3 persons 17.9%, 4 persons 23.6%, 5 persons 11.0%, 6 persons 5.2%, 7 or more persons 2.9%. Family households (1985) 30,021,000 (79.0%); nonfamily 7,967,000 (21.0%), of which 1-person 7,900,000 (20.8%).

## Type of household (1983)

Total number of dwelling units: 34,705,000

| | number of dwellings | percent of total |
|---|---|---|
| **by kind of dwelling** | | |
| exclusive entry (do not share bathroom or kitchen) | 31,935,000 | 94.0 |
| combined with nondwelling | 2,770,000 | 8.0 |
| detached house | 22,306,000 | 64.3 |
| apartment building | 9,329,000 | 26.9 |
| tenement (substandard or overcrowded building) | 2,882,000 | 8.3 |
| **by legal tenure of householder** | | |
| owned | 21,650,000 | 62.4 |
| rented | 12,951,000 | 37.3 |
| by government | 2,645,000 | 7.6 |
| by private owner | 8,487,000 | 24.5 |
| other | 1,819,000 | 5.2 |
| **by kind of amenities** | | |
| running water | 32,637,000 | 94.0 |
| flush toilet | 20,198,000 | 58.2 |
| bathroom | 30,633,000 | 88.3 |
| **by year of construction** | | |
| prior to 1945 | 3,670,000 | 10.6 |
| 1945–60 | 4,738,000 | 13.7 |
| 1961–70 | 8,870,000 | 25.6 |
| 1971–80 | 14,473,000 | 41.7 |
| 1981–83 | 2,705,000 | 7.8 |

*Immigration* (1985): permanent immigrants/registered aliens admitted 850,612, from South Korea 80.3%, Taiwan 8.8%, United States 3.4%, Philippines 1.4%, United Kingdom 0.8%, Vietnam 0.5%, West Germany 0.4%.

## Vital statistics

*Birth rate* per 1,000 population (1986): 11.4 (world avg. 26.0); (1980) legitimate 99.2%; illegitimate 0.8%.
*Death rate* per 1,000 population (1986): 6.2 (world avg. 9.9).
*Natural increase rate* per 1,000 population (1986): 5.2 (world avg. 16.1).
*Total fertility rate* (avg. births per childbearing woman; 1986): 1.8.
*Marriage rate* per 1,000 population[8] (1985): 6.1.
*Divorce rate* per 1,000 population[8] (1985): 1.4.
*Life expectancy* at birth (1986): male 75.1 years; female 80.8 years.
*Major causes of death* per 100,000 population (1986): malignant neoplasms (cancers) 157.5; heart diseases 117.1; cerebrovascular diseases 106.2; pneumonia and bronchitis 43.6; accidents and adverse effects 23.3; senility without mention of psychosis 22.0; suicide 21.1; cirrhosis of the liver 13.9; nephritis, nephrotic syndrome, and nephrosis 11.5; hypertensive diseases 9.6.

## Social indicators

*Educational attainment* (1980). Percent of population aged 15 years and over having: no schooling 0.3%; primary and lower secondary education 38.5%; higher secondary 38.0%; junior college and technical college 5.7%; university and postgraduate 8.0%; still in school 9.5%.

## Distribution of income (1980)

percent of average household income by decile

| 1 | 2 | 3 | 4 | 5 | 6 | 7 | 8 | 9 | 10 (highest) |
|---|---|---|---|---|---|---|---|---|---|
| 35.8 | 53.6 | 64.6 | 73.5 | 82.9 | 93.2 | 105.2 | 120.4 | 145.4 | 224.8. |

*Quality of working life.* Average workweek (1986): 46.7 hours (11.9% overtime). Annual rate of industrial deaths per 100,000 workers (1984): 3.7. Proportion of labour force insured for damages or income loss resulting from injury, permanent disability, and death (1987): 47.8%. Average mandays lost to labour stoppages per 1,000 workdays (1985): 0.2. Average duration of journey to work[9] (1983): 32 minutes (26.7% private automobile,

67.4% public transportation, 5.5% taxi, 0.4% other). Rate per 1,000 workers of discouraged (unemployed no longer seeking work; 1982): 64.7.
*Access to services* (1983). Proportion of households having access to: gas supply (1980) 63.0%; safe public water supply 93.7%; public sewage collection 89.4%.
*Social participation.* Eligible voters participating in last national election (1986): 69.9%. Population 15 years and over participating in social service activities on a voluntary basis (1981): 26.0%. Trade union membership in total work force (1986): 28.9%.
*Social deviance* (1986). Offense rate per 100,000 population for: violent crime (murder, rape, robbery, and assault) 37.8; larceny and theft 1,130.1; other felony 5.9. Incidence in general population of: alcoholism, n.a.; drug and substance abuse, n.a. Rate of suicide per 100,000 population (1986) 21.1.

### Leisure/use of personal time

**Daily activities (1981)**
(both sexes)

| Social activities | daily average hrs./min. | % of day |
|---|---|---|
| Work | 4.35 | 19.1 |
| Meals | 1.50 | 7.6 |
| Housekeeping and childcare | 1.49 | 7.6 |
| Commuting to work/school | .36 | 2.5 |
| Schoolwork | .32 | 2.2 |
| Shopping | .22 | 1.5 |
| **Personal activities** | | |
| Sleep | 7.57 | 33.1 |
| Rest and relaxation | 1.19 | 5.5 |
| Personal care and grooming | .57 | 4.0 |
| Transportation (excluding commuting) | .12 | .8 |

**Recreational activities (1981)**

| | weekday hrs./min. | % of total leisure time | weekend hrs./min. | % of total leisure time |
|---|---|---|---|---|
| **Males** | | | | |
| Personal associations and friendships | 2.30 | 18.7 | 3.20 | 18.2 |
| Television, radio, newspapers, and magazines | 2.27 | 18.4 | 2.59 | 16.3 |
| Study and research (excluding schoolwork) | 2.23 | 17.9 | 2.45 | 15.0 |
| Hobbies and amusements | 2.12 | 16.5 | 3.18 | 18.1 |
| Voluntary social activities | 2.11 | 16.3 | 3.04 | 16.8 |
| Sports | 1.38 | 12.2 | 2.51 | 15.6 |
| **Females** | | | | |
| Television, radio, newspapers, and magazines | 2.29 | 19.1 | 2.37 | 16.3 |
| Study and research (excluding schoolwork) | 2.24 | 18.4 | 2.34 | 16.0 |
| Voluntary social activities | 2.21 | 18.1 | 2.32 | 15.7 |
| Hobbies and amusements | 2.07 | 16.3 | 2.48 | 17.4 |
| Personal associations and friendships | 2.06 | 16.1 | 2.51 | 17.7 |
| Sports | 1.34 | 12.0 | 2.43 | 16.9 |

*Material well-being* (1986). Households possessing: automobile 67.4%; telephone, virtually 100%; colour television receiver 98.9%; refrigerator 98.4%; air conditioner 54.6%; washing machine 99.6%; vacuum cleaner 98.2%; videocassette recorder 33.5%; camera 83.8%; microwave oven 45.3%.

## National economy

*Gross national product* (at current market prices; 1985): U.S.$1,366,040,000,-000 (U.S.$11,310 per capita).

### Structure of gross domestic product and labour force

| | 1985 | | 1986 | |
|---|---|---|---|---|
| | in value ¥'000,000,000 | % of total value | labour force | % of labour force |
| Agriculture | 9,949.0 | 3.2 | 4,950,000 | 8.2 |
| Mining | 1,225.7 | 0.4 | 80,000 | 0.1 |
| Manufacturing | 94,257.3 | 29.8 | 14,440,000 | 24.0 |
| Construction | 23,128.9 | 7.3 | 5,340,000 | 8.9 |
| Public utilities | 10,549.1 | 3.3 | 320,000 | 0.5 |
| Transportation and communication | 19,652.4 | 6.2 | 3,530,000 | 5.9 |
| Trade | 43,313.3 | 13.7 | 13,390,000 | 22.2 |
| Finance | 48,778.8 | 15.4 | 2,250,000 | 3.7 |
| Pub. admin., defense | 14,358.1 | 4.5 | 1,970,000 | 3.3 |
| Services | 62,882.4 | 19.9 | 12,050,000 | 20.0 |
| Other | −11,980.5[10] | −3.8[10] | 1,880,000[11] | 3.1 |
| TOTAL | 316,114.5 | 100.0[7] | 60,200,000 | 100.0[7] |

*Budget* (1987)[12]. Revenue: ¥54,101,000,000,000 (income tax 30.5%; corporation tax 21.9%; public bonds 19.4%; liquor tax 3.6%; stamp duties 3.3%; custom duties 0.9%). Expenditures: ¥54,101,000,000,000 (national debt 20.9%; transfers to local governments 18.8%; social security 18.7%; public works 11.2%; culture, education, and science promotion 9.0%; national defense 6.5%; pensions 3.5%; economic cooperation 1.2%; foodstuff control 1.0%; measures for energy 0.9%; small enterprises 0.4%).
*Public debt* (1986): U.S.$900,100,000,000.
*Population economically active* (1987[13]): total 61,470,000; activity rate of total population 50.3% (participation rates: ages 15–64, 63.2%; female, 40.1%; unemployed 2.6%).

### Price and earnings indexes (1980 = 100)

| | 1981 | 1982 | 1983 | 1984 | 1985 | 1986 | 1987 |
|---|---|---|---|---|---|---|---|
| Consumer price index | 104.9 | 107.8 | 109.9 | 112.3 | 114.6 | 115.3 | 115.2[13] |
| Monthly earnings index | 105.1 | 110.6 | 115.0 | 119.8 | 124.6 | 129.2 | 130.3[14] |

*Household income and expenditure*[15] (1986). Average household size 3.8; average annual income per household ¥5,435,300 (U.S.$32,250); sources of income: wages and salaries 94.3%, of which regular income of household head 64.4%, temporary income and bonuses of household head 18.0%, income of other household members 11.9%; expenditure: food 20.4%, transportation 7.9%, reading and recreation 7.1%, clothing and footwear 5.6%, fuel, light, and water charges 4.6%, housing 3.9%, education 3.6%, furniture and household utensils 3.2%, medical care 1.9%, net savings 14.0%.

### Manufacturing, mining, and construction enterprises (1984)

| | no. of establishments | avg. no. of persons engaged | monthly as a % of avg. of all contract wages | annual value added (¥'000,000,000) |
|---|---|---|---|---|
| Electrical machinery | 32,966 | 1,795,000 | 88.6 | 14,537 |
| Nonelectrical machinery | 41,174 | 1,085,000 | 106.6 | 9,077 |
| Transport equipment | 14,959 | 924,000 | 108.8 | 8,599 |
| Food products | 51,536 | 1,129,000 | 74.4 | 8,115 |
| Chemical products | 5,342 | 396,000 | 123.0 | 7,805 |
| Fabricated metal products | 48,413 | 755,000 | 91.0 | 4,974 |
| Iron and steel | 6,760 | 396,000 | 123.7 | 4,893 |
| Printing and publishing | 28,758 | 503,000 | 124.6 | 4,352 |
| Ceramic, stone, and clay | 21,226 | 473,000 | 91.2 | 3,881 |
| Textiles | 36,267 | 626,000 | 66.9 | 3,022 |
| Paper and paper products | 11,810 | 276,000 | 99.4 | 2,243 |
| Nonferrous metal products | 4,227 | 181,000 | 106.0 | 1,802 |
| Precision instruments | 7,692 | 259,000 | 92.2 | 1,649 |
| Apparel products | 29,673 | 522,000 | 51.1 | 1,559 |
| Lumber and wood products | 22,816 | 282,000 | 72.6 | 1,339 |
| Furniture and fixtures | 17,759 | 229,000 | 79.5 | 1,186 |
| Petroleum and coal products | 989 | 38,000 | 140.7 | 1,166 |
| Rubber products | 5,496 | 159,000 | 100.0 | 1,107 |
| Leather products | 5,625 | 75,000 | 72.2 | 352 |
| Mining | 890 | 48,903 | 107.9 | 340 |
| Construction | 297,027[16] | 5,299,000 | 96.5 | 71,334[16] |

*Tourism* (1985): receipts from visitors U.S.$1,137,000,000; expenditures by nationals abroad U.S.$4,814,000,000.

### Financial aggregates

| | 1981 | 1982 | 1983 | 1984 | 1985 | 1986 | 1987 (8 mo) |
|---|---|---|---|---|---|---|---|
| Exchange rate[17] ¥ per: | | | | | | | |
| U.S. dollar | 220.54 | 249.08 | 237.51 | 237.52 | 238.54 | 168.52 | 147.56 |
| £ | 419.57 | 379.41 | 336.83 | 290.40 | 289.62 | 247.2 | 235.4 |
| SDR | 255.95 | 259.23 | 243.10 | 246.13 | 220.23 | 194.61 | 184.14 |
| International reserves (U.S.$)[17] | | | | | | | |
| Total (excl. gold; '000,000) | 28,208 | 23,334 | 24,602 | 26,429 | 26,719 | 42,257 | 70,394 |
| SDRs ('000,000) | 1,934 | 2,091 | 1,935 | 1,927 | 2,116 | 2,218 | 2,332 |
| Reserve pos. in IMF ('000,000) | 1,558 | 2,071 | 2,303 | 2,219 | 2,275 | 2,382 | 2,763 |
| Foreign exchange ('000,000) | 24,716 | 19,172 | 20,364 | 22,283 | 22,328 | 37,657 | 65,299 |
| Gold ('000,000 fine troy oz) | 24.23 | 24.23 | 24.23 | 24.23 | 24.23 | 24.23 | 24.23 |
| % world reserves | 2.5 | 2.6 | 2.6 | 2.6 | 2.6 | 2.6 | 2.6 |
| Interest and prices | | | | | | | |
| Central bank discount (%) | 5.50 | 5.50 | 5.00 | 5.00 | 5.00 | 3.00 | 2.50 |
| Gov't. bond yield (%) | 8.66 | 8.06 | 7.42 | 6.81 | 6.34 | 4.94 | 4.44[13] |
| Industrial share prices (1980 = 100) | 116.3 | 115.8 | 136.5 | 172.1 | 210.2 | 279.2 | 458.0[13] |
| Balance of payments (U.S.$'000,000,000) | | | | | | | |
| Balance of visible trade | 20.0 | 18.1 | 31.5 | 44.4 | 56.0 | 92.7 | ... |
| Imports, f.o.b. | 129.6 | 119.6 | 114.0 | 123.9 | 118.0 | 112.9 | ... |
| Exports, f.o.b. | 149.5 | 137.7 | 145.5 | 168.3 | 174.0 | 205.6 | ... |
| Balance of invisibles | −13.6 | −9.9 | −9.1 | −7.8 | −5.2 | −4.6 | ... |
| Balance of payments, current account | 4.8 | 6.9 | 20.8 | 35.0 | 49.2 | 86.0 | ... |

*Production* (metric tons except as noted). Agriculture, forestry, fishing (1986): rice 11,647,000, potatoes 4,073,000, radishes 2,655,000, mandarin oranges 2,168,000, cabbages 1,666,000, sweet potatoes 1,507,000, Chinese cabbages 1,503,000, onions 1,252,000, cucumbers 1,040,000, apples 986,100, wheat 876,000, watermelons 840,400, tomatoes 816,200, carrots 670,400, Welsh onions 574,200, lettuce 500,900, Japanese pears 480,600, spinach 385,-400, taro 384,900, grapes 301,300, persimmons 290,500, summer oranges 287,800, pumpkins 277,700, burdocks 268,800, peaches 219,200, turnips 211,500, strawberries 200,500, Spanish paprika 177,800, cauliflowers 140,-600, soybeans 113,600, string beans 99,300, string beans 65,700, cow's milk 7,457,000 (of which marketed as fluid milk 4,324,000), hen's eggs 2,225,000; livestock (number of live animals) 11,061,000 pigs, 4,742,000 cattle (of which 2,103,000 dairy cows), 48,000 goats, 23,000 horses, 180,947,000 hens, 155,647,000 broiler chickens; roundwood (1985) 65,582,000 cu m, of which coniferous species 20,558,000 cu m, broadleaved species 12,386,000 cu m; fish catch 12,677,000, of which sardines 4,215,000, mackerel 1,067,000 (jack mackerel 10.5%), bonito 408,000, tuna 335,000, sauries 211,000, salmon and trout 168,000, squid 87,000, yellowtails 33,000. Mining and quarrying (1986): limestone 162,368,000; quicklime 7,454,000[18]; gypsum 6,300,000[18]; dolomite 4,268,000[19]; fire clay 1,146,316[18]; pyrophyllite 1,073,-000[19]; iron ore 338,000; zinc 222,071; talc 84,522; barite 66,018; lead 48,374; copper 34,934; chromium 7,420; silver 339,659 kg; gold 3,100 kg. Manufacturing (1986): crude steel 98,275,000; semifinished steel 91,508,000; hot-rolled steel products 78,136,000; pig iron 74,651,000; cement 71,264,000; cold-rolled steel strips 20,706,000; tubes and pipes 12,046,000; paper pulp 9,067,600; sulfuric acid 6,562,400; plastic products 4,494,900, of which film 1,257,400; compound fertilizers 3,545,600; spun yarn 1,136,200; raw silk 833,600; finished products (in number of units) 311,468,000 fluorescent lamps, 200,819,000 watches, 147,517,000 motor vehicle tires, 64,211,000 electronic desk calculators, 31,272,000 videocassette recorders, 17,738,000 35-mm cameras, 12,958,000 colour television receivers, 8,441,000 microwave ovens, 7,809,700 passenger cars, 7,293,900 trucks and buses, 4,697,-000 electric refrigerators, 4,661,000 automatic washing machines, 4,173,000 typewriters, 3,396,000 copying machines, 2,627,900 motorcycles. Construction (floor area started; 1986): residential 111,004,000 sq m; nonresidential 207,682,000 sq m, of which government and public owned 20,527,000 sq m, private owned 187,155,000 sq m.

## Retail and wholesale trade and services (1985)

| | no. of establish-ments | avg. no. of em-ployees | annual sales (¥'000,000,000) |
|---|---|---|---|
| Retail trade | 1,628,620 | 6,329,000 | 101,716 |
| Food and beverages | 671,838 | 2,352,000 | 31,843 |
| Grocery | 92,667 | 622,000 | 12,852 |
| Liquors | 106,707 | 294,000 | 5,045 |
| General merchandise | 3,504 | 388,000 | 13,847 |
| Department stores | 1,824 | 381,000 | 13,689 |
| Gasoline service stations | 74,446 | 357,000 | 11,108 |
| Apparel and accessories | 229,634 | 755,000 | 10,721 |
| Motor vehicles and bicycles | 83,931 | 464,000 | 10,271 |
| Furniture and home furnishings | 172,781 | 586,000 | 8,774 |
| Eating and drinking places | 838,449 | 1,965,000 | 8,686 |
| Wholesale trade | 413,002 | 3,977,000 | 426,506 |
| General merchandise | 826 | 56,000 | 83,688 |
| Machinery and equipment | 85,098 | 961,000 | 76,705 |
| General machinery except electrical | 40,407 | 393,000 | 23,873 |
| Motor vehicles and parts | 13,756 | 195,000 | 19,575 |
| Minerals and metals | 21,049 | 245,000 | 60,011 |
| Farm, livestock, and fishery products | 39,197 | 379,000 | 51,792 |
| Food and beverages | 54,081 | 496,000 | 34,849 |
| Textiles, apparel, and accessories | 41,008 | 460,000 | 30,783 |
| Building materials | 56,055 | 355,000 | 20,560 |
| Chemicals | 15,564 | 149,000 | 17,754 |
| Drugs and toilet goods | 16,816 | 238,000 | 12,657 |
| Medical services[19] | 157,879 | 173,000 | ... |
| Educational services[19] | 82,059 | 222,000 | ... |

Energy production (consumption): electricity (kW-hr; 1986) 601,520,000,000 (537,740,000,000); coal (metric tons; 1986) 16,012,000 (106,404,000); crude petroleum (barrels; 1986) 3,849,000 (3,987,000,000); petroleum products (metric tons; 1985) 150,994,000, of which (by volume) heavy fuel oil 39.2%, gasoline 22.0%, kerosene and jet fuel 17.2%, diesel 15.3%, naphtha 6.2% (165,063,000 of which [by volume] heavy fuel oil 37.2%, gasoline 20.1%, kerosene and jet fuel 15.2%, diesel 14.0%, naphtha 13.4%); natural gas (cu m; 1986) 2,105,000,000 (2,208,000,000).
*Land use* (1984): forested 67.0%; meadows and pastures 1.7%; agricultural and under permanent cultivation 12.9%; other 18.4%.

## Foreign trade[20]

### Balance of trade (current prices)

| | 1981 | 1982 | 1983 | 1984 | 1985 | 1986 |
|---|---|---|---|---|---|---|
| ¥'000,000,000 | +4,603 | +4,473 | +7,373 | +10,674 | +13,238 | +15,519 |
| % of total | 7.4% | 6.9% | 11.8% | 20.9% | 18.7% | 28.2% |

*Imports* (1986): ¥21,550,700,000,000 (crude petroleum 15.9%; food 15.0%, of which fish 5.0%; machinery and equipment 10.3%; chemicals 6.2%; metal ores and scrap 4.6%, of which iron ore 2.2%; nonferrous metal ores 4.5%; coal 3.9%; petroleum products 3.9%; textiles 3.9%; wood 3.2%). *Major import sources:* United States 23.0%; Indonesia 5.8%; Australia 5.5%; China 4.5%; South Korea 4.2%; Saudia Arabia 4.1%; Canada 3.9%; Taiwan 3.7%; West Germany 3.4%; Malaysia 3.0%; U.S.S.R. 1.6%.
*Exports* (1986): ¥35,289,700,000,000 (motor vehicles 20.4%; iron and steel 6.1%; office machinery 5.4%; tape recorders 4.7%; chemicals 4.5%, of which plastic materials 1.4%; scientific and optical equipment 4.1%; textiles and allied products 3.5%; electron tubes 3.1%; vessels 2.3%; power-generating machinery 2.3%; metalworking machinery 1.7%; radio receivers 1.3%; television receivers 0.8%). *Major export destinations:* United States 38.5%; South Korea 5.0%; West Germany 5.0%; China 4.7%; Taiwan 3.8%; Hong Kong 3.4%; United Kingdom 3.2%; Canada 2.6%; Australia 2.5%.

### Trade by commodity group (1986)

| SITC group | imports U.S.$'000,000 | % | exports U.S.$'000,000 | % |
|---|---|---|---|---|
| 00 Food and live animals | 15,577 | 12.3 | 1,317 | 0.6 |
| 01 Beverages and tobacco | | | | |
| 02 Crude materials, excluding fuels | 18,538[21] | 14.7[21] | 1,455[21] | 0.7[21] |
| 03 Mineral fuels, lubricants, and related materials | 55,895 | 44.2 | 576 | 0.3 |
| 04 Animal and vegetable oils, fats, and waxes | 21 | 21 | 21 | 21 |
| 05 Chemicals and related products, n.e.s. | 7,933 | 6.3 | 7,542 | 3.6 |
| 06 Basic manufactures | 17,284[22] | 13.7[22] | 43,775[22] | 20.9[22] |
| 07 Machinery and transport equipment | 10,575 | 8.4 | 119,199 | 57.0 |
| 08 Miscellaneous manufactured articles | 22 | 22 | 22 | 22 |
| 09 Goods not classified by kind | 606 | 0.5 | 35,287 | 16.9 |
| TOTAL | 126,408 | 100.0[7] | 209,151 | 100.0 |

### Direction of trade (1986)

| | imports U.S.$'000,000 | % | exports U.S.$'000,000 | % |
|---|---|---|---|---|
| Africa | 3,934 | 3.1 | 4,457 | 2.1 |
| Asia | 53,479 | 42.3 | 60,708 | 29.0 |
| South America | 3,998 | 3.2 | 3,182 | 1.5 |
| North America and Central America | 36,207 | 28.6 | 92,301 | 44.2 |
| United States | 29,054 | 23.0 | 80,456 | 38.5 |
| other North and Central Am. | 7,153 | 5.6 | 11,845 | 5.7 |
| Europe | 20,437 | 16.2 | 41,498 | 19.9 |
| EEC | 13,989 | 11.1 | 30,675 | 14.7 |
| U.S.S.R. | 1,972 | 1.6 | 3,150 | 1.5 |
| other Europe | 4,476 | 3.5 | 7,673 | 3.7 |
| Oceania | 8,353 | 6.6 | 7,005 | 3.3 |
| TOTAL | 126,408 | 100.0 | 209,151 | 100.0 |

## Transport and communications

*Transport.* Railroads (1985): length 16,506 mi, 26,564 km; rolling stock (1984) locomotives 3,829, passenger cars 46,831, freight cars 49,423; passengers carried 18,987,000,000; passenger-mi 205,101,000,000, passenger-km 330,097,000,000; short ton-mi cargo 15,161,000,000, metric ton-km cargo 22,134,000,000. Roads (1985): total length 700,600 mi, 1,127,500 km (paved 58%). Vehicles (1986): passenger cars 27,844,580; trucks 17,139,806; buses 231,228. Merchant marine (1986): vessels (100 gross tons and over) 10,011; total deadweight tonnage 59,978,976. Air transport (1985): passengers carried 50,337,000; passenger-mi 40,716,000,000, passenger-km 65,527,000,000; short ton-mi cargo 2,116,320,000, metric ton-km cargo 3,089,770,000; airports (1987) with scheduled flights 65. Shares of domestic passenger traffic by mode of transportation (1985): automobiles 44.8%; railway 38.5%; buses 12.2%; ships and airplanes 4.5%.

### Distribution of traffic (1985)

| | cargo carried ('000,000 tons) | % of nat'l total | passengers carried ('000,000) | % of nat'l total |
|---|---|---|---|---|
| Road | 5,048.0 | 90.1 | 34,679.0 | 47.8 |
| Rail (intercity) | 100.0 | 1.8 | 18,989.0 | 26.2 |
| Urban transport | — | — | 18,649.0 | 25.7 |
| road | — | — | 7,702.0 | 10.6 |
| rail | — | — | 10,947.0 | 15.1 |
| Inland water | 452.0 | 8.1 | 154.0 | 0.2 |
| Air | 0.5 | 0.0 | 44.0 | 0.1 |
| TOTAL | 5,600.5 | 100.0 | 72,515.0 | 100.0 |

*Communications.* Daily newspapers (1986): total number 124; total circulation 68,653,000; circulation per 1,000 population 569. Radio (1986): 94,700,-000 receivers (1 per 1.3 persons). Television (1986): 31,346,000 receivers (1 per 3.9 persons). Telephones (1985): 66,636,000 (1 per 1.8 persons).

### Other communication media (1985)

| Print | titles | Electronic | traffic ('000) |
|---|---|---|---|
| Books (new) | 31,221 | Telegram | 42,168 |
| of which | | Domestic | 40,656 |
| Social sciences | 7,178 | International | 1,512 |
| Fiction | 6,290 | Telex | 50,000 |
| Business | 1,266 | | |
| Children's | 2,310 | | |
| Natural sciences | 2,605 | | |
| History | 1,983 | Post | |
| Arts | 3,107 | Mail | 17,160,000 |
| Magazines/journals | 3,683 | Domestic | 16,920,000 |
| Weekly | 98 | International | 240,000 |
| Monthly | 2,435 | Parcels | 155,000 |
| | | Domestic | 151,000 |
| Cinema | | International | 4,000 |
| Feature films (greater than 1,600 m) | 319 | | |

*Radio and television broadcasting* (1986): total radio stations 1,132, of which commercial 829; total television stations 13,172, of which commercial 6,910. Commercial broadcasters' broadcasting hours (by percentage of programs; 1984): reports—radio 13.3%, television 15.5%; education—radio 5.1%, television 12.0%; culture—radio 18.6%, television 24.0%; entertainment—radio 21.4%, television 42.7%; music—radio 34.7%, television 0%; sports—radio 5.9%, television 4.4%; other—radio 1.0%, television 1.4%. Advertisements (daily avg.; 1984): radio 166, television 235.

## Education and health

### Education (1986)

| | schools | teachers | students | student/teacher ratio |
|---|---|---|---|---|
| Primary (age 6–11) | 24,982 | 455,000 | 10,666,000 | 23.4 |
| Secondary (age 12–17) | 16,681 | 561,000 | 11,365,000 | 20.3 |
| Higher | 1,075 | 136,000 | 2,326,000 | 17.1 |

*Literacy* (1987): total population age 15 and over literate 97,150,000 (100%); males literate 47,230,000 (100%); females literate 49,920,000 (100%).
*Health* (1985): physicians 179,000 (1 per 670 persons); dentists (1984) 63,145 (1 per 1,901 persons); nurses[23] (1984) 303,734 (1 per 395 persons); pharmacists (1984) 129,700 (1 per 925 persons); midwives (1984) 24,649 (1 per 4,869 persons); hospital beds 1,495,000 (1 per 81.0 persons), of which general 71.6%, mental 22.6%, tuberculosis 4.1%, other 1.7%; infant mortality rate per 1,000 live births (1986) 5.3.
*Food* (1985): daily per capita caloric intake 2,088 (vegetable products 79%, animal products 21%); (1983) 119% of FAO recommended minimum.

## Military

*Total active duty personnel* (1986): 243,000 (army 63.8%, navy 18.1%, air force 18.1%). *Military expenditure as percent of GNP* (1984): 1.0% (world 5.9%); per capita expenditure U.S.$102.

[1]Oct. 1, 1986. [2]Excludes Lake Naka (38 sq mi [98 sq km]), which is part of both Tottori and Shimane prefectures. [3]Excludes Lake Towada (23 sq mi [60 sq km]), which is part of both Akita and Aomori prefectures. [4]Part of Kanto geographical region. [5]Part of Kinki geographical region. [6]1985 survey; includes Lake Naka and Lake Towada. [7]Detail does not add to total given because of rounding. [8]Figures relate only to Japanese nationals in Japan. [9]Applies to passengers carried within the metropolitan areas of Tōkyō, Ōsaka, and Nagoya only. [10]Import duties and statistical discrepancy less imputed bank service charge. [11]Includes unemployed. [12]Initial budget. [13]July. [14]May. [15]Worker's household. [16]1983. [17]End of period. [18]1985. [19]1984. [20]Import figures are f.o.b. in balance of trade and c.i.f. in commodities and trading partners. [21]Crude materials includes animal and vegetable oils, fats, and waxes. [22]Basic manufactures includes miscellaneous manufactured articles. [23]Clinical nurses only.

# Jordan

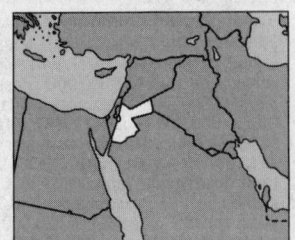

*Official name:* al-Mamlakah al-Urdunnīyah al-Hāshimīyah (al-Urdun) (Hashemite Kingdom of Jordan).
*Form of government:* constitutional monarchy with two legislative houses (Senate [30 appointed by king]; House of Deputies [130 elected]).
*Chief of state:* Monarch.
*Head of government:* Prime Minister.
*Capital:* Amman.
*Official language:* Arabic.
*Official religion:* Islam.
*Monetary unit:* 1 Jordan Dinar (JD) = 1,000 fils; valuation (Oct. 5, 1987) JD 1.00 = U.S.$2.89 = £1.78.

### Area and population

| | | area | | population |
|---|---|---|---|---|
| Governorates | Capitals | sq mi | sq km | 1986 estimate[1] |
| 'Ammān | Amman | ... | ... | 1,160,000 |
| al-Balqā' | aṣ-Ṣalt | ... | ... | 193,800 |
| Irbid | Irbid | ... | ... | 680,200 |
| al-Karak | al-Karak | ... | ... | 120,100 |
| Ma'ān | Ma'ān | ... | ... | 97,500 |
| al-Mafraq | al-Mafraq | ... | ... | 98,600 |
| aṭ-Ṭafīlah | aṭ-Ṭafīlah | ... | ... | 41,400 |
| az-Zarqā' | az-Zarqā' | ... | ... | 404,500 |
| TOTAL | | 34,443 | 89,206 | 2,796,100 |

## Demography

*Population* (1987): 2,853,000.
*Density* (1987): persons per sq mi 82.8, persons per sq km 32.0.
*Urban–rural* (1986): urban 69.6%; rural 30.4%.
*Sex distribution* (1986): male 52.31%; female 47.69%.
*Age breakdown* (1986): under 15, 48.1%; 15–29, 27.4%; 30–44, 12.5%; 45–59, 8.0%; 60–74, 3.1%; 75 and over, 0.9%.
*Population projection:* (1990) 3,202,000; (2000) 4,705,000.
*Doubling time:* 19 years.
*Ethnic composition* (1983): Arab 99.2%; Circassian 0.5%; Armenian 0.1%; Turk 0.1%; Kurd 0.1%.
*Religious affiliation* (1980): Sunnī Muslim 93.0%; Christian 4.9%; other 2.1%.
*Major cities* (1986): Amman 833,500; az-Zarqā' 285,000; Irbid 150,000; ar-Ruṣayfah 65,560; aṣ-Ṣalt 42,690.

## Vital statistics

*Birth rate* per 1,000 population (1980–85): 44.7 (world avg. 29.0).
*Death rate* per 1,000 population (1980–85): 7.9 (world avg. 11.0).
*Natural increase rate* per 1,000 population (1980–85): 36.8 (world avg. 18.0).
*Total fertility rate* (avg. births per childbearing woman; 1980–85): 7.4.
*Marriage rate* per 1,000 population (1986): 6.9.
*Divorce rate* per 1,000 population (1986): 1.2.
*Life expectancy* at birth (1980–85): male 61.9 years; female 65.5 years.
*Major causes of death* per 100,000 population: n.a.; however, major diseases include tuberculosis, typhoid, and paratyphoid fevers, salmonella, hepatitis, and dysentery; nonvenereal syphilis is widespread in the southern desert region.

## National economy

*Budget* (1986). Revenue: JD 821,225,000 (foreign grants and loans 37.0%; indirect taxes 31.2%, of which import duties 13.8%, excise taxes 6.6%, fees 5.3%; direct taxes 7.2%). Expenditures: JD 1,002,633,000 (finance administration 26.6%; defense 20.8%; economic development 19.8%; social welfare 11.3%; internal security 5.5%; communication and transport 2.3%).
*Tourism* (1985): receipts from visitors U.S.$555,000,000; expenditures by nationals abroad U.S.$166,000,000.
*Production* (metric tons except as noted). Agriculture, forestry, fishing (1986): tomatoes 220,565, citrus fruit 87,358, cucumbers 64,263, watermelons 51,292, eggplants 50,568, squash 36,850, olives 31,781, wheat 30,842, cauliflower 24,553, grapes 23,186, green peppers 11,221, barley 9,004; livestock (number of live animals) 930,000 sheep, 439,200 goats, 31,100 cattle, 14,300 camels; roundwood (1985) 9,000 cu m; fish catch (1985) 22. Mining and quarrying (1986): phosphate ore 6,249,200; potash 1,103,700. Manufacturing (1986): cement 1,837,100; chemical acids 1,024,800; fertilizer 551,100; steel 209,600; fodder 44,600; detergents 27,600; metallic pipes 12,-500; cigarettes 3,327,700,000 units; liquid batteries 55,400 units; alcoholic beverages 5,322,600 litres. Construction (1986): residential 1,709,300 sq m; nonresidential 557,300 sq m. Energy production (consumption): electricity (kW-hr; 1985) 2,473,000,000 (2,473,000,000); coal, none (n.a.); crude petroleum (barrels; 1985) 13,800 (18,396,000); petroleum products (metric tons; 1985) 2,320,000 (2,287,000); natural gas, none (n.a.).
*Population economically active* (1984): total 552,357; activity rate of total population 21.3% (participation rates: over age 15, 40.9%; female 11.1%; unemployed 6.0%).

### Price and earnings indexes (1980 = 100)

| | 1981 | 1982 | 1983 | 1984 | 1985 | 1986 | 1987[2] |
|---|---|---|---|---|---|---|---|
| Consumer price index | 107.7 | 115.7 | 121.5 | 126.2 | 130.0 | 130.0 | 130.0 |
| Daily earnings index | 106.7 | ... | ... | ... | ... | ... | ... |

*Household income and expenditure.* Average household size (1984) 6.9; income per household (1979)[3] JD 1,820 (U.S.$6,055); sources of income: n.a.; expenditure (1985): food and beverages 37.5%; housing 6.3%; transportation 5.8%; clothing and footwear 5.5%; household durable goods 4.7%; health care 4.0%; education 3.3%; other goods and services 32.9%.
*Public debt* (external, outstanding; 1985): U.S.$2,692,800,000.
*Gross national product* (at current market prices; 1985): U.S.$4,010,000,000 (U.S.$1,520 per capita).

### Structure of gross domestic product and labour force

| | 1986 | | 1984 | |
|---|---|---|---|---|
| | in value JD '000,000 | % of total value | labour force | % of labour force |
| Agriculture | 116.2 | 7.2 | 22,455 | 4.1 |
| Mining | 53.0 | 3.3 | 6,658 | 1.2 |
| Manufacturing | 193.9 | 12.0 | 35,945 | 6.5 |
| Construction | 112.5 | 7.0 | 56,836 | 10.3 |
| Public utilities | 37.7 | 2.3 | 2,370 | 0.4 |
| Transportation and communication | 161.6 | 10.0 | 46,971 | 8.5 |
| Trade | 243.1 | 15.1 | 58,369 | 10.6 |
| Finance | 164.6 | 10.2 | 15,835 | 2.9 |
| Pub. admin., defense | 281.9 | 17.5 | 273,956 | 49.6 |
| Services | 35.7 | 2.2 | | |
| Other | 213.4 | 13.2 | 32,962[4] | 5.9[4] |
| TOTAL | 1,613.6 | 100.0 | 552,357 | 100.0 |

*Land use* (1984): forested 0.4%; meadows and pastures 1.0%; agricultural and under permanent cultivation 4.2%; wasteland (mostly desert), built-on, and other 94.4%.

## Foreign trade

### Balance of trade (current prices)[5]

| | 1981 | 1982 | 1983 | 1984 | 1985 | 1986 |
|---|---|---|---|---|---|---|
| JD '000,000 | −805 | −878 | −893 | −781 | −763 | −594 |
| % of total | 52.9% | 52.9% | 61.0% | 45.7% | 55.1% | 53.7% |

*Imports* (1986): JD 850,199,200 (electrical and nonelectrical machinery 12.1%; crude petroleum 10.9%; transport equipment and spare parts 8.6%; iron and steel 4.9%; wheat, wheat flour, and rice 3.0%; fruits, vegetables, and nuts 3.0%; meat 2.9%; clothing and footwear 2.6%). *Major import sources:* Iraq 9.1%; United States 8.9%; United Kingdom 8.1%; Japan 7.8%; West Germany 7.7%; Italy 5.9%; Saudi Arabia 5.8%.
*Exports* (1986)[6]: JD 225,615,100 (natural phosphate fertilizer 29.3%; food [mostly assorted vegetables, tomatoes, olives, citrus fruit, and spices] and live animals 18.6%; chemical fertilizer 12.9%; pharmaceuticals 6.8%). *Major export destinations:* Iraq 18.8%; India 15.1%; Saudi Arabia 12.3%; Kuwait 3.9%; Yugoslavia 3.4%; Indonesia 3.4%; China 3.4%; Romania 3.3%.

## Transport and communications

*Transport.* Railroads (1985): route length 385 mi, 619 km; passenger traffic, n.a.; short ton-mi cargo 864,000,000, metric ton-km cargo 1,262,000,000. Roads (1984): total length 3,934 mi, 6,332 km (paved 74.4%). Vehicles (1982): passenger cars 118,852; trucks and buses 48,884. Merchant marine (1986): vessels (100 gross tons and over) 5; total deadweight tonnage 61,427. Air transport (1985): passenger-mi 2,224,000,000, passenger-km 3,578,635,-000; short ton-mi cargo 327,336,000, metric ton-km cargo 477,902,000; airports (1987) with scheduled flights 2.
*Communications.* Daily newspapers (1986): total number 5; total circulation 195,100; circulation per 1,000 population 71.0. Radio (1986): total number of receivers 700,000 (1 per 4.3 persons). Television (1986): total number of receivers 240,000 (1 per 12 persons). Telephones (1984): 113,663 (1 per 22 persons).

## Education and health

### Education (1985–86)

| | schools | teachers | students | student/ teacher ratio |
|---|---|---|---|---|
| Primary (age 6–11) | 1,239 | 16,979 | 530,906 | 31.3 |
| Secondary (age 12–17) | 1,671 | 17,074 | 305,046 | 17.9 |
| Voc., teacher tr. | 52 | 1,012 | 27,042 | 26.7 |
| Higher | 3 | 1,295 | 26,711 | 20.6 |

*Educational attainment* (1979). Percent of population age 14 and over having: no formal schooling 47.9%; primary education 19.8%; secondary 26.4%; higher 5.9%. *Literacy* (1986): total population age 15 and over literate 1,451,100 (79.4%); males literate 761,900 (81.7%); females literate 689,200 (73.9%).
*Health* (1986): physicians 3,114 (1 per 881 persons); hospital beds 5,246 (1 per 523 persons); infant mortality rate per 1,000 live births (1985) 49.
*Food* (1979–81): daily per capita caloric intake 2,498 (vegetable products 89%, animal products 11%); 102% of FAO recommended minimum requirement.

## Military

*Total active duty personnel* (1986): 70,200 (army 89.4%, navy 0.4%, air force 10.2%). *Military expenditure as percent of GNP* (1984): 18.5% (world 5.9%); per capita expenditure U.S.$294.

---

[1]End of year. [2]August. [3]Households involved in nonagricultural activities only. [4]Unemployed persons. [5]Includes reexports. [6]Domestic exports only.

# Kampuchea

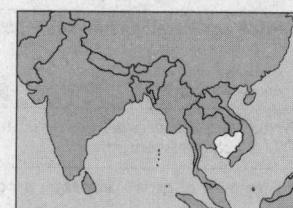

*Official name:* Sathearanakrath Pracheachon Kampuchea (People's Republic of Kampuchea)[1].
*Form of government:* single-party people's republic with one legislative house (National Assembly [117]).
*Chief of state:* President, Council of State.
*Head of government:* Prime Minister.
*Capital:* Phnom Penh.
*Official language:* Khmer.
*Official religion:* none.
*Monetary unit:* 1 riel = 100 sen; valuation (Dec. 31, 1983) 1 U.S.$ = 4.00 riels; 1 £ = 5.81 riels.

## Area and population

| Provinces | Capitals | area sq mi | area sq km | population 1981 census |
|---|---|---|---|---|
| Bătdâmbâng | Bătdâmbâng | 7,407 | 19,184 | 719,000 |
| Kâmpóng Cham | Kâmpóng Cham | 3,783 | 9,799 | 1,070,000 |
| Kâmpóng Chhnăng | Kâmpóng Chhnăng | 2,132 | 5,521 | 221,000 |
| Kâmpóng Saôm | Kâmpóng Saôm | 26 | 68 | 53,000 |
| Kâmpóng Spœ | Kâmpóng Spœ | 2,709 | 7,017 | 340,000 |
| Kâmpóng Thum | Kâmpóng Thum | 10,657[2] | 27,602[2] | 379,000 |
| Kâmpôt | Kâmpôt | 2,320 | 6,008 | 354,000 |
| Kândal | ... | 1,472 | 3,812 | 720,000 |
| Kaôh Kŏng | Krŏng Kaôh Kŏng | 4,309 | 11,161 | 25,000 |
| Krâchéh | Krâchéh | 4,283 | 11,094 | 157,000 |
| Môndól Kiri | Senmonorom | 5,517 | 14,288 | 16,000 |
| Phnom Penh | Phnom Penh | 18 | 46 | 329,000 |
| Poŭthisăt | Poŭthisăt | 4,900 | 12,692 | 175,000 |
| Preăh Vihéar | Phnum Tbêng Meanchey | 2 | 2 | 70,000 |
| Prey Vêng | Prey Vêng | 1,885 | 4,883 | 672,000 |
| Rôtânôkiri | Lumphăt | 4,163 | 10,782 | 45,000 |
| Siĕmréab | Siĕmréab | 6,354 | 16,457 | 477,000 |
| Stœng Trêng | Stœng Trêng | 4,283 | 11,092 | 39,000 |
| Svay Riĕng | Svay Riĕng | 1,145 | 2,966 | 292,000 |
| Takêv | Takêv | 1,376 | 3,563 | 531,000 |
| TOTAL LAND AREA | | 68,721 | 177,987 | 6,684,000 |
| INLAND WATER | | 1,177 | 3,048 | |
| TOTAL AREA | | 69,898 | 181,035 | |

## Demography

*Population* (1987): 7,688,000.
*Density*[3] (1987): persons per sq mi 111.9, persons per sq km 43.2.
*Urban–rural* (1985): urban 15.6%; rural 86.4%.
*Sex distribution* (1985): male 49.73%; female 50.27%.
*Age breakdown* (1985): under 15, 32.5%; 15–29, 33.5%; 30–44, 19.6%; 45–59, 9.9%; 60–74, 4.0%; 75 and over 0.5%.
*Population projection:* (1990) 8,246,000; (2000) 9,772,000.
*Doubling time:* 28 years.
*Ethnic composition* (1983): Khmer 88.1%; Chinese 4.6%; Vietnamese 4.6%; (although recent Vietnamese immigration may have raised their proportion to as much as 8%); other 2.7%.
*Religious affiliation* (1980): Buddhist 88.4%; Muslim 2.4%; other 9.2%.
*Major cities* (1971): Phnom Penh 600,000[4]; Kâmpóng Cham 34,706; Kâmpóng Chhnăng 15,813; Kratié 14,765; Pursat 14,736; Svay Riĕng 13,766.

## Vital statistics

*Birth rate* per 1,000 population (1986): 42.3 (world avg. 26.0); legitimate, n.a.; illegitimate, n.a.
*Death rate* per 1,000 population (1986): 17.6 (world avg. 9.9).
*Natural increase rate* per 1,000 population (1986): 24.7 (world avg. 16.1).
*Total fertility rate* (avg. births per childbearing woman; 1986): 4.8.
*Marriage rate* per 1,000 population: n.a.
*Divorce rate* per 1,000 population: n.a.
*Life expectancy* at birth (1986): male 45.3 years; female 48.2 years.
*Major causes of death* per 100,000 population (registered deaths only; 1966): tuberculosis of the respiratory system 154; all accidents other than vehicle accidents 111; malaria 55; pneumonia 51.

## National economy

*Budget.* The lack, since the mid-1970s, of a taxable domestic economic base or of any income-earning export markets has left Kampuchea without a central governmental budget other than the dispersal of foreign aid and the management of development investments.
*Public debt:* (1985): 508,000,000.
*Tourism:* none.
*Production* (metric tons except as noted). Agriculture, forestry, fishing (1985): rice 1,900,000, roots and tubers 139,000, cassava 100,000, corn (maize) 78,000, beans 35,000, sweet potatoes 30,000, rubber 16,000, tobacco 9,000; livestock (number of live animals) 1,500,000 cattle, 1,200,000 pigs, 685,000 buffalo, 6,000,000 chickens; roundwood 5,303,000 cu m; fish catch 68,000. Mining and quarrying (1985): salt 40,000. Manufacturing (1985): cement 50,000[4]; pork 23,000; beef and veal 16,000; sawn wood 43,000 cu m[5]; plywood 2,000 cu m[5]; cigarettes 4,100,000,000 units[4]. Construction: n.a. Energy production (consumption): electricity (kW-hr; 1985) 80,000,000 (80,000,000); coal, n.a. (n.a.); crude petroleum, n.a. (n.a.); petroleum products (metric tons; 1985), none (12,000); natural gas, n.a. (n.a.).
*Household income and expenditure.* Average household size (1980) 5.6; income per household: n.a.; sources of income: n.a.; expenditure: n.a.

---

*Gross national product* (at current market prices; 1981): U.S.$600,000,000 (U.S.$90 per capita).

## Structure of gross domestic product and labour force

| | 1966 in value '000,000 riels | 1966 % of total value | 1980 labour force | 1980 % of labour force |
|---|---|---|---|---|
| Agriculture | 13,100 | 40.9 | 2,454,000 | 74.4 |
| Mining and manufacturing | 3,300 | 10.3 | | |
| Construction | 1,700 | 5.3 | | |
| Public utilities | 400 | 1.3 | 220,000 | 6.7 |
| Transportation and communication | 700 | 2.2 | | |
| Trade | 7,300 | 22.8 | | |
| Public admin., defense | 3,900 | 12.2 | 625,000 | 18.9 |
| Services | 1,600 | 5.0 | | |
| TOTAL | 32,000 | 100.0 | 3,299,000 | 100.0 |

*Population economically active* (1985): total 3,602,000; activity rate of total population 49.5% (participation rates: ages 15–64, 64.5%; female 39.9%; unemployed, n.a.).

## Price and earnings indexes (1970 = 100)

| | 1967 | 1968 | 1969 | 1970 | 1971 | 1972 | 1973 |
|---|---|---|---|---|---|---|---|
| Consumer price index[6] | 79.5 | 84.1 | 89.4 | 100.0 | 172.0 | 215.2 | 556.1 |
| Earnings index | ... | ... | ... | ... | ... | ... | ... |

*Land use* (1984): forested 75.8%; meadows and pastures 3.3%; agricultural and under permanent cultivation 17.2%; other 3.7%.

## Foreign trade[7]

### Balance of trade (current prices)

| | 1978 | 1979 | 1980 | 1981 | 1982 | 1983 |
|---|---|---|---|---|---|---|
| U.S.$'000,000 | ... | ... | ... | −60 | ... | −20 |
| % of total | ... | ... | 41.1% | ... | 67.0% | |

*Imports* (1973): 14,200,100,000 old riels (agricultural and food products 54.4%, textiles 12.4%, mineral products 11.7%, pharmaceuticals 9.8%, metals and metal products 9.0%, chemicals 2.3%). *Major import sources* (1972): Japan 17.8%; Thailand 16.5%; Hong Kong 14.9%; France 14.4%; United States 10.1%; Singapore 5.3%.
*Exports* (1973): 2,732,500,000 old riels (rubber 93.1%, haricot beans 4.4%, sesame seeds 2.0%, rice 0.5%). *Major export destinations* (1972): South Vietnam 54.8%; Hong Kong 18.3%; Singapore 10.2%; Japan 4.1%; France 4.1%; United States 3.0%.

## Transport and communications

*Transport.* Railroads (1981): length 403 mi, 649 km; passenger-mi 33,554,000, passenger-km 54,000,000; short ton-mi cargo 6,850,000, metric ton-km cargo 10,000,000. Roads (1981): total length 8,296 mi, 13,351 km (paved 20%). Vehicles (1981): passenger cars 700; trucks 1,800. Merchant marine (1986): vessels (100 gross tons and over) 3; total deadweight tonnage 3,839. Air transport (1977): passenger-mi 26,098,800, passenger-km 42,000,000; short ton-mi cargo 274,000, metric ton-km cargo 400,000; airports (1987) with scheduled flights 1.
*Communications.* Daily newspapers (1984): total number 16; total circulation, n.a. Radio (1985): total number of receivers 200,000 (1 per 36 persons). Television (1985): total number of receivers 52,000 (1 per 140 persons). Telephones (1981): 7,315 (1 per 790 persons).

## Education and health

### Education (1983–84)

| | schools | teachers | students | student/ teacher ratio |
|---|---|---|---|---|
| Primary (age 6–11) | 3,629[8] | 36,520 | 1,504,840 | 41.2 |
| Secondary | 207 | 4,494 | 145,730 | 32.4 |
| Voc., teacher tr. | 13 | 278 | 7,334 | 26.4 |
| Higher | 2[9] | ... | 586[9] | ... |

*Educational attainment,* n.a. *Literacy* (1980): total population age 15 and over literate 48.0%.
*Health* (1984): physicians 200 (1 per 36,000 persons); hospital beds 16,200 (1 per 441 persons); infant mortality rate per 1,000 live births (1986) 140.0.
*Food* (1981–83): daily per capita caloric intake 1,930 (vegetable products 95%, animal products 5%); (1983) 85% of FAO recommended minimum requirement.

## Military

*Total active duty personnel* (1986): 35,000[10]. *Military expenditure as percent of GNP:* n.a.; per capita expenditure, n.a.

---

[1]The UN continues to seat Democratic Kampuchea (DK), whose present leadership calls itself the Coalition Government of Democratic Kampuchea and is composed of Khmer People's National Liberation Front, the DK (Khmer Rouge), and the organization of Norodom Sihanouk. [2]Area of Preăh Vihéar included with Kâmpóng Thum. [3]Based on land area. [4]1982. [5]1984. [6]Phnom Penh only. [7]In 1981 imports were estimated to be U.S.$103,000,000; exports were estimated to be U.S.$43,000,000. Major trading partners are the U.S.S.R., Vietnam, Czechoslovakia, Bulgaria, East Germany, Hungary, Cuba, Poland, Mongolia, and Laos. [8]1981–82. [9]1982–83. [10]Excludes about 160,000 Vietnamese troops and about 35,000 opposition forces of Democratic Kampuchea.

# Kenya

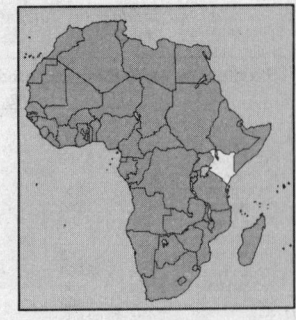

*Official name:* Jamhuri ya Kenya (Swahili); Republic of Kenya (English).
*Form of government:* unitary single-party republic with one legislative house (National Assembly [182[1]]).
*Head of state and government:* President.
*Capital:* Nairobi.
*Official languages:* Swahili; English.
*Official religion:* none.
*Monetary unit:* 1 Kenyan shilling (K Sh) = 100 cents; valuation (Oct. 5, 1987) 1 U.S.$ = K Sh 16.63; 1 £ = K Sh 27.00.

| Area and population | | area | | population |
|---|---|---|---|---|
| | | | | 1984 |
| Provinces | Provincial headquarters | sq mi | sq km | estimate |
| Central | Nyeri | 5,087 | 13,176 | 2,926,200 |
| Coast | Mombasa | 32,279 | 83,603 | 1,688,000 |
| Eastern | Embu | 61,734 | 159,891 | 3,423,500 |
| Nairobi | Nairobi | 264 | 684 | 1,103,600 |
| North Eastern | Garissa | 48,997 | 126,902 | 484,700 |
| Nyanza | Kisumu | 6,240 | 16,162 | 3,508,500 |
| Rift Valley | Nakuru | 67,131 | 173,868 | 4,132,400 |
| Western | Kakamega | 3,228 | 8,360 | 2,269,400 |
| TOTAL LAND AREA | | 220,625 | 571,416 | 19,536,300 |
| INLAND WATER | | 4,336 | 11,230 | |
| TOTAL AREA | | 224,961 | 582,646 | |

## Demography

*Population* (1987): 22,020,000.
*Density*[2] (1987): persons per sq mi 99.8, persons per sq km 38.5.
*Urban-rural* (1985): urban 19.7%; rural 80.3%.
*Sex distribution* (1985): male 49.77%; female 50.23%.
*Age breakdown* (1984): under 15, 52.0%; 15–29, 22.7%; 30–44, 12.6%; 45–59, 7.9%; 60–74, 3.6%; 75 and over, 0.9%.
*Population projection:* (1990) 24,810,000; (2000) 36,950,000.
*Doubling time:* 17 years.
*Ethnic composition* (1979): Kenyan 98.8% (Kikuyu 20.9%, Luhya 13.8%, Luo 12.8%, Kamba 11.3%, Kalenjin 10.8%, other Kenyan 29.2%); other 1.2%.
*Religious affiliation* (1980): Christian 73.0%, of which Protestant 26.5%, Roman Catholic 26.4%, African Indigenous 17.6%, Orthodox 2.5%; traditional beliefs 18.9%; Muslim 6.0%; other 2.1%.
*Major cities* (1984): Nairobi 1,162,000[3]; Mombasa 425,600; Kisumu 167,100; Nakuru 101,700; Machakos 92,300[4].

## Vital statistics

*Birth rate* per 1,000 population (1980–85): 55.1 (world avg. 29.0).
*Death rate* per 1,000 population (1980–85): 14.0 (world avg. 11.0).
*Natural increase rate* per 1,000 population (1980–85): 41.1 (world avg. 18.0).
*Total fertility rate* (avg. births per childbearing woman; 1984): 7.7.
*Life expectancy* at birth (1980–85): male 51.2 years; female 54.7 years.
*Major causes of death* per 100,000 population: n.a.; however, major infectious diseases include malaria, gastroenteritis, venereal diseases, diarrhea and dysentery, trachoma, amebiasis, and schistosomiasis.

## National economy

*Budget*[5] (1985–86). Revenue: K Sh 26,262,000,000 (income tax 24.6%, sales tax 23.3%, import duties 12.9%, internal borrowing 11.0%, excise duties 7.3%). Expenditures: K Sh 27,953,000,000 (economic services 24.8%, education 20.3%, public administration 14.4%, defense 7.2%, health 5.3%).
*Production* (metric tons except as noted). Agriculture, forestry, fishing (1985): sugarcane 3,960,000, corn (maize) 2,650,000, potatoes 650,000, cassava 400,000, sweet potatoes 280,000, plantains 260,000, wheat 250,000, pulses 200,000, pineapples 158,000, tea 147,000, bananas 144,000, coffee 130,000, sorghum 100,000, coconuts 70,000, barley 50,000, millet 50,000, sisal 50,000, seed cotton 23,000, sunflower seeds 17,000, cottonseed 15,000, tomatoes 15,000, cashew nuts 12,000, copra 10,000; livestock (number of live animals) 12,000,000 cattle, 8,200,000 goats, 7,000,000 sheep; roundwood (1984) 31,115,000 cu m; total fish catch 91,740, of which freshwater fish 92.9%. Mining and quarrying (1985): soda ash 227,760; fluorspar 58,174; lime and limestone 39,040[6]; salt 34,348; corundum (ruby) 98 kilograms[4]. Manufacturing (1985): wheat flour 292,600; corn meal 242,300; canned fruits 156,000; pyrethrum extract 120; rubber sandals 6,000,000 pairs; textbooks 3,500,000 units; floor and wall tiles 1,600,000 units; leather shoes 1,300,000 pairs; wheel barrows 15,000 units; assembled vehicles 8,860 units, of which coaches and buses 401 units; water meters 5,374 units. Construction (1982): residential 252,000 sq m; nonresidential 91,000 sq m. Energy production (consumption): electricity (kW-hr; 1985) 2,155,000,000 (2,014,000,000); coal (metric tons; 1985) none (87,000); crude petroleum (barrels; 1985) none (14,220,000); petroleum products (metric tons; 1985) 1,942,000 (1,566,000).
*Public debt* (external, outstanding; 1985): U.S.$2,857,400,000.
*Household income and expenditure.* Average household size (1980) 6.2; average annual income per household: n.a.; sources of income: n.a.; expenditure (1980): food 46.5%, housing 10.0%, furniture and utensils 9.4%, transportation 8.4%, clothing and footwear 7.7%, health 2.2%, education 1.0%.
*Population economically active* (1985): total 8,389,000; activity rate of total population 41.3% (participation rates: ages 15–64, n.a.; female [1981] 33.5; unemployed, n.a.).

| Price and earnings indexes (1980 = 100) | | | | | | | |
|---|---|---|---|---|---|---|---|
| | 1980 | 1981 | 1982 | 1983 | 1984 | 1985 | 1986[7] |
| Consumer price index | 100.0 | 111.8 | 134.7 | 150.2 | 165.4 | 187.0 | 198.8 |
| Annual earnings index | 100.0 | 116.6 | 124.5 | 132.7 | 145.3 | 157.4 | ... |

*Gross national product* (at current market prices; 1985): U.S.$5,632,000,000 (U.S.$280 per capita).

| Structure of gross domestic product and labour force | | | | |
|---|---|---|---|---|
| | 1985 | | | |
| | in value K Sh '000,000 | % of total value | labour force[8] | % of labour force |
| Agriculture | 25,467.2 | 26.7 | 240,900 | 20.5 |
| Mining | 200.8 | 0.2 | 4,800 | 0.4 |
| Manufacturing | 10,368.0 | 10.9 | 158,800 | 13.5 |
| Construction | 4,525.6 | 4.8 | 49,900 | 4.3 |
| Public utilities | 1,782.2 | 1.9 | 17,700 | 1.5 |
| Transp. and commun. | 5,282.2 | 5.5 | 55,700 | 4.7 |
| Trade | 10,494.2 | 11.0 | 89,700 | 7.6 |
| Finance | 12,070.0 | 12.7 | 53,400 | 4.6 |
| Pub. admin., defense | 12,020.6 | 12.6 | 158,600 | 13.5 |
| Services | 2,986.0 | 3.1 | 344,900 | 29.4 |
| Other | 10,068.0[9] | 10.6[9] | — | — |
| TOTAL | 95,264.8 | 100.0 | 1,174,400 | 100.0 |

*Tourism:* receipts from visitors (1985) U.S.$128,000,000; expenditures by nationals abroad (1984) U.S.$16,000,000.
*Land use* (1984): forested 6.6%; meadows and pastures 6.6%; agricultural and under permanent cultivation 4.1%; other 82.7%.

## Foreign trade[10]

| Balance of trade (current prices) | | | | | | |
|---|---|---|---|---|---|---|
| | 1981 | 1982 | 1983 | 1984 | 1985 | 1986 |
| K Sh '000,000 | −5,446 | −4,383 | −2,514 | −3,511 | −4,609 | −3,271 |
| % of total | 20.4% | 16.2% | 8.8% | 10.2% | 12.6% | 7.7% |

*Imports* (1985): K Sh 24,022,540,000 (crude petroleum 29.1%; machinery and transport equipment 24.4%, of which transport equipment 10.2%; chemicals 15.6%, of which fertilizers 4.3%, pharmaceuticals 1.9%; iron and steel 5.4%). *Major import sources:* Saudi Arabia 18.6%; U.K. 13.7%; Japan 10.0%; W.Ger. 8.0%; U.S. 5.5%; Iran 4.5%; United Arab Emirates 4.1%; Italy 3.5%.
*Exports* (1985): K Sh 16,046,860,000 (domestic exports 96.7%, of which coffee [not roasted] 29.7%, tea 24.7%, petroleum products 15.4%, vegetables and fruit 6.8% [of which canned pineapples 3.1%], soda ash 2.1%, cement 2.0%; reexports 3.3%). *Major export destinations:* U.K. 16.9%; W.Ger. 11.6%; Uganda 8.7%; U.S. 6.7%; The Netherlands 6.6%.

## Transport and communications

*Transport.* Railroads (1985): route length (1986) 1,649 mi, 2,654 km; passenger-mi 370,600,000, passenger-km 596,400,000; short ton-mi cargo 1,273,000,000, metric ton-km cargo 1,858,000,000. Roads (1985): total length 33,700 mi, 54,200 km (paved 12%). Vehicles (1984): passenger cars 122,300; trucks and buses 96,575. Merchant marine (1986): vessels (100 gross tons and over) 29; total deadweight tonnage 6,431. Air transport[11] (1985): passenger-mi 715,500,000, passenger-km 1,151,500,000; short ton-mi cargo 93,400,000, metric ton-km cargo 136,300,000; airports (1987) with scheduled flights 15.
*Communications.* Daily newspapers: total number (1985) 5; total circulation (1984) 255,000; circulation per 1,000 population (1984) 13. Radio (1986): 2,100,000 receivers (1 per 10 persons). Television (1986): 192,000 receivers (1 per 110 persons). Telephones (1983): 216,674 (1 per 87 persons).

## Education and health

| Education (1984) | schools | teachers | students | student/ teacher ratio |
|---|---|---|---|---|
| Primary (age 5–11) | 12,539 | 122,788 | 4,380,232 | 35.7 |
| Secondary (age 12–17) | 2,396 | 19,368 | 510,943 | 26.4 |
| Voc., teacher tr. | 40 | 1,551 | 24,984 | 16.1 |
| Higher | 4 | ... | 19,798 | ... |

*Educational attainment* (1979). Percent of population over age 25 having: no formal schooling 58.6%; primary education 32.2%; some secondary 7.9%; complete secondary and higher 1.3%. *Literacy* (1985): total population over age 15 literate 5,758,000 (59.2%); males literate 3,311,000 (69.6%); females literate 2,447,000 (49.2%).
*Health* (1985): physicians 2,752 (1 per 7,387 persons); hospital beds 30,936 (1 per 657 persons); infant mortality rate per 1,000 live births (1984) 92.
*Food* (1981–83): daily per capita caloric intake 2,026 (vegetable products 89%, animal products 11%); (1983) 87% of FAO recommended minimum requirement.

## Military

*Total active duty personnel* (1986): 13,650 (army 95.2%; navy 4.8%; air force reorganized as part of army since 1982, air force personnel about 2,300 in 1983). *Military expenditure as percent of GNP* (1984): 3.4% (world 5.9%); per capita expenditure U.S.$10.

[1]Includes 14 nonelective seats. [2]Land area only. [3]1985. [4]1983. [5]Budget for 1986-87: Revenue K Sh 36,337,000,000; Expenditure K Sh 36,337,000,000. [6]Excludes limestone used in making cement. [7]Third quarter. [8]Employed persons only. [9]Indirect taxes less subsidies and imputed bank service charges. [10]Import figures are f.o.b. in balance of trade and c.i.f. in commodities and trading partners. [11]Kenya Airways only.

# Kiribati

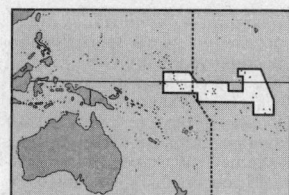

*Official name:* Republic of Kiribati.
*Form of government:* unitary republic with one legislature (House of Assembly [39]).
*Head of state and government:* President.
*Capital:* Bairiki, on Tarawa Atoll.
*Official language:* English.
*Official religion:* none.
*Monetary unit:* 1 Australian Dollar ($A) = 100 cents; valuation (Oct. 5, 1987) 1 U.S.$ = $A 1.40; 1 £ = $A 2.27.

### Area and population

| Island Groups Islands | Capitals | area[1] sq mi | sq km | population 1985 census |
|---|---|---|---|---|
| Gilberts Group | Bairiki Islet | 110 | 285 | 61,226 |
| Abaiang | Tuarabu | 7 | 17 | 4,386 |
| Abemama | Kariatebike | 11 | 27 | 2,966 |
| Aranuka | Takaeang | 4 | 12 | 984 |
| Arorae | Roreti | 4 | 9 | 1,470 |
| Banaba | Anteeren | 2 | 6 | 46 |
| Beru | Taubukinberu | 7 | 18 | 2,702 |
| Butaritari | Butaritari | 5 | 13 | 3,622 |
| Kuria | Tabontebike | 6 | 15 | 1,052 |
| Maiana | Tebangetua | 6 | 17 | 2,141 |
| Makin | Makin | 3 | 8 | 1,777 |
| Marakei | Rawannawi | 5 | 14 | 2,693 |
| Nikunau | Rungata | 7 | 19 | 2,061 |
| Nonouti | Teuabu | 8 | 20 | 2,930 |
| Onotoa | Buariki | 6 | 16 | 1,927 |
| Tabiteuea North | Utiroa | 10 | 26 | 3,171 |
| Tabiteuea South | Buariki | 5 | 12 | 1,322 |
| Tamana | Bakaka | 2 | 5 | 1,378 |
| Tarawa North | Abaokoro | 6 | 15 | 3,205 |
| Tarawa South | Bairiki | 6 | 16 | 21,393 |
| Line Group | Kiritimati | 207 | 535 | 2,633 |
| Northern | | 167 | 432 | 2,633 |
| Kiritimati (Christmas) | London | 150 | 388 | 1,737 |
| Tabuaeran (Fanning) | Paelau | 13 | 34 | 445 |
| Teraina (Washington) | Washington | 4 | 10 | 451 |
| Southern (Caroline, Flint, Malden, Starbuck, Vostok) | | 40 | 103 | — |
| Phoenix Group (Birnie, Enderbury, Kanton [Canton], McKean, Manra [Sydney], Nikumaroro [Gardner], Orona [Hull], Rawaki [Phoenix]) | Kanton | 11 | 29 | 24 |
| TOTAL | | 328 | 849 | 63,883 |

## Demography

*Population* (1987): 66,000.
*Density*[2] (1987): persons per sq mi 234.7, persons per sq km 90.7.
*Urban–rural* (1985): urban 33.4%; rural 66.6%.
*Sex distribution* (1985): male 49.56%; female 50.44%.
*Age breakdown* (1985)[3]: under 15, 38.9%; 15–29, 29.9%; 30–44, 16.1%; 45–59, 9.3%; 60–74, 4.9%; 75 and over, 0.9%.
*Population projection:* (1990) 68,000; (2000) 77,000.
*Doubling time:* 40 years.
*Ethnic composition* (1985): I-Kiribati 96.1%; mixed (part I-Kiribati and other) 2.6%; Tuvaluan 0.7%; European 0.4%; other 0.2%.
*Religious affiliation* (1985)[3]: Roman Catholic 52.6%; Kiribati Protestant (Congregational) 40.9%; Baha'i 2.4%; Seventh-day Adventist 1.4%; other 2.7%.
*Major cities* (1985): Urban Tarawa 21,393.

## Vital statistics

*Birth rate* per 1,000 population (1980–85): 34.9 (world avg. 29.0); legitimate, n.a.; illegitimate, n.a.
*Death rate* per 1,000 population (1980–85): 13.9 (world avg. 11.0).
*Natural increase rate* per 1,000 population (1980–85): 21.0 (world avg. 18.0).
*Total fertility rate* (avg. births per childbearing woman; 1984): 4.4.
*Marriage rate* per 1,000 population (1973): 4.5.
*Divorce rate* per 1,000 population: n.a.
*Life expectancy* at birth (1983): male 50.6 years; female 55.6 years.
*Major causes of death* per 100,000 population: n.a.; however, the major causes include tuberculosis, diarrheal and respiratory diseases, and nutritional disorders.

## National economy

*Budget* (1984). Revenue: $A 18,791,000 (current revenue 81.8%, of which taxes 34.0%, nontax revenue 47.8%; external aid and income 18.2%). Expenditures: $A 18,737,000 (current expenditure 83.2%, of which education 14.4%, health 10.0%[4], police 6.6%[4]; capital expenditure 16.8%).
*Public debt:* n.a.
*Tourism* (1977): visitors 796.
*Production* (metric tons except as noted). Agriculture, forestry, fishing (1985): coconuts 93,000, roots and tubers 13,000 (of which taro 3,000), copra 8,500, fruit 5,000, vegetables and melons 5,000, bananas 4,000; livestock (number of live animals) 10,000 pigs, 191,000 chickens[4]; fish catch 29,965. Mining and quarrying: none[5]. Manufacturing (1985): copra $A 4,718,400; other important products are processed fish, baked goods, cloth-

ing, boats, and handicrafts. Energy production (consumption): electricity (kW-hr; 1985) 6,000,000 (6,000,000) coal: none (n.a.); crude petroleum: none (n.a.); petroleum products (metric tons; 1985) none (9,000); natural gas: none (n.a.).
*Gross national product* (at current market prices; 1984): U.S.$30,000,000 (U.S.$480 per capita).

### Structure of gross domestic product and labour force

| | 1984 in value $A '000 | 1984 % of total value | 1985 labour force[6] | 1985 % of labour force |
|---|---|---|---|---|
| Agriculture | 10,021 | 37.1 | 327 | 5.2 |
| Mining | — | — | 13 | 0.2 |
| Manufacturing | 574 | 2.1 | 87 | 1.4 |
| Construction | 739 | 2.7 | 411 | 6.5 |
| Public utilities | 779 | 2.9 | 231 | 3.6 |
| Transportation and communication | 3,864 | 14.3 | 1,011 | 16.0 |
| Trade | 3,126 | 11.6 | 902 | 14.3 |
| Finance | 733 | 2.7 | 80 | 1.3 |
| Pub. admin., defense Services | 6,915 | 25.6 | 3,258 | 51.5 |
| Other | 283 | 1.0 | ... | ... |
| TOTAL | 27,034[7] | 100.0 | 6,320 | 100.0 |

*Population economically active* (1985): total 26,337; activity rate of total population 41.2% (participation rates: over age 15, 67.8%; female 36.1%, unemployed 2.4%).

### Price and earnings indexes (1980 = 100)

| | 1979 | 1980 | 1981 | 1982 | 1983 | 1984 | 1985 |
|---|---|---|---|---|---|---|---|
| Consumer price index | 86.1 | 100.0 | 107.7 | 113.7 | 120.8 | 128.1 | 134.6 |
| Monthly earnings index | ... | ... | ... | ... | ... | ... | ... |

*Household income and expenditure.* Average household size (1985) 6.1; income per household: n.a.; sources of income (1978): agriculture 35.9%, wages only 27.5%, wages and other 19.3%, agriculture and other 12.6%, other 4.7%; expenditure (1982): food 50.0%, tobacco and alcohol 14.0%, clothing 8.0%, transportation 8.0%, housing, energy, and household operation 7.5%.
*Land use* (1984): forested 2.8%; agricultural and under permanent cultivation 50.7%; other 46.5%.

## Foreign trade

### Balance of trade (current prices)

| | 1978 | 1979 | 1980 | 1981 | 1982 | 1983 | 1984 |
|---|---|---|---|---|---|---|---|
| $A '000 | +7,281 | +5,664 | −14,422 | −16,312 | −15,681 | −15,900 | −10,381 |
| % of total | 20.5% | 15.4% | 74.8% | −71.2% | 77.2% | 65.4% | 28.5% |

*Imports* (1984): $A 23,387,000 (machines and transport equipment 36.6%, food and live animals 23.2%, basic manufactured goods 13.4%, petroleum products 9.5%, miscellaneous manufactured articles 5.7%, beverages and tobacco 5.0%, chemicals 4.8%). *Major import sources:* Australia 35.9%; Japan 15.5%; New Zealand 7.8%; Italy 2.5%; United Kingdom 2.5%.
*Exports* (1984): $A 13,006,000 (copra 53.7%, fish and fish preparations 17.6%). *Major export destinations:* Western Europe 97%; Asia 3%.

## Transport and communications

*Transport.* Roads (1984): total length 398 mi, 640 km (paved, n.a.). Vehicles (1978): passenger cars and trucks 163; motorcycles 2,822. Merchant marine (1986): vessels (100 gross tons and over) 6; total deadweight tonnage 2,685. Air transport (1986): passenger-mi 6,184,000, passenger-km 9,953,000; short ton-mi cargo 32,000, metric ton-km cargo 47,000; airports (1987) with scheduled flights 18.
*Communications.* Daily newspapers: none. Radio (1986): total number of receivers 10,000 (1 per 6.4 persons). Television: none. Telephones (1984): 1,400 (1 per 45.7 persons).

## Education and health

### Education (1986)

| | schools | teachers | students | student/ teacher ratio |
|---|---|---|---|---|
| Primary (age 6–13) | 112 | 457 | 13,331 | 29.2 |
| Secondary (age 14–18) | 8 | 128 | 2,167 | 16.9 |
| Voc., teacher tr. | 3 | 43 | 534 | 12.4 |
| Higher[8] | — | — | — | — |

*Educational attainment* (1985)[3]: Percent of population age 25 and over having: no schooling 5.8%; less than full primary education 56.1%; primary 22.3%; some secondary 15.3%; secondary 0.5%. *Literacy* (1985): total population age 15 and over literate 90%.
*Health* (1982): physicians 19 (1 per 3,210 persons); hospital beds 283 (1 per 215 persons); infant mortality rate per 1,000 live births 82.
*Food* (1981–83): daily per capita caloric intake 2,630 (vegetable products 89%, animal products 11%); (1983) 117% of FAO recommended minimum requirement.

[1]Includes uninhabited islands. [2]Density based on inhabited island areas (280 sq mi, 726 sq km). [3]Indigenous population only, who constitute 98.7% of the total population. [4]1982. [5]Mining of phosphates on Banaba (Ocean Island) ceased in 1979. [6]Indigenous population active in cash economy only. [7]At factor cost. [8]85 students overseas.

# Korea, North

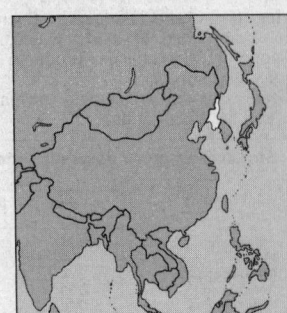

*Official name:* Chosŏn Minjujuŭi In'min Konghwaguk (Democratic People's Republic of Korea).
*Form of government:* unitary single-party republic with one legislative house (Supreme People's Assembly [615]).
*Chief of state:* President.
*Head of government:* Premier.
*Capital:* P'yŏngyang.
*Official language:* Korean.
*Official religion:* none.
*Monetary unit:* 1 won = 100 chon; valuation (Oct. 5, 1987) 1 U.S.$ = 0.94 won; 1 £ = 1.53 won.

### Area and population

| Provinces | Capitals | area[1] sq mi | sq km | population 1968 estimate |
|---|---|---|---|---|
| Chagang-do | Kanggye | 6,300 | 16,200 | 780,000 |
| Hamgyŏng-namdo | Hamhŭng | 7,400 | 19,200 | 1,315,000 |
| Hamgyŏng-pukto | Ch'ŏngjin | 6,100 | 15,900 | 1,110,000 |
| Hwanghae-namdo | Haeju | 2,900 | 7,600 | 1,340,000 |
| Hwanghae-pukto | Sariwŏn | 3,300 | 8,600 | 1,060,000 |
| Kangwŏn-do | Wŏnsan | 4,100 | 10,700 | 1,030,000 |
| P'yŏngan-namdo | P'yŏngsan | 4,700 | 12,300 | 2,250,000 |
| P'yŏngan-pukto | Sinŭiju | 4,600 | 12,000 | 1,760,000 |
| Yanggang-do | Hyesan | 5,400 | 14,100 | 435,000 |
| **Special cities** | | | | |
| Ch'ŏngjin-si | — | 700 | 1,900 | 385,000 |
| Hamhŭng-si | — | 300 | 800 | 530,000 |
| P'yŏngyang-si | P'yŏngyang | 700 | 1,800 | 1,275,000 |
| **Special district** | | | | |
| Kaesŏng-chigu | Kaesŏng | 500 | 1,200 | 289,000 |
| **TOTAL** | | 47,300[2] | 122,400[2] | 13,559,000 |

## Demography

*Population* (1987): 21,390,000.
*Density* (1987): persons per sq mi 452.2, persons per sq km 174.8.
*Urban–rural* (1985): urban 62.0%; rural 38.0%.
*Sex distribution* (1985): male 49.58%; female 50.42%.
*Age breakdown* (1985): under 15, 38.1%; 15–29, 29.4%; 30–44, 16.6%; 45–59, 9.9%; 60–74, 4.9%; 75 and over, 1.1%.
*Population projection:* (1990) 22,939,000; (2000) 28,166,000.
*Doubling time:* 29 years.
*Ethnic composition* (1983): Korean 99.8%; Chinese 0.2%.
*Religious affiliation* (1980): atheist or nonreligious 67.9%; traditional beliefs 15.6%; Ch'ŏndogyo 13.9%; Buddhist 1.7%; Christian 0.9%.
*Major cities* (1981): P'yŏngyang 1,283,000; Hamhŭng-Hŭngnam 775,000; Ch'ŏngjin 490,000; Kaesŏng 240,000; Wŏnsan 240,000.

## Vital statistics

*Birth rate* per 1,000 population (1984): 30.0 (world avg. 29.0).
*Death rate* per 1,000 population (1984): 6.0 (world avg. 11.0).
*Natural increase rate* per 1,000 population (1984): 24.0 (world avg. 18.0).
*Total fertility rate* (avg. births per childbearing woman; 1984): 3.8.
*Marriage rate* per 1,000 population: n.a.
*Divorce rate* per 1,000 population: n.a.
*Life expectancy* at birth (1984): male 65 years; female 72 years.
*Major causes of death:* n.a.; however, major diseases include endemic diseases (typhoid fever, dysentery, clonorchiasis [liver fluke], paragonimiasis [lung fluke], encephalitis, poliomielitis, diphteria, measles, tuberculosis of respiratory system, bronchitis, malignant neoplasms (cancers), hypertensive and ischemic heart diseases, and intestinal obstruction and hernia.

## National economy

*Budget* (1986). Revenue: 28,481,500,000 won (1984; turnover tax 55.0%, payments by state enterprises 30%). Expenditures: 28,481,500,000 won (1984; national economy 63.3%, social and cultural affairs 20.0%, defense 14.6%, other 2.1%).
*Production* (metric tons except as noted). Agriculture, forestry, fishing (1985): rice 5,600,000, vegetables 2,821,000, corn (maize) 2,680,000, potatoes 1,850,000, apples 580,000, millet 555,000, barley 550,000, sweet potatoes 470,000, soybeans 425,000, pulses 290,000, sugarcane 181,000, sorghum 180,000, pears 98,000, peaches 85,000, tobacco 56,000, dry onions 37,000, seed cotton 15,000, sesame seed 8,000, avocado 7,000; livestock (number of live animals) 2,800,000 pigs, 1,100,000 cattle, 350,000 sheep, 265,000 goats, 18,000,000 chickens; roundwood 4,543,000 cu m; fish catch 1,700,000. Mining and quarrying (1985): iron ore 8,000,000; crude magnesite 1,900,000; phosphate rock 500,000; sulfur 230,000; zinc 160,000; lead (metal content) 110,000; gypsum 82,000; fluorspar 40,000; graphite 25,000; silver 1,600,000 troy oz; gold 160,000 troy oz. Manufacturing (1984): cement 8,910,000; pig iron 5,750,000; chemical fertilizers 3,900,000[3]; crude steel 3,500,000; steel semimanufactures 3,400,000; television sets 200,000 units; machine tools 29,000 units; cars 18,000 units; textile fabrics 600,000,000 m. Construction: n.a. Energy production (consumption): electricity (kW-hr; 1985) 48,000,-000 (48,000,000); coal (metric tons; 1985) 51,000,000 (51,400,000); crude petroleum (barrels; 1985) none (19,000,000); petroleum products (metric tons; 1985) 2,490,000 (2,980,000); natural gas, none (n.a.).

*Population economically active* (1985): total 9,084,000; activity rate of total population 44.6% (participation rates: ages 15–64, 75.3%; female 34.5%; unemployed, n.a.).
*Price and earnings indexes:* n.a.
*Public debt* (external, outstanding; 1984): U.S.$3,600,000,000.
*Household income and expenditure.* Average household size (1980) 5.7; average annual income per household 3,677 won (U.S.$4,275); sources of income: n.a.; expenditure[4] (1984): food 46.5%; clothing 29.9%; furniture 3.8%; energy 3.3%; housing 0.6%.
*Gross national product* (1985): U.S.$20,000,000,000 (U.S.$1,000 per capita).

### Structure of gross domestic product and labour force

| | 1982 in value '000,000 won | % of total value | labour force | % of labour force |
|---|---|---|---|---|
| Agriculture | ... | ... | 3,276,000 | 44.1 |
| Mining and manufacturing | ... | ... | } 2,790,000 | 33.0 |
| Construction | ... | ... | | |
| Public utilities | ... | ... | | |
| Transp. and commun. | ... | ... | 418,000 | 4.9 |
| Trade | ... | ... | | |
| Finance | ... | ... | | |
| Pub. admin., defense | ... | ... | } 1,521,000 | 18.0 |
| Services | ... | ... | | |
| Other | ... | ... | | |
| **TOTAL** | 11,800 | 100.0 | 8,455,000 | 100.0 |

*Land use* (1984): forested 74.5%; meadows and pastures 0.4%; agricultural and under permanent cultivation 19.2%; other 5.9%.
*Tourism:* n.a.

## Foreign trade

### Balance of trade (current prices)

| | 1974 | 1976 | 1978 | 1979 | 1980 | 1981 |
|---|---|---|---|---|---|---|
| '000,000 won | −601 | −176 | −53 | +165 | −256 | −285 |
| % of total | 31.6% | 11.5% | 3.3% | 6.3% | 9.4% | 10.3% |

*Imports* (1984): U.S.$1,390,000,000 (crude petroleum, coal and coke, industrial machinery and transport equipment [including trucks], industrial chemicals, textile yarn and fabrics, and grain are among the major imports). *Major import sources* (1981): U.S.S.R. 22.0%; Japan 18.0%; China 17.0%; East European countries 7.6%.
*Exports* (1984): U.S.$1,340,000,000 (minerals [including lead, magnesite, and zinc], metallurgical products [iron and steel, nonferrous metals], cement, agricultural products [including fish, grain, fruit and vegetables, tobacco], and manufactured goods [textile fabrics, clothing], are among the major exports). *Major export destinations* (1981): U.S.S.R. 26.0%; China 17.0%; Japan 9.0%; Saudi Arabia 9.0%; India 5.0%.

## Transport and communications

*Transport.* Railroads (1985): length 2,779 mi, 4,473 km; passengers, n.a.; cargo, n.a. Roads (1985): total length 13,670 mi, 22,000 km (paved 2%). Vehicles (1982): passenger cars 180,000. Merchant marine (1986): vessels (100 gross tons and over) 71; total deadweight tonnage 615,292. Air transport (1979): passenger-mi 52,200,000, passenger-km 84,000,000; short ton-mi cargo 1,370,000, metric ton-km cargo 2,000,000; airports (1987) with scheduled flights 1.
*Communications.* Daily newspapers (1984): total number 10; total circulation, n.a. Radio (1984): total number of receivers 4,100,000 (1 per 5 persons). Television (1984): total number of receivers 1,050,000 (1 per 19 persons). Telephones (1983): 10,000 (1 per 2,000 persons).

## Education and health

### Education (1982)

| | schools | teachers | students | student/ teacher ratio |
|---|---|---|---|---|
| Primary (age 5–9) | 4,700[5] | c. 100,000 | c. 2,500,000 | ... |
| Secondary (age 10–15) | ... | | c. 2,500,000[6] | ... |
| Voc., teacher tr. | ... | | ... | ... |
| Higher | 175 | 9,244 | 200,000 | 21.6 |

*Educational attainment,* n.a. *Literacy* (1979): 90%.
*Health* (1982): physicians 45,000 (1 per 417 persons); hospital beds 244,000 (1 per 77 persons); infant mortality rate per 1,000 live births (1984) 28.
*Food* (1981–83): daily per capita caloric intake 3,116 (vegetable products 94%, animal products 6%); (1983) 127% of FAO recommended minimum requirement.

## Military

*Total active duty personnel* (1986): 840,000 (army 89.3%, navy 4.2%, air force 6.5%). *Military expenditure as percent of GNP* (1984): 22.6% (world 5.9%); per capita expenditure U.S.$254.

[1]Areas approximate. [2]Detail does not add to total given because of rounding. [3]1983. [4]Workers and clerical workers only. [5]1976. [6]Includes vocational students.

# Korea, South

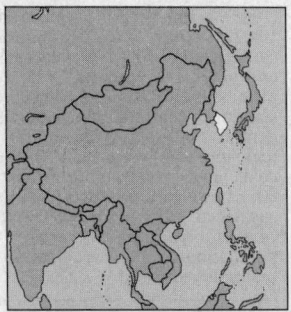

*Official name:* Taehan Min'guk
(Republic of Korea).
*Form of government:* unitary republic
with a National Assembly (276
members).
*Chief of state:* President.
*Head of government:* Prime Minister.
*Capital:* Seoul.
*Official language:* Korean.
*Official religion:* none.
*Monetary unit:* 1 won (W) = 100 chon;
valuation (Oct. 5, 1987)
1 U.S.$ = W 804; 1 £ = W 1,305.

## Area and population

| Provinces | Capitals | area sq mi | area sq km | population 1985 census |
|---|---|---|---|---|
| Cheju-do | Cheju | 705 | 1,825 | 489,458 |
| Chŏlla-namdo | Kwangju | 4,729 | 12,249 | 3,748,442 |
| Chŏlla-pukto | Chŏnju | 3,108 | 8,050 | 2,202,218 |
| Ch'ungch'ŏng-namdo | Taejŏn | 3,411 | 8,835 | 3,001,538 |
| Ch'ungch'ŏng-pukto | Ch'ŏngju | 2,870 | 7,433 | 1,391,084 |
| Kangwŏn-do | Ch'unch'ŏn' | 6,523 | 16,894 | 1,726,029 |
| Kyŏnggi-do | Inch'ŏn[1] | 4,193 | 10,859 | 4,794,240 |
| Kyŏngsang-namdo | Masan | 4,577 | 11,855 | 3,013,276 |
| Kyŏngsang-pukto | Taegu[1] | 7,506 | 19,441 | 3,519,121 |
| **Special cities** | | | | |
| Inch'ŏn-si | Inch'ŏn | 80 | 207 | 1,387,475 |
| Pusan-si | Pusan | 168 | 435 | 3,516,768 |
| Sŏul-t'ŭkpyŏlsi | Seoul | 234 | 605 | 9,645,824 |
| Taegu-si | Taegu | 176 | 455 | 2,030,649 |
| TOTAL | | 38,279[2] | 99,143 | 40,466,577[3] |

## Demography

*Population* (1987): 42,082,000.
*Density* (1987): persons per sq mi 1,099.9, persons per sq km 424.7.
*Urban–rural* (1985): urban 65.4%; rural 34.6%.
*Sex distribution* (1987): male 50.42%; female 49.58%.
*Age breakdown* (1985): under 15, 30.6%; 15–29, 31.0%; 30–44, 19.4%; 45–59, 12.3%; 60–74, 5.4%; 75 and over, 1.3%.
*Population projection:* (1990) 43,773,000; (2000) 49,914,000.
*Doubling time:* 46 years.
*Ethnic composition* (1982): Korean 99.9%; other 0.1%.
*Religious affiliation* (1983): Buddhist 48.2%; Protestant 34.2%; Roman Catholic 10.2%; Confucian 5.0%; Wonbulgyo 0.6%; Ch'ondogyo 0.4%; other 1.4%.
*Major cities* (1985): Seoul 9,645,932; Pusan 3,516,807; Taegu 2,030,672; Inch'ŏn 1,387,491; Kwangju 906,129.

## Vital statistics

*Birth rate* per 1,000 population (1986): 21.8 (world avg. 26.0).
*Death rate* per 1,000 population (1986): 6.3 (world avg. 9.9).
*Natural increase rate* per 1,000 population (1986): 15.5 (world avg. 16.1).
*Total fertility rate* (avg. births per childbearing woman; 1986): 2.1.
*Marriage rate* per 1,000 population (1982): 8.3.
*Divorce rate* per 1,000 population (1982): 0.6.
*Life expectancy* at birth (1986): male 65.2 years; female 71.5 years.
*Major causes of death* per 100,000 population: n.a.

## National economy

*Budget* (1987). Revenue: W 15,559,600,000,000 (internal tax 59.9%, customs duties 13.9%, defense surtax 13.1%, monopoly profits 6.1%). Expenditures: W 15,559,600,000,000 (defense 31.6%, economic development and social programs 25.1%, education 20.1%).
*Tourism* (1985): receipts from visitors U.S.$784,000,000; expenditures by nationals abroad U.S.$606,000,000.
*Production* (metric tons except as noted). Agriculture, forestry, fishing (1985): rice 5,626,000, cabbages 2,790,000, radishes 1,586,000, potatoes 1,362,000, barley 571,000, apples 533,000, onions 524,000, watermelon 473,000, oranges 371,000; livestock (number of live animals) 2,943,000 cattle, 2,853,000 pigs, 318,000 goats, 51,081,000 chickens; roundwood 8,573,000 cu m; fish catch 3,103,000. Mining and quarrying (1986): iron ore 528,000; zinc ore 77,366; lead ore 20,061; tungsten ore 4,081; refined silver (1985) 126,123 kg. Manufacturing (1986): cement 23,403,000; pig iron 9,017,000; crude steel 4,081,000; chemical fertilizers 2,859,000; man-made fabrics 1,116,200,000 sq m; steel cargo ships 1,835,587 gross tons; television receivers 11,268,823 units; passenger cars 456,994 units. Construction (1986): residential 22,518,000 sq m; nonresidential 21,024,000 sq m. Energy production (consumption): electricity (kW-hr; 1985) 62,716,000,000 (62,716,000,000); coal (metric tons; 1985) 22,543,000 (41,395,000); crude petroleum (barrels; 1985) none (201,406,000); petroleum products (metric tons; 1985) 23,217,000 (21,834,000).
*Household income and expenditure* (1985). Average household size 4.2; income per household W 4,538,700 (U.S.$5,150); sources of income: wages and salaries 60.3%, other 39.7%; expenditure: food and tobacco 44.6%, housing, utilities, and furnishings 15.9%, transport and communication 9.7%, education and recreation 9.6%, clothing and footwear 6.6%, health care 4.3%, other 9.3%.
*Gross national product* (at current market prices; 1986): U.S.$90,600,000,000 (U.S.$2,180 per capita).

## Structure of gross domestic product and labour force

| | 1985 in value W '000,000,000 | 1985 % of total value | 1985 labour force | 1985 % of labour force |
|---|---|---|---|---|
| Agriculture | 7,893.4 | 14.5 | 3,909,000 | 26.1 |
| Mining | 794.0 | 1.5 | 142,000 | 0.9 |
| Manufacturing | 16,757.8 | 30.7 | 3,351,000 | 22.4 |
| Construction | 4,632.7 | 8.5 | 903,000 | 6.1 |
| Public utilities | 1,740.1 | 3.2 | 36,000 | 0.2 |
| Transportation and communication | 4,164.9 | 7.6 | 663,000 | 4.4 |
| Trade | 7,073.7 | 13.0 | 3,148,000 | 21.0 |
| Finance | 6,197.8 | 11.4 | 500,000 | 3.3 |
| Pub. admin., defense | 3,186.0 | 5.8 | } 1,765,000 | 11.8 |
| Services | 2,677.6 | 4.9 | | |
| Other | −5,732[4] | −1.1[4] | 567,000[5] | 3.8[5] |
| TOTAL | 54,544.8 | 100.0 | 14,984,000 | 100.0 |

*Population economically active* (1986): total 16,116,000; activity rate of total population 38.8% (participation rates: age 15 and over, 57.1%; female, n.a.; unemployed 3.8%).

## Price and earnings indexes (1980 = 100)

| | 1981 | 1982 | 1983 | 1984 | 1985 | 1986 | 1987[6] |
|---|---|---|---|---|---|---|---|
| Consumer price index | 121.3 | 130.1 | 134.5 | 137.6 | 141.0 | 144.2 | 148.2 |
| Monthly earnings index | 120.0 | 137.7 | 154.4 | 167.3 | 186.9 | 200.6 | ... |

*Public debt* (external, outstanding; 1985): U.S.$29,126,000,000.
*Land use* (1984): forested 66.7%; meadows and pastureland 0.8%; agricultural and under permanent cultivation 22.1%; other 10.4%.

## Foreign trade

### Balance of trade (current prices)

| | 1981 | 1982 | 1983 | 1984 | 1985 | 1986 |
|---|---|---|---|---|---|---|
| US$'000,000 | −3,628 | −2,400 | −1,970 | −1,386 | −853 | 4,236 |
| % of total | 8.1% | 5.4% | 3.9% | 2.3% | 1.4% | 7.4% |

*Imports* (1986): U.S.$31,583,900,000 (machinery and transport equipment 33.7%, mineral fuels and related products 16.0%, crude materials except fuels 13.6%, chemicals and chemical products 11.1%). *Major import sources:* Japan 34.4%; United States 20.7%; West Germany 3.8%; Australia 3.4%; Malaysia 2.9%; Canada 2.2%; France 2.2%; Saudi Arabia 2.0%; United Kingdom 1.4%; China 1.4%; Indonesia 1.4%.
*Exports* (1986): U.S.$34,714,500,000 (manufactured goods 55.5%, machinery and transport equipment 33.6%, food and live animals 4.5%, chemicals and chemical products 3.1%). *Major export destinations:* United States 40.0%; Japan 15.6%; Hong Kong 4.9%; Canada 3.6%; West Germany 3.6%; United Kingdom 3.0%; Saudi Arabia 2.5%; France 1.6%.

## Transport and communications

*Transport.* Railroads (1986): length 3,914 mi, 6,299 km; passenger-mi (1985) 14,007,000,000, passenger-km 22,542,000,000; short ton-mi cargo 8,672,000,000, metric ton-km cargo 12,661,000,000. Roads (1986): total length 32,475 mi, 52,264 km (paved 50%). Vehicles (1986): passenger cars 556,659; trucks and buses 541,048. Merchant marine (1986): vessels (100 gross tons and over) 1,837; total deadweight tonnage 11,561,917. Air transport (1985): passenger-mi 6,386,594,000, passenger-km 10,278,246,000; short ton-mi cargo 1,413,851,000, metric ton-km cargo 2,064,318,000; airports (1987) with scheduled flights 4.
*Communications.* Daily newspapers (1986): total number 26; total circulation 11,000,000; circulation per 1,000 population 24. Radio (1984): total number of receivers 10,250,000 (1 per 4.0 persons). Television (1985): total number of receivers 8,272,300 (1 per 5.0 persons). Telephones (1985): 6,517,395 (1 per 6.2 persons).

## Education and health

### Education (1986–87)

| | schools | teachers | students | student/ teacher ratio |
|---|---|---|---|---|
| Primary (age 6–13) | 6,535 | 126,677 | 4,798,323 | 37.9 |
| Secondary (age 14–19) | 3,408 | 114,658 | 4,111,043 | 35.9 |
| Vocational | 736 | 34,189 | 1,007,272 | 29.5 |
| Higher | 459 | 35,573 | 1,332,455 | 37.5 |

*Educational attainment* (1980). Percent of population age 25 and over having: no formal schooling 19.7%; primary education 34.5%; secondary 36.9%; postsecondary 8.9%. *Literacy* (1981): total population age 15 and over literate 13,191,432 (92.7%); males literate 6,937,242 (97.5%); females literate 6,254,190 (87.9%).
*Health* (1985): physicians 29,596 (1 per 1,387 persons); hospital beds 74,265 (1 per 553 persons); infant mortality rate per 1,000 live births (1986): 27.0.
*Food* (1981–83): daily per capita caloric intake 2,804 (vegetable products 90%, animal products 10%); (1983) 118% of FAO recommended minimum requirement.

## Military

*Total active duty personnel* (1986): 601,000 (army 86.5%, navy 8.0%, air force 5.5%). *Military expenditure as percent of GNP* (1986): 5.5% (world *c.* 6.0%); per capita expenditure: U.S.$107.

---

[1]During 1981–82 Inch'ŏn and Taegu also became special cities. [2]Detail does not add to total given because of rounding. [3]Includes 455 people not distributed by provinces. [4]Includes import duties less imputed bank service charges. [5]Unemployed. [6]June.

# Kuwait

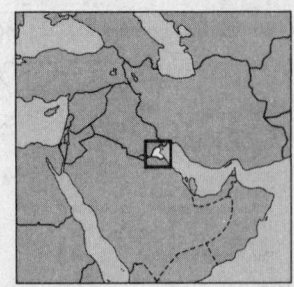

*Official name:* Dawlat al-Kuwayt (State of Kuwait).
*Form of government:* Constitutional monarchy with a single parliamentary house (National Assembly [64])[1].
*Chief of state:* Emir.
*Head of government:* Prime Minister.
*Capital:* Kuwait City.
*Official language:* Arabic.
*Official religion:* Islam.
*Monetary unit:* 1 Kuwaiti dinar (KD) = 1,000 fils; valuation (Oct. 5, 1987) 1 KD = U.S.$3.53 = £2.18.

### Area and population

| Governorates | Capitals | area | | population 1987 estimate |
|---|---|---|---|---|
| | | sq mi | sq km | |
| al-Ahmadi | al-Ahmadi | 1,984 | 5,138 | 345,783 |
| al-Jahra' | al-Jahra' | 4,372 | 11,324 | 329,588 |
| Capital | Kuwait City | 38 | 98 | 160,860 |
| Hawalli | Hawalli | 138 | 358 | 1,036,337 |
| Islands[2] | — | 348 | 900 | ... |
| TOTAL | | 6,880 | 17,818 | 1,872,568 |

## Demography

*Population* (1987): 1,873,000.
*Density* (1987): persons per sq mi 272.2, persons per sq km 105.1.
*Urban-rural* (1985): urban 93.7%; rural 6.3%.
*Sex distribution* (1985): male 56.87%; female 43.13%.
*Age breakdown* (1985): under 15, 36.8%; 15–29, 28.3%; 30–44, 24.1%; 45–59, 8.6%; 60 and over, 2.2%.
*Population projection:* (1990) 2,143,000; (2000) 3,007,000.
*Doubling time:* 26 years.
*Ethnic composition* (1983): non-Kuwaiti Arab 48.7%; Kuwaiti 41.9%; Persian 3.6%; Indian 2.4%; Pakistani 1.2%; Armenian 0.6%; Thai 0.6%; other 1.0%.
*Religious affiliation* (1980): Muslim 91.5% (Sunni about 80%, Shi'ah about 20%); Christian 6.4%; other 2.1%.
*Major cities* (1985): as-Salimiyah 153,369; Hawalli 145,126; al-Jahra' 111,222; al-Farwaniyah 68,701; Kuwait City 44,335.

## Vital statistics

*Birth rate* per 1,000 population (1986): 29.5 (world avg. 26.0); legitimate, n.a.; illegitimate, n.a.
*Death rate* per 1,000 population (1986): 2.4 (world avg. 9.9).
*Natural increase rate* per 1,000 population (1986): 27.1 (world avg. 16.1).
*Total fertility rate* (avg. births per childbearing woman; 1980–85): 6.2.
*Marriage rate* per 1,000 population (1986): 5.3.
*Divorce rate* per 1,000 population (1986): 1.6.
*Life expectancy* at birth (1980–85): male 68.0 years; female 72.9 years.
*Major causes of death* per 100,000 population (1984): circulatory diseases 82.2; accidents, poisonings, and violence 44.6; malignant neoplasms (cancers) 30.6; certain causes of perinatal morbidity and mortality 26.9; congenital anomalies 20.9; respiratory diseases 16.7; symptoms and ill-defined conditions 15.3; infectious and parasitic diseases 11.6; endocrine, nutritional, and metabolic diseases 9.0; diseases of the digestive system 5.3

## National economy

*Budget* (1987–88). Revenue: KD 1,979,400,000 (oil revenue 87.2%). Expenditures: KD 3,355,900,000 (wages and salaries 24.9%, construction and expropriations 22.3%, goods and services 7.9%, reserve fund for future generations 5.9%, transport equipment 0.7%).
*Public debt:* none.
*Tourism* (1985): receipts from visitors U.S.$103,000,000; expenditures by nationals abroad U.S.$1,988,000,000.
*Gross national product* (at current market prices; 1985): U.S.$24,760,000,000 (U.S.$14,460 per capita).

### Structure of gross domestic product and labour force

| | 1986 | | 1985 | |
|---|---|---|---|---|
| | in value KD '000,000 | % of total value | labour force | % of labour force |
| Agriculture | 51.9 | 1.0 | 12,632 | 2.0 |
| Mining (oil sector) | 1,841.8 | 37.0 | 7,033 | 1.1 |
| Manufacturing | 554.7 | 11.1 | 51,089 | 7.6 |
| Construction | 156.0 | 3.1 | 124,156 | 18.5 |
| Public utilities | −94.1 | −1.9 | 7,466 | 1.1 |
| Transportation and communication | 269.7 | 5.4 | 37,205 | 5.5 |
| Trade | 390.2 | 7.8 | 75,931 | 11.3 |
| Finance | 233.5 | 4.7 | 20,347 | 3.0 |
| Pub. admin., defense, services | 1,579.8 | 31.7 | 326,729 | 48.7 |
| Other | | | 7,797 | 1.2 |
| TOTAL | 4,983.5 | 100.0[3] | 670,385 | 100.0 |

*Production* (metric tons except as noted). Agriculture, forestry, fishing (1985): tomatoes 15,000, melons 2,000, dates 2,000, onions 2,000, pumpkins and squash 1,000, cucumbers and gherkins 1,000, garlic 1,000; livestock (number of live animals) 600,000 sheep, 320,000 goats, 160,000 cattle, 7,000 camels, 8,000,000 chickens; fish catch (1984) 4,568. Mining and quarrying

(1985): sulfur 202,377; asphalt 945,000 barrels. Manufacturing (1986): flour 144,221; concrete 47,728; bran 35,285; salt 26,166; asbestos pipes 20,984; cattle feed 17,500; liquefied caustic soda 13,693; chlorine gas 11,593; fats and oil 10,176; biscuits 2,125; detergents 1,333; hydrochloric acid 495,000 gallons; hydrogen gas 3,849,000 cu m; sodium hydrochloride 18,573 cu m; standard accumulators (batteries) 10,514 units. Construction (1986): residential 2,493,000 sq m; nonresidential 247,000 sq m. Energy production (consumption): electricity (kW-hr; 1985) 15,417,000,000 (13,159,000,000); coal, none (none); crude petroleum (barrels: 1985) 387,363,000 (215,560,-000); petroleum products (metric tons; 1985) 26,530,000 (3,918,000); natural gas (cu m; 1985) 5,831,600,000 (5,067,000,000).
*Population economically active* (1985): total 670,385; activity rate of total population 39.5% (participation rates: over age 15, 62.5%; female 19.7%; unemployed 0.1%).

### Price and earnings indexes (1980 = 100)

| | 1980 | 1981 | 1982 | 1983 | 1984 | 1985 | 1986 |
|---|---|---|---|---|---|---|---|
| Consumer price index | 100.0 | 107.4 | 115.7 | 121.2 | 122.6 | 124.4 | 125.6 |
| Monthly earnings index | ... | ... | ... | ... | ... | ... | ... |

*Household income and expenditure.* Average household size (1985) 7.2; annual income per household (1973)[4] KD 4,246 (U.S.$12,907); sources of income: wages and salaries 53.8%, self-employment 20.8%, other 25.4%; expenditure (1983): food 35.7%, housing and maintenance 18.7%, transportation 15.3%, household appliances 11.0%, clothing and footwear 10.0%, other 9.3%.
*Land use* (1984): forested 0.1%; meadows and pastures 7.5%; agricultural and under permanent cultivation 0.1%; other, built-up, and wasteland 92.3%.

## Foreign trade

### Balance of trade (current prices)

| | 1981 | 1982 | 1983 | 1984 | 1985 | 1986 |
|---|---|---|---|---|---|---|
| KD '000,000 | +2,585.0 | +885.0 | +1,204.0 | +1,590.0 | +1,367.2 | +444.7 |
| % of total | 39.9% | 16.8% | 23.1% | 28.0% | 27.7% | 11.6% |

*Imports* (1986): KD 1,698,400,000 (1984; machinery and transport equipment 43.6%, manufactured goods 22.1%, miscellaneous manufactured articles 15.3%, food and live animals 12.3%, chemicals 3.6%). *Major import sources:* Japan 21.1%; United States 11.2%; West Germany 7.9%; United Kingdom 7.5%; Italy 5.8%; France 5.0%.
*Exports* (1986): KD 2,143,100,000 (1984; crude petroleum 49.7%, refined petroleum 37.1%). *Major export destinations:* Japan 15.9%; Italy 11.2%; United States 3.6%; West Germany 2.3%; France 2.1%; United Kingdom 1.2%.

## Transport and communications

*Transport.* Railroads: none. Roads (1984): total length 1,208 mi, 1,944 km (paved 100%). Vehicles (1986): passenger cars 412,399; trucks and buses 145,310. Merchant marine (1986): vessels (100 gross tons and over) 239; total deadweight tonnage 4,121,279. Air transport (1986): passenger-mi 2,304,410,000, passenger-km 3,708,595,000; short ton-mi cargo 235,040,000, metric ton-km cargo 343,152,000; airports (1987) with scheduled flights 1.
*Communications.* Daily newspapers (1985): total number 8; total circulation 453,000; circulation per 1,000 population 253. Radio (1986): total number of receivers 500,000 (1 per 3.6 persons). Television (1986): total number of receivers 450,000 (1 per 3.9 persons). Telephones (1985): 221,882 (1 per 7.7 persons).

## Education and health

### Education (1986–87)

| | schools | teachers | students | student/ teacher ratio |
|---|---|---|---|---|
| Primary (age 6–10) | 282 | 9,704 | 175,767 | 18.1 |
| Secondary (age 11–18) | 401 | 19,158 | 245,865 | 12.8 |
| Voc., teacher tr.[5] | 6 | 788 | 12,272 | 15.6 |
| Higher | 1 | 887 | 17,414 | 19.6 |

*Educational attainment* (1985). Percent of population age 15 and over having: no formal schooling 44.4%; primary education 9.2%; some secondary 19.6%; complete secondary 18.2%; higher 8.6%. *Literacy* (1985): total population age 10 and over literate 964,324 (77.5%); males literate 591,683 (81.9%); females literate 372,641 (73.1%).
*Health* (1985): physicians 3,095 (1 per 553 persons); hospital beds 5,440[6] (1 per 314 persons); infant mortality rate per 1,000 live births 22.0.
*Food* (1981–83): daily per capita caloric intake 3,288 (vegetable products 74%, animal products 26%); (1983) 142% of FAO recommended minimum requirement.

## Military

*Total active duty personnel* (1986): 13,100 (army 76.3%, navy 8.4%, air force 15.3%). *Military expenditure as percent of GNP* (1984): 5.3% (world 5.9%); per capita expenditure U.S.$878.

[1]Parliament dissolved on July 3, 1986, and several articles of the constitution were suspended, under pressure from the Persian Gulf war and falling oil prices. [2]Bubian Island and Warba Island. [3]Detail does not add to total given because of rounding. [4]Kuwaiti households only. [5]1985–86. [6]Government hospitals only.

# Laos

*Official name:* Sathalanalat Paxathipatai Paxaxôn Lao (Lao People's Democratic Republic).
*Form of government:* unitary single-party people's republic with one legislative house (National Congress of People's Representatives [264]).
*Chief of state:* President.
*Head of government:* Prime Minister.
*Capital:* Vientiane.
*Official language:* Lao.
*Official religion:* none.
*Monetary unit:* 1 new kip (KN) = 100 at; valuation (preferential rate; Oct. 5, 1987) 1 U.S.$ = KN 35.00; 1 £ = KN 56.84.

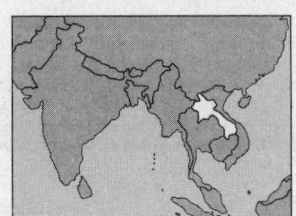

### Area and population

| Provinces | Capitals | area | | population |
|---|---|---|---|---|
| | | sq mi | sq km | 1985 census |
| Attapu | Attapu | ... | ... | 69,631 |
| Bokeo | Houayxay | ... | ... | 54,925 |
| Bolikhamxay | Pakxan | ... | ... | 122,300 |
| Champasak | Pakxé | ... | ... | 403,041 |
| Houaphan | Xam Nua | ... | ... | 209,921 |
| Khammouan | Thakhek | ... | ... | 213,462 |
| Louang Namtha | Louang Namtha | ... | ... | 97,028 |
| Louangphrabang | Louangphrabang | ... | ... | 295,475 |
| Oudomxay | Xay | ... | ... | 187,115 |
| Phôngsali | Phôngsali | ... | ... | 122,984 |
| Saravan | Saravan | ... | ... | 187,515 |
| Savannakhét | Savannakhét | ... | ... | 543,611 |
| Vientiane | Vientiane | ... | ... | 264,277 |
| Xaignabouri | Xaignabouri | ... | ... | 223,611 |
| Xékong | Thong | ... | ... | 50,909 |
| Xiangkhoang | Phônsavan | ... | ... | 161,589 |
| **Municipalities** | | | | |
| Vientiane | — | ... | ... | 377,409 |
| TOTAL | | 91,400 | 236,800 | 3,584,803 |

## Demography

*Population* (1987): 3,757,000.
*Density* (1987): persons per sq mi 41.1, persons per sq km 15.9.
*Urban–rural* (1985): urban 15.9%; rural 84.1%.
*Sex distribution* (1985): male 49.02%; female 50.98%.
*Age breakdown* (1985): under 15, 42.8%; 15–29, 26.5%; 30–44, 16.1%; 45–59, 9.6%; 60–74, 4.3%; 75 and over, 0.7%.
*Population projection:* (1990) 4,010,000; (2000) 4,906,000.
*Doubling time:* 29 years.
*Ethnic composition* (1983): Lao 67.1%; Palaung-Wa 11.9%; Tai 7.9%; Miao (Hmong) and Man (Yao) 5.2%; Mon-Khmer 4.6%; other 3.3%.
*Religious affiliation* (1980): Buddhist 57.8%; tribal religionist 33.6%; Christian 1.8%, of which Roman Catholic 0.8%, Protestant 0.2%; Muslim 1.0%; atheist 1.0%; Chinese folk-religionist 0.9%; none 3.8%; other 0.1%.
*Major cities* (1975): Vientiane 200,000[1]; Savannakhét 53,000; Pakxé 47,000; Louangphrabang 46,000.

## Vital statistics

*Birth rate* per 1,000 population (1986): 41.9 (world avg. 26.0).
*Death rate* per 1,000 population (1986): 17.9 (world avg. 9.9).
*Natural increase rate* per 1,000 population (1986): 24.0 (world avg. 16.1).
*Total fertility rate* (avg. births per childbearing woman; 1986): 5.8.
*Marriage rate* per 1,000 population: n.a.
*Divorce rate* per 1,000 population: n.a.
*Life expectancy* at birth (1986): male 45.4 years; female 49.3 years.
*Major causes of death* per 100,000 population: n.a; however, during the 1970s malaria, influenza, dysentery, and pneumonia were among the country's major health problems.

## National economy

*Budget* (1984). Revenue: KN 4,947,300,000 (state enterprises 77.2%, private sector taxes 22.8%). Expenditures: KN 8,384,300,000 (current expenditure 49.2%, capital expenditure 50.8%).
*Public debt* (external, outstanding; 1985): U.S.$458,000,000.
*Tourism* (1982): total number of tourists 29,000.
*Population economically active* (1980): total 1,839,900; activity rate of total population 49.9% (participation rates: ages 15–64, 86.4%; female 46.2%; unemployed, n.a.).

### Price and earnings indexes (1976 = 100)

| | 1980 |
|---|---|
| Consumer price index | 793 |
| Monthly earnings index | ... |

*Production* (metric tons except as noted). Agriculture, forestry, fishing (1985): rice 1,400,000, cassava 80,000, potatoes 49,000, corn (maize) 45,000, pineapples 40,000, sweet potatoes 40,000, onions 39,000, melons 36,000, sugarcane 35,000, oranges 28,000; livestock (number of live animals) 1,450,000 pigs, 915,000 water buffalo, 615,000 cattle, 65,000 goats, 6,000,000 chickens; roundwood 4,051,000 cu m; fish catch 20,000. Mining and quarrying (1985): gypsum 82,000; rock salt 10,000; tin (metal content)

540. Manufacturing (1983): domestic animal feed 3,000; washing powder 970; plastic products 185; textiles 1,451,400 metres; clothing 474,900 pieces; cigarettes 12,000,000 packets; bricks 10,900,000 units; rubber tires and tubes 1,000,000 units; beer 13,000 hectolitres; soft drinks 12,370 hectolitres. Construction: n.a. Energy production (consumption): electricity (kW-hr; 1985) 1,350,000,000 (647,000,000); coal (metric tons; 1981) 1,000 (1,000); crude petroleum, n.a. (n.a.); petroleum products (metric tons; 1985) none (55,000); natural gas, n.a. (n.a.).
*Gross national product* (at current market prices; 1984): U.S.$765,000,000 (U.S.$220 per capita).

### Structure of gross domestic product and labour force

| | 1984 | | 1983 | |
|---|---|---|---|---|
| | in value KN '000,000[2] | % of total value | labour force | % of labour force |
| Agriculture | 9,105 | 75.2 | 1,342,000 | 72.0 |
| Manufacturing | } 553[3] | 4.6[3] | | |
| Mining | | | | |
| Construction | 620 | 5.1 | | |
| Public utilities | 3 | 3 | | |
| Transportation and communication | 178 | 1.5 | 521,000 | 28.0 |
| Trade | 1,470 | 12.1 | | |
| Finance | } 180 | 1.5 | | |
| Pub. admin., defense | | | | |
| Services | | | | |
| TOTAL | 12,106 | 100.0 | 1,863,000 | 100.0 |

*Household income and expenditure.* Average household size (1980) 5.3; average annual income per household KN 3,710 (U.S.$371); sources of income: n.a.; expenditure: n.a.
*Land use* (1984): forested 55.0%; meadows and pastures 3.5%; agricultural and under permanent cultivation 3.9%; other 37.6%.

## Foreign trade

### Balance of trade (current prices)

| | 1980 | 1981 | 1982 | 1983 | 1984 | 1985 |
|---|---|---|---|---|---|---|
| U.S.$'000,000 | −100.0 | −68.1 | −61.9 | −66.8 | −36.7 | −44.7 |
| % of total | 68.2% | 66.8% | 54.7% | 56.7% | 61.9% | 54.2% |

*Imports* (1985): U.S.$63,566,000 (important imports include cereals, other food products, petroleum products, and agricultural and general machinery). *Major import sources:* Thailand 34.2%; Japan 20.4%; Singapore 17.2%; France 2.4%; Sweden 1.5%; Vietnam 1.3%; United Kingdom 1.2%; unspecified countries 21.8%.
*Exports* (1985): U.S.$18,899,000 (electricity [67.0% of all exports in 1984], wood [76.5% of all exports in 1980], coffee, and tin). *Major export destinations:* China 45.6%; Singapore 8.3%; Japan 6.5%; Thailand 4.9%; Australia 4.8%; United States 4.8%; Belgium–Luxembourg 3.3%; Iran 2.7%; unspecified countries 19.1%.

## Transport and communications

*Transport.* Railroads: none. Roads (1985): total length 8,067 mi, 12,983 km (paved 31%). Vehicles (1982): passenger cars 15,000; trucks and buses 3,000. Merchant marine: none. Air transport (1985): passenger-mi 6,000,000, passenger-km 9,000,000; short ton-mi cargo 685,000, metric ton-km cargo 1,000,000; airports (1987) with scheduled flights 7.
*Communications.* Daily newspapers (1983): total number 2; total circulation 12,500; circulation per 1,000 population 3.0. Radio (1986): total number of receivers 232,000 (1 per 16 persons). Television (1986): total number of receivers 31,000 (1 per 119 persons). Telephones (1985): 8,136 (1 per 443 persons).

## Education and health

### Education (1983–84)

| | schools | teachers | students | student/ teacher ratio |
|---|---|---|---|---|
| Primary (age 6–10) | 6,544 | 17,789 | 485,741 | 27.3 |
| Secondary (age 11–16) | 419 | 6,219 | 88,775 | 14.3 |
| Voc., teacher tr. | 60 | 2,200 | 16,237 | 7.4 |
| Higher[4] | 51[5] | 452 | 4,790 | 10.6 |

*Educational attainment,* n.a. *Literacy* (1980): total population age 15 and over literate 997,600 (45.2%); males literate 586,600 (52.8%); females literate 412,500 (37.6%).
*Health* (1985): physicians 430 (1 per 8,336 persons); hospital beds 11,650 (1 per 307.7 persons); infant mortality rate per 1,000 live births (1986) 137.0.
*Food* (1981–83): daily per capita caloric intake 2,185 (vegetable products 90%, animal products 10%); (1983) 88% of FAO recommended minimum requirement.

## Military

*Total active duty personnel* (1986): 53,000 (army 94.3%, navy 1.9%, air force 3.8%). *Military expenditure as percent of GNP* (1984): 10.5% (world 5.9%); per capita expenditure U.S.$16.

[1]1984. [2]At constant prices of 1982. [3]Manufacturing includes public utilities. [4]Includes third-level vocational. [5]Includes 1 university and 50 third-level vocational institutions.

# Lebanon

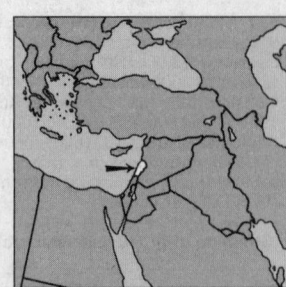

*Official name:* al-Jumhūrīyah
al-Lubnānīyah (Republic of Lebanon).
*Form of government:* multiparty
republic with one legislative house
(National Assembly [99][1]).
*Chief of state:* President.
*Head of government:* Prime Minister.
*Capital:* Beirut.
*Official language:* Arabic.
*Official religion:* none.
*Monetary unit:* 1 Lebanese pound
(LL) = 100 piastres; valuation (Oct. 5,
1987) 1 U.S.$ = LL 284.95;
1 £ = LL 462.73.

| Area and population | | area | | population |
|---|---|---|---|---|
| | | sq mi | sq km | 1970 estimate |
| Governorates | Capitals | | | |
| Bayrūt | Beirut (Bayrūt) | 7 | 18 | 474,870 |
| al-Biqāʿ | Zaḥlah | 1,653 | 4,280 | 203,520 |
| Jabal Lubnān | Bʿabdā | 753 | 1,950 | 833,055 |
| al-Janūb | Sidon (Ṣaydā) | 364 | 943 | 249,945 |
| an-Nabaṭīyah | an-Nabaṭīyah | 408 | 1,058 | ... |
| ash-Shamāl | Tripoli (Ṭarābulus) | 765 | 1,981 | 364,935 |
| TOTAL | | 3,950 | 10,230 | 2,126,325 |

## Demography

*Population* (1987): 2,762,000.
*Density* (1987): persons per sq mi 699.2, persons per sq km 270.0.
*Urban–rural* (1985): urban 83.7%; rural 16.3%.
*Sex distribution* (1985): male 48.53%; female 51.47%.
*Age breakdown* (1984): under 15, 35.6%; 15–29, 30.4%; 30–44, 15.0%; 45–59,
11.0%; 60–74, 6.0%; 75 and over, 2.0%.
*Population projection:* (1990) 2,967,000; (2000) 3,617,000.
*Doubling time:* during the 1971–75 prewar period the average growth rate
was 2.6%; however, since 1976 continuing dislocation of the population by
the civil war has rendered both the absolute size and principal components
of population change (births, deaths, migration) highly problematic.
*Ethnic composition* (1983): Lebanese 82.6%; Palestinian 9.6%; Armenian
4.9%; Syrian, Kurd, and other 2.9%.
*Religious affiliation:* no official data exist subsequent to the 1932 census,
when Christians (predominantly Maronite Roman Catholic) were a slight
majority; it is thought that Muslims today constitute the majority but by
what margin is highly uncertain. An unofficial estimate (1984) indicated
that the main religious groups were distributed as follows: Shīʿī Muslim
32%; Maronite Christian 24.5%; Sunnī Muslim 21%; Druze 7%; Greek
Orthodox 6.5%; Greek Catholic 4%; Armenian Christian 4%; other 1.0%.
*Major cities* (1985): Beirut 1,500,000; Tripoli 500,000; Zaḥlah 200,000; Sidon
(Ṣaydā) 100,000; an-Nabaṭīyah 100,000.

## Vital statistics

*Birth rate* per 1,000 population (1984): 29.8 (world avg. 29.0); legitimate,
n.a.; illegitimate, n.a.
*Death rate* per 1,000 population (1984): 8.8 (world avg. 11.0).
*Natural increase rate* per 1,000 population (1984): 21.0 (world avg. 18.0).
*Total fertility rate* (avg. births per childbearing woman; 1984): 3.8.
*Marriage rate* per 1,000 population (1973): 7.0.
*Divorce rate* per 1,000 population (1973): 0.6.
*Life expectancy* at birth (1980–85): male 65.0 years; female 68.9 years.
*Major causes of death* (mid-1970s): heart ailments and gastrointestinal dis-
eases, including typhoid fever and dysentery; violence and acts of war have
been principal causes of mortality for the last decade.

## National economy

*Budget* (1986). Revenue: LL 12,700,000,000 (customs duties c. 33%). Expenditure: LL 17,900,000,000 (defense 20.7%, internal debt service 30.2%).
*Public debt* (external, outstanding; 1985): U.S.$172,000,000.
*Production* (metric tons except as noted). Agriculture, forestry, fishing
(1985): oranges 200,000, grapes 165,000, tomatoes 125,000, potatoes 120,-
000, sugar beets 80,000, cucumbers and gherkins 70,000, lemons and limes
40,000, watermelons 30,000, onions 27,000, peaches and nectarines 22,000,
cabbages 20,000, olives 20,000, eggplants 18,000, wheat 15,000, bananas
13,000, pears 12,000, centrifugal sugar (raw value) 11,000, pulses 9,000;
livestock (number of live animals) 450,000 goats, 135,000 sheep, 45,000 cattle, 10,000,000 chickens; roundwood 473,000 cu m; fish catch 1,500. Mining
and quarrying (1985): gypsum 3,000. Manufacturing (1983): cement 1,000,-
000; wheat flour 190,000; paper and paperboard 45,000; quicklime 18,000.
Construction (1981): 5,863,000 sq m. Energy production (consumption):
electricity (kW-hr; 1985) 1,355,000,000 (1,395,000,000); coal, n.a. (none);
crude petroleum (barrels; 1985) n.a. (4,582,000); petroleum products (metric tons; 1985) 615,000 (1,846,000); natural gas, none (n.a.).
*Population economically active* (1984): total 701,783; activity rate of total
population 26.5% (participation rates: over age 15, 42.4%; female 20.5%;
unemployed [1987] 25.0%).

| Price and earnings indexes (1980 = 100) | | | | | | | |
|---|---|---|---|---|---|---|---|
| | 1978 | 1979 | 1980 | 1981 | 1982 | 1983 | 1984 |
| Consumer price index | 65.4 | 80.9 | 100.0 | 119.4 | 141.5 | 149.9 | 164.4 |
| Monthly earnings index[2] | ... | 77.8 | 100.0 | 118.5 | 137.0 | ... | ... |

*Tourism* (1980): number of tourist arrivals 135,548.
*Household income and expenditure.* Average household size (1980) 5.3; income per household: n.a.; sources of income: n.a.; expenditure: n.a.
*Gross national product* (at current market prices; 1983): U.S.$4,600,000,000–
$5,500,000,000 (U.S.$1,636–$1,956 per capita).

| Structure of gross domestic product and labour force | | | | |
|---|---|---|---|---|
| | 1984 | | 1982 | |
| | in value LL '000,000 | % of total value | labour force | % of labour force |
| Agriculture | 814.0 | 8.4 | 238,188 | 20.7 |
| Mining | } 1,277.0 | } 13.2 | ... | ... |
| Manufacturing | | | 223,136 | 19.4 |
| Construction | 331.2 | 3.4 | 71,698 | 6.2 |
| Public utilities | 516.4 | 5.3 | 8,503 | 0.7 |
| Transportation and communication | 741.4 | 7.6 | 62,161 | 5.4 |
| Finance | 1,218.0 | 12.5 | } 203,258 | } 17.7 |
| Trade | 2,722.6 | 28.0 | | |
| Pub. admin., defense | 1,060.2 | 10.9 | } 342,057 | } 29.8 |
| Services | 1,036.5 | 10.7 | | |
| Other | ... | ... | ... | ... |
| TOTAL | 9,717.3 | 100.0 | 1,149,001 | 100.0[3] |

*Land use* (1984): forested 7.9%; meadows and pastures 0.9%; agricultural
and under permanent cultivation 28.7%, wasteland, built-up, and other
areas 62.5%.

## Foreign trade

| Balance of trade (current prices) | | | | | | |
|---|---|---|---|---|---|---|
| | 1981 | 1982 | 1983 | 1984 | 1985 | 1986 |
| LL '000,000 | −8,906 | −9,890 | −12,461 | −13,987 | −25,581 | −59,090 |
| % of total | 45.0% | 48.5% | 69.0% | 64.9% | 61.8% | 60.6% |

*Imports* (1984): LL 14,800,000,000 (1982; consumer goods 40.0%; machinery
and transport equipment 35.0%; petroleum products 20.0%). *Major import
sources:* Italy 14.9%; United States 10.5%; France 8.9%; Romania 7.2%;
Japan 5.3%; Turkey 4.2%; Belgium 4.0%.
*Exports* (1984): LL 2,462,000,000 (1982; agricultural products 21.3%, of
which vegetables 15.9%; textile products 11.3%; metal products 8.5%; precious metals, jewelry, and coins 5.0%). *Major export destinations:* Saudi
Arabia 28.8%; Kuwait 8.4%; Egypt 4.8%; Switzerland 4.4%; Italy 3.8%; Syria
3.4%; Jordan 2.9%.

## Transport and communications

*Transport.* Railroads (1982): length (1986) 259 mi, 417 km; passenger-mi
5,325,000, passenger-km 8,570,000; short ton-mi cargo 28,770,000, metric
ton-km cargo 42,010,000. Roads (1982): total length 4,300 mi, 7,000 km
(paved 80%). Vehicles (1982): passenger cars 460,400; trucks and buses 35,-
000. Merchant marine (1986): vessels (100 gross tons and over) 228; total
deadweight tonnage 766,784. Air transport[4] (1984): passenger-mi 516,117,-
000, passenger-km 830,612,000; short ton-mi cargo 13,544,000, metric ton-
km cargo 19,774,000; airports (1987) with scheduled flights 1.
*Communications.* Daily newspapers (1986): total number 38; total circulation 582,734; circulation per 1,000 population 215.0. Radio (1986): total
number of receivers 2,000,000 (1 per 1.4 persons). Television (1986): total
number of receivers 500,000 (1 per 5.4 persons). Telephones (1973): 227,000
(1 per 12 persons).

## Education and health

| Education (1981–82) | | | | student/ |
|---|---|---|---|---|
| | schools | teachers | students | teacher ratio |
| Primary (age 5–9) | 1,116 | } 53,450 | 398,977 | ... |
| Secondary (age 10–16) | 1,405 | | 250,028 | ... |
| Voc., teacher tr. | 181 | 3,563 | 39,045 | 11.0 |
| Higher | 18 | 7,976 | 70,314 | 8.8 |

*Educational attainment* (1970). Percent of population age 25 and over having: no formal schooling 45.6%; ability to read and write 35.6%; primary
education 10.8%; secondary 4.9%; higher 3.1%. *Literacy* (1980): total population age 10 and over literate 1,183,000 (73.4%); males literate 643,000
(82.6%); females literate 540,000 (64.2%).
*Health* (1982): physicians 3,000 (1 per 1,000 persons); hospital beds 11,400
(1 per 263 persons); infant mortality rate per 1,000 live births (1984) 44.4.
*Food* (1979–81): daily per capita caloric intake 2,995 (vegetable products
84%, animal products 16%); (1983) 120% of FAO recommended minimum requirement.

## Military

*Total active duty personnel* (1987): 15,000 (army 96.7%, navy 3.3%); principal
factional militias[5]: Maronite Christian (Lebanese Forces [Phalange]) 5,000;
Maronite Christian/Shīʿī Muslim (75%/25%; South Lebanese Army) 1,200;
Druze 5,000; Sunnī Muslim (Islamic Unification Movement) 1,000; Shīʿī
Muslim (pro-Syria Amal) 5,000; Shīʿī Muslim (pro-Iran Hezbollah) 3,500;
occupying Syrian military forces (c. 12,500) play a nominal peacekeeping
role. *Military expenditure as percent of GNP* (1983): 8.2% (world 6.1%); per
capita expenditure: U.S.$201.

---

[1]Elected 1972; 79 remain living. [2]Excludes banking sector. [3]Detail does not add to
total given because of rounding. [4]International flights only. [5]Active duty personnel
only. Palestine Liberation Organization excluded.

# Lesotho

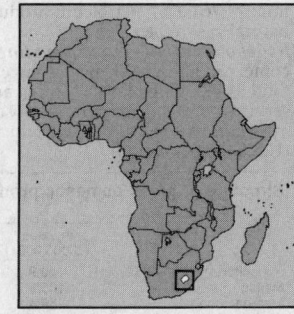

*Official name:* Lesotho (Sotho); Kingdom of Lesotho (English).
*Form of government:* constitutional monarchy with two legislative houses (National Assembly [80]; Senate [30])[1].
*Chief of state:* King.
*Head of government:* Chairman of the Military Council.
*Capital:* Maseru.
*Official languages:* Sotho; English.
*Official religion:* Christianity.
*Monetary unit:* 1 loti (plural maloti [M]) = 100 lisente; valuation (Oct. 5, 1987) 1 U.S.$ = M 2.08; 1 £ = M 3.38.

### Area and population

| Districts | Capitals | area sq mi | area sq km | population 1986 census |
|---|---|---|---|---|
| Berea | Teyateyaneng | 858 | 2,222 | 194,631 |
| Butha-Buthe | Butha-Buthe | 682 | 1,767 | 100,644 |
| Leribe | Leribe | 1,092 | 2,828 | 257,988 |
| Mafeteng | Mafeteng | 818 | 2,119 | 195,591 |
| Maseru | Maseru | 1,652 | 4,279 | 311,159 |
| Mohale's Hoek | Mohale's Hoek | 1,363 | 3,530 | 164,392 |
| Mokhotlong | Mokhotlong | 1,573 | 4,075 | 74,676 |
| Qacha's Nek | Qacha's Nek | 907 | 2,349 | 63,984 |
| Quthing | Quthing | 1,126 | 2,916 | 110,376 |
| Thaba-Tseka | Thaba-Tseka | 1,649 | 4,270 | 104,095 |
| TOTAL | | 11,720 | 30,355 | 1,577,536 |

## Demography

*Population* (1987): 1,628,000.
*Density* (1987): persons per sq mi 138.9, persons per sq km 53.6.
*Urban–rural* (1985): urban 5.8%; rural 94.2%.
*Sex distribution* (1986): male 48.21%; female 51.79%.
*Age breakdown* (1985): under 15, 42.3%; 15–29, 25.9%; 30–44, 16.2%; 45–59, 9.9%; 60–74, 4.7%; 75 and over, 1.0%.
*Population projection:* (1990) 1,760,000; (2000) 2,281,800.
*Doubling time:* 27 years.
*Ethnic composition* (1983): Sotho 99.7%; other 0.3%.
*Religious affiliation* (1980): Roman Catholic 43.5%; Protestant (mostly Lesotho Evangelical) 29.8%; Anglican 11.5%; other Christian 8.0%; tribal 6.2%; other 1.0%.
*Major urban centres* (1976): Maseru 55,031 (Maseru-Roma-Morija metropolitan area [1986] 109,382); Maputsoe 15,823; Teyateyaneng 8,589.

## Vital statistics

*Birth rate* per 1,000 population (1980–85): 41.8 (world avg. 29.0); legitimate, n.a.; illegitimate, n.a.
*Death rate* per 1,000 population (1980–85): 16.5 (world avg. 11.0).
*Natural increase rate* per 1,000 population (1980–85): 25.3 (world avg. 18.0).
*Total fertility rate* (avg. births per childbearing woman; 1980–85): 5.8.
*Life expectancy* at birth (1980–85): male 46.3 years; female 52.3 years.
*Major causes of death:* n.a.; however, major diseases include malaria, typhoid fever, and infectious and parasitic diseases.

## National economy

*Budget* (1986–87). Revenue: M 289,400,000 (tax revenue 77.4%, of which customs receipts 49.9%, sales tax 15.0%, income tax 7.2%, company tax 3.4%; nontax revenue 11.5%; grants 11.1%). Expenditures: M 380,200,000 (recurrent expenditure 65.5%, of which personal emoluments 30.2%, interest payments 6.6%, subsidies and transfers 5.5%, other goods and services 23.1%; capital expenditure 34.5%).
*Production* (metric tons except as noted). Agriculture, forestry, fishing (1986): corn (maize) 86,488, sorghum 33,458, vegetables and melons 29,000, fruit 18,000, wheat 11,000, pulses 10,000[2], roots and tubers 6,000[2], peas 3,779, beans 1,502; livestock (number of live animals; 1985) 1,400,000 sheep, 1,000,000 goats, 590,000 cattle, 107,000 horses, 107,000 asses, 80,000 pigs, 1,000,000 chickens; roundwood (1984) 293,000 cu m; fish catch 22. Mining and quarrying (1982)[3]: diamonds 42,000 carats. Manufacturing (total value added; 1985): M 40,300,000; food processing, textile and leather production, building materials, and handicrafts were the main manufacturing activities. Construction: n.a. Energy production (consumption): electricity (kW-hr; 1985) 1,000,000 (n.a.); coal, none (n.a.); petroleum, none (n.a.); natural gas, none (n.a.).
*Public debt* (external, outstanding; 1985): U.S.$172,200,000.
*Tourism* (1985): receipts from visitors U.S.$9,000,000; expenditures by nationals abroad, n.a.
*Population economically active* (1985): total 514,704[4]; activity rate of total population 33.3% (participation rates: age 12 and over, 55.8%; female, n.a.; unemployed 23%).

### Price and earnings indexes (1980 = 100)

| | 1980 | 1981 | 1982 | 1983 | 1984 | 1985 | 1986 |
|---|---|---|---|---|---|---|---|
| Consumer price index | 100.0 | 114.9 | 125.9 | 147.1 | 164.0 | 188.2 | 228.5[5] |
| Annual earnings index[6] | 100.0 | 145.6 | 311.2 | 441.8 | 518.8 | 577.6 | 597.8 |

*Household income and expenditure.* Average household size (1980) 4.4; average annual income per household (1979–80) M 1,550 (U.S.$1,150); sources of income (1978–79): agriculture 49.2%, wages and salaries 42.0%

(of which migrant workers' remittances 32.4%), home industry 2.4%, other 6.4%; expenditure (1975)[7]: food 34.0%, clothing 19.3%, housing 16.7%, transportation 9.5%, education 4.1%, health 1.8%.
*Gross national product* (at current market prices; 1985): U.S.$730,000,000 (U.S.$470 per capita).

### Structure of gross domestic product and labour force

| | 1985 in value M '000,000 | 1985 % of total value | 1985 labour force | 1985 % of labour force |
|---|---|---|---|---|
| Agriculture | 104.7 | 18.3 | | |
| Mining | 0.6 | 0.1 | | |
| Manufacturing | 56.3[8] | 9.9[8] | | |
| Construction | 50.0 | 8.8 | | |
| Public utilities | 3.9 | 0.7 | 396,192 | 77.0 |
| Transp. and commun. | 9.7 | 1.7 | | |
| Trade | 83.0 | 14.5 | | |
| Finance | 68.5 | 12.0 | | |
| Pub. admin., defense | 56.0 | 9.8 | | |
| Services | 41.3 | 7.2 | | |
| Other | 97.4[9] | 17.0[9] | 118,512[10] | 23.0[10] |
| TOTAL | 571.4 | 100.0 | 514,704[11] | 100.0 |

*Land use* (1984): meadows and pastures 65.9%; agricultural and under permanent cultivation 9.8%; other 24.3%.

## Foreign trade[12]

### Balance of trade (current prices)

| | 1979 | 1980 | 1981 | 1982 | 1983 | 1984 | 1985 |
|---|---|---|---|---|---|---|---|
| M '000,000 | −273.9 | −327.0 | −405.9 | −528.1 | −594.0 | −684.5 | −746.9 |
| % of total | 78.3% | 78.3% | 82.5% | 87.1% | 89.9% | 89.5% | 88.2% |

*Imports* (1981): M 449,060,000 (manufactured goods [excluding chemicals, machinery, and transport equipment] 37.4%, of which clothing 8.4%, blankets and traveling rugs 3.6%, footwear 3.3%; food and live animals 18.9%, of which cereals [all forms] 5.9%, sugar [all forms] 2.6%; machinery and transport equipment 17.0%, of which trucks and vans 3.5%; petroleum products 8.6%). *Major import sources:* Customs Union of Southern Africa 97.1%; European Economic Community 1.5%.
*Exports* (1981): M 43,124,000 (diamonds 42.1%; food and live animals 10.3%; umbrellas, brooms, brushes, and basketwork 8.1%; mohair 8.0%; road vehicles 3.1%; footwear 3.0%). *Major export destinations:* Customs Union of Southern Africa 46.7%; Switzerland 41.8%; West Germany 7.0%.

## Transport and communications

*Transport.* Railroads (1985): length 1 mi, 2 km. Roads (1985): total length 2,640 mi, 4,250 km (paved 12%). Vehicles (1982): passenger cars 5,129; trucks and buses 11,962. Merchant marine: vessels (100 gross tons and over) none. Air transport (1986): passenger-mi 7,770,000, passenger-km 12,510,000; short ton-mi cargo 70,000, metric ton-km cargo 100,000; airports (1987) with scheduled flights 15.
*Communications.* Daily newspapers (1985): total number 3; total circulation 44,000; circulation per 1,000 population 28. Radio (1986): total number of receivers 100,000 (1 per 16 persons). Television (1986): total number of receivers 1,000 (1 per 1,586 persons). Telephones (1983): 5,409 (1 per 271 persons).

## Education and health

### Education (1984–85)[13]

| | schools | teachers | students | student/ teacher ratio |
|---|---|---|---|---|
| Primary (age 6–12) | 1,141 | 5,663 | 314,003 | 55.4 |
| Secondary (age 13–17) | 143 | 1,676 | 35,423 | 21.1 |
| Voc., teacher tr. | 9 | 221 | 2,221 | 10.0 |
| Higher[14] | 1 | 146 | 1,119 | 7.7 |

*Educational attainment* (1976). Percent of population age 10 and over having: no formal education 28.8%; primary 64.6%; secondary 2.3%; higher 0.6%. *Literacy* (1985): total population age 15 and over literate 655,400 (73.6%); males literate 273,800 (62.4%); females literate 381,600 (84.5%).
*Health* (1982): physicians 114 (1 per 12,265 persons); hospital beds 2,300 (1 per 608 persons); infant mortality rate per 1,000 live births (1983) 109.
*Food* (1981–83): daily per capita caloric intake 2,322 (vegetable products 93%, animal products 7%); (1983) 104% of FAO recommended minimum requirement.

## Military

*Total active duty personnel* (1985): 1,500[15]. *Military expenditure as percent of GNP* (1984): 6.5% (world 5.9%); per capita expenditure U.S.$37.

[1]Following a military coup in January 1986, it was announced that executive and legislative powers were to be vested in the King, assisted by a six-member Military Council and a Council of Ministers. The 1966 independence constitution, suspended in 1970 and reinstated in 1983, was again suspended in 1986 following the coup, terminating all legislative organs. [2]1985. [3]Mining activities ended in late 1982 with the closure of Lesotho's one commercial mine. Plans to reopen the mine were being considered in 1985. [4]Age 12 and over. [5]October. [6]Based on Basotho miners working in South Africa. [7]Weights of consumer price index components. [8]Includes handicrafts. [9]Indirect taxes less subsidies. [10]Unemployed. [11]In 1986, 140,950 workers, or 19% of the total labour force, were employed in South Africa, mostly as gold miners. [12]Import figures are f.o.b. in balance of trade and c.i.f. in commodities and trading partners. [13]Excludes private schools. [14]January. [15]Lesotho Paramilitary Force.

# Liberia

*Official name:* Republic of Liberia.
*Form of government:* multiparty
republic with two legislative houses
(Senate [26]; House of Representatives
[64]).
*Head of state and government:*
President.
*Capital:* Monrovia.
*Official language:* English.
*Official religion:* none.
*Monetary unit:* 1 Liberian dollar
(L$) = 100 cents; valuation (Oct. 5,
1987) 1 U.S.$ = L$1.00; 1 £ = L$1.62.

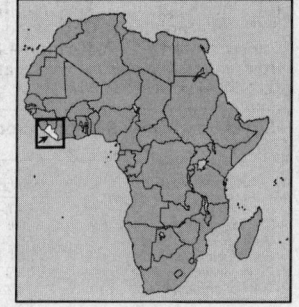

### Area and population

| Counties | Capitals | area sq mi | area sq km | population 1984 census |
|---|---|---|---|---|
| Bong | Gbarnga | 3,127 | 8,099 | 255,813 |
| Grand Bassa | Buchanan | 3,382 | 8,759 | 159,648 |
| Grand Cape Mount | Robertsport | 2,250 | 5,827 | 79,322 |
| Grand Gedeh | Zwedru | 6,575 | 17,029 | 102,810 |
| Grand Kru[1] | Barclayville | [2] | [2] | [2] |
| Lofa | Voinjama | 7,475 | 19,360 | 247,641 |
| Margibi[3] | Kakata | 1,260 | 3,263 | 97,992 |
| Maryland | Harper | 2,066[2] | 5,351[2] | 132,058[2] |
| Montserrado | Bensonville | 1,058 | 2,740 | 544,878 |
| Nimba | Saniquillie | 4,650 | 12,043 | 313,050 |
| Sinoe | Greenville | 3,959 | 10,254 | 64,147 |
| **Territories** | | | | |
| Bomi | Tubmanburg | 755 | 1,955 | 66,420 |
| Rivercess | Rivercess City | 1,693 | 4,385 | 37,849 |
| **TOTAL** | | **38,250** | **99,067[4]** | **2,101,628** |

## Demography

*Population* (1987): 2,356,000.
*Density* (1987): persons per sq mi 61.6, persons per sq km 23.8.
*Urban–rural* (1984): urban 38.8%; rural 61.2%.
*Sex distribution* (1984): male 50.59%; female 49.41%.
*Age breakdown* (1984): under 15, 43.2%; 15–29, 28.2%; 30–44, 14.7%; 45–59, 7.7%; 60–74, 4.4%; 75 and over, 1.8%.
*Population projection:* (1990) 2,605,000; (2000) 3,641,000.
*Doubling time:* 21 years.
*Ethnic composition* (1984): Kpelle 19.4%; Bassa 13.8%; Grebo 9.0%; Gio 7.8%; Kru 7.3%; Mano 7.1%; other 35.6%.
*Religious affiliation* (1984): Christian 67.7%; Muslim 13.8%; traditional beliefs and other 18.5%.
*Major cities* (1974): Monrovia 425,000[5]; Buchanan 23,999; Congo Town 21,495; Yekepa 14,189; Tubmanburg 14,089; Harbel 11,445.

## Vital statistics

*Birth rate* per 1,000 population (1984–89): 46.8 (world avg. 26.0).
*Death rate* per 1,000 population (1984–89): 12.6 (world avg. 9.9).
*Natural increase rate* per 1,000 population (1984–89): 34.2 (world avg. 16.1).
*Total fertility rate* (avg. births per childbearing woman; 1984–89): 6.9.
*Marriage rate* per 1,000 population: n.a.
*Divorce rate* per 1,000 population: n.a.
*Life expectancy* at birth (1984–89): male 53.9 years; female 56.3 years.
*Major causes of death* per 100,000 population[6] (1984): complications during pregnancy 632.6; malaria 123.5; anemia 76.0; pneumonia 74.4; measles 55.8; malnutrition 23.3.

## National economy

*Budget* (1986). Revenue: L$173,300,000 (income and profits taxes 28.7%; import duties and consular fees 24.6%; excise tax 12.5%; tax on foreign vessels 11.9%). Expenditures: L$272,000,000 (current expenditure 81.5%, of which wages and salaries 38.5%, interest on public debt 14.5%, goods and services 4.3%, subsidies and grants 2.0%; development expenditure 18.4%).
*Public debt* (external, outstanding; 1985): U.S.$879,300,000.
*Tourism:* n.a.
*Population economically active* (1984): total 669,330; activity rate of total population 31.8% (participation rates: ages 15–59, 62.9%; female [1981] 31.4%; unemployed 12.5%).

### Price and earnings indexes (1980 = 100)

| | 1980 | 1981 | 1982 | 1983 | 1984 | 1985 | 1986[7] |
|---|---|---|---|---|---|---|---|
| Consumer price index | 100.0 | 107.6 | 114.0 | 117.2 | 118.6 | 117.9 | 127.1 |
| Monthly earnings index | ... | ... | ... | ... | ... | ... | ... |

*Production* (metric tons except as noted). Agriculture, forestry, fishing (1985): cassava 320,000, rice 252,000, sugarcane 155,000, bananas 80,000, natural rubber 75,000, plantains 33,000, sweet potatoes 18,000, yams 18,000, green coffee 10,000, oranges 7,000, pineapples 7,000, cocoa beans 6,000; livestock (number of live animals) 238,000 sheep, 235,000 goats, 127,000 pigs, 42,000 cattle, 4,000,000 chickens; roundwood 4,262,000 cu m; fish catch (1984) 14,650. Mining and quarrying (1986): iron ore 14,600,000; diamonds 138,000 carats[8]; gold 4,867 troy oz[8]. Manufacturing (1982): cement 79,000; palm oil 20,000; cigarettes 20,000,000 units; beer 161,000 hectolitres[9]. Construction: n.a. Energy production (consumption): electricity (kW-hr; 1985) 904,000,000 (904,000,000); coal, none (n.a.); crude petroleum (barrels; 1985)

none (4,764,000); petroleum products (metric tons; 1985) 632,000 (507,000); natural gas, none (n.a.).
*Household income and expenditure.* Average household size (1980) 5.8; income per household: n.a.; sources of income: n.a.; expenditure (1963)[10]: food 34.4%, rent 14.9%, clothing and footwear 13.8%, household goods and services 6.1%, beverages and tobacco 5.7%, fuel and light 5.0%.
*Gross national product* (at current market prices; 1985): U.S.$1,050,000,000 (U.S.$470 per capita).

### Structure of gross domestic product and labour force

| | 1984 in value L$'000,000[11] | 1984 % of total value | 1984 labour force | 1984 % of labour force |
|---|---|---|---|---|
| Agriculture | 149.9 | 20.9 | 481,177 | 71.9 |
| Mining | 105.8 | 14.8 | 17,500 | 2.6 |
| Manufacturing | 59.4 | 8.3 | 10,699 | 1.6 |
| Construction | 26.3 | 3.7 | 4,072 | 0.6 |
| Public utilities | 28.7 | 4.0 | 2,878 | 0.4 |
| Transportation and communication | 50.6 | 7.1 | 13,986 | 2.1 |
| Trade | 60.5 | 8.5 | 46,850 | 7.0 |
| Finance | 105.4 | 14.7 | 2,117 | 0.3 |
| Pub. admin., defense | 122.5 | 17.1 ⎫ | 61,168 | 9.2 |
| Services | 31.6 | 4.4 ⎭ | | |
| Other | −24.7[12] | −3.5[12] | 28,883 | 4.3 |
| TOTAL | 716.0 | 100.0 | 669,330 | 100.0 |

*Land use* (1984): forested 39.0%; meadows and pastures 2.5%; agricultural and under permanent cultivation 3.9%; other 54.6%.

## Foreign trade

### Balance of trade (current prices)

| | 1980 | 1981 | 1982 | 1983 | 1984 | 1985 |
|---|---|---|---|---|---|---|
| L$'000,000 | +138.6 | +146.5 | +107.4 | +73.8 | +137.6 | +189.4 |
| % of total | 13.0% | 16.1% | 12.7% | 9.4% | 17.1% | 27.8% |

*Imports* (1985): L$284,460,000 (food and live animals 27.7%, machinery and transportation equipment 21.6%, petroleum and petroleum products 19.2%, basic manufactures 13.1%, chemicals 7.0%, miscellaneous manufactured articles 5.5%, beverages and tobacco 1.7%, animal and vegetable oils 1.6%). *Major import sources* (1983): United States 24.9%; West Germany 12.3%; The Netherlands 9.9%; Japan 8.1%; United Kingdom 5.2%; France 3.6%; China 3.3%; Denmark 2.3%; Belgium–Luxembourg 1.4%.
*Exports* (1985): L$435,660,000 (iron ore 64.1%, rubber 17.7%, coffee 6.3%, logs and timber 5.7%, cocoa 2.6%, diamonds 1.1%). *Major export destinations* (1983): West Germany 30.6%; United States 17.9%; Italy 17.6%; France 7.0%; The Netherlands 5.3%; Spain 4.9%; Belgium–Luxembourg 4.7%; United Kingdom 2.8%; Japan 1.5%.

## Transport and communications

*Transport.* Railroads[13] (1985): route length 304 mi, 490 km; short ton-mi cargo 2,056,000,000[14], metric ton-km cargo 3,002,000,000[14]. Roads (1984): total length 4,138 mi, 6,659 km (paved 7%). Vehicles (1984): passenger cars 12,747; trucks and buses 8,288. Merchant marine (1986): vessels (100 gross tons and over) 1,658; total deadweight tonnage 101,587,640. Air transport (1980): passenger-mi 10,600,000, passenger-km 17,000,000; short ton-mi cargo 68,000, metric ton-km cargo 100,000; airports (1987) with scheduled flights 8.
*Communications.* Daily newspapers (1986): total number 4; total circulation 282,500; circulation per 1,000 population 124. Radio (1986): total number of receivers 500,000 (1 per 4.6 persons). Television (1986): total number of receivers 42,000 (1 per 54 persons). Telephones (1984): 7,326[15] (1 per 291 persons).

## Education and health

### Education (1980)[16]

| | schools | teachers | students | student/ teacher ratio |
|---|---|---|---|---|
| Primary (age 6–12) | 1,232 | 9,099 | 227,431 | 25.0 |
| Secondary (age 13–18) | 419 | 1,129 | 51,666 | 45.8 |
| Voc., teacher tr. | 6 | 63 | 2,322 | 36.9 |
| Higher | 3 | 190 | 3,789 | 19.9 |

*Educational attainment,* n.a. *Literacy* (1984): total population age 15 and over literate 273,670 (22.4%); males literate 164,059 (27.4%); females literate 109,611 (18.4%).
*Health* (1981): physicians 236 (1 per 8,305 persons); hospital beds 3,000 (1 per 653 persons); infant mortality rate per 1,000 live births (1984–89) 122.0.
*Food* (1981–83): daily per capita caloric intake 2,368 (vegetable products 95%, animal products 5%); (1983) 102% of FAO recommended minimum requirement.

## Military

*Total active duty personnel* (1986): 6,750 (army 93.3%[17], navy 6.7%). *Military expenditure as percent of GNP* (1984): 2.3% (world 5.9%); per capita expenditure U.S.$10.

---

[1]New county created from Kru Coast and Sasstown territories and part of Maryland County. [2]Figures for Grand Kru included in Maryland. [3]New county created from Marshall and Gibi territories. [4]Detail does not add to total given because of rounding. [5]1984. [6]Hospital inpatient morbidity rates. [7]October. [8]1985. [9]1980. [10]Monrovia only. [11]At current factor cost. [12]Imputed bank service charges. [13]For iron-ore transport only. [14]Lamco and Bong Mining Company railroads only. [15]Number of subscribers. [16]1984 totals: schools 1,772; teachers 8,083; students 285,968; student/teacher ratio 35.4. [17]Army includes 250 air force personnel.

# Libya

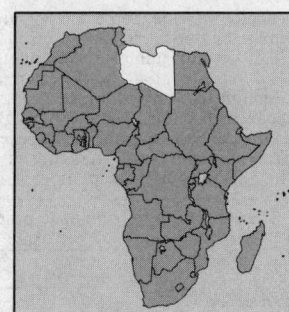

*Official name:* al-Jamāhīrīyah al-ʿArabīyah al-Lībīyah ash-Shaʿbīyah al-Ishtirākīyah (Socialist People's Libyan Arab Jamahiriya).
*Form of government:* socialist state with one policy-making body (General People's Congress [approx. 1,000]).
*Chief of state*[1]: Muʿammar al-Qadhdhafi.
*Head of government:* Secretary-general of the General People's Committee (premier).
*Capital:* Tripoli[2].
*Official language:* Arabic.
*Official religion:* Islam.
*Monetary unit:* 1 Libyan dinar (LD) = 1,000 dirhams; valuation (Oct. 5, 1987) 1 Libyan dinar = U.S.$3.33 = £2.04.

### Area and population

| Baladīyāt | Capitals | area sq mi | area sq km | population 1984 census |
|---|---|---|---|---|
| Ajdābiyā | Ajdābiyā | ... | ... | 100,547 |
| Awbāri | Awbāri | ... | ... | 48,701 |
| al-ʿAzīzīyah | al-ʿAzīzīyah | ... | ... | 85,068 |
| Banghāzi | Banghāzi | ... | ... | 485,386 |
| Darnah | Darnah | ... | ... | 105,031 |
| al-Fataḥ | al-Marj | ... | ... | 102,763 |
| Ghadamis | Ghadamis | ... | ... | 52,247 |
| Gharyān | Gharyān | ... | ... | 117,073 |
| al-Jabal al-Akhḍar | al-Baydāʾ | ... | ... | 120,662 |
| al-Khums | al-Khums | ... | ... | 149,642 |
| al-Kufrah | al-Kufrah | ... | ... | 25,139 |
| Marzuq | Marzuq | ... | ... | 42,294 |
| Miṣrātah | Miṣrātah | ... | ... | 178,295 |
| Niqāt al-Khums | Zuwārah | ... | ... | 181,584 |
| Sabhā | Sabhā | ... | ... | 76,171 |
| Sawfajjin | Bani Walīd | ... | ... | 45,195 |
| ash-Shāṭi | Birāk | ... | ... | 46,749 |
| Surt | Surt | ... | ... | 110,996 |
| Ṭarābulus | Tripoli (Ṭarābulus) | ... | ... | 990,697 |
| Tarhunah | Tarhunah | ... | ... | 84,640 |
| Ṭubruq | Ṭubruq | ... | ... | 94,006 |
| Yafran | Yafran | ... | ... | 73,420 |
| az-Zāwiyah | az-Zāwiyah | ... | ... | 220,075 |
| Zlīṭan | Zlīṭan | ... | ... | 101,107 |
| TOTAL | | 685,524 | 1,775,500 | 3,637,488 |

## Demography

*Population* (1987): 4,132,000.
*Density* (1987): persons per sq mi 6.0, persons per sq km 2.3.
*Urban–rural* (1985): urban 64.5%; rural 35.5%.
*Sex distribution* (1985): male 52.72%; female 47.28%.
*Age breakdown* (1985): under 15, 45.0%; 15–29, 25.6%; 30–44, 17.2%; 45–59, 8.4%; 60–74, 3.2%; 75 and over, 0.6%.
*Population projection:* (1990) 4,710,000; (2000) 7,292,000.
*Doubling time:* 20 years.
*Ethnic composition* (1983): Libyan Arab 83.8%; Egyptian and Tunisian 6.9%; Berber 5.2%; other 4.1%.
*Religious affiliation* (1982): Sunnī Muslim 97.0%; other 3.0%.
*Major cities* (1979): Tripoli 587,400; Banghāzī 267,700; Miṣrātah 52,200.

## Vital statistics

*Birth rate* per 1,000 population (1980–85): 47.3 (world avg. 29.0).
*Death rate* per 1,000 population (1980–85): 12.7 (world avg. 11.0).
*Natural increase rate* per 1,000 population (1980–85): 34.6 (world avg. 18.0).
*Total fertility rate* (avg. births per childbearing woman; 1980–85): 7.4.
*Marriage rate* per 1,000 population (1981): 4.3[3].
*Divorce rate* per 1,000 population (1981): 1.1[3].
*Life expectancy* at birth (1980–85): male 56.6 years; female 60.0 years.
*Major causes of death* per 100,000 population: n.a.; however, major diseases include trachoma, tuberculosis, malaria, and dysentery.

## National economy

*Budget* (1987). Revenue and expenditure: LD 4,060,000,000 (development expenditures 34.5%, trade 33.7%, current spending 30.5%).
*Public debt* (external, outstanding; 1982): U.S.$844,000,000.
*Production* (metric tons except as noted). Agriculture, forestry, fishing (1985): tomatoes 245,000, wheat 149,000, watermelons 140,000, olives 128,000, roots and tubers 110,000, potatoes 110,000, dates 100,000, onions 85,000, barley 80,000, oranges 70,000, grapes 20,000, pulses 11,000; livestock (number of live animals) 5,500,000 sheep, 900,000 goats, 200,000 cattle, 170,000 camels, 60,000 asses; roundwood (1984) 633,000 cu m; fish catch (1984) 7,800. Mining and quarrying (1985): gypsum 180,000; salt 12,000. Manufacturing (1985): lime 270,000,000; cement 4,600,000; urea 668,300; ammonia 495,000; methanol 495,000; ethylene 247,500; asphalt 150,000; crude steel 10,000. Construction (gross value in LD; 1981): residential 61,671,000; nonresidential 256,904,000. Energy production (consumption): electricity (kW-hr; 1985) 8,170,000,000 (8,170,000,000); coal (metric tons; 1985) none (1,000); crude petroleum (barrels; 1985) 375,277,000 (60,195,000); petroleum products (metric tons; 1985) 6,430,000 (6,162,000); natural gas (cu m; 1985) 3,997,812,000 (2,863,587,000).

*Gross national product* (at current market prices; 1985): U.S.$27,000,000,000 (U.S.$7,130 per capita).

### Structure of gross domestic product and labour force

| | 1984 in value LD '000,000 | 1984 % of total value | 1985 labour force | 1985 % of labour force |
|---|---|---|---|---|
| Agriculture | 266.4 | 3.6 | 178,000 | 16.8 |
| Mining | 3,039.1 | 40.4 | 24,500 | 2.3 |
| Manufacturing | 359.9 | 4.8 | 112,000 | 10.5 |
| Construction | 819.5 | 10.9 | 256,500 | 24.2 |
| Public utilities | 92.0 | 1.2 | 25,500 | 2.4 |
| Transportation and communication | 392.5 | 5.2 | 93,000 | 8.7 |
| Trade | 554.5 | 7.4 | 41,000 | 3.9 |
| Finance | 273.5 | 3.6 | 13,000 | 1.2 |
| Pub. admin., defense | 1,395.5 | 18.6 | 69,000 | 6.5 |
| Services | 84.7 | 1.1 | 183,500 | 17.3 |
| Other | 244.1 | 3.2 | 66,000 | 6.2 |
| TOTAL | 7,521.7 | 100.0 | 1,062,000 | 100.0 |

*Tourism* (1984): receipts from visitors U.S.$2,000,000; expenditures by nationals abroad U.S.$494,000,000.
*Population economically active* (1985): total 1,062,000; activity rate of total population 29.3% (participation rates: working age, n.a.; female 9.4%; unemployed, n.a.).

### Price and earnings indexes (1975 = 100)

| | 1973 | 1974 | 1975 | 1976 | 1977 | 1978 | 1979 |
|---|---|---|---|---|---|---|---|
| Consumer price index | 85.3 | 91.6 | 100.0 | 105.4 | 112.1 | 145.0 | 137.1 |
| Monthly earnings index | ... | ... | ... | ... | ... | ... | ... |

*Household income and expenditure.* Average household size (1980) 5.1; income per household: n.a.; sources of income: n.a.; expenditure (1977): food 37.2%, housing 32.2%, transportation 9.4%, education and recreation 8.5%, clothing 6.9%, medical care 3.3%.
*Land use* (1984): forested 0.4%; meadows and pastures 7.6%; agricultural and under permanent cultivation 1.2%; desert and built-up areas 90.8%.

## Foreign trade

### Balance of trade (current prices)

| | 1980 | 1981 | 1982 | 1983 | 1984 | 1985 |
|---|---|---|---|---|---|---|
| LD '000,000 | +4,674 | +2,238 | +1,894 | +1,348 | +1,486.2 | +1,790.5 |
| % of total | 56.3% | 32.0% | 29.8% | 25.9% | 69.4% | 38.3% |

*Imports* (1982): LD 2,124,323,000 (machinery and transport equipment 36.8%, consumer goods 27.1%, food and live animals 14.2%, chemicals 3.9%, animal and vegetable oil and fats 1.3%). *Major import sources* (1984): Italy 26.6%; West Germany 12.9%; Japan 6.6%; United Kingdom 5.3%; Austria 1.6%.
*Exports* (1982): LD 4,131,000,000 (crude petroleum 99.9%). *Major export destinations* (1984): Italy 24.0%; West Germany 19.0%; Spain 9.2%; Switzerland 3.8%; The Netherlands 3.5%; United Kingdom 1.8%.

## Transport and communications

*Transport.* Railroads: none. Roads (1984): total length 15,954 mi, 25,675 km (paved 56%). Vehicles (1982): passenger cars 415.509; trucks and buses 334,405. Merchant marine (1986): vessels (100 gross tons and over) 104; total deadweight tonnage 1,459,615. Air transport[4] (1985): passenger-mi 1,139,000,000, passenger-km 1,672,000,000; short ton-mi cargo 3,700,000, metric ton-km cargo 5,400,000; airports (1987) with scheduled flights 9.
*Communications.* Daily newspapers (1986): total number 1; circulation 40,000; circulation per 1,000 population 10. Radio (1986): total number of receivers 500,000 (1 per 8.0 persons). Television (1986): total number of receivers 235,300 (1 per 17 persons). Telephones (1976): 59,000 (1 per 42.0 persons).

## Education and health

### Education (1982–83)

| | schools | teachers | students | student/ teacher ratio |
|---|---|---|---|---|
| Primary (age 6–12) | 2,744 | 42,202 | 741,502 | 17.6 |
| Secondary (age 13–18) | 1,555 | 25,044 | 301,415 | 12.0 |
| Voc., teacher tr. | 195 | 3,883 | 50,363 | 12.9 |
| Higher[5] | 8 | 1,340[6] | 25,700 | ... |

*Educational attainment* (1973). Percent of population age 25 and over having: no formal schooling (illiterate) 72.7%; ability to read and write 18.8%; primary education 3.5%; secondary 4.0%; higher 1.0%. *Literacy* (1985): total population age 10 and over literate 2,701,446 (74.4%); males literate 1,666,170 (85.0%); females literate 1,035,276 (62.0%).
*Health* (1982): physicians 5,210[7] (1 per 637 persons); hospital beds 16,051 (1 per 207 persons); infant mortality rate per 1,000 live births (1980–85) 107.0.
*Food* (1981–83): daily per capita caloric intake 3,678 (vegetable products 84%, animal products 16%); (1983) 155% of FAO recommended minimum requirement.

## Military

*Total active duty personnel* (1986): 71,500 (army 76.9%, navy 9.1%, air force 14.0%). *Military expenditure as percent of GNP* (1984): 17.8% (world 5.9%); per capita expenditure U.S.$1,408.

---

[1]No formal titled office exists. [2]Al-Jufur, designated new capital on Jan. 1, 1986, is located 650 km south of Tripoli. [3]Incomplete. [4]International scheduled flights only. [5]1981–82. [6]1979–80. [7]Personnel in government services only.

# Liechtenstein

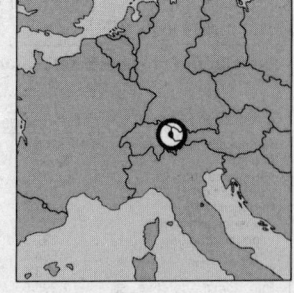

*Official name:* Fürstentum
Liechtenstein (Principality of
Liechtenstein).
*Form of government:* constitutional
monarchy with one legislative house
(Diet [15]).
*Chief of state:* Prince.
*Head of government:* Head of the
Government.
*Capital:* Vaduz.
*Official language:* German.
*Official religion:* none.
*Monetary unit:* 1 Swiss franc
(Sw F) = 100 centimes; valuation (Oct.
5, 1987) 1 U.S.$ = Sw F 1.53;
1 £ = Sw F 2.49.

### Area and population

| Communes | area | | population 1986 estimate |
|---|---|---|---|
| | sq mi | sq km | |
| Balzers | 7.6 | 19.6 | 3,477 |
| Eschen | 4.0 | 10.3 | 2,844 |
| Gamprin | 2.4 | 6.1 | 907 |
| Mauren | 2.9 | 7.5 | 2,713 |
| Planken | 2.0 | 5.3 | 290 |
| Ruggell | 2.9 | 7.4 | 1,362 |
| Schaan | 10.4 | 26.8 | 4,757 |
| Schellenberg | 1.4 | 3.5 | 672 |
| Triesen | 10.2 | 26.4 | 3,180 |
| Triesenberg | 11.5 | 29.8 | 2,277 |
| Vaduz | 6.7 | 17.3 | 4,920 |
| TOTAL | 61.8[1] | 160.0 | 27,399 |

## Demography

*Population* (1987): 27,490.
*Density* (1987): persons per sq mi 444.8, persons per sq km 171.8.
*Urban–rural:* n.a.
*Sex distribution* (1986): male 48.89%; female 51.11%.
*Age breakdown* (1986): under 15, 20.1%; 15–29, 26.7%; 30–44, 25.3%; 45–59,
14.3%; 60–74, 9.8%; 75 and over, 3.8%.
*Population projection:* (1990) 28,300; (2000) 31,000.
*Doubling time:* not applicable; doubling time exceeds 100 years.
*Ethnic composition* (1986): Liechtensteiner 63.5%; Swiss 15.6%; Austrian
7.9%; German 4.0%; other 9.0%.
*Religious affiliation* (1986): Roman Catholic 87.1%; Protestant 8.6%; other
4.3%.
*Major cities* (1986): Vaduz 4,920; Schaan 4,757.

## Vital statistics

*Birth rate* per 1,000 population (1986): 12.8 (world avg. 26.0); legitimate
93.4%; illegitimate 6.6%.
*Death rate* per 1,000 population (1986): 6.7 (world avg. 9.9).
*Natural increase rate* per 1,000 population (1986): 6.1 (world avg. 16.1).
*Total fertility rate:* n.a.
*Marriage rate* per 1,000 population (1986): 10.8.
*Divorce rate* per 1,000 population (1984): 7.3.
*Life expectancy* at birth (1980–84): male 77.6 years; female 82.6 years.
*Major causes of death* per 100,000 population (1986): diseases of the circu-
latory system 229.9, of which heart disease 127.7 (including ischemic heart
disease 54.7); malignant neoplasms (cancers) 171.5; accidents, poisonings,
and acts of violence 54.7; diseases of the respiratory system 32.8.

## National economy

*Budget* (1986). Revenue: Sw F 337,257,584 (taxes and interest 69.6%; post,
telephone, and telegraph 17.6%; other revenue sources include real estate capital-gains taxes and death and estate taxes). Expenditures: Sw F
311,604,845 (financial affairs 45.0%; education 13.7%; post, telephone, and
telegraph 13.4%; social affairs 9.8%).
*Public debt:* none.
*Tourism* (1986): 76,440 tourist arrivals; receipts from visitors, n.a.; expenditures by nationals abroad, n.a.
*Population economically active* (1986): total 13,112; activity rate of total
population 47.9% (participation rates: ages 15–64, 67.6%; female 35.6%;
unemployed 0.3%).

### Price and earnings indexes (December 1982 = 100)

| | 1980 | 1981 | 1982 | 1983 | 1984 | 1985 | 1986 |
|---|---|---|---|---|---|---|---|
| Consumer price index[2] | 87.1 | 92.8 | 98.0 | 100.9 | 103.8 | 107.4 | 108.2 |
| Monthly earnings index | ... | ... | ... | ... | ... | ... | ... |

*Household income and expenditure.* Average household size (1980) 3.0;
income per household: n.a.; sources of earned income (1986): wages and
salaries 92.9%, self-employment 7.1%; expenditure (1985)[3]: food 21.2%,
rent 17.4%, education and self-improvement 16.5%, transportation 13.8%,
health 7.3%, clothing 6.3%.
*Production* (metric tons except as noted). Agriculture, forestry, fishing
(1986): silo corn (maize) 29,400, milk 13,339, potatoes 1,194, barley 480,
wheat 360; livestock (number of live animals; 1987) 6,487 cattle, 2,606
pigs, 2,337 sheep; commercial timber (1985) 8,413 cu m. Mining and
quarrying: n.a. Manufacturing (1986): whipped cream 1,449; yogurt 56;

cheese 8; wine 100,242 kilograms; small-scale precision manufacturing
includes optical lenses, electron microscopes, electronic equipment, and
high-vacuum pumps; metal manufacturing is also important. Construction
(1985): residential 202,105 cu m; nonresidential 376,836 cu m. Energy production (consumption): electricity (kW-hr; 1985) 47,125,000 (171,234,000);
coal (metric tons; 1985) none (123); petroleum products (metric tons; 1985)
none (45,595); natural gas (metric tons; 1985) none (2,610,000).
*Gross national product* (at current market prices; 1985): *c.* U.S.$450,000,000
(*c.* U.S.$16,500 per capita).

### Structure of gross domestic product and labour force

| | 1980 | | 1987[4] | |
|---|---|---|---|---|
| | in value Sw F '000 | % of total value | labour force | % of labour force |
| Agriculture | ... | ... | 367 | 2.8 |
| Mining | ... | ... | 58 | 0.4 |
| Manufacturing | ... | ... | 4,483 | 34.2 |
| Construction | ... | ... | 1,060 | 8.1 |
| Public utilities | ... | ... | 129 | 1.0 |
| Transportation and communication | ... | ... | 395 | 3.0 |
| Trade | ... | ... | 1,619 | 12.3 |
| Finance | ... | ... | 826 | 6.3 |
| Pub. admin., defense | ... | ... | 615 | 4.7 |
| Services | ... | ... | 3,284 | 25.0 |
| Other | ... | ... | 276[5] | 2.1[5] |
| TOTAL | 876,000 | 100.0 | 13,112 | 100.0[1] |

*Land use* (1987): forested 34.8%; meadows and pastures 15.7%; agricultural
and under permanent cultivation 24.3%; other 25.2%.

## Foreign trade

### Balance of trade (current prices)

| | 1980 | 1981 | 1982 | 1983 | 1984 | 1985 |
|---|---|---|---|---|---|---|
| Sw F '000,000 | +454.6 | +531.9 | +523.5 | +560.7 | +625.4 | +755.6 |
| % of total | 34.1% | 38.6% | 39.3% | 41.6% | 41.8% | 46.4% |

*Imports* (1985): Sw F 436,475,000 (machinery and transport equipment
33.2%; hardware 14.6%; unrefined and semifabricated metal 5.7%; limestone, cement, and other building materials 5.4%; chemical products 5.1%;
food, beverages, and tobacco 2.4%, of which fruits and vegetables 0.9%;
wood and cork 1.3%). *Major import sources:* n.a.
*Exports* (1985): Sw F 1,192,054,000 (machinery and transport equipment
45.2%; other finished goods 23.6%; hardware 21.2%; chemical products
6.2%; limestone, cement, and other building materials 2.4%). *Major export
destinations:* European Economic Community countries 33.5%; Switzerland 20.0%; other European Free Trade Association countries 7.5%.

## Transport and communications

*Transport.* Railroads (1987): length 11.5 mi, 18.5 km; passenger and cargo
traffic, n.a. Roads (1986): total length 201 mi, 323 km. Vehicles (1986):
passenger cars 14,452; trucks and buses 1,634. Merchant marine: none. Air
transport: none.
*Communications.* Daily newspapers (1987): total number 2; total circulation
15,000; circulation per 1,000 population 546. Radio (1986): total number
of receivers 9,218 (1 per 3.0 persons). Television (1986): total number of
receivers 8,674 (1 per 3.1 persons). Telephones (1986): 26,529 (1 per 1.0
persons).

## Education and health

### Education (1987–88)

| | schools | teachers | students | student/ teacher ratio |
|---|---|---|---|---|
| Primary (age 7–12) | 14 | 102 | 1,754 | 17.2 |
| Secondary (age 13–19) | 9 | 98 | 1,707 | 17.4 |
| Vocational[6] | 1 | 30[7] | 117[7] | ... |

*Educational attainment,* n.a.; 9 years of formal education are compulsory,
however. *Literacy:* virtually 100%.
*Health* (1985): physicians 22 (1 per 1,222 persons); hospital beds 100 (1 per
269 persons); infant mortality rate per 1,000 live births (1984) 7.4.
*Food* (1981–83)[8]: daily per capita caloric intake 3,490 (vegetable products
61%, animal products 39%); (1983) 129% of FAO recommended minimum requirement.

## Military

*Total active duty personnel:* none. *Military expenditure as percent of GNP:*
none.

---

[1]Detail does not add to total given because of rounding. [2]The index is for Switzerland,
which is united with Liechtenstein in a customs and monetary union. [3]Household
expenditures are taken from a 1985 Swiss sample survey; a similarity of consumption
patterns is assumed. [4]January 1. [5]Includes 43 unemployed persons. [6]One evening
school with part-time teachers. [7]1986–87. [8]Figures are derived from statistics for
Switzerland and Austria.

# Luxembourg

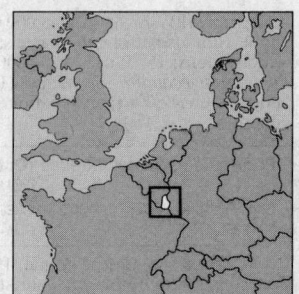

*Official name:* Grand-Duché de Luxembourg (French); Grossherzogtum Luxemburg (German) (Grand Duchy of Luxembourg).
*Form of government:* constitutional monarchy with one legislative house (Chamber of Deputies [64]).
*Chief of state:* Grand Duke.
*Head of government:* Prime Minister.
*Capital:* Luxembourg.
*Official languages:* French; German.
*Official religion:* none.
*Monetary unit:* 1 Luxembourg franc (LFr., plural LFr.) = 100 centimes; valuation (Oct. 5, 1987) 1 U.S.$ = LFr. 38.24; 1 £ = LFr. 62.10.

### Area and population

| Districts Cantons | area sq mi | area sq km | population 1986 estimate[1] |
|---|---|---|---|
| Diekirch | 447 | 1,157 | 54,420 |
| Clervaux | 128 | 332 | 9,710 |
| Diekirch | 92 | 239 | 22,390 |
| Redange | 103 | 267 | 10,500 |
| Vianden | 21 | 54 | 2,790 |
| Wiltz | 102 | 265 | 9,030 |
| Grevenmacher | 203 | 525 | 40,030 |
| Echternach | 72 | 186 | 10,990 |
| Grevenmacher | 82 | 211 | 16,910 |
| Remich | 49 | 128 | 12,130 |
| Luxembourg | 349 | 904 | 272,250 |
| Capellen | 77 | 199 | 28,790 |
| Esch | 94 | 243 | 112,250 |
| Luxembourg (Ville et Campagne) | 92 | 238 | 113,570 |
| Mersch | 86 | 224 | 17,640 |
| TOTAL | 999 | 2,586 | 366,700 |

## Demography

*Population* (1987): 367,000.
*Density* (1987): persons per sq mi 367.4, persons per sq km 141.9.
*Urban-rural* (1985): urban 77.6%; rural 22.4%.
*Sex distribution* (1986): male 48.64%; female 51.36%.
*Age breakdown* (1985): under 15, 17.3%; 15–29, 23.6%; 30–44, 21.9%; 45–59, 19.0%; 60–74, 12.6%; 75 and over, 5.6%.
*Population projection:* (1990) 368,500; (2000) 372,200.
*Doubling time:* n.a.; doubling time exceeds 100 years.
*Ethnic composition* (1986): Luxemburger 70.3%; Portuguese 8.6%; Italian 5.9%; French 4.0%; German 2.8%; other 8.4%.
*Religious affiliation* (1980): Roman Catholic 93.0%; Protestant 1.3%; other 5.7%.
*Major cities[2]* (1986): Luxembourg 86,200; Esch-sur-Alzette 24,900; Differdange 16,450; Dudelange 14,080.

## Vital statistics

*Birth rate* per 1,000 population (1985): 11.2 (world avg. 29.0); (1985) legitimate 91.3%; illegitimate 8.7%.
*Death rate* per 1,000 population (1985): 11.0 (world avg. 11.0).
*Natural increase rate* per 1,000 population (1985): 0.2 (world avg. 18.0).
*Total fertility rate* (avg. births per childbearing woman; 1985): 1.4.
*Marriage rate* per 1,000 population (1985): 5.3.
*Divorce rate* per 1,000 population (1985): 1.8.
*Life expectancy* at birth (1980–82): male 70.0 years; female 76.7 years.
*Major causes of death* per 100,000 population (1985): circulatory diseases 533.1, of which cerebrovascular disease 187.3, ischemic heart disease 179.6; malignant neoplasms (cancers) 272.2; accidents and suicides 69.8, of which suicide 15.0.

## National economy

*Budget* (1986). Revenue: LFr. 78,625,858,000 (income and excise taxes 51.7%, customs taxes 11.6%). Expenditures[3]: LFr. 78,280,400,000 (social security 24.8%, transport and power 20.2%, education and arts 12.8%, debt service 12.2%, administration 7.7%, defense 2.8%).
*Public debt* (1986): U.S.$374,230,000.
*Tourism:* Number of tourist arrivals 447,600[4].
*Production* (metric tons except as noted). Agriculture, forestry, fishing (1985): barley 61,196, oats 31,820, potatoes 29,088, wheat 28,324; livestock (number of live animals) 223,108 cattle, 69,954 pigs; roundwood (1984) 336,000 cu m. Mining and quarrying (1984): metal ores, none; nonmetals 10,465,-000, of which stone 4,460,000, sand and gravel 3,900,000, gypsum 450,000. Manufacturing (1985): steel ingots and castings 3,945,275; finished rolled products 3,878,295; pig iron 2,753,800; meat products 20,535, of which beef and veal 14,005, pork 6,530; wine 107,000 hectolitres. Construction (1984): residential and semiresidential 331,192 sq m; nonresidential 126,238 sq m. Energy production (consumption): electricity (kW-hr; 1985) 939,045,000 (3,873,097,000); coal (metric tons; 1985) none (199,000); crude petroleum, none (n.a.); petroleum products (metric tons; 1985) none (1,072,924); natural gas (cu m; 1985) none (344,856,000).
*Gross national product* (at current market prices; 1985): U.S.$4,900,000,000 (U.S.$13,380 per capita).

### Structure of gross domestic product and labour force

| | 1985 in value LFr. '000,000 | % of total value | labour force | % of labour force |
|---|---|---|---|---|
| Agriculture | 6,270 | 2.6 | 6,900 | 4.2 |
| Mining | 240 | 0.1 | | |
| Manufacturing | 71,600 | 29.7 | 38,500 | 23.5 |
| Construction | 12,780 | 5.3 | 13,600 | 8.3 |
| Public utilities | 6,030 | 2.5 | 1,400 | 0.9 |
| Transp. and commun. | 13,500 | 5.6 | 10,700 | 6.5 |
| Trade | 38,570 | 16.0 | 55,100 | 33.7 |
| Finance | 32,300 | 13.4 | 11,000 | 6.7 |
| Pub. admin., defense | 28,210 | 11.7 | 19,400 | 11.9 |
| Services | 31,580 | 13.1 | 4,400 | 2.7 |
| Other | ... | ... | 2,600[5] | 1.6[5] |
| TOTAL | 241,075[6] | 100.0 | 163,600 | 100.0 |

*Population economically active* (1985): total 163,600; activity rate of total population 44.6% (participation rates: ages 15–64 [1981] 61.3%; female 34.1%; unemployed 1.6%).

### Price and earnings indexes (1980 = 100)

| | 1981 | 1982 | 1983 | 1984 | 1985 | 1986 | 1987[7] |
|---|---|---|---|---|---|---|---|
| Consumer price index | 109.3 | 118.2 | 128.4 | 135.7 | 141.2 | 141.6 | 141.7 |
| Hourly earnings index[8] | 104.6 | 116.9 | 127.6 | 137.6 | ... | ... | ... |

*Household income and expenditure.* Average household size (1982) 2.8; income per household LFr. 751,800 (U.S.$16,455); sources of income (1985): wages and salaries 88.1%, self-employment 9.4%, transfer payments 2.5%; expenditure (1984): food and beverages 18.1%, transportation and communication 17.8%, housing 17.3%, household goods and furniture 7.8%, health 7.1%, clothing and footwear 6.6%.
*Land use* (1984): forested 31.7%; meadows and pastures 27.3%; agricultural and under permanent cultivation 21.6%; other 19.4%.

## Foreign trade

### Balance of trade (current prices)

| | 1980 | 1981 | 1982 | 1983 | 1984 | 1985 |
|---|---|---|---|---|---|---|
| LFr. '000,000 | −12,704 | −17,192 | −15,868 | −16,492 | −14,503 | −9,093 |
| % of total | 6.7% | 8.8% | 7.2% | 6.9% | 4.7% | 2.6% |

*Imports* (1985): LFr. 177,137,000,000 (metal products, machinery, and transport equipment 38.0%, of which electrical machinery 12.5%, transport equipment 8.0%; mineral products 17.5%; chemical products 9.5%; food, beverages, and tobacco 6.0%). *Major import sources:* Belgium 36.9%; West Germany 29.3%; France 11.9%; The Netherlands 4.8%; United States 3.2%; Italy 2.4%.
*Exports* (1985): LFr. 168,044,000,000 (metal products, machinery, and transport equipment 62.2%, of which electrical machinery 8.7%; plastic materials and rubber manufactures 12.8%; textile yarn, fabrics, and related products 5.0%; chemical products 5.0%; food, beverages, and tobacco 2.0%). *Major export destinations:* West Germany 26.5%; Belgium 17.1%; France 13.5%; The Netherlands 6.1%; United States 5.5%; United Kingdom 4.8%; Italy 3.6%.

## Transport and communications

*Transport.* Railroads (1986): route length 168 mi, 270 km; passenger-mi 171,000,000, passenger-km 276,000,000; short ton-mi cargo 411,000,000, metric ton-km cargo 600,000,000. Roads (1985): total length 3,209 mi, 5,164 km (paved 99%). Vehicles (1986): passenger cars 156,048; trucks and buses 14,108. Merchant marine: vessels (100 gross tons and over) n.a.; total deadweight tonnage, n.a. Air transport (1985): passenger arrivals 398,019, departures 399,479; cargo loaded and unloaded 70,378 metric tons; airports (1987) with scheduled flights 1.
*Communications.* Daily newspapers (1984): total number 6; total circulation 130,000; circulation per 1,000 population 365. Radio (1985): 228,000 receivers (1 per 1.6 persons). Television (1985): 91,300 receivers (1 per 4.0 persons). Telephones (1985): 151,525 (1 per 2.4 persons).

## Education and health

### Education (1985–86)

| | schools | teachers | students | student/ teacher ratio |
|---|---|---|---|---|
| Primary (age 6–15) | ... | 1,713 | 24,183 | 14.1 |
| Secondary (age 12–18) | ... | 3,482[10,11] | 8,584[9] | ... |
| Voc., teacher tr. | ... | | 16,507[9] | ... |
| Higher | ... | | 934[9] | ... |

*Educational attainment,* n.a. *Literacy* (1985): virtually 100% literate.
*Health* (1985): physicians 663 (1 per 553 persons); hospital beds 4,587 (1 per 80 persons); infant mortality rate per 1,000 live births 9.0.
*Food* (1981–83): daily per capita caloric intake[12] 3,679; (vegetable products 60%, animal products 40%); (1983) 139% of FAO recommended minimum requirement.

## Military

*Total active duty personnel* (1986): 690 (army 100.0%). *Military expenditure as percent of GNP* (1984): 0.9% (world 5.9%); per capita expenditure U.S.$106.

[1]January 1. [2]From country register. [3]Percentage breakdown is for 1984 expenditure of LFr. 73,607,500,000. [4]Hotel arrivals; excludes an equivalent number of campers. [5]Unemployed only. [6]Detail does not add to total given because of rounding. [7] March. [8]Manufacturing only. [9]1984–85. [10]1982–83. [11]Includes part-time teachers. [12]Figures for Belgium–Luxembourg.

# Macau

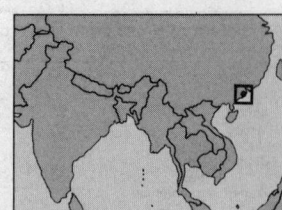

*Official name:* Macau.
*Political status:* overseas territory
(Portugal).
*Head of state and government:*
Governor (appointed).
*Capital:* Macau.
*Official language:* Portuguese.
*Official religion:* Roman Catholicism.
*Monetary unit:* 1 pataca[1] = 100 avos;
valuation (Oct. 5, 1987)
1 U.S.$ = 8.04 patacas; 1 £ = 13.05
patacas.

### Area and population

| Districts | Capital | area | | population |
|---|---|---|---|---|
| | | sq mi | sq km | 1986 estimate |
| **Parishes** | | | | |
| Marine Area | — | — | — | ... |
| Islands | | 4.2 | 10.9 | 10,200 |
| São Francisco Xavier (Coloane) | — | 2.7 | 7.1 | 3,700 |
| Nossa Senhora Carmo (Taipa) | — | 1.5 | 3.8 | 6,500 |
| Macau | Macau | 2.4 | 6.1 | 416,200 |
| Santo António | — | ... | ... | ... |
| São Lázaro | — | ... | ... | ... |
| São Lourenço | — | ... | ... | ... |
| Sé | — | ... | ... | ... |
| Nossa Senhora Fátima | — | ... | ... | ... |
| TOTAL | | 6.5[2] | 16.9[2] | 426,400 |

## Demography

*Population* (1987): 452,000.
*Density* (1987): persons per sq mi 69,538, persons per sq km 26,746.
*Urban–rural* (1981): urban 94.9%[3].
*Sex distribution* (1986): male 51.74%; female 48.26%.
*Age breakdown* (1986): under 15, 24.7%; 15–29, 32.2%; 30–44, 24.8%; 45–59, 9.7%; 60 and over, 8.6%.
*Population projection:* (1990) 539,000; (2000) 837,000.
*Doubling time:* 48 years.
*Nationality* (1981): Chinese 73.5%; Portuguese 20.3%; English 0.9%; other 5.3%.
*Religious affiliation* (1984): Buddhist and Taoist 69.9%; Roman Catholic 6.2%; nonreligious 14.1%; other 9.8%.
*Major city* (1986): Macau 416,200.

## Vital statistics

*Birth rate* per 1,000 population (1986): 17.9 (world avg. 26.0); legitimate, n.a.; illegitimate, n.a.
*Death rate* per 1,000 population (1986): 3.2 (world avg. 9.9).
*Natural increase rate* per 1,000 population (1986): 14.7 (world avg. 11.1).
*Total fertility rate* (avg. births per childbearing woman; 1980–85): 3.8.
*Marriage rate* per 1,000 population (1986): 6.8.
*Divorce rate* per 1,000 population (1986): 0.1.
*Life expectancy* at birth (1979): male 68.0 years; female 73.0 years.
*Major causes of death* per 100,000 population (1986): diseases of the circulatory system 36.5; malignant neoplasms (cancers) 21.1; diseases of the respiratory system 11.9.

## National economy

*Budget* (1986). Revenue: 2,237,090,000 patacas (gambling revenue 41.1%, direct taxes 12.9%, indirect taxes 9.7%). Expenditures: 2,063,500,000 patacas (1983; security forces 14.1%, health and social welfare 4.6%, education 4.0%).
*Gross national product* (at current market prices; 1985): U.S.$1,030,000,000 (U.S.$2,680 per capita).

### Structure of labour force

| | 1981 | |
|---|---|---|
| | labour force | % of labour force |
| Agriculture | 7,551 | 6.0 |
| Mining | 71 | 0.1 |
| Manufacturing | 56,304 | 45.0 |
| Construction | 9,937 | 7.9 |
| Public utilities | 876 | 0.7 |
| Transportation and communication | 5,776 | 4.6 |
| Trade | 14,134 | 11.3 |
| Finance | 2,191 | 1.8 |
| Public administration | 4,056 | 3.2 |
| Services | 8,714 | 7.0 |
| Other | 15,450 | 12.4 |
| TOTAL | 125,060 | 100.0 |

*Production* (metric tons except as noted). Agriculture, forestry, and fishing (1985): grapes 5,000, eggs 625; livestock (number of live animals) 8,000 cattle, 6,000 pigs; fish catch 12,400. Mining and quarrying (1982): granite 656,920. Manufacturing (1983): clothing 27,184; knitwear 13,230; meat 9,021; furniture 2,335; wine 796; explosive and pyrotechnic products 586; footwear 376; optical materials 312. Construction (1986): residential 294,-300 sq m; nonresidential 375,000 sq m. Energy production (consumption):

electricity (kW-hr; 1985) 445,000,000 (492,000,000); coal (metric tons; 1985) none (none); petroleum (barrels; 1981) none (2,559); petroleum products (metric tons; 1985) none (204,000); natural gas, none (n.a.).
*Population economically active* (1981): total 127,359; activity rate of total population 42.7% (participation rates: over age 10, 61.5%; female 37.1%; unemployed 2.4%).

### Price and earnings indexes (Oct. 1982–Sept. 1983 = 100)

| | 1983[4] | 1984[4] | 1985[4] | 1986 |
|---|---|---|---|---|
| Consumer price index | 100 | 112.2 | 115.9 | 118.5 |
| Earnings index | ... | ... | ... | ... |

*Public debt* (long-term, external, 1985): U.S.$91,000,000.
*Tourism* (1986): number of tourist arrivals 4,238,300.
*Household income and expenditure.* Average household size (1980): 4.8; income per household: n.a.; sources of income: n.a.; expenditure (1982–83): food 42.0%, rent 21.2%, education, health, and other services 8.1%, clothing and footwear 7.3%, transportation 4.9%.
*Land use* (1979): forested 50.0%; agricultural and under permanent cultivation 4.0%; built-on area, wasteland, and other 46.0%.

## Foreign trade

### Balance of trade (current prices)

| | 1981 | 1982 | 1983 | 1984 | 1985 | 1986 |
|---|---|---|---|---|---|---|
| '000,000 patacas | −112.2 | +38.5 | +250.3 | +919.4 | +1,002 | +1,312 |
| % of total | −1.4% | 0.4% | 2.3% | 6.7% | 7.5% | 8.2% |

*Imports* (1986): 7,318,200,000 patacas (industrial raw materials 65.3%, nonedible consumer goods 12.7%, capital goods 10.0%, food and beverages 6.7%, fuels and lubricants 5.2%). *Major import sources:* Hong Kong 45.9%; China 19.7%; Japan 9.9%; European Economic Community 6.6%; United States 6.1%.
*Exports* (1986): 8,630,200,000 patacas (textiles and garments 69.7%, toys 11.8%, electronics 4.1%, artificial flowers 2.8%, leather articles 2.0%, ceramics 0.8%, optical products 0.8%). *Major export destinations:* United States 33.3%; Hong Kong 15.6%; France 11.9%; West Germany 11.4%; United Kingdom 7.2%; China 3.8%; Australia 2.4%; Japan 1.5%.

## Transport and communications

*Transport.* Railroads: none. Roads (1984): total length 56 mi, 90 km (paved 100%). Vehicles (1986): passenger cars 19,513; trucks and buses 4,773. Merchant marine (1986): vessels 581[5]; total gross tonnage 22,689. Air transport: none.
*Communications.* Daily newspapers (1986): total number 14; total circulation 242,000; circulation per 1,000 population 568. Radio (1986): total number of receivers 84,000 (1 per 4.9 persons). Television (1979): total number of receivers 59,000 (1 per 4.8 persons). Telephones (1986): 47,591 (1 per 9.0 persons).

## Education and health

### Education (1985–86)

| | schools | teachers | students | student/ teacher ratio |
|---|---|---|---|---|
| Primary (age 6–11) | 74 | 1,080 | 31,669 | 29.3 |
| Secondary (age 12–18) | 31 | 769 | 13,849 | 18.0 |
| Teacher tr. | 2 | 13 | 52 | 4.0 |
| Higher | 5 | 75 | 5,840 | 77.9 |

*Educational attainment* (1981). Percent of economically active population age 10 and over having: no formal schooling 13.8%; primary education 22.6%; some secondary 27.2%; complete secondary 20.5%; some postsecondary 13.0%; higher 2.9%. *Literacy* (1981): total population age 10 and over literate 127,359 (61.3%); males literate 80,102 (76.4%); females literate 47,257 (46.2%).
*Health* (1986): physicians 697 (1 per 612 persons); hospital beds 1,258 (1 per 339 persons); infant mortality rate per 1,000 live births 7.2.
*Food* (1981–83): daily per capita caloric intake 2,008 (vegetable products 74%, animal products 26%); (1983) 107% of FAO recommended minimum requirement.

## Military

*Total active duty personnel* (1987): the Portuguese garrison has been replaced by a paramilitary force of 1,800 men drawn from the Chinese residents only.

---

[1]The pataca free floats with the Hong Kong dollar and has a parity of 1.03 patacas = HK$1.00. [2]Detail does not add to total given because of rounding. [3]5.1% of Macau's population live on sampans and other vessels. [4]March. [5]All registered vessels including barges, tugboats, floating casinos, sampans, dredgers, but excluding barges used for restaurants and recreation.

# Madagascar

*Official name:* Repoblika Demokratika Malagasy (Malagasy); République Démocratique de Madagascar (French) (Democratic Republic of Madagascar).
*Form of government:* multiparty republic with one legislative house (National People's Assembly [137]).
*Chief of state:* President.
*Head of government:* Prime Minister.
*Capital:* Antananarivo.
*Official languages:* Malagasy; French.
*Official religion:* none.
*Monetary unit:* 1 franc (FMG) = 100 centimes; valuation (Oct. 5, 1987) 1 U.S.$ = FMG 1,152; 1 £ = FMG 1,870.

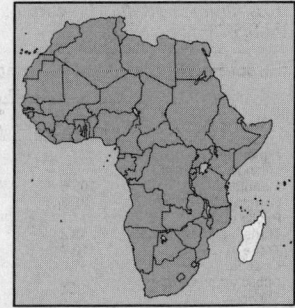

### Area and population

| Provinces | Capitals | area sq mi | area sq km | population 1985 estimate |
|---|---|---|---|---|
| Antananarivo | Antananarivo | 22,503 | 58,283 | 3,195,800 |
| Antsiranana | Antsiranana | 16,620 | 43,046 | 689,800 |
| Fianarantsoa | Fianarantsoa | 39,526 | 102,373 | 2,209,700 |
| Mahajanga | Mahajanga | 57,924 | 150,023 | 1,075,300 |
| Toamasina | Toamasina | 27,765 | 71,911 | 1,444,700 |
| Toliara | Toliara | 62,319 | 161,405 | 1,396,700 |
| TOTAL | | 226,658 | 587,041 | 10,012,000 |

## Demography

*Population* (1987): 10,605,000.
*Density* (1987): persons per sq mi 46.8, persons per sq km 18.1.
*Urban–rural* (1985): urban 21.8%; rural 78.2%.
*Sex distribution* (1985): male 49.61%; female 50.39%.
*Age breakdown* (1985): under 15, 44.0%; 15–29, 25.4%; 30–44, 15.5%; 45–59, 9.6%; 60–74, 4.6%; 75 and over, 0.9%.
*Population projection:* (1990) 11,575,000; (2000) 15,550,000.
*Doubling time:* 25 years.
*Ethnic composition* (1983): Malagasy 98.9%, of which Merina 26.6%, Betsimisaraka 14.9%, Betsileo 11.7%, Tsimihety 7.4%, Sakalava 6.4%; Antandroy 5.3%; Comorian 0.3%; Indian and Pakistani 0.2%; French 0.2%; Chinese 0.1%; other 0.3%.
*Religious affiliation* (1980): Christian 51.0%, of which Roman Catholic 26.0%, Protestant 22.8%; traditional beliefs 47.0%; Muslim 1.7%; other 0.3%.
*Major cities* (1980): Antananarivo 662,600[1]; Toamasina 95,505; Fianarantsoa 83,250; Mahajanga 80,881.

## Vital statistics

*Birth rate* per 1,000 population (1985–90): 44.1 (world avg. 26.0); legitimate, n.a.; illegitimate, n.a.
*Death rate* per 1,000 population (1985–90): 15.2 (world avg. 9.9).
*Natural increase rate* per 1,000 population (1985–90): 28.9 (world avg. 16.1).
*Total fertility rate* (avg. births per childbearing woman; 1985–90): 6.1.
*Marriage rate* per 1,000 population: n.a.
*Divorce rate* per 1,000 population: n.a.
*Life expectancy* at birth (1985–90): male 50.8 years; female 52.3 years.
*Major causes of death* per 100,000 population: n.a.; however, major diseases include malaria, leprosy, and tuberculosis.

## National economy

*Budget* (1985). Revenue: FMG 241,000,000,000 (no breakdown available). Expenditures: FMG 436,200,000,000 (current expenditure 71.8%, of which education 15.5%, defense 10.7%, health 5.9%, agriculture 1.9%, public works 0.9%).
*Public debt* (external, outstanding; 1985): U.S.$2,340,000,000.
*Tourism:* receipts from visitors (1985) U.S.$5,000,000; expenditures by nationals abroad (1983) U.S.$38,000,000.
*Production* (metric tons except as noted). Agriculture, forestry, fishing (1985): roots and tubers 2,949,000 (of which cassava 2,142,000, sweet potatoes 450,-000, potatoes 301,000), rice 2,178,000, sugarcane 1,744,000, fruit 736,000, vegetables and melons 299,000, bananas 225,000, corn (maize) 140,000, coffee 82,000, pulses 55,000, peanuts (groundnuts) 32,000, sisal 20,000, cloves 12,031[2], black pepper 2,618[2], cacao 2,000, vanilla 628[2]; livestock (number of live animals) 10,400,000 cattle, 1,500,000 goats, 1,400,000 pigs, 600,000 sheep; roundwood (1984) 6,262,000 cu m; fish catch (1984) 56,000. Mining and quarrying (1985): chromite concentrate 126,157; graphite 14,718; industrial calcite 2,000; mica 734; beryl 46,000 kg; celestite 30,000 kg; tourmaline 27,000 kg; jasper 17,000 kg; agate 9,300 kg. Manufacturing (1985): raw sugar 92,994; gasoline 72,247; cement 28,383; soap 12,321; cigarettes 2,368; chewing tobacco 1,034; beer 241,491 hectolitres. Construction (1984): residential 12,600 sq m; nonresidential 7,700 sq m. Energy production (consumption): electricity (kW-hr; 1985) 449,000,000 (449,000,000); coal (metric tons; 1985) none (8,000); crude petroleum (barrels; 1985) none (1,540,000); petroleum products (metric tons; 1985) 211,000 (243,000); natural gas, none (n.a.).
*Land use* (1984): forested 26.2%; meadows and pastures 58.5%; agricultural and under permanent cultivation 5.2%; other 10.1%.
*Population economically active:* total (1985) 4,510,000; activity rate of total population 45.1% (participation rates: ages 15–64, 74.9%; female 40.4%; unemployed [1982] 0.6%).

### Price and earnings indexes (1980 = 100)

| | 1981 | 1982 | 1983 | 1984 | 1985 | 1986 | 1987[3] |
|---|---|---|---|---|---|---|---|
| Consumer price index | 130.5 | 172.0 | 205.3 | 225.5 | 249.3 | 285.5 | 301.7 |
| Earnings index | ... | ... | ... | ... | ... | ... | ... |

*Gross national product* (at current market prices; 1984): U.S.$2,510,000,000 (U.S.$250 per capita).

### Structure of gross domestic product and labour force

| | 1983 in value U.S.$'000,000 | 1983 % of total value | 1982 labour force | 1982 % of labour force |
|---|---|---|---|---|
| Agriculture | 1,011 | 44.3 | 3,335,000 | 75.0 |
| Mining | 6 | 0.3 | 89,000 | 2.0 |
| Manufacturing | 251 | 11.0 | | |
| Construction | 103 | 4.5 | 445,000 | 10.0 |
| Public utilities | 26 | 1.1 | | |
| Transportation and communication | | | | |
| Trade | 883 | 38.7 | 578,000 | 13.0 |
| Finance | | | | |
| Services | | | | |
| Pub. admin., defense | | | | |
| TOTAL | 2,280 | 100.0[4] | 4,447,000[5] | 100.0 |

*Household income and expenditure.* Average household size (1980) 4.7; average annual income per household (1981) FMG 4,485 (U.S.$1,650); sources of income: n.a.; expenditure[6]: food 60.4%, fuel and light 9.1%, clothing and footwear 8.6%, household goods and utensils 2.4%.

## Foreign trade[7]

### Balance of trade

| | 1979 | 1980 | 1981 | 1982 | 1983 | 1984 | 1985 |
|---|---|---|---|---|---|---|---|
| FMG '000,000,000 | −25.7 | −17.9 | −37.8 | −19.3 | −25.0 | +15.1 | −39.1 |
| % of total | 13.3% | 9.5% | 18.1% | 8.2% | 9.9% | 4.1% | 9.7 |

*Imports* (1985): FMG 265,916,000,000[8] (mineral products 27.5%, of which crude petroleum 16.1%; chemical products 12.2%; vehicles and parts 10.5%; machinery 10.3%; metal products 7.1%; electrical equipment 4.2%; textiles 1.0%). *Major import sources:* France 32.5%; Soviet Union 8.7%; West Germany 6.1%; Qatar 5.7%; United States 5.6%; United Kingdom 4.4%; Saudi Arabia 3.9%; Thailand 2.8%; Japan 2.5%; Italy 2.0%.
*Exports* (1985): FMG 181,630,400,000 (coffee 35.0%; vanilla 15.9%; cloves and clove oil 14.8%; petroleum products 2.2%; sugar 1.3%). *Major export destinations:* France 36.6%; United States 13.8%; Japan 10.5%; Indonesia 7.6%; West Germany 7.1%; Italy 5.5%; The Netherlands 4.4%.

## Transport and communications

*Transport.* Railroads (1984): route length 644 mi, 1,036 km; passenger-mi 127,000,000, passenger-km 205,000,000; short ton-mi cargo 153,000,000, metric ton-km cargo 224,000,000. Roads (1985): total length 10,700 mi, 17,300 km (paved 30%). Vehicles: passenger cars (1983) 23,412; trucks and buses (1984) 14,159. Merchant marine (1986): vessels (100 gross tons and over) 71; total deadweight tonnage 96,587. Air transport (1985): passenger-mi 241,300,000, passenger-km 388,402,000; short ton-mi cargo 38,075,000, metric ton-km cargo 55,593,000; airports (1987) with scheduled flights 35.
*Communications.* Daily newspapers (1985): total number 7; total circulation 46,000[9]; circulation per 1,000 population 5.0[9]. Radio (1986): total number of receivers 2,020,000 (1 per 5 persons). Television (1986): total number of receivers 96,000 (1 per 104 persons). Telephones (1983): 37,100 (1 per 255 persons).

## Education and health

### Education (1984)

| | schools | teachers | students | student/ teacher ratio |
|---|---|---|---|---|
| Primary (age 6–13) | 13,973 | 42,462 | 1,625,216 | 38.3 |
| Secondary (14–18) | 104[10] | 10,383 | 288,543 | 27.8 |
| Voc., teacher tr. | 126 | 1,302 | 11,041 | 8.5 |
| Higher | 3[11] | 1,059 | 37,746 | 35.6 |

*Educational attainment,* n.a. *Literacy* (1985): total population age 15 and over literate 3,778,000 (67.5%); males literate 2,004,000 (73.7%); females literate 1,774,000 (61.6%).
*Health* (1982): physicians 940 (1 per 9,851 persons); hospital beds 20,800 (1 per 442 persons); infant mortality rate per 1,000 live births (1984) 110.
*Food* (1981–83): daily per capita caloric intake 2,544 (vegetable products 92%, animal products 8%); (1983) 112% of FAO recommended minimum requirement.

## Military

*Total active duty personnel* (1986): 21,100 (army 94.8%, navy 2.8%, air force 2.4%). *Military expenditure as percent of GNP* (1984): 2.6% (world 5.9%); per capita expenditure U.S.$7.

[1]1985. [2]Quantity exported. [3]April. [4]Detail does not add to total given because of rounding. [5]Includes unemployed. [6]Weights of consumer price index components in Antananarivo only; housing not included. [7]Import figures are f.o.b. in balance of trade and c.i.f. in commodities and trading partners. [8]Excludes gold and military equipment. [9]1984. [10]1971–72. [11]Two colleges and one university with six regional centres.

# Malaŵi

*Official name:* Malaŵi (Chewa);
Republic of Malaŵi (English).
*Form of government:* single-party
republic with one legislative house
(National Assembly [101]).
*Head of state and government:*
President.
*Capital:* Lilongwe.
*Official languages:* Chewa; English.
*Official religion:* none.
*Monetary unit:* 1 Malaŵi kwacha
(MK) = 100 Tambala; valuation
(Oct. 5, 1987) 1 U.S.$ = MK 2.26;
1 £ = MK 3.67.

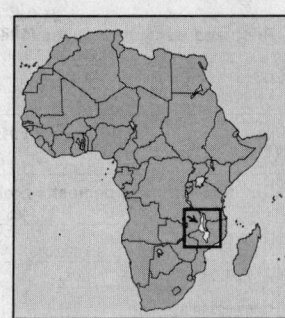

### Area and population

| Regions Districts | Capitals | area sq mi | area sq km | population 1986 estimate |
|---|---|---|---|---|
| Central | Lilongwe | 13,742 | 35,592 | 2,938,300 |
| Dedza | Dedza | 1,399 | 3,624 | 409,300 |
| Dowa | Dowa | 1,174 | 3,041 | 339,100 |
| Kasungu | Kasungu | 3,042 | 7,878 | 266,800 |
| Lilongwe | Lilongwe | 2,378 | 6,159 | 964,900 |
| Mchinji | Mchinji | 1,296 | 3,356 | 217,400 |
| Nkhotakota | Nkhotakota | 1,644 | 4,259 | 129,300 |
| Ntcheu | Ntcheu | 1,322 | 3,424 | 310,300 |
| Ntchisi | Ntchisi | 639 | 1,655 | 120,200 |
| Salima | Salima | 848 | 2,196 | 181,000 |
| Northern | Mzuzu | 10,398 | 26,931 | 815,000 |
| Chitipa | Chitipa | 1,353 | 3,504 | 90,500 |
| Karonga | Karonga | 1,141 | 2,955 | 134,500 |
| Mzimba | Mzimba | 4,027 | 10,430 | 378,300 |
| Nkhata Bay | Nkhata Bay | 1,579 | 4,090 | 133,000 |
| Rumphi | Rumphi | 2,298 | 5,952 | 78,700 |
| Southern | Blantyre | 12,260 | 31,753 | 3,525,600 |
| Blantyre | Blantyre | 777 | 2,012 | 522,500 |
| Chikwawa | Chikwawa | 1,836 | 4,755 | 248,500 |
| Chiradzulu | Chiradzulu | 296 | 767 | 225,600 |
| Machinga | Machinga | 2,303 | 5,964 | 437,200 |
| Mangochi | Mangochi | 2,422 | 6,272 | 386,800 |
| Mulanje | Mulanje | 1,332 | 3,450 | 611,300 |
| Mwanza | Mwanza | 886 | 2,295 | 91,700 |
| Nsanje | Nsanje | 750 | 1,942 | 139,300 |
| Thyolo | Thyolo | 662 | 1,715 | 411,800 |
| Zomba | Zomba | 996 | 2,580 | 450,900 |
| TOTAL LAND AREA | | 36,400 | 94,276[1] | |
| INLAND WATER | | 9,347 | 24,208 | |
| TOTAL | | 45,747 | 118,484 | 7,278,900 |

## Demography

*Population* (1987): 7,499,000.
*Density*[2] (1987): persons per sq mi 206.0, persons per sq km 79.5.
*Urban-rural* (1985): urban 12.3%; rural 87.7%.
*Sex distribution* (1985): male 48.54%; female 51.46%.
*Age breakdown* (1986): under 15, 47.8%; 15–29, 25.5%; 30–44, 14.4%; 45–59,
8.1%; 60–74, 3.5%; 75 and over, 0.6%.[1]
*Population projection:* (1990) 8,289,000; (2000) 11,631,000.
*Doubling time:* 23 years.
*Ethnic composition* (1983): Maravi (including Nyanja, Chewa, Tonga, and
Tumbuka) 58.3%; Lomwe 18.4%; Yao 13.2%; Ngoni 6.7%; other 3.4%.
*Religious affiliation* (1980): Christian 64.5%, of which Protestant 33.7%, Ro-
man Catholic 27.6%; traditional beliefs 19.0%; Muslim 16.2%; other 0.3%.
*Major cities* (1986): Blantyre 378,100; Lilongwe 202,900; Mzuzu 97,600.

## Vital statistics

*Birth rate* per 1,000 population (1984): 54.0 (world avg. 29.0).
*Death rate* per 1,000 population (1984): 22.0 (world avg. 11.0).
*Natural increase rate* per 1,000 population (1984): 32.0 (world avg. 18.0).
*Total fertility rate* (avg. births per childbearing woman; 1985): 7.6.
*Marriage rate* per 1,000 population (1977): 7.8.
*Divorce rate* per 1,000 population (1977): 1.4.
*Life expectancy* at birth (1984): male 44.0 years; female 46.0 years.
*Major causes of death* per 100,000 population[3] (1983): infectious and para-
sitic diseases 56.0, of which measles 17.4, malaria 13.7, diarrheal diseases
11.4; pneumonia 17.5; malnutrition 15.9; anemia 12.1.

## National economy

*Budget* (1986–87). Revenue: MK 665,100,000 (income tax 23.7%, surtax
21.5%, external loans 14.8%, import duties 12.6%). Expenditures: MK 733,-
100,000 (recurrent expenditures 74.6%, agriculture 7.2%, transportation and
communications 6.9%, education 2.6%, health 1.4%).
*Public debt* (external, outstanding; 1985): U.S.$774,900,000.
*Tourism:* receipts from visitors (1985) U.S.$7,700,000; expenditures by na-
tionals abroad (1982) U.S.$7,000,000.
*Production* (metric tons except as noted). Agriculture (1985): sugarcane
1,700,000, corn (maize) 1,420,000, cassava 300,000, potatoes 274,000,
peanuts (groundnuts) 180,000, sorghum 150,000, tobacco 75,000, tea 40,000;
livestock (number of live animals) 920,000 cattle, 680,000 goats, 230,000
pigs, 175,000 sheep; roundwood 6,588,000 cu m; fish catch 62,100. Mining
and quarrying (1985): limestone 110,000; cement 61,672. Manufacturing
(1985): raw sugar 69,000; beer 657,000 hectolitres; cigarettes 859,000,000
units. Construction (value in MK; 1983)[4]: residential 2,923,000; nonresidential 1,661,000. Energy production (consumption): electricity (kW-hr;
1985) 476,401,800 (398,815,000); coal (metric tons; 1985) none (29,000);
petroleum products (metric tons; 1985) none (116,000).

*Gross national product* (at current market prices; 1985): U.S.$1,160,000,000
(U.S.$170 per capita).

### Structure of gross domestic product and labour force

| | 1986 in value MK '000,000 | 1986 % of total value | 1984 labour force[5] | 1984 % of labour force |
|---|---|---|---|---|
| Agriculture | 323.1 | 37.9 | 177,688 | 46.7 |
| Mining | ... | ... | 298 | 0.1 |
| Manufacturing | 105.6 | 12.4 | 49,239 | 12.9 |
| Construction | 35.3 | 4.1 | 25,935 | 6.8 |
| Public utilities | 17.2 | 2.0 | 4,871 | 1.3 |
| Transp. and commun. | 48.2 | 5.7 | 21,986 | 5.8 |
| Trade | 110.7 | 13.0 | 31,695 | 8.3 |
| Finance | 91.4 | 10.7 | 11,548 | 3.0 |
| Public administration | 105.0 | 12.3 | | |
| Services | 36.7 | 4.3 | 57,593 | 15.1 |
| Other | −20.8[6] | −2.4[6] | | |
| TOTAL | 852.4[7] | 100.0 | 380,853 | 100.0 |

*Population economically active* (1985): total 3,074,000; activity rate of total
population 44.3% (participation rates: ages 15–64 [1983] 89.4%; female
42.6%; unemployed 1.0%[8]).

### Price and earnings indexes (1980 = 100)

| | 1979 | 1980 | 1981 | 1982 | 1983 | 1984 | 1985 |
|---|---|---|---|---|---|---|---|
| Consumer price index | 84.0 | 100.0 | 111.8 | 122.8 | 139.4 | 167.3 | 174.1 |
| Monthly earnings index | 85.7 | 100.0 | 112.9 | 131.9 | 124.3 | 125.1 | ... |

*Household income and expenditure* (1979–80). Average household size[9] 4.5;
income per household MK 1,934 (U.S.$2,419); sources of income: wages
83.3%, household enterprise 6.0%; expenditure (1985)[10]: food 32.9%, transportation 17.6%, housing 13.3%, clothing and footwear 10.7%, household
operation 9.6%, beverages and tobacco 6.4%.
*Land use* (1984): forested 49.2%; meadows and pastures 19.6%; agricultural
and under permanent cultivation 24.9%; other 6.3%.

## Foreign trade[11]

### Balance of trade (current prices)

| | 1980 | 1981 | 1982 | 1983 | 1984 | 1985 |
|---|---|---|---|---|---|---|
| MK '000,000 | −126.2 | −69.7 | −65.5 | −93.1 | +64.7 | −53.0 |
| % of total | 21.5% | 12.5% | 11.3% | 14.7% | 7.8% | 5.8% |

*Imports* (1985): MK 492,553,000 (basic manufactures 36.3%; machinery and
equipment 14.3%; transport equipment 12.8%; consumer goods 12.6%;
mineral oils, fuels, and lubricants 11.9%; building materials 6.1%). *Major
import sources:* South Africa 38.1%; U.K. 15.0%; Japan 7.8%; Zimbabwe
5.8%; W.Ger. 5.6%.
*Exports* (1985): MK 419,146,000[12] (tobacco 43.9%; tea 23.1%; sugar 10.6%;
corn 7.0%; unbleached cotton fabric 2.1%). *Major export destinations:*
U.K. 33.9%; U.S. 10.3%; W.Ger. 8.3%; Zambia 6.4%; South Africa 6.4%.

## Transport and communications

*Transport.* Railroads (1985–86): route length 515 mi, 829 km; passenger-mi
76,200,000, passenger-km 122,700,000; short ton-mi cargo 76,000,000, metric ton-mi cargo 111,300,000. Roads (1985): total length 7,576 mi, 12,192
km (paved 21%). Vehicles (1985): passenger cars 13,559; trucks and buses
14,545. Merchant marine (1986): vessels (100 gross tons and over) 1; total
deadweight tonnage 300. Air transport (1985): passenger-mi 52,200,000,
passenger-km 84,000,000; short ton-mi cargo 616,000, metric ton-km cargo
948,000; airports (1987) with scheduled flights 5.
*Communications.* Daily newspapers (1985): total number 2; total circulation
32,000; circulation per 1,000 population 4.5. Radio (1986): total number of
receivers 1,060,000 (1 per 6.9 persons). Television (1985): total number of
receivers, n.a. Telephones (1985): 43,436 (1 per 162 persons).

## Education and health

### Education (1984–85)

| | schools | teachers | students | student/ teacher ratio |
|---|---|---|---|---|
| Primary (age 6–13) | 3,962 | 23,132 | 899,459 | 38.9 |
| Secondary (age 14–18) | 73 | 1,150 | 24,343 | 21.2 |
| Teacher tr., voc. | 10[13] | 173 | 2,420 | 14.0 |
| Higher | 4 | 270 | 1,964 | 7.3 |

*Educational attainment* (1977). Percent of population age 25 and over having: primary education 4.7%; secondary 2.5%; higher 0.2%. *Literacy* (1985):
total population over age 15 literate 1,555,000 (41.2%).
*Health:* physicians (1983) 161 (1 per 41,108 persons); hospital beds (1986)
12,119 (1 per 600 persons); infant mortality rate (1985) 152.0.
*Food* (1981–83): daily per capita caloric intake 2,423 (vegetable products 96%,
animal products 4%); 104% of FAO recommended minimum requirement.

## Military

*Total active duty personnel* (1986): 5,250 (army 95.2%, navy 1.9%, air force
2.9%). *Military expenditure as percent of GNP* (1984): 1.7% (world 5.9%);
per capita expenditure U.S.$3.

[1]Detail does not add to total given because of rounding. [2]Based on land area.
[3]Reported inpatient deaths in hospitals. [4]New construction in the cities of Blantyre
and Lilongwe only. [5]Employed persons only. [6]Less imputed bank service charges. [7]At
1978 prices. [8]Registered. [9]Based on sample survey of the city of Blantyre. [10]Weights
of consumer price index components, cities of Blantyre and Lilongwe only. [11]Import
figures are f.o.b. in balance of trade and c.i.f. in commodities and trading partners.
Reexports included in balance of trade, excluded from commodities and trading
partners. [12]Reexports accounted for 2.5% of total exports. [13]1982–83.

# Malaysia

*Official name:* Malaysia.
*Form of government:* federal constitutional monarchy with two legislative houses (Senate [69[1]]; House of Representatives [177]).
*Chief of state:* Yang di-Pertuan Agong.
*Head of government:* Prime Minister.
*Capital:* Kuala Lumpur.
*Official language:* Malay.
*Official religion:* Islam.
*Monetary unit:* 1 ringgit, or Malaysian dollar (M$) = 100 cents; valuation (Oct. 5, 1987) 1 U.S.$ = M$2.55; 1 £ = M$4.13.

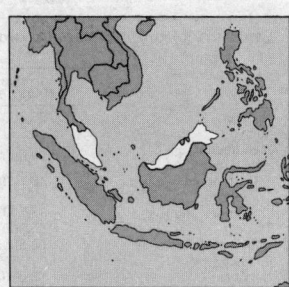

### Area and population

| Regions States | Capitals | area sq mi | area sq km | population 1985 estimate |
|---|---|---|---|---|
| **East Malaysia** | | | | |
| Sabah[2] | Kota Kinabalu | 28,460 | 73,711 | 1,222,718 |
| Sarawak | Kuching | 48,050 | 124,449 | 1,477,428 |
| **West Malaysia** | | | | |
| Johor | Johor Baharu | 7,330 | 18,985 | 1,867,333 |
| Kedah | Alor Setar | 3,639 | 9,425 | 1,263,155 |
| Kelantan | Kota Baharu | 5,765 | 14,931 | 1,048,420 |
| Melaka | Melaka | 640 | 1,658 | 524,028 |
| Negeri Sembilan | Seremban | 2,565 | 6,646 | 647,159 |
| Pahang | Kuantan | 13,884 | 35,960 | 921,360 |
| Pinang | Pinang | 398 | 1,031 | 1,049,282 |
| Perak | Ipoh | 8,110 | 21,005 | 2,020,135 |
| Perlis | Kangar | 307 | 795 | 166,948 |
| Selangor | Shah Alam | 3,072 | 7,956 | 1,731,090 |
| Terengganu | Kuala Terengganu | 5,002 | 12,955 | 638,830 |
| **Federal Territory** | | | | |
| Kuala Lumpur | — | 94 | 243 | 1,103,228 |
| TOTAL LAND AREA | | 127,317 | 329,750 | 15,681,114 |
| INLAND WATER | | 264 | 684 | |
| TOTAL AREA | | 127,581 | 330,434 | |

## Demography

*Population* (1987): 16,538,000.
*Density* (1987): persons per sq mi 129.9, persons per sq km 50.2.
*Urban-rural* (1985): urban 38.2%; rural 61.8%.
*Sex distribution* (1985): male 50.36%; female 49.64%.
*Age breakdown* (1985): under 15, 38.0%; 15–29, 29.3%; 30–44, 17.2%; 45–59, 9.7%; 60–74, 4.5%; 75 and over, 1.3%.
*Population projection:* (1990) 17,894,000; (2000) 23,271,000.
*Doubling time:* 28 years.
*Ethnic composition* (1985): Malay 59.0%; Chinese 32.0%; Indian 9.0%.
*Religious affiliation* (1980): Muslim 52.9%; Buddhist 17.3%; Chinese folk-religionist 11.6%; Hindu 7.0%; Christian 6.4%; other 4.8%.
*Major cities* (1980): Kuala Lumpur 1,103,200[3]; Ipoh 293,849; Pinang 248,241; Johor Baharu 246,395; Petaling Jaya 207,805.

## Vital statistics

*Birth rate* per 1,000 population (1986): 30.6 (world avg. 26.0).
*Death rate* per 1,000 population (1986): 5.7 (world avg. 9.9).
*Natural increase rate* per 1,000 population (1986): 24.9 (world avg. 16.1).
*Total fertility rate* (avg. births per childbearing woman; 1986): 3.8.
*Marriage rate* per 1,000 population (1985): 1.7.
*Divorce rate* per 1,000 population (1979): 0.02.
*Life expectancy* at birth (1986): male 67.0 years; female 71.2 years.
*Major causes of death* per 100,000 population (1981)[4]: heart disease 29.1; infectious and parasitic diseases 19.2; malignant neoplasms (cancers) 18.6; cerebrovascular diseases 14.4; pneumonia 10.6.

## National economy

*Budget* (1986). Revenue: M$22,121,000,000 (income tax 39.8%, import and export duties 21.9%, sales and excise taxes 14.1%). Expenditures: M$29,564,000,000 (economic development 25.7%, debt service 20.0%, education 13.7%, administration 8.3%, defense 8.1%, internal security 5.0%, health 4.0%).
*Tourism:* receipts from visitors (1985) U.S.$545,000,000; expenditures by nationals abroad (1984) U.S.$1,119,000,000.
*Land use* (1984): forested 61.8%; meadows and pastures 0.1%; agricultural and under permanent cultivation 13.2%; other 24.9%.
*Production* (metric tons except as noted). Agriculture (1986): palm oil 4,544,000, rice 1,743,000, rubber 1,540,000, palm kernels 1,200,000, pineapples 147,000, cacao 128,000, peppers 16,000; livestock (number of live animals; 1985) 2,100,000 pigs, 570,000 cattle, 345,000 goats, 260,000 buffalo, 65,000 sheep, 55,000,000 chickens; roundwood 29,400,000 cu m; fish catch (1985) 632,185. Mining and quarrying (1986): bauxite 566,170; iron ore 207,963; copper 115,304; tin concentrates 29,135. Manufacturing (1986): cement 3,176,000; processed palm oil 2,255,000; iron and steel products 362,000; paints 37,062,000 litres; plywood 503,000 cu m; tires 3,846,000 units; television receivers 863,000 units; air conditioners 337,000 units; road motor vehicles 153,000 units. Construction (housing completion; 1986)[5]: residential 8,809,100 sq m; nonresidential 959,900 sq m. Energy production (consumption): electricity (kW-hr; 1985) 14,915,000,000 (14,973,000,000); coal (metric tons; 1985) none (544,000); petroleum (barrels; 1985) 166,207,000 (54,839,000); petroleum products (metric tons; 1985) 6,877,000 (8,974,000); natural gas (cu m; 1985) 16,391,000,000 (10,325,000,000).
*Gross national product* (1985): U.S.$31,930,000,000 (U.S.$2,040 per capita).

### Structure of gross domestic product and labour force

| | in value[6] M$'000,000 | % of total value | labour force[7] | % of labour force |
|---|---|---|---|---|
| | 1986 | | | |
| Agriculture | 12,242 | 21.2 | 1,789,000 | 32.1 |
| Mining | 6,434 | 11.1 | 36,000 | 0.6 |
| Manufacturing | 12,028 | 20.8 | 818,000 | 14.7 |
| Construction | 2,488 | 4.3 | 371,000 | 6.7 |
| Public utilities | 1,029 | 1.8 | 41,000 | 0.7 |
| Transp. and commun. | 3,810 | 6.6 | 235,000 | 4.2 |
| Trade | 6,701 | 11.6 | 1,005,000 | 18.1 |
| Finance | 4,734 | 8.2 | 170,000 | 3.1 |
| Pub. admin., defense | 7,096 | 12.3 | 832,000 | 14.9 |
| Services | 1,300 | 2.3 | 273,000 | 4.9 |
| Other | −141[8] | −0.2[8] | ... | ... |
| TOTAL | 57,721 | 100.0 | 5,570,000 | 100.0 |

*Public debt* (external, outstanding; 1985): U.S.$13,834,100,000.
*Population economically active* (1985): total 5,575,900; activity rate of total population 35.6% (participation rates: over age 15, 58.8%; female [1980] 33.6%; unemployed 6.2%).

### Price and earnings indexes (1980 = 100)

| | 1981 | 1982 | 1983 | 1984 | 1985 | 1986 | 1987[9] |
|---|---|---|---|---|---|---|---|
| Consumer price index | 109.7 | 116.1 | 120.4 | 125.1 | 125.5 | 126.4 | 127.9 |

*Household income and expenditure.* Average household size (1980) 5.2; income per household: n.a.; sources of income: n.a.; expenditure (1980): food 36.2%, housing 24.1%, transportation 16.6%, recreation and education 6.7%, clothing and footwear 4.7%, health 1.3%.

## Foreign trade[10]

### Balance of trade (current prices)

| | 1981 | 1982 | 1983 | 1984 | 1985 | 1986 |
|---|---|---|---|---|---|---|
| M$'000,000 | +3,141 | +1,961 | +5,028 | +8,954 | +10,664 | +10,480 |
| % of total | 6.1% | 3.6% | 8.3% | 13.1% | 16.2% | 17.1% |

*Imports* (1986): M$27,990,000,000 (intermediate goods for manufacturing 34.8%; machinery and transport equipment 13.9%; food, beverages, and tobacco 6.8%; metal products 5.3%; consumer durables 5.1%; intermediate goods for agriculture and construction 4.6%). *Major import sources:* Japan 20.5%; U.S. 18.8%; Singapore 15.0%; West Germany 4.5%; U.K. 4.5%; Australia 4.2%.
*Exports* (1986): M$35,791,000,000 (crude and partly refined petroleum 15.1%; saw logs and sawn lumber 11.6%; rubber 8.9%; palm oil 8.5%; LNG 5.3%; tin 1.8%). *Major export destinations:* Japan 22.7%; Singapore 17.1%; U.S. 16.6%; South Korea 5.2%; West Germany 3.6%; U.K. 3.5%.

## Transport and communications

*Transport.* Railroads (1984): route length 1,666 mi, 2,681 km; passenger-mi 872,000,000[11], passenger-km 1,404,000,000[11]; short ton-mi cargo 697,000,000[11], metric ton-km cargo 1,020,000,000[11]. Roads (1985): total length 19,144 mi, 30,809 km (paved 80%). Vehicles (1985): passenger cars 1,173,968; trucks and buses 138,343. Merchant marine (1986): vessels (100 gross tons and over) 498; total deadweight tonnage 2,506,631. Air transport (1985): passenger-mi 3,892,000,000, passenger-km 6,264,000,000; short ton-mi cargo 142,917,000, metric ton-km cargo 208,656,000; airports (1987) with scheduled flights 35.
*Communications.* Daily newspapers (1985): total number 42; circulation 1,670,000[12]; circulation per 1,000 population 109[12]. Radio (1983): total number of receivers 282,893[13] (1 per 52.5 persons). Television (1983): total number of receivers 1,672,845[13] (1 per 8.9 persons). Telephones (1985): 1,278,751 (1 per 12 persons).

## Education and health

### Education (1986)

| | schools | teachers | students | student/ teacher ratio |
|---|---|---|---|---|
| Primary (age 7–12) | 6,652 | 98,061 | 2,232,575 | 22.8 |
| Secondary (age 13–19) | 1,136 | 58,223 | 1,297,734 | 22.3 |
| Voc., teacher tr. | 54 | 1,909 | 21,337 | 11.2 |
| Higher[3] | 41 | 8,415 | 96,212 | 11.4 |

*Educational attainment* (1980). Percent of population age 25 and over having: no formal schooling 36.6%; primary education 42.1%; secondary 19.4%; higher 1.9%. *Literacy* (1980): total population age 15 and over literate 5,719,358 (72.6%); males 3,195,031 (82.2%); females 2,524,327 (63.2%).
*Health* (1983): physicians 4,508 (1 per 3,301 persons); hospital beds 35,139 (1 per 502 persons); infant mortality rate per 1,000 live births (1986) 27.0.
*Food* (1981–83): daily per capita caloric intake 2,557 (vegetable products 86%, animal products 14%); (1983) 111% of FAO recommended minimum requirement.

## Military

*Total active duty personnel* (1986): 110,000 (army 81.8%, navy 8.2%, air force 10.0%). *Military expenditure as percent of GNP* (1983): 8.1% (world 6.1%); per capita expenditure U.S.$160.

[1]Includes 43 nonelective seats. [2]Includes Labuan federal territory. [3]1985. [4]Medically certified deaths only. [5]Results of the Central Bank Survey of four major towns: Kuala Lumpur, Shah Alam, Kelang, and Seberang Prai. [6]At constant prices of 1978. [7]Employed only. [8]Includes import duties and bank service charges. [9]June. [10]Import figures are f.o.b. (free on board) in balance of trade and c.i.f. (cost, insurance, and freight) for commodities and trading partners. [11]Peninsular Malaysia and Singapore; 1985. [12]1984. [13]Licenses issued and renewed.

# Maldives

*Official name:* Divehi Jumhuriyya
(Republic of Maldives).
*Form of government:* republic with
one legislative house (People's
Council [48[1]]).
*Head of state and government:*
President.
*Capital:* Male.
*Official language:* Divehi.
*Official religion:* Islam.
*Monetary unit:* 1 Maldivian Rufiyaa
(Rf) = 100 laaris; valuation (Oct. 5,
1987) 1 U.S.$ = Rf 7.00;
1 £ = Rf 11.37.

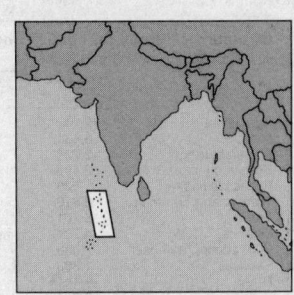

### Area and population[2]

| Administrative atolls | Capitals | area sq mi | area sq km | population 1985 census |
|---|---|---|---|---|
| Haa-Alifu | Dhidhdhoo | ... | ... | 9,891 |
| Haa-Dhaalu | Nolhivaranfaru | ... | ... | 10,848 |
| Shaviyani | Farukolhu Funadhoo | ... | ... | 7,529 |
| Noonu | Manadhoo | ... | ... | 6,874 |
| Raa | Ugoofaaru | ... | ... | 9,516 |
| Baa | Eydhafushi | ... | ... | 6,945 |
| Lhaviyani | Naifaru | ... | ... | 6,402 |
| Kaafu | Male | ... | ... | 54,908 |
| Alifu | Mahibadhoo | ... | ... | 7,695 |
| Vaavu | Felidhoo | ... | ... | 1,423 |
| Meemu | Muli | ... | ... | 3,493 |
| Faafu | Magoodhoo | ... | ... | 2,148 |
| Dhaalu | Kudahuvadhoo | ... | ... | 3,576 |
| Thaa | Veymandhoo | ... | ... | 6,942 |
| Laamu | Hithadhoo | ... | ... | 7,158 |
| Gaafu-Alifu | Viligili | ... | ... | 6,081 |
| Gaafu-Dhaalu | Thinadhoo | ... | ... | 8,870 |
| Gnyaviyani | Foah Mulah | ... | ... | 6,189 |
| Seenu | Hithadhoo | ... | ... | 14,965 |
| TOTAL | | 115 | 298 | 181,453 |

## Demography

*Population* (1987): 195,000.
*Density* (1987): persons per sq mi 1,695.7, persons per sq km 654.4.
*Urban-rural* (1985): urban 25.5%; rural 74.5%.
*Sex distribution* (1986): male 51.84%; female 48.16%.
*Age breakdown* (1985): under 15, 44.4%; 15–29, 27.0%; 30–44, 13.5%; 45–59, 11.2%; 60 and over, 3.9%.
*Population projection:* (1990) 215,000; (2000) 283,000.
*Doubling time:* 17 years.
*Ethnic composition:* the majority is principally of Sinhalese and Dravidian extraction; Arab, African, and Negrito influences are also present.
*Religious affiliation:* virtually 100% Sunnī Muslim.
*Major cities* (1985): Male 46,334.

## Vital statistics

*Birth rate* per 1,000 population (1985): 49.5 (world avg. 29.0); legitimate, n.a.; illegitimate, n.a.
*Death rate* per 1,000 population (1985): 8.8 (world avg. 11.0).
*Natural increase rate* per 1,000 population (1985): 40.7 (world avg. 18.0).
*Total fertility rate* (avg. births per childbearing woman; 1986): 6.5.
*Marriage rate* per 1,000 population (1981): 34.6.
*Divorce rate* per 1,000 population (1981): 25.5.
*Life expectancy* at birth (1986): male 57.4 years; female 58.4 years.
*Major causes of death* per 100,000 population: n.a.; however, waterborne diseases (including gastroenteritis, cholera, and typhoid fever) are principal health problems, as are malaria, shigellosis, filariasis, leprosy, and tuberculosis.

## National economy

*Budget* (1985). Revenue: Rf 177,318,000 (import duties 29.4%, tourism 21.7%, civil aviation 9.9%, state trading organization profits 6.8%, foreign aid 5.4%). Expenditures: Rf 199,340,000 (main airport 16.2%, education 11.2%, defense 9.9%, home office and social services 6.9%, health 6.7%, finance 4.7%, atolls administration 4.6%, Islamic centre 4.6%, reclamation 4.3%).
*Public debt* (external, outstanding; 1985) U.S.$52,100,000.
*Production* (metric tons except as noted). Agriculture, forestry, fishing (1985): vegetables and melons 18,000, coconuts 10,000, roots and tubers 8,000 (including cassava, sweet potatoes, and yams), fruits excluding melons 8,000, copra 2,000; fish catch 61,900, of which skipjack tuna 42,600, yellow-fin tuna 6,100. Mining and quarrying: coral for construction materials. Manufacturing: details n.a.; however, major industries include boat building and repairing, coir yarn and mat weaving, coconut and fish processing, lacquer work, garment manufacturing, and handicrafts. Construction: n.a. Energy production (consumption): electricity (kW-hr; 1985) 12,896,577 (12,896,-577); coal, none (n.a.); petroleum products (metric tons; 1984) none (8,000); natural gas, none (n.a.).
*Tourism:* receipts from visitors (1985) U.S.$37,000,000; expenditures by nationals abroad (1983) U.S.$3,000,000.
*Household income and expenditure.* Average household size (1985) 6.1; income per household: n.a.; sources of income: n.a.; expenditure: n.a.
*Gross national product* (at current market prices; 1985): U.S.$50,000,000 (U.S.$270 per capita).

### Structure of gross domestic product and labour force

| | 1985 in value Rf '000[3] | 1985 % of total value | 1980 labour force[4] | 1980 % of labour force |
|---|---|---|---|---|
| Agriculture[5] | 236,300 | 34.6 | 35,900 | 54.9 |
| Mining | 6,600 | 1.0 | ... | ... |
| Manufacturing | 28,000 | 4.1 | 13,600 | 20.8 |
| Public utilities | | | 200 | 0.3 |
| Construction | 40,700 | 6.0 | 3,100 | 4.7 |
| Transportation and communication | 33,700 | 4.9 | 3,300 | 5.0 |
| Trade | 55,300 | 8.1 | 2,000 | 3.1 |
| Pub. admin., defense | 108,800 | 15.9 | ... | ... |
| Finance | | | ... | ... |
| Services | 173,600 | 25.4 | 5,300 | 8.1 |
| Other | | | 2,000 | 3.1 |
| TOTAL | 683,000 | 100.0 | 65,400 | 100.0 |

*Population economically active* (1980): total 65,410; activity rate of total population 42.2% (participation rates: ages 15–59, 79.8%; female 38.8%; unemployed, n.a.).
*Land use* (1984): forested 3.3%; meadows and pastures 3.3%; agricultural and under permanent cultivation 10.0%; built-on, wasteland, and other 83.4%.

## Foreign trade[6]

### Balance of trade (current prices)

| | 1980 | 1981 | 1982 | 1983 | 1984 | 1985 |
|---|---|---|---|---|---|---|
| Rf '000,000 | −119.9 | −35.6 | −91.2 | −269.9 | −217.5 | −177.5 |
| % of total | 50.5% | 21.4% | 39.4% | 58.7% | 46.7% | 35.3% |

*Imports* (1985): U.S.$47,891,000 (food, beverages, and tobacco 28.6%, of which tobacco and beverages 6.4%, rice 3.3%, sugar and sugar products 1.9%; machinery and transport equipment 17.8%; petroleum products 15.5%; textiles 12.8%; chemicals 6.2%; iron and steel 3.4%; wood and wood products 2.6%). *Major import sources* (1983): Singapore 62.1%; Japan 11.4%; Sri Lanka 7.9%; India 4.5%; Hong Kong 3.1%; United Kingdom 1.9%.
*Exports* (1985): U.S.$23,027,000 (fresh skipjack tuna 38.2%; clothing and wearing apparel 32.5%; dried skipjack 13.3%; canned fish 10.0%; salted reef fish [including grouper, perch, and snapper] 9.3%; dried shark fins 1.3%). *Major export destinations:* Thailand 29.4%; United States 24.3%; Sri Lanka 20.3%; Japan 10.1%; Canada 7.9%; West Germany 3.2%.

## Transport and communications

*Transport.* Railroads: none. Roads: total length, n.a. Vehicles (1985): passenger cars 336; trucks 338. Merchant marine (1986): vessels (100 gross tons and over) 30; total deadweight tonnage 132,978. Air transport (1985): passenger arrivals 123,609, passenger departures 122,315; cargo loaded 343 metric tons, cargo unloaded 2,391 metric tons; airports (1987) with scheduled flights 1.
*Communications.* Daily newspapers (1985): total number 2; circulation, n.a. Radio (1985): total number of receivers 19,146 (1 per 9.6 persons). Television (1985): total number of receivers 3,686 (1 per 50 persons). Telephones (1985): 2,485 (1 per 74 persons).

## Education and health

### Education (1986)

| | schools | teachers | students | student/ teacher ratio |
|---|---|---|---|---|
| Primary (age 6–11) | 243 | 1,138 | 41,812 | 36.7 |
| Secondary (age 11–18) | 9 | 291 | 3,581 | 12.3 |
| Voc., teacher tr. | 10 | 52 | 462 | 8.9 |
| Higher | — | — | — | — |

*Educational attainment* (1977). Percent of population age 25 and over having: no formal schooling or no standard passed 80.2%; primary standard 15.1%; secondary standard 3.9%; postsecondary 0.1%; higher 0.1%; not stated 0.6%. *Literacy* (1982): total population age 15 and over literate 62,-365 (81.1%); males literate 31,896 (80.2%); females literate 30,469 (82.0%).
*Health* (1985): physicians 23 (1 per 7,957 persons); hospital beds[7] 121 (1 per 1,512 persons); infant mortality rate per 1,000 live births 63.0.
*Food* (1979–81): daily per capita caloric intake 1,983 (vegetable products 91%, animal products 9%); 90% of FAO recommended minimum requirement.

## Military

*Total active duty personnel:* Maldives maintains a single security force numbering about 700–1,000; it performs both army and police functions.

---

[1]Includes eight nonelective seats. [2]Maldives is divided into 19 administrative districts corresponding to atoll groups; arrangement shown here is from north to south; total area excludes 34,634 sq mi (89,702 sq km) of tidal waters. [3]At 1984 prices. [4]Employed persons only. [5]Primarily fishing. [6]Import figures are f.o.b. (free on board) in balance of trade and c.i.f. (cost, insurance, and freight) for commodities and trading partners. [7]In government establishments only.

# Mali

*Official name:* République du Mali
(Republic of Mali).
*Form of government:* unitary
single-party republic with one
legislative house (National Assembly
[82]).
*Head of state and government:*
President.
*Capital:* Bamako.
*Official language:* French.
*Official religion:* none.
*Monetary unit:* 1 CFA franc
(CFAF)[1] = 100 centimes; valuation
(Oct. 5, 1987) 1 U.S.$ = CFAF 306.67;
1 £ = CFAF 498.00.

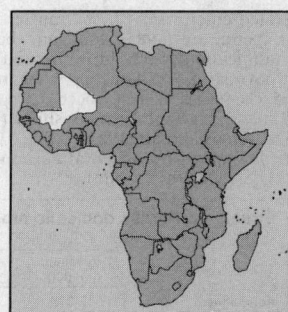

### Area and population

| Regions | Capitals | area sq mi | area sq km | population 1987 census |
|---|---|---|---|---|
| Gao | Gao | 124,323 | 321,996 | 383,734 |
| Kayes | Kayes | 76,356 | 197,760 | 1,058,575 |
| Koulikoro | Koulikoro | 34,685 | 89,833 | 1,180,260 |
| Mopti | Mopti | 34,257 | 88,752 | 1,261,383 |
| Ségou | Ségou | 21,671 | 56,127 | 1,328,250 |
| Sikasso | Sikasso | 29,529 | 76,480 | 1,308,828 |
| Tombouctou[2] | Tombouctou | 157,907 | 408,977 | 453,032 |
| **District** | | | | |
| Bamako | Bamako | 103 | 267 | 646,163 |
| TOTAL | | 478,841 | 1,240,192 | 7,620,225 |

## Demography

*Population* (1987): 7,653,000.
*Density* (1987): persons per sq mi 16.0, persons per sq km 6.2.
*Urban–rural* (1983): urban 20.2%; rural 79.8%.
*Sex distribution* (1987): male 48.9%; female 51.1%.
*Age breakdown* (1983): under 15, 42.7%; 15–29, 26.1%; 30–44, 16.1%; 45–59, 9.4%; 60–74, 4.6%; 75 and over, 1.1%.
*Population projection:* (1990) 8,052,000; (2000) 9,541,000.
*Doubling time:* 25 years.
*Ethnic composition* (1983): Bambara 31.9%; Fulani 13.9%; Senufo 12.0%; Soninke 8.8%; Tuareg 7.3%; Songhai 7.2%; Malinke 6.6%; Dogon 4.0%; Dyula 2.9%; Bobo 2.4%; Arab 1.2%; other 1.8%.
*Religious affiliation* (1983): Muslim 90%; traditional beliefs 9%; Christian 1%.
*Major cities* (1976): Bamako 646,163[3]; Ségou 65,400; Mopti 53,300; Sikasso 46,500; Kayes 49,400.

## Vital statistics

*Birth rate* per 1,000 population (1980–85): 50.6 (world avg. 29.0); legitimate, n.a.; illegitimate, n.a.
*Death rate* per 1,000 population (1980–85): 22.5 (world avg. 11.0).
*Natural increase rate* per 1,000 population (1980–85): 28.1 (world avg. 18.0).
*Total fertility rate* (avg. births per childbearing woman; 1980–85): 6.7.
*Marriage rate* per 1,000 population (1983): 2.8.
*Divorce rate* per 1,000 population: n.a.
*Life expectancy* at birth (1980–85): male 40.4 years; female 43.6 years.
*Major causes of death* per 100,000 population: n.a.; morbidity ([notified cases of illness] percent of all reported illness; 1983): malaria 66.5%; syphilis and gonococcal infections 8.7%; amebiasis and schistosomiasis 8.3%; measles 5.1%; influenza 3.8%.

## National economy

*Budget* (1986). Revenue: CFAF 69,180,000,000 (indirect taxes 35.8%, direct taxes 16.3%, customs duties 15.4%, carryover revenue from previous fiscal years 9.7%). Expenditures: CFAF 69,080,000,000 (defense 18.7%, education 12.6%, foreign affairs 3.3%, commerce and finance 2.9%).
*Tourism:* receipts from visitors (1984) U.S.$12,000,000; expenditures by nationals abroad (1983) U.S.$17,000,000.
*Population economically active* (1976): total 2,266,000; activity rate of total population 35.4% (participation rates: ages 15–64, 52.3%; female 17.0%; unemployed 1.3%[4]).

### Price and earnings indexes (1970 = 100)

| | 1980 | 1981 | 1982 | 1983 | 1984 | 1985 | 1986 |
|---|---|---|---|---|---|---|---|
| Consumer price index[5] | 382.7 | 429.5 | 439.4 | 482.6 | ... | ... | ... |
| Hourly earnings index[6] | 100.0 | 100.0 | 113.1 | 113.1 | 113.1 | 113.1 | 113.1 |

*Production* (metric tons except as noted). Agriculture, forestry, fishing (1985): millet 1,100,000, vegetables 235,000, rice 187,000, seed cotton 176,-000, peanuts (groundnuts) in shell 120,000, cottonseed 110,000, sugarcane 107,000, corn (maize) 90,000, cassava 73,000, pulses 57,000, sweet potatoes 55,000, cotton lint 54,000, yams 18,000, fruit 12,000, wheat 2,000, tobacco 1,100; livestock (number of live animals) 6,460,000 sheep, 6,080,000 goats, 5,800,000 cattle, 800,000 asses, 400,000 camels, 75,000 horses, 54,000 pigs, 14,000,000 chickens; roundwood 4,892,000 cu m; fish catch 60,000. Mining and quarrying (1986): gold 16,100 troy oz, salt 4,500. Manufacturing (1985): cotton fibre 67,900; goat, mutton, and lamb meat 45,000; soft drinks 43,-700; beef and veal 36,000; cement 24,800; sugar 24,000; molasses 8,400; beer 9,500 hectolitres[7]. Construction: n.a. Energy production (consumption): electricity (kW-hr; 1986) 170,846,000 (117,060,000[8]); coal, none (n.a.);

crude petroleum, none (n.a.); petroleum products (metric tons; 1985) none (173,000); natural gas, none (n.a.).
*Gross national product* (at current market prices; 1985): U.S.$1,070,000,000 (U.S.$130 per capita).

### Structure of gross domestic product and labour force

| | 1984 in value CFAF '000,000,000 | 1984 % of total value | 1982 labour force | 1982 % of labour force |
|---|---|---|---|---|
| Agriculture | 244.0 | 51.9 | 3,355,300 | 85.9 |
| Mining | } 32.0 | 6.8 | 195,300 | 5.0 |
| Manufacturing | | | | |
| Construction | 23.0 | 4.9 | | |
| Public utilities | 9 | 9 | | |
| Transportation and communication | 24.0 | 5.1 | | |
| Trade | 73.0 | 15.5 | } 355,400 | 9.1 |
| Finance | 9 | 9 | | |
| Pub. admin., defense | 37.0 | 7.9 | | |
| Services | 22.0[9] | 4.7[9] | | |
| Other | 15.0 | 3.2 | | |
| TOTAL | 470.0 | 100.0 | 3,906,000 | 100.0 |

*Public debt* (external, outstanding; 1985): U.S.$1,327,400,000.
*Household income and expenditure.* Average household size (1980) 5; average annual income per household: n.a.; sources of income: n.a.; expenditure: n.a.
*Land use* (1984): forested 7.1%; meadows and pastures 24.6%; agricultural and under permanent cultivation 1.7%; other 66.6%.

## Foreign trade

### Balance of trade (current prices)

| | 1980 | 1981 | 1982 | 1983 | 1984 | 1985 |
|---|---|---|---|---|---|---|
| CFAF '000,000,000 | −25.6 | −35.7 | −33.0 | −36.9 | −35.3 | −43.8 |
| % of total | 22.8% | 29.8% | 25.6% | 22.7% | 17.4% | 22.1% |

*Imports* (1983): U.S.$254,900,000 (machinery, appliances, and transportation equipment 35.5%; petroleum products 19.1%; construction materials 11.8%; food products 10.5%; chemicals and pharmaceutical products 10.5%). *Major import sources* (1985): France 34.3%; Côte d'Ivoire 19.2%; United States 9.1%; West Germany 8.1%; Italy 6.5%; Senegal 4.7%; Spain 3.1%; United Kingdom 2.8%; The Netherlands 2.8%; Belgium–Luxembourg 2.8%; China 2.6%; Hong Kong 1.9%; Japan 1.5%; Pakistan 1.2%; Switzerland 0.5%.
*Exports* (1983): U.S.$166,800,000 (raw cotton and cotton products 40.9%; live animals 30.4%; salted, dried, or smoked fish 1.2%; peanuts 1.0%). *Major export destinations* (1985): France 18.2%; West Germany 15.3%; Belgium–Luxembourg 12.3%; United Kingdom 6.8%; Portugal 6.5%; Côte d'Ivoire 4.5%; Italy 4.3%; The Netherlands 3.2%; Niger 1.5%.

## Transport and communications

*Transport.* Railroads (1985): route length (1986) 401 mi, 646 km; passenger-mi 107,349,000, passenger-km 172,761,000; short ton-mi cargo 165,301,000, metric ton-km cargo 241,335,000. Roads (1986): total length 9,756 mi, 15,700 km (paved 11%). Vehicles (1985): passenger cars 23,209; trucks and buses 6,802. Merchant marine: vessels (100 gross tons and over) none. Air transport (1983): passenger-mi 68,000,000; passenger-km 110,000,000; short ton-mi cargo 411,000, metric ton-km cargo 600,000; airports (1987) with scheduled flights 9.
*Communications.* Daily newspapers (1985): total number 1; total circulation 40,000; circulation per 1,000 population 4.9. Radio (1985): total number of receivers 110,000 (1 per 75 persons). Television (1985): total number of receivers 500 (1 per 16,420 persons). Telephones (1983): 9,537 (1 per 789 persons).

## Education and health

### Education (1982–83)

| | schools | teachers | students | student/ teacher ratio |
|---|---|---|---|---|
| Primary (age 6–14) | 1,558 | 10,912 | 348,373 | 31.9 |
| Secondary (age 15–17) | 20 | 3,870 | 64,148 | 16.6 |
| Voc., teacher tr. | 11 | 890 | 12,612 | 14.2 |
| Higher | 7 | 499 | 5,792 | 11.6 |

*Educational attainment* (1976). Percent of adult population age 25 and over having: no formal schooling 95.4%; primary education 3.8%; secondary 0.6%; postsecondary and higher 0.2%. *Literacy* (1980): total population age 15 and over literate 361,800 (10.1%); males literate 329,200 (18.6%); females literate 32,600 (1.8%).
*Health* (1983): physicians 283 (1 per 26,879 persons); hospital beds 4,215 (1 per 1,805 persons); infant mortality rate per 1,000 live births (1985–90) 127.
*Food* (1981–83): daily per capita caloric intake 1,889 (vegetable products 92%, animal products 8%); (1983) 68% of FAO recommended minimum requirement.

## Military

*Total active duty personnel* (1987): 5,050 (army 91.1%, navy 1.0%, air force 7.9%). *Military expenditure as percent of GNP* (1984): 5.0% (world 5.9%); per capita expenditure U.S.$7.

[1]In June 1984, the Mali franc (MF) was replaced by the CFA franc at the rate of 1 CFA franc = 2 Mali francs; older data may be reported in Mali francs. [2]Area for Tombouctou region is estimated as a residue between total reported area and the remainder of the regions. [3]1987 census. [4]Urban areas, estimated. [5]Food index for Bamako only. [6]Minimum hourly wages of industrial workers. [7]1983. [8]1985. [9]Services includes finance and public utilities.

# Malta

*Official name:* Repubblika ta' Malta
(Maltese); Republic of Malta (English).
*Form of government:* unitary multiparty
republic with one legislative house
(House of Representatives [65]).
*Chief of state:* President.
*Head of government:* Prime Minister.
*Capital:* Valletta.
*Official languages:* Maltese; English.
*Official religion:* Roman Catholicism.
*Monetary unit:* 1 Maltese lira
(Lm) = 100 cents = 1,000 mils;
valuation[1] (Oct. 5, 1987)
1 Lm = U.S.$2.86 = £1.76.

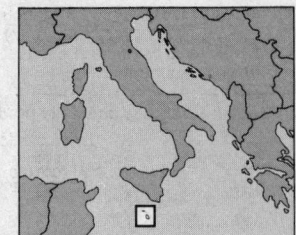

### Area and population

| Census regions[3] | area sq mi | area sq km | population 1987 estimate[2] |
|---|---|---|---|
| Gozo and Comino | 27 | 70 | 25,112 |
| Inner Harbour | 6 | 15 | 97,765 |
| Northern | 30 | 78 | 31,738 |
| Outer Harbour | 12 | 32 | 101,631 |
| South Eastern | 20 | 53 | 42,653 |
| Western | 27 | 69 | 44,435 |
| TOTAL | 122 | 316[4] | 343,334 |

## Demography

*Population* (1987): 345,000.
*Density* (1987): persons per sq mi 2,827.9, persons per sq km 1,092.7.
*Urban–rural* (1985): urban 85.3%; rural 14.7%.
*Sex distribution* (1987): male 49.28%; female 50.72%.
*Age breakdown* (1987): under 15, 24.1%; 15–29, 22.8%; 30–44, 23.6%; 45–59, 15.1%; 60–74, 10.5%; 75 and over, 3.9%.
*Population projection:* (1990) 353,000; (2000) 370,000.
*Doubling time:* 92 years.
*Ethnic composition* (1980): Maltese 95.7%; British 2.1%; other 2.2%.
*Religious affiliation* (1980): Roman Catholic 97.3%; Anglican 1.2%; other 1.5%.
*Major cities* (1987): Birkirkara 20,300; Qormi 18,413; Hamrun 13,651; Sliema 13,650; Valletta 9,263.

## Vital statistics

*Birth rate* per 1,000 population (1986): 16.4 (world avg. 26.0); legitimate 98.8%; illegitimate 1.2%.
*Death rate* per 1,000 population (1986): 8.2 (world avg. 9.9).
*Natural increase rate* per 1,000 population (1986): 8.2 (world avg. 16.1).
*Total fertility rate* (avg. births per childbearing woman; 1980–85): 2.0.
*Marriage rate* per 1,000 population (1986): 7.6.
*Divorce rate* per 1,000 population: n.a.
*Life expectancy* at birth (1985): male 70.8 years; female 76.0 years.
*Major causes of death* per 100,000 population (1986): diseases of the circulatory system 524.2; malignant neoplasms (cancers) 148.0; endocrine, nutritional, and metabolic diseases of the blood and blood-forming organs 61.5; diseases of the respiratory system 48.0; diseases of the digestive system 21.1; accidents, poisoning, and violence 17.8.

## National economy

*Budget* (1986). Revenue: Lm 225,853,000 (national insurance 23.2%, income tax 19.5%, customs and excise taxes 19.4%, property income 10.6%). Expenditures: Lm 195,654,000 (national insurance benefits 27.1%, health 11.3%, education 8.8%).
*Public debt* (1985): U.S.$165,120,000.
*Production* (value added in Lm except where noted). Agriculture, forestry, fishing (1983): vegetables 7,912,000 (of which tomatoes 2,751,000, melons 387,000, onions 223,000), cereals 2,417,000 (of which wheat 920,000, barley 333,000), fruits 1,900,000 (of which citrus fruits 731,000, strawberries 553,-000), potatoes 1,617,000; livestock (number of live animals) 53,366 pigs, 12,794 cattle, 3,395 sheep, 1,062,900 chickens; fish catch (1985) 1,217,983. Mining and quarrying (1984): quarrying 978,000. Manufacturing (1984): textiles and wearing apparel 36,957,000, of which clothing 29,022,000, textiles 4,399,000, footwear 3,536,000; machinery and transport equipment 20,773,000; food and beverages 18,994,000; wood, cork, and furniture 5,349,000; chemicals 3,579,000; tobacco and tobacco products 3,131,000; plastics 1,741,000. Construction (1984): 19,009,000. Energy production (consumption): electricity (kW-hr; 1985) 784,000,000 (784,000,000); coal (metric tons; 1985) none (218,000); crude petroleum, none (n.a.); petroleum products (metric tons; 1985) none (189,000); natural gas, none (n.a.).
*Population economically active* (1985): total 122,685; activity rate of total population 36.7% (participation rates: ages 15–64, n.a.; female 24.3%; unemployed 7.7%).

### Price and earnings indexes (1980 = 100)

| | 1981 | 1982 | 1983 | 1984 | 1985 | 1986 | 1987[5] |
|---|---|---|---|---|---|---|---|
| Consumer price index | 111.5 | 118.0 | 117.0 | 116.5 | 116.2 | 118.5 | 118.4 |
| Annual earnings index | 108.7 | 120.2 | ... | ... | ... | ... | ... |

*Household income and expenditure.* Average household size (1982) 3.6; average annual income per household Lm 4,736 (U.S.$11,399); sources of income (1985): wages and salaries 49.8%, professional and unincorpo-

rated enterprises 17.7%, transfer payments 14.4%, property income 12.1%; expenditure (1985): food and beverages 34.0%, transportation and communication 15.3%, furniture and household operations 8.8%, clothing and footwear 8.7%, housing 6.0%, recreation, entertainment, and education 5.7%, health 3.3%, tobacco 3.3%.
*Tourism:* receipts from visitors (1985) U.S.$149,000,000; expenditures by nationals abroad (1984) U.S.$50,000,000.
*Gross national product* (at current market prices; 1985): U.S.$1,190,000,000 (U.S.$3,300 per capita).

### Structure of gross domestic product and labour force

| | 1985 in value Lm '000 | 1985 % of total value | 1985 labour force | 1985 % of labour force |
|---|---|---|---|---|
| Agriculture | 19,375 | 4.5 | 5,433 | 4.4 |
| Manufacturing | 126,929 | 29.5 | 33,911 | 27.6 |
| Mining Construction } | 20,758 | 4.8 | 6,645 | 5.4 |
| Public utilities | 22,278 | 5.2 | 1,383 | 1.1 |
| Transportation and communication | 23,955 | 5.5 | 8,072 | 6.6 |
| Trade | 66,696 | 15.5 | 11,599 | 9.5 |
| Finance | 21,916 | 5.1 | 3,533 | 2.9 |
| Pub. admin., defense | 58,534 | 13.6 | 28,543 | 23.3 |
| Services | 34,894 | 8.1 | 13,628 | 11.1 |
| Other | 35,215 | 8.2 | 9,938[6] | 8.1[6] |
| TOTAL | 430,550 | 100.0 | 122,685 | 100.0 |

*Land use* (1983): agricultural and under permanent cultivation 41.2%; other (infertile clay soil with underlying limestone) 58.8%.

## Foreign trade

### Balance of trade (current prices)

| | 1981 | 1982 | 1983 | 1984 | 1985 | 1986 |
|---|---|---|---|---|---|---|
| Lm '000,000 | −125.6 | −123.8 | −128.1 | −149.1 | −114.1 | −167.6 |
| % of total | 26.6% | 26.8% | 28.9% | 29.1% | 21.8% | 31.7% |

*Imports* (1986): Lm 347,909,000 (semimanufactures 29.3%, of which textile fabrics and yarn 12.8%, metal and metal manufactures 7.2%; machinery and transport equipment 27.7%, of which electrical equipment 11.6%, transport equipment 4.8%; food and beverages 11.2%, of which cereals 2.3%, meats 1.8%, fruits and vegetables 1.7%; chemicals 8.0%; fuels 6.0%; tobacco 1.7%). *Major import sources:* Italy 23.3%; United Kingdom 17.7%; West Germany 18.9%; United States 5.2%; France 4.2%; The Netherlands 3.0%; Spain 2.2%.
*Exports* (1986): Lm 180,316,000 (clothing and footwear 35.6%; machinery and transport equipment 25.0%, of which electrical equipment 18.3%; semimanufactures 11.2%, of which rubber 3.1%; printed material 5.2%; food and beverages 3.6%; chemicals 1.3%). *Major export destinations:* West Germany 32.9%; United Kingdom 14.2%; Italy 11.1%; United States 7.9%; Libya 4.9%; The Netherlands 4.9%; U.S.S.R. 4.5%.

## Transport and communications

*Transport.* Railroads: none. Roads (1985): total length 830 mi, 1,335 km (paved 92%). Vehicles (1985): passenger cars 82,259; trucks and buses 18,-187. Merchant marine (1986): vessels (100 gross tons and over) 246; total deadweight tonnage 3,415,403. Air transport (1986): passenger-mi 462,000,-000, passenger-km 744,000,000; short ton-mi cargo 3,049,000, metric ton-km cargo 4,452,000; airports (1987) with scheduled flights 1.
*Communications.* Daily newspapers (1981): total number 4; total circulation 81,000; circulation per 1,000 population 245. Radio (1985): total number of receivers 92,363 (1 per 3.6 persons). Television (1985): total number of receivers 116,541 (1 per 2.9 persons). Telephones (1985): 122,267 (1 per 2.8 persons).

## Education and health

### Education (1984–85)

| | schools | teachers | students | student/ teacher ratio |
|---|---|---|---|---|
| Primary (age 5–13) | 124 | 1,777 | 35,411 | 19.9 |
| Secondary (age 11–20) | 65 | 1,624 | 21,759 | 13.4 |
| Voc., teacher tr. | 23 | 555 | 6,140 | 11.1 |
| Higher | 1 | 156 | 1,408 | 9.0 |

*Educational attainment,* n.a. *Literacy* (1980): total population age 15 and over literate 261,900 (81.4%); males literate 129,500 (83.4%); females literate 132,400 (79.7%).
*Health* (1984): physicians 413 (1 per 786 persons); hospital beds 3,142 (1 per 93 persons); infant mortality rate per 1,000 live births (1986) 10.1.
*Food* (1981–83): daily per capita caloric intake 2,682 (vegetable products 74%, animal products 26%); 108% of FAO recommended minimum requirement.

## Military

*Total active duty personnel* (1987): 910 (army 100%). *Military expenditure as percent of GNP* (1984): 1.0% (world 5.9%); per capita expenditure U.S.$32.

---

[1]The Maltese lira is tied to the currencies of several principal trading partners. [2]January 1. [3]Malta has no first-order administrative subdivisions; data are reported according to census regions. [4]Detail does not add to total given because of rounding. [5]August. [6]Mostly unemployed.

# Martinique

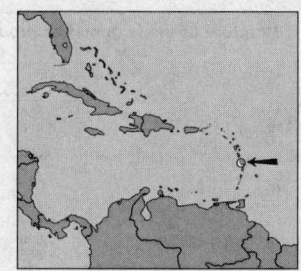

*Official name:* Département de la Martinique (Department of Martinique).
*Political status:* overseas department (France) with two legislative houses (General Council [44]; Regional Council [41]).
*Chief of state:* President of France.
*Heads of government:* Commissioner of the Republic (for France); President of the General Council (for Martinique); President of the Regional Council (for Martinique).
*Capital:* Fort-de-France.
*Official language:* French.
*Official religion:* none.
*Monetary unit:* 1 Franc (F) = 100 centimes; valuation (Oct. 5, 1987) 1 U.S.$ = F 6.13; 1 £ = F 9.96.

### Area and population

| Arrondissements | Capitals | area sq mi | area sq km | population 1982 census |
|---|---|---|---|---|
| Fort-de-France | Fort-de-France | 141 | 365 | 176,749 |
| Le Marin | Le Marin | 154 | 399 | 78,329 |
| La Trinité | La Trinité | 126 | 327 | 73,488 |
| TOTAL | | 421 | 1,091 | 328,566[1] |

## Demography

*Population* (1987): 329,000[2].
*Density* (1987): persons per sq mi 781.5, persons per sq km 301.6.
*Urban–rural* (1982): urban 57.1%; rural 42.9%.
*Sex distribution* (1982): male 48.49%; female 51.51%.
*Age breakdown* (1982): under 15, 28.3%; 15–29, 30.3%; 30–44, 16.2%; 45–59, 13.2%; 60–74, 8.5%; 75 and over, 3.3%; not specified, 0.2%.
*Population projection*[2,3]: (1990) 331,000; (2000) 337,000.
*Doubling time:* 60 years[3].
*Ethnic composition* (1983): mulatto 93.7%; French (metropolitan and Martinique white) 2.6%; East Indian 1.7%; other 2.0%.
*Religious affiliation* (1980): Roman Catholic 91.4%; Protestant (mostly Seventh-day Adventist) 4.7%; syncretist 1.6%; nonreligious 1.2%; other 1.1%.
*Major cities* (1982): Fort-de-France 96,649; Schoelcher 16,412; Le Lamentin 6,872; Saint-Pierre 4,923.

## Vital statistics

*Birth rate* per 1,000 population (1986): 18.1 (world avg. 26.0); (1985) legitimate 36.1%; illegitimate 63.9%.
*Death rate* per 1,000 population (1986): 6.4 (world avg. 9.9).
*Natural increase rate* per 1,000 population (1986): 11.7 (world avg. 16.1).
*Total fertility rate* (avg. births per childbearing woman; 1985–90): 2.1.
*Marriage rate* per 1,000 population (1985–86): 3.8.
*Divorce rate* per 1,000 population (1985–86): 1.0.
*Life expectancy* at birth (1980–85): male 71.0 years; female 75.5 years.
*Major causes of death* per 100,000 population (1982): diseases of the circulatory system 192.3; malignant neoplasms (cancers) 100.2; mental disorders (including deaths associated with chronic alcoholism) 30.6; accidents 25.4; diseases of the respiratory system 24.5; diabetes mellitus 23.9.

## National economy

*Budget* (1987). Revenue: F 1,354,000,000 (receipts from French central government 41.3%, health and social service receipts from local administrative bodies 13.6%, public works subsidies 6.6%, new loans 4.3%, unspecified sources 34.2%). Expenditures: F 1,354,000,000 (health and social assistance 47.0%, improvements to public works and property 22.7%, other administrative services 10.9%, debt payments 2.7%).
*Production* (metric tons except as noted). Agriculture, forestry, fishing (1985): sugarcane 245,000[4], bananas 190,000, pineapples 25,000, yams 10,000, sweet potatoes 7,000, carrots 5,000, tomatoes 4,000, cucumbers 3,000, avocados 1,724[4,5], limes 712[4,5], pimientos 123[4,5]; livestock (number of live animals) 73,000 sheep, 52,000 cattle, 42,000 pigs, 27,000 goats; roundwood 11,000 cu m; fish catch 5,200. Mining and quarrying (1985): pumice 165,000; sand and gravel for local construction. Manufacturing (1986): petroleum products 428,000[6]; cement 191,000[6]; sugar 8,400; pineapple compote 2,190; pineapple juice 1,390; rum 97,200 hectolitres; other products include clothing, fabricated metals, and yawls and sails. Construction (buildings authorized; 1985): residential, n.a.; nonresidential 56,000 sq m. Energy production (consumption): electricity (kW-hr; 1986) 477,000,000 (415,000,000); coal, none (none); crude petroleum (barrels; 1985) none (3,523,000); petroleum products (metric tons; 1985) 428,000 (190,000); natural gas, none (none).
*Population economically active* (1982): total 130,500; activity rate of total population 39.9% (participation rates: ages 15–64, 62.2%; female 44.7%; unemployed [1985] 28.0%).

### Price and earnings indexes (1980 = 100)[7]

| | 1980 | 1981 | 1982 | 1983 | 1984 | 1985 | 1986[8] |
|---|---|---|---|---|---|---|---|
| Consumer price index | 100.0 | 115.4 | 126.9 | 140.6 | 151.6 | 161.0 | 164.4 |
| Monthly earnings index[9] | 100.0 | 113.5 | 137.0 | 147.9 | 153.9 | 163.9 | 164.5 |

*Tourism* (1984): receipts from visitors U.S.$87,000,000; expenditures by nationals abroad, n.a.
*Public debt* (external, outstanding; 1984[10]): U.S.$32,000,000.
*Gross national product* (at current market prices; 1983): U.S.$1,330,000,000 (U.S.$4,070 per capita).

### Structure of gross domestic product and labour force

| | 1982 in value F '000,000 | 1982 % of total value | 1982 labour force | 1982 % of labour force |
|---|---|---|---|---|
| Agriculture | 720 | 8.1 | 9,844 | 7.5 |
| Mining | } 552 | 6.2 | 1,853 | 1.4 |
| Manufacturing | | | 4,001 | 3.1 |
| Construction | 324 | 3.6 | 7,832 | 6.0 |
| Public utilities | 96 | 1.1 | 1,006 | 0.8 |
| Transportation and communication | 390 | 4.4 | 5,197 | 4.0 |
| Trade, restaurants, hotels | 1,541 | 17.4 | 9,864 | 7.6 |
| Finance, real estate | 630 | 7.1 | 17,878 | 13.7 |
| Pub. admin., defense, services | 4,267 | 48.1 | 29,382 | 22.5 |
| Other | 354 | 4.0 | 43,643[11] | 33.4 |
| TOTAL | 8,874 | 100.0 | 130,500 | 100.0 |

*Household income and expenditure.* Average household size (1982) 3.8; income per household (1979) F 70,009 (U.S.$17,415); sources of income (1979): salaries 74.2%, industrial and commercial profits 10.0%, pensions and rents 4.8%, other 11.0%; expenditure (1980)[12]: food and beverages 31.7%, transportation 13.3%, housing 11.2%, clothing and footwear 8.2%, recreation 7.5%, household furnishings 7.4%, health 3.5%, energy 2.7%, other 14.5%.
*Land use* (1984): forested 26.4%; meadows and pastures 31.1%; agricultural and under permanent cultivation 17.9%; other 24.6%.

## Foreign trade

### Balance of trade (current prices)

| | 1980 | 1981 | 1982 | 1983 | 1984 | 1985 | 1986 |
|---|---|---|---|---|---|---|---|
| F '000,000 | −3,011 | −3,211 | −3,819 | −4,359 | −4,632 | −4,593 | −4,569 |
| % of total | 73.1% | 62.2% | 65.3% | 62.4% | 63.2% | 61.2% | 60.4% |

*Imports* (1986): F 6,065,400,000 (food products 22.8%, electrical machinery and equipment 12.7%, mineral fuels 10.6%, transport equipment 9.9%, chemical products 8.4%, metal manufactures 6.6%). *Major import sources* (1985): France 58.4%; other EEC countries 9.9%; Venezuela 7.8%; Saudi Arabia 6.0%; United States 3.0%.
*Exports* (1986): F 1,496,400,000 (bananas 48.1%, petroleum products 20.0%, rum 9.4%, canned pineapple 3.2%, fertilizer 2.1%). *Major export destinations* (1985): France 65.3%; Guadeloupe 23.1%; other EEC countries 3.0%.

## Transport and communications

*Transport.* Railroads: none. Roads (1985): total length 1,156 mi, 1,861 km (paved 85%). Vehicles (1985): passenger cars 135,269; trucks and buses 7,328. Fishing fleet (1985): vessels (100 gross tons and over) 2. Air transport (1986): passenger arrivals 424,646, passenger departures 423,792; cargo unloaded 5,957 metric tons, cargo loaded 4,966 metric tons; airports (1987) with scheduled flights 1.
*Communications.* Daily newspapers (1985): total number 1; total circulation 30,000; circulation per 1,000 population 92. Radio (1986): total number of receivers 55,000 (1 per 6.0 persons). Television (1986): total number of receivers 45,000 (1 per 7.3 persons). Telephones (1983): 83,600 (1 per 3.9 persons).

## Education and health

### Education (1983–84)

| | schools | teachers | students | student/ teacher ratio |
|---|---|---|---|---|
| Primary (age 6–11) | 224 | 2,024 | 39,050 | 19.3 |
| Secondary (age 12–18) | ... | 2,416 | 31,912 | 13.2 |
| Vocational[13] | ... | 653 | 15,410 | 23.6 |
| Higher | 1 | 40 | 1,220 | 30 |

*Educational attainment* (1982). Percent of population age 25 and over having: no formal schooling 9.8%; primary education 62.7%; secondary 21.2%; higher 6.3%. *Literacy* (1982): total population age 15 and over literate 206,807 (92.5%); males literate 97,538 (91.8%); females literate 109,269 (93.2%).
*Health:* physicians (1982) 394 (1 per 829 persons); hospital beds (1984) 4,200 (1 per 78 persons); infant mortality rate per 1,000 live births (1985–86) 13.0.
*Food* (1981–83): daily per capita caloric intake 2,681 (vegetable products 80%, animal products 20%); 110% of FAO recommended minimum requirement.

## Military

*Total active duty personnel* (1984): 2,800[14].

[1]De jure (legally resident, but not necessarily present) census result 326,717. [2]Based on de jure population. [3]Net migration to metropolitan France nearly outweighs natural increase rate. [4]1986. [5]Production for export only. [6]1985. [7]All figures are end of year unless otherwise indicated. [8]End of September. [9]Based on minimum-level wage in public administration. [10]Includes external long-term private debt not guaranteed by the government. [11]Includes 35,936 unemployed. [12]Weights of consumer price index components. [13]1982–83. [14]Includes police.

# Mauritania

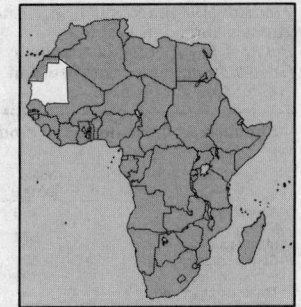

*Official name:* al-Jumhūrīyah
al-Islāmīyah al-Mūrītānīyah (Arabic),
République Islamique de Mauritanie
(French) (Islamic Republic of
Mauritania).
*Form of government:* military regime.
*Head of state and government:*
President assisted by Military
Committee for National Salvation
(24).
*Capital:* Nouakchott.
*Official languages:* Arabic; French.
*Official religion:* Islam.
*Monetary unit:* 1 Mauritanian Ouguiya
(UM) = 5 khoums; valuation (Oct. 5,
1987) 1 U.S.$ = UM 74.73;
1 £ = UM 121.36.

### Area and population

| Regions | Capitals | area sq mi | area sq km | population 1987 estimate[1] |
|---|---|---|---|---|
| el-'Açâba | Kiffa | 13,900 | 36,000 | 160,000 |
| Adrar | Atar | 83,100 | 215,300 | 70,000 |
| Brakna | Aleg | 14,000 | 37,100 | 169,000 |
| Dakhlet Nouadhibou | Nouadhibou | 11,600 | 30,000 | 33,000 |
| Gorgol | Kaédi | 5,400 | 14,000 | 188,000 |
| Guidimaka | Sélibaby | 4,000 | 10,000 | 115,000 |
| Hodh ech-Chargui | Néma | 64,000 | 166,000 | 267,000 |
| Hodh el-Gharbi | 'Ayoûn el-'Atroûs | 22,000 | 57,000 | 140,000 |
| Inchiri | Akjoujt | 19,000 | 49,000 | 26,000 |
| Tagant | Tidjikdja | 36,000 | 93,000 | 80,000 |
| Tiris Zemmour | Fdérik | 98,600 | 255,300 | 37,000 |
| Trarza | Rosso | 26,000 | 67,000 | 249,000 |
| **District** | | | | |
| Nouakchott | Nouakchott | 400 | 1,000 | 285,000 |
| TOTAL | | 398,000 | 1,030,700 | 1,819,000 |

## Demography

*Population* (1987): 1,844,000.
*Density* (1987): persons per sq mi 4.6, persons per sq km 1.8.
*Urban–rural* (1983): urban 25.0%; rural 75.0%[2].
*Sex distribution* (1985): male 49.48%; female 50.52%.
*Age breakdown* (1985): under 15, 46.4%; 15–29, 26.0%; 30–44, 14.6%; 45–59, 8.4%; 60–74, 3.9%; 75 and over, 0.7%.
*Population projection:* (1990) 1,999,000; (2000) 2,673,000.
*Doubling time:* 37 years.
*Ethnic composition* (1983): Moor 81.5%; Wolof 6.8%; Tukulor 5.3%; Soninke 2.8%; Fulani 1.1%; other 2.5%.
*Religious affiliation* (1980): Muslim 99.4%; Christian 0.4%; other 0.2%.
*Major cities* (1981): Nouakchott 350,000[3]; Nouadhibou 22,000; Kaédi 21,-000; Zouérate (Zouîrât) 17,500[4].

## Vital statistics

*Birth rate* per 1,000 population (1985–90): 50.0 (world avg. 26.0); legitimate, n.a.; illegitimate, n.a.
*Death rate* per 1,000 population (1985–90): 19.2 (world avg. 9.9).
*Natural increase rate* per 1,000 population (1985–90): 30.8 (world avg. 16.1).
*Total fertility rate* (avg. births per childbearing woman; 1984): 6.2.
*Marriage rate* per 1,000 population (1984)[5]: 1.1.
*Divorce rate* per 1,000 population (1984)[5]: 0.1.
*Life expectancy* at birth (1984): male 45.0 years; female 48.0 years.
*Morbidity* (notified cases of illness per 100,000 population; 1984): enteritis and diarrhea 10,566; conjunctivitis 7,080; malaria 2,897; scarlet fever 2,476; measles 714.0; chicken pox 306.4.

## National economy

*Budget* (1986). Revenue: UM 18,600,000,000 (1984; tax revenue 63.4%). Expenditures: UM 18,600,000,000 (1984; administration 75.8%, public debt service 10.1%, investments 6.2%).
*Public debt* (external, outstanding; 1985): U.S.$1,363,000,000.
*Tourism:* receipts from visitors (1985) U.S.$7,000,000; expenditures by nationals abroad (1983) U.S.$22,000,000.
*Land use* (1984): forested 14.7%; meadows and pastures 38.1%; agricultural and under permanent cultivation 0.2%; desert 47.0%.
*Production* (metric tons except as noted). Agriculture, forestry, fishing (1985): millet 32,000, pulses 24,000, rice 15,000, dates 12,000, vegetables 9,000, roots and tubers 6,000, sweet potatoes 2,000, peanuts (groundnuts) 2,000, corn (maize) 1,000; livestock (number of live animals) 5,200,000 sheep, 3,250,000 goats, 1,350,000 cattle, 785,000 camels, 161,000 horses and asses, 4,000,000 chickens; roundwood 12,000 cu m; fish catch 57,000. Mining and quarrying (1985): iron ore (gross weight) 9,333,000; gypsum 5,470. Manufacturing (1985): milk 93,000; hydraulic cement 75,000; meat 43,000, of which fresh beef and veal 17,000, fresh mutton and lamb 7,000, goat meat 5,300; hides and skins 5,200; cheese 1,700; butter 700. Construction (1984): 42,478 sq m. Energy production (consumption): electricity (kW-hr; 1985) 103,000,000 (103,000,000); coal (metric tons; 1985) none (7,000); crude petroleum, none (n.a.); petroleum products (metric tons; 1985) none (197,000); natural gas, none (n.a.).
*Gross national product* (at current market prices; 1985): U.S.$700,000,000 (U.S.$420 per capita).

### Structure of gross domestic product and labour force

| | 1984 in value UM '000,000 | 1984 % of total value | 1981 labour force | 1981 % of labour force |
|---|---|---|---|---|
| Agriculture | 8,564 | 19.2 | 353,000 | 69.0 |
| Mining | 4,426 | 9.9 | | |
| Manufacturing | 3,808 | 8.6 | 40,000 | 8.0 |
| Public utilities | | | | |
| Construction | 3,505 | 7.9 | | |
| Transportation and communication | 3,188 | 7.2 | | |
| Trade and finance | 5,688 | 12.8 | 118,000 | 23.0 |
| Pub. admin., defense | 7,800 | 17.5 | | |
| Services | 2,685 | 6.0 | | |
| Other | 4,836 | 10.9 | | |
| TOTAL | 44,500 | 100.0 | 511,000 | 100.0 |

*Population economically active* (1985): total 590,000; activity rate of total population 31.2% (participation rates: ages 15–64, 57.4%; female 13.0%; unemployed, n.a.).

### Price and earnings indexes (1980 = 100)

| | 1978 | 1979 | 1980 | 1981 | 1982 | 1983 | 1984 |
|---|---|---|---|---|---|---|---|
| Consumer price index | 82.8 | 90.3 | 100.0 | 119.1 | 134.1 | 135.3 | 144.9 |
| Earnings index | ... | ... | ... | ... | ... | ... | ... |

*Household income and expenditure.* Average household size (1980) 5.0; income per household: n.a.; sources of income: n.a.; expenditure[5] (1983): food and beverages 61.0%; housing 24.0%; clothing and footwear 5.2%.

## Foreign trade

### Balance of trade (current prices)

| | 1981 | 1982 | 1983 | 1984 | 1985 | 1986 |
|---|---|---|---|---|---|---|
| UM '000,000 | +1,178 | −530 | +4,969 | +7,877 | +13,129 | +10,122 |
| % of total | 4.9% | 2.1% | 18.4% | 27.0% | 29.4% | 24.2% |

*Imports* (1984): UM 10,620,000,000 (1983; machinery and transport equipment 40.0%, food 25.0%, crude petroleum and petroleum products 18.6%). *Major import sources:* France 21.9%; Spain 19.8%; West Germany 9.6%; United States 7.6%; Senegal 6.9%; Algeria 6.0%; Thailand 5.7%; China 3.0%; Egypt 3.0%; Italy 2.7%; Belgium–Luxembourg 2.6%; The Netherlands 2.5%; Japan 1.4%; Denmark 1.3%; United Kingdom 1.1%; Canada 0.9%; Côte d'Ivoire 0.8%; India 0.8%; South Korea 0.4%.
*Exports* (1984): UM 15,982,000,000 (fish 50.3%, iron ore 49.7%). *Major export destinations:* Italy 23.9%; Japan 22.1%; Belgium 17.9%; France 15.1%; Spain 7.3%; United Kingdom 5.0%; West Germany 3.2%; Algeria 1.5%; Portugal 1.0%; Senegal 0.9%; Greece 0.9%; Turkey 0.6%; United States 0.4%.

## Transport and communications

*Transport.* Railroads (1984): route length 428 mi, 689 km; passenger-mi 4,350,000, passenger-km 7,000,000; short ton-mi cargo 4,207,000,000, metric ton-km cargo 6,142,000,000. Roads (1985): total length 4,557 mi, 7,335 km (paved 22%). Vehicles (1985): passenger cars 15,017; trucks and buses 2,188. Merchant marine (1986): vessels (100 gross tons and over) 73; total deadweight tonnage 10,230. Air transport[6] (1985): passenger-mi 144,226,-000, passenger-km 232,109,000; short ton-mi cargo 27,422,000, metric ton-km cargo 40,035,000; airports (1987) with scheduled flights 9.
*Communications.* Daily newspapers (1986): total number 1; total circulation, n.a. Radio (1986): total number of receivers 200,000 (1 per 8.5 persons). Television (1986): total number of receivers 1,000 (1 per 1,691 persons). Telephones (1984): 3,791 (1 per 450 persons).

## Education and health

### Education (1983–84)

| | schools | teachers | students | student/ teacher ratio |
|---|---|---|---|---|
| Primary (age 6–11) | 756 | 2,629 | 119,337 | 45.4 |
| Secondary (age 12–17) | 30 | 1,013 | 27,924 | 27.6 |
| Voc., teacher tr. | 13 | 372 | 3,572 | 9.6 |
| Higher | 7 | 25[7] | 4,340 | ... |

*Educational attainment,* n.a. *Literacy* (1978): total adult population literate 17.0%.
*Health* (1984): physicians 170 (1 per 9,547 persons); hospital beds 1,325 (1 per 1,225 persons); infant mortality rate per 1,000 live births 133.0.
*Food* (1981–83): daily per capita caloric intake 2,162 (vegetable products 76%, animal products 24%); (1983) 92% of FAO recommended minimum requirement.

## Military

*Total active duty personnel* (1986): 8,470 (army 94.4%, navy 3.8%, air force 1.8%). *Military expenditure as percent of GNP* (1983): 5.8% (world 6.1%); per capita expenditure U.S.$25.

---

[1]January 1. [2]The percentage of nomads in Mauritania declined from about 80% of the total population in 1970 to about 25% of the total population in 1983. [3]1984. [4]1977. [5]Nouakchott only. [6]Includes part of Air Afrique traffic. [7]1980–81.

# Mauritius

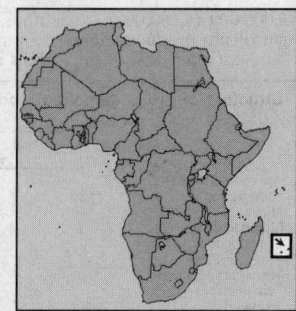

*Official name:* Mauritius.
*Form of government:* constitutional monarchy with one legislative house (Legislative Assembly [70[1]]).
*Chief of state:* British Monarch represented by governor-general.
*Head of government:* Prime Minister.
*Capital:* Port Louis.
*Official language:* English.
*Official religion:* none.
*Monetary unit:* 1 Mauritian Rupee (Mau Re; plural Mau Rs) = 100 cents; valuation (Oct. 5, 1987) 1 U.S.$ = Mau Rs 13.09; 1 £ = Mau Rs 21.25.

### Area and population

| Islands Districts | area sq mi | area sq km | population 1986 estimate[2] |
|---|---|---|---|
| Mauritius | 720 | 1,865 | 998,471 |
| Black River | 100 | 259 | 38,336 |
| Flacq | 115 | 298 | 111,551 |
| Grand Port | 101 | 262 | 96,146 |
| Moka | 89 | 230 | 63,028 |
| Pamplemousses | 69 | 179 | 93,647 |
| Plaines Wilhems | 78 | 202 | 313,025 |
| Port Louis | 17 | 44 | 138,272 |
| Rivière du Rampart | 57 | 148 | 83,856 |
| Savanne | 94 | 243 | 60,610 |
| Rodrigues | 40 | 104 | 35,284 |
| Agelega Saint Brandon } | 27 | 71 | 500 |
| TOTAL | 788[3] | 2,040 | 1,034,255 |

## Demography

*Population* (1987): 1,040,000.
*Density* (1987): persons per sq mi 1,319.8, persons per sq km 509.6.
*Urban-rural* (1986)[4]: urban 41.1%; rural 58.9%.
*Sex distribution* (1986)[4]: male 49.95%; female 50.05%.
*Age breakdown* (1985)[4]: under 15, 31.3%; 15–29, 31.5%; 30–44, 18.9%; 45–59, 10.9%; 60–74, 6.1%; 75 and over, 1.3%.
*Population projection:* (1990) 1,075,000; (2000) 1,202,000.
*Doubling time:* 58 years.
*Ethnolinguistic composition* (1983): Creole 55.5%; Indian 39.6%; European 3.8%; Chinese 0.6%; other 0.5%.
*Religious affiliation* (1983)[4]: Hindu 52.5%; Roman Catholic 25.7%; Muslim 12.9%; Protestant 4.4%; Buddhist 0.4%; other 4.1%.
*Major cities* (1983): Port Louis 148,040; Beau Bassin–Rose Hill 87,520; Quatre Bornes 56,676; Vacoas–Phoenix 56,011; Curepipe 57,613.

## Vital statistics

*Birth rate* per 1,000 population (1985): 19.0 (world avg. 29.0).
*Death rate* per 1,000 population (1985): 6.8 (world avg. 11.0).
*Natural increase rate* per 1,000 population (1985): 12.2 (world avg. 18.0).
*Total fertility rate* (avg. births per childbearing woman; 1985)[4]: 1.9.
*Marriage rate* per 1,000 population (1985): 11.0.
*Divorce rate* per 1,000 population (1983)[4]: 0.4.
*Life expectancy* at birth (1982–84): male 64.4 years; female 71.2 years.
*Major causes of death* per 100,000 population (1985): diseases of the circulatory system 308.2; diseases of the respiratory system 60.2; endocrine and metabolic disorders 33.0; malignant neoplasms (cancers) 24.0.

## National economy

*Budget* (1987–88). Revenue: Mau Rs 6,324,000,000 (tax revenue 79.1%, of which import and stamp duties 38.7%, personal and corporate taxes 9.6%; nontax revenue and grants 20.9%). Expenditures: Mau Rs 8,005,000,000 (current expenditure 73.8%, of which debt servicing 25.2%, education 9.0%, social security 6.8%, health 5.2%, police 3.8%; development expenditure 26.2%).
*Public debt* (external, outstanding; 1985): U.S.$404,100,000.
*Tourism* (1985): receipts from visitors U.S.$65,000,000; expenditures by nationals abroad U.S.$18,900,000.
*Gross national product* (at current market prices; 1985): U.S.$1,110,000,000 (U.S.$1,090 per capita).

### Structure of gross domestic product and labour force

| | 1986 in value Mau Rs '000,000[5] | % of total value | labour force[6] | % of labour force |
|---|---|---|---|---|
| Agriculture | 2,145 | 14.3 | 52,032 | 21.8 |
| Mining | 20 | 0.1 | 179 | 0.1 |
| Manufacturing | 3,320 | 22.1 | 83,941 | 35.2 |
| Construction | 845 | 5.6 | 6,417 | 2.7 |
| Public utilities | 485 | 3.2 | 3,704 | 1.6 |
| Transportation and communication | 1,575 | 10.5 | 9,089 | 3.8 |
| Trade | 2,015 | 13.4 | 10,107 | 4.2 |
| Finance | 2,295 | 15.2 | 5,338 | 2.2 |
| Pub. admin., defense | 1,590 | 10.6 } | 63,034 | 26.5 |
| Services | 750 | 5.0 } | | |
| Other | ... | ... | 4,444 | 1.9 |
| TOTAL | 15,040 | 100.0 | 238,285 | 100.0 |

*Production* (metric tons except as noted). Agriculture, forestry, fishing (1985): sugarcane 5,583,000, green tea 45,300, potatoes 23,300, tomatoes 9,000, black tea 8,100, bananas 7,100, corn (maize) 4,900, onions 3,000, cabbages 3,000, peanuts (groundnuts) 2,200, tobacco 835; livestock (number of live animals) 71,000 goats, 60,000 cattle, 11,000 pigs, 4,000 sheep; roundwood 30,000 cu m; fish catch 12,512. Manufacturing (1985): articles of apparel and clothing 2,539[7]; watches and clocks 146[7]; sugar, refined 645,800; molasses 160,000; iron bars 13,700; processed tea 8,100; beer and stout 171,900 hectolitres; rum 42,900 hectolitres. Construction (1985): residential 315,000 sq m; nonresidential 102,000 sq m. Energy production (consumption): electricity (kW-hr; 1985) 521,000,000 (521,000,000); coal (metric tons; 1985) none (27,000); crude petroleum, none (none); petroleum products (metric tons; 1985) none (181,000); natural gas, none (none).
*Population economically active* (1984): total 367,000; activity rate of total population 38.0% (participation rates: over age 15, 58.5%; female 15.1%; unemployed 19.1%).

### Price and earnings indexes (1980 = 100)

| | 1981 | 1982 | 1983 | 1984 | 1985 | 1986 | May 1987 |
|---|---|---|---|---|---|---|---|
| Consumer price index | 114.5 | 127.5 | 134.7 | 144.6 | 154.3 | 157.2 | 159.0 |
| Monthly earnings index | 117.9 | 129.9 | 138.7 | 144.5 | 148.1 | ... | ... |

*Household income and expenditure.* Average household size (1983)[4] 4.7; income per household (1979) Mau Rs 15,540 (U.S.$2,430); sources of income (1984): salaries and wages 53.1%, entrepreneurial income 32.4%, transfer payments 7.3%, interest and dividends 4.3%, other 2.9%; expenditure (current weights of consumer price index components): food, beverages, and tobacco 50.4, clothing and footwear 10.5%, housing 10.4%, transportation 10.0%, energy 6.4%, health care 3.0%, other 9.3%.
*Land use* (1984): forested 31.4%; meadows and pastures 3.4%; agricultural and under permanent cultivation 57.8%; other 7.4%.

## Foreign trade[8]

### Balance of trade (current prices)

| | 1980 | 1981 | 1982 | 1983 | 1984 | 1985 |
|---|---|---|---|---|---|---|
| Mau Rs '000,000 | −560.7 | −1,260.9 | −330.0 | −161.6 | −482.8 | −352.0 |
| % of total | 7.7% | 17.4% | 4.0% | 1.8% | 4.5% | 2.6% |

*Imports* (1985): Mau Rs 8,041,200,000 (manufactured goods classified chiefly by material 32.3%, food 16.8%, mineral fuels and lubricants 14.3%, machinery and transport equipment 13.3%, chemicals 6.9%, inedible crude materials excluding fuels 4.9%, animal and vegetable oils and fats 3.3%). *Major import sources:* France 12.7%; South Africa 8.6%; United Kingdom 8.0%; Kuwait 7.4%; Japan 6.0%; China 5.4%; Bahrain 4.7%.
*Exports* (1985): Mau Rs 6,636,500,000 (sugar 43.2%, clothing 38.5%, tea 2.7%, watches and clocks 2.2%, fish and fish preparations 2.1%, pearls and precious and semiprecious stones 1.9%, textile yarn and fabric 1.4%). *Major export destinations:* United Kingdom 43.5%; France 20.8%; United States 15.1%; West Germany 6.3%; Italy 3.2%; Belgium 1.7%; Réunion 1.7%.

## Transport and communications

*Transport.* Railroads: none. Roads (1985): total length 1,108 mi, 1,783 km (paved 92%). Vehicles (1985): passenger cars 31,265; trucks and buses 14,224. Merchant marine (1986): vessels (100 gross tons and over) 26; total deadweight tonnage 257,529. Air transport (1984): passenger-mi 276,000,000, passenger-km 444,000,000; short ton-mi cargo 5,712,400, metric ton-km cargo 8,340,000; airports (1987) with scheduled flights 2.
*Communications.* Daily newspapers (1986): total number 8; total circulation 77,000; circulation per 1,000 population 74. Radio (1986): 200,000 receivers (1 per 5.2 persons). Television (1986): 110,000 receivers (1 per 9.4 persons). Telephones (1985): 64,597 (1 per 15 persons).

## Education and health

### Education (1986)

| | schools | teachers | students | student/ teacher ratio |
|---|---|---|---|---|
| Primary (age 5–12) | 273 | 6,161 | 138,765 | 22.5 |
| Secondary (age 12–20) | 125 | 3,572 | 68,604 | 19.2 |
| Voc., teacher tr.[9] | 7 | 69[10] | 444 | ... |
| Higher[9] | 2 | 184[10] | 344 | ... |

*Educational attainment* (1983). Percent of population age 25 and over having: no formal education 24.4%, less than complete primary 0.1%, primary 51.5%, secondary 20.4%, higher 3.6%. *Literacy* (1983)[4]: total population age 15 and over literate 544,940 (83.1%); males literate 291,635 (90.0%); females literate 253,305 (76.4%).
*Health* (1985): physicians 711 (1 per 1,404 persons)[4]; hospital beds 2,850 (1 per 350 persons)[4]; infant mortality rate per 1,000 live births 25.1.
*Food* (1981–83): daily per capita caloric intake 2,717 (vegetable products 89%, animal products 11%); (1983) 118% of FAO recommended minimum requirement.

## Military

*Total active duty personnel:* none; however, a special police mobile unit ensures internal security. *Military expenditure as percent of GNP* (1984): 0.3% (world 5.9%); per capita expenditure U.S.$3.

[1]Includes 8 nonelective seats. [2]Year beginning figure. [3]Detail does not add to total given because of rounding. [4]Island of Mauritius only. [5]At factor cost. [6]Employed persons in establishments employing 10 or more persons. [7]Export earnings in Mau Rs '000,000. [8]Import figures are f.o.b. (free on board) in balance of trade and c.i.f. (cost, insurance, and freight) for commodities and trading partners. [9]1984. [10]1982.

# Mayotte

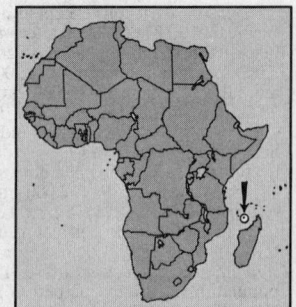

*Official name:* Collectivité Territoriale de Mayotte (Territorial Collectivity of Mayotte).
*Political status:* overseas dependency of France with one legislative house (General Council [17])[1].
*Chief of state:* President of France.
*Head of government:* Commissioner of the Republic (for France); President of the General Council (for Mayotte).
*Capital:* Dzaoudzi (Capital designate, Mamoudzou).
*Official language:* French.
*Official religion:* none.
*Monetary unit:* 1 French (metropolitan) franc (F) = 100 centimes; valuation (Oct. 5, 1987) 1 U.S.$ = F 6.13; 1 £ = F 9.96.

### Area and population

| Islands Communes | Capitals | area sq mi | area sq km | population 1985 census |
|---|---|---|---|---|
| **Grande Terre** | | | | |
| Acoua | Acoua | 4.9 | 12.6 | 2,708 |
| Bandraboua | Bandraboua | 12.5 | 32.4 | 3,533 |
| Bandrele | Bandrele | 14.1 | 36.5 | 2,974 |
| Boueni | Boueni | 5.4 | 14.1 | 3,004 |
| Chiconi | Chiconi | 3.2 | 8.3 | 4,025 |
| Chirongui | Chirongui | 10.9 | 28.3 | 3,387 |
| Dembeni | Dembeni | 15.0 | 38.8 | 2,322 |
| Kani-Keli | Kani-Keli | 7.9 | 20.5 | 2,792 |
| Koungou | Koungou | 11.0 | 28.4 | 3,479 |
| Mamoudzou | Mamoudzou | 16.2 | 41.9 | 12,086 |
| Mtsamboro | Mtsamboro | 5.3 | 13.7 | 3,918 |
| M'tsangamouji | M'tsangamouji | 8.4 | 21.8 | 3,249 |
| Ouangani | Ouangani | 7.3 | 19.0 | 2,575 |
| Sada | Sada | 4.3 | 11.2 | 4,137 |
| Tsingoni | Tsingoni | 13.4 | 34.8 | 3,007 |
| **Petite Terre** | | | | |
| Dzaoudzi- Labattoir | Dzaoudzi | 2.6 | 6.7 | 5,865 |
| Pamandzi | Pamandzi | 1.7 | 4.3 | 4,106 |
| **TOTAL** | | 144.1 | 373.2[2] | 67,167 |

## Demography

*Population* (1987): 73,700.
*Density* (1987): persons per sq mi 511.5, persons per sq km 197.5.
*Urban–rural:* n.a.
*Sex distribution* (1978): male 49.94%; female 50.06%.
*Age breakdown* (1978): under 15, 50.2%; 15–29, 23.4%; 30–44, 13.9%; 45–59, 7.0%; 60–74, 3.8%; 75 and over, 1.7%.
*Population projection:* (1990) 85,000; (2000) 111,000.
*Doubling time:* 14 years.
*Ethnic composition* (1985): Comorian (a mixture of Bantu, Arab, and Malagasy peoples) 96.9%; Europeans 2.5%; other 0.5%.
*Religious affiliation* (1985): Sunnī Muslim 96.9%; Christian, principally Roman Catholic, 3.0%; other 0.1%.
*Major towns* (1985)[3]: Mamoudzou 12,026; Dzaoudzi 5,865.

## Vital statistics

*Birth rate* per 1,000 population (1985): 45.0 (world avg. 29.0); (1978) legitimate (monogamous marriage) 70.8%, legitimate (polygamous marriage) 18.4%, illegitimate 10.8%.
*Death rate* per 1,000 population (1985): 17.0 (world avg. 11.0).
*Natural increase rate* per 1,000 population (1985): 28.0 (world avg. 18.0).
*Total fertility rate* (avg. births per childbearing woman): n.a.
*Marriage rate* per 1,000 population: n.a.; *marital status of adult population* (1978): monogamous marriage 51.8%; unmarried 27.3%; polygamous marriage 11.0%; divorced 6.6%; widowed 3.3%.
*Divorce rate* per 1,000 population: n.a.
*Life expectancy* at birth: n.a.
*Morbidity* (percent of reported cases of illness; 1985): malaria 29.4%; syphilis 25.0%; gonorrhea 24.2%; tuberculosis 5.6%; typhoid 5.6%; leprosy 4.8%.

## National economy

*Budget* (1987). Revenue: F 220,708,000 (subsidies 41.5%, indirect taxes 18.3%, loans 6.6%, direct taxes 5.3%). Expenditures: F 220,708,000 (general administrative services 42.0%, investments 29.5%, debt service 3.5%).
*Public debt:* n.a.
*Tourism:* n.a.
*Production* (metric tons except as noted). Agriculture, forestry, fishing (1986): rice 2,500, mangoes 1,500[4], bananas 1,300[4], breadfruit 700[4], citrus fruit 600[4], cassava 500[4], pineapples 200[4], corn (maize) 150[4], coffee 35,000 kilograms[5], ylang-ylang 21,100 kilograms[5], copra 6,600 kilograms[5], vanilla 3,500 kilograms[5], cloves 1,050 kilograms[5], cinnamon 573 kilograms[5]; coconut palm trees (number of producing trees) 350,000; livestock (number of live animals; 1985) 15,000 goats, 3,000 cattle, 1,200 sheep; roundwood, n.a.; fish catch *c.* 800. Mining and quarrying: negligible. Manufacturing (1983): mostly involves processing of agricultural products for export. Construction (gross value in F '000; 1985): residential, none; nonresidential 50,200. Energy production (consumption): electricity (kW-hr; 1986)

6,000,000 (6,000,000); coal, none (none); crude petroleum, none (none); petroleum products, none (n.a.); natural gas, none (none).
*Gross national product* (at current market prices): n.a.

### Structure of gross domestic product and labour force

| | 1978 in value | 1978 % of total value | 1978 labour force | 1978 % of labour force |
|---|---|---|---|---|
| Agriculture, forestry, and fishing | ... | ... | 9,298 | 61.6 |
| Mining | ... | ... | 19 | 0.1 |
| Manufacturing | ... | ... | 833 | 5.5 |
| Construction | ... | ... | 1,361 | 9.0 |
| Public utilities | ... | ... | 133 | 0.9 |
| Transportation and communication | ... | ... | 287 | 1.9 |
| Trade | ... | ... | 672 | 4.5 |
| Finance | ... | ... | 220 | 1.5 |
| Pub. admin., defense | ... | ... | 218 | 1.4 |
| Education, health | ... | ... | 348 | 2.3 |
| Other | ... | ... | 1,697[6] | 11.2 |
| TOTAL | | | 15,086 | 100.0[2] |

*Population economically active* (1978): total 15,086; activity rate of total population 31.9% (participation rates: ages 15–64, 65.7%; female 35.9%; unemployed 5.8%).

### Price and earnings indexes (1982 = 100)[7,8]

| | 1982 | 1983 | 1984 | 1985 | 1986[9] |
|---|---|---|---|---|---|
| Consumer price index | 108.9 | 116.6 | 123.2 | 132.3 | 138.3 |
| Hourly earnings index[10] | 106.0 | 116.9 | 130.0 | 140.8 | 162.7 |

*Household income and expenditure.* Average household size (1978) 4.7; income per household: n.a.; sources of income: n.a.; expenditure: n.a.
*Land use* (1985): agricultural 64.3%, of which 21.4% is under permanent cultivation; other 35.7%.

## Foreign trade

### Balance of trade (current prices)

| | 1981 | 1982 | 1983 | 1984 | 1985 | 1986 |
|---|---|---|---|---|---|---|
| F '000,000 | −96 | −110 | −140 | −173 | −185 | −188 |
| % of total | 83.9% | 91.1% | 90.1% | 89.6% | 89.1% | 85.5% |

*Imports* (1985): F 196,047,000 (food products 26.5%; mineral fuels 15.5%; metals and metal products 14.9%; machinery 11.9%; chemical products 7.0%; transport equipment 6.5%; wood and wood products 3.8%; textiles and clothing 3.7%). *Major import sources:* France 56.1%; South Africa 11.4%; Bahrain 9.4%; Thailand 6.6%; Réunion 4.2%.
*Exports* (1985): F 10,693,000 (reexports [including rice products, clothing, cigarettes, and chemical products] 64.2%; domestic exports 35.8%, of which ylang-ylang 22.5%, vanilla 11.2%, coffee 2.0%). *Major export destinations:* Comoros 64.2%; France 34.0%; Réunion 1.8%.

## Transport and communications

*Transport.* Railroads: none. Roads (1984): total length 143 mi, 230 km (paved 49%). Vehicles (1984): 1,528. Merchant marine: n.a. Air transport (1986): passenger arrivals 14,009, passenger departures 14,140; cargo unloaded 570 metric tons, cargo loaded 327 metric tons; airports (1987) with scheduled flights 1.
*Communications.* Daily newspapers (1985): total number 1; total circulation, n.a. Radio (1986): total number of receivers 30,000 (1 per 2.3 persons). Television: total number of receivers, n.a.[11]. Telephones: (1985): 970 (1 per 69 persons).

## Education and health

### Education (1984–85)

| | schools | teachers | students | student/ teacher ratio |
|---|---|---|---|---|
| Primary (age 6–11) | 72 | 429[12] | 15,625[12] | 36.4[12] |
| Secondary (age 12–18) | 3 | 66 | 1,374 | 20.0 |
| Voc., teacher tr. | | | | |
| Higher | — | — | — | — |

*Educational attainment* (1978). Percent of population age 20 and over having: no formal education 86.2%; some primary 8.3%; early secondary 3.4%; late secondary 1.5%; postsecondary and higher 0.6%. *Literacy* (1978): total population age 15 and over literate 4,279 (18.0%); males literate 3,230 (27.5%); females literate 1,049 (8.7%).
*Health* (1985): physicians (1980) 9 (1 per 5,857 persons); hospital beds 102 (1 per 655 persons); infant mortality rate per 1,000 live births 110.0.
*Food:* daily per capita caloric intake, n.a.

## Military

*Total active duty personnel* (1985): 300 French troops.

---

[1]Final status of Mayotte is not yet determined; it is claimed by the Comoros as an integral part of that country. [2]Detail does not add to total given because of rounding. [3]Populations cited are for communes, not towns. [4]1983. [5]Export production only. [6]Includes 872 unemployed. [7]Base period is January 1982. [8]All indexes are for December except where footnoted. [9]September. [10]Skilled workers. [11]Television transmission began in 1986. [12]1985–86.

# Mexico

*Official name:* Estados Unidos
Mexicanos (United Mexican States).
*Form of government:* federal republic
with two legislative houses (Senate
[64]; Chamber of Deputies [400]).
*Chief of state and head of government:*
President.
*Capital:* Mexico City.
*Official language:* Spanish.
*Official religion:* none.
*Monetary unit:* 1 peso (Mex$) = 100
centavos; valuation (Oct. 5, 1987)
1 U.S.$ = Mex$1,582;
1 £ = Mex$2,569.

### Area and population

| States | Capitals | area[1] sq mi | sq km | population 1986 estimate |
|---|---|---|---|---|
| Aguascalientes | Aguascalientes | 2,112 | 5,471 | 647,700 |
| Baja California Norte | Mexicali | 26,997 | 69,921 | 1,348,500 |
| Baja California Sur | La Paz | 28,369 | 73,475 | 291,000 |
| Campeche | Campeche | 19,619 | 50,812 | 553,000 |
| Chiapas | Tuxtla Gutiérrez | 28,653 | 74,211 | 2,435,300 |
| Chihuahua | Chihuahua | 94,571 | 244,938 | 2,206,000 |
| Coahuila | Saltillo | 57,908 | 149,982 | 1,840,900 |
| Colima | Colima | 2,004 | 5,191 | 405,500 |
| Durango | Durango | 47,560 | 123,181 | 1,347,100 |
| Guanajuato | Guanajuato | 11,773 | 30,491 | 3,404,400 |
| Guerrero | Chilpancingo | 24,819 | 64,281 | 2,469,500 |
| Hidalgo | Pachuca | 8,036 | 20,813 | 1,771,300 |
| Jalisco | Guadalajara | 31,211 | 80,836 | 5,049,700 |
| México | Toluca | 8,245 | 21,355 | 10,650,300 |
| Michoacán | Morelia | 23,138 | 59,928 | 3,281,900 |
| Morelos | Cuernavaca | 1,911 | 4,950 | 1,194,200 |
| Nayarit | Tepic | 10,417 | 26,979 | 824,200 |
| Nuevo León | Monterrey | 25,067 | 64,924 | 3,032,400 |
| Oaxaca | Oaxaca | 36,275 | 93,952 | 2,609,500 |
| Puebla | Puebla | 13,090 | 33,902 | 3,923,300 |
| Querétaro | Querétaro | 4,420 | 11,449 | 905,900 |
| Quintana Roo | Chetumal | 19,387 | 50,212 | 351,600 |
| San Luis Potosí | San Luis Potosí | 24,351 | 63,068 | 1,951,100 |
| Sinaloa | Culiacán | 22,521 | 58,328 | 2,254,500 |
| Sonora | Hermosillo | 70,291 | 182,052 | 1,743,700 |
| Tabasco | Villahermosa | 9,756 | 25,267 | 1,252,600 |
| Tamaulipas | Ciudad Victoria | 30,650 | 79,384 | 2,207,800 |
| Tlaxcala | Tlaxcala | 1,551 | 4,016 | 643,900 |
| Veracruz | Jalapa | 27,683 | 71,699 | 6,389,700 |
| Yucatán | Mérida | 14,827 | 38,402 | 1,254,000 |
| Zacatecas | Zacatecas | 28,283 | 73,252 | 1,235,200 |
| **Federal District** | | | | |
| Distrito Federal | — | 571 | 1,479 | 10,051,500 |
| TOTAL | | 756,066 | 1,958,201 | 79,579,900[2] |

## Demography

*Population* (1987): 81,323,000.
*Density*[3] (1987): persons per sq mi 107.6, persons per sq km 41.5.
*Urban–rural* (1986): urban 69.7%; rural 30.3%.
*Sex distribution* (1986): male 50.22%; female 49.78%.
*Age breakdown* (1986): under 15, 39.7%; 15–29, 30.2%; 30–44, 16.1%; 45–59,
8.7%; 60–74, 4.1%; 75 and over, 1.2%.
*Population projection:* (1990) 86,215,000; (2000) 99,604,000.
*Doubling time:* 31 years.
*Ethnic composition* (1981): mestizo 55.0%; Amerindian 29.0%; Caucasian
15.0%; black 0.5%; other 0.5%.
*Religious affiliation* (1980): Roman Catholic 92.6%; Protestant (including
Evangelical) 3.3%; Jewish 0.1%; other 0.9%; none 3.1%.
*Major cities* (1980): Mexico City 8,831,079; Guadalajara 1,626,152; Ciudad
Netzahualcóyotl 1,341,230; Monterrey 1,090,009; Puebla 835,759; León
593,002; Juárez 544,496; Tijuana 429,500; Mérida 400,142; Chihuahua
385,603.
*Place of birth* (1980): 98.4% native-born; 1.6% foreign-born and unknown.
*Mobility* (1970). Population living in the same state as in 1960: 87.2%;
different state 12.8%.
*Households* (1980). Total households 12,074,609; average household size 5.5;
1 person 5.4%, 2 persons 10.2%, 3 persons 12.4%, 4 persons 14.3%, 5 persons 13.5%, 6 persons 11.7%, 7 or more persons 32.5%. Family households:
11,421,286 (94.6%); nonfamily 653,323 (5.4%).
*Immigration* (1980): permanent immigrants admitted 73,260.
*Emigration* (1984): legal immigrants to the United States 57,600.

## Vital statistics

*Birth rate* per 1,000 population (1986): 27.3 (world avg. 26.0); (1978) legiti-
mate 91.0%, illegitimate 7.9%, unspecified 1.1%.
*Death rate* per 1,000 population (1986): 5.0 (world avg. 9.9).
*Natural increase rate* per 1,000 population (1986): 22.3 (world avg. 16.1).
*Total fertility rate* (avg. births per childbearing woman; 1986): 3.4.
*Marriage rate* per 1,000 population (1983): 6.8.
*Divorce rate* per 1,000 population (1982): 0.4.
*Life expectancy* at birth (1985): male 64.9 years; female 71.4 years.
*Major causes of death* per 100,000 population (1983): diseases of the circula-
tory system 96.0; accidents 81.2; infectious parasitic diseases 71.5; diseases
of the respiratory system 65.8; diseases of the digestive system 45.2; ma-
lignant neoplasms (cancers) and nonmalignant tumours 43.4; conditions
originating in the perinatal period 32.0; ill-defined conditions 30.0.

## Social indicators

*Educational attainment* (1980). Percent of population age 25 and over having: no primary education 38.0%; some primary 31.7%; completed primary
17.3%; some secondary 8.1%; some postsecondary 4.9%.

### Distribution of income (1977)

percent of household income by quintile

| 1 | 2 | 3 | 4 | 5 (highest) |
|---|---|---|---|---|
| 2.9 | 7.0 | 12.0 | 20.4 | 57.7 |

*Quality of working life.* Average workweek (1984): 46.1 hours. Annual rate
(1984) per 100,000 workers for: temporary disability 2,626; indemnification
for injury 131; death 6. Labour conflicts (1985): 51,207, involving 57,697
workers. Labour stoppages (1985): 417, involving 27,729 workers. Average
duration of journey to work: n.a. Method of transport: n.a. Rate per 1,000
workers of discouraged (unemployed no longer seeking work): n.a.
*Access to services* (1980). Proportion of dwellings having access to: electricity
74.6%; safe public water supply 71.2%; public sewage collection 49.2%.
*Social participation.* Eligible voters participating in last national election: *c.*
50%. Population participating in voluntary work: n.a. Trade union membership in total work force: n.a. Practicing religious population in total
affiliated population (1970): weekly 10% of urban dwellers, 25% of rural
dwellers; yearly 55% of urban dwellers, 73% of rural dwellers.
*Social deviance* (1983). Criminal cases tried by local authorities per 100,-
000 population for: murder 8.4; rape 1.9; other assault 76.9; theft 31.2.
Incidence per 100,000 in general population of: alcoholism, n.a.; drug and
substance abuse, n.a.[4]; suicide 1.47[5].
*Leisure* (1982). Favourite leisure activities (average daily attendance): cinema 430,486; museums and archaeological sites 29,220; live theatre 7,676;
sporting events 5,056; bullfights 330.
*Material well-being* (1970). Households possessing: radio 46.3%; television
1.8%; radio and television 29.4%.

## National economy

*Gross national product* (1985): U.S.$163,790,000,000 (U.S.$2,100 per capita).

### Structure of gross domestic product and labour force

| | 1985 in value U.S.$'000,000 | 1985 % of total value | 1984 labour force | 1984 % of labour force |
|---|---|---|---|---|
| Agriculture | 16,825 | 9.4 | 5,342,000 | 24.0 |
| Mining | 6,747 | 3.8 | 271,000 | 1.2 |
| Manufacturing | 43,810 | 24.6 | 2,361,000 | 10.6 |
| Construction | 8,373 | 4.7 | 1,468,000 | 6.6 |
| Public utilities | 3,292 | 1.8 | 68,000 | 0.3 |
| Transportation and communication | 13,645 | 7.7 | 1,023,000 | 4.6 |
| Trade | 42,473 | 23.8 | 2,744,000 | 12.3 |
| Finance | 15,973 | 9.0 | 480,000 | 2.2 |
| Pub. admin., defense | 6,633 | 3.7 | 1,121,000 | 5.0 |
| Services | 20,518 | 11.5 | 6,335,000 | 28.5 |
| Other | — | — | 1,039,000[6] | 4.7[6] |
| TOTAL | 178,289[7] | 100.0 | 22,252,000 | 100.0 |

*Budget* (1985). Revenue: Mex$7,896,100,000,000 (revenue from state
petroleum company 45.5%, income taxes 23.9%, value added taxes 16.2%,
import duties 5.1%, excise taxes 4.8%). Expenditures: Mex$11,478,200,000,-
000 (interest on public debt 36.9%, transfer payments and subsidies 29.6%,
goods and services 18.2%).
*Public debt* (external, outstanding; 1985): U.S.$97,700,000,000.
*Tourism* (1985): receipts from visitors U.S.$1,727,000,000; expenditures by
nationals abroad U.S.$694,300,000.

### Manufacturing, mining, and construction enterprises (1985)

| | no. of enter- prises | no. of employees ('000) | yearly wages as a % of avg. of all wages[5] | annual income (Mex$'000,000) |
|---|---|---|---|---|
| Manufacturing | 127,539 | 2,303.6 | 166.2 | 16,492,900 |
| Food, beverages, and tobacco | 46,260 | 476.2 | 130.0 | 4,281,300 |
| Chemicals | 4,476 | 264.8 | ... | 2,777,800 |
| Nonelectrical machinery and transport equipment | 6,879 | 264.9 | ... | 2,456,200 |
| Textiles and apparel | 15,753 | 399.9 | 122.8 | 1,462,700 |
| Iron and steel | 1,013 | 113.0 | ... | 1,364,200 |
| Electrical machinery | 2,084 | 220.3 | ... | 1,066,600 |
| Nonmetallic mineral products | 9,173 | 127.7 | ... | 903,000 |
| Paper and printing | 6,750 | 118.7 | ... | 871,100 |
| Metal products | 18,750 | 173.5 | ... | 830,800 |
| Wood and wood products | 14,852 | 108.6 | ... | 297,800 |
| Other manufactures | 1,549 | 36.0 | ... | 181,400 |
| Mining | 466 | 59.5 | 198.2 | 374,700 |
| Construction | 4,648 | 336.4 | 131.8 | 1,449,100 |

*Production* (metric tons except as noted). Agriculture, forestry, fishing
(1986): sugarcane 37,800,000[8], corn (maize) 13,600,000, sorghum 5,861,000,
wheat 3,347,000, bananas 1,668,000, tomatoes 1,665,000[8], oranges 1,587,-
000, dry beans 1,083,000, potatoes 840,000[8], grapes 779,000, mangoes 725,-
000, lemons 675,000, soybeans 633,000, barley 580,000, pineapples 491,000,
avocados 416,000, rice 406,000, apples 350,000, cottonseed 300,000, coffee
269,000[8], cotton lint 196,000[8], tobacco 62,000; livestock (number of live
animals; 1985) 37,450,000 cattle, 19,000,000 pigs, 10,500,000 goats, 6,500,-
000 sheep, 6,135,000 horses, 3,183,000 asses, 3,130,000 mules, 200,000,000
chickens; roundwood (1985) 21,317,000 cu m; fish catch (1985) 1,226,-
244, of which sardines 372,344, anchovies 147,116. Mining and quarrying
(metals by metal content; 1985): iron ore 5,161,000; copper 290,000; zinc
273,840; lead 206,640; manganese 150,647; silver 69,453,000 troy oz; gold
233,438 troy oz; (nonmetals; 1985) sulfur 2,151,000; fluorite 695,000; phosphate rock 600,000; barite 435,000; graphite 42,910. Manufacturing (value

added Mex$'000,000; 1986): machinery and transport equipment 952,700, of which transport equipment 396,600, electrical machinery 334,600; food and beverages 838,000; chemical products 538,200; printed and published materials 274,000; textiles 268,400; metal products 251,500; iron and steel products 228,400; paper and paper products 210,100; wearing apparel and footwear 151,000; rubber products 67,500. Construction (gross value of new construction in Mex$'000,000; 1983): residential 781.026; nonresidential 103.089.

### Trade and service enterprises (1985)

| | no. of establishments | no. of employees | yearly wage as a % of avg. of all wages[5] | annual income (Mex$'000,000) |
|---|---|---|---|---|
| Trade | 618,059 | 1,780,700 | ... | 14,348,200 |
| Wholesale | 30,264 | 329,100 | ... | 5,205,700 |
| Retail | 587,795 | 1,451,600 | ... | 9,142,500 |
| Boutiques (excluding food products) | 223,601 | 600,200 | ... | 3,022,900 |
| Food and tobacco speciality stores | 339,736 | 588,500 | ... | 2,050,800 |
| Automobiles, tires, and auto parts dealers | 16,768 | 104,400 | ... | 1,737,600 |
| Small supermarkets and grocery stores | 4,512 | 96,400 | ... | 1,227,300 |
| Gasoline stations | 2,395 | 23,900 | ... | 708,700 |
| Other | 783 | 38,200 | ... | 395,200 |
| Services | 341,436 | 1,401,500 | 85.2 | 3,476,900 |
| Professional services | 21,040 | 193,000 | 77.9 | 645,700 |
| Food and beverages services | 109,108 | 341,400 | ... | 620,600 |
| Transportation and travel agencies | 3,058 | 41,000 | 133.4 | 353,400 |
| Lodging | 7,819 | 111,500 | ... | 283,900 |
| Automotive repair | 55,850 | 148,500 | ... | 209,800 |
| Educational services (private) | 8,227 | 124,200 | 134.3 | 166,000 |
| Medical and social assistance | 38,606 | 101,000 | 206.4 | 151,700 |
| Amusement services (cinemas and theatres) | 2,915 | 29,500 | 148.9 | 144,500 |
| Recreation | 8,323 | 41,000 | ... | 139,500 |
| Other repair | 36,031 | 64,200 | ... | 86,500 |
| Commercial and professional organizations | 3,209 | 41,900 | 77.9 | 67,400 |
| Other | 47,250 | 164,300 | 49.9 | 607,900 |

Energy production (consumption): electricity (kW-hr; 1985) 93,405,000,000 (93,363,000,000); coal (metric tons; 1985) 14,743,000 (15,294,000); crude petroleum (barrels; 1986) 886,610,000 (446,000,000[8]); petroleum products (metric tons; 1985) 66,338,000 (62,741,000); natural gas (cu m; 1986) 39,-038,000,000 (23,908,000,000[8]).

*Population economically active* (1984): total 22,252,000; activity rate of total population 29.2% (participation rates: ages 15–64, 57.1%[9]; female 27.8%[9]; unemployed 9.7%.)

### Price and earnings indexes (1980 = 100)

| | 1981 | 1982 | 1983 | 1984 | 1985 | 1986 | 1987[10] |
|---|---|---|---|---|---|---|---|
| Consumer price index | 127.9 | 203.3 | 410.2 | 679.0 | 1,071.2 | 1,994.9 | 4,607.8 |
| Earnings index | 125.3 | 259.3 | 385.0 | 605.8 | ... | ... | ... |

*Household income and expenditure.* Average household size (1986) 5.3; income per household: n.a. Sources of income: n.a.; expenditure (1984): food, beverages, and tobacco 35.8%, housing (includes household furnishings) 20.2%, transportation and communication 12.0%, clothing and footwear 10.3%, recreation and entertainment 5.0%, health and medical services 5.0%.

*Land use* (1984): forested 23.8%; meadows and pastures 38.7%; agricultural and under permanent cultivation 12.8%; other 24.7%.

### Financial aggregates[11]

| | 1982 | 1983 | 1984 | 1985 | 1986 | 1987[12] |
|---|---|---|---|---|---|---|
| Exchange Rate, Mex$ per: | | | | | | |
| U.S. Dollar | 56.40 | 120.09 | 167.83 | 256.87 | 611.77 | 1,459.63 |
| £ | 98.73 | 182.18 | 224.89 | 332.98 | 897.46 | 2,141.28 |
| SDR | 62.27 | 128.38 | 171.80 | 408.28 | 1,129.62 | 1,943.52 |
| International reserves (U.S.$) | | | | | | |
| Total (excl. gold; '000,000) | 834 | 3,913 | 7,272 | 4,906 | 5,607 | 11,700[13] |
| SDRs ('000,000) | 6 | 23 | 3 | — | 9 | 455 |
| Reserve pos. in IMF ('000,000) | — | 95 | — | — | — | — |
| Foreign exchange | 828 | 3,795 | 7,269 | 4,906 | 5,661 | 11,326[13] |
| Gold ('000,000 fine troy oz) | 2.07 | 2.31 | 2.42 | 2.36 | 2.57 | 2.52[13] |
| % world reserves | 0.22 | 0.24 | 0.26 | 0.25 | 0.33 | 0.32[13] |
| Interest and prices | | | | | | |
| Treasury bill rate | 45.75 | 59.19 | 49.47 | 63.36 | 98.30 | ... |
| Balance of payments (U.S.$'000,000) | | | | | | |
| Balance of visible trade, | +6,795 | +13,762 | +12,941 | +8,451 | +4,599 | ... |
| of which: | | | | | | |
| Imports, f.o.b. | 14,435 | 7,721 | 11,255 | 13,460 | 11,432 | ... |
| Exports, f.o.b. | 22,081 | 22,228 | 24,196 | 21,867 | 16,031 | ... |
| Balance of invisibles | −13,660 | −9,654 | −9,112 | −8,317 | −6,359 | ... |
| Balance of payments, current account | −5,753 | +5,208 | +4,240 | +540 | −1,270 | ... |

### Foreign trade

### Balance of trade (current prices)

| | 1981 | 1982 | 1983 | 1984 | 1985 | 1986 |
|---|---|---|---|---|---|---|
| Mex$'000,000 | −4,099 | +6,792 | +13,762 | +12,947 | +8,451 | +4,599 |
| % of total | 9.3% | 19.3% | 44.6% | 36.5% | 24.2% | 16.7% |

*Imports* (1986): Mex.$11,384,500,000 (machinery and transport equipment 44.5%, of which electrical machinery 11.5%; transport equipment 11.2%,

chemical products 14.9%; unprocessed agricultural products 6.9%, of which soybeans 1.5%; corn 1.4%, sorghum 0.6%; livestock and fish 1.4%). *Major import sources* (1985): United States 68.5%; Japan 5.6%; West Germany 4.0%; Italy 1.9%; United Kingdom 1.7%; Canada 1.6%; France 1.5%.

*Exports* (1986): Mex.$15,759,300,000 (crude petroleum 35.1%; machinery and transport equipment 19.4%; unprocessed agricultural products [including livestock] 13.4%, of which coffee 5.2%, tomatoes 2.7%, live cattle 1.6%; chemical products 5.3%; petroleum products 4.0%). *Major export destinations* (1985): United States 62.6%; Japan 6.8%; Spain 6.6%; France 2.9%; Canada 2.6%; United Kingdom 2.5%; Brazil 1.4%; Israel 1.0%.

### Trade by commodity group (1985)

| | imports | | exports | |
|---|---|---|---|---|
| SITC group | U.S.$'000,000 | % | U.S.$'000,000 | % |
| 00 Food and live animals | 1,619 | 12.0 | 1,323 | 6.2 |
| 01 Beverages and tobacco | — | — | 747 | 3.5 |
| 02 Crude materials, excluding fuels | 209 | 1.6 | 514 | 2.4 |
| 03 Mineral fuels, lubricants, and related materials | 1,341 | 10.0 | 15,281 | 71.7 |
| 04 Animal and vegetable oils, fats, and waxes | — | — | — | — |
| 05 Chemicals and related products, n.e.s. | 1,373 | 10.2 | 676 | 3.2 |
| 06 Basic manufactures | 4,726 | 35.4 | 1,118 | 5.2 |
| 07 Machinery and transport equipment | 1,404 | 10.5 | 1,564 | 7.3 |
| 08 Miscellaneous manufactured articles | 2,581 | 19.2 | 91 | 0.4 |
| 09 Goods not classified by kind | 151 | 1.1 | 6 | 0.1 |
| TOTAL[14] | 13,440 | 100.0 | 21,320 | 100.0 |

### Direction of trade (1985)

| | imports | | exports | |
|---|---|---|---|---|
| SITC group | U.S.$'000,000 | % | U.S.$'000,000 | % |
| Africa | 66 | 0.4 | 84 | 0.4 |
| Asia | 1,066 | 6.6 | 2,155 | 9.0 |
| South America | 470 | 2.9 | 619 | 2.6 |
| North and Central America | 11,440 | 70.4 | 16,355 | 68.1 |
| United States | 11,132 | 68.5 | 15,029 | 62.6 |
| other North and Central Am. | 308 | 1.9 | 1,326 | 5.5 |
| Europe | 2,295 | 14.1 | 4,049 | 16.8 |
| EEC | 1,851 | 11.4 | 3,869 | 16.1 |
| U.S.S.R. | 7 | — | 6 | — |
| other Europe | 437 | 2.7 | 174 | 0.7 |
| Oceania | 105 | 0.6 | 32 | 0.1 |
| unknown | 810 | 5.0 | 725 | 3.0 |
| freight and insurance charges | | | — | — |
| TOTAL | 16,252 | 100.0 | 24,019 | 100.0 |

### Transport and communications

*Transport.* Railroads (1986): route length 15,979 mi, 25,716 km; passenger-mi 3,606,000,000, passenger-km 5,803,000,000; short ton-mi cargo 33,041,000,-000, metric ton-km cargo 48,239,000,000. Roads (1985): total length 109,820 mi, 176,738 km (paved 50%). Vehicles (1984): passenger cars 5,028,604; trucks and buses 2,167,000. Merchant marine (1986): vessels (100 gross tons and over) 642; total deadweight tonnage 2,206,643. Air transport[15] (1986): passenger-mi 10,491,000,000, passenger-km 16,884,000,000; short ton-mi cargo 109,458,000, metric ton-km cargo 159,816,000; airports (1986) 72.

*Communications.* Daily newspapers (1983): total number, more than 350; total circulation, n.a.; circulation per 1,000 population, n.a. Radio (1986): 25,278,000 receivers (1 per 3.2 persons). Television (1986): 9,490,000 receivers (1 per 8.4 persons). Telephones (1985): 7,329,416 (1 per 11 persons).

### Education and health

### Education (1986–87)

| | schools | teachers | students | student/teacher ratio |
|---|---|---|---|---|
| Primary (age 6–12) | 75,184 | 444,620 | 14,951,302 | 33.6 |
| Secondary (age 12–18) | 16,426 | 224,732[16] | 4,384,616 | ... |
| Voc., teacher tr.[16] | 5,811 | 139,391 | 2,088,292 | 15.0 |
| Higher[16] | 1,347 | 98,061 | 1,072,764 | 13.7 |

*Literacy* (1986): total population age 15 and over literate 44,116,332 (92.0%); males literate, n.a.; females literate n.a.

*Health:* physicians (1980) 53,053 (1 per 1,308 persons); hospital beds (1984) 72,000 (1 per 1,070 persons); infant mortality rate per 1,000 live births (1985) 53.0.

*Food* (1981–83): daily per capita caloric intake 2,966 (vegetable products 86%, animal products 14%); (1983) 124% of FAO recommended minimum.

### Military

*Total active duty personnel* (1986): 139,500 (army 75.3%, navy 20.1%, air force 4.6%). *Military expenditure as percent of GNP* (1984): 0.3% (world 5.9%); per capita expenditure U.S.$7.

[1]Total land area is 754,107 sq mi (1,953,128 sq km); the area shown for the states, federal district, and the grand total includes both land and water area. [2]Official estimate includes 52,700 not assigned by state. [3]Based on land area. [4]Through 1982, cannabis remained the most abused drug. [5]1984. [6]Includes unemployed. [7]At 1984 prices. [8]1985. [9]1980. [10]July. [11]Exchange rates and treasury bill rates are expressed in period averages; international reserves are expressed in end-of-period rates. [12]August. [13]May. [14]Totals include adjustments of unspecified nature. [15]All scheduled traffic of Mexicana and AeroMexico airlines. [16]1985–86.

# Micronesia, Federated States of

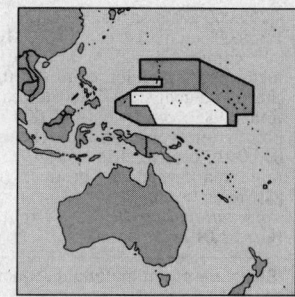

*Official name:* Federated States of Micronesia.
*Political status:* federal republic in free association with the United States with one legislative house (National Congress [14])[1].
*Head of state and government:* President.
*Capital:* Kolonia.
*Official language:* none.
*Official religion:* none.
*Monetary unit:* 1 U.S. dollar (U.S.$) = 100 cents; valuation (Oct. 5, 1987) 1£ = U.S.$1.62.

### Area and population

| States<br>Major Islands | area | | population<br>1985<br>estimate |
|---|---|---|---|
| | sq mi | sq km | |
| Kosrae | 42.3 | 109.6 | 6,462 |
| Kosrae Island | 42.3 | 109.6 | 6,462 |
| Pohnpei | 133.3 | 345.2 | 27,871 |
| Pohnpei Island | 129.0 | 334.1 | 24,788 |
| Truk | 49.1 | 127.2 | 46,159 |
| Moen Islands | 7.0 | 18.1 | 14,218 |
| Yap | 45.9 | 118.9 | 10,948 |
| Yap Island | 38.7 | 100.2 | 6,951 |
| TOTAL | 270.8[2] | 701.4[2] | 91,440 |

## Demography

*Population* (1987): 97,400.
*Density* (1987): persons per sq mi 359.7, persons per sq km 138.9.
*Urban–rural* (1980): urban 19.4%; rural 80.6%.
*Sex distribution* (1980): male 51.12%; female 48.88%.
*Age breakdown* (1980): under 15, 46.4%; 15–29, 26.8%; 30–44, 12.6%; 45–59, 8.5%; 60–74, 4.5%; 75 and over, 1.2%.
*Population projection:* (1990) 107,800; (2000) 151,200.
*Doubling time:* 26 years.
*Ethnic composition* (1980): Trukese 41.1%; Pohnpeian 25.9%; Mortlockese 8.3%; Kosraean 7.4%; Yapese 6.0%; Ulithian, or Woleaian, 4.0%; Pingelapese, or Mokilese, 1.2%; Western Trukese 1.0%; Palauan 0.4%; Filipino 0.2%; other 4.5%.
*Religious affiliation:* Christianity is the predominant religious tradition, with the Kosraeans, Pohnpeians, and Trukese being mostly Protestant and the Yapese mostly Roman Catholic.
*Major cities* (1980): Moen 10,351; Tol 6,705; Kolonia 5,549; Sokehs 3,632; Kitti 3,401.

## Vital statistics

*Birth rate* per 1,000 population (1984): 29.4 (world avg. 29.0); legitimate, n.a.; illegitimate, n.a.
*Death rate* per 1,000 population (1984)[3]: 2.7 (world avg. 11.0).
*Natural increase rate* per 1,000 population (1984): 26.7 (world avg. 18.0).
*Total fertility rate* (avg. births per childbearing woman; 1985)[4]: 5.3.
*Marriage rate* per 1,000 population: n.a.
*Divorce rate* per 1,000 population: n.a.
*Life expectancy* at birth (1985)[3]: male 64.0 years; female 68.1 years.
*Major causes of death* per 100,000 population (1984): diseases of the cerebrovascular system 53.2; pulmonary diseases 47.5; suicide and accidents 23.8.

## National economy

*Budget* (1985). Revenue: U.S.$80,965,900 (U.S. Department of the Interior 49.8%, other U.S. government grants and federal program funds 40.2%, local revenue sources 10.0%). Expenditures: n.a.
*Public debt* (external, outstanding): n.a.
*Tourism* (1985): number of visitors 11,805.
*Production* (metric tons except as noted). Agriculture, forestry, fishing (1985): n.a.; however, Micronesia's major crops include coconuts (from which more than 4,000 tons of copra is produced), cassava, sweet potatoes, and a variety of tropical fruits (including bananas); livestock comprises mostly pigs and poultry; fish catch, n.a., however, tuna is one of the major natural resources of Micronesia. Mining and quarrying: quarrying of sand and aggregate for local construction only. Manufacturing: n.a.; however, copra is the most important product, and the manufacture of handicrafts and personal items (clothing, mats, boats, etc.) by individuals is also important. Construction: n.a. Energy production (consumption): electricity[5] (kW-hr; 1984) 150,000,000 (150,000,000); coal, none (n.a.); crude petroleum, none (n.a.); petroleum products (metric tons; 1984) none (50,000[5]); natural gas, none (n.a.).
*Price and earnings indexes:* n.a.
*Household income and expenditure:* average household size (1980) 7.0; average annual income per household, n.a.; sources of income (as percent of workers over age 16): wage and salary workers (private) 22.8%, wage and salary workers (government) 51.5%, self-employed persons 2.7%, primarily subsistence workers 5.7%; expenditure (1985): food and beverages 73.5%.
*Land use* (1984)[5]: forested 22.5%; meadows and pastures 13.5%; agricultural and under permanent cultivation 33.5%; other 30.5%.

*Gross national product* (at current market prices; 1983): U.S.$106,500,000 (U.S.$1,250 per capita).

### Structure of gross domestic product and labour force

| | 1983 | | 1980 | |
|---|---|---|---|---|
| | in value<br>U.S.$'000,000 | % of total<br>value | labour<br>force | % of labour<br>force |
| Nonmonetarized<br>Agriculture | 40.6 | 38.1 | 5,055 | 35.4 |
| Monetarized<br>Agriculture | 4.3 | 4.1 | 196 | 1.4 |
| Trade | 12.7 | 11.9 | 864 | 6.1 |
| Public administration | 31.5 | 29.6 | 1,763 | 12.3 |
| Manufacturing | | | 115 | 0.8 |
| Construction and<br>mining | | | 946 | 6.6 |
| Transportation,<br>communication,<br>and public utilities | 17.4 | 16.3 | 472 | 3.3 |
| Finance | | | 121 | 0.8 |
| Services | | | 3,086 | 21.6 |
| Other | | | 1,680[6] | 11.7 |
| TOTAL | 106.5 | 100.0 | 14,298 | 100.0 |

*Population economically active* (1982): total 41,535[7]; activity rate of total population 51.4% (participation rates: ages 15–64, 50.9%; female 48.9%; unemployed 5.0%).

## Foreign trade

### Balance of trade (current prices)

| | 1978 | 1979 | 1980 | 1981 | 1982 | 1983 |
|---|---|---|---|---|---|---|
| U.S.$'000,000 | ... | ... | ... | ... | ... | −54.94 |
| % of total | ... | ... | ... | ... | ... | 88.4% |

*Imports* (1983): U.S.$58,530,000 (much of Micronesia's food must be imported, including fruits, vegetables, meat, and fish; nearly all manufactured goods must be imported, including such necessities as medicine and fuel oil. *Major import sources:* United States; Japan; Guam; Australia.
*Exports* (1983): U.S.$3,590,000 (primarily from copra, but black pepper, handicrafts, and a few marine products are also exported). *Major export destinations:* United States; Japan.

## Transport and communications

*Transport.* Railroads: none. Roads (1985): total length 19 mi[8], 31 km[8]. Vehicles: passenger cars, trucks, and buses, n.a. Merchant marine: n.a. Air transport: n.a.; airports (1987) with scheduled flights 4.
*Communications.* Daily newspapers (1985): there are no private newspapers. Radios (1984): total number of receivers 15,800 (1 per 5.4 persons). Television (1984): total number of receivers 500 (1 per 170.8 persons). Telephones: n.a.

## Education and health

### Education (1980–81)

| | schools | teachers | students | student/<br>teacher ratio |
|---|---|---|---|---|
| Elementary (age 3–5) | ... | ... | 1,690 | ... |
| Elementary (age 6–13) | ... | ... | 13,866 | ... |
| Elementary (over age 14) | ... | ... | 1,557 | ... |
| High school (age 12–18) | ... | ... | 3,104 | ... |
| High school (over age 18) | ... | ... | 777 | ... |
| College[9] | ... | ... | 720 | ... |

*Educational attainment* (1980). Percent of population age 25 and over having: no formal schooling 24.8%; some primary education 38.2%; primary 11.7%; some secondary 7.7%; secondary 9.6%; higher 8.0%. *Literacy* (1980): total population age 15 and over literate 30,074 (76.7%); males literate 13,710 (67.0%); females literate 16,364 (87.2%).
*Health* (1985): physicians 36[10] (1 per 2,540 persons); hospital beds, n.a.; infant mortality rate per 1,000 live births (1984) 36.5.
*Food:* daily per capita caloric intake, n.a.

## Military

External security is provided by the United States.

[1]On Nov. 3, 1986, the United States unilaterally terminated the UN trusteeship it held over the Federated States of Micronesia, the Republic of the Marshall Islands, the Republic of Palau, and the Commonwealth of the Northern Mariana Islands, thus formally initiating their free-association political status. The United Nations has thus far not recognized the termination of the trusteeship. [2]Detail does not add to total given because of rounding. [3]For registered deaths only. [4]Includes other islands in geographic Micronesia. [5]Includes the area formerly comprising the U.S. Trust Territory of the Pacific Islands. [6]Includes unemployed. [7]Includes more than 18,000 persons "not working" but not considered to be unemployed. [8]Paved road only. [9]In 1985, 1,200 students were enrolled in colleges and universities in the United States. [10]Excludes medical officers.

# Mongolia

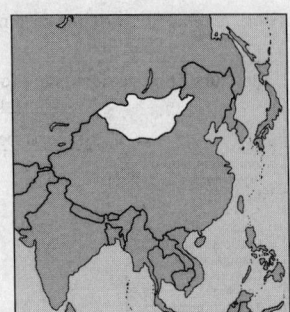

Official name: Büged Nayramdah
Mongol Arad Ulas (Mongolian
People's Republic).
Form of government: unitary
single-party republic with one
legislative house (People's Great
Hural [370]).
Chief of state: Chairman of
the Presidium of the People's
Great Hural.
Head of government: Premier.
Capital: Ulaanbaatar (Ulan Bator).
Official language: Khalkha Mongolian.
Official religion: none.
Monetary unit: 1 tugrik = 100 möngös;
valuation (Oct 5, 1987) 1 U.S.$ = 3.36
tugriks; 1 £ = 5.45 tugriks.

### Area and population

| Provinces | Capitals | area sq mi | area sq km | population 1984 estimate |
|---|---|---|---|---|
| Arhangay | Tsetserleg | 21,000 | 55,000 | 83,800 |
| Bayanhongor | Bayanhongor | 45,000 | 116,000 | 69,500 |
| Bayan-Ölgiy | Ölgiy | 18,000 | 46,000 | 84,000 |
| Bulgan | Bulgan | 19,000 | 49,000 | 46,000 |
| Dornod | Choybalsan | 47,000 | 122,000 | 67,800 |
| Dornogovi | Saynshand | 43,000 | 111,000 | 47,400 |
| Dundgovi | Mandalgov | 30,000 | 78,000 | 44,100 |
| Dzavhan | Uliastay | 32,000 | 82,000 | 88,100 |
| Govi-Altay | Altay | 55,000 | 142,000 | 62,500 |
| Hentiy | Öndörhaan | 32,000 | 82,000 | 60,500 |
| Hovd | Hovd | 29,000 | 76,000 | 71,600 |
| Hövsgöl | Mörön | 39,000 | 101,000 | 96,600 |
| Ömnögovi | Dalandzadgad | 64,000 | 165,000 | 35,500 |
| Övörhangay | Arvayheer | 24,000 | 63,000 | 93,200 |
| Selenge | Sühbaatar | 16,000 | 42,000 | 76,400 |
| Sühbaatar | Baruun-urt | 32,000 | 82,000 | 47,200 |
| Töv | Dzuunmod | 31,000 | 81,000 | 90,200 |
| Uvs | Ulaangom | 27,000 | 69,000 | 81,400 |
| **Autonomous municipalities** | | | | |
| Darhan | — | 100 | 200 | 63,600 |
| Erdenet | — | 300 | 800 | 40,500 |
| Ulaanbaatar | — | 800 | 2,000 | 470,500 |
| TOTAL | | 604,000[1] | 1,565,000 | 1,820,400 |

## Demography

Population (1987): 1,989,000.
Density (1987): persons per sq mi 3.3, persons per sq km 1.3.
Urban–rural (1986): urban 51.8%; rural 48.2%.
Sex distribution (1986): male 50.08%; female 49.92%.
Age breakdown (1985): under 15, 42.7%; 15–29, 26.2%; 30–44, 16.1%; 45–59, 9.7%; 60–74, 4.4%; 75 and over, 0.9%.
Population projection: (1990) 2,146,000; (2000) 2,764,000.
Doubling time: 26 years.
Ethnic composition (1979): Khalkha Mongol 77.5%; Kazakh 5.3%; Dörbed Mongol 2.8%; Bayad 2.0%; Buryat Mongol 1.9%; Dariganga Mongol 1.5%; other 9.0%.
Religious affiliation: Although formal freedom of worship, or of propagandization against religion, exists, all traditional religious practice (lamaistic Buddhism, shamanism, Islam, and others) has become vastly attenuated during the 20th century; reliable data on the current situation do not exist.
Major cities (1985): Ulaanbaatar (Ulan Bator) 488,200; Darhan 69,800; Erdenet 42,900.

## Vital statistics

Birth rate per 1,000 population (1985): 36.8 (world avg. 29.0); legitimate, n.a.; illegitimate, n.a.
Death rate per 1,000 population (1985): 9.9 (world avg. 11.0).
Natural increase rate per 1,000 population (1985): 26.9 (world avg. 18.0).
Total fertility rate (avg. births per childbearing woman; 1986): 4.6.
Marriage rate per 1,000 population (1985): 6.6.
Divorce rate per 1,000 population (1985): 0.4.
Life expectancy at birth (1986): male 61.1 years; female 65.2 years.
Major causes of death per 100,000 population: n.a.; however, major diseases include brucellosis, helminthiasis (an infection with worms), bacillary dysentery and amoebiasis, enteritis and other diarrheal diseases, cerebrospinal meningitis, trachoma, and tuberculosis of the respiratory system. Typhus, diphtheria, and acute poliomyelitis, formerly widespread, have reportedly been eliminated.

## National economy

Budget (1986). Revenue: 5,865,000,000 tugriks (turnover tax 66.3%, deductions from profits 26.3%, social insurance contributions 3.6%, forestry and hunting 3.1%). Expenditures: 5,855,000,000 tugriks (social and cultural services 41.3%, economy 39.4%, defense 13.5%, administration and other 4.1%).
Public debt (1985): U.S.$4,160,000,000.
Tourism (1983): number of tourists 170,000; receipts from visitors, n.a.; expenditures by nationals abroad, n.a.
Production (metric tons except as noted). Agriculture, forestry, fishing (1985): wheat 482,000, potatoes 114,000, barley 94,000, oats 53,000, vegetables 41,300; livestock (number of live animals; 1986) 13,249,000 sheep,

4,299,000 goats, 2,408,000 cattle, 1,971,000 horses, 56,100 pigs; roundwood 1,500,000 cu m; fish catch 400. Mining and quarrying (1985): fluorspar 787,000; copper 120,000. Manufacturing (1985): flour 175,800; cement 151,000; meat 62,500; woolen cloth 2,100,000 sq m; leather shoes 2,900,000 pairs; sheep and goat skins 2,880,000 sq m; beer 88,500,000 hectolitres. Construction (1985): residential 240,000 sq m; nonresidential 1,066 units. Energy production (consumption): electricity (kW-hr; 1985) 2,788,000,000 (3,050,000,000); coal (metric tons; 1985) 6,518,000 (6,518,000); crude petroleum, none (n.a.); petroleum products (metric tons; 1985) none (765,000); natural gas, none (n.a.).
Gross national product (at current market prices; 1985): U.S.$1,911,000,000 (U.S.$1,010 per capita).

### Structure of net material product and labour force

| | 1985 value | % of total value | labour force | % of labour force |
|---|---|---|---|---|
| Agriculture | ... | 16.2 | 321,000 | 47.8 |
| Mining and manufacturing | ... | 32.6 | 91,000 | 13.6 |
| Construction | ... } | 5.0 | 29,200 | 4.4 |
| Public utilities | ... } | | 17,400 | 2.6 |
| Transportation and communication | ... | 11.5 | 36,400 | 5.4 |
| Trade | ... | 33.0 | 41,600 | 6.2 |
| Services[2] | ... | ... | 105,600 | 15.7 |
| Other | ... | 1.7 | 28,900 | 4.3 |
| TOTAL | ... | 100.0 | 671,100 | 100.0 |

Population economically active (1985): total 671,000; activity rate of total population 35.5% (participation rates: ages 15–64, 55.9%; female 51.3%; unemployed, n.a.)
Price and earnings indexes: n.a.
Household income and expenditure. Average household size (1980) 5.0; income per household: n.a.; sources of income: n.a.; expenditure: n.a.
Land use (1984): forested 9.7%; meadows and pastures 78.8%; agricultural and under permanent cultivation 0.8%; other 10.7%.

## Foreign trade

### Balance of trade (current prices)

| | 1980 | 1981 | 1982 | 1983 | 1984 | 1985 |
|---|---|---|---|---|---|---|
| U.S.$'000,000 | −138.7 | −225.7 | −220.0 | −305.0 | −230.0 | −388.0 |
| % of total | 15.2% | 20.1% | 17.0% | 20.7% | 18.1% | 22.7% |

Imports (1985): U.S.$1,048,000,000 (machinery and equipment 36.3%; fuels, minerals, and metals 28.7%; consumer goods 18.8%; food products 10.5%; chemical products, fertilizers, and rubber 7.3%). Major import sources: U.S.S.R. and socialist countries 99.0%; capitalist countries 1.0%.
Exports (1985): U.S.$660,000,000 (minerals and metals 42.0%; raw materials and food products 40.3%; consumer goods 16.8%; chemicals and related products 0.7%). Major export destinations: U.S.S.R. and socialist countries 96.1%; capitalist countries 3.9%.

## Transport and communications

Transport. Railroads (1985): length 1,086 mi, 1,748 km; passenger-mi 270,900,000, passenger-km 436,000,000; short ton-mi cargo 4,082,000,000, metric ton-km cargo 5,960,000,000. Roads (1986): total length 29,000 mi, 47,600 km (paved 2%). Vehicles: n.a. Merchant marine: vessels (100 gross tons and over) none. Air transport (1985): passenger-mi 183,000,000, passenger-km 295,000,000; short ton-mi cargo 4,500,000, metric ton-km cargo 6,500,000; airports (1987) with scheduled flights 1.
Communications. Daily newspapers (1985): total number 2; total circulation 96,000; circulation per 1,000 population 85.0. Radio (1986): total number of receivers 194,000 (1 per 9.7 persons). Television (1986): total number of receivers 88,100 (1 per 21 persons). Telephones (1986): 49,300 (1 per 38 persons).

## Education and health

### Education (1985–86)

| | schools | teachers | students | student/ teacher ratio |
|---|---|---|---|---|
| Primary and secondary (age 8–18) | 678 | 17,000 | 428,000 | 25.2 |
| Voc., teacher tr. | 40 | 1,200 | 27,700 | 23.1 |
| Higher | 8 | 1,500 | 24,500 | 16.4 |

Educational attainment (1979). Percent of population age 10 and over having: primary education 48.0%; some secondary 29.7%; complete secondary 9.5%; vocational secondary 7.0%; some higher and complete higher 5.8%.
Literacy (1980): total population age 15 and over literate 849,000 (89.5%); males literate 443,000 (93.4%); females literate 406,000 (85.5%).
Health (1986): physicians 4,400 (1 per 430 persons); hospital beds 21,200 (1 per 89 persons); infant mortality rate per 1,000 live births 47.0.
Food (1981–83): daily per capita caloric intake 2,744 (vegetable products 67%, animal products 33%); (1983) 117% of FAO recommended minimum requirement.

## Military

Total active duty personnel (1986): 25,500 (army 86.3%; navy, none; air force 13.7%). Military expenditure as percent of GNP (1984): 11.5% (world 5.9%); estimated foreign military assistance $600,000; per capita expenditure U.S.$200.

[1]Detail does not add to total given because of rounding. [2]Services includes finance, public administration, and defense.

# Morocco

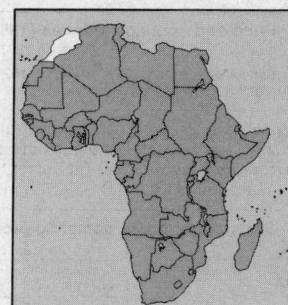

*Official name:* al-Mamlakah al-Maghribīyah (Kingdom of Morocco).
*Form of government:* constitutional monarchy with one legislative house (House of Representatives [306]).
*Chief of state:* King.
*Head of government:* Prime Minister.
*Capital:* Rabat.
*Official language:* Arabic.
*Official religion:* Islam.
*Monetary unit:* 1 Moroccan dirham (DH) = 100 Moroccan francs; valuation (Oct. 5, 1987) 1 U.S.$ = DH 8.37; 1 £ = DH 13.57.

### Area and population[1]

| Provinces | Capitals | area sq mi | area sq km | population 1985 estimate |
|---|---|---|---|---|
| Agadir | Agadir | 2,282 | 5,910 | 647,000 |
| Azilal | Azilal | 3,880 | 10,050 | 399,000 |
| Béni Mellal | Béni Mellal | 2,732 | 7,075 | 749,000 |
| Ben Slimane | Ben Slimane | 1,066 | 2,760 | 185,000 |
| Boulemane | Boulemane | 5,558 | 14,395 | 140,000 |
| Chaouen (Chefchaouen) | Chaouen (Chefchaouen) | 1,680 | 4,350 | 328,000 |
| Essaouira | Essaouira | 2,446 | 6,335 | 409,000 |
| Fès | Fès | 2,085 | 5,400 | 877,000 |
| Figuig | Figuig | 21,618 | 55,990 | 105,000 |
| Guelmim | Guelmim | 11,100 | 28,750 | 141,000 |
| al-Hoceima | al-Hoceima | 1,371 | 3,550 | 331,000 |
| Ifrane | Ifrane | 1,278 | 3,310 | 106,000 |
| el-Jadida | el-Jadida | 2,317 | 6,000 | 818,000 |
| el-Kelaa des Srarhna | el-Kelaa Srarhna | 3,888 | 10,070 | 614,000 |
| Kénitra | Kénitra | 1,832 | 4,745 | 781,000 |
| Khémisset | Khémisset | 3,207 | 8,305 | 430,000 |
| Khénifra | Khénifra | 4,757 | 12,320 | 390,000 |
| Khouribga | Khouribga | 1,641 | 4,250 | 473,000 |
| Marrakech | Marrakech | 5,697 | 14,755 | 1,355,000 |
| Meknès | Meknès | 1,542 | 3,995 | 670,000 |
| Nador | Nador | 2,367 | 6,130 | 655,000 |
| Ouarzazate | Ouarzazate | 16,043 | 41,550 | 572,000 |
| Oujda | Oujda | 7,992 | 20,700 | 843,000 |
| er-Rachidia | er-Rachidia | 23,006 | 59,585 | 450,000 |
| Safi | Safi | 2,813 | 7,285 | 754,000 |
| Settat | Settat | 3,764 | 9,750 | 728,000 |
| Sidi Kacem | Sidi Kacem | 1,568 | 4,060 | 545,000 |
| Tangier | Tangier | 461 | 1,195 | 477,000 |
| Tan-Tan | Tan-Tan | 6,678 | 17,295 | 51,000 |
| Taounate | Taounate | 2,156 | 5,585 | 559,000 |
| Taroudannt | Taroudannt | 6,355 | 16,460 | 593,000 |
| Tata | Tata | 10,010 | 25,925 | 103,000 |
| Taza | Taza | 5,799 | 15,020 | 649,000 |
| Tétouan | Tétouan | 2,326 | 6,025 | 757,000 |
| Tiznit | Tiznit | 2,687 | 6,960 | 336,000 |
| **Prefectures** | | | | |
| Ain Chok–Hay Hassani | — | | | 339,000 |
| Ain Sebaa–Hay Mohammadi | — | | | 471,000 |
| Ben Msik–Sidi Othmane | — | 623 | 1,615 | 737,000 |
| Casablanca–Anfa | — | | | 976,000 |
| Mohammadia–Znata | — | | | 173,000 |
| Rabat–Salé | — | 492 | 1,275 | 1,169,000 |
| TOTAL | | 177,117 | 458,730 | 21,885,000 |

## Demography

*Population* (1987): 23,119,000[1].
*Density* (1987): persons per sq mi 130.5, persons per sq km 50.4.
*Urban–rural* (1985): urban 43.9%; rural 56.1%.
*Sex distribution* (1985): male 50.06%; female 49.94%.
*Age breakdown* (1985): under 15, 41.6%; 15–29, 28.7%; 30–44, 14.5%; 45–59, 9.3%; 60–74, 4.5%; 75 and over, 1.4%.
*Population projection:* (1990) 25,100,000; (2000) 33,018,000.
*Doubling time:* 21 years.
*Ethnic composition* (1982): Arab–Berber 99.1%; other 0.9%.
*Religious affiliation* (1982): Muslim (mostly Sunnī) 98.7%; Christian 1.1%.
*Major cities* (1984): Casablanca 2,600,000; Fès 852,000; Rabat 556,000.

## Vital statistics

*Birth rate* per 1,000 population (1980–85): 44.1 (world avg. 29.0).
*Death rate* per 1,000 population (1980–85): 11.7 (world avg. 11.0).
*Natural increase rate* per 1,000 population (1980–85): 32.4 (world avg. 18.0).
*Total fertility rate* (avg. births per childbearing woman; 1980–85): 6.4.
*Life expectancy* at birth (1980–85): male 56.1 years; female 59.4 years.
*Major causes of death* per 100,000 population (1985): parasitic and infectious diseases 75.0.

## National economy

*Budget* (1986). Revenue: DH 55,420,000,000 (loans 38.7%). Expenditures: DH 68,310,000,000 (current 32.5%, investment 30.0%).
*Public debt* (external, outstanding; 1985): U.S.$11,230,500,000.
*Tourism:* receipts from visitors (1985) U.S.$600,000,000; expenditures by nationals abroad (1984) U.S. $70,000,000.
*Production* (metric tons except as noted). Agriculture, forestry, fishing (1985): wheat 2,400,000, barley 2,100,000, oranges 758,000, potatoes 570,000; livestock (number of live animals) 12,000,000 sheep, 4,500,000 goats, 2,600,000 cattle; roundwood 1,643,000 cu m; fish catch 473,056. Mining and quarrying (1985): phosphate rock 20,778,900; iron ore 190,500; lead 152,500; copper 59,200; zinc 27,200. Manufacturing (value in DH; 1985): foodstuffs

16,662,000,000; chemicals 9,450,000,000; textiles and leather 6,146,000,000. Construction (value added in DH; 1985): 4,510,000,000. Energy production (consumption): electricity (kW-hr; 1985) 6,950,000,000 (6,950,000,000); coal (metric tons; 1985) 900,000 (1,050,000); crude petroleum (barrels; 1986) 200,000 (34,000,000[2]); petroleum products (metric tons; 1985) 4,062,000 (4,103,000); natural gas (cu m; 1986) 74,000,000 (85,000,000[2]).
*Gross national product* (at current market prices; 1985): U.S.$13,390,000,000 (U.S.$610 per capita).

### Structure of gross domestic product and labour force

| | 1985 in value DH '000,000 | 1985 % of total value | 1982 labour force | 1982 % of labour force |
|---|---|---|---|---|
| Agriculture | 21,996 | 18.4 | 2,351,629 | 39.2 |
| Mining | 8,094 | 6.8 | 63,360 | 1.1 |
| Manufacturing | 19,842 | 16.6 | 930,615 | 15.5 |
| Construction | 7,814 | 6.5 | 437,464 | 7.3 |
| Public utilities | 2,250 | 1.9 | 22,465 | 0.4 |
| Transp. and commun. | 6,010 | 5.0 | 140,981 | 2.3 |
| Trade | 16,024 | 13.4 | 498.130 | 8.3 |
| Finance | 3,676 | 3.1 | ... | ... |
| Pub. admin., defense | 14,276 | 11.9 | 532,803 | 8.9 |
| Services | 15,475 | 12.9 | 474,109 | 7.9 |
| Other | 4,201 | 3.5 | 547,704 | 9.1 |
| TOTAL | 119,658 | 100.0 | 5,999,260 | 100.0 |

*Population economically active* (1982): total 5,999,260; activity rate of total population 29.6% (participation rates: over age 15, 47.9%; female 18.1%; unemployed 4.7%).

### Price and earnings indexes (1980 = 100)

| | 1980 | 1981 | 1982 | 1983 | 1984 | 1985 | 1986[3] |
|---|---|---|---|---|---|---|---|
| Consumer price index | 100.0 | 112.5 | 124.4 | 132.1 | 148.5 | 160.0 | 175.7 |
| Hourly earnings index[4] | 100.0 | 111.9 | 132.7 | 150.3 | ... | ... | ... |

*Household income and expenditure.* Average household size (1982) 5.8; income per household: n.a.; sources of income: n.a.; expenditure (1972–73)[5]: food 54.0%, clothing 8.5%, housing 7.0%, transportation 6.9%.
*Land use* (1984): forested 11.6%; meadows and pastures 28.0%; agricultural and under permanent cultivation 18.7%; other 41.7%.

## Foreign trade[6]

### Balance of trade (current prices)

| | 1981 | 1982 | 1983 | 1984 | 1985 | 1986 |
|---|---|---|---|---|---|---|
| DH '000,000 | −7,406 | −10,405 | −8,173 | −12,190 | −13,454 | −9,201 |
| % of total | 23.1% | 29.5% | 22.2% | 24.2% | 23.6% | 17.1% |

*Imports* (1985): DH 38,675,074,000 (petroleum 25.7%; food, beverages, and tobacco 13.2%; vegetable oil 3.6%; chemical products 3.2%). *Major import sources:* France 22.8%; Saudi Arabia 14.9%; Spain 7.1%.
*Exports* (1985): DH 21,740,090,000 (food, beverages, and tobacco 25.3%; phosphates 22.2%; phosphoric acid 14.4%; clothing 5.6%). *Major export destinations:* France 23.6%; Spain 7.4%; West Germany 6.9%; India 5.8%.

## Transport and communications

*Transport.* Railroads (1985): route length (1986) 1,105 mi, 1,779 km; passenger-km 1,932,000,000; metric ton-km cargo 4,560,000,000. Roads (1985): total length 35,747 mi, 57,530 km (paved 46%). Vehicles (1985): passenger cars 491,144; trucks and buses 232,689. Merchant marine (1986): vessels (100 gross tons and over) 294; total deadweight tonnage 595,364. Air transport (1985): passenger-km 2,124,000,000; metric ton-km cargo 38,796,000; airports (1987) 14.
*Communications.* Daily newspapers (1986): total number 8; total circulation 282,000; circulation per 1,000 population 12.4. Radio (1986): 3,000,000 receivers (1 per 7.6 persons). Television (1986): 1,098,645 receivers (1 per 20.6 persons). Telephones (1985): 311,138 (1 per 70 persons).

## Education and health

### Education (1985–86)

| | schools | teachers | students | student/ teacher ratio |
|---|---|---|---|---|
| Primary (age 7–12) | 3,443[7] | 79,300[8] | 2,279,887 | ... |
| Secondary (age 14–21) | 1,145[7] | 56,106[8] | 1,200,383 | ... |
| Voc., teacher tr. | 17[9] | 952 | 7,674 | ... |
| Higher | 19[10] | 4,456 | 134,640 | 30.2 |

*Educational attainment* (1982). Percent of population age 25 and over having: no formal education 47.8%; some primary education 47.8%; some secondary 3.8%; higher 0.6%; not specified 2.3%. *Literacy* (1980): total population over age 15 literate 7,655,000 (70.7%); males literate 4,459,000 (82.4%); females literate 3,196,000 (58.7%).
*Health* (1984): physicians 2,957 (1 per 7,727 persons); hospital beds 26,538 (1 per 805 persons); infant mortality rate per 1,000 live births (1980–85) 97.0.
*Food* (1981–83): daily per capita caloric intake 2,706 (vegetable products 93%, animal products 7%); (1983) 105% of FAO recommended minimum requirement.

## Military

*Total active duty personnel* (1986): 170,000 (army 88.2%, navy 4.1%, air force 7.7%). *Military expenditure as percent of GNP* (1984): 5.0% (world 5.9%); per capita expenditure U.S.$31.

[1]Excludes Western Sahara. [2]1985. [3]September. [4]Minimum wages in nonagricultural activities. [5]Weights of consumer price index components. [6]Import figures are f.o.b. in balance of trade and c.i.f. in commodities and trading partners. [7]1984–85. [8]Public schools only. [9]Teacher's training establishments. [10]1982.

# Mozambique

*Official name:* República Popular de Moçambique (People's Republic of Mozambique).
*Form of government:* people's republic with a single legislative house (People's Assembly [250]).
*Chief of state and head of government:* President.
*Capital:* Maputo.
*Official language:* Portuguese.
*Official religion:* none.
*Monetary unit:* 1 metical (Mt., plural meticais) = 100 centavos; valuation (Oct. 5, 1987) 1 U.S.$ = Mt. 403.65; 1 £ = Mt. 655.49.

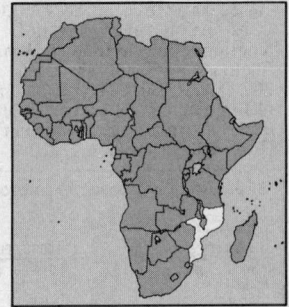

### Area and population

| Provinces | Capitals | area[1] | | population 1987 estimate[2] |
|---|---|---|---|---|
| | | sq mi | sq km | |
| Cabo Delgado | Pemba | 31,902 | 82,625 | 1,109,900 |
| Gaza | Xai-Xai | 29,231 | 75,709 | 1,138,700 |
| Inhambane | Inhambane | 26,492 | 68,615 | 1,167,000 |
| Manica | Chimoio | 23,807 | 61,661 | 756,900 |
| Maputo | Maputo | 9,944 | 25,756 | 544,700 |
| Nampula | Nampula | 31,508 | 81,606 | 2,837,900 |
| Niassa | Lichinga | 49,829 | 129,056 | 607,700 |
| Sofala | Beira | 26,262 | 68,018 | 1,257,700 |
| Tete | Tete | 38,890 | 100,724 | 981,300 |
| Zambézia | Quelimane | 40,544 | 105,008 | 2,952,200 |
| **City** | | | | |
| Maputo | — | 232 | 602 | 1,006,800 |
| TOTAL LAND AREA | | 303,623 | 786,380 | 14,360,800 |
| INLAND WATER | | 5,019 | 13,000 | |
| TOTAL AREA | | 308,642[3] | 799,380 | |

## Demography

*Population* (1987): 14,516,000.
*Density*[4] (1987): persons per sq mi 47.8, persons per sq km 18.5.
*Urban–rural* (1980): urban 13.2%; rural 86.8%.
*Sex distribution* (1986): male 48.81%; female 51.19%.
*Age breakdown* (1980): under 15, 44.4%; 15–29, 26.7%; 30–44, 15.9%; 45–59, 8.7%; 60–74, 3.6%; 75 and over, 0.7%.
*Population projection:* (1990) 15,696,000; (2000) 20,463,000.
*Doubling time:* 26 years.
*Ethnic composition* (1983): Makua 47.3%; Tsonga 23.3%; Malawi 12.0%; Shona 11.3%; Yao 3.8%; Swahili 0.8%; Makonde 0.6%; Portuguese 0.2%; other 0.7%.
*Religious affiliation* (1980): traditional beliefs 47.8%; Christian 38.9%, of which Roman Catholic 31.4%; Muslim 13.0%; other 0.3%.
*Major cities* (1986): Maputo 882,800; Beira 269,700; Nampula 182,600.

## Vital statistics

*Birth rate* per 1,000 population (1980–85): 45.1 (world avg. 29.0); (1974) legitimate 73.1%; illegitimate 26.9%.
*Death rate* per 1,000 population (1980–85): 19.7 (world avg. 11.0).
*Natural increase rate* per 1,000 population (1975–80): 25.4 (world avg. 18.0).
*Total fertility rate* (avg. births per childbearing woman; 1980–85): 6.1.
*Marriage rate* per 1,000 population (1974): 0.7.
*Divorce rate* per 1,000 population (1973): 0.01.
*Life expectancy* at birth (1980–85): male 44.4 years; female 46.2 years.
*Major infectious diseases* (certified cases per 100,000 population; 1980): measles 227.4; pulmonary tuberculosis 55.9; viral hepatitis 19.2; leprosy 13.8; cholera 4.6; tetanus 4.5.

## National economy

*Budget* (1986). Revenue: Mt. 20,300,000,000 (indirect taxes 42.8%, direct taxes 31.0%, profits from state enterprises 10.8%). Expenditures: Mt. 27,400,000,000 (education 16.8%, health 6.6%).
*Production* (metric tons except as noted). Agriculture, forestry, fishing (1985): cassava 3,180,000, sugarcane 800,000, coconut 400,000, corn (maize) 340,000, sorghum 180,000, bananas 70,000, peanuts (groundnuts) 60,000; livestock (number of live animals) 1,330,000 cattle, 360,000 goats, 145,000 pigs, 115,000 sheep, 19,000,000 chickens; roundwood 15,231,000 cu m; fish catch 37,700. Mining and quarrying (1985): marine salt 28,000; hydraulic lime 10,000; bauxite 5,037; bentonite 361; copper 118[5]; garnet 1,500 kg. Manufacturing (value added in Mt.[6]; 1986): clothing and footwear 2,093,594; processed fish products 1,528,450; alcoholic beverages 1,284,516; flour 1,219,008; textiles 1,110,831; machinery and transport equipment 921,364, of which electrical equipment 410,650; tobacco 788,036; wood 702,419; cotton 520,780; soaps and oils 515,009; cashews 418,624; rubber 411,925; furniture 296,207; dairy products 279,250. Construction (1974): residential 247,000 sq m; nonresidential 121,000. Energy production (consumption): electricity (kW-hr; 1985) 1,945,000,000 (1,540,000,000); coal (metric tons; 1985) 380,000 (420,000); crude petroleum (barrels; 1985) none (3,960,000); petroleum products (metric tons; 1985) 507,000 (483,000); natural gas, none (none).
*Public debt* (external, outstanding; 1985)[7]: U.S.$1,224,000,000.
*Population economically active* (1980): total 5,671,290; activity rate of total population 48.6% (participation rates: over age 15, 87.3%; female 52.4%; unemployed 1.7%).

### Price and earnings indexes (1980 = 100)

| | 1980 | 1981 | 1982 | 1983 | 1984 | 1985 | 1986 |
|---|---|---|---|---|---|---|---|
| Consumer price index | 100 | 102 | 120 | 155 | 202 | 261 | 305 |
| Monthly earnings index | ... | ... | ... | ... | ... | ... | ... |

*Household income and expenditure.* Average household size (1980) 4.2; income per household: n.a.; sources of income: n.a.; expenditure: n.a.
*Gross national product* (at current market prices; 1985): U.S.$2,200,000,000 (U.S.$160 per capita).

### Structure of gross domestic product and labour force

| | 1986[6] | | 1980 | |
|---|---|---|---|---|
| | in value Mt. '000,000 | % of total value | labour force | % of labour force |
| Agriculture | 25,000 | 44.5 | 4,754,831 | 83.8 |
| Mining | } 14,800 | 26.3 | 346,794 | 6.1 |
| Manufacturing | | | | |
| Construction | 6,200 | 11.0 | 42,121 | 0.7 |
| Public utilities | ... | ... | 8 | 8 |
| Transportation and communication | 4,600 | 8.2 | 77,025 | 1.4 |
| Trade and finance | | | 112,244 | 2.0 |
| Pub. admin., defense | } 5,600 | 10.0 } | 243,449[8] | 4.3[8] |
| Services | | | | |
| Other | | | 94,826 | 1.7 |
| TOTAL | 56,200 | 100.0 | 5,671,290 | 100.0 |

*Tourism:* n.a.
*Land use* (1984): forested 19.4%; meadows and pastures 56.1%; agricultural and under permanent cultivation 3.9%; other 20.6%.

## Foreign trade

### Balance of trade (current prices)

| | 1981 | 1982 | 1983 | 1984 | 1985 | 1986 |
|---|---|---|---|---|---|---|
| Mt. '000,000 | −18,392 | −22,918 | −20,286 | −18,843 | −18,989 | −18,739 |
| % of total | 48.1% | 57.0% | 65.7% | 70.6% | 69.4% | 74.6% |

*Imports* (1986): Mt. 21,937,180,000 (foodstuffs 27.5%, capital equipment 16.1%, machinery and spare parts 12.5%, crude petroleum and derivatives 8.8%, chemicals 7.1%, metals 4.0%). *Major import sources:* United States 12.4%; U.S.S.R. 12.1%; South Africa 11.7%; Italy 6.3%; France 6.1%; Portugal 6.1%.
*Exports* (1986): Mt. 3,198,385,000 (shrimps 48.4%, cashew nuts 21.1%, sugar 10.2%, petroleum products 5.1%, citrus fruit 2.8%, copra 2.6%, tea 1.6%). *Major export destinations:* Japan 22.6%; United States 22.1%; Spain 21.3%; East Germany 7.7%; Portugal 2.9%.

## Transport and communications

*Transport.* Railroads (1986): track length 2,182 mi, 3,512 km; passenger-mi 163,793,000, passenger-km 263,600,000; short ton-mi cargo 207,743,000, metric ton-km cargo 303,300,000. Roads (1984): total length 12,420 mi, 19,990 km (paved 25%). Vehicles (1981): passenger cars 99,400; trucks and buses 24,700. Merchant marine (1986): vessels (100 gross tons and over) 104; total deadweight tonnage 38,811. Air transport (1985): passenger-mi 291,000,000, passenger-km 468,000,000; short ton-mi cargo 7,175,000, metric ton-km cargo 10,476,000; airports (1987) with scheduled flights 7.
*Communications.* Daily newspapers (1986): total number 2; total circulation 77,000; circulation per 1,000 population 5.4. Radio (1986): total number of receivers 500,000 (1 per 28 persons). Television (1986): total number of receivers 20,000 (1 per 705 persons). Telephones (1985): 60,232 (1 per 229 persons).

## Education and health

### Education (1985–86)

| | schools | teachers | students | student/ teacher ratio |
|---|---|---|---|---|
| Primary (age 5–9)[9] | 4,382 | 20,756 | 1,251,391 | 60.3 |
| Secondary (age 10–16) | 208 | 3,422 | 144,012 | 42.1 |
| Voc., teacher tr. | 34 | 864 | 10,485 | 12.2 |
| Higher | 2 | 330 | 1,569 | 4.8 |

*Educational attainment* (1980). Percent of population age 25 and over having: no formal schooling 80.7%; primary education 18.2%; secondary 0.9%; higher 0.2%. *Literacy* (1985): total population age 15 and over literate 1,270,389 (16.6%); males literate 743,101 (20.0%); females literate 527,288 (13.3%).
*Health* (1986): physicians 279 (1 per 50,817 persons); hospital beds 12,270 (1 per 1,155 persons); infant mortality rate per 1,000 live births (1980–85) 153.0.
*Food* (1981–83): daily per capita caloric intake 1,735 (vegetable products 97%, animal products 3%); (1983) 71% of FAO recommended minimum requirement.

## Military

*Total active duty personnel* (1986): 15,800 (army 88.6%, navy 5.1%, air force 6.3%). *Military expenditure as percent of GNP* (1984): 8.4% (world 5.9%); per capita expenditure U.S.$17.

---

[1]Total area is shown for the provinces. [2]January 1. [3]Detail does not add to total given because of rounding. [4]Density is based on land area. [5]Metal content only. [6]At prices of 1980. [7]Includes external long-term private debt not guaranteed by the government. [8]Services includes Public utilities. [9]Includes initiation classes in which pupils learn Portuguese.

# Nauru

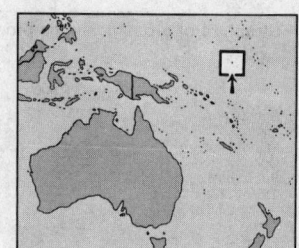

*Official name:* Naoero (Republic of Nauru).
*Form of government:* republic with one legislative house (Parliament [18]).
*Head of state and government:* President.
*Capital:* Yaren[1].
*Official language:* Nauruan.
*Official religion:* none.
*Monetary unit:* 1 Australian dollar ($A) = 100 cents; valuation (Oct. 5, 1987) 1 U.S.$ = $A 1.40; 1 £ = $A 2.27.

| Area and population | area | | population |
|---|---|---|---|
| Districts | sq mi | sq km | 1983 census[2] |
| Aiwo | 0.4 | 1.1 | 812[23] |
| Anabar | 0.6 | 1.5 | 226 |
| Anetan | 0.4 | 1.0 | 265 |
| Anibare | 1.2 | 3.1 | 87 |
| Baitsi | 0.5 | 1.2 | 363 |
| Boe | 0.2 | 0.5 | 578 |
| Buada | 1.0 | 2.6 | 467 |
| Denigomodu | 0.3 | 0.9 | 2,600[3] |
| Ewa | 0.5 | 1.2 | 269 |
| Ijuw | 0.4 | 1.1 | 132 |
| Meneng | 1.2 | 3.1 | 1,024 |
| Nibok | 0.6 | 1.6 | 338 |
| Uaboe | 0.3 | 0.8 | 272 |
| Yaren | 0.6 | 1.5 | 559 |
| TOTAL | 8.2 | 21.2 | 8,043[4] |

## Demography

*Population* (1987): 8,100.
*Density* (1987): persons per sq mi 987.8, persons per sq km 382.1.
*Urban–rural* (1985): urban 100%; rural 0%.
*Sex distribution[5]* (1981): male 51.30%; female 48.70%.
*Age breakdown[5]* (1981): under 15, 43.8%; 15–24, 23.0%; 25–34, 13.7%; 35–44, 8.2%; 45–55, 6.1%; 55–64, 3.1%; 65 and over, 2.1%.
*Population projection:* (1990) 8,200; (2000) 8,600.
*Doubling time:* n.a.; doubling time exceeds 100 years[6].
*Ethnic composition* (1983): Nauruan 61.7%; other Pacific islander 26.5%; Asian 8.5%; Caucasian 3.3%.
*Religious affiliation* (1980): Nauruan Protestant Church (Congregational) 54.5%; Roman Catholic 24.0%; Chinese folk-religionist 8.4%; Anglican 3.1%; Buddhist 1.7%; Baha'i 1.7%; nonreligious 6.6%.
*Major cities:* none.

## Vital statistics

*Birth rate* per 1,000 population (1983): 31.2 (world avg. 29.0); legitimate, n.a.; illegitimate, n.a.
*Death rate* per 1,000 population (1983): 5.8 (world avg. 11.0).
*Natural increase rate* per 1,000 population (1983): 25.4 (world avg. 18.0).
*Total fertility rate* (avg. births per childbearing woman): n.a.
*Marriage rate* per 1,000 population[5] (1977): 6.3.
*Divorce rate* per 1,000 population[5] (1977): 0.3.
*Life expectancy* at birth[5] (1976–81): male 48.9 years; female 62.1 years.
*Major causes of death* per 100,000 population (1976–81)[5, 7]: accidents, suicide, and violence 116.0; diseases of the circulatory system 89.0; diseases of the digestive system 53.0; malignant neoplasms (cancers) 38.0; infectious and parasitic diseases 33.0.

## National economy

*Budget* (1985–86). Revenue: $A 103,946,100[8] (no breakdown available). Expenditures: $A 76,782,500 (no breakdown available).
*Public debt* (external, outstanding): none.
*Tourism:* receipts from visitors, n.a.; expenditures by nationals abroad, n.a.
*Gross national product* (at current market prices; 1984): U.S.$160,000,000 (U.S.$20,000 per capita).

| Distribution of gross domestic product and labour force | 1982 | | 1981 | |
|---|---|---|---|---|
| | value in $A '000,000 | % of total value | labour force | % of labour force |
| Agriculture | ... | ... | ... | ... |
| Mining | ... | ... | ... | ... |
| Manufacturing | ... | ... | ... | ... |
| Construction | ... | ... | ... | ... |
| Public utilities | ... | ... | ... | ... |
| Transportation and communications | ... | ... | ... | ... |
| Trade | ... | ... | ... | ... |
| Finance | ... | ... | ... | ... |
| Services | ... | ... | ... | ... |
| Pub. admin., defense | ... | ... | ... | ... |
| Other | ... | ... | ... | ... |
| TOTAL | 100 | 100.0 | 4,769[9] | 100.0 |

*Production* (metric tons except as noted). Agriculture, forestry, fishing (1985): coconuts 2,000, and noncommercial quantities of bananas, pineapples, and vegetables are produced, but most foodstuffs and beverages are imported; livestock (number of live animals) 2,000 pigs; roundwood, none;

fish catch, n.a. (fish caught are for local consumption only). Mining and quarrying (1985): phosphate rock 1,508,000. Manufacturing: none. Construction (1977): 65 units. Energy production (consumption): electricity (kW-hr; 1985) 28,000,000 (28,000,000); coal, none (n.a.); crude petroleum, none (n.a.); petroleum products (metric tons; 1985) none (41,000); natural gas, none (n.a.).
*Population economically active[5]* (1981): total 1,758; activity rate of total population 35.2% (participation rates: over age 15, 61.5%; female, n.a.; unemployed, n.a.).
*Price and earnings indexes:* n.a.
*Household income and expenditure.* Average household size (1977) 8.0; income per household: [10]; sources of income: n.a.; expenditure: n.a.
*Land use* (1983): forested 40%; meadows and pastures, nil; agricultural and under permanent cultivation, nil; built-on, wasteland, and other c. 60%[11].

## Foreign trade

| Balance of trade (current prices) | 1978 | 1979 | 1980 | 1981 | 1982 | 1983 |
|---|---|---|---|---|---|---|
| $A '000,000 | +42.9 | +66.8 | +81.6 | +61.9 | ... | +98.6 |
| % of total | 65.4% | 75.9% | 59.2% | 67.5% | ... | 57.4% |

*Imports* (1979): $A 10,600,000 (food, fuel, water, machinery for phosphate industry, and building materials). *Major import sources:* Australia 58.0%; United Kingdom, New Zealand, and Japan.
*Exports* (1979): $A 77,400,000 (phosphate 100%). *Major export destinations* (1985): Australia 61.3%; New Zealand 22.5%; Philippines 15.2%; South Korea 1.0%.

## Transport and communications

*Transport.* Railroads (1985): length 3 mi, 5 km; (1983–84) passenger traffic, n.a.; short ton-mi cargo 4,670,000, metric ton-km cargo 6,820,000. Roads (1985): total length 12 mi, 19 km (paved 100%). Vehicles (1984): passenger cars, trucks, and buses 1,788. Merchant marine (1986): vessels 8; total deadweight tonnage, 93,391. Air transport (1982): passenger-mi 147,886,-000, passenger-km 238,000,000; short ton-mi cargo 1,096,000, metric ton-km cargo 1,600,000; airports (1987) with scheduled flights 1.
*Communications.* Daily newspapers: none; 1 bimonthly, total circulation 750; circulation per 1,000 population, about 95. Radio (1985): total number of receivers 4,000 (1 per 2.1 persons). Television: no broadcast TV; videotaped television is commonplace, however. Telephones (1979): 1,500 (1 per 5.3 persons).

## Education and health

| Education (1985) | schools | teachers | students | student/ teacher ratio |
|---|---|---|---|---|
| Primary (age 6–13) | 7 | 102 | 1,451 | 14.2 |
| Secondary (age 14–17) | 2 | 36 | 465 | 12.9 |
| Vocational | 1 | 4 | 60 | 15.0 |
| Teacher training (at second level)[12] | 1 | 1 | 10 | 10.0 |
| Higher | — | — | 88[13] | — |

*Educational attainment.* n.a. *Literacy* (1979): total population age 15 and over literate 99.0%.
*Health* (1980): physicians, 11 (1 per 700 persons); hospital beds 200 (1 per 40.0 persons); infant mortality rate per 1,000 live births (1981) 31.2.
*Food* (1978–80): daily per capita caloric intake 3,202 (vegetable products 64%, animal products 36%); 120% of FAO recommended minimum requirement.

## Military

*Total active duty personnel* (1985): Nauru does not have any military establishment. The defense is assured by Australia, but no formal agreement exists. There is a police force of about 57 Nauruans.

[1]Seat of government. [2]Preliminary. [3]Includes expatriates and their dependents. [4]Total includes 51 Nauruans unable to complete census forms; not distributable by district. [5]Nauruan population only. [6]The high natural growth rate of population is being minimized by emigration. [7]Average for the period. Of the 191 deaths during the six years, the leading specific causes by actual number were: motor vehicle accidents 31; viral hepatitis 17; acute cerebrovascular disease 16; diabetes mellitus 11; drownings 9; cirrhosis 8; diabetes 6. [8]Largely from phosphate exports. [9]The Nauruan economy is heavily dependent on contract immigrant labour, largely engaged in phosphate production. In 1981 Nauruans constituted only 36.9% of the employment structure (most of whom worked in the administrative–governmental sector); foreign contract labour as a percent of labour force included I-Kiribati 26.7%, Tuvaluans 17.0%, Chinese 8.0%, Filipinos 3.6%, and others 7.8%. Government employed 1,700 people, Nauru Phosphate Corporation employed 2,832 in 1981. [10]Individual landowner-ship, distribution of phosphate royalties according to landownership, and sequential working of phosphate deposits have combined to produce considerable inequities in income distribution among Nauruans. Similar inequities exist between the Nauru-ans and the alien work force, especially the phosphate workers from Kiribati and Tuvalu. Minimum Nauruan annual salary was $A 4,503 in 1981. [11]About 80% of Nauru's land area is classified as phosphate-bearing, of which about 60% had been mined out by the early 1980s. [12]1980. [13]Nauruans studying overseas at secondary and tertiary levels.

# Nepal

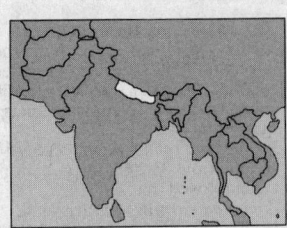

*Official name:* Nepāl Adhirājya
(Kingdom of Nepal).
*Form of government:* constitutional
monarchy with one legislative house
(National Panchayat [140]).
*Chief of state:* King.
*Head of government:* Prime Minister.
*Capital:* Kāthmāndu.
*Official language:* Nepālī.
*Official religion:* none.
*Monetary unit:* 1 Nepalese rupee
(NRs) = 100 paisa (pice); valuation
(Oct. 5, 1987) 1 U.S.$ = NRs 20.98;
1 £ = NRs 34.07.

### Area and population

| Development regions Geographic regions | Capitals | area sq mi | area sq km | population 1981 census |
|---|---|---|---|---|
| Eastern | Dhankūtā | 10,987 | 28,456 | 3,708,923 |
| Mountain | | | | 338,439 |
| Hill | | | | 1,257,042 |
| Tarai | | | | 2,113,442 |
| Central | Kāthmāndu | 10,583 | 27,410 | 4,909,357 |
| Mountain | | | | 413,143 |
| Hill | | | | 2,108,433 |
| Tarai | | | | 2,387,781 |
| Western | Pokharā | 11,351 | 29,398 | 3,128,859 |
| Mountain | | | | 19,951 |
| Hill | | | | 2,150,939 |
| Tarai | | | | 957,969 |
| Mid-western | Surkhet | 16,362 | 42,378 | 1,955,611 |
| Mountain | | | | 242,486 |
| Hill | | | | 1,042,365 |
| Tarai | | | | 670,760 |
| Far-western | Dipāyal | 7,544 | 19,539 | 1,320,089 |
| Mountain | | | | 288,877 |
| Hill | | | | 604,336 |
| Tarai | | | | 426,876 |
| TOTAL | | 56,827 | 147,181 | 15,022,839 |

## Demography

*Population* (1987): 17,567,000.
*Density* (1987): persons per sq mi 309.1, persons per sq km 119.4.
*Urban–rural* (1985): urban 8.0%; rural 92.0%.
*Sex distribution* (1986): male 51.45%; female 48.55%.
*Age breakdown* (1986): under 15, 42.2%; 15–29, 25.6%; 30–44, 17.3%; 45–59, 10.0%; 60–74, 4.2%; 75 and over, 0.7%.
*Population projection:* (1990) 18,910,000; (2000) 23,176,000.
*Doubling time:* 27 years.
*Ethnic composition* (1981): Nepalese 58.4%; Bihārī (including Maithilī and Bhojpurī) 18.7%; Tharu 3.6%; Tamang 3.5%; Newār 3.0%; other 12.8%.
*Religious affiliation* (1981): Hindu 89.5%; Buddhist 5.3%; Muslim 2.7%; Jain 0.1%; other 2.4%.
*Major cities* (1981): Kāthmāndu 235,160; Birātnagar 93,544; Lalitpūr 79,875; Bhaktapūr 48,472; Pokharā 46,642.

## Vital statistics

*Birth rate* per 1,000 population (1986): 42.2 (world avg. 26.0).
*Death rate* per 1,000 population (1986): 16.0 (world avg. 9.9).
*Natural increase rate* per 1,000 population (1986): 26.2 (world avg. 16.1).
*Total fertility rate* (avg. births per childbearing woman; 1986): 6.0.
*Marriage rate* per 1,000 population: n.a.
*Divorce rate* per 1,000 population: n.a.
*Life expectancy* at birth (1986): male 53.4 years; female 50.6 years.
*Major causes of death* per 100,000 population: n.a.; however, major diseases include malaria, tuberculosis, cholera, and typhoid.

## National economy

*Budget* (1985–86). Revenue: NRs 4,624,700,000 (taxes on goods and services 38.7%, customs duties 21.0%, income tax 9.9%, interest on loans 9.0%, registration taxes 6.5%, land revenue 6.0%, government services 5.2%). Expenditures: NRs 4,307,200,000 (loan repayment 22.2%, defense 16.5%, general administration 12.6%, economic services 8.6%, social services 7.9%, education 4.3%, revenue and economic administration 4.2%).
*Public debt* (external, outstanding; 1986): U.S.$711,100,000.
*Tourism:* receipts from visitors (1985) U.S.$40,463,000; expenditures by nationals abroad (1984) U.S.$24,000,000.
*Production* (metric tons except as noted). Agriculture, forestry, fishing (1985): rice 2,800,000, corn (maize) 710,000, wheat 534,000, potatoes 420,000, sugarcane 408,000, millet 125,000, jute 33,000, tobacco 6,000, milk (cow, buffalo, goat) 812,000, eggs 17,500; livestock (number of live animals) 7,500,000 cattle, 4,500,000 buffalo, 2,650,000 goats, 2,480,000 sheep, 400,000 pigs; roundwood 15,776,000 cu m; fish catch 9,076. Mining and quarrying (1984–85): limestone 56,000; magnesite 19,851; talc 6,015; garnet 27,300 kg. Manufacturing (1984–85): cement 31,800; jute 18,504; sugar 11,048; soap 7,476; tea 806; plywood 2,541,000 square feet; cigarettes 4,250,000,000 units; shoes 83,000 pairs. Construction: n.a. Energy production (consumption): electricity (kW-hr; 1985) 408,000,000 (472,000,000); coal (metric tons; 1985) none (60,000); petroleum products (metric tons; 1985) none (117,000); natural gas, none (none).
*Gross national product* (at current market prices; 1985): U.S.$2,610,000,000 (U.S.$160 per capita).

### Structure of gross domestic product and labour force

| | 1983–84 in value NRs '000,000 | 1983–84 % of total value | 1981 labour force | 1981 % of labour force |
|---|---|---|---|---|
| Agriculture | 22,087 | 57.8 | 6,244,289 | 91.1 |
| Mining | 96 | 0.3 | 971 | [1] |
| Manufacturing | 1,650 | 4.3 | 33,029 | 0.5 |
| Construction | 2,502 | 6.6 | 2,022 | [1] |
| Public utilities | 140 | 0.4 | 3,013 | [1] |
| Transportation and communication | 2,306 | 6.0 | 7,424 | 0.1 |
| Trade | 1,355 | 3.5 | 109,446 | 1.6 |
| Finance | | | 9,850 | 0.1 |
| Services | 8,048[2] | 21.1[2] | 313,570 | 4.6 |
| Other | | | 127,272[3] | 1.9[3] |
| TOTAL | 38,184 | 100.0 | 6,850,886 | 100.0[4] |

*Population economically active* (1986): total 7,760,155; activity rate of total population 45.5% (participation rates: ages 15–64, 82.5%; female 34.7%; unemployed [1980] 5.5%).

### Price and earnings indexes (1980 = 100)

| | 1981 | 1982 | 1983 | 1984 | 1985 | 1986 | 1987[5] |
|---|---|---|---|---|---|---|---|
| Consumer price index | 111.1 | 124.1 | 139.5 | 143.4 | 155.0 | 184.5 | 204.2 |
| Monthly earnings index | ... | ... | ... | ... | ... | ... | ... |

*Household income and expenditure.* Average family size (1981) 5.8; income per family (1976–77) NRs 5,914 (U.S.$473); sources of income (1973–74)[6]: wages and salaries 39.2%, self-employment 33.6%, owner-occupied dwellings 17.5%; expenditure (1973–75)[6]: food and beverages 48.0%, housing 20.0%, clothing and footwear 8.8%, fuel and power 4.2%, recreation 3.4%, education 3.2%.
*Land use* (1985): forested 37.6%; meadows and pastures 13.4%; agricultural and under permanent cultivation 18.0%; other 31.0%.

## Foreign trade[7]

### Balance of trade (current prices)

| | 1981 | 1982 | 1983 | 1984 | 1985 | 1986 |
|---|---|---|---|---|---|---|
| NRs '000,000 | −2,601.2 | −3,827.2 | −5,064.2 | −4,411.4 | −5,048.0 | −6,275.7 |
| % of total | 42.9% | 62.2% | 65.0% | 51.1% | 46.3% | 51.0% |

*Imports* (1984–85): NRs 7,742,100,000 (basic manufactured goods 30.7%; machinery and transport equipment 21.6%; mineral fuels 11.9%; chemicals 11.7%; food and live animals, chiefly for food 10.1%; miscellaneous manufactured articles 5.8%; crude materials except fuels 5.5%). *Major import sources:* India 50.3%; Japan 11.5%; Soviet Union 5.8%; South Korea 5.2%; United Kingdom 3.3%; China 3.3%.
*Exports* (1984–85): NRs 2,740,600,000 (food and live animals, chiefly for food 36.2%; basic manufactures 23.7%; machinery, transport equipment, and other manufactured articles 19.9%; crude materials except fuels 17.8%; animal and vegetable oils 2.1%). *Major export destinations:* India 58.4%; United States 17.6%; West Germany 5.3%; United Kingdom 3.8%; Soviet Union 3.5%.

## Transport and communications

*Transport.* Railroads (1983–84): route length 32 mi, 52 km; passengers carried 1,192,000; freight handled 18,100 tons. Roads (1984–85): total length 3,682 mi, 5,925 km (paved 46%). Vehicles (1978): passenger cars 14,201; trucks and buses 9,988. Merchant marine: none. Air transport[8] (1986): passenger-mi 186,000,000, passenger-km 300,000,000; short ton-mi cargo 4,266,000, metric ton-km cargo 6,228,000; airports (1987) with scheduled flights 5.
*Communications.* Daily newspapers (1985): total number 58; total circulation, n.a.; circulation per 1,000 population, n.a. Radio (1986): 2,012,000 receivers (1 per 8.5 persons). Television (1986): 18,000 receivers (1 per 952 persons). Telephones (1984): 23,500 (1 per 692 persons).

## Education and health

### Education (1985–86)

| | schools | teachers | students | student/ teacher ratio |
|---|---|---|---|---|
| Primary (age 6–11) | 11,873 | 51,266 | 1,812,098 | 35.3 |
| Secondary (age 12–17) | 4,899 | 18,362 | 496,821 | 27.1 |
| Vocational | 5 | 117 | 648 | 5.5 |
| Higher | 116 | 4,165 | 67,555 | 16.2 |

*Educational attainment* (1981). Percent of adult population age 25 and over having: no formal schooling 41.2%; primary education 29.4%; secondary 22.7%; higher 6.8%. *Literacy* (1981): total population age 15 and over literate 1,822,718 (20.7%); males literate 1,425,241 (31.9%); females literate 397,477 (9.2%).
*Health* (1986): physicians 692 (1 per 24,770 persons); hospital beds 3,767 (1 per 4,550 persons); infant mortality rate per 1,000 live births 111.5.
*Food* (1981–83): daily per capita caloric intake 2,008 (vegetable products 93%, animal products 7%); (1983) 93% of FAO recommended minimum.

## Military

*Total active duty personnel* (1986): 30,000 (army 100.0%). *Military expenditure as percent of GNP* (1984): 1.3% (world 5.9%); per capita expenditure U.S.$2.

[1]Less than 0.1%. [2]Includes indirect taxes less subsidies. [3]Includes activities not adequately defined. [4]Detail does not add to total given because of rounding. [5]July. [6]For Kāthmāndu only. [7]Import figures are f.o.b. (free on board) in balance of trade and c.i.f. (cost, insurance, and freight) for commodities and trading partners. [8]International flights only.

# Netherlands, The

*Official name:* Koninkrijk der Nederlanden (Kingdom of The Netherlands).
*Form of government:* constitutional monarchy with two legislative houses (First Chamber [75]; Second Chamber [150]).
*Chief of state:* Monarch.
*Head of government:* Prime Minister.
*Seat of government:* The Hague.
*Capital:* Amsterdam.
*Official language:* Dutch.
*Official religion:* none.
*Monetary unit:* 1 Netherlands guilder (f.) = 100 cents; valuation (Oct. 5, 1987) 1 U.S.$ = f. 2.07; 1 £ = f. 3.37.

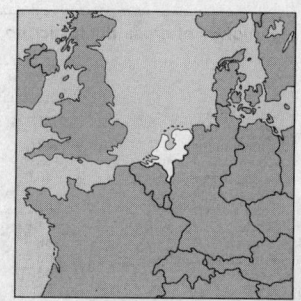

### Area and population

| Provinces | Capitals | area sq mi | area sq km | population 1986 estimate[1] |
|---|---|---|---|---|
| Drenthe | Assen | 1,025 | 2,654 | 431,997 |
| Flevoland | Lelystad | 548 | 1,420 | 177,334 |
| Friesland | Leeuwarden | 1,295 | 3,357 | 598,068 |
| Gelderland | Arnhem | 1,935 | 5,011 | 1,761,492 |
| Groningen | Groningen | 905 | 2,344 | 560,029 |
| Limburg | Maastricht | 838 | 2,170 | 1,088,331 |
| Noord-Brabant | 's-Hertogenbosch | 1,910 | 4,946 | 2,124,656 |
| Noord-Holland | Haarlem | 1,031 | 2,672 | 2,322,708 |
| Overijssel | Zwolle | 1,289 | 3,339 | 998,751 |
| Utrecht | Utrecht | 514 | 1,331 | 944,372 |
| Zeeland | Middelburg | 691 | 1,790 | 355,781 |
| Zuid-Holland | The Hague | 1,123 | 2,908 | 3,164,652 |
| TOTAL LAND AREA | | 13,105[2] | 33,943[2] | 14,529,430 |
| INLAND WATER | | 3,028 | 7,842 | |
| TOTAL AREA | | 16,133[2] | 41,785[2] | |

## Demography

*Population* (1987): 14,615,000.
*Density* (1987): persons per sq mi 1,115.2, persons per sq km 430.6.
*Urban–rural* (1986): urban 88.4%; rural 11.6%.
*Sex distribution* (1986): male 49.45%; female 50.55%.
*Age breakdown* (1986): under 15, 19.2%; 15–29, 25.6%; 30–44, 22.7%; 45–59, 15.7%; 60–74, 11.7%; 75 and over, 5.1%.
*Population projection:* (1990) 14,739,000; (2000) 15,245,000.
*Doubling time:* n.a.; vital rates and net migration in near balance.
*Ethnic composition* (by nationality; 1986): Netherlander 96.2%; Turkish 1.0%; Moroccan 0.8%; German 0.3%; other 1.7%.
*Religious affiliation* (1984): Roman Catholic 36.2%; Dutch Reformed Church 18.1%; Reformed Churches 8.3%; other 2.7%; no religion 34.7%.
*Major cities* (1986): Amsterdam 679,140; Rotterdam 571,372; The Hague 443,961; Utrecht 229,933; Eindhoven 190,839.

## Vital statistics

*Birth rate* per 1,000 population (1985): 12.3 (world avg. 29.0); legitimate 91.7%; illegitimate 8.3%.
*Death rate* per 1,000 population (1985): 8.5 (world avg. 11.0).
*Natural increase rate* per 1,000 population (1985): 3.8 (world avg. 18.0).
*Total fertility rate* (avg. births per childbearing woman; 1984): 1.5.
*Marriage rate* per 1,000 population (1985): 5.7.
*Divorce rate* per 1,000 population (1985): 2.3.
*Life expectancy* at birth (1985): male 73.1 years; female 79.7 years.
*Major causes of death* per 100,000 population (1985): malignant neoplasms (cancers) 226.3, of which lung cancer 56.0; ischemic heart diseases 176.1; cerebrovascular diseases 80.9; accidents, poisoning, and violence 37.3.

## National economy

*Budget* (1985). Revenue: f. 140,368,000,000 (income and corporate taxes 35.2%, natural gas royalties 10.9%, excise and import taxes 7.4%). Expenditures: f. 170,037,000,000 (social security and public health 18.7%, education and culture 17.1%, defense 7.9%).
*Public debt* (1986): U.S.$108,912,000,000.
*Tourism* (1985): receipts from visitors U.S.$1,503,000,000; expenditures by nationals abroad U.S.$3,118,000,000.
*Production* (metric tons except as noted). Agriculture (1985): potatoes 7,150,-000, sugar beets 6,335,000, vegetables and melons 2,820,000, wheat 851,000; livestock (number of live animals) 12,383,000 pigs, 5,248,000 cattle, 814,000 sheep; roundwood 1,139,000 cu m; fish catch (1984) 462,413. Manufacturing (value of sales in f. '000,000; 1984): foodstuffs 73,300; synthetic fibres 41,400; petroleum products 31,200; electrical machinery 12,800; transport equipment 11,800. Construction (1982): residential 58,947,000 cu m; non-residential 51,620,000 cu m. Energy production (consumption): electricity (kW-hr; 1985) 62,947,000,000 (64,059,000,000); coal (metric tons; 1985) 132,000 (10,638,000); crude petroleum (barrels; 1985) 25,548,000 (292,-489,000); petroleum products (metric tons; 1985) 46,915,000 (25,229,000); natural gas (cu m; 1985) 80,721,000,000 (20,084,000,000).
*Household income and expenditure.* Average household size (1985) 2.6; income per household (1984) f. 74,500 (U.S.$23,200); sources of income: wages 40.0%, transfer payments 28.2%, self-employment 19.6%, other 12.2%; expenditure (1985): housing 27.3%, food 17.6%, clothing 6.8%.
*Gross national product* (at current market prices; 1985): U.S.$132,920,000,-000 (U.S.$9,180 per capita).

### Structure of gross domestic product and labour force

| | 1985 in value f. '000,000 | % of total value | labour force | % of labour force |
|---|---|---|---|---|
| Agriculture | 13,840 | 4.1 | 268,100 | 4.5 |
| Mining | 33,570 | 10.0 | 11,300 | 0.2 |
| Manufacturing | 62,900 | 18.8 | 993,400 | 16.8 |
| Construction | 18,700 | 5.6 | 385,700 | 6.5 |
| Public utilities | 5,350 | 1.6 | 44,200 | 0.8 |
| Transportation and communication | 22,920 | 6.8 | 322,600 | 5.5 |
| Trade | 51,020 | 15.2 | 906,500 | 15.4 |
| Pub. admin., defense | 46,880 | 14.0 | . . .[3] | . . .[3] |
| Finance | } 96,940 | 28.9 | 457,300 | 7.8 |
| Services | | | 1,716,100[3] | 29.1[3] |
| Other | −16,710[4] | −5.0[4] | 790,000[5] | 13.4[5] |
| TOTAL | 335,410 | 100.0 | 5,895,200 | 100.0 |

*Population economically active* (1985): total 5,895,200; activity rate of total population 40.7% (participation rates: ages 15–64, 59.4%; female 34.8%; unemployed 12.7%).

### Price and earnings indexes (1980 = 100)

| | 1980 | 1981 | 1982 | 1983 | 1984 | 1985 | 1986 |
|---|---|---|---|---|---|---|---|
| Consumer price index | 100.0 | 106.7 | 113.0 | 116.2 | 120.0 | 122.7 | 122.9 |
| Hourly earnings index | 100.0 | 103.0 | 110.0 | 113.0 | 115.0 | 120.0 | 122.0 |

*Land use* (1984): forested 8.8%; meadows and pastures 33.6%; agricultural and under permanent cultivation 25.8%; other 31.8%.

## Foreign trade

### Balance of trade (current prices)

| | 1981 | 1982 | 1983 | 1984 | 1985 | 1986 |
|---|---|---|---|---|---|---|
| f. '000,000 | 9,704 | 12,453 | 12,410 | 17,792 | 18,284 | 12,627 |
| % of total | 3.2% | 4.0% | 3.8% | 4.8% | 4.6% | 3.3% |

*Imports* (1986): f. 184,791,000,000 (manufactured goods 31.3%; machinery and transport equipment 25.5%, of which transport equipment 6.8; foodstuffs, beverages, and tobacco 13.0%; mineral fuels 11.9; chemicals 10.4%). *Major import sources:* West Germany 21.0%; Belgium–Luxembourg 10.3%; United Kingdom 8.3%; United States 7.9%; France 6.3%.
*Exports* (1986): f. 197,418,000,000 (manufactured goods 23.6%, of which metal products 6.4%; food and beverages 19.7%; chemical products 17.1%; machinery and transport equipment 16.9%; mineral fuels 15.4%). *Major export destinations:* West Germany 28.4%; Belgium–Luxembourg 13.0%; France 9.6%; United Kingdom 8.3%; Italy 5.0%.

## Transport and communications

*Transport.* Railroads (1985): length 2,867 km; passenger-km 9,228,000,000; metric ton-km cargo 3,216,000,000. Roads (1984): total length 111,891 km (paved 86.9%). Vehicles (1985): passenger cars 4,901,000; trucks and buses 401,630. Merchant marine (1986): vessels (100 gross tons and over) 1,334; total deadweight tonnage 5,993,883. Air transport[6]: passenger-km (1985) 18,240,000,000; metric ton-km cargo (1986) 1,596,000,000; airports (1987) 5.
*Communications.* Daily newspapers (1984): total number 79; total circulation 4,500,000; circulation per 1,000 population 312. Radio (1986): total number of receivers 4,808,728 (1 per 3.0 persons). Television (1986): total number of receivers 4,632,846 (1 per 3.1 persons). Telephones (1985): 8,840,000 (1 per 1.6 persons).

## Education and health

### Education (1984–85)

| | schools | teachers | students | student/ teacher ratio |
|---|---|---|---|---|
| Primary (age 6–12) | 9,467 | 75,998 | 1,193,338 | 15.8 |
| Secondary (age 12–18) | 1,409 | 53,375 | 822,615 | 15.4 |
| Voc., teacher tr. | 2,031 | 54,560 | 640,737 | 11.7 |
| Higher | 456 | 30,396 | 305,126 | 10.0 |

*Educational attainment* (1985). Percent of population[7] ages 25–64 having: primary education 16.7%; secondary 61.8%; higher 20.0%. *Literacy* (1986): virtually 100% literate.
*Health* (1985): physicians (1986) 32,193 (1 per 452 persons); hospital beds 68,461 (1 per 212 persons); infant mortality rate per 1,000 live births 8.0.
*Food* (1981–83): daily per capita caloric intake 3,541 (vegetable products 58%, animal products 42%); (1983) 129% of FAO recommended minimum requirement.

## Military

*Total active duty personnel* (1986): 105,134 (army 63.0%, navy 16.2%; air force 17.1%, other[8] 3.7%). *Military expenditure as percent of GNP* (1984): 3.2% (world 5.9%); per capita expenditure U.S.$276.

[1]January 1st estimate; includes about 1,259 persons having no fixed municipality of residence. [2]Detail does not add to total given because of rounding. [3]Services include Public administration, defense. [4]Imputed bank service charge. [5]Includes 750,700 unemployed persons. [6]KLM (Royal Dutch Airlines) only. [7]Economically active population (4,612,000) only. [8]Composed of 3,909 military police.

# Netherlands Antilles

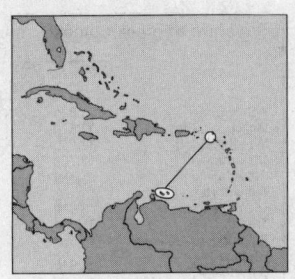

*Official name:* Nederlandse Antillen (Netherlands Antilles).
*Political status:* nonmetropolitan territory of The Netherlands with one legislative house (States of the Netherlands Antilles [22])[1].
*Chief of state:* Dutch Monarch represented by the governor.
*Head of government:* Prime Minister.
*Capital:* Willemstad.
*Official language:* Dutch.
*Official religion:* none.
*Monetary unit:* 1 Netherlands Antillean guilder (NA f.) = 100 cents; valuation (Oct. 5, 1987) 1 U.S.$ = NA f. 1.80; 1 £ = NA f. 2.92.

| Area and population | | area | | population |
|---|---|---|---|---|
| | | sq mi | sq km | 1981 census |
| Island councils | Capitals | | | |
| Leeward Islands | | | | |
| Bonaire | Kralendijk | 111 | 288 | 8,753 |
| Curaçao | Willemstad | 171 | 444 | 147,388 |
| Windward Islands | | | | |
| Saba | The Bottom | 5 | 13 | 965 |
| Sint Eustatius or Statia | Oranjestad | 8 | 21 | 1,358 |
| Sint Maarten (Dutch part only) | Philipsburg | 13 | 34 | 13,156 |
| TOTAL | | 308 | 800 | 171,620 |

## Demography

*Population* (1987): 176,000.
*Density* (1987): persons per sq mi 571.4, persons per sq km 220.0.
*Urban–rural* (1985)[2]: urban 92.4%; rural 7.6%.
*Sex distribution* (1981): male 48.25%; female 51.75%.
*Age breakdown* (1981): under 15, 30.0%; 15–29, 29.9%; 30–44, 19.5%; 45–59, 11.3%; 60–74, 6.7%; 75 and over, 2.6%.
*Population projection:* (1990) 178,000; (2000) 185,000.
*Doubling time:* 47 years.
*Ethnic composition* (1980)[2]: Netherlands Antillean (Dutch/Spanish/black/Amerindian) creole 84.0%; white 6.1%; other West Indian 4.9%; Suriname creole 2.9%; other 2.1%.
*Religious affiliation* (1981): Roman Catholic 83.8%; Protestant 10.2%, of which Lutheran/Reformed tradition 3.3%, Methodist 3.2%, Seventh-day Adventist 1.5%; Jewish 0.3%; nonreligious 2.6%; other 3.1%.
*Major cities* (1980): Willemstad (urban area) 100,000; Philipsburg 10,000.

## Vital statistics

*Birth rate* per 1,000 population (1982): 20.7 (world avg. 29.0); legitimate 52.3%, illegitimate 47.7%[3].
*Death rate* per 1,000 population (1982): 5.5 (world avg. 11.0).
*Natural increase rate* per 1,000 population (1982): 15.2 (world avg. 18.0).
*Total fertility rate* (avg. births per childbearing woman; 1984)[2]: 3.4.
*Marriage rate* per 1,000 population (1982): 5.6.
*Divorce rate* per 1,000 population (1982): 2.8.
*Life expectancy* at birth (1981)[4]: male 71.1 years; female 75.7 years.
*Major causes of death* per 100,000 population (1983): diseases of the circulatory system 206.0; malignant neoplasms (cancers) 128.6; accidents 40.4; diseases of the digestive system 31.2; diseases of the respiratory system 27.1; nephritis and nephrosis 23.7.

## National economy

*Budget* (1984). Revenue: NA f. 342,300,000[5] (tax revenue 50.7%, of which import duties 24.0%, taxes on goods and services 18.9%, foreign exchange commission 6.8%; revenue sharing transfers from island governments 28.7%). Expenditures: NA f. 394,500,000 (current expenditures 97.9%; development expenditures 2.1%).
*Public debt* (external, outstanding; 1984)[2, 6]: U.S.$853,000,000.
*Tourism:* receipts from visitors (1986) U.S.$257,000,000, of which Sint Maarten U.S.$162,000,000, Curaçao U.S.$89,000,000, Bonaire U.S.$6,000,000; expenditures by nationals abroad (1983)[2] U.S.$107,000,000.
*Production* (metric tons except as noted). Agriculture, forestry, fishing (value of production in NA f. '000; 1982): eggs 3,863, fruits and vegetables 2,850[7], pork 1,250, goat meat 555; livestock (number of live animals; 1985[2]) 23,000 goats, 9,000 cattle, 9,000 sheep, 8,000 pigs; roundwood, n.a.; fish (1984) 1,800. Mining and quarrying (1985): unrefined salt 390,000. Manufacturing (1985): residual fuel oil 6,800,000[2, 8]; beer 134,000 hectolitres[2, 9]; curaçao liqueur 780 hectolitres; other manufactures include electronic parts, cigarettes, textiles, and rum. Construction: n.a. Energy production (consumption): electricity (kW-hr; 1985[2]) 2,400,000,000 (2,400,000,000); coal, none (none); crude petroleum (barrels; 1985[2, 8]) none (74,400,000); petroleum products (metric tons; 1985[2, 8]) 9,670,000 (1,991,000); natural gas, none (none).
*Household income and expenditure.* Average household size (1981) 3.7; income per household: n.a.; sources of income: n.a.; expenditure (1984)[10, 11]: food 22.1%, transportation and communication 19.4%, housing 18.8%, household furnishings 10.0%, clothing and footwear 8.7%, recreation and education 5.9%, beverages and tobacco 2.3%, health 2.2%, other 10.6%.
*Gross national product* (at current market prices; 1985)[2]: U.S.$1,610,000,000 (U.S.$6,810 per capita).

## Structure of gross domestic product and labour force

| | 1980[2] | | 1981[12] | |
|---|---|---|---|---|
| | in value NA f. '000,000 | % of total value | labour force | % of labour force |
| Agriculture | } 22.7 | 0.9 | 280 | 0.5 |
| Mining | | | 173 | 0.3 |
| Manufacturing | 543.3 | 22.3 | 6,408 | 11.2 |
| Construction | 188.2 | 7.7 | 5,147 | 9.0 |
| Public utilities | 40.9 | 1.7 | 1,213 | 2.1 |
| Transportation and communication | 361.1 | 14.8 | 4,599 | 8.0 |
| Trade | 511.8 | 21.0 | 14,145 | 24.8 |
| Finance | 289.0 | 11.9 | 3,896 | 6.8 |
| Pub. admin., defense | 402.4 | 16.5 } | 21,150 | 37.0 |
| Services | 145.7 | 6.0 } | | |
| Other | −69.2[13] | −2.8[13] | 143 | 0.3 |
| TOTAL | 2,435.9 | 100.0 | 57,154 | 100.0 |

*Population economically active* (1981): total 70,207; activity rate of total population 40.9% (participation rates: ages 15–64, 63.5%; female 40.6%; unemployed [1986] 25.0%, of which Curaçao 28.0%, Bonaire 16.0%, Windward Islands 1.0%).

## Price and earnings indexes[2] (1980 = 100)

| | 1979 | 1980 | 1981 | 1982 | 1983 | 1984 | 1985[14] |
|---|---|---|---|---|---|---|---|
| Consumer price index | 87.2 | 100.0 | 112.2 | 119.0 | 122.4 | 125.0 | 125.4 |
| Monthly earnings index[15] | 88.9 | 100.0 | 114.7 | 127.8 | 129.4 | 129.9 | ... |

*Land use* (1984): forested, negligible; meadows and pastures, negligible; agricultural and under permanent cultivation 8.3%; other (dry savanna) 91.7%.

## Foreign trade[4, 16]

| Balance of trade (current prices) | | | | | |
|---|---|---|---|---|---|
| | 1980 | 1981 | 1982 | 1983 | 1984 |
| NA f. '000,000 | −898 | ... | −427 | −167 | −580 |
| % of total | 10.0% | ... | 5.2% | 2.2% | 8.9% |

*Imports* (1983): NA f. 3,824,000,000 (crude petroleum 78.0%, basic and miscellaneous manufactures 7.0%, machinery and transport equipment 5.5%, food 4.6%, petroleum products 2.7%). *Major import sources* (1984): Venezuela 50.0%; Mexico 15.4%; United States 10.3%; Libya 3.9%; The Netherlands 3.4%.
*Exports* (1983): NA f. 3,657,000,000 (petroleum products 90.0%, crude petroleum 6.7%, organic chemicals 1.2%). *Major export destinations* (1984): United States 17.4%; Jamaica 9.3%; Puerto Rico 8.7%; Cuba 8.4%; The Netherlands 6.0%; Colombia 5.3%.

## Transport and communications

*Transport.* Railroads: none. Roads (1984): total length 510 mi, 820 km (paved, n.a.). Vehicles (1982)[2]: passenger cars 55,000; trucks and buses 8,000. Merchant marine vessels (100 gross tons and over) n.a. Air transport (1982)[17]: passenger-mi 234,000,000, passenger-km 377,000,000; short ton-mi cargo 1,243,000, metric ton-km cargo 1,815,000; airports (1987) with scheduled flights 5.
*Communications.* Daily newspapers (1986): total number 5; total circulation 65,700; circulation per 1,000 population 375. Radio (1986): 149,000 receivers (1 per 1.2 persons). Television (1986): 54,000 receivers (1 per 3.3 persons). Telephones (1985)[2]: 49,600 (1 per 3.5 persons).

## Education and health

| Education (1983) | schools | teachers | students | student/ teacher ratio |
|---|---|---|---|---|
| Primary (age 6–12) | 91 | 1,248 | 24,578 | 19.7 |
| Secondary (age 12–17) | 22 | 633 | 8,623 | 13.6 |
| Voc., teacher tr. | 3 | 79 | 732 | 9.3 |
| Higher | 1 | 53 | 677 | 12.8 |

*Educational attainment* (1981). Percent of population age 25 and over having: no formal schooling or incomplete primary education 29.7%; completed primary 31.5%; completed vocational or secondary 37.6%; completed higher 1.2%. *Literacy* (1985): total population age 15 and over literate 95.0%.
*Health* (1985): physicians 184 (1 per 950 persons); hospital beds 1,500 (1 per 117 persons); infant mortality rate per 1,000 live births (1982) 8.4.
*Food* (1981–83)[2]: daily per capita caloric intake 2,807 (vegetable products 65%, animal products 35%); (1983) 116% of FAO recommended minimum requirement.

## Military

*Total active duty personnel* (1986): A small Dutch naval contingent is stationed permanently in the Netherlands Antilles.

[1]Aruba withdrew from the Netherlands Antilles on Jan. 1, 1986, becoming an autonomous member of the Kingdom of The Netherlands, the same status as the whole of the Netherlands Antilles. [2]Includes Aruba. [3]Excludes Sint Eustatius. [4]Curaçao only. [5]Excludes development aid from The Netherlands. [6]Includes external long-term private debt not guaranteed by the government. [7]Mostly tomatoes, beans, cucumbers, gherkins, melons, and lettuce grown on hydroponic farms; aloes grown for export, divi-divi pods, and sour orange fruit are non-hydroponic crops. [8]Curaçao's oil refinery was operational in early 1987, but the oil refinery on Aruba was closed in March 1985. [9]1981. [10]Weights of consumer price index components. [11]Curaçao and Bonaire only. [12]Employed persons only. [13]Less imputed bank service charges. [14]First quarter average. [15]Minimum wages in manufacturing as of January 1 of each year. [16]Imports c.i.f.; exports f.o.b. [17]ALM airlines only.

# New Caledonia

*Official name:* Territoire de la Nouvelle-Calédonie et Dépendances (Territory of New Caledonia and Dependencies).
*Political status:* overseas territory (France) with four autonomous regional councils forming one advisory legislative house (Territorial Congress [46])[1].
*Chief of state:* President of France.
*Head of government:* High Commissioner (for France); President of Territorial Congress assisted by the presidents of the four autonomous regional councils (for New Caledonia)[1].
*Capital:* Nouméa.
*Official language:* French.
*Official religion:* none.
*Monetary unit:* 1 franc of the Comptoirs français du Pacifique (CFPF) = 100 centimes; valuation (Oct. 5, 1987) 1 U.S.$ = CFPF 108.38; 1 £ = CFPF 176.00.

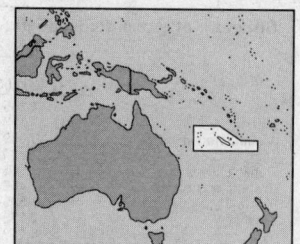

### Area and population

| | | area | | population |
| Regions | Capitals | sq mi | sq km | 1983 census |
|---|---|---|---|---|
| Loyauté | ... | 765 | 1,981 | 15,510 |
| Nord | ... | 2,837 | 7,348 | 21,512 |
| Nouméa | Nouméa | 637 | 1,650 | 85,098 |
| Sud | ... | 2,995 | 7,757 | 23,248 |
| TOTAL | | 7,233[2, 3] | 18,734[2, 3] | 145,368 |

## Demography

*Population* (1987): 152,000.
*Density* (1987): persons per sq mi 21.2, persons per sq km 8.2.
*Urban–rural* (1983): urban 58.5%; rural 41.5%.
*Sex distribution* (1983): male 51.10%; female 48.90%.
*Age breakdown* (1983): under 15, 36.2%; 15–29, 26.9%; 30–44, 19.5%; 45–59, 11.2%; 60–74, 5.1%; 75 and over, 1.1%.
*Population projection:* (1990) 157,000; (2000) 175,000.
*Doubling time:* 40 years.
*Ethnic composition* (1983): Melanesian 43.4%; European 37.1%; Polynesian 12.2%, of which Wallisian 8.4%, Tahitian 3.8%; Indonesian 3.7%; Vietnamese 1.6%; other 2.0%.
*Religious affiliation* (1984): Roman Catholic 62.7%; other (mostly Protestant) 37.3%.
*Major cities* (1983)[4]: Nouméa 60,112; Mont-Doré 14,614; Dumbéa 5,538.

## Vital statistics

*Birth rate* per 1,000 population (1984): 22.8 (world avg. 29.0); (1980) legitimate 57.5%; illegitimate 42.5%.
*Death rate* per 1,000 population (1984): 5.3 (world avg. 11.0).
*Natural increase rate* per 1,000 population (1984): 17.5 (world avg. 18.0).
*Total fertility rate* (avg. births per childbearing woman; 1984): 3.5.
*Marriage rate* per 1,000 population (1983): 5.7.
*Divorce rate* per 1,000 population (1983): 1.1.
*Life expectancy* at birth (1980–85): male 64.6 years; female 68.5.
*Major causes of death* per 100,000 population (1978): malignant neoplasms (cancers) 35.1; perinatal mortality 24.9; cerebrovascular diseases 24.1; heart diseases 13.9; cranial fractures 13.9.

## National economy

*Budget* (1986). Revenue: CFPF 39,255,000,000 (French government grants 34.7%; indirect taxes 27.4%; direct taxes 11.4%; loans 8.2%). Expenditures: CFPF 39,255,000,000 (current expenditure 91.8%, of which general administration 45.5%, grants and subsidies to regions 34.8%, public debt 8.9%; capital expenditure 8.2%).
*Public debt* (external, outstanding; 1984[5]): U.S.$201,000,000.
*Tourism* (1983): receipts from visitors U.S.$46,000,000[6]; expenditures by nationals abroad, n.a.
*Production* (metric tons except as noted). Agriculture, forestry, fishing (1985): coconuts 11,000, vegetables and melons 5,000, roots and tubers 4,000, bananas 2,000, corn (maize) 1,638, plantains 1,000, coffee 520, sorghum 443, wheat 367; livestock (number of live animals) 122,000 cattle, 40,000 pigs, 18,000 goats; roundwood 12,000 cu m; fish catch 3,500, of which trochus shells 300. Mining and quarrying (1985): nickel ore 3,075,000[7] (ferronickel [metal content] 42,161[7], nickel matte [metal content] 8,905); chromite ore 149,496 (concentrate 78,820); cobalt (metal content) 750. Manufacturing (1985): cement 31,200; copra 452; soap 363; refined coconut oil 129; beer 44,183 hectolitres. Construction (dwellings authorized; 1984): residential 45,900 sq m; nonresidential, n.a. Energy production (consumption): electricity (kW-hr; 1985) 1,120,000,000 (1,113,000,000); coal (metric tons; 1985) none (177,000); crude petroleum, none (none); petroleum products (metric tons; 1985) none (308,000); natural gas, none (none).
*Population economically active* (1983): total 58,154; activity rate of total population 40.0% (participation rates: ages 15–64, n.a.; female, n.a.; unemployed 6.0%).

### Price and earnings indexes (1980 = 100)[8]

| | 1980 | 1981 | 1982 | 1983 | 1984 | 1985 | 1986[9] |
|---|---|---|---|---|---|---|---|
| Consumer price index | 100.0 | 115.9 | 131.3 | 145.8 | 156.2 | 164.3 | 162.8 |
| Earnings index[10] | 100.0 | 115.9 | 138.3 | 153.2 | 164.2 | 172.3 | 173.1 |

*Land use* (1984): forested 37.7%; meadows and pastures 14.5%; agricultural and under permanent cultivation 1.1%; other 46.7%.
*Gross national product* (at current market prices; 1983): U.S.$1,210,000,000 (U.S.$8,300 per capita).

### Structure of gross domestic product and labour force

| | 1983 | | | |
| | in value CFPF '000,000 | % of total value | labour force | % of labour force |
|---|---|---|---|---|
| Agriculture | 2,155 | 1.9 | 19,700 | 33.9 |
| Mining | 5,303 | 4.6 | | |
| Manufacturing | 11,180 | 9.8 | 7,244 | 12.5 |
| Construction | 5,290 | 4.6 | | |
| Public utilities | 2,318 | 2.0 | 593 | 1.1 |
| Transportation and communication | 4,917 | 4.3 | 2,659 | 4.6 |
| Trade | 30,483[11] | 26.7 | 4,370[12] | 7.5[12] |
| Finance | 19,814[11] | 17.4 | 1,025 | 1.7 |
| Services | | | | |
| Pub. admin., defense | 31,537 | 27.6 | 18,922[12] | 32.5[12] |
| Other | 1,164 | 1.0 | 3,641[13] | 6.3[13] |
| TOTAL | 114,161 | 100.0[2] | 58,154 | 100.0[2] |

*Household income and expenditure.* Average household size (1983) 4.1; average annual income per household (1980) CFPF 1,670,000 (U.S.$20,600); sources of income (1980): salaries 71.6%, welfare 5.1%, pensions 4.5%, other 18.8%; expenditure (1980): food 28.4%, transportation and communication 15.1%, housing 13.3%, energy 8.3%, recreation 6.4%, clothing and footwear 5.6%, household supplies 3.7%, health 2.6%, other 16.6%.

## Foreign trade

### Balance of trade (current prices)

| | 1982 | 1983 | 1984 | 1985 | 1986 |
|---|---|---|---|---|---|
| CFPF '000,000 | −16,323 | −18,971 | −12,902 | −11,993 | −35,667 |
| % of total | 22.9% | 28.4% | 14.9% | 12.0% | 39.5% |

*Imports* (1986): CFPF 62,939,000,000 (mineral products 19.6%, transportation equipment 19.0%, food 14.5%, machinery and electrical goods 12.4%, chemicals 6.5%). *Major import sources:* France 50.3%; other EEC countries 13.2%; Australia 7.4%; Japan 5.2%; United States 4.9%.
*Exports* (1986) CFPF 27,272,000,000 (ferronickel and nickel matte 66.2%, nickel ore 9.1%, chromite 3.7%). *Major export destinations* (1985): France 58.7%; United States 20.7%; Australia 5.2%.

## Transport and communications

*Transport.* Railroads: none. Roads (1985): total length 3,422 mi, 5,507 km (paved, n.a.). Vehicles (1985): passenger cars 42,000; trucks and buses 2,500. Merchant marine: vessels (100 gross tons and over) n.a. Air transport (1986)[14]: passenger-mi 15,000,000, passenger-km 24,000,000; short ton-mi cargo, n.a.; airports (1987) with scheduled flights 10.
*Communications.* Daily newspapers (1986): total number 2; total circulation 24,000; circulation per 1,000 population 159. Radio (1986): total number of receivers 85,000 (1 per 1.8 persons). Television (1986): total number of receivers 35,000 (1 per 4.3 persons). Telephones (1984): 32,010 (1 per 4.6 persons).

## Education and health

### Education (1987)

| | schools | teachers | students | student/teacher ratio |
|---|---|---|---|---|
| Primary (age 6–10) | 276 | 1,564 | 32,205 | 20.6 |
| Secondary (age 11–17) | 47 | 1,179 | 13,540 | 11.5 |
| Vocational | 28 | 200 | 5,887 | 29.4 |
| Higher | 6 | 40 | 853 | 21.3 |

*Educational attainment* (1983). Percent of population age 20 and over having: no formal schooling 17.4%; primary education 51.8%; secondary 25.9%; higher 4.8%. *Literacy* (1976): total population age 14 and over literate 75,819 (89.4%); males literate 40,296 (90.1%); females literate 35,523 (88.7%).
*Health* (1983): physicians 194 (1 per 751 persons); hospital beds 1,224 (1 per 121 persons); infant mortality rate per 1,000 live births 16.8.
*Food* (1981–83): daily per capita caloric intake 2,889 (vegetable products 79%, animal products 21%); (1983) 104% of FAO recommended minimum requirement.

## Military

*Total active duty personnel* (1986): 4,900 French troops. *Military expenditure as percent of GNP:* n.a.

---

[1]Interim governmental structure effective as of Nov. 18, 1985. [2]Detail does not add to total given because of rounding. [3]Total area per new survey equals 7,172 sq mi (18,576 sq km); regional areas are not available. [4]Populations cited are for communes. [5]Includes external long-term private debt not guaranteed by the government. [6]Number of visitors: (1983) 90,335; (1984) 91,512; (1985) 51,190. [7]1986. [8]All figures are end of year unless footnoted. [9]September. [10]Based on minimum hourly wage. [11]Finance/Services includes restaurants and hotels. [12]Services/Pub. admin., defense includes restaurants and hotels. [13]Includes 3,500 unemployed. [14]Air Calédonie only.

# New Zealand

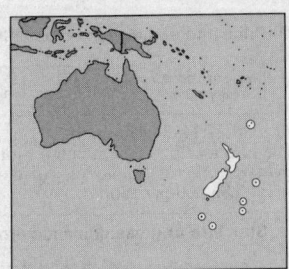

*Official name:* New Zealand.
*Form of government:* constitutional monarchy with one legislative house (House of Representatives [97]).
*Chief of state:* British Monarch, represented by governor-general.
*Head of government:* Prime Minister.
*Capital:* Wellington.
*Official language:* English.
*Official religion:* none.
*Monetary unit:* 1 New Zealand dollar ($NZ) = 100 cents; valuation (Oct. 5, 1987) 1 U.S.$ = $NZ 1.54; 1 £ = $NZ 2.50.

| Area and population | area | | population |
|---|---|---|---|
| Statistical areas[1] | sq mi | sq km | 1986 census |
| North Island | | | |
| Central Auckland | 2,154 | 5,578 | 889,225 |
| East Coast | 4,212 | 10,908 | 48,364 |
| Hawke's Bay | 4,356 | 11,283 | 150,744 |
| Northland | 4,883 | 12,646 | 127,558 |
| South Auckland– | | | |
| Bay of Plenty | 14,240 | 36,881 | 518,721 |
| Taranaki | 3,754 | 9,724 | 108,979 |
| Wellington | 10,715 | 27,751 | 598,024 |
| South Island | | | |
| Canterbury[2] | 16,691 | 43,230 | 431,421 |
| Marlborough | 4,243 | 10,989 | 38,087 |
| Nelson | 6,768 | 17,530 | 81,160 |
| Otago | 14,209 | 36,801 | 186,142 |
| Southland[3] | 11,160 | 28,905 | 104,817 |
| Westland | 5,903 | 15,289 | 23,842 |
| TOTAL | 103,288 | 267,515 | 3,307,084 |

## Demography

*Population* (1987): 3,341,000.
*Density* (1987): persons per sq mi 32.3, persons per sq km 12.5.
*Urban–rural* (1985): urban 83.7%; rural 16.3%.
*Sex distribution* (1986): male 49.66%; female 50.34%.
*Age breakdown* (1986): under 15, 23.3%; 15–29, 25.6%; 30–44, 21.2%; 45–59, 14.3%; 60–74, 11.3%; 75 and over, 4.3%.
*Population projection:* (1990) 3,423,000; (2000) 3,712,000.
*Doubling time:* 100 years.
*Ethnic composition* (1981): European 85.8%; Maori 8.9%; Pacific Island Polynesian 2.8%; other and not specified 2.5%.
*Religious affiliation* (1981): Anglican 25.7%; Presbyterian 16.5%; Roman Catholic 14.4%; Methodist 4.7%; other 38.7%.
*Major cities* (1986): Manukau 177,248; Christchurch 168,200; Auckland 149,046; Wellington 137,495; Waitemata 96,365.

## Vital statistics[4]

*Birth rate* per 1,000 population (1985): 15.8 (world avg. 29.0); legitimate 76.2%; illegitimate 23.8%.
*Death rate* per 1,000 population (1985): 8.4 (world avg. 11.0).
*Natural increase rate* per 1,000 population (1985): 7.4 (world avg. 18.0).
*Total fertility rate* (avg. births per childbearing woman; 1987): 1.9.
*Marriage rate* per 1,000 population (1985): 7.5.
*Divorce rate* per 1,000 population (1984): 0.3.
*Life expectancy* at birth (1987): male 71.8 years; female 77.8 years.
*Major causes of death* per 100,000 population (1984): diseases of the circulatory system 368.8, of which ischemic heart diseases 220.8; malignant neoplasms (cancers) 180.7; accidents 40.7; pneumonia 32.6.

## National economy

*Budget* (1984–85). Revenue: $NZ 12,539,100,000 (income tax 66.6%; customs, sales tax, and beer duty 20.5%; interest and profits 5.0%; highways tax 2.7%). Expenditures: $NZ 15,322,600,000 (social services 29.1%; debt services and investment 17.7%; health 12.5%; education 11.3%; development of industry 11.2%).
*Public debt* (external, outstanding; 1985): U.S.$12,409,500,000.
*Tourism* (1985): receipts from visitors U.S.$276,000,000; expenditures by nationals abroad U.S.$401,000,000.
*Production* (metric tons except as noted). Agriculture, forestry, fishing (1985): barley 644,400, fruits 397,000, wheat 309,600, potatoes 272,000, corn (maize) 174,600, oats 51,000; livestock (number of live animals; 1986) 68,132,000 sheep, 8,237,000 cattle, 454,000 pigs, 136,000 goats; roundwood (1984) 8,934,000 cu m; fish catch (1984) 132,300. Mining and quarrying (1984): limestone 3,718,700; aluminum 243,100; serpentine 76,900; lead 6,000; gold 21,605 troy oz. Manufacturing (value added, $NZ '000; 1983–84): food, beverages, and tobacco 1,919,781, of which meat 764,844, dairy products 242,391, wine 26,883; fabricated metal products, machinery, and equipment 1,772,307; paper and paper products 830,033; textiles, wearing apparel, and leather 725,006; chemicals and chemical, petroleum, coal, rubber, and plastic products 669,410; wood and wood products 478,729. Construction ($NZ '000; 1986): residential 1,715,988; nonresidential 1,648,095. Energy production (consumption): electricity (kW-hr; 1985) 26,765,000,000 (23,994,000,000); coal (metric tons; 1985) 2,408,500 (2,345,800); petroleum (barrels; 1985) 17,151,000 (34,098,000); petroleum products (metric tons; 1985) 3,345,000 (3,345,000); natural gas[5] (cu m; 1985) 3,700,900,000 (2,880,920,000[6]).
*Gross national product* (1985): U.S.$23,720,000,000 (U.S.$7,290 per capita).

| Structure of gross domestic product and labour force | 1986 | | 1984 | |
|---|---|---|---|---|
| | in value $NZ '000,000 | % of total value | labour force | % of labour force |
| Agriculture | 4,165 | 9.3 | 143,000 | 10.4 |
| Mining | 513 | 1.1 | 5,000 | 0.4 |
| Manufacturing | 10,059 | 22.4 | 302,000 | 22.0 |
| Construction | 2,536 | 5.7 | 88,000 | 6.4 |
| Public utilities | 1,383 | 3.1 | 16,000 | 1.2 |
| Transp. and commun. | 3,463 | 7.7 | 103,000 | 7.5 |
| Trade | 8,539 | 19.0 | 221,000 | 16.1 |
| Finance | 7,663 | 17.1 | 99,000 | 7.2 |
| Pub. admin., defense | 5,113 | 11.4 } | 302,000 | 22.0 |
| Services | 2,065 | 4.6 } | | |
| Other | −631[7] | −1.4[7] | 92,000[8] | 6.7 |
| TOTAL | 44,868[9] | 100.0 | 1,371,000 | 100.0[9] |

*Population economically active* (1984): total 1,371,000; activity rate of total population 41.9% (participation rates: ages 15–64 [1981] 65.4%; female 35.2%; unemployed 5.7%).

| Price and earnings indexes (1980 = 100) | 1981 | 1982 | 1983 | 1984 | 1985 | 1986 | 1987[10] |
|---|---|---|---|---|---|---|---|
| Consumer price index | 115.3 | 134.0 | 143.8 | 152.7 | 176.2 | 194.6 | 213.0 |
| Weekly earnings index | 119.0 | 133.0 | 134.0 | 137.0 | 149.0 | 171.0[11] | ... |

*Household income and expenditure.* Average household size (1981) 3.2; income per household $NZ 15,810 (U.S.$13,755); sources of income: n.a.; expenditure (1984–85): housing 20.3%, transportation 19.7%, food 17.1%, household durable goods 14.2%, clothing 6.0%, recreation 3.8%, education 2.2%, health 1.5%.
*Land use* (1984): forested 38.3%; meadows and pastures 52.5%; agricultural and under permanent cultivation 1.7%; other 7.5%.

## Foreign trade

| Balance of trade (current prices) | 1981 | 1982 | 1983 | 1984 | 1985 | 1986 |
|---|---|---|---|---|---|---|
| $NZ '000,000 | +383.6 | +351.1 | +811.5 | +425.9 | −868.5 | −895.3 |
| % of total | 3.1% | 2.4% | 5.3% | 2.5% | 3.6% | 4.1% |

*Imports* (1986): $NZ 11,467,000,000 (machinery and electrical equipment 23.8%; transport equipment 11.5%; mineral fuels 10.9%, of which petroleum 2.0%; chemicals 10.3%; textiles, clothing, and footwear 5.8%; iron, steel, and nonferrous metals 5.2%. *Major import sources:* Japan 19.1%; United States 15.9%; Australia 15.1%; United Kingdom 8.6%; West Germany 5.4%.
*Exports* (1986): $NZ 10,571,700,000 (food and live animals 44.6%, of which meat and meat preparations 16.4%, dairy products and eggs 13.0%, wool 12.1%; crude materials except fuels 20.7%, of which forest products 6.9%; chemicals 5.1%). *Major export destinations:* Australia 17.3%; United States 15.6%; Japan 14.5%; United Kingdom 8.8%; Iran 2.8%; U.S.S.R. 2.3%.

## Transport and communications

*Transport.* Railroads (1984): length 2,692 mi, 4,332 km; passenger-mi 284,687,000, passenger-km 458,160,000; short ton-mi cargo 2,168,000,000, metric ton-km cargo 3,165,000,000. Roads (1985): total length 57,811 mi, 93,054 km (paved 54%). Vehicles (1986): passenger cars 1,558,307; trucks and buses 318,197. Merchant marine (1986): vessels (100 gross tons and over) 118; total deadweight tonnage 344,796. Air transport (1986): passenger-mi 5,428,000,000, passenger-km 8,736,000,000; short ton-mi cargo 229,900,000, metric ton-km cargo 335,700,000; airports (1987) with scheduled flights 36.
*Communications.* Daily newspapers (1985): total number 34; total circulation 1,055,000; circulation per 1,000 population 324. Radio (1985): total number of receivers 2,800,000 (1 per 1.2 persons). Television (1985): total number of receivers 947,155 (1 per 3.4 persons). Telephones (1983): 1,939,488 (1 per 1.7 persons).

## Education and health

| Education (1985) | schools | teachers | students | student/ teacher ratio |
|---|---|---|---|---|
| Primary (age 5–12) | 2,500 | 18,188 | 452,426 | 24.9 |
| Secondary (age 13–17) | 428 | 13,045 | 230,970 | 17.7 |
| Voc., teacher tr. | 28 | 2,989 | 131,044 | 43.8 |
| Higher[12] | 7 | 2,935 | 34,431 | 11.7 |

*Educational attainment* (1981). Percent of population age 25 and over having: no formal schooling 1.2%; primary education 41.5%; secondary 26.6%; vocational, postsecondary, and higher 30.6%[9]. *Literacy* (1983): total population age 15 and over literate (virtually 100.0%).
*Health* (1985): physicians (1984) 7,750 (1 per 421 persons); hospital beds 31,273 (1 per 104 persons); infant mortality rate per 1,000 live births 10.8.
*Food* (1981–83): daily per capita caloric intake 3,517 (vegetable products 55%, animal products 45%); (1983) 132% of FAO recommended minimum.

## Military

*Total active duty personnel* (1986): 12,615 (army 46.1%, navy 20.7%, air force 33.2%). *Military expenditure as percent of GNP* (1984): 1.8% (world 5.9%); per capita expenditure U.S.$124.

[1]The statistical areas listed have no administrative significance; adjacent islands and land reclamations are included where appropriate. [2]Includes Chatham Island county. [3]Includes Stewart Island county. [4]Vital statistics figures are for December 1985. [5]Since 1979, data include manufactured gas. [6]1984. [7]Includes import duties less imputed bank service charges. [8]Includes unemployed. [9]Detail does not add to total given because of rounding. [10]January. [11]September. [12]Universities only.

# Nicaragua

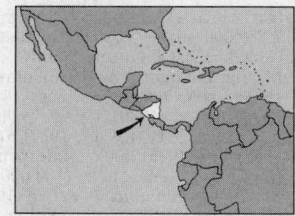

*Official name:* República de Nicaragua (Republic of Nicaragua).
*Form of government:* unitary multiparty republic with one legislative house (National Assembly [96]).
*Head of state and government:* President.
*Capital:* Managua.
*Official language:* Spanish.
*Official religion:* none.
*Monetary unit:* 1 Nicaraguan córdoba (C$) = 100 centavos; valuation (Oct. 5, 1987) 1 U.S.$ = C$2,000[1]; 1 £ = C$3,248[1].

### Area and population

| Zones Departments | Capitals | area[2] sq mi | sq km | population 1985 estimate |
|---|---|---|---|---|
| Atlantic | | | | |
| Río San Juan | San Carlos | 2,876 | 7,448 | 34,330 |
| Zelaya | Bluefields | 22,816 | 59,094 | 325,454 |
| North Central | | | | |
| Boaco | Boaco | 1,924 | 4,982 | 97,432 |
| Chontales | Juigalpa | 1,910 | 4,947 | 111,786 |
| Estelí | Estelí | 849 | 2,199 | 115,333 |
| Jinotega | Jinotega | 3,697 | 9,576 | 143,264 |
| Madriz | Somoto | 756 | 1,958 | 80,268 |
| Matagalpa | Matagalpa | 2,623 | 6,794 | 263,649 |
| Nueva Segovia | Ocotal | 1,290 | 3,341 | 139,116 |
| Pacific | | | | |
| Carazo | Jinotepe | 398 | 1,032 | 97,106 |
| Chinandega | Chinandega | 1,800 | 4,662 | 285,506 |
| Granada | Granada | 372 | 964 | 136,068 |
| León | León | 2,021 | 5,234 | 257,815 |
| Managua | Managua | 1,389[3] | 3,597[3] | 903,998[3] |
| Masaya | Masaya | 224 | 581 | 179,114 |
| Rivas | Rivas | 830 | 2,149 | 101,825 |
| **National District** | | | | |
| Distrito Nacional | | 3 | 3 | 3 |
| TOTAL LAND AREA | | 45,775 | 118,558 | 3,272,064 |
| INLAND WATER | | 3,588 | 9,291 | |
| TOTAL AREA | | 49,363 | 127,849 | |

## Demography

*Population* (1987): 3,502,000.
*Density* (1987)[4]: persons per sq mi 76.5, persons per sq km 29.5.
*Urban–rural* (1986): urban 58.0%; rural 42.0%.
*Sex distribution* (1985): male 50.00%; female 50.00%.
*Age breakdown* (1985): under 15, 46.7%; 15–29, 27.5%; 30–44, 14.2%; 45–59, 7.5%; 60–74, 3.4%; 75 and over, 0.7%.
*Population projection:* (1990) 3,871,000; (2000) 5,261,000.
*Doubling time:* 21 years.
*Ethnic composition* (1980): mestizo (Spanish/Indian) 68.8%; white 14.0%; black 8.0%; Zambo (black/Indian) 5.0%; Amerindian 4.0%; other 0.2%.
*Religious affiliation* (1984): Roman Catholic 86.9%; other 13.1%.
*Major cities* (1985): Managua 682,111; León 100,982; Granada 88,636; Masaya 74,946; Chinandega 67,792.

## Vital statistics

*Birth rate* per 1,000 population (1985): 44.2 (world avg. 29.0).
*Death rate* per 1,000 population (1985): 9.7 (world avg. 11.0).
*Natural increase rate* per 1,000 population (1985): 34.5 (world avg. 18.0).
*Total fertility rate* (avg. births per childbearing woman; 1984): 5.7.
*Marriage rate* per 1,000 population (1985): 3.6.
*Divorce rate* per 1,000 population (1985): 0.4.
*Life expectancy* at birth (1985): male 58.7 years; female 61.0 years.
*Major causes of death* per 100,000 population (1978): diseases of the circulatory system 62.1; accidents, poisoning, and violence 59.2; infectious and parasitic diseases 52.3.

## National economy

*Budget* (1984)[5]. Revenue: C$15,850,000,000 (sales tax 41.2%, import duties 16.2%, social security 10.2%, property tax 7.8%). Expenditures: C$26,740,-000,000 (current expenditures 81.0%, development expenditures 19.0%).
*Tourism:* receipts from visitors (1984) U.S.$5,000,000; expenditures by nationals abroad (1983) U.S.$7,000,000.
*Production* (metric tons except as noted). Agriculture, forestry, fishing (1985): sugarcane 2,831,000, corn (maize) 234,000, sorghum 194,000, seed cotton 180,000, rice 156,000, bananas 114,000[6], dry beans 104,000[6], plantains 85,000, oranges 55,000[6], coffee 44,000[6]; livestock (number of live animals) 1,890,000 cattle, 540,000 pigs, 5,000,000 chickens; roundwood 3,581,000 cu m; fish catch 4,939, of which shrimp 2,285. Mining and quarrying (1985): gold 24,000 troy oz; salt 20,000. Manufacturing (value added in C$'000,000; 1984): beverages 3,044; processed foods 2,675; petroleum products 1,417; tobacco products 966; nonindustrial chemical products 887; textiles 880; metal products 790. Construction (buildings authorized[7]; 1985): residential 62,700 sq m; nonresidential 15,300 sq m. Energy production (consumption): electricity (kW-hr; 1985) 1,059,000,000 (1,246,000,000); coal, none (none); crude petroleum (barrels; 1985) none (3,650,000); petroleum products (metric tons; 1985) 490,000 (629,000); natural gas, none (none).
*Gross national product* (at current market prices; 1985): U.S.$2,760,000,000 (U.S.$840 per capita).

### Structure of gross domestic product and labour force

| | 1985 in value C$'000,000 | % of total value | 1980 labour force | % of labour force |
|---|---|---|---|---|
| Agriculture | 9,340 | 22.7 | 391,963 | 45.4 |
| Mining | 190 | 0.4 | 6,566 | 0.7 |
| Manufacturing | 11,334 | 27.5 | 91,403 | 10.6 |
| Construction | 1,764 | 4.3 | 37,322 | 4.3 |
| Public utilities | 471 | 1.1 | 6,652 | 0.8 |
| Transportation and communication | 2,096 | 5.1 | 30,064 | 3.4 |
| Trade | 7,160 | 17.4 | 105,053 | 12.2 |
| Finance, real estate | 2,679 | 6.5 | 16,761 | 2.0 |
| Pub. admin., defense | 4,358 | 10.6 } | 158,789 | 18.4 |
| Services | 1,824 | 4.4 } | | |
| Other | — | — | 19,352 | 2.2 |
| TOTAL | 41,216 | 100.0 | 863,925 | 100.0 |

*Public debt* (external, outstanding; 1985): U.S.$4,752,800,000.
*Population economically active* (1980): total 863,925; activity rate of total population 29.8% (participation rates: ages 15–64, 54.0%; female 21.6%; unemployed [1985] 30.0%).

### Price and earnings indexes (1980 = 100)

| | 1979 | 1980 | 1981 | 1982 | 1983 | 1984 | 1985 |
|---|---|---|---|---|---|---|---|
| Consumer price index | 73.9 | 100.0 | 123.9 | 154.6 | 202.6 | 274.4 | 876.7 |
| Hourly earnings index[8] | 77.7 | 100.0 | 125.1 | ... | ... | ... | ... |

*Household income and expenditure.* Average household size (1980) 6.9; income per household: n.a.; sources of income: n.a.; expenditure (1985)[7]: food, beverages, and tobacco 40.4%, clothing and footwear 20.9%, housing, energy, and household furnishings 19.7%, other 19.0%.
*Land use* (1984): forested 34.0%; meadows and pastures 42.9%; agricultural and under permanent cultivation 10.7%; other 12.4%.

## Foreign trade[9]

### Balance of trade (current prices)

| | 1981 | 1982 | 1983 | 1984 | 1985 | 1986 |
|---|---|---|---|---|---|---|
| U.S.$'000,000 | −491.2 | −370.0 | −375.1 | −439.8 | −592.7 | −661.4 |
| % of total | 32.6% | 31.3% | 30.3% | 36.3% | 49.6% | 60.2% |

*Imports* (1985): U.S.$894,200,000 (crude petroleum and petroleum products 12.6%, chemical and pharmaceutical products 10.4%, industrial machinery 10.4%, fertilizers 8.0%, food products 6.6%, road motor vehicles 5.4%). *Major import sources* (1986): Socialist bloc 51.0%; EEC 14.0%; CACM 6.0%; United States 0.6%; not specified 28.4%.
*Exports* (1985): U.S.$301,500,000 (coffee 39.3%, cotton 30.5%, bananas 5.5%, shrimp and lobster 4.3%, fresh beef 3.7%). *Major export destinations* (1986): EEC 55.0%; Socialist bloc 13.9%; CACM 5.0%; not specified 26.1%.

## Transport and communications

*Transport.* Railroads (1984): length (1986) 214 mi, 344 km; passenger-mi 37,566,000, passenger-km 60,465,000; short ton-mi cargo 3,253,000, metric ton-km cargo 4,750,000. Roads (1985): total length 9,104 mi, 14,651 km (paved 11%). Vehicles (1985): passenger cars 33,094; trucks and buses 42,229. Merchant marine (1986): vessels (100 gross tons and over) 24; total deadweight tonnage 31,947. Air transport (1985): passenger arrivals 126,972, passenger departures 134,471; cargo unloaded 3,384, metric tons, cargo loaded 2,595 metric tons; airports (1985) with scheduled flights 7.
*Communications.* Daily newspapers (1986): total number 3; total circulation 143,500; circulation per 1,000 population 42. Radio (1986): 300,000 receivers (1 per 11 persons). Television (1986): 171,000 receivers (1 per 20 persons). Telephones (1984): 50,459 (1 per 63 persons).

## Education and health

### Education (1985)

| | schools | teachers | students | student/ teacher ratio |
|---|---|---|---|---|
| Primary (age 7–12) | 4,102 | 15,273 | 524,020 | 34.3 |
| Secondary (age 13–18) Voc., teacher tr. } | 431 | 4,778 | 151,269 | 31.7 |
| Higher | 16 | 2,527 | 29,001 | 11.5 |

*Educational attainment.* n.a. *Literacy* (1983): total population age 15 and over literate 88.0%.
*Health* (1985): physicians (1984) 2,172 (1 per 1,456 persons); hospital beds 5,083 (1 per 644 persons); infant mortality rate per 1,000 live births 76.4.
*Food* (1979–81): daily per capita caloric intake 2,188 (vegetable products 84%, animal products 16%); (1983) 102% of FAO recommended minimum requirement.

## Military

*Total active duty personnel* (1986): 72,000 (army 95.8%, navy 1.4%, air force 2.8%). *Military expenditure as percent of GNP* (1984): 13.4% (world 5.9%); per capita expenditure U.S.$150.

[1]Market rate only; complex exchange rate structures were introduced on June 1, 1987. [2]Total land area only is shown for the departments and the national district; the total area (both land and water) is shown only in the grand total. [3]Distrito Nacional is included with Managua. [4]Based on land area. [5]*Budget* (1987). Revenue: C$263,520,000,000. Expenditures: C$384,960,000,000 (current expenditures 90.5%, development expenditures 9.5%). [6]1986. [7]Managua only. [8]Nonagricultural activities. [9]Import figures are c.i.f.

# Niger

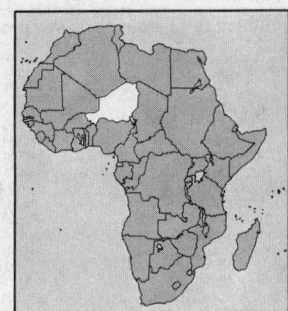

*Official name:* République du Niger
(Republic of Niger).
*Form of government:* military
government with one advisory
body (National Development
Council[1] [150]).
*Head of state and government:*
President in conjunction with the
Supreme Military Council.
*Capital:* Niamey.
*Official language:* French.
*Official religion:* none.
*Monetary unit:* 1 CFA franc
(CFAF) = 100 centimes;
valuation (Oct. 5, 1987)
1 U.S.$ = CFAF 306.67;
1 £ = CFAF 498.00.

### Area and population

| Departments | Capitals | area sq mi | area sq km | population 1987[2] estimate |
|---|---|---|---|---|
| Agadez | Agadez | 244,869 | 634,209 | 174,000 |
| Diffa | Diffa | 54,138 | 140,216 | 203,000 |
| Dosso | Dosso | 11,970 | 31,002 | 876,000 |
| Maradi | Maradi | 14,896 | 38,581 | 1,243,000 |
| Niamey | Niamey | 34,862 | 90,293 | 1,585,000 |
| Tahoua | Tahoua | 41,188 | 106,677 | 1,234,000 |
| Zinder | Zinder | 56,151 | 145,430 | 1,298,000 |
| TOTAL | | 458,075[3] | 1,186,408 | 6,613,000 |

## Demography

*Population* (1987): 6,947,000.
*Density* (1987): persons per sq mi 15.2, persons per sq km 5.9.
*Urban–rural* (1987): urban 19.8%; rural 80.2%.
*Sex distribution* (1985): male 49.53%; female 50.47%.
*Age breakdown* (1985): under 15, 46.7%; 15–29, 25.6%; 30–44, 14.9%; 45–59, 8.0%; 60–74, 3.9%; 75 and over, 0.9%.
*Population projection:* (1990) 7,702,000; (2000) 10,832,000.
*Doubling time:* 26 years.
*Ethnic composition* (1983): Hausa 52.0%; Zerma 14.7%; Fulani 10.4%; Kanuri 8.7%; Songhai 8.1%; Tuareg 3.0%; French 0.1%; other 3.0%.
*Religious affiliation* (1983): Sunnī Muslim 97.5%; other 2.5%.
*Major cities* (1983): Niamey 399,100; Zinder 82,800; Maradi 65,100; Tahoua 41,900.

## Vital statistics

*Birth rate* per 1,000 population (1980–85): 51.0 (world avg. 29.0).
*Death rate* per 1,000 population (1980–85): 22.9 (world avg. 11.0).
*Natural increase rate* per 1,000 population (1980–85): 28.1 (world avg. 18.0).
*Total fertility rate* (avg. births per childbearing woman; 1980–85): 7.1.
*Marriage rate* per 1,000 population: n.a.
*Divorce rate* per 1,000 population: n.a.
*Life expectancy* at birth (1980–85): male 40.9 years; female 44.1 years.
*Major causes of death* per 100,000 population (1976): malaria 317; measles 229; meningitis 145; other major diseases include bacillary dysentery and amebiasis, typhoid fever, enteritis and other diarrheal diseases, avitaminoses and other nutritional deficiency diseases, tuberculosis of the respiratory system, and bronchitis.

## National economy

*Budget* (1987). Revenue: CFAF 198,073,000,000 (external aid 32.5%; new debt 27.4%; import and export duties 16.6%; excise taxes 9.6%; personal income taxes 7.2%). Expenditures: CFAF 162,400,000,000 (capital expenses 46.7%; administration 33.2%, of which education 10.6%, health 4.8%, defense 2.6%; national debt 20.1%).
*Public debt* (external, outstanding; 1985): U.S.$791,300,000.
*Tourism* (1985): receipts from visitors U.S.$3,000,000; expenditures by nationals abroad, n.a.
*Gross national product* (at current market prices; 1985): U.S.$1,250,000,000 (U.S.$190 per capita).

### Structure of gross domestic product and labour force

| | 1985 in value CFAF '000,000 | 1985 % of total value | labour force | % of labour force |
|---|---|---|---|---|
| Agriculture | 298,200 | 45.2 | 2,849,000 | 88.9 |
| Mining | 51,700 | 7.8 | | |
| Manufacturing | 25,900 | 3.9 | | |
| Construction | 18,600 | 2.8 | | |
| Public utilities | 13,700 | 2.1 | | |
| Transportation and communication | 28,300 | 4.3 | 354,000 | 11.1 |
| Trade and finance | 82,500 | 12.5 | | |
| Pub. admin., defense | 55,400 | 8.4 | | |
| Services | 56,900 | 8.6 | | |
| Other | 28,500 | 4.3 | | |
| TOTAL | 659,700 | 100.0[3] | 3,203,000 | 100.0 |

*Production* (metric tons except as noted). Agriculture, forestry, fishing (1985): millet 1,450,000, sorghum 330,000, roots and tubers 222,000, pulses 215,-000, vegetables and melons 158,000, sugarcane 145,000, onions 120,000, rice 56,000, peanuts (groundnuts) 40,000, corn (maize) 15,000, cotton 10,-

000, wheat 2,000, tobacco leaves 1,000; livestock (number of live animals) 7,530,000 goats, 3,530,000 cattle, 3,530,000 sheep, 505,000 asses, 414,000 camels, 290,000 horses; roundwood 3,920,000 cu m; fish catch (1984) 6,840. Mining and quarrying (1986): uranium 3,108. Manufacturing (1982): cement 16,000; soap 6,600; beverages 101,000 hectolitres; beer 97,000 hectolitres. Construction (1980): CFAF 75,937,000,000. Energy production (consumption): electricity (kW-hr; 1985) 51,000,000 (338,000,000); coal (metric tons; 1985) 61,000 (61,000); crude petroleum, none (n.a.); petroleum products (metric tons; 1985) none (184,000); natural gas, none (n.a.).
*Population economically active* (1985): total 3,203,000; activity rate of total population 49.3% (participation rates: ages 15–64 [1982] 51.0%; female, n.a.; unemployed, n.a.).

### Price index (1980 = 100)

| | 1981 | 1982 | 1983 | 1984 | 1985 | 1986 | 1987[4] |
|---|---|---|---|---|---|---|---|
| Consumer price index | 122.9 | 137.2 | 133.8 | 145.0 | 143.7 | 139.1 | 127.5 |
| Hourly earnings index[5] | 107.3 | 107.2 | 107.3 | 107.3 | 107.3 | 107.3 | ... |

*Household income and expenditure.* Average household size (1980) 5.2; income per household: n.a.; sources of income (1977): self-employment 59.5%, family 30.1%, salary or wages 4.8%, employer 0.7%; (1983): food and beverages 50.5%, household expenses 19.1%, clothing 7.3%.
*Land use* (1984): forested 2.1%; meadows and pastures 7.3%; agricultural and under permanent cultivation 3.0%; other 87.6%.

## Foreign trade

### Balance of trade (current prices)

| | 1978 | 1979 | 1980 | 1981 | 1982 | 1983 |
|---|---|---|---|---|---|---|
| CFAF '000,000 | −5,200 | −2,800 | −5,900 | −14,900 | −55,500 | −9,392 |
| % of total | 3.9% | 1.5% | 2.4% | 5.7% | 19.8% | 4.0% |

*Imports* (1983): CFAF 123,288,000,000 (food products 28.3%, of which cereals 13.8%, sugar 2.8%; chemical products 13.1%; petroleum products 12.8%; nonelectrical machinery 7.3%; cotton thread and fabrics 2.2%). *Major import sources:* France 32.8%; Nigeria 31.7%; United States 4.6%; Côte d'Ivoire 4.2%; West Germany 3.6%; Japan 2.9%.
*Exports* (1983): CFAF 113,896,000,000 (uranium 82.7%; foodstuffs 11.7%, of which vegetables 6.9%, live animals 4.1%). *Major export destinations:* France 48.1%; Japan 22.8%; Nigeria 11.1%; Spain 5.2%; West Germany 4.5%.

## Transport and communications

*Transport.* Railroads (1984): none[6]. Roads (1984): total length 11,891 mi, 19,137 km (paved 17%). Vehicles (1984): passenger cars 23,102; trucks and buses 9,052. Air transport (1985)[7]: passenger-mi 144,226,000, passenger-km 232,109,000; short ton-mi cargo 47,538,000, metric ton-km cargo 69,404,-000; airports (1987) with scheduled flights 1.
*Communications.* Daily newspapers (1986): total number 1; total circulation 3,000; circulation per 1,000 population 0.4. Radio (1986): total number of receivers 300,000 (1 per 22 persons). Television (1986): total number of receivers 25,000 (1 per 269 persons). Telephones (1985): 11,824 (1 per 549 persons).

## Education and health

### Education (1980–81)

| | schools | teachers | students | student/ teacher ratio |
|---|---|---|---|---|
| Primary (age 7–12) | 1,664 | 5,518 | 228,855 | 41.5 |
| Secondary (age 13–19) | 64 | 1,371 | 32,892 | 24.0 |
| Voc., teacher tr. | 8 | 120 | 2,351 | 19.6 |
| Higher[8] | 1 | 189 | 1,825 | 9.7 |

*Educational attainment* (1977). Percent of population age 9 and over having: no formal schooling 88.6%; primary education 10.3%; secondary 0.9%; higher 0.2%. *Literacy* (1980): total population age 15 and over literate 278,-000 (9.8%); males literate 195,000 (14.0%); females literate 83,000 (5.8%).
*Health:* physicians (1980) 136 (1 per 40,209 persons); hospital beds (1979) 3,261 (1 per 1,633 persons); infant mortality rate per 1,000 live births (1980–85) 146.0.
*Food* (1981–83): daily per capita caloric intake 2,380 (vegetable products 93%, animal products 7%); (1983) 97% of FAO recommended minimum requirement.

## Military

*Total active duty personnel* (1986): 2,270 (army 94.7%, air force 5.3%). *Military expenditure as percent of GNP* (1984): 0.7% (world 5.9%); per capita expenditure U.S.$2.

[1]The legislature (National Assembly) was suspended in 1974. In 1983 the National Development Council assumed the role of a constituent assembly. A national charter (constitution) restoring some civilian control was approved by referendum June 14, 1987. [2]January 1. [3]Detail does not add to total given because of rounding. [4]June. [5]Guaranteed minimum wage for professionals. [6]Niger is a cofounder of the Common Benin–Niger Organization for Railroads and Transport, currently maintaining rail operations only in Benin, but having the purpose of extending rail services from the sea at Cotonou, Benin, to Dosso and, ultimately, Niamey, Niger. [7]Air Afrique. [8]Université de Niamey.

# Nigeria

*Official name:* Federal Republic of Nigeria.
*Form of government:* federal republic (constitution suspended in part Dec. 31, 1983); temporarily governed under emergency powers by Armed Forces Ruling Council (AFRC).
*Head of state and government:* President.
*Capital:* Lagos[1].
   (Capital designate: Abuja).
*Official language:* English.
*Official religion:* none.
*Monetary unit:* 1 Nigerian naira (₦) = 100 kobo; valuation (Oct. 5, 1987) 1 U.S.$ = ₦4.16; 1 £ = ₦6.75.

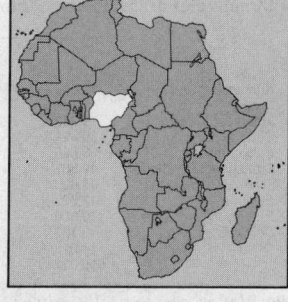

## Area and population

| | | area | | population |
| --- | --- | --- | --- | --- |
| States | Capitals | sq mi | sq km | 1984 estimate |
| Anambra | Enugu | 6,824 | 17,675 | 6,029,500 |
| Bauchi | Bauchi | 24,944 | 64,605 | 4,075,800 |
| Bendel | Benin City | 13,707 | 35,500 | 4,125,500 |
| Benue | Makurdi | 17,442 | 45,174 | 4,068,600 |
| Borno | Maiduguri | 44,942 | 116,400 | 5,025,000 |
| Cross River | Calabar | 10,516 | 27,237 | 5,830,800 |
| Gongola | Yola | 35,286 | 91,390 | 4,367,600 |
| Imo | Owerri | 4,575 | 11,850 | 6,157,000 |
| Kaduna | Kaduna | 27,122 | 70,245 | 6,868,800 |
| Kano | Kano | 16,712 | 43,285 | 9,681,000 |
| Kwara | Ilorin | 25,818 | 66,869 | 2,884,400 |
| Lagos | Ikeja | 1,292 | 3,345 | 2,825,200 |
| Niger | Minna | 25,111 | 65,037 | 1,961,800 |
| Ogun | Abeokuta | 6,472 | 16,762 | 2,596,000 |
| Ondo | Akure | 8,092 | 20,959 | 4,617,200 |
| Oyo | Ibadan | 14,558 | 37,705 | 8,732,300 |
| Plateau | Jos | 22,405 | 58,030 | 3,397,500 |
| Rivers | Port-Harcourt | 8,436 | 21,850 | 2,883,300 |
| Sokoto | Sokoto | 39,589 | 102,535 | 7,608,900 |
| **Federal Capital Territory** | | 2,824 | 7,315 | ... |
| TOTAL | | 356,669[2] | 923,768 | 93,736,200 |

## Demography

*Population* (1987): 100,595,700.
*Density* (1987): persons per sq mi 282.0, persons per sq km 108.9.
*Urban-rural* (1985): urban 16.1%; rural 83.9%.
*Sex distribution* (1985): male 49.50%; female 50.50%.
*Age breakdown* (1985): under 15, 48.3%; 15–29, 25.8%; 30–44, 14.1%; 45–59, 7.8%; 60–74, 3.4%; 75 and over, 0.6%.
*Population projection:* (1990) 108,430,000; (2000) 139,200,000.
*Doubling time:* 28 years.
*Ethnic composition* (1983): Hausa 21.3%; Yoruba 21.3%; Igbo (Ibo) 18.0%; Fulani 11.2%; Ibibio 5.6%; Kanuri 4.2%; Edo 3.4%; Tiv 2.2%; Ijaw 1.8%; Bura 1.7%; Nupe 1.2%; other 8.1%.
*Religious affiliation* (1980): Muslim 45.0%; Protestant 26.3%; Roman Catholic 12.1%; African indigenous 10.6%; traditional beliefs 5.6%; other 0.4%.
*Major cities* (1983): Lagos 1,097,000; Ibadan 1,060,000; Ogbomosho 527,400; Kano 487,100; Oshogbo 344,500.

## Vital statistics

*Birth rate* per 1,000 population (1980–85): 50.4 (world avg. 29.0).
*Death rate* per 1,000 population (1980–85): 17.1 (world avg. 11.0).
*Natural increase rate* per 1,000 population (1980–85): 33.3 (world avg. 18.0).
*Total fertility rate* (avg. births per childbearing woman; 1980–85): 7.1.
*Marriage rate* per 1,000 population: n.a.
*Life expectancy* at birth (1980–85): male 46.9 years; female 50.2 years.
*Major causes of death* per 100,000 population: n.a.; major diseases include malaria, tuberculosis, trypanosomiasis, onchocerciasis, and leprosy.

## National economy

*Budget* (1986). Revenue ₦14,189,900,000 (petroleum revenues 58.1%; import duties 12.2%; special funds 10.6%). Expenditures: ₦12,524,100,000 (recurrent expenditure 61.0%, of which debt service 40.8%, defense 9.0%, education 7.8%, police 5.4%, health 3.3%; capital expenditure 39.0%).
*Public debt* (1985): U.S.$13,015,600,000.
*Production* (metric tons except as noted). Agriculture, forestry, fishing (1986): sorghum 5,455,000, yams 5,209,000, millet 4,111,000, cassava 1,564,000, corn (maize) 1,336,000, plantains 1,127,000, sugarcane 897,000, beans 732,000, palm oil 650,000, peanuts (groundnuts) 640,000, palm kernels 350,000, rice 283,000, rubber 190,000, cacao 123,000; livestock (number of live animals 1985) 12,000,000 cattle, 26,000,000 goats, 12,850,000 sheep; roundwood 92,562,000 cu m; fish catch 246,000. Mining and quarrying (1985): limestone 1,800,000; marble 1,200,000; tin metal 858. Manufacturing (value added in producers' prices ₦'000,000; 1980): beverages and tobacco 737.9; transport equipment 717.5, of which motor vehicles 688.7; chemical products 417.1, of which drugs and medicines 116.2; textiles 334.9; food products 315.7; rubber products 43.3. Construction (1980): residential ₦5,964; nonresidential ₦1,592. Energy production (consumption): electricity (kW-hr; 1985) 9,000,000,000 (8,860,000,000); coal (metric tons; 1985) 50,000 (50,000); crude petroleum (barrels; 1985) 535,414,000 (65,835,000); petroleum products (metric tons; 1985) 8,200,000 (9,351,000); natural gas (cu m; 1985) 5,638,000,000 (5,638,000,000).

*Tourism* (1984): receipts from visitors U.S.$102,000,000; expenditures by nationals abroad U.S.$235,000,000.
*Gross national product* (at current market prices; 1985): U.S.$75,940,000,000 (U.S.$790 per capita).

## Structure of gross domestic product and labour force

| | 1985 | | | |
| --- | --- | --- | --- | --- |
| | in value ₦'000,000[3] | % of total value | labour force | % of labour force |
| Agriculture | 6,948 | 26.6 | 20,865,000 | 57.8 |
| Mining | 5,185 | 19.8 | 144,000 | 0.4 |
| Manufacturing | 2,434 | 9.3 | 6,570,000 | 18.2 |
| Construction | 1,347 | 5.1 | 433,000 | 1.2 |
| Public utilities | 214 | 0.8 | | 0.2 |
| Transp. and commun. | 746 | 2.8 | 216,600 | 0.6 |
| Trade | 5,143 | 19.7 | 5,776,000 | 16.0 |
| Finance | 916 | 3.5 } | | |
| Pub. admin., defense | 2,140 | 8.2 } | 2,095,400 | 5.6 |
| Other (including services) | 1,086 | 4.2 } | | |
| TOTAL | 26,159 | 100.0 | 36,100,000 | 100.0 |

*Population economically active* (1984): total 33,708,000; activity rate of total population 36.1% (participation rates: ages 15–64, 58.2%; female [1983] 31.9%; unemployed [registered] 0.5%).

## Price and earnings indexes (1980 = 100)

| | 1980 | 1981 | 1982 | 1983 | 1984 | 1985 | 1986 |
| --- | --- | --- | --- | --- | --- | --- | --- |
| Consumer price index | 100.0 | 120.8 | 130.1 | 160.3 | 223.8 | 236.1 | 248.8 |
| Earnings index[4] | 100.0 | ... | ... | ... | ... | ... | ... |

*Household income and expenditure.* Average household size (1982) 5.0; average annual income per household (1981) ₦2,300 (U.S.$3,745)[5]; sources of income (1979): self-employment 49.4%, wages and salaries 36.2%, interest 5.4%, rent 4.7%, transfer payments 4.3%; expenditures (1979): food 53.0%, of which beverages and tobacco 4.9%; fuel and light 11.4%, clothing 6.0%, transportation 4.7%, household goods 3.8%, other 21.1%.
*Land use* (1984): forested 16.7%; meadows and pastures 23.0%; agricultural and under permanent cultivation 34.1%; other 26.2%.

## Foreign trade

### Balance of trade (current prices)

| | 1981 | 1982 | 1983 | 1984 | 1985 | 1986 |
| --- | --- | --- | --- | --- | --- | --- |
| ₦'000,000 | −647 | −1,523 | −540 | +2,604 | +4,049 | +3,043 |
| % of total | 2.8% | 8.5% | 3.5% | 16.7% | 22.0% | 21.8% |

*Imports* (1986): ₦5,469,700,000 (machinery and transport equipment 46.0%; manufactured goods 19.3% [mostly iron and steel products, textiles, and paper products]; chemicals 13.2%; food 9.8%; mineral fuels 0.6%). *Major import sources* (1983): U.K. 21.0%; U.S. 14.2%; West Germany 13.3%; France 12.5%; Japan 9.3%; The Netherlands 4.7%; Italy 4.4%.
*Exports* (1986): ₦8,513,000,000 (crude petroleum 97.2%; other significant exports include cocoa, rubber, and palm kernels). *Major export destinations* (1982): U.S. 46.2%; The Netherlands 12.1%; France 10.1%; West Germany 6.6%; U.K. 2.3%; Ghana 1.2%.

## Transport and communications

*Transport.* Railroads (1985): length 2,178 mi, 3,505 km; passenger-km 1,950,000,000; metric ton-km cargo 1,530,000,000[7]. Roads (1984): total length 77,000 mi, 124,000 km (paved 48%). Vehicles (1981): passenger cars 262,550; trucks 90,731. Merchant marine (1986): vessels (100 gross tons and over) 206; total deadweight tonnage 809,278. Air transport (1986): passenger-km 2,261,000,000; metric ton-km cargo 44,364,000; airports (1987) with scheduled flights 16.
*Communications.* Daily newspapers (1986): total number 19; total circulation 898,000[8]; circulation per 1,000 population 9.1[8]. Radio (1986): 15,680,000 receivers (1 per 6.2 persons). Television (1986): 500,000 receivers (1 per 195 persons). Telephones (1986): 265,000 (1 per 368 persons).

## Education and health

### Education (1982–83)

| | schools | teachers | students | student/ teacher ratio |
| --- | --- | --- | --- | --- |
| Primary (age 6–12) | 37,692 | 424,717 | 15,021,100 | 35.4 |
| Secondary (age 12–17) | 5,498 | 78,117 | 2,421,625 | 31.0 |
| Voc., teacher tr. | 475 | 13,414[9] | 395,732 | ... |
| Higher | 80 | | 124,247 | ... |

*Educational attainment,* n.a. *Literacy* (1985): total population age 15 and over literate 20,208,000 (42.4%); males literate 12,551,000 (53.8%); females literate 7,657,000 (31.5%).
*Health* (1983): physicians 11,294 (1 per 8,059 persons); hospital beds 60,840 (1 per 1,496 persons); infant mortality rate per 1,000 live births (1980–85) 114.0.
*Food* (1981–83): daily per capita caloric intake 2,203 (vegetable products 96%, animal products 4%); (1983) 86% of FAO recommended minimum.

## Military

*Total active duty personnel* (1986): 94,000 (army 85.1%, navy 5.3%, air force 9.6%). *Military expenditure as percent of GNP* (1984): 1.7% (world 5.9%); per capita expenditure U.S.$13.

[1]It is presently planned to move the capital from Lagos to Abuja in the Federal Capital Territory in 1990. [2]Detail does not add to total given because of rounding. [3]At prices of 1977–78. [4]For wages earned in nonagricultural activities only. [5]Urban households only. [6]1984. [7]1983. [8]For 9 newspapers only. [9]1981–82.

# Norway

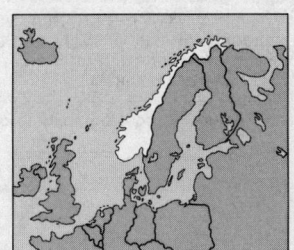

*Official name:* Kongeriket Norge
(Kingdom of Norway).
*Form of government:* constitutional
monarchy with one legislative house
(Parliament [157]).
*Chief of state:* King.
*Head of government:* Prime Minister.
*Capital:* Oslo.
*Official language:* Norwegian.
*Official religion:* Evangelical Lutheran.
*Monetary unit:* 1 Norwegian krone
(NKr) = 100 øre; valuation (Oct. 5,
1987) 1 U.S.$ = NKr 6.73;
1 £ = NKr 10.93.

| Area and population | | area[1] | | population |
|---|---|---|---|---|
| Counties | Capitals | sq mi | sq km | 1987[2] estimate |
| Akershus | — | 1,898 | 4,917 | 399,797 |
| Aust-Agder | Arendal | 3,557 | 9,212 | 95,475 |
| Buskerud | Drammen | 5,763 | 14,927 | 221,384 |
| Finnmark | Vardø | 18,779 | 48,637 | 74,690 |
| Hedmark | Hamar | 10,575 | 27,388 | 186,305 |
| Hordaland | Bergen | 6,036 | 15,634 | 402,343 |
| Møre og Romsdal | Molde | 5,832 | 15,104 | 237,489 |
| Nordland | Bodø | 14,798 | 38,327 | 241,048 |
| Nord-Trøndelag | Steinkjer | 8,673 | 22,463 | 126,648 |
| Oppland | Lillehammer | 9,753 | 25,260 | 181,620 |
| Oslo | Oslo | 175 | 454 | 449,220 |
| Østfold | Moss | 1,615 | 4,183 | 235,813 |
| Rogaland | Stavanger | 3,529 | 9,141 | 326,611 |
| Sogn og Fjordane | Leikanger | 7,195 | 18,634 | 105,966 |
| Sør-Trøndelag | Trondheim | 7,271 | 18,831 | 247,354 |
| Telemark | Skien | 5,913 | 15,315 | 162,595 |
| Troms | Tromsø | 10,021 | 25,954 | 146,595 |
| Vest-Agder | Kristiansand | 2,811 | 7,281 | 141,284 |
| Vestfold | Tønsberg | 856 | 2,216 | 192,934 |
| TOTAL | | 125,050 | 323,878 | 4,175,171[3] |

## Demography

*Population* (1987): 4,180,000.
*Density* (1987): persons per sq mi 33.4, persons per sq km 12.9.
*Urban–rural* (1985): urban 80.3%; rural 19.7%.
*Sex distribution* (1986): male 49.44%; female 50.56%.
*Age breakdown* (1986): under 15, 19.8%; 15–29, 23.2%; 30–44, 21.3%; 45–59,
14.4%; 60–74, 14.7%; 75 and over, 6.6%.
*Population projection:* (1990) 4,220,000; (2000) 4,356,000.
*Doubling time:* n.a.; doubling time exceeds 100 years.
*Ethnic composition* (by country of citizenship; 1986): Norway 97.6%; Den-
mark 0.4%; United Kingdom 0.3%; United States 0.2%; Pakistan 0.2%;
Sweden 0.2%; other 1.1%.
*Religious affiliation* (1980): Lutheran 87.9%; nonreligious 3.2%; other 8.9%.
*Major cities* (1987[2]): Oslo 449,220; Bergen 208,915; Trondheim 134,654;
Stavanger 95,619; Baerum 86,223; Kristiansand 63,393; Drammen 51,481.

## Vital statistics

*Birth rate* per 1,000 population (1986): 12.6 (world avg. 26.0); (1985) legiti-
mate 74.2%; illegitimate 25.8%.
*Death rate* per 1,000 population (1986): 10.5 (world avg. 9.9).
*Natural increase rate* per 1,000 population (1986): 2.1 (world avg. 16.1).
*Total fertility rate* (avg. births per childbearing woman; 1985): 1.7.
*Marriage rate* per 1,000 population (1985): 4.8.
*Divorce rate* per 1,000 population (1985): 1.9.
*Life expectancy* at birth (1984–85): male 72.8 years; female 79.5 years.
*Major causes of death* per 100,000 population (1985): ischemic heart disease
280.1; malignant neoplasms (cancers) 231.9; cerebrovascular disease 129.1.

## National economy

*Budget* (1986). Revenue: NKr 175,895,000,000 (value added taxes 32.3%, tax
on petroleum extraction 20.3%, taxes on petroleum income 15.5%, taxes
on interest and dividends 15.2%, ordinary income tax 7.4%). Expenditures:
NKr 134,739,000,000 (social security and welfare 17.3%, debt service 13.1%,
education 12.6%, defense 12.0%).
*Tourism* (1986): receipts from visitors U.S.$853,000,000; expenditures by
nationals abroad U.S.$2,088,000,000.
*Production* (metric tons except as noted). Agriculture, forestry, fishing (1985):
barley 685,000, potatoes 470,000, oats 420,000; livestock (number of live
animals; 1986) 2,339,100 sheep, 967,500 cattle, 837,800 pigs; roundwood
10,620,000 cu m; fish catch (1986) 1,851,520, of which herring 326,123,
blue whiting 281,001, capelin 272,420, Atlantic cod 202,949, prawn and
shrimp 57,743. Mining and quarrying (1986): iron ore 2,379,000[4], titanium
803,622[4], zinc 52,727[4], copper 21,887[4]. Manufacturing (value added in
NKr '000,000; 1985): machinery and equipment 23,187, of which transport
equipment 5,008, electrical equipment 4,324; paper and paper products
9,826; food products 9,137; chemical products 7,477; wood and wood products 4,639. Construction (1984): residential 4,808,000 sq m; nonresidential
2,354,000 sq m. Energy production (consumption): electricity (kW-hr; 1985)
103,189,000,000 (102,627,000,000); coal (metric tons; 1985) 569,000 (1,191,-
000); crude petroleum (barrels; 1985) 288,985,000 (56,170,000); petroleum
products (metric tons; 1985) 7,865,000 (7,448,000); natural gas (cu m; 1985)
26,471,000,000 (1,229,000,000).
*Gross national product* (at current market prices; 1985): U.S.$57,580,000,000
(U.S.$13,930 per capita).

## Structure of gross domestic product and labour force

| | 1986 | | | |
|---|---|---|---|---|
| | in value NKr '000,000 | % of total value | labour force | % of labour force |
| Agriculture | 19,089 | 3.7 | 151,000 | 7.1 |
| Mining | 54,636 | 10.6 | 22,000 | 1.0 |
| Manufacturing | 79,263 | 15.4 | 358,000 | 16.8 |
| Construction | 30,424 | 5.9 | 155,000 | 7.3 |
| Public utilities | 23,895 | 4.6 | 21,000 | 1.0 |
| Transp. and commun. | 49,567 | 9.6 | 179,000 | 8.4 |
| Trade | 66,626 | 12.9 | 364,000 | 17.1 |
| Finance | 42,320 | 8.2 | 142,000 | 6.7 |
| Pub. admin., defense | 99,050 | 19.2 | } 736,000[5] | 34.6 |
| Services | 40,133 | 7.8 | | |
| Other | 11,019 | 2.1 | | |
| TOTAL | 516,022 | 100.0 | 2,128,000 | 100.0 |

*Population economically active* (1986): total 2,128,000; activity rate of total
population 51.1% (participation rates: ages 15–64 [1985] 75.8%; female
43.8%; unemployed 1.9%).

| Price and earnings indexes (1980 = 100) | | | | | | | |
|---|---|---|---|---|---|---|---|
| | 1981 | 1982 | 1983 | 1984 | 1985 | 1986 | 1987[6] |
| Consumer price index | 113.6 | 126.2 | 141.1 | 149.9 | 154.2 | 165.2 | 179.3 |
| Hourly earnings index | 110.0 | 121.0 | 132.0 | 143.0 | 154.0 | 170.0 | ... |

*Public debt* (1985): U.S.$15,755,000,000.
*Household income and expenditure.* Average household size (1982) 2.7; consumption expenditure per household NKr 88,000 (U.S.$13,600); sources
of income (1984): wages and salaries 61.8%, social security 19.5%, self-
employment and property income 17.5%, other 1.2%; expenditure (1986):
food 19.7%, transportation 17.6%, housing 17.1%, recreation 8.7%, clothing
8.2%, household furniture and equipment 8.1%.
*Land use* (1984): forested 27.1%; meadows and pastures 0.3%; agricultural
and under permanent cultivation 2.8%; built-up and other 69.8%.

## Foreign trade

| Balance of trade (current prices) | | | | | | |
|---|---|---|---|---|---|---|
| | 1981 | 1982 | 1983 | 1984 | 1985 | 1986 |
| NKr '000,000 | 16,508 | 15,486 | 35,569 | 43,764 | 41,498 | −11,374 |
| % of total | 8.6% | 7.3% | 15.6% | 16.6% | 13.8% | 4.0% |

*Imports* (1986): NKr 150,052,300,000 (machinery and transport equipment
25.7%, of which road vehicles 10.1%; raw materials 11.8%, of which fuels
5.9%; metals and metal products 10.4%, of which iron and steel 3.7%; food
products 5.7%, of which fruits and vegetables 1.4%). *Major import sources:*
Sweden 18.0%; West Germany 16.9%; U.K. 8.8%; Japan 7.4%.
*Exports* (1986): NKr 133,847,400,000 (fuels and fuel products 42.4%, of
which crude petroleum 21.2%, natural gas 20.0%; metals and metal products 13.0%, of which aluminum 5.7%, iron and steel 3.4%; machinery and
transport equipment 7.6%; food products 7.4%, of which fish and fish
products 6.1%). *Major export destinations:* U.K. 27.5%; West Germany
18.9%; Sweden 10.0%; The Netherlands 6.1%.

## Transport and communications

*Transport.* Railroads (1986): length 2,622 mi, 4,219 km; passenger-mi 1,379,-
000,000, passenger-km 2,220,000,000; short ton-mi cargo 2,006,000,000[7],
metric ton-km cargo 2,928,000,000[7]. Roads (1985): total length 53,365 mi,
85,882 km (paved 65%). Vehicles (1986): passenger cars 1,592,195; trucks
and buses 282,805. Merchant marine (1986): vessels (100 gross tons and
over) 2,107; total deadweight tonnage 14,202,683. Air transport (1986): passenger-mi 2,460,000,000, passenger-km 3,959,000,000; short ton-mi cargo
94,054,000, metric ton-km cargo 137,316,000; airports (1986) 41.
*Communications.* Daily newspapers (1986): total number 63; total circulation 2,008,000; circulation per 1,000 population 482. Radio (1986): total
number of receivers 1,510,000 (1 per 2.8 persons). Television (1986): total number of receivers 1,443,020 (1 per 2.9 persons). Telephones (1985):
2,578,812 (1 per 1.6 persons).

## Education and health

| Education (1985–86) | schools | teachers | students | student/ teacher ratio |
|---|---|---|---|---|
| Primary (age 7–15) | 3,525 | 31,459 | 534,000 | 17.0 |
| Secondary (age 14–18) and vocational[8] | 920 | 17,087 | 204,199 | 12.0 |
| Higher[8] | 228 | 6,961 | 93,535 | 13.4 |

*Educational attainment* (1980). Percent of population age 16 and over having: lower secondary education 55.7%; higher secondary 31.4%; some postsecondary 9.6%; university 1.3%. *Literacy* (1986): virtually 100% literate.
*Health* (1985): physicians 10,110 (1 per 411 persons); hospital beds (1986)
24,776 (1 per 168 persons); infant mortality rate per 1,000 live births 8.5.
*Food* (1981–83): daily per capita caloric intake 3,295 (vegetable products
62%, animal products 38%); (1983) 115% of FAO recommended minimum.

## Military

*Total active duty personnel* (1986): 37,300 (army 53.6%, navy 20.4%, air force
25.2%). *Military expenditure as percent of GNP* (1984): 2.8% (world avg.
5.9%); per capita expenditure U.S.$375.

[1]Excludes Svalbard and Jan Mayen (24,360 sq mi [63,080 sq km]). [2]January 1.
[3]Includes the Norwegian population of Svalbard and Jan Mayen registered as residents in municipalities on the mainland. [4]Metal content only. [5]Includes 39,690
unemployed. [6]June. [7]1985. [8]1984–85.

# Oman

*Official name:* Salṭanat 'Umān
(Sultanate of Oman).
*Form of government:* monarchy with a
consultative council (55) appointed by
the Sultan.
*Head of state and government:* Sultan.
*Capital:* Muscat.
*Official language:* Arabic.
*Official religion:* Islam.
*Monetary unit:* 1 rial Omani
(RO) = 1,000 baizas; valuation (Oct. 5,
1987) 1 RO = U.S.$2.63 = £1.61.

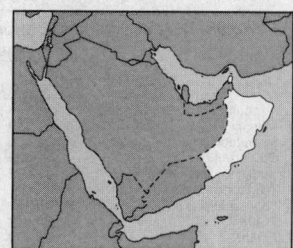

### Area and population

| Region | area[1] sq mi | sq km | population[2] 1987 estimate |
|---|---|---|---|
| **Area** | | | |
| Dhofar | 40,000 | 100,000 | ... |
| Southern | | | ... |
| Musandam (R'ūs al-Jibāl) | 800 | 2,000 | 13,000 |
| Musandam | | | ... |
| Other | 79,200 | 198,000 | ... |
| al-Baṭinah | ... | ... | ... |
| al-Jaww and al-Buraymi | ... | ... | ... |
| Dhahirah (az-Ẓāhirah) | ... | ... | ... |
| Capital | ... | ... | ... |
| Eastern al-Hajar | ... | ... | ... |
| Ja'lān and Sur (Ja'lān) | ... | ... | ... |
| Sharqiyah | ... | ... | ... |
| 'Uman Interior | ... | ... | ... |
| Western al-Ḥajar | ... | ... | ... |
| TOTAL | 120,000 | 300,000 | 1,331,000 |

## Demography

*Population* (1987): 1,331,000.
*Density* (1987): persons per sq mi 11.1, persons per sq km 4.4.
*Urban–rural* (1985): urban 8.8%; rural 91.2%.
*Sex distribution* (1985): male 52.85%; female 47.15%.
*Age breakdown* (1984): under 15, 44.1%; 15–29, 24.9%; 30–44, 18.1%; 45–59,
8.8%; 60–74, 3.5%; 75 and over, 0.6%.
*Population projection:* (1990) 1,430,000; (2000) 1,909,000.
*Doubling time:* 33 years.
*Ethnic composition* (1984): Omani Arab 77%; Indian 15%; Pakistani (mostly
Baluchi) 3½%; Bengali 2½%; other 2%.
*Religious affiliation* (1984): Muslim 86%; Hindu 13%; other 1%.
*Major city* (1981): Muscat 50,000.

## Vital statistics

*Birth rate* per 1,000 population (1980–85): 47.0 (world avg. 29.0).
*Death rate* per 1,000 population (1980–85): 14.3 (world avg. 11.0).
*Natural increase rate* per 1,000 population (1980–85): 32.7 (world avg. 18.0).
*Total fertility rate* (avg. births per childbearing woman; 1980–85): 7.1.
*Marriage rate* per 1,000 population: n.a.
*Divorce rate* per 1,000 population: n.a.
*Life expectancy* at birth (1980–85): male 51.0 years; female 53.7 years.
*Morbidity* (reported cases of illness per 100,000 population; 1985): malaria
12,200; influenza 7,357; dysentery 649; chicken pox 479; measles 296;
tuberculosis 87.

## National economy

*Budget* (1986). Revenue: RO 1,666,000,000 (oil revenue 84.6%, customs
duties 2.3%, gas revenue 2.2%, corporate income tax 1.5%, interest from
investments 1.5%). Expenditures: RO 1,886,800,000 (defense 35.3%, financing of civil ministries 34.4%, development 28.2%).
*Gross national product* (1985): U.S.$8,360,000,000 (U.S.$6,730 per capita).

### Structure of gross domestic product and labour force

| | 1985 in value RO '000,000 | % of total value | labour force[3] | % of labour force[3] |
|---|---|---|---|---|
| Agriculture | 98.5 | 2.9 | 10,251 | 3.6 |
| Mining | 1,654.1 | 48.4 | 3,618 | 1.3 |
| Manufacturing | 115.9 | 3.4 | 7,150 | 2.5 |
| Construction | 242.2 | 7.1 | 168,183 | 59.2 |
| Public utilities | 36.8 | 1.1 | 141 | 0.1 |
| Transportation and communication | 99.6 | 2.9 | 2,930 | 1.0 |
| Trade | 428.0 | 12.5 | 65,120 | 22.9 |
| Finance | 289.7 | 8.5 | 5,136 | 1.8 |
| Pub. admin., defense | 477.9 | 14.0 } | 13,260 | 4.6 |
| Services | 36.0 | 1.1 } | | |
| Other | −63.2[4] | −1.9[4] | 8,544 | 3.0 |
| TOTAL | 3,415.5 | 100.0 | 284,333 | 100.0 |

*Public debt* (external, outstanding; 1985): U.S.$1,945,500,000.
*Tourism* (1983): receipts from visitors U.S.$4,248,000,000; expenditures by
nationals abroad, n.a.
*Household income and expenditure.* Average household size (1980) 5.5; income per household: n.a.; sources of income: n.a.; food expenditure (1978):
meat and eggs 20.6%, cereals 15.2%, fruits and nuts 12.4%, vegetables
11.9%, dairy products 10.3%, other foods 29.6%.
*Production* (metric tons except as noted). Agriculture, forestry, fishing (1985):
vegetables and melons 158,000, dates 75,000, bananas 35,000, watermelons
10,000, onions 10,000, mangoes 4,000, tobacco leaf 2,000, wheat 1,000,

roots and tubers 1,000, potatoes 1,000. livestock (number of live animals)
700,000 goats, 130,000 sheep, 130,000 cattle, 1,000,000 chickens; fish catch
101,180. Mining and quarrying (1982): stone 6,220,000; sand and gravel
1,343,000; marble 50,000; copper 13,276[5]. Manufacturing (1985): major
products include cement blocks and floors, furniture, aluminum products,
household utensils, fertilizers, and fibreglass products. Construction (1986):
number of residential permits 1,043; nonresidential permits 156. Energy
production (consumption): electricity (kW-hr; 1986) 2,187,800,000 (2,332,-
700,000); coal, none (none); crude petroleum (barrels; 1986) 204,300,000
(16,643,000[5]); petroleum products (metric tons; 1985) 6,480,000 (5,650,000);
natural gas (cu m; 1985) 4,950,000,000 (4,600,000,000).
*Population economically active* (1984): total 269,410; activity rate of total
population 22.6% (participation rates: over age 15, 40.8%; female, n.a.;
unemployed, n.a.).

### Price and earnings indexes (1978 = 100)

| | 1979 | 1980 | 1981 | 1982 | 1983 | 1984 | 1985 |
|---|---|---|---|---|---|---|---|
| Consumer price index[6] | 108.5 | 119.3 | 122.7 | 124.0 | 118.6 | 108.8 | 107.8 |
| Annual earnings index | 167.9 | 514.1 | 487.7 | 521.1 | 788.0 | 681.8 | 704.3 |

*Land use* (1984): meadows and pastures 4.7%; agricultural and under permanent cultivation 0.2%; other (mostly desert and developed area) 95.1%.

## Foreign trade

### Balance of trade (current prices)

| | 1980 | 1981 | 1982 | 1983 | 1984 | 1985 |
|---|---|---|---|---|---|---|
| RO '000,000 | +696.3 | +831.6 | +600.4 | +634.9 | +417.2 | +552.0 |
| % of total | 36.8% | 34.5% | 24.5% | 29.2% | 18.0% | 20.2% |

*Imports* (1985): RO 1,088,900,000 (machinery and transport equipment
41.4%, manufactured goods 22.1%, food 11.4%, petroleum products 1.8%,
beverages and tobacco 1.6%). *Major import sources:* United Arab Emirates
21.1%; Japan 20.2%; United Kingdom 16.4%; West Germany 7.8%; United
States 5.7%; France 3.7%; The Netherlands 3.1%; India 2.3%..
*Exports* (1985): RO 1,717,200,000 (crude petroleum 93.0%, fish 0.5%, copper
0.4%, fruits and vegetables 0.2%). *Major export destinations:* Japan 64.3%;
United Arab Emirates 20.5%; Saudi Arabia 7.1%; Jordan 3.5%; Bahrain
2.0%.

## Transport and communications

*Transport.* Railroads: none. Roads (1986): total length 13,563 mi, 21,827 km
(paved 15%). Vehicles (1986): private vehicles 105,000, commercial vehicles 97,987. Merchant marine (1986): vessels (100 gross tons and over) 29;
total deadweight tonnage 12,953. Air transport (1983)[7]: passenger-mi 553,-
268,000, passenger-km 890,400,000; short ton-mi cargo 16,313,000, metric
ton-km cargo 23,817,000; airports (1987) with scheduled flights 6.
*Communications.* Daily newspapers (1986): total number 3; total circulation
30,000; circulation per 1,000 population 24. Radio (1986): total number
of receivers 500,000 (1 per 2.6 persons). Television (1986): total number
of receivers 400,000 (1 per 3.2 persons). Telephones (1986): 41,320 (1
per 50.5 persons).

## Education and health

### Education (1985–86)

| | schools | teachers | students | student/ teacher ratio |
|---|---|---|---|---|
| Primary (age 6–11) | 351 | 7,109 | 177,685 | 25.0 |
| Secondary (age 12–17) | 290 | 4,840 | 48,828 | 10.1 |
| Voc., teacher tr. | 14 | 707 | 3,141 | 4.4 |
| Higher | none | none | 2,316[8] | ... |

*Educational attainment,* n.a. *Literacy* (1979): total population age 6 and
over literate 38%; males literate 55%; females literate 20%.
*Health* (1986): physicians 581 (1 per 1,792 persons); hospital beds 2,861 (1
per 444 persons); infant mortality rate per 1,000 live births (1984) 113.4.
*Food:* daily capita caloric intake, n.a.

## Military

*Total active duty personnel* (1986): 21,500 (army 76.7%, navy 9.3%, air force
14.0%); foreign troops 3,700. *Military expenditure as percent of GNP* (1984):
27.7% (world 5.9%); per capita expenditure U.S.$1,769.

---

[1]Cadastral areas have not been calculated. [2]No census has ever been taken in Oman;
the total given is an unofficial estimate. For planning purposes the Omani government uses a 1985 estimate of 2,000,000. [3]Civilian employees and non-Omani workers
only. [4]Less imputed bank service charges. [5]1985. [6]Applies to food and beverages in
the capital area only. [7]International flights only. [8]Omani students studying abroad.

# Pakistan

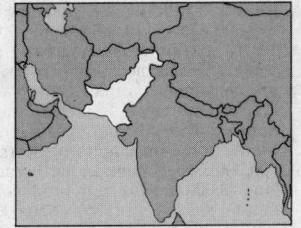

*Official name:* Islām-ī Jamhūrīya–e Pākistān (Islamic Republic of Pakistan).
*Form of government:* federal republic with two legislative houses (Senate [87]; National Assembly [237]).
*Head of state:* President.
*Head of government:* Prime Minister.
*Capital:* Islāmābād.
*Official language:* Urdū.
*Official religion:* Islam.
*Monetary unit:* 1 Pakistan Rupee (PRs) = 100 paisa; valuation (Oct. 5, 1987) 1 U.S.$ = PRs 17.18; 1 £ = PRs 27.90.

### Area and population

| Provinces | Capitals | area sq mi | area sq km | population 1983 estimate[1] |
|---|---|---|---|---|
| Baluchistān | Quetta | 134,050 | 347,188 | 4,611,000 |
| North–West Frontier | Peshāwar | 28,773 | 74,522 | 11,658,000 |
| Punjab | Lahore | 79,284 | 205,345 | 50,460,000 |
| Sind | Karāchi | 54,407 | 140,913 | 20,312,000 |
| **Federally Administered Tribal Areas** | ... | 10,510 | 27,221 | 2,329,000 |
| **Federal Capital Area** Islāmābād | ... | 350 | 906 | 359,000 |
| TOTAL | | 307,374 | 796,095 | 89,729,000 |

## Demography

*Population* (1987): 106,187,000[1].
*Density* (1987): persons per sq mi 345.5, persons per sq km 133.4.
*Urban–rural* (1985): urban 29.8%; rural 70.2%.
*Sex distribution* (1981): male 52.47%; female 47.53%.
*Age breakdown* (1981): under 15, 45.2%; 15–29, 23.9%; 30–44, 15.0%; 45–59, 9.2%; 60–74, 5.1%; 75 and over, 1.6%.
*Population projection:* (1990) 112,236,000; (2000) 137,651,000.
*Doubling time:* 26 years.
*Linguistic composition* (1981): Punjābī 48.2%; Pashto 13.1%; Sindhī 11.8%; Saraiki 9.8%; Urdū 7.6%; other 9.5%.
*Religious affiliation* (1981): Muslim 96.7%; Christian 1.6%; Hindu 1.5%; other 0.2%.
*Major cities* (1981): Karāchi 5,208,100; Lahore 2,952,700; Faisalābād 1,104,200; Rāwalpindi 806,000; Hyderābād 795,000.

## Vital statistics

*Birth rate* per 1,000 population (1986): 41.4 (world avg. 26.0).
*Death rate* per 1,000 population (1986): 14.8 (world avg. 9.9).
*Natural increase rate* per 1,000 population (1986): 26.6 (world avg. 16.1).
*Total fertility rate* (avg. births per childbearing woman; 1986): 5.5.
*Marriage rate* per 1,000 population (1975–80): 10.7.
*Divorce rate* per 1,000 population (1975–80): 0.3.
*Life expectancy* at birth (1986): male 52.4 years; female 50.6 years.
*Major causes of death* per 100,000 population: n.a.; however, major diseases include tuberculosis, cancer, poliomyelitis, typhoid, and dysentery.

## National economy

*Budget* (1986–87). Revenue: PRs 105,396,900,000 (customs duties 29.4%, excise taxes 15.3%, income taxes 8.2%, general sales tax 5.2%). Expenditures: PRs 106,109,300,000 (national defense 36.4%, interest on public debt 27.8%, grants to provinces 9.7%, subsidies 6.8%, education and health 4.8%, general administration 2.9%).
*Tourism* (1985): receipts from visitors U.S.$186,000,000; expenditures by nationals abroad U.S.$207,000,000.
*Production* (metric tons except as noted). Agriculture, forestry, fishing (1985–86): sugarcane 26,769,000, wheat 13,500,000, rice 3,051,000, cottonseed (1984–85) 1,800,000, cotton 1,208,000, corn (maize) 1,009,000, tobacco 87,000; livestock (number of live animals) 30,800,000 goats, 25,800,000 sheep, 16,700,000 cattle, 13,400,000 buffalo, 900,000 camels, 128,700,000 poultry; roundwood (1985) 20,233,000 cu m; fish catch (1984–85) 390,600. Mining and quarrying (1984–85): limestone 4,634,000; dolomite 120,867; fire clay 76,551; barite 20,827; feldspar 5,661; chromite 3,090; bauxite 2,035; magnesite 3,137. Manufacturing (1985–86): cement 4,980,000; chemical fertilizers 2,733,906, of which urea 1,820,214; steel products 2,207,159; refined sugar 1,138,358; chemicals 260,198; jute textiles 100,042; blended tea 44,236; paper and paperboard 42,792; cotton textiles 253,480,000 sq m; beverages 1,029,853,000 bottles; cigarettes 39,593,000,000 units; biscuits 447,760 units; road motor vehicles 93,070 units. Construction (value in PRs; 1983): residential 7,767,000,000; nonresidential 11,285,000,000. Energy production (consumption): electricity (kW-hr; 1985) 25,732,000,000 (25,732,000,000); coal (metric tons; 1985) 2,162,000 (2,169,000); crude petroleum (barrels; 1985) 9,532,500 (39,142,500); petroleum products (metric tons; 1985) 4,909,000 (7,422,000); natural gas (cu m; 1985) 9,081,000,000 (9,081,000,000).
*Household income and expenditure.* Average household size (1981) 6.7; income per household PRs 20,530 (U.S.$2,075); sources of income (1979): self-employment 53.1%, wages and salaries 30.7%, property 11.2%, other 5.0%; expenditure (1979): food 50.8%, housing 17.5%, clothing and footwear 9.6%, recreation 0.4%, other 21.7%.
*Gross national product* (at current market prices; 1985): U.S.$36,230,000,000 (U.S.$360 per capita).

### Structure of gross domestic product and labour force

| | 1985–86 in value PRs '000,000 | 1985–86 % of total value | 1984–85 labour force | 1984–85 % of labour force |
|---|---|---|---|---|
| Agriculture | 119,168 | 24.9 | 14,490,000 | 50.7 |
| Mining | 11,610 | 2.4 | 27,000 | 0.1 |
| Manufacturing | 83,460 | 17.4 | 3,693,000 | 12.9 |
| Construction | 22,929 | 4.8 | 1,319,000 | 4.6 |
| Public utilities | 10,639 | 2.2 | 311,000 | 1.1 |
| Transportation and communication | 38,991 | 8.1 | 1,261,000 | 4.4 |
| Trade | 82,013 | 17.1 | 3,281,000 | 11.5 |
| Finance | 29,209 | 6.1 | 225,000 | 0.8 |
| Pub. admin., defense | 42,356 | 8.9 } | 2,800,000 | 9.7 |
| Services | 38,674 | 8.1 } | | |
| Other | ... | ... | 1,189,000[2] | 4.2 |
| TOTAL | 479,049[3] | 100.0 | 28,596,000 | 100.0 |

*Public debt* (external, outstanding; 1985): U.S.$10,681,400,000.
*Population economically active* (1984–85): total 28,596,000; activity rate of total population 30.2% (participation rates: ages 15–64, 45.1%; female 5.3%; unemployed 3.9%).

### Price and earnings indexes (1980 = 100)

| | 1981 | 1982 | 1983 | 1984 | 1985 | 1986 | 1987[4] |
|---|---|---|---|---|---|---|---|
| Consumer price index | 111.9 | 118.5 | 125.8 | 134.1 | 141.9 | 147.1 | 151.2 |
| Monthly earnings index[5] | 106.0 | ... | ... | ... | ... | ... | ... |

*Land use* (1984): forested 3.9%; meadows and pastures 6.4%; agricultural and under permanent cultivation 26.0%; built-on, wasteland, and other 63.7%.

## Foreign trade[6]

### Balance of trade (current prices)

| | 1981 | 1982 | 1983 | 1984 | 1985 | 1986 |
|---|---|---|---|---|---|---|
| PRs '000,000 | −22,374 | −30,823 | −23,475 | −38,927 | −42,029 | −25,214 |
| % of total | 28.2% | 35.3% | 22.5% | 35.1% | 32.5% | 18.3% |

*Imports* (1985–86): PRs 90,978,800,000 (mineral fuels and lubricants 18.4%, nonelectrical machinery 14.8%, transport equipment 10.1%, vegetable oils 7.6%, grains, pulses, and flour 5.2%, electrical goods 5.0%, iron and steel 4.0%, drugs and medicines 2.5%). *Major import sources:* Japan 14.9%; United States 11.9%; West Germany 8.6%; Saudi Arabia 7.4%; Kuwait 6.6%; United Kingdom 6.6%; Malaysia 3.8%; Italy 3.8%.
*Exports* (1985–86): PRs 49,592,200,000 (raw cotton 16.7%, rice 11.1%, cotton fabrics 10.2%, cotton yarn 9.2%, leather 5.8%, carpets and rugs 5.4%, fish and fish preparations 2.7%). *Major export destinations:* United States 10.4%; Japan 9.6%; Saudi Arabia 7.0%; West Germany 6.0%; United Kingdom 5.5%; Italy 4.4%; France 2.8%; Hong Kong 2.6%.

## Transport and communications

*Transport.* Railroads (1985–86): route length (1986) 5,663 mi, 9,113 km; passenger-mi 10,469,000,000, passenger-km 16,848,000,000; short ton-mi cargo 5,666,000,000, metric ton-km cargo 8,272,000,000. Roads (1986): total length 64,823 mi, 104,323 km (paved 44%). Vehicles (1985): passenger cars 248,060; trucks and buses 71,615. Merchant marine (1986): vessels (100 gross tons and over) 78; total deadweight tonnage 623,182. Air transport (1985–86): passenger-km 7,054,057,000; metric ton-km cargo 309,922,000; airports (1987) with scheduled flights 30.
*Communications.* Daily newspapers (1985): total number 121; total circulation 1,991,000[7]; circulation per 1,000 population 22[7]. Radio (1986): total number of receivers 5,250,000 (1 per 20 persons). Television (1986): total number of receivers 1,880,000 (1 per 55 persons). Telephones (1985): 516,834 (1 per 194 persons).

## Education and health

### Education (1985–86)

| | schools | teachers | students | student/ teacher ratio |
|---|---|---|---|---|
| Primary (age 5–9) | 86,142 | 199,700 | 7,735,000 | 38.7 |
| Secondary (age 10–14) | 11,099 | 153,400 | 2,571,000 | 16.8 |
| Voc., teacher tr. | 293 | 4,190 | 59,000 | 14.1 |
| Higher | 590 | 22,737 | 498,613 | 21.9 |

*Educational attainment* (1981). Percent of population age 25 and over having: no formal schooling 78.9%; some primary education 8.7%; some secondary 10.5%; postsecondary 1.9%. *Literacy* (1981): total population age 15 and over literate 11,938,790 (25.6%); males literate 8,709,162 (36.0%); females literate 3,229,628 (15.2%).
*Health* (1986): physicians 46,494 (1 per 2,225 persons); hospital beds 57,709 (1 per 1,792 persons); infant mortality rate per 1,000 live births 126.0.
*Food* (1981–83): daily per capita caloric intake 2,236 (vegetable products 89%, animal products 11%); (1983) 95% of FAO recommended minimum requirement.

## Military

*Total active duty personnel* (1986): 480,600 (army 93.6%, navy 2.7%, air force 3.7%). *Military expenditure as percent of GNP* (1984): 5.9% (world 5.9%); per capita expenditure U.S.$20.

---

[1]Provincial estimates exclude and 1987 estimate includes Afghan refugees and residents of Pakistani-occupied Jammu and Kashmir. [2]Includes unemployed. [3]At factor cost. [4]May. [5]In manufacturing. [6]Import figures are f.o.b. (free on board) in balance of trade and c.i.f. (cost, insurance, and freight) for commodities and trading partners. [7]1983.

# Panama

*Official name:* República de Panamá (Republic of Panama).
*Form of government:* multiparty republic with one legislative house (Legislative Assembly [67]).
*Head of state and government:* President.
*Capital:* Panama City.
*Official language:* Spanish.
*Official religion:* none.
*Monetary unit:* 1 balboa (B) = 100 cents; valuation (Oct. 5, 1987) 1 U.S.$ = B 1.00; 1 £ = B 1.62.

### Area and population

| Provinces | Capitals | area sq mi | area sq km | population 1987 estimate |
|---|---|---|---|---|
| Bocas del Toro | Bocas del Toro | 3,443 | 8,917 | 77,500 |
| Chiriquí | David | 3,381 | 8,758 | 360,300 |
| Coclé | Penonomé | 1,944 | 5,035 | 164,500 |
| Colón | Colón | 1,915 | 4,961 | 163,100 |
| Darién | La Palma | 6,488 | 16,803 | 38,400 |
| Herrera | Chitré | 937 | 2,427 | 101,300 |
| Los Santos | Las Tablas | 1,493 | 3,867 | 81,300 |
| Panamá | Panama City | 4,642 | 12,022 | 1,037,400 |
| Veraguas | Santiago | 4,280 | 11,086 | 210,000 |
| **Special territory** | | | | |
| Comarca de San Blas | El Porvenir | 1,238 | 3,206 | 40,600 |
| TOTAL AREA | | 29,762[1] | 77,082 | 2,274,400 |

## Demography

*Population* (1987): 2,274,400.
*Density* (1987): persons per sq mi 76.4, persons per sq km 29.5.
*Urban–rural* (1985): urban 52.5%; rural 47.5%.
*Sex distribution* (1985): male 50.97%; female 49.03%.
*Age breakdown* (1985): under 15, 37.5%; 15–29, 29.4%; 30–44, 16.9%; 45–59, 9.5%; 60–74, 5.2%; 75 and over, 1.5%.
*Population projection:* (1990) 2,418,000; (2000) 2,893,000.
*Doubling time:* 33 years.
*Ethnic composition* (1980): mestizo/mulatto 59.5%; black 14.0%; white 12.0%; Amerindian 7.5%; East Indian 4.0%; other 3.0%.
*Religious affiliation* (1980): Roman Catholic 89.0%; Protestant 5.0%; Muslim 4.5%; Baha'í 1.0%; Hindu 0.3%; other 0.2%.
*Major cities* (1987): Panama City 439,996; San Miguelito 231,920; Colón 68,688; David 49,472[2].

## Vital statistics

*Birth rate* per 1,000 population (1985): 26.0 (world avg. 29.0); (1980) legitimate 28.6%; illegitimate 71.4%.
*Death rate* per 1,000 population (1985): 5.0 (world avg. 11.0).
*Natural increase rate* per 1,000 population (1985): 21.0 (world avg. 18.0).
*Total fertility rate* (avg. births per childbearing woman; 1984): 3.3.
*Marriage rate* per 1,000 population (1985): 4.6.
*Divorce rate* per 1,000 population (1985): 0.4.
*Life expectancy* at birth (1980–85)[3]: male 69.2 years; female 72.9 years.
*Major causes of death* per 100,000 population (1985): diseases of the circulatory system 102.9, of which ischemic heart diseases 42.1, cerebrovascular disease 35.9; malignant neoplasms (cancers) 48.8; accidents 31.8; infectious and parasitic diseases 23.8.

## National economy

*Budget* (1986). Revenue: B 1,649,000,000 (loans 36.8%; direct taxes 21.8%; indirect taxes 21.7%, income from state enterprises 5.5%; income from state assets 2.2%). Expenditures: B 1,649,000,000 (current expenditure 92.3%, of which payments on public debt 51.0%, education 10.2%, home affairs and justice 7.7%, health 4.8%; development expenditure 7.7%).
*Public debt* (external, outstanding; 1985): U.S.$3,274,500,000.
*Tourism* (1985): receipts from visitors U.S.$200,000,000; expenditures by nationals abroad U.S.$65,000,000.
*Production* (metric tons except as noted). Agriculture, forestry, fishing (1986): sugarcane 2,000,000[4], bananas 1,100,000, rice 172,000, corn (maize) 70,000[4], plantains 40,000[4], oranges 34,000, mangoes 28,000, coffee 16,000, cacao 1,000; livestock (number of live animals; 1985) 1,423,000 cattle, 215,000 pigs; roundwood (1985) 2,047,000 cu m; fish catch (1985) 245,539, of which shrimp 8,629. Mining and quarrying (1985): limestone 294,000; salt 16,000. Manufacturing (value of production in B; 1984): processed food 749,867,000, of which prepared meat 149,387,000, refined sugar and products 80,670,000, milk products 76,830,000, products of grains 67,283,000; garments 54,078,000; plastics 48,393,000. Construction (buildings authorized; 1984): residential 378,000 sq m; nonresidential 302,000 sq m. Energy production (consumption): electricity (kW-hr; 1985) 2,570,000,000 (2,570,000,000); coal (metric tons; 1985) none (6,000); crude petroleum (barrels; 1985) none (9,243,000); petroleum products (metric tons; 1985) 1,200,000 (823,000).
*Household income and expenditure.* Average household size (1980) 4.8; median income per household (1980) B 2,950 (U.S.$2,950); sources of income (1979): wages and salaries 85.3%, transfers 9.2%, other 5.5%; expenditure (1978): food 47.3%, housing and energy 12.7%, household furnishings 8.5%, transportation 6.8%, health care 4.9%, other 19.8%.

*Gross national product* (at current market prices; 1985): U.S.$4,400,000,000 (U.S.$2,020 per capita).

### Structure of gross domestic product and labour force

| | 1984[5] in value B '000,000 | 1984[5] % of total value | 1985 labour force[6] | 1985 % of labour force |
|---|---|---|---|---|
| Agriculture | 192.0 | 10.3 | 185,200 | 29.4 |
| Mining | 4.4 | 0.2 | 1,100 | 0.2 |
| Manufacturing | 176.0 | 9.5 | 67,200 | 10.7 |
| Construction | 96.7 | 5.2 | 33,500 | 5.3 |
| Public utilities | 65.5 | 3.5 | 9,100 | 1.4 |
| Transportation and communication | 359.6 | 19.4 | 37,600 | 6.0 |
| Trade | 284.2 | 15.3 | 87,100 | 13.8 |
| Finance, real estate | 269.5 | 14.5 | 24,500 | 3.9 |
| Pub. admin., defense | 249.8 | 13.5 | 169,600 | 26.9 |
| Services | 193.2 | 10.4 | | |
| Other | −33.97 | −1.8 | 14,800[8] | 2.4 |
| TOTAL | 1,857.0 | 100.0 | 629,700 | 100.0 |

*Population economically active* (1985)[3,9]: total 714,225; activity rate of total population 35.5% (participation rates: ages 15–69 [1983] 57.7%; female [1983] 29.8%; unemployed [1986] 10.2%).

### Price and earnings indexes (1980 = 100)

| | 1981 | 1982 | 1983 | 1984 | 1985 | 1986 | 1987[10] |
|---|---|---|---|---|---|---|---|
| Consumer price index | 107.3 | 111.9 | 114.2 | 116.0 | 117.2 | 117.2 | 118.1 |
| Monthly earnings index | 105.1 | 110.5 | 116.0 | ... | ... | ... | ... |

*Land use* (1984): forested 53.3%; meadows and pastures 15.3%; agricultural and under permanent cultivation 7.4%; other 24.0%.

## Foreign trade

### Balance of trade (current prices)

| | 1979 | 1980 | 1981 | 1982 | 1983 | 1984 |
|---|---|---|---|---|---|---|
| B '000,000 | −760.03 | −928.41 | −1,064.86 | −1,032.59 | −943.67 | −993.79 |
| % of total | 55.6% | 56.3% | 61.9% | 57.9% | 59.4% | 64.3% |

*Imports* (1984): B 1,269,820,000 (crude petroleum 22.7%, machinery and transport equipment 20.8%, manufactured products 17.7%, chemical products 12.6%, food products 8.2%). *Major import sources* (1985): United States 30.7%; Colón Free Zone 11.9%; Japan 8.9%; Mexico 7.9%; Venezuela 6.3%.
*Exports* (1984): B 276,030,000 (bananas 27.0%, shrimp 16.9%, sugar 12.1%, reexports 7.9%, coffee 4.7%). *Major export destinations* (1985)[11]: United States 60.5%; Costa Rica 5.8%; West Germany 5.8%; Belgium–Luxembourg 4.6%; Puerto Rico 3.6%.

## Transport and communications

*Transport.* Railroads: route length (1986) 359 mi, 578 km; passengers carried 40,767[12]. Roads (1985): total length 6,024 mi, 9,694 km (paved 33%). Vehicles (1984): passenger cars 120,995; trucks and buses 41,753. Merchant marine (1986): vessels (100 gross tons and over) 5,252; total deadweight tonnage 68,349,383. Panama Canal traffic (1986): oceangoing transits 12,023; cargo 142,374,423 metric tons. Air transport (1985): passenger-mi 342,433,000, passenger-km 551,094,000; short ton-mi cargo 38,221,000, metric ton-km cargo 55,802,000; airports (1987) with scheduled flights 6.
*Communications.* Daily newspapers (1986): total number 9; total circulation 197,200; circulation per 1,000 population 89. Radio (1986): 900,000 receivers (1 per 2.5 persons). Television (1986): 300,000 receivers (1 per 7.4 persons). Telephones (1985): 223,235 (1 per 9.8 persons).

## Education and health

### Education (1986)

| | schools | teachers | students | student/ teacher ratio |
|---|---|---|---|---|
| Primary (age 6–11) | 2,574 | 14,176 | 341,914 | 24.1 |
| Secondary (age 12–17) | 334 | 10,113 | 187,312 | 18.5 |
| Voc., teacher tr. | 70 | 644 | 10,548 | 16.4 |
| Higher | 8 | 4,650 | 56,227 | 12.1 |

*Educational attainment* (1980). Percent of population age 25 and over having: no formal schooling 17.4%; incomplete primary education 27.3%; complete primary education 23.4%; secondary 23.5%; higher 8.4%. *Literacy* (1980): total population age 15 and over literate 955,300 (85.6%); males literate 487,200 (86.3%); females literate 468,100 (84.9%).
*Health* (1985): physicians 2,484 (1 per 878 persons); hospital beds 7,602 (1 per 287 persons); infant mortality rate per 1,000 live births 23.0.
*Food* (1981–83): daily per capita caloric intake 2,305 (vegetable products 81%, animal products 19%); (1983) 98% of FAO recommended minimum requirement.

## Military

*Total active duty personnel* (1985): 12,000 (army 95.8%, navy 2.5%, air force 1.7%). *Military expenditure as percent of GNP* (1984): 2.4% (world 5.9%); per capita expenditure U.S.$46.

---

[1]Detail does not add to total given because of rounding. [2]1980. [3]Excludes former Canal Zone. [4]1985. [5]Prices of 1970. [6]Employed persons only. [7]Less imputed bank service charges. [8]Employed persons within former Canal Zone. [9]Excludes indigenous areas. [10]April. [11]Excludes reexports. [12]Chiriquí National Railroad only; 1985.

# Papua New Guinea

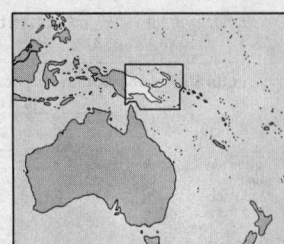

*Official name:* Papua New Guinea.
*Form of government:* constitutional monarchy with one legislative house (National Parliament [109]).
*Chief of state:* British Monarch represented by governor-general.
*Head of government:* Prime Minister.
*Capital:* Port Moresby.
*Official language:* English.
*Official religion:* none.
*Monetary unit:* 1 Papua New Guinea kina (K) = 100 toea; valuation (Oct. 5, 1987) 1 U.S.$ = K 0.89; 1 £ = K 1.45.

### Area and population

| Provinces | Administrative centres | area sq mi | area sq km | population 1986 estimate[1] |
|---|---|---|---|---|
| Central | Port Moresby | 11,400 | 29,500 | 132,800 |
| Chimbu | Kundiawa | 2,350 | 6,100 | 186,400 |
| Eastern Highlands | Goroka | 4,300 | 11,200 | 306,300 |
| East New Britain | Rabaul | 6,000 | 15,500 | 154,200 |
| East Sepik | Wewak | 16,550 | 42,800 | 254,900 |
| Enga | Wabag | 4,950 | 12,800 | 178,600 |
| Gulf | Kerema | 13,300 | 34,500 | 71,600 |
| Madang | Madang | 11,200 | 29,000 | 245,700 |
| Manus | Lorengau | 800 | 2,100 | 29,900 |
| Milne Bay | Alotau | 5,400 | 14,000 | 150,600 |
| Morobe | Lae | 13,300 | 34,500 | 357,100 |
| National Capital District | Port Moresby | 100 | 240 | 141,500 |
| New Ireland | Kavieng | 3,700 | 9,600 | 77,200 |
| Northern | Popondetta | 8,800 | 22,800 | 90,300 |
| North Solomons | Kieta | 3,600 | 9,300 | 154,500 |
| Southern Highlands | Mendi | 9,200 | 23,800 | 259,500 |
| Western | Daru | 38,350 | 99,300 | 91,700 |
| Western Highlands | Mount Hagen | 3,300 | 8,500 | 300,200 |
| West New Britain | Kimbe | 8,100 | 21,000 | 107,700 |
| West Sepik | Vanimo | 14,000 | 36,300 | 128,300 |
| TOTAL | | 178,703[2] | 462,840 | 3,441,200[3] |

## Demography

*Population* (1987): 3,500,000[1].
*Density* (1987): persons per sq mi 19.6, persons per sq km 7.6.
*Urban-rural* (1985): urban 14.3%; rural 85.7%.
*Sex distribution* (1985): male 52.09%; female 47.91%.
*Age breakdown* (1985): under 15, 41.6%; 15–29, 27.5%; 30–44, 16.0%; 45–59, 9.3%; 60–74, 4.5%; 75 and over, 1.0%[2].
*Population projection:* (1990) 3,741,000; (2000) 4,673,000.
*Doubling time:* 31 years.
*Ethnic composition* (1983): New Guinea Papuan 84.0%; New Guinea Melanesian 15.0%; other 1.0%.
*Religious affiliation* (1980): Protestant 58.4%; Roman Catholic 32.8%; Anglican 5.4%; traditional beliefs 2.5%; Bahā'ī 0.6%; other 0.3%.
*Major cities* (1986): Port Moresby 145,500; Lae 75,800; Madang 24,000; Wewak 22,500; Goroka 21,100.

## Vital statistics

*Birth rate* per 1,000 population (1985): 35.0 (world avg. 29.0); legitimate, n.a.; illegitimate, n.a.
*Death rate* per 1,000 population (1985): 12.5 (world avg. 11.0).
*Natural increase rate* per 1,000 population (1985): 22.5 (world avg. 18.0).
*Total fertility rate* (avg. births per childbearing woman; 1986): 5.2.
*Marriage rate* per 1,000 population: n.a.
*Divorce rate* per 1,000 population: n.a.
*Life expectancy* at birth (1986): male 52.6 years; female 54.2 years.
*Major causes of death* per 100,000 population: n.a.; however, major infectious diseases include malaria, intestinal infections, and tuberculosis.

## National economy

*Budget* (1986). Revenue: K 800,649,000 (foreign government grants 25.6%, customs and excise taxes 25.3%, personal income tax 17.9%, loans 6.8%, company income tax 6.7%). Expenditures: K 845,751,000 (no breakdown available).
*Public debt* (external, outstanding; 1985): U.S.$1,061,100,000.
*Tourism:* receipts from visitors (1985) U.S.$13,000,000; expenditures by nationals abroad (1984) U.S.$31,000,000.
*Production* (metric tons except as noted). Agriculture, forestry, fishing (1985): bananas 940,000, coconuts 850,000, sweet potatoes 469,000, sugarcane 350,000, taro 184,000, yams 172,000, copra 160,000, palm oil 140,000, cassava 103,000, coffee 50,000, palm kernels 48,800, cocoa 30,000, pineapples 10,000, tea 9,000; livestock (number of live animals) 1,476,000 pigs, 123,000 cattle, 16,000 goats, 4,000,000 chickens; roundwood (1984) 6,910,000 cu m; fish catch (1984) 6,047. Mining and quarrying (1985): copper 175,048; silver 46,112 kg; gold 36,908 kg. Manufacturing (value added in K; 1984): food, beverages, and tobacco 365,387,000; metals, metal products, machinery, and equipment 85,444,000; wood and wood products 56,962,000. Construction (value[4]; 1985): residential K 28,279,000; nonresidential K 11,018,000. Energy production (consumption): electricity (kW-hr; 1985) 1,565,000,000 (1,565,000,000); coal, none (n.a.); crude petroleum (barrels; 1981) none (4,266,060); petroleum products (metric tons; 1985) none (692,000); natural gas, none (n.a.).
*Gross national product* (at current market prices; 1985): U.S.$2,470,000,000 (U.S.$740 per capita).

### Structure of gross domestic product and labour force

| | 1983 in value K '000,000 | 1983 % of total value | 1980 labour force | 1980 % of labour force |
|---|---|---|---|---|
| Agriculture | 647.8 | 32.8 | 564,500 | 77.0 |
| Mining | 210.8 | 10.7 | 4,300 | 0.6 |
| Manufacturing | 178.8 | 9.1 | 14,000 | 1.9 |
| Construction | 84.7 | 4.3 | 21,600 | 2.9 |
| Public utilities | 28.8 | 1.5 | 2,800 | 0.4 |
| Transportation and communication | 68.3 | 3.5 | 17,400 | 2.4 |
| Trade | 156.6 | 7.9 | 25,100 | 3.4 |
| Finance | 187.4 | 9.5 | 4,500 | 0.6 |
| Pub. admin., defense | 147.1 | 7.5 | 77,100 | 10.5 |
| Services | 225.8 | 11.4 | | |
| Other | 37.6 | 1.9 | 1,500 | 0.2 |
| TOTAL | 1,973.7 | 100.0[2] | 732,800 | 100.0[2] |

*Population economically active* (1980): total 1,148,000; activity rate of total population 38.2% (participation rates: ages 15–64, 67.1%; female 37.5%; unemployed 12.8%[5]).

### Price and earnings indexes (1980 = 100)

| | 1980 | 1981 | 1982 | 1983 | 1984 | 1985 | 1986 |
|---|---|---|---|---|---|---|---|
| Consumer price index | 100.0 | 108.1 | 114.0 | 123.0 | 132.2 | 144.6 | 152.5 |
| Monthly earnings index | ... | ... | ... | ... | ... | ... | ... |

*Household income and expenditure.* Average household size (1980) 4.6; income per household (1975–76) K 2,771 (U.S.$3,483); sources of income: n.a.; expenditure (1977): food, beverages, and tobacco 60.9%, transportation and communication 13.0%, housing and public utilities 7.2%, clothing and footwear 6.2%, household equipment and operation 5.3%.
*Land use* (1984): forested 84.8%; agricultural and under permanent cultivation 0.8%; meadows and pastures 0.2%; other 14.2%.

## Foreign trade[6]

### Balance of trade (current prices)

| | 1980 | 1981 | 1982 | 1983 | 1984 | 1985 | 1986 |
|---|---|---|---|---|---|---|---|
| K '000,000 | +7.5 | −173.7 | −180.8 | −138.0 | −64.7 | +35.9 | −45.0 |
| % of total | 0.5% | 13.3% | 13.7% | 9.2% | 3.9% | 2.0% | 2.7% |

*Imports* (1985): K 874,774,000 (machinery and transport equipment 30.0%; mineral fuels, lubricants, and related materials 17.6%; food and live animals 17.6%; manufactured goods 15.4%). *Major import sources* (1984): Australia 39.8%; Japan 15.7%; Singapore 11.8%; United States 10.3%; United Kingdom 3.5%; Hong Kong 2.3%.
*Exports* (1985): K 910,205,000 (copper ore and concentrates 33.2%; gold 19.3%; coffee 12.9%; cocoa beans 6.7%; palm oil 6.7%; timber 6.3%; copra 3.7%; copra oil 2.5%). *Major export destinations* (1984): Japan 28.3%; West Germany 20.5%; United Kingdom 11.2%; Australia 9.8%; Spain 3.4%; United States 3.4%.

## Transport and communications

*Transport.* Railroads: none. Roads (1985): total length 12,263 mi, 19,736 km (paved 6%). Vehicles (1984): passenger cars 22,757; trucks and buses 39,481. Merchant marine (1986): vessels (100 gross tons and over) 88; total deadweight tonnage 37,670. Air transport (1985): passenger-mi 283,000,000, passenger-km 456,000,000; short ton-mi cargo 6,830,000, metric ton-km cargo 9,972,000; airports (1987) with scheduled flights 177.
*Communications.* Daily newspapers (1986): total number 1; total circulation 28,000; circulation per 1,000 population 8.2. Radio (1986): total number of receivers 225,000 (1 per 15 persons). Television (1985): total number of receivers 230,000 (1 per 14 persons). Telephones (1985): 57,863 (1 per 58 persons).

## Education and health

### Education (1985)

| | schools | teachers | students | student/ teacher ratio |
|---|---|---|---|---|
| Primary (age 7–12) | 2,392 | 11,723 | 356,729 | 30.4 |
| Secondary (age 13–16) | 119 | 2,152 | 49,067 | 22.8 |
| Voc., teacher tr. | 105 | 761 | 10,458 | 13.7 |
| Higher | 2 | 379 | 3,635 | 9.6 |

*Educational attainment* (1980). Percent of population age 25 and over having: no formal schooling 82.6%; some primary education 8.2%; completed primary 5.0%; some secondary 4.2%. *Literacy* (1980): total population age 15 and over literate 757,500 (42.3%); males literate 490,100 (52.4%); females literate 267,400 (31.3%).
*Health* (1984): physicians 280 (1 per 11,635 persons); hospital beds 14,661 (1 per 222 persons); infant mortality rate per 1,000 live births (1985) 68.0.
*Food* (1980–82): daily per capita caloric intake 2,074 (vegetable products 90%, animal products 10%); (1983) 75% of FAO recommended minimum requirement.

## Military

*Total active duty personnel* (1986): 3,232 (army 88.0%, navy 9.3%, air force 2.7%). *Military expenditure as percent of GNP* (1984): 1.7% (world 5.9%); per capita expenditure U.S.$12.

---

[1]De jure. [2]Detail does not add to total given because of rounding. [3]Includes 22,200 noncitizens. [4]Private only. [5]1977; in six urban centres. [6]Import figures are f.o.b. (free on board) in balance of trade and c.i.f. (cost, insurance, and freight) for commodities and trading partners.

# Paraguay

*Official name:* República del Paraguay (Republic of Paraguay).
*Form of government:* republic with two legislative houses (Senate [30]; Chamber of Deputies [60]).
*Head of state and government:* President.
*Capital:* Asunción.
*Official language:* Spanish.
*Official religion:* Roman Catholicism.
*Monetary unit:* 1 Paraguayan Guaraní (₲) = 100 céntimos; valuation[1] (Oct. 5, 1987) 1 U.S.$ = ₲320.02; 1 £ = ₲519.71.

### Area and population

| Regions Departments | Capitals | area sq mi | area sq km | population 1985 estimate |
|---|---|---|---|---|
| Occidental | | 95,338 | 246,925 | 50,400 |
| Alto Paraguay | Fuerte Olimpio | 17,754 | 45,982 | 10,100 |
| Boquerón | Dr. Pedro P. Peña | 18,034 | 46,708 | 12,000 |
| Chaco | Mayor Pablo Lagerenza | 14,041 | 36,367 | 300 |
| Nueva Asunción | General Eugenio A. Garay | 17,359 | 44,961 | 200 |
| Presidente Hayes | Pozo Colorado | 28,150 | 72,907 | 27,800 |
| Oriental | | 61,710 | 159,827 | 3,228,600 |
| Alto Paraná | Puerto Presidente Stroessner | 5,751 | 14,895 | 255,000 |
| Amambay | Pedro Juan Caballero | 4,994 | 12,933 | 69,400 |
| Asunción | Asunción | 45 | 117 | 477,100 |
| Caaguazú | Coronel Oviedo | 4,430 | 11,474 | 333,000 |
| Caazapá | Caazapá | 3,666 | 9,496 | 111,400 |
| Canendiyú | Salto del Guairá | 5,663 | 14,667 | 77,100 |
| Central | Asunción | 952 | 2,465 | 572,500 |
| Concepción | Concepción | 6,970 | 18,051 | 143,000 |
| Cordillera | Caacupé | 1,910 | 4,948 | 194,000 |
| Guairá | Villarrica | 1,485 | 3,846 | 149,600 |
| Itapúa | Encarnación | 6,380 | 16,525 | 284,500 |
| Misiones | San Juan Bautista | 3,690 | 9,556 | 80,100 |
| Ñeembucú | Pilar | 4,690 | 12,147 | 69,500 |
| Paraguarí | Paraguarí | 3,361 | 8,705 | 201,900 |
| San Pedro | San Pedro | 7,723 | 20,002 | 210,500 |
| TOTAL | | 157,048 | 406,752 | 3,279,000 |

## Demography

*Population* (1987): 3,897,000.
*Density* (1987): persons per sq mi 24.8, persons per sq km 9.6.
*Urban–rural* (1985): urban 43.9%; rural 56.1%.
*Sex distribution* (1984): male 50.20%; female 49.80%.
*Age breakdown* (1982): under 15, 41.1%; 15–29, 28.1%; 30–44, 15.4%; 45–59, 9.1%; 60–74, 4.8%; 75 and over, 1.5%.
*Population projection:* (1990) 4,231,000; (2000) 5,405,000.
*Doubling time:* 24 years.
*Ethnic composition* (1980): mestizo (Spanish–Guaraní) 90.8%; Amerindian 3.0%; German 1.7%; other 4.5%.
*Religious affiliation* (1980): Roman Catholic 96.0%; Protestant 2.1%; other 1.9%.
*Major cities* (1985): Asunción 477,000; Lambaré 84,000; Fernando de la Mora 80,000; Puerto Presidente Stroessner 64,000.

## Vital statistics

*Birth rate* per 1,000 population (1985): 33.1[2] (world avg. 29.0); legitimate 68.7%[2]; illegitimate 31.3%[2].
*Death rate* per 1,000 population (1985): 3.8[2] (world avg. 11.0).
*Natural increase rate* per 1,000 population (1985): 29.3 (world avg. 18.0).
*Total fertility rate* (avg. births per childbearing woman; 1980–85): 4.9.
*Marriage rate* per 1,000 population (1985): 5.0[2].
*Divorce rate* per 1,000 population: n.a.
*Life expectancy* at birth (1980–85): male 62.8 years; female 67.5 years.
*Major causes of death* per 100,000 population (1984): diseases of the circulatory system 113.2; malignant neoplasms (cancers) 39.2; perinatal causes 19.2; ill-defined conditions 70.6.

## National economy

*Budget* (1986). Revenue: ₲133,102,600,000 (domestic taxes on goods and services 38.3%, income tax 15.2%, customs duties 11.5%, sales tax 10.1%, alcohol tax 5.1%, pension funds 4.9%, real estate taxes 4.4%). Expenditures: ₲131,164,100,000 (defense 15.3%, education 13.3%, public debt 13.3%, ministry of interior 9.8%, public health 3.7%, public works 2.8%).
*Public debt* (external, outstanding; 1985): U.S.$1,524,900,000.
*Production* (metric tons except as noted). Agriculture, forestry, fishing (1985): cassava 2,200,000, sugarcane 1,700,000, soybeans 700,000, corn (maize) 500,000, seed cotton 485,000, bananas 325,000, oranges 235,000, lint cotton 160,000, sweet potatoes 120,000; livestock (number of live animals) 6,400,000 cattle, 1,400,000 pigs, 15,000,000 chickens; roundwood 7,560,000 cu m; fish catch 7,500. Mining and quarrying (1984): limestone 175,000; kaolin 50,000; gypsum 6,000. Manufacturing (1985): beef and veal 100,000; sugar 78,135; cement 45,580; hides 10,938; tung oil 9,379; edible coconut oil 4,695; coconut pulp 3,207; woven cotton fabrics 9,201,000 metres; beer 767,910 hectolitres; alcohol 39,410 hectolitres[3]; matches 9,159,000 boxes[3]. Construction (1982): residential 116,800 sq m; nonresidential 210,600 sq m. Energy production (consumption): electricity (kW-hr; 1985) 1,535,000,000 (1,710,000,000); coal, none (none); crude petroleum (barrels; 1985) none (1,466,000); petroleum products (metric tons; 1985) 193,000 (497,000); natural gas, none (none).

*Tourism* (1985): receipts from visitors U.S.$80,000,000; expenditures by nationals abroad U.S.$47,000,000.
*Gross national product* (1985): U.S.$3,180,000,000 (U.S.$860 per capita).

### Structure of gross domestic product and labour force

| | 1985 in value ₲'000,000 | 1985 % of total value | 1982 labour force | 1982 % of labour force |
|---|---|---|---|---|
| Agriculture | 403,261 | 28.9 | 445,720 | 43.3 |
| Mining | 5,672 | 0.4 | 1,130 | 0.1 |
| Manufacturing | 226,115 | 16.2 | 124,840 | 12.1 |
| Construction | 82,888 | 6.0 | 67,170 | 6.5 |
| Public utilities | 30,896 | 2.2 | 2,540 | 0.3 |
| Transp. and commun. | 57,974 | 4.2 | 26,230 | 2.6 |
| Trade | 360,391 | 25.9 | 78,650 | 7.6 |
| Finance | | | 29,140 | 2.8 |
| Pub. admin., defense | 226,693[4] | 16.3[4] | 168,980 | 16.4 |
| Services | | | 85,110 | 8.3 |
| Other | | | | |
| TOTAL | 1,393,890 | 100.0[5] | 1,029,510 | 100.0 |

*Population economically active* (1982): total 1,029,510; activity rate of total population 33.9% (participation rates: ages 15–64, 57.1%; female 11.8%; unemployed 29.0%).

### Price and earnings indexes (1980 = 100)

| | 1980 | 1981 | 1982 | 1983 | 1984 | 1985 | 1986[6] |
|---|---|---|---|---|---|---|---|
| Consumer price index | 100.0 | 114.0 | 121.7 | 138.0 | 166.1 | 207.9 | 277.1 |
| Monthly earnings index | | | | | | | |

*Household income and expenditure:* average household size (1982) 5.2; sources of income (1982): self-employment and business profits 56.0%, wages and salaries 40.8%, transfer payments from government 3.2%.
*Land use* (1984): forested 51.3%; meadows and pastures 39.0%; agricultural and under permanent cultivation 4.9%; other 4.8%.

## Foreign trade

### Balance of trade (current prices)

| | 1981 | 1982 | 1983 | 1984 | 1985 | 1986 |
|---|---|---|---|---|---|---|
| ₲'000,000 | −26,532 | −32,301 | −26,519 | −42,316 | −75,892 | −150,210 |
| % of total | 26.3% | 25.5% | 23.5% | 21.7% | 28.2% | 44.9% |

*Imports* (1985): U.S.$420,355,538 (fuels and lubricants 14.3%; food and beverages 10.3%; transport equipment 10.3%; machines, apparatus, and engines 9.7%; chemicals and pharmaceuticals 9.0%; power generating equipment 7.0%.). *Major import sources:* Brazil 38.8%; Argentina 12.2%; Greenland 8.8%; Algeria 6.2%; West Germany 5.5%; Japan 5.2%.
*Exports* (1985): U.S.$294,081,663 (cotton fibres 48.2%; soybeans 31.1%; vegetable oils 4.7%, of which tung oil 2.2%; timber 3.3%; tobacco 2.0%; perfume oils 1.9%; leather 1.8%). *Major export destinations:* Brazil 22.9%; West Germany 15.5%; The Netherlands 10.2%; France 8.1%; Greece 7.3%; Switzerland 7.3%; Argentina 6.0%.

## Transport and communications

*Transport.* Railroads (1980): route length (1987) 274 mi, 441 km; passenger-mi 13,900,000, passenger-km 22,400,000; short ton-mi cargo 23,600,000, metric ton-km cargo 34,400,000. Roads (1985): total length 9,186 mi, 14,783 km (paved 13%). Vehicles (1985): passenger cars 84,986; trucks and buses 41,986. Merchant marine (1986): vessels (100 gross tons and over) 41; total deadweight tonnage 51,540. Air transport (1982): passenger-mi 290,000,000, passenger-km 466,000,000; short ton-mi cargo 1,400,000, metric ton-km cargo 2,000,000; airports (1987) with scheduled flights 1.
*Communications.* Daily newspapers (1985): total number 5; total circulation 198,000; circulation per 1,000 population 60. Radio (1986): 624,000 receivers (1 per 6.1 persons). Television (1984): 266,200 receivers (1 per 12 persons). Telephones (1985): 88,730 (1 per 41 persons).

## Education and health

### Education (1985)

| | schools | teachers | students | student/ teacher ratio |
|---|---|---|---|---|
| Primary (age 7–12) | 3,993 | 22,764 | 570,775 | 25.1 |
| Secondary (age 13–18) | 740 | 9,044[3,7] | 172,132[7] | 19.0 |
| Higher | 2 | 2,694 | 29,154 | 10.8 |

*Educational attainment* (1982). Percent of population age 25 and over having: no formal schooling 13.6%; primary education 64.7%; secondary 15.5%; higher 3.4%; not stated 2.8%. *Literacy* (1982): total population age 15 and over literate 1,534,810 (85.7%); males literate 782,560 (88.7%); females literate 752,250 (82.9%).
*Health:* physicians (1982) 2,201 (1 per 1,379 persons); hospital beds (1985) 3,380 (1 per 1,089 persons); infant mortality rate (1984) 52.9.
*Food* (1981–83): daily per capita caloric intake 2,817 (vegetable products 81%, animal products 19%); (1983) 122% of FAO recommended minimum requirement.

## Military

*Total active duty personnel* (1986): 15,970 (army 78.3%, navy 15.6%, air force 6.1%). *Military expenditure as percent of GNP* (1983): 1.9% (world 6.1%); per capita expenditure U.S.$25.

---

[1]Official rate only; nonofficial rate is 167.2% higher. [2]Civil Registry records only. [3]1984. [4]Includes hotels and restaurants. [5]Detail does not add to total given because of rounding. [6]August. [7]Includes vocational education and teacher training.

# Peru

*Official name:* República del Perú
(Spanish) (Republic of Peru).
*Form of government:* unitary multiparty
republic with two legislative
houses (Senate [60]; Chamber of
Deputies [180]).
*Head of state and government:*
President.
*Capital:* Lima.
*Official languages:* Spanish; Quechua.
*Official religion:* Roman Catholicism.
*Monetary unit:* 1 Inti (I/.) =
100 céntimos = 1,000 soles;
valuation (Oct. 5, 1987) 1 U.S.$ =
I/. 15.89; 1 £ = I/. 25.81.

### Area and population

| Departments | Capitals | area sq mi | area sq km | population 1987 estimate |
|---|---|---|---|---|
| Amazonas | Chachapoyas | 15,945 | 41,297 | 311,800 |
| Ancash | Huaraz | 14,158 | 36,669 | 936,600 |
| Apurimac | Abancay | 7,934 | 20,550 | 361,400 |
| Arequipa | Arequipa | 24,528 | 63,528 | 884,200 |
| Ayacucho | Ayacucho | 17,058 | 44,181 | 553,000 |
| Cajamarca | Cajamarca | 13,486 | 34,930 | 1,200,000 |
| Cuzco | Cuzco | 29,471 | 76,329 | 980,600 |
| Huancavelica | Huancavelica | 8,139 | 21,079 | 371,400 |
| Huánuco | Huánuco | 13,088 | 33,897 | 571,600 |
| Ica | Ica | 8,205 | 21,251 | 508,200 |
| Junin | Huancayo | 15,944 | 41,296 | 1,037,500 |
| La Libertad | Trujillo | 8,973 | 23,241 | 1,150,900 |
| Lambayeque | Chiclayo | 5,304 | 13,737 | 854,600 |
| Lima | Lima | 13,058 | 33,821 | 6,116,700 |
| Loreto | Iquitos | 146,342 | 379,025 | 605,900 |
| Madre de Dios | Puerto Maldonado | 30,271 | 78,403 | 44,500 |
| Moquegua | Moquegua | 6,065 | 15,709 | 123,400 |
| Pasco | Cerro de Pasco | 9,356 | 24,233 | 264,800 |
| Piura | Piura | 14,055 | 36,403 | 1,374,200 |
| Puno | Puno | 27,947 | 72,382 | 984,500 |
| San Martín | Moyobamba | 20,197 | 52,309 | 414,500 |
| Tacna | Tacna | 5,881 | 15,232 | 188,300 |
| Tumbes | Tumbes | 1,827 | 4,732 | 131,700 |
| Ucayali | Pucallpa | 38,931 | 100,831 | 211,700 |
| **Constitutional Province** | | | | |
| Callao | Callao | 57 | 148 | 545,100 |
| TOTAL | | 496,225[1] | 1,285,216[1] | 20,727,100 |

## Demography

*Population* (1987): 20,727,000.
*Density* (1987): persons per sq mi 41.8, persons per sq km 16.1.
*Urban–rural* (1985): urban 70.2%; rural 29.8%.
*Sex distribution* (1985): male 50.38%; female 49.62%.
*Age breakdown* (1985): under 15, 40.5%; 15–29, 28.2%; 30–44, 16.3%; 45–59, 9.5%; 60–74, 4.5%; 75 and over, 1.0%.
*Population projection:* (1990) 22,332,000; (2000) 27,952,000.
*Doubling time:* 27 years.
*Ethnic composition* (1981): Quechua 47.1%; mestizo 32.0%; white 12.0%; Aymara 5.4%; jungle Amerindian 1.7%; other 1.8%.
*Religious affiliation* (1984): Roman Catholic 92.4%; other 7.6%.
*Major cities* (1987): Lima 5,330,800; Arequipa 572,000; Callao 545,000; Trujillo 476,000; Chiclayo 379,000.

## Vital statistics

*Birth rate* per 1,000 population (1985): 35.5[2] (world avg. 29.0); (1977) legitimate 57.8%; illegitimate 42.2%.
*Death rate* per 1,000 population (1985): 10.0[2] (world avg. 11.0).
*Natural increase rate* per 1,000 population (1985): 25.5[2] (world avg. 18.0).
*Total fertility rate* (avg. births per childbearing woman; 1985): 4.7.
*Marriage rate* per 1,000 population (1982): 6.0[2].
*Life expectancy* at birth (1985): male 58.3 years; female 62.2 years.
*Major causes of death* per 100,000 population (1982): respiratory diseases 97.9, of which pneumonia 68.1; infectious and parasitic diseases 88.2; diseases of the circulatory system 58.0; birth trauma and other perinatal causes 42.5; malignant neoplasms (cancers) 33.5.

## National economy

*Budget* (1986). Revenue: I/. 45,331,000,000 (tax on fuel 23.8%; income taxes 21.7%; tax on external trade 20.8%; tax on goods and services 11.5%; property tax 4.6%). Expenditures: I/. 75,995,000,000 (current expenditure 61.8%, of which wages 19.4%, defense 14.1%, transfer payments 12.3%, interest payments 11.5%; public debt amortization 23.6%).
*Public debt* (external, outstanding; 1985): U.S.$10,526,800,000.
*Tourism* (1985): receipts from visitors U.S.$277,000,000; expenditures by nationals abroad U.S.$165,000,000.
*Production* (metric tons except as noted). Agriculture, forestry, fishing (1986): sugarcane 6,272,800, potatoes 1,661,400, corn (maize) 864,300, rice 744,800, plantains 574,700, cassava 361,500, seed cotton 303,800, coffee 97,000; livestock (number of live animals; 1985) 13,500,000 sheep, 3,900,000 cattle, 2,050,000 pigs, 41,000,000 chickens; roundwood (1985) 7,723,000 cu m; fish catch 5,266,000. Mining and quarrying (1986): iron ore 3,353,000; zinc 569,000; copper 397,000; lead 194,000; silver 1,916 kg. Manufacturing (value added in I/. '000,000; 1981): food, beverages, and tobacco 629.3; chemicals and pharmaceuticals 250.4; textiles 249.6; nonferrous metals

219.7; transport equipment 180.7. Construction (value added in I/. '000; 1984): buildings 1,882,000[3]. Energy production (consumption): electricity (kW-hr; 1985) 12,115,000,000 (12,115,000,000); coal (metric tons; 1985) 110,000 (160,000); crude petroleum (barrels; 1985) 68,855,000 (60,737,000); petroleum products (metric tons; 1985) 7,894,000 (6,092,000); natural gas (cu m; 1985) 1,141,052,000 (1,141,052,000).
*Gross national product* (1985): U.S.$17,830,000,000 (U.S.$910 per capita).

### Structure of gross domestic product and labour force

| | 1986 in value I/. '000[4] | 1986 % of total value | 1984 labour force | 1984 % of labour force |
|---|---|---|---|---|
| Agriculture | 52,084 | 14.5 | 2,381,700 | 37.5 |
| Mining | 32,930 | 9.2 | 133,400 | 2.1 |
| Manufacturing | 83,969 | 23.4 | 666,900 | 10.5 |
| Construction | 16,438 | 4.6 | 241,300 | 3.8 |
| Public utilities | | | 19,100 | 0.3 |
| Transp. and commun. | } 145,524 | } 40.6 | 273,100 | 4.3 |
| Trade | | | 889,200 | 14.0 |
| Finance | | | 152,800 | 2.4 |
| Services[5] | 27,519 | 7.7 | 1,594,200 | 25.1 |
| TOTAL | 358,464 | 100.0 | 6,351,300 | 100.0 |

*Population economically active* (1985): total 6,569,800; activity rate of total population 33.4% (participation rates: over age 15, 56.2%; female 16.2%; unemployed 11.8%).

### Price and earnings indexes (1980 = 100)

| | 1982 | 1983 | 1984 | 1985 | 1986 | 1987[6] |
|---|---|---|---|---|---|---|
| Consumer price index | 288.4 | 609.0 | 1,280.2 | 3,372.0 | 5,999.5 | 10,390.0 |
| Monthly earnings index[7] | 313.2 | 542.4 | 1,041.8 | 2,403.9 | 5,410.5 | ... |

*Household income and expenditure.* Average household size (1981) 4.8; income per household (1971–72) S/.[8] 51,170 (U.S.$1,322); sources of income: n.a.; expenditure (1983)[7]: food, drink, and tobacco 38.1%, rent and utilities 15.6%, transportation 9.8%, recreation and education 7.4%.
*Land use* (1984): forest 54.6%; pasture 21.2%; agricultural 2.7%; other 21.5%.

## Foreign trade

### Balance of trade (current prices)

| | 1981 | 1982 | 1983 | 1984 | 1985 | 1986 |
|---|---|---|---|---|---|---|
| I/. '000,000 | +134.2 | +457.8 | +1,845.0 | +5,206.6 | +17,914.2 | +6,439 |
| % of total | 5.2% | 11.0% | 22.7% | 31.2% | 37.5% | 10.2% |

*Imports* (1986): U.S.$2,525,000,000 (raw and intermediate materials 50.7%; capital goods 27.4%, of which private sector 21.1%, public sector 6.3%; consumer goods 13.9%). *Major import sources:* U.S. 26.9%; Japan 8.8%; W.Ger. 8.6%; Argentina 7.7%; Brazil 6.6%; Switzerland 3.8%; U.K. 2.8%.
*Exports* (1986): U.S.$2,509,000,000 (mineral products 40.8%; agricultural products 16.2%; fish products 12.6%; petroleum and derivatives 9.4%; textiles 9.2%). *Major destinations:* U.S. 30.1%; Japan 10.6%; Belgium–Luxem. 6.7%; W.Ger. 5.6%; U.K. 4.7%; U.S.S.R. 3.8%; Italy 3.2%; Brazil 2.9%.

## Transport and communications

*Transport.* Railroads (1983): route length (1986) 2,144 mi, 3,451 km; passenger-km 563,024,000; metric ton-km cargo 839,718,000. Roads (1984): total length 40,400 mi, 65,000 km (paved 11%). Vehicles (1982): passenger cars 359,700; trucks and buses 196,013. Merchant marine (1986): vessels (100 gross tons and over) 632; total deadweight tonnage 997,089. Air transport (1985): passenger-km 1,601,210,000; metric ton-km cargo 192,301,000; airports (1987) 22.
*Communications.* Daily newspapers (1985): total number 66; total circulation 1,121,909[9]; circulation per 1,000 population 57[9]. Radio (1986): 3,969,000 receivers (1 per 5.1 persons). Television (1986): 1,701,000 receivers (1 per 12 persons). Telephones (1985): 599,964 (1 per 33 persons).

## Education and health

### Education (1986)

| | schools | teachers | students | student/ teacher ratio |
|---|---|---|---|---|
| Primary (age 6–11) | 31,186 | 123,000 | 4,060,000 | 33.0 |
| Secondary (age 12–16) | 4,831 | 74,000 | 1,676,000 | 22.6 |
| Voc., teacher tr. | 288 | 7,000 | 151,000 | 21.6 |
| Higher | 46 | 22,000 | 394,000 | 17.9 |

*Educational attainment* (1981). Percent of population age 25 and over having: no formal schooling 20.1%; less than primary education 33.2%; primary 21.1%; secondary 20.8%; higher 4.8%. *Literacy* (1981): total population age 15 and over literate 8,152,451 (81.6%); males 4,440,071 (89.9%); females 3,712,380 (73.5%).
*Health* (1982): physicians 14,751 (1 per 1,236 persons); hospital beds 29,991 (1 per 608 persons); infant mortality rate per 1,000 live births (1986) 90.5
*Food* (1981–83): daily per capita caloric intake 2,150 (vegetable products 87%, animal products 13%); (1983) 85% of FAO recommended minimum.

## Military

*Total active duty personnel* (1986): 127,000 (army 66.9%, navy 21.3%, air force 11.8%). *Military expenditure as percent of GNP* (1984): 7.1% (world 5.9%); per capita expenditure U.S.$76.

[1]Detail does not add to total given because of rounding. [2]Excludes Indian jungle population; based on incomplete information. [3]Includes new construction and capital repairs. [4]At prices of 1970. [5]Services includes public administration and defense. [6]June. [7]Estimate for Lima metropolitan area only. [8]Peruvian sol, the currency prior to 1985. [9]Partial circulation.

# Philippines

*Official name:* Republika ñg Pilipinas (Pilipino); Republic of the Philippines (English).
*Form of government:* unitary republic with two legislative houses (Senate [24]; House of Representatives [200]).
*Chief of state and head of government:* President.
*Capital:* Manila.
*Official languages:* Pilipino; English.
*Official religion:* none.
*Monetary unit:* 1 Philippine peso (₱) = 100 centavos; valuation (Oct. 5, 1987) 1 U.S.$ = ₱ 20.01; 1 £ = ₱ 32.50.

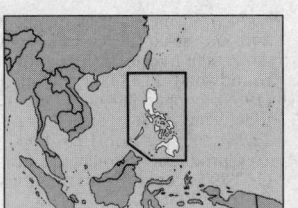

| Area and population | area | | population |
|---|---|---|---|
| | sq mi | sq km | 1985 estimate |
| **Regions** | | | |
| Bicol | 6,808 | 17,633 | 4,104,000 |
| Cagayan Valley | 14,055 | 36,403 | 2,648,000 |
| Central Luzon | 7,039 | 18,231 | 5,726,000 |
| Central Mindanao | 8,994 | 23,293 | 2,733,000 |
| Central Visayas | 5,773 | 14,951 | 4,362,000 |
| Eastern Visayas | 8,275 | 21,432 | 3,185,000 |
| Ilocos | 8,328 | 21,568 | 4,056,000 |
| National Capital Region | 246 | 636 | 7,354,000 |
| Northern Mindanao | 10,937 | 28,328 | 3,350,000 |
| Southern Mindanao | 12,237 | 31,693 | 4,032,000 |
| Southern Tagalog | 18,117 | 46,924 | 7,490,000 |
| Western Mindanao | 7,214 | 18,685 | 2,994,000 |
| Western Visayas | 7,808 | 20,223 | 5,323,000 |
| TOTAL | 115,800[1] | 300,000 | 57,357,000 |

## Demography

*Population* (1987): 57,357,000.
*Density* (1987): persons per sq mi 495.3, persons per sq km 191.2.
*Urban–rural* (1987): urban 41.0%; rural 59.0%.
*Sex distribution* (1987): male 50.20%; female 49.80%.
*Age breakdown* (1984): under 15, 39.0%; 15–29, 30.5%; 30–44, 17.0%; 45–59, 8.7%; 60–74, 4.0%; 75 and over, 0.8%.
*Population projection:* (1990) 61,483,000; (2000) 74,057,000.
*Doubling time:* 27 years.
*Ethnic composition* (by mother tongue; 1980): Tagalog 29.7%; Cebuano 24.2%; Ilocano 10.3%; Hiligaynon Ilongo 9.2%; Bicol 5.6%; Samar-Leyte 4.0%; Pampango 2.8%; Pangasinan 1.8%; other 12.5%[1].
*Religious affiliation* (1980): Roman Catholic 84.1%; Aglipayan (Philippine Independent Church) 6.2%; Muslim 4.3%; Protestant 3.5%; other 1.9%.
*Major cities* (1984): Manila 1,728,400; Quezon City 1,326,000; Cebu 552,200; Caloocan 524,600; Makati 409,000.

## Vital statistics

*Birth rate* per 1,000 population (1986): 33.8 (world avg. 26.0); (1980) legitimate 96.3%; illegitimate 3.7%.
*Death rate* per 1,000 population (1986): 8.2 (world avg. 9.9).
*Natural increase rate* per 1,000 population (1986): 25.6 (world avg. 16.1).
*Total fertility rate* (avg. births per childbearing woman; 1986): 4.5.
*Marriage rate* per 1,000 population (1983): 6.8.
*Life expectancy* at birth (1987): male 61.9 years; female 65.5 years.
*Major causes of death* per 100,000 population (1984): pneumonia 89.3; heart diseases 61.0; tuberculosis 52.9; vascular diseases 39.6; malignant neoplasms (cancers) 30.2; diarrhea 27.8; accidents 16.8; malnutrition 13.4.

## National economy

*Budget* (1986). Revenue: ₱ 87,500,000,000 (tax revenue 82.9%, of which tax on foreign trade 30.1%, tax on domestic goods and services 28.8%, income tax 19.1%; nontax revenue 9.4%). Expenditures: ₱ 92,888,000,000 (interest on debt 25.3%; education 12.5%; transport and communications 9.4%; defense 8.7%; health 4.4%; agriculture 4.1%; public services 4.1%).
*Public debt* (external, outstanding; 1985): U.S.$13,561,400,000.
*Tourism* (1985): receipts from visitors U.S.$507,000,000; expenditures by nationals abroad U.S.$37,000,000.
*Production* (metric tons except as noted). Agriculture, forestry, fishing (1985): rice 8,200,100, bananas 3,697,800, corn (maize) 3,438,800, coconut 2,964,800, sugarcane 2,747,600, pineapple 1,448,600, mango 384,300; livestock (number of live animals) 2,980,000 buffalo, 1,785,000 cattle, 2,191,000 goats, 7,158,000 pigs, 52,098,000 chickens; roundwood 36,614,000 cu m; fish catch (1984) 2,207,000. Mining and quarrying (1985): limestone 4,000,-000; chromite 257,600; copper 226,200; silver 52,800 kilograms; gold 25,200 kilograms. Manufacturing (gross value added in constant prices of 1972 in ₱ '000,000; 1983): food items 9,246; chemicals and chemical products 2,315; electrical machinery 1,717; coal and petroleum products 1,351; footwear and wearing apparel 1,247; tobacco manufactures 1,117. Construction[2] (authorized; 1984): residential 3,129,000 sq m; nonresidential 1,912,000 sq m. Energy production (consumption): electricity (kW-hr; 1985) 21,018,000,000 (21,018,000,000); coal (metric tons; 1985) 1,227,000 (1,742,000); petroleum (barrels; 1985) 4,087,000 (60,634,000); petroleum products (metric tons; 1985) 7,834,000 (8,779,000); natural gas, n.a. (n.a.).
*Land use* (1984): forested 40.1%; meadows and pastures 3.8%; agricultural and under permanent cultivation 37.9%; other 18.2%.
*Gross national product* (at current market prices; 1985): U.S.$32,630,000,000 (U.S.$600 per capita).

| Structure of gross domestic product and labour force | | | | |
|---|---|---|---|---|
| | 1985 | | | |
| | in value ₱ '000,000 | % of total value | labour force | % of labour force |
| Agriculture | 161,405 | 26.5 | 9,698,000 | 45.4 |
| Mining | 13,707 | 2.2 | 127,000 | 0.6 |
| Manufacturing | 150,523 | 24.7 | 1,921,000 | 9.0 |
| Construction | 26,691 | 4.4 | 691,000 | 3.2 |
| Public utilities | 8,700 | 1.4 | 71,000 | 0.3 |
| Transp. and commun. | 38,258 | 6.3 | 931,000 | 4.4 |
| Trade | 125,869 | 20.6 | 2,611,000 | 12.2 |
| Finance | | | 342,000 | 1.6 |
| Services } | 84,910 | 13.9 | 3,448,000 | 16.1 |
| Other | | | 1,517,000[3] | 7.1[3] |
| TOTAL | 610,063 | 100.0 | 21,357,000 | 100.0[1] |

*Population economically active* (1985): total 21,357,000; activity rate of total population 39.1% (participation rates: over age 15, 63.5%; female 24.5%; unemployed 7.1%).

| Price and earnings indexes (1980 = 100) | | | | | | | |
|---|---|---|---|---|---|---|---|
| | 1981 | 1982 | 1983 | 1984 | 1985 | 1986 | 1987[4] |
| Consumer price index | 113.1 | 124.6 | 137.1 | 206.2 | 253.8 | 255.7 | 261.2 |

*Household income and expenditure.* Average household size (1985) 5.7; income per family (1985) ₱ 30,748 (U.S.$1,616); sources of income (1971): wages and salaries 44.8%, self-employment 40.3%, owner-occupied dwellings 7.1%, pensions, social security, and related benefits 2.1%, other 5.7%; expenditure (1984): food, beverages, and tobacco 56.2%, household furnishings and operations 14.0%, clothing 6.2%, fuel and power 4.4%, transport and communication 3.3%.

## Foreign trade[5]

| Balance of trade (current prices) | | | | | | |
|---|---|---|---|---|---|---|
| | 1981 | 1982 | 1983 | 1984 | 1985 | 1986 |
| ₱ '000,000 | −18,153 | −22,674 | −28,566 | −10,907 | −8,113 | −2,974 |
| % of total | 16.9% | 20.9% | 20.7% | 5.8% | 4.5% | 1.5% |

*Imports* (1985): U.S.$5,110,673,000 (mineral fuels and lubricants 28.4%; nonelectrical machinery 7.2%; electrical machinery 5.7%; cereals 5.4%; chemicals 4.3%; base metals 3.5%; explosives 2.9%). *Major import sources:* United States 25.1%; Japan 14.4%; Malaysia 7.2%; China 5.4%; Saudi Arabia 5.3%; Kuwait 4.3%; South Korea 4.0%.
*Exports* (1985): U.S.$4,628,954,000 (1984: electrical and electronic equipment and components 23.6%; coconut products 13.5%, of which coconut oil 10.8%; clothing 11.1%; fruits and vegetables 7.3%; sugar and sugar products 6.1%; forest products 6.0%; mineral products 4.9%). *Major export destinations:* United States 35.0%; Japan 18.9%; Singapore 5.4%; Hong Kong 4.0%; West Germany 3.8%; Malaysia 3.8%; United Kingdom 3.6%.

## Transport and communications

*Transport.* Railroads (1986): route length 658 mi, 1,059 km; passenger-mi 104,000,000, passenger-km 168,000,000; short ton-mi cargo 41,000,000, metric ton-km cargo 60,000,000. Roads (1985): total length 100,481 mi, 161,709 km (paved 13%). Vehicles (1985): passenger cars 753,779; trucks and buses 108,674. Merchant marine (1986): vessels (100 gross tons and over) 1,131; total deadweight tonnage 11,668,566. Air transport[6] (1985): passenger-mi 4,853,801,000, passenger-km 7,811,451,000; short ton-mi cargo 662,243,000, metric ton-km cargo 966,859,000; airports (1987) with scheduled flights 42.
*Communications.* Daily newspapers (1984): total number 25; circulation 2,379,145; circulation per 1,000 population 44. Radio (1986): 7,500,000 receivers (1 per 7.5 persons). Television (1986): 3,997,000 receivers (1 per 14 persons). Telephones (1985): 820,271 (1 per 67 persons).

## Education and health

| Education (1984–85) | | | | |
|---|---|---|---|---|
| | schools | teachers | students | student/ teacher ratio |
| Primary (age 7–12) | 32,791 | 286,246 | 8,793,773 | 30.7 |
| Secondary (age 13–16) | 5,388 | 103,493 | 3,323,063 | 32.1 |
| Voc., teacher tr. Higher } | 1,178 | 33,935 | 1,127,968 | 33.2 |

*Educational attainment* (1980). Percent of population age 25 and over having: no grade completed 11.7%; elementary education 53.8%; secondary 18.8%; college 15.2%; not stated 0.5%. *Literacy* (1980): total population age 15 and over literate 25,139,700 (88.7%); males literate 12,772,200 (89.9%); females literate 12,367,500 (87.5%).
*Health:* physicians (1982) 46,579 (1 per 1,090 persons); hospital beds (1985) 79,703 (1 per 756 persons); infant mortality rate per 1,000 live births (1986) 59.0.
*Food* (1981–83): daily per capita caloric intake 2,411 (vegetable products 90%, animal products 10%); (1983) 106% of FAO recommended minimum requirement.

## Military

*Total active duty personnel* (1986): 113,000 (army 62.0%, navy 23.0%, air force 15.0%). *Military expenditure as percent of GNP* (1984): 1.2% (world 5.9%); per capita expenditure U.S.$7.

[1]Detail does not add to total given because of rounding. [2]Private only. [3]Includes unemployed. [4]May. [5]Import figures are f.o.b. (free on board) in balance of trade and c.i.f. (cost, insurance, and freight) for commodities and trading partners. [6]Philippines Airlines only.

# Poland

*Official name:* Polska Rzeczpospolita
Ludowa (Polish People's Republic).
*Form of government:* unitary
single-party socialist republic with one
legislative house (Sejm [460]).
*Chief of state:* President (Chairman).
*Head of government:* Prime Minister.
*Capital:* Warsaw.
*Official language:* Polish.
*Official religion:* none.
*Monetary unit:* 1 złoty (Zl) = 100
groszy; valuation (Oct. 5, 1987)
1 U.S.$ = Zl 297.70; 1 £ = Zl 483.43.

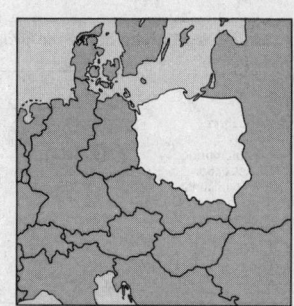

### Area and population

| | | area | | population |
|---|---|---|---|---|
| Provinces | Capitals | sq mi | sq km | 1986 estimate |
| Biała Podlaska | Biała Podlaska | 2,065 | 5,348 | 297,900 |
| Białystok | Białystok | 3,882 | 10,055 | 671,600 |
| Bielsko | Bielsko Biala | 1,430 | 3,704 | 873,600 |
| Bydgoszcz | Bydgoszcz | 3,996 | 10,349 | 1,083,800 |
| Chełm | Chełm | 1,493 | 3,866 | 240,800 |
| Ciechanów | Ciechanów | 2,456 | 6,362 | 418,100 |
| Częstochowa | Częstochowa | 2,387 | 6,182 | 767,400 |
| Elbląg | Elbląg | 2,356 | 6,103 | 466,700 |
| Gdańsk | Gdańsk | 2,855 | 7,394 | 1,401,500 |
| Gorzów | Gorzów Wielkopolski | 3,276 | 8,484 | 482,200 |
| Jelenia Góra | Jelenia Góra | 1,690 | 4,378 | 510,300 |
| Kalisz | Kalisz | 2,514 | 6,512 | 696,400 |
| Katowice | Katowice | 2,568 | 6,650 | 3,916,400 |
| Kielce | Kielce | 3,556 | 9,211 | 1,107,900 |
| Konin | Konin | 1,984 | 5,139 | 459,300 |
| Koszalin | Koszalin | 3,270 | 8,470 | 489,800 |
| Kraków | Kraków | 1,256 | 3,254 | 1,209,300 |
| Krosno | Krosno | 2,202 | 5,702 | 475,200 |
| Legnica | Legnica | 1,559 | 4,037 | 490,600 |
| Leszno | Leszno | 1,604 | 4,154 | 375,600 |
| Łódź | Łódź | 588 | 1,523 | 1,149,100 |
| Łomża | Łomża | 2,581 | 6,684 | 338,700 |
| Lublin | Lublin | 2,622 | 6,792 | 985,400 |
| Nowy Sącz | Nowy Sącz | 2,153 | 5,576 | 667,400 |
| Olsztyn | Olsztyn | 4,759 | 12,327 | 725,700 |
| Opole | Opole | 3,295 | 8,535 | 1,013,700 |
| Ostrołęka | Ostrołęka | 2,509 | 6,498 | 384,200 |
| Piła | Piła | 3,168 | 8,205 | 465,400 |
| Piotrków | Piotrków Trybunalski | 2,419 | 6,266 | 633,100 |
| Płock | Płock | 1,976 | 5,117 | 509,300 |
| Poznań | Poznań | 3,147 | 8,151 | 1,298,000 |
| Przemyśl | Przemyśl | 1,713 | 4,437 | 395,900 |
| Radom | Radom | 2,816 | 7,294 | 729,700 |
| Rzeszów | Rzeszów | 1,698 | 4,397 | 691,300 |
| Siedlce | Siedlce | 3,281 | 8,499 | 636,500 |
| Sieradz | Sieradz | 1,880 | 4,869 | 401,200 |
| Skierniewice | Skierniewice | 1,529 | 3,960 | 409,500 |
| Słupsk | Słupsk | 2,878 | 7,453 | 396,100 |
| Suwałki | Suwałki | 4,050 | 10,490 | 449,000 |
| Szczecin | Szczecin | 3,854 | 9,981 | 942,600 |
| Tarnobrzeg | Tarnobrzeg | 2,426 | 6,283 | 580,500 |
| Tarnów | Tarnów | 1,603 | 4,151 | 641,500 |
| Toruń | Toruń | 2,065 | 5,348 | 640,600 |
| Wałbrzych | Wałbrzych | 1,609 | 4,168 | 735,800 |
| Warszawa | Warszawa | 1,463 | 3,788 | 2,412,200 |
| Włocławek | Włocławek | 1,700 | 4,402 | 425,900 |
| Wrocław | Wrocław | 2,427 | 6,287 | 1,113,900 |
| Zamość | Zamość | 2,695 | 6,980 | 487,900 |
| Zielona Góra | Zielona Góra | 3,424 | 8,868 | 646,000 |
| TOTAL | | 120,727 | 312,683 | 37,340,500 |

## Demography

*Population* (1987): 37,769,000.
*Density* (1987): persons per sq mi 312.8, persons per sq km 120.8.
*Urban–rural* (1986): urban 60.2%; rural 39.8%.
*Sex distribution* (1986): male 48.77%; female 51.23%.
*Age breakdown* (1985): under 15, 25.4%; 15–29, 23.3%; 30–44, 20.9%; 45–59,
16.6%; 60–74, 9.9%; 75 and over, 3.9%.
*Population projection:* (1990) 38,726,000; (2000) 42,094,000.
*Ethnic composition* (1986): Polish 98.7%; Ukrainian 0.6%; other 0.7%.
*Religious affiliation* (1986): Roman Catholic 94.2%; other 5.8%.
*Major cities* (1986): Warsaw 1,659,400; Łódź 847,900; Kraków 740,100.

## Vital statistics

*Birth rate* per 1,000 population (1985): 18.2 (world avg. 29.0).
*Death rate* per 1,000 population (1985): 10.3 (world avg. 11.0).
*Natural increase rate* per 1,000 population (1985): 7.9 (world avg. 18.0).
*Total fertility rate* (avg. births per childbearing woman; 1984): 2.3.
*Marriage rate* per 1,000 population (1985): 7.2.
*Divorce rate* per 1,000 population (1985): 1.3.
*Life expectancy* at birth (1985): male 66.5 years; female 74.8 years.
*Major causes of death* per 100,000 population (1984): diseases of the circu-
latory system 492.9; malignant neoplasms (cancers) 179.0.

## National economy

*Budget* (1985). Revenue: Zl 4,043,453,000,000 (turnover tax 31.8%, tax
on state enterprises 30.0%). Expenditures: Zl 4,078,600,000,000 (economy
39.2%, education 9.9%, health 8.8%, defense 8.6%).
*Public debt* (external, outstanding; 1985): U.S.$25,800,000,000.
*Tourism:* receipts (1984) U.S.$106,000,000; expenditures (1983) U.S.$195,-
000,000.

*Production* (metric tons except as noted). Agriculture (1985): potatoes 36,-
546,000, sugar beets 14,644,000, rye 7,600,000, wheat 6,461,000, barley
4,086,000; livestock (live animals; 1986) 17,614,000 pigs, 11,055,000 cattle;
roundwood 23,184,000 cu m; fish catch 686,000. Mining and quarrying
(1986): copper 388,000; zinc 179,000; lead 88,300; iron ore 8,800. Manufacturing (1986): crude steel 17,144,000; cement 15,831,000; rolled steel
12,341,000; pig iron 10,574,000. Construction (1985): 13,182,000 sq m. Energy production (consumption): electricity ('000,000 kW-hr; 1986) 140,094
(147,890); coal ('000 metric tons; 1986) 259,337 (224,983); crude petroleum
(barrels; 1986) 1,224,000 (1,327,600); petroleum products (metric tons; 1986)
14,298,000 (17,500,000); natural gas ('000,000 cu m; 1986) 5,825 (12,960).
*Gross national product* (1985): U.S.$78,960,000,000 (U.S.$2,120 per capita).

### Structure of net material product and labour force

| | 1985 | | | |
|---|---|---|---|---|
| | in value Zl '000,000 | % of total value | labour force | % of labour force[1] |
| Agriculture | 1,398.7 | 16.3 | 5,112,200 | 29.8 |
| Mining | | | 547,600 | 3.2 |
| Manufacturing | 4,181.9 | 48.7 | 4,320,900 | 25.2 |
| Public utilities | | | 166,100 | 1.0 |
| Construction | 1,064.5 | 12.4 | 1,282,400 | 7.5 |
| Transp. and commun. | 579.0 | 6.7 | 1,302,900 | 7.6 |
| Trade | 1,207.2 | 14.1 | 1,386,000 | 8.1 |
| Finance | — | — | 368,300 | 2.1 |
| Public admin., defense | — | — | | |
| Services | — | — | 2,496,800 | 14.6 |
| Other | 155.1[2] | 1.8 | 153,600 | 0.9 |
| TOTAL | 8,586.4 | 100.0 | 17,136,800 | 100.0 |

*Population economically active* (1985): total 18,007,000; activity rate of total
population 48.6% (participation rates: ages 15–64, 74.6%; female 45.9%).

### Price and earnings indexes (1980 = 100)

| | 1981 | 1982 | 1983 | 1984 | 1985 | 1986 | 1987[3] |
|---|---|---|---|---|---|---|---|
| Consumer price index | 121.2 | 243.4 | 297.2 | 341.8 | 393.4 | 463.0 | 512.0 |
| Monthly earnings index | 127.4 | 198.8 | 253.5 | 288.2 | 345.6 | 418.5 | 441.9 |

*Household income and expenditure.* Average household size (1983) 3.4; average annual income Zl 1,453,000 (U.S.$3,600); sources of income: wages
82.9%, social welfare 17.1%; expenditure (1983): food 43.1%, clothing 12.7%,
housing 12.3%, recreation 8.8%, transport 5.8%.
*Land use* (1984): forested 27.9%; meadows 13.0%; agricultural and under
permanent cultivation 47.3%; other 11.8%.

## Foreign trade

### Balance of trade (current prices)

| | 1980 | 1981 | 1982 | 1983 | 1984 | 1985 | 1986 |
|---|---|---|---|---|---|---|---|
| Zl '000,000,000 | −6.4 | −7.5 | +82.2 | +90.0 | +126.2 | +96.1 | +151.6 |
| % of total | 5.8% | 7.7% | 4.5% | 4.4% | 5.0% | 2.9% | 7.2% |

*Imports* (1985): Zl 1,594,889,000,000 (machinery and transport equipment
33.5%, fuel and power 22.1%, chemicals 13.1%, iron and steel products
9.1%, food 6.9%). *Major import sources:* U.S.S.R. 34.4%; W.Ger. 9.0%;
E.Ger. 6.1%; Czechoslovakia 6.0%; Yugoslavia 3.9%.
*Exports* (1985): Zl 1,690,994,000,000 (machinery and transport equipment
39.4%, fuel and power 15.6%, chemicals 10.6%, food 6.6%, textiles and
clothing 5.9%). *Major export destinations:* U.S.S.R. 28.4%; W.Ger. 8.7%;
Czechoslovakia 6.2%; E.Ger. 4.8%; U.K. 4.3%; Hungary 3.2%.

## Transport and communications

*Transport.* Railroads (1985): length 27,095 km; passenger-km 51,997,700,000;
metric ton-km cargo 120,642,000,000. Roads (1986): total length 254,000
km (paved 61%). Vehicles (1985): passenger cars 3,179,000; trucks and
buses 732,000. Merchant marine (1986): vessels (100 gross tons and over)
749; total deadweight tonnage 4,694,249. Air transport (1986): passenger-
km 2,196,000,000; metric ton-km cargo 12,048,000; airports (1987) 12.
*Communications.* Daily newspapers (1985): 45; circulation 7,714,000. Radio
(1986): 9,466,000 (1 per 4.0 persons). Television (1986): 10,076,000 (1 per
3.7 persons). Telephones (1986): 4,215,000 (1 per 8.9 persons).

## Education and health

### Education (1985–86)

| | schools | teachers | students | student/ teacher ratio |
|---|---|---|---|---|
| Primary (age 7–15) | 16,791 | 267,600 | 4,879,100 | 18.2 |
| Secondary (age 15–19) | 896 | 21,300 | 338,000 | 15.9 |
| Voc., teacher tr. | 7,328 | 82,900 | 1,359,800 | 16.4 |
| Higher | 92 | 57,300 | 265,800 | 4.6 |

*Educational attainment* (1978). Percent of population age 25 and over having: no formal schooling 2.8%; less than full primary education 12.7%;
primary 44.9%; secondary 33.9%; higher 5.7%. *Literacy* (1983): total population age 15 and over literate 27,352,000 (99.2%).
*Health* (1986): physicians 72,900 (1 per 514 persons); hospital beds 211,500
(1 per 177 persons); infant mortality rate per 1,000 live births (1985) 18.5.
*Food* (1981–83): daily per capita caloric intake 3,301 (vegetable products
69%, animal products 31%); (1983) 127% of FAO recommended minimum.

## Military

*Total active duty personnel* (1986): 402,000 (army 73.4%, navy 4.7%, air force
21.9%). *Military expenditure as percent of GNP* (1984): 5.7% (world 5.9%);
per capita expenditure U.S.$352.

---

[1]Employed. [2]Other material activities. [3]First quarter average.

# Portugal

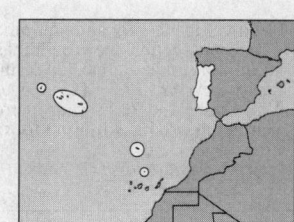

*Official name:* República Portuguesa (Republic of Portugal).
*Form of government:* parliamentary state with one legislative house (Assembly of the Republic [250]).
*Chief of state:* President.
*Head of government:* Prime Minister.
*Capital:* Lisbon.
*Official language:* Portuguese.
*Official religion:* none.
*Monetary unit:* 1 Escudo (Esc) = 100 centavos; valuation (Oct. 5, 1987) 1 U.S.$ = Esc 145.02; 1 £ = Esc 235.50.

### Area and population

| Continental Portugal Districts | Capitals | area sq mi | area sq km | population 1986 estimate[1] |
|---|---|---|---|---|
| Aveiro | Aveiro | 1,084 | 2,808 | 655,100 |
| Beja | Beja | 3,948 | 10,225 | 182,000 |
| Braga | Braga | 1,032 | 2,673 | 756,300 |
| Bragança | Bragança | 2,551 | 6,608 | 186,400 |
| Castelo Branco | Castelo Branco | 2,577 | 6,675 | 228,300 |
| Coimbra | Coimbra | 1,524 | 3,947 | 445,700 |
| Évora | Évora | 2,854 | 7,393 | 176,900 |
| Faro | Faro | 1,915 | 4,960 | 337,200 |
| Guarda | Guarda | 2,131 | 5,518 | 200,400 |
| Leiria | Leiria | 1,357 | 3,515 | 434,200 |
| Lisboa | Lisbon (Lisboa) | 1,066 | 2,761 | 2,119,600 |
| Portalegre | Portalegre | 2,342 | 6,065 | 139,600 |
| Porto | Porto | 925 | 2,395 | 1,644,400 |
| Santarém | Santarém | 2,605 | 6,747 | 460,500 |
| Setúbal | Setúbal | 1,955 | 5,064 | 742,200 |
| Viana do Castelo | Viana do Castelo | 871 | 2,255 | 264,900 |
| Vila Real | Vila Real | 1,671 | 4,328 | 265,300 |
| Viseu | Viseu | 1,933 | 5,007 | 426,500 |
| **Azores (Açores) Autonomous Region** | Ponta Delgada | 868 | 2,247 | 252,200 |
| **Madeira Autonomous Region** | Funchal | 306 | 794 | 267,400 |
| TOTAL | | 35,672[2] | 92,389[2] | 10,185,100 |

## Demography

*Population* (1987): 10,312,000.
*Density* (1987): persons per sq mi 289.1, persons per sq km 111.6.
*Urban–rural* (1981): urban 29.6%; rural 70.4%.
*Sex distribution* (1986): male 48.27%; female 51.73%.
*Age breakdown* (1985): under 15, 23.8%; 15–29, 24.2%; 30–44, 18.3%; 45–59, 16.9%; 60–74, 12.3%; 75 and over, 4.5%.
*Population projection:* (1990) 10,548,000; (2000) 10,877,000.
*Nationality* (1981): Portuguese 98.9%; Angolan 0.2%; Cape Verdean 0.2%; French 0.1%; Brazilian 0.1%; Spanish 0.1%; other 0.4%.
*Religious affiliation* (1981): Christian 96.0%, of which Roman Catholic 94.5%, Protestant 0.6%, other Christian (mostly Apostolic Catholic and Jehovah's Witness) 0.9%; nonreligious 3.8%; Jewish 0.1%; Muslim 0.1%.
*Major cities* (1985): Lisbon 827,800; Porto 344,500; Amadora 95,518[3].

## Vital statistics

*Birth rate* per 1,000 population (1985): 12.8 (world avg. 29.0); legitimate 87.7%; illegitimate 12.3%.
*Death rate* per 1,000 population (1985): 9.6 (world avg. 11.0).
*Natural increase rate* per 1,000 population (1985): 3.2 (world avg. 18.0).
*Total fertility rate* (avg. births per childbearing woman; 1980–85): 2.3.
*Marriage rate* per 1,000 population (1985): 6.7.
*Divorce rate* per 1,000 population (1985): 0.9.
*Life expectancy* at birth (1985): male 68.6 years; female 75.3 years.
*Major causes of death* per 100,000 population (1985): circulatory diseases 415.6, of which cerebrovascular diseases 237.4, ischemic heart disease 83.1; malignant neoplasms (cancers) 158.2; respiratory diseases 68.9.

## National economy

*Budget* (1985). Revenue: Esc 716,895,000,000 (indirect taxes 53.5%; direct taxes 41.7%; property income 1.6%). Expenditures: Esc 1,320,579,000,000 (public debt 30.7%; education 9.2%; health 8.7%; defense 6.5%; public works 3.9%).
*Public debt* (external, outstanding; 1985): U.S.$10,802,800,000.
*Tourism* (1985): receipts from visitors U.S.$1,137,000,000; expenditures by nationals abroad U.S.$235,000,000.
*Production* (metric tons except as noted). Agriculture, forestry, fishing (1985): potatoes 1,171,000, grapes 1,150,000, tomatoes 829,000, corn (maize) 570,000, wheat 385,000, olives 215,000, rice 147,000, oats 141,000, cork 121,800[4]; livestock (number of live animals) 5,050,000 sheep, 3,477,000 pigs, 1,010,000 cattle; roundwood (1984) 9,224,000 cu m; fish catch 229,268. Mining and quarrying (1985): copper pyrites 355,000; anthracite 237,000; kaolin 53,900; tungsten 2,975. Manufacturing (value of production in Esc '000,000; 1986): refined petroleum 235,848; cotton and synthetic fibres 178,141; animal feedstuffs 101,071; clothing 97,653; knitted fabrics 73,677; radio, television, and telecommunications equipment 65,585; iron and steel 57,418; motor vehicles 54,168; dairy products 50,088; cement 39,875; alcoholic beverages 23,165. Construction (1985): residential 5,430,841 sq m; nonresidential 1,349,282 sq m. Energy production (consumption): electricity (kW-hr; 1985) 19,007,000,000 (21,253,000,000); coal (metric tons;

1985) 238,000 (1,633,000); crude petroleum (barrels; 1985) none (52,880,-000); petroleum products (metric tons; 1985) 6,339,000 (7,016,000); natural gas, none (n.a.).
*Gross national product* (1985): U.S.$20,140,000,000 (U.S.$1,970 per capita).

### Structure of gross domestic product and labour force

| | 1984 in value Esc '000,000 | 1984 % of total value | 1985 labour force | 1985 % of labour force |
|---|---|---|---|---|
| Agriculture | 256,600 | 9.2 | 1,012,900 | 21.6 |
| Mining | 889,100 | 31.8 | 23,700 | 0.5 |
| Manufacturing | | | 1,053,200 | 22.4 |
| Construction | 172,300 | 6.2 | 359,600 | 7.7 |
| Public utilities | 61,700 | 2.2 | 29,600 | 0.6 |
| Transp. and commun. | 550,900 | 19.7 | 188,200 | 4.0 |
| Trade | | | 596,200 | 12.7 |
| Finance | 172,800 | 6.2 | 116,900 | 2.5 |
| Pub. admin., defense | 329,400 | 11.8 | 918,900 | 19.6 |
| Services | | | | |
| Other | 359,900 | 12.9 | 396,500[5] | 8.4 |
| TOTAL | 2,792,700 | 100.0 | 4,695,700 | 100.0 |

*Population economically active* (1985): total 4,695,700; activity rate of total population 46.1% (participation rates: ages 15–64, 67.8%; female 41.6%; unemployed 8.3%).

### Price and earnings indexes (1980 = 100)

| | 1980 | 1981 | 1982 | 1983 | 1984 | 1985 | 1986[6] |
|---|---|---|---|---|---|---|---|
| Consumer price index | 100.0 | 120.0 | 147.3 | 184.3 | 237.6 | 284.2 | 317.6 |
| Daily earnings index | 100.0 | 121.6 | 148.0 | 172.7 | 203.6 | 244.1 | 295.7 |

*Household income and expenditure.* Average household size (1981) 3.8; income per household: n.a.; sources of income (1985): property and entrepreneurial income 42.3%; wages and salaries 36.4%, transfer payments 12.1%; expenditure (1981): food 34.8%, transportation and communication 14.6%, housing 13.2%, clothing and footwear 11.2%, cafes and hotels 8.8%, health 4.3%, recreation 3.9%, other 9.2%.
*Land use* (1984): forested 39.7%; meadows and pastures 5.8%; agricultural and under permanent cultivation 38.7%; other 15.8%.

## Foreign trade

### Balance of trade (current prices)

| | 1981 | 1982 | 1983 | 1984 | 1985 | 1986 |
|---|---|---|---|---|---|---|
| Esc '000,000 | −352,100 | −422,240 | −390,740 | −377,210 | −248,260 | −336,500 |
| % of total | 40.7% | 38.9% | 27.8% | 19.9% | 11.4% | 13.5% |

*Imports* (1985): Esc 1,412,578,565,000 (machinery and transport equipment 18.0%, of which road vehicles 10.3%; crude petroleum 15.2%; chemicals 9.5%; cereals 2.8%). *Major import sources:* West Germany 14.1%; Spain 11.0%; France 10.0%; Italy 7.9%; U.K. 7.5%; U.S. 6.8%.
*Exports* (1985): Esc 1,076,078,848,000 (clothing 10.2%; paper products 6.6%; chemicals 4.8%; alcoholic beverages 3.6%; cork products 3.5%; petroleum 3.3%; iron and steel products 2.9%). *Major export destinations:* France 15.2%; W.Ger. 14.7%; U.K. 14.3%; U.S. 7.0%; The Netherlands 6.7%.

## Transport and communications

*Transport.* Railroads (1986): route length 2,245 mi, 3,613 km; passenger-km 5,808,000,000; metric ton-km cargo 1,452,000,000. Roads (1981): total length 32,282 mi, 51,953 km (paved 86%). Vehicles (1984): passenger cars 1,600,738; trucks and buses 103,285. Merchant marine (1986): vessels (100 gross tons and over) 355; total deadweight tonnage 1,747,097. Air transport (1985)[7]: passenger-km 4,236,000,000; metric ton-km cargo 142,884,000; airports (1987) 20.
*Communications.* Daily newspapers (1985): total number 28; total circulation 593,900[8]; circulation per 1,000 population 58[8]. Radio (1985): 2,165,000 receivers (1 per 4.7 persons). Television (1985): 1,530,000 receivers (1 per 6.6 persons). Telephones (1985): 1,835,331 (1 per 5.5 persons).

## Education and health

### Education (1983–84)

| | schools | teachers | students | student/ teacher ratio |
|---|---|---|---|---|
| Primary (age 5–11) | 13,111 | 74,320 | 1,288,163 | 17.3 |
| Secondary (age 12–19) | 510 | 36,628 | 568,839 | 15.5 |
| Voc., teacher tr. | 345 | 2,971 | 27,946 | 9.4 |
| Higher | 51 | 10,930 | 95,414 | 8.7 |

*Educational attainment* (1981). Percent of population age 25 and over having: no formal schooling 4.4%; primary education 76.2%; secondary 19.0%; postsecondary 0.1%; higher 0.3%. *Literacy* (1981): total population age 15 and over literate 5,818,135 (79.4%); males literate 2,933,526 (84.8%); females literate 2,884,609 (74.6%).
*Health* (1986): physicians 24,629 (1 per 416 persons); hospital beds (1985) 53,566 (1 per 190 persons); infant mortality rate per 1,000 live births 11.6.
*Food* (1981–83): daily per capita caloric intake 3,063 (vegetable products 79%, animal products 21%); (1983) 124% of FAO recommended minimum requirement.

## Military

*Total active duty personnel* (1986): 68,252 (army 58.6%, navy 21.2%, air force 20.2%). *Military expenditure as percent of GNP* (1984): 3.2% (world 5.9%); per capita expenditure U.S.$62.

[1]January 1. [2]Includes 156 sq mi (404 sq km) of inland water. [3]1981. [4]1984. [5]Mostly unemployed. [6]June. [7]TAP (Air Portugal) only. [8]For 16 newspapers only.

# Puerto Rico

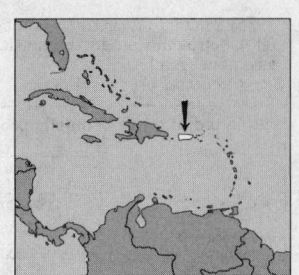

*Official name:* Estado Libre
Asociado de Puerto Rico (Spanish);
Commonwealth of Puerto Rico
(English).
*Political status:* self-governing
commonwealth associated with the
United States, having two legislative
houses (Senate [27]; House of
Representatives [51]).
*Chief of state:* President of the
United States.
*Head of government:* Governor.
*Capital:* San Juan.
*Official languages:* Spanish; English.
*Official religion:* none.
*Monetary unit:* 1 U.S. dollar
(U.S.$) = 100 cents; valuation (Oct. 5,
1987) 1 U.S.$ = £0.62.

### Population 1984 estimate

| Municipio | population | Municipio | population | Municipio | population |
|---|---|---|---|---|---|
| Adjuntas | 18,900 | Fajardo | 33,200 | Naguabo | 21,300 |
| Aguada | 32,400 | Florida | 7,600 | Naranjito | 25,100 |
| Aguadilla | 55,000 | Guánica | 18,800 | Orocovis | 20,900 |
| Agunas Buenas | 23,000 | Guayama | 40,300 | Patillas | 17,900 |
| Aibonito | 22,500 | Guayanilla | 21,000 | Peñuelas | 20,200 |
| Añasco | 24,400 | Guaynabo | 85,100 | Ponce | 190,900 |
| Arecibo | 87,000 | Gurabo | 25,000 | Quebradillas | 19,700 |
| Arroyo | 18,200 | Hatillo | 30,400 | Rincón | 12,400 |
| Barceloneta | 19,600 | Hormigueros | 15,200 | Río Grande | 37,700 |
| Barranquitas | 22,800 | Humacao | 52,400 | Sabana Grande | 21,100 |
| Bayamón | 202,500 | Isabela | 38,200 | Salinas | 26,600 |
| Cabo Rojo | 35,000 | Jayuya | 15,000 | San Germán | 34,200 |
| Caguas | 121,100 | Juana Díaz | 43,600 | San Juan | 428,900 |
| Camuy | 26,200 | Juncos | 27,000 | San Lorenzo | 33,300 |
| Canóvanas | 32,400 | Lajas | 21,300 | San Sebastián | 36,100 |
| Carolina | 165,700 | Lares | 28,000 | Santa Isabel | 19,500 |
| Cataño | 25,900 | Las Marías | 8,600 | Toa Alta | 33,400 |
| Cayey | 43,300 | Las Piedras | 23,100 | Toa Baja | 77,700 |
| Ceiba | 15,100 | Loíza | 24,600 | Trujillo Alto | 50,800 |
| Ciales | 17,200 | Luquillo | 15,400 | Utuado | 34,600 |
| Cidra | 29,600 | Manatí | 38,000 | Vega Alta | 30,000 |
| Coamo | 32,200 | Maricao | 6,700 | Vega Baja | 48,800 |
| Comerio | 18,400 | Maunabo | 11,800 | Vieques | 7,800 |
| Corozal | 29,600 | Mayagüez | 101,000 | Villalba | 22,500 |
| Culebra | 1,300 | Moca | 29,900 | Yabucoa | 31,400 |
| Dorado | 26,700 | Morovis | 21,900 | Yauco | 39,200 |
| | | | | TOTAL | 3,270,000 |

## Demography

*Area:* 3,515 sq mi, 9,104 sq km.
*Population* (1987): 3,300,000.
*Density* (1987): persons per sq mi 938.8, persons per sq km 362.5.
*Urban–rural* (1985): urban 70.7%; rural 29.3%.
*Sex distribution* (1980): male 48.70%; female 51.30%.
*Age breakdown* (1980): under 15, 31.6%; 15–29, 26.5%; 30–44, 18.4%; 45–59,
12.3%; 60–74, 8.3%; 75 and over, 2.9%.
*Population projection:* (1990) 3,327,000; (2000) 3,417,000.
*Doubling time:* 57 years.
*Ethnic composition* (1980): white 80.0%; black 20.0%.
*Religious affiliation* (1984): Roman Catholic 85.3%; Protestant 4.7%; other
10.0%.
*Major cities* (municipio; 1984): San Juan 428,900; Bayamón 202,500; Ponce
190,900; Carolina 165,700; Caguas 121,100.

## Vital statistics

*Birth rate* per 1,000 population (1985): 18.9 (world avg. 29.0); (1980) legiti-
mate 79.0%; illegitimate 21.0%.
*Death rate* per 1,000 population (1985): 6.6 (world avg. 11.0).
*Natural increase rate* per 1,000 population (1985): 12.3 (world avg. 18.0).
*Total fertility rate* (avg. births per childbearing woman; 1984): 2.4.
*Marriage rate* per 1,000 population (1983): 9.1.
*Divorce rate* per 1,000 population (1983): 4.0.
*Life expectancy* at birth (1980–85): male 70.5 years; female 77.6 years.
*Major causes of death* per 100,000 population (1983): diseases of the cir-
culatory system 260.7, of which ischemic heart diseases 99.0, diseases of
pulmonary circulation 60.6; malignant neoplasms (cancers) 105.3; diseases
of the respiratory system 72.5.

## National economy

*Budget* (1983–84). Revenue: U.S.$3,771,000,000 (income taxes 33.1%, federal
grants 18.2%, local excise taxes 15.9%, federal excise taxes 9.7%). Expenditures: U.S.$3,688,000,000 (health and welfare 32.2%, education 28.1%,
public safety 9.2%, debt payment 7.4%, general government 6.9%).
*Public debt* (outstanding; 1985): U.S.$8,832,000,000.
*Tourism* (1985): receipts from visitors U.S.$710,000,000; expenditures by
nationals abroad U.S.$618,000,000.
*Production* (value of production in U.S.$'000,000 except as noted). Agricul-
ture, forestry, fishing (1985): milk 172, starchy vegetables 57, coffee 57,
beef 50, poultry 47, fruit 29, sugar 28, eggs 25; livestock (number of live
animals) 580,000 cattle, 210,000 pigs; roundwood, n.a.; fish catch (1984)
1,256 metric tons. Mining (1984): stone 28. Manufacturing (net income in
U.S.$'000,000; 1985): chemicals 2,769; electrical machinery and equipment
1,068; food products 646; professional and scientific equipment 530; non-

electrical machinery and equipment 498; clothing 429; petroleum products
171. Construction (new buildings authorized; 1984): residential 1,453,000
sq m; nonresidential 40,900 sq m. Energy production (consumption): electricity (kW-hr; 1985) 12,316,000,000 (12,316,000,000); coal (metric tons;
1985) none (50,000); crude petroleum (barrels; 1985) none (36,283,000);
petroleum products (metric tons; 1985) 5,250,000 (5,780,000); natural gas,
none (none).
*Gross national product* (at current market prices; 1985): U.S.$15,940,000,000
(U.S.$4,860 per capita).

### Structure of gross domestic product and labour force

| | 1985 | | 1984 | |
|---|---|---|---|---|
| | in value US$'000,000 | % of total value | labour force | % of labour force |
| Agriculture | 380.2 | 1.9 | 39,000 | 4.1 |
| Manufacturing | 7,701.5 | 39.1 | 143,000 | 15.0 |
| Mining } | | | 2,000 | 0.2 |
| Construction } | 376.0 | 1.9 | 34,000 | 3.6 |
| Public utilities } | | | 11,000 | 1.2 |
| Transp. and commun. } | 1,589.8 | 8.1 | 30,000 | 3.2 |
| Trade | 2,828.3 | 14.4 | 145,000 | 15.2 |
| Finance, real estate | 2,566.7 | 13.0 | 22,000 | 2.3 |
| Pub. admin., defense | 2,328.1 | 11.8 | 177,000 | 18.6 |
| Services | 1,842.0 | 9.4 | 140,000 | 14.7 |
| Other | 68.2 | 0.4 | 209,000[1] | 21.9[1] |
| TOTAL | 19,680.8 | 100.0 | 952,000 | 100.0 |

*Population economically active* (1986): total 962,519; activity rate of total
population 29.3% (participation rates: ages 16–64, 47.6%; female 35.6%;
unemployed 20.3%).

### Price and earnings indexes (1980 = 100)

| | 1981 | 1982 | 1983 | 1984 | 1985 | 1986 | 1987[2] |
|---|---|---|---|---|---|---|---|
| Consumer price index | 109.8 | 113.9 | 114.6 | 116.8 | 117.3 | 117.0 | 119.0 |
| Earnings index[3] | 109.2 | 115.4 | 120.1 | 124.9 | 128.9 | ... | ... |

*Household income and expenditure.* Average family size (1985) 4.1; income
per family U.S.$17,634; sources of income (1985): wages and salaries 54.6%,
transfers 29.8%, self-employment 6.5%, rent 6.5%, other 2.6%; expenditure
(1984): food and beverages 30.2%, transportation 16.2%, housing and energy 16.1%, clothing 9.0%, household furnishings 6.6%, health care 5.1%,
recreation 4.7%, education 2.2%, other 9.9%.
*Land use* (1984): forested 20.1%; meadows and pastures 37.6%; agricultural
and under permanent cultivation 14.8%; other 27.5%.

## Foreign trade

### Balance of trade (current prices)

| | 1979 | 1980 | 1981 | 1982 | 1983 | 1984 | 1985 |
|---|---|---|---|---|---|---|---|
| U.S.$'000,000 | −1,295 | −2,442 | −2,282 | +721 | −466 | −690 | +925 |
| % of total | 9.0% | 15.7% | 13.9% | 4.2% | 2.7% | 3.3% | 4.4% |

*Imports* (1985): U.S.$10,162,000,000 (1983–84; petroleum products 13.1%,
chemicals [all forms] 11.9%, food 11.9%, crude petroleum 9.2%, automobiles 5.9%, textiles [all forms] 5.6%). *Major import sources* (1985–86):
United States 60.6%; Japan 8.9%; Ecuador 3.5%; Venezuela 3.2%.
*Exports* (1985): U.S.$11,087,000,000 (1983–84; chemicals, crude petroleum,
and petroleum products 33.5%, metal products and machinery 23.1%, food
and alcoholic beverages 17.4%, textiles [all forms] 8.3%). *Major export
destinations* (1985–86): United States 87.3%; U.S. Virgin Islands 1.6%; Dominican Republic 1.6%.

## Transport and communications

*Transport.* Railroads (1985)[4]: length 59 mi, 96 km. Roads (1985): total length
5,813 mi, 9,355 km (paved 86%). Vehicles (1985): passenger cars 1,102,155;
trucks and buses 197,012. Merchant marine: n.a. Air transport (1985–86):
passenger arrivals 2,513,537, passenger departures 2,556,032; cargo loaded
and unloaded 128,171 metric tons; airports (1987) with scheduled flights 8.
*Communications.* Daily newspapers (1986): total number 5; total circulation
577,000; circulation per 1,000 population 175. Radio (1986): 2,000,000 receivers (1 per 1.6 persons). Television (1986): 820,000 receivers (1 per 4.0
persons). Telephones (1985): 772,006 (1 per 4.3 persons).

## Education and health

### Education (1985–86)

| | schools | teachers | students | student/ teacher ratio |
|---|---|---|---|---|
| Primary (age 5–12) | 1,542 | 18,359 | 427,582 | 23.3 |
| Secondary (age 13–18) | 395 | 13,612 | 334,661 | 24.6 |
| Voc., teacher tr. | 52 | ... | 149,191 | ... |
| Higher | 45 | 9,045 | 156,818 | 17.3 |

*Educational attainment* (1980). Percent of population age 25 and over
having: no formal schooling 8.0%; primary education 39.8%; secondary
33.8%; higher 18.4%. *Literacy* (1980): total population age 15 and over
literate 1,948,151 (89.1%); males literate 935,553 (89.7%); females literate
1,012,598 (88.5%).
*Health* (1984): physicians (1983) 7,133 (1 per 458 persons); hospital beds
12,493 (1 per 262 persons); infant mortality rate per 1,000 live births 15.7.
*Food:* daily per capita caloric intake, n.a.

## Military

*Total active duty personnel* (1986): 3,600 U.S. personnel.

[1]Unemployed. [2]March. [3]Hourly earnings in manufacturing. [4]Privately owned railway
for sugarcane transport only.

# Qatar

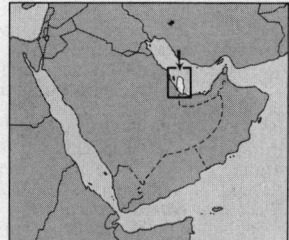

*Official name:* Dawlat Qaṭar (State of Qatar).
*Form of government:* constitutional monarchy; Islamic law is the basis of legislation in the state.
*Head of state and government:* Emir.
*Capital:* Doha.
*Official language:* Arabic.
*Official religion:* Islam.
*Monetary unit:* 1 riyal (QR) = 100 dirhams; valuation (Oct. 5, 1987) 1 U.S.$ = QR 3.63; 1 £ = QR 5.89.

### Area and population

| | area | | population[1] |
|---|---|---|---|
| Municipalities[1] | sq mi | sq km | 1986 census |
| Doha | ... | ... | 217,294 |
| al-Guwayrīyah | ... | ... | 1,629 |
| Jerīān al-Baṭnah | ... | ... | 2,727 |
| al-Jumaylīyah | ... | ... | 7,217 |
| al-Khawr | ... | ... | 8,993 |
| ar-Rayyān | ... | ... | 91,996 |
| ash-Shamāl | ... | ... | 4,380 |
| Umm aṣ-Ṣilāl | ... | ... | 11,161 |
| al-Wakrah | ... | ... | 23,682 |
| TOTAL | 4,400 | 11,400 | 369,079 |

## Demography

*Population* (1987): 414,000.
*Density* (1987): persons per sq mi 94.1, persons per sq km 36.3.
*Urban–rural* (1985): urban 88.0%; rural 12.0%.
*Sex distribution* (1986): male 67.15%; female 32.85%.
*Age breakdown* (1986): under 15, 27.8%; 15–29, 29.3%; 30–44, 32.3%; 45–59, 8.6%; 60 and over, 2.0%.
*Population projection:* (1990) 406,000; (2000) 514,000.
*Doubling time:* 29 years.
*Ethnic composition* (1983): South Asian 34%; Qatari 20%; other Arab 25%; Iranian 16%; other 5%.
*Religious affiliation* (1980): Muslim 92.4% (mostly Sunnī), Christian 5.9%; Hindu 1.1%; Bahā'ī 0.2%; other 0.4%.
*Major cities* (1983): Doha 190,000; Musay'īd 40,000.

## Vital statistics

*Birth rate* per 1,000 population (1986): 26.9 (world avg. 26.0); legitimate, n.a.; illegitimate, n.a.
*Death rate* per 1,000 population (1986): 2.1 (world avg. 9.9).
*Natural increase rate* per 1,000 population (1986): 24.8 (world avg. 16.1).
*Total fertility rate* (avg. births per childbearing woman; 1984): 4.6.
*Marriage rate* per 1,000 population (1986): 3.2.
*Divorce rate* per 1,000 population (1986): 0.8.
*Life expectancy* at birth (1980–85): male 66.9 years; female 71.6 years.
*Major causes of death* per 100,000 population (1986): diseases of the circulatory system 51.2; injury and poisoning 42.0; malignant neoplasms (cancers) 20.9; certain conditions originating in the perinatal period 14.4; diseases of the respiratory system 10.8; endocrine, nutritional, and metabolic diseases and immunity disorders 7.0; diseases of the digestive system 6.2; signs, symptoms, and ill-defined conditions 30.1.

## National economy

*Budget* (1987–88). Revenue: QR 6,745,000,000 (crude oil 85.0%). Expenditures: QR 12,217,000,000 (wages and salaries 34.3%; state capital development projects 22.6%, of which electricity and water 4.6%, housing and public buildings 4.4%, education 2.2%, communication and transport 2.1%, social services 0.9%, health 0.8%).
*Public debt:* none.
*Production* (metric tons except as noted). Agriculture, forestry, fishing (1986): tomatoes 5,799, melons 3,531, barley 1,847, eggplants 1,119, cabbage 1,014, cauliflower 678, cucumbers 660, lettuce 637, onions 494, radishes 231, turnips 230, wheat 130; livestock (number of live animals) 118,692 sheep, 68,000 goats, 18,637 camels, 7,713 cattle, 2,415 deer; roundwood, n.a.; fish catch (1984) 3,173. Mining and quarrying (1983): limestone 1,600,000; clay, sand, and gypsum are also mined for local use. Manufacturing (1986): urea 746,892; ammonia 658,328; steel reinforcing bars 493,000; ethylene 258,349; cement 165,895; clinker 151,243; sulfur 44,734. Construction (1986): residential 391,400 sq m; nonresidential 167,600 sq m. Energy production (consumption): electricity (kW-hr; 1985) 3,515,000,000 (3,515,000,000); coal, none (n.a.); crude petroleum (barrels; 1985) 107,145,000 (21,825,000); petroleum products (metric tons; 1985) 3,815,000 (530,000); natural gas (cu m; 1985) 4,303,000,000 (4,303,000,000).
*Tourism* (1986): receipts and expenditures, n.a.; total number of tourists staying in hotels 106,730.
*Population economically active* (1985): total 146,000; activity rate of total population 44.9% (participation rates: over age 15, 46.3%; female 8.6%; unemployed, n.a.).

### Price and earnings indexes (1981 = 100)

| | 1981 | 1982 | 1983 | 1984 | 1985 | 1986 |
|---|---|---|---|---|---|---|
| Consumer price index | 100.0 | 105.7 | 108.6 | 109.8 | 111.9 | 113.7 |
| Earnings index | ... | ... | ... | ... | ... | ... |

*Household income and expenditure.* Average family size (1984) 6.4; income per family: n.a.; sources of income: n.a.; expenditure (1982–83): food 39.1%, household durable goods 24.4%, recreation and personal effects 15.1%, housing 10.7%, clothing 4.4%, transportation and communication 3.7%, education 1.6%, energy and water 0.8%, health 0.2%.
*Gross national product* (at current market prices; 1985): U.S.$5,110,000,000 (U.S.$15,723 per capita).

### Structure of gross domestic product and labour force

| | 1986 | | 1984 | |
|---|---|---|---|---|
| | in value QR '000,000 | % of total value | labour force | % of labour force |
| Agriculture | 220 | 1.2 | 267 | 0.2 |
| Mining | 5,560 | 30.9 | 6,658 | 5.9 |
| Manufacturing | 1,781 | 9.9 | 12,763 | 11.3 |
| Construction | 1,247 | 6.9 | 28,347 | 25.1 |
| Public utilities | 203 | 1.1 | 6,998 | 6.2 |
| Transportation | 433 | 2.4 | 4,737 | 4.2 |
| Trade | 1,146 | 6.4 | 16,151 | 14.3 |
| Finance | 1,817 | 10.1 | 3,713 | 3.3 |
| Pub. admin., defense | } | | ... | ... |
| Services | 5,611 | 31.1 | 33,515 | 29.5 |
| Other | | | ... | ... |
| TOTAL | 18,018 | 100.0 | 113,149 | 100.0 |

*Land use* (1984): meadows and pastures 4.5%; agricultural and under permanent cultivation 0.3%; built-up, desert, and other 95.2%.

## Foreign trade[2]

### Balance of trade (current prices)

| | 1981 | 1982 | 1983 | 1984 | 1985 | 1986 |
|---|---|---|---|---|---|---|
| QR '000,000 | +15,757 | +9,138 | +7,419 | +12,698 | +8,440 | +2,710 |
| % of total | 61.4% | 41.9% | 43.9% | 63.0% | 50.4% | 25.3% |

*Imports* (1986): QR 4,000,000,000 (machinery and transport equipment 37.1%, manufactured goods 18.9%, food and live animals 17.2%, chemicals and chemical products 5.7%, beverages and tobacco 2.4%). *Major import sources:* Japan 17.0%; United Kingdom 16.5%; West Germany 9.6%; United States 6.0%; Italy 5.3%; France 5.1%; The Netherlands 2.6%; United Arab Emirates 2.6%.
*Exports* (1986): QR 6,710,000,000 (1985: crude petroleum 91.1%, liquefied gas and other nonpetroleum exports 8.9%). *Major export destinations* (1985): Japan 56.6%; France 8.9%; Singapore 3.8%; Italy 2.2%; Australia 2.0%; The Netherlands 2.0%; United Kingdom 1.1%; China 0.9%.

## Transport and communications

*Transport.* Railroads: none. Roads (1983): total length 671 mi, 1,080 km (paved, n.a.). Vehicles (1985) new passengers cars 10,001; trucks and buses 3,558. Merchant marine (1986): vessels (100 gross tons and over) 55; total deadweight tonnage 457,500. Air transport[3] (1986): passenger-mi 720,723,-000, passenger-km 1,159,892,000; short ton-mi cargo 21,485,000, metric ton-km cargo 31,368,000; airports (1987) with scheduled flights 1.
*Communications.* Daily newspapers (1986): total number 5; total circulation 51,500; circulation per 1,000 population 147. Radio (1986): total number of receivers 120,000 (1 per 2.9 persons). Television (1986): total number of receivers 150,000 (1 per 2.3 persons). Telephones (1985): 110,458 (1 per 2.9 persons).

## Education and health

### Education (1985–86)[4]

| | schools | teachers | students | student/ teacher ratio |
|---|---|---|---|---|
| Primary (age 6–11) | 90 | 2,764 | 31,844 | 11.5 |
| Secondary (age 12–17) | 68 | 2,250 | 19,506 | 8.7 |
| Vocational | 3 | 105 | 700 | 6.7 |
| Higher[5] | 1 | 431 | 5,057 | 11.7 |

*Educational attainment* (1981). Percent of population age 10 and over having: no formal education (including illiterates) 48.9%; primary 15.0%; preparatory (lower secondary) 11.7%; secondary 12.8%; postsecondary 11.6%. *Literacy* (1981): total population age 10 and over literate 96,565 (51.1%); males literate 65,151 (51.2%); females literate 31,414 (50.1%).
*Health* (1986): physicians 514 (1 per 718 persons); hospital beds 915 (1 per 403 persons); infant mortality rate per 1,000 live births (1985) 35.0.
*Food:* daily per capita caloric intake, n.a.

## Military

*Total active duty personnel* (1986): 6,000 (army 83.3%, navy 11.7%, air force 5.0%). *Military expenditure as percent of GNP* (1981): 13.1% (world 5.7%); per capita expenditure U.S.$3,896.

[1]Total population excludes 2,784 Qataris residing abroad. [2]Import figures are f.o.b. (free on board) in balance of trade and c.i.f. (cost, insurance, and freight) for commodities and trading partners. [3]Apportionment of one-fourth of international flights of Gulf Air. [4]Figures are for government-sponsored education; there were, however, 16,019 students and 911 teachers in private schools. [5]There were also 916 Qatari university students studying abroad.

# Réunion

*Official name:* Département de la Réunion (Department of Reunion).
*Political status:* overseas department (France) with two legislative houses (General Council [36]; Regional Council [45]).
*Chief of state:* President of France.
*Heads of government:* Commissioner of the Republic (for France); President of General Council (for Réunion); President of Regional Council (for Réunion).
*Capital:* Saint-Denis.
*Official language:* French.
*Official religion:* none.
*Monetary unit:* 1 Franc ( F ) = 100 centimes; valuation (Oct. 5, 1987) 1 U.S.$ = F 6.13; 1 £ = F 9.96.

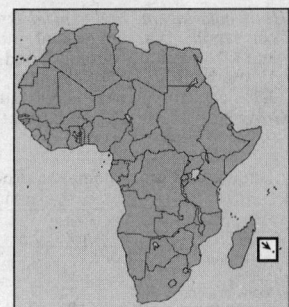

### Area and population

| Arrondissements | Capitals | area sq mi | area sq km | population 1982 census |
|---|---|---|---|---|
| Saint-Benoît | Saint-Benoît | 284 | 736 | 74,312 |
| Saint-Denis | Saint-Denis | 164 | 423 | 180,647 |
| Saint-Paul | Saint-Paul | 180 | 467 | 94,378 |
| Saint-Pierre | Saint-Pierre | 339 | 878 | 166,461 |
| TOTAL | | 969[1,2] | 2,510[1,2] | 515,798[2] |

## Demography

*Population* (1987): 565,000.
*Density* (1987): persons per sq mi 583.1, persons per sq km 225.1.
*Urban–rural* (1982): urban 52.8%; rural 47.2%.
*Sex distribution* (1982): male 49.05%; female 50.95%.
*Age breakdown* (1982): under 15, 35.6%; 15–29, 29.8%; 30–44, 17.2%; 45–59, 11.1%; 60–74, 4.6%; 75 and over, 1.7%.
*Population projection:* (1990) 595,000; (2000) 706,000.
*Doubling time:* 40 years.
*Ethnic composition* (1983): mixed race 63.5%; East Indian 28.2%; Chinese 2.2%; French 1.9%; East African 1.1%; other 3.1%.
*Religious affiliation* (1984): Roman Catholic 85.1%; other (includes Muslim, Bahá'í, Hindu, atheist, and other Christian) 14.9%.
*Major cities* (1982)[3]: Saint-Denis 126,323; Saint-Pierre 90,627; Saint-Joseph 31,141; Le Port 25,377.

## Vital statistics

*Birth rate* per 1,000 population (1986): 23.1 (world avg. 26.0); (1985) legitimate 52.9%; illegitimate 47.1%.
*Death rate* per 1,000 population (1986): 5.6 (world avg. 9.9).
*Natural increase rate* per 1,000 population (1986): 17.5 (world avg. 16.1).
*Total fertility rate* (avg. births per childbearing woman; 1984): 2.9.
*Marriage rate* per 1,000 population (1985): 5.8.
*Divorce rate* per 1,000 population (1985): 1.2.
*Life expectancy* at birth (1980–85): male 64.6 years; female 68.2 years.
*Major causes of death* per 100,000 population (1984): diseases of the circulatory system 174.0; accidents, poisoning, violence 71.1; malignant neoplasms (cancers) 46.4; diseases of the respiratory system 38.7; diseases of the digestive system 36.5; endocrine and metabolic disorders 22.4; ill-defined conditions 88.5.

## National economy

*Budget* (1987). Revenue: F 2,938,000,000 (grants from the French central government 58.9%, new loans 11.5%, taxes [including taxes on fuel, motor vehicles, and cigarettes] 9.3%, supplementary receipts from unreported sources 20.3%). Expenditures: F 2,938,000,000 (health and social services 46.1%, other administrative services 24.7%, nondepartmental investment programs 11.2%, departmental investment programs 10.3%).
*Public debt* (external, outstanding; 1984)[4]: U.S.$54,000,000.
*Tourism* (1986): number of tourist arrivals 93,476.
*Gross national product* (1984): U.S.$1,890,000,000 (U.S.$3,520 per capita).

### Structure of gross domestic product and labour force

| | 1983 in value F '000,000 | 1983 % of total value | 1982 labour force[5] | 1982 % of labour force |
|---|---|---|---|---|
| Agriculture | 841 | 6.1 | 17,390 | 14.7 |
| Mining | ... | ... | ... | ... |
| Manufacturing | 1,247 | 9.1 | 7,369 | 6.2 |
| Construction | 699 | 5.1 | 11,176 | 9.4 |
| Public utilities | 255 | 1.9 | 697 | 0.6 |
| Transportation and communication | 709 | 5.2 | 5,871 | 5.0 |
| Trade | 2,135 | 15.6 | 14,328 | 12.1 |
| Finance, real estate, insurance | 624 | 4.6 | 15,915 | 13.4 |
| Pub. admin., defense, and services | 6,797 | 49.7 | 44,576 | 37.6 |
| Other | 368 | 2.7 | 1,168 | 1.0 |
| TOTAL | 13,675 | 100.0 | 118,490 | 100.0 |

*Production* (metric tons except as noted). Agriculture, forestry, fishing (1986): sugarcane 2,113,000, corn (maize) 14,000[6], potatoes 10,824, bananas 4,520, cabbages 4,370, pineapples 3,876, mangoes 3,858, tomatoes 2,437, eggplant 1,687, tobacco 233, vanilla 58, geranium extract 24, khushkhus (vetiver) extract 12; livestock (number of live animals; 1985) 72,000 pigs, 43,000 goats, 20,000 cattle; roundwood (1985) 33,000 cu m; fish catch 1,705, of which lobster 335. Mining and quarrying (1985): gravel and sand for local use. Manufacturing (1986): sugar 243,500; cement 172,800[7]; molasses 65,300; rum 90,400 hectolitres. Construction: n.a. Energy production (consumption): electricity (kW-hr; 1986) 614,900,000 (547,000,000); coal, none (none); crude petroleum, none (none); petroleum products (metric tons; 1985) none (252,000); natural gas, none (none).
*Population economically active* (1982): total 175,595; activity rate of total population 34.0% (participation rates: ages 16–64, 57.5%; female 35.3%; unemployed [1986] 37.0%).

### Price and earnings indexes (December 1980 = 100)[8]

| | 1980 | 1981 | 1982 | 1983 | 1984 | 1985 | 1986[9] |
|---|---|---|---|---|---|---|---|
| Consumer price index | 100.0 | 113.9 | 124.3 | 134.4 | 144.0 | 152.9 | 154.9 |
| Hourly earnings index[10] | 100.0 | 114.3 | 129.8 | 140.1 | 145.8 | 155.2 | 156.6 |

*Household income and expenditure.* Average household size (1982) 4.2; income per household (1981) F 82,240 (U.S.$15,133); sources of income (1981): wages and salaries 66.4%, self-employment 17.4%, transfer payments 12.4%, other 3.8%; expenditure (1978)[11]: food and beverages 38.8%, clothing and footwear 11.5%, energy 7.4%, transportation 7.2%, housing 7.1%, household furnishings 6.2%, food away from home 2.7%, other 19.1%.
*Land use* (1984): forested 35.2%; meadows and pastures 4.0%; agricultural and under permanent cultivation 22.0%; other 38.8%.

## Foreign trade

### Balance of trade (current prices)

| | 1981 | 1982 | 1983 | 1984 | 1985 | 1986 |
|---|---|---|---|---|---|---|
| F '000,000 | −3,740 | −4,616 | −5,748 | −6,199 | −6,589 | −6,930 |
| % of total | 76.6% | 77.0% | 79.3% | 79.8% | 76.7% | 78.8% |

*Imports* (1986): F 7,860,800,000 (food and agricultural products 22.9%, electrical and nonelectrical machinery 14.1%, transport equipment 11.7%, chemical products 9.0%, mineral fuels 8.0%). *Major import sources:* France 67.0%; Bahrain 5.0%; Italy 3.0%; South Africa 3.0%; Japan 3.0%.
*Exports* (1986): F 930,400,000 (sugar 74.6%, rum 3.8%, lobster 3.0%, geranium extract 1.9%, vanilla 1.4%). *Major export destinations:* France 70.0%; United Kingdom 14.0%; Madagascar and Mayotte 3.0%.

## Transport and communications

*Transport.* Railroads, none. Roads (1985): total length 1,684 mi, 2,710 km (paved 81%). Vehicles (1985): passenger cars 138,081; trucks and buses 45,017. Merchant marine: n.a. Air transport (1986): passenger arrivals 235,426, passenger departures 234,946; cargo unloaded 7,709 metric tons, cargo loaded 3,339 metric tons; airports (1987) with scheduled flights 1.
*Communications.* Daily newspapers (1985): total number 3; total circulation 61,500; circulation per 1,000 population 113. Radio (1986): total number of receivers 123,000 (1 per 4.5 persons). Television (1986): total number of receivers 89,000 (1 per 6.2 persons). Telephones (1986): 90,015 (1 per 6.1 persons).

## Education and health

### Education (1984–85)

| | schools | teachers | students | student/ teacher ratio |
|---|---|---|---|---|
| Primary (age 6–11) | 508 | 5,087 | 113,330 | 22.3 |
| Secondary (age 12–18) Voc., teacher tr. } | 85 | 3,947 | 69,417 | 17.6 |
| Higher | 1 | 74 | 2,420 | 32.7 |

*Educational attainment* (1974). Percent of population age 20 and over having: no formal schooling 30.1%; primary education 30.2%; secondary 36.5%; higher 2.5%; not specified 0.7%. *Literacy* (1982): total population age 15 and over literate 268,300 (78.6%); males literate 126,500 (76.5%); females literate 141,800 (80.5%).
*Health* (1985): physicians (1986) 750 (1 per 734 persons); hospital beds 3,498 (1 per 156 persons); infant mortality rate per 1,000 live births 10.3.
*Food* (1981–83): daily per capita caloric intake 2,924 (vegetable products 82%, animal products 18%); (1983) 125% of FAO recommended minimum requirement.

## Military

*Total active duty personnel* (1986): 3,300 French troops[12].

---

[1]Includes 2 sq mi (6 sq km) not distributed by arrondissement. [2]Indian Ocean islets administered by France from Réunion are excluded from total. Areas of these islets, which have no permanent population, are: Îles Glorieuses 1.7 sq mi (4.3 sq km), Île Juan de Nova 1.9 sq mi (4.8 sq km), Île Tromelin 0.3 sq mi (0.8 sq km), Bassas da India 0.1 sq mi (0.2 sq km), Île Europa 7.8 sq mi (20.2 sq km). [3]Populations cited are for urban agglomerations. [4]Includes long-term private debt not guaranteed by the government. [5]Employed labour force. [6]1985. [7]1984. [8]Unless footnoted, indexes refer to December. [9]September. [10]Based on minimum-level wage in public administration. [11]Weights of consumer price index components. [12]Includes troops stationed on Mayotte.

# Romania

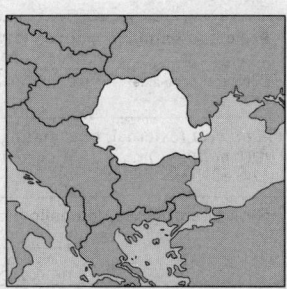

*Official name:* Republika Socialistă România (Socialist Republic of Romania).
*Form of government:* unitary single-party socialist republic with one legislative house (Grand National Assembly [369]).
*Chief of state:* President.
*Head of government:* Prime Minister.
*Capital:* Bucharest.
*Official language:* Romanian.
*Official religion:* none.
*Monetary unit:* 1 Romanian leu (plural lei) = 100 bani; valuation (Oct. 5, 1987) 1 U.S.$ = 10.05[1] lei; 1 £ = 16.32[1] lei.

### Area and population

| Districts | Capitals | area | | population |
|---|---|---|---|---|
| | | sq mi | sq km | 1985 estimate |
| Alba | Alba Iulia | 2,406 | 6,231 | 423,600 |
| Arad | Arad | 2,954 | 7,652 | 502,500 |
| Argeş | Piteşti | 2,626 | 6,801 | 666,300 |
| Bacău | Bacău | 2,551 | 6,606 | 710,200 |
| Bihor | Oradea | 2,909 | 7,535 | 653,400 |
| Bistriţa-Năsăud | Bistriţa | 2,048 | 5,305 | 316,000 |
| Botoşani | Botoşani | 1,917 | 4,965 | 463,300 |
| Brăila | Brăila | 1,824 | 4,724 | 398,300 |
| Braşov | Braşov | 2,066 | 5,351 | 682,400 |
| Buzău | Buzău | 2,344 | 6,072 | 520,000 |
| Caraş-Severin | Resita | 3,283 | 8,503 | 404,000 |
| Călăraşi | Calaraşi | 1,959 | 5,074 | 345,600 |
| Cluj | Cluj-Napoka | 2,568 | 6,650 | 741,800 |
| Constanţa | Constanţa | 2,724 | 7,055 | 698,700 |
| Covasna | Sfintu Gheorghe | 1,431 | 3,705 | 229,500 |
| Dîmboviţa | Tîrgovişte | 1,559 | 4,036 | 557,900 |
| Dolj | Craiova | 2,862 | 7,413 | 771,500 |
| Galaţi | Galaţi | 1,708 | 4,425 | 629,200 |
| Giurgiu | Giurgiu | 1,404 | 3,636 | 345,500 |
| Gorj | Tirgu Tiu | 2,178 | 5,641 | 373,600 |
| Harghita | Miercurea-Ciuc | 2,552 | 6,610 | 356,600 |
| Hunedoara | Deva | 2,709 | 7,016 | 554,400 |
| Ialomiţa | Slobozia | 1,718 | 4,449 | 302,400 |
| Iaşi | Iaşi | 2,112 | 5,469 | 784,100 |
| Maramureş | Baia Mare | 2,400 | 6,215 | 538,700 |
| Mehedinţi | Drobeta-Turnu-Severin | 1,892 | 4,900 | 328,600 |
| Mureş | Tirgu Mureş | 2,585 | 6,696 | 613,800 |
| Neamţ | Piatra Neamţ | 2,274 | 5,890 | 566,500 |
| Olt | Slatina | 2,126 | 5,507 | 531,000 |
| Prahova | Ploieşti | 1,812 | 4,694 | 861,500 |
| Sălaj | Zalău | 1,486 | 3,850 | 409,200 |
| Satu Mare | Satu Mare | 1,701 | 4,405 | 267,200 |
| Sibiu | Sibiu | 2,093 | 5,422 | 506,300 |
| Suceava | Suceava | 3,303 | 8,555 | 674,600 |
| Teleorman | Alexandria | 2,224 | 5,760 | 507,900 |
| Timiş | Timişoara | 3,356 | 8,692 | 716,400 |
| Tulcea | Tulcea | 3,255 | 8,430 | 267,100 |
| Vaslui | Vaslui | 2,045 | 5,297 | 455,300 |
| Vilcea | Rimnicu Vilcea | 2,203 | 5,705 | 424,700 |
| Vrancea | Focşani | 1,878 | 4,863 | 385,700 |
| **Muncipality** | | | | |
| Bucharest | Bucharest | 654 | 1,695 | 2,239,500 |
| TOTAL | | 91,699 | 237,500 | 22,724,800 |

## Demography

*Population* (1987): 22,913,000.
*Density* (1987): persons per sq mi 249.9, persons per sq km 96.5.
*Urban–rural* (1985): urban 50.8%; rural 49.2%.
*Sex distribution* (1985): male 49.35%; female 50.65%.
*Age breakdown* (1985): under 15, 24.6%; 15–29, 22.6%; 30–44, 19.6%; 45–59, 18.8%; 60–74, 10.7%; 75 and over, 3.7%.
*Population projection:* (1990) 23,994,000; (2000) 25,728,000.
*Ethnic composition* (1983): Romanian 88.4%; Hungarian 7.7%; other 3.9%.
*Religious affiliation* (1980): Romanian Orthodox 70.0%; Greek Orthodox 10.0%; Muslim 1.0%; atheist 7.0%; other 3.0%; none 9.0%.
*Major cities* (1985): Bucharest 1,975,800; Braşov 346,600; Constanţa 323,200; Timişoara 319,000; Iaşi 314,200.

## Vital statistics

*Birth rate* per 1,000 population (1985): 15.8 (world avg. 29.0).
*Death rate* per 1,000 population (1985): 10.9 (world avg. 11.0).
*Natural increase rate* per 1,000 population (1985): 4.9 (world avg. 18.0).
*Total fertility rate* (avg. births per childbearing woman; 1982): 2.4.
*Marriage rate* per 1,000 population (1985): 7.1.
*Divorce rate* per 1,000 population (1985): 1.4.
*Life expectancy* at birth (1982–84): male 67.0 years; female 72.6 years.
*Major causes of death* per 100,000 population (1984): diseases of the circulatory system 603.7; malignant neoplasms (cancers) 128.4.

## National economy

*Budget* (1985). Revenue: 300,125,600,000 lei (corporate tax 43.0%, turnover tax 28.3%, income tax 15.7%). Expenditures: 281,985,200,000 lei (national economy 61.2%, social services 32.1%, defense 4.3%).
*Tourism* (1984): receipts from visitors U.S.$230,000,000; expenditures by nationals abroad U.S.$85,000,000.
*Production* (metric tons except as noted). Agriculture (1985): corn (maize) 15,238,300, sugar beets 6,445,600, potatoes 6,280,000, wheat and rye 5,711,-

500; livestock (number of live animals; 1986) 18,609,000 sheep, 14,319,000 pigs, 7,077,000 cattle; roundwood 23,118,000 cu m; fish catch (1984) 253,-000. Mining and quarrying (1985): iron ore 2,287,000; bauxite 548,000; lead and zinc 72,000. Manufacturing (1985): crude steel 13,795,000; cement 12,238,000; rolled steel 9,900,000; fertilizers 3,097,000; plastics and synthetic rubber 627,900. Construction (1985): 8,591,000 sq m. Energy production (consumption): electricity (kW-hr; 1985) 71,819,000,000 (71,223,-000,000); coal (metric tons; 1985) 46,851,000 (46,851,000); crude petroleum (barrels, 1985) 80,449,000 (190,232,000); petroleum products (metric tons; 1985) 21,066,000 (12,700,000); natural gas (cu m; 1985) 38,904,000,000 (41,800,000,000).
*Public debt* (external, outstanding; 1985): U.S.$6,090,000,000.
*Gross national product* (at current market prices; 1986): U.S.$137,346,000,-000[2] (U.S.$6,109[2] per capita).

### Structure of net material product and labour force

| | 1985 | | | |
|---|---|---|---|---|
| | in value '000,000 lei | % of total value | labour force | % of labour force |
| Agriculture | 112,600 | 15.0 | 3,059,500 | 28.9 |
| Mining, manufacturing, and public utilities | 470,800 | 62.7 | 3,927,800 | 37.1 |
| Construction | 58,600 | 7.8 | 787,600 | 7.4 |
| Transp. and commun. | 45,000 | 6.0 | 720,600 | 6.8 |
| Trade | 3 | 3 | 617,400 | 5.8 |
| Pub. admin., defense | ... | ... | 56,800 | 0.5 |
| Services | ... | ... | 1,262,400 | 11.9 |
| Other | 63,800[3] | 8.5[3] | 154,000 | 1.5 |
| TOTAL | 750,800 | 100.0 | 10,586,100 | 100.0[4] |

*Population economically active* (1985): total 10,586,100; activity rate of total population 46.6% (participation rates: over age 15, 61.8%; female 45.9%; unemployed, n.a.).

### Price and earnings indexes (1980 = 100)

| | 1980 | 1981 | 1982 | 1983 | 1984 | 1985 | 1986 |
|---|---|---|---|---|---|---|---|
| Consumer price index | 100.0 | 102.2 | 119.5 | 125.7 | 127.1 | 126.6 | 126.5 |
| Monthly earnings index | 100.0 | 103.7 | 110.8 | 113.9 | 122.6 | 123.3 | 123.6 |

*Household income and expenditure.* Average household size (1984) 3.1; income per household 62,310 lei (U.S.$3,500); sources of income (1982): wages 62.6%, other 37.4%; expenditure (1980): food 62.7%, clothing 13.8%.
*Land use* (1985): forested 26.7%; meadows and pastures 18.5%; agricultural and under permanent cultivation 43.3%; other 11.5%.

## Foreign trade

### Balance of trade (current prices)

| | 1979 | 1980 | 1981 | 1982 | 1983 | 1984 | 1985 |
|---|---|---|---|---|---|---|---|
| '000,000 lei | −5,325 | −8,043 | +3,031 | +26,987 | +34,379 | +67,300 | +43,934 |
| % of total | 5.8% | 7.3% | 0.9% | 9.8% | 12.4% | 17.3% | 12.9% |

*Imports* (1985): 148,361,400,000 lei (mineral fuels 56.1%, machinery 22.2%, chemicals 6.8%). *Major import sources:* U.S.S.R. 22.4%; East Germany 5.8%; Poland 5.5%; Iraq 4.7%; China 3.7%; West Germany 3.4%.
*Exports* (1985): 192,295,200,000 lei (machinery and transport equipment 29.9%, fuels 28.3%, chemicals 10.7%). *Major export destinations:* U.S.S.R. 21.4%; Italy 7.5%; West Germany 7.5%; East Germany 4.2%; China 4.0%.

## Transport and communications

*Transport.* Railroads (1985): length 7,002 mi, 11,269 km; passenger-km 31,082,000,000; metric ton-km cargo 74,215,000,000. Roads (1986): length 72,799 km (paved 64%). Vehicles (1980): cars 250,000; trucks and buses 130,000. Merchant marine (1986): vessels (100 gross tons and over) 426; total deadweight tonnage 4,843,345. Air transport (1985): passenger-km 3,403,000,000; metric ton-km cargo 73,000,000; airports (1987) 15.
*Communications.* Daily newspapers (1985): total number 36; total circulation 3,077,700; circulation per 1,000 population 135. Radio (1986): 2,569,-665 (1 per 8.8 persons). Television (1986): 3,878,665 (1 per 5.9 persons). Telephones (1985): 1,962,681 (1 per 11 persons).

## Education and health

### Education (1985–86)

| | schools | teachers | students | student/ teacher ratio |
|---|---|---|---|---|
| Primary (age 6–13) | 14,076 | 147,147 | 3,030,666 | 20.6 |
| Secondary and vocational (age 14–17) | 1,734 | 50,210 | 1,514,745 | 30.2 |
| Higher | 44 | 12,961 | 159,738 | 12.3 |

*Educational attainment* (1977). Percent of population age 25 and over having: primary education 55.6%; secondary 39.8%; postsecondary 4.6%.
*Literacy* (1983) 95.8%.
*Health* (1986): physicians 40,050 (1 per 567 persons); hospital beds 212,953 (1 per 107 persons); infant mortality rate per 1,000 live births 25.6.
*Food* (1981–83): daily per capita caloric intake 3,341 (vegetable products 76%, animal products 24%); 126% of FAO recommended minimum.

## Military

*Total active duty personnel* (1986): 189,700 (army 79.1%, navy 4.0%, air force 16.9%). *Military expenditure as percent of GNP* (1984): 4.4% (world 5.9%); per capita expenditure U.S.$228.

[1]Noncommercial rate. [2]Constant 1986 dollars; Western estimate. [3]Includes trade and other material activities. [4]Detail does not add to total given because of rounding.

# Rwanda

*Official name:* Repubulika y'u Rwanda
(Rwanda); République Rwandaise
(French) (Republic of Rwanda).
*Form of government:* republic with
one legislative house (National
Development Council [70]).
*Head of state and government:*
President.
*Capital:* Kigali.
*Official languages:* Rwanda; French.
*Official religion:* none.
*Monetary unit:* 1 Rwanda franc (RF);
valuation (Oct. 5, 1987)
1 U.S.$ = RF 79.80; 1 £ = RF 129.59.

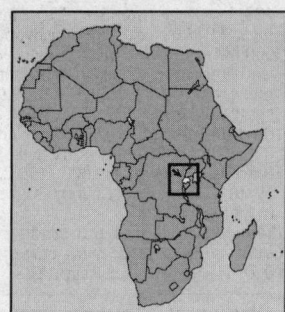

### Area and population

| Prefectures | Capitals | area sq mi | area sq km | population 1983 estimate |
|---|---|---|---|---|
| Butare | Butare | 707 | 1,830 | 682,500 |
| Byumba | Byumba | 1,925 | 4,987 | 623,600 |
| Cyangugu | Cyangugu | 859 | 2,226 | 343,500 |
| Gikongoro | Gikongoro | 846 | 2,192 | 401,900 |
| Gisenyi | Gisenyi | 925 | 2,395 | 566,400 |
| Gitarama | Gitarama | 865 | 2,241 | 706,200 |
| Kibungo | Kibungo | 1,596 | 4,134 | 420,200 |
| Kibuye | Kibuye | 510 | 1,320 | 500,600 |
| Kigali | Kigali | 1,255 | 3,251 | 835,400 |
| Ruhengeri | Ruhengeri | 680 | 1,762 | 581,200 |
| TOTAL | | 10,169[1] | 26,338 | 5,661,400[1] |

## Demography

*Population* (1987): 6,488,000.
*Density* (1987): persons per sq mi 638.0, persons per sq km 246.3.
*Urban–rural* (1985): urban 5.1%; rural 94.9%.
*Sex distribution* (1985): male 49.37%; female 50.63%.
*Age breakdown* (1985): under 15, 48.7%; 15–29, 25.8%; 30–44, 13.4%; 45–59, 7.9%; 60–74, 3.5%; 75 and over, 0.7%.
*Population projection:* (1990) 7,179,000; (2000) 10,123,000.
*Doubling time:* 22 years.
*Ethnic composition* (1985): Hutu 90%; Tutsi 9%; Twa 1%.
*Religious affiliation* (1985): Roman Catholic 56%; Protestant 12%; Muslim 9%; traditional belief systems 23%.
*Major cities* (1978): Kigali 156,700[2]; Butare 21,691; Ruhengeri 16,025; Gisenyi 12,436.

## Vital statistics

*Birth rate* per 1,000 population (1984): 52.0 (world avg. 29.0); legitimate, n.a.; illegitimate, n.a.
*Death rate* per 1,000 population (1984): 19.0 (world avg. 11.0).
*Natural increase rate* per 1,000 population (1984): 33.0 (world avg. 18.0).
*Total fertility rate* (avg. births per childbearing woman; 1984): 8.0.
*Marriage rate* per 1,000 population (1984): 2.5[3].
*Divorce rate* per 1,000 population: n.a.
*Life expectancy* at birth (1984): male 46.0 years; female 49.0 years.
*Major causes of death* per 100,000 population[4] (1984): complications of pregnancy, childbirth, and birth injury 192.4; infectious and parasitic diseases (including malaria, typhoid fever, trypanosomiasis [sleeping sickness], pneumonia, tuberculosis of the respiratory system, bacillary dysentery and amoebiasis, diphtheria, meningococcal infection, and acute poliomyelitis) 11.8; diseases of the digestive system 10.3; diseases of the nervous system 10.1; accidents, poisoning, and violence 5.2.

## National economy

*Budget* (1986). Revenue: RF 22,354,000,000 (1984; import and export duties 39.6%, taxes on goods and services 25.3%, income tax 18.1%, property taxes 1.9%). Expenditures: RF 22,354,000,000 (1984; education 28.0%, defense 14.7%, general administration 14.8%, economy and finance 13.3%, health 5.3%).
*Production* (metric tons except as noted). Agriculture, forestry, fishing (1985): plantains 2,100,000, roots and tubers 1,560,000 (of which sweet potatoes 900,000, cassava 350,000, potatoes 270,000), cereals 311,000 (of which sorghum 200,000, corn [maize] 100,000), coffee 26,000, tea 8,000, tobacco 3,000; livestock (number of live animals) 970,000 goats, 660,000 cattle, 330,000 sheep, 100,000 pigs; roundwood 5,461,000 cu m; fish catch 786. Mining and quarrying (1985): cassiterite (tin ore) 1,162; wolframite (tungsten ore) 310; gold 238 troy oz. Manufacturing (value added at producers' prices in RF '000,000; 1983): food, beverages, and tobacco products 20,800; textile industry 1,534; building materials 1,168; nonmetal minerals 1,099; wood products 667; industrial chemicals 510; printing and published materials 211. Construction (1981): residential 59,600 sq m; nonresidential 34,400 sq m. Energy production (consumption): electricity (kW-hr; 1985) 163,000,000 (174,000,000); coal, none (n.a.); petroleum products (metric tons; 1985) none (125,000); natural gas (cu m; 1985) 1,025,100 (1,025,100).
*Tourism:* receipts from visitors (1984) U.S.$4,100,000; expenditures by nationals abroad (1981) U.S.$12,000,000.
*Land use* (1984): forested 10.4%; meadows and pastures 17.6%; agricultural and under permanent cultivation 40.5%; other 31.5%.
*Population economically active* (1985): total 3,063,000; activity rate of total population 50.5% (participation rates: ages 15–64 89.4%; female 48.6%; unemployed, n.a.).

### Price and earnings indexes (1980 = 100)

| | 1980 | 1981 | 1982 | 1983 | 1984 | 1985 | 1986[5] |
|---|---|---|---|---|---|---|---|
| Consumer price index | 100.0 | 106.6 | 119.9 | 127.7 | 134.6 | 137.0 | 138.8 |
| Earnings index | ... | ... | ... | ... | ... | ... | ... |

*Public debt* (external, outstanding; 1984): U.S.$307,706,000.
*Gross national product* (at current market prices; 1985): U.S.$1,730,000,000 (U.S.$290 per capita).

### Structure of gross domestic product and labour force

| | 1984 in value RF '000,000 | 1984 % of total value | 1983 labour force | 1983 % of labour force |
|---|---|---|---|---|
| Agriculture | 68,692 | 43.2 | 2,394,000 | 88.1 |
| Mining | 572 | 0.3 | | |
| Manufacturing | 26,053 | 16.4 | | |
| Construction | 7,885 | 5.0 | | |
| Public utilities | 910 | 0.6 | | |
| Transportation and communication | 4,425 | 2.8 | 324,000 | 11.9 |
| Trade | 21,725 | 13.7 | | |
| Finance | 7,119 | 4.5 | | |
| Pub. admin., defense | 16,908 | 10.6 | | |
| Services | | | | |
| Other | 4,641 | 2.9 | | |
| TOTAL | 158,930 | 100.0 | 2,718,000 | 100.0 |

*Household income and expenditure:* Average household size (1983) 5.2; average annual income per household RF 122,870 (U.S.$1,300); sources of income (1977): self-employment (profits, interest, etc.) 71.0%, salaries and wages 16.5%, transfers 9.5%; expenditure: n.a.

## Foreign trade

### Balance of trade (current prices)

| | 1980 | 1981 | 1982 | 1983 | 1984 | 1985 |
|---|---|---|---|---|---|---|
| RF '000,000 | −15,740 | −15,810 | −16,650 | −17,980 | −11,580 | −7,840 |
| % of total | 53.5% | 50.0% | 49.7% | 55.2% | 27.1% | 22.9% |

*Imports* (1984): RF 27,121,815,200 (machinery and transport equipment 25.5%, of which transport equipment 12.7%, electrical equipment 4.2%; mineral fuels and lubricants 12.4%; textiles, clothing, and footwear 11.4%; food 9.6%; construction materials 9.3%). *Major import sources:* Belgium–Luxembourg 14.4%; Kenya 12.7%; Japan 10.1%; France 9.3%; China 8.2%; Iran 6.4%; West Germany 5.6%; United States 2.5%; The Netherlands 2.3%; Italy 2.0%.
*Exports* (1984): RF 15,542,600,000 (coffee 82.9%; tin ores and concentrates 6.2%; tea 3.7%). *Major export destinations:* Mombasa consignment 82.0%; Belgium–Luxembourg 7.6%; Kenya 3.2%; Italy 2.2%; West Germany 1.1%.

## Transport and communications

*Transport.* Railroads: none. Roads (1984): total length 7,500 mi, 12,070 km (paved 5.0%). Vehicles (1986): passenger cars 7,396; trucks and buses 10,357. Merchant marine: none. Air transport (1984): passenger arrivals 46,029, passenger departures 46,586; metric ton cargo loaded 15,204; metric ton cargo unloaded 12,003; airports (1987) with scheduled flights 2.
*Communications.* Daily newspapers (1984): total number 1; total circulation per 1,000 population, n.a. Radio (1986): total number of receivers 250,000 (1 per 25 persons). Television: none. Telephones (1984): 6,598 (1 per 894 persons).

## Education and health

### Education (1984–85)

| | schools | teachers | students | student/ teacher ratio |
|---|---|---|---|---|
| Primary (age 7–15) | 1,573 | 14,394 | 790,198 | 54.9 |
| Secondary (age 16–19)[6] | ... | 1,082 | 45,158[7] | ... |
| Voc., teacher tr. | ... | ... | 4,015[7] | ... |
| Higher | 3 | 186[8] | 1,570 | ... |

*Educational attainment* (1978). Percent of population age 25 and over having: no formal schooling 76.9%; some primary education 16.8%; complete primary education 4.0%; some secondary and complete secondary education 2.0%; some postsecondary vocational and higher education 0.3%.
*Literacy* (1980): total population age 15 and over literate 1,295,900 (49.4%); males literate 798,800 (62.2%); females literate 497,100 (37.2%).
*Health* (1984): physicians 177[9] (1 per 33,170 persons); hospital beds 9,046 (1 per 649 persons); infant mortality rate per 1,000 live births 128.0.
*Food* (1981–83): daily per capita caloric intake 2,207 (vegetable products 97%, animal products 3%); (1983) 98% of FAO recommended minimum requirement.

## Military

*Total active duty personnel* (1986): 5,200 (army 97.1%; navy, none; air force 2.9%). *Military expenditure as percent of GNP* (1984): 2.0% (world 5.9%); per capita expenditure U.S.$5.

[1]Detail does not add to total given because of rounding. [2]1981. [3]Excludes marriages not registered in court. [4]In hospitals only. [5]August. [6]1983–84. [7]Secondary includes agricultural and technical vocational students. [8]1982–83. [9]Excludes foreign physicians.

# Saint Christopher and Nevis

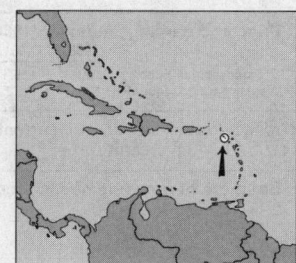

*Official name:* Federation of Saint Christopher and Nevis[1].
*Form of government:* constitutional monarchy with one legislative house (National Assembly [15][2]).
*Chief of state:* British Monarch represented by governor-general.
*Head of government:* Prime Minister.
*Capital:* Basseterre.
*Official language:* English.
*Official religion:* none.
*Monetary unit:* 1 Eastern Caribbean dollar (EC$) = 100 cents; valuation (Oct. 5, 1987) 1 U.S.$ = EC$2.70; 1 £ = EC$4.38.

### Area and population

| Islands Parishes | Capitals | area sq mi | sq km | population 1980 census |
|---|---|---|---|---|
| Saint Christopher | Basseterre | 67.2 | 174.1 | 33,881 |
| Christ Church Nichola Town | | 7.2 | 18.6 | 1,989 |
| Saint Anne Sandy Point | | 4.9 | 12.8 | 3,145 |
| Saint George Basseterre | | 11.1 | 28.7 | 14,283 |
| Saint John Capisterre | | 9.6 | 24.8 | 3,163 |
| Saint Mary Cayon | | 5.8 | 15.1 | 3,308 |
| Saint Paul Capisterre | | 5.3 | 13.8 | 2,080 |
| Saint Peter Basseterre | | 8.0 | 20.7 | 2,497 |
| Saint Thomas Middle Island | | 9.4 | 24.3 | 2,255 |
| Trinity Palmetto Point | | 6.0 | 15.4 | 1,161 |
| Nevis | Charlestown | 35.7 | 92.5 | 9,428 |
| Saint George Gingerland | | 7.1 | 18.5 | 2,295 |
| Saint James Windward | | 12.0 | 31.1 | 1,691 |
| Saint John Figtree | | 8.2 | 21.3 | 2,224 |
| Saint Paul Charlestown | | 1.4 | 3.5 | 1,243 |
| Saint Thomas Lowland | | 7.0 | 18.1 | 1,975 |
| TOTAL | | 102.9 | 266.6 | 43,309 |

## Demography

*Population* (1987): 46,500.
*Density* (1987): persons per sq mi 451.9, persons per sq km 174.4.
*Urban–rural* (1980): urban 35.8%; rural 64.2%.
*Sex distribution* (1980): male 48.12%; female 51.88%.
*Age breakdown* (1980): under 15, 37.2%; 15–29, 30.4%; 30–44, 9.5%; 45–59, 9.4%; 60–74, 10.0%; 75 and over, 3.5%.
*Population projection:* (1990) 48,000; (2000) 51,000.
*Doubling time:* 55 years.
*Ethnic composition* (1980): black 94.3%; mixed 3.3%; white 0.9%, other 1.3%.
*Religious affiliation* (1985): Protestant 76.4%, of which Anglican 36.2%, Methodist 32.3%; Roman Catholic 10.7%; other 12.9%.
*Major towns* (1985): Basseterre 18,500; Charlestown 1,700.

## Vital statistics

*Birth rate* per 1,000 population (1985): 22.3 (world avg. 29.0); (1980) legitimate 18.6%; illegitimate 81.4%.
*Death rate* per 1,000 population (1985): 9.6 (world avg. 11.0).
*Natural increase rate* per 1,000 population (1985): 12.7 (world avg. 18.0).
*Total fertility rate* (avg. births per childbearing woman; 1984): 3.2.
*Marriage rate* per 1,000 population (1977): 3.5.
*Divorce rate* per 1,000 population (1977): 0.2.
*Life expectancy* at birth (1983): male 62.0 years; female 67.0 years.
*Major causes of death* per 100,000 population (1984): diseases of the circulatory system 462.7, of which cerebrovascular disease 175.4; malignant neoplasms (cancers) 114.0; diseases of the respiratory system 41.7; infectious and parasitic diseases 35.1; ill-defined conditions 142.5.

## National economy

*Budget* (1984). Revenue: EC$55,600,000 (charges on electricity, telephones, ice, and cold storage 28.8%, import duties 19.4%, consumption taxes 18.0%, income taxes 7.7%, grants 6.7%). Expenditures: EC$70,400,000 (current expenditure 86.4%, development expenditure 13.6%).
*Public debt* (external, outstanding; 1985): U.S.$20,400,000.
*Production* (metric tons except as noted). Agriculture, forestry, fishing (1985): sugarcane 300,000, coconuts 2,000, fruits 2,000, vegetables 1,000, sweet potatoes 600[3], peanuts (groundnuts) 300[3], cotton 30[4]; livestock (number of live animals) 14,000 sheep, 10,000 pigs, 10,000 goats, 6,000 cattle; roundwood, n.a.; fish catch (1984) 1,100. Mining and quarrying: excavation of sand for local use. Manufacturing (value of production in EC$'000; 1982): sugar 29,291[5]; clothing 4,597[5,6]; assembly of electrical appliances 3,781[5]; footwear 1,851[5,6]; molasses 1,429[5]; aerated water 26,500 hectolitres; beer 10,460 hectolitres. Construction: n.a. Energy production (consumption): electricity (kW-hr; 1985) 35,000,000 (35,000,000); coal, none (none); crude petroleum, none (none); petroleum products (metric tons; 1985) none (17,-000); natural gas, none (none).
*Household income and expenditure.* Average household size (1980) 3.7; income per household: n.a.; sources of income: n.a.; expenditure (1978)[7]: food, beverages, and tobacco 55.6%, household supplies 9.4%, housing 7.6%, clothing and footwear 7.5%, fuel and light 6.6%, transportation 4.3%, other 9.0%.

*Gross national product* (at current market prices; 1985): U.S.$70,000,000 (U.S.$1,530 per capita).

### Structure of gross domestic product and labour force

| | 1984 in value EC$'000,000 | % of total value | labour force[8] | % of labour force |
|---|---|---|---|---|
| Agriculture | 25.6 | 17.2 | 4,380 | 29.6 |
| Mining | 0.3 | 0.2 | — | — |
| Manufacturing | 19.8 | 13.3 | 2,170 | 14.7 |
| Construction | 12.3 | 8.3 | 400 | 2.7 |
| Public utilities | 1.6 | 1.1 | 1,030 | 7.0 |
| Transportation and communication | 19.3 | 13.0 | 450 | 3.0 |
| Trade | 22.0 | 14.8 | 940 | 6.3 |
| Finance, real estate | 25.7[9] | 17.3[9] | 280 | 1.9 |
| Pub. admin., defense | 28.4 | 19.1 } | 4,700 | 31.7 |
| Services | [9] | [9] } | | |
| Other | −6.4[10] | −4.3[10] | 460 | 3.1 |
| TOTAL | 148.6 | 100.0 | 14,810 | 100.0 |

*Population economically active* (1980): total 17,125; activity rate of total population 39.5% (participation rates: ages 15–64, 69.5%; female 41.0%; unemployed[11]).

### Price and earnings indexes (1980 = 100)

| | 1978 | 1979 | 1980 | 1981 | 1982 | 1983 | 1984 |
|---|---|---|---|---|---|---|---|
| Consumer price index | 77.2 | 85.4 | 100.0 | 111.2 | 117.8 | 121.2 | ... |
| Annual earnings index[12] | 72.7 | 80.0 | 100.0 | 110.0 | 113.3 | 115.0 | 117.3 |

*Tourism:* receipts from visitors (1985) U.S.$31,000,000; expenditures by nationals abroad, n.a.
*Land use* (1984): forested 17.0%; meadows and pastures 3.0%; agricultural and under permanent cultivation 39.0%; other 41.0%.

## Foreign trade[13]

### Balance of trade (current prices)

| | 1980 | 1981 | 1982 | 1983 | 1984 | 1985 |
|---|---|---|---|---|---|---|
| EC$'000,000 | −55.9 | −63.3 | −67.2 | −86.3 | −87.5 | −75.3 |
| % of total | 30.0% | 32.6% | 39.8% | 45.2% | 45.4% | 38.3% |

*Imports* (1983): EC$138,700,000 (manufactured goods 22.7%; food 19.6%; machinery 19.0%; mineral fuels 9.8%; chemicals 8.0%). *Major import sources:* United States 35.0%; United Kingdom 15.4%; Trinidad and Tobago 10.0%; Canada 6.1%; Puerto Rico 5.9%.
*Exports* (1983): EC$52,400,000 (domestic exports 95.0%, of which sugar 55.2%, clothing 9.4%, footwear 8.8%, electronic goods 8.3%, beer and ale 5.5%; reexports 5.0%). *Major export destinations:* United States 47.9%; United Kingdom 18.5%; Trinidad and Tobago 13.4%.

## Transport and communications

*Transport.* Railroads (1985): length 36 mi, 58 km[14]. Roads (1985): total length 198 mi, 318 km (paved 44%). Vehicles (1985): passenger cars 3,540; trucks and buses 690. Merchant marine (1986): vessels (100 gross tons and over) 1; total deadweight tonnage 91. Air transport: passenger arrivals (1985) 66,590, passenger departures (1982) 52,410; cargo handled, n.a.; airports (1987) with scheduled flights 2.
*Communications.* Daily newspapers (1986): none. Radio (1986): total number of receivers 22,500 (1 per 2.0 persons). Television (1986): total number of receivers 7,000 (1 per 6.6 persons). Telephones (1985): 3,805 (1 per 12 persons).

## Education and health

### Education (1984–85)

| | schools | teachers | students | student/ teacher ratio |
|---|---|---|---|---|
| Primary (age 5–12) | 32 | 339 | 7,655 | 22.6 |
| Secondary (age 13–17) | 7 | 286 | 4,436 | 15.5 |
| Voc., teacher tr. | 2 | 29 | 240 | 8.3 |
| Higher | — | — | — | — |

*Educational attainment* (1980)[15]. Percent of population age 25 and over having: no formal schooling 1.1%; primary education 29.6%; secondary 67.2%; higher 2.1%. *Literacy* (1980): total population age 15 and over literate 24,887 (91.5%); males literate 11,533 (90.8%); females literate 13,354 (92.2%).
*Health* (1985): physicians 20 (1 per 2,300 persons); hospital beds 248 (1 per 185 persons); infant mortality rate per 1,000 live births 30.2.
*Food* (1981–83): daily per capita caloric intake 2,252 (vegetable products 73%, animal products 27%); (1983) 93% of FAO recommended minimum requirement.

## Military

*Total active duty personnel* (1986): the country maintains a police force and a small defense force of volunteers.

[1]Saint Kitts and Nevis and Federation of Saint Kitts and Nevis are both officially acceptable, variant, short- and long-form names of the country. [2]Includes 4 nonelective seats. [3]1984. [4]1986. [5]Export figure. [6]1981. [7]Weights of consumer price index components. [8]Employed persons only. [9]Finance, real estate includes Services. [10]Less imputed bank service charges. [11]1985: unemployment during tourist and sugarcane-harvesting seasons *c.* 10.0%; off-season *c.* 20.0%. [12]Average wages paid sugar industry employees. [13]Imports c.i.f. (cost, insurance, freight); exports f.o.b. (free on board), including reexports. [14]Light railway serving the sugar industry on Saint Christopher. [15]Includes Anguilla.

# Saint Lucia

*Official name:* Saint Lucia.
*Form of government:* constitutional
monarchy with two legislative houses
(Senate [11]; House of Assembly [17]).
*Chief of state:* British Monarch
represented by governor-general.
*Head of government:* Prime Minister.
*Capital:* Castries.
*Official language:* English.
*Official religion:* none.
*Monetary unit:* 1 Eastern Caribbean
Dollar (EC$) = 100 cents; valuation
(Oct. 5, 1987) 1 U.S.$ = EC$2.70;
1 £ = EC$4.38.

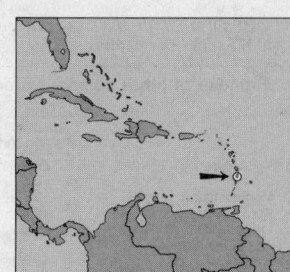

### Area and population

| Quarters | Capitals | area | | population 1986 estimate |
|---|---|---|---|---|
| | | sq mi | sq km | |
| Anse-la-Raye | Anse-la-Raye | } 18.1 | 46.9 | 6,111 |
| Canaries | Canaries | | | 2,566 |
| Castries | Castries | 30.7 | 79.5 | 52,868 |
| Choiseul | Choiseul | 12.1 | 31.3 | 7,995 |
| Dennery | Dennery | 26.9 | 69.7 | 11,874 |
| Gros Islet | Gros Islet | 39.2 | 101.5 | 12,503 |
| Laborie | Laborie | 14.6 | 37.8 | 8,483 |
| Micoud | Micoud | 30.9 | 80.0 | 14,678 |
| Soufrière | Soufrière | 19.5 | 50.5 | 8,972 |
| Vieux Fort | Vieux Fort | 16.9 | 43.8 | 13,479 |
| TOTAL | | 238[1] | 616[1] | 139,529 |

## Demography

*Population* (1987): 143,000.
*Density* (1987): persons per sq mi 600.8, persons per sq km 232.1.
*Urban–rural* (1982): urban 52.1%; rural 47.9%.
*Sex distribution* (1985): male 48.06%; female 51.94%.
*Age breakdown* (1985): under 15, 43.5%; 15–29, 27.4%; 30–44, 12.2%; 45–59,
8.7%; 60–74, 6.0%; 75 and over, 2.2%.
*Population projection:* (1990) 152,000; (2000) 186,000.
*Doubling time:* 25 years.
*Ethnic composition* (1982): black 90.3%; mixed 5.5%; East Indian 3.2%;
white 0.8%; other 0.2%.
*Religious affiliation* (1980): Roman Catholic 86.3%; Protestant 11.3%, of
which Anglican 3.0%, Seventh-day Adventist 2.5%; Rastafarian 2.2%; other
0.2%.
*Major cities* (1986): Castries 52,868; Vieux Fort (1984) 12,951.

## Vital statistics

*Birth rate* per 1,000 population (1985): 30.6 (world avg. 29.0); legitimate
15.9%; illegitimate 84.1%.
*Death rate* per 1,000 population (1985): 5.9 (world avg. 11.0).
*Natural increase rate* per 1,000 population (1985): 24.7 (world avg. 18.0).
*Total fertility rate* (avg. births per childbearing woman; 1985): 3.9.
*Marriage rate* per 1,000 population (1985): 3.1.
*Divorce rate* per 1,000 population (1985): 0.3.
*Life expectancy* at birth (1985): male 68.6 years; female 75.5 years.
*Major causes of death* per 100,000 population (1984): ischemic heart disease
92.5; malignant neoplasms (cancers) 73.8; cerebrovascular diseases 68.6;
diseases of the respiratory system 35.1; conditions originating in the peri-
natal period 35.1; diabetes mellitus 20.9; ill-defined conditions 56.7.

## National economy

*Budget* (1984–85). Revenue: EC$137,200,000 (tax revenue 78.9%, of which
income taxes 26.1%, import duties 16.9%, consumption taxes 12.6%, stamp
duties 10.6%; grants 13.1%). Expenditures: EC$147,300,000 (current expen-
diture 83.2%, of which interest payments 4.8%; capital expenditure 16.8%).
*Public debt* (external, outstanding; 1983[2]): U.S.$34,000,000.
*Production* (metric tons except as noted). Agriculture, forestry, fishing (1985):
bananas 80,000, mangoes 45,000, coconuts 31,000, yams 4,000, plantains
2,000, sweet potatoes 1,000, citrus fruits 784[3], vegetables (mostly tomatoes
and cabbages) 710[3], ginger 115[3], cocoa beans 54; livestock (number of live
animals) 15,000 sheep, 12,000 cattle, 12,000 pigs, 11,000 goats; roundwood,
n.a.; fish catch 1,044. Mining and quarrying: excavation of sand for local
construction and pumice. Manufacturing (value of production in EC$'000;
1985): cardboard boxes 22,000[3]; clothing 12,639; alcoholic beverages and
tobacco 9,586; nonalcoholic beverages 7,438; raw coconut oil 6,581; refined
coconut oil 4,117; other manufactures include soap, electrical components,
scuba-diving suits, and wooden toys. Construction (buildings authorized;
1985): residential 39,000 sq m; nonresidential 19,300 sq m. Energy production (consumption): electricity (kW-hr; 1985) 59,300,000 (49,900,000); coal,
none (none); crude petroleum, none (none); petroleum products (metric
tons; 1985) none (40,000); natural gas, none (none).
*Household income and expenditure.* Average household size (1980) 4.6;
income per household: n.a.; sources of income: n.a.; expenditure (1984)[4]:
food 46.8%, housing 13.5%, clothing and footwear 6.5%, transportation
and communication 6.3%, household furnishings 5.8%, fuel and light 4.5%,
recreation and entertainment 3.2%, beverages and tobacco 2.8%, health
care 2.3%, other 8.3%.
*Population economically active* (1980): total 49,451; activity rate of total
population 41.1% (participation rates: ages 15–64, n.a.; female 55.2%; unemployed [1984] 22.0%).

### Price and earnings indexes (1980 = 100)

| | 1980 | 1981 | 1982 | 1983 | 1984 | 1985 | 1986[5] |
|---|---|---|---|---|---|---|---|
| Consumer price index | 100.0 | 115.1 | 120.4 | 122.2 | 123.7 | 125.3 | 127.7 |
| Weekly earnings index[6] | 100.0 | ... | 115.0 | ... | ... | ... | ... |

*Gross national product* (at current market prices; 1985): U.S.$170,000,000
(U.S.$1,240 per capita).

### Structure of gross domestic product and labour force

| | 1985 | | 1983[7] | |
|---|---|---|---|---|
| | in value EC$'000,000 | % of total value | labour force | % of labour force |
| Agriculture | 58.3 | 15.0 | | |
| Mining | 2.3 | 0.6 } | 13,000 | 29.7 |
| Manufacturing | 33.0 | 8.5 | 2,600 | 5.9 |
| Construction | 27.0 | 6.9 | 1,500 | 3.4 |
| Public utilities | 15.0 | 3.9 | | |
| Transportation and communication | 40.4 | 10.4 | | |
| Trade | 88.4 | 22.7 } | 15,800 | 36.1 |
| Finance | 43.8 | 11.3 | | |
| Pub. admin., defense | 84.0 | 21.6 | | |
| Services | 19.0 | 4.9 | | |
| Other | −22.4[8] | −5.8[8] | 10,900[9] | 24.9[9] |
| TOTAL | 388.8 | 100.0 | 43,800 | 100.0 |

*Tourism* (1985): receipts from visitors U.S.$69,000,000; expenditures by na-
tionals abroad U.S.$44,000,000.
*Land use* (1984): forested 13.0%; meadows and pastures 5.0%; agricultural
and under permanent cultivation 28.0%; other 54.0%.

## Foreign trade[10]

### Balance of trade (current prices)

| | 1981 | 1982 | 1983 | 1984 | 1985 | 1986 |
|---|---|---|---|---|---|---|
| EC$'000,000 | −237.6 | −206.0 | −160.1 | −190.9 | −188.0 | −206.8 |
| % of total | 51.6% | 47.8% | 38.4% | 42.5% | 40.2% | 32.8% |

*Imports* (1985): EC$337,500,000 (food 21.7%, of which cereal and cereal
preparations 5.8%, meat and meat preparations 5.7%; machinery and transport equipment 18.4%, of which road vehicles 5.7%; chemicals and chemical products 11.7%; crude petroleum and petroleum products 9.4%; paper
and paper products 5.1%; clothing 4.5%; metal manufactures 4.0%). *Major
import sources:* United States 30.7%; United Kingdom 15.6%; Trinidad and
Tobago 9.3%; Japan 6.2%; France 3.9%.
*Exports* (1985): EC$140,500,000[11] (bananas 58.0%; cardboard boxes 9.6%;
clothing 8.1%; electrical components and parts 2.7%; refined coconut oil
2.2%; beer and ale 2.2%). *Major export destinations:* United Kingdom
64.1%; United States 13.3%; Barbados 5.1%; Trinidad and Tobago 2.4%.

## Transport and communications

*Transport.* Railroads: none. Roads (1984): total length 426 mi, 686 km (paved
65%). Vehicles (1984): passenger cars 7,049; trucks and buses 2,084. Merchant marine (1986): vessels (100 gross tons and over) 8; total deadweight
tonnage 3,415. Air transport (1985): passenger arrivals 136,063, passenger
departures 134,236; cargo unloaded 1,301 metric tons, cargo loaded 2,501
metric tons; airports (1987) with scheduled flights 2.
*Communications.* Daily newspapers: none. Radio (1986): total number of
receivers 92,500 (1 per 1.5 persons). Television (1985): total number of
receivers 5,000 (1 per 27 persons). Telephones (1985): 11,965 (1 per 11
persons).

## Education and health

### Education (1986–87)

| | schools | teachers | students | student/ teacher ratio |
|---|---|---|---|---|
| Primary (age 5–11) | 83 | 1,103 | 32,944 | 29.9 |
| Secondary (age 12–16) | 12 | 298 | 5,691 | 19.1 |
| Voc., teacher tr. | 4 | 39 | 817 | 20.9 |
| Higher | 1 | 16 | 123 | 7.7 |

*Educational attainment* (1980). Percent of population age 25 and over having: no formal schooling 17.5%; primary education 74.4%; secondary 6.8%;
higher 1.3%. *Literacy* (1984): total population age 15 and over literate
44,484 (59.7%).
*Health* (1984): physicians 58 (1 per 2,311 persons); hospital beds 522 (1 per
257 persons); infant mortality rate per 1,000 live births (1983–85 avg.) 21.7.
*Food* (1981–83): daily per capita caloric intake 2,387 (vegetable products 78%,
animal products 22%); 98% of FAO recommended minimum requirement.

## Military

*Total active duty personnel* (1985):[12].

---

[1]Rounded total includes the uninhabited 29.0 sq-mi (75-sq-km) Central Forest Preserve. [2]Includes external long-term private debt not guaranteed by the government.
[3]1982. [4]Weights of consumer price index components. [5]Average of second and third
quarters only. [6]Wages in nonagricultural activities excluding mining. [7]Wage earners
and self-employed. [8]Less imputed bank charges. [9]Unemployed. [10]Imports c.i.f. (cost,
insurance, freight); exports f.o.b. (free on board). Reexports included in balance of
trade and commodities, excluded in trading partners. [11]Reexports constitute 8.8% of
all exports. [12]The 500-member police force includes a specially trained paramilitary
unit.

# Saint Vincent and the Grenadines

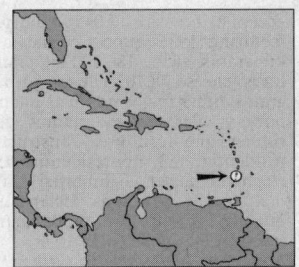

*Official name:* Saint Vincent and the Grenadines.
*Form of government:* constitutional monarchy with one legislative house (House of Assembly [19][1]).
*Chief of state:* British Monarch represented by governor-general.
*Head of government:* Prime Minister.
*Capital:* Kingstown.
*Official language:* English.
*Official religion:* none.
*Monetary unit:* 1 Eastern Caribbean Dollar (EC$) = 100 cents; valuation (Oct. 5, 1987) 1 U.S.$ = EC$2.70; 1 £ = EC$4.38.

## Area and population

| Census divisions[2] | area sq mi | area sq km | population 1985 estimate |
|---|---|---|---|
| Island of Saint Vincent | | | |
| Barrouallie | 14.2 | 36.8 | 5,187 |
| Bridgetown | 7.2 | 18.6 | 7,515 |
| Calliaqua | 11.8 | 30.6 | 19,379 |
| Chateaubelair | 30.0 | 77.7 | 6,786 |
| Colonarie | 13.4 | 34.7 | 8,015 |
| Georgetown | 22.2 | 57.5 | 7,221 |
| Kingstown (city) | 1.9 | 4.9 | 18,378 |
| Kingstown (suburbs) | 6.4 | 16.6 | 9,570 |
| Layou | 11.1 | 28.7 | 6,123 |
| Marriaqua | 9.4 | 24.3 | 9,341 |
| Sandy Bay | 5.3 | 13.7 | 3,186 |
| Saint Vincent Grenadines | | | |
| Northern Grenadines | 9.0 | 23.3 | 5,263 |
| Southern Grenadines | 7.5 | 19.4 | 2,784 |
| TOTAL | 150.3[3] | 389.3[3] | 108,748 |

## Demography

*Population* (1987): 112,000.
*Density* (1987): persons per sq mi 745.2, persons per sq km 287.7.
*Urban–rural*[4] (1985): urban 25.7%; rural 74.3%.
*Sex distribution* (1984): male 48.45%; female 51.55%.
*Age breakdown* (1985): under 15, 37.4%; 15–29, 32.7%; 30–44, 14.9%; 45–59, 7.5%; 60–74, 5.6%; 75 and over, 1.9%.
*Population projection*: (1990) 116,000; (2000) 132,000.
*Doubling time*: 36 years.
*Ethnic composition* (1983): black 74.0%; mulatto 19.0%; white 3.0%; Amerindian/black 2.0%; East Indian 2.0%.
*Religious affiliation* (1980): Protestant 77.3%, of which Anglican 36.0%, Methodist 20.4%, Seventh-day Adventist 4.1%, Plymouth Brethren 3.9%; Roman Catholic 19.3%; other 3.4%.
*Major city* (1984): Kingstown 18,378.

## Vital statistics

*Birth rate* per 1,000 population (1984): 26.2 (world avg. 29.0); legitimate, n.a.; illegitimate, n.a.
*Death rate* per 1,000 population (1984): 6.5 (world avg. 11.0).
*Natural increase rate* per 1,000 population (1984): 19.7 (world avg. 18.0).
*Total fertility rate* (avg. births per childbearing woman; 1984): 3.2.
*Marriage rate* per 1,000 population (1984): 3.6.
*Divorce rate* per 1,000 population (1980): 0.2.
*Life expectancy* at birth (1980–85): male 67.5 years; female 71.4 years.
*Major causes of death* per 100,000 population (1984): diseases of the circulatory system 192.3, of which hypertensive disease 90.6; malignant neoplasms (cancers) 78.6; endocrine and metabolic disorders 37.0; homicide and other violence 36.0; infectious and parasitic diseases 28.7.

## National economy

*Budget* (1985). Revenue: EC$96,900,000 (tax revenue 81.2%, of which import duties 37.5%, taxes on income, profits, and capital gains 23.0%, taxes on goods and services 10.0%; nontax revenue 18.8%). Expenditures: EC$91,600,000 (education 17.8%; general public services 17.7%; economic services 17.7%; health 13.4%; police and defense 6.4%).
*Public debt* (external, outstanding; 1986): U.S.$29,000,000.
*Tourism:* receipts from visitors (1986) U.S.$27,000,000; expenditures by nationals abroad (1983) U.S.$8,000,000.
*Production* (metric tons except as noted). Agriculture, forestry, fishing (1985): bananas 37,600[5], roots and tubers 25,000, coconuts 20,000, plantains 2,000, mangoes 2,000, arrowroot 314[5], ginger 122[6], tobacco 41[6], soursops, guavas, and papaws are other important fruits; livestock (number of live animals) 13,000 sheep, 8,000 cattle, 7,000 pigs; roundwood, n.a.; fish catch 547. Mining and quarrying: sand and gravel for local use. Manufacturing (1984): copra 2,000; cigarettes 20,000,000 units; rum 3,068 hectolitres; other products include flour, carbonated drinks, beer, packing boxes for bananas, boats, and electronic components. Construction (1984): 42,765 sq m. Energy production (consumption): electricity (kW-hr; 1985) 30,000,000 (30,000,000); coal, none (none); crude petroleum, none (none); petroleum products (metric tons; 1985) none (13,000); natural gas, none (none).
*Gross national product* (at current market prices; 1985): U.S.$100,000,000 (U.S.$910 per capita).

## Structure of gross domestic product and labour force

| | 1986[7] in value EC$'000,000 | 1986[7] % of total value | 1970 labour force | 1970 % of labour force |
|---|---|---|---|---|
| Agriculture | 22.0 | 17.1 | 6,882 | 29.0 |
| Mining | 0.4 | 0.3 | 48 | 0.2 |
| Manufacturing | 11.8 | 9.2 | 1,851 | 7.8 |
| Construction | 13.7 | 10.6 | 2,871 | 12.1 |
| Public utilities | 4.5 | 3.5 | 214 | 0.9 |
| Transportation and communication | 27.0 | 21.0 | 1,068 | 4.5 |
| Trade | 19.8 | 15.4 | 2,871 | 12.1 |
| Finance | 14.0[8] | 10.9[8] | } 7,190 | } 30.3 |
| Pub. admin., defense | 19.5 | 15.2 | | |
| Services | 8 | 8 | | |
| Other | −4.1[9] | −3.2[9] | 736 | 3.1 |
| TOTAL | 128.6 | 100.0 | 23,731 | 100.0 |

*Population economically active* (1980)[10]: total 32,617; activity rate of total population 31.7% (participation rates: ages 14–64, 57.2%; female 34.5%; unemployed [1986] 30.0%).

## Price and earnings indexes (1980 = 100)

| | 1980 | 1981 | 1982 | 1983 | 1984 | 1985 | 1986 |
|---|---|---|---|---|---|---|---|
| Consumer price index | 100.0 | 112.7 | 120.9 | 127.5 | 130.9 | 133.6 | 135.11[11] |
| Weekly earnings index[12] | 100.0 | 117.5 | 143.0 | 150.1 | ... | ... | ... |

*Household income and expenditure.* Average household size (1978) 5.0; income per household: n.a.; sources of income: n.a.; expenditure (1981)[13]: food, beverages, and tobacco 62.6%, clothing 7.7%, household furnishings 6.6%, housing 6.3%, energy 6.2%, other 10.6%.
*Land use* (1984): forested 41.0%; meadows and pastures 6.0%; agricultural and under permanent cultivation 50.0%; other 3.0%.

## Foreign trade[14]

### Balance of trade (current prices)

| | 1981 | 1982 | 1983 | 1984 | 1985 | 1986 |
|---|---|---|---|---|---|---|
| EC$'000,000 | −91.2 | −77.1 | −79.1 | −62.2 | −43.1 | −63.2 |
| % of total | 40.9% | 30.6% | 26.3% | 17.7% | 11.2% | 15.5% |

*Imports* (1986): EC$235,600,000 (1984; food 24.6%; machinery and transport equipment 18.2%; chemicals and chemical products 10.8%; mineral fuels 8.6%; miscellaneous manufactured goods 31.0%). *Major import sources* (1984): United States 37.0%; United Kingdom 14.8%; Trinidad and Tobago 11.4%; Japan 5.4%; Canada 3.1%.
*Exports* (1986): EC$172,400,000 (eddoes, dasheens, yams, plantains, and tanias 38.8%; bananas 28.3%; flour 11.3%). *Major export destinations* (1984): Trinidad and Tobago 45.4%; United Kingdom 24.1%; United States 10.6%; Saint Lucia 5.3%; Antigua and Barbuda 3.3%.

## Transport and communications

*Transport.* Railroads: none. Roads (1985): total length 463 mi, 745 km (paved 58%). Vehicles (1984): passenger cars 4,460; trucks and buses 2,040. Merchant marine (1986): vessels (100 gross tons and over) 103; total deadweight tonnage 833,209. Air transport (1984): passenger arrivals 72,970, passenger departures 72,769; airports (1987) with scheduled flights 4.
*Communications.* Daily newspapers: none. Radio (1986): total number of receivers 66,000 (1 per 1.7 persons). Television (1986): total number of receivers 10,000 (1 per 11 persons). Telephones (1985): 8,520 (1 per 13 persons).

## Education and health

### Education (1982–83)

| | schools | teachers | students | student/ teacher ratio |
|---|---|---|---|---|
| Primary (age 5–15) | 62 | 1,251 | 24,551 | 19.6 |
| Secondary (age 11–19) | 19 | 292 | 5,170 | 17.7 |
| Voc., teacher tr. | 5 | 39 | 275 | 7.1 |
| Higher | 1 | 19 | 105 | 5.5 |

*Educational attainment* (1980). Percent of population age 25 and over having: no formal schooling 2.4%; primary education 88.0%; secondary 8.2%; higher 1.4%. *Literacy* (1983): total population age 15 and over literate 54,000 (85.0%).
*Health:* physicians (1986) 25 (1 per 4,400 persons); hospital beds (1984) 350 (1 per 309 persons); infant mortality rate per 1,000 live births (1982–84 avg.) 35.1.
*Food* (1981–83): daily per capita caloric intake 2,353 (vegetable products 86%, animal products 14%); (1983) 97% of FAO recommended minimum requirement.

## Military

*Total active duty personnel* (1986): part of the 489-member police force is being trained for defense purposes. *Military expenditure as percent of GNP:* n.a.

[1]Includes six nonelective seats. [2]For statistical purposes only; no civil administrative subdivisions exist. [3]Includes 0.9 sq mi (2.5 sq km) not distributed by census division. [4]Urban defined as Kingstown and suburbs. [5]1986. [6]1984. [7]At prices of 1977; GDP at current prices is EC$255,500,000. [8]Finance includes services. [9]Less imputed service charges. [10]Based on projection of 1970 census except for unemployment rate. [11]Average of second and third quarters. [12]Wages in selected manufacturing and service occupations. [13]Weights of consumer price index components. [14]Imports c.i.f; exports f.o.b.

# San Marino

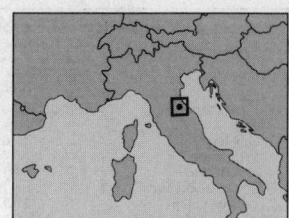

*Official name:* Serenissima Repubblica di San Marino (Most Serene Republic of San Marino).
*Form of government:* unitary multiparty republic with one legislative house (Great and General Council [60]).
*Head of state and government:* Captains-Regent (2).
*Capital:* San Marino.
*Official language:* Italian.
*Official religion:* none.
*Monetary unit:* 1 Italian lira (Lit; plural lire) = 100 centesimi; valuation (Oct. 5, 1987) 1 U.S.$ = Lit 1,329; 1 £ = Lit 2,158.

### Area and population

| Castles | Capitals | area sq mi | area sq km | population 1987 estimate[1] |
|---|---|---|---|---|
| Acquaviva | Acquaviva | 1.88 | 4.86 | 1,148 |
| Borgo Maggiore | Borgo | 3.48 | 9.01 | 4,421 |
| Citta | San Marino | 2.74 | 7.09 | 4,179 |
| Chiesanuova | Chiesanuova | 2.11 | 5.46 | 724 |
| Domagnano | Domagnano | 2.56 | 6.62 | 1,855 |
| Faetano | Faetano | 2.99 | 7.75 | 738 |
| Fiorentino | Fiorentino | 2.53 | 6.56 | 1,478 |
| Montegiardino | Montegiardino | 1.28 | 3.31 | 577 |
| Serravalle/Dogano | Serravalle | 4.07 | 10.53 | 6,995 |
| TOTAL | | 23.63[2] | 61.19 | 22,115 |

## Demography

*Population* (1987): 22,100.
*Density* (1987): persons per sq mi 935.3, persons per sq km 361.2.
*Urban–rural* (1987): urban 90.1%; rural 9.9%.
*Sex distribution* (1987): male 50.00%; female 50.00%.
*Age breakdown* (1987): under 15, 18.2%; 15–29, 25.3%; 30–44, 21.4%; 45–59, 17.4%; 60–74, 13.0%; 75 and over, 4.7%.
*Population projection:* (1990) 22,000; (2000) 23,000.
*Doubling time:* not applicable; natural population growth is negligible, averaging only 0.2% during 1982–86.
*Ethnic composition* (1987): Sammarinesi 87.1%; Italian 12.4%; other 0.4%[2].
*Religious affiliation* (1980): Roman Catholic 95.2%; no religion 3.0%; other 1.8%.
*Major cities* (1986): Serravalle/Dogano 4,655; San Marino 2,397; Borgo Maggiore 2,074; Murata 1,334; Domagnano 903.

## Vital statistics

*Birth rate* per 1,000 population (1986): 8.1 (world avg. 26.0); (1984) legitimate 94.6%; illegitimate 5.4%.
*Death rate* per 1,000 population (1986): 7.7 (world avg. 9.9).
*Natural increase rate* per 1,000 population (1986): 0.4 (world avg. 16.1).
*Total fertility rate* (avg. births per childbearing woman; 1984): 1.3.
*Marriage rate* per 1,000 population (1986): 6.8.
*Divorce rate* per 1,000 population (1986): 0.4.
*Life expectancy* at birth (1980–85): male 70.7 years; female 76.2 years.
*Major causes of death* per 100,000 population (1986): diseases of the circulatory system 334.6; malignant neoplasms (cancers) 262.3; accidents, violence, and suicide 54.3.

## National economy

*Budget* (1985). Revenue: Lit 207,193,000,000 (mainly receipts from postage stamp sales, tourism, and customs duties [collected by Italy and paid as a subsidy]). Expenditures: Lit 207,193,000,000 ([3]finance and economic planning 31.0%, internal affairs 11.3%, health and social security 9.0%, education and culture 7.1%, public works 6.3%).
*Public debt:* n.a.
*Tourism:* number of tourist arrivals (1986) 2,787,614; receipts from visitors (1983) U.S.$56,454,000; expenditures by nationals abroad, n.a.
*Gross national product* (at current market prices; 1980): U.S.$176,760,000 (U.S.$8,250 per capita).

### Structure of labour force (1987)

| | labour force | % of labour force |
|---|---|---|
| Agriculture | 347 | 3.0 |
| Manufacturing | 4,120 | 35.6 |
| Construction and public utilities | 896 | 7.7 |
| Transportation and communication | 131 | 1.1 |
| Trade | 1,614 | 13.9 |
| Finance and insurance | 221 | 1.9 |
| Services | 627 | 5.4 |
| Public administration and defense | 1,798 | 15.5 |
| Other | 1,827[4] | 15.8[4] |
| TOTAL | 11,581 | 100.0[2] |

*Production* (metric tons except as noted). Agriculture, forestry, fishing[3]: wheat *c.* 4,400; grapes *c.* 700; barley *c.* 500; livestock (number of live animals; 1985) 1,046 cattle (of which 539 dairy cattle), 1,598 pigs, 1,447 sheep, 81 horses[5], 12,045 rabbits[5], 50,040 quails[5], 19,479 chickens[5]. Manufacturing (1986): processed meats 440,168 kilograms, of which beef 209,160 kilograms, swine 186,890 kilograms, veal 17,705 kilograms; milk 1,269,464 litres; cheese 78,102 kilograms; butter 15,081 kilograms; yogurt 8,890 kilograms; other major products include textiles, cement, paper, leather, bricks, pottery, tiles, postage stamps, gold and silver jewelry, paints, synthetic rubber, and furniture. Construction (new units completed; 1986): urban residential 153; nonresidential 75. Energy production (consumption): all electrical power is imported via electrical grid from Italy, consumption n.a.; coal (metric tons; 1985) none (n.a); crude petroleum (barrels; 1985) none (n.a.); petroleum products (metric tons; 1985) none (n.a.); natural gas (cu m; 1985) none (n.a.).
*Population economically active* (1987): total 11,581; activity rate of total population 52.4% (participation rates: ages 15–64, n.a.; female 38.5%; unemployed 6.4%).

### Price and earnings indexes (1980 = 100)

| | 1981 | 1982 | 1983 | 1984 | 1985 | 1986 |
|---|---|---|---|---|---|---|
| Consumer price index | 139.2 | 150.1 | 165.1 | 174.9 | 196.1 | 204.4 |
| Monthly earnings index | ... | ... | ... | ... | ... | ... |

*Household income and expenditure.* Total number of households (1987): 7,612; average household size (1987) 2.9; income per household: n.a.; sources of income: n.a.; expenditure[6] (1985): food, beverages, and tobacco 30.4%; transportation and communication 14.5%; housing, fuel, and electrical energy 9.7%; clothing and footwear 8.8%; recreation, entertainment, education, and culture 8.1%; furniture, appliances, and goods and services for the home 7.5%; health and sanitary services 5.1%; other goods and services 15.9%.
*Land use* (1985): agricultural and under permanent cultivation 74%; meadows and pastures 22%; forested, built-on, wasteland, and other 4%.

## Foreign trade

*Balance of trade:* n.a. San Marino and Italy form a single customs area; separate figures for San Marino are not available.
*Imports* (1985): manufactured goods of all kinds, oil, and gold. *Major import source:* Italy.
*Exports* (1985): wine, wheat, woolen goods, furniture, wood, ceramics, building stone, dairy products, meat, and postage stamps. *Major export destination:* Italy.

## Transport and communications

*Transport.* Railroads: none (nearest rail terminal is at Rimini, Italy, 17 mi [27 km] northeast). Roads (1980): total length 137 mi, 220 km. Vehicles (1987): passenger cars 16,540; trucks and buses 1,760. Merchant marine: vessels (100 gross tons and over) none. Air transport: airports with scheduled flights, none; however, there is a heliport that provides passenger and cargo service between San Marino and Rimini, Italy, during the summer months.
*Communications.* Daily newspapers (1985): none; however, there are several journals of lesser frequency; total circulation of the oldest of these, *Il Nuovo Titano,* 1,300; circulation per 1,000 population 58.1. Radio (1982): total number of receivers 8,994 (1 per 2.4 persons). Television (1982): total number of receivers 5,882 (1 per 3.7 persons). Telephones (1986): 11,707 (1 per 1.9 persons).

## Education and health

### Education (1985–86)

| | schools | teachers | students | student/ teacher ratio |
|---|---|---|---|---|
| Primary (age 6–10) | 13 | 158 | 1,411 | 8.9 |
| Secondary (age 11–18) | 4 | 183 | 1,248 | 6.8 |
| Vocational | ... | ... | 701[7] | ... |
| Teacher tr. | ... | ... | 48[7] | ... |
| Higher | ... | ... | 343[7] | ... |

*Educational attainment* (1987). Percent of the adult labour force having: basic literacy or primary education 35.5%; secondary 32.6%; some postsecondary 26.3%; higher degree 5.6%. *Literacy* (1985): total population age 15 and over literate 17,852 (98.0%); males literate 8,842 (98.6%); females literate 9,010 (97.5%).
*Health:* physicians (1979) 108[8] (1 per 2,115 persons); hospital beds (1980) 61 (1 per 351 persons); infant mortality rate per 1,000 live births (1982–86) 6.4.
*Food* (1981–83): daily per capita caloric intake 3,642 (vegetable products 74%, animal products 26%); (1983) 140% of FAO recommended minimum requirement.

## Military

*Total active duty personnel* (1984): none[9]. *Military expenditure as a percent of national budget* (1984): 2.0% (world 5.9%); per capita expenditure (1984) *c.* U.S.$2.

---

[1]January 1. [2]Detail does not add to total given because of rounding. [3]Early 1980s. [4]Includes 742 unemployed persons. [5]1975. [6]Weighting coefficients for component expenditures are those of the 1985 official Italian consumer price index. [7]In Italy. [8]Panel physicians only. [9]Defense is provided by a public security force of about 50; all fit males 16–55 constitute a militia.

# São Tomé and Príncipe

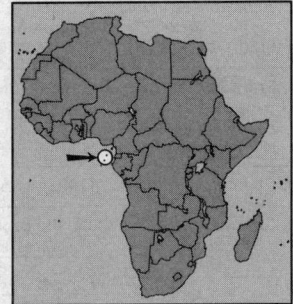

*Official name:* República democrática de São Tomé e Príncipe (Democratic Republic of São Tomé and Príncipe).
*Form of government:* republic with one legislative house (National People's Assembly [40]).
*Head of state and government:* President.
*Capital:* São Tomé.
*Official language:* Portuguese.
*Official religion:* Roman Catholicism.
*Monetary unit:* 1 dobra (Db) = 100 cêntimos; valuation (Oct. 5, 1987) 1 U.S.$ = Db 35.32; 1 £ = Db 57.36.

### Area and population

| Islands Districts | Capitals | area sq mi | area sq km | population 1984 estimate |
|---|---|---|---|---|
| Príncipe | São António | 55 | 142 | 5,671 |
| Paguê | Príncipe | 55 | 142 | 5,671 |
| São Tomé | | 332 | 859 | 98,693 |
| Aqua Grande | São Tomé | 7 | 17 | 34,997 |
| Cantagalo | Santana | 46 | 119 | 11,270 |
| Caué | São João Angolares | 103 | 267 | 4,972 |
| Lemba | Neves | 88 | 229 | 8,537 |
| Lobata | Guadalupe | 41 | 105 | 12,717 |
| Mé-zóchi | Trinidade | 47 | 122 | 26,200 |
| TOTAL | | 386 | 1,001 | 104,364 |

## Demography

*Population* (1987): 112,500.
*Density* (1987): persons per sq mi 291.5, persons per sq km 112.4.
*Urban–rural* (1981): urban 33.5%; rural 66.5%.
*Sex distribution* (1981): male 49.72%; female 50.28%.
*Age breakdown* (1981): under 15, 46.3%; 15–29, 25.0%; 30–44, 11.6%; 45–59, 10.0%; 60–74, 5.3%; 75 and over, 1.8%.
*Population projection:* (1990) 122,000; (2000) 157,000.
*Doubling time:* 27 years.
*Ethnic composition:* mestiços, angolares (descendants of Angolan slaves), forros (descendants of freed slaves), serviçais (alien contract labourers), tongas (children of serviçais), and Europeans.
*Religious affiliation* (1985): Roman Catholic, about 80%; remainder mostly Protestant, predominantly Seventh-day Adventist and an indigenous Evangelical Church.
*Major city* (1984): São Tomé 34,997.

## Vital statistics

*Birth rate* per 1,000 population (1985): 36.3 (world avg. 29.0); legitimate, n.a.; illegitimate, n.a.
*Death rate* per 1,000 population (1985): 8.8 (world avg. 11.0).
*Natural increase rate* per 1,000 population (1985): 27.5 (world avg. 18.0).
*Total fertility rate* (avg. births per childbearing woman; 1980–85): 5.3.
*Marriage rate* per 1,000 population: n.a.
*Divorce rate* per 1,000 population: n.a.
*Life expectancy* at birth (1985–90): male 48.2 years; female 51.6 years.
*Major causes of death* per 100,000 population (1972): senility without mention of psychosis, and ill-defined and unknown causes 367.5; gastritis, duodenitis, enteritis, and colitis, except diarrhea of the newborn, 95.5; pneumonia 62.4; heart disease 51.7; malaria 49.1.

## National economy

*Budget* (1984). Revenue: Db 654,900,000 (1977; indirect taxes 26.1%, import duties 13.5%, direct taxes 7.5%, export duties 6.3%, other sources 66.4%). Expenditures: Db 921,000,000 (1977; services 64.4%, wages and salaries 35.0%, interest on the public debt 0.5%).
*Tourism:* virtually nonexistent in the mid-1980s, although development planners expected to establish a centre at Praia das Concas (on São Tomé), with an initial capacity of 400 tourists per week.
*Public debt* (external, outstanding; 1985): U.S.$72,100,000.
*Production* (metric tons except as noted). Agriculture, forestry, fishing (1985): coconuts 35,000, cacao 5,000, copra 4,000, melons 4,000, bananas 3,000, cassava 3,000, palmetto 3,000, vegetables 3,000, cereals 1,000, palm kernels 500; livestock (number of live animals) 4,000 goats, 3,000 cattle, 3,000 pigs, 2,000 sheep, 123,000 poultry; roundwood 6,000 cu m; fish catch 4,355, principally marine fish and shellfish. Mining and quarrying: some quarrying to support local construction industry. Manufacturing (1975): sawn wood 3,000 cu m[1]; bread and biscuits 1,831; soap 470; palm oil 250[2]; ice 191; limes 22; corn (maize) flour 18; other products include soft drinks, beer, clothing, and bricks and clay products. Construction: (1972) buildings authorized 44 (5,561 sq m, of which residential 3,698, mixed residential-commercial 1,361, commercial 502). Energy production (consumption): electricity (kW-hr; 1985) 15,000,000 (15,000,000); coal, none (n.a.); crude petroleum, none (n.a.); petroleum products (metric tons; 1985) none (11,-000); natural gas, none (n.a.).
*Household income and expenditure:* average household size: n.a.; income per household: n.a.; sources of income: n.a.; expenditure: n.a.
*Gross national product* (at current market prices; 1985): U.S.$30,000,000 (U.S.$280 per capita).

### Structure of gross domestic product and labour force

| | 1982 in value Db '000,000 | 1982 % of total value | 1981 labour force | 1981 % of labour force |
|---|---|---|---|---|
| Agriculture | 859.7 | 50.9 | 16,486 | 54.4 |
| Mining | 4.9 | 0.3 | ... | ... |
| Manufacturing | 80.8 | 4.8 | 1,629 | 5.4 |
| Construction | 55.9 | 3.3 | 1,805 | 6.0 |
| Public utilities | 12.8 | 0.8 | 287 | 1.0 |
| Transportation and communication | 45.3 | 2.7 | 1,036 | 3.4 |
| Trade | 156.0 | 9.2 | 2,040 | 6.7 |
| Pub. admin., defense | 368.7 | 21.8 | 5,902 | 19.5 |
| Finance | 94.7 | 5.6 | 187 | 0.6 |
| Services | 11.1 | 0.6 | 1,235 | 4.1 |
| TOTAL | 1,689.9[3] | 100.0 | 30,289 | 100.0 |

*Population economically active* (1981): total 30,607; activity rate of total population 31.7% (participation rates: ages 15–64, 61.1%; female 32.4%; unemployed, n.a.).

### Price and earnings indexes (1974 = 100)

| | 1974 | 1975 | 1976 | 1977 | 1978 | 1979 |
|---|---|---|---|---|---|---|
| Consumer price index | 100.0 | ... | ... | 126.0 | 139.0 | 146.7 |
| Earnings index | ... | ... | ... | ... | ... | ... |

*Land use* (1985): meadows and pastures 1.0%; agricultural and under permanent cultivation 37.5%; forest, built-on, wasteland, and other 61.5%.

## Foreign trade

### Balance of trade (current prices)

| | 1980 | 1981 | 1982 | 1983 | 1984 | 1985 |
|---|---|---|---|---|---|---|
| U.S.$'000,000 | −11.7 | −12.6 | −15.9 | −3.6 | −4.9 | −7.6 |
| % of total | 22.5% | 31.5% | 47.7% | 23.1% | 25.4% | 42.7% |

*Imports* (1984): Db 485,900,000 (food and other agricultural products 27.4%, mineral fuels and lubricants 16.3%, consumer goods 14.7%, machinery and transport equipment 12.9%, construction materials 8.6%). *Major import sources* (1985): Portugal 40.9%; Angola 12.6%; United Kingdom 10.2%; France 7.9%; East Germany 6.3%; Spain 6.3%; Belgium–Luxembourg 3.9%; The Netherlands 3.9%; Japan 2.0%; Norway 1.6%.
*Exports* (1984): Db 539,600,000 (cacao 80.0%, copra 15.0%, coffee 1.0%, palm kernels 0.4%). *Major export destinations* (1985): East Germany 47.0%; The Netherlands, 15.6%; Portugal 15.6%; United Kingdom 5.9%; Italy 5.9%; France 3.9%; Austria 2.0%; Switzerland 2.0%.

## Transport and communications

*Transport.* Railroads: none. Roads (1975): total length 179 mi, 288 km (paved 69%). Vehicles (1975): passenger cars 1,774; trucks and buses 265. Merchant marine (1986): vessels (100 gross tons and over) 3; total deadweight tonnage 1,172. Air transport (1985): passenger-mi 3,800,000, passenger-km 6,100,000; short ton-mi cargo 70,000, short ton-km cargo 100,000; airports (1987) with scheduled flights 1.
*Communications.* Daily newspapers: none; 3 government weeklies (circulation, n.a.). Radio (1986): total number of receivers 28,000 (1 per 4.0 persons). Television: none. Telephones (1986): 2,200 (1 per 50 persons).

## Education and health

### Education (1984–85)

| | schools | teachers | students | student/ teacher ratio |
|---|---|---|---|---|
| Primary (age 6–13) | 63 | 517 | 19,086 | 36.9 |
| Secondary (age 14–18) | 11 | 300 | 6,186 | 20.6 |
| Voc., teacher tr. | 2 | 35 | 370 | 10.6 |
| Higher | ... | ... | 700[4] | |

*Educational attainment* (1981). Percent of population age 25 and over having: no formal schooling 56.6%; some primary education 18.0%; primary 19.2%; some secondary 4.6%; secondary 1.3%; postsecondary 0.3%. *Literacy* (1981): total population age 15 and over literate 28,114 (54.2%); males literate 17,689 (70.2%); females literate 10,425 (39.1%).
*Health* (1985): physicians 53 (1 per 2,016 persons); hospital beds (1978) 665 (1 per 129 persons); infant mortality rate per 1,000 live births 61.7.
*Food* (1981–83): daily per capita caloric intake 2,511 (vegetable products 87%, animal products 13%); (1983) 97% of FAO recommended minimum requirement.

## Military

*Total active duty personnel* (1985): 700 Angolan and 400 Cuban troops (distribution by branch of service, n.a.). *Military expenditure as percent of GNP* (1980): 1.8% (world 5.6%).

[1]1983. [2]1982. [3]At factor cost. [4]Students abroad, 1982–83.

# Saudi Arabia

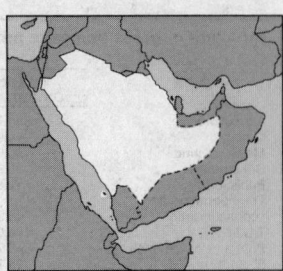

*Official name:* al-Mamlakah
al-'Arabīyah as-Sa'ūdīyah (Kingdom of
Saudi Arabia).
*Form of government:* monarchy.
*Chief of state:* King.
*Head of government:* Prime Minister.
*Capital:* Riyadh.
*Official language:* Arabic.
*Official religion:* Islam.
*Monetary unit:* 1 Saudi riyal
(SRls) = 100 halalah; valuation (Oct.
5, 1987) 1 U.S.$ = SRls 3.75;
1 £ = SRls 6.09.

| Area and population | | area | | population |
|---|---|---|---|---|
| | | | | 1985 |
| **Regions** | | | | |
| **Administrative Districts** | **Capitals** | sq mi | sq km | estimate |
| al-Gharbīyah (Western) | — | ... | ... | 3,043,189 |
| al-Bāḥah | al-Bāḥah | ... | ... | |
| al-Madīnah | Medina (al-Madīnah) | ... | ... | |
| Makkah | Mecca (Makkah) | ... | ... | |
| al-Janūbīyah (Southern) | — | ... | ... | 625,017 |
| 'Asīr | Abha | ... | ... | |
| Jīzān | Jīzān | ... | ... | |
| Najrān | Najrān | ... | ... | |
| ash-Shamālīyah (Northern) | — | ... | ... | 679,476 |
| al-Jawf | Sakākah | ... | ... | |
| al-Ḥudūd ash-Shamālīyah (Northern Borders) | 'Ar'ar | ... | ... | |
| al-Qurayyāt | an-Nabk | ... | ... | |
| Tabūk | Tabūk | ... | ... | |
| ash-Sharqiyah (Eastern) | — | ... | ... | 3,030,765 |
| ash-Sharqiyah (Eastern) | ad-Dammām | ... | ... | |
| al-Wūsṭā (Central) | — | ... | ... | 3,632,092 |
| Ḥā'il | Ḥā'il | ... | ... | |
| al-Qaṣim | Buraydah | ... | ... | |
| ar-Riyāḍ | Riyadh (ar-Riyāḍ) | ... | ... | |
| TOTAL | | 865,000 | 2,240,000 | 11,010,539 |

## Demography

*Population* (1987): 12,483,000.
*Density* (1987): persons per sq mi 14.4, persons per sq km 5.6.
*Urban–rural* (1985): urban 73.0%; rural 27.0%.
*Sex distribution* (1985): male 54.59%; female 45.41%.
*Age breakdown* (1984): under 15, 44.7%; 15–29, 28.7%; 30–44, 15.1%; 45–59, 7.8%; 60 and over, 3.7%.
*Population projection:* (1990) 13,988,000; (2000) 19,824,000.
*Doubling time:* 21 years.
*Ethnic composition* (1983): Saudi 82.0%; Yemeni 9.6%; other Arab 3.4%; other 5.0%.
*Religious affiliation* (1980): Muslim (mostly Sunnī) 98.8%; Christian 0.8%; other 0.4%.
*Major cities* (1980): Riyadh 1,308,000[1]; Jidda (Jiddah) 1,500,000[2]; Mecca 550,000; aṭ-Ṭa'if 300,000.

## Vital statistics

*Birth rate* per 1,000 population (1980–85): 42.1 (world avg. 29.0).
*Death rate* per 1,000 population (1980–85): 8.9 (world avg. 11.0).
*Natural increase rate* per 1,000 population (1980–85): 33.2 (world avg. 18.0).
*Total fertility rate* (avg. births per childbearing woman; 1980–85): 7.1.
*Marriage rate* per 1,000 population: n.a.
*Divorce rate* per 1,000 population: n.a.
*Life expectancy* at birth (1980–85): male 59.2 years; female 62.7 years.
*Major causes of death* per 100,000 population: n.a.; however, major diseases include cholera, cerebrospinal meningitis, yellow fever, typhoid, tuberculosis, lung infections, and asphyxia.

## National economy

*Budget* (1987–88). Revenue: SRls 117,280,000,000 (oil revenues 66.7%). Expenditures: SRls 170,000,000,000 (defense and security 35.7%, public administration and other government spending 14.6%, human resources development 14.0%, transport and communications 7.0%).
*Public debt:* none.
*Production* (metric tons except as noted). Agriculture, forestry, fishing (1985): wheat 1,700,000, watermelons 509,000, tomatoes 367,000, dates 235,000, sorghum 87,000, grapes 79,000, onions 75,000, pumpkins, squash, and gourds 40,000, eggplants 25,000, cucumbers and gherkins 23,000, barley 12,000, potatoes 10,000, millet 8,000, pulses 7,000; livestock (number of live animals) 2,454,000 goats, 2,270,000 sheep, 540,000 cattle, 171,000 camels, 110,000 asses, 34,000,000 poultry; fish catch 43,696. Mining and quarrying (1984): gypsum 300,000; lime 12,000. Manufacturing (1985): cement 10,-167,000; methanol 1,287,000; steel rods and bars 948,000; ethylene 927,900; urea 825,000; ethylene glycol 310,000; industrial ethanol 200,000; ethylene dichloride 190,000; styrene 125,000; caustic soda 125,000; nitrogen 82,000; citric acid 75,000; oxygen 55,000; melamine 14,000. Construction (value added in SRls; 1981): 51,689,000,000. Energy production (consumption): electricity (kW-hr; 1985) 41,904,000,000 (41,904,000,000); coal, n.a. (n.a.); crude petroleum (barrels; 1985) 1,158,800,000 (310,780,000); petroleum products (metric tons; 1984) 43,005,000 (27,307,000); natural gas (cu m; 1985) 1,511,993,000 (1,511,993,000).
*Land use* (1984): forested 0.6%; meadows and pastures 39.5%; agricultural and under permanent cultivation 0.5%; other, built-on, and waste 59.4%.

*Population economically active* (1984): total 2,673,316; activity rate of total population 24.5% (participation rates: over age 15, 44.3%; female 2.3%; unemployed, n.a.).

| Price and earnings indexes (1980 = 100) | | | | | | | |
|---|---|---|---|---|---|---|---|
| | 1981 | 1982 | 1983 | 1984 | 1985 | 1986 | 1987[3] |
| Consumer price index | 102.7 | 102.1 | 101.5 | 100.3 | 97.0 | 94.1 | 93.5 |
| Monthly earnings index | ... | ... | ... | ... | ... | ... | ... |

*Gross national product* (1985): U.S.$102,120,000,000 (U.S.$8,850 per capita).

| Structure of gross domestic product and labour force | | | | |
|---|---|---|---|---|
| | 1985–86 | | 1984 | |
| | in value SRls '000,000 | % of total value | labour force | % of labour force |
| Agriculture | 12,589 | 4.4 | 223,383 | 8.3 |
| Mining | 1,745 | 0.6 | 163,979 | 6.1 |
| Oil sector | 91,808 | 32.0 | | |
| Manufacturing | 15,418 | 5.4 | 408,058 | 15.3 |
| Construction | 34,612 | 12.1 | 515,175 | 19.3 |
| Public utilities | 769 | 0.3 | 61,591 | 2.3 |
| Transportation and communication | 20,516 | 7.2 | 116,629 | 4.4 |
| Trade | 24,165 | 8.4 | 730,124 | 27.3 |
| Finance | 23,308 | 8.1 | 104.330 | 3.9 |
| Pub. admin., defense | 27,827 | 9.7 | 350,047 | 13.1 |
| Services and other | 33,930 | 11.8 | | |
| TOTAL | 286,687 | 100.0 | 2,673,316 | 100.0 |

*Tourism* (1981): receipts from visitors U.S.$1,573,000,000; expenditures by nationals abroad U.S.$2,761,000,000.
*Pilgrims to Mecca from abroad* (1987): 960,386.
*Household income and expenditure.* Average household size (1984) 6.6; income per household: n.a.; sources of income: n.a.; expenditure (1980): food 52.2%, housing 17.2%, clothing 6.6%, furniture and utensils 5.9%, transport and communication 4.5%, health care 2.1%.

## Foreign trade

| Balance of trade (current prices) | | | | | | |
|---|---|---|---|---|---|---|
| | 1980 | 1981 | 1982 | 1983 | 1984 | 1985 | 1986 |
| SRls '000,000 | +262.5 | +286.2 | +131.8 | +23.0 | +13.6 | +14.0 | +3.6 |
| % of total | 56.7% | 54.5% | 32.1% | 7.8% | 5.4% | 7.5% | 2.5% |

*Imports* (1986): SRls 70,779,600,000 (machinery and appliances 20.7%, foodstuffs and tobacco 16.8%, transport equipment 13.3%, textiles and clothing 10.3%, metals and metal articles 9.2%, chemicals 6.9%, scientific instruments 4.2%). *Major import sources:* United States 17.5%; Japan 15.7%; West Germany 8.1%; Italy 7.3%; United Kingdom 7.3%; France 5.6%; South Korea 4.1%; Taiwan 3.2%; The Netherlands 2.4%; Switzerland 2.0%; Belgium 1.7%; Spain 1.7%; Sweden 1.1%; Canada 0.6%.
*Exports* (1986): SRls 74,377,000,000 (crude petroleum 89.7%, refined petroleum 10.3%). *Major export destinations:* Japan 20.4%; United States 16.7%; Italy 7.6%; France 5.6%; The Netherlands 4.9%; Bahrain 4.4%; Brazil 4.0%; Taiwan 3.8%; West Germany 3.0%; United Kingdom 2.8%; Singapore 2.7%; Spain 2.6%; South Korea 2.0%.

## Transport and communications

*Transport.* Railroads (1986–87): route length 544 mi, 875 km; (1986) passenger-mi 43,931,000, passenger-km 70,700,000; short ton-mi cargo 220,-000,000, metric ton-km cargo 321,190,000. Roads (1986): total length 52,733 mi, 84,866 km (paved 36%). Vehicles (1985): passenger cars 2,165,675; trucks and buses 1,966,172. Merchant marine (1986): vessels (100 gross tons and over) 380; total deadweight tonnage 4,954,572. Air transport (1986): passenger-mi 9,331,797,000, passenger-km 15,018,101,000; short ton-mi cargo 299,423,000, metric ton-km cargo 437,150,000; airports (1987) with scheduled flights 21.
*Communications.* Daily newspapers (1986): total number 10; total circulation 488,000; circulation per 1,000 population 41.8. Radio (1986): 3,230,000 receivers (1 per 3.7 persons). Television (1986): 3,700,000 receivers (1 per 3.2 persons). Telephones (1986): 980,231 (1 per 11.9 persons).

## Education and health

| Education (1985–86) | schools | teachers | students | student/ teacher ratio |
|---|---|---|---|---|
| Primary (age 6–12) | 7,566 | 77,480 | 1,285,433 | 16.6 |
| Secondary (age 13–18) | 2,946 | 37,096 | 524,738 | 14.1 |
| Voc., teacher tr. | 31 | 2,350 | 21,110 | 8.9 |
| Higher | 77[4] | 9,724 | 102,709 | 10.6 |

*Educational attainment,* n.a. *Literacy* (1984): total population age 15 and over literate 2,946,026 (48.8%); males literate 2,124,781 (58.0%); females literate 821,245 (34.6%).
*Health* (1986): physicians 13,996 (1 per 857 persons); hospital beds 23,862 (1 per 503 persons); infant mortality rate per 1,000 live births (1984) 109.8.
*Food* (1981–83): daily per capita caloric intake 3,048 (vegetable products 82%, animal products 18%); (1983) 134% of FAO recommended minimum.

## Military

*Total active duty personnel* (1986): 67,500 (army 59.3%, navy 5.2%, air force 20.7%, national guard 14.8%). *Military expenditure as percent of GNP* (1984): 21.3% (world 5.9%); per capita expenditure U.S.$2,003.

[1]1981 estimate. [2]1983 estimate. [3]July. [4]Includes colleges, institutions of advanced study, and universities.

# Senegal

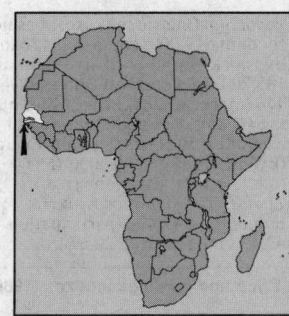

*Official name:* République du Sénégal
(Republic of Senegal).
*Form of government:* republic with
one legislative house (National
Assembly [120]).
*Head of state and government:*
President.
*Capital:* Dakar.
*Official language:* French.
*Official religion:* none.
*Monetary unit:* 1 CFA franc
(CFAF) = 100 centimes; valuation
(Oct. 5, 1987) 1 U.S.$ = CFAF 306.67;
1 £ = CFAF 498.00.

### Area and population

| Regions | Capitals | area sq mi | area sq km | population 1984 estimate |
|---|---|---|---|---|
| Dakar | Dakar | 212 | 550 | 1,380,700 |
| Diourbel | Diourbel | 1,683 | 4,359 | 501,000 |
| Fatick | Fatick | 3,064 | 7,935 | 506,500 |
| Kaolack | Kaolack | 6,181 | 16,010 | 741,600 |
| Kolda | Kolda | 8,112 | 21,011 | 517,600 |
| Louga | Louga | 11,270 | 29,188 | 493,900 |
| Saint-Louis | Saint-Louis | 17,038 | 44,127 | 612,100 |
| Tambacounda | Tambacounda | 23,012 | 59,602 | 355,000 |
| Thiès | Thiès | 2,549 | 6,601 | 837,900 |
| Ziguinchor | Ziguinchor | 2,834 | 7,339 | 361,000 |
| TOTAL | | 75,955 | 196,722 | 6,307,300 |

## Demography

*Population* (1987): 6,793,000.
*Density* (1987): persons per sq mi 89.4, persons per sq km 34.5.
*Urban–rural* (1984): urban 35.0%; rural 65.0%.
*Sex distribution* (1984): male 49.61%; female 50.39%.
*Age breakdown* (1984): under 15, 47.0%; 15–29, 25.7%; 30–44, 14.8%; 45–59, 8.2%; 60 and over, 4.3%.
*Population projection:* (1990) 7,377,000; (2000) 9,765,000.
*Doubling time:* 23 years.
*Ethnic composition* (1983): Wolof 36.2%; Fulani (Peul) 17.8%; Serer 17.0%; Tukulor 9.7%; Diola (Jola) 8.1%; Mandingo 6.5%; Soninke 2.1%; Arabs 1.0%; other 1.6%.
*Religious affiliation* (1980): Sunnī Muslim 91.0%; Roman Catholic 5.6%; traditional beliefs 3.2%; other 0.2%.
*Major cities* (1984): Dakar 671,000; Thiès 126,886[1]; Kaolack 126,900; Ziguinchor 105,200; Saint-Louis 96,594[1].

## Vital statistics

*Birth rate* per 1,000 population (1984): 48.6 (world avg. 29.0).
*Death rate* per 1,000 population (1984): 18.5 (world avg. 11.0).
*Natural increase rate* per 1,000 population (1984): 30.1 (world avg. 18.0).
*Total fertility rate* (avg. births per childbearing woman; 1984): 7.0.
*Marriage rate* per 1,000 population: n.a.
*Divorce rate* per 1,000 population: n.a.
*Life expectancy* at birth (1984): male 45.0 years; female 48.0 years.
*Major causes of death* per 100,000 population (officially confirmed transmissible diseases only; 1983): malaria 5.9; meningitis 5.5; tetanus 3.7; tuberculosis of respiratory system 1.9; measles 1.7.

## National economy

*Budget* (1986–87). Revenue: CFAF 319,679,000,000 (new debt 34.6%; import and export duties 27.2%; excise taxes 19.6%; personal income taxes 15.7%). Expenditures: CFAF 319,679,000,000 (current account 64.5%, of which education 14.7%, defense 8.9%, health 3.4%, social security and public aid 0.9%; capital account 35.5%).
*Production* (metric tons except as noted). Agriculture, forestry, fishing (1985–86): millet and sorghum 949,570, sugarcane 800,000, peanuts (groundnuts) 587,000, paddy rice 147,000, corn (maize) 146,900, beans 79,700, pulses 66,000, cotton 46,000, onions 31,000, tomatoes 28,000, cotton seed 28,000, cotton lint 18,000, oranges 18,000, bananas 6,000, coconuts 5,000; livestock (number of live animals) 2,200,000 cattle, 2,950,000 sheep, 1,080,000 goats, 190,000 pigs; roundwood 4,106,000 cu m; fish catch 244,002. Mining and quarrying (1985): calcium phosphate 1,809,800; cement 395,300; aluminum phosphate 365,640. Manufacturing (1984): peanut oil 217,000; wheat flour 86,600; refined sugar 51,800; soap 35,000; canned fish 28,700; woven cotton fabrics 11,500; nitrogenous fertilizers 6,000; carbonated beverages 257,800 hectolitres; beer 185,500 hectolitres; footwear 3,234,000 pairs. Construction (authorized; 1984): residential 251,400 sq m; nonresidential 24,500 sq m. Energy production (consumption): electricity (kW-hr; 1985) 696,000,-000 (696,000,000); coal, none (n.a.); crude petroleum (barrels; 1985) none (2,270,000); petroleum products (metric tons; 1985) 336,000 (742,000); natural gas, none (n.a.).
*Population economically active* (1985): total 3,095,000; activity rate of total population 47.1% (participation rates: ages 15–64, 78.1%; female 41.8%; unemployed, n.a.).

### Price and earnings indexes (1980 = 100)

| | 1981 | 1982 | 1983 | 1984 | 1985 | 1986 | 1987[2] |
|---|---|---|---|---|---|---|---|
| Consumer price index | 105.9 | 124.2 | 138.7 | 155.1 | 175.2 | 186.1 | 174.6 |
| Hourly earnings index | 105.0 | 105.0 | 113.6 | 113.6 | ... | ... | ... |

*Household income and expenditure*[3]. Average household size (1980) 4.8; average annual income per household (1975) CFAF 1,105,800 (U.S.$5,160); sources of income: wages and salaries 51.6%, remittances and gifts 17.5%, pensions, social security, and related benefits 12.5%, other 18.4%; expenditure (1979): food and tobacco 57.5%, housing, maintenance, and utilities 18.4%, clothing 11.9%, transport 5.4%, other 6.8%.
*Public debt* (external, outstanding; 1985): U.S.$1,989,200,000.
*Gross national product* (at current market prices; 1985): U.S.$2,400,000,000 (U.S.$370 per capita).

### Structure of gross domestic product and labour force

| | 1984 in value CFAF '000,000,000 | 1984 % of total value | 1982 labour force[4] | 1982 % of labour force |
|---|---|---|---|---|
| Agriculture | 174.1 | 17.1 | 10,654 | 9.1 |
| Mining | | | 1,918 | 1.6 |
| Manufacturing | 280.5 | 27.6 | 30,736 | 26.4 |
| Public utilities | | | 3,221 | 2.8 |
| Construction | | | 8,402 | 7.2 |
| Transportation and communication | 79.0 | 7.8 | 24,789 | 21.2 |
| Trade | 203.3 | 20.0 | 14,648 | 12.6 |
| Finance | 111.6 | 11.0 | 7,921 | 6.8 |
| Services | | | | |
| Pub. admin., defense | 153.4 | 15.1 | 14,339 | 12.3 |
| Other | 13.6 | 1.4 | | |
| TOTAL | 1,015.5 | 100.0 | 116,628 | 100.0 |

*Tourism:* receipts from visitors (1985) U.S.$81,000,000; expenditures by nationals abroad (1984) U.S.$45,000,000.
*Land use* (1984): forested 30.9%; meadows and pastures 29.7%; agricultural and under permanent cultivation 27.2%; other 12.2%.

## Foreign trade

### Balance of trade (current prices)

| | 1980 | 1981 | 1982 | 1983 | 1984 | 1985 |
|---|---|---|---|---|---|---|
| CFAF '000,000,000 | −121.5 | −156.5 | −145.9 | −174.4 | −203.1 | −100.1 |
| % of total | 37.6% | 36.5% | 28.8% | 27.5% | 30.3% | 21.4% |

*Imports* (1985): CFAF 283,093,000,000 (crude petroleum and petroleum products 22.6%; machinery and transport equipment 17.8%, of which transport equipment 7.2%; metal products 12.3%; cereals 9.8%; pharmaceutical and chemical products 5.0%). *Major import sources:* France 31.6%; Nigeria 11.4%; United States 5.7%; West Germany 4.3%; Côte d'Ivoire 4.1%; Spain 3.3%; Italy 2.9%; Japan 2.5%; The Netherlands 2.4%.
*Exports* (1985): CFAF 182,987,000,000 (petroleum products 19.3%, calcium phosphate 9.9%, canned fish 9.6%, fresh or frozen fish 7.5%, fresh or frozen crustaceans 4.9%, cotton fabrics 4.1%, peanut oilcake 2.0%, footwear 0.6%). *Major export destinations:* France 27.7%; Côte d'Ivoire 5.2%; Mauritania 3.8%; United Kingdom 3.8%; Italy 3.2%; Spain 3.0%; Japan 2.7%; Mali 2.1%.

## Transport and communications

*Transport.* Railroads (1984): route length 737 mi, 1,186 km; passenger-mi 46,197,000[5], passenger-km 74,347,000[5]; short ton-mi cargo 246,000,000[5], metric ton-km cargo 344,570,000[5]. Roads (1983): total length 8,679 mi, 13,968 km (paved 26%). Vehicles (1984): passenger cars 73,665; trucks and buses 36,144. Merchant marine (1986): vessels (100 gross tons and over) 148; total deadweight tonnage 41,651. Air transport[6] (1985): passenger-mi 207,800,000, passenger-km 253,000,000; short ton-mi cargo 12,600,000, metric ton-km cargo 18,400,000; airports (1987) with scheduled flights 12.
*Communications.* Daily newspapers (1984): total number 1; total circulation 31,000; circulation per 1,000 population 4.9. Radio (1985): total number of receivers 450,000 (1 per 15 persons). Television (1986): total number of receivers 55,000 (1 per 122 persons). Telephones (1984): 32,997 (1 per 193 persons).

## Education and health

### Education (1985–86)

| | schools | teachers | students | student/ teacher ratio |
|---|---|---|---|---|
| Primary (age 6–11) | 2,171 | 11,513 | 583,507 | 41.2 |
| Secondary (age 12–18) | 162 | 2,346[7] | 113,653 | ... |
| Voc., teacher tr. | 5 | ... | 3,515 | ... |
| Higher | 7 | 497[7] | 13,450 | ... |

*Educational attainment* (1970). Percent of population age 6 and over having: no formal schooling 95.3%; primary education 3.9%; secondary 0.7%; higher 0.1%. *Literacy* (1980): total population age 15 and over literate 1,274,000 (22.5%); males literate 1,755,000 (31.0%); females literate 804,000 (14.2%).
*Health* (1982): physicians 470 (1 per 12,987 persons); hospital beds 6,200 (1 per 973 persons); infant mortality rate per 1,000 live births (1980–85) 141.0.
*Food* (1981–83): daily per capita caloric intake 2,390 (vegetable products 93%, animal products 7%); (1983) 82% of FAO recommended minimum requirement.

## Military

*Total active duty personnel* (1986): 9,700 (army 87.6%, navy 7.2%, air force 5.2%). *Military expenditure as percent of GNP* (1984): 2.8% (world 5.9%); per capita expenditure U.S.$10.

[1]1979. [2]April. [3]Traditional African households in Dakar. [4]Private sector only. [5]1982–83. [6]International flights only. [7]1983–84.

# Seychelles

*Official name:* Republic of Seychelles
(English); République des Seychelles
(French); Repiblik Sesel (Creole).
*Form of government:* unitary
single-party republic with one
legislative house (People's Assembly
[25]).
*Head of state and government:*
President.
*Capital:* Victoria.
*Official languages:* English; French;
Creole.
*Official religion:* none.
*Monetary unit:* 1 Seychelles rupee
(SR) = 100 cents; valuation (Oct. 5,
1987) 1 U.S.$ = SR 5.54;
1 £ = SR 9.00.

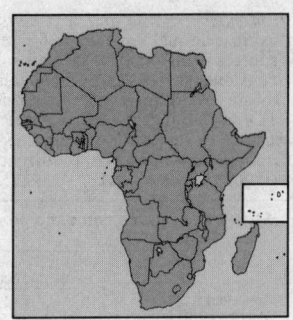

### Area and population

| Island Groups | Capital | area | | population |
|---|---|---|---|---|
| | | sq mi | sq km | 1984 estimate |
| Central (Granitic) group | | | | |
| La Digue and satellites | — | 6 | 15 | 2,000 |
| Mahé and satellites | Victoria | 61 | 158 | 57,400 |
| Praslin and satellites | — | 16 | 42 | 4,650 |
| Silhouette | — | 8 | 20 | 200 |
| Other islands | — | 2 | 4 | 50 |
| Outer (Coralline) islands | — | 83 | 214 | 400 |
| TOTAL | | 175[1] | 453 | 64,700 |

## Demography

*Population* (1987): 65,967.
*Density* (1987): persons per sq mi 377.0, persons per sq km 145.6.
*Urban–rural* (1977): urban 37.2%; rural 62.8%.
*Sex distribution* (1985): male 49.87%; female 50.13%.
*Age breakdown* (1985): under 15, 36.5%; 15–29, 32.2%; 30–44, 12.6%; 45–59,
9.7%; 60–74, 6.7%; 75 and over 2.3%.
*Population projection:* (1990) 66,900; (2000) 70,200.
*Doubling time:* 38 years.
*Ethnic composition* (1983): Seychellois Creole (mixture of Asian, African,
and European 89.1%; Indian 4.7%; Malagasy 3.1%; Chinese 1.6%; English
1.5%.
*Religious affiliation* (1986): Roman Catholic 90.0%; Anglican 8.0%; other
2.0%.
*Major city* (1977): Victoria 23,012.

## Vital statistics

*Birth rate* per 1,000 population (1986): 26.2 (world avg. 26.0); (1984) legiti-
mate 33.2%; illegitimate 66.8%.
*Death rate* per 1,000 population (1986): 7.5 (world avg. 9.9).
*Natural increase rate* per 1,000 population (1986): 18.6 (world avg. 16.1).
*Total fertility rate* (avg. births per childbearing woman; 1985): 3.3.
*Marriage rate* per 1,000 population (1984): 6.0.
*Divorce rate* per 1,000 population (1985): 0.7.
*Life expectancy* at birth (1980–85): male 66.2 years; female 73.5 years.
*Major causes of death* per 100,000 population (1985): diseases of the cir-
culatory system 200.8, of which cerebrovascular disease 69.0; malignant
neoplasms (cancers) 115.0; diseases of the respiratory system 64.4, of which
pneumonia 42.9; diseases of the digestive system 35.2; accidents and adverse effects 55.2.

## National economy

*Budget* (1986). Revenue: SR 492,500,000 (customs taxes and duties 49.5%;
income taxes 19.7%, of which personal 13.6%, companies 6.1%; administrative fees 8.1%; rents and royalties 4.6%; dividends and interest 3.6%).
Expenditures: SR 569,700,000 (education and information 23.7%; defense
10.8%; health and social services 7.5%; tourism and transport 7.2%; national development 4.8%; service on external debt 4.7%).
*Gross national product* (at current market prices; 1985): U.S.$160,000,000
(U.S.$2,450 per capita).

### Structure of gross domestic product and labour force

| | 1985 | | | |
|---|---|---|---|---|
| | in value SR '000,000 | % of total value | labour force[2] | % of labour force |
| Agriculture | 77.0 | 6.6 | 2,282 | 9.5 |
| Mining and manufacturing | 106.9 | 9.2 | 1,672 | 7.0 |
| Construction | 57.2 | 4.9 | 1,063 | 4.4 |
| Public utilities | 31.7 | 2.7 | 633 | 2.6 |
| Transportation and communication | 482.6[3] | 41.3[3] | 2,256 | 9.4 |
| Trade | 103.0 | 8.8 | 3,054 | 12.8 |
| Finance | 87.7 | 7.5 | 814 | 3.4 |
| Public admin., defense | 192.3 | 16.4 } | 3,587 | 15.0 |
| Services | 29.8 | 2.6 } | | |
| Other | ... | ... | 8,582[4] | 35.8 |
| TOTAL | 1,168.2 | 100.0 | 23,943 | 100.0[1] |

*Tourism* (1985): receipts from visitors U.S.$51,000,000; expenditures by na-
tionals abroad U.S.$9,000,000.
*Public debt* (external, outstanding; 1985): U.S.$54,000,000.

*Production* (metric tons except as noted). Agriculture, forestry, fishing (1985):
coconuts 19,000, copra 3,734, bananas 2,000, cinnamon bark 1,326, tea 87;
livestock (number of live animals) 15,000 pigs, 4,000 goats, 3,000 cattle,
185,200 chickens; fish catch 4,064, of which jack 1,339, snapper 542, bonito
446, mackerel 264. Mining and quarrying (1984): guano 4,700. Manufacturing (1986): beer and stout 41,480 hectolitres; soft drinks 38,860 hectolitres;
cigarettes 59,600,000 units. Energy production (consumption): electricity
(kW-hr; 1986) 66,600,000 (66,600,000); coal, none (n.a.); petroleum, none
(n.a.); natural gas, none (n.a.).
*Population economically active* (1985): total 27,700; activity rate of total
population 42.4% (participation rates: ages 15 and over 66.8%; female
42.4%; unemployed 20.6%).

### Price and earnings indexes (1980 = 100)

| | 1980 | 1981 | 1982 | 1983 | 1984 | 1985 | 1986 |
|---|---|---|---|---|---|---|---|
| Consumer price index | 100.0 | 110.6 | 109.6 | 116.3 | 121.0 | 122.0 | 122.4 |
| Monthly earnings index | 100.0 | 111.0 | 120.2 | 129.5 | 132.3 | 134.2 | ... |

*Household income and expenditure.* Average household size (1982) 4.8; average annual income per household (1978) SR 18,480 (U.S.$2,658); sources
of income: wages and salaries 88.8%, agricultural sales 3.8%, pensions 1.9%;
expenditure (1984): food 34.0%, housing 19.9%, beverages and tobacco
18.8%, clothing and footwear 8.6%, household and personal goods 7.1%,
transportation 6.6%, services and recreation 4.9%.
*Land use* (1984): forested 18.5%; agricultural and under permanent cultivation 25.9%; built-on, wasteland, and other 55.6%.

## Foreign trade

### Balance of trade (current prices)

| | 1981 | 1982 | 1983 | 1984 | 1985 | 1986 |
|---|---|---|---|---|---|---|
| SR '000,000 | −403.8 | −457.6 | −379.3 | −356.6 | −422.1 | −447.2 |
| % of total | 65.1% | 69.6% | 58.0% | 49.6% | 52.0% | 66.1% |

*Imports* (1986)[5]: SR 663,680,000 (machinery and transport equipment 30.4%;
manufactured goods 19.4%; petroleum, petroleum products, and related
materials 15.5%; food, beverages, and tobacco 14.7%; nonmetallic mineral
manufactures 9.8%; chemicals and related products 5.7%; textile yarn, fabrics, and finished articles 1.1%). *Major import sources:* United Kingdom
24.4%; France 16.7%; South Africa 10.0%; Italy 5.3%; Singapore 5.1%; The
Netherlands 5.0%; Japan 4.9%; United States 4.3%; Bahrain 2.8%; U.S.S.R.
2.1%.
*Exports* (1986): SR 114,920,000[6] (petroleum products 73.9%[7]; fish 3.8%; copra 3.5%; cinnamon bark 3.5%). *Major export destinations*[8] (1984): Pakistan
38.6%; Japan 26.1%; Réunion 14.9%; United Kingdom 4.9%; France 2.7%.

## Transport and communications

*Transport.* Railroads: none. Roads (1987): total length 164 mi, 264 km
(paved 61%). Vehicles (1984): passenger cars 3,318; trucks and buses
1,005. Merchant marine (1986): vessels (100 gross tons and over) 7; total
deadweight tonnage 2,491. Air transport (1986): passenger arrivals 71,000,
passenger departures 71,000; metric ton cargo unloaded 1,083, metric ton
cargo loaded 216; airports (1987) with scheduled flights 5.
*Communications.* Daily newspapers (1986): total number 1; total circulation
3,200; circulation per 1,000 population 48.4. Radio (1986): total number
of receivers 19,000 (1 per 3.5 persons). Television (1986): total number of
receivers 3,800 (1 per 17.4 persons). Telephones (1985): 11,333 (1 per 5.8
persons).

## Education and health

### Education (1987)

| | schools[9] | teachers | students | student/ teacher ratio |
|---|---|---|---|---|
| Primary (age 6–15) | 26 | 698 | 14,553 | 20.8 |
| Secondary (age 16–18) | 4 | 204 | 2,590 | 12.7 |
| Voc., teacher tr. | 1 | 163 | 1,412 | 8.7 |

*Educational attainment* (1977). Percent of population age 15 and over having: no formal schooling 13.7%; primary education 50.1%; some secondary
32.4%; complete secondary 1.4%; postsecondary 1.8%. *Literacy* (1971): total
population age 15 and over literate 17,066 (57.3%); males literate 8,103
(54.9%); females literate 8,963 (59.6%).
*Health* (1986): physicians[10] 40 (1 per 1,640 persons); hospital beds 331 (1
per 198 persons); infant mortality rate per 1,000 live births 17.4.
*Food* (1981–83): daily per capita caloric intake, 2,324 (vegetable products
84%, animal products 16%); FAO recommended minimum requirement,
n.a.

## Military

*Total active duty personnel* (1986): 1,200 (army 83.4%, navy 8.3%, air force
8.3%). *Military expenditure as percent of GNP* (1984): 5.6% (world 5.9%);
per capita expenditure U.S.$125.

---

[1]Detail does not add to total given because of rounding. [2]Excludes self-employed and
domestic workers. [3]Includes import duties. [4]Includes 5,713 unemployed. [5]Imports
c.i.f. (cost, insurance, and freight). [6]Includes SR 98,000,000 of reexports. [7]Items
reexported. [8]Domestic export only. [9]1986. [10]Includes dentists.

# Sierra Leone

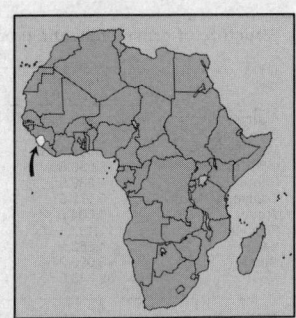

*Official name:* Republic of Sierra Leone.
*Form of government:* a unitary single-party republic with one legislative house (House of Representatives [127[1]]).
*Head of state and government:* President.
*Capital:* Freetown.
*Official language:* English.
*Official religion:* none.
*Monetary unit:* 1 leone (Le) = 100 cents; valuation (Oct. 5, 1987) 1 U.S.\$ = Le 21.80; 1 £ = Le 35.40.

| Area and population | | area | | population |
|---|---|---|---|---|
| **Provinces** | | | | **1985** |
| **Districts** | **Capitals** | **sq mi** | **sq km** | **census[2]** |
| Eastern Province | Kenema | 6,005 | 15,553 | 960,551 |
| Kailahun | Kailahun | 1,490 | 3,859 | 233,839 |
| Kenema | Kenema | 2,337 | 6,053 | 337,055 |
| Kono | Sefadu | 2,178 | 5,641 | 389,657 |
| Northern Province | Makeni | 13,875 | 35,936 | 1,262,226 |
| Bombali | Makeni | 3,083 | 7,985 | 315,914 |
| Kambia | Kambia | 1,200 | 3,108 | 186,231 |
| Koinaduga | Kabala | 4,680 | 12,121 | 183,286 |
| Port Loko | Port Loko | 2,208 | 5,719 | 329,344 |
| Tonkolili | Magburaka | 2,704 | 7,003 | 247,451 |
| Southern Province | Bo | 7,604 | 19,694 | 740,510 |
| Bo | Bo | 2,015 | 5,219 | 268,671 |
| Bonthe (incl. Sherbro) | Bonthe | 1,339 | 3,468 | 105,007 |
| Moyamba | Moyamba | 2,665 | 6,902 | 250,514 |
| Pujehun | Pujehun | 1,585 | 4,105 | 116,318 |
| Western Area | Freetown | 215 | 557 | 554,243 |
| TOTAL | | 27,699 | 71,740 | 3,517,530 |

## Demography

*Population* (1987): 3,803,000.
*Density* (1987): persons per sq mi 137.3, persons per sq km 53.0.
*Urban–rural* (1985): urban 28.3%; rural 71.7%.
*Sex distribution* (1985): male 49.01%; female 50.99%.
*Age breakdown* (1985): under 15, 41.4%; 15–29, 26.1%; 30–44, 17.1%; 45–59, 10.3%; 60–74, 4.5%; 75 and over, 0.6%.
*Population projection:* (1990) 4,024,000; (2000) 4,858,000.
*Doubling time:* 40 years.
*Ethnic composition* (1983): Mende 34.6%; Temne 31.7%; Limba 8.4%; Kono 5.2%; Bullom 3.7%; Fulani 3.7%; Koranko 3.5%; Yalunka 3.5%; Kissi 2.3%; other 3.4%.
*Religious affiliation* (1980): traditional beliefs 51.5%; Sunnī Muslim 39.4%; Protestant 4.7%; Roman Catholic 2.2%; Anglican 1.2%; other 1.0%.
*Major cities* (1985): Freetown 469,776; Koidu-New Sembehun 80,000; Bo 26,000; Kenema 13,000; Makeni 12,000.

## Vital statistics

*Birth rate* per 1,000 population (1980–85): 47.4 (world avg. 29.0); legitimate, n.a.; illegitimate, n.a.
*Death rate* per 1,000 population (1980–85): 29.7 (world avg. 11.0).
*Natural increase rate* per 1,000 population (1980–85): 17.7 (world avg. 18.0).
*Total fertility rate* (avg. births per childbearing woman; 1980–85): 6.1.
*Marriage rate* per 1,000 population: n.a.
*Divorce rate* per 1,000 population: n.a.
*Life expectancy* at birth (1980–85): male 46.7 years; female 50.0 years.
*Major causes of death* per 100,000 population: n.a.; however, the major diseases are malaria, tuberculosis, leprosy, whooping cough, measles, tetanus, and diarrhea.

## National economy

*Budget* (1984–85). Revenue: Le 282,935,000 (import duties 36.9%, direct taxes 27.1%, excise taxes 22.0%, export duties 2.2%, other including grants 11.8%). Expenditures: Le 350,795,000 (public debt charges 33.9%, education and social welfare 25.7%, general administration 20.5%, health 8.9%, construction and development 8.4%, defense 7.0%, police and justice 6.9%, agriculture development 4.6%).
*Public debt* (external, outstanding; 1984): U.S.\$390,000,000.
*Production* (metric tons except as noted). Agriculture, forestry, fishing (1985): rice 500,000, cassava 110,000, palm oil 44,000, pulses 33,000, palm kernels 30,000, millet 20,000, sorghum 20,000, corn (maize) 20,000, peanuts (groundnuts) 14,000, sweet potatoes 13,000, coffee 10,000, cocoa beans 9,000; livestock (number of live animals) 330,000 cattle, 320,000 sheep, 170,000 goats, 44,000 pigs, 5,000,000 chickens; roundwood 7,774,000 cu m; fish catch (1984) 52,500. Mining and quarrying (1986): bauxite 1,242,200; rutile (a titanium ore) 97,101; iron ore 325,000[3]; diamonds 62,453 carats. Manufacturing (1984): salt 19,200; nails 2,300; paint 1,140 hectolitres; beer and stout 35,670 hectolitres; plastic footwear 477,000 pairs[4]; cigarettes 1,346,000 units. Construction (value added in Le; 1981): 56,000,000. Energy production (consumption): electricity (kW-hr; 1985) 278,000,000 (278,000,-000); coal, none (n.a.); crude petroleum (barrels; 1985) none (1,759,000); petroleum products (metric tons; 1985) 210,000 (182,000); natural gas, none (n.a.).
*Household income and expenditure.* Average household size (1980) 4.9; average annual income per household (1984): U.S.\$320; sources of income (1984): self-employment 61.6%, wages and salaries 27.9%, other 10.5%;

expenditure (1984): food, beverages, and tobacco 55.1%, clothing and footwear 12.9%, transport and communication 9.2%, furniture, furnishings, and household durable goods 8.0%, housing 7.4%, recreation, entertainment, and education 3.8%, health 1.3%.
*Tourism* (1984): receipts from visitors U.S.\$7,000,000; expenditures by nationals abroad U.S.\$5,000,000.
*Gross national product* (at current market prices; 1985): U.S.\$1,380,000,000 (U.S.\$380 per capita).

| Structure of gross domestic product and labour force | | | | |
|---|---|---|---|---|
| | 1981–82 | | 1983–84 | |
| | in value Le '000,000 | % of total value | labour force[5] | % of labour force |
| Agriculture | 460.4 | 33.1 | 5,835 | 7.9 |
| Mining | 71.2 | 5.1 | 6,075 | 8.2 |
| Manufacturing | 66.4 | 4.8 | 8,046 | 10.9 |
| Construction | 78.1 | 5.6 | 8,986 | 12.2 |
| Public utilities | 7.4 | 0.5 | 2,134 | 2.9 |
| Transportation and communication | 184.8 | 13.3 | 7,211 | 9.8 |
| Trade | 180.4 | 13.0 } | 6,161 | 8.3 |
| Finance | 141.0 | 10.1 } | | |
| Pub. admin., defense | 147.7 | 10.6 } | 23,821 | 32.2 |
| Services | 61.6 | 4.4 } | | |
| Other | −7.2[6] | −0.5[6] | 5,639[7] | 7.6[7] |
| TOTAL | 1,391.8[8] | 100.0 | 73,908 | 100.0 |

*Population economically active* (1985): total 1,352,000; activity rate of total population 36.9% (participation rates: ages 15–64 62.9%; female 33.7%; unemployed [registered; 1984] 7.6%).

| Price index (1980 = 100) | | | | | | | |
|---|---|---|---|---|---|---|---|
| | 1981 | 1982 | 1983 | 1984 | 1985 | 1986 | 1987[9] |
| Consumer price index | 123.3 | 156.5 | 263.8 | 439.4 | 776.0 | 870.3 | 4,904.0 |

*Land use* (1984): forested 29.2%; meadows and pastures 30.8%; agricultural and under permanent cultivation 24.7%; other 15.3%.

## Foreign trade

| Balance of trade (current prices) | | | | | | |
|---|---|---|---|---|---|---|
| | 1980 | 1981 | 1982 | 1983 | 1984 | 1985 |
| Le '000,000 | −230.1 | −205.9 | −231.5 | −85.0 | −46.7 | −249.0 |
| % of total | 34.6% | 40.0% | 45.8% | 17.4% | 5.9% | 18.7% |

*Imports* (1985): Le 788,654,000 (food and live animals 29.8%; machinery and transport equipment 23.3%; minerals, fuels, and lubricants 21.3%; basic manufactured goods 13.4%; chemicals 4.2%). *Major import sources* (1984): United Kingdom 11.4%; West Germany 11.0%; Japan 6.1%; The Netherlands 5.0%; France 4.9%; United States 4.6%; China 2.3%.
*Exports* (1985): Le 649,266,000 (rutile 21.8%; coffee 20.3%; diamonds 18.8%; bauxite 17.4%; cacao 15.6%; gold 4.2%). *Major export destinations:* The Netherlands 30.9%; United Kingdom 14.6%; West Germany 11.2%; United States 9.5%.

## Transport and communications

*Transport.* Railroads (1982): length 52 mi, 84 km. Roads (1980): total length 4,635 mi, 7,459 km (paved 16%). Vehicles (1984): passenger cars 19,040; trucks and buses 6,763. Merchant marine (1986): vessels (100 gross tons and over) 29; total deadweight tonnage 1,752. Air transport[10] (1984): passenger-mi 75,698,000, passenger-km 121,825,000; short ton-mi cargo 1,337,000, metric ton-km cargo 1,952,000; airports (1987) with scheduled flights 6.
*Communications.* Daily newspapers (1986): total number 1; total circulation 10,000; circulation per 1,000 population 2.7. Radio (1986): total number of receivers 225,000 (1 per 17 persons). Television (1986): total number of receivers 25,000 (1 per 150 persons). Telephones (1981): 220,000 (1 per 15.4 persons).

## Education and health

| Education (1984–85) | | | | student/ |
|---|---|---|---|---|
| | schools | teachers | students | teacher ratio |
| Primary (age 5–11) | 1,219 | 10,451 | 350,160 | 33.5 |
| Secondary (age 12–18) | 171 | 3,829 | 81,879 | 21.4 |
| Voc., teacher tr. | 12 | 406 | 4,774 | 11.8 |
| Higher | 2 | 296 | 2,445 | 8.3 |

*Educational attainment* (1974). Percent of population age 5 and over having: no formal schooling 81.3%; primary education 12.1%; secondary 5.9%; higher 0.7%. *Literacy* (1980): total population age 15 and over literate 460,-300 (23.6%); males literate 294,500 (31.2%); females literate 165,800 (16.5%).
*Health* (1983): physicians 197 (1 per 17,906 persons); hospital beds 4,754 (1 per 742 persons); infant mortality rate per 1,000 live births 134.0.
*Food* (1981–83): daily per capita caloric intake 2,010 (vegetable products 96%, animal products 4%); (1983) 91% of FAO recommended minimum requirement.

## Military

*Total active duty personnel* (1986): 3,100 (army 96.8%, navy 3.2%, air force, none). *Military expenditure as percent of GNP* (1984): 0.7% (world 5.9%); per capita expenditure U.S.\$2.

---

[1]Includes 22 nonelective seats. [2]Preliminary. [3]1984. [4]1982. [5]Registered employment only. [6]Import duties less imputed bank service charge. [7]Registered unemployed. [8]At factor cost. [9]June. [10]International flights only.

# Singapore

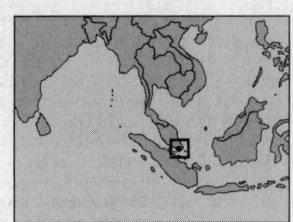

*Official name:* Hsin-chia-p'o
Kung-ho-kuo (Mandarin Chinese);
Republik Singapura (Malay);
Singapore Kudiyarasu (Tamil);
Republic of Singapore (English).
*Form of government:* unitary multiparty
republic with one legislative house
(Parliament [79]).
*Chief of state:* President.
*Head of government:* Prime Minister.
*Capital:* Singapore.
*Official languages:* Chinese; Malay;
Tamil; English.
*Official religion:* none.
*Monetary unit:* 1 Singapore dollar
(S$) = 100 cents; valuation (Oct. 5,
1987) 1 U.S.$ = S$2.10; 1 £ = S$3.41.

| Area and population | area | | population |
|---|---|---|---|
| Census areas[1] | sq mi | sq km | 1984 estimate |
| Central city area | 3 | 8 | 157,000 |
| City periphery | 17 | 46 | 942,800 |
| North | 7 | 19 | 228,100 |
| Northeast | 3 | 9 | 301,500 |
| West | 7 | 18 | 413,200 |
| Suburbs | 49 | 127 | 754,700 |
| East | 7 | 19 | 195,000 |
| North | 13 | 34 | 309,900 |
| West | 29 | 74 | 249,800 |
| Outlying areas | 169 | 437 | 674,600 |
| East | 46 | 118 | 301,100 |
| North | 53 | 137 | 177,500 |
| West | 70 | 182 | 196,000 |
| TOTAL | 240[2] | 622[2] | 2,529,100 |

## Demography

*Population* (1987): 2,616,000.
*Density* (1987): persons per sq mi 6,777.2, persons per sq km 4,205.8.
*Urban–rural* (1987): urban 100.0%.
*Sex distribution* (1986): male 50.92%; female 49.08%.
*Age breakdown* (1986): under 15, 23.9%; 15–29, 31.1%; 30–44, 24.0%; 45–59, 13.0%; 60 and over, 8.0%.
*Population projection:* (1990) 2,706,000; (2000) 3,030,000.
*Doubling time:* 71 years.
*Ethnic composition* (1986): Chinese 76.3%; Malay 15.0%; Indian[3] 6.4%; other 2.3%.
*Religious affiliation* (1980): Taoist 29.3%; Buddhist 26.7%; Muslim 16.3%; Christian 10.3%; Hindu 3.6%; nonreligious 13.2%; other 0.6%.
*Major cities:* Singapore is a unitary city-state having no separately defined cities within its borders.

## Vital statistics

*Birth rate* per 1,000 population (1986): 14.8 (world avg. 26.0).
*Death rate* per 1,000 population (1986): 5.0 (world avg. 9.9).
*Natural increase rate* per 1,000 population (1986): 9.8 (world avg. 16.1).
*Total fertility rate* (avg. births per childbearing woman; 1986): 1.4.
*Marriage rate* per 1,000 population (1986): 7.8.
*Divorce rate* per 1,000 population (1986): 0.9.
*Life expectancy* at birth (1986): male 69.9 years; female 76.2 years.
*Major causes of death* per 100,000 population (1985): diseases of the circulatory system 177.5, of which heart and hypertensive diseases 118.8; malignant neoplasms (cancers) 112.5; diseases of the respiratory system 84.8, of which pneumonia 48.6; accidents, poisoning, and violence 48.9.

## National economy

*Budget* (1986–87). Revenue: S$14,552,911,000 (premiums on land sales 44.8%; income tax 17.5%; interest and dividends 12.5%; import and excise duties 6.0%; property tax 5.8%; sales of goods and services 4.3%; motor vehicle taxes 4.0%). Expenditures: S$22,193,618,000 (social welfare and housing 42.4%; defense, justice, and police 12.0%; transport and communication 9.2%; education 8.1%; agricultural, industrial, and commercial development 4.6%; general services 4.0%; health 2.4%).
*Tourism* (1985): receipts from visitors U.S.$1,754,000,000; expenditures by nationals abroad U.S.$615,000,000.
*Production* (metric tons except as noted). Agriculture, forestry, fishing (1985): vegetables 28,648, fruits 5,610, sugarcane 370, tobacco 16; livestock (number of live animals) 810,000 pigs, 1,000 cattle, 1,000 goats, fish catch (1986) 20,279. Mining and quarrying (value added in S$; 1986): granite 78,-900,000. Manufacturing (value added in S$; 1986): electronic products and components 3,615,100,000; transport equipment 1,094,100,000; fabricated metal products except machinery and equipment 718,400,000; nonelectrical machinery 701,300,000; paints, pharmaceuticals, and chemical products 610,500,000; printing and publishing 523,100,000; petroleum refining and petroleum products 515,200,000. Construction (1985): residential 9,222,000 sq m; nonresidential 2,202,000 sq m. Energy production (consumption): electricity (kW-hr; 1986) 10,576,500,000 (9,475,800,000); coal, none (none); crude petroleum (barrels; 1985) none (260,882,000); petroleum products (metric tons; 1985) 32,236,000 (13,609,000); natural gas, none (none).
*Land use* (1984): forested 4.6%; agricultural and under permanent cultivation 9.5%; built-up area 47.6%; other 38.3%.
*Gross national product* (1985): U.S.$18,970,000,000 (U.S.$7,420 per capita).

## Structure of gross domestic product and labour force

| | 1986 | | | |
|---|---|---|---|---|
| | in value S$'000,000[4] | % of total value | labour force | % of labour force |
| Agriculture | 260.8 | 0.7 | 9,602 | 0.8 |
| Quarrying | 94.3 | 0.2 | 1,329 | 0.1 |
| Manufacturing | 9,955.8 | 25.1 | 290,114 | 25.2 |
| Construction | 3,230.8 | 8.2 | 99,504 | 8.7 |
| Public utilities | 839.9 | 2.1 | 7,797 | 0.7 |
| Transp. and commun. | 5,679.5 | 14.3 | 114,145 | 9.9 |
| Trade | 6,604.2 | 16.7 | 265,645 | 23.1 |
| Finance | 11,197.9 | 28.2 | 99,905 | 8.7 |
| Services | 4,863.9 | 12.3 | 259,177 | 22.6 |
| Other | −3,086.2[5] | −7.8[5] | 1,805 | 0.2 |
| TOTAL | 39,640.9 | 100.0 | 1,149,023 | 100.0 |

*Population economically active* (1986): total 1,149,023; activity rate of total population 44.4% (participation rates: age 15 and over, 58.4%; female 21.9%; unemployed 4.2%).

| Price and earnings indexes (1980 = 100) | | | | | | | |
|---|---|---|---|---|---|---|---|
| | 1980 | 1981 | 1982 | 1983 | 1984 | 1985 | 1986 |
| Consumer price index | 100.0 | 108.3 | 112.4 | 113.8 | 116.8 | 117.3 | 115.7 |
| Weekly earnings index | 100.0 | 113.8 | 128.3 | 137.2 | 149.0 | 156.9 | ... |

*Household income and expenditure.* Average household size (1984) 3.9; income per household S$20,800 (U.S.$9,700); sources of income (1977–78): wages and salaries 75.4%, self-employment 18.7%, transfer payments 2.0%, other 3.9%; expenditure (1984): food 25.0%, transportation and communication 13.9%, recreation and education 11.7%, housing 9.3%, furniture and household equipment 8.8%, clothing and footwear 8.1%, health 3.0%.
*Public debt* (external, outstanding; 1986): U.S.$2,120,100,000.

## Foreign trade[6]

| Balance of trade (current prices) | | | | | | |
|---|---|---|---|---|---|---|
| | 1981 | 1982 | 1983 | 1984 | 1985 | 1986 |
| S$'000,000 | −10,973 | −12,361 | −10,140 | −6,497 | −4,521 | −3,384 |
| % of total | 11.0% | 12.2% | 9.9% | 6.0% | 4.3% | 3.3% |

*Imports* (1986): S$55,545,400,000 (crude petroleum 14.8%, petroleum products 5.0%, telecommunications apparatus 4.1%, office machines 3.7%, electric power machinery 3.3%, woven textile fabrics 3.0%, ships, boats, and oil rigs 2.3%, scientific and optical instruments 2.3%). *Major import sources:* Japan 19.9%; United States 15.0%; Malaysia 13.3%; China 5.6%; Taiwan 4.0%; Kuwait 3.8%; United Kingdom 3.4%; West Germany 3.3%.
*Exports* (1986): S$48,985,500,000 (petroleum products 20.5%, office machines 9.0%, telecommunications apparatus 6.6%, electrical circuit apparatus 3.1%, clothing 3.0%, crude rubber 2.7%, scientific and optical instruments 1.5%). *Major export destinations:* United States 23.3%; Malaysia 14.8%; Japan 8.6%; Hong Kong 6.5%; Thailand 3.6%; West Germany 3.1%; Australia 3.1%; United Kingdom 2.6%.

## Transport and communications

*Transport.* Railroads (1985): length 16 mi, 26 km. Roads (1985): total length 1,643 mi, 2,644 km (paved 95%). Vehicles (1986): passenger cars 234,557; trucks and buses 114,281. Merchant marine (1986): vessels (100 gross tons and over) 716; total deadweight tonnage 10,603,737. Air transport (1986): passenger-mi 14,212,000,000, passenger-km 22,872,000,000; short ton-mi cargo 791,421,000, metric ton-km cargo 1,155,456,000; airports (1987) with scheduled flights 1.
*Communications.* Daily newspapers (1986): total number 7; total circulation 697,500; circulation per 1,000 population 270. Radio (1986): 111,568[7] receivers (1 per 23 persons). Television (1986): 398,340[7] receivers (1 per 6.5 persons). Telephones (1986): 1,074,000 (1 per 2.4 persons).

## Education and health

| Education (1986) | schools | teachers | students | student/ teacher ratio |
|---|---|---|---|---|
| Primary (age 6–13) | 236 | 10,515 | 268,820 | 25.6 |
| Secondary (age 12–18) | 157 | 8,695 | 203,088 | 23.4 |
| Voc., teacher tr. | 16 | 2,718 | 20,873 | 7.7 |
| Higher | 5 | 3,812 | 42,007 | 11.0 |

*Educational attainment* (1980). Percent of population age 25 and over having: no schooling 43.7%; primary education 38.3%; secondary 14.6%; postsecondary 3.4%. *Literacy* (1980): total population age 15 and over literate 1,459,828 (82.9%); males literate 818,864 (91.6%); females literate 640,964 (74.0%).
*Health* (1985): physicians 2,631 (1 per 972 persons); hospital beds 9,866 (1 per 259 persons); infant mortality rate per 1,000 live births (1986) 9.4.
*Food* (1981–83): daily per capita caloric intake 2,683 (vegetable products 75%, animal products 25%); (1983) 115% of FAO recommended minimum requirement.

## Military

*Total active duty personnel* (1986): 55,500 (army 81.1%, navy 8.1%, air force 10.8%). *Military expenditure as percent of GNP* (1984): 5.3% (world 5.9%); per capita expenditure U.S.$401.

---

[1]The census areas have no administrative function. [2]Includes 2 sq mi (4 sq km) not distributable by census areas. [3]Includes Sri Lankan. [4]At prices of 1985. [5]Less imputed bank service charges. [6]Import figures are f.o.b. (free on board) in balance trade and c.i.f. (cost, insurance, and freight) for commodities and trading partners. [7]Licenses only.

# Solomon Islands

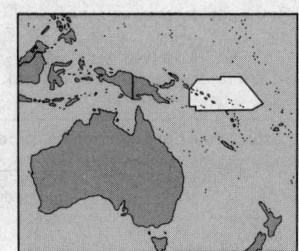

*Official name:* Solomon Islands.
*Form of government:* parliamentary
state with one legislative house
(National Parliament [38]).
*Chief of state:* British Monarch
represented by governor-general.
*Head of government:* Prime Minister.
*Capital:* Honiara.
*Official language:* English.
*Official religion:* none.
*Monetary unit:* 1 Solomon Islands
dollar (SI$) = 100 cents; valuation
(Oct. 5, 1987) 1 U.S.$ = SI$2.01;
1 £ = SI$3.27.

### Area and population

| Provinces | Capitals | area sq mi | area sq km | population 1986 census[1] |
|---|---|---|---|---|
| Central Islands | Tulagi | 493 | 1,276 | 18,522 |
| Guadalcanal | Honiara | 2,047 | 5,302 | 50,327 |
| Isabel | Buala | 1,550 | 4,014 | 14,564 |
| Makira | Kira Kira | 1,231 | 3,188 | 21,646 |
| Malaita | Auki | 1,638 | 4,243 | 80,183 |
| Temotu | Santa Cruz | 358 | 926 | 14,683 |
| Western | Gizo | 3,310 | 8,573 | 55,372 |
| **Capital Territory** | | | | |
| Honiara | — | 13 | 34 | 30,499 |
| TOTAL | | 10,640[2] | 27,556 | 285,796 |

## Demography

*Population* (1987): 291,800.
*Density* (1987): persons per sq mi 27.4, persons per sq km 10.6.
*Urban–rural* (1986): urban 15.7%; rural 84.3%.
*Sex distribution* (1986): male 51.76%; female 48.24%.
*Age breakdown* (1985): under 15, 49.1%; 15–29, 24.2%; 30–49, 16.4%; 50–59, 4.8%; 60 and over, 5.5%.
*Population projection:* (1990) 323,700; (2000) 457,300.
*Doubling time:* 21 years.
*Ethnic composition* (1976): Melanesian 93.3%; Polynesian 4.0%; Micronesian 1.4%; European 0.7%; Chinese 0.2%; other 0.4%.
*Religious affiliation* (1980): Christian 95.3%, of which Protestant 76.2%, Roman Catholic 19.1%; traditional beliefs 4.0%; other 0.7%.
*Major cities* (1986)[3]: Honiara 30,499; Gizo 3,727; Auki 3,262; Kira Kira 2,585; Buala 1,913.

## Vital statistics

*Birth rate* per 1,000 population (1982): 44.6 (world avg. 29.0).
*Death rate* per 1,000 population (1982): 11.7 (world avg. 11.0).
*Natural increase rate* per 1,000 population (1982): 32.9 (world avg. 18.0).
*Total fertility rate* (avg. births per childbearing woman; 1982): 7.3.
*Marriage rate* per 1,000 population: n.a.
*Divorce rate* per 1,000 population: n.a.
*Life expectancy* at birth (1982): male 54 years; female 54 years.
*Major causes of death* per 100,000 population: n.a.; however, major diseases include malaria, tuberculosis, and leprosy[4].

## National economy

*Budget* (1984). Revenue: SI$65,500,000 (recurrent revenue SI$53,300,000, of which import duties 32.1%, government earnings 22.8%, export duties 18.9%; foreign aid grants 5.2%). Expenditures: SI$66,400,000 (recurrent expenditure SI$50,500,000, of which administrative infrastructure 51.1%, education 11.1%, health 6.3%; development expenditure 23.9%, of which commerce and industry 6.9%, natural resources 6.1%).
*Public debt* (external, outstanding; 1985): U.S.$59,900,000.
*Tourism* (1986): tourist arrivals 7,503.
*Gross national product* (at current market prices; 1986): U.S.$197,000,000 (U.S.$700 per capita).

### Structure of gross domestic product and labour force

| | 1985 in value SI$'000,000 | 1985 % of total value | 1986 labour force[5] | 1986 % of labour force |
|---|---|---|---|---|
| Agriculture | ... | [6] | 8,411 | 33.9 |
| Mining | ... | ... | 101 | 0.4 |
| Manufacturing | ... | ... | 1,771 | 7.1 |
| Construction | ... | ... | 1,385 | 5.6 |
| Public utilities | ... | ... | 328 | 1.3 |
| Transportation and communication | ... | ... | 1,888 | 7.6 |
| Trade | ... | ... | 2,491 | 10.0 |
| Finance | ... | ... | 604 | 2.5 |
| Pub. admin., defense | ... | ...⎫ | 7,047 | 28.4 |
| Services | ... | ...⎭ | | |
| Other | ... | ... | 800 | 3.2 |
| TOTAL | 211.5[7] | 100.0 | 24,826 | 100.0 |

*Household income and expenditure.* Average household size (1986) 6.4; average annual income per household (1983) SI$1,010[8] (U.S.$1,160); sources of income (1983): wages and salaries 74.1%, self-employment, remittances, gifts, and other assistance 25.9%; expenditure (1984)[9]: food 47.0%, housing 15.5%, drink and tobacco 9.5%, clothing 5.0%, transportation 1.1%.

*Population economically active* (1985): total 23,996[5]; activity rate of total population 42.7% (participation rates: ages 15–64, 86.3%; female 16.8%[5]; unemployed, n.a.).

### Price and earnings indexes (1980 = 100)

| | 1981 | 1982 | 1983 | 1984 | 1985 | 1986 | 1987[10] |
|---|---|---|---|---|---|---|---|
| Consumer price index | 116.4 | 131.5 | 140.5 | 155.9 | 170.9 | 193.1 | 206.9 |
| Annual earnings index[8] | 108.0 | 118.8 | 131.4 | 145.9 | 154.0 | 154.2 | ... |

*Production* (metric tons except as noted). Agriculture, forestry, fishing (1985): coconuts 311,000, sweet potatoes 50,000, copra 41,904, taro 22,000, palm oil 20,000, yams 19,000, paddy rice 5,945, cocoa 1,715; livestock (number of live animals; 1983) 48,000 pigs, 19,750 cattle; roundwood (1986) 471,300 cu m; fish catch (1986) 44,207. Mining and quarrying (1983): gold 34 kilograms; silver 8 kilograms. Manufacturing (1986): processed fish 44,042, palm oil 14,560; milled rice 2,282; other major industries include soap and tobacco manufacturing, weaving, wood carving, fibreglass products, boatbuilding, and leather working. Construction (gross value in SI$; 1980): residential 1,858,000; nonresidential 693,000. Energy production (consumption): electricity (kW-hr; 1985) 29,000,000 (29,000,000); coal, none (n.a.); petroleum products (metric tons; 1985) none (44,000); natural gas, none (n.a.).
*Land use* (1984): forested 93.0%; meadows and pastures 1.4%; agricultural and under permanent cultivation 2.0%; other 3.6%.

## Foreign trade

### Balance of trade (current prices)

| | 1981 | 1982 | 1983 | 1984 | 1985 | 1986 |
|---|---|---|---|---|---|---|
| SI$'000 | −8,419 | −929 | +592 | +34,725 | +1,142 | +10,562 |
| % of total | 6.8% | 0.8% | 0.4% | 17.2% | 0.6% | 4.8% |

*Imports* (1986): SI$104,325,000 (machinery and transport equipment 29.5%; mineral fuels and lubricants 18.9%; food 16.7%; manufactured goods 15.7%; chemicals 4.7%). *Major import sources:* Australia 40.0%; Japan 16.9%; Singapore 8.2%; New Zealand 7.7%; West Germany 5.5%; United Kingdom 4.1%; China 3.5%; Hong Kong 3.0%; United States 2.3%.
*Exports* (1986): SI$114,889,000 (food 52.3%; crude materials, inedible 37.7%; animal and vegetable oils and fats 4.9%). *Major export destinations:* Japan 37.0%; Thailand 23.1%; Australia 12.4%; United Kingdom 8.5%; South Korea 4.3%; Papua New Guinea 4.0%; West Germany 3.5%; Hong Kong 3.0%; The Netherlands 2.5%; Norway 1.2%; Sweden 1.2%.

## Transport and communications

*Transport.* Railroads (1985): none. Roads[11] (1984): total length 1,300 mi, 2,100 km (paved 12%). Vehicles (1982): passenger cars 1,122; trucks and buses 1,323. Merchant marine (1986): vessels (100 gross tons and over) 27; total deadweight tonnage 5,150. Air transport (1984)[12]: passenger-mi 6,852,000, passenger-km 11,027,000; short ton-mi cargo 25,000, metric ton-km cargo 37,000; airports (1987) with scheduled flights 25.
*Communications.* Daily newspapers[13] (1986): none. Radio (1986): total number of receivers 40,000 (1 per 7.0 persons). Television (1986): none. Telephones (1985): 3,827 (1 per 71 persons).

## Education and health

### Education (1984)

| | schools | teachers | students | student/ teacher ratio |
|---|---|---|---|---|
| Primary (age 7–12) | 423 | 1,536 | 37,522 | 24.4 |
| Secondary (age 13–18) | 20 | 267 | 5,118 | 19.2 |
| Voc., teacher tr. | 2 | 63 | 1,142 | 18.1 |
| Higher | — | — | — | — |

*Educational attainment* (1976)[14]. Percent of population age 25 and over having: no schooling 55.5%; primary education 39.5%; secondary 3.3%; higher 1.6%. *Literacy* (1976): total population age 15 and over literate 55,500 (54.1%); males 33,600 (62.4%); females 21,900 (44.9%).
*Health:* physicians (1985) 32 (1 per 8,509 persons); hospital beds (1983) 1,398 (1 per 183 persons); infant mortality rate per 1,000 live births (1982) 46.
*Food* (1981–83): daily per capita caloric intake 2,119 (vegetable products 89%, animal products 11%); (1983) 80% of FAO recommended minimum requirement.

## Military

*Total active duty personnel:* no military forces are maintained, but a police force of about 500 provides internal security.

---

[1]November 23–24; provisional. [2]Detail does not add to total given because of rounding. [3]Ward populations. [4]Reported cases of these diseases in 1983 were: malaria 84,343, tuberculosis 302, and leprosy 33. [5]Wage earners only. 635–40% of the GDP is generated by subsistence agriculture. [7]Provisional. [8]Public service earnings. [9]Consumer price index components. [10]April. [11]Includes 500 mi (800 km) of privately maintained roads mainly for plantation use. [12]Solair only. [13]In 1985 there were two weekly newspapers with a combined circulation of 6,700. [14]Indigenous population only.

# Somalia

*Official name:* Jamhuuriyadda
Dimuqraadiga Soomaaliya
(Somali); Jumhūriyah aṣ-Ṣumāl
ad-Dīmuqrāṭīyah (Arabic) (Somali
Democratic Republic).
*Form of government:*
military-dominated, single-party
republic with one legislative house
(People's Assembly [177][1]).
*Chief of state:* President.
*Head of government:* Prime Minister.
*Capital:* Mogadishu.
*Official languages:* Somali; Arabic.
*Official religion:* Islam.
*Monetary unit:* 1 Somali shilling
(So.Sh.) = 100 cents; valuation (Oct. 5,
1987) 1 U.S.$ = So.Sh. 120.21;
1 £ = So.Sh. 195.21.

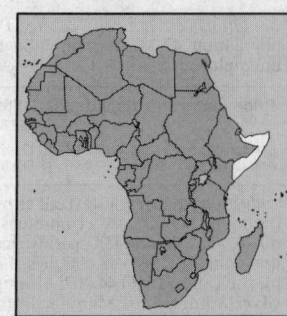

### Area and population

| Regions | Capitals | area sq mi | area sq km | population 1980 estimate |
|---|---|---|---|---|
| Bakool | Xuddur | 10,000 | 27,000 | 148,700 |
| Banaadir | Mogadishu | 400 | 1,000 | 520,100 |
| Bari | Boosaaso | 27,000 | 70,000 | 222,300 |
| Bay | Baydhabo | 15,000 | 39,000 | 451,000 |
| Galguduud | Dhuusa Mareeb | 17,000 | 43,000 | 255,900 |
| Gedo | Garbahaarrey | 12,000 | 32,000 | 235,000 |
| Hiiraan | Beled Weyne | 13,000 | 34,000 | 219,300 |
| Jubbada Dhexe | Bu'aale | 9,000 | 23,000 | 147,800 |
| Jubbada Hoose | Kismaayo | 24,000 | 61,000 | 272,400 |
| Mudug | Gaalkacyo | 27,000 | 70,000 | 311,200 |
| Nugaal | Garoowe | 19,000 | 50,000 | 112,200 |
| Sanaag | Ceerigaabo | 21,000 | 54,000 | 216,500 |
| Shabeellaha Dhexe | Towhar | 8,000 | 22,000 | 352,000 |
| Shabeellaha Hoose | Marca | 10,000 | 25,000 | 570,700 |
| Togdheer | Burko | 16,000 | 41,000 | 383,900 |
| Woqooyi Galbeed | Hargeysa | 17,000 | 45,000 | 655,000 |
| TOTAL | | 246,000[2] | 637,000 | 5,074,000 |

## Demography

*Population* (1987): 6,160,000.
*Density* (1987): persons per sq mi 25.0, persons per sq km 9.7.
*Urban–rural* (1984): urban 33.0%; rural 67.0%.
*Sex distribution* (1985): male 45.78%; female 54.22%.
*Age breakdown* (1985): under 15, 43.7%; 15–29, 25.0%; 30–44, 14.7%; 45–59,
10.1%; 60–74, 5.9%; 75 and over, 0.6%.
*Population projection:* (1990) 6,476,000; (2000) 7,134,000.
*Doubling time:* 23 years.
*Ethnic composition* (1983): Somali 98.3%; Arab 1.2%; Bantu 0.4%; other
0.1%.
*Religious affiliation* (1980): Sunnī Muslim 99.8%; Christian 0.1%; other 0.1%.
*Major cities* (1981): Mogadishu 500,000; Hargeysa 70,000; Kismaayo 70,000;
Berbera 65,000; Marca 60,000.

## Vital statistics

*Birth rate* per 1,000 population (1984): 49.0 (world avg. 29.0); legitimate,
n.a.; illegitimate, n.a.
*Death rate* per 1,000 population (1984): 20.0 (world avg. 11.0).
*Natural increase rate* per 1,000 population (1984): 29.0 (world avg. 18.0).
*Total fertility rate* (avg. births per childbearing woman; 1984): 6.8.
*Marriage rate* per 1,000 population: n.a.
*Divorce rate* per 1,000 population: n.a.
*Life expectancy* at birth (1984): male 44.0 years; female 47.0 years.
*Major causes of death* per 100,000 population: n.a.; however, major diseases
include leprosy, malaria, tetanus, and tuberculosis.

## National economy

*Budget* (1985). Revenue: So.Sh. 7,753,500,000 (taxes on international transactions 36.1%, import duties 29.4%, income from government property
7.6%, income tax 1.3%). Expenditures: So.Sh. 7,753,500,000 (finance and
central services 38.9%, defense 23.3%, economic services 12.8%, education
6.9%, foreign affairs 5.5%, health 2.3%, general administration 1.8%).
*Tourism:* receipts from visitors (1985) U.S.$8,000,000; expenditures by na-
tionals abroad (1983) U.S.$13,000,000.
*Production* (metric tons except as noted). Agriculture, forestry, fishing (1986):
corn (maize) 382,000, sugarcane 278,000, sorghum 251,000, bananas 87,000,
sesame seed 52,000, roots and tubers 41,000, vegetables 32,000, citrus fruits
22,000, rice 18,000, beans 13,000, dates 10,000, seed cotton 3,000, peanuts
(groundnuts) 1,000; livestock (number of live animals; 1985) 18,500,000
goats, 11,100,000 sheep, 6,000,000 camels, 4,400,000 cattle; roundwood
(1985) 4,435,000 cu m; fish catch (1985) 16,100. Mining and quarrying
(1984): salt 30,000. Manufacturing (value added in So.Sh. '000,000; 1984):
food and beverages 315.2; public utilities 131.8; petroleum products 90.6;
printing and publishing 87.5; textiles 53.0; clothing and footwear 36.9. Construction (value added in So.Sh.; 1982): 1,687,200,000. Energy production
(consumption): electricity (kW-hr; 1985) 145,000,000 (145,000,000); coal,
none (n.a.); crude petroleum (barrels; 1985) n.a. (2,713,000); petroleum
products (metric tons; 1985) 341,000 (358,000); natural gas, none (n.a.).
*Household income and expenditure.* Average household size (1980) 4.9;
income per household: n.a.; sources of income: n.a.; expenditure[3] (1983):

food and tobacco 62.3%, housing 15.3%, clothing 5.6%, energy 4.3%, other
12.1%.
*Public debt* (external, outstanding; 1985): U.S.$1,308,500,000.
*Gross national product* (at current market prices; 1985): U.S.$1,470,000,000
(U.S.$250 per capita).

### Structure of gross domestic product and labour force

| | 1985 in value So.Sh. '000,000[4] | 1985 % of total value | 1985 labour force | 1985 % of labour force |
|---|---|---|---|---|
| Agriculture | 4,202 | 57.5 | 1,468,000 | 73.5 |
| Mining | 21 | 0.3 | | |
| Manufacturing | 348 | 4.8 | | |
| Construction | 233 | 3.2 | | |
| Public utilities | 8 | 0.1 | | |
| Transportation and communication | 472 | 6.5 | 531,000 | 26.5 |
| Trade | 674 | 9.2 | | |
| Finance | 409 | 5.6 | | |
| Pub. admin., defense | 474 | 6.5 | | |
| Services | 189 | 2.6 | | |
| Other | 273 | 3.7 | — | — |
| TOTAL | 7,303 | 100.0 | 1,999,000 | 100.0 |

*Population economically active* (1985): total 1,999,000; activity rate of total population 42.9% (participation rates: ages 15–64, n.a.; female [1980]
22.1%; unemployed, n.a.).

### Price and earnings indexes (1980 = 100)

| | 1980 | 1981 | 1982 | 1983 | 1984 | 1985 | 1986[5] |
|---|---|---|---|---|---|---|---|
| Consumer price index | 100.0 | 144.4 | 178.5 | 241.4 | 464.1 | 639.5 | 901.6 |
| Earnings index | | | | | | | |

*Land use* (1984): forested 14.3%; meadows and pastures 65.2%; agricultural
and under permanent cultivation 1.7%; other 18.8%.

## Foreign trade

### Balance of trade (current prices)

| | 1980 | 1981 | 1982 | 1983 | 1984 | 1985 |
|---|---|---|---|---|---|---|
| So.Sh. '000,000 | −1,069.9 | −1,841.4 | −73.5 | −1,421.4 | −995.3 | −275.0 |
| % of total | 39.0% | 48.9% | 1.8% | 33.3% | 35.8% | 3.7% |

*Imports* (1984): So.Sh. 5,135,000,000 (food 25.5%; machinery and transport
equipment 22.0%, of which transport equipment 15.1%, electrical equipment 2.5%; construction materials 20.4%; mineral fuels 7.8%; manufacturing raw materials 5.6%; beverages and tobacco 2.0%; chemical products
1.72%; clothing and footwear 1.5%). *Major import sources:* Italy 35.5%;
United States 9.1%; West Germany 6.6%; France 6.3%; United Kingdom
4.8%; Kenya 3.2%; Thailand 2.3%; Japan 1.6%; Singapore 1.2%; China 1.0%.
*Exports* (1984): So.Sh. 1,273,800,000 (live animals 59.6%, of which goats
30.9%, sheep 27.5%; bananas 7.9%; undressed hides, skins, and furs 0.9%).
*Major export destinations:* Saudi Arabia 78.7%; Italy 2.9%; China 0.1%.

## Transport and communications

*Transport.* Railroads: none. Roads (1984): total length 13,242 mi, 21,311
km (paved 12%). Vehicles (1981): passenger cars 17,754; trucks and buses
9,533. Merchant marine (1986): vessels (100 gross tons and over) 26; total
deadweight tonnage 14,960. Air transport (1985): passenger-mi 147,500,000,
passenger-km 237,400,000; short ton-mi cargo 2,300,000, metric ton-km
cargo 3,300,000; airports (1987) with scheduled flights 9.
*Communications.* Daily newspapers (1986): total number 1; total circulation,
n.a. Radio (1986): total number of receivers 250,000 (1 per 24 persons).
Television[6]: total number of receivers, n.a. Telephones (1981): 4,800 (1
per 782 persons).

## Education and health

### Education (1984–85)

| | schools | teachers | students | student/ teacher ratio |
|---|---|---|---|---|
| Primary (age 6–14) | 1,121 | 14,521 | 274,610 | 18.9 |
| Secondary (age 15–18) | 80 | 2,522 | 65,186 | 25.8 |
| Voc., teacher tr. | 23 | 725 | 10,203 | 14.1 |
| Higher | 1 | 262[7] | 3,405 | ... |

*Educational attainment,* n.a. *Literacy* (1975): total population age 10 and
over literate 54.8%; males literate 60.9%; females literate 47.9%.
*Health* (1985): physicians 321 (1 per 18,156 persons); hospital beds 5,536 (1
per 1,053 persons); infant mortality rate per 1,000 live births 152.0.
*Food* (1981–83): daily per capita caloric intake 2,129 (vegetable products
71%, animal products 29%); (1983) 89% of FAO recommended minimum
requirement.

## Military

*Total active duty personnel* (1987): 65,000 (army 94.3%, navy 1.8%, air force
3.9%). *Military expenditure as percent of GNP* (1984): 6.5% (world 5.9%);
per capita expenditure U.S.$19.

[1]Including 6 nonelective seats. [2]Detail does not add to total given because of
rounding. [3]Capital city only. [4]At prices of 1977. [5]December. [6]Since the end of 1983
television service covers Mogadishu area and Hargeysa. [7]1980–81.

# South Africa

*Official name:* Republiek van
Suid-Afrika (Afrikaans); Republic of
South Africa (English).
*Form of government:* multiparty
republic with three legislative houses
(House of Assembly [178]; House
of Representatives [85]; House of
Delegates [45][1]).
*Head of state and government:* State
President.
*Capitals:* Pretoria (executive);
Bloemfontein (judicial); Cape Town
(legislative).
*Official languages:* Afrikaans; English.
*Official religion:* none.
*Monetary unit:* 1 rand (R) = 100 cents;
valuation (Oct. 5, 1987)
1 U.S.$ = R 2.08; 1 £ = R 3.38.

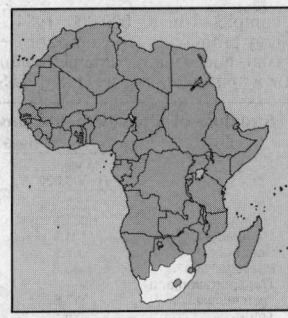

### Area and population[2]

| Provinces | Capitals | area[3] sq mi | sq km | population[4] 1983 estimate | 1985 census |
|---|---|---|---|---|---|
| Cape | Cape Town | 247,638 | 641,379 | 5,374,000 | 5,041,137 |
| Natal | Pietermaritzburg | 22,608 | 58,555 | 2,842,000 | 2,145,018 |
| Orange Free State | Bloemfontein | 49,233 | 127,513 | 2,080,000 | 1,776,903 |
| Transvaal | Pretoria | 88,197 | 228,429 | 8,950,000 | 7,532,179 |
| **National states** | | | | | |
| Gazankulu | Giyani | 2,606 | 6,750 | 585,000 | 497,213 |
| KaNgwane | Louieville | 1,436 | 3,720 | 184,000 | 392,782 |
| KwaNdebele | Siyabuswa | 355 | 920 | 200,000 | 235,855 |
| KwaZulu | Ulundi | 12,664 | 32,800 | 3,792,000 | 3,747,015 |
| Lebowa | Lebowakgomo | 8,757 | 22,680 | 1,869,000 | 1,835,984 |
| Qwaqwa | Phuthaditjhaba | 185 | 480 | 306,000 | 181,559 |
| TOTAL | | 433,679 | 1,123,226 | 26,182,000 | 23,385,645 |

## Demography

*Population* (1987): 28,881,000[4].
*Density* (1987): persons per sq mi 66.6, persons per sq km 25.7.
*Urban–rural* (1985)[5]: urban 55.9%; rural 44.1%.
*Sex distribution* (1985): male 49.37%; female 50.63%.
*Age breakdown* (1985)[5]: under 15, 41.0%; 15–29, 26.9%; 30–44, 16.1%; 45–59, 9.8%; 60–74, 5.0%; 75 and over, 1.2%.
*Population projection*[5]: (1990) 37,984,000; (2000) 50,494,000.
*Doubling time:* 28 years.
*Ethnic composition* (1984): black 68.2%, of which Zulu 23.7%, North Sotho 9.8%, Xhosa 9.7%, South Sotho 7.3%, Tswana 5.7%, other 12.0%; white 18.0%; Coloured 10.5%; Asian 3.3%.
*Religious affiliation* (1980): traditional beliefs 20.4%; Afrikaans Reformed 15.5%; Roman Catholic 9.5%; Methodist 8.5%; Anglican 6.5%; other 39.6%.
*Major cities* (municipality; 1985): Cape Town 1,911,521; Johannesburg 1,609,408; Durban 982,075; Pretoria 822,925.

## Vital statistics

*Birth rate* per 1,000 population (1983): 33.6 (world avg. 29.0); (1978) legitimate 75.9%[6]; illegitimate 24.1%[6].
*Death rate* per 1,000 population (1983): 11.0 (world avg. 11.0).
*Natural increase rate* per 1,000 population (1983): 22.6 (world avg. 18.0).
*Total fertility rate* (avg. births per childbearing woman; 1980–85)[5]: 5.1.
*Life expectancy* at birth (1980–85)[5]: male 51.8 years; female 55.2 years.
*Major causes of death* per 100,000 population (1977)[6]: heart disease 215.3; malignant neoplasms (cancers) 107.3; cerebrovascular disease 90.2; pneumonia 75.2.

## National economy

*Budget* (1986–87). Revenue: R 34,430,000,000 (income tax 58.8%, sales tax 27.4%, customs duty and excise tax 7.4%). Expenditures: R 37,751,000,000 (development 17.5%, education 16.2%, defense 14.0%, debt service 13.9%, health 7.4%).
*Production* (metric tons except as noted). Agriculture, forestry, fishing (1985): sugarcane 20,736,000, corn (maize) 7,550,000, wheat 1,600,000; livestock (number of live animals) 30,256,000 sheep, 12,733,000 cattle; forestry 18,944,000 cu m; fish catch 649,947. Mining and quarrying (1986): iron ore 24,288,000; manganese ore 3,719,294; chrome 3,452,541; gold 638,050 kg; silver 222,240 kg; platinum 115,000 kg; diamonds 10,228,467 carats. Manufacturing (value added in R '000,000; 1984): metals and metal products 5,327, of which iron and steel 2,706; machinery and transport equipment 4,269, of which electrical machinery 1,519, transport equipment 1,366; chemicals 4,243; food and beverages 3,110; textiles 1,024; printing and publishing 839; clothing and footwear 826. Construction (1986): residential 4,710,735 sq m; nonresidential 2,579,563 sq m. Energy production (consumption): electricity[7] (kW-hr; 1986) 130,345,000,000 (130,345,000,000); coal[7] (metric tons; 1985) 173,728,000 (129,389,000); petroleum[7] (barrels; 1985) none (2,180,000); petroleum products[7] (metric tons; 1985) 13,820,000 (10,523,000); natural gas, none (none).
*Household income and expenditure.* Average household size (1980) 5.1; average annual income per household R 8,829 (U.S.$11,349); sources of income (1984): wages and salaries 82.7%, transfer payments 4.8%, other 12.5%; expenditure (1984): food and beverages 32.7%, transp. and commun. 17.6%, housing 11.9%, clothing and footwear 8.3%, health 4.2%.
*Gross national product* (1985): U.S.$65,320,000,000 (U.S.$2,010 per capita).

### Structure of gross domestic product and labour force

| | 1986 in value R '000,000 | 1986 % of total value | 1985 labour force | 1985 % of labour force |
|---|---|---|---|---|
| Agriculture | 7,100 | 5.8 | 1,179,590 | 13.6 |
| Mining | 20,136 | 16.4 | 743,065 | 8.6 |
| Manufacturing | 26,690 | 21.8 | 1,379,518 | 15.8 |
| Construction | 3,840 | 3.1 | 556,339 | 6.4 |
| Public utilities | 4,912 | 4.0 | 92,720 | 1.1 |
| Transp. and commun. | 11,135 | 9.1 | 418,156 | 4.8 |
| Trade | 14,217 | 11.6 | 941,867 | 10.8 |
| Finance | 14,504 | 11.8 | 339,204 | 3.9 |
| Pub. admin., defense | 15,512 | 12.6 | 1,965,040 | 22.6 |
| Services | 2,034 | 1.7 } | 1,076,864 | 12.4 |
| Other | 2,595 | 2.1 } | | |
| TOTAL | 122,675 | 100.0 | 8,692,363 | 100.0 |

*Population economically active* (1985): total 8,692,363; activity rate of total population 37.2% (participation rates: ages 15–64 [1970] 68.3%; female [1981] 34.4%; unemployed 8.4%).

### Price and earnings indexes (1980 = 100)

| | 1981 | 1982 | 1983 | 1984 | 1985 | 1986 | 1987[8] |
|---|---|---|---|---|---|---|---|
| Consumer price index | 115.2 | 132.1 | 148.4 | 165.7 | 192.6 | 228.5 | 270.1 |
| Monthly earnings index | 121.5 | 149.0 | 158.1 | ... | ... | ... | ... |
| white (black) | (120.6) | (156.6) | (158.7) | ... | ... | ... | ... |

*Total debt* (external; 1986): U.S.$1,742,000,000.
*Tourism* (1985): receipts from visitors U.S.$378,000,000; expenditures by nationals abroad, n.a.
*Land use* (1984): forested 3.4%; meadows and pastures 65.2%; agricultural and under permanent cultivation 11.2%; other 20.2%.

## Foreign trade

### Balance of trade (current prices)

| | 1981 | 1982 | 1983 | 1984 | 1985 | 1986[9] |
|---|---|---|---|---|---|---|
| R '000,000 | −231 | +914 | +4,479 | +3,705 | +13,748 | +3,784 |
| % of total | 0.6% | 2.4% | 12.1% | 7.9% | 23.0% | 14.5% |

*Imports* (1986): R 27,010,000,000 (machinery and transport equipment 36.4%, of which motor vehicles 7.1%; chemicals 12.6%; metal products 4.5%; food 2.9%). *Major import sources* (1985): U.S. 16.9%; W.Ger. 16.6%; U.K. 12.0%; Japan 9.9%.
*Exports* (1986): R 41,508,700,000 (gold 40.2%; metals and metal products 11.8%; diamonds 7.0%; food and tobacco 5.4%; wool 3.8%). *Major export destinations* (1985): U.S. 9.5%; Japan 7.6%; U.K. 5.8%; The Netherlands 3.7%; Switzerland 3.6%; W.Ger. 3.4%.

## Transport and communications

*Transport.* Railroads (1986): length 14,392 mi, 23,612 km; passenger-km 17,826,100,000; metric ton-km cargo 92,859,199,000. Roads (1985): total length 114,243 mi, 183,851 km (paved 28%). Vehicles (1985): passenger cars 2,936,083; trucks and buses 1,228,740. Merchant marine (1986): vessels 271; total deadweight tonnage 661,706. Air transport (1985): passenger-km 8,738,430,000; metric ton-km cargo 397,476,000; airports (1987) 40.
*Communications.* Daily newspapers (1986): total number 21; total circulation 1,162,400; circulation per 1,000 population 41.6. Radio (1986): 10,000,000 receivers (1 per 2.8 persons). Television (1986): 2,700,000 receivers (1 per 10.3 persons). Telephones (1984): 3,471,519 (1 per 7.4 persons).

## Education and health

### Education (1986)

| | schools[10] | teachers | students | student/ teacher ratio |
|---|---|---|---|---|
| Primary (age 6–12) | 17,180[11] | 267,680[11] | 6,450,439[11] | 24.1[11] |
| Secondary (age 13–17) | 11 | 11 | 11 | ... |
| Vocational | 132 | 18,000 | 133,421 | 7.4 |
| Higher | 84 | 27,193 | 230,441 | 8.5 |

*Educational attainment* (1985). Percent of economically active population having: no formal schooling or incomplete primary 49.4%; complete primary education 9.1%; some secondary 27.5%; complete secondary 12.4%; postsecondary degree 1.6%. *Literacy*[5] (1984): percent of adult population literate 50%; white 93%; Asians 69%; Coloured 62%; black 32%.
*Health:* physicians (1986) 22,525 (1 per 1,510 persons); hospital beds (1980) 98,308 (1 per 246 persons); infant mortality rate (1980–85) 83.0.
*Food* (1981–83): daily per capita caloric intake 2,929 (vegetable products 85%, animal products 15%); (1983) 117% of FAO recommended minimum.

## Military

*Total active duty personnel* (1987): 97,000 (army 77.3%, navy 9.3%, air force 13.4%). *Military expenditure as percent of GNP* (1986): 3.7% (world [1984] 5.9%); per capita expenditure U.S.$69.

[1]For representation of whites, Coloureds, and Asians (mainly Indians), respectively. [2]Data exclude Bophuthatswana, Ciskei, Transkei, and Venda, which are recognized as sovereign nations by the South African government. Together these entities have an area of 36,773 sq mi (95,137 sq km) and a population (1983) of 5,122,000. [3]1983; data for subsequent redistribution of territory between the provinces and the national states not available. [4]Preliminary 1985 census data indicate very substantial underenumeration. 1983 and 1987 estimates are continuations of a demographic series incorporating the 1980 census but antedating the 1985 census. [5]Includes Bophuthatswana, Ciskei, Transkei, and Venda. [6]Whites, Asians, and Coloureds only. [7]Data apply to the Customs Union of Southern Africa comprising South Africa, Botswana, Lesotho, South West Africa/Namibia, and Swaziland. [8]August. [9]Third quarter. [10]1985. [11]Primary includes secondary.

# South West Africa/ Namibia

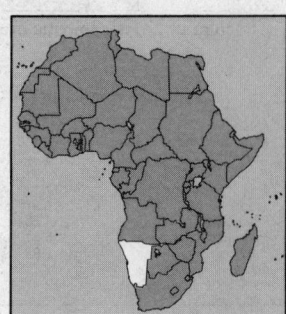

*Official name:* Suidwes-Afrika/Namibië (Afrikaans); South West Africa/ Namibia (English).
*Political status:* dependency of South Africa with one legislative house (National Assembly [62]).
*Head of state and government:* Administrator-General[1].
*Capital:* Windhoek.
*Official languages:* Afrikaans; English.
*Official religion:* none.
*Monetary unit:* 1 South African rand (R) = 100 cents; valuation (Oct. 5, 1987) 1 U.S.$ = R 2.08; 1 £ = R 3.38.

| Area and population[2] | | area | | population |
|---|---|---|---|---|
| **Magisterial Districts** | **Capitals** | sq mi | sq km | 1987 estimate[3] |
| Bethanien | Bethanien | 6,951 | 18,004 | 3,000 |
| Boesmanland | Tsumkwe | 7,131 | 18,468 | 3,000 |
| Caprivi Oos | Katima Mulilo | 4,453 | 11,533 | 44,000 |
| Damaraland | Khorixas | 17,977 | 46,560 | 28,000 |
| Gobabis | Gobabis | 16,003 | 41,447 | 25,000 |
| Grootfontein | Grootfontein | 10,239 | 26,520 | 25,000 |
| Hereroland-Oos | Otjinene | 20,058 | 51,949 | 22,000 |
| Hereroland-Wes | Okakarara | 6,371 | 16,500 | 18,000 |
| Kaokoland | Opuwo | 22,467 | 58,190 | 20,000 |
| Karasburg | Karasburg | 14,717 | 38,116 | 11,000 |
| Karibib | Karibib | 5,108 | 13,230 | 10,000 |
| Kavango | Rundu | 19,674 | 50,955 | 122,000 |
| Keetmanshoop | Keetmanshoop | 14,788 | 38,302 | 20,000 |
| Lüderitz | Lüderitz | 20,488 | 53,063 | 16,000 |
| Maltahöhe | Maltahöhe | 9,874 | 25,573 | 6,000 |
| Mariental | Mariental | 18,413 | 47,689 | 24,000 |
| Namaland | Gibeon | 8,154 | 21,120 | 15,000 |
| Okahandja | Okahandja | 6,811 | 17,640 | 15,000 |
| Omaruru | Omaruru | 3,253 | 8,425 | 6,000 |
| Otjiwarongo | Otjiwarongo | 7,934 | 20,550 | 19,000 |
| Outjo | Outjo | 14,951 | 38,722 | 10,000 |
| Owambo | Ondangwa | 20,000 | 51,800 | 520,000 |
| Rehoboth | Rehoboth | 5,476 | 14,182 | 33,000 |
| Swakopmund | Swakopmund | 17,258 | 44,697 | 18,000 |
| Tsumeb | Tsumeb | 6,340 | 16,420 | 22,000 |
| Windhoek | Windhoek | 12,930 | 33,489 | 129,000 |
| TOTAL | | 317,818 | 823,144 | 1,184,000 |

## Demography

*Population* (1987): 1,198,000.
*Density* (1987): persons per sq mi 3.8, persons per sq km 1.5.
*Urban–rural* (1987): urban *c.* 25%; rural *c.* 75%.
*Sex distribution* (1985): male 49.35%; female 50.65%.
*Age breakdown* (1985): under 15, 45.1%; 15–29, 25.9%; 30–44, 15.3%; 45–59, 8.7%; 60–74, 4.1%; 75 and over, 0.9%.
*Population projection:* (1990) 1,288,000; (2000) 1,639,000.
*Doubling time:* 21 years.
*Ethnic composition* (1986): Ovambo 49.6%; Kavango 9.3%; Herero 7.5%; Damara 7.5%; white 6.6%; Nama 4.8%; other 14.7%.
*Religious affiliation* (1981): Lutheran 51.2%; Roman Catholic 19.8%; Dutch Reformed 6.1%; Anglican 5.0%; other 17.9%.
*Major cities* (1983): Windhoek 105,100; Rundu 15,000; Rehoboth 14,000; Swakopmund 13,500; Keetmanshoop 12,000.

## Vital statistics

*Birth rate* per 1,000 population (1980–85): 44.9 (world avg. 29.0).
*Death rate* per 1,000 population (1980–85): 11.5 (world avg. 11.0).
*Natural increase rate* per 1,000 population (1980–85): 33.5 (world avg. 18.0).
*Total fertility rate* (avg. births per childbearing woman; 1980–85): 6.0.
*Marriage rate* per 1,000 population: n.a.
*Life expectancy* at birth (1980–85): male 46.6 years; female 49.9 years.
*Major causes of death* per 100,000 population: n.a.; however, major diseases include malaria, tuberculosis, and trypanosomiasis (sleeping sickness).

## National economy

*Budget* (1987–88). Revenue[4]: R 1,589,200,000 (grants from South Africa 32.5%, taxes 30.7%, customs and duties 24.4%). Expenditures: R 1,896,-600,000 (administration 18.2%, education 14.7%, national defense 10.5%, health and welfare 8.9%, transportation 8.0%).
*Public debt* (external, outstanding; 1984): U.S.$352,000,000.
*Tourism* (1981): receipts from visitors U.S.$45,960,000; expenditures by nationals abroad, n.a.
*Production* (metric tons except as noted). Agriculture, forestry, fishing (1985): roots and tubers 220,000, corn [maize] 48,000, millet 41,000, vegetables and melons 27,000, fruit 25,000[5], sorghum 7,000; pulses 6,000, wool 1,848[5], karakul pelts 1,460,600 units[6]; livestock (number of live animals; 1987) 2,936,700 cattle, 2,003,400 sheep, 1,603,900 goats; fish catch[7] 479,360, of which anchovies 376,581, South African pilchard 63,660, mackerel 33,379. Mining and quarrying (1985): diamonds 910,000 carats, of which gem quality 865,000 carats; salt 152,300; copper 48,036; lead 34,640; limestone and marble 31,600; zinc 30,232; uranium 4,000; gold 6,237 troy oz; silver 3,400 troy oz. Manufacturing (gross output in R '000,000; 1976): food and beverages 140.8; metal products 34.2; wood products 6.6; chemical products 3.6; printing and publishing 2.4; other 12.4. Construction (value of buildings

completed in R '000,000; 1984): residential 19.4; nonresidential 11.5. Energy production (consumption): electricity (kW-hr; 1986) 692,000,000 (n.a.); coal, none (n.a.); crude petroleum, none (n.a.); natural gas, none (n.a).
*Gross national product* (1985): U.S.$990,000,000 (U.S.$870 per capita).

| Structure of gross domestic product and labour force | | | | |
|---|---|---|---|---|
| | 1986 | | 1981 | |
| | in value R '000,000 | % of total value | labour force | % of labour force |
| Agriculture | 222.2 | 7.6 | 71,402 | 35.0 |
| Mining | 1,061.2 | 36.1 | 15,515 | 7.6 |
| Manufacturing | 131.9 | 4.5 | 8,017 | 3.9 |
| Construction | 65.9 | 2.2 | 17,654 | 8.7 |
| Public utilities | 53.9 | 1.8 | 1,922 | 0.9 |
| Transportation and communication | 217.6 | 7.4 | 9,615 | 4.7 |
| Trade | 328.5 | 11.2 | 22,253 | 10.9 |
| Finance | 187.3 | 6.4 | 3,764 | 1.8 |
| Services | 54.0 | 1.8 | 22,417 | 11.0 |
| Public admin., defense | 532.5 | 18.1 | 31,079 | 15.2 |
| Other | 82.5 | 2.8 | 360 | 0.2 |
| TOTAL | 2,937.5 | 100.0[8] | 203,998 | 100.0[8] |

*Population economically active:* total (1985) 477,000; activity rate of total population 40.8% (participation rates: ages 15–64, n.a.; female [1977] 38.8%; unemployed 12.0%).

| Price and earnings indexes (1980 = 100)[9] | | | | | | | |
|---|---|---|---|---|---|---|---|
| | 1980 | 1981 | 1982 | 1983 | 1984 | 1985 | 1986 |
| Consumer price index | 100.0 | 114.8 | 132.7 | 148.5 | 165.5 | 182.8 | 206.5 |
| Earnings index | ... | ... | ... | ... | ... | ... | ... |

*Household income and expenditure.* Average household size (1981) 4.8; average annual income per household (1980) R 3,223 (U.S.$4,143); sources of income (1986): wages and salaries 76.0%, income from property 20.4%, transfer payments 3.6%; expenditure: n.a.
*Land use* (1984): forested 22.4%; meadows and pastures 64.3%; agricultural and under permanent cultivation 0.8%; other 12.5%.

## Foreign trade

| Balance of trade (current prices) | | | | | | |
|---|---|---|---|---|---|---|
| | 1981 | 1982 | 1983 | 1984 | 1985 | 1986 |
| R '000,000 | −199.9 | −97.4 | −68.1 | −82.9 | 324.2 | 511.7 |
| % of total | 9.9% | 4.6% | 3.5% | 3.6% | 11.3% | 14.8% |

*Imports* (1986): R 1,479,300,000 (detail unavailable). *Major import sources:* South Africa (nearly 100%).
*Exports* (1986): R 1,991,000,000 (minerals 82.6%, of which diamonds 30.9%; agricultural products 7.7%, of which cattle 4.1%, karakul pelts 0.9%). *Major export destinations:* South Africa; United States; West Germany.

## Transport and communications

*Transport.* Railroads: length (1985) 1,454 mi, 2,340 km; (1981) metric ton-km cargo 1,900,000,000. Roads (1985): total length 28,748 mi, 46,266 km (paved 9.0%). Number of registered vehicles (1985): 120,408. Merchant marine: vessels (100 gross tons and over), none. Air transport (1985)[10]: passengers handled 300,000; cargo handled 2,200 metric tons[5]; airports (1987) with scheduled flights 9.
*Communications.* Daily newspapers (1986): total number 3; total circulation 20,700; circulation per 1,000 population 18.0. Radio (1986): 200,000 receivers (1 per 5.8 persons). Television (1986): 17,000 receivers (1 per 70 persons). Telephones (1986): 69,273 (1 per 17 persons).

## Education and health

| Education (1986) | | | | |
|---|---|---|---|---|
| | schools | teachers | students | student/ teacher ratio |
| Primary (age 6–12) | 1,114 | 11,121 | 273,500 | 31.5 |
| Secondary (age 13–19) | | | 76,580 | |
| Voc., teacher tr.[11] | 6 | 81 | 1,200 | 14.8 |
| Higher[11] | 4 | 137 | 537 | 3.9 |

*Educational attainment,* n.a. *Literacy* (1985): total population age 15 and over literate 474,000 (72.5%); males literate 239,000 (74.2%); females literate 235,000 (70.8%).
*Health* (1987): physicians 317 (1 per 3,780 persons); hospital beds 7,430 (1 per 161 persons); infant mortality rate per 1,000 live births (1985) 110.
*Food* (1979–81): daily per capita caloric intake 2,197 (vegetable products 77%, animal products 23%); 96% of FAO recommended minimum requirement.

## Military

*Total active duty personnel[12]* (1986): 21,000 (army 100%). *Military expenditure as percent of GNP* (1984): 7.7% (world 5.9%); per capita expenditure U.S.$113.

[1]In June 1985 most executive authority was formally transferred to a cabinet; the role of the South African-appointed administrator-general was nominally downgraded to that of a constitutional figurehead, but the South African State President retains veto power over acts of the Assembly. [2]Excludes area and population of Walvis Bay (part of South Africa), administered as part of South West Africa/Namibia until 1977. [3]January 1. [4]Percentage breakdown of revenue is for 1986–87. [5]1984. [6]1983. [7]The fishing season concludes in August. [8]Detail does not add to total given because of rounding. [9]Windhoek only. [10]South West Africa/Namibia's two largest airports only. [11]1982. [12]The South West Africa Territory Force (SWATF), largely controlled by the Republic of South Africa.

# Spain

*Official name:* Reino de España (Kingdom of Spain).
*Form of government:* constitutional monarchy with two legislative houses (Senate [257]; Congress of Deputies [350]).
*Chief of state:* King.
*Head of government:* Prime Minister.
*Capital:* Madrid.
*Official language:* Spanish.
*Official religion:* none.
*Monetary unit:* 1 peseta (Pta) = 100 céntimos; valuation (Oct. 5, 1987) 1 U.S.$ = Ptas 122.21; 1 £ = Ptas 198.45.

### Area and population

| Autonomous communities | Capitals | area sq mi | area sq km | population 1986 estimate |
|---|---|---|---|---|
| Andalucía | Seville (Sevilla) | 33,694 | 87,268 | 6,735,600 |
| Aragón | Zaragoza | 18,398 | 47,650 | 1,215,600 |
| Asturias | Oviedo | 4,079 | 10,565 | 1,140,100 |
| Baleares | Palma de Mallorca | 1,936 | 5,014 | 675,400 |
| Canarias | Santa Cruz de Tenerife | 2,796 | 7,242 | 1,442,500 |
| Cantabria | Santander | 2,042 | 5,289 | 527,400 |
| Castilla-La Mancha | Toledo | 30,591 | 79,230 | 1,670,100 |
| Castilla-León | Valladolid | 36,368 | 94,193 | 2,602,300 |
| Cataluña | Barcelona | 12,328 | 31,930 | 6,057,200 |
| Extremadura | Mérida | 16,063 | 41,602 | 1,084,400 |
| Galicia | Santiago de Compostela | 11,365 | 29,434 | 2,870,900 |
| La Rioja | Logroño | 1,944 | 5,034 | 263,100 |
| Madrid | Madrid | 3,087 | 7,995 | 4,907,100 |
| Murcia | Murcia | 4,370 | 11,317 | 1,007,500 |
| Navarra | Pamplona | 4,023 | 10,421 | 522,500 |
| País Vasco | Vitoria | 2,803 | 7,261 | 2,176,800 |
| Valencia | Valencia | 8,998 | 23,305 | 3,790,200 |
| TOTAL SPAIN | | 194,885 | 504,750 | 38,688,400[1] |
| **Enclaves in Northern Morocco** | | | | |
| Ceuta | — | 7.1 | 18.5 | 71,400 |
| Melilla | — | 5.4 | 14 | 58,600 |
| Chafarinas | — | .24 | .61 | ... |
| Vélez de la Gomera | — | .02 | .04 | ... |
| Alhucemas | — | .004 | .01 | ... |
| TOTAL | | 194,897.79[1] | 504,783.16 | 38,818,400[1] |

## Demography

*Population* (1987): 38,832,000.
*Density* (1987): persons per sq mi 199.2, persons per sq km 76.9.
*Urban–rural* (1985): urban 75.8%; rural 24.2%.
*Sex distribution* (1985): male 49.19%; female 50.81%.
*Age breakdown* (1985): under 15, 24.6%; 15–29, 24.2%; 30–44, 18.5%; 45–59, 16.8%; 60–74, 11.6%; 75 and over, 4.3%.
*Population projection:* (1990) 39,322,000; (2000) 40,746,000.
*Doubling time:* n.a.; doubling time exceeds 100 years.
*Ethnic composition* (1984): Spanish 72.8%; Catalan 16.4%; Galician 8.2%; Basque 2.3%; other 0.3%.
*Religious affiliation* (1980): Roman Catholic 96.9%; Protestant 0.1%; nonreligious and atheist 2.9%.
*Major cities* (1986)[2]: Madrid 3,053,101; Barcelona 1,699,231; Valencia 728,-622; Sevilla 651,299.

## Vital statistics

*Birth rate* per 1,000 population (1984): 11.9 (world avg. 29.0).
*Death rate* per 1,000 population (1984): 7.7 (world avg. 11.0).
*Natural increase rate* per 1,000 population (1984): 4.2 (world avg. 18.0).
*Total fertility rate* (avg. births per childbearing woman; 1980–85): 2.1.
*Marriage rate* per 1,000 population (1984): 5.0.
*Life expectancy* at birth (1980–85): male 71.3 years; female 77.5 years.
*Major causes of death* per 100,000 population (1980): circulatory diseases 354.7; malignant neoplasms (cancers) 156.3; respiratory diseases 71.6.

## National economy

*Budget* (1985). Revenue: Ptas 4,422,000,000,000 (indirect taxes 41.0%, personal income taxes 34.4%, direct taxes on enterprises 15.6%). Expenditures: Ptas 4,867,000,000,000[3] (current transfers 57.0%, wages and salaries 31.0%).
*Production* (metric tons except as noted). Agriculture, forestry, fishing (1985): barley 10,680,000, sugar beets 7,349,000, potatoes 5,770,000, grapes 5,345,000, wheat 5,326,000, corn (maize) 3,331,000, tomatoes 2,418,000, oranges 1,884,000, onions 1,263,000, apples 1,056,000, oats 719,000; livestock (number of live animals) 5,050,000 cattle, 12,400,000 pigs, 2,400,000 goats, 1,660,000 sheep; roundwood 13,696,000 cu m; fish catch 1,337,738. Mining and quarrying (metal content in metric tons; 1986): iron ore 3,042,000, zinc 223,200, lead 79,560, copper 46,920. Manufacturing (1986): crude steel 12,168,000; pig iron and ferroalloys 5,088,000; sulfuric acid 3,402,000; wine 3,327,000[4]; wheat flour 2,630,000[5]; sugar 960,000[4]; fertilizers 1,301,000[6], of which nitrogenous 852,000[6]; plastic resin 1,250,000[6]. Construction (1986): residential dwellings 196,228. Energy production (consumption): electricity (kW-hr; 1985) 125,560,000,000 (124,486,000,000); coal (metric tons; 1985) 40,040,000 (48,434,000); crude petroleum (barrels; 1985) 16,383,000 (327,-380,000); petroleum products (metric tons; 1985) 38,812,000 (31,179,000); natural gas (cu m; 1985) 273,978,000 (2,801,774,000).
*Gross national product* (1985): U.S.$168,820,000,000 (U.S.$4,360 per capita).

### Structure of gross domestic product and labour force

| | 1984 in value Ptas '000,000 | 1984 % of total value | 1985 labour force | 1985 % of labour force |
|---|---|---|---|---|
| Agriculture | 1,651,000 | 6.6 | 2,007,000 | 15.0 |
| Mining | | | 90,900 | 0.7 |
| Manufacturing | 6,845,000 | 27.3 | 2,862,100 | 21.4 |
| Public utilities | 775,000 | 3.1 | 91,300 | 0.7 |
| Construction | 1,710,000 | 6.8 | 1,138,200 | 8.5 |
| Transp. and commun. | 1,564,000 | 6.2 | 671,300 | 5.0 |
| Trade | 4,981,000 | 19.9 | 2,475,300 | 18.5 |
| Finance | | | 494,200 | 3.7 |
| Pub. admin., defense | 7,527,000 | 30.1 | 2,340,700 | 17.5 |
| Services | | | | |
| Other | | | 1,174,400[7] | 8.8[7] |
| TOTAL | 25,053,000 | 100.0 | 13,345,500[1] | 100.0[1] |

*Public debt* (1983): Ptas 6,332,300,000,000 (U.S.$40,410,000,000).
*Tourism* (1985): receipts from visitors U.S.$8,151,000,000; expenditures by nationals abroad U.S.$1,010,000,000.
*Population economically active* (1985): total 13,345,500; activity rate of total population 34.7% (participation rates: ages 15–64, 56.8%; female 30.7%; unemployed 19.9%).

### Price and earnings indexes (1980 = 100)

| | 1981 | 1982 | 1983 | 1984 | 1985 | 1986 | 1987 |
|---|---|---|---|---|---|---|---|
| Consumer price index | 114.6 | 131.1 | 147.0 | 163.6 | 178.0 | 193.6 | 204.2[8] |
| Monthly earnings index | 119.9 | 138.1 | 158.8 | 178.7 | 197.3 | 217.3 | 238.8[9] |

*Household income and expenditure.* Average household size (1983) 2.8; income per household Ptas 1,250,000 (U.S.$8,700); sources of income (1984): wages and salaries 52.3%, profits and self-employment 28.6%, social security 16.8%; expenditure (1982): food 30.2%, housing 12.8%, transportation 11.6%, clothing and footwear 8.9%, health 5.9%, education 2.0%.
*Land use* (1984): forested 31.3%; meadows and pastures 21.3%; agricultural and under permanent cultivation 41.1%; other 6.3%.

## Foreign trade

### Balance of trade (current prices)

| | 1981 | 1982 | 1983 | 1984 | 1985 | 1986 |
|---|---|---|---|---|---|---|
| Ptas '000,000 | −920.1 | −1,031.7 | −1,105.5 | −588.3 | −686.9 | −814.5 |
| % of total | 19.6% | 18.6% | 16.3% | 7.2% | 7.7% | 9.7% |

*Imports* (1985): Ptas 5,073,200,000,000 (petroleum and petroleum products 35.6%; machinery and transport equipment 20.7%, of which cars and trucks 4.6%; food 11.1%; chemicals, plastics, and rubber 10.0%; metals and metal products 6.8%). *Major import sources:* U.S. 10.9%; West Germany 10.6%; France 9.3%; Middle East 9.3%; U.K. 6.5%.
*Exports* (1985): Ptas 4,099,200,000,000 (machinery and transport equipment 27.1%, of which cars and trucks 13.0%; metals and metal products 15.4%; food 15.3%; petroleum products 10.7%). *Major export destinations:* France 15.5%; U.S. 10.0%; West Germany 9.6%; U.K. 8.6%; Italy 7.1%.

## Transport and communications

*Transport.* Railroads (1986): route length 7,917 mi, 12,742 km; passenger-km 15,646,000,000; metric ton-km cargo 11,299,000,000. Roads (1985): total length 198,211 mi, 318,991 km (paved 56%). Vehicles (1985): passenger cars 9,273,710; trucks and buses 1,610,623. Merchant marine (1986): vessels (100 gross tons and over) 2,397; total deadweight tonnage 9,286,019. Air transport (1986): passenger-km 19,152,000,000; metric ton-km cargo 568,524,000; airports (1987) with scheduled flights 29.
*Communications.* Daily newspapers (1983): total number 113; total circulation 3,400,000; circulation per 1,000 population 89. Radio (1986): 10,810,-000 receivers (1 per 3.6 persons). Television (1986): 9,920,000 receivers (1 per 3.9 persons). Telephones (1986): 14,258,928 (1 per 2.7 persons).

## Education and health

### Education (1984–85)

| | schools | teachers | students | student/ teacher ratio |
|---|---|---|---|---|
| Primary (age 6–13) | 23,105[10] | 193,788 | 5,644,717 | 29.2 |
| Secondary (age 14–17) | 2,583 | 72,919 | 1,314,518 | 18.0 |
| Vocational | 2,334 | 47,601 | 725,057 | 15.2 |
| Higher | 33[11] | 43,037[12] | 788,173 | ... |

*Educational attainment* (1981). Percent of population age 25 and over having: less than primary education 46.1%, of which illiterate or no formal schooling 34.5%; primary 34.0%; lower secondary 9.3%; upper secondary 3.3%; higher 7.1%. *Literacy* (1983): total population age 15 and over literate 26,004,225 (92.8%); males literate 12,950,282 (95.9%); females literate 13,053,943 (89.9%).
*Health* (1984): physicians 121,362 (1 per 314 persons); hospital beds (1986) 193,996 (1 per 199 persons); infant mortality rate per 1,000 live births 9.2.
*Food* (1981–83): daily per capita caloric intake 3,335 (vegetable products 72%, animal products 28%); (1983) 132% of FAO recommended minimum.

## Military

*Total active duty personnel* (1987): 325,000 (army 70.8%, navy 19.2%, air force 10.0%). *Military expenditure as percent of GNP* (1985): 2.2% (world [1984] 5.9%); per capita expenditure U.S.$94.

[1]Detail does not add to total given because of rounding. [2]For *municipios,* which may contain rural areas as well as the urban city proper. [3]Percentage breakdown is for 1984. [4]1985. [5]1984. [6]1983. [7]Unemployed persons not previously employed. [8]August. [9]July. [10]1982–83. [11]1986. [12]1983–84.

# Sri Lanka

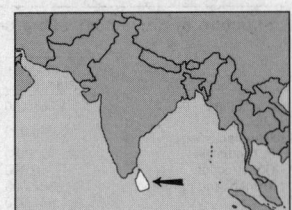

*Official name:* Sri Lankā Praja-
thanthrika Samajavadi Janarajaya
(Democratic Socialist Republic of
Sri Lanka).
*Form of government:* unitary multiparty
republic with one legislative house
(Parliament [168]).
*Head of state and government:*
President.
*Capitals:* Colombo (administrative),
Sri Jayawardenapura (legislative and
judicial).
*Official language:* Sinhalese.
*Official religion:* none.
*Monetary unit:* 1 Sri Lanka rupee
(SL Rs) = 100 cents; valuation (Oct. 5,
1987) 1 U.S.$ = SL Rs 29.68;
1 £ = SL Rs 48.20.

### Area and population

| Districts | Capitals | area sq mi | area sq km | population 1986 estimate |
|---|---|---|---|---|
| Amparai | Amparai | 1,778 | 4,604 | 439,000 |
| Anuradhapura | Anuradhapura | 2,809 | 7,275 | 659,000 |
| Badulla | Badulla | 1,090 | 2,822 | 668,000 |
| Batticaloa | Batticaloa | 1,017 | 2,633 | 379,000 |
| Colombo | Colombo | 268 | 695 | 1,836,000 |
| Galle | Galle | 652 | 1,689 | 881,000 |
| Gampaha | Gampaha | 540 | 1,399 | 1,466,000 |
| Hambantota | Hambantota | 1,013 | 2,623 | 477,000 |
| Jaffna | Jaffna | 833 | 2,158 | 915,000 |
| Kalutara | Kalutara | 624 | 1,615 | 892,000 |
| Kandy | Kandy | 833 | 2,158 | 1,188,000 |
| Kegalle | Kegalle | 642 | 1,663 | 720,000 |
| Kurunegala | Kurunegala | 1,844 | 4,776 | 1,333,000 |
| Mannar | Mannar | 778 | 2,014 | 120,000 |
| Matale | Matale | 768 | 1,989 | 392,000 |
| Matara | Matara | 481 | 1,247 | 717,000 |
| Monaragala | Monaragala | 2,188 | 5,666 | 320,000 |
| Mullaitivu | Mullaitivu | 798 | 2,066 | 86,000 |
| Nuwara Eliya | Nuwara Eliya | 555 | 1,437 | 514,000 |
| Polonnaruwa | Polonnaruwa | 1,332 | 3,449 | 294,000 |
| Puttalam | Puttalam | 1,172 | 3,036 | 552,000 |
| Ratnapura | Ratnapura | 1,251 | 3,239 | 868,000 |
| Trincomalee | Trincomalee | 1,048 | 2,714 | 292,000 |
| Vavuniya | Vavuniya | 1,021 | 2,645 | 108,000 |
| TOTAL | | 25,332[1] | 65,610[1] | 16,117,000[1] |

## Demography

*Population* (1987): 16,353,000.
*Density* (1987): persons per sq mi 645.5, persons per sq km 249.2.
*Urban–rural* (1985): urban 21.1%; rural 78.9%.
*Sex distribution* (1985): male 50.55%; female 49.45%.
*Age breakdown* (1985): under 15, 35.3%; 15–29, 29.6%; 30–44, 17.9%; 45–59, 10.6%; 60–74, 5.2%; 75 and over, 1.4%.
*Population projection:* (1990) 17,081,000; (2000) 19,752,000.
*Doubling time:* 40 years.
*Ethnic composition* (1981): Sinhalese 74.0%; Tamil 18.2%; Sri Lankan Moor 7.1%; other 0.7%.
*Religious affiliation* (1981): Buddhist 69.3%; Hindu 15.5%; Muslim 7.6%; Christian 7.5%; other 0.1%.
*Major cities* (1984): Colombo 643,000; Dehiwala–Mount Lavinia 184,000; Moratuwa 138,000; Jaffna 133,000; Kandy 120,000.

## Vital statistics

*Birth rate* per 1,000 population (1986): 23.9 (world avg. 26.0).
*Death rate* per 1,000 population (1986): 6.2 (world avg. 9.9).
*Natural increase rate* per 1,000 population (1986): 17.7 (world avg. 16.1).
*Total fertility rate* (avg. births per childbearing woman; 1986): 2.8.
*Marriage rate* per 1,000 population (1983): 7.9.
*Divorce rate* per 1,000 population (1983): 0.1.
*Life expectancy* at birth (1986): male 68.0 years; female 71.2 years.
*Major causes of death* per 100,000 population (1980): senility without mention of psychosis 116.9; diseases of the circulatory system 99.0; infectious and parasitic diseases 74.5; respiratory diseases 47.2.

## National economy

*Budget* (1986). Revenue: SL Rs 39,088,800,000 (general sales and turnover tax 26.5%, import duties 20.7%, income taxes 13.8%, selective sales taxes 12.1%, receipts of trading enterprises 6.2%). Expenditures: SL Rs 60,790,-100,000 (public debt service 15.0%, individual transfer payments 9.8%, education 7.7%, civil administration 7.7%, health 4.7%).
*Public debt* (external, outstanding; 1985): U.S.$2,815,200,000.
*Tourism* (1985): receipts from visitors U.S.$70,000,000; expenditures by nationals abroad U.S.$50,000,000.
*Production* (metric tons except as noted). Agriculture, forestry, fishing (1985): rice 2,661,000, coconuts 2,100,000, cassava 750,000, tea 214,000, copra 180,000, sweet potatoes 140,000, natural rubber 138,000, mangoes 95,000; livestock (number of live animals) 1,750,000 cattle, 990,000 buffalo, 535,000 goats; roundwood (1984) 8,497,000 cu m; fish catch 168,000. Mining and quarrying (1984): clays 131,890[2]; salt 110,000; ilmenite 102,000; rutile 6,000; graphite 6,000; gemstones SL Rs 936,783,600[2]. Manufacturing (value added in SL Rs; 1985): food, beverages, and tobacco 6,166,000,000; textile and wearing apparel 2,594,000,000; petrochemicals 1,402,000,000;

nonmetallic mineral products 1,089,000,000. Construction (1983): residential 914,200 sq m. Energy production (consumption): electricity (kW-hr; 1985) 2,464,000,000 (2,060,600,000); coal (metric tons; 1985) none (1,000); crude petroleum (barrels; 1985) none (12,380,000); petroleum products (metric tons; 1985) 1,345,000 (1,021,000); natural gas, none (n.a.).
*Gross national product* (1985): U.S.$5,980,000,000 (U.S.$360 per capita).

### Structure of gross domestic product and labour force

| | 1985 in value SL Rs '000,000 | 1985 % of total value | 1980–81 labour force | 1980–81 % of labour force |
|---|---|---|---|---|
| Agriculture | 41,069 | 27.7 | 2,374,870 | 48.2 |
| Mining | 3,328 | 2.2 | 66,170 | 1.3 |
| Manufacturing | 21,849 | 14.7 | 531,065 | 10.8 |
| Construction | 11,640 | 7.9 | 223,750 | 4.5 |
| Public utilities | 2,042 | 1.4 | 18,999 | 0.4 |
| Transp. and commun. | 16,554 | 11.2 | 208,470 | 4.2 |
| Trade | 29,261 | 19.7 | 497,855 | 10.1 |
| Finance | 9,855 | 6.6 | 48,093 | 1.0 |
| Pub. admin., defense, and services | 12,723 | 8.6 | 650,981 | 13.2 |
| Other | ... | ... | 310,092 | 6.3 |
| TOTAL | 148,321 | 100.0 | 4,930,345 | 100.0 |

*Population economically active:* total (1985) 5,920,000; activity rate of total population 36.5% (participation rates: over age 15, 48.3%; female 13.0%; unemployed [1981] 13.5%).

### Price and earnings indexes (1980 = 100)

| | 1980 | 1981 | 1982 | 1983 | 1984 | 1985 | 1986 |
|---|---|---|---|---|---|---|---|
| Consumer price index | 100.0 | 117.9 | 130.7 | 149.0 | 173.8 | 176.3 | 190.4 |
| Average wage index[3] | 100.0 | 100.2 | 118.0 | 129.3 | 162.9 | 178.0 | 187.5 |

*Household income and expenditure.* Average household size (1981) 5.2; income per household (1973) SL Rs 3,936 (U.S.$611); sources of income (1982): wages 49.0%, property income 38.8%, government transfers 9.1%; expenditure (1983): food 50.8%, transportation 14.6%, beverages and tobacco 9.3%, housing 9.2%, clothing 5.9%, recreation 3.9%, health 1.6%.
*Land use* (1984): forested 36.8%; meadows and pastures 6.8%; agricultural and under permanent cultivation 34.0%; other 22.4.

## Foreign trade

### Balance of trade (current prices)

| | 1981 | 1982 | 1983 | 1984 | 1985 | 1986 |
|---|---|---|---|---|---|---|
| SL Rs '000,000 | −10,766 | −15,021 | −14,519 | −3,933 | −9,890 | −12,773 |
| % of total | 20.4% | 25.9% | 22.4% | 5.1% | 12.0% | 15.8% |

*Imports* (1985): SL Rs 52,916,500,000 (petroleum 20.8%, machinery and transport equipment 13.7%, textiles including clothing 7.2%, wheat 5.2%, sugar 3.8%). *Major import sources:* Japan 14.5%; Saudi Arabia 8.9%; Iran 8.6%; U.S. 6.6%; West Germany 5.1%.
*Exports* (1985): SL Rs 36,206,600,000 (tea 33.2%, garments 21.3%, petroleum products 10.7%, rubber 7.1%, desiccated coconut 3.7%). *Major export destinations:* U.S. 21.2%; U.K. 6.2%; W.Ger. 5.2%; Japan 4.9%; Iraq 4.1%.

## Transport and communications

*Transport.* Railroads (1985): track length 1,208 mi, 1,944 km; passenger-mi 1,312,000,000, passenger-km 2,111,000,000; short ton-mi cargo 169,229,000, metric ton-km cargo 247,070,000. Roads (1984): total length 53,573 mi, 86,218 km (paved 35%). Vehicles (1985): passenger cars 148,587; trucks and buses 137,164. Merchant marine (1986): vessels (100 gross tons and over) 91; total deadweight tonnage 972,049. Air transport (1986): passenger mi 1,312,000,000, passenger-km 2,112,000,000; short ton-mi cargo 38,456,000, metric ton-km cargo 56,148,000; airports (1987) with scheduled flights 1.
*Communications.* Daily newspapers (1985): total number 15; total circulation 850,000; circulation per 1,000 population 53. Radio (1984): 2,073,432[4] receivers (1 per 7.5 persons). Television (1984): 415,308[4] receivers (1 per 46 persons). Telephones (1984): 108,950 (1 per 135 persons).

## Education and health

### Education (1983)

| | schools | teachers | students | student/ teacher ratio |
|---|---|---|---|---|
| Primary (age 5–10) | 3,983 | 18,693 | 593,009 | 31.7 |
| Secondary (age 11–17) | 5,629 | 113,148 | 2,930,070 | 25.9 |
| Voc., teacher tr. | 25 | 466 | 8,382 | 18.0 |
| Higher | 8[5] | 5,629 | 63,460[6] | 11.3 |

*Educational attainment* (1981). Percent of population age 25 and over having: no schooling 15.5%; less than complete primary education 12.1%; complete primary 52.3%; postprimary 14.7%; secondary 3.0%; higher 1.1%; unspecified 1.3%. *Literacy* (1981): population age 15 and over literate 86.1%; males literate 90.8%; females literate 81.2%.
*Health* (1985): physicians 2,151 (1 per 7,363 persons); hospital beds 45,211 (1 per 350 persons); infant mortality rate per 1,000 live births 23.5.
*Food* (1981–83): daily per capita caloric intake 2,217 (vegetable products 96%, animal products 4%); (1983) 104% of FAO recommended minimum.

## Military

*Total active duty personnel* (1986): 37,660 (army 79.7%, navy 10.5%, air force 9.8%). *Military expenditure as percent of GNP* (1984): 1.5% (world 5.9%); per capita expenditure U.S.$6.

[1]Detail does not add to total given because of rounding. [2]1983. [3]Agricultural minimum rates. [4]Licensed. [5]Universities only. [6]Full-time students only.

# Sudan, The

*Official name:* Jumhūrīyat as-Sūdān (Republic of the Sudan).
*Form of government:* multiparty republic with one legislative house (People's Assembly [301]).
*Chief of state:* [1].
*Head of government:* Prime Minister.
*Capital:* Khartoum.
*Official language:* Arabic.
*Official religion:* Islam.
*Monetary unit:* 1 Sudanese pound (LSd) = 100 piastres; valuation (Oct. 5, 1987) 1 U.S.$ = LSd 2.50; 1 £ = LSd 4.06.

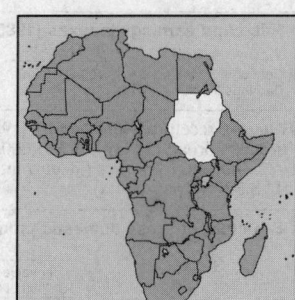

### Area and population

| Regions Provinces | Capitals | area sq mi | area sq km | population 1983 census[2] |
|---|---|---|---|---|
| A'ālī an-Nīl (Upper Nile) | Malakāl | 92,198 | 238,792 | 1,599,605 |
| A'ālī an-Nīl (Upper Nile) | Nāṣir | 45,231 | 117,148 | 802,354 |
| Junqulī (Jongley) | Bor | 46,781 | 121,164 | 797,251 |
| Baḥr al-Ghazāl (Bahr el-Ghazal) | Wāu | 77,566 | 200,894 | 2,265,510 |
| Baḥr al-Ghazāl al-Gharbīyah (Western Bahr el-Ghazal) | Raga | | | |
| Baḥr al-Ghazāl ash-Sharqīyah (Eastern Bahr el-Ghazal) | Uwayl | 51,960 | 134,576 | 1,492,597 |
| al-Buḥayrāh (El Buheyrah) | Rumbek | 25,606 | 66,318 | 772,913 |
| Dārfūr (Darfur) | al-Fāshir | 196,404 | 508,684 | 3,093,699 |
| Dārfūr al-Janūbiyah (Southern Darfur) | Nyala | 62,753 | 162,529 | 1,765,752 |
| Dārfūr ash-Shamālīyah (Northern Darfur) | al-Fāshir | 133,651 | 346,155 | 1,327,947 |
| al-Istiwā'iyah (Equatoria) | Jūbā | 76,436 | 197,969 | 1,406,181 |
| al-Istiwā'iyah al Gharbīyah (Western Equatoria) | Yambio | 30,398 | 78,732 | 359,056 |
| al-Istiwā'iyah ash-Sharqiyah (Eastern Equatoria) | Jūbā | 46,038 | 119,237 | 1,047,125 |
| Kurdufān (Kordofan) | al-Ubayyiḍ | 146,817 | 380,255 | 3,093,294 |
| Kurdufān al-Janūbiyah (Southern Kordofan) | Kāduqlī | 61,141 | 158,355 | 1,287,525 |
| Kurdufān ash-Shamālīyah (Northern Kordofan) | al-Ubayyiḍ | 85,676 | 221,900 | 1,805,769 |
| ash-Shamālīyah (Northern) | ad-Dāmir | 183,800 | 476,040 | 1,083,024 |
| an-Nīl (Nile) | ad-Dāmir | 49,167 | 127,343 | 649,633 |
| ash-Shamālīyah (Northern) | Dunqulah | 134,633 | 348,697 | 433,391 |
| ash-Sharqīyah (Eastern) | Kassalā | 128,987 | 334,074 | 2,208,209 |
| al-Baḥr al-Aḥmar (Red Sea) | Port Sudan | 84,912 | 219,920 | 695,874 |
| Kassalā (Kassala) | Kassalā | 44,075 | 114,154 | 1,512,335 |
| al-Wāstā (Central) | Wad Madanī | 53,675 | 139,017 | 4,012,543 |
| an-Nīl al-Abyaḍ (White Nile) | ad-Duwaym | 16,149 | 41,825 | 933,136 |
| al-Jazirah (El-Gezira) | Wad Madanī | 13,536 | 35,057 | 2,023,094 |
| an-Nīl al-Azraq (Blue Nile) | ad-Damazin | 23,990 | 62,135 | 1,056,313 |
| **National Capital** | | | | |
| Kharṭūm (Khartoum) | Khartoum | 10,875 | 28,165 | 1,802,299 |
| **TOTAL** | | 966,757[3] | 2,503,890 | 20,564,364 |

## Demography

*Population* (1987): 25,562,000.
*Density* (1987): persons per sq mi 26.4, persons per sq km 10.2.
*Urban–rural* (1983): urban 30.6%; rural 69.4%.
*Sex distribution* (1983): male 50.98%; female 49.02%.
*Age breakdown* (1985): under 15, 44.6%; 15–29, 26.0%; 30–44, 15.7%; 45–59, 8.9%; 60–74, 4.0%; 75 and over, 0.8%.
*Population projection:* (1990) 24,949,800; (2000) 32,885,000.
*Doubling time:* 25 years.
*Ethnic composition* (1983): Sudanese Arab 49.1%; Dinka 11.5%; Nuba 8.1%; Beja 6.4%; Nuer 4.9%; Azandi 2.7%; Bari 2.5%; Fur 2.1%; Shilluk 1.7%; Lotuko 1.5%; other 9.5%.
*Religious affiliation* (1980): Sunnī Muslim 73.0%; traditional beliefs 16.7%; Roman Catholic 5.6%; Anglican 2.3%; other 2.4%.
*Major cities* (1983): Omdurman 526,287; Khartoum 476,218; Khartoum North 341,146; Port Sudan 206,727.

## Vital statistics

*Birth rate* per 1,000 population (1980–85): 45.9 (world avg. 29.0).
*Death rate* per 1,000 population (1980–85): 17.4 (world avg. 11.0).
*Natural increase rate* per 1,000 population (1980–85): 28.5 (world avg. 18.0).
*Total fertility rate* (avg. births per childbearing woman; 1980–85): 6.6.
*Life expectancy* at birth (1980–85): male 46.6 years; female 49.0 years.
*Major causes of death* per 100,000 population (1979)[4]: pneumonia 26.4; tuberculosis 1.8; meningitis 1.3; infectious hepatitis 1.1.

## National economy

*Budget* (1987–88). Revenue: LSd 3,905,500,000 (tax revenue 60.9%; nontax revenue 34.5%). Expenditures: LSd 6,790,000,000 (current expenditures 77.1%; development budget 22.6%, of which agriculture 6.2%, transport and communications 3.5%, energy and mining 0.5%).
*Public debt* (external, outstanding; 1985): U.S.$5,086,000,000.
*Tourism* (1985): receipts from visitors U.S.$58,000,000; expenditures by nationals abroad U.S.$44,000,000.
*Production* (metric tons except as noted). Agriculture, forestry, fishing (1985): sugarcane 4,800,000, sorghum 4,271,000, seed cotton 560,000, millet 558,000, peanuts (groundnuts) 344,000, sesame seeds 228,000, cotton lint 196,000, cassava 128,000, yams 115,000; livestock (number of live animals) 20,000,000 cattle, 19,000,000 sheep, 13,500,000 goats, 2,750,000 camels;

roundwood 19,524,000 cu m; fish catch 26,290. Mining and quarrying (1984): hydraulic cement 176,000; salt 75,000; chromite concentrate 20,000; gypsum and anhydrite 8,000. Manufacturing (1985–86): raw sugar 451,500; wheat flour 280,300; cement 150,500; shoes 9,000,000 pairs; cigarettes 2,900,000,000 units; tires and tubes 555,000 units. Construction: n.a. Energy production (consumption): electricity (kW-hr; 1985) 1,037,000,000 (1,037,000,000); crude petroleum (barrels; 1985) none (8,097,000); petroleum products (metric tons; 1985) 1,001,000 (1,021,000).
*Gross national product* (1985): U.S.$7,350,000,000 (U.S.$310 per capita).

### Structure of gross domestic product and labour force

| | 1984–85 in value LSd '000,000 | 1984–85 % of total value | 1979–80 labour force | 1979–80 % of labour force |
|---|---|---|---|---|
| Agriculture | 2,929.0 | 28.2 | 3,432,600 | 65.8 |
| Mining Manufacturing | 960.0 | 9.2 | 183,300 | 3.5 |
| Construction | 577.0 | 5.5 | 107,600 | 2.1 |
| Public utilities | 244.0 | 2.3 | 59,200 | 1.1 |
| Transp. and commun. | 1,058.0 | 10.1 | 198,800 | 3.8 |
| Trade | 2,442.0 | 23.4 | 220,800 | 4.2 |
| Finance | ... | ... | | |
| Pub. admin., defense | 1,190.0 | 11.5 | | |
| Services | 1,021.0 | 9.8 | 679,800 | 13.0 |
| Other | ... | ... | 340,500 | 6.5 |
| TOTAL | 10,421.0 | 100.0 | 5,222,600 | 100.0 |

*Population economically active* (1981): total 5,973,000; activity rate of total population 31.6% (participation rates: over age 15, 53.1%; female 10.9%; unemployed, n.a.).

### Price indexes (1980 = 100)

| | 1979 | 1980 | 1981 | 1982 | 1983 | 1984 | 1985 |
|---|---|---|---|---|---|---|---|
| Consumer price index | 79.8 | 100.0 | 124.6 | 156.6 | 204.5 | 274.3 | 398.8 |

*Household income and expenditure.* Average household size (1980) 5.3; income per household: n.a.; sources of income: n.a.; expenditure (1980)[5]: food, beverages, and tobacco 66.5%, education, health, transportation, and recreation 15.2%, housing 12.4%, clothing 5.9%.
*Land use* (1984): forested 20.1%; meadows and pastures 23.6%; agricultural and under permanent cultivation 5.2%; desert and other 51.1%.

## Foreign trade

### Balance of trade (current prices)

| | 1981 | 1982 | 1983 | 1984 | 1985 | 1986 |
|---|---|---|---|---|---|---|
| LSd '000,000 | −407.3 | −621.3 | −791.6 | −550.6 | −786.5 | −1,569 |
| % of total | 36.3% | 36.8% | 32.8% | 25.2% | 31.8% | 48.5% |

*Imports* (1986): LSd 2,402,237,000 (machinery and transport equipment 35.0%, of which transport equipment 18.1%; manufactured goods 20.0%; food and tobacco 15.6%; chemicals 14.2%; crude materials 12.2%, of which petroleum products 10.7%; textiles 3.0%). *Major import sources:* Saudi Arabia 14.9%; U.K. 11.8%; West Germany 8.5%; U.S. 7.7%; Japan 5.0%.
*Exports* (1986): LSd 833,205,000 (cotton 44.0%; gum arabic 14.7%; sheep and lambs 8.0%; sesame seeds 7.0%; hides and skins 4.0%). *Major export destinations:* Saudi Arabia 13.5%; Thailand 12.2%; United Arab Emirates 8.1%; Italy 7.1%; Yugoslavia 6.9%; Japan 6.7%.

## Transport and communications

*Transport.* Railroads (1986–87): route length, 4,786 km; passenger-km 1,149,000[6]; metric ton-km cargo 1,600,000,000[6]. Roads (1982): total length 6,599 km (paved 59%). Vehicles (1985): passenger cars 99,400; trucks and buses 17,211. Merchant marine (1986): vessels (100 gross tons and over) 23; total deadweight tonnage 126,381. Air transport (1982): passenger-km 657,000,000; metric ton-km cargo 6,000,000; airports (1987) with scheduled flights 8.
*Communications.* Daily newspapers (1986): total number 2; total circulation 120,000; circulation per 1,000 population 4.9. Radio (1986): 1,500,000 receivers (1 per 16 persons). Television (1986): 250,000 receivers (1 per 98 persons). Telephones (1985): 77,920 (1 per 304 persons).

## Education and health

### Education (1985)

| | schools | teachers | students | student/ teacher ratio |
|---|---|---|---|---|
| Primary (age 7–12) | 6,707 | 47,750 | 1,653,491 | 34.6 |
| Secondary (age 13–18) | 2,167 | 17,591 | 490,583 | 27.9 |
| Voc., teacher tr. | 98 | 968[7] | 29,650 | ... |
| Higher | 16 | 1,934[8] | 35,596 | ... |

*Educational attainment,* n.a. *Literacy* (1980): total population age 15 and over literate 2,507,200 (21.6%); males 36.5%; females 6.5%.
*Health* (1981): physicians[9] 2,169 (1 per 9,369 persons); hospital beds 17,328 (1 per 1,110 persons); infant mortality rate (1980–85) 118.
*Food* (1981–83): daily per capita caloric intake 2,246 (vegetable products 81%, animal products 19.0%); (1983) 90% of FAO recommended minimum.

## Military

*Total active duty personnel* (1986): 56,750 (army 93.4%, navy 1.3%, air force 5.3%). *Military expenditure as percent of GNP* (1984): 2.1% (world 5.9%); per capita expenditure U.S.$6.

[1]The collective head of state is a Supreme Council composed of a chairman (president) and four members. [2]Preliminary. [3]Detail does not add to total given because of rounding. [4]Reported by hospitals and dispensaries. [5]Low-income households. [6]1981–82. [7]Vocational only. [8]1980. [9]Includes dentists.

# Suriname

*Official name:* Republiek Suriname (Republic of Suriname).
*Form of government:* military dictatorship with one appointive advisory body (National Assembly [31][1]).
*Head of state and government:* Chairman of the Supreme Council.
*Capital:* Paramaribo.
*Official language:* Dutch.
*Official religion:* none.
*Monetary unit:* 1 Suriname guilder (Sf) = 100 cents; valuation (Oct. 5, 1987) 1 U.S.$ = Sf 1.79; 1 £ = Sf 2.90.

### Area and population

| Districts | Capitals | area[2] | | population |
|---|---|---|---|---|
| | | sq mi | sq km | 1980 census[3] |
| Brokopondo | Brokopondo | 8,278 | 21,440 | 20,249 |
| Commewijne | Nieuw Amsterdam | 1,587 | 4,110 | 14,351 |
| Coronie | Tottness | 626 | 1,620 | 2,777 |
| Marowijne | Albina | 17,753 | 45,980 | 23,402 |
| Nickerie | Nieuw Nickerie | 24,946 | 64,610 | 34,480 |
| Para | Onverwacht | 378 | 980 | 14,867 |
| Saramacca | Groningen | 9,042 | 23,420 | 10,335 |
| Suriname | ... | 629 | 1,628 | 166,494 |
| **Town district** | | | | |
| Paramaribo | Paramaribo | 12 | 32 | 67,905 |
| TOTAL | | 63,251 | 163,820 | 354,860 |

## Demography

*Population* (1987): 415,000.
*Density* (1987): persons per sq mi 6.6, persons per sq km 2.5.
*Urban–rural* (1985): urban 45.2%; rural 54.8%.
*Sex distribution* (1985): male 49.60%; female 50.40%.
*Age breakdown* (1985): under 15, 40.2%; 15–29, 36.1%; 30–44, 9.2%; 45–59, 8.4%; 60–74, 4.6%; 75 and over, 1.5%.
*Population projection:* (1990) 448,000; (2000) 579,000.
*Doubling time:* 30 years.
*Ethnic composition* (1983): Indo-Pakistani 37.0%; Suriname Creole 31.3%; Javanese 14.2%; Bush Negro 8.5%; Amerindian 3.1%; Chinese 2.8%; Dutch 1.4%; other 1.7%.
*Religious affiliation* (1980): Hindu 27.4%; Roman Catholic 22.8%; Muslim 19.6%; Protestant (mostly Moravian) 18.8%; other 11.4%.
*Major cities* (1980): Paramaribo 67,905; Nieuw Nickerie 6,078; Meerzorg 5,355; Marienburg 3,633.

## Vital statistics

*Birth rate* per 1,000 population (1985): 29.7 (world avg. 29.0); legitimate, n.a.; illegitimate, n.a.
*Death rate* per 1,000 population (1985): 6.8 (world avg. 11.0).
*Natural increase rate* per 1,000 population (1985): 22.9 (world avg. 18.0).
*Total fertility rate* (avg. births per childbearing woman; 1985): 6.1.
*Marriage rate* per 1,000 population (1985): 6.1.
*Divorce rate* per 1,000 population (1985): 1.5.
*Life expectancy* at birth (1980–85): male 65.6 years; female 70.6 years.
*Major causes of death* per 100,000 population (1982): diseases of the circulatory system 192.3, of which cerebrovascular disease 52.3, diseases of the pulmonary circulation 51.2, ischemic heart disease 39.4; malignant neoplasms (cancers) 57.3; accidents 50.7; infectious and parasitic diseases 42.1; diseases of the respiratory system 39.1; ill-defined conditions 82.1.

## National economy

*Budget* (1985). Revenue: Sf 491,780,000 (individual income tax 23.0%, import duties 19.0%, corporate tax 11.0%, property income tax 8.6%, export duties 6.2%). Expenditures: Sf 803,350,000 (1984; general public services 24.5%, economic services 22.9%, education 11.9%, social security 5.8%, defense 5.4%, health 0.3%).
*Public debt* (external, outstanding; 1985): U.S.$24,000,000.
*Production* (metric tons except as noted). Agriculture, forestry, fishing (1985): rice 299,100, sugarcane 118,000, bananas 45,000, oranges 8,000, palm oil 7,000, coconuts 7,000, plantains 5,000, cassava 4,000, tomatoes 2,000, cucumbers 1,000; livestock (number of live animals) 60,000 cattle, 21,000 pigs, 10,000 goats; roundwood 217,000 cu m; fish catch 3,412. Mining and quarrying (1985): bauxite 3,738,000; gravel and crushed stone 66,000[4]; clay 100,000[4]; gold 141 troy oz. Manufacturing (1985): alumina 1,242,000; cement 79,500; aluminum 28,800; sugar 6,700; plywood 13,900 cu m; shoes 253,000 pairs; soft drinks 302,000 hectolitres; beer 140,000 hectolitres; cigarettes 514,000,000 units. Construction (1984): residential Sf 32,600,000; nonresidential Sf 10,600,000. Energy production (consumption): electricity (kW-hr; 1985) 1,300,000,000 (1,300,000,000); hard coal (metric tons; 1985) none (1,000); crude petroleum (barrels; 1985) 416,000 (416,000); petroleum products (metric tons; 1985) none (324,000); natural gas, none (none).
*Land use* (1984): forested 96.5%; meadows and pastures 0.2%; agricultural and under permanent cultivation 0.4%; other 2.9%.
*Population economically active* (1984): total 99,240; activity rate of total population 25.9% (participation rates [1980]: ages 15–64, 38.7%; female 27.2%; unemployed [1986] 25.0%).

### Price and earnings indexes (1980 = 100)

| | 1980 | 1981 | 1982 | 1983 | 1984 | 1985 | 1986[5] |
|---|---|---|---|---|---|---|---|
| Consumer price index[6] | 100.0 | 108.7 | 116.6 | 121.8 | 126.2 | 140.0 | 144.9 |
| Earnings index | ... | ... | ... | ... | ... | ... | ... |

*Tourism:* receipts from visitors (1985) U.S.$20,000,000; expenditures by nationals abroad (1983) U.S.$35,000,000.
*Gross national product* (at current market prices; 1985): U.S.$980,000,000 (U.S.$2,490 per capita).

### Structure of gross domestic product and labour force

| | 1985 | | 1984 | |
|---|---|---|---|---|
| | in value Sf '000,000[7] | % of total value | labour force | % of labour force |
| Agriculture, forestry | 143 | 9.2 | 16,700 | 16.8 |
| Mining | 95 | 6.1 | 4,600 | 4.7 |
| Manufacturing | 206 | 13.2 | 10,960 | 11.1 |
| Construction | 97 | 6.2 | 2,800 | 2.8 |
| Public utilities | 66 | 4.2 | 1,420 | 1.4 |
| Transportation and communication | 128 | 8.2 | 3,830 | 3.9 |
| Trade | 268 | 17.2 | 12,840 | 12.9 |
| Finance, real estate | 239 | 15.3 | 2,100 | 2.1 |
| Pub. admin., defense | 384 | 24.7 | 40,190 | 40.5 |
| Services | 21 | 1.4 | 3,800 | 3.8 |
| Other | −89[8] | −5.7[8] | — | — |
| TOTAL | 1,558 | 100.0 | 99,240 | 100.0 |

*Household income and expenditure.* Average household size (1980) 3.9; income per household: n.a.; sources of income: n.a.; expenditure[6] (1968–69): food and beverages 40.0%, household furnishings 12.3%, clothing and footwear 11.0%, transport and communications 9.5%, health care and personal effects 6.2%, housing 5.9%, energy 5.5%, recreation 5.3%, other 4.3%.

## Foreign trade[9]

### Balance of trade (current prices)

| | 1980 | 1981 | 1982 | 1983 | 1984 | 1985 |
|---|---|---|---|---|---|---|
| Sf '000,000 | −30.4 | −195.9 | −200.8 | −162.7 | −48.3 | −15.9 |
| % of total | 1.7% | 10.7% | 12.0% | 11.5% | 3.6% | 1.3% |

*Imports* (1984): Sf 699,000,000 (raw materials and semimanufactured goods 36.7%, petroleum products 27.9%, machinery and equipment 12.1%). *Major import sources:* United States 30.0%; Trinidad and Tobago 14.2%; The Netherlands 13.7%; Netherlands Antilles 11.7%.
*Exports* (1984): Sf 650,700,000 (alumina 54.5%, bauxite 12.9%, aluminum 11.6%, rice 11.4%, shrimp 3.0%, bananas 2.5%). *Major export destinations:* United States 27.6%; The Netherlands 22.0%; Norway 13.4%; Venezuela 9.6%; United Kingdom 7.0%.

## Transport and communications

*Transport.* Railroads (1985): length 54 mi, 87 km; passengers, n.a.; cargo, n.a. Roads (1985): total length 5,541 mi, 8,917 km (paved 26%). Vehicles (1986): passenger cars 35,052; trucks and buses 14,600. Merchant marine (1986): vessels (100 gross tons and over) 25; total deadweight tonnage 15,285. Air transport (1985): passenger arrivals 66,200, passenger departures 70,700; airports (1987) with scheduled flights 5.
*Communications.* Daily newspapers (1987): total number 2; total circulation, n.a. Radio (1986): total number of receivers 246,000 (1 per 1.6 persons). Television (1986): total number of receivers 48,000 (1 per 8.4 persons). Telephones (1985): 36,125 (1 per 11 persons).

## Education and health

### Education (1984–85)

| | schools | teachers | students | student/ teacher ratio |
|---|---|---|---|---|
| Primary (age 6–12) | 321 | 3,880 | 89,624 | 23.1 |
| Secondary (age 13–17) | 63 | 839 | 22,814 | 27.2 |
| Voc., teacher tr.[10] | 64 | 1,178 | 15,428 | 13.1 |
| Higher | 6 | 357 | 1,704 | 4.8 |

*Educational attainment,* n.a. *Literacy* (1980): total population age 15 and over literate 170,817 (79.2%); males literate 88,351 (83.8%); females literate 82,466 (74.8%).
*Health* (1985): physicians 219 (1 per 1,798 persons); hospital beds 1,964 (1 per 200 persons); infant mortality rate per 1,000 live births 27.6.
*Food* (1981–83): daily per capita caloric intake 2,421 (vegetable products 86%, animal products 14%); (1983) 108% of FAO recommended minimum requirement.

## Military

*Total active duty personnel* (1986): 2,535[11] (army 92.7%, navy 4.9%, air force 2.4%). *Military expenditure as percent of GNP* (1984): 2.3% (world 5.9%); per capita expenditure U.S.$63.

[1]New constitution approved by referendum on Sept. 30, 1987, provided for the election of a 51-member National Assembly, held on Nov. 25, 1987; the Assembly was to elect a State Council (cabinet) and president. [2]Area excludes 6,809 sq mi (17,635 sq km) of territory disputed with Guyana. [3]Preliminary. [4]1984. [5]Third quarter. [6]For Paramaribo and environs. [7]At factor cost. [8]Less imputed bank charges. [9]Import figures are c.i.f. (cost, insurance, and freight); export figures are f.o.b. (free on board). Exports include reexports. [10]1983–84. [11]All services are part of the army.

# Swaziland

*Official name:* Umbuso weSwatini (Swazi); Kingdom of Swaziland (English).
*Form of government:* monarchy with two legislative houses (Senate [20]; House of Assembly [50]).
*Chief of state:* King.
*Head of government:* Prime Minister.
*Capitals:* Mbabane (administrative); Lobamba (royal and legislative).
*Official languages:* Swazi; English.
*Official religion:* none.
*Monetary unit:* 1 lilangeni (plural emalangeni [E]) = 100 cents; valuation (Oct. 5, 1987) 1 U.S.$ = E 2.08[1]; 1 £ = E 3.38.

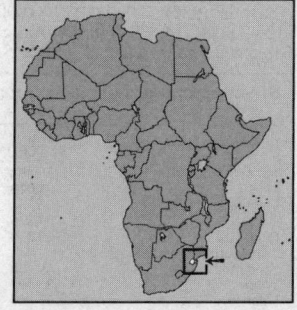

### Area and population

| Districts | Capitals | area sq mi | area sq km | population 1986 census[2] |
|---|---|---|---|---|
| Hhohho | Mbabane | 1,378 | 3,569 | 179,193 |
| Lubombo | Siteki | 2,296 | 5,947 | 152,408 |
| Manzini | Manzini | 1,571 | 4,068 | 190,613 |
| Shiselweni | Nhlangano | 1,459 | 3,780 | 153,875 |
| TOTAL | | 6,704 | 17,364 | 706,137[3] |

## Demography

*Population* (1987): 716,000.
*Density* (1987): persons per sq mi 106.8, persons per sq km 41.2.
*Urban–rural* (1985): urban 26.3%; rural 73.7%.
*Sex distribution* (1986): male 48.13%; female 51.87%.
*Age breakdown* (1985): under 15, 46.1%; 15–29, 25.7%; 30–44, 14.6%; 45–59, 8.6%; 60–74, 4.2%; 75 and over, 0.8%.
*Population projection:* (1990) 828,000; (2000) 1,098,000.
*Doubling time:* 23 years.
*Ethnic composition* (1983): Swazi 84.3%; Zulu 9.9%; Tsonga 2.5%; Indian 0.8%; Pakistani 0.8%; Portuguese 0.2%; other 1.5%.
*Religious affiliation* (1980): Christian 77.0%, of which Protestant 37.3%, Roman Catholic 10.8%; African indigenous 28.9%; traditional beliefs 20.9%; other 2.1%.
*Major cities* (1986): Manzini 52,000; Mbabane 40,000; Nhlangano 3,000; Siteki 1,800; Hlatikulu 1,600.

## Vital statistics

*Birth rate* per 1,000 population (1980–85): 47.5 (world avg. 29.0); legitimate, n.a.; illegitimate, n.a.
*Death rate* per 1,000 population (1980–85): 17.2 (world avg. 11.0).
*Natural increase rate* per 1,000 population (1980–85): 30.2 (world avg. 18.0).
*Total fertility rate* (avg. births per childbearing woman; 1980–85): 6.5.
*Marriage rate* per 1,000 population: n.a.
*Divorce rate* per 1,000 population: n.a.
*Life expectancy* at birth (1980–85): male 45.3 years; female 52.2 years.
*Major causes of death* (1982)[4]: infectious intestinal diseases 15.6%; tuberculosis 13.2%; diseases of the circulatory system 8.7%; diseases of the respiratory system 7.4%; diseases of the digestive system 5.5%; nutritional deficiencies 4.8%; malignant neoplasms (cancers) 4.4%.

## National economy

*Budget* (1986–87). Revenue: E 260,700,000 (receipts from Customs Union of Southern Africa 46.0%; tax on income and profits 23.7%; sales tax 14.2%; property income 6.0%; foreign aid grants 4.7%; fees, services, and fines 1.3%). Expenditures: E 304,700,000 (education 20.9%; transportation and communications 17.9%; general administration 11.9%; health 10.2%; public debt payments 8.5%; defense 4.9%).
*Tourism:* receipts from visitors (1985) U.S.$12,000,000; expenditures by nationals abroad (1984) U.S.$11,000,000.
*Public debt* (external, outstanding; 1985): U.S.$181,700,000.
*Gross national product* (at current market prices; 1985): U.S.$490,000,000 (U.S.$740 per capita).

### Structure of gross domestic product and labour force

| | 1983 in value E '000,000 | 1983 % of total value | 1985 labour force | 1985 % of labour force |
|---|---|---|---|---|
| Agriculture | 101.5 | 25.3 | 23,024 | 31.6 |
| Mining | 10.7 | 2.7 | 2,415 | 3.3 |
| Manufacturing | 94.0 | 23.5 | 10,600 | 14.5 |
| Construction | 17.4 | 4.3 | 3,632 | 5.0 |
| Public utilities | 5.0 | 1.3 | 1,324 | 1.8 |
| Transportation and communication | 22.1 | 5.5 | 5,413 | 7.4 |
| Trade | 35.8 | 8.9 | 7,051 | 9.7 |
| Finance | 26.3 | 6.6 | 3,264 | 4.5 |
| Pub. admin., defense | 69.8 | 17.4 | | |
| Services | 14.3 | 3.6 | 16,151 | 22.2 |
| Other | 3.7 | 0.9 | | |
| TOTAL | 400.5[5] | 100.0 | 72,874 | 100.0 |

*Population economically active* (1985): total 273,000; activity rate of total population 41.4% (participation rates: ages 15–64, n.a.; female [1982] 51.7%; unemployed [1983] 4.0%).

### Price and earnings indexes (1980 = 100)

| | 1981 | 1982 | 1983 | 1984 | 1985 | 1986 | 1987[6] |
|---|---|---|---|---|---|---|---|
| Consumer price index | 119.8 | 133.9 | 148.8 | 168.0 | 201.2 | 224.9 | 246.1 |
| Monthly earnings index[7] | 136.4 | 172.1 | 181.3 | ... | ... | ... | ... |

*Production* (metric tons except as noted). Agriculture, forestry, fishing (1985): sugarcane 3,500,000, fruit excluding melons 157,000, cereals 121,000 (of which corn [maize] 115,000, rice 3,000, sorghum 2,000), pineapples 45,000, seed cotton 32,000, roots and tubers 11,000 (of which potatoes 6,000, sweet potatoes 5,000), lint cotton 11,000, pulses 3,000; livestock (number of live animals) 620,000 cattle, 310,000 goats, 37,000 sheep, 19,000 pigs, 1,000,000 chickens; roundwood (1984) 2,223,000 cu m; fish catch (1984) 44. Mining and quarrying (1986): asbestos 23,093; diamonds 39,144 carats. Manufacturing (value added in E; 1982): food products and beverages 44,567,000; industrial chemicals 18,486,000; paper products 18,337,000; wood products, furniture, and fixtures 8,134,000; metal products 4,918,000; textiles 2,252,000. Construction (value in E; 1985)[8]: residential 2,992,000; nonresidential 1,784,300. Energy production (consumption): electricity (kW-hr; 1986) 375,500,000 (590,000,000[9]); coal (metric tons; 1986) 172,199 (27,479[9]); crude petroleum, n.a. (n.a.); petroleum products, n.a. (n.a.); natural gas, n.a. (n.a.).
*Household income and expenditure.* Average household size (1980) 5.0; income per household: n.a.; sources of income: n.a.; expenditure[10]: food, beverages, and tobacco 39.3%, transportation and communication 15.3%, clothing and footwear 10.0%, furniture and utensils 9.0%, health and education 8.0%, energy and water 6.5%.
*Land use* (1984): forested 5.8%; meadows and pastures 66.9%; agricultural and under permanent cultivation 8.4%; other 18.9%.

## Foreign trade[11]

### Balance of trade (current prices)

| | 1981 | 1982 | 1983 | 1984 | 1985 | 1986 |
|---|---|---|---|---|---|---|
| E '000,000 | −102.4 | −100.5 | −177.4 | −157.7 | −202.3 | −161.0 |
| % of total | 13.1% | 12.0% | 20.7% | 17.3% | 20.7% | 13.8% |

*Imports* (1985): E 706,681,000 (mineral fuels and lubricants 27.1%; machinery and transport equipment 23.3%; manufactured goods 17.4%; food and live animals 7.6%; chemicals 5.1%; beverages and tobacco 2.4%; animal and vegetable oils and fats 0.2%). *Major import sources* (1983–84): South Africa 84.7%; United States 7.0%; United Kingdom 2.3%; Japan 1.3%; West Germany 0.9%.
*Exports* (1985): E 368,880,000[12] (sugar 37.8%; wood and wood products 27.2%, of which woodpulp 16.9%; canned fruit and juices 7.2%; citrus fruits 6.3%; chrysotile asbestos 6.0%; coal 2.1%; meat and meat products 1.1%; diamonds 1.1%). *Major export destinations* (1983): South Africa 32.4%; United Kingdom 22.1%.

## Transport and communications

*Transport.* Railroads (1986): route length 230 mi, 370 km; passengers, n.a.; short ton-mi cargo 73,300,000[13], metric ton-km cargo 107,000,000[13]. Roads (1983): total length 1,692 mi, 2,723 km (paved 23%). Vehicles (1985): passenger cars 18,360; trucks and buses 10,218. Merchant marine: none; landlocked state. Air transport (1984)[14]: passenger-mi 13,977,000, passenger-km 22,494,000; short ton-mi cargo 1,508,000, metric ton-km cargo 2,201,000; airports (1987) with scheduled flights 1.
*Communications.* Daily newspapers (1985): total number 3; total circulation 23,000; circulation per 1,000 population 35. Radio (1986): total number of receivers 96,000 (1 per 7.1 persons). Television (1986): total number of receivers 12,400 (1 per 55 persons). Telephones (1985): 17,795 (1 per 39 persons).

## Education and health

### Education (1986)

| | schools | teachers | students | student/ teacher ratio |
|---|---|---|---|---|
| Primary (age 6–13) | 937 | 8,397 | 281,551 | 33.5 |
| Secondary (age 14–18) | 194 | 3,353 | 62,297 | 18.6 |
| Voc., teacher tr. | 2 | 100 | 1,257 | 12.6 |
| Higher | 2 | 291 | 2,997 | 10.3 |

*Educational attainment* (1976). Percent of population age 25 and over having: no formal schooling 53.6%; some primary education 25.4%; complete primary 9.2%; some secondary 7.9%; secondary and higher 3.9%. *Literacy* (1985): total population age 15 and over literate 238,400 (67.9%); males literate 119,500 (70.3%); females literate 118,900 (65.7%).
*Health* (1984): physicians 80 (1 per 7,971 persons); hospital beds 1,608 (1 per 396 persons); infant mortality rate per 1,000 live births (1985–90) 118.
*Food* (1981–83): daily per capita caloric intake 2,534 (vegetable products 87%, animal products 13%); (1983) 111% of FAO recommended minimum requirement.

## Military

*Total active duty personnel* (1983): 2,657. *Military expenditure as percent of GNP* (1984): 1.6% (world 5.9%); per capita expenditure U.S.$17.

---

[1]The lilangeni is at par with the South African rand. [2]Preliminary. [3]Includes 30,048 residents abroad. [4]Percentage of deaths of known cause at government, mission, and private hospitals. [5]At factor cost, prices of 1980; detail does not add to total given because of rounding. [6]April. [7]Based on earnings of skilled male workers in manufacturing. [8]Urban areas under the jurisdiction of the Manzini and Mbabane town councils only. [9]1985. [10]Weights of consumer price index components. [11]Import figures are f.o.b. in balance of trade and c.i.f. in commodities and trading partners. [12]Reexports accounted for 5.0% of all exports. [13]1984. [14]Royal Swazi National Airways only.

# Sweden

*Official name:* Konungariket Sverige (Kingdom of Sweden).
*Form of government:* constitutional monarchy and parliamentary state with one legislative house (Parliament [349]).
*Chief of state:* King.
*Head of government:* Prime Minister.
*Capital:* Stockholm.
*Official language:* Swedish.
*Official religion:* Church of Sweden (Lutheran).
*Monetary unit:* 1 Swedish krona (SKr) = 100 ore; valuation (Oct. 5, 1987) 1 U.S.$ = SKr 6.45; 1 £ = SKr 10.48.

### Area and population

| Counties | Capitals | area sq mi | area sq km | population 1987 estimate[1] |
|---|---|---|---|---|
| Älvsborg | Vänersborg | 4,400 | 11,395 | 427,638 |
| Blekinge | Karlskrona | 1,136 | 2,941 | 150,258 |
| Gävleborg | Gävle | 7,024 | 18,191 | 287,691 |
| Göteborg och Bohus | Göteborg | 1,985 | 5,141 | 721,553 |
| Gotland | Visby | 1,212 | 3,140 | 56,174 |
| Halland | Halmstad | 2,106 | 5,454 | 242,250 |
| Jämtland | Östersund | 19,090 | 49,443 | 133,543 |
| Jönköping | Jönköping | 3,839 | 9,944 | 301,413 |
| Kalmar | Kalmar | 4,313 | 11,170 | 237,417 |
| Kopparberg | Falun | 10,886 | 28,194 | 283,191 |
| Kristianstad | Kristianstad | 2,350 | 6,087 | 280,609 |
| Kronoberg | Växjö | 3,266 | 8,458 | 173,853 |
| Malmöhus | Malmö | 1,907 | 4,938 | 753,075 |
| Norrbotten | Luleå | 38,191 | 98,913 | 261,039 |
| Örebro | Örebro | 3,289 | 8,519 | 269,620 |
| Östergötland | Linköping | 4,078 | 10,562 | 394,753 |
| Skaraborg | Mariestad | 3,065 | 7,937 | 270,111 |
| Södermanland | Nyköping | 2,340 | 6,060 | 249,479 |
| Stockholm | Stockholm | 2,505 | 6,488 | 1,593,333 |
| Uppsala | Uppsala | 2,698 | 6,989 | 254,938 |
| Värmland | Karlstad | 6,789 | 17,584 | 278,861 |
| Västerbotten | Umeå | 21,390 | 55,401 | 245,204 |
| Västernorrland | Härnösand | 8,370 | 21,678 | 261,089 |
| Västmanland | Västerås | 2,433 | 6,302 | 254,423 |
| TOTAL LAND AREA | | 158,661[2] | 410,929 | 8,381,515 |
| INLAND WATER | | 15,071 | 39,035 | |
| TOTAL | | 173,732[2] | 449,964 | |

## Demography

*Population* (1987): 8,387,000.
*Density* (1987)[3]: persons per sq mi 52.9, persons per sq km 20.4.
*Urban–rural* (1985): urban 83.4%; rural 16.6%.
*Sex distribution* (1987): male 49.36%; female 50.64%.
*Age breakdown* (1986): under 15, 18.1%; 15–29, 20.7%; 30–44, 22.1%; 45–59, 16.0%; 60–74, 15.7%; 75 and over, 7.4%.
*Population projection:* (1990) 8,421,000; (2000) 8,534,000.
*Ethnic composition* (1986): Swedish 91.1%; Finnish 3.1%; other 5.8%.
*Religious affiliation* (1985): Church of Sweden 91.5% (nominally; about 30% nonpracticing); Roman Catholic 1.4%; Pentecostal 1.2%; other 5.9%.
*Major cities* (1987): Stockholm 663,217; Göteborg 429,339; Malmö 230,056; Uppsala 157,675; Norrköping 118,801.

## Vital statistics

*Birth rate* per 1,000 population (1986): 12.2 (world avg. 26.0); (1984) legitimate 56.4%; illegitimate 43.6%.
*Death rate* per 1,000 population (1986): 11.2 (world avg. 9.9).
*Natural increase rate* per 1,000 population (1986): 1.0 (world avg. 16.1).
*Total fertility rate* (avg. births per childbearing woman; 1984): 1.6.
*Marriage rate* per 1,000 population (1986): 4.6.
*Divorce rate* per 1,000 population (1986): 2.3.
*Life expectancy* at birth (1980–84): male 73.3 years; female 79.4 years.
*Major causes of death* per 100,000 population (1984): heart disease 422.2; malignant neoplasms (cancers) 231.1; cerebrovascular disease 113.2.

## National economy

*Budget* (1986–87). Revenue: SKr 293,189,800,000 (value-added tax 22.6%, income and capital gains taxes 21.4%, social security contributions 20.2%, nontax revenue 11.6%). Expenditures: SKr 336,392,400,000 (health and social affairs 25.4%, interest on national debt 19.3%, education and culture 12.6%, defense 7.8%, manpower 5.9%).
*Public debt* (1985): U.S.$78,220,000,000.
*Tourism* (1985): receipts from visitors U.S.$1,332,000,000; expenditures by nationals abroad U.S.$2,270,000,000.
*Production* (metric tons except as noted). Agriculture, forestry, fishing (1985): barley 2,309,170, sugar beets 2,156,340, oats 1,667,900, wheat 1,337,880, potatoes 1,265,740; livestock (number of live animals) 1,837,000 cattle, 2,500,000 pigs, 425,000 sheep; roundwood 22,800,000 cu m; fish catch 225,900, of which Baltic herring 103,100. Mining and quarrying (1986): iron ore 20,490,000, zinc 396,000[4], copper 353,000[4], lead 130,000[4]. Manufacturing (1985): crude and manufactured steel 8,421,000; paper and paperboard 5,832,000; wood pulp 2,298,000; cement 2,101,000; automobiles 314,600 vehicles[5]. Construction (1985): 32,925 dwellings completed. Energy production (consumption): electricity (kW-hr; 1985) 136,543,000,000 (135,-010,000,000); coal (metric tons; 1985) 12,000 (4,153,000); crude petroleum

(barrels; 1985) 60,000 (105,100,000); petroleum products (metric tons; 1985) 12,423,000 (14,839,000); natural gas (cu m; 1985) none (79,126,000).
*Gross national product* (1985): U.S.$99,050,000,000 (U.S.$11,860 per capita).

### Structure of gross domestic product and labour force

| | 1984 in value SKr '000,000 | 1984 % of total value | 1985 labour force | 1985 % of labour force |
|---|---|---|---|---|
| Agriculture | 25,498 | 3.3 | 208,000 | 4.7 |
| Mining | 4,018 | 0.5 | 15,000 | 0.3 |
| Manufacturing | 167,182 | 21.8 | 968,000 | 21.9 |
| Construction | 51,875 | 6.8 | 260,000 | 5.9 |
| Public utilities | 20,319 | 2.6 | 40,000 | 0.9 |
| Transportation and communication | 44,452 | 5.8 | 300,000 | 6.8 |
| Trade | 83,592 | 10.9 | 591,000 | 13.4 |
| Finance | 90,880 | 11.8 | 321,000 | 7.3 |
| Pub. admin., defense | 165,841 | 21.6 } | 1,594,000 | 36.0 |
| Services | 29,382 | 3.9 } | | |
| Other | 84,112 | 11.0 | 125,000[6] | 2.8 |
| TOTAL | 767,151 | 100.0 | 4,424,000[2] | 100.0 |

*Population economically active* (1985): total 4,424,000; activity rate of total population 53.0% (participation rates: ages 15–64, 82.6%; female 47.1%; unemployed 2.8%).

### Price and earnings indexes (1980 = 100)

| | 1981 | 1982 | 1983 | 1984 | 1985 | 1986 | 1987[7] |
|---|---|---|---|---|---|---|---|
| Consumer price index | 112.1 | 121.7 | 132.6 | 143.2 | 153.8 | 160.3 | 165.2 |
| Hourly earnings index | 110.2 | 118.2 | 127.4 | 141.2 | 154.1 | ... | ... |

*Household income and expenditure.* Average household size (1980) 2.4; income per household (1983) SKr 98,400 (U.S.$15,165); sources of income (1984): wages and salaries 61.5%, transfer payments 21.4% (includes social security 15.0%), self-employed 17.1%; expenditure (1984): housing 32.6%, food 24.9%, transportation 15.4%, recreation 9.8%.
*Land use* (1984): forested 64.2%; meadows and pastures 1.5%; agricultural and under permanent cultivation 7.3%; other 27.0%.

## Foreign trade

### Balance of trade (current prices)

| | 1981 | 1982 | 1983 | 1984 | 1985 | 1986 |
|---|---|---|---|---|---|---|
| SKr '000,000 | −1,160 | −5,800 | 10,150 | 24,710 | 16,080 | 37,910 |
| % of total | 0.4% | 1.7% | 2.5% | 5.4% | 3.2% | 7.7% |

*Imports* (1986): SKr 232,270,000,000 (machinery and transport equipment 36.0%, of which transport equipment 10.9%, electrical machinery 8.7%; chemicals 9.7%; food and tobacco products 7.0%; clothing and footwear 5.6%). *Major import sources:* West Germany 20.4%; United Kingdom 10.4%; United States 7.8%; Denmark 6.8%; Finland 6.8%; Norway 5.6%.
*Exports* (1986): SKr 265,100,000,000 (machinery and transport equipment 43.8%, of which transport equipment 17.3%, electrical machinery 7.8%; paper products 10.4%; wood and wood pulp 6.9%; chemicals 6.7%; iron and steel products 6.2%). *Major export destinations:* West Germany 11.6%; United States 11.3%; Norway 11.2%; United Kingdom 10.4%; Denmark 8.0%.

## Transport and communications

*Transport.* Railroads (1985): length 7,130 mi, 11,745 km; passenger-mi 4,094,000, passenger-km 6,588,000; short ton-mi cargo 12,050,000, metric ton-km cargo 17,592,000. Roads (1985): total length 81,207 mi, 130,691 km (paved 69%). Vehicles (1985): passenger cars 3,151,195; trucks and buses 231,442. Merchant marine (1986): vessels (100 gross tons and over) 660; total deadweight tonnage 3,033,436. Air transport (1986): passenger-mi 3,342,000,000, passenger-km 5,378,000,000; short ton-mi cargo 130,758,000, metric ton-km cargo 190,903,000; airports (1987) 36.
*Communications.* Daily newspapers (1985): total number 188; total circulation 4,837,400; circulation per 1,000 population 579. Radio (1986): 3,330,-000 receivers (1 per 2.5 persons). Television (1986): 3,265,500 receivers (1 per 2.6 persons). Telephones (1984): 7,410,000 (1 per 1.1 persons).

## Education and health

### Education (1984–85)

| | schools | teachers[8] | students | student/ teacher ratio |
|---|---|---|---|---|
| Primary (age 7–9) | 4,770 | 100,748 | 959,627 | ... |
| Secondary (age 10–18) | 520 | 28,636 | 267,477 | ... |
| Higher | ... | 17,608 | 221,200 | ... |

*Educational attainment* (1979). Percent of population age 25 and over having: lower secondary education 7.3%; higher secondary 35.7%; some postsecondary 15.4%. *Literacy* (1986): virtually 100%.
*Health* (1984): physicians 20,200 (1 per 413 persons); hospital beds 115,859 (1 per 72 persons); infant mortality rate per 1,000 live births (1985) 6.7.
*Food* (1981–83): daily per capita caloric intake 3,186 (vegetable products 57%, animal products 43%); (1983) 112% of FAO recommended minimum requirement.

## Military

*Total active duty personnel* (1986): 64,650 (army 72.7%, navy 14.9%, air force 12.4%). *Military expenditure as percent of GNP* (1984): 3.0% (world 5.9%); per capita expenditure U.S.$341.

[1]January 1. [2]Detail does not add to total given because of rounding [3]Density based on land area only. [4]Ore concentrates. [5]1984. [6]Unemployed only. [7]May. [8]1983–84.

# Switzerland

*Official name:* Confédération
Suisse (French); Schweizerische
Eidgenossenschaft (German);
Confederazione Svizzera (Italian)
(Swiss Confederation).
*Form of government:* federal state with
two legislative houses (Council of
States [46]; National Council [200]).
*Head of state and government:*
President.
*Capital:* Bern.
*Official languages:* French; German;
Italian.
*Official religion:* none.
*Monetary unit:* 1 Swiss Franc
(Sw F) = 100 centimes; valuation
(Oct. 5, 1987) 1 U.S.$ = Sw F 1.53;
1 £ = Sw F 2.49.

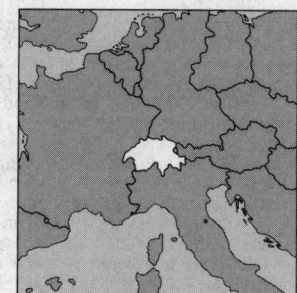

### Area and population

| Cantons | Capitals | area sq mi | area sq km | population 1987 estimate[1] |
|---|---|---|---|---|
| Aargau | Aarau | 542 | 1,405 | 472,500 |
| Appenzell Ausser-Rhoden[2] | Herisau | 94 | 243 | 49,500 |
| Appenzell Inner-Rhoden[2] | Appenzell | 66 | 172 | 13,200 |
| Basel-Landschaft[2] | Liestal | 165 | 428 | 226,600 |
| Basel-Stadt[2] | Basel | 14 | 37 | 194,500 |
| Bern | Bern | 2,335 | 6,049 | 925,300 |
| Fribourg | Fribourg | 645 | 1,670 | 194,600 |
| Genève | Geneva | 109 | 282 | 364,100 |
| Glarus | Glarus | 264 | 684 | 36,500 |
| Graubünden | Chur | 2,744 | 7,106 | 166,500 |
| Jura | Delémont | 323 | 837 | 64,800 |
| Luzern | Luzern | 576 | 1,492 | 305,800 |
| Neuchâtel | Neuchâtel | 308 | 797 | 155,700 |
| Nidwalden[2] | Stans | 107 | 276 | 31,100 |
| Obwalden[2] | Sarnen | 189 | 491 | 27,600 |
| Sankt Gallen | Sankt Gallen | 778 | 2,014 | 404,200 |
| Schaffhausen | Schaffhausen | 115 | 298 | 69,800 |
| Schwyz | Schwyz | 351 | 908 | 103,300 |
| Solothurn | Solothurn | 305 | 791 | 219,500 |
| Thurgau | Frauenfeld | 391 | 1,013 | 192,500 |
| Ticino | Bellinzona | 1,085 | 2,811 | 277,200 |
| Uri | Altdorf | 416 | 1,076 | 33,400 |
| Valais | Sion | 2,018 | 5,226 | 232,200 |
| Vaud | Lausanne | 1,243 | 3,219 | 550,000 |
| Zug | Zug | 92 | 239 | 81,600 |
| Zürich | Zürich | 668 | 1,729 | 1,131,100 |
| TOTAL | | 15,943 | 41,293 | 6,523,100[3] |

## Demography

*Population* (1987): 6,586,000.
*Density* (1987): persons per sq mi 413.1, persons per sq km 159.5.
*Urban–rural* (1985): urban 58.2%; rural 41.8%.
*Sex distribution* (1986): male 48.73%; female 51.27%.
*Age breakdown* (1986): under 15, 17.5%; 15–29, 23.1%; 30–44, 22.7%; 45–59, 17.6%; 60–74, 12.8%; 75 and over, 6.3%.
*Population projection:* (1990) 6,670,000; (2000) 6,940,000.
*Ethnolinguistic composition* (1980)[3]: German 65.0%; French 18.4%; Italian 9.8%; Spanish 1.6%; Romansch 0.8%; Turkish 0.6%; other 3.8%.
*Religious affiliation* (1980): Roman Catholic 47.6%; Protestant 44.3%; Jewish 0.3%; other 7.8%.
*Major cities* (1986): Zürich 351,545; Basel 174,606; Geneva 159,895.

## Vital statistics

*Birth rate* per 1,000 population (1986): 11.7 (world avg. 26.0); (1985) legitimate 94.4%; illegitimate 5.6%.
*Death rate* per 1,000 population (1986): 9.2 (world avg. 9.9).
*Natural increase rate* per 1,000 population (1986): 2.5 (world avg. 16.1).
*Total fertility rate* (avg. births per childbearing woman; 1985): 1.8.
*Marriage rate* per 1,000 population (1985): 5.9.
*Divorce rate* per 1,000 population (1985): 1.7.
*Life expectancy* at birth (1980–85): male 72.8 years; female 79.7 years.
*Major causes of death* per 100,000 population (1985): circulatory system diseases 364.2; malignant neoplasms (cancers) 233.1.

## National economy

*Budget* (1985). Revenue: Sw F 22,185,500,000 (taxes on consumption 52.8%, of which turnover tax 30.5%, customs duties 15.5%; taxes on income and wealth 39.8%). Expenditures: Sw F 22,881,300,000 (social security 21.4%; defense 20.1%; communications and energy 14.5%; education 8.0%).
*Public debt* (1984): U.S.$10,733,000,000.
*Tourism* (1985): receipts from visitors U.S.$3,145,000,000; expenditures by nationals abroad U.S.$2,399,000,000.
*Production* (metric tons except as noted). Agriculture, forestry, fishing (1985): potatoes 848,000, sugar beets 790,000, wheat 547,000, apples 318,000, barley 270,000, grapes 162,000; livestock (number of live animals) 1,988,000 pigs, 1,926,000 cattle, 361,000 sheep; roundwood 4,561,000 cu m; fish catch (1984) 3,985. Mining and quarrying (1986): salt 400,000; gypsum 75,000. Manufacturing (1985): cement 4,254,000; refined sugar 142,000; wine 118,000; chocolate 82,563; aluminum 73,000; woolen fabrics 8,696,000 m; 25,137,000 watches; 8,032,000 pairs of shoes. Construction (buildings completed; 1985): residential 17,537; nonresidential 8,879. Energy production (consumption)[4]: electricity (kW-hr; 1985) 53,872,000,000

(45,174,000,000); coal (metric tons; 1985) none (640,000); crude petroleum (barrels; 1985) none (27,839,000); petroleum products (metric tons; 1985) 4,068,000 (11,038,000); natural gas (cu m; 1985) 17,888,000 (1,511,275,000).
*Gross national product* (at current market prices; 1985): U.S.$105,180,000,000 (U.S.$16,100 per capita).

### Gross domestic product and structure of labour force

| | 1985 in value Sw F '000 | % of total value | labour force | % of labour force |
|---|---|---|---|---|
| Agriculture | ... | ... | 209,700 | 6.6 |
| Mining | ... | ... } | 950,600 | 29.9 |
| Manufacturing | ... | ... | | |
| Construction | ... | ... | 223,900 | 7.1 |
| Public utilities | ... | ... | 29,500 | 0.9 |
| Transp. and commun. | ... | ... | 196,000 | 6.2 |
| Trade | ... | ... | 595,900 | 18.8 |
| Finance | ... | ... | 165,200 | 5.2 |
| Pub. admin., defense | ... | ... | 268,400 | 8.5 |
| Services | ... | ... | 531,700 | 16.8 |
| TOTAL | 227,760,000 | 100.0 | 3,170,900 | 100.0 |

*Population economically active* (1985): total 3,170,900; activity rate of total population 48.5% (participation rates: age 15 and over [1984] 58.9%; female 36.9%; unemployed 1.0%).

### Price and earnings indexes (1980 = 100)

| | 1981 | 1982 | 1983 | 1984 | 1985 | 1986 | 1987[5] |
|---|---|---|---|---|---|---|---|
| Consumer price index | 106.5 | 112.5 | 115.9 | 119.3 | 123.4 | 124.3 | 125.7 |
| Annual earnings index | 106.4 | 114.0 | 118.4 | 121.5 | 125.3 | ... | ... |

*Household income and expenditure.* Average household size (1981) 2.5; average income per household (1982) Sw F 61,000 (U.S.$30,045); sources of income (1984): wages and salaries 63.9%, self-employment 21.3%, social security 12.0%; expenditure (1985): food and beverages 29.0%, housing 13.8%, transportation 11.8%, education 9.7%, health 8.8%, utilities 6.8%.
*Land use* (1984): forested 26.4%; meadows and pastures 40.5%; agricultural and under permanent cultivation 10.4%; other 22.7%.

## Foreign trade

### Balance of trade (current prices)

| | 1980 | 1981 | 1982 | 1983 | 1984 | 1985 |
|---|---|---|---|---|---|---|
| Sw F '000,000 | −11,251 | −7,272 | −5,401 | −7,341 | −8,370 | −8,126 |
| % of total | 10.2% | 6.4% | 4.9% | 6.4% | 6.4% | 5.7% |

*Imports* (1985): Sw F 74,750,300,000 (machinery and transport equipment 22.2%, clothing and textiles 9.6%, mineral fuels 9.2%, precious metals and jewelry 7.6%, chemical products 5.9%). *Major import sources:* W.Ger. 30.6%; France 11.2%; Italy 9.7%; U.K. 7.2%; U.S. 5.9%; The Netherlands 4.6%.
*Exports* (1985): Sw F 66,623,700,000 (nonelectrical machinery 19.6%, electrical machinery 10.6%, precious-metal articles and jewelry 8.3%, pharmaceuticals 7.5%, watches 6.5%). *Major export destinations:* W.Ger. 19.7%; U.S. 10.3%; France 8.3%; U.K. 8.0%; Italy 7.4%.

## Transport and communications

*Transport.* Railroads (1986)[6]: length[7] 3,158 mi, 5,028 km; passenger-km 9,204,000,000; metric ton-km cargo 6,967,000,000. Roads (1985): total length 43,855 mi, 70,578 km. Vehicles (1985): passenger cars 2,617,164; trucks and buses 211,308. Merchant marine (1986): vessels (100 gross tons and over) 34; total deadweight tonnage 550,711. Air transport (1986): passenger-km 12,875,000,000; metric ton-km cargo 725,275,000; airports (1987) 5.
*Communications.* Daily newspapers (1986): total number 102; total circulation 3,229,158; circulation per 1,000 population 494. Radio (1986): 2,512,882 receivers (1 per 2.6 persons). Television (1986): 2,215,808 receivers (1 per 3.0 persons). Telephones (1985): 5,435,820 (1 per 1.2 persons).

## Education and health

### Education (1986–87)

| | schools | teachers | students | student/ teacher ratio |
|---|---|---|---|---|
| Primary (age 6–11) | ... | ... | 405,800 | ... |
| Secondary (age 11–18) | ... | ... | 368,600 | ... |
| Voc., teacher tr. | ... | ... | 249,900 | ... |
| Higher | ... | ... | 117,000 | ... |

*Educational attainment* (1970). Percent of population age 25 and over having: no formal schooling 0.4%; primary and lower-secondary education 73.1%; higher-secondary 7.2%; some postsecondary 10.2%; university degree 3.1%. *Literacy:* virtually 100.0%.
*Health:* physicians (1984) 14,712 (1 per 442 persons); hospital beds (1983) 66,192 (1 per 98 persons); infant mortality rate (1985) 6.9.
*Food* (1981–83): daily per capita caloric intake 3,492 (vegetable products 60%, animal products 40%); (1983) 129% of FAO recommended minimum.

## Military

*Total active duty personnel*[8] (1986): 625,000 (army 92.8%, air force 7.2%).
*Military expenditure as percent of GNP* (1984): 2.1% (world 5.9%); per capita expenditure U.S.$301.

---

[1]January 1. [2]Demicanton; functions as a full canton and has the same legal prerogatives as a full canton. [3]Includes resident aliens but excludes seasonal workers. [4]Figures include Liechtenstein. [5]June. [6]Swiss Federal Railways only. [7]1984. [8]Mobilized personnel.

# Syria

*Official name:* al-Jumhūrīyah al-'Arabīyah as-Sūrīyah (Syrian Arab Republic).
*Form of government:* unitary multiparty[1] republic with one legislative house (People's Council [195]).
*Chief of state:* President.
*Head of government:* Prime Minister.
*Capital:* Damascus.
*Official language:* Arabic.
*Official religion:* none[2].
*Monetary unit:* 1 Syrian Pound (LS) = 100 piastres; valuation (Oct. 5, 1987) 1 U.S.$ = LS 3.93; 1£ = LS 6.37.

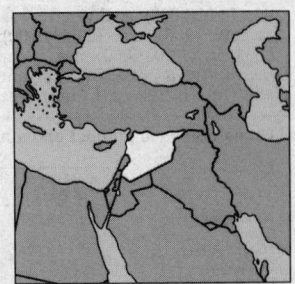

### Area and population

| Governorates | Capitals | area sq mi | area sq km | population 1987 estimate |
|---|---|---|---|---|
| Dar'ā | Dar'ā | 1,440 | 3,730 | 460,000 |
| Dayr az-Zawr | Dayr az-Zawr | 12,765 | 33,060 | 487,000 |
| Dimashq | al-Iarmouk | 6,962 | 18,032 | 1,127,000 |
| Ḥalab | Aleppo | 7,143 | 18,500 | 2,269,000 |
| Ḥamāh | Ḥamāh | 3,430 | 8,883 | 890,000 |
| al-Ḥasakah | al-Ḥasakah | 9,009 | 23,334 | 810,000 |
| Ḥimş | Homs | 16,302 | 42,223 | 1,007,000 |
| Idlib | Idlib | 2,354 | 6,097 | 721,000 |
| al-Lādhiqiyah | Latakia | 887 | 2,297 | 668,000 |
| al-Qunayţirah | al-Qunayţirah | 719[3] | 1,861[3] | 34,000 |
| ar-Raqqah | ar-Raqqah | 7,574 | 19,616 | 422,000 |
| as-Suwaydā' | as-Suwaydā' | 2,143 | 5,550 | 240,000 |
| Ţarţūs | Tartous | 730 | 1,892 | 542,000 |
| **Municipality** | | | | |
| Dimashq | Damascus | 41 | 105 | 1,292,000 |
| TOTAL | | 71,498[3] | 185,180[3] | 10,969,000 |

## Demography

*Population* (1987): 10,969,000.
*Density* (1987): persons per sq mi 153.4, persons per sq km 59.2.
*Urban-rural* (1986): urban 49.1%; rural 50.9%.
*Sex distribution* (1986): male 51.07%; female 48.93%.
*Age breakdown* (1986): under 15, 49.3%; 15–29, 22.4%; 30–44, 14.3%; 45–59, 7.5%; 60–74, 4.8%; 75 and over, 1.7%.
*Population projection:* (1990) 12,310,000; (2000) 18,082,000.
*Doubling time:* 18 years.
*Ethnic composition* (1981): Arab 88.8%; Kurdish 6.3%; other 4.9%.
*Religious affiliation* (1980): Muslim (mostly Sunnī) 89.6%; Christian 8.9%; other 1.5%.
*Major cities* (1987): Damascus 1,292,000; Aleppo 1,216,000; Homs 431,000; Latakia 241,000; Ḥamāh 214,000.

## Vital statistics

*Birth rate* per 1,000 population (1985)[4]: 44.2 (world avg. 29.0).
*Death rate* per 1,000 population (1985)[4]: 5.0 (world avg. 11.0).
*Natural increase rate* per 1,000 population (1985)[4]: 39.2 (world avg. 18.0).
*Total fertility rate* (avg. births per childbearing woman; 1980–85): 7.2.
*Marriage rate* per 1,000 population (1985)[4]: 9.4.
*Divorce rate* per 1,000 population (1985)[4]: 0.7.
*Life expectancy* at birth (1984): male 63.3 years; female 67.0 years.
*Major causes of death* per 100,000 population (1981): signs, symptoms, and ill-defined conditions 207.3; diseases of the circulatory system 60.7; infectious and parasitic diseases 15.1.

## National economy

*Budget* (1986). Revenue: LS 43,841,000,000 (taxes and duties 27.5%, budget surplus carryover 23.0%, loans and assistances 17.5%, special revenues 5.9%). Expenditures: LS 43,841,000,000 (defense 31.0%, administration 18.2%, agriculture 9.7%, education 9.0%, transport and communication 5.0%).
*Public debt* (external, outstanding; 1985): U.S.$2,750,900,000.
*Tourism* (1985): receipts from visitors U.S.$154,000,000; expenditures by nationals abroad U.S.$118,000,000.
*Gross national product* (at current market prices; 1985): U.S.$17,060,000,000 (U.S.$1,660 per capita).

### Structure of gross domestic product and labour force

| | 1985 in value LS '000,000 | 1985 % of total value | 1984 labour force | 1984 % of labour force |
|---|---|---|---|---|
| Agriculture | 22,481 | 16.4 | 1,064,331 | 44.7 |
| Mining | 39,452 | 28.8 | 18,216 | 0.8 |
| Manufacturing | | | 280,103 | 11.8 |
| Construction | 14,814 | 10.8 | 219,680 | 9.2 |
| Public utilities | ... | ... | 6,829 | 0.3 |
| Transportation and communication | 12,916 | 9.4 | 110,645 | 4.6 |
| Trade | 19,296 | 14.1 | 248,281 | 10.4 |
| Finance | 5,015 | 3.7 | 21,373 | 0.9 |
| Pub. admin. | 19,937 | 14.5 | 345,058 | 14.5 |
| Services | 3,044 | 2.2 | | |
| Other | 73 | 0.1 | 67,270[5] | 2.8[5] |
| TOTAL | 137,028 | 100.0 | 2,381,786 | 100.0 |

## Production

*Production* (metric tons except as noted). Agriculture, forestry, fishing (1985): wheat 1,714,000, barley 1,037,000, tomatoes 796,000, watermelons 673,000, grapes 486,000, potatoes 394,000, cucumbers 272,000, melons 258,000, cotton 180,000; livestock (number of live animals) 13,665,000 sheep, 1,060,000 goats, 740,000 cattle; roundwood 44,000 cu m; fish catch 5,000. Mining and quarrying (1985): phosphate rock 1,224,000; salt 62,000; asphalt 52,000; sand and gravel 14,077,000 cu m; stone 576,000 cu m; gypsum 255,000 cu m. Manufacturing (1985): cement 4,357,000; flour 1,161,000; fertilizers 104,000; sugar 54,000; silk and cotton textiles 22,000. Construction (1985): residential 5,223,000 sq m; nonresidential 787,000 sq m. Energy production (consumption): electricity (kW-hr; 1985) 7,316,000,000 (7,176,000,000); coal (metric tons; 1985) none (2,000); crude petroleum (barrels; 1985) 63,137,000 (82,716,000); petroleum products (metric tons; 1985) 9,774,000 (8,555,000); natural gas (cu m; 1985) 153,763,000 (153,763,000).
*Population economically active* (1984): total 2,381,786; activity rate of total population 23.6% (participation rates: over age 15, 46.5%; female 9.8%; unemployed [1983] 5.1%).

### Price and earnings indexes (1980 = 100)

| | 1979 | 1980 | 1981 | 1982 | 1983 | 1984 | 1985 |
|---|---|---|---|---|---|---|---|
| Consumer price index | 84.1 | 100.0 | 118.4 | 135.3 | 143.4 | 156.6 | 183.9 |
| Annual earnings index[6] | 60.6 | 100.0 | 123.4 | 153.3 | 173.2 | 180.6 | 203.0 |

*Average household size* (1984): 6.4.
*Land use* (1984): steppe and pasture 45.2%; cultivable 30.7%; forested 2.7%; other 21.4%.

## Foreign trade

### Balance of trade (current prices)

| | 1980 | 1981 | 1982 | 1983 | 1984 | 1985 |
|---|---|---|---|---|---|---|
| LS '000,000 | −6,647 | −9,977 | −6,569 | −10,281 | −8,879 | −7,857 |
| % of total | 28.7% | 37.7% | 29.2% | 40.5% | 37.9% | 37.9% |

*Imports* (1985): LS 15,570,452,000 (crude petroleum and natural gas 26.2%; chemicals and chemical products 15.0%; food, beverages, and tobacco 11.2%; basic metals industries 7.1%; paper and paper products 2.2%). *Major import sources:* Iran 17.8%; West Germany 8.2%; Libya 7.1%; Italy 6.9%; United States 6.1%; France 4.5%.
*Exports* (1985): LS 6,426,521,000 (crude petroleum and natural gas 48.5%; chemicals and chemical products 28.6%; textiles, wearing apparel, and leather 16.8%; food, beverages, and tobacco 1.3%). *Major export destinations:* Italy 31.3%; Romania 24.3%; U.S.S.R. 16.8%; France 5.2%; United Kingdom 2.7%.

## Transport and communications

*Transport.* Railroads (1985): route length 1,250 mi, 2,013 km; passenger-mi 586,733,000, passenger-km 944,257,000; short ton-mi cargo 857,049,000, metric ton-km cargo 1,251,270,000. Roads (1985): total length 16,561 mi, 26,652 km (paved 80%). Vehicles (1985): passenger cars 108,367; trucks and buses 120,905. Merchant marine (1986): vessels (100 gross tons and over) 57; total deadweight tonnage 92,480. Air transport (1985): passenger-mi 585,000,000, passenger-km 942,000,000; short ton-mi cargo 10,744,000, metric ton-km cargo 15,687,000; airports (1987) with scheduled flights 5.
*Communications.* Daily newspapers (1986): total number 9; total circulation 201,400; circulation per 1,000 population 19.0. Radio (1986): total number of receivers 2,000,000 (1 per 5.3 persons). Television (1986): total number of receivers 400,000 (1 per 26.5 persons). Telephones (1985): 616,000 (1 per 16.7 persons).

## Education and health

### Education (1986–87)

| | schools | teachers | students | student/ teacher ratio |
|---|---|---|---|---|
| Primary (age 6–11) | 8,945 | 77,456 | 1,995,183 | 25.8 |
| Secondary (age 12–18) | 1,816 | 46,443 | 798,208 | 17.2 |
| Voc., teacher tr. | 155 | 7,840 | 59,085 | 7.5 |
| Higher | 80 | 1,456 | 169,155 | 116.2 |

*Educational attainment* (1984). Percent of population having: no schooling 32.0%; knowledge of reading and writing 28.4%; primary education 31.3%; secondary 4.9%; certificate 2.0%; higher 1.9%. *Literacy* (1984): total population age 15 and over literate 2,284,264 (44.6%); males literate 1,661,453 (64.8%); females literate 622,811 (24.3%).
*Health* (1985): physicians 5,543 (1 per 1,666 persons); hospital beds 11,891 (1 per 863 persons); infant mortality rate per 1,000 live births (1980–85) 59.0.
*Food* (1981–83): daily per capita caloric intake 3,103 (vegetable products 86%, animal products 14%); 127% of FAO recommended minimum requirement.

## Military

*Total active duty personnel* (1986): 392,500 (army 81.5%, navy 0.6%, air force 17.9%). *Military expenditure as percent of GNP* (1984): 22.4% (world 5.9%); per capita expenditure U.S.$428.

---

[1]Parties other than the Communist Party form a coalition (National Progressive Front). [2]Islam is required to be the religion of the head of state and is the basis of the legal system. [3]Includes territory in the Golan Heights recognized internationally as part of Syria (located between the 1949 Israel–Syria Armistice line [west] and the 1974 UN Disengagement of Forces zone [east]) that has been occupied by Israel since 1967. Israel's unilateral annexation of this territory in December 1981 has received no international recognition. [4]Syrian Arabs only. [5]Seeking work for the first time. [6]Public sector only.

# Taiwan

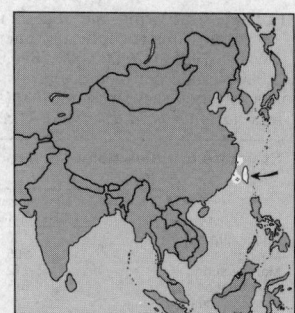

*Official name:* Chung-hua Min-kuo (Republic of China).
*Form of government:* unitary republic with a National Assembly (946)[1].
*Chief of state:* President.
*Head of government:* Premier.
*Capital:* Taipei.
*Official language:* Mandarin Chinese.
*Official religion:* none.
*Monetary unit:* 1 New Taiwan dollar (NT$) = 100 cents; valuation (Oct. 5, 1987) 1 U.S.$ = NT$29.88; 1 £ = NT$48.53.

### Area and population

| Counties | Capitals | area sq mi | sq km | population 1987 estimate[2] |
|---|---|---|---|---|
| Chang-hua | Chang-hua | 415 | 1,074 | 1,226,231 |
| Chia-i | Chia-i | 734 | 1,902 | 564,338 |
| Hsin-chu | Hsin-chu | 551 | 1,428 | 367,019 |
| Hua-lien | Hua-lien | 1,787 | 4,629 | 359,340 |
| I-lan | I-lan | 825 | 2,137 | 448,418 |
| Kao-hsiung | Feng-shan | 1,078 | 2,793 | 1,080,197 |
| Miao-li | Miao-li | 703 | 1,820 | 548,187 |
| Nan-t'ou | Nan-t'ou | 1,585 | 4,106 | 534,920 |
| P'eng-hu | Ma-kung | 49 | 127 | 100,927 |
| P'ing-tung | P'ing-tung | 1,072 | 2,776 | 897,714 |
| T'ai-chung | Feng-yuan | 792 | 2,051 | 1,161,025 |
| T'ai-nan | Hsin-ying | 778 | 2,016 | 1,003,275 |
| T'ai-pei | Pan-ch'iao | 792 | 2,052 | 2,727,510 |
| T'ai-tung | T'ai-tung | 1,357 | 3,515 | 272,477 |
| T'ao-yüan | T'ao-yüan | 471 | 1,221 | 1,232,209 |
| Yün-lin | Tou-liu | 498 | 1,291 | 783,526 |
| **Municipalities** | | | | |
| Chia-i | — | 23 | 60 | 254,001 |
| Chi-lung | — | 51 | 133 | 349,616 |
| Hsin-chu | — | 40 | 104 | 306,088 |
| Kao-hsiung | — | 59 | 154 | 1,320,552 |
| T'ai-chung | — | 63 | 163 | 695,562 |
| T'ai-nan | — | 68 | 176 | 646,298 |
| Taipei | — | 105 | 272 | 2,575,180 |
| **TOTAL** | | 13,900[3] | 36,000 | 19,454,610 |

## Demography

*Population* (1987): 19,630,000.
*Density* (1987): persons per sq mi 1,412.2, persons per sq km 545.3.
*Urban–rural* (1985): urban 72.1%; rural 27.9%.
*Sex distribution* (1986): male 51.88%; female 48.12%.
*Age breakdown* (1985): under 15, 29.6%; 15–29, 30.1%; 30–44, 19.5%; 45–59, 12.6%; 60–74, 6.8%; 75 and over, 1.4%.
*Population projection:* (1990) 20,476,000; (2000) 23,569,000.
*Doubling time:* 63 years.
*Ethnic composition* (1986): Taiwanese 84.0%; mainland Chinese 14.0%; aborigine 2.0%.
*Religious affiliation* (1980): Chinese folk-religionist 48.5%; Buddhist 43.0%; Christian 7.4%; Muslim 0.5%; other 0.6%.
*Major cities* (1986): Taipei 2,507,620; Kao-hsiung 1,302,849; T'ai-chung 674,936; T'ai-nan 639,888; Chi-lung 351,524; Hsin-chu 304,010.

## Vital statistics

*Birth rate* per 1,000 population (1986): 15.9 (world avg. 26.0).
*Death rate* per 1,000 population (1986): 4.9 (world avg. 9.9).
*Natural increase rate* per 1,000 population (1986): 11.0 (world avg. 16.1).
*Total fertility rate* (avg. births per childbearing woman; 1985): 1.9.
*Marriage rate* per 1,000 population (1986): 7.5.
*Divorce rate* per 1,000 population (1986): 1.2.
*Life expectancy* at birth (1985): male 70.8 years; female 75.8 years.
*Major causes of death* per 100,000 population (1985): diseases of the circulatory system 138.0; malignant neoplasms (cancers) 85.0; accidents and suicide 70.9.

## National economy

*Budget* (1985). Revenue: NT$574,538,000,000 (taxes 60.7%, of which income taxes 13.2%; customs duties 11.6%; surplus of public enterprises 13.4%). Expenditures: NT$563,729,000,000 (general administration and defense 35.0%; education 19.8%; reconstruction and communications 17.2%; social welfare and relief 15.7%).
*Tourism* (1985): receipts from visitors U.S.$963,000,000; expenditures by nationals abroad, n.a.
*Public debt* (domestic and foreign; 1985): U.S.$1,273,233,000[6].
*Production* (metric tons except as noted). Agriculture, forestry, fishing (1985): sugarcane 6,823,094, vegetables 3,243,364, rice 2,173,536, citrus fruits 418,864, sweet potatoes 369,461, corn (maize) 226,010, bananas 198,596, pineapple 149,745, peanuts 89,105; livestock (number of live animals) 6,673,983 pigs, 231,139 goats, 195,194 cattle; timber 474,584 cu m; fish catch 1,037,721. Mining and quarrying (1985): silver 11,386 kilograms; gold 953 kilograms. Manufacturing (1986): paperboard 18,916,400; cement 14,806,100; crude steel 1,813,700; man-made fibre 1,358,000; fertilizers 1,295,300; sulfuric acid 814,600; plastics and resins 794,000; electronic calculators 46,336,462 units; audio recorders 16,217,942 units; television receivers 5,748,352 units. Construction (1986): total residential and nonresidential 25,959,000 sq m. Energy production (consumption): electricity (kW-hr; 1986) 59,028,000,000 (38,487,089,000[4]); coal (metric tons; 1986)

1,725,024 (3,642,880[5]); petroleum (barrels; 1985) 743,187 (n.a.); natural gas (cu m; 1986) 1,022,539,000 (n.a.).
*Gross national product* (1986): U.S.$72,621,000,000 (U.S.$3,750 per capita).

### Structure of gross domestic product and labour force

| | 1986 in value NT$'000,000 | % of total value | labour force[7] | % of labour force |
|---|---|---|---|---|
| Agriculture | 152,906 | 5.7 | 1,317,000 | 17.0 |
| Mining | 14,299 | 0.5 | 33,000 | 0.4 |
| Manufacturing | 1,152,096 | 43.1 | 2,614,000 | 33.8 |
| Construction | 109,148 | 4.1 | 525,000 | 6.8 |
| Public utilities | 104,629 | 3.9 | 34,000 | 0.4 |
| Transp. and commun. | 159,093 | 5.9 | 407,000 | 5.3 |
| Trade | 366,823 | 13.7 | 1,382,000 | 17.9 |
| Finance | 237,514 | 8.9 | 212,000 | 2.8 |
| Pub. admin., defense | 251,454 | 9.4 ⎫ | 1,208,000 | 15.6 |
| Services | 183,821 | 6.9 ⎭ | | |
| Other | −56,169[8] | −2.1[8] | 1,000 | ... |
| TOTAL | 2,675,614 | 100.0 | 7,733,000 | 100.0 |

*Population economically active* (1986): total 13,161,000; activity rate of total population 68.0% (participation rates: age 15 and over 60.6%; female 22.8%; unemployed 2.7%).

### Price and earnings indexes (1981 = 100)

| | 1980 | 1981 | 1982 | 1983 | 1984 | 1985 | 1986 |
|---|---|---|---|---|---|---|---|
| Consumer price index | 86.0 | 100.0 | 103.0 | 104.4 | 104.3 | 104.2 | 104.9 |
| Monthly earnings index[9] | 84.2 | 100.0 | 109.7 | 116.6 | 134.6 | 132.1 | 145.4 |

*Household income and expenditure* (1985). Average household size 4.6; income per household NT$320,495 (U.S.$8,032[6]); sources of income: mixed entrepreneurial and property income 35.0%, mixed wages and entrepreneurial income 32.5%, wages 23.7%, entrepreneurial income 8.8%; expenditure: food 38.2%, energy 23.5%, recreation and education 9.5%, transportation 8.3%, clothing 5.9%, health 5.3%, household equipment 4.1%.
*Land use* (1980): forested 55.0%; agricultural and under permanent cultivation 25.2%; other 19.8%.

## Foreign trade

### Balance of trade (current prices)

| | 1980 | 1981 | 1982 | 1983 | 1984 | 1985 | 1986 |
|---|---|---|---|---|---|---|---|
| NT$'000,000 | 762 | 51,123 | 128,164 | 191,518 | 333,836 | 421,057 | 587,927 |
| % of total | 0.1% | 3.2% | 8.0% | 10.5% | 16.1% | 20.8% | 24.3% |

*Imports* (1986): NT$916,421,000,000 (petroleum and petroleum products 9.1%, electronic components 7.6%, nonelectrical machinery 2.4%; unmilled grains 2.1%, telecommunication equipment 2.1%, iron and steel 1.7%).
*Major import sources:* Japan 34.1%; United States 22.4%; West Germany 4.7%; Saudi Arabia 3.8%; Australia 3.7%; Canada 2.0%.
*Exports* (1986): NT$1,504,349,000,000 (electronic products and appliances 12.6%; articles of plastic 9.3%, articles of apparel and clothing 9.1%, textile yarns and fabrics 5.3%, processed food 2.2%, dolls and toys 1.8%). *Major export destinations:* United States 47.8%; Japan 11.4%; Hong Kong 7.3%; Canada 3.2%; West Germany 3.2%.

## Transport and communications

*Transport.* Railroads (1985): track length 4,800 km; passenger-km 8,316,324,000; metric ton-km cargo 2,365,460,000. Roads (1985): total length 19,857 km (paved 84%). Vehicles (1986): passenger cars 1,046,660; trucks and buses 439,910. Merchant marine (1986): vessels (100 gross tons and over) 587; total gross tonnage 4,272,795. Air transport (1986): passenger-km 12,270,996,000; metric ton-km cargo 2,537,497,000; airports (1987) 9.
*Communications.* Daily newspapers (1984): total number 31; total circulation 4,917,000; circulation per 1,000 population 259. Radio (1985): 13,500,000 receivers (1 per 1.4 persons). Television (1986): 6,085,000 receivers (1 per 3.2 persons). Telephones (1985): 5,653,000 (1 per 3.4 persons).

## Education and health

### Education (1985–86)

| | schools | teachers | students | student/ teacher ratio |
|---|---|---|---|---|
| Primary (age 6–12) | 2,459 | 71,853 | 2,313,240 | 32.2 |
| Secondary (age 13–18) | 839 | 60,346 | 1,250,840 | 20.7 |
| Vocational | 200 | 15,783 | 420,212 | 26.6 |
| Higher | 105 | 20,848 | 428,576 | 20.6 |

*Educational attainment* (1985). Percent of total population age 25 and over having: no formal schooling 13.4%; less than primary education 10.7%; primary education 33.5%; secondary 31.9%; higher 10.5%. *Literacy* (1985): total population age 15 and over literate 11,560,400 (89.9%); males literate 6,131,700 (95.2%); females literate 5,428,700 (84.6%).
*Health* (1985): physicians 16,931 (1 per 1,130 persons); hospital beds 70,806 (1 per 270 persons); infant mortality rate per 1,000 live births 6.8.
*Food* (1983): daily per capita caloric intake 2,874 (vegetable products 77%, animal products 23%); 118% of FAO recommended minimum requirement.

## Military

*Total active duty personnel* (1986): 424,000 (army 63.7%, navy 18.1%, air force 18.2%). *Military expenditure as percent of GNP* (1984): 6.6% (world 5.9%); per capita expenditure U.S.$205.

[1]As of Sept. 4, 1987. [2]As of Jan. 1, 1987, for Taiwan area only. [3]Detail does not add to total given because of rounding. [4]By industry only. [5]1985. [6]Based on the 1985 average exchange rate of NT$39.90 = U.S.$1.00. [7]Employed persons only. [8]Imputed bank service charge. [9]In manufacturing.

# Tanzania

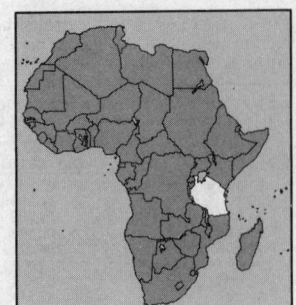

*Official name:* Jamhuri ya Mwungano wa Tanzania (Swahili); United Republic of Tanzania (English).
*Form of government:* unitary single-party republic with one legislative house (National Assembly [244[1]]).
*Chief of state:* President.
*Head of government:* Prime Minister.
*Seat of government:* Dar es Salaam (Capital designate, Dodoma).
*Official languages:* Swahili; English.
*Official religion:* none.
*Monetary unit:* 1 Tanzanian shilling (T Sh) = 100 cents; valuation (Oct. 5, 1987) 1 U.S.$ = T Sh 69.74; 1 £ = T Sh 113.25.

### Area and population

| Regions | Capitals | area sq mi | area sq km | population 1987 estimate |
|---|---|---|---|---|
| Arusha | Arusha | 31,698 | 82,098 | 1,274,000 |
| Bukoba | Bukoba | 10,987 | 28,456 | 1,397,000 |
| Dar es Salaam | Dar es Salaam | 538 | 1,393 | 1,605,000 |
| Dodoma | Dodoma | 15,950 | 41,311 | 1,239,000 |
| Iringa | Iringa | 21,950 | 56,850 | 1,167,000 |
| Kigoma | Kigoma | 14,301 | 37,040 | 828,000 |
| Kilimanjaro | Moshi | 5,116 | 13,250 | 1,159,000 |
| Lindi | Lindi | 25,498 | 66,040 | 631,000 |
| Mara | Musoma | 8,402 | 21,760 | 908,000 |
| Mbeya | Mbeya | 23,301 | 60,350 | 1,421,000 |
| Morogoro | Morogoro | 27,268 | 70,624 | 1,202,000 |
| Mtwara | Mtwara | 6,452 | 16,710 | 916,000 |
| Mwanza | Mwanza | 7,600 | 19,683 | 1,836,000 |
| Pemba North | Wete | | | |
| Pemba South | Chake Chake | 380 | 984 | [2] |
| Pwani | Dar es Salaam | 12,566 | 32,547 | 600,000 |
| Rukwa | Sumbawanga | 26,500 | 68,635 | 656,000 |
| Ruvuma | Songea | 24,583 | 63,669 | 725,000 |
| Shinyanga | Shinyanga | 19,598 | 50,760 | 1,779,000 |
| Singida | Singida | 19,050 | 49,340 | 770,000 |
| Tabora | Tabora | 29,402 | 76,150 | 1,185,000 |
| Tanga | Tanga | 10,300 | 26,677 | 1,305,000 |
| Zanzibar North | Mkokotoni | | | |
| Zanzibar South and Central | Koani | 641 | 1,660 | 605,000[2] |
| Zanzibar West | Zanzibar | | | |
| TOTAL LAND AREA | | 342,081 | 885,987 | 23,208,000 |
| INLAND WATER | | 22,800 | 59,050 | |
| TOTAL | | 364,881 | 945,037 | |

## Demography

*Population* (1987): 23,217,000.
*Density*[3] (1987): persons per sq mi 67.9, persons per sq km 26.2.
*Urban–rural* (1987): urban 17.9%; rural 82.1%.
*Sex distribution* (1985): male 49.32%; female 50.68%.
*Age breakdown* (1985): under 15, 48.8%; 15–29, 25.5%; 30–44, 14.2%; 45–59, 7.7%; 60–74, 3.2%; 75 and over, 0.6%.
*Population projection:* (1990) 25,635,000; (2000) 36,008,000.
*Doubling time:* 20 years.
*Ethnic composition* (1983): Nyamwezi and Sukuma 21.1%; Swahili 8.8%; Hehet and Bena 6.9%; Makonde 5.9%; Haya 5.9%; other 51.4%.
*Religious affiliation* (1984): Christian 40%, of which Roman Catholic 26%; Muslim 30%; traditional beliefs and other 30%.
*Major cities* (1984): Dar es Salaam 1,400,000; Mwanza 110,553[4].

## Vital statistics

*Birth rate* per 1,000 population (1984): 50.0 (world avg. 29.0).
*Death rate* per 1,000 population (1984): 16.0 (world avg. 11.0).
*Natural increase rate* per 1,000 population (1984): 34.0 (world avg. 18.0).
*Total fertility rate* (avg. births per childbearing woman; 1984): 7.0.
*Marriage rate* per 1,000 population (1967): 9.8.
*Life expectancy* at birth (1984): male 50.0 years; female 53.0 years.
*Major causes of death* per 100,000 population: n.a.; however, the major diseases include malaria, bilharziasis, tuberculosis, and sleeping sickness.

## National economy

*Budget* (1985–86). Revenue: T Sh 18,031,000,000 (sales tax 54.5%, income tax 23.5%, customs and excise tax 8.3%). Expenditures: T Sh 19,908,000,000 (economic development 37.8%, public administration 23.5%, defense 18.5%, education 10.1%, health 4.9%).
*Public debt* (external, outstanding; 1985): U.S.$2,981,700,000.
*Tourism* (1984): receipts from visitors U.S.$13,000,000; expenditures by nationals abroad U.S.$12,000,000.
*Production* (metric tons except as noted). Agriculture (1985): cassava 5,500,000, corn (maize) 2,093,000, sorghum 724,000, sweet potatoes 530,000, rice 427,000, coconuts 320,000, millet 300,000, dry beans 282,000, potatoes 200,000, seed cotton 140,000, cottonseed 87,000, unshelled peanuts (groundnuts) 59,000; livestock (number of live animals) 14,000,000 cattle, 6,450,000 goats, 4,100,000 sheep, 26,000,000 chickens; roundwood 45,540,000 cu m; fish catch 270,850. Mining and quarrying (1985): diamonds 255,715 carats; phosphate minerals 21,000. Manufacturing (1984): cement 369,000; fertilizer 51,565; wheat flour 30,000; iron sheets 23,012; rolled steel 12,104[5]; sisal twine and ropes 11,273[5]; aluminum 6,000; textiles 69,194,000 sq m. Construction: n.a. Energy production (consumption): electricity (kW-hr; 1985) 875,000,000 (875,000,000); coal (metric tons; 1985) 1,000 (1,000); crude petroleum (barrels; 1985) none (4,470,000); petroleum products (metric tons; 1985) 520,000 (569,000).
*Gross national product* (1985): U.S.$5,840,000,000 (U.S.$270 per capita).

### Structure of gross domestic product and labour force

| | 1985 in value T SH '000,000 | 1985 % of total value | 1982 labour force[6] | 1982 % of labour force |
|---|---|---|---|---|
| Agriculture | 57,180 | 58.5 | 137,419 | 20.3 |
| Mining | 265 | 0.3 | 7,231 | 1.1 |
| Manufacturing | 5,112 | 5.2 | 118,234 | 17.5 |
| Construction | 1,895 | 1.9 | 51,377 | 7.6 |
| Public utilities | 878 | 0.9 | 21,460 | 3.2 |
| Transportation and communication | 6,544 | 6.7 | 60,166 | 8.9 |
| Trade | 13,088 | 13.4 | 38,030 | 5.6 |
| Finance | | | 16,900 | 2.5 |
| Pub. admin., defense, Services | 12,805[7] | 13.1[7] | 225,170 | 33.3 |
| Other | | | | |
| TOTAL | 97,767[8] | 100.0 | 676,017 | 100.0 |

*Population economically active* (1985): total 10,913,000; activity rate of total population 48.5% (participation rates: ages 15–64, 85.7%; female 48.9%; unemployed, n.a.).

### Price and earnings indexes (1980 = 100)

| | 1982 | 1983 | 1984 | 1985 | 1986 | 1987[9] |
|---|---|---|---|---|---|---|
| Consumer price index | 162.0 | 205.8 | 280.2 | 373.5 | 495.3 | 598.8 |
| Monthly earnings index | | | | | | |

*Household income and expenditure.* Average household size (1980) 5.1; income per household: n.a.; sources of income: n.a.; expenditures (1981): food, beverages, and tobacco 54.1%, housing 8.6%, clothing 10.8%, energy 6.6%, transportation 6.4%.
*Land use* (1984): forested 47.2%; meadows and pastures 39.5%; agricultural and under permanent cultivation 5.9%; other 7.4%.

## Foreign trade

### Balance of trade (current prices)

| | 1980 | 1981 | 1982 | 1983 | 1984 | 1985 |
|---|---|---|---|---|---|---|
| T Sh '000,000 | −4,730.0 | −4,853.0 | −4,917.0 | −3,384.0 | −5,506.0 | −10,314 |
| % of total | 36.1% | 34.1% | 36.8% | 29.5% | 32.3% | 51.0% |

*Imports* (1984): T Sh 11,953,000,000 (machinery 32.2%, fuel 20.1%, consumer goods 14.3%, transport equipment 11.7%, construction materials 11.0%). *Major import sources:* United Kingdom 9.7%; Japan 9.4%; West Germany 8.2%; Italy 7.9%; United States 5.2%; Thailand 4.2%; India 3.4%.
*Exports* (1984): T Sh 5,750,000,000 (coffee 38.6%, cotton 12.4%, cashew nuts 7.6%, tea 5.7%, diamonds 5.7%, sisal 2.5%, cloves 2.4%, tobacco 1.9%). *Major export destinations:* West Germany 19.9%; United Kingdom 11.4%; India 7.3%; Algeria 4.7%; Japan 3.4%; Hong Kong 2.8%; United States 2.5%.

## Transport and communications

*Transport.* Railroads (1985): length 1,615 mi, 2,600 km; passenger-mi 736,900,000[10], passenger-km 1,186,000,000[10]; short ton-mi cargo 527,000,000[10], metric ton-km cargo 770,000,000[10]. Roads (1984): length 50,887 mi, 81,895 km. Vehicles (1984): cars, trucks, and buses 84,190. Merchant marine (1986): vessels (100 gross tons and over) 41; deadweight tonnage 59,048. Air transport (1985): passenger-mi 162,253,000, passenger-km 261,123,000; short ton-mi cargo 18,576,000, metric ton-km 27,122,000; airports (1987) 19.
*Communications.* Daily newspapers (1984): total number 3; total circulation 101,000; circulation per 1,000 population 5.0. Radio (1986): 2,000,000 receivers (1 per 11 persons). Television (1986)[11]: 10,000 receivers (1 per 2,246 persons). Telephones (1985): 113,902 (1 per 191 persons).

## Education and health

### Education (1985)

| | schools | teachers | students | student/teacher ratio |
|---|---|---|---|---|
| Primary (age 7–13) | 10,173 | 93,157 | 3,169,759 | 34.0 |
| Secondary (age 14–19) | 193 | 4,329 | 83,098 | 19.2 |
| Voc., teacher tr. | 41 | 1,152 | 13,760 | 11.9 |
| Higher | 2 | 877 | 3,414 | 3.9 |

*Educational attainment* (1978). Percent of population age 10 and over having: no schooling 48.6%; some primary education 40.7%; completed primary 8.7%; secondary and higher 1.9%. *Literacy* (1987): 85%.
*Health* (1984): physicians 1,065 (1 per 19,775 persons); hospital beds 22,800 (1 per 924 persons); infant mortality rate per 1,000 live births 111.
*Food* (1981–83): daily per capita caloric intake 2,353 (vegetable products 94%, animal products 6%); (1983) 98% of FAO recommended minimum.

## Military

*Total active duty personnel* (1986): 40,350 (army 95.4%, navy 2.1%, air force 2.5%). *Military expenditure as percent of GNP* (1984): 3.3% (world 5.9%); per capita expenditure U.S.$10.

[1]Includes 75 nonelective seats. [2]Pemba North and Pemba South are included with Zanzibar. [3]Based on land area. [4]1978. [5]1982. [6]Employed persons only. [7]Includes indirect taxes, net of subsidies less imputed bank service charges. [8]Excludes Zanzibar. [9]March. [10]For Tanzania Railways Corporation only. [11]In Zanzibar only.

# Thailand

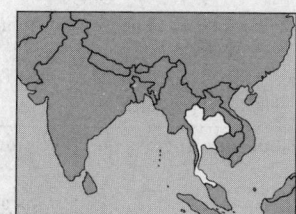

*Official name:* Muang Thai, or Prathet Thai (Kingdom of Thailand).
*Form of government:* constitutional monarchy with a multiparty National Assembly (Senate [261]; House of Representatives [347]).
*Chief of state:* King.
*Head of government:* Prime Minister.
*Capital:* Bangkok.
*Official language:* Thai.
*Official religion:* Buddhism.
*Monetary unit:* 1 Thai Baht (B) = 100 stangs; valuation (Oct. 5, 1987) 1 U.S.$ = B 25.49; 1 £ = B 41.40.

| Area and population | area | | population |
|---|---|---|---|
| Regions | sq mi | sq km | 1986 estimate |
| Bangkok Metropolis | 604 | 1,565 | 5,363,378 |
| Central[1] | 7,236 | 18,742 | 3,552,602 |
| Eastern | 14,481 | 37,507 | 3,963,061 |
| Northeastern | 65,195 | 168,854 | 18,060,945 |
| Northern | 65,500 | 169,644 | 10,391,368 |
| Southern | 27,303 | 70,715 | 6,441,186 |
| Western | 17,795 | 46,088 | 4,023,111 |
| TOTAL | 198,115[2] | 513,115 | 51,795,651 |

## Demography

*Population* (1987): 53,722,000.
*Density* (1987): persons per sq mi 271.2, persons per sq km 104.7.
*Urban–rural* (1985): urban 19.8%; rural 80.2%.
*Sex distribution* (1987): male 50.07%; female 49.93%.
*Age breakdown* (1985): under 15, 36.2%; 15–29, 30.7%; 30–44, 17.2%; 45–59, 10.2%; 60–69, 3.5%; 70 and over, 2.2%.
*Population projection:* (1990) 56,300,000; (2000) 64,132,000.
*Doubling time:* 39 years.
*Ethnic composition* (1983): Thai 79.5%, of which Siamese 52.6%, Lao 26.9%; Chinese 12.1%; Malay 3.7%; Khmer 2.7%; other 2.0%.
*Religious affiliation* (1980): Buddhist 95.0%; Muslim 3.8%; Christian 0.5%; other 0.7%.
*Major cities* (1983): Bangkok 5,363,378[3]; Chiang Mai 150,499; Hat Yai 113,964; Khon Kaen 115,515; Nakhon Ratchasima 190,692.

## Vital statistics

*Birth rate* per 1,000 population (1986): 25.3 (world avg. 26.0).
*Death rate* per 1,000 population (1986): 7.4 (world avg. 9.9).
*Natural increase rate* per 1,000 population (1986): 17.9 (world avg. 16.1).
*Total fertility rate* (avg. births per childbearing woman; 1986): 3.0.
*Marriage rate* per 1,000 population (1983): 7.7.
*Divorce rate* per 1,000 population (1979): 0.5.
*Life expectancy* at birth (1986): male 61.3 years; female 67.3 years.
*Major causes of death* per 100,000 population (1984): heart disease 35.2; accidents, poisonings, and violence 31.7; malignant neoplasms (cancers) 26.0; tuberculosis 10.1; pneumonia 7.4; malaria 4.4.

## National economy

*Budget* (1986–87). Revenue: B 227,500,000,000 (taxes 72.6%, of which indirect taxes 55.3%, direct taxes 17.4%; borrowing, state enterprises, and sale of assets and services 27.4%). Expenditures: B 227,500,000,000 (debt service 24.7%; education 18.1%; defense 18.0%; economic services 15.6%; public utilities and health 10.8%; internal security 4.8%; general administration 2.7%).
*Tourism* (1985): receipts from visitors U.S.$1,171,000,000; expenditures by nationals abroad U.S.$280,000,000.
*Production* (metric tons except as noted). Agriculture, forestry, fishing (1985): sugarcane 25,690,000, tapioca root 19,985,000, rice 19,521,000, corn (maize) 4,686,000, coconuts 1,121,000, rubber 680,000, cotton 101,000, tobacco 90,000, coffee 23,000; livestock (number of live animals) 6,250,000 buffalo, 4,800,000 cattle, 4,300,000 pigs, 74,000 goats, 79,000,000 chickens; roundwood 41,276,000 cu m; fish catch (1984) 2,250,000. Mining and quarrying (1985): limestone 9,845,000; gypsum 1,273,500; fluorite 263,100; barite 231,000; iron ore 93,800; tin 23,000. Manufacturing (1985): cement 7,916,000; refined sugar 2,294,000; tin plate 68,200; galvanized iron sheets 130,600; commercial vehicles 74,910 units[4]. Construction (1984): residential 6,122,000 sq m; nonresidential 5,605,000 sq m. Energy production (consumption): electricity (kW-hr; 1985) 23,039,000,000 (21,460,000,000); coal (metric tons; 1985) 5,190,000 (5,326,000); crude petroleum (barrels; 1985) 7,826,000 (53,672,000); petroleum products (metric tons; 1985) 8,025,000 (10,385,000); natural gas (cu m; 1985) 2,790,730,000 (2,790,730,000).
*Land use* (1984): forested 29.9%; meadows and pastures 0.6%; agricultural and under permanent cultivation 38.4%; other 31.1%.
*Population economically active* (1984): total 26,580,000; activity rate of total population 53.7% (participation rates: over age 15 [1982] 83.1%; female [1982] 47.1%; unemployed 5.1%).

| Price and earnings indexes (1980 = 100) | | | | | | | |
|---|---|---|---|---|---|---|---|
| | 1980 | 1981 | 1982 | 1983 | 1984 | 1985 | 1986[5] |
| Consumer price index | 100.0 | 112.7 | 118.6 | 123.0 | 124.1 | 127.1 | 130.3 |
| Monthly earnings index | ... | ... | ... | ... | ... | ... | ... |

*Public debt* (external, outstanding; 1985): U.S.$9,799,900,000.
*Gross national product* (at current market prices; 1985): U.S.$42,100,000,000 (U.S.$810 per capita).

| Structure of gross domestic product and labour force | | | | |
|---|---|---|---|---|
| | 1985 | | 1984 | |
| | in value B '000,000 | % of total value | labour force[6] | % of labour force |
| Agriculture | 182,279 | 17.4 | 20,387,124 | 72.6 |
| Mining | 29,279 | 2.8 | 17,429 | 0.1 |
| Manufacturing | 207,691 | 19.8 | 1,866,258 | 6.6 |
| Construction | 53,758 | 5.1 | 680,920 | 2.4 |
| Public utilities | 21,645 | 2.1 | 89,335 | 0.3 |
| Transportation and communication | 96,254 | 9.2 | 475,831 | 1.7 |
| Trade | 190,676 | 18.2 | 2,109,762 | 7.5 |
| Finance | 103,457 | 9.9 | 160,427 | 0.6 |
| Pub. admin., defense | 47,058 | 4.5 | 2,249,751 | 8.0 |
| Services | 115,467 | 11.0 | | |
| Other | ... | ... | 33,876 | 0.1 |
| TOTAL | 1,047,564 | 100.0 | 28,070,713 | 100.0[2] |

*Household income and expenditure.* Average household size (1983) 5.3; median income per household (1983) B 43,476 (U.S.$1,890); sources of income (1981): wages and salaries 45.4%, business profits 23.5%, nonmoney income 19.4%, transfer payments 5.5%, income from farming 4.5%, property income 0.9%, other 0.8%; expenditure (1981): food 41.4%, housing 23.1%, transportation and communication 7.9%, clothing and footwear 5.9%, medical and personal care 5.6%, education and recreation 5.2%, beverages and tobacco 3.6%, other 7.3%.

## Foreign trade[7]

| Balance of trade (current prices) | | | | | | |
|---|---|---|---|---|---|---|
| | 1980 | 1981 | 1982 | 1983 | 1984 | 1985 |
| B '000,000 | −36,637 | −42,090 | −17,244 | −66,497 | −45,425 | −33,285 |
| % of total | 12.1% | 12.1% | 5.1% | 18.5% | 11.5% | 7.9% |

*Imports* (1985): B 251,169,435,000 (mineral fuels and oils 22.7%, boiler machinery 13.3%, iron and steel 9.3%, electrical machinery 7.4%, motor vehicles 4.6%, organic chemicals 3.8%). *Major import sources:* Japan 26.5%; United States 11.3%; Singapore 7.5%; Malaysia 5.9%; West Germany 5.4%; Taiwan 3.1%; Saudi Arabia 2.8%; France 2.7%; United Kingdom 2.5%; China 2.4%.
*Exports:* (1985): B 193,365,507,000 (rice 11.6%, tapioca products 7.7%, rubber 7.0%, canned fish 4.0%, corn 3.9%, sugar and sugar products 3.7%, unwrought tin 3.1%, shrimps 1.8%). *Major export destinations:* United States 19.7%; Japan 13.4%; Singapore 7.9%; The Netherlands 7.1%; Malaysia 5.0%; Hong Kong 4.0%; China 3.8%; West Germany 3.7%; United Kingdom 2.4%; Saudi Arabia 2.3%.

## Transport and communications

*Transport.* Railroads (1986)[8]: route length 2,321 mi, 3,735 km; passenger-mi 5,734,000,000, passenger-km 9,228,000,000; short ton-mi cargo 1,767,000,000, metric ton-km cargo 2,580,000,000. Roads (1985): total length 22,515 mi, 36,235 km (paved 86%). Vehicles (1983): passenger cars 411,982; trucks and buses 789,837. Merchant marine (1986): vessels (100 gross tons and over) 243; total deadweight tonnage 772,437. Air transport (1986): passenger-mi 7,009,000,000, passenger-km 11,280,000,000; short ton-mi cargo 332,812,000, metric ton-km cargo 485,928,000; airports (1987) with scheduled flights 22.
*Communications.* Daily newspapers (1985): total number 31; total circulation 2,564,500[9]; circulation per 1,000 population 50[9]. Radio (1985): 7,759,709 receivers (1 per 6.7 persons). Television (1984): 3,000,000 receivers (1 per 17 persons). Telephones (1985): 754,581 (1 per 69 persons).

## Education and health

| Education (1983) | schools[10] | teachers[11] | students | student/teacher ratio |
|---|---|---|---|---|
| Primary (age 7–12) | 33,712 | 355,984 | 7,272,153 | 20.4 |
| Secondary (age 13–18) | 1,437 | 85,081 | 1,754,925 | 20.6 |
| Voc., teacher tr. | 1,528 | 19,795 | 436,788 | 22.1 |
| Higher | 62 | 28,865 | 1,120,084 | 38.8 |

*Educational attainment* (1980). Percent of population age 25 and over having: no formal schooling 20.5%; primary education 67.3%; secondary 9.3%; postsecondary 2.9%. *Literacy* (1980): total population age 15 and over literate 24,133,418 (87.3%); males literate 12,429,957 (91.6%); females literate 11,703,461 (83.1%).
*Health* (1984): physicians 8,058 (1 per 6,277 persons); hospital beds 80,620 (1 per 627 persons); infant mortality rate per 1,000 live births (1986) 52.0.
*Food* (1981–83): daily per capita caloric intake 2,319 (vegetable products 94%, animal products 6%); 105% of FAO recommended minimum requirement.

## Military

*Total active duty personnel* (1986): 256,000 (army 64.8%, navy 16.4%, air force 18.8%). *Military expenditure as percent of GNP* (1983): 4.1% (world 6.1%); per capita expenditure U.S.$33.

[1]Excluding Bangkok Metropolis. [2]Detail does not add to total given because of rounding. [3]1986. [4]1984. [5]September. [6]Economically active persons 11 years and over. [7]Import figures are f.o.b. (free on board) in balance of trade and c.i.f. (cost, insurance, and freight) for commodities and trading partners. [8]Traffic data refer to fiscal year ending September 30. [9]Excludes circulation for two dailies. [10]1980. [11]Except for higher education, data on teachers refer to public education only.

# Togo

*Official name:* République Togolaise
(Republic of Togo).
*Form of government:* republic with
one legislative body (National
Assembly [77]).
*Head of state and government:*
President.
*Capital:* Lomé.
*Official language:* French.
*Official religion:* none.
*Monetary unit:* 1 CFA franc
(CFAF) = 100 centimes; valuation
(Oct. 5, 1987) 1 U.S.$ = CFAF 306.67;
1 £ = CFAF 498.00.

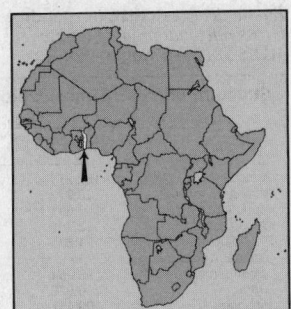

| Area and population | | area | | population |
|---|---|---|---|---|
| **Regions** | | | | 1981 |
| **Prefectures** | **Capitals** | sq mi | sq km | census |
| Centrale | Sokodé | | | 269,174 |
| Sotouboua | Sotouboua | 2,892 | 7,490 | 128,617 |
| Tchamba | Tchamba | 1 | 1 | 44,912 |
| Tchaoudjo | Sokodé | 2,198[1] | 5,692[1] | 95,645 |
| De la Kara | Kara | | | 432,626 |
| Assoli | Bafilo | 362 | 938 | 32,444 |
| Bassar | Bassar | 2,444 | 6,330 | 118,345 |
| Binah | Pagouda | 180 | 465 | 50,077 |
| Doufelgou | Niamtougou | 432 | 1,120 | 66,120 |
| Kéran | Kandé | 653 | 1,692 | 44,762 |
| Kozah | Kara | 419 | 1,085 | 120,878 |
| Des Plateaux | Atakpamé | | | 561,656 |
| Amou | Amlamé | 1,692[2] | 4,382[2] | 72,951 |
| Haho | Notsé | 1,412 | 3,658 | 109,995 |
| Kloto | Kpalimé | 1,077 | 2,790 | 106,429 |
| Ogou | Atakpamé | 2,372 | 6,145 | 163,906 |
| Wawa | Badou | 2 | 2 | 108,375 |
| Des Savanes | Dapaong | | | 326,826 |
| Oti | Sansanné-Mango | 1,453 | 3,762 | 77,747 |
| Tône | Dapaong | 1,869 | 4,840 | 249,079 |
| Maritime | Lomé | | | 1,039,700 |
| Golfe | Lomé | 133 | 345 | 438,110 |
| Lacs | Aného | 275 | 712 | 140,006 |
| Vo | Vogan | 290 | 750 | 150,313 |
| Yoto | Tabligbo | 483 | 1,250 | 100,387 |
| Zio | Tsévié | 1,289 | 3,339 | 210,884 |
| TOTAL | | 21,925 | 56,785 | 2,700,982[3] |

## Demography

*Population* (1987): 3,158,000.
*Density* (1987): persons per sq mi 144.0, persons per sq km 55.6.
*Urban–rural* (1981): urban 15.2%; rural 84.8%.
*Sex distribution* (1981): male 48.20%; female 51.80%.
*Age breakdown* (1980): under 15, 46.2%; 15–29, 25.8%; 30–44, 14.8%; 45–59, 8.6%; 60–74, 3.9%; 75 and over, 0.7%.
*Population projection:* (1990) 3,431,000; (2000) 4,522,000.
*Doubling time:* 24 years.
*Ethnic composition* (1983): Ewe 45.4%; Kabre 23.9%; Gurma 10.5%; Tem 7.3%; other African 8.5%; native 3.6%; European 0.8%.
*Religious affiliation* (1980): traditional beliefs 45.8%; Christian 37.0%; Sunnī Muslim 17.0%; other 0.2%.
*Major cities* (1983): Lomé 366,476; Sokodé 48,098[4]; Kpalimé 27,669[4].

## Vital statistics

*Birth rate* per 1,000 population (1980–85): 45.2 (world avg. 29.0); legitimate, n.a.; illegitimate, n.a.
*Death rate* per 1,000 population (1980–85): 15.7 (world avg. 11.0).
*Natural increase rate* per 1,000 population (1980–85): 29.5 (world avg. 18.0).
*Total fertility rate* (avg. births per childbearing woman; 1980–85): 6.1.
*Marriage rate* per 1,000 population (1979): 2.3.
*Divorce rate* per 1,000 population: n.a.
*Life expectancy* at birth (1980–85): male 48.8 years; female 52.2 years.
*Morbidity* (reported cases of illness per 100,000 population; 1978): infectious and parasitic diseases 26,926; diseases of the respiratory system 9,296; diseases of the digestive system 8,007; accidents, poisoning, and traumas 7,172.

## National economy

*Budget* (1987). Revenue: CFAF 89,691,000,000 (personal income taxes 39.3%; import and export taxes 37.2%; excise taxes 10.9%). Expenditures: CFAF 89,691,000,000 (current account 69.6%, of which education 18.4%, defense 13.3%, health 4.4%; debt service 26.8%; capital account 3.7%).
*Public debt* (external, outstanding; 1985): U.S.$787,000,000.
*Tourism:* receipts from visitors (1985) U.S.$20,000,000; expenditures by nationals abroad (1979) U.S.$19,000,000.
*Production* (metric tons except as noted). Agriculture, forestry, fishing (1985): roots and tubers 805,000, cassava 439,000, tomatoes 420,000, yams 336,000, corn (maize) 208,000, sorghum 110,000, millet 71,000, pulses 41,-000, cottonseed 30,000, peanuts (groundnuts) 22,000, cacao beans 16,000, rice 16,000, bananas 16,000, palm kernels 15,000, coconuts 14,000, palm oil 13,800, coffee 10,000; livestock (number of live animals) 850,000 sheep, 850,000 goats, 240,000 pigs, 240,000 cattle, 4,000,000 chickens; roundwood 765,000 cu m; fish catch 15,544. Mining and quarrying (1984): phosphate rock 2,700,000; salt 600,000[5]; marble 15,087[5]. Manufacturing (1983): cement 232,000; beer 392,000 hectolitres; woven cotton fabrics 18,000,000 sq m[5]; footwear 1,155,000 pairs[6]. Construction (value added in CFAF; 1981):

11,000,000,000. Energy production (consumption): electricity (kW-hr; 1986) 29,547,000 (229,750,000); crude petroleum, none (n.a.); petroleum products (metric tons; 1985) none (75,000).
*Gross national product* (at current market prices; 1985): U.S.$750,000,000 (U.S.$250 per capita).

### Structure of gross domestic product and labour force

| | 1983 | | 1985 | |
|---|---|---|---|---|
| | in value CFAF '000,000 | % of total value | labour force | % of labour force |
| Agriculture | 90.1 | 32.0 | 883,000 | 71.0 |
| Mining | 28.7 | 10.2 | | |
| Manufacturing | 20.1 | 7.1 | | |
| Construction | 8.1 | 2.9 | | |
| Public utilities | 5.7 | 2.0 | | |
| Transp. and commun. | 18.1 | 6.4 | 361,000 | 29.0 |
| Trade | 61.9 | 22.0 | | |
| Finance | ... | ... | | |
| Pub. admin., defense | 27.8 | 10.0 | | |
| Services | ... | ... | | |
| Other | 20.8 | 7.4 | | |
| TOTAL | 281.3 | 100.0 | 1,244,000 | 100.0 |

*Population economically active:* total (1985) 1,244,000; activity rate of total population 41.6% (participation rates: over age 15 [1981] 76.7%; female [1980] 34.9%; unemployed [1980] 2.3%).

### Price and earnings indexes (1980 = 100)

| | 1981 | 1982 | 1983 | 1984 | 1985 | 1986 | 1987[7] |
|---|---|---|---|---|---|---|---|
| Consumer price index | 119.7 | 133.0 | 145.5 | 140.3 | 137.8 | 143.5 | 144.6 |
| Hourly earning index | 100.0 | 110.0 | 110.0 | 110.0 | 110.0 | 110.0 | ... |

*Household income and expenditure.* Average household size (1980) 5.6; average annual income per household CFAF 102,000 (U.S.$452); sources of income: n.a.; expenditure (1985): food 47.9%, housing 14.9%, clothing 7.7%, services 6.6%; other 22.9%.
*Land use* (1984): forested 27.6%; meadows and pastures 3.7%; agricultural and under permanent cultivation 26.2%; other 42.5%.

## Foreign trade

### Balance of trade (current prices)

| | 1979 | 1980 | 1981 | 1982 | 1983 | 1984 |
|---|---|---|---|---|---|---|
| CFAF '000,000,000 | −63.8 | −45.1 | −60.3 | −70.2 | −46.2 | −18.2 |
| % of total | 40.7% | 24.0% | 34.4% | 37.6% | 27.2% | 9.8% |

*Imports* (1984): CFAF 118,460,000,000 (food and food products 19.6%, cotton textiles 9.4%, transport equipment and parts 8.3%, machinery and mechanical equipment 7.9%). *Major import sources:* France 32.3%; The Netherlands 10.3%; Côte d'Ivoire 7.1%; West Germany 6.9%; United Kingdom 5.6%; Japan 5.2%.
*Exports* (1984): CFAF 83,588,000,000 (phosphates 49.0%, cacao beans 25.1%, raw cotton 8.9%, clinker and cement 4.7%, coffee 3.6%). *Major export destinations:* The Netherlands 23.2%; France 21.1%; Yugoslavia 8.3%; U.S.S.R. 5.9%; Poland 4.7%; Tunisia 2.8%.

## Transport and communications

*Transport.* Railroads (1982): length 326 mi, 525 km; passenger-mi 65,000,-000, passenger-km 105,000,000; short ton-mi cargo 11,000,000, metric ton-km cargo 16,000,000. Roads (1985): total length 4,349 mi, 7,000 km (paved 23%). Vehicles (1985): passenger cars 2,570; trucks and buses 288. Merchant marine (1986): vessels (100 gross tons and over) 11; total deadweight tonnage 78,009. Air transport (1985): passenger-mi 150,000,000, passenger-km 241,000,000; short ton-mi cargo 12,500,000, metric ton-km cargo 18,-600,000; airports (1987) with scheduled flights 1.
*Communications.* Daily newspapers (1986): total number 2; total circulation 10,000[8]; circulation per 1,000 population 3.3[8]. Radio (1986): 250,000 receivers (1 per 12 persons). Television (1986): 17,000 receivers (1 per 181 persons). Telephones (1983): 11,105 (1 per 255 persons).

## Education and health

### Education (1986–87)

| | schools | teachers | students | student/ teacher ratio |
|---|---|---|---|---|
| Primary (age 6–11) | 2,345 | 10,209 | 474,998 | 46.5 |
| Secondary (age 12–18) | 248[9] | 4,200[10] | 86,327 | ... |
| Voc., teacher tr. | 18 | 198 | 5,050 | 25.5 |
| Higher | 1 | 308 | 4,500 | 14.6 |

*Educational attainment* (1981). Percent of population age 15 and over having: no formal schooling 76.5%; primary education 13.5%; secondary 8.7%; higher 1.3%. *Literacy* (1985): total population age 15 and over literate 631,-700 (39.1%); males literate 401,800 (51.7%); females literate 229,900 (27.5%).
*Health:* physicians (1985) 230 (1 per 12,992 persons); hospital beds (1982) 3,655 (1 per 752 persons); infant mortality rate (1980–85) 102.0.
*Food* (1981–83): daily per capita caloric intake 2,213 (vegetable products 96%, animal products 4%); 94% of FAO recommended minimum requirement.

## Military

*Total active duty personnel* (1986): 5,110[11] (army[11] 93.0%, navy 1.9%, air force 5.1%). *Military expenditure as percent of GNP* (1984): 2.5% (world 5.9%); per capita expenditure U.S.$6.

[1]Tchaoudjo includes Tchamba. [2]Amou includes Wawa. [3]Total includes 71,000 persons not counted separately. [4]1981. [5]1982. [6]1980. [7]April. [8]For one daily only. [9]1981–82. [10]1983. [11]Includes gendarmerie.

# Tonga

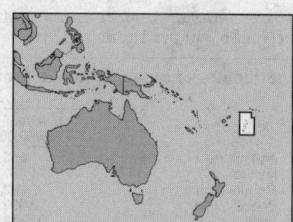

*Official name:* Pule'anga Fakatu'i 'o Tonga (Tongan); Kingdom of Tonga (English).
*Form of government:* constitutional monarchy with one legislative house (Legislative Assembly [28][1]).
*Head of state and government:* King.
*Capital:* Nukualofa.
*Official languages:* Tongan; English.
*Official religion:* none.
*Monetary unit:* 1 pa'anga (T$)[2] = 100 seniti; valuation (Oct. 5, 1987) 1 U.S.$ = T$1.40; 1 £ = T$2.27.

### Area and population

| Divisions | | area | | population |
|---|---|---|---|---|
| Districts | Capitals | sq mi | sq km | 1986 census |
| Eua | Ohonua | 33.7 | 87.4 | 4,393 |
| Eua Foou | | ... | ... | 1,995 |
| Eua Proper | | ... | ... | 2,398 |
| Haapai | Pangai | 42.5 | 110.0 | 8,979 |
| Foa | | ... | ... | 1,409 |
| Haano | | ... | ... | 892 |
| Lulunga | | ... | ... | 1,588 |
| Muomua | | ... | ... | 897 |
| Pangai | | ... | ... | 2,840 |
| Uiha | | ... | ... | 1,353 |
| Niuas | Hihifo | 27.7 | 71.7 | 2,379 |
| Niuafoou | | ... | ... | 763 |
| Niuatoputapu | | ... | ... | 1,616 |
| Tongatapu | Nukualofa | 100.6 | 260.5 | 63,614 |
| Kolofoou | | ... | ... | 15,782 |
| Kolomotua | | ... | ... | 13,117 |
| Kolovai | | ... | ... | 4,023 |
| Lapaha | | ... | ... | 6,992 |
| Nukunuku | | ... | ... | 5,790 |
| Tatakamotonga | | ... | ... | 6,778 |
| Vaini | | ... | ... | 11,132 |
| Vavau | Neiafu | 46.0 | 119.2 | 15,170 |
| Hahake | | ... | ... | 2,292 |
| Hihifo | | ... | ... | 2,095 |
| Leimatua | | ... | ... | 2,875 |
| Motu | | ... | ... | 1,387 |
| Neiafu | | ... | ... | 5,273 |
| Pangaimotu | | ... | ... | 1,248 |
| TOTAL LAND AREA | | 289.5[3] | 749.9[3] | 94,535 |
| INLAND WATER | | 11.4 | 29.6 | |
| TOTAL | | 300.9 | 779.5 | |

## Demography

*Population* (1987): 94,800.
*Density*[4] (1987): persons per sq mi 327.5, persons per sq km 126.4.
*Urban–rural* (1980): urban 31.8%; rural 68.2%.
*Sex distribution* (1986): male 50.34%; female 49.66%.
*Age breakdown* (1985): under 15, 39.6%; 15–29, 31.1%; 30–44, 14.2%; 45–59, 9.4%; 60–74, 4.7%; 75 and over, 1.0%.
*Population projection:* (1990) 96,200; (2000) 100,900.
*Doubling time:* 28 years.
*Ethnic composition* (1976): Tongan 98.3%; other 1.7%.
*Religious affiliation* (1976): Free Wesleyan 47.4%; Roman Catholic 16.1%; Free Church of Tonga 13.7%; Latter-day Saints 9.3%; Church of Tonga 8.9%; Seventh-day Adventist 2.1%; other 2.5%.
*Major city* (1986): Nukualofa 28,899.

## Vital statistics

*Birth rate* per 1,000 population (1985): 28.9 (world avg. 29.0); legitimate, n.a.; illegitimate, n.a.
*Death rate* per 1,000 population (1985): 3.5 (world avg. 11.0).
*Natural increase rate* per 1,000 population (1985) 25.4 (world avg. 18.0).
*Total fertility rate* (avg. births per childbearing woman; 1980–85): 4.3.
*Marriage rate* per 1,000 population (1985): 6.6.
*Divorce rate* per 1,000 population (1985): 0.6.
*Life expectancy* at birth (1980–85): male 61.0 years; female 64.8 years.
*Major causes of death* per 100,000 population: n.a.; however, major diseases include gastroenteritis, infantile diarrhea, and acute respiratory infections.

## National economy

*Budget* (1981)[5]. Revenue: T$12,230,000 (import duties 31.4%; income and wealth tax 13.6%; licenses, stamp duties, registration fees 1.3%). Expenditures: T$16,275,000 (investments 37.2%; social services 22.2%; economic services 13.9%; defense 2.7%).
*Tourism:* receipts from visitors (1984) U.S.$6,000,000; expenditures by nationals abroad (1983) U.S.$1,000,000.
*Production* (metric tons except as noted). Agriculture, forestry, fishing (1985): coconuts 47,000, yams 35,000, taro 30,000, sweet potatoes 17,000, cassava 17,000, fruits excluding melons 12,000, copra 5,000, bananas 3,000; livestock (number of live animals) 65,000 pigs, 11,000 goats, 9,000 horses, 8,000 cattle; roundwood 3,000 cu m; fish catch 1,993. Mining and quarrying (1982): coral 150,000; sand 25,000. Manufacturing (value added in T$; 1983): food products and beverages 2,623,000; furniture fixtures and wood products 328,000; metal products 252,000; glass and china products 203,000; paper and products 26,000. Construction (value in T$; 1984): residential 9,552,300; nonresidential 11,377,100. Energy production (consumption): electricity (kW-hr; 1985) 12,000,000 (12,000,000); coal, none

(n.a.); petroleum, none (n.a.); petroleum products (metric tons; 1985) n.a. (15,000); natural gas, none (n.a.).
*Gross national product* (at current market prices; 1985): U.S.$70,000,000 (U.S.$720 per capita).

### Structure of gross domestic product and labour force

| | 1983 | | 1976 | |
|---|---|---|---|---|
| | in value T$'000 | % of total value | labour force | % of labour force |
| Agriculture | 35,790 | 41.5 | 9,529 | 44.5 |
| Mining | 394 | 0.5 | 16 | 0.1 |
| Manufacturing | 4,271 | 4.9 | 386 | 1.8 |
| Construction | 3,354 | 3.9 | 1,153 | 5.4 |
| Public utilities | 404 | 0.5 | 114 | 0.5 |
| Transportation and communication | 4,950 | 5.7 | 829 | 3.9 |
| Trade | 12,774 | 14.8 | 825[6] | 3.8[6] |
| Finance | 5,189 | 6.0 | 61 | 0.3 |
| Pub. admin., defense | ... | ... | } 4,082 | 19.0 |
| Services | ... | ... | | |
| Other | 19,149[7] | 22.2[7] | 4,440[8] | 20.7[8] |
| TOTAL | 86,275 | 100.0 | 21,435 | 100.0 |

*Public debt* (external, outstanding; 1982): U.S.$16,000,000.
*Population economically active* (1984): total 30,900; activity rate of total population 32.1% (participation rates: ages 15–64, n.a.; female [1976] 14.7%; unemployed 4.5%).

### Price and earnings indexes (1980 = 100)

| | 1980 | 1981 | 1982 | 1983 | 1984 | 1985 | 1986 |
|---|---|---|---|---|---|---|---|
| Consumer price index | 100.0 | 114.9 | 127.4 | 139.8 | 140.0 | 167.4 | 203.9 |
| Earnings index | 100.0 | 120.3 | ... | ... | ... | ... | ... |

*Household income and expenditure.* Average household size (1986) 6.3; income per household: n.a.; sources of income: n.a.; expenditure (1983)[9]: food 55.1%, household goods 12.4%, tobacco and beverages 8.5%, clothing and footwear 6.2%, transportation 6.1%, housing 3.8%.
*Land use* (1984): forested 11.9%; meadows and pastures 6.0%; agricultural and under permanent cultivation 80.6%; other 1.5%.

## Foreign trade

### Balance of trade (current prices)

| | 1980 | 1981 | 1982 | 1983 | 1984 | 1985 |
|---|---|---|---|---|---|---|
| T$'000,000 | −23.0 | −27.3 | −37.0 | −35.2 | −36.6 | −51.8 |
| % of total | 61.7% | 63.9% | 81.5% | 73.2% | 64.7% | 78.3% |

*Imports* (1985): T$58,929,518 (food and live animals 22.5%, machinery and transport equipment 19.1%, basic manufactures 18.4%, mineral fuels 12.9%, chemicals 6.5%, beverages and tobacco 5.3%). *Major import sources:* New Zealand 39.0%; Australia 24.5%; Japan 7.8%; Spain 5.7%; United States 5.7%; Fiji 5.3%.
*Exports* (1985): T$7,169,812 (coconut oil products 23.1%, bananas 10.8%, desiccated coconut 6.8%). *Major export destinations:* New Zealand 48.4%; Australia 34.8%.

## Transport and communications

*Transport.* Railroads: none. Roads (1986): total length 269 mi, 433 km (paved 65%). Vehicles (1983): passenger cars 443, commercial vehicles 1,343. Merchant marine (1986): vessels (100 gross tons and over) 19; total deadweight tonnage 21,141. Air transport (1985): passenger-mi 621,000, passenger-km 1,000,000; cargo traffic, n.a.; airports (1987) with scheduled flights 6.
*Communications.* Daily newspapers: none. Radio (1985): total number of receivers 66,000 (1 per 1.5 persons). Television: total number of receivers, n.a.[10]. Telephones (1984): 3,996 (1 per 24.1 persons).

## Education and health

### Education (1984)

| | schools | teachers | students | student/ teacher ratio |
|---|---|---|---|---|
| Primary (age 6–10) | 111 | 810 | 16,921 | 20.9 |
| Secondary (age 13–18) | 50 | 789 | 14,549 | 18.4 |
| Voc., teacher tr. | 12 | 14[11] | 635 | ... |
| Higher[12] | 1 | ... | 125 | ... |

*Educational attainment* (1976). Percent of population age 25 and over having: no formal schooling 0.4%; incomplete primary education 37.3%; complete primary 12.4%; lower secondary 45.6%; secondary 0.1%; postsecondary 0.1%; higher 0.6%; special education 2.4%; other 1.1%. *Literacy* (1976): total population age 15 and over literate 46,456 (92.8%); males 23,372 (92.9%); females 23,084 (92.8%).
*Health* (1986): physicians 39 (1 per 2,510 persons); hospital beds 307 (1 per 319 persons); infant mortality rate per 1,000 live births (1983) 26.0.
*Food* (1981–83): daily per capita caloric intake 3,134 (vegetable products 85%, animal products 15%); (1983) 117% of FAO recommended minimum.

## Military

*Total active duty personnel:* Tonga had a national defense force of about 250 in the early 1980s.

[1]Includes 19 nonelective seats. [2]The pa'anga is at par with the Australian dollar. [3]Also includes 39.0 sq mi (101.1 sq km) of uninhabited islands. [4]Density is based on land area. [5]Estimated budget for 1985–86 was: revenue T$25,489,000; expenditures T$25,708,000. [6]Trade includes hotels and restaurants. [7]Includes indirect taxes less subsidies. [8]Includes 2,809 persons seeking work for the first time. [9]Current weight of CPI components. [10]Tonga has no authorized television service, but a "pirate" station began transmitting in mid-1984. [11]1983. [12]1982.

# Trinidad and Tobago

*Official name:* Republic of Trinidad and Tobago.
*Form of government:* multiparty republic with two legislative houses (Senate [31]; House of Representatives [36]).
*Chief of state:* President.
*Head of government:* Prime Minister.
*Capital:* Port-of-Spain.
*Official language:* English.
*Official religion:* none.
*Monetary unit:* 1 Trinidad and Tobago dollar (TT$) = 100 cents; valuation (Oct. 5, 1987) 1 U.S.$ = TT$3.60; 1 £ = TT$5.85.

| Area and population | | area | | population |
|---|---|---|---|---|
| | | | | 1986 |
| Counties | Capitals | sq mi | sq km | estimate |
| Caroni | Chaguanas | 213 | 552 | 164,800 |
| Nariva/Mayaro | Rio Claro | 350 | 906 | 32,800 |
| St. Andrew/St. David | Sangre Grande | 364 | 943 | 56,900 |
| St. George | ... | 350 | 907 | 429,400 |
| St. Patrick | Siparia | 255 | 660 | 138,000[1] |
| Tobago | Scarborough | 117 | 303 | 43,700 |
| Victoria | Princes Town | 314 | 814 | 215,500 |
| **City** | | | | |
| Port-of-Spain | — | 4 | 10 | 57,400 |
| **Boroughs** | | | | |
| Arima | — | 3 | 7 | 28,200 |
| Point Fortin | — | 6 | 16 | [1] |
| San Fernando | — | 2 | 6 | 32,600 |
| TOTAL | | 1,978 | 5,124 | 1,199,300 |

## Demography

*Population* (1987): 1,221,000.
*Density* (1987): persons per sq mi 617.3, persons per sq km 238.3.
*Urban-rural* (1986): urban 49.1%; rural 50.9%.
*Sex distribution* (1985): male 49.90%; female 50.10%.
*Age breakdown* (1985): under 15, 32.9%; 15–29, 30.6%; 30–44, 16.9%; 45–59, 11.2%; 60–74, 6.8%; 75 and over, 1.6%.
*Population projection:* (1990) 1,289,000; (2000) 1,544,000.
*Doubling time:* 31 years.
*Ethnic composition* (1980): black 40.8%; East Indian 40.7%; mixed 16.3%; white 0.9%; Chinese 0.5%; Arab 0.1%; other 0.7%.
*Religious affiliation* (1980): Christian 62.0%, of which Roman Catholic 32.9%, Protestant 28.3% (including Anglican 14.7%, Presbyterian 3.8%, Pentecostal 3.5%, Seventh-day Adventist 2.5%); Hindu 24.9%; Muslim 6.0%; other (including Rastafarian and Yoruba syncretist) 7.1%.
*Major cities* (1986): Port-of-Spain 57,400; San Fernando 32,600; Arima 28,200; Point Fortin 16,710[2].

## Vital statistics

*Birth rate* per 1,000 population (1983): 29.2 (world avg. 29.0); (1979) legitimate 56.9%; illegitimate 43.1%.
*Death rate* per 1,000 population (1983): 6.6 (world avg. 11.0).
*Natural increase rate* per 1,000 population (1983): 22.6 (world avg. 18.0).
*Total fertility rate* (avg. births per childbearing woman; 1984): 2.8.
*Marriage rate* per 1,000 population (1984): 7.2.
*Divorce rate* per 1,000 population (1984): 0.8.
*Life expectancy* at birth (1980–85): male 66.2 years; female 71.3 years.
*Major causes of death* per 100,000 population (1983): ischemic heart disease 114.3; cerebrovascular disease 83.2; malignant neoplasms (cancers) 74.5; diabetes mellitus 63.9; diseases of the respiratory system 48.5.

## National economy

*Budget* (1985): Revenue: TT$6,300,400,000 (non-oil sector 60.8%, of which tax revenue 53.2% [including individual income taxes 22.3%, taxes on goods and services 11.9%, import duties 9.7%]; oil sector 39.2%, of which corporation taxes 29.7%, royalties 7.2%). Expenditure: TT$7,543,600,000 (current expenditure 78.5%, of which education 13.2%, welfare 8.3%, health 7.4%, public debt 4.7%, defense 0.9%; development expenditure 21.5%).
*Public debt* (external, outstanding; 1985): U.S.$1,087,400,000.
*Tourism* (1985): receipts from visitors U.S.$197,000,000; expenditures by nationals abroad U.S.$219,500,000.
*Production* (metric tons except as noted). Agriculture, forestry, fishing (1985): sugarcane 1,062,000[3], coconuts 60,000, tomatoes 8,000, oranges 7,000, grapefruit 7,000, rice 4,000, cocoa 1,426[3], coffee 1,334[3]; livestock (number of live animals) 83,000 pigs, 77,000 cattle, 50,000 goats; roundwood 63,000 cu m; fish catch (1984) 3,552. Mining and quarrying (1985): natural asphalt 21,300. Manufacturing (1986): nitrogenous fertilizers 1,888,000; methanol 358,200[4]; cement 338,000; iron and steel billets 166,900[4]; urea 155,000[4]; iron and steel rods 102,900[4]; sugar 85,500[5]; 15,400 locally assembled television receivers; 10,750 locally assembled motor vehicles; rum 87,400 hectolitres. Construction (new building authorized; 1984): residential 474,000 sq m; nonresidential 168,300 sq m. Energy production (consumption): electricity (kW-hr; 1986) 3,182,000,000 (3,035,000,000[4]); coal, none (none); crude petroleum (barrels; 1986) 61,600,000 (34,832,000[4]); petroleum products (metric tons; 1985) 4,748,000 (1,541,000); natural gas (cu m; 1985) 2,812,000,000 (2,812,000,000).

*Gross national product* (at current market prices; 1985): U.S.$7,140,000,000 (U.S.$6,040 per capita).

| Structure of gross domestic product and labour force | | | | |
|---|---|---|---|---|
| | 1985 | | | |
| | in value[6] TT$'000,000 | % of total value | labour force | % of labour force |
| Agriculture | 653 | 3.4 | 44,000 | 9.5 |
| Mining | 4,461[7] | 23.5 | 65,400 | 14.1 |
| Manufacturing | 1,282 | 6.8 | | |
| Construction | 2,099 | 11.1 | 101,500 | 21.8 |
| Public utilities | 419 | 2.2 | | |
| Transp. and commun. | 1,917 | 10.1 | 30,400 | 6.5 |
| Trade | 1,769 | 9.3 | 105,200 | 22.6 |
| Finance | 1,912 | 10.1 | | |
| Pub. admin., defense | 2,910 | 15.3 | 107,800 | 23.2 |
| Services | 1,550 | 8.2 | | |
| Other | — | — | 10,700 | 2.3 |
| TOTAL | 18,972 | 100.0 | 465,000 | 100.0 |

*Population economically active* (1985): total 465,000; activity rate of total population 39.4% (participation rates: ages 15–64, 64.5%; female 33.3%; unemployed [1986] 17.0%).

| Price and earnings indexes (1980 = 100) | | | | | | | |
|---|---|---|---|---|---|---|---|
| | 1981 | 1982 | 1983 | 1984 | 1985 | 1986 | 1987[8] |
| Consumer price index | 114.3 | 127.4 | 148.7 | 168.6 | 181.4 | 195.4 | 214.6 |
| Weekly earnings index | 118.4 | 139.8 | 167.9 | 192.2 | 201.7 | 209.7[9] | ... |

*Household income and expenditure.* Average household size (1980) 4.2; income per household: n.a.; sources of income: n.a.; expenditure (1981–82): food and beverages 27.7%, housing 22.7%, clothing and footwear 15.5%, transportation 13.2%, household furnishings 8.8%, health 2.2%, education 1.5%, recreation 1.4%, energy 1.1%, other 5.9%.
*Land use* (1984): forested 44.1%; meadows and pastures 2.1%; agricultural and under permanent cultivation 31.2%; other 22.6%.

## Foreign trade[10]

| Balance of trade (current prices) | | | | | | |
|---|---|---|---|---|---|---|
| | 1981 | 1982 | 1983 | 1984 | 1985 | 1986 |
| TT$'000,000 | +2,103 | −694 | +77 | +1,079 | +1,920 | +633 |
| % of total | 13.2% | 4.5% | 0.7% | 11.5% | 21.5% | 6.8% |

*Imports* (1985): TT$3,738,975,000 (machinery and transport equipment 30.1%; food 15.2%; base metals and products 9.0%; chemical products 8.0%). *Major import sources:* United States 37.7%; Japan 9.6%; United Kingdom 9.2%; Canada 7.2%; Argentina 4.4%
*Exports* (1985): TT$5,247,127,000 (domestic exports 96.6%, of which crude petroleum 46.7%, petroleum products 32.6%, anhydrous ammonia 7.6%, urea 2.4%, methanol 1.6%; reexports [mostly aircraft parts and oil-mining machinery] 3.4%). *Major export destinations:* United States 62.6%; Italy 3.9%; United Kingdom 3.9%; Guyana 3.0%; Barbados 2.8%.

## Transport and communications

*Transport.* Railroads: none. Roads (1985): total length 4,909 mi, 7,900 km (paved 46%). Vehicles (1985): passenger cars 241,595; trucks and buses 82,361. Merchant marine (1986): vessels (100 gross tons and over) 51; total deadweight tonnage 12,801. Air transport (1986)[11]: passenger-mi 1,339,000,000, passenger-km 2,155,000,000; short ton-mi cargo 8,605,000, metric ton-km cargo 12,563,000; airports (1987) with scheduled flights 2.
*Communications.* Daily newspapers (1986): total number 4; total circulation 172,800; circulation per 1,000 population 144. Radio (1986): 552,000 receivers (1 per 2.2 persons). Television (1986): 345,000 receivers (1 per 3.5 persons). Telephones (1984): 109,477 (1 per 11 persons).

## Education and health

| Education (1984–85) | schools | teachers | students | student/ teacher ratio |
|---|---|---|---|---|
| Primary (age 5–11) | 468 | 7,627 | 168,308 | 22.1 |
| Secondary (age 12–19) | 93[12] | 4,744 | 92,595 | 19.5 |
| Voc., teacher tr. | ... | ... | ... | ... |
| Higher | 1 | ... | 2,684 | ... |

*Educational attainment* (1980). Percent of population age 25 and over having: no formal schooling 7.1%; primary education 66.5%; secondary 21.7%; higher 2.7%; other 2.0%. *Literacy* (1980): total population age 15 and over literate 653,122 (95.1%); males literate 328,645 (96.7%); females literate 324,477 (93.6%).
*Health* (1985): physicians 1,103 (1 per 1,071 persons); hospital beds 4,087 (1 per 289 persons); infant mortality rate per 1,000 live births (1981–83 avg.) 14.9.
*Food* (1981–83): daily per capita caloric intake 2,905 (vegetable products 80%, animal products 20%); (1983) 129% of FAO recommended minimum requirement.

## Military

*Total active duty personnel:* 2,130 (army 100.0%). *Military expenditure as percent of GNP* (1984): 2.7% (world 5.9%); per capita expenditure U.S.$162.

[1]St. Patrick includes the population of the borough of Point Fortin. [2]1980. [3]1986. [4]1985. [5]1987. [6]At factor cost. [7]Includes petroleum refining. [8]May. [9]Average of 2nd and 3rd quarters. [10]Import figures are f.o.b. (free on board) in balance of trade and c.i.f. (cost, insurance, and freight) in commodities and trading partners. [11]BWIA International airways only. [12]1983–84.

# Tunisia

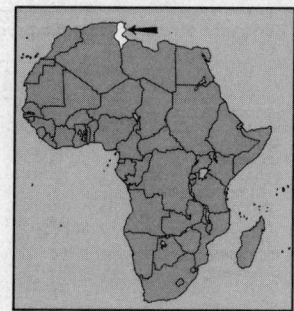

*Official name:* al-Jumhūrīyah at-Tūnisīyah (Republic of Tunisia).
*Form of government:* multiparty republic with one legislative house (Chamber of Deputies [138]).
*Head of state and government:* President.
*Capital:* Tunis.
*Official language:* Arabic.
*Official religion:* Islam.
*Monetary unit:* 1 dinar (D) = 1,000 millimes; valuation (Oct. 5, 1987) D 1.00 = U.S.$2.26 = £1.39.

### Area and population

| Governorates | Capitals | area sq mi | area sq km | population 1986 estimate |
|---|---|---|---|---|
| Aryānah | Aryānah | 602 | 1,558 | 415,800 |
| Bājah | Bājah | 1,374 | 3,558 | 286,000 |
| Banzart | Banzart | 1,423 | 3,685 | 412,700 |
| Bin 'Arūs | Bin 'Arūs | 294 | 761 | 271,600 |
| Jundūbah | Jundūbah | 1,198 | 3,102 | 379,800 |
| al-Kāf | al-Kāf | 1,917 | 4,965 | 256,000 |
| Madanīyīn | Madanīyīn | 3,316 | 8,588 | 324,400 |
| al-Mahdīyah | al-Mahdīyah | 1,145 | 2,966 | 290,400 |
| al-Munastir | al-Munastir | 393 | 1,019 | 297,700 |
| Nābul | Nābul | 1,076 | 2,788 | 489,600 |
| Qābis | Qābis | 2,770 | 7,175 | 264,000 |
| Qafşah | Qafşah | 3,471 | 8,990 | 253,300 |
| al-Qaşrayn | al-Qaşrayn | 3,114 | 8,066 | 322,700 |
| al-Qayrawān | al-Qayrawān | 2,591 | 6,712 | 451,000 |
| Qibilī | Qibilī | 8,527 | 22,084 | 104,200 |
| Şafāqis | Şafāqis | 2,913 | 7,545 | 627,000 |
| Sīdī Bū Zayd | Sīdī Bū Zayd | 2,700 | 6,994 | 314,500 |
| Silyānah | Silyānah | 1,788 | 4,631 | 232,700 |
| Sūsah | Sūsah | 1,012 | 2,621 | 346,000 |
| Taţāwīn | Taţāwīn | 15,015 | 38,889 | 109,600 |
| Tawzar | Tawzar | 1,822 | 4,719 | 73,900 |
| Tūnis | Tunis (Tūnis) | 134 | 346 | 815,600 |
| Zaghwān | Zaghwān | 1,069 | 2,768 | 126,400 |
| TOTAL | | 59,664 | 154,530 | 7,464,900 |

## Demography

*Population* (1987): 7,636,000.
*Density* (1987): persons per sq mi 128.0, persons per sq km 49.4.
*Urban–rural* (1984): urban 52.8%; rural 47.2%.
*Sex distribution* (1986): male 50.93%; female 49.07%.
*Age breakdown* (1986): under 15, 39.2%; 15–29, 28.7%; 30–44, 15.0%; 45–59, 10.4%; 60–74, 5.4%; 75 and over, 1.3%.
*Population projection:* (1990) 7,989,000; (2000) 9,856,000.
*Doubling time:* 28 years.
*Ethnic composition* (1983): Arab 98.2%; Berber 1.2%; French 0.2%; Italian 0.1%; other 0.3%.
*Religious affiliation* (1980): Sunnī Muslim 99.4%; Christian 0.3%; Jewish 0.1%; other 0.2%.
*Major cities* (commune; 1984): Tunis 596,654; Şafāqis 231,911; Aryānah 98,655; Banzart 94,509; Sūsah 83,509.

## Vital statistics

*Birth rate* per 1,000 population (1986): 31.1 (world avg. 26.0); (1974) legitimate 99.8%; illegitimate 0.2%.
*Death rate* per 1,000 population (1986 est.): 8.7 (world avg. 9.9).
*Natural increase rate* per 1,000 population (1986): 24.7 (world avg. 16.1).
*Total fertility rate* (avg. births per childbearing woman; 1984): 4.3.
*Marriage rate* per 1,000 population (1986): 12.8.
*Divorce rate* per 1,000 population (1985): 0.8.
*Life expectancy* at birth (1980–85): male 60.1 years; female 61.1 years.
*Major causes of death* per 100,000 population: n.a.; however, major illnesses include intestinal infections, trachoma, hepatitis, tuberculosis, and syphilis.

## National economy

*Budget* (1985): Revenue: D 1,822,147,000 (indirect taxes 51.4%, investment 25.7%, direct taxes 16.4%). Expenditures: D 1,263,318,000 (education 22.7%, finance 15.9%, health 10.7%, interior affairs 8.4%, defense 8.0%, agriculture 6.6%).
*Tourism:* receipts from visitors (1985) U.S.$551,000,000; expenditures by nationals abroad (1982) U.S.$102,000,000.
*Land use* (1984): forested 3.6%; meadows and pastures 19.5%; agricultural and under permanent cultivation 30.2%; other 46.7%.
*Production* (metric tons except as noted). Agriculture, forestry, fishing (1986): olives 525,000, wheat 474,000, tomatoes 418,000, watermelons and melons 340,000, sugar beets 182,000, potatoes 170,000, oranges 151,500, grapes 101,000, dates 85,000, almonds 42,000, alfalfa 38,000, tobacco 4,100; livestock (number of live animals; 1984) 5,409,000 sheep, 1,046,000 goats, 625,000 cattle; roundwood (1985) 2,768,000 cu m; fish catch 93,000. Mining and quarrying (1986): phosphate rock 5,800,000; iron ore 476,000; zinc 13,400; lead 5,000. Manufacturing (1986): cement 2,961,900; phosphoric acid 572,000; flour 516,600; crude steel 149,300; mineral water 423,700 hectolitres. Construction (1982): residential building authorized 2,679,000 sq m. Energy production (consumption): electricity (kW-hr; 1986) 3,749,600,000 (3,302,000,000); coal (metric tons; 1985) none (21,000); crude petroleum (barrels; 1985) 41,582,000 (12,433,000); petroleum products (metric tons; 1986) 1,548,200 (2,793,200); natural gas (cu m; 1986) 373,200,000 (373,200,000).

*Gross national product* (at current market prices; 1985): U.S.$8,730,000,000 (U.S.$1,220 per capita).

### Structure of gross domestic product and labour force

| | 1985 in value D '000,000 | 1985 % of total value | 1984 labour force | 1984 % of labour force[1] |
|---|---|---|---|---|
| Agriculture | 1,040.0 | 15.2 | 475,400 | 26.6 |
| Mining | 697.0 | 10.2 | 22,500 | 1.3 |
| Manufacturing | 827.0 | 12.1 | 345,100 | 19.3 |
| Construction | 392.0 | 5.7 | 237,500 | 13.3 |
| Public utilities | 103.0 | 1.5 | 15,500 | 0.9 |
| Transportation and communication | 365.0 | 5.3 | 86,700 | 4.9 |
| Trade | 1,485 | 21.6 | 153,900 | 8.6 |
| Finance | 272.0 | 4.0 | 13,100 | 0.7 |
| Pub. admin., defense | 792.0 | 11.5 | 305,600 | 17.1 |
| Services | ... | ... | 36,000 | 2.0 |
| Other | 887.0 | 12.9 | 95,100 | 5.3 |
| TOTAL | 6,860.0 | 100.0 | 1,786,400 | 100.0 |

*Public debt* (external, outstanding; 1985): U.S.$4,442,000,000.
*Population economically active* (1985): total 2,224,000, activity rate of total population 31.4% (participation rates: age 15 and over 51.6%; female 23.6%; unemployed 8.5%).

### Price and earnings indexes (1980 = 100)

| | 1980 | 1981 | 1982 | 1983 | 1984 | 1985 | 1986 |
|---|---|---|---|---|---|---|---|
| Consumer price index | 100.0 | 108.9 | 123.8 | 134.9 | 146.2 | 158.0 | 167.0 |
| Monthly earnings index[2] | 100.0 | 123.6 | 147.2 | ... | ... | ... | ... |

*Household income and expenditure.* Average household size (1984) 5.5; income per household: n.a.; sources of income: n.a.; expenditure (1983): food and beverages 42.8%, clothing and footwear 10.9%, housing 9.3%, transportation 8.0%, recreation 6.1%, household durable goods 5.7%, utilities 5.6%, health care 3.7%, education 1.7%.

## Foreign trade

### Balance of trade (current prices)

| | 1981 | 1982 | 1983 | 1984 | 1985 | 1986 |
|---|---|---|---|---|---|---|
| D '000,000 | −632.9 | −840.0 | −845.0 | −1,075.7 | −844.0 | −1,404 |
| % of total | 20.4% | 26.4% | 25.0% | 27.8% | 22.6% | 24.3% |

*Imports* (1986): D 2,303,678,000 (petroleum and petroleum products 7.7%, textiles 6.3%, plastic material 2.6%, chemical products 2.6%, pharmaceutical products 2.4%). *Major import sources:* France 27.5%; West Germany 13.0%; Italy 10.7%; United States 6.9%; Algeria 2.8%; The Netherlands 2.5%; United Kingdom 1.9%.
*Exports* (1986): D 1,403,704,000 (clothing and accessories 24.1%, petroleum and petroleum products 22.6%, electrical machinery 3.2%, cotton textiles 2.2%, shoes 1.8%, rugs and tapestries 0.4%). *Major export destinations:* France 23.3%; West Germany 15.0%; Italy 14.5%; Spain 3.6%; United States 0.7%.

## Transport and communications

*Transport.* Railroads (1986): route length 1,316 mi, 2,118 km; passenger-mi 469,800,000, passenger-km 756,000,000; short ton-mi cargo 1,282,000,000, metric ton-km cargo 1,872,000,000. Roads (1985): total length 16,312 mi, 26,252 km (paved 54%). Vehicles (1985): passenger cars 174,902; trucks and buses 179,741. Merchant marine (1986): vessels (100 gross tons and over) 71; total deadweight tonnage 449,685. Air transport (1985): passenger-mi 932,000,000, passenger-km 1,500,000,000; short ton-mi cargo 11,457,000; metric ton-km cargo 16,728,000; airports (1987) with scheduled flights 5.
*Communications.* Daily newspapers (1986): total number 5; total circulation 272,000; circulation per 1,000 population 36. Radio (1986): total number of receivers 1,160,000 (1 per 6.4 persons). Television (1986): total number of receivers 400,000 (1 per 19 persons). Telephones (1985): 297,659 (1 per 24 persons).

## Education and health

### Education (1986–87)

| | schools | teachers | students | student/ teacher ratio |
|---|---|---|---|---|
| Primary (age 6–11) | 3,503 | 40,978 | 1,326,541 | 32.4 |
| Secondary (age 12–18) | 420 | 21,561 | 459,034 | 21.3 |
| Voc., teacher tr. | ... | ... | ... | ... |
| Higher | ... | 5,171 | 40,830 | 7.9 |

*Educational attainment* (1984). Percent of population age 25 and over having: no formal schooling 65.8%; Qur'anic education 1.2%; primary 17.5%; secondary 11.2%; vocational 0.8%; higher 1.7%; unspecified 1.8%. *Literacy* (1984): total population age 15 and over literate 2,023,500 (48.2%); males literate 1,282,700 (60.4%); females literate 740,800 (35.7%).
*Health* (1986): physicians 3,453 (1 per 2,162 persons); hospital beds 15,838 (1 per 471 persons); infant mortality rate per 1,000 live births 12.1.
*Food* (1981–83): daily per capita caloric intake 2,837 (vegetable products 92%, animal products 8%); (1983) 121% of FAO recommended minimum requirement.

## Military

*Total active duty personnel* (1986): 40,300 (army 74.4%, navy 8.7%, air force 8.7%, paramilitary 8.2%). *Military expenditure as percent of GNP* (1984): 3.2% (world 5.9%); per capita expenditure U.S.$39.

[1]Employed only. [2]Government workers only.

# Turkey

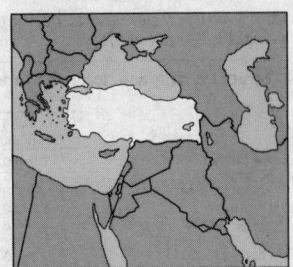

*Official name:* Türkiye Cumhuriyeti (Republic of Turkey).
*Form of government:* multiparty republic with one legislative house (Turkish Grand National Assembly [450]).
*Chief of state:* President.
*Head of government:* Prime Minister.
*Capital:* Ankara.
*Official language:* Turkish.
*Official religion:* none.
*Monetary unit:* 1 Turkish lira (LT) = 100 kurush; valuation (Oct. 5, 1987) 1 U.S.$ = LT 932.00; 1 £ = LT 1,513.00.

## Area and population

| Geographical regions | area | | population 1985 census |
|---|---|---|---|
| | sq mi | sq km | |
| Akdeniz kıyısı (Mediterranean Coast) | 22,933 | 59,395 | 4,653,426 |
| Batı Anadolu (West Anatolia) | 29,742 | 77,031 | 3,538,253 |
| Doğu Anadolu (East Anatolia) | 68,074 | 176,311 | 6,290,086 |
| Güneydoğu Anadolu (Southeast Anatolia) | 15,347 | 39,749 | 2,413,593 |
| İç Anadolu (Central Anatolia) | 91,254 | 236,347 | 12,193,155 |
| Karadeniz kıyısı (Black Sea Coast) | 31,388 | 81,295 | 6,652,172 |
| Marmara ve Ege kıyıları (Marmara and Aegean coasts) | 33,035 | 85,560 | 9,834,576 |
| Trakya (Thrace) | 9,175 | 23,764 | 5,089,197 |
| TOTAL | 300,948 | 779,452 | 50,664,458 |

## Demography

*Population* (1987): 52,845,000.
*Density* (1987): persons per sq mi 175.6, persons per sq km 67.8.
*Urban–rural* (1985): urban 53.0%; rural 47.0%.
*Sex distribution* (1980): male 50.73%; female 49.27%.
*Age breakdown* (1980): under 15, 38.5%; 15–29, 27.7%; 30–44, 16.0%; 45–59, 11.2%; 60–64, 1.8%; 65 and over, 4.8%[1].
*Population projection:* (1990) 56,941,000; (2000) 73,029,000.
*Doubling time:* 33 years.
*Ethnic composition* (1983): Turkish 85.7%; Kurdish 10.6%; Arab 1.6%; other 2.1%.
*Religious affiliation* (1980): Sunnī Muslim 99.2%; Eastern Orthodox 0.3%; other 0.5%.
*Major cities* (1985): Istanbul 5,475,982; Ankara 2,235,000; İzmir 1,489,772; Adana 777,554; Bursa 612,500.

## Vital statistics

*Birth rate* per 1,000 population (1980–85): 33.6 (world avg. 29.0).
*Death rate* per 1,000 population (1980–85): 9.3 (world avg. 11.0).
*Natural increase rate* per 1,000 population (1980–85): 24.3 (world avg. 18.0).
*Total fertility rate* (avg. births per childbearing woman; 1980–85): 4.5.
*Marriage rate* per 1,000 population (1983): 6.4.
*Divorce rate* per 1,000 population (1983): 0.4.
*Life expectancy* at birth (1985–90): male 62.5 years; female 65.8 years.
*Major causes of death* per 100,000 population (1983): heart disease 87.0; malignant neoplasms (cancers) 25.0; birth injury and difficult labour 19.7; cerebrovascular disease 17.8.

## National economy

*Budget* (1986). Revenue: LT 7,197,000,000,000 (direct taxes 43.3%, indirect taxes 39.7%). Expenditures: LT 8,270,000,000,000 (investment 22.1%, personnel 22.0%, interest on foreign loans 8.2%).
*Public debt* (external, outstanding; 1985): U.S.$17,821,000,000.
*Tourism* (1986): receipts from visitors U.S.$950,000,000; expenditures by nationals abroad U.S.$313,000,000.
*Production* (metric tons except as noted). Agriculture, forestry, fishing (1986): wheat 19,000,000, sugar beets 10,662,000, barley 7,000,000, potatoes 4,000,000, grapes 3,000,000, corn (maize) 2,300,000, apples 1,865,000, dry onions 1,300,000, olives 1,010,000, sunflower seed 940,000, lentils 850,000, tea leaves 712,000, chick-peas 630,000, oranges 600,000, rye 350,000, oats 300,000, rice 168,000; livestock (number of live animals; 1985) 40,391,000 sheep, 17,300,000 cattle, 13,100,000 goats; roundwood 18,446,000 cu m, fuelwood 12,488,000 cu m; fish catch (1984) 566,933. Mining and quarrying (1986): iron 3,912,000; chrome ore 893,000. Manufacturing (1986): cement 20,004,000; commercial fertilizers 6,813,000; steel ingot 3,596,000; crude iron 3,579,000; pig iron 347,000; beer 189,007,000 litres; wine 19,215,000 litres. Construction (1985): residential 27,049,000 sq m; nonresidential 6,700,000 sq m. Energy production (consumption): electricity (kW-hr; 1985) 33,313,000,000 (35,450,000,000); coal (metric tons; 1985) 39,094,-000 (42,557,000); crude petroleum (barrels; 1985) 15,471,000 (131,360,000); petroleum products (metric tons; 1985) 15,800,000 (15,449,000); natural gas (cu m; 1985) 65,169,000 (65,169,000).
*Household income and expenditure*[2]. Average household size (1980) 5.2; income per household (1978–79) LT 11,880 (U.S.$471); sources of income: self-employment 46.8%, wages and salaries 38.9%, transfer grants 9.4%, other 4.9%; expenditure (1979): food 41.2%, housing 25.2%, clothing 14.8%, recreation and entertainment 6.1%, transportation 5.5.%, health 3.3%, other 3.9%.
*Gross national product* (at current market prices; 1985): U.S.$56,060,000,000 (U.S.$1,110 per capita).

## Structure of gross domestic product and labour force

| | 1986 | | | |
|---|---|---|---|---|
| | in value LT '000,000 | % of total value | labour force | % of labour force |
| Agriculture | 6,485,000 | 16.5 | 9,364,000 | 48.3 |
| Mining | 760,000 | 1.9 | 128,000 | 0.7 |
| Manufacturing | 9,006,000 | 23.0 | 1,902,000 | 9.8 |
| Construction | 1,411,000 | 3.6 | 652,000 | 3.4 |
| Public utilities | 1,599,000 | 4.1 | 140,000 | 0.7 |
| Transportation and communication | 3,645,000 | 9.3 | 566,000 | 3.0 |
| Trade | 6,027,000 | 15.4 | 813,000 | 4.2 |
| Finance | 2,536,000 | 6.5 | 235,000 | 1.2 |
| Pub. admin., defense | 2,073,000 | 5.3 } | 2,484,000 | 12.8 |
| Services | 1,907,000 | 4.9 | | |
| Other | 3,742,000[3] | 9.5[3] | 3,088,000 | 15.9 |
| TOTAL | 39,191,000 | 100.0 | 19,372,000 | 100.0 |

*Population economically active* (1982): total 19,027,000; activity rate of total population 41.1% (participation rates: over age 15, 66.3%; female 32.9%; unemployed 17.7%).

## Price and earnings indexes (1980 = 100)

| | 1981 | 1982 | 1983 | 1984 | 1985 | 1986 |
|---|---|---|---|---|---|---|
| Consumer price index | 136.6 | 178.7 | 230.8 | 352.4 | 510.9 | 687.7 |
| Daily earnings index[4] | 127.4 | 161.8 | 221.2 | 306.1 | ... | ... |

*Land use* (1984): forested 26.2%; meadows and pastures 11.7%; agricultural and under permanent cultivation 35.6%; other 26.5%.

## Foreign trade

### Balance of trade (current prices)

| | 1981 | 1982 | 1983 | 1984 | 1985 | 1986 |
|---|---|---|---|---|---|---|
| U.S.$'000,000 | −4,230 | −3,097 | −3,507 | −3,624 | −3,386 | −3,648 |
| % of total | 31.0% | 21.2% | 23.4% | 20.3% | 17.5% | 19.7% |

*Imports* (1986): U.S.$11,105,000,000 (machinery 14.1%, fuels 13.3%, chemicals 9.5%, iron and steel 6.8%). *Major import sources:* West Germany 16.0%; United States 10.6%; Italy 7.8%; Iraq 6.9%; Japan 6.2%; France 4.9%; United Kingdom 4.7%.
*Exports* (1986): U.S.$7,457,000,000 (textiles 17.9%, agricultural products 14.7%, livestock and animal products 5.1%, chemical products 3.5%). *Major export destinations:* West Germany 19.4%; Italy 7.8%; Iran 7.6%; United States 7.4%; Iraq 7.4%; Saudi Arabia 4.8%; United Kingdom 4.5%.

## Transport and communications

*Transport.* Railroads (1985): route length (1987) 5,076 mi, 8,169 km; passenger-mi 4,032,000,000, passenger-km 6,489,000,000; short ton-mi cargo 5,307,000,000, metric ton-km cargo 7,748,000,000. Roads (1983): total length 188,136 mi, 302,776 km (paved, n.a.). Vehicles (1986): passenger cars 1,086,675; trucks and buses 588,491. Merchant marine (1986): vessels (100 gross tons and over) 825; total deadweight tonnage 5,712,544. Air transport (1986): passenger-mi 1,626,598,000, passenger-km 2,617,761,000; short ton-mi cargo 31,144,000, metric ton-km cargo 45,469,000; airports (1987) with scheduled flights 14.
*Communications.* Daily newspapers (1986)[5]: total number 338; total circulation 4,188,262; circulation per 1,000 population 81.3. Radio (1986): total number of receivers 8,227,000 (1 per 6.3 persons). Television (1986): total number of receivers 5,010,000 (1 per 10 persons). Telephones (1986): 2,780,000 (1 per 18 persons).

## Education and health

### Education (1984–85)

| | schools | teachers | students | student/ teacher ratio |
|---|---|---|---|---|
| Primary (age 5–12) | 47,192 | 209,911 | 6,527,036 | 31.1 |
| Secondary (age 13–18) | 4,358 | 42,653 | 1,576,875 | 36.9 |
| Voc., teacher tr. | 1,995 | 90,261 | 1,169,500 | 12.9 |
| Higher[6] | 153 | 16,454 | 225,622 | 13.7 |

*Educational attainment* (1980). Percent of population age 25 and over having: no formal schooling 52.4%; primary education 35.3%; secondary 8.7%; higher 3.6%. *Literacy* (1980): total population age 15 and over literate 8,561,370 (65.6%); males literate 6,530,035 (81.3%); females literate 2,031,335 (49.8%).
*Health* (1985): physicians 36,427 (1 per 1,391 persons); hospital beds 103,918 (1 per 488 persons); infant mortality rate per 1,000 live births 84.0.
*Food* (1981–83): daily per capita caloric intake 3,150 (vegetable products 90%, animal products 10%); (1983) 123% of FAO recommended minimum requirement.

## Military

*Total active duty personnel* (1986): 654,375 (army 82.8%, navy 8.4%, air force 8.8%). *Military expenditure as percent of GNP* (1984): 4.5% (world 5.9%); per capita expenditure U.S.$50.

[1]Including those of unknown age. [2]Urban areas only. [3]Other includes income from abroad and indirect taxes. [4]Insured workers only. [5]Principal daily newspapers only. [6]1983–84.

# Tuvalu

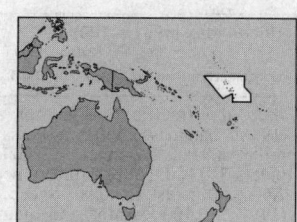

*Official name:* Tuvalu.
*Form of government:* constitutional monarchy with one legislative house (Parliament [13][1]).
*Chief of state:* British Monarch, represented by governor-general.
*Head of government:* Prime Minister.
*Capital:* Fongafale, on Funafuti atoll.
*Official language:* English.
*Official religion:* none.
*Monetary unit*[2]: 1 Tuvalu Dollar = 1 Australian Dollar ($T = $A) = 100 Tuvalu and Australian cents; valuation (Oct. 5, 1987)
1 U.S.$ = $A 1.40; 1 £ = $A 2.27.

### Area and population

| Islands[3] | area | | population 1985 census |
|---|---|---|---|
| | sq mi | sq km | |
| Funafuti | 0.91 | 2.36 | 2,810 |
| Nanumaga | 1.00 | 2.59 | 672 |
| Nanumea | 1.38 | 3.57 | 879 |
| Niulakita | 0.16 | 0.41 | 74 |
| Niutao | 0.82 | 2.12 | 904 |
| Nui | 1.27 | 3.29 | 604 |
| Nukufetau | 1.18 | 3.06 | 694 |
| Nukulaelae | 0.64 | 1.66 | 315 |
| Vaitupu | 1.89 | 4.90 | 1,231 |
| TOTAL | 9.25 | 23.96 | 8,229[4] |

## Demography

*Population* (1987): 8,200.
*Density* (1987): persons per sq mi 886.5, persons per sq km 342.2.
*Urban–rural* (1985): urban 34.2%; rural 65.8%.
*Sex distribution* (1985): male 47.42%; female 52.58%.
*Age breakdown* (1979): under 15, 33.8%; 15–29, 31.0%; 30–44, 14.3%; 45–59, 13.2%; 60–74, 6.1%; 75 and over, 1.6%.
*Population projection:* (1990) 8,200; (2000) 8,200.
*Doubling time:* 54 years[5].
*Ethnic composition* (1979): Tuvaluan (Polynesian) 91.2%; mixed (Polynesian/Micronesian/other) 7.2%; European 1.0%; other 0.6%.
*Religious affiliation* (1979): Church of Tuvalu (Congregational) 96.9%; Seventh-day Adventist 1.4%; Bahá'í 1.0%; Roman Catholic 0.2%; other 0.5%.
*Major city* (1985): Fongafale, on Funafuti atoll 2,810.

## Vital statistics

*Birth rate* per 1,000 population (1985): 23.8 (world avg. 29.0); legitimate 82.2%; illegitimate 17.8%.
*Death rate* per 1,000 population (1985): 10.7 (world avg. 11.0).
*Natural increase rate* per 1,000 population (1985): 13.1 (world avg. 18.0).
*Total fertility rate* (avg. births per childbearing woman; 1985): 2.7.
*Marriage rate* per 1,000 population: n.a.
*Divorce rate* per 1,000 population: n.a.
*Life expectancy* at birth (1979): male 56.9 years; female 60.1 years.
*Major causes of death* per 100,000 population (1985): diseases of the digestive system 170.1; diseases of the circulatory system 145.8; diseases of the respiratory system 121.5; diseases of the nervous system 121.5; malignant neoplasms (cancers) 72.9; infectious and parasitic diseases 36.5; endocrine and metabolic disorders 24.3.

## National economy

*Budget* (1987). Revenue: $A 13,498,000 (current revenue 31.1%, of which local sources 25.4%, British grants 5.7%; capital [development] revenue 68.9%, all from foreign grants and loans). Expenditures: $A 13,498,000 (current expenditures 31.1%; capital [development] expenditures 68.9%, of which marine transport 20.7%, education 13.0%, fisheries 5.6%, health 3.1%).
*Gross domestic product* (at current market prices; 1983): U.S.$3,400,000 (U.S.$410 per capita).

### Structure of gross domestic product and labour force

| | 1979 | | | |
|---|---|---|---|---|
| | in value $A | % of total value | labour force[6] | % of labour force |
| Agriculture | 597,100 | 16.0 | 42 | 4.5 |
| Mining | — | — | 1 | 0.1 |
| Manufacturing | 37,300 | 1.0 | 62 | 6.6 |
| Construction | 485,200 | 13.0 | 229 | 24.5 |
| Public utilities | ... | ... | 14 | 1.5 |
| Transportation and communication | 149,300 | 4.0 | 111 | 11.9 |
| Trade | 1,268,900 | 34.0 | 100 | 10.7 |
| Finance | } | | 13 | 1.4 |
| Pub. admin., defense | } 1,194,200 | 32.0 | 182 | 19.4 |
| Services | } | | 181 | 19.3 |
| Other | ... | ... | 1 | 0.1 |
| TOTAL | 3,732,000 | 100.0 | 936 | 100.0 |

*Production* (metric tons except as noted). Agriculture[7], forestry, fishing (1985): coconuts 3,000, hens' eggs 13, honey 2, other agricultural products include breadfruit, pulaka (taro), bananas, pandanus fruit, and pawpaws; livestock (number of live animals) 7,000 pigs[8]; forestry, n.a.; fish catch

793. Mining and quarrying: n.a. Manufacturing (1983): copra 200 metric tons; handicrafts; beche-de-mer; baked goods. Construction: n.a. Energy production (consumption): electricity (kW-hr; 1981) 3,000,000 (3,000,000); coal, none (none); crude petroleum, none (none); petroleum products, none (n.a.); natural gas, none (none).
*Public debt:* n.a.
*Tourism* (1979): number of visitors 474.
*Population economically active* (1979)[9]: total 4,010; activity rate of total population 55.2% (participation rates: over age 15, 81.1%; female 51.3%; unemployed 4.0%).

### Price and earnings indexes (1978 = 100)

| | 1979 | 1980 | 1981 | 1982 | 1983 | 1984 | 1985 |
|---|---|---|---|---|---|---|---|
| Consumer price index | 104.1 | 117.9 | 129.2 | 141.2 | 150.7 | 156.0 | 167.1 |
| Monthly earnings index | | | | | | | |

*Household income and expenditure.* Average household size (1979) 6.4; average annual income per household: $A 2,575; sources of income: agriculture and other 61.2%, cash economy only 17.9%, agriculture only 14.9%, other 6.0%; expenditure (1983)[10]: food 45.5%, housing and household operations 11.5%, transportation 10.5%, alcohol and tobacco 10.5%, clothing 7.5%, other 14.5%.
*Land use* (1983): agricultural and under permanent cultivation 75%[11]; other 25%.

## Foreign trade

### Balance of trade (current prices)

| | 1979 | 1980 | 1981 | 1982 | 1983 | 1984 |
|---|---|---|---|---|---|---|
| $A '000 | −1,594 | −3,061 | −2,556 | −2,853 | −2,877 | −3,653 |
| % of total | 75.6% | 94.7% | 98.6% | 97.5% | 95.0% | 85.4% |

*Imports* (1984): $A 3,965,000 (food and live animals 24.8%, manufactured goods 22.0%, machinery and transport equipment 14.8%, petroleum and petroleum products 11.7%, chemicals 5.1%, beverages and tobacco 4.1%, animal and vegetable oils and fats 0.4%). *Major import sources:* Australia 38.9%; New Zealand 17.3%; United Kingdom 7.0%; Japan 4.7%; United States 3.0%.
*Exports* (1984): $A 312,000 (copra 80.0%, developed cinema film 20.0%). *Major export destinations* (1982): Fiji 47.5%; Australia 39.7%; New Zealand 5.3%.

## Transport and communications

*Transport.* Railroads: none. Roads (1985): total length 5 mi, 8 km (paved, none). Vehicles: passenger cars, n.a.; trucks and buses, n.a.[12] Merchant marine (1986): vessels (100 gross tons and over) 2; total deadweight tonnage 458. Air transport (1977): passenger arrivals (Funafuti) 1,443; cargo, n.a.; airports (1987) with scheduled flights 1.
*Communications.* Daily newspapers: none. Radio (1986): total number of receivers 2,200 (1 per 3.7 persons). Television: none. Telephones (1985): 150 (1 per 55 persons).

## Education and health

### Education (1984)

| | schools | teachers | students | student/ teacher ratio |
|---|---|---|---|---|
| Primary (age 6–14) | 11 | 61 | 1,349 | 22.1 |
| Secondary (age 12–18) | 1 | 15[13] | 243 | ... |
| Vocational[13] | 8 | 16 | 354 | 22.1 |
| Higher | — | — | — | — |

*Educational attainment* (1979). Percent of population age 25 and over having: no formal schooling 0.4%; primary education 93.0%; secondary 6.1%; higher 0.5%. *Literacy* (1983): total population literate 5,509 (95.5%); males literate 2,443 (95.5%); females literate 3,066 (95.5%).
*Health* (1985): physicians 4 (1 per 2,050 persons); hospital beds (1984) 36 (1 per 231 persons); infant mortality rate per 1,000 live births 35.0.
*Food:* daily per capita caloric intake, n.a.

## Military

*Total active duty personnel* (1986): There is a police force of 31 men.

---

[1]Includes one nonelective seat. [2]The value of the Tuvalu Dollar is pegged to the value of the Australian Dollar, which is also legal currency in Tuvalu. [3]Local government councils have been established on all islands except Niulakita. [4]Total includes 46 persons unaccounted for in island populations. [5]No consistent population trend is apparent because of seasonal and long-term emigration. [6]Employment in the cash economy only. Excludes 114 phosphate workers in Nauru and 255 people employed on foreign ships. [7]Because of poor soil quality, only limited subsistence agriculture is possible on the islands. [8]Other livestock include goats. [9]Based on indigenous de facto population only. [10]Weights of consumer price index components. [11]Capable of supporting coconut palms, pandanus, and breadfruit. [12]There are several cars, tractors, trailers, and light lorries on Funafuti; a few motorcycles are in use on most islands. [13]1982–83.

# Uganda

*Official name:* Republic of Uganda.
*Form of government:* republic[1].
*Chief of state:* President.
*Head of government:* Prime Minister.
*Capital:* Kampala.
*Official language:* English.
*Official religion:* none.
*Monetary unit:* 1 Uganda
shilling (U Sh) = 100 cents;
valuation (Oct. 5, 1987)
1 U.S.$ = U Sh 60.00[2];
1 £ = U Sh 98.00.

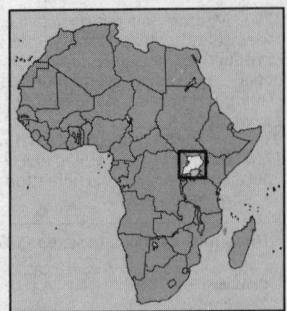

### Area and population

| Provinces Districts | Capitals | area sq mi | area sq km | population 1985 estimate |
|---|---|---|---|---|
| Busoga | Jinja | 7,030[3] | 18,200[3] | 1,408,600 |
| Iganga | Bulamogi | 5,060 | 13,110 | 755,100 |
| Jinja | Jinja | 280 | 730 | 253,400 |
| Kamuli | Namwendwa | 1,680 | 4,350 | 400,100 |
| Central | Kampala | 2,470 | 6,400 | 1,298,800 |
| Kampala | Kampala | 70 | 180 | 560,800 |
| Mpigi | Mpigi | 2,400 | 6,220 | 738,000 |
| Eastern | Mbale | 8,400[3] | 21,760 | 2,316,000 |
| Kapchorwa | Kaptanya | 670 | 1,740 | 83,100 |
| Kumi | Kumi | 1,100 | 2,860 | 273,100 |
| Mbale | Bunkoko | 980 | 2,550 | 647,400 |
| Soroti | Soroti | 3,880 | 10,060 | 545,300 |
| Tororo | Sukulu | 1,760 | 4,550 | 767,100 |
| Karamoja | Moroto | 10,550 | 27,320 | 405,600 |
| Kotido | Kotido | 5,100 | 13,210 | 194,700 |
| Moroto | Katikekile | 5,450 | 14,110 | 210,900 |
| Nile | Arua | 6,070 | 15,730 | 921,500 |
| Arua | Olaki | 3,020 | 7,830 | 543,300 |
| Moyo | Moyo | 1,930 | 5,010 | 119,600 |
| Nebbi | Nebbi | 1,120 | 2,890 | 258,600 |
| North Buganda | Bombo | 13,030 | 33,750 | 1,802,800 |
| Luwero | Luwero | 3,550 | 9,200 | 477,800 |
| Mubende | Bageza | 3,980 | 10,310 | 616,500 |
| Mukono | Kawuga Mukono | 5,500 | 14,240 | 708,500 |
| Northern | Gulu | 16,070[3] | 41,610[3] | 1,459,200 |
| Apac | Apac | 2,510 | 6,490 | 369,000 |
| Gulu | Bungatira | 4,530 | 11,740 | 305,500 |
| Kitgum | Labongo | 6,230 | 16,140 | 354,100 |
| Lira | Lira | 2,810 | 7,250 | 430,600 |
| South Buganda | Masaka | 8,220 | 21,300 | 1,071,200 |
| Masaka | Kaswa Bukoto | 6,300 | 16,330 | 741,600 |
| Rakai | Byakabanda | 1,920 | 4,970 | 329,600 |
| Southern | Mbarara | 8,290[3] | 21,480 | 2,270,500 |
| Bushenyi | Bumbaire | 2,080 | 5,400 | 600,300 |
| Kabale | Rubale | 960 | 2,490 | 503,700 |
| Mbarara | Kakika | 4,180 | 10,840 | 829,100 |
| Rukungiri | Kagunga | 1,060 | 2,750 | 337,400 |
| Western | Butebe | 12,910 | 33,440 | 1,725,600 |
| Bundibugyo | Busaru | 900 | 2,340 | 134,500 |
| Hoima | Hoima | 3,820 | 9,900 | 358,400 |
| Kabarole | Karambe | 3,230 | 8,360 | 630,500 |
| Kasese | Rukoki | 1,240 | 3,200 | 342,400 |
| Masindi | Nyangeya | 3,720 | 9,640 | 259,800 |
| TOTAL LAND AREA | | 76,080 | 197,040 | 14,679,800 |
| INLAND WATER[4] | | 16,990 | 44,000 | |
| TOTAL | | 93,070[3] | 241,040[3] | |

## Demography

*Population* (1987): 15,514,000.
*Density*[5] (1987): persons per sq mi 203.9, persons per sq km 78.7.
*Urban–rural* (1985): urban 14.4%; rural 85.6%.
*Sex distribution* (1985): male 49.54%; female 50.46%.
*Age breakdown* (1985): under 15, 48.5%; 15–29, 25.8%; 30–44, 14.1%; 45–59, 7.4%; 60–74, 3.6%; 75 and over, 0.6%.
*Population projection:* (1990) 16,948,000; (2000) 22,400,000.
*Doubling time:* 21 years.
*Ethnic composition* (1983): Ganda 17.8%; Teso 8.9%; Nkole 8.2%; Soga 8.2%; Gisu 7.2%; Chiga 6.8%; Lango 6.0%; Rwanda 5.8%; Acholi 4.6%; other 26.5%.
*Religious affiliation* (1980): Roman Catholic 49.6%; Protestant 28.7%; Muslim 6.6%; other 15.1%.
*Major cities* (1980): Kampala 458,503; Jinja 45,060; Masaka 29,123; Mbale 28,039; Mbarara 23,160.

## Vital statistics

*Birth rate* per 1,000 population (1984): 50.0 (world avg. 29.0).
*Death rate* per 1,000 population (1984): 16.0 (world avg. 11.0).
*Natural increase rate* per 1,000 population (1984): 34.0 (world avg. 18.0).
*Total fertility rate* (avg. births per childbearing woman; 1984): 6.9.
*Life expectancy* at birth (1984): male 49.0 years; female 53.0 years.
*Major causes of death* per 100,000 population: n.a.; however, major diseases include malaria, measles, venereal diseases, and dysentery.

## National economy

*Budget* (1987–88). Revenue: U Sh 44,700,000,000 (direct taxes 62.0%, others [mostly loans and grants] 38.0%). Expenditures[6]: U Sh 53,200,000,000 (percentage breakdown not available).
*Tourism:* receipts from visitors (1984) U.S.$8,000,000; expenditures by nationals abroad (1983) U.S.$10,000,000.
*Population economically active* (1985): total 5,866,000; activity rate of total population 40.0% (participation rates: ages 15–64, 80.4[7]; female 33.2%).

### Price index (1981 = 100)

| | 1980 | 1981 | 1982 | 1983 | 1984 | 1985 | 1986 |
|---|---|---|---|---|---|---|---|
| Consumer price index | 83.2 | 100.0 | 200.3 | 248.3 | 343.3 | 799.8 | 2,217.8 |

*Production* (metric tons except as noted). Agriculture, forestry, fishing (1985): bananas 7,330,000, cassava 4,000,000, sweet potatoes 2,000,000, millet 500,000, sugarcane 420,000, corn (maize) 400,000, sorghum 400,000, pulses 312,000, coffee 210,000, peanuts 100,000; livestock: 5,200,000 cattle, 2,600,000 goats, 1,500,000 sheep; roundwood 12,488,000 cu m; fish catch (1984) 212,100. Mining and quarrying (1984): copper ore (metal content) 1,100. Manufacturing (1985): meat 166,000; cement 30,000[8]; tea 7,000; raw sugar 6,000; soap and detergents 200[9]; fabrics 14,304,000 sq m[8]; cigarettes 965,000,000 units[8]; beer 148,160 hectolitres[8]. Construction: n.a. Energy production (consumption): electricity (kW-hr; 1985) 653,000,000 (621,000,-000); petroleum products (metric tons; 1985) none (213,000).
*Gross national product* (1984): U.S.$3,290,000,000 (U.S.$230 per capita).

### Structure of gross domestic product and labour force

| | 1982 in value U Sh '000,000 | 1982 % of total value | 1980 labour force | 1980 % of labour force |
|---|---|---|---|---|
| Agriculture | 99,257 | 75.8 | 5,290,000 | 85.9 |
| Manufacturing and mining | 5,310 | 4.2 | | |
| Construction | 594 | 0.4 | 272,000 | 4.4 |
| Public utilities | 451 | 0.3 | | |
| Transp. and commun. | 2,353 | 1.8 | | |
| Trade | 6,796 | 5.2 | | |
| Finance | 7,526 | 5.7 | 600,000 | 9.7 |
| Pub. admin., defense | 6,697 | 5.1 | | |
| Services | 2,010 | 1.5 | | |
| TOTAL | 130,994 | 100.0 | 6,162,000 | 100.0 |

*Public debt* (external, outstanding; 1985): U.S.$725,900,000.
*Household size.* Average household size (1980) 5.2; income per household: n.a.; expenditure[10] (1981): food 58.0%, clothing 14.0%, transportation 10.0%, fuel and lighting 6.0%.
*Land use* (1984): forested 29.3%; meadows and pastures 25.0%; agricultural and under permanent cultivation 32.6%; other 13.1%.

## Foreign trade

### Balance of trade (current prices)

| | 1979 | 1980 | 1981 | 1982 | 1983 | 1984 |
|---|---|---|---|---|---|---|
| U Sh '000,000 | +2,068 | +818 | +3,347 | +858 | +6,997 | +27,245 |
| % of total | 46.7% | 19.0% | 12.1% | 1.3% | 6.3% | 10.9% |

*Imports* (1984): U Sh 111,508,000,000 (sugar 16.0%, motor vehicles 10.8%, clothing and fabrics 9.6%, construction materials 8.0%, food 5.4%). *Major import sources* (1983): Kenya and Tanzania 29.0%; West Germany 8.6%; United Kingdom 8.2%; India 4.7%.
*Exports* (1984): U Sh 138,753,000,000 (unroasted coffee 91.8%). *Major export destinations* (1983): United States 27.0%; United Kingdom 10.9%; France 9.6%; West Germany 9.3%; Spain 8.8%; Japan 4.4%.

## Transport and communications

*Transport.* Railroads (1986): route length 1,286 km; passengers (1984) 2,100,000; cargo 331,000 metric tons. Roads (1985): total length 28,372 km (paved 22%). Vehicles (1985): passenger cars 32,155. Merchant marine (1986): vessels (100 gross tons and over) 3; total deadweight tonnage 8,600. Air transport[11] (1985): passenger-km 75,828,000; metric ton-km cargo 17,-927,000; airports (1987) 5.
*Communications.* Daily newspapers (1986): total number 1; total circulation 25,000; circulation per 1,000 population 1.6. Radio (1986): 600,000 receivers (1 per 26 persons). Television (1986): 90,000 receivers (1 per 174 persons). Telephones (1983): 54,439 (1 per 260 persons).

## Education and health

### Education (1984)

| | schools | teachers | students | student/ teacher ratio |
|---|---|---|---|---|
| Primary (age 5–11) | 6,420 | 58,377 | 1,908,564 | 32.7 |
| Secondary (age 12–15) | 297 | 5,603 | 114,828 | 20.5 |
| Voc., teacher tr. | 118 | 1,039 | 23,335 | 22.5 |
| Higher | 14 | 934 | 8,216 | 8.8 |

*Educational attainment* (1969). Percent of population age 25 and over having: no formal schooling, or less than one full year 58.2%; primary education 33.9%; lower secondary 5.0%; upper secondary 2.5%; higher 0.4%.
*Literacy* (1985): population age 15 and over literate 4,822,000 (57.0%); males literate 2,880,000 (69.7%); females literate 1,942,000 (45.3%).
*Health:* physicians (1982) 665 (1 per 20,562 persons); hospital beds (1983) 20,343 (1 per 683 persons); infant mortality rate (1984) 110.0.
*Food* (1981–83): daily per capita caloric intake 2,320 (vegetable products 94%, animal products 6%); (1983) 101% of FAO recommended minimum.

## Military

*Total active duty personnel* (1985): 18,000 (army 100%). *Military expenditure as percent of GNP* (1984): 1.1% (world 5.9%); per capita expenditure U.S.$5.

[1]Constitution of 1967 suspended July 1985; National Assembly [156 seats] dissolved July 1985 and a Council of National Resistance [25 members] established (Feb. 1986). [2]In May 1987 the Uganda shilling was fixed at a par value of U Sh 60.00 to 1 $U.S. [3]Detail does not add to total given because of rounding. [4]Includes swamps. [5]Based on land area. [6]Includes U Sh 26,400,000,000 of capital expenditures for development. [7]1980. [8]1984. [9]1982. [10]Middle income families only. [11]Uganda Airlines only.

# Union of Soviet Socialist Republics

*Official name:* Soyuz Sovetskykh Sotsialisticheskikh Respublik (Sovetsky Soyuz) (Union of Soviet Socialist Republics [Soviet Union]).
*Form of government:* federal socialist republic with one legislative house (Supreme Soviet) comprising two chambers (Soviet of the Union [750] and Soviet of the Nationalities [750]).
*Chief of state:* President (Chairman of the Supreme Soviet).
*Head of government:* Premier (Chairman of the Council of Ministers).
*Capital:* Moscow.
*Official language:* Russian.
*Official religion:* none.
*Monetary unit:* 1 ruble = 100 kopecks; valuation (Oct. 5, 1987) 1 ruble = U.S.$1.69 = £1.04.

| Area and population | | area | | population |
|---|---|---|---|---|
| Soviet Federated Socialist Republic | Capitals | sq mi | sq km | 1986 estimate |
| Russian S.F.S.R. | Moscow | 6,592,800 | 17,075,400 | 144,080,000 |
| Soviet Socialist Republics | | | | |
| Armenian | Yerevan | 11,500 | 29,800 | 3,362,000 |
| Azerbaijan | Baku | 33,400 | 86,600 | 6,708,000 |
| Belorussian | Minsk | 80,200 | 207,600 | 10,008,000 |
| Estonian | Tallinn | 17,400 | 45,100 | 1,542,000 |
| Georgian | Tbilisi | 26,900 | 69,700 | 5,234,000 |
| Kazakh | Alma-Ata | 1,049,200 | 2,717,300 | 16,028,000 |
| Kirgiz | Frunze | 76,600 | 198,500 | 4,051,000 |
| Latvian | Riga | 24,600 | 63,700 | 2,622,000 |
| Lithuanian | Vilnius | 25,200 | 65,200 | 3,603,000 |
| Moldavian | Kishinyov | 13,000 | 33,700 | 4,147,000 |
| Tadzhik | Dushanbe | 55,300 | 143,100 | 4,648,000 |
| Turkmen | Ashkhabad | 188,500 | 488,100 | 3,270,000 |
| Ukrainian | Kiev | 233,100 | 603,700 | 50,994,000 |
| Uzbek | Tashkent | 172,700 | 447,400 | 18,487,000 |
| TOTAL LAND AREA | | 8,600,400 | 22,274,900 | 278,784,000 |
| INLAND WATER | | 49,100 | 127,300 | |
| TOTAL | | 8,649,500 | 22,402,200 | |

## Demography

*Population* (1987): 282,811,000.
*Density*[1] (1987): persons per sq mi 32.9, persons per sq km 12.7.
*Urban–rural* (1986): urban 65.6%; rural 34.4%.
*Sex distribution* (1986): male 46.98%; female 53.02%.
*Age breakdown* (1985): under 15, 24.8%; 15–29, 24.8%; 30–44, 18.4%; 45–59, 18.9%; 60–74, 9.4%; 75 and over, 3.7%.
*Population projection:* (1990) 290,761,000; (2000) 318,909,000.
*Doubling time:* 74 years.
*Ethnic composition* (1983): Russian 51.9%; Ukrainian 15.8%; Uzbek 5.1%; Belorussian 3.6%; Kazakh 2.6%; Tatar 2.4%; Azerbaijani 2.2%; Armenian 1.7%; Georgian 1.4%; Tadzhik 1.2%; Moldavian 1.1%; Lithuanian 1.1%; other 9.9%.
*Religious affiliation* (1987): Christian 36.4%, of which Orthodox 31.5%, Protestant 3.1%, Roman Catholic 1.8%; Muslim 11.2%; Jewish 1.1%; nonreligious 29.7%; atheist 21.4%; other 0.2%.
*Major cities* (1986): Moscow 8,714,000; Leningrad 4,904,000; Kiev 2,495,000; Tashkent 2,077,000; Baku 1,722,000; Kharkov 1,567,000; Minsk 1,510,000; Gorky 1,409,000; Novosibirsk 1,405,000; Sverdlovsk 1,315,000; Kuybyshev 1,267,000; Tbilisi 1,174,000; Dnepropetrovsk 1,166,000.

| Other principal cities (1986) | | | | | |
|---|---|---|---|---|---|
| | population | | population | | population |
| Alma-Ata | 1,088,000 | Krasnoyarsk | 885,000 | Tolyatti | 610,000 |
| Barnaul | 586,000 | Krivoy Rog | 691,000 | Tula | 534,000 |
| Chelyabinsk | 1,107,000 | Lvov | 753,000 | Ufa | 1,077,000 |
| Donetsk | 1,081,000 | Novokuznetsk | 583,000 | Ulyanovsk | 566,000 |
| Dushanbe | 567,000 | Odessa | 1,132,000 | Ustinov | 620,000 |
| Frunze | 617,000 | Omsk | 1,122,000 | Vilnius | 555,000 |
| Irkutsk | 601,000 | Orenburg | 527,000 | Vladivostok | 608,000 |
| Karaganda | 624,000 | Penza | 532,000 | Volgograd | 981,000 |
| Kazan | 1,057,000 | Perm | 1,065,000 | Voronezh | 860,000 |
| Kemerovo | 514,000 | Riga | 890,000 | Yaroslavl | 630,000 |
| Khabarovsk | 584,000 | Rostov-na-Donu | 992,000 | Yerevan | 1,148,000 |
| Kishinyov | 643,000 | Samarkand | 580,000 | Zaporozhye | 863,000 |
| Krasnodar | 615,000 | Saratov | 907,000 | Zhdanov | 525,000 |

*Place of birth* (1983): 99.9% native-born; 0.1% foreign-born.
*Mobility* (1985). Population living in the same residence from birth: 57.0%; 15 years and more 20.1%; 14–10 years 5.7%; 9–6 years 5.1%; 5–2 years 7.2%; less than 2 years 4.9%.
*Households*[2] (1979). Average household size 3.5; 2 persons 29.7%, 3 persons 28.8%, 4 persons 23.0%, 5 persons 9.5%, 6 persons 4.1%, 7 or more persons 4.9%. Family households population: 232,075,245 (86.9%), nonfamily population 30,360,755 (13.1%).
*Emigration:* (1985) 1,140; (1979) 51,230.

## Vital statistics

*Birth rate* per 1,000 population (1986): 19.6 (world avg. 26.0); legitimate, n.a.; illegitimate, n.a.
*Death rate* per 1,000 population (1986): 9.7 (world avg. 9.9).
*Natural increase rate* per 1,000 population (1986): 9.9 (world avg. 16.1).
*Total fertility rate* (avg. births per childbearing woman; 1984): 2.3.
*Marriage rate* per 1,000 population (1985): 9.8.
*Divorce rate* per 1,000 population (1985): 3.4.
*Life expectancy* at birth (1986): male 64.0 years; female 73.0 years.
*Major causes of death* per 100,000 population (1983): diseases of the circulatory system 554.3, of which cardiovascular atherosclerosis 228.2, cerebrovascular disease 121.6, hypertensive heart disease 82.7, ischemic heart disease 73.0, other diseases of the circulatory system 48.8; malignant neoplasms (cancers) 148.1.

## Social indicators

*Educational attainment* (1984). Percent of population age 10 and over having: less than full primary education 0.2%; primary or secondary 91.0%, of which secondary 60.4%; some postsecondary and higher 8.2%; postgraduate 0.6%.
*Distribution of wealth:* n.a.
*Quality of working life* (1986). Average workweek: 39.0 hours (5.0% overtime). Annual rate per 100,000 workers for: injury or accident, n.a.; industrial illness, n.a.; death, n.a. Proportion of labour force insured for damages or income loss resulting from: injury 100.0%; permanent disability 100.0%; death 100.0%. Average days lost to labour stoppages per 1,000 workdays: n.a. Average duration of journey to work: 58–68 minutes (mostly by public transportation and foot). Rate per 1,000 workers of discouraged (unemployed no longer seeking work): n.a.
*Access to services*[3] (1985). Proportion of dwellings having access to: electricity, virtually 100%; safe public water supply 91.8%; public sewage collection 89.7%; central heating 88.9%; gas 78.3%; hot water 71.2%; bathroom 83.2%.
*Social participation.* Eligible voters participating in last national election (1984): 99.9%. Population participating in voluntary work (1984): 76.5%. Trade union membership in total work force: 100.0%. Practicing religious population in total affiliated population: n.a; estimated at 10%.
*Social deviance.* Offense rate per 100,000 population for: murder, n.a.; rape, n.a.; other assault, n.a.; grand and auto theft, n.a.; burglary and housebreaking, n.a. Incidence per 100,000 in general population of: alcoholism, n.a.; drug and substance abuse (1986) 165; suicide, n.a.
*Leisure* (1985). Favourite leisure activities (annual attendance): movies 4,100,000,000; lectures 301,700,000; museums 186,000,000; concerts 138,-700,000; theatre 124,900,000.
*Material well-being* (1986). Households possessing: automobile, 15.0%; telephone 28.5%; television receiver 97.0%; refrigerator 91.0%; air conditioner, none; washing machine 70.0%; motorcyle 14.0%; bicycle 55.0%; tape recorder 37.0%.

## National economy

*Global social product* (at current market prices; 1985): U.S.$2,046,000,000,-000 (U.S.$7,400 per capita).

| Structure of net material product and labour force | | | | |
|---|---|---|---|---|
| | 1985 | | | |
| | in value '000,000,000 rubles | % of total value | labour force | % of labour force |
| Agriculture | 112.2 | 19.4 | 25,198,000 | 19.3 |
| Mining and manufacturing | 263.6 | 45.6 | 38,103,000 | 29.2 |
| Public utilities | | | 4,894,000 | 3.8 |
| Construction | 61.7 | 10.7 | 11,492,000 | 8.8 |
| Transp. and commun. | 35.1 | 6.1 | 12,549,000 | 9.6 |
| Trade | 105.1 | 18.2 | 10,031,000 | 7.7 |
| Finance | ... | ... | 679,000 | 0.5 |
| Pub. admin., defense | ... | ... | 2,633,000 | 2.0 |
| Services | ... | ... | 23,069,000 | 17.7 |
| Other | ... | ... | 1,622,000 | 1.2 |
| TOTAL | 577.7 | 100.0 | 130,300,000[4] | 100.0[4] |

*Public debt* (1985): U.S.$27,000,000,000.
*Land use* (1985): forested 35.7%; meadows and pastures 16.8%; agricultural and under permanent cultivation 10.2%; other 37.3%.

| Manufacturing, mining, and construction enterprises (1982) | | | | |
|---|---|---|---|---|
| | no. of enterprises | no. of employees | monthly wages as a % of avg. of all wages | annual gross output ('000,000 rubles) |
| Manufacturing | | | | |
| Machinery and metal products | 8,180 | 15,011,000 | 111.2 | 182,400 |
| Food products | 7,538 | 2,717,000 | 99.2 | 104,100 |
| Chemicals and chemical products | 1,493 | 1,148,000 | 112.8 | 75,500 |
| Textiles | 1,996 | 2,210,000 | 88.4 | 72,700 |
| Clothing | 5,118 | 2,250,000 | 88.4 | 30,900 |
| Nonmetallic products | 3,200 | 2,088,000 | 103.8 | 24,800 |
| Wood, furniture, and paper | 2,275 | 1,619,000 | 112.8 | 22,300 |
| Beverages | 1,726 | 374,000 | 95.5 | 7,700 |
| Iron and steel | 408 | 1,044,000 | 131.1 | 6,200 |
| Footwear | 406 | 494,000 | 95.8 | 5,500 |
| Leather and leather products | 266 | 199,000 | 95.9 | 4,200 |
| Tobacco | 88 | 40,000 | 95.5 | 3,800 |
| Glass and pottery | 333 | 376,000 | 99.3 | 3,300 |
| Building materials | 3,938 | ... | 107.1 | 2,300 |
| Rubber and plastic | ... | 433,000 | 103.5 | ... |
| Mining | | | | |
| Petroleum and gas | 853 | 1,105,000 | 161.1 | 34,400 |
| Coal | | | 153.9 | |
| Metal ores | 1,070 | 194,000 | 153.9 | 15,900 |
| Construction | ... | 11,299,000 | 103.3 | |

*Budget* (1985). Revenue: 390,600,000,000 rubles (share in profits of state enterprises 31.2%, turnover tax 25.0%, income tax 7.7%). Expenditures: 386,500,000,000 rubles (national economy 56.8%, education and science 12.8%, social welfare 8.2%, defense 4.9%, health 4.6%).

*Tourism:* tourist arrivals (1984) 7,249,000; tourists abroad (1982) 4,500,000.

*Production* (metric tons except as noted). Agriculture, forestry, fishing (1986): potatoes 87,200,000; sugar beets 79,300,000; wheat 78,100,000[5], barley 46,500,000; vegetables 29,700,000; oats 20,500,000; rye 15,700,000[5], corn (maize) 14,400,000[5]; flax fibre 9,200,000[5]; raw cotton 8,230,000; grapes 7,500,000[5], sunflower seeds 5,300,000; rice 2,510,000; tobacco 360,000[5]; livestock (number of live animals; 1987) 147,300,000 sheep, 121,900,000 cattle, 80,000,000 pigs, 6,500,000 goats, 5,800,000 horses, 1,143,000,000 poultry; roundwood 296,000,000 cu m; fish catch 10,700,000. Mining and quarrying (1986): iron ore 250,000,000; phosphate rock 76,900,000; salt 16,100,000; potash salts 9,600,000; bauxite 4,600,000; chromium ore 3,500,000; manganese (metal content) 2,800,000; magnesite 2,500,000; asbestos 2,700,000; zinc 810,000; copper 620,000; lead 440,000; nickel 185,000; molybdenum 11,400; tungsten 9,200; mercury 66,000 flasks; diamonds 10,900,000 carats. Manufacturing (1986): crude steel 161,000,000; cement 132,000,000; pig iron 114,000,000; rolled steel 112,000,000; mineral fertilizers 34,700,000; sulfuric acid 27,900,000; steel pipes 19,800,000; meat 17,900,000; sugar 12,700,000; paper and paperboard 6,200,000; canned fish 5,600,000; resins and plastics 5,300,000; soda ash 4,900,000; caustic soda 3,200,000; vegetable oil 2,900,-000; cotton fibre 2,750,000[5]; cotton yarn 1,710,000[5]; butter 1,515,000; man-made fibres 1,500,000; margarine 1,500,000; synthetic detergents 1,200,000; soap 1,100,000; insecticides 600,000; woolen yarn 465,000; woolen fibre 421,000[5]; flax fibre 214,000[5]; leather 127,000[5]; cotton fabrics 7,677,000,000 sq m; silk fabrics 1,936,000,000 sq m; linen fabrics 802,000,000 sq m; woolen fabrics 666,000,000 sq m; agricultural equipment 4,000,000,000 rubles; machine tools 2,900,000,000 rubles; food-processing equipment 1,800,000,000 rubles; chemical equipment 966,000,000 rubles; forge press machines 693,-000,000 rubles; oil equipment 247,000,000 rubles; leather footwear 801,000,-000 pairs; tires 66,000,000 units; television receivers 9,400,000 units; radio receivers 8,800,000 units; refrigerators 5,900,000 units; bicycles 5,500,000 units; washing machines 5,400,000 units; passenger cars 1,300,000 units; motorcycles 1,100,000 units; buses 85,315 units; railroad freight cars 58,433 units[5]; railroad passenger cars 1,814 units[5]; beer 42,952,000 hectolitres; wine 22,815,000 hectolitres. Construction (1986): residential 118,200,000 sq m, of which urban 115,800,000 sq m, rural 2,400,000 sq m.

### Service enterprises (1985)

| | no. of enter- prises | no. of employees | monthly wages as a % of all wages |
|---|---|---|---|
| Public utilities | ... | 3,957,000 | 77.1 |
| Electrical power | 1,517 | 937,000 | 116.7 |
| Transport: rail | ... | 2,639,000 | 111.1 |
| Transport: road | ... | 7,788,000 | 116.1 |
| Transport: water | ... | 451,000 | 138.3 |
| Communication | 91,600 | 1,671,000 | 83.9 |
| Finance | ... | 679,000 | 95.2 |
| Wholesale trade | } | | 78.5 |
| Retail trade | 709,900 } | 7,760,000 | 78.5 |
| Tourism | ... | ... | ... |
| Education | 183,000 | 9,887,000 | 78.9 |
| Public services and administration | ... | 2,663,000 | 87.5 |
| Other services | 292,900 | 13,182,000 | ... |

Energy production (consumption): electricity (kW-hr; 1986) 1,599,000,-000,000 (1,514,000,000,000[5]); coal (metric tons; 1986) 751,000,000 (679,-000,000[5]); crude petroleum (barrels; 1986) 4,616,000,000 (3,921,000,000[5]); petroleum products (metric tons; 1984) 409,260,000 (348,010,000); natural gas (cu m; 1986) 686,000,000,000 (536,000,000,000[5]).

*Population economically active* (1986): total 131,300,000; activity rate of total population 46.9% (participation rates: ages [male] 15–60, [female] 15–55, 51.8%; female 45.7%; unemployed, n.a.).

### Price and earnings indexes (1980 = 100)

| | 1979 | 1980 | 1981 | 1982 | 1983 | 1984 | 1985 |
|---|---|---|---|---|---|---|---|
| Consumer price index | 96.9 | 100.0 | 101.2 | 104.5 | 105.2 | 104.0 | 105.0 |
| Monthly earnings index | 97.3 | 100.0 | 102.3 | 105.4 | 107.3 | 108.8 | 109.2 |

*Household income and expenditure.* Average household size (1985) 3.2; average annual income per household 6,100 rubles (U.S.$8,700); sources of income: wages and salaries 70.1%, social welfare 24.2%, other 5.7%; expenditure (1985): food 29.8%, clothing 16.0%, education and culture 15.7%, taxes 8.3%, household durable goods 7.7%, housing 2.7%.

## Foreign trade

### Balance of trade (current prices)

| | 1979 | 1980 | 1981 | 1982 | 1983 | 1984 | 1985 |
|---|---|---|---|---|---|---|---|
| '000,000,000 rubles | 4.6 | 5.2 | 4.5 | 6.7 | 8.3 | 9.1 | 3.4 |
| % of total | 5.7% | 5.5% | 4.1% | 5.6% | 6.5% | 6.5% | 2.4% |

*Imports* (1985): 69,102,000,000 rubles (machinery and transport equipment 37.2%; cereals and food products 21.2%; consumer goods 12.4%; raw materials 8.4%; mineral fuels and lubricants 5.3%; chemicals and related products 5.0%; textiles and clothing 1.7%). *Major import sources:* East Germany 10.9%; Czechoslovakia 9.5%; Bulgaria 8.8%; Poland 8.0%; Hungary 7.0%; Cuba 6.0%; Yugoslavia 4.8%; West Germany 4.5%; Finland 3.9%; United States 3.4%; Japan 3.3%; Romania 3.3%; France 2.3%; India 2.2%.

*Exports* (1985): 72,464,000,000 rubles (crude petroleum and petroleum products 40.4%; machinery and transport equipment 13.6%; mineral fuels and natural gas 12.4%; raw materials 7.5%; chemicals, fertilizers, and resins 3.9%; wood and paper products 3.0%). *Major export destinations:* East

Germany 10.6%; Czechoslovakia 9.4%; Poland 9.0%; Bulgaria 8.9%; Hungary 6.3%; West Germany 5.5%; Cuba 5.3%; Yugoslavia 3.7%; Italy 3.4%; Finland 3.2%; France 3.0%; Romania 2.7%; India 2.2%; United Kingdom 1.7%; Vietnam 1.6%; Mongolia 1.5%; Belgium 1.2%; Afghanistan 0.8%.

### Trade by commodity group (1985)

| | | imports | | exports | |
|---|---|---|---|---|---|
| SITC Group | | '000 rubles | % | '000 rubles | % |
| 00 | Food and live animals | 14,650,000 | 21.2 | 1,087,000 | 1.5 |
| 02 | Raw materials, excluding fuels | 5,804,000 | 8.4 | 5,435,000 | 7.5 |
| 03 | Mineral fuels, lubricants, and related materials | 3,662,000 | 5.3 | 38,261,000 | 52.8 |
| 05 | Chemicals and related products | 3,455,000 | 5.0 | 2,826,000 | 3.9 |
| 65 | Textile yarn, fabrics and related materials | 1,175,000 | 1.7 | 942,000 | 1.3 |
| 07 | Machinery and transport equipment | 25,706,000 | 37.2 | 9,855,000 | 13.6 |
| 08 | Miscellaneous manufactured articles | 8,569,000 | 12.4 | 1,449,000 | 2.0 |
| 09 | Goods not classified by kind | 6,081,000 | 8.8 | 12,609,000 | 17.4 |
| TOTAL | | 69,102,000 | 100.0 | 72,464,000 | 100.0 |

### Direction of trade (1985)

| | imports | | exports | |
|---|---|---|---|---|
| | '000 rubles | % | '000 rubles | % |
| Communist | | | | |
| Comecon | 37,640,000 | 54.5 | 40,053,000 | 55.3 |
| Other | 4,570,000 | 6.6 | 4,231,000 | 5.8 |
| Market Economy | | | | |
| Industrial countries | 19,268,000 | 27.9 | 18,579,000 | 25.6 |
| Developing countries | 7,624,000 | 11.0 | 9,601,000 | 13.3 |
| TOTAL | 69,102,000 | 100.0 | 72,464,000 | 100.0 |

## Transport and communications

*Transport.* Railroads (1986): length 90,037 mi, 144,900 km; passenger-mi 242,000,000,000, passenger-km 390,000,000,000; short ton-mi cargo 2,547,-000,000,000, metric ton-km cargo 3,718,400,000,000. Roads (1986): total length 604,000 mi, 971,500 km (paved 84%). Vehicles (1980): passenger cars 8,255,000; trucks and buses 7,254,000. Inland waterways (1986): length 78,670 mi, 126,600 km; passenger-mi 3,670,000,000[5], passenger-km 5,900,000,000[5]; short ton-mi cargo 179,100,000,000, metric ton-km cargo 261,500,000,000. Merchant marine (1986): vessels (100 gross tons and over) 6,726; total deadweight tonnage 28,145,633. Air transport (1986): passenger-mi 121,800,000,000, passenger-km 196,000,000,000; short ton-mi cargo 2,294,000,000[5], metric ton-km cargo 3,350,000,000[5]; airports (1987) with scheduled flights 52. Shares of domestic passenger traffic by mode of transportation (1985): buses 43.9%; railway 36.7%; ships and airplanes 19.4%. Oil and gas pipelines (1986): length 158,400 mi, 255,000 km; short ton-mi cargo 1,673,300,000,000[5], metric ton-km cargo 2,443,100,000,000[5].

### Distribution of traffic (1985)

| | cargo carried ('000,000 tons) | % of nat'l total | passengers carried ('000,000) | % of nat'l total |
|---|---|---|---|---|
| Road | 6,320.0 | 52.6 | 47,000.0 | 43.9 |
| Rail | 3,951.2 | 32.9 | 4,166.0 | 3.9 |
| Urban transport | — | — | 55,720.0 | 52.0 |
| road | — | — | 32,800.0 | 30.6 |
| rail | — | — | 22,920.0 | 21.4 |
| Inland water | 633.0 | 5.3 | 132.0 | 0.1 |
| Air | 3.1 | 0.0 | 112.6 | 0.1 |
| Pipeline | 1,113.0 | 9.2 | — | — |
| TOTAL | 12,020.4[4] | 100.0 | 107,130.6 | 100.0 |

*Communications.* Daily newspapers (1986): total number 727; total circulation 96,414,000; circulation 1,000 population 345. Radio (1986): 182,790,000 receivers (1 per 1.5 persons). Television (1986): 82,400,000 receivers (1 per 3.4 persons). Telephones (1986): 31,100,000 (1 per 9.0 persons).

## Education and health

### Education (1985–86)

| | schools | teachers | students | student/ teacher ratio |
|---|---|---|---|---|
| Primary (age 6–13) | 66,800 | } 2,800,000 | 36,300,000 | ... |
| Secondary (age 14–17) | 60,900 | | 4,500,000 | ... |
| Vocational | 4,495 | 246,000 | 2,866,000 | 11.7 |
| Higher | 894 | 377,000 | 2,763,000 | 7.3 |

*Literacy* (1984): total population age 15 and over literate 99.0%.
*Health* (1987): physicians 1,202,000[6] (1 per 239 persons); hospital beds 3,669,000 (1 per 77 persons); infant mortality rate per 1,000 live births (1986) 26.0.
*Food* (1985): daily per capita caloric intake 3,390 (vegetable products 74%, animal products 26%); (1983) 132% of FAO recommended minimum.

## Military

*Total active duty personnel* (1987): 5,130,000 (army 38.8%, command and general support troops 28.4%, paramilitary forces 11.1%, navy 8.8%, air force 8.8%, forces abroad 4.1%). *Military expenditure as percent of GDP* (1986): 12–17%[7] (world [1984] 5.9%); per capita expenditure (1984) U.S.$1,000.

[1]Based on land area. [2]Family households only. [3]Only urban dwellings. [4]Detail does not add to total given because of rounding. [5]1985. [6]Includes dentists. [7]Estimated by Western sources.

# United Arab Emirates

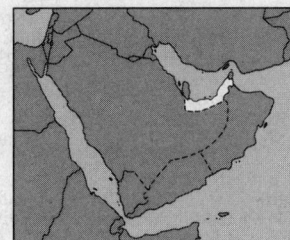

*Official name:* Ittiḥād al-Imārāt al-'Arabīyah (United Arab Emirates).
*Form of government:* monarchy; federal union of seven emirates with one legislative house (Federal National Council [40][1]).
*Chief of state:* President.
*Head of government:* Prime Minister.
*Capital:* Abu Dhabi[2].
*Official language:* Arabic.
*Official religion:* Islam.
*Monetary unit:* 1 U.A.E. Dirham (Dh) = 100 fils; valuation (Oct. 5, 1987) 1 U.S.$ = Dh 3.67; 1 £ = Dh 5.96.

### Area and population

| Emirates | Capitals | area sq mi | area sq km | population 1985 census |
|---|---|---|---|---|
| Abu Dhabi (Abū Ẓaby) | Abu Dhabi | 26,000 | 67,350 | 670,125 |
| Ajman ('Ajmān) | Ajman | 100 | 250 | 64,318 |
| Dubai (Dubayy) | Dubai | 1,510 | 3,900 | 419,104 |
| Fujairah (Al-Fujayrah) | Fujairah | 440 | 1,150 | 54,425 |
| Ras al-Khaimah (Ra's al-Khaymah) | Ras al-Khaimah | 660 | 1,700 | 116,470 |
| Sharjah (Ash-Shāriqah) | Sharjah | 1,000 | 2,600 | 268,722 |
| Umm al-Qaiwain (Umm al-Qaywayn) | Umm al-Qaiwain | 290 | 750 | 29,229 |
| TOTAL | | 30,000 | 77,700 | 1,622,393 |

## Demography

*Population* (1987): 1,856,000.
*Density* (1987): persons per sq mi 61.9, persons per sq km 23.9.
*Urban–rural* (1985): urban 77.8%; rural 22.2%.
*Sex distribution* (1985): male 67.82%; female 32.18%.
*Age breakdown* (1985): under 15, 31.0%; 15–29, 25.5%; 30–44, 31.0%; 45–59, 9.5%; 60–74, 2.4%; 75 and over, 0.6%.
*Population projection:* (1990) 2,419,000; (2000) 5,849,000.
*Doubling time:* 27 years.
*Ethnic composition* (1983): Arab 87.1%, of which Arab from United Arab Emirates 30.7%; Pakistani and Indian 9.1%; Persian 1.7%; Baluchi 0.8%; African 0.8%; British 0.2%; American 0.1%; other 0.2%.
*Religious affiliation* (1980): Muslim 94.9% (Sunnī 80%, Shī'ī 20%); Christian 3.8%; other 1.3%.
*Major cities* (1980): Dubai 266,000; Abu Dhabi 243,000; Sharjah 125,000; al-'Ayn 102,000; Ras al-Khaimah 42,000.

## Vital statistics

*Birth rate* per 1,000 population (1980–85): 29.8 (world avg. 29.0); legitimate, n.a.; illegitimate, n.a.
*Death rate* per 1,000 population (1980–85): 4.3 (world avg. 11.0).
*Natural increase rate* per 1,000 population (1980–85): 25.5 (world avg. 18.0).
*Total fertility rate* (avg. births per childbearing woman; 1980–85): 5.9.
*Marriage rate* per 1,000 population (1984): 3.3[3].
*Divorce rate* per 1,000 population (1984): 1.4[3].
*Life expectancy* at birth (1980–85): male 65.4 years; female 69.8 years.
*Major causes of death* per 100,000 population (1985)[3]: accident and poisonings 48.9; cardiovascular diseases 45.1; malignant neoplasms (cancers) 22.1; congenital anomalies 19.1; respiratory diseases 12.5.

## National economy

*Budget* (1987). Revenue: U.S.$7,250,000,000 (oil revenue 85.5%). Expenditures: U.S.$9,000,000,000 (current expenditure 64.4%, development 16.7%).
*Gross national product* (at current market prices; 1985): U.S.$26,400,000,000 (U.S.$16,970 per capita).

### Structure of gross domestic product and labour force

| | 1984 in value Dh '000,000 | % of total value | labour force | % of labour force |
|---|---|---|---|---|
| Agriculture | 1,349 | 1.4 | 35,895 | 4.9 |
| Mining | 46,958 | 46.6 | 14,866 | 2.0 |
| Manufacturing | 9,965 | 9.9 | 47,178 | 6.4 |
| Construction | 10,100 | 10.0 | 187,720 | 25.4 |
| Public utilities | 2,021 | 2.0 | 14,082 | 1.9 |
| Transportation and communication | 4,369 | 4.3 | 54,530 | 7.4 |
| Trade | 8,710 | 8.7 | 99,722 | 13.5 |
| Finance | 10,508 | 10.4 | 21,920 | 3.0 |
| Pub. admin., defense | 10,069 | 10.0 | ... | ... |
| Services | 1,604 | 1.6 | 260,520 | 35.3 |
| Other | −4,943[4] | −4.9[4] | 1,545[5] | 0.2[5] |
| TOTAL | 100,710 | 100.0 | 737,978 | 100.0 |

*Public debt* (external, outstanding; 1982): U.S.$1,117,000,000.
*Production* (metric tons except as noted). Agriculture, forestry, fishing (1985): tomatoes 80,000, dates 60,000, watermelons 30,000, cantaloupes and other melons 18,000, cabbages 15,000, cucumbers and gherkins 13,000, eggplants 11,000, pumpkins and squash 10,000, cauliflowers 9,000, lemons and limes 5,000, mangoes 4,000, eggs 4,000, green peppers 3,000, livestock (number of live animals) 450,000 goats, 155,000 sheep, 70,000 camels, 31,000 cattle, 4,000,000 chickens; fish catch 72,380. Mining and quarrying (1985): lime 45,000; also marble, shale for ceramic applications, and aggregate

for cement. Manufacturing (1985): cement 4,050,000; aluminum 156,000; sulfur 1,460; mutton and lamb meat 5,000; cow milk 5,000; beef and veal meat 3,000; goat meat 2,000; butter and ghee 156. Construction (value added in Dh; 1982): 11,015,000,000. Energy production (consumption): electricity (kW-hr; 1985) 6,690,000,000 (6,690,000,000); coal, none (n.a.); crude petroleum (barrels; 1985) 435,291,000 (49,742,000); petroleum products (metric tons; 1985) 10,958,000 (5,884,000); natural gas (cu m; 1985) 3,844,050,000 (800,844,000).
*Tourism* (1983): 16,351 rooms for tourists.
*Population economically active* (1984): total 737,978; activity rate of total population 54.5% (participation rates: over age 15, 76.1%; female 18.3%; unemployed, n.a.).
*Price and earnings indexes:* n.a.
*Household income and expenditure:* Average household size (1980) 3.8; income per household: n.a.; sources of income: n.a.; expenditure: n.a.
*Land use* (1984): forested, none; meadows and pastures 2.4%; agricultural and under permanent cultivation 0.2%; built-up, wasteland, and other 97.4%.

## Foreign trade

### Balance of trade (current prices)

| | 1980 | 1981 | 1982 | 1983 | 1984 | 1985 |
|---|---|---|---|---|---|---|
| Dh '000,000 | +25,673 | +14,668 | +18,187 | +24,430 | +27,238 | +25,516 |
| % of total | 32.6% | 26.1% | 31.6% | 28.5% | 36.7% | 36.0% |

*Imports* (1984): Dh 25,856,000,000 (machinery and transport equipment 32.3%, basic manufactures 22.8%, food and live animals 13.5%, mineral fuels 7.8%, chemicals 5.6%, crude minerals 1.9%). *Major import sources:* Japan 17.8%; United States 12.1%; United Kingdom 9.9%; Italy 7.1%; West Germany 6.7%; Bahrain 5.4%; France 4.6%; The Netherlands 2.8%; Australia 2.3%; Singapore 1.7%; China 1.6%; Belgium–Luxembourg 1.5%; Switzerland 1.4%; Saudi Arabia 0.9%; Thailand 0.9%; Turkey 0.6%.
*Exports* (1984): Dh 50,743,000,000 (crude petroleum 87.1%, nonpetroleum exports 12.9%). *Major export destinations:* Japan 49.4%; United States 8.2%; France 6.0%; Singapore 4.2%; Oman 3.1%; Italy 2.5%; Pakistan 2.1%; West Germany 1.8%; Australia 1.5%; Saudi Arabia 1.1%; Portugal 1.1%; Bangladesh 0.8%; United Kingdom 0.8%; The Netherlands 0.4%; Belgium–Luxembourg 0.3%; Bahrain 0.2%.

## Transport and communications

*Transport.* Railroads: none. Roads (1984): total length 2,709 mi, 4,360 km (paved [1981] 61%). Vehicles (1984): passenger cars 61,146; trucks and buses 16,618. Merchant marine (1986): vessels (100 gross tons and over) 220; total deadweight tonnage 1,018,926. Air transport (1983): passenger-mi 2,213,000,000, passenger-km 3,562,000,000; short ton-mi cargo 65,300,000, metric ton-km cargo 95,300,000; airports (1987) with scheduled flights 2.
*Communications.* Daily newspapers (1986): total number 12; total circulation 291,000; circulation per 1,000 population 171. Radio (1986): total number of receivers 434,000 (1 per 3.9 persons). Television (1986): total number of receivers 145,000 (1 per 12 persons). Telephones (1984): 308,793 (1 per 4.6 persons).

## Education and health

### Education (1985–86)

| | schools | teachers | students | student/ teacher ratio |
|---|---|---|---|---|
| Primary (age 6–11) Secondary (age 12–18) | 327 | 6,123[6] 3,967[6] | 152,125 61,468 | ... ... |
| Vocational[7] | 9 | 273 | 2,442 | 8.9 |
| Higher[8] | ... | 449 | 6,326 | 14.1 |

*Educational attainment* (1975). Percent of population age 25 and over having: no formal schooling 72.2%; primary education 5.2%; secondary 16.6%; higher 6.0%. *Literacy* (1984): total population age 15 and over literate 689,845 (71.2%); males literate 534,182 (72.7%); females literate 155,663 (66.3%).
*Health* (1984): physicians 1,840 (1 per 666 persons); hospital beds 4,853 (1 per 252 persons); infant mortality rate per 1,000 live births (1985) 35.0.
*Food* (1981–83): daily per capita caloric intake 3,635 (vegetable products 75%, animal products 25%); (1983) 150% of FAO recommended minimum requirement.

## Military

*Total active duty personnel* (1986): 43,000 (army 93.0%, navy 3.5%, air force 3.5%). *Military expenditure as percent of GNP* (1984): 7.4% (world 5.9%); per capita expenditure U.S.$1,357.

---

[1]All appointed seats. [2]Provisional. [3]Abu Dhabi Emirate only. [4]Includes imputed bank service charge and subsidies. [5]Unemployed seeking work for the first time. [6]Public schools only. [7]1983–84. [8]1984–85.

# United Kingdom

*Official name:* United Kingdom of Great Britain and Northern Ireland.
*Form of government:* constitutional monarchy with two legislative houses (House of Lords [1,180]; House of Commons [650]).
*Chief of state:* Sovereign.
*Head of government:* Prime Minister.
*Capital:* London.
*Official language:* English.
*Official religion:* Churches of England and Scotland "established" (protected and maintained by the state, but not "official") in their respective countries; no established church in Northern Ireland or Wales.
*Monetary unit:* 1 pound sterling (£) = 100 new pence; valuation (Oct. 5, 1987) 1 £ = U.S.$1.62.

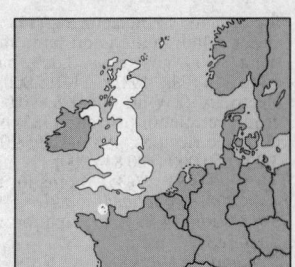

| Area and population | | area | | population |
|---|---|---|---|---|
| | | sq mi | sq km | 1986 estimate |
| **Countries** | **Capitals** | | | |
| England | London | 50,363 | 130,439 | 47,254,500 |
| **Counties** | | | | |
| Avon | | 520 | 1,346 | 946,600 |
| Bedfordshire | | 477 | 1,235 | 521,000 |
| Berkshire | | 486 | 1,259 | 734,100 |
| Buckinghamshire | | 727 | 1,883 | 612,900 |
| Cambridgeshire | | 1,316 | 3,409 | 635,200 |
| Cheshire | | 899 | 2,329 | 946,500 |
| Cleveland | | 225 | 583 | 557,600 |
| Cornwall[1] | | 1,376 | 3,564 | 448,200 |
| Cumbria | | 2,629 | 6,810 | 486,600 |
| Derbyshire | | 1,016 | 2,631 | 916,800 |
| Devon | | 2,591 | 6,711 | 999,000 |
| Dorset | | 1,025 | 2,654 | 638,200 |
| Durham | | 941 | 2,436 | 599,600 |
| East Sussex | | 693 | 1,795 | 689,700 |
| Essex | | 1,418 | 3,672 | 1,512,100 |
| Gloucestershire | | 1,020 | 2,643 | 517,100 |
| Greater London[2] | | 610 | 1,579 | 6,775,200 |
| Greater Manchester[2] | | 497 | 1,287 | 2,579,500 |
| Hampshire | | 1,458 | 3,777 | 1,527,700 |
| Hereford & Worcester | | 1,516 | 3,927 | 654,500 |
| Hertfordshire | | 631 | 1,634 | 985,700 |
| Humberside | | 1,356 | 3,512 | 848,500 |
| Isle of Wight | | 147 | 381 | 124,600 |
| Kent | | 1,441 | 3,731 | 1,500,900 |
| Lancashire | | 1,183 | 3,064 | 1,380,700 |
| Leicestershire | | 986 | 2,553 | 875,000 |
| Lincolnshire | | 2,284 | 5,915 | 567,300 |
| Merseyside[2] | | 252 | 652 | 1,467,600 |
| Norfolk | | 2,073 | 5,368 | 727,800 |
| Northamptonshire | | 914 | 2,367 | 554,400 |
| Northumberland | | 1,943 | 5,032 | 301,000 |
| North Yorkshire | | 3,208 | 8,309 | 699,800 |
| Nottinghamshire | | 836 | 2,164 | 1,006,400 |
| Oxfordshire | | 1,007 | 2,608 | 574,700 |
| Shropshire | | 1,347 | 3,490 | 392,700 |
| Somerset | | 1,332 | 3,451 | 448,900 |
| South Yorkshire[2] | | 602 | 1,560 | 1,297,900 |
| Staffordshire | | 1,049 | 2,716 | 1,021,000 |
| Suffolk | | 1,466 | 3,797 | 628,600 |
| Surrey | | 648 | 1,679 | 1,011,400 |
| Tyne and Wear[2] | | 208 | 540 | 1,135,500 |
| Warwickshire | | 765 | 1,981 | 480,700 |
| West Midlands[2] | | 347 | 899 | 2,632,300 |
| West Sussex | | 768 | 1,989 | 694,700 |
| West Yorkshire[2] | | 787 | 2,039 | 2,053,100 |
| Wiltshire | | 1,344 | 3,480 | 545,200 |
| Northern Ireland[3] | Belfast | 5,452 | 14,120 | 1,567,000 |
| Scotland | Edinburgh | 30,418[4] | 78,783 | 5,121,000 |
| **Regions** | | | | |
| Borders | | 1,814 | 4,698 | 101,800 |
| Central | | 1,042 | 2,700 | 271,800 |
| Dumfries and Galloway | | 2,481 | 6,425 | 146,800 |
| Fife | | 509 | 1,319 | 343,800 |
| Grampian | | 3,379 | 8,752 | 502,800 |
| Highland | | 10,092 | 26,137 | 200,800 |
| Lothian | | 683 | 1,770 | 741,900 |
| Strathclyde | | 5,318 | 13,773 | 2,344,600 |
| Tayside | | 2,951 | 7,643 | 392,400 |
| **Island areas[5]** (TOTAL) | | 2,149 | 5,566 | 74,300 |
| Wales | Cardiff | 8,019 | 20,768 | 2,821,000 |
| **Counties** | | | | |
| Clwyd | | 937 | 2,427 | 399,600 |
| Dyfed | | 2,227 | 5,768 | 339,000 |
| Gwent | | 531 | 1,376 | 441,800 |
| Gwynedd | | 1,494 | 3,869 | 234,600 |
| Mid Glamorgan | | 393 | 1,018 | 534,500 |
| Powys | | 1,960 | 5,077 | 112,400 |
| South Glamorgan | | 161 | 416 | 395,700 |
| West Glamorgan | | 316 | 817 | 363,400 |
| TOTAL | | 94,251 | 244,110 | 56,763,500 |

## Demography

*Population* (1987): 56,878,000.
*Density* (1987): persons per sq mi 603.5, persons per sq km 233.0.
*Urban-rural* (1985): urban 91.5%; rural 8.5%.
*Sex distribution* (1987): male 48.70%; female 51.30%.
*Age breakdown* (1987): under 15, 18.8%; 15–29, 23.7%; 30–44, 20.5%; 45–59, 16.2%; 60–74, 14.2%; 75 and over, 6.6%.
*Population projection:* (1990) 57,224,000; (2000) 58,392,000.

*Doubling time:* more than 100 years.
*Ethnic composition* (1985): white 94.4%; Asian Indian 1.3%; West Indian 1.0%; Pakistani 0.8%; African 0.2%; Chinese 0.2%; Bangladeshi 0.2%; Arab 0.1%; other and not stated 1.8%.
*Religious affiliation* (1980): Christian 86.9%, of which Anglican 56.8%, Roman Catholic 13.1%, Presbyterian 7.0%, Methodist 4.3%, Baptist 1.4%; Muslim 1.4%; Jewish 0.8%; Hindu 0.7%; Sikh 0.4%; nonreligious 8.8%; other 1.0%.
*Major cities* (1985): Greater London 6,767,500; Birmingham 1,008,000; Glasgow 733,800; Leeds 710,000; Sheffield 539,000; Liverpool 492,000; Bradford 464,400; Manchester 451,100; Edinburgh 439,700; Bristol 394,000.
*Place of birth* (1985): 93.5% (50,720,000) native-born; 5.9% foreign-born, of which Ireland 1.0%, India 0.7%, Caribbean 0.5%, Pakistan 0.4%; not stated 0.6%
*Mobility* (1981). Population living in the same residence as 1980: 90.9%; different residence, same country (of the U.K.) 8.2%; different residence, different country within the U.K. 0.4%; from outside the U.K. 0.5%.
*Households[6]* (1985). Average household size 2.7 (3.1); 1 person 24% (20%), 2 persons 33% (26%), 3 persons 17% (16%), 4 persons 18% (17%), 5 persons 6% (10%), 6 or more persons 3% (11%). Family households (1984): 16,079,-300 (74.3%), nonfamily 5,593,100 (25.7%, of which 1-person 22.5%).
*Immigration* (1985): permanent residents 232,000, from EEC 22.8%, Australia, New Zealand, and Canada 13.4%, United States 9.9%, South Africa 7.3%, Middle East 6.5%, Bangladesh and India 5.6%, Pakistan 3.9%.

## Vital statistics

*Birth rate* per 1,000 population (1986): 13.3 (world avg. 26.0); legitimate (1985) 81.1%; illegitimate 18.9%.
*Death rate* per 1,000 population (1986): 12.2 (world avg. 9.9).
*Natural increase rate* per 1,000 population (1986): 1.1 (world avg. 16.1).
*Total fertility rate* (avg. births per childbearing woman; 1986): 1.8.
*Marriage rate* per 1,000 population (1986): 6.9.
*Divorce rate* per 1,000 population (1985): 2.8.
*Life expectancy* at birth (1982–84): male 71.4 years; female 77.2 years.
*Major causes of death* per 100,000 population (1985): diseases of the circulatory system 568.5, of which ischemic heart disease 329.6, cerebrovascular disease 147.8; malignant neoplasms (cancers) 281.7; diseases of the respiratory system 131.2, of which pneumonia 59.1; diseases of the digestive system 36.4; accidents 26.5; diseases of the endocrine system 18.8, of which diabetes mellitus 14.3; diseases of the genitourinary system 16.3.

## Social indicators

*Educational attainment* (1981): Percent of population age 25 and over having: primary or secondary education only 89.7%; some postsecondary 4.8%; bachelor's or equivalent degree 4.9%; higher university degree 0.6%.

| Distribution of disposable income (1984) | | | | |
|---|---|---|---|---|
| percent of household income by quintile | | | | |
| 1 | 2 | 3 | 4 | 5 (highest) |
| 8.2 | 11.4 | 17.2 | 24.0 | 39.2 |

*Quality of working life* (1985). Average workweek (hours): male 41.9, female 37.3 (overtime male 8.8%, female 2.1%). Annual rate per 100,000 workers for: injury or accident 63.1; industrial diseases 0.5[7]; death 2.3. Proportion of labour force (employed persons) insured for damages or income loss resulting from: injury 100%; permanent disability 100%; death 100%. Average days lost to labour stoppages per 1,000 employee workdays: 0.3. Principal means of transport to work (1982): 55% private automobile, 20.5% public transportation, 15% foot, 2.5% bicycle, 7% other.
*Access to services* (1982). Proportion of households having access to: bath or shower 96%; toilet 95%; central heating 63%.
*Social participation.* Eligible voters participating in last national election: 75.4%. Population age 16 and over participating in voluntary work (1983): 23%. Trade union membership in total work force (1984) 40.9%.
*Social deviance* (1985). Offense rate per 100,000 population for: theft and handling stolen goods 3,874.2; burglary 1,721.3; fraud and forgery 278.3; violence against the person 243.1; robbery 71.5; sexual offense 48.3. Incidence per 100,000 population of: notified drug addicts 9.6[8]; suicide 9.0.
*Leisure* (1984). Favourite leisure activities (hours weekly): watching television 9.6; listening to radio 8.7; reading 2.6; cultural activities 1.5.
*Material well-being* (1985). Households possessing: automobile 62%, telephone 81%, television receiver 97% (colour 86%), refrigerator 95%, central heating 69%, washing machine 81%.

## National economy

*Gross national product* (at current market prices; 1985): U.S.$474,190,000,-000 (U.S.$8,380 per capita).

| Structure of gross domestic product and labour force | | | | |
|---|---|---|---|---|
| | 1986 | | | |
| | in value £'000,000 | % of total value | labour force | % of labour force |
| Agriculture | 5,902 | 1.8 | 329,000 | 1.2 |
| Mining | 24,445[9] | 7.5[9] | 230,000 | 0.8 |
| Manufacturing | 79,111 | 24.2 | 5,239,000 | 18.9 |
| Construction | 20,061 | 6.1 | 992,000 | 3.6 |
| Public utilities | [9] | [9] | 309,000 | 1.1 |
| Transp. and commun. | 23,727 | 7.3 | 1,341,000 | 4.8 |
| Trade | 45,770 | 14.0 | 4,403,000 | 15.9 |
| Finance | 70,386 | 21.6 | 2,203,000 | 7.9 |
| Pub. admin., defense | 23,578 | 7.3 | 1,984,000 | 7.1 |
| Services | 50,473 | 15.5 | 4,548,000 | 16.4 |
| Other | −17,404[10] | −5.3[10] | 6,194,000[11] | 22.3[11] |
| TOTAL | 326,049 | 100.0 | 27,772,000 | 100.0 |

*Budget* (1986–87). Revenue[12]: £164,400,000,000 (taxes on expenditures 38.6%, income tax 35.3%, national insurance contributions 16.3%). Expenditures: £164,400,000,000 (social security benefits 27.0%, debt interest 14.5%, military defense 11.3%, national health service 10.6%, education and science 9.7%).
*Total national debt* (1986): £171,000,000,000.

### Financial aggregates

| | 1981 | 1982 | 1983 | 1984 | 1985 | 1986 | 1987[13] |
|---|---|---|---|---|---|---|---|
| Exchange rate: | | | | | | | |
| U.S. Dollar per £ | 2.03 | 1.75 | 1.52 | 1.34 | 1.30 | 1.47 | 1.59 |
| SDRs per £ | 1.64 | 1.46 | 1.39 | 1.18 | 1.32 | 1.20 | 1.26 |
| International reserves (U.S.$) | | | | | | | |
| Total (excl. gold; '000,000,000) | 15.24 | 12.40 | 11.34 | 9.44 | 12.86 | 18.42 | 29.10 |
| SDRs ('000,000,000) | 0.99 | 1.17 | 0.52 | 0.50 | 1.13 | 1.55 | 1.61 |
| Reserve pos. in IMF ('000,000,000) | 1.44 | 1.55 | 2.10 | 1.97 | 1.99 | 1.98 | 1.82 |
| Foreign exchange ('000,000,000) | 12.81 | 9.67 | 8.72 | 6.97 | 9.74 | 14.89 | 26.65 |
| Gold ('000,000 fine troy oz) | 19.03 | 19.01 | 19.01 | 19.03 | 19.03 | 19.01 | 19.01 |
| % world reserves | 2.0 | 2.0 | 2.0 | 2.0 | 2.0 | 2.0 | 2.0 |
| Interest and prices | | | | | | | |
| Central bank discount (%) | ... | ... | ... | ... | ... | ... | ... |
| Gov't. Bond yield (%) long term | 14.74 | 12.88 | 10.81 | 10.69 | 10.62 | 9.87 | 9.23 |
| Industrial share prices (1980 = 100) | 112.8 | 130.7 | 164.9 | 196.2 | 242.2 | 304.5[14] | ... |
| Balance of payments (U.S.$'000,000) | | | | | | | |
| Balance of visible trade, | +7,170 | +3,906 | −1,312 | −5,851 | −2,440 | −12,144 | ... |
| Imports, f.o.b. | 95,594 | 93,175 | 93,391 | 99,472 | 103,458 | 118,887 | ... |
| Exports, f.o.b. | 102,765 | 97,081 | 92,078 | 93,621 | 101,017 | 106,743 | ... |
| Balance of invisibles | 11,190 | 8,578 | 10,043 | 9,693 | 12,116 | 15,323 | ... |
| Balance of payments, current account | 12,955 | 6,927 | 5,177 | 1,939 | 4,905 | −240 | ... |

*Tourism* (1985): receipts from visitors U.S.$6,988,000,000; expenditures by nationals abroad U.S.$6,253,000,000.

### Manufacturing, mining, and construction enterprises (1984)

| | no. of enterprises | no. of employees | annual wages as a % of avg. of all wages | annual value added (£'000,000) |
|---|---|---|---|---|
| Manufacturing | | | | |
| Food, beverages, and tobacco | 3,282 | 556,700 | 103.0 | 9,672.8 |
| Mechanical engineering | 3,023 | 623,500 | 108.4 | 8,822.7 |
| Electrical and electronic engineering | 2,412 | 527,500 | 96.8 | 7,819.6 |
| Chemical engineering | 1,354 | 291,700 | 118.1 | 7,353.9 |
| Paper and paper products; printing and publishing | 3,237 | 379,900 | 133.8 | 6,974.5 |
| Transport equipment | 1,671 | 637,300 | ... | 3,807.4 |
| Metal manufacturing | 901 | 303,400 | 102.8 | 2,588.7 |
| Rubber and plastic | 1,529 | 179,000 | 118.1 | 2,617.1 |
| Clothing and footwear | 2,727 | 245,500 | 85.6 | 2,290.7 |
| Timber and wood products | 2,091 | 139,800 | 98.1 | 2,025.4 |
| Textiles | 1,883 | 217,500 | 79.2 | 2,169.4 |
| Mining | | | | |
| Extraction of coal, mineral oil, and natural gas | | | 118.1 | 19,529.7 |
| Extraction of minerals other than fuels | 1,649 | 292,000 | 103.1 | 13,927.0 |
| Mineral oil processing | | | 118.1 | 1,252.0 |
| Construction | 166,184 | 989,000 | ... | 11,174.0 |

*Production* (metric tons except as noted). Agriculture, forestry, fishing (1985): wheat 12,050,000, barley 9,740,000, sugar beets 7,715,000, potatoes 6,895,000, turnips and rutabagas 3,300,000, corn (maize) 770,000, oats 615,-000; livestock (number of live animals; 1986) 24,540,000 sheep, 12,507,000 cattle, 7,981,000 pigs; roundwood 4,300,000 cu m; fish catch 737,700. Mining (metric tons; 1985): iron ore 147,000; zinc 53,600; tin 4,100; lead 4,000. Manufacturing (total sales in £'000,000; 1986): motor vehicles and parts 11,708; aerospace equipment 6,839; electronic data processing and telecommunication equipment 2,974; radios and electronic goods 2,791; telephone and telegraph equipment 1,749; mechanical lifting and handling equipment 1,603; boilers 1,511; precision instruments 1,507; constructional steelwork 1,419. Construction (value in £; 1986): residential 6,184,000,000; nonresidential 10,943,000,000, of which public 4,153,000,000, industrial 1,998,000,000, commercial 4,792,000,000.

### Retail trade enterprises (1984)

| | no. of enterprises | no. of employees | weekly wage as a % of all wages | annual turnover (£'000,000)[15] |
|---|---|---|---|---|
| Food and grocery, of which | 77,486 | 850,000 | ... | 31,360 |
| large grocery | 100 | 424,000 | ... | 20,436 |
| other grocery | 32,130 | 137,000 | ... | 3,966 |
| meats | 15,573 | 83,000 | ... | 2,710 |
| Household goods, of which | 39,379 | 282,000 | ... | 12,000 |
| electrical and musical goods | 9,606 | 91,000 | ... | 4,626 |
| furniture | 9,447 | 68,000 | ... | 3,156 |
| Drink, confectionery, and tobacco, of which | 41,992 | 260,000 | ... | 8,686 |
| tobacco and confectionery | 37,602 | 223,000 | ... | 6,575 |
| Clothing and footwear, of which | 28,684 | 285,000 | ... | 7,476 |
| women's, girls', and infants' wear | 15,246 | 107,000 | ... | 2,642 |
| footwear | 3,353 | 84,000 | ... | 1,868 |
| men's and boys' wear | 3,443 | 43,000 | ... | 1,495 |
| Mail order | 24 | 42,000 | ... | 2,737 |
| Pharmaceuticals | 8,060 | 66,000 | ... | 2,458 |

Energy production (consumption): electricity (kW-hr; 1985) 294,722,000,000 (294,722,000,000); coal (metric tons; 1985) 94,046,000 (105,701,000); crude petroleum (barrels; 1985) 914,000,000 (517,000,000); natural gas (cu m; 1985) 47,185,000,000 (62,196,000,000).

*Population economically active* (1986): total 27,772,000; activity rate of total population 48.9% (participation rates [1985]: ages 15–64, 74.3%; female 44.9%; unemployed 11.6%).

### Price and earnings indexes (1980 = 100)

| | 1981 | 1982 | 1983 | 1984 | 1985 | 1986 | 1987 |
|---|---|---|---|---|---|---|---|
| Consumer price index | 111.9 | 121.5 | 127.1 | 133.4 | 141.5 | 146.3 | 150.5[13] |
| Monthly earnings index | 113.4 | 126.3 | 137.1 | 144.9 | 161.1 | 174.1 | 186.3[16] |

*Household income and expenditure* (1984). Average household size (1985) 2.7; average annual income per household £8,133 (U.S.$10,868); sources of income: wages and salaries 66.4%, social security benefits 13.9%, rent, dividends, and interest 8.8%, income from self-employment 6.1%; expenditure (1986): food 18.5%, transport and communication 17.8%, housing 15.3%, recreation, entertainment, and education 8.8%, clothing and footwear 7.5%, household goods and services 6.3%, energy 6.2%.
*Land use* (1984): forested 9.4%; meadows and pastures 48.2%; agricultural and under permanent cultivation 28.9%; other 13.5%.

## Foreign trade

### Balance of trade (current prices)

| | 1981 | 1982 | 1983 | 1984 | 1985 | 1986 |
|---|---|---|---|---|---|---|
| £'000,000 | +7,170 | +3,906 | −1,312 | −5,851 | −2,440 | −12,144 |
| % of total | 3.6% | 2.0% | 0.7% | 3.0% | 1.2% | 5.4% |

*Imports* (1986): £86,066,700,000 (machinery and transport equipment 33.4%, of which road vehicles 9.2%, data-processing equipment 5.3%; food and live animals 10.1%, of which vegetables and fruits 2.5%, meat and meat preparations 1.7%; chemicals and chemical products 8.5%, of which organic chemicals 2.1%; petroleum and petroleum products 5.1%; textile yarn and fabrics 3.7%; paper and paperboard 3.1%; apparel and clothing accessories 2.5%; nonferrous metals 2.1%). *Major import sources:* West Germany 16.4%; United States 9.8%; France 8.5%; The Netherlands 7.7%; Japan 5.7%; Italy 5.4%; Belgium and Luxembourg 4.7%; Norway 3.8%; Ireland 3.5%; Sweden 3.2%.
*Exports* (1986): £73,009,000,000 (machinery and transport equipment 34.7%, of which road vehicles 5.4%, data-processing equipment 4.9%, power generating machinery and equipment 4.4%, machinery specialized for particular industries 4.2%; chemicals and chemical products 13.3%, of which organic chemicals 3.5%; petroleum and petroleum products 11.3%; nonmetallic mineral manufactures 3.5%; professional, scientific, and controlling instruments 3.1%; iron and steel 2.6%). *Major export destinations:* United States 14.2%; West Germany 11.7%; France 8.5%; The Netherlands 7.4%; Belgium and Luxembourg 5.2%; Ireland 4.9%; Italy 4.8%; Sweden 3.2%; Switzerland 2.2%.

## Transport and communications

*Transport.* Railroads[17] (1985): length 24,512 mi, 39,448 km; passenger-mi 16,447,000,000, passenger-km 29,688,000,000; short ton-mi cargo 10,776,-000,000, metric ton-km cargo 15,732,000,000. Roads (1985): total length 216,450 mi, 348,344 km (paved 97%). Vehicles (1985): passenger cars 16,453,000; trucks and buses 2,742,000. Merchant marine (1986): vessels (100 gross tons and over) 2,256; total deadweight tonnage 16,871,643. Air transport (1985): passenger-mi 32,064,200,000, passenger-km 51,602,400,-000; short ton-mi cargo 1,203,858,000, metric ton-km cargo 1,757,604,000; airports (1987) with scheduled flights 40.
*Communications.* Daily newspapers (1984): total number 112; total circulation 30,412,400; circulation per 1,000 population 538. Radio (1986): total number of licenses 63,528,000 (1 per 0.9 person). Television (1986): total number of licenses 18,705,000 (1 per 3 persons). Telephones (1984): 29,-336,000 (1 per 1.9 persons).

## Education and health

### Education (1984–85)[18]

| | schools | teachers | students | student/ teacher ratio |
|---|---|---|---|---|
| Primary (age 5–10) | 24,993 | 205,000 | 4,513,600 | 22.0 |
| Secondary (age 11–19) | 5,262 | 267,700 | 4,243,600 | 15.9 |
| Voc., teacher tr.[19] | 748 | 93,000 | 486,140 | c. 5.2 |
| Higher | 46[20] | 31,043 | 345,760 | 11.1 |

*Literacy* (1987): total population literate, virtually 100%.
*Health* (1985): physicians 84,700 (1 per 668 persons); hospital beds 419,000 (1 per 135 persons); infant mortality rate per 1,000 live births 9.3.
*Food* (1981–83): daily per capita caloric intake 3,162 (vegetable products 63%, animal products 37%); (1983) 128% of FAO recommended minimum requirement.

## Military

*Total active duty personnel* (1986): 323,800 (army 50.1%, navy 21.1%, air force 28.8%). *Military expenditure as percent of GNP* (1984): 5.3% (world 5.9%); per capita expenditure U.S.$450.

[1]Includes separately administered Isles of Scilly (area 6 sq mi [16 sq km]; pop. 1,900). [2]Geographical entity only; since April 1, 1986, the administrative functions of the former metropolitan county councils have been dispersed among other local authorities. [3]Comprises 26 local government districts not shown separately. [4]Detail does not add to total given because of rounding. [5]Includes three separately administered island groups (Orkney 377 sq mi, pop. 19,400; Shetland 553 sq mi, pop. 23,400; Western Isles 1,119 sq mi, pop. 31,500). [6]Figures in parentheses are for Northern Ireland (1984). [7]1982. [8]1984. [9]Mining includes Public utilities. [10]Less imputed bank service charges. [11]Includes self-employed and unemployed. [12]Revenue percentages are from 1985 budget. [13]July. [14]Third quarter. [15]Includes value-added taxes. [16]April. [17]British railways only. [18]Public sector only. [19]Third level. [20]Universities only.

# United States

*Official name:* United States of
America.
*Form of government:* federal republic
with two legislative houses (Senate
[100]; House of Representatives
[435]).
*Head of state and government:*
President.
*Capital:* Washington, D.C.
*Official language:* English.
*Official religion:* none.
*Monetary unit:* 1 dollar (U.S.$) = 100
cents; valuation (Oct. 5, 1987)
1 U.S.$ = £0.62; 1 £ = U.S.$1.62.

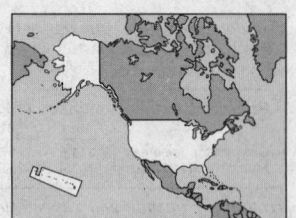

1.3%, Pakistan 1.0%, Romania 0.9.%, Portugal 0.6%. Refugee arrivals
(1987): 70,000.
*Major cities* (1986): New York 7,262,700; Los Angeles 3,259,300; Chicago
3,009,530; Houston 1,728,910; Philadelphia 1,642,900; Detroit 1,086,220;
San Diego 1,015,190; Dallas 1,003,520; San Antonio 914,350; Phoenix
894,070.

### Other principal cities (1986)

| | population | | population | | population |
|---|---|---|---|---|---|
| Akron | 222,060 | Fort Worth | 429,550 | Omaha | 349,270 |
| Albuquerque | 366,750 | Fresno | 284,660 | Pittsburgh | 387,490 |
| Anaheim | 240,730 | Honolulu | 372,330 | Portland (Ore.) | 387,870 |
| Anchorage | 235,000 | Indianapolis | 719,820 | Richmond | 217,700 |
| Arlington (Tex.) | 249,770 | Jacksonville | 610,030 | Rochester (N.Y.) | 235,970 |
| Atlanta | 421,910 | Jersey City | 219,480 | Sacramento | 323,550 |
| Aurora (Colo.) | 217,990 | Kansas City (Mo.) | 441,170 | St. Louis | 426,300 |
| Austin | 466,550 | Lexington (Ky.) | 213,600 | St. Paul | 263,680 |
| Baltimore | 752,800 | Long Beach | 396,280 | St. Petersburg | 239,480 |
| Baton Rouge | 241,130 | Louisville | 287,460 | San Francisco | 749,000 |
| Birmingham | 277,510 | Memphis | 652,640 | San Jose | 712,080 |
| Boston | 573,600 | Mesa | 251,340 | Santa Ana | 236,780 |
| Buffalo | 324,820 | Miami | 373,940 | Seattle | 486,200 |
| Charlotte | 352,070 | Milwaukee | 605,090 | Shreveport | 220,380 |
| Cincinnati | 369,750 | Minneapolis | 356,840 | Tampa | 277,580 |
| Cleveland | 535,830 | Nashville | 473,670 | Toledo | 340,680 |
| Colorado Springs | 272,000 | Newark | 316,300 | Tucson | 358,850 |
| Columbus | 566,030 | New Orleans | 554,500 | Tulsa | 373,750 |
| Corpus Christi | 263,900 | Norfolk | 274,800 | Virginia Beach | 333,400 |
| Denver | 505,000 | Oakland | 356,960 | Washington, D.C. | 626,000 |
| El Paso | 491,800 | Oklahoma City | 466,120 | Wichita | 288,000 |

*Households* (1986). Total households 88,458,000 (married-couple families
50,993,000 [57.6%]). Average household size 2.7; 1 person 23.9%, 2 persons
31.6%, 3 persons 17.8%, 4 persons 15.8%, 5 persons 6.9%, 6 persons 2.6%,
7 or more persons 1.4%. Family households: 63,558,000 (71.9%), nonfamily
24,900,000 (28.1%, of which 1-person 23.9%).

## Vital statistics

*Birth rate* per 1,000 population (1987[3]): 15.5 (world avg. 26.0); (1985) legiti-
mate 77.8%; illegitimate 22.2%.
*Death rate* per 1,000 population (1987[3]): 8.9 (world avg. 9.9).
*Natural increase rate* per 1,000 population (1987[3]): 6.6 (world avg. 16.1).
*Total fertility rate* (avg. births per childbearing woman; 1986): 1.8.
*Marriage rate* per 1,000 population (1987[3]): 9.7; median age at first mar-
riage, men 25.7 years, women 23.1 years.
*Divorce rate* per 1,000 population (1987[3]): 4.8.
*Life expectancy* at birth (1986): white male 72.0 years, black male 65.5 years;
white female 78.9 years, black female 73.6 years.
*Major causes of death* per 100,000 population (1987): cardiovascular diseases 396.0, of which ischemic heart diseases 212.2, other forms of heart
disease 84.6, cerebrovascular diseases 61.2, atherosclerosis 9.3, other cardiovascular diseases 9.4; malignant neoplasms (cancers) 194.2; diseases of
the respiratory system 59.3, of which pneumonia 27.6; accidents and adverse effects 38.9, of which motor-vehicle accidents 19.8; diabetes mellitus
15.4; suicide 12.6; chronic liver disease and cirrhosis 10.7; nephritis and
nephrosis 9.2; homicide 8.7.
*Morbidity rates of infectious diseases* per 100,000 population (1984): gonorrhea 374.7; chicken pox 138.4; syphilis 29.8; salmonellosis 17.3; hepatitis B
(serum) 11.1; tuberculosis 9.4; hepatitis A (infectious) 9.3; shigellosis 7.4;
acquired immune deficiency syndrome (AIDS) 1.9; mumps 1.3; measles
(rubeola) 1.1.
*Incidence of chronic health conditions* per 1,000 population (per 1,000 population over age 65) (1983): chronic sinusitis 134.2 (149.6); arthritis 131.3
(471.6); hypertension 121.3 (387.9); hearing impairment 90.3 (314.8); heart
conditions 82.8 (303.0).

## Social indicators

*Educational attainment* (1985). Percent of population age 25 and over
having: less than full primary education 7.5%; primary 6.4%; less than
full secondary 12.2%; secondary 38.2%; some postsecondary 16.3%; 4-year
higher degree and more 19.4%, of which postgraduate 6.9%. Number of
earned degrees (1986–87): bachelor's degree 950,000; master's degree 276,-
000; doctor's degree 33,700; first-professional degrees (in fields such as
medicine, theology, and law) 78,000.

### Distribution of income (1983)

percent of national household income by quintile

| 1 | 2 | 3 | 4 | 5 (highest) |
|---|---|---|---|---|
| 4.7 | 11.2 | 17.1 | 24.3 | 42.7 |

*Quality of working life* (1986). Average workweek: 40.7 hours (8.1% overtime). Annual rate per 100,000 workers for (1985): injury or accident 2,000;
death 11.0. Proportion of labour force insured for damages or income
loss resulting from: injury, permanent disability, and death (1984) 59.8%.
Average days lost to labour stoppages per 1,000 workdays (1986): 0.8.
Average duration of journey to work (1979): 22.5 minutes (85.7% private
automobile, 5.9% public transportation, 1.3% bicycle or motorcycle, 3.9%
foot, 2.3% work at home, 0.9% other). Rate per 1,000 workers of discouraged (unemployed no longer seeking work; 1983): 53.5.
*Access to services* (1984). Proportion of dwellings having access to: electricity
virtually 100.0%; safe public water supply 98.2%; public sewage collection
(1983) 98.1%; public fire protection, n.a.
*Social participation.* Eligible voters participating in last national election
(1986): 33.4%. Population age 14 and over participating in voluntary work
(1985): 48.0%. Trade union membership in total work force (1985): 18.0%.
Practicing religious population in total affiliated population (weekly church

### Area and population

| | | area[1] | | population |
|---|---|---|---|---|
| States | Capitals | sq mi | sq km | 1986 estimate |
| Alabama | Montgomery | 51,705 | 133,915 | 4,053,000 |
| Alaska | Juneau | 591,004 | 1,530,693 | 534,000 |
| Arizona | Phoenix | 114,000 | 295,259 | 3,317,000 |
| Arkansas | Little Rock | 53,187 | 137,754 | 2,372,000 |
| California | Sacramento | 158,706 | 411,047 | 26,981,000 |
| Colorado | Denver | 104,091 | 269,594 | 3,267,000 |
| Connecticut | Hartford | 5,018 | 12,997 | 3,189,000 |
| Delaware | Dover | 2,044 | 5,294 | 633,000 |
| Florida | Tallahassee | 58,664 | 151,939 | 11,675,000 |
| Georgia | Atlanta | 58,910 | 152,576 | 6,104,000 |
| Hawaii | Honolulu | 6,471 | 16,760 | 1,062,000 |
| Idaho | Boise | 83,564 | 216,430 | 1,003,000 |
| Illinois | Springfield | 57,871 | 149,885 | 11,553,000 |
| Indiana | Indianapolis | 36,413 | 94,309 | 5,504,000 |
| Iowa | Des Moines | 56,275 | 145,752 | 2,851,000 |
| Kansas | Topeka | 82,277 | 213,096 | 2,461,000 |
| Kentucky | Frankfort | 40,409 | 104,659 | 3,728,000 |
| Louisiana | Baton Rouge | 47,752 | 123,677 | 4,501,000 |
| Maine | Augusta | 33,265 | 86,156 | 1,174,000 |
| Maryland | Annapolis | 10,460 | 27,091 | 4,463,000 |
| Massachusetts | Boston | 8,284 | 21,455 | 5,832,000 |
| Michigan | Lansing | 97,102 | 251,493 | 9,145,000 |
| Minnesota | St. Paul | 86,614 | 224,329 | 4,214,000 |
| Mississippi | Jackson | 47,689 | 123,514 | 2,625,000 |
| Missouri | Jefferson City | 69,697 | 180,514 | 5,066,000 |
| Montana | Helena | 147,046 | 380,847 | 819,000 |
| Nebraska | Lincoln | 77,355 | 200,349 | 1,598,000 |
| Nevada | Carson City | 110,561 | 286,352 | 963,000 |
| New Hampshire | Concord | 9,279 | 24,032 | 1,027,000 |
| New Jersey | Trenton | 7,787 | 20,168 | 7,620,000 |
| New Mexico | Santa Fe | 121,593 | 314,924 | 1,479,000 |
| New York | Albany | 52,735 | 136,583 | 17,772,000 |
| North Carolina | Raleigh | 52,669 | 136,412 | 6,331,000 |
| North Dakota | Bismarck | 70,702 | 183,117 | 679,000 |
| Ohio | Columbus | 44,787 | 115,998 | 10,752,000 |
| Oklahoma | Oklahoma City | 69,956 | 181,185 | 3,305,000 |
| Oregon | Salem | 97,073 | 251,418 | 2,698,000 |
| Pennsylvania | Harrisburg | 46,043 | 119,251 | 11,889,000 |
| Rhode Island | Providence | 1,212 | 3,139 | 975,000 |
| South Carolina | Columbia | 31,113 | 80,582 | 3,378,000 |
| South Dakota | Pierre | 77,116 | 199,730 | 708,000 |
| Tennessee | Nashville | 42,144 | 109,152 | 4,803,000 |
| Texas | Austin | 266,807 | 691,027 | 16,682,000 |
| Utah | Salt Lake City | 84,899 | 219,887 | 1,665,000 |
| Vermont | Montpelier | 9,614 | 24,900 | 541,000 |
| Virginia | Richmond | 40,767 | 105,586 | 5,787,000 |
| Washington | Olympia | 68,139 | 176,479 | 4,463,000 |
| West Virginia | Charleston | 24,231 | 62,758 | 1,919,000 |
| Wisconsin | Madison | 66,215 | 171,496 | 4,785,000 |
| Wyoming | Cheyenne | 97,809 | 253,324 | 507,000 |
| **District** | | | | |
| Dist. of Columbia | — | 69 | 179 | 626,000 |
| TOTAL | | 3,679,192[2] | 9,529,063 | 241,077,000[2] |

## Demography

*Population* (1987): 243,773,000.
*Density* (1987): persons per sq mi 66.3, persons per sq km 25.6.
*Urban–rural* (1980): urban 73.7%; rural 26.3%.
*Sex distribution* (1986): male 48.68%; female 51.32%.
*Age breakdown* (1986): under 15, 21.6%; 15–29, 25.4%; 30–44, 22.4%; 45–59,
13.9%; 60–74, 11.8%; 75 and over, 4.9%.
*Population projection:* (1990) 249,657,000; (2000) 267,955,000.
*Doubling time:* 99 years.
*Composition* by race (1986): white 84.8%; black 12.2%; other races 3.0%.
*Religious affiliation* (1980): Protestant 40.0%; Roman Catholic 30.0%; Jewish
3.2%; Eastern Orthodox 2.1%; Muslim 0.8%; Hindu 0.2%; nonreligious and
atheist 6.9%; other 16.8%.
*Place of birth* (foreign-born; 1980): Mexico 2,199,221; Germany (East and
West) 849,384; Canada 842,859; Italy 831,922; United Kingdom 669,149;
Cuba 607,814; Philippines 501,440; Poland 418,128; U.S.S.R. 406,022; South
Korea 289,885; China 286,120; Vietnam (South) 231,120; Japan 221,794;
Portugal 211,614; Greece 210,998; India 206,087.
*Mobility* (1985). Population living in the same residence as in 1980: 58.3%;
different residence, same county 22.1%; different county, same state 9.1%;
different state 8.7%; moved from abroad 1.8%.
*Immigration* (1985): permanent immigrants admitted 570,000, from
Caribbean countries 14.6%, Mexico 10.7%, Philippines 8.4%, South Amer-
ica 6.9%, Korea 6.2%, India 4.6%, Central America 4.6%, China 4.4%,
African countries 3.0%, Iran 2.8%, Taiwan 2.6%, United Kingdom 2.4%,
Kampuchea 2.4%, Canada 2.0%, Laos 1.6%, Poland 1.6%, West Germany

attendance; 1984): Roman Catholic 52%; Protestant 39%, of which Baptist 41%, Methodist 37%, Lutheran 35%, Episcopal 30%, Presbyterian 28%.
*Social deviance* (1986). Offense rate per 100,000 population for: murder 8.6; rape 37.5; robbery 225.1; aggravated assault 346.1; motor vehicle theft 507.8; burglary and housebreaking 1,344.6; larceny-theft 3,010.3. Adult drug and substance users (1985): alcohol 65.0%; marijuana 12.0%; hallucinogens 1.2%[4]; tranquilizers 1.2%[4]; heroin 0.6%[4]. Rate per 100,000 population of suicide (1987) 12.6.

### Crime rates per 100,000 population in metropolitan areas (1986)

| | violent crime | | | | |
| | total | murder | rape | robbery | assault |
|---|---|---|---|---|---|
| Atlanta | 860.7 | 13.3 | 57.3 | 361.4 | 428.8 |
| Baltimore | 1,101.6 | 13.2 | 48.8 | 434.6 | 605.1 |
| Boston | 689.1 | 5.3 | 31.9 | 293.7 | 358.3 |
| Chicago | 1,217.4 | 13.4 | 36.2 | 548.3 | 619.5 |
| Dallas | 1,067.0 | 19.9 | 74.8 | 478.6 | 493.8 |
| Detroit | 1,041.1 | 18.1 | 64.3 | 509.2 | 449.5 |
| Houston | 805.9 | 15.9 | 61.3 | 391.9 | 336.8 |
| Los Angeles | 1,392.0 | 16.9 | 53.2 | 593.5 | 728.4 |
| Miami | 1,791.2 | 21.6 | 51.3 | 805.6 | 912.7 |
| Minneapolis | 453.6 | 3.4 | 43.3 | 182.1 | 224.8 |
| New York | 1,754.5 | 19.3 | 44.1 | 983.8 | 707.4 |
| Philadelphia | 609.0 | 9.7 | 38.0 | 273.7 | 287.5 |
| Pittsburgh | 364.7 | 3.9 | 24.2 | 189.4 | 147.2 |
| St. Louis | 697.0 | 13.5 | 27.0 | 217.8 | 438.7 |
| San Francisco | 883.9 | 9.9 | 42.4 | 380.3 | 451.3 |
| Washington, D.C. | 622.9 | 8.5 | 33.8 | 269.3 | 311.3 |

| | property crime | | | | |
| | total | burglary | larceny | auto theft | arson |
|---|---|---|---|---|---|
| Atlanta | 6,585.3 | 1,844.4 | 4,012.1 | 281.6 | 87.0 |
| Baltimore | 5,317.2 | 1,441.0 | 3,296.9 | 579.2 | 96.7 |
| Boston | 4,613.6 | 1,019.7 | 2,364.2 | 1,229.8 | 21.8 |
| Chicago | 5,771.3 | 1,359.6 | 3,377.7 | 1,034.0 | 87.4 |
| Dallas | 9,796.3 | 2,757.8 | 6,012.1 | 1,026.5 | 92.2 |
| Detroit | 6,666.9 | 1,788.8 | 3,494.0 | 1,384.1 | 139.1 |
| Houston | 6,745.9 | 2,114.9 | 3,280.9 | 1,350.1 | 105.9 |
| Los Angeles | 6,013.9 | 1,725.1 | 3,063.1 | 1,225.7 | 166.1 |
| Miami | 9,958.2 | 2,763.5 | 5,661.4 | 1,533.3 | 52.5 |
| Minneapolis | 5,250.1 | 1,350.2 | 3,485.6 | 414.3 | 83.2 |
| New York | 6,366.5 | 1,597.2 | 3,693.6 | 1,075.8 | 94.3 |
| Philadelphia | 3,662.1 | 937.9 | 2,200.6 | 523.5 | 20.3 |
| Pittsburgh | 2,833.4 | 736.0 | 1,397.5 | 700.0 | 92.5 |
| St. Louis | 4,577.3 | 1,281.3 | 2,748.7 | 547.3 | 122.7 |
| San Francisco | 5,169.1 | 1,108.8 | 3,454.5 | 605.9 | 55.3 |
| Washington, D.C. | 4,640.3 | 1,033.2 | 3,024.9 | 582.1 | 43.5 |

*Leisure* (1976). Favourite leisure activities (weekly hours): watching television 9.6; social time 7.6; reading 3.7; cultural activities 1.5; recreation 1.2.
*Material well-being* (1986). Occupied dwellings with householder possessing: automobile 86.1%[4]; telephone 92.2%; radio receiver 99.0%; television receiver 98.0%; freezer 36.7%; refrigerator 99.7%; air conditioner 59.5%; washing machine 72.8%; videocassette recorder 36.0%.
*Recreational expenditures* (1985): U.S.$176,289,000,000 (television and radio receivers 19.9%; toys and sport supplies 11.6%; golfing, bowling, and other participatory activities 8.3%; magazines and newspapers 7.5%; spectator amusements 5.5%, of which movies 2.1%, theatre and opera 1.7%, spectator sports 1.7%; parimutuel receipts 1.5%).

## National economy
*Budget* (1987). Revenue: U.S.$831,176,000,000 (individual income tax 45.9%, social insurance taxes and contributions 36.7%, corporation income tax 9.0%, excise taxes 3.9%, customs duties 1.5%). Expenditures: U.S.$975,-090,000,000 (defense 28.9%, social security and medicare 28.2%, interest on debt 14.3%, income security 12.4%, health 3.7%, education 2.9%, veteran benefits and services 2.7%).
*Total national debt* (1987)[5]: U.S.$2,370,388,000,000.

### Manufacturing, mining, and construction enterprises (1986)

| | no. of enter-prises [6] | no. of employees | weekly wage as a % of all wages | annual value of shipments (U.S.$'000,000) |
|---|---|---|---|---|
| **Manufacturing** | | | | |
| Food and related products | 20,208 | 1,617,000 | 99.8 | 314,500 |
| Transportation equipment | 8,466 | 2,015,000 | 146.2 | 314,081 |
| Machinery, except electrical | 48,947 | 2,060,000 | 120.9 | 205,804 |
| Electrical and electronic machinery | 15,116 | 2,113,000 | 110.2 | 205,613 |
| Chemical and related products | 11,363 | 1,023,000 | 136.8 | 198,345 |
| Apparel and other related products | 21,367 | 1,106,000 | 66.7 | 153,075 |
| Fabricated metal products | 32,793 | 1,431,000 | 112.9 | 135,974 |
| Petroleum and coal products | 2,165 | 169,000 | 161.9 | 129,600 |
| Paper and related products | 6,160 | 674,000 | 127.6 | 103,834 |
| Primary metals | 7,048 | 753,000 | 135.4 | 101,733 |
| Rubber and plastic products | 12,348 | 790,000 | 99.7 | 72,170 |
| Instruments and related products | 7,661 | 707,000 | 108.1 | 60,860 |
| Stone, clay, and glass products | 15,591 | 586,000 | 114.7 | 56,787 |
| Textile-mill products | 6,192 | 705,000 | 79.1 | 54,607 |
| Tobacco products | 117 | 59,000 | 146.7 | 18,016 |
| Leather and leather products | 2,558 | 151,000 | 67.6 | ... |
| Lumber and wood | 28,293 | 711,000 | 95.1 | ... |
| Furniture and fixtures | 9,160 | 497,000 | 85.2 | ... |
| Miscellaneous manufacturing industries | 14,532 | 1,817,000 | 86.1 | ... |
| **Mining** | | | | |
| Oil and gas extraction | 23,577 | 457,000 | | |
| Coal mining | 4,133 | | 139.6 | 122,300 |
| Metal mining | 985 | 326,000 | | |
| Nonmetallic, except fuels | 5,126 | | | |
| **Construction** | | | | |
| General contractors and operative builders | 112,963 | 1,293,000 | | |
| Heavy construction contractors | 29,055 | 1,250,000 | 155.2 | 152,500 |
| Special trade contractors | 243,729 | 2,361,000 | | |

*Gross national product* (at current market prices; 1986): U.S.$4,235,000,000,-000 (U.S.$17,600 per capita).

### Gross national product and national income
in U.S.$000,000,000

| | 1982 | 1983 | 1984 | 1985 | 1986 |
|---|---|---|---|---|---|
| Gross national product | 3,069.3 | 3,304.8 | 3,774.7 | 4,010.3 | 4,235.0 |
| By type of expenditure | | | | | |
| Personal consumption expenditures | 1,984.9 | 2,155.9 | 2,423.0 | 2,629.4 | 2,799.8 |
| Durable goods | 245.1 | 279.8 | 331.1 | 368.7 | 402.4 |
| Nondurable goods | 757.5 | 801.7 | 872.4 | 913.1 | 939.4 |
| Services | 982.2 | 1,074.4 | 1,219.6 | 1,347.5 | 1,458.0 |
| Gross private domestic investment | 414.9 | 471.6 | 674.0 | 641.6 | 671.0 |
| Fixed investment | 441.0 | 485.1 | 607.0 | 631.6 | 655.2 |
| Changes in business inventories | −26.1 | −13.5 | 67.1 | 10.0 | 15.7 |
| Net exports of goods and services | 19.0 | −8.3 | −59.2 | −79.2 | −105.5 |
| Exports | 348.4 | 336.2 | 384.6 | 369.9 | 376.2 |
| Imports | 329.4 | 344.4 | 443.8 | 449.2 | 481.7 |
| Government purchases of goods and services | 650.5 | 685.5 | 736.8 | 818.6 | 869.7 |
| Federal | 258.9 | 269.7 | 312.9 | 353.9 | 366.2 |
| State and local | 391.5 | 415.8 | 423.9 | 464.7 | 503.5 |
| By major type of product | | | | | |
| Goods output | 1,276.8 | 1,355.7 | 1,506.4 | 1,637.9 | 1,693.8 |
| Durable goods | 499.9 | 555.3 | 665.4 | 704.3 | 726.8 |
| Nondurable goods | 776.9 | 800.4 | 851.0 | 933.6 | 967.0 |
| Services | 1,510.8 | 1,639.3 | 1,615.4 | 1,969.3 | 2,116.2 |
| Structures | 281.7 | 309.8 | 370.2 | 403.1 | 425.1 |
| National income | 2,446.8 | 2,646.7 | 3,039.3 | 3,229.9 | 3,422.0 |
| By type of income | | | | | |
| Compensation of employees | 1,864.2 | 1,984.9 | 2,221.3 | 2,370.8 | 2,504.9 |
| Proprietors' income | 111.1 | 121.7 | 183.6 | 257.3 | 289.8 |
| Rental income of persons | 51.5 | 58.3 | 54.0 | 54.0 | 62.2 |
| Corporate profits | 159.1 | 225.2 | 273.3 | 277.6 | 284.4 |
| Net interest | 260.9 | 256.6 | 300.2 | 315.3 | 326.1 |
| By industry division | | | | | |
| Agriculture, forestry, fishing | 89.6 | 74.3 | 94.0 | 90.6 | 93.0 |
| Mining and construction | 259.0 | 268.0 | 290.9 | 302.6 | 293.2 |
| Manufacturing | 634.6 | 683.2 | 771.9 | 799.3 | 824.3 |
| Durable | 385.6 | 451.1 | 469.9 | 469.9 | 478.5 |
| Nondurable | 272.1 | 297.6 | 320.8 | 329.3 | 345.8 |
| Transportation | 110.8 | 120.5 | 133.5 | 140.5 | 144.1 |
| Communications | 85.6 | 96.0 | 102.2 | 109.3 | 115.3 |
| Public utilities | 92.0 | 103.5 | 118.7 | 126.5 | 132.0 |
| Wholesale and retail trade | 506.5 | 542.9 | 613.9 | 663.7 | 702.5 |
| Finance, insurance, real estate | 475.1 | 536.4 | 572.8 | 622.8 | 695.0 |
| Services | 463.6 | 515.5 | 580.2 | 643.7 | 700.2 |
| Government and government enterprise | 380.3 | 410.5 | 442.5 | 477.4 | 506.6 |
| Other | 51.2 | 49.9 | 47.4 | 39.8 | 33.7 |

### Structure of gross domestic product and labour force

| | 1986 | | | |
| | in value U.S.$'000,000,000 | % of total value | labour force | % of labour force |
|---|---|---|---|---|
| Agriculture | 93.0 | 2.2 | 3,163,000 | 2.6 |
| Mining | 95.3 | 2.3 | 783,000 | 0.7 |
| Manufacturing | 824.3 | 19.6 | 18,994,000 | 15.9 |
| Construction | 197.9 | 4.7 | 4,904,000 | 4.1 |
| Public utilities | 132.0 | 3.1 | | |
| Transportation and communication | 259.4 | 6.2 | 5,244,000 | 4.4 |
| Trade | 702.5 | 16.7 | 23,580,000 | 19.7 |
| Finance | 695.0 | 16.5 | 6,297,000 | 5.3 |
| Public administration, defense | 506.6 | 12.1 | 16,711,000 | 14.0 |
| Services | 700.2 | 16.7 | 23,099,000 | 19.3 |
| Other | −4.9[7] | −0.1 | 16,765,000[8] | 14.0 |
| TOTAL | 4,201.3 | 100.0 | 119,540,000 | 100.0 |

*Business activity* (1983): number of businesses 15,245,000 (sole proprietorships 70.2%, active corporations 19.7%, active partnerships 10.1%), of which services 4,646,000, wholesaling and retailing 2,415,000; business receipts $7,043,000,000,000 (active corporations 89.9%, sole proprietorships 6.6%, active partnerships 3.4%), of which wholesaling and retailing $195,-672,000,000, services $124,455,000,000; net profit $246,100,000,000 (active corporations 76.5%, sole proprietorships 23.5%), of which services $50,400,-000,000, wholesaling and retailing $44,900,000,000. New business concerns and business failures (1986): total number of new incorporations 702,101, total failures 61,183; failure rate per 10,000 concerns 87; current liabilities of failed concerns $43,961,000,000, average liability $718,500. Business expenditures for new plant and equipment (1986): total $395,100,000,000, of which manufacturing businesses $151,800,000,000 (nondurable goods 53.2%, durable 46.8%), trade, services, and communication $161,900,000,-000, public utilities $48,500,000,000, transportation $19,000,000,000, mining $13,900,000,000.
*Production* (metric tons except as noted). Agriculture, forestry, fishing (1986): corn (maize) 209,626,200,000, wheat 56,756,000,000, soybeans 54,590,400,-000, sugarcane 29,821,000, sugar beets 25,229,000, sorghum 23,735,000, potatoes 16,163,700, barley 12,100,000, oats 8,393,000, oranges 7,800,000, rice 6,129,400, grapes 5,595,900, cottonseed 4,628,000, apples 3,579,280, cotton 2,222,600, grapefruit 2,130,980, peanuts (groundnuts) 1,683,000, onions 1,535,000, peaches and pears 1,270,000, sunflower seeds 1,215,700, cabbages 1,213,000, green peas 1,120,000, carrots 1,030,000[9], dry beans 1,010,050[9], tobacco 546,300, rye 524,200[9], strawberries 462,117[9], almonds 335,480, milk 64,954,000,000[9], cheese 2,543,456,000[9], butter 571,576,000[9], eggs 4,041,400,-000[9]; livestock (number of live animals) 102,031,000 cattle, 50,960,000 pigs, 10,580,000 horses, 10,328,000 sheep, 1,550,000 goats, 1,155,000,000 poultry; roundwood (1985) 448,488,000 cu m; fish catch (1985) 2,897,100,000. Mining and quarrying (1986): iron ore 42,374,000; phosphate rock 40,200,000; copper 1,149,700; bauxite 500,000; lead 337,800; zinc 201,100; molybdenum

40,000; tin 11,000; uranium 6,300; nickel 2,000; silver 1,080; gold 112. Manufacturing (1986): crude steel 72,864,000; cement 71,112,000; paper and paper products 63,931,000; wood pulp 51,541,000; pig iron 43,952,000; sulfuric acid 33,404,000; gypsum and gypsum products 14,800,000; plastic and resins 14,595,000; nitrogenous and phosphate fertilizers 14,410,000; caustic soda 10,200,000; newsprint 5,108,400; man-made fibre 3,544,800; synthetic rubber 1,985,000; aluminum 1,738,000; machine tools U.S.$5,102,000,000; industrial material handling equipment U.S.$4,571,000,000; cotton fabric 3,248,000 sq m; footwear 252,000,000 pairs; motor vehicle tires 190,289,-000 units; radio receivers 58,684,000 units[9]; television receivers 40,606,000 units[9]; major household appliances 45,072,000 units, of which 12,444,000 microwave ovens, 6,510,000 refrigerators, 5,765,000 washing machines, 4,245,000 clothes dryers, 3,918,000 dishwashers, 3,729,000 water heaters. Construction (1986): private U.S.$316,600,000,000, of which residential U.S.$187,100,000,000, commercial and industrial U.S.$78,000,000,000, other U.S.$51,500,000,000; federal, state, and local U.S.$72,200,000,000.

### Retail and wholesale trade and services (1986)

| | no. of enter-prises[4] | no. of employees[10] | weekly wage as a % of all wages[10] | annual sales (U.S.$'000,000) |
|---|---|---|---|---|
| Retail trade | 1,923,228 | 18,207,000 | 57.1 | 1,445,567 |
| Durable goods | ... | ... | ... | 563,095 |
| Automotive dealers | 91,068 | 1,943,000 | 91.1 | 337,162 |
| Building materials, hardware, garden supply, and mobile home dealers | 34,002 | 743,100 | 81.7 | 85,790 |
| Furniture, home furnishings, equipment stores | 93,734 | 789,800 | 78.3 | 76,508 |
| Nondurable goods | ... | ... | ... | 882,472 |
| Food stores | 176,219 | 2,934,600 | 66.5 | 293,686 |
| General merchandise group stores | 34,145 | 2,320,100 | 58.6 | 165,793 |
| Eating and drinking places | 319,873 | 6,091,100 | ... | 141,649 |
| Gasoline service stations | 116,188 | 608,600 | 59.9 | 86,189 |
| Apparel and accessory stores | 133,920 | 1,083,700 | 47.4 | 75,283 |
| Drugstores and proprietary stores | 49,527 | 583,400 | 52.2 | 49,141 |
| Liquor stores | 34,861 | 124,500 | ... | 17,671 |
| Wholesale trade | 415,829 | 5,769,000 | 117.3 | 1,379,092 |
| Durable goods | 256,103 | 3,403,000 | 119.9 | 659,546 |
| Machinery, equipment, and supplies | 99,250 | 1,446,000 | 128.9 | 165,416 |
| Motor vehicles, automotive equipment | 39,460 | 433,600 | 105.5 | 148,268 |
| Electrical goods | 29,170 | 489,100 | 124.0 | 92,678 |
| Metals and minerals, except petroleum | 10,121 | 132,800 | 133.1 | 56,847 |
| Lumber and other construction materials | 17,041 | 229,700 | 116.5 | 50,144 |
| Hardware, plumbing, heating equipment and supplies | 20,815 | 262,400 | 113.0 | 43,387 |
| Furniture and home furnishings | 12,498 | 137,100 | 78.3 | 25,129 |
| Sporting, recreational, photographic, and hobby goods | 7,266 | 79,800 | 112.0 | 18,370 |
| Miscellaneous durable goods | 20,482 | 192,200 | 93.5 | 59,802 |
| Nondurable goods | 159,726 | 2,366,000 | 113.6 | 719,546 |
| Groceries and related products | 38,516 | 758,100 | 115.7 | 233,385 |
| Farm-products raw materials | 13,872 | 130,200 | ... | 80,873 |
| Apparel, piece goods, and notions | 14,289 | 191,200 | 107.5 | 40,701[9] |
| Beer, wine, and distilled alcoholic beverages | 6,378 | 153,400 | 127.4 | 40,301 |
| Paper and paper products | 13,967 | 192,200 | 121.3 | 38,536 |
| Chemicals and allied products | 10,724 | 132,800 | 149.8 | 26,380 |
| Drugs, drug proprietaries, and druggists' sundries | 3,851 | 172,600 | 129.3 | 28,604 |
| Miscellaneous nondurable goods | 39,434 | 444,600 | 92.3 | 110,102 |
| Services[11] | 1,261,698 | 24,093,000 | 87.3 | 363,134 |
| Business | 215,125 | 5,062,600 | 92.1 | 168,350 |
| Health, except hospitals | 346,565 | 6,812,200 | 68.6 | 143,959 |
| Legal | 115,407 | 780,000 | 129.3 | 51,209 |
| Engineering, architectural, and surveying | 45,341 | 696,700 | 162.8 | 40,934 |
| Hotels, motels, and other lodging places | 41,231 | 1,447,200 | 60.3 | 43,485 |
| Amusement and recreation, including motion pictures | 67,215 | 1,024,900 | 63.4 | 47,754 |
| Automotive repair, services, garages | 115,481 | 791,400 | 92.1 | 45,576 |
| Personal | 167,749 | 1,140,300 | 67.9 | 37,690 |
| Accounting, auditing, and bookkeeping | 51,900 | 444,600 | 119.7 | 22,620 |
| Miscellaneous repair services | 54,421 | 320,300 | 109.0 | 20,278 |

Energy production (consumption): electricity (kW-hr; 1986) 2,487,310,000,-000 (2,361,423,000,000); coal (metric tons; 1986) 805,556,000 (727,243,000); crude petroleum (barrels; 1986) 3,163,900,000 (5,967,400,000); petroleum products (metric tons; 1986) 632,170,000 (662,127,000); natural gas (cu m; 1986) 452,138,000,000 (453,000,000,000). Domestic production of energy by source (1986): coal 30.3%, crude oil 28.6%, natural gas 25.7%, nuclear power 7.0%, hydroelectric power 4.7%, other 3.7%.
Energy consumption by end use (in quads [quadrillion, or '000,000,000,-000,000, British thermal units]; 1986): total 73.93 (industrial 25.98; electric power utilities 26.79 [coal 54.0%, nuclear 16.7%, hydroelectric and nontraditional energy sources 12.9%, natural gas 10.1%]; residential and commercial 27.25 [natural gas 52.6%, electricity 29.6%]).
*Household income and expenditure.* Average household size (1986) 2.7; average annual income per household U.S.$29,460; sources of income: wages and salaries 59.5%, transfer payments 14.7%, personal interest income 13.6%, proprietors' income 8.0%, other labour income 6.0%; expenditure (1986)[12]: food 17.8%, housing, electricity, and gas 25.6%, clothing 6.0%, health 11.4%, transportation 12.9%, education and recreation 14.9%.
*Selected household characteristics* (1986). Total number of households 88,-458,000, of which: (by race and Spanish origin[13]; 1985) white 86.8%, black 10.9%, other 2.3%, Spanish origin 5.6%; (by location; 1983) in metropoli-

tan areas 68.4% (central cities 29.6%), outside metropolitan areas 31.6% (farms 1.9%); (by tenure; 1985) owned 55,812,400 (64.3%), rented 30,-987,600 (35.7%); family households 63,558,000, of which married couple 80.1%, female head with children under age 18 (1985), 9.6%, other 10.1%; nonfamily households 24,900,000, of which female householder 57.2%, male 42.8%. Work disability status of householder (1985): having no work disability 91.9%, having work disability 8.1%; having retirement or disability income 7.9%.

### Financial aggregates

| | 1981 | 1982 | 1983 | 1984 | 1985 | 1986 | 1987 |
|---|---|---|---|---|---|---|---|
| Exchange rate, U.S.$ per: | | | | | | | |
| £[14] | 2.03 | 1.75 | 1.52 | 1.34 | 1.30 | 1.47 | 1.63 |
| SDR[14] | 1.18 | 1.10 | 1.07 | 1.03 | 1.02 | 1.17 | 1.29 |
| International reserves (U.S.$)[15] | | | | | | | |
| Total (excl. gold; '000,000,000) | 18.92 | 22.81 | 22.63 | 23.84 | 32.10 | 37.45 | 34.07 |
| SDRs ('000,000,000) | 4.10 | 5.25 | 5.03 | 5.64 | 7.29 | 8.39 | 8.86 |
| Reserve pos. in IMF ('000,000,000) | 5.05 | 7.35 | 11.31 | 11.54 | 11.95 | 11.73 | 11.31 |
| Foreign exchange ('000,000,000) | 9.77 | 10.21 | 6.29 | 6.66 | 12.86 | 17.33 | 13.90 |
| Gold ('000,000 fine troy oz) | 264.11 | 264.03 | 263.39 | 262.79 | 262.65 | 262.04 | 262.15 |
| % world reserves | 27.70 | 27.83 | 27.80 | 27.77 | 27.68 | 27.63 | ... |
| Interest and prices | | | | | | | |
| Central bank discount (%)[15] | 12.00 | 8.50 | 8.50 | 8.00 | 7.50 | 5.5 | 5.5 |
| Gov't. bond yield (%)[14] | 14.44 | 12.92 | 10.45 | 11.89 | 9.64 | 7.06 | 7.82 |
| Industrial share prices[14] (1980 = 100) | 107.2 | 99.3 | 134.2 | 134.7 | 154.5 | 194.9 | 259.9 |
| Balance of payments ($'000,000,000) | | | | | | | |
| Balance of visible trade | −27.97 | −36.45 | −67.08 | −112.51 | −124.44 | −144.34 | −36.29 |
| Imports, f.o.b. | 265.07 | 247.65 | 268.89 | 332.41 | 338.86 | 368.70 | 94.72 |
| Exports, f.o.b. | 237.10 | 211.20 | 201.81 | 219.90 | 214.42 | 224.36 | 58.43 |
| Balance of invisibles | 41.78 | 36.27 | 29.88 | 18.19 | 21.65 | 18.56 | 5.39 |
| Balance of payments, current account | 6.37 | −9.05 | −46.68 | −106.49 | −117.76 | −141.46 | −33.86[3] |

*Population economically active* (1986): total 119,540,000; activity rate of total population 49.6% (participation rates: ages 16 and over 76.7%; female 43.3%, unemployed 7.1%).

### Price and earnings indexes (1980 = 100)

| | 1981 | 1982 | 1983 | 1984 | 1985 | 1986 | 1987[16] |
|---|---|---|---|---|---|---|---|
| Consumer price index | 110.4 | 117.1 | 120.9 | 126.1 | 130.5 | 133.1 | 137.8 |
| Hourly earnings index | 109.9 | 116.9 | 121.5 | 126.2 | 131.1 | 133.7 | 135.9 |

### Average employee earnings

| | average hourly earnings in U.S.$ | | average weekly earnings in U.S.$ | |
|---|---|---|---|---|
| | 1985 | 1986 | 1985 | 1986 |
| Manufacturing | | | | |
| Durable goods | 10.10 | 10.29 | 416.12 | 424.98 |
| Lumber and wood products | 8.22 | 8.33 | 327.98 | 335.70 |
| Furniture and fixtures | 7.17 | 7.46 | 282.50 | 296.91 |
| Stone, clay, and glass products | 9.84 | 10.05 | 412.30 | 424.11 |
| Primary metal industries | 11.67 | 11.86 | 484.31 | 496.93 |
| Fabricated metal products | 9.70 | 9.89 | 400.61 | 408.46 |
| Machinery, except electrical | 10.29 | 10.59 | 427.04 | 440.54 |
| Electrical and electronic equipment | 9.47 | 9.65 | 384.08 | 395.65 |
| Instruments and related products | 9.17 | 9.47 | 375.97 | 388.27 |
| Miscellaneous manufacturing | 7.30 | 7.54 | 287.62 | 298.58 |
| Nondurable goods | 8.71 | 8.94 | 344.92 | 356.71 |
| Food and kindred products | 8.57 | 8.74 | 342.80 | 349.60 |
| Tobacco manufactures | 11.96 | 12.85 | 444.91 | 480.59 |
| Textile mill products | 6.70 | 6.93 | 256.99 | 284.82 |
| Apparel and other textile products | 5.73 | 5.84 | 208.57 | 214.33 |
| Paper and allied products | 10.82 | 11.18 | 466.77 | 482.98 |
| Printing and publishing | 9.71 | 9.99 | 367.04 | 379.62 |
| Chemicals and allied products | 11.57 | 11.98 | 484.36 | 501.96 |
| Petroleum and coal products | 14.06 | 14.18 | 604.58 | 621.08 |
| Rubber and miscellaneous plastics products | 8.54 | 8.73 | 350.99 | 360.55 |
| Leather and leather products | 5.83 | 5.92 | 216.88 | 218.45 |
| Nonmanufacturing | | | | |
| Metal mining | 11.98 | 12.44 | 519.93 | ... |
| Coal mining | 15.30 | ... | 581.39 | ... |
| Oil and gas extraction | 10.99 | ... | 484.66 | ... |
| Nonmetallic minerals, except fuels | 10.11 | ... | 463.04 | ... |
| Construction | 12.3 | 12.47 | 464.46 | 466.38 |
| Transportation and public utilities | 11.40 | 11.70 | 450.30 | 458.64 |
| Wholesale trade | 9.16 | 9.35 | 351.74 | 359.04 |
| Retail trade | 5.94 | 6.03 | 174.64 | 176.08 |
| Finance, insurance, and real estate | 7.94 | 8.35 | 289.02 | 303.94 |
| Hotels, motels, and tourist courts | 5.72 | ... | 176.18 | ... |
| Health services | 8.11 | ... | 265.20 | ... |
| Legal services | 10.49 | ... | 364.00 | ... |
| Miscellaneous services | 11.51 | ... | 447.74 | ... |

*Tourism* (1986): receipts from visitors U.S.$12,913,000,000; expenditures by nationals abroad U.S.$17,627,000,000; number of foreign visitors 8,860,000 (3,722,000 from western Europe, 1,104,000 from Central America and the Caribbean, 944,000 from South America); number of nationals traveling abroad 11,562,000 (5,126,000 to Europe and the Mediterranean, 3,800,000 to Central America and the Caribbean, 616,000 to South America).
*Land use* (1985): forested 33.1%; meadows and pastures 26.2%; agricultural and under permanent cultivation 20.9%; other 19.8%.

### Foreign trade

#### Balance of trade (current prices)

| | 1981 | 1982 | 1983 | 1984 | 1985 | 1986 |
|---|---|---|---|---|---|---|
| U.S.$'000,000,000 | −28.0 | −36.5 | −67.1 | −112.5 | −122.1 | −144.3 |
| % of total | 5.6% | 7.9% | 14.3% | 20.4% | 22.0% | 24.3% |

*Imports* (1986): U.S.$387,081,500,000 (machinery and transport equipment 42.9%, of which new passenger cars 12.0%, telecommunications and sound recording and reproducing apparatus 5.5%, office machinery and automatic data-processing machines 3.9%, transport equipment parts 3.2%; basic and miscellaneous manufactures 28.8%, of which clothing 4.6%; iron and steel mill products 2.3%; mineral fuels and lubricants 10.3%, of which crude petroleum 6.2%, petroleum products 3.2%; food 5.8%). *Major import sources:* Japan 22.1%; Canada 17.7%; West Germany 5.6%; Taiwan 5.5%; Mexico 4.5%; United Kingdom 4.1%; South Korea 3.5%; Italy 2.9%; France 2.7%; Hong Kong 2.4%; Brazil 1.9%; Venezuela 1.4%; Singapore 1.3%; Indonesia 0.9%; Israel 0.6%; India 0.6%.

*Exports* (1986): U.S.$206,376,200,000 (machinery 29.3%, of which office machinery and computers 7.5%, special-purpose machinery 4.4%, power-generating machinery 4.4%; transport equipment 16.9%, of which motor vehicles and parts 9.0%, aircraft and parts 7.3%; basic and miscellaneous manufactures 15.1%, of which professional, scientific, and controlling instruments and apparatus 3.3%; chemicals and related products 10.6%; food 8.2%, of which grain and cereal preparations 3.6%). *Major export destinations:* Canada 20.9%; Japan 13.3%; Mexico 5.7%; United Kingdom 5.5%; West Germany 5.1%; The Netherlands 3.8%; France 3.5%; South Korea 2.9%; Australia 2.6%; Belgium–Luxembourg 2.5%; Taiwan 2.5%; Italy 2.2%; Saudi Arabia 1.6%; China 1.4%.

### Trade by commodity group (1986)

| SITC Group | imports (c.i.f.) U.S.$'000,000 | % | exports (f.a.s.)[17] U.S.$'000,000 | % |
|---|---|---|---|---|
| 00 Food and live animals | 22,395.1 | 5.8 | 17,302.6 | 8.4 |
| 01 Beverages and tobacco | 4,226.4 | 1.1 | 2,920.2 | 1.4 |
| 02 Crude materials, excluding fuels | 11,176.1 | 2.9 | 17,323.8 | 8.4 |
| 03 Mineral fuels, lubricants, and related materials | 39,838.1 | 10.3 | 8,114.5 | 3.9 |
| 04 Animal and vegetable oils, fat, and waxes | 580.8 | 0.2 | 1,014.9 | 0.5 |
| 05 Chemicals and related products, n.e.s. | 15,804.4 | 4.1 | 22,765.8 | 11.0 |
| 06 Basic manufactures | 51,699.9 | 13.3 | 14,005.0 | 6.8 |
| 07 Machinery and transport equipment | 166,240.2 | 42.9 | 95,289.5 | 46.2 |
| 08 Miscellaneous manufactured articles | 60,078.7 | 15.5 | 16,629.2 | 8.1 |
| 09 Goods not classified by kind | 15,041.8 | 3.9 | 11,010.7 | 5.3 |
| TOTAL | 387,081.5 | 100.0 | 206,376.2 | 100.0 |

### Direction of trade (1986)

| | imports (c.i.f.) U.S.$'000,000 | % | exports (f.a.s.)[18] U.S.$'000,000 | % |
|---|---|---|---|---|
| Africa | 10,348.1 | 2.7 | 5,978.2 | 2.7 |
| South Africa | 2,364.5 | 0.6 | 1,158.3 | 0.5 |
| Other | 7,983.6 | 2.1 | 4,819.9 | 2.2 |
| Americas | 113,483.1 | 29.3 | 76,504.5 | 35.2 |
| Canada | 68,662.4 | 17.7 | 45,332.6 | 20.9 |
| Caribbean countries and Central America | 6,749.7 | 1.8 | 6,830.5 | 3.1 |
| Mexico | 17,558.3 | 4.5 | 12,391.6 | 5.7 |
| South America | 20,512.7 | 5.3 | 11,949.8 | 5.5 |
| Asia | 162,667.8 | 42.0 | 64,531.8 | 29.7 |
| China | 5,240.5 | 1.3 | 4,780.7 | 2.2 |
| Japan | 85,456.7 | 22.1 | 28,881.6 | 13.3 |
| Middle East | 8,594.2 | 2.2 | 6,953.7 | 3.2 |
| Other Asia | 63,376.4 | 16.4 | 23,915.8 | 11.0 |
| Europe | 96,502.2 | 24.9 | 63,631.2 | 29.3 |
| EEC | 79,520.2 | 20.5 | 53,154.0 | 24.5 |
| Other Western Europe | 14,776.4 | 3.8 | 8,488.0 | 3.9 |
| U.S.S.R. | 605.5 | 0.2 | 1,247.5 | 0.6 |
| Eastern Europe | 1,600.1 | 0.4 | 741.7 | 0.3 |
| Oceania | 4,080.3 | 1.1 | 6,658.5 | 3.1 |
| Australia | 2,872.6 | 0.8 | 5,551.2 | 2.6 |
| Other | 1,207.7 | 0.3 | 1,107.3 | 0.5 |
| TOTAL | 387,081.5 | 100.0 | 217,304.2 | 100.0 |

### Transport and communications

*Transport.* Railroads (1985): length 184,235 mi, 296,497 km; passenger-mi (1984) 15,590,000,000, passenger-km 25,090,000,000; short ton-mi cargo 898,000,000,000, metric ton-km cargo 1,310,000,000,000. Roads (1986): total length 3,861,934 mi, 6,214,972 km (paved 88%). Vehicles (1986): passenger cars 135,700,000; trucks and buses 40,800,000. Merchant marine (1986): vessels (100 gross tons and over) 6,496; total deadweight tonnage 28,850,637. Air transport (1986)[19]: passenger-mi 319,118,000,000, passenger-km 513,571,000,000; short ton-mi cargo 11,447,900,000, metric ton-km cargo 18,423,593,000; airports (1986) with scheduled flights 824. Shares of intercity passenger and freight traffic by mode of transportation (1985): automobiles 81.9%; airplanes 16.0%; buses 1.4%; railway 0.7%.

### Distribution of commercial traffic (1982)

| | cargo carried ('000,000 tons) | % of nat'l total | passengers carried ('000,000) | % of nat'l total |
|---|---|---|---|---|
| Rail | 1.932 | 37.9 | 304 | 2.9 |
| Road | 493 | 9.6 | 482 | 4.6 |
| Urban transport | — | — | ... | ... |
| Road | — | — | 5,705 | 54.5 |
| Electric railway | — | — | 2,233 | 21.3 |
| Heavy rail | — | — | 1,433 | 13.7 |
| Inland water | 1,777 | 34.8 | 25 | 0.2 |
| Air | 4 | 0.1 | 294 | 2.8 |
| Pipeline | 897 | 17.6 | — | — |
| TOTAL | 5,103 | 100.0 | 10,476 | 100.0 |

*Communications.* Daily newspapers (1986): total number 1,657; total circulation 62,502,036; circulation per 1,000 population 259. Radio (1986): total number of receivers 478,000,000 (1 per 0.5 persons). Television (1985): total number of receivers 145,000,000 (1 per 1.7 persons). Telephones (1984): 181,091,000 (1 per 1.3 persons).

### Other communication media (1986)

| Print | titles | | titles |
|---|---|---|---|
| Books (new) | 42,793 | Home economics | 90 |
| of which | | Industrial arts | 106 |
| Agriculture | 445 | Journalism and | |
| Art | 1,316 | communication | 90 |
| Biography | 1,729 | Labour and industrial | |
| Business | 1,349 | relations | 70 |
| Education | 841 | Law | 273 |
| Fiction | 4,877 | Library and information | |
| General works | 1,970 | sciences | 118 |
| History | 1,936 | Literature and language | 158 |
| Home economics | 894 | Mathematics and science | 238 |
| Juvenile | 3,812 | Medicine | 182 |
| Language | 562 | Philosophy and religion | 130 |
| Law | 1,077 | Physical education and | |
| Literature | 1,800 | recreation | 151 |
| Medicine | 2,731 | Political science | 136 |
| Music | 292 | Psychology | 138 |
| Philosophy, psychology | 1,369 | Sociology and anthropology | 149 |
| Poetry, drama | 1,056 | Zoology | 94 |
| Religion | 2,212 | | |
| Science | 2,570 | **Cinema** | |
| Sociology, economics | 6,471 | Feature films | 361 |
| Sports, recreation | 962 | | |
| Technology | 2,110 | | traffic |
| Travel | 412 | | (units, '000) |
| Periodicals | 3,371 | **Electronic**[3] | |
| of which | | Telegrams | 53,000 |
| Agriculture | 153 | Domestic | 42,000 |
| Business and economics | 262 | International | 11,000 |
| Chemistry and physics | 170 | Telex | 69,559 |
| Children's periodicals | 78 | | |
| Education | 203 | **Post**[6] | (pieces of mail) |
| Engineering | 265 | Mail | 140,098,000 |
| Fine and applied arts | 145 | Domestic | 139,269,000 |
| General interest | 181 | International | 829,000 |
| History | 151 | | |

### Education and health

### Education (1986–87)

| | schools | teachers | students | student/ teacher ratio |
|---|---|---|---|---|
| Primary and preprimary (age 5–12) | 101,050 | 1,469,000 | 31,555,000 | 21.5 |
| Secondary and vocational (age 14–17) | | 1,061,000 | 13,703,000 | 12.9 |
| Higher, including teacher-training colleges | 3,280 | 690,000 | 12,164,000 | 17.6 |

*Literacy* (1980): total population age 15 and over literate 166,497,565 (95.5%); males literate 79,161,126 (95.7%); females literate 87,336,439 (95.3%); other studies indicate adult "functional" literacy may not exceed 85%.

*Health:* physicians (1985) 527,900 (1 per 452 persons), specialties (1983) internal medicine 15.9%, general practice 12.4%, general surgery 7.0%, pediatrics 6.3%, psychiatry 5.9%, obstetrics and gynecology 5.6%, anesthesiology 3.8%, orthopedics 3.1%, pathology 2.9%, ophthalmology 2.8%, radiology 2.0%, other 32.3%; hospital beds (1984) 1,339,000 (1 per 177 persons), of which nonfederal 91.6% (short-term general and special 76.2%, psychiatric 13.1%, long-term general and special 2.2%, tuberculosis 0.1%), federal 8.4%; infant mortality rate per 1,000 live births (1987) 10.2[3].

*Food* (1981–83): daily per capita caloric intake 3,647 (vegetable products 65%, animal products 35%); (1983) 138% of FAO recommended minimum requirement. Per capita consumption of major food groups (pounds annually; 1985): dairy products 596.2; flour and cereal products 173.3; sweeteners 169.7; meat 153.2; fruits and vegetables 230.7, of which fresh fruits 88.2, fresh vegetables 81.4; citrus fruit juices 49.7; fats and oils 64.0; poultry 58.0; fish 14.5.

### Military

*Total active duty personnel* (1986): 2,143,955 (army 36.0%, navy 26.5%, air force 28.3%, marine 9.2%). *Military expenditure as percent of GNP* (1984): 6.4% (world 5.9%); per capita expenditure U.S.$1,001. *Military aid* (1985): total $5,801,000,000 (Middle East and South Asia 73.2%, of which Israel 24.1%, Egypt 20.3%, Turkey 12.1%, Greece 8.6%, Pakistan 5.6%, Jordan 1.6%; Europe 9.2%, of which Spain 6.9%, Portugal 2.2%; East Asia 7.2%, of which South Korea 4.0%, Thailand 1.8%; Africa 4.8%, of which Tunisia 1.2%, Morocco 0.9%, Sudan 0.8%; Latin America 4.6%, of which El Salvador 2.3%, Honduras 1.2%; international organizations 1.1%).

[1]Total area excluding Great Lakes is 3,618,770 sq mi (9,372,571 sq km). [2]Detail does not add to total given because of rounding. [3]First six months only. [4]1982. [5]October 20. [6]1984. [7]Statistical discrepancy. [8]Includes 8,775,100 unemployed. [9]1985. [10]May 1987. [11]Figures for annual sales of services are for 1984. [12]Personal consumption expenditure. [13]Persons of Spanish origin may be of any race. [14]Annual average. [15]End of year. [16]July. [17]Domestic export only; value in f.a.s. (free alongside ship). [18]Includes reexports valued at U.S.$10,928,000,000. [19]Major carriers.

# Uruguay

*Official name:* República Oriental del Uruguay (Oriental Republic of Uruguay).
*Form of government:* republic with two legislative houses (Senate [31]; Chamber of Representatives [99]).
*Head of state and government:* President.
*Capital:* Montevideo.
*Official language:* Spanish.
*Official religion:* none.
*Monetary unit:* 1 Uruguayan new peso (NUr$) = 100 centésimos; valuation (Oct. 5, 1987) 1 U.S.$ = NUr$247.78; 1 £ = NUr$402.37.

### Area and population

| Departments | Capitals | area sq mi | area sq km | population 1985 census[1] |
|---|---|---|---|---|
| Artigas | Artigas | 4,605 | 11,928 | 68,400 |
| Canelones | Canelones | 1,751 | 4,536 | 359,700 |
| Cerro Largo | Melo | 5,270 | 13,648 | 78,000 |
| Colonia | Colonia del Sacramento | 2,358 | 6,106 | 112,100 |
| Durazno | Durazno | 4,495 | 11,643 | 54,700 |
| Flores | Trinidad | 1,986 | 5,144 | 24,400 |
| Florida | Florida | 4,022 | 10,417 | 65,400 |
| Lavalleja | Minas | 3,867 | 10,016 | 61,700 |
| Maldonado | Maldonado | 1,851 | 4,793 | 93,000 |
| Montevideo | Montevideo | 205 | 530 | 1,309,100 |
| Paysandú | Paysandú | 5,375 | 13,922 | 104,500 |
| Río Negro | Fray Bentos | 3,584 | 9,282 | 47,500 |
| Rivera | Rivera | 3,618 | 9,370 | 88,400 |
| Rocha | Rocha | 4,074 | 10,551 | 68,500 |
| Salto | Salto | 5,468 | 14,163 | 107,300 |
| San José | San José de Mayo | 1,927 | 4,992 | 91,900 |
| Soriano | Mercedes | 3,478 | 9,008 | 77,500 |
| Tacuarembó | Tacuarembó | 5,961 | 15,438 | 82,600 |
| Treinta y Tres | Trienta y Tres | 3,679 | 9,529 | 45,500 |
| TOTAL LAND AREA | | 67,574 | 175,016 | 2,940,200 |
| INLAND WATER | | 463 | 1,199 | |
| TOTAL AREA | | 68,037 | 176,215 | |

## Demography

*Population* (1987): 3,058,000.
*Density* (1987)[2]: persons per sq mi 45.3, persons per sq km 17.5.
*Urban–rural* (1985): urban 86.2%; rural 13.8%.
*Sex distribution* (1985): male 48.68%; female 51.32%.
*Age breakdown* (1985): under 15, 26.6%; 15–29, 22.9%; 30–44, 18.3%; 45–59, 16.5%; 60–74, 11.4%; 75 and over, 4.3%.
*Population projection:* (1990) 3,128,000; (2000) 3,364,000.
*Doubling time:* 91 years.
*Ethnic composition* (1980): mixed Spanish–Italian 85.9%; mestizo 3.0%; Italian 2.6%; Jewish 1.7%; mulatto 1.2%; other 5.6%.
*Religious affiliation* (1980): Christian 62.9%, of which Roman Catholic 59.5%; nonreligious and atheist 35.1%; Jewish 1.7%; other 0.3%.
*Major cities* (1985): Montevideo 1,246,500; Salto 77,400; Paysandú 75,200; Las Piedras 61,300; Rivera 55,400.

## Vital statistics

*Birth rate* per 1,000 population (1984): 17.9 (world avg. 29.0); (1981) legitimate 74.4%; illegitimate 25.6%.
*Death rate* per 1,000 population (1984): 10.2 (world avg. 11.0).
*Natural increase rate* per 1,000 population (1984): 7.7 (world avg. 18.0).
*Total fertility rate* (avg. births per childbearing woman; 1982): 2.6.
*Marriage rate* per 1,000 population (1983): 6.5.
*Divorce rate* per 1,000 population (1983): 1.0.
*Life expectancy* at birth (1981): male 69.1 years; female 73.8 years.
*Major causes of death* per 100,000 population (1984): diseases of the circulatory system 419.7; malignant neoplasms (cancers) 213.1; symptoms and ill-defined conditions 73.5; respiratory diseases 39.6; accidents 38.5.

## National economy

*Budget* (1986). Revenue: NUr$149,851,600,000 (direct taxes 73.5%, receipts from foreign trade 15.7%). Expenditures: NUr$161,170,400,000 (social security and welfare 57.8%, general public services 15.8%, interest on public debt 10.4%, capital investments 8.9%, subsidies 6.2%).
*Public debt* (external, outstanding; 1986): U.S.$2,759,300,000.
*Production* (metric tons except as noted). Agriculture, forestry, fishing (1985): sugarcane 552,000, wheat 440,000, rice 423,000, sugar beets 177,000, sorghum 152,000, potatoes 150,000, grapes 120,000, corn (maize) 108,000; livestock (number of live animals) 20,600,000 sheep, 9,948,000 cattle, 500,000 horses; roundwood 2,975,000 cu m; fish catch 139,078. Mining and quarrying (1985): clays 150,000; gypsum 100,000. Manufacturing (value added in NUr$'000,000; 1984): food products excluding beverages 16,559; petroleum products 12,217; textiles (other than clothing, footwear, or leather products) 10,441; clothing and footwear 7,961; beverages 5,558; tobacco 5,213; chemicals and chemical products 4,826; transport equipment 4,820; minerals 2,970. Construction (1984): residential 238,800 sq m; nonresidential 139,200 sq m. Energy production (consumption): electricity (kW-hr; 1985) 6,602,000,000 (3,924,000,000); coal, none (none); crude petroleum (barrels; 1985) none (8,232,000); petroleum products (metric tons; 1985) 996,000 (933,000); natural gas, none (n.a.).
*Gross national product* (1985): U.S.$4,980,000,000 (U.S.$1,650 per capita).

### Structure of gross domestic product and labour force

| | 1985 in value NUr$'000,000 | % of total value | 1985 labour force | % of labour force |
|---|---|---|---|---|
| Agriculture | 49,329 | 9.6 | 179,200 | 15.3 |
| Mining | } 123,864 | 24.2 | 1,900 | 0.2 |
| Manufacturing | | | 211,600 | 18.0 |
| Construction | 10,537 | 2.1 | 63,300 | 5.4 |
| Public utilities | 13,060 | 2.5 | 17,100 | 1.5 |
| Transp. and commun. | 33,419 | 6.5 | 59,100 | 5.0 |
| Trade | 53,151 | 10.4 | 136,800 | 11.7 |
| Finance | 58,847 | 11.5 | 42,100 | 3.6 |
| Pub. admin., defense | 45,309 | 8.8 } | 326,800 | 27.9 |
| Services | 56,620 | 11.0 } | | |
| Other | 68,451[3] | 13.4[3] | 134,400 | 11.4 |
| TOTAL | 512,587 | 100.0 | 1,172,300 | 100.0 |

*Tourism* (1984): receipts from visitors U.S.$107,000,000; expenditures by nationals abroad U.S.$154,000,000.
*Population economically active* (1985): total 1,172,300; activity rate of total population 39.9% (participation rates: ages 15–64 [1975] 59.6%; female [1975] 17.1%; unemployed 12.8%).

### Price and earnings indexes (1980 = 100)

| | 1981 | 1982 | 1983 | 1984 | 1985 | 1986 | 1987[4] |
|---|---|---|---|---|---|---|---|
| Consumer price index | 134.0 | 159.5 | 238.0 | 369.6 | 636.5 | 1,122.7 | 1,946.9 |
| Monthly earnings index[5] | 143.6 | 169.9 | 190.1 | 283.4 | 563.8 | ... | ... |

*Household income and expenditure.* Average household size (1985) 3.3; average annual income per household (1984): NUr$180,276 (U.S.$2,922); sources of income: wages 47.6%, self-employment 18.0%, pensions, transfer payments, and other 34.4%[6]; expenditure (1971–72)[7]: food 45.1%, household durable goods 13.4%, clothing 13.2%, housing 10.1%, transport and communication 5.4%, education 0.8%, personal effects and other 12.0%.
*Land use* (1984): forested 3.6%; meadows and pastures 78.5%; agricultural and under permanent cultivation 8.3%; other 9.6%.

## Foreign trade[8]

### Balance of trade (current prices)

| | 1981 | 1982 | 1983 | 1984 | 1985 | 1986 |
|---|---|---|---|---|---|---|
| U.S.$'000,000 | −284.5 | −15.3 | +305.4 | +183.6 | +179.1 | +305.2 |
| % of total | 10.5% | 0.7% | 17.1% | 11.0% | 11.7% | 16.3% |

*Imports* (1986): U.S.$869,980,000 (mineral products 20.4%; machinery and appliances 17.5%; chemical products 17.4%; synthetic plastic, resins, and rubber 8.0%; transport equipment 7.4%; vegetable products 6.9%; base metals and products 5.4%). *Major import sources* (1984): Brazil 17.2%; Nigeria 14.4%; Argentina 11.2%; United States 8.4%; West Germany 6.2%.
*Exports* (1986): U.S.$1,087,823,000 (textiles and textile products 29.1%; live animals and live animal products 27.1%; hides and skins 13.7%; vegetable products 12.3%; food, beverages, and tobacco 3.4%; synthetic plastics, resins, and rubber 1.9%). *Major export destinations* (1984): Brazil 15.6%; United States 13.3%; Argentina 9.5%; West Germany 8.5%; Iran 5.3%.

## Transport and communications

*Transport.* Railroads (1984): route length (1986) 3,001 km; passenger-km 330,000,000; metric ton-km cargo 273,000,000. Roads (1981): length 49,813 km (paved 20%). Vehicles (1981): passenger cars 281,275; trucks and buses 49,813. Merchant marine (1986): vessels (100 gross tons and over) 89; deadweight tonnage 224,854. Air transport (1985): passenger-km 386,903,000; metric ton-km cargo 36,856,000; airports (1987) 7.
*Communications.* Daily newspapers (1985): total number 21; total circulation 556,100[9]; circulation per 1,000 population 185[9]. Radio (1985): total receivers 1,700,000 (1 per 1.8 persons). Television (1985): total receivers 500,000 (1 per 6.0 persons). Telephones (1985): 374,438 (1 per 8.0 persons).

## Education and health

### Education (1985–86)

| | schools | teachers | students | student/ teacher ratio |
|---|---|---|---|---|
| Primary (age 6–12) | 2,360 | 14,193 | 356,002 | 25.1 |
| Secondary | 332 | ... | 188,176 | ... |
| Vocational[10] | 93 | 5,632 | 55,359 | 9.8 |
| Higher[10] | 1 | 4,537 | 63,734 | 14.0 |

*Educational attainment* (1975). Percent of population age 25 and over having: no formal schooling 9.9%; less than primary education 36.7%; primary 29.6%; secondary 17.4%; higher 6.3%. *Literacy* (1985): total population age 10 and over literate 95.3%; males 1,102,000 (94.8%); females 1,196,400 (95.8%).
*Health* (1984): physicians 5,756 (1 per 519 persons); hospital beds (1983) 23,400 (1 per 127 persons); infant mortality rate per 1,000 live births 30.3.
*Food* (1981–83): daily per capita caloric intake 2,706 (vegetable products 62%, animal products 38%); (1983) 99% of FAO recommended minimum.

## Military

*Total active duty personnel* (1987): 26,200 (army 71.8%, navy 16.8%, air force 11.4%). *Military expenditure as percent of GNP* (1984): 2.9% (world 5.9%); per capita expenditure U.S.$48.

---

[1]Preliminary. [2]Based on land area. [3]Includes indirect taxes less subsidies. [4]August. [5]Salaried employees only. [6]Urban only. [7]Weights of consumer price index components. [8]Import figures are f.o.b. in balance of trade and c.i.f. for commodities and trading partners. [9]Partial circulation only. [10]1984.

# Vanuatu

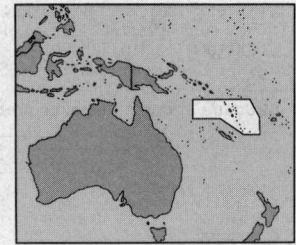

*Official name:* Ripablik blong Vanuatu (Bislama); République de Vanuatu (French); Republic of Vanuatu (English).
*Form of government:* republic with a single legislative house (Parliament [39]).
*Chief of state:* President.
*Head of government:* Prime Minister.
*Capital:* Vila.
*Official languages:* Bislama; French; English.
*Official religion:* none.
*Monetary unit:* vatu (VT); valuation (Oct. 5, 1987) 1 U.S.$ = VT 106.53; 1 £ = VT 173.00.

### Area and population

| Local Government Regions | Capitals | area sq mi | area sq km | population 1987 estimate |
|---|---|---|---|---|
| Ambrym | Eas | 257 | 666 | 8,100 |
| Ambae/Maéwo | Longana | 270 | 699 | 11,780 |
| Banks/Torres | Sola | 341 | 882 | 6,400 |
| Éfaté | Vila | 356 | 923 | 28,590 |
| Épi | Ringdove | 172 | 446 | 3,090 |
| Malekula | Lakatoro | 793 | 2,053 | 18,850 |
| Paama | Liro | 23 | 60 | 2,420 |
| Pentecost | Loltong | 193 | 499 | 11,780 |
| Santo/Malo | Luganville | 1,640 | 4,248 | 26,310 |
| Shepherd | Morua | 33 | 86 | 5,160 |
| Taféa | Isangel | 629 | 1,628 | 22,400 |
| TOTAL | | 4,707 | 12,190 | 144,880 |

## Demography

*Population* (1987): 145,000.
*Density* (1987): persons per sq mi 30.8, persons per sq km 11.9.
*Urban–rural* (1987): urban 14.5%[1]; rural 85.5%.
*Sex distribution* (1979): male 53.10%; female 46.90%.
*Age breakdown* (1985): under 15, 45.1%; 15–29, 26.3%; 30–44, 16.5%; 45–59, 8.3%; 60–74, 3.0%; 75 and over, 0.8%.
*Population projection:* (1990) 159,000; (2000) 216,000.
*Doubling time:* 21 years.
*Ethnic composition* (1979): Ni-Vanuatu 93.8%; European 2.2%; part-European 0.9%; Polynesian and Micronesian 0.9%; Asian 0.6%; other Melanesian 0.4%; other 1.2%.
*Religious affiliation* (1979): Christian 81.5%, of which Presbyterian 36.7%, Anglican 15.1%, Roman Catholic 14.8%, Seventh-day Adventist 6.2%; traditional beliefs (mostly followers of cargo cults) 7.6%; nonreligious 1.1%; unknown 9.8%.
*Major cities* (1987): Vila (Port-Vila) 15,100; Luganville (Santo) 5,900; Port Olry 884[2]; Isangel 752[2].

## Vital statistics

*Birth rate* per 1,000 population (1984): 45.0 (world avg. 29.0).
*Death rate* per 1,000 population (1984): 12.0 (world avg. 11.0).
*Natural increase rate* per 1,000 population (1984): 33.0 (world avg. 18.0).
*Total fertility rate* (avg. births per childbearing woman; 1984): 6.5.
*Marriage rate* per 1,000 population: n.a.
*Divorce rate* per 1,000 population: n.a.
*Life expectancy* at birth (1984): male 56.2 years; female 53.7 years.
*Major causes of death* per 100,000 population: n.a.; however, major diseases include malaria, infantile diarrhea, influenza, hookworm, and tuberculosis.

## National economy

*Budget* (1984). Revenue: VT 2,798,000,000 (current revenue 78.6%, of which taxes 63.7%, nontax revenue 14.9%; foreign aid 21.4%, of which grants 17.5%, loans 3.9%). Expenditures: VT 2,798,000,000 (current expenditure 98.8%, of which development expenditure 15.5%; capital expenditure 1.2%).
*Public debt* (external, outstanding; 1985): U.S.$6,900,000.
*Tourism* (1980): receipts from visitors, U.S.$9,800,000; expenditures by nationals abroad, n.a.
*Production* (metric tons except as noted). Agriculture, forestry, fishing (1985): coconuts 326,000, copra 47,000, roots and tubers 30,000, vegetables and melons 7,000, peanuts (groundnuts) 2,000, bananas 1,000, cocoa beans 1,000, corn (maize) 1,000; livestock (number of live animals) 100,000 cattle, 71,000 pigs, 8,000 goats; roundwood (1984) 38,000 cu m; fish catch (1984) 2,920, of which marine mollusks (mostly trochuses) 880, marine crustaceans 490. Mining and quarrying (1985)[3]: small quantities of coral reef limestone, crushed stone, sand, and gravel. Manufacturing (value added in '000 VT; 1984): food, beverages, and tobacco 358,000; wood products 96,000; fabricated metal products 60,000; paper products, including printing and publishing 48,800; nonmetallic mineral products 24,600; handicrafts 14,600; textiles, clothing, and leather 12,900. Construction (approvals in Vila and Luganville; 1985): residential 7,120 sq m; nonresidential 12,450 sq m. Energy production (consumption): electricity (kW-hr; 1985) 25,000,000 (25,000,000); coal, none (none); crude petroleum, none (none); petroleum products (metric tons; 1985) none (19,000); natural gas, none (none).
*Population economically active* (1979): total 51,130; activity rate of total population 46.0% (participation rates: ages 15–64, 84.3%; female 43.4%; unemployed, n.a.).

### Price and earnings indexes (1980 = 100)

| | 1980 | 1981 | 1982 | 1983 | 1984 | 1985 | 1986[4] |
|---|---|---|---|---|---|---|---|
| Consumer price index | 100.0 | 127.5 | 135.3 | 137.6 | 145.2 | 146.3 | 153.9 |
| Monthly earnings index | ... | ... | ... | ... | ... | ... | ... |

*Land use* (1984): forested 1.1%; meadows and pastures 1.7%; agricultural 6.4%; limestones, volcanic rock, and other 90.8%.
*Gross national product* (at current market prices; 1985): U.S.$118,000,000 (U.S.$880 per capita).

### Structure of gross domestic product and labour force

| | 1982 in value VT '000,000 | 1982 % of total value | 1979 labour force | 1979 % of labour force |
|---|---|---|---|---|
| Agriculture | 1,889 | 20.0 | 39,296 | 76.8 |
| Mining | 755[5] | 8.0[5] | 76 | 0.1 |
| Manufacturing | 472 | 5.0 | 990 | 1.9 |
| Construction | 189 | 2.0 | 1,103 | 2.2 |
| Public utilities | [5] | [5] | 61 | 0.1 |
| Transportation and communication | 283 | 3.0 | 1,323 | 2.6 |
| Trade | 944 | 10.0 | 2,178 | 4.3 |
| Finance | | | 326 | 0.6 |
| Pub. admin., defense } | 4,910 | 52.0 } | 5,502 | 10.8 |
| Services | | | | |
| Other | — | — | 308 | 0.6 |
| TOTAL | 9,442 | 100.0 | 51,163 | 100.0 |

*Household income and expenditure.* Average household size (1979) 5.0; income per household: n.a.; sources of income: n.a.; expenditure (1975)[1,6]: food and beverages 55.9%[7]; clothing and footwear 14.1%; health, education, and recreation 10.0%; transportation and communication 9.8%, household furnishings 8.0%, housing and energy 2.2%.

## Foreign trade[8]

### Balance of trade (current prices)

| | 1981 | 1982 | 1983 | 1984 | 1985 | 1986 |
|---|---|---|---|---|---|---|
| VT '000,000 | −2,283 | −3,462 | −3,352 | −2,416 | −4,274 | −4,587 |
| % of total | 28.7% | 44.0% | 36.3% | 21.6% | 39.6% | 60.2% |

*Imports* (1986): VT 6,105,000,000 (basic and miscellaneous manufactures 30.8%, machinery and transport equipment 24.6%, food and live animals 17.8%, mineral fuels 9.4%, chemicals 6.0%, beverages and tobacco 4.1%). *Major import sources:* Australia 36%; Japan 13%; New Zealand 10%; France 8%; New Caledonia 6%.
*Exports* (1986): VT 1,518,000,000 (domestic exports 61.6%, of which copra 29.2%, cocoa 12.9%, beef and veal 8.6%, timber 4.2%; reexports 38.4%, of which fish 8.3%). *Major export destinations*[9]: The Netherlands 34%; France 27%; Japan 17%; Belgium–Luxembourg 4%; New Caledonia 3%.

## Transport and communications

*Transport.* Railroads: none. Roads (1981): total length 660 mi, 1,062 km; (paved 4%). Vehicles (1981): passenger cars 3,000; trucks and buses 2,500. Merchant marine (1986): vessels (100 gross tons and over) 47; total deadweight tonnage 274,074. Air transport (1986): domestic passenger arrivals 86,940, international passenger arrivals 22,758, international cargo unloaded 357 metric tons; airports (1987) with scheduled flights 25.
*Communications.* Daily newspapers (1986): none. Radio (1986): total number of receivers 18,000 (1 per 7.8 persons). Television (1986): none. Telephones (1985): 3,000 (1 per 45 persons).

## Education and health

### Education (1983)

| | schools | teachers | students | student/ teacher ratio |
|---|---|---|---|---|
| Primary (age 6–11) | 246[10] | 934 | 23,465[10] | ... |
| Secondary (age 11–18) | 9 | 126[11] | 2,186 | ... |
| Voc., teacher tr. | 2 | 40[11] | 718 | ... |
| Higher | ... | ... | ... | ... |

*Educational attainment* (1979). Percent of population age 25 and over having: no formal schooling 37.2%; incomplete primary education 34.3%; complete primary 6.5%, lower-level secondary 14.7%, upper-level secondary and higher 7.3%. *Literacy* (1979): total population age 15 and over literate 32,120 (52.9%); males 18,550 (57.3%); females 13,570 (47.8%).
*Health* (1984): physicians 19 (1 per 6,968 persons); hospital beds (1983) 437 (1 per 294 persons); infant mortality rate per 1,000 live births 94.
*Food* (1981–83): daily per capita caloric intake 2,206 (vegetable products 79%, animal products 21%); (1983) 81% of FAO recommended minimum requirement.

## Military

*Total active duty personnel:* Vanuatu has a paramilitary force of about 300.

---

[1]Vila and Luganville only. [2]1979. [3]An opencut manganese mine 55 mi (34 km) northwest of Vila remained closed throughout the year. [4]Average of second quarter. [5]Mining includes Public utilities. [6]Weights of consumer price index components for low-income households only. [7]Includes tobacco. [8]Imports c.i.f.; exports f.o.b. [9]Domestic exports only. [10]1984. [11]1982.

# Venezuela

*Official name:* República de Venezuela (Republic of Venezuela).
*Form of government:* federal multiparty republic with two legislative houses (Senate [47]; Chamber of Deputies [200]).
*Head of state and government:* President.
*Capital:* Caracas.
*Official language:* Spanish.
*Official religion:* none.
*Monetary unit:* 1 bolívar (B, plural Bs) = 100 céntimos; valuation[1] (Oct. 5, 1987) 1 U.S.$ = Bs 4.30; 1 £ = Bs 6.98.

### Area and population

| States | Capitals | area sq mi | area sq km | population 1987 estimate |
|---|---|---|---|---|
| Anzoátegui | Barcelona | 16,700 | 43,300 | 820,274 |
| Apure | San Fernando de Apure | 29,500 | 76,500 | 239,296 |
| Aragua | Maracay | 2,700 | 7,014 | 1,196,817 |
| Barinas | Barinas | 13,600 | 35,200 | 428,453 |
| Bolívar | Ciudad Bolívar | 91,900 | 238,000 | 895,607 |
| Carabobo | Valencia | 1,795 | 4,650 | 1,443,464 |
| Cojedes | San Carlos | 5,700 | 14,800 | 178,255 |
| Falcón | Coro | 9,600 | 24,800 | 599,017 |
| Guárico | San Juan de Los Morros | 25,091 | 64,986 | 457,133 |
| Lara | Barquisimeto | 7,600 | 19,800 | 1,155,411 |
| Mérida | Mérida | 4,400 | 11,300 | 580,277 |
| Miranda | Los Teques | 3,070 | 7,950 | 1,837,762 |
| Monagas | Maturín | 11,200 | 28,900 | 475,487 |
| Nueva Esparta | La Asunción | 440 | 1,150 | 254,643 |
| Portuguesa | Guanare | 5,900 | 15,200 | 553,898 |
| Sucre | Cumaná | 4,600 | 11,800 | 705,515 |
| Táchira | San Cristóbal | 4,300 | 11,100 | 800,879 |
| Trujillo | Trujillo | 2,900 | 7,400 | 526,183 |
| Yaracuy | San Felipe | 2,700 | 7,100 | 356,355 |
| Zulia | Maracaibo | 24,400 | 63,100 | 2,071,058 |
| **Other federal entities** | | | | |
| Amazonas | Puerto Ayacucho | 67,900 | 175,750 | 76,889 |
| Delta Amacuro | Tucupita | 15,500 | 40,200 | 89,458 |
| Dependencias Federales | — | 50 | 120 | ... |
| Distrito Federal | Caracas | 745 | 1,930 | 2,530,026 |
| TOTAL | | 352,144[2] | 912,050 | 18,272,157 |

## Demography

*Population* (1987): 18,272,157.
*Density* (1987): persons per sq mi 51.9, persons per sq km 20.0.
*Urban–rural* (1985): urban 85.7%; rural 14.3%.
*Sex distribution* (1985): male 50.00%; female 50.00%.
*Age breakdown* (1985): under 15, 41.0%; 15–29, 28.7%; 30–44, 16.8%; 45–59, 8.8%; 60–74, 4.0%; 75 and over, 0.8%[2].
*Population projection:* (1990) 19,735,000; (2000) 24,715,000.
*Doubling time:* 29 years.
*Ethnic composition* (1981): mestizo 69%; white 20%; black 9%; Indian 2%.
*Religious affiliation* (1983): Roman Catholic 90.7%; other 9.3%.
*Major cities* (1987): Caracas 1,246,677; Maracaibo 1,124,432; Valencia 856,455; Barquisimeto 661,265; Maracay 496,662.

## Vital statistics

*Birth rate* per 1,000 population (1985): 29.0 (world avg. 29.0); (1974) legitimate 47.0%; illegitimate 53.0%.
*Death rate* per 1,000 population (1985): 4.6 (world avg. 11.0).
*Natural increase rate* per 1,000 population (1985): 24.4 (world avg. 18.0).
*Total fertility rate* (avg. births per childbearing woman; 1985–90): 3.8.
*Marriage rate* per 1,000 population (1985): 5.4.
*Divorce rate* per 1,000 population (1983): 0.3.
*Life expectancy* at birth (1980–85): male 65.1 years; female 70.6 years.
*Major causes of death* per 100,000 population (1983): circulatory diseases 132.0; accidents, poisonings, and violence 71.3; malignant neoplasms 54.3; infectious and parasitic diseases 47.4; respiratory diseases 35.6.

## National economy

*Budget* (1985). Revenue: Bs 118,039,000,000 (oil revenues 52.6%, indirect taxes 18.3%, direct taxes 10.8%, nontax revenues 9.7%). Expenditures: Bs 113,307,000,000 (1984; economic services 22.7%, education 17.7%, social welfare 7.6%, health 7.6%, housing 7.1%, defense 6.1%, public services 5.5%).
*Public debt* (external, outstanding; 1985): U.S.$16,649,800,000.
*Tourism* (1984): receipts from visitors U.S.$343,000,000; expenditures by nationals abroad U.S.$995,000,000.
*Production* (metric tons except as noted). Agriculture, forestry, fishing (1985): sugarcane 5,673,000, bananas 989,000, corn (maize) 900,000, sorghum 590,000, rice 472,000, coffee 64,000, seed cotton 46,000, sesame seed 34,000, cacao 11,000; livestock (number of live animals) 12,486,000 cattle; roundwood (1984) 1,322,000 cu m; fish catch (1984) 265,010. Mining and quarrying (1985): iron ore 15,481,000; gold 72,919 troy ounces; diamonds 215,000 carats; coal 40,400; salt 350,000. Manufacturing (1985): cement 5,121,000; steel 2,723,000; fertilizers 650,000; paper and cardboard 550,000; refined sugar 457,000; aluminum 407,000; motor vehicles 116,000 units. Construction (1984)[3]: residential 2,173,600 sq m; nonresidential 899,900 sq m. Energy production (consumption): electricity (kW-hr; 1985) 45,400,000,000 (45,392,000,000); coal (metric tons; 1985) 40,400 (301,000); crude

petroleum (barrels; 1985) 604,511,000 (299,913,000); petroleum products (metric tons; 1985) 43,153,000 (18,243,000); natural gas (cu m; 1985) 16,310,000,000 (16,310,000,000).
*Gross national product* (1985): U.S.$53,800,000,000 (U.S.$3,110 per capita).

### Structure of gross domestic product and labour force

| 1985 | in value Bs '000,000[4] | % of total value | labour force | % of labour force |
|---|---|---|---|---|
| Agriculture | 5,180 | 7.3 | 845,732 | 14.5 |
| Mining | 4,832 | 6.8 | 78,284 | 1.3 |
| Manufacturing | 14,590 | 20.5 | 913,478 | 15.7 |
| Construction | 2,208 | 3.1 | 499,551 | 8.6 |
| Public utilities | 2,646 | 3.7 | 72,755 | 1.2 |
| Transp. and commun. | 9,213 | 13.0 | 378,699 | 6.5 |
| Trade | 6,456 | 9.1 | 1,089,933 | 18.7 |
| Finance | ... | ... | 287,724 | 4.9 |
| Pub. admin., defense | 10,160 | 14.3 | 1,533,763 | 26.3 |
| Services | 15,804 | 22.2 | | |
| Other | | | 127,731 | 2.2 |
| TOTAL | 71,089 | 100.0 | 5,827,650 | 100.0[2] |

*Population economically active* (1986): total 6,107,115; activity rate of total population 34.1% (participation rates: over age 15, 56.1%; female [1984] 15.3%; unemployed 10.5%).

### Price and earnings indexes (1980 = 100)

| | 1981 | 1982 | 1983 | 1984 | 1985 | 1986 | 1987[5] |
|---|---|---|---|---|---|---|---|
| Consumer price index | 116.2 | 127.3 | 135.3 | 151.8 | 169.1 | 188.6 | 219.2 |
| Monthly earnings index | ... | ... | ... | ... | ... | ... | ... |

*Household income and expenditure:* average household size (1981) 5.3; average annual income per household (1979) Bs 2,897 (U.S.$512); sources of income: n.a.; expenditure (1984): food 55.6%, transport and communication 10.8%, rent and utilities 9.3%, education 5.9%, household furnishings and maintenance 5.1%, medical care 4.4%, clothing 4.1%.
*Land use* (1984): forested 36.2%; meadows and pastures 19.7%; agricultural and under permanent cultivation 4.3%; other 39.8%.

## Foreign trade

### Balance of trade (current prices)

| | 1981 | 1982 | 1983 | 1984 | 1985 | 1986 |
|---|---|---|---|---|---|---|
| Bs '000,000 | +35,706 | +20,765 | +31,427 | +49,665 | +36,786 | +11,429 |
| % of total | 26.0% | 17.2% | 31.8% | 34.3% | 25.0% | 7.8% |

*Imports* (1986): Bs 74,651,000,000 (1981; machinery and transport equipment 43.4%, of which road motor vehicles 12.2%; chemicals and related products 10.4%; electrical machinery, apparatus, and equipment 9.5%; iron and steel 5.9%; cereals and cereal preparations 5.0%). *Major import sources* (1985): U.S. 49.5%; Italy 6.3%; Japan 5.2%; W.Ger. 5.2%; France 4.6%; Brazil 4.4%; Canada 3.5%.
*Exports* (1986): Bs 78,682,000,000 (1981; crude petroleum oils and crude oils obtained from bituminous materials 78.7%; petroleum products, refined 14.1%). *Major export destinations* (1985): U.S. 41.1%; Netherlands Antilles 16.6%; W.Ger. 7.1%; Canada 5.2%; Italy 3.9%; Dominican Republic 2.3%.

## Transport and communications

*Transport.* Railroads (1985): route length (1986) 273 mi, 439 km; passenger-mi 4,936,000, passenger-km 7,944,000; short ton-mi cargo 9,364,000, metric ton-km cargo 13,671,000. Roads (1985): total length 47,082 mi, 75,772 km (paved 32%). Vehicles (1985): passenger cars 2,289,000; trucks and buses 1,094,000. Merchant marine (1986): vessels (100 gross tons and over) 279; total deadweight tonnage 1,428,634. Air transport (1985): passenger-mi 1,531,313,000, passenger-km 2,464,414,000; short ton-mi cargo 147,385,000, metric ton-km cargo 215,178,000; airports (1987) with scheduled flights 39.
*Communications.* Daily newspapers (1982): total number 61; total circulation 2,739,000; circulation per 1,000 population 172. Radio (1986): 6,747,000 receivers (1 per 2.6 persons). Television (1985): 2,880,800 receivers (1 per 6.0 persons). Telephones (1985): 1,451,450 (1 per 12 persons).

## Education and health

### Education (1984–85)

| | schools | teachers | students | student/ teacher ratio |
|---|---|---|---|---|
| Primary (age 7–12) | 14,277 | 125,140 | 3,256,554 | 26.0 |
| Secondary (age 13–17)[6] | 2,241 | 58,056 | 1,007,642 | 17.4 |
| Higher | 81 | 30,123 | 381,575 | 12.7 |

*Educational attainment* (1981). Percent of population age 25 and over having: no formal schooling 23.5%; primary education 47.2%; secondary 22.3%; higher 7.0%. *Literacy* (1985): total population age 15 and over literate 9,332,788 (88.4%); males 4,786,841 (90.3%); females 4,545,947 (86.5%).
*Health:* physicians (1983) 21,502 (1 per 762 persons); hospital beds (1979) 43,650 (1 per 333 persons); infant mortality rate (1985) 26.1.
*Food* (1981–83): daily per capita caloric intake 2,664 (vegetable products 79%, animal products 21%); (1983) 111% of FAO recommended minimum.

## Military

*Total active duty personnel* (1986): 71,000 (army 78.9%, navy 14.1%, air force 7.0%). *Military expenditure as percent of GNP* (1984): 1.6% (world 5.9%); per capita expenditure U.S.$63.

[1]Essential imports rate only; free market rate is 643.4% higher. [2]Detail does not add to total given because of rounding. [3]Private construction only. [4]In prices of 1968. [5]April. [6]Includes vocational and teacher training.

# Vietnam

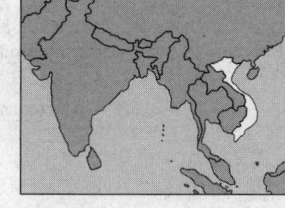

*Official name:* Cong Hoa Xa Hoi Chu Nghia Viet Nam (Socialist Republic of Vietnam).
*Form of government:* unitary single-party socialist republic with one legislative house (National Assembly [496]).
*Chief of state:* Chairman of the State Council (President).
*Head of government:* Chairman of the Council of Ministers.
*Capital:* Hanoi.
*Official language:* Vietnamese.
*Official religion:* none.
*Monetary unit:* 1 dong (D) = 10 hao = 100 xu; valuation (Oct. 5, 1987) 1 U.S.$ = D 80.00; 1 £ = D 129.80.

| Area and population | | area | | population |
|---|---|---|---|---|
| | | sq mi | sq km | 1979 census |
| **Provinces** | **Capitals** | | | |
| An Giang | Long Xuyen | 1,349 | 3,493 | 1,532,362 |
| Bac Thai | Thai Nguyen | 2,521 | 6,530 | 815,105 |
| Ben Tre | Ben Tre | 859 | 2,225 | 1,041,838 |
| Binh Tri Thien | Hue | 7,081 | 18,340 | 1,901,713 |
| Cao Bang | Cao Bang | 3,261 | 8,445 | 479,823 |
| Cuu Long | Vihn Long | 1,488 | 3,854 | 1,504,215 |
| Dac Lac | Buon Me Thoat | 7,645 | 19,800 | 490,198 |
| Dong Nai | Bien Hoa | 2,926 | 7,578 | 1,304,799 |
| Dong Thap | Cao Lamh | 1,309 | 3,391 | 1,182,787 |
| Gia Lai-Cong Tum | Cong Tum | 9,860 | 25,536 | 595,906 |
| Ha Bac | Bac Giang | 1,780 | 4,609 | 1,662,671 |
| Ha Nam Ninh | Nam Dinh | 1,453 | 3,763 | 2,781,409 |
| Ha Son Binh | Hanoi | 2,308 | 5,978 | 1,537,190 |
| Ha Tuyen | Ha Giang | 5,219 | 13,518 | 782,453 |
| Hai Hung | Hai Duong | 986 | 2,555 | 2,145,662 |
| Hau Giang | Can Tho | 2,365 | 6,126 | 2,232,891 |
| Hoang Lien Son | Lao Cai | 5,734 | 14,852 | 778,217 |
| Kien Giang | Rach Gia | 2,455 | 6,358 | 994,673 |
| Lai Chau | Lai Chau | 6,586 | 17,068 | 322,077 |
| Lam Dong | Da Lat | 3,835 | 9,933 | 396,657 |
| Lang Son | Lang Son | 3,161 | 8,187 | 484,657 |
| Long An | Tan An | 1,681 | 4,355 | 957,264 |
| Minh Hai | Bac Lieu | 2,972 | 7,697 | 1,219,595 |
| Nghe Tinh | Vinh | 8,688 | 22,502 | 3,111,989 |
| Nghia Binh | Qui Nhon | 4,595 | 11,900 | 2,095,354 |
| Phu Khanh | Nha Trang | 3,785 | 9,804 | 1,188,637 |
| Quang Nam-Da Nang | Da Nang | 4,629 | 11,989 | 1,529,520 |
| Quang Ninh | Hai Duong | 2,293 | 5,938 | 750,055 |
| Son La | Son La | 5,586 | 14,468 | 487,793 |
| Song Be | Thu Dau Mo | 3,807 | 9,859 | 659,093 |
| Tay Ninh | Ho Chi Minh City | 1,556 | 4,030 | 684,006 |
| Thai Binh | Thai Binh | 577 | 1,495 | 1,506,235 |
| Thanh Hoa | Thanh Hoa | 4,300 | 11,138 | 2,532,261 |
| Thuan Hai | Phan Thiet | 4,392 | 11,374 | 938,255 |
| Tien Giang | My Tho | 918 | 2,377 | 1,264,498 |
| Vinh Phu | Viet Tri | 1,786 | 4,626 | 1,488,348 |
| **Municipalities** | | | | |
| Haiphong | — | 585 | 1,515 | 1,279,067 |
| Hanoi | — | 826 | 2,139 | 2,570,905 |
| Ho Chi Minh City | — | 787 | 2,029 | 3,419,978 |
| **Special zone** | | | | |
| Vung Tau-Con Dao | — | 108 | 279 | 91,610 |
| **TOTAL** | | 128,052 | 331,653 | 52,741,766 |

## Demography

*Population* (1987): 62,468,000.
*Density* (1987): persons per sq mi 487.8; persons per sq km 188.4.
*Urban–rural* (1986): urban 19.0%; rural 81.0%.
*Sex distribution* (1986): male 48.91%; female 51.09%.
*Age breakdown* (1985): under 15, 40.8%; 15–29, 30.8%; 30–44, 13.5%; 45–59, 9.3%; 60–74, 4.4%; 75 and over, 1.2%.
*Population projection:* (1990) 66,573,000; (2000) 82,310,000.
*Doubling time:* 30 years.
*Ethnic composition* (1979): Vietnamese 88.0%; Chinese (Hoa) 1.9%; Tai 1.5%; Khmer 1.2%; Muong 1.2%; Thai 1.2%; Nung 0.9%; other 4.1%.
*Religious affiliation* (1980): Buddhist 55.3%; Roman Catholic 7.0%; Muslim 1.0%; other 36.7%.
*Major cities* (1979): Ho Chi Minh City 2,441,185; Hanoi 2,961,000[1]; Haiphong 330,755; Da Nang 318,655; Bien Hoa 190,086.

## Vital statistics

*Birth rate* per 1,000 population (1986): 33.6 (world avg. 26.0).
*Death rate* per 1,000 population (1986): 10.3 (world avg. 9.9).
*Natural increase rate* per 1,000 population (1986): 23.3 (world avg. 16.1).
*Total fertility rate* (avg. births per childbearing woman; 1986): 4.4.
*Life expectancy* at birth (1986): male 58.1 years; female 62.5 years.
*Major causes of death* per 100,000 population (1979): diseases of the circulatory system 123.8; malignant neoplasms (cancers) 54.0; infectious and parasitic diseases 48.0.

## National economy

*Budget* (1982). Revenue: U.S.$4,120,000,000. Expenditures: U.S.$5,560,000,000.
*Public debt* (external, outstanding; 1985): U.S.$6,700,000,000.
*Gross national product* (1984): U.S.$18,100,000,000 (U.S.$310 per capita).

| Structure of net material product and labour force | | | | |
|---|---|---|---|---|
| | 1983 | | 1985 | |
| | by value | % of total value | labour force | % of labour force |
| Agriculture | ... | 57.6 | 17,502,000 | 60.9 |
| Mining and manufacturing | ... | 23.7[2] | 870,000 | 3.0 |
| Construction | ... | 3.0 | 517,000 | 1.8 |
| Public utilities | ... | [2] | 37,100 | 0.1 |
| Transp. and commun. | ... | 1.9 | 188,000 | 0.7 |
| Trade | ... | 11.7 | 447,000 | 1.6 |
| Services | ... | ... | 927,400 | 3.2 |
| Other | ... | 2.1[3] | 8,266,500[4] | 28.7[4] |
| TOTAL | ... | 100.0 | 28,755,000 | 100.0 |

*Tourism.* Receipts from visitors (1987 est.) U.S.$15,000,000; expenditures by nationals abroad, n.a.
*Production* (metric tons except as noted). Agriculture, forestry, fishing (1985): rice 16,069,000, sugarcane 4,800,000, fruits 3,550,000, cassava 3,000,000, soybeans 3,000,000, vegetables 2,594,000, sweet potatoes 2,000,000, corn (maize) 587,000, coconuts 400,000, potatoes 189,000; livestock (number of live animals; 1986) 11,807,000 pigs, 5,188,000 cattle, 403,000 sheep and goats, 91,200,000 poultry; roundwood 24,872,000 cu m; fish catch 800,000. Mining and quarrying (1985): salt 800,000; phosphate rock 220,000; chromite 15,000; bauxite 6,000; zinc ore 5,000. Manufacturing (1985): cement 1,436,000; fertilizers 516,000; sugar 384,000; paper and paperboard 79,300; crude steel 57,500; soap 52,500; textiles 367,000,000 sq m; beer 840,000 hectolitres; leather footwear 210,000 pairs; cigarettes 20,600,000,000 units. Construction: n.a. Energy production (consumption): electricity (kW-hr; 1985) 5,228,000,000 (5,228,000,000); coal (metric tons; 1985) 5,432,000 (5,432,000); crude petroleum, none (n.a.); petroleum products (metric tons; 1985) none (1,370,000); natural gas, none (n.a.).
*Population economically active* (1985): total 28,755,000; activity rate of total population 48.0% (participation rates: ages 15–64, 55.0%[5]; female 45.5%[5]; unemployed, n.a.).
*Land use* (1984): forested 40.4%; meadows and pastures 0.8%; agricultural and under permanent cultivation 23.3%; other 35.5%.

## Foreign trade

| Balance of trade (current prices) | | | | | | |
|---|---|---|---|---|---|---|
| | 1979 | 1980 | 1981 | 1982 | 1983 | 1984 |
| U.S.$'000,000 | −1,012 | −759 | −931 | −843 | −702 | −710 |
| % of total | 46.3% | 41.4% | 49.9% | 41.6% | 39.5% | 36.4% |

*Imports* (1986): c. U.S.$1,000,000,000 (1980; fuel and raw materials 44.7%, machinery 23.2%, wheat flour and food products 17.2%). *Major import sources:* U.S.S.R. 23.0%; Japan 21.9%; Hong Kong 13.6%; Singapore 13.2%; India 12.4%; France 5.0%; United States 4.1%; Hungary 3.0%; Sweden 3.0%.
*Exports* (1986): c. U.S.$800,000,000 (1980; manufactured goods 72.8%, handicrafts 18.6%, agricultural products 8.6%). *Major export destinations:* Hong Kong 31.6%; Japan 18.3%; Singapore 17.5%; U.S.S.R. 9.7%; France 3.0%; Hungary 2.4%.

## Transport and communications

*Transport.* Railroads (1985): length 1,568 mi, 2,523 km; passenger-mi 2,087,000,000, passenger-km 3,359,000,000; short ton-mi cargo 595,000,000, metric ton-km cargo 869,000,000. Roads (1984): total length 37,282 mi, 60,000 km (paved 16%[6]). Vehicles (1976): passenger cars 100,000; trucks and buses 200,000. Merchant marine (1986): vessels (100 gross tons and over) 150; total deadweight tonnage 507,975. Air transport (1985): passenger-mi 183,300,000, passenger-km 295,000,000; short ton-mi cargo 4,100,000, metric ton-km cargo 6,000,000; airports (1987) with scheduled flights 3.
*Communications.* Daily newspapers (1984): 4; total circulation 500,000; circulation per 1,000 population 8.6. Radio (1985): 6,045,000 receivers (1 per 10 persons). Television (1984): 2,250,000 receivers (1 per 26 persons). Telephones (1982): 1,165,000 (1 per 48.1 persons).

## Education and health

| Education (1985–86) | schools | teachers | students | student/ teacher ratio |
|---|---|---|---|---|
| Primary and secondary (age 7–18) | 13,596 | 414,000 | 12,203,000 | 29.5 |
| Vocational | 298 | 11,400 | 128,000 | 11.2 |
| Higher | 97 | 18,800 | 88,600 | 4.7 |

*Educational attainment* (1983). Percent of state-employed population having[7]: vocational education 12.9%; higher 7.4%. *Literacy* (1979): total population age 15 and over literate 28,903,500 (94.0%).
*Health* (1986): physicians 19,100[8] (1 per 3,200 persons); hospital beds 216,000 (1 per 283 persons); infant mortality rate per 1,000 live births 69.
*Food* (1981–83): daily per capita caloric intake 2,185 (vegetable products 94%, animal products 6%); (1983) 92% of FAO recommended minimum.

## Military

*Total active duty personnel* (1986): 1,155,000 (army 86.6%, navy 4.7%, air force 8.7%). *Military expenditure as percent of GNP:* n.a. *Foreign military aid* (1983): U.S.$200,000,000.

[1]1985 estimate. [2]Mining and manufacturing includes public utilities. [3]Other material activities. [4]Includes finance and public administration and defense. [5]1983. [6]1981. [7]Total state-employed 3,868,000. [8]Includes dentists.

# Virgin Islands (U.S.)

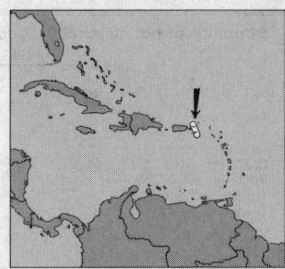

*Official name:* Virgin Islands of the
United States.
*Political status:* organized
unincorporated territory
of the United States with
one legislative house (Senate [15]).
*Chief of state:* President of the
United States.
*Head of government:* Governor.
*Capital:* Charlotte Amalie.
*Official language:* English.
*Official religion:* none.
*Monetary unit:* 1 U.S. dollar
(U.S.$) = 100 cents; valuation (Oct. 5,
1987) 1 U.S.$ = £0.62.

### Area and population

| | | area | | population |
|---|---|---|---|---|
| Islands[1] | Capitals | sq mi | sq km | 1986 estimate |
| St. Croix | Christiansted | 84 | 217 | 54,300 |
| St. John | Cruz Bay | 20 | 52 | 2,940 |
| St. Thomas | Charlotte Amalie | 32 | 83 | 52,260 |
| TOTAL | | 136 | 352 | 109,500 |

## Demography

*Population* (1987): 112,000.
*Density* (1987): persons per sq mi 823.5, persons per sq km 318.2.
*Urban–rural* (1985): urban 45.2%; rural 54.8%.
*Sex distribution* (1980): male 47.85%; female 52.15%.
*Age breakdown* (1980): under 15, 36.0%; 15–29, 24.2%; 30–44, 21.5%; 45–59,
11.1%; 60–74, 5.8%; 75 and over, 1.4%.
*Population projection:* (1990) 118,000; (2000) 143,000.
*Doubling time:* 35 years.
*Ethnic composition* (1980)[2]: black 79.7%, of which Spanish or Hispanic
origin 10.3%; white 14.8%, of which Spanish or Hispanic origin 2.3%; other
5.5%, of which Spanish or Hispanic origin 3.7%.
*Religious affiliation* (1980): Christian 98.0%, of which Protestant 63.2%
(Anglican 17.4%, Pentecostal *c.* 12.0%, Moravian *c.* 9.0%, Methodist *c.*
8.0%, Lutheran *c.* 3.0%), Roman Catholic 33.6%; Bahā'ī 0.5%; Jewish 0.3%;
nonreligious 1.2%.
*Major cities* (1980): Charlotte Amalie 11,842; Christiansted 2,914; Cruz Bay
1,928; Frederiksted 1,046.

## Vital statistics

*Birth rate* per 1,000 population (1983): 24.9 (world avg. 29.0); (1981) legiti-
mate 48.7%; illegitimate 51.3%.
*Death rate* per 1,000 population (1983): 4.7 (world avg. 11.0).
*Natural increase rate* per 1,000 population (1983): 20.2 (world avg. 18.0).
*Total fertility rate* (avg. births per childbearing woman; 1985): 2.9.
*Marriage rate* per 1,000 population (1983): 12.9.
*Divorce rate* per 1,000 population (1983): 3.0.
*Life expectancy* at birth (1980–85): male 66.7 years; female 70.7 years.
*Major causes of death* per 100,000 population (1981): diseases of the circula-
tory system 209.8, of which ischemic heart disease 127.3, cerebrovascular
disease 35.6, malignant neoplasms (cancers) 83.5; accidents 50.9; diseases
of the digestive system 34.6; violence 33.6; nephritis and nephrosis 23.4.

## National economy

*Budget.* Revenue (1985): U.S.$263,347,000 (1983; personal income tax
38.6%, gross receipts tax 13.8%, corporate income tax 11.1%, property tax
9.3%, excise tax 3.5%). Expenditures (1983): U.S.$231,000,000 (education
25.4%, health 15.7%, executive branch 12.5%, public works 7.7%, public
safety 5.7%, College of the Virgin Islands 3.8%, Territorial Court 2.7%,
legislature 2.0%).
*Tourism* (1985): receipts from visitors U.S.$532,000,000; expenditures by
nationals abroad, n.a.
*Production* (value of sales in U.S.$ except as noted). Agriculture, forestry,
fishing (1982): milk 923,000, beef and veal 489,000, poultry and eggs
316,000, ornamental plants and other nursery products 89,700, bananas
63,000, onions 51,000, mangoes 49,000 (other agricultural products include
sorghum and bay leaves); livestock (number of live animals; 1985) 8,000
cattle, 6,000 pigs, 6,000 goats, 5,000 sheep; roundwood, n.a.; fish catch
(1983) 611 metric tons. Mining and quarrying (1984): sand and traprock
for local use. Manufacturing (1985): food and related products 28,771,-
000[3]; watches, clocks, and watchcases 13,845,000[3]; printing, publishing,
and allied industries 5,206,000[3]; heavy oils 10,400,000 metric tons; gasoline
1,750,000 metric tons; jet fuel 655,000 metric tons; kerosene 450,000 metric
tons; liquefied petroleum gas 40,000 metric tons; rum 88,100 hectolitres[4].
Construction (1982): general building 64,775,000; heavy construction 52,-
414,000; special trade construction 24,776,000; buildings completed (1979)
residential 908, nonresidential 262. Energy production (consumption): electricity (kW-hr; 1985) 900,000,000 (900,000,000); coal, none (none); crude
petroleum (barrels; 1985) none (115,814,000); petroleum products (metric
tons; 1985) 13,295,000 (2,441,000); natural gas, none (none).
*Household income and expenditure:* average household size (1980) 3.4; average annual income per household (1979) U.S.$14,453; sources of income
(1984): wages and salaries 65.7%, transfer payments 13.0%, interest, dividends, and rent 12.7%, self-employment 2.6%; expenditure: n.a.

*Gross national product* (at current market prices; 1985)[5]: U.S.$1,030,000,000
(U.S.$9,300 per capita).

### Structure of gross domestic product and labour force

| | 1985 | | 1984 | |
|---|---|---|---|---|
| | in value U.S.$'000,000 | % of total value | labour force | % of labour force |
| Agriculture | ... | ... | 522 | 1.2 |
| Manufacturing | ... | ... | 2,080 | 4.9 |
| Construction and mining | ... | ... | 2,390 | 5.7 |
| Transportation and public utilities | ... | ... | 2,310 | 5.5 |
| Trade, hotels, restaurants | ... | ... | 10,970 | 26.1 |
| Finance, insurance, real estate | ... | ... | 1,770 | 4.2 |
| Pub. admin., defense | ... | ... | 12,900 | 30.6 |
| Services | ... | ... | 4,090 | 9.7 |
| Other | ... | ... | 5,088[6] | 12.1 |
| TOTAL | 1,030[7] | 100.0 | 42,120 | 100.0 |

*Public debt:* U.S.$172,000,000.
*Population economically active* (1980): total 38,082; activity rate of total
population 39.4% (participation rates: ages 15–64, 65.1%; female 45.5%;
unemployed [1985] 5.8%).

### Price and earnings indexes (1980 = 100)

| | 1980 | 1981 | 1982 | 1983 | 1984 | 1985 | 1986 |
|---|---|---|---|---|---|---|---|
| Consumer price index[8] | 100.0 | 110.4 | 117.1 | 120.9 | 126.1 | 130.5 | 133.1 |
| Annual earnings index[9] | 100.0 | 112.0 | 118.3 | 123.0 | 131.0 | 137.6 | ... |

*Land use* (1984): forested 6.0%; meadows and pastures 26.0%; agricultural
and under permanent cultivation 21.0%; other 47.0%.

## Foreign trade

### Balance of trade (current prices)

| | 1980 | 1981 | 1982 | 1983 | 1984 | 1985 |
|---|---|---|---|---|---|---|
| U.S.$'000,000 | −604.4 | +54.6 | −300.2 | −1,019.5 | −786.4 | −383.5 |
| % of total | 6.5% | 0.5% | 2.9% | 12.2% | 9.0% | 5.4% |

*Imports* (1985): U.S.$3,740,600,000 (crude petroleum from the United States
41.9%; foreign crude petroleum 40.3%; products imported for resale to
tourists [mostly jewelry and perfume] 1.4%). *Major import sources:* United
States 54.3%; other countries 45.7%.
*Exports* (1985): U.S.$3,357,100,000 (petroleum products to the United States
94.1%; rum, watch movements, alumina[10], and other exports to the United
States 2.2%; foreign exports 3.7%). *Major export destinations:* United States
96.3%; other countries 3.7%.

## Transport and communications

*Transport.* Railroads: none. Roads (1986): total length 532 mi, 856 km. Registered motor vehicles (1985): 43,901. Merchant marine, n.a. Air transport
(1985)[11]: passenger arrivals 635,557, passenger departures 606,958; cargo
unloaded 2,558 metric tons, cargo loaded 674 metric tons; airports (1987)
with scheduled flights 6[12].
*Communications.* Daily newspapers (1986): total number 2; total circulation
18,800; circulation per 1,000 population 165. Radio (1986): total number
of receivers 85,000 (1 per 1.3 persons). Television (1986): total number of
receivers 31,000 (1 per 3.7 persons). Telephones (1985): 52,314 (1 per 2.1
persons).

## Education and health

### Education (1986–87)[13]

| | schools | teachers | students | student/ teacher ratio |
|---|---|---|---|---|
| Primary (age 4.5–12) | 41 | 781[14] | 14,723 | ... |
| Secondary (age 12–18) | 10 | 506[14] | 10,903 | ... |
| Voc., teacher tr.[15] | 3 | 27 | 775 | 28.7 |
| Higher | 1 | 97 | 757 | 8.3 |

*Educational attainment* (1980): Percent of population age 25 and over having: no formal schooling 1.5%; primary education 34.1%; secondary 40.0%;
higher 24.4%. *Literacy* (1982): total population age 15 and over literate 90%.
*Health* (1985): physicians 167 (1 per 622 persons); hospital beds 507 (1 per
205 persons); infant mortality rate per 1,000 live births (1983) 20.9.
*Food:* daily per capita caloric intake, n.a.

## Military

*Total active duty personnel:* No domestic military force is maintained; the
United States is responsible for defense and security.

---

[1]For administrative purposes, the U.S. Virgin Islands is divided into two legislative
districts, St. Croix and St. Thomas/St. John. [2]*Place of birth:* U.S. Virgin Islands
44.8%; United States 12.4%; Puerto Rico 5.2%; other West Indies 29.2%, of which St.
Christopher and Nevis 6.8%, Antigua and Barbuda 5.1%, British Virgin Islands 3.4%;
not reported 5.6%. [3]1982. [4]1984. [5]Gross domestic product. [6]Includes 2,480 self-
employed and unpaid family workers and 2,608 unemployed. [7]Tourism accounts for
more than 70% of GDP. [8]U.S. mainland. [9]Annual average gross pay. [10]The alumina
plant on St. Croix closed in 1985. [11]St. Croix and St. Thomas airports. [12]Scheduled
services at 2 airports, 3 seaplane bases, and 1 heliport. [13]Excludes 19 combined primary–secondary schools. [14]Private school teachers not included in total. [15]1983–84.

# Western Samoa

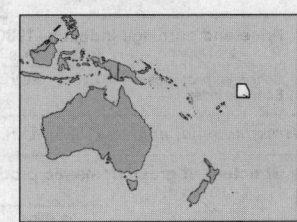

*Official name:* Malo Sa'oloto
  Tuto'atasi o Samoa i Sisifo (Samoan);
  Independent State of Western Samoa
  (English).
*Form of government:* constitutional
  monarchy[1] with one legislative house
  (Legislative Assembly [47]).
*Chief of state:* Head of State.
*Head of government:* Prime Minister.
*Capital:* Apia.
*Official languages:* Samoan; English.
*Official religion:* none.
*Monetary unit:* 1 tala (WS$, plural
  tala) = 100 sene; valuation (Oct. 5,
  1987) 1 U.S.$ = WS$2.03;
  1 £ = WS$3.30.

### Area and population

| Islands Political Districts | area[2] sq mi | area[2] sq km | population 1981 census[3] |
|---|---|---|---|
| Savaii | 659 | 1,707 | 43,150 |
| Fa'aseleleaga | | | 11,876 |
| Gaga'emauga | | | 3,893 |
| Gaga'ifomauga | | | 5,304 |
| Lealataua | | | 1,934 |
| Palauli | | | 9,234 |
| Satupa'itea | | | 5,391 |
| Vaisigano | | | 5,518 |
| Upolu | 432 | 1,119 | 113,199 |
| A'ana | | | 13,149 |
| A'ana-i-Sisifo | | | 3,363 |
| Aiga-i-le-Tai | | | 3,960 |
| Aleipata | | | 4,236 |
| Anoama'a | | | 7,816 |
| Fagaloa | | | 1,519 |
| Falealili | | | 4,727 |
| Faleata | | | 16,821 |
| Gaga'emauga | | | 2,750 |
| Lefaga | | | 3,776 |
| Lepa and Lotofaga | | | 3,058 |
| Safata | | | 6,711 |
| Sagaga | | | 12,253 |
| Vaimauga | | | 29,060 |
| TOTAL | 1,093 | 2,831 | 156,349[4] |

## Demography

*Population* (1987): 161,300.
*Density* (1987): persons per sq mi 147.6, persons per sq km 57.0.
*Urban–rural* (1981): urban 21.2%; rural 78.8%.
*Sex distribution* (1986): male 52.00%; female 48.00%.
*Age breakdown* (1981): under 15, 44.3%; 15–29, 29.1%; 30–44, 12.2%; 45–59,
  9.0%; 60–74, 3.8%; 75 and over, 1.6%.
*Population projection:* (1990) 163,900; (2000) 173,300.
*Doubling time:* 88 years.
*Ethnic composition* (1982): Samoan (Polynesian) *c.* 88%; Euronesian *c.* 10%;
  European *c.* 2%.
*Religious affiliation* (1981): Congregational 47.3%; Roman Catholic 21.7%;
  Methodist 16.2%; Latter Day Saints 8.3%; other 6.5%.
*Major city* (1981): Apia 33,170.

## Vital statistics

*Birth rate* per 1,000 population (1984): 10.2[5] (world avg. 29.0); (1978) legiti-
  mate 43.5%; illegitimate 56.5%.
*Death rate* per 1,000 population (1984): 2.3[5] (world avg. 11.0).
*Natural increase rate* per 1,000 population (1984): 7.9 (world avg. 18.0).
*Total fertility rate* (avg. births per childbearing woman; 1986): 4.4.
*Marriage rate* per 1,000 population (1984): 5.0[5].
*Divorce rate* per 1,000 population (1984): 0.1[5].
*Life expectancy* at birth (1986): male 62.6 years; female 65.6 years.
*Major causes of death* per 100,000 population[5] (1984): diseases of the circu-
  latory system 47.2; diseases of the respiratory system 22.6; diseases of the
  intestinal and digestive systems 20.7; malignant neoplasms (cancers) 17.6.

## National economy

*Budget* (1984)[6]. Revenue: WS$77,800,000 (current revenue 62.8%, of which
  taxes 53.5%, nontax revenue 9.3%; foreign aid grants 26.7%; domestic
  borrowing 9.8%). Expenditures: WS$77,800,000 (capital expenditure 59.4%,
  of which development 22.2%; current expenditure 40.6%, of which social
  services 15.9%, general administration 8.7%, economic services 6.9%).
*Public debt* (external, outstanding; 1985): U.S.$65,200,000.
*Tourism* (1984): number of visitors 40,337; number of nationals abroad, n.a.
*Land use* (1984): forested 47.0%; meadows and pastures 0.3%; agricultural
  and under permanent cultivation 42.8%; other 9.9%.
*Production* (metric tons except as noted). Agriculture, forestry, fishing
  (1985): coconuts 200,000; taro 38,000, copra 23,000, bananas 22,000, papayas 11,000, mangoes 6,000, pineapples 6,000, avocados 2,000, cacao
  2,000, milk 1,000; livestock (number of live animals) 62,000 pigs, 27,000
  cattle, 1,000,000 chickens; roundwood 131,000 cu m; fish catch 3,641. Mining and quarrying: n.a. Manufacturing (1985): coconut oil 11,766, copra
  meal 6,098, copra 2,731, sawn wood 21,000 cu m[7], veneer sheets 1,061 cu
  m[8]; other products include coconut cream, beverages, tobacco products,
  aluminum products, concrete blocks, handicrafts, and kava. Construction
  (permits issued in WS$; 1984): residential 1,628,000; commercial, indus-

trial, and other 4,135,600. Energy production (consumption): electricity
  (kW-hr; 1985) 42,000,000 (42,000,000); coal, none (n.a.); crude petroleum,
  none (n.a.); petroleum products (metric tons; 1985) none (37,000).
*Gross national product* (1985): U.S.$110,000,000 (U.S.$690 per capita).

### Structure of gross domestic product and labour force

| | 1972 in value WS$ | 1972 % of total value | 1981 labour force | 1981 % of labour force |
|---|---|---|---|---|
| Agriculture | 15,207,000 | 50.2 | 25,050 | 60.4 |
| Mining | — | — | 9 | — |
| Manufacturing | 858,900 | 2.8 | 757 | 1.8 |
| Construction | 1,146,800 | 3.8 | 2,279 | 5.5 |
| Public utilities | ... | ... | 447 | 1.1 |
| Transp. and commun. | 666,600 | 2.2 | 1,353 | 3.3 |
| Trade | 2,861,100 | 9.5 | 1,821 | 4.4 |
| Finance | 1,761,800 | 5.8 | 1,305 | 3.1 |
| Pub. admin., defense, government services | 6,346,700 | 21.0 | 1,842 | 4.4 |
| Other services | 646,000 | 2.1 | 6,374 | 15.4 |
| Other | 769,400 | 2.5 | 269 | 0.6 |
| TOTAL | 30,264,300 | 100.0[9] | 41,506 | 100.0 |

*Population economically active* (1981): total 41,506; activity rate of total
  population 26.5% (participation rates: ages 15–64, 48.6%; female 15.0%).

### Price and earnings indexes (1980 = 100)

| | 1981 | 1982 | 1983 | 1984 | 1985 | 1986 | 1987[10] |
|---|---|---|---|---|---|---|---|
| Consumer price index | 120.5 | 142.6 | 166.0 | 185.7 | 202.2 | 214.2 | 221.4 |
| Monthly earnings index[11] | 112.8 | ... | 146.6 | 163.0 | ... | ... | ... |

*Household income and expenditure.* Average household size (1976) 5.9;
  income per household (1972) WS$1,518 (U.S.$2,200); sources of income:
  wages 49.4%, self-employment 22.8%, remittances, gifts, and other assistance 18.0%, land rent 8.7%, other 1.1%; expenditure (1980)[12]: food 58.8%,
  transportation 9.0%, housing and furnishings 5.1%, fuel and light 5.0%,
  clothing 4.2%, other goods and services 1.9%, other 16.0%.

## Foreign trade[13]

### Balance of trade (current prices)

| | 1981 | 1982 | 1983 | 1984 | 1985 | 1986 |
|---|---|---|---|---|---|---|
| WS$'000 | −41,937 | −38,402 | −45,719 | −48,024 | −66,772 | −72,388 |
| % of total | 65.3% | 54.2% | 45.5% | 39.5% | 46.9% | 60.6% |

*Imports* (1985): WS$115,074,000 (1983; food 21.3%, machinery 21.0%,
  petroleum products 18.4%, miscellaneous manufactured articles 7.4%,
  chemicals 5.9%, animal oils and fats 0.5%). *Major import sources:* New
  Zealand 32.1%; Australia 19.8%; Fiji 15.8%; Japan 13.7%; U.S. 3.7%.
*Exports* (1985): WS$36,180,000 (coconut oil 45.1%, taro 14.6%, coconut
  cream 7.9%, beverages and tobacco 5.5%, copra and copra meal 4.2%,
  timber 2.1%). *Major export destinations:* U.S. 61.5%; New Zealand 18.1%;
  Australia 9.0%; American Samoa 2.1%; West Germany 1.1%.

## Transport and communications

*Transport.* Railroads: none. Roads (1983): total length[14] 1,296 mi, 2,085
  km (paved 14%). Vehicles (1984): passenger cars 1,795; trucks and buses
  2,494. Merchant marine (1986): vessels (100 gross tons and over) 6; total
  deadweight tonnage 34,751. Air transport (1985): passengers, n.a.; cargo,
  n.a.; airports (1987) with scheduled flights 3.
*Communications.* Daily newspapers: none. Radio (1985): 70,000 receivers
  (1 per 2.3 persons). Television (1985): 2,800 receivers (1 per 57 persons).
  Telephones (1984): 6,037 (1 per 26 persons).

## Education and health

### Education (1983)

| | schools | teachers | students | student/ teacher ratio |
|---|---|---|---|---|
| Primary (age 5–11) | 164 | 1,502[15] | 31,447 | 20.9 |
| Secondary (age 12–18) | 38[8] | 520 | 20,404 | 39.2 |
| Voc., teacher tr. | 4 | 69 | 651 | 9.4 |
| Higher | 6 | 37 | 562 | 15.2 |

*Educational attainment* (1976). Percent of population age 25 and over having: no formal schooling 60.0%; primary education 31.5%; secondary 6.3%;
  higher 2.2%. *Literacy* (1971): total population age 15 and over literate
  71,206 (97.8%); males 36,447 (97.8%); females 34,759 (97.9%).
*Health:* physicians (1981) 63 (1 per 2,476 persons); hospital beds (1982) 735
  (1 per 215 persons); infant mortality rate per 1,000 live births (1986) 52.0.
*Food:* daily per capita caloric intake (1981–83) 2,389 (vegetable products
  81%, animal products 19%); (1980–82) 95% of FAO recommended minimum requirement.

## Military

No military forces are maintained; New Zealand is responsible for defense.

[1]According to provisions in the constitution, the current Head of State, paramount
chief HH Malietoa Tanumafili II, will hold office for life. Upon his death, the monarchy will functionally cease, and future Heads of State will be elected by the Legislative
Assembly. [2]Includes 2 sq mi (5 sq km) of uninhabited islands. [3]Preliminary. [4]The
provisional total for the 1986 census is 158,940. [5]Registered only. [6]1987 budget estimate: Revenue WS$82,200,000; Expenditures WS$87,700,000. [7]1984. [8]1982. [9]Detail
does not add to total given because of rounding. [10]June. [11]Government employees
only. [12]Consumer price index components. [13]Import figures are f.o.b. in balance of
trade and c.i.f. in commodities and trading partners. [14]Total length includes 733 mi
(1,180 km) of plantation roads. [15]Includes some secondary teachers.

# Yemen (Aden)

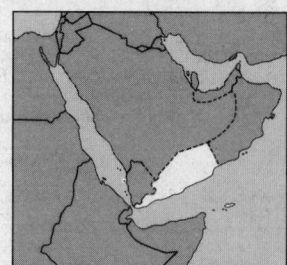

*Official name:* Jumhūrīyat al-Yaman ad-Dimuqrāṭīyah ash-Sha'bīyah (People's Democratic Republic of Yemen).
*Form of government:* single-party republic with one legislative house (Supreme People's Council [111]).
*Head of state:* Chairman of the Presidium of the Supreme People's Council.
*Head of government:* Prime Minister.
*Capital:* Aden.
*Official language:* Arabic.
*Official religion:* Islam.
*Monetary unit:* 1 Yemeni dinar (YD) = 1,000 fils; valuation (Oct. 5, 1987) 1 YD = U.S.$2.92 = £1.80.

### Area and population

| | | area | | population |
|---|---|---|---|---|
| Governorates | Capitals | sq mi | sq km | 1984 estimate |
| Abyān | Zinjibār | 8,297 | 21,489 | 412,574 |
| 'Adan | Aden | 2,695 | 6,980 | 386,364 |
| Hadramawt | al-Mukallā | 59,991 | 155,376 | 651,469 |
| Lahij | Lahij | 4,928 | 12,766 | 362,809 |
| al-Mahrah | al-Ghaydah | 25,618 | 66,350 | 80,722 |
| Shabwah | 'Atāq | 28,536 | 73,908 | 214,767 |
| TOTAL | | 130,066[1] | 336,869 | 2,108,705 |

## Demography

*Population* (1987): 2,278,000.
*Density* (1987): persons per sq mi 17.5, persons per sq km 6.8.
*Urban–rural* (1984): urban 33.2%; rural 66.8%.
*Sex distribution* (1987): male 49.47%; female 50.53%.
*Age breakdown* (1985): under 15, 44.4%; 15–29, 29.2%; 30–44, 14.0%; 45–59, 8.2%; 60–74, 3.7%; 75 and over, 0.5%.
*Population projection:* (1990) 2,460,000; (2000) 3,180,000.
*Doubling time:* 23 years.
*Ethnic composition* (1983): Arab 95.7%; Indo-Pakistani 1.8%; Somali 1.4%; Amhara and Swahili 0.7%; Jews 0.1%; Persian 0.1%; other 0.2%.
*Religious affiliation* (1980): predominantly Sunnī Muslim 99.5%; Hindu 0.2%; Christian 0.1%; nonreligious 0.1%; other 0.1%.
*Major cities* (1984): Aden 318,000; al-Mukallā 59,100; Saywūn 25,400; ash-Shiḥr 23,000; Tarīm 22,500.

## Vital statistics

*Birth rate* per 1,000 population (1980–85): 47.0 (world avg. 29.0); legitimate, n.a.; illegitimate, n.a.
*Death rate* per 1,000 population (1980–85): 17.4 (world avg. 11.0).
*Natural increase rate* per 1,000 population (1980–85): 29.6 (world avg. 18.0).
*Total fertility rate* (avg. births per childbearing woman; 1980–85): 6.8.
*Marriage rate* per 1,000 population: n.a.
*Divorce rate* per 1,000 population: n.a.
*Life expectancy* at birth (1980–85): male 46.9 years; female 49.9 years.
*Major causes of death* per 100,000 population: n.a.; however, major diseases include poliomyelitis, diphtheria, schistosomiasis, typhoid and paratyphoid fevers, yellow fever, hepatitis, asphyxia, trachoma, heart ailments, gastrointestinal diseases, respiratory diseases, salmonella, leprosy, measles, whooping cough, cholera, pulmonary tuberculosis, intestinal bilharzia, influenza, anemia and malnutrition, shigellosis, and malaria.

## National economy

*Budget* (1986). Revenue: YD 7,200,000,000 (custom duties and indirect taxes 83.3%). Expenditures: YD 9,900,000,000 (ordinary expenditures 60.6%, development 39.4%).
*Tourism* (1981): receipts from visitors U.S.$4,000,000; expenditures by nationals abroad U.S.$10,000,000.
*Production* (metric tons except as noted). Agriculture, forestry, fishing (1985): millet 80,000, watermelons 57,000, bananas 24,000, roots and tubers 17,000, potatoes 17,000, corn (maize) 16,000, wheat 15,000, tomatoes 14,000, dates 11,000, cottonseed 10,000, onions 9,000, lint cotton 5,000, sesame seed 3,000, barley 2,000, tobacco 1,000, coffee 1,000; livestock (number of live animals) 1,380,000 goats, 940,000 sheep, 170,000 asses, 96,000 cattle, 90,000 camels, 2,000,000 chickens; roundwood (1984) 276,000 cu m; fish catch 80,000. Mining and quarrying (1984): salt 76,000. Manufacturing (value added in YD '000; 1984): food, beverages, and tobacco 61,586; electricity 14,100; chemicals, petroleum, coal, rubber, and plastic products 9,469; clothing and apparel industries 5,164; fabricated metal products, machinery, and equipment 5,097; nonmetallic mineral products except petroleum and coal 2,918; paper and paper products, printing, and publishing 2,022; wood and wood products including furniture 1,950. Construction: n.a. Energy production (consumption): electricity (kW-hr; 1985) 285,000,000 (285,000,000); coal, none (n.a.); crude petroleum (barrels; 1985) none (25,662,000); petroleum products (metric tons; 1983) 3,465,000 (1,520,000); natural gas, none (n.a.).
*Household income and expenditure.* Average household size (1984) 7.4; income per household: n.a.; sources of income: n.a.; expenditure: n.a.
*Population economically active* (1984): total 450,183; activity rate of total population 21.4% (participation rates: over age 15, 41.2%; female 5.3%; unemployed, n.a.).

### Price and earnings indexes (1980 = 100)

| | 1978 | 1979 | 1980 | 1981 | 1982 | 1983 | 1984 |
|---|---|---|---|---|---|---|---|
| Consumer price index | 79.8 | 90.9 | 100.0 | 103.8 | 113.7 | 125.9 | 127.8 |
| Earnings index | ... | ... | ... | ... | ... | ... | ... |

*Gross national product* (1985): U.S.$1,130,000,000 (U.S.$490 per capita).

### Structure of gross domestic product and labour force

| | 1983 | | 1984 | |
|---|---|---|---|---|
| | in value YD '000,000 | % of total value | labour force | % of labour force |
| Agriculture | 31.5 | 8.9 | 165,897 | 36.8 |
| Mining | 0.5 | 0.1 | 8,453 | 1.9 |
| Manufacturing | 43.0 | 12.2 | 37,506 | 8.3 |
| Construction | 36.0 | 10.2 | 42,268 | 9.4 |
| Public utilities | 4.1 | 1.3 | 9,064 | 2.0 |
| Transportation and communication | 33.8 | 9.6 | 29,299 | 6.5 |
| Trade | 43.4 | 12.3 | 39,420 | 8.8 |
| Finance | 13.7 | 3.8 | 298 | 0.1 |
| Pub. admin., defense | 80.0 | 22.6 | ... | ... |
| Services | 1.7 | 0.5 | 117,978 | 26.2 |
| Other | 65.8[2] | 18.4[2] | ... | ... |
| TOTAL | 353.5 | 100.0[1] | 450,183 | 100.0 |

*Public debt* (external, outstanding; 1985): U.S.$1,446,300,000.
*Land use* (1984): forested 4.7%; meadows and pastures 27.2%; agricultural 0.5%; built-up, wasteland, and other 67.6%.

## Foreign trade

### Balance of trade (current prices)

| | 1978 | 1979 | 1980 | 1981 | 1982 | 1983 | 1984 |
|---|---|---|---|---|---|---|---|
| YD '000,000 | −110.7 | −123.8 | −234.1 | −252.9 | −248.3 | −250.4 | −278.7 |
| % of total | 45.4% | 27.7% | 30.4% | 37.6% | 31.1% | 35.0% | 38.5% |

*Imports* (1984): YD 501,600,000 (machinery and transport equipment 30.9%; food and live animals 27.4%; manufactured goods 16.0%; mineral fuels 10.1%; chemicals 4.2%; animal oils and fats 3.1%; crude minerals 2.9%; beverages and tobacco 0.8%. *Major import sources* (1985): Australia 9.2%; United Kingdom 6.5%; Japan 5.7%; The Netherlands 5.2%; France 4.7%; Italy 3.2%; West Germany 3.1%; Denmark 2.8%; Singapore 2.7%; Pakistan 2.6%; United States 1.3%; Thailand 1.2%; Belgium–Luxembourg 1.1%; Norway 0.9%; Spain 0.9%; Sweden 0.7%; Austria 0.4%; Ireland 0.4%; Greece 0.3%; Switzerland 0.3%.
*Exports* (1984): YD 222,900,000 (petroleum products 95.9%). *Major export destinations* (1985): Italy 33.0%; Japan 11.3%; New Zealand 11.3%; France 10.3%; West Germany 6.0%; Singapore 5.3%; United Kingdom 2.6%; The Netherlands 1.8%.

## Transport and communications

*Transport.* Railroads: none. Roads (1984): total length 6,793 mi, 10,932 km (paved 18%). Vehicles (1984): passenger cars 24,657; commercial vehicles 27,227. Merchant marine (1986): vessels (100 gross tons and over) 29; total deadweight tonnage 13,215. Air transport (1982): passenger-km 100,000,000; metric ton-km cargo 1,700,000; airports (1987) with scheduled flights 8.
*Communications.* Daily newspapers (1986): total number 2; total circulation 25,000; circulation per 1,000 population 10.6. Radio (1986): total number of receivers 300,000 (1 per 7.9 persons). Television (1986): total number of receivers 44,000 (1 per 18.6 persons). Telephones (1984): 16,200 (1 per 130 persons).

## Education and health

### Education (1983–84)

| | schools | teachers | students | student/ teacher ratio |
|---|---|---|---|---|
| Primary (age 7–12) | 900 | 10,986 | 237,904 | 21.7 |
| Secondary (age 13–18) | 51 | 1,555 | 27,908 | 17.9 |
| Voc., teacher tr. | 29 | 528[3] | 5,601 | ... |
| Higher | 1 | 486[3] | 4,791 | ... |

*Educational attainment,* n.a. *Literacy* (1980): total population age 15 and over literate 411,900 (38.9%); males literate 354,700 (66.6%); females literate 57,200 (10.9%).
*Health* (1984): physicians 492 (1 per 4,287 persons); hospital beds 3,354 (1 per 629 persons); infant mortality rate per 1,000 live births 137.0.
*Food* (1981–83): daily per capita caloric intake 2,277 (vegetable products 84%, animal products 16%); (1983) 94% of FAO recommended minimum requirement.

## Military

*Total active duty personnel* (1986): 27,500 (army 87.3%, navy 3.6%, air force 9.1%). *Military expenditure as percent of GNP* (1984): 17.0% (world 5.9%); per capita expenditure U.S.$44.9.

[1]Detail does not add to total given because of rounding. [2]Import duties. [3]1982–83.

# Yemen (Ṣan‘ā’)

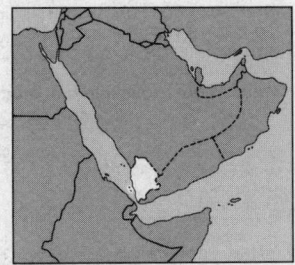

*Official name:* al-Jumhūrīyah al-‘Arabīyah al-Yamanīyah (Yemen Arab Republic).
*Form of government:* unitary single-party republic with one legislative house (Constituent People's Assembly [159]).
*Head of state and government:* President.
*Capital:* Ṣan‘ā’.
*Official language:* Arabic.
*Official religion:* Islam.
*Monetary unit:* 1 Yemen Rial (YRl) = 100 fils; valuation (Oct. 5, 1987) 1 U.S.$ = YRls 10.22; 1 £ = YRls 16.60.

## Area and population

| Governorates | Capitals | area sq mi | area sq km | population 1986 census |
|---|---|---|---|---|
| al-Baydā’ | al-Baydā’ | 4,310 | 11,170 | 381,249 |
| Dhamār | Dhamār | 3,430 | 8,870 | 812,981 |
| Ḥajjah | Ḥajjah | 3,700 | 9,590 | 897,814 |
| al-Ḥudaydah | al-Ḥudaydah | 5,240 | 13,580 | 1,294,359 |
| Ibb | Ibb | 2,480 | 6,430 | 1,511,879 |
| al-Jawf | al-Jawf | ... | ... | 87,299 |
| al-Maḥwit | al-Maḥwit | 830 | 2,160 | 322,226 |
| Ma‘rib | Ma‘rib | 15,400 | 39,890 | 121,437 |
| Ṣa‘dah | Ṣa‘dah | 4,950 | 12,810 | 344,152 |
| Ṣan‘ā’ | Ṣan‘ā’ | 7,840 | 20,310 | 1,856,876 |
| Ta‘izz | Ta‘izz | 4,020 | 10,420 | 1,643,901 |
| TOTAL | | 52,210[1,2] | 135,230[2] | 9,274,173[3] |

## Demography

*Population* (1987)[4]: 8,386,000.
*Density* (1987): persons per sq mi 160.6, persons per sq km 62.0.
*Urban–rural* (1984): urban 14.4%; rural 85.6%.
*Sex distribution* (1986): male 50.11%; female 49.89%.
*Age breakdown* (1984): under 15, 47.4%; 15–29, 25.4%; 30–44, 13.2%; 45–59, 9.3%; 60–74, 3.9%; 75 and over, 0.8%.
*Population projection*[4]: (1990) 9,029,000; (2000) 11,550,000.
*Doubling time:* 26 years.
*Ethnic composition* (1984): predominantly Arab.
*Religious affiliation* (1980): Shī‘ī Muslim 60%; Sunnī Muslim 40%.
*Major cities* (1986): Ṣan‘ā’ 427,150; Ta‘izz 178,043; al-Ḥudaydah 155,110.

## Vital statistics

*Birth rate* per 1,000 population (1984): 49.4 (world avg. 29.0); legitimate, n.a.; illegitimate, n.a.
*Death rate* per 1,000 population (1984): 22.2 (world avg. 11.0).
*Natural increase rate* per 1,000 population (1984): 27.2 (world avg. 18.0).
*Total fertility rate* (avg. births per childbearing woman; 1984): 7.1.
*Marriage rate* per 1,000 population: n.a.
*Divorce rate* per 1,000 population: n.a.
*Life expectancy* at birth (1980–85): male 46.9 years; female 49.9 years.
*Major causes of death* per 100,000 population: n.a.; however, major infectious diseases include malaria, tuberculosis, intestinal infections, leprosy, schistosomiasis, typhoid and paratyphoid fevers, viral hepatitis, and filarial infections.

## National economy

*Budget* (1986–87). Revenue: YRls 7,179,029,000 (1984; indirect taxes 64.3%, of which import duties 32.8%; nontax revenue 19.1%; direct taxes 16.6%). Expenditures: YRls 9,944,396,000 (1984; defense 26.7%; general public services 19.0%; education 13.2%; health 1.9%).
*Public debt* (external, outstanding; 1985): U.S.$1,867,900,000.
*Production* (metric tons except as noted). Agriculture, forestry, fishing (1985): sorghum 450,000, vegetables and melons 335,000, potatoes 165,000, grapes 74,000, pulses 60,000, barley 50,000, wheat 40,000, corn (maize) 40,000, dates 11,000, tobacco 7,000, sesame seed 5,000, coffee 3,000, cotton lint 2,000, sugarcane 1,000, milk 60,000, eggs 12,144; livestock (number of live animals) 2,230,000 goats, 1,850,000 sheep, 950,000 cattle, 520,000 asses, 60,000 camels; fish catch 20,958. Mining and quarrying (1984): salt 167,000; rock 509,000 cu m. Manufacturing (value added in YRls '000,000; 1984): food, beverages, and tobacco 1,218.0; wood and wood products 108.4[5]; textile and wearing apparel 104.0; paper and paper products 48.8[5]. Construction (value added in '000,000 YRls; 1982): 1,161. Energy production (consumption): electricity (kW-hr; 1985) 295,000,000 (295,000,000); coal, none (n.a.); crude petroleum, none (n.a.); petroleum products (metric tons; 1985) none (880,000,000); natural gas, none (n.a.).
*Tourism:* receipts from visitors (1985) U.S.$17,000,000; expenditures by nationals abroad (1983) U.S.$72,000,000.
*Population economically active* (1984): total 1,471,917; activity rate of total population 21.3% (participation rates: ages 15–64, 41.4%; female 12.5%; unemployed, n.a.).

## Price and earnings indexes (1980 = 100)

| | 1978 | 1979 | 1980 | 1981 | 1982 | 1983 | 1984 |
|---|---|---|---|---|---|---|---|
| Consumer price index | 75.0 | 95.0 | 100.0 | 105.0 | 108.0 | 114.0 | 128.0 |
| Earnings index | ... | ... | ... | ... | ... | ... | ... |

*Household income and expenditure.* Average household size (1984) 5.6; income per household: n.a.; sources of income: n.a.; expenditure (1972): food, beverages, and tobacco 65.0%, housing and household operations 21.1% (of which utilities 7.2%, rent and water 6.1%, durable goods 4.1%, furniture 2.1%, cleaning items 1.6%), clothing 5.8%, medical care, health, and hygiene 4.0%, transportation 3.2%, education 0.9%.
*Gross national product* (at current market prices; 1985): U.S.$4,140,000,000 (U.S.$600 per capita).

## Structure of gross domestic product and labour force

| | 1986 in value YRls '000,000 | 1986 % of total value | 1981 labour force | 1981 % of labour force |
|---|---|---|---|---|
| Agriculture | 4,126 | 20.4 | 830,400 | 69.1 |
| Mining | 397 | 2.0 | 1,300 | 0.1 |
| Manufacturing | 2,662 | 13.1 | 52,900 | 4.4 |
| Construction | 857 | 4.2 | 72,000 | 6.0 |
| Public utilities | 286 | 1.4 | 3,900 | 0.3 |
| Transportation and communication | 2,549 | 12.6 | 31,600 | 2.6 |
| Trade | 2,728 | 13.5 | 71,100 | 6.0 |
| Finance | 2,597 | 12.8 | 4,500 | 0.4 |
| Pub. admin., defense } Services | 2,513 | 12.4 | 133,900 | 11.1 |
| Other | 1,539[6] | 7.6 | ... | ... |
| TOTAL | 20,254 | 100.0 | 1,201,600 | 100.0 |

*Land use* (1984): forested 8.2%; meadows and pastures 35.9%; agricultural and under permanent cultivation 6.9%; other 49.0%.

## Foreign trade

### Balance of trade (current prices)

| | 1981 | 1982 | 1983 | 1984 | 1985 | 1986 |
|---|---|---|---|---|---|---|
| YRls '000,000 | −7,662 | −8,235 | −9,439 | −8,449 | −7,782 | −8,466 |
| % of total | 82.7% | 78.4% | 83.1% | 79.0% | 77.2% | 78.4% |

*Imports* (1982): YRls 6,939,800,000 (food and live animals 29.3%; manufactured goods 21.6%; machinery and transport equipment 19.3%; chemical products 6.5%; beverages and tobacco 1.7%). *Major import sources* (1985): Italy 9.7%; Japan 8.7%; United Kingdom 8.3%; The Netherlands 6.2%; West Germany 5.9%; France 5.2%; China 2.7%; United States 2.7%; Belgium–Luxembourg 2.4%; Australia 2.4%; Singapore 2.1%; Austria 1.5%; Sweden 1.4%; Greece 1.3%; Denmark 0.7%.
*Exports* (1982): YRls 179,963,000 (cotton, cotton fabric, and cotton yarn 23.6%; cereals 20.7%; hides and skins 3.7%; coffee 1.6%). *Major export destinations* (1985): United States 41.4%; Japan 12.6%; The Netherlands 6.9%; France 3.5%; Italy 3.5%; United Kingdom 2.6%; West Germany 1.7%; Singapore 0.2%.

## Transport and communications

*Transport.* Railroads: none. Roads (1985): total length 23,078 mi, 37,141 km (paved 6%). Vehicles (1985): passenger cars 117,756; trucks and buses 169,267. Merchant marine (1986): vessels (100 gross tons and over) 11; total deadweight tonnage 6,100. Air transport (1985): passenger-mi 358,012,000, passenger-km 576,165,000; short ton-mi cargo 43,533,000, metric ton-km cargo 63,557,000; airports (1987) with scheduled flights 5.
*Communications.* Daily newspapers (1986): total number 2; total circulation, n.a.; circulation per 1,000 population, n.a. Radio (1986): total number of receivers 200,000 (1 per 35.2 persons). Television (1986): total number of receivers 50,000 (1 per 140.9 persons). Telephones (1984): 63,255 (1 per 104.0 persons).

## Education and health

### Education (1985–86)

| | schools | teachers | students | student/teacher ratio |
|---|---|---|---|---|
| Primary (age 7–12) | 5,824 | 15,092 | 904,487 | 59.9 |
| Secondary (age 13–18) | 942 | 5,298 | 121,922 | 23.0 |
| Voc., teacher tr. | 73 | 445[7] | 11,616 | ... |
| Higher[7] | 1 | 245 | 9,024 | 36.8 |

*Educational attainment* (1975). Percent of population age 10 and over having: no formal schooling, 82.6%; reading ability only 5.3%; reading and writing ability 10.6%; primary education, 0.8%; secondary education 0.2%; higher 0.1%; not specified 0.4%. *Literacy* (1980): total population age 15 and over literate 350,600 (8.3%); males literate 340,100 (15.9%); females literate 10,500 (0.5%).
*Health* (1986): physicians 1,234 (1 per 6,631 persons); hospital beds 5,986 (1 per 1,367 persons); infant mortality rate per 1,000 live births 164.0.
*Food* (1981–83): daily per capita caloric intake 2,214 (vegetable products 89%, animal products 11%); (1983) 89% of FAO recommended minimum requirement.

## Military

*Total active duty personnel* (1986): 36,550 (army 95.8%, navy 1.5%, air force 2.7%). *Military expenditure as percent of GNP* (1984): 12.7% (world 5.9%); per capita expenditure U.S.$86.

[1]Detail does not add to total given because of rounding. [2]Area shown is according to the Swiss Technical Co-operation Service. The major part of the eastern boundary with Saudi Arabia and Yemen (Aden) is not officially delimited or demarcated; however, the government of Yemen (Ṣan‘ā’) uses a higher estimate of 77,200 sq mi (200,000 sq km). [3]Includes nationals abroad. [4]Based on reported 1986 census result of 8,105,974 resident population. [5]1983. [6]Includes import duties. [7]1983–84.

# Yugoslavia

*Official name:* Socijalistična
Federativna Republika Jugoslavija
(Slovenian); Socijalistička Federativna
Republika Jugoslavija (Macedonian,
Serbo-Croatian) (Socialist Federal
Republic of Yugoslavia).
*Form of government:* single-party
federal socialist republic with two
legislative houses (Chamber of
Republics and Provinces [88] and
Federal Chamber [220]).
*Head of state and government:*
President.
*Capital:* Belgrade.
*Official languages:* Slovenian;
Macedonian; Serbo-Croatian.
*Official religion:* none.
*Monetary unit:* 1 Yugoslav dinar
(Din) = 100 paras; valuation
(Oct. 5, 1987) 1 U.S.$ = Din 970.00;
1 £ = Din 1,575.00.

| Area and population | | area | | population |
|---|---|---|---|---|
| | | sq mi | sq km | 1986 estimate |
| Socialist republics | Capitals | | | |
| Bosnia and Hercegovina | Sarajevo | 19,741 | 51,129 | 4,356,000 |
| Croatia | Zagreb | 21,829 | 56,538 | 4,665,000 |
| Macedonia | Skopje | 9,928 | 25,713 | 2,041,000 |
| Montenegro | Titograd | 5,333 | 13,812 | 619,000 |
| Serbia | Belgrade | 21,609 | 55,968 | 5,803,000 |
| Slovenia | Ljubljana | 7,819 | 20,251 | 1,934,000 |
| Autonomous provinces[1] | | | | |
| Kosovo | Priština | 4,203 | 10,887 | 1,804,000 |
| Vojvodina | Novi Sad | 8,304 | 21,506 | 2,049,000 |
| TOTAL | | 98,766 | 255,804 | 23,271,000 |

## Demography

*Population* (1987): 23,433,000.
*Density* (1987): persons per sq mi 237.3, persons per sq km 91.6.
*Urban–rural* (1985): urban 46.5%; rural 53.5%.
*Sex distribution* (1985): male 49.36%; female 50.64%.
*Age breakdown* (1985): under 15, 23.5%; 15–29, 23.9%; 30–44, 21.0%; 45–59,
18.8%; 60–74, 9.4%; 75 and over, 3.4%.
*Population projection:* (1990) 23,925,000; (2000) 25,641,000.
*Doubling time:* 99 years.
*Ethnic composition* (1981): Serb 36.3%; Croat 19.7%; Bosnian Muslim 8.9%;
Slovenian 7.8%; Albanian 7.7%; Macedonian 6.0%; Montenegrin 2.6%;
other 11.0%.
*Religious affiliation* (1980): Serbian Orthodox 34.6%; Roman Catholic 26.0%;
Crypto-Christian 11.3%; Muslim 10.4%; other 17.7%.
*Major cities* (1981): Belgrade 1,087,915; Zagreb 649,586; Skopje 408,143;
Sarajevo 319,017; Ljubljana 224,817.

## Vital statistics

*Birth rate* per 1,000 population (1986): 15.4 (world avg. 26.0); (1982) legiti-
mate 91.6%; illegitimate 8.4%.
*Death rate* per 1,000 population (1986): 9.0 (world avg. 9.9).
*Natural increase rate* per 1,000 population (1986): 6.4 (world avg. 16.1).
*Total fertility rate* (avg. births per childbearing woman; 1984): 2.1.
*Marriage rate* per 1,000 population (1986): 6.9.
*Divorce rate* per 1,000 population (1984): 0.9.
*Life expectancy* at birth (1982–83): male 66.0 years; female 74.0 years.
*Major causes of death* per 100,000 population (1982): diseases of the circu-
latory system 448.8; malignant neoplasms (cancers) 135.2; diseases of the
respiratory system 51.7; diseases of the digestive system 39.3.

## National economy

*Budget* (1985). Revenue: Din 696,035,100,000 (share in profit of state enterprises 74.0%, import duties 21.6%, other revenue 4.4%). Expenditures: Din
696,035,100,000 (national defense 66.0%, social welfare and health 18.7%).
*Public debt* (external, outstanding; 1985): U.S.$9,912,200,000.
*Tourism:* receipts from visitors (1985) U.S.$1,050,000,000; expenditures by
nationals abroad (1983) U.S.$107,000,000.
*Production* (metric tons except as noted). Agriculture (1986): corn (maize)
12,502,000, sugar beets 5,615,000, wheat 4,776,000, potatoes 2,519,000,
grapes 1,141,000, barley 710,000, plums 708,000, apples 605,000, tomatoes
497,000, melons 451,000, sunflower seeds 449,000, oats 252,000, rye 89,000,
tobacco 88,000, rice 36,000; livestock (number of live animals) 7,821,-
000 pigs, 7,693,000 sheep, 5,034,000 cattle, 78,281,000 poultry; roundwood
(1985) 22,428,000 cu m; fish catch (1985) 75,126,000. Mining and quarrying
(1985): copper ore 26,166,000; iron ore 5,478,000; lead and zinc ore 4,590,-
000; bauxite 3,250,000; antimony 71,000; manganese 29,000; silver (refined)
156. Manufacturing (1986): cement 9,200,000; crude steel 4,550,000; rolled
steel 4,230,000; pulp and paper 3,100,000; pig iron 3,100,000; sulfuric acid
1,594,800; plastics and resins 644,000; automobile tires 11,628,000 units;
radio and television receivers 799,000 units; leather 21,000,000 cu m; cotton fabrics 361,000,000 sq m. Construction (1985): residential 13,597,000
sq m; industrial 1,664,000 sq m; commercial 798,000 sq m. Energy production (consumption): electricity (kW-hr; 1986) 77,900,000 (75,429,000,000[2]);
coal (metric tons; 1986) 71,200,000 (62,085,000[2]); crude petroleum (barrels;

1986) 30,412,000 (98,138,000[2]); petroleum products (metric tons; 1985) 13,-
189,000 (13,189,000); natural gas (cu m; 1985) 2,400,000,000 (6,667,000,000).
*Gross national product* (1985): U.S.$47,900,000,000 (U.S.$2,070 per capita).

| Structure of gross material product and labour force | | | | |
|---|---|---|---|---|
| | 1985 | | 1981 | |
| | in value Din '000,000 | % of total value | labour force | % of labour force |
| Agriculture | 1,384,567 | 12.3 | 2,682,828 | 28.7 |
| Mining and manufacturing | 5,461,478 | 48.4 | 2,209,693[3] | 23.6[3] |
| Construction | 780,604 | 6.9 | 689,291 | 7.4 |
| Public utilities | 127,471 | 1.2 | [3] | [3] |
| Transp. and commun. | 826,579 | 7.3 | 445,362 | 4.8 |
| Trade | 2,327,983 | 20.6 | 827,575 | 8.8 |
| Finance | ... | ... | 204,866 | 2.2 |
| Pub. admin., defense, and services | ... | ... | 1,585,205 | 16.9 |
| Other | 366,505[4] | 3.3[4] | 713,851[5] | 7.6[5] |
| TOTAL | 11,275,187 | 100.0 | 9,358,671 | 100.0 |

*Population economically active* (1981): total 9,359,000; activity rate of total
population 43.4% (participation rates: ages 15–64, 68.7%; female 38.7%;
unemployed [1986] 10.6%).

| Price and earnings indexes (1980 = 100) | | | | | | |
|---|---|---|---|---|---|---|
| | 1980 | 1981 | 1982 | 1983 | 1984 | 1985 | 1986[6] |
| Consumer price index | 100.0 | 139.7 | 185.7 | 258.4 | 401.6 | 700.5 | 1,049.6 |
| Monthly earnings index | 100.0 | 137.0 | 175.0 | 223.0 | 324.0 | 440.0 | ... |

*Household income and expenditure.* Average household size (1983) 3.6; income per household (1984) Din 540,404 (U.S.$3,540); sources of income
(1985): wages 56.9%, receipts from abroad and interest 12.9%, welfare
11.6%, other 18.6%; expenditure (1984): food 33.8%, transportation 12.3%,
beverages and tobacco 11.0%, clothing and footwear 10.4%, housing 8.2%,
household utilities 8.2%, recreation 3.9%, health 3.6%.
*Land use* (1985): forested 36.6%; meadows and pastures 25.0%; agricultural
and under permanent cultivation 30.6%; other 7.8%.

## Foreign trade

| Balance of trade (current prices) | | | | | | |
|---|---|---|---|---|---|---|
| | 1981 | 1982 | 1983 | 1984 | 1985 | 1986 |
| Din '000,000,000[7] | −114.4 | −747 | −564 | −437 | −407.9 | −432 |
| % of total | 12.9% | 12.5% | 9.9% | 7.6% | 6.8% | 7.3% |

*Imports* (1986): Din 3,173,800,000,000 (machinery and transport equipment 27.9%, of which nonelectrical machinery 10.2%; mineral fuels 23.1%;
chemicals 13.4%; raw materials 10.5%; food products 5.7%). *Major import
sources:* U.S.S.R. 16.3%; West Germany 14.4%; Italy 8.0%; Iraq 7.3%;
United States 5.9%; Czechoslovakia 5.7%; Austria 3.7%; France 3.7%.
*Exports* (1985): Din 2,742,000,000,000 (machinery and transport equipment
33.5%; manufactured goods 17.1%; chemicals 11.8%; food products 8.0%;
raw materials 3.8%; mineral fuels 2.1%). *Major export destinations:* U.S.S.R.
30.0%; Italy 9.0%; West Germany 8.9%; Czechoslovakia 5.7%.

## Transport and communications

*Transport.* Railroads (1986): length 5,768 mi, 9,283 km; passenger-km
12,384,000,000; metric ton-km cargo 27,564,000,000. Roads (1986): total
length 117,744 km (paved 57%). Vehicles (1986): passenger cars 2,824,267;
trucks and buses 264,593. Merchant marine (1986): vessels (100 gross
tons and over) 490; total deadweight tonnage 4,476,264. Air transport
(1985): passenger-km 6,336,000,000; metric ton-km cargo 92,547,000; airports (1987) 17.
*Communications.* Daily newspapers (1986): 28; total circulation 2,498,000;
circulation per 1,000 population 107. Radio (1985): 4,706,000 receivers (1
per 4.9 persons). Television (1985): 4,062,000 receivers (1 per 5.7 persons).
Telephones (1986): 3,332,000 (1 per 6.9 persons).

## Education and health

| Education (1985–86) | schools | teachers | students | student/ teacher ratio |
|---|---|---|---|---|
| Primary (age 7–14) | 12,447 | 137,776 | 2,351,187 | 17.1 |
| Secondary (age 15–18) | 6,153 | 61,288 | 1,448,562 | 15.2 |
| Higher | 234 | 25,882 | 359,175 | 13.9 |

*Educational attainment* (1981). Percent of population age 15 and over
having: less than full primary education 44.7%; primary 24.2%; secondary
25.5%; higher 5.6%. *Literacy* (1981): total population age 15 and over
literate 15,172,877 (89.6%); males 95.5%; females 83.9%.
*Health* (1985): physicians 38,205 (1 per 601 persons); hospital beds 139,745
(1 per 164 persons); infant mortality rate per 1,000 live births (1986) 27.1.
*Food* (1981–83): daily per capita caloric intake 3,621 (vegetable products
77%, animal products 23%); (1983) 141% of FAO minimum requirement.

## Military

*Total active duty personnel* (1986): 210,000 (army 76.9%, navy 6.0%, air force
17.1%). *Military expenditure as percent of GNP* (1984): 3.6% (world 5.9%);
per capita expenditure U.S.$78.

---

[1]The autonomous provinces are administratively part of the Socialist Republic of Ser-
bia. [2]1985. [3]Public utilities included with mining and manufacturing. [4]Other material
activities. [5]Includes unemployed. [6]First quarter. [7]At the parity 1 U.S.$ = Din 264.53.

# Zaire

*Official name:* République du Zaïre
(Republic of Zaire).
*Form of government:* single party
republic with one legislative house
(Legislative Council [210]).
*Head of state and government:*
President.
*Capital:* Kinshasa.
*Official language:* French.
*Official religion:* none.
*Monetary unit:* 1 zaïre (Z) = 100
makuta (singular likuta) = 10,000
sengi; valuation (Oct. 5, 1987)
1 U.S.$ = Z 121.03; 1 £ = Z 196.54.

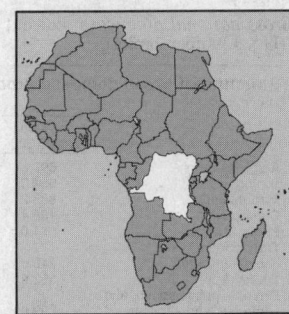

### Area and population

| Regions | Capitals | area sq mi | area sq km | population 1984 census |
|---|---|---|---|---|
| Bandundu | Bandundu | 114,154 | 295,658 | 3,682,845 |
| Bas-Zaire | Matadi | 20,819 | 53,920 | 1,971,520 |
| Equateur | Mbandaka | 155,712 | 403,293 | 3,405,512 |
| Haut-Zaire | Kisangani | 194,302 | 503,239 | 4,206,069 |
| Kasai Occidental | Kananga | 60,605 | 156,967 | 2,287,416 |
| Kasai Oriental | Mbuji-Mayi | 64,949 | 168,216 | 2,402,603 |
| Kivu | Bukavu | 99,098 | 256,662 | 5,187,865 |
| Shaba (Katanga) | Lubumbashi | 191,879 | 496,965 | 3,874,019 |
| **Neutral City** | | | | |
| Kinshasa | | 3,848 | 9,965 | 2,653,558 |
| TOTAL | | 905,365[1] | 2,344,885 | 29,671,407 |

## Demography

*Population* (1987): 31,804,000.
*Density* (1987): persons per sq mi 35.1, persons per sq km 13.7.
*Urban–rural* (1985): urban 44.2%; rural 55.8%.
*Sex distribution* (1984): male 49.18%; female 50.82%.
*Age breakdown* (1985): under 15, 45.2%; 15–29, 26.0%; 30–44, 15.5%; 45–59, 8.7%; 60–74, 3.9%; 75 and over, 0.7%.
*Population projection:* (1990) 34,138,000; (2000) 42,980,000.
*Doubling time:* 24 years.
*Ethnic composition* (1983): Luba 18.0%; Kongo 16.1%; Mongo 13.5%; Rwanda 10.3%; Azande 6.1%; Bangi and Ngale 5.8%; Rundi 3.8%; Teke 2.7%; Boa 2.3%; Chokwe 1.8%; Lugbara 1.6%; Banda 1.4%; Konzo 1.4%; other 15.2%.
*Religious affiliation* (1980): Roman Catholic 48.4%; Protestant 29.0%; indigenous Christian 17.1%; traditional beliefs 3.4%; Muslim 1.4%; other 0.7%.
*Major cities* (1984): Kinshasa 2,653,558; Lubumbashi 543,268; Mbuji-Mayi 423,363; Kananga 290,898; Kisangani 282,650.

## Vital statistics

*Birth rate* per 1,000 population (1980–85): 45.1 (world avg. 29.0).
*Death rate* per 1,000 population (1980–85): 15.8 (world avg. 11.0).
*Natural increase rate* per 1,000 population (1980–85): 29.3 (world avg. 18.0).
*Total fertility rate* (avg. births per childbearing woman; 1980–85): 6.1.
*Marriage rate* per 1,000 population (1977): 0.07[2].
*Divorce rate* per 1,000 population (1977): 0.02.
*Life expectancy* at birth (1980–85): male 48.3 years; female 51.7 years.
*Major causes of death* per 100,000 population[3] (1977): measles 9.6; meningitis 1.1; influenza 0.4; whooping cough 0.3.

## National economy

*Budget*[4] (1984). Revenue: Z 20,768,000,000 (direct and indirect taxes 84.3%, government investments 10.9%, administrative and judicial receipts 4.7%). Expenditures: Z 23,568,000,000 (service of external debt 37.5%, government salaries 21.3%, service of internal debt 7.9%).
*Public debt* (external, outstanding; 1985): U.S.$4,821,000,000.
*Tourism:* receipts from visitors (1985) U.S.$32,000,000; expenditures by nationals abroad (1983) U.S. $38,000,000.
*Production* (metric tons except as noted). Agriculture, forestry, fishing (1985): cassava 15,500,000; fruit excluding melons 2,540,000, plantains 1,490,000, sugarcane 970,000, corn (maize) 750,000, peanuts (groundnuts) 380,000, sweet potatoes 360,000, bananas 330,000, rice 290,000, yams 215,000, papayas 165,000, pineapples 165,000, mangoes 147,000, oranges 146,000, pulses 121,000, coffee 90,000, seed cotton 77,000, palm kernels 75,000; livestock (number of live animals) 2,920,000 goats, 1,350,000 cattle, 770,000 pigs, 765,000 sheep, 18,000,000 chickens; roundwood 30,491,000 cu m; fish catch 102,000. Mining and quarrying (1985): copper 471,500; lime 110,000; zinc 67,900; cobalt 10,600; tin 3,100; silver 1,516,000 troy oz; gold 63,022 troy oz; industrial diamonds 16,127,000 carats; gem diamonds 4,032,000 carats. Manufacturing (1984): corn flour 78,291; cotton textiles 78,820,000 sq m; cigarettes 3,475,000,000 units; bicycles 13,970 units; trucks 2,335 units; beer 3,699,000 hectolitres; carbonated beverages 828,000 hectolitres; leather shoes 2,556,000 pairs. Construction (1984): residential 13,000 sq m; nonresidential 18,000 sq m. Energy production (consumption): electricity (kW-hr; 1985) 4,615,000,000 (4,500,000,000); coal (metric tons; 1985) 130,000 (165,000); crude petroleum (barrels; 1985) 9,296,000 (2,306,000); petroleum products (metric tons; 1985) 313,000 (743,000); natural gas, none (n.a.).
*Household income and expenditure.* Average household size (1982) 6.0; average annual income per household Z 1,200 (U.S.$209); sources of income: wages and salaries, small-scale trading; expenditure (1975)[5]: food 60.6%,

---

housing and energy 12.5%, clothing and footwear 9.5%, transportation 5.7%, furniture and utensils 4.7%, medical care 2.5%, recreation 2.1%, personal care 1.7%, education 0.8%.
*Gross national product* (1985): U.S.$5,220,000,000 (U.S.$170 per capita).

### Structure of gross domestic product and labour force

| | 1984 in value Z '000,000 | 1984 % of total value | 1982 labour force | 1982 % of labour force |
|---|---|---|---|---|
| Agriculture | 31,584.7[6] | 31.7 | 8,712,000 | 70.0 |
| Mining | 24,713.4 | 24.8 | 622,000 | 5.0 |
| Manufacturing | 1,953.2 | 2.0 | 1,244,000 | 10.0 |
| Construction | 5,012.4[7] | 5.1 | | |
| Public utilities | 46.7 | [8] | | |
| Transp. and commun. | 999.7 | 1.0 | | |
| Trade | 18,523.9 | 18.6 | | |
| Finance | | | 1,867,000 | 15.0 |
| Pub. admin., defense | 15,221.4 | 15.3 | | |
| Services | | | | |
| Other | 1,528.0[9] | 1.5[9] | | |
| TOTAL | 99,583.4 | 100.0 | 12,445,000 | 100.0 |

*Population economically active* (1984): total 13,145,000; activity rate of total population 44.3% (participation rates; age 15–64, n.a.; female [1981] 42.5%; unemployed, n.a.).

### Price and earnings indexes (1980 = 100)

| | 1981 | 1982 | 1983 | 1984 | 1985 | 1986 | 1987[10] |
|---|---|---|---|---|---|---|---|
| Consumer price index | 134.9 | 183.8 | 325.5 | 495.6 | 613.6 | 900.3 | 1,552.5 |
| Monthly earnings index | ... | ... | ... | ... | ... | ... | ... |

*Land use* (1984): forested 77.7%; meadows and pastures 4.1%; agricultural and under permanent cultivation 2.9%; other 15.3%.

## Foreign trade[11]

### Balance of trade (current prices)

| | 1981 | 1982 | 1983 | 1984 | 1985 | 1986 |
|---|---|---|---|---|---|---|
| Z '000,000 | −565.6 | −445.4 | +7,102.7 | +11,554.3 | +13,339.7 | +13,228 |
| % of total | 10.6% | 9.0% | 34.2% | 18.9% | 16.4% | 11.3% |

*Imports* (1986): Z 51,959,000,000 (1982; primary manufactures and semifinished products 22.0%; energy 13.0%; consumer goods 11.0%, of which food and tobacco products 5.6%, textiles and clothing 1.0%). *Major import sources* (1985): Belgium–Luxembourg 22.0%; France 11.4%; U.S. 9.8%; West Germany 8.3%; Japan 4.1%.
*Exports* (1986): Z 65,187,000,000 (1984; copper 36.4%; crude petroleum 17.4%; cobalt 11.9%; coffee 11.4%). *Major export destinations* (1985): Belgium–Luxembourg 31.8%; U.S. 24.0%; West Germany 12.1%; France 5.4%.

## Transport and communications

*Transport.* Railroads (1985)[12]: length 3,263 mi, 5,252 km; passenger-mi 181,150,000, passenger-km 291,534,000; short ton-mi cargo 1,339,047,000, metric ton-km cargo 1,954,976,000. Roads (1981): total length 28,379 mi, 45,671 km (paved 18%). Vehicles (1981): passenger cars 89,471; trucks and buses 16,807. Merchant marine (1986): vessels (100 gross tons and over) 31; total deadweight tonnage 91,012. Air transport (1986)[13]: passenger-mi 237,439,000, passenger-km 382,121,000; short ton-mi cargo 8,336,000, metric ton-km cargo 12,170,000; airports (1987) with scheduled flights 22.
*Communications.* Daily newspapers (1986): total number 4; total circulation 45,000[14]; circulation per 1,000 population 1.6[14]. Radio (1986): 525,000 receivers (1 per 59 persons). Television (1986): 15,000 receivers (1 per 2,072 persons). Telephones (1985): 31,855 (1 per 953 persons).

## Education and health

### Education (1985–86)

| | schools | teachers | students | student/ teacher ratio |
|---|---|---|---|---|
| Primary (age 6–11)[14] | 10,065 | 112,077 | 4,993,523 | 44.6 |
| Secondary (age 12–17) | 3,972[14] | 43,459[14] | 3,198,051 | ... |
| Voc., teacher tr. | 20[15] | ... | 319,805 | ... |
| Higher | 36 | 3,072 | 37,706 | 12.3 |

*Educational attainment,* n.a. *Literacy* (1985): total population age 15 and over literate 11,004,000 (61.2%); males literate 6,872,000 (78.6%); females literate 4,132,000 (44.7%).
*Health* (1982): physicians 2,000 (1 per 14,092 persons); hospital beds 74,000 (1 per 385 persons); infant mortality rate per 1,000 live births (1983) 106.
*Food* (1981–83): daily per capita caloric intake 2,157 (vegetable products 97%, animal products 3%); (1983) 96% of FAO recommended minimum.

## Military

*Total active duty personnel* (1986): 25,400 (army 86.6%, navy 3.5%, air force 9.8%). *Military expenditure as percent of GNP* (1984): 1.2% (world 5.9%); per capita expenditure U.S.$3.

---

[1]Detail does not add to total given because of rounding. [2]Registered marriages only. [3]Infectious diseases only. [4]Budget for 1985 was: Revenue Z 30,700,000,000 (no breakdown available); Expenditures Z 34,700,000,000 (no breakdown available). Budget estimate for 1986 without breakdown was: Revenue Z 50,460,000,000; Expenditures Z 53,100,000,000. [5]Consumer price index components. [6]Includes Z 18,069,500,000 in the subsistence sector. [7]Includes Z 1,670,800,000 in the subsistence sector. [8]Less than 0.1%. [9]Import taxes and duties less imputed bank service charge. [10]April. [11]Import figures are f.o.b. (free on board) in balance of trade and c.i.f. (cost, insurance, and freight) for commodities and trading partners. [12]Traffic statistics are for services operated by the Zaire National Railways (SNCZ), which controls more than 90% of the country's total rail facility. [13]Air Zaire only. [14]1983–84. [15]1977–78.

# Zambia

*Official name:* Republic of Zambia.
*Form of government:* republic with
one legislative house (National
Assembly [136]).
*Head of state and government:*
President.
*Capital:* Lusaka.
*Official language:* English.
*Official religion:* none.
*Monetary unit:* 1 Zambian kwacha
(K) = 100 ngwee; valuation (Oct.
5, 1987) 1 U.S.$ = K 7.82;
1 £ = K 12.70.

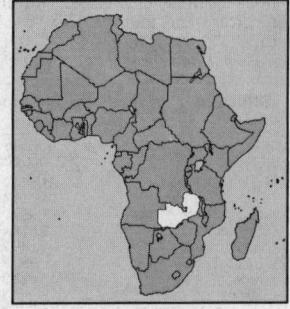

| Area and population | | area | | population |
|---|---|---|---|---|
| | | sq mi | sq km | 1980 census |
| Provinces | Capitals | | | |
| Central | Kabwe | 36,446 | 94,395 | 513,835 |
| Copperbelt | Ndola | 12,096 | 31,328 | 1,248,888 |
| Eastern | Chipata | 26,682 | 69,106 | 656,381 |
| Luapula | Mansa | 19,524 | 50,567 | 412,798 |
| Lusaka | Lusaka | 8,454 | 21,896 | 693,878 |
| Northern | Kasama | 57,076 | 147,826 | 677,894 |
| North-Western | Solwezi | 48,582 | 125,827 | 301,677 |
| Southern | Livingstone | 32,928 | 85,283 | 686,469 |
| Western | Mongu | 48,798 | 126,386 | 487,988 |
| TOTAL | | 290,586 | 752,614 | 5,679,808 |

## Demography

*Population* (1987): 7,135,000.
*Density* (1987): persons per sq mi 24.6, persons per sq km 9.5.
*Urban–rural* (1985): urban 49.5%; rural 50.5%.
*Sex distribution* (1985): male 49.69%; female 50.31%.
*Age breakdown* (1985): under 15, 49.3%; 15–29, 26.5%; 30–44, 13.0%; 45–59,
7.2%; 60–74, 3.3%; 75 and over, 0.7%.
*Population projection:* (1990) 7,912,000; (2000) 11,237,000.
*Doubling time:* 20 years.
*Ethnic composition* (1983): Bemba tribes (including Bemba, Lala, Ushi,
Lamba) 35.2%; Tonga tribes 16.5%; Maravi tribes (including Chewa,
Nsenga, Ngoni) 13.6%; Lozi tribes 9.6%; Lunda tribes (including Lunda,
Luvale [or Lwena]) 11.5%; other 13.6%.
*Religious affiliation* (1980): Christian 72.0%, of whom Protestant 34.2%,
Roman Catholic 26.2%, African Christian 8.3%; traditional beliefs 27.0%;
Muslim 0.3%; other 0.7%.
*Major cities* (1980): Lusaka 538,469; Kitwe 314,794; Ndola 282,439; Luan-
shya 132,164; Mufulira 149,778.

## Vital statistics

*Birth rate* per 1,000 population (1980–85): 48.1 (world avg. 29.0); legitimate,
n.a.; however, marriage is both early and universal, suggesting that legiti-
mate births are a relatively high proportion of all births.
*Death rate* per 1,000 population (1980–85): 15.1 (world avg. 11.0).
*Natural increase rate* per 1,000 population (1980–85): 33.0 (world avg. 18.0).
*Total fertility rate* (avg. births per childbearing woman; 1980–85): 6.8.
*Marriage rate* per 1,000 population: n.a.
*Divorce rate* per 1,000 population: n.a.
*Life expectancy* at birth (1980–85): male 49.6 years; female 53.1 years.
*Major causes of death* per 100,000 population: n.a.; however, among the
nearly 7,000,000 visits to outpatient clinics in 1982, nearly two-thirds of
the reported illnesses were related to nutritional deficiencies and infectious
and parasitic diseases.

## National economy

*Budget* (1987). Revenue: K 4,801,000,000 (customs duties and excise taxes
43.8%; mineral revenue 18.7%; income tax 15.1%). Expenditures: K 5,758,-
000,000 (constitutional and statutory expenditures 52.6%; other, including
education, health, land development, and police 47.4%).
*Production* (metric tons except as noted). Agriculture, forestry, fishing (1985):
sugarcane 1,120,000, corn (maize) 880,000, fruits and vegetables 330,000
(of which tomatoes 27,000, onions 24,000, oranges 3,000), cassava 210,000,
sunflower seeds 40,000, sweet potatoes 22,000, peanuts (groundnuts) 20,000,
sorghum 20,000, lint cotton 18,000, millet 13,000, pulses 5,000, tobacco
3,000; livestock (number of live animals) 2,600,000 cattle, 360,000 goats,
285,000 pigs, 32,000 sheep, 20,000,000 chickens; roundwood (1984) 9,921,-
000; fish catch (1984) 64,621. Mining and quarrying (1985): copper 543,000;
zinc 32,000; lead 15,000; cobalt 4,400; gold 7,903 oz. Manufacturing (1983):
cement 392,000; sulfuric acid 271,000; raw sugar 132,000; nitrogen fertilizer
86,013. Construction (value in K; 1983): residential 116,000,000; nonresidential 46,900,000. Energy production (consumption): electricity (kW-hr;
1985) 10,090,000,000 (7,010,000,000); coal (metric tons; 1985) 510,000 (510,-
000); crude petroleum (barrels; 1985) none (4,838,000); petroleum products
(metric tons; 1985) 640,000 (596,000); natural gas, none (n.a.).
*Population economically active* (1984): total 2,272,000; activity rate of total
population 35.2% (participation rates: ages 15–64, 59.7%; female 27.9%;
unemployed [1981] 0.9%).

| Price and earnings indexes (1980 = 100) | | | | | | | |
|---|---|---|---|---|---|---|---|
| | 1981 | 1982 | 1983 | 1984 | 1985 | 1986 | 1987[1] |
| Consumer price index | 114.0 | 128.2 | 153.4 | 184.1 | 253.0 | 383.6 | 518.4 |
| Monthly earnings index | ... | ... | ... | ... | ... | ... | ... |

*Gross national product* (at current market prices; 1985): U.S.$2,620,000,000
(U.S.$390 per capita).

| Structure of gross domestic product and labour force | | | | |
|---|---|---|---|---|
| | 1984 | | | |
| | in value K '000,000 | % of total value | labour force | % of labour force |
| Agriculture | 697.8 | 16.3 | 1,452,000 | 63.9 |
| Mining | 664.0 | 15.5 | 58,500 | 2.6 |
| Manufacturing | 988.2 | 23.0 | 48,200 | 2.1 |
| Construction | 135.4 | 3.2 | 33,600 | 1.5 |
| Public utilities | 71.0 | 1.7 | 7,900 | 0.3 |
| Transportation and communication | 248.6 | 5.8 | 24,600 | 1.1 |
| Trade | 592.8 | 13.8 | 30,300 | 1.3 |
| Finance, public admin. and defense, and services | 799.8 | 18.6 | 617,200 | 27.2 |
| Other | 92.4[2] | 2.1[2] | ... | ... |
| TOTAL | 4,290.0 | 100.0 | 2,272,300 | 100.0 |

*Household income and expenditure.* Average household size (1981) 5.8; average annual income per household K 1,041 (U.S.$908); sources of income:
wages and salaries 94.0%, other 6.0%; expenditure (1977): food 37.7%, housing 11.0%, clothing 8.3%, transportation 4.3%, education 2.1%, health 1.0%.
*Public debt* (external, outstanding; 1985): U.S.$3,213,900,000.
*Tourism:* receipts from visitors (1984) U.S.$49,000,000; expenditures by na-
tionals abroad (1983) U.S.$43,000,000.
*Land use* (1984): forested 39.8%; meadows and pastures 47.2%; agricultural
and under permanent cultivation 7.0%; other 6.0%.

## Foreign trade

| Balance of trade (current prices) | | | | | | |
|---|---|---|---|---|---|---|
| | 1981 | 1982 | 1983 | 1984 | 1985 | 1986 |
| K '000,000 | 12.1 | 20.5 | 154.4 | 80.4 | −124.0 | −1,372.6 |
| % of total | 0.7% | 1.1% | 8.0% | 3.5% | 4.0% | 18.2% |

*Imports* (1982): K 930,000,000 (machinery and transport equipment 34.5%;
mineral fuels, lubricants, and electricity 20.8%; basic manufactures 17.8%;
chemicals 16.0%; food 5.3%). *Major import sources:* Saudi Arabia 13.1%;
United Kingdom 12.9%; Bahrain 10.0%; United States 8.3%; West Germany 7.5%; Japan 6.1%; Italy 5.2%; Zimbabwe 4.4%; India 2.2%.
*Exports* (1982): K 950,400,000 (copper 89.2%; cobalt 4.2%; zinc 2.0%; lead
0.5%). *Major export destinations:* Japan 20.2%; France 11.3%; Italy 10.0%;
United Kingdom 6.6%; India 5.8%; West Germany 5.2%; Yugoslavia 4.7%;
China 3.9%; United States 2.7%.

## Transport and communications

*Transport.* Railroads (1985): length[3] 1,359 mi, 2,187 km; passenger-mi
346,834,000, passenger-km 558,176,000; short ton-mi cargo 1,072,208,000,
metric ton-km cargo 1,565,496,000. Roads (1985): total length 23,183 mi,
37,310 km (paved 15%). Vehicles (1982): passenger cars 105,783; trucks and
buses 94,780. Merchant marine: vessels (100 gross tons and over) none.
Air transport (1986): passenger-mi 391,974,000, passenger-km 630,822,000;
short ton-mi cargo 16,750,000, metric ton-km cargo 24,455,000; airports
(1987) with scheduled flights 14.
*Communications.* Daily newspapers (1986): total number 2; total circulation
109,000; circulation per 1,000 population 15.8. Radio (1986): total number
of receivers 528,000 (1 per 13 persons). Television (1986): total number
of receivers 66,000 (1 per 105 persons). Telephones (1985): 74,574 (1
per 89 persons).

## Education and health

| Education (1984) | | | | |
|---|---|---|---|---|
| | schools | teachers | students | student/ teacher ratio |
| Primary (age 7–13)[4] | 2,894 | 23,870 | 1,121,769 | 47.0 |
| Secondary (age 14–18)[4] | 142 | 4,602 | 104,859 | 22.8 |
| Voc., teacher tr. | 28 | 1,041 | 9,563 | 9.2 |
| Higher | 1 | 650 | 3,621 | 5.6 |

*Educational attainment* (1969). Percent of population age 15 and over having: no formal schooling 51.4%; primary education 39.3%; secondary 6.5%;
higher 0.5%; other 2.3%. *Literacy* (1980): total population literate 2,128,500
(68.6%); males literate 1,207,300 (79.3%); females literate 921,200 (58.3%).
*Health:* physicians (1982) 839 (1 per 7,186 persons); hospital beds (1981)
21,257 (1 per 274 persons); infant mortality rate per 1,000 live births
(1980–85) 88.0.
*Food* (1981–83): daily per capita caloric intake 2,008 (vegetable products
94%, animal products 6%); (1983) 83% of FAO recommended minimum
daily requirement.

## Military

*Total active duty personnel* (1986): 16,200 (army 92.6%; navy, none; air force
7.4%). *Military expenditure as percent of GNP* (1984): 6.6% (world 5.9%);
per capita expenditure U.S.$13.

[1]May. [2]Includes import duties and bank service charges. [3]1984. [4]1982.

# Zimbabwe

*Official name:* Republic of Zimbabwe.
*Form of government:* unitary multiparty republic with two legislative houses (Senate [40[1]]; House of Assembly [100]).
*Chief of state:* President.
*Head of government:* Prime Minister.
*Capital:* Harare.
*Official language:* English.
*Official religion:* none.
*Monetary unit:* 1 Zimbabwe Dollar (Z$) = 100 cents; valuation (Oct. 5, 1987) 1 U.S.$ = Z$1.71; 1 £ = Z$2.77.

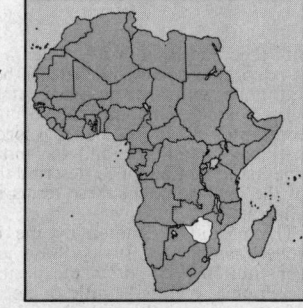

| Area and population | | area | | population |
|---|---|---|---|---|
| | | | | 1982 |
| Provinces | Capitals | sq mi | sq km | census |
| Manicaland | Mutare | 13,463 | 34,870 | 1,099,202 |
| Mashonaland Central | Bindura | 10,534 | 27,284 | 563,407 |
| Mashonaland East | Harare | 9,627 | 24,934 | 1,495,984 |
| Mashonaland West | Chinhoyi | 23,346 | 60,467 | 858,962 |
| Masvingo (Victoria) | Masvingo | 17,108 | 44,310 | 1,031,697 |
| Matabeleland North | Bulawayo | 28,393 | 73,537 | 885,339 |
| Matabeleland South | Gwanda | 25,633 | 66,390 | 519,636 |
| Midlands | Gweru | 22,767 | 58,967 | 1,091,844 |
| TOTAL | | 150,873[2] | 390,759 | 7,546,071 |

## Demography

*Population* (1987): 8,640,000.
*Density* (1987): persons per sq mi 57.3, persons per sq km 22.1.
*Urban–rural* (1982): urban 25.7%; rural 74.3%.
*Sex distribution* (1987): male 49.07%; female 50.93%.
*Age breakdown* (1987): under 15, 44.9%; 15–29, 29.2%; 30–44, 14.6%; 45–59, 7.3%; 60–74, 3.1%; 75 and over, 0.9%.
*Population projection:* (1990) 9,369,000; (2000) 11,943,000.
*Doubling time:* 20 years.
*Ethnolinguistic composition* (1982): African 97.6%, of which Shona-speaking Bantu 70.8%; Ndebele-speaking Bantu 15.8%; European 2.0%; Asian 0.1%; other 0.3%.
*Religious affiliation* (1980): Christian 44.8%, of which Protestant (including Anglican) 17.5%, African indigenous 13.6%, Roman Catholic 11.7%; animist 40.4%; other 14.8%.
*Major cities* (1983): Harare 681,000; Bulawayo 429,000; Chitungwiza 202,-000; Gweru 78,900[3]; Mutare 69,600[3].

## Vital statistics

*Birth rate* per 1,000 population (1983): 53.0 (world avg. 29.0).
*Death rate* per 1,000 population (1983): 13.0 (world avg. 11.0).
*Natural increase rate* per 1,000 population (1983): 40.0 (world avg. 18.0).
*Total fertility rate* (avg. births per childbearing woman; 1983): 7.0.
*Marriage rate* per 1,000 population: n.a.
*Divorce rate* per 1,000 population: n.a.
*Life expectancy* at birth (1987): male 57.9 years; female 61.4 years.
*Major causes of death* per 100,000 population[4] (1982): accidents and violence 46.6; infectious and parasitic diseases 32.2; diseases of the respiratory system 25.4; diseases of the circulatory system 24.5; malnutrition 15.5.

## National economy

*Budget* (1986–87). Revenue: Z$3,056,500,000 (income tax 40.7%, sales tax 16.3%, customs duties 14.4%, excise tax 9.5%, international aid grants 5.4%, revenue from investments and property 5.0%, pension contributions 2.5%). Expenditures: Z$4,675,400,000 (education 15.4%, defense 13.9%, debt service 12.8%, health 5.2%, social security and welfare 1.0%).
*Tourism:* receipts from visitors (1985) U.S.$26,000,000; expenditures by nationals abroad (1983) U.S.$180,000,000.
*Population economically active* (1982): total 2,484,070; activity rate of total population 33.1% (participation rates: over age 15, 63.5%; female 39.2%; unemployed, n.a.).

| Price and earnings indexes (1980 = 100) | | | | | | | |
|---|---|---|---|---|---|---|---|
| | 1981 | 1982 | 1983 | 1984 | 1985 | 1986 | 1987[5] |
| Consumer price index | 113.1 | 125.2 | 154.1 | 185.2 | 200.9 | 229.7 | 253.4 |
| Monthly earnings index | 127.3 | 155.1 | 168.5 | 168.8 | 170.0 | ... | ... |

*Production* (value of production in Z$ except as noted). Agriculture, forestry, fishing (1986–87): tobacco 365,035,000, corn (maize) 283,586,000, cotton 183,919,000, beef 148,908,000, sugar 146,940,000, milk and dairy products 86,882,000, wheat 74,107,000, coffee 73,890,000, soybeans 28,059,000; livestock (number of live animals; 1986) 5,364,000 cattle, 1,880,000 goats, 457,000 sheep, 194,000 pigs, 9,000,000 chickens; roundwood 7,109,000 cu m; fish catch (1984) 16,400 metric tons. Mining and quarrying (1986): gold 292,770,000; coal 89,144,000; asbestos 85,789,000; nickel 60,672,000; copper 43,272,000; chrome 39,698,000; iron ore 21,144,000; tin 10,658,000; silver 10,612,000. Manufacturing (1983–84): foodstuffs 967,100,000; metals and metal products 709,700,000; chemicals and petroleum products 557,-100,000; beverages and tobacco 422,300,000; textiles, canvas, and yarns 329,900,000; clothing and footwear 200,800,000; paper, printing and publishing 192,100,000; transport equipment 145,400,000; wood and furniture 110,100,000; nonmetallic mineral products 107,500,000; other manufactured goods 43,500,000. Construction (Z$; 1985): residential 52,902,000; nonresidential 100,460,000. Energy production (consumption): electricity

(kW-hr; 1986) 4,339,500,000 (8,498,000,000); coal (metric tons; 1985) 3,114,-000 (2,270,000); crude petroleum, none (none); petroleum products (metric tons; 1985) none (574,000); natural gas, none (none).
*Public debt* (external, outstanding; 1985): U.S.$1,526,100,000.
*Household income and expenditure.* Average household size (1980) 5.8; income per household Z$1,689 (U.S.$2,628); sources of income: n.a.; expenditure (1985): food and nonalcoholic beverages 25.3%, clothing, footwear, and textiles 12.2%, public utilities, coal, and petroleum products 10.7%, alcohol and tobacco 10.2%, hotel accommodations and travel 9.5%, household equipment 7.6%, housing 7.4%, education 3.2%, cleaning materials, medicines, and drugs 2.0%, health service 1.6%, books and newspapers 1.4%.
*Gross national product* (at current market prices; 1985): U.S.$5,450,000,000 (U.S.$650 per capita).

| Structure of gross domestic product and labour force | | | | |
|---|---|---|---|---|
| | 1986 | | 1985 | |
| | in value Z$'000,000 | % of total value | labour force[6] | % of labour force |
| Agriculture | 935 | 11.4 | 276,800 | 26.1 |
| Mining | 571 | 6.9 | 54,100 | 5.1 |
| Manufacturing | 2,489 | 30.2 | 171,400 | 16.2 |
| Construction | 239 | 2.9 | 45,700 | 4.3 |
| Public utilities | 463 | 5.6 | 7,800 | 0.7 |
| Transp. and commun. | 467 | 5.7 | 50,400 | 4.8 |
| Trade | 1,071 | 13.0 | 78,800 | 7.4 |
| Finance | 455 | 5.5 | 15,500 | 1.5 |
| Pub. admin., defense | 508 | 6.2 | 91,800 | 8.7 |
| Services | 1,224 | 14.9 | 266,400 | 25.2 |
| Other | −190[7] | −2.3[7] | — | — |
| TOTAL | 8,232 | 100.0 | 1,058,700 | 100.0 |

*Land use* (1984): forested 61.6%; meadows and pastures 12.6%; agricultural and under permanent cultivation 6.9%; other 18.9%.

## Foreign trade[8]

| Balance of trade (current prices) | | | | | | |
|---|---|---|---|---|---|---|
| | 1980 | 1981 | 1982 | 1983 | 1984 | 1985 |
| Z$'000,000 | 107.0 | 83.0 | 160.0 | 84.0 | 185.0 | 349.0 |
| % of total | 3.8% | 2.8% | 5.7% | 3.8% | 8.6% | 10.8% |

*Imports* (1985): Z$1,446,500,000 (machinery and transport equipment 29.3%; petroleum products 21.4%; chemicals 16.2%; basic manufactures 14.9%, of which textile yarns and fabrics 3.2%, iron and steel 2.0%). *Major import sources:* South Africa 18.9%; United Kingdom 10.4%; United States 10.1%; West Germany 6.9%; Japan 3.9%; France 3.4%; Italy 3.0%; Botswana 2.7%; Zambia 2.4%; The Netherlands 2.4%.
*Exports* (1985): Z$1,795,500,000 (tobacco 23.7%; ferroalloys 11.9%; cotton 9.7%; asbestos 5.2%; nickel metal 4.4%; sugar 3.4%; corn 2.2%). *Major export destinations:* United Kingdom 13.0%; South Africa 10.8%; West Germany 9.9%; United States 8.1%; Italy 5.9%; Japan 4.6%; Botswana 3.8%; Zambia 3.8%; China 3.8%; Belgium 3.4%; The Netherlands 3.1%.

## Transport and communications

*Transport.* Railroads[9] (1985): route length 2,109 mi, 3,394 km; number of passengers 2,471,000; short ton-mi cargo 4,246,000,000, metric ton-km cargo 6,200,000,000. Roads (1985): total length 48,421 mi, 77,927 km (paved 17%). Vehicles (1985): passenger cars 253,470; trucks and buses 28,839. Merchant marine: none. Air transport (1985): passenger-mi 410,700,000, passenger-km 660,900,000; short ton-mi cargo 8,861,000, metric ton-km cargo 12,937,000; airports (1987) with scheduled flights 8.
*Communications.* Daily newspapers (1985): total number 3; total circulation 191,000; circulation per 1,000 population 23. Radio (1986): 315,000 receivers (1 per 27 persons). Television (1986): 112,500 receivers (1 per 75 persons). Telephones (1984): 245,000 (1 per 32 persons).

## Education and health

| Education (1986) | | | | |
|---|---|---|---|---|
| | schools | teachers | students | student/ teacher ratio |
| Primary (age 7–13) | 4,297 | 57,823 | 2,260,367 | 39.1 |
| Secondary (age 14–19) | 1,262[10] | 19,560 | 545,841 | 27.9 |
| Voc., teacher tr. | 14[11] | 1,031[11] | 30,935 | ... |
| Higher | 1 | 431[12] | 5,866 | ... |

*Educational attainment* (1969). Percent of population age 17 and over having: no formal schooling 41.6%; some primary education 36.5%; primary 13.6%; secondary 3.3%; other 5.0%. *Literacy* (1985): total population age 15 and over literate 3,413,000 (76.0%); males literate 1,846,000 (81.5%); females literate 1,567,000 (66.8%).
*Health:* physicians (1984) 705 (1 per 11,275 persons); hospital beds (1980) 21,418 (1 per 333 persons); infant mortality rate per 1,000 live births (1985) 61.0.
*Food* (1981–83): daily per capita caloric intake 1,890 (vegetable products 92%, animal products 8%); (1983) 82% of FAO minimum requirement.

## Military

*Total active duty personnel* (1986): 42,000 (army 97.6%, air force 2.4%). *Military expenditure as percent of GNP* (1984): 6.2% (world 5.9%); per capita expenditure U.S.$44.

[1]Includes six nonelective seats. [2]Detail does not add to total given because of rounding. [3]1982. [4]Registered deaths. [5]April. [6]Wage earning workers only. [7]Imputed bank service charges. [8]Import figures are f.o.b. in balance of trade and c.i.f. in commodities and trading partners. [9]Includes operations in Botswana. [10]Includes vocational. [11]Teacher training only. [12]1984.

# Government and international organizations

This table summarizes principal facts about the governments of the countries of the world, their branches and organs, the topmost layers of local government comprising each country's chief administrative subdivisions, and the participation of their central governments in the principal intergovernmental organizations of the world.

In this table "date of independence" may refer to a variety of circumstances. In the case of the newest countries, those that attained full independence after World War II, the date given is usually just what is implied by the heading—the date when the country, within its present borders, attained full sovereignty over both its internal and external affairs. In the case of longer established countries, the choice of a single date may be somewhat more complicated, and grounds for the use of several different dates often exist. The reader interested in this subject should refer to *Macropædia* and *Micropædia* articles on national histories and relevant historical acts. In cases of territorial annexation or dissolution, the date given here refers either to the final act of union of a state comprised of smaller entities or to the final act of separation from a larger whole (*e.g.,* the separation of Bangladesh from Pakistan in 1971).

The date of the current, or last, constitution is in some ways a less complicated question, but governments sometimes do not, upon taking power, either adhere to existing constitutional forms or trouble to terminate the previous document and legitimize themselves by the installation of new constitutional forms. Often, however, the desire to legitimize extraconstitutional political activity by associating it with existing forms of long precedent leads to partial or incomplete modification, suspension, or abrogation of a constitution, so that the actual day-to-day conduct of government may be largely unrelated to the provisions of a constitution

still theoretically in force. When a date in this column is given in italics, it refers to a document that has been suspended, abolished by extraconstitutional action, or modified extensively.

The characterizations adopted under "kind of government" represent a compromise between the ideal forms provided for by the language of the national constitution and the more pragmatic language that a political scientist might adopt to describe these same systems. For an explanation of the application of these terms in the Britannica World Data, *see* the Glossary at p. 533.

The positions denoted by the terms "chief of state" and "head of government" are usually those identified with those functions by the constitution. Very often the position of chief of state will be a largely ceremonial one, with little or no authority over the day-to-day conduct of government, although the formal assent of the office to executive or legislative action may be required by the constitution. In other cases, such as in some of the Middle Eastern monarchies, the chief of state may also be the effective head of government. In certain countries, an official of a political party or a revolutionary figure entirely outside the constitutional structure may effectively exercise the powers of both positions.

Membership in the legislative house(s) of each country as given here includes all elected or appointed members, as well as ex officio members (those who by virtue of some other office or title are members of the body), whether voting or nonvoting. The legislature of a country with a unicameral system is shown as the upper house in this table.

The number of administrative subdivisions for each country is listed down to the second level. A single country may, depending on its size, complexity, and historical antecedents, have as many as five levels of

## Government and international organizations

| country | date of independence[a] | date of current or last constitution[b] | type of government | executive branch[c] chief of state | head of government | legislative branch[d] upper house (members) | lower house (members) | admin. subdivisions first-order (number) | second-order (number) | seaward claims territorial (nautical miles) | fishing/ economic (nautical miles) |
|---|---|---|---|---|---|---|---|---|---|---|---|
| Afghanistan | Aug. 19, 1919 | Nov. 30, 1987 | people's republic | ———president——— | | ... | ... | 29 | 185 | — | — |
| Albania | Nov. 28, 1912 | Dec. 27, 1976 | socialist republic | chairman PPA | chairman CM | 250 | — | 26 | 3,315 | 15 | [1] |
| Algeria | July 3, 1962 | Jan. 16, 1986 | socialist republic | ———president——— | | 295 | — | 48 | 1,111 | 12 | [1] |
| American Samoa | — | July 1, 1967 | territory (U.S.) | U.S. president | governor | 18 | 20 | 3 | 15 | 3 | 200 |
| Andorra | Dec. 6, 1288 | — | coprincipality | 3 | chief executive | 28 | — | 7 | — | — | — |
| Angola | Nov. 11, 1975 | Nov. 11, 1975 | people's republic | ———president——— | | 223 | — | 18 | 139 | 20 | 200 |
| Anguilla | — | April 1, 1982 | territory (U.K.) | British monarch | 4 | 11 | — | — | 3 | 200 | |
| Antigua and Barbuda | Nov. 1, 1981 | Nov. 1, 1981 | constitutional monarchy | British monarch | prime minister | 17 | 17 | 8 | — | 12 | 200 |
| Argentina | July 9, 1816 | July 9, 1853 | federal republic | ———president——— | | 46 | 254 | 24 | 488 | 200 | [1] |
| Aruba | — | Dec. 29, 1954 | integral part of Neth. | Dutch monarch | prime minister | 21 | — | ... | ... | 12 | 200 |
| Australia | Jan. 1, 1901 | July 9, 1900 | federal parl. state[5] | British monarch | prime minister | 76 | 148 | 8 | 866 | 3 | 200 |
| Austria | Oct. 30, 1918 | Oct. 1, 1920 | federal republic | president | chancellor | 63 | 183 | 9 | 98 | — | — |
| Bahamas, The | July 10, 1973 | July 10, 1973 | constitutional monarchy | British monarch | prime minister | 16 | 49 | — | 15 | 3 | 200 |
| Bahrain | Aug. 15, 1971 | Dec. 6, 1973 | monarchy (emirate) | emir | prime minister | x | — | 11 | — | 3 | [1] |
| Bangladesh | March 26, 1971 | Dec. 16, 1972 | republic | ———president——— | | 330 | — | 4 | 64 | 12 | 200 |
| Barbados | Nov. 30, 1966 | Nov. 30, 1966 | constitutional monarchy | British monarch | prime minister | 21 | 27 | 11 | — | 12 | 200 |
| Belgium | Oct. 4, 1830 | 1831 | constitutional monarchy | monarch | prime minister | 183 | 212 | 3 | 9 | 3 | 200[6] |
| Belize | Sept. 21, 1981 | Sept. 21, 1981 | constitutional monarchy | British monarch | prime minister | 9 | 28 | 6 | — | 3 | [1] |
| Benin | Aug. 1, 1960 | Aug. 26, 1977 | people's republic | ———president——— | | 196 | — | 6 | 84 | 200 | [1] |
| Bermuda | — | June 8, 1968 | colony (U.K.) | British monarch | 7 | 11 | 40 | 11 | — | 3 | 200 |
| Bhutan | March 24, 1910 | — | 8 | ———king——— | | 150 | — | 18 | — | — | — |
| Bolivia | Aug. 6, 1825 | February 1967 | republic | ———president——— | | 27 | 130 | 9 | 99 | — | — |
| Botswana | Sept. 30, 1966 | March 3, 1965 | republic | ———president——— | | 15[9] | 39 | 14 | — | — | — |
| Brazil | Sept. 7, 1822 | Jan. 24, 1967 | federal republic | ———president——— | | 72 | 487 | 27 | 3,963 | 200 | 200[10] |
| British Virgin Islands | — | June 1, 1977 | colony (U.K.) | British monarch | governor | 11 | — | — | 3 | 200 | |
| Brunei | Jan. 1, 1984 | Sept. 29, 1959 | monarchy (sultanate) | ———sultan——— | | 21 | — | 4 | — | 12 | 200 |
| Bulgaria | Oct. 5, 1908 | May 18, 1971 | socialist republic | chairman SC | chairman CM | 400 | — | 28 | 4,823 | 12 | 200 |
| Burkina Faso | Aug. 5, 1960 | *Nov. 27, 1977* | state | ———president——— | | x | — | 30 | 300 | — | — |
| Burma | Jan. 4, 1948 | Jan. 4, 1974 | people's republic | president | prime minister | 489 | — | 14 | 314 | 12 | 200 |
| Burundi | July 1, 1962 | Nov. 20, 1981 | republic | ———president——— | | 65 | — | 15 | 114 | — | — |
| Cameroon | Jan. 1, 1960 | June 2, 1972 | republic | ———president——— | | 120 | — | 10 | 40 | 50 | [1] |
| Canada | July 1, 1867 | April 17, 1982 | federal parl. state[5] | British monarch | prime minister | 104 | 282 | 12 | 4,740 | 12 | 200 |
| Cape Verde | July 5, 1975 | Sept. 7, 1980 | republic | president | prime minister | 83 | — | 14 | — | 12[12] | 200 |
| Cayman Islands | — | Aug. 22, 1972 | colony (U.K.) | British monarch | governor | 16 | — | 3 | 8 | 3 | 200 |
| Central African Republic | Aug. 13, 1960 | Nov. 21, 1986 | republic | ———chairman CMRN——— | | 52 | — | 17 | 47 | — | — |
| Chad | Aug. 11, 1960 | *Aug. 29, 1978* | republic | ———president——— | | x | — | 14 | 53 | — | — |
| Chile | Sept. 18, 1810 | March 11, 1981[13] | republic | ———president——— | | 13 | 51 | 12 | 200 | | |
| China | 1523 BC | Dec. 4, 1982 | people's republic | president | premier SC | 2,978 | — | 29 | 327 | 12 | [1] |
| Christmas Island | — | Oct. 1, 1958 | external territory (Aust.) | Australian GG | administrator | — | — | — | — | 3 | 200 |
| Cocos (Keeling) Islands | — | Nov. 23, 1955 | external territory (Aust.) | Australian GG | administrator | — | — | — | — | 3 | 200 |
| Colombia | July 20, 1810 | Aug. 5, 1886 | republic | ———president——— | | 114 | 199 | 32 | 990 | 12 | 200 |
| Comoros | July 6, 1975 | Oct. 1, 1978 | federal Islamic republic | ———president——— | | 42 | — | 3 | 7 | 12 | 200 |
| Congo | Aug. 15, 1960 | July 8, 1979 | people's republic | ———president——— | | 153 | — | 15 | 45 | 200 | [1] |
| Cook Islands | — | Aug. 4, 1965 | territory (N.Z.)[14] | British monarch | prime minister | 15[9] | 24 | — | 10 | 12 | 200 |
| Costa Rica | Sept. 15, 1821 | Nov. 9, 1949 | republic | ———president——— | | 57 | — | 7 | 80 | 12 | 200 |
| Côte d'Ivoire | Aug. 7, 1960 | Oct. 31, 1960 | republic | ———president——— | | 175 | — | 49 | — | 12 | 200 |
| Cuba | May 20, 1902 | Feb. 24, 1976 | socialist republic | ———president——— | | 510 | — | 15 | 169 | 12 | 200 |
| Cyprus | Aug. 16, 1960 | Aug. 16, 1960 | republic | ———president——— | | 106[15] | — | 6[15] | ... | 12 | [1] |
| Czechoslovakia | Oct. 28, 1918 | July 11, 1960 | federal socialist republic | president | premier | 150 | 200 | 2 | 12 | — | — |
| Denmark | c. 800 | June 5, 1953 | constitutional monarchy | monarch | prime minister | 179 | — | 16 | 275 | 3 | 200 |
| Djibouti | June 27, 1977 | — | republic | president | prime minister | 65 | — | 5 | 11 | 12 | 200 |
| Dominica | Nov. 3, 1978 | Nov. 3, 1978 | republic | president | prime minister | 31 | — | 10 | 27 | 12 | 200 |
| Dominican Republic | Feb. 27, 1844 | Nov. 28, 1966 | republic | ———president——— | | 30 | 120 | 30 | 97 | 6 | 200 |
| Ecuador | May 24, 1822 | Aug. 10, 1979 | republic | ———president——— | | 71 | — | 20 | 147 | 200 | [1] |
| Egypt | Feb. 28, 1922 | Sept. 11, 1971 | republic | president | prime minister | 458 | — | 26 | ... | 12 | 200 |

administrative subordination (as does the U.S.S.R.) or it may have none at all. Each level of subordination may have several kinds of subdivisions.

Finally, in the second half of the table are listed the memberships each country maintains in the principal international intergovernmental organizations of the world. This part of the table may also be utilized to provide a complete membership list for each of these organizations as of Dec. 1, 1987.

**Notes for the column headings**

a. The date may also be either that of the organization of the present form of government or the inception of the present administrative structure (federation, confederation, union, etc.).
b. Constitutions whose dates are in italic type had been wholly or substantially suspended or abolished as of late 1987.
c. For abbreviations used in this column see the list on the facing page.
d. When a legislative body has been adjourned or otherwise suspended, figures in parentheses indicate the number of members in the legislative body as provided for in the constitution. If the provision for the legislative body in the constitution has been abrogated then the space has been marked with an "X".
e. Vatican City also a member.
f. States contributing funds to or receiving aid from UNICEF in 1986.
g. Palestine (Liberation Organization) also a member.

**International organizations, conventions**

- ACP African, Caribbean, and Pacific (Lomé III) convention
- ASEAN Association of South East Asian Nations
- COMECON Council for Mutual Economic Assistance
- EC The European Communities
- ECOWAS Economic Community of West African States
- EEC European Economic Community
- FAO Food and Agriculture Organization
- GATT General Agreement on Tariffs and Trade
- I-ADB Inter-American Development Bank
- IAEA International Atomic Energy Agency
- IBRD International Bank for Reconstruction and Development
- ICAO International Civil Aviation Organization
- ICJ International Court of Justice
- IDA International Development Association
- IDB Islamic Development Bank
- IFC International Finance Corporation
- ILO International Labour Organisation
- IMF International Monetary Fund
- IMO International Maritime Organization
- ITU International Telecommunication Union
- LAS League of Arab States
- NATO North Atlantic Treaty Organization
- OAS Organization of American States
- OAU Organization of African Unity
- OPEC Organization of Petroleum Exporting Countries
- SPC South Pacific Commission
- UNCTAD United Nations Conference on Trade and Development
- UNESCO United Nations Educational Scientific and Cultural Organization
- UNICEF United Nations Children's Fund
- UNIDO United Nations Industrial Development Organization
- UPU Universal Postal Union
- WHO World Health Organization
- WIPO World Intellectual Property Organization
- WMO World Meteorological Organization
- WTO Warsaw Treaty of Friendship, Co-operation and Mutual Assistance (The Warsaw Pact)

**Abbreviations used in the executive branch column**

- AFRC Armed Forces Ruling Council
- CM Council of Ministers
- CMRN Military Committee for National Recovery
- CMSN Military Committee for National Salvation
- CP Collective Presidency
- CS Council of State
- FEC Federal Executive Council
- GG Governor-general
- GPC General People's Committee
- MC Military Council
- PC Presidential Council Administrative Council
- PNDC Provisional National Defense Council
- PPA Presidium, People's Assembly
- PPGH Presidium, People's Great Hural
- PRC People's Redemption Council
- PSPC Presidium, Supreme People's Council
- PSSU Presidium, Supreme Soviet of the U.S.S.R.
- RC Revolutionary Council
- SC State Council
- SMC Supreme Military Council
- SUC Supreme Council

membership in international organizations

| United Nations (date of admission) | UN organs★ and affiliated intergovernmental organizations | | | | | | | | | | | | | | | | | | | | Commonwealth of Nations | regional multi-purpose | | | | | | economic | | | | | | | military | | country |
|---|---|---|---|---|---|---|---|---|---|---|---|---|---|---|---|---|---|---|---|---|---|---|---|---|---|---|---|---|---|---|---|---|---|---|---|---|---|
| | UNCTAD★[e] | UNICEF★[f] | ICJ★ | FAO | GATT | IAEA[e] | IBRD | ICAO | IDA | IFC | ILO | IMF | IMO | ITU[e] | UNESCO | UNIDO | UPU[e] | WHO | WIPO[e] | WMO | | ASEAN | EC | LAS[g] | OAS | OAU | SPC | ACP | COMECON | ECOWAS | EEC | I-ADB | IDB[g] | OPEC | NATO | WTO | |
| 1946 | ● | ● | ● | ● | | ● | ● | ● | ● | ● | ● | ● | | ● | ● | ● | ● | ● | | ● | | | | | | | | | | | | | ● | | | | Afghanistan |
| 1955 | ● | | ● | ● | | ● | | | | | | | | ● | ● | | ● | ● | | ● | | | | | | | | | | | | | | | | | Albania |
| 1962 | ● | ● | ● | ● | ●2 | ● | ● | ● | ● | | ● | ● | ● | ● | ● | ● | ● | ● | ● | ● | | | | ● | | ● | | | | | | | ● | ● | | | Algeria |
| — | | | | | | | | | | | | | | | | | ● | | | | | | | | | | ● | | | | | | | | | | American Samoa |
| — | | | | | | | | | | | | | | | | | | | | | | | | | | | | | | | | | | | | | Andorra |
| 1976 | ● | ● | ● | ● | ●2 | | | ● | | | ● | | ● | ● | ● | ● | ● | ● | ● | ● | | | | | | ● | | ● | | | | | | | | | Angola |
| — | | | | | | | | | | | | | | | | | ● | | | ● | ● | | | | | | | | | | | | | | | | Anguilla |
| 1981 | ● | ● | ● | ● | | | ● | ● | | ● | ● | ● | ● | | ● | | ●2 | ● | | | ● | | | | ● | | | ● | | | | | | | | | Antigua and Barbuda |
| 1945 | ● | ● | ● | ● | ● | ● | ● | ● | ● | ● | ● | ● | ● | ● | ● | ● | ● | ● | ● | ● | | | | | ● | | | | | | | ● | | | | | Argentina |
| — | | | | | | | | | | | | | | | ● | | ● | | | ● | | | | | | | | | | | | | | | | | Aruba |
| 1945 | ● | ● | ● | ● | ● | ● | ● | ● | ● | ● | ● | ● | ● | ● | ● | ● | ● | ● | ● | ● | ● | | | | | | ● | | | | | | | | | | Australia |
| 1955 | ● | ● | ● | ● | ● | ● | ● | ● | ● | ● | ● | ● | ● | ● | ● | ● | ● | ● | ● | ● | | | | | | | | | | | | ● | | | | | Austria |
| 1973 | ● | ● | ● | ● | ●2 | | ● | ● | | ● | ● | ● | ● | ● | ● | ● | ● | ● | ● | ● | ● | | | | ● | | | ● | | | | ● | | | | | Bahamas, The |
| 1971 | ● | ● | ● | ● | ●2 | | ● | ● | | | ● | ● | ● | ● | ● | ● | ● | ● | | ● | | | | ● | | | | | | | | | ● | | | | Bahrain |
| 1974 | ● | ● | ● | ● | ● | ● | ● | ● | ● | ● | ● | ● | ● | ● | ● | ● | ● | ● | ● | ● | ● | | | | | | | | | | | | ● | | | | Bangladesh |
| 1966 | ● | ● | ● | ● | ● | | ● | ● | | ● | ● | ● | ● | ● | ● | ● | ● | ● | ● | ● | ● | | | | ● | | | ● | | | | ● | | | | | Barbados |
| 1945 | ● | ● | ● | ● | ● | ● | ● | ● | ● | ● | ● | ● | ● | ● | ● | ● | ● | ● | ● | ● | | | ● | | | | | | | | ● | ● | | | ● | | Belgium |
| 1981 | ● | ● | ● | ● | ●2 | | ● | | ● | ● | ● | ● | | ● | ● | ● | ● | | | ● | ● | | | | | | | ● | | | | | | | | | Belize |
| 1960 | ● | ● | ● | ● | ● | | ● | ● | ● | ● | ● | ● | ● | ● | ● | ● | ● | ● | ● | ● | | | | | | ● | | ● | | ● | | | ● | | | | Benin |
| — | | | | | | | | | | | | | | ● | | | ● | | | ● | ● | | | | | | | | | | | | | | | | Bermuda |
| 1971 | ● | ● | ● | ● | | | ● | | ● | | | ● | | | ● | ● | ● | ● | | | | | | | | | | | | | | | | | | | Bhutan |
| 1945 | ● | ● | ● | ● | | ● | ● | ● | ● | ● | ● | ● | | ● | ● | ● | ● | ● | ● | ● | | | | | ● | | | | | | | ● | | | | | Bolivia |
| 1966 | ● | ● | ● | ● | ●2 | | ● | ● | ● | ● | ● | ● | | ● | ● | ● | ● | ● | | ● | ● | | | | | ● | | ● | | | | | | | | | Botswana |
| 1945 | ● | ● | ● | ● | ● | ● | ● | ● | ● | ● | ● | ● | ● | ● | ● | ● | ● | ● | ● | ● | | | | | ● | | | | | | | ● | | | | | Brazil |
| — | | ● | | | | | | | | | | | | | ●11 | | ● | | | ● | ● | | | | | | | | | | | | | | | | British Virgin Islands |
| 1984 | ● | | ● | | | ● | | ● | | | | | ● | ● | | | ● | ● | | ● | ● | ● | | | | | | | | | | | ● | | | | Brunei |
| 1955 | ● | ● | ● | ● | | ● | | ● | | | ● | | ● | ● | ● | ● | ● | ● | ● | ● | | | | | | | | | ● | | | | | | | ● | Bulgaria |
| 1960 | ● | ● | ● | ● | ● | | ● | ● | ● | ● | ● | ● | | ● | ● | ● | ● | ● | ● | ● | | | | | | ● | | ● | | ● | | | ● | | | | Burkina Faso |
| 1948 | ● | ● | ● | ● | ● | ● | ● | ● | ● | ● | ● | ● | ● | ● | ● | | ● | ● | | ● | | | | | | | | | | | | | | | | | Burma |
| 1962 | ● | ● | ● | ● | ● | | ● | ● | ● | ● | ● | ● | | ● | ● | ● | ● | ● | ● | ● | | | | | | ● | | ● | | | | | | | | | Burundi |
| 1960 | ● | ● | ● | ● | ● | ● | ● | ● | ● | ● | ● | ● | ● | ● | ● | ● | ● | ● | ● | ● | | | | | | ● | | ● | | | | | ● | | | | Cameroon |
| 1945 | ● | ● | ● | ● | ● | ● | ● | ● | ● | ● | ● | ● | ● | ● | ● | ● | ● | ● | ● | ● | ● | | | | | | | | | | | ● | | | ● | | Canada |
| 1975 | ● | ● | ● | ● | ●2 | | ● | ● | ● | | ● | ● | ● | ● | ● | ● | ● | ● | | ● | | | | | | ● | | ● | | ● | | | | | | | Cape Verde |
| — | | | | | | | | | | | | | | | | | ● | | | ● | ● | | | | | | | | | | | | | | | | Cayman Islands |
| 1960 | ● | ● | ● | ● | ● | | ● | ● | ● | | ● | ● | | ● | ● | ● | ● | ● | ● | ● | | | | | | ● | | ● | | | | | | | | | Central African Republic |
| 1960 | ● | ● | ● | ● | ● | | ● | ● | ● | | ● | ● | | ● | ● | | ● | ● | ● | ● | | | | | | ● | | ● | | | | | ● | | | | Chad |
| 1945 | ● | ● | ● | ● | ● | ● | ● | ● | ● | ● | ● | ● | ● | ● | ● | ● | ● | ● | ● | ● | | | | | ● | | | | | | | ● | | | | | Chile |
| 1945 | ● | ● | ● | ● | | ● | ● | ● | ● | ● | ● | ● | ● | ● | ● | ● | ● | ● | ● | ● | | | | | | | | | | | | | | | | | China |
| — | | | | | | | | | | | | | | | | | ● | | | | ● | | | | | | | | | | | | | | | | Christmas Island |
| — | | | | | | | | | | | | | | | | | ● | | | | ● | | | | | | | | | | | | | | | | Cocos (Keeling) Islands |
| 1945 | ● | ● | ● | ● | ● | ● | ● | ● | ● | ● | ● | ● | ● | ● | ● | ● | ● | ● | ● | ● | | | | | ● | | | | | | | ● | | | | | Colombia |
| 1975 | ● | ● | ● | ● | | | ● | ● | ● | | ● | ● | | ● | ● | ● | ● | ● | | ● | | | | | | ● | | ● | | | | | ● | | | | Comoros |
| 1960 | ● | ● | ● | ● | ● | | ● | ● | ● | ● | ● | ● | ● | ● | ● | ● | ● | ● | ● | ● | | | | | | ● | | ● | | | | | | | | | Congo |
| — | | ● | | ● | | | | | | | | | | | | | ● | ● | | | ● | | | | | | ● | | | | | | | | | | Cook Islands |
| 1945 | ● | ● | ● | ● | | ● | ● | ● | ● | ● | ● | ● | ● | ● | ● | ● | ● | ● | ● | ● | | | | | ● | | | | | | | ● | | | | | Costa Rica |
| 1960 | ● | ● | ● | ● | ● | ● | ● | ● | ● | ● | ● | ● | ● | ● | ● | ● | ● | ● | ● | ● | | | | | | ● | | ● | | ● | | | | | | | Côte d'Ivoire |
| 1945 | ● | ● | ● | ● | ● | ● | | ● | | | ● | | ● | ● | ● | ● | ● | ● | ● | ● | | | | | ● | | | | ● | | | | | | | | Cuba |
| 1960 | ● | ● | ● | ● | ● | ● | ● | ● | ● | ● | ● | ● | ● | ● | ● | ● | ● | ● | ● | ● | ● | | | | | | | | | | ●11 | | | | | | Cyprus |
| 1945 | ● | ● | ● | ● | ● | ● | | ● | | | ● | | ● | ● | ● | ● | ● | ● | ● | ● | | | | | | | | | ● | | | | | | | ● | Czechoslovakia |
| 1945 | ● | ● | ● | ● | ● | ● | ● | ● | ● | ● | ● | ● | ● | ● | ● | ● | ● | ● | ● | ● | | | ● | | | | | | | | ● | ● | | | ● | | Denmark |
| 1977 | ● | ● | ● | ● | | | ● | ● | ● | ● | ● | ● | ● | ● | | | ● | ● | | ● | | | | ● | | ● | | ● | | | | | ● | | | | Djibouti |
| 1978 | ● | ● | ● | ● | ●2 | | ● | | ● | ● | ● | ● | ● | | ● | ● | ● | ● | | ● | ● | | | | ● | | | ● | | | | | | | | | Dominica |
| 1945 | ● | ● | ● | ● | ● | ● | ● | ● | ● | ● | ● | ● | ● | ● | ● | ● | ● | ● | ● | ● | | | | | ● | | | | | | | ● | | | | | Dominican Republic |
| 1945 | ● | ● | ● | ● | | ● | ● | ● | ● | ● | ● | ● | ● | ● | ● | ● | ● | ● | ● | ● | | | | | ● | | | | | | | ● | | ● | | | Ecuador |
| 1945 | ● | ● | ● | ● | ● | ● | ● | ● | ● | ● | ● | ● | ● | ● | ● | ● | ● | ● | ● | ● | | | | ●2 | | ● | | | | | | | ● | | | | Egypt |

## Government and international organizations (continued)

| country | date of independence[a] | date of current or last constitution[b] | type of government | executive branch[c] chief of state | head of government | legislative branch[d] upper house (members) | lower house (members) | admin. subdivisions first-order (number) | second-order (number) | seaward claims territorial (nautical miles) | fishing/economic (nautical miles) |
|---|---|---|---|---|---|---|---|---|---|---|---|
| El Salvador | Jan. 30, 1841 | Dec. 20, 1983 | republic | —————president————— | | 60 | — | 14 | 261 | 200 | 1 |
| Equatorial Guinea | Oct. 12, 1968 | Oct. 12, 1982 | republic | —————president————— | | 60 | — | 7 | — | 12 | 1 |
| Ethiopia | c. 1000 BC | Sept. 12, 1987 | people's republic | —————chairman CM————— | | 835 | — | 14 | 103 | 12 | 1 |
| Faeroe Islands | — | March 23, 1948 | part of Danish realm | Danish monarch [16] | | 32 | — | 7 | 50 | 3 | 200 |
| Falkland Islands | — | Oct. 3, 1985 | colony (U.K.) | British monarch [4] | | 10 | — | — | — | 3 | 200 |
| Fiji | Oct. 10, 1970 | *Oct. 10, 1970* | republic | president | prime minister | ... | ... | 4 | 14 | 12[12] | 200 |
| Finland | Dec. 6, 1917 | July 17, 1919 | republic | president | prime minister | 200 | — | 12 | 461 | 4 | 12 |
| France | August 843 | Oct. 4, 1958 | republic | president | prime minister | 319 | 577 | 22 | 96 | 12 | 200 |
| French Guiana | — | March 19, 1946 | overseas dept. (Fr.) | French president [17] | | 19 | 31 | 2 | 20 | 12 | 200 |
| French Polynesia | — | Sept. 6, 1984 | overseas territory (Fr.) | French president [18] | | 41 | — | 5 | 48 | 12 | 200 |
| Gabon | Aug. 17, 1960 | Feb. 21, 1961 | republic | president | prime minister | 120 | — | 9 | 37 | 100 | 150 |
| Gambia, The | Feb. 18, 1965 | April 24, 1970 | republic | —————president————— | | 36 | — | 7 | 35 | 200 | 1 |
| Gaza Strip | — | — | Israeli military | ——— area commander ——— | | — | — | 3 | — | — | — |
| Germany, East | Oct. 11, 1949 | April 9, 1968 | socialist republic | chairman CS | chairman CM | 500 | — | 15 | 227 | 12 | 200 |
| Germany, West | May 5, 1955 | May 23, 1949 | federal republic | president | chancellor | 45 | 520 | 11 | 30 | 3 | 200 |
| Ghana | March 6, 1957 | *Sept. 24, 1979* | republic | —————chairman PNDC————— | | (...) | — | 10 | 154 | 200 | 1 |
| Gibraltar | — | Aug. 11, 1969 | colony (U.K.) | British monarch | governor | 18 | — | — | — | 3 | 200 |
| Greece | Feb. 3, 1830 | June 11, 1975 | republic | president | prime minister | 300 | — | 15 | 51 | 6 | 1 |
| Greenland | — | May 1, 1979 | part of Danish realm | Danish monarch [20] | | 27 | — | 3 | 18 | 3 | 21 |
| Grenada | Feb. 7, 1974 | March 3, 1967 | constitutional monarchy | British monarch | prime minister | 13 | 15 | 7 | — | 12 | 200 |
| Guadeloupe | — | March 19, 1946 | overseas dept. (Fr.) | French president [17] | | 43 | 41 | 3 | 34 | 12 | 200 |
| Guam | — | Aug. 1, 1950 | territory (U.S.) | U.S. president | governor | 21 | — | 19 | — | 3 | 200 |
| Guatemala | Sept. 15, 1821 | Jan. 14, 1986 | republic | —————president————— | | 100 | — | 22 | 327 | 12 | 200 |
| Guernsey | — | Jan. 1, 1949 | crown dependency (U.K.) | British monarch | bailiff | 59 | — | 10 | — | 3 | 200 |
| Guinea | Oct. 2, 1958 | *May 14, 1982* | republic | —————president————— | | x | — | 8 | 33 | 12 | 200 |
| Guinea-Bissau | Sept. 10, 1974 | May 16, 1984 | republic | —————president————— | | 150 | — | 9 | 37 | 12 | 200 |
| Guyana | May 26, 1966 | Oct. 6, 1980 | cooperative republic | president | prime minister | 65 | — | 10 | 98 | 12 | 200 |
| Haiti | Jan. 1, 1804 | *Aug. 27, 1983* | republic | —————president————— | | (59) | — | 9 | 41 | 12 | 200 |
| Honduras | Nov. 5, 1838 | Jan. 20, 1982 | republic | —————president————— | | 134 | — | 18 | 282 | 12 | 200 |
| Hong Kong | — | — | colony (U.K.) | British monarch | governor | 57 | 30 | 3 | 18 | 3 | 1 |
| Hungary | Nov. 16, 1918 | Aug. 20, 1949 | socialist republic | president PC | prime minister | 386 | — | 25 | 103 | — | — |
| Iceland | June 17, 1944 | June 17, 1944 | republic | president | prime minister | 21 | 42 | 24 | 229 | 12 | 200 |
| India | Aug. 15, 1947 | Jan. 26, 1950 | federal republic | president | prime minister | 244 | 544 | 32 | 386 | 12 | 200 |
| Indonesia | Aug. 17, 1945 | Aug. 17, 1945 | republic | —————president————— | | 1,000 | 500 | 27 | 301 | 12[12] | 200 |
| Iran | Oct. 7, 1906 | Dec. 2–3, 1979 | Islamic republic | president | prime minister | 270 | — | 24 | 195 | 12 | 50[22] |
| Iraq | Oct. 3, 1932 | Sept. 22, 1968 | republic | —————president————— | | 250 | — | 18 | 157 | 12 | 1 |
| Ireland | Dec. 6, 1921 | Dec. 29, 1937 | republic | president | prime minister | 60 | 166 | 27 | 49 | 3 | 200 |
| Isle of Man | — | 1961 | crown dependency (U.K.) | British monarch | chairman | 11 | 24 | 26 | — | 3 | 200 |
| Israel | May 14, 1948 | June 1950[23] | republic | president | prime minister | 120 | — | 6 | 13 | 6 | 1 |
| Italy | March 17, 1861 | Jan. 1, 1948 | republic | president | prime minister | 323 | 630 | 20 | 94 | 12 | 1 |
| Jamaica | Aug. 6, 1962 | Aug. 6, 1962 | constitutional monarchy | British monarch | prime minister | 21 | 60 | 14 | — | 12 | 1 |
| Japan | c. 660 BC | May 3, 1947 | constitutional monarchy | emperor | prime minister | 252 | 512 | 47 | 3,256 | 12[24] | 200 |
| Jersey | — | Jan. 1, 1949 | crown dependency (U.K.) | British monarch | bailiff | 57 | — | 12 | — | 3 | 200 |
| Jordan | March 22, 1946 | Jan. 1, 1952 | constitutional monarchy | king | prime minister | 30 | 130 | 5 | 14 | 3 | 1 |
| Kampuchea | Nov. 9, 1953 | June 1981 | people's republic | president CS | prime minister | 117 | — | 20 | ... | 12 | 200 |
| Kenya | Dec. 12, 1963 | Dec. 12, 1963 | republic | —————president————— | | 172 | — | 8 | 40 | 12 | 200 |
| Kiribati | July 12, 1979 | July 12, 1979 | republic | —————president————— | | 41 | — | 23 | — | 12 | 200 |
| Korea, North | Sept. 9, 1948 | Dec. 27, 1972 | socialist republic | president | premier | 655 | — | 13 | 152 | 12 | 200 |
| Korea, South | Aug. 15, 1948 | Oct. 27, 1980 | republic | president | prime minister | 276 | — | 13 | 97 | 12[25] | 12 |
| Kuwait | June 19, 1961 | Nov. 16, 1962 | const. mon. (emirate) | emir | prime minister | (64) | — | 4 | — | 12 | 1 |
| Laos | Oct. 23, 1953 | *May 11, 1947* | people's republic | president | chairman CM | 264 | — | 17 | ... | — | — |
| Lebanon | Nov. 26, 1941 | May 23, 1926 | republic | president | prime minister | 99 | — | 6 | 26 | 12 | 1 |
| Lesotho | Oct. 4, 1966 | *Aug. 16, 1983* | monarchy | king | chairman MC | (30) | (80) | 10 | 22 | — | — |
| Liberia | July 26, 1847 | July 20, 1984 | republic | —————president————— | | 26 | 64 | 13 | 50 | 200 | 1 |
| Libya | Dec. 24, 1951 | March 2, 1977 | socialist state[26] | rev. leader | sec. gen. GPC | 1,112 | — | 24 | 201 | 12[27] | 1 |
| Liechtenstein | July 12, 1806 | Oct. 5, 1921 | constitutional monarchy | prince | head of gov't. | 15 | — | 11 | — | — | — |
| Luxembourg | May 10, 1867 | Oct. 17, 1868 | constitutional monarchy | grand duke | prime minister | 21[9] | 64 | 3 | 12 | — | — |
| Macau | — | August 1976 | overseas terr. (Port.) | Port. president | governor | 17 | — | 3 | 5 | 6 | 12 |
| Madagascar | June 26, 1960 | Dec. 30, 1975 | republic | president | prime minister | 137 | — | 6 | 18 | 50 | 150 |
| Malawi | July 6, 1964 | July 6, 1966 | republic | —————president————— | | 123 | — | 3 | 24 | — | — |
| Malaysia | Aug. 31, 1957 | Aug. 31, 1957 | fed. const. monarchy | paramount ruler | prime minister | 69 | 177 | 14 | 126 | 12 | 200 |
| Maldives | July 26, 1965 | Nov. 11, 1968 | republic | —————president————— | | 48 | — | 19 | 202 | 12, 28 | 28 |
| Mali | Sept. 22, 1960 | June 19, 1979 | republic | —————president————— | | 82 | — | 8 | 42 | — | — |
| Malta | Sept. 21, 1964 | Sept. 21, 1964 | republic | president | prime minister | 69 | — | — | — | 12 | 25 |
| Martinique | — | March 19, 1946 | overseas dept. (Fr.) | French president [17] | | 44 | 41 | 3 | 34 | 12 | 200 |
| Mauritania | Nov. 28, 1960 | *May 20, 1961* | republic | —————president CMSN————— | | x | — | 13 | 44 | 70 | 200 |
| Mauritius | March 12, 1968 | March 12, 1968 | constitutional monarchy | British monarch | prime minister | 70 | — | 10 | ... | 12 | 200 |
| Mayotte | — | Dec. 24, 1976 | terr. collectivity (Fr.) | French president [29] | | 17 | — | 17 | — | 12 | 200 |
| Mexico | Sept. 16, 1810 | Feb. 5, 1917 | federal republic | —————president————— | | 64 | 400 | 32 | 2,389 | 12 | 200 |
| Monaco | Feb. 2, 1861 | Dec. 17, 1962 | constitutional monarchy | prince | min. of state | 18 | — | 1 | 4 | 12 | 1 |
| Mongolia | March 13, 1921 | July 6, 1960 | people's republic | chairman PPGH | premier | 370 | — | 21 | 331 | — | — |
| Montserrat | — | Jan. 1, 1960 | colony (U.K.) | British monarch | governor | 11 | — | 3 | — | 3 | 200 |
| Morocco | March 2, 1956 | March 10, 1972 | constitutional monarchy | king | prime minister | 306 | — | 38 | 133 | 12 | 200 |
| Mozambique | June 25, 1975 | June 25, 1975 | people's republic | —————president————— | | 250 | — | 11 | 112 | 12 | 200 |
| Nauru | Jan. 31, 1968 | Jan. 31, 1968 | republic | —————president————— | | 18 | — | — | — | 12 | 200 |
| Nepal | Nov. 13, 1769 | Dec. 16, 1962 | constitutional monarchy | king | prime minister | 140 | — | 14 | 75 | — | — |
| Netherlands, The | March 30, 1814 | March 29, 1814 | constitutional monarchy | monarch | prime minister | 75 | 150 | 12 | 912 | 12 | 200 |
| Netherlands Antilles | — | Dec. 29, 1954 | integral part of Neth. | Dutch monarch | prime minister | 22 | — | 5 | — | 12 | 200 |
| New Caledonia | — | Aug. 23, 1985 | overseas territory (Fr.) | French president [18] | | 46 | — | 4 | ... | 12 | 200 |
| New Zealand | Sept. 26, 1907 | June 30, 1852[23] | constitutional monarchy | British monarch | prime minister | 97 | — | 239 | — | 12 | 200 |
| Nicaragua | April 30, 1838 | *Jan. 9, 1987* | republic | —————president————— | | (96) | — | 17 | 136 | 200 | 1 |
| Niger | Aug. 3, 1960 | *Nov. 8, 1960*[31] | republic | —————president SMC————— | | 150 | — | 7 | 32 | — | — |
| Nigeria | Oct. 1, 1960 | Oct. 1, 1979 | federal republic | —————president AFRC————— | | x | x | 20 | 271 | 30 | 200 |
| Niue | — | Oct. 19, 1974 | territory (N.Z.)[14] | British monarch | premier | 20 | — | 14 | — | 12 | 200 |
| Norfolk Island | — | May 30, 1979 | external territory (Aust.) | Australian GG | administrator | 9 | — | — | — | 3 | 200 |

| membership in international organizations | | | | | | | | | | | | | | | | | | | | | | | | | | | | | | | | | | | | | country |
|---|---|---|---|---|---|---|---|---|---|---|---|---|---|---|---|---|---|---|---|---|---|---|---|---|---|---|---|---|---|---|---|---|---|---|---|---|---|
| United Nations (date of admission) | UN organs★ and affiliated intergovernmental organizations | | | | | | | | | | | | | | | | | | | | Common-wealth of Nations | regional multi-purpose | | | | | | economic | | | | | | | military | | |
| | UNCTAD★[a] | UNICEF★[f] | ICJ★ | FAO | GATT | IAEA[g] | IBRD | ICAC | IDA | IFC | ILO | IMF | IMO | ITU[e] | UNESCO | UNIDO | UPU[e] | WHO | WIPO[g] | WMO | | ASEAN | EC | LAS[g] | OAS | OAU | SPC | ACP | COMECON | ECOWAS | EEC | I-ADB | IDB[g] | OPEC | NATO | WTO | |
| 1945 | • | • | • | • | | • | • | • | • | • | • | • | • | • | • | • | • | • | • | • | | | | | • | | | | | | | • | | | | | El Salvador |
| 1968 | • | • | • | • | •2 | | • | • | • | • | • | • | • | • | • | • | • | • | • | • | | | | | | • | | • | | | | | | | | | Equatorial Guinea |
| 1945 | • | • | • | • | | • | • | • | • | • | • | • | • | • | • | • | • | • | • | • | | | | | | • | | • | | | | | | | | | Ethiopia |
| — | | | | | | | | | | | | | | | | | • | | | | • | | | | | | | | | | | | | | | | Faeroe Islands |
| — | | | | | | | | | | | | | | | | | • | | | | | | | | | | | | | | | | | | | | Falkland Islands |
| 1970 | • | • | • | • | •2 | | • | • | • | • | • | • | • | • | • | • | • | • | • | • | | | | | | | • | • | | | | | | | | | Fiji |
| 1955 | • | • | • | • | • | • | • | • | • | • | • | • | • | • | • | • | • | • | • | • | | | • | | | | | | | | • | • | | | | | Finland |
| 1945 | • | • | • | • | • | • | • | • | • | • | • | • | • | • | • | • | • | • | • | • | | | • | | | | | | | | • | | | | • | | France |
| — | | | | | | | | | | | | | | | | | • | | | | | | | | | | • | | | | | | | | | | French Guiana |
| — | | | | | | | | | | | | | | | | | • | | | • | | | | | | | • | | | | | | | | | | French Polynesia |
| 1960 | • | • | • | • | | | • | • | • | • | • | • | • | • | • | • | • | • | • | • | | | | | | • | | • | | | | • | • | | | | Gabon |
| 1965 | • | • | • | • | | | • | • | • | • | • | • | • | • | • | • | • | • | • | • | • | | | | | • | | • | | | | • | | | | | Gambia, The |
| — | | | | | | | | | | | | | | | | | • | | | | | | | | | | | • | | | | | | | | | Gaza Strip |
| 1973 | • | • | • | • | | • | • | • | • | • | • | • | • | • | • | • | • | • | • | • | | | | | | • | | | • | | • | | | | • | | Germany, East |
| 1973 | • | • | • | • | • | • | • | • | • | • | • | • | • | • | • | • | • | • | • | • | | | • | | | • | | | | | • | | | | • | | Germany, West |
| 1957 | • | • | • | • | • | | • | • | • | • | • | • | • | • | • | • | • | • | • | • | • | | | | | • | | • | | • | | | | | | | Ghana |
| — | | | | | | | | | | | | | | | | | • | | | | | | | | | | | | | | | | | | | | Gibraltar |
| 1945 | • | • | • | • | • | • | • | • | • | • | • | • | • | • | • | • | • | • | • | • | | | • | | | | | | | | • | | | | •19 | | Greece |
| — | | | | | | | | | | | | | | | | | • | | | | | | | | | | | | | | | | | | | | Greenland |
| 1974 | • | • | • | • | •2 | | • | • | • | • | • | • | • | • | • | • | • | • | • | • | • | | | | • | | | • | | | | • | | | | | Grenada |
| — | | | | | | | | | | | | | | | | | • | | | | | | | | | | • | | | | | | | | | | Guadeloupe |
| — | | | | | | | | | | | | | | | | | • | | | | | | | | • | | • | | | | | • | | | | | Guam |
| 1945 | • | • | • | • | | • | • | • | • | • | • | • | • | • | • | • | • | • | • | • | | | | | • | | | | | | | • | | | | | Guatemala |
| — | | | | | | | | | | | | | | | | | • | | | | | | | | | | | | | | | • | | | | | Guernsey |
| 1958 | • | • | • | • | | | • | • | • | • | • | • | • | • | • | • | • | • | • | • | | | | | | • | | • | | • | | | | | | | Guinea |
| 1974 | • | • | • | • | •2 | | • | • | • | • | • | • | • | • | • | • | • | • | • | • | | | | | | • | | • | | • | | • | | | | | Guinea-Bissau |
| 1966 | • | • | • | • | • | | • | • | • | • | • | • | • | • | • | • | • | • | • | • | • | | | | | | | • | | | | • | | | | | Guyana |
| 1945 | • | • | • | • | | • | • | • | • | • | • | • | • | • | • | • | • | • | • | • | | | | | • | | | | | | | • | | | | | Haiti |
| 1945 | • | • | • | • | • | | • | • | • | • | • | • | • | • | • | • | • | • | • | • | | | | | • | | | | | | | • | | | | | Honduras |
| — | | • | | | • | | | | | | | | | | •11 | | | | | • | | | | | | | | | | | | | | | | | Hong Kong |
| 1955 | • | • | • | • | • | • | • | • | • | • | • | • | • | • | • | • | • | • | • | • | | | | | | | | | • | | | | | | | • | Hungary |
| 1946 | • | • | • | • | • | • | • | • | • | • | • | • | • | • | • | • | • | • | • | • | | | | | | | | | | | • | | | | • | | Iceland |
| 1945 | • | • | • | • | • | • | • | • | • | • | • | • | • | • | • | • | • | • | • | • | • | | | | | | | | | | | • | • | | | | India |
| 1950 | • | • | • | • | | • | • | • | • | • | • | • | • | • | • | • | • | • | • | • | | • | | | | | | | | | | | • | • | | | Indonesia |
| 1945 | • | • | • | • | | • | • | • | • | • | • | • | • | • | • | • | • | • | • | • | | | | | | | | | | | | | • | • | | | Iran |
| 1945 | • | • | • | • | | • | • | • | • | • | • | • | • | • | • | • | • | • | • | • | | | | • | | | | | | | | | • | • | | | Iraq |
| 1955 | • | • | • | • | • | • | • | • | • | • | • | • | • | • | • | • | • | • | • | • | • | | • | | | | | | | | • | | | | | | Ireland |
| — | | | | | | | | | | | | | | | | | • | | | | | | | | | | | | | | | | | | | | Isle of Man |
| 1949 | • | • | • | • | • | • | • | • | • | • | • | • | • | • | • | • | • | • | • | • | | | | | | | | | | | • | | • | | • | | Israel |
| 1955 | • | • | • | • | • | • | • | • | • | • | • | • | • | • | • | • | • | • | • | • | | | • | | | | | | | | • | | | | • | | Italy |
| 1962 | • | • | • | • | • | | • | • | • | • | • | • | • | • | • | • | • | • | • | • | • | | | | • | | | • | | | | • | | | | | Jamaica |
| 1956 | • | • | • | • | • | • | • | • | • | • | • | • | • | • | • | • | • | • | • | • | | | | | | | | | | | | | • | | | | Japan |
| — | | | | | | | | | | | | | | | | | • | | | | | | | | | | | | | | | | | | | | Jersey |
| 1955 | • | • | • | • | | | • | • | • | • | • | • | • | • | • | • | • | • | • | • | | | | • | | | | | | | | | • | | | | Jordan |
| 1955 | • | • | • | • | •2 | | • | • | • | • | • | • | • | • | • | • | • | • | • | • | | | | | | | | | | | | | | | | | Kampuchea |
| 1963 | • | • | • | • | | | • | • | • | • | • | • | • | • | • | • | • | • | • | • | • | | | | | • | | • | | | | | | | | | Kenya |
| — | | • | | • | •2 | | | • | | | • | | • | • | • | | • | • | | • | • | | | | | | • | • | | | | | | | | | Kiribati |
| — | | • | | • | | | | • | | | • | | • | • | • | | • | • | | • | | | | | | | | | | | | | | | | | Korea, North |
| — | • | • | | • | | • | • | • | • | • | • | • | • | • | • | • | • | • | • | • | | | | | | | | | | | | | • | • | | | Korea, South |
| 1963 | • | • | • | • | | | • | • | • | • | • | • | • | • | • | • | • | • | • | • | | | | • | | | | | | | | | | • | | | Kuwait |
| 1955 | • | • | • | • | | | • | • | • | • | • | • | • | • | • | • | • | • | • | • | | | | | | | | | | | | | • | | | | Laos |
| 1945 | • | • | • | • | | | • | • | • | • | • | • | • | • | • | • | • | • | • | • | | | | • | | | | | | | | | • | | | | Lebanon |
| 1966 | • | • | • | • | •2 | | • | • | • | • | • | • | • | • | • | • | • | • | • | • | • | | | | | • | | • | | | | • | | | | | Lesotho |
| 1945 | • | • | • | • | | | • | • | • | • | • | • | • | • | • | • | • | • | • | • | | | | | | • | | | | | | • | | | | | Liberia |
| 1955 | • | • | • | • | | | • | • | • | • | • | • | • | • | • | • | • | • | • | • | | | | • | | • | | | | | | • | • | | | Libya |
| — | • | | • | | | | | | | | | | | | | | • | | | • | | | | | | | | | | | | | | | | | Liechtenstein |
| 1945 | • | • | • | • | • | • | • | • | • | • | • | • | • | • | • | • | • | • | • | • | | | • | | | | | | | | • | | | | • | | Luxembourg |
| — | | | | | | | | | | | | | | | | | • | | | | | | | | | | | | | | | | | | | | Macau |
| 1960 | • | • | • | • | | | • | • | • | • | • | • | • | • | • | • | • | • | • | • | | | | | | • | | • | | | | | • | | | | Madagascar |
| 1964 | • | • | • | • | | | • | • | • | • | • | • | • | • | • | • | • | • | • | • | • | | | | | • | | • | | | | | • | | | | Malawi |
| 1957 | • | • | • | • | • | | • | • | • | • | • | • | • | • | • | • | • | • | • | • | • | • | | | | | | | | | | | • | | | | Malaysia |
| 1965 | • | • | • | • | | | • | • | • | • | • | • | • | • | • | • | • | • | • | • | • | | | | | | | | | | | | • | | | | Maldives |
| 1960 | • | • | • | • | •2 | | • | • | • | • | • | • | • | • | • | • | • | • | • | • | | | | | | • | | • | | | | • | | | | Mali |
| 1964 | • | • | • | • | | | • | • | • | • | • | • | • | • | • | • | • | • | • | • | • | | | | | | | | | | | •11 | | | | | Malta |
| — | | | | | | | | | | | | | | | | | • | | | | | | | | | | | • | | | | | | | | | Martinique |
| 1961 | • | • | • | • | • | | • | • | • | • | • | • | • | • | • | • | • | • | • | • | | | | | • | • | | • | | • | | • | | | | | Mauritania |
| 1968 | • | • | • | • | • | | • | • | • | • | • | • | • | • | • | • | • | • | • | • | • | | | | | • | | • | | | | • | | | | | Mauritius |
| — | | | | | | | | | | | | | | | | | • | | | | | | | | | | | | | | | | | | | | Mayotte |
| 1945 | • | • | • | • | | | • | • | • | • | • | • | • | • | • | • | • | • | • | • | | | | | • | | | | | | | • | | | | | Mexico |
| — | • | | • | | | | | | | | | | | | | | • | | | • | | | | | | | | | | | | | | | | | Monaco |
| 1961 | • | • | • | • | | | | | • | | • | | | • | • | • | • | • | • | • | | | | | | | | | • | | | | | | | | Mongolia |
| — | | | | | | | | | | | | | | | | | • | | | | • | | | | | | | | | | | | | | | | Montserrat |
| 1956 | • | • | • | • | •2 | | • | • | • | • | • | • | • | • | • | • | • | • | • | • | | | | • | | • | | • | | | | • | | | | | Morocco |
| 1975 | • | • | • | • | | | | | | | • | | • | • | • | • | • | • | • | • | | | | | | • | | • | | | | • | | | | | Mozambique |
| — | | | | | | | | | | | | | | | | | • | | | | •30 | | | | | | • | | | | | | • | | | | Nauru |
| 1955 | • | • | • | • | | | • | • | • | • | • | • | • | • | • | • | • | • | • | • | | | | | | | | | | | | • | • | | | | Nepal |
| 1945 | • | • | • | • | • | • | • | • | • | • | • | • | • | • | • | • | • | • | • | • | | | • | | | | | | | | • | • | | | • | | Netherlands, The |
| — | | | | | | | | | | | | | | | •11 | | | • | | • | | | | | | | | • | | | | | | | | | Netherlands Antilles |
| — | | | | | | | | | | | | | | | | | • | | | • | | | | | | | • | | | | | | | | | | New Caledonia |
| 1945 | • | • | • | • | • | | • | • | • | • | • | • | • | • | • | • | • | • | • | • | • | | | | | | • | | | | | | | | | | New Zealand |
| 1945 | • | • | • | • | | | • | • | • | • | • | • | • | • | • | • | • | • | • | • | | | | | • | | | | | | | • | | | | | Nicaragua |
| 1960 | • | • | • | • | | | • | • | • | • | • | • | • | • | • | • | • | • | • | • | | | | | | • | | • | | • | | • | | | | | Niger |
| 1960 | • | • | • | • | | | • | • | • | • | • | • | • | • | • | • | • | • | • | • | • | | | | | • | | • | | • | | | | • | | | Nigeria |
| — | | | | | | | | | | | | | | | | | • | | | | • | | | | | | | | | | | | | | | | Niue |
| — | | | | | | | | | | | | | | | | | • | | | | • | | | | | | • | | | | | | | | | | Norfolk Island |

## Government and international organizations (continued)

| country | date of independence[a] | date of current or last constitution[b] | type of government | executive branch[c] chief of state | head of government | legislative branch[d] upper house (members) | lower house (members) | admin. subdivisions first-order (number) | second-order (number) | seaward claims territorial (nautical miles) | fishing/economic (nautical miles) |
|---|---|---|---|---|---|---|---|---|---|---|---|
| Norway | June 7, 1905 | May 17, 1814 | constitutional monarchy | king | prime minister | 157 | — | 19 | 454 | 4 | 200 |
| Oman | Dec. 20, 1951 | — | monarchy (sultanate) | —————sultan————— | | 55 | — | 11 | 41 | 12 | 200 |
| Pacific Is., Trust Terr. of | | | | | | | | | | | |
| Marshall Islands | Oct. 21, 1986 | May 1, 1979 | republic | —————president | | 12[9] | 33 | 26 | — | 3 | 200 |
| Micronesia, F.S. of | Nov. 3, 1986 | May 10, 1979 | federal republic | —————president————— | | 14 | — | 4 | ... | 3 | 200 |
| Northern Mariana Is. | Nov. 3, 1986 | Jan. 9, 1978 | commonwealth (U.S.) | U.S. president | governor | 9 | 14 | 4 | — | 3 | 200 |
| Palau | — | Jan. 1, 1981 | republic | —————president————— | | 16 | 18 | 16 | — | 3 | 200 |
| Pakistan | Aug. 14, 1947 | Aug. 14, 1973 | federal Islamic republic | —————president————— | | 87 | 237 | 6 | 16 | 12 | 200 |
| Panama | Nov. 3, 1903 | Oct. 11, 1972 | republic | —————president————— | | 67 | — | 10 | 65 | 200 | 1 |
| Papua New Guinea | Sept. 16, 1975 | Sept. 16, 1975 | constitutional monarchy | British monarch | prime minister | 109 | — | 20 | 86 | 12[12] | 200 |
| Paraguay | May 14, 1811 | Aug. 25, 1967 | republic | —————president————— | | 30 | 60 | 20 | 190 | 200 | 1 |
| Peru | July 28, 1821 | July 28, 1980 | republic | —————president————— | | 60 | 180 | 25 | 152 | 200 | 1 |
| Philippines | July 4, 1946 | Feb. 11, 1987 | republic | —————president————— | | 24 | 200 | 73 | 1,500 | 28 | 200 |
| Pitcairn Island | — | Nov. 30, 1838 | colony (U.K.) | British monarch | isl. magistrate | 10 | — | — | — | 3 | 200 |
| Poland | Nov. 10, 1918 | July 22, 1952 | socialist republic | chairman CS | chairman CM | 460 | — | 49 | 261 | 12 | 200 |
| Portugal | c. 1140 | April 25, 1976 | republic | president | prime minister | 250 | — | 20 | 305 | 12 | 200 |
| Puerto Rico | July 25, 1952 | July 25, 1952 | commonwealth (U.S.) | U.S. president | governor | 27 | 51 | 78 | ... | 3 | 200 |
| Qatar | Sept. 3, 1971 | July 1970[32] | constitutional monarchy | —————emir————— | | — | — | — | — | 3 | 33 |
| Réunion | — | March 19, 1946 | overseas dept. (Fr.) | French president | 17 | 36 | 45 | 4 | 24 | 12 | 200 |
| Romania | May 21, 1877 | Aug. 21, 1965 | socialist republic | president | prime minister | 369 | — | 41 | 237 | 12 | 200 |
| Rwanda | July 1, 1962 | Dec. 20, 1978 | republic | —————president————— | | 70 | — | 10 | 143 | — | — |
| St. Christopher and Nevis | Sept. 19, 1983 | Sept. 19, 1983 | constitutional monarchy | British monarch | prime minister | 15 | — | 14 | — | 12 | 200 |
| St. Helena and Ascension | — | Jan. 1, 1967 | colony (U.K.) | British monarch | governor | 15[34] | — | 3 | — | 3 | 200 |
| St. Lucia | Feb. 22, 1979 | Feb. 22, 1979 | constitutional monarchy | British monarch | prime minister | 11 | 17 | 10 | — | 3 | 12 |
| St. Pierre and Miquelon | — | June 1985 | terr. collectivity (Fr.) | French president | 29 | 14 | — | 2 | — | 12 | 200 |
| St. Vincent | Oct. 27, 1979 | Oct. 27, 1979 | constitutional monarchy | British monarch | prime minister | 19 | — | — | — | 3 | 12 |
| San Marino | 855 | Oct. 8, 1600 | republic | —————captains-regent (2)————— | | 60 | — | 9 | — | — | — |
| São Tomé and Príncipe | July 12, 1975 | Dec. 15, 1982 | republic | —————president————— | | 40 | — | 2 | 7 | 12[6] | 200 |
| Saudi Arabia | Sept. 23, 1932 | — | monarchy | —————king————— | | — | — | 14 | — | 12 | — |
| Senegal | Aug. 20, 1960 | March 7, 1963 | republic | —————president————— | | 120 | — | 10 | 30 | 12 | 200 |
| Seychelles | June 29, 1976 | June 5, 1979 | republic | —————president————— | | 25 | — | — | — | 12 | 200 |
| Sierra Leone | April 27, 1961 | June 14, 1978 | republic | —————president————— | | 127 | — | 4 | 12 | 200 | 1 |
| Singapore | Aug. 9, 1965 | June 3, 1959 | republic | president | prime minister | 79 | — | — | — | 3 | 12 |
| Solomon Islands | July 7, 1978 | July 7, 1978 | constitutional monarchy | British monarch | prime minister | 38 | — | 8 | 174 | 12[12] | 200 |
| Somalia | July 1, 1960 | Aug. 25, 1979 | republic | —————president————— | | 177 | — | 16 | 60 | 200 | 1 |
| South Africa | May 31, 1910 | Sept. 3, 1984 | republic | state president | prime minister[35] | 308 | — | 10 | 358 | 12 | 200 |
| Bophuthatswana | Dec. 6, 1977[36] | Dec. 6, 1977 | republic | —————president————— | | 108 | — | 12 | 76 | — | — |
| Ciskei | Dec. 4, 1981[36] | Dec. 4, 1981 | republic | —————president————— | | 69 | — | 7 | 42 | — | — |
| KwaNdebele | — | — | self-governing homeland | state president | chief minister | 72 | — | ... | ... | — | — |
| Transkei | Oct. 26, 1976[36] | Dec. 1963 | republic | president | prime minister | 150 | — | 28 | 123 | — | — |
| Venda | Sept. 13, 1979[36] | Sept. 13, 1979 | republic | —————president————— | | 92 | — | 4 | — | — | — |
| South West Africa/Namibia | — | — | dependency of S.Af. | state president | 37 | 62 | — | 26 | — | 6 | 12 |
| Spain | 1492 | Dec. 29, 1978 | constitutional monarchy | king | prime minister | 257 | 350 | 17 | 50 | 12 | 200 |
| Sri Lanka | Feb. 4, 1948 | Sept. 7, 1978 | republic | —————president————— | | 168 | — | 24 | 682 | 12 | 200 |
| Sudan, The | Jan. 1, 1956 | May 8, 1973 | republic | president SUC | prime minister | (301) | — | 8 | 19 | 12 | 1 |
| Suriname | Nov. 25, 1975 | Nov. 25, 1987 | republic | —————chairman SUC————— | | 51 | — | 9 | — | 12 | 200 |
| Swaziland | Sept. 6, 1968 | Sept. 6, 1968 | monarchy | king | prime minister | 20 | 50 | 4 | 40 | — | — |
| Sweden | before 836 | Jan. 1, 1975 | constitutional monarchy | king | prime minister | 349 | — | 24 | 279 | 12 | 200 |
| Switzerland | Sept. 22, 1499 | May 29, 1874 | federal state | —————president————— | | 46 | 200 | 26 | 177 | — | — |
| Syria | April 17, 1946 | March 12, 1973 | republic | president | prime minister | 195 | — | 14 | 41 | 35 | 1 |
| Taiwan | Oct. 25, 1945 | Oct. 25, 1947 | republic | president | premier | 946 | — | 23 | — | 12 | 200 |
| Tanzania | Dec. 9, 1961 | April 25, 1977 | republic | president | prime minister | 244 | — | 25 | 105 | 50 | 1 |
| Thailand | 1350 | Dec. 22, 1978 | constitutional monarchy | king | prime minister | 261 | 347 | 72 | 576 | 12 | 200 |
| Togo | April 27, 1960 | Jan. 13, 1980 | republic | —————president————— | | 77 | — | 5 | 21 | 30 | 200 |
| Tokelau | — | 1948 | territory (N.Z.) | New Zealand GG | administrator | — | — | 3 | — | 12 | 200 |
| Tonga | June 4, 1970 | 1875 | constitutional monarchy | —————monarch————— | | 28 | — | 5 | 23 | 12 | 200 |
| Trinidad and Tobago | Aug. 31, 1962 | Aug. 1, 1976 | republic | president | prime minister | 31 | 36 | 11 | 30 | 12 | 200 |
| Tunisia | March 20, 1956 | June 1, 1959 | republic | —————president————— | | 138 | — | 23 | 243 | 12 | 1 |
| Turkey | Oct. 29, 1923 | Nov. 7, 1982 | republic | president | prime minister | 400 | — | 67 | 580 | 12[38] | 200[38] |
| Turks and Caicos Islands | — | Aug. 30, 1976 | colony (U.K.) | British monarch | governor | (19) | — | 3 | — | 3 | 200 |
| Tuvalu | Oct. 1, 1978 | Oct. 1, 1978 | constitutional monarchy | British monarch | prime minister | 13 | — | 9 | — | 12 | 200 |
| Uganda | Oct. 9, 1962 | Sept. 8, 1967 | republic | president | prime minister | (156) | — | 10 | 34 | — | — |
| U.S.S.R. | c. 900 | Oct. 7, 1977 | fed. socialist republic | chairman PSSU | chairman CM | 750 | 750 | 15 | 167 | 12 | 200 |
| United Arab Emirates | Dec. 2, 1971 | Dec. 2, 1971[32] | federation of emirates | —————president————— | | 40 | — | 7 | — | 3[40] | 200 |
| United Kingdom | Oct. 14, 1066 | 35 | constitutional monarchy | monarch | prime minister | 1,180 | 650 | 4 | ... | 3 | 200 |
| United States | July 4, 1776 | March 4, 1789 | federal republic | —————president————— | | 100 | 435 | 51 | 3,137 | 3 | 200 |
| Uruguay | Aug. 25, 1828 | Feb. 15, 1967 | republic | —————president————— | | 31 | 99 | 19 | ... | 200 | 1 |
| Vanuatu | July 30, 1980 | July 30, 1980 | republic | president | prime minister | 39 | — | 4 | 11 | 12[12] | 200 |
| Venezuela | July 5, 1811 | Jan. 23, 1961 | federal republic | —————president————— | | 47 | 200 | 23 | 156 | 12 | 200 |
| Vietnam | Sept. 2, 1954 | Dec. 18, 1980 | socialist republic | chairman CS | chairman CM | 496 | — | 40 | 391 | 12 | 200 |
| Virgin Islands (U.S.) | — | — | territory (U.S.) | U.S. president | governor | 15 | — | 2 | — | 3 | 200 |
| Wallis and Futuna | — | July 29, 1961 | overseas territory (Fr.) | French president | 41 | 20 | — | 3 | — | 12 | 200 |
| West Bank | — | — | Israeli military | —— area commander | | — | — | 7 | — | — | — |
| Western Sahara | — | — | annexture of Morocco | | 43 | — | — | 4 | — | 12 | 200 |
| Western Samoa | Jan. 1, 1962 | Oct. 28, 1960 | | head of state | prime minister | 47 | — | 21 | — | 12 | 200 |
| Yemen (Aden) | Nov. 30, 1967 | Dec. 27, 1978 | people's republic | chairman PSPC | prime minister | 111 | — | 6 | 27 | 12 | 200 |
| Yemen (Şan'ā') | December 1918 | June 19, 1974[32] | republic | president | prime minister | 159 | 1,000 | 11 | 41 | 12 | 1 |
| Yugoslavia | Dec. 1, 1918 | Feb. 21, 1974 | federal socialist republic | president CP | president FEC | 88 | 220 | 8 | 527 | 12 | 1 |
| Zaire | June 30, 1960 | Feb. 15, 1978 | republic | —————president————— | | 210 | — | 9 | 41 | 12 | 200 |
| Zambia | Oct. 24, 1964 | Aug. 25, 1973 | republic | —————president————— | | 136 | — | 9 | 53 | — | — |
| Zimbabwe | April 18, 1980 | April 18, 1980 | republic | president | prime minister | 40 | 100 | 8 | — | | |

[1]Territorial sea claim assumed to claim fishing/economic rights within the same zone. [2]Full membership pending. [3]President of France and Bishop of Urgel, Spain. [4]Executive responsibilities divided between (for the U.K.) the governor and (locally) the chief officer of the Executive Council. [5]Formally a constitutional monarchy. [6]Defined by equidistant line. [7]Executive responsibilities divided between (for the U.K.) the governor and (locally) the premier of the Cabinet. [8]Resembles a constitutional monarchy without a formal constitution. [9]Body with limited legislative authority. [10]Exclusive fishing zone within 100 nautical miles (nm). [11]Associate member. [12]Measured from claimed archipelagic baselines. [13]Not fully effective until 1989. [14]Self-governing state in free association with New Zealand. [15]Includes Turkish Federated State of Cyprus. [16]Executive responsibilities divided between (for Denmark) the State Commissioner and (locally) the Head of the Home Government. [17]Executive responsibilities divided among (for France) the Commissioner and (locally) the President of the General Council and the President of the Regional Council. [18]Executive responsibilities divided between (for France) the High Commissioner and (locally) the President of the Territorial Assembly (called Territorial Congress in New Caledonia). [19]Suspended from full participation. [20]Executive responsibilities divided between (for Denmark) the High Commissioner and (locally) the Prime Minister. [21]In part 12 nm or specific coordinates. [22]Sea of Oman only; median line boundaries in the Persian Gulf.

| United Nations (date of admission) | UNCTAD | UNICEF | ICJ | FAO | GATT | IAEA | IBRD | ICAC | IDA | IFC | ILO | IMF | IMO | ITU | UNESCO | UNIDO | UPU | WHO | WIPO | WMO | Commonwealth of Nations | ASEAN | EC | LAS | OAS | OAU | SPC | ACP | COMECON | ECOWAS | EEC | I-ADB | IDB | OPEC | NATO | WTO | country |
|---|---|---|---|---|---|---|---|---|---|---|---|---|---|---|---|---|---|---|---|---|---|---|---|---|---|---|---|---|---|---|---|---|---|---|---|---|---|
| 1945 | • | • | • | • | • | • | • | • | • | • | • | • | • | • | • | • | • | • | • | • | | | | | | | | | | | | • | | | • | | Norway |
| 1971 | • | • | • | • | | • | • | | • | | • | • | • | • | • | • | • | • | | • | | | | • | | | | | | | | | • | | | | Oman |
| — | | • | | | | | | | | | | | | | | | | | | | | | | | | | • | | | | | | | | | | Pacific Is., Trust Terr. of Marshall Islands |
| — | | • | | | | | | | | | | | | | | | | | | | | | | | | | • | | | | | | | | | | Micronesia, F.S. of |
| — | | • | | | | | | | | | | | | | | | | | | | | | | | | | • | | | | | | | | | | Northern Mariana Is. |
| — | | • | | | | | | | | | | | | | | | | | | | | | | | | | • | | | | | | | | | | Palau |
| 1947 | • | • | • | • | • | • | • | • | • | • | • | • | • | • | • | • | • | • | • | • | | | | | | | | | | | | | • | | | | Pakistan |
| 1945 | • | • | • | • | • | • | • | • | • | • | • | • | • | • | • | • | • | • | • | • | | | | | • | | | | | | | • | | | | | Panama |
| 1975 | • | • | • | • | •[2] | • | • | | • | • | • | • | • | • | • | • | • | • | • | • | • | | | | | | • | • | | | | | | | | | Papua New Guinea |
| 1945 | • | • | • | • | • | • | • | • | • | • | • | • | • | • | • | • | • | • | • | • | | | | | • | | | | | | | • | | | | | Paraguay |
| 1945 | • | • | • | • | • | • | • | • | • | • | • | • | • | • | • | • | • | • | • | • | | | | | • | | | | | | | • | | | | | Peru |
| 1945 | • | • | • | • | • | • | • | • | • | • | • | • | • | • | • | • | • | • | • | • | | • | | | | | | | | | | | | | | | Philippines |
| — | | | | | | | | | | | | | | | | | | | | | | | | | | | • | | | | | | | | | | Pitcairn Island |
| 1945 | • | • | • | • | | • | • | • | | | • | | • | • | • | • | • | • | • | • | | | | | | | | | • | | | | | | | • | Poland |
| 1955 | • | • | • | • | • | • | • | • | • | • | • | • | • | • | • | • | • | • | • | • | | | • | | | | | | | | • | • | | | • | | Portugal |
| — | | | | | | | | | | | | | | | | | | | | | | | | | | | | | | | | | | | | | Puerto Rico |
| 1971 | • | • | • | • | •[2] | • | • | | • | | • | • | • | • | • | • | • | • | | • | | | | • | | | | | | | | | • | • | | | Qatar |
| — | | | | | | | | | | | | | | | | | | | | | | | | | | | | | | | | | | | | | Réunion |
| 1955 | • | • | • | • | | • | • | • | | | • | | • | • | • | • | • | • | • | • | | | | | | | | | • | | | • | | | | • | Romania |
| 1962 | • | • | • | • | | • | • | | • | • | • | • | • | • | • | • | • | • | | • | | | | | | • | | • | | | | | | | | | Rwanda |
| 1983 | • | • | • | • | •[2] | | • | | • | | • | • | • | • | • | | • | • | | • | • | | | | • | | | • | | | | | | | | | St. Christopher and Nevis |
| — | | • | | | | | | | | | | | | | | | | | | | • | | | | | | | • | | | | | | | | | St. Helena and Ascension |
| 1979 | • | • | • | • | •[2] | | • | | • | • | • | • | • | • | • | | • | • | | • | • | | | | • | | | • | | | | | | | | | St. Lucia |
| — | | | | | | | | | | | | | | | | | | | | | | | | | | | • | | | | | | | | | | St. Pierre and Miquelon |
| 1980 | • | • | • | • | •[2] | | • | | • | • | • | • | • | • | • | | • | • | | • | • | | | | • | | | • | | | | | | | | | St. Vincent |
| — | | • | • | | | | | | | | | | | • | • | | • | • | • | | | | | | | | | | | | | | | | | | San Marino |
| 1975 | • | • | • | • | | • | • | | • | | • | • | • | • | • | • | • | • | • | • | | | | | | • | | • | | | | | | | | | São Tomé and Príncipe |
| 1945 | • | • | • | • | | • | • | • | • | • | • | • | • | • | • | • | • | • | • | • | | | | • | | | | | | | | | • | • | | | Saudi Arabia |
| 1960 | • | • | • | • | • | • | • | • | • | • | • | • | • | • | • | • | • | • | • | • | | | | | | • | | • | | • | | | • | | | | Senegal |
| 1976 | • | • | • | • | •[2] | | • | | • | • | • | • | • | • | • | • | • | • | | • | • | | | | | • | | • | | | | | | | | | Seychelles |
| 1961 | • | • | • | • | • | • | • | • | • | • | • | • | • | • | • | • | • | • | • | • | • | | | | | • | | • | | • | | | | | | | Sierra Leone |
| 1965 | • | • | • | • | • | • | • | • | • | • | • | • | • | • | • | • | • | • | • | • | • | • | | | | | | | | | | | | | | | Singapore |
| 1978 | • | • | • | • | •[2] | | • | | • | • | • | • | • | • | • | • | • | • | | • | • | | | | | | • | • | | | | | | | | | Solomon Islands |
| 1960 | • | • | • | • | • | • | • | • | • | • | • | • | • | • | • | • | • | • | • | • | | | | • | | • | | • | | | | | • | | | | Somalia |
| 1945 | • | • | • | • | • | • | • | • | • | • | | • | • | • | | | | • | • | • | | | | | | | | | | | | | | | | | South Africa |
| — | | | | | | | | | | | | | | | | | | | | | | | | | | | | | | | | | | | | | Bophuthatswana |
| — | | | | | | | | | | | | | | | | | | | | | | | | | | | | | | | | | | | | | Ciskei |
| — | | | | | | | | | | | | | | | | | | | | | | | | | | | | | | | | | | | | | KwaNdebele |
| — | | | | | | | | | | | | | | | | | | | | | | | | | | | | | | | | | | | | | Transkei |
| — | | | | | | | | | | | | | | | | | | | | | | | | | | | | | | | | | | | | | Venda |
| — | | • | | | | | | | | | | • | | | • | | •[11] | • | • | • | | | | | | | | | | | | | | | | | South West Africa/Namibia |
| 1955 | • | • | • | • | • | • | • | • | • | • | • | • | • | • | • | • | • | • | • | • | | | | | • | | | | | | • | • | | | • | | Spain |
| 1955 | • | • | • | • | • | • | • | • | • | • | • | • | • | • | • | • | • | • | • | • | • | | | | | | | | | | | | | | | | Sri Lanka |
| 1956 | • | • | • | • | • | • | • | • | • | • | • | • | • | • | • | • | • | • | • | • | | | | • | | • | | • | | | | | • | | | | Sudan, The |
| 1975 | • | • | • | • | •[2] | | • | | • | • | • | • | • | • | • | • | • | • | • | • | | | | | • | | | • | | | | • | | | | | Suriname |
| 1968 | • | • | • | • | •[2] | | • | | • | • | • | • | • | • | • | • | • | • | | • | • | | | | | • | | • | | | | • | | | | | Swaziland |
| 1946 | • | • | • | • | • | • | • | • | • | • | • | • | • | • | • | • | • | • | • | • | | | | | | | | | | | | • | | | | | Sweden |
| — | | • | • | • | • | • | • | • | • | • | • | • | • | • | • | • | • | • | • | • | | | | | | | | | | | | • | | | | | Switzerland |
| 1945 | • | • | • | • | | • | • | • | • | • | • | • | • | • | • | • | • | • | • | • | | | | • | | | | | | | | | | | | | Syria |
| — | | | | | | | | • | | | | | | | | | | | | | | | | | | | | | | | | | | | | | Taiwan |
| 1961 | • | • | • | • | • | • | • | • | • | • | • | • | • | • | • | • | • | • | • | • | • | | | | | • | | • | | | | | | | | | Tanzania |
| 1946 | • | • | • | • | • | • | • | • | • | • | • | • | • | • | • | • | • | • | • | • | | • | | | | | | | | | | | | | | | Thailand |
| 1960 | • | • | • | • | • | • | • | • | • | • | • | • | • | • | • | • | • | • | • | • | | | | | | • | | • | | • | | | | | | | Togo |
| — | | | | | | | | | | | | | | | | | | | | | | | | | | | • | | | | | | | | | | Tokelau |
| 1962 | • | • | • | • | •[2] | | • | | • | • | • | • | • | • | • | | • | • | | • | • | | | | | | • | • | | | | | | | | | Tonga |
| 1962 | • | • | • | • | •[2] | | • | | • | • | • | • | • | • | • | • | • | • | | • | • | | | | • | | | • | | | | • | | | | | Trinidad and Tobago |
| 1956 | • | • | • | • | •[2] | • | • | • | • | • | • | • | • | • | • | • | • | • | • | • | | | | • | | • | | | | | | | • | | | | Tunisia |
| 1945 | • | • | • | • | • | • | • | • | • | • | • | • | • | • | • | • | • | • | • | • | | | | | | | | | | | •[11] | | • | | • | | Turkey |
| — | | | | | | | | | | | | | | | | | | | | | | | | | | | | | | | | | | | | | Turks and Caicos Islands |
| — | | • | • | | | | | •[2] | | | | • | | | • | | • | | | | •[30] | | | | | | • | • | | | | | | | | | Tuvalu |
| 1962 | • | • | • | • | •[2] | • | • | | • | • | • | • | • | • | • | • | • | • | • | • | • | | | | | • | | • | | | | | • | | | | Uganda |
| 1945[39] | •[39] | •[39] | •[39] | | •[39] | •[39] | | | | | •[39] | | | •[39] | •[39] | •[39] | •[39] | •[39] | •[39] | •[39] | | | | | | | | | • | | | | | | | • | U.S.S.R. |
| 1971 | • | • | • | • | | • | • | | • | • | • | • | • | • | • | • | • | • | | • | | | | • | | | | | | | | | • | • | | | United Arab Emirates |
| 1945 | • | • | • | • | • | • | • | • | • | • | • | • | • | • | • | • | • | • | • | • | • | | • | | | | | | | | • | • | | | • | | United Kingdom |
| 1945 | • | • | • | • | • | • | • | • | • | • | • | • | • | • | | • | • | • | • | • | | | | | • | | | | | | | • | | | • | | United States |
| 1945 | • | • | • | • | • | • | • | • | • | • | • | • | • | • | • | • | • | • | • | • | | | | | • | | | | | | | • | | | | | Uruguay |
| 1981 | • | • | • | • | | | • | | • | • | • | • | • | • | • | • | • | • | | • | • | | | | | | • | • | | | | | | | | | Vanuatu |
| 1945 | • | • | • | • | • | • | • | • | • | • | • | • | • | • | • | • | • | • | • | • | | | | | • | | | | | | | • | | • | | | Venezuela |
| 1977 | • | • | • | • | | • | • | | • | • | • | • | • | • | • | • | • | • | | • | | | | | | | | | • | | | | | | | | Vietnam |
| — | | | | | | | | | | | | | | | | | • | | | | | | | | | | | | | | | | | | | | Virgin Islands (U.S.) |
| — | | | | | | | | | | | | | | | | | • | | | | | | | | | | • | | | | | | | | | | Wallis and Futuna |
| — | | | | | | | | | | | | | | | | | | | | | | | | | | | | | | | | | | | | | West Bank |
| 1976 | • | • | • | | • | | | | | | | • | | | • | | • | • | | | | | | | | •[42] | | • | | | | | | | | | Western Sahara |
| — | • | • | • | • | | | • | | • | • | | • | | • | • | | • | • | | • | • | | | | | | • | • | | | | | | | | | Western Samoa |
| 1967 | • | • | • | • | •[2] | | • | | • | • | • | • | • | • | • | • | • | • | | • | | | | • | | • | | • | | | | | • | | | | Yemen (Aden) |
| 1947 | • | • | • | • | | | • | | • | • | • | • | • | • | • | • | • | • | | • | | | | • | | | | | | | | | • | | | | Yemen (Şan'ā') |
| 1945 | • | • | • | • | • | • | • | • | • | • | • | • | • | • | • | • | • | • | • | • | | | | | | | | | | | •[11] | • | | | | | Yugoslavia |
| 1960 | • | • | • | • | | • | • | • | • | • | • | • | • | • | • | • | • | • | | • | | | | | | • | | • | | | | | | | | | Zaire |
| 1964 | • | • | • | • | •[2] | • | • | • | • | • | • | • | • | • | • | • | • | • | • | • | • | | | | | • | | • | | | | | | | | | Zambia |
| 1980 | • | • | • | • | | • | • | • | • | • | • | • | • | • | • | • | • | • | • | • | • | | | | | • | | • | | | | | | | | | Zimbabwe |

[23]Evolving body of constitutional law.   [24]3 nm in 5 straits.   [25]3 nm in Korean Strait.   [26]Formally a *jamahiriya*, translatable as "the masses of people."   [27]Based on Gulf of Sidra closing line (32°30′ N), in part.   [28]Zone defined by geographical coordinates.   [29]Executive responsibilities divided between (for France) the Commissioner and (locally) the President of the General Council.   [30]Special member.   [31]National charter, antecedent to future constitution approved by referendum June 14, 1987.   [32]Provisional constitution.   [33]Limits of continental shelf or median line boundaries.   [34]Excludes local councils on Ascension and Tristan da Cunha.   [35]Based on evolving body of statutes and common law.   [36]Recognized by South Africa and each other only.   [37]Executive responsibilities divided between (for South Africa) the administrator-general and (locally) the Cabinet.   [38]Black Sea only; complex maritime dispute exists with Greece in Aegean Sea.   [39]Belorussian and Ukrainian S.S.R.s are also members.   [40]12 nm for Sharjah.   [41]Executive responsibilities divided between (for France) the Superior Administrator and (locally) the President of the Territorial Assembly.   [42]Membership held by the Sahrawi Arab Democratic Republic.   [43]Mixed political system approximating a constitutional monarchy.

# Area and population

This table provides the area and population for each of the countries of the world and for all political dependencies with a permanent civilian population. Only countries such as the Vatican City State, the British Indian Ocean Territory, and similar anomalous cases are omitted. The data represent the latest published and unpublished data for both the surveyed area of the countries and their populations, the latter both as of a single year (1987) to provide the best comparability and as of the most recent census to provide the fullest comparison of certain demographic measures that are not always available in estimated form between successive national censuses. The 1987 estimates represent a combination of national, United Nations (UN) or other international organization, and *Encyclopædia Britannica* estimates so as to give the best fit to available published series, to take account of unpublished information received in correspondence, and to incorporate the results of very recent censuses for which published analyses and projections based upon them are not yet available.

One principal point to bear in mind when studying these statistics is that all of them, whatever degree of precision may be implied by the exactness of the numbers, are estimates—all of varying, and some of suspect accuracy. Even a country like the United States—which has a long tradition both of census taking and of the use of the most sophisticated analytical tools in processing the data—is unable to determine within 2.5% its total population nationally. And that is an average underenumeration. In larger cities, where enumeration of certain populations, both legal and illegal, is most difficult, the accuracy of the enumerated count may be off considerably more than 5%. When a country like Nigeria, the most populous in Africa, does not know within 20% its real population and is delayed or prevented from measuring it by political circumstances, both the amount and the margin of error are likely to increase. The editors have tried to take account of the range of variation and accuracy in published data, but it is difficult to establish a value for many sources of inaccuracy unless some country or agency has made a conscientious effort to establish both the relative accuracy (precision) of its estimate and the absolute magnitude of the quantity it is trying to measure—for example, the number of people in Kampuchea (Cambodia) who died at the hands of the Khmer Rouge. Was it 1,000,000, 2,000,000, 3,000,000? If a figure of 1,000,000 is cited, what is its accuracy: ± 1%, 10%, 50%? Is the source of the figure Vietnam (potential bias on the high side to justify its invasion), China (potential bias on the low side because of its political connection with the Khmer Rouge), the United States (habitually unable to obtain or produce by analysis accurate data about Southeast Asia, complicated by political bias)?

Many similar problems exist and in endless variations: What is the extent of southern European immigration to western Europe in search of jobs? How many refugees from Uganda or Afghanistan are there in surrounding countries? How many illegal immigrants are there in the United States? How many Palestinians are there in the Middle East (they are politically inconvenient to enumerate everywhere)? How many Amerindians exist in the countries of South America (any accurate answer to that question raises the question, "Where did they go?")? How many people have died or emigrated as a result of the civil violence in Central America?

Still, much information is accurate, well founded, and updated regularly. The sources of these data are censuses; national population registers (cu-

## Area and population

| country | area square miles | area square kilometres | rank | population (latest estimate) total midyear 1987 | rank | density per sq mi | density per sq km | % annual growth rate 1982–87 | population (most recent census) census year | total | male (%) | female (%) | urban (%) |
|---|---|---|---|---|---|---|---|---|---|---|---|---|---|
| Afghanistan | 251,825 | 652,225 | 40 | 14,184,000 | 53 | 56.3 | 21.7 | −1.2 | 1979 | 13,051,358[1] | 51.4 | 48.6 | 15.1 |
| Albania | 11,100 | 28,748 | 126 | 3,087,000 | 109 | 278.1 | 107.4 | 2.1 | 1982 | 2,786,100 | 51.6 | 48.4 | 33.6 |
| Algeria | 919,595 | 2,381,741 | 10 | 23,116,000 | 36 | 25.1 | 9.7 | 3.1 | 1987[3] | 22,971,558 | 49.7[4] | 50.3[4] | 40.6[5] |
| American Samoa | 77 | 199 | 195 | 37,000 | 191 | 480.5 | 185.9 | 1.9 | 1980 | 32,297 | 50.7 | 49.3 | 17.5 |
| Andorra | 181 | 468 | 177 | 48,800 | 187 | 269.6 | 104.3 | 5.4 | 1986 | 45,877 | 53.1 | 46.9 | 64.7 |
| Angola | 481,350 | 1,246,700 | 21 | 9,105,000 | 67 | 18.9 | 7.3 | 3.0 | 1970 | 5,673,046 | 52.1 | 47.9 | 14.2 |
| Anguilla | 35 | 91 | 203 | 6,700 | 207 | 191.4 | 73.6 | 0.2 | 1984 | 6,987 | 49.1 | 50.9 | — |
| Antigua and Barbuda | 171 | 442 | 179 | 82,400 | 177 | 481.9 | 186.4 | 1.3 | 1970 | 65,525 | 47.2[3] | 52.8[3] | 30.8[4] |
| Argentina | 1,073,399 | 2,780,092 | 8 | 31,497,000 | 29 | 29.3 | 11.3 | 1.6 | 1980 | 27,947,446 | 49.2 | 50.8 | 86.3 |
| Aruba | 75 | 193 | 196 | 65,200 | 182 | 869.3 | 337.8 | 1.2 | 1981 | 60,312 | 48.6 | 51.4 | ... |
| Australia | 2,966,200 | 7,682,300 | 6 | 16,188,000 | 48 | 5.5 | 2.1 | 1.3 | 1981 | 14,576,330 | 49.9 | 50.1 | 89.0 |
| Austria | 32,376 | 83,855 | 109 | 7,554,000 | 77 | 233.3 | 90.1 | −0.1 | 1981 | 7,555,338 | 47.4 | 52.6 | 55.1 |
| Bahamas, The | 5,382 | 13,939 | 140 | 245,000 | 156 | 45.5 | 17.6 | 2.4 | 1980 | 209,505[6] | 48.8 | 51.2 | 54.4 |
| Bahrain | 267 | 691 | 169 | 481,000 | 142 | 1,801.5 | 696.1 | 5.2 | 1981 | 350,798 | 58.4 | 41.6 | 80.7 |
| Bangladesh | 55,598 | 143,998 | 90 | 105,307,000 | 9 | 1,894.1 | 731.3 | 2.5 | 1981 | 89,912,000 | 51.5 | 48.5 | 15.7 |
| Barbados | 166 | 430 | 180 | 254,000 | 155 | 1,530.1 | 590.7 | 0.3 | 1980 | 248,983 | 47.6 | 52.4 | 40.1[2] |
| Belgium | 11,783 | 30,518 | 124 | 9,861,000 | 66 | 836.9 | 323.1 | −0.0 | 1981 | 9,848,647 | 48.7 | 51.3 | 72.4[2] |
| Belize | 8,867 | 22,965 | 133 | 176,000 | 163 | 19.8 | 7.7 | 2.7 | 1980 | 145,353 | 50.6 | 49.4 | 52.0 |
| Benin | 43,450 | 112,600 | 96 | 4,307,000 | 97 | 99.1 | 38.3 | 3.1 | 1979 | 3,331,210 | 47.9 | 52.1 | 38.3 |
| Bermuda | 21 | 54 | 206 | 57,900 | 185 | 2,757.1 | 1,072.2 | 0.9 | 1980[7] | 54,050 | 48.9 | 51.1 | 100.0 |
| Bhutan | 18,150 | 47,000 | 118 | 1,338,000 | 126 | 73.7 | 28.5 | 2.0 | 1969 | 931,514 | 51.4[2] | 48.6[2] | 3.9 |
| Bolivia | 424,164 | 1,098,581 | 27 | 6,799,000 | 81 | 16.0 | 6.2 | 2.8 | 1976 | 4,613,486 | 49.1 | 50.9 | 41.7 |
| Botswana | 224,607 | 581,730 | 45 | 1,168,000 | 131 | 5.2 | 2.0 | 3.7 | 1981 | 941,027 | 47.1 | 52.9 | 15.9 |
| Brazil | 3,286,488 | 8,511,965 | 5 | 141,302,000 | 6 | 43.0 | 16.6 | 2.2 | 1980[3] | 119,002,706 | 49.7 | 50.3 | 67.6 |
| British Virgin Islands | 59 | 153 | 199 | 12,200 | 201 | 206.8 | 79.7 | 1.5 | 1980[9] | 10,985 | 51.1 | 49.9 | 12.0 |
| Brunei | 2,226 | 5,765 | 150 | 241,000 | 158 | 108.3 | 41.8 | 3.6 | 1981 | 192,832 | 53.4 | 46.6 | 59.4 |
| Bulgaria | 42,823 | 110,912 | 98 | 8,983,000 | 68 | 209.8 | 81.0 | 0.3 | 1985 | 8,942,976 | 49.5 | 50.5 | 58.0[10] |
| Burkina Faso | 105,869 | 274,200 | 68 | 8,308,000 | 73 | 78.5 | 30.3 | 3.2 | 1985[3] | 7,976,019 | 48.3 | 51.7 | 9.0[10] |
| Burma | 261,228 | 676,577 | 39 | 39,218,000 | 24 | 150.1 | 58.0 | 2.0 | 1983 | 35,313,905 | 49.6 | 50.4 | 24.0 |
| Burundi | 10,747 | 27,834 | 128 | 4,989,000 | 92 | 464.2 | 179.2 | 2.8 | 1979[11] | 4,114,135 | 48.3 | 51.7 | 5.3[2] |
| Cameroon | 179,714 | 465,468 | 49 | 10,759,000 | 59 | 59.9 | 23.1 | 3.0 | 1976 | 7,663,246 | 49.0 | 51.0 | 28.5 |
| Canada | 3,849,675 | 9,970,610 | 2 | 25,853,000 | 31 | 6.7 | 2.6 | 1.0 | 1981 | 24,343,181 | 49.6 | 50.4 | 76.4 |
| Cape Verde | 1,557 | 4,033 | 152 | 350,000 | 149 | 224.8 | 86.8 | 2.4 | 1980[3] | 295,073 | 46.3 | 53.7 | 35.1 |
| Cayman Islands | 102 | 264 | 191 | 22,800 | 195 | 223.5 | 86.4 | 4.1 | 1979 | 16,677[12] | 48.6 | 51.4 | 100.0 |
| Central African Republic | 240,324 | 622,436 | 42 | 2,774,000 | 112 | 11.5 | 4.5 | 2.5 | 1975 | 2,054,610 | 48.0 | 52.0 | 34.6 |
| Chad | 495,755 | 1,284,000 | 20 | 5,265,000 | 90 | 10.6 | 4.1 | 2.4 | 1975 | 4,029,917 | 47.7 | 52.3 | 16.0 |
| Chile | 292,135 | 756,626 | 37 | 12,536,000 | 55 | 42.9 | 16.6 | 1.8 | 1982 | 11,329,736 | 49.0 | 51.0 | 82.2 |
| China | 3,696,100 | 9,572,900 | 3 | 1,072,330,000 | 1 | 290.1 | 112.0 | 1.2 | 1982 | 1,008,175,288 | 51.5 | 48.5 | 21.2 |
| Christmas Island | 52 | 135 | 200 | 2,000 | 212 | 38.5 | 14.8 | −8.0 | 1981 | 2,871 | 66.8 | 33.2 | — |
| Cocos (Keeling) Islands | 5.6 | 14.4 | 211 | 600 | 214 | 107.1 | 41.7 | 1.8 | 1986 | 616 | 53.7[13] | 46.3[13] | ... |
| Colombia | 440,831 | 1,141,748 | 26 | 28,655,000 | 30 | 65.0 | 25.1 | 1.7 | 1985 | 27,867,326 | 49.5 | 50.5 | 63.6[14] |
| Comoros | 719 | 1,862 | 158 | 422,000 | 145 | 586.9 | 226.6 | 3.4 | 1980 | 335,150 | 49.9 | 50.1 | 23.2 |
| Congo | 132,047 | 342,000 | 57 | 2,180,000 | 120 | 16.5 | 6.4 | 3.9 | 1984 | 1,912,429 | 48.5[15] | 51.5[15] | 51.1 |
| Cook Islands | 91 | 236 | 194 | 17,300 | 198 | 190.1 | 73.3 | −0.2 | 1981 | 17,754 | 51.7 | 48.3 | ... |
| Costa Rica | 19,730 | 51,100 | 116 | 2,613,000 | 115 | 132.4 | 51.1 | 2.5 | 1984 | 2,416,809 | 50.0 | 50.0 | 43.9 |
| Côte d'Ivoire | 123,847 | 320,763 | 63 | 11,154,000 | 57 | 90.1 | 34.8 | 4.2 | 1975 | 6,702,866 | 51.8 | 48.2 | 32.0 |
| Cuba | 42,804 | 110,861 | 99 | 10,302,000 | 63 | 240.7 | 92.9 | 1.0 | 1981 | 9,723,605 | 50.6 | 49.4 | 69.0 |
| Cyprus | 3,572 | 9,251 | 147 | 719,000 | 138 | 201.3 | 77.7 | 1.9 | 1982[3] | 642,731 | 49.7 | 50.3 | 63.5 |
| Czechoslovakia | 49,384 | 127,905 | 92 | 15,591,000 | 49 | 315.7 | 121.9 | 0.3 | 1980 | 15,283,095 | 48.7 | 51.3 | 65.5 |
| Denmark | 16,638 | 43,092 | 119 | 5,127,000 | 91 | 308.2 | 119.0 | −0.0 | 1987[16] | 5,124,794 | 49.3 | 50.7 | 84.3[17] |
| Djibouti | 8,950 | 23,200 | 132 | 470,000 | 143 | 52.5 | 20.3 | 4.7 | 1960–61 | 81,200 | ... | ... | 75.0[18] |
| Dominica | 290 | 750 | 166 | 87,700 | 176 | 302.4 | 116.9 | 2.0 | 1981[17] | 73,795 | 49.8 | 50.2 | ... |
| Dominican Republic | 18,704 | 48,443 | 117 | 6,708,000 | 83 | 358.6 | 138.5 | 2.5 | 1981 | 5,647,977 | 50.1 | 49.9 | 52.0 |
| Ecuador | 103,930 | 269,178 | 69 | 9,923,000 | 65 | 95.5 | 36.9 | 2.9 | 1982 | 8,060,712 | 49.9 | 50.1 | 49.2 |
| Egypt | 385,229 | 997,739 | 29 | 49,143,000 | 21 | 127.6 | 49.3 | 2.7 | 1986 | 50,455,049[3] | 50.1[3] | 49.9[3] | 43.8[19, 20] |

mulated periodically); registration of migration, births, and deaths, and so on; sample surveys to establish demographic conditions; and the like.

The statistics provided for area and population by country are ranked, and the population densities based on those values are also provided. The population densities, for purposes of comparison within this table, are calculated on the bases of the 1987 population estimate as shown and of total area of the country. Elsewhere in individual country presentations the reader may find densities calculated on more specific population figures and more specialized area bases: land area for Finland (because of its many lakes), or ice-free area for Greenland (most of which is ice cap). The data in this section conclude with the estimated growth rate for the country (including both natural growth and net migration) during 1981–86, calculated mainly from country sources.

In the section containing census data, information supplied includes the census total (usually de facto, the population actually present, rather than de jure, the population legally resident, who might be anywhere); the male–female breakdown; the proportion that is urban (according to the country's own definition of the term "urban," which differs very much from country to country); and finally an analysis of the age structure of the population by 15-year age groups. This last analysis may be particularly useful in distinguishing the general type of population being recorded— young, fast-growing nations show a high proportion of people under 30 (some countries like Jordan or Mayotte have more than 50% of their population under 15 years), while other nations (for example Sweden, which suffered no age-group losses in World War II) exhibit quite uniform proportions among age groups.

Finally, a section is provided giving the population of each country at the end of each decade from 1930 to 2000. The data for years past represent the best available analysis of the published data by the country itself, by the demographers of the United Nations, or by the editors of Britannica. The projections for 1990 and 2000, similarly, represent the best fit of available data through the mid-1980s with projected population structure and growth rates during the next 15 years. The evidence of the last 15 years with respect to similar estimates published around 1970, however, shows how cloudy is the glass through which these numbers are read. In 1970 no respectable Western analyst would have imagined proposing that mainland China could achieve the degree of birth control that it has since then (as evidenced in the 1982 census); on the other hand, even the Chinese admit that their methods have been somewhat Draconian and that they expect some backlash in terms of higher birth-rates among those who have so far postponed larger families. How much is "some" by 2000? Compound that problem with all the social, economic, political, and biological factors that can affect 200 countries' populations, and the difficulty facing the prospective compiler of such projections may be appreciated.

Specific data about the vital rates affecting the data in this table may be found in great detail in both the country statistical boxes in "The Nations of the World" section and in the *Vital statistics, marriage, family* table, beginning at page 764.

Percentages in this table for male and female population will always total 100.0, but percentages by age group may not for reasons such as nonresponse on census forms, "don't know" responses, which are common in countries with poor birth registration systems, and the like.

| 0–14 | 15–29 | 30–44 | 45–59 | 60–74 | 75 and older | 1930 | 1940 | 1950 | 1960 | 1970 | 1980 | 1990 projection | 2000 projection | country |
|---|---|---|---|---|---|---|---|---|---|---|---|---|---|---|
| 44.5 | 26.9 | 15.8 | 8.6 | 3.6 | 0.6 | ... | ... | 8,958 | 10,775 | 13,623 | 15,372 | 14,805 | 17,081 | Afghanistan |
| 37.3[2] | 28.9[2] | 16.6[2] | 10.2[2] | 5.5[2] | 1.5[2] | 1,003 | 1,088 | 1,215 | 1,607 | 2,136 | 2,671 | 3,286 | 4,044 | Albania |
| 46.0[4] | 27.2[4] | 12.8[4] | 8.3[4] | 4.4 | 1.4 | 6,489 | 7,628 | 8,753 | 10,800 | 14,330 | 18,741 | 25,280 | 34,064 | Algeria |
| 40.9 | 28.8 | 16.0 | 9.4 | 4.0 | 0.9 | 10 | 13 | 19 | 20 | 27 | 32 | 40 | 48 | American Samoa |
| 19.0 | 27.3 | 26.4 | 14.8 | 9.4 | 3.1 | 5 | 5 | 6 | 8 | 19 | 33 | 57 | 96 | Andorra |
| 41.7 | 23.2 | 17.0 | 7.4 | 3.8 | 1.0 | 3,344 | 3,738 | 4,145 | 4,841 | 5,673 | 7,426 | 9,978 | 13,280 | Angola |
| 34.9 | 28.5 | 13.6 | 8.9 | 10.1 | 4.0 | ... | ... | 6 | 6 | 7 | 7 | 7 | 7 | Anguilla |
| 44.0 | 24.2 | 12.0 | 11.7 | ——8.0—— | | 30 | 34 | 45 | 55 | 66 | 75 | 86 | 98 | Antigua and Barbuda |
| 30.4 | 23.9 | 18.8 | 15.1 | 9.0 | 2.8 | 11,896 | 14,169 | 17,150 | 20,611 | 23,788 | 28,237 | 32,880 | 37,197 | Argentina |
| 25.9 | 30.6 | 21.3 | 12.7 | 7.4 | 2.1 | 16 | 31 | 51 | 57 | 58 | 60 | 68 | 76 | Aruba |
| 25.1 | 25.3 | 20.5 | 15.2 | 10.4 | 3.5 | 6,503 | 7,079 | 8,219 | 10,315 | 12,552 | 14,698 | 16,913 | 19,078 | Australia |
| 19.9 | 23.6 | 20.1 | 17.1 | 13.2 | 6.1 | 6,435 | 6,684 | 6,935 | 7,048 | 7,447 | 7,549 | 7,549 | 7,530 | Austria |
| 38.1 | 27.8 | 17.9 | 9.8 | 5.1 | 1.3 | 61 | 70 | 79 | 113 | 169 | 210 | 262 | 327 | Bahamas, The |
| 32.9 | 34.5 | 20.0 | 8.8 | 3.1 | 0.7 | ... | 90 | 127 | 162 | 215 | 337 | 527 | 715 | Bahrain |
| 46.6 | 24.6 | 14.9 | 8.2 | ——5.7—— | | 35,353 | 41,259 | 45,482 | 54,699 | 68,171 | 88,507 | 113,005 | 139,693 | Bangladesh |
| 28.9 | 32.3 | 14.2 | 11.2 | ——13.3—— | | 159 | 179 | 209 | 232 | 235 | 249 | 256 | 263 | Barbados |
| 20.0 | 23.7 | 19.1 | 18.6 | 12.8 | 5.8 | 8,129 | 8,301 | 8,639 | 9,153 | 9,690 | 9,859 | 9,864 | 9,875 | Belgium |
| 46.2 | 27.1 | 11.8 | 8.4 | 4.7 | 1.8 | 51 | 56 | 68 | 90 | 120 | 145 | 190 | 249 | Belize |
| 45.9[2] | 25.4[2] | 15.1[2] | 8.6[2] | 3.9[2] | 0.9[2] | 1,099 | 1,355 | 1,538 | 1,990 | 2,686 | 3,494 | 4,733 | 6,532 | Benin |
| 22.7 | 27.5 | 22.2 | 15.7 | 9.0 | 2.9 | 28 | 31 | 37 | 43 | 53 | 55 | 59 | 65 | Bermuda |
| 39.2[8] | 26.5[8] | 16.3[8] | 10.9[8] | ——7.1[8]—— | | 440 | 500 | 726 | 853 | 1,045 | 1,165 | 1,420 | 1,731 | Bhutan |
| 41.5 | 27.0 | 15.4 | 9.8 | 4.6 | 1.7 | 2,153 | 2,508 | 2,765 | 3,405 | 4,265 | 5,600 | 7,400 | 9,837 | Bolivia |
| 56.5 | 19.9 | 10.2 | 6.6 | 3.4 | 3.4 | 212 | 278 | 387 | 522 | 650 | 889 | 1,303 | 1,817 | Botswana |
| 39.1 | 28.6 | 16.4 | 10.0 | ——5.9—— | | 33,718 | 41,525 | 52,901 | 71,539 | 93,139 | 121,286 | 150,368 | 179,487 | Brazil |
| 34.0 | 29.0 | 18.7 | 9.7 | 6.3 | 2.3 | 5 | 7 | 7 | 7 | 10 | 11 | 13 | 15 | British Virgin Islands |
| 38.5 | 32.7 | 16.4 | 7.9 | ——4.5—— | | 30 | 36 | 48 | 84 | 129 | 187 | 269 | 388 | Brunei |
| 21.8[10] | 22.4[10] | 20.6[10] | 18.6[10] | 13.0[10] | 3.4[10] | 5,997 | 6,624 | 7,273 | 7,906 | 8,515 | 8,829 | 9,050 | 9,276 | Bulgaria |
| 47.4[10] | 21.1[10] | 16.1[10] | 9.3[10] | ——6.1[10]—— | | ... | ... | 3,584 | 4,350 | 5,412 | 6,604 | 8,994 | 11,719 | Burkina Faso |
| 37.6[4] | 28.4[4] | 17.6[4] | 9.8[4] | 5.6[4] | 1.1[4] | 14,282 | 16,119 | 18,489 | 22,063 | 26,997 | 33,938 | 41,114 | 48,553 | Burma |
| 42.4 | 29.4 | 13.4 | 8.2 | 4.8 | 1.8 | ... | ... | 2,435 | 2,908 | 3,350 | 4,120 | 5,425 | 7,170 | Burundi |
| 43.4 | 24.3 | 16.6 | 9.9 | 4.3 | 1.5 | ... | ... | 4,888 | 5,609 | 6,727 | 8,727 | 11,757 | 15,801 | Cameroon |
| 23.4 | 28.9 | 20.0 | 15.0 | 9.6 | 3.1 | 10,498 | 11,693 | 13,737 | 17,909 | 21,324 | 24,070 | 26,599 | 29,243 | Canada |
| 46.0 | 27.6 | 9.1 | 9.0 | 6.3 | 2.0 | 146 | 181 | 147 | 200 | 272 | 296 | 377 | 479 | Cape Verde |
| 29.1 | 25.8 | 22.1 | 13.1 | 7.3 | 2.6 | 6 | 7 | 7 | 8 | 11 | 17 | 26 | 38 | Cayman Islands |
| 43.5 | 23.5 | 17.1 | 12.4 | 2.7 | 0.8 | ... | ... | 1,311 | 1,500 | 1,793 | 2,333 | 2,987 | 3,823 | Central African Republic |
| 40.6 | 28.3 | 17.2 | 9.5 | ——4.4—— | | ... | 2,351 | 2,639 | 3,032 | 3,643 | 4,477 | 5,668 | 7,308 | Chad |
| 31.9 | 29.1 | 19.1 | 11.7 | 6.3 | 1.9 | 4,365 | 5,063 | 6,091 | 7,585 | 9,368 | 11,104 | 13,218 | 15,768 | Chile |
| 33.6 | 29.1 | 17.5 | 12.2 | 6.3 | 1.3 | 500,000 | 530,000 | 556,613 | 682,024 | 838,396 | 981,235 | 1,112,000 | 1,253,000 | China |
| 25.9 | 26.4 | 35.8 | 10.8 | ——1.1—— | | ... | ... | 1 | 3 | 3 | 3 | 2 | 1 | Christmas Island |
| 27.4[13] | 28.3[13] | 27.2[13] | 11.2[13] | ——5.9[13]—— | | ... | ... | 1 | 1 | 1 | 1 | 1 | 1 | Cocos (Keeling) Islands |
| 36.1 | 31.2 | 17.2 | 9.5 | 4.6 | 1.4 | 7,280 | 9,097 | 11,268 | 15,321 | 20,884 | 25,559 | 30,095 | 35,436 | Colombia |
| 47.2 | 23.2 | 14.8 | 7.6 | 5.1 | 1.8 | ... | ... | 177 | 245 | 333 | 466 | 650 | | Comoros |
| 45.6[15] | 22.2[15] | 15.5[15] | 11.3[15] | 4.7[15] | 0.7[15] | ... | ... | 736 | 933 | 1,182 | 1,664 | 2,447 | 3,600 | Congo |
| 42.7 | 26.6 | 13.7 | 10.4 | 5.2 | 1.3 | 11 | 13 | 15 | 18 | 18 | 18 | 17 | 17 | Cook Islands |
| 37.9 | 31.5 | 15.8 | 9.2 | 4.4 | 1.2 | 499 | 619 | 866 | 1,250 | 1,737 | 2,206 | 2,811 | 3,587 | Costa Rica |
| 44.5 | 27.0 | 16.7 | 7.8 | 2.8 | 1.2 | 2,075 | 2,350 | 2,775 | 3,865 | 5,550 | 8,320 | 12,657 | 16,194 | Côte d'Ivoire |
| 30.3 | 27.6 | 19.1 | 12.1 | 8.2 | 2.7 | 3,837 | 4,566 | 5,752 | 7,019 | 8,565 | 9,724 | 10,614 | 11,727 | Cuba |
| 25.0 | 26.6 | 20.1 | 13.8 | ——14.5—— | | 357 | 413 | 494 | 573 | 615 | 628 | 762 | 926 | Cyprus |
| 24.3 | 22.9 | 19.8 | 17.2 | 11.5 | 4.3 | 13,964 | 14,713 | 12,389 | 13,654 | 14,334 | 15,265 | 15,728 | 16,194 | Czechoslovakia |
| 17.9 | 22.8 | 22.7 | 16.2 | 13.8 | 6.6 | 3,542 | 3,832 | 4,271 | 4,581 | 4,929 | 5,123 | 5,137 | 5,165 | Denmark |
| 38.0[18] | 34.0[18] | 17.0[18] | ——11.0[18]—— | | | 70 | 44 | 60 | 78 | 158 | 355 | 513 | 690 | Djibouti |
| 39.8 | 28.6 | 11.9 | 9.2 | 7.4 | 3.1 | 41 | 45 | 51 | 60 | 70 | 74 | 93 | 114 | Dominica |
| 43.9[2] | 29.3[2] | 14.2[2] | 8.2[2] | 3.5[2] | 1.0[2] | 1,400 | 1,759 | 2,313 | 3,160 | 4,343 | 5,643 | 7,223 | 9,247 | Dominican Republic |
| 41.9 | 28.1 | 15.4 | 8.6 | 4.5 | 1.5 | 2,102 | 2,546 | 3,307 | 4,421 | 5,958 | 8,123 | 10,782 | 13,939 | Ecuador |
| 39.9[19,20] | 26.7[19,20] | 16.6[19,20] | 10.6[19,20] | 5.2[19,20] | 1.0[19,20] | 14,822 | 16,942 | 20,461 | 26,085 | 33,329 | 40,642 | 52,536 | 63,941 | Egypt |

## Area and population (continued)

| country | area | | | population (latest estimate) | | | | | population (most recent census) | | | | |
|---|---|---|---|---|---|---|---|---|---|---|---|---|---|
| | square miles | square kilo-metres | rank | total midyear 1987 | rank | density per sq mi | per sq km | % annual growth rate 1982–87 | census year | total | male (%) | female (%) | urban (%) |
| El Salvador | 8,124 | 21,041 | 134 | 4,974,000 | 93 | 612.3 | 236.4 | 1.3 | 1971 | 3,554,648 | 49.6 | 50.4 | 39.4 |
| Equatorial Guinea | 10,831 | 28,051 | 127 | 328,000 | 153 | 30.3 | 11.7 | 2.2 | 1983 | 300,000 | 48.1 | 51.9 | 27.6 |
| Ethiopia | 472,400 | 1,223,500 | 23 | 45,997,000 | 22 | 97.4 | 37.6 | 2.6 | 1984 | 42,184,966 | 49.8 | 50.2 | 10.2 |
| Faeroe Islands | 540 | 1,399 | 160 | 46,500 | 188 | 86.1 | 33.2 | 1.0 | 1987 | 46,369 | 52.3 | 47.7 | 96.2 |
| Falkland Islands | 4,700 | 12,173 | 142 | 2,100 | 210 | 0.4 | 0.2 | 1.0 | 1980[21] | 1,813 | 54.7 | 45.3 | 56.8 |
| Fiji | 7,056 | 18,274 | 137 | 726,000 | 137 | 102.9 | 39.7 | 2.0 | 1986 | 715,375 | 50.7 | 49.3 | 38.7 |
| Finland | 130,559 | 338,145 | 58 | 4,942,000 | 94 | 37.9 | 14.6 | 0.5 | 1980 | 4,784,710 | 48.3 | 51.7 | 59.9 |
| France | 210,026 | 543,965 | 46 | 55,623,000 | 17 | 264.8 | 102.3 | 0.4 | 1982 | 54,334,871 | 49.0 | 51.0 | 73.22 |
| French Guiana | 33,399 | 86,504 | 108 | 88,800 | 175 | 2.7 | 1.0 | 3.7 | 1982 | 73,022 | 52.7 | 47.3 | 73.4 |
| French Polynesia | 1,359 | 3,521 | 153 | 183,000 | 161 | 134.7 | 52.0 | 2.6 | 1983 | 166,753 | 51.1 | 48.9 | 39.7 |
| Gabon | 103,347 | 267,667 | 70 | 1,195,000 | 130 | 11.6 | 4.5 | 1.8 | 1960–61 | 448,564 | 49.1[2] | 50.9[2] | 35.8[2] |
| Gambia, The | 4,127 | 10,689 | 145 | 787,000 | 136 | 190.7 | 73.6 | 3.1 | 1983 | 695,886 | 50.7[14] | 49.3[14] | 21.2 |
| Gaza Strip | 140 | 363 | 184 | 548,000 | 141 | 3,914.3 | 1,509.6 | 3.0 | 1985[16] | 509,900 | 49.9 | 50.1 | ... |
| Germany, East | 41,827 | 108,333 | 101 | 16,598,000 | 44 | 396.8 | 153.2 | −0.1 | 1981 | 16,705,635 | 47.0 | 53.0 | 76.4 |
| Germany, West | 96,026 | 248,708 | 74 | 60,924,000 | 13 | 634.4 | 245.0 | −0.2 | 1986[16] | 61,020,500 | 47.8 | 52.2 | 85.54 |
| Ghana | 92,098 | 238,533 | 78 | 13,482,000 | 54 | 146.4 | 56.5 | 2.6 | 1984 | 12,205,574 | 49.1 | 50.9 | 31.3 |
| Gibraltar | 2.3 | 5.8 | 213 | 29,000 | 193 | 12,608.7 | 5,000.0 | −0.1 | 1981[22] | 26,479 | 52.2 | 47.8 | ... |
| Greece | 50,949 | 131,957 | 91 | 10,010,000 | 64 | 196.5 | 75.9 | 0.5 | 1981 | 9,740,417 | 49.1 | 50.9 | 58.1 |
| Greenland | 840,000 | 2,175,600 | 13 | 54,100 | 186 | 0.06 | 0.02 | 0.9 | 1987[16] | 53,733 | 54.4 | 45.6 | 79.4 |
| Grenada | 133 | 345 | 186 | 104,000 | 172 | 782.0 | 301.4 | 3.1 | 1981 | 89,088 | 47.1[2] | 52.9[2] | 25.3[24] |
| Guadeloupe | 687 | 1,780 | 159 | 335,000 | 151 | 487.6 | 188.2 | 0.4 | 1982[3] | 327,002 | 49.0 | 51.0 | 43.5[2] |
| Guam | 209 | 541 | 173 | 124,000 | 168 | 593.3 | 229.2 | 2.2 | 1980 | 105,979 | 52.2 | 47.8 | 39.5 |
| Guatemala | 42,042 | 108,889 | 100 | 8,434,000 | 70 | 200.6 | 77.5 | 2.9 | 1981[3] | 6,043,559 | 49.8 | 50.2 | 34.3 |
| Guernsey | 30 | 78 | 204 | 60,000 | 184 | 2,000.0 | 769.2 | 1.0 | 1976[25] | 54,381 | 48.3 | 51.7 | ... |
| Guinea | 94,926 | 245,857 | 75 | 6,380,000 | 86 | 67.2 | 26.0 | 2.4 | 1983 | 5,781,014 | 48.6 | 51.4 | 26.0 |
| Guinea-Bissau | 13,948 | 36,125 | 122 | 912,000 | 133 | 65.4 | 25.2 | 2.2 | 1979 | 767,739 | 48.2 | 51.8 | 14.0 |
| Guyana | 83,000 | 215,000 | 81 | 802,000 | 135 | 9.7 | 3.7 | 0.8 | 1980 | 758,619 | 49.7[24] | 50.3[24] | 31.9[24] |
| Haiti | 10,579 | 27,400 | 130 | 5,532,000 | 89 | 522.9 | 201.9 | 1.9 | 1982 | 5,053,792 | 48.5 | 51.5 | 20.6 |
| Honduras | 43,277 | 112,088 | 97 | 4,657,000 | 95 | 107.6 | 41.5 | 3.3 | 1974 | 2,656,948 | 49.5 | 50.5 | 37.5 |
| Hong Kong | 400 | 1,037 | 162 | 5,602,000 | 88 | 14,005.0 | 5,402.1 | 1.3 | 1986[26] | 5,396,000 | 51.4 | 48.6 | 93.1 |
| Hungary | 35,921 | 93,036 | 105 | 10,608,000 | 60 | 295.3 | 114.0 | −0.2 | 1980 | 10,709,463 | 48.4 | 51.6 | 53.2 |
| Iceland | 39,769 | 103,000 | 102 | 245,000 | 157 | 6.2 | 2.4 | 0.9 | 1986[16] | 243,698 | 50.2 | 49.8 | 89.7 |
| India | 1,222,559 | 3,166,414 | 7 | 783,044,000 | 2 | 640.5 | 247.3 | 1.8 | 1981 | 685,184,692 | 50.3 | 49.7 | 23.7 |
| Indonesia | 741,101 | 1,919,443 | 15 | 172,245,000 | 5 | 232.4 | 89.7 | 2.2 | 1980 | 147,490,298 | 49.7 | 50.3 | 22.3 |
| Iran | 636,372 | 1,648,196 | 17 | 49,930,000 | 20 | 78.5 | 30.3 | 3.6 | 1976 | 33,708,744 | 51.5 | 48.5 | 47.0 |
| Iraq | 169,235 | 438,317 | 53 | 16,476,000 | 46 | 97.4 | 37.4 | 3.3 | 1977 | 12,000,497 | 51.5 | 48.5 | 63.7 |
| Ireland | 27,137 | 70,285 | 113 | 3,560,000 | 103 | 131.2 | 50.7 | 0.5 | 1986 | 3,537,195 | 50.2[13] | 49.8[13] | 55.6[13] |
| Isle of Man | 221 | 572 | 172 | 64,200 | 183 | 290.5 | 112.2 | −0.1 | 1986[3] | 64,282 | 47.9 | 52.1 | 51.1 |
| Israel[27] | 7,992 | 20,700 | 135 | 4,449,000 | 96 | 556.7 | 214.9 | 2.1 | 1983[3, 28] | 4,037,620 | 49.8 | 50.2 | 86.9 |
| Italy | 116,324 | 301,278 | 65 | 57,256,000 | 15 | 492.2 | 190.0 | 0.2 | 1981[3] | 56,556,911 | 48.6 | 51.4 | 66.5[2] |
| Jamaica | 4,244 | 10,991 | 144 | 2,372,000 | 116 | 558.9 | 215.8 | 1.5 | 1982 | 2,190,357 | 49.1 | 50.9 | 47.8 |
| Japan | 145,870 | 377,801 | 56 | 122,100,000 | 7 | 837.0 | 323.2 | 0.6 | 1985 | 121,047,196 | 49.2 | 50.8 | 76.7 |
| Jersey | 45 | 116 | 201 | 78,100 | 178 | 1,735.6 | 673.3 | 0.4 | 1981[3] | 76,050 | 48.0 | 52.0 | ... |
| Jordan[29] | 34,443 | 89,206 | 107 | 2,853,000 | 111 | 82.8 | 32.0 | 3.9 | 1979 | 2,132,997 | 52.3 | 47.7 | 59.5 |
| Kampuchea | 69,898 | 181,035 | 85 | 7,688,000 | 74 | 110.0 | 42.5 | 2.9 | 1981 | 6,684,000 | 50.0[30] | 50.0[30] | 10.3[30] |
| Kenya | 224,961 | 582,646 | 44 | 22,020,000 | 38 | 97.9 | 37.8 | 4.0 | 1979 | 15,327,061 | 49.7 | 50.3 | 15.1 |
| Kiribati | 328 | 849 | 164 | 66,800 | 180 | 203.7 | 78.7 | 2.0 | 1985 | 63,980 | 49.6 | 50.4 | 33.5 |
| Korea, North | 47,250 | 122,370 | 94 | 21,390,000 | 39 | 452.7 | 174.8 | 2.5 | 31 | 31 | 49.6[4] | 50.4[4] | 63.8[4] |
| Korea, South | 38,279 | 99,143 | 103 | 42,082,000 | 23 | 1,099.3 | 424.5 | 1.4 | 1985[3] | 40,466,577 | 50.1 | 49.9 | 65.4 |
| Kuwait | 6,880 | 17,818 | 138 | 1,873,000 | 122 | 272.2 | 105.1 | 4.5 | 1985 | 1,697,301 | 56.9 | 43.1 | 100.0 |
| Laos | 91,400 | 236,800 | 80 | 3,757,000 | 102 | 41.1 | 15.9 | 2.0 | 1985 | 3,584,803 | 50.4[4] | 49.6[4] | 15.9[4] |
| Lebanon | 3,950 | 10,230 | 146 | 2,762,000 | 113 | 699.2 | 270.0 | 0.9 | 1970 | 2,126,325 | 50.8 | 49.2 | 60.1 |
| Lesotho | 11,720 | 30,355 | 125 | 1,628,000 | 125 | 138.9 | 53.6 | 2.6 | 1986[3] | 1,577,536 | 48.2 | 51.8 | 17.2[20] |
| Liberia | 38,250 | 99,067 | 104 | 2,356,000 | 117 | 61.6 | 23.8 | 3.4 | 1984 | 2,101,628 | 50.6 | 49.4 | 38.8 |
| Libya | 685,524 | 1,775,500 | 16 | 4,132,000 | 99 | 6.0 | 2.3 | 4.4 | 1984 | 3,637,488 | 53.0[14] | 47.0[14] | 59.8[14] |
| Liechtenstein | 62 | 160 | 198 | 27,500 | 194 | 443.5 | 171.9 | 0.9 | 1980 | 25,215 | 49.6 | 50.4 | ... |
| Luxembourg | 999 | 2,586 | 155 | 367,000 | 148 | 367.4 | 141.9 | 0.1 | 1981 | 364,602 | 48.8 | 51.2 | 77.6[2] |
| Macau | 6.5 | 16.9 | 210 | 452,000 | 144 | 69,538.5 | 26,745.6 | 7.5 | 1981[3] | 241,729 | 50.9 | 49.1 | 95.4 |
| Madagascar | 226,658 | 587,041 | 43 | 10,605,000 | 61 | 46.8 | 18.1 | 2.8 | 1974–75 | 7,603,790 | 50.0 | 50.0 | 16.3 |
| Malawi | 45,747 | 118,484 | 95 | 7,499,000 | 78 | 163.9 | 63.3 | 3.2 | 1977 | 5,547,460 | 48.2 | 51.8 | 8.5 |
| Malaysia | 127,581 | 330,434 | 61 | 16,538,000 | 45 | 129.6 | 50.0 | 1.3 | 1980 | 13,136,109 | 50.2 | 49.8 | 34.2 |
| Maldives | 115 | 298 | 188 | 195,000 | 159 | 1,695.7 | 654.4 | 3.3 | 1985 | 181,453 | 51.8 | 48.2 | 25.5 |
| Mali | 478,841 | 1,240,192 | 22 | 7,653,000 | 76 | 16.0 | 6.2 | 1.7 | 1987 | 7,620,225 | 48.9 | 51.1 | 16.8[20] |
| Malta | 122 | 316 | 187 | 345,000 | 150 | 2,827.9 | 1,091.8 | 1.2 | 1985 | 345,418 | 49.2 | 50.8 | 94.3[32] |
| Martinique | 421 | 1,091 | 161 | 329,000 | 152 | 781.5 | 301.6 | 0.2 | 1982[3] | 326,717 | 48.5 | 51.5 | 57.1 |
| Mauritania | 398,000 | 1,030,700 | 28 | 1,844,000 | 124 | 4.6 | 1.8 | 2.5 | 1976–77 | 1,419,939 | 50.1 | 49.9 | 21.9 |
| Mauritius | 788 | 2,040 | 157 | 1,040,000 | 132 | 1,319.8 | 509.8 | 1.1 | 1983 | 1,002,178 | 49.8 | 50.2 | 41.7[33] |
| Mayotte | 144 | 373 | 183 | 73,700 | 179 | 511.8 | 197.6 | 5.0 | 1985 | 67,167 | 49.9[34] | 50.1[34] | 53.3[34] |
| Mexico | 756,066 | 1,958,201 | 14 | 81,323,000 | 11 | 107.6 | 41.5 | 2.2 | 1980 | 66,846,833 | 49.4 | 50.6 | 66.3 |
| Monaco | 0.7 | 1.9 | 215 | 29,000 | 192 | 41,428.6 | 15,263.2 | 1.2 | 1982 | 27,063 | 46.6 | 53.4 | 100.0 |
| Mongolia | 604,000 | 1,565,000 | 18 | 1,989,000 | 121 | 3.3 | 1.3 | 2.6 | 1979 | 1,594,800 | 50.1 | 49.9 | 51.2 |
| Montserrat | 40 | 102 | 202 | 12,000 | 202 | 300.0 | 117.6 | 0.5 | 1980 | 11,606 | 48.1 | 51.9 | 13.2 |
| Morocco | 177,117 | 458,730 | 51 | 23,119,000 | 35 | 130.5 | 50.4 | 2.8 | 1982 | 20,419,555[35] | 50.1 | 49.9 | 42.7 |
| Mozambique | 308,642 | 799,380 | 34 | 14,516,000 | 52 | 47.0 | 18.2 | 2.6 | 1980 | 12,130,000 | 48.7 | 51.3 | 13.2 |
| Nauru | 8.2 | 21.2 | 209 | 8,100 | 205 | 987.8 | 382.1 | −0.7 | 1983 | 8,042 | 52.1[5, 36] | 47.9[5, 36] | — |
| Nepal | 56,827 | 147,181 | 89 | 17,567,000 | 43 | 309.1 | 119.4 | 2.6 | 1981 | 15,022,839 | 51.2 | 48.8 | 6.4 |
| Netherlands, The | 16,133 | 41,785 | 120 | 14,615,000 | 51 | 905.9 | 349.8 | 0.4 | 1986[16] | 14,529,430 | 49.4 | 50.6 | 88.4 |
| Netherlands Antilles | 308 | 800 | 165 | 176,000 | 162 | 571.4 | 220.0 | 0.4 | 1981 | 171,620 | 48.3 | 51.7 | ... |
| New Caledonia | 7,233 | 18,734 | 136 | 152,000 | 165 | 21.0 | 8.1 | 1.1 | 1983 | 145,368 | 51.8 | 48.2 | 58.5 |
| New Zealand | 103,288 | 267,515 | 71 | 3,341,000 | 106 | 32.3 | 12.5 | 0.8 | 1986 | 3,307,084 | 49.7[13] | 50.3[13] | 83.6[13] |
| Nicaragua | 49,363 | 127,849 | 93 | 3,502,000 | 104 | 70.9 | 27.4 | 3.4 | 1971 | 1,877,952 | 48.3 | 51.7 | 48.0 |
| Niger | 458,074 | 1,186,408 | 25 | 6,947,000 | 80 | 15.2 | 5.9 | 3.4 | 1977 | 5,098,427 | 49.3 | 50.7 | 11.8 |
| Nigeria | 356,669 | 923,768 | 31 | 100,596,000 | 10 | 282.0 | 108.9 | 2.5 | 1963[37] | 55,670,055 | 50.5 | 49.5 | 16.1 |
| Niue | 100 | 258 | 192 | 2,600 | 209 | 26.0 | 10.1 | −4.2 | 1984 | 2,887 | 51.2 | 48.8 | ... |
| Norfolk Island | 14 | 35 | 207 | 2,000 | 211 | 142.9 | 57.1 | 1.4 | 1986[3] | 1,977 | 50.7 | 49.3 | — |

| 0–14 | 15–29 | 30–44 | 45–59 | 60–74 | 75 and older | 1930 | 1940 | 1950 | 1960 | 1970 | 1980 | 1990 projection | 2000 projection | country |
|---|---|---|---|---|---|---|---|---|---|---|---|---|---|---|
| 46.2 | 25.1 | 15.2 | 8.2 | 4.3 | 1.0 | 1,350 | 1,550 | 1,931 | 2,527 | 3,534 | 4,508 | 5,171 | 6,717 | El Salvador |
| 38.1[4] | 26.0[4] | 17.7[4] | 11.5[4] | 5.6[4] | 1.1[4] | ... | ... | 211 | 244 | 291 | 281 | 351 | 445 | Equatorial Guinea |
| 46.6 | 22.7 | 15.6 | 8.9 | 4.5 | 1.7 | ... | ... | 16,675 | 20,024 | 24,068 | 38,521 | 50,087 | 66,509 | Ethiopia |
| 24.8 | —45.7— | | 13.8 | —15.7— | | 24 | 27 | 31 | 35 | 39 | 43 | 48 | 53 | Faeroe Islands |
| 25.4 | 22.6 | —38.0— | | —14.0— | | 2 | 2 | 2 | 2 | 2 | 2 | 2 | 2 | Falkland Islands |
| 38.2 | 29.5 | 17.8 | 9.6 | 3.8 | 0.8 | 181 | 218 | 289 | 394 | 520 | 634 | 770 | 936 | Fiji |
| 20.2 | 24.4 | 22.1 | 16.8 | 12.4 | 4.1 | 3,449 | 3,698 | 4,009 | 4,430 | 4,606 | 4,780 | 5,013 | 5,255 | Finland |
| 22.0 | 23.5 | 19.6 | 17.3 | 11.6 | 6.0 | 41,150 | 41,300 | 41,736 | 45,684 | 50,770 | 53,880 | 56,320 | 58,707 | France |
| 34.2 | 29.2 | 19.9 | 9.8 | 5.1 | 1.8 | 30 | 30 | 27 | 33 | 49 | 69 | 99 | 142 | French Guiana |
| 38.5 | 29.7 | 16.5 | 10.3 | 4.2 | 0.8 | 39 | 50 | 62 | 84 | 109 | 151 | 197 | 256 | French Polynesia |
| 33.4[2] | 24.5[2] | 19.0[2] | 13.5[2] | 7.7[2] | 1.8[2] | ... | ... | ... | ... | 950 | 1,064 | 1,273 | 1,603 | Gabon |
| 41.3[14] | 26.5[14] | 17.6[14] | 8.3[14] | 4.3[14] | 1.7[14] | 211 | 193 | 232 | 357 | 458 | 632 | 860 | 1,156 | Gambia, The |
| 47.7 | 29.2 | 11.0 | 7.8 | —4.3— | | ... | ... | ... | ... | 370 | 451 | 596 | 789 | Gaza Strip |
| 19.4 | 24.2 | 20.0 | 17.3 | 12.8 | 6.3 | 15,400 | 16,800 | 18,387 | 17,240 | 17,058 | 16,737 | 16,530 | 16,303 | Germany, East |
| 15.0 | 24.4 | 20.1 | 20.1 | 13.5 | 6.9 | 37,500 | 40,600 | 49,986 | 55,433 | 60,714 | 61,566 | 60,500 | 59,107 | Germany, West |
| 46.7[4] | 26.1[4] | 14.5[4] | 8.2[4] | 3.8[4] | 0.7[4] | 3,110 | 3,636 | 5,297 | 6,958 | 8,789 | 11,294 | 14,545 | 18,730 | Ghana |
| 21.4 | 22.2 | 22.3 | 17.7 | 12.6 | 3.8 | 16 | 14 | 23 | 24 | 26 | 30 | 29 | 29 | Gibraltar |
| 21.3[23] | 22.0[23] | 19.1[23] | 19.8[23] | 12.4[23] | 5.4[23] | 6,367 | 7,319 | 7,566 | 8,327 | 8,793 | 9,643 | 10,145 | 10,608 | Greece |
| 24.6 | 33.0 | 23.6 | 12.8 | 4.8 | 1.1 | 16 | 19 | 23 | 33 | 41 | 50 | 56 | 61 | Greenland |
| 39.4[2] | 31.2[2] | 10.1[2] | 9.2[2] | 7.3[2] | 2.8[2] | 68 | 71 | 76 | 90 | 95 | 91 | 111 | 134 | Grenada |
| 31.1 | 29.2 | 16.6 | 12.0 | 7.8 | 2.8 | 151 | 180 | 206 | 265 | 320 | 327 | 339 | 353 | Guadeloupe |
| 34.9 | 30.6 | 19.4 | 10.5 | 3.9 | 0.5 | 19 | 22 | 59 | 67 | 85 | 107 | 132 | 165 | Guam |
| 44.9 | 26.8 | 14.8 | 8.5 | 3.9 | 1.1 | 1,771 | 2,201 | 3,024 | 4,005 | 5,263 | 6,917 | 9,197 | 12,222 | Guatemala |
| 21.6 | 22.2 | 17.6 | 17.7 | 15.2 | 5.6 | 40 | 44 | 44 | 45 | 51 | 55 | 62 | 69 | Guernsey |
| 43.1[4] | 26.2[4] | 16.3[4] | 9.6[4] | 4.2[4] | 0.7[4] | ... | ... | 3,245 | 3,660 | 4,388 | 5,407 | 6,876 | 8,879 | Guinea |
| 44.3 | 25.5 | 15.1 | 8.2 | 4.7 | 2.2 | ... | 341 | 411 | 520 | 653 | 787 | 972 | 1,200 | Guinea-Bissau |
| 47.1[24] | 25.1[24] | 13.4[24] | 9.0[24] | 4.4[24] | 1.0[24] | 309 | 344 | 423 | 560 | 702 | 759 | 821 | 888 | Guyana |
| 39.2 | 26.9 | 15.6 | 10.0 | 5.4 | 2.9 | 2,422 | 2,827 | 3,097 | 3,723 | 4,234 | 4,922 | 5,863 | 7,118 | Haiti |
| 48.1 | 25.8 | 13.9 | 7.8 | 3.6 | 0.9 | 948 | 1,146 | 1,390 | 1,873 | 2,553 | 3,691 | 5,105 | 6,978 | Honduras |
| 23.1 | 29.9 | 21.2 | 14.3 | 9.1 | 2.4 | 821 | 1,786 | 1,974 | 3,074 | 3,942 | 5,063 | 5,814 | 6,665 | Hong Kong |
| 21.8 | 20.7 | —40.6— | | —16.9— | | 8,649 | 9,280 | 9,338 | 9,984 | 10,353 | 10,708 | 10,553 | 10,369 | Hungary |
| 25.5 | 26.1 | 20.8 | 13.2 | 9.9 | 4.5 | 107 | 121 | 143 | 176 | 204 | 228 | 252 | 277 | Iceland |
| 39.5 | 25.9 | 17.4 | 10.7 | —6.5— | | 278,000 | 317,000 | 352,664 | 427,802 | 543,132 | 687,057 | 814,749 | 941,008 | India |
| 40.8 | 27.0 | 16.4 | 10.2 | 4.5 | 1.1 | 60,750 | 70,500 | 75,449 | 92,701 | 119,467 | 148,040 | 183,457 | 222,753 | Indonesia |
| 44.5 | 25.2 | 14.8 | 10.1 | 3.8 | 1.0 | 12,400 | 14,000 | 16,913 | 21,554 | 28,359 | 38,715 | 52,745 | 64,822 | Iran |
| 48.9 | 24.5 | 12.3 | 8.2 | 4.2 | 1.9 | ... | 3,745 | 5,180 | 6,847 | 9,356 | 13,108 | 18,165 | 25,151 | Iraq |
| 30.3[13] | 24.6[13] | 17.2[13] | 13.1[13] | 10.9[13] | 3.8[13] | 2,927 | 2,958 | 2,969 | 2,834 | 2,954 | 3,415 | 3,618 | 3,817 | Ireland |
| 17.6 | 20.2 | 19.0 | 16.0 | 17.4 | 9.2 | 50 | 52 | 55 | 49 | 52 | 64 | 64 | 63 | Isle of Man |
| 32.6 | 26.4 | 18.0 | 12.3 | 9.4 | 3.1 | ... | ... | ... | 2,114 | 2,958 | 3,896 | 4,739 | 5,475 | Israel[27] |
| 21.4 | 22.4 | 20.0 | 18.7 | 12.7 | 4.7 | 40,293 | 43,840 | 46,769 | 50,223 | 53,565 | 56,232 | 57,361 | 57,388 | Italy |
| 38.4 | 28.8 | 13.8 | 9.4 | 6.9 | 2.6 | 1,009 | 1,212 | 1,403 | 1,629 | 1,891 | 2,133 | 2,481 | 2,882 | Jamaica |
| 21.5 | 20.7 | 23.9 | 19.2 | 10.8 | 3.9 | 64,450 | 73,075 | 83,200 | 93,419 | 103,720 | 116,807 | 124,275 | 132,589 | Japan |
| 16.9 | 24.7 | 21.6 | 17.0 | 13.8 | 5.9 | 50 | 51 | 57 | 63 | 68 | 76 | 79 | 82 | Jersey |
| 51.6 | 23.4 | 13.4 | 7.4 | 3.1 | 1.1 | ... | ... | 1,095 | 1,384 | 1,795 | 2,181 | 3,202 | 4,705 | Jordan[29] |
| 43.8[30] | 24.9[30] | 16.8[30] | 9.8[30] | 4.1[30] | 0.6[30] | 2,800 | 3,400 | 4,163 | 5,364 | 7,060 | 6,400 | 8,246 | 9,772 | Kampuchea |
| 51.4 | 24.8 | 13.2 | 7.0 | 3.0 | 0.6 | 3,400 | 4,470 | 6,018 | 8,115 | 11,225 | 16,667 | 24,810 | 36,950 | Kenya |
| 38.9 | 29.9 | 16.1 | 9.3 | 4.9 | 0.9 | 27 | 29 | 33 | 41 | 49 | 59 | 68 | 77 | Kiribati |
| 38.7[4] | 29.2[4] | 16.6[4] | 9.8[4] | 4.7[4] | 1.0[4] | ... | ... | 9,740 | 10,526 | 13,892 | 18,025 | 22,939 | 28,166 | Korea, North |
| 29.9 | 31.1 | 19.5 | 12.6 | 5.5 | 1.3 | ... | ... | 21,147 | 25,142 | 32,976 | 38,124 | 43,773 | 49,914 | Korea, South |
| 36.8 | 28.3 | 24.1 | 8.6 | 1.8 | 0.4 | ... | ... | 145 | 292 | 748 | 1,370 | 2,143 | 3,007 | Kuwait |
| 42.5[4] | 26.6[4] | 16.2[4] | 9.7[4] | 4.3[4] | 0.7[4] | 930 | 1,075 | 1,949 | 2,382 | 2,962 | 3,292 | 4,010 | 4,906 | Laos |
| 42.6 | 23.8 | 16.7 | 9.1 | —7.7— | | ... | 965 | 1,364 | 1,786 | 2,470 | 2,669 | 2,967 | 3,617 | Lebanon |
| 39.1[20] | 25.5[20] | 15.5[20] | 10.4[20] | 5.2[20] | 2.3[20] | 537 | 566 | 766 | 885 | 1,043 | 1,358 | 1,760 | 2,282 | Lesotho |
| 43.2 | 28.2 | 14.7 | 7.7 | 4.4 | 1.8 | ... | ... | 758 | 1,004 | 1,393 | 1,864 | 2,605 | 3,642 | Liberia |
| 44.3[14] | 22.2[14] | 15.4[14] | 8.2[14] | 4.0[14] | 1.6[14] | 800 | 900 | 1,029 | 1,349 | 1,982 | 3,043 | 4,710 | 7,292 | Libya |
| 23.0 | 26.5 | 24.1 | 14.1 | 9.2 | 3.1 | 10 | 11 | 14 | 16 | 21 | 26 | 28 | 31 | Liechtenstein |
| 18.5 | 23.7 | 21.2 | 18.7 | 12.8 | 5.1 | 297 | 296 | 296 | 314 | 339 | 364 | 369 | 372 | Luxembourg |
| 22.9 | 36.2 | 16.7 | 12.7 | 8.8 | 2.6 | 196 | 375 | 188 | 169 | 221 | 284 | 539 | 837 | Macau |
| 44.4 | 25.7 | 14.2 | 10.0 | 4.6 | 1.1 | 3,722 | 4,034 | 4,330 | 5,370 | 6,720 | 8,714 | 11,575 | 15,550 | Madagascar |
| 44.6 | 25.7 | 14.2 | 9.0 | 4.3 | 2.0 | 1,394 | 1,696 | 3,033 | 3,481 | 4,511 | 6,046 | 8,289 | 11,631 | Malawi |
| 39.5 | 29.1 | 16.5 | 9.2 | 4.6 | 1.1 | ... | ... | 6,187 | 7,908 | 10,466 | 13,765 | 17,894 | 23,271 | Malaysia |
| 44.6[5] | 24.8[5] | 16.4[5] | 9.6[5] | 3.5[5] | 0.6[5] | 78 | 81 | 82 | 106 | 128 | 155 | 215 | 283 | Maldives |
| 44.0[20] | 24.9[20] | 16.1[20] | 8.7[20] | 4.8[20] | 1.5[20] | 2,815 | 3,388 | 3,426 | 4,224 | 5,690 | 7,653 | 8,052 | 9,541 | Mali |
| 24.1 | 23.2 | 23.0 | 15.4 | 10.5 | 3.8 | 239 | 270 | 308 | 329 | 326 | 319 | 352 | 370 | Malta |
| 30.5 | 29.3 | 15.9 | 13.0 | 8.2 | 3.0 | 175 | 200 | 222 | 252 | 287 | 326 | 331 | 337 | Martinique |
| 45.7 | 26.1 | 14.8[2] | 8.7[2] | 4.0[2] | 0.6[2] | ... | ... | 781 | 970 | 1,245 | 1,548 | 1,999 | 2,673 | Mauritania |
| 32.6 | 31.7 | 17.8 | 10.9 | 5.7 | 1.3 | 413 | 428 | 479 | 662 | 824 | 957 | 1,075 | 1,202 | Mauritius |
| 50.2[34] | 23.4[34] | 13.9[34] | 7.0[34] | 3.8[34] | 1.7[34] | ... | ... | ... | ... | ... | 52 | 85 | 111 | Mayotte |
| 43.0 | 27.8 | 14.9 | 8.4 | 4.0 | 1.8 | 16,589 | 19,815 | 26,606 | 36,369 | 50,313 | 69,655 | 86,215 | 99,604 | Mexico |
| 12.7[10] | 17.8[10] | 18.6[10] | 19.9[10] | 20.7[10] | 10.0[10] | 23 | 20 | 22 | 23 | 24 | 27 | 30 | 34 | Monaco |
| 43.1[2] | 26.2[2] | 16.3[2] | 9.2[2] | 4.1[2] | 0.9[2] | 725 | 750 | 747 | 931 | 1,248 | 1,663 | 2,146 | 2,764 | Mongolia |
| 31.5 | 27.2 | 13.8 | 10.7 | 11.6 | 5.3 | 13 | 15 | 14 | 12 | 12 | 12 | 12 | 13 | Montserrat |
| 42.2 | 28.3 | 14.1 | 9.2 | 4.8 | 1.5 | 6,980 | 7,750 | 8,953 | 11,640 | 15,126 | 19,082 | 25,100 | 33,018 | Morocco |
| 44.4 | 26.7 | 15.9 | 8.7 | 3.6 | 0.7 | 3,890 | 5,086 | 5,742 | 7,046 | 9,140 | 12,103 | 15,696 | 20,463 | Mozambique |
| 44.1[5,36] | 33.1[5,36] | 11.4[5,36] | 8.5[5,36] | 1.9[5,36] | 1.0[5,36] | 3 | 3 | 4 | 5 | 7 | 8 | 8 | 7 | Nauru |
| 41.4 | 25.5 | 17.4 | 10.0 | 4.7 | 1.0 | 6,250 | 7,000 | 8,000 | 9,180 | 11,232 | 14,642 | 18,910 | 23,176 | Nepal |
| 19.2 | 25.6 | 22.7 | 14.8 | 11.7 | 5.1 | 7,936 | 8,834 | 10,027 | 11,417 | 12,958 | 14,150 | 14,739 | 15,245 | Netherlands, The |
| 30.0 | 29.9 | 19.5 | 11.3 | 6.7 | 2.6 | 61 | 77 | 112 | 136 | 163 | 171 | 178 | 186 | Netherlands Antilles |
| 36.2 | 26.9 | 19.5 | 11.2 | 5.1 | 1.1 | 54 | 53 | 59 | 79 | 110 | 140 | 157 | 175 | New Caledonia |
| 26.7[13] | 25.9[13] | 19.1[13] | 14.3[13] | 10.5[13] | 3.5[13] | 1,491 | 1,636 | 1,908 | 2,372 | 2,820 | 3,100 | 3,423 | 3,712 | New Zealand |
| 48.1 | 25.6 | 14.1 | 7.4 | 3.8 | 1.1 | 700 | 825 | 1,109 | 1,472 | 1,972 | 2,771 | 3,871 | 5,261 | Nicaragua |
| 45.9[2] | 25.6[2] | 14.7[2] | 8.2[2] | 4.6[2] | 1.0[2] | 1,490 | 1,700 | 2,291 | 2,913 | 4,016 | 5,510 | 7,702 | 10,832 | Niger |
| 43.0 | 31.9 | 16.5 | 5.1 | 2.5 | 1.0 | ... | ... | 33,320 | 42,366 | 56,346 | 84,446 | 108,430 | 139,230 | Nigeria |
| 38.2 | 26.9 | 14.4 | 11.3 | 6.3 | 2.8 | 4 | 4 | 4 | 4 | 4 | 3 | 2 | 2 | Niue |
| 24.2 | 16.5 | 22.7 | 20.0 | —16.7— | | 1 | 1 | 1 | 1 | 2 | 2 | 2 | 2 | Norfolk Island |

## Area and population (continued)

| country | area | | | population (latest estimate) | | | | | population (most recent census) | | | | |
|---|---|---|---|---|---|---|---|---|---|---|---|---|---|
| | square miles | square kilo- metres | rank | total midyear 1987 | rank | density | | % annual growth rate 1982–87 | census year | total | male (%) | female (%) | urban (%) |
| | | | | | | per sq mi | per sq km | | | | | | |
| Norway | 125,050 | 323,878 | 62 | 4,180,000 | 98 | 33.4 | 12.9 | 0.3 | 1986[16] | 4,159,187 | 49.4 | 50.6 | 70.3[38] |
| Oman | 120,000 | 300,000 | 66 | 1,331,000 | 127 | 11.1 | 4.4 | 4.1 | [31] | [31] | 52.9[4] | 47.1[4] | 8.8[4] |
| Pacific Is., Trust Territory of the | | | | | | | | | | | | | |
| Marshall Islands | 70 | 181 | 197 | 40,600 | 190 | 580.0 | 224.3 | 4.0 | 1980 | 30,873 | 51.3 | 48.7 | 47.8 |
| Micronesia, Federated States of | 271 | 702 | 168 | 97,400 | 173 | 359.4 | 138.7 | 3.4 | 1980 | 73,160 | 51.1 | 48.9 | 19.4 |
| Northern Mariana Islands | 184 | 477 | 176 | 21,200 | 197 | 115.2 | 44.4 | 2.9 | 1980 | 16,780 | 52.5 | 47.5 | 16.0 |
| Palau | 188 | 488 | 175 | 14,200 | 200 | 75.5 | 29.1 | 2.3 | 1986 | 13,873 | 53.3 | 46.7 | 51.4[38] |
| Pakistan | 307,374 | 796,095 | 35 | 106,187,000 | 8 | 345.5 | 133.4 | 3.0 | 1981[39] | 84,253,644 | 52.5 | 47.5 | 28.3 |
| Panama | 29,762 | 77,082 | 111 | 2,274,000 | 119 | 76.4 | 29.5 | 2.2 | 1980 | 1,831,399 | 50.7 | 49.3 | 49.7 |
| Papua New Guinea | 178,704 | 462,840 | 50 | 3,500,000 | 105 | 19.6 | 7.6 | 2.3 | 1980 | 3,010,727 | 52.3 | 47.7 | 13.1 |
| Paraguay | 157,048 | 406,752 | 54 | 3,897,000 | 100 | 24.8 | 9.6 | 2.9 | 1982 | 3,035,360 | 50.1 | 49.9 | 42.8 |
| Peru | 496,225 | 1,285,216 | 19 | 20,727,000 | 40 | 41.8 | 16.1 | 2.6 | 1981 | 17,005,210 | 49.7 | 50.3 | 64.9 |
| Philippines | 115,800 | 300,000 | 67 | 57,357,000 | 14 | 495.3 | 191.2 | 2.5 | 1980 | 48,098,460 | 50.2 | 49.8 | 37.3 |
| Pitcairn Island | 1.8 | 4.5 | 214 | 44 | 215 | 24.4 | 9.8 | –4.1 | 1987 | 68 | 54.7[13] | 45.3[13] | ... |
| Poland | 120,727 | 312,683 | 64 | 37,769,000 | 26 | 312.8 | 120.8 | 0.8 | 1978 | 35,061,450 | 48.7 | 51.3 | 57.5 |
| Portugal | 35,672 | 92,389 | 106 | 10,312,000 | 62 | 289.1 | 111.6 | 0.8 | 1981[3] | 9,833,014 | 48.2 | 51.8 | 29.7 |
| Puerto Rico | 3,515 | 9,104 | 148 | 3,277,000 | 107 | 932.3 | 360.0 | 0.1 | 1980 | 3,196,520 | 48.7 | 51.3 | 66.8 |
| Qatar | 4,400 | 11,400 | 143 | 414,000 | 147 | 94.1 | 36.3 | 9.3 | 1986 | 369,079 | 67.2 | 32.8 | 88.0[4] |
| Réunion | 982 | 2,544 | 156 | 565,000 | 140 | 575.4 | 222.1 | 1.7 | 1982[3] | 515,798 | 49.1 | 50.9 | 52.8 |
| Romania | 91,699 | 237,500 | 79 | 22,913,000 | 37 | 249.9 | 96.5 | 0.4 | 1977 | 21,559,910 | 49.3 | 50.7 | 47.5 |
| Rwanda | 10,169 | 26,338 | 131 | 6,488,000 | 85 | 638.0 | 246.3 | 3.4 | 1978 | 4,830,984 | 48.9 | 51.1 | 4.5 |
| St. Christopher and Nevis | 103 | 267 | 190 | 46,500 | 188 | 451.5 | 174.2 | 0.6 | 1980 | 43,309 | 48.1 | 51.9 | 37.1 |
| St. Helena and Ascension | 159 | 412 | 181 | 7,200 | 206 | 45.3 | 17.5 | 1.5 | 1976[40] | 5,866 | 52.0 | 48.0 | 25.8 |
| St. Lucia | 238 | 617 | 171 | 142,000 | 167 | 596.6 | 230.1 | 2.0 | 1980 | 120,300 | 47.2 | 52.8 | ... |
| St. Pierre and Miquelon | 93 | 242 | 193 | 6,000 | 208 | 64.5 | 24.8 | 0.0 | 1982 | 6,041 | 49.4 | 50.6 | ... |
| St. Vincent and the Grenadines | 150 | 389 | 182 | 112,000 | 169 | 746.7 | 287.9 | 1.2 | 1980 | 97,845 | 48.5[2] | 51.5[2] | 25.7[2] |
| San Marino | 24 | 61 | 205 | 22,100 | 196 | 920.8 | 362.3 | 0.2 | 1976 | 19,149 | 50.4 | 49.6 | 90.1[41] |
| São Tomé and Príncipe | 386 | 1,001 | 163 | 112,000 | 170 | 290.2 | 111.9 | 2.6 | 1981 | 96,611 | 49.7 | 50.3 | ... |
| Saudi Arabia | 865,000 | 2,240,000 | 12 | 12,483,000 | 56 | 14.4 | 5.6 | 4.0 | 1974 | 6,726,466 | 53.2 | 46.8 | 65.9[2] |
| Senegal | 75,955 | 196,722 | 82 | 6,793,000 | 82 | 89.4 | 34.5 | 2.6 | 1976 | 4,907,057 | 49.5 | 50.5 | 26.7 |
| Seychelles | 175 | 453 | 178 | 66,000 | 181 | 377.1 | 145.7 | 0.5 | 1977 | 61,898 | 50.4 | 49.6 | 37.2 |
| Sierra Leone | 27,699 | 71,740 | 112 | 3,803,000 | 101 | 137.3 | 53.0 | 1.9 | 1985 | 3,517,530 | 49.6 | 50.4 | 28.3[4] |
| Singapore | 240 | 622 | 170 | 2,616,000 | 114 | 10,900.1 | 4,205.8 | 1.1 | 1980 | 2,413,945 | 51.0 | 49.0 | 100.0 |
| Solomon Islands | 10,640 | 27,556 | 129 | 292,000 | 154 | 27.4 | 10.6 | 3.5 | 1976 | 196,823 | 52.2 | 47.8 | 9.3 |
| Somalia | 246,000 | 637,000 | 41 | 6,160,000 | 87 | 25.0 | 9.7 | 2.8 | 1975 | 3,253,024[1] | 49.4[2] | 50.6[2] | 30.2[2] |
| South Africa[42] | 470,412 | 1,218,363 | 24 | 34,975,000 | 27 | 74.3 | 28.7 | 2.7 | 1985[43] | 23,149,790[43] | 49.0[44] | 49.0[44] | 53.2[45] |
| Bophuthatswana | 15,444 | 40,000 | — | 1,606,000 | — | 101.3 | 39.1 | 2.7 | 1980 | 1,287,814 | 46.9[24] | 53.1[24] | 14.2[24] |
| Ciskei | 2,080 | 5,386 | — | 1,140,000 | — | 383.8 | 148.2 | 7.5 | 1985 | 831,636 | 47.3 | 52.7 | 49.8 |
| KwaNdebele | 355 | 920 | — | 278,000 | — | 783.1 | 302.2 | 8.3 | 1985 | 235,855 | 45.2[38] | 54.8[38] | 9.7[38] |
| Transkei | 16,816 | 43,553 | — | 2,832,000 | — | 163.9 | 63.3 | 2.8 | 1980 | 2,334,946 | 41.2[24] | 58.8[24] | 3.2[24] |
| Venda | 2,393 | 6,198 | — | 516,000 | — | 187.3 | 72.3 | 5.8 | 1985 | 459,986 | 41.0[38] | 59.0[38] | 2.1[38] |
| South West Africa/Namibia | 317,818 | 823,144 | 33 | 1,198,000 | 129 | 3.8 | 1.5 | 2.4 | 1981 | 1,040,708 | 49.2 | 50.8 | 26.0 |
| Spain | 194,898 | 504,783 | 48 | 38,832,000 | 25 | 199.2 | 76.9 | 0.4 | 1981 | 37,746,260 | 49.1 | 50.9 | 72.8[2] |
| Sri Lanka | 25,332 | 65,610 | 114 | 16,353,000 | 47 | 645.5 | 249.2 | 1.5 | 1981 | 14,848,364 | 50.8 | 49.2 | 21.5 |
| Sudan, The | 966,757 | 2,503,890 | 9 | 25,562,000 | 32 | 26.4 | 10.2 | 3.9 | 1983 | 20,564,364 | 50.8 | 49.2 | 20.6[4] |
| Suriname | 63,251 | 163,820 | 87 | 415,000 | 146 | 6.6 | 2.5 | 2.7 | 1980 | 354,860 | 49.5 | 50.5 | 44.8[2] |
| Swaziland | 6,704 | 17,364 | 139 | 716,000 | 139 | 106.8 | 41.2 | 3.7 | 1986 | 676,089 | 46.7[20] | 53.3[20] | 15.2[20] |
| Sweden | 173,732 | 449,964 | 52 | 8,387,000 | 71 | 48.3 | 18.6 | 0.1 | 1986[16] | 8,381,515 | 49.4 | 50.6 | 83.1[38] |
| Switzerland | 15,943 | 41,293 | 121 | 6,586,000 | 84 | 413.1 | 159.5 | 0.4 | 1980[46] | 6,365,960 | 48.9 | 51.1 | 57.1 |
| Syria | 71,498 | 185,180 | 84 | 10,969,000 | 58 | 153.4 | 59.2 | 3.3 | 1981 | 9,052,628 | 51.1 | 48.9 | 47.0 |
| Taiwan | 13,900 | 36,000 | 123 | 19,630,000 | 41 | 1,412.2 | 545.3 | 1.4 | 1980[3] | 17,968,797 | 52.2 | 47.8 | 70.6[2] |
| Tanzania | 364,881 | 945,037 | 30 | 23,217,000 | 34 | 63.6 | 24.6 | 3.2 | 1978 | 17,512,611 | 49.0 | 51.0 | 13.8 |
| Thailand | 198,115 | 513,115 | 47 | 53,722,000 | 18 | 271.2 | 104.7 | 1.9 | 1980 | 44,824,540 | 49.8 | 50.2 | 17.0 |
| Togo | 21,925 | 56,785 | 115 | 3,158,000 | 108 | 144.0 | 55.6 | 2.8 | 1981 | 2,705,250 | 48.7 | 51.3 | 15.2 |
| Tokelau | 4.7 | 12.2 | 212 | 1,600 | 213 | 340.4 | 131.1 | 0.3 | 1981 | 1,572 | 49.4 | 50.6 | — |
| Tonga | 288 | 747 | 167 | 94,800 | 174 | 329.2 | 126.9 | 0.5 | 1986 | 94,535 | 50.3 | 49.7 | 24.7[20] |
| Trinidad and Tobago | 1,978 | 5,124 | 151 | 1,221,000 | 128 | 617.3 | 238.3 | 1.8 | 1980 | 1,079,791 | 50.0 | 50.0 | 56.9[2] |
| Tunisia | 59,664 | 154,530 | 88 | 7,662,000 | 75 | 128.4 | 49.6 | 2.6 | 1984 | 6,975,450 | 50.8 | 49.2 | 52.8 |
| Turkey | 300,948 | 779,452 | 36 | 52,845,000 | 19 | 175.6 | 67.8 | 2.5 | 1985 | 50,664,558 | 50.7[38] | 49.3[38] | 53.7 |
| Turks and Caicos Islands | 193 | 500 | 174 | 10,300 | 203 | 53.4 | 20.6 | 6.8 | 1980 | 7,413 | 48.3 | 51.7 | — |
| Tuvalu | 9.3 | 24.0 | 208 | 8,200 | 204 | 881.7 | 341.7 | 1.3 | 1985 | 8,229 | 47.4 | 52.6 | ... |
| Uganda | 93,070 | 241,040 | 77 | 15,514,000 | 50 | 166.7 | 64.4 | 2.8 | 1980 | 12,636,179 | 49.5 | 50.5 | 8.1 |
| U.S.S.R. | 8,649,500 | 22,402,200 | 1 | 282,811,000 | 3 | 32.7 | 12.6 | 0.9 | 1979 | 262,436,227 | 46.6 | 53.4 | 62.3 |
| United Arab Emirates | 30,000 | 77,700 | 110 | 1,856,000 | 123 | 61.9 | 23.9 | 8.9 | 1985 | 1,622,464 | 64.9 | 35.1 | 80.8[13] |
| United Kingdom | 94,251 | 244,110 | 76 | 56,878,000 | 16 | 603.5 | 233.0 | 0.2 | 1981[48] | 56,379,000 | 48.6 | 51.4 | 89.6 |
| United States | 3,679,192 | 9,529,063 | 4 | 243,773,000 | 4 | 66.3 | 25.6 | 1.0 | 1980[49] | 226,545,805 | 48.6 | 51.4 | 73.7 |
| Uruguay | 68,037 | 176,215 | 86 | 3,058,000 | 110 | 44.9 | 17.4 | 0.8 | 1985 | 2,940,200 | 48.7 | 51.3 | 86.2 |
| Vanuatu | 4,707 | 12,190 | 141 | 145,000 | 166 | 30.8 | 11.9 | 3.2 | 1979 | 111,251 | 53.1 | 46.9 | 17.8 |
| Venezuela | 352,144 | 912,050 | 32 | 18,272,000 | 42 | 51.9 | 20.0 | 2.8 | 1981 | 14,516,735 | 50.0 | 50.0 | 85.7 |
| Vietnam | 128,052 | 331,653 | 60 | 62,468,000 | 12 | 487.8 | 188.4 | 2.2 | 1979 | 52,741,766 | 48.5 | 51.5 | 19.2 |
| Virgin Islands (U.S.) | 136 | 352 | 185 | 112,000 | 171 | 823.5 | 318.2 | 1.9 | 1980 | 96,569 | 47.8 | 52.2 | 29.6 |
| Wallis and Futuna | 106 | 274 | 189 | 15,000 | 199 | 141.5 | 54.7 | 4.7 | 1983 | 12,408 | 50.5 | 49.5 | ... |
| West Bank | 2,270 | 5,900 | 149 | 844,000 | 134 | 371.8 | 143.1 | 2.6 | 1985[16] | 793,400 | 49.8 | 50.2 | ... |
| Western Sahara | 97,344 | 252,120 | 73 | 185,000 | 160 | 1.9 | 0.7 | 2.6 | 1970 | 76,425 | ... | ... | ... |
| Western Samoa | 1,093 | 2,831 | 154 | 161,000 | 164 | 147.3 | 56.9 | 0.6 | 1981 | 156,349 | 51.8 | 48.2 | 21.2 |
| Yemen (Aden) | 130,066 | 336,869 | 59 | 2,285,000 | 118 | 17.6 | 6.8 | 2.6 | 1973 | 1,590,275 | 49.5 | 50.5 | 33.3 |
| Yemen (Ṣan'ā') | 75,300 | 195,000 | 83 | 8,386,000 | 72 | 111.4 | 43.0 | 2.5 | 1986 | 9,274,173[50] | 47.3[13] | 52.7[13] | 10.2[13] |
| Yugoslavia | 98,766 | 255,804 | 72 | 23,433,000 | 33 | 237.3 | 91.6 | 0.7 | 1981 | 22,424,711 | 49.4 | 50.6 | 47.3 |
| Zaire | 905,365 | 2,344,885 | 11 | 31,804,000 | 28 | 35.1 | 13.6 | 2.2 | 1984 | 29,671,407 | 49.2 | 50.8 | 36.6[4] |
| Zambia | 290,586 | 752,614 | 38 | 7,135,000 | 79 | 24.6 | 9.5 | 3.4 | 1980 | 5,679,808 | 49.0 | 51.0 | 43.0 |
| Zimbabwe | 150,873 | 390,759 | 55 | 8,640,000 | 69 | 57.3 | 22.1 | 2.8 | 1982 | 7,532,000 | 49.3 | 50.7 | 23.0 |

[1]Settled population only.   [2]1980 estimate.   [3]Data are for de jure population.   [4]1985 estimate.   [5]1977 census.   [6]Includes residents abroad; excludes visitors.   [7]Excludes institutional population.   [8]1982 estimate.   [9]Excludes institutional population, residents abroad, and visitors.   [10]1975 census.   [11]Includes residents abroad and visitors.   [12]Excludes visitors.   [13]1981 census.   [14]1973 census.   [15]1974 census.   [16]Civil register; not a census.   [17]1985 register.   [18]1983 estimate.   [19]Excludes the Sinai and residents abroad.   [20]1976 census.   [21]Excludes marine detachment.   [22]Excludes visitors, transients, and family members of British servicemen.   [23]1984 estimate.   [24]1970 census.   [25]Data exclude Alderney (1981 estimated population 2,100) and Sark (1981 estimated population 500).   [26]Excludes residents abroad, visitors, and Vietnamese refugees.   [27]Excluding territory occupied after 1967.   [28]Includes East Jerusalem and Israeli residents in the occupied territories.

| 0–14 | 15–29 | 30–44 | 45–59 | 60–74 | 75 and older | 1930 | 1940 | 1950 | 1960 | 1970 | 1980 | 1990 projection | 2000 projection | country |
|---|---|---|---|---|---|---|---|---|---|---|---|---|---|---|
| | | age distribution (%) | | | | population (by decade, '000s) | | | | | | | | |
| 19.8 | 23.2 | 21.3 | 14.4 | 14.7 | 6.6 | 2,807 | 2,973 | 3,265 | 3,581 | 3,877 | 4,086 | 4,220 | 4,356 | Norway |
| 44.3[4] | 24.8[4] | 18.0[4] | 8.9[4] | 3.5[4] | 0.6[4] | ... | ... | 390 | 494 | 657 | 984 | 1,457 | 1,973 | Oman |
| | | | | | | | | | | | | | | Pacific Is., Trust Territory of the |
| 50.5 | 25.2 | 12.1 | 7.0 | 4.2 | 1.0 | 10 | ... | 11 | 15 | 22 | 31 | 46 | 67 | Marshall Islands |
| 46.4 | 26.8 | 12.6 | 8.5 | 4.5 | 1.1 | 32 | ... | 30 | 40 | 57 | 77 | 108 | 151 | Micronesia, Federated States of |
| 40.6 | 27.9 | 17.8 | 9.2 | 3.8 | 0.8 | 19 | 48 | 6 | 9 | 10 | 17 | 23 | 31 | Northern Mariana Islands |
| 35.0 | 29.6 | 17.9 | 9.6 | 6.0 | 1.9 | 8 | 25 | 6 | 9 | 11 | 12 | 15 | 19 | Palau |
| 44.5 | 23.9 | 15.4 | 9.3 | 5.3 | 1.6 | 23,600 | 28,300 | 36,450 | 45,851 | 64,449 | 86,143 | 112,236 | 137,651 | Pakistan |
| 39.1 | 28.1 | 16.7 | 9.5 | 5.1 | 1.5 | 523 | 620 | 800 | 1,082 | 1,458 | 1,956 | 2,418 | 2,893 | Panama |
| 43.0 | 25.9 | 17.0 | 10.4 | 3.5 | 0.2 | 1,306 | 1.308 | 1,613 | 1,920 | 2,419 | 2,999 | 3,741 | 4,673 | Papua New Guinea |
| 41.1 | 28.1 | 15.4 | 9.1 | 4.8 | 1.5 | 880 | 1,111 | 1,371 | 1,778 | 2,290 | 3,168 | 4,231 | 5,405 | Paraguay |
| 41.2 | 27.9 | 15.6 | 9.3 | 4.4 | 1.6 | 5,752 | 6,784 | 7,975 | 9,993 | 13,248 | 17,295 | 22,332 | 27,952 | Peru |
| 42.0 | 28.5 | 15.6 | 8.6 | 4.3 | 1.0 | 13,094 | 16,459 | 20,988 | 27,561 | 36,850 | 48,316 | 61,483 | 74,057 | Philippines |
| 32.1[13] | 13.2[13] | 18.9[13] | 13.2[13] | 9.4[13] | 13.2[13] | 0.19 | 0.20 | 0.14 | 0.14 | 0.09 | 0.06 | ... | ... | Pitcairn Island |
| 23.9 | 27.4 | 18.5 | 16.9 | 9.9 | 3.4 | 29,500 | 31,500 | 24,824 | 29,561 | 32,657 | 35,578 | 38,726 | 42,094 | Poland |
| 25.5 | 23.5 | 18.0 | 17.2 | 11.9 | 3.9 | 6,804 | 7,696 | 8,405 | 8,826 | 9,040 | 9,781 | 10,547 | 10,877 | Portugal |
| 31.6 | 26.4 | 18.5 | 12.3 | 8.3 | 2.9 | 1,552 | 1,880 | 2,219 | 2,358 | 2,718 | 3,206 | 3,285 | 3,312 | Puerto Rico |
| 27.8 | 29.3 | 32.3 | 8.6 | 1.6 | 0.4 | ... | ... | 47 | 59 | 151 | 225 | 444 | 560 | Qatar |
| 35.6 | 29.8 | —27.6— | | —6.9— | | 198 | 221 | 244 | 338 | 447 | 507 | 595 | 706 | Réunion |
| 25.7 | 23.7 | 19.6 | 17.1 | 10.9 | 3.0 | 14,141 | 15,907 | 16,311 | 18,407 | 20,799 | 22,201 | 23,181 | 24,098 | Romania |
| 47.7[2] | 25.7[2] | 14.2[2] | 8.4[2] | 3.4[2] | 0.6[2] | 1,600 | 1,910 | 2,189 | 2,740 | 3,679 | 5,144 | 7,179 | 10,123 | Rwanda |
| 37.2 | 30.4 | 9.5 | 9.4 | 10.0 | 3.5 | 38 | 43 | 49 | 51 | 46 | 44 | 48 | 51 | St. Christopher and Nevis |
| 34.0 | 27.5 | 16.7 | 10.8 | 8.4 | 2.6 | 4 | 5 | 5 | 5 | 5 | 6 | 8 | 9 | St. Helena and Ascension |
| 49.6 | 21.3 | 11.6 | 9.8 | 5.5 | 2.2 | 60 | 70 | 79 | 94 | 100 | 124 | 151 | 185 | St. Lucia |
| 28.7 | 26.0 | 20.4 | 13.2 | 8.5 | 3.2 | 4 | 4 | 5 | 5 | 5 | 6 | 6 | 6 | St. Pierre and Miquelon |
| 41.7[2] | 33.3[2] | 11.5[2] | 7.3[2] | 5.2[2] | 1.0[2] | 53 | 61 | 67 | 80 | 86 | 103 | 116 | 132 | St. Vincent and the Grenadines |
| 24.4 | 23.0 | 19.9 | 17.4 | 11.4 | 3.9 | 10 | 10 | 13 | 15 | 19 | 21 | 22 | 23 | San Marino |
| 46.3 | 25.0 | 11.6 | 10.0 | 5.3 | 1.8 | ... | 60 | 60 | 64 | 74 | 93 | 122 | 157 | São Tomé and Príncipe |
| 46.7 | 23.9 | 15.2 | 7.9 | —6.3— | | ... | ... | 3,200 | 4,175 | 6,120 | 9,372 | 13,988 | 19,824 | Saudi Arabia |
| 43.1 | 26.2 | 15.3 | 9.1 | 4.6 | 1.5 | ... | ... | 2,600 | 3,076 | 4,267 | 5,672 | 7,377 | 9,765 | Senegal |
| 39.6 | 26.3 | 14.0 | 10.8 | 6.8 | 2.1 | 27 | 32 | 34 | 42 | 54 | 63 | 67 | 70 | Seychelles |
| 40.7[15] | 24.8[15] | 17.4[15] | 9.2[15] | —7.9[15]— | | 1,600 | 1,700 | 1,809 | 2,165 | 2,692 | 3,333 | 4,025 | 4,861 | Sierra Leone |
| 27.0 | 34.7 | 19.8 | 11.3 | 5.9 | 1.3 | 596 | 751 | 1,022 | 1,639 | 2,075 | 2,414 | 2,706 | 3,030 | Singapore |
| 47.8 | 24.1 | 14.5 | 8.4 | 3.6 | 1.3 | 94 | 94 | 104 | 125 | 163 | 229 | 324 | 457 | Solomon Islands |
| 44.1[2] | 25.5[2] | 15.8[2] | 9.5[2] | 4.3[2] | 0.7[2] | ... | ... | 1,826 | 2,226 | 2,790 | 5,074 | 6,693 | 8,827 | Somalia |
| 37.7[45] | —46.3[45]— | | —14.7[45]— | | 1.3[45] | 8,541 | 10,353 | 12,458 | 15,925 | 22,460 | 29,077 | 37,984 | 50,494 | South Africa[42] |
| 52.6[24] | 21.3[24] | 10.4[24] | —13.6[24]— | | 2.1[24] | ... | ... | ... | ... | 880 | 1,335 | 1,738 | 2,263 | Bophuthatswana |
| 44.9 | 26.2 | 15.0 | 6.9 | 5.5 | 1.5 | ... | ... | ... | ... | 530 | 678 | 1,424 | 2,992 | Ciskei |
| ... | ... | ... | ... | ... | ... | ... | ... | ... | ... | ... | 156 | 356 | 809 | KwaNdebele |
| 43.7[24] | 21.5[24] | 13.3[24] | —20.3[24]— | | 1.2[24] | ... | ... | ... | ... | 1,746 | 2,336 | 3,076 | 4,050 | Transkei |
| 43.3[24] | 20.3[24] | 12.4[24] | —22.7[24]— | | 1.3[24] | ... | ... | ... | ... | 269 | 345 | 613 | 1,091 | Venda |
| 44.0[2] | 26.0[2] | 15.5[2] | 9.3[2] | 4.3[2] | 0.9[2] | 283 | 336 | 405 | 522 | 761 | 989 | 1,288 | 1,639 | South West Africa/ Namibia |
| 25.6[3] | 23.2[3] | 17.9[3] | 17.6[3] | 11.4[3] | 4.2[3] | 23,445 | 25,757 | 27,868 | 30,303 | 33,779 | 37,386 | 39,322 | 40,747 | Spain |
| 35.3 | 29.6 | 17.9 | 10.6 | 5.2 | 1.4 | 5,253 | 5,972 | 7,678 | 9,889 | 12,514 | 14,747 | 17,081 | 19,752 | Sri Lanka |
| 45.1[4] | 26.1[4] | 15.6[4] | 8.7[4] | 3.8[4] | 0.7[4] | 7,500 | 8,500 | 9,322 | 11,256 | 14,090 | 19,553 | 28,651 | 41,905 | Sudan, The |
| 39.3 | 29.5 | 13.8 | 10.0 | 4.5 | 2.8 | 170 | 193 | 215 | 247 | 292 | 357 | 448 | 579 | Suriname |
| 47.7[20] | 25.2[20] | 13.7[20] | 7.9[20] | 3.7[20] | 1.4[20] | 139 | 154 | 253 | 320 | 409 | 559 | 828 | 1,098 | Swaziland |
| 17.9 | 20.7 | 22.2 | 16.1 | 15.5 | 7.6 | 6,142 | 6,371 | 7,041 | 7,498 | 8,081 | 8,310 | 8,432 | 8,539 | Sweden |
| 19.2 | 23.1 | 22.0 | 17.4 | 12.7 | 5.6 | 4,066 | 4,234 | 4,715 | 5,429 | 6,270 | 6,385 | 6,666 | 6,939 | Switzerland |
| 47.5[2] | 27.4[2] | 12.4[2] | 7.9[2] | 3.6[2] | 1.1[2] | ... | 2,597 | 3,495 | 4,561 | 6,305 | 8,704 | 12,107 | 16,827 | Syria |
| 32.1 | 32.1 | 16.5 | 12.6 | 5.7 | 1.0 | 4,614 | 5,987 | 7,619 | 10,792 | 14,676 | 17,642 | 20,476 | 23,569 | Taiwan |
| 46.2 | 24.9 | 14.4 | 8.5 | 4.5 | 1.6 | ... | ... | 7,892 | 10,073 | 13,273 | 18,580 | 25,635 | 36,008 | Tanzania |
| 38.3 | 30.1 | 16.1 | 10.1 | 4.3 | 1.1 | 11,838 | 15,296 | 20,010 | 26,392 | 35,745 | 46,961 | 56,300 | 64,132 | Thailand |
| 44.4[2] | 25.8[2] | 15.6[2] | 9.1[2] | 4.3[2] | 0.8[2] | 750 | 834 | 1,201 | 1,465 | 1,954 | 2,601 | 3,431 | 4,522 | Togo |
| 42.9 | 22.5 | 12.7 | 10.2 | 7.2 | 4.5 | 1.1 | 1.3 | 1.5 | 1.8 | 1.7 | 1.6 | 1.6 | 1.7 | Tokelau |
| 44.4[20] | 26.2[20] | 14.8[20] | 9.5[20] | 4.0[20] | 1.1[20] | 28 | 37 | 50 | 65 | 80 | 92 | 96 | 101 | Tonga |
| 34.2 | 30.9 | 16.3 | 10.0 | 6.2 | 1.7 | 408 | 503 | 668 | 828 | 941 | 1,082 | 1,289 | 1,544 | Trinidad and Tobago |
| 39.7 | 28.8 | 14.2 | 10.7 | 5.4 | 1.2 | 2,381 | 2,887 | 3,530 | 4,221 | 5,137 | 6,392 | 8,285 | 10,751 | Tunisia |
| 39.0[38] | 27.7[38] | 15.5[38] | 10.9[38] | 5.0[38] | 1.5[38] | 14,448 | 17,723 | 20,809 | 27,509 | 35,321 | 44,438 | 56,941 | 73,029 | Turkey |
| 41.4 | 26.7 | 11.8 | 11.0 | 7.0 | 2.2 | 5 | 6 | 6 | 6 | 6 | 7 | 11 | 13 | Turks and Caicos Islands |
| 31.8[47] | 31.7[47] | 15.2[47] | 13.2[47] | 6.3[47] | 1.7[47] | 4 | 4 | 5 | 5 | 6 | 8 | 8 | 8 | Tuvalu |
| 47.8[2] | 26.0[2] | 14.0[2] | 8.0[2] | 3.5[2] | 0.6[2] | ... | ... | 5,969 | 7,551 | 9,806 | 12,786 | 16,928 | 22,400 | Uganda |
| 24.3[2] | 26.6[2] | 19.0[2] | 16.9[2] | 9.6[2] | 3.4[2] | 179,000 | 195,000 | 180,075 | 214,335 | 241,700 | 265,542 | 290,761 | 318,909 | U.S.S.R. |
| 31.9[4] | 24.9[4] | 32.1[4] | 8.7[4] | 1.9[4] | 0.5[4] | ... | ... | 70 | 90 | 223 | 980 | 2,419 | 5,849 | United Arab Emirates |
| 20.6 | 22.8 | 19.4 | 16.9 | 14.4 | 5.8 | 46,038 | 48,226 | 50,290 | 52,372 | 55,632 | 56,330 | 57,224 | 58,392 | United Kingdom |
| 22.6 | 27.4 | 19.1 | 15.2 | 11.3 | 4.4 | 123,616 | 132,594 | 152,271 | 180,671 | 204,879 | 227,757 | 249,657 | 267,995 | United States |
| 26.6 | 22.8 | 18.3 | 16.5 | 11.4 | 4.3 | 1,734 | 1,974 | 2,194 | 2,531 | 2,824 | 2,908 | 3,128 | 3,364 | Uruguay |
| 45.3 | 27.5 | 15.0 | 7.7 | 3.4 | 1.1 | ... | ... | 43 | 52 | 65 | 86 | 118 | 159 | 215 | Vanuatu |
| 40.5 | 29.9 | 15.8 | 8.7 | 4.0 | 1.1 | 2,980 | 3,740 | 5,145 | 7,635 | 10,559 | 15,020 | 19,735 | 24,715 | Venezuela |
| 42.5[2] | 28.6[2] | 13.2[2] | 9.6[2] | 5.0[2] | 1.1[2] | ... | ... | 24,600 | 30,200 | 40,064 | 53,722 | 66,573 | 82,310 | Vietnam |
| 36.0 | 24.2 | 21.5 | 11.1 | 5.7 | 1.4 | 22 | 25 | 27 | 32 | 75 | 98 | 118 | 143 | Virgin Islands (U.S.) |
| 45.8 | 24.8 | 13.8 | 9.0 | 5.7 | 0.9 | ... | ... | 7 | 8 | 9 | 11 | 17 | 26 | Wallis and Futuna |
| 46.6 | 30.1 | 9.5 | 8.2 | —5.7— | | ... | ... | ... | ... | 608 | 721 | 909 | 1,162 | West Bank |
| 42.9 | 27.2 | 16.3 | 7.4 | 4.4 | 1.8 | ... | ... | 14 | 32 | 76 | 155 | 200 | 257 | Western Sahara |
| 44.3 | 29.1 | 12.2 | 9.0 | 3.8 | 1.0 | 45 | 61 | 82 | 111 | 143 | 155 | 164 | 173 | Western Samoa |
| 47.3 | 20.8 | 15.8 | 8.6 | —6.6— | | ... | ... | 907 | 1,109 | 1,436 | 1,910 | 2,468 | 3,191 | Yemen (Aden) |
| 45.7[13] | 23.2[13] | 15.1[13] | 10.5[13] | 4.7[13] | 0.8[13] | ... | ... | 3,622 | 4,429 | 4,840 | 7,059 | 9,029 | 11,550 | Yemen (San'ā') |
| 24.5 | 25.0 | 19.8 | 18.3 | 8.3 | 3.5 | 14,360 | 16,425 | 16,346 | 18,402 | 20,371 | 22,304 | 23,925 | 25,643 | Yugoslavia |
| 45.2[4] | 25.9[4] | 15.5[4] | 8.7[4] | 3.9[4] | 0.7[4] | 8,764 | 10,370 | 13,055 | 16,151 | 21,368 | 27,406 | 34,138 | 42,980 | Zaire |
| 46.9[2] | 25.7[2] | 14.7[2] | 8.3[2] | 3.6[2] | 0.7[2] | 1,272 | 1,484 | 2,473 | 3,219 | 4,295 | 5,648 | 7,912 | 11,237 | Zambia |
| 51.0 | 26.3 | 13.4 | 6.5 | 1.2 | 1.6 | 1,100 | 1,461 | 2,276 | 3,538 | 5,308 | 7,100 | 9,369 | 11,943 | Zimbabwe |

[29]Excluding West Bank.   [30]1962 census.   [31]No census ever taken.   [32]1967 census.   [33]Island of Mauritius only.   [34]1978 census.   [35]Including 163,868 in Western Sahara.   [36]Indigenous population only.   [37]A census was taken in 1973, but the results were repudiated.   [38]1980 census.   [39]Excludes Afghan refugees.   [40]Excludes the island of Tristan da Cunha and military personnel.   [41]1987 estimate.   [42]Includes Black states shown separately.   [43]Excludes Bophuthatswana, Ciskei, KwaNdebele, Transkei, and Venda.   [44]1980 census; excludes Bophuthatswana, Ciskei, Transkei, and Venda.   [45]1980 census; excludes Bophuthatswana, Transkei, and Venda.   [46]Includes resident aliens; excludes seasonal workers.   [47]1979 census.   [48]Includes residents abroad and foreign military personnel; excludes visitors.   [49]Excludes 515,000 armed forces overseas.   [50]Includes national abroad.

# Major cities and national capitals

The following table lists the principal cities or municipalities (those exceeding 100,000 in population) of the countries of the world, together with figures for each national capital (indicated by a ★), regardless of size.

Most of the populations given refer to a so-called city proper, that is, a legally defined, incorporated or chartered area defined by administrative boundaries and by national or state law as a "city" (in some cases, only as a locality that is "urban" in nature, or perhaps, in the smallest countries, simply as "the settlement"). There are many variations on this basic concept, however. One that is encountered frequently is the municipality, or commune, similar to the medieval city-state in that the city is governed together with its immediately adjoining, economically dependent areas, whether urban or rural in nature. Some countries define no other demographic or legal entities within such communes or municipalities, but many identify a centre, seat, head (*cabecera*), or locality that corresponds to the most densely populated, compact, contiguous core of the municipality. Secondary centres may also be defined, and in certain countries these may be places of considerable size, depending on how long the municipality's boundaries have gone unchanged. Because the amount of work involved in defining these "centres" carefully may be considerable, the necessary manpower, employment and commuting data, and cartographic resources usually exist only at the time of a national census (generally five or ten years apart). Between censuses, therefore, it may be possible only to track the growth of the municipality as a whole. Thus, in order to provide the most up-to-date data for cities in this table, figures referring to municipalities or communes may be given (identified by the abbreviation "MU"), even though the country itself may define a smaller, more closely knit city proper. Specific identification of municipalities is provided in this table *only* when the country also publishes data for a more narrowly defined city proper; it is *not* provided when the sole published figure is the municipality, whether or not this is the proper local administrative term for the entity.

Since many national capitals are first-order administrative subdivisions (equivalent to a U.S. state) in their national hierarchy of local government, care has been taken to provide data referring to the actual urban core of the subdivision (the demographic "city proper"). Thus, data are provided for the city of Brasília, or Kuala Lumpur, but not for the national or federal capital areas that contain them. Problems also exist in the identification of cities in terms of named legal entities. There is, for example, a single municipality (*commune*) named Brussel (Brussels) at the centre of the Brussels agglomeration in Belgium; the *commune* numbers only about 140,000 population, while the agglomeration, which is understood by most people to constitute the city, numbers nearly a million. Both are shown so as to apprise the reader of the existence of a problem.

For certain countries, more than one form of the name of the city is given, usually to permit recognition of recent place name changes or of *forms* of the place name likely to be encountered in press stories if the title of the city's entry in the *Encyclopædia Britannica* is spelled according to a different romanization or spelling policy. One such case is China, for which city names are spelled first according to a long-established scholarly system called Wade–Giles, while current press references are likely to be spelled according to the more recent Chinese romanization system, Pinyin. (Peking in Wade–Giles, for example, would be spelled Pei-ching; in Pinyin, Beijing.) The use of the conventional Western spelling Peking in this table is supplemented by provision of the Pinyin alternative spelling.

Sources for this data were usually the national census and statistical abstracts of the countries concerned, supplemented by correspondence with most national statistical offices to solicit data not yet issued as part of the national publishing program.

## Major cities and national capitals

| country<br>city | population |
|---|---|
| **Afghanistan** (1984 est.) | |
| Herāt | 159,804 |
| ★ Kābul | 1,179,341 |
| Mazār-e Sharīf | 117,723 |
| Qandahār | 203,177 |
| **Albania** (1983 est.) | |
| ★ Tiranë | 206,100 |
| **Algeria** (1987) | |
| ★ Algiers | 1,483,000 |
| Annaba | 310,000 |
| Batna | 182,000 |
| Bejaïa | 124,122[1] |
| Blida (el-Boulaida) | 165,000 |
| Boufarik | 112,000[2] |
| ech-Cheliff | 118,996[1] |
| Constantine (Qacentina) | 438,000 |
| Oran (Wahran) | 590,000 |
| Sétif | 168,000 |
| Sidi bel Abbes | 146,653[1] |
| Skikda | 141,159[1] |
| Tizi Ouzou | 100,749[1] |
| Tlemcen (Tilimsen) | 146,089[1] |
| **American Samoa** (1985 est.) | |
| ★ Pago Pago | 3,400 |
| **Andorra** (1986) | |
| ★ Andorra la Vella | 15,639 |
| **Angola** (1987 est.) | |
| ★ Luanda | 1,134,000 |
| Lubango | 105,000[3] |
| **Anguilla** (1984) | |
| ★ The Valley | 1,042 |
| **Antigua and Barbuda** (1982 est.) | |
| ★ Saint John's | 30,000 |
| **Argentina** (1980) | |
| Almirante Brown | 332,548 |
| Avellaneda | 330,654 |
| Bahía Blanca | 220,765 |
| Berazategui | 200,926 |
| ★ Buenos Aires | 2,922,829 |
| Caseros | 340,343 |
| Córdoba | 968,829 |
| Corrientes | 180,612 |
| Esteban Echeverría | 187,969 |
| Florencio Varela | 172,654 |
| General San Martín | 384,306 |
| General Sarmiento | 499,648 |
| Godoy Cruz | 141,553 |
| Guaymallén | 157,334 |
| La Plata | 454,884 |
| Lanús | 465,891 |
| Lomas de Zamora | 508,620 |
| Mar del Plata | 407,024 |
| Mendoza | 118,427 |
| Merlo | 282,828 |
| Moreno | 193,626 |
| Morón | 596,769 |
| Paraná | 161,638 |
| Posadas | 143,889 |
| Quilmes | 441,780 |
| Resistencia | 218,438 |
| Río Cuarto | 110,254 |
| Rosario | 875,664 |
| Salta | 260,744 |
| San Fernando | 134,156 |
| San Isidro | 287,048 |
| San Juan | 117,731 |
| San Justo | 946,715 |
| San Miguel de Tucumán | 392,888 |
| San Salvador de Jujuy | 124,950 |
| Santa Fe | 287,240 |
| Santiago del Estero | 148,758 |
| Tigre | 205,926 |
| Vicente López | 289,815 |
| **Aruba** (1986 est.) | |
| ★ Oranjestad | 19,800 |
| **Australia** (1986 est.)[4] | |
| Adelaide | 993,100 |
| Brisbane | 1,171,300 |
| ★ Canberra | 285,800 |
| Geelong | 148,300 |
| Gold Coast | 219,300 |
| Hobart | 180,300 |
| Melbourne | 2,942,000 |
| Newcastle | 429,300 |
| Perth | 1,025,300 |
| Sydney | 3,430,600 |
| Townsville | 103,700 |
| Wollongong | 237,600 |
| **Austria** (1981) | |
| Graz | 243,166 |
| Innsbruck | 117,287 |
| Linz | 199,910 |
| Salzburg | 139,426 |
| ★ Vienna | 1,531,346 |
| **Bahamas, The** (1980) | |
| ★ Nassau | 110,000 |
| **Bahrain** (1987 est.) | |
| ★ al-Manāmah | 146,994 |
| **Bangladesh** (1981)[5] | |
| Bākerganj (Barisāl) | 159,298 |
| Chittagong | 1,388,476 |
| Comilla | 126,130 |
| ★ Dhākā (Dacca) | 3,458,602 |
| Jessore | 149,426 |
| Khulna | 623,184 |
| Mymensingh | 107,863 |
| Pābna | 101,080 |
| Rājshāhi | 171,600 |
| Rangpur | 155,964 |
| Saidpur | 128,085 |
| Sirājganj | 104,522 |
| Sylhet | 166,847 |
| **Barbados** (1980) | |
| ★ Bridgetown | 7,552 |
| **Belgium** (1986 est.) | |
| Antwerp | 483,199 |
| Brugge (Bruges) | 117,799 |
| ★ Brussels | 137,211[3] |
| Agglomeration | 976,536 |
| Charleroi | 210,234 |
| Ghent | 234,251 |
| Liège (Luik) | 201,749 |
| Namur | 102,501 |
| Schaerbeek | 105,346[3] |
| **Belize** (1985 est.) | |
| ★ Belmopan | 4,500 |
| **Benin** (1982 est.) | |
| ★ Cotonou (official) | 487,020 |
| ★ Porto-Novo (de facto) | 208,258 |
| **Bermuda** (1985 est.) | |
| ★ Hamilton | 1,676 |
| **Bhutan** (1985 est.) | |
| ★ Paro (administrative) | 3,000 |
| ★ Thimphu (official) | 20,000 |
| **Bolivia** (1985 est.) | |
| Cochabamba | 317,251 |
| ★ La Paz (administrative) | 992,592 |
| Oruro | 178,393 |
| Potosí | 109,876[3] |
| Santa Cruz | 441,717 |
| ★ Sucre (judicial) | 86,609 |
| **Botswana** (1986 est.) | |
| ★ Gaborone | 96,100 |
| **Brazil** (1980) | |
| Americana | 121,794 |
| Anápolis | 160,520 |
| Aracaju | 288,106 |
| Araçatuba | 113,486 |
| Barra Mansa | 123,421 |
| Bauru | 178,861 |
| Belém | 758,117 |
| Belo Horizonte | 1,442,483 |
| Blumenau | 144,819 |
| ★ Brasília | 411,305 |
| Campina Grande | 222,229 |
| Campinas | 566,517 |
| Campo Grande | 282,844 |
| Campos | 174,218 |
| Canoas | 214,115 |
| Carapicuíba | 185,763 |
| Caruaru | 137,636 |
| Cascavel | 100,351 |
| Caxias do Sul | 198,824 |
| Contagem | 111,697 |
| Cuiabá | 167,894 |
| Curitiba | 843,733 |
| Diadema | 228,594 |
| Divinópolis | 108,344 |
| Duque de Caxias | 306,057 |
| Feira de Santana | 225,003 |
| Florianópolis | 153,547 |
| Fortaleza | 648,815 |
| Franca | 143,630 |
| Goiânia | 703,263 |
| Governador Valadares | 173,699 |
| Guarulhos | 395,117 |
| Imperatriz | 111,818 |
| Ipatinga | 105,083 |
| Itabuna | 129,938 |
| Jacareí | 103,652 |
| João Pessoa | 290,424 |
| Joinville | 217,074 |
| Juàzeiro do Norte | 125,248 |
| Juiz de Fora | 299,728 |
| Jundiaí | 210,015 |
| Lages | 108,768 |
| Limeira | 137,812 |
| Londrina | 258,054 |
| Maceió | 376,479 |
| Manaus | 613,068 |
| Marília | 103,904 |
| Maringá | 158,047 |
| Mauá | 205,817 |
| Mogi das Cruzes | 122,265 |
| Montes Claros | 151,881 |
| Mossoró | 118,007 |
| Natal | 376,552 |
| Nilópolis | 103,033 |
| Niterói | 386,185 |
| Nova Iguaçu | 491,802 |
| Novo Hamburgo | 132,066 |
| Olinda | 266,392 |
| Osasco | 473,856 |
| Passo Fundo | 103,121 |
| Pelotas | 197,092 |
| Petrópolis | 149,427 |
| Piracicaba | 179,395 |
| Ponta Grossa | 171,111 |
| Porto Alegre | 1,108,883 |
| Porto Velho | 101,644 |
| Presidente Prudente | 127,623 |
| Recife | 1,184,215 |
| Ribeirão Prêto | 300,704 |
| Rio Claro | 103,174 |
| Rio de Janeiro | 5,090,700 |
| Rio Grande | 124,706 |
| Salvador | 1,506,602 |
| Santa Maria | 151,202 |
| Santarém | 101,534 |
| Santo Andre | 549,278 |
| Santos | 411,023 |
| São Bernardo do Campo | 381,261 |
| São Caetano do Sul | 163,030 |
| São Carlos | 109,231 |
| São Gonçalo | 221,278 |
| São João de Meriti | 210,548 |
| São José do Rio Prêto | 171,982 |
| São José dos Campos | 268,073 |
| São Luís | 182,466 |
| São Paulo | 7,033,529 |
| São Vicente | 192,770 |
| Sorocaba | 254,718 |
| Taubaté | 155,371 |
| Teresina | 339,264 |
| Uberaba | 180,296 |
| Uberlândia | 230,400 |
| Vitória | 144,143 |
| Vitória da Conquista | 125,717 |
| Volta Redonda | 177,772 |
| **British Virgin Islands** (1980) | |
| ★ Road Town | 2,525 |
| **Brunei** (1985 est.) | |
| ★ Bandar Seri Begawan | 55,000 |
| **Bulgaria** (1986 est.) | |
| Burgas | 182,570 |
| Pleven | 129,782 |
| Plovdiv | 342,131 |
| Ruse | 183,746 |
| Shumen | 100,122 |
| ★ Sofia | 1,114,962 |
| Sliven | 102,455 |
| Stara Zagora | 150,906 |
| Tolbukhin | 109,069 |
| Varna | 302,211 |
| **Burkina Faso** (1985) | |
| Bobo Dioulasso | 231,162 |
| ★ Ouagadougou | 442,223 |
| **Burma** (1983) | |
| Bassein | 144,092 |
| Mandalay | 532,895 |
| Monywa | 106,873 |
| Moulmein | 219,991 |
| Pegu | 150,447 |
| ★ Rangoon | 2,458,712 |
| Sittwe (Akyab) | 107,907 |
| Taunggye | 107,607 |
| **Burundi** (1986 est.) | |
| ★ Bujumbura | 272,622 |
| **Cameroon** (1985 est.) | |
| Douala | 852,700 |
| Maroua | 100,200 |
| Nkongsamba | 105,200 |
| ★ Yaoundé | 583,500 |
| **Canada** (1981) | |
| Brampton | 149,030 |
| Burlington | 114,853 |
| Burnaby | 136,494 |
| Calgary | 592,743 |
| East York | 101,974 |
| Edmonton | 532,246 |
| Etobicoke | 298,713 |
| Halifax | 114,594 |
| Hamilton | 306,434 |
| Kitchener | 139,734 |
| Laval | 268,335 |
| London | 254,280 |
| Longueuil | 124,320 |
| Mississauga | 315,056 |
| Montreal | 980,354 |
| North York | 559,521 |
| Oshawa | 117,519 |
| ★ Ottawa | 295,163 |
| Quebec | 166,474 |
| Regina | 162,613 |
| Saint Catharines | 124,018 |
| Saskatoon | 154,210 |
| Scarborough | 443,353 |
| Thunder Bay | 112,486 |
| Toronto | 599,217 |
| Vancouver | 414,281 |
| Windsor | 192,083 |
| Winnipeg | 564,473 |
| York | 134,617 |
| **Cape Verde** (1985 est.) | |
| ★ Praia | 49,500 |
| **Cayman Islands** (1987 est.) | |
| ★ George Town | 11,500 |
| **Central African Republic** (1985 est.) | |
| ★ Bangui | 473,817 |

| country<br>city | population |
|---|---|
| **Chad** (1986 est.) | |
| ★ N'Djamena | 511,700 |
| Sarh | 100,000 |
| **Chile** (1987 est.; MU) | |
| Antofagasta | 204,577 |
| Arica | 169,774 |
| Calama | 109,645 |
| Chillán | 148,805 |
| Concepción | 294,375 |
| Coquimbo | 105,252 |
| Iquique | 132,948 |
| La Serena | 106,617 |
| Los Angeles | 126,122 |
| Osorno | 122,462 |
| Puente Alto | 165,534 |
| Puerto Montt | 113,488 |
| Punta Arenas | 111,724 |
| Quilpué | 103,004 |
| Rancagua | 172,489 |
| San Bernardo | 168,534 |
| ★ Santiago | 421,900 |
| Greater Santiago | 4,858,342 |
| Talca | 164,482 |
| Talcahuano | 231,356 |
| Temuco | 217,789 |
| Valdívia | 117,205 |
| Valparaíso | 278,762 |
| Viña del Mar | 297,294 |
| **China** (1985 est.)[6] | |
| An-ch'ing (Anqing) | 207,200 |
| An-shan (Anshan) | 1,088,900 |
| An-shun (Anshun) | 126,700 |
| An-ta (Anda) | 150,000 |
| An-yang (Anyang) | 348,100 |
| Canton (Guangzhou) | 2,486,100 |
| Chan-chiang (Zhanjiang) | 312,300 |
| Ch'ang-chi (Changji) | 100,800 |
| Chang-chia-k'ou (Zhangjiakou) | 483,200 |
| Ch'ang-chih (Changzhi) | 261,200 |
| Ch'ang-chou (Changzhou) | 446,900 |
| Chang-chou (Zhangzhou) | 155,300 |
| Ch'ang-ch'un (Changchun) | 1,424,500 |
| Ch'ang-sha (Changsha) | 919,200 |
| Ch'ang-shu (Changshu) | 245,600 |
| Ch'ang-te (Changde) | 170,500 |
| Ch'ao-an (Chao'an) | 130,000 |
| Chao-ch'ing (Zhaoqing) | 137,600 |
| Ch'ao-chou (Chaozhou) | 257,500 |
| Ch'ao-hu (Chaohu) | 111,500 |
| Ch'ao-yang (Chaoyang) | 168,200 |
| Chen-chiang (Zhenjiang) | 319,300 |
| Chen-chou (Chenzhou) | 138,900 |
| Cheng-chou (Zhengzhou) | 962,500 |
| Ch'eng-te (Chengde) | 222,600 |
| Ch'eng-tu (Chengdu) | 1,523,400 |
| Chi-an (Ji'an) | 127,900 |
| Chi-hsi (Jixi) | 626,300 |
| Chi-lin (Jilin) | 882,700 |
| Chi-nan (Jinan) | 1,110,500 |
| Chi-ning (Jining) (*Inner Mongolia*) | 141,000 |
| Chi-ning (Jining) (*Shantung*) | 207,200 |
| Ch'i-t'ai-ho (Qitaihe) | 151,700 |
| Chia-hsing (Jiaxing) | 168,300 |
| Chia-mu-ssu (Jiamusi) | 419,700 |
| Chiang-men (Jiangmen) | 159,800 |
| Chiao-tso (Jiaozuo) | 320,000 |
| Ch'ih-feng (Chifeng) | 270,300 |
| Chin-chou (Jinzhou) | 584,800 |
| Chin-hua (Jinhua) | 132,600 |
| Ch'in-huang-tao (Qinhuangdao) | 293,900 |
| Ch'ing-chiang (Qingjiang) | 150,000 |
| Ching-men (Jingmen) | 211,700 |
| Ch'ing-tao (Qingdao) | 1,140,000 |
| Ching-te-chen (Jingdezhen) | 294,700 |
| Chiu-chiang (Jiujiang) | 243,900 |
| Chou-k'ou (Zhoukou) | 102,200 |
| Chou-k'ou-chen (Zhoukouzhen) | 150,000 |
| Ch'u-ching (Qujing) | 124,600 |
| Chu-chou (Zhuzhou) | 333,700 |
| Ch'ü-chou (Quzhou) | 102,100 |
| Ch'u-chou (Chuzhou) | 110,100 |
| Ch'ü-hsien (Quxian) | 120,000 |
| Ch'üan-chou (Quanzhou) | 150,000 |
| Chungking (Chongqing) | 2,030,800 |
| Chung-shan (Zhongshan) | 208,900 |
| E-chou (Ezhou) | 195,800 |
| Feng-ch'eng (Fengcheng) | 100,000 |
| Fo-shan (Foshan) | 229,700 |
| Fu-chou (Fuzhou) (*Kiangsi*) | 105,100 |
| Fu-chou (Fuzhou) | 754,500 |
| Fu-hsin (Fuxin) | 551,300 |
| Fu-shun (Fushun) | 1,077,300 |
| Fu-yang (Fuyang) | 118,900 |
| Ha-mi (Hami) | 141,100 |
| Hai-k'ou (Haikou) | 198,900 |
| Hai-la-erh (Hailar) | 149,000 |
| Han-chung (Hanzhong) | 148,900 |
| Han-ku (Hangu) | 100,000 |
| Han-tan (Handan) | 727,500 |
| Hang-chou (Hangzhou) | 973,400 |
| Harbin | 2,217,300 |
| Heng-yang (Hengyang) | 401,900 |
| Ho-fei (Hefei) | 594,200 |
| Ho-kang (Hegang) | 472,000 |
| Ho-pi (Hebi) | 156,000 |
| Ho-tse (Heze) | 109,300 |
| Hsi-ch'ang (Xichang) | 101,300 |
| Hsi-ning (Xining) | 473,000 |
| Hsia-men (Xiamen) | 328,100 |
| Hsiang-fan (Xiangfan) | 294,400 |
| Hsiang-t'an (Xiangtan) | 377,100 |
| Hsiao-kan (Xiaogan) | 109,000 |
| Hsien-ning (Xianning) | 124,600 |
| Hsien-yang (Xianyang) | 272,800 |
| Hsin-hsiang (Xinxiang) | 397,100 |
| Hsin-t'ai (Xintai) | 143,500 |
| Hsin-yang (Xinyang) | 159,800 |
| Hsin-yu (Xinyu) | 120,200 |
| Hsing-t'ai (Xingtai) | 251,400 |
| Hsü-ch'ang (Xuchang) | 156,700 |
| Hsü-chou (Xuzhou) | 709,400 |
| Hsüan-hua (Xuanhua) | 140,000 |
| Hu-chou (Huzhou) | 184,900 |
| Hu-ho-hao-t'e (Hohhot) | 542,800 |
| Huai-nan (Huainan) | 603,200 |
| Huai-pei (Huaibei) | 272,300 |
| Huai-yin (Huaiyin) | 191,700 |
| Huang-shih (Huangshi) | 380,200 |
| Hui-chou (Huizhou) | 107,700 |
| Hun-chiang (Hunjiang) | 436,100 |
| I-ch'ang (Yichang) | 317,100 |
| I-ch'un (Yichun) | 758,200 |
| I-ning (Yining) | 150,700 |
| I-pin (Yibin) | 214,400 |
| I-yang (Yiyang) | 150,900 |
| K'ai-feng (Kaifeng) | 447,800 |
| Kan-chou (Ganzhou) | 185,300 |
| Kashgar (Kashi) | 138,800 |
| Ko-chiu (Gejiu) | 189,900 |
| K'o-erh-ch'in-yu-i-ch'ien-ch'i (Horqin Youyi Qianqi) | 100,000 |
| Kuei-lin (Guilin) | 314,100 |
| Kuei-yang (Guiyang) | 871,300 |
| K'un-ming (Kunming) | 950,000 |
| Lai-wu (Laiwu) | 132,700 |
| Lan-chou (Lanzhou) | 1,144,500 |
| Lang-fang (Langfang) | 113,300 |
| Le-shan (Leshan) | 295,500 |
| Leng-shui-chiang (Lengshuijiang) | 150,000 |
| Liao-ch'eng (Liaocheng) | 114,800 |
| Liao-yang (Liaoyang) | 430,100 |
| Liao-yüan (Liaoyuan) | 319,100 |
| Lien-yün-kang (Lianyungang) | 277,400 |
| Lin-fen (Linfen) | 151,900 |
| Lin-i (Linyi) | 176,000 |
| Liu-chou (Liuzhou) | 501,000 |
| Liu-p'an-shui (Liupanshui) | 317,100 |
| Lo-yang (Luoyang) | 624,000 |
| Long-yen (Longyan) | 102,200 |
| Lu-chou (Luzhou) | 228,000 |
| Lü-ta (Lüda) | 1,270,000[1] |
| Ma-an-shan (Ma'anshan) | 249,100 |
| Man-chou-li (Manzhouli) | 104,100 |
| Mao-ming (Maoming) | 103,100 |
| Mei-hsien (Meixian) | 154,600 |
| Mien-yang (Mianyang) | 220,700 |
| Mu-tan-chiang (Mudanjiang) | 486,900 |
| Nan-ch'ang (Nanchang) | 880,500 |
| Nan-ch'ung (Nanchong) | 149,900 |
| Nan-ning (Nanning) | 564,900 |
| Nan-p'ing (Nanping) | 153,000 |
| Nan-t'ung (Nantong) | 297,000 |
| Nan-yang (Nanyang) | 180,600 |
| Nanking (Nanjing) | 1,865,100 |
| Nei-chiang (Neijiang) | 179,500 |
| Ning-po (Ningbo) | 422,000 |
| Pai-ch'eng (Baicheng) | 193,500 |
| Pang-pu (Bengbu) | 390,900 |
| Pao-chi (Baoji) | 278,700 |
| Pao-ting (Baoding) | 411,300 |
| Pao-t'ou (Baotou) | 866,200 |
| Pei-an (Bei'an) | 197,400 |
| Pei-hai (Beihai) | 115,700 |
| Pei-p'iao (Beipiao) | 100,000 |
| ★ Peking (Beijing) | 4,983,000 |
| Pen-hsi (Benxi) | 678,500 |
| P'ing-hsiang (Pingxiang) | 332,400 |
| P'ing-ting-shan (Pingdingshan) | 338,000 |
| Po-shan (Boshan) | 100,000 |
| P'u-ling (Puling) | 138,400 |
| P'u-yang (Puyang) | 113,700 |
| San-ming (Sanming) | 141,700 |
| Sha-shih (Shashi) | 213,400 |
| Shan-t'ou (Shantou) | 476,600 |
| Shao-hsing (Shaoxing) | 148,700 |
| Shao-kuan (Shaoguan) | 286,100 |
| Shao-yang (Shaoyang) | 210,900 |
| Shang-ch'iu (Shangqiu) | 129,800 |
| Shang-jao (Shangrao) | 111,200 |
| Shanghai | 6,725,700 |
| Shen-chen (Shenzhen) | 152,600 |
| Shen-yang (Shenyang) | 3,173,200 |
| Shih-chia-chuang (Shijiazhuang) | 902,000 |
| Shih-ho-tzu (Shihezi) | 294,500 |
| Shih-tsui-shan (Shizuishan) | 199,200 |
| Shih-yen (Shiyan) | 203,900 |
| Shuang-ya-shan (Shuangyashan) | 340,700 |
| Sian (Xi'an) | 1,686,300 |
| Ssu-p'ing (Siping) | 274,400 |
| Su-chou (Suzhou) (*Anhui*) | 114,400 |
| Su-chou (Suzhou) | 611,500 |
| Sui-chou (Suizhou) | 147,500 |
| Sui-hua (Suihua) | 195,800 |
| Ta-ch'ing (Daqing) | 500,900 |
| Ta-hsien (Daxian) | 132,500 |
| Ta-li (Dali) | 110,000 |
| Ta-lien (Dalian) | 1,334,300 |
| Ta-t'ung (Datong) | 688,200 |
| T'ai-an (Tai'an) | 194,500 |
| T'ai-chou (Taizhou) | 135,300 |
| T'ai-yüan (Taiyuan) | 1,355,900 |
| Tan-tung (Dandong) | 449,800 |
| T'ang-shan (Tangshan) | 921,100 |
| Te-chou (Dezhou) | 153,400 |
| Te-yang (Deyang) | 171,100 |
| T'ieh-ling (Tieling) | 313,000 |
| T'ien-shui (Tianshui) | 121,400 |
| Tientsin (Tianjin) | 4,123,800 |
| Tsa-lan-t'un (Zalantun) | 109,100 |
| Ts'ang-chou (Cangzhou) | 190,800 |
| Tsao-chuang (Zaozhuang) | 269,400 |
| Tsitsihar (Qiqihar) | 955,200 |
| Tsun-i (Zunyi) | 233,700 |
| Tu-k'ou (Dukou) | 355,900 |
| Tu-yün (Duyun) | 121,100 |
| T'ung-ch'uan (Tongchuan) | 234,300 |
| T'ung-hua (Tonghua) | 285,100 |
| T'ung-liao (Tongliao) | 184,400 |
| T'ung-ling (Tongling) | 169,500 |
| Tung-ying (Dongying) | 163,600 |
| Tzu-kung (Zigong) | 353,400 |
| Tzu-po (Zibo) | 762,500 |
| Wan-hsien (Wanxian) | 134,100 |
| Wei-fang (Weifang) | 296,500 |
| Wei-nan (Weinan) | 102,000 |
| Wen-chou (Wenzhou) | 365,600 |
| Wu-chou (Wuzhou) | 190,300 |
| Wu-hai (Wuhai) | 226,600 |
| Wu-han (Wuhan) | 2,899,000 |
| Wu-hsi (Wuxi) | 696,300 |
| Wu-hu (Wuhu) | 385,800 |
| Wu-lu-mu-ch'i (Ürümqi) | 947,000 |
| Ya-k'o-she (Yakeshe) | 323,100 |
| Yang-chou (Yangzhou) | 286,600 |
| Yang-ch'üan (Yangquan) | 291,400 |
| Yen-an (Yan'an) | 150,000 |
| Yen-ch'eng (Yancheng) | 248,300 |
| Yen-chi (Yanji) | 167,500 |
| Yen-t'ai (Yantai) | 311,200 |
| Yin-ch'uan (Yinchuan) | 256,200 |
| Ying-k'ou (Yingkou) | 355,700 |
| Yü-lin (Yulin) | 109,000 |
| Yü-men (Yumen) | 150,000 |
| Yü-tz'u (Yuci) | 168,600 |
| Yüeh-yang (Yueyang) | 228,300 |
| **Christmas Island** (1980 est.) | |
| ★ The Settlement at Flying Fish Cove | 1,200 |
| **Cocos (Keeling) Islands** (1985 est.) | |
| ★ West Island | 233 |
| **Colombia** (1985) | |
| Armenia | 180,221 |
| Barrancabermeja | 137,406 |
| Barranquilla | 896,649 |
| Bello | 206,297 |
| ★ Bogotá | 3,974,813 |
| Bucaramanga | 341,513 |
| Buenaventura | 160,342 |
| Cali | 1,323,944 |
| Cartagena | 491,368 |
| Cúcuta | 357,026 |
| Floridablanca | 137,975 |
| Ibagué | 269,495 |
| Itagüí | 135,797 |
| Manizales | 275,067 |
| Medellín | 1,418,554 |
| Montería | 157,466 |
| Neiva | 178,130 |
| Palmira | 175,186 |
| Pasto | 197,407 |
| Pereira | 233,271 |
| Popayán | 141,964 |
| Santa Marta | 177,922 |
| Sincelejo | 120,537 |
| Soledad | 164,494 |
| Valledupar | 142,771 |
| Villavicencio | 161,166 |
| **Comoros** (1980) | |
| ★ Moroni | 17,267 |
| **Congo** (1984) | |
| ★ Brazzaville | 585,812 |
| Pointe-Noire | 294,203 |
| **Cook Islands** (1981) | |
| ★ Rarotonga Island | 9,530 |
| **Costa Rica** (1984) | |
| ★ San José | 241,464 |
| **Côte d'Ivoire** (1984 est.) | |
| ★ Abidjan | 1,850,000 |
| Bouaké | 220,000 |
| Yamoussoukro | 120,000 |
| **Cuba** (1986 est.) | |
| Bayamo | 105,302 |
| Camagüey | 260,782 |
| Cienfuegos | 109,304 |
| Guantánamo | 174,383 |
| Holguín | 194,728 |
| ★ Havana | 2,014,806 |
| Matanzas | 105,382 |
| Pinar del Río | 100,906 |
| Santa Clara | 178,278 |
| Santiago de Cuba | 358,764 |
| **Cyprus** (1982) | |
| Limassol | 100,254 |
| ★ Nicosia | 123,298[7] |
| **Czechoslovakia** (1986 est.) | |
| Bratislava | 417,103 |
| Brno | 385,684 |
| Košice | 222,175 |
| Liberec | 100,919 |
| Olomouc | 106,086 |
| Ostrava | 327,791 |
| Plzen | 175,244 |
| ★ Prague | 1,193,513 |
| **Denmark** (1985) | |
| Ålborg | 113,865 |
| Århus | 194,348 |
| ★ Copenhagen | 1,358,540[4] |
| Odense | 136,803 |
| **Djibouti** (1985 est.) | |
| ★ Djibouti | 200,000 |
| **Dominica** (1981) | |
| ★ Roseau | 8,346 |
| **Dominican Republic** (1983 est.) | |
| La Romana | 101,000 |
| Santiago de los Caballeros | 285,000 |
| ★ Santo Domingo | 1,410,000 |
| **Ecuador** (1987 est.) | |
| Ambato | 126,067 |
| Cuenca | 201,490 |
| Guayaquil | 1,572,615 |
| Machala | 144,396 |
| Portoviejo | 141,568 |
| ★ Quito | 1,137,705 |
| **Egypt** (1986 est.) | |
| Alexandria | 2,893,000 |
| Aswān | 195,700 |
| Asyūt | 291,300 |
| Banhā | 120,200 |
| Bani Suwayf | 162,500 |
| Būr Sa'īd (Port Said) | 382,000 |
| ★ Cairo | 6,325,000 |
| Damanhūr | 225,900 |
| Damyāt | 121,200 |
| al-Fayyūm | 227,300 |
| Hulwan (Helwan) | 352,300 |
| al-Ismā'īlīyah | 236,200 |
| al-Jīzah (Giza) | 1,670,800 |
| Kafr ad-Dawwar | 160,554[1] |
| Kafr ash-Shaykh | 104,200 |
| al-Maḥallah al-Kubrā | 385,300 |
| al-Manṣūrah | 357,800 |
| al-Minya | 203,300 |
| Qinā | 141,700 |
| Sawhāj | 141,500 |
| Shibīn al-Kawm | 135,900 |
| Shubrā al-Khaymah | 533,300 |
| as-Suways (Suez) | 265,000 |
| Ṭanṭa | 373,500 |
| al-Uqṣur (Luxor) | 147,900 |
| az-Zaqāzīq | 274,400 |
| **El Salvador** (1985 est.) | |
| ★ San Salvador | 459,902 |
| Santa Ana | 137,879 |
| **Equatorial Guinea** (1983) | |
| ★ Malabo | 30,710 |
| **Ethiopia** (1984) | |
| ★ Addis Ababa | 1,423,111 |
| Asmera | 275,385 |
| **Faeroe Islands** (1987 est.) | |
| ★ Tórshavn | 15,287 |
| **Falkland Islands** (1986 est.) | |
| ★ Stanley | 1,100 |
| **Fiji** (1986) | |
| ★ Suva | 69,481 |
| **Finland** (1987 est.) | |
| Espoo | 162,106 |
| ★ Helsinki | 487,749 |
| Tampere | 170,097 |
| Turku | 160,974 |
| Vantaa | 147,225 |
| **France** (1982) | |
| Aix-en-Provence | 100,221 |
| Amiens | 130,302 |
| Angers | 135,293 |
| Besançon | 112,023 |
| Bordeaux | 201,965 |
| Boulogne-Billancourt | 102,582 |
| Brest | 154,110 |
| Caen | 112,332 |
| Clermont-Ferrand | 145,901 |
| Dijon | 139,188 |
| Grenoble | 156,437 |
| Le Havre | 198,700 |
| Le Mans | 145,976 |
| Lille | 167,791 |
| Limoges | 137,809 |
| Lyon | 410,455 |
| Marseille | 868,435 |
| Metz | 113,236 |
| Montpellier | 190,423 |
| Mulhouse | 111,742 |
| Nantes | 237,789 |
| Nice | 331,165 |
| Nîmes | 120,515 |
| ★ Paris | 2,165,892 |
| Perpignan | 107,812 |
| Reims | 176,419 |
| Rennes | 190,861 |
| Roubaix | 101,488 |
| Rouen | 100,696 |
| Saint-Étienne | 193,938 |
| Strasbourg | 247,068 |
| Toulon | 177,443 |
| Toulouse | 344,917 |
| Tours | 131,265 |
| Villeurbanne | 115,378 |
| **French Guiana** (1982) | |
| ★ Cayenne | 37,097 |
| **French Polynesia** (1983) | |
| ★ Papeete | 23,496 |
| **Gabon** (1985 est.) | |
| ★ Libreville | 235,700 |
| Port Gentil | 124,400 |
| **Gambia, The** (1986) | |
| ★ Banjul | 44,188[1] |
| Serekunda | 102,600 |
| **Gaza Strip** (1979 est.) | |
| Gaza (Ghazzah) | 120,000 |
| **Germany, East** (1986 est.) | |
| ★ Berlin (East) | 1,215,586 |
| Cottbus | 124,752 |
| Dessau | 103,569 |
| Dresden | 519,769 |
| Erfurt | 216,046 |
| Gera | 131,843 |
| Halle | 235,169 |
| Jena | 107,401 |
| Karl-Marx-Stadt | 315,452 |
| Leipzig | 553,660 |
| Magdeburg | 288,965 |
| Potsdam | 139,497 |
| Rostock | 244,444 |
| Schwerin | 127,538 |
| Zwickau | 120,206 |

## Major cities and national capitals (continued)

| country city | population |
|---|---|
| **Germany, West** (1987 est.) | |
| Aachen | 239,170 |
| Augsburg | 245,962 |
| Bergisch Gladbach | 101,776 |
| Berlin (West) | 1,879,225 |
| Bielefeld | 299,360 |
| Bochum | 381,216 |
| ★ Bonn | 291,439 |
| Bottrop | 112,256 |
| Braunschweig | 247,836 |
| Bremen | 521,976 |
| Bremerhaven | 132,194 |
| Cologne (Köln) | 914,336 |
| Darmstadt | 133,572 |
| Dortmund | 568,164 |
| Duisburg | 514,628 |
| Düsseldorf | 560,572 |
| Erlangen | 100,200 |
| Essen | 615,421 |
| Frankfurt am Main | 592,411 |
| Freiburg im Breisgau | 186,156 |
| Gelsenkirchen | 283,560 |
| Göttingen | 133,796 |
| Hagen | 206,070 |
| Hamburg | 1,571,267 |
| Hamm | 165,957 |
| Hannover | 505,718 |
| Heidelberg | 136,227 |
| Heilbronn | 111,713 |
| Herne | 171,274 |
| Hildesheim | 100,558 |
| Karlsruhe | 268,309 |
| Kassel | 184,353 |
| Kiel | 243,626 |
| Koblenz | 110,277 |
| Krefeld | 216,598 |
| Leverkusen | 154,703 |
| Lübeck | 209,159 |
| Ludwigshafen | 152,162 |
| Mainz | 189,005 |
| Mannheim | 294,648 |
| Mönchengladbach | 255,087 |
| Mülheim an der Ruhr | 170,392 |
| Munich (München) | 1,274,716 |
| Münster | 267,628 |
| Neuss | 143,832 |
| Nürnberg | 467,392 |
| Oberhausen | 221,542 |
| Offenbach am Main | 107,078 |
| Oldenburg | 139,256 |
| Osnabrück | 153,776 |
| Paderborn | 110,296 |
| Pforzheim | 104,452 |
| Recklingshausen | 117,585 |
| Regensburg | 123,821 |
| Remscheid | 121,005 |
| Saarbrücken | 184,353 |
| Salzgitter | 105,392 |
| Siegen | 107,319 |
| Solingen | 157,401 |
| Stuttgart | 565,486 |
| Ulm | 100,745 |
| Wiesbaden | 266,542 |
| Witten | 102,232 |
| Wolfsburg | 121,951 |
| Wuppertal | 376,217 |
| Würzburg | 127,050 |
| **Ghana** (1984) | |
| ★ Accra | 859,640 |
| Kumasi | 348,880 |
| Tamale | 136,828 |
| **Gibraltar** (1987 est.) | |
| ★ Gibraltar | 29,166 |
| **Greece** (1981) | |
| ★ Athens | 885,737 |
| Iráklion | 102,398 |
| Kallithéa | 117,319 |
| Larissa | 102,426 |
| Pátrai (Patras) | 142,163 |
| Peristérion | 140,858 |
| Piraiévs (Piraeus) | 196,389 |
| Thessaloníki | 406,413 |
| **Greenland** (1987 est.) | |
| ★ Nuuk (Godthåb) | 11,209 |
| **Grenada** (1981) | |
| ★ Saint George's | 4,788 |
| **Guadeloupe** (1982) | |
| ★ Basse-Terre | 13,397 |
| **Guam** (1980) | |
| ★ Agana | 896 |
| **Guatemala** (1981) | |
| ★ Guatemala City | 754,243 |
| **Guernsey** (1976) | |
| ★ St. Peter Port | 16,982 |
| **Guinea** (1983) | |
| ★ Conakry | 705,280 |
| **Guinea-Bissau** (1979) | |
| ★ Bissau | 109,214 |
| **Guyana** (1980) | |
| ★ Georgetown | 167,839 |
| **Haiti** (1987 est.) | |
| ★ Port-au-Prince | 472,895 |
| **Honduras** (1985 est.) | |
| San Pedro Sula | 372,800 |
| ★ Tegucigalpa | 571,400 |
| **Hong Kong** (1987 est.) | |
| Hong Kong | 5,602,000[8] |
| **Hungary** (1986 est.) | |
| ★ Budapest | 2,076,000 |
| Debrecen | 211,800 |
| Győr | 129,000 |
| Kecskemét | 102,900 |
| Miskolc | 211,700 |
| Nyíregyháza | 116,800 |
| Pécs | 177,100 |
| Szeged | 182,100 |
| Székesfehérvár | 111,500 |
| **Iceland** (1986 est.) | |
| ★ Reykjavík | 91,394 |
| **India** (1981) | |
| Ādoni | 108,939 |
| Agartala | 132,186 |
| Āgra | 694,191 |
| Ahmadābād | 2,059,725 |
| Ahmadnagar | 143,937 |
| Ajmer | 375,593 |
| Akola | 225,412 |
| Aligarh | 320,861 |
| Allahābād | 616,051 |
| Alleppey | 169,940 |
| Alwar | 145,795 |
| Ambāla | 104,565 |
| Ambattur | 114,915 |
| Amrāvati | 261,404 |
| Amritsar | 594,844 |
| Amroha | 112,682 |
| Anantapur | 119,531 |
| Arrah | 125,111 |
| Asansol | 183,375 |
| Aurangābād | 284,607 |
| Avadi | 124,574 |
| Bally | 147,735 |
| Bālurghāt | 104,648 |
| Bangalore | 2,476,355 |
| Baranagar | 170,343 |
| Bareilly | 386,734 |
| Barrackpur | 115,253 |
| Belgaum | 274,430 |
| Bellary | 201,579 |
| Bhāgalpur | 225,062 |
| Bharatpur | 105,274 |
| Bharūch | 110,070 |
| Bhatinda | 124,453 |
| Bhātpāra | 260,761 |
| Bhavnagar | 307,121 |
| Bhilai (Nagar) | 290,090 |
| Bhīlwāra | 122,625 |
| Bhimavaram | 101,894 |
| Bhiwandi | 115,298 |
| Bhiwāni | 101,277 |
| Bhopāl | 671,018 |
| Bhubaneswar | 219,211 |
| Bhusāwal | 123,133 |
| Bihār | 151,343 |
| Bijāpur | 147,313 |
| Bikaner | 253,174 |
| Bilāspur | 147,218 |
| Bokaro Steel City | 224,099 |
| Bombay (Greater) | 8,243,405 |
| Brahmapur | 162,550 |
| Bulandshahr | 103,436 |
| Burdwān | 167,364 |
| Burhānpur | 140,986 |
| Calcutta | 3,305,006 |
| Chandernagore | 101,925 |
| Chandīgarh | 373,789 |
| Chandrapur | 115,777 |
| Chāpra | 111,564 |
| Cochin | 513,249 |
| Coimbatore | 704,514 |
| Cuddalore | 127,625 |
| Cuddapah | 103,125 |
| Cuttack | 269,950 |
| Darbhanga | 176,301 |
| Dāvangere | 196,621 |
| Dehra Dūn | 211,416 |
| Delhi | 4,884,234 |
| Dhānbād | 120,221 |
| Dhārwār-Hubli | 527,108 |
| Dhūlia | 210,759 |
| Dindigul | 164,103 |
| Dombivli | 103,222 |
| Durg | 114,637 |
| Durgāpur | 311,798 |
| Elūru | 168,154 |
| Erode | 142,252 |
| Etāwah | 212,174 |
| Faizābād | 101,873 |
| Farīdābād | 330,864 |
| Farrukhābād-Fatehgarh | 145,793 |
| Firozābād | 202,338 |
| Gadag-Betigeri | 117,368 |
| Gangānagar | 123,692 |
| Garden Reach | 191,107 |
| Gaya | 247,075 |
| Ghāziābād | 271,730 |
| Gondia | 100,423 |
| Gorakhpur | 290,814 |
| Gulbarga | 221,325 |
| Guntūr | 367,699 |
| Gwalior | 539,015 |
| Hāpur | 102,837 |
| Hardwār | 114,180 |
| Hissār | 131,309 |
| Howrah (Haora) | 744,429 |
| Hugli Chinsurah | 125,193 |
| Hyderābād | 2,150,580 |
| Ichalkaranji | 133,751 |
| Imphāl | 156,622 |
| Indore | 829,327 |
| Jabalpur | 614,162 |
| Jadabpur | 251,968 |
| Jaipur | 977,165 |
| Jālgaon | 145,335 |
| Jālna | 122,276 |
| Jammu | 206,135 |
| Jāmnagar | 277,615 |
| Jamshedpur | 438,385 |
| Jaunpur | 105,140 |
| Jhānsi | 246,172 |
| Jodhpur | 506,345 |
| Jullundur | 408,196 |
| Junāgadh | 118,646 |
| Kākināda | 226,409 |
| Kalyān | 136,052 |
| Kāmārhāti | 234,951 |
| Kānchipuram | 130,926 |
| Kānpur | 1,481,789 |
| Karnāl | 132,107 |
| Katihār | 104,781 |
| Khandwa | 114,725 |
| Kharagpur | 150,475 |
| Kolhāpur | 340,625 |
| Kota | 358,241 |
| Kozhikode (Calicut) | 394,447 |
| Kumbakonam | 132,832 |
| Kurnool | 206,362 |
| Lātūr | 111,986 |
| Lucknow | 895,721 |
| Ludhiāna | 607,052 |
| Madras | 3,276,622 |
| Madurai | 820,891 |
| Mālegaon | 245,883 |
| Mandya | 100,285 |
| Mangalore | 172,252 |
| Masulipatam | 138,530 |
| Mathura | 147,493 |
| Meerut | 417,395 |
| Miraj | 105,455 |
| Mirzāpur-cum-Vindhyachal | 127,787 |
| Monghyr | 129,260 |
| Morādābād | 330,051 |
| Muzaffarnagar | 171,816 |
| Muzaffarpur | 190,416 |
| Mysore | 441,754 |
| Nabadwīp | 109,108 |
| Nadiād | 142,689 |
| Nāgercoil | 171,648 |
| Nāgpur | 1,219,461 |
| Naihāti | 114,607 |
| Nānded | 191,269 |
| Nāsik (Nashik) | 262,428 |
| Navsāri | 106,793 |
| Nellore | 237,065 |
| ★ New Delhi | 273,036 |
| Nizāmābād | 183,061 |
| Pālghāt | 111,245 |
| Pānihāti | 205,718 |
| Pānīpat | 137,927 |
| Parbhani | 109,364 |
| Pathānkot | 110,039 |
| Patiāla | 205,141 |
| Patna | 776,371 |
| Pimpri-Chinchwad | 220,966 |
| Pondicherry | 162,639 |
| Porbandar | 115,182 |
| Proddatūr | 107,070 |
| Pune | 1,203,351 |
| Puri | 100,942 |
| Quilon | 137,943 |
| Raichūr | 124,762 |
| Raipur | 338,245 |
| Rājahmundry | 203,358 |
| Rājapālaiyam | 101,640 |
| Rājkot | 445,076 |
| Rāmpur | 204,610 |
| Rānchi | 489,626 |
| Ratlām | 142,319 |
| Raurkela Steel Township | 206,821 |
| Rewa | 100,641 |
| Rohtak | 166,767 |
| Sāgar | 160,392 |
| Sahāranpur | 295,355 |
| Salem | 361,394 |
| Sambalpur | 110,282 |
| Sambhal | 108,232 |
| Sāngli | 152,389 |
| Secunderābād (Cantonment) | 135,994 |
| Shāhjahānpur | 185,396 |
| Shillong | 109,244 |
| Shimoga | 151,783 |
| Sholāpur (Solapur) | 511,103 |
| Shrīrāmpur | 127,304 |
| Sikar | 102,970 |
| Silīguri | 154,378 |
| Sītāpur | 101,210 |
| Sonepat | 109,369 |
| South Dum-Dum | 230,266 |
| South Suburban | 378,765 |
| Srīnagar | 586,038 |
| Surat | 776,583 |
| Tamkūr | 108,670 |
| Tenāli | 119,257 |
| Thāna (Thane) | 309,897 |
| Thanjāvūr | 184,015 |
| Tiruchchirāppalli | 362,045 |
| Tirunelveli | 128,850 |
| Tirupati | 115,292 |
| Tiruppūr | 165,223 |
| Tiruvottiyūr | 134,014 |
| Titāgarh | 104,534 |
| Trivandrum | 483,086 |
| Tumkūr | 108,670 |
| Tuticorin | 192,949 |
| Udaipur | 232,588 |
| Ujjain | 278,454 |
| Ulhāsnagar | 273,668 |
| Vadodara (Baroda) | 734,473 |
| Valparai | 115,452 |
| Vārānasi (Benares) | 708,647 |
| Vellore | 174,247 |
| Vijayawāda | 454,577 |
| Vishākhapatnam | 565,321 |
| Vizianagaram | 114,806 |
| Warangal | 335,150 |
| Yamunānagar | 109,304 |
| **Indonesia** (1980) | |
| Ambon | 208,898 |
| Balikpapan | 280,675 |
| Bandung | 1,462,637 |
| Banjarmasin | 381,286 |
| Bogor | 247,409 |
| Cirebon | 223,776 |
| ★ Jakarta | 6,503,449 |
| Jambi | 230,373 |
| Jember | 122,712 |
| Kediri | 221,830 |
| Madiun | 150,562 |
| Magelang | 123,484 |
| Malang | 511,780 |
| Manado | 217,159 |
| Medan | 1,378,955 |
| Padang | 480,922 |
| Pakanbaru | 186,262 |
| Palembang | 787,187 |
| Pekalongan | 132,558 |
| Pematangsiantar | 150,376 |
| Pontianak | 304,778 |
| Probolinggo | 100,296 |
| Samarinda | 264,718 |
| Semarang | 1,026,671 |
| Sukabumi | 109,994 |
| Surabaya | 2,027,913 |
| Surakarta | 469,888 |
| Tanjung Karang-Telukbetung | 284,275 |
| Tegal | 131,728 |
| Ujung Pandang | 709,038 |
| Yogyakarta | 398,727 |
| **Iran** (1985 est.) | |
| Ahvāz | 508,500 |
| Āmol | 106,500 |
| Arāk | 244,300 |
| Ardabīl | 258,100 |
| Bakhtarān | 536,500 |
| Bandar 'Abbās | 212,300 |
| Borūjerd | 162,800 |
| Dezfūl | 123,000 |
| Gorgān | 113,200 |
| Hamadan | 262,200 |
| Isfahan (Eşfahān) | 1,121,200 |
| Karaj | 431,900 |
| Kāshān | 136,000 |
| Kermān | 266,800 |
| Khorramābād | 235,600 |
| Meshed (Mashhad) | 1,103,300 |
| Orūmīyeh | 298,400 |
| Qazvīn | 205,900 |
| Qom | 637,700 |
| Rasht | 266,300 |
| Sabzevār | 129,600 |
| Sanandaj | 207,500 |
| Shīrāz | 834,800 |
| Tabrīz | 929,200 |
| ★ Tehrān | 5,751,500 |
| Yazd | 223,300 |
| Zāhedān | 220,500 |
| Zanjān | 205,900 |
| **Iraq** (1985 est.) | |
| al-Amārah | 131,758 |
| ★ Baghdad | 4,648,609 |
| Ba'qūbah | 114,516 |
| Basra | 616,700 |
| al-Ḥillah | 215,249 |
| Irbīl | 333,903 |
| Karbalā' | 184,574 |
| Kirkūk | 207,900[9] |
| Mosul | 570,926 |
| an-Najaf | 242,603 |
| an-Nasiriyah | 138,842 |
| ar-Ramādī | 137,388 |
| as-Sulaymaniyah | 279,424 |
| **Ireland** (1986) | |
| Cork | 133,196 |
| ★ Dublin | 502,337 |
| **Isle of Man** (1986) | |
| ★ Douglas | 20,368 |
| **Israel** (1983) | |
| Bat Yam | 129,700 |
| Beersheba (Be'er Sheva') | 111,100 |
| Haifa (Ḥefa) | 227,900 |
| Ḥolon | 133,900 |
| ★ Jerusalem (Yerushalayim, Al-Quds) | 431,800 |
| Netanya | 101,600 |
| Petaḥ Tiqwa | 124,600 |
| Ramat Gan | 117,600 |
| Rishon le-Ẕiyyon | 102,500 |
| Tel Aviv-Yafo | 330,400 |
| **Italy** (1986 est.; MU) | |
| Ancona | 104,600 |
| Bari | 363,970 |
| Bergamo | 119,251 |
| Bologna | 435,248 |
| Bolzano | 101,841 |
| Brescia | 200,227 |
| Cagliari | 222,897 |
| Catania | 371,749 |
| Catanzaro | 103,533 |
| Cosenza | 105,958 |
| Ferrara | 144,504 |
| Florence (Firenze) | 428,443 |
| Foggia | 158,949 |
| Forlì | 110,578 |
| Genoa (Genova) | 731,484 |
| La Spezia | 109,673 |
| Lecce | 100,093 |
| Livorno | 174,590 |
| Messina | 267,782 |
| Milan (Milano) | 1,507,877 |
| Modena | 177,369 |
| Monza | 122,476[3] |
| Naples (Napoli) | 1,204,021 |
| Novara | 102,719 |
| Padua (Padova) | 226,998 |
| Palermo | 722,095 |
| Parma | 176,347 |
| Perugia | 146,101 |
| Pescara | 131,292 |
| Piacenza | 105,894 |
| Pisa | 104,477 |
| Prato | 161,705[3] |
| Ravenna | 136,116 |
| Reggio di Calabria | 178,778 |
| Reggio nell'Emilia | 130,198 |
| Rimini | 129,506[3] |
| ★ Rome (Roma) | 2,823,927 |
| Salerno | 155,539 |
| Sassari | 119,888 |
| Siracusa | 121,286 |
| Taranto | 244,533 |
| Terni | 111,288 |
| Torre del Greco | 104,654[3] |
| Turin (Torino) | 1,030,011 |
| Trieste | 239,978 |
| Udine | 100,372 |
| Venice (Venezia) | 332,762 |
| Verona | 259,636 |
| Vicenza | 110,869 |
| **Jamaica** (1982) | |
| ★ Kingston | 104,041 |
| **Japan** (1986 est.) | |
| Abiko | 113,044 |
| Ageo | 181,794 |
| Aizuwakamatsu | 118,561 |
| Akashi | 263,031 |
| Akita | 298,139 |
| Amagasaki | 507,882 |
| Anjō | 134,818 |
| Aomori | 293,969 |
| Asahikawa | 365,843 |
| Ashikaga | 168,134 |
| Atsugi | 180,150 |
| Beppu | 134,071 |
| Chiba | 796,668 |
| Chigasaki | 188,217 |
| Chōfu | 193,951 |
| Daitō | 123,541 |
| Fuji | 216,188 |
| Fujieda | 113,627 |
| Fujinomiya | 113,447 |
| Fujisawa | 333,622 |
| Fukui | 251,324 |
| Fukuoka | 1,175,707 |
| Fukushima | 272,305 |
| Fukuyama | 361,828 |
| Funabashi | 512,973 |
| Futyu | 205,252 |
| Gifu | 411,299 |
| Habikino | 111,798 |
| Hachinohe | 241,920 |
| Hachiōji | 432,431 |
| Hadano | 145,086 |
| Hakodate | 318,734 |
| Hamamatsu | 518,787 |
| Higashi-Kurume | 111,011 |
| Higashi-Murayama | 127,301 |

| country city | population |
|---|---|
| Higashi-Ōsaka | 522,144 |
| Himeji | 453,636 |
| Hino | 158,609 |
| Hirakata | 385,525 |
| Hiratsuka | 232,485 |
| Hirosaki | 176,084 |
| Hiroshima | 1,055,176 |
| Hitachi | 205,672 |
| Hōfu | 118,225 |
| Ibaraki | 253,493 |
| Ichihara | 240,790 |
| Ichikawa | 407,548 |
| Ichinomiya | 259,123 |
| Ikeda | 101,862 |
| Imabari | 124,574 |
| Iruma | 122,157 |
| Ise | 105,336 |
| Isesaki | 113,121 |
| Ishinomaki | 123,740 |
| Itami | 183,476 |
| Iwaki | 351,508 |
| Iwakuni | 111,894 |
| Iwatsuki | 101,338 |
| Izumi (*Miyagi Pref.*) | 129,329 |
| Izumi (*Osaka Pref.*) | 140,223 |
| Joetsu | 130,912 |
| Kadoma | 141,221 |
| Kagoshima | 531,188 |
| Kakamigahara | 125,870 |
| Kakogawa | 230,397 |
| Kamakura | 175,975 |
| Kanazawa | 433,012 |
| Kariya | 114,649 |
| Kashihara | 113,578 |
| Kashiwa | 279,892 |
| Kasugai | 259,689 |
| Kasukabe | 174,940 |
| Katsuta | 104,214 |
| Kawagoe | 289,218 |
| Kawaguchi | 407,520 |
| Kawanishi | 137,936 |
| Kawasaki | 1,106,148 |
| Kiryū | 130,537 |
| Kisarazu | 120,824 |
| Kishiwada | 186,330 |
| Kita-Kyūshū | 1,053,010 |
| Kitami | 107,434 |
| Kobe | 1,422,922 |
| Kochi | 313,204 |
| Kodaira | 159,831 |
| Kofu | 202,565 |
| Koganei | 105,275 |
| Komaki | 114,860 |
| Komatsu | 106,269 |
| Koriyama | 304,435 |
| Koshigaya | 261,150 |
| Kumagaya | 145,082 |
| Kumamoto | 560,263 |
| Kurashiki | 414,737 |
| Kure | 225,357 |
| Kurume | 224,480 |
| Kushiro | 216,313 |
| Kyōto | 1,480,355 |
| Machida | 328,567 |
| Maebashi | 279,877 |
| Matsubara | 136,465 |
| Matsudo | 432,677 |
| Matsue | 140,749 |
| Matsumoto | 198,496 |
| Matsusaka | 117,047 |
| Matsuyama | 430,396 |
| Minakoyojō | 131,722 |
| Minō | 116,796 |
| Misato | 110,668 |
| Mishima | 101,044 |
| Mitaka | 166,876 |
| Mito | 230,695 |
| Miyazaki | 281,526 |
| Moriguchi | 159,157 |
| Morioka | 234,688 |
| Muroran | 138,663 |
| Musashino | 139,199 |
| Nagano | 339,086 |
| Nagaoka | 183,981 |
| Nagareyama | 127,952 |
| Nagasaki | 448,554 |
| Nagoya | 2,130,632 |
| Naha | 305,727 |
| Nara | 333,222 |
| Narashino | 139,061 |
| Neyagawa | 259,280 |
| Niigata | 477,782 |
| Niihama | 131,621 |
| Niiza | 130,792 |
| Nishinomiya | 423,131 |
| Nobeoka | 135,510 |
| Noda | 107,288 |
| Numazu | 211,315 |
| Obihiro | 164,292 |
| Odawara | 187,352 |
| Ogaki | 146,411 |
| Ōita | 395,346 |
| Okayama | 577,910 |
| Okazaki | 289,028 |
| Okinawa | 102,669 |
| Ōme | 113,047 |
| Ōmiya | 378,108 |
| Ōmuta | 158,171 |
| Onomichi | 100,019 |
| Ōsaka | 2,643,213 |
| Ōta | 134,772 |
| Otaru | 174,695 |
| Ōtsu | 238,000 |
| Oyama | 135,218 |
| Saga | 168,760 |
| Sagamihara | 491,224 |
| Sakai | 818,537 |
| Sakata | 101,169 |
| Sakura | 124,205 |
| Sapporo | 1,567,724 |
| Sasebo | 249,973 |
| Sayama | 147,295 |
| Sendai | 692,404 |
| Seto | 124,437 |
| Shimizu | 241,406 |
| Shimonoseki | 268,667 |
| Shizuoka | 470,025 |
| Sōka | 195,333 |
| Suita | 351,681 |
| Suzuka | 166,949 |
| Tachikawa | 149,015 |
| Takamatsu | 328,210 |
| Takaoka | 175,895 |
| Takarazuka | 197,493 |
| Takasaki | 233,090 |
| Takatsuki | 351,988 |
| Tama | 127,641 |
| Tokorozawa | 282,869 |
| Tokushima | 259,293 |
| Tokuyama | 112,525 |
| ★ Tokyo | 8,379,385 |
| Tomakomai | 158,324 |
| Tondabayashi | 103,917 |
| Tottori | 138,080 |
| Toyama | 315,338 |
| Toyohashi | 325,451 |
| Toyokawa | 108,180 |
| Toyonaka | 416,829 |
| Toyota | 314,222 |
| Tsu | 151,135 |
| Tsuchiura | 120,794 |
| Tsuruoka | 100,021 |
| Ube | 175,367 |
| Ueda | 116,795 |
| Uji | 168,550 |
| Urawa | 382,440 |
| Utsunomiya | 411,056 |
| Wakayama | 401,117 |
| Yachiyo | 142,205 |
| Yaizu | 109,358 |
| Yamagata | 246,128 |
| Yamaguchi | 125,371 |
| Yamato | 180,685 |
| Yao | 276,797 |
| Yatsushiro | 108,901 |
| Yokkaichi | 265,974 |
| Yokohama | 3,049,782 |
| Yokosuka | 427,690 |
| Yonago | 131,856 |
| Zama | 101,292 |
| **Jersey** (1981) | |
| ★ St. Helier | 25,698 |
| **Jordan** (1986 est.) | |
| ★ Amman | 833,500 |
| az-Zarqā' | 285,000 |
| Irbid | 150,000 |
| **Kampuchea** (1982 est.) | |
| ★ Phnom Penh | 600,000 |
| **Kenya** (1984 est.) | |
| Kisumu | 167,100 |
| Mombasa | 425,600 |
| ★ Nairobi | 1,103,600 |
| Nakuru | 101,700 |
| **Kiribati** (1985) | |
| ★ Bairiki | 21,393 |
| **Korea, North** (1981 est.) | |
| Ch'ŏngjin | 490,000 |
| Haeju | 213,000[1] |
| Hamhŭng-Hungnam | 775,000 |
| Kaesŏng | 240,000 |
| Kimch'aek (Songjin) | 490,000[1] |
| ★ P'yŏngyang | 1,283,000 |
| Sinŭiju | 200,000 |
| Wŏnsan | 240,000 |
| **Korea, South** (1985) | |
| Andong | 114,340 |
| Anyang | 361,530 |
| Ch'angwŏn | 111,676[10] |
| Cheju | 203,298 |
| Chinhae | 121,406 |
| Chinju | 227,441 |
| Ch'ŏnan | 170,088 |
| Ch'ŏngju | 350,279 |
| Chŏnju | 426,498 |
| Ch'unch'ŏn | 163,217 |
| Ch'ungju | 113,345 |
| Inch'ŏn | 1,387,491 |
| Iri | 192,275 |
| Kangnŭng | 132,995 |
| Kumi | 142,148 |
| Kunsan | 185,661 |
| Kwangju | 906,129 |
| Kyŏngju | 127,684 |
| Masan | 449,247 |
| Mokp'o | 236,078 |
| P'ohang | 261,256 |
| Puch'ŏn | 456,318 |
| Pusan | 3,516,807 |
| Sŏngnam | 447,839 |
| ★ Seoul (Sŏul) | 9,645,932 |
| Sunch'ŏn | 121,938 |
| Suwŏn | 430,834 |
| Taegu | 2,030,672 |
| Taejŏn | 886,695 |
| Tonghae | 104,310[10] |
| Uijŏngbu | 162,701 |
| Ulsan | 551,320 |
| Wŏnju | 151,372 |
| Yŏsu | 171,929 |
| **Kuwait** (1985) | |
| Ḩawallī | 145,126 |
| ★ Kuwait (al-Kuwayt) | 44,335 |
| as-Sālimīyah | 153,369 |
| **Laos** (1984 est.) | |
| ★ Vientiane | 200,000 |
| **Lebanon** (1985 est.) | |
| ★ Beirut (Bayrūt) | 1,500,000 |
| an-Nabaṭīyah | 100,000 |
| Sidon (Ṣaydā) | 100,000 |
| Tripoli (Ṭarābulus) | 500,000 |
| Zaḩlah | 200,000 |
| **Lesotho** (1986)[4] | |
| ★ Maseru | 109,382 |
| **Liberia** (1984 est.) | |
| ★ Monrovia | 425,000 |
| **Libya** (1981 est.) | |
| Banghāzī | 367,600 |
| Misrātah | 116,900 |
| ★ Tripoli (Ṭarābulus) | 858,500 |
| **Liechtenstein** (1986) | |
| ★ Vaduz | 4,927 |
| **Luxembourg** (1986 est.) | |
| ★ Luxembourg | 86,200 |
| **Macau** (1986 est.) | |
| ★ Macau (Santo Nome de Deus) | 416,200 |
| **Madagascar** (1985 est.) | |
| ★ Antananarivo | 662,600 |
| **Malaŵi** (1986 est.) | |
| Blantyre | 378,100 |
| ★ Lilongwe | 202,900 |
| **Malaysia** (1980) | |
| Ipoh | 293,849 |
| Johor Baharu | 246,395 |
| Kelang | 192,080 |
| Kota Baharu | 167,872 |
| ★ Kuala Lumpur | 565,329 |
| Kuala Terengganu | 180,296 |
| Kuantan | 131,547 |
| Petaling Jaya | 207,805 |
| Pinang (George Town) | 248,241 |
| Port Kelang | 192,080 |
| Seremban | 132,911 |
| Taiping | 146,002 |
| **Maldives** (1985) | |
| ★ Male | 46,334 |
| **Mali** (1985 est.) | |
| ★ Bamako | 801,910 |
| **Malta** (1986 est.) | |
| ★ Valletta | 9,263 |
| **Martinique** (1982) | |
| ★ Fort-de-France | 96,649 |
| **Mauritania** (1984 est.) | |
| ★ Nouakchott | 350,000 |
| **Mauritius** (1987 est.) | |
| ★ Port Louis | 139,730 |
| **Mayotte** (1985) | |
| ★ Dzaoudzi | 5,865 |
| Mamoudzou (★ designate) | 12,026 |
| **Mexico** (1980) | |
| Acapulco | 301,902 |
| Aguascalientes | 293,152 |
| Atizapán de Zaragoza (Ciudad López Mateos) | 188,497 |
| Campeche | 128,434 |
| Celaya | 141,675 |
| Chihuahua | 385,603 |
| Ciudad Madero | 132,444 |
| Ciudad Obregón | 165,572 |
| Ciudad Victoria | 140,161 |
| Coatzacoalcos | 127,170 |
| Cuernavaca | 192,770 |
| Culiacán | 304,826 |
| Ensenada | 120,483 |
| Durango | 257,915 |
| Gómez Palacio | 116,967 |
| Guadalajara | 1,626,152 |
| Guadalupe | 370,524 |
| Hermosillo | 297,175 |
| Irapuato | 170,138 |
| Jalapa | 204,594 |
| Juárez | 544,496 |
| León | 593,002 |
| Los Mochis | 122,531 |
| Matamoros | 188,745 |
| Mazatlán | 199,830 |
| Mérida | 400,142 |
| Mexicali | 341,559 |
| ★ Mexico City | 8,831,079 |
| Minatitlán | 106,765 |
| Monclova | 115,786 |
| Monterrey | 1,090,009 |
| Morelia | 297,544 |
| Nezahualcóyotl | 1,341,230 |
| Nuevo Laredo | 201,731 |
| Oaxaca | 154,223 |
| Orizaba | 114,848 |
| Pachuca | 110,351 |
| Poza Rica | 166,799 |
| Puebla | 835,759 |
| Querétaro | 215,976 |
| Reynosa | 194,693 |
| Saltillo | 284,937 |
| San Luis Potosí | 362,371 |
| San Nicolás de los Garza | 280,696 |
| Tampico | 267,957 |
| Tepic | 145,741 |
| Tijuana | 429,500 |
| Tlaquepaque | 133,500 |
| Toluca | 199,778 |
| Torreón | 328,086 |
| Tuxtla | 131,096 |
| Uruapan | 122,828 |
| Veracruz | 284,822 |
| Villahermosa | 158,216 |
| Zapopan | 345,390 |
| **Monaco** (1982) | |
| ★ Monaco | 27,063[8] |
| **Mongolia** (1985 est.) | |
| ★ Ulaanbaatar Bator | 488,200 |
| **Montserrat** (1980) | |
| ★ Plymouth | 1,568 |
| **Morocco** (1982) | |
| Agadir | 110,479 |
| Casablanca (Dar el-Beida) | 2,139,204 |
| Fès (Fez) | 448,823 |
| Kenitra | 188,194 |
| Khouribga | 127,181 |
| Marrakech | 439,728 |
| Meknès | 319,783 |
| Mohammedia | 105,120 |
| Oujda | 260,082 |
| ★ Rabat | 518,616 |
| Safi | 197,309 |
| Salé | 289,391 |
| Tanger | 266,346 |
| Tétouan | 199,615 |
| **Mozambique** (1986 est.) | |
| Beira | 269,700 |
| ★ Maputo (Lourenço Marques) | 882,814 |
| Nampula | 182,553 |
| **Nauru** (1983) | |
| ★ Yaren | 559 |
| **Nepal** (1981) | |
| ★ Kathmandu | 235,160 |
| **Netherlands, The** (1986 est.) | |
| ★ Amsterdam (capital) | 679,140 |
| Apeldoorn | 145,773 |
| Arnhem | 127,968 |
| Breda | 119,174 |
| Dordrecht | 106,968 |
| Eindhoven | 190,839 |
| Enschede | 144,048 |
| Groningen | 168,006 |
| Haarlem | 149,776 |
| Leiden | 105,262 |
| Maastricht | 114,579 |
| Nijmegen | 147,182 |
| Rotterdam | 571,372 |
| ★ The Hague (seat of government) | 443,961 |
| Tilburg | 153,703 |
| Utrecht | 229,933 |
| Zaanstad | 128,248 |
| **Netherland Antilles** (1980 est.)[4] | |
| ★ Willemstad | 100,000 |
| **New Caledonia** (1983; MU) | |
| ★ Nouméa | 60,112 |
| **New Zealand** (1986) | |
| Auckland | 149,046 |
| Christchurch | 168,200 |
| Manukau | 177,248 |
| ★ Wellington | 137,495 |
| **Nicaragua** (1985 est.) | |
| León | 100,982 |
| ★ Managua | 682,111 |
| **Niger** (1983 est.) | |
| ★ Niamey | 399,100 |
| **Nigeria** (1983 est.) | |
| Aba | 216,000 |
| Abeokuta | 308,800 |
| Ado-Ekiti | 265,800 |
| Akure | 117,300 |
| Benin City | 165,900 |
| Calabar | 126,000 |
| Ede | 221,900 |
| Effon-Alaiye | 110,600 |
| Enugu | 228,400 |
| Gusau | 114,100 |
| Ibadan | 1,060,000 |
| Ife | 214,500 |
| Ijebu-Ode | 113,110 |
| Ikare | 101,700 |
| Ikerre | 176,800 |
| Ilesha | 273,400 |
| Ilobu | 143,800 |
| Ilorin | 343,900 |
| Iseyin | 157,000 |
| Iwo | 261,600 |
| Jos | 149,000 |
| Kaduna | 202,000 |
| Kano | 487,100 |
| Katsina | 149,300 |
| Kumo | 107,000 |
| ★ Lagos | 1,097,000 |
| Maiduguri | 230,900 |
| Mushin | 240,700 |
| Offa | 142,300 |
| Ogbomosho | 527,400 |
| Oka | 103,500 |
| Ondo | 122,600 |
| Onitsha | 268,700 |
| Oshogbo | 344,500 |
| Oyo | 185,300 |
| Port Harcourt | 296,200 |
| Sapele | 100,600 |
| Shaki | 125,800 |
| Shomolu | 106,800 |
| Sokoto | 148,000 |
| Zaria | 274,000 |
| **Niue** (1984) | |
| ★ Alofi | 894 |
| **Norfolk Island** | |
| ★ Kingston | ... |
| **Norway** (1987 est.) | |
| Bergen | 209,299 |
| ★ Oslo | 451,484 |
| Trondheim | 135,005 |
| **Oman** (1981 est.) | |
| ★ Muscat | 50,000 |
| **Pacific Islands, Trust Territory of the** | |
| **Marshall Is.** (1985 est.) | |
| ★ Majuro | 14,267 |
| **Micronesia, Federated States of** (1980) | |
| ★ Kolonia | 5,549 |
| **Northern Mariana Is.** (1985 est.) | |
| ★ Saipan | 17,840 |
| **Palau** (1986) | |
| ★ Koror | 9,442 |
| **Pakistan** (1981) | |
| Bahāwalpur | 180,263 |
| Chiniot | 105,559 |
| Dera Ghāzi Khān | 102,007 |
| Faisalābād (Lyallpur) | 1,104,209 |
| Gujrānwāla | 658,753 |
| Gujrāt | 155,058 |
| Hyderābād | 751,529 |
| ★ Islamābād | 204,364 |
| Jhang | 195,558 |
| Jhelum | 106,462 |
| Karāchi | 5,208,132 |
| Kasūr | 155,523 |
| Lahore | 2,952,689 |
| Lahore Cantonment | 237,000 |
| Lārkāna | 123,890 |
| Mardān | 147,977 |
| Mīrpur Khās | 124,371 |
| Multān | 730,070 |
| Nawābshāh | 102,139 |
| Okāra | 153,483 |
| Peshāwar | 566,248 |
| Quetta | 285,719 |
| Rahīm Yār Khān | 119,036 |
| Rāwalpindi | 794,843 |
| Sāhīwāl | 150,954 |
| Sargodha | 291,362 |
| Sheikhūpura | 141,168 |
| Siālkot | 302,009 |
| Sukkur | 190,551 |
| Wāh Cantonment | 122,335 |
| **Panama** (1987 est.) | |
| ★ Panama City | 439,996 |
| San Miguelito | 231,920 |
| **Papua New Guinea** (1987 est.) | |
| ★ Port Moresby | 152,100 |
| **Paraguay** (1985 est.) | |
| ★ Asunción | 477,065 |
| **Peru** (1987 est.) | |
| Arequipa | 572,000 |
| Callao | 545,000 |
| Chiclayo | 379,000 |
| Chimbote | 270,000 |
| Cuzco | 245,000 |
| Huancayo | 195,000 |
| Ica | 140,000 |
| Iquitos | 237,000 |
| ★ Lima | 375,957[11] |
| Metro Lima-Callao | 5,875,900 |
| Piura | 284,000 |

## Major cities and national capitals (continued)

| country<br>city | population |
|---|---|
| Pucallpa | 134,000 |
| Tacna | 131,000 |
| Trujillo | 476,000 |
| **Philippines** (1984 est.) | |
| Angeles | 213,305 |
| Bacolod | 287,830 |
| Baguio | 133,726 |
| Batangas | 155,064[1] |
| Butuan | 172,489 |
| Cabanatuan | 153,899 |
| Cadiz | 133,791[1] |
| Cagayan de Oro | 275,938 |
| Calbayog | 113,594 |
| Caloocan | 524,624 |
| Cebu | 552,155 |
| Dagupan | 103,401 |
| Davao | 179,521 |
| General Santos | 183,255 |
| Iligan | 181,865 |
| Iloilo | 263,422 |
| Las Piñas | 190,364 |
| Legaspi | 108,864 |
| Lipa | 133,540 |
| Lucena | 124,355 |
| Makati | 408,991 |
| Malabon | 212,930 |
| Mandaluyong | 226,670 |
| Mandaue | 137,300 |
| ★ Manila | 1,728,441 |
| Metro Manila | 6,720,050 |
| Marikina | 248,183 |
| Muntilupa | 172,421 |
| Navotas | 146,899 |
| Olongapo | 173,701 |
| Ormoc | 116,474 |
| Parañaque | 252,791 |
| Pasay | 320,889 |
| Pasig | 318,853 |
| Quezon City | 1,326,035 |
| San Carlos | 107,080 |
| San Juan del Monte | 139,126 |
| San Pablo | 143,023 |
| Tacloban | 117,243 |
| Tagig | 130,719 |
| Toledo | 102,565 |
| Valenzuela | 275,725 |
| Zamboanga | 379,194 |
| **Pitcairn Island** (1987) | |
| ★ Adamstown | 44[8] |
| **Poland** (1986 est.) | |
| Białystok | 250,800 |
| Bielsko-Biała | 175,900 |
| Bydgoszcz | 366,400 |
| Bytom | 238,900 |
| Chorzów | 142,000 |
| Czestochowa | 249,100 |
| Dąbrovo Górnicza | 138,000 |
| Elbląg | 118,500 |
| Gdańsk | 468,600 |
| Gdynia | 246,500 |
| Gliwice | 209,700 |
| Gorzów Wielkopolski | 115,700 |
| Jastrzębie-Zdrój | 100,500 |
| Kalisz | 104,100 |
| Katowice | 363,300 |
| Kielce | 203,400 |
| Koszalin | 101,300 |
| Kraków | 740,100 |
| Łódź | 847,900 |
| Lublin | 327,000 |
| Olsztyn | 149,900 |
| Opole | 126,100 |
| Płock | 114,700 |
| Poznań | 575,100 |
| Radom | 216,500 |
| Ruda Śląska | 166,100 |
| Rybnik | 137,600 |
| Rzeszów | 141,900 |
| Sosnowiec | 256,500 |
| Szczecin | 392,300 |
| Tarnów | 115,900 |
| Toruń | 119,300 |
| Tychy | 183,800 |
| Wałbrzych | 138,700 |
| ★ Warsaw (Warszawa) | 1,659,400 |
| Włocławek | 116,700 |
| Wodzislaw Śląskie | 109,200 |
| Wrocław | 637,200 |
| Zabrze | 198,400 |
| Zielona Góra | 109,900 |
| **Portugal** (1985 est.) | |
| ★ Lisbon | 827,800 |
| Porto | 344,500 |
| **Puerto Rico** (1984 est.; MU) | |
| Bayamón | 202,500 |
| Caguas | 121,100 |
| Carolina | 165,700 |
| Ponce | 190,900 |
| ★ San Juan | 428,900 |
| **Qatar** (1986) | |
| ★ Doha | 217,294 |
| **Réunion** (1982) | |
| ★ Saint-Denis | 84,400 |
| **Romania** (1985 est.) | |
| Arad | 185,892 |
| Bacău | 175,299 |
| Baia Mare | 135,536 |
| Botoşani | 104,836 |
| Brăila | 234,600 |
| Braşov | 346,640 |
| ★ Bucharest | 1,975,808 |
| Buzău | 132,311 |
| Cluj-Napoca | 309,843 |
| Constanţa | 323,236 |
| Craiova | 275,098 |
| Galaţi | 292,805 |
| Iaşi | 314,156 |
| Oradea | 208,507 |
| Piatra Neamţ | 107,581 |
| Piteşti | 154,112 |
| Ploieşti | 234,021 |
| Reşiţa | 104,362 |
| Satu Mare | 128,115 |
| Sibiu | 176,928 |
| Timişoara | 318,955 |
| Tirgu Mureş | 157,411 |
| **Rwanda** (1981 est.) | |
| ★ Kigali | 156,700 |
| **St. Christopher and Nevis** (1985 est.) | |
| ★ Basseterre | 18,500 |
| **St. Helena and Ascension** (1978 est.) | |
| ★ Jamestown | 1,500 |
| **St. Lucia** (1986 est.) | |
| ★ Castries | 52,868 |
| **St. Pierre and Miquelon** (1982) | |
| ★ Saint-Pierre | 5,415 |
| **St. Vincent and The Grenadines** (1984 est.) | |
| ★ Kingstown | 18,378 |
| **San Marino** (1986 est.) | |
| ★ San Marino | 2,397 |
| **São Tomé and Príncipe** (1984 est.) | |
| ★ São Tomé | 34,997 |
| **Saudi Arabia** (1980 est.) | |
| ad-Dammām | 200,000[12] |
| Jiddah | 1,308,000[11] |
| Mecca (Makkah) | 550,000 |
| Medina (al-Madinah) | 290,000 |
| ★ Riyadh (ar-Riyad) | 1,000,000[11] |
| aṭ-Ṭā'if | 300,000 |
| **Senegal** (1984 est.) | |
| ★ Dakar | 671,000 |
| Kaolack | 126,900 |
| Thiès | 126,900[13] |
| Ziguinchor | 105,200 |
| **Seychelles** (1977) | |
| ★ Victoria | 23,012 |
| **Sierra Leone** (1985) | |
| ★ Freetown | 469,776 |
| **Singapore** (1987 est.)[8] | |
| ★ Singapore | 2,616,000 |
| **Solomon Islands** (1986 est.; MU) | |
| ★ Honiara | 30,499 |
| **Somalia** (1981 est.) | |
| ★ Mogadishu | 500,000 |
| **South Africa** (1986) | |
| ★ Bloemfontein (judicial) | 104,381 |
| Boksburg | 110,832 |
| ★ Cape Town (legislative) | 776,617 |
| Metro Cape Town | 1,911,521 |
| Durban | 634,301 |
| Metro Durban | 982,075 |
| Germiston | 116,718 |
| Johannesburg | 632,369 |
| Metro Johannesburg | 1,609,408 |
| Pietermaritzburg | 133,809 |
| Port Elizabeth | 272,844 |
| ★ Pretoria (executive) | 443,059 |
| Metro Pretoria | 822,925 |
| Roodepoort | 141,764 |
| Soweto | 864,000[10] |
| **Bophuthatswana** | |
| ★ Mmabatho | ... |
| **Ciskei** (1986 est.) | |
| ★ Bisho | 2,850 |
| Mdantsane | 242,823 |
| **KwaNdebele** | |
| ★ Siyabuswa | ... |
| **Transkei** (1978 est.) | |
| ★ Umtata | 30,000 |
| **Venda** | |
| ★ Thohoyandou | ... |
| **South West Africa/Namibia** (1985 est.) | |
| ★ Windhoek | 110,000 |
| **Spain** (1986 est.; MU) | |
| Albacete | 126,594 |
| Alcalá de Henares | 142,862[11] |
| Alcorcón | 140,657[11] |
| Alicante | 258,707 |
| Almería | 154,242 |
| Badajoz | 119,220 |
| Badalona | 227,744[11] |
| Barcelona | 1,699,231 |
| Bilbao | 379,107 |
| Burgos | 158,610 |
| Cádiz | 155,219 |
| Castellón de la Plana | 127,578 |
| Córdoba | 296,075 |
| Coruña, La | 239,505 |
| Gerona | 126,030[11] |
| Getafe | 127,060[11] |
| Gijón | 255,969[11] |
| Granada | 256,528 |
| Hospitalet de Llobregat | 294,033[11] |
| Huelva | 135,576 |
| Jaén | 103,291 |
| La Laguna | 112,635[11] |
| Leganés | 163,426[11] |
| León | 135,014 |
| Lérida | 107,787 |
| Logroño | 115,922 |
| ★ Madrid | 3,053,101 |
| Málaga | 566,480 |
| Móstoles | 149,649[11] |
| Murcia | 304,185 |
| Orense | 100,430 |
| Oviedo | 185,920 |
| Palma (de Mallorca) | 295,351 |
| Palmas de Gran Canaria, Las (Is. Canarias) | 356,730 |
| Pamplona | 184,340 |
| Sabadell | 194,943[11] |
| Salamanca | 152,766 |
| San Sebastián | 175,267 |
| Santa Coloma de Gramanet | 140,588[11] |
| Santa Cruz de Tenerife | 212,523 |
| Santander | 186,456 |
| Sevilla (Seville) | 651,299 |
| Tarragona | 106,361 |
| Terrassa | 155,360[11] |
| Valencia | 728,622 |
| Valladolid | 327,786 |
| Vigo | 258,724[11] |
| Vitoria | 199,936 |
| Zaragoza (Saragossa) | 573,711 |
| **Sri Lanka** (1984 est.) | |
| ★ Colombo | 643,000 |
| Dehiwala-Mount Lavinia | 184,000 |
| Jaffna | 133,000 |
| Kandy | 120,000 |
| Kotte | 102,000 |
| Moratuwa | 138,000 |
| **Sudan, The** (1983) | |
| ★ Khartoum | 476,218 |
| Khartoum North | 341,146 |
| Port Sudan | 206,727 |
| Omdurman | 526,287 |
| **Suriname** (1986 est.) | |
| ★ Paramaribo | 77,558 |
| **Swaziland** (1986 est.) | |
| ★ Mbabane | 48,000 |
| **Sweden** (1987 est.; MU) | |
| Borås | 100,054 |
| Göteborg | 429,339 |
| Helsingborg | 106,275 |
| Jönköping | 108,235 |
| Linköping | 117,835 |
| Malmö | 230,056 |
| Norrköping | 118,801 |
| Örebro | 118,443 |
| ★ Stockholm | 663,217 |
| Uppsala | 157,675 |
| Västerås | 117,732 |
| **Switzerland** (1986 est.) | |
| Basel (Bâle) | 174,606 |
| ★ Bern (Berne) | 138,574 |
| Geneva (Genève) | 159,895 |
| Lausanne | 125,004 |
| Zürich | 351,545 |
| **Syria** (1987 est.) | |
| Aleppo (Halab) | 1,216,000 |
| ★ Damascus (Dimashq) | 1,292,000 |
| Hamāh | 214,000 |
| Homs (Hims) | 431,000 |
| Latakia (al-Ladhiqiyah) | 241,000 |
| **Taiwan** (1986 est.) | |
| Chang-hua | 201,103 |
| Chi-lung (Keelung) | 351,524 |
| Chia-i | 253,573 |
| Chung-ho | 324,930 |
| Chung-li | 237,271 |
| Feng-shan (Kao-hsiung-hsien) | 267,022 |
| Fêng-yüan | 139,747 |
| Hsin-chu | 304,010 |
| Hsin-chuang | 232,438 |
| Hsin-tien | 190,579 |
| Hua-lien | 105,177 |
| Kao-hsiung | 1,302,849 |
| Pan-ch'iao (T'ai-pei-hsien) | 479,748 |
| P'ing-tung | 200,441 |
| San-chu'ung | 353,957 |
| T'ai-chung | 674,936 |
| T'ai-nan | 639,888 |
| T'ai-tung | 111,206 |
| ★ Taipei (T'ai-pei) | 2,507,620 |
| T'ao-yuan | 204,700 |
| Yung-ho | 232,438 |
| **Tanzania** (1978) | |
| ★ Dar es Salaam | 769,445 |
| Mwanza | 110,553 |
| Tanga | 103,399 |
| Zanzibar | 110,506 |
| **Thailand** (1983 est.) | |
| ★ Bangkok | 5,018,327 |
| Chiang Mai | 150,499 |
| Hat Yai | 113,964 |
| Khon Kaen | 115,515 |
| Nakhon Ratchasima | 190,692 |
| Ubon Ratchathani | 100,255 |
| **Togo** (1983) | |
| ★ Lomé | 366,476 |
| **Tokelau** | |
| — | — |
| **Tonga** (1986) | |
| ★ Nukualofa | 28,899 |
| **Trinidad and Tobago** (1986 est.) | |
| ★ Port-of-Spain | 57,400 |
| **Tunisia** (1984) | |
| Şafāqis (Sfax) | 231,911 |
| ★ Tunis | 596,654 |
| **Turkey** (1985) | |
| Adana | 777,554 |
| Adapazari | 155,041 |
| ★ Ankara | 2,235,000 |
| Antakya | 109,233 |
| Antalya | 258,139 |
| Balıkesir | 152,402 |
| Batman | 114,210 |
| Bursa | 612,500 |
| Denizli | 171,360 |
| Diyarbakır | 305,259 |
| Elazığ | 181,523 |
| Erzurum | 252,648 |
| Eskişehir | 367,328 |
| Gaziantep | 466,302 |
| İçel | 314,105 |
| İskenderun | 173,607 |
| Isparta | 101,784 |
| İstanbul | 5,475,982 |
| İzmir | 1,489,772 |
| İzmit | 236,144 |
| Kahramanmaraş | 212,206 |
| Kayseri | 378,458 |
| Konya | 438,839 |
| Kütahya | 120,354 |
| Malatya | 251,257 |
| Manisa | 126,319 |
| Osmaniye | 107,748 |
| Samsun | 280,068 |
| Şanlıurfa | 206,385 |
| Sivas | 197,266 |
| Trabzon | 155,960 |
| Van | 121,306 |
| Zonguldak | 119,125 |
| **Turks and Caicos Islands** (1980) | |
| ★ Cockburn Town | 3,124 |
| **Tuvalu** (1985 est.) | |
| ★ Funafuti | 2,810 |
| **Uganda** (1980) | |
| ★ Kampala | 458,503 |
| **Union of Soviet Socialist Republics** (1986 est.) | |
| Abakan | 148,000 |
| Achinsk | 120,000 |
| Aktyubinsk | 239,000 |
| Alma-Ata | 1,088,000 |
| Almalyk | 117,000 |
| Almetyevsk | 125,000 |
| Andizhan | 281,000 |
| Andropov | 252,000 |
| Angarsk | 259,000 |
| Angren | 126,000 |
| Anzhero-Sudzhensk | 111,000 |
| Arkhangelsk | 412,000 |
| Armavir | 170,000 |
| Arzamas | 107,000 |
| Ashkhabad | 366,000 |
| Astrakhan | 503,000 |
| Baku | 1,114,000 |
| Balakovo | 184,000 |
| Balashikha | 130,000 |
| Baranovichi | 152,000 |
| Barnaul | 586,000 |
| Batumi | 133,000 |
| Belaya Tserkov | 187,000 |
| Belgorod | 286,000 |
| Belovo | 117,000 |
| Beltsy | 151,000 |
| Bendery | 126,000 |
| Berdyansk | 131,000 |
| Berezniki | 198,000 |
| Biysk | 228,000 |
| Blagoveshchensk | 199,000 |
| Bobruysk | 227,000 |
| Borisov | 136,000 |
| Bratsk | 245,000 |
| Brest | 230,000 |
| Brezhnev | 459,000 |
| Bryansk | 437,000 |
| Bukhara | 214,000 |
| Chardzhou | 162,000 |
| Cheboksary | 402,000 |
| Chelyabinsk | 1,107,000 |
| Cherepovets | 309,000 |
| Cherkassy | 280,000 |
| Cherkessk | 105,000 |
| Chernigov | 285,000 |
| Chernovtsy | 249,000 |
| Chimkent | 379,000 |
| Chirchik | 156,000 |
| Chita | 342,000 |
| Daugavpils | 126,000 |
| Dimitrovgrad | 119,000 |
| Dneprodzerzhinsk | 275,000 |
| Dnepropetrovsk | 1,166,000 |
| Donetsk | 1,081,000 |
| Dushanbe | 567,000 |
| Dzerzhinsk | 277,000 |
| Dzhambul | 308,000 |
| Dzhezkazgan | 103,000 |
| Ekibastuz | 130,000 |
| Elektrostal | 149,000 |
| Engels | 180,000 |
| Fergana | 199,000 |
| Frunze | 617,000 |
| Gomel | 478,000 |
| Gorky | 1,409,000 |
| Gorlovka | 343,000 |
| Grodno | 255,000 |
| Grozny | 399,000 |
| Guryev | 147,000 |
| Irkutsk | 601,000 |
| Ivano-Frankovsk | 218,000 |
| Ivanovo | 476,000 |
| Izhevsk | 620,000 |
| Kalinin | 442,000 |
| Kaliningrad | 389,000 |
| Kaliningrad (*Moscow obl.*) | 144,000 |
| Kaluga | 302,000 |
| Kamensk-Uralsky | 202,000 |
| Kamyshin | 118,000 |
| Kansk | 106,000 |
| Karaganda | 624,000 |
| Karshi | 137,000 |
| Kaunas | 410,000 |
| Kazan | 1,057,000 |
| Kemerovo | 514,000 |
| Kerch | 170,000 |
| Khabarovsk | 584,000 |
| Kharkov | 1,567,000 |
| Kherson | 352,000 |
| Khimki | 127,000 |
| Khmelnitsky | 223,000 |
| Kiev | 2,495,000 |
| Kineshma | 105,000 |
| Kirov | 415,000 |
| Kirovabad | 265,000 |
| Kirovakan | 167,000 |
| Kirovograd | 266,000 |
| Kiselevsk | 127,000 |
| Kishinyov | 643,000 |
| Kislovodsk | 108,000 |
| Klaipėda | 197,000 |
| Kokand | 169,000 |
| Kokchetav | 123,000 |
| Kolomna | 158,000 |
| Kolpino | 131,000 |
| Kommunarsk | 125,000 |
| Komsomolsk-na-Amure | 309,000 |
| Konstantinovka | 114,000 |
| Kostroma | 273,000 |
| Kovrov | 155,000 |
| Kramatorsk | 195,000 |
| Krasnodar | 615,000 |
| Krasnoyarsk | 885,000 |
| Krasny Luch | 111,000 |
| Kremenchug | 227,000 |
| Krivoy Rog | 691,000 |
| Kurgan | 348,000 |
| Kursk | 426,000 |
| Kustanay | 207,000 |
| Kutaisi | 217,000 |
| Kuybyshev | 1,267,000 |
| Kzyl-Orda | 185,000 |
| Leninabad | 153,000 |
| Leninakan | 226,000 |
| Leningrad | 4,359,000 |
| Leninsk-Kuznetsky | 167,000 |
| Liepaja | 113,000 |
| Lipetsk | 456,000 |
| Lisichansk | 123,000 |
| Lutsk | 179,000 |
| Lvov | 753,000 |
| Lyubertsy | 162,000 |
| Magadan | 145,000 |
| Magnitogorsk | 425,000 |
| Makeyevka | 453,000 |
| Makhachkala | 311,000 |
| Margilan | 124,000 |
| Maykop | 142,000 |
| Melitopol | 172,000 |
| Mezhdurechensk | 103,000 |
| Miass | 162,000 |
| Michurinsk | 103,000 |
| Minsk | 1,510,000 |
| Mogilyov | 351,000 |
| ★ Moscow | 8,527,000 |
| Murmansk | 426,000 |

| country city | population |
|---|---|
| Murom | 122,000 |
| Mytishchi | 151,000 |
| Nakhodka | 152,000 |
| Nalchik | 231,000 |
| Namangan | 283,000 |
| Navoi | 103,000 |
| Nevinnomyssk | 115,000 |
| Nikolayev | 493,000 |
| Nikopol | 156,000 |
| Nizhnekamsk | 177,000 |
| Nizhnevartovsk | 200,000 |
| Nizhny Tagil | 423,000 |
| Noginsk | 121,000 |
| Norilsk | 181,000 |
| Novgorod | 224,000 |
| Novocheboksarsk | 106,000 |
| Novocherkassk | 187,000 |
| Novokuybyshevsk | 111,000 |
| Novokuznetsk | 583,000 |
| Novomoskovsk (*Tula obl.*) | 147,000 |
| Novorossiysk | 177,000 |
| Novoshakhtinsk | 106,000 |
| Novosibirsk | 1,405,000 |
| Novotroitsk | 104,000 |
| Nukus | 146,000 |
| Odessa | 1,132,000 |
| Odintsovo | 118,000 |
| Oktyabrsky | 104,000 |
| Omsk | 1,122,000 |
| Ordzhonikidze | 308,000 |
| Orekhovo-Zuyevo | 136,000 |
| Orenburg | 527,000 |
| Orsha | 120,000 |
| Orsk | 270,000 |
| Oryol | 331,000 |
| Osh | 204,000 |
| Panevėžys | 119,000 |
| Pavlodar | 302,000 |
| Pavlograd | 122,000 |
| Penza | 532,000 |
| Perm | 1,065,000 |
| Pervouralsk | 138,000 |
| Petropavlovsk | 229,000 |
| Petropavlovsk-Kamchatsky | 248,000 |
| Petrouralsk | 138,000 |
| Petrozavodsk | 259,000 |
| Pinsk | 113,000 |
| Podolsk | 208,000 |
| Poltava | 305,000 |
| Prokopyevsk | 276,000 |
| Pskov | 197,000 |
| Pyatigorsk | 120,000 |
| Riga | 890,000 |
| Rostov-na-Donu | 992,000 |
| Rovno | 226,000 |
| Rubtsovsk | 167,000 |
| Rudny | 116,000 |
| Rustavi | 145,000 |
| Ryazan | 500,000 |
| Salavat | 151,000 |
| Samarkand | 380,000 |
| Saransk | 315,000 |
| Sarapul | 110,000 |
| Saratov | 907,000 |
| Semipalatinsk | 324,000 |
| Serov | 103,000 |
| Serpukhov | 142,000 |
| Sevastopol | 345,000 |
| Severodonetsk | 125,000 |
| Severodvinsk | 234,000 |
| Shakhty | 223,000 |
| Shchelkovo | 106,000 |
| Shevchenko | 152,000 |
| Šiauliai | 137,000 |
| Simferopol | 333,000 |
| Slavyansk | 143,000 |
| Smolensk | 334,000 |
| Sochi | 313,000 |
| Solikamsk | 107,000 |
| Stakhanov | 110,000 |
| Stary Oskol | 161,000 |
| Stavropol | 299,000 |
| Sterlitamak | 245,000 |
| Sukhumi | 128,000 |
| Sumgait | 228,000 |
| Sumy | 262,000 |
| Surgut | 215,000 |
| Sverdlovsk (*Sverdlovsk obl.*) | 1,315,000 |
| Syktyvkar | 218,000 |
| Syzran | 173,000 |
| Taganrog | 291,000 |
| Taldy-Kurgan | 109,000 |
| Tallinn | 472,000 |
| Tambov | 300,000 |
| Tartu | 111,000 |
| Tashauz | 107,000 |
| Tashkent | 2,077,000 |
| Tbilisi | 1,174,000 |

| country city | population |
|---|---|
| Temirtau | 226,000 |
| Ternopol | 189,000 |
| Tiraspol | 166,000 |
| Tolyatti (Togliatti) | 610,000 |
| Tomsk | 483,000 |
| Tselinograd | 269,000 |
| Tula | 534,000 |
| Tyumen | 440,000 |
| Ufa | 1,077,000 |
| Ukhta | 102,100 |
| Ulan-Ude | 342,000 |
| Ulyanovsk | 566,000 |
| Uralsk | 197,000 |
| Urgench | 120,000 |
| Usolye-Sibirskoye | 109,000 |
| Ussuriysk | 157,000 |
| Ust-Ilimsk | 101,000 |
| Ust-Kamenogorsk | 313,000 |
| Uzhgorod | 108,000 |
| Velikiye Luki | 111,000 |
| Vilnius | 555,000 |
| Vinnitsa | 375,000 |
| Vitebsk | 340,000 |
| Vladimir | 336,000 |
| Vladivostok | 608,000 |
| Volgodonsk | 172,000 |
| Volgograd | 981,000 |
| Vologda | 273,000 |
| Volzhsky | 250,000 |
| Vorkuta | 110,000 |
| Voronezh | 860,000 |
| Voroshilovgrad | 503,000 |
| Votkinsk | 100,000 |
| Yakutsk | 184,000 |
| Yaroslavl | 630,000 |
| Yelets | 117,000 |
| Yenakiyevo | 117,000 |
| Yerevan | 1,148,000 |
| Yevpatoriya | 104,000 |
| Yoshkar-Ola | 236,000 |
| Yuzhno-Sakhalinsk | 163,000 |
| Zagorsk | 112,000 |
| Zaporozhye | 863,000 |
| Zelenograd | 144,000 |
| Zhdanov | 525,000 |
| Zhitomir | 282,000 |
| Zlatoust | 205,000 |
| **United Arab Emirates** (1980) | |
| ★ Abu Dhabi (Abū Ẓaby) | 243,000 |
| Al-'Ayn | 102,000 |
| Dubai (Dubayy) | 266,000 |
| Sharjah (ash-Shāriqah) | 125,000 |
| **United Kingdom** (1981) | |
| Aberdeen, Scot. | 190,465 |
| Belfast, N.Ire. | 354,400 |
| Birmingham | 1,024,118 |
| Blackburn | 110,254 |
| Blackpool | 149,012 |
| Bolton | 143,921 |
| Bournemouth | 148,382 |
| Bradford | 295,048 |
| Brighton | 137,985 |
| Bristol | 420,234 |
| Cardiff, Wales | 266,267 |
| Coventry | 322,573 |
| Derby | 220,681 |
| Dudley | 187,367 |
| Dundee, Scot. | 174,345 |
| Edinburgh, Scot. | 420,169 |
| Glasgow, Scot. | 765,030 |
| Gloucester | 108,150 |
| Huddersfield | 148,544 |
| Ipswich | 131,131 |
| Kingston upon Hull | 325,485 |
| Leeds | 451,841 |
| Leicester | 328,835 |
| Liverpool | 544,861 |
| ★ London | 6,677,928 |
| Luton | 164,743 |
| Manchester | 448,604 |
| Middlesbrough | 159,421 |
| Newcastle upon Tyne | 203,591 |
| Newport | 116,658 |
| Northampton | 155,694 |
| Norwich | 173,286 |
| Nottingham | 277,203 |
| Oldbury/Smethwick | 153,461 |
| Oldham | 107,830 |
| Oxford | 119,909 |
| Peterborough | 114,733 |
| Plymouth | 242,560 |
| Poole | 124,974 |
| Portsmouth | 177,905 |
| Preston | 168,405 |
| Reading | 198,341 |
| Rotherham | 123,312 |
| St. Helens | 114,822 |
| Sheffield | 477,257 |

| country city | population |
|---|---|
| Slough | 106,822 |
| Southampton | 214,802 |
| Southend-on-Sea | 156,969 |
| Stockport | 136,792 |
| Stoke-on-Trent | 275,168 |
| Sunderland | 195,896 |
| Sutton Coldfield | 103,097 |
| Swansea, Wales | 175,172 |
| Swindon | 128,493 |
| Walsall | 178,852 |
| West Bromwich | 154,531 |
| Wolverhampton | 265,631 |
| York | 126,377 |
| **United States** (1986 est.) | |
| Abilene (*Tex.*) | 112,430 |
| Akron (*Ohio*) | 222,060 |
| Albuquerque (*N.M.*) | 366,750 |
| Alexandria (*Va.*) | 107,800 |
| Allentown (*Pa.*) | 104,360 |
| Amarillo (*Tex.*) | 165,850 |
| Anaheim (*Calif.*) | 240,730 |
| Anchorage (*Alsk.*) | 235,000 |
| Ann Arbor (*Mich.*) | 107,800 |
| Arlington (*Tex.*) | 249,770 |
| Atlanta (*Ga.*) | 421,910 |
| Aurora (*Colo.*) | 217,990 |
| Austin (*Tex.*) | 466,550 |
| Bakersfield (*Calif.*) | 150,400 |
| Baltimore (*Md.*) | 752,800 |
| Baton Rouge (*La.*) | 241,130 |
| Beaumont (*Tex.*) | 119,900 |
| Berkeley (*Calif.*) | 104,110 |
| Birmingham (*Ala.*) | 277,510 |
| Boise City (*Idaho*) | 108,390 |
| Boston (*Mass.*) | 573,600 |
| Bridgeport (*Conn.*) | 141,860 |
| Brownsville (*Tex.*) | 102,110 |
| Buffalo (*N.Y.*) | 324,820 |
| Cedar Rapids (*Iowa*) | 108,370 |
| Charlotte (*N.C.*) | 352,070 |
| Chattanooga (*Tenn.*) | 162,170 |
| Chesapeake (*Va.*) | 134,400 |
| Chicago (*Ill.*) | 3,009,530 |
| Chula Vista (*Calif.*) | 118,840 |
| Cincinnati (*Ohio*) | 369,750 |
| Cleveland (*Ohio*) | 535,830 |
| Colorado Springs (*Colo.*) | 272,000 |
| Columbus (*Ga.*) | 180,180 |
| Columbus (*Ohio*) | 566,030 |
| Concord (*Calif.*) | 105,980 |
| Corpus Christi (*Tex.*) | 263,900 |
| Dallas (*Tex.*) | 1,003,520 |
| Dayton (*Ohio*) | 178,920 |
| Denver (*Colo.*) | 505,000 |
| Des Moines (*Iowa*) | 192,060 |
| Detroit (*Mich.*) | 1,086,220 |
| Durham (*N.C.*) | 113,890 |
| El Paso (*Tex.*) | 491,800 |
| Elizabeth (*N.J.*) | 106,560 |
| Erie (*Pa.*) | 115,270 |
| Eugene (*Ore.*) | 105,410 |
| Evansville (*Ind.*) | 129,480 |
| Flint (*Mich.*) | 145,590 |
| Fort Lauderdale (*Fla.*) | 148,660 |
| Fort Wayne (*Ind.*) | 172,900 |
| Fort Worth (*Tex.*) | 429,550 |
| Fremont (*Calif.*) | 153,580 |
| Fresno (*Calif.*) | 284,660 |
| Fullerton (*Calif.*) | 108,750 |
| Garden Grove (*Calif.*) | 134,850 |
| Garland (*Tex.*) | 176,510 |
| Gary (*Ind.*) | 136,790 |
| Glendale (*Ariz.*) | 125,820 |
| Glendale (*Calif.*) | 153,660 |
| Grand Rapids (*Mich.*) | 186,530 |
| Greensboro (*N.C.*) | 176,650 |
| Hampton (*Va.*) | 126,000 |
| Hartford (*Conn.*) | 137,980 |
| Hayward (*Calif.*) | 101,520 |
| Hialeah (*Fla.*) | 161,760 |
| Hollywood (*Fla.*) | 120,940 |
| Honolulu (*Ha.*) | 372,330 |
| Houston (*Tex.*) | 1,728,910 |
| Huntington Beach (*Calif.*) | 183,620 |
| Huntsville (*Ala.*) | 163,420 |
| Independence (*Mo.*) | 112,950 |
| Indianapolis (*Ind.*) | 719,820 |
| Inglewood (*Calif.*) | 102,550 |
| Irving (*Tex.*) | 128,530 |
| Jackson (*Miss.*) | 208,440 |
| Jacksonville (*Fla.*) | 610,030 |
| Jersey City (*N.J.*) | 219,480 |
| Kansas City (*Kan.*) | 162,070 |
| Kansas City (*Mo.*) | 441,170 |
| Knoxville (*Tenn.*) | 173,210 |
| Lakewood (*Colo.*) | 122,140 |
| Lansing (*Mich.*) | 128,980 |
| Laredo (*Tex.*) | 117,060 |
| Las Vegas (*Nev.*) | 193,240 |

| country city | population |
|---|---|
| Lexington (*Ky.*) | 213,600 |
| Lincoln (*Neb.*) | 183,050 |
| Little Rock (*Ark.*) | 181,030 |
| Livonia (*Mich.*) | 100,540 |
| Long Beach (*Calif.*) | 396,280 |
| Los Angeles (*Calif.*) | 3,259,300 |
| Louisville (*Ky.*) | 287,460 |
| Lubbock (*Tex.*) | 186,400 |
| Macon (*Ga.*) | 118,420 |
| Madison (*Wis.*) | 175,850 |
| Memphis (*Tenn.*) | 652,640 |
| Mesa (*Ariz.*) | 251,430 |
| Miami (*Fla.*) | 373,940 |
| Milwaukee (*Wis.*) | 605,090 |
| Minneapolis (*Minn.*) | 356,840 |
| Mobile (*Ala.*) | 203,260 |
| Modesto (*Calif.*) | 132,940 |
| Montgomery (*Ala.*) | 194,290 |
| Nashville (*Tenn.*) | 473,670 |
| New Haven (*Conn.*) | 123,450 |
| New Orleans (*La.*) | 554,500 |
| New York City (*N.Y.*) | 7,262,700 |
| Newark (*N.J.*) | 316,300 |
| Newport News (*Va.*) | 161,700 |
| Norfolk (*Va.*) | 274,800 |
| Oakland (*Calif.*) | 356,960 |
| Odessa (*Tex.*) | 101,210 |
| Oklahoma City (*Okla.*) | 466,120 |
| Omaha (*Neb.*) | 349,270 |
| Ontario (*Calif.*) | 114,310 |
| Orange (*Calif.*) | 100,740 |
| Orlando (*Fla.*) | 145,940 |
| Oxnard (*Calif.*) | 130,800 |
| Pasadena (*Calif.*) | 129,900 |
| Pasadena (*Tex.*) | 118,050 |
| Paterson (*N.J.*) | 139,160 |
| Peoria (*Ill.*) | 110,290 |
| Philadelphia (*Pa.*) | 1,642,900 |
| Phoenix (*Ariz.*) | 894,070 |
| Pittsburgh (*Pa.*) | 387,490 |
| Plano (*Tex.*) | 111,030 |
| Pomona (*Calif.*) | 115,540 |
| Portland (*Ore.*) | 387,870 |
| Portsmouth (*Va.*) | 111,000 |
| Providence (*R.I.*) | 157,200 |
| Pueblo (*Colo.*) | 101,240 |
| Raleigh (*N.C.*) | 180,430 |
| Reno (*Nev.*) | 111,420 |
| Richmond (*Va.*) | 217,700 |
| Riverside (*Calif.*) | 196,750 |
| Roanoke (*Va.*) | 101,900 |
| Rochester (*N.Y.*) | 235,970 |
| Rockford (*Ill.*) | 135,760 |
| Sacramento (*Calif.*) | 323,550 |
| St. Louis (*Mo.*) | 426,300 |
| St. Paul (*Minn.*) | 263,680 |
| St. Petersburg (*Fla.*) | 239,480 |
| Salt Lake City (*Utah*) | 158,440 |
| San Antonio (*Tex.*) | 914,350 |
| San Bernardino (*Calif.*) | 138,610 |
| San Diego (*Calif.*) | 1,015,190 |
| San Francisco (*Calif.*) | 749,000 |
| San Jose (*Calif.*) | 712,080 |
| Santa Ana (*Calif.*) | 236,780 |
| Savannah (*Ga.*) | 146,800 |
| Scottsdale (*Ariz.*) | 111,140 |
| Seattle (*Wash.*) | 486,200 |
| Shreveport (*La.*) | 220,380 |
| South Bend (*Ind.*) | 107,190 |
| Spokane (*Wash.*) | 172,890 |
| Springfield (*Mass.*) | 149,410 |
| Springfield (*Ill.*) | 100,290 |
| Springfield (*Mo.*) | 139,360 |
| Stamford (*Conn.*) | 101,080 |
| Sterling Heights (*Mich.*) | 111,960 |
| Stockton (*Calif.*) | 183,430 |
| Sunnyvale (*Calif.*) | 112,130 |
| Syracuse (*N.Y.*) | 160,750 |
| Tacoma (*Wash.*) | 158,950 |
| Tallahassee (*Fla.*) | 119,480 |
| Tampa (*Fla.*) | 277,580 |
| Tempe (*Ariz.*) | 136,840 |
| Toledo (*Ohio*) | 340,680 |
| Topeka (*Kan.*) | 118,580 |
| Torrance (*Calif.*) | 135,570 |
| Tucson (*Ariz.*) | 358,850 |
| Tulsa (*Okla.*) | 373,750 |
| Virginia Beach (*Va.*) | 333,400 |
| Waco (*Tex.*) | 105,220 |
| Warren (*Mich.*) | 149,800 |
| ★ Washington D.C. | 626,000 |
| Waterbury (*Conn.*) | 102,300 |
| Wichita (*Kan.*) | 288,070 |
| Winston-Salem (*N.C.*) | 148,080 |
| Worcester (*Mass.*) | 157,770 |
| Yonkers (*N.Y.*) | 186,080 |
| Youngstown (*Ohio*) | 104,690 |
| **Uruguay** (1985 est.) | |
| ★ Montevideo | 1,246,000 |

| country city | population |
|---|---|
| **Vanuatu** (1987 est.) | |
| ★ Vila | 15,100 |
| **Venezuela** (1987 est.) | |
| Acarigua | 119,611 |
| Barcelona | 216,964 |
| Barinas | 158,309 |
| Barquisimeto | 661,265 |
| Baruta | 256,058 |
| Cabimas | 162,097 |
| ★ Caracas | 1,246,677 |
| Ciudad Bolívar | 240,954 |
| Ciudad Guayana (San Felix de Guayana) | 458,789 |
| Coro | 124,317 |
| Cumaná | 218,413 |
| Guarenas | 101,742[11] |
| Los Teques | 148,602 |
| Maracaibo | 1,124,432 |
| Maracay | 496,662 |
| Maturín | 205,076 |
| Mérida | 188,160 |
| Petare | 494,196 |
| San Cristóbal | 234,905 |
| Turmero | 110,186[11] |
| Valencia | 856,455 |
| Valera | 131,279 |
| **Vietnam** (1979) | |
| Bien Hoa | 190,086 |
| Can Tho | 182,856 |
| Da Nang | 318,655 |
| Haiphong | 330,755 |
| ★ Hanoi | 819,913 |
| Ho Chi Minh City (Saigon) | 2,441,185 |
| Hon Gai | 115,312 |
| Hue | 165,865 |
| Long Xuyen | 112,488 |
| My Tho | 101,496 |
| Nam Dinh | 161,180 |
| Nha Trang | 172,663 |
| Quy Nhon | 130,534 |
| Tha Nguyen | 138,023 |
| Thanh Hoa | 103,981 |
| Vinh | 154,040 |
| **Virgin Islands (U.S.)** (1980) | |
| ★ Charlotte Amalie | 11,842 |
| **Wallis and Futuna** (1983) | |
| ★ Matautu | 815 |
| **West Bank** | |
| ★ — | — |
| **Western Sahara** (1982) | |
| ★ El Aaiún (Laayoune) | 93,875 |
| **Western Samoa** (1981) | |
| ★ Apia | 33,170 |
| **Yemen (Aden)** (1984 est.) | |
| ★ Aden | 318,000 |
| **Yemen (Ṣan'ā')** (1986) | |
| Al-Ḥudaydah | 155,110 |
| ★ Ṣan'ā' | 427,185 |
| Ta'izz | 178,430 |
| **Yugoslavia** (1981) | |
| Banja Luka | 123,937 |
| ★ Belgrade (Beograd) | 1,087,915 |
| Ljubljana | 224,817 |
| Maribor | 106,113 |
| Niš | 161,376 |
| Novi Sad | 170,020 |
| Osijek | 104,775 |
| Priština | 108,083 |
| Rijeka | 159,433 |
| Sarajevo | 319,017 |
| Skopje (Skoplje) | 408,143 |
| Split | 169,322 |
| Subotica | 100,516 |
| Zagreb | 649,586 |
| **Zaire** (1984) | |
| Bukavu | 171,064 |
| Kananga | 290,898 |
| Kikwit | 146,784 |
| ★ Kinshasa | 2,653,558 |
| Kisangani | 282,650 |
| Likasi | 194,465 |
| Lubumbashi | 543,268 |
| Matadi | 144,742 |
| Mbandaka | 125,263 |
| Mbuji-Mayi | 423,363 |
| **Zambia** (1980) | |
| Chingola | 145,869 |
| Kabwe | 143,635 |
| Kitwe | 314,794 |
| Luanshya | 132,164 |
| ★ Lusaka | 538,469 |
| Mufulira | 149,778 |
| Ndola | 282,439 |
| **Zimbabwe** (1983 est.) | |
| Bulawayo | 429,000 |
| Chitungwiza | 202,000 |
| ★ Harare | 681,000 |

[1]1983. [2]1977. [3]1984. [4]All populations cited are for officially defined, widest agglomerations of metropolitan areas. [5]Chittagong, Dhākā, Khulna, and Rājshāhi are metropolitan areas. Others are urban agglomerations (not cities proper). [6]Excludes the agricultural population of the named civil division. [7]Excludes population of Lefkoşe (Turkish-occupied Nicosia), estimated at 37,400 in 1985. [8]No separate areas within the state are distinguished administratively as cities. [9]1970. [10]1980. [11]1981. [12]1978. [13]1979.

# Language

This table presents data on the principal language communities of each of the countries of the world. The countries, and the principal languages used in each, are listed alphabetically; a bullet (●) indicates those languages that are designated as official by each country. The sum of the estimated populations for each language community and of the "Other" group equals the estimated de facto population of the country given in the *Area and population* table.

The estimates represent, so far as national data collection systems permit, the distribution of mother tongues (a mother tongue being the language spoken first and, usually, most fluently by an individual). Many countries do not collect data on this basis, however, and for these countries a variety of techniques have been used to approximate mother-tongue distribution. Some countries compile data on ethnic or "national" groups; for such countries ethnic distribution was often assumed to conform roughly to the distribution of language communities. This approach, however, must be used with caution, because a minority population is not always free to educate its children in its own language and because better economic opportunities often draw minority group members into the majority-language community. For some countries, a given individual may only be visible in national statistics as a passport-holder of a foreign nation, however long he may remain resident. Such persons, often guest workers, have sometimes had to be assumed to be speakers of the principal language of their home country. For example, since The Netherlands does not collect language data, holders of Moroccan passports were assumed to be speakers of Arabic (although perhaps a quarter of them might be of Berber heritage). For other countries, the language mosaic may be so complex, the language communities so minute in size, scholarly study so inadequate, and the census base so obsolete that it was possible only to assign percentages to groups of related languages, despite their mutual unintelligibility (Papuan and Melanesian languages in Papua New Guinea, for instance). For some countries in the Americas, so few speakers of any single indigenous language remain that it was necessary to combine these groups as *Amerindian* so as to give a fair impression of their aggregate size within their respective countries.

No systematic attempt has been made to account for populations that may legitimately be described as bilingual, unless the country itself collects data on that basis, as does Bolivia or the Comoros, for example. Where a nonindigenous official or excolonial language constitutes a lingua franca of the country, however, speakers of the language as a second tongue are shown in italics, even though very few may speak it as a mother tongue. Similarly, no attempt has been made to distinguish between degrees of dialectal variance among communities *usually* classified as belonging to the same language—*e.g.,* between French and Occitan (the dialect of southern France), or between the various dialects of Chinese.

In giving the names of Bantu languages, grammatical particles specific to a language's autonym (name for itself) have been omitted (the form *Rwanda* is used here, for example, rather than *kinyaRwanda,* and *Tswana* instead of *seTswana*). Parenthetical alternatives are given for a number of languages that differ markedly from the name of the people speaking them (such as Kurukh, spoken by the Oraon tribes of India) or that may be combined with other groups sometimes distinguishable in national data but appearing here under the name of the largest member—*e.g.,* "Tamil (and other Indian languages)" combining data on South Asian Indian populations in Singapore. The term *patois* as used here refers to distinguishable dialectal communities related to a national, official, or former colonial language (such as the French patois that survives in Grenada from the end of French rule in 1783).

## Language

| Major languages by country | Number of speakers | Major languages by country | Number of speakers | Major languages by country | Number of speakers | Major languages by country | Number of speakers | Major languages by country | Number of speakers |
|---|---|---|---|---|---|---|---|---|---|
| **Afghanistan**[1] | | **Aruba** | | Somba | 230,000 | Mande | 730,000 | **Cape Verde** | |
| ● Dari (Persian), of which | | ● Dutch | ... | Yoruba (Nago) | 380,000 | Mossi | 3,990,000 | Crioulo (Portuguese | |
| Chahar Aimaq | 410,000 | Papiamento | 59,000 | Other | 280,000 | Senufo | 440,000 | Creole) | 350,000 |
| Hazāra | 1,240,000 | Other | 7,000 | | | Tuareg | 280,000 | ● Portuguese | ... |
| Tadzhik | 2,880,000 | | | **Bermuda** | | Other | 210,000 | | |
| ● Pashto | 7,410,000 | **Australia** | | ● English | 54,000 | | | **Cayman Islands** | |
| Turkmen | 290,000 | ● English | 15,992,000 | Other | 4,000 | **Burma**[1] | | ● English | 23,000 |
| Uzbek | 1,240,000 | Other (including | | | | ● Burmese | 26,670,000 | | |
| Other (including | | Aboriginal | | **Bhutan**[1] | | Karen | 2,590,000 | **Central African Republic**[1] | |
| other Dari) | 720,000 | languages) | 196,000 | Assamese | 177,000 | Rakhine | | Banda | 790,000 |
| | | | | ● Dzongkha (Bhutia) | 836,000 | (Arakanese) | 1,730,000 | Baya (Gbaya) | 680,000 |
| **Albania**[1] | | **Austria** | | Gurung | 207,000 | Shan | 3,490,000 | ● French | 320,000 |
| ● Albanian | 2,987,000 | Czech | 10,000 | Other | 118,000 | Other | 4,750,000 | Kare | 70,000 |
| Greek | 58,000 | ● German | 7,370,000 | | | | | Mbaka | 120,000 |
| Macedonian | 10,000 | Hungarian | 19,000 | **Bolivia** | | **Burundi**[1] | | Mbum | 110,000 |
| Montenegrin | 5,000 | Serbo-Croatian | 32,000 | ● Aymara | 512,000 | ● French | 340,000 | Ngbandi | 290,000 |
| Romanian | 16,000 | Slovene | 23,000 | ● Quechua | 927,000 | ● Rundi | 4,940,000 | Sango (lingua franca) | ... |
| Other | 11,000 | Other | 99,000 | ● Spanish | 2,474,000 | Other[3] | 50,000 | Sara | 190,000 |
| | | | | Spanish-Aymara | 1,416,000 | | | Zande (Azande) | 270,000 |
| **Algeria**[1] | | **Bahamas, The** | | Spanish-Quechua | 1,113,000 | **Cameroon**[1] | | Other | 240,000 |
| ● Arabic | 19,080,000 | ● English | ... | Spanish-Aymara- | | Bamileke-Widekum- | | | |
| Berber | 3,920,000 | English Creole | 208,000 | Quechua | 179,000 | Bamum | 2,000,000 | **Chad**[1] | |
| French | 30,000 | French (Haitian) Creole | 25,000 | Aymara-Quechua | 85,000 | Duala-Lunda-Basa | 1,580,000 | Arabic | 1,374,000 |
| Other | 80,000 | Other | 12,000 | Spanish-others | 82,000 | ● English | ... | Dagu | 121,000 |
| | | | | Other | 11,000 | Fang | 2,110,000 | ● French | 310,000 |
| **American Samoa** | | **Bahrain** | | | | ● French | 1,620,000 | Hausa | 121,000 |
| ● English | 1,000 | ● Arabic | 350,000 | **Botswana**[1] | | Fulani | 1,030,000 | Kanuri | 121,000 |
| ● Samoan | 33,000 | Other | 130,000 | ● English | ... | Maka | 420,000 | Kotoko | 110,000 |
| Other | 3,000 | | | Khoikhoin (Hottentot) | 29,000 | Mandara | 610,000 | Masa | 121,000 |
| | | **Bangladesh**[1] | | Ndebele | 15,000 | Tikar | 800,000 | Masalit, Maba, | |
| **Andorra** | | ● Bengali | 102,920,000 | San (Bushmen) | 41,000 | Other | 2,210,000 | and Mimi | 330,000 |
| ● Catalan | 15,000 | Chakma | 390,000 | Shona | 145,000 | | | Mbum | 341,000 |
| French | 3,000 | Garo | 90,000 | Tswana | 881,000 | **Canada** | | Mubi | 220,000 |
| Castilian Spanish | 29,000 | Khasi | 80,000 | Other | 57,000 | Amerindian, of which | 132,000 | Sara, Bagirmi, | |
| Other | 2,000 | Magh | 200,000 | | | Cree | 70,000 | and Kreish | 1,605,000 |
| | | Santal | 70,000 | **Brazil**[1] | | Ojibway | 21,000 | Tama | 330,000 |
| **Angola**[1] | | Tippera | 70,000 | Amerindian languages | 240,000 | Arabic | 54,000 | Teda (Tubu) | 385,000 |
| Ambo (Ovambo) | 220,000 | Other | 1,470,000 | German | 780,000 | Chinese | 240,000 | Other | 86,000 |
| Chokwe | 380,000 | | | Italian | 590,000 | Czech | 26,000 | | |
| Herero | 70,000 | **Barbados** | | Japanese | 680,000 | Danish | 28,000 | **Chile**[1] | |
| Kongo | 1,200,000 | English Creole | 232,000 | ● Portuguese | 137,700,000 | Dutch | 160,000 | Amerindian languages | |
| Luchazi | 220,000 | ● English | 20,000 | Other | 1,310,000 | ● English | 15,837,000 | (mostly Araucanian) | 860,000 |
| Luimbe-Nganguela | 490,000 | Other | 2,000 | | | Eskimo (Inuktitut) | 21,000 | ● Spanish | 11,490,000 |
| Lunda | 110,000 | | | **British Virgin Islands** | | Finnish | 36,000 | Other | 190,000 |
| Luvale (Luena) | 330,000 | **Belgium**[1] | | ● English | 11,000 | ● French | 6,632,000 | | |
| Mbunda | 110,000 | ● Dutch | 5,770,000 | Other | 1,000 | German | 553,000 | **China**[1] | |
| Mbundu | 1,970,000 | ● French | 3,310,000 | | | Greek | 132,000 | Achang | 21,000 |
| Nyaneka-Humbe | 490,000 | ● German | 60,000 | **Brunei**[1] | | Hungarian | 90,000 | Bulan (Blang) | 62,000 |
| Ovimbundu | 3,380,000 | Italian | 260,000 | Chinese | 48,000 | Italian | 571,000 | Ch'iang (Qiang) | 109,000 |
| ● Portuguese | ... | Other | 460,000 | ● English | ... | Japanese | 21,000 | ● Chinese (Han) | 1,000,510,000 |
| Other | 140,000 | | | ● Malay | 156,000 | Norwegian | 21,000 | Chingpo (Jingpo) | 100,000 |
| | | **Belize** | | Other | 37,000 | Pilipino | 41,000 | Chuang (Zhuang) | 14,295,000 |
| **Anguilla** | | Black Carib (Garifuna) | 16,000 | | | Polish | 137,000 | Daghur (Daur) | 101,000 |
| ● English | 7,000 | ● English | ... | **Bulgaria**[1] | | Portuguese | 176,000 | Evenk (Ewenki) | 20,000 |
| | | English Creole | 90,000 | ● Bulgarian | 7,660,000 | Punjābī | 57,000 | Gelo | 948,000 |
| **Antigua and Barbuda** | | German | 4,000 | Romany | 220,000 | Russian | 34,000 | Hani (Woni) | 1,131,000 |
| ● English | 79,000 | Mayan | 23,000 | Turkish | 760,000 | Serbo-Croatian | 41,000 | Hui | 7,721,000 |
| Other | 3,000 | Spanish | 44,000 | Other | 330,000 | Slovak | 21,000 | Kazakh | 969,000 |
| | | | | | | Spanish | 75,000 | Kirgiz | 121,000 |
| **Argentina** | | **Benin**[1] | | **Burkina Faso**[1,2] | | Ukrainian | 305,000 | Korean | 1,885,000 |
| Guaraní | 280,000 | Bariba | 420,000 | Bobo | 570,000 | Vietnamese | 31,000 | Lahu | 325,000 |
| Italian | 850,000 | Fon | 2,820,000 | ● Fulani | 490,000 | Yiddish | 34,000 | Li | 948,000 |
| ● Spanish | 30,140,000 | ● French | 670,000 | Fulani | 690,000 | Other | 349,000 | Lisu | 515,000 |
| Other | 220,000 | Fulani (Peul) | 170,000 | Grusi | 430,000 | | | Manchu | 4,598,000 |
| | | | | Gurma | 400,000 | | | Maonan | 41,000 |
| | | | | Lobi | 580,000 | | | Miao | 5,364,000 |

| Major languages by country | Number of speakers |
|---|---|
| Mongol | 3,644,000 |
| Mulam | 97,000 |
| Nakhi (Naxi) | 269,000 |
| Nu | 25,000 |
| Pai (Bai) | 1,210,000 |
| Pumi | 26,000 |
| Puyi (Chung-chia) | 2,264,000 |
| Salar | 74,000 |
| She | 398,000 |
| Shui | 307,000 |
| Sibo (Xibe) | 89,000 |
| Tadzhik | 28,000 |
| Tai (Dai) | 896,000 |
| Tibetan | 4,110,000 |
| Tu | 171,000 |
| T'u-chia (Tujia) | 3,030,000 |
| T'ung (Dong) | 1,524,000 |
| Tung-hsiang (Dongxiang) | 298,000 |
| Uighur | 6,370,000 |
| Wa (Va) | 318,000 |
| Yao | 1,508,000 |
| Yi | 5,825,000 |
| Other | 957,000 |
| **Christmas Island[1]** | |
| Chinese | 1,300 |
| ● English | ... |
| Malay | 600 |
| Other | 100 |
| **Cocos (Keeling) Islands** | |
| ● English | 200 |
| Malay | 400 |
| **Colombia** | |
| Arawakan | 181,000 |
| Cariban | 83,000 |
| Chibchan | 186,000 |
| ● Spanish | 28,136,000 |
| Other | 69,000 |
| **Comoros** | |
| ● Arabic | |
| Comorian | 317,000 |
| Comorian-French | 54,000 |
| Comorian-Malagasy | 23,000 |
| Comorian-Arabic | 7,000 |
| Comorian-Swahili | 2,000 |
| Comorian-French-other | 16,000 |
| ● French | 20,000 |
| Other | 2,000 |
| **Congo** | |
| Bubangi | 26,000 |
| ● French | 640,000 |
| Kongo | 1,122,000 |
| Kota | 20,000 |
| Lingala (lingua franca) | ... |
| Maka | 40,000 |
| Mbete | 106,000 |
| Mboshi | 251,000 |
| Monokutuba (lingua franca) | ... |
| Punu | 66,000 |
| Sanga | 60,000 |
| Teke | 376,000 |
| Other | 113,000 |
| **Cook Islands** | |
| ● English | ... |
| ● Maori | 16,000 |
| Other | 2,000 |
| **Costa Rica** | |
| ● Spanish | 2,540,000 |
| Spanish-Chibchan | 10,000 |
| Chibchan | 5,000 |
| Chinese | 5,000 |
| English Creole | 52,000 |
| **Côte d'Ivoire[1]** | |
| Akan | 4,620,000 |
| ● French | 2,930,000 |
| Kru | 1,860,000 |
| Malinke | 1,660,000 |
| Southern Mande | 1,140,000 |
| Voltaic (including Senufo) | 1,750,000 |
| Other | 130,000 |
| **Cuba** | |
| ● Spanish | 10,302,000 |
| **Cyprus[1]** | |
| ● Greek | 570,000 |
| ● Turkish | 130,000 |
| Other | 20,000 |
| **Czechoslovakia[1]** | |
| ● Czech | 9,852,000 |
| German | 56,000 |
| Hungarian | 596,000 |
| Polish | 72,000 |
| Russian | 8,000 |
| ● Slovak | 4,910,000 |
| Ukrainian | 47,000 |
| Other | 51,000 |

| Major languages by country | Number of speakers |
|---|---|
| **Denmark[1]** | |
| ● Danish | 4,999,000 |
| English | 15,000 |
| German | 8,000 |
| Norwegian | 10,000 |
| Swedish | 8,000 |
| Turkish | 23,000 |
| Other | 64,000 |
| **Djibouti[1]** | |
| Afar | 174,000 |
| ● Arabic | 28,000 |
| ● French | 40,000 |
| Issa | 221,000 |
| Other | 47,000 |
| **Dominica** | |
| ● English | ... |
| French Creole | 62,000 |
| French Creole-English | 26,000 |
| **Dominican Republic** | |
| French (Haitian) Creole | 130,000 |
| ● Spanish | 6,570,000 |
| **Ecuador** | |
| Quechuan (and other Indian languages) | 690,000 |
| ● Spanish | 9,230,000 |
| **Egypt[1]** | |
| ● Arabic | 48,550,000 |
| Other | 590,000 |
| **El Salvador** | |
| ● Spanish | 4,974,000 |
| **Equatorial Guinea[1]** | |
| Bubi | 48,000 |
| Duala | 9,000 |
| Fang | 236,000 |
| Ibibio | 4,000 |
| Maka | 4,000 |
| ● Spanish | ... |
| Other[4] | 26,000 |
| **Ethiopia** | |
| ● Amharic | 17,340,000 |
| Gurage | 1,470,000 |
| Oromo (Galla) | 16,280,000 |
| Tigrinya | 3,860,000 |
| Other | 7,040,000 |
| **Faeroe Islands** | |
| ● Danish | ... |
| ● Faeroese | 46,000 |
| **Falkland Islands** | |
| ● English | 2,000 |
| **Fiji[1]** | |
| ● English | ... |
| Fijian | 334,000 |
| Hindi | 354,000 |
| Other | 38,000 |
| **Finland** | |
| ● Finnish | 4,626,000 |
| ● Swedish | 306,000 |
| Other | 10,000 |
| **France** | |
| Arabic[5] | 1,450,000 |
| ● French[5,6,7] | 51,850,000 |
| Basque | 80,000 |
| Breton | 550,000 |
| Catalan (Rousillonais) | 200,000 |
| Corsican | 160,000 |
| Dutch (Flemish) | 100,000 |
| German (Alsatian) | 1,270,000 |
| Occitan | 1,510,000 |
| Italian[5] | 340,000 |
| Polish[5] | 70,000 |
| Portuguese[5] | 780,000 |
| Spanish[5] | 330,000 |
| Turkish[5] | 130,000 |
| Other[5] | 670,000 |
| **French Guiana** | |
| Amerindian languages | 3,000 |
| English Creole | 1,000 |
| ● French | ... |
| French Creoles | 81,000 |
| Other | 4,000 |
| **French Polynesia** | |
| ● French[8] | 12,000 |
| Tahitian[8] | 127,000 |
| Other[8] | 44,000 |
| French speakers | 150,000 |
| **Gabon[1]** | |
| Fang | 420,000 |
| ● French | 400,000 |
| Mbete | 170,000 |
| Mpongwe | 180,000 |
| Punu | 140,000 |
| Other | 280,000 |

| Major languages by country | Number of speakers |
|---|---|
| **Gambia, The** | |
| Dyola | 81,000 |
| ● English | ... |
| Fulani | 148,000 |
| Malinke | 318,000 |
| Soninke | 65,000 |
| Wolof | 115,000 |
| Other | 61,000 |
| **Gaza Strip** | |
| Arabic | 539,000 |
| Hebrew | ... |
| Other | 9,000 |
| **Germany, East[1]** | |
| ● German | 16,550,000 |
| Other | 50,000 |
| **Germany, West[1]** | |
| Dutch | 300,000 |
| English | 120,000 |
| ● German | 57,090,000 |
| Greek | 370,000 |
| Italian | 610,000 |
| Spanish | 180,000 |
| Turkish | 1,040,000 |
| Other | 1,220,000 |
| **Ghana[1]** | |
| Akan | 7,070,000 |
| ● English | ... |
| Ewe | 1,600,000 |
| Ga-Adangme | 1,050,000 |
| Mossi | 2,140,000 |
| Other | 1,630,000 |
| **Gibraltar** | |
| ● English | 10,000 |
| Spanish | 11,000 |
| Other | 9,000 |
| **Greece[1]** | |
| Albanian | 60,000 |
| ● Greek | 9,560,000 |
| Macedonian | 150,000 |
| Turkish | 90,000 |
| Other | 140,000 |
| **Greenland** | |
| ● Danish | 5,000 |
| ● Greenlandic | 49,000 |
| **Grenada** | |
| ● English | 100,000 |
| Other | 4,000 |
| **Guadeloupe** | |
| French Creole and French | 319,000 |
| ● French | ... |
| Other | 16,000 |
| **Guam** | |
| Chamorro | 43,000 |
| ● English | 44,000 |
| Japanese | 2,000 |
| Palauan | 1,000 |
| Philippine languages | 21,000 |
| Other | 13,000 |
| **Guatemala** | |
| Mayan languages | 2,843,000 |
| Cakchiquel | 534,000 |
| Kekchí | 343,000 |
| Quiché | 1,127,000 |
| ● Spanish | 5,572,000 |
| Black Carib (Garífuna) | 19,000 |
| **Guernsey** | |
| ● English | 60,000 |
| ● French | ... |
| **Guinea[1]** | |
| ● French | 540,000 |
| Fulani (Peul) | 2,460,000 |
| Kissi | 380,000 |
| Mande, of which | 3,250,000 |
| Malinke | 1,480,000 |
| Susu | 700,000 |
| Other | 1,070,000 |
| **Guinea-Bissau[1]** | |
| Balante | 250,000 |
| Fulani | 210,000 |
| Malinke | 110,000 |
| Mandyako | 100,000 |
| Pepel | 90,000 |
| ● Portuguese | ... |
| Other | 160,000 |
| **Guyana** | |
| Amerindian languages | 15,000 |
| Arawakan | 6,000 |
| Cariban | 10,000 |
| ● English | ... |
| English Creole | 626,000 |
| Other (includes Caribbean Hindi and English) | 160,000 |

| Major languages by country | Number of speakers |
|---|---|
| **Haiti** | |
| ● French | 50,000 |
| French-French Creole | 670,000 |
| French Creole | 4,820,000 |
| **Honduras** | |
| ● Spanish | 4,531,000 |
| Black Carib (Garífuna) | 95,000 |
| Miskito | 14,000 |
| English Creole | 15,000 |
| Other | 2,000 |
| **Hong Kong[1]** | |
| ● Chinese (Cantonese)[10] | 5,433,000 |
| ● English | ... |
| Pilipino | 37,000 |
| Other | 132,000 |
| **Hungary[1]** | |
| ● Hungarian | 10,540,000 |
| Other | 60,000 |
| **Iceland[1]** | |
| ● Icelandic | 237,000 |
| Other | 8,000 |
| **India** | |
| Anga (Angika) | 580,000 |
| Assamese | 12,820,000 |
| Baghēlkhandī | 330,000 |
| Bāgri | 1,510,000 |
| Banjārī | 670,000 |
| Barel | 330,000 |
| Bengali | 63,690,000 |
| Bhīlī (Bhilali) | 350,000 |
| Bhīlī (Bhilodi) | 1,790,000 |
| Bhojpuri | 20,510,000 |
| Boḍo | 730,000 |
| Bundēlkhandī | 540,000 |
| Chhattisgarhī | 9,580,000 |
| Ḍōgrī | 1,860,000 |
| ● English | ... |
| Garhwālī | 1,830,000 |
| Gāṙo | 590,000 |
| Gojri | 470,000 |
| Gōṇḍī | 2,210,000 |
| Gujarātī | 36,700,000 |
| Halbī | 500,000 |
| Hārautī | 480,000 |
| ● Hindī | 219,920,000 |
| Hō | 1,070,000 |
| Kachchī | 670,000 |
| Kannaḍa | 30,860,000 |
| Kashmiri | 3,460,000 |
| Khāsī | 550,000 |
| Khortha (Khotta) | 720,000 |
| Kōṅkaṇī | 2,180,000 |
| Kōrkū | 410,000 |
| Kōyā | 300,000 |
| Kui | 500,000 |
| Kumaunī | 1,770,000 |
| Kurukh (Oraon) | 1,770,000 |
| Lamani (Banjārī) | 1,720,000 |
| Lushai (Mizo) | 390,000 |
| Maghī (Magadhī) | 9,500,000 |
| Maithilī | 8,760,000 |
| Malayāḷam | 31,350,000 |
| Mālvī | 920,000 |
| Maṇḍeālī | 350,000 |
| Marāṭhī | 59,690,000 |
| Mārwāṛī | 6,740,000 |
| Meithei (Manipurī) | 1,120,000 |
| Mēwāṛī | 1,170,000 |
| Mikir | 290,000 |
| Muṇḍa | 310,000 |
| Muṇḍārī | 1,100,000 |
| Nagpuri | 480,000 |
| Nepali (Gōrkhālī) | 1,840,000 |
| Nimāḍī | 1,140,000 |
| Oriyā | 28,220,000 |
| Pahāṛī | 1,820,000 |
| Punjābī | 19,890,000 |
| Rajāsthānī | 3,000,000 |
| Sadānī (Sadrī) | 1,150,000 |
| Santālī | 5,280,000 |
| Savara (Sōrā) | 320,000 |
| Sindhī | 1,720,000 |
| Surgujia | 770,000 |
| Tamil | 53,780,000 |
| Telugu | 63,960,000 |
| Tripuri | 380,000 |
| Tuḷu | 1,660,000 |
| Urdū | 40,910,000 |
| Other | 11,070,000 |
| **Indonesia** | |
| ● Bahasa Indonesia | 20,700,000 |
| Balinese | 3,510,000 |
| Banjarese | 2,310,000 |
| Batak | 3,670,000 |
| Bugi | 3,310,000 |
| Javanese | 69,070,000 |
| Madurese | 8,280,000 |
| Minang | 4,340,000 |
| Sundanese | 26,270,000 |
| Other | 30,780,000 |

| Major languages by country | Number of speakers |
|---|---|
| **Iran[1]** | |
| Armenian | 240,000 |
| Iranian languages | 36,990,000 |
| Bakhtyārī (Lurī) | 840,000 |
| Baluchi | 1,140,000 |
| ● Farsī (Persian) | 22,780,000 |
| Gilaki | 2,640,000 |
| Kurdish | 4,560,000 |
| Lurī | 2,160,000 |
| Māzandarānī | 1,800,000 |
| Other | 1,080,000 |
| Semitic languages | 1,200,000 |
| Arabic | 1,080,000 |
| Other | 120,000 |
| Turkic languages | 11,130,000 |
| Afshari | 560,000 |
| Azerbaijani | 8,390,000 |
| Qashqa'i | 630,000 |
| Shahsavani | 300,000 |
| Turkish (mostly Pishagchi, Bayat, and Qajar) | 360,000 |
| Turkmen | 780,000 |
| Other | 100,000 |
| Other | 370,000 |
| **Iraq[1]** | |
| ● Arabic | 12,700,000 |
| Assyrian | 140,000 |
| Kurdish | 3,130,000 |
| Persian | 140,000 |
| Turkish | 60,000 |
| Turkmen | 220,000 |
| Other | 100,000 |
| **Ireland** | |
| ● English | 3,380,000 |
| ● Irish | 180,000 |
| **Isle of Man** | |
| ● English | 64,000 |
| **Israel** | |
| ● Arabic | 818,000 |
| English | 53,000 |
| French | 36,000 |
| German | 29,000 |
| ● Hebrew | 3,060,000 |
| Hungarian | 25,000 |
| Romanian | 69,000 |
| Russian | 77,000 |
| Spanish | 38,000 |
| Yiddish | 95,000 |
| Other | 148,000 |
| **Italy[1]** | |
| Albanian | 120,000 |
| Catalan | 30,000 |
| French | 300,000 |
| German | 300,000 |
| Greek | 40,000 |
| ● Italian | 53,850,000 |
| Rhaetian | 730,000 |
| Friulian | 710,000 |
| Ladin | 20,000 |
| Sardinian | 1,520,000 |
| Slovene | 120,000 |
| Other | 230,000 |
| **Jamaica** | |
| Chinese | 22,000 |
| ● English | 635,000 |
| English Creoles | 1,660,000 |
| Hindi and other Indian languages | 49,000 |
| Spanish | 5,000 |
| **Japan[1]** | |
| Chinese | 60,000 |
| ● Japanese | 121,370,000 |
| Korean | 580,000 |
| Other | 90,000 |
| **Jersey** | |
| ● English | 78,000 |
| French | ... |
| **Jordan[1]** | |
| ● Arabic | 2,830,000 |
| Other | 20,000 |
| **Kampuchea[1]** | |
| Chinese | 360,000 |
| ● Khmer | 6,770,000 |
| Vietnamese | 360,000 |
| Other[11] | 200,000 |
| **Kenya** | |
| Arabic | 57,000 |
| Bajun (Rajun) | 53,000 |
| Basuba | 86,000 |
| Boran | 99,000 |
| Degodia | 134,000 |
| Embu | 260,000 |
| Gabbra | 44,000 |
| Gurreh | 119,000 |
| Gusii (Kisii) | 1,356,000 |
| Kalenjin | 2,374,000 |
| Kamba | 2,479,000 |

## Language (continued)

| Major languages by country | Number of speakers |
|---|---|
| Kikuyu | 4,602,000 |
| Kuria | 128,000 |
| Luhya | 3,045,000 |
| Luo | 2,810,000 |
| Masai | 346,000 |
| Mbere | 88,000 |
| Meru | 1,207,000 |
| Nyika (Mijikenda) | 1,053,000 |
| Ogaden | 37,000 |
| Orma | 46,000 |
| Pokomo | 57,000 |
| Sambur | 106,000 |
| Somali | 225,000 |
| ● Swahili | 13,200,000 |
| Taita | 220,000 |
| Teso | 189,000 |
| Turkana | 297,000 |
| Other[12] | 502,000 |
| **Kiribati**[1] | |
| ● English | ... |
| Kiribati (Gilbertese) | 65,200 |
| Tuvaluan (Ellice) | 400 |
| Other | 400 |
| **Korea, North**[1] | |
| ● Korean | 21,347,000 |
| Chinese | 43,000 |
| **Korea, South**[1] | |
| ● Korean | 42,040,000 |
| Other | 42,000 |
| **Kuwait**[1] | |
| ● Arabic | 1,697,000 |
| Other | 176,000 |
| **Laos**[1] | |
| ● Lao | 2,520,000 |
| Miao (Hmong)- | |
| Man (Yao) | 200,000 |
| Mon-Khmer | 170,000 |
| Palaung-Wa | 450,000 |
| Tai | 290,000 |
| Other[13] | 130,000 |
| **Lebanon**[1] | |
| ● Arabic | 2,513,000 |
| Armenian | 19,000 |
| French | 660,000 |
| Kurdish | 14,000 |
| Other | 215,000 |
| **Lesotho**[1] | |
| ● English | ... |
| ● Sesotho | 1,623,000 |
| Other | 5,000 |
| **Liberia**[1] | |
| ● English | 350,000 |
| Kwa (Kru) | |
| Bassa | 326,000 |
| Belle | 12,000 |
| Dey | 8,000 |
| Grebo | 211,000 |
| Krahn | 89,000 |
| Kru | 173,000 |
| Mande (Northern) | |
| Gbandi | 66,000 |
| Kpelle | 458,000 |
| Loma | 133,000 |
| Mandingo | 120,000 |
| Mende | 18,000 |
| Vai | 84,000 |
| Mande (Southern) | |
| Gio | 185,000 |
| Mano | 167,000 |
| West Atlantic (Mel) | |
| Gola | 93,000 |
| Kissi | 95,000 |
| Other | 116,000 |
| **Libya**[1] | |
| ● Arabic | 3,746,000 |
| Berber | 217,000 |
| Other[14] | 169,000 |
| **Liechtenstein**[1] | |
| ● German | 23,000 |
| Other | 4,000 |
| **Luxembourg**[1] | |
| Belgian | 10,000 |
| ● French | 15,000 |
| ● German | 10,000 |
| Italian | 22,000 |
| Luxembourgish | 258,000 |
| Portuguese | 31,000 |
| Other | 21,000 |
| **Macau** | |
| Chinese | 442,000 |
| ● Portuguese | ... |
| Other | 10,000 |
| **Madagascar**[1] | |
| ● French | 1,090,000 |
| Malagasy | 10,490,000 |
| Other | 110,000 |

| Major languages by country | Number of speakers |
|---|---|
| **Malaŵi** | |
| ● Chewa (Maravi) | 4,370,000 |
| ● English | ... |
| Lomwe | 1,380,000 |
| Ngoni | 500,000 |
| Yao | 990,000 |
| Other | 260,000 |
| **Malaysia** | |
| Bajau | 104,000 |
| Chinese | 958,000 |
| Chinese and others | 542,000 |
| Dusan | 172,000 |
| English | 83,000 |
| English and others | 184,000 |
| Iban | 394,000 |
| Iban and others | 64,000 |
| ● Malay | 7,130,000 |
| Malay and others | 2,534,000 |
| Tamil | 642,000 |
| Tamil and others | 10,000 |
| Other | 3,723,000 |
| **Maldives** | |
| ● Divehi (Maldivian) | 195,000 |
| **Mali**[1] | |
| Bambara | 2,770,000 |
| Bobo | 210,000 |
| Dogon | 350,000 |
| Dyula | 250,000 |
| ● French | 690,000 |
| Fulani | 1,210,000 |
| Malinke | 580,000 |
| Senufo | 1,040,000 |
| Songhai | 620,000 |
| Soninke | 760,000 |
| Tuareg | 640,000 |
| Other | 260,000 |
| **Malta**[1] | |
| ● English | 7,000 |
| ● Maltese | 330,000 |
| Other | 8,000 |
| **Martinique** | |
| French Creole and | |
| French | 318,000 |
| ● French | ... |
| Other | 11,000 |
| **Mauritania**[1] | |
| ● Arabic | ... |
| ● French | 100,000 |
| Fulani | 20,000 |
| Hassānīyah Arabic | 1,500,000 |
| Soninke | 50,000 |
| Tukulor | 100,000 |
| Wolof | 120,000 |
| Other | 50,000 |
| **Mauritius** | |
| Bhojpurī | 205,000 |
| ● English | 2,000 |
| French | 38,000 |
| French Creole | 577,000 |
| Hindī | 116,000 |
| Tamil | 37,000 |
| Urdū | 25,000 |
| Other | 41,000 |
| **Mayotte** | |
| Comorian | |
| (related to Swahili) | 74,000 |
| ● French | ... |
| **Mexico** | |
| Aztec (Nahuatl) | 1,948,000 |
| Chinantec | 109,000 |
| Chol | 137,000 |
| English | ... |
| Huastec | 147,000 |
| Huichol | 73,000 |
| Mazahua | 275,000 |
| Mazatec | 176,000 |
| Mayo | 80,000 |
| Mixtec | 457,000 |
| Mixe | 105,000 |
| Otomi | 433,000 |
| ● Spanish | 73,995,000 |
| Tarahumara | 89,000 |
| Tarasco | 168,000 |
| Tlapanec | 78,000 |
| Totonac | 277,000 |
| Tzeltal | 304,000 |
| Tzotzil | 189,000 |
| Yucatec (Maya) | 941,000 |
| Zapotec | 599,000 |
| Other | 745,000 |
| **Monaco**[1] | |
| English | 1,000 |
| ● French | 17,000 |
| Italian | 5,000 |
| Monegasque | 4,000 |
| Other | 2,000 |

| Major languages by country | Number of speakers |
|---|---|
| **Mongolia**[1] | |
| Bayad | 40,000 |
| Buryat | 38,000 |
| Dariganga | 30,000 |
| Dörbed | 56,000 |
| Dzakhchin | 24,000 |
| Kazakh | 105,000 |
| ● Khalkha (Mongolian) | 1,541,000 |
| Ould | 12,000 |
| Torgut | 10,000 |
| Uryankhai | 24,000 |
| Other | 109,000 |
| **Montserrat** | |
| ● English | 12,000 |
| **Morocco**[1] | |
| ● Arabic | 17,177,000 |
| Berber | 5,780,000 |
| Other[11] | 162,000 |
| **Mozambique**[1] | |
| Makua | 6,870,000 |
| Malaŵi | 1,740,000 |
| ● Portuguese | ... |
| Shona | 1,640,000 |
| Tsonga | 3,380,000 |
| Yao | 550,000 |
| Other | 340,000 |
| **Nauru** | |
| ● Nauruan | 4,900 |
| Other[12] | 3,100 |
| **Nepal** | |
| Bhojpurī | 1,337,000 |
| Bhutia (Sherpa) | 88,000 |
| Gurung | 204,000 |
| Hindī (Awadhi dialect) | 274,000 |
| Limbu | 151,000 |
| Magar | 249,000 |
| Maithili | 1,952,000 |
| ● Nepālī | 10,252,000 |
| Newari | 525,000 |
| Rai, Kirati | 258,000 |
| Tamang | 611,000 |
| Thārū | 638,000 |
| Other | 1,028,000 |
| **Netherlands, The**[1] | |
| Arabic | 120,000 |
| ● Dutch | 14,081,000 |
| Dutch and Frisian | 400,000 |
| German | 41,000 |
| Turkish | 158,000 |
| Other | 237,000 |
| **Netherlands Antilles** | |
| ● Dutch | ... |
| English | 14,000 |
| Papiamento | 151,000 |
| Other | 11,000 |
| **New Caledonia**[1] | |
| ● French | 58,000 |
| Melanesian languages | 64,000 |
| Wallisian | 13,000 |
| Other | 18,000 |
| **New Zealand** | |
| ● English | 3,120,000 |
| Maori | 107,000 |
| Other | 114,000 |
| **Nicaragua** | |
| ● Spanish | 3,318,000 |
| Misumalpan languages | |
| Miskito | 138,000 |
| Sumo | 8,000 |
| English Creole | 35,000 |
| Other | 3,000 |
| **Niger**[1] | |
| ● French | 340,000 |
| Fulani | 720,000 |
| Hausa | 3,610,000 |
| Kanuri | 600,000 |
| Songhai | 570,000 |
| Tuareg | 200,000 |
| Zerma and Dendi | 1,020,000 |
| Other | 220,000 |
| **Nigeria**[1] | |
| Arabic | 300,000 |
| Bura | 1,600,000 |
| Edo | 3,400,000 |
| ● English | ... |
| Fulani | 11,300,000 |
| Hausa | 21,500,000 |
| Ibibio | 5,700,000 |
| Igbo (Ibo) | 18,100,000 |
| Ijaw | 1,800,000 |
| Kanuri | 4,200,000 |
| Nupe | 1,200,000 |
| Tiv | 2,300,000 |
| Yoruba | 21,500,000 |
| Other | 7,900,000 |

| Major languages by country | Number of speakers |
|---|---|
| **Niue** | |
| ● English | ... |
| Niuean | 3,000 |
| **Norfolk Island** | |
| ● English | 2,000 |
| **Norway**[1] | |
| Danish | 16,000 |
| English | 23,000 |
| ● Norwegian | 4,078,000 |
| Swedish | 10,000 |
| Other | 53,000 |
| **Oman**[1] | |
| ● Arabic (Omani) | 1,020,000 |
| Bengali | 30,000 |
| Indian | 200,000 |
| Pakistani (mostly | |
| Baluchi) | 50,000 |
| Other | 30,000 |
| **Pacific Islands, Trust Territory of the Marshall Islands** | |
| ● English | 700 |
| ● Marshallese | 37,500 |
| Other | 2,800 |
| **Micronesia, Federated States of** | |
| ● English | 500 |
| Kosraean | 7,100 |
| Mortlockese | 7,400 |
| Palauan | 400 |
| Ponapean | 23,000 |
| Trukese | 40,300 |
| Woleaian | 3,600 |
| Yapese | 5,600 |
| Other | 9,100 |
| **Northern Mariana Islands** | |
| Chamorro | 11,500 |
| ● English | 1,100 |
| Palauan | 800 |
| Philippine languages | 2,900 |
| Woleaian | 2,400 |
| Other | 2,300 |
| **Palau** | |
| ● English | 100 |
| ● Palauan | 10,100 |
| Other | 1,800 |
| **Pakistan** | |
| Baluchi | 3,200,000 |
| Brahui | 1,270,000 |
| Pashto | 13,950,000 |
| Punjābī, of which | |
| Punjābī | 51,150,000 |
| Hindko | 2,580,000 |
| Sindhī, of which | |
| Sindhī | 12,500,000 |
| Siraiki | 10,440,000 |
| ● Urdū | 8,070,000 |
| Other[12] | 3,030,000 |
| **Panama** | |
| Amerindian languages | 106,000 |
| Chibchan | 95,000 |
| Cuna | 42,000 |
| Guaymí | 54,000 |
| Choco | 11,000 |
| Chinese | 7,000 |
| English Creoles | 318,000 |
| ● Spanish | 1,840,000 |
| Other | 3,000 |
| **Papua New Guinea**[1] | |
| ● English | ... |
| Papuan languages | 2,940,000 |
| Melanesian | |
| languages | 530,000 |
| Other[15] | 30,000 |
| **Paraguay** | |
| Guarani | 1,578,000 |
| Guarani and Spanish | 1,695,000 |
| ● Spanish | 152,000 |
| Other | 472,000 |
| **Peru** | |
| Aymara | 601,000 |
| ● Quechua | 5,509,000 |
| ● Spanish | 14,092,000 |
| Other | 524,000 |
| **Philippines** | |
| Aklanon | 560,000 |
| Bicol | 3,990,000 |
| Bolinao (Zambal) | 250,000 |
| Cebuano | 13,990,000 |
| Chavacano | 300,000 |
| Chinese | 140,000 |
| Davaweno | 170,000 |
| ● English | 20,000 |
| Hamtikanon | 470,000 |
| Hiligaynon/Ilongo | 5,730,000 |
| Ibanag | 340,000 |
| Ifugao | 180,000 |
| Ilocano | 6,390,000 |

| Major languages by country | Number of speakers |
|---|---|
| Kangkanai | 210,000 |
| Maguindanao | 690,000 |
| Manobo | 180,000 |
| Maranao | 820,000 |
| Masbate | 420,000 |
| Pampango | 1,970,000 |
| Pangasinan | 1,290,000 |
| ● Pilipino | |
| (Tagalog) | 13,660,000 |
| Romblon | 240,000 |
| Samal | 330,000 |
| Samar-Leyte | |
| (Waray-Waray) | 2,650,000 |
| Subanon | 190,000 |
| Sulu-Moro (Tau Sug) | 450,000 |
| Other | 1,730,000 |
| **Pitcairn Island** | |
| ● English | 44 |
| **Poland** | |
| Belorussian | 190,000 |
| ● Polish | 37,280,000 |
| Ukrainian | 230,000 |
| Other | 80,000 |
| **Portugal**[1] | |
| ● Portuguese | 10,199,000 |
| Other | 113,000 |
| **Puerto Rico** | |
| ● English | 12,000 |
| ● Spanish | 1,859,000 |
| Spanish and English | 1,360,000 |
| Other | 46,000 |
| **Qatar**[1] | |
| ● Arabic | 344,000 |
| Other | 35,000 |
| **Réunion** | |
| ● French | 170,000 |
| French Creole | 510,000 |
| Other[16] | 60,000 |
| **Romania**[1] | |
| Bulgarian | 10,000 |
| German | 363,000 |
| Hebrew | 26,000 |
| Hungarian | 1,764,000 |
| ● Romanian | 20,263,000 |
| Romany | 232,000 |
| Russian | 32,000 |
| Serbian | 34,000 |
| Slovak | 22,000 |
| Tatar | 23,000 |
| Turkish | 23,000 |
| Ukrainian | 55,000 |
| Other | 65,000 |
| **Rwanda** | |
| ● French | 440,000 |
| ● Rwanda | 6,490,000 |
| **St. Christopher and Nevis** | |
| ● English | ... |
| English Creole | 46,000 |
| **St. Helena and Ascension** | |
| ● English | 7,000 |
| **St. Lucia** | |
| ● English | ... |
| French/English Creole | 134,000 |
| Other | 8,000 |
| **St. Pierre and Miquelon**[1] | |
| ● French | 5,900 |
| Other | 100 |
| **St. Vincent and the Grenadines** | |
| ● English | ... |
| English Creole | 111,000 |
| Other | 1,000 |
| **San Marino**[1] | |
| ● Italian | 22,000 |
| **São Tomé and Príncipe** | |
| Crioulo (Portuguese | |
| Creole) | 112,000 |
| ● Portuguese | ... |
| **Saudi Arabia**[1] | |
| ● Arabic | 11,860,000 |
| Other | 620,000 |
| **Senegal**[1] | |
| Arabic | 70,000 |
| Dyola | 550,000 |
| ● French | 340,000 |
| Fulani | 1,210,000 |
| Mandingo (Malinke) | 440,000 |
| Serer | 1,150,000 |
| Soninke | 140,000 |
| Tukulor | 660,000 |
| Wolof | 2,460,000 |
| Other | 120,000 |

| Major languages by country | Number of speakers |
|---|---|
| **Seychelles** | |
| ● English | ... |
| ● French | 10,000 |
| French Creole | 63,000 |
| Other | 3,000 |
| **Sierra Leone**[1] | |
| Bullom | 142,000 |
| ● English | ... |
| Fulani | 142,000 |
| Kissi | 87,000 |
| Kono | 197,000 |
| Koranko | 132,000 |
| Krio (English Creole [lingua franca]) | ... |
| Limba | 318,000 |
| Mende | 1,314,000 |
| Temne | 1,205,000 |
| Yalunka | 132,000 |
| Other | 134,000 |
| **Singapore**[1] | |
| ● Bahasa Malaysia | 392,000 |
| Chinese | 1,995,000 |
| ● English | ... |
| ● Mandarin Chinese | ... |
| ● Tamil (and other Indian languages) | 169,000 |
| Other | 61,000 |
| **Solomon Islands**[1] | |
| ● English | ... |
| Melanesian languages | 248,000 |
| Papuan languages | 25,000 |
| Polynesian languages | 12,000 |
| Other[17] | 8,000 |
| **Somalia**[1] | |
| ● Arabic | ... |
| English | ... |
| ● Somali | 6,060,000 |
| Other | 100,000 |
| **South Africa**[18] | |
| ● Afrikaans | 5,003,000 |
| ● English | 1,851,000 |
| Nguni | 11,750,000 |
| Shangana-Tsonga | 870,000 |
| Sotho | 6,184,000 |
| Venda | 475,000 |
| Other | 2,471,000 |
| **Bophuthatswana** | |
| ● Afrikaans | ... |
| ● English | ... |
| ● Tswana | 1,089,000 |
| Other | 517,000 |
| **Ciskei** | |
| ● English | ... |
| ● Xhosa | 1,136,000 |
| Other | 4,000 |
| **KwaNdebele** | |
| Afrikaans | ... |
| English | ... |
| Ndebele | 180,000 |
| Sotho | 46,000 |
| Swazi | 18,000 |
| Other | 34,000 |
| **Transkei** | |
| ● English | ... |
| ● Xhosa | 2,668,000 |
| Other | 164,000 |
| **Venda** | |
| ● Afrikaans | ... |
| ● English | ... |
| ● Venda | 464,000 |
| Other | 52,000 |
| **South West Africa/Namibia** | |
| ● Afrikaans | ... |
| Bergdama (Damara) | 90,000 |
| East Caprivian (mostly Lozi) | 45,000 |
| ● English | 128,000 |
| German | ... |
| Herero | 90,000 |
| Kavango (Okavango) | 111,000 |
| Nama | 58,000 |
| Ovambo (Ambo [Kwanyama]) | 594,000 |
| San (Bushmen) | 34,000 |
| Other | 176,000 |

| Major languages by country | Number of speakers |
|---|---|
| **Spain** | |
| Basque | 890,000 |
| ● Castilian Spanish | 28,270,000 |
| Catalan | 6,370,000 |
| Galician | 3,180,000 |
| Other | 120,000 |
| **Sri Lanka** | |
| English | 11,000 |
| English and Sinhalese | 899,000 |
| English and Tamil | 186,000 |
| English, Sinhalese, and Tamil | 590,000 |
| ● Sinhalese | 9,869,000 |
| Sinhalese and Tamil | 1,527,000 |
| Tamil | 3,213,000 |
| Other | 56,000 |
| **Sudan, The**[1] | |
| ● Arabic | 12,620,000 |
| Azande | 690,000 |
| Bari | 630,000 |
| Beja | 1,630,000 |
| Dinka | 2,950,000 |
| Fur | 530,000 |
| Lotuko | 380,000 |
| Nubian | 2,070,000 |
| Nuer | 1,260,000 |
| Shilluk | 440,000 |
| Other | 2,380,000 |
| **Suriname** | |
| ● Dutch | ... |
| ● English | ... |
| Sranantonga | 170,000 |
| Sranantonga-other | 170,000 |
| Other (mostly Hindi, Javanese, and Saramacca) | 80,000 |
| **Swaziland**[1] | |
| ● English | ... |
| ● Swazi | 600,000 |
| Zulu | 70,000 |
| Other[19] | 40,000 |
| **Sweden**[1] | |
| Finnish | 263,000 |
| ● Swedish | 7,643,000 |
| Other | 481,000 |
| **Switzerland** | |
| ● French | 1,213,000 |
| ● German | 4,284,000 |
| ● Italian | 643,000 |
| Romansh | 53,000 |
| Other | 393,000 |
| **Syria**[1] | |
| ● Arabic | 9,740,000 |
| Armenian | 307,000 |
| Kurdish | 691,000 |
| Other | 230,000 |
| **Taiwan**[1] | |
| South Fukien Chinese | 13,152,000 |
| Hakka and Hokkien Chinese | 1,963,000 |
| ● Mandarin Chinese | 4,103,000 |
| Other | 412,000 |
| **Tanzania**[1] | |
| Chagga (Chaga), Pare | 1,140,000 |
| ● English | ... |
| Gogo | 910,000 |
| Ha | 800,000 |
| Haya | 1,370,000 |
| Hehet | 1,600,000 |
| Iramba | 660,000 |
| Luguru | 1,140,000 |
| Luo | 190,000 |
| Makonde | 1,370,000 |
| Masai | 230,000 |
| Ngoni | 310,000 |
| Nyakyusa | 1,250,000 |
| Nyamwezi (Sukuma) | 4,900,000 |
| Shambala | 990,000 |
| ● Swahili | 2,050,000 |
| Tatoga | 170,000 |
| Yao | 570,000 |
| Other | 3,570,000 |

| Major languages by country | Number of speakers |
|---|---|
| **Thailand**[1] | |
| Chinese | 6,510,000 |
| Karen | 190,000 |
| Malay | 1,950,000 |
| Mon-Khmer languages | 1,440,000 |
| Khmer | 680,000 |
| Kuy | 570,000 |
| Other | 190,000 |
| Thai languages | 43,000,000 |
| Lao | 14,430,000 |
| ● Thai (Siamese) | 28,200,000 |
| Other | 370,000 |
| Other | 550,000 |
| **Togo**[1] | |
| Ewe | 1,432,000 |
| ● French | 540,000 |
| Gurma | 332,000 |
| Kabre | 756,000 |
| Tem | 229,000 |
| Other | 408,000 |
| **Tokelau** | |
| ● English | ... |
| Tokelauan | 2,000 |
| **Tonga** | |
| ● English | ... |
| ● Tongan | 93,000 |
| Other | 2,000 |
| **Trinidad and Tobago** | |
| ● English | ... |
| English Creole | 1,221,000 |
| French Creole | ... |
| Hindi | ... |
| Spanish | ... |
| **Tunisia** | |
| ● Arabic | 5,358,000 |
| Arabic-French | 2,010,000 |
| Arabic-French-English | 241,000 |
| Arabic-other | 9,000 |
| Other-no Arabic | 21,000 |
| Other | 22,000 |
| **Turkey**[1] | |
| Arabic | 840,000 |
| Kurdish | 5,590,000 |
| ● Turkish | 45,270,000 |
| Other | 1,150,000 |
| **Turks and Caicos Islands** | |
| ● English | 9,000 |
| **Tuvalu** | |
| ● English | ... |
| Kiribati (Gilbertese) | 600 |
| Tuvaluan (Ellice) | 7,400 |
| **Uganda**[1] | |
| Acholi | 720,000 |
| Chiga (Kiga) | 1,060,000 |
| ● English | ... |
| Ganda (Luganda) | 2,760,000 |
| Gisu | 1,110,000 |
| Gwere | 450,000 |
| Karamojong | 320,000 |
| Lango | 930,000 |
| Lugbara | 590,000 |
| Nkole | 1,270,000 |
| Nyoro | 510,000 |
| Rundi | 480,000 |
| Rwanda | 900,000 |
| Soga | 1,270,000 |
| Teso | 1,380,000 |
| Toro | 500,000 |
| Other[3] | 1,260,000 |
| **U.S.S.R.** | |
| Armenian | 4,063,000 |
| Avar | 509,000 |
| Azerbaijani | 5,786,000 |
| Bashkir | 991,000 |
| Belorussian | 7,577,000 |
| Bulgarian | 265,000 |
| Buryat | 344,000 |
| Chechen | 804,000 |
| Chuvashi | 1,544,000 |
| Dargin | 304,000 |
| Estonian | 1,049,000 |

| Major languages by country | Number of speakers |
|---|---|
| Gagauz | 167,000 |
| Georgian | 3,788,000 |
| German | 1,191,000 |
| Greek | 141,000 |
| Hebrew | 277,000 |
| Hungarian | 176,000 |
| Ingush | 195,000 |
| Kabardinian | 340,000 |
| Kara-Kalpak | 314,000 |
| Kazakh | 6,897,000 |
| Kirgiz | 2,014,000 |
| Komi | 269,000 |
| Komi-Permyak | 126,000 |
| Korean | 232,000 |
| Kumyk | 242,000 |
| Lak | 102,000 |
| Latvian | 1,475,000 |
| Lezgian | 376,000 |
| Lithuanian | 3,012,000 |
| Mari | 582,000 |
| Moldavian | 2,985,000 |
| Mordovinian | 934,000 |
| Ossetian | 516,000 |
| Polish | 361,000 |
| ● Russian | 165,639,000 |
| Tadzhik | 3,058,000 |
| Tatar | 5,855,000 |
| Turkmenian | 2,160,000 |
| Tuvinian | 177,000 |
| Udmurt | 589,000 |
| Uighur | 196,000 |
| Ukrainian | 37,836,000 |
| Uzbek | 13,240,000 |
| Yakut | 337,000 |
| Other | 3,776,000 |
| **United Arab Emirates**[1] | |
| ● Arabic | 1,620,000 |
| Other | 240,000 |
| **United Kingdom** | |
| ● English | 52,860,000 |
| Scots-Gaelic | 70,000 |
| Welsh | 520,000 |
| Other | 3,420,000 |
| **United States** | |
| American Indian or Alaska Native languages | 417,000 |
| Arabic | 269,000 |
| Armenian | 114,000 |
| Asian Indian languages | 306,000 |
| Chinese | 741,000 |
| Czech | 137,000 |
| Dutch | 174,000 |
| ● English | 216,180,000 |
| Finnish | 78,000 |
| French | 1,828,000 |
| German | 1,837,000 |
| Greek | 468,000 |
| Hungarian | 201,000 |
| Italian | 1,836,000 |
| Japanese | 391,000 |
| Korean | 330,000 |
| Lithuanian | 81,000 |
| Norwegian | 126,000 |
| Persian | 126,000 |
| Philippine languages | 586,000 |
| Polish | 917,000 |
| Portuguese | 416,000 |
| Russian | 197,000 |
| Serbo-Croatian | 173,000 |
| Slovak | 96,000 |
| Spanish | 13,627,000 |
| Swedish | 113,000 |
| Thai | 110,000 |
| Ukrainian | 137,000 |
| Vietnamese | 238,000 |
| Yiddish | 358,000 |
| Other | 1,165,000 |
| **Uruguay** | |
| ● Spanish | 2,952,000 |
| Other | 106,000 |
| **Vanuatu** | |
| Bislama (English Creole) | 120,000 |
| ● English | ... |
| ● French | 40,000 |
| Melanesian languages | 137,000 |
| Other | 8,000 |

| Major languages by country | Number of speakers |
|---|---|
| **Venezuela** | |
| ● Spanish | 17,800,000 |
| Other | 480,000 |
| **Vietnam**[1] | |
| Bahnar | 120,000 |
| Chinese | 1,040,000 |
| Jarai | 220,000 |
| Khmer | 860,000 |
| Muong | 490,000 |
| Nung | 670,000 |
| Rhadé | 160,000 |
| Tai | 920,000 |
| Tay (Tho) | 1,070,000 |
| ● Vietnamese | 54,650,000 |
| Yao | 410,000 |
| Other | 1,850,000 |
| **Virgin Islands (U.S.)** | |
| ● English | 91,000 |
| French | 3,000 |
| Spanish | 15,000 |
| Other | 3,000 |
| **Wallis and Futuna** | |
| ● French | ... |
| Wallisian | 15,000 |
| **West Bank** | |
| Arabic | 815,000 |
| Hebrew | 29,000 |
| **Western Sahara** | |
| Arabic | 185,000 |
| **Western Samoa** | |
| ● English | 1,000 |
| ● Samoan | 77,000 |
| Samoan and English | 83,000 |
| Other | 200 |
| **Yemen (Aden)**[1] | |
| ● Arabic | 2,190,000 |
| Other | 100,000 |
| **Yemen (Şan'ā')**[1] | |
| ● Arabic | 8,250,000 |
| Other | 140,000 |
| **Yugoslavia**[1] | |
| Albanian | 1,810,000 |
| Hungarian | 450,000 |
| ● Macedonian | 1,400,000 |
| ● Serbo-Croatian | 16,310,000 |
| ● Slovenian | 1,830,000 |
| Other | 1,640,000 |
| **Zaire**[1] | |
| Azande | 1,940,000 |
| Boa | 740,000 |
| Chokwe | 580,000 |
| ● French | 2,470,000 |
| Kongo | 5,100,000 |
| Luba | 5,720,000 |
| Lugbara | 510,000 |
| Mongo | 4,290,000 |
| Ngala and Bangi | 1,840,000 |
| Rundi | 1,220,000 |
| Rwanda | 3,270,000 |
| Teke | 870,000 |
| Other | 5,720,000 |
| **Zambia**[1] | |
| Bemba | 2,520,000 |
| ● English | ... |
| Lozi | 690,000 |
| Luena | 370,000 |
| Lunda | 460,000 |
| Malawi | 970,000 |
| Ngoni | 260,000 |
| Tonga | 1,180,000 |
| Other[20] | 700,000 |
| **Zimbabwe** | |
| ● English | 669,000 |
| Ndebele (Nguni) | 1,362,000 |
| Nyanja | 448,000 |
| Shona | 6,121,000 |
| Other | 41,000 |

[1]Figures given represent ethnolinguistic groups.   [2]Majority of population speak Moré (language of the Mossi); Dyula is language of commerce.   [3]Swahili also spoken.   [4]Pidgin English and Portuguese patois also spoken.   [5]Based on "nationality" at 1982 census.   [6]Includes naturalized citizens.   [7]French is the universal language throughout France; traditional dialects and minority languages are retained regionally in the approximate numbers shown, however.   [8]Mother tongue.   [9]Mostly non-Tahitian Polynesian and Chinese languages bilingual or multilingual with French or Tahitian.   [10]Includes some Kan-Hakka and Mandarin speakers.   [11]French also spoken.   [12]English also spoken.   [13]English and French also spoken.   [14]English and Italian also spoken.   [15]About half the population also speaks Pisin (Pidgin English); English and Hiri (Police Motu) also spoken.   [16]Gujarāti and Chinese also spoken.   [17]Solomon Islands Pidgin (English) is the lingua franca.   [18]Excludes the Black states shown separately.   [19]Afrikaans and Portuguese also spoken.   [20]Swahili, Tshiluba, Lingala, and Kikongo are national languages.

# Religion

The following table presents statistics on religious affiliation for each of the countries of the world. An assessment was made for each country of the available data on distribution of religious communities within the total population; the best available figures, whether originating as census data, membership figures of the churches concerned, or estimates by external analysts in the absence of reliable local data, were applied as percentages to the estimated 1987 midyear population of the country to obtain the data shown below.

Several concepts govern the nature of the available data, each useful separately but none the basis of any standard of international practice in the collection of such data. The word "affiliation" was used above to describe the nature of the relationship joining the religious bodies named and the populations shown. This term implies some sort of formal, usually documentary, connection between the religion and the individual (a baptismal certificate, a child being assigned the religion of its parents on a census form, maintenance of one's name on the tax rolls of a state religion, etc.) but says nothing about the nature of the individual's personal religious practice, in that the individual may have lapsed, never been confirmed as an adult, joined another religion, or may have joined an organization that is formally atheist.

The user of these statistics should be careful to note that not only does the nature of the affiliation (with an organized religion) differ greatly from country to country, but the social context of religious practice does also. A country in which a single religion has long been predominant will often show more than 90% of its population to be *affiliated*, while in actual fact, no more than 10% may actually *practice* that religion on a regular basis. Such a situation often leads to undercounting of minority religions (where someone [head of household, communicant, child] is counted at all), blurring of distinctions seen to be significant elsewhere (a Hindu country may not distinguish Protestant [or even Christian] denominations; a Christian country may not distinguish among its Muslim or Buddhist citizens), or double-counting in countries where an individual may conscientiously practice more than one "religion" at a time.

Communist countries consciously attempt to ignore, suppress, or render invisible religious practice within their boundaries. Countries with large numbers of adherents of traditional, often animist, religions and belief systems usually have little or no formal methodology for defining the nature of local religious practice. On the other hand, countries with strong missionary traditions, or good census organizations, or few religious sensitivities may have very good, detailed, and meaningful data.

The most authoritative work available is DAVID B. BARRETT (ed.), *World Christian Encyclopedia* (1982); it examines both the theoretical and practical problems of collecting and analyzing religious statistics, assembles a mine of national detail, and establishes a basis for further study.

## Religion

| Religious affiliation | 1986 population |
|---|---|
| **Afghanistan** | |
| Sunnī Muslim | 10,500,000 |
| Shīʽī Muslim | 3,550,000 |
| other | 140,000 |
| **Albania** | |
| Muslim | 630,000 |
| Christian[1] | 170,000 |
| atheist | 580,000 |
| nonreligious | 1,710,000 |
| **Algeria** | |
| Sunnī Muslim | 22,910,000 |
| other | 210,000 |
| **American Samoa** | |
| Congregational | 20,000 |
| other | 17,000 |
| **Andorra** | |
| Roman Catholic | 46,000 |
| other | 3,000 |
| **Angola** | |
| Christian[1] | 8,190,000 |
| traditional beliefs | 860,000 |
| other | 50,000 |
| **Anguilla** | |
| Anglican | 2,800 |
| Methodist | 2,300 |
| other | 1,700 |
| **Antigua and Barbuda** | |
| Anglican | 36,000 |
| other Protestant | 35,000 |
| Roman Catholic | 8,000 |
| other | 3,000 |
| **Argentina** | |
| Roman Catholic | 29,240,000 |
| other | 2,260,000 |
| **Aruba** | |
| Roman Catholic | 57,500 |
| other | 7,400 |
| **Australia**[2] | |
| Anglican | 4,230,000 |
| Roman Catholic | 4,210,000 |
| Uniting Church | 790,000 |
| Presbyterian | 710,000 |
| Methodist | 550,000 |
| Orthodox | 470,000 |
| other Protestant | 1,310,000 |
| nonreligious | 1,750,000 |
| other | 2,170,000 |
| **Austria** | |
| Roman Catholic | 6,370,000 |
| Protestant | 420,000 |
| atheist and nonreligious | 450,000 |
| other | 310,000 |
| **Bahamas, The** | |
| Anglican | 50,000 |
| other Protestant | 120,000 |
| Roman Catholic | 60,000 |
| other | 10,000 |
| **Bahrain** | |
| Shīʽī Muslim | 290,000 |
| Sunnī Muslim | 120,000 |
| other | 80,000 |
| **Bangladesh** | |
| Muslim | 91,250,000 |
| Hindu | 12,770,000 |
| other | 1,290,000 |
| **Barbados** | |
| Anglican | 101,000 |
| other Protestant | 65,000 |
| other | 88,000 |
| **Belgium** | |
| Roman Catholic | 8,870,000 |
| other | 990,000 |
| **Belize** | |
| Roman Catholic | 109,000 |
| Anglican | 21,000 |
| other | 47,000 |
| **Benin** | |
| traditional beliefs | 2,640,000 |
| Roman Catholic | 800,000 |
| Muslim | 650,000 |
| other | 200,000 |
| **Bermuda** | |
| Anglican | 22,000 |
| Methodist | 9,000 |
| Roman Catholic | 8,000 |
| other | 19,000 |
| **Bhutan** | |
| Buddhist | 930,000 |
| Hindu | 330,000 |
| other | 80,000 |
| **Bolivia** | |
| Roman Catholic | 6,390,000 |
| other | 410,000 |
| **Botswana** | |
| Christian[1] | 590,000 |
| traditional beliefs | 570,000 |
| other | 10,000 |
| **Brazil** | |
| Roman Catholic | 124,060,000 |
| Protestant | 8,620,000 |
| Afro-American Spiritist | 2,830,000 |
| Spiritist | 2,400,000 |
| atheist and nonreligious | 1,980,000 |
| other | 1,410,000 |
| **British Virgin Islands** | |
| Methodist | 5,000 |
| Anglican | 3,000 |
| other | 4,000 |
| **Brunei** | |
| Muslim | 150,000 |
| Buddhist | 30,000 |
| other | 60,000 |
| **Bulgaria** | |
| Eastern Orthodox | 2,400,000 |
| Muslim | 670,000 |
| atheist | 5,790,000 |
| other | 110,000 |
| **Burkina Faso** | |
| traditional beliefs | 3,720,000 |
| Muslim | 3,570,000 |
| Christian[1] | 1,010,000 |
| **Burma** | |
| Buddhist | 35,080,000 |
| Christian | 1,930,000 |
| Muslim | 1,500,000 |
| other | 710,000 |
| **Burundi** | |
| Roman Catholic | 3,910,000 |
| traditional beliefs | 670,000 |
| other | 400,000 |
| **Cameroon** | |
| Roman Catholic | 3,770,000 |
| Protestant | 2,210,000 |
| traditional beliefs | 2,320,000 |
| Muslim | 2,370,000 |
| other | 90,000 |
| **Canada** | |
| Roman Catholic | 12,020,000 |
| Protestant | 10,650,000 |
| Eastern Orthodox | 390,000 |
| Jewish | 310,000 |
| Muslim | 100,000 |
| Sikh | 80,000 |
| Hindu | 80,000 |
| nonreligious | 1,910,000 |
| other | 310,000 |
| **Cape Verde** | |
| Roman Catholic | 342,000 |
| Protestant | 8,000 |
| **Cayman Islands** | |
| Presbyterian | 8,000 |
| Church of God | 5,000 |
| other | 10,000 |
| **Central African Republic** | |
| Protestant | 1,390,000 |
| Roman Catholic | 920,000 |
| traditional beliefs | 330,000 |
| other | 130,000 |
| **Chad** | |
| Muslim | 2,320,000 |
| Christian[1] | 1,740,000 |
| traditional beliefs | 1,200,000 |
| other | 10,000 |
| **Chile** | |
| Roman Catholic | 9,930,000 |
| other | 2,600,000 |
| **China** | |
| nonreligious | 634,800,000 |
| Chinese folk-religionist | 215,500,000 |
| atheist | 128,700,000 |
| Buddhist | 64,300,000 |
| Muslim | 25,700,000 |
| other | 3,200,000 |
| **Christmas Island** | |
| Buddhist | 700 |
| Muslim | 500 |
| Christian | 400 |
| other | 500 |
| **Cocos (Keeling) Islands** | |
| Muslim | 340 |
| Christian | 130 |
| other | 120 |
| **Colombia** | |
| Roman Catholic | 27,170,000 |
| other | 1,480,000 |
| **Comoros** | |
| Sunnī Muslim | 421,000 |
| Christian | 1,000 |
| **Congo** | |
| Roman Catholic | 1,180,000 |
| Protestant | 540,000 |
| African Christian | 310,000 |
| other | 150,000 |
| **Cook Islands** | |
| Congregational | 12,000 |
| other | 6,000 |
| **Costa Rica** | |
| Roman Catholic | 2,410,000 |
| other | 200,000 |
| **Côte d'Ivoire** | |
| traditional beliefs | 4,890,000 |
| Christian[1] | 3,570,000 |
| Muslim | 2,680,000 |
| other | 20,000 |
| **Cuba** | |
| Roman Catholic | 4,080,000 |
| nonreligious | 5,020,000 |
| atheist | 660,000 |
| other | 540,000 |
| **Cyprus** | |
| Greek Orthodox | 548,000 |
| Muslim | 133,000 |
| other | 38,000 |
| **Czechoslovakia** | |
| Roman Catholic | 10,230,000 |
| atheist | 3,130,000 |
| Czechoslovak Church | 690,000 |
| other | 1,540,000 |
| **Denmark** | |
| Evangelical Lutheran | 4,670,000 |
| other | 460,000 |
| **Djibouti** | |
| Sunnī Muslim | 442,000 |
| Christian[1] | 28,000 |
| **Dominica** | |
| Roman Catholic | 68,000 |
| other | 21,000 |
| **Dominican Republic** | |
| Roman Catholic | 6,290,000 |
| other | 420,000 |
| **Ecuador** | |
| Roman Catholic | 9,140,000 |
| other | 780,000 |
| **Egypt** | |
| Sunnī Muslim | 40,200,000 |
| Christian[1] | 8,750,000 |
| other | 200,000 |
| **El Salvador** | |
| Roman Catholic | 4,560,000 |
| other | 410,000 |
| **Equatorial Guinea** | |
| Roman Catholic | 270,000 |
| other | 60,000 |
| **Ethiopia** | |
| Ethiopian Orthodox | 24,150,000 |
| Muslim (mostly Sunnī) | 14,440,000 |
| traditional beliefs | 5,240,000 |
| other | 2,160,000 |
| **Faeroe Islands** | |
| Evangelical Lutheran | 34,000 |
| other | 12,000 |
| **Falkland Islands** | |
| Anglican | 1,000 |
| other | 1,000 |
| **Fiji** | |
| Christian | 384,000 |
| Hindu | 277,000 |
| Muslim | 57,000 |
| other | 8,000 |
| **Finland** | |
| Lutheran | 4,420,000 |
| other | 520,000 |
| **France** | |
| Roman Catholic | 42,500,000 |
| nonreligious | 6,790,000 |
| atheist | 1,890,000 |
| Muslim | 1,670,000 |
| other | 2,770,000 |
| **French Guiana** | |
| Roman Catholic | 77,000 |
| other | 12,000 |
| **French Polynesia** | |
| Protestant | 100,000 |
| Roman Catholic | 72,000 |
| other | 11,000 |
| **Gabon** | |
| Roman Catholic | 780,000 |
| other | 410,000 |
| **Gambia, The** | |
| Muslim (mostly Sunnī) | 751,000 |
| other | 36,000 |
| **Gaza Strip** | |
| Muslim | 540,000 |
| other | 8,000 |
| **German Democratic Republic** | |
| Protestant | 7,800,000 |
| Roman Catholic | 1,160,000 |
| unaffiliated and other | 7,640,000 |
| **Germany, Federal Republic of** | |
| Protestant | 28,820,000 |
| Roman Catholic | 26,680,000 |
| other Christian | 1,040,000 |
| nonreligious | 2,250,000 |
| Muslim | 1,460,000 |
| atheist | 550,000 |
| other | 120,000 |
| **Ghana** | |
| Christian[1] | 8,440,000 |
| traditional beliefs | 2,890,000 |
| Muslim | 2,120,000 |
| other | 40,000 |
| **Gibraltar** | |
| Roman Catholic | 22,000 |
| other | 7,000 |
| **Greece** | |
| Greek Orthodox | 9,770,000 |
| Muslim | 150,000 |
| other | 90,000 |
| **Greenland** | |
| Evangelical Lutheran | 53,000 |
| other | 1,000 |
| **Grenada** | |
| Roman Catholic | 67,000 |
| Anglican | 22,000 |
| other | 15,000 |
| **Guadeloupe** | |
| Roman Catholic | 302,000 |
| other | 32,000 |
| **Guam** | |
| Roman Catholic | 99,000 |
| Protestant | 21,000 |
| other | 4,000 |
| **Guatemala** | |
| Roman Catholic | 6,300,000 |
| Protestant | 2,100,000 |
| **Guernsey** | |
| Anglican | 39,000 |
| other | 21,000 |
| **Guinea** | |
| Muslim | 4,400,000 |
| traditional beliefs | 1,880,000 |
| other | 100,000 |
| **Guinea-Bissau** | |
| traditional beliefs | 590,000 |
| Muslim | 270,000 |
| Christian | 50,000 |
| **Guyana** | |
| Hindu | 280,000 |
| Christian[1] | 420,000 |
| Muslim | 70,000 |
| other | 40,000 |
| **Haiti** | |
| Roman Catholic | 4,440,000 |
| Baptist | 540,000 |
| other (mostly Protestant) | 550,000 |
| **Honduras** | |
| Roman Catholic | 4,480,000 |
| other | 180,000 |
| **Hong Kong** | |
| Buddhist (some Confucianist and Taoist) | 5,120,000 |
| Christian | 480,000 |
| **Hungary** | |
| Roman Catholic | 5,720,000 |
| Protestant | 2,290,000 |
| nonreligious | 920,000 |
| atheist | 760,000 |
| other | 920,000 |
| **Iceland** | |
| Lutheran | 237,000 |
| other | 8,000 |
| **India** | |
| Hindu | 647,090,000 |
| Muslim | 88,880,000 |
| Christian | 19,030,000 |
| Sikh | 15,390,000 |
| Buddhist | 5,550,000 |
| Jain | 3,770,000 |
| other | 3,330,000 |
| **Indonesia** | |
| Muslim | 150,030,000 |
| Protestant | 9,990,000 |
| Roman Catholic | 5,170,000 |
| Hindu | 3,440,000 |
| Buddhist | 1,550,000 |
| other | 2,070,000 |

| Religious affiliation | 1986 population |
|---|---|
| **Iran** | |
| Shīʻī Muslim | 46,430,000 |
| Sunnī Muslim | 2,500,000 |
| other | 1,000,000 |
| **Iraq** | |
| Shīʻī Muslim | 8,810,000 |
| Sunnī Muslim | 6,970,000 |
| other | 700,000 |
| **Ireland** | |
| Roman Catholic | 3,313,000 |
| other | 248,000 |
| **Isle of Man** | |
| Anglican | 40,000 |
| other | 24,000 |
| **Israel** | |
| Jewish | 3,670,000 |
| Muslim (mostly Sunnī) | 600,000 |
| other | 180,000 |
| **Italy** | |
| Roman Catholic | 47,640,000 |
| nonreligious | 7,790,000 |
| atheist | 1,490,000 |
| other | 340,000 |
| **Jamaica** | |
| Protestant | 1,900,000 |
| Roman Catholic | 230,000 |
| other | 240,000 |
| **Japan** | |
| Shintoist[3] | 113,740,000 |
| Buddhist[3] | 90,260,000 |
| Christian | 1,680,000 |
| other | 14,590,000 |
| **Jersey** | |
| Anglican | 48,000 |
| Roman Catholic | 18,000 |
| other | 12,000 |
| **Jordan** | |
| Sunnī Muslim | 2,650,000 |
| other | 200,000 |
| **Kampuchea** | |
| Buddhist | 6,800,000 |
| other | 890,000 |
| **Kenya** | |
| Roman Catholic | 5,810,000 |
| Anglican | 1,590,000 |
| other Protestant | 4,250,000 |
| African Christian | 3,880,000 |
| traditional beliefs | 4,160,000 |
| Muslim | 1,320,000 |
| other | 1,000,000 |
| **Kiribati** | |
| Roman Catholic | 35,000 |
| Congregational | 27,000 |
| other | 5,000 |
| **Korea, North** | |
| atheist and nonreligious | 14,520,000 |
| traditional beliefs | 3,340,000 |
| Ch'ŏndogyo | 2,970,000 |
| other | 550,000 |
| **Korea, South** | |
| Buddhist | 20,280,000 |
| Protestant | 14,390,000 |
| Confucian | 2,100,000 |
| Roman Catholic | 4,290,000 |
| Ch'ŏndogyo | 170,000 |
| Wonbulgyo | 250,000 |
| other | 590,000 |
| **Kuwait** | |
| Sunnī Muslim | 1,370,000 |
| Shīʻī Muslim | 340,000 |
| other | 160,000 |
| **Laos** | |
| Buddhist | 2,170,000 |
| traditional beliefs | 1,260,000 |
| other | 320,000 |
| **Lebanon** | |
| Shīʻī Muslim | 880,000 |
| Maronite Christian | 680,000 |
| Sunnī Muslim | 580,000 |
| Druze | 190,000 |
| other | 430,000 |
| **Lesotho** | |
| Roman Catholic | 710,000 |
| Protestant | 680,000 |
| other | 240,000 |
| **Liberia** | |
| Christian | 1,600,000 |
| traditional beliefs | 440,000 |
| Muslim | 330,000 |
| **Libya** | |
| Sunnī Muslim | 4,010,000 |
| other | 120,000 |
| **Liechtenstein** | |
| Roman Catholic | 23,500 |
| other | 3,500 |
| **Luxembourg** | |
| Roman Catholic | 341,000 |
| other | 26,000 |
| **Macau** | |
| Buddhist and Taoist | 316,000 |
| other | 136,000 |
| **Madagascar** | |
| Christian[1] | 5,410,000 |
| traditional beliefs | 4,980,000 |
| other | 210,000 |
| **Malaŵi** | |
| Christian[1] | 4,840,000 |
| traditional beliefs | 1,420,000 |
| Muslim | 1,210,000 |
| other | 20,000 |
| **Malaysia** | |
| Muslim | 8,750,000 |
| Buddhist | 2,860,000 |
| Chinese folk-religionist | 1,920,000 |
| Hindu | 1,160,000 |
| Christian | 1,060,000 |
| other | 790,000 |
| **Maldives** | |
| Sunnī Muslim | 195,000 |
| **Mali** | |
| Muslim | 7,820,000 |
| traditional beliefs | 780,000 |
| Christian | 90,000 |
| **Malta** | |
| Roman Catholic | 336,000 |
| other | 9,000 |
| **Martinique** | |
| Roman Catholic | 301,000 |
| other | 28,000 |
| **Mauritania** | |
| Sunnī Muslim | 1,830,000 |
| other | 10,000 |
| **Mauritius** | |
| Hindu | 550,000 |
| Roman Catholic | 270,000 |
| Muslim | 130,000 |
| other | 90,000 |
| **Mayotte** | |
| Sunnī Muslim | 72,000 |
| Christian | 2,000 |
| **Mexico** | |
| Roman Catholic | 75,310,000 |
| Protestant | 2,680,000 |
| nonreligious | 2,520,000 |
| other | 810,000 |
| **Monaco** | |
| Roman Catholic | 26,000 |
| other | 3,000 |
| **Mongolia** | |
| atheist and nonreligious | 1,300,000 |
| traditional beliefs | 610,000 |
| other | 70,000 |
| **Montserrat** | |
| Anglican | 4,400 |
| Methodist | 2,500 |
| other | 5,100 |
| **Morocco** | |
| Muslim (mostly Sunnī) | 22,820,000 |
| other | 300,000 |
| **Mozambique** | |
| traditional beliefs | 6,940,000 |
| Muslim | 1,890,000 |
| Roman Catholic | 4,560,000 |
| other | 1,130,000 |
| **Nauru** | |
| Congregational | 4,400 |
| Roman Catholic | 1,900 |
| other | 1,700 |
| **Nepal** | |
| Hindu | 15,720,000 |
| Buddhist | 930,000 |
| Muslim | 470,000 |
| other | 440,000 |
| **Netherlands, The** | |
| Roman Catholic | 5,300,000 |
| Dutch Reformed Church | 2,650,000 |
| Reformed Churches | 1,210,000 |
| nonreligious | 5,080,000 |
| other | 400,000 |
| **Netherlands Antilles** | |
| Roman Catholic | 153,000 |
| other | 23,000 |
| **New Caledonia** | |
| Roman Catholic | 110,000 |
| Protestant | 28,000 |
| other | 14,000 |
| **New Zealand** | |
| Anglican | 860,000 |
| Presbyterian | 550,000 |
| Roman Catholic | 480,000 |
| Methodist | 160,000 |
| other | 1,290,000 |
| **Nicaragua** | |
| Roman Catholic | 3,040,000 |
| other | 460,000 |
| **Niger** | |
| Sunnī Muslim | 6,770,000 |
| other | 170,000 |
| **Nigeria** | |
| Muslim | 45,270,000 |
| Protestant | 26,460,000 |
| Roman Catholic | 12,170,000 |
| African Christian | 10,660,000 |
| traditional beliefs | 5,630,000 |
| other | 400,000 |
| **Niue** | |
| Congregational | 1,900 |
| other | 700 |
| **Norfolk Island** | |
| Anglican | 800 |
| other | 1,200 |
| **Norway** | |
| Lutheran | 3,674,000 |
| other | 506,000 |
| **Oman** | |
| Muslim | 1,140,000 |
| Hindu | 170,000 |
| other | 10,000 |
| **Pacific Islands, Trust Territory of the** | |
| Protestant | 84,000 |
| Roman Catholic | 78,000 |
| other | 9,000 |
| **Pakistan** | |
| Muslim | 102,790,000 |
| other | 3,400,000 |
| **Panama** | |
| Roman Catholic | 2,024,000 |
| other | 250,000 |
| **Papua New Guinea** | |
| Protestant | 2,233,000 |
| Roman Catholic | 1,148,000 |
| other | 120,000 |
| **Paraguay** | |
| Roman Catholic | 3,741,000 |
| other | 156,000 |
| **Peru** | |
| Roman Catholic | 19,160,000 |
| other | 1,570,000 |
| **Philippines** | |
| Roman Catholic | 48,240,000 |
| Aglipayan | 3,560,000 |
| Protestant | 2,240,000 |
| Muslim | 2,470,000 |
| other | 850,000 |
| **Pitcairn Island** | |
| Seventh-day Adventist | 40 |
| Anglican | 4 |
| **Poland** | |
| Roman Catholic | 35,580,000 |
| other | 2,190,000 |
| **Portugal** | |
| Roman Catholic | 9,740,000 |
| other | 570,000 |
| **Puerto Rico** | |
| Roman Catholic | 2,800,000 |
| other | 480,000 |
| **Qatar** | |
| Muslim (mostly Sunnī) | 350,000 |
| other | 29,000 |
| **Réunion** | |
| Roman Catholic | 481,000 |
| other | 84,000 |
| **Romania** | |
| Romanian Orthodox | 16,040,000 |
| Greek Orthodox | 2,290,000 |
| atheist | 1,600,000 |
| nonreligious | 2,060,000 |
| other | 920,000 |
| **Rwanda** | |
| Roman Catholic | 3,630,000 |
| Protestant | 780,000 |
| Muslim | 580,000 |
| traditional beliefs | 1,490,000 |
| **St. Christopher and Nevis** | |
| Anglican | 17,000 |
| Methodist | 15,000 |
| other | 14,000 |
| **St. Helena and Ascension** | |
| Anglican | 6,100 |
| other | 900 |
| **St. Lucia** | |
| Roman Catholic | 123,000 |
| other | 19,000 |
| **St. Pierre and Miquelon** | |
| Roman Catholic | 5,900 |
| other | 100 |
| **St. Vincent and the Grenadines** | |
| Anglican | 40,000 |
| Methodist | 23,000 |
| Roman Catholic | 22,000 |
| other | 28,000 |
| **San Marino** | |
| Roman Catholic | 21,000 |
| other | 1,000 |
| **São Tomé and Príncipe** | |
| Roman Catholic | 90,000 |
| Protestant | 20,000 |
| **Saudi Arabia** | |
| Muslim (mostly Sunnī) | 12,330,000 |
| other | 150,000 |
| **Senegal** | |
| Sunnī Muslim | 6,180,000 |
| other | 610,000 |
| **Seychelles** | |
| Roman Catholic | 59,000 |
| other | 6,000 |
| **Sierra Leone** | |
| traditional beliefs | 1,960,000 |
| Sunnī Muslim | 1,500,000 |
| other | 344,000 |
| **Singapore** | |
| Taoist | 766,000 |
| Buddhist | 698,000 |
| Muslim | 426,000 |
| Christian | 269,000 |
| nonreligious | 345,000 |
| other | 110,000 |
| **Solomon Islands** | |
| Protestant | 223,000 |
| Roman Catholic | 56,000 |
| other | 13,000 |
| **Somalia** | |
| Sunnī Muslim | 6,148,000 |
| other | 12,000 |
| **South Africa[4]** | |
| Afrikaans Reformed (NGK) | 4,430,000 |
| Roman Catholic | 2,710,000 |
| Black independent churches | 5,830,000 |
| other Christian churches | 8,960,000 |
| Hindu | 590,000 |
| Muslim | 370,000 |
| nonreligious[5] | 5,390,000 |
| other | 340,000 |
| **Bophuthatswana** | |
| Christian | 1,450,000 |
| traditional beliefs | 150,000 |
| **Ciskei** | |
| Christian | 820,000 |
| traditional beliefs | 320,000 |
| **KwaNdebele** | |
| Christian | 280,000 |
| **Transkei** | |
| Christian | 1,990,000 |
| traditional beliefs | 840,000 |
| **Venda** | |
| traditional beliefs | 400,000 |
| Christian | 120,000 |
| **South West Africa/Namibia** | |
| Lutheran | 613,000 |
| Roman Catholic | 237,000 |
| other | 347,000 |
| **Spain** | |
| Roman Catholic | 37,670,000 |
| other | 1,160,000 |
| **Sri Lanka** | |
| Buddhist | 11,333,000 |
| Hindu | 2,535,000 |
| Muslim | 1,243,000 |
| Christian | 1,226,000 |
| other | 16,000 |
| **Sudan, The** | |
| Sunnī Muslim | 18,660,000 |
| traditional beliefs | 4,270,000 |
| Christian[1] | 2,330,000 |
| other | 310,000 |
| **Suriname** | |
| Hindu | 114,000 |
| Roman Catholic | 95,000 |
| Muslim | 81,000 |
| Protestant | 78,000 |
| other | 47,000 |
| **Swaziland** | |
| Christian[1] | 550,000 |
| traditional beliefs | 150,000 |
| other | 20,000 |
| **Sweden** | |
| Church of Sweden | 7,670,000 |
| other | 717,000 |
| **Switzerland** | |
| Roman Catholic | 3,135,000 |
| Protestant | 2,920,000 |
| other | 531,000 |
| **Syria** | |
| Muslim (mostly Sunnī) | 9,830,000 |
| Christian | 980,000 |
| other | 160,000 |
| **Taiwan** | |
| Chinese folk-religionist | 9,520,000 |
| Buddhist | 8,440,000 |
| Christian[1] | 1,450,000 |
| other | 220,000 |
| **Tanzania** | |
| Christian | 9,290,000 |
| Muslim | 6,970,000 |
| traditional beliefs | 6,970,000 |
| **Thailand** | |
| Buddhist | 51,040,000 |
| Muslim | 2,040,000 |
| other | 650,000 |
| **Togo** | |
| traditional beliefs | 1,450,000 |
| Christian[1] | 1,170,000 |
| Sunnī Muslim | 540,000 |
| other | 10,000 |
| **Tokelau** | |
| Congregational | 1,100 |
| other | 500 |
| **Tonga** | |
| Free Wesleyan | 45,000 |
| Roman Catholic | 15,000 |
| other | 34,000 |
| **Trinidad and Tobago** | |
| Roman Catholic | 402,000 |
| Protestant | 346,000 |
| Hindu | 304,000 |
| other | 168,000 |
| **Tunisia** | |
| Sunnī Muslim | 7,620,000 |
| other | 50,000 |
| **Turkey** | |
| Muslim (mostly Sunnī) | 52,420,000 |
| other | 420,000 |
| **Turks and Caicos Islands** | |
| Baptist | 3,700 |
| Methodist | 1,700 |
| Anglican | 1,600 |
| other | 1,900 |
| **Tuvalu** | |
| Congregational | 7,750 |
| other | 250 |
| **Uganda** | |
| Roman Catholic | 7,690,000 |
| Protestant | 4,440,000 |
| traditional beliefs | 1,950,000 |
| Muslim (mostly Sunnī) | 1,020,000 |
| other | 410,000 |
| **U.S.S.R.** | |
| Christian | 102,940,000 |
| Orthodox | 89,060,000 |
| Protestant | 8,770,000 |
| Roman Catholic | 5,090,000 |
| Muslim | 31,670,000 |
| Jewish | 3,110,000 |
| nonreligious | 83,990,000 |
| atheist | 60,520,000 |
| other | 570,000 |
| **United Arab Emirates** | |
| Sunnī Muslim | 1,410,000 |
| Shīʻī Muslim | 350,000 |
| other | 90,000 |
| **United Kingdom** | |
| Christian[1] | 49,430,000 |
| Church of England | 32,310,000 |
| Roman Catholic | 7,450,000 |
| nonreligious | 5,010,000 |
| Muslim | 800,000 |
| Jewish | 460,000 |
| other | 1,190,000 |
| **United States** | |
| Christian[1] | 214,520,000 |
| Protestant | 135,780,000 |
| Roman Catholic | 73,130,000 |
| Eastern Orthodox | 5,360,000 |
| Jewish | 7,800,000 |
| atheist and nonreligious | 16,820,000 |
| other | 4,630,000 |
| **Uruguay** | |
| Roman Catholic | 1,820,000 |
| other | 1,230,000 |
| **Vanuatu** | |
| Presbyterian | 53,000 |
| Anglican | 22,000 |
| Roman Catholic | 22,000 |
| other | 48,000 |
| **Venezuela** | |
| Roman Catholic | 16,570,000 |
| other | 1,710,000 |
| **Vietnam** | |
| Buddhist | 34,540,000 |
| atheist and nonreligious | 11,560,000 |
| Roman Catholic | 4,370,000 |
| other | 11,990,000 |
| **Virgin Islands (U.S.)** | |
| Protestant | 72,000 |
| Roman Catholic | 38,000 |
| other | 2,000 |
| **Wallis and Futuna** | |
| Roman Catholic | 15,000 |
| **West Bank** | |
| Muslim (mostly Sunnī) | 680,000 |
| Jewish | 100,000 |
| Christian and other | 70,000 |
| **Western Sahara** | |
| Sunnī Muslim | 185,000 |
| **Western Samoa** | |
| Congregational | 76,000 |
| Roman Catholic | 35,000 |
| other | 50,000 |
| **Yemen (Aden)** | |
| Muslim (mostly Sunnī) | 2,274,000 |
| other | 11,000 |
| **Yemen (Ṣanʻāʼ)** | |
| Shīʻī Muslim | 5,030,000 |
| Sunnī Muslim | 3,350,000 |
| **Yugoslavia** | |
| Orthodox | 8,110,000 |
| Roman Catholic | 6,090,000 |
| Crypto-Christian | 2,650,000 |
| Muslim | 2,440,000 |
| atheist and nonreligious | 3,910,000 |
| other | 230,000 |
| **Zaire** | |
| Roman Catholic | 15,390,000 |
| Protestant | 9,220,000 |
| African Christian | 5,440,000 |
| traditional beliefs | 1,080,000 |
| other | 670,000 |
| **Zambia** | |
| Christian[1] | 5,140,000 |
| traditional beliefs | 1,930,000 |
| other | 70,000 |
| **Zimbabwe** | |
| Christian[1] | 5,010,000 |
| traditional beliefs | 3,500,000 |
| other | 130,000 |

[1]Includes affiliated and nominal Christians. [2]Based on self-identification of respondent at 1981 census. [3]Many Japanese adhere to both Shintoism and Buddhism. [4]Excludes Black republics listed separately. [5]Includes traditional beliefs and religion not known.

# Vital statistics, marriage, family

This table provides some of the basic measures that control the size, rate, and direction of population change within a country. The accuracy of these data is principally a function of the effectiveness of each respective national system for collecting information about vital and civil events (birth, death, marriage, etc.) and of the sophistication of the analysis that can be brought to bear upon the data so compiled. Calculating life expectancy, for example, requires detailed information about age structure and mortality experience, but the calculation can be made in different ways upon a single information base.

Thus data on birth rates depend not only on the completeness of registration of births in a particular country but also on the conditions under which those data are collected: Do all births take place in a hospital? Are the births reported comparably in all parts of the country? Are the records of the births tabulated in a central location with an effort to eliminate inconsistent reporting of birth events, perinatal mortality, etc.? The same difficulties apply to death rates but with the added complication of having to identify "cause of death" in a country with, say, only one physician for every 1,000 population: too few to perform autopsies to assess accurately the cause of death after the fact and also too few to provide ongoing care at a level where records would permit inference about cause of death based on prior condition or diagnosis.

Calculating natural increase, which at its most basic is simply the difference between the birth and death rates, may be complicated by the differing degrees of completeness of birth and death registrations for a given country. The total fertility rate may be understood as the average number of children that would be borne per woman if all childbearing

women lived to the end of their childbearing years and bore children at each age at the average rate for that age. Calculating the fertility rate is complicated by changing age structure of the population over time, changing mortality rates among mothers, and changing medical practice at births, each improvement leading to greater numbers of live-born children and greater numbers of children who survive their first year (the basis for measurement of infant mortality, another basic control on the growth of a population).

As indicated above, data for causes of death are not only particularly difficult to obtain, since many countries are not well equipped to collect the data, but are also difficult to assess, as their accuracy may be suspect and their meaning may be subject to varying interpretation. Take the case of a citizen of a less developed country who dies of what is clearly a lung infection: Was the death complicated by chronic malnutrition, itself complicated by a parasitic infestation, these last two together so weakening the subject that he died of an infection that he might have survived had his general health been better? Similarly, in a developed country: Someone may die from what is identified in an autopsy as a cerebrovascular accident, but if that accident occurred in a vascular system that was weakened by diabetes, what was the actual cause of death? Statistics on causes of death seek to identify the "underlying" cause (that which sets the final train of events leading to death in motion) but often must settle for the most proximate cause or symptom. Even this kind of analysis may be misleading for those charged with interpreting the data with a view to ordering health-care priorities for a particular country. The eight main groups of causes of death include most, but not all, of the causes classified

## Vital statistics, marriage, family

| country | vital rates | | | | | | causes of death (rate per 100,000 population) | | | | | | | | |
|---|---|---|---|---|---|---|---|---|---|---|---|---|---|---|---|
| | year | birth rate per 1,000 population | death rate per 1,000 population | infant mortality rate per 1,000 live births | rate of natural increase per 1,000 population | total fertility rate | year | infectious and parasitic diseases | malignant neoplasms (cancers) | endocrine and metabolic disorders | diseases of the nervous system | diseases of the circulatory system | diseases of the respiratory system | diseases of the digestive system | accidents, poisoning, and violence |
| Afghanistan | 1980–85 | 48.9 | 27.3 | 194.0 | 21.6 | 6.9 | ... | ... | ... | ... | ... | ... | ... | ... | ... |
| Albania | 1985 | 26.2 | 5.8 | 44.0[2] | 20.4 | 3.6[3] | ... | ... | ... | ... | ... | ... | ... | ... | ... |
| Algeria | 1984 | 40.2 | 8.6 | 81.2 | 31.6 | 6.1 | ... | ... | ... | ... | ... | ... | ... | ... | ... |
| American Samoa | 1985 | 43.0 | 4.4 | 11.1 | 38.6 | 4.2 | 1985 | 8.4 | 75.8 | 14.0 | ... | 112.4 | 22.5 | ... | 53.4 |
| Andorra | 1984 | 11.4 | 4.0 | 16.0[3] | 7.4 | ... | ... | ... | ... | ... | ... | ... | ... | ... | ... |
| Angola | 1984 | 47.0 | 25.0 | 144.0 | 22.0 | 6.4 | 1973 | 73.2 | 6.5 | 4.9 | 3.6 | 19.2 | 24.6 | 3.6 | 89.0 |
| Anguilla | 1986 | 22.2 | 9.0 | 19.5 | 13.2 | 1.9[4] | 1985 | — | 159.5 | 14.5 | 14.5 | 435.1 | 232.1 | 29.0 | ... |
| Antigua and Barbuda | 1985 | 14.8 | 5.0 | 19.8 | 9.8 | 2.1[6] | 1983 | 21.7 | 46.0 | 34.5 | 26.4[7] | 171.3 | 40.3[7] | 18.1[7] | 31.1[8] |
| Argentina | 1985 | 25.0 | 9.0 | 36.0[6] | 16.0 | 3.4 | 1981 | 29.5 | 148.8 | 8.2 | 10.1 | 371.9 | 45.7 | 43.8 | 58.4 |
| Aruba | 1983 | 16.9 | 5.1 | 8.0 | 11.8 | 3.4,[6,9] | ... | ... | ... | ... | ... | ... | ... | ... | ... |
| Australia | 1986 | 15.7 | 7.4 | 10.0 | 8.3 | 1.9[10] | 1984 | 3.3 | 167.8 | 15.2 | 9.8 | 349.0 | 50.2 | 23.5 | 46.6 |
| Austria | 1986 | 11.6 | 11.9 | 11.2[10] | −0.3 | 1.5[10] | 1985 | 5.2 | 253.9 | 18.1 | 14.9 | 634.0 | 65.0 | 60.1 | 54.6 |
| Bahamas, The | 1984 | 22.2 | 5.0 | 23.1[11] | 17.2 | 3.1[6] | 1984 | 12.8 | 102.2 | 25.2 | 14.6 | 128.8 | 52.7 | 28.8 | 65.5 |
| Bahrain | 1984 | 36.8 | 5.9 | 30.0[10] | 30.9 | 5.3 | 1983 | 4.7 | 23.9 | 6.2 | 3.9 | 97.3 | 17.2 | 6.5 | 30.2 |
| Bangladesh | 1986 | 42.7 | 16.3 | 133.0 | 26.4 | 5.7 | 1976 | 15.5 | 19.8 | ... | ... | 5.9 | 25.7 | ... | ... |
| Barbados | 1986 | 16.1 | 8.2 | 9.2 | 7.9 | 1.9[4] | 1984 | 20.6 | 142.1 | 56.0 | 12.7 | 364.7 | 38.9 | 21.0 | 36.9 |
| Belgium | 1986 | 11.8 | 11.1 | 9.4[10] | 0.7 | 1.6 | 1984 | 7.7 | 273.5 | 27.0 | 22.1 | 480.0 | 81.2 | 43.0 | 74.8 |
| Belize | 1985 | 40.1 | 4.0 | 18.9 | 36.1 | 4.6[6] | 1983 | 43.1 | 38.7 | 25.4 | 16.5 | 95.1 | 52.0 | 12.7 | 26.6 |
| Benin | 1984 | 49.0 | 17.0 | 116.0 | 32.0 | 6.5 | 1977 | ... | ... | ... | ... | 206.5 | 200.7 | ... | ... |
| Bermuda | 1986 | 15.6 | 7.3 | 13.5 | 8.3 | 1.7 | 1984 | 3.5 | 163.0 | 50.0[8] | 7.0[8] | 354.0 | 37.0 | 19.6[7] | 39.0 |
| Bhutan | 1986 | 37.8 | 17.3 | 137.0 | 20.5 | 5.5 | ... | ... | ... | ... | ... | ... | ... | ... | ... |
| Bolivia | 1980–85 | 44.0 | 15.9 | 110.0[10] | 28.1 | 6.3 | ... | ... | ... | ... | ... | ... | ... | ... | ... |
| Botswana | 1986 | 45.6 | 11.1 | 68.4[12] | 34.5 | 6.8 | 1977 | 23.9 | 6.0 | 8.7 | 3.0 | 8.4 | ... | ... | ... |
| Brazil | 1985 | 32.0 | 7.0 | 64.0 | 25.0 | 3.6[6] | 1980[13] | 57.4 | 49.3 | 8.7 | 3.0 | 156.2 | 36.9 | 10.3 | 57.9 |
| British Virgin Islands | 1984 | 19.2 | 5.6 | 13.3 | 13.6 | ... | 1984 | 17.1 | 25.6 | 17.1 | — | 273.3 | 85.4 | 25.6 | 25.6 |
| Brunei | 1985 | 30.1 | 3.6 | 12.1 | 26.5 | 4.4[4] | 1985 | 48.0 | 64.0 | ... | ... | 132.0 | 25.0 | 3.1[12] | 21.0 |
| Bulgaria | 1985 | 13.2 | 12.0 | 15.8 | 1.2 | 2.0[6] | 1984 | 7.6 | 160.6 | 17.2 | 5.5 | 673.0 | 82.0 | 34.7 | 41.6 |
| Burkina Faso | 1980–85 | 47.8 | 20.1 | 137.0[10] | 27.7 | 6.5 | ... | ... | ... | ... | ... | ... | ... | ... | ... |
| Burma | 1985 | 33.2 | 13.7 | 106.0 | 19.5 | 4.5 | 1978 | 32.6 | 6.5 | 6.1 | ... | 14.1 | 19.8 | 1.7 | 7.3 |
| Burundi | 1980–85 | 47.2 | 19.0 | 124.0 | 28.2 | 6.4 | ... | ... | ... | ... | ... | ... | ... | ... | ... |
| Cameroon | 1980–85 | 42.9 | 15.8 | 103.0 | 27.1 | 5.8 | ... | ... | ... | ... | ... | ... | ... | ... | ... |
| Canada | 1986 | 14.8 | 7.3 | 9.3[6] | 7.5 | 1.7[6] | 1984 | 4.0 | 178.2 | 17.5 | 18.3 | 311.3 | 51.2 | 26.4 | 37.2 |
| Cape Verde | 1986 | 32.0 | 8.7 | 76.5[10] | 13.1 | 2.4[4] | 1980 | 153.7 | 43.8 | 20.6 | 16.5 | 135.8 | 72.3 | 27.7 | 30.1 |
| Cayman Islands | 1986 | 16.7 | 6.0 | 11.1 | 10.7 | ... | 1979 | 18.2 | 60.1 | 52.0 | ... | 204.6 | 54.1 | ... | 102.1 |
| Central African Republic | 1983 | 41.0 | 17.0 | 142.0 | 24.0 | 5.5 | 1978 | 59.0 | ... | ... | ... | ... | ... | ... | ... |
| Chad | 1984 | 43.0 | 21.0 | 139.0 | 22.0 | 5.6 | ... | ... | ... | ... | ... | ... | ... | ... | ... |
| Chile | 1985 | 21.7 | 6.1 | 19.6 | 15.6 | 3.0[12] | 1984 | 23.1[14] | 100.9 | 13.6[14] | 8.5[14] | 177.6 | 65.8 | 56.6[14] | 76.6 |
| China | 1985 | 17.8 | 6.6 | 39.0[4] | 11.2 | 2.4[4] | 1981[15] | 23.7 | 113.0 | 6.3 | 9.4 | 251.1 | 43.0 | 25.9 | 31.3 |
| Christmas Island | 1985 | 15.4 | 1.8 | ... | 13.6 | ... | ... | ... | ... | ... | ... | ... | ... | ... | ... |
| Cocos (Keeling) Islands | 1981 | 14.4 | 1.8 | — | 12.6 | ... | ... | ... | ... | ... | ... | ... | ... | ... | ... |
| Colombia | 1982 | 30.6 | 5.8 | 60.9[12] | 24.8 | 2.2[10] | 1977[17] | 86.6 | 54.1 | 7.2 | 5.9 | 129.2 | 60.7 | 9.9 | 70.1 |
| Comoros | 1985 | 44.0 | 15.0 | 111.0 | 29.0 | 7.0 | ... | ... | ... | ... | ... | ... | ... | ... | ... |
| Congo | 1980–85 | 44.5 | 18.6 | 81.0 | 25.9 | 6.0 | ... | ... | ... | ... | ... | ... | ... | ... | ... |
| Cook Islands | 1985 | 24.6 | 6.9 | 25.9 | 17.7 | 4.1 | 1976–78 | 54.0 | 38.0 | 27.0 | 0.0 | 197.0 | 110.0 | 18.0 | 49.0 |
| Costa Rica | 1984 | 31.4 | 4.1 | 18.9 | 27.3 | 3.3 | 1983 | 17.5 | 78.4 | 8.7 | 1.9 | 111.5 | 39.5 | 8.5 | 37.2 |
| Côte d'Ivoire | 1984 | 45.0 | 14.0 | 106.0 | 31.0 | 6.5 | ... | ... | ... | ... | ... | ... | ... | ... | ... |
| Cuba | 1986 | 16.3 | 6.1 | 13.6 | 10.2 | 2.0[6] | 1985 | 12.7 | 116.6 | 15.3 | 8.3 | 252.2 | 48.4 | 21.2 | 63.8 |
| Cyprus | 1986 | 19.5 | 7.9 | 11.6 | 12.6[6] | 2.5[14] | ... | ... | ... | ... | ... | ... | ... | ... | ... |
| Czechoslovakia | 1986 | 14.2 | 11.8 | 14.0 | 2.4 | 2.3[2] | 1985 | 4.1 | 234.0 | ... | 7.8 | 665.5 | 86.4 | ... | 79.6 |
| Denmark | 1986 | 10.8 | 11.4 | 7.9[10] | −0.6 | 1.4 | 1985 | 4.9 | 283.9 | 19.5 | 11.6 | 523.8 | 89.3 | 37.1 | 78.3 |
| Djibouti | 1980–85 | 49.2 | 18.3 | c. 200 | 30.9 | 6.8 | ... | ... | ... | ... | ... | ... | ... | ... | ... |
| Dominica | 1984 | 20.8 | 5.2 | 16.3[11] | 15.6 | 3.4 | 1984 | 13.4 | 88.6 | 26.7 | 14.6 | 197.8 | 27.9 | 9.7 | 8.5 |
| Dominican Republic | 1985–90 | 30.9 | 7.1 | 67.0 | 23.8 | 4.2[10] | 1982 | 47.0 | 26.8 | 14.9 | 10.6 | 85.6 | 29.4 | 22.1 | 34.7 |
| Ecuador | 1984 | 36.8 | 8.1 | 68.4 | 28.7 | 4.8[10] | 1980 | 122.1 | 41.7 | 10.8 | 10.5 | 87.4 | 103.2 | 28.0 | 70.6 |
| Egypt | 1984 | 37.4 | 10.9 | 93.0[10] | 26.5 | 5.4 | 1980 | 25.2 | 19.2 | 7.6 | 10.4 | 200.1 | 165.6 | 254.5 | 21.6 |

by the World Health Organization and would not, thus, aggregate to the country's crude death rate for the same year. Among the lesser causes excluded by the present classification are: benign neoplasms; nutritional disorders; anemias; mental disorders; kidney and genitourinary diseases not classifiable under the main groups; maternal deaths (for which data *are* provided, however, in the "Health services" table); diseases of the skin and musculoskeletal systems; congenital and perinatal conditions; and general senility and other ill-defined (ill-diagnosed) conditions, a kind of "other" category.

Expectation of life is probably the most accurate single measure of the quality of life in a given society. It summarizes in a single number all of the natural and social stresses that operate upon individuals in that society. The number may range from as few as 40 years of life in the least developed countries to as much as 80 years for women in the most developed nations. The lost potential in the years separating those two numbers is prodigious, regardless of how the loss arises—wars and civil violence, poor public health services, or poor individual health practice in matters of nutrition, exercise, stress management, and so on.

Data on marriages and marriage rates probably are less meaningful in terms of international comparisons than some of the measures mentioned above because the number, timing, and kinds of social relationships that substitute for marriage depend on many kinds of social variables—income, degree of social control, heterogeneity of the society (race, class, language communities), or level of development of civil administration (if one must travel for a day or more to obtain a legal civil ceremony, one may forgo it). Nevertheless, the data for a single country say specific things about local practice in terms of the age at which a man or woman typically marries, and the overall rate will at least define the number of legal civil marriages, though it cannot say anything about other, less formal arrangements (here the figure for the legitimacy rate for children in the next section may identify some of the societies in which economics or social constraints may operate to limit the number of marriages that are actually confirmed on civil registers). The available data usually include both first marriages and remarriages after annulment, divorce, widowhood, or the like.

The data for families provide information about the average size of a family unit (individuals related by blood or civil register) and the average number of children under a specified age (set here at 15 to provide a consistent measure of social minority internationally, though legal minority depends on the laws of each country). When well-defined family data are not collected as part of a country's national census or vital statistics surveys, data for households are substituted on the assumption that most households worldwide represent families in some conventional sense. In the older countries of Europe and North America increasing numbers of households are composed of unrelated individuals (unmarried heterosexual couples, aged [or younger] groups sharing limited [often fixed] incomes for reasons of economy, or homosexual couples); such arrangements are not yet so common in the rest of the world that they represent great numbers overall. Very few census programs, even in developed countries, make adequate provision for identifying these households.

| expectation of life at birth (latest year) | | nuptiality, family, and family planning | | | | | | | | | | | | | country |
|---|---|---|---|---|---|---|---|---|---|---|---|---|---|---|---|
| | | marriages | | | age at marriage (latest) | | | | | | families (F), households (H) (latest) | | | | |
| | | | | | groom (percent) | | | bride (percent) | | | families (households) | | children | | legal abortions | |
| male | female | year | total number | rate per 1,000 population | 19 and under | 20–29 | 30 and over | 19 and under | 20–29 | 30 and over | total ('000) | size | number under age 15 | percent legitimate | number | ratio per 100 live births | |
| 36.6 | 37.3 | 1970 | 6,212 | 0.4 | | | | | | | H 2,110 | H 6.2 | H 2.8[1] | ... | ... | ... | Afghanistan |
| 67.9 | 72.9 | 1984 | 26,397 | 9.1 | 2.0 | 81.2 | 16.8 | 23.0 | 73.7 | 3.4 | ... | F 5.4 | ... | ... | ... | ... | Albania |
| 61.6 | 63.3 | 1983 | 143,169 | 6.2 | 3.4 | 68.3 | 28.3 | 37.7 | 53.5 | 8.8 | ... | H 4.9 | ... | ... | ... | ... | Algeria |
| 67.5 | 73.1 | 1982 | 362 | 10.7 | 5.6 | 65.5 | 28.8 | 24.5 | 60.5 | 15.0 | H 4 | H 7.1 | H 2.9 | 86.0 | ... | ... | American Samoa |
| —70.0— | | 1984 | 130 | 3.1 | ... | ... | ... | ... | ... | ... | | | | | ... | ... | Andorra |
| 40.4 | 43.6 | 1972 | 26,278 | 4.5 | ... | ... | ... | ... | ... | ... | ... | H 4.8 | | | ... | ... | Angola |
| 68.6 | 71.9 | 1986 | 154 | 22.2 | 1.7[5] | 56.7[5] | 41.6[5] | 10.7[5] | 58.0[5] | 31.3[5] | H 1.6 | H 4.1 | H 1.8 | 34.4 | ... | ... | Anguilla |
| 70.4 | 74.2 | 1984 | 203 | 2.6 | 0.5 | 41.1 | 58.5 | 10.6 | 54.8 | 34.6 | H 15 | H 4.2 | H 1.9 | 18.7 | ... | ... | Antigua and Barbuda |
| 67.3 | 74.0 | 1983 | 177,010 | 6.0 | 5.6 | 71.5 | 22.9 | 26.0 | 58.6 | 15.4 | H 7,104 | H 3.9 | H 1.2 | 70.2 | ... | ... | Argentina |
| 71.6 | 76.8 | 1982 | 470 | 7.7 | | | | | | | ... | H 3.6 | | 41.3 | ... | ... | Aruba |
| 72.6 | 79.1 | 1985 | 108,655 | 7.0 | 1.9 | 64.8 | 33.3 | 10.8 | 66.0 | 23.2 | F 4,140 | F 3.1 | F 0.5 | 84.5 | ... | ... | Australia |
| 69.2 | 76.4 | 1985 | 44,867 | 5.9 | 2.7 | 67.5 | 29.8 | 12.5 | 69.5 | 18.0 | F 2,020 | F 3.7 | F 0.7 | 77.6 | ... | ... | Austria |
| 66.9 | 70.9 | 1984 | 1,681 | 7.4 | 3.6 | 62.4 | 34.0 | 17.6 | 59.3 | 23.1 | H 40 | H 4.3 | H 1.8 | 37.8 | ... | ... | Bahamas, The |
| 68.3 | 73.0 | 1983 | 2,396 | 6.2 | 6.2 | 74.4 | 19.4 | 45.9 | 48.5 | 5.6 | H 61 | H 6.7 | H 3.0 | ... | ... | ... | Bahrain |
| 50.2 | 49.2 | 1982 | | 9.4 | | | | | | | ... | H 5.8 | | | ... | ... | Bangladesh |
| 70.0 | 75.4 | 1983 | 1,252 | 5.0 | 0.6 | 49.9 | 49.5 | 5.5 | 66.7 | 27.8 | H 67 | H 3.7 | H 1.5 | 27.9 | ... | ... | Barbados |
| 70.0 | 76.8 | 1985 | 57,200 | 5.8 | 4.3 | 79.8 | 15.9 | 22.1 | 67.1 | 10.8 | F 3,613 | F 2.7 | F 0.5 | 93.9 | ... | ... | Belgium |
| 63.3 | 67.1 | 1984 | 860 | 5.3 | ... | ... | ... | ... | ... | ... | H 29 | H 5.2 | H 2.4 | 46.1 | ... | ... | Belize |
| 47.0 | 51.0 | 1980–85 | | 12.8 | ... | ... | ... | ... | ... | ... | ... | H 5.4 | | | ... | ... | Benin |
| 68.8 | 76.3 | 1985 | 696 | 12.2 | — | 42.4 | 57.5 | 2.1 | 53.1 | 44.9 | H 18 | H 2.7 | H 0.7 | 68.7 | 92 | 11.0 | Bermuda |
| 47.7 | 46.3 | | | | | | | | | | ... | H 5.4 | | | ... | ... | Bhutan |
| 48.6 | 53.0 | 1980 | 26,990 | 4.8 | 8.3 | 75.1 | 16.6 | 26.1 | 55.4 | 18.5 | H 1,050 | H 4.4 | H 1.8 | 80.9 | ... | ... | Bolivia |
| 54.7 | 61.2 | | | | ... | ... | ... | ... | ... | ... | H 125 | H 5.7 | H 2.0 | 28.0 | ... | ... | Botswana |
| 62.3 | 67.6 | 1984 | 936,070 | 7.1 | 7.4 | 69.1 | 23.5 | 33.4 | 51.7 | 14.9 | F 31,076 | F 4:1 | H 1.6 | ... | ... | ... | Brazil |
| 68.6 | 71.9 | 1984 | 149 | 12.7 | — | 43.6 | 56.4 | 2.0 | 56.4 | 41.6 | H 3 | H 3.3 | H 1.1 | 43.8 | ... | ... | British Virgin Islands |
| 70.1 | 72.7 | 1984 | 1,626 | 7.5 | 10.0 | 72.8 | 17.2 | 18.4 | 71.5 | 10.1 | H 23 | H 5.8 | H 2.5 | 99.3 | ... | ... | Brunei |
| 68.3 | 73.5 | 1985 | 66,227 | 7.4 | 6.4 | 75.6 | 18.0 | 37.7 | 51.4 | 10.9 | F 2,627 | F 3.3 | F 0.7 | 89.1 | 131,140 | 107.2 | Bulgaria |
| 43.7 | 46.8 | 1975 | | 9.4 | ... | ... | ... | ... | ... | ... | ... | H 4.9 | | | ... | ... | Burkina Faso |
| 51.2 | 54.3 | | | | | | | | | | ... | H 5.1 | | | ... | ... | Burma |
| 44.9 | 48.1 | | | | | | | | | | ... | H 4.9 | | | ... | ... | Burundi |
| 49.2 | 52.6 | | | | | | | | | | ... | H 5.2 | | | ... | ... | Cameroon |
| 73.0 | 79.0 | 1985 | 180,200 | 7.1 | 3.1 | 68.1 | 28.8 | 13.3 | 67.3 | 19.4 | H 9,255 | H 2.8 | H 1.4 | 91.0 | 61,750 | 16.5 | Canada |
| 59.9 | 63.3 | 1975 | 1,604 | 5.4 | ... | ... | ... | ... | ... | ... | F 59 | F 5.1 | | 55.2 | ... | ... | Cape Verde |
| —74.5— | | 1986 | 216 | 10.0 | ... | ... | ... | ... | ... | ... | H 4 | H 3.8 | H 1.1 | 66.8 | ... | ... | Cayman Islands |
| 46.0 | 49.0 | | | | | | | | | | ... | H 4.3 | | | ... | ... | Central African Republic |
| 43.0 | 45.0 | | | | | | | | | | ... | H 3.9 | | | ... | ... | Chad |
| 68.1 | 75.1 | 1985 | 91,099 | 7.5 | 6.5 | 74.4 | 19.1 | 26.4 | 60.7 | 12.9 | H 1,690 | H 4.5 | H 2.0 | 72.4 | 2,346 | 1.0 | Chile |
| 66.4 | 69.3 | 1985 | 8,290,588 | 8.0 | ... | ... | ... | ... | ... | ... | H 241.3[16] | H 4.3 | | | ... | ... | China |
| 63.0 | 66.5 | 1982 | 25 | 8.3 | — | 90.9 | 9.1 | 45.5 | 36.4 | 18.1 | — | H 5.8 | H 1.5 | 97.1 | ... | ... | Christmas Island |
| 63.0 | 66.5 | 1981 | 6 | 10.8 | — | 100.0 | — | — | 100.0 | — | — | H 6.3 | H 2.6 | 93.3 | 2 | 40.0 | Cocos (Keeling) Islands |
| 62.6 | 67.2 | 1977 | 88,401 | 3.5 | 5.6 | 69.5 | 24.9 | 33.6 | 55.3 | 11.1 | F 4,772 | F 5.4 | F 2.5 | 75.2 | ... | ... | Colombia |
| 50.3 | 53.8 | 1964 | 1,959 | 8.5 | ... | ... | ... | ... | ... | ... | ... | H 5.3 | | | ... | ... | Comoros |
| 44.9 | 48.1 | | | | ... | ... | ... | ... | ... | ... | H 326 | H 4.7 | H 2.0 | ... | ... | ... | Congo |
| 64.0 | 70.0 | 1985 | 105 | 6.1 | 1.2 | 63.4 | 35.4 | 22.0 | 51.2 | 26.8 | H 3 | H 5.6 | H 2.4 | ... | ... | ... | Cook Islands |
| 70.5 | 75.7 | 1983 | 19,171 | 7.9 | 9.2 | 69.3 | 21.5 | 36.2 | 51.1 | 12.7 | F 472 | F 5.0 | F 1.7 | 64.9 | ... | ... | Costa Rica |
| 51.0 | 54.0 | | | | | | | | | | ... | H 4.5 | | | ... | ... | Côte d'Ivoire |
| 72.6 | 76.1 | 1985 | 79,800 | 8.1 | 11.3 | 57.7 | 31.0 | 31.9 | 47.0 | 21.1 | F 2,002 | F 4.2 | H 1.6 | ... | 116,956 | 70.8 | Cuba |
| 72.6 | 76.1 | 1984 | 5,100 | 7.8 | 1.3 | 75.5 | 23.2 | 18.2 | 70.2 | 11.6 | F 160 | H 3.5 | H 1.1 | 99.7 | ... | ... | Cyprus |
| 67.2 | 74.4 | 1985 | 121,340 | 7.7 | 6.7 | 73.1 | 20.2 | 27.3 | 57.4 | 15.3 | F 4,187 | F 3.6 | F 0.9 | 93.1 | 119,325 | 52.8 | Czechoslovakia |
| 71.6 | 77.5 | 1985 | 29,322 | 5.7 | 0.6 | 48.8 | 50.6 | 3.1 | 61.9 | 35.0 | F 2,563 | F 2.0 | F 0.4 | 58.1 | 20,742 | 40.0 | Denmark |
| —45.0— | | 1982 | 2,500 | 6.7 | ... | ... | ... | ... | ... | ... | ... | H 5.6 | | 96.8 | ... | ... | Djibouti |
| 72.8 | 76.5 | 1969 | 234 | 3.3 | ... | ... | ... | ... | ... | ... | H 18 | H 4.3 | H 2.2 | 35.0 | ... | ... | Dominica |
| 60.7 | 64.6 | 1985 | 21,301 | 3.4 | 8.0 | 63.0 | 29.0 | 29.7 | 51.0 | 19.3 | H 753 | H 5.1 | H 2.5 | 32.8 | ... | ... | Dominican Republic |
| 59.8 | 63.6 | 1984 | 53,800 | 5.9 | 13.0 | 65.7 | 21.3 | 39.1 | 47.9 | 13.0 | ... | H 5.1 | | 67.9 | ... | ... | Ecuador |
| 58.0 | 61.1 | 1980 | 384,941 | 9.4 | 8.7 | 61.6 | 29.7 | 46.4 | 42.1 | 11.5 | H 8,411 | H 5.4 | H 2.1 | ... | ... | ... | Egypt |

## Vital statistics, marriage, family (continued)

| country | vital rates | | | | | | causes of death (rate per 100,000 population) | | | | | | | | |
|---|---|---|---|---|---|---|---|---|---|---|---|---|---|---|---|
| | year | birth rate per 1,000 population | death rate per 1,000 population | infant mortality rate per 1,000 live births | rate of natural increase per 1,000 population | total fertility rate | year | infectious and parasitic diseases | malignant neoplasms (cancers) | endocrine and metabolic disorders | diseases of the nervous system | diseases of the circulatory system | diseases of the respiratory system | diseases of the digestive system | accidents, poisoning, and violence |
| El Salvador | 1984 | 29.8 | 6.0 | 35.1 | 23.8 | 5.3 | 1984 | 60.0 | 21.6 | 9.9 | 9.0 | 63.9 | 34.8 | 26.1 | 124.6 |
| Equatorial Guinea | 1980–85 | 42.5 | 21.0 | 137.0[14] | 21.5 | 5.7 | ... | ... | ... | ... | ... | ... | ... | ... | ... |
| Ethiopia | 1985 | 49.7 | 23.1 | 155.0 | 26.6 | 6.7 | 1978 | 39.5 | 3.8 | 24.6 | 2.7 | 5.6 | 16.3 | 28.9 | 15.8 |
| Faeroe Islands | 1986 | 17.0 | 7.8 | 9.5[10] | 9.2 | 2.2[10] | 1985 | 2.2 | 173.4 | 6.6 | 8.8 | 399.5 | 37.3 | 21.9 | 46.1 |
| Falkland Islands | 1981 | 15.0 | 5.0 | ... | 10.0 | ... | ... | ... | ... | ... | ... | ... | ... | ... | ... |
| Fiji | 1985 | 27.9 | 5.3 | 18.5 | 22.6 | 3.3 | 1983 | 22.2 | 44.8 | 22.6 | 4.9 | 185.9 | 41.8 | 18.9 | 45.2 |
| Finland | 1986 | 12.4 | 9.6 | 6.3[10] | 2.8 | 1.6 | 1986 | 8.1 | 198.6 | 12.0 | 11.9 | 531.5 | 79.7 | 26.7 | 79.7 |
| France | 1986 | 14.1 | 9.9 | 8.0 | 4.2 | 1.8[6] | 1984 | 12.6 | 238.3 | 21.8 | 18.3 | 356.7 | 59.3 | 59.7 | 91.6 |
| French Guiana | 1985 | 30.0 | 5.8 | 20.6[18] | 24.2 | 3.1[19] | 1981 | 43.5 | 49.1 | 16.8 | 26.7 | 119.3 | 29.5 | 47.7 | 89.8 |
| French Polynesia | 1986 | 28.9 | 5.1 | 20.2[20] | 23.8 | 3.5[10] | 1984 | 21.2 | 67.7 | 10.0 | 19.4 | 120.1 | 36.5 | 17.7 | 58.9 |
| Gabon | 1980–85 | 33.8 | 18.1 | 121.6 | 15.7 | 4.5 | ... | ... | ... | ... | ... | ... | ... | ... | ... |
| Gambia, The | 1980–85 | 48.4 | 29.0 | 174.0 | 19.4 | 6.4 | ... | ... | ... | ... | ... | ... | ... | ... | ... |
| Gaza Strip | 1984 | 48.3 | 8.1 | ... | 40.2 | ... | ... | ... | ... | ... | ... | ... | ... | ... | ... |
| Germany, East | 1986 | 13.7 | 13.5 | 10.0[6] | −0.2 | 1.6 | 1984 | 4.9 | 215.1 | 36.4 | 9.9 | 774.0 | 77.6 | 30.6 | 37.3 |
| Germany, West | 1986 | 10.2 | 11.5 | 8.9 | −1.3 | 1.3[6] | 1985 | 8.0 | 266.3 | 20.6 | 13.3 | 588.3 | 72.9 | 54.1 | 58.0 |
| Ghana | 1980–85 | 46.9 | 14.6 | 98.0 | 32.3 | 6.5 | ... | ... | ... | ... | ... | ... | ... | ... | ... |
| Gibraltar | 1986 | 17.4 | 9.9 | ... | 7.5 | ... | ... | ... | ... | ... | ... | ... | ... | ... | ... |
| Greece | 1986 | 11.3 | 9.2 | 14.1[10] | 2.1 | 2.2[10] | 1985 | 6.7 | 182.6 | 35.8 | 13.5 | 450.8 | 55.5 | 32.5 | 49.1 |
| Greenland | 1985 | 19.2 | 7.8 | 24.6 | 11.4 | 2.2 | 1985 | 30.1 | 120.4 | — | 3.8 | 182.4 | 82.7 | 30.1 | 223.8 |
| Grenada | 1983 | 31.4 | 6.9 | 16.5[21] | 24.5 | 3.5[6] | 1981 | 26.7 | 90.9 | 48.3 | ... | 186.3 | 41.5 | 31.4 | 30.0 |
| Guadeloupe | 1984 | 20.2 | 6.8 | 17.4 | 13.4 | 2.1 | 1983 | 13.0 | 105.8 | 31.2 | 16.4 | 243.0 | 22.7 | 33.9 | 80.0 |
| Guam | 1985 | 17.8 | 3.4 | 10.6 | 14.4 | 3.2[3] | 1983 | ... | 53.0 | 13.2 | 13.2 | 140.4 | 15.0 | ... | 63.0 |
| Guatemala | 1985 | 41.7 | 7.5 | 56.0 | 34.2 | 5.8[6] | 1981 | 256.8 | 28.2 | 12.4 | 11.3 | 57.2 | 143.2 | 24.8 | 195.9 |
| Guernsey | ... | ... | ... | ... | ... | ... | ... | ... | ... | ... | ... | ... | ... | ... | ... |
| Guinea | 1980–85 | 46.8 | 23.5 | 159.0 | 23.3 | 6.2 | ... | ... | ... | ... | ... | ... | ... | ... | ... |
| Guinea-Bissau | 1980–85 | 40.7 | 21.7 | 143.0 | 19.0 | 5.4 | ... | ... | ... | ... | ... | ... | ... | ... | ... |
| Guyana | 1984 | 29.3 | 7.6 | 41.0[10] | 21.7 | 3.3 | 1977 | 88.1 | 45.6 | 46.4 | 10.4 | 236.2 | 69.3 | 35.9 | 67.3 |
| Haiti | 1985 | 36.0 | 13.0 | 107.0 | 23.0 | 4.5[6] | ... | ... | ... | ... | ... | ... | ... | ... | ... |
| Honduras | 1985 | 41.0 | 8.0 | 73.0 | 33.0 | 6.2[6] | 1981 | 80.9 | 14.9 | 4.9 | 9.8 | 53.1 | 31.9 | 21.6 | 53.9 |
| Hong Kong | 1986 | 13.0 | 4.7 | 7.6 | 8.3 | 1.8[6] | 1986 | 14.7 | 146.0 | 5.6 | 3.4 | 136.2 | 76.8 | 19.7 | 29.3 |
| Hungary | 1986 | 12.1 | 13.8 | 20.4 | −1.7 | 1.7[6] | 1985 | 10.4 | 267.6 | 20.5 | 10.8 | 749.1 | 71.1 | 75.6 | 124.7 |
| Iceland | 1985 | 16.0 | 6.9 | 5.7 | 9.1 | 1.9 | 1984 | 4.2 | 162.0 | 5.0 | 10.9 | 293.9 | 79.8 | 18.4 | 53.4 |
| India | 1986 | 29.6 | 11.5 | 111.0 | 18.1 | 3.9 | ... | ... | ... | ... | ... | ... | ... | ... | ... |
| Indonesia | 1986 | 29.8 | 11.7 | 77.0 | 18.1 | 3.7 | ... | ... | ... | ... | ... | ... | ... | ... | ... |
| Iran | 1985 | 39.7 | 11.4 | 111.0 | 28.3 | 5.4 | ... | ... | ... | ... | ... | ... | ... | ... | ... |
| Iraq | 1980–85 | 44.4 | 8.7 | 73.0[10] | 35.7 | 6.7 | ... | ... | ... | ... | ... | ... | ... | ... | ... |
| Ireland | 1986 | 17.4 | 9.5 | 10.1[6] | 7.9 | 3.2[4] | 1983 | 7.0 | 185.7 | 11.4 | 15.7 | 475.2 | 128.2 | 22.9 | 45.3 |
| Isle of Man | 1985 | 10.0 | 14.9 | 0.1 | −4.9 | ... | 1985 | 7.1 | 314.1 | 14.3 | — | 809.4 | 188.4 | 17.1 | 71.4 |
| Israel | 1986 | 23.1 | 6.7 | 11.2 | 16.4 | 2.9[10] | 1984 | 13.1 | 122.5 | 10.3 | 8.6 | 280.4 | 42.8 | 18.8 | 40.5 |
| Italy | 1985 | 10.1 | 9.5 | 10.9 | 0.6 | 1.8[6] | 1984 | 5.9 | 226.0 | 36.1 | 14.0 | 429.7 | 60.9 | 54.7 | 46.0 |
| Jamaica | 1985 | 24.3 | 6.0 | 13.2[6] | 18.3 | 3.3[6] | 1978 | 39.3 | 74.8 | 40.5[22] | 12.0 | 210.9 | 41.7 | 21.4 | 28.0 |
| Japan | 1986 | 11.4 | 6.2 | 5.3 | 5.2 | 1.8[6] | 1985 | 9.6 | 155.5 | 9.1 | 5.2 | 245.5 | 60.3 | 31.5 | 46.7 |
| Jersey | 1984 | 12.2 | 10.7 | ... | 1.5 | ... | ... | ... | ... | ... | ... | ... | ... | ... | ... |
| Jordan | 1980–85 | 44.7 | 7.9 | 49.0[10] | 36.8 | 7.4 | ... | ... | ... | ... | ... | ... | ... | ... | ... |
| Kampuchea | 1986 | 42.3 | 17.6 | 140.0 | 24.3 | 4.8 | ... | ... | ... | ... | ... | ... | ... | ... | ... |
| Kenya | 1980–85 | 55.1 | 14.0 | 92.0[6] | 41.1 | 7.7[6] | ... | ... | ... | ... | ... | ... | ... | ... | ... |
| Kiribati | 1980–85 | 34.9 | 13.9 | 82.0[2] | 21.0 | 4.4[6] | ... | ... | ... | ... | ... | ... | ... | ... | ... |
| Korea, North | 1984 | 30.0 | 6.0 | 28.0 | 24.0 | 3.8 | ... | ... | ... | ... | ... | ... | ... | ... | ... |
| Korea, South | 1986 | 21.8 | 6.3 | 27.0 | 15.5 | 2.1 | ... | ... | ... | ... | ... | ... | ... | ... | ... |
| Kuwait | 1986 | 29.5 | 2.4 | 22.0[10] | 27.1 | 5.2[4] | 1985 | 10.3 | 29.7 | 6.6 | 5.7 | 79.9 | 18.6 | 7.0 | 44.7 |
| Laos | 1986 | 41.9 | 17.9 | 116.0[10] | 24.0 | 5.8 | ... | ... | ... | ... | ... | ... | ... | ... | ... |
| Lebanon | 1984 | 29.8 | 8.8 | 44.4 | 21.0 | 3.8 | ... | ... | ... | ... | ... | ... | ... | ... | ... |
| Lesotho | 1980–85 | 41.8 | 16.5 | 109.0[14] | 25.3 | 5.8 | ... | ... | ... | ... | ... | ... | ... | ... | ... |
| Liberia | 1984–89 | 46.8 | 12.2 | 122.0 | 34.2 | 6.9 | ... | ... | ... | ... | ... | ... | ... | ... | ... |
| Libya | 1980–85 | 47.3 | 12.7 | 107.0 | 34.6 | 7.4 | ... | ... | ... | ... | ... | ... | ... | ... | ... |
| Liechtenstein | 1986 | 12.8 | 6.7 | 7.4[6] | 6.1 | ... | 1986 | 11.3 | 171.5 | 18.8 | — | 229.9 | 32.8 | 52.5 | 54.7 |
| Luxembourg | 1985 | 11.2 | 11.0 | 9.0 | 0.2 | 1.4 | 1985 | 4.4 | 271.6 | 21.8 | 17.5 | 533.1 | 64.6 | 54.0 | 73.6 |
| Macau | 1985 | 19.6 | 3.8 | 12.6 | 15.8 | 3.4[4] | 1983 | 31.4 | 80.8 | 12.2 | 2.4 | 138.7 | 40.2 | 21.0 | 36.9 |
| Madagascar | 1985–90 | 44.1 | 15.2 | 110.0[6] | 28.9 | 6.1 | ... | ... | ... | ... | ... | ... | ... | ... | ... |
| Malawi | 1984 | 54.0 | 22.0 | 152.0[10] | 32.0 | 7.6[10] | 1982[24] | 45.9 | 3.6 | 16.0 | 4.7 | 3.6 | 18.6 | 2.8 | 6.1 |
| Malaysia | 1986 | 30.6 | 5.7 | 27.0 | 24.9 | 3.8 | 1981[25] | 19.2 | 18.6 | 2.7 | 1.5 | 43.5 | 10.6 | 3.3 | 21.0 |
| Maldives | 1985 | 49.5 | 8.8 | 63 | 40.7 | 6.5 | ... | ... | ... | ... | ... | ... | ... | ... | ... |
| Mali | 1980–85 | 50.2 | 22.4 | 149.0 | 27.8 | 6.7 | ... | ... | ... | ... | ... | ... | ... | ... | ... |
| Malta | 1985 | 15.9 | 8.3 | 13.6 | 7.6 | 2.0[4] | 1985 | 0.6 | 100.8 | 65.7 | 4.8 | 308.8 | 28.2 | 20.2 | 18.7 |
| Martinique | 1985–86 | 18.1 | 6.5 | 13.0 | 11.6 | 2.1[4] | 1982 | 12.9 | 100.2 | 29.4 | 12.3 | 192.3 | 24.5 | 22.1 | 35.8 |
| Mauritania | 1985–90 | 50.0 | 19.2 | 133.0[6] | 30.8 | 6.2[6] | ... | ... | ... | ... | ... | ... | ... | ... | ... |
| Mauritius | 1986 | 18.3 | 6.7 | 23.8[10] | 11.6 | 1.9[10] | 1985 | 17.3 | 24.0 | 33.0 | ... | 308.2 | 60.2 | 22.0 | ... |
| Mayotte | 1985 | 45.0 | 17.0 | 110.0 | 28.0 | ... | ... | ... | ... | ... | ... | ... | ... | ... | ... |
| Mexico | 1984 | 33.2 | 5.4 | 53.0[10] | 27.8 | 4.0[4] | 1982 | 68.4 | 40.3 | 30.9 | 8.7 | 95.1 | 66.3 | 44.9 | 92.5 |
| Monaco | 1983 | 19.6 | 16.6 | ... | 3.0 | ... | ... | ... | ... | ... | ... | ... | ... | ... | ... |
| Mongolia | 1985 | 36.8 | 9.9 | 47.0[27] | 26.9 | 4.0[27] | ... | ... | ... | ... | ... | ... | ... | ... | ... |
| Montserrat | 1985 | 21.0 | 11.5 | 17.0 | 9.5 | 2.2 | 1985 | 67.5 | 75.9 | 8.4 | 8.4 | 615.9 | 59.1 | 67.5 | 33.7 |
| Morocco | 1980–85 | 44.1 | 11.7 | 97.0 | 32.4 | 6.4 | ... | ... | ... | ... | ... | ... | ... | ... | ... |
| Mozambique | 1980–85 | 45.1 | 19.7 | 153.0 | 25.4 | 6.1 | ... | ... | ... | ... | ... | ... | ... | ... | ... |
| Nauru | 1983 | 31.2 | 5.8 | 31.2[12] | 25.4 | ... | 1976–81[28] | 33.0 | 38.0 | 24.0 | 13.0 | 89.0 | 16.0 | 53.0 | 116.0 |
| Nepal | 1986 | 42.2 | 16.0 | 111.5 | 26.2 | 6.0 | ... | ... | ... | ... | ... | ... | ... | ... | ... |
| Netherlands, The | 1986 | 12.7 | 8.3 | 8.0[10] | 4.4 | 1.5[10] | 1984 | 4.4 | 227.5 | 15.9 | 13.4 | 369.6 | 58.5 | 29.2 | 41.7 |
| Netherlands Antilles | 1982 | 20.7 | 5.5 | 8.2 | 15.2 | 3.4[6,9] | 1983 | 20.8 | 128.6 | 17.9 | 5.2 | 206.0 | 27.1 | 31.2 | 57.1 |
| New Caledonia | 1984 | 22.8 | 5.3 | 19.3[21] | 17.5 | 3.5[6] | ... | ... | ... | ... | ... | ... | ... | ... | ... |
| New Zealand | 1986 | 16.3 | 8.3 | 10.8[10] | 8.0 | 1.9 | 1984 | 4.7 | 180.6 | 13.4 | 11.9 | 368.4 | 79.6 | 21.1 | 54.3 |
| Nicaragua | 1985 | 44.2 | 9.7 | 76.4 | 34.5 | 5.7[6] | 1978 | 52.3 | 13.5 | 2.9 | 4.5 | 62.1 | 18.6 | 14.2 | 59.2 |
| Niger | 1980–85 | 51.0 | 22.9 | 146.0 | 28.1 | 7.1 | ... | ... | ... | ... | ... | ... | ... | ... | ... |
| Nigeria | 1980–85 | 50.4 | 17.1 | 114.0 | 33.3 | 7.1 | ... | ... | ... | ... | ... | ... | ... | ... | ... |
| Niue | 1984 | 22.5 | 7.2 | 19.1[33] | 15.3 | ... | ... | ... | ... | ... | ... | ... | ... | ... | ... |
| Norfolk Island | 1986 | 12.6 | 7.6 | ... | 5.0 | ... | ... | ... | ... | ... | ... | ... | ... | ... | ... |

| expectation of life at birth (latest year) | | nuptiality, family, and family planning | | | | | | | | | | | | | | | country |
| male | female | marriages | | | age at marriage (latest) | | | | | | families (F), households (H) (latest) | | | | | | |
| | | year | total number | rate per 1,000 population | groom (percent) | | | bride (percent) | | | families (households) | | children | | legal abortions | | |
| | | | | | 19 and under | 20-29 | 30 and over | 19 and under | 20-29 | 30 and over | total ('000) | size | number under age 15 | percent legitimate | number | ratio per 100 live births | |
|---|---|---|---|---|---|---|---|---|---|---|---|---|---|---|---|---|---|
| 61.7 | 65.3 | 1984 | 16,786 | 3.5 | 7.2 | 57.2 | 35.6 | 27.1 | 49.1 | 23.8 | H 686 | H 5.4 | H 2.4 | 32.5 | ... | ... | El Salvador |
| 42.4 | 45.6 | 1966 | 209 | 0.8 | | | | | | | | H 4.5 | | | | | Equatorial Guinea |
| 39.5 | 42.6 | | ... | | | | | | | | | H 4.5 | | | | | Ethiopia |
| 73.4 | 78.7 | 1985 | 188 | 4.1 | — | 67.3 | 32.7 | 13.4 | 74.3 | 12.3 | F 14 | F 3.0 | F 0.9 | 67.1 | 26 | 3.3 | Faeroe Islands |
| ... | ... | 1980 | 11 | | | | | | | | H 1 | H 3.3 | H 0.9 | 75.0 | ... | ... | Falkland Islands |
| 67.8 | 72.1 | 1985 | 6,593 | 10.1 | 7.3 | 72.5 | 20.2 | 14.4 | 75.0 | 10.6 | F 97 | F 6.0 | F 2.5 | 82.7 | | | Fiji |
| 70.3 | 78.6 | 1985 | 25,727 | 5.3 | 2.5 | 68.5 | 29.0 | 10.6 | 69.4 | 20.0 | F 1,163 | F 2.8 | F 0.9 | 84.9 | 13,642 | 21.0 | Finland |
| 70.9 | 79.0 | 1986 | 265,340 | 4.8 | 1.8 | 75.4 | 22.8 | 14.2 | 70.2 | 15.6 | H 19,590 | H 2.7 | H 1.0 | 82.2 | 181,735 | 23.9 | France |
| 63.4 | 69.7 | 1985 | 244 | 3.0 | | | | | | | H 12 | H 3.3 | H 1.4 | 23.0 | ... | ... | French Guiana |
| 64.4 | 69.2 | 1986 | 1,119 | 6.2 | 11.3[5] | 75.8[5] | 12.9[5] | 41.5[5] | 52.5[5] | 6.0[5] | H 32 | H 5.0 | H 2.0 | 45.1 | ... | ... | French Polynesia |
| 48.0 | 51.4 | | | | | | | | | | H 136 | H 4.0 | ... | ... | | | Gabon |
| 40.9 | 44.1 | | ... | | | | | | | | H 123 | H 4.9 | H 3.4 | | | | Gambia, The |
| | | | | | | | | | | | | | | | | | Gaza Strip |
| 69.6 | 75.4 | 1985 | 133,898[6] | 7.8 | 4.1 | 71.9 | 24.0 | 18.5 | 65.0 | 16.5 | F 4,781 | F 3.5 | F 0.7 | 66.4 | 80,100 | 35.0 | Germany, East |
| 71.2 | 77.8 | 1985 | 364,684 | 6.0 | 2.2 | 63.2 | 34.6 | 11.3 | 66.7 | 22.0 | F 22,882 | F 2.7 | F 0.5 | 90.4 | 86,298 | 14.8 | Germany, West |
| 50.3 | 53.8 | | | | | | | | | | H 2,272 | H 5.1 | H 2.2 | | ... | ... | Ghana |
| 71.4 | 75.5 | 1986 | 177 | 6.1 | | | | | | | H 7 | H 3.8 | H 1.0 | 97.1 | | | Gibraltar |
| 72.2 | 76.4 | 1985 | 62,547 | 6.3 | 2.0 | 65.6 | 32.4 | 29.1 | 57.1 | 13.8 | H 2,990 | H 3.3 | H 0.7 | 98.2 | 220 | 0.2 | Greece |
| 60.4 | 66.3 | 1985 | 344 | 6.5 | 0.9 | 46.8 | 52.3 | 6.7 | 62.5 | 30.8 | F 27 | F 2.0 | F 0.4 | 32.3 | 539 | 51.3 | Greenland |
| 65.4 | 69.4 | 1979 | 360 | 3.9 | | | | | | | H 20 | H 2.9 | H 2.2 | 22.5 | ... | ... | Grenada |
| 67.8 | 73.2 | 1984 | 1,653 | 5.0 | 0.9 | 63.1 | 36.0 | 19.2 | 58.7 | 22.1 | H 70 | H 3.7 | H 1.9 | 43.4 | 561 | 8.7 | Guadeloupe |
| 69.6 | 74.5 | 1985 | 1,370 | 11.3 | 7.9 | 59.1 | 33.0 | 16.9 | 63.2 | 19.9 | H 25 | H 4.5 | H 1.5 | 64.5 | ... | ... | Guam |
| 56.8 | 61.3 | 1985 | 38,199 | 4.8 | 18.3 | 55.7 | 26.0 | 46.2 | 36.2 | 17.6 | H 1,185 | H 4.5 | H 2.7 | 34.8 | | | Guatemala |
| ... | ... | | ... | | | | | | | | H 18 | H 2.9 | ... | ... | | | Guernsey |
| 38.7 | 41.8 | | | | | | | | | | H 1,064 | H 4.7 | ... | ... | | | Guinea |
| 41.4 | 44.6 | | | | | | | | | | H 124 | H 4.1 | H 2.8 | 11.3 | ... | ... | Guinea-Bissau |
| 66.9 | 70.9 | 1968 | 2,760 | 4.2 | | | | | | | H 178 | H 5.0 | H 2.5 | 61.4 | | | Guyana |
| 51.2 | 54.4 | 1980 | | 0.7 | | | | | | | H 1,147 | H 1.8 | ... | | | | Haiti |
| 58.2 | 61.7 | 1983 | 19,875 | 4.9 | 7.7 | 65.1 | 27.2 | 27.9 | 58.5 | 13.6 | H 463 | H 5.7 | H 2.8 | ... | ... | ... | Honduras |
| 73.2 | 79.0 | 1986 | 43,280 | 8.0 | 1.1 | 60.8 | 38.1 | 6.4 | 72.9 | 20.7 | H 1,245 | H 3.9 | H 1.0 | 90.4 | 10,600 | 12.0 | Hong Kong |
| 65.6 | 73.6 | 1985 | 73,238 | 6.9 | 6.9 | 69.3 | 23.8 | 31.0 | 51.8 | 17.2 | F 3,028 | F 3.4 | F 0.8 | 91.2 | 82,191 | 65.6 | Hungary |
| 74.7 | 80.2 | 1985 | 1,252 | 5.2 | 2.4 | 75.8 | 21.8 | 11.1 | 73.4 | 15.5 | H 49 | H 3.3 | H 1.3 | 52.9 | 687 | 15.7 | Iceland |
| 56.2 | 57.0 | | ... | | | | | | | | H 97,093 | H 5.6 | H 2.4 | ... | 492,696 | 2.0 | India |
| 53.9 | 56.7 | 1984 | | 7.2 | | | | | | | H 30,263 | H 4.9 | H 2.0 | ... | | | Indonesia |
| 58.0 | 58.3 | 1984 | 384,876 | 8.9 | | | | | | | H 6,709 | H 4.3 | H 2.2 | | | | Iran |
| 61.5 | 63.3 | 1982 | 56,440 | 4.0 | 4.0 | 49.1 | 46.9 | 23.9 | 47.2 | 28.9 | H 2,128 | H 6.9 | H 3.2 | ... | | | Iraq |
| 70.1 | 75.6 | 1985 | 18,590[6] | 5.2 | 5.2 | 77.1 | 17.7 | 14.9 | 75.2 | 9.9 | H 726 | H 3.9 | H 1.3 | 92.2 | ... | ... | Ireland |
| ... | ... | 1985 | 333 | 5.1 | 2.4 | 60.7 | 36.9 | 8.7 | 65.8 | 25.5 | | | | 79.4 | | | Isle of Man |
| 73.5 | 77.1 | 1985 | 29,158 | 6.9 | 3.3 | 75.4 | 21.3 | 24.0 | 65.2 | 10.8 | H 1,026 | H 3.7 | H 1.3 | 97.5 | 18,948 | 19.2 | Israel |
| 71.0 | 77.8 | 1985 | 295,990 | 5.2 | 1.7 | 75.2 | 23.1 | 18.7 | 70.1 | 11.2 | F 17,615 | F 3.2 | F 0.7 | 94.7 | 227,809 | 38.9 | Italy |
| 67.9 | 71.9 | 1985 | 11,800 | 5.1 | | | | | | | H 509 | H 4.3 | H 2.0 | ... | ... | ... | Jamaica |
| 75.1 | 80.8 | 1985 | 735,900 | 6.1 | 1.0[5] | 64.2[5] | 34.8[5] | 3.5[5] | 82.0[5] | 14.5[5] | F 22,240 | F 5.4 | F 1.2 | 99.2 | 598,100 | 37.9 | Japan |
| ... | ... | | | | | | | | | | H 27 | H 2.5 | ... | | | | Jersey |
| 61.9 | 65.5 | 1984 | 18,189 | 7.1 | 6.0 | 71.6 | 22.4 | 46.7 | 47.8 | 5.5 | H 375 | H 6.9 | H 3.4 | ... | ... | ... | Jordan |
| 45.3 | 48.2 | | ... | | | | | | | | | H 5.6 | | | | | Kampuchea |
| 51.2 | 54.7 | | ... | | | | | | | | H 1,938 | H 6.2 | H 2.7 | ... | ... | ... | Kenya |
| 50.6 | 55.6 | 1973 | 291[23] | 4.5 | 9.9 | 66.7 | 23.5 | 34.7 | 54.5 | 10.8 | H 10 | H 6.3 | F 2.0 | ... | | | Kiribati |
| 65.0 | 72.0 | | | | | | | | | | | H 5.7 | | | | | Korea, North |
| 65.2 | 71.5 | 1982 | 326,004 | 8.3 | 1.7 | 81.4 | 16.9 | 10.1 | 85.2 | 4.7 | F 7,969 | F 4.8 | F 1.6 | ... | | | Korea, South |
| 68.0 | 72.9 | 1985 | 9,426 | 5.3 | 5.3 | 69.3 | 25.4 | 39.9 | 50.0 | 10.1 | H 143 | H 7.2 | H 1.6 | ... | | | Kuwait |
| 49.4 | 52.4 | | | | | | | | | | | H 5.3 | | | ... | ... | Laos |
| 65.0 | 68.9 | 1973 | 18,601 | 7.0 | | | | | | | H 405 | H 5.3 | H 2.2 | ... | ... | ... | Lebanon |
| 46.3 | 52.3 | | ... | | | | | | | | H 242 | H 4.4 | H 2.0 | ... | | | Lesotho |
| 53.9 | 56.3 | | | | | | | | | | | H 5.8 | ... | ... | | | Liberia |
| 56.6 | 60.0 | 1979 | 17,236 | 6.0 | | | | | | | F 383 | F 5.4 | F 2.9 | ... | ... | ... | Libya |
| 77.6 | 82.6 | 1986 | 296 | 10.8 | 1.7 | 68.2 | 30.1 | 10.2 | 71.9 | 17.9 | H 8 | H 3.0 | H 0.7 | 93.4 | ... | ... | Liechtenstein |
| 70.0 | 76.7 | 1985 | 1,962 | 5.3 | 0.4 | 44.7 | 54.9 | 4.3 | 73.5 | 22.2 | H 128 | H 2.8 | H 0.5 | 91.8 | ... | ... | Luxembourg |
| 68.0 | 73.0 | 1985 | 3,254 | 8.5 | 14.5 | 60.3 | 25.2 | 49.5 | 36.9 | 13.6 | H 50 | H 4.8 | H 1.8 | 99.3 | | | Macau |
| 48.9 | 50.4 | 1975 | 19,800 | 2.6 | ... | ... | ... | ... | ... | ... | H 1,709 | H 4.7 | H 2.0 | ... | | | Madagascar |
| 44.0 | 46.0 | 1977 | 4,300 | 7.8 | | | | | | | | | | | | | Malawi |
| 67.0 | 71.2 | 1979[26] | 23,030 | 1.7 | 0.5[26] | 65.3[26] | 34.2[26] | 7.9[26] | 77.0[26] | 15.1[26] | | H 5.2 | | | ... | ... | Malaysia |
| 57.4 | 58.4 | 1982 | 1,404 | 8.9 | 12.3 | 54.1 | 33.6 | 39.5 | 41.4 | 19.1 | H 23 | H 6.1 | H 2.7 | ... | | | Maldives |
| 40.4 | 43.6 | 1983 | 21,785 | 2.8 | | | | | | | H 1,254 | H 5.1 | ... | ... | | | Mali |
| 70.8 | 76.0 | 1985 | 2,549 | 7.5 | 1.9 | 79.2 | 18.9 | 11.3 | 77.8 | 10.9 | H 76 | H 3.6 | H 1.2 | 99.3 | | | Malta |
| 71.0 | 75.5 | 1985 | 1,331 | 4.1 | 0.3 | 60.5 | 39.2 | 12.9 | 60.4 | 26.7 | H 71 | H 3.8 | | 36.1 | | | Martinique |
| 45.0 | 48.0 | | ... | | | | | | | | H 246 | H 5.3 | H 2.2 | ... | ... | ... | Mauritania |
| 64.4 | 71.2 | 1985 | 11,245 | 11.0 | 1.6 | 56.8 | 41.6 | 24.4 | 57.9 | 17.7 | F 155 | F 5.3 | F 2.0 | 55.4 | | | Mauritius |
| ... | ... | | | | | | | | | | H 10 | H 4.7 | H 2.3 | 89.2 | | | Mayotte |
| 64.9 | 71.4 | 1982 | 528,963 | 7.2 | 17.3 | 63.5 | 19.2 | 40.7 | 46.9 | 12.4 | H 9,851 | H 5.3 | H 2.3 | 91.0 | ... | ... | Mexico |
| ... | ... | 1981 | 190 | 7.3 | | | | | | | H 10 | H 2.3 | H 0.3 | 96.8 | | | Monaco |
| 61.1 | 65.2 | 1985 | 12,500 | 6.6 | | | | | | | F 311 | F 5.1 | ... | ... | ... | ... | Mongolia |
| 68.6 | 71.9 | 1985 | 55 | 4.6 | — | 41.8 | 58.2 | 9.1 | 45.5 | 45.5 | H 4 | H 3.1 | | 23.4 | | | Montserrat |
| 56.1 | 59.4 | | | | | | | | | | H 2,819 | H 5.8 | H 2.5 | ... | | | Morocco |
| 44.4 | 46.2 | 1974 | 6,037 | 0.7 | | | | | | | F 1,860 | F 4.4 | F 2.0 | 73.1 | | | Mozambique |
| 48.9 | 62.1 | 1977 | 43[29] | 6.3 | | | | | | | H 1 | H 8.0 | H 2.6 | ... | | | Nauru |
| 50.6 | 53.4 | | | | | | | | | | | F 5.8 | H 2.2 | ... | ... | ... | Nepal |
| 73.1 | 79.7 | 1985 | 82,747 | 5.7 | 0.4 | 68.7 | 30.9 | 3.9 | 76.4 | 19.7 | H 5,509 | H 2.6 | H 0.6 | 91.7 | 19,623 | 11.5 | Netherlands, The |
| 71.1[30] | 75.7[30] | 1982 | 959 | 5.6 | 4.0 | 77.0 | 18.9 | 22.2 | 61.1 | 16.7 | H 41 | H 3.7 | H 2.1 | 52.3 | ... | ... | Netherlands Antilles |
| 64.6 | 68.5 | 1983 | 831 | 5.7 | 3.6 | 70.2 | 26.2 | 31.4 | 53.4 | 15.2 | | H 4.1 | | 57.5 | | | New Caledonia |
| 71.8 | 77.8 | 1985 | 24,657 | 7.5 | 1.6 | 64.3 | 34.1 | 9.4 | 67.0 | 23.6 | H 1,004 | H 3.2 | H 0.8 | 76.2 | 7,275 | 14.1 | New Zealand |
| 58.7 | 61.0 | 1985 | 11,822 | 3.6 | —18.1[31]— | | 81.9[32] | —48.2[31]— | | 51.8[32] | | H 6.9 | | ... | ... | ... | Nicaragua |
| 40.9 | 44.1 | | ... | | | | | | | | H 1,029 | H 5.2 | H 2.4 | ... | ... | ... | Niger |
| 46.9 | 50.2 | | | | | | | | | | | H 5.0 | | | | | Nigeria |
| 63.0 | 66.5 | 1982 | 12 | 3.5[34] | | | | | | | F 1 | F 4.1 | F 1.9 | 58.2 | | | Niue |
| 58.0 | 59.9 | 1983 | 10 | 4.8 | — | 56.3 | 43.7 | 6.3 | 50.0 | 43.7 | ... | ... | ... | 73.9 | ... | ... | Norfolk Island |

## Vital statistics, marriage, family   (continued)

| country | vital rates | | | | | | causes of death (rate per 100,000 population) | | | | | | | | |
|---|---|---|---|---|---|---|---|---|---|---|---|---|---|---|---|
| | year | birth rate per 1,000 population | death rate per 1,000 population | infant mortality rate per 1,000 live births | rate of natural increase per 1,000 population | total fertility rate | year | infectious and parasitic diseases | malig-nant neo-plasms (cancers) | endocrine and metabolic disorders | diseases of the nervous system | diseases of the circula-tory system | diseases of the respira-tory system | diseases of the digestive system | accidents, poisoning, and violence |
| Norway | 1986 | 12.6 | 10.5 | 8.5 | 2.1 | 1.7 | 1985 | 7.5 | 231.9 | 13.0 | 16.1 | 518.5 | 105.2 | 30.4 | 65.0 |
| Oman | 1980–85 | 47.0 | 14.3 | 113.4[6] | 32.7 | 7.1 | ... | ... | ... | ... | ... | ... | ... | ... | ... |
| Pacific Is., Trust Terr. of the | | | | | | | | | | | | | | | |
|   Marshall Islands | 1984 | 39.2 | 5.1 | 33.0 | 34.1 | 5.0[3] | 1984 | 46.0 | 34.5 | 60.3 | 11.5 | 80.5 | 77.6 | 14.4 | 23.0 |
|   Micronesia, Fed. States of | 1984 | 29.4 | 2.7 | 95.0 | 26.7 | ... | 1984 | 20.4 | 27.1 | 6.8 | 4.5 | 53.2 | 47.5 | 5.7 | 23.8 |
|   Northern Mariana Islands | 1984 | 31.4 | 5.5 | 23.8 | 25.9 | ... | 1984 | 20.5 | 66.7 | 25.6 | 5.1 | 143.6 | 25.6 | 35.9 | 97.4 |
|   Palau | 1984 | 27.7 | 6.9 | 32.6 | 20.8 | 3.9[4] | 1984 | 32.9 | 73.9 | 24.6 | 32.9 | 90.3 | 98.6 | — | 180.7 |
| Pakistan | 1986 | 41.4 | 14.8 | 126.0 | 26.6 | 5.5 | ... | ... | ... | ... | ... | ... | ... | ... | ... |
| Panama | 1985 | 26.0 | 5.0 | 23.0 | 21.0 | 3.3[6] | 1985 | 23.8 | 48.8 | 9.5 | 3.4 | 102.9 | 23.1 | 6.5 | 45.3 |
| Papua New Guinea | 1985 | 35.0 | 12.5 | 68.0 | 22.5 | 5.2[27] | ... | ... | ... | ... | ... | ... | ... | ... | ... |
| Paraguay | 1980–85 | 36.0 | 7.2 | 52.9[6] | 28.8 | 4.9 | 1984 | 40.5 | 25.6 | 14.3 | 6.5 | 95.7 | 30.0 | 13.4 | 26.0 |
| Peru | 1985 | 35.5 | 10.0 | 92.7 | 25.5 | 4.7 | 1982 | 88.2 | 33.5 | 13.5 | 10.5 | 58.0 | 97.9 | 24.1 | 30.5 |
| Philippines | 1986 | 33.8 | 8.2 | 59.0 | 25.6 | 4.2 | 1984 | 179.8 | 30.2 | 13.4 | ... | 100.6 | ... | ... | 16.8 |
| Pitcairn Island | 1982 | — | — | — | — | ... | ... | ... | ... | ... | ... | ... | ... | ... | ... |
| Poland | 1986 | 16.9 | 10.0 | 18.5[10] | 6.9 | 2.3[6] | 1984 | 11.4 | 179.0 | 16.2 | 9.5 | 492.9 | 52.0 | 34.0 | 72.4 |
| Portugal | 1985 | 12.8 | 9.6 | 11.6 | 3.2 | 2.3[6] | 1985 | 9.3 | 158.3 | 20.4 | 9.2 | 424.7 | 69.2 | 47.5 | 70.1 |
| Puerto Rico | 1985 | 18.9 | 6.6 | 15.7[6] | 12.3 | 2.4[6] | 1983 | 11.6 | 105.3 | 35.0 | 9.1 | 260.7 | 72.5 | 43.6 | 54.8 |
| Qatar | 1985 | 30.6 | 2.6 | 35.0 | 28.0 | 4.6[6] | 1985 | 6.0 | 27.6 | 11.3 | 3.3 | 45.8 | 10.6 | 8.0 | 61.5 |
| Réunion | 1985 | 24.1 | 5.6 | 10.3 | 18.5 | 2.9[6] | 1984 | 9.5 | 46.4 | 22.4 | ... | 174.0 | 38.7 | 36.5 | 71.1 |
| Romania | 1985 | 15.8 | 10.9 | 25.6 | 4.9 | 2.4[2] | 1984 | 8.4 | 128.4 | 7.4 | 8.3 | 603.7 | 115.4 | 50.0 | 66.3 |
| Rwanda | 1984 | 52.0 | 19.0 | 128.0 | 33.0 | 8.0 | ... | ... | ... | ... | ... | ... | ... | ... | ... |
| St. Christopher and Nevis | 1985 | 22.3 | 9.6 | 30.2 | 12.7 | 3.2[6] | 1984 | 35.1 | 114.0 | 37.9[14] | 6.8[3] | 462.7 | 41.7 | 6.6 | 28.5 |
| St. Helena and Ascension | 1982 | 24.6 | 10.0 | 16.3 | 14.6 | ... | ... | ... | ... | ... | ... | ... | ... | ... | ... |
| St. Lucia | 1985 | 30.6 | 5.9 | 21.7[18] | 24.7 | 3.9 | 1984 | 19.4 | 73.8 | 25.4 | 6.7 | 193.9 | 35.1 | 14.2 | 39.5 |
| St. Pierre and Miquelon | 1984 | 21.0 | 9.5 | 12.3[14] | 11.5 | ... | 1977 | 72.9 | 108.3 | 102.1 | 25.0 | 366.7 | 45.8 | 39.6 | 39.6 |
| St. Vincent and the Grenadines | 1984 | 26.2 | 6.5 | 35.1[11] | 19.7 | 3.2[6] | 1984 | 28.7 | 78.6 | 37.0 | 10.2 | 192.3 | 26.8 | 22.2 | 45.3 |
| San Marino | 1986 | 8.1 | 7.7 | 6.4[36] | 0.4 | 1.3[6] | 1982–86[28] | — | 256.2 | 10.0 | — | 297.9 | 27.2 | 22.6 | 48.9 |
| São Tomé and Príncipe | 1985 | 36.3 | 8.8 | 61.7 | 27.5 | 5.1[4] | ... | ... | ... | ... | ... | ... | ... | ... | ... |
| Saudi Arabia | 1980–85 | 42.1 | 8.9 | 109.8[6] | 33.2 | 7.1 | ... | ... | ... | ... | ... | ... | ... | ... | ... |
| Senegal | 1984 | 48.6 | 18.5 | 131.0[4] | 30.1 | 7.0 | ... | ... | ... | ... | ... | ... | ... | ... | ... |
| Seychelles | 1986 | 26.2 | 7.6 | 17.4 | 18.6 | 3.5[6] | 1985 | 40.2 | 115.0 | 6.1 | 19.9 | 200.8 | 64.4 | 35.3 | 69.0 |
| Sierra Leone | 1980–85 | 47.4 | 29.7 | 134.0[6] | 17.7 | 6.1 | ... | ... | ... | ... | ... | ... | ... | ... | ... |
| Singapore | 1986 | 14.8 | 5.0 | 9.4 | 9.9 | 1.4 | 1985 | 14.2 | 112.5 | 19.0 | 3.4 | 177.5 | 84.8 | 15.1 | 48.9 |
| Solomon Islands | 1982 | 44.6 | 11.7 | 46.0 | 32.9 | 7.3 | ... | ... | ... | ... | ... | ... | ... | ... | ... |
| Somalia | 1984 | 49.0 | 20.0 | 152.0[10] | 29.0 | 6.8 | ... | ... | ... | ... | ... | ... | ... | ... | ... |
| South Africa | 1983 | 33.6 | 11.0 | 83.0 | 22.6 | 5.1 | ... | ... | ... | ... | ... | ... | ... | ... | ... |
|   Bophuthatswana | ... | ... | ... | ... | ... | ... | ... | ... | ... | ... | ... | ... | ... | ... | ... |
|   Ciskei | 1982 | ... | ... | 89.0 | ... | ... | ... | ... | ... | ... | ... | ... | ... | ... | ... |
|   KwaNdebele | ... | ... | ... | ... | ... | ... | ... | ... | ... | ... | ... | ... | ... | ... | ... |
|   Transkei | 1984 | ... | ... | 89.0 | ... | ... | ... | ... | ... | ... | ... | ... | ... | ... | ... |
|   Venda | ... | ... | ... | ... | ... | ... | ... | ... | ... | ... | ... | ... | ... | ... | ... |
| South West Africa/ Namibia | 1980–85 | 44.9 | 11.5 | 110.0 | 33.5 | 6.0 | ... | ... | ... | ... | ... | ... | ... | ... | ... |
| Spain | 1984 | 12.1 | 7.7 | 9.0 | 4.4 | 2.1[4] | 1982 | 14.2 | 153.7 | 20.5 | 11.8 | 361.2 | 67.4 | 42.7 | 43.2 |
| Sri Lanka | 1986 | 23.9 | 6.2 | 23.5 | 17.7 | 2.8 | 1980 | 49.1 | 27.9 | 8.3 | 46.2 | 99.0 | 47.2 | 14.4 | 69.2 |
| Sudan, The | 1980–85 | 45.9 | 17.4 | 118.0 | 28.5 | 6.6 | ... | ... | ... | ... | ... | ... | ... | ... | ... |
| Suriname | 1985 | 29.7 | 6.8 | 27.6 | 22.9 | 3.0[4] | 1982 | 42.1 | 57.3 | 17.6 | 5.2 | 192.3 | 39.1 | 30.3 | 76.0 |
| Swaziland | 1980–85 | 47.5 | 17.2 | 129.0 | 30.3 | 6.5 | ... | ... | ... | ... | ... | ... | ... | ... | ... |
| Sweden | 1986 | 12.2 | 11.2 | 6.8[10] | 1.0 | 1.7[10] | 1985 | 7.9 | 235.6 | 18.4 | 10.2 | 614.6 | 92.5 | 29.5 | 59.2 |
| Switzerland | 1986 | 11.7 | 9.2 | 6.9[10] | 2.5 | 1.8[10] | 1985 | 5.6 | 250.5 | 24.7 | 15.2 | 417.8 | 50.1 | 29.6 | 75.7 |
| Syria | 1985 | 44.2 | 5.0 | 48[4] | 39.2 | 6.8[4] | 1981 | 15.1 | 8.4 | 5.0 | 4.0 | 60.7 | 13.2 | 4.5 | 20.0 |
| Taiwan | 1986 | 15.9 | 4.9 | 6.8[10] | 11.0 | 1.9[10] | 1985 | 11.2 | 85.0 | 14.2 | ... | 138.0 | 13.1 | 16.7 | 70.9 |
| Tanzania | 1984 | 50.0 | 16.0 | 111.0 | 34.0 | 7.0 | ... | ... | ... | ... | ... | ... | ... | ... | ... |
| Thailand | 1986 | 25.3 | 7.4 | 52.0 | 17.9 | 3.0 | 1984 | 29.2 | 26.1 | ... | ... | 68.3 | 10.2 | 20.1 | 37.4 |
| Togo | 1980–85 | 45.2 | 15.7 | 102.0 | 29.5 | 6.1 | ... | ... | ... | ... | ... | ... | ... | ... | ... |
| Tokelau | 1982 | 27.7 | 10.3 | — | 17.4 | 4.3 | ... | ... | ... | ... | ... | ... | ... | ... | ... |
| Tonga | 1985 | 28.9 | 3.5 | 26.0[14] | 25.4 | 6.6 | ... | ... | ... | ... | ... | ... | ... | ... | ... |
| Trinidad and Tobago | 1983 | 29.2 | 6.6 | 14.9[21] | 22.6 | 2.8[6] | 1983 | 16.3 | 74.5 | 71.8 | 10.2 | 271.1 | 48.5 | 29.3 | 59.4 |
| Tunisia | 1985 | 31.3 | 6.7 | 71.0[4] | 24.6 | 4.3[6] | 1980 | 18.2 | 8.9 | 3.9 | 5.2 | 29.3 | 10.0 | 6.2 | 12.4 |
| Turkey | 1980–85 | 33.6 | 9.3 | 84.0[10] | 24.3 | 4.5 | 1983 | 16.8 | 25.2 | 2.3 | 1.4 | 107.3 | 19.8 | 3.9 | 7.4 |
| Turks and Caicos Islands | 1983 | 27.5 | 3.9 | 10.2[2] | 23.6 | ... | ... | ... | ... | ... | ... | ... | ... | ... | ... |
| Tuvalu | 1985 | 23.8 | 10.7 | 35.0 | 13.1 | 2.7 | 1985 | 40.0 | 70.0 | 20.0 | 120.0 | 140.0 | 120.0 | 160.0 | — |
| Uganda | 1984 | 50.0 | 16.0 | 110.0 | 34.0 | 7.0 | ... | ... | ... | ... | ... | ... | ... | ... | ... |
| U.S.S.R. | 1986 | 19.6 | 9.7 | 26.0 | 9.9 | 2.3[6] | 1983 | ... | 148.1 | ... | ... | 554.3 | ... | ... | ... |
| United Arab Emirates | 1980–85 | 29.8 | 4.3 | 35.0[10] | 25.5 | 5.9 | ... | ... | ... | ... | ... | ... | ... | ... | ... |
| United Kingdom | 1986 | 13.3 | 12.2 | 9.3 | 1.1 | 1.8 | 1985 | 4.2 | 281.7 | 14.2 | 20.2 | 568.5 | 131.2 | 36.4 | 40.1 |
| United States | 1987 | 15.5 | 8.9 | 10.2 | 6.6 | 1.8[27] | 1986–87 | 15.7 | 194.8 | 15.1 | 0.6 | 394.9 | 59.4 | 15.6 | 60.4 |
| Uruguay | 1984 | 17.9 | 10.2 | 30.3 | 7.7 | 2.6[2] | 1984 | 24.3 | 213.1 | 21.1 | ... | 419.7 | 39.6 | 10.0 | 49.7 |
| Vanuatu | 1984 | 45.0 | 12.0 | 94.0 | 33.0 | 6.5 | 1985 | 71.0 | 23.4 | 16.6 | 12.1 | 38.5 | 61.9 | 12.8 | 24.2 |
| Venezuela | 1985 | 29.0 | 4.6 | 27.3[6] | 24.4 | 3.8[4] | 1983 | 47.4 | 54.3 | 17.4 | 10.0 | 132.0 | 35.6 | 19.0 | 71.4 |
| Vietnam | 1986 | 33.6 | 10.3 | 69.0 | 23.3 | 4.4 | 1979 | 48.0 | 54.0 | ... | ... | 123.8 | ... | ... | ... |
| Virgin Islands (U.S.) | 1985 | 21.6 | 4.9 | 20.2[14] | 16.7 | 2.9[10] | 1981 | 6.1 | 83.5 | 25.5 | 5.1 | 209.8 | 20.4 | 34.6 | 84.5 |
| Wallis and Futuna | 1978 | 41.1 | 10.6 | 40.5 | 30.5 | ... | ... | ... | ... | ... | ... | ... | ... | ... | ... |
| West Bank | 1984 | 39.1 | 8.2 | ... | 30.9 | ... | ... | ... | ... | ... | ... | ... | ... | ... | ... |
| Western Sahara | 1980–85 | 29.0 | 4.5 | 5.3 | 24.5 | ... | ... | ... | ... | ... | ... | ... | ... | ... | ... |
| Western Samoa | 1984 | 10.2 | 2.3 | 52.0[27] | 7.9 | 4.5[10] | 1984 | 6.9 | 17.6 | 4.4 | 1.9 | 47.2 | 22.6 | 20.7 | 9.4 |
| Yemen (Aden) | 1980–85 | 47.0 | 17.4 | 137.0[6] | 29.6 | 6.8 | ... | ... | ... | ... | ... | ... | ... | ... | ... |
| Yemen (Ṣanʿāʾ) | 1980–85 | 48.6 | 18.4 | 135.0 | 30.2 | 7.0 | ... | ... | ... | ... | ... | ... | ... | ... | ... |
| Yugoslavia | 1986 | 15.4 | 9.0 | 27.1 | 6.4 | 2.1[6] | 1982 | 13.5 | 135.8 | 9.1 | 6.9 | 450.7 | 52.3 | 39.5 | 63.0 |
| Zaire | 1980–85 | 45.1 | 15.8 | 106.0[14] | 29.3 | 6.1 | ... | ... | ... | ... | ... | ... | ... | ... | ... |
| Zambia | 1980–85 | 48.1 | 15.1 | 88.0 | 33.0 | 6.8 | ... | ... | ... | ... | ... | ... | ... | ... | ... |
| Zimbabwe | 1983 | 53.0 | 13.0 | 61.0[10] | 40.0 | 7.0 | 1979 | 7.3 | 152.9 | 7.0 | 1.6 | 310.6 | 64.7 | 6.6 | 102.4 |

| expectation of life at birth (latest year) male | female | nuptiality: marriages — year | total number | rate per 1,000 population | age at marriage (latest): groom (percent) 19 and under | 20–29 | 30 and over | bride (percent) 19 and under | 20–29 | 30 and over | families (F), households (H) (latest): total ('000) | size | children: number under age 15 | percent legitimate | legal abortions: number | ratio per 100 live births | country |
|---|---|---|---|---|---|---|---|---|---|---|---|---|---|---|---|---|---|
| 72.8 | 79.5 | 1985 | 20,221 | 4.8 | 1.4 | 65.9 | 32.7 | 8.1 | 71.8 | 20.1 | F 1,684 / H 161 | F 2.4 / H 5.5 | F 0.6 | 74.2 | 14,599 | 28.0 | Norway |
| 51.0 | 53.7 | … | … | … | … | … | … | … | … | … | … | … | … | … | … | … | Oman |
| … | … | … | … | … | … | … | … | … | … | … | H 4 | H 8.0 | … | … | … | … | Pacific Is., Trust Terr. of the Marshall Islands |
| … | … | … | … | … | … | … | … | … | … | … | H 11 | H 7.0 | … | … | … | … | Micronesia, Fed. States of |
| 59.0 | 64.0 | … | … | … | … | … | … | … | … | … | H 3 | H 5.4 | … | … | … | … | Northern Mariana Islands |
| 58.9 | 62.5 | … | … | … | … | … | … | … | … | … | H 2 | H 5.9 | … | … | … | … | Palau |
| 52.0 | 50.2 | 1971 | 62,900 | 10.7[19] | … | … | … | … | … | … | … | H 6.7 | … | … | … | … | Pakistan |
| 69.2 | 72.9 | 1985 | 9,986 | 4.6 | 4.6[35] | 55.6[35] | 39.8[35] | 19.2[35] | 53.6[35] | 27.2[35] | F 347 | F 4.9 | … | 28.6 | 12 | — | Panama |
| 52.6 | 54.2 | … | … | … | … | … | … | … | … | … | H 674 | H 4.6 | … | … | … | … | Papua New Guinea |
| 62.8 | 67.5 | 1985 | 18,370 | 5.8 | 3.2 | 64.3 | 32.5 | 32.5 | 47.7 | 19.8 | H 345 | H 5.2 | … | 68.7 | … | … | Paraguay |
| 58.3 | 62.2 | 1982 | 109,200 | 6.0 | 5.5 | 60.4 | 34.1 | 25.9 | 51.4 | 22.6 | H 2,772 | H 4.8 | … | 57.8 | … | … | Peru |
| 61.9 | 65.5 | 1983 | 351,663 | 6.8 | 10.4 | 70.3 | 19.3 | 30.0 | 58.0 | 12.0 | F 9,566 | F 5.7 | F 2.4 | 96.3 | … | … | Philippines |
| 63.0 | 66.5 | 1972 | 2 | … | … | … | … | … | … | … | … | … | … | … | … | … | Pitcairn Island |
| 66.5 | 74.8 | 1985 | 266,800 | 7.2 | 3.5 | 79.0 | 17.5 | 19.2 | 68.2 | 12.6 | F 9,435 | F 3.6 | F 0.9 | 95.3 | 132,844 | 19.0 | Poland |
| 68.6 | 75.3 | 1985 | 68,461 | 6.7 | 6.8 | 76.3 | 16.9 | 28.3 | 60.0 | 11.7 | H 2,954 | H 3.8 | H 0.8 | 88.5 | … | … | Portugal |
| 70.8 | 76.9 | 1983 | 29,632 | 9.1 | 11.5 | 56.5 | 32.0 | 28.0 | 48.9 | 23.1 | F 563 | H 4.1 | F 1.8 | 79.0 | … | … | Puerto Rico |
| 66.9 | 71.6 | 1985 | 1,092 | 3.6 | 4.7 | 71.2 | 24.1 | 39.7 | 54.5 | 5.8 | … | H 6.4 | … | … | … | … | Qatar |
| 64.6 | 68.2 | 1985 | 3,185 | 5.8 | 2.3 | 73.6 | 24.1 | 29.0 | 56.6 | 14.4 | H 121 | H 4.2 | H 2.3 | 52.9 | 3,838 | 32.5 | Réunion |
| 67.0 | 72.6 | 1985 | 161,094 | 7.1 | 3.3 | 74.9 | 21.8 | 37.2 | 48.2 | 14.6 | H 7,115 | H 3.1 | … | … | 404,000 | 99.0 | Romania |
| 46.0 | 49.0 | 1980 | 13,890 | 2.7 | … | … | … | … | … | … | H 894 | H 5.2 | … | … | … | … | Rwanda |
| 62.0 | 67.0 | 1977 | 150 | 3.5 | … | … | … | … | … | … | H 11 | H 3.7 | H 1.9 | 18.6 | … | … | St. Christopher and Nevis |
| … | … | 1982 | 29 | 5.2 | 8.3 | 58.4 | 33.3 | 38.9 | 44.4 | 16.7 | H 1 | H 4.4 | H 1.6 | 56.5 | … | … | St. Helena and Ascension |
| 68.6 | 75.5 | 1985 | 423 | 3.1 | 0.7 | 46.9 | 52.4 | 8.8 | 53.6 | 37.6 | H 27 | H 4.6 | … | 15.9 | … | … | St. Lucia |
| 65.8 | 71.6 | 1984 | 33 | 5.4 | … | … | … | … | … | … | H 2 | H 3.3 | H 0.9 | 83.0 | … | … | St. Pierre and Miquelon |
| 67.5 | 71.4 | 1984 | 394 | 3.6 | 0.7 | 44.2 | 55.1 | 11.1 | 57.2 | 31.7 | H 20 | H 5.0 | … | … | … | … | St. Vincent and the Grenadines |
| 70.7 | 76.2 | 1985 | 202 | 9.0 | 2.8 | 80.8 | 16.4 | 19.9 | 72.6 | 7.5 | F 6 | F 3.2 | F 0.8 | 94.6 | … | … | San Marino |
| 48.2 | 51.6 | … | … | … | … | … | … | … | … | … | … | … | … | … | … | … | São Tomé and Príncipe |
| 59.2 | 62.7 | … | … | … | … | … | … | … | … | … | H 1,513 | H 6.6 | … | … | … | … | Saudi Arabia |
| 45.0 | 48.0 | … | … | … | … | … | … | … | … | … | H 1,167 | H 4.8 | … | … | … | … | Senegal |
| 66.2 | 73.5 | 1984 | 390 | 6.0 | 1.8 | 55.9 | 42.3 | 15.6 | 60.8 | 23.6 | H 13 | H 4.8 | H 1.9 | 33.2 | 221 | 12.7 | Seychelles |
| 46.7 | 50.0 | … | … | … | … | … | … | … | … | … | H 722 | H 4.9 | … | … | … | … | Sierra Leone |
| 69.9 | 76.2 | 1986 | 20,075 | 7.8 | 0.6 | 72.0 | 27.4 | 7.7 | 80.1 | 12.2 | H 510 | H 3.9 | H 1.3 | … | 19,100 | 47.1 | Singapore |
| 54.0 | 54.0 | … | … | … | … | … | … | … | … | … | F 41 | F 5.6 | F 2.3 | … | … | … | Solomon Islands |
| 44.0 | 47.0 | … | … | … | … | … | … | … | … | … | … | H 4.9 | … | … | … | … | Somalia |
| 51.8 | 55.2 | 1977 | 64,979[37] | … | 3.5[37] | 69.4[37] | 27.1[37] | 22.1[37] | 58.6[37] | 19.3[37] | F 1,403 | H 5.1 | … | 75.9 | … | … | South Africa |
| … | … | … | … | … | … | … | … | … | … | … | … | … | … | … | … | … | Bophuthatswana |
| … | … | … | … | … | … | … | … | … | … | … | H 144 | H 6.2 | … | … | … | … | Ciskei |
| … | … | … | … | … | … | … | … | … | … | … | … | … | … | … | … | … | KwaNdebele |
| —57.0— | | … | … | … | … | … | … | … | … | … | … | … | … | … | … | … | Transkei |
| … | … | … | … | … | … | … | … | … | … | … | H 70 | H 5.4 | … | … | … | … | Venda |
| 46.6 | 49.9 | … | … | … | … | … | … | … | … | … | … | H 4.8 | … | … | … | … | South West Africa/Namibia |
| 71.3 | 77.5 | 1983 | 183,490 | 4.8 | 5.7 | 80.8 | 13.5 | 20.8 | 71.7 | 7.5 | F 10,665 | F 3.5 | … | 97.9 | … | … | Spain |
| 68.0 | 71.2 | 1983 | 121,553 | 7.9 | 0.4 | 72.4 | 27.2 | 17.8 | 73.4 | 8.8 | H 2,721 | H 5.2 | H 1.9 | 92.5 | … | … | Sri Lanka |
| 49.0 | 46.6 | … | … | … | … | … | … | … | … | … | H 3,471 | H 5.3 | … | … | … | … | Sudan, The |
| 63.2 | 67.0 | 1985 | 2,400[3] | 6.1 | … | … | … | … | … | … | … | H 3.9 | … | … | … | … | Suriname |
| 45.3 | 52.2 | … | … | … | … | … | … | … | … | … | H 112 | H 5.0 | … | … | 1,145 | … | Swaziland |
| 73.3 | 79.4 | 1985 | 38,297 | 4.6 | 0.5 | 44.6 | 54.9 | 2.4 | 58.2 | 39.4 | H 3,498 | H 2.4 | H 0.5 | 56.4 | 30,755 | 32.8 | Sweden |
| 72.8 | 79.7 | 1985 | 38,776 | 5.9 | 0.3 | 59.0 | 40.7 | 3.8 | 71.3 | 24.9 | H 2,500 | H 2.5 | … | 94.4 | … | … | Switzerland |
| 63.3 | 67.0 | 1984[38] | 81,460 | 8.2 | … | … | … | … | … | … | F 1,151 | H 6.2 | F 2.4 | … | … | … | Syria |
| 70.8 | 75.8 | 1986 | 145,592 | 7.5 | 2.4 | 76.6 | 21.0 | 11.2 | 81.5 | 7.3 | H 4,288 | H 4.6 | H 0.5 | … | … | … | Taiwan |
| 50.0 | 53.0 | 1967 | 3,475 | 9.8 | … | … | … | … | … | … | H 3,435 | H 5.1 | H 2.3 | … | … | … | Tanzania |
| 61.3 | 67.3 | 1985 | 343,134 | 6.6 | … | … | … | … | … | … | H 8,419 | H 5.3 | H 2.0 | … | … | … | Thailand |
| 48.8 | 52.2 | 1979[39] | 5,753 | 2.3 | … | … | … | … | … | … | H 479 | H 5.6 | … | … | … | … | Togo |
| 63.0 | 66.5 | 1981 | 9 | 6.0 | — | 83.3 | 16.7 | — | 100.0 | — | … | H 5.5 | … | … | … | … | Tokelau |
| 61.0 | 64.8 | 1983 | 699 | 6.7 | … | … | … | … | … | … | F 15 | F 6.1 | F 2.7 | … | … | … | Tonga |
| 66.2 | 71.3 | 1984 | 8,403 | 7.2 | 3.8 | 65.2 | 31.0 | 23.4 | 57.9 | 18.7 | H 193 | H 4.2 | H 2.1 | 56.9 | … | … | Trinidad and Tobago |
| 60.1 | 61.1 | 1985 | 50,000 | 7.0 | 1.4 | 72.5 | 26.1 | 35.9 | 54.7 | 9.4 | H 1,313 | H 5.5 | … | 99.8 | 20,500 | 9.5 | Tunisia |
| 62.5 | 65.8 | 1983 | 308,256 | 6.4 | 7.7[40] | 72.4[40] | 19.9[40] | 35.9[40] | 52.1[40] | 12.0[40] | H 8,601 | H 5.2 | H 2.0 | … | … | … | Turkey |
| 68.6 | 71.9 | 1980 | 27 | 3.6 | … | … | … | … | … | … | … | H 4.3 | H 2.0 | 82.4 | … | … | Turks and Caicos Islands |
| 56.9 | 60.1 | … | … | … | … | … | … | … | … | … | H 1 | H 6.4 | H 2.2 | 82.2 | … | … | Tuvalu |
| 49.0 | 53.0 | … | … | … | … | … | … | … | … | … | … | H 5.2 | … | … | … | … | Uganda |
| 64.0 | 73.0 | 1985 | 2,717,800 | 9.8 | 3.9 | 78.6 | 17.5 | 25.0 | 58.0 | 17.0 | F 66,307 | F 3.9 | … | … | 10,000,000 | 230.0 | U.S.S.R. |
| 65.4 | 69.8 | … | … | … | … | … | … | … | … | … | … | H 3.8 | … | … | … | … | United Arab Emirates |
| 71.4 | 77.2 | 1985 | 393,117 | 6.9 | 7.7[31] | 59.3[41] | 33.0 | 20.9[31] | 55.3[41] | 23.8 | H 21,672 | H 2.7 | H 1.7 | 81.1 | 145,497[42] | 20.7[42] | United Kingdom |
| 72.0 | 78.9 | 1986 | 2,433,000 | 9.7 | 8.5 | 59.5 | 32.0 | 21.1 | 55.8 | 23.1 | F 63,558 | F 2.6 | F 1.0 | 77.8 | 1,553,900 | 42.8 | United States |
| 69.1 | 73.8 | 1983 | 19,168 | 6.5 | 8.3 | 62.7 | 29.0 | 28.3 | 51.7 | 20.0 | H 829 | H 3.4 | … | 74.4 | … | … | Uruguay |
| 56.2 | 53.7 | … | … | … | … | … | … | … | … | … | H 23 | H 5.0 | … | … | … | … | Vanuatu |
| 65.1 | 70.6 | 1985 | 93,939 | 5.4 | 10.7[1] | 66.0[1] | 23.3[1] | 37.3[1] | 49.3[1] | 13.4[1] | … | H 5.3 | … | 47.0 | … | … | Venezuela |
| 58.1 | 62.5 | … | … | … | … | … | … | … | … | … | … | … | … | … | … | … | Vietnam |
| 66.7 | 70.7 | 1983 | 1,341 | 12.9 | 3.1 | 44.6 | 52.3 | 12.7 | 50.9 | 36.4 | H 28 | H 3.4 | H 1.3 | 48.7 | … | … | Virgin Islands (U.S.) |
| 59.2 | 62.9 | 1980 | 60 | 5.6 | … | … | … | … | … | … | … | H 6.6 | H 3.0 | 78.3 | … | … | Wallis and Futuna |
| … | … | … | … | … | … | … | … | … | … | … | … | … | … | … | … | … | West Bank |
| … | … | 1972 | 459 | 4.9 | … | … | … | … | … | … | … | … | … | … | … | … | Western Sahara |
| 62.6 | 65.6 | 1984 | 555 | 5.0 | 0.9 | 58.7 | 40.4 | 7.2 | 68.8 | 24.0 | F 20 | F 7.8 | F 3.8 | 43.5 | … | … | Western Samoa |
| 46.9 | 49.9 | … | … | … | … | … | … | … | … | … | … | H 5.5 | … | … | … | … | Yemen (Aden) |
| 42.7 | 44.8 | … | … | … | … | … | … | … | … | … | … | H 5.8 | … | … | … | … | Yemen (Şan'ā') |
| 66.0 | 74.0 | 1984 | 168,290 | 7.3 | 2.9 | 76.2 | 20.9 | 27.2 | 60.9 | 11.9 | H 6,187 | H 3.6 | H 0.9 | 91.6 | 288,100 | 74.0 | Yugoslavia |
| 48.3 | 51.7 | 1975 | 185,300 | 7.5 | … | … | … | … | … | … | … | H 6.0 | … | … | … | … | Zaire |
| 49.6 | 53.1 | … | … | … | … | … | … | … | … | … | H 873 | H 5.8 | H 2.1 | … | … | … | Zambia |
| 57.9 | 61.4 | … | … | … | … | … | … | … | … | … | … | H 5.8 | … | 95.8 | … | … | Zimbabwe |

[1]Excludes nomadic tribes. [2]1982. [3]1980. [4]1985–90. [5]First marriages only. [6]1984. [7]1977. [8]1978. [9]Netherlands Antilles includes Aruba. [10]1985. [11]1982–84 average. [12]1981. [13]Data exclude deaths of unknown cause. [14]1983. [15]Estimates based on rural survey. [16]Millions of households. [17]Based on burial permits. [18]1983–85 comparative. [19]1975–80. [20]1984–86 average. [21]1981–83 average. [22]Includes nutritional disorders. [23]1968. [24]Reported inpatient deaths only. [25]Medically certified deaths only. [26]Includes Sarawak; refers to non-Muslim civil marriages and Christian ritual marriages only. [27]1986. [28]Annual average rates for the period. [29]1973. [30]Curaçao only. [31]Less than 21 years of age. [32]Over 21 years of age. [33]1981–85 average. [34]1976. [35]Excludes tribal Indians. [36]1982–86 average. [37]Whites, Asians, and Coloureds only. [38]Syrian Arabs only. [39]African population only. [40]Urban areas only. [41]21–29 years of age. [42]Excludes Northern Ireland.

# National product and accounts

The national product and accounts table furnishes breakdowns of how the aggregate income (output) of a nation is produced, distributed, and spent by its population and of the principal elements of a country's balance of payments (merchandise trade, invisibles, and tourism).

**Measures of national output.** The two most commonly used measures of national output (except for certain centrally planned economies) are GNP and GDP. Each of these measures represents an aggregate value of goods and services produced within a specific country. The GDP, the more basic of these, is a measure of the value of goods and services produced entirely within each country. It is equal to the sum of all factor costs (factor incomes) or all value added provided by the combined productive capabilities of labour and capital within each economic system. The GNP, the more comprehensive value, is composed of both domestic production and the net value added (net factor income) from transactions with other countries. When the factor income value received from other countries is greater than the value paid, a country's GNP is greater than its GDP. In theory, if all national accounts could be equilibrated, the global summation of GDP (each country's value added to the world economy) would equal the total of all GNP values.

In the first section of the table, data are provided for the nominal GNP (value in current prices for the year indicated), together with the per capita value of this product, both denominated in U.S. dollars for ease of comparison. Beside these are given figures for GDP denominated in the national currency, first as a nominal value, then as a "real" value (adjusted, that is, to eliminate the effect of recent inflation [most often] or, occasionally, of deflation). The real values are obtained by dividing the nominal GDP by a GDP deflator (essentially a consumer price index that covers price changes in the whole economy) and are adjusted to a common base year of 1980. GNP per capita provides a rough measure of annual monetary income per person, but values should be compared cautiously, as they are subject to a number of distortions, notably of purchasing power parity (the ability of any two currencies to purchase goods in their respective domestic markets differing by more than a simple exchange rate) and in the existence of elements of national production that do not enter the monetary economy (*e.g.,* food, clothing, or housing produced and consumed within families or in communal groups).

In a number of countries with centrally planned economies the conventional concept for the aggregated national income/product is net material product (NMP) and includes only material goods and "productive" services. The GDP values presented in this table for free market economies are not directly comparable to the official NMP measures published by the centrally planned economies. The GDP value is more comprehensive and covers a number of sectors (especially services) excluded from the NMP value. Estimated GNPs have been supplied for most countries (including the centrally planned), based either on the country's own, or on external, analysis.

**The origin, distribution, and spending of the national product.** Even though GNP/GDP values allow a general comparison of relative economic development, more information is provided when these aggregates are analyzed according to their component kinds of expenditure, cost components, and industrial sectors of origin.

There are three major domestic expenditure components of GDP: pri-

## National product and accounts

| country | gross national product (GNP), 1985 nominal ('000,000 U.S.$) | per capita (U.S.$) | gross domestic product (GDP), 1985 nominal ('000,000,000 national currency) | real (constant prices of 1980; '000,000,000 national currency) | GDP by type of expenditure, 1984 (%) consumption private | government | gross domestic investment | foreign trade exports | imports | cost components of GDP, 1984 (%) net indirect taxes | consumption of fixed capital | compensation of employees | net operating surplus |
|---|---|---|---|---|---|---|---|---|---|---|---|---|---|
| Afghanistan | 3,520 | 230 | ... | 100.4[1,2] | ... | ... | ... | ... | ... | ... | ... | ... | ... |
| Albania | 2,580[6] | 930[6] | ... | ... | ... | ... | ... | ... | ... | ... | ... | ... | ... |
| Algeria | 55,230 | 2,530 | 202.0[7] | ... | 45 | 16 | 38 | 26 | −25 | 20[5] | 8[5] | 37[5] | 35[5] |
| American Samoa | 190 | 5,340 | ... | ... | ... | ... | ... | ... | ... | ... | ... | ... | ... |
| Andorra | 360[7] | 9,000[7] | ... | ... | ... | ... | ... | ... | ... | ... | ... | ... | ... |
| Angola | 6,930[10] | 830[10] | 202.0[7] | ... | 58[7] | 27[7] | 9[7] | 45[7] | −39[7] | ... | ... | ... | ... |
| Anguilla | ... | ... | ... | ... | ... | ... | ... | ... | ... | ... | ... | ... | ... |
| Antigua and Barbuda | 160 | 1,990 | 0.435[10] | 0.316[10] | 68 | 19 | 27 | 91 | −104 | ... | ... | ... | ... |
| Argentina | 65,080 | 2,130 | 0.683[7] | 0.026[7] | 72 | 14 | 14 | 13 | −9 | 8[7] | 11 | 34[7] | 57[7,11] |
| Aruba | 12 | 12 | 0.817 | | 12 | 12 | 12 | 12 | 12 | 12 | 12 | 12 | 12 |
| Australia | 171,170 | 10,860 | 222.0 | 148.2 | 60 | 17 | 24 | 15 | −16 | 13 | 8 | 52 | 28 |
| Austria | 69,060 | 9,140 | 1,366.6 | 1,076.3 | 57 | 19 | 24 | 39 | −39 | 14 | 12 | 53 | 21 |
| Bahamas, The | 1,670 | 7,140 | 1.978[10] | ... | 61 | 13 | 18 | 64 | −56 | ... | ... | ... | ... |
| Bahrain | 4,040 | 9,290 | 1.876 | ... | 30[7] | 17[7] | 45[7] | 78[7] | −70[7] | 3[6] | 9[6] | 28[6] | 60[6] |
| Bangladesh | 14,770 | 150 | 417.0 | 238.7 | 89 | 8 | 13 | 6 | −16 | ... | ... | ... | ... |
| Barbados | 1,180 | 4,660 | 2.474 | 1.682 | 62 | 17 | 16 | 74 | −69 | 14[5] | 6[5] | 57[5] | 24[5] |
| Belgium | 83,230 | 8,440 | 4,812.0 | 3,604.0 | 66 | 18 | 16 | 75 | −75 | 10 | 9 | 56 | 25 |
| Belize | 180 | 1,080 | 0.368[10] | 0.335[10] | 70 | 24 | 16 | 56 | −66 | 12 | 9 | —79— | |
| Benin | 1,080 | 270 | 439.4[7] | ... | 78 | 10 | 7 | 18 | −28 | 9[15] | 7[15] | 23[15] | 61[15] |
| Bermuda | 1,030 | 18,100 | 1.058 | ... | 68 | 12 | 20 | 60 | −60 | ... | ... | ... | ... |
| Bhutan | 190 | 150 | 2.013[10] | 1.850[10] | ... | ... | ... | ... | ... | ... | ... | ... | ... |
| Bolivia | 3,010 | 470 | 2.769 | 0.109 | 76 | 8 | 11 | 23 | −18 | 10[5] | 6[5] | 36[5] | 47[5] |
| Botswana | 900 | 830 | 1.524 | 1.171 | 49 | 27 | 25 | 60 | −61 | 13[6] | 11[6] | 39[6] | 37[6] |
| Brazil | 222,010 | 1,640 | 1,406.065 | 13.750 | —74— | | 19 | 16 | −9 | 10[6] | 5[6] | —85[6]— | |
| British Virgin Islands | ... | 7,130[18] | 0.085 | ... | 43[7] | 18[7] | 38[7] | 114[7] | −115[7] | 12[15] | 11 | 53[15] | 36[11,15] |
| Brunei | 3,940 | 17,570 | 7.529 | ... | ... | ... | ... | ... | ... | ... | ... | ... | ... |
| Bulgaria | 25,530 | 2,860 | 25.45[12] | 24.61[02] | 58 | 11 | 24 | —7— | | ... | ... | ... | ... |
| Burkina Faso | 1,080 | 140 | 363.8[10] | 260.0[10] | 89 | 16 | 21 | 21 | −47 | 8[7] | 7[7] | 24[7] | 61[7] |
| Burma | 7,080 | 190 | 56.081 | 49.852 | 88 | — | 16 | 6 | −9 | 8 | 9 | 38 | 45 |
| Burundi | 1,110 | 240 | 139.640 | 103.668 | 83 | 13 | 18 | 11 | −25 | 10[6] | 2[6] | 21[6] | 66[6] |
| Cameroon | 8,300 | 810 | 3,195.0[10] | ... | 63 | 10 | 26 | 20 | −19 | 13[7] | 5[7] | 27[7] | 54[7] |
| Canada | 347,360 | 13,700 | 476.4 | 351.4 | 57 | 20 | 20 | 29 | −25 | 10 | 12 | 54 | 24 |
| Cape Verde | 140 | 420 | 0.104[7,23] | ... | 67 | 23 | 83 | 46 | −119 | ... | ... | ... | ... |
| Cayman Islands | ... | 12,100[18] | 0.213 | ... | ... | ... | ... | ... | ... | ... | ... | ... | ... |
| Central African Republic | 700 | 270 | 318.7 | 202.7 | 91 | 13 | 12 | 25 | −41 | 12[24] | — | 24[24] | 64[24] |
| Chad | 560[10] | 110[10] | 0.612[7,23] | ... | 83[7] | 24[7] | 7[7] | —147— | | 6[19] | 7[19] | 13[19] | 75[19] |
| Chile | 17,230 | 1,430 | 2,576.6 | 1,054.6 | 73 | 14 | 14 | 24 | −25 | 14[6] | 11[6] | 42[6] | 34[6] |
| China | 318,920 | 310 | 682.2[27] | 558.3[27] | —71[2,7]— | | 30[2,7] | —12[2,7]— | | ... | ... | ... | ... |
| Christmas Island | ... | ... | ... | ... | ... | ... | ... | ... | ... | ... | ... | ... | ... |
| Cocos (Keeling) Islands | ... | ... | ... | ... | ... | ... | ... | ... | ... | ... | ... | ... | ... |
| Colombia | 37,610 | 1,360 | 4,865.1 | 1,753.2 | 71 | 11 | 19 | 12 | −12 | 9 | 11 | 44 | 47[11] |
| Comoros | 110 | 280 | 48.750 | ... | 66[7] | 22[7] | 32[7] | —207— | | ... | ... | ... | ... |
| Congo | 1,910 | 950 | 920.1[10] | 574.0[10] | 36 | 14 | 27 | 57 | −33 | 13 | 14 | 28 | 45 |
| Cook Islands | 20[5] | 1,110[5] | ... | ... | 80[24] | 32[24] | 26[24] | 32[24] | −71[24] | ... | ... | ... | ... |
| Costa Rica | 3,340 | 1,340 | 192.425 | 42.093 | 61 | 16 | 23 | 34 | −34 | 15 | 3 | 46 | 36 |
| Côte d'Ivoire | 6,250 | 610 | 2,855.8[10] | ... | 62 | 16 | 11 | 45 | −35 | 23[16] | 8[16] | 33[16] | 36[16] |
| Cuba | 26,920[10] | 2,690[10] | 13,940.3[2] | 14,779.7[2] | 78 | 8 | 26 | —12— | | ... | ... | ... | ... |
| Cyprus | 2,650 | 3,980 | 1.423 | 0.967 | 62 | 16 | 35 | 56 | −68 | 7 | 11 | —82— | |
| Czechoslovakia | 85,960 | 5,550 | 548.7[2] | 524.3[2] | 55 | 10 | 26 | —9— | | ... | ... | ... | ... |
| Denmark | 57,330 | 11,210 | 605.3 | 414.3 | 54 | 26 | 18 | 37 | −36 | 15 | 9 | 55 | 22 |
| Djibouti | 300[10] | 740[10] | 67.2[25] | ... | 72[7] | 38[7] | 25[7] | —35[7]— | | 17[25] | 11 | 35[25] | 48[11,25] |
| Dominica | 90 | 1,070 | 0.231[10] | 0.203[10] | 71 | 25 | 39 | 37 | −72 | ... | ... | ... | ... |
| Dominican Republic | 5,050 | 790 | 14.477 | 7.155 | 73 | 8 | 21 | 13 | −15 | 7 | 6 | —87— | |
| Ecuador | 10,880 | 1,160 | 1,111.7 | 326.4 | 66 | 12 | 18 | 25 | −22 | 8 | 11 | 21 | 71[11] |
| Egypt | 32,220 | 690 | 32.516 | ... | 69 | 18 | 24 | 22 | −33 | 6[6] | 11 | 36[6] | 59[6,11] |

vate consumption (analyzed in greater detail in the "Household budgets and consumption" table), government spending, and gross domestic investment. The fourth, nondomestic, component of GDP expenditure is net foreign trade; value is given for both exports (a positive value) and imports (a negative value, representing obligations to other countries). The sum of these five percentages, excluding statistical discrepancies and rounding, should be 100% of the GDP.

The distribution of GDP by cost components usually comprises four general categories: indirect taxes (excise or value-added taxes), consumption of fixed capital (depreciation), and two income categories: (a) compensation of employees (salaries, wages, etc.) and (b) net operating surplus ("profits," interests, rent, etc.).

The distribution of GDP for ten industrial sectors is aggregated into three major industrial groups:

1. The primary sector, comprised of agriculture and mineral production (including fossil fuels).
2. The secondary sector, composed of manufacturing, construction, and public utilities.
3. The tertiary sector, which includes transportation and communication, trade (wholesale and retail), financial services (including banking, real estate, etc.), other (personal and business) services, and government.

Percentages in this section of the table may not add to 100 because the value of each industry is calculated as a percentage of the total GDP, which may contain significant monetary adjustments that are not distributable to all industries.

**Average annual growth rate of real GDP.** The columns show average annual growth rates of real product for the decade from 1970 to 1980, as well as for the five years from 1980 to 1985. Real GDP growth rates give an overall impression of the growth in final output achieved by various countries during the periods indicated.

**Balance of payments (external account transactions).** The external account records the sum (net) of all economic transactions of a current nature between one country and the rest of the world. The account shows a country's net of overseas receipts and obligations, including not only the trade of goods and services but also such invisible items as interest and dividends, short- and long-term investments, tourism, transfers to or from overseas residents, etc. Each transaction gives rise either to a foreign claim for payment, recorded as a deficit (e.g., from imports, capital outflows), or a foreign obligation to pay, recorded as a surplus (e.g., from exports, capital inflows) or a domestic claim on another country. A deficit transaction in the balance of payment of one country is automatically accompanied by a surplus in that of another. Values are given in U.S. dollars for comparability.

**Tourist trade.** Income from tourism is often a significant element in a country's economic balance. Receipts from foreign nationals reflect payments for goods and services from foreign currency resources by tourists in the given country. Expenditures by nationals abroad are also payments for goods and services, but in this case made by the residents of the given country as tourists abroad. The U.S. dollar is used as the common currency for comparability by the World Tourism Organization.

| origin of GDP by economic sector, 1984 (%) | | | | | | | | | | avg. annual growth rate of real GDP (%) | | balance of payments, 1986 (current external transactions; '000,000 U.S.$) | | | tourist trade, 1985 ('000,000 U.S.$) | | country |
|---|---|---|---|---|---|---|---|---|---|---|---|---|---|---|---|---|---|
| primary | | secondary | | | tertiary | | | | | 1970–1980 | 1980–1985 | net transfers | | current balance of payments | receipts from foreign nationals | expenditures by nationals abroad | |
| agriculture | mining | manufacturing | construction | public utilities | transp., communication | trade | financial svcs. | other svcs. | govt. | | | goods-merchandise | invisibles | | | | |
| 65[2] | 3 | 15[2,3] | 4[2] | 3 | 4[2] | 10[2] | 2[2] | | | 2.1[2] | 2.2[2,4] | -200[5] | 7[5] | -193[5] | 1 | ... | Afghanistan |
| ... | ... | ... | ... | ... | ... | ... | ... | | | 6.3[2] | 5.7[2,4] | ... | ... | ... | ... | ... | Albania |
| 8[7] | 31[7] | 11[7] | 15[7] | 17 | 6[7] | 16[7] | 13[7] | | | 7.8 | -1.9[8] | 4,223[9] | -3,208[9] | 1,015[9] | 143 | 574 | Algeria |
| ... | ... | ... | ... | ... | ... | ... | ... | | | ... | ... | -96[9] | | | ... | ... | American Samoa |
| ... | ... | ... | ... | ... | ... | ... | ... | | | ... | ... | ... | ... | ... | ... | ... | Andorra |
| 28[7] | 23[7] | 4[7] | 3[7] | 17 | 41[7] | | | | | -2.2 | -2.5[4] | -34[6] | -175[6] | -209[6] | ... | ... | Angola |
| ... | ... | ... | ... | ... | ... | ... | ... | | | ... | ... | ... | ... | ... | 9 | ... | Anguilla |
| 5 | 1 | 5 | 6 | 3 | 17 | 28 | 19 | 5 | 16 | 2.3 | 3.0[4] | -157 | 81 | -76 | 84 | 67 | Antigua and Barbuda |
| 16 | 3 | 24 | 4 | 4 | 12 | 13 | 8 | 17 | | 2.4 | -2.1 | 4,877[9] | -5,831[9] | -954[9] | 673 | 681[10] | Argentina |
| 12 | 12 | 12 | 12 | 12 | 12 | 12 | 12 | 12 | 12 | 12 | 12 | 12 | 12 | 12 | 111 | 17 | Aruba |
| 5 | 5 | 18 | 6 | 4 | 8 | 13 | 23 | 17 | 4 | 3.3 | 3.1 | -2,170 | -7,062 | -9,232 | 1,051 | 1,813 | Australia |
| 4 | 13 | 28[13] | 7 | 3 | 6 | 16 | 14 | 3 | 14 | 3.7 | 1.6 | -4,394 | 4,366 | -28 | 6,041 | 3,333 | Austria |
| 4 | 3 | 1[13] | 3 | 3 | 11 | 27 | 12 | 16 | 17 | 6.3 | | -727 | 723 | -4 | 870 | 106[10] | Bahamas, The |
| 1 | 19 | 11 | 10 | ... | 10 | 10 | 15 | 24 | | 4.6 | 5.3[4] | -159 | 181[9] | 196[9] | 101 | 997 | Bahrain |
| 48 | 13 | 9[13] | 5 | 1 | 7 | 9 | 2 | 16 | 4 | 4.5 | 3.8 | -1,374 | 737 | -637 | 38 | 23[7] | Bangladesh |
| 6 | 1 | 11 | 6 | 3 | 7 | 27 | 12 | 17 | | 4.3 | -0.5 | -259[9] | 299[9] | 40[9] | 312 | 267 | Barbados |
| 2 | 1 | 24 | 5 | 4 | 8 | 20 | 5 | 20 | 8 | 3.3 | 0.6 | -1,121[14] | 2,483[14] | 3,604[14] | 1,661 | 2,048 | Belgium |
| 21 | — | 15 | 6 | 2 | 11 | 17 | 11 | 11 | 10 | 4.9 | -0.5[4] | -17 | 38 | 21 | 11 | ... | Belize |
| 35[6] | 3 | 6[3,6] | 7[6] | 3 | 10[6] | 20[6] | 8[6] | | 14[6] | 3.9 | 3.4 | -156[16] | 104[16] | -52[16] | 10 | 4[10] | Benin |
| 1[16] | — | 4[16] | 5[16] | 2[16] | 7[16] | 33[16] | 22[16] | 18[16] | 8[16] | 3.0 | -1.4[4] | -348[9] | 344[9] | -4[9] | 349 | ... | Bermuda |
| 50 | — | 4 | 13 | ... | 2 | 11 | 9 | | 11 | 4.1 | 5.6[4] | -52[17] | -27[17] | -79[17] | 2 | ... | Bhutan |
| 27 | 5 | 21 | 4 | 1 | 5 | 14 | 10 | 4 | 8 | 4.5 | -2.3 | 161[9] | -443[9] | -282[9] | 36 | 38 | Bolivia |
| 6 | 32 | 7 | 4 | 3 | 2 | 23 | 4 | 4 | 16 | 15.8 | 11.2 | 272 | -103 | 169 | 51 | 16[7] | Botswana |
| 10[9] | 19 | 28[9] | 6 | 9[9] | 8[9] | 16[9] | 10[9] | 11[9] | 7[9] | 8.6 | 1.8 | 12,466[9] | -12,739[9] | -273[9] | 1,739 | 1,145 | Brazil |
| 9[15] | 13 | 6[13,15] | 12[15] | 2[15] | 10[15] | 27[15] | 17[15] | 1[15] | 10[15] | 3.7 | -0.4[4] | -14[19] | 13[19] | -1[19] | 92 | ... | British Virgin Islands |
| 1 | 61 | 10 | 3 | — | 3 | 11 | 11 | | | 8.9 | -3.0[4] | | | | ... | ... | Brunei |
| 18[2] | 3 | 57[2,3] | 10[2] | 3 | 8[2] | 5[2] | 2[2,20] | | | 6.7[2] | 4.0[2] | | | | 343 | ... | Bulgaria |
| 43 | — | 14 | 1 | 1 | 6 | 12 | 22 | | | 5.3 | 2.4 | -196[7] | 136[7] | -60[7] | 4 | 23[10] | Burkina Faso |
| 48 | 1 | 9 | 2 | — | 4 | 25 | 11 | | | 4.3 | 5.3 | -202[9] | -49 | -206[9] | 12 | 5 | Burma |
| 52 | 1[21] | 5 | 6 | 21 | 3 | 9 | 2 | 5 | 8 | 4.0 | 4.0 | -11 | — | — | 27[10] | 18[7] | Burundi |
| 22 | 16 | 11 | 6 | 1 | 5 | 13 | 12 | 2 | 7 | 4.5 | 5.7[22] | 524[10] | -689[10] | -165[10] | 59[10] | 707 | Cameroon |
| 3 | 6 | 17 | 4 | 4 | 7 | 9 | 50 | | | 4.1 | 2.5 | 7,718 | -13,708 | -5,990 | 3,056 | 4,125 | Canada |
| 21[7] | 17 | 5[7] | 16[7] | 3[7] | 47 | | | | | -0.2 | 3.1[4] | -66[16] | 64[16] | -21[6] | ... | ... | Cape Verde |
| ... | ... | ... | ... | ... | ... | ... | ... | | | ... | ... | -96[7] | 153[7] | 57[7] | 86 | ... | Cayman Islands |
| 41[9] | 2[9] | 7[9] | 2[9] | 1[9] | 4[9] | 21[9] | 20[9] | | | 2.6 | 1.5 | -37[9] | -8[9] | -45[9] | 3[25] | 26[7] | Central African Republic |
| 52[7] | — | 7[7] | 1[7] | — | 39[7] | | | | | 0.5 | ... | -105[9] | 18[9] | -87[9] | 2[25] | 19[10] | Chad |
| 10[26] | 8[26] | 21[26] | 6[26] | 3[26] | 6[26] | 17[26] | 30[26] | | | 2.8 | -0.1 | 1,100 | -2,191 | -1,091 | 115 | 269 | Chile |
| 44[27] | 3 | 41[3,27] | 5[27] | 3 | 3[27] | 7[27] | | | | 5.8 | 9.8 | -13,123[9] | 1,706[9] | -11,417[9] | 1,290 | ... | China |
| ... | ... | ... | ... | ... | ... | ... | ... | | | ... | ... | ... | ... | ... | ... | ... | Christmas Island |
| ... | ... | ... | ... | ... | ... | ... | ... | | | ... | ... | ... | ... | ... | ... | ... | Cocos (Keeling) Islands |
| 18 | 3 | 22 | 5 | 2 | 8 | 14 | 27 | | | 5.5 | 2.1 | 1,890 | -1,467 | 423 | 286 | 168 | Colombia |
| 37[9] | ... | 4[9] | 10[9] | ... | 4[9] | 25[9] | ... | 20[9] | | 2.0 | 4.0[4] | -10[9] | -4[9] | -14[9] | ... | ... | Comoros |
| 8 | 43 | 5 | 7 | 1 | 7 | 11 | 18 | | | 4.7 | 7.8 | 651[10] | -441[10] | 210[10] | 13 | 55 | Congo |
| 26[5] | — | 11[5] | 9[5] | 2[5] | 7[5] | 14[5] | 3[5] | ... | ... | -2.6 | 3.2[4] | | | | 46 | ... | Cook Islands |
| 21 | 13 | 23[13] | 4 | 3 | 5 | 20 | 25 | | | 5.7 | 0.5 | 41 | -227 | -186 | 118 | 36[7] | Costa Rica |
| 28 | 3 | 12 | 2 | 1 | 7 | 47 | | | | 6.5 | -1.7 | 1,388[9] | -1,338[9] | 50[9] | 74 | 180[7] | Côte d'Ivoire |
| 10[2] | 3 | 35[2,3] | 10[2] | 3 | 8[2] | 37[2] | 12,20 | | | 5.8[2] | 8.5[2] | | | | 88 | ... | Cuba |
| 9 | 1 | 16 | 10 | 2 | 9 | 18 | 35 | | | 4.2 | 4.5[4] | -696 | 682 | -14 | 298 | 53[10] | Cyprus |
| 8[2] | 3 | 60[2,3] | 11[2] | 3 | 4[2] | 16[2] | 12,20 | | | 4.6[2] | 1.7[2] | | | | 307 | 229[7] | Czechoslovakia |
| 6 | 1 | 20 | 6 | 1 | 8 | 15 | 2 | 19 | 23 | 2.4 | 2.1 | -1,178 | -3,143 | -4,321 | 1,326 | 1,410 | Denmark |
| 4 | — | 8 | 7 | 3 | 10 | 16 | 11 | 2 | 27 | 0.9 | 2.8[4] | -100[6] | 75[6] | -25[6] | ... | ... | Djibouti |
| 30 | 1 | 7 | 8 | 3 | 11 | 9 | 10 | 1 | 24 | 2.9 | 6.2[4] | -11 | 7 | -4 | 5 | 0.7[7] | Dominica |
| 17 | 4 | 18 | 7 | 2 | 8 | 16 | 9 | 9 | 10 | 7.0 | 1.6 | -544 | 425 | -119 | 297 | 87[7] | Dominican Republic |
| 14 | 16 | 19 | 5 | 1 | 7 | 17 | 6 | 8 | 7 | 9.1 | 2.2 | 555 | -1,168 | -613 | 130 | 155[10] | Ecuador |
| 18 | 13 | 33[13] | 5 | 3 | 4 | 11 | 25 | | | 7.1 | 5.2 | -4,503[9] | 2,258[9] | -2,245[9] | 990 | 146[10] | Egypt |

## National product and accounts (continued)

| country | gross national product (GNP), 1985 | | gross domestic product (GDP), 1985 | | GDP by type of expenditure, 1984 (%) | | | | | cost components of GDP, 1984 (%) | | | |
|---|---|---|---|---|---|---|---|---|---|---|---|---|---|
| | nominal ('000,000 U.S.$) | per capita (U.S.$) | nominal ('000,000,000 national currency) | real (constant prices of 1980; '000,000,000 national currency) | consumption private | consumption government | gross domestic investment | foreign trade exports | foreign trade imports | net indirect taxes | consumption of fixed capital | compensation of employees | net operating surplus |
| El Salvador | 3,940 | 820 | 14.331 | 8.115 | 79 | 16 | 12 | 22 | −29 | 8 | 4 | —87— | |
| Equatorial Guinea | 60[7] | 200[7] | 0.019[7,23] | ... | 116[7] | 53[7] | 117[7] | —79[7]— | | ... | ... | ... | ... |
| Ethiopia | 4,630 | 110 | 10.031[7] | 9.583[7] | 79 | 18 | 13 | 13 | −23 | ... | ... | ... | ... |
| Faeroe Islands | 510 | 11,200 | 5.099 | ... | ... | ... | ... | ... | ... | ... | ... | ... | ... |
| Falkland Islands | ... | ... | ... | ... | ... | ... | ... | ... | ... | ... | ... | ... | ... |
| Fiji | 1,190 | 1,700 | 1.212 | 0.954 | 63 | 19 | 19 | 43 | −44 | 10 | 7 | 48 | 36 |
| Finland | 53,450 | 10,900 | 334.9 | 219.4 | 53 | 19 | 24 | 31 | −29 | 11 | 14 | 54 | 21 |
| France | 526,630 | 9,550 | 4,597.2 | 2,937.8 | 65 | 17 | 19 | 24 | −24 | 13 | 12 | 55 | 20 |
| French Guiana | 180[7] | 2,340[7] | ... | ... | ... | ... | ... | ... | ... | ... | ... | ... | ... |
| French Polynesia | 1,300[10] | 7,660[10] | 136.953[6] | 87.193[6] | 68[6] | 34[6] | 32[6] | 12[6] | −45[6] | 6[6] | 17[6] | 46[6] | 31[6] |
| Gabon | 3,330 | 2,890 | 1,455.6[10] | 982.2[10] | 31[7] | 13[7] | 33[7] | —23[7]— | | 18[16] | 14[16] | 30[16] | 37[16] |
| Gambia, The | 170 | 230 | 0.491[6] | 0.418[6] | 102[7] | 27[7] | 37[7] | —66[7]— | | ... | ... | ... | ... |
| Gaza Strip | 494[10] | 950[10] | 0.082 | 0.001 | 130 | 21 | 36 | 43 | −130 | ... | ... | ... | ... |
| Germany, East | 93,631[10] | 5,600[10] | | 233.6[2] | 57 | 11 | 18 | —13— | | 10[2,6] | 9[2,6] | 40[2,6] | 41[2,6] |
| Germany, West | 667,970 | 10,950 | 1,839.9 | 1,580.9 | 57 | 20 | 21 | 34 | −31 | 11 | 13 | 54 | 22 |
| Ghana | 4,960 | 390 | 373.0 | 41.9 | 90 | 6 | 7 | 8 | −11 | 5[15] | 3[15] | —91[15]— | |
| Gibraltar | 130 | 4,550 | 0.074 | ... | ... | ... | ... | ... | ... | ... | ... | ... | ... |
| Greece | 35,250 | 3,550 | 4,614.2 | 1,826.3 | 67 | 20 | 22 | 23 | −31 | 12 | 9 | 41 | 38 |
| Greenland | 390 | 7,330 | ... | ... | ... | ... | ... | ... | ... | ... | ... | ... | ... |
| Grenada | 90 | 900 | 0.260 | 0.189 | 76 | 26 | 34 | 45 | −82 | ... | ... | ... | ... |
| Guadeloupe | 1,180[7] | 3,580[7] | 8.486[7] | ... | 96[7] | 33[7] | 24[7] | 7[7] | −60[7] | 11[5] | 11 | 70[5] | 19[5,11] |
| Guam | 670 | 5,660 | ... | ... | ... | ... | ... | ... | ... | ... | ... | ... | ... |
| Guatemala | 9,890 | 1,240 | 11.130 | 7.443 | 84 | 8 | 10 | 13 | −15 | ... | ... | ... | ... |
| Guernsey | 1,350[30] | 9,900[30] | ... | ... | ... | ... | ... | ... | ... | ... | ... | ... | ... |
| Guinea | 1,950 | 320 | 2.367[7,23] | ... | 73 | 14 | 10 | 25 | −22 | ... | ... | ... | ... |
| Guinea-Bissau | 150 | 170 | 0.083[7,23] | ... | 75 | 26 | 23 | 6 | −30 | ... | ... | ... | ... |
| Guyana | 460 | 580 | 1.700[10] | | 58 | 32 | 23 | 55 | −68 | 17 | 7 | —76— | |
| Haiti | 1,900 | 360 | 10.047 | 6.828 | 84 | 12 | 16 | 24 | −35 | 10[6] | 3[6] | —87[6]— | |
| Honduras | 3,190 | 730 | 6.959 | 5.347 | 72 | 15 | 21 | 26 | −34 | 11 | 5 | —84— | |
| Hong Kong | 33,770[18] | 6,190[18] | 266.6 | 182.2 | 64 | 7 | 24 | 106 | −102 | 4 | —96— | | |
| Hungary | 20,720 | 1,950 | 1,033.7 | 786.7 | 61 | 10 | 26 | 41 | −38 | ... | ... | ... | ... |
| Iceland | 2,580 | 10,700 | 111.023 | 15.292 | 59 | 17 | 23 | 42 | −42 | 22 | 13 | —65— | |
| India | 194,820 | 260 | 2,435.5 | 1,665.9 | 68 | 11 | 25 | 7 | −9 | 11 | 7 | —82— | |
| Indonesia | 86,590 | 520 | 96,066.4 | 56,543.0 | 58 | 11 | 27 | 27 | −23 | 1 | 5 | —94— | |
| Iran | 159,138[7] | 3,830[7] | 15,305.8 | 9,044.3 | 54 | 14 | 32 | 10 | −11 | 2 | 7 | —91— | |
| Iraq | 34,470[10] | 2,310[10] | 12.617[6] | ... | —91[6]— | | 42[6] | 24[6] | −57[6] | 4[19] | 7[19] | 21[19] | 68[19] |
| Ireland | 17,250 | 4,900 | 17.254 | 10.226 | 57 | 19 | 24 | 61 | −61 | 12 | 9 | 56 | 23 |
| Isle of Man | 380 | 5,430 | 0.162[7] | ... | ... | ... | ... | ... | ... | ... | ... | ... | ... |
| Israel | 21,140 | 4,910 | 25.966 | 0.119 | 57 | 32 | 21 | 38 | −48 | 10 | 13 | 51 | 28 |
| Italy | 371,050 | 6,500 | 684,843.0 | 334,679.0 | 64 | 20 | 19 | 24 | −26 | 9 | 10 | 56 | 25 |
| Jamaica | 2,090 | 900 | 11.263 | 4.764 | 65 | 17 | 22 | 55 | −60 | 11[6] | 10[6] | 58[6] | 22[6] |
| Japan | 1,366.040 | 11,310 | 316,115.0 | 291,207.0 | 59 | 10 | 29 | 17 | −14 | 6 | 14 | 55 | 24 |
| Jersey | 1,350[30] | 9,900[30] | 0.510[10] | ... | ... | ... | ... | ... | ... | ... | ... | ... | ... |
| Jordan | 4,010 | 1,520 | 1.573 | 1.210 | 92 | 25 | 32 | 50 | −99 | 12 | 8 | 43 | 36 |
| Kampuchea | 600[25] | 900[25] | ... | ... | ... | ... | ... | ... | ... | ... | ... | ... | ... |
| Kenya | 5,960 | 290 | 94.836 | 60.226 | 62 | 18 | 22 | 27 | −29 | 14 | 11 | 37 | 50[11] |
| Kiribati | 30[10,18] | 480[10,18] | 0.021[5] | | 93[5] | 36[5] | 44[5] | 23[5] | −96[5] | 5[5] | 5[5] | 30[5] | 61[5] |
| Korea, North | 14,700[10] | 760[10] | 11.8[6] | | ... | ... | ... | ... | ... | ... | ... | ... | ... |
| Korea, South | 88,440 | 2,150 | 75,511.0 | 54,674.0 | 59 | 10 | 31 | 38 | −38 | 13 | 9 | 41 | 38 |
| Kuwait | 24,760 | 14,460 | 5.943 | ... | 46 | 21 | 21 | 59 | −47 | ... | ... | ... | ... |
| Laos | 765[10] | 220[10] | ... | ... | ... | ... | ... | ... | ... | ... | ... | ... | ... |
| Lebanon | 5,000[7] | 1,900[7] | 12.599[6] | | —110[16]— | | 18[16] | —28[16]— | | 8[35] | 5[35] | —88[35]— | |
| Lesotho | 730 | 470 | 0.432[7] | 0.293[7] | 192[7] | 25[7] | 34[7] | 11[7] | −161[7] | 22[7] | 3[7] | 45[7] | 30[7] |
| Liberia | 1,040 | 470 | 0.811 | 0.797 | 47 | 24 | 19 | 60 | −50 | 14[6] | —86[6]— | | |
| Libya | 27,000 | 7,130 | 8.846[6] | 8.682[6] | 31[7] | 34[7] | 23[7] | 43[7] | −31[7] | 4[6] | 5[6] | 30[6] | 61[6] |
| Liechtenstein | 524[5] | 20,960[5] | ... | ... | ... | ... | ... | ... | ... | ... | ... | ... | ... |
| Luxembourg | 4,900 | 13,360 | 195.3[10] | 142.4[10] | 59 | 15 | 26 | 93 | −93 | 12 | 11 | 58 | 19 |
| Macau | 1,030 | 2,680 | ... | ... | ... | ... | ... | ... | ... | ... | ... | ... | ... |
| Madagascar | 2,510 | 250 | 1,553.4 | | 78 | 14 | 13 | 15 | −19 | 12[16] | 1[16] | —87[16]— | |
| Malawi | 1,160 | 170 | 2.024 | 1.105 | 67 | 16 | 15 | 28 | −25 | 9[16] | 7[16] | 27[16] | 58[16] |
| Malaysia | 31,930 | 2,040 | 77.547 | 68.443 | 50 | 15 | 34 | 54 | −52 | 16[15] | 11 | 32[15] | 52[11,15] |
| Maldives | 50 | 270 | 0.537[10] | 0.511[10] | 63 | 18 | 31 | 68 | −80 | ... | ... | ... | ... |
| Mali | 1,070 | 130 | 790.7[7] | | 75[7] | 27[7] | 17[7] | 23[7] | −41[7] | 8[6] | 7[6] | 25[6] | 60[6] |
| Malta | 1,190 | 3,540 | 0.476 | 0.426 | 69 | 17 | 29 | 70 | −85 | 9 | 5 | 47 | 40 |
| Martinique | 1,330[7] | 4,070[7] | 9.963[7] | | 90[7] | 36[7] | 19[7] | 13[7] | −58[7] | 10[5] | 11 | 66[5] | 24[5,11] |
| Mauritania | 700 | 420 | 44.500 | ... | 75 | 23 | 37 | 42 | −76 | 9[19] | 6[19] | 27[19] | 58[19] |
| Mauritius | 1,110 | 1,090 | 16.380 | ... | 69 | 13 | 21 | 50 | −52 | 16 | 11 | 42 | 42[11] |
| Mayotte | ... | ... | ... | ... | ... | ... | ... | ... | ... | ... | ... | ... | ... |
| Mexico | 163,790 | 2,100 | 45,588.8 | 4,630.0 | 61 | 10 | 22 | 18 | −10 | 10 | 6 | 28 | 56 |
| Monaco | ... | ... | ... | ... | ... | ... | ... | ... | ... | ... | ... | ... | ... |
| Mongolia | 1,820[10] | 1,000[10] | ... | ... | ... | ... | ... | ... | ... | ... | ... | ... | ... |
| Montserrat | 30 | 2,530 | 0.100 | 0.073 | 96 | 21 | 26 | 14 | −57 | ... | ... | ... | ... |
| Morocco | 13,390 | 610 | 119.7 | 80.6 | 70 | 18 | 23 | 25 | −36 | 14[5] | 11 | 33[5] | 53[5,11] |
| Mozambique | 2,200 | 160 | 111.5[7] | | 83[7] | 17[7] | 8[7] | 15[7] | −24[7] | ... | ... | ... | ... |
| Nauru | 160[10] | 20,000[10] | ... | ... | ... | ... | ... | ... | ... | ... | ... | ... | ... |
| Nepal | 2,610 | 160 | 41.738 | 28.263 | 82 | 8 | 19 | 11 | −20 | 6 | 5 | —89— | |
| Netherlands, The | 132,920 | 9,170 | 412.5 | 345.2 | 59 | 17 | 19 | 63 | −58 | 9 | 10 | 53 | 28 |
| Netherlands Antilles | 1,610[12] | 6,810[12] | 2.558[6] | | 55[5,12] | 24[5,12] | 21[5,12] | 110[5,12] | −109[5,12] | 6[5,12] | 10[5,12] | 68[5,12] | 16[5,12] |
| New Caledonia | 1,210 | 8,300 | 114.2[5] | | 60[7] | 35[7] | 17[7] | 27[7] | −39[7] | 3[7] | 9[7] | 59[7] | 29[7] |
| New Zealand | 23,720 | 7,290 | 44.255 | 26.056 | 56 | 15 | 32 | 33 | −37 | 10 | 8 | 49 | 33 |
| Nicaragua | 2,760 | 840 | 35.783[7] | 23.939[7] | 55 | 35 | 18 | 18 | −25 | 9[15] | 4[15] | 56[15] | 31[15] |
| Niger | 1,250 | 190 | 697.2[7] | | 82[7] | 11[7] | 19[7] | 22[7] | −35[7] | 9[5] | 7[5] | 16[5] | 68[5] |
| Nigeria | 75,940 | 790 | 56.716[17] | 41.754[17] | 71 | 10 | 12 | 17 | −10 | 4[7] | 2[7] | 29[7] | 65[7] |
| Niue | 4[5] | 1,160[5] | ... | ... | ... | ... | ... | ... | ... | ... | ... | ... | ... |
| Norfolk Island | ... | ... | ... | ... | ... | ... | ... | ... | ... | ... | ... | ... | ... |

| agriculture | mining | manufacturing | construction | public utilities | transp., communication | trade | financial svcs. | other svcs. | govt. | real GDP 1970–1980 | real GDP 1980–1985 | goods-merchandise | invisibles | current balance of payments | receipts from foreign nationals | expenditures by nationals abroad | country |
|---|---|---|---|---|---|---|---|---|---|---|---|---|---|---|---|---|---|
| 21 | — | 15 | 3 | 2 | 4 | 26 | 9 | 8 | 11 | 3.4 | -1.8 | -216[9] | 187[9] | -29[9] | 10 | 74[7] | El Salvador |
| 41[7] | 28 | 12[7,28] | 28 | 28 | 28 | 47[7] | | | | -9.4 | 1.2[4] | -15[25] | -3[25] | -18[25] | ... | ... | Equatorial Guinea |
| 44 | — | 11 | 4 | 1 | 7 | 11 | 4 | 7 | 9 | 2.6 | 0.3 | -383[10] | 251[10] | -132[10] | 9 | 4[10] | Ethiopia |
| 24[5] | 13 | 16[5,13] | 10[5] | 2[5] | 9[5] | 12[5] | 12[5] | 16[5] | | ... | ... | ... | ... | ... | ... | ... | Faeroe Islands |
| ... | ... | ... | ... | ... | ... | ... | ... | ... | ... | ... | ... | ... | ... | ... | ... | ... | Falkland Islands |
| 19 | 1 | 10 | 6 | 2 | 10 | 18 | 14 | 24 | | 3.9 | 1.3 | -122 | 127 | 5 | 157 | 18[7] | Fiji |
| 8 | — | 25 | 7 | 3 | 7 | 10 | 14 | 5 | 14 | 3.7 | 2.6 | 1,664 | -2,718 | -867 | 501 | 776 | Finland |
| 4 | 2 | 26 | 6 | 3 | 5 | 10 | 12 | 33 | | 3.6 | 1.5 | -2,247 | 5,747 | 3,500 | 7,942 | 4,557 | France |
| 5[16] | ... | 4[16] | 8[16] | — | 6[16] | 12[16] | 9[16] | ... | 56[16] | 2.9 | -4.8[4] | ... | ... | ... | ... | ... | French Guiana |
| 5[6] | ... | 8[6] | 9[6] | 1[6] | 6[6] | 24[6] | | 23[6] | 24[6] | 5.4 | 5.3[4] | -379[6] | 337[6] | -42[6] | 98 | ... | French Polynesia |
| 6[7] | 47[7] | 4[7] | 7[7] | 2[7] | 4[7] | 8[7] | 1[7] | 7[7] | 8[7] | 7.5 | -0.2[22] | 1,097[9] | -1,260[9] | -163[9] | 4[10] | 92[7] | Gabon |
| 27[7] | — | 7[7] | 8[7] | ... | 8[7] | 24[7] | 11[7] | 3[7] | 14 | 2.2 | 4.5[4] | -35[7] | 27 | -33[7] | 5 | 27 | Gambia, The |
| 13 | 13 | 12[13] | 22 | ... | 53 | | | | | 7.1[29] | 0.2[4] | -163[9] | 163[9] | —9 | 4 | 8 | Gaza Strip |
| 8[2] | 3 | 70[2,3] | 6[2] | 3 | 4[2] | 9[2] | ... | 32, 20 | | 4.9[2] | 4.2[2,4] | ... | ... | ... | ... | ... | Germany, East |
| 2 | 1 | 31 | 6 | 3 | 6 | 11 | 41 | | | 2.7 | 1.3 | 53,630 | -17,860 | 35,770 | 5,899 | 14,607 | Germany, West |
| 41[9] | 19 | 11[9] | 3[9] | 19 | 7[9] | 28[9] | 8[9] | | | 1.3 | -0.4 | 61 | -104 | -43 | 2 | 25[7] | Ghana |
| ... | ... | ... | ... | ... | ... | ... | ... | ... | ... | ... | ... | -84[9] | ... | ... | 28 | ... | Gibraltar |
| 18 | 2 | 18 | 6 | 2 | 8 | 13 | 3 | 7 | 17 | 4.8 | 1.3 | -5,053[9] | 1,779[9] | -3,276[9] | 1,428 | 368 | Greece |
| ... | ... | ... | ... | ... | ... | ... | ... | ... | ... | ... | ... | ... | ... | ... | ... | ... | Greenland |
| 22 | 1 | 3 | 8 | 2 | 8 | 23 | 7 | 6 | 22 | 3.4 | 2.2 | -47 | 37 | -10 | 21 | 3 | Grenada |
| 7[5] | 13 | 6[5,13] | 4[5] | — | 4[5] | 18[5] | 11[5] | 20[5] | 29[5] | 5.2 | 1.2[4] | -627[5] | 458[5] | -169[5] | 95 | ... | Guadeloupe |
| — | — | 31[5] | 7[5] | ... | 2[5] | 40[5] | 7[5] | 135 | | ... | ... | ... | ... | ... | 175[7] | ... | Guam |
| 26 | — | 16 | 2 | 2 | 7 | 26 | 22 | | | 5.7 | -0.9 | -17[9] | -229[9] | -246[9] | 67 | 77 | Guatemala |
| ... | ... | ... | ... | ... | ... | ... | ... | ... | ... | ... | ... | ... | ... | ... | ... | ... | Guernsey |
| 40[9] | 13[9] | 2[9] | 6[9] | — | 1[9] | 21[9] | 3[9] | 12[9] | | 2.7 | 0.9 | ... | ... | ... | ... | ... | Guinea |
| 49[7] | 1[7] | 1[7] | 3[7] | — | 46[7] | | | | | 1.4 | 2.8[4] | -41[7] | 15[7] | -26[7] | ... | ... | Guinea-Bissau |
| 20 | 4 | 11[31] | 6 | 31 | 6 | 7 | 46 | | | 1.8 | -5.6[22] | 59 | -102[9] | -97[9] | 4 | 11[7] | Guyana |
| 32 | — | 17 | 6 | 1 | 2 | 18 | 5 | 8 | 11 | 4.8 | -1.0 | -135 | 72 | -63 | 69 | 39[7] | Haiti |
| 24 | 2 | 13 | 5 | 2 | 7 | 12 | 11 | 8 | 5 | 4.8 | 1.0 | -1 | -154 | -155 | 24 | 23[10] | Honduras |
| 1 | — | 25 | 5 | 2 | 8 | 21 | 27 | 16 | | 9.6 | 5.8 | 74 | ... | ... | 1,831 | ... | Hong Kong |
| 13[2] | 3 | 38[2,3] | 11[2] | 3 | 7[2] | 12[2] | 20[2, 20] | | | 5.0 | 1.7 | -529 | -760 | -1,289 | 512 | 208 | Hungary |
| 24 | ... | 16 | 10 | 32 | 9 | 17[32] | 32 | 25 | | 4.9 | 0.3 | 73 | -90 | -17 | 41 | 76 | Iceland |
| 33 | 5 | 23 | | | 6 | 16 | 6 | 6 | 6 | 3.3 | 5.5 | -5,616[9] | 1,439[9] | -4,177[9] | 1,098 | 227[7] | India |
| 24 | 18 | 13 | 6 | 1 | 6 | 16 | 17 | | | 8.0 | 4.5 | 5,822[9] | -7,662[9] | -1,840[9] | 488 | 577[7] | Indonesia |
| 17 | 11 | 8 | 7 | 1 | 8 | 21 | 27 | | | 3.6 | 5.7 | 2,358[10] | -2,772[10] | -414[10] | 27 | ... | Iran |
| 14 | 23 | 10 | 9 | 1 | 6 | 11 | 25 | | | 9.3 | -3.1[4] | ... | ... | ... | 181 | ... | Iraq |
| 11 | 33 | 35[33] | 33 | 33 | 19 | | 28 | | 7 | 4.6 | 1.8 | 1,307 | -1,752 | -445 | 549[34] | 422 | Ireland |
| ... | ... | ... | ... | ... | ... | ... | ... | ... | ... | ... | ... | ... | ... | ... | 62[7] | ... | Isle of Man |
| 4 | 13 | 23[13] | 5 | 2 | 6 | 13 | 46 | | | 3.4 | 2.3 | -1,924 | 3,186 | 1,262 | 1,109 | 531 | Israel |
| 5 | 3 | 24 | 8 | 5 | 7 | 16 | 13 | 8 | 14 | 3.2 | 1.6 | -4,341 | 216 | 4,557 | 8,758 | 2,283 | Italy |
| 6 | 9 | 18 | 9 | 3 | 7 | 20 | 15 | 1 | 12 | -0.7 | 0.1 | -246 | 138 | -108 | 407 | 20[10] | Jamaica |
| 3 | — | 30 | 7 | 3 | 6 | 14 | 15 | 19 | 5 | 4.7 | 4.0 | 92,820 | -6,990 | 85,830 | 1,137 | 4,814 | Japan |
| 67 | — | 47 | | | 90[7] | | | | | ... | ... | ... | ... | ... | 223[7] | ... | Jersey |
| 6 | 3 | 24 | 12 | 2 | 14 | 12 | 6 | 3 | 13 | 7.1 | 4.3 | -1,426 | 1,386 | -40 | 555 | 452 | Jordan |
| ... | ... | ... | ... | ... | ... | ... | ... | ... | ... | -8.8 | -2.1[4] | ... | ... | ... | ... | ... | Kampuchea |
| 27 | — | 11 | 5 | 2 | 5 | 11 | 7 | 9 | 12 | 6.1 | 2.7 | -291 | 189 | -102 | 128 | 16[10] | Kenya |
| 37 | — | 2 | 3 | 3 | 14 | 12 | 3 | 27 | | 0.6 | 3.9[4] | ... | ... | ... | ... | ... | Kiribati |
| ... | ... | ... | ... | ... | ... | ... | ... | ... | ... | 5.9[2] | 8.5[2,4] | ... | ... | ... | ... | ... | Korea, North |
| 14[9] | ... | 31[9] | 8[9] | 9[9] | 8[9] | 13[9] | 11[9] | 5[9] | 6[9] | 8.3 | 7.6 | 4,206 | 411 | 4,617 | 784 | 606 | Korea, South |
| — | 46[9] | 6[9] | 3[9] | 9[9] | 4[9] | 10[9] | 10[9] | 19[9] | | 2.3 | 0.3 | 1,979 | 4,181 | 6,160 | 103 | 1,988 | Kuwait |
| ... | ... | ... | ... | ... | ... | ... | ... | ... | ... | 0.8 | 2.4[4] | ... | ... | ... | ... | ... | Laos |
| 9[19] | 13 | 13[13,19] | 31[9] | 5[19] | 8[19] | 28[19] | 23[19] | | 10[19] | 1.5 | -8.6[4] | ... | ... | ... | ... | ... | Lebanon |
| 18[9] | — | 10[9] | 9[9] | 1[9] | 2[9] | 14[9] | 12[9] | 24[9] | 10[9] | 9.0 | 0.5 | -318 | 309 | -9 | 9 | 5[10] | Lesotho |
| 17 | 17 | 8 | 2 | 3 | 6 | 6 | 41 | | | 0.6 | -2.7 | 184[9] | -109[9] | 75[9] | 6 | ... | Liberia |
| 2[6] | 48[6] | 3[6] | 12[6] | 1[6] | 4[6] | 6[6] | 23[6] | | | 7.5 | -6.1 | 4,640[9] | -2,750[9] | 1,890[9] | 12 | 405[7] | Libya |
| ... | ... | ... | ... | ... | ... | ... | ... | ... | ... | ... | ... | ... | ... | ... | ... | ... | Liechtenstein |
| 3 | 13 | 30[13] | 6 | 3 | 6 | 17 | 36 | | | 4.4 | 1.7[4] | 14 | 14 | 14 | ... | ... | Luxembourg |
| ... | ... | ... | ... | ... | ... | ... | ... | ... | ... | ... | ... | ... | ... | ... | ... | ... | Macau |
| 42[9] | 33 | 16[9,33] | 33 | 33 | 42[9] | | | | | 0.7 | -0.8 | 137 | -164[7] | -151[7] | 5[10] | 38[7] | Madagascar |
| 36[9] | — | 12[9] | 4[9] | 2[9] | 6[9] | 18[9] | 7[9] | 4[9] | 13[9] | 5.1 | 2.0 | 28[6] | -101[6] | -73[6] | 6[10] | ... | Malawi |
| 21 | 5 | 18 | 5 | 3 | 8 | 14 | 8 | 3 | 13 | 8.1 | 5.2 | 3,369 | -3,665 | -296 | 545 | 1,119[10] | Malaysia |
| 29 | 1 | 5[31] | 8 | 31 | 6 | 10 | 42 | | | 13.2 | 9.5[4] | -36[9] | 279 | -99[9] | 41 | 5 | Maldives |
| 52 | 13 | 7[13] | 5 | — | 5 | 16 | 8 | | 8 | 0.3 | -0.5 | -115 | -34 | -149 | 12 | 18[7] | Mali |
| 5 | 33 | 30 | 3 | 6 | 6 | 16 | 4 | 8 | 13 | 10.6 | 2.3 | -261 | 267 | 6 | 149 | 33[10] | Malta |
| 6[25] | 13 | 5[13,25] | 4[25] | 2[25] | 4[25] | 17[25] | 63[25] | | | 3.9 | 0.1[4] | -736[5] | 581[5] | -155[5] | 93 | ... | Martinique |
| 19 | 10 | 9[21] | 8 | 21 | 7 | 13 | 34 | | | 2.2 | 0.2 | 38[9] | -147[9] | -109[9] | 7 | 22[7] | Mauritania |
| 12 | — | 15 | 5 | 2 | 9 | 11 | 45 | | | 5.9 | 3.9 | 69 | 36 | 105 | 65 | 19 | Mauritius |
| ... | ... | ... | ... | ... | ... | ... | ... | ... | ... | ... | ... | ... | ... | ... | ... | ... | Mayotte |
| 9 | 10 | 24 | 5 | 1 | 7 | 23 | 22 | | | 6.6 | 1.7 | 4,599 | -5,869 | -1,270 | 2,900 | 2,262 | Mexico |
| ... | ... | ... | ... | ... | ... | ... | ... | ... | ... | ... | ... | ... | ... | ... | ... | ... | Monaco |
| 18[2] | 33 | 38[2,33] | 33 | 33 | 11[2] | 33[2] | ... | | | 6.3[2] | 7.1[2,4] | ... | ... | ... | ... | ... | Mongolia |
| 4 | 1 | 6 | 7 | 4 | 10 | 17 | 51 | | | 4.6 | 2.1 | -8[9] | 7[9] | -19 | 8 | ... | Montserrat |
| 17 | 7 | 16 | 7 | 1 | 5 | 14 | — | 13 | 12 | 5.6 | 2.8 | -1,368[9] | 477[9] | -891[9] | 600 | 70[10] | Morocco |
| 40[25] | — | 8[25] | 6[25] | 1[25] | 4[25] | 24[25] | | ... | 8[25] | -0.6 | -9.6 | -372[7] | 178[7] | -194[7] | ... | ... | Mozambique |
| ... | ... | ... | ... | ... | ... | ... | ... | ... | ... | ... | ... | ... | ... | ... | ... | ... | Nauru |
| 58 | — | 4 | 7 | — | 6 | 4 | 21 | | | 2.1 | 4.0 | -297 | 184 | -113 | 33 | 23[10] | Nepal |
| 5 | 9 | 18 | 6 | 2 | 7 | 15 | 29 | | 15 | 3.4 | 0.7 | 6,999 | -2,351 | 4,648 | 1,503 | 3,118 | Netherlands, The |
| 15, 12 | | 22[5,12] | 8[5,12] | 25[12] | 15[5,12] | 21[5,12] | 32[5,12] | | | 3.5[12] | -2.6[4,12] | -37[12] | 94[7,12] | 91[7,12] | 225 | 107[7] | Netherlands Antilles |
| 2[7] | 57 | 10[7] | 5[7] | 2[7] | 4[7] | 27[7] | 17[7] | | 28[7] | 0.7 | -2.0[4] | -106[7] | 273[7] | 167[7] | 26 | ... | New Caledonia |
| 9 | 1 | 23 | 5 | 3 | 9 | 21 | 15 | 4 | 12 | 2.4 | 2.5 | 239 | -1,674 | -1,435 | 276 | 401 | New Zealand |
| 24 | 1 | 25 | 3 | 2 | 6 | 19 | 7 | 5 | 9 | 1.8 | 0.2 | -540[9] | -205[9] | -745[9] | 5 | 77 | Nicaragua |
| 44 | 9 | 4 | 3 | 2 | 4 | 13 | | 8 | 9 | 3.9 | -3.6 | -41 | 35 | -6 | 3 | ... | Niger |
| 25[7] | 20[7] | 5[7] | 7[7] | 1[7] | 4[7] | 22[7] | 16[7] | | | 4.9 | -3.4 | 2,535 | -2,170 | 365 | 102 | 454[7] | Nigeria |
| ... | ... | ... | ... | ... | ... | ... | ... | ... | ... | ... | ... | ... | ... | ... | ... | ... | Niue |
| ... | ... | ... | ... | ... | ... | ... | ... | ... | ... | ... | ... | ... | ... | ... | ... | ... | Norfolk Island |

## National product and accounts (continued)

| country | gross national product (GNP), 1985 nominal ('000,000 U.S.$) | per capita (U.S.$) | gross domestic product (GDP), 1985 nominal ('000,000,000 national currency) | real (constant prices of 1980; '000,000,000 national currency) | consumption private | government | gross domestic investment | exports | imports | net indirect taxes | consumption of fixed capital | compensation of employees | net operating surplus |
|---|---|---|---|---|---|---|---|---|---|---|---|---|---|
| Norway | 57,580 | 13,870 | 501.8 | 336.4 | 47 | 19 | 26 | 47 | -38 | 11 | 14 | 48 | 27 |
| Oman | 8,360 | 6,730 | 3.575 | ... | 30 | 25 | 29 | 48 | -32 | 1[25] | —99[25]— | | |
| Pacific Is., Trust Terr. of the | 160[10] | 1,030[10] | ... | ... | ... | ... | ... | ... | ... | ... | ... | ... | ... |
|   Marshall Islands | ... | ... | | | | | | | | | | | |
|   Micronesia, F.S. of | ... | ... | | | | | | | | | | | |
|   Northern Mariana Is. | ... | ... | | | | | | | | | | | |
|   Palau | ... | ... | | | | | | | | | | | |
| Pakistan | 36,230 | 360 | 478.0 | 322.5 | 82 | 12 | 17 | 11 | -22 | 10 | 6 | —85— | |
| Panama | 4,400 | 2,020 | 4.882 | 4.070 | 63 | 22 | 17 | 36 | -37 | 8 | 8 | 50 | 34 |
| Papua New Guinea | 2,470 | 740 | 2.292 | ... | 63 | 23 | 28 | 41 | -55 | 8 | 10 | 40 | 42 |
| Paraguay | 3,180 | 860 | 1,393.9 | 627.1 | 78 | 6 | 23 | 18 | -25 | 5 | 10 | 32 | 53 |
| Peru | 17,830 | 910 | 157,977 | 4.842 | 68 | 11 | 16 | 22 | -18 | 9[7] | 7[7] | 31[7] | 53[7] |
| Philippines | 32,630 | 600 | 609.5 | 257.6 | 75 | 7 | 19 | 22 | -22 | 8 | 10 | —82— | |
| Pitcairn Island | ... | ... | ... | ... | | | | | | | | | |
| Poland | 78,960 | 2,120 | 10,367.2 | ... | 63 | 10 | 26 | 18 | -16 | ... | ... | ... | ... |
| Portugal | 20,140 | 1,980 | 3,524.8 | 1,319.5 | 71 | 14 | 23 | 36 | -45 | 10 | 4 | 47 | 39 |
| Puerto Rico | 15,940 | 4,860 | 21.109 | 17.657 | 75 | 15 | 12 | 59 | -61 | 7 | 6 | 45 | 42 |
| Qatar | 5,110 | 15,720 | 23.542[7] | ... | 24[7] | 35[7] | 22[7] | 54[7] | -35[7] | ... | ... | ... | ... |
| Réunion | 1,890[10] | 3,520[10] | 14.933[10] | ... | 85[5] | 33[5] | 23[5] | 7[5] | -47[5] | 10[5] | 11 | 65[5] | 25[5,11] |
| Romania | 45,536[10] | 2,020[10] | ... | 300.0[2] | 48 | 7 | 36 | —9— | | ... | ... | ... | ... |
| Rwanda | 1,730 | 290 | 158.9[10] | ... | 77 | 16 | 15 | 10 | -17 | 7 | 4 | 19 | 69 |
| St. Christopher | 70 | 1,530 | 0.167[10] | 0.146[10] | 78 | 22 | 32 | 56 | -87 | 17[37] | 4[37] | 67[37] | 13[37] |
| St. Helena | ... | ... | | | | | | | | | | | |
| St. Lucia | 160 | 1,170 | 0.408[10] | 0.342[10] | 62 | 25 | 35 | 64 | -86 | ... | ... | ... | ... |
| St. Pierre and Miquelon | ... | ... | | | | | | | | | | | |
| St. Vincent | 100 | 910 | 0.269[10] | 0.199[10] | 57 | 29 | 31 | 71 | -89 | 17[16] | 8[16] | 49[16] | 26[16] |
| San Marino | 175[5] | 8,250[5] | ... | ... | | | | | | | | | |
| São Tomé and Príncipe | 30 | 280 | 1.178[7] | ... | 36[7] | 30[7] | 22[7] | —127—[7] | | ... | ... | ... | ... |
| Saudi Arabia | 102,120 | 8,850 | 330.9 | 353.2 | 39 | 33 | 31 | 45 | -47 | — | 11 | 17[5] | 83[5,11] |
| Senegal | 2,400 | 370 | 1,186.9 | 763.1 | 79 | 20 | 13 | 36 | -49 | 17[25] | 6[25] | —77[25]— | |
| Seychelles | 160 | 2,450 | 1.074[10] | 879.2[10] | 60 | 31 | 21 | 64 | -76 | 18 | 6 | 39 | 37 |
| Sierra Leone | 1,380 | 380 | 1.939[7] | 1.277[7] | 102 | 7 | 9 | 9 | -28 | 9[5] | 10[5] | 27[5] | 55[5] |
| Singapore | 18,970 | 7,420 | 38.521 | 33.647 | 43 | 11 | 48 | —2— | | ... | ... | ... | ... |
| Solomon Islands | 140 | 510 | 0.178[7] | 0.128[7] | ... | ... | ... | ... | | 9[5] | 12[5] | 25[5] | 54[5] |
| Somalia | 1,450 | 250 | 1.102[7,23] | ... | 69[7] | 32[7] | 11[7] | —127— | | ... | ... | ... | ... |
| South Africa | 65,320 | 1,990 | 120.175 | 65.511 | 55 | 17 | 24 | 27 | -25 | 8 | 15 | 54 | 23 |
|   Bophuthatswana | 1,736[1,10] | 950[1,10] | ... | ... | | | | | | | | | |
|   Ciskei | 377 | 490 | 0.397 | ... | | | | | | | | | |
|   KwaNdebele | ... | ... | | | | | | | | | | | |
|   Transkei | 1,471[1,10] | 470[1,10] | ... | ... | | | | | | | | | |
|   Venda | 201[1,10] | 490[1,10] | ... | ... | | | | | | | | | |
| S.W. Africa/Namibia | 990 | 870 | 1,952[10] | 1.316[10] | ... | ... | ... | ... | ... | ... | ... | ... | ... |
| Spain | 168,820 | 4,370 | 25,935.0[10] | 16,129.0[10] | 67 | 12 | 18 | 23 | -20 | 6 | 12 | 48 | 34 |
| Sri Lanka | 5,980 | 380 | 157.763 | 87.678 | 72 | 8 | 26 | 29 | -35 | 13[7] | 5[7] | 45[7] | 37[7] |
| Sudan, The | 7,350 | 310 | 6.218[7] | ... | 91 | 12 | 11 | 10 | -23 | 11[15] | 7[15] | 39[15] | 43[15] |
| Suriname | 1,010 | 2,570 | 1.719[10] | 1.542[10] | 67 | 25 | 12 | 44 | -48 | 14 | 10 | 68 | 9 |
| Swaziland | 490 | 740 | 0.716[10] | ... | 80 | 24 | 24 | 74 | -103 | 20[25] | 6[25] | 44[25] | 30[25] |
| Sweden | 99,050 | 11,860 | 862.5 | 574.2 | 50 | 28 | 18 | 36 | -32 | 11 | 12 | 58 | 19 |
| Switzerland | 105,180 | 16,100 | 227.8 | 168.3 | 62 | 13 | 24 | 38 | -38 | 6 | 10 | 63 | 22 |
| Syria | 17,060 | 1,660 | 79.549 | 57.094 | 65 | 23 | 24 | 13 | -24 | 4 | 3 | —93— | |
| Taiwan | 60,380 | 3,160 | 2,357.1 | ... | 51 | 16 | 21 | 58 | -46 | 13[25] | 8[25] | 50[25] | 28[25] |
| Tanzania | 5,840 | 270 | 108.091 | 43.931 | 82 | 12 | 15 | 8 | -17 | 11 | 2 | 15 | 72 |
| Thailand | 42,100 | 810 | 1,047.6 | 885.9 | 66 | 13 | 24 | 24 | -27 | 11 | 8 | 27 | 54 |
| Togo | 750 | 250 | 281.3[7] | 206.6[7] | 82[7] | 15[7] | 19[7] | 36[7] | -51[7] | 14[6] | 7[6] | 28[6] | 51[6] |
| Tokelau | 0.9[5] | 560[5] | ... | ... | | | | | | | | | |
| Tonga | 70 | 720 | 0.073[7] | 0.073[7] | 96[7] | 18[7] | 28[7] | —41[7]— | | 11[7] | 3[7] | 37[7] | 48[7] |
| Trinidad and Tobago | 7,140 | 6,040 | 18.140 | 12.472 | 58 | 22 | 22 | 32 | -33 | -1 | 7 | 58 | 36 |
| Tunisia | 8,730 | 1,200 | 6.859 | 4.320 | 63 | 17 | 32 | 34 | -46 | 14 | 10 | —76— | |
| Turkey | 56,060 | 1,110 | 27,509.0 | 5,465.7 | 79 | 10 | 20 | 12 | -21 | 4 | 5 | —90— | |
| Turks and Caicos Is. | ... | 3,510[7,18] | 0.028[7] | ... | ... | ... | ... | ... | | | | | |
| Tuvalu | 5[25] | 680[25] | 0.004[7] | ... | ... | ... | ... | ... | | ... | ... | ... | ... |
| Uganda | 3,290[10] | 230[10] | 518.8[25] | ... | 86[7] | 14[7] | 9[7] | —97—[7] | | 16[19] | 8[19] | 26[19] | 49[19] |
| U.S.S.R. | 1,925,000[10] | 7,000[10] | 567.9[2] | 540.4[2] | —72[2,7]— | | 26[2,7] | —22[2,7]— | | ... | ... | ... | ... |
| United Arab Emirates | 26,400 | 16,970 | 101.5[10] | 101.8[10] | 25 | 18 | 30 | 59 | -32 | -3 | 17 | 24 | 61 |
| United Kingdom | 474,190 | 8,380 | 351.6 | 252.8 | 61 | 22 | 17 | 29 | -29 | 14 | 12 | 57 | 18 |
| United States | 3,915,350 | 16,360 | 3,957.0 | 3,162.3 | 65 | 18 | 20 | 8 | -10 | 8 | 13 | 60 | 19 |
| Uruguay | 4,980 | 1,650 | 520.158 | 78.967 | 75 | 12 | 9 | 25 | -20 | 12 | 3 | —85— | |
| Vanuatu | 118 | 880 | 7.742[25] | ... | ... | ... | ... | ... | | ... | ... | ... | ... |
| Venezuela | 53,800 | 3,110 | 372.0 | 238.2 | 60 | 13 | 16 | 30 | -19 | 6 | 8 | 37 | 50 |
| Vietnam | 18,100[10] | 310[10] | 20.742[15] | ... | ... | ... | ... | ... | | ... | ... | ... | ... |
| Virgin Islands (U.S.) | ... | 9,300[19] | 1.030 | ... | ... | ... | ... | ... | | ... | ... | ... | ... |
| Wallis and Futuna | 10[6] | 920[6] | ... | ... | | | | | | | | | |
| West Bank | 1,062[10] | 1,360[10] | 0.236[10] | 0.004[10] | 105 | 15 | 25 | 26 | -71 | ... | ... | ... | ... |
| Western Sahara | ... | ... | | | | | | | | | | | |
| Western Samoa | 110 | 690 | ... | ... | ... | ... | ... | ... | | ... | ... | ... | ... |
| Yemen (Aden) | 1,130 | 490 | 0.311[6] | ... | 106[5] | 42[5] | 49[5] | 14[5] | -111[5] | 16[5] | 8[5] | 58[5] | 19[5] |
| Yemen (Ṣan'ā') | 4,140 | 600 | 17.950[10] | 14.996[10] | 82 | 40 | 21 | 7 | -50 | 15[6] | 2[6] | 31[6] | 52[6] |
| Yugoslavia | 47,900 | 2,070 | 11,951.3 | ... | 52 | 15 | 36 | 20 | -22 | ... | ... | ... | ... |
| Zaire | 5,220 | 170 | 147.214 | 18.294 | 35 | 15 | 29 | 77 | -56 | 9[19] | 7[19] | —84[19]— | |
| Zambia | 2,620 | 390 | 7.049 | 3.193 | 56 | 25 | 15 | 37 | -33 | 14 | 13 | 44 | 30 |
| Zimbabwe | 5,450 | 670 | 8.099 | 4.419 | 58[9] | 19[9] | 23[9] | 26[9] | -26[9] | 11[6] | 11 | 58[6] | 31[6,11] |

[1]Real prices of 1978. [2]Net material product. [3]Manufacturing includes mining and public utilities. [4]1980–84. [5]1980. [6]1982. [7]1983. [8]1980–82. [9]1985. [10]1984. [11]Net operating surplus includes consumption of fixed capital. [12]Netherlands Antilles includes Aruba. [13]Manufacturing includes mining. [14]Data refer to the Belgium-Luxembourg Economic Union (BLEU) and exclude transactions between the two countries. [15]1978. [16]1979. [17]1984–85. [18]GDP. [19]1977. [20]Activities in the material sphere not elsewhere specified. [21]Mining includes public utilities.

| origin of GDP by economic sector, 1984 (%) — primary | | secondary | | | tertiary | | | | | avg. annual growth rate of real GDP (%) | | balance of payments, 1986 (current external transactions; '000,000 U.S.$) — net transfers | | current balance of payments | tourist trade, 1985 ('000,000 U.S.$) | | country |
|---|---|---|---|---|---|---|---|---|---|---|---|---|---|---|---|---|---|
| agri-culture | mining | manu-factur-ing | con-struc-tion | public util-ities | transp., commu-nication | trade | finan-cial svcs. | other svcs. | govt. | 1970–1980 | 1980–1985 | goods-merchan-dise | invisibles | | receipts from foreign nationals | expendi-tures by nationals abroad | |
| 4 | 20 | 14 | 5 | 4 | 9 | 13 | 8 | 8 | 14 | 4.8 | 3.4 | 4,680[9] | -1,754[9] | 2,926[9] | 828 | 1,925 | Norway |
| 3 | 48 | 3 | 7 | 1 | 3 | 12 | 9 | 1 | 15 | 3.6 | 4.0 | 607 | -1,576 | -969 | ... | ... | Oman |
| ... | ... | ... | ... | ... | ... | ... | ... | ... | ... | ... | ... | ... | ... | ... | ... | ... | Pacific Is., Trust. Terr. of |
| ... | ... | ... | ... | ... | ... | ... | ... | ... | ... | ... | ... | ... | ... | ... | ... | ... | Marshall Islands |
| ... | ... | ... | ... | ... | ... | ... | ... | ... | ... | ... | ... | ... | ... | ... | ... | ... | Micronesia, F.S of |
| ... | ... | ... | ... | ... | ... | ... | ... | ... | ... | ... | ... | ... | ... | ... | 121 | ... | Northern Mariana Is. |
| ... | ... | ... | ... | ... | ... | ... | ... | ... | ... | ... | ... | ... | ... | ... | ... | ... | Palau |
| 25 | 1 | 20 | 5 | 2 | 8 | 17 | 3 | 8 | 8 | 4.7 | 6.6 | -2,819 | 2,119 | -700 | 186 | 207 | Pakistan |
| 9 | — | 9 | 5 | 4 | 20 | 14 | 17 | 10 | 15 | 5.6 | 2.8 | -542 | 984 | 442 | 200 | 65 | Panama |
| 33[7] | 11[7] | 9[7] | 4[7] | 1[7] | 4[7] | 8[7] | 10[7] | 13[7] | 8[7] | 4.0 | 1.3 | -50[10] | -274[10] | -324[10] | 13 | 311[10] | Papua New Guinea |
| 29 | | 16 | 6 | 2 | 4 | 25 | ——17—— | | | 8.6 | 2.4 | -192[9] | -34[9] | -226[9] | 80 | 47 | Paraguay |
| 8 | 11 | 25 | 3 | 2 | 8 | 17 | ——27—— | | | 3.5 | -0.3 | -16 | -1,014 | -1,030 | 277 | 165 | Peru |
| 25 | 2 | 25 | 6 | 1 | 6 | 18 | 8 | ——9—— | | 6.1 | -0.5 | -202 | 1,224 | 1,022 | 507 | 37 | Philippines |
| ... | ... | ... | ... | ... | ... | ... | ... | ... | ... | ... | ... | ... | ... | ... | ... | ... | Pitcairn Island |
| 17[2] | 3 | 50[2,3] | 12[2] | 3 | 6[2] | 14[2] | ——22,20—— | | | 5.6[2] | -0.8[2] | 902[36] | -1,209[36] | -307[36] | 118 | 195[7] | Poland |
| 9 | 13 | 32[13] | 6 | 2 | ——20—— | | 6 | 13 | 12 | 4.8 | 1.0 | -1,634 | 2,778 | 1,144 | 1,137 | 235 | Portugal |
| 2 | — | 39 | 2 | 3 | 5 | 15 | ——34—— | | | 4.9 | 2.2 | -720[10] | -1,668[10] | -2,388[10] | 710 | 618 | Puerto Rico |
| 2[9] | — | 12[9] | 11[9] | 1[9] | 49 | 11[9] | 14[9] | 2[9] | 46[9] | 4.0 | -2.2[4] | 1,842[7] | -1,432[7] | 410[7] | ... | ... | Qatar |
| 7[6] | ... | 10[6] | 6[6] | 2[6] | 5[6] | 15[6] | 24[6] | ——32[6]—— | | 6.0 | 4.4[4] | -699[6] | 696[6] | -3[6] | ... | ... | Réunion |
| 15[2] | 3 | 61[2,3] | 8[2] | 3 | 6[2] | ——10[2]—— | | | | 9.2[2] | 4.4[2] | 1,917[36] | -509 | 1,408[36] | 153 | 85[10] | Romania |
| 43 | — | 16 | 5 | 1 | 3 | 14 | ——18—— | | | 3.0 | 1.8 | -75 | 6 | -69 | 4[25] | 11[10] | Rwanda |
| 17 | — | 13 | 8 | 1 | 13 | 15 | 17 | ——16—— | | 3.0 | 2.7 | -287 | 147 | -147 | 13 | 3[7] | St. Christopher |
| ... | ... | ... | ... | ... | ... | ... | ... | ... | ... | ... | ... | ... | ... | ... | ... | ... | St. Helena |
| 14 | 1 | 10 | 7 | 4 | 11 | 22 | 7 | 10 | 21 | 5.8 | 2.9[4] | -477 | 36[7] | -117 | 69 | 44 | St. Lucia |
| ... | ... | ... | ... | ... | ... | ... | ... | ... | ... | ... | ... | ... | ... | ... | ... | ... | St. Pierre and Miquelon |
| 17 | — | 10 | 11 | 3 | 16 | 14 | 10 | 3 | 20 | 2.8 | 5.2 | -23[7] | 20[7] | -37 | 23 | 8[7] | St. Vincent |
| ... | ... | ... | ... | ... | ... | ... | ... | ... | ... | ... | ... | ... | ... | ... | ... | ... | San Marino |
| 51[6] | — | 5[6] | 3[6] | 1[6] | 3[6] | 9[6] | 6[6] | 1[6] | 22[6] | -1.1 | 1.5[4] | -6[7] | -2[7] | -8[7] | ... | ... | São Tomé and Príncipe |
| 2 | 41 | 4 | 14 | — | 8 | 10 | 7 | 3 | 11 | 11.1 | -1.5 | 7,032[9] | -20,287[9] | -13,255[9] | 2,378 | 3,152[7] | Saudi Arabia |
| 17 | 33 | 28[33] | 33 | 33 | ——55—— | | | | | 2.0 | 3.3 | -379[6] | -21[6] | -400[6] | 81 | 45[10] | Senegal |
| 7 | 13 | 9[13] | 5 | 2 | 42 | 8 | 8 | 3 | 16 | 6.2 | -1.6[4] | -87 | 55 | -32 | 51 | 9 | Seychelles |
| 33[6] | 5[6] | 5[6] | 6[6] | 1[6] | 13[6] | 13[6] | 10[6] | 4[6] | 11[6] | 2.0 | 2.1 | -99 | 179 | 89[7] | 7 | 4[7] | Sierra Leone |
| 1 | — | 24 | 11 | 2 | 14 | 18 | 23 | ——13—— | | 9.2 | 6.1 | -2,328 | 2,807 | 479 | 1,754 | 615 | Singapore |
| 59[38] | 3 | 1[3,38] | 2[38] | 3 | 2[38] | 8[38] | ——8[38]—— | | 14[38] | 8.6 | 4.7[4] | 1[9] | -20[9] | -19[9] | 2[15] | ... | Solomon Islands |
| 52 | | 5 | 3 | 1 | 6 | 7 | 6 | 11 | 9 | 1.7 | 4.9 | -240[9] | 143[9] | -97[9] | 13[6] | 137 | Somalia |
| 5 | 13 | 23 | 4 | 4 | 10 | 12 | 14 | 4 | 13 | 3.4 | 1.2 | 7,063 | -3,869 | 3,194 | 630[7] | 651[10] | South Africa |
| 6[5] | 33 | 69[5,33] | 33 | 33 | ——25[5]—— | | | | | | | ... | ... | ... | ... | ... | Bophuthatswana |
| 9[5] | — | 20[5] | 10[5] | ... | 3[5] | ——58[5]—— | | | | 9.1 | 9.6 | ... | ... | ... | ... | ... | Ciskei |
| ... | ... | ... | ... | ... | ... | ... | ... | ... | ... | ... | ... | ... | ... | ... | ... | ... | KwaNdebele |
| 27[5] | 33 | 12[5,33] | 33 | 33 | ——61[5]—— | | | | | ... | ... | ... | ... | ... | ... | ... | Transkei |
| ... | ... | ... | ... | ... | ... | ... | ... | ... | ... | ... | ... | ... | ... | ... | ... | ... | Venda |
| 7 | 26 | 5 | 3 | 4 | 7 | 14 | 8 | 2 | 21 | 4.8 | -0.7[4] | ... | ... | ... | 46[25] | ... | S.W. Africa/Namibia |
| 7 | 13 | 27[13] | 7 | 3 | 6 | 20 | ——30—— | | | 3.8 | 1.6 | -6,251 | 10,348 | 4,097 | 8,151 | 1,010 | Spain |
| 24 | 1 | 17 | 8 | 2 | 11 | 20 | 4 | ——6—— | | 4.7 | 5.1 | -555 | 143 | -412 | 70 | 50 | Sri Lanka |
| 28 | 13 | 9[13] | 6 | 2 | 10 | 23 | ... | 10 | 12 | 2.2 | -0.7 | -307 | 289 | -18 | 58 | 44 | Sudan, The |
| 7 | 5 | 12 | 6 | 5 | 6 | 16 | ——43—— | | | 5.2 | -0.9[4] | 16[9] | -39[9] | -23[9] | 20 | 35[7] | Suriname |
| 25[7] | 3[7] | 23[7] | 4[7] | 17 | 6[7] | 9[7] | 7[7] | 4[7] | 17[7] | 6.9 | 3.9[8] | -88 | 37 | -51 | 12 | 11[10] | Swaziland |
| 3 | — | 22 | 7 | 3 | 6 | 11 | 12 | 15 | 22 | 2.0 | 1.8 | 5,098 | -4,278 | 820 | 1,332 | 2,270 | Sweden |
| ... | ... | ... | ... | ... | ... | ... | ... | ... | ... | 1.3 | 1.4 | -1,561[9] | 7,767[9] | 6,206[9] | 3,145 | 2,399 | Switzerland |
| 20 | 8 | 9 | 7 | — | 8 | 23 | ——25—— | | | 9.9 | 2.3 | -1,951[9] | 999[9] | -952[9] | 154 | 118 | Syria |
| 7 | 1 | 42 | 4 | 4 | 6 | 14 | 9 | 6 | 10 | 9.7 | 6.0 | 16,857 | -640 | 16,217 | 1,066[10] | 1,229[7] | Taiwan |
| 49 | — | 6 | 2 | 1 | 5 | 12 | ——24—— | | | 5.4 | 0.8 | -350[25] | 71[25] | -279[25] | 13 | 12[7] | Tanzania |
| 20 | 2 | 20 | 5 | 2 | 8 | 22 | ——21—— | | | 6.9 | 5.0 | -1,332[9] | -205[9] | -1,537[9] | 1,171 | 280 | Thailand |
| 32[7] | 7[7] | 5[7] | 5[7] | 2[7] | ——49[7]—— | | | | | 3.2 | -4.2[2] | -94 | -20 | -114 | 20 | 23[8] | Togo |
| ... | ... | ... | ... | ... | ... | ... | ... | ... | ... | ... | ... | ... | ... | ... | ... | ... | Tokelau |
| 41[7] | — | 5[7] | 4[7] | — | 6[7] | 15[7] | 6[7] | ——22[7]—— | | 4.1 | 8.6[4] | -21[9] | 15[9] | -6[9] | 6 | 1[7] | Tonga |
| 3 | 25 | 7 | 13 | 2 | 11 | 9 | 10 | 7 | 14 | 4.4 | -4.1 | 765[9] | -843[9] | -78[9] | 197 | 219 | Trinidad and Tobago |
| 13 | 11 | 12 | 6 | 1 | 5 | 18 | ——34—— | | | 7.1 | 4.1 | -936 | 316 | -620 | 551 | 657 | Tunisia |
| 19 | 2 | 25 | 4 | 3 | 10 | 17 | ——20—— | | | 5.2 | 4.5 | -3,081 | 1,553 | -1,528 | 1,482 | 324 | Turkey |
| ... | ... | ... | ... | ... | ... | ... | ... | ... | ... | 5.6 | -0.2[4] | ... | ... | ... | 12 | ... | Turks and Caicos Is. |
| 16[16] | | 1[16] | 13[16] | ... | 4[16] | 34[16] | ——32[16]—— | | | ... | ... | ... | ... | ... | ... | ... | Tuvalu |
| 76[6] | — | 4[6] | | — | 2[6] | 5[6] | 6[6] | 2[6] | 5[6] | -1.6 | 1.1 | -49[25] | 57[25] | 8[25] | 8[10] | 10[7] | Uganda |
| 20[2] | 3 | 46[2,3] | 11[2] | 3 | 6[2] | 18[2] | ... | | | 5.1[2] | 3.5[2] | ... | ... | ... | ... | ... | U.S.S.R. |
| 1 | 46 | 10 | 10 | 2 | 4 | 9 | ——18—— | | | 15.1 | -2.8 | ... | ... | ... | ... | ... | United Arab Emirates |
| 2 | 13 | 24[13] | 6 | 11 | 7 | 13 | 19 | 16 | 7 | 2.0 | 1.9 | -12,144 | 11,904 | -240 | 6,988 | 6,253 | United Kingdom |
| 3 | 3 | 21 | 4 | 3 | 6 | 17 | 16 | 15 | 12 | 2.5 | 2.6 | -144,340 | 2,880 | -141,460 | 11,663 | 17,043 | United States |
| 12 | 13 | 20[13] | 3 | 3 | 6 | 12 | 13 | 10 | 8 | 3.1 | -3.0 | 297 | -205 | 91 | 129 | 304[7] | Uruguay |
| 20[6] | 8[6,21] | 5[6] | 26 | 21 | 3[6] | 10[6] | ——52[6]—— | | | 3.5 | 7.6[4] | -38 | 35 | -3 | 2[15] | ... | Vanuatu |
| 7 | 20 | 19 | 3 | 2 | 11 | 11 | ——27—— | | | 4.1 | -1.3 | 986 | -2,614 | 1,628 | 367 | 995[10] | Venezuela |
| 58[2] | 3 | 24[2,3] | 3[2] | 3 | 2[2] | 12[2] | ——22,20—— | | | 0.5[2] | 10.7[2,4] | ... | ... | ... | ... | ... | Vietnam |
| ... | ... | ... | ... | ... | ... | ... | ... | ... | ... | 3.1 | -3.2[4] | ... | ... | ... | 532 | ... | Virgin Islands (U.S.) |
| ... | ... | ... | ... | ... | ... | ... | ... | ... | ... | ... | ... | ... | ... | ... | ... | ... | Wallis and Futuna |
| 20 | 13 | 8[13] | 15 | ... | ——57—— | | | | | 10.2[29] | 1.1[4] | -217[9] | 217[9] | -9 | 7 | 35 | West Bank |
| ... | ... | ... | ... | ... | ... | ... | ... | ... | ... | ... | ... | ... | ... | ... | ... | ... | Western Sahara |
| ... | ... | ... | ... | ... | ... | ... | ... | ... | ... | 3.0 | -3.2[22] | -32 | 39 | 7 | 7 | ... | Western Samoa |
| 10[5] | — | 12[5] | 8[5] | 1[5] | 10[5] | 13[5] | 11[5] | 15 | 23[5] | 1.2 | 1.6 | -794[10] | 426[10] | -368[10] | 7 | 12[7] | Yemen (Aden) |
| 26[6] | 16 | 7[6] | 8[6] | 1[6] | 4[6] | 17[6] | ——37[6]—— | | | 8.0 | 4.5 | -1,016 | 860 | -156 | 17 | 58 | Yemen (San'ā') |
| 11[9] | 11[9] | 34[9] | 7[9] | 2[9] | 7[9] | 11[9] | ——24[9]—— | | | 5.8 | 0.8 | -1,231[7] | 1,506[7] | 275[7] | 1,050 | 86[7] | Yugoslavia |
| 32 | 25 | 2 | 5 | — | 1 | 19 | ——15—— | | | 0.5 | 1.3 | 940[10] | -563[10] | 377[10] | 23[10] | 38[7] | Zaire |
| 16 | 15 | 23 | 3 | 2 | 6 | 14 | ——19—— | | | 1.4 | 0.9 | 209[9] | -493[9] | -284[9] | 49[10] | 43[7] | Zambia |
| 14 | 6 | 27 | 4 | 3 | 7 | 14 | 6 | 16 | 8 | 3.5 | 5.3 | 315 | -262 | 53 | 26 | 104[7] | Zimbabwe |

[22] 1980–83. [23] U.S. dollars. [24] 1970. [25] 1981. [26] 1986. [27] National income. [28] Manufacturing includes mining, construction, public utilities, and transportation and communication. [29] 1968–80. [30] Guernsey and Jersey. [31] Manufacturing includes public utilities. [32] Trade includes public utilities and finance. [33] Manufacturing includes mining, construction, and public utilities. [34] Includes Northern Ireland. [35] 1973. [36] Transactions in convertible currencies only. [37] 1975. [38] 1972.

# Employment and labour

This table provides international comparisons of the world's national labour forces—giving their size; composition by demographic component, employment status, and industry; and overall growth rates.

The first part of the table focuses on the concept of "economically active population," which the International Labour Organisation (ILO) defines as persons of all ages who are either employed or looking for work. In general, "economically active population" does not include students, persons occupied solely in domestic duties, retired persons, persons living entirely on their own means, and persons wholly dependent on others. Persons engaged in illegal economic activities—smugglers, prostitutes, drug dealers, bootleggers, black marketeers, and others—also fall outside the purview of the ILO definition. Countries differ markedly in their treatment, as part of the labour force, of such groups as members of the armed forces, inmates of institutions, persons seeking their first job, seasonal and international migrant workers, and persons engaged in part-time economic activities. Some countries include some or all of these groups among the economically active population, while other countries treat them as inactive.

Three principal breakdowns of the economically active total are given: (1) participation rate, or the proportion of the economically active who possess some particular characteristic, is given for women and for those of working age (ages 15 to 64), (2) activity rate, the proportion of the total population who are economically active, is given for both sexes and as a

total, and (3) employment status, usually (and here) grouped as employers, self-employed, employees, family workers (usually unpaid), and others.

Each of these measures indicates certain characteristics in a given national labour market; none should be interpreted in isolation, however, as each is influenced by a variety of incentives and constraints—demographic structure and change, social or religious customs, educational opportunity, sexual differentiation in employment patterns, degree of technological development, and the like. Participation and activity rates, for example, may be high in a particular country because it possesses an older population with few children, hence a higher proportion of working age, or, because, despite a young population with many below working age, the economy attracts eligible immigrant workers, themselves almost exclusively of working age. At the same time, low activity and participation rates might be characteristic of a country having a young population with poor employment possibilities or of a country with a good job market distorted by the presence of large numbers of "guest" or contract workers who are not part of the domestic labour force. An illiterate woman in a strongly sex-differentiated labour force is likely to begin and end as a family or traditional agricultural worker. Loss of working-age men to war, civil violence, or emigration for job opportunities may also affect the structure of a particular labour market.

The distribution of the economically active population by employment status reveals that a large percentage of economically active persons in

## Employment and labour

| country | year | economically active population | | | | | | | | | | | employed population by economic sector | | | |
|---|---|---|---|---|---|---|---|---|---|---|---|---|---|---|---|---|
| | | total ('000) | participation rate (%) | | activity rate (%) | | | employment status (%) | | | | | agriculture, forestry, fishing | | mining, quarrying | |
| | | | female | ages 15–64 | total | male | female | employers, self-employed | employees | unpaid family workers | other | | number ('000) | % of labour force | number ('000) | % of labour force |
| Afghanistan | 1979 | 3,946 | 7.9 | 49.1 | 30.2 | 54.1 | 4.9 | ... | ... | ... | ... | | 2,369 | 61.3 | 59 | 1.5 |
| Albania[2] | 1983 | 698 | 42.5 | 41.8[3] | 24.6 | 27.2 | 21.8 | ... | ... | ... | ... | | 152 | 21.8 | ... | ... |
| Algeria | 1984[4] | 3,758 | 6.8[5] | 31.0[6,7] | 18.0[5] | 33.8[5] | 2.4[5] | 21.0 | 72.2 | 6.4 | 0.4 | | 857 | 22.8 | [8] | [8] |
| American Samoa | 1980 | 9 | 39.2 | 46.1 | 26.4 | 31.6 | 21.0 | 2.4 | 97.3 | 0.2 | 0.1 | | 0.1 | 1.4 | — | — |
| Andorra | 1986 | 21 | ... | ... | 46.8 | ... | ... | ... | ... | ... | ... | | 0.1 | 0.6 | 0.6 | 2.7 |
| Angola | 1980 | 3,414 | 40.6 | 73.4 | 44.2 | 53.4 | 35.3 | ... | ... | ... | ... | | 2,518 | 73.8 | [8] | [8] |
| Anguilla | 1984 | 2.8 | 40.5 | 73.6 | 41.6 | 50.8 | 32.9 | 17.2 | 56.4 | — | 26.4 | | 0.2 | 8.5 | — | 0.1 |
| Antigua and Barbuda | 1983 | 31 | 39.6 | 56.2[12] | 39.4 | 49.6 | 30.0 | 12.3[13] | 69.9[13] | 0.6[13] | 17.2[13] | | 2.1[7] | 9.07 | 0.1[7] | 0.37 |
| Argentina | 1985 | 11,452 | 26.8 | 59.2 | 37.5 | 55.3 | 19.9 | 25.1[14] | 71.2[14] | 3.3[14] | 0.4[14] | | 1,201[14] | 12.0[14] | 471[14] | 0.5[14] |
| Aruba | 1981 | 26 | 36.7 | 62.0 | 43.2 | 56.1 | 30.9 | ... | ... | ... | ... | | — | 0.2 | — | — |
| Australia | 1985 | 7,217 | 38.5 | 68.9 | 60.2 | 75.2 | 45.7 | 14.7 | 77.0 | 0.4 | 7.9 | | 435 | 6.3 | 107 | 1.5 |
| Austria | 1985 | 3,355 | 39.5 | 65.5 | 44.4 | 56.7 | 33.3 | 10.2 | 85.5 | 4.3 | ... | | 294 | 8.8 | 15 | 0.4 |
| Bahamas, The | 1980 | 87 | 44.5 | 70.5 | 41.6 | 47.4 | 36.0 | 81.4 | 3.4 | 0.5 | 14.8 | | 5 | 5.6 | 0.3 | 0.4 |
| Bahrain | 1984 | 177 | 13.7 | 65.9 | 43.1 | 63.2 | 14.4 | 9.8[15] | 88.7[15] | 0.1[15] | 1.4[15] | | 4 | 2.1 | 5 | 2.9 |
| Bangladesh | 1984 | 28,493 | 8.9 | 49.4 | 29.9 | 53.5 | 5.4 | 38.1 | 44.1 | 15.6 | 2.2 | | 16,448 | 58.8 | 46 | 0.2 |
| Barbados | 1985 | 113 | 46.5 | 73.7[16] | 45.6[16] | 52.2[16] | 39.7[16] | 8.8[7] | 76.4[7] | 0.2[7] | 14.6[7] | | 8 | 8.1 | — | — |
| Belgium | 1984 | 4,214 | 39.2 | 60.6[14] | 42.8 | 53.3 | 32.8 | 11.9 | 71.1 | 3.2 | 13.8 | | 106 | 2.9 | 26 | 0.7 |
| Belize | 1980 | 47 | 22.7 | 63.0 | 32.6 | 49.7 | 15.0 | 27.2[17] | 64.1[17] | 8.7[17] | — | | 15 | 37.1 | — | 0.1 |
| Benin | 1985 | 1,964 | 48.3 | 86.6 | 48.5 | 51.1 | 46.0 | ... | ... | ... | ... | | 1,093[7] | 64.0[7] | [8] | [8] |
| Bermuda | 1985 | 32 | 45.8 | 82.1[14,18] | 56.6 | 62.8 | 50.7 | 7.7[14] | 88.6[14] | 0.5[14] | 3.2[14] | | 0.2 | 0.7 | 0.1 | 0.4 |
| Bhutan | 1982 | 574[14] | 33.6[14] | 69.4[14] | 44.8[14] | 57.8[14] | 31.0[14] | ... | ... | ... | ... | | 613 | 94.3 | [8] | [8] |
| Bolivia | 1985 | 1,996 | 23.4 | 53.2 | 31.1 | 48.1 | 14.4 | 48.9[20] | 38.2[20] | 9.1[20] | 3.8[20] | | 806[17,21] | 47.3[17,21] | 80[17,21] | 4.7[17,21] |
| Botswana | 1985 | 368 | 53.0 | 72.7 | 37.0 | 38.1 | 36.0 | 3.1[15] | 41.0[15] | 45.4[15] | 10.5[15] | | 154[15] | 54.0[15] | 11[15] | 3.9[15] |
| Brazil | 1984 | 52,433 | 33.1 | 49.2[6,14] | 39.5 | 53.0 | 26.1 | 27.0[14] | 65.3[14] | 5.2[14] | 2.5[14] | | 14,974 | 29.8 | 7,998[22] | 15.9[22] |
| British Virgin Islands | 1980 | 5 | 38.5 | 72.8 | 45.4 | 54.6 | 35.8 | 18.5 | 79.7 | 0.8 | 1.0 | | 0.2 | 5.3 | — | — |
| Brunei | 1982 | 71[15] | 23.8[15] | 61.1[15] | 36.7[15] | 52.3[15] | 18.7[15] | 7.4[15] | 88.4[15] | 0.6[15] | 3.6[15] | | 3 | 5.0 | 4 | 5.7 |
| Bulgaria | 1985 | 4,802 | 47.6 | 75.3[24] | 51.0[24] | 54.3[24] | 47.6[24] | ... | 99.2 | ... | 0.8 | | 816 | 17.0 | [8] | [8] |
| Burkina Faso | 1985 | 3,765 | 47.0 | 88.6 | 54.2 | 58.0 | 50.5 | ... | ... | ... | ... | | 2,964[14] | 86.7[14] | [8] | [8] |
| Burma | 1984 | 14,497 | 39.1[14] | 71.0[14] | 45.0[14] | 54.7[14] | 35.2[14] | ... | ... | ... | ... | | 9,590 | 66.2 | 85 | 0.5 |
| Burundi | 1984 | 2,752 | 52.6 | 94.4[25] | 60.9 | 59.5 | 62.2 | 35.7[25] | 5.6[25] | 58.5[25] | 0.2[25] | | 2,246[25] | 93.1[25] | 1.4[25] | 0.1[25] |
| Cameroon | 1982 | 3,543 | 37.5 | 65.6 | 39.9 | 50.0 | 29.8 | 60.2 | 14.6 | 18.0 | 7.1 | | 2,595 | 76.7 | 2 | 0.1 |
| Canada | 1985 | 12,639 | 42.6 | 65.2[26] | 49.8 | 57.9 | 42.0 | 9.0 | 89.4 | 0.8 | 0.8 | | 659 | 5.3 | 210 | 1.7 |
| Cape Verde | 1985 | 121 | 28.9 | 60.0 | 37.1 | 54.4 | 17.7 | ... | ... | ... | ... | | 53[14] | 52.0[14] | [8] | [8] |
| Cayman Islands | 1979 | 8 | 42.0 | ... | 48.7 | 58.1 | 39.8 | 10.6 | 80.7 | — | 8.7 | | 0.1 | 1.7 | — | — |
| Central African Republic | 1985 | 1,282 | 47.0 | 81.6 | 49.8 | 54.5 | 45.3 | ... | ... | ... | ... | | 543[24] | 83.7[24] | 7[24] | 1.0[24] |
| Chad | 1985 | 1,790 | 21.7 | 57.4 | 35.7 | 56.7 | 15.3 | ... | ... | ... | ... | | 1,361 | 83.3 | [8] | [8] |
| Chile | 1984 | 3,890 | 30.7 | 52.9 | 33.0 | 46.8 | 19.9 | 23.6 | 51.5 | 10.9 | 13.9 | | 567 | 15.1 | 71 | 1.9 |
| China | 1986 | 513,625[7] | 44.1[7] | 83.2[7] | 51.2[7] | 55.7[7] | 46.4[7] | 0.9 | 24.8 | —73.4— | | | 311,870 | 62.5 | 1,060 | 0.2 |
| Christmas Island | 1981 | 1.6 | 9.8 | 76.4 | 56.3 | 76.0 | 16.6 | ... | ... | ... | ... | | — | 0.1 | 1.1 | 68.2 |
| Cocos (Keeling) Islands | 1981 | 0.3 | 29.6 | 69.4 | 50.5 | 63.8 | 31.1 | ... | ... | ... | ... | | 0.1 | 21.8 | — | — |
| Colombia | 1985 | 9,558 | 32.8 | 49.4[27] | 34.3 | 46.6 | 22.3 | ... | ... | ... | ... | | 2,412[14] | 28.5[14] | 50[14] | 0.6[14] |
| Comoros | 1985 | 117 | 26.2 | 53.1 | 29.6 | 43.5 | 15.6 | 47.6[14] | 25.6[14] | —26.8[14]— | | | 53[14] | 53.3[14] | 0.1[14] | 0.1[14] |
| Congo | 1985 | 710 | 39.3 | 69.4 | 40.8 | 50.2 | 31.6 | ... | ... | ... | ... | | 405[14] | 62.5[14] | [8] | [8] |
| Cook Islands | 1981 | 6 | 30.3 | 63.1 | 33.7 | 45.6 | 21.1 | 11.0 | 65.7 | 3.7 | 19.6 | | 2 | 29.2 | — | 0.3 |
| Costa Rica | 1985 | 887 | 26.1 | 55.8[29] | 35.7 | 53.2 | 18.5 | 20.0 | 69.1 | 4.1 | 6.8 | | 249[17] | 31.4[17] | 1.5[17] | 0.2[17] |
| Côte d'Ivoire | 1985 | 4,053 | 34.7 | 71.4 | 41.3 | 52.8 | 29.3 | ... | ... | ... | ... | | 2,792 | 70.9 | [8] | [8] |
| Cuba | 1985 | 3,618[15] | 31.5[15] | 58.5[15] | 37.2[15] | 50.5[15] | 23.7[15] | 9.9[13] | 88.2[13] | 1.3[13] | 0.6[13] | | 581[2] | 18.3[2] | 709[2,22] | 22.3[2,22] |
| Cyprus | 1984 | 248 | 36.9 | 67.2[14] | 37.0 | 47.1 | 27.1 | 21.1[7] | 56.0[7] | 10.8[7] | 12.1[7] | | 43 | 18.1 | 1.1 | 0.5 |
| Czechoslovakia | 1985 | 7,649 | 46.1 | 78.9[14] | 49.3 | 54.6 | 44.3 | 0.1[14] | 91.2[14] | 8.5[14] | 0.2[14] | | 1,040 | 13.7 | 191 | 2.5 |
| Denmark | 1985 | 2,753 | 45.6 | 79.6 | 53.9 | 59.4 | 48.6 | 9.3 | 87.9 | 2.3 | 0.5 | | 176 | 6.4 | 5 | 0.2 |
| Djibouti | 1982[21] | ... | ... | ... | ... | ... | ... | ... | ... | ... | ... | | 0.1 | 0.4 | — | — |
| Dominica | 1981 | 25 | 34.1 | 61.7 | 34.3 | 45.4 | 23.3 | 29.4 | 49.8 | 1.9 | 18.9 | | 7.8 | 38.1 | — | — |
| Dominican Republic | 1981 | 1,915 | 28.9 | 53.6 | 33.9 | 48.1 | 19.7 | 36.5 | 51.3 | 3.3 | 8.9 | | 420 | 21.4 | 5 | 0.3 |
| Ecuador | 1982 | 2,346 | 20.6 | 49.6 | 29.1 | 46.3 | 12.0 | 37.3 | 47.6 | 5.8 | 9.3 | | 787 | 34.8 | 7 | 0.3 |
| Egypt | 1984 | 11,133 | 7.0 | 41.9 | 24.5 | 44.8 | 3.5 | 26.0[16] | 51.5[16] | 16.0[16] | 6.6[16] | | 4,348 | 41.2 | 40 | 0.4 |

some less developed countries falls under the heading "employers, self-employed." This occurs because the countries involved have poor, largely agrarian economies in which the average worker is a farmer who tills his own small plot of land. In countries with well-developed economies, "employees" will usually constitute the largest portion of the economically active.

Caution should be exercised when using the economically active data to make intercountry comparisons, as countries often differ in their choices of classification schemes, definitions, and coverage of groups and in their methods of collection and tabulation of data. Data on female labour-force activity, in particular, often lacks comparability. In many less developed countries, particularly those dominated by the Islamic faith, a cultural bias favouring traditional roles for women results in the undercounting of economically active females.

The next major section of the table provides data on the distribution by industrial sector of the "employed population," which consists of all persons above a specific age who, during a specified period, were either at work or formally attached to a job. Whenever possible the "employed population" has been taken to be the actively working fraction of the labour force, *i.e.,* excluding those who are unemployed or under- and fractionally (or seasonally) employed. The data usually include such groups as unpaid family workers and members of the armed forces and usually exclude such groups as the unemployed and the severely underemployed.

The table's categorization of industrial sectors is based largely on the divisions listed in the International Standard Industrial Classification of All Economic Activities. The category "services, other" includes such activities as public administration and defense, educational services, medical and dental services, motion-picture and other entertainment services, domestic services, and activities not adequately defined.

Finally, regarding the section on labour-force growth, it should be recognized that for many economies changes in age and sex structure, in patterns and volume of unemployment and underemployment, in international and internal migration, or in technological development may significantly alter the projections.

A substantial part of the data presented in this table is summarized from various issues of the ILO's *Yearbook of Labour Statistics.* The ILO compiles its statistics both from official publications and from information submitted directly by national authorities. The editors have supplemented and updated ILO data with statistical information from Britannica's statistical holdings of official publications and from direct correspondence with, relevant authorities. The *World Development Report,* published annually by the World Bank, furnishes the data for the table's last section, "average annual growth of labour force."

| manufacturing, construction | | electricity, gas, water | | transportation, communications | | trade, hotels, restaurants | | finance, real estate | | services, other | | avg. annual growth of labour force | | | country |
|---|---|---|---|---|---|---|---|---|---|---|---|---|---|---|---|
| number ('000) | % of labour force | number ('000) | % of labour force | number ('000) | % of labour force | number ('000) | % of labour force | number ('000) | % of labour force | number ('000) | % of labour force | 1965– 1980 (%) | 1980– 1985 (%) | 1985– 2000 (%) | |
| 474 | 12.3 | 11 | 0.3 | 66 | 1.7 | 138 | 3.6 | 1 | 1 | 749[1] | 19.3[1] | 1.7 | ... | ... | Afghanistan |
| 333 | 47.8 | ... | ... | 33 | 4.8 | 54 | 7.7 | ... | ... | 125 | 17.9 | 2.8 | 2.9 | 2.4 | Albania[2] |
| 1,234[8] | 32.8[8] | 8 | 8 | 240 | 6.4 | 373 | 9.9 | 1 | 1 | 1,055[1] | 28.1[1] | 2.2 | 3.6 | 3.7 | Algeria |
| 2.5 | 31.1 | 9 | 9 | 0.7[9] | 8.7[9] | 0.9 | 11.5 | 0.2 | 2.6 | 3.6 | 44.7 | ... | ... | ... | American Samoa |
| 2.7 | 12.7 | 1.3 | 5.9 | 1.8 | 8.5 | 5.8[10] | 26.9[10] | 1.3 | 6.0 | 7.9[10] | 36.7[10] | ... | ... | ... | Andorra |
| 326[8] | 9.6[8] | 8 | 8 | 11 | 11 | 11 | 11 | 11 | 11 | 569[11] | 16.7[11] | 2.2 | 1.7 | 2.1 | Angola |
| 0.5 | 25.0 | — | 0.5 | 0.2 | 7.9 | 0.4 | 19.7 | 1 | 1 | 0.8[1] | 38.3[1] | ... | ... | ... | Anguilla |
| 4.3[7] | 18.5[7] | 0.3[7] | 1.5[7] | 2.6[7] | 11.1[7] | 5.2[7] | 22.4[7] | 0.8[7] | 3.3[7] | 7.9[7] | 33.9[7] | ... | ... | ... | Antigua and Barbuda |
| 2,989[14] | 30.0[14] | 103[14] | 1.0[14] | 460[14] | 4.6[14] | 1,702[14] | 17.0[14] | 396[14] | 4.0[14] | 3,090[14] | 30.9[14] | 1.1 | 1.1 | 1.5 | Argentina |
| 3.9 | 16.6 | 0.5 | 2.1 | 1.3 | 5.4 | 7.7 | 32.7 | 1.0 | 4.4 | 9.1 | 38.6 | ... | ... | ... | Aruba |
| 1,673 | 24.1 | 141 | 2.0 | 541 | 7.8 | 1,389 | 20.0 | 680 | 9.8 | 1,982 | 28.5 | 2.4 | 1.8 | 1.3 | Australia |
| 1,237 | 36.9 | 42 | 1.3 | 212 | 6.3 | 606 | 18.1 | 182 | 5.4 | 767 | 22.9 | 0.2 | 0.8 | 0.1 | Austria |
| 12 | 14.4 | 1.3 | 1.6 | 6 | 7.7 | 24 | 30.3 | 6 | 8.0 | 26 | 32.0 | ... | ... | ... | Bahamas, The |
| 52 | 29.9 | 3 | 1.9 | 16 | 9.2 | 24 | 13.5 | 7 | 3.8 | 64 | 36.7 | ... | ... | ... | Bahrain |
| 2,970 | 10.6 | 64 | 0.2 | 1,088 | 3.9 | 3,255 | 11.6 | 136 | 0.5 | 3,965 | 14.2 | 1.9 | 2.8 | 3.0 | Bangladesh |
| 19 | 20.8 | 2 | 2.4 | 5 | 5.6 | 20 | 22.1 | 3 | 3.4 | 35 | 37.6 | ... | 0.3 | ... | Barbados |
| 1,025 | 27.9 | 33 | 0.9 | 263 | 7.2 | 697 | 19.0 | 271 | 7.4 | 1,248 | 34.0 | 0.7 | 0.7 | 0.1 | Belgium |
| 6 | 14.9 | 0.6 | 1.5 | 2 | 4.3 | 6 | 14.2 | 0.4 | 0.9 | 11 | 27.0 | ... | ... | ... | Belize |
| 172[7,8] | 10.1[7,8] | 8 | 8 | 11 | 11 | 11 | 11 | 11 | 11 | 442[7,11] | 25.9[7,11] | 1.9 | 2.0 | 2.5 | Benin |
| 3.6 | 11.0 | 0.4 | 1.3 | 2.2 | 6.8 | 11 | 34.2 | 4 | 13.6 | 10 | 32.0 | ... | ... | ... | Bermuda |
| 6[8] | 0.9[8] | 8 | 8 | 19 | 19 | 9 | 1.4 | 19 | 19 | 22[19] | 3.4[19] | 1.8 | 1.9 | 1.9 | Bhutan |
| 198[17,21] | 11.6[17,21] | 8[17,21] | 0.5[17,21] | 95[17,21] | 5.6[17,21] | 126[17,21] | 7.4[17,21] | 15[17,21] | 0.9[17,21] | 378[17,21] | 22.0[17,21] | 2.0 | 2.7 | 2.7 | Bolivia |
| 22[15] | 7.6[15] | 2[15] | 0.8[15] | 3[15] | 1.1[15] | 12[15] | 4.3[15] | 1[15] | 0.5[15] | 79[15] | 27.7[15] | 2.4 | 3.5 | 3.4 | Botswana |
| 2,926[23] | 5.8[23] | 22 | 22 | 1,818 | 3.6 | 5,354 | 10.7 | 1 | 1 | 17,138[1] | 34.2[1] | 3.3 | 2.3 | 2.1 | Brazil |
| 0.3 | 6.2 | 0.6 | 12.0 | 0.1 | 2.8 | 0.4 | 8.1 | 0.3 | 5.8 | 1.1 | 22.7 | ... | ... | ... | British Virgin Islands |
| 15 | 22.6 | 2 | 2.9 | 4 | 6.6 | 7 | 10.8 | 2 | 3.0 | 29 | 43.4 | ... | ... | ... | Brunei |
| 2,154[8] | 44.9[8] | 8 | 8 | 326 | 6.8 | 397 | 8.3 | 1 | 1 | 1,108[1] | 23.1[1] | 0.2 | 0.0 | 0.2 | Bulgaria |
| 146[8,14] | 4.3[8,14] | 8 | 8 | 11 | 11 | 11 | 11 | 11 | 11 | 310[11,14] | 9.1[11,14] | 1.6 | 1.9 | 2.2 | Burkina Faso |
| 1,423 | 9.8 | 16 | 0.1 | 480 | 3.3 | 1,413 | 9.7 | 872 | 6.0 | 618 | 4.4 | 2.2 | 1.9 | 1.8 | Burma |
| 51[25] | 2.1[25] | 1.7[25] | 0.1[25] | 6[25] | 0.3[25] | 21[25] | 0.9[25] | 1.3[25] | 0.1[25] | 84[25] | 3.5[25] | 1.2 | 2.0 | 2.4 | Burundi |
| 222 | 6.6 | 3 | 0.1 | 47 | 1.4 | 141 | 4.2 | 8 | 0.2 | 363 | 10.7 | 1.7 | 1.8 | 2.2 | Cameroon |
| 2,936 | 23.4 | 131 | 1.0 | 821 | 6.6 | 2,196 | 17.5 | 1,219 | 9.7 | 4,359 | 34.8 | 3.2 | 1.4 | 0.9 | Canada |
| 23[8,14] | 22.5[8,14] | 8 | 8 | 11 | 11 | 11 | 11 | 11 | 11 | 26[11,14] | 25.5[11,14] | ... | ... | ... | Cape Verde |
| 2 | 23.4 | 0.1 | 1.8 | 0.2 | 3.1 | 0.7 | 9.6 | 0.5 | 7.2 | 4 | 53.2 | ... | ... | ... | Cayman Islands |
| 18[24] | 2.8[24] | 1[24] | 0.2[24] | 5[24] | 0.8[24] | 27[24] | 4.1[24] | 0.6[24] | 0.1[24] | 47[24] | 7.3[24] | 1.2 | 1.3 | 1.8 | Central African Republic |
| 76[8,14] | 4.7[8,14] | 8 | 8 | 11 | 11 | 11 | 11 | 11 | 11 | 197[11,14] | 12.1[11,14] | 1.6 | 1.8 | 2.1 | Chad |
| 714 | 18.9 | 29 | 0.8 | 236 | 6.3 | 698 | 18.5 | 124 | 3.3 | 1,330 | 35.3 | 2.2 | 2.6 | 1.7 | Chile |
| 104,180 | 20.9 | 4,370 | 0.9 | 12,220 | 2.5 | 23,630 | 4.7 | 1,380 | 0.3 | 40,020 | 8.0 | 2.4 | 2.5 | 1.4 | China |
| 0.1 | 3.4 | — | 0.6 | 0.1 | 4.5 | 0.1 | 4.1 | | 1.5 | 0.3 | 17.1 | ... | ... | ... | Christmas Island |
| 0.1 | 25.7 | | 2.1 | | 5.3 | | 4.6 | | 0.2 | 0.2 | 40.3 | ... | ... | ... | Cocos (Keeling) Islands |
| 1,379[14] | 16.3[14] | 44[14] | 0.5[14] | 353[14] | 4.2[14] | 1,540[14,28] | 18.1[14,28] | 28 | 28 | 2,689[14] | 31.8[14] | 2.6 | 2.8 | 2.3 | Colombia |
| 7[14] | 7.3[14] | 0.1[14] | 0.1[14] | 2[14] | 2.1[14] | 2[14] | 1.9[14] | 0.2[14] | 0.2[14] | 35[14] | 35.0[14] | ... | ... | ... | Comoros |
| 77[8,14] | 11.9[8,14] | 8 | 8 | 11 | 11 | 11 | 11 | 11 | 11 | 166[11,14] | 25.6[11,14] | 2.0 | 1.8 | 2.2 | Congo |
| 0.7 | 12.1 | 0.1 | 2.4 | 0.7 | 12.3 | 0.5 | 9.2 | 0.1 | 2.3 | 2 | 31.4 | ... | ... | ... | Cook Islands |
| 148[17] | 18.6[17] | 9[17] | 1.1[17] | 20[17] | 2.6[17] | 88[17] | 11.0[17] | 20[17] | 2.6[17] | 258[17] | 32.5[17] | 3.8 | 3.1 | 2.4 | Costa Rica |
| 347[8] | 8.8[8] | 8 | 8 | 11 | 11 | 11 | 11 | 11 | 11 | 799[11] | 20.3[11] | 2.7 | 2.6 | 2.6 | Côte d'Ivoire |
| 315[2,23] | 9.9[2,23] | 22 | 22 | 216[2] | 6.8[2] | 367[2] | 11.6[2] | 19[2] | 0.7[2] | 801[2] | 25.3[2] | 2.3 | 2.3 | 1.7 | Cuba |
| 66 | 27.8 | 1.5 | 0.6 | 12 | 4.8 | 41 | 17.1 | 9 | 3.6 | 65 | 27.5 | ... | ... | ... | Cyprus |
| 3,214 | 42.3 | 70 | 0.9 | 507 | 6.7 | 858 | 11.3 | 284 | 3.7 | 1,442 | 18.9 | 0.9 | 0.4 | 0.7 | Czechoslovakia |
| 739 | 27.0 | 19 | 0.7 | 188 | 6.9 | 419 | 15.3 | 199 | 7.3 | 993 | 36.2 | 1.2 | 0.6 | 0.2 | Denmark |
| 3 | 18.8 | 0.5 | 2.9 | 3 | 17.0 | 3 | 19.5 | 1.3 | 8.0 | 5 | 33.5 | ... | ... | ... | Djibouti |
| 3.7 | 18.1 | 0.2 | 1.2 | 0.9 | 4.4 | 1.6 | 7.8 | 0.3 | 1.2 | 6.0 | 29.1 | ... | ... | ... | Dominica |
| 305 | 17.1 | 14 | 0.8 | 40 | 2.3 | 192 | 10.8 | 22 | 1.3 | 785 | 44.0 | 2.8 | 3.5 | 2.9 | Dominican Republic |
| 445 | 19.6 | 13 | 0.6 | 101 | 4.5 | 272 | 12.0 | 44 | 1.9 | 594 | 26.2 | 2.7 | 3.1 | 2.9 | Ecuador |
| 2,292 | 21.7 | 77 | 0.7 | 616 | 5.8 | 954 | 9.0 | 123 | 1.2 | 2,099 | 20.0 | 2.2 | 2.6 | 2.7 | Egypt |

## Employment and labour (continued)

| country | year | economically active population | | | | | | | | | | employed population by economic sector | | | |
| --- | --- | --- | --- | --- | --- | --- | --- | --- | --- | --- | --- | --- | --- | --- | --- |
| | | total ('000) | participation rate (%) | | activity rate (%) | | | employment status (%) | | | | agriculture, forestry, fishing | | mining, quarrying | |
| | | | female | ages 15–64 | total | male | female | employers, self-employed | employees | unpaid family workers | other | number ('000) | % of labour force | number ('000) | % of labour force |
| El Salvador | 1980 | 1,593 | 34.8 | 62.4 | 35.4 | 47.5 | 24.0 | 28.2 | 59.2 | 10.9 | 1.7 | 637 | 40.6 | 4 | 0.3 |
| Equatorial Guinea | 1980 | 159 | 40.9 | 72.2 | 45.2 | 54.1 | 36.1 | ... | ... | ... | ... | 104 | 65.8 | [8] | [8] |
| Ethiopia | 1984 | 18,492 | 39.2 | 74.3 | 43.9 | 53.5 | 34.3 | ... | ... | ... | ... | ... | ... | ... | ... |
| Faeroe Islands | 1977 | 18 | 27.2 | 64.2[30] | 41.9 | 58.2 | 23.9 | 11.1 | 86.3 | ... | 2.6 | 3 | 18.8 | 0.1 | 0.6 |
| Falkland Islands | 1980 | 0.95 | 22.5 | 70.3[26] | 52.5 | 74.3 | 26.1 | ... | ... | ... | ... | ... | ... | ... | ... |
| Fiji | 1986 | 241 | 21.2 | 54.6[26] | 33.7 | 52.4 | 14.5 | 33.6 | 42.2 | 16.3 | 7.9 | 106 | 48.0 | 1 | 0.6 |
| Finland | 1985 | 2,630 | 47.5 | 78.0 | 53.6 | 58.2 | 49.3 | 12.6 | 84.0 | 1.4 | 2.0 | 295 | 11.3 | [8] | [8] |
| France | 1984 | 23,880 | 40.9 | 65.1 | 43.5 | 52.7 | 34.8 | 14.3 | 75.9 | ... | 9.8 | 1,659 | 7.8 | 122 | 0.6 |
| French Guiana | 1982 | 31 | 37.2 | 67.2 | 42.7 | 51.0 | 33.5 | 14.9 | 61.5 | 3.0 | 20.6 | 4 | 13.4 | 0.2 | 0.6 |
| French Polynesia | 1983 | 58[31] | 31.6[31] | 66.0[31,32] | 34.7[31] | 45.5[31] | 22.9[31] | 19.7[33] | 76.3[33] | 3.4[33] | 0.6[33] | 8 | 13.9 | — | ... |
| Gabon | 1985 | 518 | 38.4 | 68.2 | 45.0 | 56.4 | 34.0 | ... | ... | ... | ... | 379[14] | 75.5[14] | [8] | [8] |
| Gambia, The | 1983 | 326 | 46.3 | 78.2 | 47.3 | 51.1 | 43.6 | ... | ... | ... | ... | 240 | 73.7 | 0.1 | — |
| Gaza Strip | 1985 | 92.0 | 4.6 | 33.0[34] | 17.5 | ... | ... | ... | ... | ... | ... | ... | ... | ... | ... |
| Germany, East | 1985 | 8,539 | 49.3 | ... | 51.3 | 55.0 | 48.0 | ... | ... | ... | ... | 922 | 10.8 | [8] | [8] |
| Germany, West | 1985 | 29,012 | 39.4 | 67.1 | 47.6 | 60.3 | 35.9 | 8.8 | 87.2 | 3.1 | 0.9 | 1,416 | 5.2 | 329 | 1.2 |
| Ghana | 1985 | 4,963 | 40.6 | 68.1 | 36.5 | 43.8 | 29.4 | ... | ... | ... | ... | 2,143[17] | 45.0[17] | [8] | [8] |
| Gibraltar | 1985 | 12 | 29.7 | 67.4[15] | 42.2 | 58.2 | 25.6 | 5.9[15] | 93.8[15] | ... | 0.3[15] | — | — | — | — |
| Greece | 1984 | 3,868 | 34.6 | 57.4 | 39.1 | 52.0 | 26.6 | 32.9 | 45.1 | 13.9 | 8.1 | 1,047 | 27.9 | 27 | 0.7 |
| Greenland | 1976 | 21 | 33.4 | ... | 43.1 | 53.0 | 31.4 | 12.6 | 82.5 | 0.4 | 4.5 | 3 | 15.1 | 0.3 | 1.5 |
| Grenada | 1984 | 46 | ... | ... | 48.2 | ... | ... | 21.3[15] | 77.7[15] | 1.0[15] | — | 8.0[15] | 28.7[15] | 0.1[15] | 0.3[15] |
| Guadeloupe | 1982 | 124 | 42.5 | 63.7 | 37.9 | 44.5 | 31.6 | ... | ... | ... | ... | 13 | 14.1 | 7[35] | 7.2[35] |
| Guam | 1980 | 44 | 34.8 | 66.6[12] | 42.0 | 52.4 | 30.6 | 2.3 | 96.6 | 0.1 | 1.0 | 0.3 | 0.7 | — | — |
| Guatemala | 1981 | 1,696 | 14.6 | 49.1 | 28.0 | 48.0 | 8.1 | 42.5 | 47.2 | 6.8 | 3.5 | 909 | 53.9 | 2 | 0.1 |
| Guernsey | 1976 | 26 | ... | ... | 47.7 | 62.4 | 34.0 | 17.9 | 82.1 | — | — | 5 | 17.7 | 0.2 | 0.8 |
| Guinea | 1980 | 2,626 | 41.7 | 77.9 | 48.6 | 57.3 | 40.0 | ... | ... | ... | ... | 2,119 | 80.6 | [8] | [8] |
| Guinea-Bissau | 1979 | 213 | 3.6 | 41.0 | 38.7 | 78.4 | 2.6 | ... | ... | ... | ... | 153 | 71.9 | 0.1 | — |
| Guyana | 1980[36] | 239 | 24.7 | 57.3 | 31.5 | 47.9 | 15.5 | 19.8[13] | 77.6[13] | 2.1[13] | 0.5[13] | 49 | 25.0 | 9 | 4.8 |
| Haiti | 1983 | 2,264 | 42.9 | 69.1 | 44.2 | 52.1 | 36.9 | 59.3 | 16.6 | 10.5 | 13.6 | 1,299 | 65.4 | 20 | 1.0 |
| Honduras | 1984 | 1,256 | 16.7 | 53.6 | 29.7 | 49.3 | 9.9 | ... | ... | ... | ... | 719 | 57.2 | 4 | 0.3 |
| Hong Kong | 1985 | 2,637 | 36.3 | 70.6 | 50.0 | 61.9 | 37.4 | 10.0 | 84.5 | 1.9 | 3.6 | 45 | 1.7 | 0.3 | — |
| Hungary | 1986 | 4,877 | 45.9 | 72.5[14] | 45.8 | 51.3 | 40.7 | 3.2[37] | 80.2[37] | 2.5[37] | 14.1[37] | 1,113[37] | 22.7[37] | [8] | [8] |
| Iceland | 1984 | 117 | 31.5[16] | 79.1[3] | 48.7 | 60.6[3] | 44.5[3] | ... | ... | ... | ... | 24 | 20.3 | ... | ... |
| India | 1981[38] | 244,605 | 26.0 | 57.4[26] | 36.8 | 52.7 | 19.8 | 10.0[39] | 17.1[39] | 3.3[39] | 69.6[39] | 153,015 | 62.6 | 1,264 | 0.5 |
| Indonesia | 1982 | 59,599 | 36.1 | 64.6 | 35.5[14] | 48.0[14] | 23.2[14] | 20.6 | 53.9 | 22.5 | 3.0 | 31,593 | 54.7 | 391 | 0.7 |
| Iran | 1976 | 9,796 | 14.8 | 50.2 | 29.1 | 48.1 | 8.9 | 30.5 | 48.4 | 10.4 | 10.6 | 3,615 | 38.1 | 90 | 0.9 |
| Iraq | 1985 | 4,259 | 19.9 | 50.2 | 26.8 | 42.1 | 10.9 | 25.4[33] | 59.5[33] | 11.4[33] | 3.7[33] | 1,122[17] | 29.9[17] | 47[17] | 1.3[17] |
| Ireland | 1984 | 1,314 | 29.4 | 60.4 | 37.2 | 52.3 | 21.9 | 18.4 | 72.2 | 2.6 | 6.8 | 186 | 14.5 | 11 | 0.9 |
| Isle of Man | 1981 | 28 | 38.2 | 67.7 | 42.6 | 55.1 | 31.2 | 14.0 | 79.8 | — | 6.2 | 1.4 | 5.5 | 3.5[35] | 13.4[35] |
| Israel | 1985 | 1,467 | 38.1 | 61.2[40] | 34.4 | 42.6 | 26.2 | 18.2 | 73.8 | 1.3 | 6.7 | 80 | 5.6 | 326[35] | 23.0[35] |
| Italy | 1985 | 23,364 | 35.3 | 58.2[30] | 41.1 | 54.6 | 28.2 | 21.3 | 63.4 | 4.7 | 10.6 | 2,296 | 11.0 | 209 | 1.0 |
| Jamaica | 1984 | 971 | 46.6 | 72.2[30] | 42.6 | 49.6 | 40.4 | 31.2[13] | 67.1[13] | 1.7[13] | — | 237 | 32.7 | 7 | 0.9 |
| Japan | 1985 | 59,630 | 39.7 | 68.8 | 49.4 | 60.5 | 38.6 | 15.4 | 72.3 | 9.4 | 2.9 | 5,090 | 8.8 | 90 | 0.2 |
| Jersey | 1981 | 37 | 40.7 | ... | 51.2 | 63.5 | 40.0 | 13.4 | 86.6 | — | — | 2 | 5.9 | 0.2 | 0.6 |
| Jordan | 1984 | 552 | 11.1 | 42.2 | 21.3 | 36.1 | 5.0 | 22.8[25] | 67.2[25] | 0.8[25] | 9.2[25] | 22 | 4.3 | 7 | 1.3 |
| Kampuchea | 1962 | 2,500 | 42.0 | 74.4 | 43.6 | 50.6 | 36.7 | 36.4 | 12.2 | 50.0 | 1.4 | 2,008 | 80.2 | 2 | 0.1 |
| Kenya | 1985 | 8,389 | 40.9 | 76.2 | 40.7 | 48.4 | 33.2 | ... | ... | ... | ... | 241[21] | 20.5[21] | 5[21] | 0.4[21] |
| Kiribati | 1985 | 26 | 36.1 | 67.8[26] | 41.2 | 53.1 | 29.5 | 71.0 | 26.5 | ... | 2.5 | 0.5 | 6.9 | ... | 0.2 |
| Korea, North | 1985 | 9,084 | 46.0 | 75.3 | 44.6 | 48.6 | 40.6 | ... | ... | ... | ... | 3,355[14] | 42.8[14] | [8] | [8] |
| Korea, South | 1985 | 15,554 | 38.4 | 56.7 | 37.9 | 46.3 | 29.3 | 30.0 | 52.0 | 14.0 | 4.0 | 3,722 | 24.9 | 154 | 1.0 |
| Kuwait | 1985 | 670 | 19.7 | 62.5[26] | 39.5 | 55.8 | 18.1 | 10.0[14] | 88.4[14] | 0.1[14] | 1.5[14] | 13 | 1.9 | 7 | 1.1 |
| Laos | 1980 | 1,839 | 46.2 | 86.4 | 49.9 | 53.3 | 46.5 | ... | ... | ... | ... | 1,393 | 75.7 | [8] | [8] |
| Lebanon | 1984 | 702 | 25.6 | 46.2 | 26.5 | 40.9 | 13.2 | ... | ... | ... | ... | 238[7] | 20.7[7] | 223[7,35] | 19.4[7,35] |
| Lesotho | 1976 | 424 | 32.3 | 56.1 | 34.8 | 48.9 | 21.7 | 7.5 | 50.0 | 36.8 | 5.7 | 99 | 23.3 | 129 | 30.5 |
| Liberia | 1984 | 669 | 31.4[15] | 62.9[41] | 31.8 | ... | ... | ... | ... | ... | ... | 481 | 71.9 | 18 | 2.6 |
| Libya | 1985 | 1,062 | 7.3[14] | 50.9[14] | 24.1[42] | 42.3[42] | 3.5[42] | 23.7[42] | 69.6[42] | 4.2[42] | 2.6[42] | 178 | 16.8 | 25 | 2.3 |
| Liechtenstein | 1986 | 13 | 35.6 | 67.6 | 47.9 | 63.0 | 33.4 | 9.0[14] | 87.2[14] | 3.8[14] | ... | 0.4 | 2.8 | 0.1 | 0.4 |
| Luxembourg | 1985 | 164 | 33.3[15] | 61.3[15] | 42.2[15] | 57.7[15] | 27.4[15] | 9.4[15] | 85.1[15] | 3.5[15] | 2.0[15] | 7 | 4.3 | 0.2 | 0.1 |
| Macau | 1981 | 127 | 37.1 | 61.5[6] | 48.6 | ... | ... | 9.9 | 86.4 | 3.5 | 0.2 | 0.6 | 0.1 | 0.1 | 0.1 |
| Madagascar | 1985 | 4,510 | 40.4 | 74.9 | 45.1 | 54.2 | 36.1 | ... | ... | ... | ... | 3,314[14] | 80.9[14] | [8] | [8] |
| Malawi | 1985 | 3,074 | 42.6 | 74.3 | 44.3 | 51.9 | 36.9 | 79.9[33] | 17.8[33] | 0.3[33] | 2.0[33] | 178[21] | 46.7[21] | 0.3[21] | 0.1[21] |
| Malaysia | 1980 | 4,924 | 33.7 | 62.1 | 37.5 | 49.6 | 25.3 | 28.7 | 54.3 | 10.2 | 6.7 | 1,855 | 40.4 | 47 | 1.0 |
| Maldives | 1985 | 79 | 37.2[33] | 78.3[33] | 43.6 | 56.2[33] | 37.1[33] | 86.4[33] | 13.4[33] | ... | 0.2[33] | 36 | 45.5 | — | — |
| Mali | 1976 | 2,266 | 17.0 | 52.3 | 35.4 | 60.2 | 11.8 | 45.8 | 4.1 | 42.5 | 7.5 | 1,862 | 84.9 | 8 | 0.4 |
| Malta | 1985 | 123 | 24.3 | 52.2[14] | 36.7 | 57.0 | 17.4 | 14.1[16] | 77.4[16] | ... | 8.5[16] | 5 | 4.8 | 1.5 | 1.3 |
| Martinique | 1982 | 131 | 44.7 | 62.6 | 39.9 | 45.6 | 34.6 | 12.3 | 57.4 | 0.3 | 30.0 | 10 | 10.4 | 2 | 2.0 |
| Mauritania | 1985 | 590 | 21.0 | 55.7 | 31.2 | 49.8 | 13.0 | ... | ... | ... | ... | 358[14] | 69.4[14] | [8] | [8] |
| Mauritius | 1986 | 367[17] | 25.8[17] | 59.0[17] | 37.6[17] | 55.8[17] | 19.4[17] | 10.3[7] | 73.7[7] | 0.9[7] | 15.1[7] | 52[21] | 21.8[21] | 0.2[21] | 0.1[21] |
| Mayotte | 1978 | 15.1 | 35.9 | 65.7 | 31.9 | 41.0 | 22.9 | 51.0 | 27.9 | 21.0 | — | 9.3 | 65.4 | — | 0.1 |
| Mexico | 1980 | 22,066 | 27.8 | 57.1 | 33.0 | 48.2 | 18.2 | 27.0 | 44.3 | 6.6 | 22.1 | 5,700 | 26.0 | 477 | 2.2 |
| Monaco | 1975 | ... | ... | ... | ... | ... | ... | ... | ... | ... | ... | — | 0.2 | — | 0.1 |
| Mongolia | 1985 | 671 | ... | ... | ... | ... | ... | ... | ... | ... | ... | 321 | 47.8 | [43] | [43] |
| Montserrat | 1980 | 5.1 | 41.6 | 74.1 | 44.0 | 53.4 | 35.3 | 20.4[13] | 78.0[13] | 1.6[13] | — | 0.5 | 9.3 | — | 0.2 |
| Morocco | 1982 | 5,999 | 19.7 | 49.7 | 29.6 | 47.9 | 11.6 | 27.1 | 40.5 | 17.6 | 14.8 | 2,352 | 43.1 | 63 | 1.2 |
| Mozambique | 1980 | 5,671 | 52.4 | 87.3[26] | 35.8[13] | 53.4[13] | 18.7[13] | 44.4[13] | 40.0[13] | 14.5[13] | 1.1[13] | 4,755 | 85.3 | 347[35] | 6.2[35] |
| Nauru | 1977 | 2.2 | ... | ... | 30.5 | ... | ... | ... | ... | ... | ... | ... | ... | ... | ... |
| Nepal | 1986 | 7,760 | 34.7 | 82.5 | 45.5 | 57.8 | 32.5 | 86.2[15] | 9.1[15] | 2.5[15] | 2.2[15] | 6,244[15] | 91.1[15] | 1.0[15] | — |
| Netherlands, The | 1986 | 6,022 | 35.6 | 60.1 | 41.2[17] | 54.2[17] | 28.5[17] | 7.8[37] | 77.4[37] | 2.0[37] | 12.8[37] | 268[37] | 5.2[37] | 11[37] | 0.2[37] |
| Netherlands Antilles[44] | 1983 | 104 | 39.2 | 63.7 | 42.0 | 52.5 | 32.1 | ... | ... | ... | ... | 0.4 | 0.4 | 0.2 | 0.2 |
| New Caledonia | 1983 | 45 | 37.6 | 63.6 | 30.8 | 37.7 | 23.7 | 20.5 | 58.8 | 12.8 | 8.0 | 10 | 22.1 | [43] | [43] |
| New Zealand | 1981 | 1,332 | 34.2 | 66.1 | 42.4 | 56.1 | 28.8 | 12.9 | 81.7 | 0.5 | 4.9 | 144 | 10.8 | 5 | 0.4 |
| Nicaragua | 1980 | 864 | 21.6 | 54.0 | 29.8 | 46.8 | 13.9 | ... | ... | ... | ... | 392 | 45.4 | 7 | 0.7 |
| Niger | 1985 | 3,203 | 47.4 | 89.7 | 52.4 | 55.6 | 49.2 | ... | ... | ... | ... | 2[21] | 8.2[21] | 5[21] | 24.1[21] |
| Nigeria | 1983 | 29,453 | 31.9 | 59.4 | 32.0 | 43.1 | 20.6 | ... | ... | ... | ... | 9,296 | 33.5 | 103 | 0.4 |
| Niue | 1984 | 1.0 | 35.7 | 57.3[26] | 35.4 | 44.5 | 25.9 | 9.1 | 71.5 | 10.9 | 8.5 | 0.2 | 21.3 | — | 1.2 |
| Norfolk Island | 1981 | 1.3 | 51.5 | ... | 72.2 | ... | ... | ... | ... | ... | ... | — | 3.0 | — | 0.3 |

| manufacturing, construction number ('000) | % of labour force | electricity, gas, water number ('000) | % of labour force | transportation, communications number ('000) | % of labour force | trade, hotels, restaurants number ('000) | % of labour force | finance, real estate number ('000) | % of labour force | services, other number ('000) | % of labour force | avg. annual growth of labour force 1965–1980 (%) | 1980–1985 (%) | 1985–2000 (%) | country |
|---|---|---|---|---|---|---|---|---|---|---|---|---|---|---|---|
| 328 | 21.0 | 10 | 0.6 | 66 | 4.2 | 256 | 16.3 | 16 | 1.0 | 250 | 16.0 | 3.3 | 2.9 | 3.3 | El Salvador |
| 18[8] | 11.4[8] | [8] | [8] | [11] | [11] | [11] | [11] | [11] | [11] | 36[11] | 22.8[11] | ... | ... | ... | Equatorial Guinea |
| ... | ... | ... | ... | ... | ... | ... | ... | ... | ... | ... | ... | 2.1 | 1.7 | 2.2 | Ethiopia |
| 6 | 31.7 | 0.1 | 0.8 | 1.9 | 11.0 | 2 | 11.9 | 0.3 | 1.9 | 4 | 23.3 | ... | ... | ... | Faeroe Islands |
| ... | ... | ... | ... | ... | ... | ... | ... | ... | ... | ... | ... | ... | ... | ... | Falkland Islands |
| 30 | 13.5 | 2 | 1.0 | 13 | 5.9 | 26 | 11.7 | 6 | 2.7 | 37 | 16.6 | ... | ... | ... | Fiji |
| 842[8] | 32.3[8] | [8] | [8] | 194 | 7.4 | 374 | 14.4 | 159 | 6.1 | 741 | 28.5 | 0.7 | 0.9 | 0.3 | Finland |
| 6,571 | 30.9 | 217 | 1.0 | 1,370 | 6.4 | 3,454 | 16.3 | 1,656 | 7.8 | 6,206 | 29.2 | 0.8 | 0.9 | 0.5 | France |
| 4 | 15.2 | 0.4 | 1.4 | 1.3 | 4.9 | 2 | 7.3 | 4 | 13.3 | 12 | 43.9 | ... | ... | ... | French Guiana |
| 10 | 17.7 | 0.4 | 0.7 | 3 | 5.9 | 14 | 23.7 | 1 | 2.2 | 21 | 35.7 | ... | ... | ... | French Polynesia |
| 54[8,14] | 10.8[8,14] | [8] | [8] | [11] | [11] | [11] | [11] | [11] | [11] | 69[11,14] | 13.7[11,14] | ... | ... | ... | Gabon |
| 13 | 3.8 | 1 | 0.4 | 8 | 2.5 | 17 | 5.1 | [1] | [1] | 47[1] | 14.5[1] | ... | ... | ... | Gambia, The |
| ... | ... | ... | ... | ... | ... | ... | ... | ... | ... | ... | ... | ... | ... | ... | Gaza Strip |
| 4,077[8] | 47.8[8] | [8] | [8] | 630 | 7.4 | 869 | 10.2 | [1] | [1] | 2,041 | 23.9[1] | 0.5 | 0.9 | 0.2 | Germany, East |
| 10,350 | 37.7 | 239 | 0.9 | 1,561 | 5.7 | 4,158 | 15.2 | 1,715 | 6.3 | 7,664 | 27.8 | 0.3 | 0.7 | −0.5 | Germany, West |
| 380[8,17] | 8.0[8,17] | [8] | [8] | [11] | [11] | [11] | [11] | [11] | [11] | 2,240[11,17] | 47.0[11,17] | 1.9 | 2.7 | 2.9 | Ghana |
| 5[21] | 41.0[21] | 0.2[21] | 1.9[21] | 0.6[21] | 5.1[21] | 2[21] | 20.8[21] | 0.6[21] | 5.1[21] | 3[21] | 26.1[21] | ... | ... | ... | Gibraltar |
| 1,007 | 26.9 | 31 | 0.8 | 279 | 7.4 | 569 | 15.2 | 131 | 3.5 | 656 | 17.6 | 0.5 | 0.6 | 0.3 | Greece |
| 6 | 27.2 | 0.2 | 1.2 | 1.8 | 8.7 | 3 | 12.5 | 0.3 | 1.6 | 7 | 32.2 | ... | ... | ... | Greenland |
| 4.4[15] | 15.9[15] | 0.4[15] | 1.3[15] | 1.7[15] | 6.1[15] | 3.9[15] | 14.0[15] | 0.4[15] | 1.3[15] | 9.0[15] | 32.4[15] | ... | ... | ... | Grenada |
| 10[23] | 10.8[23] | 0.7 | 0.7 | 5 | 5.2 | 10 | 10.9 | 1.5 | 16.4 | 32 | 34.7 | ... | ... | ... | Guadeloupe |
| 5 | 11.0 | [9] | [9] | 3[9] | 7.7[9] | 8 | 17.2 | 1.6 | 3.6 | 27 | 59.8 | ... | ... | ... | Guam |
| 264 | 15.7 | 8 | 0.5 | 43 | 2.6 | 147 | 8.7 | 21 | 1.3 | 290 | 17.2 | 2.3 | 2.8 | 3.3 | Guatemala |
| 4 | 14.5 | 0.5 | 2.0 | 2 | 8.5 | 6 | 24.6 | 1 | 4.2 | 7 | 27.7 | ... | ... | ... | Guernsey |
| 237[8] | 9.0[8] | [8] | [8] | [11] | [11] | [11] | [11] | [11] | [11] | 270[11] | 10.3[11] | 1.7 | 1.6 | 1.8 | Guinea |
| 5 | 2.2 | 0.1 | 0.1 | 2 | 1.2 | 5 | 2.3 | 0.1 | — | 47 | 22.3 | ... | ... | ... | Guinea-Bissau |
| 35 | 17.7 | 2 | 1.5 | 9 | 4.7 | 15 | 7.5 | 3 | 1.5 | 73 | 37.3 | ... | ... | ... | Guyana |
| 152 | 7.6 | 2 | 0.1 | 18 | 0.9 | 303 | 15.3 | 5 | 0.2 | 188 | 9.5 | 1.0 | 2.0 | 2.2 | Haiti |
| 211 | 16.8 | 5 | 0.4 | 38 | 3.0 | 107 | 8.5 | 12 | 1.0 | 160 | 12.8 | 2.8 | 3.9 | 3.9 | Honduras |
| 1,131 | 43.2 | 19 | 0.7 | 215 | 8.2 | 601 | 23.0 | 151 | 5.8 | 454 | 17.4 | 3.9 | 2.5 | 1.4 | Hong Kong |
| 1,896[8,37] | 38.6[8,37] | [8] | [8] | 396[37] | 8.1[37] | 509[37] | 10.4[37] | [1] | [1] | 999[1,37] | 20.2[1,37] | 0.1 | 0.0 | 0.3 | Hungary |
| 39 | 33.9 | [9] | [9] | | | 17 | 14.5 | | | 37 | 31.3 | ... | ... | ... | Iceland |
| 28,708 | 11.7 | 974 | 0.4 | 6,069 | 2.5 | 12,165 | 5.0 | 1,764 | 0.7 | 40,645 | 16.6 | 1.7 | 2.0 | 1.8 | India |
| 8,168 | 14.1 | 62 | 0.1 | 1,796 | 3.1 | 8,554 | 14.8 | 113 | 0.2 | 7,126 | 12.3 | 2.1 | 2.4 | 2.2 | Indonesia |
| 2,884 | 30.3 | 61 | 0.7 | 433 | 4.6 | 672 | 7.0 | 101 | 1.1 | 1,640 | 17.3 | 3.2 | 3.3 | 3.2 | Iran |
| 739[17] | 19.8[17] | 30[17] | 0.8[17] | 229[17] | 6.1[17] | 286[17] | 7.6[17] | 40[17] | 1.1[17] | 1,252[17] | 33.4[17] | 3.6 | 3.7 | 4.0 | Iraq |
| 359 | 28.0 | 16 | 1.2 | 74 | 5.8 | 210 | 16.4 | 82 | 6.4 | 342 | 26.8 | 0.8 | 1.6 | 1.6 | Ireland |
| 2.9[23] | 11.3[23] | 0.5 | 1.9 | 2.3 | 8.9 | 5.5 | 21.4 | [1] | [1] | 9.7[1] | 37.6[1] | ... | ... | ... | Isle of Man |
| 82[23] | 5.7[23] | 12 | 0.8 | 89 | 6.3 | 177 | 12.5 | 135 | 9.5 | 518 | 36.6 | 3.0 | 2.2 | 2.1 | Israel |
| 6,687 | 32.0 | ... | ... | 1,091 | 5.2 | 4,365 | 20.9 | 716 | 3.4 | 5,530 | 26.5 | 0.3 | 0.7 | 0.2 | Italy |
| 125 | 17.2 | [9] | [9] | 33[9] | 4.6[9] | 103 | 14.2 | ... | ... | 220 | 30.3 | 2.0 | 2.9 | 2.4 | Jamaica |
| 19,830 | 34.1 | 330 | 0.6 | 3,430 | 5.9 | 13,180 | 22.7 | 3,920 | 6.8 | 12,200 | 21.0 | 1.0 | 0.9 | 0.5 | Japan |
| 6 | 17.2 | 0.6 | 1.6 | 3 | 6.9 | 6 | 15.8 | 3 | 9.2 | 16 | 42.8 | ... | ... | ... | Jersey |
| 93 | 17.9 | 2 | 0.5 | 47 | 9.0 | 58 | 11.2 | 16 | 3.0 | 274 | 52.8 | 1.7 | 4.4 | 4.2 | Jordan |
| 91 | 3.6 | 2 | 0.1 | 29 | 1.2 | 144[28] | 5.8[28] | [28] | [28] | 224 | 9.0 | 1.2 | ... | ... | Kampuchea |
| 209[21] | 17.8[21] | 18[21] | 1.5[21] | 56[21] | 4.7[21] | 90[21] | 7.6[21] | 53[21] | 4.5[21] | 504[21] | 42.9[21] | 3.6 | 3.5 | 3.7 | Kenya |
| 0.6 | 8.2 | 0.2 | 3.3 | 1.1 | 15.0 | 1.1 | 16.1 | 0.1 | 1.3 | 3.4 | 48.7 | ... | ... | ... | Kiribati |
| 2,373[8,14] | 30.3[8,14] | [8] | [8] | [11] | [11] | [11] | [11] | [11] | [11] | 2,110[11,14] | 26.9[11,14] | 2.7 | 3.0 | 2.8 | Korea, North |
| 4,408 | 29.5 | 41 | 0.3 | 698 | 4.7 | 3,370 | 22.6 | 561 | 3.8 | 1,980 | 13.3 | 2.8 | 2.7 | 1.9 | Korea, South |
| 175 | 26.4 | 7 | 1.1 | 37 | 5.6 | 76 | 11.5 | 20 | 3.1 | 327 | 49.3 | 6.9 | 6.2 | 3.5 | Kuwait |
| 130[8] | 7.1[8] | [8] | [8] | [11] | [11] | [11] | [11] | [11] | [11] | 316[11] | 17.2[11] | 1.6 | 1.8 | 2.2 | Laos |
| 72[7,23] | 6.2[7,23] | 9[7] | 0.7[7] | 62[7] | 5.4[7] | 203[7] | 17.7[7] | [1] | [1] | 342[1,7] | 29.8[1,7] | 1.7 | ... | ... | Lebanon |
| 23 | 5.5 | 1 | 0.2 | 4 | 1.1 | 8 | 2.0 | — | 0.1 | 159 | 37.4 | 1.8 | 2.0 | 2.1 | Lesotho |
| 15 | 2.2 | 3 | 0.4 | 14 | 2.1 | 47 | 7.0 | 2 | 0.3 | 90 | 13.5 | 2.6 | 2.2 | 2.7 | Liberia |
| 368 | 34.7 | 26 | 2.4 | 93 | 8.7 | 41 | 3.9 | 13 | 1.2 | 318 | 30.0 | 3.6 | 3.7 | 3.5 | Libya |
| 5.5 | 42.3 | 0.1 | 1.0 | 0.4 | 3.0 | 1.6 | 12.3 | 0.8 | 6.3 | 4.2 | 31.8 | ... | ... | ... | Liechtenstein |
| 52 | 32.4 | 1.4 | 0.9 | 11 | 6.6 | 35 | 22.0 | 18 | 11.0 | 36 | 22.7 | ... | ... | ... | Luxembourg |
| 66 | 53.0 | 0.9 | 0.7 | 6 | 4.6 | 23 | 18.5 | 2 | 1.8 | 19 | 15.4 | ... | ... | ... | Macau |
| 244[8,14] | 6.0[8,14] | [8] | [8] | [11] | [11] | [11] | [11] | [11] | [11] | 539[11,14] | 13.1[11,14] | 2.1 | 1.9 | 2.3 | Madagascar |
| 75[21] | 19.7[21] | 5[21] | 1.3[21] | 22[21] | 5.8[21] | 32[21] | 8.3[21] | 12[21] | 3.0[21] | 58[21] | 15.1[21] | 2.2 | 2.6 | 2.6 | Malawi |
| 804 | 17.5 | 8 | 0.2 | 161 | 3.5 | 560 | 12.2 | 80 | 1.7 | 1,078 | 23.5 | 3.4 | 2.9 | 2.6 | Malaysia |
| 24 | 30.5 | 0.4 | 0.5 | 5 | 6.1 | 2.5 | 3.2 | [1] | [1] | 11[1] | 14.3[1] | ... | ... | ... | Maldives |
| 26 | 1.2 | 1.2 | 0.1 | 12 | 0.5 | 45 | 2.0 | 0.2 | — | 239 | 10.9 | 1.7 | 2.5 | 2.7 | Mali |
| 39 | 34.6 | 1.4 | 1.2 | 8 | 7.2 | 12 | 10.3 | 4 | 3.1 | 42 | 37.4 | ... | ... | ... | Malta |
| 12 | 12.5 | 1.0 | 1.1 | 5 | 5.5 | 10 | 10.4 | 18 | 18.9 | 37 | 39.2 | ... | ... | ... | Martinique |
| 46[8,14] | 8.9[8,14] | [8] | [8] | [11] | [11] | [11] | [11] | [11] | [11] | 112[11,14] | 21.7[11,14] | 1.8 | 2.7 | 3.1 | Mauritania |
| 90[21] | 37.9[21] | 4[21] | 1.6[21] | 9[21] | 3.8[21] | 10[21] | 4.2[21] | 5[21] | 2.2[21] | 67[21] | 28.4[21] | 2.6 | 3.3 | 2.1 | Mauritius |
| 2.2 | 15.4 | 0.1 | 0.9 | 0.3 | 2.0 | 0.7 | 4.7 | 0.2 | 1.5 | 1.4 | 9.9 | ... | ... | ... | Mayotte |
| 3,871 | 17.6 | 116 | 0.5 | 672 | 3.1 | 1,729 | 7.9 | 406 | 1.8 | 8,970 | 40.9 | 3.9 | 3.2 | 3.0 | Mexico |
| 1 | 11.8 | — | 0.8 | 0.6 | 6.0 | 3 | 26.1 | 0.9 | 9.4 | 4 | 45.6 | ... | ... | ... | Monaco |
| 120[43] | 18.0[43] | 17 | 2.6 | 36 | 5.4 | 42 | 6.2 | ... | ... | 135 | 20.0 | 2.7 | 3.0 | 2.8 | Mongolia |
| 1.1 | 22.3 | 0.1 | 1.7 | 0.2 | 4.5 | 0.4 | 8.1 | 0.1 | 1.7 | 2.7 | 52.2 | ... | ... | ... | Montserrat |
| 1,368 | 25.1 | 22 | 0.4 | 141 | 2.6 | 498 | 9.1 | [1] | [1] | 1,007[1] | 18.5[1] | 2.9 | 3.3 | 3.1 | Morocco |
| 42[23] | 0.8[23] | ... | ... | 77 | 1.3 | 112 | 2.0 | ... | ... | 243 | 4.4 | 3.2 | ... | ... | Mozambique |
| ... | ... | ... | ... | ... | ... | ... | ... | ... | ... | ... | ... | ... | ... | ... | Nauru |
| 36[15] | 0.5[15] | 3.0[15] | — | 7[15] | 0.1[15] | 109[15] | 1.6[15] | 10[15] | 0.1[15] | 441[15] | 6.4[15] | 1.6 | 2.3 | 2.3 | Nepal |
| 1,379[37] | 26.8[37] | 44[37] | 0.9[37] | 323[37] | 6.3[37] | 907[37] | 17.6[37] | 457[37] | 8.9[37] | 1,756[37] | 34.1[37] | 1.4 | 1.4 | 0.5 | Netherlands, The |
| 15 | 18.1 | 1.8 | 2.2 | 6 | 7.3 | 21 | 25.5 | 5 | 6.0 | 34 | 40.2 | ... | ... | ... | Netherlands Antilles[44] |
| 7[43] | 16.2[43] | 0.6 | 1.3 | 3 | 5.9 | 10 | 23.2 | 1.0 | 2.3 | 15 | 30.2 | ... | ... | ... | New Caledonia |
| 397 | 29.8 | 15 | 1.1 | 108 | 8.1 | 218 | 16.4 | 92 | 6.9 | 354 | 26.5 | 1.9 | 1.8 | 1.2 | New Zealand |
| 129 | 14.9 | 7 | 0.8 | 30 | 3.4 | 105 | 12.2 | 17 | 2.0 | 178 | 20.6 | 2.9 | 3.8 | 3.9 | Nicaragua |
| 52[21] | 22.8[21] | 3[21] | 11.3[21] | 2[21] | 8.7[21] | 2[21] | 8.8[21] | 1[21] | 6.2[21] | 2[21] | 10.0[21] | 1.8 | 2.3 | 2.6 | Niger |
| 2,252 | 8.1 | 318 | 1.1 | 1,123 | 4.0 | 6,534 | 23.5 | 204 | 0.7 | 7,946 | 28.6 | 3.0 | 2.6 | 2.9 | Nigeria |
| 0.2 | 21.3 | — | 1.7 | — | 4.6 | 0.1 | 9.5 | — | 0.1 | 0.4 | 40.4 | ... | ... | ... | Niue |
| 0.1 | 14.8 | — | 0.7 | 0.1 | 7.6 | 0.3 | 27.8 | — | 4.8 | 0.4 | 41.1 | ... | ... | ... | Norfolk Island |

## Employment and labour (continued)

| country | year | economically active population total ('000) | participation rate (%) female | participation rate (%) ages 15–64 | activity rate (%) total | activity rate (%) male | activity rate (%) female | employment status (%) employers, self-employed | employment status (%) employees | employment status (%) unpaid family workers | employment status (%) other | employed population by economic sector — agriculture, forestry, fishing number ('000) | % of labour force | mining, quarrying number ('000) | % of labour force |
|---|---|---|---|---|---|---|---|---|---|---|---|---|---|---|---|
| Norway | 1985 | 2,063 | 43.5 | 75.8[18] | 49.9[14] | 69.1[14] | 40.9[14] | 9.0 | 86.3 | 2.0 | 2.7 | 147 | 7.2 | 24 | 1.2 |
| Oman | 1982 | 231 | 7.1[14] | 50.1[14] | 28.5[14] | 50.8[14] | 4.2[14] | ... | ... | ... | ... | 9 | 3.9 | 4 | 1.6 |
| Pacific Is., Trust Terr. of the | | | | | | | | | | | | | | | |
|   Marshall Islands | 1980 | 4 | 25.2 | 30.0[12] | 14.3 | 20.8 | 7.4 | 4.2 | 80.8 | 0.5 | 14.5 | 0.1 | 1.2 | — | — |
|   Micronesia, Fed. States of | 1980 | 10 | 29.8 | 26.1[12] | 13.4 | 18.4 | 8.2 | 2.9 | 77.8 | 0.4 | 18.9 | 0.2 | 2.5 | — | — |
|   Northern Mariana Islands | 1980 | 6 | 34.3 | 63.6[12] | 36.3 | 45.5 | 26.3 | 2.1 | 97.0 | 0.1 | 0.8 | 0.1 | 2.1 | — | — |
|   Palau | 1980 | 3 | 34.3 | 41.6[12] | 23.9 | 30.3 | 17.0 | 3.1 | 91.3 | — | 5.6 | 0.1 | 2.9 | — | — |
| Pakistan | 1985 | 28,596 | 11.5 | 51.0 | 30.2 | 51.5 | 7.2 | 40.9 | 27.5 | 27.7 | 3.9 | 14,490 | 52.7 | 27 | 0.1 |
| Panama | 1984 | 683 | 30.9 | 52.2[14] | 32.1[14] | 45.8[14] | 18.2[14] | 25.6 | 66.1 | 4.0 | 4.3 | 178 | 27.2 | 0.9 | 0.1 |
| Papua New Guinea | 1980 | 749 | 39.5 | 35.6[6] | 24.9 | 28.8 | 20.6 | 71.1 | 27.9 | — | 1.0 | 564 | 77.0 | 4 | 0.6 |
| Paraguay | 1982 | 1,039 | 19.7 | 57.5 | 34.3 | 54.8 | 13.6 | 43.1 | 37.7 | 9.2 | 10.0 | 446 | 43.2 | 1.4 | 0.1 |
| Peru | 1982 | 5,978 | 28.6 | 53.1[15] | 31.8 | 45.4 | 18.2 | 49.1 | 45.1 | 5.8 | ... | 2,296 | 38.4 | 68 | 1.2 |
| Philippines | 1985 | 21,643 | 30.1 | 65.4 | 36.9[3] | 46.3[3] | 27.5[3] | 36.3 | 42.1 | 15.5 | 6.1 | 10,085 | 49.6 | 129 | 0.6 |
| Pitcairn Island | 1981 | 0.035 | ... | ... | ... | ... | ... | ... | ... | ... | ... | 0.003 | 8.6 | — | — |
| Poland | 1985 | 17,137 | 45.4[3] | 73.7[3] | 51.2[3] | 57.4[3] | 45.4[3] | 13.2[3] | 74.0[3] | 12.1[3] | 0.7[3] | 5,112 | 29.8 | 548 | 3.2 |
| Portugal | 1985 | 4,696 | 41.6 | 67.8 | 46.1 | 56.0 | 37.0 | 24.0 | 62.4 | 5.3 | 8.3 | 1,013 | 23.6 | 24 | 0.6 |
| Puerto Rico | 1986 | 963 | 35.6 | 47.6[18] | 29.5[37] | 39.2[37] | 20.3[37] | 13.7 | 84.1 | 0.9 | 1.4 | 56 | 5.9 | 0.9 | 0.1 |
| Qatar | 1984 | 113 | 9.8 | 63.8 | 40.3 | 60.8 | 9.8 | ... | ... | ... | ... | 0.3 | 0.2 | 7 | 5.9 |
| Réunion | 1982 | 176 | 35.3 | 57.5[18] | 34.0 | 44.9 | 23.6 | 10.4 | 56.3 | 1.1 | 32.2 | 17[21] | 14.7[21] | 7[21,35] | 6.2[21,35] |
| Romania | 1985 | 10,586 | 45.6[33] | 75.6[33] | 50.1[33] | 55.2[33] | 45.1[33] | ... | ... | ... | ... | 3,060 | 28.9 | [8] | [8] |
| Rwanda | 1978 | 2,661 | 51.5 | 94.3 | 55.1 | 54.6 | 55.6 | 38.8 | 7.2 | 53.8 | 0.2 | 2,472 | 92.9 | 12 | 0.4 |
| St. Christopher and Nevis | 1984 | 17[14] | 41.0[14] | 69.5[14] | 39.5[14] | 48.5[14] | 31.3[14] | 12.4[13] | 86.6[13] | 1.1[13] | — | 4 | 29.6 | — | — |
| St. Helena and Ascension | 1976 | 2.6 | ... | ... | 50.7 | ... | ... | ... | ... | ... | ... | 0.1 | 6.3 | [8] | [8] |
| St. Lucia | 1980 | 49 | 55.2 | 54.4[13] | 41.1 | 39.0 | 43.0 | 27.3[13] | 70.8[13] | 2.0[13] | ... | 10.4 | 35.9 | ... | 0.1 |
| St. Pierre and Miquelon | 1982 | 2 | 31.8 | 60.6 | 39.4 | 54.5 | 24.7 | 12.5 | 76.8 | ——10.7—— | | 0.1 | 3.1 | 0.2[35] | 11.6[35] |
| St. Vincent | 1970 | 24 | 35.9 | 58.9[30] | 27.5 | 37.6 | 18.7 | 16.0 | 82.5 | 1.5 | — | 6.9 | 29.0 | ... | 0.2 |
| San Marino | 1986 | 11 | 40.2 | 70.3 | 50.0 | 59.3 | 40.6 | 20.6 | 78.2 | 1.2 | — | 0.4 | 3.5 | [8] | [8] |
| São Tomé and Príncipe | 1981 | 31 | 32.4 | 61.1 | 31.7 | 43.1 | 20.4 | 15.9 | 79.9 | 0.1 | 4.1 | 16 | 56.2 | 2[35] | 5.5[35] |
| Saudi Arabia | 1984 | 2,673 | 3.9 | 45.1 | 24.5 | 40.9 | 2.3 | ... | ... | ... | ... | 223 | 8.4 | 164 | 6.1 |
| Senegal | 1985 | 3,095 | 41.8 | 78.1 | 47.1 | 55.3 | 39.1 | ... | ... | ... | ... | 117[21] | 9.1[7,21] | 2[7,21] | 1.6[7,21] |
| Seychelles | 1985 | 28 | 42.4 | 66.8[27] | 42.4 | 49.0 | 35.9 | 10.7[15] | 76.6[15] | 0.3[15] | 12.4[15] | 5[15] | 19.5[15] | ... | ... |
| Sierra Leone | 1985 | 1,352 | 33.7 | 62.9 | 37.5 | 50.8 | 24.8 | ... | ... | ... | ... | 617[21] | 8.5[17,21] | 6[17,21] | 8.9[17,21] |
| Singapore | 1985 | 1,204 | 36.4 | 65.6 | 47.1 | 59.8 | 34.3 | 13.0 | 80.9 | 1.9 | 4.1 | 8 | 0.7 | 2.4 | 0.2 |
| Solomon Islands | 1985[21] | 25 | 16.8 | 86.3 | 42.7 | ... | ... | ... | ... | ... | ... | 8 | 32.4 | 0.1 | 0.3 |
| Somalia | 1985 | 1,999 | 39.7 | 72.8 | 43.0 | 52.5 | 33.7 | ... | ... | ... | ... | 1,366[14] | 75.6[14] | [8] | [8] |
| South Africa | 1980 | 8,690 | 32.3 | 68.3[13] | 34.7 | 46.2 | 22.8 | ... | ... | ... | ... | 1,306 | 15.0 | 836 | 9.6 |
|   Bophuthatswana | 1979 | 405 | ... | ... | 31.5 | ... | ... | 0.7 | ... | ... | ... | 36 | 8.9 | 12 | 33.8 |
|   Ciskei | 1984 | 90 | 41.3[14] | ... | 20.4[14] | 25.5[14] | 15.9[14] | 12.1[25] | 77.0[25] | 10.9[25] | — | 10 | 10.9 | 1.1 | 1.2 |
|   KwaNdebele | ... | ... | ... | ... | ... | ... | ... | ... | ... | ... | ... | ... | ... | ... | ... |
|   Transkei | 1978 | 121 | ... | ... | ... | ... | ... | ... | ... | ... | ... | 5 | 3.8 | 4 | 3.0 |
|   Venda | 1980 | 30 | 38.5 | ... | 8.6 | 12.9 | 5.6 | ... | ... | ... | ... | 7.2 | 28.2 | 0.3 | 1.4 |
| South West Africa/Namibia | 1985 | 477 | 23.9 | 55.4 | 30.8 | 47.3 | 14.6 | ... | ... | ... | ... | 185[14] | 43.4[14] | [8] | [8] |
| Spain | 1985 | 13,346 | 30.7 | 56.8[18] | 35.7[16] | 52.0[16] | 20.0[16] | 18.0 | 67.3 | 5.6 | 9.1 | 2,007 | 16.5 | 91 | 0.7 |
| Sri Lanka | 1981 | 5,017 | 25.5 | 53.6 | 44.4 | 64.8 | 23.1 | 24.7 | 55.2 | 2.2 | 17.9 | 1,876 | 45.5 | 34 | 0.8 |
| Sudan, The | 1980 | 5,973[15] | 20.0[42] | 55.1[26,42] | 29.4[42] | 46.7[42] | 11.9[42] | 59.2[42] | 25.3[42] | 9.9[42] | 5.6[42] | 3,433 | 65.8 | 183[35] | 3.5[35] |
| Suriname | 1984 | 99 | 27.9[14] | 38.7[14] | 25.9 | ... | ... | ... | ... | ... | ... | 17 | 16.8 | 5 | 4.7 |
| Swaziland | 1985 | 273 | 39.9 | 72.1 | 42.0 | 51.2 | 33.1 | ... | ... | ... | ... | 23[21] | 31.6[21] | 2[21] | 3.3[21] |
| Sweden | 1985 | 4,424 | 47.1 | 82.6[18] | 52.3[7] | 56.9[7] | 47.9[7] | 6.8 | 90.1 | 0.3 | 2.8 | 208 | 4.8 | 15 | 0.3 |
| Switzerland | 1980 | 3,092 | 36.2 | 70.7 | 48.6 | 63.4 | 34.4 | 9.6 | 90.3 | ... | ... | 218 | 7.2 | 6 | 0.2 |
| Syria | 1984 | 2,384 | 10.6 | 47.7 | 23.6 | 41.5 | 5.1 | 34.0[16] | 56.2[16] | 7.4[16] | 2.4[16] | 1,064 | 46.0 | 18 | 0.8 |
| Taiwan | 1985 | 9,234 | 36.4 | 71.1 | 47.9 | 58.8 | 36.2 | 21.5 | 66.6 | 11.9 | — | 2,232 | 24.7 | 41 | 0.5 |
| Tanzania | 1985 | 10,913 | 48.9 | 85.7 | 48.5 | 50.2 | 46.8 | ... | ... | ... | ... | 1377[7,21] | 20.3[7,21] | 77[21] | 1.1[7,21] |
| Thailand | 1982 | 25,749 | 47.6 | 83.1[26] | 53.0 | 55.2 | 50.6 | 29.1 | 24.1 | 43.3 | 3.5 | 16,985 | 68.4 | 65 | 0.3 |
| Togo | 1985 | 1,244 | 37.5 | 69.5 | 42.0 | 53.3 | 31.1 | ... | ... | ... | ... | 813[14] | 73.0[14] | [8] | [8] |
| Tokelau | 1981 | 0.8 | 51.2 | 88.3 | 48.5 | 47.9 | 49.2 | ... | ... | ... | ... | 0.1 | 16.1 | | |
| Tonga | 1976 | 21 | 15.7 | 43.7 | 23.8 | 39.3 | 7.6 | 32.7 | 33.3 | 13.1 | 20.9 | 9.5 | 51.2 | — | 0.1 |
| Trinidad and Tobago | 1985 | 465 | 33.3 | 64.5 | 39.4 | 52.6 | 26.2 | 18.0 | 74.5 | 5.3 | 2.2 | 44 | 9.7 | 65[35] | 14.4[35] |
| Tunisia | 1982 | 1,810[14] | 20.1[14] | 51.4[14] | 28.4[14] | 45.1[14] | 11.5[14] | 24.7[14] | 50.1[14] | 10.5[14] | 14.7[14] | 539 | 30.2 | 16 | 0.9 |
| Turkey | 1980 | 19,212 | 36.1 | 68.2 | 42.9 | 54.1 | 31.4 | 23.2 | 32.1 | 40.9 | 3.8 | 11,105 | 60.0 | 132 | 0.7 |
| Turks and Caicos Islands | 1980 | 2.9 | 42.8 | 69.4 | 39.2 | 46.5 | 32.5 | ... | ... | ... | ... | 0.4 | 13.9 | | |
| Tuvalu | 1979[46] | 4.0 | 51.3 | 81.0[26] | 55.2 | 57.6 | 53.1 | 0.3 | 22.2 | ——77.5—— | | — | 4.2[21] | — | 0.1[21] |
| Uganda | 1985 | 7,054 | 41.9 | 78.9 | 45.6 | 53.4 | 37.9 | ... | ... | ... | ... | 5,292[14] | 85.9[14] | [8] | [8] |
| U.S.S.R. | 1985 | 135,424[25] | 49.8[25] | 72.7[14] | 51.7[25] | 55.7[25] | 48.1[25] | ... | 82.8[24] | ... | 17.2[24,47] | 25,198 | 19.3 | [8] | [8] |
| United Arab Emirates | 1984 | 738 | 5.8 | 77.0 | 54.5 | 74.6 | 10.2 | 6.8[14] | 92.7[14] | 0.1[14] | 0.5[14] | 36 | 4.9 | 15 | 2.0 |
| United Kingdom | 1984 | 27,012 | 40.1 | 71.9[15] | 47.8 | 58.8 | 37.4 | 8.4 | 80.4 | ... | 11.2 | 628 | 2.6 | 327 | 1.4 |
| United States | 1985 | 117,167 | 43.7 | 72.2 | 49.1 | 56.8 | 41.8 | 8.1 | 90.6 | 0.4 | 0.9 | 3,603 | 3.1 | 1,036 | 0.9 |
| Uruguay | 1985 | 1,172 | 29.6[14] | 60.3[14] | 39.0[14] | 55.6[14] | 22.8[14] | ... | ... | ... | ... | 179 | 15.3 | 2 | 0.2 |
| Vanuatu | 1979 | 51 | 43.4 | 84.3 | 46.0 | 49.0 | 42.5 | ... | ... | ... | ... | 39 | 76.8 | 0.1 | 0.1 |
| Venezuela | 1985 | 5,828 | 27.3 | 57.8 | 33.9 | 48.8 | 18.7 | 25.6 | 57.2 | 3.2 | 14.0 | 846 | 14.8 | 78 | 1.4 |
| Vietnam | 1985 | 28,755 | 47.2 | 80.1 | 48.2 | 52.3 | 44.2 | ... | ... | ... | ... | 17,502 | 60.9 | 870[35] | 3.0[35] |
| Virgin Islands (U.S.) | 1980 | 38 | 45.5 | 65.1 | 39.4 | 44.9 | 34.4 | 9.5 | 90.2 | 0.3 | — | 0.5 | 1.3 | — | 0.1 |
| Wallis and Futuna | 1976 | 3.3 | 35.8 | 65.2 | 36.5 | 46.9 | 26.1 | 42.2 | 18.3 | 39.5 | — | 2.7 | 79.2 | — | — |
| West Bank | 1985 | 159.2 | 13.6 | 35.9[34] | 19.6 | ... | ... | ... | ... | ... | ... | ... | ... | ... | ... |
| Western Sahara | ... | ... | ... | ... | ... | ... | ... | ... | ... | ... | ... | ... | ... | ... | ... |
| Western Samoa | 1981 | 42 | 15.0 | 48.6 | 26.5 | 43.5 | 8.3 | 21.1 | 43.5 | 35.0 | 0.4 | 25 | 60.4 | — | — |
| Yemen (Aden) | 1984 | 450 | 6.8 | 43.0 | 19.2 | 40.2 | 2.9 | 29.8[42] | 34.2[42] | 15.1[42] | 20.9[42] | 166 | 36.9 | 8 | 1.9 |
| Yemen (Ṣanʿāʾ) | 1984 | 1,472 | 12.5 | 41.4 | 21.3 | 38.8 | 5.1 | 45.2[24] | 34.0[24] | 19.1[24] | 1.7[24] | 830[15] | 69.1[15] | 1.3[15] | 0.1[15] |
| Yugoslavia | 1981 | 9,359 | 38.7 | 68.7 | 43.4 | 54.3 | 32.9 | 17.2 | 65.7 | 10.5 | 6.6 | 2,683 | 30.6 | [8] | [8] |
| Zaire | 1980 | 10,434 | 37.6 | 67.8 | 40.4 | 51.3 | 29.8 | ... | ... | ... | ... | 7,460 | 71.5 | [8] | [8] |
| Zambia | 1984 | 2,032 | 27.9 | 59.2[26] | 31.6 | 46.0 | 17.4 | ... | ... | ... | ... | 1,462[16] | 64.6[16] | 58[16] | 2.5[16] |
| Zimbabwe | 1985 | 2,484[7] | 39.2[7] | 63.5[7,26] | 33.1[7] | 41.1[7] | 25.4[7] | ... | ... | ... | ... | 277[21] | 26.1[21] | 54[21] | 5.1[21] |

[1]Services includes finance, real estate. [2]State sector only. [3]1978. [4]Excludes Algerians abroad. [5]1983. [6]Over age 10. [7]1982. [8]Manufacturing, construction includes mining, quarrying and electricity, gas, water. [9]Transportation, communications includes electricity, gas, water. [10]Services includes hotels. [11]Services includes transportation, communications; trade, hotels, restaurants; and finance, real estate. [12]Over age 16. [13]1970. [14]1980. [15]1981. [16]1983. [17]1984. [18]Ages 16–64. [19]Services includes transportation, communications and finance, real estate. [20]1976. [21]Wage earners only. [22]Mining, quarrying includes manufacturing, and electricity, gas, water. [23]Construction only. [24]1975. [25]1979. [26]Over age 15. [27]Over age 12.

| manufacturing, construction number ('000) | % of labour force | electricity, gas, water number ('000) | % of labour force | transportation, communications number ('000) | % of labour force | trade, hotels, restaurants number ('000) | % of labour force | finance, real estate number ('000) | % of labour force | services, other number ('000) | % of labour force | avg. annual growth of labour force 1965–1980 (%) | 1980–1985 (%) | 1985–2000 (%) | country |
|---|---|---|---|---|---|---|---|---|---|---|---|---|---|---|---|
| 525 | 25.6 | 21 | 1.0 | 174 | 8.5 | 351 | 17.1 | 133 | 6.5 | 676 | 32.9 | 1.8 | 0.8 | 0.7 | Norway |
| 54 | 23.7 | 2 | 0.9 | 6 | 2.6 | 101 | 43.9 | 4 | 1.6 | 50 | 21.8 | 3.8 | 5.2 | 2.7 | Oman |
| | | | | | | | | | | | | | | | Pacific Is., Trust Terr. of the |
| 0.5 | 12.4 | [9] | [9] | 0.3[9] | 7.1[9] | 0.6 | 12.8 | — | 0.7 | 2.9 | 65.7 | ... | ... | ... | Marshall Islands |
| 1.1 | 11.6 | [9] | [9] | 0.5[9] | 5.1[9] | 0.9 | 9.2 | 0.1 | 1.3 | 6.9 | 70.4 | ... | ... | ... | Micronesia, Fed. States of |
| 1.1 | 18.4 | [9] | [9] | 0.5[9] | 8.7[9] | 0.9 | 15.3 | 0.2 | 2.7 | 3.2 | 52.8 | ... | ... | ... | Northern Mariana Islands |
| 0.6 | 19.5 | [9] | [9] | 0.2[9] | 8.0[9] | 0.3 | 11.8 | — | 1.6 | 1.6 | 56.2 | ... | ... | ... | Palau |
| 5,012 | 18.2 | 311 | 1.1 | 1,261 | 4.6 | 3,281 | 11.9 | 225 | 0.8 | 2,874 | 10.6 | 2.6 | 3.2 | 2.8 | Pakistan |
| 103 | 15.7 | 9 | 1.3 | 39 | 5.9 | 99 | 15.1 | 24 | 3.7 | 202 | 30.9 | 2.7 | 3.0 | 2.6 | Panama |
| 26 | 4.8 | 3 | 0.4 | 17 | 2.4 | 25 | 3.4 | 4 | 0.6 | 79 | 10.8 | 1.9 | 2.2 | 2.0 | Papua New Guinea |
| 196 | 18.8 | 3 | 0.3 | 31 | 3.0 | 86 | 8.3 | 18 | 1.7 | 254 | 24.6 | 3.2 | 3.1 | 2.8 | Paraguay |
| 992 | 16.6 | 13 | 0.2 | 282 | 4.7 | 976 | 16.3 | 105 | 1.8 | 1,245 | 20.8 | 2.9 | 2.9 | 2.8 | Peru |
| 2,604 | 12.8 | 79 | 0.4 | 913 | 4.5 | 2,650 | 13.0 | 351 | 1.7 | 3,516 | 17.3 | 2.5 | 2.5 | 2.4 | Philippines |
| — | — | 0.002 | 5.7 | 0.005 | 14.3 | 0.002 | 5.7 | 0.016 | 45.7 | 0.007 | 20.0 | | | | Pitcairn Island |
| 5,603 | 32.7 | 166 | 1.0 | 1,303 | 7.6 | 1,386 | 8.1 | 368 | 2.1 | 2,650 | 15.5 | 1.1 | 0.7 | 0.7 | Poland |
| 1,413 | 32.9 | 30 | 0.7 | 188 | 4.4 | 596 | 13.9 | 117 | 2.7 | 920 | 21.2 | 1.2 | 1.0 | 0.8 | Portugal |
| 230 | 24.2 | 14 | 1.5 | 43 | 4.5 | 176 | 18.6 | 31 | 3.3 | 397 | 41.9 | ... | ... | ... | Puerto Rico |
| 41 | 36.3 | 7 | 6.2 | 5 | 4.2 | 16 | 14.3 | 4 | 3.3 | 34 | 29.6 | ... | ... | ... | Qatar |
| 11[21,23] | 9.4[21,23] | 0.7[21] | 0.6[21] | 6[21] | 4.9[21] | 14[21] | 12.1[21] | 16[21] | 13.8[21] | 45[21] | 38.3[21] | ... | ... | ... | Réunion |
| 4,716[8] | 44.5[8] | [8] | [8] | 721 | 6.8 | 617 | 5.8 | ... | — | 1,474 | 14.0 | 0.2 | 0.7 | 0.7 | Romania |
| 61 | 2.3 | 1 | — | 7 | 0.3 | 26 | 1.0 | 1 | — | 81 | 3.1 | 2.9 | 2.8 | 2.9 | Rwanda |
| 3 | 17.4 | 1 | 7.0 | 0.5 | 3.0 | 0.9 | 6.3 | 0.3 | 1.9 | 5 | 34.8 | ... | ... | ... | St. Christopher and Nevis |
| 0.3[8] | 12.0[8] | [8] | [8] | 0.1 | 4.5 | 0.1 | 4.1 | 0.7 | 29.0 | 1.0 | 44.2 | ... | ... | ... | St. Helena and Ascension |
| 5.2 | 17.8 | 0.5 | 1.7 | 1.1 | 3.7 | 3.1 | 10.6 | — | — | 8.7 | 30.0 | ... | ... | ... | St. Lucia |
| 0.1[23] | 6.0[23] | — | 1.8 | 0.2 | 9.5 | 0.6 | 29.0 | — | 2.3 | 0.8 | 36.8 | ... | ... | ... | St. Pierre and Miquelon |
| 4.7 | 19.9 | 0.2 | 0.9 | 1.1 | 4.5 | 2.9 | 12.1 | 1 | 1 | 7.9[1] | 33.4[1] | ... | ... | ... | St. Vincent |
| 4.98 | 46.8[8] | [8] | [8] | 0.1 | 1.2 | 1.6 | 15.1 | 0.2 | 1.9 | 3.3 | 31.6 | ... | ... | ... | San Marino |
| 2[23] | 6.1[23] | 0.3 | 1.0 | 1 | 3.5 | 2 | 6.9 | 0.2 | 0.6 | 6 | 20.1 | ... | ... | ... | São Tomé and Príncipe |
| 923 | 34.5 | 62 | 2.3 | 117 | 4.4 | 730 | 27.3 | 104 | 3.9 | 350 | 13.1 | 4.9 | 4.4 | 3.5 | Saudi Arabia |
| 39[7,21] | 33.6[7,21] | 3[7,21] | 2.8[7,21] | 25[7,21] | 21.3[7,21] | 15[7,21] | 12.6[7,21] | 8[7,21] | 6.8[7,21] | 14[7,21] | 12.3[7,21] | 3.1 | 1.9 | 2.1 | Senegal |
| 6[15] | 23.2[15] | 0.2[15] | 0.8[15] | 2[15] | 8.4[15] | 4[15] | 15.6[15] | 0.5[15] | 1.8[15] | 8[15] | 30.5[15] | ... | ... | ... | Seychelles |
| 17[17,21] | 24.9[17,21] | 2[17,21] | 3.1[17,21] | 7[17,21] | 10.6[17,21] | 6[17,21,28] | 9.0[17,21,28] | 28 | 28 | 24[17,21] | 34.9[17,21] | 0.9 | 1.1 | 1.4 | Sierra Leone |
| 397 | 34.4 | 8 | 0.7 | 117 | 10.1 | 271 | 23.5 | 101 | 8.7 | 251 | 21.7 | 4.2 | 1.9 | 0.8 | Singapore |
| 3 | 12.9 | 0.3 | 1.3 | 2 | 8.7 | 3 | 10.3 | 0.5 | 2.1 | 8 | 32.0 | ... | ... | ... | Solomon Islands |
| 152[8,14] | 8.4[8,14] | [8] | [8] | 11 | 11 | 11 | 11 | 11 | 11 | 290[11,14] | 16.0[11,14] | 3.1 | 2.0 | 1.7 | Somalia |
| 1,925 | 22.2 | 80 | 0.9 | 428 | 4.9 | 1,011 | 11.6 | 287 | 3.3 | 2,816 | 32.4 | 1.8 | 2.8 | 2.8 | South Africa |
| | | | | | | | | | | | | | | | Bophuthatswana |
| 31 | 34.0 | 0.5 | 0.5 | 5 | 5.3 | 12 | 13.8 | 1.1 | 1.2 | 30 | 33.0 | ... | ... | ... | Ciskei |
| | | | | | | | | | | | | | | | KwaNdebele |
| 19 | 16.0 | ... | ... | 3 | 2.6 | 8 | 6.5 | 1 | 0.9 | 81 | 67.2 | ... | ... | ... | Transkei |
| 2.8 | 11.0 | 0.1 | 0.3 | 0.8 | 3.3 | 2.6 | 10.0 | 0.1 | 0.4 | 12 | 45.4 | ... | ... | ... | Venda |
| 93[8,14] | 21.8[8,14] | [8] | [8] | 11 | 11 | 11 | 11 | 11 | 11 | 148[11,14] | 34.7[11,14] | ... | ... | ... | South West Africa/Namibia |
| 4,000 | 32.9 | 91 | 0.8 | 671 | 5.5 | 2,475 | 20.3 | 494 | 4.1 | 2,341 | 19.2 | 0.6 | 1.3 | 0.8 | Spain |
| 543 | 13.2 | 16 | 0.4 | 200 | 4.8 | 437 | 10.6 | 57 | 1.4 | 957 | 23.3 | 2.2 | 1.6 | 1.6 | Sri Lanka |
| 108[23] | 2.1[23] | 59 | 1.1 | 199 | 3.8 | 221[28] | 4.2[28] | 28 | 28 | 1,020 | 19.5 | 2.4 | 2.8 | 3.1 | Sudan, The |
| 14 | 13.9 | 1.4 | 1.4 | 4 | 3.9 | 13 | 12.9 | 2 | 2.1 | 44 | 44.3 | ... | ... | ... | Suriname |
| 14[21] | 19.5[21] | 1[21] | 1.8[21] | 5[21] | 7.4[21] | 7[21] | 9.7[21] | 3[21] | 4.5[21] | 16[21] | 22.2[21] | ... | ... | ... | Swaziland |
| 1,228 | 28.6 | 40 | 0.9 | 300 | 7.0 | 591 | 13.7 | 321 | 7.5 | 1,594 | 37.2 | 1.1 | 0.3 | 0.3 | Sweden |
| 1,162 | 38.5 | 22 | 0.7 | 180 | 6.0 | 586 | 19.4 | 246 | 8.2 | 592 | 19.6 | 0.8 | 0.7 | -0.1 | Switzerland |
| 500 | 21.6 | 7 | 0.3 | 111 | 4.8 | 248 | 10.7 | 21 | 0.9 | 345 | 14.9 | 3.3 | 3.5 | 4.0 | Syria |
| 2,867 | 31.8 | 58 | 0.6 | 420 | 4.6 | 1,241 | 13.7 | 200 | 2.2 | 1,968 | 21.8 | ... | 2.9 | ... | Taiwan |
| 170[7,21] | 25.1[7,21] | 2[7,21] | 3.2[7,21] | 60[7,21] | 8.9[7,21] | 38[7,21] | 5.6[7,21] | 17[7,21] | 2.5[7,21] | 225[7,21] | 33.3[7,21] | 2.8 | 2.8 | 3.0 | Tanzania |
| 2,527 | 10.2 | 76 | 0.3 | 501 | 2.0 | 2,298 | 9.3 | 11 | 11 | 2,378 | 9.6 | 2.8 | 2.5 | 1.7 | Thailand |
| 110[8,14] | 9.9[8,14] | [8] | [8] | 11 | 11 | 11 | 11 | 11 | 11 | 190[11,14] | 17.1[11,14] | 2.7 | 2.3 | 2.5 | Togo |
| | | | | — | 0.9 | — | 3.0 | | | 0.6 | 80.0 | | | | Tokelau |
| 1.5 | 8.3 | 0.1 | 0.6 | 0.8 | 4.5 | 0.8 | 4.4 | 0.1 | 0.3 | 5.7 | 30.7 | | | | Tonga |
| 35[45] | 35[45] | 102[45] | 22.3[45] | 30 | 6.7 | 105 | 23.1 | | | 109 | 23.8 | 1.9 | 2.5 | 2.1 | Trinidad and Tobago |
| 561 | 31.5 | 10 | 0.6 | 65 | 3.6 | 155 | 8.7 | 11 | 0.6 | 346 | 19.4 | 2.8 | 3.1 | 2.8 | Tunisia |
| 2,741 | 14.8 | 33 | 0.2 | 531 | 2.9 | 1,084 | 5.9 | 294 | 1.6 | 2,602 | 13.9 | 1.7 | 2.3 | 2.0 | Turkey |
| 0.3 | 10.8 | — | 0.4 | 0.1 | 2.6 | 0.1 | 4.3 | — | 1.0 | 1.9 | 65.9 | ... | ... | ... | Turks and Caicos Islands |
| 0.3[21] | 31.7[21] | — | 1.6[21] | 0.1[21] | 3.7[21] | 0.1[21] | 11.9[21] | — | 1.2[21] | 0.3[21] | 38.5[21] | ... | ... | ... | Tuvalu |
| 272[8,14] | 4.4[8,14] | [8] | [8] | 11 | 11 | 11 | 11 | 11 | 11 | 599[11,14] | 9.7[11,14] | 3.0 | 2.7 | 3.0 | Uganda |
| 54,489[8] | 41.8[8] | [8] | [8] | 12,549 | 9.6 | 10,031 | 7.7 | 679 | 0.5 | 27,324 | 21.0 | 1.2 | 0.9 | 0.5 | U.S.S.R. |
| 235 | 31.9 | 14 | 1.9 | 55 | 7.4 | 100 | 13.5 | 22 | 3.0 | 261 | 35.4 | ... | 5.2 | 2.1 | United Arab Emirates |
| 7,222 | 30.4 | 333 | 1.4 | 1,426 | 6.0 | 4,753 | 20.0 | 2,033 | 8.5 | 7,071 | 29.7 | 0.3 | 0.5 | 0.2 | United Kingdom |
| 30,435 | 26.2 | 1,529 | 1.3 | 6,387 | 5.5 | 24,027 | 20.7 | 11,562 | 10.0 | 37,496 | 32.3 | 2.2 | 1.2 | 0.8 | United States |
| 275 | 23.4 | 17 | 1.5 | 59 | 5.0 | 137 | 11.7 | 42 | 3.6 | 461 | 39.3 | 0.4 | 0.6 | 0.9 | Uruguay |
| 2 | 4.1 | 0.1 | 0.1 | 1 | 2.6 | 2 | 4.3 | 0.3 | 0.6 | 6 | 11.3 | ... | ... | ... | Vanuatu |
| 1,413 | 24.7 | 73 | 1.3 | 379 | 6.6 | 1,090 | 19.0 | 288 | 5.0 | 1,557 | 27.2 | 4.2 | 3.5 | 3.0 | Venezuela |
| 517[23] | 1.8[23] | 37 | 0.1 | 188 | 0.7 | 447 | 1.6 | 1 | 1 | 9,194[1] | 32.0[1] | 1.8 | ... | ... | Vietnam |
| 6.8 | 19.1 | 0.6 | 1.8 | 2.8 | 7.9 | 9.0 | 25.3 | 1.9 | 5.3 | 14.0 | 39.2 | ... | ... | ... | Virgin Islands (U.S.) |
| 0.2 | 5.5 | — | 0.1 | — | 1.2 | 0.1 | 1.5 | — | — | 0.4 | 12.5 | ... | ... | ... | Wallis and Futuna |
| ... | ... | ... | ... | ... | ... | ... | ... | ... | ... | ... | ... | | | | West Bank |
| | | | | | | | | | | | | | | | Western Sahara |
| 3 | 7.3 | 0.5 | 1.1 | 1 | 3.2 | 2 | 4.4 | 1 | 3.1 | 8 | 20.4 | ... | ... | ... | Western Samoa |
| 80 | 17.7 | 9 | 2.0 | 29 | 6.5 | 39 | 8.8 | 0.3 | 0.1 | 118 | 26.2 | 1.6 | 2.8 | 3.1 | Yemen (Aden) |
| 125[15] | 10.4[15] | 4[15] | 0.3[15] | 32[15] | 2.6[15] | 71[15] | 6.0[15] | 5[15] | 0.4[15] | 134[15] | 11.1[15] | 0.7 | 2.6 | 3.4 | Yemen (Şan'ā') |
| 2,899[8] | 33.0[8] | [8] | [8] | 445 | 5.1 | 828 | 9.4 | 205 | 2.3 | 1,720 | 19.6 | 0.9 | 1.0 | 0.7 | Yugoslavia |
| 1,346[8] | 12.9[8] | [8] | [8] | 11 | 11 | 11 | 11 | 11 | 11 | 1,629[11] | 15.6[11] | 1.7 | 2.3 | 2.5 | Zaire |
| 81[16] | 3.6[16] | 8[16] | 0.3[16] | 24[16] | 1.1[16] | 30[16] | 1.3[16] | 22[16] | 1.0[16] | 578[16] | 25.6[16] | 2.7 | 3.2 | 3.5 | Zambia |
| 217[21] | 20.5[21] | 8[21] | 0.7[21] | 50[21] | 4.8[21] | 79[21] | 7.4[21] | 16[21] | 1.5[21] | 358[21] | 33.9[21] | 3.0 | 2.7 | 3.0 | Zimbabwe |

[28]Trade includes finance, real estate. [29]Ages 15–69. [30]Ages 14–64. [31]Excludes unemployed. [32]Ages 15–60. [33]1977. [34]Over age 14. [35]Mining, quarrying includes manufacturing. [36]Economically active figures pertain to persons aged 15–64 only. [37]1985. [38]Excludes Assam. [39]1971. [40]Ages 18–64. [41]Ages 15–59. [42]1973. [43]Manufacturing, construction includes mining, quarrying. [44]Netherlands Antilles includes Aruba. [45]Electricity, gas, water includes construction. [46]De facto indigenous population only. [47]Includes communal workers and their families. [48]Ages 20–64.

# Agriculture and land use

This table provides data on the structure of national agricultural sectors from the perspective of farms and farmland use. The data are taken mainly from national agricultural censuses and surveys, supplemented by reports of the United Nations Food and Agriculture Organization's (FAO's) *World Census of Agriculture.* Many of these national censuses, of course, were taken under guidelines established by the FAO for the *World Census of Agriculture* programs (the 1980 census was the fourth, and it included national censuses taken during the decade 1976–85). It represents a cooperative effort by FAO member countries to collect agricultural data within a general framework that permits international harmonization of concepts and definitions; transfer of technical expertise; and increased effectiveness in the collection, analysis, publication, and policy-related use of such statistics. Some 92 countries participated in the 1980 round; more than 100 countries were expected to participate in the 1990 round of censuses.

All agricultural statistics are subject to quality-control problems, including errors or biases arising from such factors as incomplete or inaccurate lists of holdings, ambiguous questions, respondents who inadvertently or willfully give inaccurate information, failure to record data for all parts of fragmented holdings, respondents' misunderstandings of the definitions of land use and cropping methods, or a failure to report livestock tem-

porarily absent from the holding on public or common pasture land or in transit. Frequently subjects studied, classificational schemes, and definitions vary from the FAO guidelines from country to country (economic planners need different information about a commercial, high-technology, multicrop agricultural sector than they do for a family-subsistence, low-technology, one-crop sector). When a complete census of agriculture is impossible, a sample survey may be taken. This is a limited census of a predetermined number of carefully screened holdings. From these results, nationwide projections may be prepared, but these are often of uncertain reliability.

With respect to the first section of the table, number and size of farms, many countries impose a minimum size limit for holdings that may be covered in their census reports, and this cutoff, if not sufficiently low, can result in a substantial undercount of smaller holdings; conversely Soviet bloc nations often publish statistics only on state collective or cooperative farms and exclude privately held plots of land, even though in some instances these provide a significant fraction of agricultural output.

The land tenure statistics classify farms according to the rights under which the farmer holds the land. Owner-operated includes two types of ownership: outright ownership in which the holder has title and has the right to determine use and transfer of the land; and ownerlike possession

## Agriculture and land use

| country | year | number of farms ('000) | size of holding: average (ha) | size class (%): under 1 ha | 1–5 ha | 5–10 ha | 10–20 ha | 20–50 ha | 50–200 ha | over 200 ha | tenure (% of farms): owner-operated individual/family | corporate/state | socialized/collective | rented (including share-croppers) | tribal/communal | other |
|---|---|---|---|---|---|---|---|---|---|---|---|---|---|---|---|---|
| Afghanistan | 1981 | 126[1] | 3.5[1] | 44.8[1] | 35.2[1] | —————20.0[1]————— | | | | | 55.1[1] | — | — | 25.1[1] | — | 19.8[1] |
| Albania | 1979 | 0.4 | 1,281 | ... | ... | ... | ... | ... | ... | ... | — | ————100.0———— | | ... | ... | ... |
| Algeria | 1973 | 899 | 6.2 | 1.1 | 12.7 | 15.8 | 21.7 | 25.6 | 18.0 | 5.1 | ... | ... | ... | ... | ... | ... |
| American Samoa | 1980 | 1.3 | 1.8 | 49.2[5] | 45.5[6] | ——4.9[7]—— | | ——0.4[8]—— | | | 85.9 | — | — | 5.0 | — | 9.1 |
| Andorra | ... | ... | ... | ... | ... | ... | ... | ... | ... | ... | ... | ... | ... | ... | ... | ... |
| Angola | 1970 | 1,067 | 3.9 | 3.3 | 13.5 | 9.3 | 11.3 | 13.7 | 19.2 | 29.7 | 80.5 | 1.1 | — | — | 18.2 | 0.2 |
| Anguilla | ... | ... | ... | ... | ... | ... | ... | ... | ... | ... | ... | ... | ... | ... | ... | ... |
| Antigua and Barbuda | 1981 | 2.1 | 0.8 | 53.5 | ——46.5—— | | ... | ... | ... | ... | ... | ... | ... | ... | ... | ... |
| Argentina | 1974 | 510 | 399 | ——19.4—— | | 8.2 | 9.5 | 16.7 | 25.1 | 21.1 | 73.8[9] | — | — | 11.7[9] | — | 14.5[9] |
| Aruba | ... | ... | ... | ... | ... | ... | ... | ... | ... | ... | ... | ... | ... | ... | ... | ... |
| Australia | 1984 | 174 | 2,796 | 0.7[11] | 7.2[11] | 5.2[11] | 6.3[11] | 11.9[11] | 26.2[11] | 42.6[11] | 95.7[11] | 3.7[11] | — | — | — | 0.6[11] |
| Austria | 1980[13] | 303 | 24.2 | 3.7 | 31.0 | 17.3 | 21.0 | 21.2 | 5.2 | 0.6 | 59.0 | — | — | 2.3 | — | 38.7 |
| Bahamas, The | 1978 | 4.2 | 8.5 | 55.2[5] | 30.1[6] | ——12.3[7]—— | | 1.1[14] | 0.4[15] | 1.0[16] | 74.9 | 0.6 | — | 4.0 | — | 20.5 |
| Bahrain | 1980 | 0.8 | 4.4 | 19.4 | 52.9 | 17.4 | 8.2 | 2.0 | ——0.1—— | | 37.9 | 0.1 | — | 62.0 | — | — |
| Bangladesh | 1980 | 6,853 | 1.3 | 54.1 | ——45.9—— | | | | | | 53.2 | — | — | 0.5 | ... | 46.3 |
| Barbados | 1969 | 0.2 | 95.8 | ... | ... | ... | ... | ... | ... | ... | ... | ... | ... | ... | ... | ... |
| Belgium | 1984 | 102 | 13.6 | 2.3 | 38.1 | 15.6 | 21.2 | 18.7 | ——4.1—— | | 27.7[9,18] | — | 0.8[9,18] | 71.5[9,18] | — | — |
| Belize | 1974 | 8.9 | 26.7 | ——69.4—— | | | 16.7 | 8.6 | 4.4 | 0.9 | 43.6 | 56.4 | — | — | — | — |
| Benin | 1983 | ... | ... | ... | ... | ... | ... | ... | ... | ... | ... | ... | ... | ... | ... | ... |
| Bermuda | 1981 | ... | ... | ... | ... | ... | ... | ... | ... | ... | ... | ... | ... | ... | ... | ... |
| Bhutan | 1982 | ... | 1.6 | 51.3[5] | 42.9[6] | —————5.8[20]————— | | | | | ... | ... | ... | ... | ... | ... |
| Bolivia | 1980 | 700 | 25.0[22] | ... | ... | ... | ... | ... | ... | ... | 80.0[22] | — | — | ... | ... | 20.0[22] |
| Botswana | 1985 | 81.0 | 3.2 | 32.1 | 49.9 | 12.6 | ——————5.4——— | | | | — | 0.6 | — | — | 99.4 | — |
| Brazil | 1980 | 5,160 | 70.7 | 9.1 | 27.5 | 13.8 | 15.0 | 16.6 | 12.6 | 5.4 | 61.3 | — | — | 17.2 | — | 21.5[25] |
| British Virgin Islands | 1980 | 0.3 | ... | ... | ... | ... | ... | ... | ... | ... | ... | ... | ... | ... | ... | ... |
| Brunei | 1964 | 6.3 | 2.6 | 44.1[5] | 40.4[6] | —————15.5[20]————— | | | | | 52.3 | 1.0 | — | 22.0 | — | 24.7 |
| Bulgaria | 1973 | 0.170[27] | 25,700[27] | ... | ... | ... | ... | ... | ... | ... | ... | ... | ... | ... | ... | ... |
| Burkina Faso | ... | ... | ... | ... | ... | ... | ... | ... | ... | ... | ... | ... | ... | ... | ... | ... |
| Burma | 1981 | 4,300 | 2.3[22] | 61.0[22,28] | —————39.0[29]————— | | | | | | ... | ... | ... | ... | ... | ... |
| Burundi | 1983 | ... | ... | ... | ... | ... | ... | ... | ... | ... | ... | ... | ... | ... | ... | ... |
| Cameroon | 1973 | 926 | 1.6 | 42.7 | 53.8 | 3.2 | 0.3 | — | — | — | 2.4 | — | — | 5.2 | 59.5 | 32.9 |
| Canada | 1981 | 318 | 207 | 1.5[5] | ——6.8[31]—— | | 5.3 | 14.0 | 40.5 | 31.9 | 63.3 | — | — | 6.2 | — | 30.5 |
| Cape Verde | 1979 | ... | ... | ... | ... | ... | ... | ... | ... | ... | ... | ... | ... | ... | ... | ... |
| Cayman Islands | 1984 | 0.2 | ... | — | 5.0 | 80.0 | — | 10.0 | 3.0 | 2.0 | ————90.0———— | | | ————10.0———— | | |
| Central African Republic | 1974 | 283 | 1.7 | 32.2 | 65.2 | 2.5 | — | — | — | — | 0.3[9] | — | — | 0.1[9] | 98.6[9] | 1.2[9] |
| Chad | 1973 | 366 | 2.6 | 19.7 | 69.5 | 10.0 | ——0.8—— | | | | ... | ... | ... | ... | ... | ... |
| Chile | 1976 | 306 | 94.1 | ... | ... | ... | ... | ... | ... | ... | ... | ... | ... | ... | ... | ... |
| China | 1985 | 1,650[21] | ... | ... | ... | ... | ... | ... | ... | ... | — | 10.0[11] | 90.0[11] | — | — | — |
| Christmas Island | ... | ... | ... | ... | ... | ... | ... | ... | ... | ... | ... | ... | ... | ... | ... | ... |
| Cocos (Keeling) Islands | ... | ... | ... | ... | ... | ... | ... | ... | ... | ... | ... | ... | ... | ... | ... | ... |
| Colombia | 1971 | 1,177 | 26.3 | 22.8 | 36.7 | 13.6 | 10.0 | 8.5 | 6.3 | 2.1 | 68.7 | — | — | 5.8 | 4.1 | 21.4 |
| Comoros | 1965 | ... | 25 | ... | ... | ... | ... | ... | ... | ... | — | 42.1 | — | 57.9 | — | — |
| Congo | 1973 | 143 | 1.4 | 37.3 | 62.2 | 0.5 | — | — | — | — | ... | ... | ... | ... | ... | ... |
| Cook Islands | 1975[34] | 1.1 | 2.3 | ... | ... | ... | ... | ... | ... | ... | ... | ... | ... | ... | ... | ... |
| Costa Rica | 1973 | 82 | 38.3 | 23.3 | 25.5 | 11.2 | 10.8 | 15.2 | 10.7 | 3.3 | 97.9 | 1.7 | — | 0.1 | — | 0.3 |
| Côte d'Ivoire | 1975 | 550 | 5.0 | 9.5 | 54.4 | 24.9 | 9.4 | 1.7 | 0.1 | — | ... | ... | ... | ... | ... | ... |
| Cuba | 1985 | ... | ... | ... | ... | ... | ... | ... | ... | ... | ... | ... | ... | ... | ... | ... |
| Cyprus | 1977 | 43.8 | 5.3 | 17.9 | 58.1 | 16.0 | 6.1 | 1.7 | ——0.2—— | | 69.6 | — | — | 23.7 | 0.3 | 6.4 |
| Czechoslovakia | 1980 | 1,391 | 8.1 | 89.9[35] | —————9.9[36]————— | | | | 0.0[37] | 0.2[38] | 6.0[9] | 30.8[9] | 63.2[9] | — | 0.6 | — |
| Denmark | 1986 | 90 | 31.4 | ——19.4—— | | | ——64.4—— | | ——16.2—— | | ... | ... | ... | ... | ... | ... |
| Djibouti | ... | ... | ... | ... | ... | ... | ... | ... | ... | ... | ... | ... | ... | ... | ... | ... |
| Dominica | 1986 | ... | ... | ... | ... | ... | ... | ... | ... | ... | ... | ... | ... | ... | ... | ... |
| Dominican Republic | 1971 | 305 | 9.0 | 23.0 | 54.0 | 11.1 | 2.4 | 7.1 | 1.9 | 0.4 | 54.7 | — | — | 10.1 | 20.0 | 15.1 |
| Ecuador | 1974 | 517 | 15.4 | 27.8 | 38.8 | 10.6 | 8.0 | 8.2 | 5.6 | 0.9 | 70.3 | 0.3 | — | 7.7 | 7.4 | 14.3 |
| Egypt | 1983 | ... | ... | ... | ... | ... | ... | ... | ... | ... | ... | ... | ... | ... | ... | ... |
| El Salvador | 1971 | 271 | 5.4 | 48.9 | 37.9 | 5.8 | 3.4 | 2.6 | 1.2 | 0.2 | 41.5 | — | — | 28.2 | 6.3 | 24.1 |
| Equatorial Guinea | ... | ... | ... | ... | ... | ... | ... | ... | ... | ... | ... | ... | ... | ... | ... | ... |
| Ethiopia | 1977 | 4,893 | 1.4 | 49.9 | 46.5 | 3.4 | 0.2 | — | — | — | 98.4 | 1.6 | — | — | — | — |
| Faeroe Islands | ... | ... | ... | ... | ... | ... | ... | ... | ... | ... | ... | ... | ... | ... | ... | ... |
| Falkland Islands | 1982 | 0.041 | 32,586[39] | ————————————————100.0 | | | | | | | — | 75.0[39] | — | — | — | 25.0[39] |

in which the holder lacks the legal title but uses it under perpetual lease, hereditary tenure, or leases of 30 years or more with nominal, or no, rent. Farms classed as owner-operated are divided into individual and family, corporate or state, and socialized or collective proprietorships. Rented includes sharecropping; communal/tribal includes types of customary or traditional arrangements in which title or goods do not change hands.

Statistics on types of farms by commodities produced refer to FAO categories. The terms "mainly crops" and "mainly livestock" indicate that more than half of the for-sale production was that indicated, and farms not fitting either category were defined as mixed.

The section on technology provides some principal measures of the extent to which modern technology plays a role in the farm activities of each country (although, of course, irrigation may employ technology developed in ancient times).

The classification of farmland by economic use is also subject to differing interpretations. Some countries classify land under permanent crops (those not needing to be replanted each year) as cropland or arable land; that is, land rotated between different crops. Land under temporary crops includes land requiring replanting after each harvest, but some crops have biennial or longer growing cycles and so are sometimes arbitrarily placed under temporary and sometimes under permanent cropland. Permanently

cropped land may include trees, such as cacao (cocoa) or coffee, but other trees may be grown to shade these; temporarily cropped land is sometimes simultaneously planted with permanent crops, causing confusion in classification. Many countries do not distinguish similarly between temporary and permanent meadow or pasture (land used permanently for livestock forage), and some include grassland and meadows under cropland. Land left temporarily fallow or land subject to changing use may be inconsistently classified. Forests and woodlands may have commercial potential but also may be used for grazing livestock.

Measurements of area are given in hectares (1 hectare is equal to 2.4711 acres). The following notes further define the column headings:
a. All properties used wholly or partly for agricultural production. A property need not have agricultural land to be considered a farm; piggeries, hatcheries, and poultry batteries are farms because they engage in agricultural production, i.e., raise livestock and produce livestock products.
b. All forms of tenure not included in the preceding categories. Includes land operated by schools, religious bodies, squatters, seasonally by nomads, and built-on, waste, and similar types of alienation.
... Not available, or no agricultural census or survey ever taken.
—None, less than half the smallest unit shown, or not applicable.

| activity (% of farms) | | | technology (% of farms using) | | | | land in farms | | cropland | | | | meadows and pastures | woodland and forest | other[b] | country |
|---|---|---|---|---|---|---|---|---|---|---|---|---|---|---|---|---|
| mainly crops | mainly livestock | mixed/other | tractor | electricity | irrigation works | artificial fertilizer (kg/ha) | total ('000 ha) | % of total land area | permanent crops | temporary crops | fallow | total cropland | | | | |
| ... | ... | ... | ... | ... | 33[2] | 2.5 | 39,810 | 61.0 | 1.8 | 46.3 | 51.9 | 19.9 | 75.4 | 4.8 | — | Afghanistan |
| ... | ... | ... | 15[3] | ... | 54[2] | 155[4] | 697 | 24.2 | 16.3 | —83.7— | | 100.00 | ... | ... | ... | Albania |
| ... | ... | ... | 7[3] | ... | 4[2] | 22[4] | 5,544 | 2.3 | 4.1 | 65.1 | 30.8 | 93.9 | 2.3 | 3.9 | ... | Algeria |
| 5.6 | 1.0 | 93.4 | 3[3] | 39.7 | ... | ... | 2.4 | 12.2 | ... | ... | 10.7 | 78.0 | 5.1 | — | 16.9 | American Samoa |
| ... | ... | ... | ... | ... | ... | ... | ... | ... | ... | ... | ... | ... | ... | ... | ... | Andorra |
| ... | ... | ... | 3[3] | ... | 89.3 | 2[4] | 4,180 | 3.4 | 36.8 | 63.2 | — | 1.7 | 82.0 | — | 16.2 | Angola |
| ... | ... | ... | ... | ... | ... | ... | ... | ... | ... | ... | ... | ... | ... | ... | ... | Anguilla |
| ... | ... | ... | 29[3] | ... | ... | ... | 1.5 | 3.4 | ... | ... | ... | ... | ... | ... | ... | Antigua and Barbuda |
| 10.6 | 78.9 | 10.5 | 6[3] | ... | 5[2] | 3[4] | 203,345 | 73.1 | ... | ... | ... | 10.6 | 78.9 | 4.8 | 5.7 | Argentina |
| ... | ... | ... | 10 | ... | ... | ... | ... | ... | ... | ... | ... | ... | ... | ... | ... | Aruba |
| 29.4[12] | 70.6[12] | — | 7[3] | ... | 4[2] | 25[4] | 486,600 | 63.3 | 0.8 | —99.2— | | 9.9 | 90.1 | — | — | Australia |
| ... | ... | ... | 71 | ... | ... | 252[4] | 7,326 | 87.4 | 6.6 | 87.4 | 6.0 | 21.3 | 26.0 | 41.5 | 11.2 | Austria |
| ... | ... | ... | 8[3] | ... | 10.3 | 122[4] | 36.2 | 2.6 | 23.3 | 59.9 | 16.8 | 23.3 | 6.9 | 25.7 | 44.0 | Bahamas, The |
| ... | ... | ... | ... | 21.3 | 50[2] | 57[4] | 3.5 | 5.2 | 50.7 | 49.3 | ... | 45.9 | — | — | 54.1 | Bahrain |
| 91.3[17] | 8.7[17] | — | 1[3] | ... | 20[2] | 51.0 | 8,887 | 61.7 | 2.1 | 96.3 | 1.5 | 88.7 | — | —11.3— | | Bangladesh |
| ... | ... | ... | 17[3] | ... | ... | 197[4] | 19.8 | 45.9 | ... | ... | ... | 13.7 | | —86.3— | | Barbados |
| ... | ... | ... | 139[3,19] | ... | ... | 547[4,19] | 1,396 | 45.7 | 7.4[18] | 92.6[18] | | 62.8[18] | 34.2[18] | 0.7[18] | 2.3[18] | Belgium |
| ... | ... | ... | 25[3] | ... | 4[2] | 32[4] | 233 | 10.0 | 13.1 | 81.1 | 5.8 | 36.5 | 15.9 | 36.1 | 11.6 | Belize |
| ... | ... | ... | ... | ... | 1[2] | 3[4] | 3,300 | 29.3 | ... | ... | ... | 100.0 | — | — | — | Benin |
| ... | ... | ... | ... | ... | ... | ... | 0.3 | 6.6 | 24.2 | 63.0 | 12.7 | 83.8 | 10.8 | 5.4 | — | Bermuda |
| ... | ... | ... | ... | ... | 5[2] | 3[4] | 150 | 3.0 | 14.2[21] | —85.8[21]— | | 100.0 | — | — | — | Bhutan |
| 13.6 | 27.9 | 58.5 | 63 | ... | 1[2] | 1.7[23] | 84,060 | 76.3 | 19.3 | 80.7 | | 1.4 | 49.4 | 49.2 | ... | Bolivia |
| 80.0[26] | 16.2[26] | 3.8[26] | ... | ... | 1[2] | 1.7[23] | 343[24] | 5.9[24] | ... | 100.00[24] | | 83.5[24] | ... | ... | ... | Botswana |
| 80.0[26] | 16.2[26] | 3.8[26] | 10[3] | 4.1[26] | 3[2] | 30[4] | 364,854 | 42.9 | 18.2 | 66.9 | 14.9 | 15.8 | 47.8 | 24.2 | 12.2 | Brazil |
| ... | ... | ... | 1[3] | ... | ... | ... | ... | ... | ... | ... | ... | ... | ... | ... | ... | British Virgin Islands |
| ... | ... | ... | 10[3] | ... | 14[2] | ... | 16.4 | 2.8 | 78.0 | 22.0 | — | 54.8 | 0.1 | 16.4 | 28.7 | Brunei |
| ... | ... | ... | 14[3] | ... | 29[2] | 244[4] | 6,071 | 53.0 | ... | ... | ... | 70.0 | 24.0 | — | 6.0 | Bulgaria |
| ... | ... | ... | ... | ... | 1[2] | 5[4] | ... | ... | ... | ... | ... | ... | ... | ... | ... | Burkina Faso |
| ... | ... | ... | 1[3] | ... | 10[2] | 16[4] | 10,300 | 15.2 | —80.2[30]— | | 19.8[30] | 14.8[30] | ... | 14.0[30] | 71.2[30] | Burma |
| ... | ... | ... | ... | ... | 4[2] | 2[4] | 2,388 | 85.8 | —73.8— | | 26.2 | 56.7 | 37.7 | 5.6 | — | Burundi |
| ... | ... | ... | ... | ... | —[2] | 60.0[12] | 1,490 | 3.3 | ... | ... | ... | 100.0 | — | — | — | Cameroon |
| 35.3[26] | 61.4[26] | 3.3[26] | 14[3] | ... | 1[2] | 49[4] | 65,889 | 7.1 | —50.0— | | 16.3 | 63.3 | 6.7 | 5.4 | 24.6 | Canada |
| ... | ... | ... | 1[3] | ... | 5[2] | — | 25[32] | 6.2[32] | 20.8[32] | 79.1[32] | ... | 100.0[32] | ... | ... | ... | Cape Verde |
| 2.4 | 7.1 | 90.5 | 90.0 | ... | ... | ... | ... | ... | ... | ... | ... | ... | ... | ... | ... | Cayman Islands |
| ... | ... | ... | ... | ... | —[2] | 1[4] | 491 | 0.8 | 11.8 | 88.2 | — | 100.0 | — | — | — | Central African Republic |
| ... | ... | ... | ... | ... | ... | 2[4] | 23,877[33] | 45.8[33] | 50.0[33] | —50.0[33]— | | 23.7[33] | 76.3[33] | ... | ... | Chad |
| ... | ... | ... | 6[3] | ... | 23[2] | 25[4] | 28,800 | 39.1 | 6.1 | 65.5 | 28.4 | 11.5 | 42.3 | 20.7 | 25.4 | Chile |
| ... | ... | ... | 8[3] | ... | 45[2] | 124 | 143,600 | 15.0 | 2.6 | —97.4— | | 100.0 | ... | ... | ... | China |
| ... | ... | ... | ... | ... | ... | ... | ... | ... | ... | ... | ... | ... | ... | ... | ... | Christmas Island |
| ... | ... | ... | ... | ... | ... | ... | ... | ... | ... | ... | ... | ... | ... | ... | ... | Cocos (Keeling) Islands |
| ... | ... | ... | 5[3] | ... | 6[2] | 47[4] | 30,993 | 27.0 | 30.6 | 27.6 | 41.8 | 24.7 | 56.4 | — | 18.9 | Colombia |
| ... | ... | ... | ... | ... | ... | ... | 115 | 50.0 | ... | ... | ... | 34.8 | 9.4 | 10.9 | 44.9 | Comoros |
| ... | ... | ... | 1[3] | ... | 1[2] | 2[4] | 197 | 0.6 | 49.5 | 50.5 | ... | 100.0 | — | — | — | Congo |
| ... | ... | ... | 22[3] | ... | ... | ... | ... | ... | 55.9 | 21.9 | 22.2 | 100.0 | — | — | — | Cook Islands |
| ... | ... | ... | 10[3] | ... | 4[2] | 132[4] | 3,122 | 60.0 | 42.2 | 57.8 | — | 15.7 | 49.9 | 22.9 | 11.4 | Costa Rica |
| ... | ... | ... | 1[3] | ... | 2[2] | 11[4] | 2,753 | 8.6 | 65.9 | 34.1 | ... | 100.0 | ... | ... | ... | Côte d'Ivoire |
| ... | ... | ... | 21[3] | ... | 32[2] | 164[4] | 8,589 | 77.5 | 12.7 | —87.3— | | 34.4 | 34.2 | 29.5 | 1.9 | Cuba |
| 98.0 | 2.0 | ... | 26[3] | ... | 22[2] | 46[4] | 234 | 25.3 | 35.4 | 53.2 | 11.4 | 76.1 | 1.6 | 1.7 | 20.6 | Cyprus |
| 34.3 | 24.4 | 41.3 | 26[3] | 100.0 | 4[2] | 344[4] | 6,924 | 54.1 | 2.6 | —97.4— | | 75.3 | 24.7 | — | — | Czechoslovakia |
| 49.2 | 24.0 | 26.8 | 98.6 | ... | 15.2 | 267[4] | 2,819 | 65.4 | 1.2 | 98.7 | 0.1 | 92.4 | 7.6 | — | — | Denmark |
| ... | ... | ... | ... | ... | ... | ... | ... | ... | ... | ... | ... | ... | ... | ... | ... | Djibouti |
| ... | ... | ... | 5[3] | ... | ... | 135[4] | 20 | 26.3 | ... | ... | ... | ... | ... | ... | ... | Dominica |
| ... | ... | ... | 2[3] | ... | 12[2] | 29[4] | 2,736 | 56.5 | 27.8 | 54.3 | 18.0 | 41.8 | 45.8 | 11.6 | 0.8 | Dominican Republic |
| 67.8 | 12.4 | 19.8 | 3[3] | ... | 22[2] | 21[4] | 7,955 | 29.6 | 32.8 | 51.5 | 15.7 | 32.8 | 32.2 | 29.0 | 6.0 | Ecuador |
| ... | ... | ... | 17[3] | ... | 100[2] | 361[4] | 2,731 | 3.0 | 3.5 | 96.5 | ... | 100.0 | ... | ... | ... | Egypt |
| 95.3 | 4.7 | — | 5[3] | ... | 15[2] | 113[4] | 1,452 | 69.0 | 25.1 | 58.6 | 16.4 | 44.9 | 38.2 | 11.6 | 5.3 | El Salvador |
| ... | ... | ... | ... | ... | ... | ... | ... | ... | ... | ... | ... | ... | ... | ... | ... | Equatorial Guinea |
| ... | ... | ... | ... | ... | 1[2] | 3[4] | 6,971 | 5.7 | 7.4 | 76.8 | 15.8 | 86.9 | 9.1 | — | 4.0 | Ethiopia |
| ... | ... | ... | ... | ... | ... | ... | ... | ... | ... | ... | ... | ... | ... | ... | ... | Faeroe Islands |
| ... | ... | ... | ... | ... | ... | ... | 1,173[39] | 96.4[39] | ... | ... | ... | ... | ... | ... | ... | Falkland Islands |

## Agriculture and land use (continued)

| country | year | number of farms ('000) | average (ha) | under 1 ha | 1–5 ha | 5–10 ha | 10–20 ha | 20–50 ha | 50–200 ha | over 200 ha | individual/ family | corporate/ state | socialized/ collective | rented (including share-croppers) | tribal/ com-munal | other |
|---|---|---|---|---|---|---|---|---|---|---|---|---|---|---|---|---|
| | | | | size class (%) | | | | | | | owner-operated | | | | | |
| Fiji | 1979 | 66 | 4.2 | 64.3 | 20.6 | 8.1 | 3.7 | 2.1 | —1.2— | | — | — | — | 3.5 | 95.1 | 1.4 |
| Finland | 1985 | 200 | 60.0 | — | 15.2 | 25.6 | 30.2 | 23.2 | —5.8— | | 79.9 | 0.7 | — | 19.3 | — | 0.1 |
| France | 1980 | 1,263 | 26.6 | 9.5 | 18.8 | 13.2 | 19.3 | 27.5 | —11.7— | | 65.2[11] | | — | 33.5[11] | — | 1.2[11] |
| French Guiana | 1981 | 2.2 | 3.3 | 50.4 | 41.2 | 4.4 | —————4.0———— | | | | ... | ... | ... | ... | ... | ... |
| French Polynesia | ... | ... | ... | ... | ... | ... | ... | ... | ... | ... | ... | ... | ... | ... | ... | ... |
| Gabon | 1975 | 71 | 1.0 | 68.0 | —32.0— | | — | — | — | — | 81.8 | — | — | 0.3 | 5.3 | 12.5 |
| Gambia, The | ... | ... | ... | ... | ... | ... | ... | ... | ... | ... | ... | ... | ... | ... | ... | ... |
| Gaza Strip | 1980 | ... | ... | ... | ... | ... | ... | ... | ... | ... | ... | ... | ... | ... | ... | ... |
| Germany, East | 1982 | 5.0 | ... | ... | ... | ... | ... | ... | ... | ... | — | 9.6 | 90.4 | — | — | — |
| Germany, West | 1983 | 887 | 13.6 | 16.0 | 26.4 | 15.4 | 18.8 | 19.5 | 3.9 | | 39.5 | — | — | 6.7 | — | 53.8 |
| Ghana | 1970 | 805 | 3.2 | 36.6 | 48.7 | 9.0 | 3.9 | 1.8 | | | ... | ... | ... | ... | ... | ... |
| Gibraltar | | | | | | | | | | | | | | | | |
| Greece | 1981 | 999 | 3.5 | 24.7 | 54.2 | 15.0 | 4.7 | 1.2 | —0.2— | | ... | ... | ... | ... | ... | ... |
| Greenland | | | | | | | | | | | | | | | | |
| Grenada | 1981 | 8 | 1.7 | 88.3[28] | 6.9[41] | 3.3[42] | 0.7 | 0.4[14] | —0.3[43]— | | ————73.2———— | | | 14.1 | — | 12.7 |
| Guadeloupe | 1981 | 19 | 3.7 | 32.1 | 58.6 | 7.1 | —————2.2———— | | | | 46.6[44] | — | — | 19.1[44] | — | 34.3[44] |
| Guam | 1978 | 2 | 5.8 | 75.6 | 19.6 | 2.5 | 1.0 | 0.8 | —0.5— | | 80.5 | — | — | 5.8 | — | 13.7 |
| Guatemala | 1979 | 600 | 6.8 | 39.7[45] | 39.8[46] | 8.2[47] | 2.0[48] | —0.2[49]— | | | ————74.0[50]———— | | | 6.3[50] | 5.8[50] | 13.9[50] |
| Guernsey | 1987 | 0.106 | 18.6 | 6.7[51] | 24.0[51] | 23.1[51] | —46.1[51]— | | — | — | 31.1[9] | — | — | 68.9[9] | — | — |
| Guinea | | | | | | | | | | | | | | | | |
| Guinea-Bissau | 1961 | 87 | 3.0 | 13.4 | 73.3 | 10.0 | 3.0 | 0.3 | | | ... | ... | ... | ... | ... | ... |
| Guyana | 1964 | | | | | | | | | | — | 90.0 | — | ... | ... | 10.0 |
| Haiti | 1971 | 617 | 1.4 | 58.7 | 37.5 | —3.8— | | | | | 66.6 | — | — | 25.0 | — | 8.4 |
| Honduras | 1974 | 195 | 13.5 | 17.3 | 46.6 | 14.5 | 9.8 | 7.8 | 3.3 | 0.8 | 99.7 | 0.1 | — | — | 0.2 | — |
| Hong Kong | 1986 | 11 | 0.3 | 97.5 | 2.3 | 0.1 | —0.1— | | — | — | —————9.0———— | | | 77.0 | — | 14.0 |
| Hungary | 1981 | 798 | 8.3 | ... | ... | ... | ... | ... | ... | ... | 6.8 | 13.3 | 74.5 | — | — | — |
| Iceland | 1981 | 7.0 | ... | 15.7 | 9.3 | 11.7 | 23.7 | 35.8 | —3.7— | | ... | ... | ... | ... | ... | ... |
| India | 1977 | 81,569 | 2.0 | 54.6 | 35.8 | 6.6 | 2.4 | 0.5 | —0.1— | | 92.7 | — | — | 1.2 | — | 6.1 |
| Indonesia[53] | 1973 | 14,374 | 1.0 | 70.4 | 27.4 | 1.6 | 0.6 | — | — | — | 74.8 | — | — | 3.2 | — | 22.1 |
| Iran | 1973 | ... | ... | ... | ... | ... | ... | ... | ... | ... | ... | ... | ... | ... | ... | ... |
| Iraq | 1971 | 591 | 9.7 | 20.2 | 29.3 | 21.4 | 18.5 | 9.0 | 1.3 | 0.3 | 52.5 | — | — | 40.9 | — | 6.6 |
| Ireland | 1980 | 279[26] | 25.0 | 2.7[26] | —37.8[26]— | | —52.4[26]— | | 7.1[26] | | ... | ... | ... | ... | ... | ... |
| Isle of Man | 1983 | 0.8 | 59.3 | 26.3[54] | 13.0[55] | 18.1[14] | 24.6[15] | —18.0[16]— | | — | 60.0[12] | — | — | ... | — | 40.0[12] |
| Israel | 1984 | 40[11] | 13.4[11] | 25.9[11, 53] | 62.5[11, 53] | 8.1[11, 53] | —3.5[11, 53]— | | — | — | 77.5[11] | — | 1.8[11] | — | — | 20.7[11] |
| Italy | 1983 | 3,271 | 7.2 | 18.0[39] | 30.2[39] | 37.7[39] | 3.1[39] | 9.2[39] | 1.8[39] | | 81.5[26] | — | — | 6.7[26] | — | 11.8[26] |
| Jamaica | 1979 | 184 | 2.9 | 32.5[56] | 60.7[57] | 4.8[42] | 0.9 | 0.4[14] | 0.3[15] | 0.4[16] | 99.5[58] | 0.2[58] | —[58] | —[58] | —[58] | 0.3[58] |
| Japan | 1985 | 4,376 | 1.2 | 69.9 | 28.4 | —1.7— | | | | | 79.4[26] | ... | ... | ... | ... | 20.6[26] |
| Jersey | 1984 | 0.7 | 9.0 | —44.4— | | 20.6 | 22.1 | —13.0— | | | 31.4[59] | ... | ... | 68.6[59] | — | — |
| Jordan | 1983 | 57 | 6.3 | 25.3 | 44.6 | 15.6 | 8.6 | 4.5 | 1.3 | 0.1 | 80.5 | — | — | 13.1 | 0.3 | 6.1 |
| Kampuchea | ... | ... | ... | ... | ... | ... | ... | ... | ... | ... | ... | ... | ... | ... | ... | ... |
| Kenya | 1975 | 1,487 | 4.1 | 31.8 | 58.1 | 9.9 | — | — | 0.1 | 0.1 | ... | ... | ... | ... | ... | ... |
| Kiribati | ... | ... | ... | ... | ... | ... | ... | ... | ... | ... | ... | ... | ... | ... | ... | ... |
| Korea, North | ... | ... | ... | ... | ... | ... | ... | ... | ... | ... | ... | ... | ... | ... | ... | ... |
| Korea, South | 1983 | 2,000 | 1.1 | 66.2 | —33.8— | | — | — | — | — | 82.5[26] | — | — | 17.4[26] | — | 0.1[26] |
| Kuwait | 1986 | 1.9 | 2.4 | 48.6[26] | 25.4[26] | 10.2[26] | 8.7[26] | 4.0[26] | 3.1[26] | | 95.3 | — | — | ... | ... | 4.7 |
| Laos | ... | ... | ... | ... | ... | ... | ... | ... | ... | ... | ... | ... | ... | ... | ... | ... |
| Lebanon | 1970 | 143 | 4.3 | 47.7 | —44.5— | | —6.5— | | 1.2 | 0.1 | ... | ... | ... | ... | ... | ... |
| Lesotho | 1970 | 187 | 2.0 | 27.0 | 67.5 | —5.5— | | — | — | — | ... | ... | ... | ... | ... | ... |
| Liberia[64] | 1971 | 122 | 3.0 | 52.8 | 31.0 | 12.0 | —3.7— | | —0.5— | | 40.0[9] | — | — | — | 43.3[9] | 16.7[9] |
| Libya | 1977 | 170 | 11.0 | 5.0[65] | —40.0[65]— | | —42.0[65, 66]— | | —13.0[65, 67]— | | ... | ... | ... | ... | ... | ... |
| Liechtenstein | 1980 | 0.5 | 8.0 | 27.5 | 30.4 | 16.2 | 14.2 | 10.5 | 1.2 | — | 86.2 | — | — | 13.6 | — | 0.2 |
| Luxembourg | 1985 | 4.4 | 29 | —26.3— | | 9.0 | 11.8 | 30.5 | —22.3— | | 52.2[9] | —0.7[9]— | | 47.1[9] | — | — |
| Macau | ... | ... | ... | ... | ... | ... | ... | ... | ... | ... | ... | ... | ... | ... | ... | ... |
| Madagascar | 1971 | 940 | 1.0 | 65.0 | 35.0 | ... | — | — | — | — | ... | ... | ... | ... | ... | ... |
| Malawi | 1981 | 1,136 | 1.2 | 54.9 | 45.1 | ... | — | — | — | — | ... | ... | ... | ... | ... | ... |
| Malaysia[68] | 1980 | 920[69] | 2.2[69, 70] | ... | ... | ... | ... | ... | ... | ... | 53.2[26, 69] | 18.2[26, 71] | ... | 19.6[26, 69] | ... | 9.0[26, 69] |
| Maldives | 1985 | ... | ... | ... | ... | ... | ... | ... | ... | ... | ... | ... | ... | ... | ... | ... |
| Mali | 1980 | 481 | 4.0 | 19.2 | 55.2 | 18.2 | —7.5— | | — | — | 94.2[9, 73] | 1.7[9] | — | — | 4.1[9] | — |
| Malta | 1983 | 4.4[74] | 3.0[74] | 38.7[74] | 53.3[74] | 6.9[74] | 1.1[74] | — | — | — | 29.6 | — | — | 70.4 | — | — |
| Martinique | 1981 | 19.6 | 3.1 | 67.5 | 26.4 | 3.4 | —2.1— | | —0.6— | | ... | ... | ... | ... | ... | ... |
| Mauritania | 1976 | ... | ... | ... | ... | ... | ... | ... | ... | ... | ... | ... | ... | ... | ... | ... |
| Mauritius | 1980 | 32.5 | 1.1 | 61.3 | 36.2 | 1.9 | 0.3 | 0.2 | —0.1— | | 95.8 | — | — | 4.2 | — | — |
| Mayotte | 1978 | 4.8 | 1.7 | ... | ... | ... | ... | ... | ... | ... | ... | ... | ... | ... | ... | ... |
| Mexico | 1970 | 1,020 | 137 | 33.5 | 26.2 | 10.0 | 6.7 | 9.2 | 8.1 | 6.3 | 97.6[75] | 0.2 | — | — | 2.2[75] | — |
| Monaco | ... | ... | ... | ... | ... | ... | ... | ... | ... | ... | ... | ... | ... | ... | ... | ... |
| Mongolia | 1983 | 0.3 | ... | ... | ... | ... | ... | ... | ... | ... | — | 19.6[24, 76] | 80.4[24, 76] | — | — | — |
| Montserrat | 1979 | 0.8 | 1.2 | 62.5[56] | 28.0[77] | —9.5[29]— | | | | | 14.6 | — | — | 84.4 | — | 1.0 |
| Morocco | 1984 | 1,900[60] | 3.9[60] | —75.0[60]— | | —25.0[60]— | | | | | ... | ... | ... | ... | ... | ... |
| Mozambique | 1973 | 1,605 | 3.1 | —89.7[78]— | | —10.0[79]— | | —0.3— | | | 0.2 | 0.1 | — | — | 99.7 | — |
| Nauru | ... | ... | ... | ... | ... | ... | ... | ... | ... | ... | ... | ... | ... | ... | ... | ... |
| Nepal | 1982 | 2,194 | 1.1 | 66.7 | 29.9 | 2.7 | —0.7— | | | | 97.5 | — | — | 1.6 | — | 0.9 |
| Netherlands, The | 1986 | 134 | 15.0 | 11.2 | 21.6 | 16.6 | 23.1 | 23.9 | —3.6— | | —47.0[80]— | | | 12.9[80] | — | 40.1[80] |
| Netherlands Antilles | ... | ... | ... | ... | ... | ... | ... | ... | ... | ... | ... | ... | ... | ... | ... | ... |
| New Caledonia[53] | 1976 | 2.3 | 145 | 2.3 | 9.0 | 11.3 | 22.6 | 25.4 | 17.8 | 11.7 | 45.7 | — | — | — | — | — |
| New Zealand | 1985 | 79 | 271 | —12.5— | | 10.3 | 8.4 | —46.5— | | 22.3 | 85.7 | 10.9 | — | — | — | 3.4 |
| Nicaragua | ... | ... | ... | ... | ... | ... | ... | ... | ... | ... | ... | ... | ... | ... | ... | ... |
| Niger | 1980[81] | 699 | 4.9 | 3.8 | 54.1 | 37.8 | —4.3— | | | | ... | ... | ... | ... | ... | ... |
| Nigeria | 1971 | ... | ... | 92 | 7.8 | 0.2 | — | — | — | — | ... | ... | ... | ... | ... | ... |
| Niue | ... | ... | ... | ... | ... | ... | ... | ... | ... | ... | ... | ... | ... | ... | ... | ... |
| Norfolk Island | ... | ... | ... | ... | ... | ... | ... | ... | ... | ... | ... | ... | ... | ... | ... | ... |
| Norway | 1986 | 102 | 9.4 | 11.9[28] | 26.4[82] | 27.5 | 24.6 | 9.1 | —0.7— | | 97.4[9, 18] | 1.8[9, 18] | — | — | — | 0.8[9, 18] |
| Oman | 1979 | 65 | 1.3 | ... | ... | ... | ... | ... | ... | ... | ... | ... | ... | ... | ... | ... |
| Pacific Is., Trust Terr. of | 1970 | 4.0 | 10.3 | 7.4 | 53.4 | 22.4 | 7.8 | 5.5 | 3.6 | — | 90.8 | — | — | 1.4 | — | 7.8 |
| Marshall Islands | ... | ... | ... | ... | ... | ... | ... | ... | ... | ... | ... | ... | ... | ... | ... | ... |
| Micronesia, F.S. of | ... | ... | ... | ... | ... | ... | ... | ... | ... | ... | ... | ... | ... | ... | ... | ... |

| activity (% of farms) | | | technology (% of farms using) | | | | farm land use — land in farms | | cropland | | | | meadows and pastures | woodland and forest | other[b] | country |
|---|---|---|---|---|---|---|---|---|---|---|---|---|---|---|---|---|
| mainly crops | mainly live-stock | mixed/ other | tractor | electri-city | irriga-tion works | artificial fertilizer (kg/ha) | total ('000 ha) * | % of total land area | perma-nent crops | tempo-rary crops | fallow | total crop-land | | | | |
| ... | ... | ... | 19[3] | ... | ... | 46[4] | 277 | 15.2 | ... | ... | ... | ... | ... | ... | ... | Fiji |
| ... | ... | ... | 99[3] | 100.0[26] | 3[2] | 222[4] | 12,025 | 39.5 | 0.3[26] | 97.6[26] | 2.1[26] | 20.1 | 1.1 | 58.1 | 20.7 | Finland |
| ... | ... | ... | 74.8 | ... | 6[2] | 312[4] | 33,649 | 61.8 | 7.4 | 90.6 | 2.0 | 53.6 | 34.1 | 8.2 | 4.1 | France |
| ... | ... | ... | 30[3] | ... | ... | 199[4] | 7.3 | 0.1 | 10.4 | 52.5 | 37.3 | 89.6 | 10.4 | ... | ... | French Guiana |
| ... | ... | ... | 2[3] | ... | ... | 13[4] | ... | ... | ... | ... | ... | ... | ... | ... | ... | French Polynesia |
| ... | ... | ... | 3[3] | ... | —[2] | 5[4] | 73.0 | 0.3 | ... | ... | ... | ... | ... | ... | ... | Gabon |
| ... | ... | ... | ... | ... | 21[2] | 16[4] | ... | ... | ... | ... | ... | ... | ... | ... | ... | Gambia, The |
| ... | ... | ... | 16[3] | ... | 52.8[40] | ... | 19.3 | 53.2 | 74.6 | 25.4 | ... | 100.0 | ... | ... | ... | Gaza Strip |
| 28.7 | 71.3 | — | 31[3] | ... | 3[2] | 290[4] | 6,259 | 57.8 | ... | ... | ... | 75.6 | 20.1 | ... | 4.3 | Germany, East |
| ... | ... | ... | 198[3] | ... | 4[2] | 421[4] | 12,026 | 48.4 | 1.2[18] | —97.8[18]— | | 51.7[18] | 32.6[18] | 11.5[18] | 4.2[18] | Germany, West |
| ... | ... | ... | 1[3] | ... | 1[2] | 8[4] | 2,574 | 10.8 | 61.4 | 38.6 | — | 100.0 | ... | ... | ... | Ghana |
| ... | ... | ... | ... | ... | ... | ... | ... | ... | ... | ... | ... | ... | ... | ... | ... | Gibraltar |
| ... | ... | ... | 42[3] | ... | 57.3 | 161[4] | 3,546 | 26.9 | 29.2 | 61.1 | 9.7 | 98.1 | 1.9 | — | — | Greece |
| ... | ... | ... | ... | ... | ... | ... | ... | ... | ... | ... | ... | ... | ... | ... | ... | Greenland |
| ... | ... | ... | 2[3] | ... | ... | ... | 13.9 | 40.2 | ... | ... | ... | ... | ... | ... | ... | Grenada |
| 60.6 | 18.1 | 21.3 | 3.2 | ... | 5[2] | 255 | 70 | 39.6 | 23.0 | 73.3 | 3.7 | 56.2 | 25.2 | 7.6 | 11.0 | Guadeloupe |
| ... | ... | ... | 7[3] | 88.4 | ... | ... | 11.6 | 20.5 | —94.8— | | 5.2 | 49.5 | 41.2 | ... | 9.3 | Guam |
| — | 100.0 | — | 2[3] | ... | 4[2] | 51[4] | 4,147 | 38.1 | 27.6 | —72.4— | | 42.0 | 27.3 | 27.2 | 3.4 | Guatemala |
| — | 100.0 | — | ... | ... | ... | ... | 2 | 31.2 | — | 100.0 | | 7.6 | 92.4 | ... | — | Guernsey |
| ... | ... | ... | ... | ... | 4[2] | 1[4] | ... | ... | ... | ... | ... | ... | ... | ... | ... | Guinea |
| ... | ... | ... | ... | ... | ... | 8[4] | 169 | 4.7 | ... | ... | ... | ... | ... | ... | ... | Guinea-Bissau |
| ... | ... | ... | 7[3] | ... | 26[2] | 21[4] | 10,652 | 26.2 | ... | ... | ... | 8.4 | 91.6 | ... | ... | Guyana |
| ... | ... | ... | 1[3] | ... | 8[2] | 4[4] | 1,579 | 57.0 | ... | ... | ... | 54.4 | 33.3 | 12.3 | —* | Haiti |
| ... | ... | ... | 2[3] | ... | 5[2] | 16[4] | 2,630 | 23.5 | 15.4[18] | 34.6[18] | 50.0[18] | 52.0[18] | 48.0[18] | — | —* | Honduras |
| 56.3 | 37.3 | 6.4 | 22.7 | ... | 90.0 | 100.0[23] | 7.3 | 6.8 | 7.4 | 37.0 | 55.6 | 100.0 | ... | ... | ... | Hong Kong |
| ... | ... | ... | 11[3] | ... | 3[2] | 300[4] | 7,413 | 79.7 | 11.8 | 86.1 | 2.1 | 71.7 | 17.3 | ... | 11.0 | Hungary |
| ... | ... | ... | 1,750[3] | 87.0[33] | ... | 4,413[4] | ... | ... | ... | ... | ... | ... | ... | ... | ... | Iceland |
| ... | ... | ... | 3[3] | ... | 23[2] | 39[4] | 163,343 | 49.7 | | —88.3— | 11.7 | 96.0[52] | 1.5[52] | —2.5[52]— | | India |
| 86.8 | — | 13.2 | 1[3] | ... | 27[2] | 74[4] | 14,168 | 7.4 | 21.6 | 71.1 | 7.3 | 89.5 | 0.6 | 1.4 | 8.5 | Indonesia[53] |
| ... | ... | ... | 5[3] | ... | 29[2] | 76[4] | 20,235 | 12.3 | ... | ... | ... | ... | ... | ... | ... | Iran |
| 87.9 | 11.2 | 0.8 | 6[3] | ... | 32[2] | 17[4] | 5,732 | 13.1 | 3.0 | 62.4 | 34.6 | 87.2 | 0.7 | 0.2 | 11.9 | Iraq |
| ... | ... | ... | 152[3] | ... | ... | 697[4] | 5,790 | 84.0 | 0.5 | 99.5 | | 8.0 | 60.1 | —31.8— | | Ireland |
| ... | ... | ... | ... | ... | ... | ... | 47 | 83.0 | 2.1 | 84.2 | 13.7 | 12.3 | 87.7 | — | — | Isle of Man |
| 43.1[11,53] | 30.2[11,53] | 26.7[11,53] | 63[3] | ... | 50[2] | 183[4] | 584 | 28.2 | 22.0 | 78.0 | | 70.5 | ... | ... | 29.6 | Israel |
| ... | ... | ... | 95[3] | ... | 25.7 | 168[4] | 17,249 | 57.2 | 26.3[39] | —73.7[39]— | | 52.4[39] | 21.2[39] | 17.1[39] | 9.3[39] | Italy |
| 80.8[20] | —19.2[20]— | | 11[3] | ... | 12[2] | 47[4] | 603[58] | 54.8[58] | 22.2[58] | 72.2[58] | 5.6[58] | 41.3[58] | 21.6[58] | 13.5[58] | 23.6[58] | Jamaica |
| ... | ... | ... | 330[3] | ... | 67[2] | 437[4] | 4,996[24] | 13.2[24] | 10.9[24] | 84.8[24] | 4.3[24] | 86.4[24] | 13.6[24] | ... | ... | Japan |
| 85.1[60] | 14.9[60] | — | ... | ... | ... | ... | 6.7[60] | 5.8[60] | — | 100.0[60] | | 64.6[60] | 34.7[60] | ... | 0.7[60] | Jersey |
| 58.2[39,61] | 14.9[39,61] | 26.9[39,61] | 5.0 | 1.5 | 19.2 | 35.5[23] | 364 | 4.1 | 13.3 | 63.0 | 23.7 | 87.7 | 1.0 | 0.3 | 11.0 | Jordan |
| ... | ... | ... | ... | ... | 3[2] | 2[4] | ... | ... | ... | ... | ... | ... | ... | ... | ... | Kampuchea |
| ... | ... | ... | 3[3] | ... | 2[2] | 38[4] | 6,132 | 10.8 | 29.5[62] | 70.5[62] | ... | 21.5[62] | 47.1[62] | 4.9[62] | 26.5[62] | Kenya |
| ... | ... | ... | ... | ... | ... | ... | ... | ... | ... | ... | ... | ... | ... | ... | ... | Kiribati |
| ... | ... | ... | 27[3] | ... | 46[2] | 345[4] | ... | ... | ... | ... | ... | ... | ... | ... | ... | Korea, North |
| 94.0[58] | 0.4[58] | 5.6[58] | 0.4 | 10.3[63] | 55[2] | 331[4] | 2,026[24] | 20.4[24] | 6.0[24] | —94.0— | | 98.3[24] | 1.7[24] | ... | ... | Korea, South |
| 36.7 | 61.8 | 1.5 | 100.0 | 100.0 | 100 | 420[4] | 44.7 | 2.5 | ... | ... | ... | 100.0 | ... | ... | ... | Kuwait |
| ... | ... | ... | 1[3] | ... | 13[2] | 1[4] | ... | ... | ... | ... | ... | ... | ... | ... | ... | Laos |
| 77.0[61] | 8.1[61] | 14.9[61] | 10[3] | ... | 29[2] | 119[4] | 275[24] | 27.0[24] | 36.7[24] | 39.7[24] | 23.6[24] | 100.0[24] | ... | ... | ... | Lebanon |
| 5.3[61] | 93.3[61] | 1.4[61] | 5[3] | ... | —[2] | 15[4] | 372 | 12.3 | | 89.6 | 10.4 | 98.8 | — | — | 1.2 | Lesotho |
| ... | ... | ... | 1[3] | ... | 1[2] | 8[4] | 370[12] | 3.8[12] | 66.2[12] | 33.8[12] | | 98.3[12] | — | 1.7[12] | — | Liberia[64] |
| ... | ... | ... | 13[3] | ... | 11[2] | 43[4] | 8,800[12] | 5.1[12] | | —33.3[12]— | 66.7[12] | 20.5[12] | 79.5[12] | — | — | Libya |
| 20.9 | 68.8 | 10.3 | 113[3] | ... | ... | ... | 3.9 | 24.3 | 1.8 | —98.2— | | 26.1 | 58.3 | 14.1 | 1.5 | Liechtenstein |
| ... | ... | ... | 164[3] | ... | ... | 19 | 126 | 48.8 | 2.7 | 96.7 | 0.7 | 44.4 | 55.6 | — | — | Luxembourg |
| ... | ... | ... | ... | ... | ... | ... | ... | ... | ... | ... | ... | ... | ... | ... | ... | Macau |
| ... | ... | ... | 1[3] | ... | 33[2] | 5[4] | 2,200[30] | 3.8[30] | 19.0[30] | 81.0[30] | — | 100.0[30] | ... | ... | ... | Madagascar |
| 22.1 | ... | 77.9 | 1[3] | ... | 0.2[40] | 18[4] | 1,332 | 14.2 | 0.2 | 99.8 | | 94.8 | — | 5.2 | — | Malawi |
| ... | ... | ... | 2[3,72] | ... | 8[2,72] | 107[4,72] | 4,100[59] | 31.2[59] | 84.8[59] | 15.2[59] | — | 100.0[59] | ... | ... | ... | Malaysia[68] |
| ... | ... | ... | ... | ... | ... | ... | 19 | 63.5 | ... | ... | ... | ... | ... | ... | ... | Maldives |
| ... | ... | ... | ... | ... | 16[2] | 7[4] | 41,500 | 34.0 | — | 18.0 | 82.0 | 28.0 | 72.0 | — | ... | Mali |
| ... | ... | ... | 34[3] | ... | 8[2] | 684[4] | 10.9 | 34.1 | 4.2 | 85.0 | 10.8 | 100.0 | ... | ... | ... | Malta |
| ... | ... | ... | 46[3] | ... | 26[2] | 669[4] | 75.4 | 71.1 | 39.6 | 60.0 | 0.4 | 36.9 | 33.6 | 10.0 | 19.5 | Martinique |
| ... | ... | ... | 2[3] | ... | 4[2] | 2[4] | 167 | 0.2 | — | ... | ... | 100.0 | — | — | — | Mauritania |
| ... | ... | ... | 3[3] | ... | 16[2] | 254[4] | 97.8[60] | 52.5[60] | 3.3[18] | 96.7[18] | — | 100.0[18] | — | — | — | Mauritius |
| ... | ... | ... | ... | ... | ... | ... | 8.0 | 21.0 | ... | ... | ... | ... | ... | ... | ... | Mayotte |
| 66.4[61] | 25.0[61] | 8.6[61] | 6[3] | ... | 21[2] | 59[4] | 139,868 | 72.7 | 6.3 | 58.1 | 35.6 | 16.5 | 53.3 | 14.2 | 16.0 | Mexico |
| ... | ... | ... | ... | ... | ... | ... | ... | ... | ... | ... | ... | ... | ... | ... | ... | Monaco |
| ... | ... | ... | 8[3] | ... | 3[2] | 12[4] | 124,977 | 79.9 | — | 53.0 | 47.0 | 2.0 | 98.0 | — | — | Mongolia |
| ... | ... | ... | 7[3] | ... | ... | ... | 1.6[21] | 15.3[21] | 32.1[21] | 67.9[21] | — | 46.9[21] | 53.1[21] | — | — | Montserrat |
| ... | ... | ... | 3[3] | ... | 6[2] | 29[4] | 7,814 | 17.0 | 6.6 | 63.5 | 29.9 | 100.0 | ... | ... | ... | Morocco |
| ... | ... | ... | 2[3] | ... | 2[2] | 8[4] | 13,626 | 17.8 | | —44.9— | 55.1 | 55.0 | 45.0 | — | — | Mozambique |
| ... | ... | ... | ... | ... | ... | ... | ... | ... | ... | ... | ... | ... | ... | ... | ... | Nauru |
| 31.4 | 55.6 | 13.0 | 1[3] | ... | 39 | 14[4] | 2,683[21] | 18.2[21] | 1.3 | 97.1 | 1.6 | 94.0 | 1.7 | 0.6 | 3.7 | Nepal |
| ... | ... | ... | 217[3] | ... | 59[2] | 788[4] | 2,013 | 48.2 | 11.6 | 87.7 | 0.7 | 43.3 | 56.7 | — | — | Netherlands, The |
| ... | ... | ... | 153[3,10] | ... | ... | ... | ... | ... | ... | ... | ... | ... | ... | ... | ... | Netherlands Antilles |
| ... | ... | ... | 69[3] | ... | ... | 50[4] | 333 | 17.8 | ... | ... | ... | ... | ... | ... | ... | New Caledonia[53] |
| 12.6 | 51.1 | 36.3 | 197[3] | ... | 7.2[44] | 1,147[4] | 21,377 | 79.7 | ... | ... | ... | 3.4 | 63.9 | 5.1 | 27.5 | New Zealand |
| ... | ... | ... | 2[3] | ... | 6[2] | 56[4] | ... | ... | ... | ... | ... | ... | ... | ... | ... | Nicaragua |
| ... | ... | ... | ... | ... | 1[2] | 1[4] | 3,407 | 2.9 | ... | ... | ... | ... | ... | ... | ... | Niger |
| ... | ... | ... | ... | ... | 4[2] | 9[4] | 34,290 | 37 | | —20.0— | 80.0 | 31.4 | 27.5 | 41.1 | — | Nigeria |
| ... | ... | ... | 1[3] | ... | ... | ... | ... | ... | ... | ... | ... | ... | ... | ... | ... | Niue |
| ... | ... | ... | ... | ... | ... | ... | ... | ... | ... | ... | ... | ... | ... | ... | ... | Norfolk Island |
| ... | ... | ... | 169[3] | ... | 9[2] | 201 | 954 | 2.9 | ... | ... | ... | 44.9 | 55.1 | ... | ... | Norway |
| ... | ... | ... | 2[3] | ... | 95[2] | 36[4] | 83 | 0.3 | 68.6 | 31.4 | ... | 49.2 | | —50.8— | | Oman |
| ... | ... | ... | 1[3] | ... | ... | ... | 40 | 21.1 | 54.2 | 9.8 | 36.0 | 68.7 | 17.5 | — | 13.7 | Pacific Is., Trust Terr. of Marshall Islands |
| ... | ... | ... | ... | ... | ... | ... | ... | ... | ... | ... | ... | ... | ... | ... | ... | Micronesia, F.S. of |

## Agriculture and land use (continued)

| country | year | number of farms ('000) | average (ha) | under 1 ha | 1-5 ha | 5-10 ha | 10-20 ha | 20-50 ha | 50-200 ha | over 200 ha | individual/family | corporate/state | socialized/collective | rented (including share-croppers) | tribal/communal | other |
|---|---|---|---|---|---|---|---|---|---|---|---|---|---|---|---|---|
| | | | | | | | | | | | owner-operated | | | | | |
| Northern Mariana Is. | 1980 | 0.3 | 16.5 | 32.8[28] | 34.1[41] | 33.1[20] | | | | | 75.6 | ... | ... | 12.4 | ... | 12.0 |
| Palau | ... | ... | ... | | | | | | | | | | | | | |
| Pakistan | 1980 | 4,070 | 4.7 | 17.2 | 56.2 | 17.4 | 6.5 | 2.7 | | | 64.1[9] | 0.3[9] | — | 35.6[9] | — | — |
| Panama | 1980 | 153 | 14.7 | 41.0 | 25.0 | 9.3 | 9.0 | 9.0 | 5.6 | 1.0 | 23.2 | — | — | 2.0 | — | 74.8[25] |
| Papua New Guinea[83] | 1983 | 0.9 | 467 | 26.8 | | | | | 28.3 | 44.9 | 26.9[9] | 71.0[9] | — | 2.1[9] | — | — |
| Paraguay | 1981 | 249 | 86 | 8.9 | 27.9 | 18.5 | 23.0 | 14.6 | 4.6 | 2.5 | 93.5[9] | 0.1[9] | — | 1.8[9] | — | 4.6[9] |
| Peru | 1984 | 1,574 | 9.5 | 22.0[13] | 47.7 | 13.2 | 6.7 | 5.5 | 2.8 | | 75.5 | — | — | 0.8 | 6.8 | 16.9 |
| Philippines | 1980 | 3,420 | 2.6 | 22.7 | 63.3 | 10.5 | 3.5 | | | | 58.3 | — | — | 27.4 | — | 14.3 |
| Pitcairn Island | ... | ... | ... | | | | | | | | ... | ... | ... | ... | ... | ... |
| Poland | 1983 | 3,958 | 4.8 | 58.6 | | 25.5 | 15.8 | | | 0.1 | 71.4[9] | — | 28.6[9] | | | |
| Portugal | 1979 | 784 | 6.6 | 44.5 | 41.9 | 7.7 | 3.3 | 1.5 | 0.7 | 0.4 | 68.1 | — | | 8.7 | — | 23.2 |
| Puerto Rico | 1982 | 22 | 17.7 | 5.3[5,60] | 28.0[60,84] | 20.4[60] | 20.3[60] | 12.8[60] | 10.8[60] | 2.5[60] | 79.3 | — | — | 7.4 | — | 13.3 |
| Qatar | 1985 | 0.8[60] | 42.5[80] | 79.1[24,85] | | | | | 20.9[24,86] | | | | | | | |
| Réunion | 1981 | 21 | 3.6 | 50.9 | 41.6 | 5.3 | 1.8 | | 0.3 | | 46.1[87] | | | 22.5[87] | — | 31.4[87] |
| Romania | 1985 | 4.8[88] | 3,141[88] | ... | ... | ... | ... | ... | ... | ... | | 13.7[9] | 60.8[9] | — | 25.5[9] | |
| Rwanda | 1979 | 104 | 9.5 | ... | ... | ... | ... | ... | ... | ... | ... | ... | ... | ... | ... | ... |
| St. Christopher | 1981 | ... | ... | ... | ... | ... | ... | ... | ... | ... | 46.8[9] | 48.0[9] | — | 5.2[9] | — | — |
| St. Helena | 1983 | ... | ... | | | | | | | | — | — | — | 100.0 | — | — |
| St. Lucia | 1974 | 11 | 2.7 | 47.8[56] | 44.9[57] | 4.3[42] | 1.8 | 0.5[14] | 0.2[15] | 0.8[16] | 69.1 | — | — | 18.3 | — | 12.6 |
| St. Pierre and Miquelon | ... | ... | ... | | | | | | | | | | | | | |
| St. Vincent | 1983 | 8[44] | 1.8[44] | 48.0[44,56] | 40.7[44,77] | 8.5[41,44] | 2.4[7,44] | | 0.5[8,44] | | 62.0[44] | — | — | 8.8[44] | — | 19.2[44] |
| San Marino | 1975 | 0.7 | 7.0 | 21.3 | 47.8 | 24.7 | | 5.1 | 1.1 | | 39.9[9] | 15.5[9] | — | 29.9[9] | — | 14.7[9] |
| São Tomé and Príncipe | 1964 | 11.1 | 8.7 | 88.5 | 9.8 | 0.7 | 0.2 | 0.2 | 0.2 | 0.4 | 77.2 | — | — | 20.5 | — | 2.3 |
| Saudi Arabia | 1983 | 212 | 10.1 | 36.6 | 35.8 | 11.3 | 8.2 | 5.0 | 2.6 | 0.5 | 85.9 | — | — | 2.6 | — | 11.5 |
| Senegal | 1976 | 362 | 7.0 | 99.4 | | | | | 0.6 | | ... | | 0.6 | ... | — | 99.4 |
| Seychelles | 1977 | 4.9 | 1.5 | ... | ... | ... | ... | ... | ... | ... | ... | ... | ... | ... | ... | ... |
| Sierra Leone | 1971 | 286 | 1.8 | 38.8 | 55.0 | 6.1 | | 0.1 | | | 93.6 | — | — | 6.4 | — | — |
| Singapore | 1973 | 16 | 0.8 | 77.4 | 22.2 | 0.3 | 0.1 | | | | 7.4 | — | — | 88.8 | — | 3.8 |
| Solomon Islands | 1975[69] | 92 | 1.0 | ... | ... | ... | ... | ... | ... | ... | — | — | — | — | 100.0 | — |
| Somalia | 1984 | 198 | 3.6 | ... | ... | ... | ... | ... | ... | ... | 99.9 | 0.1 | — | | | |
| South Africa | 1978 | 72 | 1,193 | ... | ... | ... | ... | ... | ... | ... | ... | ... | ... | ... | ... | ... |
| Bophuthatswana | 1976 | ... | ... | | | | | | | | | | | | | |
| Ciskei | 1978 | ... | ... | | | | | | | | | | | | | |
| KwaNdebele | ... | ... | ... | | | | | | | | | | | | | |
| Transkei | 1976 | ... | ... | | | | | | | | | | | | | |
| Venda | 1976 | 53.3 | 9.3 | ... | ... | ... | ... | ... | ... | ... | ... | ... | ... | ... | ... | ... |
| S.W. Africa/Namibia | 1983 | ... | ... | | | | | | | | | | | | | |
| Spain | 1982 | 2,375 | 18.7 | 26.4 | 37.1 | 14.0 | 10.2 | 7.1 | 3.9 | 1.3 | 75.4 | ... | ... | 4.0 | — | 20.6 |
| Sri Lanka | 1982 | 1,817 | 1.1 | 77.5[5] | 22.2[89] | | 0.1[90] | 0.1[14] | 0.1[91] | | 77.1[87] | 6.4[87] | 0.1[87] | 14.4[87] | — | 2.0[87] |
| Sudan, The | 1982 | ... | | | | | | | | | 22.3 | 2.2 | — | 28.0 | 42.0 | 5.5 |
| Suriname | 1981 | 22 | 7.5 | 21.9[58] | 61.2[58] | 11.1[58] | 3.6[58] | 1.6[58] | 0.3[58] | 0.3[58] | 20.2[58] | 0.9[58] | — | 49.5[58] | — | 29.4[58] |
| Swaziland | 1972 | 39 | 19.5 | 26.2 | 60.4 | 12.0 | | | | 1.4 | 86.1 | — | — | 3.4 | — | 10.5 |
| Sweden | 1986 | 106[92] | 27.4[92] | | 16.3[82,92] | 20.1[92] | 22.2[92] | 27.6[92] | 13.8[92] | | 47.8[92,93] | — | — | 16.1[92,93] | — | 36.1[92,93] |
| Switzerland | 1985 | 119 | 9.1 | 23.1 | 18.7 | 14.6 | 27.5 | 15.2 | 0.9 | — | 36.2[24] | — | 0.8[24] | 58.5[24] | — | 4.5[24] |
| Syria | 1985 | 485[12] | 11.5[12] | 51.0[12,85] | | | 42.0[12,94] | | 6.2[12,95] | 0.8[12,96] | 99.2[12,73] | — | 0.8[12] | ... | | |
| Taiwan | 1985 | 791 | 1.1 | 73.2[24] | 26.2[24] | 0.5[24] | 0.1[24] | —[24] | —[24] | —[24] | 93.5 | — | — | 6.5 | — | — |
| Tanzania | 1972 | 2,489 | 3.0 | 59.7 | 37.7 | 2.1 | 0.4 | 0.1 | | 0.2 | 87.3 | — | — | 3.6 | — | 9.1 |
| Thailand | 1983 | 4,471 | 3.6 | 14.7 | 70.2[97] | 15.1[98] | | | | | 72.4 | — | — | 5.5 | — | 22.1 |
| Togo | 1983 | 263 | 1.5 | 48.8 | 38.6[99] | 12.7[100] | | | | | 70.7[9] | — | — | 21.1[9] | 8.2[9] | — |
| Tokelau | ... | ... | ... | | | | | | | | ... | ... | ... | ... | ... | ... |
| Tonga | 1976 | 9.1 | 7.6 | 0.7 | 37.7 | 1.6 | | | | | 8.4 | 8.4 | — | 83.2 | — | — |
| Trinidad and Tobago | 1982 | 30.6 | 4.3 | 35.1 | 50.7 | 9.6 | 4.1 | | 0.4 | 0.1 | 52.1 | — | — | 36.5 | — | 11.4 |
| Tunisia | 1985 | ... | | | | | | | | | | | | | | |
| Turkey | 1980 | 3,651 | 6.2 | 15.8 | 46.3 | 20.2 | 11.6 | 5.3 | 0.8 | — | 88.6 | ... | ... | 12.1 | — | 1.2 |
| Turks and Caicos Is. | ... | ... | ... | | | | | | | | | | | | | |
| Tuvalu | 1976 | 1.5 | 1.7 | | | | | | | | 99.9 | | | | 0.1 | |
| Uganda | 1964 | 1,171 | 3.9 | 20.7 | 59.8 | 11.2 | 8.3 | | | | 97.4 | — | — | — | — | 2.6 |
| U.S.S.R. | 1984 | 48.2[88] | 11,558[88] | — | — | — | — | — | — | 100.0[88] | — | 46.1 | 53.9 | — | — | [102] |
| United Arab Emirates | 1980 | 3.1[103] | 5.1[103] | ... | ... | ... | ... | ... | ... | ... | ... | ... | ... | ... | ... | ... |
| United Kingdom | 1985 | 258 | 67.2 | 5.4[28] | 7.8[82] | 12.9 | 16.8 | 25.4 | 26.0 | 5.8 | 70.2[104] | | — | 29.8[104] | | |
| United States | 1982 | 2,241 | 180.0 | 8.4[57] | | 20.0[7] | | 31.8[105] | 23.5[106] | 16.3[107] | 75.2 | 12.7 | — | 11.6 | — | 0.5 |
| Uruguay | 1980 | 68 | 234.4 | — | 12.2 | 14.4 | 14.6 | 16.6 | 21.0 | 21.2 | 59.1 | | — | 17.3 | — | 23.6 |
| Vanuatu | 1983 | ... | | | | | | | | | 65.3[24] | 34.7[24] | — | | | |
| Venezuela | 1971 | 288 | 91.9 | 5.8 | 37.7 | 17.2 | 14.4 | 11.3 | 7.9 | 5.7 | 61.5 | — | — | 6.1 | — | 31.3[25] |
| Vietnam | 1983 | ... | | | | | | | | | | | | | | |
| Virgin Islands (U.S.) | 1978 | 0.4 | 26.1 | 24.1[5] | 41.8[84] | 15.1 | 5.3 | 5.6 | 6.0 | 2.1 | 84.7 | ... | — | 7.4 | — | 7.9 |
| Wallis and Futuna | 1983 | ... | ... | | | | | | | | | | | | | |
| West Bank | 1980 | ... | ... | | | | | | | | | | | | | |
| Western Sahara | 1983 | ... | ... | | | | | | | | | | | | | |
| Western Samoa | 1975 | ... | ... | | | | | | | | | | | | 86.0 | 14.0 |
| Yemen (Aden) | 1977 | 0.08[88] | 604[88] | ... | ... | | | | | | ... | 44.3[88] | 55.7[88] | ... | | |
| Yemen (Şan'ā') | 1977–83 | 591 | 2.3 | 57.5 | 30.9 | 7.4 | 3.3 | 0.8 | 0.1 | | 90.3[9] | — | — | 9.4[9] | — | 0.3[9] |
| Yugoslavia | 1981 | 2,680 | 4.2 | 30.4 | 48.4 | 16.4 | 3.8 | 0.9 | 0.1 | | 99.9 | — | 0.1 | | | |
| Zaire | 1970 | 2,538 | 2.3 | 41.6 | 57.3 | 1.0 | 0.2 | | | | 4.2 | 0.1 | — | | 95.6 | 0.1 |
| Zambia | 1971 | 768 | 3.1 | 50.5 | 45.2 | 3.8 | | | 0.5 | | | | | | | |
| Zimbabwe | 1974 | 765 | 38.7 | 16.7[108] | | | 52.8[109] | 29.8[110] | 0.7[67] | | 2.0 | | — | — | 98.0 | — |

[1]1967. [2]Irrigated land as percentage of area of arable land, not percentage of number of farms; 1982/83. [3]Tractors per 1,000 hectares of arable land; 1982/83. [4]Kilograms per hectare of arable land; 1982/83. [5]Less than 1.2 hectares. [6]1.2 to 4.0 hectares. [7]4.0 to 20 hectares. [8]20 hectares or more. [9]Based on area, not number of holdings. [10]Netherlands Antilles includes Aruba. [11]1971. [12]1981. [13]Excludes holdings without land. [14]20 to 40 hectares. [15]40 to 81 hectares. [16]81 hectares or more. [17]1977. [18]1979. [19]Belgium includes Luxembourg. [20]4.0 hectares or more. [21]1984. [22]Family farms only. [23]Percentage of farms using artificial fertilizer. [24]1980. [25]Almost all squatters. [26]1970. [27]Government agro-industrial complexes. [28]Less than 2.0 hectares. [29]2.0 hectares or more. [30]1976. [31]1.2 to 10 hectares. [32]Irrigated land only. [33]1968. [34]Rarotonga only. [35]Less than 0.5 hectare. [36]0.5 to 50 hectares. [37]50 to 1,000 hectares. [38]1,000 hectares or more. [39]1975. [40]Irrigated land as percentage of all farmland. [41]2.0 to 4.0 hectares. [42]2.0 to 10 hectares. [43]10 hectares or more. [44]1972. [45]Less than 0.7 hectare. [46]0.7 to 7.1 hectares. [47]7.1 to 45 hectares. [48]45 to 452 hectares. [49]452 hectares or more. [50]Excludes holdings of 0.04 hectare (400 square metres) or less. [51]1974. [52]Excludes state of Punjab. [53]Does not include estates, collective farms, or traditional farms. [54]Less than 8.0 hectares. [55]8.0 to 20 hectares. [56]Less than 0.4 hectare. [57]0.4 to 4.0 hectares. [58]1969. [59]1982. [60]1978. [61]Farms producing mainly for cash sales. [62]3,611 large farms only, occupying 2,502,400 hectares; 1984. [63]Percentage of

| mainly crops | mainly livestock | mixed/other | tractor | electricity | irrigation works | artificial fertilizer (kg/ha) | total ('000 ha) | % of total land area | permanent crops | temporary crops | fallow | total cropland | meadows and pastures | woodland and forest | other[b] | country |
|---|---|---|---|---|---|---|---|---|---|---|---|---|---|---|---|---|
| ... | ... | ... | | | | | | | | | | | | | | Northern Mariana Is. |
| ... | ... | ... | | | | | | | | | | | | | | Palau |
| ... | ... | ... | 35.8 | ... | 32.4 | 59[4] | 19,109 | 24.0 | ——83.7—— | | 16.3 | 93.8 | — | 0.6 | 5.6 | Pakistan |
| ... | ... | ... | 3.9[11] | 0.5[11] | 5[2] | 40[4] | 2,259 | 29.3 | 21.6 | 43.3 | 35.0 | 24.6 | 57.4 | 15.6 | 2.4 | Panama |
| ... | ... | ... | 4[3] | | | 18[4] | 397 | 0.9 | 97.5 | 2.5 | — | 35.9 | 23.6 | — | 40.5 | Papua New Guinea[83] |
| 33.0 | ——67.0—— | | 4[3] | | 3[2] | 5[4] | 21,426 | 52.7 | | | | | | | | Paraguay |
| 4.9 | 93.0 | 2.1 | 8.1 | 6.5 | 38.8 | 25.0 | 14,893 | 11.6 | 24.1 | 75.9 | | 27.1 | 47.5 | 19.8 | 5.6 | Peru |
| 98.2 | 1.5 | 0.3 | 4.0[11] | | 21.2[11] | 30[4] | 9,034 | 30.1 | 57.5 | 42.5 | — | 86.3 | 6.8 | ——6.9—— | | Philippines |
| ... | ... | ... | | | | | | | | | | | | | | Pitcairn Island |
| ... | ... | ... | 51[3] | | 1[2] | 231[4] | 18,985 | 60.7 | 1.6 | ——98.4—— | | 86.1 | 13.3 | ——0.6—— | | Poland |
| ... | ... | ... | 58 | | 79 | 66[4] | 5,183 | 56.1 | 26.1 | 44.6 | 29.3 | 52.6 | 3.2 | 34.5 | 9.7 | Portugal |
| ... | ... | ... | 6.2 | | 3.7 | | 386 | 43.6 | ——74.0—— | | 26.0 | 28.7 | 49.6 | 16.8 | 4.9 | Puerto Rico |
| 99.7 | 0.3 | — | 27[3] | | 100.0 | 279[4] | 33 | 2.9 | 43.6 | 56.4 | | 10.2 | 1.5 | — | 88.3 | Qatar |
| ... | ... | ... | 3.0 | | 15.6[40,87] | 321[4] | 74 | 29.1 | 5.0 | 86.3 | 8.7 | 61.2 | 11.6 | 13.8 | 13.4 | Réunion |
| ... | ... | ... | 16[3] | | 19.7[40] | 158[4] | 15,020 | 63.2 | 6.0 | 94.0 | | 70.7 | 29.3 | — | — | Romania |
| ... | ... | ... | | | 0.2[40] | 1[4] | 1,460 | 57.1 | 30.7 | ——69.3—— | | 67.7 | 32.3 | — | — | Rwanda |
| ... | ... | ... | 15[3] | | | 171[4] | 12 | 45.3 | 31.5 | ——68.5—— | | 58.1 | — | ——41.9—— | | St. Christopher |
| ... | ... | ... | 3[3] | | — | | 4 | 12.9 | — | ——100.0—— | | 50.0 | 50.0 | — | — | St. Helena |
| 25.0 | ——75.0—— | | 2[3] | | 5.8 | 95[4] | 29 | 47.3 | 68.5 | ——31.5—— | | 57.9 | 10.2 | 26.4 | 5.5 | St. Lucia |
| ... | ... | ... | | | | | | | | | | | | | | St. Pierre and Miquelon |
| ... | ... | ... | 4[3] | | 2.2[44] | 229[4] | 11 | 28.8 | 75.0 | ——25.0—— | | 82.1 | 17.9 | — | — | St. Vincent |
| ... | ... | ... | | | | | 4.7 | 76.5 | 60.9 | 6.5 | 32.6 | 69.2 | 6.2 | 8.2 | 16.4 | San Marino |
| ... | ... | ... | 3[3] | | 6.2[40] | | 96 | 100.0 | 99.4 | ——0.6—— | | 38.3 | — | 59.7 | 2.0 | São Tomé and Príncipe |
| ... | ... | ... | 60.3 | | 43.8 | 217[4] | 2,135 | 1.0 | 4.1 | 18.7 | 77.2 | 88.5 | — | ——11.5—— | | Saudi Arabia |
| ... | ... | ... | | | 5.9[40] | 5[4] | 11,338 | 59.1 | 0.1 | ——99.9—— | | 22.4 | 77.6 | — | — | Senegal |
| 1.8 | 32.4 | 65.8 | 6[3] | | | 66[4] | 7.5 | 27.8 | 89.6 | ——10.4—— | | 100.0 | — | — | — | Seychelles |
| 50.3 | ——49.7—— | | | | 0.4[37] | 1[4] | 2,732 | 38.1 | 20.7 | ——79.3—— | | 19.3 | 80.7 | — | — | Sierra Leone |
| 12.5 | 6.2 | 81.3 | 1.4 | | 100.0 | 783[4] | 5.6[21] | 9.0[21] | 75.0 | 25.0 | | 66.7 | — | 33.3 | — | Singapore |
| 43.4 | ——56.6—— | | 0.5 | | 40.0 | | 93 | 3.4 | 40.0 | 45.2 | 14.8 | 100.0 | — | — | — | Solomon Islands |
| 20.0 | 60.0 | 20.0 | 0.5 | | 40.0 | 1 | ... | ... | ... | | | | | | | Somalia |
| ... | ... | ... | 13[3] | | 12.4 | 65[4] | 85,447 | 70.2 | 5.9 | ——94.1—— | | 11.9 | 79.7 | 1.3 | 7.1 | South Africa |
| ... | ... | ... | | | 1.1[40] | | 3,839 | 94.8 | — | 87.1 | ... | 2.4 | 97.6 | — | — | Bophuthatswana |
| ... | ... | ... | | | 0.3[40] | | 598 | 63.5 | — | 51.3 | ... | 12.6 | 87.4 | — | — | Ciskei |
| ... | ... | ... | | | | | | | | | | | | | | KwaNdebele |
| ... | ... | ... | | | 2.8[40] | | 622 | 14.9 | | | | 100.0 | ... | ... | ... | Transkei |
| ... | ... | ... | 0.3 | | 0.5[40] | 4.8 | 500 | 64.9 | 25.4 | 63.6 | 11.0 | 9.2 | 90.8 | — | | Venda |
| ... | ... | ... | 4[3] | | 0.2[40] | | 662 | 0.8 | 0.3 | ——99.7—— | | 100.0 | | | | S.W. Africa/Namibia |
| ... | ... | ... | 19 | | 45 | 71[4] | 44,312 | 87.8 | 23.8 | 55.8 | 20.4 | 40.9 | 12.5 | 21.7 | 24.9 | Spain |
| ... | ... | ... | 12[3] | | 25[2] | 77[4] | 1,967 | 30.0 | 62.4[87] | 37.6[87] | — | 88.3[87] | 0.4[87] | 2.1[87] | 9.2[87] | Sri Lanka |
| ... | ... | ... | 1[3] | | 14[2] | 7[4] | 31,500 | 13.3 | 0.8 | 88.7 | 10.5 | 23.8 | 76.2 | — | — | Sudan, The |
| 33.0[58] | 12.5[58] | 54.5[58] | 27[3] | | 78[2] | 216[4] | 165 | 1.0 | 15.0 | 53.0 | 32.0 | 40.4 | 23.1 | 19.1 | 17.4 | Suriname |
| 39.7 | ——60.3—— | | 20[3] | | 43[2] | 138[4] | 766,775 | 44.6 | 2.0 | 81.1 | 16.9 | 19.7 | 60.6 | 12.0 | 7.7 | Swaziland |
| 46.0[92,93] | ——54.0[92,93]—— | | 92[21] | | 1.8[40,80] | 160[4] | 8,558 | 19.0[93] | 0.2[93] | 96.4[93] | 3.4[93] | 31.8[93] | 6.3[93] | 50.6[93] | 11.2[93] | Sweden |
| 35.5[24] | ——64.5[24]—— | | 258[3] | | 4.3[40] | 430[4] | 1,203 | 29.1 | 6.7 | 66.2 | 27.1 | 36.1 | 53.4 | 10.5 | — | Switzerland |
| ... | ... | ... | 0.3[12] | | 14.8[21] | 32[4] | 6,127 | 33.1 | 10.0 | 60.6 | 29.4 | 91.8 | | | 8.2 | Syria |
| ... | ... | ... | | | 37.6[40] | 400[80] | 1,334[80] | 37.1[80] | 8.6[80] | 91.4[80] | | 67.0[80] | ——33.0[80]—— | | | Taiwan |
| 56.2 | ——43.8—— | | 0.3 | | 0.8[40] | 4[4] | 7,545 | 8.5 | 19.1 | 72.5 | 8.4 | 49.8 | 10.2 | 24.7 | 15.3 | Tanzania |
| ... | ... | ... | 51 | | 28.5 | 24[4] | 15,916 | 31.0 | 10.6 | ——89.4—— | | 94.0 | — | ——4.3—— | 1.7 | Thailand |
| ... | ... | ... | | | 0.4[26,40] | 2[4] | 406 | 7.1 | 17.3[17] | ——82.7[17]—— | | 71.0[17] | 29.0[17] | — | — | Togo |
| ... | ... | ... | | | | | | | | | | | | | | Tokelau |
| 8.4 | — | 91.6 | 1[3] | | — | 18[4] | 58 | 83.6 | 57.0 | ——43.0—— | | 93.1 | 6.9 | — | — | Tonga |
| 63.7[101] | ——36.3[101]—— | | 16[3] | | 0.6[40,80] | 49[4] | 132 | 25.8 | 55.9 | ——44.1—— | | 62.3 | 4.4 | 6.1 | 27.2 | Trinidad and Tobago |
| ... | ... | ... | 6[3] | | 2.3[40] | 16[4] | 4,923 | 31.9 | 39.7 | 45.2 | 15.1 | 100.0 | ... | ... | ... | Tunisia |
| 11.5 | 2.5 | 86.0 | 19[3] | | 46.9 | 63[4] | 27,541[93] | 35.3[93] | 10.7[93] | 67.4[93] | 21.9[93] | 100.0[93] | | | | Turkey |
| ... | ... | ... | | | | | | | | | | | | | | Turks and Caicos Is. |
| ... | ... | ... | | | | | | | | | | | | | | Tuvalu |
| ... | ... | ... | 1[3] | | 2.2[40,80] | | 2,262 | 11.3 | 29.8 | 70.2 | | 100.0 | | | | Uganda |
| — | ... | 100.0 | 113 | | 3.1[40] | 99[4] | 605,700 | 27.2 | ——91.6—— | | 8.4 | 37.5 | 61.6 | ——0.9—— | | U.S.S.R. |
| ... | ... | ... | | | 28.6[40] | 299[4] | 17.5[60] | 0.2[60] | 64.8[60] | 18.2[60] | 17.1[60] | 97.6[60] | — | 1.3[60] | 1.1[60] | United Arab Emirates |
| ... | ... | ... | 76[3] | | 0.8[40,80] | 375[4] | 18,703 | 76.6 | 0.8 | 98.6 | 0.6 | 37.7 | 59.4 | 1.7 | 1.2 | United Kingdom |
| 43.4 | 52.6 | 4.0 | 85.7 | 66.2 | 12.4 | 104[4] | 411,175[93] | 43.2[93] | 1.5 | 86.4 | 12.1 | 45.1 | 42.4 | 8.8 | 3.7 | United States |
| 37.1 | 58.7 | 4.2 | 23[3] | | 0.5[40] | 28[4] | 16,025 | 90.9 | 3.8 | 75.2 | 21.0 | 7.6 | 86.5 | 2.8 | 3.1 | Uruguay |
| 82.6[24] | 13.7[24] | 3.7[24] | 1[3] | | | 3[4] | 183 | 15.0 | 82.8 | 4.5 | 12.7 | 78.8 | — | ——21.2—— | | Vanuatu |
| 39.8 | 12.1 | 48.1 | 11[3] | | 1.2[40,80] | 38[4] | 26,470 | 30.0 | 19.0 | 59.0 | 22.0 | 13.2 | 57.0 | 22.8 | 7.0 | Venezuela |
| ... | ... | ... | 5[3] | | 22.8[37] | 47[4] | 7,857 | 24.1 | 8.4 | ——91.6—— | | 65.4 | 34.6 | ... | ... | Vietnam |
| 53.4 | ——46.6—— | | 12.2 | | ... | 157[4] | 9.9 | 29.1 | 63.7 | 5.9 | 30.4 | 7.0 | 77.6 | 9.9 | 5.5 | Virgin Islands (U.S.) |
| ... | ... | ... | | | | | 5.0 | 25.0 | 80.0 | ——20.0—— | | 100.0 | | | | Wallis and Futuna |
| ... | ... | ... | c.9[3] | | 4.7[40] | | 185 | 31.4 | 62.2 | 37.8 | — | 100.0 | | | | West Bank |
| ... | ... | ... | 6[3] | | | | 5,002 | 18.8 | | | | | 100.0 | | | Western Sahara |
| ... | ... | ... | | | | | 70 | 24.8 | 71.2 | 28.8 | — | 93.8 | 6.2 | — | — | Western Samoa |
| 35.5[9,30] | 56.9[9,30] | 7.6[9,30] | 5[3] | | 53.8[40] | 12[4] | 108 | 0.3 | 3.9 | 85.1 | 11.0 | 95.7 | 4.3 | — | 1.2 | Yemen (Aden) |
| ... | ... | ... | 39.2 | | 4.4 | 10[4] | 1,351 | 0.1 | 6.7 | 69.7 | 23.6 | 98.8 | — | — | — | Yemen (Şan'ā') |
| 12.7[58] | ——87.3[58]—— | | 16.5 | 4.8[63] | 2[2] | 118[4] | 12,462[58] | 48.8[58] | 8.5[58] | 84.7[58] | 6.8[58] | 52.8[58] | 26.4[58] | 16.2[58] | 4.6[58] | Yugoslavia |
| 92.3 | ——9.7—— | | 0.4 | | —[2] | 1[4] | 5,897 | 2.6 | 7.7 | ——92.3—— | | 70.6 | 20.1 | 2.0 | 7.3 | Zaire |
| 15.8 | 9.7 | 74.5 | 1[3] | | 0.3[40] | 13[4] | 938 | 13.3 | 4.5 | ——95.5—— | | 14.2 | 38.1 | ... | 47.7 | Zambia |
| 1.8[9,60] | 26.7[9,60] | 71.5[9,60] | 8[3] | | 1.5[60] | 58[4] | 29,620 | 76.6 | 2.5 | ——97.5—— | | 34.5 | 65.7 | — | — | Zimbabwe |

farms having electric motors.  [64]Excludes temporary bushland available for agricultural use to subsistence farms.  [65]Western Libya only.  [66]10 to 100 hectares.  [67]100 hectares or more.  [68]Peninsular Malaysia only; excludes shifting cultivators.  [69]Smallholder farms only.  [70]Average size of estate farm is 400 hectares.  [71]Based on total number of households on estates.  [72]All Malaysia.  [73]Includes rented farms.  [74]Excludes part-time farmers.  [75]In area, privately owned lands constitute 49.7% of Mexico's farmland, communal land (ejidos) 49.8%.  [76]In area, state lands constitute 79.1% of Mongolia's farmland, agricultural cooperatives 20.9%.  [77]0.4 to 2.0 hectares.  [78]Less than 3.0 hectares.  [79]3.0 to 50 hectares.  [80]1983.  [81]Data refer to cultivated area only.  [82]2.0 to 5.0 hectares.  [83]Large holdings only.  [84]1.2 to 5.0 hectares.  [85]Less than 7.0 hectares.  [86]7.0 hectares or more.  [87]1973.  [88]State farms and communes only.  [89]1.2 to 12 hectares.  [90]12 to 20 hectares.  [91]40 hectares or more.  [92]Holdings of arable land only.  [93]1985.  [94]7.0 to 25 hectares.  [95]25 to 300 hectares.  [96]300 hectares or more.  [97]1.0 to 6.4 hectares.  [98]6.4 hectares or more.  [99]1.0 to 3.0 hectares.  [100]3.0 hectares or more.  [101]1963.  [102]24,600,000 farm households with small plots constitute 8% of total farmland.  [103]Abu Dhabi only.  [104]Excludes Northern Ireland.  [105]20 to 72 hectares.  [106]72 to 202 hectares.  [107]202 hectares or more.  [108]Less than 8.0 hectares.  [109]8.0 to 16 hectares.  [110]16 to 100 hectares.

# Crops and livestock

This table provides comparative data for selected categories of agricultural production for the countries of the world. The data are taken mainly from the United Nations Food and Agricultural Organization's (FAO) annual *Production Yearbook*.

Although the FAO provides standardized guidelines upon which many nations have organized their data collection systems and methods, persistent variations in standards of coverage and reporting periods limit the value of country to country comparisons. The FAO depends largely on questionnaires supplied to each country, but where no official or semi-official responses are returned the FAO makes estimates, using unofficial or other data. Statistics are based on calendar year periods; that is, data for any particular crop refer to the calendar year in which the harvest (or the bulk of the harvest) occurred. In countries where intensive inter-cropping and multiple cropping are practiced, the broader parameter of food supply availability (see *Household budgets and consumption* table) may be a better indicator by which to make intercountry comparisons of agricultural production than the more specific components of agriculture presented in this table. In spite of the oftentimes tragic food shortages in a number of countries in recent years, worldwide agricultural production is probably more often under-reported than over-reported. Most countries

do not report complete domestic production; for example, the Soviet bloc, excepting Czechoslovakia, publishes, initially at least, statistics only for collective or cooperative production and excludes the production of privately held plots of land that in some instances represent a significant part of total agricultural production. Some countries report only crops that are sold commercially and ignore crops produced for family or communal subsistence.

Individual categories of crop production also display some peculiarities that may cause statistical discrepancies between national and FAO figures. The FAO's cereals statistics relate to weight or volume of crops harvested for dry grain (excluding cereal crops used for grazing; harvested for hay; or harvested green for food, feed, or silage). Some countries, however, collect their basic data on sown or cultivated areas instead and calculate production statistics from estimates of yield. Millet and sorghum, which in many European and North American countries are used primarily as livestock or poultry feed, may be reported by such countries as animal fodder only, while the U.S.S.R. and many African and Asian nations use them for human consumption and report them as cereals. Fruit statistics, especially for tropical fruits, are frequently unavailable, and coverage is not uniform, with some countries reporting both commercial fruits and

## Crops and livestock

| country | crops | | | | | | | | | | | |
|---|---|---|---|---|---|---|---|---|---|---|---|---|
| | grains | | | | roots and tubers[a] | | | | pulses[b] | | | | fruits[c] | | vegetables[d] | |
| | production ('000 metric tons) | | yield (kg/hectare) | | production ('000 metric tons) | | yield (kg/hectare) | | production ('000 metric tons) | | yield (kg/hectare) | | production ('000 metric tons) | | production ('000 metric tons) | |
| | 1975–77 average | 1986 | 1975–77 average | 1986 | 1975–77 average | 1986 | 1975–77 average | 1986 | 1975–77 average | 1986 | 1975–77 average | 1986 | 1975–77 average | 1986 | 1975–77 average | 1986 |
| Afghanistan | 4,417 | 4,042 | 1,301 | 1,294 | 250 | 330 | 13,282 | 13,200 | 33 | 40 | 1,563 | 1,633 | 860 | 994 | 611 | 784 |
| Albania | 800 | 1,075 | 2,307 | 3,060 | 113 | 136 | 7,312 | 8,774 | 18 | 24 | 320 | 404 | 140 | 198 | 163 | 186 |
| Algeria | 2,045 | 2,632 | 649 | 956 | 513 | 850 | 7,201 | 7,083 | 72 | 63 | 747 | 373 | 1,538 | 1,632 | 704 | 1,354 |
| American Samoa | ... | ... | ... | ... | 4 | 4 | 5,913 | 5,483 | ... | ... | ... | ... | 2 | 1 | — | — |
| Andorra | | | | | | | | | | | | | | | | |
| Angola | 520 | 310 | 722 | 434 | 1,937 | 2,190 | 13,507 | 14,175 | 68 | 40 | 569 | 364 | 416 | 425 | 204 | 227 |
| Anguilla | | | | | | | | | | | | | | | | |
| Antigua and Barbuda | — | — | 1,788 | 1,667 | — | — | 3,695 | 5,952 | ... | ... | ... | ... | 8 | 9 | 1 | 1 |
| Argentina | 23,168 | 27,250 | 2,008 | 2,558 | 2,149 | 2,389 | 12,696 | 16,989 | 205 | 272 | 1,076 | 1,018 | 6,615 | 5,770 | 2,337 | 2,718 |
| Aruba[2] | | | | | | | | | | | | | | | | |
| Australia | 16,553 | 24,957 | 1,250 | 1,554 | 725 | 938 | 20,620 | 25,112 | 102 | 787 | 639 | 925 | 2,046 | 2,401 | 939 | 1,276 |
| Austria | 4,065 | 5,111 | 4,006 | 4,825 | 1,559 | 982 | 23,042 | 28,186 | 5 | 1 | 2,226 | 2,325 | 986 | 1,029 | 562 | 492 |
| Bahamas, The | 1 | 1 | 1,021 | 1,262 | 1 | 2 | 8,644 | 9,312 | 1 | 1 | 1,427 | 1,300 | 11 | 13 | 26 | 28 |
| Bahrain | | | | | — | — | 23,000 | 22,935 | ... | ... | ... | ... | 36 | 48 | 19 | 30 |
| Bangladesh | 19,001 | 25,333 | 1,841 | 2,327 | 1,595 | 1,714 | 10,052 | 10,433 | 228 | 203 | 718 | 729 | 1,404 | 1,555 | 1,051 | 1,230 |
| Barbados | 2 | 2 | 2,614 | 2,500 | 12 | 6 | 10,637 | 7,967 | 1 | 1 | 1,199 | 1,246 | 2 | 3 | 6 | 9 |
| Belgium[3] | 1,772 | 2,419 | 3,939 | 6,349 | 1,286 | 1,650 | 32,131 | 33,674 | 11 | 6 | 2,677 | 3,637 | 337 | 398 | 1,083 | 1,247 |
| Belize | 22 | 23 | 1,366 | 1,753 | 2 | 3 | 19,389 | 20,000 | 1 | 3 | 541 | 761 | 56 | 93 | 2 | 4 |
| Benin | 302 | 504 | 736 | 845 | 1,200 | 1,621 | 7,914 | 8,472 | 28 | 47 | 419 | 544 | 134 | 158 | 86 | 171 |
| Bermuda | ... | ... | ... | ... | 1 | 1 | 17,082 | 9,500 | ... | ... | ... | ... | 1 | 1 | 2 | 2 |
| Bhutan | 145 | 182 | 1,417 | 1,370 | 37 | 46 | 6,642 | 6,924 | 2 | 3 | 556 | 622 | 38 | 51 | 10 | 11 |
| Bolivia | 594 | 838 | 1,134 | 1,292 | 1,141 | 1,177 | 6,733 | 5,720 | 17 | 30 | 950 | 1,177 | 570 | 562 | 352 | 278 |
| Botswana | 87 | 11 | 500 | 215 | 6 | 7 | 4,821 | 5,385 | 18 | 14 | 611 | 467 | 8 | 11 | 15 | 16 |
| Brazil | 29,431 | 37,048 | 1,419 | 1,652 | 29,152 | 28,376 | 11,892 | 12,231 | 2,204 | 2,266 | 496 | 403 | 15,005 | 26,249 | 3,518 | 5,104 |
| British Virgin Islands | ... | ... | ... | ... | ... | ... | ... | ... | ... | ... | ... | ... | — | 1 | ... | ... |
| Brunei | 7 | 3 | 2,062 | 1,500 | 2 | 1 | 6,530 | 6,626 | ... | ... | ... | ... | 4 | 6 | 6 | 9 |
| Bulgaria | 7,926 | 7,214 | 3,518 | 3,742 | 350 | 400 | 11,326 | 10,000 | 82 | 74 | 784 | 983 | 2,249 | 2,344 | 1,911 | 1,975 |
| Burkina Faso | 1,120 | 1,894 | 529 | 772 | 93 | 87 | 5,544 | 5,755 | 172 | 177 | 376 | 373 | 43 | 68 | 58 | 123 |
| Burma | 9,527 | 15,952 | 1,795 | 2,956 | 88 | 339 | 5,189 | 9,817 | 274 | 598 | 461 | 701 | 1,069 | 1,023 | 1,734 | 2,103 |
| Burundi | 303 | 464 | 1,100 | 1,189 | 1,102 | 1,222 | 7,465 | 7,526 | 365 | 332 | 1,003 | 910 | 974 | 1,336 | 131 | 186 |
| Cameroon | 928 | 911 | 929 | 986 | 2,170 | 2,260 | 2,362 | 2,457 | 98 | 123 | 600 | 568 | 1,039 | 1,207 | 408 | 429 |
| Canada | 41,352 | 59,489 | 2,198 | 2,626 | 2,359 | 2,850 | 21,744 | 25,119 | 127 | 511 | 1,305 | 1,571 | 666 | 639 | 1,493 | 1,975 |
| Cape Verde | 4 | 12 | 467 | 759 | 16 | 15 | 4,496 | 2,984 | 1 | 6 | 189 | 603 | 10 | 10 | 5 | 6 |
| Cayman Islands | ... | ... | ... | ... | — | — | 4,533 | 4,504 | ... | ... | ... | ... | 1 | 1 | — | — |
| Central African Republic | 94 | 108 | 526 | 546 | 1,100 | 966 | 3,225 | 4,019 | 6 | 6 | 500 | 492 | 154 | 175 | 39 | 51 |
| Chad | 600 | 754 | 538 | 598 | 348 | 588 | 4,191 | 5,272 | 54 | 60 | 398 | 436 | 88 | 117 | 49 | 77 |
| Chile | 1,685 | 2,675 | 1,768 | 3,355 | 743 | 799 | 9,639 | 14,890 | 116 | 147 | 912 | 946 | 1,595 | 2,405 | 1,148 | 1,253 |
| China | 242,557 | 347,800 | 2,497 | 3,858 | 144,743 | 138,300 | 13,020 | 15,324 | 6,183 | 5,600 | 1,066 | 1,273 | 9,905 | 19,101 | 69,076 | 101,240 |
| Christmas Island | | | | | | | | | | | | | | | | |
| Cocos (Keeling) Islands | ... | ... | ... | ... | ... | ... | ... | ... | ... | ... | ... | ... | ... | ... | ... | ... |
| Colombia | 2,800 | 3,178 | 2,302 | 2,570 | 3,541 | 3,522 | 9,626 | 11,094 | 126 | 163 | 597 | 702 | 3,308 | 4,212 | 1,223 | 1,411 |
| Comoros | 17 | 23 | 1,183 | 1,103 | 95 | 111 | 3,434 | 3,229 | 2 | 3 | 547 | 591 | 31 | 40 | 2 | 3 |
| Congo | 21 | 11 | 652 | 700 | 604 | 673 | 5,921 | 6,540 | 7 | 7 | 604 | 659 | 189 | 248 | 28 | 38 |
| Cook Islands | ... | ... | ... | ... | 11 | 12 | 29,790 | 32,272 | ... | ... | ... | ... | 15 | 15 | 2 | 2 |
| Costa Rica | 283 | 304 | 1,889 | 2,238 | 38 | 55 | 8,482 | 7,169 | 15 | 31 | 527 | 540 | 1,376 | 1,245 | 52 | 74 |
| Côte d'Ivoire | 810 | 992 | 775 | 927 | 3,284 | 4,767 | 4,635 | 6,516 | 8 | 8 | 625 | 672 | 1,635 | 1,980 | 257 | 458 |
| Cuba | 547 | 636 | 2,253 | 2,730 | 695 | 1,014 | 5,622 | 6,581 | 25 | 27 | 705 | 780 | 591 | 1,335 | 386 | 591 |
| Cyprus | 129 | 79 | 1,298 | 1,130 | 182 | 211 | 20,392 | 23,947 | 8 | 6 | 853 | 1,037 | 432 | 570 | 111 | 140 |
| Czechoslovakia | 9,594 | 10,803 | 3,585 | 4,301 | 3,846 | 3,512 | 15,944 | 19,388 | 120 | 215 | 1,445 | 2,079 | 657 | 960 | 1,025 | 1,093 |
| Denmark | 6,511 | 7,984 | 3,663 | 5,015 | 752 | 1,129 | 21,632 | 36,419 | 11 | 632 | 2,926 | 4,302 | 153 | 85 | 221 | 318 |
| Djibouti | ... | ... | ... | ... | ... | ... | ... | ... | ... | ... | ... | ... | ... | ... | 1 | 13 |
| Dominica | — | — | 1,311 | 1,395 | 23 | 26 | 9,813 | 9,828 | 1 | ... | 500 | 500 | 65 | 59 | 5 | 6 |
| Dominican Republic | 357 | 390 | 2,516 | 2,685 | 352 | 209 | 6,031 | 5,270 | 63 | 61 | 999 | 819 | 1,270 | 1,571 | 195 | 268 |
| Ecuador | 721 | 773 | 1,379 | 1,608 | 814 | 782 | 10,450 | 11,980 | 50 | 52 | 512 | 677 | 3,854 | 3,446 | 297 | 346 |
| Egypt | 7,925 | 8,933 | 3,948 | 4,687 | 1,017 | 1,480 | 17,271 | 18,546 | 347 | 408 | 2,030 | 2,078 | 3,520 | 4,664 | 6,506 | 8,490 |
| El Salvador | 591 | 579 | 1,529 | 1,615 | 18 | 34 | 10,326 | 15,179 | 38 | 50 | 703 | 820 | 269 | 356 | 92 | 130 |
| Equatorial Guinea | ... | ... | ... | ... | 80 | 91 | 2,722 | 2,397 | ... | ... | ... | ... | 14 | 19 | ... | ... |
| Ethiopia | 4,408 | 5,720 | 987 | 1,220 | 1,187 | 1,275 | 3,283 | 2,859 | 640 | 945 | 769 | 1,032 | 186 | 214 | 442 | 556 |
| Faeroe Islands | ... | ... | ... | ... | 1 | 1 | 13,671 | 13,686 | ... | ... | ... | ... | ... | ... | ... | ... |
| Falkland Islands | ... | ... | ... | ... | ... | ... | ... | ... | ... | ... | ... | ... | ... | ... | ... | ... |

those consumed for subsistence. Figures on wild fruits and berries tend not to be included in national reports at all. Statistical variances also occur among data for individual varieties of fruit. Some banana and plantain growers, for example, report production in terms of bunches, including the weight of the stalk; others do not. Vegetable statistics include vegetables and melons grown for human consumption only. Some countries do not make this distinction in their reports, and some exclude the production of kitchen gardens and small family plots. In certain countries, such small-scale production may account for 20 to 40 percent of total ouput.

Livestock statistics may be distorted by the timing of country reports. Ireland, for example, takes a livestock enumeration in December that is reported the following year and that appears low against data for otherwise comparable countries because of the slaughter and export of animals at the close of the grazing season. It balances this, however, with a June enumeration, when numbers tend to be high. Milk production as defined by the FAO includes whole fresh milk, excluding milk sucked by young animals but including amounts fed by farmers or ranchers to livestock. Some countries—notably Czechoslovakia, France, Hungary, Italy, and West Germany—include milk sucked by young animals in their reports. Certain countries do not distinguish between milk cows and other cattle, so that yield per cow must be estimated. Some countries do not report egg production statistics (here given in metric tons), and external estimates must be based on the numbers of chickens and reported or assumed egg-laying rates. Some other countries report egg production by number, and this must be converted to weight, using official conversion factors; but, as eggs vary in size and weight, discrepancies, again, may arise.

Metric system units used in the table may be converted to English system units as follows:

metric tons × 1.1023 = short tons
kilograms × 2.2046 = pounds
kilograms per hectare × 0.8922 = pounds per acre.

The notes that follow, keyed by references in the table headings, provide further definitional information.
a. Includes such crops as potatoes and cassava.
b. Includes beans and peas harvested for dry grain only. Does not include green beans and green peas.
c. Excludes melons.
d. Includes melons, green beans, and green peas.
e. From milk cows only.
f. From chickens only.

| livestock | | | | | | | | | | | | | | country |
|---|---|---|---|---|---|---|---|---|---|---|---|---|---|---|
| cattle | | sheep | | hogs | | chickens | | milk[e] | | | | eggs[f] | | |
| stock ('000 head) | | stock ('000 head) | | stock ('000 head) | | stock ('000 head) | | production ('000 metric tons) | | yield (kg/animal) | | production (metric tons) | | |
| 1975–77 average | 1986 | 1975–77 average | 1986 | 1975–77 average | 1986 | 1975–77 average | 1986 | 1975–77 average | 1986 | 1975–77 average | 1986 | 1975–77 average | 1986 | |
| 3,663 | 3,750 | 20,620 | 20,000 | ... | ... | 6,233 | 6,700 | 569 | 610 | 532 | 500 | 13,447 | 14,200 | Afghanistan |
| 490 | 610 | 1,163 | 1,230 | 133 | 220 | 3,067 | 5,200 | 254 | 345 | 1,441 | 1,414 | 7,347 | 13,200 | Albania |
| 1,049 | 1,557 | 9,803 | 14,795 | 4 | 5 | 16,528 | 22,000 | 453 | 539 | 964 | 975 | 16,700 | 123,000 | Algeria |
| — | — | ... | ... | 10 | 11 | 49 | 50 | — | — | 800 | 800 | 33 | 31 | American Samoa |
| ... | 11 | ... | 9[1] | ... | ... | ... | ... | ... | ... | ... | ... | ... | ... | Andorra |
| 2,817 | 3,380 | 205 | 255 | 360 | 470 | 5,000 | 5,900 | 140 | 148 | 500 | 502 | 3,450 | 3,900 | Angola |
| ... | ... | ... | ... | ... | ... | ... | ... | ... | ... | ... | ... | ... | ... | Anguilla |
| 8 | 18 | 10 | 13 | 3 | 4 | 62 | 80 | 8 | 6 | 1,230 | 1,000 | 128 | 163 | Antigua and Barbuda |
| 58,645 | 53,000 | 34,799 | 29,243 | 3,960 | 4,000 | 32,800 | 45,000 | 5,586 | 6,200 | 1,905 | 2,116 | 191,893 | 279,000 | Argentina |
| ... | ... | ... | ... | ... | ... | ... | ... | ... | ... | ... | ... | ... | ... | Aruba[2] |
| 32,587 | 23,451 | 145,219 | 155,561 | 2,200 | 2,553 | 42,339 | 52,000 | 6,344 | 6,205 | 2,767 | 3,395 | 195,547 | 183,000 | Australia |
| 2,528 | 2,655 | 166 | 243 | 3,693 | 3,921 | 12,856 | 14,473 | 3,301 | 3,700 | 3,247 | 3,728 | 88,585 | 105,000 | Austria |
| 4 | 5 | 31 | 40 | 17 | 20 | 748 | 850 | 2 | 3 | 1,000 | 1,000 | 330 | 429 | Bahamas, The |
| 5 | 6 | 3 | 7 | ... | ... | 350 | 848 | 6 | 6 | 2,800 | 2,900 | 1,750 | 3,600 | Bahrain |
| 26,060 | 23,200 | 1,138 | 1,110 | ... | ... | 50,992 | 70,800 | 759 | 950 | 250 | 264 | 32,954 | 48,500 | Bangladesh |
| 20 | 18 | 49 | 55 | 38 | 49 | 525 | 1,100 | 6 | 11 | 1,112 | 1,319 | 1,681 | 1,261 | Barbados |
| 3,045 | 3,180 | 101 | 147 | 4,809 | 5,593 | 31,807 | 31,000 | 3,861 | 4,160 | 3,655 | 3,926 | 235,500 | 173,000 | Belgium[3] |
| 48 | 49 | 3 | 4 | 18 | 25 | 310 | 650 | 4 | 4 | 1,018 | 1,024 | 623 | 1,237 | Belize |
| 720 | 930 | 856 | 1,160 | 380 | 600 | 8,533 | 22,200 | 10 | 15 | 117 | 130 | 6,120 | 16,020 | Benin |
| — | 1 | ... | ... | 1 | 3 | 56 | 50 | 1 | 2 | 3,036 | 3,071 | 318 | 520 | Bermuda |
| 272 | 325 | 39 | 44 | 61 | 77 | 125 | ... | 24 | 28 | 257 | 257 | 145 | 240 | Bhutan |
| 3,407 | 6,000 | 7,970 | 9,500 | 1,227 | 1,100 | 7,270 | 7,500 | 75 | 98 | 1,404 | 1,397 | 16,893 | 26,400 | Bolivia |
| 2,840 | 2,720 | 230 | 210 | 15 | 8 | 650 | 950 | 71 | 96 | 350 | 350 | 489 | 702 | Botswana |
| 100,489 | 128,918 | 17,946 | 18,473 | 34,979 | 33,000 | 327,477 | 500,000 | 10,166 | 11,860 | 780 | 700 | 537,891 | 1,050,000 | Brazil |
| 2 | 2 | 7 | 8 | 2 | 3 | ... | ... | ... | ... | ... | ... | ... | ... | British Virgin Islands |
| 3 | 4 | ... | ... | 11 | 14 | 618 | 1,800 | ... | ... | ... | ... | 1,420 | 1,900 | Brunei |
| 1,644 | 1,706 | 9,843 | 9,724 | 3,589 | 3,734 | 35,304 | 37,927 | 1,480 | 2,176 | 2,274 | 3,296 | 105,002 | 155,918 | Bulgaria |
| 2,550 | 3,106 | 1,650 | 2,215 | 153 | 206 | 10,200 | 21,000 | 74 | 89 | 175 | 175 | 5,724 | 14,700 | Burkina Faso |
| 7,542 | 9,981 | 194 | 347 | 1,771 | 3,116 | 16,783 | 35,000 | 217 | 601 | 245 | 245 | 23,182 | 51,000 | Burma |
| 785 | 415 | 310 | 370 | 36 | 80 | 2,700 | 3,600 | 47 | 25 | 350 | 350 | 2,052 | 2,850 | Burundi |
| 2,756 | 4,361 | 2,083 | 2,500 | 900 | 1,180 | 8,983 | 9,200 | 37 | 48 | 500 | 500 | 7,040 | 10,400 | Cameroon |
| 14,993 | 11,465 | 595 | 722 | 5,906 | 10,721 | 86,488 | 99,269 | 7,731 | 8,050 | 3,840 | 4,837 | 312,427 | 305,331 | Canada |
| 11 | 13 | 2 | 1 | 22 | 54 | 59 | 230 | 1 | — | 500 | 502 | 48 | 152 | Cape Verde |
| 4 | 5 | ... | ... | 1 | — | 16 | 21 | ... | ... | ... | ... | 82 | 85 | Cayman Islands |
| 925 | 2,135 | 68 | 112 | 160 | 360 | 1,352 | 2,300 | 3 | 5 | 110 | 110 | 890 | 985 | Central African Republic |
| 3,535 | 5,017 | 2,295 | 2,620 | 6 | 12 | 2,700 | 3,500 | 108 | 110 | 270 | 270 | 2,430 | 3,060 | Chad |
| 3,474 | 3,500 | 5,691 | 5,980 | 896 | 1,130 | 16,267 | 19,000 | 1,025 | 1,150 | 1,393 | 1,691 | 57,516 | 76,500 | Chile |
| 55,087 | 66,820 | 94,245 | 94,210 | 276,399 | 331,400 | 690,000 | 1,400,000 | 870 | 2,860 | 1,286 | 1,589 | 2,320,000 | 4,350,000 | China |
| ... | ... | ... | ... | ... | ... | ... | ... | ... | ... | ... | ... | ... | ... | Christmas Island |
| ... | ... | ... | ... | ... | ... | ... | ... | ... | ... | ... | ... | ... | ... | Cocos (Keeling) Islands |
| 23,831 | 23,590 | 2,028 | 2,750 | 1,876 | 2,440 | 25,760 | 35,000 | 2,225 | 3,017 | 961 | 973 | 119,498 | 177,150 | Colombia |
| 74 | 86 | 7 | 9 | ... | ... | 243 | 362 | 3 | 4 | 500 | 500 | 519 | 608 | Comoros |
| 58 | 71 | 53 | 63 | 43 | 44 | 885 | 1,350 | 2 | 3 | 1,500 | 1,500 | 662 | 1,050 | Congo |
| — | ... | ... | ... | 14 | 17 | 63 | ... | ... | ... | ... | ... | 82 | 110 | Cook Islands |
| 1,850 | 2,415 | 2 | 3 | 218 | 222 | 6,100 | 4,400 | 279 | 414 | 1,041 | 1,424 | 16,087 | 11,700 | Costa Rica |
| 503 | 881 | 1,010 | 1,502 | 253 | 450 | 10,733 | 15,900 | 9 | 17 | 112 | 122 | 4,800 | 11,000 | Côte d'Ivoire |
| 5,531 | 6,400 | 339 | 380 | 1,472 | 2,400 | 19,320 | 25,417 | 830 | 1,100 | 1,342 | 1,571 | 82,906 | 113,350 | Cuba |
| 32 | 41 | 460 | 500 | 147 | 221 | 3,200 | 4,200 | 24 | 75 | 3,380 | 3,333 | 4,790 | 5,870 | Cyprus |
| 4,592 | 5,073 | 804 | 1,104 | 6,741 | 6,833 | 39,765 | 46,849 | 5,464 | 7,015 | 2,920 | 3,865 | 227,157 | 277,919 | Czechoslovakia |
| 3,085 | 2,495 | 59 | 89 | 7,769 | 9,321 | 14,993 | 14,008 | 5,034 | 5,111 | 4,582 | 5,808 | 71,367 | 81,300 | Denmark |
| 28 | 47 | 367 | 410 | ... | ... | 98 | 117 | ... | ... | 1,067 | 1,000 | 234 | 274 | Djibouti |
| 4 | 4 | 3 | 4 | 8 | 9 | ... | ... | 1 | 2 | ... | ... | ... | ... | Dominica |
| 1,925 | 2,055 | 51 | 80 | 719 | 2,500 | 7,433 | 20,000 | 348 | 500 | 1,517 | 2,000 | 21,933 | 18,600 | Dominican Republic |
| 2,576 | 3,727 | 2,142 | 1,959 | 2,737 | 4,986 | 16,367 | 45,000 | 814 | 989 | 1,365 | 1,311 | 22,682 | 41,300 | Ecuador |
| 2,076 | 2,750 | 1,875 | 2,550 | 15 | 56 | 26,375 | 51,000 | 632 | 965 | 673 | 673 | 74,258 | 106,000 | Egypt |
| 1,141 | 1,010 | 4 | 4 | 453 | 400 | 3,510 | 4,300 | 258 | 283 | 1,007 | 699 | 30,697 | 38,700 | El Salvador |
| 4 | 4 | 32 | 35 | 4 | 5 | 120 | 195 | ... | ... | ... | ... | 100 | 155 | Equatorial Guinea |
| 25,662 | 26,300 | 23,081 | 23,550 | 16 | 19 | 51,200 | 56,000 | 554 | 600 | 203 | 217 | 70,249 | 77,280 | Ethiopia |
| 2 | 2 | 70 | 72 | ... | ... | ... | ... | ... | ... | ... | ... | ... | ... | Faeroe Islands |
| 9 | 7 | 642 | 699 | ... | ... | 3 | 2 | 1 | 2 | 1,000 | 1,001 | ... | ... | Falkland Islands |

## Crops and livestock (continued)

| country | grains production ('000 metric tons) 1975–77 average | grains production 1986 | grains yield (kg/hectare) 1975–77 average | grains yield 1986 | roots and tubers[a] production ('000 metric tons) 1975–77 average | roots production 1986 | roots yield (kg/hectare) 1975–77 average | roots yield 1986 | pulses[b] production ('000 metric tons) 1975–77 average | pulses production 1986 | pulses yield (kg/hectare) 1975–77 average | pulses yield 1986 | fruits[c] production ('000 metric tons) 1975–77 average | fruits production 1986 | vegetables[d] production ('000 metric tons) 1975–77 average | vegetables production 1986 |
|---|---|---|---|---|---|---|---|---|---|---|---|---|---|---|---|---|
| Fiji | 21 | 34 | 2,160 | 2,219 | 20 | 88 | 8,115 | 9,146 | 2 | 3 | 1,644 | 867 | 13 | 18 | 13 | 16 |
| Finland | 3,452 | 3,544 | 2,670 | 2,911 | 788 | 773 | 15,957 | 19,624 | 11 | 5 | 2,080 | 2,120 | 98 | 113 | 98 | 175 |
| France | 35,926 | 49,748 | 3,730 | 5,239 | 6,257 | 6,300 | 21,530 | 31,297 | 147 | 1,255 | 1,973 | 3,728 | 13,514 | 14,972 | 6,418 | 7,117 |
| French Guiana | 1 | 9 | 1,671 | 3,204 | 14 | 13 | 10,766 | 11,480 | ... | ... | ... | ... | 2 | 2 | 1 | 9 |
| French Polynesia |  |  |  |  | 18 | 13 | 12,582 | 8,554 | ... | ... | ... | ... | 6 | 5 | 5 | 8 |
| Gabon | 8 | 11 | 1,465 | 1,527 | 343 | 396 | 5,827 | 6,435 | — | — | 400 | 583 | 154 | 187 | 18 | 28 |
| Gambia, The | 70 | 138 | 834 | 1,373 | 9 | 6 | 3,278 | 3,000 | 4 | 4 | 250 | 278 | 4 | 4 | 7 | 7 |
| Gaza Strip | ... | 5 | ... | 2,808 | 3 | 8 | 17,751 | 16,667 | ... | 1 | ... | 2,571 | 257 | 168 | 50 | 75 |
| Germany, East | 8,599 | 11,662 | 3,406 | 4,639 | 8,267 | 9,859 | 14,099 | 21,478 | 71 | 103 | 1,392 | 1,845 | 577 | 1,015 | 1,059 | 1,377 |
| Germany, West | 20,666 | 26,050 | 3,912 | 5,292 | 10,676 | 8,700 | 26,057 | 37,021 | 60 | 161 | 2,731 | 2,201 | 3,946 | 5,151 | 1,823 | 2,711 |
| Ghana | 666 | 920 | 828 | 1,011 | 3,315 | 5,279 | 6,264 | 8,979 | 16 | 11 | 102 | 88 | 1,298 | 818 | 365 | 733 |
| Gibraltar |  |  |  |  |  |  |  |  |  |  |  |  |  |  |  |  |
| Greece | 3,625 | 5,228 | 2,365 | 3,552 | 974 | 943 | 15,210 | 21,331 | 98 | 60 | 1,137 | 1,264 | 4,137 | 4,802 | 3,127 | 3,791 |
| Greenland |  |  |  |  |  |  |  |  |  |  |  |  |  |  |  |  |
| Grenada | 1 | — | 899 | 987 | 3 | 4 | 4,984 | 5,074 | 1 | 1 | 1,157 | 1,504 | 28 | 19 | 2 | 1 |
| Guadeloupe | — | — | 1,400 | 1,200 | 34 | 23 | 11,536 | 11,210 | — | — | 676 | 531 | 163 | 175 | 22 | 26 |
| Guam | — | — | 1,500 | 1,500 | 1 | 2 | 14,075 | 13,273 | ... | ... | ... | ... | 2 | 1 | 1 | 1 |
| Guatemala | 1,004 | 1,281 | 1,431 | 1,602 | 62 | 53 | 3,917 | 4,565 | 84 | 123 | 594 | 651 | 560 | 968 | 222 | 283 |
| Guernsey |  |  |  |  |  |  |  |  |  |  |  |  |  |  |  |  |
| Guinea | 565 | 604 | 829 | 799 | 778 | 663 | 7,122 | 7,179 | 40 | 50 | 667 | 769 | 587 | 673 | 384 | 420 |
| Guinea-Bissau | 85 | 211 | 706 | 907 | 33 | 40 | 5,128 | 6,154 | 2 | 2 | 544 | 567 | 40 | 40 | 23 | 20 |
| Guyana | 277 | 358 | 2,170 | 3,583 | 23 | 30 | 6,826 | 6,977 | 1 | 1 | 622 | 522 | 37 | 46 | 8 | 11 |
| Haiti | 413 | 445 | 1,092 | 1,236 | 721 | 812 | 4,386 | 4,109 | 82 | 92 | 494 | 517 | 917 | 1,058 | 255 | 317 |
| Honduras | 474 | 538 | 1,006 | 1,334 | 19 | 23 | 3,372 | 7,178 | 31 | 40 | 413 | 537 | 1,297 | 1,644 | 70 | 108 |
| Hong Kong | 3 | — | 1,854 | 2,200 | 1 | — | 16,964 | 24,469 | ... | ... | ... | ... | 3 | 3 | 182 | 157 |
| Hungary | 11,970 | 14,236 | 3,899 | 4,954 | 1,562 | 1,263 | 12,697 | 18,554 | 132 | 222 | 1,681 | 2,352 | 2,415 | 2,598 | 1,837 | 1,891 |
| Iceland |  |  |  |  | 7 | 13 | 9,069 | 12,500 | ... | ... | ... | ... | — | — | 1 | 2 |
| India | 129,165 | 165,837 | 1,264 | 1,601 | 15,022 | 18,204 | 12,139 | 13,629 | 11,642 | 12,985 | 504 | 544 | 17,858 | 24,767 | 36,753 | 48,716 |
| Indonesia | 25,887 | 45,324 | 2,397 | 3,507 | 15,312 | 16,266 | 8,654 | 10,701 | 275 | 354 | 1,001 | 829 | 3,645 | 5,880 | 2,258 | 3,543 |
| Iran | 8,653 | 11,292 | 1,135 | 1,230 | 606 | 1,600 | 14,356 | 14,546 | 214 | 283 | 1,139 | 736 | 3,675 | 5,040 | 3,431 | 4,166 |
| Iraq | 1,642 | 2,586 | 874 | 1,063 | 61 | 120 | 9,687 | 16,438 | 38 | 33 | 780 | 879 | 1,721 | 1,995 | 1,811 | 2,787 |
| Ireland | 1,488 | 1,896 | 4,189 | 5,143 | 1,243 | 700 | 26,216 | 22,951 | — | 1 | 3,222 | 3,590 | 23 | 20 | 276 | 222 |
| Isle of Man |  |  |  |  |  |  |  |  |  |  |  |  |  |  |  |  |
| Israel | 276 | 190 | 1,961 | 1,895 | 185 | 211 | 32,861 | 38,411 | 8 | 10 | 1,462 | 1,151 | 2,014 | 1,873 | 736 | 833 |
| Italy | 15,942 | 18,624 | 3,236 | 3,829 | 2,992 | 2,652 | 16,588 | 19,565 | 365 | 272 | 1,236 | 1,390 | 19,957 | 22,072 | 12,104 | 13,908 |
| Jamaica | 12 | 9 | 1,957 | 2,200 | 207 | 250 | 9,994 | 11,819 | 5 | 8 | 690 | 943 | 319 | 348 | 84 | 126 |
| Japan | 16,964 | 15,805 | 5,720 | 5,898 | 5,508 | 5,951 | 22,429 | 24,931 | 167 | 132 | 1,375 | 1,641 | 7,970 | 7,047 | 14,964 | 15,374 |
| Jersey |  |  |  |  |  |  |  |  |  |  |  |  |  |  |  |  |
| Jordan | 74 | 55 | 408 | 586 | 7 | 13 | 14,826 | 19,231 | 10 | 9 | 396 | 639 | 102 | 146 | 350 | 516 |
| Kampuchea | 1,740 | 2,092 | 1,280 | 1,209 | 110 | 143 | 8,195 | 7,627 | 18 | 37 | 574 | 906 | 175 | 195 | 457 | 457 |
| Kenya | 3,164 | 3,190 | 1,590 | 1,779 | 1,188 | 1,570 | 7,680 | 9,813 | 295 | 518 | 486 | 1,080 | 480 | 682 | 382 | 454 |
| Kiribati |  |  |  |  | 10 | 13 | 8,546 | 8,973 | ... | ... | ... | ... | 4 | 5 | 4 | 5 |
| Korea, North | 7,295 | 10,990 | 3,702 | 4,406 | 1,645 | 2,377 | 12,557 | 13,109 | 260 | 291 | 796 | 866 | 727 | 1,354 | 1,944 | 2,917 |
| Korea, South | 8,970 | 8,461 | 4,559 | 5,709 | 2,364 | 1,254 | 17,243 | 22,199 | 56 | 45 | 848 | 1,115 | 1,002 | 2,110 | 7,044 | 9,336 |
| Kuwait | — | — | 1,908 | 3,288[5] | — | — | 13,467 | 15,000 | ... | ... | ... | ... | 5 | 5 | 26 | 41 |
| Laos | 786 | 1,527 | 1,278 | 2,270 | 97 | 252 | 9,500 | 10,186 | 13 | 26 | 1,444 | 2,174 | 91 | 182 | 149 | 234 |
| Lebanon | 66 | 21 | 1,114 | 1,181 | 38 | 231 | 5,524 | 22,314 | 11 | 9 | 877 | 976 | 689 | 847 | 279 | 381 |
| Lesotho | 175 | 132 | 950 | 679 | 5 | 6 | 13,061 | 15,000 | 19 | 6 | 876 | 411 | 13 | 15 | 19 | 25 |
| Liberia | 243 | 295 | 1,222 | 1,405 | 316 | 379 | 3,910 | 4,027 | 3 | 3 | 489 | 524 | 114 | 132 | 59 | 77 |
| Libya | 238 | 286 | 407 | 691 | 89 | 112 | 5,469 | 7,000 | 8 | 11 | 1,104 | 1,206 | 320 | 462 | 483 | 581 |
| Liechtenstein |  |  |  |  | 10 | 12 | 18,703 | 18,932 |  |  |  |  |  |  |  |  |
| Luxembourg[3] | ... | ... | ... | ... | ... | ... | ... | ... | ... | ... | ... | ... | ... | ... | ... | ... |
| Macau |  |  |  |  | 3 | 4 | 10,000 | 10,000 | — | — |  |  | 4 | 5 | 1 | 2 |
| Madagascar | 2,154 | 2,293 | 1,767 | 1,737 | 1,960 | 3,246 | 6,217 | 5,969 | 71 | 62 | 871 | 896 | 871 | 742 | 278 | 299 |
| Malawi | 1,333 | 1,564 | 1,141 | 1,154 | 517 | 459 | 4,519 | 4,030 | 194 | 198 | 612 | 603 | 334 | 399 | 185 | 219 |
| Malaysia | 1,983 | 1,886 | 2,650 | 2,858 | 525 | 520 | 9,843 | 9,630 | ... | ... | ... | ... | 897 | 1,022 | 448 | 461 |
| Maldives | 1 | — | 839 | 788 | 6 | 9 | 5,138 | 5,068 | — | — | 600 | 597 | 7 | 8 | 15 | 18 |
| Mali | 1,188 | 1,775 | 725 | 904 | 93 | 145 | 9,185 | 9,804 | 34 | 60 | 1,098 | 1,036 | 10 | 12 | 110 | 252 |
| Malta | 5 | 9 | 2,540 | 3,813 | 20 | 13 | 8,509 | 6,842 | 1 | 2 | 1,885 | 2,308 | 10 | 16 | 46 | 48 |
| Martinique |  |  |  |  | 32 | 40 | 9,097 | 8,448 | ... | ... | ... | ... | 278 | 246 | 30 | 27 |
| Mauritania | 42 | 112 | 470 | 496 | 6 | 6 | 1,173 | 1,937 | 20 | 24 | 365 | 324 | 16 | 19 | 4 | 8 |
| Mauritius | 2 | 5 | 2,590 | 7,684 | 11 | 26 | 15,281 | 24,702 | 1 | 1 | 476 | 625 | 7 | 9 | 24 | 32 |
| Mayotte |  |  |  |  |  |  |  |  |  |  |  |  |  |  |  |  |
| Mexico | 17,024 | 23,975 | 1,751 | 2,344 | 849 | 1,123 | 12,213 | 14,135 | 1,072 | 1,331 | 590 | 648 | 6,758 | 8,797 | 2,870 | 4,531 |
| Monaco |  |  |  |  |  |  |  |  |  |  |  |  |  |  |  |  |
| Mongolia | 423 | 871 | 937 | 1,382 | 40 | 133 | 8,316 | 11,857 | 2 | — | 518 | 1,143 | 3 | — | 21 | 47 |
| Montserrat | — | — | 1,000 | 1,652 |  |  | 2,363 | 3,332 |  |  |  |  | 1 | 1 |  |  |
| Morocco | 4,110 | 7,824 | 886 | 1,499 | 222 | 570[5] | 10,793 | 12,925[5] | 363 | 393 | 666 | 915 | 1,587 | 2,032 | 1,308 | 1,460 |
| Mozambique | 679 | 610 | 720 | 682 | 2,783 | 3,420 | 4,784 | 5,841 | 73 | 60 | 611 | 480 | 303 | 347 | 186 | 191 |
| Nauru |  |  |  |  |  |  |  |  |  |  |  |  | — | — | — | — |
| Nepal | 3,707 | 3,989 | 1,701 | 1,631 | 363 | 503 | 5,495 | 5,126 | 110 | 146 | 401 | 435 | 125 | 153 | 215 | 265 |
| Netherlands, The | 1,121 | 1,265 | 4,674 | 7,497 | 5,234 | 6,857 | 32,531 | 41,207 | 27 | 163 | 2,813 | 5,249 | 508 | 507 | 2,391 | 2,942 |
| Netherlands Antilles[2] | 1 | 2 | 653 | 714 | ... | ... | ... | ... | ... | ... | ... | ... | ... | ... | ... | ... |
| New Caledonia | 1 | 3 | 2,500 | 1,690 | 18 | 23 | 5,865 | 5,695 | — | — | 722 | 684 | 8 | 6 | 3 | 3 |
| New Zealand | 818 | 1,210 | 3,767 | 3,942 | 255 | 289 | 25,662 | 29,241 | 49 | 295 | 2,481 | 3,876 | 267 | 560 | 323 | 443 |
| Nicaragua | 319 | 572 | 1,085 | 1,628 | 25 | 50 | 4,058 | 5,993 | 47 | 71 | 753 | 608 | 334 | 307 | 44 | 49 |
| Niger | 1,242 | 1,832 | 400 | 417 | 221 | 232 | 7,322 | 7,415 | 225 | 313 | 270 | 194 | 32 | 42 | 106 | 159 |
| Nigeria | 7,660 | 12,106 | 888 | 1,185 | 28,049 | 36,261 | 10,003 | 11,426 | 711 | 1,332 | 279 | 587 | 2,035 | 2,943 | 2,490 | 4,064 |
| Niue |  |  |  |  | 2 | 2 | 2,503 | 2,602 |  |  |  |  |  |  | — | — |
| Norfolk Island |  |  |  |  |  |  |  |  |  |  |  |  |  |  |  |  |
| Norway | 897 | 1,108 | 2,988 | 3,193 | 536 | 440 | 22,363 | 24,450 | ... | ... | ... | ... | 113 | 127 | 165 | 194 |
| Oman | 4 | 2 | 1,177 | 1,826 | — | 1[5] | 1,111 | 4,063[5] | ... | ... | ... | ... | 87 | 140 | 36 | 159 |
| Pacific Is., Trust Territory of the Marshall Islands | — | — | 1,091 | 1,210 | 11 | 14 | 8,339 | 8,750 | — | — | 600 | 600 | 3 | 3 | 3 | 3 |
| Micronesia, Fed. States of | ... | ... | ... | ... | ... | ... | ... | ... | ... | ... | ... | ... | ... | ... | ... | ... |

| cattle stock ('000 head) 1975–77 average | cattle stock ('000 head) 1986 | sheep stock ('000 head) 1975–77 average | sheep stock ('000 head) 1986 | hogs stock ('000 head) 1975–77 average | hogs stock ('000 head) 1986 | chickens stock ('000 head) 1975–77 average | chickens stock ('000 head) 1986 | milk[e] production ('000 metric tons) 1975–77 average | milk[e] production ('000 metric tons) 1986 | milk yield (kg/animal) 1975–77 average | milk yield (kg/animal) 1986 | eggs[f] production (metric tons) 1975–77 average | eggs[f] production (metric tons) 1986 | country |
|---|---|---|---|---|---|---|---|---|---|---|---|---|---|---|
| 157 | 159 | ... | ... | 17 | 31 | 787 | 1,000 | 48 | 45 | 1,700 | 1,698 | 1,850 | 2,600 | Fiji |
| 1,807 | 1,576 | 113 | 116 | 1,123 | 1,211 | 8,769 | 7,000 | 3,222 | 3,044 | 4,261 | 5,048 | 83,833 | 83,100 | Finland |
| 23,986 | 22,896 | 10,806 | 10,790 | 11,664 | 10,956 | 166,037 | 188,000 | 29,814 | 33,700 | 2,911 | 3,363 | 755,667 | 925,000 | France |
| 2 | 15 | ... | ... | 4 | 10 | 121 | 100 | — | 1 | 503 | 478 | 311 | 260 | French Guiana |
| 6 | 7 | 3 | 2 | 20 | 48 | 419 | 720 | 2 | 2 | 2,833 | 2,700 | 624 | 730 | French Polynesia |
| 3 | 8 | 73 | 82 | 127 | 152 | 1,020 | 2,000 | — | 1 | 250 | 250 | 617 | 1,390 | Gabon |
| 288 | 290 | 135 | 191 | 9 | 12 | 280 | 349 | 5 | 5 | 175 | 175 | 359 | 582 | Gambia, The |
| 2 | 5 | 69 | 67 | ... | ... | 717 | 1,380 | 9 | 8 | 5,290 | 6,008 | 1,657 | 2,300 | Gaza Strip |
| 5,529 | 5,827 | 1,866 | 2,587 | 11,437 | 12,946 | 47,699 | 50,680 | 8,042 | 9,150 | 3,772 | 4,397 | 305,418 | 340,000 | Germany, East |
| 14,473 | 15,627 | 1,073 | 1,296 | 20,209 | 24,282 | 88,729 | 71,057 | 22,097 | 26,350 | 4,092 | 4,880 | 875,325 | 770,000 | Germany, West |
| 830 | 1,188 | 1,810 | 2,175 | 379 | 586 | 11,661 | 10,000 | 7 | 10 | 55 | 55 | 11,029 | 10,600 | Ghana |
| ... | ... | | | | | | | | | | | ... | ... | Gibraltar |
| 1,180 | 740 | 8,311 | 10,122 | 763 | 1,095 | 29,620 | 31,000 | 701 | 642 | 1,512 | 1,834 | 111,546 | 136,675 | Greece |
| | | 18 | 21 | | | | | | | | | | | Greenland |
| 6 | 4 | 9 | 17 | 11 | 11 | 252 | 260 | 1 | 2 | 800 | 800 | 930 | 1,000 | Grenada |
| 83 | 82 | 3 | 4 | 37 | 44 | 420 | 390 | 10 | 17 | 518 | 500 | 457 | 1,183 | Guadeloupe |
| 2 | 2 | ... | ... | 10 | 14 | 127 | 218 | ... | ... | ... | ... | 1,191 | 1,000 | Guam |
| 1,472 | 2,284 | 583 | 680 | 616 | 862 | 10,880 | 14,700 | 310 | 360 | 894 | 900 | 33,017 | 42,150 | Guatemala |
| ... | ... | | | ... | ... | | | | | | | | | Guernsey |
| 1,546 | 1,838 | 410 | 465 | 34 | 49 | 5,313 | 11,700 | 36 | 42 | 185 | 185 | 5,565 | 12,180 | Guinea |
| 266 | 333 | 146 | 200 | 210 | 286 | 357 | 712 | 8 | 10 | 170 | 170 | 252 | 514 | Guinea-Bissau |
| 265 | 200 | 108 | 120 | 125 | 180 | 10,100 | 14,600 | 12 | 23 | 771 | 798 | 3,583 | 4,200 | Guyana |
| 850 | 1,400 | 81 | 92 | 1,700 | 700 | 4,450 | 8,000 | 23 | 22 | 230 | 237 | 1,835 | 3,750 | Haiti |
| 1,839 | 2,848 | 5 | 7 | 519 | 563 | 3,885 | 5,400 | 241 | 280 | 650 | 865 | 16,100 | 21,200 | Honduras |
| 10 | 3 | — | — | 429 | 372 | 4,488 | 5,488 | 5 | 2 | 2,363 | 2,286 | 2,792 | 2,070 | Hong Kong |
| 1,936 | 1,766 | 2,137 | 2,465 | 7,700 | 8,280 | 56,072 | 56,686 | 1,961 | 2,725 | 2,768 | 3,961 | 232,123 | 223,000 | Hungary |
| 63 | 64 | 865 | 770 | 7 | 13 | 247 | 307 | 128 | 123 | 3,491 | 3,719 | 2,808 | 3,500 | Iceland |
| 180,031 | 200,000 | 40,722 | 54,460 | 7,416 | 8,700 | 147,957 | 180,000 | 11,396 | 20,100 | 513 | 703 | 495,667 | 916,500 | India |
| 6,324 | 6,465 | 3,614 | 5,193 | 2,878 | 5,643 | 102,783 | 375,475 | 66 | 220 | 735 | 1,032 | 73,980 | 344,300 | Indonesia |
| 7,283 | 8,350 | 34,333 | 34,500 | 52 | ... | 60,000 | 100,000 | 1,260 | 1,700 | 771 | 723 | 204,667 | 230,000 | Iran |
| 1,835 | 1,550 | 9,960 | 8,800 | ... | ... | 15,433 | 75,000 | 320 | 320 | 750 | 753 | 24,617 | 85,000 | Iraq |
| 6,308 | 5,779 | 2,649 | 2,774 | 888 | 994 | 8,249 | 7,417 | 4,543 | 5,687 | 3,228 | 3,922 | 39,095 | 36,000 | Ireland |
| | 35[4] | | 132[4] | | 5[4] | | 70[4] | | | | | | | Isle of Man |
| 304 | 321 | 205 | 232 | 83 | 130 | 19,000 | 29,000 | 656 | 869 | 6,289 | 8,278 | 92,410 | 92,620 | Israel |
| 8,446 | 8,910 | 8,197 | 9,718 | 8,933 | 9,169 | 106,667 | 111,000 | 9,597 | 10,865 | 3,307 | 3,598 | 658,400 | 630,000 | Italy |
| 279 | 290 | 5 | 6 | 203 | 245 | 4,300 | 5,300 | 49 | 50 | 1,000 | 1,000 | 13,500 | 17,500 | Jamaica |
| 3,747 | 4,742 | 11 | 26 | 7,758 | 11,061 | 246,031 | 342,000 | 5,319 | 7,455 | 4,159 | 5,000 | 1,858,000 | 2,225,000 | Japan |
| | | | | | | | | | | | | | | Jersey |
| 33 | 35 | 732 | 1,100 | ... | ... | 24,000 | 34,000 | 11 | 20 | 898 | 1,000 | 9,413 | 26,280 | Jordan |
| 1,050 | 1,571 | 2 | 1 | 433 | 1,299 | 4,133 | 5,900 | 18 | 16 | 170 | 170 | 6,100 | 6,500 | Kampuchea |
| 9,537 | 9,000 | 3,168 | 7,100 | 63 | 98 | 16,527 | 21,000 | 920 | 901 | 456 | 450 | 17,864 | 33,264 | Kenya |
| | | 10 | 10 | | | 154 | 220 | | | 101 | 118 | | | Kiribati |
| 850 | 1,122 | 268 | 359 | 1,700 | 2,920 | 17,316 | 18,600 | 31 | 80 | 2,000 | 2,459 | 75,473 | 129,900 | Korea, North |
| 1,684 | 2,864 | 6 | 5 | 1,561 | 2,853 | 26,829 | 51,081 | 205 | 980 | 4,546 | 4,900 | 189,920 | 325,000 | Korea, South |
| 10 | 21 | 127 | 265 | ... | ... | 5,353 | 8,000 | 13 | 40 | 2,332 | 2,500 | 2,365 | 14,500 | Kuwait |
| 327 | 593 | ... | ... | 669 | 1,516 | 4,225 | 8,300 | 5 | 8 | 200 | 200 | 18,333 | 28,100 | Laos |
| 40 | 50 | 150 | 137 | 17 | 21 | 3,867 | 10,500 | 47 | 92 | 1,799 | 2,300 | 17,317 | 55,000 | Lebanon |
| 505 | 520 | 1,197 | 1,420 | 78 | 65 | 824 | 1,000 | 17 | 23 | 290 | 290 | 775 | 798 | Lesotho |
| 35 | 43 | 176 | 246 | 93 | 131 | 2,100 | 3,700 | 1 | 1 | 100 | 100 | 1,928 | 3,600 | Liberia |
| 188 | 210 | 4,147 | 5,550 | ... | ... | 4,692 | 25,500 | 56 | 69 | 1,188 | 1,438 | 9,015 | 16,000 | Libya |
| 8 | 9 | 1 | 2 | 8 | 9 | 43 | ... | 15 | 19 | 3,213 | 3,351 | 250 | 250 | Liechtenstein |
| ... | ... | ... | ... | | | | | | | | | | | Luxembourg[3] |
| 2 | 9 | ... | ... | 7 | 6 | 353 | 450 | ... | ... | ... | ... | 535 | 635 | Macau |
| 8,799 | 10,485 | 606 | 604 | 601 | 1,350 | 13,018 | 16,000 | 31 | 41 | 700 | 700 | 10,078 | 11,760 | Madagascar |
| 689 | 930 | 84 | 180 | 174 | 240 | 7,783 | 8,350 | 30 | 40 | 415 | 460 | 9,967 | 11,440 | Malawi |
| 449 | 620 | 50 | 69 | 1,503 | 2,150 | 44,448 | 56,300 | 23 | 30 | 680 | 680 | 112,967 | 137,500 | Malaysia |
| ... | ... | | | | | | | | | | | | | Maldives |
| 4,014 | 4,676 | 5,310 | 5,500 | 30 | 58 | 12,500 | 14,500 | 80 | 94 | 200 | 200 | 6,750 | 7,830 | Mali |
| 14 | 14 | 7 | 5 | 23 | 95 | 999 | 1,100 | 28 | 28 | 3,688 | 3,889 | 6,625 | 6,600 | Malta |
| 49 | 41 | 41 | 87 | 35 | 45 | 1,117 | 2,000 | 4 | 3 | 679 | 775 | 1,020 | 800 | Martinique |
| 1,147 | 1,000 | 4,170 | 3,950 | ... | ... | 2,850 | 3,600 | 69 | 93 | 350 | 350 | 2,422 | 3,400 | Mauritania |
| 53 | 61 | 3 | 4 | 5 | 12 | 1,100 | 1,750 | 24 | 25 | 2,377 | 2,500 | 2,347 | 3,500 | Mauritius |
| | | | | | | | | | | | | | | Mayotte |
| 25,286 | 31,123 | 6,309 | 8,419 | 14,030 | 18,631 | 145,247 | 220,000 | 6,145 | 8,000 | 1,180 | 1,356 | 464,090 | 850,000 | Mexico |
| ... | ... | | | | | | | | | | | | | Monaco |
| 2,403 | 2,408 | 14,289 | 13,248 | 14 | 56 | 165 | 300 | 208 | 236 | 409 | 419 | 453 | 1,300 | Mongolia |
| 8 | 9 | 3 | 4 | 1 | 1 | 30 | 33 | 2 | 2 | 750 | 750 | 41 | 57 | Montserrat |
| 3,547 | 2,570 | 14,457 | 12,100 | 8 | 8 | 20,000 | 35,000 | 506 | 850 | 552 | 607 | 55,433 | 83,000 | Morocco |
| 1,366 | 1,340 | 100 | 116 | 117 | 150 | 14,092 | 20,000 | 58 | 65 | 170 | 170 | 7,867 | 12,500 | Mozambique |
| ... | ... | | | 2 | 2 | 3 | ... | | | | | 7 | 10 | Nauru |
| 6,634 | 6,374 | 690 | 810 | 329 | 456 | 7,450 | 9,634 | 181 | 220 | 325 | 326 | 13,300 | 13,000 | Nepal |
| 4,616 | 5,076 | 780 | 800 | 7,691 | 12,908 | 68,832 | 90,000 | 10,441 | 12,665 | 4,725 | 5,592 | 319,076 | 640,000 | Netherlands, The |
| 8 | 9 | 8 | 9 | 6 | 8 | 100 | 135 | 4 | 4 | 1,286 | 1,281 | 477 | 550 | Netherlands Antilles[2] |
| 115 | 122 | 5 | 3 | 22 | 40 | 166 | 500 | 3 | 4 | 600 | 600 | 480 | 1,200 | New Caledonia |
| 9,016 | 8,392 | 56,942 | 71,646 | 447 | 450 | 7,278 | 8,500 | 6,436 | 8,042 | 3,165 | 3,581 | 55,762 | 44,200 | New Zealand |
| 2,662 | 2,100 | 2 | 3 | 670 | 750 | 4,097 | 5,500 | 457 | 125 | 1,123 | 625 | 25,008 | 31,300 | Nicaragua |
| 2,676 | 3,300 | 2,356 | 3,500 | 27 | 37 | 8,000 | 14,000 | 76 | 106 | 177 | 200 | 5,440 | 7,820 | Niger |
| 11,267 | 12,169 | 10,400 | 13,160 | 910 | 1,351 | 90,000 | 168,600 | 310 | 359 | 275 | 295 | 125,300 | 250,000 | Nigeria |
| 1 | 1 | ... | ... | 1 | 1 | 15 | 20 | — | — | 772 | 714 | 35 | 20 | Niue |
| ... | ... | | | | | | | | | | | | | Norfolk Island |
| 927 | 970 | 1,696 | 2,502 | 689 | 695 | 3,796 | 4,100 | 1,854 | 1,971 | 4,816 | 5,327 | 38,205 | 49,471 | Norway |
| 132 | 130 | 65 | 213 | ... | ... | 800 | 827 | 16 | 16 | 420 | 420 | 483 | 1,519 | Oman |
| 7 | 11 | ... | ... | 21 | 28 | 164 | ... | ... | ... | ... | ... | 135 | 157 | Pacific Is., Trust Territory of the |
| | | | | | | | | | | | | | | Marshall Islands |
| ... | ... | ... | ... | ... | ... | ... | ... | ... | ... | ... | ... | ... | ... | Micronesia, Fed. States of |

## Crops and livestock (continued)

| country | grains production ('000 metric tons) 1975–77 average | grains production 1986 | grains yield (kg/hectare) 1975–77 average | grains yield 1986 | roots and tubers[a] production ('000 metric tons) 1975–77 average | roots production 1986 | roots yield (kg/hectare) 1975–77 average | roots yield 1986 | pulses[b] production ('000 metric tons) 1975–77 average | pulses production 1986 | pulses yield (kg/hectare) 1975–77 average | pulses yield 1986 | fruits[c] production ('000 metric tons) 1975–77 average | fruits production 1986 | vegetables[d] production ('000 metric tons) 1975–77 average | vegetables production 1986 |
|---|---|---|---|---|---|---|---|---|---|---|---|---|---|---|---|---|
| Northern Mariana Islands | ... | ... | ... | ... | ... | ... | ... | ... | ... | ... | ... | ... | ... | ... | ... | ... |
| Palau | ... | ... | ... | ... | ... | ... | ... | ... | ... | ... | ... | ... | ... | ... | ... | ... |
| Pakistan | 14,169 | 20,869 | 1,441 | 1,853 | 321 | 547 | 11,435 | 10,243 | 852 | 857 | 525 | 529 | 2,124 | 2,570 | 1,925 | 2,597 |
| Panama | 241 | 266 | 1,237 | 1,462 | 75 | 82 | 8,234 | 8,109 | 5 | 6 | 296 | 438 | 1,206 | 1,204 | 34 | 55 |
| Papua New Guinea | 3 | 3 | 1,588 | 1,415 | 1,046 | 1,180 | 6,951 | 6,969 | 1 | 2 | 500 | 500 | 981 | 1,111 | 230 | 278 |
| Paraguay | 445 | 817 | 1,401 | 1,388 | 1,690 | 2,969 | 14,021 | 14,021 | 71 | 39 | 815 | 713 | 713 | 1,047 | 207 | 218 |
| Peru | 1,592 | 1,892 | 1,901 | 2,347 | 2,375 | 2,361 | 6,987 | 8,222 | 103 | 123 | 824 | 815 | 1,608 | 1,407 | 736 | 744 |
| Philippines | 9,571 | 13,506 | 1,398 | 1,902 | 2,261 | 2,717 | 5,554 | 6,364 | 32 | 42 | 631 | 754 | 3,413 | 6,362 | 824 | 796 |
| Pitcairn Island | ... | ... | ... | ... | ... | ... | ... | ... | ... | ... | ... | ... | ... | ... | ... | ... |
| Poland | 19,940 | 24,908 | 2,532 | 3,017 | 45,843 | 39,000 | 18,378 | 18,615 | 232 | 456 | 1,146 | 1,488 | 1,648 | 2,091 | 4,005 | 4,708 |
| Portugal | 1,426 | 1,547 | 1,057 | 1,597 | 1,200 | 1,147 | 8,682 | 8,605 | 85 | 77 | 230 | 298 | 1,790 | 1,591 | 1,710 | 1,853 |
| Puerto Rico | 5 | 6 | 6,652 | 8,802 | 39 | 31 | 5,785 | 6,640 | 4 | 4 | 738 | 715 | 286 | 280 | 23 | 35 |
| Qatar | — | 2 | 3,108 | 3,258 | — | — | 9,792 | 14,091 | ... | ... | ... | ... | 3 | 12 | 6 | 18 |
| Réunion | 13 | 14 | 5,316 | 5,640 | 12 | 10 | 15,050 | 11,054 | 1 | 1 | 2,781 | 2,037 | 23 | 33 | 10 | 12 |
| Romania | 17,890 | 28,491 | 2,838 | 3,780 | 3,904 | 8,513 | 12,854 | 26,438 | 98 | 314 | 121 | 490 | 2,795 | 5,074 | 3,704 | 7,169 |
| Rwanda | 235 | 317 | 1,094 | 1,327 | 1,297 | 1,580 | 8,354 | 7,890 | 219 | 270 | 803 | 974 | 1,838 | 2,136 | 150 | 188 |
| St. Christopher and Nevis | ... | ... | ... | ... | 3 | 3 | 3,411 | 3,440 | — | — | 1,000 | 1,000 | 2 | 2 | 1 | 1 |
| St. Helena and Ascension | ... | ... | ... | ... | ... | ... | ... | ... | ... | ... | ... | ... | ... | ... | ... | ... |
| St. Lucia | — | — | 700 | 769 | 10 | 11 | 4,484 | 4,180 | — | — | 2,000 | 2,500 | 98 | 144 | 1 | 1 |
| St. Pierre and Miquelon | ... | ... | ... | ... | ... | ... | ... | ... | ... | ... | ... | ... | ... | ... | ... | ... |
| St. Vincent and the Grenadines | — | 1 | 3,214 | 3,375 | 21 | 59 | 7,674 | 6,520 | — | — | 845 | 1,013 | 30 | 54 | 1 | 1 |
| San Marino | ... | ... | ... | ... | ... | ... | ... | ... | ... | ... | ... | ... | ... | ... | ... | ... |
| São Tomé and Príncipe | 1 | 1 | 1,522 | 1,556 | 13 | 16 | 12,197 | 13,478 | ... | ... | ... | ... | 4 | 4 | 2 | 3 |
| Saudi Arabia | 289 | 2,349 | 750 | 3,826 | — | 25 | 2,545 | 20,417 | 6 | 7 | 1,717 | 1,944 | 693 | 1,165 | 686 | 1,157 |
| Senegal | 687 | 961 | 641 | 681 | 95 | 30 | 3,262 | 4,396 | 16 | 15 | 267 | 302 | 63 | 84 | 71 | 101 |
| Seychelles | ... | ... | ... | ... | — | — | 5,766 | 5,000 | ... | ... | ... | ... | 2 | 2 | 1 | 2 |
| Sierra Leone | 615 | 577 | 1,448 | 1,477 | 120 | 148 | 4,309 | 3,489 | 28 | 33 | 564 | 600 | 114 | 148 | 146 | 183 |
| Singapore | ... | ... | ... | ... | 2 | — | 11,556 | 11,188 | ... | ... | ... | ... | 17 | 5 | 38 | 21 |
| Solomon Islands | 4 | 5 | 2,750 | 2,550 | 76 | 94 | 13,450 | 16,036 | 1 | 2 | 788 | 1,100 | 11 | 14 | 5 | 6 |
| Somalia | 260 | 639 | 637 | 748 | 33 | 42 | 11,001 | 10,769 | 10 | 21 | 330 | 344 | 231 | 240 | 26 | 32 |
| South Africa[6] | 11,192 | 10,857 | 1,375 | 1,556 | 759 | 1,180 | 12,304 | 13,258 | 96 | 105 | 883 | 1,331 | 2,602 | 3,604 | 1,510 | 1,763 |
| Bophuthatswana[6] | ... | ... | ... | ... | ... | ... | ... | ... | ... | ... | ... | ... | ... | ... | ... | ... |
| Ciskei[6] | ... | ... | ... | ... | ... | ... | ... | ... | ... | ... | ... | ... | ... | ... | ... | ... |
| KwaNdebele[6] | ... | ... | ... | ... | ... | ... | ... | ... | ... | ... | ... | ... | ... | ... | ... | ... |
| Transkei[6] | ... | ... | ... | ... | ... | ... | ... | ... | ... | ... | ... | ... | ... | ... | ... | ... |
| Venda[6] | ... | ... | ... | ... | ... | ... | ... | ... | ... | ... | ... | ... | ... | ... | ... | ... |
| South West Africa/Namibia | 88 | 98 | 488 | 489 | 187 | 235 | 9,333 | 9,400 | 6 | 6 | 945 | 985 | 29 | 33 | 25 | 28 |
| Spain | 13,642 | 16,336 | 1,889 | 2,125 | 5,675 | 4,911 | 14,296 | 16,768 | 432 | 316 | 689 | 715 | 11,193 | 13,883 | 8,226 | 9,163 |
| Sri Lanka | 1,414 | 2,655 | 1,865 | 2,975 | 890 | 895 | 5,019 | 11,557 | 15 | 39 | 566 | 781 | 1,049 | 1,054 | 648 | 959 |
| Sudan, The | 2,724 | 4,386 | 669 | 663 | 287 | 314 | 3,516 | 3,411 | 89 | 109 | 1,237 | 1,309 | 792 | 963 | 768 | 877 |
| Suriname | 184 | 300 | 3,771 | 3,960 | 3 | 4 | 5,510 | 6,242 | — | — | 820 | 790 | 56 | 58 | 3 | 7 |
| Swaziland | 94 | 96 | 1,404 | 1,413 | 13 | 9 | 3,652 | 1,889 | 3 | 3 | 582 | 609 | 106 | 117 | 11 | 13 |
| Sweden | 5,332 | 5,756 | 3,394 | 3,821 | 1,058 | 1,397 | 23,363 | 36,286 | 20 | 112 | 1,868 | 2,548 | 205 | 145 | 235 | 303 |
| Switzerland | 748 | 961 | 4,268 | 5,190 | 797 | 721 | 32,562 | 35,698 | 2 | 1 | 2,983 | 3,699 | 730 | 850 | 269 | 352 |
| Syria | 2,252 | 3,171 | 823 | 1,169 | 140 | 397 | 13,129 | 17,241 | 217 | 150 | 752 | 898 | 1,386 | 1,908 | 2,232 | 3,027 |
| Taiwan | 3,565 | 3,303 | 4,264 | 5,272 | 2,341 | 5,430 | 15,146 | 13,889 | 32 | 40 | 944 | 1,887 | 1,639 | 2,165 | 2,387 | 3,531 |
| Tanzania | 2,488 | 3,777 | 1,062 | 1,112 | 5,980 | 6,239 | 9,179 | 11,030 | 218 | 362 | 459 | 539 | 1,730 | 2,721 | 911 | 1,050 |
| Thailand | 17,341 | 23,703 | 1,789 | 1,967 | 10,072 | 15,630 | 14,587 | 12,546 | 206 | 414 | 658 | 665 | 4,525 | 6,116 | 2,758 | 3,134 |
| Togo | 252 | 313 | 882 | 908 | 804 | 809 | 11,351 | 16,044 | 23 | 43 | 344 | 543 | 37 | 47 | 58 | 78 |
| Tokelau | ... | ... | ... | ... | — | — | 18,269 | 17,667 | ... | ... | ... | ... | — | — | ... | ... |
| Tonga | ... | ... | ... | ... | 94 | 99 | 6,720 | 6,774 | ... | ... | ... | ... | 11 | 13 | 7 | 7 |
| Trinidad and Tobago | 25 | 8 | 2,864 | 2,550 | 21 | 20 | 11,891 | 12,060 | 3 | 4 | 1,514 | 1,676 | 65 | 61 | 32 | 31 |
| Tunisia | 1,017 | 642 | 744 | 606 | 97 | 170 | 9,323 | 11,333 | 79 | 72 | 588 | 633 | 693 | 955 | 920 | 1,285 |
| Turkey | 23,664 | 29,358 | 1,741 | 1,991 | 2,713 | 3,900 | 14,955 | 19,499 | 749 | 1,910 | 1,188 | 1,096 | 10,553 | 13,865 | 10,924 | 16,758 |
| Turks and Caicos Islands | ... | ... | ... | ... | ... | ... | ... | ... | ... | ... | ... | ... | ... | ... | ... | ... |
| Tuvalu | ... | ... | ... | ... | ... | ... | ... | ... | ... | ... | ... | ... | — | — | — | — |
| Uganda | 1,651 | 1,100 | 1,258 | 1,230 | 5,090 | 7,880 | 4,543 | 7,726 | 382 | 528 | 671 | 788 | 8,965 | 8,483 | 251 | 312 |
| U.S.S.R. | 179,383 | 199,698 | 1,454 | 1,818 | 85,819 | 87,200 | 11,685 | 13,655 | 7,150 | 7,936 | 1,352 | 1,132 | 18,027 | 21,234 | 27,322 | 33,884 |
| United Arab Emirates | — | 4 | 6,691 | 3,306 | — | — | 17,359 | 10,370 | ... | ... | ... | ... | 36 | 201 | 35 | 321 |
| United Kingdom | 14,642 | 24,414 | 3,975 | 6,060 | 5,399 | 6,500 | 24,526 | 36,723 | 189 | 550 | 2,590 | 3,667 | 510 | 557 | 3,705 | 3,970 |
| United States | 257,983 | 316,187 | 3,561 | 4,706 | 16,228 | 16,659 | 27,780 | 31,423 | 943 | 1,329 | 1,339 | 1,762 | 26,757 | 24,991 | 24,785 | 26,699 |
| Uruguay | 953 | 964 | 1,178 | 1,988 | 198 | 156 | 4,989 | 5,032 | 5 | 6 | 892 | 981 | 292 | 400 | 149 | 190 |
| Vanuatu | 1 | 1 | 500 | 515 | 30 | 30 | 20,001 | 20,000 | ... | ... | ... | ... | 5 | 6 | 6 | 7 |
| Venezuela | 1,129 | 2,282 | 1,692 | 2,313 | 553 | 679 | 7,685 | 8,747 | 38 | 52 | 447 | 558 | 1,886 | 2,267 | 318 | 387 |
| Vietnam | 11,469 | 16,850 | 2,061 | 2,762 | 3,425 | 5,235 | 6,468 | 5,641 | 95 | 158 | 487 | 807 | 2,103 | 3,835 | 2,251 | 3,272 |
| Virgin Islands (U.S.) | ... | ... | ... | ... | ... | ... | ... | ... | ... | ... | ... | ... | ... | ... | ... | ... |
| Wallis and Futuna | ... | ... | ... | ... | 6 | 6 | 10,326 | 10,168 | ... | ... | ... | ... | 8 | 9 | — | 1 |
| West Bank | ... | ... | ... | ... | ... | ... | ... | ... | ... | ... | ... | ... | ... | ... | ... | ... |
| Western Sahara | 1 | 2 | 708 | 741 | ... | ... | ... | ... | ... | ... | ... | ... | ... | ... | ... | ... |
| Western Samoa | ... | ... | ... | ... | 35 | 44 | 6,861 | 7,154 | ... | ... | ... | ... | 53 | 58 | — | 1 |
| Yemen (Aden) | 112 | 113 | 1,628 | 1,736 | 4 | 8 | 13,187 | 15,000 | ... | — | ... | 529 | 115 | 183 | 107 | 114 |
| Yemen (Şan'ā') | 931 | 566 | 841 | 671 | 82 | 208 | 11,243 | 24,471 | 76 | 49 | 1,046 | 748 | 106 | 105 | 187 | 432 |
| Yugoslavia | 15,936 | 18,243 | 3,419 | 4,339 | 2,752 | 2,519 | 8,816 | 8,901 | 231 | 236 | 1,236 | 1,320 | 3,281 | 3,306 | 2,636 | 2,662 |
| Zaire | 770 | 1,119 | 744 | 854 | 12,557 | 16,265 | 6,878 | 7,004 | 147 | 127 | 611 | 634 | 2,457 | 2,572 | 464 | 533 |
| Zambia | 1,699 | 1,203 | 1,397 | 1,909 | 191 | 246 | 3,423 | 3,753 | 8 | 6 | 412 | 622 | 62 | 91 | 182 | 247 |
| Zimbabwe | 2,187 | 3,096 | 1,408 | 1,675 | 73 | 109 | 3,951 | 4,977 | 28 | 51 | 606 | 734 | 93 | 129 | 128 | 143 |

| cattle stock ('000 head) 1975–77 average | cattle stock ('000 head) 1986 | sheep stock ('000 head) 1975–77 average | sheep stock ('000 head) 1986 | hogs stock ('000 head) 1975–77 average | hogs stock ('000 head) 1986 | chickens stock ('000 head) 1975–77 average | chickens stock ('000 head) 1986 | milk[e] production ('000 metric tons) 1975–77 average | milk[e] production ('000 metric tons) 1986 | milk yield (kg/animal) 1975–77 average | milk yield (kg/animal) 1986 | eggs[f] production (metric tons) 1975–77 average | eggs[f] production (metric tons) 1986 | country |
|---|---|---|---|---|---|---|---|---|---|---|---|---|---|---|
| ... | ... | ... | ... | ... | ... | ... | ... | ... | ... | ... | ... | ... | ... | Northern Mariana Islands |
| ... | ... | ... | ... | ... | ... | ... | ... | ... | ... | ... | ... | ... | ... | Palau |
| 14,855 | 16,749 | 18,979 | 25,826 | ... | ... | 31,571 | 127,471 | 2,163 | 2,640 | 888 | 960 | 51,700 | 215,000 | Pakistan |
| 1,361 | 1,443 | ... | ... | 182 | 205 | 4,134 | 8,200 | 78 | 105 | 961 | 991 | 12,914 | 19,750 | Panama |
| 129 | 123 | 1 | 2 | 1,327 | 1,489 | 1,052 | 4,400 | 1 | — | 179 | 286 | 1,597 | 2,539 | Papua New Guinea |
| 5,470 | 7,151 | 370 | 388 | 1,083 | 1,403 | 9,501 | 14,569 | 128 | 190 | 1,905 | 1,900 | 18,393 | 32,519 | Paraguay |
| 4,153 | 3,820 | 15,017 | 13,500 | 2,099 | 2,170 | 36,838 | 43,000 | 818 | 829 | 1,218 | 1,260 | 53,674 | 95,100 | Peru |
| 1,753 | 1,814 | 30 | 30 | 6,395 | 7,275 | 45,820 | 53,005 | 13 | 15 | 1,027 | 1,035 | 183,982 | 234,400 | Philippines |
| ... | ... | ... | ... | ... | ... | ... | ... | ... | ... | ... | ... | ... | ... | Pitcairn Island |
| 13,051 | 10,919 | 3,513 | 4,991 | 20,070 | 18,949 | 81,354 | 62,700 | 16,610 | 15,704 | 2,754 | 2,935 | 445,391 | 465,000 | Poland |
| 1,110 | 1,099 | 3,850 | 5,100 | 1,879 | 3,092 | 16,593 | 17,500 | 684 | 842 | 2,274 | 2,406 | 47,226 | 68,750 | Portugal |
| 559 | 583 | 6 | 6 | 282 | 210 | 5,341 | 7,500 | 408 | 363 | 2,130 | 1,797 | 19,574 | 19,100 | Puerto Rico |
| 8 | 7 | 38 | 55 | ... | ... | 207 | 1,500 | 5 | 8 | 1,545 | 1,500 | ... | 950 | Qatar |
| 22 | 20 | 2 | 3 | 104 | 72 | 2,634 | 4,200 | 5 | 3 | 495 | 323 | 1,920 | 2,500 | Réunion |
| 5,938 | 6,867 | 14,042 | 18,609 | 9,191 | 14,319 | 70,700 | 124,770 | 3,832 | 4,100 | 1,837 | 2,070 | 273,950 | 385,000 | Romania |
| 651 | 670 | 253 | 343 | 76 | 104 | 762 | 1,300 | 30 | 74 | 340 | 536 | 583 | 1,400 | Rwanda |
| 6 | 6 | 14 | 14 | 9 | 10 | 74 | 85 | ... | ... | ... | ... | 255 | 350 | St. Christopher and Nevis |
| 1 | 1 | 1 | 2 | 1 | 1 | 12 | 15 | ... | ... | ... | ... | ... | ... | St. Helena and Ascension |
| 8 | 12 | 11 | 15 | 8 | 12 | 128 | 250 | 1 | 1 | 1,317 | 1,370 | 460 | 525 | St. Lucia |
| ... | ... | ... | ... | ... | ... | ... | ... | ... | ... | ... | ... | ... | ... | St. Pierre and Miquelon |
| 7 | 8 | 11 | 14 | 6 | 7 | 139 | 178 | 1 | 2 | 1,348 | 1,364 | 450 | 582 | St. Vincent and the Grenadines |
| ... | ... | ... | ... | ... | ... | ... | ... | ... | ... | ... | ... | ... | ... | San Marino |
| 2 | 3 | 1 | 2 | 5 | 3 | 70 | 100 | — | — | 170 | 170 | 132 | 172 | São Tomé and Príncipe |
| 306 | 530 | 2,221 | 3,800 | ... | ... | 5,933 | 36,000 | 153 | 395 | 1,000 | 1,129 | 15,807 | 140,000 | Saudi Arabia |
| 2,379 | 2,200 | 1,734 | 2,202 | 174 | 194 | 6,524 | 11,000 | 84 | 79 | 353 | 360 | 5,219 | 8,800 | Senegal |
| 2 | 2 | ... | ... | 10 | 15 | 109 | 290 | — | — | 512 | 526 | 394 | 1,479 | Seychelles |
| 323 | 333 | 280 | 332 | 28 | 46 | 3,360 | 4,600 | 17 | 17 | 350 | 350 | 3,864 | 5,290 | Sierra Leone |
| 1 | — | ... | ... | 1,127 | 750 | 12,600 | 8,761 | ... | ... | ... | ... | 24,787 | 18,850 | Singapore |
| 24 | 23 | ... | ... | 41 | 50 | 133 | 143 | 1 | 1 | 600 | 600 | 269 | 288 | Solomon Islands |
| 3,848 | 3,800 | 9,679 | 10,100 | 8 | 10 | 2,500 | 3,170 | 154 | 147 | 351 | 350 | 2,000 | 2,640 | Somalia |
| 12,845 | 11,750 | 31,317 | 29,481 | 1,350 | 1,445 | 26,000 | 35,000 | 2,515 | 2,600 | 2,753 | 2,826 | 143,518 | 182,000 | South Africa[6] |
| ... | ... | ... | ... | ... | ... | ... | ... | ... | ... | ... | ... | ... | ... | Bophuthatswana[6] |
| ... | ... | ... | ... | ... | ... | ... | ... | ... | ... | ... | ... | ... | ... | Ciskei[6] |
| ... | ... | ... | ... | ... | ... | ... | ... | ... | ... | ... | ... | ... | ... | KwaNdebele[6] |
| ... | ... | ... | ... | ... | ... | ... | ... | ... | ... | ... | ... | ... | ... | Transkei[6] |
| ... | ... | ... | ... | ... | ... | ... | ... | ... | ... | ... | ... | ... | ... | Venda[6] |
| 2,850 | 2,030 | 5,200 | 6,200 | 33 | 46 | 435 | 510 | 65 | 69 | 399 | 412 | 120 | 175 | South West Africa/Namibia |
| 4,442 | 5,084 | 15,864 | 17,735 | 8,486 | 10,367 | 52,280 | 53,000 | 5,344 | 6,702 | 2,872 | 3,533 | 605,517 | 689,318 | Spain |
| 1,716 | 1,783 | 28 | 29 | 35 | 86 | 5,739 | 7,000 | 161 | 210 | 428 | 478 | 16,904 | 38,000 | Sri Lanka |
| 15,289 | 22,389 | 14,830 | 20,600 | ... | ... | 23,000 | 30,000 | 860 | 1,750 | 500 | 500 | 22,967 | 40,500 | Sudan, The |
| 26 | 63 | 4 | 3 | 18 | 22 | 907 | 1,300 | 8 | 11 | 1,606 | 1,460 | 3,100 | 2,700 | Suriname |
| 630 | 620 | 32 | 38 | 19 | 20 | 507 | 1,000 | 33 | 39 | 246 | 255 | 265 | 295 | Swaziland |
| 1,873 | 1,779 | 382 | 434 | 2,571 | 2,410 | 11,398 | 11,200 | 3,221 | 3,517 | 4,853 | 5,749 | 107,000 | 117,000 | Sweden |
| 1,991 | 1,902 | 370 | 365 | 2,011 | 1,973 | 6,104 | 5,691 | 3,439 | 3,863 | 3,886 | 4,799 | 41,905 | 45,000 | Switzerland |
| 590 | 750 | 6,456 | 12,500 | 1 | 1 | 7,038 | 15,400 | 301 | 650 | 1,141 | 1,857 | 34,283 | 86,750 | Syria |
| 130 | 105 | ... | ... | 3,267 | 6,674 | 24,760 | 59,313 | 46 | 92 | 3,426 | 5,000 | 59,462 | 178,500 | Taiwan |
| 11,590 | 14,300 | 3,498 | 4,300 | 141 | 180 | 14,167 | 28,000 | 333 | 432 | 160 | 160 | 25,470 | 57,512 | Tanzania |
| 4,268 | 4,835 | 34 | 58 | 3,409 | 4,215 | 53,352 | 79,100 | 7 | 37 | 2,004 | 2,643 | 87,700 | 128,000 | Thailand |
| 222 | 276 | 796 | 850 | 260 | 288 | 2,364 | 3,700 | 6 | 7 | 225 | 225 | 1,700 | 3,789 | Togo |
| ... | ... | ... | ... | 1 | 1 | 3 | ... | ... | ... | ... | ... | 5 | 4 | Tokelau |
| 7 | 8 | ... | ... | 59 | 65 | 121 | 130 | — | — | 1,500 | 1,500 | 293 | 412 | Tonga |
| 73 | 77 | 9 | 12 | 55 | 83 | 6,700 | 8,000 | 7 | 11 | 1,726 | 1,703 | 7,540 | 8,000 | Trinidad and Tobago |
| 895 | 643 | 5,913 | 5,300 | 3 | 4 | 12,667 | 16,400 | 222 | 300 | 856 | 1,304 | 19,767 | 54,500 | Tunisia |
| 14,790 | 16,200 | 41,137 | 40,400 | 15 | 12 | 41,300 | 61,046 | 3,039 | 3,230 | 589 | 587 | 161,327 | 290,000 | Turkey |
| ... | ... | ... | ... | ... | ... | ... | ... | ... | ... | ... | ... | ... | ... | Turks and Caicos Islands |
| ... | ... | ... | ... | 6 | 9 | 10 | 21 | ... | ... | ... | ... | 8 | 15 | Tuvalu |
| 4,877 | 5,100 | 993 | 1,700 | 167 | 250 | 12,333 | 18,500 | 283 | 364 | 350 | 350 | 11,924 | 18,000 | Uganda |
| 110,167 | 120,888 | 142,192 | 140,850 | 64,409 | 77,772 | 741,000 | 1,100,000 | 91,129 | 100,650 | 2,173 | 2,348 | 3,202,000 | 4,424,000 | U.S.S.R. |
| 21 | 46 | 90 | 382 | ... | ... | 199 | 4,550 | 6 | 11 | 609 | 495 | 1,137 | 9,500 | United Arab Emirates |
| 14,182 | 12,695 | 25,524 | 24,540 | 7,886 | 7,930 | 129,763 | 111,782 | 14,518 | 16,250 | 4,383 | 4,989 | 833,333 | 715,462 | United Kingdom |
| 127,606 | 105,468 | 13,516 | 9,983 | 52,965 | 52,313 | 919,267 | 1,160,000 | 54,163 | 65,354 | 4,908 | 6,048 | 3,810,200 | 4,057,310 | United States |
| 10,676 | 9,961 | 15,560 | 24,526 | 452 | 195 | 5,217 | 6,300 | 747 | 920 | 1,698 | 1,704 | 13,099 | 21,500 | Uruguay |
| 102 | 101 | ... | ... | 63 | 72 | 131 | 180 | 2 | 2 | 197 | 209 | 208 | 252 | Vanuatu |
| 9,346 | 12,371 | 257 | 422 | 1,797 | 2,852 | 31,113 | 51,000 | 1,222 | 1,555 | 1,175 | 1,152 | 96,111 | 150,370 | Venezuela |
| 1,531 | 2,500 | 12 | 20 | 9,008 | 13,000 | 56,300 | 70,000 | 18 | 35 | 800 | 800 | 52,667 | 83,400 | Vietnam |
| 7 | 11 | 4 | 3 | 3 | 2 | 57 | 49 | 3 | 2 | 3,709 | 2,769 | 175 | 200 | Virgin Islands (U.S.) |
| — | — | ... | ... | 9 | 27 | 20 | 36 | — | — | 1,500 | 1,500 | 29 | 43 | Wallis and Futuna |
| ... | ... | ... | ... | ... | ... | ... | ... | ... | ... | ... | ... | ... | ... | West Bank |
| ... | ... | 17 | 25 | ... | ... | ... | 1,000 | ... | ... | 1,000 | 1,000 | ... | ... | Western Sahara |
| 26 | 27 | ... | ... | 50 | 64 | 487 | 560 | 1 | 1 | 1,000 | 1,000 | 130 | 179 | Western Samoa |
| 83 | 96 | 855 | 930 | ... | ... | 1,403 | 1,700 | 13 | 16 | 398 | 425 | 1,468 | 2,200 | Yemen (Aden) |
| 863 | 952 | 1,604 | 1,850 | ... | ... | 2,497 | 16,200 | 56 | 63 | 200 | 200 | 9,991 | 12,350 | Yemen (San'ā') |
| 5,756 | 5,041 | 7,830 | 7,697 | 7,511 | 7,821 | 51,232 | 77,973 | 3,857 | 4,600 | 1,429 | 1,708 | 190,933 | 239,000 | Yugoslavia |
| 1,143 | 1,400 | 722 | 770 | 680 | 780 | 11,500 | 18,000 | 6 | 7 | 792 | 855 | 6,561 | 7,700 | Zaire |
| 1,963 | 2,770 | 28 | 46 | 185 | 214 | 19,404 | 13,500 | 53 | 75 | 300 | 300 | 29,493 | 30,800 | Zambia |
| 6,356 | 4,800 | 712 | 550 | 212 | 170 | 8,400 | 9,400 | 145 | 232 | 1,160 | 1,650 | 9,543 | 12,300 | Zimbabwe |

1 1982.    2 Netherlands Antilles includes Aruba.    3 Belgium includes Luxembourg.    4 1983.    5 1985.    6 South Africa includes Bophuthatswana, Ciskei, KwaNdebele, Transkei, and Venda.

# Extractive industries

Extractive industries are generally defined as those activities involved in the exploitation of natural resources and include such industries as mining, forestry, fisheries, and agriculture; the definition is sometimes confined to nonrenewable resources. For the purposes of this table agriculture is excluded; it is covered in tables elsewhere in *Britannica World Data*.

Extractive industries are here divided into three parts: mining, forestry, and fisheries. These major headings are each divided into two main subheadings, one that treats production and one that treats foreign trade. The production sections are presented in terms of volume except for mining, and the trade sections are presented in terms of U.S. dollars. The formulation of the sections was determined by the systems of classification used in standard international sources. "Extractive," for example, implies the production of primary (unprocessed) raw materials only, but because of the way national statistical information is reported the table may occasionally include some processed and manufactured materials as well, since these are often indistinguishably associated with the extractive process (sulfur from petroleum extraction, cured or treated lumber, or "processed" fish). This is also the case in the trade sections, where individual national trade nomenclatures may not distinguish some processed and manufactured goods from unprocessed raw materials.

**Mining.** In the absence of a single international standard of practice for calculating or reporting value of mineral production, single-country sources predominantly have been used to compile mining production figures, supplemented by U.S. Bureau of Mines data and industry sources,

especially *Mining Journal*'s *Mining Annual Review*. Each country has its own methods of classifying mining data, which do not always accord with the principal mineral production categories adopted in this table; namely, "metals," "nonmetals," and "energy." The available data have therefore been adjusted to make them accord better with the definition of each group. Included in the "metal" category are all ferrous and nonferrous metallic ores, concentrates, and scrap; the "nonmetal" group includes all nonmetallic minerals (stone, clay, precious gems, etc.) except the mineral fuels; the last group, "energy," is composed predominantly of the natural hydrocarbon fuels, though it may also include manufactured gas.

The contribution (value) of each national mineral sector to its country's gross domestic product is given, as is the distribution by group of that contribution (to gross domestic product and to foreign trade), although statistics regarding the value of mineral production are less readily available in country sources than those regarding trade or volume of minerals produced. Figures for value added by mineral output, though not always available, were sought first, as they provide the most consistent standard to compare the importance of minerals both within a particular national economy and among national mineral sectors worldwide. Where value added to the gross domestic product was not available, gross value of production or sales was substituted. Figures for value of production are reported here in millions of U.S. dollars to permit comparisons to be made from country to country. Comparisons can also be made as to the relative importance of each mineral group within a given country.

## Extractive industries

| country | mining: % of GDP, 1985 | mineral production (value added): year | total ('000,000 U.S.$) | metals[a] | non-metals[b] | energy[c] | trade (value): year | exports total ('000,000 U.S.$) | exp metals[a] | exp non-metals[b] | exp energy[c] | imports total ('000,000 U.S.$) | imp metals[a] | imp non-metals[b] | imp energy[c] |
|---|---|---|---|---|---|---|---|---|---|---|---|---|---|---|---|
| Afghanistan | ... | 1982–83 | 283.8[1] | — | 0.1[1] | 99.9[1] | 1984 | 291.9[2] | 0.1[2] | 2.7[2] | 97.2[2] | — | ... | ... | ... |
| Albania | ... | ... | ... | ... | ... | ... | ... | ... | ... | ... | ... | ... | ... | ... | ... |
| Algeria | 31.0[3] | 1983 | 13,021.3 | —1.3[4]— | | 98.7[4] | 1984 | 7,611.0 | 0.4 | 0.2 | 99.4 | 147.8[3] | 9.5[3] | 21.7[3] | 68.8[3] |
| American Samoa | ... | 1985 | ... | — | 100.0 | — | 1985 | ... | — | — | — | 0.3 | — | 6.8 | 93.2 |
| Andorra | ... | ... | ... | ... | ... | ... | 1983 | ... | — | — | 100.0 | 2.1 | — | 100.0 | ... |
| Angola | 16.1[3] | 1983 | 549.0 | ... | ... | ... | 1983 | 1,365.9 | — | 0.1 | 99.9 | | | | |
| Anguilla | ... | 1981 | 7 | | | | | | ... | ... | ... | ... | ... | ... | ... |
| Antigua and Barbuda | 0.8[8] | 1984 | 1.0 | — | 100.0 | — | 1984 | ... | ... | ... | ... | ... | ... | ... | ... |
| Argentina | 2.8 | 1984 | 1,699.0 | 2.8 | 7.9 | 89.3 | 1984 | 30.2 | 53.0 | 14.1 | 33.0 | 608.8 | 22.9 | 7.7 | 69.5 |
| Aruba[10] | ... | ... | ... | ... | ... | ... | ... | ... | ... | ... | ... | ... | ... | ... | ... |
| Australia | 5.0 | 1983–84 | 7,931.0 | 31.3 | 6.5 | 62.2 | 1985 | 8,663.4 | 40.3 | 1.8 | 57.9 | 760.9 | 2.3 | 26.7 | 71.0 |
| Austria | 0.5 | 1985 | 314.2 | 6.1[9] | 15.2[9] | 78.7[9] | 1985 | 163.2 | 44.6 | 49.4 | 5.9 | 2,710.5 | 13.7 | 6.2 | 80.1 |
| Bahamas, The | 9.2[3] | 1983 | 153.2[11] | — | 10.0 | 90.0[11] | 1985 | 24.6 | — | 100.0 | — | 243.3 | — | — | 100.0 |
| Bahrain | 19.0[8] | 1984 | 947.1 | — | — | 100.0 | 1983 | 32.8 | — | 3.8 | 96.2 | 1,980.8 | — | 0.1 | 99.9 |
| Bangladesh | — | 1984–85 | 0.2 | ... | 5.7[12,13] | 94.3[12,13] | 1985 | — | — | — | — | 243.0 | — | 11.2 | 88.8 |
| Barbados | 1.8 | 1985 | 16.3 | —100.0— | | | 1985 | — | — | — | — | 1.3[3] | — | — | 100.0[3] |
| Belgium | 0.5 | 1985 | 436.2 | — | 49.8[3] | 50.2[3] | 1985[14] | 3,868.1 | 6.4 | 89.5 | 4.1 | 10,285.1 | 14.8 | 32.5 | 52.7 |
| Belize | 0.2 | 1985 | 0.4 | — | 100.0 | — | 1984 | — | — | — | — | 1.4[15] | — | 41.4[15] | 58.6[15] |
| Benin | 5.0[8] | 1983 | 2.0 | —100.0[16]— | | | 1983 | — | — | — | — | 2.0[2] | — | 100.0[2] | — |
| Bermuda | 2.0[4] | 1978–79 | 2.0 | | | | 1984 | 0.3[3] | 73.2[3] | 26.8[3] | | 1.1 | — | — | 100.0 |
| Bhutan | 0.3[8] | 1984 | 0.6[18] | | | | 1982 | | | | | ... | ... | ... | ... |
| Bolivia | 8.6 | 1985 | 380.0 | 55.8[3] | — | 44.2[3] | 1984 | 557.3 | —34.7[19]— | | 65.3 | 1.5 | 100.0[2] | — | — |
| Botswana | 31.7[3] | 1983 | 369.7 | 12.5[2,20] | 86.6[2,20] | 0.9[2,20] | 1921 | ... | | | | | | | |
| Brazil | 1.4[8] | 1984 | 3,061.7 | 25.3[3,20] | 22.1[3,20] | 52.6[3,20] | 1984 | 2,038.9[3] | 93.7[3] | 4.9[3] | 1.2[3] | 8,180.5 | 1.1 | 2.0 | 96.8 |
| British Virgin Islands | 0.1 | 1985 | 0.8 | — | 100.0 | — | 1982 | — | — | — | — | 0.8[9] | 10.3[9] | 89.7[9] | — |
| Brunei | 54.3 | 1985 | 1,918.3 | ... | ... | ... | 1984 | 2,829.2 | — | — | 100.0 | 3.7 | 21.1 | 78.9 | — |
| Bulgaria | ... | ... | ... | ... | ... | ... | ... | ... | ... | ... | ... | ... | ... | ... | ... |
| Burkina Faso | 0.1[8] | 1984 | 0.7 | — | 100.0 | — | 1983 | — | — | — | — | 2.3 | — | 100.0 | — |
| Burma | 1.1 | 1984–85 | 72.4[23] | | | | 1983 | 58.5[24] | 67.0[24] | 22.1[24] | 10.9[24] | 1.9 | — | 100.0 | — |
| Burundi | 0.5[2] | 1982 | 5.6 | | | | 1985 | 12.1[3] | 2.4[3] | 97.6[3] | — | ... | | | |
| Cameroon | 16.3[13] | 1983–84 | 1,247.1[16] | | | | 1983 | 1,012.3 | 0.2 | — | 99.8 | 29.9[2] | 66.6[2] | 33.4[2] | — |
| Canada | 6.0[8] | 1984 | 20,024.7 | 32.0[2] | 12.9[2] | 55.1[2] | 1985 | 13,529.6 | 18.8 | 11.4 | 69.8 | 5,097.1 | 24.0 | 8.4 | 67.7 |
| Cape Verde | 0.3[9] | 1981 | 0.2 | — | 100.0 | — | 1982 | 1.1 | 1.8 | 98.2 | — | 0.8[15] | — | — | 100.0[15] |
| Cayman Islands | ... | ... | ... | | | | 1983 | 3.8[24] | — | 14.1[24] | 85.9[24] | 0.4[15] | — | — | 100.0[15] |
| Central African Republic | 2.5 | 1985 | 17.4[25] | —100.0[25]— | | | 1983 | 37.3 | — | 100.0 | — | 1.4[15] | — | 100.0[15] | — |
| Chad | 0.5[3] | 1983 | 3.0 | — | 100.0 | — | 1982 | — | — | 100.0 | — | ... | | | |
| Chile | 8.4[26] | 1986 | 2,372.0 | ... | ... | ... | 1983 | 736.5 | 94.7 | 5.3 | — | 271.5 | 4.7 | 4.7 | 90.6 |
| China | ... | ... | ... | | | | 1982 | 3,923.9 | 4.1 | 4.2 | 91.7 | 773.4 | 76.4 | 15.7 | 7.9 |
| Christmas Island | ... | 1985 | ... | — | 100.0 | — | 1983 | 49.6 | — | 100.0 | — | ... | | | |
| Cocos (Keeling) Islands | ... | ... | ... | | | | 1983 | 0.1[9] | — | 100.0[9] | — | 0.2 | 100.0 | — | — |
| Colombia | 2.6[26] | 1986 | 1,008.0 | ... | ... | ... | 1984 | 171.0[28] | 47.4 | 18.1 | 34.5 | 321.6 | 2.2 | 9.8 | 88.0 |
| Comoros | ... | 1985 | ... | — | 100.0 | — | 1983 | 0.1[28] | —28[28] | 100.0[28] | ... | ... | | | |
| Congo | 43.0[8] | 1984 | 905.9[16] | | | | 1983 | 1,062.9[24] | 1.2[24] | 5.4[24] | 93.4[24] | 3.8[15] | — | 100.0[15] | ... |
| Cook Islands | — | 1979 | 75.9 | 23.6[4] | 76.4[4] | | 1983 | 0.3[24] | 100.0[24] | — | — | 0.1[15] | — | 42.1[15] | 57.9[15] |
| Costa Rica | 1.9[3] | ... | ... | ... | ... | ... | 1983 | 0.9 | 100.0 | — | — | 110.3[2] | 0.1[2] | 3.9[2] | 96.0[2] |
| Côte d'Ivoire | 2.9[8] | 1984 | 192.5[16] | | | | 1983 | 60.2 | 1.6 | 35.1 | 63.3 | 260.5 | 0.2 | 4.5 | 95.3 |
| Cuba | ... | ... | ... | | | | 1984 | 361.8 | 100.0 | — | — | 1,295.3[3] | 0.1[3] | 2.3[3] | 97.6[3] |
| Cyprus | 0.6 | 1984 | 14.7 | 9.7 | 90.3 | — | 1985 | 11.1 | 28.1 | 71.9 | — | 115.8 | — | 5.2 | 94.8 |
| Czechoslovakia | 2.3[3] | 1984 | 3,789.6 | 7.5 | 7.7 | 84.8 | 1984 | 377.1[29,30] | — | 14.1 | 85.9 | 804.2[29,31] | 66.1 | 19.2 | 14.7 |
| Denmark | 1.0 | 1984 | 377.5 | — | 13.9 | 86.1 | 1985 | 409.8 | 18.3 | 9.3 | 72.4 | 1,673.5 | 1.1 | 5.5 | 93.4 |
| Djibouti | ... | 1983 | — | — | 100.0 | — | 1983 | — | — | — | — | 22.9[3,32] | —6.8[3]— | | 93.2[3,32] |
| Dominica | 0.8 | 1984 | 0.6 | — | 100.0 | — | 1981 | 0.1[33] | — | 100.0[33] | — | 0.6 | — | 25.3 | 74.7 |
| Dominican Republic | 3.8[26] | 1986 | 327.0 | 97.0[15] | 3.0[15] | — | 1983 | 3.2 | 1.4 | 98.6 | — | 344.7 | 0.1 | 0.1 | 99.8 |
| Ecuador | 17.0 | 1985 | 2,797.7 | — | 0.1[2] | 99.9[2] | 1983 | 1,368.6[24] | — | — | 100.0[24] | 12.2 | 7.5 | 92.5 | — |
| Egypt | 23.3[3] | 1983 | 6,917.0 | 0.3[9] | 1.1[9] | 98.6[9] | 1985 | 2,008.2 | 0.1 | 0.1 | 99.7 | 194.3 | 3.9 | 26.7 | 69.4 |

Since the data for value of mineral production are obtained mostly from country sources, there is some variation (from a standard calendar year) in the time periods to which the data refer. In addition, the time period for which production data are available does not always correspond with the year for which mineral trade data are available.

The Standard International Trade Classification (SITC), Revision 3, was used to determine the commodity groupings for foreign trade statistics. The actual trade data for these groups is taken largely from the United Nations annual *Yearbook of International Trade Statistics* and national sources.

**Forestry.** Data for the production and trade sections of forestry are based on the United Nations annual *Yearbook of Forest Products.* Production of roundwood (all wood obtained in removals from forests) is the principal indicator of the volume of each country's forestry sector; this total is broken down further (as percentages of the roundwood total) into its principal components: fuelwood and charcoal, and industrial roundwood. The latter group was further divided to show its principal component, sawlogs and veneer; lesser categories of industrial roundwood could not be shown for reasons of space. These included pitprops (used in mining, a principal consumer of wood) and pulpwood (used in papermaking and plastics). Value of trade in forest products is given for both imports and exports, although exports alone tend to be the significant indicator for producing countries, while imports of wood are rarely a significant fraction of the trade of most importing countries.

**Fisheries.** Data for nominal (live weight) catches of fish, crustaceans, mollusks, etc., in all fishing areas (inland waters and marine areas) are taken from the United Nations annual *Yearbook of Fishery Statistics* (*Catches and Landings*). Total catch figures are given in metric tons; the catches in inland waters and marine areas are given as percentages of the total catch, as are the main kinds of catch—fish, crustaceans, and mollusks. The principal exclusion is marine mammals, such as whales and seals.

Figures for trade in fishery products (including processed products and preparations like oils, meals, and animal feeding stuffs) are taken from the United Nations annual *Yearbook of Fishery Statistics* (*Fishery Commodities*). Value figures for trade in fish products are given for both imports and exports.

The following notes further define the column headings:
a. Includes ferrous and nonferrous metallic ores and scraps, such as bauxite, copper, gold (except unwrought or semimanufactured), iron ore, lead, uranium, or zinc.
b. Includes natural fertilizers; stone, sand, and aggregate; and pearls, precious and semiprecious stones, worked and unworked.
c. Includes hydrocarbon solids, liquids, and gases.
1 cubic metre = 35.3147 cubic feet
1 metric ton = 1.1023 short tons

| forestry, 1985 | | | | | | fisheries, 1985 | | | | | | | | country |
|---|---|---|---|---|---|---|---|---|---|---|---|---|---|---|
| production of roundwood | | | | trade (value '000 U.S.$) | | catch (nominal) | | | | | | trade (value, '000 U.S.$) | | |
| total ('000 cubic metres) | fuelwood, charcoal (%) | industrial roundwood (%) | | exports | imports | total ('000 metric tons) | by source (%) | | by kind of catch (%) | | | exports | imports | |
| | | total | sawlogs, veneer | | | | marine | fresh-water | fish | crusta-ceans | mollusks | | | |
| 6,452 | 76.2 | 23.8 | 13.3 | ... | 29,313 | 1.5 | — | 100.0 | 100.0 | — | — | ... | ... | Afghanistan |
| 2,330 | 69.0 | 31.0 | 31.0 | 730 | 445 | 4.0 | 100.0 | — | 100.0 | — | — | ... | ... | Albania |
| 1,691 | 86.4 | 13.6 | 1.2 | 1,502[5] | 298,972 | 66.0 | 100.0 | — | 95.5 | 4.5 | — | 250 | 16,173 | Algeria |
| ... | ... | ... | ... | ... | 1,801[6] | 0.4 | 100.0 | — | 75.5 | 0.9 | — | 201,262 | 2,476 | American Samoa |
| ... | ... | ... | ... | | | | | | | | | | | Andorra |
| 9,096 | 84.2 | 15.8 | 6.1 | 98[2] | 256 | 74.5 | 89.3 | 10.7 | 98.8 | 1.2 | — | ... | 45,740 | Angola |
| ... | ... | ... | ... | ... | ... | — | 100.0 | — | 100.0 | — | — | 49[2] | ... | Anguilla |
| ... | ... | ... | ... | ... | 2,596[9] | 2.2 | 100.0 | — | 99.2 | 0.8 | — | ... | ... | Antigua and Barbuda |
| 13,429 | 63.0 | 37.0 | 17.6 | 9,262 | 94,722 | 410.9 | 98.1 | 1.9 | 90.0 | 4.1 | 5.9 | 149,426 | 9,900 | Argentina |
| ... | ... | ... | ... | | | 0.8 | 100.0 | — | 100.0 | — | — | | | Aruba[10] |
| 19,217 | 15.0 | 85.0 | 40.4 | 196,087 | 823,759 | 160.0 | 98.6 | 1.4 | 51.7 | 24.1 | 24.1 | 280,054 | 216,245 | Australia |
| 14,204 | 9.9 | 90.1 | 61.3 | 1,310,816 | 620,220 | 4.5 | — | 100.0 | 100.0 | — | — | 1,619 | 68,262 | Austria |
| 115 | — | 100.0 | 13.0 | 1,061 | 7,337 | 8.2 | 100.0 | — | 18.7 | 73.5 | 7.2 | 15,730 | 825 | Bahamas, The |
| — | — | — | — | ... | 45,786 | 7.8 | 100.0 | — | 75.4 | 24.1 | 0.5 | ... | 3,430 | Bahrain |
| 27,144 | 96.9 | 3.1 | 1.7 | 9,496 | 10,057 | 763.7 | 24.9 | 75.1 | 95.8 | 4.2 | — | 82,310 | — | Bangladesh |
| ... | ... | ... | ... | ... | 12,705 | 3.9 | 100.0 | — | 100.0 | — | — | ... | 2,045 | Barbados |
| 3,086[14] | 17.4[14] | 82.6[14] | 52.7[14] | 1,091,176[14] | 1,221,333[14] | 44.6 | 100.0 | — | 93.5 | 4.0 | 2.5 | 84,155[14] | 303,695[14] | Belgium |
| 164 | 76.8 | 23.2 | 23.2 | 1,061 | 2,011 | 1.4 | 99.9 | 0.1 | 28.0 | 56.5 | 15.5 | 7,400 | 400 | Belize |
| 4,401 | 94.9 | 5.1 | 0.5 | ... | 5,643 | 20.3 | 18.7 | 81.3 | 100.0 | — | — | 640 | 2,770 | Benin |
| ... | ... | ... | ... | ... | 2,434[17] | 0.5 | 100.0 | — | 92.1 | 7.9 | — | — | 5,630 | Bermuda |
| 3,224 | 91.4 | 8.6 | 7.4 | 501 | 143[9] | 1.0 | — | 100.0 | 100.0 | — | — | ... | ... | Bhutan |
| 1,317 | 88.7 | 11.3 | 10.3 | 5,923 | 10,900 | 4.7 | — | 100.0 | 100.0 | — | — | ... | 1,400 | Bolivia |
| 803 | 90.8 | 9.2 | — | ... | 1,640 | 1.7 | — | 100.0 | 100.0 | — | — | ... | 1,400 | Botswana |
| 225,905 | 74.4 | 25.6 | 14.1 | 800,615 | 148,385 | 959.3 | 78.0 | 22.0 | 88.8 | 10.2 | 1.0 | 172,910 | 36,716 | Brazil |
| ... | ... | ... | ... | 10[15, 22] | 181[15, 22] | 0.3 | 100.0 | — | 92.1 | 7.9 | — | 216[15] | 145[15] | British Virgin Islands |
| 294 | 26.9 | 73.1 | 70.1 | 90 | 6,915 | 3.0 | 95.3 | 4.7 | 80.3 | 19.7 | — | — | 3,258 | Brunei |
| 4,786 | 36.0 | 64.0 | 25.9 | 21,988 | 156,919 | 100.2 | 88.1 | 11.9 | 91.9 | 0.3 | 7.8 | 11,910 | 11,530 | Bulgaria |
| 6,691 | 95.4 | 4.6 | — | ... | 2,242 | 7.0 | — | 100.0 | 100.0 | — | — | — | 900 | Burkina Faso |
| 18,876 | 84.0 | 16.0 | 10.1 | 85,400 | 12,010 | 634.8 | 77.2 | 22.8 | 100.0 | — | — | 18,860 | — | Burma |
| 3,635 | 98.8 | 1.2 | 0.2 | ... | 1,342 | 14.9 | — | 100.0 | 100.0 | — | — | — | 274 | Burundi |
| 10,752 | 74.3 | 25.7 | 19.5 | 91,280 | 5,400 | 50.0 | 60.0 | 40.0 | 98.7 | 1.3 | — | 3,260 | 22,400 | Cameroon |
| 171,305 | 3.6 | 96.4 | 71.0 | 11,221,233 | 980,424 | 1,425.8 | 96.9 | 3.1 | 88.7 | 6.6 | 4.7 | 1,356,462 | 355,915 | Canada |
| ... | ... | ... | ... | ... | 1,801 | 10.2 | 100.0 | — | 99.3 | 0.7 | — | 2,460 | 78 | Cape Verde |
| ... | ... | ... | ... | ... | ... | 0.5 | 100.0 | — | — | 100.0 | — | 4,310 | 70 | Cayman Islands |
| 3,418 | 85.6 | 14.4 | 7.9 | 20,251 | 1,626 | 13.0 | — | 100.0 | 100.0 | — | — | — | 220 | Central African Republic |
| 3,567 | 85.8 | 14.2 | 0.1 | ... | 1,352 | 115.0 | — | 100.0 | 100.0 | — | — | ... | ... | Chad |
| 15,493 | 39.2 | 60.8 | 32.1 | 349,936 | 41,600 | 4,804.4 | 100.0 | — | 97.0 | 0.4 | 1.9 | 438,630 | 1,600 | Chile |
| 263,373[27] | 64.8[27] | 35.2[27] | 20.1[27] | 440,076[27] | 1,894,066[27] | 6,778.8 | 56.6 | 43.4 | 80.3 | 9.3 | 10.1 | 366,920 | ... | China |
| ... | ... | ... | ... | ... | ... | — | 100.0 | — | 100.0 | — | — | ... | ... | Christmas Island |
| ... | ... | ... | ... | ... | ... | — | 100.0 | — | 100.0 | — | — | ... | ... | Cocos (Keeling) Islands |
| 17,224 | 84.5 | 15.5 | 11.4 | 13,535 | 116,584 | 69.7 | 32.1 | 67.9 | 91.1 | 7.7 | 1.2 | 26,930 | 56,300 | Colombia |
| ... | ... | ... | ... | ... | ... | 5.2 | 100.0 | — | 99.0 | 1.0 | — | ... | 120 | Comoros |
| 2,381 | 66.5 | 33.5 | 24.0 | 48,750 | 2,532 | 33.5 | 59.6 | 40.4 | 99.9 | 0.1 | — | 3,100 | 22,800 | Congo |
| ... | ... | ... | ... | ... | ... | 0.8 | 100.0 | — | 68.5 | 0.7 | 28.4 | ... | 150 | Cook Islands |
| 3,055 | 83.5 | 16.5 | 10.3 | 16,942 | 66,848 | 14.7 | 98.0 | 2.0 | 67.4 | 31.1 | 0.4 | 30,325 | 3,319 | Costa Rica |
| 12,486 | 63.8 | 36.2 | 31.2 | 227,927 | 21,960 | 93.1 | 80.7 | 19.3 | 93.4 | 6.6 | — | 46,756 | 65,428 | Côte d'Ivoire |
| 3,344 | 84.3 | 15.7 | 5.2 | ... | 252,747 | 219.9 | 92.3 | 7.7 | 85.6 | 9.4 | 4.3 | 117,995 | 54,362 | Cuba |
| 80 | 28.8 | 71.2 | 45.0 | 156[8] | 48,265 | 2.4 | 97.8 | 2.2 | 92.4 | 0.2 | 7.4 | — | 9,138 | Cyprus |
| 19,002 | 7.3 | 92.7 | 54.2 | 375,230 | 105,330 | 19.8 | — | 100.0 | 100.0 | — | — | 2,679 | 73,388 | Czechoslovakia |
| 2,693 | 13.0 | 87.0 | 45.8 | 186.020 | 885,102 | 1,696.3 | 98.6 | 1.4 | 95.0 | 0.6 | 4.4 | 952,712 | 370,442 | Denmark |
| ... | ... | ... | ... | ... | 1,377 | 0.4 | 100.0 | — | 98.4 | 1.6 | — | — | 450 | Djibouti |
| ... | ... | ... | ... | ... | 880 | 0.4 | 100.0 | — | 100.0 | — | — | — | 685 | Dominica |
| 982 | 99.4 | 0.6 | 0.4 | 17[9] | 48,996 | 18.3 | 86.2 | 13.8 | 83.6 | 5.4 | 10.5 | 3,074 | 12,305 | Dominican Republic |
| 8,571 | 68.6 | 31.4 | 27.4 | 19,715 | 121,447 | 901.1 | 100.0 | — | 96.0 | 4.0 | — | 261,653 | — | Ecuador |
| 2,011 | 95.4 | 4.6 | — | ... | 668,098 | 138.8 | 19.1 | 80.9 | 97.0 | 2.2 | 0.8 | 681 | 55,604 | Egypt |

## Extractive industries (continued)

| country | % of GDP, 1985 | mineral production (value added) year | total ('000,000 U.S.$) | metals[a] | non-metals[b] | energy[c] | trade (value) year | exports total ('000,000 U.S.$) | metals[a] | non-metals[b] | energy[c] | imports total ('000,000 U.S.$) | metals[a] | non-metals[b] | energy[c] |
|---|---|---|---|---|---|---|---|---|---|---|---|---|---|---|---|
| El Salvador | 0.1 | 1985 | 8.4 | —100.0— | | — | 1982 | 2.4 | 8.7 | 91.3 | — | 227.0 | — | 2.1 | 97.9 |
| Equatorial Guinea | — | | | | | | 1983 | 0.7[24] | 100.0[24] | — | — | | | | |
| Ethiopia | 0.2[34] | 1984–85 | 7.9 | —100.0— | | — | 1983 | — | — | — | — | 173.3[2] | 0.2[2] | — | 99.8[2] |
| Faeroe Islands | — | 1984 | — | — | — | — | 1983 | — | — | — | — | 2.1[29] | 1.3 | 87.2 | 11.5[29] |
| Falkland Islands | ... | ... | ... | ... | ... | ... | 1983 | — | — | — | — | ... | ... | ... | ... |
| Fiji | 0.6 | 1985 | 6.9[35] | 84.0[2] | 16.0[2] | — | 1984 | 15.3[15] | 100.0[15] | — | — | 4.6[29] | — | 32.8 | 67.2[29] |
| Finland | 0.4 | 1984 | 213.0 | 51.6 | 48.4 | — | 1985 | 58.2 | 36.2 | 55.7 | 8.0 | 2,669.8 | 7.5 | 5.1 | 87.4 |
| France | 1.7 | 1984 | 4,611.5 | 4.1 | 29.9 | 66.0 | 1985 | 1,780.5 | 53.8 | 26.3 | 20.0 | 20,772.1 | 5.0 | 4.2 | 90.8 |
| French Guiana | ... | 1985 | ... | —100.0— | | — | 1985 | 0.1 | 100.0 | — | — | 1.5 | — | — | 100.0 |
| French Polynesia | ... | 1983 | ... | ... | ... | ... | 1983 | 6.3 | 1.9 | 98.1 | — | 5.1[15,29] | — | 30.7[15] | 69.3[15,29] |
| Gabon | 47.2[3] | 1983 | 1,589.5 | 8.9 | 0.1 | 91.0 | 1983 | 1,226.0 | 8.5 | — | 91.5 | 6.5 | — | 100.0 | — |
| Gambia, The | 0.1[37] | 1982–83 | 0.3 | — | 100.0 | — | 1983 | 4.2[24] | — | 100.0[24] | — | | | | |
| Gaza Strip | ... | ... | ... | ... | ... | ... | [39] | [39] | ... | ... | ... | ... | ... | ... | ... |
| Germany, East | ... | ... | ... | ... | ... | ... | | | | | | | | | |
| Germany, West | 1.0[8] | 1984 | 6,121.1 | 0.5 | 16.6 | 82.9[1] | 1985 | 3,260.8 | 25.7 | 19.2 | 55.1 | 24,378.4 | 13.0 | 4.2 | 82.9 |
| Ghana | 1.0 | 1983[40] | 547.9 | 97.7 | 2.3 | — | 1983 | 32.3[24] | 29.8[24] | 53.2[24] | 17.0[24] | 331.0[15] | 20.7[15] | 1.6[15] | 77.7[15] |
| Gibraltar | ... | ... | ... | ... | ... | ... | 1983 | 5.9[2] | 100.0[2] | — | — | 0.8 | — | 99.4 | 0.6 |
| Greece | 1.9 | 1985 | 647.3 | 18.7[9] | 40.4[9] | 40.9[9] | 1985 | 288.0 | 34.1 | 32.1 | 33.8 | 2,782.5 | 2.0 | 1.5 | 96.5 |
| Greenland | ... | 1984 | ... | —100.0— | | — | 1985 | 31.4 | 100.0 | — | — | 1.2 | — | 100.0 | — |
| Grenada | 1.1 | 1985 | 1.1 | — | 100.0 | — | 1984 | — | — | — | — | 0.1[15] | 2.7[15] | — | 97.3[15] |
| Guadeloupe | ... | 1980 | ... | — | 100.0 | — | 1985 | 0.4 | 100.0 | — | — | 5.2 | — | 24.8 | 75.2 |
| Guam | ... | 1984 | ... | — | 100.0 | — | 1983 | 0.9[24] | 100.0[24] | — | — | ... | ... | ... | ... |
| Guatemala | 0.3[26] | 1986 | 30.0[16] | ... | ... | ... | 1983 | 48.2 | 0.1 | 5.1 | 94.8 | 121.2[9] | 1.2[9] | 6.1[9] | 92.7[9] |
| Guernsey | ... | ... | ... | ... | ... | ... | | | | | | | | | |
| Guinea | 13.4 | 1983 | 299.0[43] | —100.0[43]— | | — | 1983 | 407.3[24] | 98.7[24] | 1.3[24] | — | 0.8[2] | 100.0[2] | — | — |
| Guinea-Bissau | 1.3[3] | 1983 | 1.0 | — | 100.0 | — | 1983 | 1.2[24] | 11.7[24] | 88.3[24] | — | 1.3[15] | — | 89.5[15] | 10.5[15] |
| Guyana | 7.9[26] | 1986 | 45.0[44] | ... | ... | ... | 1983 | 122.3 | 99.6 | 0.4 | — | 3.5[33] | — | 47.2[33] | 52.8[33] |
| Haiti | 0.1[26] | 1986 | 2.0[45] | —100.0[45]— | | — | 1983 | 8.5[24] | 100.0[24] | — | — | 0.9[33] | — | 99.1[33] | 0.9[33] |
| Honduras | 2.0 | 1986 | 67.0 | —100.0— | | — | 1983 | 42.4 | 100.0 | — | — | 104.6 | — | 2.4 | 97.6 |
| Hong Kong | 0.1 | 1985 | 45.7 | — | 100.0 | — | 1985 | 499.7 | 38.1 | 61.1 | 0.8 | 1,009.1 | 6.5 | 66.5 | 27.0 |
| Hungary | 8.1[3] | 1984 | 1,258.9 | 3.7 | 2.8 | 93.5 | 1985 | 17.1[24] | — | — | 100.0[24] | 1,738.6[29,32] | 3.2 | 4.7 | 92.1[29,32] |
| Iceland | —[15] | 1984 | ... | — | 100.0 | — | 1985 | 9.3 | 4.6 | 95.4 | — | 44.8 | 71.9 | 17.4 | 10.7 |
| India | 2.7 | 1984–85 | 5,216.6 | 6.0 | 8.6 | 85.4 | 1983 | 2,790.6 | 18.1 | 42.8 | 39.1 | 2,840.4 | 4.4 | 35.4 | 60.2 |
| Indonesia | 16.2 | 1985 | 14,054.8 | 2.3[2] | 0.2[2] | 97.5[2] | 1984 | 14,879.3 | 1.8 | 0.1 | 98.1 | 1,514.3 | 6.4 | 6.4 | 87.2 |
| Iran | 11.3[8] | 1983–84 | 22,601.3 | —8.2[20,37]— | | 91.8[20,37] | 1983 | 18,229.5 | 0.1 | 0.2 | 99.7 | 56.4 | 5.3 | 36.3 | 58.4 |
| Iraq | 24.7 | 1983 | 7,176.9[16] | — | 0.1 | 99.9 | 1983 | 8,645.9 | — | 0.1 | 99.9 | 47.2 | 19.8 | 39.8 | 40.4 |
| Ireland | 1.2[9] | 1981 | 211.2[46] | 18.7 | 79.8 | 1.4[46] | 1985 | 292.3 | 65.1 | 28.0 | 6.9 | 581.4 | 13.3 | 7.9 | 78.7 |
| Isle of Man | ... | ... | ... | ... | ... | ... | | | | | | | | | |
| Israel | 0.7[47] | 1982–83 | 195.4 | 5.7[47,48] | 94.3[47] | [47,48] | 1985 | 1,569.2 | 0.2 | 99.8 | — | 2,575.0 | 0.1 | 52.9 | 47.0 |
| Italy | 1.0[9] | 1982 | 2,593.0 | 3.8 | 14.8 | 81.4 | 1985 | 494.6 | 23.2 | 50.3 | 26.5 | 20,162.4 | 8.4 | 3.4 | 88.2 |
| Jamaica | 5.1 | 1985 | 102.4 | 97.6[2] | 2.4[2] | — | 1983 | 486.0 | 99.8 | 0.2 | — | 5.2 | 0.6 | — | 99.4 |
| Japan | 0.4 | 1984 | 1,431.5 | 10.9 | 24.1 | 65.0 | 1985 | 328.7 | 35.8 | 60.8 | 3.4 | 57,466.2 | 10.9 | 3.2 | 85.9 |
| Jersey | ... | ... | ... | ... | ... | ... | | | | | | | | | |
| Jordan | 3.3 | 1985 | 133.5 | — | —100.0— | | 1984 | 223.5 | 1.0 | 99.0 | — | 555.8 | 0.2 | 4.4 | 95.4 |
| Kampuchea | ... | 1985 | ... | | 100.0 | ... | 1982 | 3.8 | 100.0 | — | — | ... | ... | ... | ... |
| Kenya | 0.2 | 1985 | 12.2 | 0.8[2] | 99.2[2] | — | 1983 | 49.8[2] | 10.6[2] | 46.3[2] | 43.1[2] | 424.9 | 0.1 | 1.7 | 98.2 |
| Kiribati | — | 1982 | ... | ... | ... | ... | 1983 | — | — | — | — | 0.2[9] | 100.0[9] | — | — |
| Korea, North | ... | | | | | | | | | | | | | | |
| Korea, South | 1.5 | 1985 | 1,251.6 | 4.5[8] | 50.1[8] | 45.4[8] | 1985 | 91.3 | 22.2 | 77.4 | 0.4 | 7,929.4 | 11.5 | 3.7 | 84.8 |
| Kuwait | 50.3 | 1985 | 9,953.1 | — | 0.3[3] | 99.7[3] | 1983 | 4,415.3 | 0.7 | 0.4 | 98.9 | 206.9 | 0.9 | 11.5 | 87.6 |
| Laos | ... | 1985 | ... | —100.0— | | — | 1983 | 0.7[24] | 100.0[24] | — | — | ... | ... | ... | ... |
| Lebanon | ... | | | | | | 1983 | 37.5 | 22.0 | 78.0 | — | 187.7 | 0.4 | 21.5 | 78.1 |
| Lesotho | 0.2[13] | 1983–84 | 0.9 | — | 100.0 | — | [21] | | | | | | | | |
| Liberia | 16.9 | 1984 | 105.8 | 93.4[9,20] | 6.6[9,20] | — | 1984 | 333.8 | 83.9 | 16.1 | — | 3.2 | — | 100.0 | — |
| Libya | 50.6[3] | 1983 | 15,471.0 | — | 0.7[15] | 99.3[15] | 1983 | 10,906.2 | — | — | 100.0 | 86.7 | 80.1 | 19.9 | — |
| Liechtenstein | ... | | | | | | [14] | | | | | | | | |
| Luxembourg | 0.1[8] | 1984 | 2.9 | — | 100.0 | — | ... | ... | ... | ... | ... | ... | ... | ... | ... |
| Macau | ... | 1983 | 2.7 | — | 100.0 | — | 1983 | 4.5 | 0.4 | 99.6 | — | 4.9 | 5.0 | 38.5 | 56.5 |
| Madagascar | 0.3[3] | 1983 | 6.0 | —100.0— | | — | 1983 | 11.4[24] | 34.9[24] | 65.1[24] | — | 73.9[2] | 0.3[2] | — | 99.7[2] |
| Malawi | — | 1984 | 0.2[2] | — | 100.0 | — | 1983 | — | — | — | — | 5.9[9] | — | 45.8[9] | 54.2[9] |
| Malaysia | 9.8 | 1985 | 2,393.8 | ... | ... | ... | 1983 | 3,184.5 | 3.8 | 1.1 | 95.1 | 755.8 | 18.8 | 9.2 | 72.0 |
| Maldives | 1.2[8] | 1984 | 0.9 | — | 100.0 | — | 1985 | — | — | — | — | ... | ... | ... | ... |
| Mali | 0.2[8] | 1984 | 2.6[52] | —100.0— | | — | 1983 | 2.0 | — | 100.0 | — | 1.1[33] | 0.1[33] | 99.9[33] | ... |
| Malta | 4.4 | 1985 | 44.5 | — | 100.0 | — | 1984 | 6.1 | 33.3 | 66.7 | — | 12.5 | 1.2 | 59.9 | 38.9 |
| Martinique | ... | 1984 | ... | — | 100.0 | — | 1985 | 3.3[3] | 14.1[3] | — | 85.9[3] | 57.2 | — | — | 100.0 |
| Mauritania | 9.9[8] | 1984 | 69.4 | —100.0— | | — | 1983 | 162.1 | 99.6 | — | 0.4 | 0.1 | — | 100.0 | — |
| Mauritius | 0.1 | 1985 | 1.3 | — | 100.0 | — | 1983 | 3.4 | — | 100.0 | — | 2.5 | — | 100.0 | — |
| Mayotte | ... | | | | | | | | | | | | | | |
| Mexico | 10.0[8] | 1984 | 17,160.2 | 5.6 | 4.4 | 90.0 | 1984 | 15,745.0 | 1.7 | 1.6 | 96.7 | 575.1 | 39.9 | 17.6 | 42.5 |
| Monaco | ... | | | | | | | | | | | | | | |
| Mongolia | ... | | | | | | | | | | | | | | |
| Montserrat | 1.2 | 1985 | 0.4 | —100.0— | | — | 1983 | 0.4[24] | 100.0[24] | — | — | 0.1[4] | — | 21.7[4] | 78.3[4] |
| Morocco | 4.7 | 1985 | 558.5 | —97.1[9,20]— | | 2.9[9,20] | 1984 | 635.0 | 11.4 | 87.4 | 1.2 | 1,170.9 | 0.1 | 14.8 | 85.2 |
| Mozambique | 0.4[3] | 1983 | 18.0 | ... | 100.0 | ... | 1983 | 9.7 | 17.2 | 37.3 | 45.5 | 5.2 | — | 100.0 | — |
| Nauru | ... | 1984 | ... | — | 100.0 | — | 1984 | 125.0 | — | 100.0 | — | ... | ... | ... | ... |
| Nepal | 0.3[8] | 1983–84 | 6.4 | ... | ... | ... | 1983 | — | — | — | — | 15.7[9] | 9.6[9] | 85.6[9] | 4.8[9] |
| Netherlands, The | 8.4 | 1984 | 9,698.6 | — | 2.1[2] | 97.9[2] | 1985 | 6,548.5 | 9.3 | 5.1 | 85.6 | 11,233.2 | 7.7 | 5.1 | 87.2 |
| Netherlands Antilles[10] | ... | 1983 | ... | — | 100.0 | — | 1984[53] | 80.9 | — | 19.0 | 81.0 | 3,331.5 | — | — | 100.0 |
| New Caledonia | 9.3[3] | 1984 | 72.0 | 100.0 | — | — | 1983 | 24.7 | 100.0 | — | — | 9.2 | — | 5.4 | 94.6 |
| New Zealand | 1.1[34] | 1984–85 | 251.6 | 5.4[13] | 16.5[13] | 78.1[13] | 1985 | 117.4 | 21.7 | 4.0 | 74.3 | 401.0 | 25.3 | 26.5 | 48.2 |
| Nicaragua | 0.5[26] | 1986 | 16.0 | —100.0— | | — | 1983 | — | — | — | — | 152.1[2] | — | 1.5[2] | 98.5[2] |
| Niger | 8.7[8] | 1984 | 122.7 | 97.9[15] | 2.9[15] | –0.8[15] | 1983 | 261.7[24] | 95.0[24] | 0.4[24] | 4.6[24] | 9.6[9] | — | 100.0[9] | — |
| Niue | ... | 1983 | ... | — | 100.0 | — | 1984 | — | — | — | — | ... | ... | ... | ... |
| Norfolk Island | ... | ... | ... | ... | ... | ... | 1983 | — | — | — | — | ... | ... | ... | ... |

| forestry, 1985 — production of roundwood: total ('000 cubic metres) | fuelwood, charcoal (%) | industrial roundwood (%) total | industrial roundwood (%) sawlogs, veneer | trade ('000 U.S.$) exports | trade ('000 U.S.$) imports | fisheries, 1985 — catch (nominal) total ('000 metric tons) | by source (%) marine | by source (%) fresh-water | by kind of catch (%) fish | by kind of catch (%) crustaceans | by kind of catch (%) mollusks | trade ('000 U.S.$) exports | trade ('000 U.S.$) imports | country |
|---|---|---|---|---|---|---|---|---|---|---|---|---|---|---|
| 4,754 | 98.2 | 1.8 | 1.2 | 6,587 | 36,723 | 12.1 | 86.0 | 14.0 | 25.5 | 73.0 | 1.5 | 17,220 | 880 | El Salvador |
| 607 | 73.6 | 26.4 | 26.4 | 4,405 | ... | 3.6 | 88.9 | 11.1 | 80.5 | 12.5 | 2.8 | 420 | 2,040 | Equatorial Guinea |
| 37,896 | 95.2 | 4.8 | 0.3 | ... | 9,563 | 5.0 | 20.0 | 80.0 | 100.0 | — | — | — | 1,320 | Ethiopia |
| ... | ... | ... | ... | ... | ... | 361.6 | 100.0 | — | 95.7 | 3.3 | 1.0 | 161,708 | 1,906 | Faeroe Islands |
| ... | ... | ... | ... | ... | ... | — | 100.0 | — | 37.5 | 62.5 | — | ... | 4,197 | Falkland Islands |
| 249 | 14.9 | 85.1 | 82.3 | 5,916 | 8,050 | 27.7 | 91.4 | 8.6 | 82.7 | 5.8 | 10.0 | 13,288 | 12,209 | Fiji |
| 41,782 | 7.4 | 92.6 | 38.2 | 4,603,703 | 298,055 | 160.6 | 78.8 | 21.2 | 100.0 | — | — | 16,559 | 85,434 | Finland |
| 38,999 | 26.7 | 73.3 | 47.8 | 1,577,911 | 3,014,159 | 844.5 | 96.5 | 3.5 | 72.9 | 3.3 | 27.1 | 359,000[36] | 1,039,848[36] | France |
| 254 | 26.0 | 74.0 | 70.5 | 2,169 | 1,087 | 3.0 | 100.0 | — | 60.5 | 39.5 | — | 20,862 | 14,692 | French Guiana |
| ... | ... | ... | ... | ... | 14,695 | 2.0 | 100.0 | — | 99.9 | 0.1 | — | 7 | 4,197 | French Polynesia |
| 2,706 | 45.2 | 54.8 | 54.8 | 108,028 | 3,969 | 47.8 | 96.0 | 4.0 | 96.2 | 3.7 | 0.1 | 5,440 | 9,010 | Gabon |
| 783 | 97.3 | 2.7 | 1.8 | ... | 164 | 11.5[38] | 69.6[38] | 30.4[38] | 95.6[38] | 4.2[38] | ... | 2,210 | 3,210 | Gambia, The |
| ... | ... | ... | ... | ... | ... | 1.6 | ... | ... | 99.9 | 0.1 | — | ... | ... | Gaza Strip |
| 10,566 | 6.2 | 93.8 | 41.2 | 113,100 | 460,509 | 197.7 | 90.2 | 9.8 | 93.5 | 0.5 | 6.0 | 2,951 | 24,621 | Germany, East |
| 30,650 | 12.4 | 87.6 | 53.7 | 2,885,385 | 5,064,297 | 225.3 | 89.3 | 10.7 | 81.8 | 7.9 | 10.3 | 286,989 | 819,555 | Germany, West |
| 8,459 | 86.1 | 13.9 | 9.4 | 26,587 | 2,695 | 254.2 | 84.3 | 15.7 | 98.9 | 0.2 | 0.9 | 24,585 | 10,500 | Ghana |
|  |  |  |  |  |  |  |  |  |  |  |  |  |  | Gibraltar |
| 2,683 | 71.4 | 28.6 | 15.2 | 31,984 | 284,968 | 102.0 | 91.2 | 8.8 | 90.5 | 3.8 | 5.7 | 32,063 | 82,405 | Greece |
| — | — | — | — | ... | ... | 149.4 | 100.0 | — | 64.3 | 35.0 | 0.7 | 134,337 | 711 | Greenland |
| ... | ... | ... | ... | ... | ... | 1.2 | 100.0 | — | 98.9 | 0.2 | 0.2 | — | 570 | Grenada |
| 17 | 88.2 | 11.8 | 11.8 | 4,143[5] | 14,194 | 9.0 | 100.0 | — | 95.2 | 1.3 | 3.3 | 401 | 7,645 | Guadeloupe |
| ... | ... | ... | ... | 77[3] | 1,935[3] | 0.6 | 86.4 | 13.6 | 100.0 | — | — | 1,039[3] | 6,613[3] | Guam |
| 6,869 | 97.2 | 2.8 | 2.7 | 11,212 | 44,678 | 2.7 | 98.3 | 1.7 | 28.7 | 71.3 | — | 9,998 | 1,200 | Guatemala |
| ... | ... | ... | ... | ... | ... | [42] | [42] | [42] | [42] | [42] | [42] | ... | ... | Guernsey |
| 3,689 | 83.6 | 16.4 | 4.9 | 3,646[33] | ... | 30.0 | 93.3 | 6.7 | 100.0 | — | — | — | 2,331 | Guinea |
| 559 | 75.5 | 24.5 | 7.2 | 130 | 98 | 3.6 | 100.0 | — | 72.2 | 27.2 | 0.6 | 600 | — | Guinea-Bissau |
| 192 | 6.3 | 93.8 | 89.6 | 4,251 | 6,009 | 42.1 | 98.1 | 1.9 | 91.9 | 8.1 | — | 4,634 | — | Guyana |
| 5,902 | 96.0 | 4.0 | 3.8 | ... | 4,955 | 4.4 | 93.2 | 6.8 | 97.7 | 2.3 | — | — | 3,713 | Haiti |
| 5,082 | 89.3 | 10.7 | 10.4 | 31,080 | 20,843 | 9.6 | 98.7 | 1.3 | 11.1 | 83.7 | 5.2 | 38.462 | 3,336 | Honduras |
| 180 | 100.0 | — | — | 77,739 | 539,915 | 198.2 | 97.1 | 2.9 | 85.1 | 8.2 | 6.7 | 277,339 | 471,609 | Hong Kong |
| 6,780 | 44.2 | 55.8 | 29.3 | 84,756 | 255,247 | 36.9 | — | 100.0 | 100.0 | — | — | 4,282 | 31,183 | Hungary |
| — | — | — | — | ... | 35,782 | 1,680.2 | 100.0 | — | 97.4 | 1.6 | 1.0 | 617,355 | 4,698 | Iceland |
| 245,029 | 90.8 | 9.2 | 7.5 | 16,372 | 210,674 | 2,810.0 | 61.6 | 38.4 | 91.5 | 7.8 | 0.7 | 300,110 | — | India |
| 149,008 | 82.0 | 18.0 | 16.0 | 1,188,950 | 208,428 | 2,067.1 | 87.1 | 12.9 | 89.8 | 6.3 | 3.2 | 236,620 | 22,940 | Indonesia |
| 6,745 | 35.1 | 64.9 | 5.5 | 38 | 263,333 | 60.4 | 92.5 | 7.5 | 90.8 | 8.0 | 1.2 | 30,025 | 60,812 | Iran |
| 137 | 63.5 | 36.5 | 14.6 | ... | 158,081 | 21.5 | 25.6 | 74.4 | 100.0 | — | — | ... | ... | Iraq |
| 1,256 | 3.7 | 96.3 | 50.8 | 33,200 | 269,613 | 205.9 | 99.7 | 0.3 | 88.1 | 4.5 | 7.4 | 109,177 | 39,964 | Ireland |
| ... | ... | ... | ... | ... | ... | 7.0 | 100.0 | — | 17.9 | 0.8 | 81.3 | 3,460[3] | ... | Isle of Man |
| 118 | 9.3 | 90.7 | 22.0 | 13,311 | 186,648 | 21.0 | 35.6 | 64.4 | 99.5 | 0.5 | — | 1,747 | 35,957 | Israel |
| 9,448 | 51.8 | 48.2 | 26.0 | 719,725 | 2,652,987 | 504.1 | 91.8 | 8.2 | 74.1 | 6.6 | 19.3 | 140,920[49] | 984,990[49] | Italy |
| 93 | 14.0 | 86.0 | 72.0 | 1,452 | 49,380 | 10.0 | 95.0 | 5.0 | 100.0 | — | — | 2,784 | 11,579 | Jamaica |
| 33,465 | 1.6 | 98.4 | 57.5 | 770,543 | 5,871,528 | 11,443.7 | 98.2 | 1.8 | 86.0 | 1.7 | 11.5 | 819,840 | 4,744,277 | Japan |
| ... | ... | ... | ... | ... | ... | 3.0[42] | 100.0[42] | — | 9.4[42] | 89.3[42] | 1.3[42] | 3,075[8] | ... | Jersey |
| 9 | 55.6 | 44.4 | — | 8,056[8] | 51,118 | ... | 100.0 | — | 100.0 | — | — | ... | 6,450 | Jordan |
| 5,303 | 89.3 | 10.7 | 2.1 | 173 | 1,885 | 68.0 | 8.8 | 91.2 | 99.4 | 0.6 | — | ... | ... | Kampuchea |
| 32,409 | 95.2 | 4.8 | 1.3 | 3,255 | 18,201 | 106.0 | 5.9 | 94.1 | 99.6 | 0.3 | 0.1 | 990 | 860 | Kenya |
| ... | ... | ... | ... | ... | ... | 29.6 | 100.0 | — | 88.6 | 0.3 | 11.1 | 1,593 | 97 | Kiribati |
| 4,543 | 86.8 | 13.2 | 13.2 | ... | 1,879 | 1,700.0 | 93.5 | 6.5 | 100.0 | — | — | 27,954 | — | Korea, North |
| 8,573 | 72.1 | 27.9 | 12.0 | 131,518 | 854,848 | 2,649.9 | 98.0 | 2.0 | 69.2 | 3.0 | 26.5 | 796,878 | 89,775 | Korea, South |
| — | — | — | — | 23,387 | 114,055 | 5.2 | 100.0 | — | 81.7 | 18.3 | — | 6,258 | 7,309 | Kuwait |
| 4,051 | 94.0 | 6.0 | 3.5 | 1,533 | 816[15] | 20.0 | — | 100.0 | 100.0 | — | — | — | ... | Laos |
| 473 | 94.7 | 5.3 | 5.3 | 3,239 | 65,701 | 1.5 | 93.3 | 6.7 | 100.0 | — | — | ... | ... | Lebanon |
| 293 | 100.0 | — | — | 50 | 50 | ... | — | 100.0 | 100.0 | — | — | — | 1,160 | Lesotho |
| 4,262 | 89.4 | 10.6 | 7.4 | 35,624 | 1,352 | 11.5 | 65.2 | 34.8 | 98.4 | 1.6 | — | 1,050 | 7,050 | Liberia |
| 634 | 84.5 | 15.5 | 9.9 | ... | 110,797 | 7.8 | 100.0 | — | 100.0 | — | — | — | 19,920 | Libya |
| 8 | — | 100.0 | ... | ... | ... | — | — | 100.0 | 100.0 | — | — | [51] | [51] | Liechtenstein |
| [14] | [14] | [14] | [14] | [14] | [14] | — | — | 100.0 | 100.0 | — | — | [14] | [14] | Luxembourg |
| ... | ... | ... | ... | 183 | 7,790 | 12.4 | 100.0 | — | 24.2 | 71.8 | 4.0 | 7,667 | 8,927 | Macau |
| 6,262 | 87.1 | 12.9 | 7.5 | 46 | 6,959 | 56.0 | 25.0 | 75.0 | 87.4 | 12.0 | 0.2 | 18,273 | — | Madagascar |
| 6,588 | 94.2 | 5.8 | 2.0 | 600 | 16,720 | 62.1 | — | 100.0 | 100.0 | — | — | — | 50 | Malawi |
| 39,688 | 19.1 | 80.9 | 77.8 | 1,702,983 | 226,777 | 632.2 | 98.5 | 1.5 | 75.3 | 13.3 | 9.6 | 106,657 | 110,946 | Malaysia |
| ... | ... | ... | ... | ... | ... | 43.7 | 100.0 | — | 100.0 | — | — | 15,453 | ... | Maldives |
| 4,892 | 93.7 | 6.3 | 0.1 | ... | 1,174 | 60.0 | — | 100.0 | 100.0 | — | — | 590 | 360 | Mali |
| ... | ... | ... | ... | ... | 17,458 | 2.5 | 100.0 | — | 88.4 | 7.1 | 4.5 | 3,631 | 5,693 | Malta |
| 11 | 90.9 | 9.1 | 9.1 | ... | 10,622 | 5.2 | 100.0 | — | 96.9 | 2.1 | — | 173 | 12,839 | Martinique |
| 12 | 58.3 | 41.7 | 8.3 | ... | ... | 57.0 | 78.9 | 21.1 | 79.9 | 1.9 | 18.2 | 127,042 | 400 | Mauritania |
| 30 | 73.3 | 26.7 | 20.0 | ... | 8,685 | 12.5 | 99.8 | 0.2 | 96.5 | 0.6 | 2.9 | 9,913 | 6,644 | Mauritius |
| ... | ... | ... | ... | ... | ... | 0.7[8] | ... | ... | ... | ... | ... | ... | ... | Mayotte |
| 21,317 | 64.9 | 35.1 | 20.5 | 13,884 | 307,005 | 1,226.2 | 90.8 | 9.2 | 86.7 | 7.1 | 5.9 | 370,998 | 8,608 | Mexico |
| ... | ... | ... | ... | ... | ... | — | 100.0 | — | 100.0 | — | — | [36] | [36] | Monaco |
| 2,390 | 56.5 | 43.5 | 43.5 | 9,300 | 6,800 | 0.4 | — | 100.0 | 100.0 | — | — | — | 1,150 | Mongolia |
| ... | ... | ... | ... | ... | 367[6,9] | 0.1 | — | 100.0 | 100.0 | — | — | — | 178[15] | Montserrat |
| 1,643 | 67.8 | 32.2 | 4.1 | 23,962 | 117,221 | 473.1 | 99.7 | 0.3 | 94.0 | 0.4 | 5.6 | 220,235 | 79 | Morocco |
| 15,231 | 93.7 | 6.3 | 0.6 | 1,299 | 296 | 37.7 | 86.7 | 13.3 | 82.2 | 17.0 | 0.8 | 33,387 | 6,620 | Mozambique |
| ... | ... | ... | ... | ... | ... | — | 100.0 | — | 100.0 | — | — | ... | ... | Nauru |
| 15,776 | 96.5 | 3.5 | 3.5 | 12,000 | ... | 9.1 | — | 100.0 | 100.0 | — | — | ... | ... | Nepal |
| 1,139 | 8.8 | 91.2 | 39.5 | 862,645 | 1,872,322 | 504.2 | 99.2 | 0.8 | 76.8 | — | 23.2 | 543,666 | 308,449 | Netherlands, The |
| ... | ... | ... | ... | ... | 10,243 | 1.0 | 100.0 | — | 100.0 | — | — | — | 4,780 | Netherlands Antilles[10] |
| 12 | ... | 100.0 | 91.7 | ... | 8,840 | 3.5 | 100.0 | — | 88.0 | 2.3 | 1.1 | 350 | 1,932 | New Caledonia |
| 8,934 | 0.6 | 99.4 | 51.3 | 305,300 | 113,888 | 283.0[54] | ... | ... | 78.1[54] | 2.0[54] | 19.8[54] | 271,019[55] | 18,115[55] | New Zealand |
| 3,581 | 75.4 | 24.6 | 23.2 | 2,569 | 12,368 | 4.2 | 98.0 | 2.0 | 31.0 | 69.0 | — | 12,889 | — | Nicaragua |
| 3,920 | 93.8 | 6.2 | — | ... | 285 | 6.8 | — | 100.0 | 100.0 | — | — | — | 505 | Niger |
| 95,566 | 91.7 | 8.3 | 6.0 | 6,089 | 159,883 | 241.6 | 63.8 | 36.2 | 99.0 | 1.0 | — | 3,291 | 103,533 | Nigeria |
| ... | ... | ... | ... | ... | ... | — | 100.0 | — | 100.0 | — | — | ... | ... | Niue |
| ... | ... | ... | ... | ... | ... | — | 100.0 | — | 100.0 | — | — | ... | ... | Norfolk Island |

## Extractive industries (continued)

| country | % of GDP, 1985 | mining — mineral production (value added) year | total ('000,000 U.S.$) | by kind (%) metals[a] | non-metals[b] | energy[c] | trade (value) year | exports total ('000,000 U.S.$) | by kind (%) metals[a] | non-metals[b] | energy[c] | imports total ('000,000 U.S.$) | by kind (%) metals[a] | non-metals[b] | energy[c] |
|---|---|---|---|---|---|---|---|---|---|---|---|---|---|---|---|
| Norway | 18.7 | 1984 | 10,217.5 | 0.6 | 0.9 | 98.5 | 1985 | 9,602.3 | 1.8 | 0.7 | 97.5 | 1,151.5 | 45.8 | 9.5 | 44.7 |
| Oman | 47.9 | 1984 | 4,196.6 | — | 0.5 | 99.5 | 1985 | 3,990.0[24] | — | — | 100.0[24] | 12.4 | 6.0 | 60.9 | 33.1 |
| Pacific Is., Trust Terr. of the | ... | ... | ... | ... | ... | ... | | ... | ... | ... | ... | | | | |
|   Marshall Islands | ... | ... | ... | ... | ... | ... | 1982 | — | ... | ... | ... | 3.7[2] | — | — | 100.0[2] |
|   Micronesia, Fed. States of | — | — | — | — | — | — | ... | ... | ... | ... | ... | ... | ... | ... | ... |
|   Northern Mariana Islands | — | — | — | — | — | — | | | | | | | | | |
|   Palau | — | — | — | — | — | — | 1983 | ... | ... | ... | ... | 2.1[3] | ... | — | 100.0[3] |
| Pakistan | 2.2 | 1984–85 | 384.9 | 0.1[3,20] | 18.5[3,20] | 78.9[3,20] | 1985 | 14.5 | 37.6 | 62.4 | — | 1,032.4 | 5.9 | 2.9 | 91.2 |
| Panama | 0.1 | 1984 | 6.0 | —100.0— | | | 1983 | 97.5 | 1.5 | 92.9 | 5.6 | 353.0 | — | 0.7 | 99.3 |
| Papua New Guinea | 10.7[3] | 1983 | 252.7[57] | 100.0 | — | — | 1984 | 333.6 | 100.0 | — | — | 0.7 | — | 100.0 | — |
| Paraguay | 0.4 | 1985 | 18.6 | — | 100.0 | — | 1983 | ... | — | — | — | 74.7[33] | — | 2.9[33] | 97.1[33] |
| Peru | 9.2[26] | 1986 | 2,320.0 | 51.5[15] | 8.2[15,58] | 40.3[15,58] | 1983 | 1,012.9 | 69.5 | 1.1 | 29.4 | 10.5 | 41.4 | 32.9 | 25.7 |
| Philippines | 2.2 | 1985 | 736.6 | 91.5[9] | 6.9[9] | 1.6[9] | 1983 | 606.5 | 99.1 | 0.3 | 0.6 | 1,624.7 | 3.0 | 1.2 | 95.8 |
| Pitcairn Island | — | — | — | | | | | | | | | | | | |
| Poland | 5.4[3] | 1984 | 2,885.8 | 11.3 | 13.8 | 74.9 | 1984 | 2,055.2 | 2.1 | 17.1 | 80.8 | 2,305.9 | 11.6 | 7.0 | 81.4 |
| Portugal | 0.6[15] | 1980 | 145.8 | 30.8 | 64.7 | 4.5 | 1985 | 75.6 | 28.9 | 71.1 | — | 1,822.3 | 2.3 | 4.0 | 93.7 |
| Puerto Rico | — | 1984–85 | 12.1 | — | 100.0 | — | 1977[59] | 51.1[29] | 30.6 | 36.2 | 33.2[29] | 54.4[59] | 0.2 | 93.5 | 6.3 |
| Qatar | 45.9[3] | 1983 | 2,943.5 | — | 100.0 | — | 1983 | 3,232.8 | — | — | 100.0 | 18.5 | 94.1 | 5.9 | — |
| Réunion | ... | 1984 | ... | — | 100.0 | — | 1985 | 0.3 | 100.0 | — | — | 8.1 | — | — | 100.0 |
| Romania | ... | ... | | | | | | | | | | | | | |
| Rwanda | 0.4[8] | 1984 | 5.7 | —100.0— | | | 1983 | 2.8[24] | 100.0[24] | — | — | 3.4[15] | — | 100.0[15] | — |
| St. Christopher and Nevis | 0.3 | 1985 | 0.2 | — | 100.0 | — | 1983 | ... | — | — | — | 0.1[2] | 78.6[2] | — | 21.4[2] |
| St. Helena and Ascension | ... | ... | | | | | 1982 | ... | ... | ... | ... | 0.4 | — | 100.0 | — |
| St. Lucia | 0.7 | 1985 | 1.2 | — | 100.0 | — | 1983 | ... | ... | ... | ... | ... | | | |
| St. Pierre and Miquelon | ... | ... | | | | | 1984 | — | — | — | — | 0.8[9] | 87.0[9] | — | 13.0[9] |
| St. Vincent | 0.3 | 1985 | 0.3 | — | 100.0 | — | 1983 | ... | — | — | — | 0.6[15] | — | — | 100.0[15] |
| San Marino | ... | ... | | | | | | | | | | | | | |
| São Tomé and Principe | ... | 1983 | ... | — | 100.0 | — | 1983 | ... | — | — | — | ... | | | |
| Saudi Arabia | 40.5[34] | 1984–85 | 32,245.7 | —1.6— | | 98.4 | 1984 | 34,600.6 | 0.1 | — | 99.9 | 191.1 | 28.6 | 70.0 | 1.3 |
| Senegal | 1.5[3] | 1983 | 32.3 | ... | ... | ... | 1983 | 77.1 | 2.5 | 97.5 | — | 208.0[9] | — | — | 100.0[9] |
| Seychelles | — | 1984 | | | | | 1983 | — | 100.0[24] | — | — | 0.3[2] | — | 38.7[2] | 61.3[2] |
| Sierra Leone | 7.5[3] | 1984 | 114.0 | —100.0— | | | 1983 | 79.4 | 44.2 | 55.8 | — | 0.5 | — | 100.0 | — |
| Singapore | 0.3 | 1985 | 50.8 | — | 100.0 | — | 1985 | 283.7 | 55.4 | 17.3 | 27.3 | 6,016.5 | 1.5 | 1.4 | 97.1 |
| Solomon Islands | 0.3[3] | 1984 | ... | —100.0— | | | 1984 | 0.6[35] | 100.0[35] | — | — | 0.8[15] | — | 74.8[15] | 25.2[15] |
| Somalia | ... | 1983 | 10.8[9] | — | 100.0 | — | 1983 | ... | — | — | — | ... | | | |
| South Africa | 14.8[62] | 1985 | 8,076.5 | —85.2[1,3]— | | 14.8[1,3] | 1983[21] | 3,051.3[46] | 38.8 | 26.6 | 34.6[46] | 135.9[46] | 52.5 | 47.4 | 0.1[46] |
|   Bophuthatswana | 52.6[15] | ... | | | | | | | | | | | | | |
|   Ciskei | 0.1[15] | ... | | | | | | | | | | | | | |
|   KwaNdebele | ... | ... | | | | | | | | | | | | | |
|   Transkei | 0.6[63] | ... | | | | | | | | | | | | | |
|   Venda | 1.7[63] | ... | | | | | | | | | | | | | |
| South West Africa/Namibia | 36.1[26] | 1986 | 467.8 | —100.0— | | — | 1983 | 593.0 | 64.0 | 36.0 | — | [21] | [21] | [21] | [21] |
| Spain | 1.4[8] | 1983 | 1,759.0 | 11.9 | 16.0 | 72.1 | 1985 | 271.1 | 32.5 | 53.6 | 14.0 | 11,184.0 | 10.4 | 2.7 | 86.9 |
| Sri Lanka | 0.8 | 1984 | 47.5 | —100.0— | | — | 1984 | 36.7 | 10.8 | 89.2 | — | 428.2 | 0.2 | 3.0 | 96.9 |
| Sudan, The | —[15] | 1978–79 | 9.0 | —100.0— | | — | 1983 | ... | — | — | — | 162.7[9] | — | 0.1[9] | 99.9[9] |
| Suriname | 5.8 | 1984[20] | 277.3 | 99.8 | 0.2 | — | 1983 | 210.0 | 100.0 | — | — | 4.2 | — | — | 100.0 |
| Swaziland | 3.2[3] | 1983 | 14.0 | 9.4[15] | 77.3[15] | 13.3[15] | 1984 | 17.2 | — | 86.9 | 13.1 | [21] | [21] | [21] | [21] |
| Sweden | 0.5 | 1984 | 487.2 | 87.8 | 12.2 | — | 1985 | 675.5 | 82.0 | 12.8 | 5.2 | 3,796.4 | 11.6 | 4.5 | 83.9 |
| Switzerland | ... | 1984 | ... | — | 100.0 | — | 1985 | 1,323.5 | 5.5 | 93.9 | 0.6 | 2,475.4 | 2.7 | 56.5 | 40.8 |
| Syria | 7.4 | 1985 | 1,503.4 | — | —100.0— | | 1983 | 471.3 | — | 3.4 | 96.6 | 34.5 | 2.2 | 8.9 | 88.9 |
| Taiwan | 0.6 | 1985 | 355.8 | 0.5 | 61.1 | 38.3 | 1984 | ... | — | — | — | 4,680.6 | 19.5 | — | 80.5 |
| Tanzania | 0.2 | 1984 | 22.0 | — | 100.0 | — | 1982 | 15.3 | 50.4 | 49.6 | — | 159.6[9] | — | 3.0[9] | 97.0[9] |
| Thailand | 2.8 | 1984 | 900.7 | 18.9 | 39.6 | 41.5 | 1984 | 354.0 | 14.6 | 85.4 | 0.1 | 1,907.9 | 5.5 | 8.6 | 86.0 |
| Togo | 13.7[8] | 1984 | 92.2 | — | 100.0 | — | 1984 | 92.2 | — | 100.0 | — | 83.2[15] | — | 1.4[15] | 98.6[15] |
| Tokelau | — | 1985 | — | | | | 1983 | — | — | — | — | ... | | | |
| Tonga | 0.6[3] | 1983 | 0.4 | — | 100.0 | — | 1983 | — | — | — | — | 0.4[2] | — | 73.2[2] | 26.8[2] |
| Trinidad and Tobago | 20.6 | 1983 | 1,670.4 | — | — | 100.0 | 1984 | 961.1 | — | — | 100.0 | 28.7 | 56.5 | 42.6 | 0.9 |
| Tunisia | 10.2 | 1985 | 835.2 | 0.9[9] | 13.2[9] | 85.9[9] | 1984 | 791.2 | 0.8 | 5.7 | 93.5 | 172.5 | 2.5 | 78.2 | 19.3 |
| Turkey | 2.3 | 1984 | 1,011.8 | 14.5[2,20] | 13.9[2,20] | 71.6[2,20] | 1984 | 394.5 | 10.8 | 50.5 | 38.7 | 3,867.9 | 5.1 | 1.4 | 93.5 |
| Turks and Caicos Is. | 3.6[8] | 1983 | 1.0 | — | 100.0 | — | | | | | | | | | |
| Tuvalu | — | 1985 | — | | | | 1983 | — | — | — | — | ... | — | — | 100.0 |
| Uganda | —[9] | 1981 | 2.9 | — | 100.0 | — | 1983 | — | — | — | — | ... | | | |
| U.S.S.R. | ... | 1984 | 63,099.0 | —31.8[20]— | | 68.2[20] | 1984 | 52,690.0[64] | 10.3 | 1.4 | 88.3[64] | 10,070.0[64] | 59.3 | 2.7 | 38.0[64] |
| United Arab Emirates | 46.2[8] | 1984 | 12,786.7 | — | — | 100.0 | 1983 | 14,074.9 | 0.2 | 0.1 | 99.7 | 34.5 | 4.0 | 93.3 | 2.7 |
| United Kingdom | 7.0[8] | 1984 | 29,958.5 | 0.1[9] | 3.5[9] | 96.4[9] | 1985 | 17,468.9 | 4.8 | 11.7 | 83.5 | 12,460.1 | 14.2 | 18.3 | 67.5 |
| United States | 3.1 | 1985 | 122,800.0 | 2.4[3] | 4.5[3] | 93.1[3] | 1985 | 9,884.7 | 27.6 | 17.8 | 54.6 | 45,596.6 | 5.5 | 10.5 | 84.0 |
| Uruguay | 1.1 | 1985 | 55.8 | — | 100.0 | — | 1984 | 1.1 | — | 100.0 | — | 267.0 | — | 2.3 | 97.7 |
| Vanuatu | ... | 1984 | — | — | 100.0 | — | 1983 | — | — | — | — | 2.2[2] | — | 75.6[2] | 24.4[2] |
| Venezuela | 15.8 | 1984 | 9,926.9 | —2.0[58]— | | 98.0[58] | 1983 | 6,925.1 | 2.3 | 0.4 | 97.3 | 85.5 | 63.6 | 32.8 | 3.6 |
| Vietnam | ... | ... | | | | | | | | | | | | | |
| Virgin Islands (U.S.) | ... | 1985 | ... | — | 100.0 | — | 1982 | 1,195.2 | 99.8[65] | 0.2 | — | 1,889.9[66] | — | 0.2 | 99.8[16] |
| Wallis and Futuna | ... | ... | | | | | | | | | | | | | |
| West Bank | ... | ... | | | | | 1983[39] | 7.9[39,67] | ... | | | | | | |
| Western Sahara | ... | ... | | | | | | | | | | | | | |
| Western Samoa | ... | 1984 | ... | | | | 1984 | — | ... | | | | | | |
| Yemen (Aden) | 0.1[15] | 1982 | 1.4 | — | 100.0 | — | 1983 | 29.2[24] | — | — | 100.0[24] | 160.2 | — | — | 100.0 |
| Yemen (Şan'ā') | 1.2[68] | 1982–83 | 36.6 | — | 100.0 | — | 1983 | — | — | — | — | 3.9[9] | — | — | 100.0[9] |
| Yugoslavia | 2.8 | 1984 | 1,310.0 | 23.5 | 13.0 | 63.5 | 1985 | 85.4 | 78.2 | 19.5 | 2.3 | 3,323.9 | 6.5 | 6.1 | 87.4 |
| Zaire | 11.5[2] | 1982 | 624.9 | —100.0— | | | 1983 | 360.8[24] | 18.8[24] | 23.6[24] | 57.6[24] | 1.7[15] | 4.9[15] | 95.1[15] | — |
| Zambia | 14.2 | 1985 | 332.2 | 96.5[3] | 3.5[3] | — | 1983 | 23.4 | 55.3 | 44.7 | — | 117.1[33] | — | 2.5[33] | 97.5[33] |
| Zimbabwe | 6.5 | 1985 | 326.3 | 70.0[20] | 19.3[20] | 10.7[20] | 1983 | 73.9 | 20.3 | 79.7 | — | 10.3[2] | 98.5[2] | 1.5[2] | — |

[1]Gross value of sales. [2]1982. [3]1983. [4]1978. [5]1977. [6]Lumber only. [7]Salt exports valued at U.S.$33,000. [8]1984. [9]1981. [10]Netherlands Antilles includes Aruba, except fish catch data. [11]Includes petroleum refining. [12]Production of limestone, china clay, and natural gas only. [13]1983–84. [14]Belgium includes Luxembourg. [15]1980. [16]Mostly crude petroleum. [17]Wood, lumber, and cork only. [18]Mostly slate, limestone, and coal. [19]Mostly metals. [20]Gross value of production (output). [21]South Africa includes Botswana, Lesotho, South West Africa/Namibia, and Swaziland. [22]Charcoal only. [23]Mostly crude petroleum and natural gas. [24]1982–83 average. [25]Mostly diamonds; some gold. [26]1986. [27]China includes Taiwan. [28]Coal, emeralds, and ferronickel only. [29]Includes coke and briquettes. [30]Excludes metals, precious stones, crude petroleum, and natural gas. [31]Excludes precious stones, crude petroleum, and natural gas. [32]Includes petroleum products. [33]1979. [34]1984–85. [35]Mostly gold. [36]France includes Monaco. [37]1982–83. [38]Excludes mollusks. [39]West Bank includes Gaza Strip. [40]Enterprises

| forestry, 1985 | | | | | | fisheries, 1985 | | | | | | | | country |
|---|---|---|---|---|---|---|---|---|---|---|---|---|---|---|
| production of roundwood | | | | trade (value '000 U.S.$) | | catch (nominal) | | | | | | trade (value, '000 U.S.$) | | |
| total ('000 cubic metres) | fuelwood, charcoal (%) | industrial roundwood (%) total | sawlogs, veneer | exports | imports | total ('000 metric tons) | by source (%) marine | fresh-water | by kind of catch (%) fish | crusta-ceans | mollusks | exports | imports | |
| 10,620 | 7.5 | 92.5 | 45.3 | 807,552 | 431,589 | 2,106.8 | 100.0 | — | 94.9 | 4.4 | 0.7 | 922,460 | 70,871 | Norway |
| ... | ... | ... | ... | 352[2,17] | 55,676 | 101.2 | 100.0 | — | 97.2 | 2.0 | 0.8 | 25,374 | 2,750 | Oman |
| ... | ... | ... | ... | ... | ... | 5.5 | 100.0 | — | 100.0 | — | — | 1,160 | 185 | Pacific Is., Trust Terr. of the |
| | | | | | | | | | | | | | | Marshall Islands |
| | | | | | | | | | | | | | | Micronesia, Fed. States of |
| | | | | | | | | | | | | | | Northern Mariana Islands |
| ... | ... | ... | ... | ... | ... | 0.3[3] | 100.0[3] | ... | 98.9[3] | ... | ... | 70[3] | ... | Palau |
| 20,233 | 96.9 | 3.1 | 1.5 | ... | 103,721 | 408.4 | 81.6 | 18.4 | 93.4 | 6.6 | — | 79,810 | 79 | Pakistan |
| 2,047 | 83.4 | 16.6 | 13.6 | 1,029 | 36,881 | 282.5 | 100.0 | — | 94.2 | 5.7 | 0.1 | 79,555[56] | 5,130[56] | Panama |
| 7,623 | 72.6 | 27.4 | 24.6 | 69,123 | 5,504 | 6.1 | 100.0 | — | 67.0 | 33.0 | — | 13,833 | 23,940 | Papua New Guinea |
| 7,560 | 63.7 | 36.3 | 31.2 | 91,030 | 8,566 | 7.5 | — | 100.0 | 100.0 | — | — | — | — | Paraguay |
| 7,723 | 84.3 | 15.7 | 14.5 | 3,614 | 37,518 | 4,168.4 | 99.4 | 0.6 | 97.4 | 0.1 | 1.6 | 221,236 | 2,230 | Peru |
| 36,614 | 79.7 | 20.3 | 11.7 | 229,399 | 73,918 | 1,867.7 | 71.4 | 28.6 | 81.8 | 5.2 | 12.7 | 155,383 | 3,599 | Philippines |
| ... | ... | ... | ... | ... | ... | ... | 100.0 | — | 100.0 | — | — | ... | ... | Pitcairn Island |
| 23,340 | 15.0 | 85.0 | 44.0 | 153,625 | 174,784 | 683.5 | 95.8 | 4.2 | 85.9 | — | 14.1 | 100,147 | 55,428 | Poland |
| 9,258 | 5.4 | 94.6 | 46.6 | 540,167 | 165,667 | 298.5[54] | ... | ... | 96.2[54] | 0.6[54] | 3.2[54] | 104,728 | 199,595 | Portugal |
| ... | ... | ... | ... | ... | ... | 1.5[54] | ... | ... | 80.4[54] | 7.6[54] | 12.0[54] | 60 | 60 | Puerto Rico |
| — | — | — | — | ... | 17,625 | 2.5 | 100.0 | — | 95.9 | 3.7 | 0.4 | — | 1,201 | Qatar |
| 33 | 93.9 | 6.1 | — | ... | 19,532 | 3.0 | 100.0 | — | 66.4 | 33.6 | — | 4,213 | 13,543 | Réunion |
| 24,126 | 18.9 | 81.1 | 36.9 | 302,950 | 122,660 | 237.6 | 75.4 | 24.6 | 100.0 | — | — | — | 18,233 | Romania |
| 5,461 | 95.9 | 4.1 | 0.5 | ... | 1,774 | 0.8 | — | 100.0 | 100.0 | — | — | — | — | Rwanda |
| ... | ... | ... | ... | 11[9] | 857[9] | 1.5 | 100.0 | — | 100.0 | — | — | — | — | St. Christopher and Nevis |
| ... | ... | ... | ... | ... | ... | 0.2 | 100.0 | — | 100.0 | — | — | 1,410 | 6[8] | St. Helena and Ascension |
| ... | ... | ... | ... | 5,227[2,61] | 6,385[3] | 1.0 | 100.0 | — | 97.1 | 2.9 | — | — | 1,190 | St. Lucia |
| ... | ... | ... | ... | ... | ... | 12.5[8] | 100.0 | — | 100.0[8] | — | — | 11,963 | — | St. Pierre and Miquelon |
| ... | ... | ... | ... | ... | 2,984 | 0.5 | 100.0 | — | 100.0 | — | — | — | 690 | St. Vincent |
| ... | ... | ... | ... | ... | ... | — | — | 100.0 | 100.0 | — | — | 49 | 49 | San Marino |
| 6 | — | 100.0 | 100.0 | ... | ... | 4.4 | 100.0 | — | 98.2 | — | 1.8 | — | — | São Tomé and Príncipe |
| ... | ... | ... | ... | ... | 512,289 | 43.7 | 100.0 | — | 80.7 | 18.9 | 0.4 | 2,760 | 73,621 | Saudi Arabia |
| 4,106 | 86.7 | 13.3 | 0.5 | ... | 34,715 | 244.0 | 93.9 | 6.1 | 95.0 | 2.3 | 2.7 | 129,976 | 16,449[8] | Senegal |
| ... | ... | ... | ... | ... | ... | 4.4 | 100.0 | — | 97.8 | — | 1.1 | 1,160 | 75 | Seychelles |
| 7,774 | 98.2 | 1.8 | 0.3 | ... | 1,130 | 53.0 | 68.9 | 31.1 | 96.5 | 1.6 | 1.9 | 6,300 | 1,940 | Sierra Leone |
| ... | ... | ... | ... | 418,626 | 363,315 | 23.0 | 98.8 | 1.2 | 83.9 | 11.2 | 4.9 | 161,943 | 204,376 | Singapore |
| 512 | 41.0 | 59.0 | 59.0 | 18,881 | 2,292 | 44.5 | 100.0 | — | 98.8 | — | — | 22,202 | 655 | Solomon Islands |
| 4,435 | 98.5 | 1.5 | 0.6 | ... | 2,224 | 16.5 | 100.0 | — | 97.2 | 2.8 | — | 1,370 | 200[2] | Somalia |
| 18,944[50] | 37.0[50] | 63.0[50] | 21.8[50] | 237,858[50] | 239,769[50] | 649.9 | 99.9 | 0.1 | 97.6 | 0.9 | 0.9 | 89,819[21] | 143,017[21] | South Africa |
| ... | ... | ... | ... | ... | ... | ... | ... | ... | ... | ... | ... | ... | ... | Bophuthatswana |
| ... | ... | ... | ... | ... | ... | ... | ... | ... | ... | ... | ... | ... | ... | Ciskei |
| ... | ... | ... | ... | ... | ... | ... | ... | ... | ... | ... | ... | ... | ... | KwaNdebele |
| ... | ... | ... | ... | ... | ... | ... | ... | ... | ... | ... | ... | ... | ... | Transkei |
| ... | ... | ... | ... | ... | ... | ... | ... | ... | ... | ... | ... | ... | ... | Venda |
| 50 | 50 | 50 | 50 | 50 | 50 | 132.1 | 100.0 | — | 98.8 | 1.2 | — | 21 | 21 | South West Africa/Namibia |
| 13,696 | 13.6 | 86.4 | 26.5 | 379,819 | 584,321 | 1,337.7 | 98.0 | 2.0 | 83.3 | 2.2 | 14.5 | 354,284 | 412,790 | Spain |
| 8,577 | 91.8 | 8.2 | 2.0 | 836 | 25,325 | 175.4 | 81.3 | 18.7 | 97.3 | 2.7 | — | 16,841 | 27,473 | Sri Lanka |
| 19,524 | 90.6 | 9.4 | 0.2 | ... | 22,218 | 26.3 | 1.6 | 98.4 | 100.0 | — | — | — | 860 | Sudan, The |
| 217 | 3.7 | 96.3 | 84.3 | 4,277 | 9,710 | 3.4 | 93.3 | 6.7 | 81.5 | 18.5 | — | 26,540 | 200 | Suriname |
| 2,223 | 25.2 | 74.8 | 14.3 | 83,443 | 730 | — | — | 100.0 | 100.0 | — | — | 21 | 21 | Swaziland |
| 53,339 | 8.3 | 91.7 | 44.5 | 4,930,038 | 556,628 | 247.6 | 95.6 | 4.4 | 98.7 | 1.1 | 0.2 | 80,714 | 244,800 | Sweden |
| 4,965 | 17.5 | 82.5 | 61.3 | 379,023 | 743,664 | 4.0 | — | 100.0 | 100.0 | — | — | 4,966[51] | 193,346[51] | Switzerland |
| 44 | 25.0 | 75.0 | 34.1 | 113 | 111,026 | 5.0 | 20.0 | 80.0 | 99.5 | 0.5 | — | — | 5,710 | Syria |
| 537 | 11.6 | 88.4 | ... | ... | ... | 1,037.7 | 75.8 | 24.2 | ... | ... | ... | 286,956 | 64,985 | Taiwan |
| 42,540 | 96.8 | 3.2 | 0.7 | 758 | 18,100 | 270.9 | 15.1 | 84.9 | 99.7 | 0.1 | 0.1 | 1,080 | 190 | Tanzania |
| 41,276 | 89.8 | 10.2 | 4.4 | 39,102 | 252,817 | 2,123.6 | 92.2 | 7.8 | 73.3 | 9.1 | 10.6 | 675,063 | 138,312 | Thailand |
| 765 | 78.7 | 21.3 | 2.4 | 14[33] | 483 | 15.5 | 95.5 | 4.5 | 100.0 | — | — | 70 | 4,980 | Togo |
| ... | ... | ... | ... | ... | ... | ... | 100.0 | — | 100.0 | — | — | ... | ... | Tokelau |
| 3 | — | 100.0 | 100.0 | ... | 1,604 | 2.0 | 100.0 | — | 100.0 | — | — | 70 | 300 | Tonga |
| 63 | 34.9 | 65.1 | 61.9 | 351[8] | 100,539 | 2.9 | 100.0 | — | 87.2 | 12.8 | — | 510 | 7,891 | Trinidad and Tobago |
| 2,768 | 96.4 | 3.6 | 0.1 | 81[15] | 117,235 | 88.9 | 100.0 | — | 85.3 | 2.4 | 12.2 | 34,001 | 688 | Tunisia |
| 18,446 | 67.7 | 32.3 | 21.5 | 50,770 | 104,964 | 576.1 | 92.5 | 7.5 | 96.3 | 2.5 | 1.2 | 61,365 | 1,080 | Turkey |
| ... | ... | ... | ... | ... | ... | 1.3 | 100.0 | — | 23.1 | 20.7 | 56.2 | 3,273 | ... | Turks and Caicos Is. |
| ... | ... | ... | ... | ... | ... | 0.8 | 100.0 | — | 100.0 | — | — | — | 57[9] | Tuvalu |
| 12,488 | 86.9 | 13.1 | 0.6 | 38 | 3,499 | 212.2 | — | 100.0 | 100.0 | — | — | — | — | Uganda |
| 355,700 | 22.6 | 77.4 | 42.4 | 2,726,304 | 889,100 | 10,522.9 | 91.4 | 8.6 | 96.5 | 2.1 | 1.4 | 383,908 | 135,207 | U.S.S.R. |
| ... | ... | ... | ... | ... | ... | 72.4 | 100.0 | — | 99.8 | 0.2 | — | 2,200 | 17,173 | United Arab Emirates |
| 4,428 | 3.6 | 96.4 | 59.1 | 704,137 | 5,123,488 | 832.5 | 98.4 | 1.6 | 91.0 | 5.0 | 4.0 | 342,029 | 943,881 | United Kingdom |
| 448,488 | 22.7 | 77.3 | 47.2 | 5,335,351 | 10,550,932 | 4,766.8 | 98.4 | 1.6 | 72.8 | 7.0 | 20.0 | 1,058,052[60] | 4,051,794[60] | United States |
| 2,975 | 92.8 | 7.2 | 0.9 | 6,646 | 13,656 | 139.1 | 99.5 | 0.5 | 99.4 | 0.1 | 0.5 | 54,150 | 700 | Uruguay |
| 38 | 63.2 | 36.8 | 36.8 | 677 | 451 | 2.9 | 100.0 | — | 53.1 | 16.8 | 30.1 | 7,283 | 7,030 | Vanuatu |
| 1,302 | 51.2 | 48.8 | 46.9 | ... | 286,802 | 282.8 | 94.6 | 5.4 | 90.3 | 3.9 | 5.8 | 114,581 | 4,191 | Venezuela |
| 24,872 | 86.9 | 13.1 | 6.5 | ... | 8,669 | 800.0 | 71.2 | 28.8 | 87.3 | 8.8 | 3.9 | 59,066 | — | Vietnam |
| ... | ... | ... | ... | ... | ... | 0.6 | 100.0 | — | 91.4 | 5.8 | 2.8 | ... | 3,053[4] | Virgin Islands (U.S.) |
| ... | ... | ... | ... | ... | ... | ... | 100.0 | — | 100.0 | — | — | ... | ... | Wallis and Futuna |
| ... | ... | ... | ... | ... | ... | — | ... | ... | ... | ... | ... | ... | ... | West Bank |
| ... | ... | ... | ... | ... | ... | ... | 100.0 | — | ... | ... | ... | ... | ... | Western Sahara |
| 131 | 53.4 | 46.6 | 44.3 | 1,478 | 4,856 | 3.6 | 100.0 | — | 97.4 | 1.3 | 1.3 | ... | 1,610 | Western Samoa |
| 288 | 100.0 | — | — | 29 | 11,294 | 85.2 | 100.0 | — | 93.0 | 1.5 | 5.5 | 11,875 | 270 | Yemen (Aden) |
| ... | ... | ... | ... | ... | ... | 20.6 | 100.0 | — | 98.4 | 1.6 | — | 200 | 3,610 | Yemen (Şan'ā') |
| 15,863 | 25.9 | 74.1 | 53.6 | 402,241 | 278,223 | 75.0 | 65.8 | 34.2 | 96.9 | 0.6 | 2.5 | 14,454 | 40,986 | Yugoslavia |
| 30,491 | 91.7 | 8.3 | 1.5 | 17,846 | 5,539 | 102.0 | 1.0 | 99.0 | 100.0 | — | — | — | 47,211 | Zaire |
| 9,891 | 95.2 | 4.8 | 1.3 | ... | 21,894 | 67.7 | — | 100.0 | 100.0 | — | — | — | 310 | Zambia |
| 7,109 | 80.6 | 19.4 | 5.2 | 8,625 | 15,996 | 17.4 | — | 100.0 | 100.0 | — | — | — | 860 | Zimbabwe |

with 30 or more persons engaged. [41]Excludes quarried sand, stone, and clay. [42]Jersey includes Guernsey. [43]Mostly bauxite and diamonds. [44]Mostly bauxite. [45]Bauxite mining ceased in 1983. [46]Excludes crude petroleum. [47]1979–80. [48]Metals includes energy. [49]Italy includes San Marino. [50]South Africa includes Lesotho and South West Africa/Namibia. [51]Switzerland includes Liechtenstein. [52]Includes cement. [53]Curaçao and Aruba only. [54]Marine catch only. [55]Excludes trade with Cook Islands, Niue, and Tokelau. [56]Excludes the Free Zone of Colón and the Canal Zone. [57]Mostly copper, gold, and silver. [58]Nonmetals includes coal mining. [59]Trade with United States only. [60]United States includes Puerto Rico. [61]Paper and paperboard only. [62]South Africa includes South West Africa/Namibia. [63]1973. [64]Includes refined petroleum and electricity. [65]Bauxite only. [66]Excludes bauxite imports. [67]Exports of stone and marble to Jordan only. [68]1981–82.

# Manufacturing industries

This table summarizes the activity of the manufacturing sectors of the countries of the world, providing figures for value added, number of establishments, and the distribution of value added by size of establishment (as reckoned by number of employees). The data are organized to show the relative importance of six principal sectors for each country and the concentration of activity within each sector. Manufacturing activity is classified according to the scheme outlined in the International Standard Industrial Classification (ISIC).

The sectors for which data have been provided include: (1) food, beverages, and tobacco; (2) textiles, apparel, and leather; (3) wood, paper, chemicals, and related products; (4) primary and fabricated metals and processed minerals; (5) machinery (except electrical) and transport equipment; (6) electrical and electronic machinery. For each of these sectors (for which ISIC definitions are provided below), data are given for their respective share of total manufacturing value added (or, occasionally, some other measure of value, when value added was not reported); for the number of establishments with fewer than and more than 100 employees, and, where it was known, for the share of the sectoral value added represented by these two groups of establishments; and, finally, for the total value added in U.S.$ by all manufacturing.

The collection and publication of national manufacturing data is usually carried out by one of three methods: a full census of manufacturing (usually done every five to ten years for a given country), a periodic survey of manufacturing (usually taken at annual or other regular intervals between censuses), and the onetime sample survey (often limited in geographical, sectoral, or size-of-enterprise coverage). The full census is, naturally, the most complete, but since up to ten years may elapse between such censuses, it has often been necessary to substitute a survey of more recent date, but less complete coverage, in order to provide more timely data. For each country the initial date indicates the year of the survey.

To permit international comparisons U.S. dollar figures for total value added by manufacturing have been given, but should be used only with caution, because of inherent uncertainties with respect to national accounting methods, purchasing power parities, price structures and preferments, exchange rates, and so on.

The majority of countries collect data for establishments, generally referring to each separate physical facility, regardless of the number of separately incorporated legal entities (companies, partnerships, parastatal organizations), any of which may operate more than one facility. Other countries collect data only for enterprises, focusing on the corporate legal

## Manufacturing industries

| country | year | food, beverages, and tobacco (group 1) percent of total value added | 1-99 employees number | percent of value added | 100 or more emp. number | percent of value added | textiles, apparel, and leather (group 2) percent of total value added | 1-99 employees number | percent of value added | 100 or more emp. number | percent of value added | wood, paper, chemicals, and related products (group 3) percent of total value added | 1-99 employees number | percent of value added | 100 or more emp. number | percent of value added |
|---|---|---|---|---|---|---|---|---|---|---|---|---|---|---|---|---|
| Afghanistan[1] | 1983 | 52.0 | 67 | ... | ... | ... | 20.2 | ... | ... | 66 | ... | 22.7 | ... | ... | 61 | ... |
| Albania | 1984 | ... | ... | ... | ... | ... | ... | ... | ... | ... | ... | ... | ... | ... | ... | ... |
| Algeria[3,4] | 1978 | 26.4 | 535[5] | ... | ... | ... | 21.6 | 752[5] | ... | ... | ... | 15.5 | 433[5] | ... | ... | ... |
| American Samoa | ... | ... | ... | ... | ... | ... | ... | ... | ... | ... | ... | ... | ... | ... | ... | ... |
| Andorra | 1972 | ... | 142 | ... | ... | ... | ... | 104 | ... | ... | ... | ... | 49 | ... | ... | ... |
| Angola | 1973 | 50.2 | ... | ... | ... | ... | 6.9 | ... | ... | ... | ... | 28.0 | ... | ... | ... | ... |
| Anguilla | ... | ... | ... | ... | ... | ... | ... | ... | ... | ... | ... | ... | ... | ... | ... | ... |
| Antigua and Barbuda | 1980 | ... | 14 | 100.0 | — | — | ... | 12 | 100.0 | — | — | ... | 15 | 100.0 | — | — |
| Argentina | 1981 | 26.8 | 1,188 | ... | 92 | ... | 9.2 | 1,059 | ... | 75 | ... | 29.6 | 1,394 | ... | 101 | ... |
| Aruba[6] | ... | ... | ... | ... | ... | ... | ... | ... | ... | ... | ... | ... | ... | ... | ... | ... |
| Australia[7] | 1984 | 17.8 | 2,986 | 32.8 | 401 | 67.2 | 7.0 | 2,414 | 44.7 | 253 | 55.3 | 32.4 | 7,463 | 55.3 | 419 | 44.7 |
| Austria[9] | 1983 | 16.7 | 453 | ... | 132 | ... | 9.0 | 857 | ... | 220 | ... | 23.0 | 4,270 | ... | 300 | ... |
| Bahamas, The[11] | 1978 | 27.6 | ... | ... | ... | ... | 0.3 | ... | ... | ... | ... | 57.9 | ... | ... | ... | ... |
| Bahrain | 1982 | ... | ... | ... | ... | ... | ... | ... | ... | ... | ... | ... | ... | ... | ... | ... |
| Bangladesh[12] | 1982 | 26.3 | 525 | ... | ... | ... | 32.8 | ... | ... | 1,443 | ... | 23.1 | 712 | ... | ... | ... |
| Barbados | 1984 | 30.8 | 40 | 47.2 | 10 | 52.8 | 11.4 | 37 | 25.1 | 7 | 74.9 | 20.3 | 76 | 80.3 | 3 | 19.7 |
| Belgium[13] | 1983 | 19.0 | 6,964 | ... | ... | ... | 8.4[14] | 3,728 | ... | ... | ... | 27.3[15] | 5,883 | ... | ... | ... |
| Belize | ... | ... | ... | ... | ... | ... | ... | ... | ... | ... | ... | ... | ... | ... | ... | ... |
| Benin | 1978 | 59.7 | ... | ... | ... | ... | 12.0 | ... | ... | ... | ... | 11.7 | ... | ... | ... | ... |
| Bermuda | ... | ... | ... | ... | ... | ... | ... | ... | ... | ... | ... | ... | ... | ... | ... | ... |
| Bhutan | ... | ... | ... | ... | ... | ... | ... | ... | ... | ... | ... | ... | ... | ... | ... | ... |
| Bolivia[4,9] | 1982 | 41.5 | 274 | ... | ... | ... | 7.1 | 305 | ... | ... | ... | 7.9 | 439 | ... | ... | ... |
| Botswana[13,18] | 1984 | 51.2 | 43 | ... | ... | ... | 13.2 | 58 | ... | ... | ... | 4.8 | 67 | ... | ... | ... |
| Brazil[9] | 1980 | 17.0 | 26,226 | 38.6 | 1,272 | 61.4 | 10.9 | 14,325 | 23.8 | 1,913 | 76.2 | 30.8 | 27,752 | 30.5 | 1,925 | 69.5 |
| British Virgin Islands | 1978 | ... | 1 | 100.0 | — | — | — | — | — | ... | ... | ... | 2 | 100.0 | — | — |
| Brunei[19] | 1980 | ... | 29 | 100.0 | — | — | 13.5 | 76 | 100.0 | — | — | 5.4 | 60 | 100.0 | — | — |
| Bulgaria[4,11,20] | 1984 | 21.6 | ... | ... | 266 | ... | ... | ... | ... | 244 | ... | ... | ... | ... | 258 | ... |
| Burkina Faso[4] | 1979 | 54.7 | 14 | ... | 2 | ... | 8.0 | 4 | ... | 2 | ... | 33.6 | 27 | ... | ... | ... |
| Burma | 1983 | ... | ... | ... | ... | ... | ... | ... | ... | ... | ... | ... | ... | ... | ... | ... |
| Burundi | 1983 | ... | ... | ... | ... | ... | ... | ... | ... | ... | ... | ... | ... | ... | ... | ... |
| Cameroon[4,9,22] | 1979 | 52.4 | 30 | ... | ... | ... | 13.0 | ... | ... | 35 | ... | 12.6 | 66 | ... | ... | ... |
| Canada | 1983 | 15.6 | 2,991 | ... | 518 | ... | 6.7 | 3,302 | ... | 523 | ... | 34.6 | 11,284 | ... | 1,065 | ... |
| Cape Verde | 1983 | 100.0 | ... | ... | ... | ... | — | ... | ... | ... | ... | — | ... | ... | ... | ... |
| Cayman Islands | ... | ... | ... | ... | ... | ... | ... | ... | ... | ... | ... | ... | ... | ... | ... | ... |
| Central African Republic[4,13] | 1982 | 65.7 | 17 | ... | ... | ... | -3.7 | ... | ... | 4 | ... | 16.9 | 9 | ... | ... | ... |
| Chad | 1975 | 44.9 | ... | ... | ... | ... | 39.7 | ... | ... | ... | ... | 3.9 | ... | ... | ... | ... |
| Chile[9,23] | 1983 | 27.7 | ... | ... | 287 | ... | 6.0 | ... | ... | 165 | ... | 30.2 | ... | ... | 284 | ... |
| China[1,4] | 1983 | 14.4 | 62,547 | ... | ... | ... | 18.4 | ... | ... | 24,794 | ... | 18.9 | ... | ... | 43,569 | ... |
| Christmas Island | ... | ... | ... | ... | ... | ... | ... | ... | ... | ... | ... | ... | ... | ... | ... | ... |
| Cocos (Keeling) Islands | ... | ... | ... | ... | ... | ... | ... | ... | ... | ... | ... | — | ... | ... | — | — |
| Colombia[9,12] | 1983 | 35.0 | 1,220 | ... | ... | ... | 12.7 | 1,639 | ... | ... | ... | 28.4 | 1,563 | ... | ... | ... |
| Comoros | 1983 | ... | ... | ... | ... | ... | ... | ... | ... | ... | ... | ... | ... | ... | ... | ... |
| Congo | 1985 | 51.1 | ... | ... | ... | ... | 1.4 | ... | ... | ... | ... | 36.7 | ... | ... | ... | ... |
| Cook Islands[24] | 1978 | 100.0 | 15 | ... | 2 | ... | — | ... | ... | ... | ... | ... | ... | ... | ... | ... |
| Costa Rica[9,25] | 1983 | 41.2 | ... | ... | 44 | ... | 10.0 | ... | ... | 50 | ... | 35.2 | 119 | ... | ... | ... |
| Côte d'Ivoire[4,9,20] | 1983 | 31.2 | 298 | ... | ... | ... | 17.3 | ... | ... | 73 | ... | 28.0 | 268 | ... | ... | ... |
| Cuba[4] | 1984 | 61.8 | ... | ... | 337[26] | ... | 4.1 | ... | ... | 43 | ... | 11.8 | ... | ... | 87 | ... |
| Cyprus[9] | 1984 | 28.3 | 721 | 39.3 | 18 | 60.7 | 26.7 | 1,753 | 73.2 | 24 | 26.8 | 25.1 | 1,934 | 82.0 | 7 | 18.0 |
| Czechoslovakia[4] | 1984 | 8.3 | ... | ... | 122 | ... | 11.0 | ... | ... | 86 | ... | 18.1 | ... | ... | 136 | ... |
| Denmark[13,27] | 1984 | 24.0 | 841 | ... | ... | ... | 5.3 | 717 | ... | ... | ... | 27.9 | 2,213 | ... | ... | ... |
| Djibouti | 1983 | ... | ... | ... | ... | ... | ... | ... | ... | ... | ... | ... | ... | ... | ... | ... |
| Dominica | 1984 | ... | ... | ... | ... | ... | ... | ... | ... | ... | ... | ... | ... | ... | ... | ... |
| Dominican Republic[9,26,28] | 1983 | 60.6 | ... | ... | 1,069 | ... | 6.9 | 225 | ... | ... | ... | 21.3 | 346 | ... | ... | ... |
| Ecuador[9,12] | 1982 | 32.3 | 357 | ... | ... | ... | 13.6 | 240 | ... | ... | ... | 28.5 | 399 | ... | ... | ... |
| Egypt[9,12] | 1981 | 18.3 | 2,521 | ... | ... | ... | 25.6 | ... | ... | 1,309 | ... | 23.6 | ... | ... | 643 | ... |
| El Salvador[9] | 1983 | 35.9 | 100 | ... | ... | ... | 18.1 | 107 | ... | ... | ... | 33.6 | 134 | ... | ... | ... |
| Equatorial Guinea | ... | ... | ... | ... | ... | ... | ... | ... | ... | ... | ... | ... | ... | ... | ... | ... |
| Ethiopia[9,12] | 1982 | 50.2 | ... | ... | 164 | ... | 24.7 | ... | ... | 90 | ... | 18.5 | ... | ... | 106 | ... |
| Faeroe Islands[1] | 1977 | 45.6 | ... | ... | ... | ... | ... | ... | ... | ... | ... | ... | ... | ... | ... | ... |
| Falkland Islands | ... | ... | ... | ... | ... | ... | ... | ... | ... | ... | ... | ... | ... | ... | ... | ... |

entity but often combining data for several separate, and smaller, establishments. When only a single sectoral enterprise or establishment total was available, the *average* size of these establishments was calculated (since the total number of employees in the sector was known), and the figure for number of establishments was placed in the table above or below the 100-employee cutoff accordingly. Such figures are given in italics.

Another impediment to international comparability in terms of size of establishment is the size limit each country establishes as the minimum reporting unit for such surveys. For a small country it may be both feasible and desirable to survey all establishments, however small. For larger countries, the cost to collect and analyze data for all establishments may be prohibitively high, and, moreover, interest from a development point of view may be exclusively in middle and large-scale industry, that needed to permit replacement of imported goods with domestic manufactures. Thus, when the distributions of number of establishments are examined, it should be noted (and has been footnoted wherever possible) when such limits in coverage may be applicable.

In terms of the industrial groups implied by the names of the manufacturing sectors used here, the content of each sector is usually defined by the two- or three-digit level of classification in the ISIC system:

| group | EB category | ISIC code (-s) | remarks |
|---|---|---|---|
| 1. | Food, beverages, and tobacco | 31 | |
| 2. | Textiles, apparel, and leather | 32 | |
| 3. | Wood, paper, chemicals, and related products | 33 | wood and furniture |
| | | 34 | paper and products; printing and publishing |
| | | 35 | industrial chemicals, pharmaceuticals, petroleum and products, rubber, plastics |
| 4. | Primary and fabricated metals and processed minerals | 36 | pottery, china, glass |
| | | 37 | iron; steel; nonferrous metals |
| | | 381 | metal products |
| 5. | Machinery (except electrical) and transport equipment | 382 + 384 minus 3825 | machinery and transport equipment minus office equipment and computers |
| 6. | Electrical and electronic machinery | 383 + 3825 | electrical and electronic equipment, plus office equipment and computers |

It should be noted that these groups do not account for ISIC groups 385 and 390 (professional goods and other industries, respectively).

| primary and fabricated metals; proc. minerals (group 4) | | | | | machinery (except elec.) and transport equip. (group 5) | | | | | electrical and electronic machinery (group 6) | | | | | total manufacturing value added (U.S.$'000,-000) | country |
|---|---|---|---|---|---|---|---|---|---|---|---|---|---|---|---|---|
| percent of total value added | establishments | | | | percent of total value added | establishments | | | | percent of total value added | establishments | | | | | |
| | 1–99 employees | | 100 or more emp. | | | 1–99 employees | | 100 or more emp. | | | 1–99 employees | | 100 or more emp. | | | |
| | number | percent of value added | number | percent of value added | | number | percent of value added | number | percent of value added | | number | percent of value added | number | percent of value added | | |
| 2.3[2] | ... | ... | 16[2] | ... | 2 | ... | ... | 2 | ... | 2 | ... | ... | 2 | ... | 202 | Afghanistan |
| 36.5[5] | 337[5] | ... | ... | ... | ... | ... | ... | ... | ... | 5 | 5 | ... | ... | ... | 1,100 | Albania |
| ... | ... | ... | ... | ... | 5 | 5 | ... | ... | ... | 5 | ... | ... | ... | ... | 2,674 | Algeria |
| ... | 38 | ... | ... | ... | ... | 25 | ... | ... | ... | ... | 83 | ... | ... | ... | ... | American Samoa |
| | | | | | | | | | | | | | | | | Andorra |
| 10.9 | ... | ... | ... | ... | 3.0 | ... | ... | ... | ... | 1.1 | ... | ... | ... | ... | 593 | Angola |
| ... | ... | ... | ... | ... | ... | ... | ... | ... | ... | ... | ... | ... | ... | ... | ... | Anguilla |
| | 10 | 100.0 | — | | ... | ... | ... | ... | | — | ... | ... | — | | | Antigua and Barbuda |
| 11.0 | 206 | ... | 21 | ... | 12.1 | ... | ... | 151 | ... | 3.0 | ... | ... | 29 | ... | 15,883 | Argentina |
| | | | | | | | | | | | | | | | | Aruba[6] |
| 23.2 | 6,020 | 35.0 | 357 | 65.0 | 26.6[8] | 6,744[8] | 34.1[8] | 554[8] | 65.9[8] | 8 | 8 | 8 | 8 | 8 | 31,670 | Australia |
| 25.0 | 759 | ... | 155 | ... | 13.6[10] | 965 | ... | 202 | ... | 10.4[10] | 300 | ... | 114 | ... | 13,516 | Austria |
| 13.5 | ... | ... | ... | ... | 0.7 | ... | ... | ... | ... | | ... | ... | ... | ... | 30 | Bahamas, The |
| | ... | ... | ... | ... | | ... | ... | ... | ... | | ... | ... | ... | ... | 400 | Bahrain |
| 11.7 | 365 | ... | ... | ... | 2.3 | 153 | ... | ... | ... | 2.9 | ... | ... | 60 | ... | 666 | Bangladesh |
| 36.0[2] | 50[2] | 62.4[2] | 7[2] | 37.6[2] | 2 | 2 | 2 | 2 | 2 | 2 | 2 | 2 | 2 | 2 | 116 | Barbados |
| 41.3[2, 16] | 4,651 | ... | ... | ... | 2 | 1,343 | ... | ... | ... | 2 | ... | ... | 628 | ... | 18,272 | Belgium |
| | ... | ... | ... | ... | | ... | ... | ... | ... | — | ... | ... | — | | ... | Belize |
| 4.8 | ... | ... | ... | ... | 11.8[17] | ... | ... | ... | ... | 17 | ... | ... | ... | ... | 46 | Benin |
| ... | ... | ... | ... | ... | ... | ... | ... | ... | ... | ... | ... | ... | ... | ... | ... | Bermuda |
| ... | ... | ... | ... | ... | ... | ... | ... | ... | ... | ... | ... | ... | ... | ... | ... | Bhutan |
| 42.1 | 155 | ... | ... | ... | 0.4[10] | 26 | ... | — | | 0.4[10] | 14 | ... | ... | ... | 821 | Bolivia |
| 4.2[2] | 68[2] | ... | ... | ... | 2 | 2 | ... | — | | 2 | 2 | ... | ... | ... | 74 | Botswana |
| 17.9 | 25,084 | 25.3 | 1,641 | 74.7 | 15.6 | 9,268 | 18.0 | 1,651 | 82.0 | 5.3 | 2,245 | 48.7 | 558 | 51.3 | 77,648 | Brazil |
| ... | 4 | 100.0 | — | | — | ... | ... | — | | ... | ... | ... | ... | ... | ... | British Virgin Islands |
| | 70[2] | 100.0[2] | ... | ... | 2 | 2 | 2 | — | | ... | 2 | 2 | — | | ... | Brunei |
| 49.4[2] | ... | ... | 237 | ... | 2 | ... | ... | 932[17, 21] | ... | 2 | ... | ... | 17 | ... | ... | Bulgaria |
| 3.7 | 9 | ... | ... | ... | ... | ... | ... | ... | ... | ... | ... | ... | ... | ... | 68 | Burkina Faso |
| ... | ... | ... | ... | ... | ... | ... | ... | ... | ... | ... | ... | ... | ... | ... | 831 | Burma |
| ... | ... | ... | ... | ... | ... | ... | ... | ... | ... | ... | ... | ... | ... | ... | 110 | Burundi |
| 10.1 | ... | ... | 9 | ... | 4.7 | ... | ... | 8 | ... | 1.7 | ... | ... | 9 | ... | 340 | Cameroon |
| 16.6 | 6,862 | ... | 508 | ... | 16.4 | 2,605 | ... | 381 | ... | 7.2 | 977 | ... | 258 | ... | 66,353 | Canada |
| | ... | ... | ... | ... | — | ... | ... | ... | ... | — | ... | ... | ... | ... | 5 | Cape Verde |
| | ... | ... | ... | ... | | ... | ... | ... | ... | | ... | ... | ... | ... | ... | Cayman Islands |
| 10.9[2] | 8[2] | ... | ... | ... | 2 | 2 | ... | ... | ... | 2 | 2 | ... | ... | ... | 14 | Central African Republic |
| 11.5 | ... | ... | ... | ... | ... | ... | ... | ... | ... | ... | ... | ... | ... | ... | 77 | Chad |
| 32.5 | ... | ... | 138 | ... | 2.2 | ... | ... | 46 | ... | 1.2 | ... | ... | 22 | ... | 4,695 | Chile |
| 16.2 | ... | ... | 49,252 | ... | 26.1[17] | ... | ... | 101,649[17] | ... | 17 | ... | ... | 17 | ... | ... | China |
| | ... | ... | ... | ... | | ... | ... | ... | ... | | ... | ... | ... | ... | ... | Christmas Island |
| — | — | | — | | — | — | | — | | — | — | | — | | ... | Cocos (Keeling) Islands |
| 14.1 | 991 | ... | ... | ... | 5.0 | 505 | ... | ... | ... | 3.3 | 188 | ... | ... | ... | 6,971 | Colombia |
| ... | ... | ... | ... | ... | — | — | | — | | — | ... | ... | ... | ... | 5 | Comoros |
| 10.8[2] | ... | ... | ... | ... | 2 | ... | ... | ... | ... | 2 | ... | ... | ... | ... | 101 | Congo |
| 7.0 | 42 | ... | ... | ... | 3.2[10] | 14 | ... | ... | ... | 3.0[10] | 19 | ... | ... | ... | 657 | Cook Islands / Costa Rica |
| 21.2[2] | 79 | ... | ... | ... | 2 | 2 | ... | ... | ... | 2 | 2 | ... | ... | ... | 916 | Côte d'Ivoire |
| 5.9 | ... | ... | 82 | ... | 10.3[10] | ... | ... | 134[10] | ... | 1.1[10] | ... | ... | 18[10] | ... | 4,786 | Cuba |
| 12.7 | 860 | 71.4 | 6 | 28.6 | 4.2 | 253 | 79.4 | 2 | 20.6 | 1.6 | 40 | 74.1 | 1 | 25.9 | 365 | Cyprus |
| 22.0 | ... | ... | 151 | ... | 31.6[10] | ... | ... | 212[10] | ... | 6.4[10] | ... | ... | 47[10] | ... | ... | Czechoslovakia |
| 14.0 | 1,239 | ... | ... | ... | 18.4[10] | 1,164 | ... | ... | ... | 5.9[10] | 299 | ... | ... | ... | 9,749 | Denmark |
| ... | ... | ... | ... | ... | ... | ... | ... | ... | ... | — | ... | ... | ... | ... | 24 | Djibouti |
| ... | ... | ... | ... | ... | ... | ... | ... | ... | ... | | ... | ... | ... | ... | 5 | Dominica |
| 9.7 | 138 | ... | ... | ... | 0.5[10] | 10[10] | ... | ... | ... | 0.8[10] | 17[10] | ... | ... | ... | 1,503 | Dominican Republic |
| 17.1 | 243 | ... | ... | ... | 2.2 | 58 | ... | ... | ... | 4.4 | 47 | ... | ... | ... | 1,058 | Ecuador |
| 18.5 | ... | ... | 1,125 | ... | 7.8 | ... | ... | 118 | ... | 5.8 | ... | ... | 48 | ... | 2,652 | Egypt |
| 7.2 | 43 | ... | ... | ... | 1.4 | 14 | ... | ... | ... | 2.3 | 10 | ... | ... | ... | 580 | El Salvador |
| ... | ... | ... | ... | ... | ... | ... | ... | ... | ... | ... | ... | ... | ... | ... | ... | Equatorial Guinea |
| 6.5 | ... | ... | 56 | ... | — | — | | — | | 1.4 | 3 | ... | ... | ... | 445 | Ethiopia |
| ... | ... | ... | ... | ... | ... | ... | ... | ... | ... | ... | ... | ... | ... | ... | 122 | Faeroe Islands |
| ... | ... | ... | ... | ... | ... | ... | ... | ... | ... | ... | ... | ... | ... | ... | ... | Falkland Islands |

## Manufacturing industries (continued)

| country | year | food, beverages, and tobacco (group 1) percent of total value added | 1–99 employees number | 1–99 percent of value added | 100 or more emp. number | 100+ percent of value added | textiles, apparel, and leather (group 2) percent of total value added | 1–99 employees number | 1–99 percent of value added | 100 or more emp. number | 100+ percent of value added | wood, paper, chemicals, and related products (group 3) percent of total value added | 1–99 employees number | 1–99 percent of value added | 100 or more emp. number | 100+ percent of value added |
|---|---|---|---|---|---|---|---|---|---|---|---|---|---|---|---|---|
| Fiji[9] | 1983 | 44.8 | 120 | ... | ... | ... | 3.9 | 142 | ... | ... | ... | 30.1 | 225 | ... | ... | ... |
| Finland[13,29,30] | 1984 | 12.5 | 1,007 | ... | 141 | ... | 6.5 | 752 | ... | 186 | ... | 42.1 | 2,015 | ... | 432 | ... |
| France[9] | 1984 | 18.0 | ... | ... | ... | ... | 6.6 | ... | ... | ... | ... | 25.0 | ... | ... | ... | ... |
| French Guiana | | ... | ... | ... | ... | ... | ... | ... | ... | ... | ... | ... | ... | ... | ... | ... |
| French Polynesia | 1980 | ... | ... | ... | ... | ... | ... | ... | ... | ... | ... | ... | ... | ... | ... | ... |
| Gabon | 1978 | 17.5 | 145 | ... | ... | ... | 2.8 | 1,482[31] | ... | ... | ... | 41.9 | 64 | ... | ... | ... |
| Gambia, The[9,28] | 1982 | 74.4 | ... | ... | 13 | ... | 3.6 | 2 | ... | ... | ... | 1.7 | 4 | ... | ... | ... |
| Gaza Strip[32] | 1985 | 13.9 | 107 | ... | ... | ... | 20.4 | 536 | ... | ... | ... | 65.7[33] | 986[33] | ... | ... | ... |
| Germany, East[1,4] | 1984 | 16.3 | ... | ... | 558 | ... | 83.7[34] | ... | ... | 3,028[34] | ... | [34] | ... | ... | 34 | ... |
| Germany, West | 1983 | 12.2 | 3,439 | ... | 1,157 | ... | 4.7 | 3,886 | ... | 1,323 | ... | 26.2 | 9,001 | ... | 2,865 | ... |
| Ghana[9,35] | 1983 | 53.1 | ... | ... | 74 | ... | 5.7 | ... | ... | 55 | ... | 24.6 | ... | ... | 164 | ... |
| Gibraltar | | ... | ... | ... | ... | ... | ... | ... | ... | ... | ... | ... | ... | ... | ... | ... |
| Greece[13,22,36] | 1981 | 19.2 | 21,202 | ... | 143 | ... | 21.2 | 30,491 | ... | 254 | ... | 22.6 | 29,689 | ... | 148 | ... |
| Greenland | | ... | ... | ... | ... | ... | ... | ... | ... | ... | ... | ... | ... | ... | ... | ... |
| Grenada[1] | 1984 | 76.2 | 16 | ... | ... | ... | 15.9 | 7 | ... | ... | ... | 7.9[33] | 11[33] | ... | ... | ... |
| Guadeloupe | 1980 | ... | ... | ... | ... | ... | ... | ... | ... | ... | ... | ... | ... | ... | ... | ... |
| Guam | | ... | ... | ... | ... | ... | ... | ... | ... | ... | ... | ... | ... | ... | ... | ... |
| Guatemala[3,28] | 1984 | 42.1 | 577 | ... | ... | ... | 10.0 | 388 | ... | ... | ... | 35.5 | 545 | ... | ... | ... |
| Guernsey | | ... | ... | ... | ... | ... | ... | ... | ... | ... | ... | ... | ... | ... | ... | ... |
| Guinea | 1983 | ... | ... | ... | ... | ... | ... | ... | ... | ... | ... | ... | ... | ... | ... | ... |
| Guinea-Bissau | 1983 | ... | ... | ... | ... | ... | ... | ... | ... | ... | ... | ... | ... | ... | ... | ... |
| Guyana[28,37] | 1981 | 36.7 | 31 | ... | ... | ... | 63.3[34] | 8 | ... | ... | ... | [34] | 20 | ... | ... | ... |
| Haiti[9] | 1984 | 39.3 | 550 | ... | ... | ... | 14.7 | 138 | ... | ... | ... | 46.0[33] | 97 | ... | ... | ... |
| Honduras | 1975 | 56.1 | 233 | ... | ... | ... | 9.9 | 198 | ... | ... | ... | 23.0 | 280 | ... | ... | ... |
| Hong Kong[9,18] | 1984 | 5.2 | 1,007 | ... | ... | ... | 39.5 | 15,086 | ... | ... | ... | 16.6 | 13,343 | ... | ... | ... |
| Hungary[4,25] | 1984 | 9.6 | 1,977 | ... | 194 | ... | 11.2 | 14,483 | ... | 258 | ... | 23.5 | 5,229 | ... | 225 | ... |
| Iceland[9,20] | 1983 | 52.9 | 824 | ... | ... | ... | 7.7 | 235 | ... | ... | ... | 17.3 | 782 | ... | ... | ... |
| India[13,39] | 1982 | 10.4 | 25,597 | ... | ... | ... | 15.6 | ... | ... | 13,426 | ... | 25.5 | 17,053 | ... | ... | ... |
| Indonesia[13,40,41] | 1984 | 28.4 | ... | ... | 2,356 | ... | 15.2 | ... | ... | 1,979 | ... | 25.5 | ... | ... | 2,047 | ... |
| Iran[9,12] | 1983 | 14.8 | 1,070 | ... | ... | ... | 23.1 | ... | ... | 1,200 | ... | 16.4 | 973 | ... | ... | ... |
| Iraq | 1981 | 27.9 | 3,775 | ... | ... | ... | 15.1 | 7,797 | ... | ... | ... | 17.2 | 4,769 | ... | ... | ... |
| Ireland[13,42] | 1981 | 28.3 | 959 | ... | ... | ... | 8.3 | 722 | ... | ... | ... | 26.9 | 1,484 | ... | ... | ... |
| Isle of Man | | ... | ... | ... | ... | ... | ... | ... | ... | ... | ... | ... | ... | ... | ... | ... |
| Israel[9,19,28,43] | 1984 | 12.3 | 1,027 | ... | ... | ... | 11.2 | 1,957 | ... | ... | ... | 23.2 | 3,477 | ... | ... | ... |
| Italy[4,41] | 1982 | 5.7 | ... | ... | 2,056 | ... | 12.6 | 5,973 | ... | ... | ... | 25.4 | ... | ... | 5,834 | ... |
| Jamaica[9,22,44] | 1983 | 44.6 | 308 | ... | ... | ... | 5.0 | 157 | ... | ... | ... | 37.7 | 333 | ... | ... | ... |
| Japan[45] | 1983 | 9.6 | 49,593 | 50.1 | 1,824 | 49.9 | 5.9 | 73,918 | 70.1 | 1,610 | 29.9 | 26.1 | 92,706 | 54.3 | 2,366 | 45.7 |
| Jersey | 1984 | ... | ... | ... | ... | ... | ... | ... | ... | ... | ... | ... | ... | ... | ... | ... |
| Jordan[13] | 1983 | 21.9 | 640 | ... | ... | ... | 5.7 | 588 | ... | ... | ... | 34.6 | 981 | ... | ... | ... |
| Kampuchea | | ... | ... | ... | ... | ... | ... | ... | ... | ... | ... | ... | ... | ... | ... | ... |
| Kenya[13,23] | 1982 | 38.3 | ... | ... | 126 | ... | 12.5 | ... | ... | 121 | ... | 26.7 | ... | ... | 178 | ... |
| Kiribati | 1982 | ... | ... | ... | ... | ... | ... | ... | ... | ... | ... | ... | ... | ... | ... | ... |
| Korea, North | | ... | ... | ... | ... | ... | ... | ... | ... | ... | ... | ... | ... | ... | ... | ... |
| Korea, South[9,28,46] | 1983 | 15.8 | 4,164 | 13.0 | 281 | 87.0 | 16.6 | 8,950 | 20.7 | 1,309 | 79.3 | 25.2 | 19,642[33] | 18.2[33] | 1,817[33] | 81.8[33] |
| Kuwait[9] | 1982 | 7.3 | 488 | ... | ... | ... | 6.1 | 1,942 | ... | ... | ... | 59.2 | 510 | ... | ... | ... |
| Laos | | ... | ... | ... | ... | ... | ... | ... | ... | ... | ... | ... | ... | ... | ... | ... |
| Lebanon | | ... | ... | ... | ... | ... | ... | ... | ... | ... | ... | ... | ... | ... | ... | ... |
| Lesotho | 1983 | ... | ... | ... | ... | ... | ... | ... | ... | ... | ... | ... | ... | ... | ... | ... |
| Liberia | 1983 | ... | ... | ... | ... | ... | ... | ... | ... | ... | ... | ... | ... | ... | ... | ... |
| Libya[47] | 1979 | 15.8 | 102 | ... | ... | ... | 4.1 | 27 | ... | ... | ... | 80.1[33] | 51 | ... | ... | ... |
| Liechtenstein | 1975 | ... | 43 | ... | 1 | ... | ... | 22 | ... | 2 | ... | ... | 69 | ... | 2 | ... |
| Luxembourg[4,13,41] | 1982 | 6.2 | 33 | ... | ... | ... | 2.0 | 10 | ... | ... | ... | 19.5 | ... | ... | 37 | ... |
| Macau[9,30] | 1983 | 1.5 | 102 | ... | ... | ... | 68.0 | 546 | ... | ... | ... | 15.2 | 244 | ... | ... | ... |
| Madagascar[9] | 1982 | 28.0 | 98 | ... | ... | ... | 50.2 | ... | ... | 45 | ... | 21.8[33] | 99[33] | ... | ... | ... |
| Malawi[20,48] | 1983 | 50.4 | ... | ... | 37 | ... | 20.0 | ... | ... | 22 | ... | 20.6 | ... | ... | 34 | ... |
| Malaysia[13] | 1982 | 22.0 | 1,699 | ... | ... | ... | 6.1 | 672 | ... | ... | ... | 32.3 | 3,173 | ... | ... | ... |
| Maldives | | ... | ... | ... | ... | ... | ... | ... | ... | ... | ... | ... | ... | ... | ... | ... |
| Mali | 1981 | 30.0 | ... | ... | ... | ... | 53.0 | ... | ... | ... | ... | 17.0[33] | ... | ... | ... | ... |
| Malta[13] | 1983 | 19.4 | ... | ... | 357 | ... | 31.9 | 192 | ... | ... | ... | 18.6 | 518 | ... | ... | ... |
| Martinique[49] | 1986 | ... | 69 | ... | ... | ... | ... | 142[34] | ... | ... | ... | ... | ... | ... | 34 | ... |
| Mauritania | 1983 | ... | ... | ... | ... | ... | ... | ... | ... | ... | ... | ... | ... | ... | ... | ... |
| Mauritius[9,12,50] | 1984 | 35.2 | 196 | ... | ... | ... | 37.3 | ... | ... | 157 | ... | 11.8 | 107 | ... | ... | ... |
| Mayotte | | ... | ... | ... | ... | ... | ... | ... | ... | ... | ... | ... | ... | ... | ... | ... |
| Mexico[9,19] | 1984 | 22.8 | ... | ... | 476 | ... | 11.3 | ... | ... | 136 | ... | 35.5 | ... | ... | 341 | ... |
| Monaco | | ... | ... | ... | ... | ... | ... | ... | ... | ... | ... | ... | ... | ... | ... | ... |
| Mongolia[11] | 1983 | 25.0 | ... | ... | ... | ... | 36.9 | ... | ... | ... | ... | 21.4 | ... | ... | ... | ... |
| Montserrat | | ... | ... | ... | ... | ... | ... | ... | ... | ... | ... | ... | ... | ... | ... | ... |
| Morocco[11] | 1980 | 32.1 | ... | ... | ... | ... | 14.9 | ... | ... | ... | ... | 18.7 | ... | ... | ... | ... |
| Mozambique | 1972 | 48.1 | 769 | ... | 93 | ... | 14.9 | 5 | ... | 62 | ... | 21.4 | 194 | ... | 110 | ... |
| Nauru | | ... | ... | ... | ... | ... | ... | ... | ... | ... | ... | ... | ... | ... | ... | ... |
| Nepal[12] | 1982 | 69.8 | 3,715 | ... | 58 | ... | 11.5 | 256 | ... | 16 | ... | 12.2 | 477 | ... | 13 | ... |
| Netherlands, The[13,37] | 1980 | 14.7 | 1,242 | ... | 313 | ... | 3.7 | 1,039 | ... | 265 | ... | 46.6 | 1,444 | ... | 322 | ... |
| Netherlands Antilles[6] | 1980 | ... | ... | ... | ... | ... | ... | ... | ... | ... | ... | ... | ... | ... | ... | ... |
| New Caledonia | | ... | ... | ... | ... | ... | ... | ... | ... | ... | ... | ... | ... | ... | ... | ... |
| New Zealand | 1981 | 26.2 | 933 | ... | 106 | ... | 10.4 | 1,091 | ... | 89 | ... | 28.7 | 2,347 | ... | 129 | ... |
| Nicaragua[4,9,35] | 1984 | 50.2 | ... | ... | 84 | ... | 12.3 | ... | ... | 59 | ... | 28.0 | 90 | ... | ... | ... |
| Niger | 1980 | 32.5 | ... | ... | 26.2 | ... | ... | ... | ... | ... | ... | 27.1 | ... | ... | ... | ... |
| Nigeria[9,12] | 1980 | 30.6 | ... | ... | 315 | ... | 10.4 | ... | ... | 117 | ... | 25.1 | ... | ... | 468 | ... |
| Niue | | ... | ... | ... | ... | ... | ... | ... | ... | ... | ... | ... | ... | ... | ... | ... |
| Norfolk Island | | ... | ... | ... | ... | ... | ... | ... | ... | ... | ... | ... | ... | ... | ... | ... |
| Norway[9] | 1984 | 14.1 | 2,282 | 56.0 | 96 | 44.0 | 2.8 | 757 | 80.1 | 24 | 19.9 | 33.2 | 4,327 | 45.4 | 194 | 54.6 |
| Oman | | ... | ... | ... | ... | ... | ... | ... | ... | ... | ... | ... | ... | ... | ... | ... |
| Pacific Is., Trust Terr. of the Marshall Islands | | ... | ... | ... | ... | ... | ... | ... | ... | ... | ... | ... | ... | ... | ... | ... |
| Micronesia, Fed. States of | | ... | ... | ... | ... | ... | ... | ... | ... | ... | ... | ... | ... | ... | ... | ... |

| primary and fabricated metals; proc. minerals (group 4) | | | | | machinery (except elec.) and transport equip. (group 5) | | | | | electrical and electronic machinery (group 6) | | | | | total manufac-turing value added (U.S.$'000,000) | country |
|---|---|---|---|---|---|---|---|---|---|---|---|---|---|---|---|---|
| percent of total value added | establishments 1–99 employees number | 1–99 percent of value added | 100 or more emp. number | 100+ percent of value added | percent of total value added | establishments 1–99 employees number | 1–99 percent of value added | 100 or more emp. number | 100+ percent of value added | percent of total value added | establishments 1–99 employees number | 1–99 percent of value added | 100 or more emp. number | 100+ percent of value added | | |
| 20.2[2] | 67 | ... | | | [2] | 34 | ... | ... | ... | [2] | 9 | ... | ... | ... | 89 | Fiji |
| 13.2 | 1,024 | ... | 145 | ... | 16.5 | 896 | ... | 203 | ... | 5.9 | 139 | ... | 55 | ... | 13,419 | Finland |
| 14.5 | ... | ... | ... | ... | 25.9[10] | ... | ... | ... | ... | 7.5[10] | ... | ... | ... | ... | 124,452 | France |
| ... | ... | ... | ... | ... | ... | ... | ... | ... | ... | ... | ... | ... | ... | ... | ... | French Guiana |
| ... | ... | ... | ... | ... | ... | ... | ... | ... | ... | ... | ... | ... | ... | ... | 107 | French Polynesia |
| 37.8[2] | 444[2] | ... | ... | ... | [2] | 2 | ... | ... | ... | [2] | 2 | ... | ... | ... | 175 | Gabon |
| −0.8 | 2 | ... | ... | ... | — | — | — | — | — | — | — | — | — | — | 8 | Gambia, The |
| 33 | 33 | ... | ... | ... | 33 | 33 | ... | ... | ... | 33 | 33 | ... | ... | ... | 31 | Gaza Strip |
| 34 | ... | ... | 34 | ... | 34 | ... | ... | 34 | ... | 34 | ... | ... | 34 | ... | ... | Germany, East |
| 16.3 | 5,340 | ... | 1,044 | ... | 24.4 | 5,750 | ... | 2,590 | ... | 13.4 | 3,562 | ... | 2,063 | ... | 184,293 | Germany, West |
| 14.5 | ... | ... | 38 | ... | 1.4 | ... | ... | 12 | ... | 0.4 | 11 | ... | ... | ... | 1,615 | Ghana |
| ... | ... | ... | ... | ... | ... | ... | ... | ... | ... | ... | ... | ... | ... | ... | ... | Gibraltar |
| 21.0 | 19,921 | ... | 103 | ... | 10.2 | 21,662 | ... | 67 | ... | 5.1 | 5,272 | ... | 36 | ... | 7,409 | Greece |
| 33 | ... | ... | ... | ... | ... | ... | ... | ... | ... | ... | ... | ... | ... | ... | ... | Greenland |
| 33 | 33 | ... | ... | ... | 33 | 33 | ... | ... | ... | 33 | 33 | ... | ... | ... | 12 | Grenada |
| — | — | — | ... | ... | — | — | ... | ... | ... | — | — | ... | — | ... | 91 | Guadeloupe |
| ... | ... | ... | ... | ... | ... | ... | ... | ... | ... | ... | ... | ... | ... | ... | ... | Guam |
| 9.5 | 293 | ... | ... | ... | 0.9 | 53 | ... | ... | ... | 1.5 | 30 | ... | ... | ... | 2,137 | Guatemala |
| ... | ... | ... | ... | ... | ... | ... | ... | ... | ... | ... | ... | ... | ... | ... | ... | Guernsey |
| ... | ... | ... | ... | ... | ... | ... | ... | ... | ... | ... | ... | ... | ... | ... | 67 | Guinea |
| 34 | ... | ... | ... | ... | 34 | ... | ... | ... | ... | 34 | 1 | ... | ... | ... | 1 | Guinea-Bissau |
| 33 | 61 | ... | ... | ... | 33 | 32[17] | ... | ... | ... | 33 | 17 | ... | ... | ... | 53 | Guyana |
| 9.0 | 98 | ... | ... | ... | 0.6 | 11 | ... | ... | ... | 1.1 | 9 | ... | ... | ... | 171 | Haiti |
| 9.1 | 7,355 | ... | ... | ... | 4.1 | 4,072[10] | ... | ... | ... | 17.1 | 2,392[10] | ... | ... | ... | 416[38] | Honduras |
| ... | ... | ... | ... | ... | ... | ... | ... | ... | ... | ... | ... | ... | ... | ... | 7,655 | Hong Kong |
| 15.1 | 300 | ... | 64 | ... | 19.2[10] | 9,418[17] | ... | 312[17] | ... | 13.1[10] | 17 | ... | 17 | ... | 5,184 | Hungary |
| 20.5[2] | 635[2] | ... | ... | ... | [2] | 2 | ... | ... | ... | [2] | 2 | ... | ... | ... | 600 | Iceland |
| 20.9 | 18,056 | ... | ... | ... | 17.7 | 9,901 | ... | ... | ... | 8.7 | 3,763 | ... | ... | ... | 14,788 | India |
| 20.3 | ... | ... | 1,055 | ... | 6.9 | ... | ... | 326 | ... | 3.4 | ... | ... | 115 | ... | 4,361 | Indonesia |
| 24.1 | 3,114 | ... | ... | ... | 14.2[10] | ... | ... | 325[10] | ... | 6.7[10] | ... | ... | 144[10] | ... | 10,615 | Iran |
| 17.3 | 3,534 | ... | ... | ... | 8.7 | 98 | ... | ... | ... | 4.6 | 17 | ... | ... | ... | 6,055 | Iraq |
| 13.5 | 1,078 | ... | ... | ... | 6.3 | 409 | ... | ... | ... | 12.1 | 253 | ... | ... | ... | 5,434 | Ireland |
| ... | ... | ... | ... | ... | ... | ... | ... | ... | ... | ... | ... | ... | ... | ... | ... | Isle of Man |
| 21.9 | 2,978 | ... | ... | ... | 10.5 | 387[10] | ... | ... | ... | 18.9 | 497[10] | ... | ... | ... | 5,893 | Israel |
| 21.9 | ... | ... | 5,890 | ... | 21.9[10] | ... | ... | 3,230[10] | ... | 9.3[10] | ... | ... | 1,127[10] | ... | 75,078 | Italy |
| 12.0[2] | 361[2] | ... | ... | ... | [2] | 2 | ... | ... | ... | [2] | 2 | ... | ... | ... | 659 | Jamaica |
| 18.2 | 79,249 | 43.9 | 2,190 | 56.1 | 20.1 | 51,447 | 27.3 | 2,555 | 62.7 | 16.8 | 27,510 | 19.1 | 2,406 | 80.9 | 360,987 | Japan |
| ... | ... | ... | ... | ... | ... | ... | ... | ... | ... | ... | ... | ... | ... | ... | 27 | Jersey |
| 31.9[2] | 1,374[2] | ... | ... | ... | [2] | 2 | ... | ... | ... | [2] | 2 | ... | ... | ... | 519 | Jordan |
| ... | ... | ... | ... | ... | ... | ... | ... | ... | ... | ... | ... | ... | ... | ... | ... | Kampuchea |
| 8.5 | ... | ... | 76 | ... | 5.9[10] | ... | ... | 33[10] | ... | 7.6[10] | ... | ... | 16[10] | ... | 31 | Kenya |
| ... | ... | ... | ... | ... | ... | ... | ... | ... | ... | ... | — | — | — | — | 1 | Kiribati |
| ... | ... | ... | ... | ... | ... | ... | ... | ... | ... | ... | ... | ... | ... | ... | ... | Korea, North |
| 17.1 | 33 | 33 | 33 | 33 | 12.2 | 33 | 33 | 33 | 33 | 10.3 | 33 | 33 | 33 | 33 | 26,957 | Korea, South |
| 19.8 | 707 | ... | ... | ... | 4.1[10] | 48[10] | ... | ... | ... | 3.2[10] | 25[10] | ... | ... | ... | 1,475 | Kuwait |
| ... | ... | ... | ... | ... | ... | ... | ... | ... | ... | ... | ... | ... | ... | ... | ... | Laos |
| ... | ... | ... | ... | ... | ... | ... | ... | ... | ... | ... | ... | ... | ... | ... | ... | Lebanon |
| ... | ... | ... | ... | ... | ... | ... | ... | ... | ... | ... | ... | ... | ... | ... | 20 | Lesotho |
| 33 | 85 | ... | ... | ... | 33 | 6[17] | ... | ... | ... | 33 | 17 | ... | ... | ... | 50 | Liberia |
| ... | ... | ... | ... | ... | ... | ... | ... | ... | ... | ... | ... | ... | ... | ... | 628 | Libya |
| 60.8 | 96 | ... | 1 | ... | 10.2[10] | 4 | ... | 2 | 26[10] | 1.3[10] | 29 | ... | 2 | ... | ... | Liechtenstein |
| 1.7 | 108 | ... | 45 | ... | 1.8[10] | 44[10] | ... | ... | ... | 4.0[10] | 7[10] | ... | ... | ... | 926 | Luxembourg |
| 33 | 33 | ... | ... | ... | 33 | 33 | ... | 33 | ... | 33 | 33 | ... | ... | ... | 158 | Macau |
| 6.1 | ... | ... | 16 | ... | 1.9 | ... | ... | 2 | ... | 1.1 | 4 | ... | ... | ... | 145 | Madagascar |
| ... | ... | ... | ... | ... | ... | ... | ... | ... | ... | ... | ... | ... | ... | ... | 94 | Malawi |
| 14.8 | 1,220 | ... | ... | ... | 7.7 | 693 | ... | ... | ... | 15.8 | 255 | ... | ... | ... | 3,847 | Malaysia |
| ... | ... | ... | ... | ... | ... | ... | ... | ... | ... | ... | ... | ... | ... | ... | ... | Maldives |
| 33 | ... | ... | ... | ... | 33 | ... | ... | ... | ... | 33 | ... | ... | ... | ... | 102 | Mali |
| 8.1 | 224 | ... | ... | ... | 4.4[10] | 51[10] | ... | ... | ... | 10.5[10] | 35[10] | ... | ... | ... | 256 | Malta |
| ... | 34 | ... | ... | ... | ... | 34 | ... | ... | ... | ... | 34 | ... | ... | ... | 75 | Martinique |
| 7.0 | 59 | ... | ... | ... | 1.7[10] | 16[10] | ... | ... | ... | 1.5[10] | 18[10] | ... | ... | ... | 44 | Mauritania |
| ... | ... | ... | ... | ... | ... | ... | ... | ... | ... | ... | ... | ... | ... | ... | 128 | Mauritius |
| ... | ... | ... | ... | ... | ... | ... | ... | ... | ... | ... | ... | ... | ... | ... | ... | Mayotte |
| 15.4 | ... | ... | 230 | ... | 8.9 | ... | ... | 39 | ... | 3.7 | ... | ... | 74 | ... | 41,202 | Mexico |
| ... | ... | ... | ... | ... | ... | ... | ... | ... | ... | ... | ... | ... | ... | ... | ... | Monaco |
| 14.0[2] | ... | ... | ... | ... | [2] | ... | ... | ... | ... | [2] | ... | ... | ... | ... | ... | Mongolia |
| ... | ... | ... | ... | ... | ... | ... | ... | ... | ... | ... | ... | ... | ... | ... | ... | Montserrat |
| 14.0 | ... | ... | ... | ... | 17.8 | ... | ... | ... | ... | 6.7 | ... | ... | ... | ... | 2,250 | Morocco |
| 12.2 | 113 | ... | 50 | ... | 2.1 | 15 | ... | 16 | ... | 1.3 | 9 | ... | 6 | ... | 457 | Mozambique |
| ... | ... | ... | ... | ... | ... | ... | ... | ... | ... | ... | ... | ... | ... | ... | ... | Nauru |
| 3.3 | 201 | ... | 57 | ... | 1.2 | 42 | ... | 3 | ... | ... | ... | ... | ... | ... | 178 | Nepal |
| 13.0 | 552 | ... | 134 | ... | 10.7[10] | 2,513[17] | ... | 441[17] | ... | 9.6[10] | 17 | ... | 17 | ... | 36,497 | Netherlands, The |
| ... | ... | ... | ... | ... | ... | ... | ... | ... | ... | ... | ... | ... | ... | ... | 302 | Netherlands Antilles[6] |
| ... | ... | ... | ... | ... | ... | ... | ... | ... | ... | ... | ... | ... | ... | ... | ... | New Caledonia |
| 15.1 | 476 | ... | 29 | ... | 11.6 | 2,728 | ... | 125 | ... | 5.1 | ... | ... | ... | ... | 5,068 | New Zealand |
| 7.8 | ... | ... | 39 | ... | 0.7 | 7 | ... | ... | ... | 0.7 | 8 | ... | ... | ... | 1,324 | Nicaragua |
| 14.2[2] | ... | ... | ... | ... | [2] | ... | ... | ... | ... | [2] | ... | ... | ... | ... | 28 | Niger |
| 10.8 | ... | ... | 272 | ... | 21.1 | ... | ... | 39 | ... | 1.7 | ... | ... | 17 | ... | 6,460 | Nigeria |
| ... | ... | ... | ... | ... | ... | ... | ... | ... | ... | ... | ... | ... | ... | ... | ... | Niue |
| ... | ... | ... | ... | ... | ... | ... | ... | ... | ... | ... | ... | ... | ... | ... | ... | Norfolk Island |
| 22.5 | 2,129 | 32.4 | 101 | 67.6 | 19.8[10] | 2,012[10] | 12.2[10] | 139[10] | 87.8[10] | 6.5[10] | 367[10] | 26.5[10] | 46[10] | 73.5[10] | 7,802 | Norway |
| ... | ... | ... | ... | ... | ... | ... | ... | ... | ... | ... | ... | ... | ... | ... | ... | Oman |
| ... | ... | ... | ... | ... | ... | ... | ... | ... | ... | ... | ... | ... | ... | ... | ... | Pacific Is., Trust Terr. of the Marshall Islands |
| ... | ... | ... | ... | ... | ... | ... | ... | ... | ... | ... | ... | ... | ... | ... | ... | Micronesia, Fed. States of |

## Manufacturing industries (continued)

| country | year | food, beverages, and tobacco (group 1) percent of total value added | 1–99 employees number | 1–99 employees percent of value added | 100 or more emp. number | 100 or more emp. percent of value added | textiles, apparel, and leather (group 2) percent of total value added | 1–99 employees number | 1–99 employees percent of value added | 100 or more emp. number | 100 or more emp. percent of value added | wood, paper, chemicals, and related products (group 3) percent of total value added | 1–99 employees number | 1–99 employees percent of value added | 100 or more emp. number | 100 or more emp. percent of value added |
|---|---|---|---|---|---|---|---|---|---|---|---|---|---|---|---|---|
| Northern Mariana Islands | | ... | ... | ... | ... | ... | ... | ... | ... | ... | ... | ... | ... | ... | ... | ... |
| Palau | | ... | ... | ... | ... | ... | ... | ... | ... | ... | ... | ... | ... | ... | ... | ... |
| Pakistan | 1981 | 35.2 | ... | ... | 549 | ... | 21.3 | ... | ... | 1,311 | ... | 23.6 | 663 | ... | ... | ... |
| Panama[9,28] | 1983 | 46.3 | 321 | ... | ... | ... | 7.5 | 95 | ... | ... | ... | 32.2 | 265 | ... | ... | ... |
| Papua New Guinea | 1983 | 56.8 | 124 | ... | ... | ... | 0.5 | 19 | ... | ... | ... | 24.1 | 135 | ... | ... | ... |
| Paraguay | 1982 | 36.0 | ... | ... | ... | ... | 12.0 | ... | ... | ... | ... | 52.0[33] | ... | ... | ... | ... |
| Peru[9] | 1980 | 24.7 | 6,236 | ... | 82 | ... | 12.5 | 8,613 | ... | 106 | ... | 22.1 | 7,476 | ... | 148 | ... |
| Philippines[9] | 1981 | 33.0 | 30,299 | ... | ... | ... | 16.0 | 32,886 | ... | ... | ... | 32.0 | 8,985 | ... | ... | ... |
| Pitcairn Island | | ... | ... | ... | ... | ... | ... | ... | ... | ... | ... | ... | ... | ... | ... | ... |
| Poland[51] | 1984 | 18.6 | 10,656 | ... | ... | ... | 15.0 | 8,132 | ... | ... | ... | 19.2 | ... | ... | 5,084 | ... |
| Portugal[9,25] | 1981 | 20.4 | 10,825 | ... | 212 | ... | 24.2 | 10,387 | ... | 439 | ... | 21.7 | 11,067 | ... | 270 | ... |
| Puerto Rico | 1982 | 11.2 | 296 | 22.7 | 37 | 77.3 | 8.4 | 286 | 25.6 | 131 | 74.4 | 47.5 | 578 | 25.2 | 68 | 74.8 |
| Qatar | 1985 | ... | ... | ... | ... | ... | ... | ... | ... | ... | ... | ... | ... | ... | ... | ... |
| Réunion | 1978 | ... | 35 | ... | ... | ... | ... | 5 | ... | ... | ... | ... | 16 | ... | ... | ... |
| Romania[4,20,51] | 1984 | 11.0 | ... | ... | 299 | ... | 15.0 | ... | ... | 227 | ... | 74.0[33] | ... | ... | 205 | ... |
| Rwanda[4,11,37] | 1981 | 75.7 | ... | ... | 17 | ... | 10.1 | ... | ... | 3 | ... | 5.8 | ... | ... | 17 | ... |
| St. Christopher and Nevis | 1984 | ... | ... | ... | ... | ... | ... | ... | ... | ... | ... | ... | ... | ... | ... | ... |
| St. Helena and Ascension | | ... | ... | ... | ... | ... | ... | ... | ... | ... | ... | ... | ... | ... | ... | ... |
| St. Lucia | 1985 | ... | ... | ... | ... | ... | ... | ... | ... | ... | ... | ... | ... | ... | ... | ... |
| St. Pierre and Miquelon | | ... | ... | ... | ... | ... | ... | ... | ... | ... | ... | ... | ... | ... | ... | ... |
| St. Vincent | 1984 | ... | ... | ... | ... | ... | ... | ... | ... | ... | ... | ... | ... | ... | ... | ... |
| San Marino | 1984 | ... | 34 | ... | ... | ... | ... | 65 | ... | ... | ... | ... | 64 | ... | ... | ... |
| São Tomé and Príncipe | 1983 | ... | ... | ... | ... | ... | ... | ... | ... | ... | ... | ... | ... | ... | ... | ... |
| Saudi Arabia[50] | 1981 | ... | 2,145 | ... | 26 | ... | ... | 8,019 | ... | 2 | ... | ... | 2,751 | ... | 37 | ... |
| Senegal[9,20] | 1983 | 54.4 | ... | ... | 38 | ... | 16.8 | ... | ... | 33 | ... | 4.8 | 66 | ... | ... | ... |
| Seychelles | 1984 | 79.1 | 14 | ... | ... | ... | 2.0 | 2 | ... | ... | ... | 12.0 | 10 | ... | ... | ... |
| Sierra Leone[11] | 1973–74 | 80.3 | ... | ... | ... | ... | 2.7 | ... | ... | ... | ... | 10.8 | ... | ... | ... | ... |
| Singapore[12,13] | 1984 | 5.5 | 319 | ... | ... | ... | 4.3 | 562 | ... | ... | ... | 27.8 | 1,000 | ... | ... | ... |
| Solomon Islands | | ... | ... | ... | ... | ... | ... | ... | ... | ... | ... | ... | ... | ... | ... | ... |
| Somalia[9,11] | 1979 | 17.3 | 75 | ... | ... | ... | 20.3 | 58 | ... | ... | ... | 19.0 | 37 | ... | ... | ... |
| South Africa | 1979 | 14.8 | 1,722 | 16.5 | 457 | 83.5 | 9.8 | 1,733 | 14.9 | 556 | 85.1 | 27.4 | 3,666 | 20.7 | 649 | 79.3 |
| Bophuthatswana | | ... | ... | ... | ... | ... | ... | ... | ... | ... | ... | ... | ... | ... | ... | ... |
| Ciskei | | ... | ... | ... | ... | ... | ... | ... | ... | ... | ... | ... | ... | ... | ... | ... |
| KwaNdebele | | ... | ... | ... | ... | ... | ... | ... | ... | ... | ... | ... | ... | ... | ... | ... |
| Transkei | | ... | ... | ... | ... | ... | ... | ... | ... | ... | ... | ... | ... | ... | ... | ... |
| Venda | | ... | ... | ... | ... | ... | ... | ... | ... | ... | ... | ... | ... | ... | ... | ... |
| South West Africa/Namibia | | ... | ... | ... | ... | ... | ... | ... | ... | ... | ... | ... | ... | ... | ... | ... |
| Spain[13] | 1982 | 17.0 | 44,381 | ... | ... | ... | 9.5 | 14,228 | ... | ... | ... | 27.8 | 43,249 | ... | ... | ... |
| Sri Lanka[13] | 1981 | 32.8 | 204 | ... | ... | ... | 18.2 | ... | ... | 332 | ... | 29.0 | 365 | ... | ... | ... |
| Sudan, The | 1983 | ... | ... | ... | ... | ... | ... | ... | ... | ... | ... | ... | ... | ... | ... | ... |
| Suriname | | ... | ... | ... | ... | ... | ... | ... | ... | ... | ... | ... | ... | ... | 38 | ... |
| Swaziland[13] | 1982 | 44.2 | ... | ... | 14 | ... | 2.2 | 33 | ... | ... | ... | 44.6 | ... | ... | 38 | ... |
| Sweden[13] | 1984 | 9.7 | 696 | ... | 153 | ... | 2.4 | 583 | ... | 67 | ... | 35.4 | 2,806 | ... | 428 | ... |
| Switzerland[53] | 1985 | 17.3 | 3,352 | ... | 149 | ... | 9.0 | 2,699 | ... | 131 | ... | 32.2 | 15,395 | ... | 318 | ... |
| Syria[9,20] | 1984 | 18.6 | 8,029 | ... | ... | ... | 17.7 | 15,126 | ... | ... | ... | 29.0 | 12,783 | ... | ... | ... |
| Taiwan[13] | 1985 | 7.8 | ... | ... | ... | ... | 19.8 | ... | ... | ... | ... | 27.9 | ... | ... | ... | ... |
| Tanzania | 1981 | 20.4[54] | ... | ... | 205 | ... | 29.4[54] | ... | ... | 191 | ... | 25.2[54] | 324 | ... | ... | ... |
| Thailand[9,12] | 1980 | 19.5 | 2,152 | ... | ... | ... | 26.0 | ... | ... | 1,462 | ... | 22.8 | 2,118 | ... | ... | ... |
| Togo[4,9] | 1979 | 62.1 | ... | ... | 12 | ... | 7.4 | 3 | ... | ... | ... | 13.6 | 26 | ... | ... | ... |
| Tokelau | | ... | ... | ... | ... | ... | ... | ... | ... | ... | ... | ... | ... | ... | ... | ... |
| Tonga | 1981 | 73.8 | 33 | 100.0 | — | — | 1.1 | 11 | 100.0 | — | — | 11.7 | 23 | 100.0 | — | — |
| Trinidad and Tobago[11,55] | 1980 | 13.0 | ... | ... | 97 | ... | 4.0 | 83 | ... | ... | ... | 82.8[33] | 225 | ... | ... | ... |
| Tunisia | 1981 | 14.1 | 283 | 35.9 | 35 | 64.1 | 16.9 | 276 | 26.4 | 124 | 73.6 | 22.2 | 253 | 26.8 | 49 | 73.2 |
| Turkey[9,56] | 1984 | 20.5 | 1,595 | 16.3 | 304 | 83.7 | 15.9 | 1,521 | 18.3 | 326 | 81.7 | 29.4 | 1,432 | 9.2 | 242 | 90.8 |
| Turks and Caicos Islands | | ... | ... | ... | ... | ... | ... | ... | ... | ... | ... | ... | ... | ... | ... | ... |
| Tuvalu | | ... | ... | ... | ... | ... | ... | ... | ... | ... | ... | ... | ... | ... | ... | ... |
| Uganda[11,13] | 1971 | 43.3 | 148 | 19.7 | 24 | 39.0 | 22.8 | 48 | 8.7 | 9 | 34.1 | 13.2 | 113 | 61.8 | 21 | 38.0 |
| U.S.S.R.[3,4] | 1983 | 20.3 | 9,491 | ... | ... | ... | 17.4 | 7,842 | ... | ... | ... | 15.7 | ... | ... | 4,057 | ... |
| United Arab Emirates[12,29] | 1978 | 8.0 | 73 | ... | ... | ... | 1.7 | 67 | ... | ... | ... | 25.3 | 209 | ... | ... | ... |
| United Kingdom[13,25] | 1983 | 14.8 | 4,909 | ... | 514 | ... | 5.9 | 12,134 | ... | 1,062 | ... | 29.0 | 27,488 | ... | 1,555 | ... |
| United States[13,58] | 1983 | 11.7 | 22,994 | 24.1 | 3,890 | 75.9 | 6.2 | 30,578 | 24.8 | 6,204 | 75.2 | 29.6 | 120,525 | 29.7 | 9,646 | 70.3 |
| Uruguay[9,22,28] | 1984 | 33.5 | 2,789 | ... | ... | ... | 19.4 | 1,995 | ... | ... | ... | 34.0 | 2,897 | ... | ... | ... |
| Vanuatu | | ... | ... | ... | ... | ... | ... | ... | ... | ... | ... | ... | ... | ... | ... | ... |
| Venezuela[9,28,58] | 1983 | 24.7 | 2,138 | 25.2 | 161 | 74.8 | 7.9 | 1,778 | 44.1 | 132 | 55.9 | 39.1 | 2,085 | 34.7 | 191 | 65.3 |
| Vietnam | | ... | ... | ... | ... | ... | ... | ... | ... | ... | ... | ... | ... | ... | ... | ... |
| Virgin Islands (U.S.) | | ... | ... | ... | ... | ... | ... | ... | ... | ... | ... | ... | ... | ... | ... | ... |
| Wallis and Futuna | | ... | ... | ... | ... | ... | ... | ... | ... | ... | ... | ... | ... | ... | ... | ... |
| West Bank | 1985 | 46.6 | 233 | ... | ... | ... | 10.8 | 685 | ... | ... | ... | 20.8 | 584 | ... | ... | ... |
| Western Sahara | | ... | ... | ... | ... | ... | ... | ... | ... | ... | ... | ... | ... | ... | ... | ... |
| Western Samoa | | ... | ... | ... | ... | ... | ... | ... | ... | ... | ... | ... | ... | ... | ... | ... |
| Yemen (Aden)[28,37] | 1983 | 37.6 | 488 | ... | ... | ... | 13.1 | ... | ... | 13 | ... | 28.7 | ... | ... | 14 | ... |
| Yemen (Ṣanʿāʾ)[28,59] | 1980 | 34.2 | 442 | ... | ... | ... | 7.9 | 536 | ... | ... | ... | 13.6 | 659 | ... | ... | ... |
| Yugoslavia[4,51] | 1984 | 10.8 | ... | ... | 1,395 | ... | 19.1 | ... | ... | 1,582 | ... | 24.1 | ... | ... | 2,866 | ... |
| Zaire[11] | 1980 | 44.0 | ... | ... | ... | ... | 20.0 | ... | ... | ... | ... | 36.0[33] | ... | ... | ... | ... |
| Zambia[9,11] | 1974 | 34.5 | 172 | ... | ... | ... | 8.3 | 156 | ... | ... | ... | 22.0 | 179 | ... | ... | ... |
| Zimbabwe[13] | 1982 | 26.0 | ... | ... | ... | ... | 21.0 | ... | ... | ... | ... | 21.0 | ... | ... | ... | ... |

[1]Data in value added columns refer to gross output in value of sales. [2]Group 4 includes groups 5 and 6. [3]Data in value added columns refer to gross ouput in producer's prices. [4]Establishment data refer to enterprises. [5]Group 4 includes groups 5 and 6 and mining and public utilities; establishment data are for 1969. [6]Netherlands Antilles includes Aruba. [7]Establishments of 4 or more workers. [8]Group 5 includes group 6 and 385 and 390. [9]Value added calculated in producer's prices. [10]Group 5 includes and group 6 excludes ISIC 3825 (office machinery and computing equipment). [11]Total value and percentages calculated on sum of figures directly referable to groups 1–6; may exclude data withheld for confidentiality and minor or ambiguously classified manufacturing. [12]Establishments of 10 or more workers. [13]Data in value added columns are calculated in factor values. [14]Excludes leather and leather products. [15]Excludes synthetic fibre industry. [16]Includes professional goods. [17]Group 5 includes group 6. [18]Value added data refer to 1983. [19]Establishment data are incomplete. [20]Value added data refer to 1982. [21]Includes professional goods and industrial activities of cooperatives. [22]Establishment data are for 1978. [23]Establishments of 50 or more workers. [24]Establishment data are for 1973. [25]Establishment data are for 1980. [26]Includes sugarcane cropping. [27]Value added data refer to establishments of 20 or more workers; establishment data refer to establishments of 6 or more. [28]Establishments of 5 or more workers. [29]Establishment data are for 1981. [30]Value added data refer to establishments of 5 or more workers. [31]Includes petrochemical, rubber, and plastics industries.

Column groups:
- **primary and fabricated metals; proc. minerals (group 4)**
- **machinery (except elec.) and transport equip. (group 5)**
- **electrical and electronic machinery (group 6)**

| (g4) percent of total value added | (g4) 1–99 emp. number | (g4) 1–99 emp. percent of value added | (g4) 100 or more emp. number | (g4) 100 or more emp. percent of value added | (g5) percent of total value added | (g5) 1–99 emp. number | (g5) 1–99 emp. percent of value added | (g5) 100 or more emp. number | (g5) 100 or more emp. percent of value added | (g6) percent of total value added | (g6) 1–99 emp. number | (g6) 1–99 emp. percent of value added | (g6) 100 or more emp. number | (g6) 100 or more emp. percent of value added | total manufacturing value added (U.S.$'000,000) | country |
|---|---|---|---|---|---|---|---|---|---|---|---|---|---|---|---|---|
| ... | ... | ... | ... | ... | ... | ... | ... | ... | ... | ... | ... | ... | ... | ... | ... | Northern Mariana Islands |
| ... | ... | ... | ... | ... | ... | ... | ... | ... | ... | ... | ... | ... | ... | ... | ... | Palau |
| 11.5 | 597 | ... | ... | ... | 4.2 | 395 | ... | ... | ... | 3.5 | 185 | ... | ... | ... | 2,898 | Pakistan |
| 11.2 | 128 | ... | ... | ... | 1.1 | 21 | ... | ... | ... | 1.5 | 12 | ... | ... | ... | 578 | Panama |
| 18.6[2] | 96[2] | ... | ... | ... | [2] | ... | ... | ... | ... | [2] | ... | ... | ... | ... | 267 | Papua New Guinea |
| 22.1[33] | 98 | ... | 11 | ... | 8.0[10] | 1,774 | ... | 83 | ... | 3.1[10] | 524 | ... | 5 | ... | 816 | Paraguay |
| 8.4 | 7,633 | ... | ... | ... | 6.0 | 2,097[10] | ... | ... | ... | 3.7 | ... | ... | 280[10] | ... | 5,204 | Peru |
| ... | ... | ... | ... | ... | ... | ... | ... | ... | ... | ... | ... | ... | ... | ... | 5,063 | Philippines |
| ... | ... | ... | ... | ... | ... | ... | ... | ... | ... | ... | ... | ... | ... | ... | ... | Pitcairn Island |
| 15.8 | ... | ... | 3,093 | ... | 21.3 | ... | ... | 1,820 | ... | 7.4 | ... | ... | 755 | ... | 24,509 | Poland |
| 33.7[2] | 7,938 | ... | 226 | ... | [2] | 1,351 | ... | 112 | ... | [2] | 155 | ... | 38 | ... | 7,153 | Portugal |
| 3.1 | 351 | 53.0 | 16 | 47.0 | 6.7[10] | 104 | 13.9 | 12 | 86.1 | 13.2[10] | 112 | 18.5 | 69 | 81.5 | 8,606 | Puerto Rico |
| ... | ... | ... | ... | ... | ... | ... | ... | ... | ... | ... | ... | ... | ... | ... | 456 | Qatar |
| ... | 9 | ... | ... | ... | ... | 18[17] | ... | ... | ... | ... | 17 | ... | ... | ... | 189[52] | Réunion |
| [33] | ... | ... | 482[2] | ... | [33] | ... | ... | 2 | ... | [33] | ... | ... | 2 | ... | ... | Romania |
| 3.8 | ... | ... | 10[2] | ... | 4.4 | ... | ... | 2 | ... | 0.1 | ... | ... | 2 | ... | 134 | Rwanda |
| ... | ... | ... | ... | ... | ... | ... | ... | ... | ... | ... | ... | ... | ... | ... | 7 | St. Christopher and Nevis |
| — | — | — | — | — | — | — | — | — | — | — | — | — | — | — | ... | St. Helena and Ascension |
| — | — | — | — | — | — | — | — | — | — | — | — | — | — | — | 12 | St. Lucia |
| ... | ... | ... | ... | ... | ... | ... | ... | ... | ... | ... | ... | ... | ... | ... | ... | St. Pierre and Miquelon |
| ... | 44 | ... | ... | ... | ... | 241[17] | ... | ... | ... | ... | 17 | ... | ... | ... | 8 | St. Vincent |
| ... | ... | ... | ... | ... | ... | ... | ... | ... | ... | ... | ... | ... | ... | ... | ... | San Marino |
| ... | 9,481[2] | ... | 112[2] | ... | ... | 2 | ... | 2 | ... | ... | 2 | ... | 2 | ... | 22 | São Tomé and Príncipe |
| ... | ... | ... | ... | ... | ... | ... | ... | ... | ... | ... | ... | ... | ... | ... | ... | Saudi Arabia |
| 24.1[2] | 45[2] | ... | ... | ... | [2] | 2 | ... | ... | ... | [2] | 2 | ... | ... | ... | 170 | Senegal |
| 6.9 | 4 | ... | ... | ... | — | — | ... | ... | ... | — | — | ... | ... | ... | 14 | Seychelles |
| 6.2 | ... | ... | ... | ... | — | ... | ... | ... | ... | — | ... | ... | ... | ... | 31 | Sierra Leone |
| 11.8 | 579 | ... | ... | ... | 17.1[10] | 601[10] | ... | ... | ... | 30.9[10] | ... | ... | 324[10] | ... | 5,215 | Singapore |
| 12.3 | 37 | ... | ... | ... | ... | ... | ... | ... | ... | ... | ... | ... | ... | ... | ... | Solomon Islands |
| ... | ... | ... | ... | ... | ... | ... | ... | ... | ... | ... | ... | ... | ... | ... | 41 | Somalia |
| 27.3 | 3,585 | 15.9 | 577 | 84.1 | 13.7 | 2,117 | 23.5 | 312 | 76.5 | 5.2 | 638 | 16.7 | 117 | 83.3 | 13,409 | South Africa |
| ... | ... | ... | ... | ... | ... | ... | ... | ... | ... | ... | ... | ... | ... | ... | ... | Bophuthatswana |
| ... | ... | ... | ... | ... | ... | ... | ... | ... | ... | ... | ... | ... | ... | ... | ... | Ciskei |
| ... | ... | ... | ... | ... | ... | ... | ... | ... | ... | ... | ... | ... | ... | ... | ... | KwaNdebele |
| ... | ... | ... | ... | ... | ... | ... | ... | ... | ... | ... | ... | ... | ... | ... | ... | Transkei |
| ... | ... | ... | ... | ... | ... | ... | ... | ... | ... | ... | ... | ... | ... | ... | ... | Venda |
| ... | ... | ... | ... | ... | ... | ... | ... | ... | ... | ... | ... | ... | ... | ... | ... | South West Africa/Namibia |
| 22.9 | 35,038 | ... | ... | ... | 14.4 | 6,951 | ... | ... | ... | 7.2 | 2,550 | ... | ... | ... | 40,186 | Spain |
| 14.1 | ... | ... | 201 | ... | 2.3 | 61 | ... | ... | ... | 2.9 | 31 | ... | ... | ... | 254 | Sri Lanka |
| ... | ... | ... | ... | ... | ... | ... | ... | ... | ... | ... | ... | ... | ... | ... | 467 | Sudan, The |
| 6.4 | 34 | ... | ... | ... | 2.5[17] | ... | ... | 4[17] | ... | [17] | ... | ... | 17 | ... | 93 | Suriname |
| ... | ... | ... | ... | ... | ... | ... | ... | ... | ... | ... | ... | ... | ... | ... | ... | Swaziland |
| 17.3 | 1,889 | ... | 250 | ... | 22.8 | 1,139 | ... | 218 | ... | 10.8 | 342 | ... | 113 | ... | 23,653 | Sweden |
| 25.4 | 7,973 | ... | 228 | ... | 43.3 | 2,983 | ... | 280 | ... | ... | 2,676 | ... | 224 | ... | 12,800 | Switzerland |
| 32.4[2] | 18,254[2] | ... | ... | ... | [2] | 2 | ... | ... | ... | [2] | 2 | ... | ... | ... | 1,749 | Syria |
| 14.0 | ... | ... | ... | ... | 9.3 | ... | ... | ... | ... | 13.0 | ... | ... | ... | ... | 19,498 | Taiwan |
| 9.35[54] | ... | ... | 70 | ... | 12.2[17,54] | ... | ... | 46[17] | ... | [17] | ... | ... | 17 | ... | 354 | Tanzania |
| 24.9 | 1,208 | ... | ... | ... | 3.7 | 765 | ... | ... | ... | 0.5 | 153 | ... | ... | ... | 5,159 | Thailand |
| 16.5 | ... | ... | 9 | ... | — | — | ... | ... | ... | ... | ... | ... | ... | ... | 52 | Togo |
| — | — | — | — | — | — | — | — | — | — | — | — | — | — | — | ... | Tokelau |
| 12.8[2] | 19 | 100.0 | — | — | [2] | 7 | 100.0 | — | — | [2] | 2 | 100.0 | — | — | 4 | Tonga |
| [33] | 82 | ... | ... | ... | [33] | 27[17] | ... | ... | ... | [33] | 17 | ... | ... | ... | 735 | Trinidad and Tobago |
| 46.8 | 30 | 50.3 | 29 | 49.7 | ... | ... | ... | ... | ... | ... | ... | ... | ... | ... | 840 | Tunisia |
| 18.3 | 1,519 | 16.0 | 285 | 84.0 | 10.4 | 835 | 13.9 | 165 | 86.1 | 5.0 | 452 | 10.1 | 85 | 89.9 | 9,706 | Turkey |
| — | — | — | — | — | — | — | — | — | — | — | — | — | — | — | ... | Turks and Caicos Islands |
| — | — | — | — | — | — | — | — | — | — | — | — | — | — | — | ... | Tuvalu |
| 20.7 | 20 | 7.9 | 8 | 92.1 | ... | 64 | 77.0 | 5 | 23.0 | — | ... | ... | ... | ... | 73 | Uganda |
| 46.6[2,57] | ... | ... | 16,093[2,57] | ... | [2] | ... | ... | 2 | ... | [2] | ... | ... | 2 | ... | ... | U.S.S.R. |
| 63.9 | 285 | ... | ... | ... | 9.0 | 5 | ... | ... | ... | -8.3 | 9 | ... | ... | ... | 266 | United Arab Emirates |
| 16.1 | 15,703 | ... | 1,114 | ... | 20.8 | 23,098 | ... | 1,675 | ... | 11.1 | 4,423 | ... | 481 | ... | 125,092 | United Kingdom |
| 13.0 | 52,544 | 23.4 | 6,287 | 76.6 | 20.6 | 76,365 | 20.1 | 6,751 | 79.9 | 13.4 | 12,103 | 9.9 | 2,870 | 90.1 | 879,440 | United States |
| 7.4 | 1,538 | ... | ... | ... | 2.9 | 761 | ... | ... | ... | 2.4 | 410 | ... | ... | ... | 1,298 | Uruguay |
| ... | ... | ... | ... | ... | ... | ... | ... | ... | ... | ... | ... | ... | ... | ... | ... | Vanuatu |
| 18.7 | 2,063 | 35.0 | 126 | 65.0 | 6.1[10] | 408 | 26.1 | 65 | 73.9 | 2.5[10] | 163 | 30.5 | 40 | 69.5 | 17,287 | Venezuela |
| ... | ... | ... | ... | ... | ... | ... | ... | ... | ... | ... | ... | ... | ... | ... | ... | Vietnam |
| ... | ... | ... | ... | ... | ... | ... | ... | ... | ... | ... | ... | ... | ... | ... | ... | Virgin Islands (U.S.) |
| ... | ... | ... | ... | ... | ... | ... | ... | ... | ... | ... | ... | ... | ... | ... | ... | Wallis and Futuna |
| 15.4 | 813 | ... | ... | ... | — | ... | ... | ... | ... | ... | ... | ... | ... | ... | 142 | West Bank |
| — | — | — | — | — | — | — | — | — | — | — | — | — | — | — | ... | Western Sahara |
| ... | ... | ... | ... | ... | ... | ... | ... | ... | ... | ... | ... | ... | ... | ... | ... | Western Samoa |
| 20.4[2] | 12[2] | ... | ... | ... | [2] | 2 | ... | ... | ... | [2] | 2 | ... | ... | ... | 117 | Yemen (Aden) |
| 44.1[2] | 1,358[2] | ... | ... | ... | [2] | 2 | ... | ... | ... | [2] | 2 | ... | ... | ... | 172 | Yemen (San'ã) |
| 22.0 | ... | ... | 2,061 | ... | 15.5[10] | ... | ... | 1,186[10] | ... | 7.5[10] | ... | ... | 535[10] | ... | ... | Yugoslavia |
| [33] | ... | ... | ... | ... | [33] | ... | ... | ... | ... | [33] | ... | ... | ... | ... | 256 | Zaire |
| 12.8 | 152 | ... | ... | ... | 19.4 | 217 | ... | ... | ... | 2.9 | 21 | ... | ... | ... | 520 | Zambia |
| 30.5[2] | ... | ... | ... | ... | [2] | ... | ... | ... | ... | [2] | ... | ... | ... | ... | 1,702 | Zimbabwe |

[32]Value added data are "revenue." [33]Group 3 includes groups 4, 5, and 6. [34]Group 2 includes groups 3, 4, 5 and 6. [35]Establishments of 30 or more workers. [36]Value added data refer to establishments of 30 or more workers. [37]Establishment data are for 1979. [38]1984. [39]Establishment and value added data refer to establishments of 10 or more workers with electric power and 20 or more without power. [40]Excludes petroleum manufacturing and manufacturing on tea, tobacco, and rubber estates. [41]Establishments of 20 or more workers. [42]Establishments of 3 or more workers. [43]Excludes the diamond industry. [44]Excludes sugar factories and refineries. [45]Establishment data are for 1982. [46]Percent of value added by establishment size and number of establishments data refer to 1982. [47]Establishment data are for 1976. [48]Establishment data refer to establishments with annual sales of 100,000 kwachas or more. [49]Value added data refer to 1980. [50]Privately owned establishments only. [51]Socialized sector only. [52]1980. [53]Value added data refer to 1975. [54]Percent of gross output. [55]Establishment data are for 1975. [56]Excludes establishments in the private sector with fewer than 10 workers. [57]Includes (385) professional goods and (390) other industries. [58]Percent of value added by establishment size and number of establishments data refer to 1977. [59]Including a 10 percent sample of establishments with fewer than 5 employees.

# Energy

This table provides data about the commercial energy supplies (reserves, production, consumption, and trade) of the various countries of the world, together with data about oil pipeline networks and traffic. Many of the data and concepts used in this table are adopted from the United Nations' *Energy Statistics Yearbook*.

*Electricity.* Total installed electrical power capacity comprises the sum of the rated power capacities of all main and auxiliary generators in a country. 'Total installed capacity' (kW) is multiplied by 8,760 hours per year to yield 'Total production capacity' (kW-hr).

Production of electricity comprises the total gross production of electricity by publicly or privately owned enterprises and also that generated by industrial establishments for their own use, but usually excludes consumption by the utility itself. Measured in 1,000,000s of kilowatt-hours (kW-hr), annual production of electricity ranges generally between 30% and 40% of total production capacity. The data are further analyzed by type of generation: fossil fuels, hydroelectric power, and nuclear fuel.

The great majority of the world's electrical and other energy needs are met by the burning of fossil hydrocarbon solids, liquids, and gases, either for thermal generation of electricity or in internal combustion engines. Many renewable and nontraditional sources of energy are being developed worldwide (wood, biogenic gases and liquids, tidal, wave, and wind power, geothermal and photothermal [solar] energy, and so on), but collectively these sources are still negligible in the world's total energy consumption.

For this reason only hydroelectric and nuclear generation are considered here separately with fossil fuels.

Trade in electrical energy refers to the transfer of generated electrical output via an international grid. Total electricity consumption (residential and nonresidential) is equal to total electricity requirements less transformation and distribution losses.

*Coal.* The term coal, as used in the table, comprises all grades of anthracite, bituminous, subbituminous, and lignite that have acquired or may in the future, by reason of new technology or changed market prices, acquire an economic value. These types of coal may be differentiated according to heat content (density) and content of impurities. Most coal reserve data are based on proved recoverable reserves only, of all grades of coal. Exceptions are footnoted, with proved in-place reserves reported only when recoverable reserves are unknown. Production figures include deposits removed from both surface and underground workings as well as quantities used by the producers themselves or issued to the miners. Wastes recovered from mines or nearby preparation plants are excluded from production figures.

*Natural gas.* This term refers to any combustible gas (usually chiefly methane) of natural origin from underground sources. The data for production cover, to the extent possible, gas obtained from gas fields, petroleum fields, or coal mines that is actually collected and marketed. (Much natural gas in Middle Eastern and North African oil fields is

## Energy

| country | electricity | | | | | | | | | | | | coal | | |
|---|---|---|---|---|---|---|---|---|---|---|---|---|---|---|---|
| | installed capacity, 1985 ('000 kW) | production, 1985 | | power source, 1985 | | | trade, 1985 | | consumption | | | | reserves, latest ('000,000 metric tons) | production, 1985 ('000 metric tons) | consumption, 1985 ('000 metric tons) |
| | | capacity ('000,000 kW-hr) | amount ('000,000 kW-hr) | fossil fuel (%) | hydro-power (%) | nuclear fuel (%) | exports ('000,000 kW-hr) | imports ('000,000 kW-hr) | amount, 1985 ('000,000 kW-hr) | per capita, 1985 (kW-hr) | resi-dential, 1984 (%) | non-resi-dential, 1984 (%) | | | |
| Afghanistan | 450 | 3,942 | 1,060 | 26.6 | 73.4 | — | — | — | 1,060 | 64 | ... | ... | 66 | 151 | 151 |
| Albania | 740 | 6,482 | 3,155 | 20.8 | 79.2 | — | 600 | — | 2,555 | 838 | 24.1[3] | 75.9[3] | 15[1] | 1,790 | 2,010 |
| Algeria | 3,546 | 31,063 | 12,274 | 94.7 | 5.3 | — | 86 | 172 | 12,360 | 569 | 24.1[3] | 75.9[3] | 43 | 8 | 1,608 |
| American Samoa | 32 | 280 | 75 | 100.0 | — | — | ... | — | 75 | 2,143 | 27.5[2] | 72.5[2] | — | — | — |
| Andorra | ... | ... | ... | ... | ... | ... | ... | ... | ... | ... | ... | ... | ... | ... | ... |
| Angola | 600 | 5,256 | 1,790 | 25.4 | 74.6 | — | — | — | 1,790 | 204 | 27.5[4] | 72.5[4] | — | — | — |
| Anguilla | — | ... | ... | ... | ... | ... | ... | ... | ... | ... | ... | ... | ... | ... | ... |
| Antigua and Barbuda | 26 | 228 | 77 | 100.0 | — | — | — | — | 77 | 963 | 42.4 | 57.6 | ... | ... | ... |
| Argentina | 16,058 | 140,668 | 45,265 | 41.6 | 45.6 | 12.8 | 6 | — | 45,259 | 1,481 | 25.7 | 74.3 | 130 | 400 | 1,203 |
| Aruba[5] | ... | ... | ... | ... | ... | ... | ... | ... | ... | ... | ... | ... | ... | ... | ... |
| Australia | 31,217 | 273,461 | 118,969 | 87.9 | 12.1 | — | — | — | 118,969 | 7,579 | 30.1[4] | 69.9[4] | 65,702 | 168,484 | 82,443 |
| Austria | 15,241 | 133,511 | 43,923 | 29.4 | 70.6 | — | 7,770 | 6,051 | 42,204 | 5,626 | 23.1[4] | 83.4[4] | 64 | 3,081 | 7,019 |
| Bahamas, The | 357 | 3,127 | 854 | 100.0 | — | — | — | — | 854 | 3,713 | 33.6 | 66.4 | ... | — | — |
| Bahrain | 725 | 6,351 | 2,130 | 100.0 | — | — | — | — | 2,130 | 4,931 | — | — | ... | — | ... |
| Bangladesh | 1,308 | 11,458 | 4,870 | 84.8 | 15.2 | — | — | — | 4,870 | 48 | 25.7 | 74.3 | 1,054[1] | — | 98 |
| Barbados | 94 | 823 | 364 | 100.0 | — | — | — | — | 364 | 1,439 | 25.5 | 74.5 | ... | ... | ... |
| Belgium | 14,152 | 123,972 | 56,356 | 37.9 | 0.7 | 61.4 | 5,543 | 5,497 | 56,310 | 5,686 | 26.9[6] | 73.1[6] | 410 | 7,666 | 16,032 |
| Belize | 21 | 184 | 60 | 100.0 | — | — | — | — | 60 | 368 | ... | ... | ... | ... | ... |
| Benin | 15 | 131 | 5 | 100.0 | — | — | — | 85 | 90 | 22 | ... | ... | ... | ... | ... |
| Bermuda | 149 | 1,305 | 395 | 100.0 | — | — | — | — | 395 | 5,000 | 41.4[2] | 58.6[2] | ... | ... | ... |
| Bhutan | 17 | 149 | 30 | 73.3 | 26.7 | — | — | 5 | 35 | 25 | 29.2[2] | 69.8[2] | ... | — | 1 |
| Bolivia | 566 | 4,958 | 1,725 | 30.4 | 69.6 | — | — | 2 | 1,727 | 271 | 45.1 | 54.9 | ... | — | 1 |
| Botswana | 8 | 8 | 522[8,9] | 8 | 8 | 8 | 8 | 82[8,9] | 8 | 8 | ... | ... | 3,500 | 400[6,8] | 8 |
| Brazil | 43,804 | 383,723 | 192,945 | 7.6 | 92.4 | — | 2 | 2,781 | 195,724 | 1,444 | 20.1 | 79.9 | 2,343 | 7,712 | 16,814 |
| British Virgin Islands | 5 | 44 | 30 | 100.0 | — | — | — | — | 30 | 2,308 | ... | ... | ... | ... | ... |
| Brunei | 240 | 2,102 | 949 | 100.0 | — | — | — | — | 949 | 4,021 | 55.3 | 44.7 | — | — | — |
| Bulgaria | 10,243 | 89,729 | 41,633 | 63.1 | 5.4 | 31.5 | 1,655 | 5,959 | 45,937 | 5,064 | 41.2[2] | 58.8[2] | 3,730 | 30,880 | 38,934 |
| Burkina Faso | 40 | 350 | 115 | 100.0 | — | — | — | — | 115 | 17 | ... | ... | ... | ... | ... |
| Burma | 818 | 7,166 | 1,756 | 50.5 | 49.5 | — | — | — | 1,756 | 47 | ... | 59.1[4,10] | 2 | 78 | 258 |
| Burundi | 9 | 79 | 2 | 100.0 | — | — | — | 150 | 152 | 32 | ... | ... | ... | ... | ... |
| Cameroon | 570 | 4,993 | 2,237 | 5.0 | 95.0 | — | — | — | 2,237 | 227 | ... | ... | ... | 1 | 2 |
| Canada | 99,284 | 869,728 | 460,408 | 20.6 | 66.1 | 13.3 | 43,416 | 3,093 | 420,085 | 16,522 | 28.8 | 71.2 | 6,846 | 60,853 | 48,403 |
| Cape Verde | 4 | 35 | 26 | 100.0 | — | — | — | — | 26 | 80 | ... | ... | ... | ... | ... |
| Cayman Islands | 31 | 272 | 124 | 100.0 | — | — | — | — | 124 | 6,200 | 55.4[2] | 44.6[2] | ... | ... | ... |
| Central African Republic | 30 | 263 | 75 | 5.3 | 94.7 | — | — | — | 75 | 29 | 17.5[11] | 82.5[11] | 4 | ... | ... |
| Chad | 38 | 333 | 65 | 100.0 | — | — | — | — | 65 | 13 | ... | ... | ... | ... | ... |
| Chile | 3,355 | 29,390 | 13,893 | 25.0 | 75.0 | — | — | — | 13,893 | 1,154 | 19.7 | 80.3 | 1,181 | 1,218 | 1,764 |
| China | 82,200 | 720,072 | 410,700 | 77.5 | 22.5 | — | — | 1,050 | 411,750 | 396 | 6.1[9] | 93.9[9] | 737,100[1] | 845,000 | 839,170 |
| Christmas Island | 12 | 105 | 33 | 100.0 | — | — | — | — | 33[6] | 11,000[6] | ... | ... | ... | ... | ... |
| Cocos (Keeling) Islands | ... | ... | ... | ... | ... | ... | ... | ... | ... | ... | ... | ... | ... | ... | ... |
| Colombia | 5,648 | 49,476 | 26,800 | 27.2 | 72.8 | — | 10 | 8 | 26,798 | 933 | 45.1 | 54.9 | 1,035 | 6,500 | 5,900 |
| Comoros | 4 | 35 | 10 | 100.0 | — | — | — | — | 10 | 23 | ... | ... | ... | ... | ... |
| Congo | 149 | 1,305 | 237 | 0.8 | 99.2 | — | — | 27 | 264 | 152 | ... | ... | ... | ... | ... |
| Cook Islands | 6 | 53 | 10 | 100.0 | — | — | — | — | 10 | 500 | ... | ... | ... | ... | ... |
| Costa Rica | 825 | 7,227 | 2,826 | 2.1 | 97.9 | — | 50 | — | 2,776 | 1,068 | 43.9 | 56.1 | ... | ... | ... |
| Côte d'Ivoire | 1,163 | 10,188 | 1,785 | 23.9 | 76.1 | — | — | — | 1,785 | 182 | 15.4 | 84.6 | ... | ... | ... |
| Cuba | 3,229 | 28,286 | 12,199 | 99.6 | 0.4 | — | — | — | 12,199 | 1,215 | 29.4 | 70.6 | ... | — | 84 |
| Cyprus | 389 | 3,408 | 1,319 | 100.0 | — | — | — | — | 1,319 | 1,972 | 21.2 | 78.8 | ... | — | 74 |
| Czechoslovakia | 19,547 | 171,232 | 80,627 | 80.0 | 5.4 | 14.6 | 7,257 | 10,796 | 84,166 | 5,403 | 23.6[2] | 76.4[2] | 5,560 | 126,610 | 126,561 |
| Denmark | 8,651 | 75,783 | 29,064 | 99.7 | 0.1 | 0.2[12] | 2,695 | 3,155 | 29,524 | 5,764 | 32.5[6] | 67.5[6] | 63[1] | — | 12,146 |
| Djibouti | 40 | 350 | 150 | 100.0 | — | — | — | — | 150 | 412 | ... | ... | ... | ... | ... |
| Dominica | 7 | 61 | 18 | 11.1 | 88.9 | — | — | — | 18 | 237 | 53.5 | 46.5 | ... | ... | ... |
| Dominican Republic | 960 | 8,410 | 4,020 | 87.1 | 12.9 | — | — | — | 4,020 | 644 | ... | ... | ... | — | 19 |
| Ecuador | 1,778 | 15,575 | 4,490 | 27.8 | 72.2 | — | — | 10 | 4,500 | 480 | 41.2 | 58.8 | 18 | ... | ... |
| Egypt | 5,850 | 51,246 | 23,220 | 54.3 | 45.7 | — | — | — | 23,220 | 495 | 28.3 | 71.1 | 53 | ... | 1,200 |

flared [burned] because it is often not economical to capture and market it.) Manufactured gas is generally a by-product of industrial operations such as gasworks, coke ovens, and blast furnaces. It is usually burned at the point of production and rarely enters the marketplace. Production of manufactured gas is, therefore, only reported as a percentage of domestic gas consumption.

*Crude petroleum.* Crude petroleum is the liquid product obtained from oil wells; the term also includes shale oil, tar sand extract, and field or lease condensate. Production and consumption data in the table refer, so far as possible, to the same year so that the relationship between national production and consumption patterns can be clearly seen; both are given in barrels.

Proved reserves are that oil remaining underground in known fields whose existence has been "proved" by the evaluation of nearby producing wells or by seismic tests in sedimentary strata known to contain crude petroleum, and that is judged recoverable within the limits of present technology and economic conditions (prices). The published proved reserve figures do not necessarily reflect the true reserves of a country, because government authorities or corporations often have political or economic motives for withholding or altering such data.

The estimated exhaustion rate of petroleum reserves is an extrapolated ratio of published proved reserves to the current rate of withdrawal/production. Present world published proved reserves will last about 30 years at the present rate of withdrawal, but there are large country-to-country variations above or below the average.

Data on petroleum and product pipelines are provided because of the great importance to both domestic and international energy markets of this means of bringing these energy sources from their production or transportation points to refineries, intermediate consumption and distribution points, and final consumers. Their traffic may represent a very significant fraction of the total movement of goods within a country. Available data for petroleum pipelines are often incomplete and their basis varies internationally, some countries reporting only international shipments, others reporting domestic shipments of 50 kilometres or more, and so on.

For data in the hydrocarbons portions of the table (coal, natural gas, and petroleum), extensive use has been made of a variety of international sources, such as those of the United Nations, the International Energy Agency (of the Organization for Economic Cooperation and Development), and the World Energy Conference; of the resources of the U.S. Department of Energy; and of various industry surveys, such as those published by British Petroleum (BP *Statistical Review of World Energy*), the *International Petroleum Encyclopedia,* the *Oil and Gas Journal,* the *Petroleum Economist,* and *World Oil.*

a. Includes refined petroleum products pipelines.

| natural gas | | | | | | crude petroleum | | | | | | | country |
|---|---|---|---|---|---|---|---|---|---|---|---|---|---|
| published proved reserves, 1987 ('000,000,-000 cu m) | production | | consumption | | | reserves, 1987 | | production, 1986 ('000,000 barrels) | consumption, 1986 ('000,000 barrels) | refining capacity, 1987 ('000 barrels per day) | pipelines (latest)a | | |
| | natural gas, 1986 ('000,000 cu m) | manufac-tured gas, 1985 (% of total gas consumption) | amount, 1985 ('000,000 cu m) | resi-dential, 1984 (%) | non-resi-dential, 1984 (%) | published proved ('000,000 barrels) | years to exhaust proved reserves | | | | length (km) | traffic ('000,000 metric ton-km) | |
| 64 | 2,888 | ... | 596 | ... | ... | ... | ... | — | — | — | — | — | Afghanistan |
| 7 | 300 | ... | 436 | ... | ... | 210 | 10 | 22 | 23[2] | 40 | 182 | — | Albania |
| 3,001 | 35,065 | 52.8 | 5,055 | 26.8[4] | 73.2[4] | 4,830 | 13 | 365 | 174[2] | 465 | 6,910 | ... | Algeria |
| ... | ... | ... | ... | ... | ... | ... | ... | — | — | — | — | — | American Samoa |
| ... | ... | ... | ... | ... | ... | ... | ... | | | | | | Andorra |
| 54 | 187 | 12.6 | 115 | ... | ... | 1,950 | 19 | 103 | 11[2] | 32 | 179 | ... | Angola |
| ... | ... | ... | ... | ... | ... | ... | ... | — | — | — | — | — | Anguilla |
| 676 | 18,740 | 11.7 | 18,616 | 36.1 | 63.9 | 2,180 | 13 | 169 | 168[2] | 670 | 6,290 | — | Antigua and Barbuda |
| ... | ... | ... | ... | ... | ... | ... | ... | | | | | | Argentina |
| | | | | | | | | | | | | | Aruba[5] |
| 527 | 14,748 | 37.7 | 12,251 | ... | ... | 1,692 | 9 | 187 | 219 | 626 | 2,975 | ... | Australia |
| 11 | 1,115 | 24.4 | 5,910 | 25.7[4] | 74.3[4] | 144 | 18 | 8 | 77 | 204 | 725 | 4,463 | Austria |
| — | — | 39.9 | | | | | | — | 27[2] | | | | Bahamas, The |
| 226 | 6,108 | 2.8 | 3,568 | ... | ... | 165 | 10 | 16 | 68[2] | 250 | 72 | ... | Bahrain |
| 360 | 3,220 | 0.4 | 2,949 | 31.7 | 68.3 | — | — | — | 8[2] | 31 | | — | Bangladesh |
| — | 26 | ... | 25 | 55.6 | 44.4 | 0.5 | 0.8 | 0.7 | 2[2] | 3 | — | — | Barbados |
| — | 41[2] | 27.0 | 10,714 | 43.4[6] | 56.6[6] | ... | ... | — | 175[7] | 648 | 1,276 | 709 | Belgium |
| ... | ... | ... | ... | ... | ... | ... | ... | | | | | | Belize |
| — | ... | ... | ... | ... | ... | 100 | 39 | 3 | | | — | — | Benin |
| ... | ... | ... | ... | ... | ... | ... | ... | | | | | | Bermuda |
| ... | ... | ... | ... | ... | ... | ... | ... | — | — | — | — | — | Bhutan |
| 143 | 2,883 | 53.7 | 175 | — | 100.0 | 157 | 26 | 6 | 8[2] | 47 | 3,165 | ... | Bolivia |
| ... | ... | [8] | ... | ... | ... | — | — | — | 8 | — | — | — | Botswana |
| 95 | 5,675 | 76.5 | 2,348 | 23.4[9] | 76.6[9] | 2,358 | 11 | 216 | 399[2] | 1,321 | 2,465 | ... | Brazil |
| ... | ... | ... | ... | ... | ... | ... | ... | — | — | — | — | — | British Virgin Islands |
| 204 | 7,781 | 3.2 | 1,128 | ... | ... | 1,475 | 25 | 60 | — | 10 | 553 | ... | Brunei |
| 7 | 20 | 9.1 | 6,136 | ... | ... | 11 | 6 | 2 | 94[2] | 300 | 611 | ... | Bulgaria |
| ... | ... | ... | ... | ... | ... | ... | ... | — | — | — | — | — | Burkina Faso |
| 321 | 674 | 0.5 | 980 | — | 100.0 | 716 | 90 | 8 | 10[2] | 26 | 1,117 | — | Burma |
| ... | ... | ... | ... | ... | ... | ... | ... | | | | | | Burundi |
| 115 | — | 94.8 | ... | ... | ... | 500 | 8 | 64 | 25[2] | 43 | — | — | Cameroon |
| 2,778 | 78,359 | 22.7 | 59,115 | 20.6[4] | 79.4[4] | 4,806 | 9 | 537 | 531 | 1,760 | 23,564 | 89,800 | Canada |
| ... | ... | ... | ... | ... | ... | ... | ... | | | | | | Cape Verde |
| ... | ... | ... | ... | ... | ... | ... | ... | — | — | — | — | — | Cayman Islands |
| ... | ... | ... | ... | ... | ... | ... | ... | | | | | | Central African Republic |
| ... | ... | ... | ... | ... | ... | ... | ... | | | | | | Chad |
| 141 | 6,408 | 46.2 | 1,007 | 49.3 | 50.7 | 207 | 17 | 12 | 28[2] | 150 | 1,540 | ... | Chile |
| 416 | 14,023 | ... | 12,864 | ... | ... | 18,525 | 19 | 956 | 726 | 2,200 | 7,600 | ... | China |
| ... | ... | ... | ... | ... | ... | ... | ... | — | — | — | — | — | Christmas Island |
| ... | ... | ... | ... | ... | ... | ... | ... | | | | | | Cocos (Keeling) Islands |
| 108 | 5,165 | 10.8 | 3,891 | 0.8 | 99.2 | 1,600 | 15 | 110 | 71[2] | 226 | 4,935 | ... | Colombia |
| ... | ... | ... | ... | ... | ... | ... | ... | | | | | | Comoros |
| 68 | 34 | 37.6 | — | ... | ... | 721 | 17 | 42 | — | 21 | 25 | ... | Congo |
| — | — | 33.4 | — | ... | ... | ... | ... | — | — | 16 | 95 | — | Cook Islands |
| ... | — | ... | — | ... | ... | ... | ... | — | 3[2] | 16 | | — | Costa Rica |
| 100 | — | 49.9 | — | ... | ... | 125 | 17 | 7 | 12[2] | 73 | — | — | Côte d'Ivoire |
| ... | 6 | 98.2 | 7 | ... | ... | ... | ... | — | 44[2] | 160 | — | — | Cuba |
| — | — | 48.1 | — | ... | ... | ... | ... | — | 3[2] | 16 | — | — | Cyprus |
| 9 | 756 | 36.8 | 9,961 | — | ... | 19 | 21 | 0.9 | 117[2] | 455 | 2,948 | 8,899 | Czechoslovakia |
| 76 | 1,756 | 38.8 | 671 | ... | ... | 516 | 19 | 27 | 78 | 166 | 618 | 35 | Denmark |
| ... | ... | ... | ... | ... | ... | ... | ... | — | — | — | — | — | Djibouti |
| ... | ... | 44.4 | ... | ... | ... | — | — | — | — | — | — | — | Dominica |
| 87 | 169 | 31.3 | 140 | — | 100.0 | 1,265 | 12 | 107 | 11[2] | 44 | 104 | ... | Dominican Republic |
| 255 | 4,460 | 12.6 | 3,584 | 25.3 | 74.7 | 4,500 | 15 | 299 | 43[2] | 88 | 2,158 | ... | Ecuador |
| | | | | | | | | | 147[2] | 452 | 1,703 | ... | Egypt |

# Energy (continued)

| country | installed capacity, 1985 ('000 kW) | production, 1985 capacity ('000,000 kW-hr) | production, 1985 amount ('000,000 kW-hr) | fossil fuel (%) | hydro-power (%) | nuclear fuel (%) | exports ('000,000 kW-hr) | imports ('000,000 kW-hr) | consumption amount, 1985 ('000,000 kW-hr) | per capita, 1985 (kW-hr) | residential, 1984 (%) | non-residential, 1984 (%) | coal reserves, latest ('000,000 metric tons) | coal production, 1985 ('000 metric tons) | coal consumption, 1985 ('000 metric tons) |
|---|---|---|---|---|---|---|---|---|---|---|---|---|---|---|---|
| El Salvador | 500 | 4,380 | 1,695 | 7.1 | 53.1 | 39.8[12] | — | — | 1,695 | 305 | 45.5 | 54.5 | ... | ... | ... |
| Equatorial Guinea | 7 | 61 | 15 | 86.7 | 13.3 | — | — | — | 15 | 38 | ... | ... | ... | ... | ... |
| Ethiopia | 335 | 2,935 | 831 | 23.0 | 77.0 | — | — | — | 831 | 19 | ... | ... | 11 | — | — |
| Faeroe Islands | 68 | 596 | 178 | 71.9 | 28.1 | — | — | — | 178 | 4,238 | ... | ... | ... | ... | ... |
| Falkland Islands | 1 | 9 | 3 | 100.0 | — | — | — | — | 3 | 1,500 | ... | ... | ... | ... | ... |
| Fiji | 202 | 1,770 | 395 | 25.8 | 74.2 | — | — | — | 395 | 572 | 19.8[13] | 80.2[13] | ... | — | 16 |
| Finland | 11,313 | 99,102 | 47,098 | 36.0 | 25.8 | 38.2 | 878 | 5,565 | 51,785 | 10,588 | 18.6[4] | 81.3[4] | — | — | 5,207 |
| France | 88,800[14] | 777,888[14] | 326,400[14] | 16.0[14] | 18.8[14] | 65.3[14] | 28,800[14] | 5,400[14] | 303,000[14] | 5,545[14] | 30.3[6] | 69.7[6] | 381 | 18,964[14] | 38,820[14] |
| French Guiana | 40 | 350 | 190 | 100.0 | — | — | — | — | 190 | 2,317 | ... | 58.7[4,10] | ... | ... | ... |
| French Polynesia | 79 | 692 | 220 | 85.5 | 14.5 | — | — | — | 220 | 1,350 | ... | ... | ... | ... | ... |
| Gabon | 200 | 1,752 | 540 | 51.9 | 48.1 | — | — | — | 540 | 469 | 37.5 | 62.5 | ... | ... | ... |
| Gambia, The | 11 | 96 | 42 | 100.0 | — | — | — | — | 42 | 65 | ... | ... | ... | ... | ... |
| Gaza Strip | ... | ... | ... | ... | ... | ... | ... | ... | ... | ... | ... | ... | ... | ... | ... |
| Germany, East | 21,944 | 192,229 | 113,834 | 87.3 | 1.5 | 11.2 | 3,674 | 3,836 | 113,996 | 6,799 | 31.7[9] | 68.3[9] | 21,000 | 312,156 | 317,154 |
| Germany, West | 92,704 | 812,087 | 406,714 | 65.2 | 3.8 | 31.0 | 16,330 | 18,829 | 409,213 | 6,722 | 26.3[6] | 73.7[6] | 59,069 | 209,207 | 210,652 |
| Ghana | 1,060 | 9,286 | 3,036 | 1.4 | 98.6 | — | 270 | — | 2,766 | 204 | ... | ... | ... | — | 2 |
| Gibraltar | 21 | 184 | 63 | 100.0 | — | — | — | — | 63 | 2,032 | ... | ... | ... | ... | ... |
| Greece | 7,116 | 62,336 | 27,740 | 89.9 | 10.1 | — | 209 | 948 | 28,479 | 2,883 | 30.6[6] | 69.4[6] | 3,000 | 35,888 | 37,964 |
| Greenland | 88 | 771 | 185 | 100.0 | — | — | — | — | 185 | 3,426 | 34.1[13] | 65.9[13] | ... | ... | ... |
| Grenada | 8 | 70 | 25 | 100.0 | — | — | — | — | 25 | 223 | 46.8 | 53.2 | ... | ... | ... |
| Guadeloupe | 103 | 902 | 462 | 100.0 | — | — | — | — | 462 | 1,383 | ... | 32.9[10] | ... | ... | ... |
| Guam | 302 | 2,646 | 1,100 | 100.0 | — | — | — | — | 1,100 | 9,649 | 36.9[6] | 63.1[6] | ... | ... | ... |
| Guatemala | 777 | 6,807 | 1,755 | 61.4 | 38.6 | — | — | — | 1,755 | 220 | 27.0[4] | 73.0[4] | ... | ... | ... |
| Guernsey | ... | ... | ... | ... | ... | ... | ... | ... | ... | ... | ... | ... | ... | ... | ... |
| Guinea | 175 | 1,533 | 500 | 84.0 | 16.0 | — | — | — | 500 | 82 | ... | ... | ... | ... | ... |
| Guinea-Bissau | 7 | 61 | 14 | 100.0 | — | — | — | — | 14 | 16 | ... | ... | ... | ... | ... |
| Guyana | 168 | 1,472 | 390 | 98.7 | 1.3 | — | — | — | 390 | 409 | 32.5[15] | 67.5[15] | ... | ... | ... |
| Haiti | 126 | 1,104 | 375 | 30.7 | 69.3 | — | — | — | 375 | 57 | ... | ... | 13[1] | ... | ... |
| Honduras | 285 | 2,497 | 1,065 | 17.8 | 82.2 | — | 2 | 170 | 1,233 | 282 | 29.7 | 70.3 | 21[1] | ... | ... |
| Hong Kong | 5,580 | 48,881 | 19,235 | 100.0 | — | — | 1,050 | — | 18,185 | 3,278 | 19.9 | 80.1 | ... | ... | 5,223 |
| Hungary | 5,817 | 50,957 | 26,779 | 75.0 | 0.6 | 24.2 | 1,924 | 12,732 | 37,587 | 3,514 | 30.7[2] | 69.3[2] | 4,661 | 24,042 | 25,617 |
| Iceland | 947 | 8,296 | 4,044 | 0.1 | 95.2 | 4.7[12] | — | — | 4,044 | 16,642 | 20.9[4] | 79.1[4] | — | — | 69 |
| India | 51,180 | 448,337 | 188,479 | 66.7 | 30.8 | 2.5 | 75 | 4 | 188,408 | 248 | 12.3 | 87.7 | 1,581 | 157,485 | 160,476 |
| Indonesia | 8,826 | 77,316 | 27,797 | 91.4 | 7.8 | 0.8[12] | — | — | 27,797 | 167 | 24.9 | 75.1 | 23,232[1] | 1,492 | 918 |
| Iran | 13,404 | 117,419 | 37,300 | 82.8 | 17.2 | — | — | — | 37,300 | 836 | 21.1[9] | 78.9[9] | 193 | 900 | 1,000 |
| Iraq | 2,500 | 21,900 | 18,760 | 96.7 | 3.3 | — | — | — | 18,760 | 1,180 | 28.9[17] | 71.1[17] | ... | — | — |
| Ireland | 3,195 | 27,988 | 11,738 | 92.9 | 7.1 | — | — | — | 11,738 | 3,253 | 41.4[6] | 58.6[6] | 15 | 57 | 1,586 |
| Isle of Man | ... | ... | 188[18] | 100.0 | — | — | — | — | 172 | 2,530 | 48.1[6] | 51.9[6] | ... | ... | ... |
| Israel | 4,137 | 36,240 | 15,698 | 100.0 | — | — | 297 | — | 15,401 | 3,622 | 27.1 | 72.9 | ... | — | 2,873 |
| Italy | 54,976[19] | 481,590[19] | 182,237[19] | 72.1[19] | 22.5[19] | 3.9[19] | 1,436[19] | 25,105[19] | 205,906[19] | 3,592[19] | 25.0[6] | 75.0[6] | 39 | 1,755[19] | 24,219[19] |
| Jamaica | 740 | 6,482 | 2,400 | 93.8 | 6.2 | — | — | — | 2,400 | 1,027 | 18.1 | 81.9 | ... | ... | ... |
| Japan | 169,528 | 1,485,065 | 673,412 | 63.0 | 13.1 | 23.7 | — | — | 673,412 | 5,577 | 20.8[4] | 79.2[4] | 1,015 | 16,382 | 109,460 |
| Jersey | ... | ... | 337[18] | ... | ... | ... | ... | ... | 303[18] | 3,940[18] | ... | ... | ... | ... | ... |
| Jordan | 808 | 7,078 | 2,473 | 100.0 | — | — | — | — | 2,473 | 704 | 35.3 | 64.7 | ... | ... | ... |
| Kampuchea | 45 | 394 | 80 | 50.0 | 50.0 | — | — | — | 80 | 11 | ... | ... | ... | ... | ... |
| Kenya | 559 | 4,897 | 2,492 | 19.1 | 67.4 | 13.5[12] | — | 215 | 2,707 | 131 | 27.6 | 72.4 | ... | ... | 86 |
| Kiribati | 2 | 18 | 6 | 100.0 | — | — | — | — | 6 | 94 | ... | ... | ... | ... | ... |
| Korea, North | 8,700 | 76,212 | 48,000 | 41.7 | 58.3 | — | — | — | 48,000 | 2,355 | ... | ... | 600 | 51,000 | 51,400 |
| Korea, South | 17,670 | 154,789 | 62,716 | 67.5 | 5.8 | 26.7 | — | — | 62,716 | 1,520 | 16.8[6] | 83.2[6] | 132 | 22,543 | 41,395 |
| Kuwait | 5,230 | 45,815 | 15,689 | 100.0 | — | — | — | — | 15,689 | 8,663 | 70.4 | 29.6 | ... | ... | ... |
| Laos | 225 | 1,971 | 1,350 | 3.7 | 96.3 | — | 723 | 20 | 647 | 157 | ... | ... | ... | — | — |
| Lebanon | 668 | 5,852 | 1,355 | 56.8 | 43.2 | — | — | 40 | 1,395 | 523 | ... | ... | ... | — | — |
| Lesotho | [8] | [8] | [8] | [8] | [8] | [8] | [8] | [8] | [8] | [8] | ... | ... | ... | [8] | [8] |
| Liberia | 325 | 2,847 | 904 | 62.2 | 37.8 | — | — | — | 904 | 413 | ... | ... | ... | — | 1 |
| Libya | 1,460 | 12,790 | 8,170 | 100.0 | — | — | — | — | 8,170 | 2,266 | ... | ... | ... | ... | ... |
| Liechtenstein | [20] | [20] | [20] | [20] | [20] | [20] | [20] | [20] | [20] | [20] | ... | ... | ... | — | [20] |
| Luxembourg | 1,238 | 10,845 | 502 | 86.1 | 13.9 | — | 422 | 3,945 | 4,025 | 11,088 | 15.3[6] | 84.7[6] | ... | — | 199 |
| Macau | 137 | 1,200 | 445 | 100.0 | — | — | — | 47 | 492 | 1,249 | 75.0 | 25.0 | ... | ... | ... |
| Madagascar | 102 | 894 | 449 | 45.4 | 54.6 | — | — | — | 449 | 45 | ... | ... | 1,075[1] | — | 8 |
| Malawi | 160 | 1,402 | 514 | 5.3 | 94.7 | — | 1 | — | 513 | 74 | 14.5[2] | 85.5[2] | 12 | — | 29 |
| Malaysia | 3,897 | 34,138 | 14,915 | 75.0 | 25.0 | — | — | 58 | 14,973 | 962 | 20.3 | 79.7 | 7 | — | 544 |
| Maldives | 2 | 18 | 11 | 100.0 | — | — | — | — | 11 | 60 | 50.9[2] | 49.1[2] | ... | ... | ... |
| Mali | 56 | 491 | 164 | 17.7 | 82.3 | — | — | — | 164 | 20 | ... | ... | ... | ... | ... |
| Malta | 205 | 1,796 | 784 | 100.0 | — | — | — | — | 784 | 2,047 | 25.1[9] | 74.9[9] | ... | — | 212 |
| Martinique | 65 | 569 | 275 | 100.0 | — | — | — | — | 275 | 838 | ... | 40.9[10] | ... | ... | ... |
| Mauritania | 55 | 482 | 103 | 100.0 | — | — | — | — | 103 | 55 | ... | ... | ... | — | 7 |
| Mauritius | 274 | 2,400 | 521 | 77.9 | 22.1 | — | — | — | 521 | 496 | ... | ... | ... | — | 27 |
| Mayotte | 3 | 26 | ... | ... | ... | ... | ... | ... | ... | ... | ... | ... | ... | ... | ... |
| Mexico | 24,085 | 210,985 | 93,405 | 70.1 | 28.1 | 1.8[12] | 114 | 72 | 93,363 | 1,182 | 17.4[9] | 82.6[9] | 1,917 | 8,600 | 8,800 |
| Monaco | [14] | [14] | [14] | [14] | [14] | [14] | [14] | [14] | [14] | [14] | ... | ... | ... | [14] | [14] |
| Mongolia | 758 | 6,640 | 2,788 | 100.0 | — | — | — | 153 | 2,941 | 1,541 | 29.8[2] | 70.2[2] | 24,000[1] | 6,518 | 6,293 |
| Montserrat | 4 | 35 | 12 | 100.0 | — | — | — | — | 12 | 1,000 | 38.6 | 61.4 | ... | ... | ... |
| Morocco | 1,982 | 17,362 | 6,950 | 94.1 | 5.9 | — | — | — | 6,950 | 317 | 28.5 | 71.5 | 45 | 900 | 1,050 |
| Mozambique | 1,803 | 15,794 | 1,945 | 21.1 | 78.9 | — | 505 | 100 | 1,540 | 110 | ... | ... | 240 | 380 | 420 |
| Nauru | 10 | 88 | 28 | 100.0 | — | — | — | — | 28 | 3,500 | ... | ... | ... | ... | ... |
| Nepal | 171 | 1,498 | 408 | 6.9 | 93.1 | — | 7 | 71 | 472 | 29 | 46.7 | 53.3 | ... | 6 | 66 |
| Netherlands, The | 16,608 | 145,486 | 62,936 | 94.1 | — | 5.9 | 126 | 4,626 | 67,436 | 4,651 | 25.0 | 75.0 | 497 | 132 | 10,638 |
| Netherlands Antilles[5] | 400 | 3,504 | 2,400 | 100.0 | — | — | — | — | 2,400 | 9,091 | ... | ... | 2 | — | 177 |
| New Caledonia | 367 | 3,215 | 1,120 | 56.8 | 43.2 | — | — | — | 1,120 | 7,320 | ... | ... | ... | ... | ... |
| New Zealand | 6,382 | 55,906 | 26,764 | 19.1 | 75.1 | 5.8[12] | — | — | 26,764 | 8,066 | 37.5 | 62.5 | 243 | 2,409 | 2,039 |
| Nicaragua | 394 | 3,451 | 1,059 | 46.6 | 24.9 | 28.5[12] | 10 | 197 | 1,246 | 381 | 41.7 | 58.3 | ... | ... | ... |
| Niger | 65 | 569 | 51 | 100.0 | — | — | — | 287 | 338 | 55 | 4.9 | 95.1 | 5[1] | 61 | 61 |
| Nigeria | 4,025 | 35,259 | 9,000 | 76.2 | 23.8 | — | 140 | — | 8,860 | 93 | 37.9 | 62.1 | 169 | 50 | 50 |
| Niue | 1 | 9 | 3 | 100.0 | — | — | — | — | 3 | 1,000 | ... | ... | ... | ... | ... |
| Norfolk Island | ... | ... | ... | ... | ... | ... | ... | ... | ... | ... | ... | ... | ... | ... | ... |

| natural gas | | | | | | crude petroleum | | | | | | | country |
| published proved reserves, 1987 ('000,000,000 cu m) | production: natural gas, 1986 ('000,000 cu m) | production: manufactured gas, 1985 (% of total gas consumption) | consumption: amount, 1985 ('000,000 cu m) | consumption: residential, 1984 (%) | consumption: non-residential, 1984 (%) | reserves, 1987: published proved ('000,000 barrels) | reserves, 1987: years to exhaust proved reserves | production, 1986 ('000,000 barrels) | consumption, 1986 ('000,000 barrels) | refining capacity, 1987 ('000 barrels per day) | pipelines (latest)[a]: length (km) | pipelines (latest)[a]: traffic ('000,000 metric ton-km) | |
|---|---|---|---|---|---|---|---|---|---|---|---|---|---|
| — | — | 93.3 | — | — | — | ... | ... | — | 5[2] | 17 | — | — | El Salvador |
| ... | ... | 100.0 | — | — | — | ... | ... | — | ... | — | — | — | Equatorial Guinea |
| ... | ... | ... | — | — | — | ... | ... | — | 5[2] | 18 | — | — | Ethiopia |
| ... | ... | ... | ... | ... | ... | ... | ... | — | — | — | — | — | Faeroe Islands |
| ... | ... | ... | ... | ... | ... | ... | ... | — | — | — | — | — | Falkland Islands |
| — | — | 100.0 | ... | ... | ... | ... | ... | — | — | — | — | — | Fiji |
| — | — | 36.4 | 971 | 0.6[6] | 99.4[6] | ... | ... | — | 84 | 241 | — | — | Finland |
| 33 | 4,298 | 24.6[14] | 30,110[14] | 32.4[6] | 67.6[6] | 222 | 11 | 21 | 664 | 1,834 | 7,546 | 25,859 | France |
| ... | ... | ... | ... | ... | ... | ... | ... | — | — | — | — | — | French Guiana |
| ... | ... | ... | ... | ... | ... | ... | ... | — | — | — | — | — | French Polynesia |
| 15 | 68 | 3.4 | 201 | — | 100.0 | 646 | 11 | 60 | 9[2] | 16 | 284 | ... | Gabon |
| ... | ... | ... | ... | ... | ... | ... | ... | — | — | — | — | — | Gambia, The |
| ... | ... | ... | ... | ... | ... | ... | ... | — | — | — | — | — | Gaza Strip |
| 51 | 11,720 | 37.5 | 8,770 | ... | ... | 2 | 1 | 3 | 168[2] | 470 | 1,801 | 4,300 | Germany, East |
| 264 | 19,227 | 24.5 | 63,155 | 36.6[6] | 63.4[6] | 404 | 11 | 29 | 922 | 1,720 | 5,732 | 8,394 | Germany, West |
| — | — | 100.0 | — | — | — | 2 | 21 | 0.1 | 8[2] | 28 | 3 | ... | Ghana |
| ... | ... | ... | ... | ... | ... | ... | ... | — | ... | — | — | — | Gibraltar |
| 0.5 | 51 | 90.6 | 68 | ... | ... | 23 | 3 | 9 | 91 | 385 | 573 | ... | Greece |
| ... | ... | ... | ... | ... | ... | ... | ... | — | — | — | — | — | Greenland |
| ... | ... | ... | ... | ... | ... | ... | ... | — | — | — | — | — | Grenada |
| ... | ... | 100.0 | ... | ... | ... | ... | ... | — | — | — | — | — | Guadeloupe |
| ... | ... | ... | ... | ... | ... | ... | ... | — | 11[2] | — | — | — | Guam |
| 0.8 | 23 | 7.7 | ... | ... | ... | 23 | 13 | 2 | 5[2] | 16 | 275 | ... | Guatemala |
| ... | ... | ... | ... | ... | ... | ... | ... | — | — | — | — | — | Guernsey |
| ... | ... | ... | ... | ... | ... | ... | ... | — | — | — | — | — | Guinea |
| ... | ... | ... | ... | ... | ... | ... | ... | — | — | — | — | — | Guinea-Bissau |
| ... | ... | ... | ... | ... | ... | ... | ... | — | — | — | — | — | Guyana |
| — | — | 28.5 | — | — | — | ... | ... | — | 2[2] | 14 | — | — | Haiti |
| ... | ... | 55.1 | ... | ... | ... | ... | ... | — | — | — | — | — | Honduras |
| ... | ... | ... | ... | ... | ... | ... | ... | — | — | — | — | — | Hong Kong |
| 125 | 7,039 | 11.0 | 10,826 | 14.0[6] | 86.0[6] | 160 | 11 | 14 | 60[2] | 242 | 1,760 | 2,823 | Hungary |
| ... | ... | ... | ... | ... | ... | ... | ... | — | 4 | — | — | — | Iceland |
| 575 | 6,170 | 34.7 | 4,004 | 55.0[16] | 45.0[16] | 4,375 | 20 | 223 | 313[2] | 991 | 5,325 | ... | India |
| 1,841 | 32,731 | 11.4 | 7,169 | — | 100.0 | 8,478 | 17 | 507 | 197[2] | 636 | 2,906 | ... | Indonesia |
| 13,819 | 13,855 | 15.1 | 8,233 | — | 100.0 | 36,500 | 52 | 704 | 270[2] | 530 | 9,800 | ... | Iran |
| 748 | 595 | 47.9 | 589 | ... | ... | 40,000 | 63 | 630 | 111[2] | 319 | 4,675 | ... | Iraq |
| 53 | 1,682 | 4.3 | 2,276 | 13.9[6] | 86.1[6] | ... | ... | — | 33 | 56 | — | — | Ireland |
| ... | ... | ... | ... | ... | ... | ... | ... | — | — | — | — | — | Isle of Man |
| 1 | 68 | 93.3 | 49 | — | 100.0 | 0.7 | 19 | 0.04 | 50[2] | 180 | 998 | ... | Israel |
| 252 | 14,931 | 18.8[19] | 33,214[19] | 45.6[6] | 54.4[6] | 951 | 50 | 19 | 648 | 2,679 | 3,851 | 9,179 | Italy |
| — | — | 78.0 | — | — | — | ... | ... | — | 8[2] | 36 | 10 | ... | Jamaica |
| 32 | 2,291 | 45.8 | 38,079 | 61.3[15] | 38.7[15] | 58 | 15 | 4 | 1,611 | 4,790 | 406 | ... | Japan |
| — | — | 93.7 | — | — | — | ... | ... | — | — | — | — | — | Jersey |
| ... | ... | ... | ... | ... | ... | ... | ... | — | 18[2] | 100 | 209 | — | Jordan |
| ... | ... | ... | ... | ... | ... | ... | ... | — | — | — | — | — | Kampuchea |
| — | — | 104.8 | — | — | — | ... | ... | — | 15[2] | 95 | 483 | ... | Kenya |
| ... | ... | ... | ... | ... | ... | ... | ... | — | — | — | — | — | Kiribati |
| ... | ... | 54.8 | ... | ... | ... | ... | ... | — | 19[2] | 42 | 37 | ... | Korea, North |
| ... | ... | ... | ... | 100.0 | ... | ... | ... | — | 201[2] | 507 | 294 | ... | Korea, South |
| 1,377 | 4,089 | 37.1 | 5,416 | 21.7 | 78.3 | 94,576 | 169 | 560 | 216[2] | 618 | 917 | ... | Kuwait |
| ... | ... | ... | ... | ... | ... | ... | ... | — | ... | — | 136 | — | Laos |
| — | — | 33.3 | ... | ... | ... | ... | ... | — | 5[2] | 37 | 72 | — | Lebanon |
| — | — | [8] | ... | ... | ... | ... | ... | — | [8] | — | — | — | Lesotho |
| — | — | 50.5 | ... | ... | ... | ... | ... | — | 5[2] | 15 | — | — | Liberia |
| 626 | 4,689 | 19.0 | 2,864 | ... | ... | 22,800 | 63 | 361 | 60[2] | 329 | 4,826 | ... | Libya |
| — | — | [20] | 20 | ... | ... | ... | ... | — | — | — | — | — | Liechtenstein |
| ... | — | 53.4 | 373 | 48.0[6] | 52.0[6] | ... | ... | — | 7 | — | 48 | — | Luxembourg |
| ... | ... | ... | ... | ... | ... | ... | ... | — | — | — | — | — | Macau |
| ... | — | 100.0 | — | ... | ... | ... | ... | — | 2[2] | 16 | — | — | Madagascar |
| ... | — | 100.0 | ... | ... | ... | ... | ... | — | — | — | — | — | Malawi |
| 1,453 | 6,196 | 5.2 | 10,325 | 33.8 | 66.2 | 3,200 | 18 | 182 | 55[2] | 212 | 707 | ... | Malaysia |
| ... | ... | ... | ... | ... | ... | ... | ... | — | — | — | — | — | Maldives |
| ... | ... | ... | ... | ... | ... | ... | ... | — | — | — | — | — | Mali |
| — | — | 170.1 | — | ... | ... | ... | ... | — | 3[2] | 13 | — | — | Malta |
| ... | ... | ... | ... | ... | ... | ... | ... | — | — | — | — | — | Mauritania |
| ... | ... | ... | ... | ... | ... | ... | ... | — | — | — | — | — | Mauritius |
| ... | ... | ... | ... | ... | ... | ... | ... | — | — | — | — | — | Mayotte |
| 2,146 | 35,461 | 23.9[14] | 23,909[14] | 3.9[9] | 96.1[9] | 54,880 | 60 | 913 | 424[2] | 1,349 | 10,975 | ... | Mexico |
| ... | ... | ... | ... | ... | ... | ... | ... | — | — | — | ... | ... | Monaco |
| ... | ... | ... | ... | ... | 64.6[4,10] | ... | ... | — | — | — | — | — | Mongolia |
| ... | ... | ... | ... | ... | ... | ... | ... | — | — | — | — | — | Montserrat |
| 2 | 74 | 51.5 | 85 | — | 100.0 | 2 | 10 | 0.2 | 34[2] | 81 | 362 | ... | Morocco |
| 65 | — | 100.0 | — | ... | ... | ... | ... | — | 4[2] | 17 | 289 | ... | Mozambique |
| ... | ... | ... | ... | ... | ... | ... | ... | — | — | — | — | — | Nauru |
| ... | — | ... | ... | ... | ... | ... | ... | — | — | — | — | ... | Nepal |
| 1,815 | 74,284 | 18.4 | 33,289 | 46.8 | 53.4 | 195 | 6 | 32 | 252 | 1,401 | 1,383 | 4,202 | Netherlands, The |
| — | — | 50.0 | ... | ... | ... | ... | ... | — | 74[2] | 320 | — | — | Netherlands Antilles[5] |
| ... | ... | ... | ... | ... | ... | ... | ... | — | — | — | — | — | New Caledonia |
| 125 | 4,040 | 2.0 | 2,884 | 4.8 | 95.2 | 182 | 17 | 11 | 31 | 54 | 310 | ... | New Zealand |
| — | — | 93.7 | — | — | — | ... | ... | — | 4[2] | 15 | 56 | ... | Nicaragua |
| ... | — | — | ... | ... | ... | ... | ... | — | — | — | — | — | Niger |
| 1,303 | 2,044 | 2.0 | 5,638 | — | 100.0 | 16,000 | 30 | 537 | 66[2] | 250 | 5,042 | ... | Nigeria |
| ... | ... | ... | ... | ... | ... | ... | ... | — | — | — | — | — | Niue |
| ... | ... | ... | ... | ... | ... | ... | ... | — | — | — | — | — | Norfolk Island |

## Energy (continued)

| country | electricity — installed capacity, 1985 ('000 kW) | production, 1985 capacity ('000,000 kW-hr) | production, 1985 amount ('000,000 kW-hr) | power source, 1985 fossil fuel (%) | hydro-power (%) | nuclear fuel (%) | trade, 1985 exports ('000,000 kW-hr) | imports ('000,000 kW-hr) | consumption amount, 1985 ('000,000 kW-hr) | per capita, 1985 (kW-hr) | residential, 1984 (%) | non-residential, 1984 (%) | coal reserves, latest ('000,000 metric tons) | coal production, 1985 ('000 metric tons) | coal consumption, 1985 ('000 metric tons) |
|---|---|---|---|---|---|---|---|---|---|---|---|---|---|---|---|
| Norway | 23,236 | 203,547 | 103,190 | 0.3 | 99.7 | — | 4,618 | 4,055 | 102,627 | 24,777 | 27.0[4] | 73.0[4] | 30 | 569 | 1,191 |
| Oman | 1,083 | 9,487 | 2,846 | 100.0 | — | — | — | — | 2,846 | 1,423 | ... | ... | ... | ... | ... |
| Pacific Is., Trust Territory of the | 52 | 456 | 164 | 100.0 | — | — | — | — | 164 | 1,065 | ... | ... | ... | ... | ... |
| Marshall Islands | | | | | | | | | | | | | | | |
| Micronesia, Fed. States of | ... | ... | ... | ... | ... | ... | ... | ... | ... | ... | ... | ... | ... | ... | ... |
| Northern Mariana Islands | | | | | | | | | | | | | | | |
| Palau | ... | ... | ... | ... | ... | ... | ... | ... | ... | ... | ... | ... | ... | ... | ... |
| Pakistan | 5,894 | 51,631 | 25,732 | 39.9 | 58.6 | 1.5 | — | — | 25,732 | 256 | 28.8 | 71.2 | 102 | 2,162 | 2,169 |
| Panama | 898 | 7,866 | 2,570 | 24.9 | 75.1 | — | — | — | 2,570 | 1,178 | 26.8[9] | 73.2[9] | ... | — | 6 |
| Papua New Guinea | 467 | 4,091 | 1,565 | 73.2 | 26.8 | — | — | — | 1,565 | 446 | 8.9 | 91.1 | ... | ... | ... |
| Paraguay | 994 | 8,707 | 1,535 | 2.3 | 97.7 | — | 25 | 200 | 1,710 | 464 | 20.4[9] | 79.6[9] | 28[1] | 110 | 160 |
| Peru | 3,502 | 30,678 | 12,115 | 23.1 | 76.9 | — | — | — | 12,115 | 615 | | | 82 | 1,227 | 1,742 |
| Philippines | 6,581 | 57,650 | 21,018 | 39.0 | 35.3 | 25.7[12] | — | — | 21,018 | 386 | 19.7 | 80.3 | ... | ... | ... |
| Pitcairn Island | ... | | | | | | | | | | | | | | |
| Poland | 29,038 | 254,373 | 137,708 | 97.2 | 2.8 | — | 7,568 | 5,456 | 135,596 | 3,646 | 33.5[2] | 66.5[2] | 42,700 | 249,388 | 217,436 |
| Portugal | 6,079 | 53,252 | 19,007 | 43.4 | 56.6 | — | 1,284 | 3,530 | 21,253 | 2,081 | 36.4[4] | 63.6[4] | 52 | 238 | 1,633 |
| Puerto Rico | 4,100 | 35,916 | 12,316 | 98.8 | 1.2 | — | — | — | 12,316 | 3,569 | 31.0[9] | 69.0[9] | ... | — | 50 |
| Qatar | 1,005 | 8,804 | 3,515 | 100.0 | — | — | — | — | 3,515 | 11,159 | 69.0[16] | 31.0[16] | ... | ... | ... |
| Réunion | 149 | 1,305 | 567 | 0.9 | 99.1 | — | — | — | 567 | 1,068 | ... | ... | ... | — | — |
| Romania | 19,580 | 171,521 | 75,268 | 84.2 | 15.8 | — | 1,000 | 3,259 | 77,527 | 3,368 | 23.6[2] | 76.4[2] | 3,970[1] | 46,581 | 51,881 |
| Rwanda | 58 | 508 | 163 | 1.8 | 98.2 | — | 1 | 12 | 174 | 29 | ... | ... | ... | ... | ... |
| St. Christopher and Nevis | 15 | 131 | 35 | 100.0 | — | — | — | — | 35 | 761 | ... | ... | ... | — | — |
| St. Helena and Ascension | 2 | 18 | 2 | 100.0 | — | — | — | — | 2 | 333 | ... | ... | ... | — | — |
| St. Lucia | 20 | 175 | 73 | 100.0 | — | — | — | — | 73 | 562 | 26.6[2] | 73.4[2] | ... | — | — |
| St. Pierre and Miquelon | 22 | 193 | 35 | 100.0 | — | — | — | — | 35 | 5,833 | ... | ... | ... | — | — |
| St. Vincent and the Grenadines | 10 | 88 | 30 | 40.0 | 60.0 | — | — | — | 30 | 288 | 45.3 | 54.7 | ... | ... | ... |
| San Marino | [19] | [19] | [19] | [19] | [19] | [19] | [19] | [19] | [19] | [19] | | | | [19] | [19] |
| São Tomé and Príncipe | 6 | 53 | 19 | 46.7 | 53.3 | — | — | — | 15 | 155 | ... | ... | ... | ... | ... |
| Saudi Arabia | 13,710 | 120,100 | 32,410 | 100.0 | — | — | — | — | 32,410 | 2,808 | 67.4[16] | 32.6[16] | ... | ... | ... |
| Senegal | 180 | 1,577 | 696 | 100.0 | — | — | — | — | 696 | 108 | ... | ... | ... | ... | ... |
| Seychelles | 19 | 166 | 62 | 100.0 | — | — | — | — | 62 | 816 | ... | ... | ... | ... | ... |
| Sierra Leone | 106 | 929 | 278 | 100.0 | — | — | — | — | 278 | 77 | ... | ... | ... | ... | ... |
| Singapore | 3,160 | 27,682 | 9,876 | 100.0 | — | — | 50 | — | 9,826 | 3,840 | 18.0 | 82.0 | ... | — | 2 |
| Solomon Islands | 13 | 114 | 29 | 100.0 | — | — | — | — | 29 | 107 | 26.6 | 73.4 | ... | — | — |
| Somalia | 60 | 526 | 145 | 100.0 | — | — | — | — | 145 | 31 | ... | ... | ... | ... | ... |
| South Africa | 24,727[8] | 216,609[8] | 122,293[8] | 96.2[8] | 0.6[8] | 3.2[8] | 206[8] | 500[8] | 122,587[8] | 3,294[8] | ... | ... | 58,404 | 173,728[8] | 129,389[8] |
| Bophuthatswana | ... | ... | ... | ... | ... | ... | ... | ... | ... | ... | ... | ... | ... | ... | ... |
| Ciskei | ... | ... | ... | ... | ... | ... | ... | ... | ... | ... | ... | ... | ... | ... | ... |
| KwaNdebele | ... | ... | ... | ... | ... | ... | ... | ... | ... | ... | ... | ... | ... | ... | ... |
| Transkei | ... | ... | ... | ... | ... | ... | ... | ... | ... | ... | ... | ... | ... | ... | ... |
| Venda | ... | ... | ... | ... | ... | ... | ... | ... | ... | ... | ... | ... | ... | ... | ... |
| South West Africa/Namibia | [8] | [8] | [8] | [8] | [8] | [8] | [8] | [8] | [8] | [8] | | | ... | [8] | [8] |
| Spain | 39,205 | 343,436 | 125,560 | 52.7 | 25.0 | 22.3 | 5,001 | 3,927 | 124,486 | 3,230 | 16.7[4] | 83.2[4] | 883 | 40,040 | 48,434 |
| Sri Lanka | 949 | 8,313 | 2,464 | 2.8 | 97.2 | — | — | — | 2,464 | 152 | 16.9 | 83.1 | ... | — | 1 |
| Sudan, The | 313 | 2,742 | 1,037 | 50.6 | 49.4 | — | — | — | 1,037 | 48 | ... | ... | ... | ... | ... |
| Suriname | 415 | 3,635 | 1,300 | 29.2 | 70.8 | — | — | — | 1,300 | 3,467 | ... | ... | 1,820 | — | 1 |
| Swaziland | [8] | [8] | [8] | [8] | [8] | [8] | [8] | [8] | [8] | [8] | 18.7[15] | 81.3[15] | ... | [8] | [8] |
| Sweden | 33,168 | 290,552 | 136,543 | 4.9 | 52.1 | 43.0 | 6,675 | 5,142 | 135,010 | 16,165 | 26.4[4] | 73.6[4] | 1 | 12 | 4,143 |
| Switzerland | 15,150[20] | 132,714[20] | 53,872[20] | 1.6[20] | 58.9[20] | 39.5[20] | 23,210[20] | 14,512[20] | 45,174[20] | 7,056[20] | 26.6[6] | 73.4[6] | ... | — | 640[20] |
| Syria | 2,940 | 25,754 | 7,316 | 60.9 | 39.1 | — | 140 | ... | 7,176 | 683 | 21.2[6] | 78.8[6] | ... | — | 2 |
| Taiwan | 15,970 | 139,897 | 52,556 | 34.5 | 13.1 | 52.4 | — | — | 47,919 | 2,504 | 27.1[2] | 72.9[2] | 200 | ... | ... |
| Tanzania | 440 | 3,854 | 875 | 29.7 | 70.3 | — | — | — | 875 | 39 | ... | ... | 200 | 1 | 1 |
| Thailand | 7,215 | 63,203 | 24,179 | 84.7 | 15.3 | — | 20 | 723 | 24,882 | 484 | 24.4 | 75.6 | 879 | 5,190 | 5,326 |
| Togo | 36 | 315 | 34 | 88.2 | 11.8 | — | — | 213 | 247 | 83 | ... | ... | ... | ... | ... |
| Tokelau | ... | | | | | | | | | | | | | | |
| Tonga | 6 | 53 | 12 | 100.0 | — | — | — | — | 12 | 110 | ... | ... | ... | ... | ... |
| Trinidad and Tobago | 765 | 6,701 | 3,035 | 100.0 | — | — | — | — | 3,035 | 2,561 | 24.7 | 75.3 | ... | — | |
| Tunisia | 1,414 | 12,387 | 4,021 | 97.3 | 2.7 | — | — | — | 4,021 | 568 | 32.7 | 67.3 | ... | — | 21 |
| Turkey | 9,119 | 79,882 | 33,313 | 63.8 | 36.2 | — | — | 2,137 | 35,450 | 719 | 14.2[9] | 85.8[9] | 4,857 | 39,094 | 42,557 |
| Turks and Caicos Islands | 9 | 79 | 12 | 100.0 | — | — | — | — | 12 | 1,500 | ... | ... | ... | ... | ... |
| Tuvalu | ... | ... | ... | ... | ... | ... | ... | — | ... | ... | ... | ... | ... | ... | ... |
| Uganda | 163 | 1,428 | 653 | 1.4 | 98.6 | — | 32 | — | 621 | 40 | ... | ... | ... | ... | ... |
| U.S.S.R. | 319,293 | 2,797,007 | 1,544,000 | 75.6 | 13.3 | 11.1 | 27,246 | 300 | 1,517,054 | 5,445 | 21.6[2] | 78.4[2] | 244,700 | 680,136 | 664,524 |
| United Arab Emirates | 2,480 | 21,725 | 6,690 | 100.0 | — | — | — | — | 6,690 | 5,041 | ... | ... | ... | ... | ... |
| United Kingdom | 67,607 | 592,237 | 294,722 | 77.9 | 1.4 | 20.7 | — | — | 294.722 | 5,232 | 35.4[6] | 64.6[6] | 4,600 | 94,046 | 105,701 |
| United States | 701,875 | 6,148,425 | 2,525,191 | 73.2 | 11.2 | 15.2 | 4,965 | 45,901 | 2,566,127 | 10,781 | 34.9[6] | 65.1[6] | 263,843 | 803,850 | 736,627 |
| Uruguay | 1,301 | 11,397 | 6,602 | 2.3 | 97.7 | — | 2,678 | — | 3,924 | 1,303 | 43.4 | 56.6 | ... | ... | ... |
| Vanuatu | 11 | 96 | 25 | 100.0 | — | — | — | — | 25 | 176 | ... | ... | ... | ... | ... |
| Venezuela | 12,499 | 109,491 | 45,400 | 54.4 | 45.6 | — | 8 | — | 45,392 | 2,621 | 22.7 | 77.3 | 372 | 41 | 301 |
| Vietnam | 1,270 | 11,125 | 5,000 | 62.0 | 38.0 | — | — | — | 5,000 | 84 | 36.4[2] | 63.6[2] | 150 | 5,300 | 4,800 |
| Virgin Islands (U.S.) | 341 | 2,987 | 900 | 100.0 | — | — | — | — | 900 | 8,571 | 40.2 | 59.8 | ... | ... | ... |
| Wallis and Futuna | ... | ... | ... | ... | ... | ... | ... | ... | ... | ... | ... | ... | ... | ... | ... |
| West Bank | | | | | | | | | | | | | | | |
| Western Sahara | 56 | 491 | 78 | 100.0 | — | — | — | — | 78 | 503 | ... | ... | ... | ... | ... |
| Western Samoa | 17 | 149 | 42 | 59.5 | 40.5 | — | — | — | 42 | 258 | ... | ... | ... | ... | ... |
| Yemen (Aden) | 160 | 1,402 | 285 | 100.0 | — | — | — | — | 285 | 133 | ... | ... | 1[1] | ... | ... |
| Yemen (Şan'ā') | 115 | 1,007 | 295 | 100.0 | — | — | — | — | 295 | 43 | ... | ... | ... | ... | ... |
| Yugoslavia | 15,250 | 133,590 | 73,942 | 59.4 | 31.7 | 5.5 | 2,036 | 2,663 | 74,569 | 3,221 | 26.1[4] | 73.9[4] | 16,570 | 68,463 | 72,762 |
| Zaire | 2,166 | 18,974 | 4,615 | 2.9 | 97.1 | — | 125 | 10 | 4,500 | 150 | ... | 89.1[4,10] | 600 | 130 | 165 |
| Zambia | 1,729 | 15,146 | 10,090 | 0.3 | 99.7 | — | 3,100 | 20 | 7,010 | 1,052 | 13.6 | 86.4 | 72 | 510 | 510 |
| Zimbabwe | 1,539 | 13,482 | 4,342 | 21.9 | 78.1 | — | — | 3,000 | 7,342 | 836 | 16.3 | 83.7 | 734 | 2,350 | 2,270 |

| natural gas — published proved reserves, 1987 ('000,000,000 cu m) | production — natural gas, 1986 ('000,000 cu m) | production — manufactured gas, 1985 (% of total gas consumption) | consumption — amount, 1985 ('000,000 cu m) | consumption — residential, 1984 (%) | consumption — non-residential, 1984 (%) | crude petroleum — reserves, 1987 — published proved ('000,000 barrels) | reserves, 1987 — years to exhaust proved reserves | production, 1986 ('000,000 barrels) | consumption, 1986 ('000,000 barrels) | refining capacity, 1987 ('000 barrels per day) | pipelines (latest)[a] — length (km) | pipelines (latest)[a] — traffic ('000,000 metric ton-km) | country |
|---|---|---|---|---|---|---|---|---|---|---|---|---|---|
| 2,612 | 25,479 | 54.9 | 1,229 | ... | ... | 11,133 | 36 | 306 | 75 | 240 | 53 | 4,905 | Norway |
| 264 | 1,365 | 51.2 | 5,922 | ... | ... | 4,037 | 20 | 207 | 17[2] | 48 | 1,300 | — | Oman |
| ... | ... | ... | ... | ... | ... | ... | ... | — | — | — | — | — | Pacific Is., Trust Territory of the Marshall Islands |
| ... | ... | ... | ... | ... | ... | ... | ... | — | — | ... | — | — | Micronesia, Fed. States of |
|  |  |  |  |  |  |  |  |  |  |  |  |  |  |
| ... | ... | ... | ... | ... | ... | ... | ... | — | — | — | — | — | Northern Mariana Islands |
| ... | ... | ... | ... | ... | ... | ... | ... | — | ... | ... | — | — | Palau |
| 625 | 11,114 | 1.0 | 9,081 | 25.8 | 74.2 | 116 | 8 | 15 | 39[2] | 130 | 1,135 | — | Pakistan |
| — | — | 40.5 | — | — | — |  |  | — | 9[2] | 100 | 130 | ... | Panama |
| 14 |  | 100.0 | — | — | — | 50 | ... |  |  |  |  |  | Papua New Guinea |
|  |  |  |  |  |  |  |  |  |  |  |  |  |  |
| ... | ... | 12.5 | ... | ... | ... | ... | ... | — | 1[2] | 8 | — | — | Paraguay |
| 24 | 1,271 | 17.2 | 1,119 | ... | 71.4[10] | 535 | 8 | 65 | 61[2] | 176 | 800 | ... | Peru |
| 0.6 | — | 78.3 | ... | ... | ... | 19 | 6 | 3 | 60[2] | 286 | 357 | ... | Philippines |
| ... | ... | ... | ... | ... | ... | ... | ... | ... | ... | ... | — | — | Pitcairn Island |
| 125 | 5,825 | 36.2 | 11,578 | ... | ... | 11 | 11 | 1 | 104[2] | 385 | 2,346 | 17,836 | Poland |
|  |  |  |  |  |  |  |  |  |  |  |  |  |  |
| — | ... | 62.0 | ... | ... | ... | ... | ... | — | 73 | 294 | 69 | ... | Portugal |
| — | ... | 66.7 | ... | ... | ... | ... | ... | — | 36[2] | 121 | ... | ... | Puerto Rico |
| 4,191 | 5,839 | 20.5 | 4,303 | — | 100.0 | 3,391 | 39 | 87 | 22[2] | 62 | 235 | — | Qatar |
| ... | ... | ... | ... | ... | ... | ... | ... | — | — | — | — | — | Réunion |
| 163 | 34,269 | 8.0 | 40,112 | ... | ... | 1,362 | 17 | 80 | 190[2] | 617 | 4,229 | 4,443 | Romania |
|  |  |  |  |  |  |  |  |  |  |  |  |  |  |
| 40 | — | — | 1 | ... | ... | ... | ... | — | — | — | — | — | Rwanda |
| ... | ... | ... | ... | ... | ... | ... | ... | — | — | — | — | — | St. Christopher and Nevis |
| ... | ... | ... | ... | ... | ... | ... | ... | — | — | — | — | — | St. Helena and Ascension |
| ... | ... | ... | ... | ... | ... | ... | ... | — | — | — | — | — | St. Lucia |
| ... | ... | ... | ... | ... | ... | ... | ... | ... | ... | ... | ... | — | St. Pierre and Miquelon |
|  |  |  |  |  |  |  |  |  |  |  |  |  |  |
| ... | ... | ... | ... | ... | ... | ... | ... | — | — | — | — | — | St. Vincent and the Grenadines |
| ... | ... | [19] | [19] | ... | ... | ... | ... | — | — | — | — | — | San Marino |
| ... | ... | ... | ... | ... | ... | ... | ... | — | — | — | — | — | São Tomé and Príncipe |
| 4,108 | 9,308 | 383.9 | 1,512 | 11.1[16] | 88.9[16] | 169,576 | 91 | 1,871 | 311[2] | 1,125 | 6,550 | ... | Saudi Arabia |
| — | ... | 16.6 | ... | ... | ... | ... | ... | — | 2[2] | 30 | — | — | Senegal |
|  |  |  |  |  |  |  |  |  |  |  |  |  |  |
| ... | ... | ... | ... | ... | ... | ... | ... | — | — | — | — | — | Seychelles |
| ... | ... | ... | ... | ... | ... | ... | ... | — | 2[2] | 10 | — | — | Sierra Leone |
| — | — | 445.8 | ... | ... | ... | ... | ... | — | 261[2] | 961 | — | — | Singapore |
| ... | ... | ... | ... | ... | ... | ... | ... | — | — | — | 15 | ... | Solomon Islands |
| 6 | — | ... | ... | ... | ... | ... | ... | — | 3[2] | 10 | 15 | ... | Somalia |
|  |  |  |  |  |  |  |  |  |  |  |  |  |  |
| 28 | — | 100.0[8] | — | — | ... | 115 | ... | — | 117[2,8] | 389 | 2,679 | ... | South Africa |
| ... | ... | ... | ... | ... | ... | ... | ... | — | — | — | — | — | Bophuthatswana |
| ... | ... | ... | ... | ... | ... | ... | ... | — | — | — | — | — | Ciskei |
| ... | ... | ... | ... | ... | ... | ... | ... | — | — | — | — | — | KwaNdebele |
| ... | ... | ... | ... | ... | ... | ... | ... | — | — | — | — | — | Transkei |
|  |  |  |  |  |  |  |  |  |  |  |  |  |  |
| ... | ... | [8] | ... | ... | ... | ... | ... | — | — | — | — | — | Venda |
| — | ... | [8] | ... | ... | ... | ... | ... | — | [8] | ... | — | — | South West Africa/Namibia |
| 14 | 354 | 56.4 | 2,836 | ... | ... | 34 | 3 | 13 | 339 | 1,305 | 2,127 | 3,161 | Spain |
| — | ... | 92.9 | ... | ... | ... | ... | ... | — | 12[2] | 50 | 69 | ... | Sri Lanka |
| — | ... | 77.8 | ... | ... | ... | 300 | ... | ... | 8[2] | 24 | 815 | ... | Sudan, The |
|  |  |  |  |  |  |  |  |  |  |  |  |  |  |
| ... | ... | [8] | ... | ... | ... | 1 | 2 | 0.7 | 1[2] | — | — | — | Suriname |
| — | — | 69.7 | 82 | ... | ... | ... | ... | ... | 8 | ... | — | — | Swaziland |
| — | — | ... | ... | ... | ... | ... | ... | — | 135 | 437 | — | — | Sweden |
| — | — | 18.8[20] | 1,634[20] | 38.3[6] | 61.7[6] | ... | ... | — | 102 | 65 | 314 | 1,207 | Switzerland |
| 122 | 136 | 26.6 | 154 | ... | ... | 1,470 | 21 | 71 | 83[2] | 229 | 1,819 | ... | Syria |
|  |  |  |  |  |  |  |  |  |  |  |  |  |  |
| 21 | 980 | ... | ... | ... | ... | 10 | 10 | 1 | ... | 543 | 615 | ... | Taiwan |
| 118 | — | 100.0 | ... | ... | ... | ... | ... | ... | 4[2] | 14 | 982 | ... | Tanzania |
| 92 | 3,222 | 15.0 | 2,791 | — | 100.0 | 96 | 7 | 13 | 54[2] | 192 | 67 | ... | Thailand |
| — | ... | ... | ... | ... | ... | ... | ... | ... | ... | 20 | — | — | Togo |
| ... | ... | ... | ... | ... | ... | ... | ... | ... | ... | ... |  |  | Tokelau |
|  |  |  |  |  |  |  |  |  |  |  |  |  |  |
|  |  |  |  |  |  |  |  |  |  |  |  |  | Tonga |
| 294 | 3,545 | 11.6 | 2,818 | — | 100.0 | 567 | 9 | 64 | 35[2] | 300 | 1,051 | ... | Trinidad and Tobago |
| 71 | 436 | 3.4 | 1,041 | 4.4 | 95.6 | 1,740 | 44 | 40 | 12[2] | 34 | 883 | ... | Tunisia |
| 15 | 456 | 78.3 | 68 | ... | ... | 139 | 8 | 17 | 142 | 460 | 4,059 | 41,918 | Turkey |
| ... | ... | ... | ... | ... | ... | ... | ... | ... | ... | ... | — | — | Turks and Caicos Islands |
|  |  |  |  |  |  |  |  |  |  |  |  |  |  |
| ... | ... | ... | ... | ... | ... | ... | ... | ... | ... | ... | — | — | Tuvalu |
| ... | ... | ... | ... | ... | ... | ... | ... | ... | ... | ... | — | — | Uganda |
| 35,396 | 685,995 | 10.5 | 570,892 | ... | ... | 60,700 | 14 | 4,490 | 3,287 | 12,260 | 78,300 | 1,370,300 | U.S.S.R. |
| 3,140 | 10,254 | 299.0 | 801 | ... | ... | 33,050 | 66 | 502 | 50[2] | 185 | 830 | ... | United Arab Emirates |
| 634 | 45,461 | 13.0 | 62,195 | 52.7[6] | 47.3[6] | 5,301 | 6 | 907 | 599 | 1,780 | 3,926 | 9,678 | United Kingdom |
|  |  |  |  |  |  |  |  |  |  |  |  |  |  |
| 5,202 | 451,698 | 19.3 | 500,898 | 33.4[9] | 66.6[9] | 27,280 | 9 | 3,164 | 5,679 | 15,288 | 278,035 | 810,904 | United States |
| — | ... | 97.3 | — | — | — | ... | ... | ... | 8[2] | 45 | ... | ... | Uruguay |
| ... | ... | ... | ... | ... | ... | ... | ... | ... | ... | ... | — | — | Vanuatu |
| 2,622 | 17,418 | 14.0 | 16,310 | 8.2 | 91.8 | 55,521 | 90 | 616 | 300[2] | 1,225 | 6,850 | ... | Venezuela |
| ... | ... | ... | ... | ... | ... | ... | ... | ... | ... | ... | 150 | ... | Vietnam |
|  |  |  |  |  |  |  |  |  |  |  |  |  |  |
| — | — | 100.0 | ... | ... | ... | ... | ... | — | 116[2] | 600 | ... | ... | Virgin Islands (U.S.) |
| ... | ... | ... | ... | ... | ... | ... | ... | — | — | — | — | — | Wallis and Futuna |
| ... | ... | ... | ... | ... | ... | ... | ... | — | — | — | — | — | West Bank |
| ... | ... | ... | ... | ... | ... | ... | ... | — | — | — | — | — | Western Sahara |
| ... | ... | ... | ... | ... | ... | ... | ... | — | — | — | — | — | Western Samoa |
|  |  |  |  |  |  |  |  |  |  |  |  |  |  |
| 142 | — | 100.0 | — | — | — | ... | ... | ... | 26[2] | 170 | 32 | ... | Yemen (Aden) |
| ... | ... | ... | ... | ... | ... | 1,000 | 250 | 4 | ... | 10 | — | — | Yemen (San'ā') |
| 87 | 1,838 | 21.2 | 5,859 | ... | ... | 263 | 8 | 31 | 95[2] | 483 | 1,523 | 2,555 | Yugoslavia |
| 1 | ... | 100.0 | — | — | — | 111 | 9 | 12 | 2[2] | 17 | 390 | ... | Zaire |
| ... | ... | 100.0 | ... | ... | ... | ... | ... | ... | 5[2] | 25 | 1,724 | ... | Zambia |
|  |  |  |  |  |  |  |  |  |  |  |  |  |  |
| ... | — | 85.8 | ... | ... | ... | ... | ... | ... | ... | ... | 8 | ... | Zimbabwe |

[1]Estimated reserves in place. [2]1985. [3]1972. [4]1981. [5]Netherlands Antilles includes Aruba. [6]1983. [7]Belgium includes Luxembourg. [8]South Africa includes Botswana, Lesotho, South West Africa/Namibia, and Swaziland. [9]1982. [10]Transportation and industry only; excludes agricultural, commercial, and public service sectors. [11]1978. [12]Geothermally generated electricity. [13]1986. [14]France includes Monaco. [15]1980. [16]Residential includes agriculture. [17]1977. [18]1984. [19]Italy includes San Marino. [20]Switzerland includes Liechtenstein.

# Transportation

This table presents data on the transportation infrastructure of the various countries and dependencies of the world and on their commercial passenger and cargo traffic. Most states have roads and airports, with services corresponding to their traffic levels and to the prevailing level of economic development. A number of states, however, lack railroads or inland waterways, because of either geographic constraints or lack of development capital and technical expertise. Pipelines, one of the oldest means of bulk transport if aqueducts are considered, are today the least developed transportation mode worldwide for shipment of bulk materials. Because the principal contemporary application of pipeline technology is to facilitate the shipment of hydrocarbon liquids and gases, coverage of pipelines will be found in the "Energy" table. However, it is also true that pipelines now find increasing application for slurries of coal or other raw materials.

While the United Nations' *Statistical Yearbook* and *Monthly Bulletin of Statistics* provide much data on infrastructure and traffic and have established basic categories and classifications for transportation statistics, the number of countries covered is limited. Several commercial publications maintain substantial data bases and publishing programs for their particular areas of interest: Highway and vehicle statistics are provided by the International Road Federation's annual *Road and Motor Vehicle Statistics* and *World Road Statistics;* the International Union of Railways' *International Railway Statistics* and Jane's *World Railways* provide

similar data for railways; Lloyd's *Register of Shipping Statistical Tables* summarizes the world's merchant marine; the *Official Airline Guide,* the International Civil Aviation Organization's *Digest of Statistics,* and the International Air Transport Association's *World Air Transport Statistics* have also been used to supplement and update data collected by the UN. Because several of these agencies are commercially or insurance-oriented, their data tend to be more complete, accurate, and timely than those of intergovernmental organizations, which depend on periodic responses to questionnaires or publication of results in official sources. All of these international sources are supplemented by national statistical sources to provide additional data. Such diversity of sources, however, imposes limitations on the comparability of the statistics from country to country because the basis and completeness of data collection and the frequency and timeliness of analysis and publication may vary greatly. Data more than five years old are shown in italic.

The categories adopted in the table also have special problems of comparability. Total road length is subject to wide international variation of interpretation, as "roads" can mean anything from mere tracks to highly developed highways. Each country also has individual classifications that differ according to climate, availability of road-building materials, traffic patterns, administrative responsibility, and so on. "Paved roads," by contrast, is a much more tightly definable category, but the proportion of paved to total roads may be distorted by the less comparable total road

## Transportation

| country | roads and motor vehicles (latest) | | | | | | | | railroads (latest) | | | | | |
| | roads | | | motor vehicles | | | cargo | | track length | | traffic | | | |
| | length | | paved (per-cent) | auto-mobiles | trucks and buses | persons per vehicle | short ton-mi ('000,000) | metric ton-km ('000,000) | mi | km | passengers | | cargo | |
| | mi | km | | | | | | | | | passen-ger-mi ('000,000) | passen-ger-km ('000,000) | short ton-mi ('000,000) | metric ton-km ('000,000) |
|---|---|---|---|---|---|---|---|---|---|---|---|---|---|---|
| Afghanistan | 11,789 | 18,974 | 42 | *31,754* | *30,997* | 268 | *1,993* | *2,910* | 6 | 10 | ... | ... | ... | ... |
| Albania | *13,049* | *21,000* | *14* | *3,500* | *11,200* | *146* | ... | ... | 253 | 408 | *181* | *291* | *87* | *127* |
| Algeria | 44,795 | 72,091 | 54 | 574,506 | 360,139 | 22 | *2,148* | *3,136* | 2,576[2] | 4,146[2] | 1,140 | 1,835 | 1,802 | 2,631 |
| American Samoa | 186 | 300 | 90 | —4,818— | | 7.4 | ... | ... | — | — | — | — | — | — |
| Andorra | *137* | *220* | *55* | 26,000 | | | ... | ... | — | — | — | — | — | — |
| Angola | 45,877 | 73,830 | 51 | 56,625 | 29,000 | 97 | ... | ... | 1,834[2] | 2,952[2] | ... | ... | ... | ... |
| Anguilla | 55 | 88 | 80 | 973 | 239 | 5.4 | ... | ... | — | — | — | — | — | — |
| Antigua and Barbuda | 341 | 548 | 44 | 7,120 | 1,209 | 9.4 | ... | ... | — | — | — | — | — | — |
| Argentina | 131,321 | 211,341 | 26 | 3,773,600 | 1,396,000 | *5.9 | ... | ... | 21,233[2] | 34,172[2] | 6,674 | 10,740 | 6,510 | 9,504 |
| Aruba | 236 | 380 | ... | 23,409 | 582 | 2.5 | ... | ... | — | — | — | — | — | — |
| Australia | 500,049 | 804,753 | 47 | 8,770,899 | 1,231,359 | 1.6 | *32,964* | *48,127* | 24,389[2,7] | 39,251[2,7] | *1,359* | *2,187* | 27,017 | 39,444 |
| Austria | 66,739 | 107,406 | 100 | 2,530,800 | 234,925 | 2.8 | 5,949 | 8,685 | 4,148 | 6,676 | 4,356 | 7,010 | 8,154 | 11,904 |
| Bahamas, The | 2,548 | 4,100 | 40 | 88,000 | 5,600 | 2.4 | ... | ... | — | — | — | — | — | — |
| Bahrain | 96 | 155 | 100 | 72,253 | 23,182 | 4.3 | ... | ... | — | — | — | — | — | — |
| Bangladesh | 98,522 | 158,551 | 12 | 38,665 | 23,263 | 1,581 | ... | ... | 1,793[2] | 2,886[2] | 3,748 | 6,031 | 557 | 813 |
| Barbados | 996 | 1,603 | 90 | 32,263 | 5,363 | 6.7 | ... | ... | — | — | — | — | — | — |
| Belgium | 79,469 | 127,893 | 96 | 3,342,704 | 319,899 | 2.7 | 13,445 | 19,630 | 2,325[2] | 3,741[2] | 4,071 | 6,552 | 5,079 | 7,416 |
| Belize | 1,639 | 2,637 | 16 | 3,707 | 1,855 | 29 | ... | ... | — | — | — | — | — | — |
| Benin | 4,626 | 7,445 | 11 | 2,740 | 567 | 1,191 | ... | ... | 360 | 580 | 85 | 138 | 121 | 177 |
| Bermuda | 139 | 224 | 100 | 17,240 | 4,224 | 2.6 | ... | ... | — | — | — | — | — | — |
| Bhutan | 1,091 | 1,755 | 61 | 1,587 | 889 | 870 | ... | ... | — | — | — | — | — | — |
| Bolivia | 25,468 | 40,987 | 4 | 40,638 | 36,951 | 78 | 1,133 | 1,654 | 2,198[2] | 3,538[2] | 457 | 736 | 357 | 521 |
| Botswana | 4,987 | 8,026 | 25 | 14,283 | 23,987 | 28 | ... | ... | 442 | 712 | | | 888 | 1,297 |
| Brazil | 984,736 | 1,583,172 | 7 | 10,008,040 | 1,082,000 | 12 | 150,100 | 219,100 | 17,984[2] | 28,942[2] | 9,578 | 15,415 | 63,303 | 92,401 |
| British Virgin Islands | *86* | *138* | *69* | 2,735 | | ... | ... | ... | — | — | — | — | — | — |
| Brunei | 958 | 1,542 | 35 | 79,428 | 10,663 | 2.5 | ... | ... | 12[14] | 19[14] | — | — | — | — |
| Bulgaria | 23,384 | 37,633 | 91 | 1,030,090 | 587,400 | 5.5 | 7,071 | 10,324 | 2,670 | 4,297 | 5,536 | 8,909 | 12,446 | 18,172 |
| Burkina Faso | 8,249 | 13,276 | 11.1 | 21,182 | 6,647 | 238 | ... | ... | 321 | 517 | 422 | 680 | 322 | 470 |
| Burma | 14,333 | 23,067 | 17 | 43,300 | 44,700 | 386 | ... | ... | 1,949[2] | 3,137[2] | 2,401 | 3,864 | 427 | 624 |
| Burundi | 3,196 | 5,144 | 7 | 7,533 | 6,188 | 334 | ... | ... | — | — | — | — | — | — |
| Cameroon | 40,330 | 64,905 | 5 | 72,449 | 41,301 | 90 | 2,029 | 2,963 | 729[2] | 1,173[2] | 268 | 432 | 518 | 756 |
| Canada | 549,445 | 884,249 | 81 | 11,118,071 | 3,095,243 | 1.8 | 29,033 | 42,388 | 74,600 | 120,000 | 1,447 | 2,328 | 158,921 | 232,036 |
| Cape Verde | 1,398 | 2,250 | 29 | *4,000* | *1,343* | 54 | ... | ... | — | — | — | — | — | — |
| Cayman Islands | 110 | 177 | 68 | 7,354 | 1,757 | 2.1 | ... | ... | — | — | — | — | — | — |
| Central African Republic | 12,600 | 20,278 | 2 | *43,321* | *3,861* | 54 | ... | ... | — | — | — | — | — | — |
| Chad | 24,855 | 40,000 | 1 | 7,000 | 5,000 | 390 | ... | ... | — | — | — | — | — | — |
| Chile | 49,227 | 79,224 | 12 | 624,738 | 257,298 | 14 | ... | ... | 5,037[2] | 8,107[2] | 790 | 1,272 | 1,701 | 2,484 |
| China | 584,000 | 940,000 | ... | 794,452 | 2,231,981 | 341 | 121,235 | 177,000 | 35,200 | 56,600 | 160,440 | 258,204 | 598,945 | 874,500 |
| Christmas Island | 20 | 32 | ... | 759 | 383 | 2.9 | ... | ... | 12 | 20 | — | — | ... | ... |
| Cocos (Keeling) Islands | 15 | 24 | ... | | | | ... | ... | — | — | — | — | — | — |
| Colombia | 65,369 | 105,201 | 28 | 509,478 | 520,085 | 26 | *11,115* | *16,227* | 2,023[2] | 3,255[2] | 142 | 228 | 534 | 780 |
| Comoros | 466 | 750 | 53 | 3,600 | 2,000 | 68 | ... | ... | — | — | — | — | — | — |
| Congo | 6,835 | 11,000 | 5 | *30,500* | *78,600* | 15 | 46 | 67 | 498 | 802 | 237 | 381 | 299 | 437 |
| Cook Islands | 174 | 280 | ... | 689 | 728 | 12 | ... | ... | — | — | — | — | — | — |
| Costa Rica | 21,914 | 35,267 | 13 | 113,230 | 72,816 | 14 | ... | ... | 590 | 950 | 56 | 90 | 108.6 | 158.5 |
| Côte d'Ivoire | 34,175 | 55,000 | 9 | 182,956 | 52,491 | 41 | ... | ... | 816 | 1,314 | 533[17] | 858[17] | 363[17] | 530[17] |
| Cuba | 21,100 | 34,000 | 30 | 200,100 | 164,500 | 27 | 1,116 | 1,630 | 3,038[18] | 4,889[18] | 1,372[18] | 2,208[18] | 2,010[18] | 2,935[18] |
| Cyprus | 7,158 | 11,519 | 48 | 121,500 | 58,900 | 3.7 | ... | ... | — | — | — | — | — | — |
| Czechoslovakia | 46,535 | 74,891 | 100 | 2,694,994 | 425,174 | 5.0 | 8,033 | 11,729 | 8,149 | 13,114 | 12,327 | 19,839 | 45,345 | 66,203 |
| Denmark | 43,587 | 70,147 | 100 | 1,500,946 | 346,431 | 2.8 | 6,400 | 9,400 | 1,535 | 2,471 | 2,801 | 4,508 | 1,198 | 1,749 |
| Djibouti | 1,799 | 2,895 | 7 | —11,000— | | 41 | ... | ... | 66 | 106 | ... | ... | 90.1 | 131.6 |
| Dominica | 489 | 787 | 60 | 2,713 | 1,250 | 21 | ... | ... | — | — | — | — | — | — |
| Dominican Republic | 10,788 | 17,362 | 29 | 94,601 | 55,346 | 40 | ... | ... | 65[2,18] | 104[2,18] | — | — | ... | ... |
| Ecuador | 22,486 | 36,187 | 28 | 248,575 | 32,624 | 32 | ... | ... | 600[2] | 965[2] | 27 | 43 | 8 | 12 |
| Egypt | 18,999[20] | 30,576[20] | 50[20] | 719,199 | 292,846 | 46 | *1,079* | *1,575* | 2,700[2] | 4,346[2] | 14,977 | 24,103 | 1,779 | 2,597 |

statistics. Automobile, truck, and bus fleet statistics, which are usually based upon registration, are relatively accurate, though some countries round off figures, and unregistered vehicles may cause substantial undercount. There is also inconsistent classification of vehicle types; in some countries a vehicle may serve variously as an automobile, a truck, or a bus, or even as all three on certain occasions. Relatively few countries collect and maintain commercial road traffic statistics.

Data on national railway systems are generally given for railway track length rather than the length of routes, which may be multitracked. Siding tracks usually are not included, but some countries fail to distinguish them. The United States data include only class 1 railways, which account for about 94 percent of total track length. Passenger traffic is usually calculated from tickets sold to fare-paying passengers. Such statistics are subject to distortion if there are large numbers of nonpaying passengers, such as military personnel, or if season tickets are sold and not all the allowed journeys are utilized. Railway cargo traffic is calculated by weight hauled multiplied by the length of the journey. Changes in freight load during the journey should be accounted for but sometimes are not, leading to discrepancies.

Merchant fleet and tonnage statistics collected by Lloyd's registry service for vessels over 100 gross tons are quite accurate. Cargo statistics, however, reflect the port and customs requirements of each country and the reporting rules of each country's merchant marine authority (although

these, increasingly, reflect the recommendations of the International Maritime Organization); often, however, they are only estimates based on customs declarations and the count of vessels entered and cleared. Even when these elements are reported consistently, further uncertainties may be introduced because of ballast, bunkers, ships' stores, or transshipped goods included in the data.

Airport data are based on scheduled flights reported in the commercial *Official Airline Guide* and are both reliable and current. The comparability of civil air traffic statistics suffers from differing characteristics of the air transportation systems of different countries; data for an entire country may be two to three years behind those for a single airport.

Outside of Europe, where standardization of data on inland waterways is necessitated by the volume of international traffic, comparability of national data declines markedly. Calculations as to both the length of a country's waterway system (or route length of river, lake, and coastal traffic) and the makeup of its stock of commercially significant vessels (those for which data will be collected) are largely determined by the nature and use of the country's hydrographic net—its seasonality, relief profile, depth, access to potential markets—and inevitably differ widely from country to country. Data for coastal or island states may refer to scheduled coastwise or interisland traffic.

| merchant marine | | | | air | | | | | | | canals and inland waterways (latest) | | | | country |
|---|---|---|---|---|---|---|---|---|---|---|---|---|---|---|---|
| fleet, 1986 (vessels over 100 gross tons) | total dead-weight tonnage, 1986 ('000) | international cargo (latest) | | airports with sched-uled flights, 1987 | traffic (latest) | | | | | | length | | cargo | | |
| | | loaded metric tons ('000) | off-loaded metric tons ('000) | | passengers | | cargo | | | | mi | km | short ton-mi ('000,000) | metric ton-km ('000,000) | |
| | | | | | passenger-mi ('000,000) | passenger-km ('000,000) | short ton-mi ('000,000) | metric ton-km ('000,000) | | | | | | | |
| — | — | — | — | 1 | 871[1] | 140[1] | 5.1[1] | 7.4[1] | | | 750 | 1,200 | ... | ... | Afghanistan |
| 20 | 79.9 | 1,150 | 635 | 1 | ... | ... | ... | ... | | | 27 | 43 | ... | ... | Albania |
| 145 | 1,018.5 | 53,370 | 15,865 | 22 | 1,561[3] | 2,512[3] | 9.1[3] | 13.2[3] | | | ... | ... | ... | ... | Algeria |
| — | — | 175 | 557 | 3 | ... | ... | ... | ... | | | ... | ... | ... | ... | American Samoa |
| — | — | — | — | — | — | — | — | — | | | — | — | ... | — | Andorra |
| 100 | 127.4 | 9,675 | 912 | 19 | 606 | 975 | 23.2 | 33.9 | | | 805 | 1,295 | ... | ... | Angola |
| 15 | 5.6 | — | 18 | 1 | ... | ... | ... | ... | | | — | — | ... | ... | Anguilla |
| 5 | 1.0 | 30 | 110 | 1 | 68[4] | 109[4] | 14.8[5] | 21.6[5] | | | — | — | ... | ... | Antigua and Barbuda |
| 454 | 3,171.2 | 37,728 | 5,376 | 65 | 4,131[6] | 6,648[6] | 126.7[6] | 185.0[6] | | | 6,800 | 11,000 | 19,326 | 28,215 | Argentina |
| 8 | 261.7 | ... | ... | 1 | ... | ... | ... | ... | | | ... | ... | ... | ... | Aruba |
| 673 | 3,653.6 | 244,548 | 20,520 | 441 | 19,722 | 31,740 | 635.0 | 927.1 | | | 5,200 | 8,368 | ... | ... | Australia |
| 26 | 210.6 | — | — | 6 | 857 | 1,380 | 16.1 | 23.5 | | | 222 | 358 | 5,941 | 8,674 | Austria |
| 302 | 10,600.4 | 19,350 | 10,850 | 21 | 245[8] | 394[8] | ... | ... | | | ... | ... | ... | ... | Bahamas, The |
| 98 | 64.4 | 13,000 | 3,800 | 1 | 774[9] | 1,245[9] | 22.3[9] | 32.6[9] | | | ... | ... | ... | ... | Bahrain |
| 274 | 517.8 | 936 | 8,940 | 8 | 889 | 1,430 | 13.6 | 19.9 | | | 5,240 | 8,433 | ... | ... | Bangladesh |
| 34 | 8.1 | 240 | 665 | 1 | 93[10] | 149[10] | 0.8[11] | 1.1[11] | | | ... | ... | ... | ... | Barbados |
| 355 | 3,916.5 | 49,512 | 73,656 | 4 | 3,452 | 5,556 | 407.0 | 594.0 | | | 1,215 | 1,956 | 3,590 | 5,242 | Belgium |
| 3 | 0.8 | 165 | 80 | 8 | ... | ... | ... | ... | | | 513 | 825 | ... | ... | Belize |
| 15 | 4.9 | 79 | 807 | 5 | 144[12] | 232[12] | 27.4[12] | 40.0[12] | | | 300 | 500 | ... | ... | Benin |
| 97 | 1,759.7 | 65 | 710 | 1 | ... | ... | ... | ... | | | ... | ... | ... | ... | Bermuda |
| | | | | 1 | ... | ... | ... | ... | | | ... | ... | ... | — | Bhutan |
| 2 | 18.9 | — | — | 19 | 552 | 888 | 19.6 | 28.7 | | | 6,200 | 10,000 | 90 | 132 | Bolivia |
| — | — | — | — | 3 | 355 | 570 | 24.2 | 35.3 | | | ... | ... | ... | ... | Botswana |
| 697 | 10,277.8 | 146,364 | 48,864 | 110 | 14,719[13] | 23,688[13] | 787.7[13] | 1,150.0[13] | | | 31,000 | 50,000 | 43,408 | 63,374 | Brazil |
| 32 | 8.6 | 7 | 15 | 3 | ... | ... | ... | ... | | | ... | ... | ... | ... | British Virgin Islands |
| 5 | 1.7 | 14,550 | 796 | 1 | ... | ... | ... | ... | | | 130 | 209 | ... | ... | Brunei |
| 205 | 1,989.1 | 3,750 | 25,256 | 13 | 2,007 | 3,231 | 30.1 | 43.9 | | | 293 | 471 | 1,397 | 2,039 | Bulgaria |
| — | — | — | — | 2 | 134 | 215 | 14.5 | 21.2 | | | ... | ... | ... | ... | Burkina Faso |
| 106 | 150.9 | 1,176 | 516 | 21 | 118 | 191 | 1.6 | 2.3 | | | 7,950 | 12,800 | ... | ... | Burma |
| ... | ... | ... | ... | 1 | ... | ... | ... | ... | | | ... | ... | ... | ... | Burundi |
| 49 | 88.7 | 1,032 | 3,192 | 10 | 346 | 548 | 34.3 | 50.1 | | | 1,300 | 2,090 | ... | ... | Cameroon |
| 1,249 | 3,829.7 | 130,400 | 51,260 | 61 | 45,529 | 73,271 | 3,233 | 4,721 | | | 1,860 | 3,000 | ... | ... | Canada |
| 25 | 22.1 | 107 | 321 | 9 | ... | ... | ... | ... | | | ... | ... | ... | ... | Cape Verde |
| 282 | 2,121.7 | 615 | 705 | 3 | ... | ... | ... | ... | | | ... | ... | ... | ... | Cayman Islands |
| — | — | — | — | 1 | 106 | 170 | 20.7 | 30.2 | | | 500 | 800 | ... | ... | Central African Republic |
| — | — | — | — | 2 | 144 | 232 | 27.4 | 40.0 | | | 1,240 | 2,000 | ... | ... | Chad |
| 255 | 907.5 | 13,452 | 4,800 | 13 | 1,218 | 1,960 | 94.0 | 137.2 | | | 450 | 725 | 5,629 | 8,218 | Chile |
| 1,562 | 24,007.0[15] | 69,564 | 71,136 | 77 | 7,270 | 11,700 | 288.0 | 420.0 | | | 67,800 | 109,100 | 154,500 | 225,500 | China |
| — | — | 1,155 | 46 | 1 | ... | ... | ... | ... | | | ... | ... | ... | ... | Christmas Island |
| — | — | — | — | 1 | ... | ... | ... | ... | | | ... | ... | ... | ... | Cocos (Keeling) Islands |
| 90 | 486.4 | 11,196 | 5,628 | 78 | 2,446 | 3,936 | 127.8 | 186.6 | | | 8,900 | 14,300 | ... | ... | Colombia |
| 3 | 2.2 | 10 | 95 | 3 | ... | ... | ... | ... | | | ... | ... | ... | ... | Comoros |
| 21 | 10.8 | 3,228 | 672 | 17 | 144 | 232 | 27.4 | 40.0 | | | 700 | 1,120 | ... | ... | Congo |
| — | — | 10 | 30 | 6 | ... | ... | ... | ... | | | ... | ... | ... | ... | Cook Islands |
| 25 | 9.5 | 1,600 | 1,500 | 8 | 343[16] | 552[16] | 17.6[16] | 25.6[16] | | | 454 | 730 | ... | ... | Costa Rica |
| 58 | 151.5 | 4,830 | 4,891 | 14 | 210 | 339 | 39.3 | 57.4 | | | 460 | 740 | ... | ... | Côte d'Ivoire |
| 422 | 1,274.2 | 2,208 | 2,364 | 12 | 1,525 | 2,455 | 23.0 | 33.6 | | | 149 | 240 | ... | ... | Cuba |
| 940 | 18,763.0 | 1,920 | 3,156 | 3 | 872 | 1,404 | 19.3 | 28.1 | | | ... | ... | ... | ... | Cyprus |
| 20 | 299.3 | — | — | 14 | 1,163 | 1,872 | 14.4 | 21.0 | | | 300 | 483 | 2,983 | 4,356 | Czechoslovakia |
| 1,063 | 6,805.2 | 11,244 | 32,952 | 12 | 1,991[19] | 3,204[19] | 88.6[19] | 129.3[19] | | | 259 | 417 | 1,200 | 1,700 | Denmark |
| 7 | 2.7 | 366 | 870 | 3 | ... | ... | ... | ... | | | ... | ... | ... | ... | Djibouti |
| 7 | 3.0 | 30 | 55 | 2 | ... | ... | ... | ... | | | ... | ... | ... | ... | Dominica |
| 35 | 67.5 | 2,100 | 3,600 | 3 | 299 | 481 | 6.2 | 9.0 | | | ... | ... | ... | ... | Dominican Republic |
| 155 | 611.6 | 9,950 | 2,450 | 14 | 557 | 896 | 26.0 | 37.9 | | | 900 | 1,500 | ... | ... | Ecuador |
| 422 | 1,484.9 | 12,120 | 32,952 | 11 | 2,498 | 4,020 | 71.2 | 114.5 | | | 2,088 | 3,360 | 1,709 | 2,495 | Egypt |

## Transportation (continued)

| country | roads length mi | km | paved (percent) | motor vehicles auto-mobiles | trucks and buses | persons per vehicle | cargo short ton-mi ('000,000) | metric ton-km ('000,000) | railroads track length mi | km | traffic passengers passenger-mi ('000,000) | passenger-km ('000,000) | cargo short ton-mi ('000,000) | metric ton-km ('000,000) |
|---|---|---|---|---|---|---|---|---|---|---|---|---|---|---|
| El Salvador | 7,558 | 12,164 | 14 | 136,163 | 19,461 | 32 | ... | ... | 374[2] | 602[2] | 3 | 5 | 17 | 25 |
| Equatorial Guinea | 1,715 | 2,760 | 12 | 4,000 | 3,000 | 40 | ... | ... | — | — | — | — | — | — |
| Ethiopia | 23,532 | 37,871 | 34 | 41,250 | 19,159 | 720 | ... | ... | 485[21] | 781[21] | 217 | 350 | 86 | 125 |
| Faeroe Islands | 124 | 200 | ... | 10,942 | 2,360 | 3.4 | ... | ... | — | — | — | — | — | — |
| Falkland Islands | 45 | 73 | 22 | 732 | 230 | 2.1 | ... | ... | — | — | — | — | — | — |
| Fiji | 2,564 | 4,127 | 13 | 32,453 | 22,799 | 13 | ... | ... | 660[14] | 1,062[14] | ... | ... | ... | ... |
| Finland | 47,262 | 76,061 | 55 | 1,546,094 | 230,375 | 2.8 | 15,000 | 22,000 | 3,670[2] | 5,906[2] | 2,003 | 3,224 | 5,529 | 8,072 |
| France | 499,945 | 804,650 | 92 | 20,940,000 | 3,426,000 | 2.3 | 73,000 | 106,000 | 21,547[2] | 34,676[2] | 37,073 | 59,664 | 40,061 | 58,488 |
| French Guiana | 691 | 1,112 | 65 | 14,440 | 625 | 5.3 | ... | ... | — | — | — | — | — | — |
| French Polynesia | 495 | 797 | 33 | ... | ... | ... | ... | ... | — | — | — | — | — | — |
| Gabon | 4,400 | 7,082 | 8 | 16,043 | 10,695 | 41 | ... | ... | 210 | 338 | 12 | 19 | 71 | 103 |
| Gambia, The | 1,484 | 2,388 | 21 | 5,200 | 720 | 129 | ... | ... | — | — | — | — | — | — |
| Gaza Strip | ... | ... | ... | 15,393 | 4,760 | 25 | ... | ... | — | — | — | — | — | — |
| Germany, East | 29,440 | 47,380 | 100 | 3,306,230 | 360,821 | 4.6 | 5,122 | 7,479 | 3,732 | 14,054 | 13,950 | 22,451 | 40,182 | 58,668 |
| Germany, West | 302,764 | 487,251 | 99 | 26,099,297 | 1,557,612 | 2.3 | 90,500 | 132,200 | 42,992 | 69,190 | 25,926 | 41,724 | 41,415 | 60,468 |
| Ghana | 17,600 | 28,300 | 20 | 52,864 | 24,312 | 158 | ... | ... | 592 | 953 | 125 | 201 | 51 | 74 |
| Gibraltar | 31 | 50 | 100 | 8,519 | 1,034 | 3.0 | ... | ... | — | — | — | — | — | — |
| Greece | 64,191 | 103,306 | 83 | 1,264,375 | 620,724 | 5.4 | ... | ... | 1,534[2] | 2,469[2] | 1,036 | 1,668 | 485 | 708 |
| Greenland | 96 | 154 | 41 | 1,781 | 809 | 21 | ... | ... | — | — | — | — | — | — |
| Grenada | 609 | 980 | 66 | 4,784 | 981 | 16 | ... | ... | — | — | — | — | — | — |
| Guadeloupe | 1,284 | 2,067 | 80 | 95,962 | 28,134 | 2.7 | ... | ... | — | — | — | — | — | — |
| Guam | 419 | 674 | 100 | 57,856 | 16,521 | 1.6 | ... | ... | — | — | — | — | — | — |
| Guatemala | 11,200 | 18,000 | 16 | 188,100 | 58,500 | 31 | ... | ... | 375[2] | 603[2] | ... | ... | ... | ... |
| Guernsey | ... | ... | ... | ... | ... | ... | ... | ... | — | — | — | — | — | — |
| Guinea | 17,600 | 28,400 | 4 | 9,948 | 9,992 | 254 | ... | ... | 584[2] | 940[2] | ... | ... | ... | ... |
| Guinea-Bissau | 3,143 | 5,058 | 8 | —4,100— | | 200 | ... | ... | — | — | — | — | — | — |
| Guyana | 5,524 | 8,890 | 9 | 25,541 | 7,648 | 24 | ... | ... | 65[14] | 109[14] | — | — | ... | ... |
| Haiti | 2,299 | 3,700 | 17 | 34,669 | 11,658 | 113 | ... | ... | — | — | — | — | — | — |
| Honduras | 10,577 | 17,022 | 12 | 66,666 | 18,759 | 51 | ... | ... | 571[2] | 919[2] | ... | ... | ... | ... |
| Hong Kong | 839 | 1,350 | 100 | 177,961 | 93,092 | 20 | ... | ... | 24 | 39 | 920 | 1,480 | 64 | 93 |
| Hungary | 18,413 | 29,633 | 98 | 1,435,900 | 157,797 | 6.7 | 6,655 | 9,716 | 8,140 | 13,100 | 6,965 | 11,209 | 15,278 | 22,307 |
| Iceland | 7,189 | 11,569 | 12 | 103,100 | 13,160 | 2.0 | 318 | 464 | — | — | — | — | — | — |
| India | 1,101,000 | 1,772,000 | 47 | 1,517,000 | 952,000 | 306 | 55,500 | 81,000 | 38,200[2] | 61,478[2] | 155,500 | 250,300 | 146,200 | 213,400 |
| Indonesia | 110,539 | 177,896 | 64 | 958,919 | 1,030,809 | 87 | 17,000 | 25,000 | 4,004 | 6,444 | 3,962 | 6,376 | 805 | 1,175 |
| Iran | 67,710 | 108,970 | 31 | 2,113,465 | 389,247 | 19 | 46,750 | 68,250 | 2,837[2] | 4,567[2] | 1,560 | 2,526 | 2,645 | 3,861 |
| Iraq | 15,699 | 25,265 | 65 | 229,500 | 145,300 | 35 | ... | ... | 1,516[2] | 2,439[2] | 34 | 55 | 777 | 1,134 |
| Ireland | 57,354 | 92,303 | 94 | 709,456 | 98,829 | 4.4 | ... | ... | 1,848 | 2,975 | 589 | 948 | 378 | 552 |
| Isle of Man | 357 | 574 | 58 | —32,473— | | 2.0 | ... | ... | 37[2] | 59[2] | ... | ... | ... | ... |
| Israel | 7,930 | 12,760 | 100 | 613,680 | 126,724 | 5.8 | ... | ... | 533 | 858 | 127 | 205 | 645 | 942 |
| Italy | 187,223 | 301,307 | 100 | 22,398,000 | 1,915,830 | 2.3 | 98,720 | 144,129 | 12,257[2] | 19,726[2] | 25,165 | 40,500 | 11,999 | 17,520 |
| Jamaica | 7,680 | 12,360 | 30 | 42,037 | 23,154 | 36 | ... | ... | 215 | 346 | 24 | 40 | 89 | 129 |
| Japan | 700,600 | 1,127,500 | 58 | 27,844,580 | 17,139,806 | 2.7 | 137,546 | 200,813 | 16,506 | 26,564 | 205,101 | 330,097 | 15,061 | 22,134 |
| Jersey | ... | ... | ... | 46,717 | 7,975 | 1.4 | ... | ... | — | — | — | — | — | — |
| Jordan | 3,935 | 6,332 | 74 | 118,852 | 48,884 | 14 | 19,133 | 27,934 | 385[2] | 619[2] | 3.7 | 6.0 | 864 | 1,262 |
| Kampuchea | 8,296 | 13,351 | 20 | 700 | 1,800 | 2,600 | ... | ... | 403[2] | 649[2] | 34 | 54 | 6.8 | 10 |
| Kenya | 33,700 | 54,200 | 12 | 122,300 | 96,575 | 93 | ... | ... | 1,649 | 2,654 | 371 | 596 | 1,273 | 1,858 |
| Kiribati | 398 | 640 | ... | —163— | | 344 | ... | ... | — | — | — | — | — | — |
| Korea, North | 13,670 | 22,000 | 2 | ... | ... | ... | ... | ... | 2,779 | 4,473 | ... | ... | ... | ... |
| Korea, South | 31,692 | 51,003 | 46 | 465,119 | 483,170 | 43 | 4,841 | 7,068 | 3,905 | 6,285 | 13,853 | 22,295 | 8,422 | 12,296 |
| Kuwait | 1,208 | 1,944 | 100 | 405,405 | 114,607 | 3.2 | ... | ... | — | — | — | — | — | — |
| Laos | 8,067 | 12,983 | 31 | 15,000 | 3,000 | 217 | ... | ... | — | — | — | — | — | — |
| Lebanon | 4,350 | 7,000 | 80 | 460,400 | 35,000 | 5.3 | ... | ... | 137.9[2] | 222[2] | 5.3 | 8.6 | 29 | 42 |
| Lesotho | 2,540 | 4,250 | 12 | 5,129 | 11,962 | 82 | ... | ... | 1 | 2 | — | — | — | — |
| Liberia | 4,138 | 6,659 | 7 | 12,747 | 8,288 | 100 | ... | ... | 304[2] | 490[2] | ... | ... | 2,056[14] | 3,002[14] |
| Libya | 12,000 | 19,300 | 56 | 415,509 | 334,405 | 4.3 | ... | ... | — | — | — | — | — | — |
| Liechtenstein | 205 | 330 | ... | 14,452 | 1,634 | 1.6 | ... | ... | 12 | 19 | ... | ... | ... | ... |
| Luxembourg | 3,209 | 5,164 | 99 | 156,048 | 14,108 | 2.1 | 136 | 198 | 168[2] | 270[2] | 171 | 276 | 411 | 600 |
| Macau | 56 | 90 | 100 | 17,866 | 4,411 | 17 | ... | ... | — | — | — | — | — | — |
| Madagascar | 10,700 | 17,300 | 30 | 23,412 | 14,159 | 252 | ... | ... | 644[2] | 1,036[2] | 127 | 205 | 153 | 224 |
| Malawi | 7,576 | 12,192 | 21 | 13,559 | 14,545 | 251 | — | — | 515[2] | 829[2] | 76 | 123 | 76 | 111 |
| Malaysia | 19,144 | 30,809 | 80 | 1,173,968 | 138,343 | 12 | ... | ... | 1,666[2] | 2,681[2] | 872[30] | 1,404[30] | 1,520[30] | 2,220[30] |
| Maldives | ... | ... | ... | 338 | 336 | 270 | ... | ... | — | — | — | — | — | — |
| Mali | 9,756 | 15,700 | 11 | 22,020 | 6,422 | 280 | ... | ... | 401 | 646 | 107 | 173 | 165 | 241 |
| Malta | 830 | 1,335 | 92 | 82,259 | 18,187 | 3.4 | ... | ... | — | — | — | — | — | — |
| Martinique | 1,156 | 1,861 | 85 | 135,269 | 7,328 | 2.3 | ... | ... | — | — | — | — | — | — |
| Mauritania | 4,557 | 7,335 | 22 | 15,017 | 2,188 | 96 | ... | ... | 428[2] | 689[2] | 4 | 7 | 4,207 | 6,142 |
| Mauritius | 1,108 | 1,783 | 92 | 31,265 | 14,224 | 22 | ... | ... | — | — | — | — | — | — |
| Mayotte | 143 | 230 | 49 | —1,528— | | 40 | ... | ... | — | — | — | — | — | — |
| Mexico | 133,265 | 214,470 | 50 | 5,221,159 | 1,978,327 | 10 | ... | ... | 15,979[2] | 25,716[2] | 3,606 | 5,803 | 33,041 | 48,239 |
| Monaco | 29 | 46 | 100 | 14,528 | 3,164 | 1.5 | ... | ... | 1 | 2 | — | — | — | — |
| Mongolia | 29,000 | 46,700 | 2 | ... | ... | 5.2 | 1,325 | 1,934 | 1,086 | 1,748 | 271 | 436 | 4,082 | 5,960 |
| Montserrat | 87 | 140 | 95 | 2,200 | 57 | 5.2 | ... | ... | — | — | — | — | — | — |
| Morocco | 35,778 | 57,530 | 46 | 491,144 | 232,689 | 30 | 830 | 1,212 | 1,105[2] | 1,779[2] | 1,200 | 1,932 | 3,123 | 4,560 |
| Mozambique | 12,420 | 19,990 | 25 | 99,400 | 24,700 | 100 | ... | ... | 2,182 | 3,512 | 140 | 225 | 198 | 290 |
| Nauru | 12 | 19 | 100 | —1,788— | | 4.0 | ... | ... | — | — | — | — | ... | ... |
| Nepal | 3,682 | 5,925 | 46 | 14,201 | 9,988 | 574 | 984 | 1,437 | 322[2] | 52[2] | ... | ... | ... | ... |
| Netherlands, The | 69,525 | 111,891 | 87 | 4,901,000 | 401,630 | 2.7 | 12,624 | 18,431 | 1,781 | 2,867 | 5,734 | 9,228 | 2,203 | 3,216 |
| Netherlands Antilles | 510 | 820 | ... | 24,000 | 855 | 9.3 | ... | ... | — | — | — | — | — | — |
| New Caledonia | 3,422 | 5,507 | 14 | 42,000 | 2,500 | 3.3 | ... | ... | — | — | — | — | — | — |
| New Zealand | 57,811 | 93,054 | 54 | 1,558,307 | 318,197 | 1.8 | ... | ... | 2,692 | 4,332 | 285 | 458 | 2,168 | 3,165 |
| Nicaragua | 9,104 | 14,651 | 11 | 33,094 | 42,229 | 43 | ... | ... | 214[2] | 344[2] | 38 | 60 | 3.2 | 4.7 |
| Niger | 11,891 | 19,137 | 17 | 23,102 | 9,052 | 189 | ... | ... | — | — | — | — | — | — |
| Nigeria | 77,000 | 124,000 | 48 | 262,550 | 90,731 | 241 | ... | ... | 2,178 | 3,505 | 1,950 | 2,707 | 1,048 | 1,530 |
| Niue | 142 | 229 | 54 | 264 | 64 | 12 | ... | ... | — | — | — | — | — | — |
| Norfolk Island | 45 | 72 | 83 | 1,802 | 90 | 1.1 | ... | ... | — | — | — | — | — | — |

| merchant marine | | | | air | | | | | canals and inland waterways (latest) | | | | country |
| --- | --- | --- | --- | --- | --- | --- | --- | --- | --- | --- | --- | --- | --- |
| fleet, 1986 (vessels over 100 gross tons) | total dead-weight tonnage, 1986 ('000) | international cargo (latest) | | airports with sched-uled flights, 1987 | traffic (latest) | | | | length | | cargo | | |
| | | loaded metric tons ('000) | off-loaded metric tons ('000) | | passengers | | cargo | | mi | km | short ton-mi ('000,000) | metric ton-km ('000,000) | |
| | | | | | passenger-mi ('000,000) | passenger-km ('000,000) | short ton-mi ('000,000) | metric ton-km ('000,000) | | | | | |
| 14 | 3.3 | 384 | 1,488 | 1 | 274 | 442 | 25.4 | 37.1 | ... | ... | ... | ... | El Salvador |
| 2 | 6.7 | 96 | 59 | 2 | 4 | 7 | 0.7 | 1.0 | 104 | 167 | ... | ... | Equatorial Guinea |
| 23 | 84.8 | 631 | 1,815 | 30 | 693 | 1,116 | 58.6 | 85.6 | 70 | 113 | ... | ... | Ethiopia |
| 195 | 83.9 | 240 | 340 | 1 | ... | ... | ... | ... | ... | ... | ... | ... | Faeroe Islands |
| 5 | 4.1 | 4 | 6 | 1 | ... | ... | ... | ... | ... | ... | ... | ... | Falkland Islands |
| 56 | 26.3 | 672 | 672 | 20 | 317 | 509 | 4.4 | 6.4 | 126 | 203 | ... | ... | Fiji |
| 276 | 1,907.8 | 20,244 | 29,952 | 21 | 1,812 | 2,916 | 63.6 | 92.9 | 3,764 | 6,057 | 2,900 | 4,200 | Finland |
| 984 | 9,305.3 | 55,032 | 170,856 | 69 | 24,383[22] | 39,240[22] | 2,188.7[22] | 3,195.5[22] | 5,280 | 8,500 | 6,082 | 8,880 | France |
| — | — | 15 | 233 | 1 | ... | ... | ... | ... | 2,336 | 3,760 | ... | ... | French Guiana |
| ... | ... | 15 | 520 | 32 | ... | ... | ... | ... | ... | ... | ... | ... | French Polynesia |
| 23 | 170.2 | 6,702 | 423 | 25[23] | 267 | 430 | 18.7 | 27.3 | 1,000 | 1,600 | ... | ... | Gabon |
| 6 | 4.0 | 60 | 180 | 1 | ... | ... | ... | ... | 250 | 400 | ... | ... | Gambia, The |
| — | — | ... | ... | — | ... | ... | ... | ... | ... | ... | ... | ... | Gaza Strip |
| 403 | 1,923.6 | 9,000 | 12,100 | 4 | 1,579 | 2,541 | 49.1 | 71.6 | 1,441 | 2,319 | 1,312 | 1,916 | Germany, East |
| 1,752 | 7,744.6 | 39,324 | 93,564 | 26 | 16,553 | 26,640 | 2,026.5 | 2,958.9 | 2,705 | 4,354 | 35,614 | 51,996 | Germany, West |
| 137 | 178.3 | 1,190 | 2,596 | 4 | 185 | 299 | 6.9 | 10.0 | 803 | 1,293 | ... | ... | Ghana |
| 100 | 2,999.0 | 3 | 232 | 1 | ... | ... | ... | ... | ... | ... | ... | ... | Gibraltar |
| 2,255 | 51,294.3 | 21,396 | 26,280 | 29 | 3,967 | 6,384 | 69.4 | 101.4 | 50 | 80 | 585 | 854 | Greece |
| 50 | ... | 270 | 285 | 3 | 9 | 14 | 0.16 | 0.24 | ... | ... | ... | ... | Greenland |
| 3 | 0.6 | 25 | 55 | 3 | ... | ... | ... | ... | ... | ... | ... | ... | Grenada |
| ... | ... | 620 | 1,101 | 8 | ... | ... | ... | ... | ... | ... | ... | ... | Guadeloupe |
| ... | ... | 85 | 165 | 1 | ... | ... | ... | ... | ... | ... | ... | ... | Guam |
| 8 | 13.6 | 2,500 | 1,950 | 2 | 85 | 136 | 4.9 | 7.1 | 162 | 260 | ... | ... | Guatemala |
| — | — | ... | ... | 1 | ... | ... | ... | ... | ... | ... | ... | ... | Guernsey |
| 19 | 2.9 | 10,430 | 630 | 1 | 90 | 144 | 0.5 | 0.7 | 805 | 1,295 | ... | ... | Guinea |
| 17 | 2.8 | 35 | 115 | 1 | 5 | 8 | 0.7 | 1.0 | ... | ... | ... | ... | Guinea-Bissau |
| 103 | 22.2 | 1,500 | 585 | 18 | ... | ... | ... | ... | 3,700 | 6,000 | ... | ... | Guyana |
| 8 | 1.7 | 300 | 750 | 2 | ... | ... | ... | ... | 60 | 100 | ... | ... | Haiti |
| 424 | 827.1 | 1,420 | 1,185 | 5 | 255 | 410 | 12.0 | 17.0 | 289 | 465 | ... | ... | Honduras |
| 416 | 13,664.5 | 19,500[24] | 42,984[24] | 1 | ... | ... | ... | ... | ... | ... | ... | ... | Hong Kong |
| 22 | 122.3 | ... | ... | 4 | 710 | 1,143 | 16.2 | 23.7 | 1,008 | 1,622 | 1,112 | 1,623 | Hungary |
| 389 | 161.6 | 600 | 1,400 | 24 | 1,409 | 2,268 | 17.1 | 25.0 | ... | ... | 58 | 84 | Iceland |
| 736 | 10,691.0 | 30,358 | 40,036 | 94 | 9,580 | 15,420 | 387.7 | 566.0 | 10,054 | 16,180 | ... | ... | India |
| 1,707 | 2,927.1 | 87,815 | 24,875 | 94 | 5,704 | 9,180 | 155.0 | 226.2 | 13,409 | 21,579 | 17,000 | 25,000 | Indonesia |
| 359 | 5,064.3 | 94,100 | 12,000 | 13 | 2,963 | 4,768 | 90.4 | 132.0 | 626 | 1,008 | ... | ... | Iran |
| 149 | 1,699.6 | 97,830 | 8,638 | 3 | 917 | 1,476 | 37.5 | 54.7 | 631 | 1,015 | ... | ... | Iraq |
| 154 | 148.9 | 5,050 | 12,410 | 5 | 1,551 | 2,496 | 54.1 | 79.0 | 454 | 731 | ... | ... | Ireland |
| — | — | 3 | 170 | 1 | ... | ... | ... | ... | ... | ... | ... | ... | Isle of Man |
| 64 | 679.2 | 7,185 | 16,365 | 6 | 4,183[25] | 6,732[25] | 394.3[25] | 575.7[25] | ... | ... | ... | ... | Israel |
| 1,569 | 12,407.1 | 35,304 | 193,404 | 36 | 8,694[26] | 13,992[26] | 589.0[26] | 859.0[26] | 849 | 1,366 | 179 | 262 | Italy |
| 13 | 12.9 | 6,860 | 3,525 | 6 | 1,074 | 1,728 | 13.1 | 19.1 | ... | ... | ... | ... | Jamaica |
| 10,011 | 59,979.0 | 93,816 | 603,276 | 65 | 41,376 | 66,588 | 2,592.2 | 3,784.6 | 1,100 | 1,770 | 143,912 | 210,107 | Japan |
| — | — | ... | ... | 1 | ... | ... | ... | ... | ... | ... | ... | ... | Jersey |
| 5 | 61.4 | 9,696 | 7,152 | 2 | 2,013 | 3,240 | 113.6 | 165.9 | ... | ... | 19,202 | 28,035 | Jordan |
| 3 | 3.8 | 10 | 100 | 1 | ... | ... | ... | ... | 2,300 | 3,700 | ... | ... | Kampuchea |
| 29 | 6.4 | 1,560 | 3,792 | 15 | 753[27] | 1,212[27] | 28.3[27] | 41.4[27] | ... | ... | ... | ... | Kenya |
| 6 | 2.7 | 12 | 29 | 18 | 0.002[28] | 0.004[28] | — | — | 3 | 5 | ... | ... | Kiribati |
| 71 | 615.3 | 600 | 4,000 | 1 | 52 | 84 | 1.4 | 2.0 | 1,400 | 2,250 | ... | ... | Korea, North |
| 1,837 | 11,561.9 | 31,896 | 101,112 | 3 | 8,329 | 13,404 | 1,005.2 | 1,467.5 | 1,000 | 1,600 | 7,831 | 11,434 | Korea, South |
| 239 | 4,121.3 | 53,750 | 13,950 | 1 | 2,304 | 3,708 | 235.0 | 343.2 | ... | ... | ... | ... | Kuwait |
| — | — | — | — | 7 | 5 | 8 | 0.07 | 0.10 | 2,850 | 4,587 | ... | ... | Laos |
| 228 | 766.8 | 400 | 2,700 | 1 | 516 | 831 | 13.5 | 19.8 | ... | ... | ... | ... | Lebanon |
| — | — | — | — | 15 | 8 | 13 | 0.07 | 0.10 | — | — | — | — | Lesotho |
| 1,658 | 101,587.4 | 15,000 | 1,885 | 8 | 11 | 17 | 0.07 | 0.10 | 230 | 370 | ... | ... | Liberia |
| 104 | 1,459.6 | 50,097 | 11,602 | 9 | 831 | 1,337 | 9.0 | 13.1 | — | — | ... | ... | Libya |
| — | — | — | — | | | | 0.2 | 0.3 | 17 | 27 | ... | ... | Liechtenstein |
| | | | | 1 | 57 | 92 | | | 23 | 37 | 198 | 289 | Luxembourg |
| 14[29] | ... | 300 | 500 | — | — | — | — | — | ... | ... | ... | ... | Macau |
| 71 | 96.6 | 305 | 755 | 35 | 241 | 338 | 38.1 | 55.6 | 727 | 1,170 | ... | ... | Madagascar |
| 1 | 0.3 | ... | ... | 5 | 52 | 84 | 0.6 | 0.9 | 891 | 1,434 | ... | ... | Malawi |
| 498 | 2,506.6 | 41,810 | 25,506 | 35 | 3,892 | 6,264 | 142.9 | 208.7 | 4,534 | 7,296 | ... | ... | Malaysia |
| 30 | 133.0 | 20 | 70 | 1 | ... | ... | ... | ... | ... | ... | ... | ... | Maldives |
| — | — | — | — | 9 | 68 | 110 | 0.4 | 0.6 | 1,128 | 1,815 | 18 | 27 | Mali |
| 246 | 3,415.4 | 252 | 1,476 | 1 | 462 | 744 | 3.0 | 4.5 | ... | ... | ... | ... | Malta |
| — | — | 485 | 1,175 | 1 | ... | ... | ... | ... | ... | ... | ... | ... | Martinique |
| 73 | 10.2 | 7,815 | 575 | 9 | 144 | 232 | 27.4 | 40.0 | 500 | 800 | ... | ... | Mauritania |
| 26 | 257.5 | 722 | 936 | 2 | 276 | 444 | 5.7 | 8.3 | ... | ... | ... | ... | Mauritius |
| — | — | ... | ... | 1 | ... | ... | ... | ... | ... | ... | ... | ... | Mayotte |
| 642 | 2,206.6 | 69,540 | 10,956 | 72 | 10,491[31] | 16,884[31] | 109.5[31] | 159.8[31] | 1,800 | 2,900 | ... | ... | Mexico |
| — | — | ... | ... | 1 | ... | ... | ... | 1 | ... | ... | ... | ... | Monaco |
| 1 | 1.0 | 5 | 45 | 1 | 183 | 295 | 4.5 | 6.5 | 247 | 397 | 3.2 | 4.7 | Mongolia |
| — | — | ... | ... | 1 | ... | ... | ... | ... | ... | ... | ... | ... | Montserrat |
| 294 | 595.4 | 20,748 | 12,948 | 14 | 1,283 | 2,064 | 26.6 | 38.8 | 600 | 1,000 | 2,622 | 3,828 | Morocco |
| 104 | 38.8 | 2,565 | 2,937 | 7 | 306 | 492 | 7.6 | 11.1 | 2,330 | 3,750 | ... | ... | Mozambique |
| 8 | 93.4 | 1,425 | 40 | 1 | 148[32] | 238[32] | 1.1[32] | 1.6[32] | ... | ... | ... | ... | Nauru |
| — | — | — | — | 5 | 186[33] | 300[33] | 4.2[33] | 6.2[33] | ... | ... | ... | ... | Nepal |
| 1,334 | 5,993.9 | 78,672 | 249,660 | 5 | 11,953[34] | 19,236[34] | 1,093.0[34] | 1,596.0[34] | 2,724 | 4,384 | 4,602 | 6,719 | Netherlands, The |
| — | — | 26,700 | 26,030 | 5 | 234[35] | 377[35] | 1.2[35] | 1.8[35] | ... | ... | ... | ... | Netherlands Antilles |
| ... | ... | 1,200 | 680 | 10 | ... | ... | ... | ... | ... | ... | ... | ... | New Caledonia |
| 118 | 344.8 | 9,612 | 5,952 | 36 | 5,428 | 8,736 | 229.9 | 335.7 | 1,000 | 1,600 | 1,503 | 2,195 | New Zealand |
| 24 | 31.9 | 426 | 1,296 | 1 | 47 | 76 | 3.8 | 5.5 | 1,379 | 2,220 | ... | ... | Nicaragua |
| — | — | ... | ... | 1 | 144 | 232 | 47.5 | 69.4 | 186 | 300 | ... | ... | Niger |
| 206 | 809.3 | 55,725 | 13,931 | 6 | 1,405 | 2,261 | 30.4 | 44.4 | 5,328 | 8,575 | ... | ... | Nigeria |
| — | — | — | — | 1 | ... | ... | ... | ... | ... | ... | ... | ... | Niue |
| — | — | — | — | 1 | ... | ... | ... | ... | ... | ... | ... | ... | Norfolk Island |

## Transportation (continued)

| country | roads length mi | km | paved (per-cent) | automobiles | trucks and buses | persons per vehicle | cargo short ton-mi ('000,000) | cargo metric ton-km ('000,000) | track length mi | km | passenger-mi ('000,000) | passenger-km ('000,000) | cargo short ton-mi ('000,000) | cargo metric ton-km ('000,000) |
|---|---|---|---|---|---|---|---|---|---|---|---|---|---|---|
| Norway | 53,358 | 85,872 | 64 | 1,513,954 | 249,673 | 2.4 | 4,125 | 6,022 | 2,646[2] | 4,258[2] | 1,392 | 2,241 | 2,008 | 2,932 |
| Oman | 13,563 | 21,827 | 15 | 105,000 | 97,987 | 59 | ... | ... | — | — | — | — | — | — |
| Pacific Is., Trust Terr. of the | 1,000 | 1,600 | 25 | 4,206 | 2,311 | 20 | ... | ... | — | — | — | — | — | — |
| Marshall Islands | ... | ... | ... | ... | ... | ... | | | — | — | — | — | — | — |
| Micronesia, Fed. States of | | | | | | | | | | | | | | |
| Northern Mariana Islands | ... | ... | ... | | | | | | — | — | — | — | — | — |
| Palau | ... | ... | ... | —1,687— | | 7.2 | | | — | — | — | — | — | — |
| Pakistan | 62,324 | 100,300 | 69 | 211,752 | 66,722 | 351 | | | 5,482[2] | 8,823[2] | 11,065 | 17,808 | 4,932 | 7,200 |
| Panama | 6,024 | 9,694 | 33 | 120,995 | 41,753 | 13 | | | 359[2] | 578[2] | ... | ... | ... | ... |
| Papua New Guinea | 12,263 | 19,736 | 6 | 22,757 | 39,481 | 57 | | | — | — | — | — | — | — |
| Paraguay | 9,186 | 14,783 | 13 | 84,986 | 41,986 | 26 | | | 274[2] | 441[2] | 14 | 22 | 24 | 34 |
| Peru | 40,400 | 65,000 | 11 | 359,700 | 196,013 | 33 | | | 2,144[2] | 3,451[2] | 350 | 563 | 575 | 839 |
| Philippines | 100,481 | 161,709 | 13 | 753,779 | 108,674 | 63 | | | 658[2] | 1,059[2] | 104 | 168 | 41 | 60 |
| Pitcairn Island | 4 | 6 | — | 3 | — | 18 | | | — | — | — | — | — | — |
| Poland | 158,000 | 254,000 | 61 | 3,179,000 | 732,000 | 9.3 | 25,064 | 36,593 | 16,836 | 27,095 | 32,297 | 51,977 | 82,627 | 120,642 |
| Portugal | 32,282 | 51,953 | 86 | 1,600,738 | 103,285 | 6.9 | 4,950 | 7,220 | 2,245[2] | 3,613[2] | 3,609 | 5,808 | 994 | 1,452 |
| Puerto Rico | 5,813 | 9,355 | 86 | 1,102,155 | 197,012 | 2.5 | | | — | — | — | — | — | — |
| Qatar | 671 | 1,080 | ... | | | | | | — | — | — | — | — | — |
| Réunion | 1,684 | 2,710 | 81 | 138,081 | 45,017 | 2.1 | | | — | — | — | — | — | — |
| Romania | 45,235 | 72,799 | 64 | 250,000 | 130,000 | 58 | 4,080 | 5,957 | 7,002 | 11,269 | 19,313 | 31,082 | 50,830 | 74,215 |
| Rwanda | 7,500 | 12,070 | 5 | 6,795 | 8,564 | 408 | 140 | 200 | — | — | — | — | — | — |
| St. Christopher and Nevis | 198 | 318 | 44 | 3,540 | 690 | 11 | | | — | — | — | — | — | — |
| St. Helena and Ascension | 109 | 175 | 74 | —1,124[41]— | | 5.0[41] | | | — | — | — | — | — | — |
| St. Lucia | 426 | 686 | 65 | 7,049 | 2,084 | 22 | | | — | — | — | — | — | — |
| St. Pierre and Miquelon | 67 | 108 | 42 | 1,732 | 607 | 2.6 | | | — | — | — | — | — | — |
| St. Vincent and the Grenadines | 463 | 745 | 58 | 4,460 | 2,040 | 17 | | | — | — | — | — | — | — |
| San Marino | 137 | 220 | ... | 16,540 | 1,760 | 1.2 | | | — | — | — | — | — | — |
| São Tomé and Príncipe | 179 | 288 | 69 | 1,774 | 265 | 41 | | | — | — | — | — | — | — |
| Saudi Arabia | 51,140 | 82,300 | 42 | 2,165,675 | 1,966,172 | 2.7 | | | 544[2] | 875[2] | 44 | 71 | 220 | 321 |
| Senegal | 8,679 | 13,968 | 26 | 73,665 | 36,144 | 57 | 375 | 547 | 737[2] | 1,186[2] | 46 | 74 | 246 | 345 |
| Seychelles | 164 | 264 | 61 | 3,318 | 1,005 | 15 | | | — | — | — | — | — | — |
| Sierra Leone | 4,635 | 7,459 | 16 | 19,040 | 6,763 | 139 | 36 | 53 | 52 | 84 | ... | ... | ... | ... |
| Singapore | 1,643 | 2,644 | 95 | 233,557 | 114,281 | 7.4 | | | 16 | 26 | ... | ... | ... | ... |
| Solomon Islands | 1,300 | 2,100 | 12 | 1,122 | 1,323 | 99 | | | — | — | — | — | — | — |
| Somalia | 13,242 | 21,311 | 12 | 17,754 | 9,533 | 204 | | | — | — | — | — | — | — |
| South Africa | 114,537 | 184,330 | 27 | 2,936,083 | 1,415,184 | 6.3 | | | 14,653 | 23,581 | 12,513 | 20,137 | 63,437 | 92,616 |
| Bophuthatswana | 5,474 | 8,810 | ... | | | | | | 142 | 228 | ... | ... | ... | ... |
| Ciskei | 1,553 | 2,500 | 20 | | | | | | 78 | 125 | ... | ... | ... | ... |
| KwaNdebele | ... | ... | ... | | | | | | | | | | | |
| Transkei | 5,468 | 8,800 | ... | | | | | | 130 | 209 | ... | ... | ... | ... |
| Venda | 739 | 1,189 | 11 | | | | | | 8 | 13 | — | — | — | — |
| South West Africa/Namibia | 28,748 | 46,269 | 9 | —120,408— | | 10 | | | 1,454 | 2,340 | ... | ... | 1,300 | 1,900 |
| Spain | 198,211 | 318,991 | 56 | 9,273,710 | 1,610,263 | 3.5 | 74,000 | 108,100 | 8,435[2] | 13,575[2] | 9,693 | 15,600 | 7,906 | 11,544 |
| Sri Lanka | 53,573 | 86,218 | 35 | 148,587 | 137,164 | 55 | | | 1,208 | 1,944 | 1,312 | 2,111 | 169 | 247 |
| Sudan, The | 4,100 | 6,599 | 59 | 99,400 | 17,211 | 203 | | | 2,974 | 4,786 | 714 | 1,149 | 1,096 | 1,600 |
| Suriname | 5,541 | 8,917 | 26 | 31,560 | 12,780 | 8.0 | | | 54 | 87 | ... | ... | ... | ... |
| Swaziland | 1,692 | 2,723 | 23 | 17,238 | 8,558 | 24 | | | 230[2] | 370[2] | — | — | 73 | 107 |
| Sweden | 81,207 | 130,691 | 69 | 3,151,195 | 231,442 | 2.5 | 15,744 | 22,986 | 7,130 | 11,745 | 4,094 | 6,588 | 11,988 | 17,503 |
| Switzerland | 43,855 | 70,578 | 96 | 2,617,164 | 211,308 | 2.3 | 4,340 | 6,337 | 3,158 | 5,028 | 5,719 | 9,204 | 4,772 | 6,967 |
| Syria | 16,561 | 26,652 | 80 | 108,367 | 120,905 | 48 | 2,569 | 3,751 | 1,250 | 2,013 | 587 | 944 | 857 | 1,251 |
| Taiwan | 10,919 | 17,572 | 84 | 1,046,660 | 439,910 | 13 | 4,146 | 6,053 | 2,983 | 4,800 | 5,167 | 8,316 | 1,620 | 2,365 |
| Tanzania | 50,887 | 81,895 | 4 | —84,190— | | 250 | | | 2,222 | 3,576 | 577[46] | 929[46] | 475[46] | 694[46] |
| Thailand | 47,420 | 76,315 | 39 | 411,982 | 789,837 | 41 | | | 2,321[2] | 3,735[2] | 5,734 | 9,228 | 1,767 | 2,580 |
| Togo | 4,349 | 7,000 | 23 | 2,570 | 288 | 1,045 | | | 321 | 516 | 65 | 105 | 11 | 16 |
| Tokelau | ... | ... | ... | | | | | | — | — | — | — | — | — |
| Tonga | 269 | 433 | 65 | 443 | 1,343 | 53 | | | — | — | — | — | — | — |
| Trinidad and Tobago | 4,909 | 7,900 | 46 | 241,595 | 82,361 | 3.6 | | | — | — | — | — | — | — |
| Tunisia | 16,312 | 26,252 | 54 | 174,902 | 179,741 | 21 | 610 | 890 | 1,316[2] | 2,118[2] | 470 | 756 | 1,282 | 1,872 |
| Turkey | 188,136 | 302,776 | ... | 1,086,675 | 588,491 | 31 | 29,232 | 42,678 | 5,076[2] | 8,169[2] | 4,032 | 6,489 | 5,307 | 7,748 |
| Turks and Caicos Islands | 75 | 121 | 20 | —1,563— | | 5 | | | — | — | — | — | — | — |
| Tuvalu | 5 | 8 | — | | | | | | — | — | — | — | — | — |
| Uganda | 17,630 | 28,372 | 22 | 32,155 | 8,865 | 358 | | | 799[2] | 1,286[2] | ... | ... | ... | ... |
| U.S.S.R. | 604,000 | 971,500 | 84 | 8,255,000 | 7,254,000 | 17 | 97,000 | 142,000 | 90,037 | 144,900 | 242,000 | 390,000 | 2,547,000 | 3,718,400 |
| United Arab Emirates | 800 | 1,300 | 61 | 130,700 | 77,600 | 5.2 | | | — | — | — | — | — | — |
| United Kingdom | 216,450 | 348,344 | 97 | 16,453,000 | 2,742,000 | 2.9 | 73,200 | 106,900 | 24,512[49] | 39,448[49] | 19,126[49] | 30,780[49] | 10,915[49] | 15,936[49] |
| United States | 3,891,781 | 6,263,043 | 88 | 135,700,000 | 40,800,000 | 1.4 | 666,000 | 973,000 | 184,235 | 296,497 | 15,590 | 25,090 | 897,542 | 1,310,388 |
| Uruguay | 30,952 | 49,813 | 20 | 281,275 | 49,813 | 8.8 | 500 | 730 | 1,865[2] | 3,001[2] | 205 | 330 | 187 | 273 |
| Vanuatu | 660 | 1,062 | 4 | 3,000 | 2,500 | 8.4 | | | — | — | — | — | — | — |
| Venezuela | 47,082 | 75,772 | 38 | 2,289,000 | 1,094,000 | 5.1 | | | 273 | 439 | 4.9 | 7.9 | 9.4 | 13.7 |
| Vietnam | 37,282 | 60,000 | 16 | 100,000 | 200,000 | 163 | 1,062 | 1,550 | 1,568 | 2,523 | 2,087 | 3,359 | 595 | 869 |
| Virgin Islands (U.S.) | 532 | 856 | 100 | —43,901— | | 2.5 | | | — | — | — | — | — | — |
| Wallis and Futuna | 62 | 100 | ... | | | | | | — | — | — | — | — | — |
| West Bank | ... | ... | ... | 25,370 | 14,374 | 19 | | | ... | ... | ... | ... | ... | ... |
| Western Sahara | 3,790 | 6,100 | 8 | 6,284 | 424 | 20 | | | ... | ... | ... | ... | ... | ... |
| Western Samoa | 1,296 | 2,085 | 14 | 1,795 | 2,494 | 37 | | | — | — | — | — | — | — |
| Yemen (Aden) | 1,150 | 1,850 | ... | 16,500 | 16,300 | 57 | | | — | — | — | — | — | — |
| Yemen (Ṣan'ā') | 23,078 | 37,141 | 6 | 117,756 | 169,267 | 24 | | | — | — | — | — | — | — |
| Yugoslavia | 73,163 | 117,744 | 57 | 2,824,267 | 264,593 | 7.5 | 14,960 | 21,840 | 5,768 | 9,283 | 7,695 | 12,384 | 18,879 | 27,564 |
| Zaire | 28,379 | 45,671 | 18 | 89,471 | 16,807 | 268 | | | 3,623 | 5,252 | 181[52] | 292[52] | 1,339[52] | 1,954[52] |
| Zambia | 23,183 | 37,310 | 15 | 105,783 | 94,780 | 30 | | | 1,359 | 2,187 | 347 | 558 | 1,072 | 1,565 |
| Zimbabwe | 48,421 | 77,927 | 17 | 253,470 | 28,839 | 29 | | | 2,109[2] | 3,394[2] | ... | ... | 4,249 | 6,204 |

[1]Bakhtar Afghan Airlines only.  [2]Route length.  [3]Air Algérie international flights only.  [4]Leeward Island Air Transport Company only.  [5]Seagreen only.  [6]Aerolineas Argentinos only.  [7]Government railways only.  [8]Bahamasair only.  [9]Apportionment of ¼ of international flights of Gulf Air (jointly administered by the governments of Bahrain, Oman, Qatar, and United Arab Emirates) only.  [10]Caribbean Airways only.  [11]Caribbean Air Cargo only.  [12]Cotonou airport only.  [13]Cruzeiro do Sul, Transbrasil, VARIG, and VASP only.  [14]For industrial purposes only.  [15]China includes Taiwan.  [16]Lasca only.  [17]All traffic between Ouagadougou, Burkina Faso, and Abidjan, Côte d'Ivoire.  [18]Excludes railroads serving the sugar industry.  [19]Apportionment of 2/7 of total operations performed by SAS only.  [20]National roads only.  [21]Includes 100 km of the Chemin de Fer Djibouti–Ethiopien (CDE) in Djibouti.  [22]Air France, UTA, and Air Inter only.

| merchant marine | | international cargo (latest) | | air | traffic (latest) | | | | canals and inland waterways (latest) | | | | country |
|---|---|---|---|---|---|---|---|---|---|---|---|---|---|
| | | | | | passengers | | cargo | | length | | cargo | | |
| fleet, 1986 (vessels over 100 gross tons) | total dead-weight tonnage, 1986 ('000) | loaded metric tons ('000) | off-loaded metric tons ('000) | airports with scheduled flights, 1987 | passenger-mi ('000,000) | passenger-km ('000,000) | short ton-mi ('000,000) | metric ton-km ('000,000) | mi | km | short ton-mi ('000,000) | metric ton-km ('000,000) | |
| 2,107 | 14,202.7 | 58,428 | 17,604 | 41 | 2,460[36] | 3,960[36] | 94.0[36] | 137.3[36] | 980 | 1,577 | 7,328 | 10,698 | Norway |
| 29 | 13.0 | 19,200 | 3,600 | 6 | 553[9] | 890[9] | 16.3[9] | 23.8[9] | ... | ... | ... | ... | Oman |
| — | — | 25 | 115 | 9 | _188_ | 302 | 3.9 | 5.6 | ... | ... | ... | ... | Pacific Is., Trust Terr. of the Marshall Islands |
| ... | ... | ... | ... | ... | ... | ... | ... | ... | | | | | Micronesia, Fed. States of |
| | | | | | | | | | | | | | Northern Mariana Islands |
| ... | ... | 2 | 56 | ... | ... | ... | ... | ... | | | ... | ... | Palau |
| 78 | 623.2 | 4,812 | 15,444 | 18 | 4,429 | 7,128 | 226.4 | 330.5 | ... | ... | ... | ... | Pakistan |
| 5,252 | 68,349.4 | 924 | 2,259 | 6 | 342 | 551 | 38.2 | 55.8 | 548 | 882 | ... | ... | Panama |
| 88 | 37.7 | 1,950 | 1,530 | 177 | 291 | 468 | 7.0 | 10.2 | 6,798 | 10,940 | ... | ... | Papua New Guinea |
| 41 | 51.5 | — | — | 1 | 290 | 466 | 1.4 | 2.0 | 1,900 | 3,100 | ... | ... | Paraguay |
| 632 | 997.1 | 10,300 | 3,283 | 22 | 992[37] | 1,596[37] | 30.1[37] | 43.9[37] | 5,300 | 8,600 | ... | ... | Peru |
| 1,131 | 11,668.6 | 12,744 | 16,932 | 42 | 5,645[38] | 9,084[38] | 168.7[38] | 246.3[38] | 2,000 | 3,200 | ... | ... | Philippines |
| — | — | ... | ... | — | ... | ... | ... | ... | | | | | Pitcairn Island |
| 749 | 4,694.2 | 39,386 | 15,913 | 12 | 1,365 | 2,196 | 8.4 | 12.2 | 1,850 | 2,977 | 968 | 1,413 | Poland |
| 355 | 1,747.1 | 4,930 | 18,120 | 20 | 2,781[39] | 4,476[39] | 91.1[39] | 133.0[39] | 510 | 820 | ... | ... | Portugal |
| — | — | 40 | 40 | 8 | ... | ... | ... | ... | | | ... | ... | Puerto Rico |
| 55 | 457.5 | 17,900 | 2,200 | 1 | 721[9] | 1,160[9] | 21.4[9] | 31.4[9] | ... | ... | ... | ... | Qatar |
| — | — | 336 | 1,128 | 1 | ... | ... | ... | ... | | | ... | ... | Réunion |
| 426 | 4,843.3 | 8,600 | 28,570 | 15 | 2,115 | 3,403 | 50.0 | 73.0 | 1,031 | 1,659 | 1,655 | 2,417 | Romania |
| — | — | ... | ... | 2 | ... | ... | ... | ... | | | ... | ... | Rwanda |
| 1 | 0.1 | 30 | 40 | 2 | ... | ... | ... | ... | | | ... | ... | St. Christopher and Nevis |
| 2 | 2.8 | 1 | 16 | 1 | ... | ... | ... | ... | | | ... | ... | St. Helena and Ascension |
| 8 | 3.4 | 105 | 185 | 2 | ... | ... | ... | ... | | | ... | ... | St. Lucia |
| — | — | 20 | 55 | 1 | ... | ... | ... | ... | | | ... | ... | St. Pierre and Miquelon |
| 103 | 833.2 | 70 | 115 | 4 | ... | ... | ... | ... | | | ... | ... | St. Vincent and the Grenadines |
| — | — | — | — | — | — | — | — | — | — | — | — | — | San Marino |
| 3 | 1.2 | 11 | 18 | 1 | ... | ... | ... | ... | | | ... | ... | São Tomé and Príncipe |
| 380 | 4,954.6 | 224,000 | 41,000 | 18 | 9,604 | 15,456 | 330.2 | 482.1 | ... | ... | ... | ... | Saudi Arabia |
| 148 | 41.7 | 2,448 | 2,880 | 12 | 129 | 208 | 26.2 | 38.3 | 935 | 1,505 | ... | ... | Senegal |
| 7 | 2.5 | 6 | 210 | 5 | ... | ... | ... | ... | | | ... | ... | Seychelles |
| 29 | 1.7 | 1,588 | 534 | 6 | 76[42] | 122[42] | 1.3[42] | 1.9[42] | 500 | 800 | 447 | 652 | Sierra Leone |
| 716 | 10,603.7 | 45,708 | 67,116 | 1 | 14,212 | 22,872 | 791.4 | 1,155.4 | ... | ... | ... | ... | Singapore |
| 27 | 5.2 | 290 | 300 | 25 | 7 | 11 | 0.02 | 0.04 | ... | ... | ... | ... | Solomon Islands |
| 26 | 15.0 | 147 | 625 | 9 | 177 | 284 | 3.4 | 4.9 | ... | ... | ... | ... | Somalia |
| 271 | 661.7 | 59,750 | 27,245 | 36 | 5,674[43] | 9,132[43] | 281.9[43] | 411.5[43] | ... | ... | ... | ... | South Africa |
| — | — | — | — | 1 | — | — | — | — | | | ... | ... | Bophuthatswana |
| | | | | | | | | | | | ... | ... | Ciskei |
| ... | ... | ... | ... | 1 | ... | ... | | | | | ... | ... | KwaNdebele |
| | | | | | | | | | | | ... | ... | Transkei |
| — | — | — | — | 9 | ... | — | ... | ... | ... | ... | ... | ... | Venda |
| | | | | | | | | | | | | | South West Africa/Namibia |
| 2,397 | 9,286.0 | 45,072 | 97,368 | 29 | 11,900 | 19,152 | 389.4 | 568.5 | 649 | 1,045 | 21,836[44] | 31,880[44] | Spain |
| 91 | 972.0 | 2,112 | 4,224 | 1 | 1,312 | 2,112 | 38.5 | 56.1 | 267 | 430 | ... | ... | Sri Lanka |
| 23 | 126.4 | 1,303 | 3,047 | 8 | _408_ | 657 | 4.1 | 6.0 | 3,300 | 5,310 | ... | ... | Sudan, The |
| 25 | 15.3 | 6,000 | 1,435 | 5 | 152 | 245 | 2.5 | 3.6 | 746 | 1,200 | ... | ... | Suriname |
| — | — | — | — | 1 | 14 | 22 | 1.5 | 2.2 | ... | ... | ... | ... | Swaziland |
| 660 | 3,037.4 | 41,772 | 55,776 | 36 | 3,342[45] | 5,378[45] | 130.8[45] | 190.9[45] | 724 | 1,165 | 6,200 | 9,000 | Sweden |
| 34 | 550.7 | ... | ... | 5 | 8,000 | 12,875 | 496.8 | 725.3 | 13 | 21 | 108 | 158 | Switzerland |
| 57 | 92.5 | 7,656 | 11,124 | 5 | 585 | 942 | 10.7 | 15.7 | 418 | 672 | ... | ... | Syria |
| 587 | [15] | ... | ... | 9 | 7,624 | 12,271 | 1,737.9 | 2,537.5 | ... | ... | ... | ... | Taiwan |
| 41 | 59.0 | 932 | 2,342 | 19 | 163 | 262 | 18 | 2.6 | 726 | 1,168 | ... | ... | Tanzania |
| 243 | 772.4 | 18,516[47] | 17,376[47] | 22 | 7,009 | 11,280 | 322.8 | 485.9 | 2,500 | 4,000 | ... | ... | Thailand |
| 11 | 78.0 | 257 | 851 | 1 | 129 | 208 | 11.0 | 16.0 | 30 | 50 | ... | ... | Togo |
| — | — | — | — | — | — | — | — | — | ... | ... | | | Tokelau |
| 19 | 21.1 | 20 | 60 | 6 | ... | ... | ... | ... | ... | ... | ... | ... | Tonga |
| 51 | 12.8 | 13,450 | 6,030 | 2 | 1,339[48] | 2,155[48] | 8.6[48] | 12.6[48] | ... | ... | ... | ... | Trinidad and Tobago |
| 71 | 449.7 | 3,936 | 5,400 | 5 | 820 | 1,320 | 10.5 | 15.4 | ... | ... | ... | ... | Tunisia |
| 825 | 5,712.5 | 54,708 | 36,924 | 14 | 1,627 | 2,618 | 31.1 | 45.5 | 750 | 1,200 | 35 | 51 | Turkey |
| 13 | 3.9 | 150 | 165 | 5 | ... | ... | ... | ... | ... | ... | ... | ... | Turks and Caicos Islands |
| 2 | 0.5 | ... | ... | 1 | ... | ... | ... | ... | | | ... | ... | Tuvalu |
| 3 | 8.6 | ... | ... | 7 | 47 | 76 | 12.2 | 17.9 | ... | ... | ... | ... | Uganda |
| 6,726 | 28,145.6 | 166,483 | 75,878 | 52 | 121,800 | 196,000 | 2,294.0 | 3,350.0 | 84,900 | 136,700 | 179,000 | 262,000 | U.S.S.R. |
| 220 | 1,018.9 | 58,500 | 7,500 | 2 | 2,213[9] | 3,562[9] | 65.3[9] | 95.3[9] | ... | ... | ... | ... | United Arab Emirates |
| 2,256 | 16,871.6 | 153,696 | 147,504 | 40 | 31,697 | 51,012 | 1,286.9 | 1,878.8 | 1,461 | 2,351 | 29,600 | 43,200 | United Kingdom |
| 6,496 | 28,850.6 | 317,460[40] | 357,648[40] | 824 | 329,836 | 530,820 | 8,906.7 | 13,003.6 | 25,727 | 41,403 | 421,000 | 615,000 | United States |
| 89 | 224.9 | 855[50] | 405[50] | 7 | 230 | 370 | 1.2 | 1.8 | 1,000 | 1,600 | ... | ... | Uruguay |
| 47 | 274.1 | 60 | 55 | 25 | ... | ... | ... | ... | ... | ... | ... | ... | Vanuatu |
| 279 | 1,428.6 | 88,155 | 12,093 | 39 | 1,531 | 2,464 | 147.4 | 215.2 | 4,400 | 7,100 | ... | ... | Venezuela |
| 150 | 508.0 | 300 | 1,000 | 3 | 183 | 295 | 4.1 | 6.0 | 11,000 | 17,702 | ... | ... | Vietnam |
| — | — | 9,500 | 12,600 | 6 | ... | ... | ... | ... | | | ... | ... | Virgin Islands (U.S.) |
| | | | | 2 | ... | ... | ... | ... | | | | | Wallis and Futuna |
| — | — | 45 | 16 | 1 | ... | ... | ... | ... | | | ... | ... | West Bank |
| — | — | | | 3 | ... | ... | ... | ... | | | ... | ... | Western Sahara |
| 6 | 34.8 | 49 | 89 | | ... | ... | ... | ... | | | ... | ... | Western Samoa |
| 29 | 13.2 | 2,000 | 3,500 | 8 | _62_ | _100_ | 1.2 | 1.7 | ... | ... | ... | ... | Yemen (Aden) |
| 11 | 6.1 | 100 | 2,700 | 5 | 358[51] | 576[51] | 43.5[51] | 63.6[51] | ... | ... | ... | ... | Yemen (Şan'ā') |
| 490 | 4,476.3 | 7,476 | 24,948 | 17 | 3,937 | 6,336 | 63.4 | 92.5 | 1,243 | 2,001 | 2,956 | 4,315 | Yugoslavia |
| 31 | 91.0 | 1,950 | 1,084 | 22 | 237[53] | 382[53] | 8.3[53] | 12.2[53] | 9,300 | 15,000 | 678 | 990 | Zaire |
| — | — | ... | ... | 14 | 392 | 631 | 17.3 | 25.2 | 1,398 | 2,250 | ... | ... | Zambia |
| — | — | — | — | 8 | 410 | 661 | 10.0 | 14.6 | ... | ... | | | Zimbabwe |

[23]Includes airfields. [24]Includes transshipments. [25]El Al only. [26]Alitalia only. [27]Kenya Airways only. [28]Air Tungaru only. [29]1982. [30]Peninsular Malaysia and Singapore. [31]Aeronaves de Mexico and Mexicana only. [32]Air Nauru only. [33]International traffic only. [34]KLM and NLM only. [35]Antillean Airlines only. [36]Includes 2/7 apportionment of total operations of SAS. [37]Aeroperu and Faucett only. [38]PAL only. [39]TAP only. [40]United States includes Puerto Rico. [41]St. Helena only. [42]Sierra Leone Airlines international traffic only. [43]SAA only. [44]Coastal shipping only. [45]Includes 3/7 apportionment of total operations of SAS. [46]Tanzania Railways Corporation only. [47]Port of Bangkok only. [48]BWIA international only. [49]British Railways only; excluding Northern Ireland. [50]Port of Montevideo only. [51]Yemen Airways only. [52]Zaire National Railways only. [53]Air Zaire only.

# Communications

Virtually all the states of the world have a variety of communications media available to their citizens: newspapers (although only daily papers are included in this table), radio broadcast systems, and telephone, post office, and telegraph facilities; most also have television and telex. The focus of this table, therefore, is on the relative density and distribution of communications services. Unfortunately, the availability of information about the infrastructure and traffic volume of these national systems runs far behind the capabilities of the systems themselves. Certain countries publish no information about themselves; others publish data analyzed according to a variety of fiscal, calendar, religious, or other years; still others, while they possess such data almost simultaneously with the end of the business year, may not publish them except in company reports of limited distribution. Even when they are published in national statistical summaries, it may be only after a delay of up to several years.

The data also originate in sources of varying completeness and reliability. Data for some kinds of communications apparatus and traffic are relatively easy to track; telephones, for example, even mobile, must be installed, and service recorded so that it may be charged. But in most countries radios may be purchased by anyone and turned on whenever desired; car radios are seldom enumerated or licensed separately. As a result, data on distribution and use of radio and television apparatus may be collected in a variety of ways—on the basis of numbers of subscribers, licenses issued, periodic sample surveys, census or housing surveys, or private consumer surveys.

The United Nations Educational, Scientific and Cultural Organization (Unesco) publishes in its *Statistical Yearbook* extensive data on newspapers, radio, and television that have been collected from standardized questionnaires. The completeness and recency of its data, however, depend on the timely return of each questionnaire, and response rates depend on a variety of factors. In general, however, response rates for inquiries by international organizations in communications are better than in other fields because these organizations and the responsible authorities in each country must conduct day-to-day business and, hence, have a better ongoing relationship.

Newspaper statistics are especially difficult to collect and compare. Newspapers continually are founded, cease publication, merge, or change frequency of publication. Data on circulation, sales, and readership are often incomplete, slow to be aggregated at the national level, or regarded as proprietary for either private or governmental publications. In some countries circulation data are virtually nonexistent. In others no daily newspaper exists.

The commercially published annual *World Radio TV Handbook* (J.M.

## Communications

| country | daily newspapers (latest) number | total circulation ('000) | circulation per 1,000 population | radio, 1986 transmitters (latest) | receivers (all types) ('000) | persons per receiver | television, 1986 transmitters (latest) | receivers (all types) ('000) | persons per receiver | telephones, 1985 receivers ('000) | persons per receiver | traffic, 1985 ('000 calls) local | long-distance | international |
|---|---|---|---|---|---|---|---|---|---|---|---|---|---|---|
| Afghanistan | 12 | 106 | 7 | 14 | 150 | 115 | 1 | 20 | 860 | 32[1] | 496[1] | —110[2]— | | 18[2] |
| Albania | 2 | 145 | 52 | 14 | 210 | 14 | 176 | 50 | 60 | 4.84 | 580[4] | ... | | ... |
| Algeria | 4 | 480 | 23 | 55 | 3,250 | 6.9 | 44 | 1,540 | 15 | 769 | 28 | —1,430,954[5]— | | 880,802[5] |
| American Samoa | 2 | 9 | 237 | 1 | 16 | 2.3 | 3 | 8.0 | 4.5 | 5.9 | 6.1 | ... | | 595 |
| Andorra | 1 | ... | ... | 4 | 8.0 | 5.8 | — | 4.0 | 12 | 21[7] | 1.9[7] | ... | | ... |
| Angola | 4 | 112 | 14 | 55 | 400 | 22 | 2 | 32 | 276 | 40[4] | 197[4] | 66,080[1] | 260[1] | 320[1] |
| Anguilla | — | — | — | 4 | 2.2 | 3.1 | — | ... | ... | 1.38 | 4.9 | 624[8] | | 49 |
| Antigua and Barbuda | — | — | — | 5[11] | 35 | 2.3 | 2 | 27 | 3.0 | 117 | 7.2[7] | 36,400[5,7] | 3,600[5,7] | 3,223[12] |
| Argentina | 227 | ... | ... | 202 | 19,866 | 1.6 | 75 | 5,925 | 5.3 | 3,594[7] | 8.3[7] | 16,698,605[5,8] | 30,237[8,15] | 3,580[8] |
| Aruba | 2 | 16 | 187 | 5 | 12 | 5.1 | 1 | 6 | 10 | 16 | 16 | 16 | 16 | 16 |
| Australia | 61 | 4,740 | 308 | 284 | 30,000 | 0.5 | 386 | 4,974[17] | 3.2[17] | 8,727 | 1.8 | 6,860,064 | 1,092,312 | 27,400 |
| Austria | 33 | ... | ... | 567 | 2,619[17] | 2.9[17] | 864 | 3,024[17] | 2.5[19] | 3,720 | 2.0 | —26,064,267[12]— | | 306,499[12] |
| Bahamas, The | 3 | 32 | 136 | 5 | 120 | 2.0 | 1 | 40 | 5.9 | 97 | 2.4 | ... | | 3,642 |
| Bahrain | 5 | ... | ... | 3 | 200 | 2.2 | 1 | 135 | 3.2 | 115 | 3.6 | 122,572[4,5] | | 34,359 |
| Bangladesh | 54 | 554 | 6 | 23 | 4,120 | 25 | 8 | 302 | 340 | 122[4] | 763[4] | —347,600[21]— | | 84[12,21] |
| Barbados | 2 | 40 | 156 | 4 | 335 | 0.8 | 2 | 60 | 4.2 | 75[7] | 3.4[7] | —483,000[8]— | | 1,182 |
| Belgium | 26 | 2,204 | 224 | 41 | 4,526[17] | 2.2[17] | 31 | 3,041[17] | 3.2[17] | 4,346 | 2.3 | 1,673,686[7] | 2,389,357[5] | 97,113 |
| Belize | — | — | — | 11 | 88 | 1.9 | — | ... | ... | 8.6[8] | 18[8] | 28,382[4,5] | | 844[12] |
| Benin | 3 | ... | ... | 7 | 300 | 14 | 2 | 16 | 268 | 17 | 238 | ... | 7,103[12] | 2,603[12] |
| Bermuda | 1 | 17 | 297 | 5 | 100 | 0.6 | 2 | 67 | 0.9 | 527 | 1.1[7] | 43,805[4] | | 18,397[12] |
| Bhutan | — | — | — | 1 | 13 | 113 | ... | ... | ... | 15[4] | 89 | ... | | ... |
| Bolivia | 14 | 253 | 40 | 184 | 3,000 | 2.2 | 42 | 300 | 22 | 214[7] | 29[7] | —2,879[21]— | | 2,435[8,12] |
| Botswana | 1 | 24 | 22 | 9 | 80 | 14 | ... | ... | ... | 19[7] | 55[7] | —66,180[7,12]— | | 5,570[7,12] |
| Brazil | 279 | 8,528 | 62 | 1,818 | 50,540 | 2.7 | ... | 36,000 | 3.8 | 11,428 | 12 | 16,185,456 | 2,114,600 | 10,398 |
| British Virgin Islands | — | — | — | 1 | 6.9 | 1.8 | 1 | 2.6 | 4.7 | 3.7 | 3.2 | —4,000[5,7]— | | 2,150[12] |
| Brunei | — | — | — | 8 | 74 | 3.1 | 2 | 48 | 4.8 | 33 | 6.8 | ... | 22,720[1,5] | 7,898[12] |
| Bulgaria | 17 | 2,274 | 254 | 35 | 2,400 | 3.7 | 339 | 2,100 | 4.3 | 1,790[8] | 5.0[8] | 25,800[8] | 344[4] | 6,130[8] |
| Burkina Faso | 1 | 2 | 0.2 | 9 | 311 | 26 | 2 | 41 | 196 | 147 | 542[7] | —16,132[5,7]— | | 1,130[7,12] |
| Burma | 6 | 509 | 14 | 7 | 800 | 48 | 2 | 64 | 601 | 51[8] | 711[8] | —65,000[21]— | | 72[8] |
| Burundi | 1 | 20 | 4 | 5 | 230 | 21 | 1 | 4.0 | 1,207 | 6.0[8] | 754[8] | 1,205[8] | 533[8] | 538[8] |
| Cameroon | 1 | 35 | 4 | 19 | 800 | 12 | ... | 2.0 | 4,937 | 49[7] | 192[7] | ... | | 22,905[12] |
| Canada | 108 | 5,412 | 211 | 1,540 | 21,810 | 1.2 | 1,231 | 15,300 | 1.7 | 16,510[7] | 1.5[7] | 31,204,785[7] | 1,640,932[7] | 112,198[8] |
| Cape Verde | — | — | — | 3 | 50 | 6.8 | — | 0.5[19] | 668[19] | 2.47 | 136[7] | —126,000[7]— | | 377[7] |
| Cayman Islands | 1 | 5 | 210 | 4 | 20 | 1.1 | — | 1.2 | 19 | 13 | 1.6 | —16,353[5,7]— | | 4,412[12] |
| Central African Republic | — | — | — | 4 | 125 | 22 | ... | ... | ... | 7.0 | 377 | 9,016[12] | 3[12] | 750[12] |
| Chad | 1 | 2 | 0.3 | 7 | 100 | 51 | ... | ... | ... | 3.0 | 1,673 | 3,573[12] | 230[12] | 267[12] |
| Chile | 66 | 1,407 | 120 | 109 | 4,100 | 3.0 | 131 | 2,000 | 6.1 | 761 | 16 | 1,544,966 | 62,919 | 13,585 |
| China | 222 | ... | ... | ... | 223,730[19] | 4.6[19] | c. 5,300 | 69,000 | 15 | 6,260 | 166 | —849,500— | | 12,600 |
| Christmas Island | — | — | — | 1 | 2.5 | 0.9 | ... | ... | ... | ... | ... | ... | | ... |
| Cocos (Keeling) Islands | — | — | — | 1 | 0.15 | 4.1 | ... | ... | ... | 0.18[8] | 3.1[8] | ... | | ... |
| Colombia | 31 | 1,324 | 47 | ... | 7,980 | 3.5 | 84 | 3,800 | 7.4 | 2,097 | 13 | 12,276,900[12] | 1,059,900[12] | 32,400[12] |
| Comoros | — | — | — | 7 | 41 | 10 | ... | ... | ... | 0.50[8] | 738[8] | —940[3]— | | 14[3] |
| Congo | 3 | 24 | 11 | 10 | 200 | 10 | 1 | 5.5 | 381 | 18[8] | 104[8] | 47,582[8] | 31,722[8] | 1,979[8] |
| Cook Islands | 1 | 2 | 114 | 3 | 4.5 | 3.8 | ... | ... | ... | 2.8 | 6.2 | ... | | 270[12] |
| Costa Rica | 5 | 201 | 78 | 123 | 200 | 13 | 11 | 470 | 5.4 | 315 | 7.9 | 412,228 | 217,128 | 2,159 |
| Côte d'Ivoire | 1 | 80 | 8 | 24 | 1,210 | 8.8 | 12 | 550 | 19 | 88[1] | 99[1] | ... | | 1,600 |
| Cuba | 17 | 1,409 | 140 | 150 | 3,232 | 3.2 | 58 | 1,525 | 6.7 | 515 | 20 | —117,900— | | 1,600 |
| Cyprus | 11 | 123 | 92 | 6 | 171 | 3.9 | 29 | 88 | 7.6 | 220 | 3.0 | —713,913[5]— | | 1,031,931[5] |
| Czechoslovakia | 30 | 4,263 | 275 | 123 | 4,210[17] | 3.7[17] | 74 | 4,360[17] | 3.6[17] | 3,591 | 4.3 | 5,091,000 | 374,000 | 7,000 |
| Denmark | 47 | 1,837 | 359 | 49 | 2,052[17] | 2.5[17] | 32 | 1,953[17] | 2.6[17] | 4,005 | 1.3 | 2,445,000 | 1,510,000 | 55,000 |
| Djibouti | — | — | — | 3 | 32 | 14 | 1 | 14 | 33 | 8.1 | 53 | —7,179[5]— | | 2,106[12] |
| Dominica | — | — | — | 3 | 35 | 2.5 | ... | ... | ... | 6.9 | 12 | —6,000[5,7]— | | 779[12] |
| Dominican Republic | 9 | 208 | 33 | 188 | 800 | 8.0 | 19 | 500 | 13 | 186[7] | 33[7] | 2,017,011[4] | 8,460[4] | 2,933[4] |
| Ecuador | 7 | 538 | 57 | ... | 1,900 | 5.1 | 26 | 600 | 16 | 339 | 28 | ... | | 12,249[12] |
| Egypt | 17 | ... | ... | 154 | 15,000 | 3.2 | 74 | 2,010 | 24 | 1,155 | 40 | 3,129,000[12] | 92,000[12] | 24,800[12] |
| El Salvador | 6 | 300 | 62 | 75 | 1,200 | 4.6 | 5 | 400 | 14 | 124[7] | 42[7] | 255,147[5,7] | 170,098[5,7] | 19,072[12] |
| Equatorial Guinea | 2 | 1 | 3 | 3 | 35 | 9.1 | ... | 2.5 | 128 | 1.4[4] | 210[4] | ... | | ... |
| Ethiopia | 3 | 47 | 1 | 9 | 2,000 | 22 | 2 | 40 | 1,119 | 122 | 357 | 316,767[5] | 4,422 | 2,150[12] |
| Faeroe Islands | — | — | — | 4 | 18 | 2.6 | 23 | 10 | 4.6 | 20[7] | 2.3[7] | ... | | 444 |
| Falkland Islands | — | — | — | 2 | 1 | 2.1 | ... | ... | ... | 0.44 | 4.5 | —4— | | 1,151[12] |

Frost, editor) is a valuable source of information on broadcast media and has complete and timely coverage. It depends on data received from broadcasters, but because some do not respond, local correspondents and monitors are used in many countries, and some unconfirmed or unofficial data are included as estimates. Data on transmitters may be complicated by new or changing technology in areas like the use of low-powered relays (secondary, or repeater installations) for local rebroadcast or use of satellite relays.

The statistics on telephones, telegraph, and telex are derived mainly from the UN-affiliated International Telecommunication Union's (ITU's) *Yearbook of Common Carrier Telecommunication Statistics* with additional statistics from national and regional intergovernmental sources. A number of countries report incomplete telephone data: the national total may exclude figures for some telephone companies, or some portion of the national territory; some countries supply statistics only on telephone exchange lines; some island states report only radio telephones. A number of countries omit data on public coin-box telephones; their statistics, thus, reflect an undercount. The traffic data for telephone calls may represent any one of three quantities: "pulses," measure of mechanical activity rather than an enumeration of actual conversations; minutes of connect time; or "calls," the practical equivalent of a conversation between in-dividuals. Depending on a country's metering system, multiple counting of a single call may occur. Telegraph traffic is reported predominantly as "messages," or sometimes in words; telex traffic is usually reported in minutes of connect time, but, depending on the national metering system, it may also be given as "pulses," or minutes.

Post office statistics are collected mainly from the Universal Postal Union's annual summary *Statistique des services postaux*. Postal services, unlike the other media discussed above, tend most often to be operated by a single national service, to cover a country completely, and to record traffic data according to broadly similar schemes (although the details of *classes* of mail handled may differ). Some countries do not enumerate domestic traffic or may record only international traffic requiring handling charges.

Unesco surveys, the diverse industry sources cited above, and scores of national statistical sources have also been used in the compilation of this table because no single source is complete.

... Not available.

—None, nil, or not applicable.

| post offices, 1985 | | | telegraph, 1985 | | | telex, 1985 | | | | country |
| number | persons per office | pieces of mail handled ('000) | total traffic ('000) | national traffic ('000) | international outgoing traffic ('000) | subscriber lines | traffic ('000 minutes) total | national | international outgoing | |
| --- | --- | --- | --- | --- | --- | --- | --- | --- | --- | --- |
| 349[3] | 36,447[3] | 11,218[3] | 183[2] | 95[2] | 88[2] | 78[4] | ... | ... | 132[4] | Afghanistan |
| 292[3] | 7,328[3] | ... | ... | ... | ... | ... | ... | ... | ... | Albania |
| 2,185 | 10,516 | 358,480 | 2,966[6] | 2,695[6] | 271[6] | 7,404 | 32,338 | 23,270 | 9,068 | Algeria |
| ... | ... | ... | 19 | ... | ... | 88 | 149 | ... | ... | American Samoa |
| ... | ... | 3,483[8] | ... | ... | ... | ... | ... | ... | ... | Andorra |
| 133 | 53,263 | 7,453 | 198[1] | 154[1] | 44[1] | 587[1] | ... | ... | 1,599[1] | Angola |
| 22 | 318 | 353[9,10] | 0.9[8] | 0.004[8] | 0.9[8] | 35 | ... | ... | 27 | Anguilla |
| 15[3] | 5,333[3] | 2,262[9,10,13,14] | ... | ... | 315[6] | 108 | ... | ... | 189 | Antigua and Barbuda |
| 5,600 | 4,975 | 680,283 | 11,357[8] | 11,114[8] | 216[8] | 8,816[8] | ... | 135,982[2,5] | 9,190[8] | Argentina |
| 16 | 16 | 16 | ... | ... | 16 | 16 | 16 | 16 | 16 | Aruba |
| 4,630 | 3,379 | 3,210,331 | 3,614 | 3,009 | 605 | 45,884 | 65,094[18] | 50,336[18] | 14,758[18] | Australia |
| 2,650[20] | 2,851[20] | 2,915,155 | 1,372 | 1,137 | 235 | 25,015 | 113,344 | 76,321 | 37,023 | Austria |
| 127 | 1,649 | 40,667 | 41 | 21 | 20 | 501 | 1,317 | 68 | 1,249 | Bahamas, The |
| 11 | 31,890 | 54,200 | 141 | 18 | 123 | 2,051 | 10,678 | 2,170 | 8,508 | Bahrain |
| 7,627 | 12,980 | 546,311 | 3,998[21] | 3,470[21] | 528[21] | 701[4] | ... | 90[18,21] | 1,230[4] | Bangladesh |
| 16[8] | 15,875[8] | 17,009[8,10] | ... | ... | 29 | 353 | 741 | 2.6 | 738 | Barbados |
| 1,842[20] | 5,352[20] | 3,013,783 | 912 | 677 | 235 | 26,464 | 128,264 | 57,369 | 70,895 | Belgium |
| 105 | 1,385 | 4,619 | 208[8] | 108[8] | 108[8] | 97 | ... | ... | 138 | Belize |
| 162 | 22,962 | 2,347[22] | ... | 53 | ... | 236 | 679 | 76 | 603 | Benin |
| 15[3] | 3,333[3] | ... | ... | ... | 12[7] | 530 | ... | ... | 1,616 | Bermuda |
| 81[3] | 16,728[3] | 2,266[23] | ... | ... | ... | ... | ... | ... | ... | Bhutan |
| 458[3] | 11,572[3] | 54,609[3] | 244[8] | 210[8] | 34[8] | 930[1] | 2,087[8] | 1,152[8] | 935[8] | Bolivia |
| 147 | 7,649 | 65,859 | ... | ... | 42[8] | 451[7] | 2,283 | 896 | 1,387 | Botswana |
| 10,075 | 13,454 | 4,025,945[24] | 21,375 | 21,187 | 188 | 70,582 | 476,000 | 457,000 | 19,000 | Brazil |
| 13 | 846 | 9[25] | ... | ... | 144[6] | 58[7] | ... | ... | 77 | British Virgin Islands |
| 12 | 18,333 | 8,398 | ... | 3 | 27[6] | 491 | ... | ... | 814 | Brunei |
| 2,857[3] | 3,101[3] | ... | 7,593[8] | 7,393[8] | 199[8] | 6,030[8] | 30,733[8] | 27,463[8] | 3,270[8] | Bulgaria |
| 216 | 37,037 | 22,891 | ... | ... | 22[7] | 227[7] | ... | ... | 501[7] | Burkina Faso |
| 1,113 | 33,346 | 100,127 | 1,028[8] | 997[8] | 31[8] | 106[7] | ... | ... | 434[7] | Burma |
| 17 | 266,088 | 1,616[9] | 9[8] | 4[8] | 5[8] | 100[8] | ... | ... | 224[8] | Burundi |
| 261 | 33,823 | 64,248[23] | 917[7] | 889[7] | 28[7] | 1,650 | ... | ... | 3,002 | Cameroon |
| 7,941 | 3,204 | 7,598,103[24] | ... | 1,423[2,26] | 567[7,27] | 48,820[7] | ... | ... | 15,435[7] | Canada |
| 59[20] | 5,593[20] | 2,183 | 527 | 417 | 117 | 797 | 170[7] | 0.6[7] | 169[7] | Cape Verde |
| 20 | 1,000 | 5,285 | 104 | 0.6[1] | 396[6] | 244 | ... | ... | 463 | Cayman Islands |
| 76[8] | 32,310[8] | 34,525[28] | 64 | 48 | 16 | 139 | ... | ... | 450 | Central African Republic |
| 27 | 174,444 | 1,148[11] | 294[6] | 59[6] | 235[6] | 90 | 236 | 9 | 227 | Chad |
| 749 | 15,053 | 150,385[10] | 2,655 | 2,594 | 61 | 5,974 | 16,611 | 11,638 | 4,973 | Chile |
| 51,209 | 20,433 | 4,780,567[10,14,24] | 207,412 | 206,100 | 1,312 | 2,062 | ... | ... | 8,885 | China |
| 2[8] | 1,600[8] | ... | ... | ... | ... | ... | ... | ... | ... | Christmas Island |
| 4[8] | 154[8] | ... | ... | ... | ... | ... | ... | ... | ... | Cocos (Keeling) Islands |
| ... | ... | 209,461[28] | 19,611 | 19,520 | 89 | 5,950 | 27,364 | 21,545 | 5,819 | Colombia |
| 9[3] | 38,889[3] | 1,732[29] | ... | 173 | ... | 42[8] | ... | ... | 60[8] | Comoros |
| 133 | 14,394 | 19,770 | 260[8] | 116[8] | 144[8] | 329[8] | ... | ... | 798[8] | Congo |
| ... | ... | ... | 36[7] | 26[7] | 10[7] | 72 | ... | 11[4] | 91 | Cook Islands |
| 330 | 7,879 | 29,039 | 272 | 227 | 45 | 1,534 | 2,351 | 444 | 1,907 | Costa Rica |
| 1,145 | 8,515 | 60,817[9,10,14] | 581[2] | 508[2] | 73[2] | 1,800[7] | ... | ... | 3,433[7] | Côte d'Ivoire |
| 700[3] | 13,271[3] | 86,991[1,10] | 15,986[21] | 17,333 | 7,128[6] | 3,599 | 34,400 | 32,653 | 1,747 | Cuba |
| 697 | 943 | 35,879 | 149 | 99 | 50 | 3,344 | 6,660 | 2,164 | 4,496 | Cyprus |
| 6,635 | 2,339 | 74,410[25] | 9,533 | 9,243 | 290 | 10,818 | ... | 71,625[5] | 6,309 | Czechoslovakia |
| 1,293 | 3,956 | 1,570,051 | 329 | 211 | 118 | 13,307 | 55,673 | 17,800 | 37,873 | Denmark |
| 5[8] | 60,000[8] | 1,623[8] | 21[7] | 0.07[7] | 21[7] | 175 | 585 | 55 | 530 | Djibouti |
| 63[8] | 1,274[8] | 2,051[8] | ... | ... | 244[6] | 49 | ... | ... | 82 | Dominica |
| 154[3] | 25,807[3] | 21,741[30] | ... | ... | ... | ... | ... | ... | ... | Dominican Republic |
| 480[8] | 18,635[8] | 37,260[8] | 2,134[8] | 2,021[8] | 56 | 2,573 | 6,971[8] | 3,882[8] | 3,116 | Ecuador |
| 9,016 | 5,666 | 523,981 | 10,553 | 9,715 | 838 | 5,297 | 33,700 | 23,600 | 10,100 | Egypt |
| 400 | 13,070 | 32,538 | 1,131[7] | 1,097[7] | 34[7] | 756[7] | 1,812[7] | 1,012[7] | 800[7] | El Salvador |
| 19 | 20,473 | ... | ... | ... | ... | ... | ... | ... | ... | Equatorial Guinea |
| 480 | 68,281 | 31,221[9,10,14] | 269 | 252 | 17 | 693 | 1,833 | 774 | 1,059 | Ethiopia |
| ... | ... | ... | 278[8] | ... | 278[8] | 141[8] | ... | ... | ... | Faeroe Islands |
| ... | ... | 233[31] | ... | ... | 1.5 | 17 | 72 | 1.1 | 71 | Falkland Islands |

## Communications (continued)

| country | daily newspapers (latest) | | | radio, 1986 | | | television, 1986 | | | telephones, 1985 | | traffic, 1985 ('000 calls) | | |
|---|---|---|---|---|---|---|---|---|---|---|---|---|---|---|
| | number | total circulation ('000) | circulation per 1,000 population | transmitters (latest) | receivers (all types) ('000) | persons per receiver | transmitters (latest) | receivers (all types) ('000) | persons per receiver | receivers ('000) | persons per receiver | local | long-distance | international |
| Fiji | 2 | 53 | 76 | 12 | 400 | 1.8 | ... | ... | ... | 53 | 13 | —155,821[15]— | | 2,974[12] |
| Finland | 67 | 2,600 | 533 | 101 | 2,500 | 2.0 | 172 | 1,792[17] | 2.7[17] | 3,028 | 1.6 | 1,914,390 | 407,470 | 18,110 |
| France | 102 | 13,490 | 244 | 840 | 20,000 | 2.8 | 10,670 | 17,951[17] | 3.1[17] | 34,347 | 1.6 | —82,894,000— | | |
| French Guiana | 1 | 16 | 194 | 13 | 44 | 1.9 | 9 | 6.5 | 13 | 27 | 3.1 | —113,176— | | |
| French Polynesia | 2 | 22 | 128 | 6 | 84 | 2.1 | 10 | 26 | 6.8 | 38 | 4.6 | —42,200[5]— | | 3,000[12] |
| Gabon | 2 | 33 | 35 | 16 | 145 | 8.1 | 8 | 37 | 32 | 14[7] | 81[7] | 13,560[5,8] | 34,800[5,8] | 288,000[5,8] |
| Gambia, The | — | — | — | 3 | 110 | 7.0 | ... | ... | ... | 3.5 | 212 | 3,700 | 475 | 350 |
| Gaza Strip | ... | ... | ... | ... | ... | ... | ... | ... | ... | | | | | |
| Germany, East | 39 | 9,300 | 559 | 117 | 6,510 | 2.6 | 505 | 5,985 | 2.8 | 3,630 | 4.7 | 1,316,883 | 754,179 | 12,609 |
| Germany, West | 633 | ... | ... | 469[33] | 25,483[17] | 2.4[17] | 5,718 | 22,908[17] | 2.7[17] | 37,899 | 1.7 | 17,172,160 | 10,012,026 | 432,128 |
| Ghana | 4 | 460 | 35 | 4 | 3,000 | 4.4 | 9 | 140 | 94 | 72[7] | 174[7] | 183[7,15] | 49[7,15] | 113[7,15] |
| Gibraltar | 1 | 3 | 104 | 3 | 10 | 2.8 | 4 | 7.0 | 4.1 | 11 | 2.6 | 9,330[4] | | 2,550[12] |
| Greece | 124 | ... | ... | 55 | 4,000 | 2.5, | 84 | 1,725 | 5.8 | 3,529[7] | 2.8[7] | 4,761,691[17] | 648,702[7] | 26,338[7] |
| Greenland | — | — | — | 18 | 14 | 3.9 | 34[1] | 12 | 4.5 | 12[7] | 4.4[7] | ... | | ... |
| Grenada | — | — | — | 3 | 50 | 1.9 | 1[1] | ... | ... | 6.4 | 15 | —148[8]— | | 1,124[12] |
| Guadeloupe | 1 | 25 | 75 | 5 | 96 | 3.5 | 8 | 47 | 7.3 | 96 | 3.5 | —320,031[5]— | | |
| Guam | 1 | 18 | 149 | 6 | 102 | 1.2 | 2 | 82 | 1.5 | 31[7] | 3.7[7] | ... | | ... |
| Guatemala | 9 | ... | ... | 115 | 500 | 16 | 24 | 300 | 27 | 128 | 62 | 8,583 | 12,468 | 2,301 |
| Guernsey | 1 | 16 | 269 | ... | ... | ... | ... | ... | ... | 47 | 1.3 | —35,684— | | 341 |
| Guinea | 1 | 20 | 4 | 8 | 200 | 31 | 1 | 11 | 566 | 10[1] | 553[1] | ... | 96[8,12] | 986[8,12] |
| Guinea-Bissau | 1 | 6 | 7 | 2 | 25 | 36 | ... | ... | ... | 5.0[1] | 161[1] | | | |
| Guyana | 1 | 60 | 76 | 8 | 350 | 2.3 | ... | ... | ... | 33 | 24 | —88,458[5]— | | 289 |
| Haiti | 6 | 22 | 4 | 48 | 200 | 27 | 1 | 25 | 217 | 38[8] | 135[8] | ... | 452[4] | 818[4] |
| Honduras | 7 | 293 | 65 | 153 | 300 | 15 | 20 | 90 | 50 | 46[7] | 92[7] | 189,200[7,12] | 121,000[7,12] | 10,907[7,12] |
| Hong Kong | 69 | ... | ... | 24 | 2,740 | 2.0 | 52 | 1,312 | 4.0 | 2,315 | 2.4 | —4,100,000— | | 144,761[12] |
| Hungary | 29 | 2,512 | 236 | 51 | 5,500 | 1.9 | 98 | 3,500 | 3.0 | 1,485 | 7.2 | | | |
| Iceland | 5 | 114 | 507 | 26 | 73 | 3.3[17] | 130[17] | 65[17] | 3.7[17] | 125[7] | 1.9[7] | | | 1,323 |
| India | 1,423 | ... | ... | 162 | 50,000 | 16 | 19 | 5,000 | 155 | 3,761 | 203 | 12,069,000[5] | 202,000 | 5,350 |
| Indonesia | 89 | 2,603 | 17 | 301 | 32,800 | 5.1 | 231 | 4,900 | 34 | 720[7] | 222[7] | 4,949,040[4,5] | 10,632[4] | 2,481[4] |
| Iran | 14 | ... | ... | 193 | 10,000 | 4.6 | 478 | 2,100 | 22 | 1,884[36] | 24[36] | 7,801,075[12,36] | 617,641[12,36] | 44,990[12,36] |
| Iraq | 6 | 324 | 21 | 46 | 2,800 | 5.7 | 35 | 605 | 26 | 886 | 17 | —1,518,817[4,5]— | | 13,329[12] |
| Ireland | 7 | 709 | 200 | 21 | 996[17] | 3.6[17] | 21 | 918[17] | 3.9[17] | 942 | 3.8 | —2,329,000[37]— | | 28,000[12,38] |
| Isle of Man | — | — | — | ... | 221 | 3.0[1] | ... | 228 | 3.0[8] | | | | | |
| Israel | 25 | 843 | 196 | 63 | 700 | 6.3 | 48 | 620 | 7.1 | 1,780[36] | 2.5[36] | 1,850,000[5,36] | 4,850,000[5,36] | 41,210[12,36] |
| Italy | 66 | ... | ... | 2,151 | 15,000 | 3.8 | 2,445 | 14,521[17] | 3.9[17] | 25,615 | 2.3 | 13,151,711 | 5,363,517 | 128,156 |
| Jamaica | 2 | 84 | 36 | 19 | 910 | 2.6 | 8 | 350 | 6.7 | 126[4] | 18[4] | ... | 1,888[4] | 55,725[7,12] |
| Japan | 124 | 68,653 | 569 | 1,070 | 95,000 | 1.3 | 12,756 | 30,250 | 4.0 | 66,636 | 1.8 | —42,000,000[21]— | | 253,000[12,36] |
| Jersey | 1 | 24 | 309 | ... | ... | ... | ... | ... | ... | 64[7] | 1.2[7] | 51,652[7] | 7,766[7] | 555[7] |
| Jordan | 5 | 195 | 71 | 17 | 700 | 3.9 | 46 | 240 | 11 | 71[1] | 32[1] | ... | | |
| Kampuchea | 16 | ... | ... | 6 | 200[19] | 36[19] | 2 | 52[19] | 140[19] | 7.3[1] | 886[1] | | | |
| Kenya | 5 | 255 | 13 | 22 | 2,100 | 10 | 4 | 192 | 110 | 248[7] | 79[7] | 7,007[7] | 6,755[7,15] | 936[7] |
| Kiribati | — | — | — | 1 | 10 | 6.5 | ... | 11[4] | 5.5[4] | 1.1 | 58 | 64[4,12] | 171[12] | 43[12] |
| Korea, North | 10 | ... | ... | ... | 1,920 | 11 | ... | 175 | 119 | | | | | |
| Korea, South | 25 | 6,748 | 171 | 118 | 23,000 | 1.8 | 126 | 7,312[17] | 5.7[17] | 7,539 | 5.4 | 42,206,000[5] | 176,032[5] | 9,900 |
| Kuwait | 7 | 453 | 253 | 6 | 500 | 3.9 | 13 | 450 | 4.0 | 274[7] | 5.8[7] | ... | | 7,770[8,12] |
| Laos | 2 | 12 | 3 | 4 | 232 | 16 | 2 | 31 | 119 | 8.1 | 445 | 3,879 | 2 | 23 |
| Lebanon | 38 | 583 | 215 | 10 | 2,000 | 1.4 | 10 | 500 | 5.4 | 150[4] | 18[4] | ... | | |
| Lesotho | 3 | 44 | 28 | 4 | 100 | 16 | 1 | 1.0 | 1,586 | 14 | 110 | ... | 3,854[7,12,40] | |
| Liberia | 4 | 283 | 124 | 9[41] | 500 | 4.6 | 5 | 42 | 55 | 7.7[4] | 263[4] | ... | | |
| Libya | 1 | 40 | 10 | 20 | 500 | 7.9 | 13 | 235 | 17 | 102[4] | 33[4] | ... | | |
| Liechtenstein | 2 | 15 | 547 | ... | 9.2 | 3.0 | ... | 8.7 | 3.2 | 27[36] | 1.0[36] | 7,266[4] | 12,727[4,12] | 5,242[4,12] |
| Luxembourg | 6 | 130 | 365 | 7 | 228 | 1.6 | 3 | 91 | 4.0 | 234[7] | 1.6[7] | —165,917— | | 80,865[12] |
| Macau | 10 | ... | ... | 5 | 84 | 5.2 | 4 | ... | ... | 50 | 7.7 | | | 15,447[12] |
| Madagascar | 7 | 46 | 5 | 21 | 2,020 | 5.1 | 24 | 96 | 107 | 37[7] | 263[7] | 9,487[7] | 69[7] | 47[7] |
| Malawi | 2 | 32 | 5 | 16 | 1,060 | 6.9 | ... | ... | ... | 41 | 172 | —134,700[3,5]— | | 2,449[12] |
| Malaysia | 42 | ... | ... | 83 | 1,660[7] | 9.2[7] | 59 | 1,583 | 10 | 1,279 | 12 | —7,679,106[5]— | | 19,084[12] |
| Maldives | 2 | ... | ... | 3 | 13 | 15 | 2 | 3.7 | 51 | 2.5 | 73 | ... | 68[12] | 260[12] |
| Mali | 1 | 40 | 5 | 14 | 300 | 28 | 1 | 0.8 | 10,575 | 9.5[8] | 815[8] | ... | 90[4] | 97[4] |
| Malta | 4 | 81 | 245 | 3 | 92[17] | 3.7[17] | 4 | 116[17] | 3.0[17] | 122 | 2.7 | ... | 72,385 | 1,506 |
| Martinique | 1 | 30 | 92 | 6 | 55 | 6.0 | 10 | 45 | 7.3 | 112 | 2.9 | —280,895[5]— | | |
| Mauritania | 1 | ... | ... | 4 | 200 | 8.5 | 1 | 1.0 | 1,691 | 4.8[8] | 331[8] | 7,712[5,8] | 85[8,12] | 310[8,12] |
| Mauritius | 8 | 77 | 74 | 5 | 200 | 5.2 | 4 | 110 | 9.4 | 65 | 16 | —60,059[8]— | | 2,600[12] |
| Mayotte | 1 | ... | ... | 1 | 30 | 2.3 | ... | ... | ... | 0.45[8] | 134[8] | | | |
| Mexico | ... | ... | ... | 872 | 25,278 | 3.2 | 405 | 9,490 | 8.4 | 6,796[7] | 11[7] | 2,964,630 | 608,361 | 25,587 |
| Monaco | 2 | 11 | 408 | 12 | 9.7 | 2.9 | 5 | 17[17] | 1.6[17] | 37 | 0.8 | —13,200[5]— | | 208,700[5] |
| Mongolia | 2 | 96 | 85 | ... | 181 | 11 | ... | 60 | 32 | 43[8] | 42[8] | | | |
| Montserrat | — | — | — | 4[11] | 4.2 | 2.8 | 1 | 1.2 | 9.9 | 3.5 | 3.4[8] | —4,674[5]— | | 688[12] |
| Morocco | 8 | 282 | 12 | 36 | 3,000 | 7.6 | 51 | 1,099[17] | 21[17] | 311 | 71 | —715,594[5]— | | |
| Mozambique | 2 | 77 | 5 | 39 | 500 | 28 | 1 | 20 | 707 | 60 | 230 | 101,317[7,12] | 2,635[4] | 334 |
| Nauru | — | — | — | 1 | 4 | 2.0 | ... | ... | ... | 1.6[4] | 5.2[4] | —1,304[21]— | | 130[21] |
| Nepal | 51 | ... | ... | 7 | 2,012 | 8.5 | 1 | 18 | 952 | 18[7] | 905[7] | —4,432[12]— | | 1,002[12] |
| Netherlands, The | 79 | 4,500 | 312 | 50 | 4,809[17] | 3.0[17] | 29 | 4,633[17] | 3.1[17] | 8,840 | 1.7 | 3,255,000 | 2,639,000 | 126,758 |
| Netherlands Antilles | 4 | 34 | 188 | 11[42] | 149 | 1.2 | 2 | 54 | 3.3 | 667[7,16] | 3.5[7,16] | —7,160[2,12,16]— | | 11,671[12,16] |
| New Caledonia | 2 | 24 | 159 | 3 | 85 | 1.8 | 20 | 35 | 4.3 | 32[7] | 4.6[7] | —29,450[5]— | | 3,490[12] |
| New Zealand | 34 | 1,055 | 324 | 65 | 2,800 | 1.2 | 567 | 931[17] | 3.5[17] | 2,203[36] | 1.5[36] | —766,485[12,36]— | | 56,850[12,36] |
| Nicaragua | 3 | 144 | 42 | 87 | 300 | 11 | 7 | 171 | 20 | 50[7] | 63[7] | ... | 8,400[2,12] | 5,069[7] |
| Niger | 1 | 3 | 0.4 | 19 | 160[19] | 41[19] | 12 | 25 | 269 | 12 | 541 | —57,366[4,5]— | | 2,231[12] |
| Nigeria | 19 | ... | ... | 111 | 15,680 | 6.3 | 41 | 500 | 196 | 260 | 368 | 86,947[5] | 1,140[15] | 25,257[12] |
| Niue | — | — | — | 1 | 1.0 | 2.5 | ... | ... | ... | 0.50[7] | 5.9[7] | | | |
| Norfolk Island | — | — | — | 2 | 1.2 | 1.6 | ... | 0.4[7] | 4.7[7] | 1.09[7] | 1.8[7] | 1,200[4] | ... | 26[4] |
| Norway | 64 | 1,882 | 454 | 764 | 1,505 | 2.8 | 1,389 | 1,339.4 | 3.1 | 2,579[7] | 1.6[7] | —6,131,368[5]— | | 176,257[12] |
| Oman | 3 | 30 | 24 | 12 | 500 | 2.6 | 11 | 400 | 3.2 | 66 | 19 | 307,045[5] | 61[12] | 11,735[12] |
| Pacific Is., Trust Terr. of the | | | | | | | | | | 9.2[4] | 16[4] | | | |
|   Marshall Islands | — | — | — | 2 | ... | ... | | | | | | | | |
|   Micronesia, Fed. States of | — | — | — | 4 | 17 | 5.4 | 3 | 1.1 | 86 | | | | | |
| Northern Mariana Islands | — | — | — | 3 | 10.4 | 2.0 | 1 | 4.1 | 5.0 | ... | ... | ... | | ... |
| Palau | ... | ... | ... | 1 | ... | ... | 1 | 1.6 | 7.6 | 0.85[7] | 15[7] | | | |
| Pakistan | 118 | 1,991 | 22 | 75 | 5,250 | 20 | 19 | 1,880 | 55 | 517 | 194 | —3,107,840[5]— | | 1,888 |
| Panama | 7 | 132 | 62 | 97 | 900 | 2.5 | 16 | 300 | 7.4 | 223 | 9.8 | 472,362 | 115,227 | 3,725 |
| Papua New Guinea | 1 | 28 | 8 | 26 | 225 | 15 | ... | ... | ... | 58 | 57 | 35,510 | 19,010 | 2,740 |

| post offices, 1985 | | | telegraph, 1985 | | | telex, 1985 | | | | country |
|---|---|---|---|---|---|---|---|---|---|---|
| number | persons per office | pieces of mail handled ('000) | total traffic ('000) | national traffic ('000) | international outgoing traffic ('000) | subscriber lines | traffic ('000 minutes) | | | |
| | | | | | | | total | national | international outgoing | |
| 217 | 2,709 | 28,206[10] | 143 | 134 | 9 | 589 | ... | 997[5] | 1,126 | Fiji |
| 3,632[8] | 1,340[8] | 1,098,005[8] | 662 | 586 | 76 | 8,400 | 26,202 | 11,100 | 15,102 | Finland |
| 17,223[32] | 3,227[32] | 16,351,500[32] | 12,549 | 10,887 | 1,662 | 124,515 | 519,886 | 373,421 | 146,465 | France |
| ... | ... | ... | 21 | 19 | 2 | 265 | 677 | 578 | 99 | French Guiana |
| 91 | 1,857 | 14,636 | 88 | 71 | 17 | 214 | 633 | 8 | 625 | French Polynesia |
| ... | ... | 13,435[3] | 272[8] | 146[8] | 126[8] | 647[7] | 2,721[8] | 876[8] | 2,033[7] | Gabon |
| ... | ... | ... | 11 | 3 | 8 | 85 | 122 | 12 | 110 | Gambia, The |
| ... | ... | ... | ... | ... | ... | ... | ... | ... | ... | Gaza Strip |
| 11,977 | 1,390 | 1,457,375 | 13,340 | 11,295 | 2,045 | 16,476 | ... | ... | 9,288 | Germany, East |
| 17,967 | 3,398 | 14,645,967 | 5,710 | 3,859 | 1,851 | 161,482 | 572,856 | 383,033 | 189,823 | Germany, West |
| 990 | 12,329 | 118,125 | 1,760[21] | 3,320[6,7] | 187[7] | 310[7] | 76[18] | 6[18] | 70[18] | Ghana |
| 3 | 9,666 | 3,705 | 10 | 4 | 6 | 188 | 436 | 8 | 428 | Gibraltar |
| 1,219[20] | 8,150[20] | 418,144 | 3,427[7] | 3,167[7] | 260[7] | 18,232 | 52,964 | 32,223 | 20,741 | Greece |
| ... | ... | ... | ... | ... | ... | ... | ... | ... | ... | Greenland |
| 51[3] | 2,157[3] | ... | ... | 0.2[4] | 29 | 53 | ... | ... | 117 | Grenada |
| 44[3] | 7,500[3] | ... | 98 | 92 | 6 | 641 | 644 | 513 | 131 | Guadeloupe |
| ... | ... | ... | ... | ... | ... | ... | ... | ... | ... | Guam |
| ... | ... | 54,301[35] | ... | ... | 2,907[6] | 1,182 | ... | ... | 597[18] | Guatemala |
| 22 | 2,545 | 13,482[24] | 1.4 | 0.8 | 0.6 | 286 | ... | ... | ... | Guernsey |
| ... | ... | 30,809[13] | 50[8] | 21[8] | 29[8] | 195[8] | ... | ... | 415[8] | Guinea |
| ... | ... | ... | ... | ... | ... | ... | ... | ... | ... | Guinea-Bissau |
| 128 | 6,237 | 21,031 | ... | ... | 1,391 | 142 | 365[18] | 52[18] | 313[18] | Guyana |
| 132[3] | 33,106[3] | 1,046,472[13] | ... | ... | ... | ... | ... | ... | ... | Haiti |
| 508[3] | 7,264[3] | 60,689[3] | 19[7] | 1[7] | 18[7] | 700[7] | 2,072[7] | 1,087[7] | 985[7] | Honduras |
| 142 | 38,239 | 562,939 | 1,156 | 7 | 1,149 | 26,993 | 75,514 | 31,521 | 43,993 | Hong Kong |
| 3,216 | 3,308 | 1,855,494 | 12,110 | 11,703 | 407 | 10,782 | 172,017[2,5] | 73,525[5] | 9,718 | Hungary |
| 150[8] | 1,586[8] | 38,823[8] | 571 | 555 | 16 | 442 | 1,730 | 288 | 1,442 | Iceland |
| 144,875 | 4,729 | 12,068,468 | 63,485 | 61,519 | 1,966 | 26,287 | ... | 209,462[5] | 22,730 | India |
| 16,071 | 10,244 | 447,811 | 7,281[4] | 7,142[4] | 139[4] | 8,853[8] | ... | 440,683[4,5] | 10,480[8] | Indonesia |
| 3,815 | 12,389 | 256,751[9,10,14] | 5,613[36] | 5,543[36] | 70[36] | 4,079 | 22,746[36] | 16,272[36] | 6,474[36] | Iran |
| 288[8] | 48,995[8] | 193,996[8] | ... | 844[4] | 426 | 2,187 | 7,668 | 1,652 | 6,016 | Iraq |
| 2,096[3] | 1,662[3] | 482,153[10,13] | 235 | 188 | 47 | 7,269 | 31,097 | 24,194 | 6,903 | Ireland |
| 37 | 1,748 | 25,162 | ... | ... | ... | ... | ... | ... | ... | Isle of Man |
| 1,404 | 3,050 | 410,000 | 612[36] | 414[36] | 198[36] | 5,440[36] | 21,937[36] | 15,500[36] | 6,437[36] | Israel |
| 14,348 | 3,986 | 7,191,975 | 23,996 | 22,625 | 1,371 | 65,416 | 325,794 | 203,873 | 121,921 | Italy |
| 788 | 2,779 | ... | 273[7] | 195[7] | 78[7] | 442[7] | ... | ... | 938[7] | Jamaica |
| 23,615 | 5,131 | 17,160,121 | 41,454[36] | 40,660[36] | 794[36] | 47,000[36] | ... | 111,103[4] | 61,529[36] | Japan |
| 24 | 3,166 | 37,491 | ... | ... | ... | 431 | ... | ... | 1,525 | Jersey |
| 770 | 3,246 | 100,244 | ... | ... | ... | ... | ... | ... | ... | Jordan |
| ... | ... | 10,320[29] | ... | ... | ... | ... | ... | ... | ... | Kampuchea |
| 829 | 24,524 | 231,213[9,10,14] | ... | 1,034[8] | 3,452[6,8] | 1,856[7] | 5,424[7] | 2,220[7] | 3,204[7] | Kenya |
| 5[3] | 10,800[3] | 374[31,39] | 38 | 35 | 3 | 28 | ... | 577 | 72 | Kiribati |
| ... | ... | ... | ... | ... | ... | ... | ... | ... | ... | Korea, North |
| 2,553[20] | 16,081[20] | 1,259,958[24] | 10,868 | 10,759 | 109 | 8,938 | 11,423[18] | 3,125[18] | 8,298[18] | Korea, South |
| 51 | 33,280 | 145,876[9,10,14] | 621[8] | 86[8] | 535[8] | 3,692[8] | 12,513[8] | 3,324[8] | 9,189[8] | Kuwait |
| ... | ... | 4,496[3] | 5,066 | 4,894 | 172 | 37 | ... | ... | 47 | Laos |
| ... | ... | ... | 156 | 91 | 65 | ... | ... | ... | ... | Lebanon |
| 130 | 10,769 | 26,837[10] | 56[7] | 7[7] | 49[7] | 219 | 287 | ... | ...[1] | Lesotho |
| 54 | 38,055 | 8,453 | ... | ... | ... | ... | ... | ... | ... | Liberia |
| 317 | 10,943 | 92,348 | ... | ... | ... | ... | ... | ... | ... | Libya |
| 12 | 2,256 | 14,596[24] | ... | ... | ... | ... | ... | ... | ... | Liechtenstein |
| 107 | 3,419 | 147,925 | 46 | 18 | 28 | 2,391 | 10,474 | 2,105 | 8,369 | Luxembourg |
| 7 | 57,142 | 10,092 | ... | ... | 36 | 613 | 883 | 155 | 728 | Macau |
| 8,783 | 1,223 | 35,112[7] | 1,069[7] | 984[7] | 85[7] | 341[7] | 128[7,18] | 22[7,18] | 106[7,18] | Madagascar |
| 263 | 23,828 | 113,975 | ... | ... | 1,504[6] | 482 | ... | ... | 815 | Malawi |
| 5,689 | 2,755 | 959,197 | 1,183[7] | 657 | 5,650[6] | 10,881 | ... | ... | 9,932 | Malaysia |
| 26 | 6,978 | 1,367 | ... | ... | 6 | 150 | ... | ... | 256 | Maldives |
| 119[8] | 53,738[8] | 5,466[8] | ... | ... | ... | ... | ... | ... | ... | Mali |
| 163 | 22,500[3] | 37,366[3] | 45 | 22 | 23 | 832 | 2,440 | 285 | 2,155 | Malta |
| 44[3] | 7,273[3] | ... | 64 | 59 | 5 | 531 | 1,288 | 1,077 | 211 | Martinique |
| ... | ... | 3,035[3] | 42[8] | 28[8] | 14[8] | 227[7] | ... | 3,560[5,8] | 257[7] | Mauritania |
| 106 | 9,757 | 29,504 | ... | ... | 41 | 444 | 1,315 | 141 | 1,174 | Mauritius |
| ... | ... | ... | ... | ... | ... | 20 | ... | ... | ... | Mayotte |
| 7,076 | 10,946 | 674,990 | 25,072 | 24,805 | 267 | 23,319 | 186,932[1] | 171,343[1] | 13,306[7] | Mexico |
| ... | ... | ... | 12 | 7 | 5 | 672 | ... | ... | 2,338 | Monaco |
| 382[3] | 3,900[3] | ... | ... | ... | ... | ... | ... | ... | ... | Mongolia |
| 11 | 1,090 | 394 | 3[7] | ... | 3[7] | 33 | ... | ... | 31 | Montserrat |
| 1,095 | 19,602 | 179,615 | 1,130 | 984 | 146 | 6,444 | 3,788[18] | 1,931[18] | 1,857[18] | Morocco |
| 609 | 22,626 | 20,133 | ... | 117[21] | 40 | 680 | ... | 788[5] | 1,361 | Mozambique |
| 1 | 7,000 | 168 | ... | ... | 7[21] | 10[21] | ... | ... | 27[21] | Nauru |
| ... | ... | ... | 1,196 | 1,111 | 85 | 230 | ... | ... | 581 | Nepal |
| 2,913 | 4,987 | 5,319,300 | 767 | 435 | 332 | 39,306 | ... | 375,705[5] | 88,100 | Netherlands, The |
| 14[16] | 19,458[16] | 14,045[16] | ... | ... | 978[8,16] | 783[8,16] | 1,784[8,16] | 335[8,16] | 1,449[8,16] | Netherlands Antilles |
| 267 | 561 | 21,558 | 32 | 9 | 23 | 187 | 512[7] | 217 | 491[7] | New Caledonia |
| 1,287 | 2,464 | 639,850[9,10,14,24] | 1,988[36] | 1,573[36] | 415[36] | 6,480 | 21,434 | 11,071 | 10,363 | New Zealand |
| ... | ... | 35,890[29] | 770[7] | 755[7] | 15[7] | 391[1] | 1,572[7] | 425[7] | 1,147[7] | Nicaragua |
| 159[8] | 37,735[8] | 5,704[8] | 621 | 598 | 23 | 297 | ... | ... | 529 | Niger |
| 3,371 | 28,537 | 1,119,673[9,10] | 484 | 431 | 53 | 4,848 | ... | 11,502[5] | 3,661 | Nigeria |
| ... | ... | ... | 9 | ... | ... | ... | ... | ... | ... | Niue |
| 1[8] | 2,000[8] | 877[8] | 10[8] | — | 3[8] | ... | ... | ... | ... | Norfolk Island |
| 2,753 | 1,510 | 1,602,438 | 430 | 322 | 108 | 10,817 | 40,217 | 19,109 | 21,108 | Norway |
| 103 | 14,563 | 41,846[9] | 198 | 13 | 185 | 1,520 | 5,217 | 1,881 | 3,336 | Oman |
| 6[3] | ... | ... | ... | ... | ... | ... | ... | ... | ... | Pacific Is., Trust Terr. of the<br>  Marshall Islands |
| ... | ... | ... | ... | ... | ... | ... | ... | ... | ... | Micronesia, Fed. States of |
| ... | ... | ... | ... | ... | ... | ... | ... | ... | ... | |
| ... | ... | ... | ... | ... | ... | ... | ... | ... | ... | Northern Mariana Islands<br>  Palau |
| 11,898 | 7,875 | 702,589[24] | ... | 1,286[7] | 387 | 5,210 | ... | 30[4,18] | 2,397[18] | Pakistan |
| 268 | 6,833 | 22,247 | 670 | 646 | 24 | 1,700 | 3,656 | 763 | 2,893 | Panama |
| 116 | 33,593 | 31,824 | ... | 61[6] | 19 | 1,371 | 3,412 | 1,800 | 1,612 | Papua New Guinea |

## Communications (continued)

| country | daily newspapers (latest) | | | radio, 1986 | | | television, 1986 | | | telephones, 1985 | | traffic, 1985 ('000 calls) | | |
|---|---|---|---|---|---|---|---|---|---|---|---|---|---|---|
| | number | total circulation ('000) | circulation per 1,000 population | transmitters (latest) | receivers (all types) ('000) | persons per receiver | transmitters (latest) | receivers (all types) ('000) | persons per receiver | receivers ('000) | persons per receiver | local | long-distance | international |
| Paraguay | 5 | 198 | 60 | 56 | 624 | 6.1 | 4 | 231 | 16 | 837 | 43[7] | 260,084[5,7] | 20,053[5,7] | 1,029[7] |
| Peru | 66 | ... | ... | 189 | 3,969 | 5.1 | 138 | 1,701 | 12 | 600 | 33 | 1,804,270[12] | 165,568[12] | 19,469[12] |
| Philippines | 22 | ... | ... | 295 | 7,500 | 7.5 | 43 | 3,997 | 14 | 820 | 67 | —17,463[7]— | | 4,378[7] |
| Pitcairn Island | — | — | — | — | ... | ... | ... | ... | ... | 0.024 | 2.7[4] | | | |
| Poland | 45 | 7,714 | 207 | ... | 9,300 | 4.0 | 118 | 9,466[17] | 4.0[17] | 4,215 | 9.2 | —1,139,248[7]— | | 3,385 |
| Portugal | 28 | ... | ... | 83 | 2,439 | 4.2 | 23 | 1,585 | 6.5 | 1,835 | 5.5 | 1,794,121 | 3,244,194 | 55,334[12] |
| Puerto Rico | 5 | 577 | 175 | 90 | 2,000 | 1.6 | 14 | 820 | 4.0 | 710[7] | 4.6[7] | 1,135,406[4] | 68,538[4] | 1,375[4] |
| Qatar | 5 | 56 | 184 | 11 | 120 | 2.8 | 8 | 150 | 2.2 | 110 | 2.9 | | | 25,391[12] |
| Réunion | 3 | 62 | 113 | 25 | 123 | 4.5 | 19 | 89 | 6.2 | 115 | 4.7 | —249,411[5]— | | |
| Romania | 36 | 3,078 | 135 | 71 | 3,211 | 7.1 | 344 | 3,910 | 5.8 | 2,027[1] | 11[1] | ... | ... | ... |
| Rwanda | 1 | — | — | 8[43] | 250 | 25 | ... | ... | ... | 9.0 | 697 | 8,214[5] | 450[12] | 371[12] |
| St. Christopher and Nevis | — | — | — | 2 | 22 | 2.0 | 4 | 7.0 | 6.6 | 3.8 | 12 | ... | | 1,065[12] |
| St. Helena and Ascension | — | — | — | 4 | 3.3 | 2.1 | ... | ... | ... | 1.0 | 7.0 | | | 383 |
| St. Lucia | — | — | — | 4 | 92 | 1.5 | ... | ... | ... | 12 | 11 | —13,073[5,7]— | | 353 |
| St. Pierre and Miquelon | — | — | — | 4 | 3.0 | 2.0 | 3 | 2.6 | 2.3 | 3.9 | 1.5 | —13,099[5]— | | |
| St. Vincent and the Grenadines | — | — | — | 1 | 66 | 1.7 | ... | 10 | 11 | 8.5 | 13 | —5,500[5,7]— | | 1,169[12] |
| San Marino | — | — | — | — | 8[2] | 2.7[2] | ... | 5[1] | 4.3[1] | 12 | 1.9 | —6,840— | | 2,201 |
| São Tomé and Príncipe | — | — | — | 5 | 28 | 3.9 | ... | ... | ... | 2.57 | 42[7] | 2,384[7] | 24[7] | 18[7] |
| Saudi Arabia | 10 | 488 | 42 | ... | 3,230 | 3.7 | 121 | 3,700 | 3.2 | 1,382 | 8.4 | 2,258,000[5] | 280,611 | 41,929 |
| Senegal | 1 | 31 | 5 | 11 | 450 | 15 | 1 | 55 | 122 | 40[2] | 142[2] | | | 9,502[12] |
| Seychelles | 1 | 3 | 48 | 1 | 19 | 3.5 | 1 | 3.8 | 17 | 11 | 5.9 | —3,955— | | 671[12] |
| Sierra Leone | 1 | 10 | 3 | 3 | 225 | 17 | 2 | 25 | 149 | 16[4] | 216[4] | | | 838[12] |
| Singapore | 11 | 714 | 279 | 21 | 593[17] | 4.4[17] | 8 | 486[17] | 5.3[17] | 1,074 | 2.4 | 4,016,090 | 21,060 | 15,725 |
| Solomon Islands | — | — | ... | 3 | 60 | 4.6 | ... | ... | ... | 4.5 | 59 | 3,400 | 400 | 535[12] |
| Somalia | 1 | ... | ... | 4 | 250 | 24 | 1 | ... | ... | 4.8[1] | 1,086[1] | | | |
| South Africa | 20 | 1,277 | 47 | 301 | 8,550[44] | 3.9[44] | 465 | 2,500[44] | 13[44] | 3,890 | 8.5 | —12,636,427[5]— | | 15,444 |
| Bophuthatswana | — | — | — | 16 | [44] | [44] | 9 | [44] | [44] | 247 | 62[7] | | 716[4] | |
| Ciskei | — | — | — | 2 | [44] | [44] | ... | [44] | [44] | 5.5[8] | 134[8] | 4,344[4,5] | 1,281[4] | |
| KwaNdebele | — | — | — | 44 | [44] | [44] | ... | [44] | [44] | ... | ... | | | |
| Transkei | — | — | — | 14 | [44] | [44] | ... | [44] | [44] | ... | ... | | | |
| Venda | — | — | — | 6 | [44] | [44] | ... | [44] | [44] | ... | ... | | | |
| South West Africa/Namibia | 3 | 20 | 19 | c. 40 | 200 | 6.0 | 8 | 17 | 71 | 647 | 177 | ... | 29,146[12] | 1,017[12] |
| Spain | 113 | 3,400 | 89 | 264 | 11,410 | 3.4 | 1,027 | 10,145 | 3.8 | 14,259 | 2.7 | ... | 2,819,680 | 87,789 |
| Sri Lanka | 15 | 850 | 53 | 61 | 2,073[17] | 7.8[17] | 4 | 350 | 46 | 109[7] | 142[7] | 3,010[5,8] | 1,090[5,8] | 4,005[7,12] |
| Sudan, The | 2 | 120 | 5 | 6 | 1,500 | 16 | 20 | 250 | 93 | 78 | 304 | 122,460[4] | 999[4] | 1,654[4,12] |
| Suriname | 2 | ... | ... | 16 | 246 | 1.6 | 6 | 48 | 8.4 | 36 | 11 | —113,624[5]— | | 2,183[5] |
| Swaziland | 3 | 23 | 35 | 8 | 96 | 7.1 | 11 | 12 | 55 | 18 | 37 | 39[4] | 262[4] | 52[4] |
| Sweden | 169 | 4,782 | 574 | 340 | 3,330 | 2.5 | 803 | 3,265[17] | 2.6[17] | 7,410[7] | 1.1[7] | —22,536,865[5]— | | 6,345,114[5] |
| Switzerland | 101 | 3,208 | 491 | 215 | 2,513[17] | 2.6[17] | 825 | 2,216[17] | 3.0[17] | 5,436 | 1.2 | 5,025,000[12] | 5,895,000[12] | 730,000[12] |
| Syria | 9 | 201 | 19 | 29 | 2,000 | 5.3 | 40 | 400 | 27 | 616 | 17 | 586,000 | 70,000[12] | 15,000[12] |
| Taiwan | 31 | 4,917 | 259 | ... | 13,500 | 1.4 | 28 | 6,085 | 3.2 | 4,855[7] | 3.9[7] | 8,665,315[4] | 7,987[4] | 30,278[4,12] |
| Tanzania | 3 | 101 | 5 | 19 | 1,500 | 15 | 2 | 8 | 2,808 | 114 | 191 | 5,151[15] | 2,898[15] | 561[15] |
| Thailand | 31 | ... | ... | 217 | 7,700 | 6.8 | 74 | 3,300 | 16 | 755 | 68 | 1,229,092[5] | 64,238 | 2,507 |
| Togo | 2 | ... | ... | 11 | 250 | 12 | 4 | 17 | 181 | 127 | 239[7] | 4,572[4,5] | 54[7] | 104[7] |
| Tokelau | — | — | — | ... | ... | ... | ... | ... | ... | 0.003[4] | 525[4] | | | |
| Tonga | — | — | — | 2 | 50 | 2.0 | ... | ... | ... | 4.0[7] | 24[7] | 1,566[7] | 60[7] | 716[7] |
| Trinidad and Tobago | 4 | 173 | 144 | 5 | 552 | 2.2 | 6 | 345 | 3.5 | 109[7] | 11[7] | 2,700[8] | 8,200[8] | 550[8] |
| Tunisia | 5 | 272 | 37 | 12 | 1,160 | 6.4 | 20 | 400 | 19 | 272 | 27 | —656,156[5]— | | 511,199[5] |
| Turkey | 364 | 3,878 | 89 | 44 | 8,227 | 6.3 | 153 | 5,010 | 10 | 3,455 | 15 | —6,957,020[5]— | | 65,868[12] |
| Turks and Caicos Islands | — | — | — | 2 | ... | ... | ... | ... | ... | 1.6 | 5.2 | —4,564[5]— | | 587[12] |
| Tuvalu | — | — | — | 1 | 2.2 | 3.7 | ... | 1.1[8] | 7.6[8] | 0.15 | 55 | — | 36[12] | 3[12] |
| Uganda | 1 | 25 | 2 | 13 | 600 | 26 | 8 | 90 | 174 | 54[8] | 262[8] | | | 196[8] |
| U.S.S.R. | 727 | 96,414 | 345 | ... | 170,000 | 1.6 | 2,882 | 90,000 | 3.1 | 26,667[4] | 10[4] | | 1,454,400[4] | 2,130[4] |
| United Arab Emirates | 12 | 291 | 171 | 15[45] | 434 | 3.9 | 15[45] | 145 | 12 | 338 | 4.6 | ... | 301,477[6] | 114,694[6] |
| United Kingdom | 112 | 30,412 | 538 | 487 | 63,528 | 0.9 | 1,643 | 18,716[17] | 3.0[17] | 29,518[7] | 1.9[7] | 20,315,000 | 4,328,000 | 199,400 |
| United States | 1,657 | 62,502 | 259 | 10,808 | 507,000 | 0.5 | 6,526 | 145,000[19] | 1.7[19] | 181,091[7] | 1.3[7] | 365,304,830 | 37,525,289 | 419,725[7] |
| Uruguay | 21 | ... | ... | 94 | 1,800 | 1.7 | 33 | 500 | 6.0 | 374 | 8.1 | 624,358 | 46,141 | 4,920 |
| Vanuatu | — | — | — | 4 | 18 | 7.6 | ... | ... | ... | 3.0 | 44 | —4,329[5]— | | 96 |
| Venezuela | 61 | 2,739 | 172 | 210 | 6,747 | 2.6 | 63 | 2,750 | 6.5 | 1,451 | 12 | 9,612,000[6] | 1,212,000[6] | 75,745[6] |
| Vietnam | 4 | 500 | 9 | 39 | 6,045 | 10 | ... | 500 | 122 | 109 | 550 | —7,528[1]— | | 930[6] |
| Virgin Islands (U.S.) | 2 | 19 | 165 | 9 | 85 | 1.3 | 3 | 31 | 3.7 | 51[7] | 2.1[7] | 96,371[4] | 3,670[4] | 91[4] |
| Wallis and Futuna | — | — | — | 2 | ... | ... | ... | ... | ... | 0.34 | 40 | —255— | | 101[6] |
| West Bank | 22 | ... | ... | ... | ... | ... | ... | ... | ... | ... | ... | | | |
| Western Sahara | — | — | — | ... | ... | ... | ... | ... | ... | 1.0[4] | 143[4] | | | |
| Western Samoa | — | — | — | 6 | 18 | 8.9 | ... | 2.5[8] | 63[8] | 7.5[8] | 21[8] | ... | 78[4] | 208[4] |
| Yemen (Aden) | 2 | 25 | 11 | 6 | 300 | 7.9 | 5 | 44 | 54 | 238 | 94[8] | 40[4] | 18[4] | 71[4] |
| Yemen (Şan'ā') | 2 | ... | ... | 6 | 200 | 35 | 14 | 50 | 141 | 90[4] | 70[4] | | | |
| Yugoslavia | 28 | 2,498 | 107 | 803 | 4,460[17] | 5.2[17] | 1,040 | 4,000 | 5.8 | 3,031[7] | 7.6[7] | 3,845,000[7] | 7,978,000[7] | 2,970,000[7] |
| Zaire | 4 | 45 | 1.6 | 22 | 525 | 59 | ... | 15 | 2,072 | 32 | 949 | 788 | 684 | 3,685 |
| Zambia | 2 | 109 | 16 | 16 | 528 | 13 | 9 | 66 | 104 | 75 | 89 | —3,788[12]— | | 6,249[12] |
| Zimbabwe | 3 | 191 | 23 | 31 | 315 | 27 | 14 | 112 | 75 | 248 | 33 | 213,815[5] | 396,448[5] | 320,405[5] |

| post offices, 1985 | | | telegraph, 1985 | | | telex, 1985 | | | | country |
| --- | --- | --- | --- | --- | --- | --- | --- | --- | --- | --- |
| num-ber | per-sons per office | pieces of mail handled ('000) | total traffic ('000) | na-tional traffic ('000) | inter-national outgoing traffic ('000) | sub-scriber lines | traffic ('000 minutes) | | | |
| | | | | | | | total | national | international outgoing | |
| 382 | 7,931 | 5,610 | 295[7] | 259[7] | 36[7] | 793[7] | ... | ... | 997[7] | Paraguay |
| 2,626 | 10,084 | 65,906 | 11,752 | 11,724 | 28 | 3,336 | 22,521 | 18,008 | 4,513 | Peru |
| 2,094 | 26,743 | 427,831 | 13,456[7] | 13,243[7] | 213[7] | 12,860[7] | 11,782[7] | 3,463[7] | 8,319[7] | Philippines |
| 1 | 63 | ... | ... | ... | ... | ... | ... | ... | ... | Pitcairn Island |
| 8,262 | 4,519 | 1,685,286 | 18,256 | 17,475 | 781 | 29,606 | ... | ... | 10,098 | Poland |
| 7,999 | 1,273 | 493,783 | 1,173 | 1,062 | 111 | 18,427 | 70,927 | 50,668 | 20,259 | Portugal |
| 124[3] | 24,677[3] | ... | ... | ... | ... | ... | ... | ... | ... | Puerto Rico |
| 24 | 10,416 | 29,340[25] | 133 | 9 | 124 | 1,072 | 2,808 | 844 | 1,964 | Qatar |
| 50[3] | 10,340[3] | ... | 41 | 33 | 8 | 527 | 814 | 576 | 238 | Réunion |
| 5,046[3] | 4,429[3] | 795,199[13] | 5,393[21] | 5,150[21] | 243[21] | 6,750[1] | ... | ... | 3,683[1] | Romania |
| 24 | 262,555 | 12,752 | 17 | 14 | 3 | 100 | ... | 522[1] | 327 | Rwanda |
| 9[3] | 5,000[3] | 6,381[3] | ... | 10 | 172[6] | 59 | ... | ... | 118 | St. Christopher and Nevis |
| 10 | 600 | 128 | 5 | ... | 5 | 11 | ... | ... | 41 | St. Helena and Ascension |
| 55 | 1,818 | 4,320 | 19[4] | ... | 285[6] | 149 | ... | ... | 233 | St. Lucia |
| ... | ... | 1,714[10, 13] | 1.1 | 0.9 | 0.2 | 40 | 77 | 59 | 18 | St. Pierre and Miquelon |
| 49 | 2,632 | 1,967[25] | ... | ... | 208[6] | 93 | ... | ... | 127 | St. Vincent and the Grenadines |
| 8[8] | 2,750[8] | ... | ... | 4.7 | ... | 84 | 40[18] | 2[18] | 38[18] | San Marino |
| 57 | 1,684 | 249 | 0.5[7] | 0.2[7] | 0.3[7] | 38[7] | 55[7] | 0.1[7] | 55[7] | São Tomé and Príncipe |
| 443 | 15,830 | 572,836 | 953 | 447 | 506 | 16,535 | 50,062 | 29,830 | 20,232 | Saudi Arabia |
| 530[8] | 11,118[8] | 44,391[8] | ... | ... | 142 | 870 | ... | ... | 2,277 | Senegal |
| ... | ... | 1,618[31] | ... | ... | 2 | 172 | 325 | 78 | 247 | Seychelles |
| 113[8] | 24,661[8] | 27,262[8] | ... | 20[2] | 11 | 300 | 485 | 30 | 455 | Sierra Leone |
| 126 | 20,423 | 348,277 | 283 | 12 | 271 | 16,795 | 60,727 | 29,420 | 31,307 | Singapore |
| 99[8] | 2,121[8] | 5,595[8] | 20 | 15 | 5 | 124 | 264 | 15 | 249 | Solomon Islands |
| ... | ... | ... | ... | ... | ... | ... | ... | ... | ... | Somalia |
| 2,227[3, 44] | 13,529[3, 44] | 1,678,751[3, 44] | 8,172 | 7,900 | 272 | 32,014 | ... | 280,731[5] | 16,320 | South Africa |
| 44 | 44 | 44 | ... | ... | ... | ... | ... | ... | ... | Bophuthatswana |
| 44 | 44 | 44 | ... | ... | ... | ... | ... | ... | ... | Ciskei |
| 44 | 44 | 44 | ... | ... | ... | ... | ... | ... | ... | KwaNdebele |
| 44 | 44 | 44 | ... | ... | ... | ... | ... | ... | ... | Transkei |
| 44 | 44 | 44 | ... | ... | ... | ... | ... | ... | ... | Venda |
| 81[3] | 12,914[3] | ... | ... | ... | ... | ... | ... | ... | ... | South West Africa/Namibia |
| 12,535 | 3,075 | 4,219,486 | 7,029 | 6,642 | 387 | 36,910 | 109,622 | 64,939 | 44,683 | Spain |
| 3,690 | 4,303 | 611,978 | 2,095[4] | 1,870[4] | 193[7] | 1,040[7] | 1,826[7, 18] | 252[7, 18] | 1,574[7, 18] | Sri Lanka |
| 790 | 27,848 | 67,730 | ... | ... | ... | 775[4] | ... | ... | 1,379[4] | Sudan, The |
| ... | ... | ... | 62[7] | 6[7] | 56[7] | 289 | 449 | 117 | 332 | Suriname |
| 72[8] | 8,405[8] | 17,267[8] | 46 | 3 | 43 | 308 | 83[18] | 36[18] | 47[18] | Swaziland |
| 2,034[8] | 4,097[8] | 3,333,607 | 252 | 110 | 142 | 18,174 | 48,548 | 16,240 | 32,308 | Sweden |
| 3,796 | 1,721 | 4,240,643 | 1,733 | 1,053 | 680 | 39,011 | 157,425 | 83,261 | 74,164 | Switzerland |
| 543 | 18,909 | 22,759 | 265 | 168 | 97 | 1,961 | ... | ... | 2,186 | Syria |
| 12,441 | 1,538 | 1,327,631 | 1,029 | 878 | 151 | ... | ... | ... | ... | Taiwan |
| 707 | 30,739 | 171,354 | 1,145 | 1,103 | 42 | 1,195 | 3,140[18] | 2,684[18] | 456[18] | Tanzania |
| 4,036 | 12,833 | 477,251 | 8,197 | 8,088 | 109 | 5,372 | 12,843 | 4,817 | 8,026 | Thailand |
| 390 | 6,935 | ... | 327 | 77 | 257[7] | 387 | 518 | 110 | 408 | Togo |
| ... | ... | ... | ... | ... | ... | ... | ... | ... | ... | Tokelau |
| ... | ... | 1,063[25, 29] | 152[7] | 81[7] | 71[7] | 74[7] | ... | ... | 186[7] | Tonga |
| 229[8] | 5,126[8] | 27,230[8] | ... | 217[4] | ... | 267[8] | ... | ... | 1,053[8] | Trinidad and Tobago |
| 600 | 11,833 | 174,073 | 537 | 418 | 119 | 2,963 | 6,724 | 2,052 | 4,672 | Tunisia |
| 55,876 | 881 | 973,447 | 9,333 | 9,203 | 130 | 14,775 | ... | ... | 14,022 | Turkey |
| 7 | 1,285 | 325[9, 10] | ... | 0.1 | 40[6] | 70 | ... | ... | 90 | Turks and Caicos Islands |
| ... | ... | 2,313[13] | 17 | 5 | 12 | 4 | ... | ... | 24 | Tuvalu |
| ... | ... | 28,275[30] | 578[8] | 52[8] | 5[8] | 419[8] | 262[8, 18] | 114[8, 18] | 148[8, 18] | Uganda |
| 90,723[3] | 2,955[3] | 5,925,000[3] | 541,012[4] | 540,110[4] | 902[4] | 1,611[7] | ... | ... | 9,581[7] | U.S.S.R. |
| 53 | 30,612 | 112,264 | 533 | 55 | 478 | 6,129 | 19,438 | 7,957 | 11,481 | United Arab Emirates |
| 21,240[20] | 2,660[20] | 14,158,609 | 1,028[36] | ... | 1,028[36] | 104,886[36] | 218,746[7, 18] | 110,296[7, 18] | 342,668[36] | United Kingdom |
| 39,327 | 6,706 | 139,554,164[24] | 37,386[7] | 33,805[7] | 3,581[7] | 151,996[7] | ... | ... | 185,909[7] | United States |
| 1,277[3] | 2,323[3] | 35,356[13] | 1,104 | 1,060 | 44 | 1,489 | 2,246 | 154 | 2,092 | Uruguay |
| 6[8] | 20,833[8] | 3,000[8] | ... | ... | 4 | 104 | ... | ... | 247 | Vanuatu |
| 809[3] | 7,215[3] | 347,500[28] | 3,244 | 2,928 | 316 | 17,465 | 40,331 | 31,237 | 9,094 | Venezuela |
| ... | — | ... | ... | 5[1] | 250 | ... | ... | 10[1, 18] | 376 | Vietnam |
| 5[3] | 23,200[3] | ... | ... | ... | ... | ... | ... | ... | ... | Virgin Islands (U.S.) |
| 6 | 2,065 | 233 | 8 | 4 | 4 | 4 | ... | ... | 5 | Wallis and Futuna |
| ... | ... | ... | ... | ... | ... | ... | ... | ... | ... | West Bank |
| ... | ... | ... | ... | ... | ... | ... | ... | ... | ... | Western Sahara |
| 47 | 3,326 | 2,087[9, 25] | ... | ... | ... | ... | ... | ... | ... | Western Samoa |
| 111 | 20,243 | 4,097 | ... | 17[4] | ... | 80[7] | 371[4] | 4[4] | 447[7] | Yemen (Aden) |
| 122 | 76,017 | 17,185 | ... | ... | ... | ... | ... | ... | ... | Yemen (Ṣan'ā') |
| 3,841 | 6,043 | 1,249,797 | 12,833[7] | 11,702[7] | 1,131[7] | 11,462[7] | ... | 258,755[5, 7] | 5,005[7, 18] | Yugoslavia |
| 362[8] | 83,592[8] | ... | 52 | 43 | 9 | 1,697 | 2,068 | 66 | 2,002 | Zaire |
| 232[8] | 23,578[8] | 69,175[8] | 24,912[6] | 22,908[6] | 2,004[6] | 1,476 | 6,103 | 4,099 | 2,004 | Zambia |
| 294 | 25,561 | 184,022 | 579 | 530 | 49 | 2,065 | 89,422[5] | 12,824[5] | 3,366 | Zimbabwe |

[1]1981. [2]1980. [3]1978. [4]1982. [5]Number of pulses ('000). [6]Number of words ('000). [7]1984 [8]1983. [9]Excludes postcards. [10]Excludes small packets. [11]Excludes transmitters of the BBC and "Deutsche Welle." [12]Number of minutes ('000). [13]1977. [14]Excludes printed matter. [15]Operator-controlled calls only. [16]Netherlands Antilles includes Aruba. [17]Based on licensed sets only. [18]Number of calls ('000). [19]1985. [20]Permanent post offices only. [21]1979. [22]Excludes domestic small packets. [23]1972. [24]Domestic and foreign sent only. [25]Foreign received and foreign sent only. [26]Telegrams to U.S. are included in national. [27]Excludes telegrams to the U.S.. [28]1974. [29]1973. [30]1975. [31]1971. [32]Includes overseas departments. [33]Excludes foreign armed services network transmitters. [34]Most towns have cable service. [35]1976. [36]1986. [37]Includes traffic to the U.K. [38]Excludes traffic to the U.K. [39]Includes Tuvalu. [40]Includes traffic to South Africa. [41]Excludes eight Voice of America transmitters. [42]Excludes transmitters of Transworld Radio and "Radio Nederland." [43]Excludes transmitters of "Deutsche Welle." [44]South Africa includes Bophuthatswana, Ciskei, KwaNdebele, Transkei, and Venda. [45]Abu Dhabi only.

# Trade: external

The following table presents comparative data on the import and export trade of all the countries of the world. The table analyzes data for both imports and exports in two ways: (1) into several major commodity groups defined in accordance with the United Nations system called the Standard International Trade Classification (SITC) and (2) by direction of trade for each country with major world trading blocs and partners. These commodity groupings are defined by the SITC code numbers beneath the column headings. The single digit numbers represent broad SITC categories; the double digit numbers represent subcategories of the single digit categories (27 is a subcategory of 2), the three digit is a subcategory of the double digit (667 is a subcategory of 66). Where a plus or minus sign is used before one of these SITC numbers, the SITC category or subcategory is being added to or subtracted from the aggregate implied by the total of the preceding sections. The SITC commodity aggregations used here are listed in the table at the end of this headnote. The full SITC commodity breakdown is presented in the United Nations publication *Standard International Trade Classification, Revision 3.*

The SITC was developed by the United Nations through its Statistical Commission as an outgrowth of the need for a standard system of aggregat-

ing commodities of external trade to provide international comparability of foreign trade statistics. All member nations of the United Nations are urged to use the SITC system as far as possible in reporting their external trade statistics. The United Nations Statistical Commission has defined external merchandise trade as "all goods whose movement into or out of the customs area of a country compiling the statistics adds to or subtracts from the material resources of the country." Goods passing through a country for transport only are excluded, but goods entering for reexport, or deposited (as in a bonded warehouse, or free trade area) for reimport, are included. Statistics in this table refer only to goods and exclude purely financial transactions that are covered in the "Finance" and "National product and accounts" tables.

For purposes of comparability of data, total value of imports and exports is given in this table in U.S. dollars; conversions from other currencies are determined according to International Monetary Fund (IMF) average rates for the year for which data are supplied. The commodity categories are given in terms of percentages of the total value of the country's import or export trade (with the exclusions noted above). Value is based on transaction value: for imports, the value at which the goods were

## Trade: external

| country | year | imports total value U.S.$ (000,000) | food and agricultural raw materials (0+1+2 −27−28 +4) | mineral ores and concentrates (27+28 +667) | fuels and other energy (3) | manufactured goods total[a] (5+6 −667 +7+8 +9) | of which chemicals and related products (5) | of which machinery and transport equipment (7) | of which other[a] (6−667 +8+9) | from European Economic Community (EEC)[b] | from United States | from U.S.S.R. and Eastern Europe[c] | from Japan | from all other[d] |
|---|---|---|---|---|---|---|---|---|---|---|---|---|---|---|
| Afghanistan | 1982[1] | 622.4 | 16.4 | 0.5 | 18.0 | 65.1 | 4.5 | 24.8 | 35.8 | ... | 1.1 | 59.7 | 12.6 | 26.5 |
| Albania | 1982[2] | 373.5 | ... | ... | 33.3 | ... | 16.6 | 22.2 | ... | 28.7 | 4.6 | 35.6 | 2.8 | 28.4 |
| Algeria | 1984 | 10,288.9 | 23.1 | 0.3 | 2.1 | 74.5 | 6.7 | 31.5 | 36.4 | 60.7 | 5.6 | 3.5 | 8.1 | 22.0 |
| American Samoa | 1983[3] | 227.1 | ——61.1[4]—— | | 20.5 | 18.4[5] | 1.5 | 4.9 | 12.1[5] | 0.1[6] | 81.6[6] | —[6] | 5.3[6] | 13.1[6] |
| Andorra | 1984 | 232.5[7] | ... | ... | ... | ... | ... | ... | ... | ... | ... | ... | ... | ... |
| Angola | 1979 | 1,123.0 | ——36.9[4]—— | | ... | 63.1[5] | 2.9 | 39.2 | 21.0[5] | 45.4[2] | 9.1[2] | ... | 2.9[2] | 42.6[2] |
| Anguilla | ... | ... | ... | ... | ... | ... | ... | ... | ... | ... | ... | ... | ... | ... |
| Antigua and Barbuda | 1981 | 110.9 | 26.4 | 0.2 | 1.9 | 71.5 | 6.8 | 32.1 | 32.6 | 34.7[8] | 34.5[8] | 0.5[8] | 1.3[8] | 29.1[8] |
| Argentina | 1985 | 3,814.1 | 8.2 | 4.2 | 12.1 | 75.5 | 21.9 | 35.7 | 17.8 | 28.0 | 18.2 | 2.6 | 7.0 | 44.2 |
| Aruba | 1984 | 2,126.2 | 3.1 | — | 88.1 | 8.7 | 2.3 | 2.8 | 3.6 | 1.9 | 7.6 | — | 0.8 | 89.8 |
| Australia | 1986 | 24,448.7 | 7.3 | 0.9 | 4.7 | 87.0 | 8.7 | 41.9 | 36.4 | 24.2 | 22.0 | 0.3 | 21.8 | 31.7 |
| Austria | 1986 | 26,893.8 | 10.0 | 1.9 | 8.7 | 79.4 | 10.1 | 33.8 | 35.5 | 66.9 | 3.2 | 8.3 | 4.4 | 17.1 |
| Bahamas, The | 1985 | 3,081.1 | 6.5 | — | 73.7 | 19.8 | 3.9 | 6.5 | 9.4 | 3.6 | 27.3 | — | 1.4 | 67.6 |
| Bahrain | 1985 | 2,720.2 | 9.2 | 0.5 | 53.2 | 37.1 | 5.4 | 14.0 | 17.7 | 21.1[9] | 7.4[9] | ... | 9.9[9] | 61.5[9] |
| Bangladesh | 1985 | 2,420.5 | 29.4 | 1.1 | 16.6 | 52.9 | 11.8 | 18.3 | 22.8 | 12.6 | 12.2 | 3.9 | 12.2 | 59.2 |
| Barbados | 1986 | 587.2 | ——18.3[4]—— | | 9.3 | 72.4[5] | 8.8 | 36.3 | 27.2[5] | 20.4 | 39.8 | ... | 5.6 | 34.1 |
| Belgium[10] | 1986 | 68,649.7 | 14.3 | 8.3 | 10.6 | 66.8 | 10.4 | 27.9 | 28.5 | 72.3 | 5.0 | 2.3 | 2.8 | 17.6 |
| Belize | 1985 | 128.2 | 27.1 | 0.2 | 17.1 | 55.6 | 7.8 | 17.6 | 30.3 | 18.8[2] | 48.3[2] | 0.1[2] | 2.9[2] | 29.9[2] |
| Benin | 1982 | 475.5 | 25.4 | 0.4 | 4.7 | 69.4 | 5.3 | 22.2 | 41.9 | 60.5 | 5.1 | 2.3 | 5.5 | 26.7 |
| Bermuda | 1984 | 413.4 | 20.8 | 0.1 | 12.3 | 66.8 | 8.8 | 23.2 | 34.9 | 15.9 | 58.1 | 0.2 | 5.0 | 20.9 |
| Bhutan | 1985[11] | 66.3 | ... | ... | ... | ... | ... | ... | ... | ... | ... | ... | ... | 100.0[12] |
| Bolivia | 1982 | 485.8 | 20.2 | 0.3 | 1.9 | 77.6 | 10.7 | 37.4 | 29.4 | 36.9 | 29.1 | 1.5 | 10.9 | 21.5 |
| Botswana | 1984 | 706.8 | 20.8 | 1.9 | 10.3 | 67.1 | 6.8 | 29.2 | 31.0 | ... | 1.9 | ... | 0.3 | 97.8 |
| Brazil | 1984 | 15,208.7 | 10.9 | 1.7 | 52.8 | 34.6 | 11.2 | 15.5 | 7.9 | 12.6 | 16.6 | 3.2 | 4.0 | 63.5 |
| British Virgin Islands | 1982 | 58.5 | 28.2 | 0.4 | 10.6 | 60.8 | 4.3 | 33.0 | 23.6 | 7.8 | 42.9 | — | 0.1 | 49.2 |
| Brunei | 1984 | 621.8 | 21.7 | 0.6 | 1.6 | 76.1 | 7.8 | 35.2 | 33.1 | 16.2 | 15.3 | — | 20.1 | 48.4 |
| Bulgaria | 1985 | 13,647.0 | 9.7 | ——46.9[14]—— | | 43.4[15] | 5.8 | 33.2 | 4.4[15] | 9.4 | 1.1 | 73.7 | 0.6 | 15.2 |
| Burkina Faso | 1983 | 287.5 | 27.6 | 0.8 | 17.1 | 54.5 | 10.0 | 23.7 | 20.7 | 44.9 | 9.4 | 0.3 | 4.3 | 41.1 |
| Burma | 1984[11] | 640.7 | ——19.2—— | | | 80.8 | ... | 47.6 | ... | 25.8 | ... | 16.2 | 33.7 | 24.3 |
| Burundi | 1985 | 193.4 | 16.2 | 1.0 | 17.7 | 65.2 | 8.4 | 28.2 | 28.6 | 50.1 | 5.7 | 0.2 | 6.3 | 37.8 |
| Cameroon | 1982 | 1,243.2 | 10.2 | 2.4 | 3.7 | 83.7 | 13.2 | 34.8 | 35.7 | 67.6 | 7.6 | 1.1 | 6.1 | 17.6 |
| Canada | 1986 | 79,836.2 | 7.9 | 2.3 | 4.7 | 85.0 | 6.0 | 56.4 | 22.6 | 11.3 | 68.9 | 0.3 | 6.8 | 12.7 |
| Cape Verde | 1984 | 70.5 | 44.8[16] | —[16] | 9.1[16] | 46.0[16] | 6.6[16] | 13.9[16] | 25.5[16] | 70.1 | 2.1 | 3.3 | 1.7 | 22.8 |
| Cayman Islands | 1985 | 144.0 | 25.1 | 0.1 | 13.4 | 61.4 | 5.9 | 21.0 | 34.5 | ... | 78.3 | — | 7.0 | 14.6 |
| Central African Republic | 1984 | 87.0 | 21.8[16] | 1.7[16] | 1.8[16] | 74.7[16] | 11.8[16] | 33.9[16] | 29.1[16] | 59.3 | 4.6 | ... | 5.3 | 30.8 |
| Chad | 1984 | 171.2 | 15.9[19] | 0.6[19] | 14.2[19] | 69.3[19] | 16.4[19] | 28.8[19] | 24.1[19] | 39.3[2] | 11.2[2] | ... | 0.1[2] | 49.4[2] |
| Chile | 1983 | 2,694.8 | 21.3 | 1.6 | 21.5 | 55.6 | 13.9 | 22.5 | 19.3 | 18.5 | 25.6 | 0.2 | 5.8 | 49.9 |
| China | 1986 | 43,403.3 | 10.3 | 1.6[4] | 1.2 | 86.9[5] | 8.8 | 39.2 | 38.9[5] | 18.0 | 10.8 | 8.1 | 28.9 | 34.2 |
| Christmas Island | ... | ... | ... | ... | ... | ... | ... | ... | ... | ... | ... | ... | ... | ... |
| Cocos (Keeling) Islands | ... | ... | ... | ... | ... | ... | ... | ... | ... | ... | ... | ... | ... | ... |
| Colombia | 1984 | 4,492.4 | 13.8 | 0.9 | 10.6 | 74.7 | 18.0 | 35.0 | 21.7 | 18.2 | 34.2 | 1.6 | 9.6 | 36.4 |
| Comoros | 1985 | 36.7 | ——47.1[4, 20]—— | | 13.1[20] | 39.8[5, 20] | 3.5[20] | 17.6[20] | 18.8[5, 20] | 54.6[2] | 3.4[2] | ...[2] | 0.8[2] | 41.1[2] |
| Congo | 1985 | 598.1 | 19.7[16] | 0.9[16] | 13.9[16] | 65.5[16] | 10.1[16] | 22.5[16] | 32.9[16] | 74.5[2] | 3.5[2] | 0.6[2] | 2.7[2] | 18.6[2] |
| Cook Islands | 1986 | 26.4 | ——29.4[4]—— | | 12.0 | 58.6[5] | 7.5 | 17.3 | 33.8[5] | 6.4[16] | 5.0[16] | —[16] | 7.6[16] | 81.0[16] |
| Costa Rica | 1982 | 945.2 | 10.6 | 0.5 | 20.0 | 69.0 | 20.8 | 14.6 | 33.5 | 11.1 | 41.0 | 0.2 | 4.1 | 43.7 |
| Côte d'Ivoire | 1985 | 1,733.8 | 18.2 | 0.7 | 21.3 | 59.1 | 12.8 | 22.2 | 24.0 | 54.1 | 6.9 | 1.1 | 5.0 | 33.0 |
| Cuba | 1984 | 8,133.7 | 15.6 | 0.3[4] | 30.8 | 53.4[5] | 5.9 | 30.5 | 17.0[5] | 6.9 | — | 79.9 | 3.0 | 10.1 |
| Cyprus | 1986 | 1,275.5 | 17.1 | 0.7 | 12.6 | 69.6 | 9.0 | 24.3 | 36.3 | 60.7 | 4.2 | 4.9 | 9.3 | 21.0 |
| Czechoslovakia | 1985 | 17,616.8 | 11.8 | 3.5 | 30.7 | 54.0 | 6.8 | 31.1 | 16.0 | 8.9 | 0.2 | 74.8 | 0.3 | 15.8 |
| Denmark | 1986 | 22,737.5 | 15.3 | 0.6 | 8.9 | 75.3 | 10.5 | 31.7 | 33.1 | 51.7 | 4.8 | 2.8 | 5.7 | 35.1 |
| Djibouti | 1983 | 221.2 | 42.8 | 1.1 | 9.4 | 46.7 | 5.1 | 22.5 | 19.1 | 52.2 | 1.8 | — | 7.6 | 38.4 |
| Dominica | 1985 | 55.3 | 28.0 | 0.2 | 10.9 | 60.9 | 11.4 | 22.5 | 27.0 | 23.4 | 24.5 | 0.1 | 7.4 | 44.7 |
| Dominican Republic | 1983 | 1,279.0 | 16.6 | 0.2 | 36.2 | 46.9 | 12.5 | 16.9 | 17.5 | 11.3 | 36.4 | — | 4.3 | 48.0 |
| Ecuador | 1982 | 1,758.4 | 7.7 | 0.7 | 1.6 | 90.0 | 19.2 | 42.9 | 27.9 | 21.1 | 37.4 | 0.9 | 13.6 | 27.0 |
| Egypt | 1985 | 9,961.5 | 33.9 | 0.6 | 3.8 | 61.7 | 9.1 | 25.4 | 27.2 | 42.2 | 13.0 | 10.2 | 5.2 | 29.4 |
| El Salvador | 1983 | 963.5 | 19.2 | 0.6 | 22.6 | 57.6 | 20.7 | 12.0 | 24.9 | 10.9 | 29.4 | 0.1 | 3.2 | 56.4 |
| Equatorial Guinea | 1981 | 43.2 | ... | ... | 22.4 | ... | ... | 17.4 | ... | 92.3[2] | 1.6[2] | —[2] | —[2] | 6.1[2] |
| Ethiopia | 1985 | 988.6 | 32.8 | 0.3 | 14.8 | 52.2 | 7.4 | 28.7 | 16.1 | 35.6 | 16.1 | 20.0 | 6.0 | 22.3 |
| Faeroe Islands | 1986 | 329.2 | 14.6 | 0.7 | 9.7 | 75.0 | 4.8 | 38.5 | 31.8 | 65.2 | 2.3 | 0.8 | 4.8 | 26.9 |
| Falkland Islands | 1975 | 3.4 | 30.9 | — | 2.6 | 64.4 | 5.7 | 14.4 | 44.3 | 88.5 | — | 0.1 | 3.3 | 8.1 |

purchased by the importer plus the cost of transportation and insurance to the frontier of the importing country (c.i.f. [cost, insurance, and freight] valuation); for exports, the value at which the goods were sold by the exporter, including the cost of transportation and insurance to bring the goods onto the transporting vehicle at the frontier of the exporting country (f.o.b. [free on board] valuation).

The largest part of the information presented here comes from the United Nations' *Commodity Trade Statistics* (including microfiche format) and *International Trade Statistics Yearbook*. These publications, however, can not always provide the most recent data for all countries listed in this table and must be supplemented by national and regional sources.

a. Also includes any unallocated commodities.
b. EEC of twelve countries (Belgium, Denmark, France, West Germany, Greece, Ireland, Italy, Luxembourg, The Netherlands, Portugal, Spain, and the United Kingdom).
c. Includes Albania, Bulgaria, Czechoslovakia, East Germany, Hungary, Poland, and Romania.
d. Percentages in these columns may include value of trade shown as not available (...) in any of the four preceding columns.

... Not available.
— None, less than 0.05%, or not applicable.
Detail may not add to 100.0 or indicated subtotals because of rounding.

**SITC category codes:**

| | |
|---|---|
| 0 | food and live animals, chiefly for food. |
| 1 | beverages and tobacco. |
| 2 | crude materials, inedible, except fuels. |
| 27 | crude fertilizers and crude minerals (excluding coal, petroleum, and precious stones). |
| 28 | metalliferous ores and metal scrap. |
| 3 | mineral fuels, lubricants, and related materials (including coal, petroleum, and hydrocarbon products). |
| 4 | animal and vegetable oils, fats, and waxes. |
| 5 | chemicals and related products not specified elsewhere. |
| 6 | manufactured goods classified chiefly by material. |
| 667 | pearls, precious and semiprecious stones, unworked or worked. |
| 7 | machinery and transport equipment. |
| 8 | miscellaneous manufactured articles. |
| 9 | commodities and transactions not specified elsewhere. |

| exports | | | | | | | | | direction of trade (percent) | | | | | country |
|---|---|---|---|---|---|---|---|---|---|---|---|---|---|---|
| total value U.S.$ (000,000) | Standard International Trade Classification (SITC) categories (percent) | | | | | | | | to European Economic Community (EEC)[b] | to United States | to U.S.S.R. and Eastern Europe[c] | to Japan | to all other[d] | |
| | food and agricultural raw materials (0+1+2 −27−28 +4) | mineral ores and concentrates (27+28 +667) | fuels and other energy (3) | manufactured goods | | | | | | | | | | |
| | | | | total[a] (5+6 −667 +7+8 +9) | of which chemicals and related products (5) | of which machinery and transport equipment (7) | of which other[a] (6−667 +8+9) | | | | | | | |
| 694.3 | 44.4 | — | 39.3 | 16.3 | 1.7 | — | 14.6 | ... | 1.4 | 61.9 | 0.1 | 36.6 | Afghanistan |
| 350.7 | | 26.2 | 40.3 | | | | | 31.2 | 0.8 | 35.7 | 1.1 | 31.2 | Albania |
| 11,885.7 | 0.4 | 0.4 | 97.6 | 1.7 | 1.0 | — | 0.6 | 69.3 | 21.7 | 1.1 | 0.7 | 7.3 | Algeria |
| 177.2 | 99.9 | — | — | 0.1 | — | — | 0.1 | — | 98.9 | ... | 0.8 | 0.3 | American Samoa |
| 9.6[7] | ... | ... | ... | ... | ... | ... | ... | ... | ... | ... | ... | ... | Andorra |
| 1,102.0 | 14.9 | 10.7 | 74.0 | 0.4 | ... | ... | 0.4 | 13.5[2] | 40.1[2] | ... | 4.9[2] | 41.5[2] | Angola |
| ... | ... | ... | ... | ... | ... | ... | ... | ... | ... | ... | ... | ... | Anguilla |
| 34.2 | 3.4 | ... | — | 96.5 | 3.2 | 33.2 | 60.2 | 7.9[8] | 35.1[8] | —[8] | 1.8[8] | 55.2[8] | Antigua and Barbuda |
| 8,396.0 | 69.6 | 0.2 | 7.6 | 22.6 | 4.4 | 6.0 | 12.2 | 24.3 | 12.2 | 17.4 | 4.3 | 41.7 | Argentina |
| 2,088.6 | 0.2 | 0.7 | 98.9 | 0.3 | 0.1 | 0.1 | — | 7.9 | 63.4 | — | — | 28.6 | Aruba |
| 22,478.6 | 38.3 | 15.5 | 21.4 | 24.8 | 1.8 | 6.1 | 17.0 | 14.0 | 8.5 | 3.7 | 25.3 | 48.6 | Australia |
| 22,524.8 | 8.3 | 0.9 | 1.2 | 89.6 | 8.7 | 33.2 | 47.7 | 60.1 | 4.0 | 9.6 | 1.2 | 25.1 | Austria |
| 3,033.1 | —1.8[4]— | | 89.3 | 8.8[5] | 7.9 | 0.5 | 0.4[5] | 5.0 | 84.9 | — | 1.8 | 8.3 | Bahamas, The |
| 2,637.4 | 0.1 | 0.1 | 92.4 | 7.3 | 0.1 | 0.7 | 6.5 | 1.4[9] | 9.7[9] | ... | 11.8[9] | 77.0[9] | Bahrain |
| 973.7 | 31.2 | — | 2.5 | 66.2 | 0.2 | 1.6 | 64.5 | 16.9 | 20.6 | 6.0 | 7.2 | 49.3 | Bangladesh |
| 274.6 | —16.1[4]— | | 15.4 | 68.5[5] | 5.5 | 48.2 | 14.8[5] | 13.7 | 23.7 | ... | 1.2 | 61.3 | Barbados |
| 68,872.3 | 11.9 | 6.6 | 4.9 | 76.6 | 12.5 | 25.8 | 38.3 | 73.1 | 5.3 | 1.5 | 0.9 | 19.1 | Belgium[10] |
| 90.1 | 63.2 | — | 3.0 | 33.7 | 1.5 | 7.4 | 24.8 | 21.2[9] | 49.7[9] | —[9] | 0.1[9] | 29.0[9] | Belize |
| 42.6 | 48.4 | 0.0 | 3.9 | 47.7 | 0.4 | 3.7 | 43.5 | 32.9 | — | — | 6.9 | 60.2 | Benin |
| 40.5 | 0.9 | 0.4 | — | 98.7 | 56.9 | 20.4 | 21.4 | 43.7 | 24.7 | — | — | 31.6 | Bermuda |
| 14.5 | ... | ... | ... | ... | ... | ... | ... | ... | ... | ... | ... | 100.0[13] | Bhutan |
| 895.5 | 6.1 | 19.1 | 44.5 | 30.2 | 0.2 | 0.6 | 29.4 | 14.5 | 28.8 | 0.9 | 1.8 | 54.0 | Bolivia |
| 673.9 | 10.2 | 80.2 | — | 9.5 | 0.5 | 2.3 | 6.7 | ... | 8.2 | — | 0.1 | 91.8 | Botswana |
| 27,008.0 | 51.9 | 5.8 | 15.4 | 26.9 | 2.8 | 6.3 | 17.8 | 25.2 | 28.5 | 5.0 | 5.6 | 35.6 | Brazil |
| 1.2 | 78.1 | 2.7 | 1.5 | 17.7 | 0.1 | 10.2 | 7.4 | 4.6 | 57.4 | — | — | 38.0 | British Virgin Islands |
| 3,196.8 | 0.2 | — | 98.8 | 1.0 | 0.1 | 0.5 | 0.5 | 2.3 | 5.5 | — | 68.4 | 23.7 | Brunei |
| 13,341.0 | 18.6 | —10.0[14]— | | 71.4[15] | 5.8 | 53.4 | 12.1[15] | 6.4 | 0.2 | 73.9 | 0.2 | 19.3 | Bulgaria |
| 57.0 | 89.4 | 0.1 | — | 10.5 | 0.1 | 4.1 | 6.3 | 28.8 | 0.1 | — | 4.3 | 66.8 | Burkina Faso |
| 421.5 | 81.6 | 14.7 | — | 3.7 | — | — | 3.7 | 12.3 | — | — | 6.7 | 81.1 | Burma |
| 109.6 | 91.0 | — | — | 9.0 | — | — | 9.0 | 41.7 | 5.9 | — | 1.2 | 51.2 | Burundi |
| 1,028.9 | 43.8 | — | 47.0 | 9.2 | 1.3 | 0.9 | 7.0 | 47.6 | 40.1 | 0.4 | 1.2 | 10.7 | Cameroon |
| 84,268.3 | 18.5 | 4.7 | 9.7 | 67.1 | 4.8 | 42.0 | 20.3 | 6.8 | 77.5 | 1.3 | 4.9 | 9.5 | Canada |
| 49.7 | 4.5 | 0.5 | 86.1 | 8.9 | 0.0 | 7.3 | 1.6 | 2.5 | — | — | — | 97.5[17] | Cape Verde |
| 1.8 | 2.1[18] | 2.2[18] | —[18] | 95.8[18] | 94.1[18] | 0.5[18] | 1.2[18] | —[18] | 100.0[18] | —[18] | —[18] | —[18] | Cayman Islands |
| 85.9 | 71.2[16] | 25.0[16] | —[16] | 3.8[16] | —[16] | —[16] | 3.8[16] | 77.2 | 0.9 | ... | 0.1 | 21.8 | Central African Republic |
| 111.1 | 83.1[19] | 0.8[19] | 7.9[19] | 8.2[19] | 0.5[19] | 5.4[19] | 2.3[19] | 64.4[2] | 0.1[2] | ... | 4.3[2] | 31.3[2] | Chad |
| 3,619.6 | 28.7 | 23.0 | 1.6 | 46.6 | 2.3 | 1.1 | 43.2 | 35.7 | 26.1 | 1.7 | 9.0 | 27.5 | Chile |
| 31,336.9 | 22.8 | 1.7[4] | 11.7 | 63.8[5] | 5.6 | 3.6 | 54.6[5] | 12.9 | 8.5 | 8.4 | 15.3 | 55.0 | China |
| ... | ... | ... | ... | ... | ... | ... | ... | ... | ... | ... | ... | ... | Christmas Island |
| ... | ... | ... | ... | ... | ... | ... | ... | ... | ... | ... | ... | ... | Cocos (Keeling) Islands |
| 3,483.1 | 67.2 | 0.8 | 14.9 | 17.1 | 3.0 | 0.9 | 13.1 | 37.5 | 31.5 | 2.1 | 4.4 | 24.5 | Colombia |
| 15.7 | 64.1[20] | —[20] | 5.6[20] | 30.3[20] | 29.5[20] | —[20] | 0.8[20] | 53.6[2] | 39.7[2] | ...[2] | ...[2] | 6.6[2] | Comoros |
| 1,087.4 | 3.6[16] | 4.1[16] | 89.6[16] | 2.7[16] | —[16] | 0.2[16] | 2.6[16] | 38.7[2] | 54.0[2] | 0.1[2] | 0.7[2] | 6.5[2] | Congo |
| 3.1 | 44.8 | — | — | 55.2 | ... | ... | ... | ... | 0.0 | — | 12.2 | 87.7 | Cook Islands |
| 876.8 | 70.6 | — | 0.9 | 28.5 | 7.2 | 4.2 | 17.1 | 26.4 | 33.7 | 3.0 | 0.7 | 36.2 | Costa Rica |
| 2,670.0 | 79.8 | 0.1 | 9.7 | 10.3 | 2.5 | 1.8 | 6.1 | 57.5 | 12.6 | 5.8 | 1.1 | 22.9 | Côte d'Ivoire |
| 6,164.3 | 81.9 | 5.9[4] | 10.1 | 2.1[5] | ... | ... | ... | 3.9 | — | 85.4 | 0.9 | 9.8 | Cuba |
| 503.5 | 37.7 | 2.2 | 5.9 | 54.2 | 5.1 | 12.7 | 36.4 | 38.3 | 1.9 | 5.0 | 0.3 | 54.6 | Cyprus |
| 17,542.9 | 6.1 | 0.3 | 4.3 | 89.3 | 6.0 | 53.6 | 29.7 | 9.5 | 0.4 | 70.5 | 0.2 | 19.4 | Czechoslovakia |
| 20,567.1 | 35.6 | 0.6 | 3.2 | 60.6 | 8.9 | 24.3 | 27.4 | 45.3 | 8.4 | 1.9 | 3.4 | 41.1 | Denmark |
| 10.8 | 6.1[21] | —[21] | — | 93.9[21] | 0.1[21] | 1.4[21] | 92.5[21] | 42.1[18] | 5.9[18] | 0.1[18] | —[18] | 52.0[18] | Djibouti |
| 28.4 | 59.8 | — | — | 40.1 | 28.6 | 5.4 | 6.1 | 50.4 | 3.4 | — | — | 46.2 | Dominica |
| 648.3 | 75.7 | 0.3 | — | 24.1 | 4.0 | 4.5 | 15.6 | 13.9 | 66.5 | 6.7 | 2.3 | 10.5 | Dominican Republic |
| 2,290.8 | 32.7 | — | 64.3 | 3.1 | 0.3 | 0.8 | 2.0 | 4.0 | 43.1 | 1.1 | 0.7 | 51.0 | Ecuador |
| 3,714.2 | 17.7 | 0.1 | 68.2 | 14.1 | 0.8 | 0.1 | 13.2 | 43.9 | 0.9 | 20.7 | 3.1 | 31.4 | Egypt |
| 468.4 | 61.6 | 0.4 | 2.6 | 35.4 | 7.9 | 2.6 | 24.9 | 15.7 | 28.0 | 4.1 | 6.1 | 46.0 | El Salvador |
| 13.6 | 98.7 | — | — | 1.3 | — | — | 1.3 | 96.5[2] | 0.7[2] | —[2] | —[2] | 2.7[2] | Equatorial Guinea |
| 337.5 | 88.9 | 0.2 | 9.8 | 1.1 | 0.6 | — | 0.5 | 48.9 | 10.5 | 8.7 | 10.3 | 21.7 | Ethiopia |
| 242.2 | 93.7 | — | — | 6.3 | — | 6.3 | — | 68.6 | 14.0 | 0.5 | 2.0 | 15.0 | Faeroe Islands |
| 2.6 | 100.0 | — | — | — | — | — | — | 100.0 | — | — | — | — | Falkland Islands |

## Trade: external   (continued)

| country | year | total value U.S.$ (000,000) | food and agricultural raw materials (0+1+2 −27−28 +4) | mineral ores and concentrates (27+28 +667) | fuels and other energy (3) | manufactured goods total[a] (5+6 −667 +7+8 +9) | of which chemicals and related products (5) | of which machinery and transport equipment (7) | of which other[a] (6−667 +8+9) | from European Economic Community (EEC)[b] | from United States | from U.S.S.R. and Eastern Europe[c] | from Japan | from all other[d] |
|---|---|---|---|---|---|---|---|---|---|---|---|---|---|---|
| Fiji | 1985 | 440.6 | 19.0 | 0.3 | 22.7 | 58.0 | 7.6 | 18.0 | 32.3 | 9.3 | 4.1 | 0.1 | 15.1 | 71.4 |
| Finland | 1986 | 15,325.6 | 9.5 | 2.3 | 15.3 | 72.8 | 10.2 | 35.5 | 27.1 | 42.9 | 4.8 | 18.0 | 6.5 | 27.8 |
| France[22] | 1986 | 128,217.4 | 14.8 | 1.4 | 12.7 | 71.1 | 10.7 | 29.5 | 30.9 | 59.9 | 7.5 | 3.4 | 3.6 | 25.6 |
| French Guiana | 1985 | 256.3 | 24.8 | 0.1 | 15.2 | 59.8 | 6.0 | 29.5 | 24.4 | 70.1 | 4.9 | 0.2 | 4.1 | 20.8 |
| French Polynesia | 1983 | 538.3 | 21.4 | 0.3 | 11.9 | 66.3 | 5.3 | 30.1 | 30.9 | 57.9 | 15.8 | 0.1 | 4.3 | 21.9 |
| Gabon | 1983 | 685.6 | 18.5 | 1.0 | 1.8 | 78.8 | 7.5 | 38.5 | 32.7 | 74.6 | 11.0 | 0.4 | 7.4 | 6.6 |
| Gambia, The | 1983[3] | 115.4 | —34.5[4]— | | 12.2 | 53.3[5] | 6.9 | 14.4 | 32.0[5] | 46.7[2] | 5.4[2] | 6.6[2] | 4.1[2] | 37.1[2] |
| Gaza Strip | 1985 | 281.4 | ... | ... | ... | ... | ... | 26.8 | ... | 15.0[25] | 0.3[25] | 62.0[25] | 0.9[25] | 21.7[25] |
| Germany, East | 1985 | 23,432.7 | —58.6— | | | 41.4 | ... | 26.8 | ... | 15.0[25] | 0.3[25] | 62.0[25] | 0.9[25] | 21.7[25] |
| Germany, West[26] | 1986 | 190,635.5 | 16.0 | 2.4 | 11.5 | 70.1 | 9.3 | 26.5 | 34.4 | 52.3 | 6.5 | 4.4 | 5.8 | 31.0 |
| Ghana | 1981 | 1,273.3 | 10.0 | 0.6 | 30.7 | 58.7 | 11.8 | 27.1 | 19.8 | 36.1 | 11.1 | 1.6 | 3.5 | 47.8 |
| Gibraltar | 1985 | 146.7 | —23.0[4]— | | 38.3 | 38.7[5] | 3.8 | 13.2 | 21.7[5] | 77.0[27] | 4.0[27] | ...[27] | 8.3[27] | 10.6[27] |
| Greece | 1986 | 11,304.5 | 20.9 | 1.3 | 17.7 | 60.1 | 10.5 | 25.8 | 23.8 | 58.3 | 3.0 | 5.2 | 6.1 | 27.4 |
| Greenland | 1986 | 359.7 | 21.8 | 0.4 | 6.9 | 70.9 | 3.7 | 29.4 | 37.8 | 77.2 | 2.7 | 0.3 | 4.6 | 15.2 |
| Grenada | 1982 | 56.5 | —35.5[4]— | | 13.3 | 51.2[5] | 10.0 | 14.8 | 26.4[5] | 23.3 | 20.2 | 0.9 | 4.6 | 50.9 |
| Guadeloupe | 1986 | 792.1 | 24.8 | 0.2 | 7.6 | 67.4 | 9.2 | 26.7 | 31.5 | 79.8 | 2.3 | 0.3 | 2.5 | 15.0 |
| Guam | 1983 | 610.7 | 16.9 | 0.1 | 46.9 | 36.2 | 2.3 | 19.1 | 14.8 | ... | 23.4 | ... | 19.9 | 56.6 |
| Guatemala | 1983 | 1,135.0 | 10.9 | 0.4 | 16.9 | 71.8 | 24.3 | 17.6 | 29.9 | 12.7 | 34.2 | 0.4 | 5.2 | 47.5 |
| Guernsey[30] | ... | | | | | | | | | | | | | |
| Guinea | 1980 | 204.4 | —10.0— | | 30.3 | 59.7[5] | 3.0 | 39.8 | 16.9[5] | 71.0[2] | 10.2[2] | 5.8[2] | 1.7[2] | 11.3[2] |
| Guinea-Bissau | 1980 | 55.5 | 20.1 | 2.2 | 6.2 | 71.5 | 5.6 | 36.4 | 29.5 | 59.6 | 0.5 | 7.6 | 0.5 | 31.7 |
| Guyana | 1983 | 246.1 | 5.6 | 0.5 | 43.2 | 50.7 | 9.4 | 23.2 | 18.1 | 20.1 | 21.6 | 0.7 | 1.6 | 56.0 |
| Haiti | 1981[31] | 375.7 | —33.7[4]— | | 14.4 | 51.9[5] | 9.3 | 17.1 | 25.5[5] | 10.8 | 52.1 | 0.4 | 6.3 | 30.4 |
| Honduras | 1983 | 823.0 | 10.7 | 0.3 | 22.4 | 66.6 | 20.1 | 18.4 | 28.1 | 14.2 | 36.0 | 0.2 | 4.5 | 45.2 |
| Hong Kong | 1986 | 35,389.3 | 13.1 | 3.0 | 3.2 | 80.7 | 7.7 | 24.0 | 49.1 | 11.5 | 8.4 | 0.4 | 20.4 | 59.3 |
| Hungary | 1985 | 8,151.9 | 12.1 | 1.7[4] | 22.0 | 64.2[5] | 13.4 | 27.4 | 23.4[5] | 21.8 | 3.0 | 49.5 | 1.7 | 24.1 |
| Iceland | 1986 | 1,115.5 | 11.7 | 2.8 | 9.6 | 75.9 | 7.9 | 33.1 | 34.9 | 52.9 | 7.0 | 6.5 | 6.5 | 27.1 |
| India | 1983[11] | 14,859.8 | 10.2 | 7.9 | 40.2 | 41.7 | 6.9 | 18.0 | 16.8 | 23.9 | 10.0 | 12.0 | 7.6 | 46.6 |
| Indonesia | 1984 | 13,882.1 | 10.4 | 1.4 | 19.5 | 68.8 | 15.4 | 36.3 | 17.1 | 15.4 | 18.5 | 0.7 | 23.8 | 41.6 |
| Iran | 1985 | 11,635.0 | 15.4[32] | 0.4[32] | —[32] | 83.9[32] | 7.2[32] | 44.3[32] | 32.5[32] | 38.4[2] | 0.7[2] | 6.4[2] | 12.9[2] | 41.6[2] |
| Iraq | 1985 | 10,556.0 | —24.3[4,33]— | | 0.3[33] | 75.4[5,33] | 7.2[33] | 30.6[33] | 37.6[5,33] | 29.9[33] | 5.6[33] | 3.3[33] | 15.5[33] | 45.7[33] |
| Ireland | 1986 | 11,570.6 | 15.0 | 0.9 | 8.5 | 75.6 | 12.1 | 31.4 | 32.0 | 67.3 | 15.8 | 1.6 | 3.8 | 11.5 |
| Isle of Man[30] | ... | | | | | | | | | | | | | |
| Israel | 1985 | 8,319.9 | 11.7 | 16.4 | 16.3 | 55.6 | 7.3 | 25.2 | 23.1 | 44.9 | 20.2 | 0.4 | 2.2 | 32.2 |
| Italy[34] | 1986 | 102,346.5 | 20.6 | 2.3 | 17.0 | 60.1 | 10.7 | 24.1 | 25.3 | 54.7 | 5.6 | 4.8 | 2.0 | 32.9 |
| Jamaica | 1985 | 1,143.6 | 19.5 | 0.2 | 32.9 | 47.4 | 9.2 | 17.9 | 20.3 | 10.4 | 41.4 | 0.3 | 7.1 | 40.8 |
| Japan | 1986 | 126,407.8 | 24.1 | 6.4 | 29.4 | 40.1 | 7.4 | 10.0 | 22.6 | 11.1 | 23.1 | 1.8 | — | 63.9 |
| Jersey | 1980 | 537.1 | 23.9 | 0.4 | 9.3 | 66.5 | 6.5 | 24.8 | 35.2 | ... | ... | ... | ... | 100.0[35] |
| Jordan | 1985 | 2,733.0 | 19.7 | 1.0 | 20.8 | 58.5 | 6.3 | 19.3 | 32.9 | 29.5 | 11.9 | 4.7 | 6.3 | 47.6 |
| Kampuchea | ... | | | | | | | | | | | | | |
| Kenya | 1984 | 1,500.7 | 14.6 | 0.3 | 30.6 | 54.5 | 12.1 | 26.8 | 15.6 | 37.1 | 4.5 | 0.3 | 10.3 | 47.7 |
| Kiribati | 1985 | 15.1 | 33.4 | 0.1 | 15.0 | 51.5 | 5.0 | 29.4 | 17.0 | 6.2 | 2.6 | ... | 21.2 | 70.0 |
| Korea, North | 1985 | 1,620.0[2] | ... | ... | ... | ... | ... | ... | ... | 3.4[2] | ... | 53.6[2] | 15.4[2] | 27.7[2] |
| Korea, South | 1986 | 31,583.9 | 14.5 | 4.1 | 16.1 | 65.3 | 11.1 | 34.2 | 20.1 | 10.2 | 20.7 | — | 34.4 | 34.7 |
| Kuwait | 1982 | 8,283.4 | 14.5 | 0.6 | 0.6 | 84.2 | 3.6 | 43.6 | 37.0 | 36.2 | 12.7 | 1.3 | 24.1 | 25.7 |
| Laos | 1974 | 64.8 | 32.1 | 0.2 | 11.2 | 56.4 | 6.1 | 25.7 | 24.7 | 17.9 | 4.7 | — | 18.8 | 58.6 |
| Lebanon | 1983 | 3,661.2 | 21.0[32] | 7.0[32] | 6.6[32] | 65.5[32] | 4.6[32] | 21.1[32] | 39.8[32] | 47.5[2] | 14.5[2] | ... | 7.0[2] | 30.9[2] |
| Lesotho | 1981 | 504.9 | 25.1 | 0.8[4] | 9.6 | 64.5[5] | 6.4 | 17.0 | 41.1[5] | 1.5 | 0.2 | ... | — | 98.2[38] |
| Liberia | 1984 | 363.2 | 25.5 | 0.9 | 19.8 | 53.9 | 6.7 | 26.8 | 20.5 | 40.0 | 22.3 | 1.1 | 8.1 | 28.5 |
| Libya | 1981 | 8,381.7 | 19.4 | 0.3 | 1.0 | 79.3 | 4.5 | 38.2 | 36.7 | 64.8 | 6.3 | 4.6 | 7.6 | 16.7 |
| Liechtenstein | 1984 | 185.1 | 6.3 | 0.3[4] | 0.4 | 93.1[5] | 5.0 | 33.7 | 54.4[5] | | | | | |
| Luxembourg | 1984 | 2,770.0 | 13.4 | 3.8[4] | 13.6 | 69.1[5] | 14.1 | 20.6 | 34.5[5] | 90.0 | 2.9 | ... | 0.3 | 6.8 |
| Macau | 1985 | 777.2 | 18.2 | 2.2 | 6.4 | 73.3 | 4.4 | 10.3 | 58.6 | 5.0 | 7.2 | — | 10.2 | 77.7 |
| Madagascar | 1984 | 412.2 | 14.9 | 0.2 | 27.9 | 57.0 | 11.5 | 25.8 | 19.7 | 43.5 | 12.3 | 0.9 | 3.4 | 39.9 |
| Malawi | 1983 | 308.9 | —11.3[4]— | | 18.0 | 70.7[5] | 19.0 | 24.3 | 27.4[5] | 28.4 | 3.1 | 0.4 | 6.9 | 61.2 |
| Malaysia | 1985 | 12,258.5 | 12.9 | 1.8 | 12.2 | 73.1 | 8.7 | 43.6 | 20.8 | 14.4 | 15.2 | 0.4 | 23.0 | 46.9 |
| Maldives | 1983 | 56.9 | 34.2 | 2.5 | 19.7 | 43.6 | 7.1 | 16.7 | 19.8 | 5.6[2] | —[2] | —[2] | 13.0[2] | 81.4[2] |
| Mali | 1979 | 304.5 | 16.5 | 0.4 | 16.4 | 66.7 | 4.0 | 44.5 | 18.1 | 51.4 | 2.6 | 3.4 | 1.2 | 41.5 |
| Malta | 1985 | 757.3 | 17.7 | 0.8 | 12.0 | 69.5 | 7.2 | 24.1 | 38.2 | 77.4 | 5.7 | 3.3 | 1.2 | 12.4 |
| Martinique | 1986 | 879.4 | 23.7 | 0.2 | 9.7 | 66.4 | 10.2 | 23.2 | 33.0 | 83.0 | 2.4 | 0.4 | 2.6 | 11.5 |
| Mauritania | 1984 | 213.4 | 33.6[16] | ... | 11.9[16] | 54.5[16] | ... | 21.9[16] | 32.6[16] | 70.4[2] | 8.6[2] | ... | 1.5[2] | 19.5[2] |
| Mauritius | 1983 | 442.0 | 28.9 | 1.3 | 18.8 | 50.9 | 7.8 | 12.1 | 31.1 | 31.3 | 2.9 | 0.1 | 4.8 | 60.8 |
| Mayotte | 1985 | 21.8 | 26.6 | ... | 11.9 | ... | ... | ... | ... | ... | ... | ... | ... | 100.0[39] |
| Mexico | 1984 | 11,254.3 | 21.3 | 2.9 | 4.3 | 71.4 | 14.3 | 34.3 | 22.8 | 13.8 | 65.7 | 0.3 | 4.5 | 15.8 |
| Monaco[22] | ... | | | | | | | | | | | | | |
| Mongolia | 1985 | 1,442.0[2] | 10.4 | —28.7[14]— | | 59.5[15] | 6.0 | 36.2 | 17.3[15] | ... | —[2] | 97.2[2] | 0.1[2] | 2.7[2] |
| Montserrat | 1985 | 18.4 | —31.2[4]— | | 11.8 | 57.0[5] | 6.6 | 21.1 | 29.3[5] | 19.6[9] | 38.5[9] | —[9] | 4.7[9] | 37.1[9] |
| Morocco | 1984 | 3,906.7 | 25.6 | 4.4 | 26.1 | 43.8 | 7.3 | 19.7 | 16.8 | 42.6 | 12.5 | 6.6 | 3.1 | 35.2 |
| Mozambique | 1984 | 487.2 | —25.0[4]— | | 18.7 | 56.4[5] | 4.6 | 17.3 | 34.4[5] | 32.1 | 5.8 | 25.7 | 3.2 | 33.2 |
| Nauru | 1981[41] | 17.7 | —34.4[4]— | | 1.9 | 63.8[5] | 5.3 | 14.8 | 43.7[5] | | | | | |
| Nepal | 1985[3] | 442.1 | 16.2 | 0.6 | 11.6 | 71.6 | 13.4 | 19.6 | 38.6 | 7.0 | 1.3 | 0.7 | 11.8 | 79.2 |
| Netherlands, The | 1986 | 75,580.2 | 17.4 | 1.8 | 11.9 | 68.8 | 10.4 | 28.4 | 30.0 | 63.9 | 7.9 | 2.5 | 3.3 | 22.5 |
| Netherlands Antilles | 1984[42] | 1,898.2 | 5.5 | 0.1 | 81.8 | 12.6 | 2.3 | 3.7 | 6.7 | 6.2 | 9.5 | 0.1 | 1.0 | 83.3 |
| New Caledonia | 1983 | 303.4 | 23.7 | 0.2 | 23.1 | 53.0 | 6.0 | 20.6 | 26.4 | 48.0 | 10.2 | 0.1 | 5.6 | 36.1 |
| New Zealand | 1986 | 6,133.6 | 7.8 | 2.3 | 8.7 | 81.2 | 11.8 | 39.4 | 30.1 | 22.6 | 17.4 | 0.2 | 21.1 | 38.7 |
| Nicaragua | 1982 | 774.9 | 12.6 | 0.3 | 32.9 | 63.9 | 15.8 | 23.2 | 24.9 | 17.0 | 19.0 | 7.6 | 2.4 | 54.0 |
| Niger | 1981 | 509.7 | 24.8 | 1.9 | 14.8 | 58.4 | 6.9 | 25.7 | 25.8 | 48.0 | 3.7 | 0.4 | 2.5 | 45.4 |
| Nigeria | 1985 | 6,204.6 | 20.5 | 2.6 | 0.9 | 76.0 | 15.7 | 34.2 | 26.2 | 53.1 | 13.4 | 3.5 | 7.4 | 22.6 |
| Niue | 1985 | 1.9 | 40.5 | 0.1 | 19.9 | 39.5 | 3.7 | 19.6 | 16.2 | — | 0.1 | — | 13.3 | 86.6 |
| Norfolk Island | 1986[3] | 16.3 | 20.1 | 0.1 | 9.6 | 70.2 | 5.4 | 14.4 | 50.4 | ... | ... | ... | ... | 100.0[43] |
| Norway | 1986 | 20,305.3 | 8.5 | 3.1 | 5.9 | 82.5 | 6.7 | 40.5 | 35.2 | 49.3 | 6.8 | 1.8 | 7.4 | 34.7 |
| Oman | 1985 | 3,152.7 | 14.5 | 0.3 | 1.8 | 83.4 | 4.0 | 41.8 | 37.7 | 36.7 | 5.7 | ... | 20.2 | 37.4 |
| Pacific Is., Trust Territory of the | 1978[3] | 38.9 | —46.2[4]— | | 12.9 | 40.9[5] | 4.8 | 12.5 | 23.5[5] | —[32] | 34.7[32] | —[32] | 25.2[32] | 40.1[32] |
|   Marshall Islands | ... | | | | | | | | | | | | | |
|   Micronesia, Fed. States of | ... | | | | | | | | | | | | | |

| exports total value U.S.$ (000,000) | Standard International Trade Classification (SITC) categories (percent) | | | | | | | direction of trade (percent) | | | | | country |
|---|---|---|---|---|---|---|---|---|---|---|---|---|---|
| | food and agricultural raw materials (0+1+2 −27−28 +4) | mineral ores and concentrates (27+28 +667) | fuels and other energy (3) | manufactured goods | | | | to European Economic Community (EEC)[b] | to United States | to U.S.S.R. and Eastern Europe[c] | to Japan | to all other[d] | |
| | | | | total[a] (5+6−667 +7+8 +9) | of which chemicals and related products (5) | of which machinery and transport equipment (7) | of which other[a] (6−667 +8+9) | | | | | | |
| 235.4 | 58.1 | 0.1 | 20.0 | 21.8 | 0.9 | 3.4 | 17.5 | 31.6 | 4.7 | — | 2.3 | 61.3 | Fiji |
| 16,325.6 | 14.1 | 0.4 | 2.4 | 83.2 | 5.5 | 27.6 | 50.1 | 37.8 | 5.4 | 21.7 | 1.5 | 33.7 | Finland |
| 119,345.3 | 18.4 | 1.0 | 2.8 | 77.8 | 14.0 | 34.7 | 29.1 | 57.9 | 7.4 | 2.3 | 1.4 | 31.1 | France[22] |
| 36.7 | 73.9 | 0.2 | — | 25.9 | 1.1 | 8.4 | 16.4 | 23.0 | 37.7 | — | 16.7 | 22.6 | French Guiana |
| 41.2 | 14.4 | 15.2 | — | 70.4 | 2.4 | 17.2 | 50.7 | 70.4 | 12.6 | — | 4.9 | 12.1 | French Polynesia |
| 1,475.4 | 7.5 | 7.0 | 79.5 | 6.0 | 1.2 | 0.6 | 4.1 | 54.6 | 25.6 | 1.8 | 0.3 | 17.6 | Gabon |
| 48.5 | 78.0[16] | —[16] | —[16] | 22.0[16] | —[16] | —[16] | 22.0[16] | 55.2[2] | 0.2[2] | —[2] | —[2] | 44.6[2] | Gambia, The |
| 116.9 | ... | ... | ... | ... | ... | ... | ... | ... | ... | ... | ... | 100.0[24] | Gaza Strip |
| 25,267.6 | —27.7— | | | 72.3 | ... | 46.6 | ... | ...[25] | ...[25] | ...[25] | ...[25] | ...[25] | Germany, East |
| 243,195.2 | 6.3 | 0.6 | 1.6 | 91.4 | 12.8 | 47.8 | 30.8 | 50.9 | 10.5 | 3.7 | 1.7 | 33.3 | Germany, West[26] |
| 872.9 | 55.2 | 2.1 | 12.2 | 30.5 | — | 2.0 | 28.4 | 38.9 | 25.2 | 7.3 | 12.9 | 15.6 | Ghana |
| 62.7 | —10.8[4]— | | 77.7 | 11.5[5] | 2.1 | 4.7 | 4.7[5] | 17.3 | 0.2 | ... | ... | 82.5[28] | Gibraltar |
| 5,660.4 | 33.3 | 3.3 | 6.6 | 56.8 | 3.3 | 2.9 | 50.5 | 63.6 | 7.1 | 4.9 | 0.7 | 23.7 | Greece |
| 236.1 | 89.4 | 5.9 | 1.4 | 3.3 | — | 2.6 | 0.7 | 95.5 | 0.2 | ... | ... | 4.3 | Greenland |
| 18.6 | 84.5[29] | —[29] | —[29] | 15.5[29] | —[29] | —[29] | 15.5[29] | 57.5[29] | 2.4[29] | 3.9[29] | —[29] | 36.2[29] | Grenada |
| 108.6 | 85.7 | 0.3 | 0.2 | 13.8 | 3.1 | 6.1 | 4.6 | 78.9 | 2.3 | — | ... | 18.9 | Guadeloupe |
| 39.2 | 23.5 | 2.7 | 3.5 | 70.3 | 5.6 | 11.5 | 53.2 | ... | 24.9 | — | 4.8 | 70.4 | Guam |
| 1,179.6 | 68.8 | 0.2 | 6.0 | 25.0 | 10.3 | 1.1 | 13.6 | 14.7 | 35.9 | 1.7 | 3.7 | 44.0 | Guatemala |
| ... | ... | ... | ... | ... | ... | ... | ... | ... | ... | ... | ... | ... | Guernsey[30] |
| 466.7 | 3.0 | 96.8 | ... | 0.2 | ... | ... | 0.2 | 45.4[2] | 23.5[2] | 21.4[2] | —[2] | 9.6[2] | Guinea |
| 11.4 | 87.1 | 0.3 | — | 12.6 | 0.3 | — | 12.3 | 57.0 | — | — | ... | 43.0 | Guinea-Bissau |
| 188.7 | 52.9 | 36.4 | 0.2 | 10.5 | 2.9 | 3.4 | 4.4 | 37.1 | 17.3 | 4.0 | 8.0 | 33.6 | Guyana |
| 153.3 | 36.6[19] | 12.2[19] | —[19] | 51.2[19] | 5.0[19] | 7.2[19] | 39.0[19] | 22.6 | 73.4 | 0.1 | ... | 3.9 | Haiti |
| 660.1 | 84.2 | 6.4 | 0.6 | 8.8 | 3.3 | — | 5.4 | 18.3 | 55.1 | 1.7 | 6.0 | 18.9 | Honduras |
| 35,465.7 | 6.1 | 1.4 | 0.6 | 91.9 | 4.2 | 22.2 | 65.4 | 14.7 | 31.3 | 0.3 | 4.7 | 48.9 | Hong Kong |
| 8,555.2 | 23.6 | 0.9[4] | 5.1 | 70.3[5] | 11.5 | 33.5 | 25.4[5] | 16.0 | 2.3 | 52.4 | 0.3 | 28.8 | Hungary |
| 1,095.8 | 80.6 | 0.9 | — | 18.6 | — | 1.3 | 17.2 | 54.2 | 21.7 | 5.5 | 4.8 | 13.8 | Iceland |
| 9,143.5 | 28.3 | 16.4 | 14.1 | 41.2 | 4.0 | 6.6 | 30.6 | 16.7 | 10.5 | 23.0 | 9.5 | 40.3 | India |
| 21,887.8 | 14.0 | 1.4 | 73.3 | 11.4 | 0.8 | 1.0 | 9.6 | 5.0 | 20.6 | 0.7 | 47.3 | 26.4 | Indonesia |
| 11,635.0 | ... | ... | 98.0 | ... | ... | ... | ... | 35.2[2] | 5.2[2] | ... | 17.1[2] | 42.5[2] | Iran |
| 10,349.0[2] | —0.4[4]— | | 99.6[2] | 0.1[5] | —— | — | —[5] | 43.8[2] | 4.3[2] | ... | 5.5[2] | 46.3[2] | Iraq |
| 12,605.7 | 28.0 | 2.1 | 0.8 | 69.2 | 13.0 | 30.5 | 25.7 | 72.0 | 8.7 | 0.8 | 1.8 | 16.6 | Ireland |
| ... | ... | ... | ... | ... | ... | ... | ... | ... | ... | ... | ... | ... | Isle of Man[30] |
| 6,256.4 | 14.0 | 25.1 | — | 60.8 | 15.6 | 20.2 | 25.0 | 31.6 | 34.2 | 0.4 | 3.4 | 30.4 | Israel |
| 97,834.3 | 8.3 | 0.4 | 2.8 | 88.5 | 7.2 | 33.6 | 47.7 | 53.6 | 10.7 | 3.0 | 1.4 | 31.4 | Italy[34] |
| 568.6 | 25.1 | 51.7 | 4.8 | 18.4 | 3.2 | 5.4 | 9.8 | 23.9 | 33.2 | 5.3 | 1.3 | 36.3 | Jamaica |
| 209,151.2 | 1.3 | 0.2 | 0.3 | 98.2 | 4.5 | 70.0 | 23.7 | 14.8 | 38.8 | 1.8 | — | 44.6 | Japan |
| 209.2 | 27.6 | 4.3[36] | — | 68.0 | 1.2 | 31.1 | 35.7 | ... | ... | ... | ... | 100.0[37] | Jersey |
| 789.9 | 15.6 | 31.6 | — | 52.6 | 16.6 | 14.4 | 21.9 | 6.5 | 0.2 | 5.4 | 2.1 | 85.7 | Jordan |
| ... | ... | ... | ... | ... | ... | ... | ... | ... | ... | ... | ... | ... | Kampuchea |
| 1,084.4 | 68.7 | 2.0 | 18.4 | 10.9 | 3.0 | 1.3 | 6.6 | 45.2 | 5.0 | 0.6 | 0.8 | 48.4 | Kenya |
| 4.2 | 94.7 | — | — | 5.3 | — | — | 5.3 | 30.1 | 8.2 | — | 1.7 | 60.1 | Kiribati |
| 1,290.0[2] | ... | ... | ... | ... | ... | ... | ... | 5.7[2] | ... | 45.4[2] | 13.7[2] | 35.2[2] | Korea, North |
| 34,714.5 | 5.5 | 0.3 | 1.9 | 92.3 | 3.1 | 33.6 | 55.6 | 12.4 | 40.1 | — | 15.6 | 31.9 | Korea, South |
| 10,861.3 | 1.6 | 0.2 | 75.6 | 22.6 | 8.4 | 6.5 | 7.7 | 18.8 | 0.3 | — | 14.2 | 66.6 | Kuwait |
| 11.3 | 84.0 | 11.9 | — | 4.1 | — | — | 4.1 | 0.3 | — | — | 3.7 | 96.0 | Laos |
| 690.9 | 20.1[32] | 0.5[32] | —[32] | 79.2[32] | 9.6[32] | 11.4[32] | 58.2[32] | 5.9[2] | 2.3[2] | ... | 0.2[2] | 91.6[2] | Lebanon |
| 49.6 | 28.8 | 42.6 | 0.1 | 28.5 | 0.9 | 3.3 | 24.3 | 10.3 | 0.1 | ... | — | 89.6 | Lesotho |
| 449.1 | 34.1 | 64.8 | — | 1.1 | 0.1 | 0.3 | 0.8 | 70.5 | 20.2 | 1.9 | 1.3 | 6.1 | Liberia |
| 15,571.1 | ... | ... | 99.6 | 0.4 | 0.4 | — | — | 52.7 | 27.4 | 4.4 | 2.1 | 13.3 | Libya |
| 451.3 | 0.3 | —[4] | 0.2 | 99.5[5] | 7.8 | 47.2 | 44.4[5] | 35.3 | ... | ... | ... | 64.7 | Liechtenstein |
| 2,519.0 | 6.2 | 1.5[4] | 0.4 | 91.9[5] | 16.8 | 13.3 | 61.7[5] | 74.4 | 5.8 | ... | 0.1 | 19.7 | Luxembourg |
| 903.3 | 2.6 | 0.2 | — | 97.2 | 0.6 | 5.4 | 91.2 | 31.8 | 32.4 | 1.3 | 2.0 | 32.6 | Macau |
| 339.9 | 85.6 | 2.8 | 2.3 | 9.3 | 2.3 | 1.0 | 5.9 | 61.8 | 14.7 | 0.9 | 8.4 | 14.1 | Madagascar |
| 246.1 | —94.1[4]— | | 0.1 | 5.8[5] | 0.6 | 1.4 | 3.8[5] | 47.8 | 6.3 | — | 4.9 | 41.0 | Malawi |
| 15,310.8 | 35.5 | 0.9 | 31.7 | 32.0 | 1.1 | 18.6 | 12.3 | 14.5 | 12.9 | 1.5 | 24.4 | 46.7 | Malaysia |
| 13.4 | 51.9 | 1.4 | — | 46.7 | — | — | 46.7 | 5.8 | 41.5 | 0.7 | 18.8 | 33.3 | Maldives |
| 106.2 | 76.4 | — | — | 23.6 | 0.3 | 0.5 | 22.8 | 71.1 | — | — | 3.0 | 25.9 | Mali |
| 400.1 | 7.2 | 1.3 | 3.5 | 88.0 | 1.3 | 22.1 | 64.7 | 66.7 | 6.4 | 7.8 | 0.2 | 19.0 | Malta |
| 208.9 | 66.7 | 0.2 | 18.4 | 14.7 | 3.4 | 3.6 | 7.7 | 69.2 | 0.3 | — | — | 30.5 | Martinique |
| 297.3 | 50.2 | 49.1 | — | 0.7 | — | — | 0.7 | 65.1[2] | 0.3[2] | ... | 12.5[2] | 22.1[2] | Mauritania |
| 368.3 | 68.6 | 1.2 | — | 30.2 | 0.4 | 0.9 | 28.8 | 83.3 | 8.5 | 0.2 | — | 8.0 | Mauritius |
| 0.6 | 24.6 | — | — | 75.4 | 41.5 | ... | 33.9 | ... | ... | ... | ... | 100.0[40] | Mayotte |
| 24,053.6 | 9.0 | 2.2 | 68.1 | 20.8 | 3.9 | 7.7 | 9.2 | 18.5 | 58.1 | 0.2 | 7.8 | 15.5 | Mexico |
| ... | ... | ... | ... | ... | ... | ... | ... | ... | ... | ... | ... | ... | Monaco[22] |
| 570.0[2] | 39.9 | —42.6[14]— | | 17.5[15] | ... | 0.1 | 17.4[15] | ... | 0.7[2] | 90.5[2] | 1.4[2] | 7.4[2] | Mongolia |
| 2.9 | 5.8 | — | 0.3 | 93.9 | 0.2 | 20.5 | 73.2 | ... | 55.6[29] | ... | ... | 44.4[29] | Montserrat |
| 2,171.9 | 24.8 | 28.9 | 4.0 | 42.3 | 23.1 | 0.9 | 18.4 | 59.5 | 1.5 | 5.5 | 3.8 | 29.7 | Morocco |
| 86.4 | 79.3 | 1.4[4] | 6.3 | 13.0[5] | — | — | 13.0[5] | 26.9 | 14.6 | 15.4 | 11.9 | 31.2 | Mozambique |
| 89.2 | — | 100.0 | — | — | — | — | — | ... | ... | ... | ... | ... | Nauru |
| 128.5 | 40.7 | 0.2 | — | 59.1 | 3.5 | — | 55.6 | 15.2 | 21.7 | 4.2 | 0.5 | 58.4 | Nepal |
| 80,554.8 | 24.9 | 1.2 | 15.4 | 58.5 | 17.1 | 19.8 | 21.6 | 74.9 | 4.7 | 1.3 | 0.7 | 18.3 | Netherlands, The |
| 1,639.6 | — | 0.1 | 97.6 | 2.2 | 1.6 | 0.3 | 0.3 | 15.6 | 17.4 | — | 0.4 | 66.6 | Netherlands Antilles |
| 155.1 | 1.6 | 15.9 | 0.1 | 82.3 | 0.3 | 4.5 | 77.5 | 47.1 | 6.9 | — | 23.7 | 22.3 | New Caledonia |
| 5,943.0 | 67.5 | 0.6 | 0.8 | 31.1 | 5.2 | 5.5 | 20.4 | 19.8 | 16.2 | 2.3 | 14.7 | 47.0 | New Zealand |
| 390.7 | 90.8 | 0.1 | 1.3 | 7.8 | 5.0 | 0.1 | 2.6 | 29.4 | 25.0 | 7.4 | 1.1 | 26.7 | Nicaragua |
| 454.8 | 17.1 | 79.7 | 0.9 | 2.3 | — | 0.5 | 1.8 | 46.6 | — | — | 17.7 | 35.7 | Niger |
| 13,134.3 | 2.2 | — | 96.7 | 1.0 | — | — | 1.0 | 64.5 | 18.1 | 0.3 | 0.1 | 17.1 | Nigeria |
| 0.1 | 61.9 | — | — | 38.1 | — | — | 38.1 | ... | 1.3 | — | — | 98.7 | Niue |
| 1.8 | 24.0 | — | — | 76.0 | 1.0 | 12.0 | 63.0 | ... | ... | ... | ... | 100.0[44] | Norfolk Island |
| 18,234.0 | 9.8 | 1.5 | 42.9 | 45.8 | 6.9 | 17.6 | 21.3 | 64.9 | 5.4 | 0.9 | 1.2 | 27.6 | Norway |
| 5,032.8 | 1.2 | 0.1 | 93.1 | 5.6 | 0.1 | 3.8 | 1.7 | 2.7[2] | 0.9[2] | —[2] | 55.9[2] | 40.6[2] | Oman |
| 19.3 | —96.5[4]— | | — | 3.5[5] | — | — | 3.5[5] | ... | ... | ... | ... | ... | Pacific Is., Trust Territory of the Marshall Islands |
| ... | ... | ... | ... | ... | ... | ... | ... | ... | ... | ... | ... | ... | Micronesia, Fed. States of |

## Trade: external  (continued)

| country | year | imports total value U.S.$ (000,000) | Standard International Trade Classification (SITC) categories (percent) | | | | | | | direction of trade (percent) | | | | |
|---|---|---|---|---|---|---|---|---|---|---|---|---|---|---|
| | | | food and agricultural raw materials (0+1+2 −27−28 +4) | mineral ores and concentrates (27+28 +667) | fuels and other energy (3) | manufactured goods total[a] (5+6 −667 +7+8 +9) | of which chemicals and related products (5) | of which machinery and transport equipment (7) | of which other[a] (6−667 +8+9) | from European Economic Community (EEC)[b] | from United States | from U.S.S.R. and Eastern Europe[c] | from Japan | from all other[d] |
| Northern Mariana Islands | ... | ... | ... | ... | ... | ... | ... | ... | ... | ... | ... | ... | ... | ... |
| Palau | ... | ... | ... | ... | ... | ... | ... | ... | ... | ... | ... | ... | ... | ... |
| Pakistan | 1986 | 5,377.0 | 21.8 | 1.6 | 14.3 | 62.3 | 15.1 | 32.0 | 15.2 | 26.4 | 13.2 | 2.3 | 16.2 | 41.9 |
| Panama | 1983 | 1,411.4 | 11.2 | 0.2 | 27.8 | 60.9 | 11.8 | 23.0 | 26.0 | 8.7 | 32.3 | 0.2 | 7.8 | 50.9 |
| Papua New Guinea | 1984 | 968.4 | ——20.3[4]—— | | 18.0 | 61.6[5] | 7.9 | 28.1 | 25.7[5] | 6.7[2] | 10.3 | —[2] | 15.7 | 67.2[2] |
| Paraguay | 1981 | 506.1 | ——13.8—— | | 18.8 | 67.4 | 6.1 | 35.9 | 25.3 | 18.5 | 9.8 | 0.6 | 8.3 | 62.8 |
| Peru | 1982 | 2,940.3 | 19.6 | 0.3 | 1.7 | 78.4 | 12.0 | 44.2 | 22.2 | 21.0 | 36.8 | 0.6 | 12.5 | 29.1 |
| Philippines | 1986 | 5,394.3 | 13.2 | 1.8 | 17.0 | 68.0 | 14.4 | 15.5 | 38.0 | 11.3 | 24.9 | 0.4 | 17.2 | 46.2 |
| Pitcairn Island | ... | ... | ... | ... | ... | ... | ... | ... | ... | ... | ... | ... | ... | ... |
| Poland | 1985 | 10,836.4 | 15.4 | 3.9 | 22.2 | 58.4 | 8.9 | 30.5 | 19.0 | 19.5 | 1.2 | 47.9 | 0.6 | 30.7 |
| Portugal | 1986 | 9,396.5 | 19.4 | 1.3 | 15.3 | 64.0 | 11.3 | 29.3 | 23.3 | 58.9 | 6.8 | 1.1 | 3.6 | 29.6 |
| Puerto Rico | 1984[3] | 9,528.5 | ——20.3[4]—— | | 22.2 | 57.5[5] | 12.0 | 16.6 | 28.9[5] | 6.7 | 57.3 | 0.1 | 5.9 | 30.1 |
| Qatar | 1984 | 1,162.0 | 22.6 | 2.4 | 0.9 | 74.1 | 5.8 | 35.3 | 32.9 | 39.3 | 9.1 | 0.5 | 19.2 | 31.0 |
| Réunion | 1986 | 1,141.2 | 24.6 | 0.2 | 6.6 | 68.5 | 9.4 | 26.4 | 32.7 | 77.9 | 0.4 | — | 2.7 | 19.0 |
| Romania | 1985 | 12,167.0 | 10.6 | ——56.1[14]—— | | 33.3[15] | 6.8 | 22.2 | 4.3[15] | 10.2 | 3.1 | 43.1 | 1.1 | 42.6 |
| Rwanda | 1982 | 276.4 | ——17.6[4]—— | | 11.9 | 70.5[5] | 6.4 | 26.0 | 38.1[5] | 39.4 | 3.7 | 1.4 | 12.8 | 42.8 |
| St. Christopher and Nevis | 1982 | 43.8 | 26.2 | — | 11.3 | 62.5 | 9.3 | 18.9 | 34.3 | 19.8 | 36.3 | — | 3.8 | 40.1 |
| St. Helena and Ascension | 1984 | 4.3 | 39.0 | — | 11.7 | 49.2 | 6.8 | 15.7 | 26.7 | 57.0 | — | — | 0.2 | 42.8 |
| St. Lucia | 1983 | 106.8 | 28.4 | 0.2 | 12.2 | 59.2 | 12.0 | 17.2 | 30.0 | 19.2 | 35.4 | 0.2 | 4.7 | 40.5 |
| St. Pierre and Miquelon | 1984 | 43.9 | 19.4 | 0.1 | 29.9 | 50.6 | 4.3 | 27.4 | 18.8 | 46.1 | 0.3 | — | — | 53.5 |
| St. Vincent and the Grenadines | 1985 | 79.3 | 29.3 | 0.4[4] | 8.0 | 62.3[5] | 13.4 | 16.9 | 32.0[5] | 27.2 | 36.3 | 0.2 | 4.5 | 31.8 |
| San Marino[34] | ... | ... | ... | ... | ... | ... | ... | ... | ... | ... | ... | ... | ... | ... |
| São Tomé and Príncipe | 1977 | 14.8 | 46.5 | 3.0[14] | 1.9 | 45.7[15] | 10.1 | 12.8 | 22.8[15] | 89.1[2,21] | —[2,21] | —[2,21] | 0.5[2,21] | 10.4[2,21] |
| Saudi Arabia | 1985 | 23,622.6 | 15.6 | 0.4 | 0.5 | 83.5 | 6.5 | 35.8 | 41.3 | 35.2 | 17.0 | 0.6 | 19.0 | 28.2 |
| Senegal | 1981 | 1,077.4 | 28.3 | — | 30.4 | 41.3 | 7.6 | 17.5 | 16.2 | 48.6 | 4.5 | 2.6 | 1.3 | 43.0 |
| Seychelles | 1984 | 87.3 | 21.8 | 0.1 | 30.2 | 47.9 | 5.8 | 18.7 | 23.3 | 29.3 | 3.1 | 3.4 | 6.4 | 57.8 |
| Sierra Leone | 1983 | 165.7 | 28.5 | 0.4 | 34.7 | 36.4 | 5.5 | 14.9 | 15.9 | 40.7 | 3.5 | 0.7 | 4.6 | 50.5 |
| Singapore | 1986 | 25,511.7 | 12.2 | 0.6 | 19.8 | 67.4 | 5.8 | 37.4 | 24.1 | 11.6 | 15.0 | 0.3 | 19.9 | 53.2 |
| Solomon Islands | 1984 | 65.5 | 21.8 | 0.8 | 22.7 | 54.7 | 6.0 | 23.9 | 24.8 | 6.3 | 3.3 | 0.1 | 15.0 | 75.3 |
| Somalia | 1981 | 512.9 | 26.6 | — | 2.3 | 71.1 | 2.0 | 50.0 | 19.1 | 66.0 | 4.3 | 0.1 | 1.8 | 27.8 |
| South Africa[46] | 1982 | 16,941.1 | 5.6 | 1.5 | 0.4[47] | 92.4[48] | 8.6 | 42.9 | 41.0[48] | 38.2 | 14.6 | 0.4 | 10.1 | 36.8 |
| Bophuthatswana[46] | ... | ... | ... | ... | ... | ... | ... | ... | ... | ... | ... | ... | ... | ... |
| Ciskei[46] | ... | ... | ... | ... | ... | ... | ... | ... | ... | ... | ... | ... | ... | ... |
| KwaNdebele[46] | ... | ... | ... | ... | ... | ... | ... | ... | ... | ... | ... | ... | ... | ... |
| Transkei[46] | ... | ... | ... | ... | ... | ... | ... | ... | ... | ... | ... | ... | ... | ... |
| Venda[46] | ... | ... | ... | ... | ... | ... | ... | ... | ... | ... | ... | ... | ... | ... |
| South West Africa/Namibia[46] | 1985 | 560.1 | ... | ... | ... | ... | ... | ... | ... | ... | ... | ... | ... | ... |
| Spain | 1985 | 30,001.5 | 15.4 | 4.9 | 36.2 | 43.5 | 8.4 | 21.7 | 13.4 | 36.7 | 10.9 | 2.4 | 3.4 | 46.6 |
| Sri Lanka | 1984 | 1,847.5 | 16.8 | 0.8 | 25.7 | 56.7 | 8.3 | 24.3 | 24.1 | 14.3 | 8.9 | 0.7 | 16.6 | 59.4 |
| Sudan, The | 1983 | 1,354.4 | 18.6 | 0.3 | 26.6 | 54.6 | 11.0 | 26.6 | 17.0 | 38.3 | 9.1 | 1.5 | 3.2 | 47.9 |
| Suriname | 1976 | 281.0 | 11.9 | 2.3[14] | 27.2 | 57.7[15] | 11.5 | 29.8 | 16.4[15] | 22.2[50] | 28.3[50] | 1.2[50] | 6.2[50] | 42.2[50] |
| Swaziland | 1985 | 323.8 | ——12.6[4]—— | | 27.1 | 60.3 | 5.1 | 23.3 | 31.9 | ... | ... | ... | ... | ... |
| Sweden | 1986 | 32,509.0 | 10.0 | 1.8 | 10.8 | 77.5 | 9.7 | 36.1 | 31.6 | 57.2 | 7.8 | 3.7 | 5.5 | 25.7 |
| Switzerland | 1986 | 41,258.5 | 10.0 | 4.9 | 5.9 | 79.2 | 11.6 | 29.6 | 38.0 | 73.0 | 5.4 | 2.0 | 4.7 | 14.9 |
| Syria | 1984 | 4,115.8 | 21.4 | 0.3 | 34.3 | 44.0 | 7.4 | 19.1 | 17.4 | 28.2 | 3.4 | 14.1 | 4.6 | 49.6 |
| Taiwan | 1986 | 23,840.3 | 16.4 | 3.0 | 13.0 | 67.6 | 14.5 | 32.4 | 20.7 | 11.3 | 22.4 | — | 34.1 | 32.2 |
| Tanzania | 1981 | 867.3 | 7.6 | 0.6 | 30.8 | 61.0 | 10.0 | 35.0 | 16.1 | 42.5 | 1.8 | 1.1 | 11.5 | 43.2 |
| Thailand | 1984 | 10,525.9 | 9.1 | 2.5 | 23.5 | 64.8 | 12.5 | 30.0 | 22.3 | 12.5 | 13.4 | 1.1 | 26.9 | 46.0 |
| Togo | 1981 | 435.8 | 27.2 | 0.6 | 8.4 | 63.7 | 6.1 | 21.3 | 36.3 | 65.8 | 4.2 | 1.1 | 5.6 | 23.4 |
| Tokelau | 1982 | 0.6 | 55.7 | — | 33.4 | 11.1 | 5.7 | 1.1 | 4.3 | ... | ... | ... | ... | 100.0 |
| Tonga | 1984 | 41.0 | 35.0 | 0.7 | 14.0 | 50.4 | 6.0 | 13.6 | 30.7 | 2.8 | 5.5 | — | 11.4 | 80.3 |
| Trinidad and Tobago | 1985 | 1,526.1 | 25.5 | 1.4 | 3.3 | 69.8 | 9.5 | 30.4 | 29.9 | 18.7 | 39.1 | 0.1 | 9.5 | 32.6 |
| Tunisia | 1986 | 2,900.6 | 18.2 | 6.6 | 6.8 | 68.4 | 9.6 | 25.1 | 33.7 | 67.7 | 7.0 | 3.9 | 1.6 | 19.9 |
| Turkey | 1986 | 11,020.2 | 9.1 | 3.2 | 19.9 | 67.7 | 14.4 | 36.6 | 16.8 | 41.0 | 10.6 | 6.9 | 6.2 | 35.4 |
| Turks and Caicos Islands | 1984[11] | 26.3 | ——32.1[4]—— | | 11.6 | 56.3[5] | ... | ... | ... | ... | 74.7 | ... | ... | 25.3 |
| Tuvalu | 1983 | 2.7 | 36.8 | 0.2 | 14.0 | 49.0 | 6.9 | 12.3 | 29.7 | 2.5 | 0.5 | — | 2.1 | 94.9 |
| Uganda | 1984 | 344.1 | 8.7[20] | 0.7[20] | 29.6[20] | 61.0[20] | 11.1[20] | 26.8[20] | 23.0[20] | 32.7[2] | 1.0[2] | — | 5.5[2] | 60.8[2] |
| U.S.S.R. | 1986 | 88,906.0 | ——19.7—— | | | 80.3 | 7.4 | 40.7 | 32.3 | 11.5 | 1.8 | 53.2 | 3.5 | 29.9 |
| United Arab Emirates | 1982 | 9,439.9 | 10.3 | 0.5 | 6.0 | 83.1 | 5.4 | 40.6 | 37.1 | 37.9 | 13.8 | 0.4 | 19.2 | 28.7 |
| United Kingdom[30] | 1986 | 126,259.8 | 15.8 | 3.7 | 7.3 | 73.2 | 8.5 | 33.4 | 31.2 | 51.8 | 9.8 | 1.8 | 5.7 | 30.9 |
| United States[52] | 1986 | 387,054.0 | 9.0 | 2.0 | 10.3 | 78.7 | 4.0 | 43.0 | 31.7 | 20.5 | — | 0.6 | 22.1 | 56.8 |
| Uruguay | 1984 | 775.7 | 13.6 | 0.8 | 36.3 | 49.3 | 17.7 | 18.5 | 13.1 | 17.4 | 8.5 | 3.9 | 1.8 | 68.3 |
| Vanuatu | 1983 | 51.2 | 26.5 | 0.2 | 11.0 | 62.2 | 6.3 | 21.0 | 34.9 | 14.2 | 1.1 | — | 12.2 | 72.5 |
| Venezuela | 1982 | 13,393.2 | 16.3 | 1.4 | 0.6 | 81.6 | 8.9 | 43.3 | 29.4 | 21.9 | 45.8 | 0.2 | 10.2 | 22.0 |
| Vietnam | 1985 | 2,152.0[2] | ... | ... | ... | ... | ... | ... | ... | 2.8[2] | 1.0[2] | 70.5[2] | 7.7[2] | 18.0[2] |
| Virgin Islands (U.S.) | 1978 | 667.4 | 11.9 | — | 58.5 | 29.6 | 3.7 | 8.2 | 17.6 | 0.9 | 58.0 | 0.1 | 0.2 | 40.7 |
| Wallis and Futuna | 1981 | 6.4 | ——25.6[4]—— | | 18.1 | 56.4[5] | 26.0 | 16.3 | 14.1[5] | ... | ... | ... | ... | ... |
| West Bank | 1985 | 386.5 | ... | ... | ... | ... | ... | ... | ... | ... | ... | ... | ... | 100.0[53] |
| Western Sahara | ... | ... | ... | ... | ... | ... | ... | ... | ... | ... | ... | ... | ... | ... |
| Western Samoa | 1983 | 52.6 | 24.3 | 0.3 | 17.5 | 57.9 | 7.4 | 22.9 | 27.6 | 5.5 | 11.0 | — | 11.4 | 72.2 |
| Yemen (Aden) | 1977 | 544.0 | ——18.1[4]—— | | 46.6 | 35.2[5] | 2.0 | 22.7 | 10.6[5] | 18.4 | — | 4.0 | 11.3 | 66.4 |
| Yemen (San'ā') | 1981 | 1,608.8 | 32.2 | 0.1 | 8.3 | 59.4 | 5.6 | 25.4 | 28.4 | 30.8 | 2.8 | 1.2 | 17.7 | 47.5 |
| Yugoslavia | 1986 | 11,749.1 | 14.4 | 3.1 | 22.2 | 60.4 | 13.5 | 28.0 | 18.9 | 32.9 | 5.7 | 32.3 | 1.3 | 27.9 |
| Zaire | 1983 | 494.4 | 22.4[8] | 1.2[8] | 7.6[8] | 68.8[8] | 10.3[8] | 31.7[8] | 26.9[8] | 50.8 | 6.9 | 0.3 | 3.0 | 39.0 |
| Zambia | 1982 | 1,000.2 | 7.5 | 0.4 | 20.8 | 71.4 | 16.0 | 34.5 | 20.8 | 28.8 | 9.5 | 0.8 | 6.2 | 54.6 |
| Zimbabwe | 1984 | 959.4 | 10.8 | 0.3 | 21.4 | 67.5 | 14.8 | 31.1 | 21.6 | 28.9 | 9.3 | — | 5.3 | 56.5 |

[1]Year ending March 20.  [2]Estimated based on trading partners' information.  [3]Year ending June 30.  [4]Excluding precious stones, etc. (667).  [5]Including precious stones, etc. (667).  [6]Excluding fish imported for canneries.  [7]Trade with France and Spain only.  [8]1978.  [9]1984.  [10]Figures for Belgium–Luxembourg Economic Union (Luxembourg is also shown separately).  [11]Year ending March 31.  [12]Includes 87.9% from India.  [13]Includes 95.9% to India.  [14]Including metals.  [15]Excluding metals.  [16]1980.  [17]Includes 94.7% for ships' bunkers and stores.  [18]1981.  [19]1975.  [20]1976.  [21]1979.  [22]Figures for France include Monaco.  [23]Includes 91.9% from Israel.  [24]Includes 82.2% to Israel.  [25]Import figures refer to total trade turnover (figures are not available separately for imports and for exports).  [26]Excluding trade with East Germany (1.6% of total imports and 1.4% of total exports).  [27]Excluding petroleum products.  [28]Includes 77.7% for ships' bunkers.  [29]Domestic exports only.  [30]Figures for United Kingdom include Guernsey, Isle of Man, and Jersey (the latter is also shown separately).  [31]Year ending September 30.  [32]1977.  [33]Commercial imports only (excluding oil

| total value U.S.$ (000,000) | food and agricultural raw materials (0+1+2-27-28+4) | mineral ores and concentrates (27+28+667) | fuels and other energy (3) | manufactured goods total[a] (5+6-667+7+8+9) | of which chemicals and related products (5) | of which machinery and transport equipment (7) | of which other[a] (6-667+8+9) | to European Economic Community (EEC)[b] | to United States | to U.S.S.R. and Eastern Europe[c] | to Japan | to all other[d] | country |
|---|---|---|---|---|---|---|---|---|---|---|---|---|---|
| ... | ... | ... | ... | ... | ... | ... | ... | ... | ... | ... | ... | ... | Northern Mariana Islands |
| ... | ... | ... | ... | ... | ... | ... | ... | ... | ... | ... | ... | ... | Palau |
| 3,384.0 | 31.4 | 0.5 | 0.7 | 67.4 | 0.8 | 2.9 | 63.7 | 28.0 | 10.8 | 4.0 | 9.8 | 47.4 | Pakistan |
| 302.6 | 77.1 | 0.5 | 12.1 | 10.3 | 2.0 | 0.2 | 8.1 | 14.2 | 54.2 | 0.1 | 0.3 | 31.2 | Panama |
| 899.0 | 40.1[45] | 50.5[45] | 0.1[45] | 9.3[45] | 0.1[45] | 1.8[45] | 7.4[45] | 45.4[2] | 2.7 | 0.7[2] | 29.3 | 21.9[2] | Papua New Guinea |
| 295.5 | 90.6 | — | — | 9.4 | 4.1 | — | 5.2 | 25.9 | 5.6 | 0.3 | 8.4 | 59.7 | Paraguay |
| 2,812.8 | 16.2 | 15.3 | 26.4 | 42.1 | 1.6 | 1.2 | 39.3 | 20.2 | 35.8 | 1.6 | 15.1 | 27.3 | Peru |
| 5,680.1 | 33.5 | 5.4 | 1.5 | 59.6 | 4.9 | 7.9 | 46.7 | 18.9 | 35.5 | 0.4 | 17.6 | 27.7 | Philippines |
| ... | ... | ... | ... | ... | ... | ... | ... | ... | ... | ... | ... | ... | Pitcairn Island |
| 11,489.4 | 11.8 | 3.8 | 15.7 | 68.8 | 6.1 | 39.4 | 23.2 | 22.6 | 2.0 | 40.7 | 0.5 | 34.2 | Poland |
| 7,160.2 | 16.5 | 1.2 | 3.3 | 79.0 | 6.1 | 15.7 | 57.2 | 68.3 | 7.0 | 1.1 | 0.8 | 22.8 | Portugal |
| 9,146.0 | —17.64— | | 5.8 | 76.6[5] | 27.7 | 21.4 | 27.5[5] | 4.4 | 82.7 | — | 0.2 | 12.8 | Puerto Rico |
| 4,512.6 | —18 | —18 | 93.9[18] | 6.1[18] | 3.9[18] | —18 | 2.2[18] | 43.2[18] | 0.2[18] | —18 | 33.3[18] | 23.4[18] | Qatar |
| 130.5 | 86.2 | 0.1 | 0.3 | 13.4 | 4.3 | 5.0 | 4.1 | 88.2 | 0.2 | — | 2.3 | 9.3 | Réunion |
| 11,267.0 | 12.6 | —28.3[14]— | | 59.0[15] | 10.7 | 29.9 | 18.4[15] | 24.1 | 5.8 | 36.1 | 0.6 | 33.5 | Romania |
| 102.9 | —98.9— | | — | 1.1 | — | — | 1.1 | 48.1 | 33.3 | — | 1.4 | 17.3 | Rwanda |
| 18.8 | 68.6 | — | — | 31.4 | 0.6 | 14.7 | 16.1 | 45.5 | 28.1 | — | — | 26.4 | St. Christopher and Nevis |
| 0.04 | 100.0 | — | — | — | — | — | — | ... | ... | ... | ... | ... | St. Helena and Ascension |
| 47.5 | 57.2 | 0.1 | 0.1 | 42.6 | 1.5 | 13.7 | 27.4 | 41.2 | 10.6 | — | — | 48.1 | St. Lucia |
| 7.8 | 99.9 | — | — | 0.1 | — | — | 0.1 | 7.7 | 74.3 | — | — | 18.0 | St. Pierre and Miquelon |
| 63.2 | 85.7 | —4 | — | 14.2[5] | 0.8 | 4.0 | 9.4[5] | 28.2 | 9.7 | — | — | 62.1 | St. Vincent and the Grenadines |
| ... | ... | ... | ... | ... | ... | ... | ... | ... | ... | ... | ... | ... | San Marino[34] |
| 24.1 | 99.8 | ... | ... | 0.2 | — | 0.1 | 0.1 | 82.7[2,21] | —2,21 | —2,21 | —2,21 | 17.3[2,21] | São Tomé and Principe |
| 27,480.1 | 0.5 | 0.1 | 94.4 | 5.0 | 2.8 | 1.4 | 0.8 | 22.3[2] | 6.7[2] | 1.7[2] | 34.1[2] | 35.2[2] | Saudi Arabia |
| 560.8 | 28.8 | 14.1 | 37.4 | 19.7 | 6.0 | 4.0 | 9.7 | 32.9 | 0.2 | 0.8 | 1.6 | 64.5 | Senegal |
| 25.6 | 12.1 | 0.1 | 78.9 | 8.9 | 0.3 | 7.6 | 1.0 | 4.7 | 7.0 | — | 3.2 | 85.1 | Seychelles |
| 91.5 | 33.1 | 62.0 | 3.9 | 1.1 | 0.1 | — | 1.0 | 91.0 | 2.4 | — | — | 6.6 | Sierra Leone |
| 22,494.5 | 12.3 | 0.6 | 20.7 | 66.4 | 5.8 | 38.6 | 22.0 | 11.1 | 23.4 | 0.9 | 8.6 | 56.0 | Singapore |
| 92.5 | 96.7 | — | — | 3.3 | — | — | 3.3 | 34.1 | — | — | 33.2 | 32.6 | Solomon Islands |
| 152.0 | 99.4 | — | 0.2 | 0.4 | — | 0.1 | 0.2 | 6.2 | — | — | — | 93.7 | Somalia |
| 17,804.3 | 12.4 | 10.7 | 6.5 | 70.4[49] | 2.5 | 2.6 | 65.4[49] | 21.5 | 6.9 | 0.1 | 8.6 | 62.8 | South Africa[46] |
| ... | ... | ... | ... | ... | ... | ... | ... | ... | ... | ... | ... | ... | Bophuthatswana[46] |
| ... | ... | ... | ... | ... | ... | ... | ... | ... | ... | ... | ... | ... | Ciskei[46] |
| ... | ... | ... | ... | ... | ... | ... | ... | ... | ... | ... | ... | ... | KwaNdebele[46] |
| ... | ... | ... | ... | ... | ... | ... | ... | ... | ... | ... | ... | ... | Transkei[46] |
| | | | | | | | | | | | | | Venda[46] |
| 716.3 | ... | ... | ... | ... | ... | ... | ... | ... | ... | ... | ... | ... | South West Africa/Namibia[46] |
| 24,267.3 | 16.9 | 1.0 | 9.5 | 72.7 | 8.5 | 27.2 | 37.0 | 52.0 | 9.9 | 3.0 | 1.3 | 33.7 | Spain |
| 1,453.8 | 63.0 | 2.5 | 9.0 | 25.5 | 0.5 | 1.4 | 23.5 | 17.4 | 19.3 | 6.2 | 4.3 | 52.9 | Sri Lanka |
| 623.5 | 93.9 | 0.3 | 2.7 | 3.1 | — | 2.2 | 0.9 | 25.2 | 2.0 | 7.7 | 5.4 | 59.7 | Sudan, The |
| 274.6 | 21.6 | 32.7[14] | — | 45.7[15] | 43.1 | 0.5 | 2.1[15] | 35.7[50] | 19.3[50] | —50 | 3.7[50] | 41.2[50] | Suriname |
| 176.4 | 63.8[45] | —45 | 0.8[45] | 35.3[45] | 15.8[45] | 4.3[45] | 15.2[45] | ... | ... | ... | ... | ... | Swaziland |
| 37,221.9 | 9.8 | 1.7 | 2.9 | 85.7 | 6.7 | 43.8 | 35.2 | 50.0 | 11.4 | 2.2 | 1.4 | 35.0 | Sweden |
| 37,608.6 | 4.0 | 4.5 | 0.2 | 91.3 | 21.6 | 32.5 | 37.2 | 54.9 | 9.5 | 3.0 | 3.2 | 29.4 | Switzerland |
| 1,853.4 | 22.2 | 1.4 | 63.1 | 13.3 | 3.6 | 0.9 | 8.8 | 39.3 | 0.1 | 43.1 | 0.1 | 17.3 | Syria |
| 39,135.0 | 7.4 | 0.2 | 1.0 | 91.3 | 2.7 | 29.1 | 59.5 | 10.7 | 47.8 | — | 11.4 | 30.1 | Taiwan |
| 564.3 | 82.4 | 10.1 | 0.2 | 7.3 | 0.7 | 2.5 | 4.1 | 45.5 | 3.5 | 2.7 | 2.8 | 45.5 | Tanzania |
| 7,412.9 | 60.0 | 4.8 | 0.7 | 34.5 | 1.0 | 7.3 | 26.2 | 20.7 | 17.2 | 1.4 | 13.0 | 47.7 | Thailand |
| 208.2 | 32.1 | 50.6 | 1.3 | 16.0 | — | 1.4 | 14.6 | 60.8 | — | 1.5 | 0.4 | 37.3 | Togo |
| 0.1 | 100.0 | — | — | ... | ... | ... | ... | ... | ... | ... | ... | ... | Tokelau |
| 9.2 | 86.7 | — | 0.1 | 13.2 | 0.1 | 3.6 | 9.5 | 6.6 | 8.8 | — | 0.1 | 84.5 | Tonga |
| 2,141.7 | 2.2 | 0.3 | 79.7 | 17.8 | 12.2 | 2.9 | 2.7 | 13.6 | 60.9 | — | 0.1 | 25.5 | Trinidad and Tobago |
| 1,759.6 | 13.0 | 2.7 | 24.3 | 60.1 | 20.0 | 5.3 | 34.8 | 73.8 | 0.7 | 3.6 | 0.1 | 21.8 | Tunisia |
| 7,456.7 | 34.6 | 3.3 | 2.5 | 59.6 | 5.5 | 5.6 | 48.6 | 43.8 | 7.4 | 3.8 | 1.3 | 43.7 | Turkey |
| 3.0 | 100.0 | — | — | — | — | — | — | — | 100.0 | — | — | — | Turks and Caicos Islands |
| 0.1 | 78.8 | — | — | 21.2 | — | — | 21.2 | — | — | — | — | 100.0[51] | Tuvalu |
| 398.6 | 96.6[20] | 0.2[20] | 0.8[20] | 2.4[20] | — | — | 2.4[20] | 55.5[2] | 22.2[2] | — | 6.7[2] | 15.6[2] | Uganda |
| 97,164.0 | 6.6 | 2.4[4] | 47.3 | 43.7[5] | 3.1 | 15.0 | 25.5[5] | 13.2 | 0.5 | 52.6 | 1.4 | 32.4 | U.S.S.R. |
| 17,333.2 | 0.9 | — | 92.2 | 6.8 | 0.2 | 1.9 | 4.7 | 13.2 | 3.8 | — | 33.8 | 49.1 | United Arab Emirates |
| 107,104.3 | 9.2 | 3.4 | 11.9 | 75.5 | 13.3 | 34.7 | 27.5 | 48.0 | 14.2 | 1.6 | 1.6 | 34.5 | United Kingdom[30] |
| 217,335.9 | 16.3 | 2.2 | 3.8 | 77.8 | 10.3 | 45.7 | 21.7 | 24.1 | — | 0.9 | 12.2 | 62.7 | United States[52] |
| 924.9 | 61.9 | 0.1 | 0.3 | 37.6 | 3.8 | 1.4 | 32.4 | 21.3 | 13.6 | 8.0 | 2.8 | 54.4 | Uruguay |
| 29.6 | 99.3[29] | —29 | —29 | 0.7[29] | —29 | —29 | 0.7[29] | 46.2 | 18.2 | — | 12.6 | 23.0 | Vanuatu |
| 16,498.8 | 0.6 | 0.9 | 94.7 | 3.8 | 0.8 | 0.4 | 2.5 | 17.9 | 28.6 | 0.2 | 3.4 | 50.0 | Venezuela |
| 734.0[2] | ... | ... | ... | ... | ... | ... | ... | 2.8[2] | —2 | 55.2[2] | 8.1[2] | 33.9[2] | Vietnam |
| 2,512.1 | — | — | 91.3 | 8.7 | 6.2 | — | 2.5 | 1.0 | 96.8 | 1.3 | 0.1 | 0.8 | Virgin Islands (U.S.) |
| ... | ... | ... | ... | ... | ... | ... | ... | ... | ... | ... | ... | ... | Wallis and Futuna |
| 166.4 | ... | ... | ... | ... | ... | ... | ... | ... | ... | ... | ... | 100.0[54] | West Bank |
| ... | ... | ... | ... | ... | ... | ... | ... | ... | ... | ... | ... | ... | Western Sahara |
| 18.6 | 90.6 | — | — | 9.4 | — | 5.8 | 3.6 | 11.6 | 31.7 | — | 3.6 | 53.1 | Western Samoa |
| 180.8 | —15.5[54]— | | 84.0 | 0.5[5] | — | 0.4 | 0.1[5] | 1.8 | — | — | 9.6 | 88.6 | Yemen (Aden) |
| 47.5 | 23.8 | — | — | 76.2 | 1.6 | 64.5 | 10.2 | 24.6 | 3.0 | 0.1 | 0.1 | 72.3 | Yemen (Şan'ā') |
| 10,297.5 | 12.2 | 0.6 | 2.0 | 85.2 | 11.6 | 33.9 | 39.6 | 25.2 | 5.5 | 47.8 | 0.2 | 21.3 | Yugoslavia |
| 1,559.5 | 13.0 | 70.8 | 11.1 | 5.0 | — | — | ... | 51.8[2] | 22.0[2] | —2 | 4.9[2] | 21.3[2] | Zaire |
| 1,021.8 | 0.4[21] | 0.6[21] | 1.2[21] | 97.7[21,55] | 0.2[21] | 0.3[21] | 97.2[21,55] | 41.0 | 2.6 | 0.5 | 21.3 | 34.5 | Zambia |
| 1,004.3 | 47.9 | 7.3 | 1.3 | 43.4 | 1.9 | 1.8 | 39.8 | 34.7 | 6.2 | — | 5.2 | 53.8 | Zimbabwe |

companies' imports). [34]Figures for Italy include San Marino. [35]Includes 84.9% from United Kingdom. [36]Including coins. [37]Includes 67.3% to United States. [38]Includes 97.1% from Customs Union of Southern Africa. [39]Includes 52.9% from France in 1984. [40]Includes 70.2% to France. [41]Based on trade with Australia and New Zealand only; year ending June 30. [42]Curaçao only. [43]Includes 49.2% from Australia. [44]Includes 62.6% to Australia. [45]1982. [46]Figures for South Africa refer to Customs Union of Southern Africa (includes South Africa, Botswana, Lesotho, and Swaziland, also shown separately; also South West Africa/Namibia, Bophuthatswana, Ciskei, KwaNdebele, Transkei, and Venda). [47]Excluding crude oil. [48]Including crude oil (included in "special transactions" accounting in total for 23.4%. [49]Including gold (included in "special transactions" accounting in total for 54.4%. [50]1983. [51]All to Fiji. [52]Figures for United States include Virgin Islands (U.S.), American Samoa, Puerto Rico, and Guam, also shown separately. [53]Includes 87.8% from Israel. [54]Includes 57.8% to Israel, 41.6% to Jordan. [55]Includes copper 81.8%.

# Trade: domestic

The following table presents data relating to domestic wholesale and retail trade for the countries of the world. The section on wholesale trade is based for the most part on establishments engaged primarily in selling goods to retailers and distributors for resale or to purchasers who buy for business and farm uses. The retail trade section is based on businesses engaged in selling merchandise for personal or household consumption; restaurants are, when possible, included, hotels excluded.

The data presented here are based on information received from a variety of direct country and international sources. The direct country sources include such items as correspondence, statistical abstracts, annual reports, and censuses of business and trade. Among the more useful international sources are the various compilations of the United Nations dealing with domestic trade and Euromonitor's *Retail Trade International* (2 vols.).

Since there is no single published source or common international methodology for the compilation of data on wholesale and retail trade, nor a single current year on which, by common agreement, the various national reports would be based, allowance must be made for variations in the meaning and recency of the information provided for any single country and for its comparability internationally. Variations occur in part because of the ways in which countries define wholesale and retail trade; the conventional capitalist, or free-enterprise, distinctions between wholesale and retail activity (of a single enterprise or an entire national trade sector) may not exist in the business practice of some countries, and data may overlap in their final reports. Variations also exist in the kind and level of detail reported. For example, countries may design surveys differently according to the size (number of employees, sales, surface area) of establishments surveyed, their profitability, or other less direct criteria, such as ownership or location. The depth of analysis to which the data are subjected may also vary. The structure of a national trade sector is also affected by the degree of government involvement, which may range from total control of wholesale distribution in some socialist countries, to partial involvement in some strategic sectors, or to relative noninvolvement in fully private trade sectors of capitalist countries. In some smaller countries data may refer to a single trading enterprise.

At the table's extreme left, preceding the year to which the trade data refer, the combined value of the country's wholesale and retail trade as a percentage of gross domestic product or net material product is given. Unless otherwise noted, GDP data include restaurants and exclude hotels.

Both the wholesale and retail sections of the table provide similar detail: establishments or outlets, employees, sales, and derived values for relationships among these measures; the retail section provides an additional breakdown of sales by an end-use classification of retail sales outlets.

Although all sales figures are given in U.S. dollars, the comparability of these dollar figures may differ considerably; for instance, the purchasing power of various national currencies in domestic transactions may bear only a distant relationship to the exchange rate of the same currency in international transactions. The price of goods may also vary, depending on the degree to which they are subject to direct subsidies and artificial cost controls such as tax, investment, or free-trade preferences by a central government seeking to influence social or economic conditions.

## Trade: domestic

| country | domestic trade as percentage of GDP, 1984 | year | wholesale trade | | | | | retail trade | | |
|---|---|---|---|---|---|---|---|---|---|---|
| | | | establishments[a] | employees[b] | sales[c] $'000,000 | employees per establishment | sales per establishment $'000 | outlets[a] | employees[b] | sales[c] $'000,000 |
| Afghanistan | 10.1[1,2] | 1979–80 | ... | [3] | ... | ... | ... | ... | 146,075[3,4] | ... |
| Albania | 9.5[5] | 1983 | ... | ... | ... | ... | ... | 10,585[6] | ... | 994[6] |
| Algeria | 9.2[7] | 1971 | ... | [3] | ... | ... | ... | 3,600[8] | 65,917[3,9] | 12,607[10] |
| American Samoa | ... | 1985 | 40 | 77[11] | ... | ... | ... | 300 | 499[11] | ... |
| Andorra | 25.2[7] | 1972 | ... | ... | ... | ... | ... | 592 | 2,264 | ... |
| Angola | 4.8[12] | 1973 | [3] | ... | ... | ... | ... | 29,138[3] | ... | ... |
| Anguilla | ... | 1984 | [3] | [3] | ... | [3] | ... | 92[3] | 291[3] | ... |
| Antigua and Barbuda | 27.6[2] | 1980 | 25 | 350 | ... | 14.0 | ... | 199 | 1,000 | 23[10] |
| Argentina | 12.7[13] | 1974 | 45,700 | 275,000[4] | 10,922[14] | 6.0[4] | ... | 445,798[15] | 930,000[4,15] | 15,540[10] |
| Aruba | ... | 1983 | ... | [3] | ... | ... | ... | ... | 3,192[3,16] | 17 |
| Australia | 13.4 | 1979–80 | 39,319[18] | 361,000[4,18] | 84,798[18] | 9.2[4,18] | 2,157[18] | 110,500 | 737,378[4] | 43,952 |
| Austria | 16.1[2] | 1984 | 15,330[10] | 168,572[4,10] | 34,819[10] | 11.0[4,10] | 2,271[10] | 42,491[10] | 249,646[4,10] | 17,015[10] |
| Bahamas, The[19] | 26.2[2] | 1980 | 23 | 1,066 | 143 | 46.3 | 6.235 | 132 | 4,059 | 2577 |
| Bahrain | 9.3[7] | 1983 | [3] | [3] | ... | [3] | ... | 255[3] | 12,551[3] | 1,601 |
| Bangladesh | 8.8 | 1983 | ... | [3] | ... | ... | ... | ... | 146,000[3,20] | 4,800 |
| Barbados | 26.9[2] | 1979 | ... | [3] | ... | ... | ... | 1,911 | 5,800[3,15] | 264[10] |
| Belgium | 19.7[15] | 1984 | 57,079[7] | 166,900[12] | 65,286[7] | 3.0[12] | 1,144[7] | 121,690[7] | 159,848[7] | 26,497 |
| Belize | 15.5[2] | 1983 | ... | ... | ... | ... | ... | ... | ... | 23 |
| Benin | 22.4[2,10] | 1979 | ... | ... | ... | ... | ... | 170[8] | 1,910[4,8] | 150[10] |
| Bermuda | ... | 1985 | 60[21] | 820 | ... | ... | ... | 310[8,12] | 4,342[15] | 116[15,22] |
| Bhutan | 2.9[7] | 1982 | ... | [3] | ... | ... | ... | ... | 9,000[3,4] | ... |
| Bolivia | 13.8 | 1983 | ... | [3] | ... | ... | ... | ... | 17,414[3,23] | 1,818 |
| Botswana | 22.8[2] | 1982–83 | 164[21] | 1,800 | 447 | 9.8[21] | 2,933[21] | 1,333[21] | 5,200 | 149 |
| Brazil | 16.4[2] | 1980 | 45,969 | 370,000 | 91,331 | 8.0 | 1,987 | 885,558 | 1,435,000 | 82,481 |
| British Virgin Islands | 26.7[2,5] | 1982 | ... | ... | ... | ... | ... | ... | 366 | 5[12] |
| Brunei | 11.2[2] | 1984 | [3] | [3] | ... | [3] | ... | 887[3,27] | 3,883[3,27] | ... |
| Bulgaria | 5.3[1,2] | 1983 | ... | 7,600 | ... | ... | ... | 44,127[15] | 93,600[15] | 11,060[15] |
| Burkina Faso | 12.9[2,10] | 1975 | ... | [3] | ... | ... | ... | ... | 19,354[3,4] | ... |
| Burma | 24.3[15] | 1983 | ... | ... | ... | ... | ... | ... | ... | 2,116 |
| Burundi | 8.5[2] | 1981 | ... | ... | ... | ... | ... | ... | 1 | 445 |
| Cameroon | 13.0[2] | 1980 | ... | ... | ... | ... | ... | 1,312[8] | 13,776[4,8] | 753[10] |
| Canada | 9.3[2] | 1985 | ... | 451,665[10] | 65,813[7] | ... | ... | ... | 1,138,500[15] | 102,643 |
| Cape Verde | ... | ... | ... | ... | ... | ... | ... | ... | ... | ... |
| Cayman Islands | 17.0[16] | 1979 | ... | [3] | ... | ... | ... | ... | 1,518[3] | ... |
| Central African Republic | 27.3[5] | 1978[2] | [3] | [3] | [3] | ... | [3] | 102[3,8] | 26,659[3,4,28] | 252[3,8] |
| Chad | 30.1[2,9] | 1983 | ... | [3] | [3] | ... | ... | ... | 1,661[3,8,23] | 497[3] |
| Chile | 16.7[2,13] | 1983 | 561[8] | 15,300[8] | 2,312[8] | 27.2[8] | 4,121[8] | 1,125[8,15] | 21,700[8,15] | 1,403[8,15] |
| China | 4.6[2,10] | 1985 | 67,000 | 1,067,000[4] | ... | 15.9[4] | ... | 7,783,000[15] | 17,960,000[4,15] | 145,534[15,22] |
| Christmas Island | ... | 1981 | — | [3] | — | — | — | 5 | 65[3] | ... |
| Cocos (Keeling) Islands | ... | 1981 | ... | [3] | ... | ... | ... | 1 | 13[3] | ... |
| Colombia | 14.0[2] | 1983 | ... | ... | ... | ... | ... | ... | ... | 6,285 |
| Comoros | 14.8[2,7] | 1974 | ... | [3] | ... | ... | ... | ... | 983[3,8,30] | ... |
| Congo | 10.7[2] | ... | ... | ... | ... | ... | ... | ... | ... | ... |
| Cook Islands | 24.0[5] | 1982[31] | [3] | [3] | [3] | ... | [3] | 109[3] | 369[3] | 31[3] |
| Costa Rica | 19.6[2] | 1975 | 332[32] | 4,073[32] | 35[32] | 12.3[32] | 104[32] | 9,713 | 26,486 | 475[10] |
| Côte d'Ivoire | 17.1[2,11] | 1981 | ... | ... | [3] | ... | ... | 2,023[8] | 16,720[8] | 1,548[3,10] |
| Cuba | 37.4[1,2] | 1985 | ... | ... | 11,079 | ... | ... | 56,916 | ... | 8,530 |
| Cyprus | 17.8[2] | 1983 | 1,538 | 8,000 | 1,128 | 5.2 | 733 | 8,312 | 8,500 | 1,044 |
| Czechoslovakia | 16.3[1,2] | 1984 | ... | ... | ... | ... | ... | 63,503 | 247,284 | 42,740 |
| Denmark | 12.4[2] | 1983 | 5,692 | 124,000 | 27,933 | 21.8 | 4,907 | 50,826[12] | 116,000[12] | 15,796[12] |
| Djibouti | 15.6[2] | 1985 | 28 | 371[7] | ... | ... | ... | 431 | 1,877[7] | ... |
| Dominica | 8.9[2] | 1983 | ... | [3] | ... | ... | ... | ... | 1,597[3,12] | 4 |
| Dominican Republic | 16.6[15] | 1983 | 670 | ... | 3,136 | ... | 4,681 | 11,220[7] | ... | 1,259[7] |
| Ecuador | 16.5[2] | 1980[2] | 2,450 | 15,591[4] | 2,805 | 6.4[4] | 1,145 | 102,981 | 179,847[4] | 5,922 |
| Egypt | 12.8[2,33] | 1980–81[8] | 1,766 | 42,300[4] | 3,216 | 24.0[4] | 1,821 | 2,136 | 48,200[4] | 2,015 |

The data on distribution of retail sales by kind of consumer goods may have their origin in several different types of data or analysis: One country may aggregate sales data by kind of establishment only (this may be perfectly satisfactory in a country of small, independent outlets); another may aggregate data directly by kind of goods (most easily done in a country with well-developed statistical, tax-reporting, and commercial systems). Other countries may find it impolitic to publish data that reflect the poverty of their distribution network or their supply of consumer goods and may aggregate or publish data for only a few sectors: food or nonfood goods, for example. For countries with only a few trading enterprises in a particular sector, detail must often be withheld to preserve the confidentiality of individual businesses.

The notes that follow further define the various headings.

a. The number of establishments or outlets refers to economic units that operate at a single physical location in one principal kind of activity, whether singly owned or part of a multiunit firm. Such units are not necessarily identical with a company or enterprise.

b. Number of employees refers to full-time and part-time paid workers, including salaried managers and officers; it usually excludes owner-operators, partners, vendors, and unpaid relatives.

c. Total sales (also called turnover) includes the value of merchandise sold for cash or credit; amounts received from customers for layaway purchases; receipts from rental or leasing of vehicles, equipment, tools, instruments, etc.; receipts for delivery, installation, maintenance, repair, alteration, storage, and other services.

d. Outlets engaged primarily in the sale of food and nonalcoholic beverages, such as grocery stores, meat and fish markets, and bakeries.

e. Outlets engaged primarily in the sale of clothing and shoes; also includes outlets that sell accessory items, such as millinery, furs, and leather goods.

f. Outlets engaged primarily in the sale of home furnishings, including furniture, draperies, floor coverings, household appliances, and home entertainment equipment.

g. Outlets that primarily serve food and drink, including restaurants, lunchrooms, cafeterias, social caterers, refreshment places, contract feeders, ice cream parlors, and bars and taverns.

h. Outlets engaged primarily in the sale of pharmaceuticals, cosmetics, and perfumes.

i. Outlets engaged primarily in the sale of building materials, hardware, garden supplies, paint, electrical supplies, and farm equipment.

j. Outlets engaged primarily in the sale of motor vehicles, motorcycles, bicycles, and tires, batteries, and other automotive supplies and parts; includes service stations.

k. Outlets engaged in the sale of multiple lines of merchandise, such as department stores, variety stores, and rural general stores.

l. Miscellaneous specialized outlets such as those engaged primarily in the sale of liquors, sporting goods, books, jewelry, photographic and optical goods, gifts, flowers, tobacco products, home fuels, and newspapers.

| retail trade (continued) | | | | | | | | | | | | country |
|---|---|---|---|---|---|---|---|---|---|---|---|---|
| percent breakdown of sales | | | | | | | | | employees per outlet | sales per outlet $'000 | population per outlet | |
| food[d] | clothing, shoes[e] | home furnishings[f] | eating, drinking[g] | drugs, pharmaceuticals[h] | building materials[i] | automobile parts[j] | general merchandise[k] | other[l] | | | | |
| ... | ... | ... | ... | ... | ... | ... | ... | ... | ... | ... | ... | Afghanistan |
| 61.5 | | | | 38.5 | | | | | ... | 936[6] | 268[6] | Albania |
| ... | ... | ... | ... | ... | ... | ... | ... | ... | 5.0[8] | ... | 5,146[8] | Algeria |
| ... | ... | ... | ... | ... | ... | ... | ... | ... | ... | ... | 119 | American Samoa |
| ... | ... | ... | ... | ... | ... | ... | ... | ... | 3.8 | ... | 39 | Andorra |
| ... | ... | ... | ... | ... | ... | ... | ... | ... | ... | ... | ... | Angola |
| ... | ... | ... | ... | ... | ... | ... | ... | ... | 3.2[3] | ... | 733[3] | Anguilla |
| ... | ... | ... | ... | ... | ... | ... | ... | ... | 5.0 | 100 | 378 | Antigua and Barbuda |
| ... | ... | ... | ... | ... | ... | ... | ... | ... | 2.1[4,15] | ... | 58[15] | Argentina |
| ... | ... | ... | ... | ... | ... | ... | ... | ... | ... | ... | ... | Aruba |
| 28.8 | 7.0 | 6.5 | 6.3[2] | 2.8 | 1.1 | 30.0 | 9.6 | 7.9 | 6.7[4] | 398 | 132 | Australia |
| 30.0 | 14.5 | 10.3 | ... | 4.8 | ... | 13.7 | 10.1 | 16.6 | 5.9[4,10] | 400[10] | 178 | Austria |
| 24.4[7] | 7.7[7] | 7.1[7] | — | 3.7[7] | 8.4[7] | 30.1[7] | 7.6[7] | 11.0[7] | 30.8 | 1,881 | 1,026 | Bahamas, The[19] |
| ... | ... | ... | ... | ... | ... | ... | ... | ... | 49.2[3] | ... | 1,507[3] | Bahrain |
| ... | ... | ... | ... | ... | ... | ... | ... | ... | ... | ... | ... | Bangladesh |
| ... | ... | ... | ... | ... | ... | ... | ... | ... | ... | ... | 130 | Barbados |
| 35.1 | | | | 64.9 | | | | | 1.2[7] | 218[7] | 817 | Belgium |
| ... | ... | ... | ... | ... | ... | ... | ... | ... | ... | ... | ... | Belize |
| ... | ... | ... | ... | ... | ... | ... | ... | ... | 11.3[4,8] | ... | 19,871[8] | Benin |
| ... | ... | ... | ... | ... | ... | ... | ... | ... | 11.0[10,15] | ... | 178[8,12] | Bermuda |
| ... | ... | ... | ... | ... | ... | ... | ... | ... | ... | ... | ... | Bhutan |
| ... | ... | ... | ... | ... | ... | ... | ... | ... | ... | ... | ... | Bolivia |
| ... | ... | ... | ... | ... | ... | ... | ... | ... | 2.7[21] | 120[21] | 645[21] | Botswana |
| 15.0[22,24] | 7.2[22] | 13.0[22,25] | ... | 4.7[22] | [25] | 27.3[22,26] | 19.3[22] | 13.5[22] | 1.6 | 93 | 137 | Brazil |
| ... | ... | ... | ... | ... | ... | ... | ... | ... | ... | ... | ... | British Virgin Islands |
| ... | ... | ... | ... | ... | ... | ... | ... | ... | 4.4[3,27] | ... | 2463[3,27] | Brunei |
| 43.9[12] | 8.5[12] | 4.0[12] | ... | 6.3[12] | ... | ... | 19.0[12] | 18.3[12] | 2.1[15] | 251[15] | 203[15] | Bulgaria |
| ... | ... | ... | ... | ... | ... | ... | ... | ... | ... | ... | ... | Burkina Faso |
| ... | ... | ... | ... | ... | ... | ... | ... | ... | ... | ... | ... | Burma |
| ... | ... | ... | ... | ... | ... | ... | ... | ... | ... | ... | ... | Burundi |
| ... | ... | ... | ... | ... | ... | ... | ... | ... | 10.5[4,8] | ... | 6,481[8] | Cameroon |
| 23.0 | 5.0 | 2.3 | 8.4 | 3.9 | 0.8 | 29.1 | 12.8 | 14.7 | ... | ... | ... | Canada |
| ... | ... | ... | ... | ... | ... | ... | ... | ... | ... | ... | ... | Cape Verde |
| ... | ... | ... | ... | ... | ... | ... | ... | ... | ... | ... | ... | Cayman Islands |
| ... | ... | ... | ... | ... | ... | ... | ... | ... | ... | 2,471[3,8] | 21,774[3,8] | Central African Republic |
| ... | ... | ... | ... | ... | ... | ... | ... | ... | ... | ... | ... | Chad |
| 28.3[7] | 29[7] | 5.0[7] | 1.6[7] | 5.4[7] | 4.7[7] | 18.0[7] | 17.1[7,29] | 19.9[7] | 19.3[9,15] | 1,247[9,15] | 10,336[9,15] | Chile |
| 45.8[22] | 16.9[22] | | | 37.3[22] | | | | | 2.4[4,15] | 22[15,22] | 134[15] | China |
| ... | ... | ... | ... | ... | ... | ... | ... | ... | ... | ... | 662 | Christmas Island |
| ... | ... | ... | ... | ... | ... | ... | ... | ... | ... | ... | 569 | Cocos (Keeling) Islands |
| ... | ... | ... | ... | ... | ... | ... | ... | ... | ... | ... | ... | Colombia |
| ... | ... | ... | ... | ... | ... | ... | ... | ... | ... | ... | ... | Comoros |
| ... | ... | ... | ... | ... | ... | ... | ... | ... | ... | ... | ... | Congo |
| ... | ... | ... | ... | ... | ... | ... | ... | ... | 3.4[3] | 284[3] | 84[3] | Cook Islands |
| 37.7 | 13.5 | 6.9 | ... | 8.2 | 7.0 | 15.1 | 5.9 | 5.7 | 2.7 | 59 | 202 | Costa Rica |
| ... | ... | ... | ... | ... | ... | ... | ... | ... | 8.3[8] | ... | 4,257[8] | Côte d'Ivoire |
| 35.0 | ... | ... | 29.3 | 3.2 | ... | 3.0 | ... | 29.5 | ... | 150 | 177 | Cuba |
| 20.2[7] | 9.9[7] | 7.0[7] | ... | 1.7[7] | 9.2[7] | 37.3[7] | 4.7[7] | 10.0[7] | 1.0 | 126 | 78 | Cyprus |
| 37.7 | 15.0 | 11.4 | ... | 3.5 | 2.2 | 6.7 | ... | 23.5 | 3.9 | 673 | 243 | Czechoslovakia |
| 48.9[7] | 6.7[7] | 7.7[7] | —[7] | 0.6[7] | 2.6[7] | 15.0[7] | 8.6[7] | 9.9[7] | 2.3[12] | 311[12] | 101[12] | Denmark |
| ... | ... | ... | ... | ... | ... | ... | ... | ... | ... | ... | 998 | Djibouti |
| ... | ... | ... | ... | ... | ... | ... | ... | ... | ... | ... | ... | Dominica |
| ... | ... | ... | ... | ... | ... | ... | ... | ... | ... | 1127 | 519[7] | Dominican Republic |
| 24.2 | 29.1 | 8.1 | 3.0 | 4.8 | 4.0 | 17.8 | 3.4 | 5.6 | 1.7[4] | 58 | 79 | Ecuador |
| ... | ... | ... | ... | ... | ... | ... | ... | ... | 22.6[4] | 943 | 20,036 | Egypt |

## Trade: domestic (continued)

| country | domestic trade as percentage of GDP, 1984 | year | wholesale trade | | | | | retail trade | | |
|---|---|---|---|---|---|---|---|---|---|---|
| | | | establishments[a] | employees[b] | sales[c] $'000,000 | employees per establishment | sales per establishment $'000 | outlets[a] | employees[b] | sales[c] $'000,000 |
| El Salvador | 27.5[2] | 1982 | 384 | 6,800 | 629 | 17.7 | 1,638 | 1,435 | 10,900 | 443 |
| Equatorial Guinea | ... | ... | ... | ... | | | | ... | ... | |
| Ethiopia | 10.3 | 1973[8,35] | 375 | 3,200 | [3] | 8.5 | | 7,416 | 17,100 | 201 |
| Faeroe Islands | 11.7[2,11] | 1984 | 87 | [3] | | | | 570[2] | 1,484[2,3,11] | |
| Falkland Islands | ... | 1976 | 2 | | | | | 21 | | |
| Fiji | 16.0[2] | 1983 | 138[8] | 2,000[8] | 248[8] | 14.5[8] | 1,797[8] | 578[8] | 6,000[8] | 351[8] |
| Finland | 9.9[2] | 1984 | 8,186[7] | 85,900[4,7] | 27,300[7] | 10.5[4,7] | 3,335[7] | 36,177[7] | 166,900[4,7] | 18,173[7] |
| France | 11.8[2] | 1984 | 132,909 | 866,415 | 181,802 | 6.5 | 1,368 | 607,661 | 1,226,751 | 126,750 |
| French Guiana | | 1981 | [3] | [3] | | | | 113[3,8] | 372[3,8] | |
| French Polynesia | 24.1[2,7] | 1983 | | [3] | | | | | 1,535[3] | |
| Gabon | 8.2[10] | 1982 | ... | | | | | ... | 12,683[3,4,12] | ... |
| Gambia, The | 23.7[10] | 1983 | ... | 1,900 | | | | ... | 500 | |
| Gaza Strip | | 1985 | | [3] | | | | | 1,000[3] | |
| Germany, East | 9.6[1,2] | 1984 | | | | | | 102,900[10] | 898,500[4,10] | 39,060[10] |
| Germany, West | 10.7[2] | 1983 | 36,318[21] | 947,700[4] | 288,606 | 27.3[4,21] | 9,647 | 249,466[21] | 2,004,900[4] | 145,805 |
| Ghana | 24.3[2,10] | 1977[8] | 460 | 1,100 | 115 | 2.4 | 250 | 2,182 | 5,700 | 237 |
| Gibraltar | | 1981 | | 552 | | | | | 1,443 | |
| Greece | 11.3[15] | 1978 | 25,266 | 59,648 | | 2.4 | | 160,599 | 64,201 | 12,263[22] |
| Greenland | 8.0[21] | 1986 | | [3] | 130 | | | | 2,153[3,4,23] | 108 |
| Grenada | 21.6[2] | 1983 | | [3] | [3] | | | | 2,813[3,12] | 6[3] |
| Guadeloupe | 17.5[2,11] | 1983 | | [3] | | | | | 2,994[3,12] | 212 |
| Guam | | 1982 | 89 | 981 | 165 | 11.0 | 1,853 | 802 | 5,400 | 413 |
| Guatemala | 26.0[15] | 1982 | | [3] | | | | 88,200 | 51,700[3,4,11] | 712[10] |
| Guernsey | ... | 1976 | | [3] | | | | | 2,805[3] | |
| Guinea | 21.5[13] | 1979 | | [3] | | | | | 12,808[3,30] | |
| Guinea-Bissau | | 1977 | [3] | [3] | | | | 685[3] | 516[3] | 443[3,23] |
| Guyana | 7.4[15] | 1980[8] | | | | | | 147 | | 93[10] |
| Haiti | 17.8[2] | 1983 | | [3] | | | | 653[8,28] | 3,900[3,4,16] | 174 |
| Honduras | 11.6[15] | 1983 | | | | | | | 45,900[9] | 401 |
| Hong Kong | 20.4[2] | 1985[37] | 11,709 | 58,655[4] | 6,694[11] | 5.0[4] | 711[11] | 48,933 | 170,088[4] | 9,200[10] |
| Hungary | 11.6[1,2] | 1984 | 206[7] | 122,600[7] | 13,121[12] | 595[7] | | 37,141[38] | 170,516[38] | 9,989[38] |
| Iceland | 9.4[2,11] | 1983 | 1,509[39] | 5,132[12] | 598[39] | | 396[39] | 1,956[39] | 7,052[12] | 644[39] |
| India | 13.2[2] | 1980 | [3] | [3] | | | | 3,132,000[3,15] | 3,615,000[3,15] | 108,300[10] |
| Indonesia | 16.0[15] | 1983 | | [3] | | | | | 1,000,063[3,7] | 44,816 |
| Iran | 21.3[2] | 1972–73 | 18,210 | 31,688 | 2,429 | 1.7 | 133 | 218,132 | 80,055 | 27,814[10] |
| Iraq | 11.2[2] | 1975–76 | 1,532[27] | 2,700[27] | | 1.8[27] | | 77,766[27] | 106,800[27] | 11,378[10] |
| Ireland | 11.0[2,10] | 1977 | 3,073 | 40,584 | 4,593 | 13.2 | 1,495 | 32,332 | 79,870 | 4,170 |
| Isle of Man | 12.0[10] | 1981 | | 775 | | | | | 3,146 | |
| Israel | 12.7[2] | 1983 | 3,836[9] | 36,490[13] | | 8.7[9] | | 2,207[8,9] | 43,272[13,15] | 10,578 |
| Italy | 15.6[2] | 1983 | | [3] | | | | 1,033,725 | 1,369,200[3] | 122,978 |
| Jamaica | 20.5 | 1979 | | 1,830[8] | | | | 10,150[11] | 11,230[8] | 1,457[10] |
| Japan | 14.3[15] | 1985 | 413,002 | 3,997,000[4] | 2,214,396 | 9.7[4] | 5,362 | 1,628,620[15] | 6,329,000[4,15] | 426,411[15] |
| Jersey | | 1981 | | 909[4] | | | | | 4,154 | |
| Jordan | 17.2[2] | 1977 | 788[8] | 1,075[8] | | 13.8[8] | | 189[8] | 2,436[8] | 2,210[10] |
| Kampuchea | | ... | | | | | | | | |
| Kenya | 11.3[2] | 1984 | 2,277 | 28,259 | | 12.4 | | 5,732 | 35,967 | ... |
| Kiribati | 15.8[7] | 1985 | | 440[4] | | | | 35[23] | 569[3] | 7[23] |
| Korea, North | | | | | | | | | | |
| Korea, South | 12.9[2] | 1982 | 45,568 | 112,427 | 9,693 | 2.5 | 213 | 749,628 | 409,222 | 20,889 |
| Kuwait | 10.3[2] | 1982 | 2,391 | 22,000 | 5,554 | 9.2 | 2,323 | 12,882 | 44,000 | 6,489 |
| Laos | ... | | | | | | | | | |
| Lebanon | 28.3[2,9] | 1983 | | | | | | | | 1,662 |
| Lesotho | 11.5[2,10] | | | | | | | | | |
| Liberia | 7.2[2] | | | | | | | | | |
| Libya | 5.9[2,7] | 1973 | 1,126 | 4,148[4] | | 3.7[4] | | 26,825 | 44,605[4] | 9,205[10] |
| Liechtenstein | | 1975 | 67 | 216 | | 3.2 | | 228 | 740 | |
| Luxembourg | 17.1[2] | 1984 | 1,226 | 7,472[5] | 2,134 | 5.9[5] | 1,698 | 3,749 | 11,381[5] | 1,499 |
| Macau | | 1981 | | 482[4] | | | | | 13,652[4] | |
| Madagascar | | 1976 | 1,104 | | | | | 1,570 | | 696[12] |
| Malawi | 12.6[2] | 1983 | 588[8] | 17,300[8] | 455[8,12] | 29[8] | 1,103[8,12] | 708[8] | 7,500[8] | 176[8,12] |
| Malaysia | 12.3[2] | 1980 | 19,663 | 116,200 | 15,461 | 5.9 | 786 | 95,993 | 73,000 | 6,099 |
| Maldives | 9.9[2] | 1977 | | [3] | | | | | 1,341[3,4] | |
| Mali | 16.5[2,7] | 1979 | | [3] | | | | | 5,200[3] | |
| Malta | 15.7 | | | [3] | | | | | | |
| Martinique | 17.9[2,11] | 1983 | | [3] | | | | | 3,518[3,12] | 234 |
| Mauritania | 12.8[2] | 1971[8] | 23 | 100 | 102 | 4.3 | 4,445 | 59 | 700 | 103 |
| Mauritius | 11.5[2] | 1985 | [3] | [3] | | 3 | | 1813[3,8] | 6,288[3,8] | 387[12] |
| Mayotte | | 1983 | [3] | | | | 3 | 413 | | 27[3] |
| Mexico | 22.8[2] | 1975 | 11,652 | 130,939[4] | 6,739 | 11.2[4] | 578 | 463,612 | 987,089[4] | 17,062[10] |
| Monaco | | ... | | | | | | | | |
| Mongolia | 33.0[1] | 1983[3,41] | | | | | | 4,828 | 21,100 | 1,088 |
| Montserrat | 17.1[2] | 1980 | | | | | | 160 | 200 | 11[12] |
| Morocco | 13.9 | 1972 | | | | | | 4,000[8] | 20,000[8] | 4,727[10] |
| Mozambique | | 1980 | | [3] | | | | | 63,058[3] | |
| Nauru | | | | | | | | | | |
| Nepal | 3.5[2] | 1983 | | [3] | | | | | 119,000[3,4,12] | 736 |
| Netherlands, The | 12.6[2] | 1983 | | 255,300 | | | | 89,739 | 336,000 | 28,860 |
| Netherlands Antilles | | 1983 | | [3] | | | | | 7,810[3,16,42] | 149[17] |
| New Caledonia | 26.7[2,10] | 1981 | | [3] | | | | 324 | 4,524[3] | |
| New Zealand | 18.3[2] | 1982–83 | 8,263 | 76,664 | 16,295 | 9.3 | 1,972 | 29,961[15] | 116,301[15] | 10,358[15] |
| Nicaragua | 19.2 | 1983 | | | | | | 20,610[7] | 92,100[21] | 356 |
| Niger | 13.5[2] | | | | | | | | | |
| Nigeria | 21.6[2] | 1982[8] | | [3] | | | | 22,190 | 266,280 | |
| Niue | | 1982 | 3 | [3] | | | | 22[3] | 82[3] | |
| Norfolk Island | | 1986 | | [3] | | | | | 275[3] | |

retail trade  (continued)

percent breakdown of sales

| food[d] | clothing, shoes[e] | home furnishings[f] | eating, drinking[g] | drugs, pharma- ceuticals[h] | building materials[i] | automobile parts[j] | general merchandise[k] | other[l] | employees per outlet | sales per outlet $'000 | population per outlet | country |
|---|---|---|---|---|---|---|---|---|---|---|---|---|
| 11.9[9,34] | 7.6[9,34] | 16.2[9,34] | ... | 7.9[9,34] | 6.3[9,34] | 12.4[9,34] | 28.2[9,34] | 9.5[9,34] | 7.6 | 309 | 3,483 | El Salvador |
| ... | ... | ... | ... | ... | ... | ... | ... | ... | ... | ... | ... | Equatorial Guinea |
| ... | ... | ... | ... | ... | ... | ... | ... | ... | 2.3 | 27 | ... | Ethiopia |
| ... | ... | ... | ... | ... | ... | ... | ... | ... | ... | ... | ... | Faeroe Islands |
| ... | ... | ... | ... | ... | ... | ... | ... | ... | ... | ... | 95 | Falkland Islands |
| 27.8[23] | 10.4[23] | 1.7[23] | ... | 1.0[23] | 2.6[23] | 17.1[23] | 22.7[23] | 16.7[23] | 10.4[8] | 607[8] | 1,163[8] | Fiji |
| 22.8 | 5.4 | 1.9 | ... | 2.5 | 8.2 | 27.5 | 20.6 | 11.1 | 4.6[4,7] | 502[7] | 133[7] | Finland |
| 40.9[13] | 15.9[13] | 17.6[13] | ... | 5.8[13] | ... | 4.0[13,36] | ... | 15.9[13] | 2.0 | 209 | 90 | France |
| ... | ... | ... | ... | ... | ... | ... | ... | ... | 34[3,8] | ... | 648[3,8] | French Guiana |
| ... | ... | ... | ... | ... | ... | ... | ... | ... | ... | ... | ... | French Polynesia |
| 50.5 | 9.6 | ... | ... | ... | 33.8 | 6.1 | ... | ... | ... | ... | ... | Gabon |
| ... | ... | ... | ... | ... | ... | ... | ... | ... | ... | ... | ... | Gambia, The |
| ... | ... | ... | ... | ... | ... | ... | ... | ... | ... | ... | ... | Gaza Strip |
| 32.0 | 15.1 | ... | — | 5.6 | ... | ... | ... | 47.3 | 8.7[4,10] | 380[10] | 162[10] | Germany, East |
| 28.8 | 13.5 | 10.0 | — | 6.1 | ... | 11.9 | ... | 29.7 | 8.2[4,21] | 829[21] | 246[21] | Germany, West |
| ... | ... | ... | ... | ... | ... | ... | ... | ... | 2.6 | 108 | 4,797 | Ghana |
| ... | ... | ... | ... | ... | ... | ... | ... | ... | ... | ... | ... | Gibraltar |
| 60.0[22] | 18.1[22] | 9.5[22] | ... | ... | ... | ... | ... | 12.4[22] | 0.4 | ... | 59 | Greece |
| ... | ... | ... | ... | ... | ... | ... | ... | ... | ... | ... | ... | Greenland |
| ... | ... | ... | ... | ... | ... | ... | ... | ... | ... | ... | ... | Grenada |
| ... | ... | ... | ... | ... | ... | ... | ... | ... | ... | ... | ... | Guadeloupe |
| 16.3 | 4.3 | 3.1 | 9.2 | 0.6 | 4.2 | 32.6 | 7.4 | 22.3 | 6.7 | 515 | 138 | Guam |
| ... | ... | ... | ... | ... | ... | ... | ... | ... | ... | ... | 83 | Guatemala |
| ... | ... | ... | ... | ... | ... | ... | ... | ... | ... | ... | ... | Guernsey |
| ... | ... | ... | ... | ... | ... | ... | ... | ... | ... | ... | ... | Guinea |
| ... | ... | ... | ... | ... | ... | ... | ... | ... | 0.8 | ... | 1,080[3] | Guinea-Bissau |
| 9.7 | 18.9 | 13.8 | 4.5 | 2.8 | 17.7 | 18.6 | ... | 14.0 | ... | 743 | 5,884 | Guyana |
| ... | ... | ... | ... | ... | ... | ... | ... | ... | ... | ... | 7,034[8,28] | Haiti |
| ... | ... | ... | ... | ... | ... | ... | ... | ... | ... | ... | ... | Honduras |
| 23.7[22] | 8.8[22] | ... | ... | ... | ... | ... | 5.0[22] | 62.5[22] | 3.5[4] | 205[10] | 111 | Hong Kong |
| 28.6 | 12.1 | 17.1 | ... | 0.7 | 8.7 | 9.1 | ... | 23.7 | 4.6[38] | 269[38] | 287[38] | Hungary |
| 24.6 | 8.8 | 10.1 | — | 5.6 | — | — | 31.1 | 19.8 | ... | 329[39] | 121[39] | Iceland |
| ... | ... | ... | ... | ... | ... | ... | ... | ... | 1.2[3,15] | ... | 219[3,15] | India |
| ... | ... | ... | ... | ... | ... | ... | ... | ... | ... | ... | ... | Indonesia |
| ... | ... | ... | ... | ... | ... | ... | ... | ... | 0.4 | ... | 141 | Iran |
| ... | ... | ... | ... | ... | ... | ... | ... | ... | 1.4[27] | ... | 148[27] | Iraq |
| 30.4 | 4.6 | 8.9 | 10.9 | 2.6 | 3.0 | 23.9 | 4.7 | 11.0 | 2.5 | 129 | 99 | Ireland |
| ... | ... | ... | ... | ... | ... | ... | ... | ... | ... | ... | ... | Isle of Man |
| 22.0 | 7.0 | 11.0 | ... | ... | ... | 10.0 | 6.0 | 44.0 | 9.6[8,9] | ... | 1,624[8,9] | Israel |
| 50.8 | 15.1 | ... | ... | 3.4 | ... | ... | ... | 30.7 | ... | 119 | 55 | Italy |
| ... | ... | ... | ... | ... | ... | ... | ... | ... | ... | ... | 214[11] | Jamaica |
| 26.3 | 10.5 | 7.2 | — | 2.5 | 3.8 | 21.0[26] | 13.6 | 15.1 | 3.9[4,15] | 262[15] | 74[15] | Japan |
| ... | ... | ... | ... | ... | ... | ... | ... | ... | ... | ... | ... | Jersey |
| ... | ... | ... | ... | ... | ... | ... | ... | ... | 12.9[8] | ... | 792[8] | Jordan |
| ... | ... | ... | ... | ... | ... | ... | ... | ... | ... | ... | ... | Kampuchea |
| ... | ... | ... | ... | ... | ... | ... | ... | ... | 6.3 | ... | 3,408 | Kenya |
| ... | ... | ... | ... | ... | ... | ... | ... | ... | ... | 189[23] | 1,571[23] | Kiribati |
| ... | ... | ... | ... | ... | ... | ... | ... | ... | ... | ... | ... | Korea, North |
| 29.4[21,24] | 13.1[21] | 8.9[21] | 18.9[21] | 5.0[21] | 2.4[21] | 5.4[21] | 1.2[21] | 15.6[21] | 0.5 | 28 | 52 | Korea, South |
| 17.0[14] | 6.8[14] | 13.7[14] | 3.4[14] | 0.9[14] | 7.1[14] | 13.2[14] | 1.3[14] | 36.6[14] | 3.4 | 504 | 116 | Kuwait |
| ... | ... | ... | ... | ... | ... | ... | ... | ... | ... | ... | ... | Laos |
| ... | ... | ... | ... | ... | ... | ... | ... | ... | ... | ... | ... | Lebanon |
| ... | ... | ... | ... | ... | ... | ... | ... | ... | ... | ... | ... | Lesotho |
| ... | ... | ... | ... | ... | ... | ... | ... | ... | ... | ... | ... | Liberia |
| ... | ... | ... | ... | ... | ... | ... | ... | ... | 1.7[4] | ... | 84 | Libya |
| ... | ... | ... | ... | ... | ... | ... | ... | ... | 3.2 | ... | 105 | Liechtenstein |
| 32.1 | 11.3 | 10.0 | ... | 3.4 | ... | 35.0 | ... | 8.2 | 2.9[5] | 400 | 98 | Luxembourg |
| ... | ... | ... | ... | ... | ... | ... | ... | ... | ... | ... | ... | Macau |
| ... | ... | ... | ... | ... | ... | ... | ... | ... | ... | ... | 4,977 | Madagascar |
| ... | ... | ... | ... | ... | ... | ... | ... | ... | 10.6[8] | 427[8,12] | 9,348[8] | Malawi |
| 32.9[40] | 7.3[40] | 10.8[40] | ... | 2.5[40] | 1.1[40] | 33.3[26,40] | 4.4[40] | 7.7[40] | 0.8 | 64 | 143 | Malaysia |
| ... | ... | ... | ... | ... | ... | ... | ... | ... | ... | ... | ... | Maldives |
| ... | ... | ... | ... | ... | ... | ... | ... | ... | ... | ... | ... | Mali |
| ... | ... | ... | ... | ... | ... | ... | ... | ... | ... | ... | ... | Malta |
| ... | ... | ... | ... | ... | ... | ... | ... | ... | ... | ... | ... | Martinique |
| ... | ... | ... | ... | ... | ... | ... | ... | ... | 11.9 | 1,742 | 20,300 | Mauritania |
| ... | ... | ... | ... | ... | ... | ... | ... | ... | 34.7[3,8] | ... | 5,639[3,8] | Mauritius |
| ... | ... | ... | ... | ... | ... | ... | ... | ... | ... | 652[3] | 1,477[3] | Mayotte |
| 17.8 | 7.3 | 5.8 | ... | 2.8 | 7.3 | 24.5 | 16.6 | 17.9 | 2.1[4] | 41 | 130 | Mexico |
| ... | ... | ... | ... | ... | ... | ... | ... | ... | ... | ... | ... | Monaco |
| ... | ... | ... | ... | ... | ... | ... | ... | ... | 4.3 | 225 | 372 | Mongolia |
| ... | ... | ... | ... | ... | ... | ... | ... | ... | 1.2 | c. 70 | 73 | Montserrat |
| ... | ... | ... | ... | ... | ... | ... | ... | ... | 5.0[8] | ... | c. 4,000[8] | Morocco |
| ... | ... | ... | ... | ... | ... | ... | ... | ... | ... | ... | ... | Mozambique |
| ... | ... | ... | ... | ... | ... | ... | ... | ... | ... | ... | ... | Nauru |
| ... | ... | ... | ... | ... | ... | ... | ... | ... | ... | ... | ... | Nepal |
| 33.4 | —18.5— | | ... | 1.2 | ... | ... | 6.4 | 40.5 | 3.7 | 322 | 160 | Netherlands, The |
| ... | ... | ... | ... | ... | ... | ... | ... | ... | ... | ... | ... | Netherlands Antilles |
| ... | ... | ... | ... | ... | ... | ... | ... | ... | ... | ... | 439 | New Caledonia |
| 19.0[22] | 4.7[22] | 7.1[22] | 4.0[22,43] | 2.4[22] | 1.6[22] | 40.4[22] | 5.6[22] | 15.2[22,44] | 3.9[15] | 346[15] | 106[15] | New Zealand |
| ... | ... | ... | ... | ... | ... | ... | ... | ... | ... | ... | 143[7] | Nicaragua |
| ... | ... | ... | ... | ... | ... | ... | ... | ... | ... | ... | ... | Niger |
| ... | ... | ... | ... | ... | ... | ... | ... | ... | 12.0 | ... | 4,016 | Nigeria |
| ... | ... | ... | ... | ... | ... | ... | ... | ... | 3.7[3] | ... | 144[3] | Niue |
| ... | ... | ... | ... | ... | ... | ... | ... | ... | ... | ... | ... | Norfolk Island |

## Trade: domestic (continued)

| country | domestic trade as percentage of GDP, 1984 | year | wholesale trade | | | | | retail trade | | |
|---|---|---|---|---|---|---|---|---|---|---|
| | | | establish-ments[a] | employees[b] | sales[c] $'000,000 | employees per establishment | sales per establishment $'000 | outlets[a] | employees[b] | sales[c] $'000,000 |
| Norway | 11.1[2] | 1985 | 14,345 | 102,972[4] | 30,372 | 7.2[4] | 2,117 | 36,434 | 130,498[4] | 16,660 |
| Oman | 12.1[15] | 1983 | ... | 3 | ... | ... | ... | 4,731[2, 3, 5] | ... | 2,449 |
| Pacific Is., Trust Terr. of the | ... | | | | | | | | | |
|   Marshall Islands | ... | 1980 | ... | 148[4] | ... | ... | ... | ... | 395[2, 4] | ... |
|   Micronesia, Fed. States of | ... | 1980 | ... | 348[4] | ... | ... | ... | ... | 489[2, 4] | ... |
|   Northern Mariana Islands | ... | 1982 | 11 | 364 | 29 | 33 | 2,595 | 258 | 1,490 | 57 |
|   Palau | | 1983 | ... | 114[4] | | | | ... | 226[2, 4] | ... |
| Pakistan | 15.4[15] | 1983 | ... | | | | | 276,701[28] | 501,773[4, 28] | 12,848 |
| Panama | 14.3[2] | 1982[45] | 560 | 13,115 | 1,491 | 23.4 | 2,662 | 7,561 | 15,765[8] | 1,334 |
| Papua New Guinea | 8.4[11, 15] | 1985[2] | ... | | | | | ... | | 669 |
| Paraguay | 25.5[15] | 1983 | | | | | | ... | 91,900[4, 9] | 1,186 |
| Peru | 16.7[2] | 1973 | 4,210 | 34,100 | 2,163 | 8.1 | 514 | 103,010 | 72,200 | 2,015 |
| Philippines | 19.7[2] | 1981 | 20,642 | 122,717 | 4,538 | 5.9 | 220 | 279,968 | 241,872 | 4,836 |
| Pitcairn Island | | 1982 | — | — | — | — | — | 1 | | |
| Poland | 13.7[1, 2] | 1983 | ... | 124,100 | 34,652 | | | 214,330 | 441,800 | 31,247 |
| Portugal | 22.0[2, 12] | 1981[8] | 7,719 | 163,500[4] | 12,860 | 21.2[4] | 1,666 | 15,290 | 114,600[4] | 5,108 |
| Puerto Rico | 15.2[2] | 1982 | 2,282 | 30,541 | 7,133 | 13.4 | 3,126 | 34,461 | 76,370 | 6,505 |
| Qatar | 11.4[2] | 1983 | 268 | | | | | 2,848 | | 1,943 |
| Réunion | 22.8[2, 12] | 1984 | 3 | 3 | | 3 | | 6,439[3] | 11,132[3] | |
| Romania | 6.3[1, 10] | 1985 | ... | | | | | 82,707 | 457,800 | 16,164 |
| Rwanda | 13.7[2] | 1978 | | 3 | | | | | 8,014[2, 3] | ... |
| St. Christopher and Nevis | 17.4[2] | 1983 | | 3 | | | | | 568[3] | ... |
| St. Helena and Ascension | ... | 1976 | | 3 | | | | | 95[3, 4] | ... |
| St. Lucia | 22.3[2] | 1980 | | 3 | | | | | 4,770[2, 3, 4] | ... |
| St. Pierre and Miquelon | ... | 1982 | | 3 | | | | | 279[2, 3, 4] | ... |
| St. Vincent | 14.0 | | | | | | | | | |
| San Marino | ... | 1986 | 102 | 3 | | | | 867 | 838[3] | |
| São Tomé and Príncipe | ... | | | | | | | | | |
| Saudi Arabia | 9.5 | 1981 | 4,460 | 31,481[4] | | 7.1[4] | | 80,266 | 174,187[4] | 36,574[10] |
| Senegal | 25.0[2, 12] | 1982 | | 4,600[21] | | | | 510[8] | 5,610[8] | 664[10] |
| Seychelles | 24.0[2] | 1984 | 3 | 3 | | 3 | | 186[3] | 1,448[3] | |
| Sierra Leone | 13.0[2, 7] | 1977 | ... | 2,521[8] | | | | ... | 2,293[8] | 177[10] |
| Singapore | 18.7[2] | 1983 | 20,103 | 98,900 | 30,772 | 4.9 | 1,531 | 16,029 | 42,845 | 5,294 |
| Solomon Islands | 7.7[15, 16] | 1984 | ... | 272 | | | | ... | 1,709 | |
| Somalia | 7.0[2] | ... | | | | | | | | |
| South Africa | 11.0[2, 47] | 1985 | 10,106[9, 47] | 232,478[9, 47] | 28,956 | 23.0[9, 47] | 1,878[9, 47] | 58,100[10, 47] | 373,200[10, 47] | 19,945[15] |
|   Bophuthatswana | 47 | 1979[3] | ... | | | | | 1,248 | 4,195 | 110 |
|   Ciskei | 47 | 1979[3] | ... | | | | | 682 | 1,632 | 36 |
|   KwaNdebele | 47 | | | | | | | | | |
|   Transkei | 47 | 1977[3] | | | | | | ... | 5,580[4] | |
|   Venda | 47 | 1978[3] | | | | | | 485 | | |
| South West Africa/Namibia | 13.9 | 1977 | 222 | 5,035 | 377 | 22.7 | 1,698 | 1,284 | 7,569 | 254 |
| Spain | 19.9[2] | 1984 | 40,000[21] | | | | | 710,865[21] | 1,400,000[21] | 54,777 |
| Sri Lanka | 19.5[2] | 1982 | 239[8] | 21,400[8] | | 89.5[8] | | 1,400[8] | 60,000[8] | 1,394[10] |
| Sudan, The | 19.3[10] | 1981 | | | | | | ... | | 3,278 |
| Suriname | 15.8[2] | 1983 | | | | | | ... | 12,700[4, 9] | 189 |
| Swaziland | 8.9[10] | 1983 | 79 | 1,100 | | 13.9 | | 646 | 4,200 | 20[13] |
| Sweden | 10.9[2] | 1983 | 27,913 | 163,000 | 38,685 | 5.8 | 1,386 | 75,709 | 268,300 | 29,210 |
| Switzerland | ... | 1985 | 15,019 | 143,470 | | 9.6 | | 53,465 | 259,674 | 23,620[22] |
| Syria | 23.3[2] | 1985 | 2,827[28] | | | | | 81,167[28] | 110,000[4, 28] | 6,411[3, 50] |
| Taiwan | 13.9[2, 13] | 1983[37] | 55,654 | 159,215 | 5,641 | 2.9 | 101 | 355,760 | 150,625 | 11,651 |
| Tanzania | 13.3[2] | 1983 | | | | | | 1,620[8] | 16,524[8] | 945 |
| Thailand | 22.1[2] | 1980[8, 51] | 5,647 | 187,737 | 21,693 | 33.2 | 3,842 | 11,280 | 113,408 | 3,945 |
| Togo | 22.0[10] | 1980 | | | | | | 181[8] | 1,815[8] | 112 |
| Tokelau | | 1984 | | | | | | 3 | 3[12] | |
| Tonga | 14.8[2, 10] | 1976 | ... | 14[4] | | | | ... | 654[4] | ... |
| Trinidad and Tobago | 14.6[2] | 1977 | 124 | 6,786 | 509 | 54.7 | 4,102 | 370 | 15,986 | 812[10] |
| Tunisia | 21.2 | 1983 | | | | | | ... | 106,300[3, 4, 11] | 2,814 |
| Turkey | 17.1[13] | 1980 | 24,592 | 46,071 | 8,049 | 0.5 | 327 | 281,949 | 85,059 | 8,686 |
| Turks and Caicos Islands | ... | ... | | | | | | ... | | |
| Tuvalu | 34.0[21] | 1979 | | 3 | | | | | 113[3, 4] | |
| Uganda | 6.6[12] | 1977 | 226 | 4,100 | | 18.1 | | 251 | 3,200 | 5,285[12] |
| U.S.S.R. | 17.5[1, 2] | 1984 | ... | 2,358,000[10] | 240,800[10] | ... | | 1,030,400 | 7,592,000 | 363,512 |
| United Arab Emirates | 9.0[2] | 1983 | 3 | 3 | | 3 | | 13,906[2, 3, 9] | 74,332[2, 3, 4, 11] | 5,093 |
| United Kingdom | 11.6[2] | 1984 | 104,688[10, 53] | 877,000[10, 53] | 214,596[10, 53] | 8.4[10, 53] | 2,050[10, 53] | 343,153[10, 53] | 2,326,000[4, 15, 53] | 110,033[15, 53] |
| United States | 16.5[2, 13] | 1985 | 415,829[7] | 4,984,880[7] | 1,997,895[7] | 12.0[7] | 4,805[7] | 1,923,228[7] | 14,467,813[7] | 1,383,257 |
| Uruguay | 11.7 | 1984 | | | | | | ... | | 5,397[15] |
| Vanuatu | ... | 1983[54] | 18 | 187[4] | | 10.4[4] | | 256 | 1,439[4] | |
| Venezuela | 11.0[2] | 1979 | ... | | | | | ... | 161,596 | 13,366[10] |
| Vietnam | 11.7[1, 10] | 1979 | 2,400[50] | ... | | | | 2,000[50] | 50,000[50] | 7,485[9] |
| Virgin Islands (U.S.) | ... | 1982 | 104 | 1,363 | 197 | 13.1 | 1,196 | 1,191 | 6,980 | 489 |
| Wallis and Futuna | ... | 1983 | | 3 | | | | | 123[3, 4] | ... |
| West Bank | ... | 1985 | | 3 | | | | | 2,400[3] | ... |
| Western Sahara | ... | | | | | | | | | |
| Western Samoa | 9.5[2, 16] | 1975 | | 3 | | | | | 1,172[2, 3] | ... |
| Yemen (Aden) | 13.9[2, 12] | ... | | 3 | | | | | | |
| Yemen (Şan'ā') | 16.7[2, 7] | 1983 | | 3 | | | | ... | 71,100[3, 12] | 2,195 |
| Yugoslavia | 22.2[2, 55] | 1984 | 1,687[10] | 196,641[10] | 24,416 | 116.6[10] | 14,856[10] | 82,560 | 362,934 | 17,514 |
| Zaire | 18.6 | 1981 | | | | | | 3,036[8] | 33,398[8] | 3,300[10] |
| Zambia | 13.1[2] | 1974 | 494[8] | 15,500[8] | 977[8] | 31.4[8] | 1,978[8] | 1,636[8] | 13,700[8] | 768[10] |
| Zimbabwe | 13.6 | 1983 | | 3 | | | | ... | 80,600[2, 3] | 693 |

[1]Percent of net material product. [2]Includes hotels. [3]Retail trade data include wholesale trade. [4]All persons engaged including proprietors. [5]1978. [6]Excludes retail trade network of the agricultural cooperatives. [7]1982. [8]Data refer to larger establishments only. [9]1977. [10]1983. [11]1980. [12]1981. [13]1985. [14]1973. [15]Excludes restaurants (eating and drinking establishments). [16]1972. [17]Netherlands Antilles includes Aruba. [18]1981–82. [19]Data refer to New Providence Island only. [20]1974. [21]1979. [22]1984. [23]1976. [24]Includes alcohol and tobacco. [25]Home furnishings includes building materials. [26]Includes all fuels. [27]Privately owned establishments only. [28]1975. [29]General merchandise includes clothing, shoes. [30]Includes wage earners in finance and insurance. [31]Rarotonga only. [32]Wholesalers selling directly to the public only. [33]1987. [34]Selected outlets in urban areas only. [35]Excludes Addis Ababa and Asmera. [36]Motorcycles, bicycles,

retail trade (continued)

percent breakdown of sales

| food[d] | clothing, shoes[e] | home furnishings[f] | eating, drinking[g] | drugs, pharmaceuticals[h] | building materials[i] | automobile parts[j] | general merchandise[k] | other[l] | employees per outlet | sales per outlet $'000 | population per outlet | country |
|---|---|---|---|---|---|---|---|---|---|---|---|---|
| 31.6[7,24] | 9.8[7] | 7.2[7] | ... | ... | 4.6[7] | 33.0[7] | 4.7[7] | 9.1[7] | 3.6[4] | 457 | 114 | Norway |
| ... | ... | ... | ... | ... | ... | ... | ... | ... | ... | ... | 188[2,3,5] | Oman |
| ... | ... | ... | ... | ... | ... | ... | ... | ... | ... | ... | ... | Pacific Is., Trust Terr. of the Marshall Islands |
| ... | ... | ... | ... | ... | ... | ... | ... | ... | ... | ... | ... | Micronesia, Fed. States of |
| 25.1 | 1.4 | 1.0 | 10.4 | ... | 6.2 | 20.5 | 6.6 | 28.8 | 5.8 | 220 | 71 | Northern Mariana Islands |
| ... | ... | ... | ... | ... | ... | ... | ... | ... | ... | ... | ... | Palau |
| 64.0 | 12.0 | 4.0 | ... | ... | ... | ... | ... | 20.0 | 1.8[4,28] | ... | 273[28] | Pakistan |
| 33.5[46] | 10.9[46] | 9.5[46] | ... | ... | ... | ... | ... | 46.1[46] | 13.9[8] | 176 | 270 | Panama |
| ... | ... | ... | 7.1[2] | ... | ... | 26.0 | ... | 66.9 | ... | ... | ... | Papua New Guinea |
| ... | ... | ... | ... | ... | ... | ... | ... | ... | ... | ... | ... | Paraguay |
| ... | ... | ... | ... | ... | ... | ... | ... | ... | 0.7 | 20 | 145 | Peru |
| 25.4[24] | 12.3 | 6.7 | ... | ... | 11.3 | 29.5[26] | ... | 14.8 | 0.9 | 17 | 177 | Philippines |
| ... | ... | ... | ... | ... | ... | ... | ... | ... | ... | ... | 54 | Pitcairn Island |
| 31.1[38] | 9.9[38] | 11.1[38] | ... | 2.0[38] | 4.9[38] | 6.7[38] | ... | 34.3[38] | 2.1 | 146 | 171 | Poland |
| 27.5[23] | 13.1[23] | 9.1[23] | 14.6[23] | 6.9[23] | 7.8[23] | 16.2[23] | —4.8[23]— | | 7.5[4] | 334 | 645 | Portugal |
| 30.5 | 9.9 | 4.5 | 7.5 | 4.3 | 5.9 | 23.2 | 8.9 | 5.3 | 2.2 | 188 | 95 | Puerto Rico |
| ... | ... | ... | ... | ... | ... | ... | ... | ... | ... | 682 | 99 | Qatar |
| ... | ... | ... | ... | ... | ... | ... | ... | ... | 1.7[3] | ... | 83[3] | Réunion |
| 30.0 | 10.0 | 5.9 | 25.0 | 1.6 | 0.8 | ... | ... | 26.7 | 5.5 | 195 | 275 | Romania |
| ... | ... | ... | ... | ... | ... | ... | ... | ... | ... | ... | ... | Rwanda |
| ... | ... | ... | ... | ... | ... | ... | ... | ... | ... | ... | ... | St. Christopher and Nevis |
| ... | ... | ... | ... | ... | ... | ... | ... | ... | ... | ... | ... | St. Helena and Ascension |
| ... | ... | ... | ... | ... | ... | ... | ... | ... | ... | ... | ... | St. Lucia |
| ... | ... | ... | ... | ... | ... | ... | ... | ... | ... | ... | ... | St. Pierre and Miquelon |
| ... | ... | ... | ... | ... | ... | ... | ... | ... | ... | ... | 26 | St. Vincent |
| ... | ... | ... | ... | ... | ... | ... | ... | ... | ... | ... | ... | San Marino |
| ... | ... | ... | ... | ... | ... | ... | ... | ... | ... | ... | ... | São Tomé and Príncipe |
| ... | ... | ... | ... | ... | ... | ... | ... | ... | 2.2[4] | ... | 120 | Saudi Arabia |
| ... | ... | ... | ... | ... | ... | ... | ... | ... | 11.0[8] | ... | 11,839[8] | Senegal |
| ... | ... | ... | ... | ... | ... | ... | ... | ... | 7.8[3] | ... | 348[3] | Seychelles |
| ... | ... | ... | ... | ... | ... | ... | ... | ... | ... | ... | ... | Sierra Leone |
| 1.2 | 4.3 | 10.2 | 10.5 | 0.7 | 0.3 | 22.1 | —50.7— | | 2.7 | 330 | 156 | Singapore |
| ... | ... | ... | ... | ... | ... | ... | ... | ... | ... | ... | ... | Solomon Islands |
| ... | ... | ... | ... | ... | ... | ... | ... | ... | ... | ... | ... | Somalia |
| 31.3 | 9.9 | 5.6 | ... | 2.9 | ... | 29.8 | 11.1 | 9.4 | 6.4[10,47] | 383[10,47] | c. 540[10,47] | South Africa |
| ... | ... | ... | ... | ... | ... | ... | ... | ... | 3.4 | 88 | 1,041 | Bophuthatswana |
| ... | ... | ... | ... | ... | ... | ... | ... | ... | 2.4 | 53 | 972 | Ciskei |
| ... | ... | ... | ... | ... | ... | ... | ... | ... | ... | ... | ... | KwaNdebele |
| ... | ... | ... | ... | ... | ... | ... | ... | ... | ... | ... | ... | Transkei |
| ... | ... | ... | ... | ... | ... | ... | ... | ... | ... | ... | 621 | Venda |
| 31.4 | 11.9 | 5.3 | ... | 2.8 | 1.7 | ... | 41.9 | 5.0 | 5.9 | 198 | 713 | South West Africa/Namibia |
| 39.2 | 10.5 | 16.7 | ... | ... | ... | 4.2[48] | ... | 29.4 | 2.0[21] | 119[21] | 52[21] | Spain |
| ... | ... | ... | ... | ... | ... | ... | ... | ... | 42.9[8] | ... | 10,814[8] | Sri Lanka |
| ... | ... | ... | ... | ... | ... | ... | ... | ... | ... | ... | ... | Sudan, The |
| ... | ... | ... | ... | ... | ... | ... | ... | ... | ... | ... | ... | Suriname |
| 52.1[13] | 25.7[13] | 22.2[13] | ... | ... | ... | ... | ... | ... | 6.5 | ... | 955 | Swaziland |
| 32.7 | 10.5 | 9.5 | — | 5.5 | 5.1 | 19.4[49] | ... | 17.3 | 3.5 | 386 | 110 | Sweden |
| 46.4[22] | 13.5[22] | ... | ... | ... | ... | ... | ... | 40.1[22] | 4.9 | ... | 122 | Switzerland |
| 14.2[3,50] | 2.9[3,50] | ... | 4.3[3,50] | 25.1[3,50] | ... | 4.7[3,50] | 48.8[3,50] | | 1.4[4,28] | ... | 91[28] | Syria |
| 21.5[12] | 3.2[12] | 8.8[12] | ... | 4.1[12] | 3.1[12] | 8.7[12,26] | 3.1[12] | 47.5[12] | 0.3 | 33 | 52 | Taiwan |
| ... | ... | ... | ... | ... | ... | ... | ... | ... | 10.0[8] | ... | 12,600[8] | Tanzania |
| 2.6 | 2.7 | 10.8 | ... | 1.3 | 10.8 | 57.8 | 5.5 | 8.5 | 10.1 | 350 | 4,163 | Thailand |
| ... | ... | ... | ... | ... | ... | ... | ... | ... | 10.0[8] | ... | 15,600[8] | Togo |
| ... | ... | ... | ... | ... | ... | ... | ... | ... | ... | ... | 533 | Tokelau |
| ... | ... | ... | ... | ... | ... | ... | ... | ... | ... | ... | ... | Tonga |
| 18.6 | ... | 8.5 | 2.7 | ... | 10.7 | 28.2 | 15.3 | 15.9 | 43.2 | 1,467 | 2,798 | Trinidad and Tobago |
| ... | ... | ... | ... | ... | ... | ... | ... | ... | ... | ... | ... | Tunisia |
| 24.8 | 12.3 | 15.4 | ... | 3.7 | 8.8 | 11.2[52] | 0.6 | 23.2[26] | 0.3 | 30 | 158 | Turkey |
| ... | ... | ... | ... | ... | ... | ... | ... | ... | ... | ... | ... | Turks and Caicos Islands |
| ... | ... | ... | ... | ... | ... | ... | ... | ... | ... | ... | ... | Tuvalu |
| ... | ... | ... | ... | ... | ... | ... | ... | ... | 12.7 | ... | 47,200 | Uganda |
| 42.6 | 23.9 | 7.4 | 8.7 | 1.2 | 1.1 | 5.6 | ... | 9.5 | 7.4 | 353 | 267 | U.S.S.R. |
| ... | ... | ... | ... | ... | ... | ... | ... | ... | ... | ... | 49[2,3,9] | United Arab Emirates |
| 26.9 | 6.4 | 11.2[25] | ... | 2.1 | 25 | 29.3 | 12.7 | 11.4 | 6.8[4,15,53] | 321[15,53] | 165[15,53] | United Kingdom |
| 20.5 | 5.2 | 5.0 | 9.6 | 3.3 | 5.5 | 29.8 | 11.6 | 9.5 | 7.5[7] | 554[7] | 121[7] | United States |
| ... | ... | ... | ... | ... | ... | ... | ... | ... | ... | ... | ... | Uruguay |
| ... | ... | ... | ... | ... | ... | ... | ... | ... | 5.6[4] | ... | 484 | Vanuatu |
| 50.2 | 10.1 | 7.6 | ... | ... | ... | 5.0 | ... | 27.1 | ... | ... | ... | Venezuela |
| ... | ... | ... | ... | ... | ... | ... | ... | ... | 25.0[50] | ... | 26,300[50] | Vietnam |
| 26.5 | 7.1 | 3.7 | 8.6 | 2.2 | 3.8 | 13.1 | 4.6 | 30.4 | 5.9 | 411 | 97 | Virgin Islands (U.S.) |
| ... | ... | ... | ... | ... | ... | ... | ... | ... | ... | ... | ... | Wallis and Futuna |
| ... | ... | ... | ... | ... | ... | ... | ... | ... | ... | ... | ... | West Bank |
| ... | ... | ... | ... | ... | ... | ... | ... | ... | ... | ... | ... | Western Sahara |
| ... | ... | ... | ... | ... | ... | ... | ... | ... | ... | ... | ... | Western Samoa |
| ... | ... | ... | ... | ... | ... | ... | ... | ... | ... | ... | ... | Yemen (Aden) |
| ... | ... | ... | ... | ... | ... | ... | ... | ... | ... | ... | ... | Yemen (Şan'ā') |
| 26.5[10] | 11.3[10] | 4.2[10] | ... | 0.3[10] | 5.0[10] | 3.8[10] | ... | 43.5[10] | 4.4 | 212 | 278 | Yugoslavia |
| ... | ... | ... | ... | ... | ... | ... | ... | ... | 11.0[8] | ... | 9,676[8] | Zaire |
| ... | ... | ... | ... | ... | ... | ... | ... | ... | 8.4[8] | 359[8] | 2,873[8] | Zambia |
| ... | ... | ... | ... | ... | ... | ... | ... | ... | ... | ... | ... | Zimbabwe |

motor fuel, lubricants, and tires only. [37]Excludes import/export establishments. [38]Socialist sector only. [39]Excludes fuels, automobiles, alcohol and tobacco, and building materials. [40]Peninsular Malaysia only. [41]State- and cooperative-owned establishments including public catering. [42]Curaçao only. [43]Excludes bars. [44]Includes bars and hotels. [45]Excludes Colón Free Trade Zone. [46]1971. [47]South Africa includes Bophuthatswana, Ciskei, KwaNdebele, Transkei, and Venda. [48]Motor vehicles only. [49]Includes bicycles, rental vehicles, and boats. [50]State sector only. [51]Excludes combined wholesale/retail outlets. [52]Excludes all fuels. [53]Excludes motor vehicles. [54]Urban establishments only. [55]Percent of gross material product.

# Finance

This table presents major statistical aggregates comprising national financial structure or constituting the basis of certain international financial comparisons. It includes such data as international reserves, money supply, central banking activity and discount rates, commercial (or "deposit money") banking activity, and external indebtedness of the central government. The country models are broadly similar and permit comparison of internal structure and external position at a high level of generalization.

One of the principal financial criteria of the relative economic position of a country is the size of its international reserves. International reserves as represented in this table comprise the sum of a country's (1) reserve position in the International Monetary Fund (IMF), a quota subscribed in the country's own currency, constituting a level up to which transactions may be effected within the IMF system; (2) holdings of foreign exchange; (3) holdings of gold; and (4) holdings of Special Drawing Rights (SDRs; an unconditional credit allocation, within a quota system set by the IMF, of currency needed by a country to maintain stability of foreign exchange transactions or markets). At appropriate accounting intervals these four elements are valued in a single unit of account (the SDR) and summed. The portion of this reserve total comprised by foreign exchange is very significant as an indication of the country's international liquidity (ability to pay its debts immediately in hard currencies). The ratio of external debt to total reserves, however, is less susceptible of interpretation in isolation: a low ratio, for example, may characterize the situation of a country with little need to borrow or of one with substantial debt but also the means to repay it. Much higher ratios, on the other hand, may be manageable, despite small reserves, if a country's export earnings are also high.

The section on money supply for the country, both as a total and as a per capita amount, refers to one particular measure of money in circulation: M1, the sum of money in private sector demand deposit accounts and outside banks in circulation; it is distinguished from a broader measure of supply, M2, which is roughly M1 plus "quasi-money" (the time, savings, and foreign-currency deposits of residents).

The section of the table outlining banking activity and the principal monetary aggregates encompasses both central bank authorities and commercial (deposit) banks. For both, the principal component aggregates are grouped under assets and liabilities. For certain countries, the four principal aggregates under assets and liabilities do not comprise the entire total, and the percentages shown, therefore, may add to less than 100% (occasionally more, when the net of other liabilities [capital, reserves, undistributed profits, checks, and other transit items] is negative, reducing the total against which these percentages are calculated). The items excluded by the choice of categories are the least significant worldwide but may be important locally; they include such items as quasi-money, money seasonally adjusted, unused bank overdrafts, and so on. In the case of the central bank authority, data are also provided for the central bank discount rate, generally the controlling interest rate for banking and commercial activity in the country.

The largest share of assets in the case of both central and commercial

## Finance

| country | international reserves, 1987[a] total ('000,000 SDRs) | % foreign exchange | ratio of external debt to total reserves, 1985[b] | money supply, 1986[b] stock ('000,000,000 national currency) | M1 per capita | central bank authority, 1986[b] assets (%) claims on government | claims on private sector | claims on banks | claims on foreign assets | liabilities (%) reserve money | government deposits | foreign liabilities | capital accounts | central bank discount rate, 1987[a] |
|---|---|---|---|---|---|---|---|---|---|---|---|---|---|---|
| Afghanistan | 244 | 86.1 | 4.3[1] | 76.4[2] | 4,960[2] | 81.8[2,3] | 0.2[2] | 1.8[2] | 16.2[2] | 67.6[2] | 7.5[2] | 0.2[2] | 8.8[2] | ... |
| Albania | ... | ... | ... | ... | ... | ... | ... | ... | ... | ... | ... | ... | ... | ... |
| Algeria | 1,421 * | 86.3 | 4.5 | 202.2[2] | 9,250[2] | 53.5[2] | 0.1[2] | 28.0[2] | 18.4[2] | 99.9[2] | 0.6[2] | 0.3[2] | — | ... |
| American Samoa | ... | ... | ... | ... | ... | ... | ... | ... | ... | ... | ... | ... | ... | ... |
| Andorra | ... | ... | ... | ... | ... | ... | ... | ... | ... | ... | ... | ... | ... | ... |
| Angola | ... | ... | ... | ... | ... | ... | ... | ... | ... | ... | ... | ... | ... | ... |
| Anguilla | ... | ... | ... | ... | ... | ... | ... | ... | ... | ... | ... | ... | ... | ... |
| Antigua and Barbuda | 26 | 100.0 | 2.1[1,5] | 0.087 | 1,070 | 32.7 | — | — | 67.3 | 101.7 | — | ... | — | 7.0[7] |
| Argentina | 1,476 | 89.6 | 10.8 | 4.287 | 140 | 22.0[2] | — | 47.2[2] | 30.8[2] | 29.8[2] | 1.5[2] | 33.7[2] | 8.7[2] | 90.1[8,9] |
| Aruba[10] | ... | ... | ... | ... | ... | ... | ... | ... | ... | ... | ... | ... | ... | ... |
| Australia | 7,403 | 96.3 | ... | 25.974 | 1,620 | 37.2 | 0.2 | — | 62.6 | 56.8 | — | — | — | 16.6 |
| Austria | 5,875 | 87.4 | ... | 193.5 | 25,610 | 3.1 | — | 37.1 | 59.8 | 72.4 | 0.3 | — | 29.4 | 3.5 |
| Bahamas, The | 215 | 100.0 | 1.0 | 0.249 | 1,050 | 12.1 | — | — | 87.9 | 54.3 | 23.1 | — | 22.8 | 7.5 |
| Bahrain | 1,801 | 99.5 | 0.5[1] | 0.236 | 560 | — | — | — | 100.0 | 20.1 | 58.6 | 1.5 | 23.7 | 5.09 |
| Bangladesh | 538 | 99.8 | 17.6 | 49.996 | 480 | 20.4[3] | — | 54.9 | 24.7 | 54.2 | — | 36.1 | 6.2 | 11.28 |
| Barbados | 147 | 100.0 | 2.5 | 0.395 | 1,560 | 26.7 | 6.6 | 0.1 | 66.5 | 53.0 | 28.7 | 32.4 | 6.3 | 4.97 |
| Belgium | 7,276 | 83.7 | ... | 1,038.9 | 105,400 | 24.6 | — | — | 75.4 | 114.9 | — | — | — | 7.5 |
| Belize | 31 | 100.0 | 6.6 | 0.071 | 410 | 53.9 | — | — | 46.1 | 55.6 | — | 21.3 | — | 12.0 |
| Benin | 5 | 100.0 | 153.8 | 79.4 | 18,720 | 26.0 | — | 71.9 | 2.0 | 46.5 | 5.3 | 44.2 | — | 9.5 |
| Bermuda | ... | ... | ... | 0.041[2] | 720[2] | ... | ... | ... | ... | ... | ... | ... | ... | ... |
| Bhutan | ... | ... | ... | 0.050[6,12] | 40[6,12] | ... | ... | ... | ... | ... | ... | ... | ... | 8.3[2,8] |
| Bolivia | 239[9] | 87.0 | 13.9 | 207,200[2] | 31,800,000[2] | 81.6[2] | ... | 3.3[2] | 15.1[2] | 6.3[2] | 84.4[2] | 19.2[2] | ... | 149.0[2] |
| Botswana | 1,119 | 100.0 | 0.4 | 0.244 | 210 | — | — | — | 100.0 | 7.5 | 57.7 | — | 17.5 | 9.0 |
| Brazil | 3,242 | 97.6 | 6.9 | 100.363[2] | 730[2] | 31.8[2,3] | 17.0[2] | 4.2[2] | 47.0[2] | 13.9[2] | 23.3[2] | 67.7[2] | — | 95.5 |
| British Virgin Islands | ... | ... | ... | 0.020[2,13] | 1,690[2,13] | ... | ... | ... | ... | ... | ... | ... | ... | 6.7[2,8] |
| Brunei | ... | ... | ... | 1.350[11] | 6,100[11] | ... | ... | ... | ... | ... | ... | ... | ... | ... |
| Bulgaria | ... | ... | ... | ... | ... | ... | ... | ... | ... | ... | ... | ... | ... | ... |
| Burkina Faso | 224 | 100.0 | 3.6 | 85.4 | 10,330 | 12.8 | — | 7.9 | 79.3 | 77.1 | 2.7 | 18.6 | — | 9.5 |
| Burma | 46 | 80.4 | 67.1 | 16.337 | 420 | −26.5 | — | 124.7 | 1.8 | 69.5 | — | 12.5 | — | ... |
| Burundi | 44 | 97.7 | 14.0 | 20.309 | 4,170 | 62.7[3] | 0.5 | 1.2 | 35.7 | 43.4 | 10.8 | 13.0 | 16.8 | 7.0 |
| Cameroon | 51 | 98.0 | 14.7 | 445.3 | 41,980 | 33.1 | — | 59.8 | 7.1 | 65.1 | 29.0 | 3.5 | — | 8.0 |
| Canada | 4,958 | 86.7 | ... | 80.2 | 3,120 | 74.6 | — | — | 25.4 | 99.1 | — | — | — | 8.6 |
| Cape Verde | ... | ... | ... | ... | ... | ... | ... | ... | ... | ... | ... | ... | ... | ... |
| Cayman Islands | ... | ... | ... | 0.022[2] | 1,040[2] | ... | ... | ... | ... | ... | ... | ... | ... | ... |
| Central African Republic | 48 | 100.0 | 5.9 | 52.3 | 19,100 | 34.5 | — | 30.1 | 35.4 | 66.6 | 2.9 | 20.3 | — | 8.0 |
| Chad | 30 | 100.0 | 4.4 | 69.1 | 13,290 | 16.7 | — | 72.3 | 11.0 | 79.7 | 3.7 | 18.4 | — | 8.0 |
| Chile | 1,962 | 97.3 | 5.1 | 116.2[11] | 9,780[11] | 14.6[11] | 11.0[11] | 48.1[11] | 26.3[11] | 5.8[11] | 1.8[11] | 35.3[11] | 11.3[11] | 26.68 |
| China | 10,477 | 95.8 | 0.2[11] | 386.2 | 360 | ... | ... | ... | ... | ... | ... | ... | ... | ... |
| Christmas Island | ... | ... | ... | ... | ... | ... | ... | ... | ... | ... | ... | ... | ... | ... |
| Cocos (Keeling) Islands | ... | ... | ... | ... | ... | ... | ... | ... | ... | ... | ... | ... | ... | ... |
| Colombia | 2,214 | 98.4 | 5.6 | 545.3[2] | 19,140[2] | 31.5[2] | 4.4[2] | 23.9[2] | 40.2[2] | 49.1[2] | 9.0[2] | 10.6[2] | 6.3[2] | 27.0[2] |
| Comoros | ... | ... | ... | 6.145[11] | 16,100[11] | 14.7[2] | — | 41.9[2] | 30.0[2] | 57.5[2] | 2.2[2] | 3.0[2] | — | 9.0[11] |
| Congo | 5 | 80.0 | 400.1 | 95.8 | 44,780 | 53.2 | — | 43.5 | 3.4 | 49.2 | 12.6 | 35.8 | — | 8.0 |
| Cook Islands | ... | ... | ... | ... | ... | ... | ... | ... | ... | ... | ... | ... | ... | ... |
| Costa Rica | 386 | 99.5 | 7.2 | 42.487 | 16,580 | 50.4 | — | 15.6 | 34.0 | 43.3 | 8.2 | 143.4 | 4.9 | 28.0 |
| Côte d'Ivoire | 16 | 93.8 | 863.6 | 640.2 | 58,600 | 43.2 | — | 55.9 | 0.8 | 53.6 | 3.6 | 39.8 | — | 9.5 |
| Cuba | ... | ... | ... | ... | ... | ... | ... | ... | ... | ... | ... | ... | ... | ... |
| Cyprus | 598 | 97.3 | 1.5 | 0.283 | 420 | 16.1 | — | 10.9 | 73.0 | 84.1 | 3.2 | 0.3 | — | 6.0 |
| Czechoslovakia | ... | ... | ... | ... | ... | ... | ... | ... | ... | ... | ... | ... | ... | ... |
| Denmark | 6,968 | 99.2 | ... | 215.0 | 42,060 | 0.6 | 23.5 | 38.1 | 37.8 | 28.2 | 44.9 | 5.3 | — | 7.0 |
| Djibouti | ... | ... | ... | 26.084[2] | 56,340[2] | ... | ... | ... | ... | ... | ... | ... | ... | ... |
| Dominica | 12 | 100.0 | 42.0[1,5] | 0.037 | 420 | 65.5 | — | — | 34.5 | 60.4 | — | 37.9 | — | 6.57 |
| Dominican Republic | 262 | 99.6 | 7.4 | 1.355[2] | 220[2] | 32.2 | — | 29.0 | 38.8 | 69.8 | — | 174.4 | −2.8 | ... |
| Ecuador | 443 | 96.6 | 9.7 | 129.058[11] | 15,380[11] | 35.1[3] | 4.8 | 40.9 | 19.2 | 27.6 | 23.7 | 107.9 | 2.0 | 11.0[2] |
| Egypt | 797 | 89.3 | 20.1 | 15.973 | 330 | 80.7[3] | — | 9.9 | 9.4 | 77.7 | 5.3 | 15.0 | — | 13.09 |

banks is usually either claims on government and government agencies or foreign assets and holdings, though some of the latter, such as the large outstanding loans to socialist and less developed countries, have become the chief liabilities. The chief liability of a central bank is usually reserve money (the currency and notes issued by the bank). When government deposits represent a substantial share, budgetary surpluses have usually been deposited by the central government. Large foreign liabilities imply extensive foreign investment. Among the deposit money banks, loans to the private sector normally represent the largest share of assets; occasionally, a trade- or banking-oriented country such as Belgium or Hong Kong will show major foreign assets. The chief liabilities of these banks will usually be savings deposits. If the country commands a high degree of confidence internationally, foreign liabilities may comprise a substantial share of liabilities.

Because the majority of the world's countries are in the less developed bloc, and because their principal financial concern is external debt and its service, data are given for outstanding external public and publicly guaranteed long-term debt rather than for total public debt, which is the major concern in the developed countries. For comparability, the data are given in U.S. dollars. The volume of debt by itself does not create external payment problems. If the country's external debt service (interest payments plus principal repayment) needs can be met by a strong, dependable export market, by export of services, or, occasionally, by direct remittances from abroad (by residents working abroad and sending wages

home in foreign currencies, for example), no debt problem need exist. Countries whose debt service ratio (total debt service as a percent of exports of goods and services) is relatively high, however, must often base their external borrowing policy on maintenance of domestic conditions of strict efficiency and, sometimes, austerity. The failure to adhere to such policies may lead to eventual crises of financial liquidity, deflation, and slower growth.

Ideally, the data presented here should be obtained by utilizing a single international methodology to provide a universally comparable set of international statistics. No international agency, however, can collect such data for all countries because of differences, both overall and in detail, in national definitions of financial aggregates, in accounting methodology, and in the completeness with which it is possible to survey a country's financial activity. The greater part of the data presented in the table comes from the IMF's *International Financial Statistics* and the World Bank's *World Debt Tables*. These sources are supplemented by other recent data from national, regional, or other international sources. In a few cases the desired data are negligible or unavailable, as noted.

Detailed percentages may not add to 100.0 because of rounding, statistical discrepancy, or nonaccounting of negligible quantities.
—None, less than 0.5 of the last significant figure, or not applicable.
... Not available.
a. Latest month.
b. Year-end.

| deposit money banks, 1986[b] | | | | | | | | | | external public debt outstanding (long-term, disbursed only), 1985[b] | | | | | | | country |
| assets (%) | | | | liabilities | | | | | | total ('000,000 U.S.$) | creditors (%) | | debt service | | | | |
| loans to government | loans to private sector | reserves | foreign assets | deposits ('000,000,000 national currency) | composition (%) | | | | | | official | private | total ('000,000 U.S.$) | repayment (%) | | debt service ratio (%) | |
| | | | | | demand depos. | savings depos. | govt. depos. | foreign liabilities | | | | | | principal | interest | | |
|---|---|---|---|---|---|---|---|---|---|---|---|---|---|---|---|---|---|
| 4.4[2,3] | 42.4[2] | 7.0[2] | 45.5[2] | 15.455[2] | 24.0[2] | 46.3[2,4] | 0.2[2] | 5.7[2] | 1,424[1] | | | 46[1] | 56.5[1] | 43.5[1] | 15.5[1,5] | Afghanistan |
| | | | | | | | | | | | | | | | | Albania |
| 8.6[2] | 89.4[2] | 1.1[2] | 0.9[2] | 195.252[2] | 53.6[2] | 11.1[2] | 4.3[2] | 12.4[2] | 13,664.0 | 19.6 | 80.4 | 4,583.6 | 71.7 | 28.3 | 33.3 | Algeria |
| | | | | | | | | | | | | | | | | American Samoa |
| | | | | | | | | | | | | | | | | Andorra |
| — | 38.9[6] | 1.9[6] | 51.8[6] | 0.063[6] | 13.2[6] | 67.1[6] | — | 13.4[6] | 1,106[1] | | | 348[1] | 79.2[1] | 20.8[1] | 12.6[1,5] | Angola |
| | | | | | | | | | | | | | | | | Anguilla |
| 13.2[3] | 59.3 | 17.2 | 10.3 | 0.498 | 11.0 | 58.4 | — | 26.6 | 201,[5] | | | 11,[5] | | | 1.0[1,5] | Antigua and Barbuda |
| 18.0[2] | 56.9[2] | 19.6[2] | 5.4[2] | 15.796[2] | 6.3[2] | 34.2[2,4] | 15.3[2] | 34.1[2] | 35,603.9 | 11.6 | 88.4 | 4,313.8 | 19.4 | 80.6 | 41.7 | Argentina |
| | | | | | | | | | | | | | | | | Aruba[10] |
| 19.8[2,3] | 74.4[2] | 3.9[2] | 2.0[2] | 110.854[2] | 13.2[2] | 68.1[2] | 1.0[2] | 4.0[2] | | | | | | | | Australia |
| 31.9[3] | 37.1 | 2.6 | 28.4 | 2,360.0 | 4.5 | 42.9 | 3.0 | 29.6 | | | | | | | | Austria |
| 17.6[3] | 85.1 | 7.8 | −12.1 | 0.796 | 23.2 | 67.7[4] | 2.9 | | 190.2 | 12.0 | 88.0 | 51.0 | 60.6 | 39.4 | 3.6 | Bahamas, The |
| 7.9 | 39.8 | 3.3 | 48.9 | 1.421 | 11.0 | 45.7 | 19.1 | 10.7 | 847[1] | | | 164[1] | 78.0[1] | 22.0[1] | 3.9[1,5] | Bahrain |
| 31.7[3] | 54.7 | 6.8 | 5.5 | 152.243 | 20.3 | 54.4 | 3.5 | 2.4 | 5,967.8 | 98.6 | 1.4 | 214.3 | 58.7 | 41.3 | 16.7 | Bangladesh |
| 23.3 | 60.4 | 7.6 | 8.7 | 1.354 | 17.1 | 62.5 | 4.9 | 15.8 | 351.9 | 49.9 | 50.1 | 42.9 | 54.1 | 45.9 | 3.4[11] | Barbados |
| 26.0[3] | 16.2 | 0.3 | 57.5 | 8,291.6 | 7.8 | 16.0[4] | — | 70.6 | | | | | | | | Belgium |
| 24.1[3] | 57.0 | 10.8 | 8.1 | 0.210 | 14.1 | 60.9 | 7.3 | 12.5 | 94.2 | 83.3 | 16.7 | 14.8 | 52.3 | 37.8 | 11.6 | Belize |
| 3.3 | 88.1 | 1.9 | 6.7 | 111.6 | 44.7 | 27.2 | 9.8 | 16.3 | 676.7 | 51.5 | 48.5 | 22.4 | 61.2 | 38.8 | 9.25 | Benin |
| —12.3[2] | | 7.8[2] | — | 5.457[2] | —84.6[2]— | | | | 511[1] | | | 108[1] | 71.3[1] | 28.7[1] | 80.5[1,5] | Bermuda |
| | | | | 0.891[2] | | | | | | | | | | | | Bhutan |
| | 68.1[2] | 24.4[2] | 7.5[2] | 0.0004 | 7.3[2] | 12.4[2] | | 62.3[2] | 3,259.3 | 72.0 | 28.0 | 214.4 | 66.7 | 33.3 | 29.1 | Bolivia |
| 8.2[3] | 51.9 | 24.6 | 10.0 | 0.419 | 44.2 | 42.0 | — | 8.5 | 334.2 | 89.6 | 10.4 | 48.5 | 53.6 | 46.4 | 5.4 | Botswana |
| 22.3[3] | 60.4 | 10.4 | 5.5 | 917.558 | 28.9 | 25.7 | 4.8 | 21.9 | 73,893.6 | 19.0 | 81.0 | 7,776.2 | 19.2 | 80.8 | 26.6 | Brazil |
| —27.2[2]— | | 0.9[2] | 69.0[2] | 0.201[2] | 7.1[2] | 48.0[2] | — | 40.1[2] | | | | | | | | British Virgin Islands |
| —28.5[11]— | | 0.5[11] | | 3.864[11] | —69.5[11]— | | | | 236[1] | | | 1[1] | | | 0.4[1,5] | Brunei |
| | | | | | | | | | 3,170[14] | | | | | | | Bulgaria |
| 5.2 | 69.9 | 22.3 | 2.5 | 131.0 | 30.3 | 22.0 | 30.1 | 10.2 | 496.3 | 92.8 | 7.2 | 26.7 | 62.9 | 37.1 | 8.7[6] | Burkina Faso |
| 93.1[3] | 5.7 | 1.2 | | 52.909 | 2.1 | 14.1[4] | 9.1 | 14.5 | 2,946.8 | 88.8 | 11.2 | 196.6 | 64.3 | 35.7 | 37.4[11] | Burma |
| 32.8[3] | 51.7 | 4.7 | 10.4 | 11.531 | 73.5 | 7.6 | — | 12.0 | 415.3 | 93.6 | 6.4 | 21.4 | 59.3 | 40.7 | | Burundi |
| 8.3 | 84.3 | 3.8 | 3.5 | 1,169.4 | 23.9 | 32.8 | 10.3 | 9.4 | 1,974.6 | 79.5 | 20.5 | 238.0 | 60.8 | 39.2 | 8.3 | Cameroon |
| 6.1[3] | 68.8 | 1.9 | 21.0 | 325.4 | 19.7 | 50.4[4] | 0.6 | 27.7 | | | | | | | | Canada |
| | | | | | | | | | 90.6 | 98.5 | 1.5 | 4.6 | 45.7 | 54.3 | | Cape Verde |
| | | | 99.9[11] | 124.515[11] | | | | 99.9[11] | 6.5[9] | 84.9[9] | 15.1[9] | | | | | Cayman Islands |
| 0.2 | 76.7 | 0.6 | 21.7 | 41.7 | 25.4 | 14.8 | 3.9 | 3.8 | 296.0 | 92.1 | 7.9 | 13.5 | 48.9 | 51.1 | 10.0[11] | Central African Republic |
| 0.2 | 92.3 | 0.8 | 6.7 | 81.3 | 27.5 | 4.4 | 5.1 | 1.7 | 149.6 | 79.5 | 20.5 | 8.1 | 76.5 | 23.5 | 2.2[11] | Chad |
| 9.7[11] | 81.6[11] | 2.6[11] | 6.0[11] | 1,331.0[11] | 3.9[11] | 29.1[11] | 7.0[11] | 64.2[11] | 12,734.5 | 17.2 | 82.8 | 1,229.8 | 18.2 | 81.8 | 26.2 | Chile |
| —95.8[2]— | | 0.2[2] | 3.1[2] | 588.9[2] | —61.3[2]— | | 5.5[2] | 1.3[2] | 4,023.4[11] | 68.3[11] | 31.7[11] | 342.9[11] | 55.0[11] | 45.0[11] | 1.2[11] | China |
| | | | | | | | | | | | | | | | | Christmas Island |
| | | | | | | | | | | | | | | | | Cocos (Keeling) Islands |
| 4.6[2] | 65.1[2] | 23.4[2] | 3.9[2] | 1,148.7[2] | 29.7[2] | 36.4[2] | — | 16.4[2] | 9,377.0 | 55.0 | 45.0 | 1,406.8 | 46.0 | 54.0 | 29.2 | Colombia |
| | | | | | | | | | 129.1 | 99.8 | 0.2 | 2.0 | 20.0 | 80.0 | 9.6 | Comoros |
| 14.9 | 80.1 | 1.1 | 3.9 | 253.4 | 16.8 | 13.0 | 21.0 | 21.3 | 1,760.4 | 53.6 | 46.4 | 323.1 | 66.9 | 33.1 | 19.0[11] | Congo |
| | | | | | | | | | | | | | | | | Cook Islands |
| 9.2[3] | 61.1 | 23.4 | 6.6 | 65.803 | 44.1 | 74.5[4] | — | 5.5 | 3,665.2 | 47.6 | 52.4 | 464.1 | 28.1 | 71.9 | 36.6 | Costa Rica |
| 5.7 | 80.8 | 6.9 | 4.1 | 1,301.5 | 24.4 | 25.2 | 9.1 | 12.9 | 5,699.6 | 45.9 | 54.1 | 577.1 | 25.4 | 74.6 | 17.4 | Côte d'Ivoire |
| | | | | | | | | | 5,937[1] | | | 412[1] | 51.2[1] | 48.8[1] | 9.2[1,5] | Cuba |
| 9.1 | 65.3 | 18.9 | 6.8 | 1.341 | 11.3 | 59.8 | 2.3 | 17.7 | 923.2 | 48.6 | 51.4 | 159.5 | 58.7 | 41.3 | 11.9 | Cyprus |
| | | | | | | | | | 3,850[14] | | | | | | | Czechoslovakia |
| 7.2 | 66.5 | 2.5 | 24.8 | 554.2 | 36.6 | 33.6 | — | 24.4 | | | | | | | | Denmark |
| | | | | | | | | | 97.6 | 91.3 | 8.7 | 3.8 | 42.1 | 57.9 | | Djibouti |
| | | | | | | | | | 42[1,5] | | | 3[1,5] | 33.3[1,5] | 66.7[1,5] | 8.8[1,5] | Dominica |
| 14.1[3] | 44.5 | 20.3 | 20.7 | 0.193 | 15.7 | 57.0 | — | 19.5 | | | | | | | | Dominican Republic |
| 21.7[2,3] | 58.4[2] | 16.2[2] | 3.7[2] | 3.358[2] | 19.6[2] | 36.8[2] | 8.4[2] | 1.2[2] | 2,520.9 | 69.5 | 30.5 | 220.0 | 38.4 | 61.6 | 12.1[11] | Dominican Republic |
| | 83.0[11] | 14.7[11] | 2.3[11] | 214.312[11] | 38.4[11] | 13.2[11] | — | | 7,121.1 | 27.6 | 72.4 | 938.8 | 24.3 | 75.7 | 28.8 | Ecuador |
| 29.5[3] | 27.9 | 20.1 | 20.1 | 46.112 | 13.3 | 45.8[4] | 2.3 | 14.3 | 17,751.2 | 83.4 | 16.6 | 2,248.9 | 74.8 | 25.2 | 33.9 | Egypt |

**Finance** (continued)

| country | international reserves, 1987[a] | | | money supply, 1986[b] | | central bank authority, 1986[b] | | | | | | | | central bank discount rate, 1987[a] |
|---|---|---|---|---|---|---|---|---|---|---|---|---|---|---|
| | total ('000,000 SDRs) | % foreign exchange | ratio of external debt to total reserves, 1985[b] | stock ('000,000,000 national currency) | M1 per capita | assets (%) | | | | liabilities (%) | | | | |
| | | | | | | claims on government | claims on private sector | claims on banks | claims on foreign assets | reserve money | government deposits | foreign liabilities | capital accounts | |
| El Salvador | 150 | 88.7 | 7.4 | 3.047 | 620 | 42.4[3] | 1.2 | 32.2 | 24.2 | 39.1 | 18.9 | 49.8 | 9.0 | ... |
| Equatorial Guinea | 19 | 100.0[9] | 36.2 | ... | ... | ... | ... | ... | ... | ... | ... | ... | ... | ... |
| Ethiopia | 203 | 96.6 | 11.2 | 3.273 | 70 | 52.2 | — | 33.7 | 14.1 | 66.8 | 9.5 | 5.1 | 6.7 | 3.0[7] |
| Faeroe Islands | ... | ... | ... | ... | ... | ... | ... | ... | ... | ... | ... | ... | ... | ... |
| Falkland Islands | ... | ... | ... | ... | ... | ... | ... | ... | ... | ... | ... | ... | ... | ... |
| Fiji | 88 | 100.0 | 2.3 | 0.179 | 250 | 1.1[3] | — | — | 98.9 | 58.9 | 6.7 | — | 35.3 | 1.0 |
| Finland | 3,724 | 98.2 | ... | 27.838 | 5,650 | 3.1 | 16.8 | 40.9 | 39.3 | 47.3 | 5.3 | 0.1 | 17.7 | 7.0 |
| France | 27,371 | 89.5 | ... | 1,072.0[2] | 19,390[2] | 6.5 | — | 21.8 | 71.8 | 59.5 | — | 0.7 | — | 9.5 |
| French Guiana | ... | ... | ... | 2.145 | 24,590 | ... | ... | ... | ... | ... | ... | ... | ... | ... |
| French Polynesia | ... | ... | ... | 39.572 | 216,300 | ... | ... | ... | ... | ... | ... | ... | ... | ... |
| Gabon | 28 | 96.4 | 4.5 | 151.7 | 128,200 | 21.3 | — | 27.5 | 51.1 | 64.0 | 13.1 | 12.6 | — | 8.0 |
| Gambia, The | 12 | 100.0 | 81.5 | 0.166 | 210 | 33.4[3] | — | 38.2 | 28.4 | 25.6 | 28.4 | 142.9 | 14.0 | 20.0 |
| Gaza Strip | ... | ... | ... | ... | ... | ... | ... | ... | ... | ... | ... | ... | ... | ... |
| Germany, East | ... | ... | ... | ... | ... | ... | ... | ... | ... | ... | ... | ... | ... | ... |
| Germany, West | 52,073 | 93.6 | 7.4 | 340.2 | 5,600 | 10.8 | — | 41.6 | 47.6 | 78.9 | 0.5 | 10.2 | — | 3.0 |
| Ghana | 418 | 98.3 | 2.4 | 55.156 | 4,140 | 49.7[3] | — | 2.0 | 48.3 | 24.9 | 3.6 | 76.6 | — | 23.5 |
| Gibraltar | ... | ... | ... | ... | ... | ... | ... | ... | ... | ... | ... | ... | ... | ... |
| Greece | 1,263 | 90.7 | 12.1 | 897.4 | 89,620 | 55.1 | 0.9 | 20.9 | 23.2 | 71.0 | 2.4 | — | ... | 20.5 |
| Greenland | ... | ... | ... | ... | ... | ... | ... | ... | ... | ... | ... | ... | ... | ... |
| Grenada | 14 | 100.0 | 2.0 | 0.069 | 750 | 39.9 | — | — | 60.1 | 89.3 | — | 7.7 | — | 6.5[7] |
| Guadeloupe | ... | ... | ... | 4.299 | 12,850 | ... | ... | ... | ... | ... | ... | ... | ... | ... |
| Guam | ... | ... | ... | ... | ... | ... | ... | ... | ... | ... | ... | ... | ... | ... |
| Guatemala | 317 | 94.3 | 6.7 | 1.608 | 190 | 70.6[3] | — | 6.9 | 22.5 | 72.0 | 26.1 | 58.2 | 5.9 | 9.0 |
| Guernsey | ... | ... | ... | ... | ... | ... | ... | ... | ... | ... | ... | ... | ... | ... |
| Guinea | ... | ... | ... | 22.5[2] | 3,490[2] | ... | ... | ... | ... | ... | ... | ... | ... | ... |
| Guinea-Bissau | ... | ... | ... | ... | ... | ... | ... | ... | ... | ... | ... | ... | ... | ... |
| Guyana | 2 | 100.0 | 112.5 | 0.881 | 1,100 | 99.1 | — | — | 0.9 | 16.9 | — | 59.8 | 9.9 | 14.0 |
| Haiti | 36 | 97.2 | 80.9 | 1.400[11] | 270[11] | 83.6[3, 11] | 9.7[11] | 2.3[11] | 4.5[11] | 44.1[11] | 6.7[11] | 37.1[11] | 8.8[11] | ... |
| Honduras | 91 | 98.9 | 20.5 | 0.953 | 210 | 38.3[3] | — | 46.7 | 15.0 | 31.4 | 14.1 | 69.3 | 20.1 | 24.0 |
| Hong Kong | ... | ... | ... | 56.094 | 10,080 | ... | ... | ... | ... | ... | ... | ... | ... | 4.7[15] |
| Hungary | 1,808 | 95.4 | 3.2 | 289.1 | 27,220 | 13.2 | — | 60.6 | 26.1 | 32.3 | 2.2 | 79.3 | 2.5 | 10.0 |
| Iceland | 233 | 99.6 | ... | 22.555 | 91,970 | 28.7 | 0.6 | 15.6 | 55.1 | 58.2 | 12.0 | 6.9 | — | 21.0 |
| India | 5,600 | 93.5 | 3.9 | 462.7 | 600 | 76.1 | — | 9.9 | 14.0 | 69.1 | 0.1 | 8.9 | 7.4 | 10.0 |
| Indonesia | 3,304 | 96.7 | 5.2 | 11,631.0 | 68,240 | 12.0[3] | 4.4 | 51.6 | 32.1 | 31.4 | 40.9 | 0.4 | 9.2 | 15.1[16] |
| Iran | 5,376[6] | 96.1[6] | ... | 3,922.0[5] | 87,880[5] | 85.0[3, 5] | — | 2.1[5] | 12.8[5] | 68.2[5] | 17.9[5] | 1.6[5] | 3.9[5] | ... |
| Iraq | ... | ... | ... | ... | ... | ... | ... | ... | ... | ... | ... | ... | ... | ... |
| Ireland | 2,969 | 99.6 | ... | 2.382 | 670 | 16.4 | ... | — | 83.6 | 68.9 | 10.1 | — | 30.5 | 11.3 |
| Isle of Man | ... | ... | ... | ... | ... | ... | ... | ... | ... | ... | ... | ... | ... | ... |
| Israel | 3,963 | 99.1 | 4.3 | 0.987[2] | 230[2] | 51.3 | — | 3.1 | 45.5 | 18.2 | 16.5 | 0.2 | — | 79.6[2] |
| Italy | 20,097 | 88.4 | ... | 343,048.0 | 5,993,000 | 66.5 | — | 1.3 | 32.2 | 70.4 | — | 0.2 | — | 11.5 |
| Jamaica | 157 | 100.0 | 17.5 | 2.140 | 910 | 87.6 | — | 0.8 | 11.6 | 46.6 | 37.8 | 145.5 | 5.6 | 21.0 |
| Japan | 54,856 | 98.5 | ... | 98,214.0 | 806,000 | 39.5 | — | 37.1 | 23.4 | 112.2 | 4.9 | — | — | 2.5 |
| Jersey | ... | ... | ... | ... | ... | ... | ... | ... | ... | ... | ... | ... | ... | ... |
| Jordan | 205 | 82.9 | 5.8 | 0.897 | 320 | 36.0 | — | — | 64.0 | 119.0 | 1.7 | — | — | 6.2 |
| Kampuchea | ... | ... | ... | ... | ... | ... | ... | ... | ... | ... | ... | ... | ... | ... |
| Kenya | 324 | 99.1 | 7.3 | 17.522 | 810 | 43.2 | — | — | 56.8 | 80.9 | — | 58.4 | 6.4 | 12.5 |
| Kiribati | ... | ... | ... | ... | ... | ... | ... | ... | ... | ... | ... | ... | ... | ... |
| Korea, North | ... | ... | ... | ... | ... | ... | ... | ... | ... | ... | ... | ... | ... | ... |
| Korea, South | 2,614 | 99.6 | 10.1 | 8,847.0 | 211,000 | 16.5[3] | — | 66.4 | 17.2 | 30.9 | 8.8 | 8.1 | — | 7.0 |
| Kuwait | 3,796 | 97.7 | 0.1[1] | 0.979 | 530 | — | — | — | 100.0 | 42.7 | 36.5 | — | 14.9 | 6.0[2] |
| Laos | ... | ... | ... | ... | ... | ... | ... | ... | ... | ... | ... | ... | ... | ... |
| Lebanon | 440 | 56.5 | 0.1 | 13.784[11] | 5,210[11] | 30.9 | 0.4 | 1.2 | 67.5 | 22.3 | 71.7 | ... | ... | 18.1[2] |
| Lesotho | 61 | 100.0 | 3.9 | 0.155 | 100 | 9.8 | — | — | 90.2 | 91.3 | −14.9 | 5.9 | 13.3 | 9.5[9] |
| Liberia | 1 | 100.0 | 799.4 | 0.148 | 60 | 98.3[3] | 0.2 | 0.9 | 0.6 | 33.8 | 3.4 | 62.9 | 4.4 | 7.1[8] |
| Libya | 4,740 | 97.3 | 0.2[1] | 3.131 | 770 | 26.1 | 1.3 | — | 72.6 | 80.3 | 27.8 | — | — | 5.0 |
| Liechtenstein | ... | ... | ... | ... | ... | ... | ... | ... | ... | ... | ... | ... | ... | ... |
| Luxembourg | ... | ... | ... | 51.6[11] | 141,000[11] | ... | ... | ... | ... | ... | ... | ... | ... | 5.0[8] |
| Macau | ... | ... | ... | ... | ... | ... | ... | ... | ... | ... | ... | ... | ... | ... |
| Madagascar | 879 | 100.0[9] | 48.4 | 238.6[2] | 23,460[2] | 95.0[2, 3] | — | 0.7[2] | 4.3[2] | 15.2[2] | 31.2[2] | 102.7[2] | 1.3[2] | ... |
| Malawi | 16 | 100.0 | 17.2 | 0.204 | 30 | 91.5[3] | — | — | 8.5 | 57.5 | 6.9 | 66.6 | — | 11.0 |
| Malaysia | 5,450 | 98.5 | 2.8 | 14.529 | 900 | 11.2 | — | — | 88.8 | 55.1 | 3.3 | 0.2 | — | 4.1[2] |
| Maldives | 6 | 100.0 | 11.9 | 0.193 | 1,010 | 82.3[3] | — | 0.1 | 17.6 | 83.6 | 21.7 | — | 4.3 | 9.0[16] |
| Mali | 12 | 91.7 | 57.5 | 117.5 | 13,720 | 68.6 | — | 28.5 | 3.0 | 60.2 | — | 32.4 | — | 9.9 |
| Malta | 944 | 98.2 | 0.1 | 0.319 | 930 | — | — | — | 100.0 | 81.1 | 6.4 | — | — | 6.0 |
| Martinique | ... | ... | ... | 4.153 | 12,640 | ... | ... | ... | ... | ... | ... | ... | ... | ... |
| Mauritania | 32 | 100.0 | 23.0 | 11.393 | 6,670 | 33.5 | — | 38.7 | 27.8 | 38.7 | 3.2 | 71.3 | 28.5 | 6.0[2] |
| Mauritius | 181 | 99.4 | 12.7 | 2.670 | 2,580 | 64.1 | — | 0.6 | 35.3 | 41.5 | 0.1 | 41.0 | 5.5 | 10.0 |
| Mayotte | ... | ... | ... | 0.191 | 2,650 | ... | ... | ... | ... | ... | ... | ... | ... | ... |
| Mexico | 6,111 | 98.5 | 14.5 | 5,794.0 | 72,020 | 62.7 | — | 0.9 | 36.3 | 49.4 | — | 21.7 | — | 98.5[7] |
| Monaco | ... | ... | ... | ... | ... | ... | ... | ... | ... | ... | ... | ... | ... | ... |
| Mongolia | ... | ... | ... | ... | ... | ... | ... | ... | ... | ... | ... | ... | ... | ... |
| Montserrat | ... | ... | ... | 0.009[6, 13] | 800[6, 13] | ... | ... | ... | ... | ... | ... | ... | ... | 4.5[6, 8] |
| Morocco | 165 | 84.8 | 79.3 | 50.029 | 2,180 | 72.4[11] | 7.0[11] | 14.5[11] | 2.4[11] | 63.0[11] | 0.9[11] | 41.1[11] | — | 8.5[9] |
| Mozambique | ... | ... | ... | ... | ... | ... | ... | ... | ... | ... | ... | ... | ... | ... |
| Nauru | ... | ... | ... | ... | ... | ... | ... | ... | ... | ... | ... | ... | ... | ... |
| Nepal | 87 | 94.3 | 8.6 | 6.951 | 400 | 72.3[3] | 1.6 | 10.5 | 15.6 | 55.7 | 22.8 | 6.0 | — | 15.0 |
| Netherlands, The | 12,260 | 87.5 | ... | 97.2 | 6,670 | 4.4 | — | 15.5 | 80.1 | 45.6 | 8.2 | — | — | 4.5 |
| Netherlands Antilles[10] | 190 | 90.0 | ... | 0.514 | 2,160 | 20.6 | 0.1 | — | 79.3 | 74.2 | 12.3 | — | 7.1 | 6.0 |
| New Caledonia | ... | ... | ... | 35.424 | 234,000 | ... | ... | ... | ... | ... | ... | ... | ... | ... |
| New Zealand | 4,857 | 100.0 | ... | 4.668 | 1,430 | 11.8 | 6.7 | — | 81.5 | 8.8 | 49.5 | 37.6 | — | 20.0 |
| Nicaragua | 171[5] | 97.7[5] | 18.1[5] | 10.937[5] | 3,720[5] | 74.3[5] | — | 17.9[5] | 7.8[5] | 34.9[5] | −0.9[5] | 84.5[5] | 1.3[5] | ... |
| Niger | 172 | 99.4 | 5.8 | 83.0 | 12,150 | 35.3 | — | 19.5 | 45.2 | 47.1 | 21.0 | 29.8 | — | 9.5 |
| Nigeria | 665 | 96.4 | 7.7 | 13.105 | 130 | 63.0 | 5.7 | 15.6 | 15.8 | 38.1 | 12.3 | 0.4 | 3.8 | 11.0 |
| Niue | ... | ... | ... | ... | ... | ... | ... | ... | ... | ... | ... | ... | ... | ... |
| Norfolk Island | ... | ... | ... | ... | ... | ... | ... | ... | ... | ... | ... | ... | ... | ... |

| deposit money banks, 1986[b] | | | | | | | | | external public debt outstanding (long-term, disbursed only), 1985[b] | | | | | | | country |
|---|---|---|---|---|---|---|---|---|---|---|---|---|---|---|---|---|
| assets (%) | | | | liabilities | composition (%) | | | | total ('000,000 U.S.$) | creditors (%) | | debt service | | | | |
| loans to government | loans to private sector | reserves | foreign assets | deposits ('000,000,000 national currency) | demand depos. | savings depos. | govt. depos. | foreign liabilities | | official | private | total ('000,000 U.S.$) | repayment (%) principal | interest | debt service ratio (%) | |
| 6.3 | 74.1 | 12.5 | 7.1 | 6.639 | 26.4 | 62.3[4] | — | 1.6 | 1,460.4 | 89.7 | 10.3 | 195.9 | 65.1 | 34.9 | 20.3[11] | El Salvador |
| ... | ... | ... | ... | ... | ... | ... | ... | ... | 119.3 | 95.5 | 4.5 | 1.6 | 68.8 | 31.2 | ... | Equatorial Guinea |
| 55.6[3] | 10.3 | 27.5 | 4.1 | 3.630 | 45.0 | 32.9 | 3.4 | 3.3 | 1,742.2 | 83.9 | 16.1 | 104.7 | 66.3 | 33.7 | 13.5[11] | Ethiopia |
| ... | ... | ... | ... | ... | ... | ... | ... | ... | ... | ... | ... | ... | ... | ... | ... | Faeroe Islands |
| ... | ... | ... | ... | ... | ... | ... | ... | ... | ... | ... | ... | — | ... | ... | — | Falkland Islands |
| 19.5[3] | 53.9 | 7.8 | 18.8 | 0.683 | 16.9 | 59.8 | 2.6 | 18.5 | 302.2 | 75.8 | 24.2 | 55.6 | 55.6 | 44.4 | 10.6 | Fiji |
| 0.8 | 73.6 | 3.7 | 21.9 | 313.833 | 6.8 | 46.6 | 3.2 | 31.4 | ... | ... | ... | ... | ... | ... | ... | Finland |
| 4.9[2] | 59.0[2] | 1.8[2] | 34.3[2] | 3,777.0[2] | 19.1[2] | 28.7[2] | — | 34.2[2] | ... | ... | ... | ... | ... | ... | ... | France |
| ... | ... | ... | ... | ... | ... | ... | ... | ... | ... | ... | ... | ... | ... | ... | ... | French Guiana |
| ... | ... | ... | ... | ... | ... | ... | ... | ... | 127[1] | ... | ... | 11[1] | 36.4[1] | 63.6[1] | 3.0[1,5] | French Polynesia |
| 17.8 | 77.5 | 1.5 | 3.2 | 433.8 | 24.0 | 28.2 | 13.3 | 10.4 | 871.7 | 33.2 | 66.8 | 222.6 | 76.7 | 23.3 | 11.2[11] | Gabon |
| 36.8[3] | 46.1 | 10.6 | 6.5 | 0.417 | 17.5 | 26.2 | — | 4.3 | 179.4 | 83.7 | 16.3 | 8.1 | 69.1 | 30.7 | 8.3[5] | Gambia, The |
| ... | ... | ... | ... | ... | ... | ... | ... | ... | ... | ... | ... | ... | ... | ... | ... | Gaza Strip |
| ... | ... | ... | ... | ... | ... | ... | ... | ... | 13,950[14] | ... | ... | ... | ... | ... | ... | Germany, East |
| 18.4[3] | 65.0 | 3.1 | 13.5 | 2,563.8 | 8.9 | 31.4 | 1.6 | 7.3 | ... | ... | ... | ... | ... | ... | ... | Germany, West |
| 21.2[3] | 37.4 | 40.6 | 0.8 | 49.585 | 35.8 | 28.1 | 2.6 | 5.2 | 1,170.1 | 87.7 | 12.3 | 81.8 | 69.8 | 30.2 | 12.2 | Ghana |
| — | 17.4 | 0.9 | ... | 0.401 | — | 79.0 | — | ... | 85[1] | ... | ... | 19[1] | 71.1[1] | 28.9[1] | ... | Gibraltar |
| 31.9 | 43.1 | 18.5 | 6.4 | 3,866.2 | 5.8 | 64.2 | — | 24.4 | 12,452.0 | 19.6 | 80.4 | 1,759.9 | 45.6 | 54.4 | 24.8 | Greece |
| ... | ... | ... | ... | ... | ... | ... | ... | ... | ... | ... | ... | ... | ... | ... | ... | Greenland |
| 14.9[3] | 57.1 | 18.7 | 9.3 | 0.266 | 14.5 | 59.2 | — | 13.3 | 41.4 | 89.1 | 10.9 | 5.9 | 69.5 | 30.5 | 11.8 | Grenada |
| ... | ... | ... | ... | ... | ... | ... | ... | ... | 62[1] | ... | ... | 8[1] | 50.0[1] | 50.0[1] | 3.6[1,5] | Guadeloupe |
| — | 66.3[2] | ... | ... | 0.559[2] | 28.6[2] | 71.4[2] | — | — | ... | ... | ... | ... | ... | ... | ... | Guam |
| 8.8 | 66.7 | 22.9 | 1.4 | 3.361 | 22.3 | 67.4 | — | 2.8 | 2,148.1 | 63.1 | 36.9 | 254.8 | 58.0 | 42.0 | 21.3 | Guatemala |
| ... | ... | ... | ... | ... | ... | ... | ... | ... | ... | ... | ... | ... | ... | ... | ... | Guernsey |
| ... | ... | ... | ... | ... | ... | ... | ... | ... | 1,292.2 | 83.3 | 16.7 | 65.8 | 69.9 | 30.1 | ... | Guinea |
| ... | ... | ... | ... | ... | ... | ... | ... | ... | 217.4 | 78.1 | 21.9 | 10.2 | 81.4 | 18.6 | 77.8 | Guinea-Bissau |
| 48.3[3] | 23.1 | 27.1 | 1.4 | 2.925 | 12.5 | 55.0 | ... | 3.0 | 742.7 | 77.0 | 23.0 | 25.0 | 46.4 | 53.6 | 9.5 | Guyana |
| — | 59.3[11] | 30.7[11] | 10.0[11] | 1.491[11] | 26.6[11] | 66.5[11] | — | 2.9[11] | 534.2 | 87.3 | 12.7 | 20.2 | 64.9 | 35.1 | 5.7[11] | Haiti |
| 26.3 | 68.4 | 4.9 | 0.4 | 2.624 | 18.8 | 43.4[4] | — | 2.5 | 2,178.4 | 78.8 | 21.2 | 170.5 | 43.6 | 56.4 | 17.6 | Honduras |
| — | 25.0 | 1.6 | 48.7 | 1,697.5 | — | 30.3[4] | — | 49.0 | 251.1 | 18.3 | 81.7 | 71.4 | 66.2 | 33.8 | ... | Hong Kong |
| 52.8[3] | 31.1 | 12.2 | 3.9 | 806.8 | 17.7 | 32.5[4] | — | 10.5 | 10,137.8 | 12.9 | 87.2 | 2,581.8 | 68.3 | 31.7 | 25.0 | Hungary |
| 2.8 | 78.4 | 15.4 | 3.5 | 71.6[10] | 28.9 | 40.9 | — | 23.5 | ... | ... | ... | ... | ... | ... | ... | Iceland |
| 20.5 | 65.6 | 13.9 | — | 1,161.8 | 16.5 | 70.4 | — | — | 26,649.5 | 87.1 | 12.9 | 1,885.1 | 57.5 | 42.5 | 13.3 | India |
| 14.9 | 56.2 | 7.6 | 21.2 | 38,647.0 | 15.7 | 41.3[4] | 4.4 | 1.4 | 26,624.6 | 56.2 | 43.8 | 4,015.1 | 58.8 | 41.2 | 20.1 | Indonesia |
| 19.3[11] | 44.6[11] | 33.6[11] | 2.5[11] | 6,117.8[11] | 37.5[11] | 48.8[11] | — | 1.0[11] | 2,494[1] | ... | ... | 1,049[1] | 86.5[1] | 13.5[1] | 9.1[1,5] | Iran |
| ... | ... | ... | ... | ... | ... | ... | ... | ... | 7,150[1] | ... | ... | 1,982[1] | 75.7[1] | 24.3[1] | 11.6[1,5] | Iraq |
| 19.8 | 44.0 | 5.2 | 14.2 | 10.638 | 10.1 | 51.3 | 0.9 | 26.4 | ... | ... | ... | ... | ... | ... | ... | Ireland |
| ... | ... | ... | ... | ... | ... | ... | ... | ... | ... | ... | ... | ... | ... | ... | ... | Isle of Man |
| 27.8[2] | 39.0[2] | 4.9[2] | 28.3[2] | 33.786[2] | 1.5[2] | 71.3[2] | — | 43.9[2] | 15,850.4 | 71.0 | 29.0 | 2,109.9 | 37.3 | 62.7 | 19.7 | Israel |
| 22.0[2] | 42.9[2] | 13.1[2] | 12.7[2] | 611,152.0[2] | 41.0[2] | 33.7[2] | — | 16.1[2] | ... | ... | ... | ... | ... | ... | ... | Italy |
| 25.6[3] | 47.1 | 23.1 | 4.2 | 8.106 | 17.4 | 56.1 | 1.7 | 5.5 | 2,822.7 | 83.9 | 16.1 | 397.6 | 48.4 | 51.6 | 36.5 | Jamaica |
| 12.3[3] | 78.3 | 1.3 | 8.1 | 445,358.0 | 16.2 | 53.2 | — | 13.4 | ... | ... | ... | ... | ... | ... | ... | Japan |
| ... | ... | ... | ... | ... | ... | ... | ... | ... | ... | ... | ... | ... | ... | ... | ... | Jersey |
| 10.4 | 60.0 | 8.4 | 18.8 | 2.151 | 14.4 | 54.6 | 7.3 | 16.2 | 2,692.8 | 68.3 | 31.7 | 454.3 | 66.3 | 33.7 | 22.1 | Jordan |
| ... | ... | ... | ... | ... | ... | ... | ... | ... | 508[1] | ... | ... | 12[1] | — | 100.0[1] | ... | Kampuchea |
| 20.2[3] | 65.0 | 9.8 | 1.8 | 34.884 | 32.4 | 52.1[4] | 2.8 | 2.4 | 2,857.4 | 85.3 | 14.7 | 385.8 | 63.1 | 36.9 | 25.5 | Kenya |
| ... | ... | ... | ... | ... | ... | ... | ... | ... | ... | ... | ... | ... | ... | ... | ... | Kiribati |
| ... | ... | ... | ... | ... | ... | ... | ... | ... | 796[1] | ... | ... | 69[1] | 39.9[1] | 60.1[1] | ... | Korea, North |
| 5.7 | 74.3 | 2.1 | 9.9 | 62,591.0 | 8.4 | 40.0[4] | 0.3 | 20.0 | 29,126.0 | 34.9 | 65.1 | 5,030.1 | 57.2 | 42.8 | 15.2 | Korea, South |
| — | 67.2 | 3.8 | 29.0 | 7.639 | 8.4 | 46.7 | 3.0 | 15.9 | 686[1] | ... | ... | 1,057[1] | 92.8[1] | 7.2[1] | 4.3[1,5] | Kuwait |
| ... | ... | ... | ... | ... | ... | ... | ... | ... | 458[1] | ... | ... | 22[1] | 13.6[1] | 86.4[1] | 7.7[1,5] | Laos |
| 16.9[11] | 48.1[11] | 5.9[11] | 29.1[11] | 90.009[11] | 6.8[11] | 69.4[4,11] | 0.8[11] | 13.7[11] | 172.0 | 100.0 | — | 54.1 | 78.7 | 21.3 | ... | Lebanon |
| 33.5[3] | 22.1 | 23.9 | 20.4 | 0.409 | 29.9 | 48.3 | 5.9 | 2.4 | 172.2 | 95.5 | 4.5 | 18.4 | 76.6 | 23.4 | 5.7 | Lesotho |
| 26.6[3] | 31.4 | 33.5 | 7.8 | 0.236 | 34.7 | 22.7 | 8.0 | 14.6 | 879.3 | 80.5 | 19.5 | 18.0 | 44.4 | 55.6 | 4.4[11] | Liberia |
| — | 66.0 | 29.2 | 4.9 | 3.094 | 62.2 | 35.8 | 11.2 | 1.7 | 1,177[1] | ... | ... | 614[1] | 92.1[1] | 8.0[1] | 8.4[1,5] | Libya |
| ... | ... | ... | ... | ... | ... | ... | ... | ... | ... | ... | ... | ... | ... | ... | ... | Liechtenstein |
| ... | 2.2 | — | 97.8 | 7,152.6 | 1.2 | 5.5 | — | 85.6 | ... | ... | ... | ... | ... | ... | ... | Luxembourg |
| ... | ... | ... | ... | ... | ... | ... | ... | ... | 91[1] | ... | ... | 15[1] | 46.7[1] | 53.3[1] | 4.7[1,5] | Macau |
| 2.4[2] | 87.5[2] | 3.0[2] | 7.2[2] | 414.6[2] | 34.3[2] | 12.3[2] | 6.9[2] | 4.3[2] | 2,340.0 | 80.3 | 19.7 | 117.0 | 54.9 | 45.1 | 18.9[11] | Madagascar |
| 24.1[3] | 41.1 | 33.0 | 1.8 | 0.559 | 19.3 | 48.0 | — | 17.8 | 774.9 | 87.3 | 12.7 | 75.9 | 63.2 | 36.8 | 20.4[6] | Malawi |
| 11.0 | 74.0 | 5.5 | 5.5 | 69.318 | 10.1 | 57.4 | 9.1 | 8.9 | 13,834.1 | 23.6 | 76.4 | 3,969.3 | 71.5 | 28.5 | 22.3 | Malaysia |
| 23.9[3] | 47.8 | 24.0 | 4.4 | 0.380 | 11.5 | 35.4 | 0.3 | 39.0 | 52.2 | 86.6 | 13.4 | 7.8 | 79.5 | 20.5 | 8.6 | Maldives |
| 2.5 | 81.4 | 10.1 | 5.8 | 138.2 | 34.4 | 12.9 | 7.1 | 16.9 | 1,327.4 | 96.2 | 3.8 | 37.9 | 67.0 | 33.0 | 17.6 | Mali |
| 4.2 | 52.6 | 27.4 | 15.8 | 0.465 | 6.9 | 78.9 | — | 7.2 | 123.6 | 99.9 | 0.1 | 11.5 | 87.0 | 13.0 | 1.4 | Malta |
| ... | ... | ... | ... | ... | ... | ... | ... | ... | 28[1] | ... | ... | 7[1] | 50.0[1] | 50.0[1] | 1.9[1,5] | Martinique |
| 1.1 | 89.7 | 4.9 | 4.3 | 19.168 | 35.8 | 18.1 | 0.8 | 29.9 | 1,363.0 | 90.1 | 9.9 | 78.4 | 64.5 | 35.5 | 13.1[11] | Mauritania |
| 30.7 | 51.8 | 9.9 | 7.6 | 8.500 | 16.0 | 76.4 | — | 0.4 | 404.1 | 78.3 | 21.7 | 66.6 | 60.4 | 39.6 | 11.5 | Mauritius |
| ... | ... | ... | ... | ... | ... | ... | ... | ... | ... | ... | ... | ... | ... | ... | ... | Mayotte |
| 44.5[3] | 29.1 | 17.2 | 6.1 | 26,216.0 | 9.4 | 57.7[4] | — | 30.5 | 72,509.9 | 11.6 | 88.4 | 10,976.7 | 31.7 | 68.3 | 36.9 | Mexico |
| ... | ... | ... | ... | ... | ... | ... | ... | ... | ... | ... | ... | ... | ... | ... | ... | Monaco |
| ... | ... | ... | ... | ... | ... | ... | ... | ... | 4,396[1] | ... | ... | 95[1] | — | 100.0[1] | ... | Mongolia |
| ... | ... | ... | ... | ... | ... | ... | ... | ... | ... | ... | ... | ... | ... | ... | ... | Montserrat |
| — | 71.7[6] | 2.9[6] | 17.6[6] | 0.043[6] | 18.8[6] | 61.4[6] | — | 13.9[6] | 11,230.5 | 63.9 | 36.1 | 1,034.4 | 52.6 | 47.4 | 32.3 | Morocco |
| 33.5[11] | 57.8[11] | 2.2[11] | 6.5[11] | 37.271[11] | 52.0[11] | 24.2[11] | 2.8[11] | 0.9[11] | 1,224[1] | ... | ... | 149[1] | 63.1[1] | 36.9[1] | 62.3[1,5] | Mozambique |
| ... | ... | ... | ... | ... | ... | ... | ... | ... | ... | ... | ... | ... | ... | ... | ... | Nauru |
| 30.6[3] | 47.7 | 8.7 | 12.0 | 11.974 | 14.8 | 71.8 | — | 4.6 | 527.3 | 99.5 | 0.5 | 12.9 | 55.0 | 45.0 | 4.0 | Nepal |
| 15.3[3] | 50.0 | 0.4 | 34.3 | 581.4 | 11.6 | 41.3[4] | — | 31.4 | ... | ... | ... | ... | ... | ... | ... | Netherlands, The |
| 0.2[3] | 46.0 | 15.6 | 38.1 | 1.702 | 15.9 | 48.0[4] | 0.8 | 31.2 | 816[1] | ... | ... | 146[1] | 63.7[1] | 36.3[1] | ... | Netherlands Antilles[10] |
| ... | ... | ... | ... | ... | ... | ... | ... | ... | 126[1] | ... | ... | 14[1] | 42.9[1] | 57.1[1] | 5.5[1,5] | New Caledonia |
| 22.8 | 71.2 | 0.5 | 5.5 | 19.999 | 18.2 | 66.4 | — | 5.6 | ... | ... | ... | ... | ... | ... | ... | New Zealand |
| — | 84.4[5] | 13.8[5] | 1.8[5] | 20.709[5] | 26.2[5] | 20.5[4,5] | 21.6[5] | 6.5[5] | 4,752.8 | 71.8 | 28.2 | 41.1 | 53.8 | 46.2 | 17.6[5] | Nicaragua |
| 14.4 | 66.7 | 16.1 | 2.7 | 143.6 | 28.6 | 26.5 | 15.2 | 28.0 | 791.3 | 78.4 | 21.6 | 66.9 | 55.0 | 45.0 | 26.7 | Niger |
| 30.1 | 56.0 | 5.5 | 6.3 | 27.461 | 22.6 | 39.8 | 3.6 | 3.0 | 13,015.6 | 17.6 | 82.4 | 4,004.3 | 68.6 | 31.4 | 30.8 | Nigeria |
| ... | ... | ... | ... | ... | ... | ... | ... | ... | ... | ... | ... | ... | ... | ... | ... | Niue |
| ... | ... | ... | ... | ... | ... | ... | ... | ... | ... | ... | ... | ... | ... | ... | ... | Norfolk Island |

## Finance (continued)

| country | international reserves, 1987[a] | | | money supply, 1986[b] | | central bank authority, 1986[b] | | | | | | | | central bank discount rate, 1987[a] |
|---|---|---|---|---|---|---|---|---|---|---|---|---|---|---|
| | total ('000,000 SDRs) | % foreign exchange | ratio of external debt to total reserves, 1985[b] | stock ('000,000,000 national currency) | M1 per capita | assets (%) | | | | liabilities (%) | | | | |
| | | | | | | claims on government | claims on private sector | claims on banks | claims on foreign assets | reserve money | government deposits | foreign liabilities | capital accounts | |
| Norway | 10,574 | 99.6 | ... | 101.8 | 24,390 | 22.5 | — | 33.5 | 43.9 | 14.7 | 68.3 | — | — | 8.0 |
| Oman | 856 | 98.8 | 1.8 | 0.304 | 230 | 18.1 | — | — | 81.9 | 43.5 | 20.1 | 0.3 | 18.9 | 9.5[2, 8] |
| Pacific Is., Trust Terr. of the | ... | ... | ... | ... | ... | ... | ... | ... | ... | ... | ... | ... | ... | ... |
| Marshall Islands | ... | ... | ... | ... | ... | ... | ... | ... | ... | ... | ... | ... | ... | ... |
| Micronesia, Fed. States of | ... | ... | ... | ... | ... | ... | ... | ... | ... | ... | ... | ... | ... | ... |
| Northern Mariana Islands | ... | ... | ... | ... | ... | ... | ... | ... | ... | ... | ... | ... | ... | ... |
| Palau | ... | ... | ... | ... | ... | ... | ... | ... | ... | ... | ... | ... | ... | ... |
| Pakistan | 774 | 91.2 | 12.1 | 144.646 | 1,380 | 61.2 | — | 21.3 | 17.5 | 62.4 | 12.4 | 18.7 | — | 10.0 |
| Panama | 142 | 100.0 | 33.5 | 0.410[2] | 190[2] | 62.3[3] | 24.8 | — | 13.0 | 21.3 | 23.3 | 52.3 | 8.7 | ... |
| Papua New Guinea | 349 | 99.4 | 2.4 | 0.244[2] | 70[2] | 13.4[2] | — | — | 86.7[2] | 25.0[2] | 18.5[2] | 5.7[2] | 21.5[2] | 11.5[7] |
| Paraguay | 397 | 99.7 | 2.8 | 158.674 | 41,290 | 24.4[3] | 1.4 | 24.3 | 50.0 | 68.6 | 4.4 | 5.9 | 9.3 | ... |
| Peru | 1,244[9] | 94.0[9] | 5.5 | 42.713 | 2,090 | 35.7[3] | — | 25.5 | 38.7 | 72.2 | 12.3 | 21.1 | 11.5 | 72.0[2] |
| Philippines | 1,225 | 92.3 | 20.2 | 42.7 | 750 | 23.8[3] | — | 37.0 | 39.2 | 40.2 | 11.3 | 48.2 | — | 9.1 |
| Pitcairn Island | ... | ... | ... | ... | ... | ... | ... | ... | ... | ... | ... | ... | ... | ... |
| Poland | 660 | 97.6 | ... | 2,989.1 | 79,470 | 24.9 | — | 69.8 | 5.3 | 73.1 | 21.6 | 4.1 | 1.2 | 4.0 |
| Portugal | 1,935 | 63.6 | 5.0 | 801.0[11] | 80,160[11] | 29.9[11] | 2.2[11] | 2.2[11] | 65.6[11] | 38.5[11] | 4.2[11] | 12.3[11] | 7.4[11] | 15.0 |
| Puerto Rico | ... | ... | ... | ... | ... | ... | ... | ... | ... | ... | ... | ... | ... | ... |
| Qatar | 526[9] | 93.2[9] | 0.4[1] | 4.017[2] | 13,340[2] | — | ... | 0.3[2] | 99.7[2] | 73.4[2] | 31.5[2] | — | 4.6[2] | 7.0[8, 11] |
| Réunion | ... | ... | ... | 6.105 | 10,910 | ... | ... | ... | ... | ... | ... | ... | ... | ... |
| Romania | 545 | 85.0 | 16.8 | 179.7 | 7,860 | — | 42.1 | 55.9 | 2.1 | 28.2 | 28.7 | 2.9 | — | ... |
| Rwanda | 129 | 100.0 | 2.9 | 14.699[2] | 2,400[2] | 19.8[2, 3] | 1.5[2] | 15.9[2] | 59.5[2] | 53.8[2] | 17.3[2] | 10.1[2] | — | 9.0[9] |
| St. Christopher and Nevis | 11 | 100.0 | ... | 0.023[6, 13] | 520[6, 13] | ... | ... | ... | ... | ... | ... | ... | ... | ... |
| St. Helena and Ascension | ... | ... | ... | ... | ... | ... | ... | ... | ... | ... | ... | ... | ... | ... |
| St. Lucia | 22 | 100.0 | ... | 0.092 | 650 | 36.2 | — | — | 63.8 | 97.7 | — | — | — | 7.0[7] |
| St. Pierre and Miquelon | ... | ... | ... | 0.181 | 30,170 | ... | ... | ... | ... | ... | ... | ... | ... | ... |
| St. Vincent and the Grenadines | 14 | 100.0 | 1.6 | 0.062 | 570 | 19.2 | — | — | 80.8 | 98.7 | — | — | — | 6.5[7] |
| San Marino | ... | ... | ... | ... | ... | ... | ... | ... | ... | ... | ... | ... | ... | ... |
| São Tomé and Príncipe | ... | ... | ... | ... | ... | ... | ... | ... | ... | ... | ... | ... | ... | ... |
| Saudi Arabia | 16,009 | 99.0 | 0.2[1] | 81.8[2] | 7,280[2] | — | — | — | 100.0[2] | 10.6[2] | 67.0[2] | — | — | ... |
| Senegal | 8 | 87.5 | 301.4 | 227.0 | 33,860 | 50.1 | — | 48.9 | 0.9 | 38.3 | 1.8 | 57.0 | — | 9.5 |
| Seychelles | 13 | 100.0 | 6.1 | 0.158 | 2,390 | 59.1 | — | 12.0 | 28.9 | 61.8 | 16.6 | — | 8.1 | 6.0 |
| Sierra Leone | 25 | 100.0 | 35.5 | 1.852 | 490 | 89.5 | — | — | 10.5 | 64.1 | 0.6 | 400.4 | — | 16.0 |
| Singapore | 10,310 | 100.0 | 0.1 | 9.822 | 3,780 | — | — | — | 100.0 | 25.9 | 19.4 | — | — | 4.4[16] |
| Solomon Islands | 22 | 100.0 | 1.7 | 0.031 | 110 | 6.5 | — | 9.4 | 84.1 | 32.9 | 22.6 | 9.8 | 41.7 | 12.0[7] |
| Somalia | 11[9] | 90.9[9] | 396.5 | 12.211 | 2,010 | 65.7[3] | — | 24.5 | 9.9 | 49.7 | 15.0 | 138.1 | 9.0 | 12.0 |
| South Africa | 809 | 73.9 | ... | 22.928 | 670 | 17.5 | — | 9.2 | 73.3 | 81.0 | 33.1 | 30.4 | — | 9.5 |
| Bophuthatswana | ... | ... | ... | ... | ... | ... | ... | ... | ... | ... | ... | ... | ... | ... |
| Ciskei | ... | ... | ... | ... | ... | ... | ... | ... | ... | ... | ... | ... | ... | ... |
| KwaNdebele | ... | ... | ... | ... | ... | ... | ... | ... | ... | ... | ... | ... | ... | ... |
| Transkei | ... | ... | ... | ... | ... | ... | ... | ... | ... | ... | ... | ... | ... | ... |
| Venda | ... | ... | ... | ... | ... | ... | ... | ... | ... | ... | ... | ... | ... | ... |
| South West Africa/Namibia | ... | ... | ... | ... | ... | ... | ... | ... | ... | ... | ... | ... | ... | ... |
| Spain | 14,764 | 96.5 | 6.2 | 7,580.0 | 194,800 | 46.6 | — | 22.5 | 30.9 | 100.3 | 4.6 | — | 6.0 | 8.0 |
| Sri Lanka | 266 | 99.2 | 6.2 | 21.044 | 1,300 | 71.1 | — | 6.2 | 22.7 | 41.0 | — | 21.8 | — | 11.0 |
| Sudan, The | 20 | 100.0 | 420.3 | 5.830 | 230 | 94.0[3] | — | 3.5 | 2.5 | 89.6 | — | 81.1 | 0.9 | 13.5[8, 11] |
| Suriname | 21 | 90.5 | 1.7[1] | 0.880[2] | 2,280[2] | 93.8[2] | — | — | 6.2[2] | 84.5[2] | 2.0[2] | — | 4.3[2] | ... |
| Swaziland | 81 | 100.0 | 2.2 | 0.115 | 160 | 11.9 | — | 0.4 | 87.7 | 77.4 | 5.0 | 10.8 | 8.9 | 9.0 |
| Sweden | 6,671 | 96.8 | ... | ... | ... | 64.3 | — | 2.9 | 32.7 | 47.6 | — | 1.3 | — | 7.5 |
| Switzerland | 19,631 | 85.2 | ... | 75.9 | 11,550 | 6.8 | — | 10.6 | 82.6 | 74.6 | 2.1 | — | — | 3.5 |
| Syria | 61[9] | 52.5[9] | 23.4 | 46.207[11] | 4,650[11] | 94.7[3, 11] | — | 2.0[11] | 3.3[11] | 75.1[11] | 12.5[11] | 11.1[11] | 0.3[11] | 5.0[11] |
| Taiwan | ... | ... | ... | 1,137.863 | 58,370 | 0.2[3] | — | 3.3 | 96.6 | 15.6 | 3.5 | — | — | 4.5 |
| Tanzania | 51 | 100.0 | 180.7 | 20.985[11] | 980[11] | 92.8[11] | — | 3.5[11] | 3.7[11] | 84.9[11] | — | 8.0[11] | — | 11.0[8] |
| Thailand | 2,988 | 97.1 | 4.3 | 109.6 | 2,060 | 47.5[2] | — | 11.3[2] | 35.5[2] | 38.4[2] | 3.6[2] | 13.3[2] | 45.9[2] | 10.0[9] |
| Togo | 275 | 100.0 | 2.7 | 89.7 | 28,790 | 28.8 | — | 3.8 | 67.5 | 74.6 | 1.6 | 21.7 | — | 9.5 |
| Tokelau | ... | ... | ... | ... | ... | ... | ... | ... | ... | ... | ... | ... | ... | ... |
| Tonga | ... | ... | ... | ... | ... | 3.4[18] | 14.5[18] | 24.9[18] | 51.7[18] | —89.2[18]— | | 0.2[18] | 10.6[18] | ... |
| Trinidad and Tobago | 260 | 99.2 | 1.0 | 2.073 | 1,710 | 41.9 | — | — | 58.1 | 68.3 | 32.3 | — | 37.5 | 7.5 |
| Tunisia | 138 | 95.7 | 18.5 | 2.112 | 280 | 5.0 | — | 79.7 | 15.2 | 60.8 | 7.1 | 12.6 | 21.6 | 9.2 |
| Turkey | 1,247 | 89.3 | 14.8 | 5,091.1 | 97,540 | 70.3[3] | — | 4.3 | 25.4 | 26.4 | 0.7 | 69.9 | 1.1 | 52.0[2] |
| Turks and Caicos Islands | ... | ... | ... | ... | ... | ... | ... | ... | ... | ... | ... | ... | ... | ... |
| Tuvalu | ... | ... | ... | ... | ... | ... | ... | ... | ... | ... | ... | ... | ... | ... |
| Uganda | 22 | 100.0 | 11.6 | 225.608[2] | 15,160[2] | 66.2[2, 3] | — | — | 33.8[2] | 41.1[2] | 25.1[2] | 97.8[2] | — | 36.0 |
| U.S.S.R. | ... | ... | ... | ... | ... | ... | ... | ... | ... | ... | ... | ... | ... | ... |
| United Arab Emirates | 3,347 | 99.2 | 0.4[1] | 9.505[2] | 7,410[2] | 3.5[2, 3] | — | 1.2[2] | 95.3[2] | 49.5[2] | 15.6[2] | — | 35.4[2] | ... |
| United Kingdom | 23,134 | 97.1 | ... | 75.2 | 1,330 | 38.5 | — | — | 61.5 | 63.0 | — | 32.0 | — | 8.8[16] |
| United States | 35,834 | 74.4 | ... | 746.6 | 3,080 | 81.7 | — | — | 17.8 | 94.7 | 6.7 | 0.1 | — | 5.5 |
| Uruguay | 504 | 81.9 | 9.8 | 85.8 | 28,150 | 44.6 | 8.1 | 17.4 | 29.8 | 13.0 | 42.0 | 55.3 | — | 58.4[8] |
| Vanuatu | 26 | 100.0 | 0.6 | 2.810 | 19,740 | — | — | 12.7 | 87.3 | 47.9 | 27.8 | 1.2 | 12.6 | 6.5[16] |
| Venezuela | 4,961 | 91.9 | 1.6 | 98.429 | 5,460 | 2.7 | — | 4.6 | 92.7 | 59.3 | 16.2 | — | 32.8 | 12.7 |
| Vietnam | ... | ... | ... | ... | ... | ... | ... | ... | ... | ... | ... | ... | ... | ... |
| Virgin Islands (U.S.) | ... | ... | ... | ... | ... | ... | ... | ... | ... | ... | ... | ... | ... | ... |
| Wallis and Futuna | ... | ... | ... | 0.464 | 31,560 | ... | ... | ... | ... | ... | ... | ... | ... | ... |
| West Bank | ... | ... | ... | ... | ... | ... | ... | ... | ... | ... | ... | ... | ... | ... |
| Western Sahara | ... | ... | ... | ... | ... | ... | ... | ... | ... | ... | ... | ... | ... | ... |
| Western Samoa | 21 | 100.0 | 4.6 | 0.022 | 140 | 23.2 | — | 7.8 | 69.1 | 53.9 | 1.9 | 34.2 | — | 13.5[19] |
| Yemen (Aden) | 255[11] | 99.6[11] | 5.0[11] | 0.369[11] | 180[11] | 81.1[11] | — | — | 18.9[11] | 94.5[11] | — | 8.2[11] | — | ... |
| Yemen (Şan'ā') | 537 | 100.0 | 6.3 | 23.683 | 3,310 | 87.5[3] | — | — | 12.5 | 80.2 | 9.0 | 1.3 | 0.6 | 9.5[8] |
| Yugoslavia | 701 | 90.7 | 8.5 | 3,829.8 | 163,900 | 2.5 | 7.7 | 57.5 | 32.3 | 162.5 | 1.8 | 72.8 | — | 61.0 |
| Zaire | 159 | 89.3 | 23.3 | 50.048 | 1,590 | 70.0[3] | 1.1 | 3.4 | 25.4 | 29.4 | 0.7 | 64.2 | −12.0 | 26.0 |
| Zambia | 40 | 100.0 | 16.1 | 1.232[2] | 180[2] | 80.4[2] | 2.4[2] | — | 17.2[2] | 9.6[2] | — | 113.1[2] | — | 30.0 |
| Zimbabwe | 114 | 83.3 | 12.4 | 1.125 | 130 | 10.5 | 38.6 | — | 50.9 | 71.0 | 0.1 | 54.3 | — | 9.0 |

| deposit money banks, 1986[b] | | | | | | | | | external public debt outstanding (long-term, disbursed only), 1985[b] | | | | | | | country |
| assets (%) | | | | liabilities | | | | | total ('000,000 U.S.$) | creditors (%) | | debt service | | | | |
| loans to govern-ment | loans to private sector | re-serves | foreign assets | deposits ('000,000,000 national currency) | composition (%) | | | | | offi-cial | private | total ('000,000 U.S.$) | repayment (%) | | debt service ratio (%) | |
| | | | | | demand depos. | savings depos. | govt. depos. | foreign liabilities | | | | | princi-pal | inter-est | | |
|---|---|---|---|---|---|---|---|---|---|---|---|---|---|---|---|---|
| 13.7[3] | 65.1 | 0.7 | 10.8 | 466.6 | 13.9 | 41.7[4] | 0.9 | 21.1 | ... | ... | ... | ... | ... | ... | ... | Norway |
| 3.9 | 63.9 | 10.5 | 21.7 | 1.056 | 12.8 | 49.7 | 11.4 | 12.3 | 1,945.5 | 18.8 | 81.2 | 255.2 | 56.2 | 43.8 | 4.8 | Oman |
| ... | ... | ... | ... | ... | ... | ... | ... | ... | 33[1] | ... | ... | 30[1] | 86.7[1] | 13.3[1] | ... | Pacific Is., Trust Terr. of the |
| | | | | | | | | | | | | | | | | Marshall Islands |
| | | | | | | | | | | | | | | | | Micronesia, Fed. States of |
| | | | | | | | | | | | | | | | | |
| | | | | | | | | | | | | | | | | Northern Mariana Islands |
| | | | | | | | | | | | | | | | | Palau |
| 19.8[3] | 68.4 | 6.7 | 5.1 | 226.935 | 31.8 | 34.6 | 0.6 | 11.0 | 10,681.4 | 93.1 | 6.9 | 1,071.7 | 71.5 | 28.5 | 29.5 | Pakistan |
| 1.4[2] | 9.0[2] | — | 89.6[2] | 25.184[2] | 1.4[2] | 5.5[2] | — | 88.9[2] | 3,275.6 | 34.9 | 65.1 | 431.6 | 30.5 | 69.5 | 6.8 | Panama |
| 17.4[11] | 75.4[11] | 5.2[11] | 1.9[11] | 0.690[11] | 22.6[11] | 60.7[11] | 3.5[11] | 7.5[11] | 1,061.1 | 46.7 | 53.3 | 130.8 | 49.7 | 50.3 | 13.4[11] | Papua New Guinea |
| — | 55.9 | 38.4 | 5.7 | 304.596 | 22.1 | 49.5 | — | 3.3 | 1,524.9 | 67.6 | 32.4 | 152.5 | 47.9 | 52.1 | 12.9 | Paraguay |
| 1.0 | 50.1 | 44.3 | 4.6 | 49.383 | 32.0 | 43.9[4] | — | 3.2 | 10,526.8 | 45.1 | 54.9 | 298.7 | 51.0 | 49.0 | 7.9 | Peru |
| 17.9[3] | 53.2 | 9.7 | 16.6 | 213.0 | 6.3 | 45.9 | 5.8 | 30.3 | 13,561.4 | 50.7 | 49.3 | 1,257.0 | 33.9 | 66.1 | 15.8 | Philippines |
| | | | | | | | | | | | | | | | | Pitcairn Island |
| 52.0[3] | 33.8 | 9.3 | 4.9 | 13,722.0 | 13.3 | 19.1 | 0.2 | 44.7 | 29,330[14] | ... | ... | ... | ... | ... | ... | Poland |
| 6.4[11] | 66.7[11] | 13.4[11] | 13.5[11] | 2,313.6[11] 16.324[2] | 22.7[11] | 72.2[11] | 5.2[11] | 51.3[11] | 10,802.8 | 23.6 | 76.4 | 2,502.5 | 59.9 | 40.1 | 31.5 | Portugal |
| | | | | | | | | | | | | | | | | Puerto Rico |
| ... | 47.3[2] | 1.4[2] | 51.3[2] | 13.621[2] | 21.3[2] | 53.5[2] | 3.6[2] | 6.6[2] | 211[1] | ... | ... | 126[1] | 78.6[1] | 21.4[1] | 5.6[1,5] | Qatar |
| ... | ... | ... | ... | ... | ... | ... | ... | ... | 55[1] | ... | ... | 13[1] | 38.5[1] | 61.5[1] | 3.1[1,5] | Réunion |
| 30.4 | 66.1 | 1.1 | 2.5 | 670.2 | 6.5 | 25.0 | — | 14.2 | 5,800.9 | 47.1 | 52.9 | 1,772.7 | 69.4 | 30.6 | 13.6 | Romania |
| 17.9[2,3] | 62.6[2] | 6.6[2] | 12.9[2] | 20.977[2] | 30.1[2] | 39.0[2] | 8.2[2] | 11.0[2] | 324.4 | 96.4 | 3.6 | 15.2 | 71.7 | 28.3 | 5.5[11] | Rwanda |
| 2.4[6] | 60.2[6] | 2.8[6] | 14.8[6] | 0.206[6] | 9.5[6] | 68.0[6] | 1.4[6] | 5.5[6] | ... | ... | ... | ... | ... | ... | ... | St. Christopher and Nevis |
| | | | | | | | | | | | | | | | | St. Helena and Ascension |
| 9.5[3] | 59.5 | 13.7 | 17.4 | 0.463 | 11.5 | 68.0 | — | 8.8 | ... | ... | ... | ... | ... | ... | ... | St. Lucia |
| | | | | | | | | | | | | | | | | St. Pierre and Miquelon |
| 20.9[3] | 42.1 | 16.3 | 20.7 | 0.257 | 8.5 | 63.8 | — | 16.5 | 23.2 | 97.8 | 2.2 | 2.4 | 50.0 | 50.0 | 2.2[5] | St. Vincent and the Grenadines |
| | | | | | | | | | | | | | | | | San Marino |
| ... | ... | ... | ... | ... | ... | ... | ... | ... | 72.1 | 92.4 | 7.6 | 3.7 | 59.5 | 40.5 | 38.7 | São Tomé and Príncipe |
| — | 41.8[2] | 8.8[2] | 49.4[2] | 143.0[2] | 32.2[2] | 45.6[2,4] | 1.0[2] | 7.3[2] | 3,947[1] | ... | ... | 1,785[1] | 88.9[1] | 11.1[1] | 5.1[1,5] | Saudi Arabia |
| 3.5 | 86.0 | 6.5 | 3.0 | 433.0 | 27.1 | 24.6 | 5.5 | 11.2 | 1,989.2 | 87.3 | 12.7 | 88.6 | 50.9 | 49.1 | ... | Senegal |
| 66.1[3] | 20.5 | 6.2 | 7.3 | 0.444 | 17.9 | 55.6 | 7.6 | 4.6 | 54.0 | 84.3 | 15.7 | 6.0 | 68.3 | 31.7 | 4.3[2] | Seychelles |
| 31.4[3] | 20.1 | 21.6 | 26.8 | 1.837 | 45.4 | 23.6 | — | 9.2 | 390.0 | 73.5 | 26.5 | 9.9 | 73.7 | 26.3 | 10.9[11] | Sierra Leone |
| 5.9 | 51.5 | 3.5 | 39.1 | 66.993 | 7.1 | 31.5 | 3.7 | 43.6 | 1,790.8 | 21.5 | 78.5 | 721.8 | 78.5 | 21.5 | 2.4 | Singapore |
| 16.8[3] | 66.3 | 12.1 | 4.9 | 0.077 | 22.5 | 53.4 | 2.3 | 9.8 | 59.9 | 75.0 | 25.0 | 1.1 | 72.7 | 27.3 | 1.3 | Solomon Islands |
| 5.7[3] | 32.5 | 20.3 | 41.5 | 12.597 | 47.6 | 36.3 | — | — | 1,308.5 | 96.1 | 3.9 | 57.2 | 70.1 | 29.9 | 44.8 | Somalia |
| 6.3 | 87.6 | 2.8 | 3.2 | 56.385 | 33.0 | 43.0 | — | 8.3 | ... | ... | ... | ... | ... | ... | ... | South Africa |
| | | | | | | | | | | | | | | | | Bophuthatswana |
| | | | | | | | | | | | | | | | | Ciskei |
| | | | | | | | | | | | | | | | | KwaNdebele |
| | | | | | | | | | | | | | | | | Transkei |
| | | | | | | | | | | | | | | | | |
| | | | | | | | | | | | | | | | | Venda |
| 0.2[11] | 50.5[11] | 23.0[11] | — | 0.810[11] | —64.7[11]— | | 24.6[11] | 0.4[11] | ... | ... | ... | ... | ... | ... | ... | South West Africa/Namibia |
| 26.7[3] | 51.3 | 10.6 | 8.9 | 35,597.0 | 13.7 | 40.6 | 3.5 | 9.5 | ... | ... | ... | ... | ... | ... | ... | Spain |
| 4.7 | 72.7 | 11.0 | 11.6 | 59.478 | 15.7 | 51.6 | 6.5 | 8.9 | 2,815.2 | 77.0 | 23.0 | 226.3 | 52.4 | 47.6 | 13.9 | Sri Lanka |
| 1.1 | 39.7 | 40.6 | 18.6 | 6.643 | 39.4 | 27.7 | 10.3 | 7.3 | 5,086.0 | 82.0 | 18.0 | 130.4 | 48.7 | 51.3 | 15.6 | Sudan, The |
| 9.0[2] | 50.1[2] | 39.5[2] | 1.5[2] | 1.378[2] | 33.9[2] | 48.7[2] | 1.0[2] | 4.1[2] | 43[1] | ... | ... | 5[1] | 40.1[1] | 60.0[1] | 1.8[1,5] | Suriname |
| 7.0 | 44.8 | 44.4 | 3.8 | 0.360 | 24.1 | 56.3 | 3.9 | 4.0 | 181.7 | 95.1 | 4.9 | 23.3 | 67.0 | 33.0 | 8.5 | Swaziland |
| 8.0[2] | 79.2[2] | 1.3[2] | 11.4[2] | 594.8[2] | —75.6[2,4]— | | — | 24.4[2] | ... | ... | ... | ... | ... | ... | ... | Sweden |
| 2.4 | 62.0 | 3.0 | 32.6 | 576.9 | 6.1 | 38.0 | — | 23.2 | ... | ... | ... | ... | ... | ... | ... | Switzerland |
| 59.6[3,11] | 14.4[11] | 23.8[11] | 2.3[11] | 41.314[11] | 36.7[11] | 12.6[11] | 9.3[11] | 9.4[11] | 2,750.9 | 94.8 | 5.2 | 360.2 | 73.4 | 26.6 | 14.8 | Syria |
| 22.7[3] | 68.6 | 1.2[17] | 7.4 | 3,289.9 | 27.6 | 42.4[4] | 4.7 | 8.6 | 5,669[1] | ... | ... | 2,218[1] | 74.8[1] | 25.2[1] | ... | Taiwan |
| 74.5[3,11] | 18.0[11] | 4.8[11] | 2.7[11] | 28.480[11] | 36.9[11] | 33.0[11] | 3.9[11] | 23.9[11] | 2,981.7 | 80.9 | 19.1 | 61.1 | 65.5 | 34.5 | ... | Tanzania |
| 16.5[3] | 69.7 | 3.1 | 5.6 | 719.3 | 4.7 | 78.9 | 2.9 | 4.4 | 9,898.4 | 58.0 | 42.0 | 1,499.1 | 59.8 | 40.2 | 14.7 | Thailand |
| 0.5 | 49.0 | 42.0 | 8.1 | 173.6 | 24.7 | 43.7 | 18.5 | 16.4 | 787.0 | 89.0 | 11.0 | 89.3 | 56.9 | 43.1 | 27.4 | Togo |
| | | | | | | | | | | | | | | | | Tokelau |
| ... | ... | ... | ... | ... | ... | ... | ... | ... | 24[1,5] | ... | ... | 1[1,5] | ... | ... | 5.6[1,5] | Tonga |
| 7.5[3] | 73.5 | 15.4 | 3.7 | 8.070 | 15.6 | 77.3 | 1.7 | 3.2 | 1,087.4 | 20.4 | 79.6 | 183.8 | 56.4 | 43.6 | 7.1 | Trinidad and Tobago |
| 12.5 | 82.5 | 1.0 | 4.0 | 4.541 | 29.1 | 26.6 | — | 7.9 | 4,442.0 | 70.2 | 29.8 | 676.9 | 64.5 | 35.5 | 24.9 | Tunisia |
| 24.3[3] | 52.1 | 12.8 | 9.6 | 17,248.9 | 21.0 | 38.4 | 7.7 | 17.5 | 17,821.2 | 69.4 | 30.6 | 3,501.7 | 64.2 | 35.8 | 30.9 | Turkey |
| | | | | | | | | | | | | | | | | Turks and Caicos Islands |
| | | | | | | | | | | | | | | | | Tuvalu |
| 0.8 | 78.4 | 16.0 | 4.9 | 668,509 | 36.6 | 15.8 | 0.1 | 1.5 | 725.9 | 93.1 | 6.9 | 106.2 | 74.6 | 25.4 | ... | Uganda |
| | | | | | | | | | 26,400[14] | | | | | | | U.S.S.R. |
| 10.7[2,3] | 37.8[2] | 4.6[2] | 46.9[2] | 94.521[2] | 6.7[2] | 42.7[2] | 4.1[2] | 21.1[2] | 1,335[1] | ... | ... | 704[1] | 81.5[1] | 18.5[1] | 3.0[1,5] | United Arab Emirates |
| 2.1[3] | 20.1 | 0.4 | 68.6 | 702.1 | 8.8 | 15.5[4] | — | 70.3 | ... | ... | ... | ... | ... | ... | ... | United Kingdom |
| 12.5[3] | 79.1 | 3.4 | 5.1 | 3,860.3 | 14.4 | 50.8 | 1.0 | 5.4 | ... | ... | ... | ... | ... | ... | ... | United States |
| 13.1[3] | 47.2 | 18.1 | 21.5 | 759.2 | 5.6 | 47.2[4] | 2.2 | 27.7 | 2,686.0 | 16.3 | 83.7 | 406.1 | 30.6 | 69.4 | 30.6 | Uruguay |
| 0.8[3] | 9.6 | 1.0 | 87.7 | 39.568 | 4.8 | 32.4[4] | 0.7 | 52.2 | 6.9 | 75.4 | 24.6 | 0.6 | 66.7 | 33.3 | 0.7 | Vanuatu |
| 6.4[3] | 74.8 | 14.3 | 4.5 | 200.158 | 36.2 | 59.6[4] | 9.4 | 1.6 | 16,649.8 | 0.8 | 99.2 | 2,160.3 | 36.5 | 63.5 | 12.9 | Venezuela |
| | | | | | | | | | 5,302[1] | ... | ... | 154[1] | 7.8[1] | 92.2[1] | 26.8[1,5] | Vietnam |
| | | | | | | | | | | | | | | | | Virgin Islands (U.S.) |
| | | | | | | | | | | | | | | | | Wallis and Futuna |
| | | | | | | | | | | | | | | | | West Bank |
| | | | | | | | | | | | | | | | | Western Sahara |
| 19.6[3] | 35.5 | 34.7 | 10.2 | 0.075 | 16.9 | 55.4 | 9.1 | 0.1 | 65.2 | 94.6 | 5.4 | 5.2 | 67.3 | 32.7 | 19.2 | Western Samoa |
| 34.2[3,11] | 5.2[11] | 57.3[11] | 3.3[11] | 0.311[11] | 36.3[11] | 45.6[11] | 10.0[11] | 7.4[11] | 1,446.3 | 100.0 | — | 113.7 | 83.6 | 16.4 | 47.9[11] | Yemen (Aden) |
| 2.6[3] | 37.2 | 37.5 | 22.8 | 13.125 | 25.2 | 52.4 | 1.2 | 18.0 | 1,867.8 | 99.3 | 0.7 | 125.7 | 85.3 | 14.7 | 55.8 | Yemen (Şan'ā') |
| 0.2 | 61.8 | 32.3 | 5.6 | 17,650.1 | 15.0 | 48.4[4] | — | 29.4 | 9,919.2 | 45.0 | 55.0 | 1,170.5 | 37.0 | 63.0 | 9.3 | Yugoslavia |
| 2.4[3] | 32.1 | 40.5 | 24.9 | 43.562 | 37.9 | 5.9[4] | 0.4 | 7.1 | 4,821.0 | 84.2 | 15.8 | 341.0 | 35.8 | 64.2 | 14.8[11] | Zaire |
| 28.2 | 36.2 | 20.0 | 15.6 | 4.945 | 34.5 | 35.6 | 2.7 | 11.3 | 3,213.9 | 78.4 | 21.6 | 86.2 | 51.2 | 48.8 | 10.2 | Zambia |
| 42.2[3] | 46.4 | 8.7 | 1.7 | 2.509 | 29.0 | 53.5 | — | 4.3 | 1,526.1 | 42.7 | 57.3 | 325.6 | 64.6 | 35.4 | 19.9[11] | Zimbabwe |

[1]Includes external long-term private debt not guaranteed by the government. [2]1985. [3]Includes claims on nonfinancial government (public) enterprises and/or local governments. [4]Includes foreign currency deposits. [5]1983. [6]1982. [7]Treasury bill rate. [8]Time deposit rate. [9]1986. [10]External public debt data for Netherlands Antilles include Aruba. [11]1984. [12]Excludes Indian rupee currency. [13]Cash and demand deposits at local banks. [14]Gross hard currency debt to the West. [15]Six-month interbank offer rate. [16]Money market rate. [17]Cash in vaults only. [18]1977. [19]Government bond yield.

# Housing and construction

The present table summarizes data about the housing stock and the construction industries of the countries of the world. The principal focus is on the elements that are most comparable internationally: the age of the housing (by decade, so far as possible), the legal tenure of the householder, construction of exterior walls, principal physical amenities, sanitary arrangements, and the amount of space both absolutely (total area of the average dwelling in square metres [1 square metre equals 1.20 square yards, or 10.76 square feet]) and relatively (persons per room). The data on construction characterize the industry in number of new units constructed annually, their area, and the portion of the gross domestic product (GDP) represented by each country's construction industry.

Because housing patterns differ greatly from country to country, the portion of each country's housing stock for which data are compared is defined as specifically as possible. In general, the numbers refer to permanent, private dwelling units that are usually occupied year-round, whether or not actually occupied on the date of the housing census or survey. That definition implies the exclusion of certain housing that is often part of national housing censuses: vacation homes, second homes

occupied less than half the year, collective or communal dwellings, and so on. The housing unit to which the data on tenure refer may be either the individual dwelling or the household, according to the reporting practice of the country concerned.

The data are collected mostly from national housing censuses and surveys. The majority of countries combine the housing census with the population census at five- to ten-year intervals. Some countries, however, can conduct a meaningful housing census only in the capital city or in the few largest cities; others may be able to collect and process data for only a few of the most important housing characteristics even when national coverage is complete. These choices may be dictated by the lack of funding to collect data for the entire country or by the perception, particularly in a tropical, rural country where adequate dwellings can be built by hand, that no urgent housing problem exists. These choices may be complex, however, as planners are always aware that much housing is physically inadequate to protect dwellers from the elements, is disadvantageously placed in relation to tainted or disease-infested water supply or to the outfall of unprocessed sewage, or is built of materials (mud,

## Housing and construction

| country | housing stock | | | decade built (percent) | | | | | tenure[c] (percent) | | | construction of exterior walls (percent) | | | |
|---|---|---|---|---|---|---|---|---|---|---|---|---|---|---|---|
| | year | dwelling units[a] | median age[b] (years) | 1939 or earlier | 1940–49 | 1950–59 | 1960–69 | 1970 or later | owned | rented | collective, vacant, other | traditional materials | sawn/ framed wood | masonry or cement | other |
| Afghanistan | 1979 | 136,279 | ... | ... | ... | ... | ... | ... | 55.2 | 23.5 | 21.3 | ... | ... | ... | ... |
| Albania | ... | ... | ... | ... | ... | ... | ... | ... | ... | ... | ... | ... | ... | ... | ... |
| Algeria | 1977 | 2,208,712[6] | ... | ... | ... | ... | 23.7 | | 56.7 | 29.4 | 13.9 | ... | ... | ... | ... |
| American Samoa | 1980 | 4,688 | 13.4 | 4.2 | 4.8 | 7.7 | 38.4 | 44.9 | 71.2 | 25.1 | 3.7 | 4.1 | 56.3 | 34.9 | 4.7 |
| Andorra | ... | ... | ... | ... | ... | ... | ... | ... | ... | ... | ... | ... | ... | ... | ... |
| Angola | ... | ... | ... | ... | ... | ... | ... | ... | ... | ... | ... | ... | ... | ... | ... |
| Anguilla | 1984 | 1,840 | ... | ... | ... | ... | ... | ... | ... | ... | ... | — | 8.1 | 91.2 | 0.7 |
| Antigua and Barbuda | 1970 | 15,405[6] | 11.1 | 13.8 | 9.7 | 31.4 | 46.1 | — | 55.9 | 40.4 | 3.7 | ... | ... | ... | ... |
| Argentina | 1980 | 7,103,853 | 21.6 | 9.1 | 14.9 | 17.3 | 22.0 | 36.7 | 67.7 | 14.8 | 17.5 | 6.1 | 6.7 | 84.2 | 3.0 |
| Aruba | 1981 | 14,929 | 29.0 | 28.2 | —34.2— | | 14.9 | 22.7 | 49.0 | 51.0 | — | | 9.4 | 87.7 | 2.9 |
| Australia | 1981 | 5,161,163 | 26.1 | —37.9— | | 10.4 | 18.6 | 33.1 | 61.6 | 22.6 | 15.8 | ... | ... | ... | ... |
| Austria | 1981 | 3,052,037 | 63.6 | —44.5— | | 13.3 | 19.4 | 22.8 | 47.7 | 36.2 | 16.1 | ... | ... | ... | ... |
| Bahamas, The | 1980 | 54,308 | 30.7 | —54.7— | | | 25.6 | 19.7 | 51.4 | 37.4 | 11.2 | 4.0[14] | 32.3 | 54.7 | 9.0 |
| Bahrain | 1981 | 52,810 | 15.2 | 41.2 | 17.1 | 14.5 | —27.2— | | 60.6[13] | 33.6[13] | 5.8[13] | 2.1[13] | — | 95.1[13] | 2.8[13] |
| Bangladesh | 1981 | 14,790,000 | ... | ... | ... | ... | ... | ... | 89.7 | 5.0 | 5.3 | 20.0 | 11.6 | 5.0 | 63.4 |
| Barbados | 1980 | 67,138 | 18.9 | —51.3— | | | 20.6 | 28.1 | 70.2 | 21.5 | 8.3 | 0.1 | 68.9[15] | 26.3 | 4.7 |
| Belgium | 1981 | 3,599,997 | 35.2 | 48.4[16] | —17.2[17]— | | 14.2 | 16.0 | 59.2 | 38.1 | 2.7 | ... | ... | ... | ... |
| Belize | 1980 | 27,298 | ... | —24.6— | | | 30.0 | 41.0 | 56.1 | 27.2 | 16.7 | 7.5 | 73.4 | 14.0 | 5.1 |
| Benin | 1975 | 644,000 | ... | ... | ... | ... | ... | ... | ... | ... | ... | ... | ... | ... | ... |
| Bermuda | 1980 | 20,350 | 31.2 | —67.9— | | | 16.6 | 15.5 | 39.4 | 53.7 | 6.9 | — | 1.7[15] | 95.1 | 3.2 |
| Bhutan | ... | ... | ... | ... | ... | ... | ... | ... | ... | ... | ... | ... | ... | ... | ... |
| Bolivia | 1976 | 1,040,704 | ... | ... | ... | ... | 47.4 | | 69.3 | 15.1 | 15.6 | ... | ... | ... | ... |
| Botswana | 1981 | 170,262 | ... | ... | ... | ... | ... | ... | 59.9 | 17.1 | 23.0 | 65.5 | — | 28.0 | 6.5 |
| Brazil | 1984 | 29,163,724 | ... | ... | ... | ... | ... | ... | 63.4 | 22.3 | 14.3 | ... | ... | ... | ... |
| British Virgin Islands | 1980 | 3,287 | 21.6 | —39.8— | | —31.2— | | 29.0 | 47.4 | 43.0 | 9.6 | — | 21.6 | 68.0 | 10.4 |
| Brunei | 1981 | 28,676 | ... | ... | ... | ... | ... | ... | 83.8 | 11.8 | 4.4 | 0.2 | 54.8 | 36.5 | 8.5 |
| Bulgaria | 1975 | 2,734,717 | 17.9 | 47.0 | —34.9— | | 11.1 | 7.0 | 77.3 | 22.7 | — | ... | ... | ... | ... |
| Burkina Faso | ... | ... | ... | ... | ... | ... | ... | ... | ... | ... | ... | ... | ... | ... | ... |
| Burma | 1983 | 6,750,884 | ... | ... | ... | ... | ... | ... | ... | ... | ... | 83.5 | 14.8 | — | 1.7 |
| Burundi | 1979[22] | 938,000 | ... | ... | ... | ... | ... | ... | 98.7 | 1.1 | 0.2 | ... | ... | ... | ... |
| Cameroon | 1976 | 1,390,896 | ... | ... | ... | ... | ... | ... | 83.4 | 11.2 | 5.4 | 75.5 | 13.9 | 9.5 | 1.1 |
| Canada | 1981 | 8,063,000 | 14.6 | —41.2— | | 13.8 | 17.9 | 27.1 | 62.1 | 37.9 | — | ... | ... | ... | ... |
| Cape Verde | ... | ... | ... | ... | ... | ... | ... | ... | ... | ... | ... | ... | ... | ... | ... |
| Cayman Islands | 1979 | 4,426 | ... | —52.0— | | | | 48.0 | 67.8 | 32.2 | — | 1.0 | 24.0 | 74.0 | 1.0 |
| Central African Republic | 1975 | 405,399 | ... | ... | ... | ... | ... | ... | ... | ... | ... | 82.2 | 7.1 | 2.5 | 8.2 |
| Chad | ... | ... | ... | ... | ... | ... | ... | ... | ... | ... | ... | ... | ... | ... | ... |
| Chile | 1982 | 2,510,275 | 20.4 | —46.2— | | | 21.1 | 32.7 | 63.1 | 18.7 | 18.2 | 13.0 | 44.4 | 41.6 | 1.0 |
| China | 1982 | 220,100,775 | ... | ... | ... | ... | ... | ... | 18.5[1] | 81.5[1] | — | ... | ... | ... | ... |
| Christmas Island | 1984 | 1,231 | 14.0[3] | —32.2[3]— | | | 27.2[3] | 40.6[3] | — | 86.4[23] | 13.6[23] | — | 1.7[23] | 74.7[23] | 23.6[23] |
| Cocos (Keeling) Islands | 1981 | 150 | ... | ... | ... | ... | 33.3 | | —80.7— | | 19.3 | — | 6.0 | 52.0 | 42.0 |
| Colombia | 1985 | 5,266,581 | 20.6[25] | 46.7[25] | 7.9[25] | 26.2[25] | 19.2[25] | — | 67.6 | 23.6 | 8.8 | 16.7 | 7.0 | 75.6 | 0.7 |
| Comoros | 1980 | 81,791 | ... | —5.3— | | 7.7 | 21.3 | 63.7 | 87.4 | 3.1 | 9.5 | 73.5 | 1.8 | 16.9 | 7.8 |
| Congo | 1984 | 363,140 | ... | ... | ... | ... | ... | ... | 61.0 | 34.6 | 4.4 | 15.0 | 20.0 | 52.8 | 12.2 |
| Cook Islands | 1981 | 3,153[6] | 14.0 | 5.9 | 5.7 | 16.8 | 48.6 | 23.0 | 85.3[12] | 9.4[12] | 5.3[12] | ... | ... | ... | ... |
| Costa Rica | 1984 | 500,788 | ... | ... | ... | ... | 36.4[25] | | 65.8 | 20.7 | 13.5 | 1.1 | 60.1 | 35.6 | 3.2 |
| Côte d'Ivoire | 1985 | 1,146,370[26] | ... | ... | ... | ... | ... | ... | ... | ... | ... | ... | ... | ... | ... |
| Cuba | 1981 | 2,363,364 | 24.6 | 15.0[27] | 8.2[28] | 21.3[29] | 21.6 | 25.6 | ... | ... | ... | 1.4 | 37.1 | 61.5 | — |
| Cyprus | 1982 | 168,588 | 22.8 | —39.9— | | | 15.4 | 44.7 | 60.0 | 16.5 | 23.5 | 11.9 | — | 87.6 | 0.5 |
| Czechoslovakia | 1980 | 5,009,771 | 36.7 | —40.0[16]— | | 15.1[17] | 20.3 | 24.6 | 44.7 | 41.7 | 13.6 | — | 2.9 | 93.8 | 3.3 |
| Denmark | 1985 | 2,120,549 | 30.8 | 40.0 | 6.7 | 10.8 | 17.9 | 24.6 | 55.3 | 43.2 | 1.5 | ... | ... | ... | ... |
| Djibouti | 1982 | 25,000 | 27.6 | ... | ... | ... | ... | ... | ... | ... | ... | ... | 73.0[30] | 22.5 | 4.5 |
| Dominica | 1981 | 17,307 | ... | —58.4[18]— | | 16.9[18] | 21.1[18] | 3.6[18] | 64.7[18] | 26.6[18] | 8.7[18] | 0.2[18] | 88.8[18] | 10.2[18] | 0.8[18] |
| Dominican Republic | 1981 | 1,114,833[6] | ... | —12.4— | | | —87.6— | | 72.0 | 17.0 | 11.0 | 31.8[18] | 46.2[18] | 15.3[18] | 6.7[18] |
| Ecuador | 1982 | 1,576,441 | ... | ... | ... | ... | ... | ... | 66.7 | 22.9 | 10.4 | 46.9 | 9.3 | 41.4 | 2.4 |
| Egypt | 1976 | 7,311,139 | ... | ... | ... | ... | ... | ... | ... | ... | ... | ... | ... | ... | ... |
| El Salvador | 1971 | 680,456 | ... | ... | ... | ... | ... | ... | 56.7[20] | 22.3[20] | 21.0[20] | 37.9 | 9.6 | 46.9 | 5.6 |
| Equatorial Guinea | ... | ... | ... | ... | ... | ... | ... | ... | ... | ... | ... | ... | ... | ... | ... |
| Ethiopia | 1984 | 9,300,000 | ... | ... | ... | ... | ... | ... | ... | ... | ... | ... | ... | ... | ... |
| Faeroe Islands | 1977 | 11,172 | 32.5 | 33.7 | —26.4— | | 21.8 | 15.0 | 84.5 | 9.9 | 5.6 | — | 43.9 | 53.5 | 2.6 |
| Falkland Islands | 1980 | 589 | ... | ... | ... | ... | ... | ... | 38.9 | 16.6 | 44.5 | — | 86.4 | 10.9 | 2.7 |
| Fiji | 1986 | 124,098 | ... | ... | ... | ... | ... | ... | 74.4 | 14.6 | 11.0 | 9.0 | 26.4 | 29.8 | 34.8 |
| Finland | 1980 | 1,838,058 | 22.0 | 19.2 | 7.8 | 17.0 | 20.9 | 35.1 | 61.0 | 20.9 | 18.1 | ... | ... | ... | ... |
| France | 1982 | 19,590,400 | 31.0[20] | —71.9[20]— | | | 12.7[20] | 15.4[20] | 50.7 | 41.0 | 8.3 | ... | ... | ... | ... |
| French Guiana | 1982 | 21,063 | ... | ... | ... | ... | 23.2[18] | | 34.5 | 54.0 | 11.5 | 29.4[37] | —70.6— | | ... |
| French Polynesia | 1983 | ... | 13.6 | —5.0— | | 9.0 | 30.0 | 56.0 | ... | ... | ... | 38.0 | —62.0— | | ... |

skins, thatch, etc.) that may harbour pests or disease. In the developed countries, median age and the distribution of physical amenities provide strong indicators of the quality and availability of housing.

The data for construction industries refer to new construction for the most recent year in which a broad range of countries could be surveyed. The scope of the data may be limited in several respects. It may be confined to activity capable of being surveyed in the national capital region only, may be limited to private new construction only or to government and government-financed activity only, or may refer to construction mortgaged or financed through certain organizations only. Depending on national data-collection systems, it usually excludes remodeling of old premises but may include extensions or enlargements of existing buildings. The data for construction are usually taken either from the UN's *Construction Statistics Yearbook* or from official national sources that report two principal types of data: authorized new construction or certification after construction that newly built structures meet building and fire codes and the like. The figures for completed construction are naturally more meaningful but are not available for many countries, necessitating the provision of authorized construction data, which are usually available only for areas regulated by certain types of governmental authorities.

A more complete indication of total activity in a national construction industry is its contribution to the national gross domestic product, since that figure also includes civil-engineering projects, such as dams, roads and other transportation infrastructure, recreational facilities, irrigation and land reclamation works, and the like. The predominance within the "new residential" sector of multiunit housing usually indicates (in a developed country) a particularly mobile society or (in a developing country) one in which limited development resources obliges planners to concentrate available physical and manpower resources in collective projects.

a. Data refer to permanent, private dwelling units that are usually occupied year-round, whether or not occupied on the census date.

b. Data are estimates unless specifically provided by a country source.

c. Data may be either for dwellings or for households, depending on country reporting practice.

d. Data may be either for construction completed or for construction authorized, depending on country reporting practice.

| physical amenities (percent) | | | sewage disposal (percent) | | | space[b] | | | construction industry (1984) | | | | | | country |
|---|---|---|---|---|---|---|---|---|---|---|---|---|---|---|---|
| | | | | | | | | | percent of GDP | new residential[d] | | | new nonresidential[d] | | |
| piped water | electricity | inside toilet or WC | closed public sewer or septic tank | open public sewer | other | average area (sq m) | rooms per dwelling unit | persons per room | | 1- or 2-unit dwellings | multiunit dwellings | floor area ('000 sq m) | number of units | floor area ('000 sq m) | |
| 25.3[1] | 66.5[1] | 5.5[1] | 5.5 | 77.9 | 16.6 | ... | 5.5 | 2.1 | 3.9[2] | ... | ... | ... | 48[3] | 65.6[3,4] | Afghanistan |
| ... | ... | ... | | | | | | | 7.8[5] | | | | ... | ... | Albania |
| 45.8 | 49.2 | ... | 54.1 | —45.9— | | ... | 2.27 | 2.87 | 15.1[5] | | | | ... | ... | Algeria |
| 77.4 | 96.2 | ... | 83.5 | — | 16.5 | ... | 3.0 | 2.3 | ... | —194[8]— | | | 8 | ... | American Samoa |
| | | | | | | | | | 13.4[9] | —95[3]— | | 91.3[3] | 14[3] | 47.5[3] | Andorra |
| 36.9 | 64.1 | 30.1[10] | 55.7 | —44.3— | | ... | 4.8 | 0.8 | 1.7[5] | —1,587[3]— | | 585.2[3] | 210[3] | 164.5[3] | Angola |
| 85.4 | | | 17.0 | —83.0— | | ... | 3.1 | ... | ... | | | | | | Anguilla |
| 72.9 | 86.8 | 95.1 | 77.1 | —22.9— | | ... | 3.9 | 1.3 | 6.2 | | | | | | Antigua and Barbuda |
| 98.7 | 98.7 | 89.2 | ... | | | ... | 4.3 | 1.1 | 3.8[11] | —25,716[8,9]— | | 3,406[8,9] | 8 | 8 | Argentina |
| | | | —84[5]— | | | | | | ... | | | | 102[5] | | Aruba |
| 97.1[12] | 98.4[13] | 92.2 | 99.0 | —1.0— | | ... | 5.1 | 0.6 | 6.5 | 150,800 | 118,200 | 17,959 | 18,869 | 7,161 | Australia |
| 95.0 | ... | 85.5 | 94.3 | — | 5.7 | 76.5 | 2.8 | 1.0 | 7.1 | 17,500 | 1,400 | 3,400[8] | 300 | 8 | Austria |
| 63.9 | 77.9 | ... | 63.2 | 2.2 | 34.6 | ... | 4.0 | 1.2 | 2.9 | —1,046— | | | 113 | ... | Bahamas, The |
| 97.5 | 98.2 | ... | 44.7 | — | 55.3 | ... | 3.0[13] | 2.3[13] | 6.4[9] | —2,124[5]— | | | 2,445[5] | ... | Bahrain |
| 56.8 | | | 1.3 | —98.7— | | ... | 2.0 | 2.9 | 5.3 | | | | | | Bangladesh |
| 82.4 | 83.0 | 43.6 | 95.8 | 0.7 | 3.5 | ... | 4.2 | 0.8 | 5.6 | —753[12]— | | | 35[12] | ... | Barbados |
| 95.3 | 100.0 | 79.0 | 62.5[18] | —37.5[18]— | | 82.1 | 5.0 | 0.5 | 5.4 | 22,589 | 441 | 17,067 | 6,362 | 22,067 | Belgium |
| 60.1 | 59.4 | 19.7 | 21.1 | —78.9— | | ... | 2.5[19] | 1.9[19] | 5.7 | | | | | | Belize |
| ... | ... | ... | | | | | | | 4.7[5] | | | | | | Benin |
| 97.4 | ... | 96.7 | 96.7 | —3.3— | | ... | 3.2 | 0.7 | ... | 148[20] | 12[20] | 20.1[20] | 15[20] | 15.0[20] | Bermuda |
| | | | | | | | | | 13.3 | | | | | | Bhutan |
| 37.9 | 33.0 | ... | 12.5 | —87.5— | | ... | ... | ... | 4.3 | —105— | | | 1[5] | | Bolivia |
| 56.1 | 5.4 | 25.4 | 8.6 | 20.4 | 71.0 | ... | ... | ... | 4.1 | —766— | | 70.2 | 393 | 80.7 | Botswana |
| 66.2 | 79.4 | ... | 47.9 | —52.1— | | ... | 5.1[3] | 0.9[3] | 3.9 | —94,492— | | 18,191 | 7,218 | 5,296 | Brazil |
| 62.3 | 90.2 | 65.1 | 65.1 | 25.3 | 9.6 | ... | 3.9 | 1.1 | 10.1[21] | | | | | | British Virgin Islands |
| 90.3 | 64.2 | 94.2 | 57.4 | —42.6— | | ... | 4.2 | 1.6 | 3.3 | —195— | | | 5 | | Brunei |
| 74.6 | 99.8 | 33.2 | 33.2 | —67.8— | | ... | 3.6 | 1.0 | 9.5[2] | 9,561 | 1,684 | 5,518 | ... | ... | Bulgaria |
| ... | ... | ... | ... | | | | | | 1.4 | | | | | | Burkina Faso |
| ... | ... | ... | ... | | | | | | 1.8 | | | | | | Burma |
| 11.0 | 0.6 | ... | 1.6 | —98.4— | | | | | 6.1 | | | | | | Burundi |
| 22.0 | 5.9 | 2.2 | 2.2 | 70.4 | 27.6 | ... | 4.1 | 1.2 | 6.0 | 780[5] | 201[5] | 230.4[5] | 53[5] | 51.1[5] | Cameroon |
| 99.5 | 100.0 | 98.9 | 98.9 | —1.1— | | ... | 5.7 | 0.5 | 4.2 | — | 1,953[5] | ... | 10,745[5] | ... | Canada |
| | | | | | | | | | 20.3[23] | —242[9]— | | 30.5[9] | 3[9] | 0.5[9] | Cape Verde |
| 99.0 | 96.0 | 83.7 | 57.0 | —43.0— | | ... | 4.0 | 1.1 | ... | | | | | | Cayman Islands |
| | | | | | | ... | 1.1[24] | 3.4[24] | 2.6 | —124[20]— | | 18.8[20] | 57[20] | 16.6[20] | Central African Republic |
| | | | | | | | | | 1.3[5] | | | | | | Chad |
| 81.4 | 84.7 | ... | 63.2 | 36.4 | 0.4 | ... | 3.6 | 1.3 | 5.1[5] | | | 23.0 | ... | 113.0 | Chile |
| 89.4[1] | ... | 25.2[1] | 47.0[1] | —53.0[1]— | | 37.0 | 2.2 | 1.8 | 5.2 | | | 77,030 | ... | 61,060 | China |
| 100.0 | 100.0 | 100.0 | 100.0 | — | — | ... | 5.7 | 1.0 | ... | | | | | | Christmas Island |
| 35.6 | 100.0 | 100.0 | 100.0 | — | — | ... | 6.1 | 0.6 | ... | | | | | | Cocos (Keeling) Islands |
| 70.5 | 78.5 | 77.9 | 69.6 | —30.4— | | ... | 3.3 | 1.6 | 5.4 | 5,300 | 10,135 | 6,808 | 1,179 | 902.9 | Colombia |
| 12.9 | 5.7 | ... | 2.1 | —97.9— | | 33.7 | 2.5 | 2.1 | 11.5[9] | | | | | | Comoros |
| 30.5 | 8.8 | 16.6 | —86.2[1]— | | 13.8[1] | ... | 3.7[1] | 1.7[1] | 7.1 | | | | | | Congo |
| 88.3[12] | 60.6[12] | ... | 36.7[12] | —63.3[12]— | | ... | 4.0[12] | 0.7[12] | 4.5[20] | —44— | | | 32 | ... | Cook Islands |
| 86.9 | 97.3 | ... | 66.5 | —33.5— | | ... | 4.0 | 1.4 | 4.1 | —4,004— | | 304 | 1,307 | 68 | Costa Rica |
| 23.0 | 39.6 | 23.9 | —68.5— | | 31.5 | ... | ... | ... | 2.2 | | | | | | Côte d'Ivoire |
| 74.1 | 82.9 | 45.2 | 60.9 | 9.0 | 30.1 | ... | 4.1 | 1.0 | 8.9[2] | 327 | 545 | 988 | 508 | 1,145.1 | Cuba |
| 100.0 | 98.1 | 74.5 | 95.6 | —4.4— | | ... | 4.6 | 0.8 | 10.3 | —5,808— | | 239.1[8] | 839 | 8 | Cyprus |
| 91.6 | 100.0 | 70.8 | 91.2 | —8.8— | | 68.0 | 3.5 | 0.9 | 11.0[2] | 26,131 | | 7,276 | 14,449 | 3,370.0 | Czechoslovakia |
| 100.0 | 100.0 | 99.2 | 98.6[23] | —1.4[23]— | | 108.0 | 3.8 | 0.6 | 6.3 | —26,891— | | 2,904 | | | Denmark |
| 45.0 | 58.0 | 82.0 | 26.0 | 23.0 | 51.0 | ... | 1.9 | 6.9 | 7.5 | —88— | | 27.7 | 31 | 52.3 | Djibouti |
| 91.1[5] | ... | 12.3[18] | 12.3[18] | —87.7[18]— | | ... | 2.8[18] | 1.7[18] | 7.7 | | | | | | Dominica |
| 49.3 | 36.7[18] | 14.1 | 52.1[18] | 22.6[18] | 25.3[18] | ... | 2.8[18] | 1.5[18] | 6.9 | 5,371 | 486 | 692 | 430 | 312 | Dominican Republic |
| 51.8 | 47.3 | 32.7 | 34.9 | 13.3 | 51.8 | ... | 2.8 | 1.8 | 4.8 | 13,323 | 3,666 | 2,355.2 | 1,114 | 556.3 | Ecuador |
| 30.2 | 45.7 | ... | ... | | | ... | 3.2 | 1.8 | 4.8[31] | | | | | | Egypt |
| 48.0[32] | 34.1 | 6.3[13] | 20.0[32] | —80.0[32]— | | ... | 1.5[20] | 3.3[20] | 3.2 | 8,963 | 118 | 383.6 | 10 | 0.7 | El Salvador |
| | | | | | | | | | 4.9[32] | | | | | | Equatorial Guinea |
| | | | | | | ... | | 2.7[33] | 4.2 | —1,739[23]— | | 162[23] | 61[23] | 32.3[23] | Ethiopia |
| 99.7 | 99.5 | 95.0 | 89.7 | 8.1 | 2.2 | ... | 5.5 | 1.1 | 10.2[3] | | | | | | Faeroe Islands |
| 98.8 | ... | 98.8 | 98.0[34] | —2.0[34]— | | ... | 7.4 | 0.4[34] | ... | | | | | | Falkland Islands |
| 73.7 | 43.2 | 56.0 | 35.4[35] | —64.6[35]— | | ... | 3.3 | 1.8 | 6.0 | —997— | | 93 | 179 | 45 | Fiji |
| 98.5 | 95.6[18] | 88.3 | 94.9 | —5.1— | | 69.0 | 3.4 | 0.8 | 6.7 | 25,560 | 940 | 16,721[4] | 33,103 | 27,519[4] | Finland |
| 99.2 | 98.8[36] | 85.0 | 73.8[26] | —26.2[26]— | | 77.0[20] | 3.7 | 0.8 | 5.9 | 190,132[5] | 6,489[5] | ... | ... | 16,090[9] | France |
| 67.7 | 80.4 | 59.1 | 34.3 | —65.7— | | ... | 2.8 | 1.3 | ... | | | 16.9[5] | 8 | 17.6 | French Guiana |
| 86.0 | 76.0 | 76.0 | 2.0 | 67.0 | 31.0 | ... | 3.4 | 1.7[35] | 9.4[9] | —767[8]— | | | 8 | ... | French Polynesia |

## Housing and construction (continued)

| country | year | dwelling units[a] | median age[b] (years) | decade built (percent) 1939 or earlier | 1940–49 | 1950–59 | 1960–69 | 1970 or later | tenure[c] (percent) owned | rented | collective, vacant, other | construction of exterior walls (percent) traditional materials | sawn/framed wood | masonry or cement | other |
|---|---|---|---|---|---|---|---|---|---|---|---|---|---|---|---|
| Gabon | 1967[38] | 15,886 | ... | ... | ... | ... | ... | ... | —87.0— | | 13.0[39] | ... | ... | ... | ... |
| Gambia, The | 1983 | 202,199 | ... | ... | ... | ... | ... | ... | 63.9 | 21.9 | 14.2 | 82.9 | — | 12.9 | 4.2 |
| Gaza Strip | 1985 | 66,819[40] | ... | ... | ... | ... | ... | ... | 89.1[41] | 7.6[41] | 3.3[41] | ... | ... | ... | ... |
| Germany, East | 1981 | 6,562,467 | ... | —62.4— | | 6.1 | 10.1 | 21.4 | 36.3 | 63.7 | — | ... | ... | ... | ... |
| Germany, West | 1982 | 26,076,000 | ... | —53.7— | | | 20.5 | 25.8 | 36.0[20] | 64.0[20] | — | ... | ... | ... | ... |
| Ghana | 1970 | 870,036 | ... | ... | ... | ... | ... | ... | 47.7[26] | 25.3[26] | 27.0 | ... | ... | ... | ... |
| Gibraltar | 1986 | 7,846 | ... | ... | ... | ... | ... | ... | 5.9 | 94.1 | — | ... | ... | ... | ... |
| Greece | 1981 | 3,999,332 | 29.2 | —30.2[16]— | | 27.4[17] | 20.7 | 21.5 | 73.1[10] | 26.9[10] | — | ... | ... | ... | ... |
| Greenland | 1985 | 16,096 | 10.8[12] | —11.9[12]— | | 18.8[12] | 46.5[12] | 22.8[12] | 39.3 | —60.7— | | ... | ... | ... | ... |
| Grenada | 1970 | 19,642 | 18.3 | —48.0— | | 29.0 | 22.2 | 0.8 | 76.5 | 14.0 | 9.5 | 0.4 | 80.8 | 17.8 | 1.0 |
| Guadeloupe | 1982 | 85,629 | ... | ... | ... | ... | 8.1[10] | ... | 64.3 | 29.9 | 5.8 | 29.5[37] | —70.5— | | |
| Guam | 1980 | 28,091 | ... | ... | ... | ... | ... | 44.6 | 40.8 | 47.6 | 11.6[39] | ... | ... | ... | ... |
| Guatemala | 1981 | 1,259,598 | 12.5 | —62.0— | | | 10.0 | 28.0 | 64.7 | 11.3 | 24.0 | 55.6 | 21.1 | 19.3 | 4.0 |
| Guernsey | 1976 | 17,824 | ... | ... | ... | ... | ... | ... | 63.5 | 33.5 | 3.0 | ... | ... | ... | ... |
| Guinea | ... | ... | ... | ... | ... | ... | ... | ... | ... | ... | ... | ... | ... | ... | ... |
| Guinea-Bissau | 1979 | 123,936 | ... | ... | ... | ... | ... | ... | ... | ... | ... | 95.7 | 0.1 | 2.3 | 1.9 |
| Guyana | 1970 | 129,722 | ... | —45.8— | | | 31.6 | 1.0 | 56.8 | 29.8 | 13.4 | 3.1 | 87.2 | 7.1 | 2.6 |
| Haiti | 1982 | 1,130,795 | ... | ... | ... | ... | ... | 24.1 | 82.9[12] | 4.8[12] | 12.3[12] | ... | ... | ... | ... |
| Honduras | 1974 | 526,566 | ... | —43.1— | | | 37.9 | 14.2 | 71.8 | 16.5 | 12.7 | 61.0 | 26.4 | 11.7 | 0.9 |
| Hong Kong | 1981 | 1,061,086 | ... | ... | ... | ... | 13.6 | 38.3 | 27.7 | 70.4 | 1.9 | ... | ... | ... | ... |
| Hungary | 1984 | 3,774,000 | 36.2 | —40.6[16]— | | 12.8[29] | 16.9 | 29.7 | 75.1 | 24.7 | 0.2 | 30.8 | 14.3 | 54.8 | 0.1 |
| Iceland | 1984 | 70,777 | 25.6 | 18.5 | —27.5— | | —54.1— | | 70.3[19] | —29.7[19]— | | ... | ... | 71.9[19] | ... |
| India | 1981 | 142,954,921 | ... | ... | ... | ... | ... | ... | 84.6[13] | 15.4[13] | — | ... | ... | ... | ... |
| Indonesia | 1980 | 30,263,273 | ... | ... | ... | ... | ... | ... | 87.0[13] | 5.0[13] | 8.0[13] | ... | ... | ... | ... |
| Iran | 1976 | 5,331,220 | ... | —82.5— | | | | 17.5 | 70.2 | 15.0 | 14.8 | ... | ... | ... | ... |
| Iraq | 1956 | 741,000 | ... | ... | ... | ... | ... | ... | 83.0 | 12.8 | 4.2 | ... | ... | ... | ... |
| Ireland | 1981 | 875,816 | 47.2 | 45.0 | —16.3— | | 12.7 | 26.0 | 67.9 | 20.9 | 11.2 | ... | ... | ... | ... |
| Isle of Man | 1981 | 24,348[42] | ... | ... | ... | ... | ... | ... | 62.5 | 36.5 | 1.0 | ... | ... | ... | ... |
| Israel | 1983 | 1,104,270 | ... | —9.5[43]— | | —90.5[44]— | | | 72.9 | 24.6 | 2.5 | ... | ... | ... | ... |
| Italy | 1981 | 17,542,000 | 19.4 | —30.8[16]— | | 19.7[17] | 27.5[45] | 22.0 | 58.9 | 35.5 | 5.6 | ... | ... | ... | ... |
| Jamaica | 1982 | 517,297 | ... | —33.6— | | | 26.8 | 39.6 | 46.7 | 29.5 | 23.8 | 7.1 | 28.4 | 54.4 | 10.1 |
| Japan | 1983 | 34,704,500 | 13.0 | —13.5— | | 9.7 | 24.0 | 52.1 | 62.4 | 37.3 | 0.3 | — | 77.4 | 21.5 | 1.1 |
| Jersey | 1981[42] | 26,674 | ... | ... | ... | ... | ... | ... | 48.8 | 49.2 | 2.0 | ... | ... | ... | ... |
| Jordan | 1979 | 378,815[47] | ... | ... | ... | ... | ... | ... | 62.6 | 30.8 | 6.6 | ... | ... | ... | ... |
| Kampuchea | ... | ... | ... | ... | ... | ... | ... | ... | ... | ... | ... | ... | ... | ... | ... |
| Kenya | 1962[1] | 137,000[6] | ... | ... | ... | ... | ... | ... | ... | ... | ... | ... | ... | ... | ... |
| Kiribati | 1978 | 10,802 | ... | ... | ... | ... | ... | ... | 68.2 | 17.9 | 13.9 | 64.4 | —35.6— | | |
| Korea, North | ... | ... | ... | ... | ... | ... | ... | ... | ... | ... | ... | ... | ... | ... | ... |
| Korea, South | 1980 | 5,318,880 | 19.0 | —26.1— | | 15.8 | 18.2 | 39.9 | 86.9 | 11.0 | 2.1 | 11.8 | 38.8 | 49.2 | 0.2 |
| Kuwait | 1980 | 170,804 | 14.5 | —12.2— | | | 38.8 | 34.5 | 21.2 | 61.2 | 17.6 | 46.5[48] | — | 36.5[48] | 17.0[48] |
| Laos | ... | ... | ... | ... | ... | ... | ... | ... | ... | ... | ... | ... | ... | ... | ... |
| Lebanon | 1970 | 483,908[6] | ... | —30.1[49]— | | 40.2[50] | 29.4 | ... | ... | ... | ... | ... | ... | ... | ... |
| Lesotho | 1976[42] | 240,308 | ... | ... | ... | ... | ... | ... | ... | ... | ... | ... | ... | ... | ... |
| Liberia | 1974[38] | 263.333 | ... | ... | ... | ... | ... | ... | ... | ... | ... | ... | ... | ... | ... |
| Libya | 1973 | 345,836 | ... | ... | ... | ... | ... | ... | 62.5 | 28.0 | 9.5 | ... | ... | ... | ... |
| Liechtenstein | 1980 | 8,421 | 29.4 | —27.1[49]— | | 15.0[50] | 27.1 | 30.8 | 53.6 | 41.7 | 4.7 | ... | ... | ... | ... |
| Luxembourg | 1981 | 128,281[42] | ... | —62.1[43]— | | 11.8[51] | 7.8 | 18.3 | 59.2 | —40.8— | | ... | ... | ... | ... |
| Macau | 1981 | 45,158 | ... | ... | ... | ... | ... | ... | 71.8[18] | 28.2[18] | — | ... | 0.5[18] | 99.3[18] | 0.2[18] |
| Madagascar | ... | ... | ... | ... | ... | ... | ... | ... | ... | ... | ... | ... | ... | ... | ... |
| Malawi | 1977 | 1,834,118 | ... | ... | ... | ... | ... | ... | 39.6 | —60.4— | | ... | ... | ... | ... |
| Malaysia | 1980 | 2,332,563 | ... | ... | ... | ... | ... | ... | 64.0 | 23.0 | 13.0 | ... | ... | ... | ... |
| Maldives | 1985 | 29,818 | ... | ... | ... | ... | ... | ... | ... | ... | ... | ... | ... | ... | ... |
| Mali | 1976[42] | 1,253,802 | ... | ... | ... | ... | ... | ... | ... | ... | ... | ... | ... | ... | ... |
| Malta | 1967 | 87,049 | ... | —81.8[53]— | | | 18.2[54] | — | 32.4 | 63.9 | 3.7 | 93.0 | — | 92.9 | 0.2[1] |
| Martinique | 1982 | 85,265 | ... | ... | ... | ... | ... | ... | 64.1 | 31.3 | 7.3 | 20.4[37] | —79.6— | | |
| Mauritania | ... | ... | ... | ... | ... | ... | ... | ... | ... | ... | ... | ... | ... | ... | ... |
| Mauritius | 1983[55] | 158,215 | ... | —19.7— | | | 24.3[56] | 56.0[57] | 73.2 | 12.5 | 14.3 | ... | 4.2 | 66.8 | 28.9 |
| Mayotte | 1978 | 10,053 | ... | ... | ... | ... | ... | ... | 88.1 | 6.2 | 5.7 | 83.6 | —7.7— | | 8.7 |
| Mexico | 1980 | 12,216,462 | ... | —51.4— | | | 15.4 | 33.2 | 66.8 | —33.2— | | 28.2 | 9.6 | 56.2 | 6.0 |
| Monaco | 1975 | 12,625 | 28.5 | —51.4— | | 22.7 | —25.8— | | ... | ... | ... | ... | ... | ... | ... |
| Mongolia | 1969 | 242,000 | ... | ... | ... | ... | ... | ... | 100.0 | — | — | ... | ... | ... | ... |
| Montserrat | 1980 | 3,706 | ... | —47.4— | | | 24.5 | 28.1 | 69.2 | 21.9 | 8.8 | — | 60.9 | 39.0 | 0.1 |
| Morocco | 1982[42] | 3,419,282 | ... | ... | ... | ... | ... | ... | 40.8[1] | 43.7[1] | 15.5[1] | 24.5 | — | 73.5 | 1.8 |
| Mozambique | 1980 | 2,712,439 | ... | ... | ... | ... | ... | ... | ... | ... | ... | 86.5 | 2.3 | 8.3 | 2.9 |
| Nauru | 1977 | 508[58] | ... | —88.6[58]— | | | | 11.4[58] | 11.0[33] | 80.6[33] | 8.4[33] | ... | ... | ... | ... |
| Nepal | 1961[59] | 37,122 | ... | ... | ... | ... | ... | ... | 75.3 | 10.7 | 14.0 | ... | ... | ... | ... |
| Netherlands, The | 1977 | 4,573,000[6] | 20.0 | 22.0[60] | —29.0[61]— | | 24.6 | 24.4 | ... | ... | ... | ... | ... | ... | ... |
| Netherlands Antilles | 1981 | 41,101 | 21.0 | 22.4 | —27.4— | | 19.7 | 30.5 | 45.3 | 54.7 | — | — | 21.6 | 75.7 | 2.7 |
| New Caledonia | 1983 | 35,107 | 15.8 | —9.8— | | 11.2 | 32.1 | 46.9 | 53.0 | 31.1 | 15.9 | 6.3 | 21.0 | 58.1 | 14.6 |
| New Zealand | 1981 | 1,048,035 | ... | —64.6— | | | 19.2 | 16.2 | 70.8 | 25.3 | 3.9 | ... | ... | ... | ... |
| Nicaragua | 1971 | 330,422 | ... | ... | ... | ... | ... | ... | 64.4 | 20.3 | 15.3 | 30.8 | 45.6 | 21.8 | 1.8 |
| Niger | ... | ... | ... | ... | ... | ... | ... | ... | ... | ... | ... | ... | ... | ... | ... |
| Nigeria | 1961[38] | 92,900 | ... | ... | ... | ... | ... | ... | 8.0 | 80.9 | 11.1 | ... | ... | ... | ... |
| Niue | 1981 | 673 | ... | ... | ... | ... | ... | ... | 89.2 | 7.4 | 3.4 | ... | ... | ... | ... |
| Norfolk Island | 1986 | 787 | 14.8[23] | —32.8[23]— | | | 32.5[23] | 34.7[23] | 55.0 | 34.1 | 10.9 | — | 46.4 | 3.8 | 49.8 |
| Norway | 1980 | 1,523,512 | 25.3 | 35.1 | 6.9 | 16.8 | 18.7 | 22.5 | 66.6 | 23.5 | 9.9 | ... | ... | ... | ... |
| Oman | 1982 | 2,469 | ... | ... | ... | ... | ... | ... | ... | ... | ... | ... | ... | ... | ... |
| Pacific Is., Trust Terr. of the | | | | | | | | | | | | | | | |
|   Marshall Islands | 1980 | 4,163 | ... | 3.4 | 3.1 | 13.3 | 24.7 | 55.5 | 60.0 | 33.0 | 7.0 | 10.7 | 63.5 | 15.9 | 9.9 |
|   Micronesia, Fed. States of | 1980 | 11,562 | ... | 1.7 | 2.1 | 5.2 | 21.3 | 69.7 | 51.8 | 39.2 | 9.0 | 6.0 | 41.8 | 14.6 | 37.6 |
|   Northern Mariana Islands | 1980 | 3,373 | ... | 0.8 | 3.7 | 8.4 | 29.4 | 57.7 | 53.6 | 36.1 | 10.3 | 0.0 | 6.1 | 33.4 | 60.5 |
|   Palau | 1980 | 2,265 | ... | 2.5 | 3.1 | 8.6 | 29.8 | 56.0 | 78.0 | 12.1 | 9.9 | 0.7 | 23.1 | 16.7 | 59.5 |
| Pakistan | 1980 | 12,587,648 | 17.2[63] | | 17.1[49,63] | 36.7[63,64] | 24.9[63,65] | 21.3[63,66] | 78.4[63] | 7.7[63] | 13.9[63] | 49.2[63] | 2.4[63] | 41.4[63] | 7.1[63] |
| Panama | 1980 | 364,726 | 18.0 | —47.4— | | 12.8 | 18.1 | 21.7 | 70.1 | 21.1 | 8.8 | 37.1 | — | 52.2 | 10.7 |
| Papua New Guinea | 1975[1] | 42,860 | ... | ... | ... | ... | ... | ... | 40.0 | —60.0— | | ... | ... | ... | ... |

| piped water | electricity | inside toilet or WC | closed public sewer or septic tank | open public sewer | other | average area (sq m) | rooms per dwelling unit | persons per room | percent of GDP | 1- or 2-unit dwellings | multiunit dwellings | floor area ('000 sq m) | number of units | floor area ('000 sq m) | country |
|---|---|---|---|---|---|---|---|---|---|---|---|---|---|---|---|
| ... | 50.5 | ... | ... | ... | ... | ... | 3.0 | 1.3 | 7.3[5] | ---445[26]--- | | 216.1[26] | 75[26] | 119.4[26] | Gabon |
| 21.9 | ... | ... | ... | ... | ... | ... | 2.0 | 2.0 | 8.1[5] | 120[26] | 76[26] | ... | 14[26] | ... | Gambia, The |
| 97.2 | 93.5 | 97.3 | ... | ... | ... | ... | 2.6 | 2.4 | ... | ---1,223[11]--- | | 195.5[11] | ... | 31.8[11] | Gaza Strip |
| 98.2 | 100.0 | 60.1 | 90.8 | ---9.2--- | | 63.0 | 2.8 | 1.1 | 5.8[2] | ... | ... | 7,316 | ... | ... | Germany, East |
| 99.2[34] | 99.7[34] | 97.1 | 97.1 | ---2.9--- | | ... | 4.2 | 0.6 | 5.8 | 134,732 | 20,270 | 193,817[4] | 34,315 | 150,794[4] | Germany, West |
| 34.0[32] | ... | ... | ... | ... | ... | ... | ... | ... | 2.2 | ... | ... | ... | ... | ... | Ghana |
| 96.7[23] | 100.0[23] | 98.8[23] | 100.0[23] | ... | | ... | 3.2[23] | 1.2[23] | ... | ... | ... | ... | ... | ... | Gibraltar |
| 81.3[13] | 89.0[13] | 93.0[13] | ... | ... | ... | ... | 3.5[13] | 0.9[13] | 6.4 | 24,937 | 3,968 | 24,023[4] | 10,216 | 9,958[4] | Greece |
| 62.7[12] | 84.2[12] | 39.1[12] | 39.1[12] | ---60.9[12]--- | | ... | 2.8 | 1.2 | 27.4[32] | ---561[11]--- | | 41.5[11] | ... | 28.4 | Greenland |
| 86.5 | ... | 23.0 | 23.0 | ---77.0--- | | ... | 2.9 | 1.6 | 7.8 | ... | ... | ... | ... | | Grenada |
| 69.4 | 77.2 | 55.4 | 24.6 | ---75.4--- | | ... | 3.5 | 1.1 | 4.4[3] | 460[23] | 10[23] | 91.9[23] | 31[23] | 40.9[23] | Guadeloupe |
| 99.5 | ... | 96.5 | 97.5 | ---2.5--- | | ... | 4.7 | 0.7 | 7.9[9] | ... | ... | ... | ... | | Guam |
| 52.0 | 37.0 | 14.3 | 20.1 | 3.4 | 76.5 | ... | 2.4 | 2.2 | 1.8 | ---500[8]--- | | 100.6[8] | 8 | 8 | Guatemala |
| 96.5 | ... | 88.8 | 49.3 | ---50.7--- | | ... | 5.5 | 0.5 | ... | ... | ... | ... | ... | | Guernsey |
| ... | ... | ... | ... | ... | ... | ... | ... | ... | 6.4[11] | ... | ... | ... | ... | | Guinea |
| 3.7 | 3.9 | 25.6 | 25.8 | ---74.2--- | | ... | 1.4` | 4.5 | 2.6[5] | ... | ... | ... | ... | | Guinea-Bissau |
| 81.0 | ... | 26.3 | 13.0 | ---87.0--- | | ... | 2.7 | 2.1 | 5.9 | ---1,259[3]--- | | ... | 56[3] | ... | Guyana |
| 12.0[32] | 1.1[13] | ... | 2.0[32] | ---98.0[32]--- | | ... | 2.2[13] | 2.1[13] | 5.6 | ---472[8]--- | | ... | 8 | ... | Haiti |
| 55.0[32] | 25.0 | 13.0 | 14.4 | ---85.6--- | | ... | 2.4 | 2.3 | 5.5 | ---1,691--- | | 181.1 | 82 | 76.0 | Honduras |
| 85.7 | ... | 69.2[25] | 65.4[25] | ---34.6[25]--- | | 53.2[13] | 3.1[25] | 2.8[25] | 5.1 | ---470--- | | 758 | 288 | 1,171 | Hong Kong |
| 81.2 | 98.8 | 65.9 | 79.5 | ---20.5--- | | 65.0 | 2.2 | 1.3 | 10.5[2] | 35,014 | 1,391 | 26,341[4] | 3,884 | 17,331[4] | Hungary |
| 99.1[19] | 94.6[19] | 93.6[19] | 86.5[19] | ---13.5[19]--- | | ... | 4.8[19] | 0.9[19] | 9.8 | ... | ... | 812.8[4] | ... | 926.5[4] | Iceland |
| 67.0[25] | 53.5[1,25] | 20.0[25] | ... | ... | ... | ... | 2.0[13] | 2.6[13] | 5.7 | ---65,839[5]--- | | ... | 12,431[5] | ... | India |
| 11.0 | 14.2 | 26.6 | 22.8[13] | ---77.2[13]--- | | 59.0 | 3.3 | 1.7[13] | 5.8 | ---167,837--- | | ... | ... | ... | Indonesia |
| 46.8 | 48.3 | 26.7 | ... | ... | ... | 60.0 | 2.7 | 2.0 | 7.4 | 87,945[5] | 1,196[5] | 14,780[5] | 4,724[5] | 1,194[5] | Iran |
| 20.8 | 17.1 | ... | ... | ... | ... | ... | 2.4 | ... | 9.3 | ---62,615[9]--- | | 7,625[9] | 20,467[9] | ... | Iraq |
| 94.8 | 94.7[13] | 93.0 | 72.3[13] | ---27.7[13]--- | | ... | 5.1 | 0.7 | 6.4 | ... | ... | ... | ... | | Ireland |
| ... | ... | 96.8 | ... | ... | ... | ... | ... | 0.4 | ... | ... | ... | ... | ... | | Isle of Man |
| 96.5[13] | 96.5[13] | 98.8 | 99.0[10] | ---1.0[10]--- | | ... | 3.0 | 1.2 | 5.4 | 1,384 | 1,453 | 3,470 | ... | 1,520 | Israel |
| 98.7 | 99.0[13] | 94.0 | 95.7[13] | ---4.3[13]--- | | 85.3 | 4.2 | 0.8 | 7.6 | ---45,755--- | | 92,400[4] | 26,577 | 82,300[4] | Italy |
| 76.9 | 48.6 | 35.2 | ... | ... | ... | ... | 2.4[18] | 4.3 | 9.0 | ---3,432[5]--- | | ... | 235[26] | ... | Jamaica |
| 94.0 | ... | 58.2 | 61.2 | ---38.8--- | | 85.9 | 4.7 | 0.7 | 7.5 | 621,700 | 206,600 | 111,870 | 214,400 | 84,268 | Japan |
| 91.0[46] | ... | 93.0 | 91.0[46] | ... | ... | ... | ... | 0.5 | ... | ---349[5]--- | | ... | ... | ... | Jersey |
| 77.2 | 77.3 | 55.4[33] | 15.7 | ---84.3--- | | ... | ... | ... | 11.7 | ---6,947[8]--- | | 1,656.5[8] | 8 | 8 | Jordan |
| ... | ... | ... | ... | ... | ... | ... | ... | ... | 5.3[7] | ... | ... | ... | ... | | Kampuchea |
| ... | ... | ... | ... | ... | ... | ... | 1.9 | 2.5 | 5.4 | ---648--- | | 118 | 47 | 37 | Kenya |
| 21.3 | 23.7 | 15.5 | ... | ... | ... | ... | ... | ... | 4.0[9] | ... | ... | ... | ... | | Kiribati |
| ... | ... | ... | ... | ... | ... | ... | ... | ... | ... | ... | ... | ... | ... | | Korea, North |
| 51.2 | 49.9[18] | 98.4 | ... | ... | ... | ... | 3.0 | 2.3 | 8.3 | ---65,770--- | | 20,551 | 35,816 | 19,012 | Korea, South |
| 53.9 | 99.5 | ... | 35.9 | ---64.1--- | | ... | 4.0 | 1.8 | 3.8 | ---1,277--- | | 3,131 | 105 | 511 | Kuwait |
| ... | ... | ... | ... | ... | ... | ... | ... | ... | ... | ... | ... | ... | ... | | Laos |
| ... | 93.4 | 82.9 | ... | ... | ... | ... | ... | ... | 3.4[35] | ... | ... | ... | ... | | Lebanon |
| ... | ... | ... | ... | ... | ... | ... | ... | ... | 9.9[5] | ... | ... | ... | ... | | Lesotho |
| ... | ... | ... | ... | ... | ... | ... | 2.3[42] | 1.7 | 3.3 | ... | ... | ... | ... | | Liberia |
| 70.1 | 72.1 | 40.6 | 40.6 | ---59.4--- | | ... | 3.3 | 1.8 | 11.9[9] | ... | ... | ... | ... | | Libya |
| 96.5 | 96.6 | 86.7 | 90.2 | ---9.8--- | | 102.0 | 3.0 | 1.4 | ... | ... | ... | 202.1[4,11] | ... | 373.8[4,11] | Liechtenstein |
| 99.4[18] | ... | 97.2 | 93.0[18] | ---7.0[18]--- | | 86.4[18] | 5.4 | 0.5 | 5.8 | 1,101[5] | 805 | 484.6[5] | 77[5] | 121.5[5] | Luxembourg |
| 95.7 | 99.3 | 68.9 | ... | ... | ... | ... | 3.2[18] | 2.5[18] | ... | ---132--- | | 207.5 | 28 | 217.1 | Macau |
| ... | ... | ... | ... | ... | ... | ... | ... | ... | 4.5[5] | ---38[18]--- | | 12.6 | 8 | 7.7 | Madagascar |
| 12.4 | 15.7[40] | 33.0[40] | 33.0[40] | ---67.0[40]--- | | ... | 2.1 | 1.7 | 4.2 | ---108--- | | ... | 89 | ... | Malawi |
| 65.0 | 64.4 | ... | 56.4. | 4.4 | 39.2 | ... | 2.3[18, 52] | 2.6[18, 52] | 5.4 | ... | ... | ... | ... | ... | Malaysia |
| ... | 9.8[35] | ... | 2.5[35] | ---97.5[35]--- | | ... | 2.3[35] | 2.7[35] | 7.6 | ... | ... | ... | ... | ... | Maldives |
| ... | ... | ... | ... | ... | ... | ... | ... | ... | 5.7[9] | ... | ... | ... | ... | | Mali |
| ... | ... | ... | 78.5 | 15.4 | 6.1 | ... | 3.2 | 1.3 | 3.0[3] | ---1,633[5]--- | | ... | 769[5] | ... | Malta |
| 55.4 | 70.5 | 41.8 | 41.8 | ---58.2--- | | ... | 3.4 | 1.1 | 3.0[23] | ... | ... | ... | ... | 76.2 | Martinique |
| ... | ... | ... | ... | ... | ... | ... | ... | ... | 7.9 | ... | ... | ... | ... | | Mauritania |
| 79.7 | 92.6 | 51.1 | 51.1 | ---48.9--- | | ... | 5.4 | ... | 5.9 | ---4,239--- | | 394 | 341 | 61 | Mauritius |
| 27.4 | ... | 3.9 | 54.7 | ---45.3--- | | ... | 2.0 | 2.4 | ... | ... | ... | ... | ... | | Mayotte |
| 66.2 | 74.6 | 45.0 | 49.2 | ---50.8--- | | ... | 2.3 | 2.5 | 4.9 | ---285,681[23]--- | | ... | 61,386[23] | ... | Mexico |
| 100.0 | 100.0 | 98.4 | 98.4 | ---1.6--- | | ... | 2.8 | 0.4 | ... | ... | ... | ... | ... | | Monaco |
| 0.3 | 47.5 | ... | ... | ... | ... | ... | 2.2 | 2.1 | 5.1[9] | ---842--- | | 183.4[3] | ... | 113.3[3] | Mongolia |
| 78.6 | 72.1 | 49.3 | 49.3 | 30.4 | 20.4 | ... | 3.5 | 0.9 | 6.6 | ... | ... | ... | ... | ... | Montserrat |
| 30.5 | 37.2 | 50.2 | ... | ... | ... | ... | 2.7 | 2.2 | 6.5 | 19,736 | 2,694 | 5,847 | 948 | 619 | Morocco |
| 12.7 | 4.2 | ... | ... | ... | ... | ... | ... | ... | 5.6[23] | ---145[26]--- | | 51.7[26] | 20[26] | 25.0[26] | Mozambique |
| ... | 49.2 | ... | ... | ... | ... | ... | 3.6[33] | 1.6[33] | ... | ... | ... | ... | ... | | Nauru |
| 47.7 | 30.2 | 6.1 | ... | ... | ... | ... | 3.7 | 2.0 | 6.6 | ... | ... | ... | ... | | Nepal |
| 95.7[1, 13] | 94.8[1, 13] | 89.8[1, 13] | 89.8[1, 13] | ---10.2[1, 13]--- | | ... | 5.0 | 1.0 | 6.5 | ---14,335--- | | 41,717[4] | 15,922 | 52,235[4] | Netherlands, The |
| 79.6 | 96.9 | 79.6 | ... | ... | ... | ... | 4.2 | 1.0 | ... | ---1,323[62]--- | | ... | 740[62] | ... | Netherlands Antilles |
| 85.1 | 79.0[23] | 68.3 | 69.2 | ---30.8--- | | ... | 3.3 | 1.3 | 4.6[5] | ---286--- | | ... | 1 | ... | New Caledonia |
| 92.7[13] | ... | 97.1[13] | ... | ... | ... | ... | 5.6 | 0.5 | 5.2 | ... | ... | 2,686 | 8,608 | 2,788 | New Zealand |
| 27.9 | 40.9 | 19.3 | 19.2 | ---80.8--- | | ... | 2.2 | 2.1 | 3.0 | ---842--- | | 43.2 | 28 | 19.6 | Nicaragua |
| ... | ... | ... | ... | ... | ... | ... | ... | ... | 3.1 | ... | ... | ... | ... | | Niger |
| ... | 81.3 | 7.0 | ... | ... | ... | ... | 1.4 | 3.0 | 6.7 | 2,175[3] | 2,197[3] | ... | 1,592[3] | ... | Nigeria |
| 18.9 | 93.0 | 28.4 | 14.1 | ---85.9--- | | ... | 4.0 | 1.2 | ... | 6 | ... | ... | ... | | Niue |
| 8.0 | 98.3 | ... | 94.2 | --- | 5.8 | ... | 6.2 | 2.5 | ... | ... | ... | ... | ... | | Norfolk Island |
| 97.5[18] | ... | 86.8 | 86.8 | ---13.2--- | | 83.5 | 3.9 | 0.9 | 4.9 | 19,854 | 498 | 4,808 | 4,608 | 2,354 | Norway |
| ... | ... | ... | ... | ... | ... | ... | ... | ... | 7.4 | 1,269 | 117 | ... | 254 | ... | Oman |
| | | | | | | | | | | | | | | | Pacific Is., Trust Terr. of the |
| 46.3 | 48.9 | ... | 28.6 | ---71.4--- | | ... | ... | ... | ... | ... | ... | ... | ... | | Marshall Islands |
| 40.0 | 28.3 | ... | 8.0 | ---92.0--- | | ... | ... | ... | ... | ... | ... | ... | ... | | Micronesia, Fed. States of |
| 92.5 | 94.1 | ... | 54.8 | ---45.2--- | | ... | ... | ... | ... | ... | ... | ... | ... | | Northern Mariana Islands |
| 70.8 | 75.7 | ... | 19.6 | ---80.4--- | | ... | ... | ... | ... | ... | ... | ... | ... | | Palau |
| 20.3[63] | 30.6[63] | 25.1[63] | ... | ... | ... | ... | 1.9[63] | 3.3[63] | 4.8 | ... | ... | ... | ... | | Pakistan |
| 80.7 | 65.7 | 74.3 | 43.9 | ---56.1--- | | ... | 2.6 | 1.8 | 5.3 | 1,504 | 164 | 302.0 | 75 | 76.0 | Panama |
| 50.0 | 56.0 | 40.0 | ... | ... | ... | ... | ... | ... | 3.6[9] | ---629--- | | ... | ... | ... | Papua New Guinea |

## Housing and construction (continued)

| country | housing stock | | | | | | | | | | | | | |
|---|---|---|---|---|---|---|---|---|---|---|---|---|---|---|
| | year | dwelling units[a] | median age[b] (years) | decade built (percent) | | | | | tenure[c] (percent) | | | construction of exterior walls (percent) | | | |
| | | | | 1939 or earlier | 1940–49 | 1950–59 | 1960–69 | 1970 or later | owned | rented | collective, vacant, other | traditional materials | sawn/framed wood | masonry or cement | other |
| Paraguay | 1982 | 580,810[6] | 21.1 | —————56.0————— | | | 17.0 | 27.0 | 80.4 | 10.5 | 9.1 | 21.5 | 29.7 | 47.6 | 1.2 |
| Peru | 1981 | 3,257,100 | ... | —————30.9————— | | | ———69.1——— | | 68.5 | 14.8 | 14.8 | 47.4 | 7.0 | 33.1 | 12.5 |
| Philippines | 1980 | 8,607,187 | ... | | | | 21.5[18] | | 80.2 | 12.4 | 7.4 | 36.3 | 33.6 | 23.8 | 6.3 |
| Pitcairn Island | 1986 | 15 | ... | 46.7 | 20.0 | 13.3 | — | 20.0 | 100.0 | ... | ... | — | 100.0 | — | — |
| Poland | 1978 | 9,326,045 | ... | 42.1[67] | ———38.8[68]——— | | | 19.1 | ... | ... | ... | ———14.1——— | | ———85.9——— | |
| Portugal | 1981 | 3,235,630 | 33.7 | —————53.3————— | | | 17.5 | 29.2 | 56.7 | 38.8 | 4.6 | — | 0.7 | 61.0 | 38.3 |
| Puerto Rico | 1980 | 969,611 | 15.8 | 5.7 | 6.5 | 15.0 | 31.6 | 41.2 | 65.7 | 23.8 | 10.5 | — | 19.7 | 77.4 | 2.9 |
| Qatar | ... | ... | ... | ... | ... | ... | ... | ... | ... | ... | ... | ... | ... | ... | ... |
| Réunion | 1982 | 141,123 | ... | ... | ... | ... | 21.2[10] | | 54.6 | 34.5 | 10.9 | ... | ... | ... | ... |
| Romania | 1966 | 5,380,299 | ... | ... | ... | ... | ... | ... | ... | ... | ... | ... | ... | ... | ... |
| Rwanda | ... | ... | ... | ... | ... | ... | ... | ... | ... | ... | ... | ... | ... | ... | ... |
| St. Christopher and Nevis | 1980 | 11,445 | 24.2 | —————66.9————— | | | 18.2 | 14.9 | 52.7 | 32.7 | 14.6 | — | 51.3 | 21.6 | 27.1 |
| St. Helena and Ascension | 1976 | 1,147 | 23.4 | ... | ... | ... | ... | ... | 57.7 | 30.1 | 12.2 | ... | ... | ... | ... |
| St. Lucia | 1980[42] | 26,919 | ... | ——41.1[69]—— | | | 24.0[69] | 34.9[69] | 64.7 | 26.0 | 9.3 | 0.1 | 83.6[15] | 12.8 | 3.5 |
| St. Pierre and Miquelon | 1982 | 1,760 | 11.3 | —————69.0————— | | | 13.8 | 17.2 | 77.3 | 17.8 | 4.9 | ... | ... | ... | ... |
| St. Vincent and the Grenadines | 1970 | 16,940 | ... | — | ... | ... | ... | ... | 74.7 | 16.5 | 7.9 | 8.9 | 64.1 | 26.1 | 0.8 |
| San Marino | 1979 | 7,000 | ... | ... | ... | ... | ... | ... | 73.5 | 21.9 | 4.6 | ... | ... | ... | ... |
| São Tomé and Príncipe | ... | ... | ... | ... | ... | ... | ... | ... | ... | ... | ... | ... | ... | ... | ... |
| Saudi Arabia | ... | ... | ... | ... | ... | ... | ... | ... | ... | ... | ... | ... | ... | ... | ... |
| Senegal | 1955[38, 70] | 13,000 | ... | ... | ... | ... | ... | ... | ———84.6——— | | 15.4 | ... | ... | ... | ... |
| Seychelles | 1977 | 12,315 | ... | ... | ... | ... | ... | ... | 46.6 | ———53.4——— | | 4.1 | 57.2 | 38.7 | — |
| Sierra Leone | ... | ... | ... | ... | ... | ... | ... | ... | ... | ... | ... | ... | ... | ... | ... |
| Singapore | 1980 | 513,224 | ... | —————63.2————— | | | | 36.8 | 55.0 | 39.6 | 5.4 | 4.7 | ———95.3——— | | |
| Solomon Islands | 1979[38] | 3,423 | ... | ... | ... | ... | ... | ... | 27.4[12] | 43.0[12] | 29.6[12] | ... | ... | ... | ... |
| Somalia | ... | ... | ... | ... | ... | ... | ... | ... | ... | ... | ... | ... | ... | ... | ... |
| South Africa | 1970 | 1,354,520 | 18.6 | 24.6 | 16.0 | 24.2 | 35.2 | | ... | ... | ... | ... | ... | ... | ... |
| Bophuthatswana | ... | ... | ... | ... | ... | ... | ... | ... | ... | ... | ... | ... | ... | ... | ... |
| Ciskei | ... | ... | ... | ... | ... | ... | ... | ... | ... | ... | ... | ... | ... | ... | ... |
| KwaNdebele | ... | ... | ... | ... | ... | ... | ... | ... | ... | ... | ... | ... | ... | ... | ... |
| Transkei | ... | ... | ... | ... | ... | ... | ... | ... | ... | ... | ... | ... | ... | ... | ... |
| Venda | ... | ... | ... | ... | ... | ... | ... | ... | ... | ... | ... | ... | ... | ... | ... |
| South West Africa/Namibia | ... | ... | ... | ... | ... | ... | ... | ... | ... | ... | ... | ... | ... | ... | ... |
| Spain | 1981 | 12,329,929 | 39.4[3, 48] | 39.2[3, 48] | ——23.4[3, 48]—— | | 18.5[3, 48] | 18.9[3, 48] | 57.2[18] | 24.4[18] | 18.3[18] | ... | ... | ... | ... |
| Sri Lanka | 1981 | 2,811,406 | ... | ... | ... | ... | 11.1[13] | | 69.4 | 10.1 | 20.5 | ... | ... | ... | ... |
| Sudan, The | 1966[1] | 253,060 | ... | ... | ... | ... | ... | ... | 59.2 | 28.3 | 12.6 | 76.5 | 4.4 | 16.7 | 2.4 |
| Suriname | 1980 | 77,658 | ... | —————52.4————— | | | | 47.6 | ... | ... | ... | 38.9[71] | ———61.1[71]——— | | |
| Swaziland | 1976 | 86,847 | ... | ... | ... | ... | ... | ... | ... | ... | ... | 39.9 | ———60.1——— | | |
| Sweden | 1980 | 3,669,512 | 25.2 | 26.8 | 10.9 | 15.5 | 23.9 | 19.1 | 38.9 | 56.0 | 5.1 | 98.7 | ... | ... | ... |
| Switzerland | 1980 | 2,413,185 | ... | —————58.1————— | | | 22.6 | 19.3 | 29.9 | 67.1 | 3.0 | ... | ... | ... | ... |
| Syria | 1983 | 1,642,809 | ... | ... | ... | ... | 8.7[18] | — | 81.6[18] | 15.5[18] | 2.8[18] | ... | ... | ... | ... |
| Taiwan | 1980 | 3,171,876[6] | 15.3 | ——13.8[16]—— | | 14.0[17] | 42.4[72] | 29.8[73] | 79.1 | 11.8 | 9.1 | ... | ... | ... | ... |
| Tanzania | 1978 | 3,554,793 | ... | ——17.0—— | | | ———83.0——— | | 75.4 | 19.4 | 5.2 | 83.0 | ... | 16.3 | 0.7 |
| Thailand | 1980 | 8,414,648 | ... | ——22.0[18]—— | | 25.0[18] | 53.0[18] | | 83.4 | 9.1 | 7.5 | 15.1 | 70.0 | 6.3 | 8.6 |
| Togo | 1958–60[1] | 22,274 | ... | ... | ... | ... | ... | ... | ... | ... | ... | ... | ... | ... | ... |
| Tokelau | 1981 | 284 | ... | ... | ... | ... | ... | ... | 97.7[34] | 2.3[34] | — | 49.6 | 28.2 | 12.3 | 9.9 |
| Tonga | 1976 | 13,908 | 22.5 | 52.7 | ——6.7[74]—— | | 20.3[75] | 20.3[76] | 85.1 | 2.5 | 12.4 | 35.1 | 45.4 | 15.3 | 4.2 |
| Trinidad and Tobago | 1980 | 231,436 | ... | —————56.3————— | | | 14.5 | 29.2 | 64.6 | 34.0 | 1.4 | 3.3 | 32.6 | 53.8 | 10.3[15] |
| Tunisia | 1984 | 1,313,200 | ... | ... | ... | ... | ... | ... | 78.9 | 12.6 | 8.5 | ... | ... | ... | ... |
| Turkey | 1980 | 8,522,499[42] | ... | ... | ... | ... | ... | ... | 80.7[26] | 19.3[26] | — | 0.7[42] | ———99.3[42]——— | | |
| Turks and Caicos Islands | 1980 | 1,644 | 20.0 | —————45.1————— | | | 15.5 | 39.4 | 68.6 | 22.8 | 8.6 | — | 36.8 | 59.9 | 3.3 |
| Tuvalu | 1979 | 1,079 | ... | ... | ... | ... | ... | ... | 81.6 | 12.1 | 6.6 | 64.9 | 4.2 | 31.0 | — |
| Uganda | ... | ... | ... | ... | ... | ... | ... | ... | ... | ... | ... | ... | ... | ... | ... |
| U.S.S.R. | 1984 | 79,285,700[42] | ... | ... | ... | ... | ... | ... | 42.1 | 57.9 | — | ... | ... | ... | ... |
| United Arab Emirates | 1980 | 153,009 | 15.0 | — | 0.8 | 1.3 | 11.4 | 86.5 | 36.2 | 45.2 | 18.6 | 2.9 | 7.3 | 87.3 | 2.5 |
| United Kingdom | 1981[77] | 21,321,894[6] | 32.6 | ——54.0—— | | 13.0 | 16.6 | 16.4 | 51.1 | 40.3 | 8.6 | ... | ... | ... | ... |
| United States | 1983 | 91,675,000 | 22.7 | 29.9 | 9.0 | 15.6 | 19.7 | 25.8 | 64.7 | 32.6 | 2.7 | ... | ... | ... | ... |
| Uruguay | 1975 | 848,000 | ... | ... | ... | ... | ... | ... | 52.1 | 32.1 | 15.8 | ... | ... | ... | ... |
| Vanuatu | 1979 | 22,513 | ... | ... | ... | ... | ... | ... | 40.9[38] | 25.7[38] | 33.4[38] | 61.4 | 7.7 | 13.6 | 17.2 |
| Venezuela | 1981 | 2,708,674 | ... | ... | ... | ... | ... | ... | 75.1 | 17.8 | 7.1 | 11.8 | 2.1 | 78.9 | 7.2 |
| Vietnam | 1962[79] | 204,000[6] | ... | ... | ... | ... | ... | ... | 68.4 | 28.0 | 3.6 | ... | ... | ... | ... |
| Virgin Islands (U.S.) | 1980 | 32,650 | 14.7 | 6.5 | 3.5 | 8.9 | 42.7 | 38.4 | 34.6 | 52.2 | 13.2 | ... | ... | ... | ... |
| Wallis and Futuna | 1983 | 1,389 | 14.4 | ——8.0—— | | 11.0 | 24.0 | 57.0 | 94.4[12] | 0.6[12] | 5.0[12] | 67.0 | ———31.0——— | | 2.0 |
| West Bank | 1985 | 119,165[40] | ... | ... | ... | ... | ... | ... | 86.2[41] | 11.5[41] | 2.3[41] | ... | ... | ... | ... |
| Western Sahara | 1974 | 4,000 | ... | ... | ... | ... | ... | ... | 32.2[36] | 62.3[36] | 5.5[36] | ... | ... | ... | ... |
| Western Samoa | 1976 | 32,938 | ... | ... | ... | ... | ... | ... | 93.4 | 2.1 | 4.5 | 75.6 | ———24.4——— | | |
| Yemen (Aden) | ... | ... | ... | ... | ... | ... | ... | ... | ... | ... | ... | ... | ... | ... | ... |
| Yemen (Ṣan'ā') | 1975 | 863,109 | ... | ... | ... | ... | ... | ... | 85.3 | 7.0 | 7.7 | ... | ... | ... | ... |
| Yugoslavia | 1981 | 6,129,892 | ... | ——31.1—— | | 12.7 | 26.8 | 29.4 | 67.1 | 25.0 | 7.9 | ... | ———82.6——— | | 17.4 |
| Zaire | 1967[38] | 168,000 | ... | ... | ... | ... | ... | ... | 47.4 | 38.3 | 14.3 | ... | ... | ... | ... |
| Zambia | 1969 | 879,000 | ... | ... | ... | ... | ... | ... | 78.8 | 21.1 | ... | ... | ... | ... | ... |
| Zimbabwe | 1969 | 925,581 | ... | ... | ... | ... | ... | ... | 65.1[80] | 32.6[80] | 2.3[80] | 55.9[81] | ———44.1[81]——— | | |

[1]Urban areas only.  [2]Percent of net material product.  [3]1980.  [4]Volume ('000 cubic metres).  [5]1983.  [6]Occupied dwellings only; may include seasonal and temporary housing.  [7]1966.  [8]Residential includes nonresidential.  [9]1982.  [10]1974.  [11]1985.  [12]1976.  [13]1971.  [14]Stucco.  [15]Includes wood and brick, and wood and concrete.  [16]1945 and earlier.  [17]1946 to 1960.  [18]1970.  [19]1960.  [20]1983–85 average.  [21]1983.  [22]Data refer to rugos, which usually contain two to three houses each.  [23]1981.  [24]1959–60; data refer to households and are based on a demographic survey of the African population excluding Bangui town, East Dubangi, and the nomad population.  [25]1973.  [26]1975.  [27]1933 and earlier.  [28]1934–45.  [29]1946–59.  [30]Includes corrugated steel.  [31]1987.  [32]1979.  [33]1961.  [34]1972.  [35]1977.  [36]1968.  [37]Traditional houses (usually constructed of fragile tropical materials and lacking modern conveniences).  [38]Capital city only.  [39]Vacant dwellings only.  [40]1967.  [41]Excludes refugee camps.  [42]Data refer to households.  [43]1947 and earlier.  [44]1948–83.  [45]1961–71.  [46]Minimum.  [47]Includes nonconventional housing units.  [48]Data refer to buildings, not

| physical amenities (percent) | | | sewage disposal (percent) | | | space[b] | | | construction industry (1984) percent of GDP | new residential[d] | | | new nonresidential[d] | | country |
|---|---|---|---|---|---|---|---|---|---|---|---|---|---|---|---|
| piped water | electricity | inside toilet or WC | closed public sewer or septic tank | open public sewer | other | average area (sq m) | rooms per dwelling unit | persons per room | percent of GDP | 1- or 2-unit dwellings | multiunit dwellings | floor area ('000 sq m) | number of units | floor area ('000 sq m) | |
| ... | ... | 26.4 | ... | ... | ... | ... | 2.2[34] | 2.4[34] | 6.2 | 418[9] | 33[9] | 116.8[9] | 1,114[9] | 210.6[9] | Paraguay |
| 73.4 | 89.5 | 78.0 | 58.1 | —41.9— | ... | 42.4 | 2.6 | 2.0 | 5.0 | ... | ... | 910.2 | ... | ... | Peru |
| 41.4 | 46.0 | 35.0 | 44.1 | —55.9— | ... | ... | 2.4[34] | 2.3[34] | 5.7 | —28,094— | | 3,131 | 3,403 | 1,912 | Philippines |
| 100.0 | 100.0 | — | — | —100.0— | ... | 100.0 | 5.0 | 0.4 | ... | | | | | | Pitcairn Island |
| 69.7 | 96.2 | 41.4 | 67.0 | —33.0— | ... | 53.9 | 3.2 | 1.2 | 11.6[2] | 54,670 | 4,320 | 72,755[4] | 68,393 | 70,979[4] | Poland |
| 73.4 | 77.6 | 67.7 | 75.5 | —24.5— | | ... | 3.9 | 0.8 | 6.2 | 17,525 | 1,938 | 6,089 | 6,416 | 1,836 | Portugal |
| 95.2 | 97.4 | 89.7 | 89.6 | —10.4— | | ... | 4.8 | 0.8 | 1.8 | 2,684 | 31 | 1,453 | 1,131 | 40.9 | Puerto Rico |
| ... | ... | ... | ... | ... | | ... | ... | ... | 8.5 | —496— | | ... | 123 | ... | Qatar |
| 70.6 | 81.6 | 50.7 | 52.4 | —47.6— | | ... | 3.6 | 1.2 | 4.7[3] | ... | ... | ... | ... | ... | Réunion |
| ... | 48.6 | ... | 12.2 | —87.8— | | ... | 2.6 | 1.4 | 7.7[2] | ... | ... | ... | ... | ... | Romania |
| ... | ... | ... | ... | ... | | ... | ... | ... | 5.0 | —435— | | ... | 63 | ... | Rwanda |
| 96.6 | 58.3 | 33.5 | 31.8[18] | —68.2[18]— | | ... | 3.0 | 1.3 | 8.6 | | | | | | St. Christopher and Nevis |
| 58.0 | 62.6 | 46.9 | ... | ... | | ... | 4.1 | 1.1 | ... | | | | | | St. Helena and Ascension |
| 79.5[18] | 36.1[18] | ... | 11.0[18] | —89.0[18]— | | ... | 2.7[18] | 1.7[18] | 6.6 | —339[35]— | | ... | 46[35] | ... | St. Lucia |
| 99.7 | 99.8 | 99.2 | 97.6 | —2.4— | | ... | 4.6 | 0.7 | ... | | | | | | St. Pierre and Miquelon |
| 95.0[5] | ... | ... | 22.0[5] | —78.0[5]— | | ... | 2.8 | 1.8 | 11.2 | | | | | | St. Vincent and the Grenadines |
| 99.8 | 100.0 | 98.3 | 98.3 | —1.7— | | ... | 4.5 | 0.8 | ... | —156— | | ... | 55 | ... | San Marino |
| ... | ... | ... | ... | ... | | ... | ... | ... | 2.0[23] | | | | | | São Tomé and Principe |
| ... | ... | ... | ... | ... | | ... | ... | ... | 14.1 | —54,535[8,9]— | | ... | 8 | ... | Saudi Arabia |
| 87.7 | 95.9 | ... | ... | ... | | ... | 2.3 | 1.5 | 7.1 | —979— | | 251.4 | 38 | 24.6 | Senegal |
| 77.5 | 46.8 | 33.1 | 33.1 | —66.9— | | ... | 3.6 | 1.4 | 4.9 | —4,802[8,35]— | | ... | 8 | ... | Seychelles |
| ... | ... | ... | ... | ... | | ... | ... | ... | 2.6[5] | | | | | | Sierra Leone |
| 90.6[18] | 98.3 | 63.6[18] | 63.6[18] | —36.4[18]— | | ... | 1.8[18] | 2.5[18] | 11.0 | ... | ... | 10,954 | 3,835 | 3,308 | Singapore |
| 92.7[12] | 79.6[12] | 89.2 | 89.2[12] | —10.8[12]— | | 41.8[12] | 2.3[12] | 2.0[12] | ... | 1,174[3] | | ... | ... | ... | Solomon Islands |
| ... | ... | ... | ... | ... | | ... | ... | ... | 5.1[9] | | | | | | Somalia |
| ... | ... | ... | ... | ... | | ... | 3.4 | ... | 3.8 | 30,992 | 816 | | | | South Africa |
| ... | ... | ... | ... | ... | | ... | ... | ... | | | | | | | Bophuthatswana |
| ... | ... | ... | ... | ... | | ... | ... | ... | | | | | | | Ciskei |
| ... | ... | ... | ... | ... | | ... | ... | ... | | | | | | | KwaNdebele |
| ... | ... | ... | ... | ... | | ... | ... | ... | | | | | | | Transkei |
| ... | ... | ... | ... | ... | | ... | ... | ... | 3.2 | | | | | | Venda |
| ... | ... | ... | ... | ... | | ... | ... | ... | | | | | | | South West Africa/Namibia |
| 90.5[3,48] | 94.7[3,48] | ... | 87.9[3,48] | —12.1[3,48]— | | ... | 4.4[18] | ... | 6.4 | 7,400[12] | 15,700[12] | ... | ... | ... | Spain |
| 18.2 | 14.9 | 4.7 | 4.7 | —95.3— | | 18.6[18] | 2.5 | 2.1 | 7.9 | —8,904— | | 847.9 | ... | ... | Sri Lanka |
| 63.9 | 26.4 | 70.2 | 2.6 | —97.4— | | ... | 2.2 | 2.5 | 4.3[5] | | | | | | Sudan, The |
| 62.9 | 82.0 | 40.4 | 19.6[71] | —80.4[71]— | | ... | 2.1 | 1.9 | 5.9 | —1,534— | | 316[4] | 172 | ... | Suriname |
| 33.4 | ... | 20.0 | ... | ... | | ... | ... | ... | 4.3[5] | —100[9]— | | ... | 36[9] | ... | Swaziland |
| 100.0 | 96.2 | 96.2 | 96.3 | —3.7— | | ... | 4.1 | 0.6 | 6.4 | 17,847 | 885 | ... | ... | ... | Sweden |
| 100.0 | ... | 93.3 | 92.2 | — | 7.8 | 86.0 | 3.6 | 0.7 | ... | 13,212[9] | 4,466[9] | ... | 9,058[9] | ... | Switzerland |
| 40.2 | 41.7 | ... | 36.0 | —64.0— | | 90.6 | 3.0 | 2.0 | 6.6 | —16,493— | | 4,455 | 747 | 408 | Syria |
| 79.4 | ... | 94.2 | 69.3 | ... | | 85.9 | 3.7 | 1.5 | 4.4 | ... | ... | ... | ... | ... | Taiwan |
| 37.2 | 6.3 | ... | ... | ... | | ... | 2.5 | 1.9 | 2.1 | | | | | | Tanzania |
| 17.3 | 43.0 | 40.9 | 40.9[12] | 9.8[12] | 49.3[12] | ... | 1.9[12] | ... | 5.3 | ... | ... | 6,122 | ... | 5,605 | Thailand |
| 4.1 | 10.3 | ... | — | —100.0— | | ... | 1.8 | 3.4 | 2.9[5] | —153[3]— | | 43.2[3] | 12[3] | ... | Togo |
| 2.3[34] | 60.9 | 2.3[34] | ... | ... | | ... | ... | ... | ... | | | | | | Tokelau |
| 61.3 | 20.9 | 42.3 | 11.2 | —88.8— | | ... | ... | ... | 3.9[5] | —738[8,23]— | | 668[8,23] | 8 | 8 | Tonga |
| 64.3 | 83.3 | 41.1 | 41.0 | —59.0— | | ... | 3.3 | 1.4 | 12.8 | 2,980 | 30 | 514.1 | 71 | 128.1 | Trinidad and Tobago |
| 26.4 | 63.4 | 43.3 | 51.8 | —41.2— | | ... | 1.9 | 2.4 | 6.0 | —17,208[9]— | | 2,679[9] | ... | ... | Tunisia |
| 49.1[42] | 56.8[26] | 84.8[42] | ... | ... | | ... | 2.5[26] | 2.2[18] | 3.7 | 22,486 | 31,701 | 12,868 | 3,014 | 3,014 | Turkey |
| 19.9 | 47.6 | ... | 70.5 | —29.5— | | ... | 3.5 | 1.1 | ... | | | | | | Turks and Caicos Islands |
| 65.4 | 7.4 | 37.3 | ... | ... | | ... | ... | ... | 13.0[32] | | | | | | Tuvalu |
| ... | ... | ... | ... | ... | | ... | ... | ... | 0.4[23] | —179[34]— | | 37.3[34] | 65[34] | 26.8[34] | Uganda |
| 90.8[1] | 100.0[1] | 88.7[1] | 88.7[1] | —11.3[1]— | | ... | ... | ... | 10.7[2] | —2,008,000— | | 112,510 | ... | ... | U.S.S.R. |
| 30.9[36] | 24.2[36] | 84.5 | ... | ... | | ... | 2.8 | 1.8 | 9.7 | —3,197— | | ... | 133 | ... | United Arab Emirates |
| ... | ... | 99.0 | ... | ... | | ... | 3.8 | 0.6 | 5.7 | | | | | | United Kingdom |
| 97.6 | 100.0[1] | 98.1 | 98.1 | —1.9— | | ... | 5.1 | 0.6 | 4.1 | ... | ... | 214,300 | ... | 123,400 | United States |
| 63.1 | 80.7 | 62.7 | ... | ... | | ... | 3.5 | 2.1 | 2.7 | ... | ... | 238.8 | ... | 139.2 | Uruguay |
| 13.7 | 11.7 | 19.1 | ... | ... | | ... | ... | ... | ... | ... | ... | 3.2 | ... | 9.4 | Vanuatu |
| 85.3 | 88.6 | 84.4 | 71.3 | —28.7— | | ... | 3.9[13] | 1.5[13] | 3.0 | 1,883 | 368 | 2,173.6 | 609 | 899.9 | Venezuela |
| 23.7 | 71.0 | ... | ... | ... | | ... | ... | ... | 3.0[2,5] | —400[25]— | | 212.3[25] | 53[25] | 59.3[25] | Vietnam |
| 96.3 | 98.1 | 86.0 | 93.6 | —6.4— | | ... | 4.2 | 0.8 | ... | 833[32] | 75[32] | ... | 262[32] | ... | Virgin Islands (U.S.) |
| 23.0 | ... | 9.0 | 24.0 | — | 7.6 | ... | 1.8[12] | 4.0[12] | ... | | | | | | Wallis and Futuna |
| 75.2 | 91.2 | 90.1 | ... | ... | | ... | ... | 2.7 | 2.4 | —4,514[11]— | | 629.1[11] | ... | 112.5[11] | West Bank |
| 78.5 | 95.3 | ... | ... | ... | | ... | 4.5 | 1.2 | ... | | | | | | Western Sahara |
| 9.2[70] | 18.8[70] | ... | ... | ... | | ... | 3.9[70] | 1.5[70] | 13.2[9] | —97— | | ... | 140 | ... | Western Samoa |
| ... | ... | ... | ... | ... | | ... | ... | ... | 7.9[3] | | | | | | Yemen (Aden) |
| 5.7 | 4.6 | ... | ... | ... | | ... | 2.0 | 2.8 | 7.9 | —5,147[9]— | | 1,167.4[9] | ... | ... | Yemen (San'ā) |
| 67.8 | 95.7 | 53.3 | ... | ... | | 60.7 | 2.4 | 1.5 | 6.9[2,11] | 63,406 | 1,711 | 14,431 | 20,622 | 4,779 | Yugoslavia |
| ... | ... | ... | ... | ... | | ... | ... | ... | 5.1 | —97— | | 13 | 35 | 18 | Zaire |
| 12.4 | 27.5[19] | 15.1 | ... | 82.3 | | ... | 1.9 | 2.6 | 3.2 | | | | | | Zambia |
| ... | 9.3[81] | ... | ... | ... | | ... | 2.8 | 1.9 | 3.5 | —2,112— | | ... | ... | ... | Zimbabwe |

dwellings.  [49]1946 and earlier.  [50]1947–60.  [51]1948–60.  [52]Peninsular Malaysia only.  [53]1957 and earlier.  [54]1958–67.  [55]Excluding Rodrigues Island and lesser outlying islands. [56]1960–68.  [57]1969–83.  [58]Nauruan dwellings only.  [59]Data are for the cities of Kāthmandu, Lalitpur, Bhaktapur, Birātnagar, Nepālganj, and Birganj only.  [60]1930 and earlier.  [61]1931–59.  [62]Netherlands Antilles includes Aruba.  [63]Excludes Islāmābād, North-West Frontier, and Federally Administered Tribal Areas.  [64]1947–65.  [65]1966–75.  [66]1976–80.  [67]1944 and earlier.  [68]1945–70.  [69]Proportional distribution of known data.  [70]European-style dwellings only.  [71]1964.  [72]1961–75.  [73]1976 and later.  [74]1939–56.  [75]1956–66.  [76]1966–70. [77]Data exclude Northern Ireland.  [78]Data refer to "household spaces."  [79]Data refer to Ho Chi Minh City (Saigon) only.  [80]Data refer to dwellings occupied by Europeans, Asians, and Coloureds only.  [81]Data refer to dwellings occupied by Africans only.

# Household budgets and consumption

This table provides international data on household income, on the consumption expenditure of households for goods and services, and on the principal object of such expenditure (in most countries), food consumption (by kind). For purposes of this compilation, income comprises pretax monetary payments and payment in kind. The first part of the table provides data on distribution of income by households and by sources of income; the second part analyzes the largest portion of income use—consumption expenditure. Such expenditure is defined as the purchase of goods and services to satisfy current wants and needs. This definition excludes income expended on taxes, debts, savings and investments, and insurance policies. The third and last part of the table focuses on food, which usually, and often by a wide margin, represents the largest share of consumer spending worldwide. The data provided include daily available calories per capita and consumption by major food groups.

For both sources of income and consumption expenditure, the primary basis of analysis for most countries is the household, an economic unit that can be as small as a single person or as large as an extended family. For some of the countries that do not compile information by household, the table provides data on personal income and personal expenditure; i.e., the income and expenditure of all the individuals constituting a society's households. When no expenditure data at all is available, the table reports the weights of each major class of goods and services comprising a given country's consumer (or retail) price index (CPI). The weighting of the components of the CPI usually reflects household spending patterns within the country, its principal urban or rural areas, though sometimes only in the country's major city.

The data on distribution of income show, collectively for an entire country, the proportion of total income earned by households comprising the lowest quintile and highest decile (poorest 20% and wealthiest 10%) within the country. These figures show the degree to which either group represents a disproportionate share of poverty or wealth.

The data on sources of income illuminate patterns of economic structure in the gaining of an income. They indicate, for example, that in poor, agrarian countries income often derives largely from self-employment (usually farming) or that in industrial countries, with well-developed systems of salaried employment and social welfare, income derives mainly from wages and salaries and secondarily from transfer payments (see headnote a). Because household sizes and numbers of income earners vary so greatly internationally, and because the frequency and methodology of household and CPI surveys do not permit single-year comparisons for more than a few countries at once, no summary of total *household* income or expenditure was possible. Instead, U.S. dollar figures are supplied for *per capita* private final consumption expenditure (for a single, recent year) that are more comparable internationally and refer to the same date. The figures on distribution of consumption expenditure by end use reveal patterns of personal and family use of disposable income and indicate, inter alia, that in developing countries food may absorb 50% or more of disposable income, while in the larger household budgets of the developed countries, by contrast, food purchases may account for only 20–30% of spending. In either type of country, the cost of transportation often rivals that of housing, once the more basic need. Each category of expenditure betrays similar complexities of local habit, necessity, and aspiration.

The reader should exercise caution when using these data to make intercountry comparisons. Most of the information comes from single-country surveys, which often differ markedly in their coverage of economically or demographically stratified groups, in sample design, or in the methods

## Household budgets and consumption

| country | income (latest) | | | | | | consumption expenditure | | | | | | |
| | percent received by | | by source (percent) | | | | per capita private final, U.S.$ 1985 | by kind or end use (percent of household or personal budget; latest) | | | | | |
| | lowest 20% of households | highest 10% of households | wages, salaries | self-employment | transfer payments[a] | other[b] | | food[c] | housing[d] | clothing[e] | health care | energy, water | education |
|---|---|---|---|---|---|---|---|---|---|---|---|---|---|
| Afghanistan | ... | ... | 20.7 | 28.0 | 8.2 | 43.1 | 100[1] | 33.9 | 3.0 | ... | 1.1 | 0.7 | ... |
| Albania | ... | ... | ... | ... | ... | ... | ... | ... | ... | ... | ... | ... | ... |
| Algeria | ... | ... | ... | ... | ... | ... | 1,080[2] | 55.7 | 5.4 | 9.2 | 3.1 | ... | [3] |
| American Samoa | ... | ... | ... | ... | ... | ... | ... | 41.3 | 22.2[4] | 5.1 | ... | ... | 1.3 |
| Andorra | ... | ... | ... | ... | ... | ... | ... | ... | ... | ... | ... | ... | ... |
| Angola | ... | ... | ... | ... | ... | ... | 290[5] | ... | ... | ... | ... | ... | ... |
| Anguilla | ... | ... | ... | ... | ... | ... | ... | ... | ... | ... | ... | ... | ... |
| Antigua and Barbuda | ... | ... | ... | ... | ... | ... | 1,380[2] | 46.5 | 28.8[6] | 7.5 | ... | [6] | ... |
| Argentina | 4.4 | 35.2 | ... | ... | ... | ... | 1,410[5] | ... | ... | ... | ... | ... | ... |
| Aruba | ... | ... | ... | ... | ... | ... | [7] | 27.4 | 18.4 | 8.4 | 2.9 | ... | ... |
| Australia | 4.6 | 27.0 | 60.1 | 14.4 | 14.4 | 11.1 | 6,260 | 21.5 | 19.9 | 6.5 | 6.6 | 2.5 | 1.2 |
| Austria | 4.0 | 28.7 | 56.1 | ... | 24.3 | 19.6 | 4,950 | 20.4 | 12.4 | 10.8 | 4.4 | 4.9 | 0.3 |
| Bahamas, The | 3.6 | 32.1 | ... | ... | ... | ... | 5,370[2] | 20.5 | 14.1 | 4.0 | 3.2 | 3.6 | 0.1 |
| Bahrain | ... | ... | ... | ... | ... | ... | 3,700[5] | ... | ... | ... | ... | ... | ... |
| Bangladesh | 6.6 | 29.5 | 26.9 | 65.2 | 0.4 | 7.5 | 150 | 66.1 | 8.9 | 7.9 | 1.1 | 6.9 | 1.2 |
| Barbados | 6.8 | ... | ... | ... | ... | ... | 2,920 | 51.6[8] | 13.1 | 5.1 | ... | 6.2 | ... |
| Belgium | 7.9[9] | 21.5[9] | 52.9 | 10.1 | 21.6 | 15.4 | 5,380 | 23.3 | 18.0[6] | 6.1 | 9.4 | [6] | 0.2 |
| Belize | ... | ... | 84.1 | ——15.9—— | | | 790[2] | 51.5[8] | 2.3 | 11.1 | 3.4 | 6.0 | 1.5 |
| Benin | 8.0 | 39.0 | ... | ... | ... | ... | 190[2] | ... | ... | ... | ... | ... | ... |
| Bermuda | 7.2 | 24.7 | 72.2 | 6.7 | 2.4 | 18.7 | 12,690 | 17.3 | 20.8 | 5.3 | 4.1 | 4.0 | 2.8 |
| Bhutan | ... | ... | ... | ... | ... | ... | ... | 72.3 | ... | 21.2 | ... | 3.7 | ... |
| Bolivia | 4.0 | ... | ... | ... | ... | ... | 790 | 41.7 | 12.6 | 9.8 | 4.6 | 0.7 | 1.2 |
| Botswana | 4.3[9,10] | 42.0[9,10] | 65.6 | 14.8 | 19.6 | — | 350 | 40.1[8] | 13.16 | 10.8 | 1.3 | [6] | ... |
| Brazil | 2.3 | 48.3 | ... | ... | ... | ... | 1,120 | 46.8[11] | 4.2[11] | 7.5[11] | 4.4[11] | 5.0[11] | 1.9[11] |
| British Virgin Islands | ... | ... | ... | ... | ... | ... | 2,880[5] | 34.1 | 21.0 | 8.2 | 3.1 | 4.5 | 3.2 |
| Brunei | ... | ... | ... | ... | ... | ... | ... | 45.1 | 5.0[6] | 6.1 | ... | [6] | [3] |
| Bulgaria | 9.7 | 22.5 | 60.8 | 14.3 | 19.5 | 5.4 | 750[12] | 45.0 | 7.2 | 9.7 | 2.1 | ... | ... |
| Burkina Faso | ... | ... | ... | ... | ... | ... | 100[2] | 47.7[13] | 5.1[13] | 4.4[13] | 5.2[13] | 13.7[13] | [3] |
| Burma | 8.0 | ... | ... | ... | ... | ... | 160 | 49.1[13] | 10.4[13] | 15.3[13] | 2.4[13] | 4.0[13] | 5.9[13] |
| Burundi | ... | ... | ... | ... | ... | ... | 200 | 59.6[13] | 4.4[13] | 11.1[13] | ... | 5.8[13] | ... |
| Cameroon | ... | ... | ... | ... | ... | ... | 420[2] | 33.6[13] | 14.6[13] | 16.3[13] | 5.0[13] | ... | [15] |
| Canada | 6.0 | 30.1 | 65.4 | 6.9 | 15.3 | 12.4 | 7,930 | 17.8 | 22.1[6] | 6.8 | 3.5 | [6] | 2.8 |
| Cape Verde | ... | ... | ... | ... | ... | ... | 160[2] | ... | ... | ... | ... | ... | ... |
| Cayman Islands | ... | ... | ... | ... | ... | ... | ... | ... | ... | ... | ... | ... | ... |
| Central African Republic | ... | ... | ... | ... | ... | ... | 210[2] | 70.5[13] | 0.6[13] | 9.5[13] | 1.0[13] | 6.5[13] | ... |
| Chad | 8.0 | 30.0 | ... | ... | ... | ... | 110[5] | 45.3[13] | ... | 3.5[13] | 11.9[13] | 5.8[13] | ... |
| Chile | 4.4 | 34.8 | 40.8 | ... | 8.1 | 51.2 | 920 | 41.9 | 13.3 | 7.6 | ... | ... | [3] |
| China | 8.5[16] | 37.7[16,17] | ... | ... | ... | ... | 150[5] | 59.3[16] | 11.1[16] | 11.2[16] | ... | ... | ... |
| Christmas Island | ... | ... | ... | ... | ... | ... | ... | ... | ... | ... | ... | ... | ... |
| Cocos (Keeling) Islands | ... | ... | ... | ... | ... | ... | ... | ... | ... | ... | ... | ... | ... |
| Colombia | 4.0 | 43.5 | 49.3 | 36.6 | 6.2 | 7.9 | 870 | 35.7 | 11.5 | 5.9 | 6.1 | 2.0 | 1.7 |
| Comoros | ... | ... | 25.6 | 64.5 | 8.7 | 1.2 | 170[5] | 56.0 | ... | 10.0 | 5.0 | 14.4 | ... |
| Congo | 7.0 | 43.5 | ... | ... | ... | ... | 440[2] | ... | ... | ... | ... | ... | ... |
| Cook Islands | ... | ... | ... | ... | ... | ... | ... | 65.2[8,13] | 3.1[13] | 12.4[13] | ... | ... | ... |
| Costa Rica | 3.9[18] | 39.8[18] | ... | ... | ... | ... | 950 | 40.8 | 12.3 | 10.0 | — | 6.6 | ... |
| Côte d'Ivoire | 2.4 | 43.7 | 44.9 | 49.9 | ——5.2—— | | 420[2] | 51.1 | 11.6 | 8.4 | ... | 8.1 | ... |
| Cuba | ... | ... | 57.3 | ... | ... | 42.7 | 1,030 | ... | ... | ... | ... | ... | ... |
| Cyprus | 7.9[18] | ... | ... | ... | ... | ... | 2,210 | 25.6 | 5.9 | 11.6 | 2.4 | 1.9 | 0.6 |
| Czechoslovakia | 10.01[19] | 21.8[19] | 62.1 | ... | 20.2 | 17.7 | 3,720 | 29.6 | ... | 11.5 | ... | ... | ... |
| Denmark | 4.3[20] | 24.0[20] | 65.5 | 8.8 | 12.4 | 13.3 | 6,170 | 21.3 | 19.3 | 5.8 | 1.9 | 6.2 | 1.5 |
| Djibouti | ... | ... | 51.6 | 36.0 | 10.5 | 1.9 | 710[5] | 50.3 | 6.4 | 1.7 | 2.4 | 13.1 | ... |
| Dominica | ... | ... | ... | ... | ... | ... | 730[2] | 65.2 | 8.9 | 9.5 | — | 5.4 | — |
| Dominican Republic | 4.5[9] | 41.7[9] | 41.7 | 31.8 | 1.5 | 25.0 | 1,250[2] | 51.7[8] | 23.9 | 6.0 | ... | ... | ... |
| Ecuador | 2.9 | 51.5 | 26.2 | 65.8 | 4.8 | 3.2 | 1,140 | 38.6[8] | 6.8[6] | 11.4 | 3.8 | [6] | ... |
| Egypt | 5.8 | 33.2 | ... | ... | ... | ... | 690 | 49.7[18] | 8.8[18] | 14.2[18] | 1.8[18] | 3.6[18] | 2.1[18] |

employed for collection, classification, and tabulation of data. Further, the reference period of the data varies greatly; while a significant portion of the data is from 1979 or later, information for some countries dates from the early and mid-1970s. This older information is typeset in italic. Finally, intercountry comparisons of annual personal consumption expenditure may be misleading because of the distortions of price and purchasing power present when converting a national currency unit into U.S. dollars.

The table's food consumption data include total daily available calories per capita (food supply), which amounts to domestic production and imports minus exports, animal feed, and nonfood uses, and a percentage breakdown of the major food groups that make up food supply.

The data for daily available calories per capita provide a measure of the nutritional adequacy of each nation's food supply. The following list, based on estimates from the United Nations Food and Agriculture Organization (FAO), indicates the regional variation in recommended daily minimum nutritional requirements, which are defined by factors such as climatic ambience and average body weight: Africa (2,320 calories), Centrally Planned Asia (2,300 calories), Far East (2,240 calories), Latin America (2,360 calories), Near East (2,440 calories).

The breakdown of diet by food groups describes the character of a nation's food supply. A typical breakdown for a low-income country might show a diet with heavy intake of vegetable foods, such as cereals, potatoes, or cassava. In the high-income countries, a relatively larger portion of total calories derives from animal products (meat, eggs, and milk). The reader should note, however, that these data refer to total national *supply* and do not reflect the dietary differences that often exist between socioeconomic groups within a single country.

In compiling this table, Britannica editors rely on both numerous na-

tional reports and principal secondary sources such as the International Bank for Reconstruction and Development's *World Development Report* (annual), the International Labour Organisation's *Household Income and Expenditure Statistics 1968–1976* and *Statistical Sources and Methods, vol. 1 Consumer Price Indices;* the UN's *Yearbook of National Accounts Statistics* (annual) and *National Accounts Statistics: Compendium of Income Distribution Statistics;* and the FAO's *Food Balance Sheets 1975– 77 and 1979–81.*

The following terms further define the column headings:

a. Includes pensions, family allowances, unemployment payments, remittances from abroad, and social security and related benefits.
b. Includes interest and dividends, rents and royalties, and all other income not reported under the three preceding categories.
c. Includes alcoholic and nonalcoholic beverages. Excludes tobacco except as noted.
d. Rent, maintenance of dwellings, and taxes only; excludes energy and water (heat, light, power, and water) and household durables (furniture, appliances, utensils, and household operations), shown separately.
e. Includes footwear.
f. Furniture, appliances, and utensils; usually includes expenditure on household operation.
g. Includes expenditure on cultural activities other than education.
h. May include data not shown separately in preceding categories, including meals away from home.
i. Includes peas, beans, and lentils.
j. Represents pure fats and oils only.
k. Consists mainly of spices, stimulants, sugars and honey, and nuts and oilseeds.

| transportation, communication | household durable goods[f] | recreation[g] | personal effects, other[h] | food consumption daily available calories per capita | cereals | potatoes, cassava | meat, poultry | fish | eggs, milk | fruits, vegetables[i] | fats, oils[j] | other[k] | country |
|---|---|---|---|---|---|---|---|---|---|---|---|---|---|
| ... | ... | ... | 61.3 | *1,896* | *81.5* | *1.4* | *3.3* | — | *3.6* | *3.7* | *3.1* | *3.4* | Afghanistan |
| ... | ... | ... | ... | *2,657* | *66.4* | *2.6* | *5.2* | *0.1* | *6.2* | *6.5* | *6.4* | *6.6* | Albania |
| 6.7 | 6.4 | 3.4[3] | 10.2 | 2,586 | 56.8 | 2.2 | 2.0 | 0.2 | 6.4 | 6.7 | 13.1 | 12.3 | Algeria |
| 12.4 | 4 | 1.6 | 16.1 | ... | ... | ... | ... | ... | ... | ... | ... | ... | American Samoa |
| ... | ... | ... | ... | ... | ... | ... | ... | ... | ... | ... | ... | ... | Andorra |
| ... | ... | ... | ... | *2,141* | *35.3* | *33.8* | *3.2* | *0.9* | *1.9* | *7.7* | *7.2* | *10.0* | Angola |
| ... | ... | ... | ... | ... | ... | ... | ... | ... | ... | ... | ... | ... | Anguilla |
| 10.0 | ... | ... | 7.2 | 1,979 | 34.3 | 1.4 | 7.6 | 2.0 | 13.6 | 7.2 | 12.8 | 21.2 | Antigua and Barbuda |
| ... | ... | ... | ... | 3,308 | 29.8 | 4.5 | 22.6 | 0.3 | 8.3 | 5.2 | 9.7 | 19.5 | Argentina |
| 17.4 | 9.1 | 5.0 | 11.4 | 7 | 7 | 7 | 7 | 7 | 7 | 7 | 7 | 7 | Aruba |
| 15.3 | 7.2 | 6.2 | 13.1 | 3,055 | 26.1 | 3.3 | 19.5 | 0.7 | 9.7 | 5.5 | 9.6 | 25.6 | Australia |
| 16.5 | 7.3 | 5.4 | 17.6 | 3,575 | 19.6 | 4.0 | 13.7 | 0.4 | 10.5 | 5.5 | 23.8 | 22.5 | Austria |
| 15.1 | 6.0 | 6.5 | 26.9 | 2,200 | 29.1 | 1.2 | 18.3 | 0.8 | 7.1 | 8.0 | 9.7 | 25.8 | Bahamas, The |
| ... | ... | ... | ... | ... | ... | ... | ... | ... | ... | ... | ... | ... | Bahrain |
| 0.9 | ... | ... | 7.0 | 1,837 | 85.4 | 2.0 | 0.9 | 0.8 | 1.4 | 2.6 | 2.8 | 4.2 | Bangladesh |
| 4.6 | 9.6 | ... | 9.8 | 3,020 | 28.8 | 4.5 | 14.8 | 2.0 | 6.1 | 4.9 | 11.6 | 27.2 | Barbados |
| 12.9 | 12.4 | 4.6 | 13.2 | 3,639 | 19.2 | 5.5 | 19.6 | 0.8 | 9.9 | 5.2 | 20.7 | 19.3 | Belgium |
| 6.5 | 10.1 | 2.2 | 5.4 | 2,714 | 35.3 | 7.1 | 7.3 | 0.4 | 9.7 | 9.3 | 9.2 | 21.8 | Belize |
| ... | ... | ... | ... | 2,174 | 34.6 | 37.2 | 2.2 | 0.7 | 0.6 | 5.6 | 10.9 | 8.3 | Benin |
| 10.6 | 11.9 | 5.4 | 17.8 | 2,799 | 22.5 | 2.0 | 19.1 | 2.8 | 12.1 | 8.6 | 11.2 | 21.7 | Bermuda |
| ... | 0.7 | ... | 2.1 | *2,028* | *85.2* | *2.4* | *0.4* | *0.1* | *0.6* | *2.1* | *5.3* | *3.9* | Bhutan |
| 12.6 | 8.9 | 3.1 | 4.8 | 2,082 | 42.1 | 11.6 | 8.3 | 0.3 | 2.9 | 8.2 | 7.8 | 18.7 | Bolivia |
| 10.5 | 13.7 | ... | 10.5 | 2,352 | 53.1 | 1.0 | 6.0 | 0.1 | 9.0 | 9.6 | 9.2 | 12.0 | Botswana |
| 6.4[11] | 8.6[11] | 5.7[11] | 6.4[11] | 2,578 | 38.0 | 8.4 | 6.9 | 0.5 | 5.2 | 10.4 | 8.2 | 22.5 | Brazil |
| 2.3 | 13.1 | 1.6 | 8.9 | ... | ... | ... | ... | ... | ... | ... | ... | ... | British Virgin Islands |
| 17.2 | 8.3 | 8.9[3] | 9.4 | 2,594 | 50.0 | 2.7 | 6.1 | 2.0 | 6.7 | 4.9 | 8.8 | 18.7 | Brunei |
| 7.0 | 4.4 | ... | 24.6 | 3,619 | 43.7 | 1.6 | 9.0 | 0.3 | 7.5 | 6.4 | 13.8 | 17.6 | Bulgaria |
| 18.6[13] | 3.0[13] | 2.3[3, 13] | ... | 2,010 | 70.5 | 2.1 | 2.2 | 0.1 | 1.5 | 10.1 | 3.5 | 10.0 | Burkina Faso |
| 3.8[13] | 0.5[13] | 1.1[13] | 7.5[13] | 2,420 | 81.2 | 0.3 | 1.7 | 1.0 | 0.7 | 5.3 | 5.7 | 4.0 | Burma |
| ... | 6.0[13] | ... | 13.1[13, 14] | 2,353 | 25.2 | 35.4 | 1.1 | 0.3 | 1.3 | 22.5 | 3.2 | 10.8 | Burundi |
| 10.5[13] | ... | 5.1[13] | 14.9[13, 15] | 2,295 | 32.8 | 21.1 | 3.3 | 0.8 | 0.8 | 14.2 | 8.7 | 18.2 | Cameroon |
| 15.4 | 7.4 | 6.9 | 17.2 | 3,340 | 19.8 | 4.6 | 19.7 | 0.9 | 11.4 | 6.3 | 17.2 | 20.0 | Canada |
| ... | ... | ... | ... | 2,704 | 58.5 | 5.1 | 1.7 | 1.8 | 2.6 | 8.1 | 8.7 | 13.6 | Cape Verde |
| ... | ... | ... | ... | ... | ... | ... | ... | ... | ... | ... | ... | ... | Cayman Islands |
| 4.1[13] | 0.8[13] | 1.3[13] | 5.7[13] | 2,117 | 15.9 | 52.0 | 4.1 | 0.5 | 0.3 | 6.4 | 6.1 | 14.7 | Central African Republic |
| ... | ... | ... | 33.5[13] | *1,762* | *57.2* | *11.2* | *3.2* | *1.6* | *2.6* | *8.2* | *3.3* | *12.7* | Chad |
| 11.8 | 7.8 | 8.2[3] | 9.4 | 2,759 | 48.7 | 3.4 | 6.7 | 1.4 | 6.4 | 6.8 | 8.0 | 18.6 | Chile |
| ... | ... | ——18.4[16]—— | | 2,426 | 66.4 | 12.1 | 7.6 | 0.4 | 1.1 | 4.1 | 3.6 | 4.6 | China |
| ... | ... | ... | ... | ... | ... | ... | ... | ... | ... | ... | ... | ... | Christmas Island |
| ... | ... | ... | ... | ... | ... | ... | ... | ... | ... | ... | ... | ... | Cocos (Keeling) Islands |
| 14.1 | 5.3 | 4.0 | 13.8 | 2,494 | 33.2 | 9.6 | 7.4 | 0.4 | 5.3 | 11.9 | 7.1 | 25.2 | Colombia |
| 6.6 | ... | 3.0 | 5.0 | 2,219 | 38.4 | 33.3 | 2.3 | 1.2 | 1.2 | 9.0 | 3.3 | 11.3 | Comoros |
| ... | ... | ... | ... | 2,433 | 15.2 | 49.8 | 2.0 | 2.3 | 0.9 | 9.0 | 10.2 | 10.5 | Congo |
| 5.7[13] | 9.6[13] | ... | 4.0[13] | ... | ... | ... | ... | ... | ... | ... | ... | ... | Cook Islands |
| 6.5 | 8.2 | 9.2[3] | 6.4 | 2,653 | 34.3 | 1.0 | 5.9 | 0.5 | 9.7 | 9.5 | 11.0 | 28.2 | Costa Rica |
| ... | 7.3 | ... | 13.5 | 2,613 | 37.8 | 27.4 | 3.2 | 1.5 | 2.0 | 9.7 | 9.5 | 9.1 | Côte d'Ivoire |
| ... | ... | ... | ... | 2,796 | 37.6 | 6.7 | 7.0 | 1.2 | 9.9 | 7.5 | 8.8 | 21.2 | Cuba |
| 20.0 | 12.3 | 7.4 | 12.4 | 3,054 | 40.0 | 2.5 | 13.7 | 0.4 | 7.9 | 9.5 | 10.1 | 15.9 | Cyprus |
| ... | 5.0 | ... | 53.9 | 3,393 | 30.5 | 4.7 | 14.8 | 0.5 | 10.3 | 3.3 | 14.2 | 21.8 | Czechoslovakia |
| 16.5 | 6.9 | 7.9 | 12.6 | 3,548 | 18.5 | 4.3 | 19.5 | 2.9 | 11.3 | 3.4 | 18.9 | 21.1 | Denmark |
| ... | 1.5 | ... | 24.6 | ... | ... | ... | ... | ... | ... | ... | ... | ... | Djibouti |
| — | — | — | 11.0 | 2,018 | 30.1 | 17.0 | 7.4 | 1.9 | 5.8 | 13.8 | 8.2 | 15.9 | Dominica |
| ... | ... | ... | 18.4 | 2,130 | 33.0 | 3.4 | 4.8 | 0.7 | 6.6 | 20.7 | 11.1 | 19.7 | Dominican Republic |
| 12.3 | 7.0 | ... | 20.1 | 2,114 | 31.0 | 4.9 | 6.2 | 1.7 | 8.0 | 12.4 | 11.4 | 24.5 | Ecuador |
| 5.2[18] | 3.6[18] | 1.3[18] | 9.7[18] | 3,175 | 64.0 | 1.5 | 2.3 | 0.3 | 1.7 | 7.6 | 11.5 | 11.1 | Egypt |

## Household budgets and consumption   (continued)

| country | income (latest) | | | | | | consumption expenditure | | | | | | |
| --- | --- | --- | --- | --- | --- | --- | --- | --- | --- | --- | --- | --- | --- |
| | percent received by | | by source (percent) | | | | per capita private final, U.S.$ 1985 | by kind or end use (percent of household or personal budget; latest) | | | | | |
| | lowest 20% of households | highest 10% of households | wages, salaries | self-employment | transfer payments[a] | other[b] | | food[c] | housing[d] | clothing[e] | health care | energy, water | education |
| El Salvador | 5.5[9] | 29.5[9] | ... | ... | ... | ... | 960 | 42.8[18] | 11.7[18] | 8.4[18] | 2.5[18] | 3.9[18] | 3 |
| Equatorial Guinea | ... | ... | ... | ... | ... | ... | 705[5] | ... | ... | ... | ... | ... | ... |
| Ethiopia | ... | ... | ... | ... | ... | ... | 90 | 57.4[13] | [21] | 7.8[13] | 2.1[13] | ... | ... |
| Faeroe Islands | ... | ... | ... | ... | ... | ... | ... | 43.8 | 8.5 | 8.0 | ... | 18.9 | ... |
| Falkland Islands | ... | ... | ... | ... | ... | ... | ... | 46.0[13] | 10.0[13] | 13.0[13] | ... | 5.0[13] | ... |
| Fiji | 3.7 | 37.8 | 81.5 | 9.1 | — | 9.4 | 1,040 | 40.3[8] | 18.6 | 6.3 | ... | 4.9 | ... |
| Finland | 6.3[9] | 21.7[9] | 66.4 | 16.8 | 14.2 | 2.6 | 5,930 | 25.5[8] | 18.7[6] | 5.6 | 2.4 | [6] | 3 |
| France | 5.5 | 26.4 | 50.7 | 15.1 | 28.5 | 5.7 | 5,990 | 20.1 | 17.9[6] | 6.3 | 13.6 | [6] | 0.4 |
| French Guiana | ... | ... | 74.6 | —25.4— | | ... | | 50.0 | 7.3 | 8.4 | 2.2 | 4.1 | ... |
| French Polynesia | ... | ... | 48.0 | 40.9 | 9.4 | 1.6 | 4,660[1] | 36.5 | 5.9 | 9.0 | 1.0 | 8.6 | 3 |
| Gabon | 3.3 | 54.4 | ... | ... | ... | ... | 870[2] | 54.7[8,13] | 13.0[13] | 17.5[13] | 1.9[13] | ... | ... |
| Gambia, The | ... | ... | ... | ... | ... | ... | 370[5] | 58.0[22] | 5.1[22] | 17.5[22] | ... | 5.4[22] | ... |
| Gaza Strip | ... | ... | ... | ... | ... | ... | 720[2] | ... | ... | ... | ... | ... | ... |
| Germany, East | 12.2[9,23] | 17.5[9,23] | 68.3 | | 31.7 | | 5,710 | 41.4[8] | 3.3 | 15.1 | ... | 1.9 | 3 |
| Germany, West | 6.0 | 24.0 | 57.2 | [24] | 22.0 | 20.7[24] | 5,800 | 21.8 | 15.6 | 9.0 | 3.2 | 6.0 | 3 |
| Ghana | ... | ... | 41.6[25] | 47.1[25] | — | 11.3[25] | 450 | 57.4 | 11.5[6] | 14.3 | 1.3 | [6] | 3 |
| Gibraltar | ... | ... | ... | ... | ... | ... | ... | 39.0[8] | 12.6 | 11.0 | ... | ... | ... |
| Greece | ... | ... | 42.8 | [24] | 17.3 | 42.8[24] | 2,190 | 32.4 | 14.5 | 7.8 | 3.1 | 3.4 | 0.5 |
| Greenland | ... | ... | ... | ... | ... | ... | ... | 31.5 | 8.9 | 9.2 | 1.7 | 7.8 | ... |
| Grenada | ... | ... | ... | ... | ... | ... | 710[2] | 61.5[8] | 6.5 | 8.0 | ... | 6.0 | ... |
| Guadeloupe | ... | ... | —76.8— | | —23.2— | | 3,250[5] | 34.4 | 12.2 | 9.2 | — | 5.7 | 3 |
| Guam | ... | ... | ... | ... | ... | ... | ... | 24.1 | 28.6 | 10.6 | 4.8 | ... | ... |
| Guatemala | 5.3 | 42.1 | ... | ... | ... | ... | 1,160 | 57.3[18] | 12.7[6,18] | 10.4[18] | 2.1[18] | [6] | 1.0[18] |
| Guernsey | ... | ... | ... | ... | ... | ... | ... | 23.7 | 12.2 | 7.5 | ... | 8.2 | ... |
| Guinea | ... | ... | ... | ... | ... | ... | 250[2] | 61.5 | 7.3[6] | 7.9 | 11.1 | [6] | ... |
| Guinea-Bissau | ... | ... | ... | ... | ... | ... | 60[2] | ... | ... | ... | ... | ... | ... |
| Guyana | ... | ... | 73.0 | ... | 6.3 | 20.7 | 320 | 42.5[8] | 21.4 | 8.6 | — | 5.2 | 3 |
| Haiti | ... | ... | ... | ... | ... | ... | 360 | 77.9 | 8.3 | 3.2 | ... | ... | ... |
| Honduras | 3.2 | 50.6 | 52.7 | ... | 1.7 | 45.6 | 570 | 44.4 | 22.3[6] | 9.1 | 6.9 | [6] | 3 |
| Hong Kong | 4.3[20] | 37.3[20] | ... | ... | ... | ... | 4,080 | 20.6 | 15.4[6] | 19.4 | 6.2 | [6] | 1.1 |
| Hungary | 6.9[9] | 20.5[9] | 65.6 | —34.4— | | | 1,100 | 46.5[8] | ... | 9.1 | ... | 4.7 | ... |
| Iceland | 4.5 | 26.9 | —80.0— | | —20.0— | | 6,690 | 23.8 | 11.0 | 8.5 | 1.7 | 5.5 | 0.4 |
| India | 5.0 | 34.9 | 40.7 | 41.6 | ... | 17.7 | 170 | 56.8 | 2.7 | 10.8 | 1.9 | 4.8 | 2.2 |
| Indonesia | 6.6 | 34.0 | 42.1 | 41.5 | 2.5 | 13.9 | 300 | 63.3[8] | 17.4[6] | 4.6 | ... | [6] | 3 |
| Iran | 3.8 | 41.7 | 40.8 | 28.2 | 3.7 | 27.3 | 2,050 | 42.1[8] | 22.8[6] | 10.4 | 4.3 | [6] | 3 |
| Iraq | 2.1 | ... | ... | ... | ... | ... | 930[27] | 55.4 | 7.9 | 10.3 | 2.4 | 4.1 | — |
| Ireland | 4.6 | 26.5 | 61.5 | 15.8 | 19.7 | 3.0 | 2,960 | 39.5 | 6.9 | 6.2 | ... | 6.1 | 3 |
| Isle of Man | ... | ... | ... | ... | ... | ... | ... | 29.1 | 8.3 | 6.3 | ... | 11.2 | ... |
| Israel | 6.0 | 22.6 | 90.8 | 0.8 | —8.4— | | 3,260 | 30.3[8] | 18.0 | ... | ... | 3.6 | ... |
| Italy | 6.2 | 28.1 | 49.5 | 19.9 | 20.6 | 10.0 | 3,900 | 28.1 | 18.2 | 8.6 | 1.7 | 6.0 | 3 |
| Jamaica | 2.2 | ... | 70.9 | 27.3 | 1.8 | ... | 610 | 36.8 | 8.5 | 2.3 | 2.5 | 4.6 | 0.2 |
| Japan | 9.1[20] | 22.7[20] | 57.5 | 12.3 | 19.0 | 11.1 | 6,400 | 26.8 | 4.7 | 7.1 | 2.5 | 6.3 | 4.1 |
| Jersey | ... | ... | ... | ... | ... | ... | ... | 28.3 | 14.9 | 8.3 | ... | 6.5 | ... |
| Jordan | ... | ... | ... | ... | ... | ... | 1,370 | 38.8 | 6.5[6] | 6.0 | 4.0 | [6] | 3.4 |
| Kampuchea | ... | ... | ... | ... | ... | ... | ... | 53.0 | 23.0 | 9.0 | ... | ... | ... |
| Kenya | 2.6 | 45.8 | 22.4 | ... | ... | 77.6 | 190 | 46.5 | 10.0 | 7.7 | 2.2 | 2.6 | 1.0 |
| Kiribati | ... | ... | 69.8 | 21.4 | 6.0 | 2.8 | 370[27] | 64.0[8] | 1.0 | 8.0 | ... | 3.6 | ... |
| Korea, North | ... | ... | ... | ... | ... | ... | ... | 46.5[28] | 0.6[28] | 29.9[28] | 15.9[28,29] | 3.3[28] | ... |
| Korea, South | 8.0[18,30] | 24.5[18,30] | 57.8 | 18.5 | 4.7 | 19.0 | 1,230 | 44.6[8] | 11.2[6] | 6.6 | 4.3 | [6] | 3 |
| Kuwait | ... | ... | 53.8 | 20.8 | —25.4— | | 5,120 | 37.0[8] | 18.7[6] | 10.0 | 1.0 | [6] | ... |
| Laos | ... | ... | ... | ... | ... | ... | ... | ... | ... | ... | ... | ... | ... |
| Lebanon | 5.0 | 45.0 | 27.9 | ... | 3.0 | 69.1 | 1,410[27] | 42.8[13] | 16.8[13] | 8.6[13] | 7.2[13] | 4.5[13] | 3.9[13] |
| Lesotho | ... | ... | 42.0 | 51.6 | —6.4— | | 500[5] | 34.0[18] | 9.7[18] | 19.3[18] | 1.8[18] | 4.8[18] | 4.1[18] |
| Liberia | 5.3 | ... | ... | ... | ... | ... | 170 | 40.1[8,13] | 14.9[13] | 13.8[13] | ... | 5.0[13] | ... |
| Libya | 10.1 | ... | ... | ... | ... | ... | 2,790[5] | 37.2 | 32.2[6] | 6.9 | 3.3 | [6] | 3 |
| Liechtenstein | ... | ... | 92.9[31] | 7.1[31] | ... | ... | ... | 21.2[8] | 17.5 | 6.3 | 7.3 | 4.5 | 3 |
| Luxembourg | ... | ... | 79.2 | —20.8— | | | 5,680 | 17.4 | 11.7 | 6.4 | 6.8 | 8.5 | 3 |
| Macau | ... | ... | ... | ... | ... | ... | ... | 44.2[8] | 22.8 | 7.3 | ... | 4.8 | ... |
| Madagascar | 5.2 | ... | 58.8[13,32] | 14.1[13,32] | ... | 27.1[13,32] | 180 | 35.8 | ... | 12.0 | ... | ... | ... |
| Malawi | 10.4 | 40.1 | 83.3 | 6.0 | — | 11.7 | 120 | 39.3[8,33] | 13.3[33] | 10.7[33] | ... | ... | ... |
| Malaysia | 3.5 | 39.8 | ... | ... | ... | ... | 1,040 | 37.1 | 10.6[6] | 5.7 | 2.2 | [6] | 0.5 |
| Maldives | ... | ... | ... | ... | ... | ... | 270 | ... | ... | ... | ... | ... | ... |
| Mali | ... | ... | ... | ... | ... | ... | 120[5] | ... | ... | ... | ... | ... | ... |
| Malta | ... | ... | 50.8 | 15.6 | 18.9 | 14.6 | 2,120 | 34.0 | 3.9[34] | 8.7 | 3.3 | 2.1[34] | 3 |
| Martinique | ... | ... | ... | ... | ... | ... | 3,590[5] | 31.7 | 11.2 | 8.2 | 3.5 | 2.7 | ... |
| Mauritania | ... | ... | ... | ... | ... | ... | 320[2] | 61.0[13] | 24.0[13] | 5.2[13] | ... | ... | ... |
| Mauritius | 4.0 | 46.7 | 53.1 | 32.4 | 4.3 | 10.3 | 700 | 50.4[8] | 4.0 | 10.5 | 3.0 | 6.4 | 2.9 |
| Mayotte | ... | ... | ... | ... | ... | ... | ... | ... | ... | ... | ... | ... | ... |
| Mexico | 2.9 | 40.6 | 58.8 | 25.4 | —15.8— | | 1,360[2] | 35.8[8] | 8.2[6] | 10.3 | 5.0 | [6] | 3 |
| Monaco | ... | ... | ... | ... | ... | ... | ... | ... | ... | ... | ... | ... | ... |
| Mongolia | ... | ... | ... | ... | ... | ... | ... | ... | ... | ... | ... | ... | ... |
| Montserrat | ... | ... | ... | ... | ... | ... | 3,010 | 54.1[8] | 0.7 | 17.9 | ... | 1.8 | ... |
| Morocco | 4.0 | ... | ... | ... | ... | ... | 380 | 54.0 | 7.0 | 8.5 | ... | 3.0 | ... |
| Mozambique | ... | ... | ... | ... | ... | ... | 280[5] | ... | ... | ... | ... | ... | ... |
| Nauru | ... | ... | ... | ... | ... | ... | ... | ... | ... | ... | ... | ... | ... |
| Nepal | 3.1 | 50.7 | 39.2[13] | —60.8[13]— | | | 110 | 57.4[13] | 11.4[6,13] | 10.5[13] | 4.2[13] | [6] | 3 |
| Netherlands, The | 7.1 | 23.9 | 40.0 | 19.6 | 28.2 | 12.2 | 5,090 | 17.6 | 13.4[34] | 6.8 | 12.7 | 6.5[34] | 0.3 |
| Netherlands Antilles | ... | ... | ... | ... | ... | ... | 3,520[7,27] | 24.4[35] | 18.8[35] | 8.7[35] | 2.2[35] | — | 3 |
| New Caledonia | ... | ... | 63.1 | 23.9 | 13.0 | ... | 2,840[5] | 28.4 | 13.3 | 5.6 | 2.6 | 8.3 | 1.3 |
| New Zealand | 5.1[20] | 28.7[20] | ... | ... | ... | ... | 4,030 | 20.1 | 20.3 | 6.0 | 1.5 | 2.3 | 0.6 |
| Nicaragua | 3.1[16] | ... | ... | ... | ... | ... | 770[5] | 40.4[8,13] | 19.7[4,6,13] | 20.9[13] | ... | [6] | ... |
| Niger | ... | ... | ... | ... | ... | ... | 250[5] | 50.5 | 19.1[4] | 7.3 | ... | ... | ... |
| Nigeria | ... | ... | 36.2 | 49.4 | 4.3 | 10.1 | 560[2] | 53.0[8] | ... | 6.0 | ... | 11.1 | ... |
| Niue | ... | ... | ... | ... | ... | ... | ... | 54.5[8] | 5.0 | 5.0 | ... | ... | ... |
| Norfolk Island | ... | ... | ... | ... | ... | ... | ... | ... | ... | ... | ... | ... | ... |

| transportation, communication | household durable goods[f] | recreation[g] | personal effects, other[h] | daily available calories per capita | food consumption — percent of total calories derived from | | | | | | | | country |
|---|---|---|---|---|---|---|---|---|---|---|---|---|---|
| | | | | | cereals | potatoes, cassava | meat, poultry | fish | eggs, milk | fruits, vegetables[i] | fats, oils[j] | other[k] | |
| 7.7[18] | 8.5[18] | 8.7[3,18] | 5.8[18] | 2,048 | 56.9 | 0.9 | 2.4 | 0.2 | 5.3 | 8.8 | 8.4 | 17.1 | El Salvador |
| ... | ... | ... | ... | ... | ... | ... | ... | ... | ... | ... | ... | ... | Equatorial Guinea |
| 5.3[13] | 17.1[13] | 3.0[13] | 7.3[13] | 1,793 | 68.8 | 3.9 | 4.2 | — | 2.9 | 9.3 | 2.2 | 8.7 | Ethiopia |
| ... | 6.6 | ... | 14.2 | 3,135 | 29.3 | 5.5 | 15.8 | 3.9 | 7.0 | 3.3 | 18.0 | 17.2 | Faeroe Islands |
| ... | 5.0[13] | ... | 21.0[13] | ... | ... | ... | ... | ... | ... | ... | ... | ... | Falkland Islands |
| 11.3 | 7.6 | ... | 11.0 | 3,103 | 31.2 | 15.1 | 3.7 | 2.7 | 2.9 | 4.3 | 11.5 | 28.5 | Fiji |
| 18.0 | 7.3 | 9.0[3] | 13.5 | 3,079 | 23.9 | 5.3 | 15.7 | 1.8 | 17.0 | 3.9 | 14.1 | 18.3 | Finland |
| 13.6 | 8.5 | 6.0 | 13.7 | 3,529 | 22.2 | 4.4 | 17.7 | 1.0 | 11.0 | 4.8 | 18.3 | 20.7 | France |
| 7.5 | 6.7 | 4.9 | 8.9 | 2,718 | 34.1 | 5.2 | 16.9 | 2.0 | 7.1 | 8.0 | 7.1 | 19.6 | French Guiana |
| 13.1 | 9.2 | 8.6[3] | 8.1 | 2,898 | 36.0 | 9.0 | 10.0 | 2.3 | 4.9 | 4.7 | 13.8 | 19.2 | French Polynesia |
| 6.3[13] | ... | ... | 6.6[13] | 2,428 | 24.2 | 24.3 | 6.2 | 1.9 | 2.8 | 14.0 | 8.3 | 18.3 | Gabon |
| ... | ... | ... | 14.0[22] | 2,251 | 59.9 | 1.3 | 3.0 | 2.1 | 1.7 | 2.1 | 15.0 | 14.9 | Gambia, The |
| ... | ... | ... | ... | 2,554 | 51.3 | 1.6 | 4.6 | 0.2 | 4.8 | 8.8 | 13.5 | 15.2 | Gaza Strip |
| 1.2 | 27.5 | 4.4[3] | 5.2 | 3,689 | 24.6 | 7.7 | 14.2 | 0.7 | 8.7 | 4.0 | 18.4 | 21.8 | Germany, East |
| 15.1 | 9.4 | 9.7[3] | 10.2 | 3,351 | 20.8 | 4.7 | 15.2 | 0.7 | 10.2 | 5.6 | 18.7 | 24.1 | Germany, West |
| 3.3 | 3.8 | 3.9[3] | 4.5 | 1,769 | 32.8 | 36.7 | 2.2 | 2.8 | 0.5 | 9.8 | 6.8 | 8.4 | Ghana |
| 13.3 | 10.0 | ... | 14.1 | ... | ... | ... | ... | ... | ... | ... | ... | ... | Gibraltar |
| 14.4 | 7.3 | 3.3 | 13.3 | 3,668 | 31.8 | 3.5 | 10.8 | 0.8 | 9.4 | 9.5 | 17.6 | 16.6 | Greece |
| 7.8 | 5.9 | 11.8[26] | 15.4 | ... | ... | ... | ... | ... | ... | ... | ... | ... | Greenland |
| 4.0 | 6.5 | ... | 7.5 | 2,166 | 29.9 | 3.4 | 6.9 | 3.2 | 9.8 | 12.3 | 9.8 | 24.5 | Grenada |
| 16.3 | 6.0 | 6.6[3] | 9.6 | 2,491 | 37.9 | 4.2 | 9.9 | 3.5 | 7.2 | 10.1 | 9.3 | 17.9 | Guadeloupe |
| 18.0 | ... | 5.1 | 8.8 | ... | ... | ... | ... | ... | ... | ... | ... | ... | Guam |
| 5.8[18] | 6.0[18] | 1.8[18] | 3.2[18] | 2,138 | 58.0 | 0.5 | 3.5 | 0.1 | 4.5 | 8.5 | 6.8 | 18.2 | Guatemala |
| 15.7 | 8.3 | ... | 24.6 | ... | ... | ... | ... | ... | ... | ... | ... | ... | Guernsey |
| 5.1 | 2.9 | 4.1 | ... | 1,880 | 41.0 | 20.4 | 1.8 | 0.6 | 1.1 | 15.0 | 14.6 | 5.4 | Guinea |
| ... | ... | ... | ... | 2,326 | 57.7 | 8.2 | 3.9 | 0.3 | 2.3 | 6.4 | 12.6 | 8.6 | Guinea-Bissau |
| 4.8 | 2.9 | 6.4[3] | 8.2 | 2,360 | 53.2 | 1.4 | 4.4 | 1.8 | 6.0 | 4.9 | 7.5 | 20.8 | Guyana |
| ... | 4.0 | ... | 6.6 | 1,905 | 40.2 | 11.4 | 3.5 | 0.3 | 1.5 | 16.4 | 3.7 | 23.1 | Haiti |
| 3.0 | 8.3 | 2.4[3] | 3.5 | 2,135 | 54.0 | 0.6 | 2.3 | 0.1 | 4.8 | 13.0 | 8.4 | 16.7 | Honduras |
| 8.0 | 13.3 | 7.9 | 8.1 | 2,771 | 34.5 | 1.2 | 18.0 | 3.2 | 4.4 | 6.2 | 17.1 | 15.4 | Hong Kong |
| ... | 8.0 | ... | 31.7 | 3,484 | 32.5 | 3.3 | 12.7 | 0.2 | 9.6 | 4.7 | 16.4 | 20.6 | Hungary |
| 18.8 | 8.8 | 9.7 | 11.8 | 3,087 | 19.6 | 4.0 | 16.4 | 6.0 | 19.5 | 3.2 | 9.7 | 21.6 | Iceland |
| 11.0 | 4.5 | 0.7 | 4.6 | 2,056 | 66.5 | 2.0 | 0.2 | 0.2 | 3.4 | 9.0 | 7.4 | 11.1 | India |
| ... | 3.1 | ... | 11.6 | 2,118 | 68.4 | 8.3 | 0.8 | 1.0 | 0.4 | 2.2 | 6.2 | 12.7 | Indonesia |
| 6.2 | 7.1 | 1.4[3] | 5.6 | 2,986 | 64.1 | 1.2 | 3.8 | — | 2.8 | 6.4 | 8.4 | 13.3 | Iran |
| 5.3 | 6.2 | 1.2 | 7.2 | 2,155 | 60.6 | 0.5 | 3.9 | 0.2 | 3.6 | 8.8 | 5.9 | 16.5 | Iraq |
| 13.1 | 6.0 | 9.1[3] | 13.1 | 3,699 | 26.0 | 6.2 | 15.7 | 0.7 | 12.1 | 5.3 | 13.8 | 20.2 | Ireland |
| 15.0 | 6.7 | ... | 23.3 | ... | ... | ... | ... | ... | ... | ... | ... | ... | Isle of Man |
| ... | 7.2 | ... | 40.9 | 3,060 | 35.4 | 2.7 | 10.1 | 0.8 | 11.3 | 8.0 | 15.1 | 16.7 | Israel |
| 15.1 | 6.9 | 6.1[3] | 14.3 | 3,688 | 34.8 | 2.3 | 12.0 | 0.7 | 8.6 | 7.3 | 16.9 | 17.4 | Italy |
| 13.2 | 5.3 | 3.3 | 23.3 | 2,544 | 34.7 | 8.3 | 6.1 | 1.5 | 5.1 | 7.0 | 11.5 | 25.8 | Jamaica |
| 9.1 | 4.1 | 9.0 | 26.3 | 2,852 | 43.4 | 2.5 | 6.3 | 6.8 | 5.6 | 5.3 | 11.5 | 18.6 | Japan |
| 13.9 | 7.1 | ... | 21.0 | ... | ... | ... | ... | ... | ... | ... | ... | ... | Jersey |
| 5.9 | 5.0 | 2.8 | 27.6 | 2,107 | 61.8 | 1.6 | 3.7 | 0.3 | 5.2 | 4.1 | 9.1 | 14.2 | Jordan |
| ... | ... | ... | 15.0 | 1,925 | 80.5 | 1.1 | 3.7 | 1.2 | 0.4 | 5.0 | 1.9 | 6.2 | Kampuchea |
| 8.4 | 9.4 | 3.1 | 9.1 | 2,011 | 52.6 | 9.1 | 4.7 | 0.3 | 5.3 | 8.3 | 5.8 | 13.9 | Kenya |
| 8.0 | 2.9 | ... | 12.5 | 2,718 | 28.3 | 17.5 | 3.6 | 5.4 | 1.3 | 6.2 | 9.4 | 28.2 | Kiribati |
| ... | 3.8[28] | ... | ... | 2,996 | 68.9 | 5.6 | 2.7 | 2.3 | 0.9 | 8.1 | 2.5 | 9.1 | Korea, North |
| 9.7 | 4.7 | 9.6[3] | 9.3 | 3,056 | 67.7 | 2.1 | 3.6 | 2.2 | 1.3 | 6.2 | 3.8 | 13.1 | Korea, South |
| 15.3 | 11.0 | ... | 7.0 | 3,344 | 37.8 | 1.0 | 11.5 | 0.6 | 10.5 | 9.0 | 11.0 | 18.6 | Kuwait |
| ... | ... | ... | ... | 1,929 | 83.4 | 1.4 | 5.5 | 0.6 | 1.3 | 4.3 | 1.1 | 2.4 | Laos |
| 5.4[13] | 2.6[13] | 1.9[13] | 6.3[13] | 2,495 | 52.7 | 2.0 | 3.6 | 0.2 | 3.9 | 8.7 | 8.0 | 20.9 | Lebanon |
| 9.5[18] | 6.9[18] | 3.1[18] | 6.8[18] | 2,424 | 76.8 | 0.6 | 3.8 | 0.2 | 2.4 | 4.6 | 2.5 | 9.2 | Lesotho |
| ... | 6.1[13] | ... | 20.1[13] | 2,276 | 48.0 | 22.9 | 2.5 | 1.4 | 0.9 | 6.0 | 12.3 | 6.0 | Liberia |
| 9.4 | 4.6 | 8.5[3] | 2.5 | 3,812 | 40.3 | 1.5 | 6.0 | 0.5 | 6.6 | 10.3 | 20.3 | 14.5 | Libya |
| 13.8 | 6.2 | 16.5[3] | 6.7 | ... | ... | ... | ... | ... | ... | ... | ... | ... | Liechtenstein |
| 17.1 | 9.1 | 3.6[3] | 19.4 | 3,639 | 19.2 | 5.5 | 19.6 | 0.8 | 9.9 | 5.2 | 20.7 | 19.3 | Luxembourg |
| 4.9 | 2.9 | ... | 13.1 | 2,418 | 46.0 | 0.7 | 16.9 | 3.2 | 3.1 | 6.3 | 12.2 | 11.7 | Macau |
| 9.7 | ... | ... | 42.5 | 2,491 | 60.3 | 17.2 | 5.6 | 0.4 | 0.5 | 5.9 | 3.2 | 6.9 | Madagascar |
| 17.6[33] | 9.6[33] | ... | 9.5[33] | 2,208 | 69.3 | 2.4 | 1.4 | 0.8 | 0.8 | 10.8 | 3.1 | 11.4 | Malawi |
| 18.0 | 7.7 | 6.0 | 12.2 | 2,518 | 51.2 | 2.7 | 4.0 | 3.1 | 5.2 | 4.0 | 10.4 | 18.6 | Malaysia |
| ... | ... | ... | ... | 1,765 | 42.5 | 6.4 | 0.8 | 12.4 | — | 12.5 | 7.7 | 17.7 | Maldives |
| ... | ... | ... | ... | 1,893 | 73.5 | 2.5 | 4.2 | 0.8 | 2.4 | 2.9 | 5.5 | 8.2 | Mali |
| 15.3 | 8.8 | 5.7[3] | 18.2 | 2,843 | 34.5 | 1.6 | 12.5 | 1.4 | 11.6 | 5.8 | 13.7 | 19.0 | Malta |
| 13.3 | 7.4 | 7.5 | 14.5 | 2,673 | 33.0 | 4.8 | 10.0 | 3.1 | 5.1 | 11.3 | 7.2 | 25.4 | Martinique |
| ... | ... | ... | 9.8[13] | 2,074 | 50.7 | 0.6 | 6.1 | 1.7 | 16.1 | 7.9 | 7.4 | 9.6 | Mauritania |
| 10.0 | 6.4 | — | 6.4 | 2,766 | 50.0 | 1.1 | 2.6 | 1.4 | 6.5 | 4.2 | 16.6 | 17.6 | Mauritius |
| ... | ... | ... | ... | ... | ... | ... | ... | ... | ... | ... | ... | ... | Mayotte |
| 12.4 | 12.0 | 4.9[3] | 11.5 | 2,890 | 49.9 | 0.9 | 5.1 | 0.7 | 6.9 | 9.7 | 9.1 | 17.7 | Mexico |
| ... | ... | ... | ... | ... | ... | ... | ... | ... | ... | ... | ... | ... | Monaco |
| ... | ... | ... | ... | 2,774 | 52.2 | 1.5 | 25.7 | 0.1 | 5.3 | 0.6 | 5.4 | 9.1 | Mongolia |
| ... | 10.2 | ... | 15.3 | ... | ... | ... | ... | ... | ... | ... | ... | ... | Montserrat |
| 6.9 | 3.6 | ... | 17.0 | 2,606 | 63.0 | 1.3 | 2.6 | 0.5 | 2.1 | 5.0 | 11.0 | 14.5 | Morocco |
| ... | ... | ... | ... | 1,881 | 34.0 | 39.5 | 1.9 | 0.3 | 0.9 | 4.3 | 10.2 | 9.0 | Mozambique |
| ... | ... | ... | ... | ... | ... | ... | ... | ... | ... | ... | ... | ... | Nauru |
| 2.1[13] | — | 7.9[3,13] | 6.5[13] | 1,933 | 83.0 | 1.9 | 1.1 | — | 5.0 | 0.2 | 4.9 | 1.9 | Nepal |
| 10.9 | 7.4 | 9.1 | 15.4 | 3,617 | 17.4 | 4.6 | 16.9 | 0.5 | 13.5 | 4.4 | 21.6 | 21.0 | Netherlands, The |
| 19.4[35] | 10.0[35] | 6.0[3,35] | 10.6[35] | 2,712[27] | 29.8[7] | 2.3[7] | 15.4[7] | 1.3[7] | 9.6[7] | 6.3[7] | 11.8[7] | 23.5[7] | Netherlands Antilles |
| 15.1 | 3.7 | 6.4 | 15.2 | 2,842 | 36.9 | 7.9 | 10.6 | 0.4 | 5.6 | 5.7 | 11.7 | 21.3 | New Caledonia |
| 19.7 | 14.2 | 3.8 | 11.5 | 3,573 | 21.3 | 3.3 | 19.9 | 0.4 | 15.8 | 5.4 | 16.0 | 17.8 | New Zealand |
| ... | [4] | ... | 19.0[13] | 2,446 | 40.5 | 1.2 | 6.1 | ... | 7.7 | 5.1 | 9.7 | 29.7 | Nicaragua |
| ... | [4] | ... | 23.1 | 2,440 | 68.7 | 4.1 | 3.5 | 0.1 | 2.9 | 12.0 | 4.5 | 4.2 | Niger |
| 4.7 | 3.8 | ... | 21.4 | 2,378 | 42.2 | 25.4 | 1.9 | 1.2 | 1.1 | 6.3 | 11.7 | 10.2 | Nigeria |
| 17.5 | 13.0 | ... | 5.0 | ... | ... | ... | ... | ... | ... | ... | ... | ... | Niue |
| ... | ... | ... | ... | ... | ... | ... | ... | ... | ... | ... | ... | ... | Norfolk Island |

## Household budgets and consumption   (continued)

| country | income (latest) | | | | | | consumption expenditure | | | | | | |
|---|---|---|---|---|---|---|---|---|---|---|---|---|---|
| | percent received by | | by source (percent) | | | | per capita private final, U.S.$ 1985 | by kind or end use (percent of household or personal budget; latest) | | | | | |
| | lowest 20% of households | highest 10% of households | wages, salaries | self-employment | transfer payments[a] | other[b] | | food[c] | housing[d] | clothing[e] | health care | energy, water | education |
| Norway | 5.0 | 23.7 | 61.8 | 11.7 | 20.8 | 5.8 | 6,780 | 26.0[8] | 17.1[6] | 8.2 | 3.7 | [6] | [3] |
| Oman | ... | ... | ... | ... | ... | ... | 2,730 | ... | ... | ... | ... | ... | ... |
| Pacific Is., Trust Territory of the | | | | | | | | | | | | | |
|   Marshall Islands | ... | ... | ... | ... | ... | ... | ... | ... | ... | ... | ... | ... | ... |
|   Micronesia, Federated States of | ... | ... | ... | ... | ... | ... | ... | ... | ... | ... | ... | ... | ... |
|   Northern Mariana Islands | ... | ... | ... | ... | ... | ... | ... | ... | ... | ... | ... | ... | ... |
|   Palau | ... | ... | ... | ... | ... | ... | ... | ... | ... | ... | ... | ... | ... |
| Pakistan | 8.0 | ... | 30.7 | 53.1 | 1.3 | 14.9 | 250 | 53.5 | 20.2[4,6] | 9.2 | ... | [6] | ... |
| Panama | 2.0 | 44.2 | 85.3 | ... | 9.2 | 5.5 | 1,420 | 47.3 | 12.7[6] | 4.8 | 4.9 | [6] | [3] |
| Papua New Guinea | ... | ... | 72.7 | 2.5 | ... | 24.8 | 430 | 40.3[8] | 18.6 | 6.3 | ... | 4.9 | ... |
| Paraguay | ... | ... | 38.1 | ... | 2.6 | 59.3 | 940 | 48.7 | 16.4 | 9.7 | 3.4 | — | 1.5 |
| Peru | 5.9[18] | 28.4[18] | ... | ... | ... | ... | 490 | 38.1[8] | 15.6[6] | 7.3 | 2.6 | [6] | [3] |
| Philippines | 5.2 | 37.0 | 44.8 | 40.3 | 2.1 | 12.8 | 480 | 54.1 | ... | 6.2 | ... | 4.4 | ... |
| Pitcairn Island | ... | ... | ... | ... | ... | ... | ... | ... | ... | ... | ... | ... | ... |
| Poland | 10.1[19] | 20.6[19] | 82.9 | ... | ... | 17.1 | 950 | 42.8 | — | 11.1 | 6.1 | 1.1 | 5.2 |
| Portugal | 5.2 | 33.4 | 36.4 | [24] | 21.3 | 42.3[24] | 1,380 | 34.8 | 3.2 | 11.2 | 4.3 | 2.7 | 0.8 |
| Puerto Rico | 3.2 | 34.7 | 54.6 | 6.5 | 29.8 | 9.1 | 4,740 | 30.2 | 16.1[6] | 9.0 | 5.1 | [6] | 2.2 |
| Qatar | ... | ... | ... | ... | ... | ... | 5,620[5] | 39.1 | 10.7 | 4.4 | 0.2 | 0.8 | 1.6 |
| Réunion | 3.1[20] | 51.4[20] | 66.4 | 17.1 | 12.4 | 3.8 | 2,800[2] | 38.9 | 7.1 | 11.5 | ... | 7.4 | ... |
| Romania | ... | ... | 62.6 | — 37.4 — | | | 1,260 | 62.7[36] | — | 13.8[36] | 0.7[36] | 9.2[36] | [3] |
| Rwanda | ... | ... | 16.5 | 71.0 | 9.5 | 3.0 | 210[2] | ... | ... | ... | ... | ... | ... |
| St. Christopher and Nevis | ... | ... | ... | ... | ... | ... | 1,050[2] | 55.6[8] | 7.6 | 7.5 | ... | 6.6 | ... |
| St. Helena and Ascension | ... | ... | ... | ... | ... | ... | ... | 77.0 | ... | 10.0 | ... | 5.0 | ... |
| St. Lucia | ... | ... | ... | ... | ... | ... | 740[2] | 49.6[8] | 13.5 | 6.5 | 2.3 | 4.5 | [3] |
| St. Pierre and Miquelon | ... | ... | ... | ... | ... | ... | ... | ... | ... | ... | ... | ... | ... |
| St. Vincent and the Grenadines | ... | ... | ... | ... | ... | ... | 520[2] | 62.6[8] | 6.3 | 7.7 | ... | 6.2 | ... |
| San Marino | ... | ... | ... | ... | ... | ... | ... | 30.4[8] | 9.7[6] | 8.8 | 5.1 | [6] | [3] |
| São Tomé and Príncipe | ... | ... | ... | ... | ... | ... | 180[5] | ... | ... | ... | ... | ... | ... |
| Saudi Arabia | ... | ... | ... | ... | ... | ... | 3,490 | 52.2[18,37] | 17.2[18,37] | 6.6[18,37] | 2.1[18,37] | 1.8[18,37] | 1.1[18,37] |
| Senegal | 5.5 | 45.4 | 51.6 | — 48.4 — | | | 320 | 56.0[13] | 8.7[13] | 11.9[13] | ... | 5.8[13] | ... |
| Seychelles | 4.1 | 35.6 | ... | ... | ... | ... | 1,400[2] | 49.4 | 12.5 | 8.6 | 0.3 | 7.4 | ... |
| Sierra Leone | 5.6 | 37.8 | 27.9 | 61.6 | ... | 10.5 | 310[2] | 55.1[8] | 7.4[6] | 12.9 | 1.3 | [6] | [3] |
| Singapore | 6.5 | 34.4 | 75.4 | 18.7 | 2.0 | 3.9 | 3,110 | 22.7 | ... | 8.1 | 3.1 | [6] | 0.9 |
| Solomon Islands | ... | ... | 74.1 | — 25.9 — | | | 550[1] | 56.5[8,13] | 15.5[6,13] | 5.0[13] | ... | [6] | ... |
| Somalia | ... | ... | ... | ... | ... | ... | 140[5] | 62.3[8,13] | 15.3[13] | 5.6[13] | ... | 4.3[13] | ... |
| South Africa | 1.9 | 39.4 | 82.9 | ... | 4.8 | 12.3 | 870[38] | 32.2 | 11.7[6] | 8.1 | 4.2 | [6] | — |
|   Bophuthatswana | ... | ... | ... | ... | ... | ... | ... | ... | ... | ... | ... | ... | ... |
|   Ciskei | ... | ... | ... | ... | ... | ... | ... | ... | ... | ... | ... | ... | ... |
|   KwaNdebele | ... | ... | ... | ... | ... | ... | ... | ... | ... | ... | ... | ... | ... |
|   Transkei | 3.4 | 43.8 | ... | ... | ... | ... | ... | ... | ... | ... | ... | ... | ... |
|   Venda | ... | ... | 56.2 | 4.8 | 32.9 | 6.1 | ... | 51.2 | 4.3 | 11.2 | 0.5 | 4.5 | 1.9 |
| South West Africa/Namibia | ... | ... | 76.0 | ... | 3.6 | 20.4 | [38] | ... | ... | ... | ... | ... | ... |
| Spain | 6.9[9] | 24.5[9] | 53.9 | ... | 18.0 | 28.1 | 2,800[2] | 30.6 | 16.1 | 8.5 | 2.3 | 2.7 | 2.1 |
| Sri Lanka | 5.9 | 35.2 | 50.8 | ... | 12.8 | 36.4 | 270 | 54.2 | 2.7 | 6.3 | 1.4 | 3.2 | 0.6 |
| Sudan, The | 4.0 | 34.6 | 35.8 | 53.0 | ... | 11.2 | 360[2] | 66.5[8] | 12.4 | 5.9 | ... | ... | ... |
| Suriname | 9.3 | ... | 74.6 | ... | 3.2 | 22.2 | 1,680[2] | 40.0[13] | 9.5[13] | 11.0[13] | 3.6[13] | 6.9[13] | 2.6[13] |
| Swaziland | 2.8 | 54.5 | ... | ... | ... | ... | 600[2] | 39.3[8,39] | ... | 10.0[39] | 8.0[39] | 6.5[39] | ... |
| Sweden | 5.6 | 24.6 | 61.5 | 11.2 | 21.4 | 5.9 | 6,160 | 23.1 | 20.9 | 7.3 | 2.6 | 5.5 | 0.2 |
| Switzerland | 6.0[40] | 27.0[40] | 63.9 | [24] | 14.8 | 21.3[24] | 8,790 | 21.2[8] | 17.5 | 6.3 | 7.3 | 4.5 | [3] |
| Syria | 6.0 | ... | ... | ... | ... | ... | 1,210 | 48.8[8] | 17.7 | 9.1 | ... | 4.6 | [3] |
| Taiwan | 8.4 | 22.8 | 69.3 | 5.5 | 0.6 | 24.6 | 1,590 | 38.2[8] | 23.5[6] | 5.9 | 5.3 | [6] | [3] |
| Tanzania | 5.8 | 35.6 | 33.8 | 59.8 | ... | 6.4 | 250 | 54.3[8] | 8.6 | 10.8 | 4.5 | 6.6 | 0.8 |
| Thailand | 5.1 | 42.8 | 36.9 | 50.9 | 0.4 | 11.8 | 490 | 44.3 | 3.2 | 10.8 | 5.0 | 3.2 | 0.6 |
| Togo | 8.0 | 30.5 | ... | ... | ... | ... | 190[5] | 56.1 | 13.7[6] | 8.5 | 2.2 | [6] | 0.7 |
| Tokelau | ... | ... | ... | ... | ... | ... | ... | ... | ... | ... | ... | ... | ... |
| Tonga | ... | ... | ... | ... | ... | ... | 860[2] | 55.1 | 3.8 | 6.2 | ... | ... | ... |
| Trinidad and Tobago | 2.6 | 33.6 | ... | ... | ... | ... | 3,230 | 27.7 | 22.7 | 15.5 | 2.2 | 1.1 | 1.5 |
| Tunisia | 4.1 | 37.6 | ... | ... | ... | ... | 720 | 42.8 | 9.3 | 10.9 | 3.7 | 5.6 | 1.7 |
| Turkey | 3.5[9] | 41.5[9] | 38.9[18] | 46.8[18] | 9.4[18] | 4.9[18] | 810[2] | 41.2[18] | 25.2[18] | 14.8[18] | 3.3[16] | ... | ... |
| Turks and Caicos Islands | ... | ... | ... | ... | ... | ... | ... | ... | ... | ... | ... | ... | ... |
| Tuvalu | ... | ... | 17.9 | 76.1 | — 6.0 | | | 56.0[8] | 11.5 | 7.5 | ... | ... | ... |
| Uganda | 6.2 | ... | 88.3[13,41] | 1.8[13,41] | — 9.9[13,41] — | | 560[5] | 58.0[13,37] | ... | 14.0[13,37] | ... | 6.0[13,37] | ... |
| U.S.S.R. | ... | ... | 70.1 | ... | 24.2 | 5.7 | 1,860 | 34.8 | 3.2 | 18.9 | [42] | 0.2 | [42] |
| United Arab Emirates | ... | ... | ... | ... | ... | ... | 4,120 | ... | ... | ... | ... | ... | ... |
| United Kingdom | 5.8 | 24.8 | 66.4 | 6.1 | 17.8 | 9.7 | 4,880 | 16.9 | 15.4 | 6.9 | 1.1 | 5.0 | 0.8 |
| United States | 4.2[20] | 28.2[20] | 65.5 | 8.0 | 14.7 | 11.8 | 10,870 | 17.8 | 15.9 | 6.0 | 11.4 | 3.7 | ... |
| Uruguay | 6.0[9,18] | 29.3[9,18] | 49.1 | 20.8 | — 30.1 — | | 1,260 | 45.1 | 10.1 | 13.2 | ... | ... | 0.8 |
| Vanuatu | ... | ... | ... | ... | ... | ... | ... | 55.9[8,43] | 2.2[6,43] | 14.1[43] | ... | [6] | ... |
| Venezuela | 3.0 | 35.7 | ... | ... | ... | ... | 1,790 | 54.3 | 9.3[6] | 4.1 | 4.4 | [6] | [3] |
| Vietnam | ... | ... | ... | ... | ... | ... | ... | ... | ... | ... | ... | ... | ... |
| Virgin Islands (U.S.) | ... | ... | 65.7 | 2.6 | 13.0 | 12.7 | ... | 25.3[44] | 24.9[44] | 5.4[44] | ... | 6.5[44] | ... |
| Wallis and Futuna | ... | ... | ... | ... | ... | ... | ... | ... | ... | ... | ... | ... | ... |
| West Bank | ... | ... | ... | ... | ... | ... | 1,080[2] | ... | ... | ... | ... | ... | ... |
| Western Sahara | ... | ... | ... | ... | ... | ... | ... | ... | ... | ... | ... | ... | ... |
| Western Samoa | ... | ... | 71.7[18] | 8.7[18] | — | 19.6[18] | 590[5] | 58.8 | 12.0[4] | 4.2 | ... | ... | ... |
| Yemen (Aden) | ... | ... | ... | ... | ... | ... | ... | ... | ... | ... | ... | ... | ... |
| Yemen (Şan'ā') | ... | ... | 12.2 | 74.1 | 13.4 | 0.3 | 400 | ... | ... | ... | ... | ... | ... |
| Yugoslavia | 7.2 | 24.7 | 56.9 | ... | 18.9 | 24.2 | 950 | 46.6 | 8.2[6] | 10.4 | 3.6 | [6] | [3] |
| Zaire | ... | ... | ... | ... | ... | ... | 50 | 60.6 | 17.1[4,6] | 9.5 | 2.5 | [6] | 0.8 |
| Zambia | 3.4 | 46.4 | 79.9 | 17.8 | 1.3 | 1.0 | 220 | 37.7[8] | 11.0 | 8.3 | 1.0 | — | 2.1 |
| Zimbabwe | 3.0 | 55.5 | ... | ... | ... | ... | 360 | 35.3[8] | 7.3 | 12.2 | 1.6 | 8.7 | 3.2 |

[1]1982.   [2]1984.   [3]Recreation includes education.   [4]Housing includes household durable goods.   [5]1983.   [6]Housing includes energy, water.   [7]Netherlands Antilles includes Aruba.   [8]Includes tobacco.   [9]Based on post-tax income.   [10]Rural wage earners only.   [11]Urban households in the Federal District only.   [12]1981.   [13]Capital city only.   [14]Includes wage taxes.   [15]Personal effects, other includes education.   [16]Rural only.   [17]Highest 20%.   [18]Urban areas only.   [19]Based on post-tax per capita income.   [20]Excludes income in kind.   [21]Consumer price index excludes rent.   [22]Low-income population in Banjul and Kombo St. Mary only.   [23]Excludes property income and pensions.   [24]Other includes self-employment.   [25]Urban areas of eastern region only.

| transportation, communication | household durable goods[f] | recreation[g] | personal effects, other[h] | food consumption — daily available calories per capita | percent of total calories derived from — cereals | potatoes, cassava | meat, poultry | fish | eggs, milk | fruits, vegetables[i] | fats, oils[j] | other[k] | country |
|---|---|---|---|---|---|---|---|---|---|---|---|---|---|
| 17.6 | 8.1 | 8.7[3] | 10.6 | 3,391 | 24.5 | 4.8 | 11.4 | 2.4 | 16.1 | 4.2 | 17.4 | 19.1 | Norway |
| ... | ... | ... | ... | ... | ... | ... | ... | ... | ... | ... | ... | ... | Oman |
| ... | ... | ... | ... | ... | ... | ... | ... | ... | ... | ... | ... | ... | Pacific Is., Trust Territory of the |
|  |  |  |  |  |  |  |  |  |  |  |  |  | Marshall Islands |
| ... | ... | ... | ... | ... | ... | ... | ... | ... | ... | ... | ... | ... | Micronesia, Federated States of |
|  |  |  |  |  |  |  |  |  |  |  |  |  | Northern Mariana Islands |
|  |  |  |  |  |  |  |  |  |  |  |  |  | Palau |
| ... | [4] | ... | 17.1 | 2,180 | 63.1 | 0.6 | 1.8 | 0.1 | 5.9 | 4.6 | 10.5 | 13.5 | Pakistan |
| 6.8 | 8.5 | 5.8[3] | 9.2 | 2,338 | 38.9 | 3.4 | 7.8 | 0.6 | 5.6 | 9.2 | 10.9 | 23.6 | Panama |
| 11.3 | 7.6 | ... | 11.0 | 2,269 | 15.4 | 34.5 | 6.3 | 1.9 | 0.6 | 26.0 | 4.4 | 10.9 | Papua New Guinea |
| 4.5 | 6.2 | 2.3 | 7.3 | 2,839 | 30.0 | 15.7 | 14.6 | 0.1 | 4.1 | 14.7 | 7.9 | 12.9 | Paraguay |
| 9.8 | 7.0 | 7.4[3] | 12.2 | 2,195 | 43.7 | 9.6 | 4.5 | 2.2 | 4.6 | 8.2 | 8.0 | 19.1 | Peru |
| 3.3 | 14.0 | ... | 18.0 | 2,405 | 59.5 | 7.2 | 4.5 | 2.7 | 1.6 | 7.6 | 4.2 | 12.6 | Philippines |
| ... | ... | ... | ... | ... | ... | ... | ... | ... | ... | ... | ... | ... | Pitcairn Island |
| 8.4 | 12.3 | 6.4 | 6.6 | 3,479 | 35.2 | 6.8 | 10.4 | 1.0 | 12.6 | 3.8 | 13.9 | 16.1 | Poland |
| 14.6 | 10.0 | 3.9 | 14.5 | 3,204 | 39.3 | 6.1 | 10.5 | 1.5 | 4.3 | 6.8 | 15.5 | 16.1 | Portugal |
| 16.2 | 6.6 | 4.7 | 9.9 | ... | ... | ... | ... | ... | ... | ... | ... | ... | Puerto Rico |
| 3.7 | 24.4 | 15.1 |  | 3,050 | 48.8 | 0.8 | 10.1 | 0.5 | 7.1 | 11.6 | 7.8 | 13.3 | Qatar |
| 7.2 | 6.2 | ... | 21.8 | 2,782 | 48.2 | 1.7 | 8.9 | 1.7 | 4.6 | 7.0 | 13.4 | 14.6 | Réunion |
| 3.7[36] | 4.7[36] | 3.0[3,36] | 2.2[36] | 3,346 | 43.5 | 4.2 | 8.9 | 0.4 | 10.0 | 5.8 | 12.2 | 14.9 | Romania |
| ... | ... | ... | ... | 2,274 | 10.4 | 41.9 | 1.1 | — | 0.8 | 28.1 | 1.3 | 16.4 | Rwanda |
| 4.3 | 9.4 | ... | 9.0 | 2,038 | 26.3 | 6.4 | 10.5 | 2.7 | 8.5 | 5.9 | 9.8 | 29.8 | St. Christopher and Nevis |
| ... | 8.0 | ... | ... | ... | ... | ... | ... | ... | ... | ... | ... | ... | St. Helena and Ascension |
| 6.3 | 5.8 | 3.2[3] | 8.3 | 2,390 | 27.7 | 8.5 | 11.6 | 2.2 | 6.5 | 13.4 | 11.0 | 19.0 | St. Lucia |
| ... | ... | ... | ... | ... | ... | ... | ... | ... | ... | ... | ... | ... | St. Pierre and Miquelon |
| 3.7 | 6.6 | ... | 6.9 | 2,234 | 28.7 | 12.8 | 6.4 | 1.0 | 5.1 | 7.3 | 10.7 | 28.0 | St. Vincent and the Grenadines |
| 14.5 | 7.5 | 8.1[3] | 15.9 | ... | ... | ... | ... | ... | ... | ... | ... | ... | San Marino |
| ... | ... | ... | ... | 2,376 | 36.2 | 14.1 | 1.8 | 1.5 | 2.0 | 8.3 | 10.9 | 25.3 | São Tomé and Príncipe |
| 4.5[18,37] | 5.9[18,37] | ... | 8.6[18,37] | 2,940 | 44.7 | 0.7 | 7.7 | 0.6 | 7.7 | 13.8 | 10.4 | 14.4 | Saudi Arabia |
| 5.4[13] | 1.7[13] | ... | 10.5[13] | 2,346 | 65.1 | 0.7 | 2.9 | 1.8 | 2.3 | 2.6 | 13.0 | 11.6 | Senegal |
| 7.6 | 5.8 | 2.0 | 6.4 | ... | ... | ... | ... | ... | ... | ... | ... | ... | Seychelles |
| 9.2 | 8.0 | 3.8[3] | 2.3 | 1,938 | 55.0 | 5.3 | 1.3 | 2.0 | 1.2 | 7.0 | 19.6 | 8.7 | Sierra Leone |
| 13.9 | 9.2 | 11.0 | 21.5 | 3,165 | 45.6 | 2.9 | 12.6 | 2.0 | 4.7 | 7.3 | 8.5 | 16.4 | Singapore |
| 11.0[13] | ... | ... | 12.0[13] | 2,039 | 20.5 | 41.1 | 3.7 | 4.4 | 1.2 | 6.7 | 8.4 | 13.9 | Solomon Islands |
| ... | ... | ... | 12.1[13] | 1,986 | 50.9 | 1.1 | 10.5 | 0.2 | 16.8 | 4.0 | 8.6 | 8.0 | Somalia |
| 17.3 | 10.0 | 5.4 | 11.1 | 2,861 | 53.2 | 1.3 | 7.9 | 0.8 | 5.5 | 3.5 | 7.6 | 20.2 | South Africa |
| ... | ... | ... | ... | ... | ... | ... | ... | ... | ... | ... | ... | ... | Bophuthatswana |
| ... | ... | ... | ... | ... | ... | ... | ... | ... | ... | ... | ... | ... | Ciskei |
| ... | ... | ... | ... | ... | ... | ... | ... | ... | ... | ... | ... | ... | KwaNdebele |
| ... | ... | ... | ... | 2,450 | ... | ... | ... | ... | ... | ... | ... | ... | Transkei |
| 5.4 | 11.9 | 0.9 | 8.2 | ... | ... | ... | ... | ... | ... | ... | ... | ... | Venda |
| ... | ... | ... | ... | 2,183 | 47.7 | 14.5 | 13.8 | — | 4.8 | 1.8 | 10.0 | 7.4 | South West Africa/Namibia |
| 13.6 | 7.5 | 4.6 | 12.0 | 3,294 | 25.9 | 6.8 | 13.6 | 1.6 | 8.9 | 8.8 | 16.3 | 18.1 | Spain |
| 16.9 | 3.6 | 3.0 | 8.1 | 2,251 | 56.6 | 4.1 | 0.4 | 1.4 | 2.4 | 8.4 | 3.6 | 23.1 | Sri Lanka |
| ... | ... | ... | 15.2 | 2,314 | 51.7 | 1.8 | 5.2 | 0.1 | 5.8 | 5.3 | 15.5 | 14.6 | Sudan, The |
| 9.5[13] | 6.8[13] | 5.8[13] | 4.3[13] | 2,529 | 51.6 | 1.6 | 6.2 | 1.8 | 4.1 | 3.7 | 11.5 | 19.5 | Suriname |
| 15.3[39] | 9.0[39] | ... | 11.9[39] | 2,553 | 55.0 | 2.2 | 7.3 | — | 4.7 | 3.8 | 6.9 | 20.2 | Swaziland |
| 15.6 | 6.7 | 9.7 | 8.4 | 3,146 | 20.1 | 4.7 | 17.0 | 2.2 | 14.8 | 4.1 | 16.7 | 20.3 | Sweden |
| 13.8 | 6.2 | 16.5[3] | 6.7 | 3,449 | 20.9 | 2.7 | 18.6 | 0.5 | 13.5 | 6.0 | 15.8 | 22.0 | Switzerland |
| 3.8 | 5.1 | 3.1[3] | 7.8 | 3,005 | 50.4 | 1.6 | 4.0 | 0.1 | 5.5 | 11.8 | 13.1 | 13.6 | Syria |
| 8.3 | 4.1 | 9.5[3] | 5.2 | 2,749 | ... | ... | ... | ... | ... | ... | ... | ... | Taiwan |
| 6.4 | 6.3 | 1.6 | 0.1 | 1,955 | 33.5 | 31.1 | 2.9 | 1.1 | 2.4 | 13.7 | 6.0 | 9.3 | Tanzania |
| 11.8 | 6.2 | 3.6 | 11.3 | 2,330 | 66.1 | 2.7 | 3.7 | 1.6 | 0.7 | 6.2 | 2.5 | 16.5 | Thailand |
| 8.6 | 3.1 | 0.6 | 6.5 | 2,126 | 39.7 | 36.5 | 2.1 | 1.0 | 0.3 | 4.2 | 6.1 | 10.2 | Togo |
| ... | ... | ... | ... | ... | ... | ... | ... | ... | ... | ... | ... | ... | Tokelau |
| 6.1 | 12.4 | ... | 16.5 | 3,200 | 13.2 | 42.5 | 10.9 | 2.3 | 1.3 | 3.3 | 8.2 | 18.3 | Tonga |
| 13.2 | 8.8 | 1.4 | 5.9 | 2,837 | 40.2 | 3.0 | 6.7 | 0.8 | 7.2 | 7.4 | 12.0 | 22.7 | Trinidad and Tobago |
| 8.0 | 5.7 | 6.1 | 6.2 | 2,763 | 55.8 | 1.3 | 2.7 | 0.5 | 4.3 | 8.6 | 14.7 | 12.1 | Tunisia |
| 5.5[18] | ... | 6.1[18] | 3.9[18] | 2,937 | 53.7 | 3.3 | 3.5 | 0.5 | 4.3 | 10.8 | 11.5 | 12.4 | Turkey |
| ... | ... | ... | ... | ... | ... | ... | ... | ... | ... | ... | ... | ... | Turks and Caicos Islands |
| 10.5 | ... | ... | 14.5 | ... | ... | ... | ... | ... | ... | ... | ... | ... | Tuvalu |
| 10.0[13,37] | ... | ... | 12.0[13,37] | 1,784 | 30.0 | 18.5 | 3.3 | 1.3 | 2.6 | 30.3 | 1.6 | 12.3 | Uganda |
| ... | 9.1 | 18.5[42] | 15.3 | 3,360 | 38.4 | 6.3 | 9.3 | 1.8 | 9.9 | 4.3 | 10.9 | 19.2 | U.S.S.R. |
| ... | ... | ... | ... | 3,224 | 31.2 | 0.9 | 9.6 | 1.6 | 9.5 | 13.8 | 16.5 | 16.9 | United Arab Emirates |
| 16.7 | 6.9 | 8.5 | 21.8 | 3,249 | 21.1 | 6.3 | 15.8 | 0.7 | 12.0 | 4.5 | 18.1 | 21.5 | United Kingdom |
| 12.9 | 8.3 | ... | 24.1 | 3,641 | 18.2 | 2.9 | 20.6 | 0.6 | 11.7 | 5.5 | 16.6 | 24.0 | United States |
| 5.4 | 13.4 | ... | 12.0 | 2,886 | 32.5 | 3.8 | 20.0 | 0.4 | 11.3 | 4.2 | 9.7 | 18.0 | Uruguay |
| 9.8[43] | 8.0[43] | ... | 10.0[43] | 2,134 | 24.0 | 17.9 | 12.9 | 3.3 | 3.2 | 4.1 | 5.4 | 23.8 | Vanuatu |
| 10.8 | 5.1 | 5.9[3] | 6.1 | 2,646 | 36.7 | 2.5 | 9.5 | 0.8 | 9.3 | 10.4 | 10.0 | 20.9 | Venezuela |
| ... | ... | ... | ... | 2,135 | 72.9 | 8.6 | 4.8 | 2.2 | 0.1 | 3.4 | 2.0 | 6.0 | Vietnam |
| 11.7[44] | 4.3[44] | ... | 21.8[44] | ... | ... | ... | ... | ... | ... | ... | ... | ... | Virgin Islands (U.S.) |
| ... | ... | ... | ... | ... | ... | ... | ... | ... | ... | ... | ... | ... | Wallis and Futuna |
| ... | ... | ... | ... | 2,861 | 45.0 | 1.5 | 6.4 | 0.1 | 6.0 | 11.4 | 12.5 | 17.1 | West Bank |
| ... | ... | ... | ... | ... | ... | ... | ... | ... | ... | ... | ... | ... | Western Sahara |
| 9.0 | [4] | ... | 16.0 | 2,234 | 28.7 | 12.8 | 6.4 | 1.0 | 5.1 | 7.3 | 10.7 | 28.0 | Western Samoa |
| ... | ... | ... | ... | 2,273 | 60.3 | 0.2 | 2.9 | 1.5 | 4.8 | 8.6 | 9.4 | 12.4 | Yemen (Aden) |
| ... | ... | ... | ... | 2,475 | 67.3 | 1.4 | 4.3 | 0.4 | 4.5 | 10.3 | 4.9 | 6.9 | Yemen (San'ā') |
| 12.3 | 8.2 | 3.9[3] | 6.8 | 3,550 | 47.0 | 3.3 | 7.4 | 0.2 | 7.8 | 6.2 | 14.1 | 14.0 | Yugoslavia |
| 5.7 | [4] | 2.0 | 1.7 | 2,130 | 14.5 | 58.4 | 1.8 | 0.6 | 0.2 | 9.4 | 7.7 | 7.5 | Zaire |
| 4.3 | — | — | 35.6 | 2,146 | 70.0 | 4.7 | 2.9 | 0.8 | 1.5 | 2.3 | 4.3 | 13.4 | Zambia |
| 4.0 | 9.3 | 1.4 | 17.0 | 2,109 | 63.5 | 1.2 | 3.3 | 0.1 | 1.8 | 2.4 | 8.6 | 19.1 | Zimbabwe |

[26]Includes shooting, hunting, and fishing.   [27]1980.   [28]Workers and clerical workers only.   [29]Includes cultural activities.   [30]Excludes single-person households and self-employed.   [31]Earned income only.   [32]Malagasy households only.   [33]Blantyre and Lilongwe only.   [34]Housing includes water.   [35]Curaçao and Bonaire only.   [36]Rural cooperatives only.   [37]Middle-income population only.   [38]South Africa includes South West Africa/Namibia.   [39]Middle- to high-income families only.   [40]Excludes transfers and property income.   [41]Unskilled African workers only.   [42]Recreation includes health care and education; based on cost of subsidized services only.   [43]Urban, low-income households only.   [44]St. Thomas only.

# Health services

The provision of health services in most countries is a large and growing sector of the national economy as well as one of the principal determinants of the quality of life. This table summarizes the basic indicators of: health manpower; hospitals, by kind and utilization; mortality rates that are most indicative of general health services; external controls on health (adequacy of food supply and availability of safe drinking water); and sources and amounts of expenditure on health care. Each datum refers more or less directly to the availability or use of a particular health service in a country, and, while each may be an accurate measure at a national level, each may also conceal considerable differences in availability of the particular service to different segments of a population or regions of a country. In the United States, for example, the availability of physicians ranges from about one per 900 persons in the least well-served state to one per 350 in the best-served, with a rate of one per 185 in the national capital. These disparities are even more pronounced in most other countries, unless the government has made some special effort to achieve a more even distribution of manpower and facilities. In addition, even when trained manpower exists and facilities have been created, the country may lose health professionals via the "brain drain" to foreign countries; or low levels of financial support at the national level may leave facilities underserved; or lack of good transportation may prevent those most in need from reaching the clinic or hospital that could help them.

Definitions and limits of data have been made as specific as possible in the compilation of this table. For example, despite wide variation worldwide in the nature of the qualifying or certifying process that permits an individual to represent himself as a physician, organizations such as the World Health Organization (WHO) try to institute international standards for training and qualification. International statistics presented here for "physicians" refer to persons qualified according to WHO standards and exclude traditional health practitioners, whatever the local custom with regard to the designation "doctor." Statistics for health manpower in this table uniformly include all those actually working in the health service field, whether in the actual provision of services or in teaching, administration, research, or other tasks. One group of practitioners for whom this type of guideline works less well is that of midwives, whose training and qualifications vary enormously from country to country but who must be included, as they represent, after nurses, perhaps the largest and most important category of health auxiliary worldwide. The statistics here refer to those midwives working in some kind of institutional setting (a hospital, clinic, community health-care centre, or the like) and exclude rural noninstitutional midwives and traditional birth attendants.

Hospitals also differ considerably worldwide in terms of staffing and services. In this tabulation, the term hospital refers generally to a permanent facility offering inpatient services and/or nursing care and staffed by at least one physician. Establishments offering only outpatient or custodial care are excluded. These statistics are broken down into data for general hospitals (those providing care in more than one specialty), specialized facilities (with care in only one specialty), local medical centres, and rural health-care centres; the last two generally refer to institutions that provide a more limited range of medical or nursing care, often less than full-time. Hospital data are further analyzed into three categories of administrative classification: public, private nonprofit, and private for profit. Statistics on

## Health services

| country | health personnel | | | | | | | | hospitals | | | | | | | | | | hospital beds per 10,000 pop. |
|---|---|---|---|---|---|---|---|---|---|---|---|---|---|---|---|---|---|---|---|
| | year | physicians | dentists | nurses | pharmacists | midwives | population per physician | | year | number | kinds (%) | | | | ownership (%) | | | |
| | | | | | | | | | | | general | specialized | medical centres | rural | government | private nonprofit | private for profit | |
| Afghanistan | 1982 | 1,215 | 110[1] | 944[1] | 245 | 687[1] | 13,092 | | 1982 | 68 | 66.2 | 16.2 | — | 17.6 | 86.8 | 13.2 | — | 4 |
| Albania | 1982 | 3,861 | 900[4] | 6,801[5] | 532[5] | 5,098[5] | 720 | | 1977 | 928 | 5.2 | 3.1 | 82.4 | 9.3 | 100.0 | — | — | 66[4] |
| Algeria | 1985 | 10,862 | 2,664 | 24,700 | 1,584 | 3,800 | 1,967 | | 1984 | 447 | —44.3— | | 55.7 | — | 85.3[9] | 4.4[9] | 10.3[9] | 23 |
| American Samoa | 1983 | 27 | 7 | 141 | 1 | 1 | 1,270 | | 1985 | 1 | 100.0 | — | — | — | 100.0 | — | — | 38 |
| Andorra | 1984 | 53 | ... | ... | 2 | ... | 784 | | 1984 | 1 | 100.0 | — | — | — | 100.0 | — | — | 31 |
| Angola | 1980 | 436 | ... | ... | ... | ... | 17,000 | | 1980 | | | | | | | | | 28 |
| Anguilla | 1986 | 3 | 1[15] | 16[6] | 1[15] | 11[15] | 2,239 | | 1986 | 1 | — | — | — | 100.0 | 100.0 | ... | ... | 36 |
| Antigua and Barbuda | 1983 | 31 | 4 | 154 | 18 | 160[5] | 2,523 | | 1983 | 2 | 100.0 | — | — | — | 100.0 | — | — | 53 |
| Argentina | 1980 | 72,672 | ... | ... | ... | ... | 388 | | 1980 | 3,189 | 84.2 | 15.8 | — | — | 41.9 | 3.6 | 54.5 | 54 |
| Aruba | 1985 | 59 | 16 | 189 | 9 | ... | 1,043 | | 1985 | 1 | 100.0 | — | — | — | ... | ... | ... | 45 |
| Australia | 1982 | 27,500 | 5,721 | 106,600[1] | 9,800[1] | 5,900[1] | 552 | | 1985 | 1,080[20] | — | — | — | — | 69.0[20] | —31.0[20]— | | 58 |
| Austria | 1985 | 19,398 | 3,002 | 25,641 | 1,969 | 1,073[16] | 256 | | 1986 | 332 | 30.1 | 69.9 | — | ... | ... | ... | ... | 91 |
| Bahamas, The | 1983 | 218 | 31[12] | 952 | 37[12] | 120[12] | 1,018 | | 1985 | 5 | 60.0 | 20.0 | 20.0 | — | 60.0 | —40.0— | | 43 |
| Bahrain | 1985 | 518 | 35[6] | 2,374[6] | 68[6] | 276[6] | 832 | | 1982 | 12 | 42.7 | 58.3 | — | — | 75.0 | 16.7 | 8.3 | 34[17] |
| Bangladesh | 1984 | 13,500 | 248[1,25] | 5,800 | ... | 3,850 | 7,368 | | 1984 | 746 | 38.2 | 15.7 | ... | 46.1 | 78.4 | —21.6— | | 3[26] |
| Barbados | 1983 | 213 | 30[6] | 1,050[6] | ... | 366[6] | 1,179 | | 1982 | 11 | 27.3 | 18.2 | — | 54.5 | 81.8 | — | 18.2 | 84[19] |
| Belgium | 1985 | 28,828 | 5,911 | 91,263[6] | 10,608 | 4,920[6] | 342 | | 1982 | 531 | 53.3 | 46.7 | — | — | 36.3 | —63.7— | | 93[10] |
| Belize | 1985 | 78 | 12[10] | 209[10] | 17[10] | 179[1] | 2,133 | | 1985 | 12[9] | 58.3[9] | 25.0[9] | — | 16.7[9] | 100.0[9] | — | — | 35 |
| Benin | 1982 | 270 | 13[12] | 1,294[12] | 55[12] | 312[12] | 13,600 | | 1980 | 131 | 4.6 | 9.9 | 80.9 | 4.6 | 87.8 | 12.2 | — | 13[6] |
| Bermuda | 1985 | 70 | 22 | 544 | 30 | ... | 813 | | 1985 | 2 | 50.0 | 50.0 | — | — | ... | ... | ... | 57 |
| Bhutan | 1985 | 70 | ... | 129[6] | ... | 17[6] | 18,360 | | 1985 | 28 | 75.0[12] | 25.0[12] | ... | ... | 50.0 | —50.0— | | 7 |
| Bolivia | 1978 | 3,410 | 1,182[29] | 1,552[29] | 1,902[29] | ... | 1,555 | | 1978 | 400[30] | 18.0[30] | 5.5[30] | 42.5[30] | 34.0[30] | ... | ... | ... | 19 |
| Botswana | 1984 | 155 | 14 | 574[12] | 10[12] | 714[12] | 6,748 | | 1984 | 22 | —63.6— | | 36.4 | — | 72.7 | —27.3— | | 21 |
| Brazil | 1983 | 103,000 | 56,015[12] | 306,411[12] | 5,129[12] | 2,526[12] | 1,200 | | 1983 | 23,314[6] | 22.6[6] | 13.3[6] | —64.1[6]— | | 64.0[6] | —36.0[6]— | | 41 |
| British Virgin Islands | 1986 | 7 | 1[12] | 46[12] | 2[4] | 1[4] | 1,720 | | 1986 | 1 | 100.0 | — | — | — | 100.0 | — | — | 42 |
| Brunei | 1982 | 107 | 17 | 627 | 5 | 133 | 1,897 | | 1982 | 5 | 80.0 | — | — | 20.0 | 80.0 | 20.0 | — | 31 |
| Bulgaria | 1985 | 25,665 | 5,745 | 58,496 | 4,209 | 7,824 | 349 | | 1986 | 250 | 74.8 | 25.2 | — | — | ... | ... | ... | 92 |
| Burkina Faso | 1984[25] | 180 | 14[1] | 1,927[1] | 46[1] | 281[1] | 42,128 | | 1984 | 44[5] | 4.5[5] | — | 88.7[5] | 6.8[5] | 100.0[5] | — | — | 7 |
| Burma | 1985 | 9,481 | 410[1] | 6,978[1,25] | 801,25[15,543] | ... | 3,937 | | 1985 | 614[6] | 49.7[6] | 2.4[6] | — | 47.9[6] | 100.0[6] | — | — | 7 |
| Burundi | 1983 | 216 | 6 | 1,126 | 24 | 73[9] | 20,942 | | 1983 | 33 | | | | | | | | 13 |
| Cameroon | 1982 | 604 | 17 | 3,216 | 96 | 399 | 14,800 | | 1984 | 1,003[5] | 5.8[5] | 0.5[5] | 87.5[5] | 6.2[5] | 70.1[5] | 23.5[5] | 6.4[5] | 27 |
| Canada | 1982 | 45,542 | 11,484 | 239,338 | 17,039[1] | ... | 538 | | 1978 | 1,226 | 65.8 | 26.9 | 7.3 | — | 93.4 | — | 6.6 | 75[12] |
| Cape Verde | 1980 | 51[25] | 3 | 187[25] | 7[25] | 232[25] | 5,820[25] | | 1980 | 21 | 9.5 | 4.8 | 61.9 | 23.8 | 100.0 | — | — | 21 |
| Cayman Islands | 1986 | 31 | 8 | 59[17] | 3[9] | 11[17] | 706 | | 1986 | 2 | 50.0 | — | — | 50.0 | 100.0 | — | — | 29 |
| Central African Republic | 1984 | 112 | 6 | 710 | 16 | 168 | 22,997 | | 1984 | 104 | 19.2 | 4.8 | 76.0 | — | 74.0 | — | 26.0 | 15 |
| Chad | 1980 | 94 | 4,4.25 | 933[4,25] | 9[4,25] | 96[4,25] | 47,640 | | 1978 | 4 | 100.0 | — | — | — | — | — | 100.0 | 8 |
| Chile | 1984 | 6,067 | 1,643 | 25,302 | 198 | 1,956 | 1,958 | | 1985 | 202 | 51.4[6] | 19.0[6] | — | 29.6[6] | 82.2[6] | — | 17.8[6] | 27 |
| China | 1985 | 1,413,000[32] | ... | 637,000 | 33,800 | 76,000 | 737[32] | | 1985 | 59,614 | 14.7 | 5.6 | — | 79.5 | 100.0 | — | — | 24 |
| Christmas Island | 1985 | 2 | 1 | 5[1] | 1 | ... | 1,100 | | 1985 | 1 | 100.0 | — | — | — | 100.0 | — | — | 133 |
| Cocos (Keeling) Islands | 1985 | 1 | — | 4 | ... | ... | 621 | | 1984 | 2 | 50.0 | — | 50.0 | — | 100.0 | — | — | 86 |
| Colombia | 1983 | 21,778 | 7,990 | 26,415[5] | ... | ... | 1,266 | | 1980 | 849 | 84.7[9] | 15.3[9] | — | — | 82.1 | 17.9 | — | 17 |
| Comoros | 1982 | 20 | 1[4] | 108[12] | 2[4] | 13[12] | 17,300 | | 1980 | 17 | 17.7 | — | 23.5 | 58.8 | 100.0 | — | — | 22 |
| Congo | 1980 | 278 | 2[4] | 1,915[4] | 28[4] | 413[4] | 5,986 | | 1978 | 473 | 0.6 | 0.2 | 97.3 | 1.9 | 94.9 | 5.1 | — | 45 |
| Cook Islands | 1982 | 18 | 8[25] | 65[25] | 21,25 | 8[1,25] | 939 | | 1981 | 8 | 12.5 | — | — | 87.5 | 100.0 | — | — | 87 |
| Costa Rica | 1982 | 1,929 | 239[9] | 1,192[9] | 123[5,25] | ... | 1,198 | | 1980 | 39 | 48.7 | 28.2 | —23.1— | | 92.3 | — | 7.7 | 33[6] |
| Côte d'Ivoire | 1982 | 502 | 36[4] | 3,052[4] | 76[4] | 615[4] | 17,860 | | 1978 | 61[15] | 13.1[15] | 3.3[15] | — | 83.6[15] | 98.4 | —1.6— | | 13 |
| Cuba | 1986 | 25,418 | 5,530 | 42,109[17] | 61[017] | ... | 401 | | 1985 | 277 | 37.2 | —42.2— | | 20.6 | 100.0 | — | — | 55 |
| Cyprus | 1983 | 741 | 222 | 2,185 | 337[6] | 189[6] | 718 | | 1983 | 124[6] | 3.2[6] | —89.5[6]— | | 7.3[6] | 12.1[6] | 0.8[6] | 87.1[6] | 67 |
| Czechoslovakia | 1986 | 47,569 | 8,302 | 103,080[19] | 7,300 | 6,792[6] | 326 | | 1986 | 377 | 60.7 | 39.3 | — | — | 100.0 | — | — | 99 |
| Denmark | 1985 | 12,975 | 4,519 | 29,892 | 1,470 | 915 | 394 | | 1985 | 127[6] | 87.4[6] | 12.6[6] | — | — | 91.3[6] | 8.7[6] | — | 70 |
| Djibouti | 1985 | 68 | 4 | 288[1,34] | 4 | 19[1,34] | 6,323 | | 1984 | 29 | 6.9 | 3.5 | 75.8 | 13.8 | 100.0 | — | — | 30[17] |
| Dominica | 1983 | 26 | 7 | 153 | 10 | 47[4] | 2,846 | | 1983 | 48 | 2.1 | 2.1 | 91.6 | 4.2 | 100.0 | — | — | 29[10] |
| Dominican Republic | 1980[25] | 2,142 | ... | 2,431[35] | ... | ... | 2,600 | | 1973 | 339 | 80.5 | 6.8 | — | 12.7 | 40.7 | 0.3 | 59.0 | 16[12,22] |
| Ecuador | 1984 | 11,000 | 795[9] | ... | 505[9] | ... | 760 | | 1984 | 337 | 16.6 | 7.1 | 49.6 | 26.7 | 53.7[9] | 1.9[9] | 44.4[9] | 16 |
| Egypt | 1984 | 73,300 | 8,218[6] | 34,371[1] | 18,860[6] | 9,004[6,25] | 635 | | 1982 | 1,521 | 32.3 | 13.2 | 15.9 | 38.6 | 83.1 | 3.8 | 13.1 | 18[10] |

number of beds refer to beds that are maintained and staffed on a full-time basis for a succession of inpatients to whom care is provided.

Data on hospital utilization refer to institutions defined as above. Admission and discharge, the two principal points at which statistics are normally collected, are the basis for the data on the amount and distribution of care by kind of facility. The data on numbers of patients exclude babies born during a maternal confinement but include persons who die before being discharged. The bed-occupancy and average length-of-stay statistics depend on the concept of a "patient-day," which is the annual total of daily censuses of inpatients. The bed-occupancy rate is the ratio of total patient-days to potential days based on the number of beds; the average length-of-stay rate is the ratio of total patient-days to total admissions. Bed-occupancy rates may exceed 100% because stays of partial days are counted as full days.

Two measures that give an excellent indication of the level of ordinary health care in a country are those for infant mortality and for maternal mortality. The former refers to infants who die within a year of birth, the latter to deaths directly attributable to delivery or complications of pregnancy, childbirth, or puerperium (the period immediately following birth). Levels of nutrition and access to safe drinking water are two of the most basic limitations imposed by the physical environment in which health-care activities take place. The nutritional data are based on recommendations of the United Nations' Food and Agriculture Organization for the necessary daily intake (in calories) for a moderately active person of average size in a climate of a particular kind (fewer calories are needed in a hot climate) to remain in average *good* health. Excess intake in the

most developed countries ranges to more than 150% of what is required to maintain health (the excess usually being construed to diminish, rather than raise, health). The range of deficiency is less dramatic numerically but far more critical to the countries in which deficiencies are chronic, because the deficiencies lead to overall poor health (raising health service needs and costs), to decreased productivity in nearly every area of national economic life, and to the loss of social and economic potential through early mortality. By "safe" water is meant only water that has no substantial quantities of chemical or biological pollutants, *i.e.*, quantities sufficient to cause "immediate" health problems.

Two principal kinds of public health-care finance data are given: health insurance and central government expenditure. The data on insurance refer to public programs only and identify the mandated basis or extent of responsibility for costs or funding required under the relevant law of the principal participants (individuals, employers, and government). Data on public health-care expenditure refer to a consolidated statement of expenditure, budgetary and otherwise, by all elements of the central government but exclude expenditure by other levels (state, city, etc.). In a number of countries significant governmental expenditures for health-care services are made at these other levels, amounting to 2, 10, and sometimes 20 times the level of central government expenditure. These expenditures may include costs for national health insurance, family-planning programs, and workmen's compensation. Expenditures at the national level for social security are excluded.

| admissions or discharges | | | | | bed occu-pancy rate (%) | aver-age length of stay (days) | mortality | | popu-lation with access to safe water 1980 (%) | food supply (% of FAO require-ment) 1983 | financing of public health care, latest year | | | | | country |
|---|---|---|---|---|---|---|---|---|---|---|---|---|---|---|---|---|
| | | | | | | | infant mortality per 1,000 live births 1984–85 | maternal mortality per 100,000 live births 1982–83 | | | health-care insurance | | | public health expendi-tures (% of natl. budget) | public health expendi-tures per capita (U.S.$) | |
| rate per 10,000 pop. | by kinds of hospital (%) | | | | | | | | | | indiv. (% of earn-ings) | em-ployer (% of payroll) | govt. (% of covered earnings) | | | |
| | general | special-ized | medical centres | rural | | | | | | | | | | | | |
| 76[2] | 52.8[2] | 46.7[2] | — | 0.5[2] | 58.0[2] | 8[2] | 194.0 | ... | 10 | 95 | — | — | — | ... | 1.40[3] | Afghanistan |
| | ... | ... | ... | ... | | | 44.0[6] | ... | ... | 121 | — | 8.0[7] | 8 | ... | 26.20[3] | Albania |
| 568[10] | ... | ... | ... | ... | 64.1[9, 11] | 10[9, 11] | 81.2 | ... | 78 | 115 | 4.5[7] | 5.5[7] | — | ... | 26.50[3] | Algeria |
| 1,346 | 100.0 | — | — | — | 42.0 | 4 | 11.1 | ... | ... | ... | ... | ... | ... | ... | ... | American Samoa |
| | | | | | | | 16.0[12] | ... | 100 | ... | ... | ... | ... | ... | ... | Andorra |
| 296[13] | 58.5[13] | ... | ... | 41.5[13] | 44.5[13] | 16[13] | 144.0 | 113.4[14] | 17 | 82 | ... | ... | ... | ... | 14.50[3] | Angola |
| 1,097[6] | — | — | — | 100.0[6] | 52.3[4] | 6[4] | 19.5[16] | 0.6[17] | ... | ... | ... | ... | ... | 10.8 | 62.00 | Anguilla |
| 480[18] | 100.0[18] | — | — | — | 89.5[18] | 13[18] | 19.8 | 170.4 | 100[19] | 81 | 3.0[7] | 5.0[7] | — | 9.0 | 33.20 | Antigua and Barbuda |
| | | | | | | | 36.0 | 69.4[1] | 60 | 119 | 3.0 | 4.5 | ... | 1.8 | 7.90 | Argentina |
| | | | | | | | 8.0[6] | | ... | ... | ... | ... | ... | ... | ... | Aruba |
| | | | | | | | 10.0[16] | 6.2 | 97 | 115 | 21 | — | 8 | 9.5 | 273.00 | Australia |
| 2,096 | | | | | 83.4 | 17 | 11.2 | 4.5[10] | 88 | 132 | 3.2[21] | 3.2[21] | ... | 11.7 | 394.30 | Austria |
| 979[22] | 77.0 | —23.0— | | | | | 23.1 | 18.9 | 98[15] | 85 | 1.7[7, 23] | 7.37[7, 24] | ... | 17.5 | 207.50 | Bahamas, The |
| 1,104 | 74.0 | 26.0 | — | — | 72.6[20] | 9[20] | 30.0 | ... | 98[1] | ... | ... | ... | ... | 6.7 | 212.30 | Bahrain |
| 60 | | | | | | | 133.0[16] | ... | 68 | 84 | ... | ... | ... | 4.1 | 0.60 | Bangladesh |
| 842 | 93.9 | 4.6 | — | 1.5 | 89.8[22] | 34[22] | 9.2[16] | 24.1[12] | 100[6] | 132 | 1.0 | 1.0 | — | 11.5 | 161.10 | Barbados |
| 1,552 | 91.0 | 9.0 | — | — | 85.3 | 19 | 9.4 | 8.6[10] | 89 | 139 | 1.8 | 3.8 | ... | 1.7 | 73.90 | Belgium |
| | | | | | | | 18.9 | 48.8[10] | 63[1] | 117 | 3.0[7] | 4.1[7] | 8 | 9.0 | 29.70 | Belize |
| | | | | | | | 116.0 | ... | 17 | 83 | — | 0.2[27] | ... | 5.6 | 4.90[3] | Benin |
| 1,295 | 95.4 | 4.6 | — | — | 84.1 | 9.6[20] | 9.0 | ... | ... | ... | ... | ... | ... | 13.4 | 0.40 | Bermuda |
| 2,567 | | | | | | | 137.0[16] | ... | 8 | 90[12] | ... | ... | ... | 4.3[28] | 13.60[28] | Bhutan |
| | | | | | | | 110.0 | ... | 39 | 82 | 2.0 | 8.0 | — | 1.5 | 7.50 | Bolivia |
| 691[12] | 89.1[12] | 6.7[12] | 4.2[12] | | 90.0[20] | 10[20] | 68.4[1] | ... | 29[1] | 93 | — | — | — | 4.8 | 30.90 | Botswana |
| 868[12] | 100.0[12] | | | | 75.0[12] | 8[12] | 64.0 | 92.1[1 2] | 63 | 106 | 21 | 21 | 21 | 7.6 | 23.90 | Brazil |
| | | | | | | | 13.3 | ... | 90[6] | ... | ... | ... | ... | 4.0 | 42.80 | British Virgin Islands |
| 1,069 | 98.5 | — | — | 1.5 | 38.0 | 4 | 12.1 | ... | 72 | 110 | ... | ... | ... | 3.6 | 0.50 | Brunei |
| 2,118[6] | | | | | 84.4[6] | 16[6] | 12.0 | 22.0 | 100 | 146 | — | 30.0[7] | 8 | ... | 196.30[3] | Bulgaria |
| 665[5, 11] | | | | | 63.7[5, 11] | 12[5, 11] | 137.0 | ... | 14 | 85 | — | 11.5[31] | — | 5.5 | 1.10 | Burkina Faso |
| 289[6] | 75.7[6] | 10.1[6] | — | 14.2[6] | 78.1[6] | 9[6] | 106.0 | ... | 23 | 116 | 1.0 | 2.0 | 1.0 | 6.9 | 1.90 | Burma |
| | | | | | | | 124.0 | ... | 2[1] | 102 | — | — | — | ... | 1.90[3] | Burundi |
| | | | | | | | 103.0 | ... | 49 | 88 | — | 7.0[31] | — | 5.1 | 9.10 | Cameroon |
| 1,677 | 93.9 | 6.0 | 0.1 | — | 75.7[6] | 13[6] | 9.3 | 5.4 | 99 | 130 | 21 | 21 | 21 | 6.4 | 264.00 | Canada |
| 279[13] | | | | | 71.7[13] | 11[13] | 76.5 | 107.3[12] | 31 | 100 | 8.0 | 15.0 | ... | ... | ... | Cape Verde |
| 1,129[17] | 91.3[17] | — | — | 8.7[17] | 65.5[20] | 4[9] | 11.1[16] | ... | 99[9] | ... | ... | ... | ... | 12.4 | 452.70 | Cayman Islands |
| 326 | 43.9[9] | 1.0[9] | 37.9[9] | 17.2[9] | 41.9 | 7 | 142.0[19] | ... | 18 | 91 | — | 12.0[27, 31] | — | 5.1 | 3.30 | Central African Republic |
| | | | | | | | 139.0 | ... | 26 | 59 | — | 6.0[31] | ... | 4.2 | 0.60[3] | Chad |
| 962[12] | 84.9[12] | 9.3[12] | — | 5.8[12] | 75.8 | 9 | 19.6 | 40.3 | 76 | 105 | 6.0 | — | ... | 6.1 | 25.20 | Chile |
| 182 | | | | | 82.7 | 16 | 39.0 | ... | ... | 111 | — | 33 | ... | ... | 3.90 | China |
| | | | | | | | ... | ... | 100 | ... | ... | ... | ... | ... | ... | Christmas Island |
| 445 | 84.6 | — | 15.4 | | | | ... | ... | 100 | ... | ... | ... | ... | ... | ... | Cocos (Keeling) Islands |
| 613[6] | 88.9[4] | 11.1[4] | — | — | 59.3[6] | 6[6] | 60.9[1] | 133.5[5] | 64 | 110 | 2.3 | 4.7 | ... | 4.6 | 9.40 | Colombia |
| 510[4] | 63.7[4] | — | — | 36.3[4] | 67.9[4] | 11[4] | 111.0 | ... | ... | 91 | — | — | ... | 5.3 | 0.90 | Comoros |
| | | | | | | | 81.0 | ... | 13 | 109 | — | 0.2 | — | ... | 37.90 | Congo |
| 1,352 | 70.7 | — | — | 29.3 | 43.6[20] | 9[20] | 25.9 | ... | ... | ... | ... | ... | ... | ... | ... | Cook Islands |
| 1,192 | 77.8 | 16.7 | —5.5— | | 75.7 | 8 | 18.9 | 26.0 | 81 | 114 | 5.5 | 9.3 | 1.3 | 22.5 | 70.50 | Costa Rica |
| 171[15] | | | | | | | 106.0 | ... | 14 | 112 | — | 5.5[31] | ... | 3.9 | 15.40 | Côte d'Ivoire |
| 1,526 | 49.7[6] | 45.7[6] | 1.9[6] | 2.7[6] | 74.4[6] | 11[6] | 13.6[16] | 45.4 | 62 | 126 | — | 10.0 | 8 | ... | 65.30[3] | Cuba |
| 567[6, 20] | | | | | 71.1 | 8[6] | 11.6[16] | ... | 92[1] | 137 | 6.0[7] | 6.0[7] | 8 | 6.1 | 66.20 | Cyprus |
| 1,823 | 95.7 | 4.3 | — | — | 64.6 | 13 | 11.8[57] | 10.0 | 74.5[19] | 145 | — | 20.0[6] | 8 | ... | 263.50[3] | Czechoslovakia |
| 1,992 | 97.8 | 2.2 | — | — | 82.0 | 11 | 11.4 | 7.7[10] | 99 | 128 | — | — | 8 | 1.2 | 48.20 | Denmark |
| | | | | | c. 200 | | | | | | | | | 5.8 | 19.50 | Djibouti |
| 729 | | | | | | | 16.3 | 117.6[4] | 91[19] | 100 | 3.0[7] | 5.0[7] | — | 8.8 | 20.80 | Dominica |
| | 73.1[22] | 16.7[22] | — | 10.2[22] | 59.8[22] | 7[22] | 67.0 | 55.3[4] | 57 | 105 | 2.5[7] | 7.0[7] | 2.5[7] | 10.3 | 22.90 | Dominican Republic |
| 471 | —85.0[9, 36]— | | 15.0[9] | 36 | 60.4 | 8 | 68.4 | 185.9[1] | 51 | 89 | 5.0[7] | 1.0 | — | 7.5 | 14.20 | Ecuador |
| | | | | | | | 93.0 | 93.1[12] | 84 | 126 | 1.0 | 4.0 | — | 2.4 | 11.90 | Egypt |

## Health services (continued)

| country | \- health personnel | | | | | | | \- hospitals | | kinds (%) | | | | ownership (%) | | | hospital beds per 10,000 pop. |
|---|---|---|---|---|---|---|---|---|---|---|---|---|---|---|---|---|---|
| | year | physicians | dentists | nurses | pharmacists | midwives | population per physician | year | number | general | specialized | medical centres | rural | government | private non-profit | private for profit | |
| El Salvador | 1984 | 1,592[30] | 600[1] | 1,350[30] | 597[9] | ... | 3,002[30] | 1979 | 82 | 15.8 | 17.1 | 15.9 | 51.2 | 69.5 | 1.2 | 29.3 | 14[10,30] |
| Equatorial Guinea | 1975 | 5 | ... | 248 | ... | 2 | 62,000 | 1982 | 65[5] | | | | | | | | 105 |
| Ethiopia | 1984 | 539 | 16[12] | 7,547[12,37] | 216 | 37 | 78,740 | 1984 | 85 | 32.6[12] | 18.6[12] | — | 48.8[12] | 88.4[12] | 9.3[12] | 2.3[12] | 3 |
| Faeroe Islands | 1986 | 75 | 37 | 221 | 8 | 18 | 613 | 1986 | 3 | 33.3 | — | — | 66.7 | 100.0 | — | — | 76 |
| Falkland Islands | 1986 | 3 | 1 | 12 | — | 5 | 700 | 1986 | 1 | 100.0 | — | — | — | 100.0 | — | — | 133 |
| Fiji | 1985 | 408 | 61 | 1,496 | 44[12] | ... | 1,712 | 1984 | 27 | 11.1 | 33.3 | — | 55.6 | 92.6 | 7.4 | — | 25[17] |
| Finland | 1986 | 10,193 | 3,916 | 43,989 | 7,057[17] | 1,179[10] | 481 | 1985 | 367 | 79.8 | 20.2 | — | — | 94.9 | —5.1— | | 125 |
| France | 1984 | 125,000 | 34,082 | 280,745 | 44,906 | 8,955 | 439 | 1982 | 4,464[39] | —85.4[1,39]— | | — | 14.6[1,39] | 45.5 | —54.5— | | 91[19] |
| French Guiana | 1984 | 122 | 32 | 312 | 29 | 25 | 654 | 1984 | 6 | 16.7[6] | — | 66.7[6] | 16.7[6] | 33.3 | —66.7— | | 125 |
| French Polynesia | 1983 | 174 | 51[6] | 424[6,25] | 24[6] | 10[6,25] | 950 | 1981 | 34 | 8.8 | 5.9 | 52.9 | 32.4 | 94.1 | — | 5.9 | 65[19] |
| Gabon | 1980 | 265 | 20[5] | 823[5] | 28[5] | 99[40] | 4,053 | 1981 | 103 | —15.5— | | — | 84.5 | 100.0 | — | — | 44 |
| Gambia, The | 1981 | 60 | 6[4] | 179[4] | 2[4] | 90[4] | 10,900 | 1978 | 16 | 18.8 | 12.5 | — | 68.7 | 87.5 | 12.5 | — | 12[1] |
| Gaza Strip | ... | ... | ... | ... | ... | ... | ... | 1985 | 7 | | | | | 85.7 | 14.3 | — | 17 |
| Germany, East | 1986 | 37,943 | 11,757 | ... | 3,800 | ... | 439 | 1985 | 537 | | | | | 84.9 | —15.1— | | 102 |
| Germany, West | 1985 | 153,895 | 34,415 | 263,435 | 30,865 | 5,366 | 397 | 1986 | 3,098 | 44.7[12] | 55.3[12] | — | — | 35.7 | 35.6 | 30.5 | 111 |
| Ghana | 1982 | 1,435 | 95[1] | 17,758[1] | 611[1] | 6,728[1] | 8,278 | 1979 | 329 | 2.7 | 4.9 | 54.7 | 37.7 | 78.4 | 13.1 | 8.5 | 18[1] |
| Gibraltar | 1984 | 24 | 5[6] | 246 | 13[6] | 14[6] | 1,196 | 1985 | 3 | 100.0 | — | — | — | 100.0 | — | — | 91 |
| Greece | 1984 | 28,212 | 8,379 | 19,980 | ... | 1,831 | 351 | 1984 | 595 | 56.8[42] | 43.2 | 42 | 42 | 21.0 | 3.7 | 75.3 | 58 |
| Greenland | 1986 | 63 | 28 | 567 | ... | 12 | 850 | 1985 | 17[19] | 5.9[19] | — | — | 94.1[19] | 100.0 | — | — | 108 |
| Grenada | 1985 | 38 | 7[1] | 337[1] | 1[4] | 107[4] | 2,639 | 1982 | 39 | 7.7 | 7.7 | 69.2 | 15.4 | 100.0 | — | — | 33[17] |
| Guadeloupe | 1984 | 309 | 114 | 1,230[19] | 119 | 101[19] | 1,072 | 1984 | 27 | 60.0[4] | 30.0[4] | — | 10.0[4] | 37.0 | —63.0— | | 122 |
| Guam | 1982 | 83 | 23 | 396 | 30 | ... | 1,363 | 1982 | 4 | 25.0 | 25.0 | 50.0 | — | 50.0 | —50.0— | | 21[9] |
| Guatemala | 1981 | 1,250 | 275 | 4,345[9,25] | ... | ... | 5,700 | 1982 | 159[44] | 38.4[44] | 25.8[44] | 32.7[44] | 3.1[44] | 76.7[44] | — | 23.3[44] | 14 |
| Guernsey | 1982 | 53 | 21 | 592 | 15 | 31 | 1,094 | 1982 | 5 | 20.0 | 80.0 | — | — | 100.0 | — | — | 91 |
| Guinea | 1980 | 301 | 21[35] | 1,533[35] | 159[35] | 394[35] | ... | 1976 | 314 | 1.9 | — | 87.9 | 10.1 | 100.0 | — | — | 17 |
| Guinea-Bissau | 1980 | 108 | 2 | ... | 3 | ... | 7,287 | 1981 | 17 | 11.8 | — | — | 88.2 | 100.0 | — | — | 19[19] |
| Guyana | 1982 | 270 | 24 | 881[9] | 32[9] | 546[9] | 2,857 | 1979 | 55 | 20.0 | 12.7 | 27.3 | 40.0 | 87.3 | 3.6 | 9.1 | 53 |
| Haiti | 1985 | 803 | 92 | 657 | 6[9,25] | 100[9] | 6,539 | 1981 | 72 | —77.8— | | — | 22.2 | — | 61.1 | —38.9— | 7[17] |
| Honduras | 1985 | 1,900 | 380 | 3,545[12] | 497 | ... | 2,301 | 1985 | 46 | 59.1[6] | 11.4[6] | — | 29.5[6] | 45.7 | — | 54.3 | 14 |
| Hong Kong | 1986[34] | 5,147 | 1,158 | 15,229 | 588 | 981 | 1,075 | 1982 | 71 | 43.7 | 15.5 | 39.4 | 1.4 | 50.7 | 26.8 | 22.5 | 44[16] |
| Hungary | 1986 | 30,258 | 3,258 | 42,681 | 4,548 | 2,569 | 304 | 1986 | ... | | | | | | | | 98 |
| Iceland | 1985 | 574 | 191 | 2,724[37] | 168 | 37 | 420 | 1985 | 46[12] | 54.3[12] | 41.4[12] | 4.3[12] | ... | ... | ... | ... | 111 |
| India | 1985[34] | 297,000 | 8,648[1] | 165,000 | 155,621[1] | 217,981[1] | 2,520 | 1981 | 25,452 | 26.7 | 0.3 | 65.8 | 7.2 | 71.6 | —28.4— | | 8[19] |
| Indonesia | 1985 | 18,447 | 1,292[25] | 62,615[6] | 1,800[9] | 16,928[6] | 8,953 | 1985 | 1,306 | 14.7 | 8.3 | 39.4 | 37.6 | 30.2 | 23.0 | 46.8[4] | 6[17] |
| Iran | 1983 | 15,945 | 2,340 | 29,486 | 2,650 | 2,202 | 2,582 | 1982 | 581 | 71.1 | 15.5 | 9.8 | 3.6 | 66.4 | 13.9 | 19.7 | 16 |
| Iraq | 1984 | 4,428 | 984 | 6,082[6] | 952 | 2,267[6] | 3,374 | 1982 | 230[17] | 48.3 | 33.8 | 2.1 | 15.8 | 95.7 | — | 4.3 | 24[17] |
| Ireland | 1984 | 4,250 | 990 | 24,390[9,37] | 2,068[1] | 37 | 830 | 1982 | 238 | 33.5[12] | 37.8[12] | 1.4[12] | 27.3[12] | 63.2[12] | 21.5[12] | 15.3[12] | 108 |
| Isle of Man | 1986 | 82 | 19[6,25] | 750[6,25] | 30[6] | 616[6,25] | 784 | 1986 | 3 | 33.3 | 33.3 | — | 33.3 | 100.0 | — | — | 109[1] |
| Israel | 1983 | 11,895 | 2,900 | 14,785 | 2,540 | 12,110 | 345 | 1985 | 151 | 27.8 | 72.2 | — | — | 30.5 | 29.8 | 39.7 | 64 |
| Italy | 1981 | 190,196[32] | ... | 186,335[37] | 43,500[12] | 37 | ... | 1984 | 1,804 | 73.7 | 26.3 | — | — | 63.1 | —36.9— | | 85 |
| Jamaica | 1986[25] | 365 | 57 | 2,560 | 116 | 477 | 6,400 | 1986 | 37 | 83.8 | 16.2 | — | — | 83.8 | —16.2— | | 25 |
| Japan | 1985 | 181,101 | 63,145 | 595,091 | 129,700 | 24,649 | 663 | 1985 | 9,608 | 88.8[10] | 11.2[10] | — | — | 15.8[10] | 3.1[10] | 81.1[10] | 123 |
| Jersey | 1982 | 148 | 41 | 646 | 22 | 27[1] | 517 | 1984 | 7 | 14.3 | 85.7 | — | — | 100.0 | — | — | 107 |
| Jordan | 1984 | 2,310 | 486 | 830 | 800 | 266 | 1,102 | 1984 | 41 | 80.0 | 20.0 | — | — | 39.0 | —61— | | 14 |
| Kampuchea | 1984 | 200 | ... | ... | 130 | ... | 36,000 | 1984 | 146 | 84.9 | 15.1 | ... | ... | | | | 23 |
| Kenya | 1985 | 2,752 | 384 | 19,815[10] | 131[10] | ... | 7,387 | 1984 | 506 | —42.1— | | 57.9 | — | | | | 15[17] |
| Kiribati | 1985 | 12 | 1 | 129 | 3 | 213[6] | 5,332 | 1982 | 34 | 2.9 | — | 97.1 | — | 100.0 | — | — | 45 |
| Korea, North | 1982 | 45,000 | ... | ... | ... | ... | 417 | 1982 | 7,924 | 19.3 | 12.4 | —68.3— | | | | | 130 |
| Korea, South | 1985 | 29,596 | 5,436 | 59,104 | 29,866 | 6,247 | 1,387 | 1985 | 8,579 | —5.9— | | 94.1 | — | | | | 18 |
| Kuwait | 1984 | 2,692 | 291 | 8,293[6] | 714 | 128 | 548 | 1984 | 25 | 40.0[6] | 36.7[6] | 23.3[6] | — | 68.0 | — | 32.0 | 34 |
| Laos | 1985 | 430 | 15[35] | 1,028[35] | 16[35] | 352[35] | 8,336 | 1985 | 38[15] | ... | ... | ... | ... | ... | ... | ... | 32 |
| Lebanon | 1982 | 3,000 | 730[9] | 3,681[9] | 1,002[9] | 614[9] | 1,000 | 1982 | 130[44] | ... | ... | ... | ... | | | | 38 |
| Lesotho | 1982 | 114 | 6 | 452 | 7 | ... | 12,265 | 1985 | 136 | —14.7— | | 85.3 | — | 40.9[5] | 59.1[5] | — | 16 |
| Liberia | 1981 | 236 | 21[12] | 567[12] | 4[12] | 114[12] | 8,305 | 1981 | 85[12] | | | | | 60.0[12] | —40.0[12]— | | 15 |
| Libya | 1982[25] | 5,210 | 384 | 9,495 | 514 | 1,218 | 637 | 1982 | 64 | 68.8 | 31.2 | — | — | 100.0 | — | — | 48 |
| Liechtenstein | 1985 | 22 | 7 | ... | 2 | ... | 1,231 | 1985 | 1 | | | | | | | | 36 |
| Luxembourg | 1985 | 663 | 168 | 93 | 254 | 102 | 553 | 1985 | 33 | 60.6 | 39.4 | — | — | ... | ... | ... | 125 |
| Macau | 1986 | 697 | 105[1] | 605[1] | 5[1] | 1,357 | 612 | 1986 | 4[5] | 50.0[5] | 50.0[5] | — | — | ... | ... | ... | 30 |
| Madagascar | 1982 | 940 | 94[1] | 3,779[1] | 87[1] | 1,423[1] | 9,851 | 1978 | 749 | 0.8 | 1.1 | 75.7 | 22.4 | 100.0 | — | — | 23[6] |
| Malawi | 1983 | 161 | 12 | 2,149[37] | 12 | 37 | 41,108 | 1986 | 371 | 12.9 | 0.8 | —86.3— | | 67.7 | —32.3— | | 17 |
| Malaysia | 1983 | 4,508 | 957 | 29,358 | 626[6] | 14,525 | 3,301 | 1981[50] | 163 | 20.2 | 50.4 | — | 29.4 | 39.9 | — | 60.1 | 20 |
| Maldives | 1985 | 23 | ... | 74 | 13 | 141 | 7,957 | 1985 | 4 | 100.0 | — | — | — | 100.0 | — | — | 7 |
| Mali | 1983 | 283 | 14[4] | 2,058 | 24[4] | 305 | 27,350 | 1983 | 162 | 0.5[5] | 81.3[5] | — | 18.2[5] | 100.0 | — | — | 6 |
| Malta | 1984 | 413 | 57 | 2,962 | 369 | 225 | 786 | 1983 | 7 | 28.6 | 71.4 | — | — | ... | ... | ... | 101 |
| Martinique | 1982 | 394 | 107 | 1,871 | 146 | 106 | 829 | 1984 | 19 | 17.6[9] | 11.9[9] | 17.6[9] | 52.9[9] | 78.9 | —21.1— | | 128 |
| Mauritania | 1984 | 170 | 8 | 582 | 16 | 129 | 9,547 | 1984 | 13 | 8.3[5] | — | — | 91.7[5] | 100.0 | — | — | 8 |
| Mauritius | 1985 | 711 | 96 | 1,467[25] | 85 | 569[25] | 1,404 | 1984 | 17 | 41.2 | 23.5 | 23.5 | 11.8 | 88.2 | —11.8— | | 29[22] |
| Mayotte | 1980 | 9 | 1 | 51 | 1 | 2 | 5,567 | 1985 | 2 | | | | | | | | 15 |
| Mexico | 1982 | 66,373 | 1,879[29] | 40,998[29] | 112[29] | 634[29] | 1,102 | 1974 | 1,575 | 47.3 | 10.6 | 26.2 | 15.9 | | | | 9[10] |
| Monaco | 1985 | 63 | 32[6] | 391[6] | 56[6] | 6[6] | 449 | 1982 | 1 | 100.0 | — | — | — | 100.0 | — | — | 182[17] |
| Mongolia | 1986[25] | 4,400 | 200 | 7,932[19] | 300 | 963[1] | 356 | 1981 | 1,659 | 2.1 | 5.4 | 71.9 | 20.6 | 100.0 | — | — | 92[17] |
| Montserrat | 1985 | 8 | 16 | 73 | 6 | 32[4] | 1,482 | 1986 | 1 | 100.0 | — | — | — | 100.0 | — | — | 58 |
| Morocco | 1984 | 2,957 | 198 | 22,147[1] | 1,030 | 74[1] | 7,727 | 1982 | 141 | 20.6 | 24.8 | 44.0 | 10.6 | 100.0 | — | — | 12[10] |
| Mozambique | 1986 | 279 | 96[12,25] | 2,694 | 8[12,25] | 971 | 50,817 | 1986 | 250 | 4.0 | 0.8 | 84.4 | 10.8 | 100.0 | — | — | 11 |
| Nauru | 1980 | 11 | 2[40] | 61[37,40] | 140 | 37 | 700 | 1980 | 2[40] | 100.0[40] | — | — | — | 50.0[40] | 50.0[40] | — | 250 |
| Nepal | 1986 | 734[32] | ... | 742 | 427 | 1,845 | 24,554[32] | 1986 | 89 | 88.2[12] | 11.8[12] | — | — | 82.4[12] | 17.6[12] | — | 2 |
| Netherlands, The | 1986 | 32,193 | 7,118 | 34,500[4] | 1,900 | 971 | 452 | 1985 | 790 | 26.2 | 73.8 | — | — | ... | ... | ... | 122 |
| Netherlands Antilles | 1985 | 184 | 35 | ... | 21 | 12 | 950 | 1985 | 11 | —100.0— | | — | — | ... | ... | ... | 85 |
| New Caledonia | 1983 | 194 | 37 | 283[1] | 48 | 23[1] | 751 | 1981 | 38 | 10.5 | 7.9 | 39.5 | 42.1 | 92.1 | — | 7.9 | 83[19] |
| New Zealand | 1984 | 7,750 | 1,275 | 36,931 | 3,182 | 2,600[6] | 417 | 1985 | 268[6,20] | | | | | 38.8[6,20] | — | 61.2[6,20] | 97[20] |
| Nicaragua | 1984 | 2,172 | 222 | 5,649 | ... | ... | 456 | 1985 | 52 | 55.1 | 8.2 | 36.7 | ... | 46.2[35] | — | 53.8[35] | 16 |
| Niger | 1980 | 136 | 10[4] | 1,080[4] | 12[4] | 2,006[4] | 40,209 | 1978 | 212 | 1.9 | 0.5 | 94.8 | 2.8 | 97.2 | 2.8 | — | 6[9] |
| Nigeria | 1981 | 10,399 | 379 | 36,464 | 2,609 | 30,190 | 8,326 | 1981 | 2,374[12] | 25.2[12] | — | 74.8[12] | — | 70.2[52] | —29.8[52]— | | 9 |
| Niue | 1980[25] | 2 | 3 | 34 | ... | 21 | 1,600 | 1985 | 1 | 100.0 | — | — | — | 100.0 | — | — | 131[19] |
| Norfolk Island | 1985[25] | 2 | ... | 8[1] | 1 | 1[1] | 1,067 | 1985 | 1 | ... | ... | ... | ... | 100.0 | — | — | 113 |

| admissions or discharges — rate per 10,000 pop. | general | specialized | medical centres | rural | bed occupancy rate (%) | average length of stay (days) | infant mortality per 1,000 live births 1984–85 | maternal mortality per 100,000 live births 1982–83 | population with access to safe water 1980 (%) | food supply (% of FAO requirement) 1983 | health-care insurance indiv. (% of earnings) | employer (% of payroll) | govt. (% of covered earnings) | public health expenditures (% of natl. budget) | public health expenditures per capita (U.S.$) | country |
|---|---|---|---|---|---|---|---|---|---|---|---|---|---|---|---|---|
| 378[20] | ... | ... | ... | ... | 77.1[20] | 7[20] | 35.1 | 69.6[10] | 48 | 91 | 2.5 | 6.3 | ... | 5.9 | 14.10 | El Salvador |
| ... | ... | ... | ... | ... | ... | ... | 137.0[19] | ... | ... | ... | ... | ... | ... | ... | ... | Equatorial Guinea |
| ... | ... | ... | ... | ... | 33.2[38] | 11[38] | 155.0 | ... | 13 | 84 | ... | ... | ... | 3.4 | 1.00 | Ethiopia |
| 1,812 | 76.6 | — | — | 24.3 | 89.7 | 14 | 9.5 | ... | ... | ... | ... | ... | ... | ... | ... | Faeroe Islands |
| 1,790[1] | 100.0[1] | — | — | — | 41.7[1] | 8[1] | ... | ... | ... | ... | ... | ... | ... | ... | ... | Falkland Islands |
| 997[1] | 59.4[1] | 10.2[1] | — | 30.4[1] | 77.1[1] | 8[1] | 18.5 | 41.0[10] | 69 | 105 | — | 1.4 | — | 9.0 | 37.80 | Fiji |
| 2,080 | 58.9[12] | 40.8[12] | —0.3[12]— | | 81.7[10] | 19[10] | 6.3 | 3.0 | 84 | 111 | 1.0 | 1.4 | [8] | 10.4 | 320.50 | Finland |
| 1,917[39] | ... | ... | ... | ... | 81.9[39] | 14[39] | 8.0 | 15.1 | 97 | 138 | 5.5 | 8.0 | ... | 14.5 | 611.80 | France |
| 2,081 | 82.2[6,22] | ... | — | 17.8[6,22] | 79.4 | 10 | 20.6 | ... | ... | ... | ... | ... | ... | ... | ... | French Guiana |
| 1,472 | 70.9 | ... | 3.2 | 25.9 | 51.7 | 8 | 20.2 | ... | ... | 105 | ... | ... | ... | ... | ... | French Polynesia |
| 258 | ... | ... | ... | ... | 23.6 | 13 | 121.6 | ... | 11[1] | 102 | — | 4.0 | — | ... | 81.20[3] | Gabon |
| 437[20] | ... | ... | ... | ... | ... | ... | 174.0 | ... | 12[1] | 95 | — | — | — | 7.9 | 8.20 | Gambia, The |
| 1,170 | 86.2 | 13.8 | ... | ... | 65.8 | 3 | ... | ... | ... | ... | ... | ... | ... | ... | ... | Gaza Strip |
| 1,383[19] | 42.8[4] | 57.2[4] | — | — | 74.0[19] | 21[19] | 10.0 | 16.7 | 82 | 142 | 10.0[7] | 12.5[7,41] | [8] | ... | 348.00[3] | Germany, East |
| 1,871[10] | 80.5[19] | 19.5[19] | — | — | 84.8[10] | 18[10] | 8.9[16] | 10.8[10] | 99 | 129 | 3.5[23] | 3.5[23] | ... | 18.7 | 579.10 | Germany, West |
| ... | ... | ... | ... | ... | ... | ... | 98.0 | ... | 50 | 66 | 5.0[7] | 11.5[7] | ... | 9.8 | 6.50 | Ghana |
| 1,560 | 100.0 | — | — | [42] | 63.2[6] | 11[6] | ... | ... | ... | ... | ... | ... | ... | ... | 292.30 | Gibraltar |
| 1,217 | 70.5[42] | 29.5 | [42] | [42] | 69.0 | 12 | 14.1 | 14.3 | 97 | 143 | 3.7 | 3.7 | ... | 10.5 | 160.80 | Greece |
| 2,682[19] | 22.2[19] | — | ... | 77.8[19] | 66.5[10] | 10 | 24.6 | ... | ... | ... | ... | ... | ... | ... | ... | Greenland |
| 749[12] | ... | ... | ... | ... | ... | ... | 16.5[43] | ... | 85 | 93 | 4.0[7] | 4.0[7] | ... | 15.6 | 18.70 | Grenada |
| 2,420 | 58.1[22] | 41.9[22] | ... | ... | 87.1 | 15 | 17.4 | 106.4[4] | ... | 107 | ... | ... | ... | ... | ... | Guadeloupe |
| 738[9] | 97.6[9] | 2.4[9] | — | — | 78.8[9] | 8[9] | 10.6 | ... | ... | ... | ... | ... | ... | 2.7 | 32.90 | Guam |
| 317 | ... | ... | ... | ... | 70.8 | 11 | 56.0 | 105.8[1] | 42 | 95 | 2.0 | 4.0 | — | 10.9 | 15.30 | Guatemala |
| 977 | 89.0 | 11.0 | — | — | 83.9 | 28 | 8.4[45] | ... | ... | ... | ... | ... | ... | ... | ... | Guernsey |
| ... | ... | ... | ... | ... | ... | ... | 159.0 | ... | 10 | 84 | — | 3.2 | ... | ... | 3.40[3] | Guinea |
| 326 | 59.8 | — | — | 40.2 | 57.5 | 11 | 143.0 | ... | ... | 82 | ... | ... | ... | ... | ... | Guinea-Bissau |
| ... | ... | ... | ... | ... | ... | ... | 41.0 | 104.3[5] | 93 | 104 | 4.9[7] | 7.4[7] | — | 3.7 | 22.00 | Guyana |
| 123 | ... | ... | ... | ... | ... | ... | 107.0 | ... | 12 | 83 | 2.0[23] | 4.0[24] | 1.2 | 5.7 | 3.90 | Haiti |
| 429[12] | 75.6[12] | 16.7[12] | — | 7.7[12] | 70.2[12] | 8[12] | 73.0 | 82.0[9] | 55 | 94 | 2.5 | 5.0 | 2.5 | 8.0 | 9.80 | Honduras |
| 1,494 | 93.6 | 3.2 | 3.2 | — | 82.4 | 8 | 7.6[16] | 6.4[10] | ... | 117 | — | 33 | ... | ... | ... | Hong Kong |
| 2,100 | ... | ... | ... | ... | 78.3 | 13 | 20.4[16] | 14.6[10] | 44 | 135 | 3.0[23] | 24.0 | [8] | 3.6 | 36.70 | Hungary |
| 2,087 | 84.0[12] | 14.2[12] | 1.8[12] | — | 101.0 | 19[6] | 5.7 | 0.0 | 99 | 113 | 2.0 | — | [8] | 23.0 | 690.00 | Iceland |
| ... | ... | ... | ... | ... | ... | ... | 111.0[16] | ... | 41 | 96 | 2.2 | 4.4 | 25.0 | 2.4 | 1.00 | India |
| 66[4,20] | ... | ... | ... | ... | 55.1[4,20] | 94[20] | 77.0[16] | ... | 19 | 110 | 2.0 | 5.0 | — | 2.5 | 2.60 | Indonesia |
| ... | ... | ... | ... | ... | ... | ... | 111.0 | ... | 51 | 128 | 7.0[7] | 20.0[7] | 3.0[7] | 7.4 | 65.60 | Iran |
| 592 | 65.5 | 26.4 | 7.0 | 1.1 | 60.3 | 6 | 73.0 | ... | 76 | 121 | 5.0[7] | 12.0[7,46] | — | ... | 22.30[3] | Iraq |
| 1,771[47] | ... | ... | ... | ... | ... | 9[19,47] | 10.1 | 11.9 | 73 | 143 | 1.0 | 1.0 | [8] | 13.2 | 341.90 | Ireland |
| 1,274[1] | 83.9[1] | 7.0[1] | — | 9.1[1] | 81.2[1] | 25[1] | 0.1 | 131.9[9] | ... | ... | ... | ... | ... | 22.3 | 426.40 | Isle of Man |
| 1,671 | 95.9 | 4.1 | — | — | 91.0 | 13 | 11.2[16] | 2.0 | 99 | 121 | 0.8 | 5.7 | — | 3.5 | 190.90 | Israel |
| 1,679 | 91.2 | 8.8 | — | — | 69.1 | 14 | 10.9 | 13.2[1] | 86 | 140 | 1.2 | 11.9[23] | ... | 12.1 | 417.10 | Italy |
| 647[17] | 81.0[17] | 19.0[17] | — | — | 77.0 | 7 | 13.2 | 135.7[1] | 82 | 111 | 2.5[7] | 2.5[7] | ... | 5.4 | 26.70 | Jamaica |
| 643[6] | 97.9[6] | 2.1[6] | — | — | 83.3[6] | 56[6] | 5.3[16] | 15.3[10] | 98 | 113 | 4.3 | 4.3 | 16.4 | ... | 472.20[3] | Japan |
| 1,749 | 81.9 | 18.1 | — | — | 86.8[19] | 24[19] | 8.4[17,45] | ... | ... | ... | ... | ... | ... | 18.4 | 422.30 | Jersey |
| 822 | 93.6[6] | 6.4[6] | — | — | 41.0[6] | 3[6] | 49.0 | ... | 66 | 125 | — | — | — | 4.2 | 24.40 | Jordan |
| ... | ... | ... | ... | ... | ... | ... | 140.0[16] | ... | 45 | 85 | ... | ... | ... | ... | ... | Kampuchea |
| ... | ... | ... | ... | ... | ... | ... | 92.0 | ... | 24 | 83 | ... | — | — | 6.7 | 5.20 | Kenya |
| 633 | 47.6 | — | 52.4 | — | 58.0 | 15 | 82.0[6] | ... | ... | ... | ... | ... | ... | ... | ... | Kiribati |
| ... | ... | ... | ... | ... | ... | ... | 28.0 | ... | ... | 127 | ... | ... | ... | ... | 16.00[3] | Korea, North |
| 279[48] | 97.8[48] | 2.2[48] | — | — | 60.3 | 12[48] | 27.0 | ... | 79 | 118 | 1.5[23] | 1.5[23] | ... | 1.4 | 5.40 | Korea, South |
| 1,054 | 66.4[6] | 28.5[6] | 5.1[6] | — | 71.7[6] | 8[6] | 22.0 | 12.6 | 89 | ... | — | — | — | 6.5 | 388.60 | Kuwait |
| 96[15] | ... | ... | ... | ... | 19.7[15] | 7[15] | 116.0 | ... | 48[1] | 88 | ... | ... | ... | ... | 0.90[3] | Laos |
| ... | ... | ... | ... | ... | ... | ... | 44.4 | ... | 92[1] | 120 | 1.5 | 5.5 | ... | ... | 19.30[3] | Lebanon |
| 410[5] | 20.8[5] | 0.4[5] | 6.2[5] | 72.6[5] | 79.6[5,20] | 105[5,20] | 109.0[19] | ... | 23 | 104 | ... | ... | ... | 5.8 | 6.40 | Lesotho |
| ... | ... | ... | ... | ... | ... | ... | 122.0 | ... | 10 | 102 | — | — | — | 6.4 | 5.80 | Liberia |
| 719 | ... | ... | ... | ... | 52.7 | 13 | 107.0 | ... | 87 | 155 | 1.0 | 1.4 | 1.6 | ... | 106.30[3] | Libya |
| ... | ... | ... | ... | ... | ... | ... | 7.4 | ... | ... | ... | ... | ... | ... | ... | ... | Liechtenstein |
| 1,878 | 93.3 | 6.7 | — | — | 80.9 | 14 | 9.0 | 24.5 | 98 | 139 | 4.1 | 4.1 | — | 2.2 | 106.00 | Luxembourg |
| ... | ... | ... | ... | ... | ... | ... | 12.6 | ... | ... | 107 | ... | ... | ... | 5.7[28,49] | 17.30[28,49] | Macau |
| 699[20] | ... | ... | ... | ... | 57.9[20] | 2[20] | 110.0 | ... | 26 | 112 | — | 8.3[31] | — | ... | 7.20[3] | Madagascar |
| 420[19] | ... | ... | ... | ... | 53.0[19] | 8[19] | 152.0 | ... | 44 | 95 | ... | ... | ... | 7.9 | 4.80 | Malawi |
| 635[22] | ... | ... | ... | ... | ... | ... | 27.0[16] | 50.6 | 64 | 111 | ... | ... | [8] | 4.4 | 29.70 | Malaysia |
| 291 | 100.0 | — | — | — | 57.5[51] | 5[51] | 63.0 | ... | ... | 88 | ... | ... | ... | 5.8 | 8.30 | Maldives |
| 178[5] | 54.9[5] | 37.5[5] | — | 7.6[5] | 58.8[5] | 7[5] | 149.0 | ... | 23 | 68 | ... | 2.0 | — | 2.5 | 2.20 | Mali |
| 1,569[6] | ... | ... | ... | ... | 83.7[6] | 19[6] | 13.6 | 32.9 | 100 | 108 | 8.3[7] | 8.3[7] | 8.3[7] | 8.6 | 106.40 | Malta |
| 1,722 | 69.0[9] | 6.0[9] | 11.3[9] | 13.7[9] | 75.9 | 15 | 13.0 | 27.4[15] | ... | 114 | ... | ... | ... | ... | ... | Martinique |
| 115[5] | ... | ... | ... | ... | 97.8[5] | 5[5] | 133.0 | ... | 17[1] | 92 | — | 2.0 | — | 2.8 | 4.30 | Mauritania |
| 1,087[22] | ... | ... | ... | ... | 84.5[12,22] | 8[12,22] | 23.8 | 98.9 | 60 | 118 | — | — | — | 7.8 | 25.90 | Mauritius |
| 778 | 100.0 | — | — | — | 74.8 | 6 | 110.0 | ... | ... | ... | ... | ... | ... | ... | ... | Mayotte |
| ... | ... | ... | ... | ... | ... | ... | 53.0 | 86.9[1] | 59 | 126 | 2.3 | 5.6 | — | 1.5 | 8.00 | Mexico |
| 2,630 | 100.0 | — | — | — | 77.6 | 14 | ... | ... | ... | ... | ... | ... | ... | ... | ... | Monaco |
| 2,508 | 25.9 | 33.0 | 1.1 | 40.0 | 89.1 | 14 | 47.0[16] | ... | 21[15] | 117 | ... | ... | ... | ... | 16.00[3] | Mongolia |
| 718[1] | 100.0[1] | — | — | — | 30.7[1] | 5[1] | 17.0 | — | 100 | ... | ... | ... | ... | 18.0 | 93.30 | Montserrat |
| 225 | 57.1 | 25.1 | 8.2 | 9.6 | 63.5 | 12 | 97.0 | ... | 53 | 105 | 0.2 | 0.4 | — | 3.1 | 5.50 | Morocco |
| 92[12,20] | ... | ... | ... | ... | 70.2[12,20] | 9[12,20] | 101.1 | ... | 7 | 71 | ... | ... | ... | 7.1 | 0.50[3] | Mozambique |
| 2,660[40] | 100.0[40] | — | — | — | ... | ... | 31.2[1] | ... | ... | ... | ... | ... | [8] | ... | ... | Nauru |
| 46[12,20] | ... | ... | ... | ... | 61.5[12,20] | 7[12,20] | 111.5[16] | ... | 11 | 93 | ... | ... | ... | 5.0 | 1.30 | Nepal |
| 1,140 | 95.1 | 4.9 | — | — | 79.1[20] | 13[20] | 8.0 | 9.7[10] | 97 | 129 | 5.9 | 14.1 | — | 11.0 | 540.40 | Netherlands, The |
| ... | ... | ... | ... | ... | ... | ... | 5.5[6] | ... | ... | 112 | ... | ... | ... | 7.9 | 45.00 | Netherlands Antilles |
| 1,468 | 77.9 | 3.0 | 3.2 | 15.9 | 57.6 | 16 | 19.3[43] | ... | ... | 104 | ... | ... | ... | ... | ... | New Caledonia |
| ... | ... | ... | ... | ... | 78.7[19,22] | 12[6,22] | 10.8 | 19.8 | 93 | 132 | — | — | [8] | 12.6 | 347.80 | New Zealand |
| 634 | —91.7— | | 8.3 | | ... | ... | 76.4 | 65.2[4] | 46 | 102 | 4.0 | 11.0 | 0.5 | 14.6 | 33.70 | Nicaragua |
| 83[20] | ... | ... | ... | ... | 62.0[20] | 9[20] | 146.0 | — | 49 | 97 | — | 11.0[27,31] | — | 4.1 | 3.60 | Niger |
| ... | ... | ... | ... | ... | ... | ... | 114.0 | ... | 28 | 86 | 6.0[7] | 6.0[7] | — | 2.5 | 2.80 | Nigeria |
| 1,674 | 100.0 | — | — | — | 56.7[12] | 14[12] | 19.1 | ... | ... | ... | ... | ... | ... | 9.6 | 136.10 | Niue |
| ... | ... | ... | ... | ... | 37.7 | 9 | ... | ... | ... | ... | ... | ... | ... | 6.5 | 104.10 | Norfolk Island |

## Health services (continued)

| country | health personnel | | | | | | | hospitals | | | | | | | | | |
| --- | --- | --- | --- | --- | --- | --- | --- | --- | --- | --- | --- | --- | --- | --- | --- | --- | --- |
| | year | physicians | dentists | nurses | pharma-cists | midwives | population per physician | year | number | kinds (%) | | | | ownership (%) | | | hospital beds per 10,000 pop. |
| | | | | | | | | | | general | specialized | medical centres | rural | government | private non-profit | private for profit | |
| Norway | 1985 | 10,110 | 4,397 | 44,353[37] | 3,041[19] | [37] | 411 | 1985 | 1,192 | 6.2 | 91.9 | ... | 1.9 | ... | ... | ... | 165 |
| Oman | 1985 | 581 | 63[10] | 2,104[10] | 148[10] | 33[19] | 1,792 | 1985 | 40 | —37.5— | | —62.5— | | 100.0 | — | — | 23 |
| Pacific Is., Trust Terr. of the | | | | | | | | | | | | | | | | | |
| Marshall Islands | 1985 | 17 | 2 | 51 | ... | ... | 2,111 | 1985 | 2 | 100 | — | — | — | 100 | — | — | 15 |
| Micronesia, Fed. States of | 1985 | 36 | 13 | 257 | 7 | ... | 2,542 | 1984 | 4 | 100 | — | — | — | 100 | — | — | 37 |
| Northern Mariana Islands | 1985 | 18 | 6 | 125 | ... | ... | 1,111 | 1985 | 2 | 100 | — | — | — | 100 | — | — | 31 |
| Palau | 1980 | 10 | 4 | 85 | ... | ... | 1,212 | 1985 | 1 | 100 | — | — | — | 100 | — | — | ... |
| Pakistan | 1986 | 46,494 | 1,539[34] | 14,249[17, 34] | 1,770[6] | 9,947[6] | 2,225 | 1986 | 895[6, 11] | 62.3[6] | 6.1[6] | ... | 31.6[6] | 82.2[6] | 1.1[6] | 16.7[6] | 6 |
| Panama | 1985 | 2,484 | 503 | 2,269 | 157[4] | ... | 877 | 1985 | 57 | ... | ... | ... | ... | 88.4[52] | —11.6[52]— | | 36 |
| Papua New Guinea | 1984 | 280 | 16[12] | 3,228[12, 37] | 9[12] | [37] | 11,635 | 1980 | 390 | 5.1 | — | 53.6 | 41.2 | 46.2 | 53.8 | — | 45[10] |
| Paraguay | 1982 | 2,201 | 855[9] | 2,636[9] | 860[9] | 783[9] | 1,379 | 1985 | 143[15] | 63.6[15] | 4.9[15] | — | 31.5[15] | 91.6[15] | 8.4[15] | — | 9 |
| Peru | 1982 | 14,751 | 3,687[12] | 10,065[12] | 3,457[12] | 2,171[12] | 1,236 | 1977 | 437 | 66.4 | 9.1 | 24.5 | — | 60.4 | 15.6 | 24.0 | 16[6] |
| Philippines | 1982 | 46,579 | 1,090[1, 25] | 9,644[1, 25] | 539[1, 25] | 9,470[1, 25] | 1,090 | 1984 | 1,602 | ... | ... | ... | ... | 25.2 | —74.8— | | 13 |
| Pitcairn Island | 1985 | — | — | 1[25] | — | — | — | ... | ... | ... | ... | ... | ... | ... | ... | ... | ... |
| Poland | 1986 | 73,200 | 17,400 | 171,244[17] | 16,100 | 18,996[17] | 510 | 1984 | 782 | 87.9 | 12.1 | — | — | ... | ... | ... | 56[16] |
| Portugal | 1986 | 24,629 | 437[17] | 29,525[17] | 4,807 | 824[17] | 416 | 1965 | 481 | 80.7 | 19.3 | — | — | 78.8[6] | 21.2[6] | — | 53 |
| Puerto Rico | 1983 | 7,133 | 741[12] | 14,392[12] | 1,436[12] | 199[12] | 458 | 1980 | 111 | 72.1 | 27.9 | — | — | 48.6 | 19.8 | 31.5 | 38[10] |
| Qatar | 1986[25] | 514 | 53 | 1,161 | 135 | 70[1] | 605 | 1985 | 3 | 33.0 | 67.0 | — | — | 100.0 | — | — | 29[16] |
| Réunion | 1986 | 750 | 193[17] | 1,791[17] | 174[17] | 102[17] | 734 | 1984 | 21 | 36.4[5] | 18.1[5] | — | 45.5[5] | 74.2[52] | —25.8[52]— | | 64[17] |
| Romania | 1985[25] | 40,050 | 7,340 | 81,031[6] | 6,588 | 12,248[6] | 567 | 1986 | 437[1] | 56.8[1] | 32.5[1] | — | 10.8[1] | ... | ... | ... | 93 |
| Rwanda | 1984[25] | 258 | 1[1] | 936 | 6 | 616[1] | 21,943 | 1984 | 170 | —16.5— | | —83.5— | | 50.0[19] | —50.0[19]— | | 15 |
| St. Christopher and Nevis | 1985 | 20 | 5 | 225 | 7 | 123[12] | 2,300 | 1985 | 3 | ... | ... | ... | ... | 100.0 | — | — | 54 |
| St. Helena and Ascension | 1982 | 3 | 1 | 30[9] | ... | 7[9] | 1,667 | 1982 | 8 | 12.5 | 12.5 | 75.0 | — | ... | ... | ... | 110 |
| St. Lucia | 1984 | 58 | 5 | 236 | 16[19] | 66[5] | 2,311 | 1984 | 5 | 20.0[19] | 20.0[19] | — | 60.0[19] | ... | ... | ... | 39 |
| St. Pierre and Miquelon | 1983 | 11 | 2 | 20[5] | ... | 1[5] | 545 | 1983 | 1 | 100.0 | — | — | — | 100.0 | — | — | 167 |
| St. Vincent | 1984 | 24 | 1 | 290 | ... | ... | 4,300 | 1984 | 9 | 11.1 | 33.3 | 22.2 | 33.3 | 100.0 | — | — | 32 |
| San Marino | 1979 | 10[25] | ... | ... | ... | ... | 2,030 | 1980 | ... | ... | ... | ... | ... | ... | ... | ... | 28 |
| São Tomé and Príncipe | 1981 | 38 | — | 157 | 1 | 13 | 2,500 | 1978 | 16 | 12.5 | — | 87.5 | — | ... | ... | ... | 78 |
| Saudi Arabia | 1986[25] | 9,982 | 747 | 24,528 | 540 | 6,939 | 1,202 | 1986 | 181 | ... | ... | ... | ... | 77.9 | — | 22.1 | 24 |
| Senegal | 1984 | 470[6] | 50 | 2,360[1, 25] | 167 | 451 | 12,987[6] | 1984 | 87 | 18.4 | 29.9 | 51.7 | — | 100.0 | — | — | 10[6] |
| Seychelles | 1985 | 35 | 8 | 288 | 3 | 131[9] | 1,864 | 1985 | 6 | 16.7 | 16.7 | 66.7 | — | 100.0 | — | — | 51 |
| Sierra Leone | 1983 | 197 | 30[12] | 1,758[12, 37] | 8[12] | [37] | 17,906 | 1984 | 109 | 0.9[12] | 7.2[12] | 58.9[12] | 33.0[12] | 76.8[12] | 15.2[12] | 8.0[12] | 13 |
| Singapore | 1985 | 2,631 | 496 | 8,395 | 436 | 650 | 972 | 1985 | 22 | ... | ... | ... | ... | 45.5 | —54.5— | | 39 |
| Solomon Islands | 1985 | 32 | 15 | 462 | ... | ... | 8,509 | 1986 | 134 | 6.0 | — | 94.0 | — | 72.7[19] | —27.3[19]— | | 52 |
| Somalia | 1985 | 321 | 2[12] | 1,834[12] | 21[14] | 556[12] | 18,156 | 1985 | 75[14] | ... | ... | ... | ... | ... | ... | ... | 9 |
| South Africa | 1986[34] | 22,525 | 3,704 | 88,795 | 7,557 | ... | 1,510 | 1980 | 595 | ... | ... | ... | ... | 40.7 | —59.3— | | 41 |
| Bophuthatswana | 1984 | 93 | ... | 3,342 | 12[35] | ... | 16,800 | 1984 | 156 | —6.4— | | —93.6— | | ... | ... | ... | 40 |
| Ciskei | 1986[25] | 283 | 7 | 3,855 | 10 | 54 | 2,820 | 1986 | 97 | 5.2 | 1.0 | 92.8 | 1.0 | 99.0 | 1.0 | — | 41 |
| KwaNdebele | ... | ... | ... | ... | ... | ... | ... | ... | ... | ... | ... | ... | ... | ... | ... | ... | ... |
| Transkei | 1985 | 240 | ... | 4,112[4] | ... | ... | 3,412 | 1985 | 29 | ... | ... | ... | ... | ... | ... | ... | 87 |
| Venda | 1985 | 25 | ... | 839 | ... | ... | 16,920 | 1985 | 54 | 5.5 | 1.9 | —92.6— | | ... | ... | ... | 34 |
| South West Africa/Namibia | 1987 | 317 | 41[10] | 3,390[10] | ... | ... | 3,780 | 1985 | 68 | ... | ... | ... | ... | ... | ... | ... | 87 |
| Spain | 1984 | 121,362 | 4,682 | 136,992[6] | 28,748 | 4,893[6] | 316 | 1981 | 1,054 | 71.2 | 28.8 | — | — | 38.8 | 14.8 | 46.4 | 51 |
| Sri Lanka | 1985[25] | 2,151 | 275[6] | 8,091 | 441[6] | 3,808[6] | 7,363 | 1982 | 493 | 5.9 | 31.4 | 20.7 | 42.0 | 100.0 | — | — | 29[17] |
| Sudan, The | 1981[25] | 2,169 | 334 | 13,693 | 58 | 376 | 9,369 | 1981 | 160 | 21.9 | 5.6 | — | 72.5 | ... | ... | ... | 9 |
| Suriname | 1985 | 219 | 21[4] | 660[4] | 13[4] | 88[4] | 1,798 | 1980 | 17 | 29.4 | 17.6 | 47.1 | 5.9 | 58.8 | 29.4 | 11.8 | 50[17] |
| Swaziland | 1984 | 80 | 13 | 84[4] | 10[4] | 731[4] | 7,971 | 1978 | 33 | 9.1 | 9.1 | 48.5 | 33.3 | 21.2 | 57.6 | 21.2 | 25[10] |
| Sweden | 1985 | 20,200 | 9,338 | 72,386[37] | 4,107 | [37] | 413 | 1984 | 1,000[19] | 10.3[19] | 89.7[19] | — | — | ... | ... | ... | 139 |
| Switzerland | 1984 | 14,712 | 3,070 | 26,998 | 1,323 | 1,650[9] | 442 | 1983 | 372 | 52.7 | 47.3 | — | — | ... | ... | ... | 102 |
| Syria | 1985 | 6,163 | 1,975 | 8,326 | 2,621 | 2,201 | 1,666 | 1985 | 193 | 79.8 | 20.2 | — | — | 22.3 | —77.7— | | 12 |
| Taiwan | 1985 | 15,039 | 3,273 | 24,248 | 8,211 | 2,408 | 1,130 | 1985 | 1,000 | 5.5 | 5.7 | 88.8 | — | ... | ... | ... | 37 |
| Tanzania | 1984 | 1,065 | 18[4] | 8,291[6] | 25[5] | 2,887[6] | 19,775 | 1982 | 3,032 | 4.9 | — | 87.2 | 7.9 | ... | ... | ... | 11[10] |
| Thailand | 1984 | 8,058 | 1,326 | 54,012 | 3,312 | 8,573 | 6,277 | 1984 | 916 | 88.6 | 3.4 | —8.0— | | 72.9 | —27.1— | | 16 |
| Togo | 1985 | 230 | 4[12] | 1,116 | 50 | 559[12] | 12,992 | 1979 | 65 | 10.8 | 4.6 | 61.5 | 23.1 | 96.9 | 3.1 | — | 13[6] |
| Tokelau | 1985[25] | 4 | 1 | 18[6, 37] | ... | [37] | 400 | 1985 | 3 | — | — | — | 100.0 | 100.0 | — | — | 225 |
| Tonga | 1982 | 35 | 19 | 253 | 3 | 161 | 2,881 | 1982 | 9 | 44.4 | — | 55.6 | — | 100.0 | — | — | 30 |
| Trinidad and Tobago | 1985 | 1,103 | 129 | 3,344[37] | 496 | [37] | 1,071 | 1985 | 31 | 8.0[9] | 16.0[9] | 40.0[9] | 36.0[9] | 60.0[9] | — | 40.0[9] | 35 |
| Tunisia | 1986 | 3,453 | 550 | 9,353 | 1,243 | ... | 2,162 | 1985 | 125 | 23.5[6] | 20.2[6] | — | 56.3[6] | 100.0 | — | — | 21[16] |
| Turkey | 1985 | 32,263 | 6,896 | 29,216 | 11,428[6] | 12,470 | 1,495 | 1983 | 646 | 74.3 | 11.3 | — | 14.4 | 83.9 | —16.1— | | 21 |
| Turks and Caicos Islands | 1984[25] | 4 | 1 | 33[37] | ... | [37] | 2,100 | 1984 | 5 | ... | ... | ... | ... | ... | ... | ... | 24 |
| Tuvalu | 1985[25] | 4 | 2 | 36[37] | 1 | [37] | 2,075 | 1985 | 8 | 11.1 | — | — | 88.9 | 100.0 | — | — | 36 |
| Uganda | 1982 | 665 | 17[1] | 6,778[1, 37] | 27[1] | [37] | 20,562 | 1981 | 485 | 15.5 | 1.2 | 83.3 | — | 84.5 | 15.5 | — | 15[19] |
| U.S.S.R. | 1987 | 1,202,000[32] | [32] | 2,880,000[6, 37] | 86,000[10] | [37] | 235[32] | 1986 | 23,100 | ... | ... | ... | ... | 100.0 | — | — | 128 |
| United Arab Emirates | 1984[25] | 1,840 | 95[6] | 2,814[6] | 89[6] | ... | 666 | 1984 | 20[19] | 50.0[1] | 27.3[1] | 4.5[1] | 18.2[1] | 95.5[1] | 4.5[1] | — | 40 |
| United Kingdom | 1985 | 84,700 | 22,988 | 284,116[37] | 15,108[6] | [37] | 668 | 1985 | 2,501[1] | ... | ... | ... | ... | 100.0 | — | — | 74 |
| United States | 1985 | 545,986 | 132,750 | 1,485,725 | 156,960 | 2,500 | 438 | 1986 | 6,841 | 84.9 | 15.1 | — | — | 32.3 | 51.4 | 16.3 | 53 |
| Uruguay | 1984 | 5,756 | 2,535 | 15,200[9] | 584 | 300 | 519 | 1983 | 61 | —63.9— | | — | 36.1 | 100.0 | — | — | 79 |
| Vanuatu | 1984 | 19 | 2[6] | 324 | 3[6] | 5[6] | 6,726 | 1980 | 21 | 14.3 | — | 52.4 | 33.3 | 47.6 | 52.4 | — | 35[19] |
| Venezuela | 1979 | 15,359 | 4,645 | 38,061[4] | 4,063 | ... | 947 | 1979 | 446 | ... | ... | ... | ... | 42.1 | 4.3 | 53.6 | 30 |
| Vietnam | 1986 | 19,100[32] | ... | 44,080[1] | 11,900[25] | 13,700[1, 25] | 3,162[32] | 1984 | 10,768 | 14.6 | 6.5 | 78.9 | ... | 100.0 | — | — | 35[17] |
| Virgin Islands (U.S.) | 1985 | 167 | ... | 241[29] | ... | ... | 622 | 1985 | ... | ... | ... | ... | ... | ... | ... | ... | 49 |
| Wallis and Futuna | 1981[25] | 4 | 1 | 27 | 1 | 5 | 2,800 | 1982 | 3 | 33.3 | — | — | 66.7 | 100.0 | — | — | 77 |
| West Bank | ... | ... | ... | ... | ... | ... | ... | 1985 | 16 | ... | ... | ... | ... | 52.9[10] | —47.1[10]— | | 16 |
| Western Sahara[54] | 1982 | 11 | — | ... | 2 | ... | 13,000 | 1982[30] | 2 | 50.0 | — | 50.0 | — | 100.0 | — | — | 9 |
| Western Samoa | 1981 | 63 | 7 | 344 | 4 | 42[25] | 2,476 | 1984 | 30 | 3.3 | — | — | 96.7 | 100.0 | — | — | 47[6] |
| Yemen (Aden) | 1984 | 492 | 18 | 1,733 | 29 | 261 | 4,287 | 1984 | 51 | 12.2[12] | 16.4[12] | 34.7[12] | 36.7[12] | 98.0[12] | 2.0[12] | — | 17 |
| Yemen (Ṣan'ā') | 1984 | 1,069 | 41 | 2,440 | 114 | 113 | 6,435 | 1984 | 34 | 63.3[6] | 3.3[6] | — | 33.3[6] | 86.7[6] | 13.3[6] | — | 6 |
| Yugoslavia | 1985 | 38,205 | 8,021 | 67,468[10] | 5,047[10] | 7,747[10] | 601 | 1982 | 425[12] | 32.5[12] | 30.3[12] | 37.2[12] | — | ... | ... | ... | 61[10] |
| Zaire | 1982 | 2,000 | 58[9] | 14,661[9] | 414[9] | 3,043[9] | 14,092 | 1982 | 942[9] | 37.3[9] | 38.9[9] | 23.8[9] | — | 40.9[9] | 44.6[9] | 14.5[9] | 26 |
| Zambia | 1984 | 798 | 42 | 5,167 | 44 | 1,392 | 8,076 | 1987 | 965 | 8.2 | 0.3 | 19.0 | 72.5 | 80.9 | 19.1 | — | 32[10] |
| Zimbabwe | 1984 | 705 | 158[12] | 5,258[12] | 354[12] | 2,351[12] | 11,275 | 1980 | ... | ... | ... | ... | ... | ... | ... | ... | 30 |

[1]1981. [2]Excludes four specialized hospitals. [3]May include expenditures at the intermediate and local levels of government and/or the costs of additional services such as national health insurance and family-planning programs. [4]1978. [5]1977. [6]1982. [7]Includes funds for old-age retirement, incapacitating disability, work injury, and death insurance. [8]Government provides remainder of the cost of benefits. [9]1979. [10]1984. [11]Excludes medical centres. [12]1980. [13]Excludes specialized hospitals and medical centres. [14]1972. [15]1975. [16]1986. [17]1985. [18]Excludes one mental hospital. [19]1983. [20]General hospitals only. [21]Amounts vary internally. [22]Government hospitals only. [23]Minimum on a graduated scale. [24]Maximum on a graduated scale. [25]Government-employed health personnel only. [26]Includes hospital beds in dispensaries. [27]Employed women only. [28]Includes expenditures at the intermediate and local levels of government.

| admissions or discharges — rate per 10,000 pop. | by kinds of hospital (%) general | special-ized | medical centres | rural | bed occu-pancy rate (%) | average length of stay (days) | mortality infant per 1,000 live births 1984–85 | maternal per 100,000 live births 1982–83 | popu-lation with access to safe water 1980 (%) | food supply (% of FAO require-ment) 1983 | health-care insurance indiv. (% of earn-ings) | em-ployer (% of payroll) | govt. (% of covered earnings) | public health expendi-tures (% of natl. budget) | public health expendi-tures per capita (U.S.$) | country |
|---|---|---|---|---|---|---|---|---|---|---|---|---|---|---|---|---|
| 1,663 | 87.1 | —12.9— | | | 84.0 | 9 | 8.5[16] | 2.0[10] | 98 | 115 | 4.4[7] | 16.8[7] | 4.9[7] | 10.8 | 539.50 | Norway |
| 1,214 | ... | ... | ... | ... | 72.9 | 5[20] | 113.4 | | 52 | ... | | | | 4.2 | 170.60 | Oman |
| | | | | | | | 33.0 | — | | | | | | 26.1 | 120.20 | Pacific Is., Trust Terr. of the Marshall Islands |
| 2,171 | 100 | — | — | — | | | 95.0 | ... | | | | | | ... | ... | Micronesia, Fed. States of |
| 1,875 | 100 | — | — | — | | | 23.8 | | | | | | | ... | 394.20 | Northern Mariana Islands |
| | | | | | | | 32.6 | 0.7 | | | | | | | | Palau |
| 565 | ... | ... | ... | ... | 64.5[19] | 7[19] | 126.0[16] | | 29 | 95 | — | 7.0 | — | 1.1 | 0.70 | Pakistan |
| 253[20] | ... | ... | ... | ... | | | 23.0 | 49.4[10] | 83 | 98 | 1.0 | 8.0 | 0.8[7] | 13.1 | 103.60 | Panama |
| | | | | | | | 68.0 | | 16 | 75 | — | — | | 9.0 | 20.50 | Papua New Guinea |
| | | | | | | | 52.9 | 131.2 | 28 | 122 | 9.5[7] | 16.5[7] | 1.5[7] | 5.8 | 9.40 | Paraguay |
| 416 | 90.9 | 7.8 | 1.3 | — | 88.2 | 14 | 92.7 | 91.9[1] | 49 | 85 | 2.5 | 5.0 | — | 6.2 | 13.00 | Peru |
| | | | | | | | 59.0[16] | 125.0[12] | 55 | 104 | 1.3 | 1.3 | [8] | 4.8 | 4.30 | Philippines |
| | | | | | | | 18.5 | | | | | | | 15.4 | 303.00 | Pitcairn Island |
| 1,273 | | | | | 80.5[6] | 17[6] | 18.5 | 14.1[10] | 55 | 127 | — | 33.0[7] | [8] | ... | 167.60[3] | Poland |
| 902[6] | 86.8[6] | 13.4[6] | — | — | | | 11.6 | 16.1[10] | 92 | 124 | 8.0[7] | 21.0[7] | | 4.4 | 22.70 | Portugal |
| 1,227 | 95.0 | 5.0 | — | — | 64.8 | 8 | 15.7 | 4.6 | | | | | | 24.0[28,49] | 148.10[28,49] | Puerto Rico |
| 1,328[1] | 54.3[1] | 45.7[1] | — | — | | | 35.0 | | 97 | | | | | | | Qatar |
| 836[5,20] | | | | | 82.0[5,20] | 12[5,20] | 10.3 | | | 125 | | | | 0.8 | 5.30 | Réunion |
| | | | | | | | 25.6 | 170.1 | | 126 | — | 7.0[23] | [8] | | | Romania |
| 338 | | | | | 58.7 | 9 | 128.0 | | 38 | 98 | | | | 4.6 | 1.50 | Rwanda |
| 1,328[1,6] | | | | | 57.4[6,20] | 10[6,20] | 30.2 | 90.9[1] | 95 | | | | | | | St. Christopher and Nevis |
| | | | | | | | 16.3 | | | | | | | | | St. Helena and Ascension |
| 1,026 | | | | | | | 21.7[53] | | 70[1] | 102 | 5.0[7] | 5.0[7] | | | | St. Lucia |
| | | | | | | | 12.3 | | | | | | | | | St. Pierre and Miquelon |
| 772[4] | | | | | 68.3[14,20] | 9[14,20] | 35.1 | | 95[19] | 100 | — | — | | 13.4 | 41.30 | St. Vincent |
| 1,435 | | | | | 69.5 | 11 | 6.4 | | | | | | | | | San Marino |
| 1,733 | 76.1 | — | 23.9 | — | 68.7 | 12 | 61.7 | | | 97 | | | | | | São Tomé and Príncipe |
| 757[25] | | | | | | | 109.8 | | 64 | 134 | — | — | | | 540.30[3] | Saudi Arabia |
| 378[4,5] | 34.2[5] | — | 54.8[5] | 11.0[5] | 75.1[4,5] | 9.6[4,5] | 131.0 | | 35 | 82 | 3.0[24] | 3.0[24] | | 4.7 | 5.00 | Senegal |
| 9,465[20] | | | | | 67.0[20] | 6[20] | 17.4[16] | | | 100 | 5.0[7] | 10.0[7] | | 13.1 | 48.90 | Seychelles |
| 13[12,20] | | | | | 77.1[12,20] | 18[12,20] | 134.0 | | 12[1] | 91 | — | — | | 7.5 | 3.70 | Sierra Leone |
| 899[22] | 75.9[22] | 24.1[22] | — | — | 73.0[1] | 10[1] | 9.4[16] | 4.7[1] | 100 | 115 | — | — | [8] | 6.2 | 120.30 | Singapore |
| | | | | | | | 46.0[6] | | | 73 | | | | 7.4 | 12.80 | Solomon Islands |
| | | | | | | | 152.0 | | 38 | 89 | | | | 3.2 | 2.60 | Somalia |
| | | | | | | | 83.0[19] | | | 118 | | | [8] | | 11.30[3] | South Africa |
| | | | | | | | | | | | | | | | | Bophuthatswana |
| 488 | | | | | 79.0 | 16 | 89.0[6] | | | | | | | | | Ciskei |
| | | | | | | | | | | | | | | | | KwaNdebele |
| | | | | | | | 84.0 | | | | | | | | | Transkei |
| 1,130 | | | | | 102.4 | 11 | | | | | | | | | | Venda |
| | | | | | | | 110.0 | | | 82 | | | | | | South West Africa/Namibia |
| 914 | 91.7 | 8.3 | — | — | 73.0 | 15 | 9.0 | 11.1[12] | 78 | 132 | 4.8[7] | 25.8[7] | ... | 0.6 | 10.10 | Spain |
| 1,623 | 39.9 | 15.0 | 0.8 | 44.3 | 88.3 | 6 | 23.5[16] | 64.5[12] | 22 | 104 | — | — | [8] | 3.6 | 4.40 | Sri Lanka |
| 81[20] | | | | | | | 118.0 | | 46 | 90 | | | | 1.3 | 0.90 | Sudan, The |
| 820 | 83.6 | 2.4 | 8.0 | 6.0 | 41.6 | 15 | 27.6 | 71.1[1] | | 109 | | | | 0.3 | 3.20 | Suriname |
| 456[20] | | | | | | | 129.0 | | 37 | 105 | | | | 10.3 | 31.90 | Swaziland |
| 1,968 | 89.0 | 11.0 | — | — | 86.1 | 22 | 6.8 | 2.1[10] | 99 | 117 | — | 9.5 | | 1.2 | 63.30 | Sweden |
| 1,278 | 85.9 | 14.1 | — | — | 80.8 | 24 | 6.9 | 1.4[10] | 96 | 129 | 73 | — | | 13.1 | 384.70 | Switzerland |
| 433[10] | | | | | 39.6[10] | 4[10] | 48.0 | | 71 | 127 | | | | 1.1 | 1.50 | Syria |
| | | | | | | | 6.8 | | | | 1.4[7] | 5.6[7] | 3.2[7] | | 67.40[3] | Taiwan |
| 706 | 66.5 | — | 13.1 | 20.4 | | | 111.0 | | 48 | 98 | 5.0[7] | 5.0[7] | | 4.9 | 3.50 | Tanzania |
| | | | | | | | 52.0[16] | | 23 | 105 | — | — | | 5.7 | 8.80 | Thailand |
| | | | | | | | 102.0 | | 11 | 94 | — | 2.0[27] | | 3.6 | 3.30 | Togo |
| 965[6] | — | — | — | 100.0[6] | 12.0[6] | 11[6] | | | | | | | | | | Tokelau |
| 718 | 97.6 | — | 2.4 | — | 56.8 | 10 | 26.0[6] | | | 117 | | | | 5.9 | 104.70 | Tonga |
| 980[9,13] | | | | | 88.6[9,13] | 5[9,13] | 14.9[43] | 78.9[5] | 89 | 129 | 2.8[7] | 5.6[7] | [8] | 6.5 | 29.20 | Trinidad and Tobago |
| 652[10] | | | | | 65.5[10] | 8 | 71.0 | | 62 | 121 | 5.0 | 15.0 | | 1.8 | 6.80 | Tunisia |
| 462 | 78.3[1] | 19.1[1] | — | 2.6[1] | 44.1[1] | 9[1] | 84.0 | | 69 | 123 | 5.0 | 6.0 | | | | Turkey |
| | | | | | | | 10.2[6] | | | | | | | 9.1 | 137.00 | Turks and Caicos Islands |
| 1,368 | 40.9 | — | — | 59.1 | 51.5[20] | 12.2[20] | 35.0 | | | 117 | | | | | | Tuvalu |
| | | | | | | | 110.0 | | 10 | 101 | — | — | | 3.4 | 0.80 | Uganda |
| | | | | | | | 26.0 | | | 132 | | 4.4[23] | | | 177.80[3] | U.S.S.R. |
| 1,032[6] | 78.4[1] | 15.4[1] | 0.8[1] | 5.4[1] | 69.6[6] | 7[6] | 35.0 | | 88 | | | | | 6.2 | 185.00 | United Arab Emirates |
| 1,216 | | | | | 75.8 | 10 | 9.3[16] | 9.2 | 99 | 128 | 9.0 | 11.45 | | 12.5 | 343.90 | United Kingdom |
| 1,458 | 96.9[10] | 3.1[10] | — | — | 68.4 | 7 | 10.2[16] | 7.9 | 99 | 137 | 1.3 | 1.3 | | 11.3 | 461.10 | United States |
| 309 | | | | | 50.8 | 8 | 30.3 | 55.9[4] | 78 | 99 | 3.0 | 4.0 | | 4.1 | 15.70 | Uruguay |
| 912 | 40.5 | — | 14.0 | 45.5 | 33.6 | 8 | 94.0 | 3.0[17] | | 100 | | | 1.5[7] | | | Vanuatu |
| 1,587 | 12.4 | 8.1 | 56.6 | 22.9 | 80.7 | 7 | 27.3 | 64.7[12] | 81 | 99 | 2.0 | 4.25[23] | 1.5[23] | 7.6 | 55.30 | Venezuela |
| | | | | | | | 69.0[16] | | 24 | 99 | | | | | 2.40[3] | Vietnam |
| | | | | | | | 20.2[19] | 280.0[1] | | | | | | | | Virgin Islands (U.S.) |
| 1,100 | 76.0 | — | — | 24.0 | 49.4 | 13 | 40.5[4] | | | | | | | | | Wallis and Futuna |
| 929 | | | | | 76.3 | 5 | | | | | | | | | | West Bank |
| 226 | 98.2 | — | 1.8 | — | 36.9 | 5 | 5.3 | | | | | | | | | Western Sahara[54] |
| 823 | 62.0 | — | — | 38.0 | 25.4 | 7 | 52.0[16] | | | 94 | | | | 9.3 | 18.50 | Western Samoa |
| 277 | | | | | | | 137.0 | | 37 | 92 | | | | | 5.70[3] | Yemen (Aden) |
| 95 | 89.0 | 0.4 | — | 10.6 | 73.4 | 18 | 135.0 | | 4 | 94 | | | | 4.4 | 8.80 | Yemen (Şan'ā') |
| 993 | 81.0[55] | 19.0 | 55 | — | 86.3[19] | 11 | 27.1[16] | 22.4 | 58 | 141 | 8.7 | | | | 142.10[3] | Yugoslavia |
| 474[9,20] | | | | | 71.6[9,20] | 12[9,20] | 106.0[19] | | 16 | 96 | | | | 1.8 | 0.60 | Zaire |
| 1,249 | —75.7— | | —24.3— | | 68.5 | 7 | 88.0 | | 42 | 83 | 5.0[24] | 5.0[23] | | 8.4 | 20.60 | Zambia |
| 1,043 | 40.1 | 6.1 | 53.8 | — | 67.5 | 7 | 61.0 | 37.1[9] | | 82 | | | | 6.2 | 15.90 | Zimbabwe |

[29]1974.  [30]Public sector only.  [31]Includes family allowances.  [32]Includes physicians practicing dentistry.  [33]Employer provides entire cost.  [34]Registered personnel; all may not be present and working in the country.  [35]1976.  [36]General hospitals includes specialized and rural hospitals.  [37]Nurses includes midwives.  [38]Rural hospitals only.  [39]Excludes hospices and sanatoriums.  [40]1971.  [41]Excludes hazardous occupations such as mining.  [42]General hospitals includes medical centres and rural hospitals.  [43]1981–83 average.  [44]1973.  [45]Combined rate for Guernsey and Jersey.  [46]Excludes oilfield operations.  [47]Public general and specialized hospitals only.  [48]General and specialized hospitals only.  [49]Includes welfare.  [50]Peninsular Malaysia only.  [51]Central Hospital only.  [52]Based on bed ownership.  [53]1975–80 estimate.  [54]Settlements of Smara, Boudjour, and El Aaiún only.  [55]General hospitals includes medical centres.

# Social protection

This table summarizes the principal social protective activities of the countries of the world. Because the administrative structure, financing, manning, and scope of programmed tasks vary so greatly from country to country, the basis of the comparisons is most often either manpower or finance.

The provision of social security programs for specific social needs, however, is summarized simply in terms of the existence or nonexistence of a specific benefit program because of the great complexity of national programs in terms of eligibility, coverage, term, age limits, financing, payments, and so on. Activities connected with a particular type of benefit often take place at more than one governmental level or through more than one agency at the same level. The data shown here are summarized from the U.S. Social Security Administration's *Social Security Programs Throughout the World* (biennial). A bullet symbol (●) indicates that a country has at least one program within the defined area; in some cases it may have several. A blank space indicates that no program existed providing the benefit shown; ellipses [...] indicate that no information was available as to whether a program existed.

Data given for social security expenditure as a percentage of total central governmental expenditure are taken from the International Monetary Fund's *Government Finance Statistics Yearbook*, which provides the most comparable analytical series on the consolidated accounts of the central governments, governmentally administered social security funds, and independent national agencies, all usually separate accounting entities, through which these services may be provided in a given country.

Data on the finances of social security programs are taken in large part from the International Labour Office's *The Cost of Social Security* (triennial), supplemented by national data sources.

Figures for manpower in police and fire services are from a variety of national sources, principally census and manpower surveys, from the 1976–86 census period. The relative scarcity of international sources and data on these topics is in part a reflection of the fact that in many countries these functions are viewed as matters of merely local concern and, as they are not conducted or directly funded by the central government, tend to be ignored in the data collection and publication programs of the central government. The manpower figures refer, for the most part, to full-time, paid professional staff, excluding clerical support and volunteer staff. Fire fighters employed by private companies are included. Personnel in military service who perform either police or fire functions are presumed to be employed in their principal activity, military service. Figures for criminal

## Social protection

| country | social security | | | | | | finances | | | | | | | | | |
| | programs available, 1985 | | | | | expendi-tures, 1984 (% of total central govt.) | year | receipts | | | | | expenditures | | | |
| | old-age invalid-ity, death | sickness and mater-nity[a] | work injury | unem-ploy-ment | family allow-ances | | | total ('000,000 natl. cur.) | insured persons (%) | em-ployers (%) | govern-ment (%) | other (%) | total ('000,000 natl. cur.) | benefits (%) | admin-istration (%) | other (%) |
|---|---|---|---|---|---|---|---|---|---|---|---|---|---|---|---|---|
| Afghanistan | ● | ● | ● | | | ... | ... | ... | ... | ... | ... | ... | ... | ... | ... | ... |
| Albania | ... | ... | ... | ... | ... | ... | ... | ... | ... | ... | ... | ... | ... | ... | ... | ... |
| Algeria | ● | ● | ● | | ● | ... | 1984 | 11,086.0 | ... | ... | ... | ... | 11,417.0 | ... | ... | ... |
| American Samoa | ● | ... | ... | ... | ... | ... | 1980 | 2.3 | 29.3 | 40.9 | ... | 29.7 | 0.6 | 100.0 | — | — |
| Andorra | ... | ... | ... | ... | ... | ... | ... | ... | ... | ... | ... | ... | ... | ... | ... | ... |
| Angola | ... | ... | ... | ... | ... | ... | ... | ... | ... | ... | ... | ... | ... | ... | ... | ... |
| Anguilla | ... | ... | ... | ... | ... | ... | ... | ... | ... | ... | ... | ... | ... | ... | ... | ... |
| Antigua and Barbuda | ● | ● | ● | | | ... | 1983 | ... | ... | ... | ... | ... | 1.3 | ... | ... | ... |
| Argentina | ● | ● | ● | ● | ● | 35.5 | 1980 | 27,318,424.2 | 38.4 | 49.4 | 10.2 | 2.1 | 26,433,082.7 | 94.8 | 4.4 | 0.8 |
| Aruba | ● | ... | ... | ... | ... | 7 | ... | ... | ... | ... | ... | ... | ... | ... | ... | ... |
| Australia | ● | ● | ● | ● | ● | 26.1 | 1980 | 17,235.3 | 13.0 | 12.3 | 70.4 | 4.3 | 15,807.3 | 96.0 | 3.5 | 0.4 |
| Austria | ● | ● | ● | ● | ● | 44.8[8] | 1980 | 224,889.0 | 31.3 | 48.5 | 16.8 | 3.4 | 223,466.0 | 95.2 | 2.7 | 2.1 |
| Bahamas, The | ● | ● | ● | | ● | 7.3[9] | 1979 | 25.1 | ... | ... | ... | ... | 15.3 | ... | ... | ... |
| Bahrain | ● | | ● | | | 1.5[8] | 1980 | 24,596.0 | 12.5 | 43.6 | 21.1 | 22.8 | 3,626.0 | 70.7 | 20.2 | 9.2 |
| Bangladesh | | ● | ● | | | 2.6[2, 8] | 1977 | 466.7 | 2.2 | 2.2 | 93.7 | 1.9 | 445.3 | 99.6 | 0.4 | — |
| Barbados | ● | ● | ● | ● | | 17.7 | 1980 | 66.1 | 22.7 | 28.8 | 31.0 | 17.5 | 37.7 | 93.6 | 6.4 | — |
| Belgium | ● | ● | ● | ● | ● | 40.8 | 1980 | 884,343.7 | 18.3 | 43.3 | 35.3 | 3.2 | 903,666.6 | 94.3 | 4.1 | 1.5 |
| Belize | ● | ● | ● | | | 2.9 | 1982 | 5.3 | ... | ... | ... | ... | 4.2 | ... | ... | ... |
| Benin | ● | ● | ● | | ● | 8.7[8, 9] | 1977 | 3,654.7 | 7.4 | 49.4 | 41.9 | 1.3 | 3,165.6 | 91.0 | 8.3 | 0.7 |
| Bermuda | ... | ... | ... | ... | ... | ... | ... | ... | ... | ... | ... | ... | ... | ... | ... | ... |
| Bhutan | ... | ... | ... | ... | ... | ... | ... | ... | ... | ... | ... | ... | ... | ... | ... | ... |
| Bolivia | ● | ● | ● | | ● | 4.9 | 1980 | 3,628.4 | 28.8 | 53.6 | 6.2 | 11.5 | 3,673.3 | 80.4 | 19.3 | 0.4 |
| Botswana | ● | | ● | | | 4.3[8] | 1983 | — | | | | | 11.0[8] | ... | ... | ... |
| Brazil | ● | ● | ● | ● | ● | 30.5 | 1983 | 8,605,500.0 | ... | ... | ... | ... | 8,290,000.0 | ... | ... | ... |
| British Virgin Islands | ... | ... | ... | ... | ... | ... | 1982 | ... | ... | ... | ... | ... | 0.2 | ... | ... | ... |
| Brunei | ● | ... | ● | ... | ... | ... | 1981 | ... | ... | ... | ... | ... | 2.5[11] | ... | ... | ... |
| Bulgaria | ● | ● | ● | | ● | ... | 1977 | 2,609.7 | — | 53.7 | 40.2 | 6.1 | 2,506.0 | 94.9 | 0.1 | 5.0 |
| Burkina Faso | ● | ● | ● | | ● | 6.7 | 1977 | 3,727.5 | 10.1 | 61.4 | 24.8 | 3.7 | 2,635.7 | 90.5 | 9.5 | — |
| Burma | ● | ● | ● | | | 0.4 | 1977 | 340.1 | 1.4 | 40.9 | 57.7 | — | 333.1 | 99.2 | 0.8 | — |
| Burundi | ● | | ● | | ● | 0.7[11] | 1980 | 475.0 | 21.1 | 39.3 | 25.7 | 13.9 | 266.7 | 73.5 | 26.2 | 0.3 |
| Cameroon | ● | | ● | | ● | 4.2 | 1984 | 32,490.0 | ... | ... | ... | ... | 28,340.0 | ... | ... | ... |
| Canada | ● | ● | ● | ● | ● | 27.0 | 1980 | 41,921.7 | 7.4 | 12.8 | 71.2 | 8.6 | 35,523.4 | 97.5 | 2.5 | — |
| Cape Verde | ● | ● | ● | | ● | ... | ... | ... | ... | ... | ... | ... | ... | ... | ... | ... |
| Cayman Islands | ● | ... | ● | ... | ... | 1.7[8] | ... | ... | ... | ... | ... | ... | ... | ... | ... | ... |
| Central African Republic | ● | | ● | | ● | 6.2[3, 8] | 1981 | 2,009.0 | ... | ... | ... | ... | 1,675.0 | ... | ... | ... |
| Chad | ● | | ● | | ● | 1.9[12] | ... | ... | ... | ... | ... | ... | ... | ... | ... | ... |
| Chile | ● | ● | ● | ● | ● | 37.1 | 1980 | 139,950.3 | 20.5 | 38.3 | 34.2 | 7.0 | 115,545.9 | 92.5 | 7.5 | — |
| China | ● | ● | ● | | | ... | ... | ... | ... | ... | ... | ... | ... | ... | ... | ... |
| Christmas Island | ● | ● | ● | ● | ● | ... | ... | ... | ... | ... | ... | ... | ... | ... | ... | ... |
| Cocos (Keeling) Islands | ● | ● | ● | ● | ● | ... | 1985 | 0.2 | ... | ... | ... | ... | 0.2 | ... | ... | ... |
| Colombia | ● | ● | ● | | ● | 19.3[2, 8] | 1980 | 52,412.9 | 16.0 | 49.8 | 16.2 | 18.0 | 44,180.6 | 77.6 | 12.4 | 10.1 |
| Comoros | ... | ... | ... | ... | ... | ... | ... | ... | ... | ... | ... | ... | ... | ... | ... | ... |
| Congo | ● | | ● | | ● | 0.4[6] | 1980 | 5,682.0 | ... | ... | ... | ... | ... | ... | ... | ... |
| Cook Islands | ● | ... | ... | ... | ... | ... | ... | ... | ... | ... | ... | ... | ... | ... | ... | ... |
| Costa Rica | ● | ● | ● | | | 14.5[2] | 1980 | 3,408.3 | 27.6 | 45.9 | 20.4 | 6.1 | 2,927.4 | 88.8 | 6.9 | 4.4 |
| Côte d'Ivoire | ● | | ● | | ● | 3.1[8, 16] | 1980 | 34,416.0 | ... | ... | ... | ... | 18,864.0 | ... | ... | ... |
| Cuba | ... | ... | ... | ... | ... | ... | ... | ... | ... | ... | ... | ... | ... | ... | ... | ... |
| Cyprus[17] | ● | ● | ● | ● | | 16.6 | 1980 | 34.0 | 30.0 | 36.3 | 29.2 | 4.5 | 27.6 | 98.1 | 1.9 | — |
| Czechoslovakia | ● | ● | ● | | ● | ... | 1980 | 91,367.0 | ... | 3.7 | 94.6 | 1.7 | 91,367.0 | 99.6 | 0.4 | — |
| Denmark | ● | ● | ● | ● | ● | 33.8[2] | 1980 | 103,269.1 | 1.8 | 5.9 | 90.2 | 2.1 | 100,587.5 | 97.3 | 2.7 | — |
| Djibouti | ● | | ● | ... | ● | 8.3[9] | 1979 | 1,352.2 | ... | ... | ... | ... | 1,115.7 | ... | ... | ... |
| Dominica | ● | ● | ● | | | 1.4[9] | 1979 | 2.5 | ... | ... | ... | ... | 0.8 | ... | ... | ... |
| Dominican Republic | ● | ● | ● | | | 8.6 | 1980 | 136.8 | ... | ... | 43.6 | 4.4 | 123,852 | 87.2 | 8.0 | 4.8 |
| Ecuador | ● | ● | ● | | ● | 1.1[8] | 1980 | 13,643.0 | 36.9 | 43.0 | 0.1 | 19.9 | 8,585.0 | 72.0 | 28.0 | — |
| Egypt | ● | ● | ● | ● | | 11.3 | 1984 | 2,796.6 | ... | ... | ... | ... | 1,435.1 | ... | ... | ... |
| El Salvador | ● | ● | ● | | | 3.2 | 1980 | 169.7 | 23.4 | 63.0 | 0.9 | 3.4 | 134.1 | 85.9 | 14.1 | — |
| Equatorial Guinea | ... | ... | ... | ... | ... | ... | ... | ... | ... | ... | ... | ... | ... | ... | ... | ... |
| Ethiopia | ● | | ● | | | 3.4[16] | 1980 | 117.7 | 21.8 | 70.7 | 4.5 | 3.0 | 79.8 | 98.2 | 1.8 | ... |
| Faeroe Islands | ● | ... | ... | ... | ● | ... | ... | ... | ... | ... | ... | ... | ... | ... | ... | ... |
| Falkland Islands | ● | ... | ... | ... | ● | ... | ... | ... | ... | ... | ... | ... | ... | ... | ... | ... |

offenses known to police, usually excluding civil offenses and minor traffic violations, are taken in part from Interpol's *International Crime Statistics* (biennial) and a variety of national sources; supplemental information about the constitution of various national police forces may be found in JOHN ANDRADE, *World Police & Paramilitary Forces* (1985). Criminal offense data for certain countries refer to cases disposed of in court, rather than to complaints. Virtually all data on fire alarms and on expenditure for police and fire services are taken from national statistical sources. Data for fire alarms usually exclude nonemergency calls, medical emergencies, and fire code inspection visits but may include false fire alarms to which a normal response with personnel and equipment was made.

The figures for military manpower refer to full-time, active-duty military service and exclude reserve, militia, paramilitary, and similar organizations. Because of the difficulties attached to the analysis of data on military manpower and budgets (including problems such as data withheld on national security grounds, or the publication of budgetary data specifically intended to hide actual expenditure, or the complexity of long-term financing of purchases of military matériel [how much was actually spent as opposed to what was committed, offset by nonmilitary transfers, etc.]), extensive use is made of the principal international analytical tools: pub-

lications such as those of the International Institute for Strategic Studies (*The Military Balance* and *Strategic Survey*), the Stockholm International Peace Research Institute (*World Armaments and Disarmament,* SIPRI *Yearbook*), and the U.S. Arms Control and Disarmament Agency (*World Military Expenditures and Arms Transfers*).

The data on military expenditures are from the sources identified above, as well as from the IMF's *Government Finance Statistical Yearbook* and country statistical publications.

a. Sickness and maternity refers to cash benefits for sickness and maternity. Countries must provide both benefits to be included. In many countries medical care and hospital coverage are also provided for sickness and maternity.

b. A police officer is a full-time, paid professional, performing domestic security functions. Data include administrative staff, but exclude clerical employees, volunteers, and members of paramilitary groups.

c. A fire fighter is a full-time, paid, professional. Data include administrative staff, but exclude clerical employees and volunteers.

d. Includes all active-duty personnel, regular and conscript, performing national security functions. Excludes reserves, paramilitary forces, border patrols, and gendarmeries.

| police protection (latest) | | | fire protection (latest) | | | military protection — manpower, 1986[d] | | military protection — expenditure, 1984 | | | | arms trade, 1985 ('000,000 U.S.$) | | country |
|---|---|---|---|---|---|---|---|---|---|---|---|---|---|---|
| offenses (reported to police) per 100,000 population | population per police officer[b] | government expenditure per 1,000 population (U.S.$) | fire alarms per 100,000 population | population per fire fighter[c] | government expenditure per 1,000 population (U.S.$) | total ('000) | per 1,000 population | total '000,000 U.S.$ | per capita | % of national budget | % of GDP or GNP | imports | exports | |
| ... | 540[1] | ... | ... | ... | ... | 50.0 | 3.3 | 209[2] | 14[2] | 62.7[2] | 5.9[2] | 150 | 0 | Afghanistan |
| ... | 550 | ... | ... | ... | ... | 42.0 | 13.9 | 143 | 49 | 11.0 | 8.1[3] | 0 | 0 | Albania |
| 1,673 | 840 | ... | ... | ... | ... | 169.0 | 7.5 | 1,403 | 66 | 6.5 | 2.7 | 270 | 0 | Algeria |
| 5,386 | 460 | 17,676 | 180 | 850 | 8,126 | — | 4 | | | | | ... | ... | American Samoa |
| 2,930 | 220 | ... | ... | ... | ... | — | 4 | | | | | ... | ... | Andorra |
| 240 | 14[5] | ... | ... | ... | ... | 50.0 | 5.7 | 667[2] | 82[2] | 25.0[2] | 9.9[2] | 440 | 0 | Angola |
| 2,102 | 100 | 24,233 | ... | ... | ... | — | 4 | | | | | ... | ... | Anguilla |
| 4,167 | 120 | 41,624 | ... | ... | ... | 0.7[2] | 8.9[2] | | | | | ... | ... | Antigua and Barbuda |
| 1,102 | 1,270 | 8,429[6] | ... | ... | ... | 73.0 | 2.4 | 2,327 | 77 | 17.2 | 3.7 | 150 | 0 | Argentina |
| 1,631 | ... | ... | ... | ... | ... | — | 4 | | | | | ... | ... | Aruba |
| 6,897 | 450 | 16,132 | ... | ... | ... | 70.5 | 4.4 | 4,657 | 299 | 9.3 | 2.9 | 700 | 50 | Australia |
| 5,646 | 470 | ... | ... | ... | ... | 54.7 | 7.2 | 921 | 122 | 3.3 | 1.3 | 10 | 100 | Austria |
| 5,706 | 160 | ... | ... | ... | ... | — | — | 9 | 40 | 2.5 | 0.5 | ... | ... | Bahamas, The |
| 1,233 | 180 | ... | ... | ... | ... | 2.8 | 6.8 | 148 | 382 | 10.2 | 3.6 | 10 | 0 | Bahrain |
| 61 | 2,560 | 453 | ... | ... | ... | 91.3 | 0.9 | 248 | 3 | 9.7 | 1.9 | 0 | 0 | Bangladesh |
| 3,336 | 280 | ... | ... | ... | ... | — | — | 11 | 44 | 2.9 | 1.0 | 0 | 0 | Barbados |
| 2,350 | 640 | ... | ... | ... | ... | 91.4 | 9.3 | 2,669 | 271 | 5.5 | 3.1 | 240 | 180 | Belgium |
| ... | 290 | ... | ... | ... | ... | 0.6 | 3.5 | 4 | 25 | 4.0 | 2.0 | ... | ... | Belize |
| 1,234 | 3,250 | 1,138 | ... | ... | ... | 3.5 | 0.8 | 26 | 7 | 10.2 | 2.6 | 5 | 0 | Benin |
| 7,390 | 370 | 290,191 | ... | 1,030 | 471 | — | 4 | | | | | ... | ... | Bermuda |
| ... | ... | ... | ... | ... | ... | 4.0[10] | 3.1[10] | | | | | ... | ... | Bhutan |
| ... | ... | ... | ... | ... | ... | 27.6 | 4.2 | 120 | 19 | 5.4 | 2.2 | 0 | 0 | Bolivia |
| 5,046 | 750 | 6,705[8] | ... | 21,300 | ... | 3.0 | 2.7 | 25[2] | 25[2] | 6.2[2] | 3.1[2] | 0 | 0 | Botswana |
| 188 | ... | ... | 13 | 3,450 | ... | 283.4 | 2.0 | 1,778 | 13 | 2.8 | 0.8 | 20 | 60 | Brazil |
| 1,865 | 190 | ... | ... | ... | ... | — | 4 | | | | | ... | ... | British Virgin Islands |
| 1,740 | 100 | 126,103 | 279 | ... | 33,195 | 4.1 | 17.6 | 305 | 1,398 | 24.5 | 8.1 | ... | ... | Brunei |
| ... | ... | ... | ... | ... | ... | 148.5 | 16.6 | 4,532 | 508 | 19.0 | 7.8 | 500 | 240 | Bulgaria |
| ... | ... | ... | ... | ... | ... | 4.0 | 0.5 | 30 | 4 | 17.6 | 2.7 | 5 | 0 | Burkina Faso |
| 40 | 650 | ... | ... | ... | ... | 186.0 | 4.8 | 195 | 5 | 19.1 | 2.9 | 20 | 0 | Burma |
| 82 | ... | ... | ... | ... | ... | 7.2 | 1.5 | 38 | 8 | 14.2 | 3.5 | 5 | 0 | Burundi |
| ... | 1,170 | ... | ... | ... | ... | 7.3 | 0.7 | 139 | 14 | 7.9 | 1.9 | 30 | 0 | Cameroon |
| 8,938 | 370 | ... | 309 | ... | ... | 83.0 | 3.2 | 7,604 | 302 | 8.2 | 2.2 | 50 | 190 | Canada |
| ... | 460 | ... | ... | ... | ... | 1.2[10] | 3.6[10] | 13[3] | 43[3] | 13.5[3] | 11.8[3] | 10 | 0 | Cape Verde |
| 12,190 | 110 | 33,287 | 1,764 | 322 | ... | — | 4 | | | | | ... | ... | Cayman Islands |
| ... | 2,740[1] | ... | ... | ... | ... | 2.3 | 0.8 | 13[2] | 5[2] | 9.0[2] | 1.9[2] | 0 | 0 | Central African Republic |
| ... | 990 | ... | ... | ... | ... | 14.2 | 2.8 | 9 | 2 | 22.0 | 1.6 | 10 | 0 | Chad |
| 1,373 | 470 | 6,459 | ... | ... | ... | 101.0 | 8.2 | 817 | 69 | 11.9 | 4.2 | 20 | 20 | Chile |
| ... | 1,360[13] | ... | ... | ... | ... | 2,950.0 | 2.8 | 24,040 | 23 | 32.3 | 7.5 | 110 | 350 | China |
| 790[14] | 190 | ... | ... | ... | ... | — | 4 | | | | | ... | ... | Christmas Island |
| ... | ... | ... | ... | ... | ... | — | 4 | | | | | ... | ... | Cocos (Keeling) Islands |
| 687 | 420 | ... | ... | ... | ... | 66.2 | 2.3 | 574 | 21 | 10.0 | 1.4 | 10 | 0 | Colombia |
| ... | 960 | ... | ... | ... | ... | — | 15 | | | | | ... | ... | Comoros |
| 10 | 870 | ... | ... | ... | ... | 8.7 | 4.1 | 55 | 28 | 5.2 | 2.6 | 20 | 0 | Congo |
| ... | ... | ... | ... | ... | ... | — | 4 | | | | | ... | ... | Cook Islands |
| 558 | 480 | ... | ... | 953,000 | ... | — | — | 33 | 14 | 4.0 | 1.0 | 20 | 0 | Costa Rica |
| 295 | 4,640 | ... | ... | ... | ... | 13.2 | 1.2 | 78 | 8 | 4.4 | 1.3 | 20 | 0 | Côte d'Ivoire |
| ... | 650 | 2,503 | ... | ... | ... | 162.0 | 15.9 | 1,600 | 160 | ... | 5.9 | 800 | 0 | Cuba |
| 644 | 180 | 35,383 | ... | ... | ... | 13.0 | 19.3 | 36 | 55 | 4.7 | 1.5 | 5 | 0 | Cyprus[17] |
| ... | 640 | ... | ... | ... | ... | 201.0 | 12.9 | 7,642 | 494 | 18.0 | 5.8 | 390 | 825 | Czechoslovakia |
| 9,365 | 600 | 67,601 | ... | ... | 13,548 | 29.5 | 5.8 | 1,395 | 273 | 5.3 | 2.4 | 70 | 0 | Denmark |
| ... | ... | ... | ... | ... | ... | 4.5 | 9.9 | 27 | 67 | 22.4 | 8.1 | ... | ... | Djibouti |
| 18,328 | 300 | 29,740 | ... | ... | ... | — | — | | | | | ... | ... | Dominica |
| 295 | 580 | ... | ... | ... | ... | 21.3 | 3.3 | 94 | 15 | 8.3 | 1.2 | 5 | 0 | Dominican Republic |
| 292 | 260 | ... | ... | ... | ... | 42.0 | 4.4 | 204 | 22 | 11.3 | 1.6 | 20 | 0 | Ecuador |
| 2,378 | 580 | ... | ... | ... | ... | 445.0 | 9.3 | 5,122 | 113 | 25.0 | 13.5 | 1,100 | 30 | Egypt |
| ... | 1,000 | ... | ... | ... | ... | 42.6 | 8.7 | 251 | 53 | 30.6 | 6.1 | 90 | 0 | El Salvador |
| ... | 190 | ... | ... | ... | ... | 2.3 | 7.2 | 2[3] | 11[3] | 21.0[3] | 3.4[3] | 0 | 0 | Equatorial Guinea |
| 324 | 1,100 | ... | ... | ... | ... | 227.0 | 5.1 | 428 | 10 | 25.1 | 8.9 | 390 | 0 | Ethiopia |
| ... | ... | 49 | ... | ... | ... | — | 4 | | | | | ... | ... | Faeroe Islands |
| ... | 330 | 38,723 | ... | — | ... | — | 4 | | | | | ... | ... | Falkland Islands |

## Social protection (continued)

| country | social security | | | | | | finances | | | | | | | | | |
|---|---|---|---|---|---|---|---|---|---|---|---|---|---|---|---|---|
| | programs available, 1985 | | | | | expenditures, 1984 (% of total central govt.) | year | receipts | | | | | expenditures | | | |
| | old-age invalidity, death | sickness and maternity[a] | work injury | unemployment | family allowances | | | total ('000,000 natl. cur.) | insured persons (%) | employers (%) | government (%) | other (%) | total ('000,000 natl. cur.) | benefits (%) | administration (%) | other (%) |
| Fiji | • | | • | | | 7.3 | 1980 | 57.8 | 28.7 | 30.8 | 9.5 | 31.1 | 20.5 | 56.4 | 43.6 | — |
| Finland | • | • | • | • | • | 33.2[8] | 1980 | 40,435.2 | 7.9 | 44.9 | 41.4 | 5.8 | 34,646.2 | 96.5 | 3.5 | — |
| France | • | ... | • | ... | • | 44.0[2,8] | 1980 | 761,712.2 | 21.0 | 53.4 | 24.1 | 1.5 | 738,971.1 | 95.2 | 3.9 | 1.0 |
| French Guiana | • | ... | • | ... | • | ... | ... | ... | ... | ... | ... | ... | ... | ... | ... | ... |
| French Polynesia | ◐ | ... | • | ... | • | ... | ... | ... | ... | ... | ... | ... | ... | ... | ... | ... |
| Gabon | • | ... | • | ... | • | ... | 1975 | 6,770.0 | ... | ... | ... | ... | ... | ... | ... | ... |
| Gambia, The | • | ... | • | ... | | 3.5[18] | 1978 | ... | ... | ... | ... | ... | ... | ... | ... | ... |
| Gaza Strip | ... | ... | ... | ... | ... | — | | ... | ... | ... | ... | ... | ... | ... | ... | ... |
| Germany, East | • | ... | • | ... | | ... | 1980 | 29,627.0 | 21.9 | 28.3 | 49.7 | 0.1 | 29,627.0 | 99.6 | 0.4 | — |
| Germany, West | • | • | • | • | • | 50.2[8] | 1980 | 357,712.0 | 34.0 | 34.2 | 28.9 | 2.9 | 355,052.0 | 96.4 | 3.1 | 0.5 |
| Ghana | • | | • | • | | 3.7 | 1984 | ... | ... | ... | ... | ... | ... | ... | ... | ... |
| Gibraltar | • | • | ... | • | • | | | ... | ... | ... | ... | ... | ... | ... | ... | ... |
| Greece | • | • | • | ... | • | 28.8[3] | 1980 | 242,714.0 | 29.7 | 47.3 | 17.0 | 5.9 | 209,443.0 | 95.2 | 4.5 | 0.4 |
| Greenland | • | ... | ... | • | ... | | | ... | ... | ... | ... | ... | ... | ... | ... | ... |
| Grenada | • | • | | | | 5.0[8,11] | 1977 | ... | ... | ... | ... | ... | ... | ... | ... | ... |
| Guadeloupe | • | ... | ... | | • | | | ... | ... | ... | ... | ... | ... | ... | ... | ... |
| Guam | • | ... | ... | | • | | | ... | ... | ... | ... | ... | ... | ... | ... | ... |
| Guatemala | • | • | • | | | 2.6[9] | 1980 | 133.4 | 31.6 | 53.1 | 8.2 | 7.1 | 90.9 | 88.3 | 11.7 | — |
| Guernsey | ... | ... | ... | | | | | ... | ... | ... | ... | ... | ... | ... | ... | ... |
| Guinea | • | • | • | | | | 1983 | 446.5 | — | 100.0 | — | — | ... | ... | ... | ... |
| Guinea-Bissau | ... | ... | ... | | | | | ... | ... | ... | ... | ... | ... | ... | ... | ... |
| Guyana | • | • | • | | | 3.7[2] | 1980 | 85,692.0 | 29.4 | 43.0 | ... | 27.5 | 18,591.0 | 68.9 | 31.1 | ... |
| Haiti | • | • | • | | | 5.1 | 1977 | 60.5 | —26.6— | | 69.9 | 3.5 | 52.4 | 92.7 | 7.3 | — |
| Honduras | • | • | • | | | 4.5[9] | | ... | ... | ... | ... | ... | ... | ... | ... | ... |
| Hong Kong | • | • | • | • | | | 1985 | ... | ... | ... | ... | ... | 895.6 | ... | ... | ... |
| Hungary | • | • | • | • | • | 23.1 | 1980 | 106,644.0 | 14.6 | 41.1 | 43.6 | 0.7 | 106,646.0 | 99.5 | 0.5 | — |
| Iceland | • | • | • | • | •[20] | 14.2 | 1981 | 932.0 | — | 14.8 | 85.2 | — | ... | ... | ... | ... |
| India | • | • | • | | | ... | 1976 | 30,870.4 | —66.1— | | 22.8 | 11.1 | 17,842.9 | 98.4 | 0.9 | 0.7 |
| Indonesia | • | • | • | | | — | | ... | ... | ... | ... | ... | ... | ... | ... | ... |
| Iran | • | • | • | | • | 7.2 | 1983 | 217,200.0 | ... | ... | ... | ... | 217,200.0 | ... | ... | ... |
| Iraq | • | • | • | | • | | 1977 | 107.8 | 9.9 | 55.6 | 21.9 | 12.6 | 71.0 | 94.0 | 2.4 | 3.6 |
| Ireland | • | • | • | • | • | 24.9 | 1980 | 1,896.7 | 11.6 | 26.3 | 61.0 | 1.0 | 1,881.3 | 95.0 | 4.7 | 0.2 |
| Isle of Man | • | • | • | • | • | 17.2[10] | 1985 | ... | ... | ... | ... | ... | 14.4 | ... | ... | ... |
| Israel | • | • | • | • | • | 20.1 | 1980 | 7,237.6 | 16.8 | 37.0 | 36.9 | 9.2 | 6,409.9 | 84.2 | 6.8 | 9.0 |
| Italy | • | • | • | • | • | 29.7 | 1980 | 61,563,000.0 | 10.8 | 54.8 | 31.9 | 2.6 | 61,318,000.0 | 89.8 | 4.3 | 5.9 |
| Jamaica | • | | • | | | 3.2[11] | 1980 | 115.9 | 17.2 | 20.7 | 36.8 | 25.3 | 58.3 | 91.0 | 8.9 | — |
| Japan | • | • | • | • | • | ... | 1980 | 30,372,556.0 | 25.9 | 28.4 | 31.3 | 14.5 | 23,871,420.0 | 89.8 | 2.0 | 8.2 |
| Jersey | • | • | • | ... | • | 10.1[22] | 1984 | 31.3 | —58.9— | | 30.3 | 10.8 | 27.1[19] | ... | ... | ... |
| Jordan | • | | • | | • | 13.2 | 1983 | ... | ... | ... | ... | ... | ... | ... | ... | ... |
| Kampuchea | ... | • | ... | | • | | | ... | ... | ... | ... | ... | ... | ... | ... | ... |
| Kenya | • | | • | | | 0.1 | 1977 | 55.9 | 19.6 | 26.5 | 38.1 | 15.8 | 30.9 | 97.2 | 2.8 | — |
| Kiribati | • | | • | | | ... | | ... | ... | ... | ... | ... | ... | ... | ... | ... |
| Korea, North | • | • | • | | | ... | | ... | ... | ... | ... | ... | ... | ... | ... | ... |
| Korea, South | | | • | | | 5.3 | 1984 | 157,400.0 | ... | ... | ... | ... | ... | ... | ... | ... |
| Kuwait | • | | | | | 5.3 | 1984 | ... | ... | ... | ... | ... | ... | ... | ... | ... |
| Laos | ... | ... | ... | | ... | | | ... | ... | ... | ... | ... | ... | ... | ... | ... |
| Lebanon | • | • | • | | • | | | ... | ... | ... | ... | ... | ... | ... | ... | ... |
| Lesotho | • | ... | ... | | ... | 1.0 | 1983 | — | ... | ... | ... | ... | ... | ... | ... | ... |
| Liberia | • | • | • | | | 0.7 | 1984 | — | ... | ... | ... | ... | ... | ... | ... | ... |
| Libya | • | • | • | | | ... | 1977 | 192.9 | 9.1 | 28.7 | 58.7 | 3.5 | 128.2 | 96.2 | 3.2 | 0.5 |
| Liechtenstein | • | • | • | • | • | ... | | ... | ... | ... | ... | ... | ... | ... | ... | ... |
| Luxembourg | • | • | • | • | • | 47.4[2] | 1980 | 35,758.5 | 23.8 | 37.2 | 25.2 | 13.7 | 32,560.9 | 95.9 | 3.3 | 0.8 |
| Macau | | | | | | | 1981 | ... | ... | ... | ... | ... | ... | ... | ... | ... |
| Madagascar | • | ... | • | ... | • | 10.3[25] | 1982 | 19,534.0 | ... | ... | ... | ... | ... | ... | ... | ... |
| Malawi | | | • | | | 1.1 | | ... | ... | ... | ... | ... | ... | ... | ... | ... |
| Malaysia | • | | • | | | 2.6[3] | 1980 | 2,130.3 | —63.6— | | 0.3 | 36.0 | 512.7 | 85.3 | 3.4 | 11.3 |
| Maldives | | | | | • | 1.2 | 1983 | ... | ... | ... | ... | ... | ... | ... | ... | ... |
| Mali | • | • | • | • | • | 4.6[2,8] | 1980 | 4,541.0 | 8.5 | 79.4 | 10.7 | 1.4 | 4,837.0 | 58.4 | 32.9 | 8.7 |
| Malta | • | • | • | • | • | 36.7 | 1980 | 52.6 | 28.1 | 33.9 | 38.1 | — | 43.6 | 99.2 | 0.8 | — |
| Martinique | • | ... | ... | | • | | | ... | ... | ... | ... | ... | ... | ... | ... | ... |
| Mauritania | • | • | • | | | 3.7[9] | 1983 | 685.5 | ... | ... | ... | ... | 523.9 | ... | ... | ... |
| Mauritius | • | • | • | | | 16.0[8] | 1977 | 344.6 | 6.6 | 25.3 | 64.9 | 3.2 | 301.8 | 99.0 | 0.5 | 0.5 |
| Mayotte | • | ... | ... | | • | | | ... | ... | ... | ... | ... | ... | ... | ... | ... |
| Mexico | • | • | • | | • | 9.5 | 1983 | 424,500.0 | ... | ... | ... | ... | 397,300.0 | ... | ... | ... |
| Monaco | ... | ... | ... | | ... | | | ... | ... | ... | ... | ... | ... | ... | ... | ... |
| Mongolia | • | • | • | | | | | ... | ... | ... | ... | ... | ... | ... | ... | ... |
| Montserrat | • | • | ... | | | | | ... | ... | ... | ... | ... | ... | ... | ... | ... |
| Morocco | • | • | • | | • | 6.1[8] | 1980 | 1,446.7 | —89.8— | | 0.2 | 10.0 | 807.6 | 89.3 | 10.7 | 0.1 |
| Mozambique | • | ... | ... | | | | | ... | ... | ... | ... | ... | ... | ... | ... | ... |
| Nauru | | | | | | | | ... | ... | ... | ... | ... | ... | ... | ... | ... |
| Nepal | • | | | | | 0.6 | 1982 | ... | ... | ... | ... | ... | ... | ... | ... | ... |
| Netherlands, The | • | • | • | • | • | 35.8 | 1980 | 113,621.6 | 33.2 | 33.2 | 24.7 | 8.9 | 95,237.9 | 96.5 | 3.4 | 0.1 |
| Netherlands Antilles | • | • | • | ... | | 8.7[7,9] | 1982 | 124.4 | ... | ... | ... | ... | ... | ... | ... | ... |
| New Caledonia | ... | ... | ... | | • | | | ... | ... | ... | ... | ... | ... | ... | ... | ... |
| New Zealand | • | • | • | • | • | 27.4 | 1980 | 3,898.6 | 3.1 | 4.7 | 89.7 | 2.4 | 3,469.8 | 98.0 | 1.8 | 0.3 |
| Nicaragua | • | • | • | | | 3.3[16] | 1980 | 711.2 | 21.2 | 58.1 | 16.3 | 4.5 | 497.8 | 88.4 | 11.6 | ... |
| Niger | • | • | • | | • | 1.7[8,16] | 1980 | 3,823.5 | 8.4 | 80.4 | — | 11.2 | 1,594.6 | 84.1 | 15.9 | — |
| Nigeria | • | | • | | | 2.5[28] | 1978 | ... | ... | ... | ... | ... | ... | ... | ... | ... |
| Niue | • | ... | ... | | | | | ... | ... | ... | ... | ... | ... | ... | ... | ... |
| Norfolk Island | | | | | | | | ... | ... | ... | ... | ... | ... | ... | ... | ... |
| Norway | • | • | • | • | • | 35.4[8] | 1980 | 59,512.6 | 21.0 | 34.6 | 42.9 | 1.5 | 57,467.2 | 97.9 | 2.1 | — |
| Oman | | | | | | — | 1984 | ... | ... | ... | ... | ... | ... | ... | ... | ... |
| Pacific Is., Trust Territory of the | • | | | | | | | ... | ... | ... | ... | ... | ... | ... | ... | ... |
| Marshall Islands | • | | | | | | | ... | ... | ... | ... | ... | ... | ... | ... | ... |
| Micronesia, Fed. States of | • | ... | ... | | ... | | | ... | ... | ... | ... | ... | ... | ... | ... | ... |

| police protection (latest) | | | fire protection (latest) | | | military protection | | | | | | | | country |
|---|---|---|---|---|---|---|---|---|---|---|---|---|---|---|
| | | | | | | manpower, 1986[d] | | expenditure, 1984 | | | | arms trade, 1985 ('000,000 U.S.$) | | |
| offenses (reported to police) per 100,000 population | population per police officer[b] | government expenditure per 1,000 population (U.S.$) | fire alarms per 100,000 population | population per fire fighter[c] | government expenditure per 1,000 population (U.S.$) | total ('000) | per 1,000 population | total '000,000 U.S.$ | per capita | % of national budget | % of GDP or GNP | imports | exports | |
| 2,002 | 440 | 24,800 | ... | 2,600 | ... | 2.7 | 3.8 | 17 | 25 | 4.6 | 1.3 | 0 | 0 | Fiji |
| 5,449 | 640 | 44,927 | 10 | 1,300 | 4,478 | 34.9 | 7.1 | 790 | 162 | 5.0 | 1.5 | 90 | 0 | Finland |
| 6,488 | 630 | ... | ... | 2,840 | ... | 557.5 | 10.1 | 22,350 | 407 | 9.0 | 4.1 | 100 | 3,300 | France |
| ... | ... | ... | ... | ... | ... | — | [4] | — | ... | ... | | ... | ... | French Guiana |
| ... | ... | ... | ... | ... | ... | — | [4] | — | | | | ... | ... | French Polynesia |
| 134 | 1,290 | ... | ... | ... | ... | 2.7 | 2.3 | 71 | 63 | 4.9 | 2.1 | 140 | 0 | Gabon |
| ... | 3,310 | ... | ... | ... | ... | 0.5[10] | 0.6[10] | 2[3] | 3[3] | 3.6[3] | 1.3[3] | 0 | 0 | Gambia, The |
| 4,355 | ... | ... | ... | ... | ... | ... | ... | ... | ... | ... | ... | ... | ... | Gaza Strip |
| 681 | ... | ... | ... | ... | ... | 179.0 | 10.8 | 10,680 | 641 | 11.6 | 6.3 | 400 | 290 | Germany, East |
| 6,755 | ... | ... | ... | ... | ... | 485.8 | 8.0 | 22,780 | 372 | 10.5 | 3.3 | 700 | 575 | Germany, West |
| ... | 620 | ... | ... | 4,330 | ... | 11.2 | 0.9 | 361 | 29 | 5.8 | 0.6 | 0 | 0 | Ghana |
| 8,140 | 170 | ... | 814 | 220 | ... | — | [4] | — | ... | ... | [4] | ... | ... | Gibraltar |
| 3,562 | 380 | 501,048 | ... | ... | ... | 209.0 | 20.9 | 2,664 | 269 | 16.8 | 7.2 | 280 | 0 | Greece |
| 12,460 | 340 | 109,098 | ... | 3,580 | 117,380[19] | — | [4] | ... | ... | ... | — | ... | ... | Greenland |
| 1,457 | 230 | 15,202 | ... | ... | ... | — | — | ... | ... | ... | ... | ... | ... | Grenada |
| ... | ... | ... | ... | ... | ... | — | [4] | — | — | — | — | ... | ... | Guadeloupe |
| ... | ... | ... | ... | ... | ... | — | [4] | — | — | — | — | ... | ... | Guam |
| ... | 670 | ... | ... | ... | ... | 32.0 | 3.9 | 179 | 23 | 14.9 | 1.9 | 10 | 0 | Guatemala |
| ... | ... | ... | ... | ... | ... | — | [4] | — | — | — | — | ... | ... | Guernsey |
| ... | 1,140 | ... | ... | ... | ... | 9.9[10] | 1.6[10] | 57[2] | 10[2] | 7.9[2] | 3.3[2] | 20 | 0 | Guinea |
| ... | ... | ... | ... | ... | ... | 8.6 | 9.6 | 7[18] | 9[18] | 8.4[18] | 4.5[18] | 20 | 0 | Guinea-Bissau |
| 5,287 | 190 | ... | ... | ... | ... | 5.5 | 6.9 | 24 | 31 | 5.9[2] | 4.8 | 10 | 0 | Guyana |
| 701 | 400 | ... | ... | ... | ... | 6.9 | 1.3 | 27 | 5 | 8.9 | 1.6 | 20 | 0 | Haiti |
| ... | 1,040 | ... | ... | ... | ... | 19.2 | 4.3 | 124 | 29 | 16.4 | 4.2 | 20 | 0 | Honduras |
| 1,471 | 220 | 76,780 | 271 | 900 | 9,589 | — | [4] | ... | ... | ... | ... | ... | ... | Hong Kong |
| 1,556 | 710 | ... | 94 | ... | ... | 105.0 | 9.9 | 3,286 | 308 | 7.6 | 4.1 | 30 | 190 | Hungary |
| 1,550 | 940 | ... | ... | ... | ... | — | — | — | — | — | — | 0 | 0 | Iceland |
| 206 | 820 | ... | ... | ... | ... | 1,260.0 | 1.6 | 7,141 | 10 | 15.6 | 3.6 | 1,900 | 5 | India |
| 137 | 1,340 | 766 | ... | ... | ... | 281.0 | 1.7 | 2,211 | 14 | 12.4 | 2.6 | 60 | 5 | Indonesia |
| ... | [21] | 21,088 | ... | ... | ... | 704.0 | 14.5 | 11,360 | 252 | 29.9 | 7.2 | 800 | 0 | Iran |
| 518 | 140 | ... | ... | ... | ... | 845.0 | 53.0 | 14,640 | 980 | 50.8[18] | 42.5 | 2,100 | 0 | Iraq |
| 2,846 | 310 | 63,050 | ... | ... | ... | 14.1 | 4.0 | 319 | 91 | 3.0 | 1.8 | 5 | 0 | Ireland |
| ... | ... | ... | ... | ... | ... | — | [4] | ... | ... | ... | ... | ... | ... | Isle of Man |
| 5,592 | 210 | 23,099 | 425 | ... | ... | 149.0 | 34.2 | 7,206 | 1,715 | 26.1 | 27.1 | 750 | 210 | Israel |
| 3,363 | 680 | ... | ... | ... | ... | 385.1 | 6.7 | 10,110 | 177 | 4.7 | 2.7 | 120 | 725 | Italy |
| 2,296 | 400 | 15,071 | ... | ... | 2,915 | 2.1 | 0.9 | 27 | 12 | 2.1 | 0.8 | 5 | 0 | Jamaica |
| 1,710 | 480 | 55,594 | 61 | 960 | 25,990 | 243.0 | 2.0 | 12,700 | 106 | 5.4 | 1.0 | 750 | 90 | Japan |
| ... | ... | ... | ... | ... | ... | — | [4] | ... | ... | ... | ... | ... | ... | Jersey |
| 630 | 630 | 27,536 | ... | ... | ... | 70.2 | 25.5 | 749 | 294 | 36.5 | 18.5 | 380 | 0 | Jordan |
| ... | 1,980 | ... | ... | ... | ... | 35.0 | 4.7 | 68[23] | 10[23] | ... | 11.0[23] | 130 | 0 | Kampuchea |
| 434 | 1,500 | ... | ... | ... | ... | 13.7 | 0.6 | 197 | 10 | 12.6 | 3.4 | 5 | 0 | Kenya |
| 2,472 | 330 | ... | ... | 63,980 | ... | ... | ... | ... | ... | ... | ... | ... | ... | Kiribati |
| ... | 460 | ... | ... | ... | ... | 840.0 | 40.2 | 5,200 | 261 | 22.6 | 19.6 | 300 | 210 | Korea, North |
| 1,984 | 420 | ... | 19 | 5,650 | ... | 601.0 | 14.5 | 4,590 | 113 | 26.6 | 5.4 | 380 | 50 | Korea, South |
| 563 | 80 | ... | 101 | ... | ... | 12.0 | 6.7 | 1,438 | 878 | 11.7 | 5.3 | 290 | 0 | Kuwait |
| ... | 280 | ... | ... | ... | ... | 53.0 | 14.4 | 55 | 16 | 21.3 | 10.5 | 20 | 0 | Laos |
| 489 | 530 | ... | ... | ... | ... | 15.3 | 5.7 | 530[2] | 201[2] | 20.0[2] | 8.2[2] | 40 | 0 | Lebanon |
| 1,643 | 1,130 | ... | ... | ... | ... | — | — | 57 | 38 | 28.5 | 6.5 | 0 | 0 | Lesotho |
| ... | 1,570 | ... | ... | ... | ... | 6.8 | 3.0 | 22 | 10 | 7.0 | 2.3 | 10 | 0 | Liberia |
| 1,022 | ... | 26,667 | ... | ... | ... | 71.5 | 18.1 | 5,101 | 1,408 | 40.0 | 17.8 | 1,300 | 40 | Libya |
| ... | 660 | ... | ... | ... | ... | — | [24] | ... | ... | ... | ... | ... | ... | Liechtenstein |
| 3,947 | 730 | 15,067 | 299 | 3,220 | ... | 0.7 | 1.9 | 42 | 115 | 2.3 | 0.9 | 0 | 0 | Luxembourg |
| 823 | ... | ... | 17 | 1,380 | ... | — | [4] | ... | ... | ... | ... | ... | ... | Macau |
| ... | 2,900 | ... | ... | ... | ... | 21.1 | 2.0 | 72 | 7 | 10.3 | 2.6 | 20 | 0 | Madagascar |
| 1,005 | 1,670 | ... | ... | ... | ... | 5.3 | 0.7 | 21 | 3 | 5.7 | 1.7 | 5 | 0 | Malawi |
| 607 | 760 | ... | ... | ... | ... | 110.0 | 6.8 | 1,193 | 78 | 10.3 | 3.8 | 450 | 0 | Malaysia |
| 3,989 | 35,710 | 2,003 | ... | — | ... | 0.8 | 4.4 | ... | ... | ... | ... | ... | ... | Maldives |
| ... | 160 | ... | ... | ... | ... | 5.1 | 0.6 | 24 | 3 | 7.9[2] | 2.1 | 10 | 0 | Mali |
| 1,499 | 230 | 34,223 | ... | ... | ... | 0.8 | 2.3 | 12 | 36 | 2.6 | 1.0 | 0 | 0 | Malta |
| ... | ... | ... | ... | ... | ... | — | [4] | — | — | — | — | ... | ... | Martinique |
| ... | 710 | ... | ... | ... | ... | 8.5 | 5.0 | 39[2] | 25[2] | 17.1[2] | 5.3[2] | 0 | 0 | Mauritania |
| 2,366 | 240 | ... | ... | ... | ... | — | — | 3 | 3 | 0.9 | 0.3 | 0 | 0 | Mauritius |
| ... | ... | ... | ... | ... | ... | — | [4] | ... | ... | ... | ... | ... | ... | Mayotte |
| 315 | ... | ... | 24 | ... | ... | 139.5 | 1.8 | 966 | 13 | 2.6 | 0.7 | 30 | 0 | Mexico |
| 3,392 | ... | ... | ... | ... | ... | — | — | ... | ... | ... | ... | ... | ... | Monaco |
| ... | 120 | ... | ... | ... | ... | 25.5 | 13.2 | 228 | 124 | 14.0 | 11.5 | 0 | 0 | Mongolia |
| 5,626[14] | 110 | 16,901 | ... | ... | ... | — | [4] | ... | ... | ... | ... | ... | ... | Montserrat |
| 589 | 840 | ... | ... | ... | ... | 170.0 | 7.5 | 666 | 31 | 14.9 | 5.0 | 130 | 0 | Morocco |
| ... | ... | ... | ... | ... | ... | 15.8 | 1.1 | 231 | 17 | 43.3 | 8.4 | 130 | 0 | Mozambique |
| ... | 110 | ... | ... | ... | ... | — | — | ... | ... | ... | ... | ... | ... | Nauru |
| 29 | 1,000 | 497 | ... | ... | ... | 30.0 | 1.8 | 32 | 2 | 6.3 | 1.2 | 0 | 0 | Nepal |
| 7,547 | 670 | 72,251 | 230 | ... | ... | 101.2 | 7.0 | 4,510 | 313 | 5.4 | 3.2 | 410 | 60 | Netherlands, The |
| 4,684[26] | 330 | ... | ... | ... | ... | — | [4] | ... | ... | ... | ... | ... | ... | Netherlands Antilles |
| ... | ... | ... | ... | ... | ... | — | [4] | — | — | — | — | ... | ... | New Caledonia |
| 12,509 | 630 | 38,418 | 652 | 1,260 | ... | 12.6 | 3.9 | 469 | 145 | 4.5 | 1.9 | 50 | 0 | New Zealand |
| ... | 90[5] | ... | ... | ... | ... | 72.0 | 21.3 | 473 | 140 | 17.7 | 13.4 | 120 | 0 | Nicaragua |
| 32 | 2,350[27] | ... | ... | ... | ... | 2.3 | 0.3 | 11 | 2 | 4.2 | 0.8 | 0 | 0 | Niger |
| 312 | 1,140 | ... | ... | ... | ... | 94.0 | 1.0 | 1,210 | 13 | 9.0 | 1.7 | 390 | 0 | Nigeria |
| ... | 270 | 20,727 | ... | ... | ... | — | [4] | — | — | — | — | ... | ... | Niue |
| ... | 746 | 27,358 | 1,117 | — | ... | — | [4] | — | — | — | — | ... | ... | Norfolk Island |
| 3,554 | 660 | 78,262 | ... | 1,660 | 27,931 | 37.3 | 9.0 | 1,679 | 406 | 7.1 | 2.9 | 180 | 0 | Norway |
| 162[16] | 430 | ... | ... | ... | ... | 21.5 | 16.7 | 2,111 | 1,769 | 46.6 | 27.7 | 100 | 0 | Oman |
| ... | 320[29] | ... | ... | ... | ... | ... | ... | ... | ... | ... | ... | ... | ... | Pacific Is., Trust Territory of the |
| 2,273 | 400 | ... | ... | ... | ... | — | [30] | — | — | — | — | ... | ... | Marshall Islands |
| ... | ... | ... | ... | ... | ... | — | [30] | — | — | — | — | ... | ... | Micronesia, Fed. States of |

## Social protection (continued)

| country | social security — programs available, 1985 | | | | | expenditures, 1984 (% of total central govt.) | finances year | receipts total ('000,000 natl. cur.) | insured persons (%) | employers (%) | government (%) | other (%) | expenditures total ('000,000 natl. cur.) | benefits (%) | administration (%) | other (%) |
|---|---|---|---|---|---|---|---|---|---|---|---|---|---|---|---|---|
| | old-age invalidity, death | sickness and maternity[a] | work injury | unemployment | family allowances | | | | | | | | | | | |
| Northern Mariana Islands | ● | ... | ... | ... | ... | ... | ... | ... | ... | ... | ... | ... | ... | ... | ... | ... |
| Palau | ● | ... | ... | ... | ... | | | | | | | | | | | |
| Pakistan | ● | ● | ● | | | 0.2 | 1983 | | | | | | | | | |
| Panama | ● | ● | ● | | | 8.2[18] | 1977 | 213.3 | 23.8 | 49.7 | 18.3 | 8.2 | 169.4 | 89.1 | 10.9 | — |
| Papua New Guinea | ● | | ● | | | 0.4 | 1983 | — | | | | | ... | | | |
| Paraguay | ● | ● | ● | | | 30.3 | 1982 | 14,660.0 | ... | ... | ... | ... | 11,278.0 | ... | ... | ... |
| Peru | ● | ● | ● | | | — | 1982 | | | | | | | | | |
| Philippines | ● | ● | ● | ● | | 1.0 | 1980 | 4,487.5 | 30.3 | 42.2 | — | 27.5 | 1,725.9 | 81.2 | 18.8 | — |
| Pitcairn Island | ... | ... | ... | ... | ... | ... | | | | | | | | | | |
| Poland | ● | ● | ● | | ● | ... | 1980 | 325,454.0 | 2.1 | 52.2 | 44.2 | 1.5 | 304,600.0 | 98.8 | 0.5 | 0.7 |
| Portugal | ● | ● | ● | ● | ● | 26.8[8,23] | 1980 | 126,998.7 | 26.2 | 64.2 | 9.3 | 0.4 | 121,222.9 | 90.1 | 9.9 | ... |
| Puerto Rico | ● | ● | ● | ● | | | 1980 | | | | | | 1,041.3 | 100.0 | — | — |
| Qatar | ... | ... | ... | ... | ... | | | ... | ... | ... | ... | ... | ... | ... | ... | ... |
| Réunion | ... | ... | ... | ... | ... | | | | | | | | | | | |
| Romania | ● | ● | ● | | ● | 22.6 | 1980 | 59,386.7 | — | 54.4 | 45.6 | — | 51,743.8 | 100.0 | — | — |
| Rwanda | ● | | ● | | | 2.9[8,16] | 1977 | 593.9 | 24.9 | 41.4 | 25.1 | 8.6 | 191.5 | 88.2 | 11.4 | 0.4 |
| St. Christopher and Nevis | ● | ● | ● | | ... | ... | | | | | | | | | | |
| St. Helena and Ascension | ● | ... | ● | ... | ● | | | | | | | | | | | |
| St. Lucia | ● | ● | ● | | | | 1983 | | | | | | | | | |
| St. Pierre and Miquelon | ... | ... | ... | ... | ... | | | | | | | | | | | |
| St. Vincent and the Grenadines | ● | | ● | | | 2.1[8] | 1983 | — | | | | | ... | ... | ... | ... |
| San Marino | ● | ... | ... | | | ... | | | | | | | | | | |
| São Tomé and Principe | ● | ● | ● | | | ... | | | | | | | | | | |
| Saudi Arabia | ● | | ● | | | ... | | | | | | | | | | |
| Senegal | ● | | ● | | ● | 2.6[2,8] | 1980 | 13,903.2 | 18.1 | 67.0 | 5.5 | 9.5 | 11,223.9 | 78.8 | 8.6 | 12.6 |
| Seychelles | ● | | ● | | | 5.3[11] | 1977 | | | | | | | | | |
| Sierra Leone | ● | | ● | | | 1.7 | 1977 | 10.5 | —26.7— | | 73.3 | — | 10.0 | 100.0 | — | — |
| Singapore | ● | | ● | | | 0.7 | 1980 | 2,244.8 | 36.7 | 44.4 | 0.2 | 18.7 | 786.7 | 89.0 | 1.4 | 9.6 |
| Solomon Islands | ● | | ● | | | 2.6[2,8] | 1983 | — | | | | | | | | |
| Somalia | | | ● | | | 1.7[8,28] | 1978 | — | | | | | | | | |
| South Africa | ● | ● | ● | ● | ● | ... | 1982 | 243.0 | ... | ... | ... | ... | 310.0 | ... | ... | ... |
| Bophuthatswana | ... | ... | ... | ... | ... | ... | | | | | | | | | | |
| Ciskei | ... | ... | ... | ... | ... | ... | | | | | | | | | | |
| KwaNdebele | ... | ... | ... | ... | ... | ... | | | | | | | | | | |
| Transkei | ... | ... | ... | ... | ... | ... | | | | | | | | | | |
| Venda | ... | ... | ... | ... | ... | ... | | | | | | | | | | |
| South West Africa/Namibia | ● | ● | ● | ... | ... | ... | | | | | | | | | | |
| Spain | ● | ● | ● | ● | ● | 62.2[2] | 1980 | 2,400,940.9 | 12.4 | 70.7 | 15.8 | 1.1 | 2,426,506.1 | 95.7 | 2.7 | 1.6 |
| Sri Lanka | ● | ● | ● | | | 10.9[8] | 1980 | 2,092.8 | —38.8— | | 43.6 | 17.6 | 1,141.8 | 95.0 | 4.1 | 0.1 |
| Sudan, The | ● | | ● | | | 2.2[18] | 1982 | | | | | | | | | |
| Suriname | ● | ... | | ● | | 5.7 | 1980 | 46.0 | 25.4 | 32.0 | 42.6 | — | 37.1 | 99.5 | 0.5 | — |
| Swaziland | ● | | ● | | | — | 1983 | | | | | | | | | |
| Sweden | ● | ● | ● | ● | ● | 46.7[8] | 1980 | 183,851.7 | 1.0 | 45.9 | 45.3 | 7.8 | 167,315.8 | 97.5 | 2.5 | — |
| Switzerland | ● | ● | ● | | ● | 49.9 | 1980 | 25,571.1 | 41.2 | 25.5 | 25.5 | 7.8 | 23,415.8 | 93.2 | 2.8 | 4.0 |
| Syria | ● | | ● | | | 8.2[3,8] | 1981 | | | | | | | | | |
| Taiwan | ● | ● | | | | 18.2[8] | ... | | | | | | | | | |
| Tanzania | ● | | ● | | | 0.3 | 1981 | | | | | | | | | |
| Thailand | ● | | ● | | | 3.0 | 1983 | — | | | | | | | | |
| Togo | ● | | ● | | ● | 10.9[8] | 1980 | 4,814.0 | 10.4 | 77.8 | — | 11.9 | 2,350.0 | 78.1 | 21.3 | 0.6 |
| Tokelau | ... | ... | ... | ... | ... | ... | | | | | | | | | | |
| Tonga | | | | | | ... | | | | | | | | | | |
| Trinidad and Tobago | ● | ● | ● | | | 5.3[3] | 1980 | 196.1 | 18.2 | 36.0 | 26.9 | 18.9 | 110.3 | 85.4 | 13.8 | 0.9 |
| Tunisia | ● | ● | ● | ● | ● | 6.2 | 1977 | 124.5 | 25.6 | 53.9 | 3.7 | 16.8 | 67.8 | 90.0 | 6.1 | 3.9 |
| Turkey | ● | ● | ● | | | 0.4 | 1980 | 218,265.1 | 27.9 | 49.9 | 11.3 | 10.8 | 183,922.7 | 95.5 | 4.1 | 0.5 |
| Turks and Caicos Islands | ... | ... | ... | ... | ... | ... | | | | | | | | | | |
| Tuvalu | ● | ... | | | ... | | 1981 | | | | | | 0.1 | 67.6 | 32.4 | — |
| Uganda | ● | | | | | 1.6[8] | 1984 | | | | | | | | | |
| U.S.S.R. | ● | ● | ● | | ● | ... | 1977 | 54,271.0 | — | — | 96.4 | 3.6 | 54,271.0 | 100.0 | — | ... |
| United Arab Emirates | ● | ... | | | | 3.8[8] | 1981 | | | | | | | | | |
| United Kingdom | ● | ● | ● | ● | ● | 25.5[8,9] | 1980 | 35,698.0 | 15.8 | 26.5 | 54.9 | 2.9 | 34,004.0 | 95.2 | 2.8 | 2.0 |
| United States | ● | | ● | ● | ●[34] | 26.7 | 1980 | 370,597.0 | 23.4 | 40.4 | 29.8 | 6.4 | 329,582.0 | 96.1 | 3.1 | 0.8 |
| Uruguay | ● | ● | ● | ● | ● | 42.5 | 1980 | 9,779.5 | 25.1 | 34.0 | 38.3 | 2.6 | 7,550.5 | 91.5 | 7.7 | 0.8 |
| Vanuatu | ... | ... | ... | ... | ... | ... | | | | | | | | | | |
| Venezuela | ● | ● | ● | ● | | 7.6[8] | 1980 | 4,259.3 | 26.8 | 53.5 | 6.8 | 12.9 | 3,336.6 | 86.0 | 14.0 | ... |
| Vietnam | ● | | ● | | | ... | | | | | | | | | | |
| Virgin Islands (U.S.) | ● | | ● | ● | | ... | | | | | | | | | | |
| Wallis and Futuna | ... | ... | ... | ... | ... | | | | | | | | | | | |
| West Bank | ... | ... | ... | ... | ... | | | | | | | | | | | |
| Western Sahara | ... | ... | ... | ... | ... | | | | | | | | | | | |
| Western Samoa | ● | | ● | | | — | | | | | | | | | | |
| Yemen (Aden) | ... | ... | ... | ... | ... | | | | | | | | | | | |
| Yemen (San'ā') | | | | | | ... | 1983 | — | | | | | — | | | |
| Yugoslavia | ● | ● | ● | | ● | 6.3 | 1981 | | | | | | | | | |
| Zaire | ● | | ● | | ● | | 1983 | 145.9 | ... | ... | ... | ... | ... | ... | ... | ... |
| Zambia | ● | | ● | | | — | 1977 | 119.8 | —40.7— | | 47.9 | 11.4 | 89.4 | 95.4 | 4.6 | — |
| Zimbabwe | ... | ... | ● | ... | ... | 3.1 | 1980 | 9.4 | — | 48.8 | 26.0 | 25.2 | 6.8 | 64.5 | 30.6 | 4.8 |

| police protection (latest) | | | fire protection (latest) | | | military protection | | | | | | | | country |
|---|---|---|---|---|---|---|---|---|---|---|---|---|---|---|
| | | | | | | manpower, 1986[d] | | expenditure, 1984 | | | | arms trade, 1985 ('000,000 U.S.$) | | |
| offenses (reported to police) per 100,000 population | population per police officer[b] | government expenditure per 1,000 population (U.S.$) | fire alarms per 100,000 population | population per fire fighter[c] | government expenditure per 1,000 population (U.S.$) | total ('000) | per 1,000 population | total '000,000 U.S.$ | per capita | % of national budget | % of GDP or GNP | imports | exports | |
| ... | ... | ... | 323 | ... | ... | — | 4 | — | — | — | — | ... | ... | Northern Mariana Islands |
| | | | | | | — | 30 | | | | | | | Palau |
| 209 | 720 | 1,954 | ... | ... | ... | 480.6 | 4.6 | 1,990 | 20 | 27.0 | 5.9 | 390 | 30 | Pakistan |
| 448 | 180 | ... | ... | ... | ... | 12.0 | 5.4 | 98 | 46 | 3.8 | 2.4 | 10 | 0 | Panama |
| 834 | 720 | ... | ... | ... | ... | 3.2 | 0.9 | 40 | 12 | 4.7 | 1.7 | 10 | 0 | Papua New Guinea |
| ... | 310 | ... | ... | ... | ... | 16.0 | 4.2 | 118 | 33 | 14.5 | 1.7 | 10 | 0 | Paraguay |
| 424 | 730 | ... | ... | ... | ... | 127.0 | 6.3 | 1,450 | 76 | 47.3 | 7.1 | 80 | 0 | Peru |
| 334 | 1,160 | 2,423 | ... | 9,090 | ... | 113.0 | 2.0 | 396 | 7 | 9.5 | 1.2 | 30 | 0 | Philippines |
| | | | | | | — | 4 | | | | | ... | ... | Pitcairn Island |
| 1,292 | 370 | ... | 56 | ... | ... | 402.0 | 10.7 | 13,440 | 364 | 22.4 | 5.7 | 550 | 700 | Poland |
| 492 | 660 | ... | ... | ... | ... | 68.3 | 6.7 | 680 | 67 | 9.4 | 3.5 | 110 | 100 | Portugal |
| 5,484 | 380 | ... | 229 | 2,870 | ... | — | 4 | — | — | — | — | ... | ... | Puerto Rico |
| 213 | ... | ... | ... | ... | ... | 6.0 | 17.9 | 604[16] | 2,684[16] | 20.1[16] | 9.1[16] | 30 | 0 | Qatar |
| ... | 220 | ... | ... | ... | ... | — | — | | | | | | | Réunion |
| | | | | | | 189.7 | 8.3 | 5,350 | 236 | 19.5 | 4.4 | 20 | 340 | Romania |
| 359 | 4,650 | ... | ... | ... | ... | 5.2 | 0.8 | 33[2] | 6[2] | 14.0[2] | 2.1[2] | 0 | 0 | Rwanda |
| ... | 300 | ... | | | | — | — | | | | | | | St. Christopher and Nevis |
| ... | 170 | 8,368 | ... | 5,150 | — | — | 4 | | | | | | | St. Helena and Ascension |
| ... | 430 | ... | | | | | | | | | | | | St. Lucia |
| ... | ... | ... | ... | ... | ... | — | 4 | | | | | | | St. Pierre and Miquelon |
| ... | 250 | 18,008 | | | | | | | | | | | | St. Vincent and the Grenadines |
| ... | 400 | ... | ... | ... | ... | — | — | | | | | | | San Marino |
| ... | ... | ... | ... | ... | ... | ... | ... | 1[16] | 11[16] | 2.5[16] | 1.6[16] | 0 | 0 | São Tomé and Príncipe |
| 169 | 280 | 131,140 | 60 | ... | ... | 67.5 | 5.6 | 22,220 | 2,003 | 29.0 | 21.3 | 2,500 | 0 | Saudi Arabia |
| 235 | 730 | ... | ... | ... | ... | 9.7 | 1.5 | 63 | 10 | 8.3 | 2.7 | 5 | 0 | Senegal |
| 6,369 | 120 | ... | ... | 2,420 | ... | 1.2 | 18.2 | 8 | 124 | 7.4 | 5.6 | ... | ... | Seychelles |
| ... | 600 | ... | ... | ... | ... | 3.1 | 0.8 | 8 | 2 | 4.2 | 0.7 | 0 | 0 | Sierra Leone |
| 1,413 | 230 | 474,409 | 321 | 2,840 | ... | 55.5 | 21.5 | 1,015 | 401 | 20.9 | 5.3 | 70 | 10 | Singapore |
| ... | 620 | 5,112 | | | | | | | | | | | | Solomon Islands |
| ... | 540 | ... | ... | ... | ... | 42.7 | 7.1 | 106 | 19 | 27.5 | 6.5 | 30 | 0 | Somalia |
| ... | 870 | 28,460 | ... | ... | ... | 106.4 | 3.2 | 3,540 | 111 | 13.2 | 4.2 | 0 | 10 | South Africa |
| | | | | | | | | | | | | | | Bophuthatswana |
| | | | | | | | | | | | | | | Ciskei |
| | | | | | | | | | | | | | | KwaNdebele |
| | | | | | | | | | | | | | | Transkei |
| | | | | | | | | | | | | | | Venda |
| ... | ... | ... | ... | ... | ... | — | 4 | | | | | ... | ... | South West Africa/Namibia |
| 2,172 | 580 | ... | ... | ... | ... | 325.5 | 8.4 | 3,633 | 95 | 7.7 | 2.2 | 130 | 340 | Spain |
| ... | 860 | ... | ... | ... | ... | 21.6 | 1.3 | 86 | 6 | 4.7 | 1.5 | 30 | 0 | Sri Lanka |
| 1,771 | 740 | 12,049 | ... | ... | ... | 56.8 | 2.3 | 134 | 6 | 11.2 | 2.1 | 40 | 0 | Sudan, The |
| ... | 610 | 21,249 | ... | ... | ... | 2.5 | 6.2 | 24 | 63 | 5.4 | 2.4 | 0 | 0 | Suriname |
| ... | ... | ... | ... | ... | ... | 2.7[2] | 4.1[2] | 11 | 17 | 5.6 | 1.6 | 0 | 0 | Swaziland |
| 10,711 | 330 | 176,110 | 189 | 1,230 | ... | 64.7 | 7.7 | 2,928 | 351 | 6.4 | 3.1 | 60 | 210 | Sweden |
| 5,134 | 640 | 135,820 | | | | 20.0 | 3.0 | 2,203 | 339 | 10.0 | 2.0 | 90 | 40 | Switzerland |
| 1,896 | 1,970 | ... | ... | ... | ... | 392.5 | 37.0 | 4,255 | 428 | 41.7 | 22.4 | 925 | 0 | Syria |
| 317 | 720 | ... | ... | 1,040 | ... | 424.0 | 21.8 | 3,867 | 205 | 44.7 | 6.6 | 575 | 0 | Taiwan |
| 64 | 1,330 | 1,953 | ... | ... | ... | 40.4 | 1.8 | 215 | 10 | 12.8 | 3.3 | 20 | 0 | Tanzania |
| 1,155 | 530 | 4,262 | ... | ... | ... | 256.0 | 4.9 | 1,682 | 33 | 19.8 | 3.9 | 140 | 0 | Thailand |
| 11 | 1,970 | ... | ... | ... | ... | 5.1 | 1.7 | 18 | 6 | 6.2 | 2.5 | 0 | 0 | Togo |
| ... | 210 | ... | ... | ... | ... | — | 4 | | | | | | | Tokelau |
| ... | 330 | 7,139 | ... | ... | ... | — | 31 | | | | | | | Tonga |
| 3,744 | 280 | 142,083 | ... | ... | ... | 2.1 | 1.7 | 189 | 162 | 6.0 | 2.7 | 0 | 0 | Trinidad and Tobago |
| 1,408 | 340 | ... | ... | ... | ... | 37.0 | 5.0 | 274 | 39 | 7.5 | 3.2 | 300 | 0 | Tunisia |
| 179 | 1,570 | ... | ... | ... | — | 654.4 | 12.7 | 2,467 | 50 | 17.6 | 4.5 | 390 | 90 | Turkey |
| ... | 90 | 20,611 | ... | ... | ... | — | 4 | | | | | | | Turks and Caicos Islands |
| ... | 290 | 13,069 | ... | — | ... | | | | | | | | | Tuvalu |
| ... | 1,090 | 1,173 | ... | ... | ... | 18.0[10] | 1.2[10] | 78 | 6 | 16.6 | 1.1 | 0 | 0 | Uganda |
| ... | 1,050[32] | ... | 42 | ... | ... | 5,130.0 | 18.3 | 260,000 | 945 | 47.5 | 12.6 | 775 | 8,900 | U.S.S.R. |
| 1,297 | 140 | ... | ... | ... | ... | 43.0 | 25.3 | 1,932 | 1,357 | 40.2 | 7.4 | 60 | 0 | United Arab Emirates |
| 7,310 | 400 | 79,281[33] | ... | 1,430 | 18,439[33] | 323.8 | 5.7 | 25,410 | 450 | 12.7 | 5.3 | 470 | 575 | United Kingdom |
| 5,207 | 350 | 87,940 | 989 | 1,060 | 27,469 | 2,144.0 | 8.9 | 237,100 | 1,000 | 26.4 | 6.3 | 575 | 9,400 | United States |
| ... | 170 | ... | 79 | ... | ... | 31.9 | 10.5 | 144 | 48 | 10.9 | 2.9 | 0 | 0 | Uruguay |
| ... | 450 | ... | ... | ... | ... | — | — | | | | | | | Vanuatu |
| 837 | 320 | ... | ... | ... | ... | 71.0 | 4.0 | 1,067 | 63 | 5.7 | 1.6 | 330 | 0 | Venezuela |
| ... | ... | ... | ... | ... | ... | 1,155.0 | 18.9 | 1,300 | 22 | ... | 10.5[16] | 650 | 10 | Vietnam |
| 3,798 | 240 | 126,972 | 980 | 680 | ... | — | 4 | | | | | ... | ... | Virgin Islands (U.S.) |
| ... | ... | ... | ... | ... | ... | — | 4 | | | | | | | Wallis and Futuna |
| 2,226 | ... | ... | | | | | | | | | | | | West Bank |
| ... | ... | ... | ... | ... | ... | — | 4 | | | | | | | Western Sahara |
| ... | ... | 6,997 | ... | ... | ... | — | 31 | | | | | | | Western Samoa |
| ... | 1,440 | ... | ... | ... | ... | 27.5 | 11.6 | 198 | 89 | 21.0[2] | 17.0 | 210 | 0 | Yemen (Aden) |
| ... | 500 | 1,905 | ... | ... | ... | 36.6 | 5.2 | 572 | 86 | 29.0 | 12.7 | 90 | 0 | Yemen (Şan'ā') |
| 1,116 | 140 | ... | ... | ... | ... | 210.0 | 9.0 | 1,791 | 78 | 49.8 | 3.6 | 20 | 310 | Yugoslavia |
| ... | 910 | ... | ... | ... | ... | 50.4 | 1.6 | 85 | 3 | 5.2 | 1.2 | 20 | 0 | Zaire |
| 2,569 | 540 | 3,960 | ... | ... | ... | 16.2 | 2.3 | 209 | 32 | 20.9 | 6.6 | 10 | 0 | Zambia |
| 1,425 | 750 | 12,457 | ... | ... | ... | 42.0 | 5.0 | 382 | 48 | 15.0 | 6.2 | 0 | 0 | Zimbabwe |

[1]Rural areas only. [2]1983. [3]1981. [4]Political dependency; defense is the responsibility of the administering country. [5]Includes civilian militia. [6]1971. [7]Netherlands Antilles includes Aruba. [8]Includes welfare. [9]1979. [10]1985. [11]1977. [12]1976. [13]Local officers only. [14]Offenses disposed of in court. [15]Military defense is the responsibility of France. [16]1980. [17]Excludes Turkish-occupied Cyprus. [18]1982. [19]Benefits paid only. [20]Coverage is through tax system. [21]340 in urban areas; 270 in rural areas. [22]1984. [23]1975. [24]Military defense is the responsibility of Switzerland. [25]1974. [26]Curaçao only. [27]Includes paramilitary forces. [28]1978. [29]Marshall Islands and Palau only. [30]Military defense is the responsibility of the United States. [31]Military defense is the responsibility of New Zealand. [32]MVD (internal security) only. [33]England and Wales only. [34]Federal-state system.

# Education

This table presents international data on education analyzed to provide maximum comparability among the different educational systems in use among the nations of the world. The principal data are, naturally, numbers of schools, teachers, and students, arranged by four principal levels of education—the first, or primary; general second level (secondary); vocational second level; and third level (higher). The ratio of students to teachers is calculated for each level. These data are supplemented at each level by a figure for enrollment ratio, an indicator of each country's achieved capability to educate the total number of children potentially educable in the age group usually represented by that level. At the first and second levels this is given as a net enrollment ratio and at the third level as a gross enrollment ratio. Two additional comparative measures are given at the third level: students per 100,000 population and proportion (percent) of adults age 25 and over who have achieved some level of higher or postsecondary education. Data in this last group are confined as far as possible to those who have completed their educations and are no longer in school. No enrollment ratio is provided for vocational training at the second level because of the great variation worldwide in the academic level at which vocational training takes place, in the need of countries to encourage or direct students into vocational programs (to support national development), and, most particularly, in the age range of students who normally constitute a national vocational system (some will be as young as 14, having just completed a primary cycle; others will be much older). At each level of education, differences in national statistical practice, in national educational structure, public-private institutional mix, training

and deployment of teachers, and timing of cycles of enrollment or completion of particular grades or standards all contribute to the problems of comparability among national educational systems.

Reporting the number of schools in a country is not simply a matter of counting permanent red-brick buildings with classrooms in them. Often the resources of a less developed country are such that temporary or outdoor facilities are all that can be afforded, while in a developed but sparsely settled country students might have to travel 80 km (50 mi) a day to find a classroom with 20 students of the same age, leading to the institution of measures such as traveling teachers, radio or televisual instruction at home under the supervision of parents, or similar systems. According to UNESCO definitions, therefore, a "school" is defined only as "a body of students . . . organized to receive instruction . . . ."

Such difficulties also limit the comparability of statistics on numbers of teachers, with the further complications that many at any level must work part-time, or that the institutions in which they work may perform a mixture of functions that do not break down into the tidy categories required by a table of this sort. In certain countries teacher training is confined to higher education, in others as a vocational form of secondary training, and so on. For purposes of this table, teacher training at the secondary level has been treated as vocational education. At the higher level, teacher training is classified as one more specialization in higher education itself.

The number of students may conceal great variation in what each country defines as a particular educational "level." Many countries do, indeed,

## Education

| country | year | first level (primary) | | | | | general second level (secondary) | | | | | vocational second level[a] | |
|---|---|---|---|---|---|---|---|---|---|---|---|---|---|
| | | schools | teachers[c] | students[d] | student/ teacher ratio | net enroll- ment ratio | schools | teachers[c] | students[d] | student/ teacher ratio | net enroll- ment ratio | schools | teachers[c] |
| Afghanistan | 1984 | 754 | 14,865 | 545,959 | 36.7 | 14 | 332 | 6,943 | 99,729 | 14.4 | ... | 16 | 666 |
| Albania | 1984 | 1,631 | 27,387 | 540,332 | 19.7 | ... | 20 | 1,552 | 35,643 | 23.0 | ... | 313 | 5,405 |
| Algeria | 1984 | 10,266 | 109,173 | 3,336,536 | 30.6 | 84 | 1,429[2] | 61,098 | 1,452,389 | 23.8 | 28[3] | 71[4] | 2,292[4] |
| American Samoa | 1986 | 33 | 346[2] | 7,725 | 20.9[2] | ... | 7 | 186[2] | 3,187 | 16.4[2] | ... | 1[5] | 4[5] |
| Andorra | 1987 | 13 | 214[7] | 5,344 | 24.8[7] | ... | 10 | 53[7] | 2,253 | 20.5[7] | ... | 5 | 37[7] |
| Angola | 1983 | 6,308 | 32,004 | 1,178,430 | 36.8 | 66[1] | ... | 3,870[1] | 124,858 | ... | ... | ... | 410[1] |
| Anguilla | 1986 | 6 | 66 | 1,483 | 22.5 | ... | 1 | 39 | 634 | 16.3 | ... | ... | ... |
| Antigua and Barbuda | 1983 | 48 | 426 | 9,933 | 23.3 | ... | 16 | 331 | 4,197 | 12.7 | ... | 1 | ... |
| Argentina | 1984 | 20,619 | 218,520 | 4,430,513 | 20.3 | 96[9] | 1,987[10] | 86,874[10] | 656,521[10] | 7.6[10] | 42[9] | 3,117[10] | 119,309[10] |
| Aruba | 1983 | 33 | 373 | 6,763 | 18.1 | ... | 10 | 189 | 3,082 | 16.3 | ... | 3 | 65 |
| Australia | 1987 | 8,466 | 95,606 | 1,711,932 | 17.9 | 97[6] | 1,619 | 101,115 | 1,289,457 | 12.8 | 84[6] | 234[11] | 52,587[11] |
| Austria | 1987 | 3,738 | 33,100 | 350,726 | 10.6 | 86[6] | 1,714 | 52,430 | 473,467 | 9.0 | 68[12] | 1,209 | 22,880 |
| Bahamas, The | 1983 | 187 | 1,972 | 37,097 | 18.8 | ... | 38 | 1,334 | 23,202 | 17.4 | ... | ... | ... |
| Bahrain | 1985 | 114 | 2,963 | 49,644 | 16.8 | 90[6] | 21 | 951 | 32,927 | 34.6 | 61[2] | 5 | 233 |
| Bangladesh | 1985 | 44,488 | 184,575 | 10,082,000 | 54.6 | 54 | 8,649 | 97,774 | 2,638,000 | 27.0 | 17 | 158[13] | 2,851[6] |
| Barbados | 1985 | 130 | 1,464 | 30,792 | 21.0 | 99[1] | 36 | 1,449 | 28,815 | 19.9 | 89[6] | 3 | 154 |
| Belgium | 1985 | 4,790 | 45,261[6] | 768,207 | ... | 93[6] | 2,272 | 56,719[2] | 858,625 | ... | 86[6] | 209[2] | 6,364[2] |
| Belize | 1985 | 225 | 1,582 | 38,512 | 24.3 | ... | 24 | 504 | 6,676 | 13.2 | ... | 5[15] | 62[15] |
| Benin | 1984 | 2,667 | 13,269 | 444,232 | 33.5 | 46 | 133[1] | 2,409 | 112,267 | 46.6 | ... | 30[1] | 609 |
| Bermuda | 1987 | 22 | 314 | 5,258 | 16.7 | ... | 12 | 337 | 4,005 | 11.9 | ... | 16 | 16 |
| Bhutan | 1985 | 143 | 1,082 | 33,934 | 31.4 | 8[3] | 30 | 589 | 16,377 | 27.8 | ... | 8 | 103 |
| Bolivia | 1983 | 8,514 | 50,703 | 1,154,819 | 22.8 | 81[6] | 845 | 8,091 | 174,982 | 21.6 | 25[6] | ... | ... |
| Botswana | 1986 | 528 | 6,980 | 223,608 | 32.0 | 76[2] | 65 | 1,283 | 32,172 | 25.1 | 18[2] | 24 | 283 |
| Brazil | 1985 | 187,274 | 1,040,566 | 24,769,736 | 23.8 | 83[6] | 9,260 | 206,111 | 3,016,138 | 14.6 | 14[2] | ... | ... |
| British Virgin Islands | 1986 | 27 | 135 | 2,399 | 17.8 | ... | 4 | 76 | 1,140 | 15.0 | ... | — | — |
| Brunei | 1984 | 178 | 2,131 | 34,373 | 16.1 | ... | 28 | 1,526 | 18,565 | 12.2 | ... | 7[15] | 275[15] |
| Bulgaria | 1986 | 3,040 | 71,400[17] | 1,248,000[17] | 17.4[17] | 97[6] | 481 | [17] | 41,559 | [17] | 78[6] | 506 | 17,884[6] |
| Burkina Faso | 1985 | 1,037 | 5,354 | 313,520 | 58.6 | 25[6] | 68 | 1,213 | 41,559 | 26.8 | 3[6] | 27 | 504 |
| Burma | 1985 | 27,499 | 104,754 | 4,855,963 | 46.4 | 65[12] | 2,238 | 41,668 | 1,251,482 | 30.0 | 16[12] | 74 | 1,036 |
| Burundi | 1986 | 1,023 | 7,245 | 387,710 | 53.5 | 39[6] | 62 | 795 | 13,037 | 16.4 | 2[4] | 47 | 1,064 |
| Cameroon | 1985 | 5,582[6] | 32,082 | 1,638,569 | 51.1 | 75[3] | 365[6] | 8,381 | 238,075 | 28.4 | 15[5] | 199[6] | 3,239 |
| Canada | 1988 | 15,512[17] | 273,190[17] | 4,959,000[17] | 18.1[17] | 97[2] | [17] | [17] | [17] | [17] | 88[4] | [17] | [17] |
| Cape Verde | 1983 | 436 | 1,459 | 50,000 | 34.3 | 89 | 16 | 603 | 10,454 | 17.3 | ... | 4 | 76 |
| Cayman Islands | 1987 | 16 | 123 | 2,094 | 17.0 | ... | 7 | 159 | 2,278 | 14.3 | ... | 1 | 9 |
| Central African Republic | 1985 | 960 | 4,263[6] | 308,022 | ... | 60[1] | 39 | 675 | 55,787 | 82.6 | ... | 4 | 122 |
| Chad | 1984 | 783[12] | 2,610[12] | 288,478 | 77.0[12] | 25[18] | ... | 590[12] | 43,053 | 31.2[12] | ... | ... | ... |
| Chile | 1984 | 8,862 | 62,746[1] | 2,092,069 | ... | 92 | 1,401 | ... | 581,243 | ... | 46[2] | 369 | ... |
| China | 1985 | 832,309 | 5,370,000 | 133,702,000 | 24.9 | ... | 93,221 | 2,652,000 | 47,060,000 | 17.7 | ... | 11,627 | 315,000 |
| Christmas Island | 1985 | 2 | 30 | 261 | 8.7 | ... | 1 | 12 | 114 | 9.5 | ... | 1 | 7 |
| Cocos (Keeling) Islands | 1986 | 2 | 8 | 105 | 13.1 | ... | 1 | 5 | 30 | 6.0 | ... | 1 | 1 |
| Colombia | 1986 | 36,979 | 135,924 | 4,002,543 | 29.4 | 75[11] | 6,336[19] | 107,084[19] | 2,136,239[19] | 19.9[19] | ... | 19 | 19 |
| Comoros | 1981 | 236 | 1,292 | 59,709 | 46.2 | ... | 32 | 434 | 13,528 | 31.2 | ... | 4 | 27 |
| Congo | 1985 | 1,522 | 7,612 | 458,338 | 60.2 | ... | 247 | 5,188 | 199,073 | 38.4 | ... | 19 | 1,073 |
| Cook Islands | 1986 | 30 | 165 | 3,183 | 19.3 | ... | 8 | 146 | 2,156 | 14.8 | ... | ... | ... |
| Costa Rica | 1984 | 3,068 | 12,223 | 353,958 | 29.0 | 89[1] | 241[19] | 9,152[19] | 148,032[19] | 16.2[19] | 37[1] | 19 | 19 |
| Côte d'Ivoire | 1985 | 4,419[5] | 31,297[1] | 1,179,456 | ... | ... | 218[5] | 4,569[5] | 245,342 | ... | ... | 38[5] | 1,947[4] |
| Cuba | 1986 | 10,187 | 77,100 | 1,077,200 | 14.0 | 95[6] | 1,287 | 65,900 | 807,600 | 12.3 | 61[20] | 639 | 27,500 |
| Cyprus | 1986 | 380 | 2,225 | 50,990 | 22.9 | ... | 92 | 2,622 | 41,399 | 15.8 | ... | 15 | 463 |
| Czechoslovakia | 1987 | 6,274 | 97,385 | 2,088,750 | 21.4 | ... | 343 | 9,723 | 134,103 | 13.8 | ... | 561 | 17,044 |
| Denmark | 1985 | 2,557 | 34,541 | 415,148 | 12.0 | ... | 3,247 | 36,105 | 339,835 | 9.4 | 75[2] | 282 | ... |
| Djibouti | 1986 | 58 | 514 | 25,212 | 49.1 | ... | 8 | 306 | 6,234 | 20.4 | ... | 12 | 110 |
| Dominica | 1983 | 58 | 635 | 18,370 | 28.9 | ... | 8 | 145 | 3,234 | 22.3 | ... | 1 | 13 |
| Dominican Republic | 1984 | 4,846 | 20,607 | 1,121,851 | 54.4 | 73[2] | ... | ... | 352,328 | ... | ... | ... | 635 |
| Ecuador | 1985 | 15,969 | 58,584 | 1,973,445 | 33.7 | 87[3] | 2,056[19] | 49,641[19] | 860,419[19] | 17.3[19] | 28[9] | 19 | 19 |
| Egypt | 1983 | 12,613 | 170,904 | 5,349,579 | 31.3 | ... | 2,715[4] | 101,107 | 2,436,646 | 24.1 | ... | 519[4] | 48,605 |

have a primary system comprised of grades 1 through 6 (or 1 through 8) that passes students on to some kind of post-primary education. But the age of intake, the ability of parents to send their children or to permit them to finish that level, or the need to withdraw the children seasonally for agricultural work all make even a simple enrollment figure difficult to assess in isolation. All of these difficulties are compounded when a country has instruction in more than one language, or when its educational establishment is so small that higher, sometimes even secondary, education cannot take place within the country. Enrollment figures in this table may, therefore, include students enrolled outside the country.

Student-teacher ratio, however, usually provides a good measure of the ratio of trained educators to the enrolled educable. In general, at each level of education both students and teachers have been counted on the basis of full-time enrollment or employment, or full-time equivalent when country statistics permit. At the primary and secondary levels, net enrollment ratio is the ratio of the number of children within the usual age group for a particular level who are actually enrolled to the total number of children in that age group (× 100). This ratio is usually less than (occasionally, equal to) 100 and is the most accurate measure of the completeness of enrollment at that particular level. It is not always, however, the best indication of utilization of teaching staff and facilities. Utilization, provided here for higher education only, is best seen in a gross enrollment ratio, which compares total enrollment (of all ages) to the population within the normal age limits for that level. For a country with substantial adult literacy or general educational programs, the difference

may be striking: typically, for a less developed country, even one with a good net enrollment ratio of 90 to 95, the gross enrollment ratio may be 20, 25, even 30% higher, indicating the heavy use made by the country of facilities and teachers at that level.

Literacy data provided here have been compiled as far as possible from data for the population age 15 and over for the best comparability internationally. Standards as to what constitutes literacy may also differ markedly; sometimes completion of a certain number of years of school is taken to constitute literacy; elsewhere it may mean only the ability to read or write at a minimal level testable by a census taker; in other countries studies have been undertaken to distinguish among degrees of functional literacy.

Finally, the data provided for public expenditure on education are complete in that they include all levels of public expenditure (national, state, local) but are incomplete for certain countries in that they do not include data for private expenditure; in some countries this fraction of the educational establishment may be of significant size. Occasionally data for external aid to education may be included in addition to domestic expenditure.

a. Usually includes teacher training at the second level.
b. Latest.
c. Full-time.
d. Full-time; may include students registered in foreign schools.

| students[d] | student/ teacher ratio | third level (higher) | | | | | | | literacy[b] | | | | public expenditure on education (percent of GNP)[b] | country |
| | | institutions | teachers[c] | students[d] | student/ teacher ratio | gross enroll- ment ratio | students per 100,000 popula- tion[b] | percent of population age 25 and over with post- secondary education[b] | over age | total (%) | male (%) | female (%) | | |
|---|---|---|---|---|---|---|---|---|---|---|---|---|---|---|
| 7,360 | 11.1 | 5 | 1,283 | 13,450 | 10.5 | 1.4[1] | 121 | 3.0 | 15 | 20.0 | 33.2 | 5.8 | 1.8 | Afghanistan |
| 123,797 | 22.9 | 8 | 1,502 | 21,285 | 14.2 | 7.0 | 713 | ... | 15 | 71.5 | 79.9 | 63.1 | ... | Albania |
| 26,216[4] | 11.4[4] | 15[1] | 12,509 | 104,285 | 8.3 | 5.8 | 529 | 0.3 | 15 | 49.6 | 63.0 | 36.9 | 4.7 | Algeria |
| 45[5] | 11.2[5] | 1 | 48[6] | 802 | 35.7[6] | ... | ... | 12.6 | 25 | 98.5 | 98.8 | 98.3 | 8.6 | American Samoa |
| 1,248 | 18.7[7] | ... | ... | ... | ... | ... | ... | ... | 15 | 100.0 | ... | ... | ... | Andorra |
| 7,060 | ... | 1 | 316 | 2,764 | 8.7 | 0.4[1] | 33 | ... | 15 | 28.0 | 36.2 | 19.3 | 5.2 | Angola |
| ... | ... | ... | ... | ... | ... | ... | ... | 6.8[8] | 15 | 94.7 | 94.6 | 94.8 | ... | Anguilla |
| ... | ... | ... | ... | ... | ... | ... | ... | 1.3 | 15 | 90.0 | ... | ... | 3.0 | Antigua and Barbuda |
| 905,755[10] | 7.6[10] | 1,251 | 64,230 | 677,535 | 10.5 | 36.4[11] | 2,253 | 6.1 | 15 | 94.9 | 95.5 | 94.4 | 4.3 | Argentina |
| 701 | 10.8 | 1 | 20 | 180 | 9.0 | ... | ... | ... | 15 | 95.0 | ... | ... | ... | Aruba |
| 859,195[11] | 16.3[11] | 95 | 26,036 | 390,706 | 15.0 | 27.1[6] | 2,313 | 21.5 | 15 | 99.5 | ... | ... | 6.0 | Australia |
| 366,055 | 16.0 | 53 | 10,352 | 175,171 | 16.9 | 25.9[6] | 2,205 | 3.3 | 15 | 100.0 | 100.0 | 100.0 | 5.9 | Austria |
| ... | ... | 1[11] | 135[11] | 2,000[11] | 14.8[11] | ... | ... | ... | 15 | 89.0 | ... | ... | 8.0 | Bahamas, The |
| 2,846 | 12.2 | 2 | 159 | 3,650 | 22.9 | 10.4[6] | 1,031 | 3.8 | 14 | 74.0 | 81.1 | 61.8 | 3.3 | Bahrain |
| 27,624[6] | 9.9[6] | 677[6] | 15,205[6] | 436,615[6] | 28.7[6] | 4.9[6] | 443 | 0.9 | 15 | 33.1 | 43.3 | 22.2 | 1.9 | Bangladesh |
| 3,592 | 23.3 | 1 | 108 | 1,617 | 15.0 | 19.4[6] | 2,065 | 3.3 | 15 | 98.0 | 98.3 | 97.7 | 5.7 | Barbados |
| 218,717[2] | 31.9[2] | 6[14] | ... | 102,354[14] | ... | 30.6[6] | 2,486 | 7.5 | ... | 100.0 | ... | ... | 6.0 | Belgium |
| 765[15] | 12.3[15] | 15 | 15 | 15 | 15 | ... | ... | 2.3 | 15 | 93.0 | ... | ... | ... | Belize |
| 8,315 | 13.7 | 1[2] | 803[2] | 6,818[2] | 8.5[2] | 2.1[2] | 179 | 0.3 | 15 | 27.9 | 39.8 | 16.6 | 5.1 | Benin |
| 16 | 16 | 1[16] | 67[16] | 638[16] | 9.5[16] | ... | ... | 7.4 | 15 | 96.9 | 96.7 | 97.0 | 3.1 | Bermuda |
| 688 | 6.7 | 2 | 18[2] | 55[2] | 3.1[2] | 0.1[2] | 25 | ... | 15 | 18.0 | 31.0 | 9.0 | ... | Bhutan |
| ... | ... | 25 | 1,487 | 13,388 | 9.0 | 16.4[1] | 1,429 | 5.0 | 15 | 63.2 | 75.8 | 51.4 | 3.0 | Bolivia |
| 3,099 | 11.0 | 1 | 142 | 1,434 | 10.1 | 1.9[2] | 166 | 0.5 | 15 | 70.8 | 72.6 | 69.5 | 7.2 | Botswana |
| ... | ... | 859 | 122,486 | 1,367,609 | 11.2 | 11.3[2] | 1,140 | 5.0 | 15 | 79.3 | 80.4 | 78.3 | 3.3 | Brazil |
| — | — | | | | | | | 8.5 | 15 | 98.3 | 98.1 | 98.5 | 4.7 | British Virgin Islands |
| 1,362[15] | 5.0[15] | 15 | 15 | 15 | 15 | ... | ... | 9.4 | 15 | 80.3 | 86.5 | 72.8 | 1.8 | Brunei |
| 216,000 | ... | 33 | 11,800 | 80,400 | 6.8 | 16.8[6] | 1,158 | 5.2 | 15 | 95.5 | ... | ... | 6.6 | Bulgaria |
| 4,186 | 8.3 | 1 | 255 | 3,669 | 14.4 | 0.7[6] | 57 | ... | 15 | 13.2 | 20.7 | 6.1 | 2.9 | Burkina Faso |
| 14,570 | 14.1 | 35 | 5,524 | 174,279 | 31.5 | 5.1[4] | 470 | 0.2 | 15 | 65.9 | 75.9 | 56.3 | 1.6 | Burma |
| 12,902 | 12.1 | 8 | 468 | 2,783 | 5.9 | 0.7[2] | 54 | ... | 10 | 33.8 | 42.8 | 25.7 | 3.4 | Burundi |
| 77,555 | 23.9 | 1[6] | 572 | 13,753 | 24.0 | 2.2[6] | 185 | 0.3 | 15 | 55.2 | 70.2 | 41.0 | 3.6 | Cameroon |
| ... | ... | 266 | 59,300 | 795,730 | 13.4 | 44.0[6] | 4,203 | 37.4 | 14 | 95.6 | 95.6 | 95.7 | 7.4 | Canada |
| 923 | 12.1 | — | — | — | — | — | — | ... | 15 | 49.3 | 55.3 | 43.4 | 7.5 | Cape Verde |
| 122 | 13.6 | 1 | 10 | 105 | 10.5 | ... | ... | 2.9 | 15 | 97.5 | 97.5 | 97.6 | ... | Cayman Islands |
| 2,514 | 20.6 | 7[1] | 297[1] | 4,571[1] | 15.4[1] | 1.2[2] | 98 | ... | 15 | 38.5 | 58.8 | 20.4 | 5.7 | Central African Republic |
| 2,559 | ... | 1[1] | 85[1] | 550[1] | 6.5[1] | 0.4 | 34 | ... | 15 | 17.8 | 35.6 | 0.5 | 2.3 | Chad |
| 129,817 | ... | 24 | 10,372[1] | 126,197 | ... | 15.8[11] | 1,660 | 3.8 | 12 | 94.4 | 95.0 | 93.8 | 4.8 | Chile |
| 3,866,000 | 12.3 | 1,016 | 344,000 | 1,703,000 | 5.0 | 1.4[6] | 138 | 1.0 | 15 | 72.6 | 83.5 | 61.2 | 2.8 | China |
| 60 | 8.6 | — | — | — | — | — | — | ... | 15 | 80.0 | ... | ... | ... | Christmas Island |
| 9 | 9.0 | ... | ... | ... | ... | ... | ... | ... | ... | ... | ... | ... | ... | Cocos (Keeling) Islands |
| 19 | 19 | 231 | 43,447 | 402,438 | 9.3 | 12.9[11] | 1,384 | 3.3 | 18 | 69.1 | ... | ... | 3.3 | Colombia |
| 327 | 12.1 | — | — | — | — | — | — | ... | 15 | 46.3 | 54.2 | 39.0 | 5.4 | Comoros |
| 5,477 | 22.2 | 5[2] | 297[2] | 7,255[2] | 24.8 | 6.7[4] | 552 | ... | 15 | 62.9 | 71.4 | 55.4 | 6.0 | Congo |
| ... | ... | ... | 41[5] | 360[5] | 8.8[5] | ... | ... | 2.1 | ... | 91.8 | 92.1 | 91.4 | ... | Cook Islands |
| 19 | 19 | 14[2] | ... | 54,466 | ... | ... | ... | 2,381 | 5.8 | 15 | 92.6 | 92.7 | 92.6 | 6.3 | Costa Rica |
| 44,481[5] | ... | 1 | 1,204[1] | 12,755 | ... | 2.4[2] | 207 | ... | 15 | 57.3 | ... | ... | 8.4 | Côte d'Ivoire |
| 307,100 | 11.2 | 35 | 19,600 | 235,200 | 12.0 | 20.1[6] | 2,123 | 5.9 | 15 | 91.1 | 91.1 | 91.1 | 5.9 | Cuba |
| 4,907 | 10.6 | 16 | 289 | 3,134 | 10.8 | ... | 391 | 7.7 | 10 | 93.1 | 97.9 | 88.4 | 3.9 | Cyprus |
| 257,968 | 15.1 | 36 | 19,459 | 169,011 | 8.7 | 15.9[6] | 1,129 | 6.0 | 15 | 99.6 | 99.6 | 99.5 | 5.1 | Czechoslovakia |
| 144,024 | ... | 96[2] | 10,411[2] | 124,144 | ... | 29.2[2] | 2,209 | ... | 14 | 100.0 | 100.0 | 100.0 | 6.5 | Denmark |
| 1,984 | 12.5 | — | — | 161[6] | ... | ... | ... | ... | 14 | 11.9 | ... | ... | 3.9 | Djibouti |
| 121 | 9.3 | ... | 59 | 284 | 4.8 | ... | ... | 1.7 | 15 | 94.9 | ... | ... | ... | Dominica |
| 27,670 | 43.6 | 6[7,14] | 3,107[7,14] | 88,024[7,14] | 28.3[7,14] | 10.1[9] | 900 | 1.9 | 15 | 77.3 | 77.7 | 76.8 | 2.0 | Dominican Republic |
| 19 | 19 | 17[6] | 11,186[6] | 267,900[6] | 23.9[6] | 33.1[6] | 3,072 | 7.6 | 15 | 69.1 | 86.8 | 56.9 | 3.9 | Ecuador |
| 765,057 | 15.7 | 12[1] | 33,200 | 873,565 | 26.3 | 21.0[2] | 1,957 | 3.4 | 15 | 43.0 | 58.9 | 26.8 | 4.1 | Egypt |

## Education (continued)

| country | year | first level (primary) | | | | | general second level (secondary) | | | | | vocational second level[a] | |
|---|---|---|---|---|---|---|---|---|---|---|---|---|---|
| | | schools | teachers[c] | students[d] | student/ teacher ratio | net enroll- ment ratio | schools | teachers[c] | students[d] | student/ teacher ratio | net enroll- ment ratio | schools | teachers[c] |
| El Salvador | 1985 | 2,883 | 24,295 | 940,963 | 38.7 | 62[6] | 285 | 3,880 | 90,288 | 23.3 | 14[6] | 17[2] | 667[2] |
| Equatorial Guinea | 1981 | 511 | 647 | 40,110 | 62.0 | ... | 14[19] | 288[19] | 3,013[19] | 10.5[19] | ... | 19 | 19 |
| Ethiopia | 1984 | 7,096 | 46,674 | 2,497,114 | 53.5 | ... | 1,066 | 13,192 | 579,834 | 44.0 | ... | ... | ... |
| Faeroe Islands | 1987 | 76[11,17] | ... | 5,606 | ... | ... | ... | ... | 2,904 | ... | ... | 3[2] | ... |
| Falkland Islands | 1986 | 8 | 23 | 232 | 10.1 | ... | 1 | 11 | 116 | 10.5 | | — | — |
| Fiji | 1986 | 672 | 4,315 | 131,221 | 30.4 | 100[6] | 140 | 2,551 | 42,200 | 16.5 | ... | 44 | 257 |
| Finland | 1984 | 4,238 | 25,139 | 369,047 | 14.7 | ... | 1,082 | 22,356 | 316,740 | 14.2 | ... | 550 | 15,000 |
| France | 1985 | 66,107 | 300,575 | 6,652,059 | 22.1 | 97[1] | 11,181[19] | 321,128[19] | 5,310,295[19] | 16.5[19] | 81[1] | 19 | 19 |
| French Guiana | 1985 | 76 | 748 | 15,620[7] | ... | ... | 8 | 470 | 5,529[7] | ... | ... | ... | 177 |
| French Polynesia | 1985 | 198 | 1,337 | 27,401 | 20.5 | ... | ... | 804 | 13,611 | 16.9 | ... | ... | 362 |
| Gabon | 1985 | 940 | 3,837 | 178,811 | 46.6 | ... | 51 | 1,894 | 25,815 | 13.6 | ... | 29 | 720 |
| Gambia, The | 1985 | 189 | 2,640 | 66,257 | 25.1 | 63[6] | 8 | 235 | 4,348 | 18.5 | 19[6] | 16 | 502 |
| Gaza Strip | 1986 | 296[17] | 3,940[17] | 105,354 | ... | ... | 17 | 17 | 54,884 | ... | ... | 17 | 17 |
| Germany, East | 1984 | 5,666 | 54,971 | 766,745 | 13.9 | ... | 5,711 | 112,172 | 1,265,349 | 11.3 | ... | 4,500 | 56,577 |
| Germany, West | 1986 | 22,420 | 304,702 | 4,316,760 | 14.2 | 80[4] | 5,359 | 189,561 | 2,840,938 | 15.0 | ... | 8,224 | 91,215 |
| Ghana | 1985 | 8,965 | 51,631[6] | 1,464,624 | 31.8[6] | ... | 5,589 | 32,795[6] | 723,385 | 24.8[6] | ... | 61 | 1,727[4] |
| Gibraltar | 1986 | 14 | 181 | 2,931 | 16.2 | ... | 2 | 122 | 1,728 | 14.2 | ... | 1 | 25 |
| Greece | 1985 | 9,229 | 36,093 | 904,426 | 25.1 | 91[1] | 2,613 | 36,851 | 701,711 | 19.0 | 76[4] | 601 | 8,427 |
| Greenland | 1987 | 94 | ... | 7,065 | ... | ... | 37[5] | 1,136[19] | 2,072 | ... | ... | 5[5] | 19 |
| Grenada | 1984 | 64 | 775 | 20,460 | 26.4 | ... | 20[1] | 321 | 6,799 | 21.2 | ... | ... | ... |
| Guadeloupe | 1984 | 230 | 2,173 | 47,733 | 22.0 | ... | ... | 2,987[19] | 49,897[19] | 16.7[19] | ... | ... | 19 |
| Guam | 1986 | 33 | 781 | 14,552 | 18.6 | ... | 22 | 814 | 16,223 | 19.9 | ... | 4 | 146 |
| Guatemala | 1985 | 8,121 | 28,467 | 1,046,043 | 36.7 | 62[2] | 1,310[19] | 14,629[19] | 204,049[19] | 13.9[19] | 14[1] | 19 | 19 |
| Guernsey | 1984 | 23 | 224 | 4,260 | 19.0 | ... | 9 | 297 | 4,095 | 13.8 | ... | 1 | 47 |
| Guinea | 1986 | 2,285 | 7,605 | 276,438 | 36.3 | 26[6] | 233 | 3,764 | 63,016 | 16.7 | ... | ... | 744[1] |
| Guinea-Bissau | 1985 | 658 | 3,153 | 81,444 | 25.8 | 53[2] | 12 | 718 | 11,710 | 16.3 | 3[2] | 4 | 107 |
| Guyana | 1980 | 424 | 6,021 | 164,830 | 27.4 | 90[4] | 87 | 2,513 | 46,595 | 18.5 | ... | 15 | 348 |
| Haiti | 1984 | 3,403 | 18,483 | 783,070 | 42.4 | 39[2] | 314 | 5,781 | 134,278 | 23.2 | ... | 10 | ... |
| Honduras | 1985 | 6,492 | 20,724 | 858,061 | 41.4 | 87[6] | 452[19] | 6,799[19] | 130,277[19] | 19.2[19] | 20[6] | 19 | 19 |
| Hong Kong | 1987 | 714 | 19,368 | 531,993 | 27.5 | 95[6] | 397 | 18,323 | 434,145 | 23.7 | 64[6] | 27 | 1,174 |
| Hungary | 1986 | 3,546 | 88,106 | 1,297,818 | 14.7 | 97[6] | 178 | 7,923 | 105,794 | 13.4 | 71[6] | 737 | 22,120 |
| Iceland | 1983 | 187 | 2,600 | 25,000 | 9.6 | ... | 157 | ... | 21,800 | ... | ... | 44 | ... |
| India | 1985 | 519,701 | 1,458,140 | 61,168,620 | 41.9 | 92[6] | 188,713 | 1,980,694 | 64,533,244 | 32.6 | 41[6] | 5,215[15] | ... |
| Indonesia | 1985 | 136,706 | 986,638 | 26,567,688 | 26.9 | 98[6] | 20,299 | 433,750 | 7,042,001 | 16.2 | 17[9] | 2,708 | 70,026 |
| Iran | 1986 | 48,982 | 268,606 | 6,343,300 | 23.6 | 88[6] | 13,818 | 167,769 | 2,922,576 | 17.4 | ... | 1,325 | 20,683 |
| Iraq | 1985 | 10,463 | 119,734 | 2,827,109 | 23.6 | 92[1] | 2,109 | 33,466 | 996,622 | 29.8 | 49[4] | 228 | 6,266 |
| Ireland | 1985 | 3,387 | 20,933 | 566,289 | 27.0 | 89[1] | 565 | 14,078 | 249,253 | 17.7 | 79[1] | 257 | 5,126 |
| Isle of Man | 1983 | 35[11,13] | 240 | 5,193 | 21.6 | ... | 5[11,13] | 276 | 4,665 | 16.9 | ... | 1[11,13] | 32[9] |
| Israel | 1986[22] | 1,843 | 45,016 | 622,056 | 13.8 | 92[2] | 936[23] | 37,717[23] | 348,262[23] | 9.2[23] | ... | 369 | 3,654 |
| Italy | 1986 | 27,748 | 230,698 | 3,715,597 | 16.1 | 98[9] | 10,033 | 129,980 | 2,764,635 | 21.3 | 66[9] | 7,564 | 112,876 |
| Jamaica | 1985[13] | 785 | ... | 337,231 | ... | 94[2] | 132 | 7,435 | 228,241 | 30.7 | 57[5] | 11 | 501 |
| Japan | 1987 | 24,933 | 448,978 | 10,226,325 | 22.8 | 100[6] | 16,738 | 566,976 | 11,456,437 | 20.2 | 95[6] | ... | ... |
| Jersey | 1984 | 38[2] | 299 | 5,472 | 18.3 | ... | 6[2] | 403 | 5,075 | 12.6 | ... | 1[11] | ... |
| Jordan | 1986 | 1,239 | 16,979 | 530,906 | 31.3 | 88[2] | 1,671 | 17,074 | 305,046 | 17.9 | 71[1] | 52[24] | 1,012[24] |
| Kampuchea | 1984 | 3,629[1] | 36,520 | 1,504,840 | 41.2 | ... | 207 | 4,494 | 145,730 | 32.4 | ... | 13 | 278 |
| Kenya | 1984 | 12,539 | 122,788 | 4,380,232 | 35.7 | 69[4] | 2,396 | 19,368 | 510,943 | 26.4 | 8[9] | 40 | 1,551 |
| Kiribati | 1986 | 112 | 457 | 13,331 | 29.2 | ... | 8 | 128 | 2,167 | 16.9 | ... | 3 | 43 |
| Korea, North | 1982 | 4,700[18] | ... | 2,500,000 | ... | ... | ... | 100,000[19] | 2,500,000[19] | 25.0[19] | ... | ... | 19 |
| Korea, South | 1987 | 6,535 | 126,677 | 4,798,323 | 37.9 | 93[11] | 3,408 | 114,658 | 4,111,043 | 35.9 | 76[1] | 736 | 34,189 |
| Kuwait | 1987 | 282 | 9,704 | 175,767 | 18.1 | 86[6] | 401 | 19,158 | 245,865 | 12.8 | 74[1] | 6[7] | 788[7] |
| Laos | 1984 | 6,544 | 17,789 | 485,741 | 27.3 | ... | 419 | 6,219 | 88,775 | 14.3 | ... | 60 | 2,200 |
| Lebanon | 1982 | 1,116 | 26 | 398,977 | 26 | ... | 1,405 | 53,450[26] | 250,028 | 12.1[26] | ... | 181 | 3,563 |
| Lesotho | 1985[13] | 1,141 | 5,663 | 314,003 | 55.4 | 71[2] | 143 | 1,676 | 35,423 | 21.1 | 12[2] | 9 | 221 |
| Liberia | 1980 | 1,232 | 9,099 | 227,431 | 25.0 | ... | 419 | 1,129 | 51,666 | 45.8 | ... | 6 | 63 |
| Libya | 1983 | 2,744 | 42,202 | 741,502 | 17.6 | ... | 1,555 | 25,044 | 301,415 | 12.0 | ... | 195 | 3,883 |
| Liechtenstein | 1988 | 14 | 102 | 1,754 | 17.2 | ... | 9 | 98 | 1,707 | 17.4 | ... | 1 | 30[27] |
| Luxembourg | 1986 | ... | 1,713 | 24,183 | 14.1 | 88[1] | ... | 3,482[2,27,28] | 8,584[11] | ... | 59[1] | ... | 28 |
| Macau | 1986 | 74 | 1,080 | 31,669 | 29.3 | ... | 31 | 769 | 13,849 | 18.0 | ... | 2[24] | 13[24] |
| Madagascar | 1984 | 13,973 | 42,462 | 1,625,216 | 38.3 | ... | 104[29] | 10,383 | 288,543 | 27.8 | ... | 126[29] | 1,302 |
| Malawi | 1985 | 3,962 | 23,132 | 899,459 | 38.9 | 44[6] | 73 | 1,150 | 24,343 | 21.2 | ... | 10[2] | 173 |
| Malaysia | 1986 | 6,652 | 98,061 | 2,232,575 | 22.8 | ... | 1,136 | 58,223 | 1,297,734 | 22.3 | ... | 54 | 1,909 |
| Maldives | 1986 | 243 | 1,138 | 41,812 | 36.7 | ... | 9 | 291 | 3,581 | 12.3 | ... | 10 | 52 |
| Mali | 1983 | 1,558 | 10,912 | 348,373 | 31.9 | 16[1] | 20 | 3,870 | 64,148 | 16.6 | ... | 11 | 890 |
| Malta | 1986 | 124 | 1,665 | 36,240 | 21.8 | 87[2] | 65 | 1,800 | 21,421 | 11.9 | 71[2] | 24 | 592 |
| Martinique | 1984 | 224 | 2,024 | 39,050 | 19.3 | ... | ... | 2,416 | 31,912 | 13.2 | ... | ... | 653[2] |
| Mauritania | 1984 | 756 | 2,629 | 119,337 | 45.4 | ... | 30 | 1,013 | 27,924 | 27.6 | ... | 13 | 372 |
| Mauritius | 1986 | 273 | 6,161 | 138,765 | 22.5 | 97[6] | 125 | 3,572 | 68,604 | 19.2 | 34[9] | 7[6] | 69[1] |
| Mayotte | 1985 | 72 | 429[7] | 15,625[7] | 36.4[7] | ... | 3[19] | 66[19] | 1,374[19] | 20.8 | ... | 19 | 19 |
| Mexico | 1987 | 75,184 | 444,620 | 14,951,302 | 33.6 | 97[6] | 16,426 | 224,732[7] | 4,384,616 | ... | ... | 5,811[7] | 139,391[7] |
| Monaco | 1982 | 6 | 1,354 | ... | ... | ... | ... | 1,914 | ... | ... | ... | ... | ... |
| Mongolia | 1986 | 26 | 26 | 26 | 26 | 99[1] | 678[26] | 17,000[26] | 428,000[26] | 25.2[26] | 84[3] | 40 | 1,200 |
| Montserrat | 1983 | 15[4] | 66 | 1,723 | 26.1 | ... | ... | 60 | 871 | 14.5 | ... | ... | 9 |
| Morocco | 1986 | 3,443[11] | 79,300[31] | 2,279,887 | ... | 63[6] | 1,145[11] | 56,106[19,31] | 1,200,383 | ... | 20[5] | ... | 19 |
| Mozambique | 1986 | 4,382 | 20,756 | 1,251,391 | 60.3 | 43[2] | 208 | 3,422 | 144,012 | 42.1 | 4[4] | 34 | 864 |
| Nauru | 1985 | 7 | 102 | 1,451 | 14.2 | ... | 2 | 36 | 465 | 12.9 | ... | 1 | 4 |
| Nepal | 1986 | 11,873 | 51,266 | 1,812,098 | 35.3 | 56[6] | 4,899 | 18,362 | 496,821 | 27.1 | 18[6] | 5 | 117 |
| Netherlands, The | 1986 | 9,388 | 102,388 | 1,568,265 | 15.3 | 87[6] | 1,382 | 53,361 | 803,782 | 15.1 | 85[2] | 2,002 | 55,931 |
| Netherlands Antilles | 1983 | 91 | 1,248 | 24,578 | 19.7 | ... | 22 | 633 | 8,623 | 13.6 | ... | 3 | 79 |
| New Caledonia | 1987 | 276 | 1,564 | 32,205 | 20.6 | ... | 47 | 1,179 | 13,540 | 11.5 | ... | 28 | 200 |
| New Zealand | 1985 | 2,500 | 18,188 | 452,426 | 24.9 | 100[2] | 428 | 13,045 | 230,970 | 17.7 | 79[9] | 28 | 2,989 |
| Nicaragua | 1985 | 4,102 | 15,273 | 524,020 | 34.3 | 73[6] | 431[19] | 4,778[19] | 151,269[19] | 31.7[19] | 21[2] | 19 | 19 |
| Niger | 1981 | 1,708 | 5,475 | 233,441 | 42.6 | 21[5] | ... | ... | 42,967 | ... | 4[5] | ... | ... |
| Nigeria | 1983 | 37,692 | 424,717 | 15,021,100 | 35.4 | ... | 5,498 | 78,117 | 2,421,625 | 31.0 | ... | 470[4] | 12,156[4] |
| Niue | 1985 | 7 | 29 | 503 | 17.3 | ... | 1 | 31 | 321 | 10.4 | ... | — | — |
| Norfolk Island | 1986 | 2 | 11 | 120 | 10.9 | ... | 1 | 6 | 111 | 18.5 | ... | — | — |

| students[d] | student/teacher ratio | third level (higher) institutions | teachers[c] | students[d] | student/teacher ratio | gross enrollment ratio | students per 100,000 population[b] | percent of population age 25 and over with post-secondary education[b] | literacy[b] over age | total (%) | male (%) | female (%) | public expenditure on education (percent of GNP)[b] | country |
|---|---|---|---|---|---|---|---|---|---|---|---|---|---|---|
| 9,505 | ... | 34 | 3,404 | 60,994 | 17.9 | 11.9[2] | 1,095 | 2.3 | 15 | 69.0 | 73.2 | 65.3 | 3.0 | El Salvador |
| 19 | 19 | — | — | — | — | 3.8[4] | 324 | ... | ... | 55.0 | ... | ... | ... | Equatorial Guinea |
| ... | ... | 11 | 1,446 | 15,776 | 10.9 | 0.4[2] | 39 | ... | 15 | 4.8 | 9.3 | 0.5 | 4.1 | Ethiopia |
| 607[2] | ... | 6[2] | ... | 949[2] | ... | ... | ... | ... | 15 | 99.0 | ... | ... | ... | Faeroe Islands |
| — | — | ... | ... | ... | ... | — | ... | ... | 15 | 99.5 | ... | ... | ... | Falkland Islands |
| 3,793 | 14.8 | 5[2] | ... | 3,947[2] | ... | 3.3[1] | 351 | 3.3 | 15 | 85.5 | 90.2 | 80.9 | 6.4 | Fiji |
| 116,906 | 7.8 | 21[14] | 5,191[14] | 119,902[14] | 23.1[14] | 30.6[6] | 2,459 | 11.9 | 15 | 100.0 | 100.0 | 100.0 | 5.7 | Finland |
| 19 | 19 | 1,094[4] | 46,648 | 1,163,903 | 25.0 | 26.8[2] | 2,114 | ... | ... | 98.8 | 98.9 | 98.7 | 5.8 | France |
| ... | ... | 1 | ... | 239 | ... | ... | ... | 6.4 | 16 | 82.0 | 82.5 | 81.3 | 17.6 | French Guiana |
| 3,441 | 9.5 | ... | ... | 180[6] | ... | ... | ... | ... | 15 | 95.0 | 94.9 | 95.0 | 9.9 | French Polynesia |
| 13,529 | 18.8 | 1[6] | 616[6] | 3,228[6] | 5.2[6] | 3.6[2] | 290 | ... | 15 | 77.0 | ... | ... | 4.6 | Gabon |
| 10,102 | 20.1 | 9 | 177 | 1,489 | 8.4 | — | ... | 0.2 | 15 | 74.9 | 35.6 | 15.1 | 4.4 | Gambia, The |
| 919 | ... | 1[2] | 301 | 2,387[2] | ... | ... | ... | 9.5[11] | ... | ... | ... | ... | ... | Gaza Strip |
| 414,044 | 7.3 | 54 | 29,700 | 434,326 | 14.6 | 30.3 | 2,582 | 17.3 | 15 | 100.0 | 100.0 | 100.0 | 5.5 | Germany, East |
| 2,776,435 | 30.4 | 110 | 327,055 | 1,336,395 | 4.1 | 29.1[6] | 2,465 | 4.9[21] | 15 | 100.0 | 100.0 | 100.0 | 4.5 | Germany, West |
| 24,827 | 19.3[4] | 3 | 1,041[4] | 7,878 | ... | 1.5[6] | 152 | 0.4 | 15 | 53.2 | 64.1 | 42.8 | 1.5 | Ghana |
| 352 | 14.1 | — | — | — | — | ... | ... | ... | 10 | 99.0 | 99.0 | 99.0 | 6.0 | Gibraltar |
| 101,558 | 12.0 | 102 | 11,735 | 167,957 | 14.3 | 17.7[4] | 1,281 | 7.6 | 14 | 93.8 | 97.3 | 90.6 | 2.6 | Greece |
| 1,469[7] | ... | — | — | — | — | ... | ... | ... | 15 | 100.0 | 100.0 | 100.0 | ... | Greenland |
| ... | ... | 2 | 92 | 1,350 | 14.7 | ... | ... | 1.5 | 15 | 85.0 | ... | ... | 4.6 | Grenada |
| 19 | 19 | 1[7] | 92[7] | 5,212[7] | 56.7[7] | ... | ... | 5.2 | 15 | 90.1 | 89.7 | 90.5 | 14.3 | Guadeloupe |
| 4,377 | 30.0 | 1 | 175 | 2,647 | 15.1 | ... | ... | 34.4 | 15 | 96.4 | 96.4 | 96.5 | 7.5 | Guam |
| 19 | 19 | 5[2] | 4,490[2] | 51,556[2] | 11.4[2] | 7.4[1] | 647 | 1.2 | 15 | 51.1 | 58.6 | 43.5 | 1.8 | Guatemala |
| 134 | 2.9 | — | — | — | — | ... | ... | ... | 15 | 100.0 | 100.0 | 100.0 | ... | Guernsey |
| 5,411 | 8.2[4] | ... | 1,373[1] | 13,182[1] | 9.6[1] | 2.1[6] | 180 | ... | 15 | 28.3 | 39.7 | 17.2 | 3.3 | Guinea |
| 1,027 | 9.6 | ... | ... | 1,889 | ... | — | ... | 0.1 | 7 | 26.8 | ... | ... | 2.9 | Guinea-Bissau |
| 4,647 | 13.4 | 1 | ... | ... | ... | 2.0[2] | 230 | 1.8 | 15 | 95.5 | 97.1 | 94.0 | 7.4 | Guyana |
| 859 | ... | ... | 818 | 5,492 | 6.7 | 1.1[2] | 100 | 0.7 | 15 | 34.7 | 37.1 | 32.5 | 1.2 | Haiti |
| 19 | 19 | 7 | 2,692 | 34,478 | 14.0 | 9.1[6] | 798 | 3.3 | 15 | 68.6 | 71.1 | 66.2 | 4.3 | Honduras |
| 21,593 | 18.4 | 11 | 3,530 | 34,434 | 9.8 | 12.8[6] | 1,410 | 7.1 | 15 | 88.1 | 94.7 | 80.9 | 2.8 | Hong Kong |
| 316,529 | 14.3 | 58 | 14,850 | 99,344 | 6.7 | 15.2[6] | 936 | 7.0 | 15 | 98.9 | 99.2 | 98.6 | 5.4 | Hungary |
| 4,280 | ... | 4 | 280 | 4,780 | 17.1 | 22.8[6] | 2,136 | 3.7 | 15 | 100.0 | 100.0 | 100.0 | 4.1 | Iceland |
| 3,033,592[15] | ... | 15 | ... | 15 | ... | 8.7[3] | 776 | 2.5 | 15 | 40.8 | 54.8 | 25.7 | 3.2 | India |
| 1,002,465 | 14.3 | 475[5] | 74,044[6] | 806,470[6] | 10.9 | 6.5[6] | 600 | 0.8 | 15 | 74.1 | 83.0 | 65.4 | 2.2 | Indonesia |
| 277,609 | 13.4 | 114[2] | 13,698 | 145,809 | 10.6 | 4.4[6] | 409 | ... | 15 | 42.8 | 55.4 | 30.1 | 5.7 | Iran |
| 106,312 | 17.0 | 25[2] | 6,952 | 116,179 | 16.7 | 10.0[2] | 856 | ... | 15 | 45.9 | 65.9 | 26.0 | 4.3 | Iraq |
| 81,900 | 16.0 | 25 | 3,690[6] | 46,618 | ... | 22.1[1] | 1,838 | 4.6 | 15 | 100.0 | 100.0 | 100.0 | 6.9 | Ireland |
| 139[9] | 4.2[9] | ... | ... | ... | ... | ... | ... | ... | ... | ... | ... | ... | ... | Isle of Man |
| 111,674 | ... | 7[14] | 8,112 | 87,293 | 10.8 | 34.2[6] | 2,769 | 23.1 | 15 | 91.8 | 95.0 | 88.7 | 8.4 | Israel |
| 2,607,749 | 23.1 | ... | ... | 1,184,142 | ... | 26.3[6] | 2,065 | 2.6 | 15 | 97.0 | 97.9 | 96.3 | 5.7 | Italy |
| 7,856 | 15.7 | 17 | ... | 14,581 | ... | 7.4[1] | 668 | 1.1 | 14 | 88.6 | 88.2 | 89.1 | 7.5 | Jamaica |
| ... | ... | 1,097 | 138,587 | 2,597,073 | 18.7 | 29.6[6] | 2,006 | 14.3 | 15 | 100.0 | 100.0 | 100.0 | 5.7 | Japan |
| ... | ... | ... | ... | ... | ... | ... | ... | ... | ... | ... | ... | ... | 4.1 | Jersey |
| 27,042[24] | 26.7[24] | 3 | 1,295 | 26,711 | 20.6 | 37.4[2] | 1,722 | 0.8 | 15 | 79.4 | 81.7 | 64.4 | 7.1 | Jordan |
| 7,334 | 26.4 | 2[2] | ... | 586[2] | ... | ... | ... | ... | 15 | 48.0 | ... | ... | ... | Kampuchea |
| 24,984 | 16.1 | 4 | ... | 19,798 | ... | 1.4[2] | 75 | ... | 15 | 59.2 | 69.6 | 49.2 | 5.6 | Kenya |
| 534 | 12.4 | ... | ... | 85[25] | ... | ... | ... | ... | 15 | 90.0 | ... | ... | 8.7 | Kiribati |
| 19 | 19 | 175 | 9,244 | 200,000 | 21.6 | ... | ... | ... | 15 | 90.0 | ... | ... | 3.6 | Korea, North |
| 1,007,272 | 29.5 | 459 | 35,573 | 1,332,455 | 37.5 | 26.1[6] | 2,930 | 8.9 | 15 | 92.7 | 97.5 | 87.9 | 4.8 | Korea, South |
| 12,272[7] | 15.6[7] | 1 | 887 | 17,414 | 19.6 | 15.6[6] | 1,287 | 10.1 | 10 | 77.5 | 80.5 | 73.1 | 4.2 | Kuwait |
| 16,237 | 7.4 | 51 | 452 | 4,790 | 10.6 | 1.4[2] | 122 | ... | 15 | 45.2 | 52.8 | 37.6 | 0.5 | Laos |
| 39,045 | 11.0 | 18 | 7,976 | 70,314 | 8.8 | 28.9 | 2,715 | 3.1 | 15 | 73.4 | 82.6 | 64.2 | 3.0 | Lebanon |
| 2,221 | 10.0 | 1 | 146 | 1,119 | 7.7 | 1.8[6] | 155 | 0.1 | 15 | 73.6 | 62.4 | 84.5 | 3.9 | Lesotho |
| 2,322 | 36.9 | 3 | 190 | 3,789 | 19.9 | 2.5[3] | 203 | 1.5 | 15 | 22.4 | 27.4 | 18.4 | 6.3 | Liberia |
| 50,363 | 12.9 | 8 | 1,340[5] | 25,700[1] | ... | 10.8[1] | 859 | 1.0 | 10 | 74.4 | 85.0 | 62.0 | 3.7 | Libya |
| 117 | ... | — | — | — | — | ... | ... | 5.4 | 15 | 100.0 | 100.0 | 100.0 | ... | Liechtenstein |
| 16,507[11] | ... | ... | 28 | 934[11] | ... | 3.4[2] | 270 | ... | 15 | 100.0 | 100.0 | 100.0 | 5.3 | Luxembourg |
| 52[24] | 4.0[24] | 5 | 75 | 5,840 | 77.9 | ... | ... | 1.4 | 10 | 61.3 | 76.4 | 46.2 | ... | Macau |
| 11,041 | 8.5 | 3 | 1,059 | 37,746 | 35.6 | 4.6 | 388 | ... | 15 | 67.5 | 73.7 | 61.6 | 3.9 | Madagascar |
| 2,420 | 14.0 | 4 | 270 | 1,964 | 7.3 | 0.7[6] | 58 | 0.2 | 15 | 41.2 | ... | ... | 2.5 | Malawi |
| 21,337 | 11.2 | 41[11] | 8,415[11] | 96,212[11] | 11.4[11] | 6.1[6] | 614 | ... | 15 | 72.6 | 82.2 | 63.2 | 6.4 | Malaysia |
| 462 | 8.9 | ... | ... | ... | ... | ... | ... | 0.4 | 15 | 81.1 | 80.2 | 82.0 | 0.6 | Maldives |
| 12,612 | 14.2 | 7 | 499 | 5,792 | 11.6 | 0.9[1] | 78 | 0.2 | 15 | 10.1 | 18.6 | 1.8 | 3.5 | Mali |
| 6,358 | 10.7 | 1 | 156 | 1,474 | 9.4 | 4.4[6] | 372 | 2.4 | 15 | 96.0 | 96.2 | 95.9 | 3.2 | Malta |
| 15,410[2] | 23.6[2] | 1 | 40 | 1,220 | 30.5 | ... | ... | ... | 15 | 92.5 | 91.8 | 93.2 | 15.2 | Martinique |
| 3,572 | 9.6 | 7 | 254[4] | 4,434 | ... | ... | ... | ... | 6 | 17.0 | ... | ... | 8.0 | Mauritania |
| 444[6] | ... | 2[6] | 184[1] | 344 | ... | 0.6[6] | 77 | 3.6 | 15[30] | 83.1[30] | 90.0[30] | 76.4[30] | 4.2 | Mauritius |
| 19 | 19 | ... | ... | ... | ... | ... | ... | ... | 15 | 18.0 | 27.5 | 8.7 | ... | Mayotte |
| 2,088,292[7] | 15.0[7] | 1,347[7] | 98,061[7] | 1,072,764[7] | 13.7[7] | 15.2[2] | 1,425 | 4.9 | 15 | 92.0 | ... | ... | 2.8 | Mexico |
| 1,218 | ... | ... | ... | ... | ... | ... | ... | 6.8 | ... | ... | ... | ... | ... | Monaco |
| 27,700 | 23.1 | 8 | 1,500 | 24,500 | 16.4 | 25.5[4] | 2,173 | ... | 15 | 89.5 | 93.4 | 85.5 | 7.0 | Mongolia |
| 66 | 7.3 | ... | ... | ... | ... | ... | ... | 5.8 | ... | ... | ... | ... | 3.5 | Montserrat |
| 7,674 | ... | 19[1] | 4,456 | 134,640 | 30.2 | 7.8[6] | 723 | ... | 15 | 70.7 | 82.4 | 58.7 | 7.4 | Morocco |
| 10,485 | 12.2 | 2 | 330 | 1,569 | 4.8 | 0.1[11] | 11 | 0.1 | 15 | 16.6 | 20.0 | 13.3 | 1.2 | Mozambique |
| 60 | 15.0 | — | — | 88[25] | — | ... | ... | ... | 15 | 99.0 | ... | ... | ... | Nauru |
| 648 | 5.5 | 116 | 4,165 | 67,555 | 16.2 | 4.8[2] | 406 | 6.8 | 15 | 20.7 | 31.9 | 9.2 | 2.8 | Nepal |
| 635,493 | 11.4 | 453 | 30,952 | 307,537 | 9.9 | 31.4[6] | 2,737 | 7.2 | 15 | 100.0 | 100.0 | 100.0 | 7.7 | Netherlands, The |
| 732 | 9.3 | 1 | 53 | 677 | 12.8 | ... | ... | 4.4 | 15 | 95.0 | ... | ... | 10.1 | Netherlands Antilles |
| 5,887 | 29.4 | 6 | 40 | 853 | 21.3 | ... | ... | 2.0 | 14 | 89.4 | 90.1 | 88.7 | 12.5 | New Caledonia |
| 131,044 | 43.8 | 7[14] | 2,935[14] | 34,431[14] | 11.7[14] | 28.5[2] | 2,599 | 30.6 | 15 | 100.0 | 100.0 | 100.0 | 4.9 | New Zealand |
| 19 | 19 | 16 | 2,527 | 29,001 | 11.5 | 11.0[6] | 916 | ... | 15 | 88.0 | ... | ... | 6.0 | Nicaragua |
| 1,821 | ... | 1 | 322 | 2,450 | 7.6 | 0.6[6] | 48 | 0.1 | 15 | 9.8 | 14.0 | 5.8 | 4.3 | Niger |
| 359,817[4] | 29.6[4] | 80 | ... | 124,247 | ... | 3.3[2] | 204 | ... | 15 | 42.4 | 53.8 | 31.5 | 2.2 | Nigeria |
| ... | ... | ... | ... | ... | ... | ... | ... | 1.9 | 15 | 99.8 | 99.7 | 99.9 | ... | Niue |
| — | — | — | — | — | — | ... | ... | ... | 15 | 100.0 | 100.0 | 100.0 | ... | Norfolk Island |

## Education (continued)

| country | year | first level (primary) | | | | | general second level (secondary) | | | | | vocational second level[a] | |
|---|---|---|---|---|---|---|---|---|---|---|---|---|---|
| | | schools | teachers[c] | students[d] | student/teacher ratio | net enrollment ratio | schools | teachers[c] | students[d] | student/teacher ratio | net enrollment ratio | schools | teachers[c] |
| Norway | 1986 | 3,525 | 31,459 | 534,000 | 17.0 | 98[4] | 920[11,19] | 17,087[11,19] | 204,199[11,19] | 12.0[11,19] | 84[4] | 19 | 19 |
| Oman | 1986 | 351 | 7,109 | 177,685 | 25.0 | 69[6] | 290 | 4,840 | 48,828 | 10.1 | 14[4] | 14 | 707 |
| Pacific Is., Trust Territory of the | | | | | | | | | | | | | |
|   Marshall Islands | 1985 | 86 | 517[17] | 9,777 | ... | ... | 7 | [17] | 1,603 | ... | ... | ... | ... |
|   Micronesia, Fed. States of | 1981 | ... | ... | 15,423 | ... | ... | ... | ... | 3,881 | ... | ... | ... | ... |
|   Northern Mariana Islands | 1986 | 18 | 367 | 7,597 | 20.7 | ... | 8 | 235 | 3,915 | 16.7 | ... | ... | ... |
|   Palau | 1984 | ... | 310[17] | 2,893[11] | 13.2[17] | ... | ... | [17] | 1,061[11] | [17] | ... | 1 | 36 |
| Pakistan | 1986 | 86,142 | 199,700 | 7,735,000 | 38.7 | ... | 11,099 | 153,400 | 2,571,000 | 16.8 | ... | 293 | 4,190 |
| Panama | 1986 | 2,574 | 14,176 | 341,914 | 24.1 | 87[6] | 334 | 10,113 | 187,312 | 18.5 | 47[6] | 70 | 644 |
| Papua New Guinea | 1986 | 2,461 | 12,318 | 374,950 | 30.4 | ... | 122 | 2,025 | 49,974 | 24.7 | ... | 112 | 745 |
| Paraguay | 1985 | 3,993 | 22,764 | 570,775 | 25.1 | 90[1] | 740[19] | 9,044[6,19] | 172,132[19] | 16.5[6,19] | 21[3] | 19 | 19 |
| Peru | 1986 | 31,186 | 123,000 | 4,060,000 | 33.0 | 97[11] | 4,831 | 74,000 | 1,676,000 | 22.6 | ... | 288 | 7,000 |
| Philippines | 1985 | 32,791 | 286,246 | 8,793,773 | 30.7 | 88[6] | 5,388 | 103,493 | 3,323,063 | 32.1 | 51[6] | 16 | 16 |
| Pitcairn Island | 1986 | 1[17] | 1[17] | 15 | 18.0[17] | ... | [17] | [17] | 3 | [17] | ... | — | — |
| Poland | 1986 | 16,791 | 267,600 | 4,879,100 | 18.2 | 99[6] | 896 | 21,300 | 338,000 | 15.9 | 72[6] | 7,328 | 82,900 |
| Portugal | 1984 | 13,111 | 74,320 | 1,288,163 | 17.3 | 97[2] | 510 | 36,628 | 568,839 | 15.5 | 28[9] | 345 | 2,971 |
| Puerto Rico | 1986 | 1,542 | 18,359 | 427,582 | 23.3 | ... | 395 | 13,612 | 334,661 | 24.6 | ... | 52 | ... |
| Qatar | 1985[13] | 92 | 2,505 | 30,515 | 12.2 | 100[6] | 70 | 2,090 | 18,261 | 8.7 | 54[6] | 3 | 88 |
| Réunion | 1985 | 508[32] | 5,087[32] | 113,330[32] | 22.3[32] | ... | 85[19] | 3,947[19] | 69,417[19] | 17.6[19] | ... | 19 | 19 |
| Romania | 1986 | 14,076 | 147,147 | 3,030,666 | 20.6 | ... | 1,734[19] | 50,210[19] | 1,514,745[19] | 30.2[19] | ... | 19 | 19 |
| Rwanda | 1985 | 1,573 | 14,394 | 790,198 | 54.9 | 59[4] | ... | 1,082[6] | 16,549 | ... | 2[2] | ... | ... |
| St. Christopher and Nevis | 1985 | 32 | 339 | 7,655 | 22.6 | ... | 7 | 286 | 4,436 | 15.5 | ... | 2 | 29 |
| St. Helena and Ascension | 1983 | 8 | 32 | 589 | 18.4 | ... | 4 | 33 | 507 | 15.4 | ... | 2 | 10 |
| St. Lucia | 1987 | 83 | 1,103 | 32,944 | 29.9 | ... | 13 | 337 | 6,508 | 19.3 | ... | 5 | 54 |
| St. Pierre and Miquelon | 1985 | 5 | 39 | 612 | 15.7 | ... | 3[3] | 56[2] | 535[2] | 9.6[2] | ... | 2[3] | 15[2] |
| St. Vincent and the Grenadines | 1983 | 62 | 1,251 | 24,551 | 19.6 | ... | 19 | 292 | 5,170 | 17.7 | ... | 5 | 39 |
| San Marino | 1987 | 13 | 171 | 1,363 | 8.0 | ... | 5 | 179 | 1,222 | 6.8 | ... | ... | ... |
| São Tomé and Príncipe | 1985 | 63 | 517 | 19,086 | 36.9 | ... | 11 | 300 | 6,186 | 20.6 | ... | 2 | 35 |
| Saudi Arabia | 1986 | 7,566 | 77,480 | 1,285,433 | 16.6 | 53[2] | 2,946 | 37,096 | 524,738 | 14.1 | 26[2] | 22 | 881[6] |
| Senegal | 1984 | 2,150 | 12,934 | 533,394 | 42.8 | 44[6] | 192 | 4,380 | 103,510 | 23.6 | ... | ... | 600 |
| Seychelles | 1987 | 26[7] | 698 | 14,553 | 20.8 | ... | 4[7] | 204 | 2,590 | 12.7 | ... | 1[7] | 163 |
| Sierra Leone | 1985 | 1,219 | 10,451 | 350,160 | 33.5 | ... | 171 | 3,829 | 81,879 | 21.4 | ... | 12 | 406 |
| Singapore | 1986 | 236 | 10,515 | 268,820 | 25.6 | 100[6] | 157 | 8,695 | 203,088 | 23.4 | 58[3] | 16 | 2,718 |
| Solomon Islands | 1986 | 430 | 1,849 | 39,563 | 21.4 | ... | 20 | 276 | 2,718 | 9.8 | ... | 2[6] | 63[6] |
| Somalia | 1985 | 1,121 | 14,521 | 274,610 | 18.9 | 18[1] | 80 | 2,522 | 65,186 | 25.8 | 7[4] | 23 | 725 |
| South Africa | 1985 | 17,430[17] | 199,949[17] | 4,722,832 | ... | ... | [17] | [17] | 1,539,213 | ... | ... | 132 | 3,733 |
|   Bophuthatswana | 1982 | 802 | 7,221 | 373,653 | 51.7 | ... | 310 | 4,391 | 115,737 | 26.4 | ... | 18 | 360 |
|   Ciskei | 1986 | 538 | 4,559 | 194,921 | 42.8 | ... | 157 | 1,875 | 45,783 | 24.4 | ... | 2 | 32 |
|   KwaNdebele | | ... | ... | ... | ... | ... | ... | ... | ... | ... | ... | ... | ... |
|   Transkei | 1983 | ... | ... | 582,090 | ... | ... | ... | ... | 150,720 | ... | ... | ... | ... |
|   Venda | 1984 | 375 | 3,638 | 132,042 | 36.3 | ... | 134 | 1,544 | 41,253 | 26.7 | ... | 1 | 33 |
| South West Africa/Namibia | 1986 | 1,114[17] | 11,121[17] | 273,500 | 31.5[17] | ... | [17] | [17] | 76,580 | [17] | ... | 61 | 811 |
| Spain | 1985 | 23,105[2] | 221,071 | 5,640,938 | 25.5 | 100[2] | 2,595 | 73,388 | 1,182,154 | 16.1 | 75[1] | 2,397[6] | 45,339[6] |
| Sri Lanka | 1984 | 9,289 | 136,280[17] | 2,145,343[13] | ... | ... | [17] | [17] | 1,377,821[13] | ... | ... | 25[2] | 466[2] |
| Sudan, The | 1985 | 6,707 | 47,750 | 1,653,491 | 34.6 | ... | 2,167 | 17,591 | 490,583 | 27.9 | ... | 98 | 968[33] |
| Suriname | 1985 | 321 | 3,880 | 89,624 | 23.1 | 98[6] | 63 | 839 | 22,814 | 27.2 | ... | 64[6] | 1,178[6] |
| Swaziland | 1986 | 937 | 8,397 | 281,551 | 33.5 | 85[6] | 194 | 3,353 | 62,297 | 18.6 | 21[9] | 2 | 100 |
| Sweden | 1985 | 4,770 | 100,748[6] | 959,627 | ... | 96[1] | 520 | 28,636[6] | 267,477 | ... | 81[1] | ... | ... |
| Switzerland | 1987 | ... | ... | 405,800 | ... | ... | ... | ... | 368,600 | ... | ... | ... | ... |
| Syria | 1987 | 8,945 | 77,456 | 1,995,183 | 25.8 | 95[6] | 1,816 | 46,443 | 798,208 | 17.2 | 52[6] | 155 | 7,840 |
| Taiwan | 1986 | 2,459 | 71,853 | 2,313,240 | 32.2 | ... | 839 | 60,346 | 1,250,840 | 20.7 | ... | 200 | 15,783 |
| Tanzania | 1985 | 10,173 | 93,157 | 3,169,759 | 34.0 | 61[1] | 193 | 4,329 | 83,098 | 19.2 | ... | 41 | 1,152 |
| Thailand | 1983 | 33,712[5] | 355,984 | 7,272,153 | 20.4 | ... | 1,437[5] | 85,081 | 1,754,925 | 20.6 | ... | 1,528[5] | 19,795 |
| Togo | 1987 | 2,345 | 10,209 | 474,998 | 46.5 | 67[6] | 248[1] | 4,200[2] | 95,941[2] | 22.8[2] | ... | 18 | 198 |
| Tokelau | 1983 | 3[5] | 39 | 482 | 15.8 | ... | 3[5] | 6[5] | 80[5] | 13.3[5] | ... | ... | 12[5] |
| Tonga | 1984 | 111 | 810 | 16,921 | 20.9 | ... | 50 | 789 | 14,549 | 18.4 | ... | 12 | 14[2] |
| Trinidad and Tobago | 1985 | 468 | 7,627 | 168,308 | 22.1 | 91[6] | 93[6] | 4,744 | 92,595 | 19.5 | 63[6] | ... | ... |
| Tunisia | 1987 | 3,503 | 40,978 | 1,326,541 | 32.4 | 94[6] | 420 | 21,561 | 459,034 | 21.3 | 32[6] | ... | ... |
| Turkey | 1986 | 47,630 | 212,717 | 6,635,821 | 31.2 | 82[6] | 5,734 | 93,384 | 2,282,537 | 24.4 | ... | 2,075 | 44,298 |
| Turks and Caicos Islands | 1985 | 17 | 1,540 | 74 | 20.8 | ... | 3 | 51 | 707 | 13.9 | ... | — | — |
| Tuvalu | 1984 | 11 | 61 | 1,349 | 22.1 | 100[1] | 1 | 15[2] | 243 | 16.7[2] | ... | 8[2] | 16[2] |
| Uganda | 1984 | 6,420 | 58,377 | 1,908,564 | 32.7 | 40[1] | 297 | 5,603 | 114,828 | 20.5 | ... | 118 | 1,039 |
| U.S.S.R. | 1986 | 66,800 | 2,800,000[17] | 36,000,000 | ... | ... | 60,900 | [17] | 4,500,000 | ... | ... | 4,495 | 246,000 |
| United Arab Emirates | 1984 | 327[17] | 5,278[13] | 125,923 | ... | 76[6] | [17] | 3,462[13] | 50,244 | ... | ... | 9 | 273 |
| United Kingdom | 1985 | 24,993 | 205,000 | 4,513,600 | 22.0 | 93[1] | 5,262 | 267,700 | 4,243,600 | 15.9 | 81[1] | 748[34] | 93,000[34] |
| United States | 1987 | 101,050[17] | 1,469,000 | 31,555,000 | 21.5 | 96[6] | [17] | 1,061,000[19] | 13,703,000[19] | 12.9[19] | 85[6] | 19 | 19 |
| Uruguay | 1984 | 2,321 | 15,027 | 350,390 | 23.3 | 88[2] | 268 | ... | 152,300 | ... | ... | 93 | 5,632 |
| Vanuatu | 1983 | 246[6] | 934 | 23,465[6] | ... | ... | 9 | 126[1] | 2,186 | ... | ... | 2 | 40[1] |
| Venezuela | 1986 | 19,868 | 130,227 | 3,332,366 | 25.6 | 86[6] | 2,277[19] | 60,112[19] | 1,037,950[19] | 17.3[19] | 38[6] | 19 | 19 |
| Vietnam | 1986 | 13,596[17] | 414,000[17] | 12,203,000[17] | 29.5[17] | 96[5] | [17] | [17] | [17] | [17] | ... | 298 | 11,400 |
| Virgin Islands (U.S.) | 1986 | 70[17] | 1,658[17] | 31,943[17] | 19.3[17] | ... | [17] | [17] | [17] | [17] | ... | 17 | 17 |
| Wallis and Futuna | 1983 | 13[23] | 134[1] | 3,962 | ... | ... | ... | ... | 150[1,25] | ... | ... | — | — |
| West Bank | 1986[35] | 1,135[17] | 8,647[17] | 179,081 | ... | ... | [17] | [17] | 96,444 | [17] | ... | 17 | 17 |
| Western Sahara | 1985 | 24 | 428 | 13,943 | 32.6 | ... | 7 | 237 | 4,560 | 19.2 | ... | ... | ... |
| Western Samoa | 1983 | 164 | 1,502 | 31,457 | 20.9 | ... | 38[1] | 520 | 20,404 | 39.2 | ... | 4 | 69 |
| Yemen (Aden) | 1984 | 900 | 10,986 | 237,904 | 21.7 | ... | 51 | 1,555 | 27,908 | 17.9 | ... | 29 | 528[2] |
| Yemen (Ṣan'ā') | 1984 | 5,095 | 13,305 | 675,402 | 50.8 | 22[9] | 611 | 3,679 | 71,819 | 19.5 | 3[9] | 52 | 674 |
| Yugoslavia | 1985 | 12,741 | 138,633 | 2,848,470 | 20.5 | 80[5] | ... | 62,643 | 938,218 | 15.0 | 76[5] | ... | ... |
| Zaire | 1986 | 10,065[6] | 112,077[6] | 4,993,523[6] | 44.6[6] | 75[2] | 3,972[6] | 49,459[6] | 3,198,051 | ... | 49[2] | 20[20] | 20[20] |
| Zambia | 1984 | 2,894[1] | 23,870[1] | 1,121,769[1] | 47.0[1] | 84[5] | 142[1] | 4,602[1] | 104,859[1] | 22.8[1] | ... | 28 | 1,041 |
| Zimbabwe | 1986 | 4,297 | 57,823 | 2,260,367 | 39.1 | 100[6] | 1,262[19] | 19,560 | 545,841 | 27.9 | ... | 14[24] | 1,031[24] |

[1]1982.  [2]1983.  [3]1979.  [4]1981.  [5]1980.  [6]1984.  [7]1986.  [8]Age 30 and over.  [9]1975.  [10]General second level includes teacher training at the second level.  [11]1985.  [12]1977.  [13]Public schools only.  [14]Universities only.  [15]Vocational second level includes third level.  [16]Third level includes vocational second level.  [17]First level includes second level.  [18]1976.  [19]General second level includes vocational second level.  [20]1978.  [21]Completed university education.  [22]Includes East Jerusalem.  [23]Includes intermediate education (ages 12–14).  [24]Teacher training only.  [25]Students

| students[d] | student/ teacher ratio | third level (higher) — institutions | teachers[c] | students[d] | student/ teacher ratio | gross enroll-ment ratio | students per 100,000 popula-tion[b] | percent of population age 25 and over with post-secondary education[b] | literacy[b] — over age | total (%) | male (%) | female (%) | public expenditure on education (percent of GNP)[b] | country |
|---|---|---|---|---|---|---|---|---|---|---|---|---|---|---|
| [19] | 19 | 228[11] | 6,961[11] | 93,535[11] | 13.4[11] | 29.3[2] | 2,217 | 11.9 | 15 | 100.0 | 100.0 | 100.0 | 7.0 | Norway |
| 3,141 | 4.4 | — | — | 2,316[25] | ... | — | ... | ... | 6 | 38.0 | 55.0 | 20.0 | 3.9 | Oman |
|  |  |  |  |  |  |  |  |  |  |  |  |  |  | Pacific Is., Trust Territory of the |
| ... | ... | ... | ... | ... | ... | ... | ... | 7.8 | 25 | 86.3 | 89.1 | 83.2 | ... | Marshall Islands |
| ... | ... | ... | ... | 1,200[25] | ... | — | ... | 8.0 | 25 | 75.2 | 79.8 | 70.5 | ... | Micronesia, Fed. States of |
| ... | ... | 1 | 20 | 534 | 26.7 | ... | ... | 21.9 | 25 | 94.9 | 96.0 | 93.5 | ... | Northern Mariana Islands |
| 382 | 10.6 | ... | ... | ... | ... | ... | ... | 16.8 | 25 | 92.7 | 94.4 | 91.0 | ... | Palau |
| 59,000 | 14.1 | 590 | 22,737 | 498,613 | 21.9 | 2.0[3] | 182 | 1.9 | 15 | 25.6 | 36.0 | 15.2 | 2.1 | Pakistan |
| 10,548 | 16.4 | 8 | 4,650 | 56,227 | 12.1 | 25.1[6] | 2,444 | 8.4 | 15 | 85.6 | 86.3 | 84.9 | 5.5 | Panama |
| 10,078 | 13.5 | 2 | 400 | 3,029 | 7.6 | 2.1[6] | 177 | ... | 15 | 42.3 | 52.4 | 31.3 | 4.7 | Papua New Guinea |
| [19] | 19 | 2 | 2,694 | 29,154 | 10.8 | 9.7[6] | 929 | 2.0 | 15 | 85.7 | 88.7 | 82.9 | 1.6 | Paraguay |
| 151,000 | 21.6 | 46 | 22,000 | 394,000 | 17.9 | 21.5[1] | 2,001 | 10.1 | 15 | 81.6 | 89.9 | 73.5 | 3.2 | Peru |
| [16] | 16 | 1,178[16] | 33,935[16] | 1,127,968[16] | 33.2[16] | 29.1[1] | 2,781 | 15.2 | 15 | 88.7 | 89.9 | 87.5 | 1.3 | Philippines |
| — | — | ... | ... | ... | ... | ... | ... | ... | 15 | 100.0 | 100.0 | 100.0 | ... | Pitcairn Island |
| 1,359,800 | 16.4 | 92 | 57,300 | 265,800 | 4.6 | 15.9[6] | 1,241 | 5.7 | 15 | 99.2 | ... | ... | 4.1 | Poland |
| 27,946 | 9.4 | 51 | 10,930 | 95,414 | 8.7 | 11.5[1] | 989 | 1.6 | 15 | 79.4 | 84.8 | 74.6 | 4.8 | Portugal |
| 149,191 | ... | 45 | 9,045 | 156,818 | 17.3 | 45.4[3] | 3,256 | 18.4 | 15 | 89.1 | 89.7 | 88.5 | 8.2 | Puerto Rico |
| 581 | 6.6 | 1 | 401 | 4,621 | 11.5 | 18.3[6] | 1,588 | 11.6 | 10 | 51.1 | 51.2 | 50.1 | 4.7 | Qatar |
| [19] | 19 | 1 | 74 | 2,420 | 32.7 | ... | ... | ... | 15 | 78.6 | 76.5 | 80.5 | 15.6 | Réunion |
| [19] | 19 | 44 | 12,961 | 159,738 | 12.3 | 11.7[6] | 729 | 4.6 | 15 | 95.8 | ... | ... | 2.1 | Romania |
| 4,015 | ... | 3 | 184[6] | 1,570 | 6.6[6] | 0.3[2] | 30 | 0.3 | 15 | 49.4 | 62.2 | 37.2 | 3.1 | Rwanda |
| 240 | 8.3 | — | — | ... | ... | ... | ... | 2.1 | 15 | 91.5 | 90.8 | 92.2 | 6.7 | St. Christopher and Nevis |
| 48 | 4.8 | ... | ... | ... | ... | ... | ... | ... | 15 | 97.1 | 96.8 | 97.5 | ... | St. Helena and Ascension |
| 927 | 18.0 | 1 | 16 | 123 | 7.7 | ... | ... | 1.3 | 15 | 59.7 | ... | ... | 7.8 | St. Lucia |
| 216[2] | 14.4[2] | — | — | — | — | ... | ... | 7.5 | 15 | 99.5 | 99.5 | 99.5 | ... | St. Pierre and Miquelon |
| 275 | 7.1 | 1 | 19 | 105 | 5.5 | ... | ... | 1.4 | 14 | 85.0 | ... | ... | 5.0 | St. Vincent and the Grenadines |
| 744[25] | — | — | ... | 337[25] | — | ... | ... | 2.4 | 15 | 98.0 | 98.2 | 97.7 | 5.9 | San Marino |
| 370 | 10.6 | ... | ... | 700[25] | — | ... | ... | 0.3 | 15 | 54.2 | 70.2 | 39.1 | 5.9 | São Tomé and Príncipe |
| 9,938 | ... | 77 | 9,724 | 102,709 | 10.6 | 9.8[2] | 830 | ... | 15 | 48.8 | 58.0 | 34.6 | 7.1 | Saudi Arabia |
| 10,051 | 16.8 | ... | 925[4] | 11,809 | 13.5[4] | 2.2[2] | 193 | 0.1 | 15 | 22.5 | 31.0 | 14.2 | 4.7 | Senegal |
| 1,412 | 8.7 | ... | ... | ... | ... | ... | ... | 2.6 | 15 | 57.3 | 54.9 | 59.6 | 9.0 | Seychelles |
| 4,774 | 11.8 | 2 | 296 | 2,445 | 8.3 | 0.6[5] | 55 | ... | 15 | 23.6 | 31.2 | 16.5 | 3.8 | Sierra Leone |
| 20,873 | 7.7 | 5 | 3,812 | 42,007 | 11.0 | 11.8[2] | 1,406 | 3.4 | 15 | 82.9 | 91.6 | 74.0 | 4.4 | Singapore |
| 1,142[6] | 18.1[6] | 1 | ... | ... | ... | ... | ... | 1.6 | 15 | 54.1 | 62.4 | 44.9 | 3.6 | Solomon Islands |
| 10,203 | 14.1 | 1 | 262[4] | 3,405 | ... | 0.9[3] | 72 | ... | 15 | 11.6 | 18.4 | 6.5 | 1.4 | Somalia |
| 35,394 | 9.5 | 96 | 15,245 | 204,546 | 13.3 | ... | ... | 3.7[14] | 15 | 79.3 | 80.6 | 78.0 | 3.8 | South Africa |
| 6,053 | 16.8 | 1 | 36[5] | 816 | ... | ... | ... | ... | 15 | 75.0 | ... | ... | ... | Bophuthatswana |
| 240 | 7.5 | 4 | 76[6] | 1,383 | ... | ... | ... | ... | 15 | 72.0 | ... | ... | ... | Ciskei |
| ... | ... | ... | ... | ... | ... | ... | ... | ... | ... | ... | ... | ... | ... | KwaNdebele |
| ... | ... | ... | ... | 560 | ... | ... | ... | ... | ... | ... | ... | ... | ... | Transkei |
| 358 | 10.8 | 4 | 119 | 2,857 | 24.0 | ... | ... | ... | 15 | 72.5 | 74.2 | 70.8 | ... | Venda |
| 1,200[1] | 14.8[1] | 4[1] | 137[1] | 537[1] | 3.9[1] | — | ... | ... | 15 | ... | ... | ... | 1.9 | South West Africa/Namibia |
| 695,180[6] | 15.3[6] | 33[2] | 43,037[2] | 692,152[2] | 16.1[2] | 25.8[2] | 2,067 | 7.1 | 15 | 92.8 | 95.9 | 89.9 | 2.5 | Spain |
| 8,382[2] | 18.0[2] | 8[2] | 5,629[2] | 63,460[2] | 11.3[2] | 4.1[2] | 405 | 2.3 | 15 | 86.1 | 90.8 | 81.2 | 2.9 | Sri Lanka |
| 29,650 | ... | 16 | 1,934[5] | 35,596 | ... | 2.0[2] | 175 | ... | 15 | 21.6 | 36.5 | 6.5 | 4.6 | Sudan, The |
| 15,428[6] | 13.1[6] | 6 | 357 | 1,704 | 4.8 | 6.9[6] | 783 | ... | 15 | 79.2 | 83.8 | 74.8 | 7.0 | Suriname |
| 1,257 | 12.6 | 2 | 291 | 2,997 | 10.3 | 3.3[2] | 278 | ... | 15 | 67.9 | 70.3 | 65.7 | 5.3 | Swaziland |
| ... | ... | ... | 17,608[6] | 221,200 | ... | 38.2[6] | 2,651 | 15.4 | 15 | 100.0 | 100.0 | 100.0 | 8.0 | Sweden |
| 249,900 | ... | ... | ... | 117,000 | ... | 21.2[6] | 1,664 | 2.9 | 15 | 100.0 | 100.0 | 100.0 | 5.1 | Switzerland |
| 59,085 | 7.5 | 80 | 1,456 | 169,155 | 116.2 | 16.4[2] | 1,568 | 1.3 | 15 | 44.6 | 64.8 | 24.3 | 6.1 | Syria |
| 420,212 | 26.6 | 105 | 20,848 | 428,576 | 20.6 | ... | 2,225 | ... | 15 | 89.9 | 95.2 | 84.6 | 3.6 | Taiwan |
| 13,760 | 11.9 | 2 | 877 | 3,414 | 3.9 | 0.4[6] | 29 | 0.2 | 15 | 79.0 | ... | ... | 5.8 | Tanzania |
| 436,788 | 22.1 | 62[5] | 28,865 | 1,120,084 | 38.8 | 22.5[2] | 2,264 | 2.9 | 15 | 88.8 | 93.2 | 84.5 | 3.9 | Thailand |
| 5,050 | 25.5 | 1 | 308 | 4,500 | 14.6 | 1.8[6] | 156 | 1.3 | 15 | 39.1 | 51.7 | 27.5 | 5.9 | Togo |
| 197[5] | 16.4[5] | — | — | 32[25] | — | ... | ... | ... | 15 | 99.8 | 99.8 | 99.8 | ... | Tokelau |
| 635 | ... | 1[1] | ... | 125[1] | ... | — | ... | ... | 15 | 92.8 | 92.9 | 92.8 | 7.8 | Tonga |
| ... | ... | 1 | ... | 2,684 | ... | 4.4[1] | 483 | 2.9 | 15 | 95.1 | 96.7 | 93.6 | 5.1 | Trinidad and Tobago |
| ... | ... | ... | 5,171 | 40,830 | 7.9 | 5.6[6] | 559 | 2.8 | 15 | 48.2 | 60.4 | 35.7 | 4.5 | Tunisia |
| 635,847 | 14.4 | 310 | 22,968 | 449,416 | 19.6 | 8.9[6] | 863 | 3.6 | 15 | 65.9 | 81.7 | 50.0 | 2.5 | Turkey |
| — | — | ... | ... | ... | ... | ... | ... | 7.7 | 15 | 86.7 | 85.0 | 88.0 | ... | Turks and Caicos Islands |
| 354[2] | 22.1[2] | — | — | 100[4,25] | ... | ... | ... | ... | 15 | 95.5 | 95.5 | 95.5 | ... | Tuvalu |
| 23,335 | 22.5 | 14 | 934 | 8,216 | 8.8 | 0.6[1] | 52 | 0.1 | 15 | 57.3 | 69.7 | 45.3 | 1.3 | Uganda |
| 2,866,000 | 11.7 | 894 | 377,000 | 2,763,000 | 7.3 | 21.4[6] | 1,918 | 8.3 | 15 | 99.0 | ... | ... | 6.6 | U.S.S.R. |
| 2,442 | 8.9 | ... | 443 | 4,502 | 10.2 | 7.8[6] | 557 | 6.0 | 15 | 71.2 | 72.7 | 66.3 | 1.7 | United Arab Emirates |
| 486,140[34] | 5.2[34] | 46[14] | 31,043 | 345,760 | 11.1 | 20.3[2] | 1,600 | 11.0 | 15 | 100.0 | 100.0 | 100.0 | 5.3 | United Kingdom |
| [19] | 19 | 3,280 | 690,000 | 12,164,000 | 17.6 | 57.3[6] | 5,281 | 32.2 | 15 | 95.5 | 95.7 | 95.3 | 6.7 | United States |
| 55,359 | 9.8 | 1 | 4,537 | 63,734 | 14.0 | 31.7[11] | 2,588 | 6.3 | 15 | 96.3 | ... | ... | 2.4 | Uruguay |
| 718 | ... | ... | ... | ... | ... | — | ... | ... | 15 | 52.9 | 57.3 | 47.8 | ... | Vanuatu |
| [19] | 19 | 82 | 31,735 | 444,450 | 14.0 | 23.4[6] | 2,267 | 7.0 | 15 | 89.0 | 90.7 | 87.2 | 8.1 | Venezuela |
| 128,000 | 11.2 | 97 | 18,800 | 88,600 | 4.7 | 2.2[5] | 212 | ... | 15 | 94.0 | ... | ... | 3.0 | Vietnam |
| [17] | 17 | 1[11] | 84[11] | 765[11] | 9.1[11] | ... | ... | 17.6 | 15 | 90.0 | ... | ... | 7.9 | Virgin Islands (U.S.) |
| — | — | — | ... | ... | ... | ... | ... | 1.0[8] | 20 | 48.9 | 51.4 | 46.6 | ... | Wallis and Futuna |
| 1,628 | ... | 4[2] | 483[3] | 7,066[2] | ... | ... | ... | 8.1 | ... | ... | ... | ... | ... | West Bank |
| ... | ... | ... | ... | ... | ... | ... | ... | ... | ... | ... | ... | ... | ... | Western Sahara |
| 651 | 9.4 | 6 | 37 | 562 | 15.2 | ... | ... | 2.2 | 10 | 98.3 | 98.5 | 98.1 | 5.9 | Western Samoa |
| 5,601 | ... | 1 | 486[2] | 4,791 | ... | 2.3[4] | 185 | ... | 15 | 38.9 | 66.6 | 10.9 | 7.4 | Yemen (Aden) |
| 23,970 | 35.6 | 1 | 245 | 9,024 | 36.8 | 1.2[5] | 76 | ... | 15 | 8.3 | 15.9 | 0.5 | 6.6 | Yemen (Ṣanʿāʾ) |
| ... | ... | 340 | 25,882 | 359,175 | 13.9 | 20.2[2] | 1,650 | 6.8 | 15 | 89.6 | 95.5 | 83.9 | 3.9 | Yugoslavia |
| 319,805 | ... | 36 | 3,072 | 37,706 | 12.3 | 1.3 | 115 | ... | 15 | 61.2 | 78.6 | 44.7 | 5.8 | Zaire |
| 9,563 | 9.2 | 1 | 650 | 3,621 | 5.6 | 1.6[2] | 141 | 0.6 | 15 | 68.6 | 79.3 | 58.3 | 5.7 | Zambia |
| 30,935 | ... | 1 | 431[6] | 5,866 | ... | 2.6[6] | 224 | 0.6 | 15 | 76.0 | 81.5 | 66.8 | 8.3 | Zimbabwe |

registered abroad.   26General second level includes first level.   27Includes part-time teachers.   28General second level includes vocational second level and third level.   291972.   30Island of Mauritius only.   31Public school teachers only.   32Includes pre-school.   33Vocational only.   34Third level vocational and teacher training.   35Excludes East Jerusalem.

# Cultural institutions

This table supplies worldwide statistics for the principal and most comparable elements of cultural activity: publishing, libraries, cinema, performing arts, museums, and nature preservation. For the most part, the data that can be compiled and compared are those measures produced as a result of governmental activity or expenditure, such as copyright and deposit, public funding, taxation, and land-use policy.

International comparisons of such data, however, should be approached with caution. In older, more prosperous nations, where the physical necessities of life are in secure supply, more money is available for cultural activities—and, indeed, for collecting data on them—than in less developed countries. Yet a developing country with an embryonic statistical system may have a flourishing cultural life that includes theatrical performance, live music, or the practice of arts no longer central to the Western experience, such as oral storytelling, ceremonial dance, traditional community ritual, or puppetry. Such activities may be more fully integrated into the life of the people than the more measurable cultural pursuits of a developed society.

The statistics actually reported may include books published (copyrighted), cultural facilities, library holdings, seating capacities of theatres and cinemas, attendance (tickets sold), and so on. Even when these figures are recalculated on a per capita basis, apparent differences among countries may be more a function of each country's statistical reporting system than of differences in the cultural habits and preferences of the people.

Furthermore, some kinds of data cannot be given meaningfully. For example, available data on government expenditures for cultural activi-

ties represent a wide variety of government policies. Some governments provide no support for cultural activities at any level; others subsidize or support them directly. Some offer tax incentives; others employ artists as teachers, performers, scholars, or archivists. Most national data on manpower engaged in cultural activities are collected on the basis of the individual's main source of income, without regard for his or her aspirations or avocations, part-time paid or unpaid activities, or other less convenient measures. A substantial part of the data presented were obtained from periodic surveys by Unesco, and they refer to a wide range of years. Throughout the table, data given in roman type are from 1983 or later; those in italic are from before 1983.

Figures for book production generally include all works published in separate bindings except advertising works, timetables, telephone directories, price lists, catalogs of businesses or exhibitions, musical scores, maps, atlases, and the like. The figures include government publications, school texts, theses, offprints, series works, and illustrated works, even those consisting principally of illustrations. Figures refer to works actually published during the year of survey, usually by a registered publisher, and deposited for copyright. A book is defined as a work of 49 or more pages, a pamphlet as a work of from 5 to 48 pages. A work published simultaneously in more than one country is counted as having been published in each. Data for newspapers are given in the Communications table beginning on page 818.

Data on libraries are for public libraries and exclude other types of collections, such as national (except when it is the sole public library), school

## Cultural institutions

| country | book publishing | | | | | | | | public libraries | | | |
|---|---|---|---|---|---|---|---|---|---|---|---|---|
| | number of titles | | | | number of copies ('000) | | | | number | volumes ('000) | registered borrowers ('000) | loans per 1,000 population |
| | books | | periodicals | pamphlets | books | | periodicals | pamphlets | | | | |
| | total | of which school textbooks | | | total | of which school textbooks | | | | | | |
| Afghanistan | 415[3] | 108[3] | 51 | ... | 5,981[3] | ... | 1,094 | ... | 55 | 350 | 11 | ... |
| Albania | 972 | 497 | 8 | 158 | 6,012 | 3,547 | 2,894 | 494 | 45 | 3,723 | ... | ... |
| Algeria | 551 | 39 | 27 | 167 | 1,300[5] | 1,194 | 476 | ... | 35 | 165 | ... | ... |
| American Samoa | 98[3] | 24[3] | 16 | 1[3] | 33[3,7] | ... | 8 | 1[3,7] | 1 | 251 | ... | 5,400 |
| Andorra | ... | ... | 15 | ... | ... | ... | 15 | ... | 1 | ... | ... | 631 |
| Angola | 33[3] | ... | ... | 24[3] | 239[3] | ... | ... | 191[3] | 2 | 41 | ... | ... |
| Anguilla | ... | ... | ... | ... | ... | ... | ... | ... | ... | ... | ... | ... |
| Antigua and Barbuda | ... | ... | ... | ... | ... | ... | ... | ... | 1 | ... | ... | ... |
| Argentina | 4,216[8] | 243[8] | ... | 8 | 13,526[8] | 1,289[8] | ... | 8 | 1,528 | 9,532 | 4,201 | 360 |
| Aruba | 13 | | | 13 | | | | | 13 | 13 | 13 | 13 |
| Australia | 2,309 | 190 | 3,534 | 599 | ... | ... | ... | ... | 350 | 24,500 | ... | ... |
| Austria | 7,725 | 86 | 2,315 | 1,334 | ... | ... | ... | ... | 2,172 | 7,022 | 813 | 1,800 |
| Bahamas, The | ... | ... | ... | ... | ... | ... | ... | ... | 37 | 60 | ... | ... |
| Bahrain | 78 | 78 | ... | ... | 843 | 843 | ... | ... | 1 | 183 | 50 | 722 |
| Bangladesh | 542[8] | 43 | 388 | 8 | ... | ... | 657 | ... | 69 | 500 | ... | ... |
| Barbados | 18 | ... | 120 | 69 | ... | ... | ... | ... | 1[15] | 173 | 64 | 2,212 |
| Belgium | 6,584[8] | ... | 11,256 | 8 | ... | ... | ... | ... | 2,351 | 24,140 | 1,731 | 4,300 |
| Belize | ... | ... | ... | ... | ... | ... | ... | ... | 1 | 100 | ... | ... |
| Benin | 13 | ... | ... | — | 18 | ... | ... | — | 1 | 32 | ... | ... |
| Bermuda | ... | ... | ... | ... | ... | ... | ... | ... | 1 | 149 | 3 | ... |
| Bhutan | ... | ... | ... | ... | ... | ... | ... | ... | — | — | ... | — |
| Bolivia | 274 | 4[3] | 106 | 27 | ... | ... | ... | ... | 99[18] | 125 | 1,120 | 37 |
| Botswana | 70[3] | ... | ... | 27[3] | 35 | ... | ... | 33 | 1 | 108 | 30 | 190 |
| Brazil | 16,370 | ... | 3,720 | 3,718 | 181,346 | ... | 900,332 | 108,136 | 3,291 | 9,600 | 2,744 | 58 |
| British Virgin Islands | 20 | ... | 20 | ... | 3 | ... | 23 | ... | 1[15] | 35 | 10 | 2,939 |
| Brunei | 50 | 25[3] | 19 | 22 | 341 | 249[3] | 128 | 19 | 1 | 97 | 6 | 230 |
| Bulgaria | 4,440 | 1,076 | 1,758 | 927 | 54,423 | 13,874 | 10,211 | 6,510 | 5,699 | 52,100 | 2,225 | 5,800 |
| Burkina Faso | 4 | ... | ... | — | ... | ... | ... | — | ... | ... | ... | ... |
| Burma | 1,400 | ... | 26 | — | ... | ... | 823 | ... | 6 | 154 | ... | ... |
| Burundi | ... | ... | ... | ... | ... | ... | ... | ... | 2 | 34 | ... | ... |
| Cameroon | 22[3] | 7[3] | 41 | ... | 94[3] | 7[3] | ... | ... | 5 | 6 | ... | ... |
| Canada | 8,600 | ... | 1,382 | 429 | ... | ... | 59,071 | ... | 777 | 51,812 | ... | 6,216 |
| Cape Verde | ... | ... | 4 | ... | ... | ... | ... | ... | — | — | ... | ... |
| Cayman Islands | 5 | ... | ... | — | ... | ... | ... | ... | 1 | 6 | 2 | 2,300 |
| Central African Republic | ... | ... | ... | ... | ... | ... | ... | ... | — | — | ... | ... |
| Chad | ... | ... | 4 | ... | ... | ... | ... | ... | 1 | 4 | 0.2 | ... |
| Chile | 1,207 | 90 | 89 | 446 | 15,118 | 1,500 | ... | 4,770 | 179 | 783 | 18 | 367 |
| China | 34,920[8] | 5,574[8] | 3,100 | 8 | 5,444,660[8] | 2,358,720[8] | 138,852 | 8 | 1,889 | 210,000 | ... | ... |
| Christmas Island | ... | ... | ... | ... | ... | ... | ... | ... | 1 | 13 | 3 | 8,000 |
| Cocos (Keeling) Islands | ... | ... | ... | ... | ... | ... | ... | ... | 1 | ... | ... | ... |
| Colombia | 6,500 | 2,570 | 1,034 | 8,541 | 48,005 | 25,750 | ... | 70,749 | ... | ... | ... | ... |
| Comoros | ... | ... | ... | ... | ... | ... | ... | ... | 2 | 8 | ... | ... |
| Congo | 9 | ... | ... | 118 | 285 | ... | ... | 1,471 | 1 | 11 | 14 | 22 |
| Cook Islands | ... | ... | ... | ... | ... | ... | ... | ... | 1 | 15 | 3 | 1,100 |
| Costa Rica | 1,759 | 825 | 274 | ... | 641 | ... | 163 | ... | 18 | 707 | ... | ... |
| Côte d'Ivoire | 46 | 13 | ... | ... | 3,766 | 3,517 | ... | ... | 1 | 25 | 2 | 3 |
| Cuba | 1,684 | 851 | 47 | 385 | 41,204 | 22,522 | 2,279 | 3,418 | 296 | 3,711 | 554 | 1,041 |
| Cyprus | 180[30] | 12 | 35 | 957[30] | 290[30] | 120 | 93 | 1,936[30] | 130[18] | 180 | ... | 230 |
| Czechoslovakia | 8,581 | 2,981[3,31] | 926 | 1,330 | 98,325 | 19,871[31] | 22,123 | 18,625 | 9,674 | 53,963 | 2,821 | 5,900 |
| Denmark | 7,296 | 903[32] | ... | 3,364 | ... | ... | ... | ... | 249 | 33,408 | ... | 17,087 |
| Djibouti | ... | ... | 2 | ... | ... | ... | 1 | ... | 2 | 16 | ... | 64 |
| Dominica | ... | ... | ... | ... | ... | ... | ... | ... | 1 | 15 | 4 | 660 |
| Dominican Republic | 1,504 | ... | ... | 715 | 3,017 | ... | ... | 1,320 | 15 | 9 | 533 | 120 |
| Ecuador | ... | ... | 284 | ... | ... | ... | ... | ... | 97 | 324 | ... | ... |
| Egypt | 1,503 | ... | 204 | 177 | 46,620 | ... | 1,841 | 6,380 | 223 | 1,329 | 6 | 10 |

and university, private, professional, business, and government libraries, even though these may play a significant role locally or nationally. Public libraries were thought to provide the most representative set of figures. Data for "volumes" may reflect either actual holdings or an estimate based on length of occupied shelving.

Statistics on commercial cinema attendance may originate from a variety of screening facilities, including fixed, mobile, or drive-in facilities. Seating capacity is given for fixed facilities only. The data on long (or feature) films may refer to prints with a length of from 1,000 to 3,000 metres, depending on the reporting practices of the individual country. However, there is some consensus among reporting countries on a standard length (for classification purposes) of 2,000 metres.

In the performing arts, many countries (if they report such data at all) include not only the familiar Western performance modes—music, theatre, opera, musical theatre, dance—but also other types of live performance, such as traditional, ceremonial, seasonal, festival, or holiday observances and such entertainments as circuses and puppet and shadow theatre. Data on number of performances and attendance refer to both amateur and professional performances unless footnoted. Statistics on the number of theatres refer to theatre buildings and open-air theatres intended mainly for theatrical and other dramatic performances. Premises only occasionally or partly used for performances of this type, such as cultural centres, cultural houses, youth centres, sports establishments, concert halls, cinemas, university and school premises, open-air grounds, antique theatres, historic buildings, and ancient sites, are excluded.

Museum data are derived in large part from surveys by Unesco and the International Council of Museums (ICOM). The number of museums and museum attendance refer to public and private institutions whose exhibits and collections are devoted primarily to art, archaeology and history, natural history and natural science and technology, or ethnology and anthropology; they may be specialized (single theme), regional, or general. National parks and nature reserves, zoos, aquariums, and botanical gardens have not been counted with museums since they are included in the nature conservation section of the table.

Data on nature preservation facilities generally refer to those operated by the national conservation authority (though in many countries, particularly those with federal systems, authority may be lodged with other governmental levels). The data on number of facilities cover all types of facilities operated by the relevant authority, including national parks and monuments, scientific reserves, game reserves, protected landscapes, resource and anthropological reserves, and multiple-use management areas. Data on surface extent usually include only those facilities with an area of more than 10 sq km (4 sq mi).

The data on national parks and nature reserves are derived from information compiled by the International Union for Conservation of Nature and Natural Resources (IUCN) and from Britannica's holdings of published and unpublished national data. The data on zoos, aquariums, and botanical gardens are mainly from the International Species Inventory System (zoos and aquariums) and the International Association of Botanical Gardens.

| cinema | | | | | performing arts | | | | museums | | | nature preservation | | | country |
|---|---|---|---|---|---|---|---|---|---|---|---|---|---|---|---|
| annual attendance (all cinemas) | | fixed cinemas | | number of long films produced | number of facilities | number of performances | annual attendance | | number | annual attendance | | national parks and nature reserves | | zoos, botanical gardens, etc. (number[2]) | |
| number ('000,000) | per 1,000 population | number | seating capacity ('000) | | | | number ('000) | per 1,000 population | | number ('000) | per 1,000 population | number | square metres per capita[1] | | |
| 4.9 | 300 | 34 | 19 | 2 | 28 | 2,913[4] | 1,676 | 590 | 7 | 7 | 0.5 | 6 | 120 | 1 | Afghanistan |
| ... | 9,900 | 105 | 29 | 14 | ... | ... | ... | ... | 2,034 | ... | ... | 4 | 110 | ... | Albania |
| 23.8 | 1,200 | 259 | ... | 5 | ... | ... | ... | ... | 11[6] | 391[6] | 18[6] | 5 | 100 | 3 | Algeria |
| 0.1 | 3,200 | 6 | 6 | ... | ... | ... | ... | ... | 1 | 52 | 1,700 | 1 | 4,300 | ... | American Samoa |
| 0.2 | 6,900 | 5 | 2 | ... | ... | 14 | 6 | 190 | 2 | 9 | 300 | — | — | ... | Andorra |
| 6.4 | 900 | 55 | 34 | 1 | ... | ... | ... | ... | 10 | ... | ... | 5 | 1,800 | 1 | Angola |
| ... | ... | 3 | ... | ... | ... | ... | ... | ... | ... | ... | ... | ... | ... | ... | Anguilla |
| ... | ... | ... | ... | ... | ... | ... | ... | ... | 3 | ... | ... | 1 | 250 | ... | Antigua and Barbuda |
| 49.6[9,10] | 1,700[9,10] | 919[10] | 622[10] | 15 | 399 | 330 | 4,136[11] | 160[11] | 318 | 5,215[12] | 200[12] | 29 | 850 | 16 | Argentina |
| ... | ... | ... | ... | ... | ... | ... | ... | [13] | ... | ... | ... | — | — | 13 | Aruba |
| ... | ... | 703 | 333 | 10 | ... | 1,419[11] | ... | ... | 15 | 5,279[14] | 360[14] | 580 | 22,500 | 41 | Australia |
| 16.1[9] | 2,100[9] | 532 | 137 | 16 | ... | ... | ... | ... | 209 | 8,943 | 1,200 | 27 | 390 | 21 | Austria |
| ... | ... | 13 | 6 | ... | ... | ... | ... | ... | 7 | ... | ... | 4 | 5,300 | 1 | Bahamas, The |
| 1.2 | 3,100 | 313 | ... | ... | ... | ... | ... | ... | 2 | 99 | 250 | ... | ... | ... | Bahrain |
| ... | ... | 444 | 273 | 18 | ... | ... | ... | ... | 38 | ... | ... | 3 | 3 | 1 | Bangladesh |
| 1.2 | 5,200 | 6 | 5 | ... | 1 | 8 | ... | ... | 1 | 30 | 120 | 1 | 10 | ... | Barbados |
| 20.7[9] | 2,100[9] | 472 | ... | 14 | ... | ... | ... | ... | 132[16] | 3,454[16] | 350[16] | 4 | 12 | 12 | Belgium |
| ... | ... | ... | ... | ... | ... | ... | ... | ... | 5 | 9 | 64 | 2 | 320 | ... | Belize |
| 0.9[9] | 300[9] | 4[10] | 4[10] | ... | ... | ... | ... | ... | 5 | 8[17] | 2[17] | 2 | 2,100 | ... | Benin |
| 0.2 | 4,200 | 4 | 2 | ... | 3 | 64 | 17 | 320 | 14 | ... | ... | 10 | 5 | 1 | Bermuda |
| ... | ... | 12 | 5 | ... | 1 | 8 | ... | ... | 1 | 16 | 13 | 11 | 6,700 | ... | Bhutan |
| 31.1[9] | 5,700[9] | 209 | 160 | 1 | 13 | 500[11] | 123[11] | 22[11] | 28 | ... | ... | 12 | 7,300 | 4 | Bolivia |
| 0.1[10] | 200[10] | 1[10] | 0.8[10] | ... | ... | 29 | ... | ... | 2 | 52 | 59 | 8 | 107,000 | ... | Botswana |
| 136.4 | 1,100 | 2,221 | 906 | 103 | 267 | 1,563 | ... | ... | 647 | 15,656 | 121 | 50 | 880 | 31 | Brazil |
| 35.3[19] | 3,300 | 1 | 0.4 | ... | ... | 3 | 4 | 330 | 1 | 1 | 85 | 7 | 800 | ... | British Virgin Islands |
| 2.6 | 13,000 | 7 | 6 | ... | ... | 78 | 9 | 41 | 3 | 112 | 510 | ... | ... | 1 | Brunei |
| 95.6 | 10,700 | 3,253 | 715 | 31 | 63 | 17,139 | 5,800 | 650 | 206 | 15,535 | 1,700 | 12 | 62 | 4 | Bulgaria |
| 3.8 | 600 | 12 | 14 | ... | ... | ... | ... | ... | 1 | ... | ... | 6 | 1,000 | ... | Burkina Faso |
| ... | ... | 175[10] | 136[10] | 47 | ... | ... | ... | ... | 12 | ... | ... | 5 | 87 | 2 | Burma |
| 0.1 | 24 | 7 | 3 | ... | 44 | ... | 77 | 19 | 2[20] | 6[20] | 1[20] | 7 | 210 | ... | Burundi |
| ... | ... | 52 | 29 | 1 | ... | 44[21] | 39[21] | 5 | 12 | 4,641 | 560 | 15 | 2,300 | 2 | Cameroon |
| 98.6 | 4,000 | 983 | 620 | 32 | 476 | 14,882[11,22] | 5,307[11,22] | 220[11,22] | 661 | 16,165[23] | 640[23] | 78 | 9,000 | 104 | Canada |
| ... | ... | ... | ... | ... | ... | ... | ... | ... | ... | ... | ... | ... | ... | ... | Cape Verde |
| 0.2[9] | 11,700[9] | 4 | 1 | ... | ... | ... | ... | ... | ... | ... | ... | ... | ... | ... | Cayman Islands |
| ... | ... | ... | ... | ... | ... | ... | ... | ... | 65 | ... | ... | 4 | 15,000 | ... | Central African Republic |
| 25.2 | 6,000 | 13 | 12 | ... | 4 | 120[24] | ... | ... | 5 | 3[25] | 0.6[25] | 1 | 230 | ... | Chad |
| 11.7[9] | 1,000[9] | 161 | 100 | 2 | ... | 811[11] | 299[11] | — | 69 | ... | ... | 64 | 10,500 | 10 | Chile |
| 18,250 | 18,100 | 143,650[26] | ... | 112 | ... | ... | ... | ... | 409 | ... | ... | 62 | 22 | 47 | China |
| ... | ... | 2 | ... | ... | ... | ... | ... | ... | ... | ... | ... | 1 | 7,000 | ... | Christmas Island |
| ... | ... | ... | ... | ... | ... | ... | ... | ... | ... | ... | ... | ... | ... | ... | Cocos (Keeling) Islands |
| 66.4[9] | 2,400[9] | 323 | 184 | — | 14 | 159[11] | 90[11] | 3[11] | 73 | 1,442[27] | 57[27] | 30 | 1,400 | 8 | Colombia |
| ... | ... | ... | ... | ... | ... | ... | ... | ... | ... | ... | ... | ... | ... | ... | Comoros |
| ... | ... | ... | ... | 1 | 1 | 74 | ... | ... | 5[20] | 57[28] | 29[28] | 10 | 7,800 | 1 | Congo |
| ... | ... | ... | ... | ... | ... | ... | ... | ... | 1 | 6 | 320 | 1 | 7,800 | ... | Cook Islands |
| ... | ... | ... | ... | ... | 9 | 347[11] | 50[11] | 24[11] | 16 | 473[29] | 200[29] | 21 | 1,700 | 1 | Costa Rica |
| 7.0 | 900 | 72 | 42 | 2 | ... | ... | ... | ... | 1 | ... | ... | 10 | 1,800 | 2 | Côte d'Ivoire |
| 85.7 | 8,500 | 518 | 276 | 10 | 51 | 51,638 | 25,600 | 2,559 | 241 | 8,159 | 816 | 4 | 24 | 6 | Cuba |
| ... | ... | ... | ... | ... | 12 | 793 | 206 | 330 | 26 | 95 | 150 | — | — | 1 | Cyprus |
| 78.9 | 5,100 | 2,836 | 861 | 61 | 82 | 24,163[11] | 8,600[11] | 558[11] | 348 | 17,666 | 1,100 | 28 | 750 | 42 | Czechoslovakia |
| 13.8 | 2,700 | 453 | 92 | 11 | 77[33] | 9,727[11,33] | 2,522[11,33] | 490[11,33] | 277 | 7,828[34] | 1,530[34] | 23 | 250 | 19 | Denmark |
| 0.6 | 5,200 | 4 | 6 | ... | ... | ... | ... | ... | ... | ... | ... | — | — | ... | Djibouti |
| ... | ... | 3 | ... | ... | ... | ... | ... | ... | ... | ... | ... | 1 | 810 | 1 | Dominica |
| 7.0[9,10] | 1,500[9,10] | 83[10] | 46[10] | ... | 2 | 41 | 74 | 14 | 6 | ... | ... | 5 | 350 | 1 | Dominican Republic |
| ... | ... | 330 | ... | ... | 75 | 148 | ... | ... | 23 | ... | ... | 12 | 3,000 | 1 | Ecuador |
| 41.5 | 900 | 202 | 185 | 52 | ... | 1,941 | 364 | 9 | 45 | 1,613 | 44 | 1 | 4 | 9 | Egypt |

## Cultural institutions (continued)

| country | book publishing | | | | | | | | public libraries | | | |
|---|---|---|---|---|---|---|---|---|---|---|---|---|
| | number of titles | | | | number of copies ('000) | | | | number | volumes ('000) | registered borrowers ('000) | loans per 1,000 population |
| | books | | periodicals | pamphlets | books | | periodicals | pamphlets | | | | |
| | total | of which school textbooks | | | total | of which school textbooks | | | | | | |
| El Salvador | 59 | 6[3] | ... | 85 | ... | ... | ... | ... | 113 | 111 | ... | ... |
| Equatorial Guinea | ... | ... | ... | ... | ... | ... | ... | ... | 3[18] | 12 | ... | ... |
| Ethiopia | 192 | 57 | 1 | 157 | 993 | ... | 2 | 66 | 3 | 80 | ... | ... |
| Faeroe Islands | 113 | 9 | ... | ... | 11 | 1 | ... | ... | 13 | 135 | 7 | 3,238 |
| Falkland Islands | ... | ... | 3 | ... | ... | ... | 2 | ... | ... | ... | ... | ... |
| Fiji | 84 | ... | 13 | 26 | 229 | ... | ... | 44 | 9 | 91 | 33 | 520 |
| Finland | 6,268 | 604 | ... | 2,295 | ... | ... | ... | ... | 461 | 29,900 | 2,100 | 15,567 |
| France | 25,448 | ... | 13,716 | 11,741 | ... | ... | 183,379 | ... | 1,141 | 64,379 | 6,094 | 1,957 |
| French Guiana | 1[3] | — | 7 | — | 2[3] | — | 6 | 1 | 1 | 19 | 0.7 | 210 |
| French Polynesia | 56 | 8 | 17 | 16 | 92 | 40 | 25 | 10 | 1 | 17 | 1 | 220 |
| Gabon | ... | ... | ... | ... | ... | ... | ... | ... | — | — | ... | ... |
| Gambia, The | 21 | ... | 3 | 125 | 8 | ... | ... | ... | 1 | 89 | 2 | 29 |
| Gaza Strip | ... | ... | ... | ... | ... | ... | ... | ... | ... | ... | ... | ... |
| Germany, East | 5,398 | 163 | 1,191 | 777 | 103,766 | 17,892 | 23,116 | 26,130 | 7,260 | 43,016 | 3,878 | 5,200 |
| Germany, West | 42,012 | 429 | 6,702 | 6,824 | ... | ... | 255,905 | ... | 13,806[18] | 75,660 | 6,174 | 3,195 |
| Ghana | 338 | 27 | 74 | 12 | 163 | ... | 254 | 91 | 9 | 1,119 | 55 | 54 |
| Gibraltar | ... | ... | 15 | ... | ... | ... | 4 | ... | 1 | 20 | 6 | 1,541 |
| Greece | 3,618 | 114 | 868 | 430 | ... | ... | ... | ... | 498[18] | ... | ... | ... |
| Greenland | ... | ... | ... | ... | ... | ... | ... | ... | 73[36] | 403[36] | ... | 8,783[36] |
| Grenada | 2[3] | ... | ... | 8[3] | 2[3] | ... | ... | 9[3] | 1 | 15 | 0.8 | ... |
| Guadeloupe | ... | ... | 45 | ... | ... | ... | 142 | ... | 1 | 90 | 15 | 410 |
| Guam | 12[3] | ... | 28 | ... | 2[3] | ... | ... | ... | 8 | 188 | 17 | ... |
| Guatemala | 312 | ... | ... | 181 | ... | ... | ... | ... | 1 | 27 | ... | ... |
| Guernsey | ... | ... | ... | ... | ... | ... | ... | ... | ... | ... | ... | ... |
| Guinea | ... | ... | 1 | ... | ... | ... | ... | ... | 1 | 12 | ... | ... |
| Guinea-Bissau | ... | ... | ... | ... | ... | ... | ... | ... | ... | ... | ... | ... |
| Guyana | 17 | ... | 65 | 38 | ... | ... | 53 | ... | 1 | 10 | ... | ... |
| Haiti | ... | ... | ... | ... | ... | ... | ... | ... | 1 | 12 | ... | ... |
| Honduras | ... | ... | ... | ... | ... | ... | ... | ... | 1 | 20 | ... | 5 |
| Hong Kong | 3,642 | 538 | 495 | 2,039 | 27,483 | 7,771 | ... | 16,829 | 48 | 2,260 | 1,601 | 1,900 |
| Hungary | 9,128 | 959 | 1,535 | 1,293 | 100,490 | 29,052 | 13,278 | 15,103 | 10,272[40] | 46,370[40] | 2,251[40] | 4,731[40] |
| Iceland | 1,121 | ... | ... | ... | ... | ... | ... | ... | 238 | 1,426 | ... | ... |
| India | 9,954 | 362 | 19,937 | ... | ... | ... | 50,094 | ... | 17,024[18] | ... | ... | ... |
| Indonesia | 4,020 | 265 | ... | 1,234 | ... | ... | ... | ... | 275 | 468 | 2,768 | ... |
| Iran | 4,835 | ... | 180 | ... | ... | ... | ... | ... | 385 | 2,161 | ... | 8 |
| Iraq | 82 | ... | ... | ... | 452 | ... | ... | ... | 15 | 240 | 17 | ... |
| Ireland | 609 | 20 | 252 | 190 | ... | ... | 2,958 | ... | 31 | 8,221 | 651 | 4,254 |
| Isle of Man | ... | ... | ... | ... | ... | ... | ... | ... | ... | ... | ... | ... |
| Israel | 4,161 | 1,189 | 890 | 243 | 11,654[8] | 5,263[8] | ... | 8 | 983 | 12,603 | 1,063 | 4,776 |
| Italy | 12,620 | 1,103 | 8,265 | 1,692 | 123,529 | 45,940 | ... | 9,273 | 8,686 | 17,000 | 2,944 | ... |
| Jamaica | 81 | 38 | ... | 18 | ... | ... | ... | 380 | 14 | 1,170 | 656 | 980 |
| Japan | 44,253 | 2,044 | 2,138 | ... | 717,480 | 224,169 | 36,293 | ... | 1,028 | 97,172 | 10,947 | 1,579 |
| Jersey | ... | ... | ... | ... | ... | ... | ... | ... | ... | ... | ... | ... |
| Jordan | ... | ... | 41 | ... | ... | ... | 211 | ... | 1 | 70 | 1 | 6 |
| Kampuchea | ... | ... | 3 | ... | ... | ... | ... | ... | ... | ... | ... | ... |
| Kenya | 235 | ... | ... | ... | ... | ... | ... | ... | 2 | 511 | 98 | 34 |
| Kiribati | ... | ... | ... | ... | ... | ... | ... | ... | 1 | 40 | ... | ... |
| Korea, North | ... | ... | ... | ... | ... | ... | ... | ... | ... | ... | ... | ... |
| Korea, South | 33,156 | 3,497 | 870 | 2,290 | 110,498 | 43,991 | ... | 7,111 | 137 | 2,510 | 16,513 | 155 |
| Kuwait | 22 | ... | 45 | 3 | 325 | ... | 982 | 34 | 22 | 319 | ... | 60 |
| Laos | ... | ... | ... | ... | ... | ... | ... | ... | ... | ... | ... | ... |
| Lebanon | ... | ... | ... | ... | ... | ... | ... | ... | 6 | 94 | ... | ... |
| Lesotho | ... | ... | 2 | ... | ... | ... | 10 | ... | 1 | ... | 3 | 14 |
| Liberia | ... | ... | ... | ... | ... | ... | ... | ... | 3 | 78 | ... | ... |
| Libya | 481[8] | ... | ... | 8 | 2,405[8] | ... | ... | 8 | 5 | 100 | ... | ... |
| Liechtenstein | ... | ... | ... | ... | ... | ... | ... | ... | 1 | ... | 10 | 1,000 |
| Luxembourg | 297 | 6[3] | 427 | 44 | ... | ... | ... | ... | 4 | 250 | 120 | ... |
| Macau | ... | ... | ... | ... | ... | ... | ... | ... | 4 | 250 | 120 | ... |
| Madagascar | 242 | 44 | ... | 79 | 335 | 100 | ... | 158 | 56 | 76 | 69 | 2 |
| Malawi | 18 | ... | 121 | ... | 74 | ... | ... | ... | 6 | 130 | 20 | 51 |
| Malaysia | 2,348 | 392 | 1,631 | 1,627 | 7,951 | 3,040 | 1,689 | 6,122 | 20 | 2,785 | 811 | 329 |
| Maldives | 3[3] | ... | ... | ... | ... | ... | ... | — | 1 | 8 | ... | ... |
| Mali | — | ... | ... | 160[5] | — | ... | 2 | 92[5] | 46 | 552 | ... | ... |
| Malta | 220 | 17[3] | 264 | 93 | ... | ... | ... | ... | 2 | 274 | 44 | 2,000 |
| Martinique | 3[3] | ... | 8 | 18[3] | 10 | ... | 17 | 33 | 1 | 120 | ... | ... |
| Mauritania | 21 | 21 | ... | 20 | ... | ... | ... | ... | 1 | 26 | ... | ... |
| Mauritius | 65 | 27[3] | ... | 59 | 104 | 69 | ... | 63 | 4 | 210 | ... | ... |
| Mayotte | ... | ... | ... | ... | ... | ... | ... | ... | ... | ... | ... | ... |
| Mexico | 4,505 | ... | 1,964 | ... | ... | ... | ... | ... | 557 | 3,720 | 8,492 | 174 |
| Monaco | 105[8] | ... | 105 | 8 | 792[8] | ... | 792 | 8 | 1 | 150 | ... | ... |
| Mongolia | 861[8] | ... | 38 | 8 | 6,009[8] | ... | 6,200 | 8 | 397 | 8,700 | ... | ... |
| Montserrat | ... | ... | ... | ... | ... | ... | ... | ... | 1 | ... | ... | ... |
| Morocco | ... | ... | 63 | ... | ... | ... | 145 | ... | 8 | 448 | ... | ... |
| Mozambique | 87 | 41 | ... | 1 | 5,542 | 4,985 | ... | 2 | 2 | 105 | ... | ... |
| Nauru | ... | ... | ... | ... | ... | ... | ... | ... | ... | ... | ... | ... |
| Nepal | 43 | — | 94 | — | 70 | — | ... | — | 400[18] | ... | ... | ... |
| Netherlands, The | 13,209 | 2,039 | ... | ... | ... | ... | ... | ... | 470 | 41,828 | 4,162 | 11,900 |
| Netherlands Antilles | 28[13] | ... | ... | 24[13] | ... | ... | ... | ... | 1[13] | 100[13] | 10[13] | 990[13] |
| New Caledonia | 15 | ... | 15 | 7 | 7 | ... | 27 | 1 | 1 | 60 | ... | ... |
| New Zealand | 1,601 | 14 | 5,788 | 1,851 | ... | ... | ... | ... | 209 | 6,062 | 2,666 | 8,000 |
| Nicaragua | 26 | ... | ... | ... | 146 | ... | ... | ... | 41 | ... | ... | ... |
| Niger | ... | 4 | ... | ... | 8 | 8 | ... | 0.1 | ... | ... | ... | ... |
| Nigeria | 940 | 360 | ... | 896 | ... | ... | ... | ... | 18 | 481 | 206 | 2 |
| Niue | ... | ... | 2 | ... | ... | ... | ... | ... | 1 | 6 | 1 | 3,359 |
| Norfolk Island | — | — | 2 | 1 | — | — | 3 | 1 | 1 | 5 | 0.2 | 6,000 |

| cinema | | | | number of long films produced | performing arts | | | | museums | | | nature preservation | | | country |
|---|---|---|---|---|---|---|---|---|---|---|---|---|---|---|---|
| annual attendance (all cinemas) | | fixed cinemas | | | number of facilities | number of performances | annual attendance | | number | annual attendance | | national parks and nature reserves | | zoos, botanical gardens, etc. (number[2]) | |
| number ('000,000) | per 1,000 population | number | seating capacity ('000) | | | | number ('000) | per 1,000 population | | number ('000) | per 1,000 population | number | square metres per capita[1] | | |
| 15.9[9] | 3,700[9] | ... | 4 | ... | ... | ... | ... | ... | 20 | 1,333 | 290 | — | — | 1 | El Salvador |
| 0.5 | 1,600 | 10 | 4 | ... | ... | 21[11] | 16[11] | 47[11] | 1 | ... | ... | ... | ... | ... | Equatorial Guinea |
| ... | ... | 40 | 36 | ... | ... | 253 | 224 | 7 | 16[6] | 66[6] | 0.16[6] | 10 | 700 | 3 | Ethiopia |
| ... | 1,000 | 5 | 1 | ... | ... | ... | ... | ... | 3 | 14 | 308 | ... | ... | ... | Faeroe Islands |
| 18.9[19] | 10,500 | 2 | 0.5 | ... | ... | ... | ... | ... | 1 | ... | ... | ... | ... | ... | Falkland Islands |
| 0.3 | 500 | 50 | 40 | ... | 3 | 255 | 57 | 90 | 1 | 40 | 58 | 2 | 76 | 1 | Fiji |
| 7.0 | 1,400 | 378 | 86 | 15 | 47 | 11,242[11] | 2,588[11] | 527[11] | 572 | 2,897 | 590 | 33 | 1,600 | 7 | Finland |
| 191.5 | 3,500 | 6,304 | 1,311 | 131 | ... | 19,300[11,35] | 10,700[11,35] | 200[11,35] | 1,434[20] | 11,000[6] | 210[6] | 26 | 270 | 79 | France |
| ... | ... | ... | ... | ... | ... | ... | ... | ... | 1 | 12 | 190 | — | ... | ... | French Guiana |
| 0.5 | 4,000 | 6 | 3 | ... | 2 | 33[11] | 14[11] | 99[11] | 3 | ... | ... | 2 | 220 | ... | French Polynesia |
| 1.1 | 2,100 | ... | ... | ... | ... | ... | ... | ... | 1 | ... | ... | 5 | 14,000 | ... | Gabon |
| ... | ... | ... | ... | ... | ... | ... | ... | ... | ... | ... | ... | 1 | 32 | ... | Gambia, The |
| ... | ... | ... | ... | ... | ... | ... | ... | ... | ... | ... | ... | ... | ... | ... | Gaza Strip |
| 73.4 | 4,400 | 2,095 | 334 | 15 | 188 | 75,380 | 9,800 | 591 | 684 | 33,700 | 2,000 | 13 | 12 | 39 | Germany, East |
| 122.8 | 2,000 | 3,664 | 821 | 83 | 325 | 51,300[11] | 21,400[11] | 350[11] | 2,025 | 56,748 | 930 | 45 | 87 | 126 | Germany, West |
| 3.9[9] | 340[9] | 7 | 9 | 1 | 11 | 3,672 | 653 | 61 | 4 | 69 | 6 | 8 | 920 | 3 | Ghana |
| 0.2 | 6,700 | 4 | 2 | ... | 3 | 39 | 15 | 450 | 1 | 17 | 590 | ... | ... | ... | Gibraltar |
| 57.4 | 5,900 | ... | ... | 47 | 91 | 14,760 | 5,230 | 560 | 83 | 3,174 | 321 | 14 | 63 | 3 | Greece |
| ... | ... | ... | ... | ... | ... | ... | ... | ... | 11 | ... | ... | 2 | 37 | ... | Greenland |
| 1.2 | 12,500 | 6 | 4 | ... | 28 | ... | ... | ... | 1 | 8 | 86 | 1 | 140 | 2 | Grenada |
| 0.8 | 2,650 | ... | ... | ... | ... | 92 | 44 | 130 | 5 | 31[25] | 95[25] | 1 | 680 | ... | Guadeloupe |
| ... | ... | ... | ... | ... | 1 | ... | ... | ... | 4 | ... | ... | 1 | 510 | ... | Guam |
| 9.5 | 1,300 | 115 | 72 | ... | ... | 206[38] | 50[38] | 7[38] | 18 | 58[39] | 7[39] | 2 | 75 | 2 | Guatemala |
| ... | ... | ... | ... | ... | ... | ... | ... | ... | 9 | ... | ... | ... | ... | 1 | Guernsey |
| ... | ... | 4 | ... | ... | ... | ... | ... | ... | 5 | 21 | 4 | 1 | 24 | ... | Guinea |
| ... | ... | ... | ... | ... | ... | ... | ... | ... | ... | ... | ... | ... | ... | ... | Guinea-Bissau |
| 13.3[9] | 14,700[9] | 50 | 40 | 4 | 3 | ... | ... | ... | 2 | 97[25] | 130[25] | 1 | 120 | 2 | Guyana |
| 2.0 | 400 | 28 | 14 | ... | ... | ... | ... | ... | 4 | 73[17] | 16[17] | 2 | 10 | ... | Haiti |
| ... | ... | 90 | ... | ... | ... | ... | ... | ... | 3 | 22 | 7 | 4 | 970 | 3 | Honduras |
| 58.0 | 10,700 | 90 | 100 | 105 | 8 | 424[11] | 362[11] | 93[11] | 5 | 565 | 130 | ... | *... | 3 | Hong Kong |
| 71.0 | 6,700 | 3,659 | 547 | 24 | 40 | 12,898[11] | 6,000[11] | 562[11] | 594 | 19,200 | 1,800 | 36 | 400 | 14 | Hungary |
| 2.2 | 9,400 | 39 | 12 | 4 | 4 | 528 | 154 | 658 | 16 | 108 | 462 | 21 | 32,000 | 2 | Iceland |
| 4,800.0 | 6,600 | 12,284 | 5,660 | 741 | ... | ... | ... | ... | 422 | ... | ... | 239 | 140 | 42 | India |
| 144.9[9] | 1,000[9] | 1,560 | 978 | 76 | 34 | 4,600 | 2,800 | 19 | 100 | 7,171 | 45 | 140 | 830 | 12 | Indonesia |
| 165.0[9] | 4,200[9] | 398[10] | 181[10] | 24 | 19 | 84[11] | ... | ... | 44 | ... | ... | 24 | 680 | 3 | Iran |
| ... | ... | 84 | 65 | 2 | 36 | 743[11] | 228[11] | 19[11] | 13 | 63 | 4 | ... | ... | 1 | Iraq |
| 18.0 | 5,800 | 177 | ... | 2 | 34 | 10,260[11] | ... | ... | 49 | ... | ... | 3 | 57 | 5 | Ireland |
| ... | ... | ... | ... | ... | ... | ... | ... | ... | 4 | ... | ... | ... | ... | 2 | Isle of Man |
| 24.2 | 6,600 | 214 | 152 | 14 | 5 | 275[11,41] | ... | ... | 95 | 6,780[42] | 1,600[42] | 5 | 79 | 13 | Israel |
| 164.8 | 2,900 | 6,361 | ... | 128 | 313 | 64,238[11] | 18,055[11] | 320[11] | 1,122 | 22,912[43] | 410[43] | 34 | 91 | 57 | Italy |
| ... | ... | ... | ... | ... | 16 | 839 | 1,143 | 540 | 5 | 44[17] | 22[17] | 2[44] | 2 | 5 | Jamaica |
| 155 | 1,300 | 2,137 | ... | 319 | 140 | 39,768[11] | ... | ... | 571 | 57,386 | 480 | 50 | 180 | 105 | Japan |
| ... | ... | ... | ... | ... | ... | ... | ... | ... | 5 | ... | ... | ... | ... | 1 | Jersey |
| 15.0 | 4,900 | 41 | 20 | ... | 5 | 64 | 180 | 84 | 16 | 147[45] | 58[45] | 2 | 130 | ... | Jordan |
| ... | ... | ... | ... | ... | ... | ... | ... | ... | 2 | ... | ... | 1 | 15 | ... | Kampuchea |
| 9.2 | 600 | 40 | 20 | ... | ... | ... | ... | ... | 6 | 531 | 27 | 28 | 1,500 | 5 | Kenya |
| ... | ... | ... | ... | ... | — | 23[46] | ... | ... | ... | ... | ... | 2 | 870 | 2 | Kiribati |
| ... | ... | ... | ... | ... | ... | ... | ... | ... | 17 | ... | ... | ... | ... | 2 | Korea, North |
| 43.9 | 1,100 | 301 | 232 | 91 | 16 | 3,449 | 402 | 10 | 146 | 665[47] | 16[47] | 14 | 120 | 4 | Korea, South |
| 3.6 | 2,500 | 14 | 600 | ... | 5 | ... | 95 | 66 | 3 | 296 | 173 | ... | ... | 1 | Kuwait |
| ... | ... | ... | ... | ... | ... | ... | ... | ... | ... | ... | ... | ... | ... | ... | Laos |
| ... | ... | ... | ... | ... | ... | ... | ... | ... | 7 | ... | ... | ... | ... | 1 | Lebanon |
| ... | ... | ... | ... | ... | ... | ... | ... | ... | 1 | ... | ... | 1 | 45 | ... | Lesotho |
| 1.5 | 800 | 13 | 9 | ... | ... | ... | ... | ... | 7 | ... | ... | 1 | 590 | 1 | Liberia |
| 10.2 | 3,500 | 49 | 22 | 2 | 14 | 439 | 160 | 51 | 26 | 50 | 16 | 2 | 340 | 2 | Libya |
| ... | ... | ... | ... | ... | ... | ... | ... | ... | 4 | 41 | 1,500 | 6 | 410 | ... | Liechtenstein |
| 1.1 | 3,000 | ... | ... | ... | ... | 337[48] | 225[48] | 613[48] | 14 | 225 | 630 | 4 | 3,100 | ... | Luxembourg |
| 3.0 | 9,300 | 8 | 9 | ... | 4 | 84 | ... | ... | 1 | 18 | 55 | ... | ... | ... | Macau |
| ... | ... | ... | ... | ... | 70 | 140 | 60 | 7 | 4[6] | 21[6,17] | 26[6,17] | 14 | 670 | 3 | Madagascar |
| 1.5 | 300 | 4 | 2 | ... | 2 | ... | ... | ... | 2 | 80 | 12 | 9 | 1,500 | ... | Malawi |
| 34.0 | 2,700 | 425 | ... | 13 | 12 | 1,303 | 312 | 25 | 16 | ... | ... | 34 | 1,000 | 6 | Malaysia |
| ... | ... | 7 | 3 | ... | 11 | ... | ... | ... | 1 | 3 | 17 | ... | ... | ... | Maldives |
| ... | ... | ... | ... | 1 | ... | ... | ... | ... | ... | ... | ... | 6 | 1,100 | 1 | Mali |
| 1.0 | 3,000 | 22 | 16 | ... | ... | ... | ... | ... | 18 | 562 | 1,700 | 2 | 1.1 | 2 | Malta |
| 1.1 | 3,450 | ... | ... | ... | ... | ... | ... | ... | 5 | ... | ... | 1 | 2,100 | ... | Martinique |
| ... | ... | 19 | 8 | ... | ... | ... | ... | ... | ... | ... | ... | 2 | 9,000 | ... | Mauritania |
| 10.6 | 10,600 | 46 | 42 | ... | 6 | 136 | 36 | 38 | 3 | 237 | 236 | 3 | 39 | 1 | Mauritius |
| ... | ... | ... | ... | ... | 2 | ... | ... | ... | ... | ... | ... | ... | ... | ... | Mayotte |
| 292.4 | 3,900 | 2,963 | ... | 105 | 94 | 17,069[49] | 6,549[49] | 57[49] | 216 | 13,070 | 170 | 29 | 120 | 11 | Mexico |
| 0.1 | 3,800 | 3 | 1 | ... | 3 | 31 | 13 | 500 | 2 | 154 | 6,200 | ... | ... | 4 | Monaco |
| 17.7 | 9,400 | 59 | ... | 6 | 21 | ... | 3,600 | 1,700 | 4 | 7,400 | 4,400 | 4 | 24,000 | ... | Mongolia |
| ... | ... | 1 | ... | ... | 1 | 16 | 4 | 360 | 1 | 2 | 170 | ... | ... | ... | Montserrat |
| 39.8[9] | 1,800[9] | 267 | 162 | 12 | ... | ... | ... | 12 | 11 | 1,580 | 74 | 2 | 17 | 5 | Morocco |
| 9.2[9] | 700[9] | 70 | 27 | ... | ... | ... | ... | 9 | ... | ... | ... | 6 | 1,300 | 4 | Mozambique |
| ... | ... | ... | ... | ... | ... | ... | ... | ... | ... | ... | ... | ... | ... | ... | Nauru |
| ... | ... | ... | ... | 1 | 16 | 65 | ... | 5 | ... | ... | ... | 10 | 590 | 1 | Nepal |
| 15.3 | 1,060 | 471 | 117 | 11 | ... | 32,851 | 8,343 | 575 | 538 | 15,879 | 1,096 | 47 | 100 | 36 | Netherlands, The |
| ... | ... | ... | ... | ... | ... | ... | ... | 7[13] | ... | ... | ... | 3 | 625 | 2[13] | Netherlands Antilles |
| 0.3 | 2,000 | 7 | 2 | ... | 1 | 46 | ... | ... | 1 | 30 | 220 | 7 | 3,300 | 1 | New Caledonia |
| ... | ... | 172 | 103 | 9 | ... | 2,287[11] | 515[11] | 120[11] | 110 | ... | ... | 147 | 8,300 | 15 | New Zealand |
| 5.2 | 1,900 | 127 | 74 | 1 | ... | ... | ... | ... | 9 | ... | ... | 2 | 53 | 1 | Nicaragua |
| ... | ... | ... | ... | ... | ... | ... | ... | ... | 1[6] | 600[6] | 110[6] | 3 | 590 | ... | Niger |
| 8.6 | 100 | 240 | ... | 20 | 23 | ... | ... | ... | 18 | ... | ... | 3 | 90 | 8 | Nigeria |
| ... | ... | ... | ... | ... | ... | ... | ... | ... | ... | ... | ... | ... | ... | ... | Niue |
| 10[19] | 5,000 | 1 | 0.1 | ... | 1 | 7 | 2 | 1,000 | 1 | 20 | 10,000 | 1 | ... | 1 | Norfolk Island |

## Cultural institutions (continued)

| country | book publishing | | | | | | | | public libraries | | | |
|---|---|---|---|---|---|---|---|---|---|---|---|---|
| | number of titles | | | | number of copies ('000) | | | | number | volumes ('000) | registered borrowers ('000) | loans per 1,000 population |
| | books | | periodicals | pamphlets | books | | periodicals | pamphlets | | | | |
| | total | of which school textbooks | | | total | of which school textbooks | | | | | | |
| Norway | 4,152[50] | ... | 4,010 | 1,388[50] | ... | ... | ... | ... | 1,391 | 16,502 | 1,198 | 4,360 |
| Oman | ... | ... | ... | ... | ... | ... | ... | ... | 1 | 20 | ... | ... |
| Pacific Is., Trust Terr. of the | 93[3] | 26 | ... | 40[3] | 47 | 11 | ... | 80 | 5[18] | 16 | ... | ... |
| Marshall Islands | ... | ... | ... | ... | ... | ... | ... | ... | ... | ... | ... | ... |
| Micronesia, Fed. States of | | | | | | | | | | | | |
| Northern Mariana Islands | | | | | | | | | | | | |
| Palau | ... | ... | ... | ... | ... | ... | ... | ... | ... | ... | ... | ... |
| Pakistan | 1,600 | ... | 1,461 | ... | ... | ... | ... | ... | 98 | 1,340 | ... | 6 |
| Panama | 114 | 9[3] | ... | 57 | 38[3] | ... | ... | 5[3] | 18 | 26 | ... | 29 |
| Papua New Guinea | ... | ... | 72 | ... | ... | ... | ... | ... | 24 | 186 | ... | ... |
| Paraguay | ... | ... | ... | ... | ... | ... | ... | ... | 15 | 45 | ... | ... |
| Peru | 481 | 41 | 507 | 65 | ... | ... | ... | ... | 557 | 1,950 | ... | 123 |
| Philippines | 265 | 175 | ... | 277 | 14,516[5] | 14,464 | ... | 202[5] | 507[18] | ... | 194 | ... |
| Pitcairn Island | | | | | | | | | | | | |
| Poland | 7,341 | 321 | 2,718 | 1,854 | 155,288 | 32,478 | 39,057 | 74,467 | 9,700 | 113,900 | 7,397 | 4,009 |
| Portugal | 7,964 | 775[32] | 915 | 1,077 | 92,395 | 8,078[32] | ... | 4,418 | 178 | 7,546 | ... | 513 |
| Puerto Rico | ... | ... | ... | ... | ... | ... | ... | ... | 121[40] | 715 | ... | ... |
| Qatar | 316 | 219 | 16 | 21 | 2,100 | 1,533 | 191 | 105 | 7 | 263 | 11 | 67 |
| Réunion | 49 | 13 | 53 | 30 | ... | ... | 110 | ... | 3 | 315 | ... | ... |
| Romania | 5,632[8] | ... | 435 | 8 | 64,608[8] | ... | 221,000 | 8 | 6,821 | 66,672 | 4,507 | 2,300 |
| Rwanda | ... | ... | 8 | ... | ... | ... | ... | ... | 5 | ... | ... | ... |
| St. Christopher and Nevis | 2[3] | — | ... | 3[3] | — | — | ... | 2[3] | 2 | ... | ... | ... |
| St. Helena and Ascension | ... | ... | 2 | ... | ... | ... | 0.5 | ... | ... | ... | ... | ... |
| St. Lucia | 5 | 6[8] | ... | 11 | 15 | 12[8] | ... | 18 | 4 | ... | ... | ... |
| St. Pierre and Miquelon | ... | ... | ... | ... | ... | ... | ... | ... | 3 | 15 | ... | ... |
| St. Vincent | ... | ... | ... | ... | ... | ... | ... | ... | 1 | ... | ... | ... |
| San Marino | 14 | ... | 11 | 1 | ... | ... | ... | ... | ... | ... | ... | ... |
| São Tomé and Príncipe | ... | ... | ... | ... | ... | ... | ... | ... | 1 | ... | ... | ... |
| Saudi Arabia | 207 | — | 58 | 11 | ... | ... | ... | ... | 28 | 36 | ... | ... |
| Senegal | 423[3,8] | 83[3,8] | ... | 8 | 169[3,8] | 70[3,8] | ... | 3,8 | 1 | 7 | ... | ... |
| Seychelles | 23 | ... | 4 | 31[3] | ... | ... | ... | ... | 1 | 35 | ... | 1,672 |
| Sierra Leone | 17[3] | 2[3] | ... | 44[3] | 9[3] | 4[3] | ... | 12[3] | 11 | 392 | ... | ... |
| Singapore | 1,524[54] | 389 | 1,786 | 403[54] | 8,947[54] | 4,081 | ... | 2,179[54] | 1 | 2,162 | 655 | 2,372 |
| Solomon Islands | ... | ... | 2 | ... | ... | ... | 4 | ... | 8 | 22 | 5 | ... |
| Somalia | ... | ... | ... | ... | ... | ... | ... | ... | ... | ... | ... | ... |
| South Africa | ... | ... | ... | ... | ... | ... | ... | ... | 85 | 7,857 | ... | ... |
| Bophuthatswana | | | | | | | | | | | | |
| Ciskei | | | | | | | | | | | | |
| KwaNdebele | | | | | | | | | | | | |
| Transkei | | | | | | | | | | | | |
| Venda | ... | ... | ... | ... | ... | ... | 18 | ... | 1 | 10 | 3 | 11 |
| South West Africa/Namibia | ... | ... | 3 | ... | ... | ... | ... | ... | 8 | 157 | ... | ... |
| Spain | 25,518 | 2,465 | 5,508 | 5,246 | 212,874 | 37,556 | 55,352 | 37,652 | 1,396 | 11,730 | 1,308 | 170 |
| Sri Lanka | 707 | 111 | 454 | 1,244 | 12,340 | 10,895 | 42,511 | 5,273 | 650 | ... | 197 | ... |
| Sudan, The | ... | 138[57] | 25 | ... | ... | 12,905[57] | 195 | — | 7 | 36 | ... | ... |
| Suriname | ... | ... | 22 | ... | ... | ... | 44 | ... | 2 | 268 | 54 | 2,100 |
| Swaziland | ... | ... | 1 | ... | ... | ... | 2,600 | ... | 1 | 51 | ... | ... |
| Sweden | 10,373[8] | ... | 3,690 | 8 | ... | ... | ... | ... | 404 | 42,886 | ... | 9,262 |
| Switzerland | 11,806[8] | 241[32] | 1,533 | 8 | ... | ... | 31,773 | ... | 79[58] | 24,000[58] | ... | 1,400 |
| Syria | 119 | 13 | 48 | — | 553 | ... | 454 | — | ... | ... | ... | ... |
| Taiwan | 9,256 | ... | 2,661 | ... | ... | ... | ... | ... | 148 | ... | ... | ... |
| Tanzania | 166 | 12[3] | 69 | 197 | ... | ... | 646 | ... | 19 | 454 | 10 | 9 |
| Thailand | 8,392 | 319 | 1,189 | 241 | ... | ... | ... | ... | 375 | 1,599 | 31 | ... |
| Togo | ... | ... | ... | ... | ... | ... | ... | ... | 1 | 8 | ... | ... |
| Tokelau | ... | ... | ... | ... | ... | ... | ... | ... | 1 | 0.2 | ... | ... |
| Tonga | 33 | 5 | ... | 287 | 0.4 | 0.1 | ... | ... | ... | ... | ... | ... |
| Trinidad and Tobago | 101 | 7 | ... | 85 | ... | ... | ... | ... | 3 | 246 | 73 | 345 |
| Tunisia | ... | 172 | 230 | — | ... | 6,000 | ... | ... | 280 | 1,315 | 65 | 174 |
| Turkey | 6,741 | 387 | 2,568 | 259 | ... | ... | ... | ... | 638 | 6,260 | 486 | 40 |
| Turks and Caicos Islands | ... | ... | ... | ... | ... | ... | ... | ... | 1 | 26 | 3 | 1,641 |
| Tuvalu | | | | | | | | | | | | |
| Uganda | ... | ... | ... | ... | ... | ... | ... | ... | 1 | 73 | 157 | 31 |
| U.S.S.R. | 54,569 | 2,836[32] | 5,357 | 28,221 | 1,465,747 | 293,085[32] | 4,279,930 | 619,597 | 133,700 | 2,050,400 | 148,000 | 11,500 |
| United Arab Emirates | 84 | 63 | 8 | — | 1,590 | 1,535 | 25 | — | 7 | 15 | ... | ... |
| United Kingdom | 52,994 | 1,824 | 6,408 | 3,840 | ... | ... | ... | ... | 167 | 131,338 | ... | 11,300 |
| United States | 51,058[65] | ... | 3,731 | ... | ... | ... | ... | ... | 8,768 | 509,250 | ... | 4,300 |
| Uruguay | 711 | 152 | 545 | 495 | ... | ... | ... | ... | 72 | 166 | ... | ... |
| Vanuatu | ... | ... | ... | ... | ... | ... | ... | ... | 1 | 12 | 0.7 | ... |
| Venezuela | 3,596 | ... | 160 | 604 | 1,194 | ... | 4,649 | ... | 23 | 1,130 | 66 | 160 |
| Vietnam | 2,060[8] | 300[8] | 173 | 8 | 42,800[8] | 8 | 323 | 8 | 427 | 8,900 | ... | ... |
| Virgin Islands (U.S) | ... | ... | ... | ... | ... | ... | ... | ... | 1 | 90 | 10 | 707 |
| Wallis and Futuna | | | | | | | | | | | | |
| West Bank | | | | | | | | | | | | |
| Western Sahara | | | | | | | | | | | | |
| Western Samoa | 79 | ... | ... | 156 | 39 | ... | ... | 43 | 1 | 61 | ... | ... |
| Yemen (Aden) | ... | ... | ... | ... | ... | ... | ... | ... | 2 | 40 | ... | ... |
| Yemen (Ṣan'ā') | | | | | | | | | | | | |
| Yugoslavia | 8,546 | 1,387 | 1,474 | 2,372 | 46,034 | 19,769 | 4,968 | 10,378 | 1,972 | 26,424 | ... | 1,200 |
| Zaire | 194[3] | 5[3] | 106 | 37[3] | ... | ... | 225 | ... | 11 | 177 | 9 | 1 |
| Zambia | 454 | 215[3] | ... | — | 235[68] | ... | ... | — | 11 | 240 | 18 | 28 |
| Zimbabwe | 183 | 41 | ... | 10 | 2,017 | ... | ... | 134 | 6 | 523 | 18 | 74 |

1Calculations based on statutory areas, whether of land or water. 2Excludes zoological and aquatic collections in museums. 3First editions only. 4Opera and ballet, drama, and variety only. 5School textbooks, university theses, and government publications only. 6National museums only. 7Excludes school textbooks and children's books. 8Books includes pamphlets. 9Excludes drive-ins, mobile units, or both. 1016-millimetre data not available. 11Professional only. 12214 reporting. 13Netherlands Antilles includes Aruba. 1414 reporting. 15The public library also serves as the national library. 16Ministry of Flemish culture museums only. 173 reporting. 18Library service points. 19Attendance in '000s. 20National and public museums only. 21Drama, ballet, and dance only. 22Drama, opera, ballet, and dance only. 23644 reporting. 24Amateur ballet, dance, and drama only. 251 reporting. 26Film projection units. 2757 reporting. 284 reporting. 2911 reporting. 30Excludes some Turkish publications. 31Includes university theses. 32Includes school pamphlets. 33Royal theatre and regional theatres only. 34263 reporting. 35Drama and opera only. 36Includes national library and school libraries. 3713,400,000 square metres per capita; a single national park comprises about one-third of the area of Greenland. 38Drama only. 3912 reporting.

| cinema | | | | | performing arts | | | | museums | | | nature preservation | | | country |
| annual attendance (all cinemas) | | fixed cinemas | | number of long films produced | number of facilities | number of performances | annual attendance | | number | annual attendance | | national parks and nature reserves | | zoos, botanical gardens, etc. (number [2]) | |
| number ('000,000) | per 1,000 population | number | seating capacity ('000) | | | | number ('000) | per 1,000 population | | number ('000) | per 1,000 population | number | square metres per capita [1] | | |
|---|---|---|---|---|---|---|---|---|---|---|---|---|---|---|---|
| 12.8[9] | 3,100[9] | 461 | 127 | 8 | 13 | 5,098[11] | 1,073[11] | 260[11] | 434 | 4,768 | 1,150 | 55 | 2,900 | 7 | Norway |
| 0.9 | 1,100 | 12 | 1 | ... | ... | ... | ... | ... | 1 | ... | ... | 1 | 190 | ... | Oman |
| ... | ... | 52 | ... | ... | ... | ... | ... | ... | 5 | ... | ... | ... | ... | ... | Pacific Is., Trust Terr. of the |
| ... | ... | ... | ... | ... | ... | ... | ... | ... | ... | ... | ... | 1 | 93 | ... | Marshall Islands |
| ... | ... | ... | ... | ... | ... | ... | ... | ... | ... | ... | ... | — | ... | ... | Micronesia, Fed. States of |
| ... | ... | ... | ... | ... | ... | ... | ... | ... | ... | ... | ... | 2 | 370 | ... | Northern Mariana Islands |
| ... | ... | ... | ... | ... | ... | ... | ... | ... | ... | ... | ... | — | ... | ... | Palau |
| 182.0 | 2,200 | 850 | ... | 60 | 12 | ... | 48[11] | 0.6[11] | 18 | 2,270 | 23 | 52 | 650 | 6 | Pakistan |
| 7.1 | 4,800 | ... | ... | ... | 1 | 55 | ... | ... | 10 | ... | ... | 6 | 3,000 | 2 | Panama |
| ... | ... | ... | ... | ... | 7 | 122 | 265 | 91 | 2 | 100 | 32 | 2 | 9 | 3 | Papua New Guinea |
| ... | ... | ... | ... | ... | ... | ... | ... | ... | 18 | ... | ... | 9 | 3,300 | 1 | Paraguay |
| 32.9 | 1,900 | 425 | ... | 1 | 35 | 2,388 | ... | ... | 12 | 201 | 10 | 11 | 1,200 | 2 | Peru |
| ... | ... | ... | ... | 136 | 6[51] | 121[51] | 29[51] | 0.6[51] | 61 | ... | ... | 26 | 72 | 5 | Philippines |
| ... | ... | ... | ... | ... | ... | ... | ... | ... | ... | ... | ... | ... | ... | ... | Pitcairn Island |
| 128.0 | 3,400 | 1,769 | 484 | 37 | 116 | 120,000[11] | 10,600[11] | 286[11] | 525 | 19,642 | 530 | 15 | 30 | 26 | Poland |
| 24.3[9] | 2,400[9] | 477 | 197 | 10 | 76 | 3,707 | 1,126 | 120 | 139 | 3,800[52] | 380[52] | 12[53] | 380[53] | 10 | Portugal |
| ... | ... | 165 | ... | ... | ... | ... | ... | ... | 24 | ... | ... | 2 | 1 | 8 | Puerto Rico |
| 0.3 | 840 | 4 | 4 | 1 | 1 | 4 | 1 | 5 | 1 | 60 | 300 | 1 | ... | 1 | Qatar |
| ... | ... | ... | ... | ... | ... | ... | ... | ... | 2 | 79 | 150 | ... | ... | ... | Réunion |
| 216.0 | 9,500 | 5,529 | 256 | 28 | 90 | 55,056[11] | 13,100[11] | 578[11] | 456 | 16,015 | 710 | 9 | 43 | 9 | Romania |
| 0.5 | 100 | 12 | 4 | 1 | 9 | 31 | 58 | 12 | 4 | ... | ... | 2 | 430 | ... | Rwanda |
| ... | ... | 3 | ... | ... | ... | ... | ... | ... | ... | ... | ... | ... | ... | ... | St. Christopher and Nevis |
| 53.0[19] | 8,800 | 2 | 1 | ... | ... | 1 | 1 | 170 | 1 | ... | ... | ... | ... | ... | St. Helena and Ascension |
| ... | ... | 6 | ... | ... | ... | ... | ... | ... | 1 | 7 | 58 | 1 | 120 | ... | St. Lucia |
| ... | ... | ... | ... | ... | ... | ... | ... | ... | 1 | 4 | 640 | ... | ... | ... | St. Pierre and Miquelon |
| ... | ... | 2 | ... | ... | ... | ... | ... | ... | ... | ... | ... | ... | ... | 1 | St. Vincent |
| 0.1 | 4,600 | 7 | 3 | ... | 1 | 26[11] | 10[11] | 46[11] | 11 | 741 | 35,000 | ... | ... | ... | San Marino |
| ... | ... | ... | ... | ... | ... | ... | ... | ... | ... | ... | ... | ... | ... | ... | São Tomé and Príncipe |
| ... | ... | ... | ... | ... | 94 | 89[46] | 90[46] | 11[46] | 1 | 40 | 4 | 1 | 400 | 2 | Saudi Arabia |
| 3.6[9] | 700[9] | 60[10] | ... | ... | 1 | 122[11] | 52[11] | 9[11] | 4 | 55 | 10 | 9 | 3,300 | 4 | Senegal |
| ... | ... | ... | ... | ... | 2 | 6[46] | 3[46] | 40[46] | 1 | 8 | 130 | 3 | 3,400 | ... | Seychelles |
| ... | ... | ... | ... | ... | ... | ... | ... | ... | 19 | 178[25] | 55[25] | 1 | 250 | 1 | Sierra Leone |
| 27.4 | 10,800 | 51 | 58 | 4 | 3 | 523 | 645 | 270 | 3 | 940 | 390 | 1 | 10 | 4 | Singapore |
| 0.1[9] | 300[9] | 2 | 1 | ... | ... | 3 | 1 | 5 | 1 | 29 | 150 | 1 | 46 | ... | Solomon Islands |
| ... | ... | ... | ... | ... | ... | ... | ... | ... | 1 | ... | ... | 1 | 570 | ... | Somalia |
| 31.2 | 1,200 | 260 | ... | 12 | 51 | 3,597[55] | 1,348[55] | 54[55] | 22[56] | 2,477[56] | 96[56] | 136 | 2,000 | 35 | South Africa |
| ... | ... | ... | ... | ... | ... | ... | ... | ... | ... | ... | ... | 2 | 380 | ... | Bophuthatswana |
| ... | ... | ... | ... | ... | ... | ... | ... | ... | ... | ... | ... | 8 | 360 | ... | Ciskei |
| ... | ... | ... | ... | ... | ... | ... | ... | ... | ... | ... | ... | ... | ... | ... | KwaNdebele |
| ... | ... | ... | ... | ... | ... | ... | ... | ... | ... | ... | ... | 2 | 22 | ... | Transkei |
| ... | ... | ... | ... | ... | ... | ... | ... | ... | 1 | ... | ... | 1 | 75 | ... | Venda |
| ... | ... | ... | ... | ... | ... | ... | ... | ... | 9 | ... | ... | 9 | 60,000 | 1 | South West Africa/Namibia |
| 141.4[9] | 3,700[9] | 4,861 | ... | 99 | 366 | 18,862 | 6,702 | 180 | 554 | 11,697 | 320 | 56 | 440 | 22 | Spain |
| 41.6 | 2,700 | 329 | ... | 33 | 22 | 1,002[46] | 600[46] | 41[46] | 9 | 466 | 34 | 37 | 400 | 4 | Sri Lanka |
| 13.2 | 600 | 56 | 97 | 2 | ... | ... | ... | ... | 7 | 221 | 10 | 3 | 810 | 2 | Sudan, The |
| ... | ... | ... | ... | ... | ... | ... | ... | ... | 3 | ... | ... | 9 | 15,000 | 1 | Suriname |
| ... | ... | ... | ... | ... | ... | ... | ... | ... | 1 | ... | ... | 4 | 610 | ... | Swaziland |
| 18.0 | 2,200 | 1,165 | 315 | 24 | 27 | 12,009 | 2,335 | 280 | 181 | 15,800 | 1,900 | 67 | 1,800 | 18 | Sweden |
| 19.3 | 3,000 | 437 | 128 | 22 | 18[11] | 3,895[11] | 1,747[11] | 270[11] | 585 | ... | ... | 19 | 190 | 32 | Switzerland |
| 12.4 | 1,300 | 84 | 48 | 24 | 5 | 411 | 165 | 20 | 16 | 321[59] | 42[59] | ... | ... | ... | Syria |
| 128.0 | 6,500 | 602 | 516 | ... | ... | ... | ... | ... | 10 | ... | ... | 28 | 84 | 3 | Taiwan |
| 3.8 | 200 | 34 | 15 | ... | 5 | 21 | 15 | 1 | 6 | 119[60] | 7[60] | 15 | 4,900 | ... | Tanzania |
| ... | ... | 651[10] | 439[10] | 55 | ... | ... | ... | ... | 64 | ... | ... | 45 | 530 | 3 | Thailand |
| ... | ... | ... | ... | ... | ... | ... | ... | ... | 1 | 48 | 21 | 7 | 1,600 | ... | Togo |
| ... | ... | ... | ... | ... | ... | ... | ... | ... | ... | ... | ... | ... | ... | ... | Tokelau |
| 0.1 | 1,000 | 3 | 2 | ... | ... | ... | ... | ... | ... | ... | ... | 5 | 320 | ... | Tonga |
| ... | ... | 72 | 57 | ... | ... | 49[46] | ... | ... | 1 | 8 | 7 | 8 | 140 | 1 | Trinidad and Tobago |
| 4.4 | 700 | 79 | 38 | ... | 12 | 598 | 164 | 26 | 35 | 367[61] | 52[61] | 3 | 46 | 3 | Tunisia |
| 56.3 | 1,159 | 853 | 476 | 72 | ... | 3,573[11,62] | 1,160[11,62] | 24[11,62] | 127 | 5,476 | 110 | 15 | 58 | 7 | Turkey |
| ... | ... | 3 | 1 | ... | ... | 3 | 0.6 | 100 | ... | ... | ... | ... | ... | ... | Turks and Caicos Islands |
| ... | ... | ... | ... | ... | ... | ... | ... | ... | ... | ... | ... | ... | ... | ... | Tuvalu |
| 2.3[9] | 200[9] | 17[10] | 10[10] | ... | ... | ... | ... | ... | 16 | ... | ... | 18 | 900 | 2 | Uganda |
| 3,968.0 | 14,800 | 141,665 | 25,387 | 321 | 628 | 281,800[11] | 124,000[11] | 449[11] | 1,479 | 174,363 | 630 | 163 | 660 | 144 | U.S.S.R. |
| 7.1 | 10,300 | 74 | 29 | ... | 1 | 12[38] | 36[38] | 40[17] | 2 | ... | ... | ... | ... | 2 | United Arab Emirates |
| 62.0 | 1,100 | 1,327 | 505 | 39 | 404 | ... | 40,242[11,22] | 720[11,22] | 1,768[63] | c. 52,000[64] | 920 | 57 | 270 | 155 | United Kingdom |
| 1,053.1 | 4,500 | 16,032 | 5,611 | 396 | ... | 21,596 | 40,200 | 170 | 4,440 | 329,083 | 1,500 | 200 | 1,270 | 652 | United States |
| 6.1 | 2,100 | 120 | 80 | 2 | 25 | 3,097 | ... | ... | 19 | 17[66] | 6[66] | 6 | 100 | 4 | Uruguay |
| 0.1 | 1,000 | 3 | 1 | ... | ... | ... | ... | ... | ... | ... | ... | ... | ... | ... | Vanuatu |
| 22.8[9] | 4,700[9] | 535 | ... | 12 | 9 | 372 | 206 | 16 | 133 | ... | ... | 34 | 4,300 | 12 | Venezuela |
| 375.0 | 6,300 | 430 | 178 | 15 | 81 | ... | 57,400[11] | 1,000[11] | 9 | 1,918[67] | 37[67] | 12 | 27 | 2 | Vietnam |
| ... | ... | ... | ... | ... | ... | ... | ... | ... | 5 | 811 | 7,700 | 2 | 660 | 1 | Virgin Islands (U.S.) |
| ... | ... | ... | ... | ... | ... | ... | ... | ... | ... | ... | ... | 4 | ... | ... | Wallis and Futuna |
| ... | ... | ... | ... | ... | ... | ... | ... | ... | ... | ... | ... | ... | ... | ... | West Bank |
| ... | ... | ... | ... | ... | ... | ... | ... | ... | ... | ... | ... | ... | ... | ... | Western Sahara |
| 0.5 | 3,200 | 6 | 6 | ... | ... | 9 | 2 | 11 | ... | ... | ... | 1 | 180 | 1 | Western Samoa |
| 3.9[9] | 1,900[9] | 24 | 24 | ... | ... | ... | ... | ... | 5 | ... | ... | ... | ... | ... | Yemen (Aden) |
| 14.5[9] | 2,500[9] | 35 | 28 | ... | ... | ... | ... | ... | ... | ... | ... | ... | ... | ... | Yemen (Şan'ā') |
| 89.0 | 3,860 | 1,307 | 440 | 29 | 149 | 18,506 | 4,906 | 220 | 358 | 11,264 | 497 | 20 | 140 | 19 | Yugoslavia |
| ... | ... | ... | ... | ... | 4 | ... | ... | ... | 4 | ... | ... | 9 | 2,700 | 4 | Zaire |
| 1.6 | 300 | 12 | 4 | ... | ... | ... | ... | ... | 3 | 12 | 2 | 19 | 10,000 | 1 | Zambia |
| ... | ... | ... | ... | ... | ... | ... | ... | ... | 9 | 162[69] | 20[69] | 17 | 3,400 | 4 | Zimbabwe |

[40] Public educational libraries include service points and trade union libraries. [41] Opera and ballet only. [42] 67 reporting. [43] 1,083 reporting. [44] Marine parks only. [45] 10 reporting. [46] Amateur only. [47] 58 reporting. [48] Two facilities only. [49] Excludes amateur opera and musical comedy. [50] Excludes school text material. [51] Metropolitan Manila only. [52] 139 reporting. [53] Excludes the Azores and Madeira. [54] Excludes government publications. [55] Performances of state-subsidized regional performing arts councils only. [56] Museums designated "declared cultural institutions" only. [57] Includes children's books. [58] Public libraries with 50,000 or more volumes only. [59] 13 reporting. [60] 5 reporting. [61] 32 reporting. [62] State theatres only. [63] 1980. [64] 1982 estimate. [65] Excludes government publications, books sold only by subscription, dissertations, and pamphlets. [66] 2 reporting. [67] 8 reporting. [68] School textbooks and government publications only. [69] 6 reporting.

The following list indicates the principal sources used in the compilation of *Britannica World Data*. It is by no means a complete list, either for international or for national sources, but is indicative only of the range of materials to which reference has been made in preparing this compilation. For example, in addition to the kinds of works cited below, reference has also been made to the constitutions of each country, to the publications of its central or commercial banks, to unpublished information received in correspondence from the countries, and to other more specialized sources.

## International Statistical Sources

Africana Publishing Co. *Africa Contemporary Record* (annual).
Asian Development Bank. *Key Indicators of Developing Member Countries of ADB* (annual, with supplements).
Billboard Ltd. *World Radio TV Handbook* (annual).
British Petroleum. *BP Statistical Review of World Energy* (annual).
Caribbean Community and Common Market. *Caricom Statistics Digest* (annual).
Council for Mutual Economic Assistance (Comecon). *Statistichesky Yezhegodnik Stran-Chlenov Soveta Economicheskoy Vzaimopomoshchi* (Statistical Yearbook of the Council for Mutual Economic Assistance).
Europa Publications Ltd. *Africa South of the Sahara* (annual); *The Europa Year Book* (2 vol.); *The Far East and Australasia* (annual); *The Middle East and North Africa* (annual); *South America, Central America, and the Caribbean* (annual).
European Communities. *ACP: Statistical Yearbook; Basic Statistics* (annual).
Food and Agriculture Organization. *Food Balance Sheets* (irreg.); *Production Yearbook; Trade Yearbook; World Census of Agriculture* (decennial); *Yearbook of Fishery Statistics; Yearbook of Forest Products.*
Her Majesty's Stationery Office. *Yearbook of the Commonwealth.*
Holmes & Meier Publishers. *Latin America and Caribbean Contemporary Record* (annual); *Middle East Contemporary Survey* (annual).
Instituts d'Émission d'Outre-Mer et des Départements d'Outre-Mer (France). *Rapports d'Activité, Bulletin trimestriel.*
Inter-American Development Bank. *Economic and Social Progress in Latin America* (annual).
Inter-Parliamentary Union. *World Directory of Parliaments* (annual).
International Air Transport Association. *World Air Transport Statistics* (annual).
International Bank for Reconstruction and Development/The World Bank. *World Bank Atlas* (annual); *World Debt Tables* (annual); *World Development Report* (annual); *World Tables* (2 vol. [irreg.]).
International Civil Aviation Organization. *Civil Aviation Statistics of the World* (annual); *Digest of Statistics.*
International Institute for Strategic Studies. *The Military Balance* (annual).
International Labour Organisation. *Year Book of Labour Statistics.*
International Monetary Fund. *Exchange Arrangements and Exchange Restrictions* (annual); *Government Finance Statistics Yearbook; International Financial Statistics* (monthly, with supplements and yearbook).
International Road Federation. *Road and Motor Vehicle Statistics* (annual); *World Road Statistics* (annual).

Jane's Publishing Co. *Jane's World Railways* (annual).
Lloyd's Register of Shipping. *Lloyd's Register of Shipping: Statistical Tables* (annual).
Longman Group Ltd. *Keesing's Contemporary Archives* (monthly).
Macmillan Press Ltd. *The Statesman's Year-Book.*
Middle East Economic Digest Ltd. *Africa Economic Digest* (semimonthly); *Middle East Economic Digest* (semimonthly).
Mining Journal. *Mining Annual Review.*
Nordic Council. *Yearbook of Nordic Statistics.*
Official Airline Guides, Inc. *Official Airline Guide* (monthly).
Organization of Eastern Caribbean States. *Annual Digest of Statistics.*
Organization for Economic Cooperation and Development. *Economic Surveys* (annual); *Financing and External Debt of Developing Countries* (annual); *National Accounts of Developing Countries* (irreg.).
Oxford University Press. *World Christian Encyclopedia* (David B. Barrett, ed. [1982]).
Pacific Publications. *Pacific Islands Year Book* (irreg.).
PennWell Publishing Co. *International Petroleum Encyclopedia* (annual).
René Moreux et Cie. *Marchés tropicaux & Méditerranéens* (semimonthly).
South Pacific Commission. *Key Economic Indicators* (occasional); *South Pacific Economies: Statistical Summary* (biennial).
United Nations (UN). *Compendium of Human Settlements Statistics* (irreg.); *Construction Statistics Yearbook; Demographic Yearbook; International Trade Statistics Yearbook; Energy Statistics Yearbook; Industrial Statistics Yearbook* (2 vol.); *Monthly Bulletin of Statistics; Population Studies* (irreg.); *National Accounts Statistics* (3 vol.; annual); *Population and Vital Statistics Report* (quarterly); *Statistical Yearbook; Supplement to the Statistical Yearbook and the Monthly Bulletin of Statistics* (quinquennial); *World Population Prospects, Estimates and Projections as Assessed in 1984.*
UN: Conference on Trade and Development. *Handbook of International Trade and Development Statistics* (annual); *The Least Developed Countries, 1985 Report* (2 vol.; 1987).
UN: Economic Commission for Africa. *African Socio-Economic Indicators* (annual); *African Statistical Yearbook; Demographic and Related Socio-Economic Data Sheets for ECA Member States* (1982); *Survey of Economic and Social Conditions in Africa* (irreg.).
UN: Economic Commission for Europe. *Annual Bulletin of Housing and Building Statistics for Europe; Annual Bulletin of Transport Statistics for Europe.*
UN: Economic Commission for Latin America. *Economic Survey of Latin America* (2 vol.; annual); *Statistical Yearbook for Latin America.*
UN: Economic and Social Commission for Asia and the Pacific. *Foreign Trade Statistics of Asia and the Pacific* (annual); *Statistical Indicators for Asia and the Pacific* (quarterly); *Statistical Yearbook for Asia and the Pacific.*
UN: Economic and Social Commission for Western Asia. *Population Bulletin* (irreg.); *The Population Situation in the ECWA Region* (irreg.); *Statistical Abstract of the Region of the Economic and Social Commission for Western Asia* (annual).
UN: Educational, Scientific, and Cultural Organization. *Statistical Yearbook; Estimates and Projections of Illiteracy* (1978).
United States: Central Intelligence Agency, *The World Factbook* (annual); Dept. of Commerce, *Foreign Economic Trends* (irreg.), *Overseas Business Reports* (annual), *World Population* (annual); Dept. of Energy, *International Energy Annual;* Dept. of Health and Human Services, *Social Security Programs Throughout the World* (biennial); Dept. of Interior, *Minerals Yearbook*

(3 vol.); Dept. of State, *Background Notes* (irreg.).
Vatican (Central Statistics Office of the Church). *Statistical Yearbook of the Church.*
West India Committee and FT International. *The Caribbean Handbook* (annual).
World Health Organization. *World Health Statistics Annual.*
World Tourism Organization. *World Tourism Statistics* (annual).

## National Statistical Sources

**Afghanistan.** *Economic and Social Indicators* (triennial); *First Seven-Year Economic and Social Development Plan, 1355–1361 (March 1976–March 1983); Preliminary Results of the First Afghan Population Census, 1979; Review of the General Socio-economic Situation in the Democratic Republic of Afghanistan During 1358 (21 March 1979–20 March 1980); Statistical Year Book.*
**Albania.** *Directives of the 8th Congress of the PLA for the 7th Five-Year Plan (1981–85) of Economic and Cultural Development of the PSR of Albania; Portrait of Albania* (1982); *Vjetari statistikor R P SH* (Statistical Yearbook of the People's Republic of Albania [annual]); *40 années d'Albanie socialiste* (1984).
**Algeria.** *Annuaire statistique; Recensement général de la population et de l'habitat, 1977.*
**American Samoa.** *Annual Report of the Governor of American Samoa to the Secretary of the Department of the Interior; Population of American Samoa* (ESCAP; Country Monograph Series No. 7.1 [1979]); *1980 Census of Population and Housing* (U.S.); *Statistical Bulletin* (annual).
**Andorra.** *Recull Estadístic* (1985).
**Angola.** *Angola: A Country Study* (1979); *Anuário Estatístico; Recenseamento Geral da População, 1960; Situação Economica e Financeira de Angola* (annual).
**Anguilla.** *Abstract of Statistics, 1960–1982; Anguilla Census of Population 1984.*
**Antigua.** *Statistical Yearbook.*
**Argentina.** *Anuario estadístico de la República Argentina; Boletín estadístico trimestral* (quarterly); *Censo nacional de población y vivienda, 1980; Encuesta permanente de hogares* (irreg.); *Estadística Mensual* (monthly); *Indicadores industriales* (annual).
**Aruba.** *Monthly Statistical Report: International Tourism to Aruba.*
**Australia.** *Integrated Economic Censuses and Surveys (1980–81); Manufacturing Establishments: Details of Operations by Industry Class* (annual); *Monthly Summary of Statistics, Australia; National Income and Expenditure* (annual); *Overseas Trade* (annual); *Social Indicators* (irreg.); *Yearbook of the Commonwealth of Australia; 1981 Census of Population and Housing.*
**Austria.** *Österreichisches Jahrbuch* (annual); *Österreichs Volkseinkommen* (Austrian National Income); *Sozialstatistische Daten 1980; Statistisches Handbuch* (annual); *Volkserzählung, 1981.*
**Bahamas, The.** *Quarterly Statistical Summary; Social Statistics Report* (annual); *Statistical Abstract* (annual); *Vital Statistics Report* (annual); *1980 Census of Population and Housing.*
**Bahrain.** *Statistical Abstract* (annual); *1981 Census of Bahrain.*
**Bangladesh.** *Bangladesh Population Census, 1981; Population of Bangladesh* (ESCAP; Country Monograph Series No. 8 [1981]); *Statistical Pocketbook of Bangladesh* (annual); *Statistical Yearbook of Bangladesh.*
**Barbados.** *Barbados Economic Report* (annual); *Monthly Digest of Statistics; Report on the Census of Production, 1981.*
**Belgium.** *Annuaire statistique de la Belgique; Bulletin de statistique* (monthly); *Recensement de la population et des logements au 1er mars 1981; Statistiques démographiques* (quarterly).

**Belize.** *Abstract of Statistics* (annual); *Belize Economic Report* (annual); *Labour Force Survey (1983–84); 1980–81 Population Census of the Commonwealth Caribbean, Belize.*
**Benin.** *Annuaire statistique; Recensement des Entreprises 1980* (2 parts); *Recensement général de la population et de l'habitation* (1979).
**Bermuda.** *Bermuda Digest of Statistics* (annual); *Report of the Population Census, 1980; Report of the Registrar General* (annual).
**Bhutan.** *Development in a Himalayan Kingdom* (A World Bank Country Study [1983]); *Statistical Handbook of Bhutan* (annual).
**Bolivia.** *Bolivia en cifras, 1980; Censo Nacional de población y vivienda de 1976; Resumen estadístico* (annual).
**Botswana.** *1981 Population and Housing Census; Statistical Abstract* (annual).
**Brazil.** *Anuário Econômico-Fiscal; Anuário Estatístico do Brasil; Brazil: A Country Study* (1983); *Foreign Trade of Brazil* (annual); *Indicadores Sociais* (1979); *IX Recenseamento Geral do Brasil, 1980.*
**British Virgin Islands.** *Census of the British Virgin Islands, 12th May 1980 (Provisional); Statistical Abstract* (irreg.).
**Brunei.** *Annual Report; Brunei Statistical Yearbook; Report on the Census of Population, 1971.*
**Bulgaria.** *Prebroyavane—1975; resultati, perspektivi* (Census of Population—1975: Results, Perspectives); *Statisticheskii yezhgodnik* (Statistical Yearbook).
**Burkina Faso (Upper Volta).** *Annuaire Statistique; Recensement général de la population du 10 au 20 decembre 1985; Statistiques Sociales* (annual).
**Burma.** *Burma: A Country Study* (1983); 1983 *Population Census; Statistical Abstract* (irreg.).
**Burundi.** *Annuaire statistique; Recensement général de la population, 16–30 août 1979.*
**Cameroon.** *Note annuelle de statistique; Recensement général de la population et de l'habitat d'avril 1976; Tableaux économiques du Cameroun* (1983).
**Canada.** *Canada Year Book* (irreg.); *Census of Agriculture, 1981; National Income and Expenditure Accounts* (quarterly); *1981 Census of Canada.*
**Cape Verde.** *Boletím Trimestral de Estatística* (quarterly).
**Cayman Islands.** *Cayman Islands Population Census 1979; Statistical Abstract of the Cayman Islands* (annual).
**Central African Republic.** *Annuaire statistique; Recensement général de la population de décembre 1975.*
**Chad.** *Annuaire statistique.*
**Chile.** *Chile XV censo nacional de población y de vivienda, 21 de abril 1982; Compendio estadístico* (annual); *Cuentas nacionales de Chile, 1960–1980; Plan nacional indicativo de desarrollo* (quinquennial).
**China, People's Republic of.** *Almanac of China's Economy* (irreg.); *China: A Country Study* (1981); *China Official Yearbook; People's Republic of China Year-Book; Major Figures by 10 Percent Sampling on the 1982 Census of the People's Republic of China; Statistical Yearbook of China; Yearbook of the Encyclopedia of China.*
**Christmas Island.** *Annual Report; Census of Population and Housing, 30 June 1981.*
**Cocos (Keeling) Islands.** *Annual Report; Census of Population and Housing, 30 June 1981.*
**Colombia.** *Colombia estadística* (annual); *Cuentas nacionales de Colombia, 1970–1981; Industria manufacturera* (annual); *XV Censo nacional de población y IV de vivienda* (1985).
**Comoros.** *Plan interimaire de développement économique et sociale (1983–1986); Recensement général de la population et de l'habitat 15 septembre 1980.*
**Congo, People's Republic of the.** *Annuaire statistique; Recensement général de la population de 1974.*
**Cook Islands.** *Cook Islands Census of Population and Dwellings, 1981; Cook Islands Quarterly Statistical Bulletin.*
**Costa Rica.** *Anuario estadístico; Censos Nacionales de 1973; Costa Rica: A Country Study* (1984).
**Côte d'Ivoire.** *Annuaire statistique; La Côte d'Ivoire en chiffres* (annual); *L'Économie Ivoirienne* (annual); *Enquête permanente aupres des menages: resultats provisoires 1985.*
**Cuba.** *Anuario estadístico; Censo de población y viviendas, 1981; Compendio estadístico de Cuba* (annual); *Cuba Quarterly Economic Report.*
**Cyprus.** *Census of Industrial Production* (annual); *Economic Report* (annual); *Statistical Abstract* (annual).
**Czechoslovakia.** *Statistická ročenka Československé Socialistické Republiky* (Statistical Yearbook of the Czechoslovak Socialist Republic); *Sčítání lidu, domů a bytů 1980* (Census of Population and Housing).
**Denmark.** *Folke- og boligtaellingen, 1981* (Population and Housing Census); *Statistisk årbog* (Statistical Yearbook).
**Djibouti.** *Annuaire statistique de Djibouti.*
**Dominica.** *Statistical Digest.*
**Dominican Republic.** *República Dominicana en cifras* (annual); *VI Censo nacional de población y vivienda, 1981.*
**Ecuador.** *Censo agropecuario, 1974; Encuesta anual de manufactura y minería; Serie estadística* (quinquennial); *IV Censo de población: III de vivienda resultados anticipados por muestreo* (1982).
**Egypt.** *Census of Population and Housing, 1976; Egypt: A Country Study* (1982); *Statistical Yearbook.*
**El Salvador.** *Anuario estadístico; Censos económicos, 1979 (Manufactura diversa; Agroindustrias; Comercio y servicios; Electricidad, construcción, transporte comercial); El Salvador en cifras* (annual).
**Equatorial Guinea.** *Censos Nacionales, Ide Población y I de Vivienda—4 al 17 de Julio de 1983.*
**Ethiopia.** *Ethiopia: A Country Study* (1980); *Ethiopia 1984 Population and Housing Census; Ethiopia Statistical Abstract* (annual).
**Faeroe Islands.** *Arbog for Faerøerne* (Yearbook for the Faeroe Islands).
**Fiji.** *Annual Employment Survey; Census of Industrial Production* (annual); *Current Economic Statistics* (quarterly); *Report on the Census of the Population, 1976.*
**Finland.** *Annual Statistics of Agriculture; Economic Survey* (annual); *Population and Housing Census, 1980; Statistical Yearbook of Finland.*
**France.** *Annuaire statistique de la France; Données sociales* (triennial); *Le Mouvement économique en France, 1949–1979; Recensement général de la population de 1982; Métropole.*
**French Guiana.** *Annuaire statistique de la Guyane; Bulletin trimestriel de statistique; Recensement général de la population dans les Départements d'outre-mer en 9 mars 1982, Guyane.*
**French Polynesia.** *Bilan statistique de l'année; Comptes économiques* (quadrennial); *Résultats du recensement de la population de la Polynésie Française, 15 Octobre 1983; Te avei'a: Bulletin d'information statistique* (quarterly).
**Gabon.** *Situation économique, financière et sociale de la République Gabonaise* (annual).
**Gambia, The.** *The Gambia since Independence: 1965–1980, 15 years of Nationhood.*
**Gaza Strip.** *Judaea, Samaria, and Gaza Area Statistics Quarterly; Palestinian Statistical Abstract* (annual).
**Germany, East.** *Statistisches Jahrbuch der Deutschen Demokratischen Republik.*
**Germany, West.** *Federal Republic of Germany: A Country Study* (1983); *Statistisches Jahrbuch für die Bundesrepublik Deutschland; Volkszählung vom 27 Mai 1970* (Census of Population).
**Ghana.** *Economic Survey* (biennial); *Ghana: An Official Handbook* (1977); *Industrial Statistics* (biennial); *Population Census of Ghana, 1984.*
**Gibraltar.** *Abstract of Statistics* (annual); *Census of Gibraltar, 1981.*
**Greece.** *Recensement des industries manufacturières: Artisanat, du commerce et autres services* (1978); *Recensement de la population et des habitations, 1981; Statistical Yearbook of Greece.*
**Greenland.** *Grønland* (annual); *Grønlands befolkning* (Greenland Population [annual]).
**Grenada.** *Abstract of Statistics* (annual).
**Guadeloupe.** *Annuaire statistique de la Guadeloupe; Recensement général de la population dans les Departements d'Outre-mer en 9 mars 1982, Guadeloupe.*
**Guam.** *Guam Annual Economic Review; 1980 Census of Population and Housing.*
**Guatemala.** *Anuario estadístico; Censos nacionales, 1981: IX de población—IV de habitación; Guatemala: A Country Study* (1983).
**Guernsey.** *Guernsey Census 1976.*
**Guinea, Republic of.** *Situation Économique et Conjoncturelle au 31 decembre 1985 et éléments sur la mise en oeuvre de la réform économique au cours du premiere trimestre 1986.*
**Guinea-Bissau.** *Boletim Trimestral de Estatística; Recenseamento Geral da População e da Habitação, 16 de Abril de 1979.*
**Guyana.** *Annual Statistical Abstract.*
**Haiti.** *Bulletin trimestriel de statistique; Haiti: A Country Profile* (1981); *Résultats préliminaires du recensement général (Septembre 1982).*
**Honduras.** *Anuario estadístico; Censo nacional de Población, 1974; Honduras: A Country Profile* (1981); *Honduras en cifras* (annual).
**Hong Kong.** *Annual Digest of Statistics; Hong Kong* (annual); *Hong Kong 1986 By-Census; Hong Kong in Figures* (annual); *Hong Kong Social and Economic Trends* (irreg.).
**Hungary.** *Statisztikai évkönyv* (Statistical Yearbook); *1980, Évi népszámlálás* (Census of Population).
**Iceland.** *Tölfraedihandbók* (Statistical Abstract of Iceland [irreg.]); *Verslunarskýrslur* (External Trade [annual]).
**India.** *Census of India, 1981; Economic Survey* (annual); *India: A Reference Annual; Statistical Abstract* (biennial).
**Indonesia.** *Indikator ekonomi* (monthly); *Indonesia: An Official Handbook* (1984); *Sensus penduduk Indonesia, 1980* (Census of Population); *Statistical Yearbook of Indonesia.*
**Iran.** *General Census of Population and Housing, November 1976; A Statistical Reflection of the Islamic Republic of Iran* (annual); *Statistical Yearbook of the Islamic Republic of Iran.*
**Iraq.** *Iraq: A Country Study* (1979); *Statistical Abstract* (annual).
**Ireland.** *Census of Population of Ireland, 1986; National Income and Expenditure* (annual); *Statistical Abstract* (annual).
**Isle of Man.** *Isle of Man 1981 Census Report; Isle of Man Digest of Economic and Social Statistics* (annual).
**Israel.** *1983 Census of Population and Housing; Israel: A Country Study* (1979); *Statistical Abstract* (annual).
**Italy.** *Annuario di statistica agraria: Annuario di statistiche demografiche; Annuario di statistiche industriali; Annuario statistico dell'istruzione; Annuario statistico Italiano; Statistiche forestale* (annual); *Statistiche sociali* (1981); *12 Censimento general della popolazione, 1981.*
**Jamaica.** *Economic and Social Survey* (annual); *Statistical Abstract* (annual); *Statistical Yearbook of Jamaica.*
**Japan.** *Establishment Census of Japan, 1981; Japan: A Country Study* (1983); *Japan Statistical Yearbook; Statistical Indicators on Social Life* (annual); *1985 Population Census of Japan.*
**Jersey.** *Report of the Census for 1981; Statistical Digest* (annual).
**Jordan.** *Census 1979; Family Expenditure Survey* (1980); *Jordan: A Country Study* (1979); *National Accounts* (irreg.); *Statistical Yearbook.*
**Kenya.** *Economic Survey* (annual); *Kenya Statistical Digest* (quarterly); *Statistical Abstract* (annual).
**Kiribati.** *National Development Plan, 1979–1982; Report on the 1985 Census of Population.*
**Korea, North.** *North Korea: A Country Study* (1981).
**Korea, South.** *Korea Statistical Yearbook; Social Indicators in Korea* (irreg.); *South Korea: A Country Study* (1982); *The 5th Five-Year Economic and Development Plan, 1982–1986; 1980 Population and Housing Census.*
**Kuwait.** *Annual Statistical Abstract; Economic Report* (annual); *General Census of Population and Housing, 1980.*
**Lesotho.** *Annual Statistical Bulletin; 1976 Population Census Report.*
**Liberia.** *Economic Survey* (annual); *1974 Census of Population and Housing.*
**Libya.** *The Five-Year Development Plan 1981–85; Libya Population Census, 1973; Statistical Abstract for Libya* (annual).
**Liechtenstein.** *Statistisches Jahrbuch; Volkszählung, 2 Dezember 1980* (Census of Population).
**Luxembourg.** *Annuaire statistique; Bulletin du STATEC* (monthly); *Recensement général de la population du 31 mars 1981.*
**Macau.** *Anuário Estatístico; Inquerito Industrial* (annual); *XII Recenseamento Geral da População, 1981.*
**Madagascar.** *Recensement général de la population et des habitats, 1975; Situation économique* (annual).
**Malawi.** *Malawi Population Census, 1977; Malawi Statistical Yearbook; Malawi Yearbook.*
**Malaysia.** *Fourth Malaysia Plan, 1981–1985; Malaysia: A Country Study* (1985); *Malaysian Annual Statistical Bulletin; 1980 Population and Housing Census.*
**Maldives.** *Population and Housing Census, 1985, Preliminary Results; Statistical Year Book of Maldives.*

**Mali.** *Annuaire statistique du Mali; Recensement de la population, 1–16 décembre 1976.*
**Malta.** *Annual Abstract of Statistics; Census of Agriculture* (annual); *Census of Industrial Production* (annual); *Malta Trade Statistics* (quarterly).
**Martinique.** *Annuaire statistique de la Martinique; Bulletin de statistique* (quarterly); *Comptes économiques de la Martinique* (irreg.); *Recensement de la population dans les départements d'outre-mer, 9 mars 1982—Martinique.*
**Mauritania.** *Annuaire Statistique; Area Handbook for Mauritania* (1972).
**Mauritius.** *Bi-annual Digest of Statistics; 1983 Housing and Population Census of Mauritius; 1980–1982 Two-Year Plan for Economic and Social Development.*
**Mayotte.** *Recensement général de la population, 1978.*
**Mexico.** *Anuario estadístico; X Censo general de población y vivienda, 1980; La Economia Mexicana en Cifras* (1986); *Informe de Gobierno: Estadístico* (annual).
**Mongolia.** *Mongolia in Figures, 1981* (irreg.); *National Economy of the MPR, 1921–81* (1981).
**Montserrat.** *Caribbean Population Census, May 12, 1980; Statistical Digest* (annual).
**Morocco.** *Annuaire statistique du Maroc; Economic and Social Development Report, 1981; Morocco: A Country Study* (1985); *Recensement général de la population et de l'habitat de 1982.*
**Mozambique.** *Anuário Estatístico; Informação Estatística* (annual); *Mozambique: A Country Study* (1985); *1º Recenseamento Geral da População, 1980.*
**Nepal.** *Census of Manufacturing Establishments of Nepal, 1981–82; Economic Survey* (annual); *Population Monograph of Nepal* (1987); *The Sixth Plan (1980–85); Statistical Pocket Book* (irreg.).
**Netherlands, The.** *Landbouwcijfers* (Agricultural Data [annual]); *Statistical Yearbook of the Netherlands; 14e Algemene volkstelling, 28 februari 1971* (14th General Population Census).
**Netherlands Antilles.** *Tweede Algemene Volks- en Woningtelling Nederlandse Antillen: toestand per 1 Februari 1981; Statistical Yearbook of the Netherlands Antilles.*
**New Caledonia.** *Annuaire statistique; Enquête socio-économique, 1980–1981; Resultats du Recensement de la population, 15 Avril 1983.*
**New Zealand.** *New Zealand Census of Population and Dwellings, 1981; New Zealand Official Yearbook.*
**Nicaragua.** *Anuario estadístico de Nicaragua; Censos nacionales, 1971; Nicaragua: A Country Study* (1982).
**Niger.** *Annuaire statistique; Les comptes de la nation: années 1978–1979–1980* (1984); *Données de base* (1979).
**Nigeria.** *Annual Abstract of Statistics; Fourth National Development Plan* (1981); *Nigeria: A Country Study* (1981).
**Niue.** *Abstract of Statistics* (annual); *Census of Population and Housing, 1976; Niue National Development Plan, 1980–1985.*
**Norfolk Island.** *Annual Report; Census of Population and Housing, 30 June 1986.*
**Norway.** *Folke- og boligtelling 1980* (Population and Housing Census); *Industristatistikk* (annual); *Statistisk årsbok* (Statistical Yearbook).
**Oman.** *Statistical Year Book; The Second Five-Year Plan of Development, 1981–1985.*
**Pacific Islands, Trust Territory of the.** *Report of the Trusteeship Council to the Security Council on the Trust Territory of the Pacific Islands* (annual); *Report to the United Nations* (annual).
**Pakistan.** *Economic Survey* (annual); *Pakistan Year Book; Pakistan Statistical Yearbook; Population Census of Pakistan, 1981; Some Socio-Economic Trends* (annual); *10 Years of Pakistan in Statistics, 1972–1982* (1983).
**Panama.** *Indicadores económicos y sociales* (annual); *Octavo censo de población: Cuarto censo de vivienda, 11 de mayo de 1980; Panama en cifras* (annual); *Situacion económica: Cuentas nacionales* (annual); *Situacion económica: Industria* (annual).
**Papua New Guinea.** *Abstract of Statistics* (quarterly); *National Accounts Statistics—Statistical Bulletin* (quarterly); *Papua New Guinea: Selected Development Issues* (A World Bank Country Study [1982]); *Population of Papua New Guinea (ESCAP;* Country Monograph Series No. 7.2 [1982]); *Rural Industries* (annual); *Summary of Statistics* (annual); *1980 National Population Census.*
**Paraguay.** *Anuario estadístico del Paraguay; Censo nacional de población y viviendo, 1982.*
**Peru.** *Censos nacionales; VIII de población: III de vivienda, 12 de julio de 1981; Compendio estadístico* (1982); *Informe estadístico* (annual); *Peru: A Country Study* (1980).
**Philippines.** *Philippine Statistical Yearbook; Philippine Yearbook; 1980 Census of Population.*
**Poland.** *Narodowy spis powszechny z dnia 7 XII 1978 r.* (Census of Population); *Poland: A Country Study* (1984); *Rocznik statystyczny* (Statistical Yearbook).
**Portugal.** *Anuário Estatístico; Estatísticas Agricolas* (annual); *Estatísticas do Comercio Externo* (annual); *Estatísticas Demograficas* (annual); *Estatísticas Industriais* (2 vol.; annual); *Estatísticas Monetarias e Financeiras* (annual); *Recenseamento Agricola, 1979; XII Recenseamento Geral da População: II Recenseamento Geral da Habitação, 1981.*
**Puerto Rico.** *Anuario estadístico; Compendio estadísticas sociales* (annual); *Informe económico al gobernador* (Economic Report to the Governor [annual]); *1980 Census of Population* (U.S.).
**Qatar.** *Annual Statistical Abstract; Economic Survey of Qatar* (annual); *Qatar Year Book.*
**Réunion.** *Annuaire statistique de la Réunion; Comptes économiques de la Réunion* (irreg.); *Panorama de l'Économie de la Réunion* (annual); *Recensement général de la population en 1974: Départements d'outre-mer—Réunion.*
**Romania.** *Anuarul statistic al Republicii Socialiste România; Recensămîntul populației și al locuințelor, din 5 ianuarie 1977; Romania Yearbook.*
**Rwanda.** *Bulletin de Statistique: Supplement Annuel; IIIème Plan de Developpement Economique, Social et Culturel 1982–86.*
**St. Christopher and Nevis.** *Annual Digest of Statistics; St. Christopher and Nevis: Economic Report* (World Bank Country Study) (1985).
**St. Lucia.** *Annual Statistical Digest.*
**St. Pierre and Miquelon.** *Résultats du recensement de la population dans les départements d'outremer, 9 mars 1982.*
**St. Vincent and the Grenadines.** *Digest of Statistics* (annual).
**San Marino.** *Annuario statistico, 1972–1980* (4 vol.); *3 Censimento generale dell agricoltura* (1977); *5 Censimento generale della popolazione* (1979).
**Saudi Arabia.** *Saudi Arabia: A Country Study* (1985); *The Statistical Indicator* (annual); *Statistical Summary* (Saudi Arabian Monetary Agency [annual]); Statistical Year Book.
**Senegal.** *Le Sénégal en chiffres* (annual); *Situation économique* (annual).
**Seychelles.** *National Development Plan, 1985–89; Statistical Abstract* (annual); *1977 Census Report.*
**Sierra Leone.** *Sierra Leone: 12 Years of Economic Achievement and Political Consolidation under the APC and Dr. Siaka Stevens, 1968–80.*
**Singapore.** *Census of Population, 1980; Economic and Social Statistics, 1960–1982; Report on the Census of Industrial Production, 1981; Singapore Yearbook; Yearbook of Statistics Singapore.*
**Solomon Islands.** *Statistical Yearbook.*
**Somalia.** *Statistical Abstract* (annual).
**South Africa.** *Population Census 80; South Africa: Official Yearbook of the Republic of South Africa; South African Statistics* (biennial).
**South West Africa/Namibia.** *Budget 19**–19*** (annual); *Statistical/Economic Review* (annual).
**Spain.** *Anuario estadístico; Censo de población de 1981.*
**Sri Lanka.** *Census of Population and Housing, 1981; Report on the Survey on Manufacturing Industries, 1979; Sri Lanka Year Book; Statistical Pocketbook of the Democratic Socialist Republic of Sri Lanka* (annual).
**Sudan, The.** *Third Population Census, 1983.*
**Swaziland.** *Annual Statistical Bulletin; Report on the 1976 Swaziland Population Census.*
**Sweden.** *Folk- och bostadsräkningen, 1980* (Population and Housing Census); *Jordbruksstatistisk årsbok* (Yearbook of Agricultural Statistics); *Statistisk årsbok för Sverige* (Statistical Abstract of Sweden [annual]).
**Switzerland.** *Recensement fédéral de la population, 1980; Statistisches Jahrbuch* (Statistical Yearbook).
**Syria.** *Census of Agriculture, 1981; General Census of Housing and Inhabitants, 1981; Statistical Abstract* (annual).
**Taiwan.** *Industry of Free China* (monthly); *Social Indicators of the Republic of China* (annual); *Statistical Abstract* (annual); *Statistical Yearbook of the Republic of China; Taiwan Statistical Data Book* (annual); *Yearbook of Labor Statistics; 1980 Census of Population and Housing.*
**Tanzania.** *Tanzania Statistical Abstract* (annual); *1978 Population Census.*
**Thailand.** *Report of the Survey of Business Trade and Services, 1983; Foreign Trade Statistics* (monthly); *Report of the 1983 Industrial Survey, Whole Kingdom; Report of the Labor Force Survey: Whole Kingdom* (quarterly); *Statistical Handbook of Thailand* (annual); *Statistical Yearbook; 1980 Population and Housing Census.*
**Togo.** *Annuaire statistique; Plan de développement économique & social, 1981–1985; Recensement général de la population, 1970.*
**Tokelau.** *Census of Population, 1981; Report of the Administrator of Tokelau for the Year Ended: 31 March 19*** (annual).
**Tonga.** *Census of Population and Housing, 1976.*
**Trinidad and Tobago.** *Population Census, 1980; Annual Statistical Digest.*
**Tunisia.** *Annuaire statistique de la Tunisie; Recensement général de la population et des logements, 30 mars 1984.*
**Turkey.** *Dış Ticaret İstatistikleri* (Annual Foreign Trade Statistics); *Genel Sanayi ve İşyerleri Sayımı* (Census of Industry and Business Establishments [1980]); *Genel Nüfus Sayımı, 12. 10. 1985* (Census of Population); *Genel Tarım Sayımı, 1980* (Census of Agriculture); *İnşaat İstatistikleni* (Construction Statistics [annual]); *Türkiye İstatistik Yilliği* (Statistical Yearbook of Turkey).
**Turks and Caicos.** *Pocket Digest of Statistics* (irreg.).
**Tuvalu.** *Abstract of Statistics* (annual); *Census of the Population, 1979.*
**Union of Soviet Socialist Republics.** *Narodnoye Khozyaystvo SSSR* (National Economy of the U.S.S.R. [annual]).
**United Arab Emirates.** *Statistical Yearbook* (Abu Dhabi) (annual).
**United Kingdom.** *Agricultural Statistics United Kingdom* (annual); *Annual Abstract of Statistics; Britain: An Official Handbook* (annual); *National Income and Expenditure* (annual); *Census 1981; Report on the Census of Production: Summary Tables* (annual).
**United States.** *Agricultural Statistics* (annual); *Annual Energy Review; Current Population Reports* (Series P-20, P-23, P-25, P-26, P-27, P-28, P-60); *Digest of Education Statistics* (annual); *Minerals Yearbook* (3 vol.; annual); *National Transportation Statistics* (annual); *Statistical Abstract* (annual); *U.S. Exports: SIC-Based Products* (annual); *U.S. Imports: SIC-Based Products* (annual); *Vital and Health Statistics* (series 1–20); *1982 Census of Construction Industries; 1982 Census of Manufacturing; 1982 Census of Mineral Industries; 1982 Census of Retail Trade; 1982 Census of Wholesale Trade; 1982 Census of Agriculture; 1980 Census of Population and Housing.*
**Uruguay.** *Anuario Estadístico; Encuesta Nacional de Hogares* (annual).
**Vanuatu.** *Recensement de la population, 1979; Vanuatu Statistical Yearbook.*
**Venezuela.** *Anuario estadístico; Encuesta de hogares por muestreo* (annual); *Encuesta industrial* (annual); *IX Censo general de población y vivienda, 20 de octubre 1981.*
**Virgin Islands of the United States.** *Annual Report; Economic Review, 1986; 1980 Census of Population* (U.S.).
**Wallis and Futuna.** *Résultats du Recensement de la Population, 15 Février 1983.*
**West Bank.** *Judaea, Samaria, and Gaza Area Statistics Quarterly; Palestinian Statistical Abstract* (annual).
**Western Sahara.** *Recensement General de la Population et de l'Habitat* (1982 [Morocco]).
**Western Samoa.** *Annual Statistical Abstract; Census of Population and Housing, 1976.*
**Yemen, People's Democratic Republic of.** *The Yemens: Country Studies* (1986).
**Yemen Arab Republic.** *The Housing and Population Census, February 1975; Statistical Year Book.*
**Yugoslavia.** *Popis stanovištva i stanova od 31. marta 1981* (Census of Population and Housing as of March 31, 1981); *Statistički godišnjak Jugoslavije* (Statistical Yearbook of Yugoslavia).
**Zaire.** *Annuaire statistique; Plan Mobutu: Programme de relance économique, 1979–1981 (Fiches des projects; Transport; Education et santé)* (3 vol.).
**Zambia.** *Country Profile: Zambia 1985; Household Budget Survey, 1974–1975; Monthly Digest of Statistics; Third National Development Plan, 1979–83; 1980 Census of Population and Housing.*
**Zimbabwe.** *1982 Population Census: Main Demographic Features of the Population of Zimbabwe; Statistical Year-book.*

# Index

This index covers both *Britannica Book of the Year* (cumulative for ten years) and *Britannica World Data*.

**Entries in black type are titles of articles in the** *Book of the Year;* **an accompanying page number** in light type **shows where the article appears in this volume. Numbers in black type indicate the years in which such an article appears. For example, "Archaeology 125; 87:141; 86:164; 85:165.** *See* **Archaeology 84–79" indicates that the article "Archaeology" appeared every year from 1979 through 1984, and may be found in alphabetical order in each of those editions. The references for the last four years are given by page number.**

Indented entries in light type that follow black type article titles refer by page number to other places in the text where the subject of the article is discussed. Light type entries that are not indented refer by page number to subjects which are not themselves article titles. Names of people covered in biographies and obituaries are listed as references to the sections **"Biographies"** and **"Obituaries"** within the article "People of the Year"; in those sections the names appear in alphabetical order. References to illustrations are by page number, and are preceded by the abbreviation "*il.*"

The index uses word-by-word alphabetization (treating a word as one or more characters separated by a space from the next word). Names beginning with "Mc" and "Mac" are alphabetized as "Mac"; "St." is treated as "Saint."

# A

A. C. Nielson Co. (U.S.)
  advertising 212
AAA: *see* American Arbitration
  Association
ABA: *see* American Bar Association
ABB Group (Co., Eur.)
  merger 218
Abbado, Claudio: *see* **Biographies 80**
Abbott, Diane
  race relations 292
Abboud, Albert Robert: *see* **Biographies 81**
ABC: *see* American Broadcasting
  Corporation
Abdallah, Ahmed
  Comoros 387
Abdallah, Georges Ibrahim
  terrorism 143
Abdul-Jabbar, Kareem
  NBA championship 314, *il.* 313
Abdul Rahman, Tunka
  Malaysia 439
Abdulaziz, Abdullah Ibn
  Saudi Arabia 418
Abdullah, Sheikh Muhammad: *see*
  **Obituaries 83**
Abel, Iorwith Wilbur: *see* **Obituaries 88**
Abergil, Eliahu
  Judaism 302
abitur (W.Ger.)
  education 183
aborigine
  arctic regions 523
  Canadian proposal 479
abortion
  Ginsburg 484
  state governments 489
Abrahams, Harold Maurice: *see* **Obituaries 79**
Abrams, Elliot
  *contra* funds 437
Abruzzo, Anderson, and Newman: *see*
  **Biographies 79**
Abruzzo, Ben: *see* **Obituaries 86**
ABT: *see* American Ballet Theatre
Abu Dhabi (U.A.E.)
  leadership struggle 420
"Abwesenheit, Die" (Handke)
  literature 250
Academy award: *see* Oscar
Acaligenes eutrophus
  RuBPCase 242
Acanthaster planci
  population outbreak 242
Acapulco agreement (Lat.Am. treaty)
  Latin American debt 492
ACC-7: *see* Anglican Consultative Council
Acción Democrática, *or* AD (pol.
  party, Venez.)
  Venezuelan politics 509
Ace, Goodman: *see* **Obituaries 83**
acesulfame-K (sweetener)
  food processing 123
ACGB: *see* Arts Council of Great Britain
Acheampong, Ignatius Kutu: *see* **Obituaries 80**
acid rain
  environmental concerns 194
  U.S.-Canadian summit 483
  zoological study 239
Acland, Sir Hugh John Dyke: *see*
  **Obituaries 82**
acquired immune deficiency syndrome,
  *or* AIDS
  entomology 240
  epidemic (special report) 206
  health and disease 202
  industry response
    condom advertising 212
    insurance 222
    publishing 248
  library program 238
  regional effect

Africa 383
  Hungary 471
  international migration 284
  United States 489
  theatre effect 371
  veterinary research 210
  World Methodist Council 298
Action of Rational Drugs in Asia,
  *or* ARDA
  pharmaceutical patents 142
Activase: *see* tissue plasminogen activator
"Actress" (film)
  motion pictures 271
AD (pol. party, Venez.): *see* Acción
  Democrática
Adams, Ansel Easton: *see* **Obituaries 85**
Adams, Harriet Stratemeyer: *see* **Obituaries 83**
Adams, Sir John Bertram: *see* **Obituaries 85**
Adams, John Michael Geoffrey Manning-
  ham: *see* **Obituaries 86**
Adamson, Joy: *see* **Obituaries 81**
Adoula, Cyrille: *see* **Obituaries 79**
Adventist World Radio-Asia (Guam)
  Seventh Day Adventists 299
advertising 212
"Advertising Age" (internat. news.)
  industrial report 212
aerial sports 308; 87:346; 86:380; 85:374.
  *See* **Aerial Sports 84–79**
aerospace 212
"Affrontements" (Michaux)
  literature 249
Afghanistan 429; 87:471; 86:502; 85:506.
  *See* **Afghanistan 84–79**
  international affairs
    Pakistan 434
    United Nations 377
    U.S.S.R. 259
  refugees 285
  *see also* WORLD DATA
Afleet
  horse racing 330
Africa Fund
  India 433
"Africa Then: Photographs 1840–1918"
  (Monti)
  photography 279
African affairs 382; 87:421; 86:453; 85:456.
  *See* **African Affairs 84–79**
  AIDS epidemic (special report) 206
  consumer affairs 141
  economic affairs 170
  food emergency 113
  locust outbreak 240
  Middle East and North Africa 406
  military affairs 264
  refugees 284
  special reports 85, 82, 81
  tourism 230
  United Nations 377
  *see also* individual countries by name
African Development Bank
  Guinea-Bissau 391
African literature
  special report 82
African National Congress, *or* ANC
  African affairs 382
  South Africa 397
African Petroleum Producers' Association
  energy 186
African Unity, Organization of, *or* OAU
  African affairs 382
  Chad-Libya conflict 406
"Afterworlds" (MacEwen)
  literature 248
Agca, Mehmet Ali: *see* **Biographies 84**
"Age of Correggio and the Carracci:
  Emilian Painting of the Sixteenth and
  the Seventeenth Centuries, The" (art
  exhibition)
  Italian art 132
"Age of Grief, The" (Smiley)
  literature 248
"Age of Sultan Suleyman the Magnificent,

The" (art exhibition)
  Turkish art 131, *il.* 133
Ager, Milton: *see* **Obituaries 80**
Aggett, Neil Hutchin: *see* **Obituaries 83**
Agriculture, Ministry of (Eth.)
  entomology 240
Agriculture, U.S. Department of, *or* USDA
  Green Revolution 6
  pest control 240
**Agriculture and Food Supplies** 113;
  87:127; 86:150; 85:150. *See*
  **Agriculture and Food Supplies
  84–79.** *See* **Fisheries 84–79.** *See* **Food
  Processing 84–79**
  Green Revolution 5
  irradiation 142
  protectionism 172
  special report 79
  world food aid *map* 7
  *see also* WORLD DATA *and* individual
    countries by name
Agrobacterium tumefaciens
  genetic engineering 145
Agrokomerc (Co., Yugos.)
  crime 145
Agt, Andreas Antonius Maria van: *see*
  **Biographies 79**
Ahlers, Conrad: *see* **Obituaries 81**
Ahn, Philip: *see* **Obituaries 79**
AIDS: *see* acquired immune deficiency
  syndrome
"AIDS and Society" (McBride) 206
Aiken, George David: *see* **Obituaries 85**
Ailuropoda melanoleuca: *see* giant panda
air pollution
  environmental concerns 192, 194
Airbus A320 *il.* 213
Airbus Industrie (Co., Eur.)
  aviation 212
airlines
  consumer affairs 142
Aitken, Sir John William Maxwell: *see*
  **Obituaries 86**
Akashi Kaikyo Bridge (Japan)
  construction 188
AKEL (pol. party, Cyp.)
  elections 408
Akhromeyev, Sergey: *see* **Biographies 85**
Akuffo, Fred W. K.: *see* **Obituaries 80.** *See*
  **Biographies 79**
Alaska (U.S.)
  current events 522
Albania 468; 87:513; 86:541; 85:547. *See*
  **Albania 84–79**
  international affairs
    West Germany 452
    Yugoslavia 478
  *see also* WORLD DATA
Albertson, Jack: *see* **Obituaries 82**
Albright, Ivan Le Lorraine: *see* **Obituaries 84**
alcohol
  cancer link 208
Alda, Alan: *see* **Biographies 80**
Alderete, Carlos
  Argentina 493
Aldrich, Jeffrey
  pest-control study 240
Aldrich, Robert: *see* **Obituaries 84**
Alebua, Ezekiel
  Solomon Islands 517
Aleixandre, Vicente: *see* **Obituaries 85**
Alekseyef, Aleksandr: *see* **Obituaries 83**
Alemán, Miguel: *see* **Obituaries 84**
Alessandri Rodríguez, Jorge: *see* **Obituaries 87**
Alexander, Eben Roy: *see* **Obituaries 79**
Alexander, Kelly Miller, Sr.: *see* **Obituaries 86**
Alexander, Lincoln: *see* **Biographies 86**
Alexandrovich, Prince Andrew: *see*
  **Obituaries 82**
Alfonsín, Raúl: *see* **Biographies 84**
  Argentina 493, *il.*
  Papal tour 300
Algeria 407; 87:448; 86:479; 85:483. *See*
  **Algeria 84–79**
  dams 190
  Libya 415
  Morocco 416
  *see also* WORLD DATA
algorithm
  mathematics 256
Ali, Muhammad: *see* **Biographies 79**
Ali, Salim: *see* **Obituaries 88**
Alia, Ramiz: *see* **Biographies 86**
  Albania 468
Alianza Popular, *or* AP (pol. party, Sp.)
  politics 461
Alianza Popular Revolucionaria Ameri-
  cana, *or* APRA (pol. party, Peru)
  Peru 507
Alive in Mission
  Baptists 297
Allan of Kilmahew, Robert Alexander
  Allan, Baron: *see* **Obituaries 80**
Allcock, Tony
  lawn bowls 334
Allégret, Yves Edouard: *see* **Obituaries 88**
Allen, Clabon Walter: *see* **Obituaries 88**
Allen, James Browning: *see* **Obituaries 79**
Allen, William Ernest Chesney: *see*
  **Obituaries 83**
Allen, Woody: *see* **Biographies 79**
Allen of Fallowfield, Alfred Walter Henry
  Allen: *see* **Obituaries 86**
Allon, Yigal: *see* **Obituaries 81**
Almeida, Cathy

bowling 315
"Alnilam" (Dickey)
  literature 247
ALP: *see* Australian Labor Party
Alpine World Cup
  skiing 337
Alston, Walter Emmons: *see* **Obituaries 85**
alteplase: *see* tissue plasminogen activator
aluminium
  mining 267
  zoological damage 239
Álvarez Armelino, Gregorio Conrado: *see*
  **Biographies 82**
Alvin, Juliette: *see* **Obituaries 83**
Alysheba
  horse racing 329, *il.*
Alzheimer's disease
  molecular basis 208
Amalrik, Andrey Alekseyevich: *see*
  **Obituaries 81**
Ambiance Plaza, L'
  structural collapse 189
AMC: *see* American Motors Corporation
Amendola, Giorgio: *see* **Obituaries 81**
Amerasians
  repatriation to United States 443
América de Cali (soccer team, Colom.)
  soccer 323
América of Mexico City
  soccer 323
American Arbitration Association, *or* AAA
  computer industry 232
American Ballet Theatre, *or* ABT
  stage production 148
American Baptist Churches in the U.S.A.,
  *or* Northern Baptists 297
American Bar Association, *or* ABA
  Bork 483
American Broadcasting Corpora-
  tion, *or* ABC
  television programming 365
American Cup III
  synchronized swimming 339
"American Drawings and Watercolours of
  the 20th Century: Andrew Wyeth, The
  Helga Pictures" (art exhibition)
  drawings 132
American Eagle
  coins 277
American Federation of Arts
  museums 272
American Furniture Manufacturers
  Association
  furniture industry 219
American Indian Dance Theatre
  European tour 148
American Jewish Committee
  Judaism 302
American Motors Corporation, *or* AMC
  automobile industry 214, *il.*
American Samoa
  United States 519
American Stock Exchange
  stock exchanges 178
America's Cup
  sailing *il.* 336
"Amerika" (miniseries)
  broadcasting industry 366, *il.* 364
Amman summit
  Arab-Israeli relations 405
Ammodramus maritimus nigrescens: *see*
  dusky seaside sparrow
Amnesty International
  Benin 384
  Kenya 391
"Amoco Cadiz" (ship)
  follow-up study 241
amoeba
  development 243
"Amor Feliz, Um" (Mourão-Ferreira): *see*
  "Happy Love Story, A"
Amoroso, Emmanuel Ciprian: *see*
  **Obituaries 83**
Amory, Derick Heathcoat Amory, 1st
  Viscount: *see* **Obituaries 82**
amphibian
  pollution sensitivity 239
ampligen
  AIDS research 202
Amsterdam stock exchange
  stock exchanges 178
ANC: *see* African National Congress
anchovy
  fisheries 121
"And the Band Played On" (Shilts)
  literature 248
Andean Group (S.Am. org.)
  economic affairs 491
Andersch, Alfred: *see* **Obituaries 81**
Andersen, Morten
  football 326
Anderson, John Bayard: *see* **Biographies 81**
Anderson, Ken: *see* **Biographies 82**
Anderson, Maxie Leroy: *see* **Obituaries 84**
Anderson, Ottis: *see* **Biographies 80**
Anderson, Sparky: *see* **Biographies 85**
Andersson, Sven Olof Morgan: *see*
  **Obituaries 88**
Andorra 445; 87:489; 86:518; 85:523. *See*
  **Andorra 84–79**
  *see also* WORLD DATA
Andrei, Alessandro
  track and field 342
Andren, Claes
  amphibian study 239
Andreotti, Giulio
  Italy 456

# C

**E**

# F

Ljuset / Martens 897

"Ljuset" (Lindgren)
literature 251
Llewellyn, Richard: *see* **Obituaries 84**
Llewelyn-Davies, Richard Llewelyn-Davis, Baron: *see* **Obituaries 82**
Lloyd, Albert Lancaster: *see* **Obituaries 83**
Lloyd, Chris Evert: *see* Evert, Chris
Lloyd, Clive: *see* **Biographies 85**
Lloyd, Sir Hugh Pughe: *see* **Obituaries 82**
Lloyd, Norman: *see* **Obituaries 81**
Lloyd Webber, Andrew: *see* **Biographies 84**
Lloyd's of London (U.K.)
insurance industry 221
Lo Jui-ch'ing: *see* **Obituaries 79**
lobster *il.* 122
Locke, Bobby: *see* **Obituaries 88**
Lockheed F-19
aerospace 213
Lockridge, Richard: *see* **Obituaries 83**
locust
Ethiopia 389
Lodge, Henry Cabot: *see* **Obituaries 86**
"Lodz Years, The" (Janosowicz)
literature 255
Loeb, William: *see* **Obituaries 82**
Loewy, Raymond Fernand: *see* **Obituaries 87**
Lofts, Norah: *see* **Obituaries 84**
loggerhead turtle, *or* Caretta caretta
conservation efforts 198
Loma Linda University Medical Center (U.S.) 299
heart transplantation 205
Lon Nol: *see* **Obituaries 86**
London (U.K.)
classical music performances 273
London, Artur: *see* **Obituaries 87**
London, George: *see* **Obituaries 86**
London Contemporary Dance Theatre
international tour 151
"London Daily News" (Br. news.)
publishing 286
London Stock Exchange
insider trading (special report) 144
stock exchanges 180
Lonergan, The Rev. Bernard Joseph Francis: *see* **Obituaries 85**
Lonetree, Clayton
crime 146
spy scandal 482
Longo, Jeannie
cycling 322
Longo, Luigi: *see* **Obituaries 81**
Longowal, Harchand Singh: *see* **Obituaries 86**
Longworth, Alice Lee Roosevelt: *see* **Obituaries 81**
loonie
Canadian coin 277
Loos, Anita: *see* **Obituaries 82**
Lopez, Nancy: *see* **Biographies 79**
López Bravo, Gregorio: *see* **Obituaries 86**
Lopid: *see* gemfibrozil
Lopokova, Lydia Vasilievna: *see* **Obituaries 82**
Loring, Eugene: *see* **Obituaries 83**
Los Angeles (Calif., U.S.)
earthquake 157
education 184
tunnels 192
Los Angeles Lakers
NBA championship 313
Los Angeles Public Library (U.S.)
fund drive 238
"Los Angeles Times" (U.S. news.)
Pulitzer Prize 287
Losey, Joseph: *see* **Obituaries 85**
lottery
state governments 490
Lotus Development Corp. (U.S.)
computer industry 231
Lotus Mansion (China)
design 131
Louganis, Greg: *see* **Biographies 84**
diving 339
Lougheed, Edgar Peter: *see* **Biographies 82**
Loughlin, Dame Anne: *see* **Obituaries 80**
Loughran, Tommy: *see* **Obituaries 83**
Louis, Joe: *see* **Obituaries 82**
Louis Armstrong Archive
jazz 275
Louisiana State University (U.S.)
college football 324
Louisy, Allan: *see* **Biographies 80**
Louly, Mohamed Mahmoud Ould Ahmed: *see* **Biographies 80**
Louvre Accord (internat. agreement)
stock exchanges 176
lovastatin, *or* Mevacor (drug)
heart disease prevention 203, *il.* 202
low density lipoproteins, *or* LDL
lovastatin 203
Lowe, Arthur: *see* **Obituaries 83**
Lowe, John
education 182
Lowenstein, Allard K.: *see* **Obituaries 81**
Lputian, Smbat
chess 318
Lubalin, Herbert Frederick: *see* **Obituaries 82**
Lubbers, Rudolphus Franciscus Marie: *see* **Biographies 83**
Netherlands 459
Lubell, Samuel: *see* **Obituaries 88**
Lubin, Germaine: *see* **Obituaries 80**
Lucas García, Fernando Romeo: *see* **Biographies 79**
Luce, Claire Boothe: *see* **Obituaries 88**
Luce, Richard
British theatre 367
"Lucie, ou un midi en Novembre" (Ouellette)
literature 250
Ludden, Allen Ellsworth: *see* **Obituaries 82**
Ludin, Itskhak
literature 255
Ludlam, Charles: *see* **Obituaries 88**
theatre 371
Ludlum, Robert: *see* **Biographies 83**
Ludwig, Daniel K.: *see* **Biographies 83**
Luján, Néstor
literature 252
Lukas, D. Wayne
horse racing 329
Lule, Yusufu Kirolde: *see* **Obituaries 86**
lumber industry: *see* wood products
Lung, Noemi
swimming 338
"Lunga vita alla signora!" (film)
motion pictures 269
Lusinchi, Jaime: *see* **Biographies 85**
Lustiger, Msgr. Jean-Marie: *see* **Biographies 82**
Lutheran Communion 298
consolidation 296
Lutheran World Federation 298
World Methodist Council 298
Lutyens, Agnes Elisabeth: *see* **Obituaries 84**
Luxembourg 458; **87**:502; **86**:530; **85**:537. *See* **Luxembourg 84–79**
social security and welfare 304
*see also* WORLD DATA
Lyle, Sandy
golf 327
Lyme disease
transmission and symptoms 204
lymphokine-activated killer cell
cancer treatment 208
Lynch, Sir Phillip Reginald: *see* **Obituaries 85**
Lynd, Helen Merrell: *see* **Obituaries 83**
Lynde, Paul: *see* **Obituaries 83**
Lynds, Roger
cosmology 137
Lyne, Andrew
millisecond pulsar 137
Lyon, Ben: *see* **Obituaries 80**
Lyons, Dame Enid Muriel: *see* **Obituaries 82**
Lyons, Sir William: *see* **Obituaries 86**
Lyubimov, Yury Petrovich: *see* **Biographies 85**

# M

Maazel, Lorin
classical music performances 273
MacArthur, John Donald: *see* **Obituaries 79**
Macartney, Carlile Aylmer: *see* **Obituaries 79**
Macau
Portugal 461, 520
McBride, Lloyd: *see* **Obituaries 84**
McCallin, Lois
man-powered aircraft 308
McCarthy, Joseph Vincent: *see* **Obituaries 79**
McCarthy, Maggie
theatre 368
McCleskey v. Kemp
death penalty 235
McConachy, Clark: *see* **Obituaries 81**
McCormack, John William: *see* **Obituaries 81**
McCoy, Timothy John Fitzgerald: *see* **Obituaries 79**
MacCready, Paul: *see* **Biographies 82**
MacDiarmid, Hugh: *see* **Obituaries 79**
McDonald, David John: *see* **Obituaries 80**
Macdonald, Dwight: *see* **Obituaries 83**
MacDonald, Flora Isabel: *see* **Biographies 80**
McDonald, H. Gregory
fossil research 239
MacDonald, John Dann: *see* **Obituaries 87**
MacDonald, Malcolm John: *see* **Obituaries 82**
MacDonald, Ross: *see* **Obituaries 84**
McDonnell, James Smith, Jr.: *see* **Obituaries 81**
McDonnell, Kim
theatre 369
McDonnell Douglas (Co., U.S.)
air transportation 212
McDougald, John Angus: *see* **Obituaries 79**
McEnroe, John: *see* **Biographies 80**
MacEntee, Sean: *see* **Obituaries 85**
MacEwen, Gwendolyn
English-Canadian literature 248
McEwen, Sir John: *see* **Obituaries 81**
McFarlane, Robert Carl: *see* **Biographies 84**
Iran-*contra* scandal (special report) 485
McGinley, Phyllis: *see* **Obituaries 79**
McGrath, Paul: *see* **Obituaries 79**
McGraw, Tug: *see* **Biographies 81**
MacGregor, Ian: *see* **Biographies 81**
McGwire, Mark
baseball 311
Machel, Samora Moisès: *see* **Obituaries 87**. *See* **Biographies 85**
McHenry, Donald F.: *see* **Biographies 81**
machinery and machine tools 223
Machito: *see* **Obituaries 85**
Macías Nguema, Francisco: *see* **Obituaries 80**
MacInnes, Helen Clark: *see* **Obituaries 86**
Macintosh (computer)
information processing 231
McIntyre, James Francis Cardinal: *see* **Obituaries 80**
Mack Lobell
Hambletonian Stake 331
McKay, Sir Alick Benson: *see* **Obituaries 84**
McKell, Sir William John: *see* **Obituaries 86**
McKelway, St. Clair: *see* **Obituaries 81**
McKenna, Siobhan: *see* **Obituaries 87**
MacKenzie, Rachel: *see* **Obituaries 81**
McKenzie, Robert Trelford: *see* **Obituaries 82**
Mackintosh, John Pitcairn: *see* **Obituaries 79**
MacLaine, Shirley: *see* **Biographies 85**
McLaren, Norman: *see* **Obituaries 88**
MacLean, Alistair: *see* **Obituaries 88**
Maclean, Donald Duart: *see* **Obituaries 84**
MacLeish, Archibald: *see* **Obituaries 83**
Maclennon, Robert: *see* **Biographies 88**
Macleod, Joseph Todd Gordon: *see* **Obituaries 85**
Mac Liammoir, Micheal: *see* **Obituaries 79**
McLuhan, Herbert Marshall: *see* **Obituaries 81**
Macmillan, Maurice Harold 1st Earl of Stockton, Viscount Macmillan of Ovenden: *see* Stockton, Maurice Harold Macmillan, 1st Earl
McNamara, Kevin: *see* **Obituaries 88**
McNeill, James Charles: *see* **Obituaries 88**
McPherson, Don
college football 324
McPherson, Rolf
Pentecostal Churches 299
McQueen, Steve: *see* **Obituaries 81**
"MACS 3000" (ship) *il.* 227
MacSharry, Ray
Irish politics 455
McTaggart, David: *see* **Biographies 86**
McWilliams, Carey: *see* **Obituaries 81**
Madagascar 392; **87**:431; **86**:463; **85**:469. *See* **Madagascar 84–79**
*see also* WORLD DATA
Madariaga y Rojo, Salvador de: *see* **Obituaries 79**
Madonna: *see* **Biographies 88**
popular music 276
Madrid Stock Exchange (Sp.)
stock exchanges 181
Maeght, Aimé: *see* **Obituaries 82**
magainin (antibiotic)
discovery 139
Magaña Borjo, Álvaro Alfredo: *see* **Biographies 84**
magazine 287
Magdalenian hunters' camp site
archaeological site 125
Magee, Patrick: *see* **Obituaries 83**
"Magic Mirror: The Portrait of France 1700–1900, A" (art exhibition)
French art 132
Magnusson, Hans
speed skating 334
Magogo Sibilile Nantithi Ngangezinyge kaDinuzulu kaSenzangakhona, Princess Constance: *see* **Obituaries 85**
Magris, Claudio
literature 252
Mahathir bin Mohamad, Datuk Seri: *see* **Biographies 87, 82**
Malaysia 439
race relations 292
Mahdi, Sadiq al-: *see* **Biographies 87**
Mahmood Iskandar ibni al-Marhum Sultan Ismail: *see* **Biographies 85**
Mahre, Phil: *see* **Biographies 84**
Mai Chi Tho
Vietnam 442
mail order
special report **84**
Maillet, Antonine: *see* **Biographies 81**
Maine
nuclear plant 187
race relations 293
mainframe
information processing 231
Makarova, Natalia
dancing 151
Makeba, Miriam *il.* 275
Maktum, Muhammad bin Rashid bin Said al-
United Arab Emirates 420
"Mal d'aimer, Le" (film)
motion pictures 269
Malamud, Bernard: *see* **Obituaries 87**
Malawi 392; **87**:431; **86**:463; **85**:469. *See* **Malawi 84–79**
food supplies 114
Mozambican refugees 284
*see also* WORLD DATA
Malaysia 439; **87**:482; **86**:512; **85**:517. *See* **Malaysia 84–79**
agriculture 120
race relations 292
roads and highways 191
Southeast Asia 436
*see also* WORLD DATA
Malcuzynski, Karol: *see* **Obituaries 85**
Maldives 433; **87**:475; **86**:506; **85**:511. *See* **Maldives 84–79**
*see also* WORLD DATA
Mali 393; **87**:431; **86**:463; **85**:469. *See* **Mali 84–79**
*see also* WORLD DATA
Malik, Adam: *see* **Obituaries 85**
Malina, Frank Joseph: *see* **Obituaries 82**
Mallalieu, Sir Joseph Percival William: *see* **Obituaries 81**
Mallowan, Sir Max Edgar Lucien: *see* **Obituaries 79**
Malone, Dumas: *see* **Obituaries 87**
Malta 458; **87**:502; **86**:531; **85**:537. *See* **Malta 84–79**
*see also* WORLD DATA
Maltese, Michael: *see* **Obituaries 82**
Maltz, Albert: *see* **Obituaries 86**
Malvinas, Islas (Atl.O.): *see* Falkland Islands
Mamet, David: *see* **Biographies 86, 79**
motion pictures 267
Mamoulian, Rouben: *see* **Obituaries 88**
man-made fibres 228
"Man Who Owned Vermont, The" (Lott)
literature 247
Manahan, Anna Anderson: *see* **Obituaries 85**
Mandela, Nelson: *see* **Biographies 86**
Mandela, Winnie: *see* **Biographies 87**
Mandlikova, Hana
tennis 341
manic-depressive illness
genetic link 208
Manila
horse racing 330
Manley, Edna Swithenbank: *see* **Obituaries 88**
Manning, Olivia: *see* **Obituaries 81**
Mansell, Nigel
automobile racing 308
Mansour, Agnes Mary: *see* **Biographies 84**
Mansouri, Lofti: *see* **Biographies 82**
Manteuffel, Hasso von: *see* **Obituaries 79**
Mantovani: *see* **Obituaries 81**
Manuel Rodríguez Patriotic Front, *or* FPMR (Chile)
Chile 497
manufacturing: *see* Industrial Review
Mao Dun: *see* **Obituaries 82**
Mar Ignatius Yacoub III: *see* **Obituaries 81**
Mara, Kamisese
Fijian politics 514
Maracay (Venez.)
flooding disaster 510
Maradona, Diego Armando: *see* **Biographies 87, 82**
Marais, Jacob Albertus: *see* **Biographies 82**
marathon running 344
Maravall, José Maria
education 183
Marchenko, Anatoly: *see* **Obituaries 87**
Marcinkus, Msgr., Paul Casimir: *see* **Biographies 83**
bank fraud charge 296
Italy 457
Marcos, Imelda Romualdez: *see* **Biographies 79**
Marcuse, Herbert: *see* **Obituaries 80**
Marechera, Dambudzo: *see* **Obituaries 88**
Marek, Franz: *see* **Obituaries 80**
Marella, Paolo Cardinal: *see* **Obituaries 85**
Margai, Sir Albert Michael: *see* **Obituaries 81**
Margulies, Lazar: *see* **Obituaries 83**
marine biology 241
marine disasters 152
Marini, Marino: *see* **Obituaries 81**
Marino, Dan: *see* **Biographies 85**
Maris, Roger Eugene: *see* **Obituaries 86**
Marjolin, Robert Ernest: *see* **Obituaries 87**
Markevitch, Igor: *see* **Obituaries 84**
Markey, Lucille Parker: *see* **Obituaries 83**
Markham, Beryl: *see* **Obituaries 87**
Markov, Georgi: *see* **Obituaries 79**
Markov, Khristo
track and field 342
Marks, Johnny: *see* **Obituaries 86**
marksmanship: *see* shooting
Marley, Bob: *see* **Obituaries 82**
Marples, Alfred Ernest Marples, Baron: *see* **Obituaries 79**
Marquard, Richard: *see* **Obituaries 81**
Marquet, Mary: *see* **Obituaries 80**
marriage
religion 299
U.S. statistics 283
Marriner, Neville: *see* **Biographies 81**
Marriott, John Willard: *see* **Obituaries 86**
Mars
space exploration 306
Marsh, Dame Edith Ngaio: *see* **Obituaries 83**
Marshall, Christopher Lee
coast-to-coast flight 308
Marshall, Thomas Humphrey: *see* **Obituaries 82**
Marshall, Thurgood
race relations 293
Marshall Islands, Republic of
South Pacific Forum 510
U.S. trusteeship terminated 519
Martenot, Maurice Louis Eugène: *see* **Obituaries 81**
Martens, Wilfried: *see* **Biographies 80**

Now there's a way to identify all your fine books with flair and style. As part of our continuing service to you, Britannica Home Library Service, Inc. is proud to be able to offer you the fine quality item shown on the next page.

Booklovers will love the heavy-duty personalized embosser. Now you can personalize all your fine books with the mark of distinction, just the way all the fine libraries of the world do.

To order this item, please type or print your name, address and zip code on a plain sheet of paper. (Note special instructions for ordering the embosser). Please send a check or money order only (your money will be refunded in full if you are not delighted) for the full amount of purchase, including postage and handling, to:

**Britannica Home Library Service, Inc.**
**Attn: Yearbook Department**
**Post Office Box 6137**
**Chicago, Illinois 60680**

(Please make remittance payable to: Britannica Home Library Service, Inc.)

# IN THE BRITANNICA TRADITION OF QUALITY...

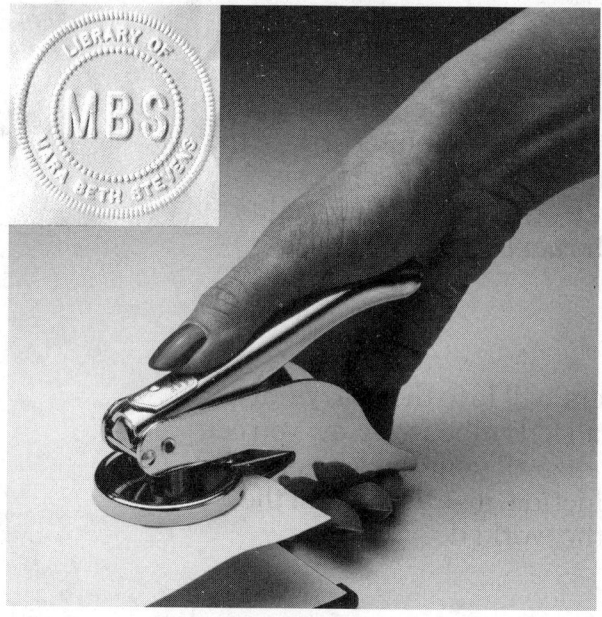

## PERSONAL EMBOSSER

A mark of distinction for your fine books. A book embosser just like the ones used in libraries. The 1½″ seal imprints "Library of _____" (with the name of your choice) and up to three centered initials. Please type or print clearly BOTH full name (up to 26 letters including spaces between names) and up to three initials.
Please allow six weeks for delivery.

Just **$20.00**

plus $2.00 shipping and handling

This offer available only in the United States.
Illinois residents please add sales tax

**Britannica Home Library Service, Inc.**